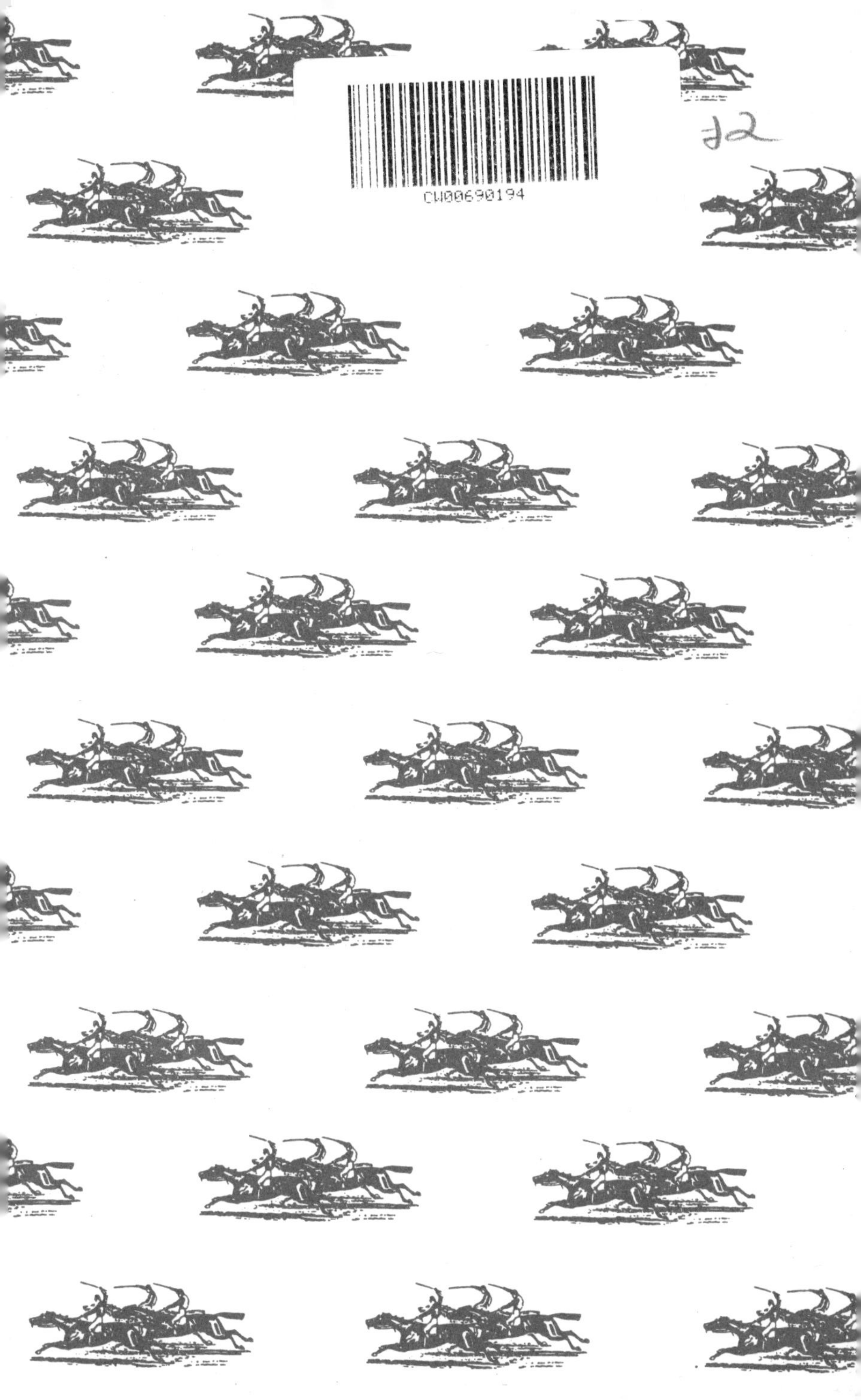
CW00690194

RUFF'S GUIDE TO THE TURF

AND

SPORTING LIFE ANNUAL

1994

Edited by
Martin Pickering

Editorial and publishing offices:
1 New Fetter Lane, London EC4A 1AR

First published 1842 by
The Sporting Life
Orbit House
1, New Fetter Lane
London EC4A 1AR

ISBN 0 901091 71 5

Editorial and Production by Martin Pickering Bloodstock Services
Jacket design and origination by P.W. Reprosharp Ltd, London EC1
Text typeset by LBJ Enterprises Ltd, Chilcompton and Aldermaston
Printed and bound by Bath Press Ltd, Bath and London
Jacket printed by Ark Litho Ltd, London SW19

Contents

FEATURES

OWNERS

TRAINERS

JOCKEYS

APPRENTICES

BREEDERS

HORSES

GENERAL AND ADMINISTRATIVE

RECORDS

BLOODSTOCK

HORSE OF THE YEAR & SPRINTER

LOCHSONG

b.m 1988 by Song, out of Peckitts Well
Owner: Jeff Smith Trainer: Ian Balding
Breeder: Littleton Stud

TWO-YEAR-OLD COLT

FIRST TRUMP

ch.c 1991 by Primo Dominie, out of Valika
Owner: Mollers Racing Trainer: Geoff Wragg
Breeders: Mrs P D Rossdale & Mrs D H Clifton

TWO-YEAR-OLD FILLY

LEMON SOUFFLE

b.f. 1991 by Salse, out of Melodrama
Owner: Lord Carnarvon Trainer: Richard Hannon
Breeder: Highclere Stud

THREE-YEAR-OLD COLT

COMMANDER IN CHIEF

b. or br.c 1990 by Dancing Brave, out of Slightly Dangerous
Owner: Khalid Abdulla Trainer: Henry Cecil
Breeder: Juddmonte Farms

THREE-YEAR-OLD FILLY

INTREPIDITY

b.f. 1990 by Sadler's Wells, out of Intrepid Lady
Owner: Sheikh Mohammed Trainer: Andre Fabre
Breeder: Mike Ryan

OLDER HORSE

Opera House

b.h. 1988 by Sadler's Wells, out of Colorspin
Owner: Sheikh Mohammed Trainer: Michael Stoute
Breeder: Meon Valley Stud

STAYER

Vintage Crop

ch.g. 1987 by Rousillon, out of Overplay
Owner: Dr Michael Smurfit Trainer: Dermot Weld
Breeders: Mr & Mrs B R Firestone

HURDLER

Granville Again

ch.g. 1986 by Deep Run, out of High Board
Owner: Eric Scarth Trainer: Martin Pipe
Breeder: M Parkhill

STEEPLECHASER

Jodami

b.g. 1985 by Crash Course, out of Masterstown Lucy
Owner: John Yeadon Trainer: Peter Beaumont
Breeder: Eamon Phelan

SPECIAL MERIT AWARD

For the person who made the greatest contribution to European racing and breeding during 1993

Francois Boutin

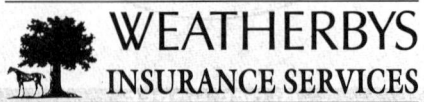

THE YEAR IN FOCUS — 1993

by Ian Carnaby

This feature first appeared in *The Sporting Life* of December 30 and 31, 1993

JANUARY

There were reports in 1992 that the *Maktoum* family was seriously considering a cutback in its British operation. However, the Maktoums were still responsible for 185 of the 554 entries for the 1994 Derby.

Anyone tempted to remark "plus ca change" might have responded in the same way where *Lord Wyatt of Weeford* and *George Walker* were concerned. The *Tote* chairman swiftly rejected the suggestion that the Tote might be handed over to the *British Horseracing Board* . . . and Walker sank further into the mire when he was charged with stealing £12.5 million from *Brent Walker*.

The new *Teletext* service, replacing *Oracle,* was roundly criticised for updating information too slowly and omitting overnight declarations. **The Sporting Life's** northern writer Jon Freeman was in no way inconvenienced and went through the seven-race card at Ayr for a 582-1 accumulator.

Jodami won the Mandarin narrowly and *Rushing Wild* was rather more impressive at Sandown. *Glencloud* came fast and late to take The Ladbroke in Ireland.

Everyone agreed when the International Classifications made *Zafonic* top two-year-old, but few could understand why *St Jovite* was rated 10lb ahead of old rival *Dr Devious*.

Former Grand National winner *Seagram* retired at 13 and the splendidly consistent *Sabin du Loir* lasted one year more. *Martin Pipe* called it a day with him after a gallant victory in the John Bull Chase at Wincanton.

Steve Cauthen failed to agree terms with *Sheikh Mohammed* for 1993. This meant that he would probably retire. The Sheikh tried unsuccessfully to recruit *Michael Kinane* and then — after lengthy deliberations — opted for champion jockey *Michael Roberts*.

Controversially, the *Jockey Club* recommended that stewards should be able to call a jockey in if he used the whip more than five times. The forehand position was still banned.

As expected, Home Secretary *Kenneth Clarke* gave the go-ahead for the evening opening of betting shops. Most sections of the industry welcomed the move, but it was bitterly opposed by some smaller firms and greyhound chiefs.

Tristram Ricketts, 46, was appointed chief executive of the British Horseracing Board. This effectively left Jockey Club chief executive *Christopher Haines* without a role to play.

Alfie Bruce resigned as chairman of the much-troubled *NARBOL,* which also lost its betting shop contracts at *United Racecourses* to *Coral* — and *William Hill* parted company with racecourse PRO *Don Payne,* promoting former jockey *David Hood* in his place.

Mighty Mogul, favourite for the Champion Hurdle, broke down at Cheltenham and was put down after a subsequent operation. *Declan Murphy* partnered *Royal Derbi* to a surprise victory in the Irish Champion Hurdle, but was also stood down for 14 days after appearing to force young *Daniel Fortt* off the course at Cheltenham. At the same venue, the impressive *National Hunt Hall of Fame* was opened.

Rod Fabricius became acting clerk of the course at Aintree, following *John Parrett's* death, and *Brendan Powell* broke his left leg for the second time in a year at Wolverhampton.

FEBRUARY

With *Frankie Dettori* apparently all set for a lucrative two-year stint in Hong Kong, *Ray Cochrane* returned as *Luca Cumani's* stable jockey. *Lester Piggott* returned to race riding in Dubai, less than four months after his horrific fall at the Breeders' Cup.

Richard Dunwoody continued to lead *Peter Scudamore,* and made it 100 for the season on *Grey Hussar* at Windsor. By stark contrast, *Dale McKeown* called it a day, winning opportunities having dried up.

The Czech horse *Quirinus* and *Cool Ground* headed the Grand National weights, but bookmakers made *Romany King,* runner-up in 1991, favourite.

A fascinating day at Sandown saw *Mole Board* spring a 33-1 surprise against *Valfinet,* and the latter's stablemate, *Rushing Wild,* beaten by *Country Member. Jimmy FitzGerald* landed a major coup with *Trainglot* in the Tote Jackpot Handicap Hurdle. Only 36 runners contested a £90,000 sponsored card at Ascot in midweek, and the executive responded by halving entry fees for the rest of the season.

Jodami beat *Chatam* cleverly in the Hennessy Irish Gold Cup. Actor *James Bolam,* part-owner of *King Credo,* saw the horse win the Tote Gold Trophy at Newbury. Less happy was *Neale Doughty,* fined £450 by the *Jockey Club* under the non-triers' rule after finishing eighth on *Thistle Monarch* at Ayr in November.

Former Gold Cup winner *Norton's Coin* was retired, and *Kim Bailey* and *Anthony Tory* parted company. *David Nicholson* sent out *Stylus* to win at 150-1 at Leicester — the longest-priced winner in Britain for two years.

Billy Newnes was relieved, and *Maxine Juster* positively radiant. Newnes won a race on the all-weather at Lingfield six months after an eye injury in Germany threatened his career, and Maxine married Kent cricketer *Graham Cowdrey*.

Milford Quay became *Martin Pipe's* 1,500th British winner, and the trainer settled his differences with the *Irish Turf Club* after a long-running dispute over the same horse's victory at Punchestown.

The Jockey Club was strongly criticised for covering up the fact that Pipe's *Her Honour* had failed a dope test at Kempton on January 22. Things went from bad to worse when Portman Square belatedly revealed that the heavily-backed *Flash of Straw* had been got at at Yarmouth six months previously. Rumours again circulated about a gang of dopers — exactly the sort of story the Jockey Club was anxious to avoid.

Trainer *Chris Trietline* was fined £1,500 after selling hurdle winner *The Hidden City* failed a test at Ludlow in November. *Racecall,* whose contract with the *Racecourse Association* had expired, withdrew sponsorship of the Racecall Gold Trophy at Redcar. The *Tote* took over.

MARCH

Britain's first Sunday point-to-point would take place on April 25 at Ashorne with *Desert Orchid* in attendance.

The *Jockey Club* predicted a fall of 8.2 per cent in horses in training in 1993, with another fall of 7.4 per cent in 1994. On the doping front, it set up *Raceguard* — a confidential, round-the-clock "hotline" — for those with information.

A split between *Mark Tompkins* and *Steve Smith Eccles* gave *Jamie Osborne* the ride on *Staunch Friend* in the Champion Hurdle. *Declan Murphy* rode a 384-1 treble at Newbury and *Rapporteur* won the race named after him at Lingfield. His 15th success at the track made him the top Flat course specialist since the war.

Ladbrokes' racing division returned increased profits of £64.8 million in 1992. Although only £300,000 up on 1991, the figure would have been £8 million higher but for the closure of 60 shops in Flanders.

At the *Tote* lunch, *Kenneth Clarke* confirmed his personal support for Sunday racing but failed to indicate when the Government might find time for the necessary legislation.

At the Cheltenham Festival, *Granville Again* won the Champion Hurdle for *Martin Pipe* and *Jodami* the Gold Cup for *Peter Beaumont*. *Shawiya* became the first filly to take the Triumph Hurdle and helped

Charlie Swan become leading rider with four winners. *Cherrykino* was killed in the Gold Cup and Ladbrokes reported that the French-trained *The Fellow* was the most heavily-backed favourite in the firm's history.

In his Budget speech, Chancellor of the Exchequer *Norman Lamont* paved the way for across-the-board VAT registration of racehorse owners.

Bill Gredley sold a half-share in *User Friendly* to a Japanese buyer and *Lord Oaksey* had a busy day at Uttoxeter. Having undertaken a bungee jump to raise £1,000 for the Injured Jockeys' Fund, he then watched his son-in-law *Mark Bradstock* saddle the winner of the William Hill Handicap Hurdle.

Peter Watson became the new chairman of the *National Association of Bookmakers* and *Len Cowburn* resigned as deputy chairman of *William Hill* and left the company.

Lingfield was chosen to stage the third Sunday meeting, on August 1 and, as the new Flat season opened, *High Premium* won the Lincoln for *Lynda Ramsden*. *Jack Berry* recorded a 1,000-1 treble on the second day.

Nick Fox, in his first year as Templegate on **The Sun**, won **The Sporting Life/Coral** Naps competition for the jumpers.

SIS announced it would begin regular transmission of British racing to the USA in April. British racecourses would benefit, receiving percentage payments based on the level of US Tote betting turnover. *Sky Sports,* in this country, would cover at least two evening fixtures each week, starting on May 20.

At the *Jockeys' Association* awards, *Michael Roberts* was voted Jockey of the Year. *Richard Dunwoody* became Jumps Jockey of the Year for the second time.

APRIL

The early part of the month was dominated by the Aintree fiasco, when two false starts resulted in the Grand National being abandoned. The phrase "laughing stock of the world" and the name of the starter, *Captain Keith Brown,* became common currency. Newspaper columnists who had seldom, if ever, commented on matters pertaining to racing, wondered how a world-famous event, beamed by satellite to 50 million people in over 20 countries, could place its trust in a long piece of elastic and two flags.

Blame flew in all directions, and senior steward Lord Hartington issued a public apology. An inquiry, headed by *Sir Michael Connell,* was set up. One likely scapegoat was "recall" man *Ken Evans,* who may or may not have raised his flag on both occasions. The committee's report on this and other issues was vague. Indeed, the report ended by being criticised almost as strongly as the antiquated starting procedure itself. All in all, a sorry episode in the history of the British Turf.

Regrettably, Aintree 1993 is unlikely to be remembered for anything else. However, it should be recorded that *Double Silk* became the first horse since *Grittar* to win the Cheltenham and Liverpool Foxhunters, and *Cab On Target* looked every inch a Gold Cup horse in the Mumm Melling Chase. Furthermore, *Graham Bradley* provided the most artistic display of jockeyship seen for many a long day when coaxing the enigmatic *Morley Street* past his full-brother Granville Again in the Martell Aintree Hurdle.

To general surprise, *Peter Scudamore* suddenly retired from the saddle at the Ascot meeting which followed. A credit to his profession and an outstanding ambassador, his final ride, on *Sweet Duke,* was a winning one. Although records are made to be broken, it seems highly unlikely that his winning tally of 1,678 will ever be matched.

On the Flat, *Zafonic* was beaten at 10-1 on by *Kingmambo* in the mud at Maisons-Laffitte. *Lester Piggott* won the Nell Gwyn on *Niche,* and *Billy Newnes* completed a full house of all 35 courses by scoring on *Queen of the Quorn* at Newcastle.

Adrian Maguire won the Scottish Champion Hurdle on *Staunch Friend,* but at a *Jockey Club* seminar *Anthony Mildmay-White* said that the jockey's whip style would have to change. The criticism was rather pointed, and Maguire considered taking legal action.

Richard Dunwoody was named as *Martin Pipe's* new stable jockey. He won two races in three days on *David Nicholson's Viking Flagship* at Punchestown, while Pipe took the Scottish National with *Run For Free.*

Tom Clarke took over from *Mike Gallemore* as editor of **The Sporting Life**. The *Stewards' Cup* was switched to a Saturday.

Sayyedati won the One Thousand Guineas. In a particularly hard-fought finish, *Richard Hills (Ajfan)* picked up a four-day ban for improper use of the whip, and a similar suspension for *Frankie Dettori (Dayflower)* made 11 days in all, causing him to miss both Chester and York.

MAY

Zafonic won the Two Thousand Guineas easily, breaking the course record in the process. *Khalid Abdulla* also seemed to hold an unbeatable hand in the Derby, although *Armiger's* narrow defeat by *Hernando* in the Prix Lupin, together with *Tenby's* workmanlike victory in the Dante, ensured that the latter would be the stable's "selected". In the event,

Tenby was joined in the Epsom line-up by another stablemate, *Commander In Chief.*

Willie Carson was fined £1,200 for dropping his hands on *Bashayer* in the Cheshire Oaks. *David Barron* and *Alex Greaves* ended their highly successful partnership.

The new arrangement between Messrs *Pipe* and *Dunwoody* was followed by various other changes. *Adrian Maguire* joined *David Nicholson* and *Mick Fitzgerald* moved to *Nicky Henderson*. *Carl Llewellyn* was confirmed as *Nigel Twiston-Davies's* number one and *Norman Williamson* just edged out *Jamie Railton* at *Kim Bailey's*.

Charles Barnett became full-time managing director at Aintree. *Cath Walwyn's* impending retirement meant that Saxon House would not be overseen by a member of the family for the first time in 50 years. David Nicholson and *Jamie Osborne* reached their respective hundreds for the season. *Roger Charlton* and *Steve Raymont* were each fined £400 under the non-triers rule after *Oare Sparrow* finished 15th at Newbury.

Lester Piggott turned up at Bath for the first time in 24 years and rode *Desert Lore* to victory for The Queen.

Barathea franked the *Zafonic* form by winning the Irish 2,000 Guineas, but *Michael Roberts* was suspended for three days for careless riding. *Nicer* won the Irish 1,000 for *Barry* and *Michael Hills*.

To nobody's great surprise, the *Royal Hong Kong Jockey Club* rejected *Frankie Dettori* following the revelation that he had been in possession of a small amount of cocaine when stopped by police in Central London. For a while it appeared that *Willie Ryan* would take his place in the colony, but he eventually decided to stay with *Henry Cecil*. No doubt bemused by all of this, local trainer *Gary Ng* finally called upon the American, *Randy Romero*.

Wolverhampton's 1993 Flat race programme was abruptly cancelled when the course was judged unraceable. Most of the meetings would go to the other RAM venue, Southwell. *Wally Pyrah* stood down after five years as *Coral* racecourse PRO. *Brian Meehan,* formerly assistant to *Richard Hannon,* saddled his first winner at Brighton.

JUNE

Commander In Chief, partnered by *Michael Kinane* and starting at 15-2, won the Derby from the 150-1 outsiders, *Blue Judge and Blues Traveller. Pat Eddery* rode the odds-on *Tenby,* who was beaten early in the straight. The paying attendance was up 20 per cent on 1992.

Opera House won the Coronation Cup, his first Group One success at the age of five, and *Intrepidity* took the Oaks. Both horses were owned by *Sheikh Mohammed* and ridden by *Michael Roberts*. *Hernando* triumphed in the Prix du Jockey-Club.

Richard Dunwoody coasted to his first National Hunt title with 173 winners and received the *MBE* in the Queen's Birthday Honours List. He also took over from *Peter Scudamore* as joint-president of the Jockeys' Association.

The *British Horseracing Board* was officially launched and announced its intention to take over the *Tote* within five years. *Sir John Sparrow, Levy Board* chairman, was reappointed for another three-year term. *Sir Thomas Pilkington* was set to succeed *Lord Hartington* as *Jockey Club* senior steward from July 1 1994.

At a generally low-key Royal Ascot, *Zafonic* missed the St James's Palace Stakes because of softish ground. Old rival *Kingmambo* triumphed in his absence, and the French also won the Coronation Stakes with *Gold Splash* and the Queen's Vase with *Infrasonic*.

Vincent O'Brien was persuaded to lead in *College Chapel* and *Lester Piggott* after their victory in the Cork and Orrery. *Drum Taps* won the Gold Cup for the second year in a row and *Robert Sangster* enjoyed a clean sweep with three of his juveniles in the Coventry, Norfolk and Chesham Stakes. *Pat Eddery* took the Ritz Club Trophy for leading rider.

Neither *Keith Brown* nor *Ken Evans* would be subjected to any form of discipline after the Grand National episode. Brown was due to retire and Evans would be officiating at Aintree again in 1994.

Jockeys' riding fees went up by two per cent from July 26, making a ride on the Flat worth £55.10 and one over jumps £75.20. *Ray Cochrane* rode his 1,000th domestic winner on Declassified at Windsor.

Coral launched its *Tote Direct* terminals, enabling betting shop patrons to place Jackpot, Placepot and Trio bets, fed straight into the Tote pool at Wigan. *Ladbrokes* and *Hills* remained unimpressed.

On a very hot day in Ireland, *Commander In Chief* galloped on too strongly for *Hernando* in the Irish Derby. Pat Eddery was back on board and Commander In Chief was very heavily backed, down to 7-4 on.

Belgian-trained *Old Hook* landed an off-course gamble when winning at Folkestone. The *Betting Office Licensees' Association* advised its members not to pay out, pending an investigation, but later gave the all-clear.

Northern jockey *David Nicholls* retired at 37. He rode 421 winners in all, the best of them the very tough sprinting mare, *Soba*.

JULY

Michael Roberts experienced an eventful month. He selected *Barathea* in the Coral-Eclipse, but *Opera House* won for *Michael Kinane*. Then, after causing "intentional interference" on *Sabrehill* at Newbury, he was suspended for ten days, making a total of 23 in 1993. An appeal failed, but Roberts received considerable support in the weighing room and the Press. The controversial Rule 153 was once again the centre of attention.

On the first day of the new whip instructions, July 5, *Jason Tate* and *Darryll Holland* were cautioned. But it was *Gary Bardwell* who received the first suspension, two days later.

Equine Viral Arteritis continued to make its presence felt with *Gavin Strang,* Shadow Agricultural Minister, accusing the Government of ignoring warnings about importing infected animals.

At Newmarket's July meeting, *Lester Piggott* won three big races, including the Falmouth Stakes on Niche. However, *Richard Hannon's* talented filly was later killed after bolting on the gallops. *Hamas* was a shock 33-1 winner of the July Cup.

Mary Reveley returned after a spell in hospital to land a 265-1 four-timer at Redcar. All were ridden by *Kevin Darley*.

Wemyss Bight turned the Epsom tables on *Intrepidity* in the Irish Oaks to give Khalid Abdulla, and Dancing Brave, another Classic success.

Baron Ferdinand was a major successful gamble in the *John Smith's Magnet Cup*. On a humbler level, the word got out about the moderate plater *Ima Red Neck,* who reached the astonishing price of 6-4 on in a 16-runner selling handicap at Nottingham. Board prices were refused in some shops on a black day for bookmaking, but Ima Red Neck finished only fourth.

David Elsworth's move from Whitsbury to *Peter Bolton's* Whitcombe Manor complex was confirmed. *The Racegoers' Club* voted Cheltenham Racecourse of the Year, thus ending Sandown's five-year sequence.

Paul Cook, claiming compensation of £280,000 for injuries sustained in the 1989 Tote Portland at Doncaster, won his case. *RTS* sued *SIS* for £800,000 over alleged breach of contract when *Chrysalis Mobiles* took over the supply of live pictures on May 1, 1992.

The *BBC North* programme **Drug Runners** claimed that a gang of dopers had stopped at least 20 horses since 1990. *The Jockey Club* said this was "just another platform to attack racing's reputation".

Opera House won the King George at Ascot, his third Group One victory in a row, and compensation for *Michael Roberts,* about to start his suspension. *Commander In Chief* finished only third and did not race again.

At Goodwood, *Zafonic* flopped badly behind *Bigstone* in the Sussex Stakes and was later found to have bled. He was retired soon afterwards and would stand at *Banstead Manor Stud*. Visibility was down to a furlong on the Thursday, when *Lochsong* and *Philidor* gave owner *Jeff Smith* a handsome double. Moving the Stewards' Cup to Saturday proved a success where betting office turnover was concerned. *Willie Carson* took advantage of Roberts' absence to score on *King's Signet.*

The Jockey Club found that most of the amateur riders in the opening race at *Newmarket* had "brought racing into disrepute" by failing to negotiate the only bend on the July Course and thereby turning the Jif Lemon Handicap into a farce.

AUGUST

A record crowd of over 10,000 attended *Lingfield's* Sunday card. Country music and a Wild West shoot-out helped to compensate for the absence of betting.

Jockeys would face random post-race dope tests from January 1, 1994, thus bringing *Britain* into line with other countries. There would be no reduction in fixtures in 1994, despite the dwindling horse population. Indeed, the *British Horseracing Board* approved 12 extra two-year-old races in April and May.

The pilot scheme of *floodlit racing* at Wolverhampton was also sanctioned. There would be no lights at Aintree, however. The recall system for the *Grand National* would involve an extra flagman, radios and dayglo colours, but no flashing lights or klaxons. Senior racecourse officials were very critical of the industry working group's recommendations.

National Hunt trainer *Owen O'Neill* landed a 3,416-1 double on the Flat at Bath, but persuaded his wife not to risk £5 on this remote possibility. *Mrs O'Neill's* thoughts were not made public.

Richard Phillips, well known for his impressions of leading racing figures, had his first training success when *Stane Street,* owned by 84-year-old *Jim Reade* (of Baulking Green fame) won at Newton Abbot.

Sayyedati proved just too good for *Ski Paradise* and *Kingmambo* in the Prix Jacques le Marois at Deauville.

A team of nine surgeons successfully battled for 13 hours to save jockey *Candy Morris'* foot after an accident at Lambourn. But *David Tegg,* recovering from two brain haemorrhages, was told he must not ride for at least a year.

Ezzoud sprang a 28-1 surprise in the Juddmonte International at York. *Sabrehill* was caught after going clear; he broke down afterwards and was retired. *Tenby* ran moderately again and was sold to Coolmore Stud. *Armiger,* very disappointing behind *Bob's Return* in the Great Voltigeur, would stand in Japan. *Sarawat* landed a gamble in the Ebor and *Lochsong* showed herself to be a genuine Group One performer with a fluent success in the Nunthorpe.

SIS signed a new media rights agreement with the *Racecourse Association,* to last at least until April, 2002. The European contract would generate up to £11m a year, to be shared among the 59 courses. SIS would NOT be going public, after all.

Lynda Ramsden and *Kieran Fallon* were each fined £700 under the non-triers rule when *Rafferty's Rules* finished tenth at Nottingham. Frankie Dettori completed a full house of all British Flat courses when Alllegsnobrain won at Edinburgh.

Snurge's victory in the Grand Prix de Deauville took the horse to within £20,000 of *Pebbles'* record as leading British-trained money winner of all time.

SEPTEMBER

Darryll Holland was suspended for eight days by the disciplinary committee after using the whip improperly three times in four days. **Timeform**, in **Chasers and Hurdlers 1992/93**, opined that the *Jockey Club's* handling of the whip issue had "done more damage to racing's public image over the years than the action of any whip-happy jockey".

Bob's Return won the 217th St Leger to give trainer *Mark Tompkins* his first Classic. *Richard Hannon* landed a treble on the opening day, and at the Doncaster Sales the turnover on yearlings was up by 48 per cent on 1992.

John Gosden won his first Group One race in Britain with *Wolfhound* in the Haydock Sprint Cup. It was finally confirmed that *Michael Roberts'* contract to ride for *Sheikh Mohammed* would not be renewed in 1994. *Frankie Dettori* became Gosden's stable jockey, and *Michael Kinane* would ride for the Sheikh in European Group races when available. Roberts shrugged off his disappointment and rode a 120-1 four-timer in the Brighton drizzle.

Dermot Browne denied that he was "The Needleman" in **Drug Runners,** but the Jockey Club was unimpressed.

Laurel Queen broke *Misty Halo's* record of 21 British victories by a mare when winning at Lingfield. The *British Horseracing Board* hired *Lee Richardson*, 36, a senior figure in the car rental world, to oversee the big promotional drive for new owners.

Bigstone won the Queen Elizabeth II Stakes at Ascot, but the Festival of British Racing crowd was well down for the second year running. *Lord Carnarvon* suffered more cruel luck at Newmarket when his *Lemon Souffle* was badly struck into in the Cheveley Park Stakes, won by *Prophecy*.

Mark Pitman retired from the saddle, aged 27, to work as assistant to his mother.

OCTOBER

The biggest-ever *Jackpot* pool of over £700,000 was shared between 1.83 tickets at Newmarket's Cambridgeshire meeting where *Penny Drops* ran away with the big handicap.

The final Prix de l'Arc de Triomphe sponsored by *CIGA* was won by *Urban Sea.* British challengers *White Muzzle* and *Opera House* - the latter sold to stand in Japan - finished second and third. *Lochsong* was a very impressive winner of the Prix de l'Abbaye.

Sheikh Mohammed bought four of *Robert Sangster's* two-year-olds for £2.8m to race in Dubai before returning to Britain for the 1994 season. *Vincent O'Brien* paid IR1.5m guineas to secure a full-brother to *Salsabil* at Goff's Sales.

The evening opening of betting shops helped turnover increase by 12.5 per cent in June compared with the same month in 1992. But there were still rumblings of discontent from staff working late. Former *William Hill* employee *Sandy Hook* lost her case for unfair dismissal when it came before an industrial tribunal.

Haydock groundsman *Alan Fyles* quite possibly averted a serious accident when discovering subsidence after heavy rain. The meeting was abandoned, as was a prestigious *Ascot* Saturday card, with the result that **Grandstand** screened three races from Worcester - including a selling hurdle.

The *Willie Carson* and *Steve Smith Eccles* autobiographies were published. Eminently readable, both were also startlingly frank in places! *Peter Scudamore* relived *Squire Osbaldeston's* remarkable feat of endurance 162 years earlier by riding 200 miles around Newmarket on a variety of steeds. *The Animal Health Trust* was the charity to benefit. *Allen Webb* retired from the saddle to become a jockeys' valet.

Aahsaylad came late to take the Cesarewitch and *Hatoof* was a very easy winner of the Champion Stakes. The veteran Beverley trainer *Alf Smith* landed a £189,000 jackpot with *Cape Marino* in the Tote Two-year-old Trophy at Redcar.

The sale of *United Racecourses* would be approved by the *Levy Board.* The buyer would guarantee the future of all three courses. A sponsor was being sought to take over the Derby, with *Ever Ready* due to withdraw after 1994.

Smart jeans became acceptable apparel in Tattersalls enclosure at *Ascot* except for the four-day royal meeting. *Nick Cheyne* was appointed clerk of the course-elect at Ascot and Lingfield won the contract to run Folkestone racecourse, taking over from *Pratt & Co.*

Frankie Dettori was fined £500 for dropping his hands when beaten on the 9-4 on chance *Southern Power* at Chester. *Barry Hills* and *Darryll Holland* ended their association. *Commander In Chief* was sold to stand in Japan. *Henry Cecil* won yet another Racing Post Trophy, this time with *King's Theatre*.

Philip Tilson, having rejected an offer of nearly £34,000 from *Ladbrokes* — he forecast the first three home in the Derby in what he understood to be a tricast bet — took his case to *Tattersalls Committee*. The committee found for Ladbrokes, who were not offering a tricast bet on the race but their own Trio. It transpired that Tilson, 17, was under age when placing the bet.

Hoax bomb warnings disrupted meetings at Lingfield and Yarmouth. *Barton Bank* won the Charlie Hall Chase at Wetherby.

Bill Wightman, John Sutcliffe and *Tommy "Squeak" Fairhurst* decided to retire.

NOVEMBER

Simon Morant, not *Gerry Scott,* was named as the new starter at Aintree. Everything went well at the November meeting, but Morant had problems at Chepstow. *Jamie Osborne* was fortunate to escape serious injury when the tape wound itself around his neck. Several jockeys had anticipated the "off".

Richard Hannon broke *Henry Cecil's* record for the number of winners in a season when *Art Tatum* took him to 181 at Yarmouth. *The Bookmakers Committee* and *Levy Board* moved inevitably towards a judgment from Home Secretary *Michael Howard* on the 33rd Levy Scheme.

Darren Biggs and *Jason Weaver* took legal action over a **News of the World** article alleging involvement with drugs. Weaver, the champion apprentice, accepted an invitation to become stable jockey to *Mark Johnston*.

Bradbury Star won the Mackeson, and *Jodami* was too good for *Cab On Target* at Haydock, even conceding him 15lb.

Francois Boutin received the Cartier Order of Merit for his "outstanding contribution to European racing and breeding". Boutin, suffering from cancer, trained the winners of eight Group One races in 1993.

Terry Ramsden, who once owned over 100 horses, received a two-year suspended sentence at the Old Bailey after pleading guilty to four charges of fraud. Ramsden was bankrupt and described by counsel as "a broken man".

Alan Munro was not offered another contract by *Fahd Salman* after his initial three-year-term. He would ride as a freelance in 1994. Salman switched sponsorship from the Middle Park Stakes to the Dewhurst, naming it after his best horse, Generous.

Lingfield took over a second management contract from *Pratt & Co.* when successful in their bid to run Brighton racecourse. Newcastle clerk of the course *David Parmley* was strongly criticised when frost and snow caused the abandonment of a Saturday programme after an early morning "all-clear". A further 11 meetings were lost during the cold snap in late November including Ascot's H & T Walker Gold Cup.

The success of *Tote Direct* in *Coral* betting shops led to a Jackpot, guaranteed for £5,000, on offer every day.

The relative authority of the *British Horseracing Board* and the *Jockey Club* became fairly clear when the board "recommended" to the club that it change Rules 28 and 153, relating to non-starters and interference. Hitherto, it had been understood that the Jockey Club retained control over this area.

Young *Daniel Fortt,* a 7lb claimer, won the Hennessy Cognac Gold Cup on *Cogent* for *Andy Turnell. SIS* paid *RTS* "a substantial sum" over the alleged breach of contract when *Chrysalis* began supplying pictures to the shops.

DECEMBER

The sport continued to be plagued by problems at the start. *Adrian Maguire, Richard Dunwoody, Peter Niven* and the claimer *Richard Davis* were all fined for anticipating the 'off' at Uttoxeter. Three horses were facing the wrong way at the time and starter *William Bennion* later resigned.

At *Kelso,* the Queen's Head Novices Chase was declared void after a fence had been dolled off following the fatal fall of one of the participants. However, six jockeys continued, thinking they were being waved on by the racecourse vet. Although the misunderstanding was a relatively minor affair — the vet's actions were strongly defended by experienced observers — the incident came at the end of a year which was notable for a variety of embarrassing mistakes.

The Budget left the rate of betting duty unchanged at seven and three-quarters per cent. *Coral* made an operating profit of £16 million for the year ended September 30, compared with £13 million the previous year. *William Hill* would be neither sold nor floated on the Stock Market after *Brent Walker* persuaded creditor banks to re-finance Hills' £325 million debt. *Ladbrokes* abandoned its much-criticised Diamond Club scheme.

Graham McCourt rode a four-timer at Windsor including *Driving Force,* the first winner for his mother Mary since she took over from *Matt McCourt,* who died in April.

Richard Dunwoody became the fourth National Hunt jockey to ride 1,000 winners when landing a double at Ludlow. Not all of them were in Britain, however. The champion made a rare error of judgment at Cheltenham, preferring *Egypt Mill Prince* to *Fragrant Dawn,* trained by *Martin Pipe,* in the Tripleprint Gold Cup. Fragrant Dawn won comfortably under *Declan Murphy*.

Robert Sangster used the Derby Awards lunch to promote the idea of an Epsom Derby which would cost owners £1 to enter and a further £2 to run. His speech at the Gimcrack Dinner the following evening was taken more seriously. Sangster pressed for a two-day Derby meeting, with the classics taking place on a Saturday.

The Tote announced a Superbet, which would be in operation before the end of 1994. The bet would involve naming the first six home in a special handicap every Saturday.

Journalists were very critical of the *Ascot* decision to convert the marathon Queen Alexandra Stakes at the royal meeting to a £30,000, ten-furlong handicap.

Diana Jones was assured of the ladies' amateur riders' title when *Captain Marmalade* won at Lingfield. National Hunt trainer *Terry Caldwell* landed a 2,625-1 double at Uttoxeter and *Francois Doumen* sent *Man To Man* from France to win the novices' hurdle for course chairman, *Stan Clarke*. *Ernie Johnson,* who won the 1969 Derby on Blakeney, retired after 25 years in the saddle.

Charles Wilson, managing director of Mirror Group Newspapers and **The Sporting Life,** was elected to the *Jockey Club*. Among five other newcomers was the former National Hunt jockey, now a successful sculptor, *Philip Blacker*.

Willie Musson and his apprentice jockey *David McCabe* were each fined £700 under the non-triers rule when *Don't Con Th' Bookie* finished seventh of nine in a Lingfield claimer. Much happier was *Nigel Twiston-Davies,* whose remarkably tough steeplechaser *Young Hustler* won the Betterware Cup at Ascot.

In the face of fierce criticism, especially from *John McCririck,* SIS reverted to its original policy of quoting a "bar" price on some opening shows. The length of time taken to compile a full show and the weakness of some markets on-course were given as the principal reasons, though several observers believed SIS had been "pressurised" by the big bookmaking firms.

Adrian Maguire and *Declan Murphy,* were suspended for whip offences after dominating the finish of an epic King George VI Tripleprint Chase at Kempton, with Maguire and *Barton Bank* getting home by a head from Murphy and *Bradbury Star*. It was Maguire's 100th winner of the season, and bookmakers began quoting a price about his beating *Peter Scudamore's* record 221 in a single campaign.

Richard Dunwoody, falling further behind in the title race, had the consolation of partnering *Riverside Boy* to an easy win in the Coral Welsh National. It was the fifth time Martin Pipe had trained the winner in the last six years.

After an 11th-hour worry about the surface, the meeting at *Wolverhampton,* with two races under floodlights, took place on Boxing Day. On this historic occasion, the programme attracted more than 10,000 racegoers, and some were even turned away. Chairman *Ron Muddle's* remark, "I hated to do that, because we are in the entertainment business" summarised quite neatly the way British racing belatedly came to regard itself in 1993.

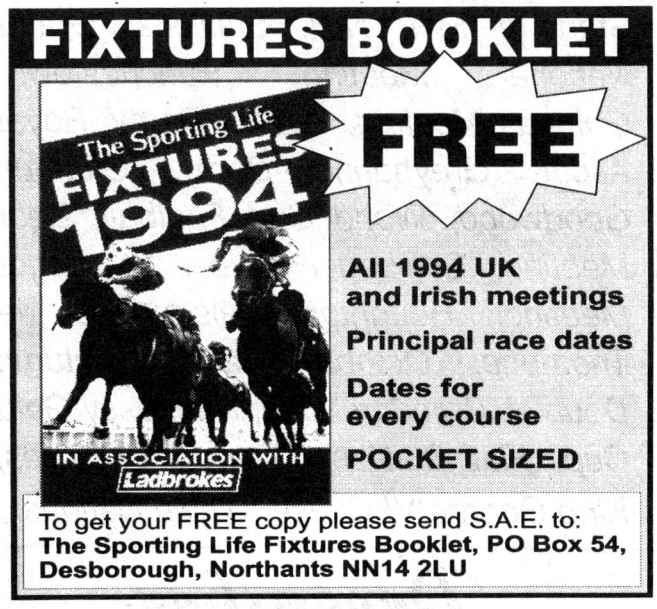

RACING PERSONALITIES LOST IN 1993

by Martin Pickering

Amended version of feature first appearing in *The Sporting Life* of December 24, 1993

M.E. "Tim" Adamthwaite, aged 77 (November). Former trainer of Courtshill Farm, Letcombe Regis, in Oxfordshire.

Charles Ashby, aged 80 (May). Scorton-based osteopath who aided the recovery of both jump jockeys and racehorses. He attended to Grand National winners Grittar, Red Alligator and Red Rum.

Clifford Atkinson, aged 78 (January). Well-known northern owner-breeder who had horses in training with Peter Easterby and Ernie Weymes. Raced Lady Mere before her sale to Robert Sangster, and her half-brother Mydrone.

John Henry Baker, aged 75 (March). Former Tiverton trainer. Recent big winners included Philosophus (Placepot Hurdle) and Star Player (Chester Cup). Son Rodney took over the stable in 1992.

Richard Beamish, aged 83 (June). An honorary member of the Turf Club and Irish National Hunt Steeplechase Committee.

Reginald Anthony Bennett, aged 52 (August). Previously assistant to Jocelyn Reavey, "Bunty" started training from his Maidenhead farm in 1988. He sent out Equinor to win the 1990 Aurelius Hurdle at Ascot.

Arthur Birch, aged 87 (September). Former Uttoxeter-based trainer of jumpers. He retired in 1985.

Lady Rohays Boyd-Rochfort, aged 76 (May). Holder of a unique place in racing history as wife of Sir Cecil Boyd-Rochfort and mother of Henry Cecil, both champion trainers.

Samuel Luther Bridge, aged 76 (January). Stourbridge amateur rider and trainer. Rode his Wild Wisdom to finish in ESB's Grand National of 1956. Trained Mac's Gift, 50-1 winner of Cheltenham's Daily Express Triumph Hurdle Trial in 1983.

Paddy Brudenell-Bruce, aged 70 (June). Former racing manager to his father-in-law Stanhope Joel and manager of his wife Dana's Snailwell Stud.

Joe Buckley, (October). Former Irish trainer from the Fifties whose reputation for bringing on young horses was legendary. His son, Pat, won the 1963 Grand National on Ayala trained by Keith Piggott (q.v.).

Albert Cammidge, aged 85 (September). Long-serving chairman of Doncaster Council's race committee. Known as "Mr Doncaster Racing", he died early on St Leger day.

Lt-Colonel John Chandos-Pole, aged 84 (December). Owner-breeder of Proverb, dual winner of the Goodwood Cup, Doncaster Cup, Chester Vase and second in the Ascot Gold Cup. He rode in point-to-points and, until 1984, was Lord Lieutenant for Northamptonshire.

Judith Chaplin, aged 53 (February). Conservative MP for Newbury. Firm advocate of fairer VAT deal for the British racing and breeding industry.

Ted Coghill, (January). The former deputy editor of *The Sporting Chronicle,* was in his late seventies. Following retirement, he was a regular racegoer in the North, especially at Haydock Park.

Keith Colson, aged 40 (September). Deputy manager of Sheikh Mohammed's Dalham Hall Stud in Newmarket.

Basil Cooper, aged 72 (February). A leading South African trainer. Both Geoff Lewis and Lester Piggott rode winners on his horses in international jockeys' challenge races during the Seventies.

Lt-Commander Wilfred Hornby Crawford, aged 77 (June). Ex-point-to-point rider and international rugby player. Stalwart Scottish National Hunt owner-breeder and trainer who gave Ron Barry his start in Britain. Equestrian artist Susan Crawford is his daughter.

Keene Daingerfield, aged 82 (September). Senior Kentucky racing official. Formerly a trainer, he was a steward for 35 years. Eclipse Award of Merit recipient in 1986.

Owen Frederick "Snowy" Davis, aged 81 (October). Joined Ryan Price after serving his time in France at Chantilly. Became travelling head lad for Josh Gifford's yard from 1970 to 1985 after Captain Price concentrated on horses for the Flat.

Frank Dempsey, aged 66 (April). Respected bloodstock agent and former stud manager. Devoted to the Thoroughbred, his deals included such as Ahonoora, King Emperor, Patch and Superlative.

Major Richard Patrick Gordon Dill, aged 69 (September). Former amateur rider, permit holder and steward at Stratford and Worcester. He owned and rode Easter Breeze to victory in the Grand Military Gold Cup at Sandown.

Don Donaldson, aged 80 (April). Ex-RAF officer and amateur rider involved in the post-war advancement of racing in the Far East.

Jack Douglas, aged 77 (September). Worked in racing in the Middleham area all his life, rising to head lad for Neville Crump, Paul Davey, James Bethell and Bill Elsey.

Roger Duchene, aged 37 (May). A top French jump jockey who was on the verge of retiring to take up training. Won 1985 French Grand National and Champion Hurdle equivalents and 1987 Breeders' Cup Chase.

Jimmy Dunn, aged 69 (January). Wrote under the pseudonym "Spiv" for the *Sheffield Star* where he was racing editor. Also a greyhound devotee, he retired in 1966 when the Star's stablemate, the *Sheffield Morning Telegraph,* ceased publication.

Mrs Mita Easton, aged 76 (June). Permit holder, anaesthetist and publican. Trained the home-bred Parkhouse, her daughter Last House and Martinstown to chase wins at Cheltenham and Sandown.

Peter Edwards, aged 65 (December). The former jockey who had over 100 rides and after retirement from the saddle became a private trainer in South Wales.

Lawrence Elliott, (July). One of Racecourse Technical Services' photo-finish operators for Midlands tracks. His brother is also employed by RTS.

John Fawkes, aged 63 (September). Course manager at Carlisle. His family had been connected with the Cumbrian racecourse for many years. He was also jockeys' man at northern meetings.

Oswald William Fletcher, aged 72 (August). Ossie was appointed editor of *The Sporting Life* in 1959 and held that position for 26 years until his retirement in 1985. He was one of Fleet Street's longest serving editors and was awarded the OBE in 1982.

Mrs Lorna A Fraser, (June). Kelso owner-breeder who had horses in training with Buster Fenningworth, Snowy Gray, John Dunlop and Denys Smith. She bred Border Bounty, the dam of prominent sire Pitcairn.

Miss Robyn E Fullelove, aged 21 (May). Stable lass and former apprentice with Richard Holder.

William Roy Herron Garland, aged 74 (May). Bill was for many years the hyper-efficient runners and riders course representative of the Press Association. Recipient of Lord Derby's Journalist of the Year award in 1983.

Lt-Commander Sir William Francis Cuthbert Garthwaite, aged 87 (December). Aviator, adventurer, and racehorse owner. His Apollo King and Sylvan Sabre were trained at Epsom by Philip Mitchell.

Ted Gifford, aged 76 (August). Skipton farmer who trained many Flat winners during the Fifties and Sixties. Prominent northern jockey Brian Henry was apprenticed to him.

Johnny Alnham Gilbert, aged 72 (July). Former ace jockey over hurdles whose own apprenticeship with Stanley Wootton prepared him in later life to train the numerous youngsters passing through the British Racing School.

Lt-Colonel Sir Martin Gilliat, aged 80 (May). Jockey Club member, racehorse owner, soldier and courtier. Private Secretary to Queen Elizabeth, the Queen Mother, for 37 years. Part owner of Padlocked, runner-up in the 1973 Triumph Hurdle.

Frank Herbert Gilman, aged 78 (August). Rutland farmer, owner-breeder and permit holder. His most successful moment came when Grittar won the 1982 Grand National, thus making him only the third man to train a National winner that he had both bred and owned.

Matt Gilsenan, aged 84 (February). The well-known and respected special duties officer to the Irish Turf Club for 14 years until he retired in 1982.

Lord Gormley, aged 75 (May). Always an ardent racing fan, he was a director of United Racecourses for five years after retirement as president of the National Union of Mineworkers from 1971 to 1982. Secured improved working conditions for stable staff.

Ted Greenway, aged 73 (June). Veterinary officer at racecourses in the North West. Previously enjoyed success as an amateur rider and trainer of point-to-pointers. Attended to the legendary Red Rum.

Eric Guerin, aged 69 (March). Rode Native Dancer to Preakness and Belmont Stakes victories in 1953. Hall of Fame jockey who also won the 1947 Kentucky Derby on Jet Pilot.

David Kenneth Harris, aged 53 (March). Enthusiastic owner-breeder who ran Brook Stud. Alerted the industry to VAT problems. Past president of the Racehorse Owners' Association, a Kempton and Brighton steward, supporter of Racing Welfare and the major stakeholder in Racing World Video.

David Heilbron, aged 76 (March). Owner of Even Keel, winner of 23 races in the Sixties and Seventies when trained by Ken Oliver.

Mrs Christine Hollinshead, aged 67 (March). Wife of Upper Longdon trainer Reg. An important team member of the family run stables for over 40 years.

Leo Hughes, aged 60 (July). Former Irish champion apprentice and respected Newmarket work rider for Geoff Wragg, Luca Cumani and Alex Scott.

Joseph Hurst, aged 62 (May). First-season permit holder from Mawbray in Cumbria. Owned the novice chaser Mils Mij, who won twice in April 1992 when ridden by his amateur rider son, William.

Phillip James, aged 55 (February). Former northern-based jockey who rode over 60 winners for Phil James and Basil Richmond.

David Charles Jermy, aged 53 (December). Somerset trainer and former amateur rider. A licence holder since 1974, his biggest success came four years later when Royal Connection won the Staff Ingham Stakes at Epsom and entered the betting for the following year's Two Thousand Guineas before failing to train on.

Noel Keating, aged 51 (April). Irish owner of horses with Jim Bolger. As chief executive of meat processing group Kepak, he was able to sponsor races at Fairyhouse and gaelic football.

Ronnie Lawson, aged 67 (July). Ex-Walter Easterby apprentice who became stable jockey for Dick McCormack in Ireland and then Geoffrey Brooke and Doug Smith in Newmarket. A work rider for Michael Stoute.

Jack Linley, aged 81 (January). Racehorse owner and a director at Sedgefield. He was widely known on the northern racecourses. The name of all his runners were prefixed by "Norton".

W.G. "Bing" Lowe, aged 88 (February). A retired permit holder, farmer and bloodstock breeder from Stow-on-the-Wold in Heythrop Hunt country. His most notable winner was Motel, hero of the 1963 Welsh National.

Donald MacRae, aged 60 (September). Newmarket farmer, landowner and owner-breeder who ran Stradishall Manor Stud. He had horses in training with Gavin Pritchard-Gordon and William Jarvis. He was a regular vendor at Doncaster, Keeneland and Tattersalls.

Frank Mahon, aged 64 (August). Senior partner of the Ridgeway Veterinary Group in Lambourn. Acknowledged by many local trainers as both a personal friend and a trusted professional.

John Smythies Mangles, aged 65 (October). Recently retired Jockey Club starter. He officiated mainly at northern meetings for 21 years and was chairman of the Sinnington Foxhounds point-to-point committee.

Michael Leo Marsh, aged 77 (February). Former permit holder who trained his Larbawn to win two consecutive Whitbread Gold Cups. A unique third Whitbread win was achieved in 1992 with Topsham Bay. The gelding was sold days prior his death and was awarded the 1993 Whitbread on the disqualification of Givus A Buck. He also owned Hennessy Cognac Gold Cup winner Broadheath. His trainers included Jack Morris (q.v.), David Nicholson and more recently David Barons.

Sydney William Martin, aged 73 (June). Bill was the cartoonist "Williams" whose work illustrated Monty Court's regular column in *The Sporting Life*.

Sir Robin McAlpine, aged 86 (February). One of the long-established English owner-breeders. His Wyck Hall Stud bred First Bloom (grandam of Royal Ascot winners Beneficial and Jeune), First Waltz, Jefferson and Torchon. He owned Oaks heroine Circus Plume and numerous winners in France. A Jockey Club member, past president and life council member of the Racehorse Owners' Association, he also served on the council of the Thoroughbred Breeders' Association.

Major Victor Hugh Harry McCalmont, aged 73 (March). Prominent Irish owner-breeder, former Turf Club senior steward and Jockey Club member. Agar's Plough won the Irish Oaks in 1955 and went on to breed several winners for his Ballylinch Stud. Other prominent winners included Fortissimo, Knockroe, London Gazette, Orchestration, Swallow Tail and Vervain.

Denis McCarthy, aged 52 (August). Former jump jockey who started a family-run yearling breaking operation at Godstone. Success followed as a trainer of pointers with Federal Trooper's win in the 1991 Horse and Hound Cup at Stratford when ridden by his son Tim.

Matthew McCourt, aged 65 (April). Wantage trainer and ex-jump jockey. His widow Mary has taken over the yard helped by their son Graham, a leading National Hunt Jockey.

Mrs Elizabeth McMahon, aged 47 (July). Owner of the Jim Bolger-trained Happy Bride (Pretty Polly Stakes) and Topanoora (Blandford Stakes). She was a member of the famous Dunne's Stores family.

Mrs Norma Moller, (January). Widow of Eric, kept the families' famous chocolate and gold silks to the fore with Young Senor and Petardia, both trained by Geoff Wragg.

Ernie Morris, aged 88 (September). Once jockey to Stanley Wootton and nicknamed "Monkey". His son "DW" was a good lightweight jockey in the Fifties and Sixties.

Jack Morris, aged 68 (January). Respected former trainer and survivor of the horse flight crash at Heathrow in 1968. His 50-plus winners included a Cheltenham first and second in the Foxhunters' and a Mildmay Chase triumph with Madras for Michael Marsh (q.v.).

Mrs Florrie Morris, aged 71 (December). Racehorse owner and supporter of the Lady Jockeys' Association. Her husband's company, Dickens Limited, sponsored the annual Invitation Stakes for lady riders at Newmarket.

Lady Murless, aged 77 (January). An accomplished horse woman, she trained and rode her own horses to success in the Thirties. Her home-bred Caergwrle won the One Thousand Guineas in 1968 when trained by husband Sir Noel. Their daughter, Julie Cecil, is now a Newmarket-based trainer.

Geoff Murphy, aged 66 (April). A noted Australian trainer who landed the Caulfield and Melbourne Cup double in 1982 with Gurner's Lane.

Ian "Jock" Murray, aged 74 (August). Served as farrier at both Nottingham and Doncaster racecourses. Attended to the charges of several Yorkshire trainers.

W.F. "Bill" Murray, aged 70 (September). Former Middleham trainer and head lad with Sam Hall. He trained the filly Altogether, a 33-1 outsider carrying 5lb overweight, to win the 1970 Chester Cup.

David Nelson, aged 62 (November). Chairman of Leicester racecourse management committee since 1985.

Jean Nielson, aged 52 (November). A secretary who had worked at the Racehorse Owners' Association for 15 years.

Philip Nunneley, aged 80 (December). Former Epsom-based handler and racegoer. His winners were all pre-war. Due to severe injuries sustained during the hostilities, he was unable to continue as a trainer.

Tom O'Leary, aged 49 (January). Irish owner of the 1992 Galway Plate winner, The Gooser. He had horses trained by Paddy Mullins, was in the crane hire business and sponsored races at Punchestown.

William J. O'Rourke. (July). Former managing director of Tattersalls (Ireland) and a veterinary officer with the Turf Club. Also a director of the Irish National Stud and Limerick racecourse. He was in his sixties.

Morris Orloff, aged 81 (December). London furrier and jeweller with horses trained by Paul Kelleway. The pair achieved success in 1980 when Sparkling Boy won the Ayr Gold Cup.

Sir William Paton, aged 76 (October). Chaired the 1970 inquiry which resulted in the current anti-doping procedures in force at British racetracks.

William Haggin Perry, aged 85 (November). Virginian owner-breeder who formed a 1960's partnership with Bull Hancock's famous Claiborne Farm. He raced 1979 Belmount winner Coastal and the champion distaffers Gamely, Lamb Chop and Revidere.

Ernest Keith Piggott, aged 89 (June). A leading jump jockey and champion jumps trainer, Lester's father continued his family's great racing traditions. In 1963, he sent out Ayala to win the Grand National.

Colonel Sir John Gawen Carew Pole, aged 90 (January). West Country landowner who in pre-war days rode his own point-to-pointers and hunter chasers. Owned Prince Brownie, an Aintree winner in 1950. Jockey Club member and a past steward at Cheltenham, Exeter and Newton Abbot.

Eamon Prendergast, aged 50 (October). Former jockey in Ireland and England under both codes. His apprenticeship was served with Seamus McGrath. Since hanging up his boots, he had assisted Dick Morgan at English bloodstock sales.

Ralph Raper, aged 69 (June). Sprotborough, South Yorkshire, commercial farmer, racehorse owner-breeder and former northern bookmaker.

Jillian Raymond, (October). Wife of jockey Bruce Raymond, she was one of Willie Stephenson's five daughters. They met and married when Bruce was apprenticed to Stephenson at Royston. She was in her late forties.

Lyle Robey, aged 51 (January). Chairman of the Kentucky State Racing Commission and former counsel for Calumet Farm.

James Keith Rogers, aged 46 (December). Wine consultant, enthusiastic racegoer and part-owner of several not very successful horses. Founder of the Bob Champion Aldaniti Cancer Fund.

R. Richards Rolapp, aged 52 (May). President of the American Horse Council since 1978. A Harvard Law School graduate, he first joined the Council in 1973 and, under his supervision, saw it reach its current position of importance.

Ken Russell, aged 42 (October). Former Queensland amateur who became one of Australia's leading jockeys. Killed in a fall at Rosehill.

E. Barry Ryan, aged 73 (March). American Jockey Club member, former owner of Normandy Farm in Kentucky and publisher. An accomplished horseman, he trained champion steeplechaser Quick Pitch and, on the Flat, Horse of the Year Roman Brother in 1965. Jeremy Tree (q.v.) trained a few horses for him.

Lt-Colonel Sir James Scott, aged 69 (November). Owner of Big Venture and Proud Pathan, part-owner of Eclipse winner Coup de Feu. He was also a bloodstock breeder and a steward at Ascot and Kempton. Alex, his son, is the Newmarket trainer.

Michael James Seely, aged 67 (August). Respected former racing correspondent of *The Times* and *Horse and Hound* contributor. Twice winner of the Clive Graham Award. His total professionalism and sense of fun will long be remembered.

Mrs Diana Senn, (March). Co-owner of 1991 Racing Post Trophy winner Seattle Rhyme, the one-time 1992 Derby favourite. Her husband Henry died in December 1991 and Seattle Rhyme died in April this year.

Charles James William Smirke, aged 87 (December). One of the leading riders this century, he never became champion jockey. His 11 British classic successes included Derby victories on Windsor Lad (1934), Mahmoud (1936), Tulyar (1952) and Hard Ridden (1958). After a 38-year career, he retired in 1959 and was rarely seen on a racecourse again.

Sir Michael Sobell, aged 100 (September). Oldest Jockey Club member, electronics magnate and philanthropist. A late convert to the joys of the Thoroughbred, his first winner was London Cry in the 1958 Chesterfield Cup and Cambridgeshire. In 1960, he purchased the famous Ballymacoll Stud in Ireland from the executors of the late Dorothy Paget. He bred Reform, Sallust and Sun Prince and as an owner-breeder achieved Classic success with Troy (Derby, Irish Derby) and Sun Princess (Oaks & St Leger). His pale blue with yellow and white check cap colours are now used by his son-in-law, Lord Weinstock, and grandson Simon.

George Spencer, aged 72 (May). Irish trainer of the one-eyed Winning Fair who, when ridden by amateur Alan Lillingston, won the Champion Hurdle at Cheltenham in 1963.

Leonard "Clippy" Stevens, aged 62 (January). Former Jerry Wilson apprentice who rode Arberoni to success in the 1952 Irish Grand National and a Galway Plate victory. Jockey for Neville Crump and at one time held a retainer from Lord Derby.

Stanley Tabiner, aged 75 (July). Pre-war Flat jockey with war-time service in Beirut where he became a leading jockey. His son, Godfrey, is a public relations officer for the Racecourse Association.

Lady (Eva Elizabeth) Thomson, aged 77 (October). Mother of Irish trainer Jim Dreaper and Eva, the wife of Michael Kauntze. Able assistant to her late husband Tom Dreaper, trainer of Arkle and Flyingbolt. Married Sir John Thomson in the late Seventies and owned many chasers, including Hard Case.

Miss Ursula D Toller, (June). Owner of this year's Wokingham Stakes winner Nagida at Royal Ascot. The four-year-old filly was trained by her nephew, James Toller.

Cliff Tonge, aged 55 (December). Herefordshire builder and long-time supporter of Frank Jordan's yard. Among his better known horses were Northern Halo, Regent Leisure and Satin Grange.

Arthur Jeremy Tree, aged 67 (March). Classic winning trainer of Only For Life, Known Fact, Juliette Marny and Scintillate. Based at famous Beckhampton for nearly 40 years, he also trained Double Jump, Sharpo, Swing Easy and the Arc winner Rainbow Quest. He was a member of The Jockey Club.

Walter Tyrrell, aged 81 (July). Former senior steward of the Irish National Hunt Steeplechase Committee and an honorary Turf Club member.

Mickey Walsh, aged 86 (August). Four times leading American steeplecase trainer of Irish origin. Recipient of the F Ambrose Clark Award and conditioner of champion King Commander.

Victor Wark, aged 79 (January). Former film director, actor, ex-amateur rider and permit holder with numerous connections in the Epsom area.

D.G. Warneck, aged 79 (April). Known as Bob Warner, his news agency provided racing and point-to-point articles to many publications in the Midlands and West Country.

Lt-Colonel Frank W.C. Weldon, aged 80 (September). Former amateur rider who later became an equestrian Gold Medal winner at the 1956 Olympic Games in Stockholm. Also won that year's RA Gold Cup at Sandown on Snowshill Jim, a feat they repeated the following year. He was director of the Badminton Horse Trials until 1988.

Mrs Valerie Wells, aged 55 (February). Longtime racehorse owner and wife of Bernard, the Kidderminster permit holder.

C.J. (Charlie) Wheatley, (January). Vale of Evesham racehorse owner and breeder. Stratford and Warwick were the venues for wins by his horses, many bearing the "Aldington" prefix. His trainers included Eddie Reavey, Martin Tate and Chris Trietline.

Kenneth E. Wheldon, (May). A scrap metal merchant from the Midlands and successful racehorse owner for 40 years. He was in his mid-sixties. His best horses were Johns Court, Persian Majesty and Major Rose.

Noel Bernard Whitcomb, aged 74 (June). Journalist and newspaper columnist, he was founder of the Daily Mirror Punters' Club, which boosted circulation and had over 600,000 members. The club's best two horses were the 13-wins jumper, Even Up, and Mirror Boy, who won the Andy Capp Handicap at Redcar.

Jack White, aged 83 (December). Veteran Irish bloodstock agent who purchased, among thousands, the Grand National winner Foinavon. Doncaster Bloodstock Sales' original Irish representative. His integrity and loyalty were legendary, as were his zest for life and sense of humour.

Frank Whitham, aged 62 (December). American racehorse owner, banker and cattle rancher died when his private plane crashed. His Argentinian-bred Bayakoa was champion North American distaffer twice. Recently, his Cleante won the Gran Premio Internacional and was declared Horse of the Year in Argentina.

Dare Wigan, aged 76 (July). Noted owner-breeder from West Blagdon in Dorset. Pelting, his foundation mare, was a prolific breeder of winners including Splashing, the dam of Bassenthwaite.

Tommy Wilkin, aged 77 (November). An amateur rider whose 40-year career ended when he was 57. The Yorkshire farmer rode 109 point-to-point winners.

Morgan Gwyn Williams, aged 69 (March). Gwent permit holder and owner-breeder of numerous National Hunt and point-to-point winners. These included Willy Wagtail, Grange Gipsy, No Boundaries, Pointer Jack and Witty Tom.

Mrs G.P. (Barbara) Williams, aged 93 (May). Aramstone, Herefordshire, owner-breeder. Her best horses were Be Hopeful (27 wins), Mabel (Yorkshire Oaks and Classic placed), May Hill (Yorkshire Oaks, Park Hill Stakes and dam of current stallion Picea) and Pasty (Cheveley Park Stakes). Recently, her horses were trained by David Arbuthnot.

Ted Williams, aged 81 (August). Initially a jump jockey, but achieved fame as an international show jumper in the Sixties with Carnival, Pegasus and Sunday Morning.

Zenya Yoshida, aged 72 (August). Leading breeder in Japan for 29 seasons via his Shadai Farms and 11 times champion sire Northern Taste. He owned White Muzzle and in recent years purchased Arc winners Carroll House and Tony Bin; Poule d'Essai des Poulains victor Hector Protector; Allez Milord, and Breeders' Cup hero Sunday Silence.

OBITUARIES OF RACEHORSES, BROODMARES AND STALLIONS DURING 1993

by Martin Pickering

Amended version of feature first appearing in *The Sporting Life* of December 23, 1993

RACEHORSES

ABNEGATION, 8: Put down the evening after breaking his neck in three places during a Wetherby steeplechase in November. Howard Johnson's gelding had previously won four hurdle races and £17,799.

ABSENT RELATIVE, 5: Brooke Sanders' winning mare was killed after being hit by a car in late November. Out of the half-sister to Cesarewitch winner Sir Michael she had won eight hurdle races and over £20,000.

AL MUTAHM, 5: Destroyed after severing his off-fore tendon in a hurdle race at Newbury during early January. An £80,000 birthday present to his wife Madeleine from Sir Andrew Lloyd Webber, the gelding had previously won 1992's Sagaro Stakes at Ascot and was being lined up for a tilt at the Champion Hurdle.

ANDREW'S FIRST, 6: Severed both flexi-tendons when challenging for the Tripleprint Feltham Novices Chase at Kempton on Boxing Day. The gelding, a previous winner of six hurdle races, was put down.

ANDREWS MINSTREL, 6: Put down a few days after a heavy fall over Southwell's all-weather hurdles in mid-January. Trainer John Jenkins had little option bearing in mind that the gelding's shoulder was fractured in four places.

ARTHURLILY, 4: Put down in December after a collision with a Reliant three-wheeler. The filly had been doing road-work from Chris Broad's Gloucestershire yard.

ASHFOLD COPSE, 7: A faller at the seventh of 19 fences in the Sun Alliance Chase at the Cheltenham Festival. The Broadsword gelding broke his neck. He had previously won a bumper, novice hurdles and steeplechases.

BITOFABANTER, 6: Arthur Moore's 1992 Swinton Hurdle winner fell and broke his neck racing at Fairyhouse at the end of November.

BORACEVA, 10: Slipped and fractured his femur when coming round from an operation to combat recurrent bouts of colic. The Salluceva gelding was put down in late June. A punters' nightmare, he did achieve 12 wins from 53 outings for £86,000. His best wins were the National Hunt Chase at the 1989 Cheltenham Festival and the following year's Rehearsal Chase at Chepstow. He was third to Givus A Buck in last season's Ritz Club Chase.

CARRICK HILL LAD, 10: Died in mid-February following a massive arterial haemorrhage on Gordon Richards's gallops while preparing for a comeback. Winner of 11 jump races and £109,293, the Royal Fountain gelding won the Timeform Chase and was second in the Welsh National. He broke down in the 1991 Gold Cup and never raced again.

CASTLEKELLY CROSS, 7: After winning the bumper at Fairyhouse on 27th November, the Michael Hourigan-trained gelding was unable to make the winners' enclosure due to the recurrence of a previous back injury. He died later that evening.

CHERRYKINO, 8: Put down in mid-March. Related to the legendary Arkle and bred and owned by Anne, Duchess of Westminster, he fractured his nearside elbow when falling at the seventh fence during the Tote Cheltenham Gold Cup. A winner of nine races over hurdles and fences he only started 13 times.

CLARE COAST, 7: John Wade's gelding fell and broke a leg during the novice chase at Kelso in December. The race was declared void.

CLASSICAL CHARM, 10: Put down after breaking a shoulder when misjudging a fence in the Proudstown Park Handicap Chase at Navan in March. The Corvaro gelding ran 20 times winning five hurdles and two chases for over £106,000. Hero of the 1988 Irish Champion

Hurdle and runner-up in Cheltenham's Champion Hurdle, he was not seen on the racecourse for nearly three years after sustaining a serious leg injury.

COWORTH PARK, 8: Broke a leg and destroyed at Kempton in late December. The Philip Mitchell trained gelding previously won three hurdle races but had not run since May 1991.

CULTURED, 4: John White's promising gelding died in late-November following two operations for a twisted gut. A winner of four hurdle races from ten starts for earnings of £17,405.

CURRENT GOLD, 22: Winner on the Flat, over hurdles and chases and one of the valiant Greystoke regulars. Successful in the 1981 Ritz Club Chase at Cheltenham, he was placed in the Scottish, Welsh and Irish Nationals. Suffered a heart attack while out hunting and died two weeks later in early December.

DANTE'S NEPHEW, 6: Matt McCormack's Le Moss gelding fell in the Novices Chase at Kempton on Boxing Day.

FATHERLAND, 3: A leading Irish juvenile who failed to score at classic age. Sent to USA, he shattered a pastern during the Hollywood Derby in November and was put down. Successful in four of his five starts in 1992, including the National Stakes, he was runner-up to Barathea in this year's Irish 2,000 Guineas before running unplaced in the Epsom Derby.

FERROMYN, 8: Collapsed and died after coming a close second in the Findus Handicap Chase at Leopardstown on Boxing Day. The gelding was the winner of five races.

FLOYD, 13: Suffered a heart attack on the gallops at Epsom in early January. Originally a stalwart performer from David Elsworth's yard, the chesnut gelding, related to Ra Nova, had recently moved to Reg Akehurst. Winner of 19 races, under both Rules, he amassed almost £200,000 in earnings. Among his Flat wins was the Queen's Prize at Kempton, while his hurdle victories included the Bula, County, Imperial Cup, Kingwell, Long Walk and a brace of Fighting Fifths.

GLEN LOCHAN, 8: The New Zealand-bred novice hurdler broke a hind leg while turned out at Henrietta Knight's establishment in May.

Prior to transfer to the northern hemisphere he won six of his 52 races in Australia. Winner of four consecutive events last winter, great expectations were placed on this grey gelding by Three Legs.

GREY TORNADO, 12: Put down following a freak accident in his paddock when he broke a femur at Dai Williams' farm during May. The Rugantino gelding had recently been retired after a career of honest endeavour as a steeplechaser.

IMA RED NECK, 4: Shattered a pastern at Salisbury in mid-August. The American-bred gelding, trained by Stan Moore, was the 6-4 on gambled-on favourite in a failed Nottingham coup during early July. Won a five-runner handicap at Southwell four days later!

IRISH SWAP, 6: Leading American handicapper put down in April after breaking his off-fore cannon bone whilst being prepared for the Californian Stakes at Santa Anita. Winner of 12 races and over $835,000.

IVANKA, 3: Humanely destroyed in February after breaking her pelvis for the second time. Clive Brittain trained this daughter of Dancing Brave to win the Ascot Fillies' Mile and chase home Armiger in the Racing Post Trophy. She was considered a leading Oaks contender.

JOINT SOVEREIGNTY, 13: Found dead in his Devon retirement paddock during September. He had experienced a massive haemorrhage. Winner of the 1989 Glynwed International Chase at Newbury followed by, a fortnight later, the Mackeson Gold Cup at Cheltenham. Ran twice in the Grand National, but unseated his rider or fell.

KOSATA, 3: Winning own-sister to Irish Derby runner-up Observation Post and half-sister to French miler Phydilla. The Barry Hills' trained filly was killed in a road accident in late September.

LARAPINTA, 5: Triple-winning novice hurdler fell at the last flight, when eight lengths clear, at Sedgefield in early December. With earnings of £6,109, he was the second horse trained by Howard Johnson to break his neck within a month (see Abnegation).

LAST 'O' THE BUNCH, 9: Gordon Richards' trained winner of 15 races fell and broke his shoulder at Wetherby on Boxing Day. The gelding was humanely destroyed.

MAJOR FOUNTAIN, 7: Suffered a heart attack during a novice chase at Sedgefield in late September.

MANGO MANILA, 8: Put down in mid-November after fracturing a knee. Con Horgan's useful performer had been castrated and was in a recovery box.

MID DAY GUN, 19: Chronic lameness decided that Michael Bell's hack be put down in early February. Trained by John Webber, the gelding started equal-favourite in the 1983 Grand National but fell at the first. He was a winner for Webber's sons Anthony and Paul.

MIDLAND LAD, 8: Died from a twisted gut in October. The Les Ayre trained gelding had won three hurdle races.

MIDNIGHT MADNESS, 15: Collapsed and died while walking back to be unsaddled after falling in a Warwick hunter chase in May. The winner of two point-to-points he had previously won 13 of his 43 starts under Rules for in excess of £45,000 including the Midlands Grand National and the Warwick National.

MIGHTY MOGUL, 6: Humanely put down in February after seriously injuring himself following an operation to rectify previous damage to his off-fore. A dual winner when trained by Jenny Pitman he was transferred to David Nicholson before the start of the season. Won all five of his outings this current term and was one-time favourite for the Champion Hurdle.

MOMENT OF TRUTH, 9: Useful chaser trained by Peter Monteith was put down in March after accidentally breaking a leg while out to grass. Winner of 17 races and £85,000, the gelding's best achievement was victory in the 1990 Northumberland Gold Cup at Newcastle.

NICHE, 3: Dropped her lad on Richard Hannon's all-weather gallops and collided with the stable farrier's van in early August. Her owner/breeder, Lord Carnarvon, held her in high esteem and had intentions of keeping her for stud after a four-year-old campaign. Winner of six races, she won both Lowther and Norfolk Stakes last year and the Nell Gwyn and Falmouth Stakes at Headquarters this season. She was a half-length second to Sayyedati in the One Thousand Guineas.

OLD APPLEJACK, 13: Broke a hind leg during racing at Newcastle in March. Winner of 14 races, the gelding was due to retire after Aintree. The Newcastle executive intend to name a race after him in memory of his eight wins at their course. His dam, Windfall VI, was put down in January (which see).

POMMES FRITES, 2: Lord Carnarvon's 'anus horribilis' continued when his filly failed to come round after a routine operation for a chipped knee sustained earlier in August. A winning daughter of Cyrano de Bergerac, she was a gallant second to Risky in Newbury's Sales Super Sprint Trophy.

PRAIRIE BAYOU, 3: This year's Preakness Stakes winner suffered a compound fracture of his near-fore cannon bone during the Belmont Stakes at Belmont Park in early June. The gelding was humanely destroyed.

RHODE ISLAND RED, 10: Killed after colliding with an oncoming lorry when returning to Charlie Moore's Brighton stables after exercise in August. The Henbit gelding's lass was taken to Sussex County Hospital purely for observation.

ROSCOE BOY, 11: Put down in March after breaking a fetlock joint. Cliff Dawson's gelding was a leading fancy for the Cheltenham Foxhunters' Chase.

ROY'S DREAM, 10: Broke down in a novice chase at Carlisle in February and was put down. John Leadbetter's Down The Hatch gelding had won at Kelso four days previously.

RUSHING WILD, 8: Humanely destroyed after breaking his pelvis during the Irish Grand National in April. Former top-rated point-to-pointer, he had won 12 races under both sets of Rules. The Martin Pipe-trained gelding had earnings of £80,000 and was second to Jodami in this year's Cheltenham Gold Cup.

SEATTLE RHYME, 4: Broke a leg on the Whitsbury gallops and was put down in April. A $55,000 yearling from Seattle Dancer's first-crop he won three races as a juvenile including the Racing Post Trophy and was third to Arazi in France's Grand Criterium. Suffered a foot injury in the spring of his classic year after being ante-post Derby favourite. Recovered to be third in the Juddmonte International. His owner, Diana Senn, died in March (which see).

SOFT DAY, 8: Shattered his near-fore fetlock during racing at Punchestown in April. He won ten of his 19 starts and had progressed from useful novice hurdler through to a promising chaser under Arthur Moore's tutelage.

SONG OF SIXPENCE, 9: Broke a hind leg during what was to be his final outing at Pontefract in October. A gelding by The Minstrel he ran 67 times under both Rules winning 12 races and was placed on 23 occasions for in excess of £130,000. Home-bred by Paul Mellon at his Rokeby Farms, the Chesterfield Cup winner had been with Ian Balding from a yearling.

SPANNER, 26: Dermot Weld's first winner as a trainer back in 1972 died on 2nd November, the same day as Vintage Crop's success in the Melbourne Cup. The horse also carried Weld to victory on three occasions in the Player Wills Amateur Riders Handicap at Galway.

TANGO TRIO, 2: The Nordance colt collapsed and died from a heart attack on the way to the winners' enclosure after victory at The Curragh in June. Owned by a syndicate he was Ben Lawlor's first winner of the season and first winner at Irish H.Q.

TERMINUS, 6: Fell and broke his neck at Southwell early in January. Bill Preece's entire was the first casualty of the new-look mini fence style hurdles.

THAKAWAH, 4: This injured horse was made to endure a long walk, despite protests, purely to be dope-tested. Two months after the bad fall at Wincanton a radiographic examination at Bristol University showed a serious break in his off-side shoulder. The Jim Old-trained gelding was put down in June.

THE ILLYWHACKER, 8: Put down in late March after the discovery that the Dawn Review gelding had sustained a hairline fracture of his near foreleg. Monitored daily, following his heavy fall in the Cathcart at Cheltenham, it was a great shock when the injury became obvious. An able chaser, this multiple winner was a gallant third to The Fellow in Kempton's King George VI Chase.

BROODMARES

BALLAQUINE, 16: Dam of the multiple Group winner Swing Low. She had a colt foal by Indian Ridge in early March but died six weeks later.

BROWN BERRY 33: Produced 19 foals, her last at the age of 26. These included Avatar (which see), French Derby winner Hours After, Stakes winner and sire Unconscious, dual French Pattern race winner and sire Monseigneur and nine other winners including the British-based stallion Komaite. Grandam of Hawkberry, she won six races including the Del Mar Debutante Stakes. She died in May.

GARDEN GREEN, 29: Unplaced herself she was dam of Wokingham Stakes hero and sire Le Johnstan, Kew Gardens and several other winners. Grandam of Tahilla and Mummy's Favourite. Her half-sister Brookfield Miss produced Fred Darling winner Littlefield and Vivante, the dual Pattern winning but savage Head for Heights, as well as the Listed winners Majestic Star and Very Sharp. She died in July.

MARMOLADA, 16: Suffered a haemorrhage in February at Sallyview Estates in Ireland. Winner of 13 races and 263,600,000 lire including Italian Oaks, Premio Lydia Tesio and three other lesser Group events. Dam of two winners including the Luca Cumani trained Masad, last year's Gran Premio d'Italia winner and Italian Derby third.

MELPOMENE, 5: Lord Carnarvon's home-bred Italian Listed race winner died in March after giving birth to a colt foal by Alzao. She was half-sister to the Cherry Hinton and Moyglare Stakes winner Lemon Souffle, herself injured during the Cheveley Park Stakes.

MY CHARMER, 24: The dam of American Triple Crown winner Seattle Slew, Two Thousand Guineas victor Lomond, Seattle Dancer and Argosy was put down in late November due to old age. She won six races from 32 starts for $34,133 and at stud bred six winners from eleven foals. In 1985 Seattle Dancer was auctioned for a world record price for a yearling of $13.1 million; he was sire of Seattle Rhyme (which see).

RICHFIELD LADY, 4: Champion Australian race mare who failed to recover from a leg operation in March. Winner of eight races from 14 outings she gleaned AUS$720,993 in stakes including the VRC Oaks. Retired after injury when fourth in the AJC Oaks, she was in foal to Last Tycoon. Substantial offers from abroad were all refused so she could be retained and her produce race in Australia.

WINDFALL VI, 25: Put down in early January she produced seven point-to-point winners including Old Applejack (which see) and Prince Pippin. A dual point-to-point winner herself and third in a Cheltenham hunter-chase she had her first foal in 1979.

STALLIONS

AVATAR, 20: Broke his neck in an accident at Frisch's Farm, Ohio, during January. Won nine races and $464,609 from 33 starts including Belmont Stakes (beating Foolish Pleasure), Santa Anita Derby and San Luis Rey Stakes. He was second to Foolish Pleasure in the Kentucky Derby. Sire of 17 Stakes winners including Honor Medal and Craelius. His dam Brown Berry (which see) produced 12 winners including four Stakes horses.

BALDSKI, 19: Half-brother to Capote and Exceller, the son of Nijinsky was put down in August after breaking a foreleg. Won seven races from three to five years and sired 36 Stakes winners.

BLETCHINGLY, 23: The big-name sire in Australian breeding of recent years died from a heart attack at Widden Stud in July. His racing career was curtailed after four wins from five outings due to weak forelegs. An immediate success at stud he was champion sire three times and champion sire of juveniles twice. Among his 46 Stakes winners was the first million-dollar earner Kingston Town, who won the prestigious W.S. Cox Plate on three occasions.

CANNONADE, 22: Victor of the 100th running of the Kentucky Derby was put down during the autumn due to old age. He won seven races and over $500,000. At stud he sired 26 Stakes winners including the Belmont hero Caveat.

CLASSIC MUSIC, 6: The unraced own-brother to Sadler's Wells and Fairy King died from a blood clot in mid-November. At 2,400,000 guineas he was the top-priced yearling of 1988. He stood at Coolmore and his first crop foals were sold in November.

DARING MARCH, 19: Put down at the Hedgeholme Stud, County Durham, in August. He won four races including the Northumberland Sprint Trophy and was Group placed five times. Sire of sound and durable racing stock, both Flat and N.H., of nearly 300 races.

DOMINION, 21: Died from a massive coronary in February after covering his second mare of the season at Aston Park Stud. A tough multiple Stakes winner in Europe and U.S.A., he won 14 times for £148,289 from 48 starts, including Prix Perth and Bernard Baruch Handicap; also second in Two Thousand Guineas. Champion juvenile sire twice and leading sire by races won for 1985 and 1987. Sire of 26 Stakes winners including Embla and the successful sires Nomination, Primo Dominie and Domynsky.

DOUBLE SCHWARTZ, 12: Died in January following a bout of colic at Ballysax Manor Stud. Champion sprinter of 1986 he won eight races and £160,397, including Prix de l'Abbaye de Longchamp, King George Stakes, Palace House Stakes and Temple Stakes. Sire of Cois na Tine, winner of the Futurity Stakes, and other Listed two-year-old winners.

K-BATTERY, 12: Put down in late-September following a four-hour operation to repair a badly fractured knee-bone. The son of Gunner B won nine races and £89,873 including the 1986 Lincoln Handicap and the following year's Earl of Sefton Stakes. Retired to stud in 1988, two of his first winners were trained, as he was, by Bill Elsey.

LORD BUD, 8: Destroyed during July after suffering from chronic peritonitis. The Listed race winning son of Lord Gayle had been re-located to Norton Grove Stud for the 1993 covering season. He won five times and was Group 1 placed at four years during a career in Ireland and U.S.A.

MORSTON, 23: Died in retirement at the Stud-on-the-Chart in late July. Unbeaten 1973 Derby winner and half-brother to Blakeney, a previous Derby winner also bred, owned and trained by Arthur Budgett. An international sire of winners including Morcon, Oraston (grandam of Island Magic), Charming Mary, Mr Fluorocarbon (which see), Valentinian and Whitstead.

MR FLUOROCARBON, 14: Striking Royal Ascot winner of the Queen Anne Stakes, three other races and Lingfield Derby Trial for £36,244. Dual purpose sire of winners under both Rules. Died during the covering season.

MUSIC BOY, 20: Died suddenly from an apparent heart attack at the Cheveley Park Stud in early May. Winner of five races as a juvenile including Gimcrack Stakes in record time and second in Flying Childers Stakes. Won King George Stakes at three for total prize money of £37,716. Sire of the winners of over 700 races world-wide worth in excess of £2,750,000. His principal winners include Mattaboy and the sprinters La Grange Music, Roaring Riva, Kind Music and Clantime.

NISHAPOUR, 18: Put down in September after suffering a recurrence of recent heart trouble. Won twice, including the 1978 French 2000 Guineas, when trained for owner/breeder the Aga Khan by Francois Mathet. Initially stood in Ireland siring French Derby victor Mouktar and Triumph Hurdle winner First Bout. Moved to Newmarket in 1987 and was responsible for this year's French Oaks heroine Shemaka. The half-brother to antipodean sensation Nassipour sired winners of over 475 races worth £2.5 million. He was buried near his paddock at Lanwades Stud.

NORTHFIELDS, 25: The Northern Dancer half-brother to Habitat died following an accident in his paddock during September. Winner of seven races and $195,071 from 30 outings he initially stood at Coolmore in Ireland and was sire of Northern Treasure, Northjet, North Stoke and Tootens. Exported to South Africa a decade ago he left his mark as a broodmare sire via such as Kooyonga and St. Jovite.

PERSIAN HEIGHTS, 8: Suffered a heart attack shortly after covering a mare at Coolmore's Castle Hyde Stud in March. Won four races and £229,142 including St. James's Palace Stakes, York's International Stakes (relegated to third), was placed second in Dubai Champion Stakes and third in Middle Park Stakes and Queen Elizabeth 11 Stakes. Champion first-season sire in 1992.

PITPAN, 24: Put down at Forke Farm Stud in March. A half-brother to Hotfoot, he won three Flat races in France and three hurdles in England. He initially stood in Ireland but returned to England in 1987. Numerous winning progeny over fences.

PRINCE REGENT, 27: Was found dead in his paddock at Collinstown Stud in May. Although semi-retired he still covered a few mares following renewed interest after the success of Remittance Man, Cybrandian and Tinryland. Trained in France, he won six races and £153,283 including the Irish Sweeps Derby and although standing in both Ireland and England failed to sire anything near his own calibre from his 400-plus winners under both Rules.

SALMON LEAP, 13: Son of Northern Dancer and half-brother to Kings Lake and Cloonlara. Died in Japan during September after spells at stud in Ireland and Australia. Won four races, £53,081, was fourth in 1983 Derby and sired 48 winners including 15 Stakes events.

SHAM, 23: Suffered a heart attack at The Walmac International establishment in U.S.A. during the spring. Won five races and $204,808 including the Santa Anita Derby and was second to Secretariat in the Kentucky Derby and Preakness Stakes. He sired Irish 2000 Guineas winner Jaazeiro and the Grade 1 winning fillies Arewehavingfunyet and Safe Play. Produced the dams of Defensive Play, Dixie Brass and Vers La Caisse.

SILENT SCREEN, 26: Humanely destroyed in March at Gainesway Farm due to chronic laminitis and old age. Juvenile champion and winner of seven races for $514,388, he sired the earners of over $15.5 million including 38 Stakes winners. Maternal sire of Peter Davies.

SOVEREIGN RED, 15: Australian-based son of Sir Tristram and foundation sire at Trans Media Park Stud in New South Wales died after a bout of colic in June. Won nine races and himself sired the winners of over 4.2 million Australian dollars including Red Express.

VAL DE L'ORNE, 21: Destroyed after an accident in the covering barn at Rockburn Farm, Virginia, in June. Won four races from five starts and 2,049,707 francs including French Derby, Prix Noailles and Prix Hocquart. Second in Grand Criterium as a juvenile. Stood initially in France, then Canada before moving to the U.S.A. Sire of Japan Cup victor Pay The Butler. A notable maternal sire.

NATIONAL HUNT STATISTICS 1992–93

Principal winners: hurdles and chases 1992–93

Owners

	Horses	Races Won	Value £
Mrs J Mould	9	18	145,788
Mrs Shirley Robins	12	16	144,375
R F Eliot	2	4	137,700
Marquesa de Moratalla	5	12	128,302
J N Yeadon	2	4	125,142
G M MacEchern	1	8	115,682
Pell-Mell Partners	22	27	114,062
G A Hubbard	31	23	105,277
P Piller	27	33	90,433
Eric Scarth	1	1	84,734
Mrs Millicent R Freethy	1	4	80,510
M & N Plant Ltd	4	10	76,720

Trainers

	Horses	Races Won	Value £
M C Pipe	143	194	808,012
D Nicholson	73	100	492,480
N A Twiston-Davies	63	76	451,332
G Richards	88	104	327,714
J T Gifford	67	49	285,899
J G FitzGerald	66	62	260,812
Mrs M Reveley	91	90	250,548
N J Henderson	77	53	242,924
G B Balding	52	38	212,445
K C Bailey	63	57	170,188
P Beaumont	22	19	162,642
Andrew Turnell	35	37	161,247

Jockeys

	1st	2nd	3rd	Unpl	Total Mts	Per cent
R Dunwoody	173	120	89	357	739	23.4
P Scudamore	129	75	47	165	416	31.0
A Maguire	124	118	97	383	722	17.2
P Niven	108	62	52	164	386	28.0
J Osborne	102	71	61	266	500	20.4
G McCourt	70	61	61	238	430	16.3
N Doughty	69	36	33	125	263	26.2
C Llewellyn	68	43	50	251	412	16.5
M Dwyer	61	58	47	150	316	19.3
C Grant	58	56	49	256	419	13.8
Peter Hobbs	51	49	37	181	318	16.0
S McNeill	51	36	47	251	385	13.2

Conditional Jockeys

	1st	2nd	3rd	Unpl	Total Mts	Per cent
M A Fitzgerald	54	51	50	271	426	12.7
D Bridgwater	39	41	42	233	355	11.0
W Marston	26	32	27	181	266	9.8
N Bentley	25	19	13	83	140	17.9
A Dobbin	23	24	14	107	168	13.7
M Foster	21	18	17	63	119	17.6
M Hourigan	21	18	18	167	224	9.4
Diane Clay	19	15	8	69	111	17.1
P Hide	19	24	10	82	135	14.1
J McCarthy	18	7	13	47	85	21.2
R Greene	17	10	23	113	163	10.4
R Hodge	17	16	12	91	136	12.5

Amateur Riders

	1st	2nd	3rd	Unpl	Total Mts	Per cent
A Thornton	26	27	12	81	146	17.8
T Jenks	20	18	19	71	128	15.6
J Greenall	12	6	2	7	27	44.4
S Swiers	12	6	3	37	58	20.7
M Buckley	9	8	8	21	46	19.6
C Burnett-Wells	9	7	6	32	54	16.7
T Byrne	9	7	2	30	48	18.8
J Durkan	9	8	6	47	70	12.9

Sires

	Winners	Races Won	Value £
Deep Run (1966) by Pampered King	51	94	622,660
Strong Gale (1975) by Lord Gayle (USA)	43	96	479,293
Crash Course (1971) by Busted	10	16	192,552
The Parson (1968) by Aureole	28	54	185,261
Furry Glen (1971) by Wolver Hollow	24	57	170,902
Over The River (FR) (1974) by Luthier	20	34	146,486
High Line (1966) by High Hat	6	15	129,895
Buckskin (FR) (1973) by Yelapa (FR)	20	36	120,845
Import (1971) by Porto Bello	1	8	115,682
Glint of Gold (1978) by Mill Reef (USA)	7	19	115,441
Ardross (1976) by Run the Gantlet	16	37	102,526
Kambalda (1970) by Right Royal V	12	34	101,859

Leading Horses

	No. of Races	Value £
Deep Sensation (8) ch g by Deep Run out of Bannow Bay	3	134,854
Jodami (8) b g by Crash Course out of Masterstown Lucy	3	122,322
Young Hustler (6) ch g by Import out of Davett	8	115,682
Granville Again (7) ch g by Deep Run out of High Board	1	84,734
Run For Free (9) b g by Deep Run out of Credit Card	4	80,510
Mighty Mogul (6) ch g by Good Thyne (USA) out of Deep Shine	5	67,385
Topsham Bay (10) b g by Proverb out of Biowen	2	62,416
Olympian (6) ch g by High Line out of Elysian	3	59,890
Valfinet (FR) (6) b g by Maiymad out of Oland (FR)	5	55,556
Sybillin (7) b g by Henbit (USA) out of Tea House	5	55,101
Sibton Abbey (8) b g by Strong Gale out of Bally Decent	4	53,638
Morley Street (9) ch g by Deep Run out of High Board	2	52,858

Winning owners: hurdles and chases 1992–93

H = Horses; R = Runners; W = Winners; 2 = Seconds; 3 = Thirds; %W-R = Percentage of winners to runners; £WIN = Win money; £W/P = Win and place money

	H	R	W	2nd	3rd	%W-R	£WIN	£W/P
QUEEN ELIZABETH THE QUEEN MOTHER	10	43	3	9	5	7.0	7,363	18,217
19th Hole Partnership	1	6	2	0	1	33.3	4,123	4,333
3 J's Racing	1	6	1	1	0	16.7	1,305	1,714
Aboobaker, NY	1	4	1	0	1	25.0	1,807	2,036
Adam, James R	4	12	1	0	0	8.3	1,446	1,446
Adams, Mrs Sue	1	3	1	0	0	33.3	1,305	1,305
Adams, S P	1	6	3	1	0	50.0	8,199	9,323
Aedean Chem & Industrial Flooring Ltd	1	7	1	2	1	14.3	1,302	2,851
A F Budge (Equine) Limited	16	32	5	10	6	15.6	12,166	21,780
Albert, Mrs Revel Guest	1	5	2	2	1	40.0	3,781	5,773
Albury Racing Limited	5	21	5	2	4	23.8	13,999	16,072
Alias Smith & Jones Racing	1	7	1	2	1	14.3	10,143	39,726
Allan, C J	1	11	3	3	0	27.3	7,269	9,620
Allen, Mrs J M	1	6	1	2	0	16.7	825	2,190
Allen, Robert	1	6	2	1	0	33.3	8,096	8,768
Allen, Mrs Richard	1	6	1	1	1	16.7	1,940	2,568
Allen, J	3	21	2	1	2	9.5	2,968	3,964
Allen, Peter J	2	5	1	0	1	20.0	2,553	3,088
Allen, M M	1	6	2	1	1	33.3	4,541	5,467
Allen, Mrs A P B	1	6	2	2	0	33.3	3,128	4,132
Allendale, Sarah Lady	1	10	5	0	0	50.0	12,335	12,501
Allison, M	2	4	1	0	1	25.0	1,424	1,595
Allison, F D	3	19	3	1	1	15.8	6,455	7,187
Allison, Miss K	1	7	1	0	0	14.3	1,480	1,480
Allright, A J	3	19	2	1	3	10.5	4,836	6,511
Al Maktoum, Sheikh Marwan	3	13	3	2	2	23.1	10,313	12,979
Alner, R	8	24	3	2	0	12.5	7,613	16,553
Al-Sabah, Mohammed	2	9	1	0	2	11.1	1,868	2,326
Alwen, Mrs Heather	2	8	1	1	0	12.5	1,714	2,509
American Technical Publishers Ltd	2	26	3	4	4	11.5	6,491	10,028
Amtrak Express Parcels Limited	2	11	4	0	1	36.4	16,418	16,677
Amy, G B	1	3	1	1	1	33.3	2,345	3,208
Anderson, N G	1	1	1	0	0	100.0	2,153	2,153
Andrews, J R	1	6	1	3	1	16.7	2,294	6,309
Andrews Freight Services Ltd	2	4	1	1	0	25.0	1,256	1,727
Anrude, S	1	5	2	0	2	40.0	5,285	7,911
Antonelli, A	1	2	1	0	0	50.0	2,058	2,058
Apollo Excellsior Racing	3	16	1	1	1	6.3	1,537	2,236
Aquarius	1	6	2	1	0	33.3	5,079	5,764
Armitage, Ian	1	5	1	0	0	20.0	2,327	2,327
Armitage, D H	1	5	2	2	0	40.0	4,149	5,459
Armstrong/Greenwell	2	12	1	1	2	8.3	1,953	3,330
Arthur, Dave	1	6	1	0	1	16.7	1,734	1,953
Askew, Mrs J N	4	27	2	2	5	7.4	4,403	7,283
Astaire, Steven	2	17	1	2	4	5.9	1,106	3,695
Atholl, Duke Of	3	30	5	3	1	16.7	15,969	25,411
Atkinson, Eric	1	1	1	0	0	100.0	1,604	1,604
Bailey, A	1	1	1	0	0	100.0	1,758	1,758
Bailey, K C	2	11	3	2	1	27.3	4,612	5,877
Bailey, Malcolm	1	3	2	0	0	66.7	3,840	3,840
Bailey, D S	1	5	1	0	0	20.0	1,778	1,778
Baines, R H	1	9	3	1	1	33.3	40,547	57,939
Baker, I A	1	4	2	2	0	50.0	4,255	5,372
Baker, Miss Deborah J	4	18	1	0	1	5.6	4,570	5,065
Bance, J F	1	7	1	3	0	14.3	2,348	4,775
Bancroft, Patrick	3	15	1	1	1	6.7	4,305	9,444
Banks, M C	4	14	2	3	1	14.3	4,358	8,162
Barber, J J	2	14	3	3	3	21.4	14,374	19,593
Barber, Mrs Marianne G	1	9	1	1	3	11.1	2,129	4,240
Barclay, Mrs C	1	5	1	2	1	20.0	2,042	3,221
Barker, Joy & Jim	2	15	2	1	1	13.3	3,008	3,557

	H	R	W	2nd	3rd	%W-R	£WIN	£W/P
Barnes, T A	2	18	2	4	2	11.1	4,250	6,878
Barnes, R H L	1	5	1	1	1	20.0	2,738	4,149
Barnes, M.	3	13	1	3	1	7.7	1,305	3,168
Barnett, George	4	21	6	2	3	28.6	11,271	13,821
Bar-One Racing	2	7	1	0	1	14.3	2,478	3,271
Barons, D H	7	24	2	3	3	8.3	3,249	5,276
Barr, F.	4	18	1	3	2	5.6	1,763	6,231
Barr, Tom	2	18	1	3	4	5.6	825	4,570
Barron, Miss N J	1	4	1	1	1	25.0	2,023	2,916
Barry, Denis	2	12	1	1	2	8.3	1,969	3,008
Barwell, Mrs M	1	8	1	1	1	12.5	3,028	6,772
B A S Limited	2	17	4	2	0	23.5	6,494	8,147
Bassett, R J	1	13	1	1	2	7.7	2,218	3,226
Bassi, S S	1	8	2	0	1	25.0	3,817	4,046
Batey, B	1	8	4	3	0	50.0	13,735	17,487
Baugh, Mrs Diane	8	34	2	1	6	5.9	2,839	4,714
Baxter, M J	1	3	1	0	0	33.3	3,078	3,078
Bayliss, Mrs M A	1	9	1	0	1	11.1	2,355	2,667
Bayman, A.	1	7	2	0	2	28.6	4,614	6,272
Beamhurst Racing	1	9	4	1	0	44.4	15,083	15,543
Beaumont, Mrs M R	3	14	1	1	3	7.1	1,165	3,092
Beavan, J O	1	11	1	1	3	9.1	3,453	5,757
Beck, J N	1	7	2	4	0	28.6	5,508	8,797
Bell, K W	3	14	1	1	4	7.1	1,996	9,165
Bell, David	3	12	4	3	1	33.3	9,568	11,775
Bennett, T H	3	16	3	1	7	18.8	8,748	13,141
Bentinck, Lady Anne	7	38	7	4	5	18.4	12,581	15,745
Bentley, D	2	11	2	1	1	18.2	3,327	4,100
Beresford, D M.	2	4	1	1	1	25.0	1,529	2,042
Berkshire Commercial Components Ltd	4	28	3	3	3	10.7	7,889	17,483
Bertram, Mrs Lorna	1	6	2	1	0	33.3	5,204	5,739
Beswick, D A	1	7	2	1	0	28.6	6,665	8,057
Bethell, R A	5	16	3	2	3	18.8	6,714	8,897
Bettaney, M A.	1	1	1	0	0	100.0	2,626	2,626
Bewley, R.	1	1	1	0	0	100.0	1,865	1,865
Bianchi, J A	6	47	3	3	6	6.4	5,687	8,557
Bill, Mrs Brenda	2	15	1	0	4	6.7	2,054	3,852
Bingdon Builders Ltd	1	4	1	0	1	25.0	1,305	1,536
Bird, Mrs M W	3	18	3	2	3	16.7	2,551	5,470
Bird, Mrs S J	1	6	1	1	0	16.7	1,523	2,395
Bird, C	1	4	1	0	0	25.0	2,788	2,788
Bird, Mrs N J	1	6	1	1	0	16.7	3,591	4,246
Birlem Oils Ltd	3	15	1	0	0	6.7	1,705	1,705
Bisgrove, Miss H A	2	26	9	4	1	34.6	28,529	43,237
Bisgrove, Mrs M A	1	8	3	2	2	37.5	7,987	15,859
Bishop, Mrs Jean R	6	23	4	4	3	17.4	8,715	13,109
Bishop, S	1	11	1	0	1	9.1	2,164	2,817
Bissill, Mrs C	1	8	2	3	1	25.0	4,033	6,527
Black, A G	2	7	1	0	1	14.3	1,632	1,769
Black, W M G	3	15	1	2	1	6.7	5,918	7,962
Black, Mrs C J	2	8	1	0	1	12.5	2,640	3,298
Blackburn, Michael	1	6	1	1	1	16.7	3,068	4,154
Blair, Nick	1	8	2	0	1	25.0	3,442	3,775
Bletsoe, M C	1	4	1	0	0	25.0	2,136	2,136
Bloodstock, PCJF	1	9	1	0	1	11.1	2,489	3,104
Bloxham, G C	1	3	1	0	0	33.3	1,763	1,763
Blue Diablo Associates	1	10	1	1	3	10.0	1,473	3,181
Boddington, M A	2	10	1	2	0	10.0	3,908	5,772
Boden, A P	1	8	1	0	1	12.5	2,794	3,522
Bolsover, John	1	3	1	0	0	33.3	1,924	1,924
Bond, David	1	8	3	0	2	37.5	7,216	7,919
Boot, Ken	1	5	1	0	0	20.0	1,830	1,830
Bostock, Mrs M	1	6	1	0	0	16.7	872	872
Bostock, J R	4	11	1	1	0	9.1	1,484	1,839
Bottomley, P	2	11	1	1	0	9.1	3,407	4,379
Bottomley, John F	2	9	1	0	0	11.1	2,128	2,128
Boucher, Mrs Eric	2	8	2	1	1	25.0	4,222	6,403
Boucher, Mrs Enid M	2	10	3	0	1	30.0	4,111	4,505
Bowden, Mrs D F	1	8	1	3	1	12.5	1,738	3,958
Bowden, R W L	2	12	3	2	2	25.0	20,271	25,633
Bowker, D	1	7	1	1	2	14.3	2,206	4,026
Bowkett, David L	1	13	2	2	4	15.4	5,784	8,466
Bowles, Lee	2	7	1	1	0	14.3	1,553	2,198
Bowling, Mark	1	7	5	0	0	71.4	14,734	15,739
Boyd, M C	3	23	4	2	6	17.4	12,554	16,952
Boyd-Rochfort, A.	1	9	3	3	0	33.3	4,764	8,060
Brackenbury, Mrs R.	2	6	2	2	0	33.3	7,175	10,083
Bradley, Paul	4	15	1	3	3	6.7	1,564	5,741
Bramall, Miss K S	1	4	1	1	0	25.0	1,872	2,752

	H	R	W	2nd	3rd	%W-R	£WIN	£W/P
Bramall, Mrs S A	14	77	8	7	7	10.4	20,125	28,267
Bramall, D C A	2	13	1	2	1	7.7	2,801	4,995
Brankin, Stuart Thomas	2	11	3	0	1	27.3	5,557	5,769
Brasher, Mrs Shirley	1	8	2	0	1	25.0	3,536	3,892
Bray, I.	3	12	2	0	3	16.7	2,951	3,856
Brazier, R	2	11	2	1	1	18.2	3,465	4,200
B R B Partners	1	4	1	0	0	25.0	2,093	2,093
Brennan, O	5	29	7	6	6	24.1	14,436	19,297
Brennan, Miss Cindy	2	17	2	4	1	11.8	5,860	7,914
Brereton, B R	2	15	1	1	3	6.7	2,741	4,752
Brewer, S H J	1	9	2	1	2	22.2	5,539	6,802
Brewis, R	4	19	2	1	4	10.5	12,179	16,992
Brian William Developments Ltd	1	2	1	0	1	50.0	1,384	1,549
Brigadier Racing	1	7	1	1	2	14.3	5,920	8,472
Briggs, E	2	10	3	1	1	30.0	7,649	13,663
Brisbane, Mrs G M	1	3	2	1	0	66.7	9,121	10,769
Britten, K R	2	11	2	1	1	18.2	5,631	7,875
Broad, Mrs A J	2	7	1	1	0	14.3	1,847	2,517
Brock, Mrs Maragaret M	1	2	1	0	1	50.0	1,488	1,722
Brookhouse, Mrs S J	1	7	1	3	0	14.3	2,285	3,663
Brooks, C P E	5	9	2	1	1	22.2	4,636	5,365
Brooks, Mrs P Margetson	2	10	1	0	1	10.0	1,772	1,877
Brooks, Ben	1	3	1	1	0	33.3	10,820	11,900
Brooks, T G	1	10	2	1	1	20.0	6,966	9,205
Brooks, Mrs M E	1	5	1	0	1	20.0	1,900	2,219
Broom, Frank J	2	9	1	1	0	11.1	2,898	3,518
Brotherton, C N	1	3	1	1	1	33.3	1,340	1,921
Broughton, Martin	1	6	1	2	0	16.7	1,484	2,178
Brown, Graham	5	20	1	1	3	5.0	2,064	3,339
Brown, Lady	1	6	1	1	2	16.7	1,172	2,436
Brown, Christopher P J	5	23	1	4	2	4.3	1,411	3,788
Brown, N	1	12	2	3	1	16.7	4,058	5,876
Brown, Mrs E	1	10	2	0	0	20.0	5,669	6,345
Brown, Mrs H	3	6	1	1	1	16.7	2,574	3,744
Brown, Mrs A L	1	10	3	3	1	30.0	8,246	12,528
Brown, J M	1	10	2	3	0	20.0	3,469	7,008
Brown, Hector H	2	4	1	2	0	25.0	1,663	2,642
Brown, Errol	1	6	1	2	1	16.7	3,084	9,711
Brown, S R	1	12	2	2	3	16.7	3,992	5,779
Brown, Mrs T	3	16	1	5	2	6.3	3,087	6,972
Brown, D H	3	13	1	4	3	7.7	2,337	5,713
Browne, J W	1	5	1	1	0	20.0	1,140	1,758
Browne, Mrs P B	1	6	2	4	0	33.3	2,955	5,508
Bryan, A G	1	1	1	0	0	100.0	1,675	1,675
Brydon, D A D	1	4	1	2	0	25.0	1,968	2,805
Buchanan, Mrs F	1	10	1	0	2	10.0	2,976	3,449
Buckle, Colin J	2	16	2	4	5	12.5	9,218	21,430
Buckle, D	1	7	2	3	0	28.6	3,611	5,788
Buckler, R H	1	1	1	0	0	100.0	1,950	1,950
Buckley, Michael	4	23	6	3	3	26.1	38,959	51,013
Buckley, C C	3	11	2	1	4	18.2	4,408	8,750
Budd, C	2	11	1	2	2	9.1	1,606	3,118
Budge, Mrs A F	1	3	1	1	0	33.3	3,056	3,734
Budge, K F	1	9	1	1	0	11.1	3,002	3,680
Bulwer-Long, Capt W H	3	6	1	1	0	16.7	3,002	3,867
Burges, Major-Gen R L T	2	12	2	3	0	16.7	7,191	9,844
Burke, Mrs Elaine M	4	15	1	1	1	6.7	1,954	2,927
Burkett, Mrs D	2	5	1	0	0	20.0	1,480	1,480
Burley, James	3	10	1	2	1	10.0	2,898	5,548
Burnard, B P	1	11	1	4	0	9.1	2,075	4,568
Burnett, Mrs June	1	9	1	0	2	11.1	1,805	2,729
Burrell, Peter	1	5	3	0	0	60.0	9,000	9,000
Burrough, B R H	1	6	2	2	0	33.3	3,275	4,501
Burt & Travica Contractors Ltd	1	10	2	2	1	20.0	3,975	6,194
Burton, Mrs A	5	32	5	1	2	15.6	8,933	10,489
Burton, Phillip	2	2	2	0	0	100.0	4,082	4,082
Bush, N D J	1	7	1	1	1	14.3	2,924	6,980
Bush, L M	1	6	1	2	0	16.7	2,110	3,180
Butler, Mrs P A L	3	10	1	0	2	10.0	1,730	2,147
Butt, H S	1	2	1	0	1	50.0	1,744	1,929
Buzzeo, Joe	2	8	2	1	1	25.0	3,430	4,531
Bychance Racing	1	8	2	1	1	25.0	8,859	10,578
C, White City All Stars C	2	8	1	0	2	12.5	1,998	2,377
Cable, J D	1	2	1	0	0	50.0	2,330	2,330
Caddy, Mrs M	2	12	1	0	0	8.3	1,305	1,305
Cadogan, Lady	1	4	1	0	0	25.0	1,206	1,206
Cadogan, Lord	6	18	3	1	2	16.7	5,496	6,564
Cadoret, Alan C	1	7	2	1	1	28.6	4,283	4,955
Cahill, Bill	3	9	3	0	0	33.3	10,005	10,005

	H	R	W	2nd	3rd	%W-R	£WIN	£W/P
Caine, Mrs Monica	1	10	3	5	0	30.0	15,149	33,489
Cairns, Alan	3	20	1	1	1	5.0	2,222	4,810
Calder Racing	1	6	2	3	0	33.3	3,647	4,939
Caldwell, T H	9	21	2	0	4	9.5	5,463	6,789
Calvert, J	1	4	2	0	0	50.0	5,324	5,621
Camis, Fred	1	8	1	0	1	12.5	1,484	1,678
Campbell, James	1	6	1	2	2	16.7	13,420	30,313
Campbell, G	2	25	3	5	4	12.0	5,581	11,292
Campbell, Mrs Angus	2	2	1	0	0	50.0	1,456	1,456
Cann, J Grant	1	1	1	0	0	100.0	3,610	3,610
Cantillon, Don	3	11	3	2	0	27.3	4,324	5,285
Carnell, H G & Son Ltd	2	5	1	1	0	20.0	2,120	2,686
Carnoustie Racing Club Ltd	1	6	2	2	1	33.3	4,027	5,389
Carr, Ken	1	10	3	2	1	30.0	7,815	10,395
Carr, Peter	2	14	3	3	0	21.4	5,386	6,852
Carr, Mrs R C	1	8	1	2	0	12.5	2,762	6,933
Carroll, Miss N	1	5	3	0	0	60.0	4,918	4,918
Carruthers, Tom	1	2	1	0	0	50.0	1,796	1,796
Carr-Walker, Mrs L M	1	4	3	0	0	75.0	8,472	8,472
Carter, E	2	7	1	1	1	14.3	1,845	5,663
Carter, O J	5	19	1	2	2	5.3	1,776	5,046
Cartwright, M F	1	6	1	0	0	16.7	1,953	1,953
Carver, L	1	14	10	2	0	71.4	16,681	17,842
Carvill, R K	1	8	1	1	1	12.5	1,435	2,170
Catherwood, Mrs Stewart	3	29	6	5	5	20.7	15,192	29,753
Catstrey, W E	1	5	1	2	0	20.0	2,374	3,461
Cavendish, Lord	2	16	4	0	4	25.0	11,492	13,164
Cawte, Mrs C M G	1	5	1	2	0	20.0	2,005	3,031
C F Hunter Ltd	1	21	5	4	2	23.8	8,188	13,639
Chadwick, S	8	42	2	1	1	4.8	4,156	5,187
Chadwick, Roy	1	6	3	1	0	50.0	32,459	36,341
Chakko, Mrs Heather	1	4	1	0	0	25.0	1,697	1,697
Champion, Mrs D F	3	8	1	0	1	12.5	3,294	3,974
Channing-Williams, S	1	2	1	0	0	50.0	1,534	1,534
Channon, M	2	10	3	3	0	30.0	3,703	5,798
Chapman, F A P	1	3	2	1	0	66.7	5,543	6,543
Chard, J	1	7	1	1	1	14.3	2,827	3,667
Charles Saunders & Partners	1	5	1	0	0	20.0	15,500	15,500
Charlton, J I A	4	15	2	1	2	13.3	3,329	6,562
Cheatle, J N	3	8	1	1	0	12.5	1,004	1,492
Cheesbrough, I D	1	5	1	2	0	20.0	2,322	4,188
Cheesbrough, P	2	13	2	1	2	15.4	9,858	10,914
Chelsea, Lord	8	40	12	7	7	30.0	26,660	33,604
Chester, J R	2	9	1	2	2	11.1	2,566	4,749
Chetwode, Lord	1	11	2	3	0	18.2	5,589	9,372
Chilcott, D W	1	11	2	3	4	18.2	2,943	5,692
Chilton, David	2	3	1	0	0	33.3	2,201	2,201
Chisholm, Gary	1	3	1	0	1	33.3	2,559	3,017
Christian, Simon	1	2	1	0	0	50.0	2,355	2,355
Christodoulou, Athos	1	3	2	0	1	66.7	30,975	46,478
C I P Racing	1	9	2	0	1	22.2	3,119	3,393
Clark, Mrs Z S	2	2	1	0	1	50.0	1,350	1,515
Clarke, Mrs H J	7	31	9	9	3	29.0	39,564	60,890
Clarke, Peter C	2	6	1	3	1	16.7	1,734	3,792
Clay, Tony	1	4	2	1	0	50.0	2,397	2,837
Clayton, J	1	12	2	3	1	16.7	4,626	6,594
Cleave, A	1	7	1	0	1	14.3	1,772	2,072
Clegg, Tony	2	3	1	0	0	33.3	1,564	1,564
Clegg, Mrs Sylvia	1	6	3	1	1	50.0	6,353	8,371
Cliff, R V	1	6	3	2	0	50.0	7,613	9,505
Clutton, Lady Sarah	2	12	5	1	1	41.7	12,121	13,135
Coard, D C	1	8	1	0	1	12.5	2,260	2,528
Coathup, Mrs J	5	22	1	2	2	4.5	1,581	3,186
Cohen, Andrew L	8	43	9	7	5	20.9	20,872	27,360
Cohen, Mrs Wendy	2	11	3	1	3	27.3	28,904	37,800
Cole, Mrs Veronica	1	8	5	1	0	62.5	20,577	21,241
Coleman, Mrs Dianne J	1	8	1	2	3	12.5	3,014	6,970
Coley, Mrs B J	1	9	1	0	1	11.1	788	1,008
Collingridge, H J	2	15	3	0	0	20.0	7,637	8,066
Collins, Jack	1	8	2	0	0	25.0	3,736	3,736
Collins, J E H	2	6	2	0	1	33.3	26,767	27,360
Collins, A K	2	10	1	1	3	10.0	2,285	3,465
Connaught Group Ltd	2	3	1	0	0	33.3	2,400	2,400
Connop, T	1	5	1	0	0	20.0	2,786	2,786
Cook, John	1	13	3	3	1	23.1	4,740	6,755
Cook, Nick	2	8	2	3	0	25.0	6,086	22,064
Cook, W R	1	7	3	1	0	42.9	10,416	10,864
Coombe, Mrs N M	1	2	2	0	0	100.0	3,276	3,276
Coombs, D W E	2	9	1	1	3	11.1	2,469	4,011

	H	R	W	2nd	3rd	%W-R	£WIN	£W/P
Cooper, John A	1	4	1	1	0	25.0	1,576	2,088
Corbett, Mrs J M	2	9	2	2	0	22.2	4,419	6,061
Corinthian Thoroughbreds Plc	1	2	1	0	0	50.0	1,953	1,953
Cornwell, C	1	4	1	2	1	25.0	1,475	2,590
Cosgrove, Mrs Joan	1	6	1	1	1	16.7	2,365	3,911
Costello, K	1	7	3	2	0	42.9	35,292	63,671
Cottrell, A J	1	9	1	0	2	11.1	2,042	3,192
Coulter, Paul	1	4	1	0	1	25.0	1,822	2,074
Courage, C J	1	11	3	1	2	27.3	16,090	17,932
Cowan, J	3	9	2	1	1	22.2	3,368	4,147
Craddock, D	1	5	1	0	1	20.0	1,710	1,915
Craggs, P F	2	3	1	0	0	33.3	6,775	6,775
Craig, J M	1	10	1	1	1	10.0	2,175	3,206
Cresswell, P S	1	6	1	0	0	16.7	2,198	2,198
Crook, Alan	1	5	1	0	1	20.0	1,660	1,909
Culley, Brian	1	6	2	0	0	33.3	4,928	4,928
Cumbrian Racing Club	2	8	3	1	0	37.5	6,515	6,943
Cundell, P D	10	33	7	5	2	21.2	12,721	16,232
Curley, Mrs B J	7	14	1	3	0	7.1	2,056	4,117
Currie, David	2	19	3	5	5	15.8	7,352	13,113
Currie Group	1	4	2	1	1	50.0	3,101	3,977
Currie, Lt Col J C	1	1	1	0	0	100.0	1,446	1,446
Curry, T M J	1	7	1	1	0	14.3	2,803	4,051
Curtis, P C N	1	10	4	3	1	40.0	8,023	10,168
Curtis, J W P	3	18	3	0	0	16.7	5,554	5,554
Cutcliffe, Miss S J	1	11	5	1	1	45.5	12,590	14,561
D A & M Lambert And Partners	1	7	1	0	2	14.3	2,008	2,438
Dagg, R B	1	6	5	0	0	83.3	9,291	9,291
Dahlawi, Sheikh Amin	1	5	2	0	1	40.0	4,278	4,563
Daley, E H	1	4	2	0	0	50.0	2,896	2,896
Dalgetty, T N	1	9	2	2	2	22.2	4,078	6,268
Dalgleish, Ian G M	2	10	2	3	1	20.0	4,089	6,088
Daniels, J	1	5	2	1	0	40.0	4,023	4,584
Darby, R	1	3	1	0	0	33.3	3,488	4,081
Dare, K L	2	9	2	0	2	22.2	3,078	3,423
Darlington, A M	2	11	1	3	0	9.1	2,411	5,532
Dartford, Mrs C M	2	13	3	3	2	23.1	6,740	10,506
Date (Bloodstock) Ltd	1	3	1	0	1	33.3	1,882	2,090
Datum Building Supplies Limited	1	4	1	0	1	25.0	1,764	2,196
Davenport, Mrs J M	4	26	4	6	3	15.4	12,025	26,171
Davies, D A	10	45	2	4	8	4.4	3,008	10,886
Davies, I L	1	4	1	0	0	25.0	830	830
Davies, M W	2	4	1	0	0	25.0	1,530	1,530
Davies, Miss L H	1	10	2	1	1	20.0	3,377	4,049
Davies, Philip	1	10	3	2	2	30.0	7,101	9,536
Davies, W	1	11	1	0	1	9.1	1,861	2,212
Davis, Miss L A	1	7	1	1	2	14.3	3,480	5,122
Davison, Mrs Gail	6	18	1	1	1	5.6	3,704	5,003
Dawes, Mike	1	5	1	1	0	20.0	1,485	2,393
Dawson, R S G	1	7	1	0	1	14.3	2,605	2,798
Dawson, Ron	2	7	2	3	2	28.6	4,227	6,020
Dawson, C D	1	1	1	0	0	100.0	2,369	2,369
Deacon, Dennis	7	42	1	5	6	2.4	2,623	7,233
Deal, P A	4	11	4	1	0	36.4	13,757	14,741
Deal, A L	2	13	1	1	4	7.7	2,399	4,506
Dean, Richard	2	22	2	1	8	9.1	3,741	6,395
Deasley, M J	2	4	1	0	1	25.0	962	1,115
Deeley, M R	2	11	5	4	0	45.5	74,551	101,548
Deer, D J	2	4	1	0	0	25.0	1,940	1,940
Delamere Partnership	1	9	2	1	3	22.2	3,363	4,446
Delton Syndicate	1	1	1	0	0	100.0	20,859	20,859
De Moratalla, Marquesa	5	26	12	1	6	46.2	128,302	153,497
Dempster, Nigel	2	6	1	1	2	16.7	2,820	5,060
Denham, Michael	1	3	1	0	0	33.3	1,688	1,688
Dening, Exors Of The Late Mr Paul	1	3	1	0	0	33.3	1,670	1,670
Denney, G	3	10	2	2	0	20.0	4,686	5,448
Denney, Exors Of The Late Mr G	2	5	1	0	0	20.0	2,716	2,716
Dennis, Russell	1	2	1	1	0	50.0	3,630	4,526
Devlin, Michael	2	8	2	1	0	25.0	5,605	6,469
Dextra Lighting Systems	1	8	2	4	0	25.0	5,947	8,757
Dibben, Mrs J M F	2	7	1	2	0	14.3	1,553	3,155
Dicarlucci, Mrs Lena	1	4	2	1	0	50.0	3,805	4,131
Dick, J	1	4	3	0	0	75.0	6,890	7,730
Dickin, Mrs C M	3	13	1	1	2	7.7	2,159	4,561
Dickinson, A	1	3	1	0	2	33.3	1,574	2,112
Dickinson, Mrs M	1	6	2	0	1	33.3	4,457	5,451
Dickinson, F A	3	13	2	2	1	15.4	5,378	8,231
Dick Richardson Horse Racing Limited	1	7	1	1	1	14.3	2,063	3,263
Disney, M J	2	13	5	2	2	38.5	12,198	14,324

	H	R	W	2nd	3rd	%W-R	£WIN	£W/P
Dixey, Charles	1	4	1	2	0	25.0	1,204	2,653
D Needham & Partners	1	10	3	1	0	30.0	7,204	8,076
Doble, G A	1	9	1	1	0	11.1	2,624	4,276
Dodgson, Mrs M	1	13	2	1	1	15.4	3,726	5,076
Dods, M J K	1	9	3	2	3	33.3	7,470	10,740
Doherty, Mrs T	1	2	1	0	1	50.0	1,893	2,198
Donnellon, Austin	1	11	2	3	2	18.2	5,711	7,818
Donnelly, T W	2	17	2	2	1	11.8	5,432	7,321
Donnelly, Oliver	2	19	1	5	3	5.3	9,990	20,284
Doocey, Michael	1	2	1	0	0	50.0	2,758	2,758
Dore, W H	10	46	4	8	3	8.7	8,720	23,859
Dougall, J	1	11	5	2	2	45.5	15,744	18,462
Douglas, Dave	1	5	1	2	0	20.0	1,165	2,772
Douglas-Pennant, Miss S	2	12	2	3	2	16.7	5,686	9,331
Drawact Ltd	1	7	3	3	0	42.9	7,965	27,506
Dresher, Mrs L M	2	11	2	2	3	18.2	4,690	8,848
Duckhaven Stud	6	29	3	3	0	10.3	5,454	6,703
Duffey, Mrs Harry J	2	15	3	1	1	20.0	12,542	13,541
Dun, Mrs T D C	2	6	1	0	0	16.7	2,297	2,622
Duncan, Graham	1	7	1	0	0	14.3	1,590	1,590
Durham Drapes Ltd	1	6	1	0	0	16.7	1,811	1,811
Dutfield, Mrs Nerys	6	26	2	3	2	7.7	4,845	8,636
Dyer, Thomas	13	70	7	11	3	10.0	14,682	24,308
Dyson, J M	1	6	1	1	0	16.7	1,674	2,040
Easterby, M H	1	10	1	0	4	10.0	2,103	3,553
East Garston Racing	1	9	1	1	4	11.1	1,826	3,197
Eaton, Mrs Cherry	1	3	1	0	1	33.3	1,602	2,147
Eaton, Miss Judy	5	18	1	0	2	5.6	3,236	4,257
Eddy, D	2	7	3	0	0	42.9	8,889	8,889
Edwards, G F	4	29	2	6	3	6.9	4,940	10,200
Edwards, A C	1	3	1	1	1	33.3	1,534	2,204
Edwards-Heathcote, Capt E J	1	5	1	2	0	20.0	3,179	4,569
Ed Weetman (Haulage & Storage) Ltd	2	20	4	3	2	20.0	7,292	9,149
Egerton, T E S	2	11	8	0	1	72.7	17,834	18,087
Elias Gale Racing	7	31	4	4	7	12.9	28,460	36,094
Eliot, R F	2	15	4	6	2	26.7	137,700	161,795
Elite Racing Club	5	14	4	1	0	28.6	12,104	13,344
Ellingham, D T	1	9	1	0	1	11.1	2,427	3,220
Elliot, Miss Ruth	1	3	1	0	1	33.3	1,484	1,743
Ellis, Mrs Eva	4	14	1	3	1	7.1	1,024	3,935
Elphick, Mrs S P	1	7	1	0	0	14.3	1,138	1,138
Elsbury, Mrs P	1	6	2	1	1	33.3	7,309	9,285
Embiricos, Mrs S N J	2	3	1	0	0	33.3	5,345	5,345
Embiricos, S N J	3	11	3	1	0	27.3	4,425	5,268
Emmerson, A	1	5	1	1	0	20.0	1,305	3,341
Ennever, Mrs Michael	1	5	4	0	0	80.0	50,918	50,918
Ennever, A M	1	4	1	0	1	25.0	3,563	4,300
Ennis, Jim	2	8	1	0	1	12.5	2,204	3,947
Enterprise Markets Ltd	1	6	3	0	0	50.0	5,595	5,595
Enticott, Malcolm	1	6	1	0	0	16.7	1,201	1,201
Errington, J W	1	5	1	1	1	20.0	1,810	2,444
Etherton, Exors Of The Late Mr J H	1	5	2	2	1	40.0	5,188	7,043
Etherton, Mrs John	2	10	1	1	3	10.0	2,580	5,440
Eubank, Mrs A	1	4	1	1	0	25.0	7,440	10,635
Eurofast Petrochemical Supplies Ltd	1	2	1	0	0	50.0	2,252	2,252
Eustace, Malcolm	1	10	2	0	1	20.0	4,722	5,038
Evans, J P Aston	1	7	1	1	1	14.3	988	1,574
Evans, Richard J	1	12	3	2	2	25.0	8,854	10,825
Evans, Gerald W	1	8	2	2	2	25.0	3,278	4,978
Evans, Patrick	2	9	1	0	1	11.1	1,616	1,778
Eve, Mrs B V	2	9	1	1	3	11.1	4,325	5,569
Express Marie Curie Racing Club	1	3	1	0	0	33.3	2,167	2,167
Eyre, J L	7	29	3	3	5	10.3	6,584	9,969
Faber, Guy	1	6	6	0	0	100.0	20,864	20,864
Fagan, W A	1	3	1	0	0	33.3	1,988	1,988
Fagan, Mrs Ann	1	6	1	0	2	16.7	2,234	3,416
Fairbrother, M J	1	10	4	0	2	40.0	10,585	11,601
Fairlord Wholesale Confectioners Ltd	1	9	2	0	1	22.2	23,831	28,322
Fairs, R G	1	7	2	0	1	28.6	5,152	5,389
Fane, John	1	10	2	2	0	20.0	4,428	5,765
Fanshawe, Mrs J	1	3	1	1	1	33.3	2,026	5,624
Faragher, Miss M	1	6	2	2	1	33.3	4,113	6,242
Farmer, E	1	11	1	3	0	9.1	2,204	4,087
Farmer, Mrs Lucia	1	7	2	1	0	28.6	3,670	4,130
Farndon, G A	6	16	1	2	0	6.3	2,560	9,680
Farrant, Frank A	1	7	5	1	0	71.4	55,556	58,616
Farrant, Mrs Alison C	2	8	3	2	1	37.5	6,694	16,629
Farrell, W A A	4	33	3	5	7	9.1	5,773	10,704
Fayers, Mrs Angela	1	7	1	0	2	14.3	1,793	2,226

	H	R	W	2nd	3rd	%W-R	£WIN	£W/P
Featherstone, J R	3	16	3	2	2	18.8	6,798	9,387
Felix Rosenstiel's Widow & Son	2	6	2	0	0	33.3	3,522	4,555
Fenwick-Smith, I C	2	5	2	0	0	40.0	3,224	3,224
Ffitch-Heyes, John	1	1	1	0	0	100.0	1,431	1,431
Fiddes, J A G	1	10	3	2	1	30.0	7,670	9,626
Findlay, A C	1	14	4	5	2	28.6	9,374	15,960
Fiorillo, Tony	1	7	2	0	0	28.6	2,849	2,849
Firth, Mrs Lynne	1	4	1	1	1	25.0	3,436	7,986
Fisher, David	1	5	1	0	0	20.0	1,996	1,996
Fitzgerald, Bill	1	3	1	0	1	33.3	1,161	1,276
Fitzgerald, M Desmond	2	19	1	4	3	5.3	2,390	5,369
FitzGerald, J G	17	42	11	11	2	26.2	20,687	36,154
F K Roofing Ltd	2	11	1	3	1	9.1	3,623	7,193
Flannigan, A	1	1	1	0	0	100.0	2,654	2,654
Flegg, R	2	21	2	3	4	9.5	2,995	5,276
Flello, Ernie	1	9	2	0	1	22.2	5,345	5,856
Fletcher, Mrs Suzanne	1	7	2	0	1	28.6	3,491	3,784
Fletcher, D E	2	9	2	0	2	22.2	5,448	6,038
Ford, T J	2	16	6	1	1	37.5	11,100	13,215
Ford, Tom	2	17	4	0	2	23.5	7,306	7,870
Ford, A E	2	21	3	4	1	14.3	14,671	18,460
Ford, David	1	2	1	0	0	50.0	1,604	1,604
Forde, Mrs M	1	12	2	2	3	16.7	4,480	6,791
Forty, A G	1	5	2	0	2	40.0	3,863	4,446
Foster, Mrs S	1	7	3	0	0	42.9	7,403	7,908
Foster, Miss V	2	10	3	1	1	30.0	5,458	7,316
Foster, Mrs J R	1	4	1	0	1	25.0	2,219	2,478
Frampton, J L	2	8	1	0	0	12.5	1,441	1,441
Francis, W D	1	3	1	1	1	33.3	1,864	2,450
Fraser, Dr Kenneth S	3	13	3	1	2	23.1	4,958	6,035
Fraser, Mrs Hugh	4	19	1	3	1	5.3	2,724	4,664
Freethy, Mrs Millicent R	1	7	4	2	0	57.1	80,510	97,880
Fretwell, J C	5	14	4	1	1	28.6	10,199	11,142
Froome, Mrs J L	2	11	4	3	2	36.4	8,786	10,999
Frost, R G	7	23	1	1	2	4.3	1,806	2,915
Fry, R P	1	6	1	0	1	16.7	2,327	2,791
Fry, Bryan	1	1	1	0	0	100.0	1,749	1,749
Full Circle Thoroughbreds H Plc	4	13	3	0	1	23.1	5,248	5,536
Fulton, Mrs J G	2	9	5	3	0	55.6	49,119	52,457
Fulton, David M	1	10	1	0	2	10.0	2,660	3,550
Futures, Alpha Financial	1	3	1	0	0	33.3	2,532	2,532
G & P Barker Ltd/Globe Engineering	1	4	1	0	0	25.0	2,113	2,113
Gainscliffe Racing	1	7	1	4	0	14.3	2,884	7,838
Gallagher Enterprises Ltd	1	7	2	0	2	28.6	3,670	4,044
Galloway, C R	1	8	2	0	4	25.0	5,440	7,205
Galvanoni, Mrs Ann	2	7	1	0	0	14.3	2,108	2,108
Galvanoni, John	2	10	1	1	1	10.0	2,355	3,479
Gantlett, Miss H L	1	7	2	1	3	28.6	4,102	5,907
Gardner, N H	1	6	1	0	1	16.7	2,790	3,070
Garrett, L J	1	4	1	0	1	25.0	3,420	6,485
Gatensbury, Brian	4	13	3	3	4	23.1	7,712	10,589
G C S Club	1	7	2	0	3	28.6	4,696	7,141
Geake, Tony	1	10	3	4	1	30.0	22,546	36,875
Gee, Brian	1	2	1	1	0	50.0	1,116	1,479
Geer, Baron G de	1	1	1	0	0	100.0	746	746
Gething, Hugh	1	14	1	1	2	7.1	2,295	3,526
Geyer Estates Limited (St Athans Hotel)	1	15	9	3	1	60.0	19,775	21,432
Gibbings, Sir Peter	2	8	3	0	1	37.5	5,482	6,307
Gibbon, Mrs Lucy	1	3	1	0	0	33.3	1,607	1,607
Gibson, James	1	7	2	0	2	28.6	5,182	5,895
Gibson, M G S	1	6	1	1	0	16.7	2,832	4,952
Gielty, M B	1	8	1	1	1	12.5	2,008	2,796
Gifford, Mrs J T	2	6	1	2	2	16.7	7,970	10,148
Gilbert, J	1	3	1	0	0	33.3	1,606	1,606
Gilbert, L	3	17	2	3	1	11.8	3,467	5,465
Giles, R A	1	8	1	4	1	12.5	2,022	5,159
Gill, D	3	17	2	3	3	11.8	5,187	7,903
Gill, N A	2	14	2	2	1	14.3	9,285	12,223
Gill, H J	1	4	1	0	1	25.0	2,761	3,137
Gill & Punter/Etec Ltd	1	8	1	2	0	12.5	1,351	2,143
Gillies, Mrs J C	1	6	2	1	1	33.3	6,172	7,407
Gillow, J Michael	2	8	5	1	0	62.5	24,850	25,332
Gilman, F H	1	6	1	2	0	16.7	2,140	2,934
Ginzel, W	1	5	2	1	0	40.0	3,479	3,809
Gleadell, Giles	2	7	2	2	1	28.6	4,430	5,987
Glove Puppet Partnership	1	3	1	1	0	33.3	2,726	4,036
Godsman, Maureen Godsman & Douglas	1	3	2	1	0	66.7	5,684	6,234
Goldman, Nigel	1	5	1	0	0	20.0	5,208	5,208
Goldsmith, Langham & Thompson Partners	1	11	5	1	2	45.5	7,705	8,664

	H	R	W	2nd	3rd	%W-R	£WIN	£W/P
Gomersall, Raymond	4	16	3	5	3	18.8	5,385	8,697
Good, J	1	3	2	0	0	66.7	3,409	3,409
Goodall, Mrs T A	1	2	1	1	0	50.0	1,302	1,795
Goodall, Mrs Betty Bate And Mr Mark	1	4	1	1	0	25.0	1,690	2,187
Gooden, W G	2	9	1	6	1	11.1	1,688	4,808
Goodfellow, Mrs J D	6	36	5	3	4	13.9	9,035	11,946
Goodfellow, J D	2	8	2	2	1	25.0	4,020	5,861
Gordon, Joseph A	2	8	3	1	0	37.5	5,957	6,469
Gordon, J D	3	25	3	4	4	12.0	10,040	14,548
Gordon, G K	1	8	1	2	2	12.5	3,074	5,308
Gordon, Miss C	1	3	1	0	1	33.3	2,268	2,439
Gormley, Peter	2	14	3	0	1	21.4	6,305	7,090
Gornall, G	1	4	1	0	0	25.0	33,800	44,794
Gorrie, Alex	1	4	2	1	0	50.0	3,247	3,857
Gowling, J S	1	7	3	0	1	42.9	4,452	4,646
Grantham, Mrs A T	1	10	2	4	1	20.0	7,639	14,492
Gray, Mrs J M	1	3	1	0	1	33.3	2,319	2,618
Gray, John J	2	13	1	4	0	7.7	1,632	5,216
Gray, Mrs Jeanne	2	13	1	2	1	7.7	1,475	2,560
Greaves, G A	2	16	2	4	1	12.5	2,881	6,015
Green, Raymond Anderson	13	64	11	9	11	17.2	29,800	42,430
Green, Paul	2	16	1	3	3	6.3	9,500	24,192
Green, Mrs Anita	1	7	3	0	1	42.9	6,215	6,623
Green, Ned	1	14	3	3	4	21.4	7,080	10,795
Greenall, J E	5	21	11	5	2	52.4	21,778	30,175
Greenwood, Geoffrey C	3	16	2	2	4	12.5	4,910	8,469
Greenwood, John	1	8	1	1	2	12.5	3,319	5,225
Gregson, G G A	1	3	1	0	0	33.3	2,443	2,443
Greig, James D	1	14	4	0	3	28.6	8,388	9,765
Greig, Colonel D C	3	7	1	1	1	14.3	2,916	3,966
Grissell, Mrs D M	2	3	1	0	0	33.3	1,475	1,694
Grist, Mrs John	2	12	4	1	3	33.3	8,264	9,689
Group 1 Racing (1991) Ltd	3	18	2	3	5	11.1	3,852	6,620
Guest Leasing & Bloodstock Co Ltd	3	11	2	1	1	18.2	5,028	6,642
Guilding, Mrs Roger	1	3	1	0	1	33.3	1,543	1,727
Guilding, R W	1	4	1	1	1	25.0	2,950	4,514
Gurr, Richard J	1	3	1	0	1	33.3	1,305	1,738
Guthrie, Mrs M	1	4	2	0	0	50.0	4,872	5,006
Gutkin, J S	1	5	1	1	1	20.0	1,644	2,562
Guy, Vivian	3	9	1	1	0	11.1	3,590	3,994
Gyle-Thompson, D C G	1	5	4	0	0	80.0	9,460	9,460
Gymcrak Thoroughbred Racing III Plc	3	22	9	1	0	40.9	19,524	25,662
H & H Racing	1	10	3	0	1	30.0	6,380	6,602
H & K Commissions	1	9	1	2	2	11.1	1,480	3,850
Hager, B W	1	6	1	0	1	16.7	1,672	1,903
Haggas, R	5	16	2	4	1	12.5	7,309	15,517
Haggas, F J	2	11	1	7	0	9.1	2,561	9,357
Hague, C	1	14	1	4	3	7.1	2,827	7,184
Haine, Mrs S C	1	6	1	0	1	16.7	1,471	1,665
Haine, Mrs Diana	3	7	1	1	0	14.3	3,522	4,167
Hale, T	1	7	1	2	2	14.3	2,109	3,363
Halewood Vintners Ltd	6	15	1	1	2	6.7	2,589	4,882
Haley, P R	1	3	2	0	0	66.7	4,884	4,884
Haley, Mrs E E	2	6	2	0	0	33.3	4,567	4,567
Halifax, Lady	1	4	2	0	1	50.0	3,569	3,852
Hall, D S	1	8	6	0	1	75.0	23,906	29,315
Hall, Mrs Janine	1	2	1	1	0	50.0	3,019	3,797
Hall, Richard	1	14	1	2	1	7.1	3,035	5,607
Hambly, Mrs Virginia	3	11	3	2	0	27.3	5,888	7,219
Hambro, Mrs R E	1	3	1	0	0	33.3	2,400	2,400
Hamilton, Jack	2	15	3	3	2	20.0	4,498	6,336
Hamilton, William	1	5	2	0	2	40.0	2,847	3,415
Hammond, R D	1	1	1	0	0	100.0	1,735	1,735
Hancock, Jeremy	2	12	4	0	3	33.3	25,188	26,408
Hancock, W	1	3	1	0	0	33.3	2,807	2,807
Hancock III, Arthur B	1	5	2	2	1	40.0	3,350	5,789
Hankinson, Jon	1	7	2	2	1	28.6	4,942	7,171
Hannigan, Mrs Violet J	2	8	3	1	0	37.5	6,318	6,947
Hannon, F O	1	1	1	0	0	100.0	30,015	30,015
Hanson, K	2	13	3	0	2	23.1	3,282	3,854
Hanson, J	7	29	4	4	2	13.8	13,640	17,534
Hardie, Timothy	3	30	4	10	6	13.3	9,885	20,157
Hardy, T C	2	5	1	0	0	20.0	1,050	1,121
Harlow, J S	1	14	2	3	1	14.3	4,402	7,071
Harrington, E	1	4	2	0	0	50.0	4,895	4,895
Harris, Mrs A E	3	6	1	1	1	16.7	1,235	1,859
Harris, Lady	7	53	5	6	6	9.4	30,445	37,453
Harrison, David Alan	1	9	3	1	0	33.3	7,209	7,833
Hartigan, P J	1	5	3	0	1	60.0	13,799	14,287

	H	R	W	2nd	3rd	%W-R	£WIN	£W/P
Hartop, Mrs Mary	1	8	1	1	1	12.5	2,427	5,362
Hartwell, R	1	4	1	0	0	25.0	1,305	1,305
Harvey, Brig C B	3	19	7	2	7	36.8	23,628	30,274
Harvey, Edward	2	7	1	1	2	14.3	2,211	4,250
Haslam, Mrs Jean	4	20	1	2	3	5.0	1,292	3,115
Haslam, Mrs P	1	2	1	0	0	50.0	1,305	1,305
Hathaway, Bernard	3	17	4	7	2	23.5	12,228	28,572
Hawes, Mrs Rosalie	4	18	3	1	0	16.7	5,569	6,045
Hawkridge Farmhouse Cheese Limited	1	2	1	0	0	50.0	1,684	1,684
Haycock, Mrs E A	1	12	1	6	1	8.3	1,856	6,902
Hayden, M	1	8	2	0	1	25.0	3,906	4,132
Haynes, A F S	1	4	1	2	0	25.0	2,763	3,577
Hayward, Miss J E	1	3	1	1	0	33.3	5,865	7,425
Hazzard, Don	3	17	2	3	5	11.8	3,131	6,381
Heath, Mrs M J	2	3	1	0	0	33.3	1,669	1,754
Heath, Christopher	7	36	6	6	4	16.7	20,325	33,320
Heat-Treatment, Pioneer	1	3	1	1	0	33.3	2,367	2,839
Heeley, Mrs R T H	1	11	1	0	1	9.1	2,208	2,454
Heenan, Dr Paul N	1	8	3	1	2	37.5	4,482	5,138
Helaissi, S A	1	7	2	2	1	28.6	2,519	3,754
Hellens, J A	8	41	3	8	4	7.3	12,257	19,327
Henderson, J R	2	10	2	3	1	20.0	5,852	9,411
Henderson, R E	1	7	1	3	1	14.3	1,848	6,571
Henderson, J (Gateshead)	3	12	1	3	2	8.3	5,117	10,488
Henderson, Mrs R G	1	6	2	1	0	33.3	15,614	26,270
Henderson, P F	2	6	1	1	1	16.7	1,514	1,990
Henderson, Mrs D A	1	2	1	0	0	50.0	1,030	1,030
Henson, Mrs Anne	2	10	1	3	1	10.0	2,301	6,089
Hepburn, R	1	9	1	3	2	11.1	2,248	3,928
Hepworth, Peter	1	4	2	0	0	50.0	3,672	3,672
Herries, Lady	1	4	1	0	1	25.0	3,132	3,367
Hewitt, H R	2	10	1	2	2	10.0	1,749	2,971
Heys, D W	1	9	3	2	0	33.3	14,161	17,463
Heywood, P C N	3	8	1	1	1	12.5	1,453	2,212
Hiatt, P W	1	10	1	2	1	10.0	1,705	2,848
Highflyers	3	17	4	3	1	23.5	9,783	11,992
Higson, Peter L	2	14	1	2	3	7.1	1,067	3,140
Higson, K	10	43	7	8	8	16.3	33,372	39,142
Hill, Andrew B	3	13	2	2	2	15.4	6,606	8,946
Hirst, Mrs A E	1	6	1	1	1	16.7	1,631	2,245
Hislop, Mrs E M	1	8	1	2	1	12.5	1,564	2,519
Hitchins, J	1	8	2	0	1	25.0	20,501	28,982
Hitchins, Mrs Elizabeth	18	83	7	10	11	8.4	14,185	29,160
Hobbs, P J	4	12	4	1	2	33.3	7,126	7,989
Hodges, R J	5	13	1	0	0	7.7	1,587	1,587
Hogg, John	2	14	2	3	3	14.3	4,750	9,189
Holder, Mrs Cheryl	2	13	3	3	1	23.1	7,221	10,398
Holder, K	1	10	1	2	2	10.0	2,186	4,480
Holland, M H	2	5	1	1	0	20.0	1,614	2,044
Holleran, Mrs M	1	12	2	2	2	16.7	3,034	4,520
Homes, Toravon	1	11	1	1	4	9.1	2,325	4,372
Honour, Fred	1	5	2	1	1	40.0	4,564	5,670
Hooley, R	1	8	2	1	2	25.0	4,923	5,868
Hooper, Tony	1	10	1	1	0	10.0	1,553	2,591
Horan, Ms M	4	14	8	2	1	57.1	18,849	20,465
Horner, Mrs Dorothy	2	8	2	1	1	25.0	3,446	4,060
Horwood, Miss Jean	2	16	1	2	1	6.3	2,374	4,263
Hoskin, M	1	1	1	0	0	100.0	1,769	1,769
Houlton, R L	2	10	1	1	2	10.0	1,537	3,119
Houlton, Mrs E	1	7	1	1	1	14.3	2,696	3,457
Houston, Mrs C	1	2	2	0	0	100.0	5,216	5,216
Howell, Mrs R	3	12	2	3	2	16.7	4,623	12,951
Hubbard, G A	31	143	23	18	16	16.1	105,277	144,531
Hubbard, Ms Jennifer	1	3	2	0	0	66.7	5,582	5,582
Huckle, J	2	11	2	3	0	18.2	14,162	25,390
Hughes, Miss N	1	3	1	0	0	33.3	2,794	2,794
Hughes, James	2	17	2	1	1	11.8	2,848	3,487
Hughes, Mrs D	1	2	1	0	0	50.0	1,631	1,631
Humphrey, Mrs Meriel	1	6	1	3	0	16.7	3,012	5,213
Humphreys, David	4	18	4	0	2	22.2	6,434	9,043
Humphries, Mrs R A	1	6	1	2	1	16.7	2,636	5,378
Humphry, C	1	10	2	2	0	20.0	4,681	5,778
Hunnisett, Mrs D R	5	35	6	4	9	17.1	20,163	25,470
Hunnisett, D R	2	8	1	1	0	12.5	2,448	2,891
Hunt, K J	1	9	2	0	0	22.2	5,559	6,122
Hunt & Co (Bournemouth) Ltd	3	8	2	2	1	25.0	17,410	61,837
Hunter, Ian	1	5	1	1	0	20.0	1,484	1,893
Hurford, Don	1	10	2	0	1	20.0	5,180	5,758
Hussein, Ahmed A	1	2	1	1	0	50.0	2,276	2,857

	H	R	W	2nd	3rd	%W-R	£WIN	£W/P
Hutchinson, Maurice	1	7	2	1	2	28.6	2,953	4,099
Hyde Sporting Promotions/Saddlehome Farm	1	4	1	0	1	25.0	1,305	1,580
Hyde Sporting Promotions Limited	1	7	1	1	1	14.3	3,200	4,576
Hyman, Mrs David	1	8	1	1	2	12.5	1,822	3,043
Ilsley, A	1	8	1	1	1	12.5	2,007	5,146
Incisa, Don Enrico	1	7	1	0	2	14.3	1,719	2,180
Inshaw, Mrs A L J	1	13	2	0	5	15.4	12,762	20,360
Insight Cartons Ltd.	1	14	1	0	2	7.1	4,403	5,342
Instantfine Ltd	1	9	1	0	0	11.1	788	788
Ivory, Frank	1	7	3	2	0	42.9	12,299	16,800
Jack-Del-Roy	1	8	2	1	1	25.0	5,633	6,964
Jackman, Mrs E	1	6	2	1	1	33.3	3,247	3,918
Jackman, G A	1	5	1	0	0	20.0	2,334	2,334
Jackson, D J	1	4	2	1	0	50.0	3,816	4,225
Jackson, Mrs D	1	4	1	0	2	25.0	1,480	2,170
J A L Racing	1	5	2	1	0	40.0	4,275	5,739
James, P G	1	9	3	2	2	33.3	9,299	12,444
Jarvis, M S	1	2	1	1	0	50.0	3,753	5,384
Jefferson, J M.	2	8	5	3	0	62.5	11,643	13,570
Jeffords, Mrs Walter M	1	1	1	0	0	100.0	9,830	9,830
Jeffreys, Miss Rosemary	1	14	1	3	5	7.1	1,954	4,973
Jenkins, C W	2	8	1	1	0	12.5	2,905	4,945
Jenks, Mrs Bryan P	1	5	1	1	1	20.0	1,534	2,479
Jenks, David	2	11	1	1	3	9.1	1,772	3,335
Jenks, W	2	16	1	4	1	6.3	1,814	4,188
Jerrard, I	1	9	1	2	1	11.1	1,599	2,524
Jewell, Mrs Linda	2	8	2	0	0	25.0	2,711	2,711
Jinks, N.	1	9	1	0	0	11.1	2,866	3,627
John Doyle Construction Limited	1	3	1	1	1	33.3	2,065	3,103
John Humphreys (Turf Accountants) Ltd	2	11	1	1	3	9.1	1,475	3,004
Johns, Roger	1	10	3	3	2	30.0	4,926	6,966
Johnsey, T A	3	18	2	2	3	11.1	4,002	6,300
Johnson, D A	4	30	5	2	6	16.7	11,516	17,537
Johnson, Geoffrey	2	15	2	1	0	13.3	5,766	6,483
Johnson, G & L	1	7	1	0	1	14.3	3,940	24,335
Johnson, J	1	6	1	3	0	16.7	1,778	3,444
Johnson, Rex	1	8	1	4	0	12.5	3,787	12,460
Johnson, Miss C D	1	2	1	0	0	50.0	1,672	1,672
Johnson, Mrs S	2	5	1	1	1	20.0	1,828	2,798
Johnson, Michael A	1	1	1	0	0	100.0	1,592	1,592
Johnston, P G	1	6	1	1	0	16.7	1,974	2,449
Jones, Peter	3	30	6	4	4	20.0	9,597	12,936
Jones, D	5	29	5	4	6	17.2	11,825	17,670
Jones, Louis	1	9	6	1	0	66.7	17,859	18,609
Jones, Malcolm B	2	10	5	2	1	50.0	11,200	13,458
Jones, R A	1	12	1	3	1	8.3	1,534	3,352
Jones, W A	1	10	2	3	0	20.0	10,967	16,757
Jones, P J	1	5	1	1	0	20.0	1,710	2,070
Jones, Frank	1	7	4	1	0	57.1	11,127	14,015
Jones, Mrs T Thomson	1	1	1	0	0	100.0	828	828
Jones, Mrs Nancy	1	4	2	0	0	50.0	4,954	4,954
Jones, Dennis C.	1	6	1	1	0	16.7	1,480	1,940
Jones, Mrs H T	1	3	1	1	0	33.3	1,958	2,313
Jones, David G	2	11	1	0	1	9.1	1,480	1,750
Jones-Bradburn, Mrs M.	1	5	1	2	0	20.0	2,255	3,014
Jonsson, L G R	1	7	1	1	2	14.3	1,530	2,327
Joseph, Jack	21	110	11	8	11	10.0	20,997	29,613
Joseph, Lady	2	6	1	1	2	16.7	4,663	6,511
Joughin, Mrs L R	3	7	1	0	0	14.3	1,987	1,987
Joyce, Mrs D	1	4	2	1	0	50.0	5,845	6,333
Joynes, Mrs P	11	45	1	4	6	2.2	2,268	7,064
Joynson, A C D	2	12	1	0	3	8.3	1,467	2,670
J Pickles (Harrogate) Limited	1	2	1	1	0	50.0	1,581	2,007
J P S Racing	1	6	2	1	0	33.3	3,980	4,414
J Smith (Chislehurst) Ltd.	1	10	2	0	3	20.0	4,650	5,210
Jubert, Mrs P	4	12	1	1	4	8.3	9,440	19,279
Julian, Marten	1	3	1	0	0	33.3	2,242	2,242
Just Racing	1	11	1	3	3	9.1	2,944	5,060
Kalman, Mrs Patricia M	1	4	1	0	0	25.0	2,323	2,323
Kane, Mrs A	1	7	3	2	0	42.9	6,429	7,914
Kaplan, Arnie	1	5	1	0	1	20.0	3,626	8,831
Kaplan, A	2	8	1	0	1	12.5	1,670	2,145
Kavanagh Roofing Southern Limited	2	16	3	5	1	18.8	8,725	13,507
Kaye, H	2	12	2	3	1	16.7	8,529	12,404
Kearns, Miss Marie	1	8	1	1	3	12.5	1,816	2,827
Keary, P J	1	4	2	0	0	50.0	4,077	4,222
Keary, J	1	4	2	0	0	50.0	6,268	6,268
Keating, M	1	6	1	0	0	16.7	4,902	5,263
Keep, T M J	1	11	1	5	2	9.1	1,562	5,424

	H	R	W	2nd	3rd	%W-R	£WIN	£W/P
Kelleway, P A	2	13	7	1	1	53.8	13,739	17,143
Kelly, Patrick	4	16	3	0	0	18.8	5,156	5,156
Kennard, L G	1	7	3	0	0	42.9	7,122	7,122
Kennedy, B	4	17	3	2	3	17.6	8,722	11,673
Kenny, T J	1	4	1	1	1	25.0	1,305	2,071
Kerr, Alan	1	9	2	1	0	22.2	3,969	4,551
Kerr-Dineen, Michael	2	15	2	2	1	13.3	5,303	9,844
Kettlewell, Mrs E A	1	2	2	0	0	100.0	4,209	4,209
Key, Mrs Ann	1	7	1	3	0	14.3	2,316	5,870
Kidd, Gerald	1	2	1	1	0	50.0	3,470	4,318
Kiely, Mrs P	1	2	1	0	1	50.0	43,435	47,597
Kilpatrick, B A	7	23	3	2	4	13.0	9,756	17,380
Kimber, L G	4	21	4	3	2	19.0	8,047	13,113
Kimber, S	1	6	2	0	1	33.3	4,433	4,953
King, A A	5	31	4	2	2	12.9	9,130	10,971
King, Mrs P M	3	6	1	0	0	16.7	1,896	1,896
King Of Clubs Ltd (Gloucester)	1	6	2	0	1	33.3	4,167	4,549
Kirby, John	1	6	1	0	0	16.7	2,442	2,442
Kirke, Mrs B	1	14	2	4	5	14.3	4,183	7,820
Knight, D	2	11	2	1	0	18.2	3,126	3,691
Knight, Miss H	1	3	2	0	0	66.7	6,064	7,104
Knightsbridge Bc	2	11	2	3	0	18.2	4,253	5,356
Knutsford, Lady	1	5	1	0	1	20.0	2,233	2,819
Konvekta Ltd	2	5	2	0	1	40.0	2,732	3,266
K P H (Equine) Ltd	1	4	2	0	0	50.0	3,718	5,098
K W Bell & Son Ltd	4	10	2	4	0	20.0	3,100	5,224
Kwiatkowski, M W	1	7	1	1	1	14.3	1,837	2,622
Kynaston, Kevan R	3	12	1	2	1	8.3	2,285	3,699
Lacey, Mrs Ann	1	3	1	1	0	33.3	929	1,416
Lads, The Blue Ball	1	1	1	0	0	100.0	1,590	1,590
Ladyswood Racing Club	6	22	2	1	3	9.1	4,177	20,345
Laing, Mrs David	1	8	1	2	1	12.5	2,190	3,887
Laing, Miss Jennifer	1	6	1	1	0	16.7	3,600	4,532
Laing, D R	1	7	1	1	0	14.3	1,837	2,400
Lake, B A J	1	6	1	1	0	16.7	3,231	4,471
Lake & Elliot Industries Ltd	1	1	1	0	0	100.0	1,757	1,757
Lamb, R R	13	43	1	3	3	2.3	2,326	4,695
Lamyman, P	4	28	1	3	3	3.6	2,890	6,799
Lane, Christopher	1	2	1	0	0	50.0	816	816
Langdon, David	1	13	3	3	2	23.1	9,257	13,357
Lansbury, G	1	8	3	2	0	37.5	14,207	26,661
Lansdown, S P	1	5	1	0	1	20.0	1,669	1,859
Laurel (Leisure) Limited	1	7	4	3	0	57.1	14,898	17,825
Lavelle, R J	2	11	2	3	1	18.2	11,031	20,463
Lavis Medical Systems	2	18	1	1	4	5.6	1,973	3,285
Leadbeater, Tim	2	11	2	4	1	18.2	5,216	10,844
Leah, R	1	6	1	2	1	16.7	1,730	3,329
Leat, Mrs Ann	1	1	1	0	0	100.0	1,872	1,872
Leckenby, Mrs K D	1	7	1	3	0	14.3	2,611	5,158
Lee, Richard	4	11	2	1	0	18.2	3,199	3,661
Lee, Mrs P J	2	8	1	1	1	12.5	1,302	2,428
Lee, P L	1	4	1	0	1	25.0	1,814	2,029
Leek, Mrs J A	1	8	1	0	2	12.5	1,480	2,113
Legouix, Mrs R	2	11	2	3	3	18.2	5,897	10,914
Lemon, John	1	3	1	1	0	33.3	1,660	2,345
Lennon, Denis	1	9	2	0	2	22.2	4,619	5,297
Leonard, P A	1	8	1	0	2	12.5	2,112	3,289
L'estrange, David	2	16	2	1	4	12.5	4,990	7,739
Lewis, Mrs Lynda	2	10	1	1	3	10.0	1,580	3,117
Lewis, David S	1	7	4	0	1	57.1	24,797	25,005
Lewis, Colin	3	13	2	1	2	15.4	3,759	6,104
Liddiard, Ron	1	4	1	1	0	25.0	1,604	1,956
Linkside Fabrications (L'pool) Ltd	1	4	1	1	1	25.0	1,903	3,064
Liscombe, D A	1	2	1	0	0	50.0	2,179	2,179
Little, Stanley	1	14	5	3	1	35.7	13,737	19,621
Llewellyn, B J	7	49	6	6	5	12.2	10,230	14,713
Lloyd, F	4	8	1	0	1	12.5	1,903	2,369
Lloyd, Mrs K	1	11	1	1	3	9.1	1,436	3,481
Lochtie, G	1	15	1	2	1	6.7	4,327	7,161
Lock, Mrs Barbara	1	12	2	0	4	16.7	4,942	6,136
Locke, Mrs Paul	3	9	3	1	1	33.3	7,798	10,405
Lockyer, M T	4	31	3	5	8	9.7	8,503	14,668
Lomas, A J	5	30	11	6	2	36.7	25,828	33,833
Longstaff, C C	1	5	2	1	0	40.0	5,309	5,788
Lousada, Mrs D	2	13	3	0	3	23.1	10,586	13,879
Lovrey, Brian	2	12	3	3	3	25.0	11,428	20,966
Lowndes, T H	3	11	1	4	2	9.1	1,858	4,072
Lowrey, Nigel	2	13	1	2	0	7.7	1,793	3,211
Luck, Guy	2	8	1	1	1	12.5	2,023	2,862

	H	R	W	2nd	3rd	%W-R	£WIN	£W/P
Ludlow, Mrs E M R	2	7	1	1	0	14.3	2,898	3,729
Lungo, Mrs B	4	21	7	4	2	33.3	12,558	15,139
Luxton, D.	1	1	1	0	0	100.0	2,295	2,295
Lyons, Terence P II	1	4	1	0	2	25.0	1,480	2,190
M & N Plant Ltd	4	30	10	4	3	33.3	76,720	87,290
Macavoy, Ian	1	10	2	1	1	20.0	3,570	4,274
Macdonald-Buchanan, Capt J	1	4	2	1	1	50.0	3,653	5,068
MacEchern, G M	1	15	8	3	1	53.3	115,682	130,035
Macfarlane, I R Scott & D J	1	3	1	0	1	33.3	2,174	2,484
Mackie, Mrs J	3	8	1	0	0	12.5	1,214	1,214
Mackrell, J A	1	3	1	0	2	33.3	2,176	2,909
Macmillan, Charles	1	12	1	0	1	8.3	2,290	2,590
Mactaggart, B	2	8	2	0	1	25.0	6,185	7,043
Madden, E R	6	32	7	4	7	21.9	25,080	30,284
Maher, Miss G	1	1	1	0	0	100.0	34,275	34,275
Mailcom Plc	1	7	2	0	1	28.6	5,559	6,075
Mailes, Miss Joy	2	4	1	1	1	25.0	1,576	2,146
Makins, Dwight	1	10	2	2	3	20.0	6,538	10,316
Maktoum, Sheikh Ahmed Bin Saeed Al	5	19	7	3	3	36.8	16,345	20,301
Malam, D A	1	5	1	0	0	20.0	2,360	2,595
Malpass Bros Ltd	1	1	1	0	0	100.0	1,723	1,723
Maltby, Mrs S J	1	4	2	0	2	50.0	4,803	5,503
Maltsword Ltd	4	31	5	4	7	16.1	15,261	23,838
Manley, K G	1	7	2	4	0	28.6	4,721	7,111
Manning, Major Ian	1	9	1	1	3	11.1	1,480	2,621
Manning, D	1	6	1	1	0	16.7	2,075	2,587
Mansell, R J	1	6	3	2	0	50.0	10,477	11,418
Manton, Lord	2	9	3	3	1	33.3	6,119	8,533
Marchant, M J	1	11	2	0	1	18.2	4,850	5,365
Mark Tompkins Racing	2	9	2	1	2	22.2	4,438	5,381
Marner, Chr.	2	14	5	1	1	35.7	15,208	16,347
Marsh, S P	4	13	1	3	1	7.7	2,128	4,421
Marsh, Mrs L A	1	6	3	0	0	50.0	5,621	5,621
Martin, Mrs A G	2	11	1	5	0	9.1	2,222	6,097
Martin, Mrs N D	1	6	1	0	1	16.7	2,989	3,583
Mason, Sydney	1	6	1	0	1	16.7	1,805	2,026
Mason, N B	18	59	1	7	7	1.7	2,850	9,341
Mathias, Richard	1	3	2	0	0	66.7	2,363	2,363
Matthews, The Hon I V	1	3	1	0	1	33.3	2,608	3,298
Mavrou, Andy	1	12	5	2	1	41.7	29,195	39,707
Maxwell-Jones, Mrs G	1	8	2	1	1	25.0	4,479	6,325
May, Mrs Jacqueline	1	9	3	1	2	33.3	8,492	9,899
Maycock, T F	1	12	1	1	2	8.3	1,474	2,741
Mazzotta, A	1	7	1	1	1	14.3	1,881	2,550
McAndrews, Neil	2	18	1	6	3	5.6	2,604	7,869
McAuley, Miss C M	3	11	1	0	0	9.1	2,107	2,107
McCaghy, J	1	5	1	0	2	20.0	30,738	42,253
McCann, J P	1	8	1	0	0	12.5	2,657	2,657
McCarthy, Mrs Susan	1	8	2	0	2	25.0	2,955	3,553
McCarthy, Jim	4	22	1	4	2	4.5	1,734	5,607
McCarthy, Jeff	1	3	1	1	0	33.3	1,587	2,125
McClelland, Mrs K	2	8	2	0	0	25.0	7,079	8,290
McCormick, Kevin	2	8	1	1	1	12.5	1,996	2,763
McCoubrey, Mrs T	3	12	1	0	4	8.3	2,287	3,892
McCune, David	5	33	2	4	9	6.1	4,471	9,811
McDonald, Mrs Susan	2	8	3	2	0	37.5	5,715	6,995
McDonald, R	3	15	1	1	0	6.7	1,935	2,290
McEwen, H F	2	8	2	1	1	25.0	5,795	6,734
McGhie, C H	1	9	6	0	1	66.7	14,029	14,309
McGilligan, N	1	9	2	2	1	22.2	2,755	3,737
McGlone, Mrs Margaret	2	7	1	2	0	14.3	9,380	31,204
McGrath, Ed	1	5	1	0	3	20.0	1,302	2,143
McGrath, Jim	2	9	2	0	0	22.2	4,022	4,022
McHarg, W G	2	12	3	2	1	25.0	7,411	11,458
McKibbin, W	3	11	1	1	1	9.1	1,910	2,629
McKinney, Mrs B M	1	10	5	0	1	50.0	22,973	26,908
McLaren, C J C	1	6	1	1	0	16.7	2,890	3,342
McMahon, Hugh	1	4	1	1	1	25.0	26,040	43,240
McManus, J P	5	11	1	1	0	9.1	2,916	3,724
Mead, Mrs B	3	15	2	2	5	13.3	6,507	9,865
Meadows, Geoff	3	13	2	3	2	15.4	4,644	9,336
Mellon, Paul	5	31	5	3	7	16.1	45,630	62,291
Mercer, Stuart M	1	4	3	1	0	75.0	15,107	26,275
Meredith, R	1	3	1	0	2	33.3	2,126	2,785
Mernagh, J F	1	6	3	1	0	50.0	4,834	5,524
Michael Jackson Bloodstock Ltd	3	17	4	4	1	23.5	61,891	82,665
Michaelson, R P B	2	5	1	2	0	20.0	2,101	4,303
Middlebrook, Mrs L	1	4	1	0	1	25.0	1,903	2,012
Middlebrook, G	1	11	4	2	2	36.4	15,036	22,552

	H	R	W	2nd	3rd	%W-R	£WIN	£W/P
Middleton, W R	1	5	1	0	0	20.0	2,080	2,080
Middx Packaging Ltd	1	14	1	3	4	7.1	1,298	4,233
Midland Markets Ltd	5	18	2	1	0	11.1	5,326	6,303
Miles, R	1	7	1	1	3	14.3	1,601	2,726
Miller, Sir Peter	1	3	1	0	1	33.3	1,702	2,032
Million In Mind Partnership (2)	2	10	5	2	1	50.0	23,961	26,338
Mills, F J	6	17	3	2	2	17.6	6,536	13,623
Mills, J V	2	13	1	3	1	7.7	1,627	3,569
Milner Cleaning Co Ltd	1	4	1	0	0	25.0	1,617	1,617
Minns, Mrs Sylvia	2	17	1	2	4	5.9	1,480	3,311
Minton-Price, R K	1	4	2	1	0	50.0	5,522	6,424
Miquel, Raymond	1	4	1	0	2	25.0	1,882	2,402
Mitchell, Trevor	1	10	2	1	2	20.0	3,650	4,458
Mitchell, N R	2	15	1	1	2	6.7	1,763	2,543
Mitchell, C W	2	10	1	0	1	10.0	2,271	2,848
Moffat, R A	1	7	2	1	0	28.6	3,658	4,354
Mohammed, Sheikh	2	9	2	1	0	22.2	4,460	8,638
Mohan, Dr G Madan	1	13	6	1	0	46.2	30,325	30,903
Moloney, J E	1	5	4	1	0	80.0	11,651	12,481
Monaghan, S	1	9	3	2	1	33.3	5,057	7,341
Monteith, Lt-Col W L	5	29	6	7	1	20.7	13,615	18,580
Monteith, P	4	26	3	1	3	11.5	7,888	11,492
Montgomery, W T	1	9	1	3	1	11.1	4,115	9,156
Moon, David O	2	5	1	2	0	20.0	1,744	2,629
Mooney, J T	1	3	1	1	0	33.3	1,182	1,606
Moorcroft, Kevin	1	3	1	0	0	33.3	1,893	1,893
Moore, A P	1	3	2	0	1	66.7	4,185	4,410
Moreton, J N G	3	23	10	1	4	43.5	41,873	47,962
Morgan-Jones, R	1	5	2	1	1	40.0	3,490	4,243
Moriarty, P	3	10	1	0	1	10.0	3,037	3,298
Morland, D	1	15	1	1	8	6.7	2,406	6,099
Morley, Mrs Anthony	1	7	3	0	1	42.9	9,979	10,309
Morrell, Mrs W	1	7	2	2	1	28.6	2,960	4,545
Morris, T	1	11	1	1	1	9.1	1,898	2,483
Morris, A W C	1	1	1	0	0	100.0	1,940	1,940
Morris, Mrs J M	1	2	1	0	1	50.0	2,618	2,957
Morrison, Miss L	1	6	1	0	1	16.7	1,564	1,862
Morton, James	2	9	2	0	2	22.2	4,745	5,490
Moss, Mrs Jill	1	4	2	1	0	50.0	11,704	24,488
Mostyn, Lord	1	5	2	3	0	40.0	11,025	15,963
Motley, Mrs Michael	1	2	1	0	0	50.0	1,679	1,679
Mould, Mrs J	9	62	18	8	10	29.0	145,788	172,978
Mountifield, Mrs J B	1	8	3	0	1	37.5	7,579	7,790
Mullins, Gerard	1	3	1	0	0	33.3	1,617	1,617
Mumford, Lady Mary	2	5	3	1	0	60.0	5,952	8,319
Murdoch, J C	1	2	1	0	0	50.0	1,188	1,188
Murdoch, J S	1	4	2	1	0	50.0	5,848	6,654
Murphy, C J	1	4	2	0	1	50.0	6,840	7,368
Murphy, Alex	1	3	1	0	0	33.3	1,679	1,679
Murphy, C	2	5	1	1	1	20.0	1,724	2,702
Murray, James (Ballymena)	2	2	1	0	1	50.0	2,091	2,266
Murray, Mrs A M	2	7	2	0	2	28.6	3,672	4,304
Murray, R G	1	6	1	1	0	16.7	1,667	2,301
Mursell, J W	2	10	1	1	3	10.0	2,028	3,430
Myburgh, Miss N	1	8	4	0	3	50.0	10,292	11,178
Myers, David	1	1	1	0	0	100.0	1,475	1,475
Nash, Mrs J P	1	2	1	0	0	50.0	1,697	1,697
Naughton, J	3	9	1	2	2	11.1	1,475	2,667
Naylor, Bill	3	12	2	0	3	16.7	6,242	9,884
N B Mason (Farms) Ltd	5	25	2	5	3	8.0	5,632	10,702
Neale, Bill	2	16	2	2	2	12.5	3,314	4,570
Nelson, W M	2	6	1	0	1	16.7	1,214	1,519
Nelson, J	1	4	1	0	3	25.0	1,712	3,252
Nelson, Peter	1	7	2	0	1	28.6	3,849	4,067
Nettley, B	2	5	3	0	1	60.0	5,439	5,969
Newsome, R J	1	11	4	2	0	36.4	9,927	11,104
Nicholls, Roger	1	6	1	2	1	16.7	1,305	2,681
Nichols, D J	1	8	4	1	1	50.0	10,413	11,226
Nixon, T F F	1	1	1	0	0	100.0	1,737	1,737
Nolan, Mrs Padraig	1	1	1	0	0	100.0	24,624	24,624
Nolan Hardman & Partners Ltd	1	7	1	3	1	14.3	3,395	7,652
Non-Stop Promotions & Marketing Ltd	2	12	1	0	1	8.3	1,480	3,851
Norman, S J	2	17	5	2	2	29.4	18,103	28,329
North, Mrs H	1	2	1	0	1	50.0	2,110	2,380
Northampton, Lord	1	9	3	3	0	33.3	11,968	21,658
North Briton Racing Club	1	7	4	1	0	57.1	20,903	21,343
North East Paper Co Ltd	1	9	2	1	1	22.2	2,790	3,756
Northover, J A	1	2	1	0	0	50.0	1,632	1,632
Noteworthy Friends	2	3	1	0	1	33.3	1,340	1,704

	H	R	W	2nd	3rd	%W-R	£WIN	£W/P
Notley, Mrs Christine	1	6	1	1	2	16.7	1,475	2,292
Nott, E C	2	15	1	3	2	6.7	2,322	4,462
Oakes, Mrs A C	1	6	1	0	0	16.7	1,302	1,302
Oberstein, M L	9	34	6	4	5	17.6	18,473	30,915
O'Byrne, D L	1	1	1	0	0	100.0	1,476	1,476
Oceala Limited	2	4	1	2	0	25.0	1,480	4,030
O'Connell, Mrs P A	1	11	3	1	1	27.3	5,360	6,399
O'Connor, Mark	3	13	3	2	2	23.1	8,117	10,837
O'Donnell, Mrs M	1	5	1	0	0	20.0	1,924	1,924
O'Donovan, J F	1	13	1	4	3	7.7	3,785	8,449
Ogden, R	5	19	7	1	3	36.8	20,258	21,668
Ogden, Keith	1	5	1	0	1	20.0	2,120	2,414
Ogden, Robert	7	16	1	3	3	6.3	4,873	10,690
O'Gorman, W H	2	18	4	5	2	22.2	13,429	37,416
O'Haire, Tom	1	6	1	2	0	16.7	1,631	2,611
Oldham, M K	4	29	2	3	4	6.9	8,666	14,645
Olds, Miss Christine	1	7	4	1	0	57.1	25,163	29,881
O'Leary, Mrs Vicky	1	2	1	0	0	50.0	1,021	1,021
Oliver, Henry	2	10	2	1	1	20.0	3,894	4,707
Ollivant, Mrs J	2	12	2	1	0	16.7	12,200	13,562
O'Mahony, Mrs Vivienne	1	3	1	0	0	33.3	1,780	2,292
O'Neill, J J	1	7	1	1	1	14.3	2,192	3,241
Opening Bid Partnership	1	7	1	0	3	14.3	2,026	2,900
Orchard, G R	5	17	2	2	2	11.8	2,609	4,056
Osborne, C D	1	5	2	1	0	40.0	3,556	4,066
Osborne House Limited	2	10	2	2	2	20.0	29,830	33,903
Oseman, Mrs K	2	10	1	0	1	10.0	2,413	3,075
Oseman, M F	1	5	1	1	1	20.0	1,941	2,840
O'Toole, Mattie	6	23	3	2	1	13.0	4,786	6,407
Owen, B.	2	16	2	3	2	12.5	4,907	8,414
Paddocks Thoroughbred Racing Ltd	1	9	3	1	1	33.3	8,300	11,237
Painting, Trevor	1	4	1	0	0	25.0	1,675	1,675
Palacegate Corporation Ltd	3	11	7	3	0	63.6	12,549	14,329
Palk, A	1	3	1	0	0	33.3	1,769	1,769
Pallister, W G	1	3	3	0	0	100.0	6,728	6,728
Palmer, Mrs Vicky	1	3	1	0	0	33.3	2,190	2,190
Palmer, Mrs S M	1	7	1	1	0	14.3	1,595	2,000
Parker, R A	2	3	1	0	1	33.3	1,488	1,731
Parker, Alan	6	23	5	2	2	21.7	41,328	49,901
Parker, Howard	4	18	2	3	4	11.1	3,144	7,170
Parker, Sir Eric	5	22	4	0	4	18.2	68,818	71,698
Parkes, J	5	17	2	0	0	11.8	5,109	5,428
Park Farm Thoroughbreds	2	10	5	0	2	50.0	8,727	9,130
Park Industrial Supplies (Wales) Ltd	1	3	1	0	2	33.3	1,302	5,537
Parr, Mrs L	1	3	2	0	0	66.7	5,001	5,206
Parr, Brian	1	8	1	0	0	12.5	1,861	1,861
Partridge, Peter	1	8	3	1	0	37.5	9,383	10,411
Patten, Mrs F	1	5	1	1	1	20.0	1,940	2,683
Pattison, Mrs Robina	1	7	2	1	1	28.6	17,850	18,583
Payne, Nigel	1	8	1	1	0	12.5	1,954	2,386
Peacock, W J	1	10	1	0	0	10.0	2,038	2,038
Peake, Mrs J A	2	11	1	1	2	9.1	2,616	3,815
Peake, R J	2	13	1	3	4	7.7	943	3,194
Pearce, Brian Arthur	5	23	1	2	3	4.3	1,364	2,989
Pearson, I H	2	16	1	2	4	6.3	2,226	5,332
Pearson, Mrs D N B	1	8	2	2	1	25.0	3,012	4,064
Pelham, H T	2	14	1	5	3	7.1	3,485	11,411
Pell-Mell Partners	22	97	27	13	14	27.8	114,062	176,250
Penny, M K	1	3	1	0	0	33.3	1,287	1,287
Penser, E.	1	7	2	1	0	28.6	3,875	4,600
Peppiatt, Mrs J J	1	8	2	1	2	25.0	2,785	4,157
Peraticos, M C	1	7	1	3	1	14.3	3,655	7,323
Perkins, Miss Charlotte A I	1	6	3	0	0	50.0	5,658	5,658
Perkins, R A H	4	30	6	3	4	20.0	15,156	22,073
Perkins, Mrs Tim	1	3	1	1	0	33.3	3,043	4,123
Perkins, Miss Melissa	2	10	2	0	0	20.0	5,231	5,231
Perry, H V	5	24	1	3	5	4.2	2,346	5,825
Perry, L.	2	6	1	0	1	16.7	1,866	2,068
Peutherer, Mrs J K	6	27	5	6	1	18.5	11,855	20,648
P F M Civil Eng Co Ltd	1	14	1	3	2	7.1	2,719	8,398
Phillips, Trevor	2	10	2	3	1	20.0	3,754	6,115
Phillips, G J	2	6	1	0	0	16.7	1,956	1,956
Phillips, A D	1	4	1	0	1	25.0	1,670	1,880
Phillips, Mrs I	1	7	2	2	1	28.6	5,590	7,843
Phillips, L.	1	7	2	1	0	28.6	3,507	3,912
Phipps, Duane & Company	1	12	1	1	3	8.3	2,192	4,510
Phipps, Mrs C	1	7	1	0	1	14.3	1,940	2,286
Pidgeon, G.	1	1	1	0	0	100.0	3,623	3,623
Piercy, J	1	7	1	2	1	14.3	3,193	5,934

	H	R	W	2nd	3rd	%W-R	£WIN	£W/P
Pike, Stewart	2	4	1	0	0	25.0	1,368	1,368
Pilkington, Lady	1	6	1	2	0	16.7	3,716	5,573
Pilkington, Mrs T D	1	5	1	0	2	20.0	2,093	2,818
Piller, P.	27	158	33	24	20	20.9	90,433	121,742
Pinfield, Keith M	1	14	5	1	1	35.7	13,415	14,211
Pinto, Maurice E.	9	28	5	1	4	17.9	19,212	23,245
Pipe, M C.	10	25	2	1	2	8.0	3,588	4,645
Piper, P W	2	13	2	4	2	15.4	5,405	8,414
Pipe Scudamore Racing Club	12	97	35	18	9	36.1	61,014	79,887
Pitman, Miss Susan	2	5	2	1	0	40.0	2,534	3,179
Plaistowe, Brian	2	6	2	0	1	33.3	4,635	4,946
Plummer, Lord	1	3	1	1	0	33.3	1,822	2,376
Pocock, I J	1	3	1	0	0	33.3	1,256	1,256
Poland, J M	1	11	1	3	1	9.1	1,382	2,934
Pond House Racing	5	40	6	9	2	15.0	10,375	15,855
Ponsonby, Rupert	1	6	2	0	0	33.3	2,925	2,925
Poore, Colin W	2	11	2	0	1	18.2	6,164	6,780
Popham, M	2	16	2	6	2	12.5	3,922	13,538
Portman, D	3	8	1	1	1	12.5	1,030	1,619
Potter, J E.	1	10	6	2	0	60.0	29,239	31,639
Pounder, C C	2	4	1	1	0	25.0	1,646	2,078
Powell, Mrs J K	3	20	5	6	0	25.0	41,037	57,084
Powell, S	7	23	1	2	3	4.3	3,213	7,791
P R D Fasteners Ltd	1	11	3	5	0	27.3	11,540	15,622
Premier Crops Limited	2	9	2	0	3	22.2	3,638	4,306
Preston, Alf	2	10	1	1	2	10.0	2,198	3,158
Price, J T	4	18	5	5	1	27.8	23,933	31,046
Price, G M	3	19	2	2	2	10.5	4,251	5,655
Principal Racing	1	7	1	2	2	14.3	1,627	2,871
Proctor, Mrs R A	1	1	1	0	0	100.0	2,653	2,653
Provan Hatch Bloodstock Ltd	1	12	1	4	1	8.3	3,583	7,999
Pryke, T R.	2	6	1	2	2	16.7	1,172	2,674
Pugh, D	3	19	3	2	4	15.8	4,619	7,092
Quesnel, Nick	1	12	3	3	2	25.0	5,308	7,808
Quicksilver Racing Partnership	1	9	1	2	2	11.1	2,738	4,450
Quinn, M	1	6	1	2	0	16.7	2,231	3,497
Quinton, M G St	1	4	1	1	0	25.0	4,760	9,120
Racing Investments	1	5	2	1	0	40.0	4,664	5,249
Rackliff, J	1	10	1	1	3	10.0	2,247	5,099
R A M Racecourses Ltd.	1	11	2	3	0	18.2	3,407	4,984
Ramsden, Jonathan	1	4	1	1	0	25.0	1,657	2,217
Ramsden, Mrs B.	7	53	6	10	10	11.3	11,158	19,789
Randall, Les	2	10	2	1	2	20.0	10,404	13,286
Rankin, Ms K	1	5	3	1	0	60.0	3,553	4,133
Rapallo Racing	1	5	1	1	0	20.0	1,590	2,240
Rapkins, Mrs Val	6	23	2	1	2	8.7	2,789	3,696
R E A Bott (Wigmore St) Ltd	3	19	3	8	2	15.8	15,711	30,223
Read, J G	1	10	3	1	3	30.0	14,124	16,105
Redford, G.	2	6	1	0	2	16.7	1,350	1,764
Reed, Guy	10	18	6	2	2	33.3	10,259	11,826
Reed, Miss Juliet E.	1	7	1	2	1	14.3	1,674	3,704
Reed, W J.	2	11	3	1	0	27.3	5,429	5,919
Reed, W G.	1	14	1	1	2	7.1	2,130	3,272
Rees, Mrs G S.	3	8	1	0	1	12.5	828	1,140
Regan, J	1	5	2	0	2	40.0	2,122	2,498
Regis, Mrs T H.	1	1	1	0	0	100.0	1,253	1,253
Reich, Mrs Philomena	2	13	2	1	1	15.4	2,909	3,712
Reid, Mrs F M	1	10	1	1	0	10.0	1,562	2,007
Reip, Mrs Jackie	2	11	2	2	3	18.2	4,507	7,208
Restoration (South West) Ltd	1	7	1	1	0	14.3	1,876	2,283
Retter, Mrs J G	3	9	2	0	0	22.2	2,934	3,138
Richard, J W M M	1	17	5	1	2	29.4	11,691	12,923
Richard Green (Fine Paintings)	3	13	5	1	2	38.5	8,645	10,264
Richards, Mrs H F	1	2	1	0	0	50.0	2,247	2,247
Richards, Ray	2	9	2	1	0	22.2	6,272	8,941
Richards, Mrs Joanne	3	14	2	5	1	14.3	13,474	18,304
Riley, P.	1	14	4	2	2	28.6	9,869	11,206
Riley-Smith, T S M S	3	11	1	0	0	9.1	1,705	1,705
Rimell, Mark G.	3	10	2	0	2	20.0	4,900	5,786
Roach Foods Limited	4	19	7	2	1	36.8	20,674	22,431
Roberts, Mrs E	4	17	3	5	2	17.6	6,077	9,591
Robertson, John	1	6	1	0	0	16.7	2,274	2,274
Robins, Mrs Shirley	12	44	16	6	3	36.4	144,375	189,428
Robinson, David G.	1	9	3	1	2	33.3	6,426	7,978
Robinson, N	1	3	1	0	1	33.3	2,280	2,971
Robinson, Dr J F.	1	2	2	0	0	100.0	5,491	5,491
Robinson Publications Limited	3	12	3	2	1	25.0	27,591	30,965
Robinson, L J.	1	8	1	1	0	12.5	2,912	3,932
Robson, John	2	12	6	1	0	50.0	22,869	27,282

	H	R	W	2nd	3rd	%W-R	£WIN	£W/P
Robson, Mrs V	2	16	1	0	4	6.3	1,918	2,741
Rocketeers, The	1	10	2	2	2	20.0	5,921	8,673
Rodford, P R	6	18	1	1	2	5.6	2,334	3,145
Rolfe, D	1	1	1	0	0	100.0	1,690	1,690
Ronan, T P	1	4	1	2	1	25.0	1,151	1,941
Roseff, Will	1	7	2	0	1	28.6	3,301	3,603
Rowe, Mrs Merrilyn	3	16	1	0	0	6.3	1,474	1,474
Rowlandsons Ltd (Jewellers)	1	10	2	0	2	20.0	12,246	18,639
Royston Racing Club Ltd	1	9	2	1	1	22.2	5,516	6,743
Rozenbroek, M J	3	9	1	1	0	11.1	1,996	2,540
Russell, Miss D S	1	13	1	3	2	7.7	2,303	4,069
Russell, R G	5	19	6	5	5	31.6	10,522	15,055
Russell, Peter J S	1	2	1	0	0	50.0	2,138	2,138
Ryall, N A	1	10	2	0	3	20.0	6,902	8,373
Ryan, J J	1	9	2	3	0	22.2	2,242	3,633
Rykens, C L	1	9	2	0	1	22.2	6,343	8,366
Rylands, P D	3	8	2	4	1	25.0	4,133	8,533
Sabey, R	1	5	1	1	1	20.0	1,475	2,286
Saccomando, A	2	18	5	3	1	27.8	13,777	16,636
Saeed, Ali	1	9	2	1	1	22.2	4,479	7,165
Sainsbury, Simon	8	28	9	5	4	32.1	35,484	41,937
Sale, B	1	13	1	0	2	7.7	1,811	2,304
Salter, Mrs J	1	13	1	0	2	7.7	1,684	2,370
Samuel, Mrs Basil	4	11	2	2	1	18.2	3,659	5,265
Sanders, Mrs Anna L	1	11	1	1	2	9.1	1,595	2,565
Sanderson, C B	1	4	1	1	0	25.0	1,625	2,072
Saunders, C R	1	4	3	0	0	75.0	4,381	4,381
Saunders, M S	6	23	3	3	1	13.0	5,611	7,527
Saunders, Miss E	2	9	1	1	1	11.1	2,120	2,828
Savill, P D	2	14	5	2	4	35.7	20,889	37,628
Scargill, Mrs Susan	1	4	2	0	1	50.0	4,013	4,313
Scarth, Eric	1	5	1	3	1	20.0	84,734	116,853
Schaverien, Keen, Murphy Partnership	1	3	3	0	0	100.0	7,741	7,741
Schlagman, Robert F	2	5	2	0	0	40.0	4,348	4,348
Schmidt-Bodner, B	3	13	8	2	0	61.5	32,409	37,745
Scholey, Mrs M B	1	7	2	2	1	28.6	6,874	10,130
Scott, Mrs J J Kirk	2	11	2	3	2	18.2	3,784	6,935
Scott, Mrs A Reid	2	7	1	0	0	14.3	1,873	1,937
Scott, J C de C	3	15	2	2	0	13.3	3,857	5,086
Scotto, Mrs H	1	7	1	1	2	14.3	1,714	3,200
Searle, R T C	1	6	3	0	0	50.0	7,799	7,799
Searle, Mrs B M	1	7	1	1	0	14.3	4,208	5,072
Sellars, P	1	3	1	0	0	33.3	1,953	1,953
Sellers, W A	4	26	2	2	1	7.7	4,837	6,306
Semple, Miss J	1	7	2	1	0	28.6	7,006	12,193
Sept, The Marston	1	10	2	3	1	20.0	5,775	9,413
Severn First Partnership	1	10	2	4	1	20.0	6,372	15,589
Sewell, Mrs L M	3	7	1	0	1	14.3	2,490	3,617
Shankland, Christopher	2	6	2	0	1	33.3	3,291	3,454
Sharp, Sir Milton	1	2	1	0	0	50.0	774	774
Shaw, R A	1	7	1	0	0	14.3	1,320	1,320
Shaw, R V	3	10	3	0	0	30.0	5,241	5,517
Shaw, I L	1	5	1	2	1	20.0	2,445	4,673
Shaw, Richard	3	13	1	4	3	7.7	2,233	6,890
Shedden, John	2	5	2	0	1	40.0	3,660	4,118
Sheffield, Col M J F	1	2	1	0	0	50.0	2,006	2,006
Shenkin, Dr Ian R	1	2	2	0	0	100.0	2,280	2,280
Sherwood, Mrs P	2	11	1	2	2	9.1	4,143	6,588
Shields, Mrs Thomas	2	14	3	1	4	21.4	6,983	8,961
Shilton, P L	1	6	1	0	0	16.7	1,749	2,379
Shone, M L	3	15	1	3	2	6.7	3,493	6,381
Short, D R	1	13	1	1	2	7.7	2,892	4,557
Short, Iain Macdonald And Jim	1	7	1	0	2	14.3	3,460	9,845
Shouler, G E	9	29	4	11	3	13.8	25,273	60,302
Shrimpton, T H	1	4	1	0	1	25.0	1,669	1,917
Sibley, Harry	1	8	1	2	2	12.5	1,732	4,178
Siddall, Miss L C	3	22	3	0	2	13.6	8,521	9,778
Silk, Dr D B A	2	9	4	2	2	44.4	6,646	8,243
Sillars Civil Engineering	1	7	3	2	0	42.9	8,066	19,804
Sills, D F	3	16	2	1	3	12.5	3,315	4,864
Simpson, P E	1	10	1	0	0	10.0	1,572	1,730
Sinclair, Robert	2	2	1	0	0	50.0	12,720	13,732
Singleton, John	2	14	1	3	4	7.1	3,270	7,471
Skan, Mrs R J	1	8	2	2	1	25.0	6,584	9,428
Skeltools Ltd	1	1	1	0	0	100.0	1,872	1,872
Skinner, Mrs T J McInnes	2	11	1	2	1	9.1	3,106	5,257
Skirton, B P	1	5	2	1	1	40.0	7,814	12,371
Slade, P	4	15	2	2	1	13.3	5,587	6,989
Slatcher, Mrs E M	1	6	1	0	1	16.7	1,145	1,307

	H	R	W	2nd	3rd	%W-R	£WIN	£W/P
Slotamatics (Bolton) Ltd	1	5	1	0	0	20.0	3,415	3,656
Sly, Mrs P	4	19	5	1	4	26.3	11,786	13,758
Small, G	2	15	3	3	2	20.0	7,829	10,883
Smith, D (Saul)	2	7	2	0	0	28.6	4,120	4,120
Smith, Mrs Wendy	1	2	1	1	0	50.0	1,590	2,170
Smith, B	2	6	1	0	1	16.7	1,298	1,682
Smith, Mrs S	11	49	2	4	4	4.1	3,074	6,136
Smith, Mrs Claire	7	32	4	7	3	12.5	8,285	17,369
Smith, Charles	1	10	3	2	2	30.0	5,563	6,892
Smith, A E	1	5	1	0	1	20.0	2,147	2,453
Smith, Mrs E R	1	10	3	2	1	30.0	9,294	12,765
Smith, David G	1	11	2	1	2	18.2	5,118	7,166
Smith, Mrs Gwen	1	14	3	2	0	21.4	6,541	7,199
Smith, Miss Judy	1	3	3	0	0	100.0	23,477	23,477
Smith, Alfred	2	15	1	4	0	6.7	1,469	3,448
Smith, Clive D	2	5	5	0	0	100.0	16,087	16,087
Smith, Sidney J	1	8	4	2	1	50.0	5,536	7,356
Smith, Mrs J	2	9	2	0	3	22.2	4,474	5,153
Smith, Miss Diane F	1	4	1	0	1	25.0	2,385	2,700
Smith, Miss H	2	5	1	0	0	20.0	2,285	2,285
Smith, John J	2	4	1	0	0	25.0	1,548	1,548
Smith, Miss T L	1	2	1	0	0	50.0	1,506	1,506
Smith, W J	5	38	1	6	1	2.6	2,265	5,741
Smith Mansfield Meat Co Ltd	1	8	1	1	3	12.5	1,480	3,074
Smiths Cleaning Service	1	3	1	1	0	33.3	1,564	2,066
Smyth-Osbourne, J G	1	3	1	0	0	33.3	2,738	2,738
Snape, Mrs J M	1	14	1	3	1	7.1	1,604	3,697
Snook, Laurie	5	13	1	1	0	7.7	1,637	2,501
Soames, M R	2	8	2	1	0	25.0	4,845	5,278
Sofroniou, Andreas	3	20	7	1	3	35.0	14,608	18,026
Solman, Geoffrey	2	22	2	4	5	9.1	4,370	10,479
Solomons, A N	1	6	2	1	2	33.3	4,177	10,469
South, J C	1	8	1	3	1	12.5	2,271	4,737
Spaceage Plastics Limited	4	20	6	5	2	30.0	18,826	23,479
Sparkler Filters (Great Britain) Ltd	1	10	2	1	1	20.0	3,018	3,756
Speirs, D A	1	4	1	0	0	25.0	2,151	2,359
Spencer, C J	1	3	1	0	0	33.3	2,063	2,063
Spencer, Roger J	1	8	1	1	1	12.5	1,602	2,315
Spensley, Mrs M A	1	5	1	3	0	20.0	1,305	3,439
Spielman, Mrs John	2	11	2	1	2	18.2	6,528	8,548
Spooner, Howard	1	3	2	0	0	66.7	6,752	6,752
Spore, M J	7	21	2	1	1	9.5	3,745	4,380
Spring, Mrs Eileen	1	12	2	0	1	16.7	3,971	4,247
Stafford, Lady Nelson Of	1	7	2	1	0	28.6	4,101	4,436
Stafford, J B	1	5	1	0	1	20.0	1,621	1,811
Stanley, Mrs Richard	2	12	2	2	0	16.7	5,280	7,413
Stanners, M	3	26	6	3	1	23.1	18,144	20,435
Staple, A	2	20	2	4	3	10.0	4,536	8,562
Star Eng Products (Shrewsbury) Ltd	1	3	1	0	1	33.3	1,350	1,590
Steed, Mrs R O	1	9	3	4	0	33.3	13,252	19,486
Steel, Miss S	1	9	3	1	2	33.3	7,526	10,456
Steers, Ian S	1	3	1	0	0	33.3	2,448	2,448
Steinmann, Mrs I M	5	13	2	2	2	15.4	6,305	8,137
Stennett, A	3	11	1	3	0	9.1	1,305	3,539
Stephenson, W A	26	49	1	1	5	2.0	1,660	3,238
Stephenson, J	1	7	1	0	2	14.3	2,794	3,687
Stern, David M	1	4	1	1	0	25.0	1,484	2,154
Steve Lilley Racing Ltd	1	7	1	1	0	14.3	828	1,376
Stevens, C H	1	8	2	2	0	25.0	3,750	4,584
Stevens, R N	1	2	2	0	0	100.0	4,966	4,966
Stevens, M H L	2	8	1	1	2	12.5	2,952	4,203
Stevens, Barry	5	16	1	0	2	6.3	1,614	2,082
Stevenson, G G	2	6	3	2	0	50.0	7,335	11,716
Steventon, John	1	6	1	1	2	16.7	1,784	2,669
Steward, Chris	2	12	1	3	1	8.3	1,954	3,627
Stewart, G P P	1	4	1	2	0	25.0	2,595	4,171
Stewart-Brown, Mrs M L	1	6	2	1	1	33.3	11,031	13,806
Stewart-Brown, B T	5	20	3	4	3	15.0	7,177	12,049
Stirk, Mrs M	2	14	3	2	3	21.4	9,076	13,015
Stocks, Mrs R E	2	9	1	2	1	11.1	3,048	5,767
Stoddart, A D	1	5	2	2	0	40.0	5,129	6,883
Stone, John	1	8	2	1	1	25.0	4,525	5,663
Stoner, P	2	16	4	3	1	25.0	12,305	14,403
Straker, Major I C	1	9	1	3	1	11.1	2,023	4,421
Strauss, Derek	1	3	1	1	0	33.3	3,835	4,520
Strawson, W H	1	11	4	3	2	36.4	10,026	13,252
Struel, Irving	1	5	2	1	0	40.0	10,303	15,923
Stuart, Mrs K A	4	24	6	7	1	25.0	14,280	21,158
Stubbings, Trevor W	1	4	1	0	0	25.0	1,302	1,302

	H	R	W	2nd	3rd	%W-R	£WIN	£W/P
Sturgis, Keith	3	18	3	4	3	16.7	5,753	8,398
Sturt, W E	7	23	7	2	5	30.4	19,923	25,682
Sullivan, J	1	3	2	0	0	66.7	3,433	3,433
Sullivan, P A	2	12	1	1	1	8.3	935	1,663
Sumner, Andrew	3	15	1	0	1	6.7	1,464	1,717
Sumner, J B	4	20	6	4	1	30.0	20,796	26,207
Sumner, Mrs B	1	5	1	2	0	20.0	1,484	2,428
Sunpak Potatoes	2	11	1	2	0	9.1	1,764	2,929
Sussex Renovations Ltd	1	1	1	0	0	100.0	2,052	2,052
Sutherland, Duke Of	1	10	3	0	2	30.0	10,927	12,505
Sweeney, G E	1	11	3	1	1	27.3	7,723	8,717
Swiers, J E	5	23	2	2	2	8.7	2,335	4,677
Swiers, W G	1	3	1	2	0	33.3	1,910	3,024
Swift, M A	1	5	2	1	0	40.0	30,096	31,464
Swinbank, G A	2	9	2	1	1	22.2	2,494	3,348
Systemcare Limited	1	6	2	1	0	33.3	4,314	4,770
Taaffe, A J	1	6	1	3	2	16.7	2,536	6,668
Tabor, M	3	18	2	5	2	11.1	3,980	44,607
Taplin, Peter	1	3	1	1	1	33.3	2,058	3,401
Tarrant, A F	1	10	2	2	2	20.0	5,996	8,378
Tate, David	2	5	1	0	1	20.0	875	1,069
Tate, R	4	17	3	1	4	17.6	4,476	6,489
Tate, Mrs Susan	2	15	4	3	4	26.7	10,727	14,035
Tavistock, Lord	1	2	1	0	0	50.0	2,532	2,532
Taylor, P A	1	5	2	1	1	40.0	3,586	4,284
Taylor, A K	1	12	1	1	0	8.3	1,480	2,000
Taylor, Mrs June	2	15	2	1	0	13.3	1,891	2,121
Taylor, Henry	2	9	2	2	0	22.2	3,153	4,038
T E F Freight (Scarborough) Ltd	1	4	2	0	1	50.0	4,020	4,385
Terry Warner Sports	2	14	3	0	0	21.4	6,686	6,686
Thackray, Brian	2	8	1	0	2	12.5	3,478	5,061
The Amigos Partnership	1	9	2	5	1	22.2	4,969	11,053
The A M W Partnership	1	1	1	0	0	100.0	1,471	1,471
The Barton Bendish Partnership	2	11	1	3	2	9.1	988	2,923
The Burford Laundry Company Ltd	2	14	2	1	2	14.3	13,553	17,024
The Caledonian Racing Club	3	13	3	2	0	23.1	6,533	7,885
The Desperate Partnership	1	5	3	0	0	60.0	7,133	7,133
The Edinburgh Woollen Mill Ltd	12	54	9	9	7	16.7	25,448	42,966
The Fairfax Partnership	1	2	1	0	1	50.0	1,375	1,571
The Fotoexpress Partnership	1	9	4	0	0	44.4	7,696	8,571
The Gradon Associates	1	9	2	2	0	22.2	4,051	5,355
The Heyfleet Partnership	2	13	2	1	0	15.4	4,434	5,377
The Ivy Syndicate	2	11	1	0	4	9.1	7,250	12,808
The Jackson Six	1	6	1	0	0	16.7	828	828
The Morley Stud	2	11	1	0	1	9.1	1,800	2,208
The Oak Tree Syndicate	1	5	1	1	0	20.0	1,467	1,822
The Pessimists	1	5	2	1	1	40.0	4,524	5,231
The Plough Partnership	1	6	2	2	1	33.3	2,959	4,696
The Roses Syndicate	1	5	2	0	2	40.0	4,932	5,975
The Scottish Trilby Racing Club	1	5	1	1	1	20.0	2,424	3,450
The Talking Horse Partnership	1	10	2	0	2	20.0	27,151	32,933
The Turf Club	1	4	1	0	0	25.0	2,898	2,898
Thomas, J L	1	5	2	0	1	40.0	3,556	7,970
Thompson, Peter S	2	12	2	0	2	16.7	4,263	5,438
Thompson, Mrs David	2	7	1	0	0	14.3	26,618	26,618
Thompson, T W	1	5	3	1	0	60.0	3,923	4,389
Thompson, David J	2	14	1	1	3	7.1	1,672	2,819
Thompson, J F	3	8	1	0	3	12.5	1,203	1,879
Thomson, A M	1	6	1	1	0	16.7	2,416	2,984
Thomson, R W	1	10	1	0	1	10.0	1,996	2,394
Thornton, David R	1	11	2	3	1	18.2	5,292	8,111
Thrift, Brian	1	6	1	1	2	16.7	1,719	2,697
Thurgood, M S C	2	13	1	1	2	7.7	1,749	2,672
Tice, R J Sunley	1	7	2	1	1	28.6	5,605	10,936
Tierney, Peter	1	5	1	2	0	20.0	1,670	2,460
Tilley, R P	1	1	1	0	0	100.0	2,039	2,039
Tindall, Ronald	2	9	2	1	2	22.2	3,514	4,421
Tindall, S P	6	34	2	6	0	5.9	4,133	7,319
Tingey, P G	1	2	1	0	0	50.0	1,537	1,537
Tinkler, Mrs Marie	1	5	2	1	1	40.0	1,843	2,501
T J Myles & Co (Contractors) Ltd	1	7	1	1	0	14.3	1,953	3,041
Tobitt, George	1	7	1	2	0	14.3	1,883	3,927
Tom Pettifer Ltd	1	12	2	1	2	16.7	5,574	7,141
Tooth, Raymond	4	19	2	1	2	10.5	5,901	9,299
Tory, G G H	1	4	1	2	0	25.0	1,900	2,648
Toulson, Miss J E	5	20	1	4	1	5.0	2,469	5,511
Towler, Mrs S	1	5	2	0	0	40.0	6,733	6,733
Townley-Berry, Mrs E J	1	7	1	1	0	14.3	1,649	2,117
Tranter, James Keith	1	10	1	2	2	10.0	2,010	3,293

	H	R	W	2nd	3rd	%W-R	£WIN	£W/P
Travail Employment Group Ltd	2	25	1	5	4	4.0	1,425	5,633
Travers-Clark, D P	1	6	1	1	0	16.7	2,948	3,764
Trietline, C C	4	21	3	7	2	14.3	4,539	8,133
Trobe, Mrs D A La	1	8	1	3	1	12.5	2,385	4,795
Tucker, Mrs E A	1	6	1	0	0	16.7	1,618	1,618
Turnbull, Mrs G A	2	7	1	1	0	14.3	1,786	2,255
Turner, Miss S J	2	9	2	2	2	22.2	4,950	7,448
Turner, Mrs A W	2	6	1	1	1	16.7	1,564	2,358
Turner, Mrs L G	2	12	1	1	0	8.3	1,800	2,442
Twiston-Davies, N A	5	24	8	1	4	33.3	15,491	18,511
T W Suiter & Son Ltd	1	6	1	0	2	16.7	1,203	1,427
Tyler, Mrs Joy	1	4	1	0	1	25.0	1,467	1,734
Tylor, P A	4	22	2	5	4	9.1	4,869	9,683
Tyrer, R	2	15	4	2	0	26.7	7,541	8,735
U K Home Computers	2	16	4	2	2	25.0	9,061	11,711
Upson, John R	21	76	11	5	9	14.5	28,278	37,391
Upson, Mrs Diane	5	27	5	6	3	18.5	47,329	53,925
Valentini, Ms K	4	16	1	1	2	6.3	2,059	2,903
Valks, David	1	6	1	0	1	16.7	809	974
Vaughan, Lawrence &	1	4	1	0	0	25.0	1,387	1,387
Vaughan, Mrs R	2	10	2	1	2	20.0	34,598	43,151
Veitch, John	1	10	2	1	2	20.0	3,962	5,664
Vernon, Mrs Pauline	1	5	1	1	1	20.0	3,501	5,036
Vestey, M W	1	5	1	1	1	20.0	2,192	3,354
Vestey, Lord	4	23	2	2	6	8.7	5,441	10,323
Vickers, Miss L J	1	2	1	0	0	50.0	1,924	1,924
Victor Chandler Ltd	1	3	1	1	1	33.3	2,846	8,404
Villiers, Hugh	1	7	1	3	1	14.3	1,636	3,083
Visual Identity Ltd-Design Studio	1	9	1	2	2	11.1	1,811	3,724
Wade, John	14	77	7	6	10	9.1	12,832	20,549
Wade, B	1	7	2	0	2	28.6	3,907	4,440
Wade-Jones, David	1	11	1	2	2	9.1	1,940	3,366
Walby, J	2	11	2	2	1	18.2	3,329	5,253
Waldie, A G	1	4	2	0	0	50.0	2,721	2,721
Wales, Mrs A	1	2	1	0	0	50.0	1,753	1,904
Waley-Cohen, Robert	4	16	3	2	0	18.8	11,439	16,664
Walker, J Wilson	2	24	6	4	2	25.0	14,813	19,819
Walker, T	1	2	1	0	0	50.0	1,756	1,756
Walker, J J H	1	11	4	2	1	36.4	7,624	9,114
Wall, Nigel	1	5	1	0	1	20.0	1,119	1,328
Walsh, D O	1	10	1	5	1	10.0	1,497	5,517
Walton, Mrs F T	11	45	2	4	4	4.4	7,012	11,367
Walwyn, Mrs F	4	19	2	3	2	10.5	8,955	25,232
Ward, Patrick	1	10	1	0	3	10.0	2,149	3,303
Ward, Mrs V C	7	25	2	0	0	8.0	4,328	4,328
Ward, Mrs B	1	6	1	1	1	16.7	1,594	2,497
Ward-Thomas, M	2	10	1	1	3	10.0	3,968	6,422
Warren, Mrs L M	1	7	2	0	2	28.6	10,592	12,564
Warren, John	2	6	2	1	0	33.3	2,823	3,380
Warren, R B	1	4	1	0	1	25.0	1,954	2,198
Waters, R	2	11	3	1	2	27.3	9,442	11,520
Watership Down Racing	2	9	3	2	1	33.3	13,366	15,614
Wates, A T A	5	17	1	1	3	5.9	8,694	12,414
Watkinson-Yull, Mrs G	2	11	1	2	3	9.1	4,163	9,303
Watson, Lady Susan	2	12	2	1	4	16.7	3,661	6,088
Watts, R C	1	5	3	0	0	60.0	6,594	6,594
Watts, Mrs S	1	8	1	2	0	12.5	2,775	3,743
Watts, N M	1	10	1	2	2	10.0	2,008	3,949
Wauchope, Mrs A D	1	3	1	1	1	33.3	2,088	2,938
Webb, S R	1	5	2	1	1	40.0	7,561	10,298
Weekes, G D	1	8	3	2	0	37.5	7,069	10,213
Weeks, H	1	3	1	0	0	33.3	3,302	3,302
Welch, Mrs S C	1	4	2	1	0	50.0	4,063	4,468
Welch, F	1	6	2	0	1	33.3	5,441	5,738
Weller, A D	2	9	2	0	1	22.2	4,259	5,822
Wells, Mrs H S	1	9	1	3	0	11.1	1,079	3,344
West, Mrs James	2	7	1	0	1	14.3	2,484	2,778
Westbrook, Sir Neil	3	16	4	3	4	25.0	10,677	21,266
Westminster, Anne Duchess Of	5	23	4	1	2	17.4	14,815	16,470
Weston, J R	1	10	2	0	1	20.0	2,595	2,825
Wetherby Racing Bureau Plc	5	27	1	6	2	3.7	2,040	7,202
Wey, E T	2	29	1	6	4	3.4	1,481	5,193
Wheatley, Exors Of The Late Mr C J	4	18	3	2	0	16.7	8,343	9,792
Wheeler, P R	1	5	1	1	0	20.0	1,764	2,524
Whelan, J J	6	27	4	7	3	14.8	16,502	31,931
Whelan, Pat	1	5	1	0	0	20.0	2,784	2,784
Whetherly, Lt Col W	1	7	6	0	1	85.7	21,287	24,740
Whettam, Mrs B	2	5	3	2	0	60.0	4,461	5,674
Whillans, Chas N	2	12	1	2	1	8.3	1,646	3,688

	H	R	W	2nd	3rd	%W-R	£WIN	£W/P
Whillans, A C	4	20	1	1	3	5.0	2,092	4,140
Whitbread, W H	3	12	2	0	4	16.7	2,971	4,172
Whitby, Sqn Ldr P G	1	3	1	0	0	33.3	1,814	1,814
White, Mrs P A	2	6	1	2	2	16.7	2,103	3,769
White, G F	3	17	1	2	3	5.9	1,918	3,694
White, Anthony	2	6	1	2	0	16.7	1,700	2,615
White, H D	1	9	2	2	2	22.2	13,182	17,001
White, Arthur	1	6	1	1	1	16.7	1,480	3,060
White, R L	2	3	1	1	0	33.3	7,400	8,248
Whitehorn, B	2	12	2	4	1	16.7	3,924	6,938
White Horse Racing Ltd	1	5	3	0	1	60.0	49,638	51,677
White Horse (United Distillers UK Plc)	1	8	1	1	2	12.5	2,710	5,278
Whitley, T J	9	39	5	4	6	12.8	12,342	22,974
Whittle, R A B	1	3	1	1	0	33.3	1,870	2,394
Whyte, David	1	5	2	0	1	40.0	4,241	4,709
Whyte, John	5	23	2	1	2	8.7	5,412	7,871
Wickett, Mrs Jane M	1	1	1	0	0	100.0	1,788	1,788
Wiegand, Peter	2	2	1	1	0	50.0	2,013	2,460
Wightman, W G R	3	18	1	1	4	5.6	1,580	3,282
Wilby, N	2	19	2	2	3	10.5	3,827	6,194
Wilde, P M de	1	8	2	1	0	25.0	6,962	7,640
Wiles, John	1	6	1	1	0	16.7	1,969	2,465
Wilkins, M A	1	5	1	0	1	20.0	1,235	1,471
Wilkins, R C	1	6	5	0	1	83.3	35,370	35,620
Wilkinson, Eddie	2	13	2	3	2	15.4	2,406	5,508
Wilkinson, Miss J	1	10	1	0	3	10.0	2,196	3,100
Wilkinson, G	1	6	3	1	1	50.0	6,563	7,480
Wilkinson, Mrs R M	1	8	3	1	1	37.5	21,128	26,565
Wilkinson, Mrs John	2	11	1	0	3	9.1	2,369	3,959
Willan, M J	2	9	2	3	2	22.2	4,132	6,633
Williams, R H	2	13	1	0	2	7.7	895	1,652
Williams, Mrs C C	2	7	4	1	0	57.1	32,556	41,047
Williams, Sid	4	11	2	1	1	18.2	5,423	6,959
Williams, D Gwyn	2	15	1	1	4	6.7	2,998	5,620
Williams, Richard	2	6	2	2	0	33.3	5,380	6,566
Williams, Rhys Thomas	3	15	1	3	1	6.7	2,332	6,215
Wilsdon, B R	1	6	1	1	1	16.7	1,719	2,622
Wilson, Fred	2	14	1	3	0	7.1	3,143	5,490
Wilson, T M	1	2	1	0	0	50.0	1,484	1,484
Wilson, Mrs M J	2	11	1	1	2	9.1	3,522	5,024
Wilson, D A	1	5	2	0	1	40.0	3,556	3,765
Wilson, Arthur	1	8	3	0	0	37.5	8,203	8,203
Wilson, Andrews &	1	3	1	1	0	33.3	1,780	3,930
Wilson, Mrs Judy	3	10	5	2	2	50.0	10,172	13,950
Wilson, Mrs Jos	1	6	2	1	1	33.3	2,942	4,018
Wilson, P	1	1	1	0	0	100.0	1,772	1,772
Wilson, Andrew	1	4	1	0	1	25.0	2,213	2,468
Wiltshire, G	13	64	8	12	9	12.5	14,018	22,079
Windrush Racing	1	11	3	2	0	27.3	10,413	14,934
Winfield, Peter S	2	8	1	1	1	12.5	1,473	2,675
Winfield, Edward P	1	7	1	1	2	14.3	5,222	23,276
Winstanley, Graham	1	4	1	0	1	25.0	1,893	2,199
Winter, J N G	1	5	2	1	0	40.0	3,982	4,441
Wintle, D J	7	13	1	1	0	7.7	1,506	1,986
Winwood Connell Partnership	1	7	2	1	1	28.6	5,785	6,602
Wood, T	3	13	4	2	1	30.8	7,740	9,400
Wood, R S	4	19	2	3	2	10.5	3,862	6,896
Woodall, M	3	8	1	2	1	12.5	1,481	2,572
Woodcock, N A	1	8	1	2	2	12.5	1,734	3,089
Woodlands (Worcestershire) Ltd	4	12	1	0	1	8.3	3,054	3,551
Woods, D	1	6	2	1	0	33.3	3,577	4,139
Woods, S P C	1	2	1	0	0	50.0	1,861	1,861
Woodward, Mrs Linda	2	5	1	0	0	20.0	1,910	1,910
Wootton, Mrs J S	1	3	1	0	1	33.3	1,756	2,185
Worcester, M	2	5	3	0	0	60.0	16,093	16,093
Wordingham, L	2	10	1	0	0	10.0	1,688	1,688
Wright, A J	1	4	1	0	1	25.0	1,604	1,816
Wright, Jerry	2	10	4	1	3	40.0	9,278	12,626
Wright, John E	1	4	1	0	0	25.0	2,220	2,220
Wright, Carleton	1	11	1	2	2	9.1	2,269	3,764
Wright, Mrs D	1	3	1	1	0	33.3	25,499	26,741
Wyatt, Mrs A	1	3	1	0	1	33.3	3,665	4,099
Yates, Tony	3	12	3	2	1	25.0	9,876	12,075
Yeadon, J N	2	12	4	7	1	33.3	125,142	146,251
York, Mrs S C	2	8	4	0	2	50.0	6,282	7,467
Zawawi, O	1	2	1	1	0	50.0	1,998	2,494
Zetland, Lord	2	11	2	0	1	18.2	4,161	4,455

Leading owners: hurdles and chases 1945–93

		Horses	Races Won	Value £
1945–46	Mr J Morant	1	2	9001
1946–47	Mr J J McDowell	1	1	10007
1947–48	Mr J Proctor	3	5	9801
1948–49	Mr W F Williamson	1	4	10350
1949–50	Mrs L Brotherton	4	7	14294
1950–51	Mr J Royle	1	3	10221
1951–52	Miss D Paget	19	50	14191
1952–53	Mr J H Griffin	2	2	10015
1953–54	Mr J H Griffin	3	4	10456
1954–55	Mrs W H E Welman	1	1	8934
1955–56	Mrs L Carver	1	5	10683
1956–57	Mrs Geoffrey Kohn	1	2	9618
1957–58	Mr D J Coughlan	1	1	13719
1958–59	Mr J E Bigg	1	3	14558
1959–60	Miss W H Wallace	1	1	13134
1960–61	Mr C Vaughan	1	2	20700
1961–62	Mr N Cohen	2	3	20852
1962–63	Mr P B Raymond	1	2	22095
1963–64	Mr J K Goodman	1	1	20280
1964–65	Mrs M Stephenson	1	4	23237
1965–66	Duchess of Westminster	1	4	24572
1966–67	Mr C P T Watkins	1	1	17630
1967–68	Mr H S Alper	3	7	18240
1968–69	Mr B P Jenks	9	25	20619
1969–70	Mr E R Courage	6	14	20001
1970–71	Mr F Pontin	3	5	24999
1971–72	Capt T A Forster	2	2	25302
1972–73	Mr N H Le Mare	3	8	34196
1973–74	Mr N H Le Mare	2	7	37386
1974–75	Mr R Guest	1	1	38005
1975–76	Mr P B Raymond	1	2	45325
1976–77	Mr N H Le Mare	1	2	41791
1977–78	Mrs O Jackson	3	13	49791
1978–79	Snailwell Stud Co Ltd	3	7	49969
1979–80	Mr H J Joel	5	16	61030
1980–81	Mr R J Wilson	1	5	77348
1981–82	Sheikh Ali Abu Khamsin	15	35	71333
1982–83	Sheikh Ali Abu Khamsin	13	32	142937
1983–84	Sheikh Ali Abu Khamsin	13	38	101080
1984–85	T Kilroe and Son Ltd	2	5	73539
1985–86	Sheikh Ali Abu Khamsin	8	18	93876
1986–87	Mr H J Joel	9	13	115560
1987–88	Miss Juliet E Reed	2	8	132526
1988–89	Mr R Burridge	2	8	163092
1989–90	Mrs Harry J Duffey	1	3	124230
1990–91	Mr P Piller	11	33	216819
1991–92	Whitcombe Manor Racing Stables Ltd	10	13	152393
1992–93	Mrs J Mould	9	18	145788

Winning trainers: hurdles and chases 1992–93

H = Horses; R = Runners; W = Winners; 2 = Seconds; 3 = Thirds; %W-R = Percentage of winners to runners; £WIN = Win money; £W/P = Win and place money

	H	R	W	2nd	3rd	%W-R	£WIN	£W/P
Aconley, Mrs V A	20	73	8	14	3	11.0	21,568	30,150
Adam, J R	4	12	1	0	0	8.3	1,446	1,446
Akehurst, R	30	104	13	15	14	12.5	58,677	89,425
Akehurst, J	20	65	9	11	9	13.8	18,275	26,688
Allan, R	17	83	6	11	15	7.2	16,701	51,287
Allen, J	4	28	2	2	4	7.1	2,968	4,897
Allison, Miss K S	4	26	4	1	1	15.4	7,935	8,667
Alner, R H	7	23	3	2	0	13.0	7,613	16,553
Anderson, K	1	4	1	0	1	25.0	1,893	2,199
Andrews, J	1	6	1	3	1	16.7	2,294	6,309
Arbuthnot, D W P	4	19	4	2	3	21.1	6,680	8,741
Armytage, R C	3	15	3	2	0	20.0	14,207	26,661
Austin, Mrs S M	7	35	2	3	5	5.7	3,863	6,115
Avison, M	6	22	3	1	4	13.6	3,282	4,789
Bailey, A	12	27	2	2	2	7.4	4,123	6,585
Bailey, K C	63	302	57	42	32	18.9	170,188	242,228
Baker, R J	23	103	6	10	6	5.8	10,009	16,963
Baker, Miss D J	4	18	1	0	1	5.6	4,570	5,065
Balding, G B	52	290	38	58	34	13.1	212,445	341,281
Balding, I A	13	46	6	6	10	13.0	47,234	68,523
Banks, M C	5	21	2	3	1	9.5	4,358	8,162
Banks, J E	8	28	3	3	1	10.7	5,293	9,929
Barker, W L	9	32	2	0	1	6.3	3,736	4,055
Barker, Mrs P A	3	19	2	2	2	10.5	3,511	5,003
Barnes, M A	11	70	7	13	9	10.0	13,089	24,668
Barnett, G	4	21	6	2	3	28.6	11,271	13,821
Barons, D H	46	211	16	19	32	7.6	94,996	126,774
Barr, R E	10	33	2	1	1	6.1	3,726	4,884
Barraclough, M F	11	49	2	0	4	4.1	3,985	5,657
Barron, T D	6	16	5	4	1	31.3	8,664	11,281
Barrow, A	18	81	4	0	7	4.9	8,144	10,294
Barwell, C R	12	43	6	3	5	14.0	12,485	17,180
Baugh, B P J	10	36	2	1	6	5.6	2,839	4,714
Beaumont, P	22	106	19	21	13	17.9	162,642	196,268
Bennett, R A	9	37	1	1	4	2.7	1,816	3,080
Benstead, C J	1	6	1	0	1	16.7	1,672	1,903
Bentley, W	9	55	7	6	5	12.7	11,886	18,909
Berry, J	2	9	1	3	1	11.1	1,730	4,169
Bevan, P J	12	42	2	5	6	4.8	3,229	8,602
Bewley, R	1	1	1	0	0	100.0	1,865	1,865
Bill, T T	6	39	2	4	6	5.1	4,402	9,934
Birkett, J J	12	53	1	3	6	1.9	2,198	5,020
Bishop, V R	3	7	2	1	0	28.6	5,845	6,333
Bishop, K	14	59	1	2	7	1.7	1,861	7,988
Bissill, W H	1	8	2	3	1	25.0	4,033	6,527
Blackford, Miss L	1	1	1	0	0	100.0	1,769	1,769
Bolton, M J	3	12	1	0	0	8.3	1,138	1,308
Bosley, J R	16	90	3	2	9	3.3	5,587	11,482
Bostock, J R	8	35	2	5	2	5.7	2,472	5,042
Bottomley, J F	5	30	3	2	1	10.0	6,839	8,365
Bowen, P	3	9	3	3	0	33.3	10,477	12,066
Bower, Miss L	10	43	1	0	5	2.3	2,196	4,071
Bowles, Lee	2	7	1	1	0	14.3	1,553	2,198
Brackenbury, Mrs R	1	1	1	0	0	100.0	3,650	3,650
Bradburne, Mrs S C	21	152	18	26	27	11.8	46,918	82,787
Bradley, J M	30	121	7	6	16	5.8	11,880	19,691
Bradley, Paul	3	9	1	1	2	11.1	1,564	3,644
Bradstock, M	14	46	4	3	8	8.7	11,544	17,079
Bramall, Mrs S A	19	120	16	13	9	13.3	42,941	56,448
Bravery, G C	5	22	4	4	6	18.2	10,292	14,287
Brennan, O	26	133	25	21	16	18.8	56,427	71,522
Brewis, R	6	26	2	1	4	7.7	12,179	16,992
Bridgwater, K S	25	96	8	7	10	8.3	17,654	25,895
Broad, C D	26	105	17	13	10	16.2	37,882	60,102

WINNING TRAINERS: HURDLES AND CHASES 1992–93

	H	R	W	2nd	3rd	%W-R	£WIN	£W/P
Bromhead, H de	2	2	1	0	0	50.0	20,859	20,859
Brooks, C P E	31	100	16	15	18	16.0	51,945	78,889
Brookshaw, S A	4	8	1	2	0	12.5	1,089	2,309
Brotherton, R	13	53	3	2	1	5.7	4,090	5,473
Brown, R L	3	20	2	3	3	10.0	3,992	6,179
Brown, Mrs Jean	2	9	4	1	2	44.4	5,126	6,159
Brown, D H	3	13	1	4	3	7.7	2,337	5,713
Brydon, D A D	1	4	1	2	0	25.0	1,968	2,805
Buckler, R H	17	77	12	6	5	15.6	25,433	31,520
Buckley, E T	7	23	4	0	0	17.4	8,193	8,193
Burchell, D	25	102	12	9	13	11.8	28,465	50,049
Burke, K R	18	79	10	9	9	12.7	19,278	30,386
Butler, P	7	24	1	3	4	4.2	2,536	7,439
Bycroft, N	8	27	3	0	1	11.1	4,513	4,825
Caldwell, T H	16	46	3	4	7	6.5	6,768	10,473
Callaghan, N A	12	38	2	6	3	5.3	2,915	43,804
Callow, R	7	28	1	2	1	3.6	2,624	5,275
Calver, P	5	21	3	3	2	14.3	6,727	9,403
Camacho, M J	3	12	5	2	2	41.7	14,377	19,850
Cambidge, B R	6	19	1	1	2	5.3	1,784	2,669
Campbell, I	16	75	7	10	11	9.3	14,665	23,720
Campbell, Mrs Angus	2	2	1	0	0	50.0	1,456	1,456
Cann, J Grant	1	1	1	0	0	100.0	3,610	3,610
Cantillon, D E	3	11	3	2	0	27.3	4,324	5,285
Carr, T J	9	41	5	5	4	12.2	9,559	12,607
Carter, O J	5	20	1	2	2	5.0	1,776	5,046
Casey, T	12	61	3	7	10	4.9	8,241	16,756
Cecil, Mrs J	2	10	5	2	1	50.0	12,350	14,789
Chadwick, S G	8	42	2	1	1	4.8	4,156	5,187
Champion, R	10	33	5	1	3	15.2	12,374	15,851
Channon, M R	8	36	6	9	3	16.7	9,555	16,474
Chapman, M C	17	103	4	11	9	3.9	7,613	18,999
Charles, M J	12	52	2	3	8	3.8	3,307	9,653
Charles-Jones, G F H	12	53	2	10	5	3.8	3,320	9,266
Charlton, J I A	23	94	9	11	12	9.6	20,328	38,628
Cheatle, J N	3	8	1	1	0	12.5	1,004	1,492
Cheesbrough, P	41	164	30	28	18	18.3	94,136	145,894
Christian, S	28	78	6	8	12	7.7	12,783	24,670
Chugg, J	6	25	1	3	3	4.0	2,636	7,070
Clarke, P C	3	15	2	5	1	13.3	4,631	8,255
Clay, Mrs L	2	11	2	3	0	18.2	2,397	4,050
Clay, W	26	142	21	17	11	14.8	40,067	52,998
Coathup, S	5	22	1	2	2	4.5	1,581	3,186
Cole, H T	2	14	5	2	1	35.7	20,577	23,982
Collingridge, H J	6	28	3	0	0	10.7	7,637	8,066
Coogan, J G	1	1	1	0	0	100.0	24,624	24,624
Cottrell, A J	1	9	1	0	2	11.1	2,042	3,192
Craggs, P F	1	1	1	0	0	100.0	6,775	6,775
Cundell, P D	12	42	8	5	3	19.0	13,866	17,539
Cunningham-Brown, K O	9	54	6	10	9	11.1	15,756	23,244
Curley, B J	11	30	1	4	2	3.3	2,056	5,398
Curtis, R	28	119	14	10	10	11.8	52,226	66,105
Curtis, J W	7	32	3	1	4	9.4	5,554	7,113
Dalgetty, T N	1	9	2	2	2	22.2	4,078	6,268
Dalton, P T	11	56	11	3	4	19.6	26,045	32,962
Davies, M W	3	8	1	0	0	12.5	1,530	1,530
Davis, N H	2	10	1	1	2	10.0	3,480	5,122
Davison, A R	11	30	1	5	3	3.3	3,704	7,615
Dawe, Mrs J C	10	44	4	4	10	9.1	8,310	14,968
Dawson, C D	1	1	1	0	0	100.0	2,369	2,369
Deacon, D J	6	41	1	5	5	2.4	2,623	7,019
Dean, R	2	22	2	1	8	9.1	3,741	6,395
Deasley, M J	1	3	1	0	1	33.3	962	1,115
Denson, A W	4	16	1	1	1	6.3	2,334	2,956
Dickin, R	25	123	15	10	17	12.2	37,254	54,394
Dixon, M	4	18	3	2	2	16.7	7,097	9,344
Dods, M	13	56	3	6	7	5.4	7,470	14,571
Donnelly, T W	9	50	4	4	5	8.0	8,551	12,248
Dooler, J	6	33	1	0	2	3.0	1,811	2,304
Doumen, F	2	5	1	0	1	20.0	44,500	60,753
Dow, S	15	55	4	8	7	7.3	8,539	16,472
Doyle, Miss Jacqueline S	8	35	4	0	2	11.4	7,306	7,870
Dufosee, J W	5	9	3	3	0	33.3	4,461	6,204
Dun, T D C	2	6	1	0	0	16.7	2,297	2,622
Dunn, A J K	10	31	4	3	2	12.9	11,651	13,739
Dutfield, Mrs P N	6	26	2	3	2	7.7	4,845	8,636
Dyer, T	12	64	6	8	3	9.4	12,835	19,316
Earnshaw, R	8	31	4	2	0	12.9	9,600	10,362

	H	R	W	2nd	3rd	%W-R	£WIN	£W/P
Easterby, M H	41	218	39	32	29	17.9	114,454	188,672
Easterby, M W	33	113	11	17	14	9.7	27,212	53,630
Eaton, Miss J	5	21	1	0	2	4.8	3,236	4,257
Eddy, D	3	15	3	1	1	20.0	8,889	9,809
Eden, G H	3	5	1	0	1	20.0	1,756	2,185
Edwards, J A C	49	253	29	44	36	11.5	77,412	140,990
Edwards, G F	4	29	2	6	3	6.9	4,940	10,200
Egerton, C R	17	56	15	7	2	26.8	36,141	41,319
Elliott, J P D	3	5	1	1	0	20.0	1,182	1,606
Ellison, B	5	22	3	2	0	13.6	6,541	7,199
Elsey, C C	4	14	1	1	0	7.1	2,330	3,692
Elsworth, D R C	25	115	18	24	13	15.7	133,170	220,658
Enright, G P	10	30	1	3	2	3.3	774	3,045
Etherington, T J	15	62	2	6	7	3.2	11,049	25,571
Etherington, J	1	3	1	0	0	33.3	1,182	1,182
Eubank, A	4	12	1	2	1	8.3	7,440	11,347
Evans, P D	19	59	6	8	9	10.2	9,981	15,605
Eyre, J L	20	74	4	4	8	5.4	8,263	12,878
Fanshawe, J R	5	17	5	2	2	29.4	10,419	19,774
Fetherston-Godley, M J	1	2	1	0	1	50.0	1,375	1,571
Ffitch-Heyes, J	17	79	9	7	13	11.4	25,150	32,825
Fisher, R F	9	27	3	3	0	11.1	6,095	8,141
FitzGerald, J G	66	268	62	49	39	23.1	260,812	356,364
Fletcher, D E	3	13	2	0	4	15.4	5,448	6,432
Flynn, P J	2	2	1	0	0	50.0	30,015	30,015
Forbes, A L	16	66	8	7	9	12.1	22,283	29,327
Ford, David	1	2	1	0	0	50.0	1,604	1,604
Forsey, B	9	26	2	1	5	7.7	3,644	5,370
Forster, Capt T A	59	217	29	21	24	13.4	95,690	122,792
Forte, A M	9	35	1	1	3	2.9	1,769	3,177
Francis, W D	1	4	1	1	1	25.0	1,864	2,450
Frost, R G	47	199	12	29	20	6.0	27,104	52,186
Gandolfo, D R	36	147	12	17	14	8.2	26,438	56,320
Garraton, D T	6	26	1	3	1	3.8	1,772	3,591
Gaselee, N A	26	121	13	16	12	10.7	65,176	87,774
Gifford, J T	67	300	49	40	41	16.3	285,899	396,356
Gill, H J	1	4	1	0	1	25.0	2,761	3,137
Glover, J A	14	63	8	6	11	12.7	16,066	25,259
Goodfellow, Mrs J D	8	44	7	5	5	15.9	13,055	17,807
Gordon, Miss C	1	3	1	0	1	33.3	2,268	2,439
Goulding, J L	5	23	1	0	0	4.3	1,305	1,305
Gray, F	8	32	1	2	1	3.1	1,475	2,560
Green, Miss Z A	5	37	1	2	8	2.7	2,976	6,715
Grissell, D M	16	70	18	16	9	25.7	35,021	54,982
Guilding, Mrs Roger	2	6	1	0	2	16.7	1,543	2,029
Hacking, W R	2	9	2	0	3	22.2	2,098	2,880
Haigh, W W	4	8	1	0	0	12.5	1,632	1,632
Haine, Mrs D	12	58	6	15	5	10.3	13,045	27,289
Haldane, J S	9	44	1	4	3	2.3	2,724	6,786
Haley, P R	2	9	4	0	0	44.4	9,451	9,451
Ham, G A	29	119	9	6	7	7.6	23,121	29,287
Hambly, A A	5	16	4	2	0	25.0	7,394	8,725
Hamilton, William	1	5	2	0	2	40.0	2,847	3,415
Hammond, M D	60	273	51	48	32	18.7	127,979	173,561
Hanmer, G D	2	2	1	0	0	50.0	2,626	2,626
Hannon, R	6	17	1	1	3	5.9	9,440	21,697
Hanson, J	6	28	4	3	2	14.3	13,640	16,534
Harris, J L	15	77	7	7	7	9.1	9,965	15,288
Harris, P W	2	6	1	1	0	16.7	1,690	2,187
Harrison, A	7	46	4	9	10	8.7	7,940	16,445
Harwood, G	14	46	12	7	8	26.1	26,332	35,572
Haslam, P C	11	24	3	4	2	12.5	4,280	7,012
Haynes, M J	7	21	1	0	0	4.8	788	788
Heaton-Ellis, M J	5	12	1	1	1	8.3	1,669	2,340
Hedger, P R	20	66	8	8	8	12.1	28,127	45,759
Hellens, J A	9	42	3	8	4	7.1	12,257	19,490
Henderson, N J	77	289	53	38	41	18.3	242,924	329,867
Henderson, Mrs R G	2	11	2	1	1	18.2	15,614	26,580
Henderson, P F	2	6	1	1	1	16.7	1,514	1,990
Herries, Lady	6	23	9	2	3	39.1	21,205	25,141
Hewitt, Mrs A R	8	39	4	2	3	10.3	15,966	20,668
Hiatt, P W	1	10	1	2	1	10.0	1,705	2,848
Hide, A	1	4	1	0	0	25.0	2,136	2,136
Hills, J W	1	4	2	0	0	50.0	2,721	2,721
Hoad, R P C	7	29	3	1	2	10.3	5,360	6,643
Hobbs, P J	76	303	37	54	33	12.2	90,097	154,500
Hodges, R J	61	258	32	22	37	12.4	90,897	129,820
Hogg, K W	3	8	1	2	0	12.5	1,700	2,615

	H	R	W	2nd	3rd	%W-R	£WIN	£W/P
Holder, R J	10	13	1	1	0	7.7	2,827	3,239
Hollinshead, R	29	96	10	8	7	10.4	18,821	24,970
Horgan, C A	4	19	2	4	2	10.5	2,786	5,522
Houghton, R F Johnson	11	41	2	7	5	4.9	6,055	18,819
Hughes, Mrs D	1	2	1	0	0	50.0	1,631	1,631
Humphrey, G L	11	41	2	4	3	4.9	4,492	10,466
Ingram, R	5	18	1	0	1	5.6	788	1,008
Jackson, C F C	5	25	1	2	1	4.0	1,710	2,923
James, C	8	33	3	3	5	9.1	6,286	8,750
James, A P	15	69	1	7	7	1.4	2,269	11,358
Jarvis, A P	12	37	2	3	4	5.4	3,522	9,268
Jefferson, J M	14	65	14	10	4	21.5	36,580	53,103
Jenkins, J R	44	213	15	31	29	7.0	38,049	78,481
Jenks, W	2	16	1	4	1	6.3	1,814	4,188
Jewell, Mrs L C	10	40	3	0	1	7.5	4,400	4,665
Johnson, J H	42	177	19	23	28	10.7	60,699	102,455
Johnson, Michael A	1	1	1	0	0	100.0	1,592	1,592
Jones, Bob	4	9	1	2	1	11.1	1,151	1,941
Jones, P J	10	45	5	8	6	11.1	6,871	14,066
Jones, A P	14	75	7	8	9	9.3	18,812	29,954
Jones, T Thomson	30	137	14	20	15	10.2	36,937	68,561
Jones, Mrs M A	1	9	6	1	0	66.7	17,859	18,609
Jones, C H	10	53	1	2	3	1.9	2,374	4,694
Jones, H Thomson	1	3	1	1	0	33.3	1,958	2,313
Jordan, F	27	131	3	5	15	2.3	4,577	12,718
Joseph, J	13	59	4	1	5	6.8	5,966	7,773
Joynes, Mrs P M	13	73	3	5	6	4.1	7,594	13,367
Juckes, R T	16	74	2	6	6	2.7	3,008	8,912
Keddy, T	4	13	1	0	0	7.7	2,349	2,349
Kelleway, P A	3	18	8	1	3	44.4	16,347	20,661
Kelleway, Miss Gay	5	21	4	4	5	19.0	7,595	10,488
Kettlewell, S E	14	51	7	7	4	13.7	38,436	48,136
Kiely, P	1	2	1	0	1	50.0	43,435	47,597
King, J S	25	121	11	18	15	9.1	24,806	44,343
Kirby, J	1	6	1	0	0	16.7	2,442	2,442
Knight, Mrs A	24	85	4	5	5	4.7	5,474	8,697
Knight, Miss H C	37	152	37	13	27	24.3	79,348	98,233
Laing, D R	3	17	1	3	1	5.9	1,837	3,524
Lamb, R R	20	61	1	3	3	1.6	2,326	4,695
Lamyman, Mrs S	6	46	1	6	4	2.2	2,890	8,372
Leach, P	12	45	10	3	8	22.2	19,538	23,886
Leadbetter, S J	8	32	2	2	3	6.3	4,382	6,392
Lee, R	37	197	29	19	31	14.7	94,525	123,002
Leigh, J P	10	42	2	4	3	4.8	4,233	8,986
Litston, Mrs J	3	11	1	6	2	9.1	1,688	5,184
Llewellyn, B J	7	49	6	6	5	12.2	10,230	14,713
Lloyd, F	2	5	1	0	1	20.0	1,903	2,239
Long, J E	10	31	2	0	2	6.5	3,472	3,853
Lungo, L	23	90	22	12	13	24.4	44,188	54,837
Luxton, D	1	1	1	0	0	100.0	2,295	2,295
Mackie, J	31	109	10	12	8	9.2	25,453	41,729
Mactaggart, B	12	47	3	1	1	6.4	8,459	9,935
Madgwick, M	9	35	4	4	1	11.4	6,696	8,705
Marks, D	3	11	1	2	1	9.1	1,881	3,114
Marvin, R F	2	13	1	0	0	7.7	1,861	1,861
Mason, N B	18	59	1	7	7	1.7	2,850	9,341
Mathias, Richard	1	3	2	0	0	66.7	2,363	2,363
Maxwell, J F C	8	12	1	1	2	8.3	1,893	3,457
McCain, D	41	148	6	14	21	4.1	14,659	36,449
McConnochie, J C	20	95	3	10	13	3.2	8,193	19,541
McCormack, M	5	18	1	3	4	5.6	2,773	6,212
McCourt, M	4	33	3	4	8	9.1	7,944	14,074
McCune, D	5	33	2	4	9	6.1	4,471	9,811
McDonald, R	4	16	1	1	0	6.3	1,935	2,290
McGovern, T P	8	32	4	3	1	12.5	5,675	7,473
McKie, Mrs I	14	42	6	7	6	14.3	16,671	23,813
McMahon, B A	12	56	1	5	3	1.8	1,484	6,096
Meade, Martyn	14	64	8	6	5	12.5	12,639	32,103
Mellor, S	28	97	4	5	5	4.1	7,238	12,812
Miller, F Bruce	1	1	1	0	0	100.0	9,830	9,830
Millman, B R	5	14	2	1	1	14.3	5,633	6,964
Mills, T G	4	6	1	1	0	16.7	1,475	2,031
Mitchell, N R	17	77	3	6	7	3.9	5,532	13,543
Mitchell, C W	2	10	1	0	1	10.0	2,271	2,848
Moffatt, D	18	73	11	10	8	15.1	22,545	32,209
Monteith, P	24	131	14	18	13	10.7	34,681	52,547
Moore, G M	40	200	29	27	20	14.5	69,815	101,041
Moore, A	42	187	13	21	29	7.0	29,299	49,778

WINNING TRAINERS: HURDLES AND CHASES 1992–93

	H	R	W	2nd	3rd	%W-R	£WIN	£W/P
Moore, J S	15	60	3	6	7	5.0	12,299	20,846
Moore, A L T	6	12	1	1	2	8.3	26,040	50,808
Morgan, K A	25	126	13	15	17	10.3	29,217	46,989
Morgan, B C	10	31	2	4	1	6.5	3,280	5,421
Morris, D	6	22	2	2	2	9.1	4,923	6,490
Muggeridge, M P	18	48	3	2	6	6.3	6,294	9,661
Muir, W R	11	39	5	5	7	12.8	8,978	13,628
Mullins, J W	8	33	1	2	0	3.0	1,617	3,185
Murphy, F	30	141	23	18	15	16.3	105,277	144,228
Murphy, Pat	1	1	1	0	0	100.0	2,794	2,794
Murphy, P G	24	105	10	6	11	9.5	36,357	46,024
Murray, B W	4	16	2	2	2	12.5	2,790	4,290
Murray, Mrs A M	1	3	2	0	0	66.7	3,672	3,672
Nash, C T	18	53	1	6	5	1.9	1,604	7,869
Naughton, T J	5	16	2	2	5	12.5	2,819	5,073
Naughton, M P	13	73	6	4	9	8.2	13,935	19,410
Nelson, W M	2	6	1	0	1	16.7	1,214	1,519
Nicholls, P F	31	132	20	19	21	15.2	54,745	81,547
Nicholson, D	73	367	100	69	43	27.2	492,480	645,934
Nolan, D A	6	18	1	1	1	5.6	2,008	2,796
Norton, J	9	35	2	3	0	5.7	1,891	2,952
O'Brien, M J P	1	1	1	0	0	100.0	34,275	34,275
O'Donoghue, J	2	10	1	2	2	10.0	1,719	3,049
O'Leary, R	11	58	4	7	9	6.9	6,563	13,930
O'Mahony, F J	3	12	3	2	2	25.0	5,058	7,270
O'Neill, J J	34	151	21	19	10	13.9	43,667	59,998
O'Neill, O	14	66	1	8	6	1.5	2,285	8,738
O'Shea, J G M	7	28	3	4	0	10.7	3,434	5,283
O'Sullivan, R J	19	87	13	9	8	14.9	26,898	34,980
Oakes, W D	1	1	1	0	0	100.0	2,153	2,153
Old, J A B	25	92	19	12	15	20.7	56,427	78,861
Oliver, J K M	15	68	1	3	6	1.5	1,924	7,751
Palling, B	7	29	2	3	1	6.9	4,051	6,078
Parker, C	23	85	14	7	14	16.5	36,015	48,126
Parkes, J	15	105	10	11	11	9.5	19,703	28,413
Parrott, Mrs H	10	46	1	4	4	2.2	2,346	6,528
Pearce, J	7	14	2	1	0	14.3	5,001	5,605
Perratt, Miss L A	17	100	12	5	7	12.0	31,245	40,560
Pidgeon, Miss Jennifer	1	1	1	0	0	100.0	3,623	3,623
Pike, S	2	4	1	0	0	25.0	1,368	1,368
Pilkington, Mrs T D	1	5	1	0	2	20.0	2,093	2,818
Pipe, M C	143	769	194	118	89	25.2	808,012	1,172,470
Pitman, Mrs J	50	242	36	38	29	14.9	117,159	230,155
Pitman, Miss Susan	2	6	2	1	1	33.3	2,534	3,457
Pocock, Mrs R	1	3	1	0	0	33.3	1,256	1,256
Popham, C L	21	118	8	11	11	6.8	22,897	36,035
Pounder, T H	2	4	1	1	0	25.0	1,646	2,078
Preece, B	18	80	2	7	5	2.5	2,564	6,900
Price, R J	21	85	10	10	9	11.8	35,134	48,919
Price, William	3	13	1	1	3	7.7	1,670	2,832
Price, G M	3	19	2	2	2	10.5	4,251	5,655
Pritchard, P A	11	51	1	1	2	2.0	3,054	4,450
Pritchard-Gordon, G A	9	23	3	2	2	13.0	5,080	6,453
Ramsden, Mrs J R	6	22	4	5	0	18.2	9,723	23,068
Reed, W G	14	87	9	11	17	10.3	20,674	32,983
Reed, W J	2	11	3	1	0	27.3	5,429	5,919
Reid, A S	7	21	2	2	0	9.5	3,099	4,020
Renfree-Barons, Mrs J R	6	11	2	1	3	18.2	4,377	8,152
Retter, Mrs J G	40	152	24	19	13	15.8	74,131	97,790
Reveley, Mrs M	91	341	90	56	49	26.4	250,548	324,160
Richards, G	88	459	104	62	53	22.7	327,714	433,789
Richards, Mrs L	1	4	1	1	0	25.0	2,204	2,874
Richmond, B	13	73	4	6	6	5.5	6,520	11,637
Rimell, Mrs M R T	2	5	1	0	2	20.0	2,866	3,752
Rodford, P R	12	89	3	9	13	3.4	6,555	14,741
Rothwell, B S	23	94	4	10	14	4.3	8,767	19,874
Rowe, R	35	167	23	24	16	13.8	51,946	77,650
Russell, Miss Lucinda V	2	3	1	0	0	33.3	2,138	2,138
Ryan, M J	10	42	5	5	4	11.9	10,397	15,130
Sanders, Miss B	13	61	9	12	7	14.8	32,031	58,170
Saunders, Miss C	11	40	13	8	5	32.5	21,754	27,385
Saunders, C R	1	4	3	0	0	75.0	4,381	4,381
Saunders, M S	6	23	3	3	1	13.0	5,611	7,527
Sawyer, H	2	5	1	0	0	20.0	1,480	1,480
Scargill, Dr J D	3	12	4	2	3	33.3	7,022	8,803
Scott, J H	4	4	1	0	1	25.0	12,720	15,182
Scudamore, M	7	27	2	1	2	7.4	4,706	6,117
Sherwood, O	51	202	37	33	23	18.3	92,844	143,932

	H	R	W	2nd	3rd	%W-R	£WIN	£W/P
Sherwood, S E	34	175	30	23	20	17.1	92,747	124,472
Siddall, Miss L C	8	54	5	3	5	9.3	13,491	18,497
Silk, Mrs D B A	2	2	1	0	0	50.0	1,605	1,605
Simpson, R	5	13	6	1	0	46.2	11,098	11,562
Skinner, Mrs T J McInnes	2	11	1	2	1	9.1	3,106	5,257
Sly, Mrs P	11	47	7	2	5	14.9	15,251	18,112
Smart, B	8	30	3	6	5	10.0	6,989	14,628
Smith, Denys	28	120	14	8	23	11.7	35,240	47,281
Smith, A	6	31	2	4	2	6.5	2,343	4,898
Smith, N A	9	28	1	4	1	3.6	1,744	5,293
Smith, Mrs S J	39	200	6	15	21	3.0	29,332	51,274
Smith, C	14	69	4	4	9	5.8	7,235	11,295
Smith, D J G Murray	15	61	6	7	3	9.8	24,746	34,435
Smith, David F	2	4	1	0	0	25.0	2,006	2,006
Smith, Sidney J	1	8	4	2	1	50.0	5,536	7,356
Smith, J P	8	38	1	3	5	2.6	1,764	5,661
Smith, Richard J	2	4	1	0	0	25.0	1,548	1,548
Smith, W	2	3	1	0	0	33.3	1,872	1,872
Smith, W J	5	38	1	6	1	2.6	2,265	5,741
Sowersby, M E	3	4	1	0	0	25.0	1,672	2,422
Spearing, J L	16	75	12	11	11	16.0	25,568	35,302
Spencer, Mrs R	1	2	1	1	0	50.0	1,116	1,479
Stamp, C D	2	5	1	0	0	20.0	1,050	1,121
Stevens, B	9	46	3	3	4	6.5	5,081	8,004
Stirk, Mrs M	2	14	3	2	3	21.4	9,076	13,015
Storey, W	17	44	3	0	3	6.8	7,928	8,660
Storey, Clive	2	4	1	1	1	25.0	2,088	2,938
Stringer, A P	10	48	4	1	9	8.3	9,289	12,830
Sutcliffe, J	1	5	1	0	0	20.0	5,208	5,208
Swiers, J E	5	23	2	2	2	8.7	2,335	4,677
Swinbank, Mrs A	17	58	5	3	5	8.6	7,910	10,815
Tate, T P	19	69	12	6	15	17.4	37,070	53,556
Tate, R	7	23	3	1	5	13.0	4,476	6,802
Thom, D T	3	9	1	1	0	11.1	1,674	2,040
Thomas, J D	8	21	1	1	1	4.8	1,302	2,428
Thompson, V	15	65	2	5	5	3.1	4,183	8,534
Thomson, A M	2	8	1	1	0	12.5	2,416	2,984
Thorner, G	10	46	4	7	4	8.7	9,749	14,955
Thornton, C W	16	38	11	6	6	28.9	20,771	26,409
Tinkler, N	33	139	25	23	17	18.0	81,987	110,397
Tompkins, M H	31	110	22	18	13	20.0	94,115	147,004
Trice-Rolph, Jon	1	5	2	1	1	40.0	3,490	4,243
Trietline, C C	23	134	7	15	12	5.2	14,346	27,268
Tucker, D R	6	26	1	1	1	3.8	1,537	2,236
Turnell, Andrew	35	157	37	20	20	23.6	161,247	244,245
Turner, D T	2	6	1	1	1	16.7	1,564	2,358
Turner, W G M	30	104	5	12	9	4.8	11,634	22,110
Turner, W G	9	27	1	1	1	3.7	1,453	2,212
Twiston-Davies, N A	63	318	76	48	35	23.9	451,332	562,941
Upson, John R	42	186	31	24	24	16.7	132,394	171,880
Usher, M D I	8	23	4	1	2	17.4	5,777	6,700
Voorspuy, R	7	33	1	6	3	3.0	1,590	4,718
Wade, J	14	77	7	6	10	9.1	12,832	20,549
Wales, W A	1	2	1	0	0	50.0	1,753	1,904
Waley-Cohen, R	3	11	2	2	0	18.2	7,267	12,235
Walford, T D	1	4	1	1	0	25.0	1,576	2,088
Walton, F T	12	51	2	4	4	3.9	7,012	11,367
Walwyn, Mrs F	17	73	11	13	6	15.1	25,760	51,653
Ward, Mrs V C	7	25	2	0	0	8.0	4,328	4,328
Warner, W J	3	10	5	2	2	50.0	10,172	13,950
Weaver, R J	11	37	2	1	7	5.4	4,440	7,804
Webber, J	30	131	10	12	14	7.6	23,671	39,776
Weedon, C	13	44	5	3	4	11.4	8,422	12,903
Wellstead, H	11	22	5	4	4	22.7	9,083	11,795
Wharton, J	17	44	1	6	5	2.3	1,631	7,938
Whillans, A C	6	32	2	3	4	6.3	3,738	7,827
White, J	65	252	38	46	32	15.1	88,877	134,919
White, K	15	63	3	6	8	4.8	5,054	11,346
White, G F	4	18	1	2	3	5.6	1,918	3,694
Whitfield, Miss A J	5	23	7	1	3	30.4	14,608	18,026
Whyte, John	5	23	2	1	2	8.7	5,412	7,871
Wightman, W G R	7	36	1	4	7	2.8	1,580	7,287
Wildman, C P	6	34	2	4	3	5.9	6,500	10,026
Wilkins, R C	1	6	5	0	1	83.3	35,370	35,620
Wilkinson, B E	7	34	5	4	6	14.7	25,747	35,082
Wilkinson, M J	17	83	10	6	15	12.0	46,607	56,563
Williams, Mrs S D	12	64	7	6	6	10.9	27,836	33,458
Williams, M	13	36	4	5	2	11.1	7,081	10,539

	H	R	W	2nd	3rd	%W-R	£WIN	£W/P
Williams, C N	3	14	3	0	0	21.4	7,403	7,908
Williams, D L	14	63	3	4	6	4.8	7,889	19,296
Williams, D G	2	13	1	0	3	7.7	2,998	4,424
Wilson, A J	15	52	2	6	5	3.8	6,942	16,546
Wilson, D A	6	31	4	3	2	12.9	7,814	10,132
Wilson, Capt J	5	11	1	0	1	9.1	828	1,140
Wilton, Miss S J	20	64	2	5	9	3.1	6,606	12,844
Wingrove, K G	9	40	1	5	4	2.5	988	3,976
Wintle, D J	33	133	10	19	16	7.5	17,810	32,398
Wonnacott, Mrs J	20	78	1	4	8	1.3	1,467	5,761
Wood, R S	4	19	2	3	2	10.5	3,862	6,896
Woodhouse, R D E	9	51	2	4	5	3.9	7,633	14,197
Woodman, S	3	6	1	0	0	16.7	33,800	44,794
Woods, S P C	3	14	3	2	2	21.4	5,437	7,073
Wordingham, L	2	10	1	0	0	10.0	1,688	1,688
Yard, W A Stephenson's	67	204	35	25	24	17.2	78,036	105,307
Yardley, F J	7	53	6	7	11	11.3	16,741	27,553

Leading jump trainers 1945–93

		Horses	Races Won	Value £
1945–46	T Rayson	2	5	933
1946–47	F T T Walwyn	36	60	11115
1947–48	F T T Walwyn	40	75	16790
1948–49	F T T Walwyn	36	64	15563
1949–50	P V F Cazalet	29	75	18427
1950–51	T F Rimell	24	60	18381
1951–52	N Crump	22	41	19357
1952–53	M V O'Brien	4	5	15515
1953–54	M V O'Brien	7	8	14274
1954–55	H R Price	24	47	13888
1955–56	W Hall	18	41	15807
1956–57	N Crump	19	39	18495
1957–58	F T T Walwyn	14	35	23013
1958–59	H R Price	29	52	26550
1959–60	P V F Cazalet	25	58	22270
1960–61	T F Rimell	28	58	34811
1961–62	H R Price	34	64	40950
1962–63	K Piggott	4	6	23091
1963–64	F T T Walwyn	30	59	67129
1964–65	P V F Cazalet	34	82	36153
1965–66	H R Price	29	65	42276
1966–67	H R Price	34	73	41222
1967–68	Denys Smith	26	55	37944
1968–69	T F Rimell	32	62	38344
1969–70	T F Rimell	35	77	61864
1970–71	F T Winter	29	73	60739
1971–72	F T Winter	31	72	62863
1972–73	F T Winter	37	85	79066
1973–74	F T Winter	41	89	101781
1974–75	F T Winter	39	81	74205
1975–76	T F Rimell	30	49	111740
1976–77	F T Winter	31	75	85202
1977–78	F T Winter	44	90	145915
1978–79	M H Easterby	24	55	146681
1979–80	M H Easterby	31	75	215173
1980–81	M H Easterby	34	70	234993
1981–82	M W Dickinson	32	84	296028
1982–83	M W Dickinson	42	120	358837
1983–84	M W Dickinson	30	86	266146
1984–85	F T Winter	43	85	218978
1985–86	N J Henderson	27	46	162234
1986–87	N J Henderson	38	67	222949
1987–88	D R C Elsworth	24	47	344210
1988–89	M C Pipe	88	208	589399
1989–90	M C Pipe	95	224	668606
1990–91	M C Pipe	94	230	957222
1991–92	M C Pipe	189	224	724380
1992–93	M C Pipe	143	194	808012

Principal NH trainers winning totals: 1976–77 to 1992–93

	1976 –77	1977 –78	1978 –79	1979 –80	1980 –81	1981 –82	1982 –83	1983 –84	1984 –85	1985 –86	1986 –87	1987 –88	1988 –89	1989 –90	1990 –91	1991 –92	1992 –93
Aconley, Mrs. V. A.	—	—	—	—	—	—	—	—	—	—	1	1	3	7	10	12	8
Akehurst, J.	—	—	—	—	—	—	—	—	—	—	—	—	—	—	6	5	9
Akehurst, R.	3	1	6	1	4	1	—	—	6	11	23	21	43	30	35	17	13
Armytage, R.	10	11	18	20	28	23	9	20	15	15	4	7	1	2	2	3	3
Bailey, K.	—	5	6	8	9	16	16	18	8	24	31	20	18	34	33	38	57
Bailey, P.	18	19	10	16	25	16	13	10	10	6	14	10	12	2	12	—	—
Baker, J. H.	7	8	11	5	7	6	6	11	11	5	5	14	15	15	16	11	—
Balding, G.	20	48	44	27	39	21	19	30	18	9	57	40	59	42	48	53	38
Barons, D.	33	29	10	16	14	16	11	18	16	20	30	29	36	40	34	25	16
Beaumont, P.	—	—	—	—	—	—	—	—	—	—	7	0	8	4	12	5	19
Bell, C. H.	13	1	2	6	12	17	22	34	5	5	—	—	—	—	—	—	—
Bill, T. T.	—	—	—	—	4	0	1	6	10	15	16	8	6	8	3	2	2
Blundell, J.	1	3	5	7	7	21	14	16	11	8	13	12	11	6	—	—	—
Bradley, J. M.	12	12	3	12	13	8	12	20	3	3	12	16	12	4	15	2	7
Brennan, O.	1	2	3	6	4	16	20	18	9	10	8	10	14	16	15	13	25
Brockbank, J. E.	—	—	—	5	2	3	8	9	1	6	0	0	3	0	2	0	—
Callaghan, N.	8	11	5	7	2	12	11	3	1	—	4	2	8	4	6	9	2
Cheesbrough, P.	—	—	—	—	—	—	—	—	—	—	—	—	—	—	—	—	30
Christian, S.	—	—	—	—	—	—	—	5	11	15	22	22	15	12	12	19	6
Clay, W.	15	7	9	17	14	9	15	14	18	4	12	4	14	11	0	5	21
Crump, N.	25	33	19	28	34	20	24	19	9	14	5	4	6	—	—	—	—
Cundell, P.	20	22	21	29	21	17	6	7	7	13	8	9	6	5	0	0	8
Dickinson, A.	53	52	64	94	—	—	—	—	—	—	—	—	—	—	—	—	—
Dickinson, M. W. ...	—	—	—	—	84	84	120	86	—	—	—	—	—	—	—	—	—
Dickinson, Mrs. M. ...	—	—	—	—	—	—	—	—	44	33	29	26	17	—	—	—	—
Easterby, M. H.	31	60	55	75	70	46	52	27	55	33	38	23	45	29	33	42	39
Easterby, M. W.	12	9	9	15	23	8	10	28	22	11	10	18	22	10	18	22	11
Edwards, J.	25	31	19	29	32	37	27	19	22	41	54	61	78	47	54	39	29
Elsworth, D.	—	—	4	7	18	24	25	26	32	37	34	47	54	24	23	20	18
Fisher, R.	—	2	8	16	15	31	38	41	23	17	17	8	6	8	1	3	3
FitzGerald, J.	6	10	7	18	20	16	28	35	41	28	73	49	59	58	45	33	62
Forster, T.	37	46	58	52	48	32	52	37	46	47	32	38	34	23	37	44	29
Fox, J.	—	—	—	—	—	6	6	22	16	1	1	2	3	—	—	—	—
Gandolfo, D.	25	44	26	33	37	28	34	24	27	16	19	13	8	14	6	14	12
Gaselee, N.	10	11	24	25	28	22	21	16	15	26	18	24	13	19	19	15	13
Gifford, J.	42	82	47	82	68	75	66	64	37	56	60	91	64	50	62	49	49
Grissell, D.	3	4	7	2	3	4	9	8	9	7	6	7	14	16	14	5	18
Hallett, T.	6	—	5	10	7	8	12	—	9	5	7	3	2	13	11	3	—
Haynes, P.	—	—	—	—	—	—	11	13	22	14	6	—	—	—	—	—	—
Henderson, N. J.	—	—	23	37	33	29	40	43	40	46	67	40	43	41	49	52	53
Hobbs, P.	—	—	—	—	—	—	—	—	—	2	12	22	24	45	33	51	37
Hodges, R.	—	1	3	1	7	6	7	19	32	19	17	21	18	19	19	21	32
Holder, R. J.	—	—	—	1	1	11	15	16	20	19	15	17	25	33	29	31	1
Hollinshead, R.	3	5	6	1	1	3	10	14	19	7	6	7	4	15	8	13	10
Jarvis, A.	10	8	10	20	26	16	11	5	15	7	4	0	—	—	—	2	2
Jenkins, J. R.	—	—	—	5	13	21	42	69	76	63	41	23	29	31	30	20	15
Jones, H.	16	18	6	3	—	—	—	—	—	—	—	—	—		—	—	—
Kelleway, P. A.	2	3	5	—	4	—	—	5	4	1	2	1	0	1	4	4	8
Kennard, L.	26	30	28	47	35	48	27	38	17	31	34	—	—	—	—	—	—
Kent, D.	18	29	23	22	22	15	—	—	—	—	—	—	—	—	—	—	—
King, J. S.	—	—	—	—	—	1	4	11	16	7	14	7	16	16	16	5	11
Lambert, M.	—	—	—	—	—	8	10	25	8	7	—	—	—	—	—	—	—
Leadbetter, S.	1	3	6	5	3	5	2	4	1	3	1	3	2	2	3	5	2
McCain, D.	6	18	14	5	1	12	7	9	6	15	4	12	13	13	8	9	6
Mellor, S.	55	45	31	22	27	20	16	23	38	25	24	6	11	21	34	8	4
Moore, A.	10	6	5	12	11	12	20	8	6	22	9	10	2	11	9	11	13
Moore, G. M.	—	—	—	—	—	—	—	—	3	16	30	47	37	53	46	38	29
Morley, D.	30	32	41	35	40	15	6	6	1	—	—	—	—	—	—	—	—
Murray Smith, D. ...	—	—	—	—	—	—	—	—	11	8	12	34	35	17	11	13	6
Naughton, M.	8	10	2	11	21	15	14	3	10	13	9	11	5	3	1	3	6
Nicholson, D.	38	34	19	28	47	67	64	50	17	22	42	50	39	42	55	63	100
Old, J.	13	11	9	16	23	21	24	23	22	10	8	6	9	2	10	21	19
Oliver, K.	20	24	10	11	6	11	9	3	10	2	6	6	7	4	4	3	1
Oliver, M.	12	17	23	7	4	9	8	13	10	10	5	8	3	5	2	—	—
O'Neill, J. J.	—	—	—	—	—	—	—	—	—	—	3	14	29	34	27	26	21

	1976 –77	1977 –78	1978 –79	1979 –80	1980 –81	1981 –82	1982 –83	1983 –84	1984 –85	1985 –86	1986 –87	1987 –88	1988 –89	1989 –90	1990 –91	1991 –92	1992 –93
Oughton, D.	—	—	—	—	—	—	8	20	16	8	5	—	—	—	—	—	—
Pipe, M. C.	5	2	6	12	14	20	23	32	51	79	106	129	208	224	230	224	194
Pitman, Mrs. J.	12	6	10	16	28	8	20	18	41	46	39	45	62	93	43	50	36
Price Ryan	8	3	1	5	7	6	6	—	—	—	—	—	—	—	—	—	—
Reveley, Mrs. M.	—	—	—	—	4	4	4	7	9	11	25	25	23	41	30	99	90
Richards, G.	50	54	33	51	54	56	39	61	64	56	59	72	69	78	118	67	104
Rimell, Mrs. M.	—	—	—	—	—	42	48	40	36	37	26	33	14	—	—	—	—
Rimell, T. F.	50	69	53	42	51	—	—	—	—	—	—	—	—	—	—	—	—
Scott, A.	2	8	14	8	8	19	22	8	16	12	—	—	—	—	—	—	—
Sherwood, O.	—	—	—	—	—	—	—	—	13	48	41	42	53	58	56	48	37
Sherwood, S.	—	—	—	—	—	—	—	—	—	—	—	—	—	—	12	17	30
Smith, Denys	12	11	18	17	19	18	26	40	37	27	32	26	20	13	21	19	14
Smith, Mrs. N.	—	2	5	2	8	13	12	12	3	7	4	—	—	—	—	—	—
Spearing, J.	5	3	10	4	5	18	24	12	27	17	14	15	6	4	9	7	12
Stephenson, W. A.	100	89	42	83	48	62	53	67	64	73	65	93	90	116	83	101	35
Sykes, Mrs W. D.	—	—	2	7	9	10	6	12	8	13	12	3	—	—	—	—	—
Tate, M.	35	31	16	28	11	22	7	15	11	4	3	2	3	2	1	1	—
Thorne, J.	11	18	13	25	16	18	19	16	18	10	—	—	—	—	—	—	—
Tinkler, N.	—	—	—	—	2	4	6	2	4	5	4	16	54	49	29	38	25
Turnell, A.	—	—	—	—	—	—	13	19	10	4	16	19	11	16	7	18	37
Turnell, R.	34	35	28	29	19	23	—	—	—	—	—	—	—	—	—	—	—
Twiston-Davies, N. A.	—	—	—	—	—	2	0	0	4	4	1	3	2	8	19	31	76
Walwyn, F.	51	63	46	36	54	45	44	46	33	30	15	26	15	18	—	—	—
Wardle, I.	9	17	14	13	7	21	8	12	7	7	3	11	6	2	—	—	—
Webber, J.	6	21	15	14	18	20	27	26	28	21	10	20	15	9	9	16	10
Wilson, J. S.	1	4	2	3	6	9	8	8	14	8	12	12	9	5	10	—	—
Winter, F.	75	90	80	86	68	68	67	90	85	41	51	32	—	—	—	—	—

[Totals given are for winners trained in Great Britain only]

Winning jockeys: hurdles and chases 1992–93

	Mounts	1st	2nd	3rd	%W-R	£WIN	£W/P
Ahern, M	65	3	7	13	4.6	3,709	12,002
Armytage, Gee	40	4	1	0	10.0	15,811	27,450
Beggan, R J	146	6	15	15	4.1	12,755	26,794
Bosley, M	110	3	4	11	2.7	5,587	13,156
Bradley, G	236	30	34	28	12.7	126,184	187,492
Brennan, M	143	23	18	16	16.1	52,911	67,266
Brennan, Helen	7	2	1	1	28.6	4,175	4,954
Brownless, C	11	1	0	1	9.1	6,873	7,690
Burchell, D J	102	13	9	12	12.7	28,879	49,807
Burrough, S	104	5	4	5	4.8	11,805	17,434
Byrne, D	154	18	25	17	11.7	62,798	101,772
Byrne, E	28	2	1	2	7.1	6,528	8,334
Caldwell, Peter	19	1	2	4	5.3	1,305	3,286
Callaghan, J	165	10	16	10	6.1	14,403	29,323
Campbell, R	102	11	14	13	10.8	26,218	42,037
Carberry, P	3	1	0	1	33.3	12,720	18,996
Carroll, A	89	14	4	7	15.7	29,398	34,376
Charlton, A	43	3	4	6	7.0	12,299	19,936
Codd, J	20	5	3	2	25.0	12,440	15,832
Comerford, K	37	4	5	3	10.8	7,233	10,677
Crosse, M	28	1	2	1	3.6	1,475	2,560
Curran, S	62	5	0	4	8.1	8,994	10,023
Davies, H	314	33	21	32	10.5	87,943	145,832
Dawe, N	26	2	1	5	7.7	5,180	7,900
Doolan, K	64	3	0	4	4.7	9,244	10,647
Doughty, N	263	69	36	33	26.2	236,149	315,591
Dowling, B	8	2	1	0	25.0	5,345	6,144
Duffy, M	3	1	0	0	33.3	1,882	1,882
Dunwoody, R	739	173	120	89	23.4	828,472	1,099,978
Dwyer, M	316	61	58	47	19.3	344,888	461,128
Earle, S	101	4	9	4	4.0	9,034	19,611
Eccles, S Smith	185	30	33	20	16.2	84,338	128,465
Frost, J	320	28	48	40	8.8	107,641	177,695
Gallagher, D	184	17	17	17	9.2	56,757	86,214
Garritty, R	181	21	17	24	11.6	67,855	104,543
Grant, C	419	58	56	49	13.8	160,594	245,383
Grantham, T	126	13	17	16	10.3	29,682	53,585
Guest, Richard	136	13	14	23	9.6	38,464	63,853
Haan, B de	124	13	22	15	10.5	36,191	100,363
Harker, G	73	3	3	7	4.1	9,042	15,605
Harley, P	70	7	11	2	10.0	14,684	22,407
Harris, J A	87	8	7	9	9.2	11,826	18,327
Harvey, L	185	19	20	22	10.3	71,283	107,590
Hawke, N	138	11	11	17	8.0	22,164	39,278
Hawkins, C	109	13	15	7	11.9	35,105	47,122
Hills, M	1	1	0	0	100.0	1,523	1,523
Hoad, M	33	4	1	3	12.1	7,108	8,625
Hobbs, Peter	318	51	49	37	16.0	113,014	173,018
Hodgson, S	43	2	6	3	4.7	4,541	12,007
Holley, P	199	21	29	19	10.6	130,496	226,275
Humphreys, W	116	5	9	8	4.3	10,714	20,454
Irvine, W	138	13	10	13	9.4	44,237	61,892
James, J	7	2	0	1	28.6	4,424	4,664
Jarvis, T	28	1	1	3	3.6	1,480	6,047
Johnson, K	160	6	8	17	3.8	28,350	44,123
Jones, K	92	2	3	6	2.2	4,686	9,099
Jones, A	59	1	7	7	1.7	2,198	9,415
Kavanagh, J R	183	23	24	22	12.6	76,780	114,237
Keightley, S	50	7	3	5	14.0	15,168	20,114
Kondrat, A	4	1	0	1	25.0	44,500	60,753
Lawrence, I	143	6	7	15	4.2	13,198	22,201
Llewellyn, C	412	68	43	50	16.5	393,323	491,023
Lodder, J	128	5	4	14	3.9	9,051	15,373

	Mounts	1st	2nd	3rd	%W-R	£WIN	£W/P
Lower, J	91	23	12	12	25.3	80,633	105,904
Lynch, M M	97	7	7	7	7.2	17,050	25,464
Lyons, S	112	6	12	11	5.4	9,925	19,721
Lyons, Gary	105	3	6	12	2.9	7,216	16,048
Mackey, S.	43	1	3	3	2.3	2,373	5,129
Maguire, A.	722	124	118	97	17.2	466,221	676,535
Maloney, M	3	1	1	0	33.3	3,020	3,464
Mann, N	170	21	11	16	12.4	44,362	61,662
Marley, R	58	1	4	4	1.7	2,128	5,443
Maude, C	133	11	18	10	8.3	51,665	75,817
McCourt, G	430	70	61	61	16.3	202,067	306,355
McDermott, P	77	1	8	6	1.3	943	6,118
McFarland, W	170	6	10	13	3.5	9,090	20,420
McKinley, E.	41	1	4	6	2.4	1,140	5,030
McLaughlin, J.	22	2	1	3	9.1	4,939	6,681
McLoughlin, P.	7	2	1	1	28.6	3,479	4,495
McNeill, S	385	51	36	47	13.2	184,938	296,998
Merrigan, A	162	7	14	14	4.3	18,003	34,264
Moloney, M	110	17	10	10	15.5	41,376	57,597
Moore, G L	153	12	16	20	7.8	33,295	48,602
Morris, D	120	15	8	9	12.5	54,430	66,575
Mulholland, A	68	3	4	8	4.4	6,584	11,281
Murphy, D	303	45	38	42	14.9	304,969	411,451
Murphy, J.	19	1	1	0	5.3	1,660	2,477
Murphy, E	110	16	12	9	14.5	35,599	55,926
Niven, P	386	108	62	52	28.0	314,482	406,017
Nolan, D.	4	1	0	0	25.0	2,008	2,008
O'Hagan, A	47	2	5	2	4.3	2,807	7,343
O'Hara, L	126	7	7	6	5.6	18,176	26,516
O'Neill, S J.	79	7	6	13	8.9	28,312	39,315
Oliver, Jacqui	37	11	2	3	29.7	27,715	35,653
Orkney, A	271	21	32	40	7.7	52,015	98,401
Osborne, J.	500	102	71	61	20.4	342,506	481,321
Perrett, M	233	27	25	19	11.6	118,078	215,883
Pitman, M.	155	22	28	19	14.2	75,569	145,256
Powell, B	207	12	15	16	5.8	27,450	49,629
Quinn, J J	44	2	3	3	4.5	4,712	7,625
Railton, J.	240	33	32	24	13.8	69,725	119,923
Ranger, M.	52	2	3	7	3.8	3,642	6,772
Reed, T	225	33	26	36	14.7	74,764	105,499
Richards, M	168	19	27	24	11.3	62,904	118,457
Scudamore, P	416	129	75	47	31.0	617,582	855,165
Sheridan, B.	9	1	1	0	11.1	2,924	17,397
Shoemark, I	78	4	4	12	5.1	8,718	13,684
Shortt, J.	4	1	0	1	25.0	24,624	26,454
Skyrme, D	129	8	6	7	6.2	14,732	22,400
Smith, V	49	4	2	2	8.2	8,787	10,210
Smith, A S	158	11	24	18	7.0	25,190	50,910
Stokell, Ann	26	1	0	2	3.8	1,119	1,539
Storey, B.	342	44	33	47	12.9	106,425	149,662
Stronge, R.	50	5	5	6	10.0	8,231	13,085
Supple, R	223	27	31	33	12.1	77,728	125,472
Swan, C	44	7	3	6	15.9	135,797	164,527
Tegg, D.	204	18	18	27	8.8	49,221	81,883
Telfer, D	41	1	5	4	2.4	2,890	8,057
Tory, A.	195	14	20	32	7.2	35,061	66,326
Turner, S.	78	4	4	5	5.1	9,976	15,724
Upton, G	217	22	21	25	10.1	53,566	79,222
Vincent, Lorna	73	8	9	6	11.0	12,815	20,566
Wall, T	182	8	15	23	4.4	18,584	35,552
Webb, A	167	11	10	23	6.6	26,470	44,895
White, J	98	7	6	6	7.1	41,170	50,208
Wilkinson, D	62	7	9	6	11.3	12,662	19,249
Williamson, N	324	41	56	36	12.7	106,120	174,405
Worthington, W	96	2	8	10	2.1	4,638	13,637
Wyer, L	259	48	39	31	18.5	181,969	260,282

Miscellaneous

	Mounts	1st	2nd	3rd	%W-R	£WIN	£W/P
King, Jeff.	3	1	0	0	33.3	1,530	1,530
O'Neill, Jonjo.	2	1	0	0	50.0	1,488	1,488
Tuck, Phil	1	1	0	0	100.0	1,544	1,544

Champion jockeys: hurdles and chases 1900–93

Season	Jockey	Wins
1900	Mr H S Sidney	53
1901	F Mason	58
1902	F Mason	67
1903	P Woodland	54
1904	F Mason	59
1905	F Mason	73
1906	F Mason	58
1907	F Mason	59
1908	P Cowley	65
1909	R Gordon	45
1910	E Piggott	67
1911	W Payne	76
1912	I Anthony	78
1913	E Piggott	60
1914	Mr J R Anthony	60
1915	E Piggott	44
1916	C Hawkins	17
1917	W Smith	15
1918	G Duller	17
1919	Mr H Brown	48
1920	F B Rees	64
1921	F B Rees	65
1922	J Anthony	78
1923	F B Rees	64
1924	F B Rees	108
1925	E Foster	76
1925–26	T Leader	61
1926–27	F B Rees	59
1927–28	W Stott	88
1928–29	W Stott	65
1929–30	W Stott	77
1930–31	W Stott	81
1931–32	W Stott	77
1932–33	G Wilson	61
1933–34	G Wilson	56
1934–35	G Wilson	73
1935–36	G Wilson	57
1936–37	G Wilson	45
1937–38	G Wilson	59
1938–39	T F Rimell	61
1939–40	T F Rimell	24
1940–41	G Wilson	22
1941–42	R Smyth	12
1942–43	No racing.	
1943–44	No racing.	
1944–45	H Nicholson	15
	T F Rimell	15
1945–46	T F Rimell	54
1946–47	J Dowdeswell	58
1947–48	B Marshall	66
1948–49	T Moloney	60
1949–50	T Moloney	95
1950–51	T Moloney	83
1951–52	T Moloney	99
1952–53	F Winter	121
1953–54	R Francis	76
1954–55	T Moloney	67
1955–56	F Winter	74
1956–57	F Winter	80
1957–58	F Winter	82
1958–59	T Brookshaw	83
1959–60	S Mellor	68
1960–61	S Mellor	118
1961–62	S Mellor	80
1962–63	J Gifford	70
1963–64	J Gifford	94
1964–65	T Biddlecombe	114
1965–66	T Biddlecombe	102
1966–67	J Gifford	122
1967–68	J Gifford	82
1968–69	B R Davies	77
	T Biddlecombe	77
1969–70	B R Davies	91
1970–71	G Thorner	74
1971–72	B R Davies	89
1972–73	R Barry	125
1973–74	R Barry	94
1974–75	T Stack	82
1975–76	J Francome	96
1976–77	T Stack	97
1977–78	J J O'Neill	149
1978–79	J Francome	95
1979–80	J J O'Neill	117
1980–81	J Francome	105
1981–82	J Francome	120
	P Scudamore	120
1982–83	J Francome	106
1983–84	J Francome	131
1984–85	J Francome	101
1985–86	P Scudamore	91
1986–87	P Scudamore	123
1987–88	P Scudamore	132
1988–89	P Scudamore	221
1989–90	P Scudamore	170
1990–91	P Scudamore	141
1991–92	P Scudamore	175
1992–93	R Dunwoody	173

Prior to the 1925-26 season the statistics show the figure of the leading jockey for the period January to December.

Principal NH jockeys' winning totals: 1976–77 to 1992–93

	1976 –77	1977 –78	1978 –79	1979 –80	1980 –81	1981 –82	1982 –83	1983 –84	1984 –85	1985 –86	1986 –87	1987 –88	1988 –89	1989 –90	1990 –91	1991 –92	1992 –93
Arnott, R.	—	—	—	—	—	—	5	9	10	5	5	7	2	3	—	—	—
Astbury, C.	4	4	5	2	—	3	2	—	—	—	—	—	—	—	—	—	—
Atkins, D.	22	19	11	13	14	7	—	—	—	—	—	—	—	—	—	—	—
Atkins, R.	23	17	18	11	9	1	3	1	1	—	2	—	—	—	—	—	—
Barnes, M.	23	13	16	12	15	13	5	9	4	6	—	—	—	—	—	—	—
Barry, R.	26	32	34	46	43	28	21	2	—	—	—	—	—	—	—	—	—
Barton, P.	18	42	23	31	28	24	35	38	32	41	14	—	—	—	—	—	—
Beggan, R. J.	—	—	—	—	—	—	—	—	12	13	30	28	24	22	13	22	6
Blacker, P.	27	39	30	33	39	19	—	—	—	—	—	—	—	—	—	—	—
Blackshaw, M.	4	—	1	—	—	—	—	—	—	—	—	—	—	—	—	—	—
Bosley, M.	—	—	—	1	—	3	—	5	3	8	10	10	4	5	8	5	3
Bradley, G.	—	—	—	4	23	38	34	38	37	39	53	36	34	30	26	29	30
Brennan, M.	—	—	—	—	5	24	22	17	14	14	21	16	17	22	17	10	23
Brown, A.	6	12	32	33	45	17	28	16	35	12	—	—	—	—	—	—	—
Brown, C.	4	7	14	10	27	34	24	38	34	33	30	23	—	—	—	—	—
Browne, D.	—	—	—	—	4	28	33	26	10	19	24	20	5	—	—	—	—
Burke, J. M.	31	35	15	4	3	12	5	12	11	—	—	—	—	—	—	—	—
Byrne, D.	—	—	—	—	—	—	—	—	—	—	3	9	29	44	21	14	18
Carmody, T.	—	2	71	86	67	1	2	1	1	4	1	1	—	1	2	—	—
Cartwright, D.	25	7	4	2	—	—	—	—	—	—	—	—	—	—	—	—	—
Champion, R.	44	56	35	7	39	21	—	—	—	—	—	—	—	—	—	—	—
Charlton, P.	9	16	15	15	11	20	26	32	34	5	—	—	—	—	—	—	—
Charlton, S.	6	12	14	17	15	13	7	16	13	13	1	—	—	—	—	—	—
Clay, N.	13	6	10	11	5	6	5	—	—	—	—	—	—	—	—	—	—
Coleman, N.	—	—	—	—	—	5	3	8	18	9	11	15	23	6	4	12	—
Crank, R.	7	12	23	3	10	10	30	22	11	19	18	9	4	1	—	—	—
Croucher, P.	—	—	—	—	1	4	7	18	28	11	20	52	—	—	—	—	—
Davies, B. R.	50	42	62	39	48	15	—	—	—	—	—	—	—	—	—	—	—
Davies, H.	—	10	15	29	52	61	85	67	50	58	40	34	50	60	51	44	33
Davies, R. F.	24	17	13	19	15	16	6	—	—	—	—	—	—	—	—	—	—
Dever, P.	—	—	—	—	—	4	8	22	14	8	13	3	1	4	2	—	—
Dickinson, M.	53	52	—	—	—	—	—	—	—	—	—	—	—	—	—	—	—
Dickman, A.	7	13	16	14	7	8	—	4	—	—	—	—	—	—	—	—	—
Double, P.	—	—	—	—	6	5	23	13	14	—	3	—	—	—	—	—	—
Doughty, N.	—	1	12	15	21	33	32	48	45	27	11	18	33	46	96	44	69
Duggan, J.	—	—	—	—	—	1	4	13	29	12	7	3	4	3	4	1	—
Dun, T. G.	1	17	26	15	21	17	22	13	22	16	17	—	—	—	—	—	—
Dunwoody, R.	—	—	—	—	—	—	4	24	46	55	70	79	91	102	127	137	173
Dutton, D.	—	—	—	—	8	35	19	22	18	13	13	11	3	—	—	—	—
Dwyer, M.	—	—	—	—	—	—	19	29	26	30	81	73	93	75	81	73	61
Earle, S. A.	—	—	—	—	—	—	—	—	13	3	6	21	13	22	16	8	4
Earnshaw, R.	—	1	3	17	18	27	46	35	38	25	5	—	—	—	—	—	—
Eccles, S Smith	14	51	34	62	59	63	58	64	56	65	56	30	45	56	56	21	30
Evans, H. J.	18	12	11	—	—	—	—	—	—	—	—	—	—	—	—	—	—
Evans, R. R.	26	26	22	17	1	—	—	—	—	—	—	—	—	—	—	—	—
Fairhurst, C.	10	7	1	3	2	—	1	1	3	4	3	—	—	—	—	—	—
Floyd, M.	20	24	34	2	16	15	2	—	—	—	—	—	—	—	—	—	—
Francome, J.	88	83	95	69	105	120	106	131	101	—	—	—	—	—	—	—	—
Frost, J.	1	—	3	—	4	8	7	12	22	14	14	30	41	46	39	41	28
Glover, J.	35	—	—	—	—	—	—	—	—	—	—	—	—	—	—	—	—
Goldstein, R.	1	4	8	12	8	11	8	11	17	12	9	20	32	21	12	—	—
Goulding, D.	11	52	24	26	15	21	12	1	—	—	—	—	—	—	—	—	—
Graham, G.	—	8	7	1	2	1	2	1	—	—	—	—	—	—	—	—	—
Grant, C.	1	2	7	33	39	36	56	26	54	41	63	80	38	94	57	78	58
Guest, Joe	5	6	5	—	—	—	—	—	—	—	—	—	—	—	—	—	—
Guest, R.	—	—	—	—	—	—	—	—	—	7	20	18	19	13	33	43	13
Haan, B de	—	—	—	12	25	5	17	29	23	22	15	16	15	29	10	4	13
Hammond M.	—	—	—	—	—	4	16	13	4	27	36	63	33	35	—	—	—
Harvey, L.	—	—	—	—	—	—	—	—	2	9	19	17	11	25	42	25	19
Hawke, N.	—	—	—	—	—	—	—	—	—	—	—	12	18	17	15	12	11
Hawkins, C.	19	27	20	31	42	26	—	31	16	30	11	17	12	11	7	4	13
Haynes, P.	13	26	20	32	21	6	—	—	—	—	—	—	—	—	—	—	—
Hobbs, Peter	—	—	—	1	5	6	5	14	15	12	20	26	47	43	9	31	51
Hobbs, Philip	13	22	20	12	20	16	16	10	6	6	—	—	—	—	—	—	—
Holland, S.	11	6	4	4	1	1	—	—	3	4	7	—	—	—	—	—	—
Holley, P.	—	—	—	—	—	—	—	—	—	1	4	6	22	11	19	11	21
Holmes, G.	16	17	22	9	3	2	3	—	—	—	—	—	—	—	—	—	—

PRINCIPAL NH JOCKEY'S WINNING TOTALS

	1976 –77	1977 –78	1978 –79	1979 –80	1980 –81	1981 –82	1982 –83	1983 –84	1984 –85	1985 –86	1986 –87	1987 –88	1988 –89	1989 –90	1990 –91	1991 –92	1992 –93
Hyett, R.	21	22	16	17	4	12	9	11	6	7	8	12	8	5	6	—	—
Jobar, S.	20	14	3	4	4	19	14	8	—	—	—	—	—	—	—	—	—
Jones, K.	—	—	—	—	—	4	14	30	7	16	4	12	1	0	2	2	2
King, J.	40	36	21	18	9	—	—	—	—	—	—	—	—	—	—	—	—
Kington, R.	1	1	1	1	1	4	7	2	2	2	—	—	—	—	—	—	—
Knight, Steve	9	9	7	20	12	20	25	20	15	9	20	14	2	—	—	—	—
Lamb, R.	14	21	58	85	44	58	27	28	30	47	48	6	—	—	—	—	—
Leach, P.	20	19	12	16	13	11	18	22	38	25	12	—	—	—	—	—	—
Linley, R.	17	33	34	30	39	36	51	35	41	9	5	4	—	—	1	—	—
Llewellyn, C.	—	—	—	—	—	—	—	—	—	2	7	41	20	19	32	53	68
Lower, J.	—	—	—	—	—	—	—	—	1	25	36	11	27	49	29	6	23
Lungo, L.	1	1	—	6	—	—	—	—	—	—	—	—	—	—	—	—	—
Maguire, A.	—	—	—	—	—	—	—	—	—	—	—	—	—	—	3	71	124
Mangan, P.	15	8	7	1	—	—	—	—	—	—	—	—	—	—	—	—	—
Mann, C.	—	6	2	2	10	5	7	13	9	14	9	7	—	—	—	—	—
Mann, N.	—	—	—	—	—	—	—	—	—	—	—	—	3	24	27	16	21
May, S.	12	8	11	4	14	4	3	1	2	1	—	—	—	—	—	—	—
McCourt, G.	13	30	9	11	17	20	35	39	30	38	33	68	86	100	83	102	70
McKeown, D.	—	—	—	—	—	—	—	—	2	1	24	17	31	30	17	16	—
McNally, G.	2	7	5	12	5	3	3	—	—	—	—	—	—	—	—	—	—
McNeill, S.	4	5	14	6	4	2	4	14	13	8	18	9	22	15	20	31	51
Mooney, K.	5	13	9	11	16	19	20	34	24	37	18	32	22	21	14	—	—
Moore, G. L.	—	2	3	12	8	10	22	11	8	14	5	5	2	9	17	11	12
Moore, S.	—	—	—	—	—	—	—	15	15	2	15	5	2	—	—	—	—
Morgan, T.	—	—	—	—	—	—	—	—	—	—	18	44	51	19	5	—	—
Morshead, S.	14	12	8	24	57	34	62	53	48	24	41	1	—	—	—	—	—
Munro, D.	23	11	—	1	—	—	—	—	—	—	—	—	—	—	—	—	—
Murphy, D. J.	—	—	—	—	—	—	—	—	6	6	18	15	19	15	29	48	45
Nicholls, P.	—	—	—	—	—	16	23	12	7	9	18	18	15	—	—	—	—
Niven, P.	—	—	—	—	—	—	—	1	—	15	28	30	49	48	86	105	108
Nolan, D.	—	—	5	10	2	3	3	5	5	4	11	4	0	6	2	0	1
O'Neill, J. J.	65	149	62	117	17	34	74	103	46	38	—	—	—	—	—	—	—
O'Neill S. J.	4	4	4	7	14	3	12	21	16	9	12	12	18	19	13	14	7
Orkney, A.	—	—	—	—	—	—	—	—	4	2	4	4	4	11	20	28	21
Osborne, J.	—	—	—	—	—	—	—	—	—	1	13	21	22	53	62	76	102
Percival, V.	5	1	—	—	—	—	—	—	—	—	—	—	—	—	—	—	—
Perrett, M.	—	—	—	1	4	5	28	29	31	—	19	24	27	52	58	22	27
Pimlott, C.	2	2	3	19	45	30	25	25	8	7	—	—	—	—	—	—	—
Pitman, M.	—	—	—	—	—	—	—	6	16	28	9	27	40	57	27	35	22
Powell, B.	—	—	—	—	—	—	1	16	27	45	48	38	64	48	38	35	12
Railton, J.	—	—	—	—	—	—	—	—	—	—	4	4	18	21	27	11	33
Read, C.	26	1	—	—	—	—	—	—	—	—	—	—	—	—	—	—	—
Reed, T.	—	—	—	1	1	2	3	4	14	14	6	16	11	14	14	19	33
Richards, M.	1	—	—	5	11	6	12	9	4	10	9	7	30	25	28	37	19
Rowe, R.	2	7	18	58	22	45	51	58	41	48	50	64	30	31	29	—	—
Rowell, R.	4	10	11	14	6	4	11	4	12	4	13	3	1	1	2	—	—
Russell, P.	3	—	—	—	—	—	—	—	—	—	—	—	—	—	—	—	—
Scudamore, P.	—	—	9	34	91	120	93	98	50	91	124	132	221	170	141	175	129
Sherwood, S.	—	—	—	—	—	9	13	23	30	79	64	54	68	—	—	—	—
Shilston, S.	4	6	9	8	12	17	11	15	13	12	11	11	1	1	—	—	—
Shortt, J.	—	—	—	—	—	—	—	—	—	—	—	—	7	11	17	13	1
Smith, C.	16	24	12	24	11	16	14	16	12	12	10	14	12	5	1	—	—
Smith, W.	46	44	35	27	33	23	20	9	—	—	—	—	—	—	—	—	—
Soane, V.	5	—	—	—	—	—	—	—	—	—	—	—	—	—	—	—	—
Storey, B.	—	—	—	—	—	7	9	13	19	20	15	25	30	32	20	40	44
Stringer, A.	—	—	—	—	16	7	18	12	16	13	10	1	—	—	—	—	—
Stronge, R.	—	—	—	4	8	11	6	11	19	16	17	4	9	2	3	10	5
Supple, R. J.	—	—	—	—	—	—	—	—	—	—	—	5	8	34	29	31	27
Suthern, J.	10	8	17	23	15	12	15	12	19	11	2	—	—	—	—	—	—
Tegg, D.	—	—	—	—	—	—	—	—	—	1	6	23	21	12	21	19	18
Thorner, G.	66	56	43	18	—	—	—	—	—	—	—	—	—	—	—	—	—
Tinkler, C.	31	55	27	32	26	12	2	—	—	—	—	—	—	—	—	—	—
Tinkler, N.	19	27	40	22	6	4	6	—	4	4	1	2	3	—	—	—	—
Tory, A. S.	—	—	—	—	—	—	—	—	—	1	—	1	15	15	32	26	14
Tuck, P.	3	5	13	24	31	27	38	41	45	37	59	71	23	5	—	—	—
Turnell, A.	28	29	21	33	23	19	2	—	—	—	—	—	—	—	—	—	—
Wakley, N.	13	3	1	—	—	—	—	—	—	—	—	—	—	—	—	—	—
Watkinson, I.	43	25	21	—	—	—	—	—	—	—	—	—	—	—	—	—	—
Webb, A.	17	13	11	10	9	26	18	21	25	24	15	20	15	10	13	14	11
Webber, A.	15	28	29	28	27	43	50	60	30	15	—	—	—	—	—	—	—
White, J.	—	—	—	—	—	—	3	12	16	19	14	15	27	31	14	11	7
Williams, John	11	12	24	13	14	11	9	8	—	—	—	—	—	—	—	—	—
Williams, M.	11	7	10	29	8	27	17	12	10	3	7	27	16	2	1	—	—
Williamson, N.	—	—	—	—	—	—	—	—	—	—	—	—	—	20	33	33	41
Wyer, L.	—	—	—	—	—	—	—	—	—	—	33	30	36	33	44	35	48

[Totals given are for winning mounts in Great Britain only]

Winning conditional jockeys: hurdles and chases 1992–93

	Mounts	1st	2nd	3rd	%W-R	£WIN	£W/P
Barry, D	49	1	3	2	2.0	2,038	3,898
Bates, A.	23	8	0	3	34.8	16,342	17,032
Bazin, G	17	1	2	3	5.9	1,679	3,383
Bellamy, R	183	15	24	20	8.2	38,736	64,586
Bentley, N	140	25	19	13	17.9	50,356	68,095
Bentley, D	138	9	18	12	6.5	17,607	32,844
Berry, M	12	1	1	1	8.3	2,036	2,765
Bohan, D	13	2	0	1	15.4	4,670	5,098
Bridgwater, D	355	39	41	42	11.0	133,244	189,671
Brown, K	9	1	0	2	11.1	3,522	4,406
Burke, J	75	10	9	6	13.3	27,466	36,749
Caddell, J	2	1	0	1	50.0	1,807	2,036
Cahill, G	21	1	2	3	4.8	1,984	3,674
Caldwell, Pat	22	2	1	2	9.1	5,463	6,626
Carey, P	14	1	1	1	7.1	1,434	2,025
Clarke, J	46	3	5	8	6.5	3,803	8,347
Clay, Diane	111	19	15	8	17.1	33,885	44,663
Clifford, B	247	16	24	29	6.5	36,640	70,239
Dace, L	33	2	6	3	6.1	3,889	8,828
Dalton, B	36	1	3	1	2.8	1,631	4,828
Darke, R	70	2	8	5	2.9	3,213	10,405
Dascombe, T	22	1	3	1	4.5	1,953	4,151
Davies, Judy	57	3	6	12	5.3	4,612	16,860
Davis, R	214	14	32	21	6.5	33,448	59,226
Dennis, C	126	3	4	4	2.4	5,342	9,121
Dicken, A	35	3	6	6	8.6	5,227	10,056
Dobbin, A.	168	23	24	14	13.7	45,626	64,306
Donohoe, S.	9	1	1	0	11.1	2,783	3,223
Driscoll, J	24	1	4	1	4.2	1,534	3,383
Dwan, W	66	10	9	4	15.2	24,062	29,336
Eccles, P Smith	35	2	3	6	5.7	4,189	7,022
Eldredge, Leanne	13	1	2	2	7.7	1,734	3,543
Eley, T.	153	14	12	16	9.2	35,510	46,290
Farrant, R	174	11	23	21	6.3	20,975	43,035
Fitzgerald, M A	426	54	51	50	12.7	153,005	225,496
Fitzgerald, M P	11	2	1	2	18.2	3,950	4,721
Flannigan, A.	64	3	8	3	4.7	5,205	9,407
Fortt, D.	37	4	6	3	10.8	8,502	13,577
Foster, M	119	21	18	17	17.6	66,967	95,393
Fry, W.	43	2	4	1	4.7	1,891	3,958
Geoghegan, D	35	2	0	0	5.7	3,830	4,033
Greene, R	163	17	10	23	10.4	35,344	51,330
Harding, B	53	2	6	6	3.8	4,013	11,836
Heaver, G	11	3	1	1	27.3	5,130	5,767
Herrington, M	6	2	1	0	33.3	3,047	3,473
Hide, P	135	19	24	10	14.1	46,281	82,991
Hobbs, D	18	1	1	3	5.6	1,861	3,164
Hodge, R	136	17	16	12	12.5	34,143	46,741
Hourigan, M	224	21	18	18	9.4	45,625	73,977
Jones, James	49	2	3	3	4.1	5,002	7,893
Kent, T	17	6	3	1	35.3	13,732	16,639
Larnach, A	146	13	17	17	8.9	31,564	52,496
Leach, N	58	5	4	3	8.6	9,512	13,020
Leahy, D	173	11	21	19	6.4	20,680	42,212
Leahy, F	22	3	2	3	13.6	4,529	6,526
Linton, A	22	1	1	2	4.5	1,956	3,317
Long, Leesa	38	3	3	4	7.9	6,369	9,012
Marston, W	266	26	32	27	9.8	54,756	84,038
Mason, S	40	7	3	4	17.5	12,626	16,506
Massey, R	15	1	0	2	6.7	1,718	2,156
Matthews, D	14	2	2	2	14.3	4,308	5,445
McCarthy, J	85	18	7	13	21.2	43,510	52,762
McGonagle, M	12	2	2	2	16.7	3,164	5,026

WINNING CONDITIONAL JOCKEYS: HURDLES AND CHASES 1992–93

	Mounts	1st	2nd	3rd	%W-R	£WIN	£W/P
McWilliams, P	28	4	2	4	14.3	6,323	8,990
Meade, D	75	4	10	7	5.3	7,936	15,064
Meredith, D	133	11	10	14	8.3	28,338	43,951
Midgley, P	78	1	9	4	1.3	1,874	8,678
Moffatt, D J	141	13	19	15	9.2	26,135	42,832
Moore, P.	18	1	1	2	5.6	1,590	2,428
Mullaney, L	13	1	1	2	7.7	937	1,868
Murphy, B	36	2	6	1	5.6	5,279	11,988
Murtagh, F	28	1	4	3	3.6	1,590	5,239
O'Hare, L	31	4	2	3	12.9	9,169	10,666
O'Sullivan, D	120	14	11	15	11.7	33,946	44,701
Perratt, F	55	9	2	6	16.4	18,991	22,517
Procter, A	57	4	7	11	7.0	14,084	21,787
Reynolds, L	15	2	0	1	13.3	5,093	5,645
Richmond, D	83	10	13	9	12.0	28,962	45,262
Roberts, Mark	10	1	0	1	10.0	1,424	1,595
Rowe, G	39	6	4	6	15.4	12,799	18,562
Ryan, D.	38	4	3	4	10.5	5,945	8,428
Ryan, J.	62	8	2	6	12.9	15,374	19,118
Salter, D	137	11	12	21	8.0	23,831	38,014
Sellars, Kate	2	1	0	0	50.0	1,277	1,277
Slattery, V.	167	10	14	12	6.0	18,582	29,094
Smith, N.	96	5	5	9	5.2	9,945	15,412
Stevens, Mark	1	1	0	0	100.0	1,630	1,630
Stevens, M	44	2	3	4	4.5	3,451	6,374
Stocks, N	18	2	2	2	11.1	5,126	7,924
Supple, J	73	1	6	3	1.4	2,850	7,042
Taylor, S.	64	7	9	7	10.9	12,983	19,759
Thompson, P	3	1	0	1	33.3	1,390	1,499
Thompson, T.	68	3	8	9	4.4	5,979	12,843
Thomson, G.	16	1	0	1	6.3	1,924	2,186
Tormey, G	39	6	6	1	15.4	14,756	18,249
Towler, D.	29	2	2	3	6.9	2,816	4,270
Waggott, P	155	12	14	29	7.7	25,429	42,523
Whelan, M	9	1	0	1	11.1	1,679	1,913
Williams, P.	138	11	22	19	8.0	27,944	54,036
Williams, S D.	60	7	2	5	11.7	14,486	18,586
Woodall, C	56	6	7	0	10.7	14,537	19,393
Wynne, S	108	12	10	5	11.1	22,317	29,457

Winning amateur riders: hurdles and chases 1992–93

	Mounts	1st	2nd	3rd	%W-R	£WIN	£W/P
Alner, Mr R	9	1	2	0	11.1	1,900	2,511
Andrews, Mr Simon	15	2	0	2	13.3	2,642	3,199
Armytage, Mr M	66	4	8	5	6.1	12,519	24,700
Bailey, Mr E	10	2	0	0	20.0	3,672	3,672
Bailey, Mrs T	3	1	0	0	33.3	3,035	3,035
Barlow, Mr D	9	1	1	2	11.1	1,864	2,694
Barraclough, Miss S	3	1	0	1	33.3	1,744	1,929
Beardsall, Mr J	17	1	1	0	5.9	1,581	2,111
Blackford, Miss L	12	1	2	1	8.3	1,769	2,902
Bonner, Mr C	51	3	3	3	5.9	5,326	7,956
Bradburne, Mr J	36	2	6	6	5.6	6,174	17,400
Bradley, Mr N	60	2	2	5	3.3	2,968	5,152
Brisby, Mr S	33	3	3	0	9.1	5,802	7,288
Brookshaw, Mr S	8	1	2	0	12.5	1,089	2,309
Brown, Mr R H	12	4	3	3	33.3	5,872	7,987
Buckley, Mr M	46	9	8	8	19.6	18,190	27,051
Burnett-Wells, Mr C	54	9	7	6	16.7	18,167	24,281
Bush, Mr S	10	1	3	1	10.0	2,898	5,370
Butler, Miss J	12	2	4	1	16.7	2,932	4,583
Byrne, Mr T	48	9	7	2	18.8	15,623	22,693
Cambidge, Mr J	14	1	1	2	7.1	1,784	2,669
Coonan, Mr A	1	1	0	0	100.0	2,682	2,682
Craggs, Mr P	3	1	0	0	33.3	6,775	6,775
Curling, Miss P	14	2	5	1	14.3	5,298	8,271
Dare, Miss A	6	3	1	0	50.0	4,535	4,959
Dawson, Mrs J	1	1	0	0	100.0	2,369	2,369
Deasley, Mr S	4	1	0	1	25.0	962	1,115
Digby, Mr J Wingfield	7	1	0	0	14.3	3,659	4,298
Duggan, Mr D	20	1	1	1	5.0	1,872	2,475
Dun, Mr J M	17	3	2	3	17.6	6,216	8,541
Durkan, Mr J	70	9	8	6	12.9	15,630	23,512
Farrell, Mrs A	42	7	8	6	16.7	14,626	21,085
Felton, Mr M	17	4	4	4	23.5	6,729	10,361
Ford, Mr R	8	1	1	2	12.5	825	2,084
Gee, Mr P	2	1	1	0	50.0	1,116	1,479
Gingell, Mr M	5	1	0	1	20.0	2,635	3,002
Goble, Mr K	3	1	1	1	33.3	1,488	2,622
Greenall, Mr J	27	12	6	2	44.4	23,023	31,896
Hacking, Mr P	16	3	0	3	18.8	3,554	4,336
Hale, Mr R	53	3	5	4	5.7	12,761	30,696
Hambly, Mr A	13	4	2	0	30.8	7,394	8,725
Hamilton, Mr B R	10	1	1	2	10.0	1,893	3,457
Hancock, Mr C	21	3	1	1	14.3	5,391	6,935
Harris, Mr N	14	3	0	3	21.4	4,110	5,188
Harvey, Mr A	7	1	1	2	14.3	2,211	4,250
Harwood, Miss A	3	1	0	0	33.3	2,013	2,013
Henderson, Mrs R	6	2	1	0	33.3	15,614	26,270
Hill, Mr A	15	5	2	3	33.3	10,172	13,285
Holmes, Miss K	5	1	0	1	20.0	1,245	1,500
Houghton, Mr G Johnson	33	2	6	4	6.1	5,543	11,030
Hughes, Mr V	3	1	0	0	33.3	1,631	1,631
Hyde, Mr T P	1	1	0	0	100.0	1,872	1,872
Jenkins, Mr P	6	1	0	0	16.7	1,646	1,646
Jenks, Mr T	128	20	18	19	15.6	57,529	77,481
Johnson, Mr P	11	2	0	0	18.2	7,012	7,487
Jones, Mr T	11	3	4	0	27.3	10,648	12,271
Leavy, Mr B	14	1	2	2	7.1	1,564	4,259
Lewis, Mr G	125	8	7	12	6.4	17,913	31,628
Lillingston, Mr Andrew	10	4	2	1	40.0	8,859	10,210
Llewellyn, Mr J L	60	6	8	8	10.0	10,773	17,044
Llewellyn, Mr J	1	1	0	0	100.0	1,800	1,800
Martin, Mr Anthony	4	2	1	0	50.0	9,440	11,665
Maundrell, Mr G	7	1	0	0	14.3	1,548	1,548

WINNING AMATEUR RIDERS: HURDLES AND CHASES 1992–93

	Mounts	1st	2nd	3rd	%W-R	£WIN	£W/P
McCain, Mr D	66	4	4	2	6.1	8,140	12,255
McCarthy, Mr T	16	1	1	2	6.3	2,553	4,050
McKie, Mr I	5	2	2	0	40.0	4,826	6,275
Miller, Miss Blythe	1	1	0	0	100.0	9,830	9,830
Miller, Mr M G	10	2	1	3	20.0	3,449	5,042
Mitchell, Miss S	14	1	0	1	7.1	1,763	2,026
Mitchell, Mr T	4	1	2	0	25.0	1,990	2,784
Moore, Mr N	23	5	2	0	21.7	10,187	11,353
Murphy, Mr Paul	21	3	2	1	14.3	8,136	10,688
Nash, Mrs P	5	2	0	0	40.0	4,024	4,024
Needham, Mrs F	24	3	1	5	12.5	4,476	6,777
Newport, Mr C	13	1	2	1	7.7	1,605	2,941
Nichol, Miss S	5	1	1	0	20.0	2,192	2,920
Ogden, Capt A	4	1	0	1	25.0	4,873	5,143
Parker, Mr D	53	4	3	5	7.5	10,130	14,412
Parker, Mr A	13	1	0	4	7.7	1,893	3,101
Pewter, Mr G	11	1	0	0	9.1	2,777	2,777
Pipe, Mr D	11	1	1	1	9.1	1,627	2,911
Pocock, Mr I	3	1	0	0	33.3	1,256	1,256
Pollock, Mr B	21	2	2	2	9.5	2,354	3,551
Ponsonby, Mr R	6	2	1	0	33.3	2,925	4,010
Pritchard, Mr J M	18	3	0	4	16.7	7,920	9,857
Rees, Mr J	11	3	2	0	27.3	4,226	5,874
Rimell, Mr M	14	3	1	2	21.4	6,546	7,928
Robson, Miss P	33	1	3	0	3.0	1,660	3,990
Russell, Mr R	19	6	5	5	31.6	10,522	15,055
Sansome, Mr A	29	5	4	3	17.2	8,761	12,287
Scott, Mr T	2	1	0	0	50.0	1,865	1,865
Sheppard, Mr M	8	1	0	2	12.5	1,543	2,121
Smith, Mr N F	7	1	0	1	14.3	2,006	2,504
Smyth-Osbourne, Mr J	6	1	0	0	16.7	2,738	2,738
Sowersby, Mr M	4	1	0	0	25.0	1,672	2,422
Stockton, Mr C	10	1	0	1	10.0	1,903	2,239
Storey, Mr C	4	1	1	1	25.0	2,088	2,938
Swiers, Mr S	58	12	6	3	20.7	24,217	33,974
Taylor, Mr C	4	1	0	0	25.0	2,626	2,626
Thomas, Miss C	12	1	1	0	8.3	1,302	1,890
Thomas, Mr C Ward	14	2	0	5	14.3	5,448	6,929
Thornton, Mr A	146	26	27	12	17.8	67,046	91,896
Thurlow, Miss J	11	1	2	1	9.1	2,566	3,904
Treloggen, Mr R	9	5	0	1	55.6	35,370	35,620
Trice-Rolph, Mr J	13	2	2	4	15.4	3,132	5,102
Trietline, Mr C	4	1	2	0	25.0	1,607	2,614
Vigors, Mr C	34	5	3	3	14.7	7,824	10,652
Wales, Mr W	3	1	0	0	33.3	1,753	1,904
Weymes, Mr J	15	1	1	0	6.7	1,033	1,515
Williams, Mr E	15	1	0	2	6.7	2,998	3,816
Wilson, Mr N	39	4	4	3	10.3	20,904	25,330
Wilson, Mr Chris	14	2	2	1	14.3	2,494	3,908
Wintle, Mr J	5	1	0	0	20.0	1,506	1,506

Leading amateur riders: hurdles and chases 1945–93

		1	2	3	Unpl	Total Mts
1945–46	Mr A B Mildmay	11	3	1	26	41
1946–47	Ld Mildmay	32	17	16	34	99
1947–48	Ld Mildmay	22	9	15	43	89
1948–49	Ld Mildmay	30	22	13	59	124
1949–50	Ld Mildmay	38	22	12	45	117
1950–51	Mr P Chisman	13	7	5	23	48
1951–52	Mr C Straker	19	10	9	29	67
1952–53	Mr A H Moralee	22	20	17	51	110
1953–54	Mr A H Moralee	22	23	13	43	101
1954–55	Mr A H Moralee	16	30	8	68	122
1955–56	Mr R McCreery	13	10	13	42	78
	Mr A H Moralee	13	19	20	40	92
1956–57	Mr R McCreery	23	11	16	89	139
1957–58	Mr J Lawrence	18	15		40	96
1958–59	Mr J Sutcliffe	18	8	6	42	74
1959–60	Mr G Kindersley	22	6	9	63	100
1960–61	Sir W Pigott-Brown ...	28	11	14	69	122
1961–62	Mr A Biddlecombe	30	25	22	128	205
1962–63	Sir W Pigott-Brown ...	20	13	4	46	53
1963–64	Mr S Davenport	32	21	19	89	131
1964–65	Mr M Gifford	15	12	15	114	126
1965–66	Mr C Collins	24	16	19	78	187
1966–67	Mr C Collins	33	16	11	66	166
1967–68	Mr R Tate	30	24	18	82	154
1968–69	Mr R Tate	17	12	10	75	114
1969–70	Mr M Dickinson	23	9	5	55	92
1970–71	Mr J Lawrence	17	15	5	23	60
1971–72	Mr W Foulkes	26	15	13	50	114
1972–73	Mr R Smith	56	49	53	164	322
1973–74	Mr A Webber	21	14	23	113	171
1974–75	Mr R Lamb	22	34	31	116	203
1975–76	Mr P Greenall	25	15	14	108	162
	Mr G Jones	25	18	29	147	219
1976–77	Mr P Greenall	27	8	10	67	112
1977–78	Mr G Sloan	23	15	13	51	102
1978–79	Mr T G Dun	26	11	13	105	155
1979–80	Mr O Sherwood	29	9	12	28	78
1980–81	Mr P Webber	32	16	24	141	213
1981–82	Mr D Browne	28	12	8	57	105
1982–83	Mr D Browne	33	21	4	59	117
1983–84	Mr S Sherwood	28	7	13	62	110
1984–85	Mr S Sherwood	30	22	17	98	167
1985–86	Mr T Thomson Jones ..	25	14	8	79	126
1986–87	Mr T Thomson Jones ..	19	13	12	71	115
1987–88	Mr T Thomson Jones ..	15	15	8	51	89
1988–89	Mr P Fenton	18	12	11	54	95
1989–90	Mr P McMahon	15	5	10	50	80
1990–91	Mr K Johnson	24	21	16	90	151
1991–92	Mr M P Hourigan	24	10	8	53	95
1992–93	Mr A Thornton	26	27	12	81	146

Winning sires: hurdles and chases in 1992–93

H = number of horses W = races won £ = win value in £

	H	W	£
ABEDNEGO	3	3	16,043.00
Absalom	5	12	25,206.80
Adonijah	3	6	12,808.50
Affirmed (USA)	1	2	3,408.70
Ahonoora	1	1	1,704.50
Akarad (FR)	1	1	1,987.50
Al Nasr (FR)	2	5	13,247.00
Al Sirat (USA)	4	7	21,720.50
Alias Smith (USA)	6	9	20,471.90
Alleged (USA)	4	5	14,355.50
Alleging (USA)	1	1	1,586.90
Alphabatim (USA)	2	2	3,359.80
Alzao (USA)	6	16	43,258.60
Anax	2	2	3,836.50
Anfield	3	4	9,022.80
Aragon	5	5	8,529.80
Arapaho	2	5	8,480.05
Arapahos (FR)	1	3	11,407.60
Arctic Tern (USA)	2	4	7,659.50
Ardoon	1	1	1,733.90
Ardross	16	37	102,526.20
Aristocracy	1	1	2,146.50
Ascertain (USA)	3	6	12,832.50
Ashford (USA)	1	1	1,305.00
Atlantic Boy	1	1	1,530.00
Auction Ring (USA)	3	3	5,814.70
Auk (USA)	1	1	2,247.00
Avocat	2	3	13,721.00
Ayyabaan	1	2	3,670.00
BABY TURK	1	1	1,625.20
Baillamont (USA)	1	3	23,477.00
Bairn (USA)	3	6	16,049.00
Balak	1	2	4,803.20
Balinger	3	4	12,386.00
Ballacashtal (CAN)	8	12	25,144.70
Balliol	1	1	2,230.80
Ballymore	1	1	1,079.00
Baptism	2	2	3,724.00
Baron Blakeney	2	5	10,554.90
Bates Motel (USA)	1	2	4,650.20
Bay Express	1	2	2,976.00
Be My Guest (USA)	5	10	21,257.35
Be My Native (USA)	10	16	53,401.00
Beau Charmeur (FR)	5	5	14,028.50
Beechcraft (NZ)	2	2	4,609.50
Beldale Flutter (USA)	6	12	51,506.20
Belfalas	3	4	7,606.70
Belfort (FR)	4	5	8,552.70
Bellypha	2	4	8,746.10
Big Spruce (USA)	1	2	6,287.00
Bikala	1	1	1,939.70
Billion (USA)	3	3	36,888.50
Bivouac	1	1	2,173.50
Black Minstrel	13	21	60,564.95
Blakeney	8	12	25,004.50
Blakeney Point	1	3	7,722.50
Blue Cashmere	3	5	9,068.10
Blue Refrain	2	5	9,665.05
Bluebird (USA)	1	1	3,817.50
Blushing Scribe (USA)	1	1	1,910.00
Bob Back (USA)	2	4	8,865.80
Boco (USA)	1	1	1,049.50
Bold Forbes (USA)	1	1	2,284.80
Bon Chat	1	3	7,987.00
Bonne Noel	1	1	2,310.00
Boreen (FR)	4	6	12,898.15
Brave Invader (USA)	1	1	2,108.70
Brezzo (FR)	1	1	2,024.00
Brilliant Invader (AUS)	1	1	1,287.00
Broadsword (USA)	7	13	38,507.50
Buckfinder (USA)	1	1	1,758.00
Buckskin (FR)	20	36	120,844.60
Bulldozer	3	4	18,630.50
Burslem	2	2	6,705.20
Busted	3	5	9,050.55
Bustineto	1	2	4,222.00
Bustino	6	9	15,800.20
Bustomi	2	2	3,167.00
Buzzards Bay	4	6	12,788.60
Bybicello	1	5	10,847.70
CAERLEON (USA)	2	3	5,790.00
Callernish	8	16	56,118.90
Camden Town	3	6	10,790.00
Candy Cane	1	2	5,869.50
Cap Martin (FR)	1	1	2,593.00
Capricorn Line	2	2	3,773.00
Cardinal Flower	1	1	1,865.00
Carlingford Castle	5	12	26,574.35
Caro	1	1	2,248.00
Carriage Way	1	1	2,175.00
Carwhite	3	5	9,558.70
Casino Boy	1	3	8,203.00
Castle Keep	5	8	14,668.20
Celestial Storm (USA)	4	6	12,065.50
Celio Rufo	2	4	18,532.25
Celtic Cone	20	30	77,179.10
Chabrias (FR)	1	1	1,593.90
Cheval	3	5	12,835.40
Chief Singer	3	6	13,991.90
Chief's Crown (USA)	2	4	6,534.60
Chukaroo	1	1	2,637.00
Church Parade	2	3	5,836.00
Cidrax (FR)	1	1	3,294.00
Cimon	1	2	2,955.00
Class Distinction	2	3	9,642.50
Claude Monet (USA)	1	2	4,208.70
Comedy Star (USA)	7	11	24,680.10
Commanche Run	6	7	12,008.80
Concorde Jr (USA)	1	1	2,036.00
Connaught	4	10	48,453.03
Conquistador Cielo (USA)	1	1	2,477.50
Cool Guy (USA)	1	2	4,077.50
Coquelin (USA)	7	16	42,566.40
Corvaro (USA)	1	3	5,797.60
Crafty Prospector (USA)	1	2	3,582.20
Cranley	1	1	3,236.00
Crash Course	10	16	192,551.90
Creetown	2	2	3,480.20
Crever	1	1	1,996.00
Crimson Beau	1	2	5,210.75
Crofthall	1	1	1,484.00
Croghan Hill	2	5	15,727.40
Crooner	3	11	22,676.90
Cruise Missile	3	4	17,454.00
Crystal Glitters (USA)	3	6	31,064.00
Cure The Blues (USA)	2	2	3,756.40
Current Magic	2	3	12,913.50
Cut Above	2	4	10,479.00
Czarist	1	1	2,916.25
DALSAAN	2	3	4,957.40
Damister (USA)	4	5	10,789.40
Dancing Brave (USA)	2	4	5,802.60
Danzig Connection (USA)	1	2	4,459.90
Dara Monarch	4	5	8,976.20
Daring March	4	6	11,503.70
Darly (FR)	1	1	1,451.50
Darshaan	1	1	2,349.00
Dawn Review	1	2	20,501.00
Day Is Done	1	1	10,698.75
Decent Fellow	4	4	8,729.45
Decoy Boy	1	1	2,105.00
Deep River	1	1	1,822.10
Deep Run	51	94	622,660.15
Denel (FR)	2	2	3,594.50
Deroulede	2	4	9,442.50
Derring Rose	4	9	28,247.50
Derrylin	8	10	21,991.00
Diagramatic (USA)	1	1	1,744.00
Diamond Prospect (USA)	1	1	2,319.00
Diamond Shoal	2	7	17,633.40
Diesis	3	5	12,501.20
Disc Jockey	1	2	3,218.30
Dixieland Band (USA)	3	9	15,417.10
Domineau (USA)	1	2	4,900.00
Dominion	7	18	82,784.20
Don	2	2	3,152.35
Don't Forget Me	2	2	2,976.00
Double Schwartz	1	1	1,637.00
Doulab (USA)	1	1	1,876.40
Down The Hatch	1	1	2,788.00
Dr Carter (USA)	1	2	3,326.50
Dreams To Reality (USA)	2	2	4,660.60
Drumalis	1	1	1,857.50
Drums Of Time (USA)	1	1	3,434.50

WINNING SIRES: HURDLES AND CHASES 1992–93

Sire	H	W	£
Dubassoff (USA)	6	17	100,519.50
Duky	2	2	5,813.75
Dunbeath (USA)	4	6	13,288.50
EFISIO	1	1	2,005.00
El Badr	1	2	4,189.90
El Gran Senor (USA)	1	4	8,387.50
Ela Mana Mou	1	1	1,729.90
Ela-Mana-Mou	8	17	44,095.90
Electric	6	11	26,076.20
Elegant Air	2	7	16,576.95
Enchantment	1	1	2,617.50
Entre Nous	1	2	4,048.20
Esprit Du Nord (USA)	1	1	2,786.25
Exceller (USA)	1	2	3,766.90
Explodent (USA)	1	1	1,996.00
FAIRY KING (USA)	2	4	8,834.00
Fappiano (USA)	1	3	4,452.00
Far North (CAN)	3	5	9,803.50
Faraway Times (USA)	1	1	4,316.75
Faustus (USA)	1	1	1,939.70
Feelings (FR)	1	1	3,678.00
Fidel	2	4	28,477.60
Final Straw	6	8	19,054.25
Fine Blade (USA)	3	3	9,365.50
Fine Blue	2	4	9,302.90
Fit To Fight (USA)	3	9	20,906.80
Fitzwilliam (USA)	1	1	1,165.00
Flash Of Steel	2	4	4,855.50
Flying Tyke	1	1	1,969.10
Foggy Bell	1	1	1,488.00
Formidable (USA)	8	15	30,537.40
Forties Field (FR)	1	1	1,614.00
Free State	1	1	1,484.00
Full Of Aces (NZ)	1	2	3,817.40
Full Of Hope	3	5	10,077.30
Full On Aces (AUS)	1	2	3,249.00
Funny Man	2	3	9,978.00
Furry Glen	24	57	170,901.50
GABITAT	1	1	1,534.00
Gaiter (NZ)	2	2	3,581.00
Gala Performance (USA)	2	3	8,733.00
Garda's Revenge (USA)	1	1	1,425.00
Garryowen	1	2	3,741.00
Gate Dancer (USA)	2	4	7,268.90
Gay Mecene (USA)	1	1	1,753.40
General Ironside	5	6	20,742.40
Giacometti	1	1	2,127.50
Ginger Boy	2	2	3,194.20
Giolla Mear	1	1	1,688.00
Gleason (USA)	3	6	14,560.25
Glen Quaich	1	2	2,960.00
Glenstal (USA)	10	22	44,928.60
Glint Of Gold	7	19	115,441.35
Glow (USA)	3	10	19,252.10
Go Marching (USA)	1	1	5,585.00
Godswalk (USA)	1	1	1,710.00
Gold Claim	1	1	1,480.00
Golden Act (USA)	2	4	9,660.00
Golden Fleece (USA)	1	2	4,750.00
Golden Love	1	1	26,040.00
Goldhill	1	1	1,607.40
Good Thyne (USA)	5	9	75,450.70
Good Times (ITY)	2	3	5,247.40
Gorytus (USA)	4	8	14,450.60
Great Nephew	1	1	2,820.00
Green Dancer (USA)	2	2	5,232.00
Green Forest (USA)	1	1	2,259.00
Green Ruby (USA)	1	1	1,670.00
Green Shoon	8	16	73,988.15
Gregorian (USA)	1	1	2,055.80
Grey Desire	2	2	3,120.50
Guest Of Honour (NZ)	1	1	2,150.00
Gunner B	1	1	4,162.50
HADEER	1	1	1,534.00
Halyudh (USA)	1	1	2,931.00
Hard Fought	1	3	10,476.50
Hardboy	1	2	10,404.00
Harvest Spirit	1	3	14,161.00
Hasty Word	1	1	2,329.50
Hatim (USA)	3	7	13,499.40
Hawaiian Return (USA)	1	3	9,299.00
He Loves Me	1	3	5,888.00
Hello Gorgeous (USA)	1	2	3,423.00
Hello Handsome	1	1	1,213.50
Henbit (USA)	8	19	86,624.60
Hero's Honor (USA)	1	3	4,267.00
High Line	6	15	129,894.85
High Top	3	3	7,672.90
Highland Park (USA)	1	1	1,484.00
Homeboy	1	2	3,478.60
Homing	1	1	2,924.00
Horage	4	7	11,305.50
Hostage (USA)	1	2	7,057.50
Hot Brandy	2	3	6,588.50
Hotfoot	3	3	11,928.00
Humdoleila	1	1	1,231.00
IDIOT'S DELIGHT	19	33	92,632.60
Ile de Bourbon (USA)	5	9	17,201.00
Ilium	1	1	1,621.00
Impecunious	1	1	1,603.60
Imperial Fling (USA)	1	1	3,522.00
Import	1	8	115,681.75
In Fijar (USA)	1	2	5,543.00
Indian King (USA)	1	1	1,411.00
Instant Fame	1	1	1,480.00
Irish River (FR)	2	3	6,616.50
Iron Duke (FR)	2	7	34,504.00
Italic (FR)	2	5	60,055.60
JALMOOD (USA)	3	5	11,031.50
Jasmine Star	2	2	4,706.00
Jefferson	1	1	4,662.50
Jellaby	1	2	5,766.00
Jester	2	2	4,628.00
Jimmy Reppin	1	2	5,225.00
Jimsun	2	3	6,745.00
John de Coombe	1	2	4,942.30
John French	1	1	1,897.60
Joshua	2	2	3,764.30
Julio Mariner	8	10	19,101.60
Jupiter Island	4	5	9,429.10
Jupiter Pluvius	1	1	1,607.40
KABOUR	1	1	2,657.00
Kala Shikari	4	12	21,209.80
Kalaglow	4	5	10,153.50
Kambalda	12	34	101,859.40
Kampala	2	4	8,026.70
Kashneb (FR)	1	1	2,469.00
Kaytu	1	1	825.00
Kemal (FR)	14	24	60,030.00
Kenmare (FR)	1	1	1,688.00
Key To The Mint (USA)	1	4	11,651.00
Kind Of Hush	5	9	17,537.75
King Among Kings	1	1	1,646.00
King Of Clubs	3	5	13,140.60
King Persian	2	2	3,054.50
King's Ride	3	6	57,154.00
Kinglet	2	2	35,280.00
Kings Lake (USA)	4	6	19,660.40
Kirrama (NZ)	1	1	2,616.00
Known Fact (USA)	1	2	5,974.50
Kris	8	11	43,482.65
L'EMIGRANT (USA)	2	3	5,689.00
Lashkari	2	4	39,373.22
Last Fandango	1	2	3,872.50
Last Tycoon	4	9	16,979.70
Latest Model	1	1	3,480.00
Law Society (USA)	5	6	8,700.70
Le Bavard (FR)	13	21	75,178.87
Le Coq D'Or	3	5	19,132.50
Le Grand Seigneur (CAN)	2	5	13,089.00
Le Moss	17	27	65,575.70
Le Nain Jaune (FR)	1	2	4,176.60
Le Solaret (FR)	2	4	7,936.10
Le Soleil	1	3	7,814.75
Lead On Time (USA)	1	1	1,569.60
Leader Of The Band (USA)	2	3	8,653.90
Leading Man	1	3	8,299.75
Leander	1	1	1,368.00
Lear Fan (USA)	1	2	5,186.75
Legal Eagle	1	3	8,343.00
Legal Tender	1	4	10,726.50
Legend Of France (USA)	1	1	4,662.50
Lemhi Gold (USA)	1	4	33,697.75
Lepanto (GER)	3	4	15,261.00
Librate	1	4	7,695.60
Lidhame	2	4	4,888.00
Lighter	9	14	30,581.35
Linkage (USA)	1	1	1,350.80
Lir	2	2	4,474.40
Little Wolf	1	2	4,541.00
Local Suitor (USA)	2	3	4,775.40
Lochnager	7	10	22,295.10
Lomond (USA)	3	4	8,367.00
Lord Durham (CAN)	1	1	2,364.95
Lord Gayle (USA)	1	3	12,257.12
Lord Ha Ha	2	4	9,917.00
Lucifer (USA)	2	2	3,564.60
Lydian (FR)	3	3	7,970.70
Lyphard (USA)	3	7	14,154.00
Lyphard's Wish (FR)	1	1	9,440.00
Lyphard's Special (USA)	3	4	7,101.50
Lypheor	3	8	14,019.90
M DOUBLE M (USA)	2	3	18,792.50
Macmillion	1	2	4,122.80
Magic Mirror	1	2	2,242.00
Main Reef	1	1	2,502.00
Maiymad	1	5	55,556.00
Majestic Maharaj	1	6	20,699.80

	H	W	£
Majestic Streak	1	2	7,079.00
Malinowski (USA)	1	3	6,739.60
Mandalus	17	28	86,644.20
Mandrake Major	4	6	26,031.00
Mari Lane	1	1	1,464.00
Marshalsea	1	1	2,286.50
Martinmas	7	14	33,716.10
Mashhor Dancer (USA)	3	8	14,404.00
Master Willie	1	1	2,190.00
Matching Pair	1	1	1,303.00
Mazaad	4	6	12,850.80
Meadowbrook	1	1	1,763.00
Meldrum	1	4	15,035.50
Melyno	1	1	1,844.60
Miami Springs	1	3	7,069.00
Midland Gayle	2	3	6,584.40
Midyan (USA)	1	2	3,839.80
Milan	1	1	2,791.80
Milford	2	3	14,784.50
Milk Of The Barley	1	1	2,999.00
Mill Reef (USA)	1	1	5,920.00
Miller's Mate	1	1	1,480.00
Miner's Lamp	1	1	828.00
Miramar Reef	2	4	7,341.80
Mirror Boy	1	1	3,047.60
Mister Majestic	1	2	3,493.60
Mister Thatch	1	1	2,259.00
Miswaki (USA)	1	4	6,493.50
Monksfield	5	6	13,812.10
Monsanto (FR)	4	6	11,385.20
Monsieure Edouarde	1	2	27,151.00
Montekin	1	1	2,126.40
Montelimar (USA)	4	5	40,831.24
Morgans Choice	1	1	1,787.50
Mouktar	2	3	5,432.00
Move Off	1	2	5,517.00
Mr Fluorocarbon	2	4	12,461.00
Mufrij	1	1	1,688.00
Mummy's Game	2	6	12,071.80
Muscatite	2	3	6,847.20
Music Boy	3	4	7,507.70
My Dad Tom (USA)	1	1	1,598.50
NAIN BLEU (FR)	1	2	4,328.00
National Trust	3	7	18,960.80
Natroun (FR)	1	2	2,720.80
Nearly A Hand	8	11	41,376.05
Nebos (GER)	1	2	4,990.00
Neltino	5	6	13,517.25
Nepotism	1	4	10,585.00
Netherkelly	3	5	9,358.50
Never So Bold	1	1	1,305.00
New Brig	2	4	18,350.50
New Member	3	6	37,611.50
Newski (USA)	2	4	12,607.00
Nicholas Bill	8	14	32,327.40
Niels	1	2	5,462.80
Night Shift (USA)	2	3	5,380.65
Nikos	1	2	3,579.60
Niniski (USA)	11	23	57,734.20
Nishapour (FR)	10	14	44,151.70
No Lute (FR)	1	1	1,675.10
Noalto	1	1	1,702.00
Nodouble (USA)	1	1	2,041.60
Noir Et Or	1	1	2,334.30
Nomination	4	12	32,797.75
Nordance (USA)	2	4	11,985.00
Nordico (USA)	1	5	9,290.80
Northern Baby (CAN)	8	15	23,809.50
Northern Guest (USA)	1	3	7,670.00
Northern Tempest (USA)	1	1	1,605.50
Northern Treat (USA)	1	2	9,618.00
Northern Value (USA)	2	2	3,819.20
Northfields (USA)	1	1	1,702.80
Norwick (USA)	9	21	47,546.05
OATS	22	38	97,090.30
Old Jocus	1	1	3,452.50
Olmeto	1	1	1,480.00
Orange Bay	2	3	6,810.00
Orchestra	3	6	13,618.80
Our Mirage	1	3	5,714.70
Our Native (USA)	1	1	3,200.00
Ovac (ITY)	2	5	23,613.20
Over The River (FR)	20	34	146,485.80
PADDY'S STREAM	7	13	32,058.55
Paico	1	1	2,196.00
Palm Track	2	5	9,048.50
Pampabird	1	1	2,658.00
Parasang	1	1	2,192.00
Pas de Seul	1	2	5,795.40
Patch	2	2	5,554.00
Pauper	1	2	5,609.25
Peacock (FR)	1	1	2,762.00
Pennine Walk	3	4	8,170.00
Persian Bold	5	12	45,462.80
Peterhof (USA)	1	1	1,749.00
Petit Montmorency (USA)	1	3	7,076.50
Petitioner	1	3	7,268.50
Petong	1	1	1,548.00
Petorius	2	5	10,815.40
Petoski	3	4	6,937.50
Phardante (FR)	4	4	6,704.00
Pharly (FR)	2	5	8,570.30
Piaffer (USA)	3	8	21,313.90
Piperhill	1	1	2,410.50
Pitpan	5	7	10,963.20
Pitskelly	1	1	1,305.00
Politico (USA)	6	8	46,867.80
Pollerton	6	15	32,242.65
Pongee	1	4	11,136.20
Pony Express	2	5	18,689.25
Porto Bello	1	1	2,264.90
Posse (USA)	1	1	2,326.50
Potent Councillor	1	3	3,922.75
Pragmatic	4	4	16,546.50
Precocious	3	3	5,601.00
Primo Dominie	3	3	4,822.30
Prince Bee	3	6	16,121.50
Prince Of Peace	1	2	5,632.80
Prince Regent (FR)	4	6	39,214.40
Prince Tenderfoot (USA)	4	5	9,451.40
Prince Vandezee	1	1	937.20
Princes Gate	1	1	1,480.00
Procida (USA)	1	1	1,305.00
Proverb	9	13	94,052.70
Pry	2	4	9,511.50
QUAYSIDE	2	2	4,558.50
R B CHESNE	1	4	24,149.00
Rabdan	1	1	2,355.00
Radical	1	2	3,672.00
Ragapan	2	4	9,185.25
Rainbow Quest (USA)	2	3	6,619.80
Raise A Cup (USA)	1	1	1,860.70
Raise You Ten	1	2	14,646.25
Raisingelle (USA)	1	3	6,594.25
Random Shot	3	7	26,496.00
Ranksborough	1	1	1,480.00
Rapid River	1	1	1,646.00
Rare One	1	1	1,467.00
Rarity	1	1	2,137.80
Reach	1	1	1,954.40
Reasonable (FR)	1	2	3,216.00
Rebel Prince	1	1	4,386.00
Record Token	1	2	3,992.20
Red Johnnie	1	4	9,868.90
Red Sunset	6	6	11,454.55
Reference Point	1	1	1,924.00
Reformed Character	1	2	12,652.50
Regal And Royal (USA)	1	1	2,046.80
Relkino	7	10	28,329.90
Remainder Man	2	5	9,876.80
Rhodomantade	1	1	3,028.00
Riboboy (USA)	2	2	4,268.50
Risk Me (FR)	3	4	7,387.00
Riverman (USA)	4	4	6,562.50
Robellino (USA)	3	6	10,481.50
Roberto (USA)	4	7	24,205.90
Roi Dagobert (FR)	1	1	2,112.00
Roi Guillaume (FR)	2	3	6,581.00
Rolfe (USA)	6	8	17,590.00
Roman Warrior	2	4	8,866.60
Rontino	1	3	5,957.30
Roscoe Blake	6	10	57,857.75
Roselier (FR)	8	9	23,672.90
Rouser	1	2	5,845.00
Rousillon (USA)	3	9	15,774.40
Royal Boxer	1	1	1,576.00
Royal Fountain	6	7	19,220.00
Royal Match	3	3	12,491.00
Royal Palace	3	6	14,034.45
Royal Vulcan	1	1	2,490.00
Rugantino	1	1	2,892.00
Runnett	1	3	3,703.00
Rushmere	1	2	17,410.00
Rusticaro (FR)	4	7	15,945.10
Rustingo	2	3	5,780.50
Rymer	2	3	9,698.00
SADLER'S WELLS (USA)	2	3	7,223.40
Sagaro	2	2	4,074.50
Saint Cyrien (FR)	3	6	18,699.60
Salluceva	1	3	10,800.00
Sallust	2	2	4,005.50
Salmon Leap (USA)	2	3	12,023.00
Sandalay	3	7	31,306.25
Sandhurst Prince	2	5	11,676.85
Saxon Farm	1	3	7,133.00
Say Primula	3	4	6,272.20
Sayf El Arab (USA)	1	1	1,302.00
Sayyaf	1	1	1,756.00
Scallywag	8	13	31,639.40
Scorpio (FR)	1	2	4,850.00
Scottish Reel	3	12	19,460.90
Sea Anchor	1	2	3,759.00
Secreto (USA)	4	10	36,170.60
Sensitive Prince (USA)	1	2	5,784.00
Sexton Blake	3	13	24,026.30
Seymour Hicks (FR)	1	1	2,074.50
Shaab	2	6	28,441.00
Shadeed (USA)	1	1	1,484.00
Shardari	3	5	9,013.20
Shareef Dancer (USA)	2	3	16,056.00
Sharpo	4	7	15,089.30
Sharrood (USA)	3	7	17,518.50

WINNING SIRES: HURDLES AND CHASES 1992–93

	H	W	£
Sheer Grit	2	4	11,557.50
Shernazar	4	6	12,393.30
Shirley Heights	6	8	16,106.50
Show-A-Leg	1	3	8,491.50
Shrivenham	1	1	2,120.25
Shy Groom (USA)	1	1	1,700.00
Shy Rambler (USA)	1	1	4,162.50
Siberian Express (USA)	3	5	16,429.50
Side Track	1	1	2,038.75
Silver Hawk (USA)	2	6	12,723.20
Silver Season	1	1	1,712.00
Simply Great (FR)	3	3	6,694.00
Sir Ivor	2	6	12,703.50
Sir Mago	1	1	1,672.00
Sit In The Corner (USA)	3	4	11,281.55
Sizzling Melody	1	5	8,204.50
Slew O' Gold (USA)	1	2	5,650.50
Slip Anchor	1	2	3,536.00
Slippered	1	1	1,576.00
Smooth Stepper	1	1	2,374.00
Solford (USA)	1	4	8,599.20
Solo Dancer (GER)	1	1	2,758.00
Song	1	1	2,007.60
Sonnen Gold	2	2	2,362.00
Sonnengold	1	2	4,022.40
Soughaan (USA)	1	1	2,026.20
Southern Music	2	3	5,862.00
Space King	2	4	38,950.00
Spanish Place (USA)	1	1	1,702.00
Sparkling Boy	1	1	1,704.50
Spartan Jester	1	1	2,295.00
Spectacular Bid (USA)	1	1	1,473.00
Spend A Buck (USA)	2	4	8,205.50
Spin Of A Coin	1	3	19,908.00
Spur On	1	2	5,181.60
St Columbus	3	5	9,300.25
Stalker	2	6	13,122.70
Stanford	1	1	3,707.00
Star Appeal	3	3	5,269.00
Star de Naskra (USA)	1	1	1,484.00
Starch Reduced	1	2	4,051.40
Step Together (USA)	1	2	7,630.50
Storm Bird (CAN)	3	5	8,764.70
Strong Gale	43	96	479,292.75
Sula Bula	2	3	4,939.20
Sunley Builds	2	2	4,409.00
Sunotra	1	2	4,614.40
Sunyboy	4	5	10,795.50
Super Concorde (USA)	1	2	6,272.00
Superlative	1	2	4,432.70
Supreme Leader	1	1	1,910.30
Sure Blade (USA)	2	3	5,215.00
Sweet Monday	2	2	3,522.00
Sweet Story	1	3	9,256.50
Swing Easy (USA)	2	3	14,956.50
TACHYPOUS	4	6	13,516.45
Takachiho	1	1	2,889.70
Tampero (FR)	1	1	1,807.40
Tap On Wood	2	2	5,996.25
Tarrago (ITY)	1	2	5,179.60
Tate Gallery (USA)	1	1	1,626.50
Taufan (USA)	5	8	17,943.35
Tawfiq (USA)	1	2	6,751.70
Teenoso (USA)	7	9	20,224.50
Telsmoss	1	1	2,027.90
Temperence Hill (USA)	1	1	1,603.60
Tender King	9	17	47,126.65
Teofane	1	1	1,856.00
Tepukei	3	7	15,063.90
Thatch (USA)	1	1	1,605.50
Thatching	3	6	15,905.70
The Minstrel (CAN)	5	6	11,597.50
The Noble Player (USA)	2	2	6,410.50
The Parson	28	54	185,260.55
The Wonder (FR)	2	4	21,896.00
Three Legs	1	4	13,442.00
Tickled Pink	1	3	8,722.45
Tilden	1	3	6,230.30
Timolin (FR)	1	1	2,605.35
Tina's Pet	5	11	38,285.20
Tinoco	1	1	1,430.70
Tip Moss (FR)	2	2	5,712.00
Tolomeo	1	1	2,521.60
Tom Noddy	1	1	1,631.00
Tom's Shu (USA)	2	5	10,628.50
Top Ville	6	12	25,431.25
Topsider (USA)	1	3	5,752.80
Torenaga	1	1	2,053.50
Torus	8	15	69,026.40
Touching Wood (USA)	9	25	78,358.95
Tower Walk	2	2	6,533.75
Town And Country	5	7	26,279.50
Transworld (USA)	2	2	11,932.50
Treasure Kay	1	1	1,719.20
Trimmingham	3	10	32,604.70
Trojan Fen	5	10	19,422.50
Troy	1	5	8,645.00
True Song	6	9	28,541.40
Try My Best (USA)	2	3	4,533.00
Tug Of War	6	9	61,514.60
Tumble Wind (USA)	4	5	9,955.50
Turn Back The Time (USA)	1	2	2,909.00
Turnpike	1	2	15,714.00
Tycoon II	2	3	7,838.40
Tyrnavos	1	2	3,276.10
UNCLE POKEY	4	4	8,697.00
Uncle Remus (NZ)	1	1	2,398.00
VACARME (USA)	1	3	6,089.00
Vaguely Noble	2	2	2,785.00
Vaguely Tender (USA)	1	1	2,251.85
Vaigly Great	4	9	18,029.40
Valiyar	3	5	8,265.00
Van Der Linden (FR)	1	2	2,807.00
Vayrann	1	2	4,253.00
Veloso (NZ)	3	5	11,868.50
Verbatim (USA)	1	1	1,649.00
Vice Regal (NZ)	1	3	6,305.30
Viking (USA)	3	7	15,733.45
Vision (USA)	5	9	15,469.90
Vital Season	1	1	1,320.00
Vivadari	1	2	5,068.00
WAFFL	1	1	1,562.00
War Hawk	1	1	1,822.10
Warpath	6	6	9,308.10
Wassl	3	3	5,163.90
Wavering Monarch (USA)	1	1	1,484.00
Welsh Captain	4	5	7,369.10
Welsh Pageant	2	4	10,871.00
Welsh Saint	1	1	2,107.40
Welsh Term	1	4	11,127.00
What A Guest	3	3	5,297.00
Where To Dance (USA)	2	2	37,344.00
Whistlefield	1	1	2,284.50
Whistling Deer	4	8	24,159.50
White Prince (USA)	1	1	2,271.00
Wind And Wuthering (USA)	1	3	9,239.25
Windjammer (USA)	3	3	4,095.20
Wolf Power (SAF)	1	2	3,979.50
Wolver Heights	2	5	11,718.30
Wolverlife	1	4	14,898.00
Worlingworth	1	2	3,863.00
YASHGAN	2	2	4,400.00
Yawa	1	2	3,011.60
Young Generation	1	1	4,142.50
Young Man (FR)	1	1	1,892.50
Young Nelson	1	1	3,582.50
ZAMAZAAN (FR)	1	3	20,264.50
Zambrano	3	5	16,649.95
Ziad (USA)	1	2	3,805.20

FLAT TURF SEASON STATISTICS 1993

Principal Flat (turf) race winners 1993

Owners

	Horses	Races Won	Value £
Sheikh Mohammed	211	144	1,703,958
K Abdulla	77	66	1,218,433
Hamdan Al-Maktoum	181	97	644,986
Maktoum Al Maktoum	68	38	638,111
R E Sangster	60	45	411,286
Mrs G A E Smith	2	3	275,271
Daniel Wildenstein	3	2	273,980
Roldvale Ltd	20	20	262,446

Trainers

	Horses	Races Won	Value £
H R A Cecil	108	94	1,248,318
R Hannon	207	182	1,229,046
M R Stoute	118	65	1,071,842
J H M Gosden	127	109	1,018,364
J L Dunlop	115	93	700,736
J Berry	117	127	540,011
G Wragg	48	35	428,417
P W Chapple-Hyam	71	52	407,059

Jockeys

	1st	2nd	3rd	Unpl	Total Mts	Per cent
Pat Eddery	169	131	83	430	813	20.8
K Darley	136	128	105	430	799	17.0
L Dettori	135	114	114	482	845	16.0
W Carson	115	93	120	509	837	13.7
M Roberts	114	96	109	396	715	15.9
G Duffield	114	91	98	450	753	15.1
J Reid	108	108	70	478	764	14.1
T Quinn	107	106	89	511	813	13.2

Apprentices

	1st	2nd	3rd	Unpl	Total Mts	Per cent
J Weaver	55	36	35	231	357	15.4
D Harrison	39	47	42	366	494	7.9
B Doyle	30	23	23	222	298	10.1
O Pears	27	25	31	183	266	10.2
S Maloney	27	22	29	206	284	9.5
D Moffatt	21	11	27	185	244	8.6
D Wright	20	23	25	303	371	5.4
S Davies	19	13	29	151	212	9.0
D McCabe	19	14	30	156	219	8.7
F Norton	19	15	20	224	278	6.8

Amateurs

	1st	2nd	3rd	Unpl	Total Mts	Per cent
Mrs L Pearce	5	3	4	22	34	14.7
T Cuff	4	2	0	12	18	22.2
Mrs M Cowdrey	4	3	4	11	22	18.2

First Season Sires

	Winners	Races Won	Value £
Warning (1985) by Known Fact (USA)	9	16	146,693
Indian Ridge (1985) by Ahonoora	9	13	85,378
Shaadi (USA) (1986) by Danzig (USA)	3	5	55,894
Danehill (USA) (1986) by Danzig (USA)	7	9	38,257
Cadeaux Genereux (1985) by Young Generation	6	8	35,156
Reprimand (1985) by Mummy's Pet	7	10	34,117
Gallic League (1985) by Welsh Saint	4	8	29,755
Rambo Dancer (CAN) (1984) by Northern Dancer	5	7	24,956

Sires

	Winners	Races Won	Value £
Sadler's Wells (USA) (1981) by Northern Dancer	20	32	994,304
Dancing Brave (USA) (1983) by Lyphard (USA)	14	30	630,631
Last Tycoon (1983) by Try My Best (USA)	8	10	474,852
Primo Dominie (1982) by Dominion	25	45	317,670
Bob Back (USA) (1981) by Roberto (USA)	4	8	299,174
Caerleon (USA) (1980) by Nijinsky (CAN)	21	29	297,856
Efisio (1982) by Formidable (USA)	22	45	277,852
Risk Me (FR) (1984) by Sharpo	15	30	272,559

Leading Horses

	No. of Races	Value £
Opera House (5) b.h. by Sadler's Wells (USA) out of Colorspin (FR)	3	502,097
Commander In Chief (3) b.c.by Dancing Brave (USA) out of Slightly Dangerous (USA)	4	461,241
Bob's Return (IRE) (3) br.c. by Bob Back (USA) out of Quality of Life	3	275,271
Bigstone (IRE) (3) b.c. by Last Tycoon out of Batave	2	273,980
Hatoof (USA) (4) ch.f. by Irish River (FR) out of Cadeaux d'Amie (USA)	1	205,707
Ezzoud (IRE) (4) b.c. by Last Tycoon out of Royal Sister II	2	178,740
Intrepidity (3) b.f. by Sadler's Wells (USA) out of Intrepid Lady (USA)	1	147,500
First Trump (2) ch.c. by Primo Dominie out of Valika	5	145,396

Trainers: Prizemoney won abroad (by courtesy of I.R.B.)

	Wins	Places	Earnings £
J L Dunlop	24	36	913,082
R Hannon	11	17	863,001
P W Chapple-Hyam	3	11	791,446
P F I Cole	11	13	541,862
C E Brittain	3	11	522,131
H R A Cecil	1	1	391,787
J H M Gosden	3	10	325,785
L M Cumani	6	8	282,423

Winning Flat race owners in 1993

H = Horses; R = Runners; W = Winners; 2 = Seconds; 3 = Thirds; %W-R = Percentage of winners to runners; £WIN = Win money; £W/P = Win and place money

	H	R	W	2	3	%W-R	£WIN	£W/P
THE QUEEN	26	120	16	23	8	13.3	97,881	191,901
A And B Racing	1	15	2	5	4	13.3	10,689	38,098
Abbey, J E	3	10	3	1	0	30.0	7,338	7,956
Abbey, Miss Gloria	2	10	1	1	1	10.0	5,254	9,774
Abbey Racing	1	8	1	0	1	12.5	3,436	3,853
Abbott Racing Partners	1	11	1	3	4	9.1	3,290	9,246
Abdulla, K	77	220	66	38	23	30.0	1,218,433	1,585,312
Abdullah, Nasser	2	6	1	0	1	16.7	3,231	4,014
Abell, J David	9	60	13	7	6	21.7	52,227	73,684
Aconley, P	3	9	1	0	0	11.1	2,758	2,758
Adams, R J	3	29	3	4	4	10.3	23,540	31,854
Adams, P B	1	5	1	0	0	20.0	3,340	3,690
Addleshaw, Mrs J	5	30	2	2	4	6.7	14,099	22,170
Adept (80) Ltd	2	16	3	3	0	18.8	11,544	16,127
Africa, Cuadra	1	6	3	0	0	50.0	13,129	14,110
Ahamad, N	3	20	3	3	1	15.0	10,937	17,904
Aird, Robert	3	27	4	1	5	14.8	14,209	21,980
Aitken, S	4	20	3	3	4	15.0	74,165	88,543
Akazawa, Yoshiki	1	5	1	0	0	20.0	4,542	5,057
Akehurst, Robin	2	10	1	1	1	10.0	2,721	3,771
Akehurst, R	1	3	1	0	0	33.3	2,070	2,070
Aldous, Miss Elizabeth	1	8	1	2	2	12.5	2,070	4,249
Alexander, William	1	3	1	0	0	33.3	2,070	2,070
Ali, Abdullah	5	29	7	6	1	24.1	27,483	37,987
Ali, Saif	4	11	1	2	2	9.1	3,553	9,595
Ali, Arashan	3	18	1	1	2	5.6	2,070	4,017
Al Jafleh, Ali K	7	36	6	2	3	16.7	21,036	25,297
Allan, Ivan	1	2	1	0	0	50.0	4,503	4,503
Allbritton, Joe L	2	16	1	4	3	6.3	1,576	8,055
Allen, B R	2	10	5	0	0	50.0	12,680	13,140
Allen, D J	5	21	1	3	2	4.8	2,758	9,450
Allen, Mrs Stephen	2	19	1	1	2	5.3	2,685	4,023
Allen, Mrs J M	1	6	1	2	2	16.7	3,184	5,829
Allen, David	3	19	2	0	1	10.5	8,686	9,471
Allen, Herbert	2	5	1	2	0	20.0	3,202	5,796
Allport, D F	2	5	2	1	0	40.0	6,937	8,822
Allright, A J	1	3	1	0	1	33.3	2,595	2,833
Al Maktoum, Sheikh Ahmed	59	216	33	29	29	15.3	150,876	252,419
Al Maktoum, Sheikh Ahmed Bin Saeed	6	27	6	7	5	22.2	32,498	48,335
Al Maktoum, Sheikh Marwan	6	20	2	2	2	10.0	6,930	12,620
Al-Maktoum, Hamdan	181	730	97	101	108	13.3	644,986	948,728
Al Maktoum, Maktoum	68	248	38	31	31	15.3	638,111	1,070,771
Al Maktoum, Mana	7	17	2	1	0	11.8	8,105	9,620
Al Maktoum, Mohammed Obaid	1	7	1	0	1	14.3	3,357	7,591
Al-Said, K	6	24	4	5	3	16.7	14,542	29,223
Altham, David	1	9	1	2	1	11.1	3,348	6,007
Alton, E C	1	11	1	0	0	9.1	3,210	3,210
A M Packaging Ltd	1	16	1	2	3	6.3	1,548	4,640
Anderson, Mrs David	1	9	1	1	1	11.1	2,700	4,992
Anderton, Colin W	1	10	1	0	2	10.0	3,132	3,831
Andrews, Anthony	1	8	1	2	2	12.5	3,340	6,014
Angus Dundee Ltd	1	2	2	0	0	100.0	6,901	6,901
Ansells Of Watford	3	24	2	0	3	8.3	8,713	12,901
Antonelli, A	1	16	2	1	2	12.5	6,377	8,174
Apollo Excellsior Racing	1	5	1	0	0	20.0	2,623	2,623
Arbib, M	4	13	2	2	2	15.4	8,054	15,225

WINNING FLAT RACE OWNERS IN 1993

	H	R	W	2	3	%W-R	£WIN	£W/P
Archer Van & Truck Hire Ltd	1	6	2	1	0	33.3	5,272	6,453
Ardsley Racing	1	6	2	1	0	33.3	4,565	5,636
Armitage, W L	1	7	1	2	2	14.3	2,898	6,158
Arnold, M W Horner, H Young, And D S	1	11	2	3	1	18.2	9,223	13,897
Asakawa, Yoshio	2	6	3	0	0	50.0	118,626	118,626
Ash, M W	1	3	1	0	0	33.3	2,959	2,959
Ashton, G G	3	18	3	2	2	16.7	9,677	12,546
Ashurst, Jack	1	7	1	2	0	14.3	3,883	6,410
Ashworth, Harvey	1	14	2	1	2	14.3	6,035	8,605
Asquith, P	10	61	5	5	7	8.2	15,504	30,082
Asquith, J	1	9	1	1	0	11.1	2,821	4,043
Astbury, John	1	1	1	0	0	100.0	2,489	2,489
Astor, Sir John	1	5	2	1	1	40.0	12,598	16,930
Atkins, A B	2	13	1	0	2	7.7	2,739	3,768
Attenborough, B T	1	9	1	0	2	11.1	6,165	8,020
Austin Stroud & Co Ltd	1	9	2	0	1	22.2	4,570	4,960
Avon Industries Ltd	4	12	1	1	0	8.3	2,835	3,703
Axford, R	1	8	1	1	1	12.5	4,110	15,255
Axon, P E	4	31	7	5	0	22.6	26,858	46,852
Azar, Nagy	2	5	1	0	0	20.0	3,850	4,053
Az Agr Associate Srl	2	9	2	2	1	22.2	5,509	7,530
Back Hill Bloodstock Ltd	5	18	1	2	1	5.6	3,494	6,373
Badger, E A	3	15	1	1	2	6.7	2,553	4,790
Baggott, J	1	5	1	0	0	20.0	3,260	3,260
Bailey, J R	3	7	1	1	1	14.3	3,524	10,324
Baker, I A	3	11	2	1	1	18.2	7,137	9,258
Baker, Dr Howard J	1	3	1	1	0	33.3	4,807	6,057
Baldwin, E	1	12	2	1	1	16.7	8,415	10,904
Barber-Lomax, C D	2	18	2	3	1	11.1	6,305	12,081
Barclay, Mrs Stella	2	10	2	0	1	20.0	5,912	6,764
Barker, G L	1	8	2	2	1	25.0	7,836	9,299
Barker, I B	1	9	1	0	1	11.1	2,232	2,628
Barker, Trevor	4	24	3	0	1	12.5	10,525	11,276
Barker, W G	4	16	1	2	1	6.3	3,290	6,660
Barnes, Dr Susan	1	7	1	3	1	14.3	2,668	5,305
Barnett, R	3	8	1	0	0	12.5	9,325	9,325
Baron, K K	1	9	1	1	1	11.1	2,724	5,525
Barr, Peter	3	19	2	0	2	10.5	5,390	6,343
Barratt, Mrs P A	6	34	1	4	4	2.9	3,407	8,308
Barrett, J W	2	20	5	5	3	25.0	14,838	20,927
Barrie, D P	1	8	1	3	0	12.5	1,380	5,546
Barrow, A	1	6	1	0	0	16.7	2,070	2,070
Barry, John Patrick	1	1	1	0	0	100.0	3,548	3,548
Barwell, Mrs M	2	12	1	1	4	8.3	5,016	8,753
Barwick, Mrs Annette	1	12	1	2	0	8.3	2,385	4,031
Bass, D	4	18	1	1	0	5.6	7,310	8,273
Bassett, Mrs Barbara	1	6	1	0	2	16.7	3,641	5,208
Batey, B	2	14	3	3	1	21.4	65,915	75,799
Baugh, Mrs Diane	1	2	1	0	0	50.0	1,725	1,725
Beaverbrook, The Dowager Lady	15	70	4	4	3	5.7	25,375	42,832
Beccle, G S	1	8	1	1	0	12.5	5,678	9,843
Beeby, Mrs J M	2	22	7	2	4	31.8	22,971	29,216
Behrens, Victor	2	9	1	2	2	11.1	3,465	5,994
Beighton, Mrs J A	1	5	1	1	1	20.0	2,301	4,670
Bell, Capt B W	1	6	1	0	1	16.7	3,132	3,884
Bell, Mrs B	1	8	1	3	2	12.5	3,002	7,990
Benjamin, Mrs Dyanne	2	21	1	2	3	4.8	5,117	8,243
Bennett, T H	4	27	2	2	3	7.4	6,311	12,553
Berenson, Richard	9	64	4	2	7	6.3	12,700	22,733
Berger, M	1	12	2	0	1	16.7	13,157	13,827
Berry, J	5	9	2	1	1	22.2	4,313	5,496
Bezwell Fixings Limited	4	18	4	4	1	22.2	15,642	20,445
Bhatia, Kamal	1	7	1	1	1	14.3	5,360	12,086
Bickenson, R D	1	14	1	1	0	7.1	3,850	5,218
Bigg, J E	5	54	3	7	10	5.6	16,819	27,136
Birkett, Mrs A	2	10	2	1	0	20.0	7,029	8,621
Birol, Yucel	2	17	2	0	2	11.8	5,819	12,515
Biswell, J W	2	4	1	0	0	25.0	3,049	3,049
Blackburn, Mrs David	6	28	1	1	3	3.6	4,557	24,290
Blacker, Mrs Philip	2	7	1	0	0	14.3	21,519	22,398
Blackpool Gazette & Herald Ltd	1	12	1	1	0	8.3	4,981	9,351
Blackwood, D H	4	23	2	3	1	8.7	5,657	8,625
Blair, Jim	2	15	1	1	1	6.7	3,158	4,935
Blake, David S	1	5	1	1	1	20.0	2,400	3,325
Bloom, Bernard	1	5	2	0	0	40.0	6,264	6,704
Boden, Miss Lucille	2	5	1	0	0	20.0	2,669	2,669
Boon, A W	1	7	1	1	0	14.3	3,623	5,131
Booth, Colin G R	5	24	1	2	4	4.2	3,028	7,445

	H	R	W	2	3	%W-R	£WIN	£W/P
Borrett, J G K	2	17	1	1	2	5.9	3,285	7,486
Bosher, Mrs S	3	16	4	2	0	25.0	17,923	20,547
Bosley, G A	3	23	2	3	2	8.7	5,649	9,196
Bowring, M P	2	19	6	4	3	31.6	16,779	22,177
Bowyer, N D	1	3	1	0	0	33.3	3,553	3,553
Brackpool, Brian	1	3	1	0	0	33.3	60,361	66,267
Bradbury, J C	1	6	2	0	1	33.3	35,075	37,405
Bradley, J M	4	23	4	5	2	17.4	13,104	18,714
Bradley, John E	1	7	1	0	0	14.3	7,245	7,382
Bramall, Miss K S	1	5	1	0	0	20.0	2,427	2,650
Bravery, Mrs F E	2	9	1	3	2	11.1	1,534	5,149
Brewis, R	1	9	1	2	1	11.1	3,348	6,717
Briam, Tony	1	8	2	0	0	25.0	5,222	5,222
Brian Gubby Ltd	7	27	1	4	2	3.7	2,553	7,151
Bridge, W J	1	7	2	0	0	28.6	5,442	5,636
Bridger, J J	4	15	1	0	0	6.7	2,406	2,406
Brittain, Mrs C E	3	13	2	0	1	15.4	37,983	45,962
Brittain, Mel	13	78	7	5	6	9.0	21,784	30,517
Brittain, C E	8	36	4	1	2	11.1	16,326	18,741
Brodrick, M J	1	9	1	3	1	11.1	10,380	19,699
Brook, Mrs S R	4	26	1	2	3	3.8	2,243	5,741
Brook, E A	1	7	1	1	0	14.3	2,322	3,094
Brotherton, D R	2	8	1	1	0	12.5	2,243	2,957
Broughton Thermal Insulation	11	61	3	7	2	4.9	11,680	22,431
Broughton Homes Ltd	1	2	1	0	0	50.0	3,582	3,875
Brown, Mrs Rita	3	28	2	2	1	7.1	9,660	13,476
Brown, J K	3	26	4	1	2	15.4	9,969	11,787
Brown, Christopher P J	2	10	1	2	1	10.0	2,900	5,373
Brown, Bill	2	11	1	0	0	9.1	4,500	4,500
Brown, Mrs E	1	4	1	1	0	25.0	8,900	12,520
Bruce, B	1	13	1	1	4	7.7	3,002	5,407
Brunton, M D	5	30	3	4	1	10.0	6,887	10,984
Bryant, Miss M	1	11	1	1	0	9.1	2,070	2,640
Bryce-Smith, N	1	10	1	0	0	10.0	2,872	3,066
Bryce-Smith, Mrs M	1	2	1	1	0	50.0	2,721	3,825
Buchanan, K J	4	16	1	3	2	6.3	3,524	8,897
Buckland Thoroughbred	1	5	1	0	0	20.0	1,380	1,380
Buckley, C C	3	18	3	0	3	16.7	8,407	9,453
Burge, Mrs K M	1	15	2	1	0	13.3	5,504	6,536
Burke, Mrs Elaine M	2	12	1	0	2	8.3	2,924	3,548
Burn, Mrs H A	1	11	2	2	2	18.2	5,503	10,678
Burrell, Mrs Mark	1	6	1	0	0	16.7	3,173	3,173
Burrowes, Mick	3	21	3	4	1	14.3	8,226	11,547
Burton Park Country Club	4	18	5	0	4	27.8	15,634	18,979
Bush, G J	1	6	1	1	1	16.7	2,534	3,879
Butler, D J	2	10	2	0	0	20.0	5,874	5,874
Butterfield, G R	2	10	2	1	0	20.0	7,152	7,998
Buxton, J W	1	7	1	1	1	14.3	3,290	5,154
Byrnes, P J	1	10	2	1	2	20.0	10,607	12,606
Cable, J D	1	10	4	1	1	40.0	16,608	18,533
Cahal, David	3	21	4	3	3	19.0	11,809	17,541
Callard, Mrs Diana	1	8	1	2	0	12.5	2,595	4,583
Calver, Mrs C	4	23	2	0	7	8.7	6,069	9,323
Calvert, J	1	7	1	0	1	14.3	3,106	3,588
Calvert, J S	1	14	1	1	1	7.1	1,702	3,346
Calzini, Mrs H I S	1	10	5	1	1	50.0	15,852	17,264
Camacho, Miss J A	1	7	3	0	1	42.9	11,559	13,509
Cameron, Ian	1	5	1	0	0	20.0	2,783	2,783
Campbell, A A	1	7	1	2	0	14.3	2,301	4,311
Campion, Mrs Lynn	1	2	1	0	0	50.0	3,080	3,080
Candy, Henry	5	20	1	0	0	5.0	2,861	3,538
Capehart, Thomas R	1	11	2	2	2	18.2	7,320	10,491
Caplan, P	2	15	1	2	2	6.7	2,660	4,281
Capon, N	1	13	1	2	1	7.7	4,235	7,548
Carnarvon, Lord	8	35	9	4	2	25.7	99,706	177,406
Carnell, H G & Son Ltd	1	5	1	0	1	20.0	5,288	5,838
Carnoustie Racing Club Ltd	1	7	1	2	1	14.3	2,385	4,672
Carr, F	2	10	1	1	2	10.0	2,005	3,907
Carrington, H P	1	8	1	1	4	12.5	2,061	13,441
Carrington-Smith, Miss M	1	7	1	1	0	14.3	3,158	4,319
Carroll, Miss N	2	12	1	1	0	8.3	6,264	12,477
Carter, E	3	10	1	1	0	10.0	2,601	3,754
Carter, Mrs Josephine	1	11	2	0	1	18.2	6,294	7,640
Carthy, M Mac	3	31	1	2	4	3.2	2,238	6,479
Cartwright, R T	1	12	1	1	1	8.3	3,287	4,406
Case, Mrs Ann	1	9	1	1	0	11.1	2,930	4,847
Cash, Mrs J	2	16	1	2	3	6.3	3,980	14,541
Castle, Charles	4	19	2	1	1	10.5	4,969	6,270

	H	R	W	2	3	%W-R	£WIN	£W/P
Castle Racing	2	11	4	1	2	36.4	33,591	37,365
Cawley, Mrs Christine	2	15	2	1	1	13.3	3,985	5,676
Cayzer, Major H S	1	11	1	0	1	9.1	5,061	7,035
Cecil, Mrs J.	3	13	3	2	2	23.1	10,746	14,581
Chakko, P F	1	12	1	1	3	8.3	3,114	6,999
Chakko, Mrs Heather	1	7	3	1	0	42.9	7,353	7,977
Chamberlain, N	5	30	1	2	3	3.3	2,960	5,866
Champion, Ray	1	6	2	2	1	33.3	6,325	8,097
Chan, Henry B H	2	12	1	4	3	8.3	3,002	7,350
Chandler, P E T	1	5	2	2	1	40.0	55,557	106,245
Chapman, David W	6	17	1	0	0	5.9	2,691	2,691
Chapman, Stephen	1	16	2	3	1	12.5	8,253	13,205
Chappell, Major D N	1	2	1	0	0	50.0	3,465	3,465
Charlesworth, T	1	15	2	1	2	13.3	6,139	8,167
Charlesworth, G	1	6	1	1	1	16.7	4,021	5,439
Charlton, M R	3	14	4	1	2	28.6	34,655	39,441
Chelgate Public Relations Ltd	1	9	3	3	1	33.3	10,324	14,932
Chelsea, Lord	2	7	1	0	0	14.3	5,380	10,216
Chesa Racing	1	8	1	0	3	12.5	4,713	6,674
Cheveley Park Stud	33	100	19	13	11	19.0	85,711	180,455
Chiang, T C	2	20	2	1	1	10.0	6,205	8,510
Child, T S	2	12	3	2	2	25.0	6,943	9,378
Chiltern Hills Racing Club	1	9	1	1	1	11.1	2,301	3,764
Ching, Brian	1	3	1	1	1	33.3	3,173	7,395
Chitty Ltd	1	7	1	1	0	14.3	5,090	6,898
Christey, P J	1	9	1	1	2	11.1	7,570	15,207
Christodoulou, Athos	5	22	4	3	5	18.2	21,724	37,864
Christofi, Mark	1	12	3	1	1	25.0	9,327	12,396
Chu, P K	1	4	2	2	0	50.0	18,390	27,498
Churm, Mrs P	2	8	2	0	0	25.0	8,193	8,661
Churston, D G	1	4	1	0	0	25.0	3,582	3,582
Circlechart Ltd	3	12	2	1	2	16.7	57,819	66,079
C I T Racing Ltd	1	2	1	0	0	50.0	2,243	2,508
Claremont Management Services	3	21	1	0	1	4.8	4,794	6,010
Clark, D B	1	11	1	1	2	9.1	3,287	7,865
Clark, John D.	1	11	2	0	1	18.2	5,271	6,781
Clarke, Mrs Margaret	2	6	1	1	1	16.7	2,781	4,659
Clarke, W H	2	11	2	0	2	18.2	6,419	7,777
Classic Racing	1	7	1	0	2	14.3	2,726	3,507
Clear Height Racing	3	24	1	2	1	4.2	2,070	3,852
Clearview Partnership	1	2	1	0	0	50.0	4,125	4,398
Cliveden Stud	4	15	2	1	2	13.3	7,031	9,353
Club 7 Racing	1	6	1	2	0	16.7	5,205	7,883
Clydesdale, Mrs M S J	1	19	3	1	0	15.8	8,030	12,254
Coathup, Mrs J	3	4	1	0	0	25.0	2,280	2,280
Cock, Exors Of The Late Mr D F	1	4	1	0	0	25.0	4,290	4,290
Cock, Mrs P R	1	6	1	0	4	16.7	2,512	6,332
Cockram, Mrs Terence A M	1	4	1	0	0	25.0	2,825	2,825
Cohen, Edwin N	2	11	5	2	0	45.5	31,542	35,210
Cohen, Lady	2	9	1	1	0	11.1	5,254	6,454
Cohn, Seymour	3	12	2	0	2	16.7	6,175	7,989
Coleman, R.	2	5	1	1	1	20.0	9,594	19,131
Coleman, W F	2	9	1	0	1	11.1	2,259	3,369
Colfax Window Systems Ltd.	3	15	1	0	1	6.7	3,494	3,971
Coller, Miss E M L	1	7	2	1	0	28.6	20,632	22,552
Collins, A K	3	18	2	2	0	11.1	8,548	11,388
Collinson, Mrs C E.	1	10	1	4	1	10.0	2,679	5,905
Colver, Miss Elizabeth	2	15	1	1	1	6.7	3,610	4,648
Computer Cab Racing Club	1	8	1	0	1	12.5	2,860	3,610
Cook, P	2	14	2	2	0	14.3	7,798	10,214
Cooper, Donald	4	12	2	0	2	16.7	5,746	7,133
Cooper, D C G	1	14	1	2	1	7.1	2,979	5,119
Coppenhall, D	1	13	1	1	1	7.7	6,255	7,781
Copyforce Ltd	4	27	4	3	4	14.8	18,053	23,426
Corbett, Mrs J M.	4	11	2	0	0	18.2	14,439	22,641
Corby, Tim	1	11	3	2	0	27.3	10,637	13,110
Cosgrove, P J	2	9	2	0	1	22.2	6,820	7,442
Cosgrove, Mrs Joan	1	5	1	0	1	20.0	3,079	3,832
Cottam, R	1	12	2	0	0	16.7	6,238	6,238
Coulter, Paul	1	7	2	1	1	28.6	4,607	5,605
Countrywide Classics Limited	3	10	1	0	0	10.0	4,175	4,417
Coupland, J F	1	18	1	2	1	5.6	2,977	4,892
Cox & Allen (Kendal) Ltd	1	18	2	1	2	11.1	5,525	9,550
Coyne, Miss Clare	1	7	3	1	0	42.9	8,939	9,737
Crawshaw, Lord	3	10	2	0	1	20.0	4,822	5,406
Crazy Horse Bloodstock	1	11	1	0	1	9.1	3,655	4,905
Crazy Horse Bloodstock II	1	8	1	2	1	12.5	2,820	5,693
Crestmart Ltd	1	16	1	3	1	6.3	3,348	6,945

WINNING FLAT RACE OWNERS IN 1993

	H	R	W	2	3	%W-R	£WIN	£W/P
Croft, Darren	3	22	1	5	2	4.5	2,623	7,101
Cronk Thoroughbred Racing Ltd	3	20	2	2	3	10.0	4,953	9,825
Crook, Mrs N K	1	1	1	0	0	100.0	3,758	3,758
Crowe, Mrs S R	2	16	1	0	0	6.3	2,574	2,835
Crown, Stephen	8	34	3	2	3	8.8	8,947	14,034
Cruden, P R	2	10	2	0	1	20.0	8,776	9,849
Cullen, Bob	2	16	1	3	2	6.3	5,186	10,220
Culling, Mike	1	14	1	1	2	7.1	2,660	4,354
Cully, W	1	13	2	3	1	15.4	4,644	8,556
Cumbrian Industrials Ltd	4	37	4	3	7	10.8	16,379	41,095
Cundell, P D	7	39	6	3	2	15.4	19,057	23,427
Cunliffe, F	1	15	1	2	2	6.7	2,474	5,373
Cunliffe-Lister, Mrs S	1	8	1	1	1	12.5	2,807	4,475
Curley, Mrs B J	2	8	1	1	0	12.5	2,847	4,127
Curran, W K	1	6	1	0	2	16.7	2,243	3,207
Currie, David	1	6	1	0	1	16.7	1,770	3,085
Cyzer, R M	34	199	19	21	20	9.5	97,871	150,693
Dahlawi, Sheikh Amin	3	14	2	1	2	14.3	13,290	15,761
Dallimore, M	1	7	1	0	1	14.3	3,261	3,932
Daniels, J	6	24	3	0	3	12.5	8,806	10,539
Dare, Miss Samantha	1	11	1	1	0	9.1	3,288	4,149
Dasmal, Khalifa	3	17	2	2	2	11.8	5,650	9,489
Davenport, Mrs J M	4	12	1	3	1	8.3	3,377	16,322
Davey, C G	1	13	2	0	1	15.4	5,492	6,231
Davey, Michael	1	4	1	0	0	25.0	3,845	3,845
Davidson-Brown, P	2	9	1	1	0	11.1	3,688	4,696
Davies, William A	2	13	1	0	0	7.7	2,512	3,012
Davies, Mrs L M	1	3	1	0	0	33.3	2,967	3,611
D'Avigdor-Goldsmid, Lady	3	16	1	0	1	6.3	15,963	16,523
Davis, J G	3	14	1	5	1	7.1	3,810	15,852
Davison, Ron	1	14	1	1	3	7.1	2,243	5,337
Dawson, Ron	4	19	3	2	4	15.8	9,317	12,689
Dawson, Richard	1	2	1	1	0	50.0	2,400	3,240
Day, Mrs Maureen	2	23	1	5	4	4.3	2,820	9,729
Deakin, Paul	1	7	2	0	1	28.6	5,320	5,837
Deal, P A	5	15	1	3	1	6.7	2,385	5,562
Deer, D J	2	5	2	0	1	40.0	9,966	10,582
De Kwiatkowski, Henryk	6	12	1	1	1	8.3	16,570	22,838
De Moratalla, Marquesa	5	20	3	4	1	15.0	20,434	29,835
Derby, Lord	5	28	8	6	4	28.6	40,715	56,814
De Rothschild, Exors Of The Late Mrs J	6	28	5	8	5	17.9	47,512	61,260
Deuters, Chris	3	17	5	4	1	29.4	27,164	36,543
Devine, Luke	1	10	1	0	3	10.0	2,269	3,481
Devonshire, Duke Of	4	15	1	1	1	6.7	3,875	9,124
De Walden, Lord Howard	25	91	15	13	11	16.5	198,627	229,548
De Walden, Lady Howard	5	19	1	1	2	5.3	2,925	4,396
Dexam International Limited	1	9	2	0	1	22.2	11,120	11,784
Dick, J	3	20	2	1	3	10.0	4,955	7,283
Digby, S Wingfield	2	13	2	2	1	15.4	31,690	42,741
Dillard, Miss Donna E	1	2	1	0	0	50.0	4,450	4,450
Dimmock, Peter	2	7	1	1	1	14.3	3,847	5,598
Dinsmore, S A B	7	25	3	0	6	12.0	8,010	10,506
Dixon, B	1	9	2	1	2	22.2	12,388	25,895
Dobson, W J	1	15	2	2	2	13.3	4,061	5,980
Dobson, Miss R	2	11	1	0	0	9.1	2,658	2,906
Dodd, Peter M	2	9	2	0	2	22.2	11,512	12,717
Dodds, Mike	1	9	1	2	1	11.1	3,106	4,795
Donovan, C G	1	8	2	1	0	25.0	7,119	7,913
Doohan, Mrs M A	1	12	1	2	2	8.3	3,063	5,400
Dooley, Mrs K	1	9	1	1	1	11.1	3,436	6,706
Doorgachurn, Mrs R J	1	8	2	0	0	25.0	5,524	5,524
Dorji, H E Lhendup	2	12	4	2	2	33.3	11,675	13,449
Douglas, Dave	1	8	1	4	1	12.5	2,243	5,093
Down And Outs Racing	2	23	2	3	2	8.7	7,076	12,618
Downes, F E	1	12	1	1	1	8.3	3,085	4,651
Dozen Dreamers Partnership	4	13	1	0	0	7.7	3,985	3,985
Drofmor Racing	1	8	2	1	0	25.0	11,499	13,446
Dubai Racing Syndicate	2	8	2	1	2	25.0	21,929	38,569
Duckhaven Stud	3	17	1	2	2	5.9	2,511	4,913
Dundas, Lady	1	4	2	0	0	50.0	5,685	5,685
Dunlop, J L	7	35	6	6	3	17.1	19,415	31,025
Durham, Lord	1	14	3	1	2	21.4	8,056	9,636
Dutfield, Mrs Nerys	8	37	1	4	1	2.7	1,957	7,438
Duxbury, Miss Betty	4	33	7	0	2	21.2	28,429	33,274
Dyer, Thomas	4	12	3	1	1	25.0	6,797	7,909
Dyke, Ken	1	3	1	0	0	33.3	3,297	3,297
Easterby, M H	4	17	2	0	2	11.8	5,621	7,487
Eastick, Brian T	2	9	3	0	0	33.3	7,181	7,181

	H	R	W	2	3	%W-R	£WIN	£W/P
East Lancs Newspapers Readers Club	1	10	3	1	1	30.0	7,580	8,559
Eaton, Mrs Cherry	1	6	1	0	1	16.7	2,794	3,395
Ecudawn	2	3	1	0	0	33.3	2,579	2,579
Edwards, S L	1	8	2	0	0	25.0	14,659	17,114
Edwards, A C	5	30	3	3	4	10.0	11,685	17,564
E H Jones (Paints) Ltd	1	10	1	0	2	10.0	3,825	5,146
Elias Gale Racing	2	16	1	1	2	6.3	3,465	5,216
Elite Racing Club	7	20	2	2	2	10.0	6,545	9,560
Elite, Mark Tompkins	2	7	2	1	1	28.6	5,108	6,397
Elliot, Alan C	2	10	1	1	3	10.0	3,699	6,365
Elliott, Miss L	3	7	1	0	0	14.3	3,845	3,845
Ellis, Hugh	2	11	3	1	2	27.3	95,284	98,465
Elsworth, D R C	2	10	1	3	2	10.0	4,079	11,349
Ennever, Mrs Michael	1	2	1	0	0	50.0	2,005	2,005
Esprit de Corps Racing	2	20	6	1	1	30.0	22,629	26,029
Etherton, Mrs John	2	11	2	0	1	18.2	5,265	6,069
Eurolink Group Plc	4	15	4	2	1	26.7	38,489	51,184
Eurostrait Ltd	3	23	2	1	3	8.7	5,634	8,553
Eustace, Mrs James	1	7	1	1	2	14.3	2,925	4,520
Evans, P J	1	11	3	3	1	27.3	8,568	10,516
Evans, Edward P	1	5	1	1	1	20.0	5,190	16,440
Ewbank, Keith H.	1	4	1	0	0	25.0	3,173	3,173
Express Marie Curie Racing Club	2	8	2	0	1	25.0	10,372	10,831
Express Newspapers Plc	2	19	1	4	3	5.3	2,070	7,032
Facchino, Mrs B.	13	79	5	5	9	6.3	19,131	36,031
Fahey, R A	1	4	1	0	1	25.0	5,901	6,887
Fairhaven, Lady	2	17	3	1	3	17.6	9,934	12,128
Fairhurst, T.	1	8	1	0	0	12.5	1,520	1,734
Faisal, Prince A A	12	56	9	8	12	16.1	100,209	161,765
Faletti, Mrs W M.	2	10	3	1	1	30.0	12,074	13,386
Falvey, John	1	8	4	1	0	50.0	14,642	15,414
Farish III, W S	2	7	2	2	2	28.6	6,667	10,122
Farndon, G A	8	43	5	2	3	11.6	15,922	21,404
Fatah, Vic	1	5	2	1	0	40.0	7,029	8,750
Faulkner, Mrs E G.	1	12	2	3	0	16.7	7,850	11,953
Fawcett, Tony	4	24	1	1	1	4.2	13,500	17,906
Fayzad Thoroughbred Limited	2	12	1	1	0	8.3	4,878	7,173
Fenwick, Mrs P T	1	3	2	0	0	66.7	5,301	5,301
Fetherston-Godley, P	2	17	2	3	3	11.8	19,049	26,076
Field, R S	1	9	2	2	0	22.2	5,064	6,300
Firth, Norman	1	8	2	1	1	25.0	7,646	8,619
Fir Trading Ltd	1	8	1	0	0	12.5	2,709	2,709
Fish, David	2	25	2	4	3	8.0	5,046	9,321
Fisher, Jack	1	10	2	0	4	20.0	6,723	8,580
Fittocks Stud Limited	4	18	3	3	0	16.7	39,605	43,716
FitzGerald, J G	6	23	1	3	2	4.3	2,217	10,455
Fitzgerald, T J.	1	12	2	1	1	16.7	5,306	6,458
Fitzgerald, Pat.	1	4	2	0	0	50.0	7,764	8,345
Flavin, P J	1	7	1	0	1	14.3	2,058	2,680
Flegg, R.	1	4	2	0	1	50.0	3,654	4,179
Fleming, J P	1	11	2	3	2	18.2	6,764	11,647
Fleming, Mrs Corinne	1	6	1	0	0	16.7	2,532	2,738
Fletcher, Mrs Sue.	1	8	2	1	1	25.0	4,844	6,482
Flynn, O G	1	8	1	2	0	12.5	2,070	4,208
Food Brokers Ltd.	3	14	1	3	1	7.1	3,558	8,281
Forbes, Mrs G S.	1	6	1	1	0	16.7	2,700	3,938
Ford, D	1	9	2	0	2	22.2	5,977	7,000
Ford, Tom	3	13	1	1	0	7.7	2,905	3,453
Foreman, T A.	2	11	1	0	0	9.1	3,287	3,287
Foster, Mrs S	2	7	2	0	0	28.6	5,601	5,601
Fotherby, J	1	14	4	2	2	28.6	10,579	13,165
Four Jays Racing Partnership	1	13	3	2	1	23.1	11,573	15,832
Foustok, A	3	19	4	2	2	21.1	14,642	20,622
Frame, A	1	8	2	1	0	25.0	6,787	7,895
Freemount Partnership	1	6	1	1	0	16.7	2,997	3,858
Friendly Society	1	6	1	1	0	16.7	2,259	3,120
Fretwell, J C	1	6	3	1	0	50.0	8,891	9,545
Freyne, Garrett J	2	9	1	3	1	11.1	4,464	11,506
Frost, T A F	1	8	1	1	0	12.5	3,079	4,289
Fulton, Mrs J G	1	6	2	0	0	33.3	20,831	21,316
Furlong, James	2	11	4	2	1	36.4	10,533	12,917
Fust, L	3	15	1	2	4	6.7	2,301	6,829
Fustok, S	5	13	6	0	1	46.2	23,631	24,902
F W Briggs/Park Lane Racing	1	14	1	2	1	7.1	3,495	5,845
Gadsden, E J S	6	32	4	9	4	12.5	12,621	22,311
Gallagher Materials Ltd	2	11	1	1	2	9.1	3,582	5,190
Gallop, D B	1	6	2	1	0	33.3	9,316	10,468
Galloway, C R	2	15	2	0	5	13.3	5,220	7,414

	H	R	W	2	3	%W-R	£WIN	£W/P
Gardiner, Mrs Linda	3	10	2	0	0	20.0	8,553	8,553
Gardner, N H	2	11	1	1	1	9.1	4,794	7,605
Garner, Mrs P A	1	9	1	0	0	11.1	3,553	3,553
Garth Thoroughbreds Ltd	2	13	1	0	0	7.7	2,163	2,384
Garthwaite, Sir Wm	2	15	3	0	2	20.0	9,342	10,247
Garthwaite, Mrs P J	2	12	1	0	0	8.3	1,553	1,553
Gaucci, Luciano	5	15	4	0	3	26.7	20,836	27,356
Gearon, Miss Katherine	1	8	1	2	0	12.5	2,793	4,811
George, Edward St	6	12	2	2	2	16.7	7,743	11,825
George, Mrs C A B St	1	9	3	0	0	33.3	6,978	6,978
Gibbons, Robert	3	22	4	1	3	18.2	18,041	23,578
Gielty, M B	2	11	1	1	1	9.1	1,646	2,602
Gill, D	5	34	2	9	2	5.9	6,032	13,900
Girls, Grandy	1	15	4	3	1	26.7	11,939	15,387
Gleadell, Giles	1	12	2	0	3	16.7	5,535	7,607
Glenton, Ian W	7	33	1	1	5	3.0	2,365	5,136
Goddard, John R	1	7	1	0	1	14.3	3,525	4,622
Godfrey, Mrs G A	1	9	2	1	2	22.2	8,206	10,492
Golding, Frank W	2	12	3	1	1	25.0	106,929	139,522
Goldman, Nigel	4	12	1	1	0	8.3	8,238	9,262
Gomersall, Raymond	4	8	1	0	2	12.5	2,927	4,034
Gomm, K C	4	30	2	3	3	6.7	7,476	11,382
Gompertz, Jeremy	1	4	1	0	0	25.0	4,978	4,978
Gonzalez, Maximo	1	19	3	4	1	15.8	12,558	25,734
Good, J R	7	45	8	6	5	17.8	21,628	31,538
Goodridge, Mrs June	1	12	1	1	3	8.3	3,080	6,477
Goody, E	5	17	1	0	2	5.9	2,070	2,610
Gorrie, Alex	8	38	1	3	5	2.6	3,106	9,492
Goulandris, P G	15	83	12	15	15	14.5	76,983	120,727
Goulandris, Mrs P G	3	11	1	2	2	9.1	3,129	7,363
Gover, Mrs Ann	1	10	2	1	1	20.0	6,766	8,008
Grace, M J	1	12	1	2	2	8.3	3,444	5,756
Graham, Mrs Tess	1	10	3	1	0	30.0	28,453	29,531
Graham, G	1	6	2	2	1	33.3	15,912	18,153
Graham, J D	6	30	1	3	0	3.3	4,092	10,014
Grant, Mrs V S	1	3	1	0	0	33.3	15,140	17,226
Grant, M W	1	5	1	1	2	20.0	5,936	9,085
G R Bailey Ltd (Baileys Horse Feeds)	3	12	3	0	2	25.0	85,541	87,713
Greaves, James E	1	14	3	2	1	21.4	10,898	14,352
Gredley, W J	20	71	4	2	6	5.6	13,255	95,820
Green, Paul	4	20	2	4	1	10.0	26,292	40,551
Green, Raymond Anderson	3	6	1	1	0	16.7	3,758	5,083
Green, Atherton And	1	9	1	0	3	11.1	3,915	5,531
Green, Peter	1	8	1	2	1	12.5	17,730	20,286
Greening, N P	1	10	1	0	0	10.0	3,106	3,106
Greenland Park Ltd	5	34	9	5	6	26.5	33,970	65,506
Greenwood, Geoffrey C	8	35	2	4	3	5.7	7,019	12,474
Greig, Neil	4	16	1	1	0	6.3	3,325	5,066
Grey, S M	1	12	1	0	4	8.3	3,365	5,090
Griffin, Reg	1	11	4	1	2	36.4	11,170	12,598
Grimes, J K	2	16	1	2	1	6.3	3,598	6,063
Group 1 Racing (1991) Ltd	6	20	1	2	2	5.0	3,340	9,476
Grubb, Murray	2	25	6	5	1	24.0	14,672	19,722
Grubmuller, Walter	3	8	3	1	1	37.5	13,599	16,270
Guest, Rae	3	12	1	1	1	8.3	1,679	2,432
Gutters, S & G	1	10	1	1	1	10.0	4,836	7,548
Haggas, B	8	32	1	6	5	3.1	3,026	12,598
Haggas, Mrs M M	2	18	3	3	2	16.7	17,368	24,779
Haim, R	3	23	2	2	4	8.7	7,283	11,385
Halifax, Lord	7	22	2	5	4	9.1	6,241	31,466
Hall, Miss S E	2	10	4	0	1	40.0	12,397	12,937
Hall, A C	5	15	1	0	1	6.7	3,266	3,739
Hall, David	1	10	1	2	0	10.0	3,850	7,490
Hall, Mrs Kate	2	14	1	2	0	7.1	2,739	5,116
Hallam, Mrs S	2	6	1	1	0	16.7	3,652	4,625
Hambleton Lodge Equine Premix Ltd	1	13	1	2	1	7.7	15,400	20,740
Hambro, Mrs Rupert	1	4	1	0	1	25.0	4,986	5,613
Hamer, C M	2	19	2	2	0	10.5	6,808	11,104
Hamilton, Les	2	10	2	3	2	20.0	6,003	10,416
Hamilton, Mrs Anne-Marie	2	17	1	2	1	5.9	3,160	5,899
Hammond, Peter	1	5	2	0	1	40.0	7,163	7,667
Hammond, S J	1	4	1	0	0	25.0	2,893	3,193
Hammy Racing	1	6	1	1	0	16.7	2,070	2,880
Hampshire, P	4	12	1	0	2	8.3	3,054	3,740
Hampson, B W	1	13	1	0	1	7.7	2,832	3,542
Hamson, Mrs C	1	11	3	2	0	27.3	17,939	21,501
Hannon, Mrs J A	1	9	1	0	0	11.1	2,873	2,873
Hansberry, J F	1	7	1	1	0	14.3	2,243	3,418

	H	R	W	2	3	%W-R	£WIN	£W/P
Hanson, J	12	41	4	8	3	9.8	16,656	41,775
Hargate Stud And Racing Limited	2	7	1	0	0	14.3	3,202	3,450
Harker, Mrs A	2	21	1	3	7	4.8	3,377	9,924
Harper, Norman	2	14	1	4	1	7.1	2,406	6,529
Harper, S	2	11	1	0	1	9.1	3,184	3,573
Harrington, E	1	6	2	2	1	33.3	6,419	8,977
Harrington, Mrs Chris	2	13	3	5	1	23.1	9,334	15,208
Harris, Mrs P W	17	76	7	14	12	9.2	27,757	63,893
Harris, Miss Karen	1	6	1	0	1	16.7	2,679	2,937
Harris, Mrs Jenny	3	16	1	4	3	6.3	3,915	24,454
Harris, Mrs F A	1	7	2	1	0	28.6	6,755	7,978
Harris, Mrs E	1	10	1	1	1	10.0	2,624	3,878
Harrison, Mrs Carol	1	11	1	0	0	9.1	2,954	2,954
Harrow, J J	1	11	1	0	1	9.1	2,532	2,868
Harsh (Tipping Gears)	1	12	5	2	2	41.7	29,754	39,114
Hart, D D	2	8	2	0	2	25.0	6,636	7,761
Hart, Peter	1	9	1	3	1	11.1	2,512	5,542
Hart, Hugh	2	7	1	1	1	14.3	4,307	6,133
Hartington, Lord	5	24	5	3	2	20.8	20,457	28,209
Hartwell, Ms Tessa	2	10	1	0	0	10.0	1,954	1,954
Harwood, G	2	12	2	0	1	16.7	7,423	8,041
Havercroft, Fred A	1	12	1	0	1	8.3	3,785	5,746
Hawes, Mrs Rosalie	6	31	9	3	5	29.0	63,930	70,806
Hawkett, Mike	2	13	2	2	0	15.4	9,742	13,532
Hawkings, L J	2	10	2	0	1	20.0	6,708	7,387
Hawkings, Mrs C A	2	7	1	2	0	14.3	3,699	5,709
Hawthorn, Ray	4	20	2	0	1	10.0	4,707	5,929
Haynes, M J	2	7	1	1	0	14.3	3,933	4,995
Hayward, Lady	1	5	2	1	0	40.0	6,521	11,203
Hazell, Mrs J	3	22	4	4	2	18.2	14,433	21,822
Hazzard, Don	2	14	1	0	1	7.1	2,700	3,458
Heathavon Stables Limited	4	29	1	1	4	3.4	3,611	6,313
Heathcote, Mrs Robert	5	36	2	5	5	5.6	17,375	30,776
Heaton, R L	1	6	2	2	1	33.3	6,372	8,802
Hedigan, Cecil J	1	7	1	2	0	14.3	2,880	10,768
Helaissi, A S	2	13	3	5	1	23.1	19,085	26,491
Helena Springfield Ltd	4	13	4	1	0	30.8	28,074	36,956
Heler, Joseph	2	18	9	3	3	50.0	33,677	42,854
Henson, Mrs Anne	5	26	2	1	1	7.7	7,292	9,123
Hern, Mrs W R	2	14	4	1	1	28.6	14,499	17,143
Herridge, G.	1	3	1	0	0	33.3	4,752	4,752
Herries, Lady	6	21	1	3	4	4.8	3,028	9,542
Hesmonds Stud	4	22	2	3	4	9.1	5,453	9,683
Hetherton, N	3	21	2	2	2	9.5	7,286	9,959
Hewitson, H	1	8	1	0	0	12.5	3,420	3,641
Hickey, Martin	1	6	3	1	0	50.0	5,641	6,211
Hide, Anthony	2	16	1	2	1	6.3	3,236	5,103
Highclere Thoroughbred Racing Ltd	4	15	1	1	3	6.7	3,176	6,762
Highflyers	7	25	2	2	1	8.0	7,570	10,471
High Point Bloodstock Ltd	1	1	1	0	0	100.0	3,202	3,202
Higson, K	39	206	18	18	19	8.7	81,651	135,863
Higson, Peter L	1	8	1	1	0	12.5	2,243	2,960
Hill, C John	13	68	11	5	2	16.2	35,990	42,080
Hill, A S	2	20	3	3	3	15.0	7,933	11,218
Hill, Miss A V	1	10	3	0	1	30.0	39,790	42,279
Hill, M.	1	10	1	1	0	10.0	3,753	4,799
Hills, B W	3	10	1	0	2	10.0	2,511	3,571
Hills, Mrs M.	1	7	1	0	1	14.3	4,630	5,412
Hill-Wood, I C.	1	5	2	0	0	40.0	15,770	15,877
Hinton, Stanley	1	12	1	0	1	8.3	3,405	6,009
Hislop, Mrs J L	2	11	2	0	0	18.2	6,374	7,513
Hitchins, Robert	2	3	1	0	1	33.3	5,936	6,552
Ho, S	1	7	2	1	2	28.6	4,004	5,383
Hobbs, P D	1	10	1	2	0	10.0	6,292	17,061
Hobbs, David A	1	18	1	2	1	5.6	3,260	7,627
Hodges, R J	5	19	2	3	5	10.5	5,834	10,661
Hodgson, K	4	39	4	2	2	10.3	15,513	18,290
Holbrook, A K	2	9	1	2	2	11.1	2,692	4,342
Holdcroft, Mrs T G	1	11	2	0	4	18.2	18,635	23,557
Holdroyd, John L	1	11	4	0	3	36.4	11,427	12,437
Hole In The Wall Breeding-Racing	1	10	1	0	1	10.0	2,058	2,429
Holland-Martin, T D	3	22	1	1	2	4.5	3,493	6,162
Holliday, L B	2	7	2	2	0	28.6	6,802	10,008
Hollinshead, R	1	2	1	0	0	50.0	2,110	2,110
Holroyd, Mrs Barbara	1	7	1	1	1	14.3	2,490	4,602
Holt, R B	1	8	2	1	1	25.0	6,933	8,479
Honour, Fred	1	2	1	0	0	50.0	3,236	3,236
Hopgood, Harry W	1	11	3	2	1	27.3	13,977	16,077

	H	R	W	2	3	%W-R	£WIN	£W/P
Horan, Ms M	5	14	3	1	2	21.4	63,931	67,328
Horgan, Jim	3	15	4	0	1	26.7	25,377	27,618
Hornall, Archie	1	8	2	0	0	25.0	6,736	7,536
Howard-Spink, G	7	36	8	3	4	22.2	61,644	79,166
Hue-Williams, Exors Of The Late Mrs V	3	16	2	1	6	12.5	8,163	15,477
Huggins, R W	6	53	10	14	5	18.9	40,711	63,648
Hughes, H B	2	14	3	1	2	21.4	16,406	20,929
Hughes, Mrs J	2	18	1	2	2	5.6	2,445	5,395
Humaid, Juma	1	4	2	1	0	50.0	32,671	51,934
Humphris, Cyril	2	7	2	1	2	28.6	9,135	12,595
Hunnisett, D R	3	15	4	0	4	26.7	26,488	33,125
Hunt, Clifton	1	15	2	1	2	13.3	6,006	8,022
Hunter, William Provan	2	14	1	5	1	7.1	3,558	10,200
Hunter, S	1	5	1	0	0	20.0	3,054	3,054
Hyman, M F	2	18	1	1	1	5.6	2,787	4,507
Imison, W B	3	48	8	6	6	16.7	24,028	33,914
Induna Racing Partners	1	5	2	1	0	40.0	5,427	7,121
Innes, Peter	1	6	1	1	2	16.7	2,540	5,540
Insight Cartons Ltd	1	3	1	0	0	33.3	4,737	4,945
Insoll, Garth	1	7	2	1	0	28.6	6,128	7,425
Invoshire Ltd	1	8	2	1	0	25.0	5,679	6,787
Irshid, Q	6	23	1	2	3	4.3	3,158	9,217
Irwin, Mrs M	1	5	2	0	0	40.0	13,071	14,689
Ison, Aubrey	1	8	2	1	0	25.0	10,584	11,964
Italia, Gerecon	12	35	6	5	8	17.1	96,222	145,896
Ivory, K T	8	53	1	5	8	1.9	2,490	11,217
Jabre, G	2	22	7	2	1	31.8	25,821	32,638
Jackman, G A	1	10	1	1	1	10.0	2,758	4,051
Jackson, A H	1	13	3	2	1	23.1	10,429	13,556
Jackson, Norman	3	18	3	2	0	16.7	8,363	12,982
Jackson, W J P	2	9	1	0	1	11.1	3,236	3,673
Jackson Construction Co Ltd	2	13	1	0	1	7.7	2,301	2,487
Jackson, F A	1	3	1	0	0	33.3	2,975	2,975
Jacobs, Paul G	3	10	1	1	0	10.0	2,685	4,865
Jansen, Mrs Francoise	2	11	1	2	1	9.1	2,286	4,972
Jarvis, Miss V R	2	12	1	1	1	8.3	3,202	5,822
Jarvis, M A	1	6	1	2	2	16.7	2,692	5,703
Jarvis, Mrs Ann	6	40	2	3	1	5.0	6,045	9,356
Jarvis, William	2	11	1	2	0	9.1	3,015	4,681
J B R Leisure Ltd	3	17	4	0	1	23.5	22,006	23,358
Jem Racing	1	3	1	0	0	33.3	3,260	3,260
Jenkinson, Robert	1	5	1	0	0	20.0	2,713	2,916
Jenks, Mrs D	1	9	1	2	2	11.1	3,015	5,312
Jerrard, I	1	7	2	0	1	28.6	6,843	7,843
Jestin, F	1	6	1	0	1	16.7	2,353	2,704
Jinks, Richard	2	20	3	3	4	15.0	28,149	38,192
Joachim, Rex	2	11	1	0	1	9.1	2,243	2,813
John, P R	1	10	2	2	1	20.0	6,700	8,970
Johnsey, T A	2	18	2	3	4	11.1	4,734	15,371
Johnson, Mrs R A	4	29	3	4	3	10.3	8,559	14,579
Johnson, D A	3	14	2	3	0	14.3	4,313	6,089
Johnson, J	1	11	2	2	1	18.2	7,570	9,606
John Stephenson & Sons (Nelson) Ltd	1	6	1	0	2	16.7	2,851	3,721
Jolliffe, Peter	1	5	1	0	0	20.0	2,070	2,070
Joly, Mrs D	2	10	2	0	1	20.0	8,079	10,992
Jones, T M	1	7	1	1	0	14.3	2,427	3,147
Jones, Mrs Dot	1	10	1	0	0	10.0	2,445	2,445
Jones, Miss Victoria	1	6	1	1	0	16.7	2,624	3,368
Jones, Ned	1	9	1	2	0	11.1	4,464	7,561
Jones, Mrs Julie	1	8	1	1	1	12.5	3,106	4,000
Jones, Peter	2	12	1	0	1	8.3	3,548	4,628
Jones, Mrs H T	2	8	1	1	0	12.5	4,988	6,376
Joyner, Ms S A	2	20	1	2	1	5.0	3,002	9,448
J P S Racing	1	3	2	0	0	66.7	6,057	6,057
Jubert, Mrs P	4	25	3	3	3	12.0	10,717	16,794
Julian Clopet And Partners	1	4	1	1	0	25.0	3,021	3,971
Julian Graves Ltd	2	17	1	0	1	5.9	2,364	2,764
Kaine, Mrs D E	2	5	1	0	0	20.0	3,379	3,379
Kalaji, Miss Maha	5	22	4	2	0	18.2	11,512	14,416
Kalla, F M	11	35	3	4	2	8.6	13,718	34,528
Kaplan, Mrs Rita J	1	18	3	3	1	16.7	9,640	19,303
Karpidas, Mrs Pauline	2	13	2	2	0	15.4	7,099	10,116
Kavanagh, Conal	2	10	4	2	0	40.0	49,727	55,496
Kavli	1	11	3	2	0	27.3	10,361	13,336
Kay, S	1	5	1	1	1	20.0	2,958	4,384
Keller, G	2	5	1	0	0	20.0	4,464	4,664
Kelleway, P A	3	7	2	1	1	28.6	8,202	9,455
Kelly, R D A	1	5	1	0	0	20.0	3,676	3,676

	H	R	W	2	3	%W-R	£WIN	£W/P
Kelly, William J	1	9	2	2	1	22.2	8,285	10,664
Kelly, W J	2	20	1	1	0	5.0	4,175	4,999
Kelsey-Fry, John	3	23	1	3	3	4.3	3,407	8,769
Kentish, M F	3	28	4	5	3	14.3	63,714	77,266
Kerman, I	1	3	1	0	0	33.3	3,054	3,282
Kerr, Miss D G	1	7	2	0	1	28.6	5,225	6,763
Kerr-Dineen, Lord de La Warr And Mrs M	1	1	1	0	0	100.0	5,436	5,436
Kersey, T	4	24	1	2	0	4.2	3,704	5,873
Keswick, Mrs Henry	2	13	1	0	3	7.7	3,611	5,026
Kettlewell, Mrs E A	1	4	2	0	1	50.0	5,562	5,855
Khaled, S	6	26	5	6	1	19.2	82,880	94,434
Khalifa, Abdulla Al	1	6	2	0	3	33.3	5,908	8,001
Khan, K F	1	10	2	2	0	20.0	7,708	10,111
Khan, M A	1	4	2	1	1	50.0	12,748	14,346
Khurbash, K	3	6	1	1	0	16.7	4,378	5,761
Kiernan, Mrs Elizabeth	1	8	1	1	0	12.5	2,259	3,627
King, A A	3	24	2	3	2	8.3	5,683	9,722
King, G J	1	4	1	1	1	25.0	3,417	4,686
King, Mrs P M	1	7	1	1	1	14.3	3,377	4,663
Kinghorn, A	1	13	1	1	0	7.7	2,243	2,813
Kingsley Partnership	1	9	2	4	0	22.2	5,524	12,077
Kitson, Sir Timothy	3	12	1	3	2	8.3	4,110	10,138
Knight Group	1	14	1	3	2	7.1	2,821	6,171
Knight, G W	1	11	1	0	0	9.1	3,758	4,865
Knipe, Mrs R F	1	10	5	0	0	50.0	28,140	29,593
Kynaston, Kevan R	2	9	2	0	1	22.2	5,127	5,506
Laidlaw, Stephen	1	10	2	1	3	20.0	15,855	20,317
Lalemant, Bob	5	15	3	0	4	20.0	30,479	33,525
Lamb, Mrs John	1	11	3	0	1	27.3	11,297	12,570
Lamb Brook Associates	1	10	1	1	2	10.0	3,054	5,006
Lamb Lane Associates	1	10	2	1	2	20.0	7,018	10,158
Lambton, Lord	1	11	1	2	0	9.1	2,557	4,761
Lancaster, Greg	1	7	1	1	0	14.3	2,406	3,844
Land, Brook	1	8	1	0	0	12.5	1,604	1,604
Landi, Ettore	5	20	4	4	0	20.0	18,389	32,852
Langley, T W	2	18	5	1	3	27.8	12,052	14,372
Lansdown, S P	1	7	2	1	2	28.6	7,958	10,132
Lansley, A G	1	13	2	3	1	15.4	11,736	17,772
Larke, Denis J	1	3	1	1	0	33.3	3,626	7,238
Latter, A D	1	6	2	1	1	33.3	10,808	16,028
Laurel (Leisure) Limited	6	51	12	9	2	23.5	44,264	60,523
Lawrance, M T	1	12	2	1	3	16.7	6,171	8,717
Lawson-Brown, John	1	11	1	4	1	9.1	2,413	5,967
Lawton, P J	1	11	2	4	0	18.2	5,899	10,948
Lazarus, Lennard	1	15	1	4	2	6.7	2,821	9,259
Lazzari, J A	3	13	3	2	0	23.1	10,138	12,471
Leach, W B	1	3	1	0	2	33.3	3,054	3,347
Leader, Rory C	1	4	2	0	1	50.0	9,191	10,501
Leatham, G H	5	29	1	3	5	3.4	2,534	8,426
Lee, Mrs C	1	3	1	0	0	33.3	2,448	2,448
Lee, Mrs John	2	9	1	0	1	11.1	10,673	11,285
Lee, F H	11	73	2	5	6	2.7	4,732	12,410
Lee, Mrs Gillian	2	18	1	2	1	5.6	2,925	6,166
Leek, J A	1	11	2	4	1	18.2	6,918	12,322
Leetham, H R	2	10	1	1	3	10.0	4,435	6,917
Leggate, David S	1	5	1	1	1	20.0	4,078	5,579
Leigh, Gerald	4	13	2	1	2	15.4	5,875	9,725
Leigh, T	1	6	1	0	3	16.7	4,191	9,442
Leonard, P A	11	37	3	2	3	8.1	63,514	73,138
Leslie, P W	1	8	1	0	0	12.5	3,878	3,878
Levinson, Mrs Paul	1	4	1	0	1	25.0	2,243	3,155
Lewis, Mrs P	2	24	1	2	5	4.2	28,543	33,590
Lewis, David S	2	2	1	0	0	50.0	2,749	2,749
Lewis, Geoff	1	2	1	0	0	50.0	1,553	1,553
Liang, Thomas T S	2	16	3	1	3	18.8	11,673	14,065
Lifetime U K Ltd	1	8	2	2	1	25.0	5,490	7,790
Liles, Mrs Margaret	1	3	1	1	0	33.3	2,601	3,279
Lines, C V	4	22	2	5	2	9.1	4,733	10,740
Linpac Group Limited	1	2	1	0	1	50.0	20,439	22,275
Lintscan Ltd (Corbett Bookmakers)	3	25	8	3	2	32.0	21,946	25,657
Lishman, John	1	15	2	1	2	13.3	7,721	10,307
Llewellyn, B J	1	2	2	0	0	100.0	4,049	4,049
Lock, T R	1	10	2	1	1	20.0	27,995	31,874
Loder, D R	2	12	2	1	3	16.7	6,632	11,029
Loder, E J	3	15	3	2	2	20.0	9,680	16,530
Long, Mrs B	1	4	1	0	0	25.0	2,512	2,512
Long, J M	2	14	1	1	2	7.1	2,364	4,352
Lonsdale, Countess Of	2	10	1	0	2	10.0	3,210	3,862

	H	R	W	2	3	%W-R	£WIN	£W/P
Lowe, P G	1	8	1	0	3	12.5	2,070	2,846
Lowry, M	1	10	1	2	2	10.0	4,221	9,950
Lucayan Stud	17	74	16	11	12	21.6	108,787	160,514
Lumley, W N	2	23	3	2	3	13.0	9,672	13,331
Lunn, N	3	18	2	6	2	11.1	10,519	17,279
Lunn, Mrs Patricia	2	10	2	0	1	20.0	5,208	5,759
Lunness, E H	2	14	2	5	0	14.3	10,990	15,520
Lury, S	2	10	1	3	2	10.0	2,579	5,278
Lynch, R N C	1	11	2	2	0	18.2	7,993	13,056
M & N Plant Ltd	4	20	6	1	2	30.0	30,202	33,836
Macdonald, Steve	1	3	1	0	0	33.3	4,935	4,935
Macfarlane, S W	1	16	1	3	2	6.3	3,184	7,537
Macgregor, Miss E G	3	11	1	2	1	9.1	5,390	11,019
Maden, D J	2	15	1	2	2	6.7	2,385	4,741
Magnier, Mrs John	1	4	1	0	0	25.0	10,029	10,971
Maguire, Billy	2	6	2	0	0	33.3	8,578	8,792
Maintenance, Prime	1	13	3	1	3	23.1	8,833	10,937
Major, C G	1	5	1	0	0	20.0	1,917	1,917
Makin, Mrs P J	4	15	3	2	0	20.0	8,374	14,263
Mallya, Vijay	1	10	3	0	1	30.0	9,020	9,313
Manana, Saeed	13	45	6	7	6	13.3	24,730	93,365
Manchester Evening News Ltd	4	20	3	0	2	15.0	12,834	13,631
Mandarin Racing	2	4	1	0	0	25.0	2,377	2,377
Mangan, E J	2	11	2	3	0	18.2	5,554	9,378
Mann, L	1	2	1	1	0	50.0	4,338	7,983
Manning, P G	1	7	1	0	2	14.3	2,070	2,685
Manny Bernstein (Racing) Ltd	1	8	3	2	1	37.5	9,327	13,616
Manton, Lady	1	11	1	0	1	9.1	3,261	4,172
Marchant, Denis	1	9	1	0	0	11.1	6,255	6,462
Marchant, R P	4	17	1	3	4	5.9	3,676	9,859
Marinopoulos, L	10	36	4	5	7	11.1	14,801	26,139
Mark Johnston Racing Ltd	2	19	2	1	2	10.5	8,525	10,987
Marks, Mrs Satu	2	15	2	1	0	13.3	5,987	7,048
Mark Tompkins Racing	4	14	2	2	2	14.3	6,453	9,846
Marriott Stables Limited	2	26	4	2	7	15.4	9,750	14,694
Marsden, J E	2	16	1	1	2	6.3	7,492	9,439
Marshall, Dave	2	19	3	4	1	15.8	8,610	13,513
Marshall, Mrs M M	1	10	1	2	2	10.0	3,818	6,164
Martin, Exors Of The Late Mr J	2	15	1	3	0	6.7	2,669	5,963
Martin, John S	1	12	2	2	1	16.7	8,376	11,432
Martin, Mrs Julie	2	15	1	1	0	6.7	3,126	4,152
Martin, Geoffrey	2	6	1	0	0	16.7	7,440	7,698
Martin, Mrs S M	1	7	1	0	0	14.3	3,262	3,262
Marucci, A	1	10	1	4	1	10.0	2,769	6,842
Mascalls Stud	2	10	1	2	1	10.0	5,754	8,326
Mason, Sydney	3	21	6	3	2	28.6	21,401	28,866
Mason, Christopher J	1	3	1	0	0	33.3	2,812	2,812
Matalon, M M	2	9	3	3	1	33.3	15,175	19,236
Matthews, Lord	12	64	5	8	9	7.8	21,086	43,730
Matthews, Lady	2	17	3	3	1	17.6	9,348	12,463
Matthews, Mrs B A	1	8	1	0	2	12.5	3,028	4,032
Matthews, P A	2	14	1	1	1	7.1	3,173	4,389
Matthews, The Hon I V	1	3	1	1	0	33.3	8,041	10,126
Maxwell, Jack	1	7	1	0	1	14.3	2,448	2,921
Mayall, Mrs R C	2	16	1	4	2	6.3	3,720	16,158
Mazza, G	7	14	1	0	1	7.1	3,285	4,716
McAllister, Mrs James	4	21	1	1	3	4.8	2,846	5,298
McAlpine, Exors Of The Late Sir Robin	6	35	8	6	6	22.9	161,774	193,640
McAlpine, R J	1	5	1	0	1	20.0	7,327	7,839
McCormack, M	3	17	2	1	3	11.8	6,190	8,299
McCreery, R J	1	7	2	2	0	28.6	16,155	18,519
McDonagh, T	1	5	1	0	0	20.0	3,553	3,553
McDuffie, David	1	10	1	2	0	10.0	2,870	4,204
McEvoy, Ms Theresa	1	5	1	1	0	20.0	3,391	4,017
McHalapar Syndicate	1	11	1	2	0	9.1	2,269	5,672
McHarg, W G	1	9	2	2	1	22.2	10,114	12,287
McIndoe, Lady	1	9	1	0	0	11.1	5,470	6,114
McKernan, P	1	11	1	0	3	9.1	2,977	4,452
McManamon, J	2	22	1	1	4	4.5	3,688	7,743
McParland, A	1	6	1	0	1	16.7	3,260	4,458
Meacock, S A	2	11	1	0	0	9.1	2,243	2,880
Mead, Rex L	2	7	1	0	0	14.3	2,843	2,843
Mellon, Paul	13	68	12	5	6	17.6	48,573	68,767
Meredith, R	2	9	1	1	2	11.1	3,718	5,826
Merrick, Mrs Pauline	1	7	5	1	0	71.4	53,039	54,347
Merritt, R Cohen & Mr A F	1	6	2	0	1	33.3	6,640	7,145
Merthyr Tydfil Car Auction Limited	3	20	1	2	3	5.0	2,982	13,334
Meyrick, Sir George	3	18	1	2	5	5.6	5,572	12,246

	H	R	W	2	3	%W-R	£WIN	£W/P
Michaelson, R P B	8	46	6	6	5	13.0	32,591	58,521
Middleton Scriven Investments Ltd	1	2	1	0	0	50.0	3,521	3,521
Midwood, D R	1	8	3	0	0	37.5	9,479	9,833
Mihalop, Mrs Judy	2	11	1	0	1	9.1	2,434	3,182
Milbank Foods Ltd	1	9	1	3	1	11.1	2,148	4,900
Miller, Mrs D	3	8	1	1	0	12.5	3,173	4,253
Miller, Mrs Celia	2	8	1	0	2	12.5	3,883	4,375
Million In Mind Partnership (2)	5	19	3	3	2	15.8	12,609	18,452
Mills, T G	10	48	3	5	8	6.3	24,650	56,642
Mills, J V	1	3	1	0	0	33.3	2,070	2,070
Mills, Mrs Lesley	2	4	2	0	0	50.0	4,038	4,038
Mills, G W	2	11	1	1	0	9.1	5,816	8,034
Milne, Gordon	1	7	1	1	0	14.3	2,637	3,514
Mines, A E T	1	9	4	3	0	44.4	11,593	13,467
Mino, S	2	15	1	3	1	6.7	12,818	19,195
Mitchell, Mrs Elaine	2	13	4	1	1	30.8	14,468	18,064
Mitchell, Mrs D M	1	18	2	6	4	11.1	5,080	12,445
Mitten, Brian	1	9	1	0	3	11.1	4,241	6,328
Moffatt, Mrs Y	1	7	1	1	0	14.3	1,912	2,663
Mohammed, Sheikh	211	767	144	107	95	18.8	1,703,958	2,602,123
Mohammed, Sultan	11	37	5	5	8	13.5	18,306	38,747
Mohammed, R A	1	9	2	0	1	22.2	8,028	11,531
Mollers Racing	8	37	11	5	7	29.7	178,719	251,369
Molossi, Terence M	1	8	1	0	0	12.5	3,077	3,077
Monteith, Lt-Col W L	4	8	3	0	0	37.5	7,558	7,558
Moore, Miss S	1	10	2	0	0	20.0	5,815	5,815
Morgan, Mrs Marion C	1	7	1	0	2	14.3	3,623	5,122
Morgan, L A	3	24	1	2	0	4.2	2,243	6,271
Morgan, Mrs B L	1	13	1	0	0	7.7	2,951	3,160
Morgan, Mrs M T	1	7	1	0	1	14.3	3,184	3,644
Morgan, Billy	1	12	1	1	0	8.3	3,761	7,301
Morris, David	1	9	1	0	0	11.1	4,890	5,268
Morrish, J K	1	6	1	2	1	16.7	2,490	4,355
Morrison, J S	2	17	2	3	3	11.8	31,082	47,750
Morriss, H H	1	9	2	2	0	22.2	7,878	11,202
Mort, David	2	10	1	1	2	10.0	10,464	23,900
Mortimer, George	2	15	2	1	4	13.3	5,404	10,743
Morton, A L R	1	1	1	0	0	100.0	3,948	3,948
Moss, Mrs Jill	1	7	1	1	0	14.3	3,623	4,683
Mountain, J A	3	15	1	0	1	6.7	3,590	3,921
Mountifield, Mrs J B	2	8	1	4	1	12.5	3,436	11,240
Mubarak, Sheikh Essa Bin	4	22	6	4	7	27.3	41,716	95,263
Multiyork Ltd	2	10	1	1	2	10.0	3,524	7,608
Mumford, Lady Mary	2	10	2	2	1	20.0	12,618	20,806
Murdoch, J C	1	12	3	2	0	25.0	9,599	11,398
Murphy, M A	1	14	1	3	2	7.1	3,366	6,930
Murphy, T H Stuart D Egan J	1	2	1	0	0	50.0	2,742	2,742
Murray, Mrs S D	2	17	2	2	2	11.8	4,661	7,219
Mursell, J W	4	33	4	4	3	12.1	73,802	100,304
Mussabah, Butti	2	9	1	1	1	11.1	4,273	9,918
Myers, Martin	4	19	3	2	2	15.8	12,694	17,454
Myers, J H	2	13	2	3	1	15.4	5,502	7,985
Myers, Mrs Nicole	2	7	1	2	0	14.3	3,377	5,865
Mytton, Gordon	4	24	1	0	2	4.2	3,494	6,137
Nabavi, P	1	4	1	0	0	25.0	2,259	2,471
Napier, Mrs N	5	22	2	2	0	9.1	14,445	17,989
Nasib, Yahya	4	26	4	2	3	15.4	11,898	15,605
Naughton, J	6	32	4	4	4	12.5	21,227	28,347
Naughton, Mrs J T	4	20	3	2	1	15.0	7,884	10,024
Neilson, Mrs Jean	1	10	1	1	1	10.0	3,095	4,555
Nelson, C R	1	6	1	0	0	16.7	2,070	2,070
Network Builders Ltd	2	11	1	0	0	9.1	3,720	4,193
Newall, Robert F S	2	7	2	0	1	28.6	6,164	7,303
Newberry, M C	1	11	1	1	1	9.1	3,290	4,479
Newbould, Mrs E E	2	10	2	0	2	20.0	4,475	5,424
Newcombe, A G	7	26	1	1	2	3.8	3,236	5,301
New Covent Garden Flower Sales	1	13	2	4	1	15.4	5,918	9,887
New House Farm Livery Stables	1	7	1	0	0	14.3	3,600	3,600
Newman, Peter	1	5	1	0	0	20.0	2,924	3,599
Newsome, Tim	2	6	1	1	0	16.7	2,406	3,024
Newson, R A	2	6	1	0	2	16.7	2,899	3,756
Newton, Dennis	2	9	1	1	1	11.1	2,448	3,879
Newton, Mrs B	1	12	3	1	5	25.0	53,954	62,384
Niarchos, S S	11	24	3	6	8	12.5	132,125	205,092
Nielsen, B E	8	48	6	14	8	12.5	89,961	216,617
Nimrod Company	1	3	1	0	0	33.3	4,435	4,435
Nixon, S	1	11	3	2	3	27.3	10,238	14,423
Nixon, J	1	3	2	0	0	66.7	4,486	4,486

WINNING FLAT RACE OWNERS IN 1993

	H	R	W	2	3	%W-R	£WIN	£W/P
Nordan, Brian	2	9	3	2	0	33.3	25,885	34,222
Norfolk, Lavinia Duchess Of	3	12	2	0	3	16.7	5,581	7,153
Normandy Developments (London)	4	27	4	4	1	14.8	15,320	25,822
North, Mrs H.	2	14	3	2	1	21.4	11,321	16,544
North Cheshire Trading & Storage Ltd	2	5	1	0	1	20.0	2,070	2,290
Northeast Press Limited	1	6	3	1	0	50.0	8,704	11,192
Norton, S G	4	20	2	2	4	10.0	5,445	9,051
Norton, Mrs Angela	2	11	2	0	0	18.2	6,446	6,446
N T C (Racing) Limited	4	29	1	3	3	3.4	4,807	20,844
Obaida, Mohamed	5	26	5	3	4	19.2	146,928	240,874
Oberstein, M L	5	24	4	1	7	16.7	11,053	15,861
O'Brien, Mrs M V	1	1	1	0	0	100.0	40,645	40,645
O'Brien, Mrs Helen	1	18	2	0	4	11.1	6,336	9,077
O'Connor, Mark	1	10	1	2	0	10.0	3,080	5,024
O'Donnell, Mrs M	8	60	5	3	3	8.3	21,724	27,792
O'Donovan, J F	1	13	1	3	2	7.7	4,175	7,700
O'Flaherty, T	1	9	1	1	0	11.1	2,406	4,302
O'Gorman, W H	2	6	1	0	0	16.7	4,280	11,183
Ohrstrom, George L	3	20	2	4	4	10.0	8,985	19,394
Olden, M	2	10	3	0	2	30.0	15,145	16,143
Oliver, J N	1	5	1	0	0	20.0	2,601	2,601
Oliver, G.	1	6	1	0	0	16.7	3,754	3,754
Olivier, Mrs R	2	13	2	0	1	15.4	6,247	7,297
Olley, C T	2	5	2	0	1	40.0	37,283	64,616
Olsson, Mrs M E.	1	12	2	1	0	16.7	6,029	7,203
Olympic Racing	2	7	1	1	0	14.3	3,392	4,713
Ong, Mrs W K	1	4	1	0	0	25.0	2,553	2,553
Oon, S T.	1	3	1	0	1	33.3	3,184	3,547
Oppenheimer, Sir Philip	15	48	10	6	7	20.8	120,608	156,580
Oppenheimer, Miss Sophie	1	6	3	0	0	50.0	18,739	19,844
Oppenheimer, A E	2	10	2	5	1	20.0	6,980	13,956
Oram, Matthew	1	3	1	1	0	33.3	4,226	7,319
Oram, Mrs W A	1	11	1	1	1	9.1	6,258	8,898
Orpen-Palmer, M B	1	5	1	0	0	20.0	2,415	2,415
Oseman, Mrs K	1	9	1	2	1	11.1	3,132	5,059
O'Sullivan, Patrick G	2	12	1	2	0	8.3	5,047	8,184
O'Toole, Starling	1	2	1	0	0	50.0	2,686	2,686
Oxton, Brian	2	22	4	3	4	18.2	19,497	27,340
P & S Lever Partners	1	9	1	1	2	11.1	21,500	29,107
Page, Mrs S	1	10	1	5	1	10.0	1,548	6,670
Painting, Trevor	4	19	2	2	0	10.5	10,435	12,861
Palacegate Corporation Ltd	7	55	12	14	7	21.8	55,362	73,547
Palmer, Keith H.	1	9	2	0	0	22.2	10,067	11,617
Palmer, Mrs M.	1	9	1	0	0	11.1	1,380	1,380
Parker, Richard	1	9	1	1	1	11.1	2,512	4,351
Parkers Of Peterborough Plc	1	6	1	3	2	16.7	2,070	5,060
Parkes, J.	1	3	1	0	0	33.3	3,371	3,371
Parrish, Malcolm	9	20	1	2	1	5.0	3,630	6,694
Pascall, M R	1	5	1	0	0	20.0	3,077	3,077
Pasquale, Terry	1	11	1	3	1	9.1	3,641	6,396
Paton, A P	2	12	1	2	0	8.3	3,641	6,067
Patrick, A J de V	1	11	1	0	3	9.1	2,070	3,173
Patrington Haven Leisure Park	1	11	1	1	2	9.1	3,106	4,569
Pattimore, M	1	8	2	0	0	25.0	4,995	4,995
Pattison, J	3	22	1	2	5	4.5	3,236	7,926
Payne, R B	2	13	2	1	2	15.4	5,550	7,936
Pearce, Henry	1	14	2	3	2	14.3	7,093	11,619
Pearce, J L C.	8	37	2	5	6	5.4	7,684	24,782
Pearson, T R.	5	14	3	1	3	21.4	9,862	12,315
Pedersen, S	5	21	2	1	2	9.5	4,143	5,829
Peebles, Roy	2	24	3	3	1	12.5	26,321	29,437
Peebles, Mrs Norma	2	19	1	5	0	5.3	1,548	5,447
Pennick, C J	1	8	3	0	4	37.5	9,309	11,220
Penser, E	1	7	2	2	0	28.6	26,932	35,504
Perratt, Miss L A	2	8	1	1	1	12.5	2,899	3,723
Perrin, Mrs K L	1	14	2	2	1	14.3	6,807	10,197
Perry, A R	2	8	1	0	1	12.5	3,028	3,414
Persian Partnership	1	5	2	0	2	40.0	11,510	19,154
Pescod, Michael	1	2	1	1	0	50.0	5,439	6,759
Peters, T C	1	10	1	0	2	10.0	3,699	5,840
Petyt, C J	1	9	1	3	2	11.1	4,241	10,082
Pharaohs Computers Ltd	1	10	1	0	2	10.0	3,339	4,222
P H Betts (Holdings) Ltd	3	17	1	2	1	5.9	4,113	12,807
Phillips, Lady Katharine	1	7	1	0	1	14.3	4,963	6,862
Pick, E	1	8	5	1	0	62.5	21,874	25,717
Pickard, J H	6	37	1	4	4	2.7	5,952	18,917
Pickering, D O.	7	29	2	1	4	6.9	7,570	10,963
Pickering, Mrs Maureen	1	8	1	3	3	12.5	6,374	24,822

	H	R	W	2	3	%W-R	£WIN	£W/P
Pickford, Mrs D.	1	10	1	1	2	10.0	2,560	4,307
Pike, Mrs Janet M	1	18	1	1	1	5.6	3,469	6,383
Pilkington, Sir Thomas	3	10	3	0	0	30.0	10,449	11,022
Pinnacle Racing Stable	4	11	2	1	0	18.2	6,316	8,086
Pin Oak Stable	2	12	3	4	1	25.0	19,450	51,668
Pipe, M C	3	9	2	0	1	22.2	5,418	5,733
P I P Electrics Limited	1	9	2	0	0	22.2	4,968	5,238
Pitts, Terry	1	7	1	0	0	14.3	3,003	3,257
Planflow (Leasing) Ltd	2	7	1	0	2	14.3	2,259	3,384
Platt, G R	3	11	1	0	0	9.1	2,511	2,872
Player, P D	2	10	3	2	1	30.0	10,773	19,819
Playforth, D	1	11	2	1	3	18.2	5,185	9,123
Pleasant Racing Club	1	11	1	1	2	9.1	2,467	4,030
Poland, Michael	4	15	5	0	0	33.3	104,873	105,109
Polglase, M J	1	14	5	2	0	35.7	16,301	18,622
Pollins, Brian	2	13	1	1	2	7.7	2,245	4,210
Ponsonby, W H	2	9	1	2	1	11.1	3,655	6,853
Poole, A.	1	9	2	0	4	22.2	4,730	5,976
Pooler, B	1	4	1	0	2	25.0	3,443	4,060
Popely, R A	3	11	5	1	0	45.5	40,526	41,562
Portman, Lady	1	6	1	1	1	16.7	3,161	5,541
Portman, Lord	3	12	3	1	1	25.0	10,981	12,875
Powell, Mrs C J	2	17	2	2	3	11.8	6,929	15,554
Pratt, Miss Vivian	1	8	3	0	0	37.5	23,262	23,418
Previte, Miss S	1	11	2	1	0	18.2	8,168	9,112
Price, Mrs Dorothy	2	4	1	0	0	25.0	2,826	3,050
Price, Mrs Diana	1	14	2	4	4	14.3	5,960	12,008
Price, J T	1	3	1	0	0	33.3	3,816	4,099
Price, T G	1	11	1	2	2	9.1	3,670	18,526
Price, Christopher	2	21	1	1	4	4.8	3,728	11,075
Pride Of Britain Limited	1	4	1	0	2	25.0	11,963	13,087
Princess Nicholas Von Preussen	1	6	1	1	1	16.7	3,436	14,349
Pritchard-Gordon, Giles W	8	47	5	5	5	10.6	16,243	36,322
Protheroe-Beynon, Mrs W	1	9	1	0	2	11.1	2,847	3,728
Pryce, Mrs Irene	1	17	2	3	3	11.8	5,630	9,236
Purcell, John	13	45	4	0	3	8.9	12,989	15,227
Pye-Jeary, Anthony	4	19	1	2	0	5.3	2,742	4,266
Quesnel, Nick	1	2	1	0	0	50.0	2,611	2,611
Quicksteel Ltd	1	11	1	2	0	9.1	2,448	3,982
Quinn, M	2	19	3	4	1	15.8	9,460	14,593
Quinn, Mrs A	1	12	1	1	2	8.3	5,381	9,075
Quintet Partnership	1	10	2	1	1	20.0	5,148	6,467
Quinton, M G St.	2	14	1	1	3	7.1	5,452	9,468
Racecourse Farm Racing	1	10	1	0	2	10.0	3,676	4,427
Ramsden, Mrs J R	3	20	1	3	2	5.0	3,287	9,589
Ramsden, Jonathan	1	18	3	0	1	16.7	20,121	20,746
Rapkins, Mrs Val.	4	34	5	6	3	14.7	17,468	26,884
Ratcliffe, J M	2	12	2	0	0	16.7	10,765	10,863
Rausing, Miss K.	5	15	2	3	1	13.3	5,505	12,500
Rawding, Miss Amanda J	2	13	1	0	1	7.7	3,454	4,382
Rawson, Mrs Christine	3	18	1	1	0	5.6	2,951	3,959
Raymond Kilgour Holdings Ltd	2	17	2	6	2	11.8	5,678	11,679
Redden, J	1	6	2	1	2	33.3	6,056	8,031
Reditt, M.	2	8	1	0	3	12.5	1,993	2,902
Redman, T S	1	17	1	3	1	5.9	3,758	6,405
Redmond, J A	7	38	3	3	3	7.9	11,380	20,062
Red Rose Partnership	1	11	1	0	1	9.1	3,210	3,719
Reece, Sir Gordon	1	11	1	0	1	9.1	2,243	2,986
Reglar, Mrs J	1	9	1	2	0	11.1	3,046	4,932
Reid, A S.	6	26	4	1	3	15.4	15,549	20,384
Reitel, E.	4	13	1	0	1	7.7	3,417	3,792
Richard Green (Fine Paintings)	6	35	2	6	1	5.7	6,973	14,243
Richards, Ray	7	38	6	2	0	15.8	37,119	41,940
Richmond, Mrs Julia	2	17	1	0	4	5.9	3,670	6,350
Richmond-Watson, S J	1	2	2	0	0	100.0	20,476	20,476
Richmond-Watson, J H	4	19	1	3	4	5.3	2,070	23,747
Riddell, N A	1	16	2	0	1	12.5	6,688	7,085
Ridley, Mrs D	2	16	3	1	1	18.8	10,058	12,278
Riley-Smith, T S M S.	7	76	11	3	3	14.5	38,314	46,790
Rizzo, Anthony	1	8	1	0	1	12.5	5,020	5,465
Roalco Limited	1	4	1	0	0	25.0	2,637	2,637
Roberts, David	1	5	1	1	0	20.0	2,579	3,149
Robertson, William	1	13	4	2	1	30.8	26,842	36,619
Robertson, A S.	1	17	2	3	3	11.8	6,189	9,909
Robins, Mrs Shirley	7	36	4	4	1	11.1	15,345	28,114
Robinson, R (Wigan)	1	11	3	2	3	27.3	7,526	11,209
Robinson, A W	2	8	1	0	1	12.5	3,496	3,901
Roborough, Lord & Lady	6	26	2	3	3	7.7	5,511	12,728

	H	R	W	2	3	%W-R	£WIN	£W/P
Robson/Pattinson Partnership	1	13	1	1	1	7.7	4,844	6,564
Rogers, M J	1	7	2	3	0	28.6	5,746	8,398
Roldvale Limited	20	108	20	11	7	18.5	262,446	361,417
Rolt, D W	1	14	3	2	1	21.4	8,218	11,079
Roots, Stephen	2	14	1	1	1	7.1	2,899	5,171
Rosario, R Del	2	8	1	0	0	12.5	2,233	2,233
Rose, J	4	15	1	1	3	6.7	3,290	6,027
Ross, Barry J	1	7	2	1	0	28.6	20,331	23,601
Roteman, Nicholas	1	7	1	0	1	14.3	4,455	5,040
Rothschild, Baron Edouard de	4	15	1	2	3	6.7	10,203	22,069
Rothschild, Sir Evelyn de.	1	5	2	0	3	40.0	8,093	10,655
Rovera, Miss P	2	5	4	0	0	80.0	20,889	20,889
Rowlands, Cliffe	2	6	1	0	0	16.7	3,005	3,005
Rowles, J W	3	15	1	0	3	6.7	3,840	5,806
Roxburghe, Duke Of	2	5	1	0	0	20.0	4,450	4,450
Ruelles Partners	1	9	1	4	1	11.1	5,385	20,927
Russell, Mrs J B	1	11	2	2	0	18.2	19,842	27,344
Ryan, Shane T	1	4	1	0	1	25.0	2,243	2,565
Ryan, M J	2	7	1	0	0	14.3	2,448	2,448
Ryan, Mrs M J	3	11	1	0	0	9.1	2,679	2,927
Saeed, Ali	4	16	2	1	3	12.5	30,057	60,728
Sage, Stephen Philip	1	5	1	0	0	20.0	2,322	2,322
Said, Wafic	2	8	1	2	2	12.5	3,818	94,878
Sainaghi, G	1	4	1	3	0	25.0	78,598	108,787
Sainsbury, F J	10	49	5	5	3	10.2	19,603	28,487
Salimeni, S E	1	6	1	0	0	16.7	3,668	3,668
Salman, Fahd	68	265	36	50	47	13.6	209,610	352,782
Salman, Faisal	3	5	1	0	0	20.0	2,868	3,521
Sampson, G C	1	8	3	1	1	37.5	9,137	14,085
Sanders, Miss Brooke	2	6	1	0	1	16.7	3,085	3,544
Sanderson, G G	1	9	2	2	0	22.2	8,690	10,322
Sandmoor Textiles Co Ltd	1	6	1	0	2	16.7	3,948	4,871
Sangster, R E	60	212	45	32	20	21.2	411,286	678,889
Saumtally, B M	1	17	2	5	2	11.8	6,217	22,471
Saunders, M S	2	11	2	1	1	18.2	5,558	7,553
Savill, P D	52	337	50	48	46	14.8	221,772	332,640
Scargill, Mrs Susan	3	11	2	4	1	18.2	5,857	9,744
Scarsdale, Lord	6	51	3	8	3	5.9	8,469	17,486
Schwarzenbach, Urs E	3	16	3	1	2	18.8	18,597	22,892
Scothern, T A	4	31	3	5	4	9.7	11,534	23,000
Scott, Mrs J J Kirk	3	26	1	4	6	3.8	3,184	9,608
Scott, A A	1	11	1	0	0	9.1	2,769	2,769
Scott, David	1	4	1	0	1	25.0	3,231	3,763
Scott-Dunn, Mrs P	1	7	1	0	1	14.3	2,243	2,848
Scuderia Golden Horse S R L	1	1	1	0	0	100.0	4,932	4,932
Scuderia Rencati Srl	3	6	1	2	0	16.7	3,080	9,398
Scullion, Mrs Elke	1	10	1	4	1	10.0	4,305	10,515
Searle, J W	1	7	1	0	0	14.3	2,763	2,763
Sevremont, Miss Therese	1	4	1	0	1	25.0	4,950	5,745
Seymour, J P	1	7	2	1	0	28.6	5,430	7,928
Shack, J	2	8	1	0	3	12.5	3,273	4,371
Shah, H R H Sultan Ahmad	7	30	5	3	1	16.7	23,242	41,971
Shannon, R J	2	13	3	0	1	23.1	9,582	10,678
Sharkey, Paul	2	7	1	2	2	14.3	3,319	6,662
Sharp, Stanley J	2	8	3	2	2	37.5	74,235	94,445
Sharratt, Mrs Christine	1	7	1	1	1	14.3	2,406	4,116
Shead, A D	1	8	1	1	1	12.5	3,028	5,045
Sheet & Roll Convertors Ltd	2	14	1	3	2	7.1	2,070	5,119
Shekells, D A	2	8	1	2	1	12.5	3,779	7,258
Shenkin, Dr Ian R	2	23	4	5	2	17.4	32,994	50,810
Shepherd, Miss E	1	8	1	0	1	12.5	2,821	3,303
Sheppard, Mrs Carol	2	11	1	3	0	9.1	1,770	3,455
Sheridan, Miss M T	1	11	1	0	0	9.1	3,391	3,826
Sheriffe, Miss M	1	6	1	1	0	16.7	3,818	6,992
Shiacolas, C	1	7	1	0	0	14.3	3,114	3,229
Short, C W Sumner And Jim	1	9	1	0	1	11.1	5,898	8,621
Shouler, G E	4	17	2	3	1	11.8	6,627	11,018
Siddall, Miss L C	6	28	2	2	5	7.1	4,476	7,797
Sieff, D	3	12	3	2	2	25.0	11,423	14,476
Sifton, Mrs June M	3	13	3	1	1	23.1	13,137	15,929
Silks, Purple	3	16	1	0	1	6.3	3,085	3,508
Sillars Civil Engineering	1	6	1	0	0	16.7	3,611	3,611
Simmons, S J	1	1	1	0	0	100.0	2,355	2,355
Simpson, Alasdair	1	9	2	1	3	22.2	7,716	12,504
Simpson, Mrs Leonard	4	19	1	0	2	5.3	5,481	6,950
Sims, Mrs A G	3	19	3	0	4	15.8	11,418	16,743
Sinanan, Mrs Margaret	1	5	1	3	1	20.0	2,905	7,130
Skelding, S	3	10	1	2	1	10.0	3,787	6,284

	H	R	W	2	3	%W-R	£WIN	£W/P
Skeltools Ltd	1	8	2	2	0	25.0	5,540	7,419
Skirton, B P	2	5	1	1	0	20.0	3,436	4,736
Skyline Racing Ltd	12	38	3	3	2	7.9	11,029	14,382
Slaney, Jeff	1	8	1	0	1	12.5	3,080	3,422
Smalley, R.	1	7	1	0	1	14.3	2,742	3,507
Smart, G M	3	17	2	1	1	11.8	9,085	13,882
Smeaton, A K.	1	9	1	2	2	11.1	2,779	6,994
Smith, Trevor J	1	14	1	1	2	7.1	2,880	4,608
Smith, Miss Judy	1	6	1	2	0	16.7	2,243	3,741
Smith, Mrs G A E.	2	8	3	0	0	37.5	275,271	275,271
Smith, M D	1	5	2	1	0	40.0	23,847	46,997
Smith, J C	22	84	14	10	11	16.7	227,700	299,042
Smith, Alex.	1	8	1	0	0	12.5	2,762	2,762
Smith, Mrs A	4	13	1	0	1	7.7	2,070	2,363
Smith, J Bryan	1	5	1	0	0	20.0	3,583	3,811
Smith, Mrs G R.	1	8	1	2	1	12.5	2,821	5,141
Smith, Willie.	1	7	1	0	0	14.3	2,243	2,448
Snook, Laurie	4	18	3	1	1	16.7	9,553	11,545
Soberg-Olsen, O	4	20	3	4	3	15.0	9,891	15,839
Solomon, W E	1	14	3	3	5	21.4	21,707	28,006
Southall, Miss Jane	2	7	1	1	1	14.3	1,380	2,265
Southam, Mrs B D	2	17	2	3	1	11.8	7,163	10,968
Southgate Racing	1	4	1	1	1	25.0	4,110	5,696
Spargo, Alan.	1	13	1	3	1	7.7	3,996	8,938
Speelman, Anthony	3	9	1	2	1	11.1	3,348	7,177
Spence, A D	4	18	4	2	1	22.2	15,663	19,190
Spence, Christopher	2	9	3	0	2	33.3	11,008	13,284
Spencer-Phillips, Mrs S H	1	4	1	1	1	25.0	8,610	10,367
Spensley, Miss Jane	1	8	2	2	1	25.0	7,182	17,160
Speyer, Alan J.	2	24	2	2	1	8.3	8,948	11,966
Sporting Partners	4	25	1	2	1	4.0	2,070	4,297
Stamp, Paul.	1	5	1	0	1	20.0	2,511	3,621
Stanley, E R W	4	12	1	1	0	8.3	6,212	8,357
Starkey, S	1	9	1	1	2	11.1	2,685	4,716
Steadfast Engineering Company Ltd	1	8	2	1	0	25.0	5,841	7,129
Steckmest, H J W	1	4	1	0	0	25.0	2,803	2,803
Steel, Miss S	1	5	1	0	0	20.0	3,210	3,210
Steele, Mrs O K.	1	13	1	1	1	7.7	7,044	8,714
Steinberg, G	8	50	2	1	5	4.0	7,973	12,701
Stelling, Dr Carlos E	4	17	5	3	1	29.4	31,133	53,229
Stevens, C H	1	7	1	0	0	14.3	3,340	3,340
Stevens, Mrs C M	1	9	1	0	2	11.1	2,070	2,937
Stevenson, R M	1	8	2	2	0	25.0	3,082	5,130
Steventon, John	1	5	1	0	0	20.0	2,469	2,634
Stewart, N M	1	6	1	2	0	16.7	3,494	13,047
Stockdale, E	1	13	2	1	1	15.4	5,857	7,725
Stoddard, A	1	7	1	2	2	14.3	3,003	6,545
Stoddart, D R.	1	5	1	0	0	20.0	2,660	2,660
Stokes, Byron J	2	9	1	1	1	11.1	2,950	5,130
Stonethorn Stud Farms Limited	1	7	1	2	0	14.3	3,782	6,072
Stovold, Mrs S J	3	16	3	2	2	18.8	15,161	21,177
Straker, Major I C.	1	5	1	1	0	20.0	3,236	4,142
Strauss, Jimmy	1	6	1	2	0	16.7	4,143	7,895
Strawbridge, George	9	36	4	8	5	11.1	20,067	35,469
Sturgess, Michael.	1	10	2	0	1	20.0	20,537	22,779
Sturgis, Keith	3	24	2	4	1	8.3	6,404	10,591
Sturman, Mrs S	1	11	1	3	3	9.1	2,847	6,752
Sturt, W E.	5	17	7	1	2	41.2	20,725	24,605
Suhail, Mohamed.	5	20	1	6	0	5.0	4,836	18,014
Suhail, Saeed.	8	36	5	5	10	13.9	23,730	40,541
Sujanani, Victor	2	8	1	0	1	12.5	3,590	4,551
Sumner, Mrs B	5	26	1	3	2	3.8	13,047	23,892
Sunley, John B	1	3	1	0	0	33.3	3,080	3,080
Swaythling, Lord	5	17	1	2	1	5.9	1,826	4,933
Swaythling, Lady	1	10	2	3	1	20.0	7,733	13,354
Swiers, J E	2	7	2	0	0	28.6	11,131	11,131
Swinburne, J A.	1	6	1	0	2	16.7	2,379	3,112
Swire, Miss B.	3	17	1	1	1	5.9	3,582	5,679
Symonds, B K	1	10	1	3	1	10.0	3,236	8,582
Taberner, S	5	19	1	0	1	5.3	2,574	2,916
Tam Racing	1	12	1	1	1	8.3	2,679	4,704
Tate, Mrs Susan	1	10	1	2	0	10.0	2,469	4,647
Tateson, C S.	1	5	1	0	0	20.0	3,262	3,484
Taverner, Miss Antonia	1	6	2	2	1	33.3	6,638	9,640
Tavistock, Lord	3	10	1	2	0	10.0	3,231	6,172
Taylor, P A.	1	7	1	0	1	14.3	3,339	3,840
Taylor, B J	1	6	2	1	1	33.3	7,765	19,859
Taylor, Geo	3	15	2	1	1	13.3	5,527	6,756

WINNING FLAT RACE OWNERS IN 1993

	H	R	W	2	3	%W-R	£WIN	£W/P
Taylor, Mrs M	1	4	1	0	1	25.0	4,710	5,569
Tennant, Lady	3	25	4	4	3	16.0	16,509	28,292
Teversham, Mrs M S	1	9	1	0	3	11.1	2,070	3,047
The 2nd Kingsley House Partnership	4	28	5	7	3	17.9	12,263	20,304
The Bloodstock Brothers	1	6	1	0	2	16.7	3,348	4,449
The Bridge Club	2	14	3	4	0	21.4	7,081	9,847
The Country Life Partnership	1	6	1	0	1	16.7	3,080	5,495
The County Group	1	7	1	2	1	14.3	2,243	3,847
The Durdans Four (II) Two	1	11	2	1	2	18.2	5,420	7,052
The Equema Partnership	1	6	1	0	1	16.7	1,941	2,335
The Exclusive Partnership	2	11	1	1	1	9.1	1,730	3,334
The Fairyhouse 1992 Partnership	4	32	4	6	3	12.5	11,252	17,613
The Fairy Story Partnership	1	7	2	1	0	28.6	12,465	13,947
The Five To Seven Partnership	1	8	3	0	0	37.5	9,638	9,638
The Gymcrak Thoroughbred Racing Club	5	17	1	1	1	5.9	2,243	5,329
The Hammond Partnership	10	62	6	3	4	9.7	21,409	33,213
The Jampot Partnership	2	12	3	1	0	25.0	26,647	30,111
The Kismetim Partnership	1	12	1	1	2	8.3	3,670	5,803
The Lime Street Racing Syndicate	1	5	1	1	0	20.0	3,210	4,145
The Losers Owners Group	1	9	1	2	2	11.1	2,489	5,278
The Mariners Partnership	1	11	1	3	2	9.1	1,380	4,185
The Monkey Racing Club Limited	10	58	4	9	6	6.9	12,558	23,875
The MSA Partnership	1	11	4	0	2	36.4	16,166	17,643
The Winning Line	1	6	1	0	1	16.7	3,036	4,399
Theobalds Stud	4	20	2	2	2	10.0	5,662	8,846
The Oh So Risky Syndicate	1	5	1	1	0	20.0	7,015	27,210
The PBT Group	2	15	2	0	2	13.3	5,375	6,472
The Pendley Associates	1	7	1	0	0	14.3	3,202	3,507
The Pendley Punters	1	4	1	0	0	25.0	3,933	4,201
The Riston Racing Partnership	1	6	1	0	0	16.7	3,688	3,929
Thesiger, Miss N F	2	10	1	1	0	10.0	2,070	2,450
The Snailwell Stud Company Limited	1	1	1	0	0	100.0	4,737	4,737
The Storm Syndicate	3	31	1	2	2	3.2	3,566	8,218
The Superlatives	1	9	1	2	1	11.1	2,977	6,031
The Sussex Stud Limited	3	17	1	1	3	5.9	5,090	8,263
The Tompkins Team	1	7	2	1	1	28.6	5,600	6,623
The Valentines	1	12	3	2	1	25.0	13,248	19,976
The Winning Team	8	43	10	4	6	23.3	43,673	57,515
Thomas, B	2	17	1	1	1	5.9	3,158	4,711
Thomas, C	1	9	1	1	1	11.1	3,366	4,453
Thomas, E R	4	28	3	3	2	10.7	8,939	12,044
Thomas, J A	1	9	1	0	2	11.1	4,878	6,203
Thomas, R J	2	30	3	2	4	10.0	11,810	17,006
Thomlinson's	1	14	2	5	2	14.3	8,688	16,390
Thompson, Mrs David	8	28	7	8	2	25.0	24,517	39,144
Thompson, Mrs Beverley	1	1	1	0	0	100.0	2,070	2,070
Thompson, David	5	20	2	3	2	10.0	6,734	23,684
Thompson, George S	3	19	2	0	1	10.5	7,882	8,912
Thompson, S	1	13	1	2	2	7.7	2,899	5,430
Thomson, Mrs J A	2	12	2	0	1	16.7	5,784	6,688
Thornhill, R	1	11	1	1	1	9.1	2,219	3,120
Threadwell, S M	1	6	2	0	0	33.3	5,491	5,491
Three Ply Racing	1	10	2	1	2	20.0	5,985	7,844
Times Of Wigan	2	12	2	0	2	16.7	5,021	5,855
Tindall, S P	4	11	1	2	1	9.1	4,342	7,698
Tinkler, Mrs Marie	1	9	1	2	1	11.1	2,070	4,141
Toller, Miss U D	1	3	1	0	1	33.3	39,640	40,466
Tomkins, C	2	23	2	0	2	8.7	6,212	7,399
Tooth, Raymond	7	33	4	1	2	12.1	14,468	18,736
Tory, R J	1	3	1	0	0	33.3	3,184	5,147
Travellers T Time Club	1	5	1	1	1	20.0	2,736	3,503
Treadwell, Mrs Penny	1	6	1	1	1	16.7	2,678	4,222
Treglown, Graham	2	23	3	3	0	13.0	10,154	12,864
Tribe, Mrs C	2	9	1	0	1	11.1	3,052	3,445
Triple Crowners I	1	7	2	3	0	28.6	9,182	15,758
Triple Crowners III	1	7	1	1	0	14.3	3,377	4,377
Trobe, Mrs D A La	1	5	1	0	1	20.0	3,231	4,720
Trojan Racing	1	8	1	0	0	12.5	2,925	2,925
Trotman, Brian	1	7	1	0	0	14.3	1,725	1,725
Trow Lane Farm	4	25	2	5	1	8.0	7,351	13,713
Truckhaven Limited	1	2	1	0	0	50.0	3,377	3,377
Tulloch, Mrs W	1	5	1	1	0	20.0	12,231	13,275
Turner, D	1	10	5	1	1	50.0	17,852	19,317
Turner, W H	1	6	1	0	2	16.7	2,201	2,930
Twigden, Ivan	1	12	2	1	0	16.7	5,875	7,432
Tyldesley, F	1	6	1	2	0	16.7	3,319	13,837
Tylor, P A	1	8	1	2	1	12.5	2,469	5,137
Ullmann, Baron G Von	1	3	1	1	1	33.3	7,505	42,182

	H	R	W	2	3	%W-R	£WIN	£W/P
Umm Qarn Racing	2	5	2	0	0	40.0	7,382	7,382
Unity Farm Holiday Centre Ltd	4	31	4	3	2	12.9	22,456	33,954
Usher, M D I	3	18	1	0	1	5.6	2,930	3,558
Valentini, Ms K	3	10	1	0	0	10.0	1,051	1,051
Vax Appliances Ltd	2	17	3	2	1	17.6	16,999	20,348
Venture Racing Ltd	1	10	1	3	0	10.0	2,950	5,623
Vestey, T & J	2	16	5	2	3	31.3	58,864	67,919
Vestey, Lord	6	25	4	4	4	16.0	51,695	82,747
Vestey, The Lady	1	2	1	0	1	50.0	4,598	6,143
Vickers, Miss L J	2	12	2	1	3	16.7	8,935	12,524
Vines, M G	2	12	1	1	1	8.3	2,951	4,101
Vintage Racing	2	16	1	1	0	6.3	4,890	6,222
Vintage Services Limited	1	9	1	0	3	11.1	2,826	4,979
Voak, B H	5	31	1	4	4	3.2	4,747	24,332
Vogt, Ian A	1	17	2	2	4	11.8	6,615	11,693
Wacker, Charles H III	2	10	2	4	2	20.0	8,465	18,379
Wakley, A G	1	15	1	5	2	6.7	3,348	10,669
Walford, Mrs C R	1	7	1	0	0	14.3	3,200	3,436
Walford, Christopher	1	6	1	3	0	16.7	3,524	6,893
Walker, Ms Christine	1	9	3	0	2	33.3	13,518	14,929
Walwyn, P T	1	1	1	0	0	100.0	0	0
Wane, Mrs H H	3	6	1	0	1	16.7	5,428	6,018
Wane, Mrs H	5	32	2	0	7	6.3	6,684	10,021
Ward, L H J	8	51	6	6	4	11.8	29,377	47,083
Ward, Mrs George	2	8	2	1	0	25.0	10,965	12,322
Ward, Mrs J E	1	6	1	0	0	16.7	2,322	2,716
Ward, George	4	6	1	1	0	16.7	4,932	5,980
Wardle, Cecil W	1	5	1	0	0	20.0	2,427	2,427
Warren, B J	1	12	4	1	1	33.3	15,475	17,368
Waters, G D	2	5	2	1	0	40.0	5,807	6,676
Wates, Mrs Michael	1	5	1	1	0	20.0	3,553	5,287
Watkins, Ron	1	5	1	2	0	20.0	2,400	3,809
Watson, Mrs R T	2	14	5	2	0	35.7	28,013	40,451
Watson, David R	1	5	1	1	2	20.0	3,915	8,507
Watson, M J	2	33	4	3	2	12.1	17,637	23,432
Watt, Michael H	2	9	1	0	2	11.1	7,310	14,025
Watt, Mrs Mary	2	10	1	4	1	10.0	2,794	6,146
Watts, Lady D M	2	15	1	1	1	6.7	6,664	9,804
Wauchope, Michael	1	7	2	1	3	28.6	6,512	8,935
Weatherby, Mrs D	1	13	5	2	0	38.5	15,220	17,015
Webster, L	1	15	3	3	4	20.0	9,100	14,343
Webster, C A	1	8	1	2	0	12.5	2,070	3,559
Weinstock, Lord	18	72	12	17	8	16.7	117,502	197,591
Welch, Mrs Carol J	1	5	2	1	0	40.0	7,578	8,769
Welfare, Racing	1	5	2	0	0	40.0	17,755	18,490
Wells, T J	1	11	1	1	1	9.1	3,377	4,663
Wentdale Const Ltd	1	7	1	2	0	14.3	3,630	15,775
Wertheimer, J	1	1	1	0	0	100.0	109,538	109,538
Wetherall, Mrs D A	1	13	2	1	1	15.4	4,775	6,198
Wetherby Racing Bureau Plc	4	24	1	1	2	4.2	3,132	5,768
Whelan, J J	1	12	1	0	2	8.3	3,641	5,280
Wheldon, K E	7	19	1	1	2	5.3	7,439	16,567
Wheldon, Exors Of The Late Mr K E	8	32	2	7	3	6.3	5,243	16,199
Whitaker, R M	5	31	4	3	6	12.9	9,917	15,810
Whitaker, W J	2	10	2	0	0	20.0	6,032	6,032
Whitcombe Manor Racing Stables Limited	2	10	2	0	1	20.0	5,434	6,611
White, P J	3	21	2	0	0	9.5	6,205	7,197
White, Michael	2	17	2	4	2	11.8	7,715	17,622
White, Anthony	7	48	2	7	3	4.2	6,667	15,613
White, Mrs P A	2	6	2	1	0	33.3	4,811	5,699
Whitehead, Ron	1	12	5	0	1	41.7	14,906	16,020
Whitehead, Miss Amanda	1	7	1	0	0	14.3	3,377	3,584
Whitelaw, Brian	1	11	1	3	1	9.1	7,570	11,270
Whitestonecliffe Racing Partnership	3	23	2	3	2	8.7	6,316	10,893
Whiting, Geoff	1	10	2	1	0	20.0	7,755	9,096
Whittle, S	1	4	1	0	0	25.0	3,002	3,002
Whitton, Harry	1	8	2	1	1	25.0	4,812	6,127
Whitwood, Mrs Carol	2	25	1	3	4	4.0	3,319	10,104
Whitworth, Robert	1	10	1	1	1	10.0	5,527	7,779
Whorton, G	1	10	2	1	0	20.0	5,024	6,144
Wickens, Martin	3	20	3	0	5	15.0	9,142	12,071
Wickham, Mrs Marion	3	43	6	3	7	14.0	19,562	25,728
Wigan, Mrs Dare	2	8	1	1	0	12.5	4,342	5,618
Wiggins, Cecil	2	16	1	5	3	6.3	4,533	11,577
Wigham, Mrs J L	3	13	1	0	0	7.7	3,236	4,058
Wight, I A N	1	9	2	1	1	22.2	26,285	37,230
Wilcox, J B	1	8	3	2	0	37.5	7,118	8,669
Wildenstein, Daniel	3	4	2	0	0	50.0	273,980	273,980

	H	R	W	2	3	%W-R	£WIN	£W/P
Wilkins, M A	4	20	4	4	2	20.0	12,616	17,751
Wilkinson, R J	2	14	2	2	3	14.3	8,419	12,502
Wilkinson, E.	1	4	1	0	0	25.0	2,601	3,767
Williams, Miss T	1	2	1	0	0	50.0	3,054	3,054
Williams, Rhys Thomas	6	15	1	3	0	6.7	3,494	7,987
Williams, C N	1	5	1	0	1	20.0	2,826	3,504
Williams, Exors Of The Late Mrs G P	1	9	2	2	0	22.2	7,105	9,298
Williams, Mrs E J	2	4	2	0	2	50.0	8,345	9,381
Williamson, Jerrard	1	7	3	1	2	42.9	23,302	36,054
Willis, P.	1	11	1	1	4	9.1	3,072	4,650
Wills, Sir David	6	33	5	6	6	15.2	55,936	73,009
Wilson, C Michael.	2	30	2	4	1	6.7	6,905	11,724
Wilson, D A	2	13	1	1	4	7.7	3,106	5,481
Wilson, David F.	1	7	1	0	0	14.3	3,558	4,146
Wilson, Tom	1	8	1	1	1	12.5	7,985	11,861
Windflower Overseas Holdings Inc	6	31	5	1	4	16.1	52,458	62,294
Windsor, Mrs L A	3	13	4	2	1	30.8	11,315	13,897
Winfield, Peter S	4	27	6	1	3	22.2	32,946	37,977
Winterford, Mr And Mrs M	1	7	3	1	1	42.9	16,574	18,220
Winton, Mrs Iva	1	8	1	1	1	12.5	3,913	5,310
Withers, Richard	2	10	2	0	1	20.0	5,714	6,326
Wong, Davie	6	21	4	0	4	19.0	15,060	18,468
Wong, Milton.	1	5	1	0	1	20.0	2,070	2,526
Woodall, M.	3	16	2	1	0	12.5	4,922	5,658
Woodall, Stephen.	1	2	1	0	0	50.0	5,047	5,047
Woods, S P C.	4	30	1	1	8	3.3	2,534	5,742
Worth, Michael	2	7	1	1	2	14.3	2,070	4,202
Wragg, A M	2	10	1	0	3	10.0	4,500	7,480
Wragg, G	2	4	1	0	0	25.0	5,340	5,340
Wright, Christopher	14	62	10	7	8	16.1	32,368	68,762
Wright, Mrs D.	2	15	1	0	1	6.7	3,816	4,526
Wright, Mrs Ann E M	1	3	1	0	1	33.3	4,557	5,303
Yarnold, Mrs J	1	4	1	0	0	25.0	3,553	3,553
Yarrow, M J	1	4	2	0	0	50.0	5,590	5,590
Yates, H S.	3	15	1	0	3	6.7	2,924	4,136
Yearley, Mrs Anne	2	9	1	0	0	11.1	2,952	2,952
Yeh, Dr Meou Tsen Geoffrey	2	11	3	1	1	27.3	11,834	13,404
Yong, N S	9	41	5	13	3	12.2	17,689	31,084
Yorkshire Racing Club Owners Group 1990	1	12	4	2	2	33.3	10,832	13,657
Young, E J G	1	8	3	0	0	37.5	14,688	14,688
Young, Mrs J E	1	10	1	0	2	10.0	3,054	4,801
Young, David C	1	13	2	1	0	15.4	6,072	7,167
Young, Derek.	1	7	1	1	1	14.3	2,479	3,532

Leading owners on the Flat: 1900–93

		Horses	Races Won	Value £
1900	H.R.H. The Prince of Wales	3	9	29585 10
1901	Sir G Blundell Maple	24	58	21370 0
1902	Mr R S Sievier	5	10	23686 0
1903	Sir James Miller	8	15	24768 0
1904	Sir James Miller	14	25	28923 0
1905	Col W Hall Walker	6	18	23687 0
1906	Ld Derby (late)	20	44	32926 0
1907	Col W Hall Walker	7	13	17910 0
1908	Mr J B Joel	10	19	26246 0
1909	Mr "Fairie"	6	23	37719 0
1910	Mr "Fairie"	7	17	35352 0
1911	Ld Derby	11	30	42781 0
1912	Mr T Pilkington	2	5	20822 0
1913	Mr J B Joel	17	31	25430 0
1914	Mr J B Joel	11	22	30724 0
1915	Mr L Neumann	7	7	13546 0
1916	Mr E Hulton	14	22	13764 0
1917	Mr "Fairie"	3	10	11751 0
1918	Lady James Douglas	2	5	14735 0
1919	Ld Glanely	10	45	30514 0
1920	Sir Robert Jardine	15	29	19385 0
1921	Mr S B Joel	21	37	33048 10
1922	Ld Woolavington	9	21	32090 0
1923	Ld Derby	13	29	40388 0
1924	H.H. Aga Khan	11	19	44367 0
1925	Ld Astor	8	20	35723 0
1926	Ld Woolavington	6	15	47256 0
1927	Ld Derby	18	37	40355 0
1928	Ld Derby	23	45	65603 0
1929	H.H. Aga Khan	20	35	39886 0
1930	H.H. Aga Khan	16	23	46259 0
1931	Mr J A Dewar	10	15	39034 10
1932	H.H. Aga Khan	14	28	57778 5
1933	Ld Derby	11	16	27559 10
1934	H.H. Aga Khan	18	45	64897 15
1935	H.H. Aga Khan	13	23	49201 0
1936	Ld Astor	9	19	38131 0
1937	H.H. Aga Khan	17	30	30655 10
1938	Ld Derby	24	50	34434 0
1939	Ld Rosebery	6	14	38464 15
1940	Lord Rothermere	2	5	6868 15
1941	Ld Glanely	9	21	8762 0
1942	His Majesty	5	10	10535 15
1943	Miss D Paget	16	26	13145 15
1944	H.H. Aga Khan	13	23	13985 0
1945	Ld Derby	13	26	25067 0
1946	H.H. Aga Khan	18	33	24118 0
1947	H.H. Aga Khan	16	28	44020 0
1948	H.H. Aga Khan	17	28	46393 0
1949	H.H. Aga Khan	19	39	68916 9
1950	M M Boussac	10	11	57044 4
1951	M M Boussac	12	17	39339 19
1952	H.H. Aga Khan	14	29	92518 13
1953	Sir Victor Sassoon	23	39	58579 7
1954	Her Majesty	10	19	40993 18
1955	Lady Zia Wernher	2	6	46345 0
1956	Maj L B Holliday	21	43	39327 0
1957	Her Majesty	16	30	62211 0
1958	Mr J McShain	2	6	63264 0
1959	Prince Aly Khan	7	13	100668 0
1960	Sir Victor Sassoon	15	29	90069 0
1961	Maj L B Holliday	25	37	39227 0
1962	Maj L B Holliday	24	39	70206 0
1963	Mr J R Mullion	5	9	68882 0
1964	Mrs H E Jackson	2	3	98270 0
1965	M J Ternynck	1	1	65301 0
1966	Lady Zia Wernher	1	2	78075 0
1967	Mr H J Joel	22	34	120925 0
1968	Mr Raymond R Guest	1	4	79075 0
1969	Mr D Robinson	42	96	92553 0
1970	Mr C Engelhard	20	30	182059 9
				£ p
1971	Mr P Mellon	11	22	138786·05
1972	Mrs J Hislop	3	10	155190·85
1973	Mr N B Hunt	8	11	124771·00
1974	Mr N B Hunt	7	8	147217·10
1975	Dr. C Vittadini	6	12	209492·90
1976	Mr D Wildenstein	5	10	244500·70
1977	Mr R Sangster	16	21	348023·10
1978	Mr R Sangster	15	27	160405·70
1979	Sir M Sobell	5	13	339751·00
1980	S Weinstock	1	4	236332·00
1981	H.H. Aga Khan	12	22	441654·00
1982	Mr R Sangster	27	38	397749·00
1983	Mr R Sangster	25	40	461488·00
1984	Mr R Sangster	24	31	395901·00
1985	Sheikh Mohammed	71	118	1082502·00
1986	Sheikh Mohammed	77	119	830532·00
1987	Sheikh Mohammed	76	126	1232255·00
1988	Sheikh Mohammed	79	122	1143310·00
1989	Sheikh Mohammed	90	130	1296052·00
1990	Hamdan Al-Maktoum	76	127	1536815·00
1991	Sheikh Mohammed	225	139	1077214·55
1992	Sheikh Mohammed	230	185	1194368·00
1993	Sheikh Mohammed	211	144	1703958·00

Winning Flat race breeders in 1993

H = number of horses W = races won £ = win value in £

	H	W	£
THE QUEEN	10	18	114,302.05
A CARR AND SON (HEXHAM) LTD	2	3	9,014.80
A J Poulton (Epping) Ltd	1	2	5,184.50
Abbey Lodge Stud	1	1	7,310.00
Abbey, Miss G	1	1	3,947.50
Abell, John David	3	7	37,503.66
Adstock Manor Stud	1	2	26,688.30
Aga Khan, H H	2	4	29,206.40
Aikin, A	1	1	2,243.00
Airlie Stud	11	20	198,814.15
Al Dahlawi Stud Co Ltd	2	3	16,336.00
Al Maktoum, Sheikh Ahmed Bin Rashid	3	3	10,656.70
Al Maktoum, Sheikh Mohammed Bin Rashid	32	47	232,860.25
Al Maktoum, Sheikh Marwan	1	1	3,611.25
Al-Maktoum, Hamdan	1	5	16,301.00
Al Maktoum, Sheikh Mohammed Obaid	1	1	3,357.00
Alamuddin, S Stanhope And Sheikh M	1	1	21,519.00
Aldershawe Stud Farm	2	5	19,791.50
Alexander, Helen C	1	1	4,449.50
Alexander, Mrs B	2	3	9,806.70
Allan, Ivan W	1	1	4,110.00
Allen E Paulson	1	3	46,626.56
Allen, B C	1	1	3,210.00
Allen, Ivan	1	1	2,668.60
Allen, M P	1	1	3,122.80
Amerivest Thoroughbred Partners	1	1	4,127.75
Anderson, Michael	1	1	2,668.00
Andrews, A And Mrs	1	1	3,340.00
Anthony, T	1	1	3,235.50
Aram, M V S And Mrs	1	2	7,578.00
Aramstone Stud Co	3	4	12,177.80
Ardenode Stud Ltd	2	2	7,898.50
Arnold, Mrs Donna C	1	3	12,375.00
Arrand, C	1	1	3,850.00
Ashford, Roy	1	2	4,921.50
Ashwood Thoroughbreds, Inc	1	2	5,856.75
Aspley Bloodstock	2	3	8,594.00
Astalon Ltd	1	4	16,165.75
Aston House Stud Incorporated	1	2	18,602.50
Aston House Stud Co	1	1	3,406.50
Aston Park Stud	4	7	22,494.80
Astor, Sir John	1	2	12,597.50
Audley Farm Incorporated	1	1	3,882.50
Auldyn Stud Ltd	1	2	6,667.00
Avon Industries Bath Ltd	1	2	5,809.50
Aykroyd, D P and D Oldrey	1	2	6,189.20
BACON, MRS F E	1	2	6,029.00
Bacton Stud	1	3	9,137.25
Badger, E A	1	1	2,553.00
Baker, Dr Howard	1	1	4,807.00
Baker, John R	1	1	2,511.00
Balding, Ian A	1	1	2,889.00
Ballinacurra Stud	1	2	14,099.40
Ballydoyle Stud	1	2	36,794.00
Ballygoran Stud	2	5	14,377.70
Ballykisteen Stud Ltd	2	3	13,326.75
Ballymacarney Stud	1	1	3,785.00
Ballymacoll Stud Farm Ltd	9	13	120,765.10
Ballymacoll Stud Co	1	2	6,822.25
Barber, R	3	4	13,846.20
Barker, W G	2	3	10,471.25
Barlage, Dale	1	1	21,500.00
Barnett, W & R Ltd	5	6	60,780.60
Baronrath Stud Ltd	2	4	279,381.10
Barratt, Mr T	1	1	3,377.25
Barratt, T	2	2	5,771.60
Barrett, Sqdn-Ldr Frank	1	2	12,387.50
Barrettstown Stud Farms Ltd	2	4	19,387.40
Barron, Mrs S C	1	1	7,440.00
Barronstown Stud	8	13	118,491.50
Barronstown Bloodstock And Swettenham Stud	1	2	13,905.00
Barronstown Bloodstock Ltd	5	5	23,300.00
Barronstown Bloodstock Ltd & Gainesway Thoroughbreds	1	1	59,407.20
Barronstown B'stock, Swettenham Stud & Roncon Ltd	1	1	4,932.00
Barry, David	2	2	5,984.75
Barry, Frank	1	2	26,249.00
Bassett, Lucy G	1	1	15,593.00
Baugh, P	1	1	2,399.80
Bavin, John	1	1	2,379.00
Beal, Bill Leach, L R French & Barry	1	2	6,666.75
Bearstone Stud	1	5	13,122.50
Beaumont, Mrs M	1	1	2,831.50
Beckett, J	1	1	5,673.00
Beechvale Stud	1	1	3,158.00
Beler, C P	1	2	9,181.50
Bell, J S	2	4	11,795.70
Belvadere Stables Inc	1	1	2,929.50
Benham Stud	2	4	51,412.90
Berger, M	1	2	13,156.50
Berkshire Equestrian Services Ltd	2	6	37,118.75
Bernard Eivers	1	1	3,600.00
Bernesq, S C E Haras Du	1	2	10,452.30
Berry, J	1	1	2,232.00
Berry, Mrs Caroline	2	3	7,809.40
Berry, Mrs J	1	1	2,713.40
Birkle, A C	3	3	9,326.10
Bishop Wilton Stud	1	2	5,305.50
Bishop's Down Farm	2	3	8,950.20
Bittersweet Farms Inc	1	1	2,889.00
Black, C R	1	1	4,500.00
Blackburn, James	1	1	3,532.00
Blacker, D S W And Partners	1	1	3,199.50
Blackwell, C A	1	2	4,812.00
Bloodstock Enterprises Ltd	1	1	7,985.20
Bloodstock Investments Ltd	1	1	2,601.40
Bloomsbury Stud	1	1	4,950.00
Blue Bear Stud Co Ltd	1	2	61,587.50
Blue Spruce Farm	1	1	11,963.00
Boland, Ronnie	1	1	3,552.75
Boon, Alan	1	1	3,622.50
Boorman, G R	1	1	2,959.00
Bosley, G A And H Clarkin	2	2	5,648.50
Botterill, D R	1	5	28,140.25
Bourke, Owen	2	2	7,164.20
Bouza, Marshall Naify And Luis F	1	1	3,720.00
Bowyer, Mrs J Murray-Smith And N	1	1	3,552.75
Bracken, Mrs T	1	1	2,763.00
Bradley, Andrew	1	1	4,751.50
Bradley, Nursery Place, Rayburg, &	1	1	4,079.25
Brady, Terry	1	2	9,614.60
Brant, E P Evans, Foxfield T'breds Inc & P M	1	1	5,190.00
Brazier, Robert	1	1	4,337.50
Brearley, J G And Mrs J M	1	1	3,444.00
Brewis, R	1	1	3,348.00
Brick Kiln Stud Farm	1	1	1,770.00
Bridges, K G	2	3	7,080.70
Brightwell, P K J And Mrs	1	1	2,905.00
Brittain, Mrs C E	1	2	37,983.00
Britton House Stud	3	5	15,424.75
Bromley, A	1	3	9,233.25
Bromley, Lt-Col R Gardner	1	1	2,070.00
Brook Bloodstock Plc	1	2	8,415.00

WINNING FLAT RACE BREEDERS IN 1993

	H	W	£
Brook Stud Ltd.	3	3	10,493.00
Brotherton, D R	1	1	2,243.00
Brown, David John	2	2	7,111.90
Bryanstown House Stud	1	2	5,819.10
Buchanan, K J And Mrs	1	1	3,523.50
Buchert, J	1	2	4,329.00
Buckram Oak Holdings	2	2	5,428.00
Buckton, C F	1	2	3,688.00
Bull, Phil	1	1	6,258.00
Burke, Mrs E M	1	1	2,427.00
Burke, W J	1	1	6,264.00
Burkett, Mrs D	1	1	2,243.00
Burns, John	1	1	2,658.00
Burns, Major-Gen Sir George	1	2	7,152.00
Burns, Mrs P H	1	1	2,406.00
Burr, Dr John L Thompson & Raymond C	1	2	6,446.00
Burrell, Mrs M	1	1	3,172.50
Buxton, Albert G Clay & Charlotte Clay	2	4	21,302.20
Bycroft, M C Collins And N	1	3	15,175.15
Byrne, Michael	1	1	21,540.00
Byrne, W J	1	1	3,325.00
CALEY, W L	3	3	11,423.30
Calumet Farm	3	7	104,222.55
Calzini, Mrs H I S	1	5	15,851.95
Camas Park Stud	1	1	3,465.00
Cambus Kenneth Farm	1	3	10,623.75
Campbell Stud	2	2	5,950.50
Campbell, Mrs E G	1	1	3,340.00
Candy, Henry	1	1	2,860.75
Capehart, Tom	1	2	7,320.00
Caradale, T Stack And	1	1	1,813.60
Carolan, P	1	2	11,380.00
Carolan, Patrick	1	1	3,699.00
Carr, Matt	1	1	2,595.00
Carrington-Smith, Miss M	2	2	5,842.50
Carson, W H F	1	2	7,630.25
Cartwright, Robert T	1	1	3,287.30
Cash, Mrs J	1	1	3,980.00
Cassidy, M J	2	3	29,020.80
Casterbridge Stud	1	2	5,434.40
Castle Farm Stud	1	2	5,484.00
Castle, Richard	2	3	11,007.80
Catridge Farm Stud Ltd.	1	1	2,259.00
Cecil Harris Bloodstock Ltd	1	2	5,841.10
Chandler, Dr John A	2	4	13,119.60
Chaplin, Miss J	1	1	2,243.00
Chapman, A L And J	1	4	27,671.85
Chapman, D W	1	1	3,817.50
Charles Nuckols Jnr & Sons	1	2	10,807.50
Charlton Down Stud	6	7	37,668.35
Chaworth, Mrs M Musters	1	1	3,172.50
Chelsea, Viscount	1	1	5,380.00
Cherry Valley Farm Inc And E A Cox Jnr	1	1	23,135.70
Cheveley Park Stud Ltd.	23	36	179,153.40
Chicago Exhibitors Corp	1	1	3,272.50
Chief's Crown Breeding Syndicate	1	2	12,299.25

	H	W	£
Chieveley Manor Enterprises	1	1	3,522.00
Chilcombe Manor Stud	1	3	10,153.50
Child, Trevor S	1	2	6,336.25
Chippenham Lodge Stud	3	4	24,008.25
Christian, Mrs M	1	1	3,669.75
Christodoulou, A	2	4	19,979.50
Chubb, Mrs M	2	2	7,073.80
Citadel Stud Establishment	1	1	4,807.00
Claiborne Farm	1	1	3,728.25
Clanville Lodge Stud	1	2	5,848.80
Clark, David B	1	1	3,287.30
Clark, W M E	1	2	5,502.20
Clark, Mrs D	1	1	2,739.00
Clark, Mrs P A	1	1	3,366.00
Clarke, David A	1	1	2,574.00
Clarke, J B	1	1	2,070.00
Clarke, W H	1	2	6,419.20
Clay, Albert G Clay & John W	1	1	2,880.00
Clay, Riverbend Farm And Robert N	1	1	3,377.25
Clay, Robert N	1	1	3,114.00
Cleaboy Farms Co	1	2	6,802.00
Clifton Lodge Stud	1	1	2,880.00
Clifton, Mrs P D Rossdale And Mrs D H	2	6	149,103.45
Cliveden Stud	4	5	21,015.15
Cloghran Stud Farm Co	1	1	5,374.00
Cloghran Stud Farm Ltd And Mrs E Burke	2	2	7,700.00
Clovelly Farms	2	2	5,890.75
Clover Stud	1	2	5,951.25
Cobhall Court Stud	1	2	5,193.00
Colby Bloodstock Agency Ltd	1	1	5,089.50
Cole, Geoffrey	1	1	3,236.00
Coller, Miss E	1	2	20,632.25
Collie, R H Cowell And Mrs R B	2	5	16,853.00
Collings, J W L	1	1	3,261.40
Collins, Leo	1	3	12,337.25
Collins, R A	4	5	17,574.55
Collins, Sean	1	3	14,207.25
Collinstown Stud Farm Ltd	5	11	56,194.21
Colver, Miss E	1	1	3,610.00
Comerford, W M	1	2	4,729.50
Condon, J C	1	1	3,080.00
Congleton & Courtney	1	1	3,465.00
Connaughton John	1	2	4,968.00
Corbett, G	1	5	11,322.60
Corbett, Thomas	1	2	9,316.25
Cordell-Lavarack, D	1	4	26,841.50
Corridan, Robert	1	2	7,739.40
Costelloe, John	1	1	4,396.00
Cotswold Stud And London Thoroughbred Services	1	1	3,201.75
Cotswold Farm 1985 Ltd.	1	2	15,459.00
Coughlan, T	1	1	3,172.50
Courtown Stud Co	2	4	13,778.15
Coval Stud Ltd	1	1	2,070.00
Cowell, R H	3	7	43,306.85
Cox, E A Jnr	2	3	71,258.30
Cox, Patrick	1	2	9,190.50
Coxland Stud	1	1	4,793.75
Craig, H F Harvey	1	1	2,880.00
Crane, G C Greenwood And P	1	2	7,019.25

	H	W	£
Crawshaw, Lord	1	2	4,822.00
Crellin, R T	1	3	8,832.75
Crepello Ltd	1	2	5,504.40
Crescent Farm	1	1	3,523.50
Crescent (UK) Ltd	3	5	16,404.25
Crest Stud Ltd	3	4	17,330.00
Crimson King Farm Inc	1	1	3,087.00
Crisp, Johnathan	1	1	2,803.00
Crockfords Stud	2	3	8,218.20
Crofts, J	1	1	6,165.00
Crook Investment Co & Swettenham Stud	3	5	60,900.50
Crystal Springs Farm & Jayeff B Stables	1	1	4,084.50
Cullen, R J	1	3	10,834.50
Cullinan, G J	2	3	11,695.00
Cummins, J	1	1	2,623.40
Cunliffe-Lister, Mrs N	1	1	2,469.00
Cyzer, C A	2	3	22,169.20
DALY, DAN	1	1	7,492.20
Dana Stud Ltd And Sussex Stud Ltd	1	1	5,089.50
Dandy, Mrs M J	3	5	22,964.50
Daniels, J	1	2	5,907.00
Danton Stud Farm Co Ltd	2	2	8,455.00
Darley Stud Management Co Ltd	10	14	118,611.25
Dasmal, Khalifa Abdulla	1	1	2,243.00
David's Farm	1	1	4,269.00
Davison, Mrs D	3	8	36,215.05
Dayspring Co Ltd	1	1	7,564.00
Dayton Ltd	1	2	273,980.00
Deepwood Farm Stud	6	7	34,216.70
Deer, D J And Mrs	3	4	17,535.25
Deer Lawn Farm, Carloss And Lamont	1	1	10,464.00
Deer Lawn Farm	1	1	2,248.00
Deerfield Farm	1	1	2,070.00
Deerpark Stud	1	1	2,595.00
Delmare Syndicate Number Two	1	2	6,294.00
Delsol Farm	1	1	2,679.00
Delta Thoroughbreds Inc.	1	1	2,469.00
Dene Investments Nv	1	2	7,712.75
Dent, N J	2	4	20,052.70
Derby Bloodstock Services Ltd	1	2	4,564.50
Derby, Exors Of The Late Lady	1	1	3,882.50
Derrinstown Stud Ltd.	1	2	7,980.00
Dick, Don	1	1	3,493.00
Dictum Enterprises Ltd.	1	4	13,292.85
Dillman, Mrs Nancy S	1	1	3,523.50
Dinnaken Farm	1	1	2,950.60
Dinwiddie Farm Ltd Partnership	1	1	3,874.50
D O B Syndicate	1	1	2,243.00
Dodford Stud	1	2	5,589.50
Doherty, Thomas	2	5	14,196.55
Dollys Grove Stud	1	1	2,511.80
Donald T Johnson	1	1	7,700.70
Donnelly, Michael	1	1	2,448.40
Donworth, B	1	1	4,342.25
Doublet Ltd	1	1	3,816.00
Downclose Stud	2	4	12,836.60

	H	W	£
Downes, F	1	1	3,084.75
Downes, Miss Amanda	1	1	3,287.30
Doyle, Michael	2	5	12,782.00
Doyle Patrick	1	1	1,957.30
Doyle, Peter	1	2	6,003.00
Due Process Stables	1	2	7,366.50
Duffy, Patrick J	1	1	2,780.60
Dullingham House Stud	1	1	2,070.00
Dunchurch Lodge Stud Co	2	2	11,488.56
Dunderry Stud	1	1	2,660.00
Dunlop, J	2	5	16,125.80
Durham, Countess Of	3	8	23,146.35
EAST RIDING SACK AND PAPER CO	1	1	3,494.25
Easterby, M H	1	1	2,448.00
Eaton Farms Inc, Tally Ho Farms & Overbrook Farm	1	2	19,837.50
Echo Valley Horse Farm & Swettenham Stud	1	1	3,406.50
Echo Valley Horse Farm Inc	1	1	4,077.50
Egan, James M	1	1	2,005.00
Eggo, R M	1	2	8,689.50
Elisha Holdings	2	5	19,433.15
Ellis, D R	1	1	4,464.00
Ellis, H	2	3	95,283.70
Elsdon Farms	1	2	5,663.60
Emmet, Lt-Comdr P S And Partner	1	2	4,106.00
Emmet, S	1	2	6,068.50
Empress Syndicate	1	2	10,688.75
Ennistown Stud	1	3	7,735.00
Entenmann, R	1	1	5,897.50
Erlengrund, Gestut	1	1	3,494.25
Ervine, W Maxwell	2	3	13,983.50
Essa, Mrs Afaf A Al	1	2	11,156.25
Etablissement Equine Investments	1	1	2,364.00
Evans, R R Bloodstock Ltd	1	1	3,184.00
Everitt, Mrs J	1	4	12,927.00
Ewar Stud Farms	1	1	3,622.50
Executive Bloodstock & Adstock Manor Stud	1	2	8,577.50
High Point Bloodstock Ltd And Victor Sujanani	1	1	3,590.00
FAIRBAIRN, MRS M	1	2	7,475.50
Fairhaven, Lord	2	4	13,381.20
Fairhurst, T	1	1	1,520.00
Falhgren, H Smoot & John T L Jones Jnr	1	1	2,511.00
Fanning, P F N	1	1	5,952.00
Fanshawe, Mrs A D	1	2	6,371.50
Fares Farm Inc	2	2	7,647.00
Fares Stables Ltd	1	1	3,557.50
Farish, W S, E J Hudson & E J Hudson Jnr	1	1	3,143.25
Farish, W S, W T Carter And E J Hudson Jnr	1	1	7,270.00
Farfellow Farms Ltd	1	1	4,163.50
Farish, William S	1	1	2,913.00
Farrell, C	2	2	5,029.80
Farrell, Mrs M E	2	3	9,884.20
Feeney, F	1	2	6,045.00
Ferry Farm Co	1	1	2,406.00
Fetherston-Godley, P And Partners	1	2	19,049.00
Field, Mrs Susan	1	1	3,297.00
Fieldspring Stud Ltd	1	4	12,815.50
Filletts Farm Stud	1	1	2,070.00
Finegan, Noel	1	1	3,106.00
Finnegan, Joseph	1	1	3,054.20
Firman, Mrs Pamela H	1	2	17,380.80
Fittocks Stud Ltd	3	8	50,805.00
Fitzgerald, Miss Louise	1	2	7,848.50
Flattery, Tommy	1	1	3,640.50
Flaxman Holdings Limited	5	6	143,339.75
Flinders Enterprises S A	1	2	6,237.70
Folkerth, Dr Theodore M	1	1	4,016.00
Folsom, John T L Jones Jnr & Robert S	2	5	32,320.00
Fonthill Stud	2	3	9,450.50
Forbes, Mrs G S	1	1	2,700.00
Forenaghts Stud Farm Ltd	1	1	3,525.00
Forte, Mrs J	1	1	4,142.50
Foundation Farm And Stud Co Ltd	1	1	3,027.50
Foundation, Woodford And St Simon Studs	1	1	3,318.75
Foustok, Ahmed M	5	8	25,099.60
Fox, J C	1	1	3,598.10
Fox, Mrs Ian	1	1	2,950.00
Fox, R M	2	2	8,025.00
Foxfield	2	2	7,664.50
Foy, C J	1	3	11,587.80
Francome, Larry Murphy, Johnathan Shack And John	1	1	2,243.00
Franks, John	3	3	8,742.50
Freeman, Keith	2	2	9,915.00
Freyne, G J	1	1	4,464.00
Fulling Mill Farm And Stud	1	1	4,191.00
Fustok, S	1	2	5,930.50
G M BREEDING FARMS INC	1	1	3,231.00
G R Smith (Thriplow) Ltd	1	3	7,353.30
Gainesway Thoroughbreds Limited	1	1	3,757.50
Gainsborough Farm Inc	10	13	254,311.25
Gainsborough Stud Management Ltd	24	32	272,311.73
Gallagher's Stud	3	5	16,896.45
Galloping Acres Farm	1	1	3,172.50
Gardner, Allen	1	3	11,672.80
Gardner, N H	1	1	4,793.75
Garthwaite, K And P J	1	1	1,553.00
Gaste, J P de	1	1	3,582.00
Gauvain, Mrs E M	1	2	5,225.00
Gee, H D And M J	2	2	6,913.10
Genesis Green Stud	1	3	34,865.40
Gentry, Mike G Rutherford & Robert A	1	2	6,772.50
Gestut Holsten, Ag	1	1	2,700.00
Gibney, Hugh C	1	3	31,269.25
Gibson, Alan	3	3	10,382.00
Gilmore, L	1	3	15,641.00
Glazeley Stud	3	6	24,684.60
Glencrest Farm	1	1	2,243.00
Golden Vale Stud	3	3	10,291.75
Good, J R And Mrs P	1	4	10,700.60
Gottlieb, Roy & North Central Bloodstock	1	3	11,506.25
Graigueshoneen Stud	1	4	16,562.00
Grange Farm (Barnby Moor) Ltd	1	1	4,737.00
Grange Stud (UK)	4	4	14,590.25
Green, B E	2	5	18,363.50
Green Park Investments Ltd	1	2	5,523.75
Green, R	1	1	4,378.00
Greenberg, Hermen	1	1	5,070.40
Greenland Park Stud	3	10	29,310.65
Greenville House Stud And J Perrot	1	3	7,883.70
Greenwood, Mrs J A Rawding And G C	1	1	3,454.00
Greetham, J M	1	1	2,490.00
Gregory, Edward	1	2	6,932.70
Grenfell, D	1	3	8,055.50
Grenfell, Exors Of The Late Comdr H	1	1	3,363.00
Griffin, G P	1	1	3,318.75
Griffin Reg And McGrath Jim	1	4	11,170.25
Griffiths, J A	1	2	6,139.40
Groves, Carolyn T	1	1	3,434.50
Groves, Franklin N	2	2	10,396.70
Grubb, Mrs P	1	1	13,500.00
Guest Leasing And Bloodstock Co	1	1	2,749.00
Guest, J	1	3	9,689.50
HADDON STUD	1	1	2,668.60
Haggas, J R	1	1	2,540.10
Hakim, G R Platt And S	1	1	2,511.00
Hale, David Barr-Thompson	1	1	3,084.75
Halifax, Lord	4	4	10,728.60
Halifax, Marquess Of Hartington And The Earl Of	1	1	4,932.00
Hall, David V	1	3	10,524.75
Hamilton Bloodstock (UK) Ltd	3	5	15,129.20
Hamilton, Mrs Emory A	1	2	6,801.80
Hamilton, William J	1	2	8,309.70
Hamwood Stud	1	2	7,929.45
Hancock, Arthur And Accommodate Partners	1	2	8,947.50
Hancock, Staci	1	1	3,201.75
Hannon, P J	1	2	6,917.50
Haras de Manneville	1	2	10,528.00
Harrington, Mrs Chris	1	3	9,334.15
Harris, D K	1	2	6,340.00
Harrison, Sir Ernest	1	1	5,287.50
Harrod, Miss N A	1	1	2,709.00
Hart, David	1	2	6,635.75
Hascombe And Valiant Studs	13	22	168,649.50
Hayes, John	1	2	6,936.80
Hayter, John	1	1	2,713.40
Haywood, G	3	3	9,611.75
Heathavon Stables Ltd	3	3	20,985.90
Hedditch, Richard	1	1	2,691.60
Heffernan, P	1	2	5,997.35

WINNING FLAT RACE BREEDERS IN 1993

	H	W	£
Heler, Joseph	2	9	33,676.65
Henry Cecil Bloodstock Ltd	1	1	2,794.00
Henson, Mrs Anne	1	2	7,292.00
Hermes Services Ltd	1	1	2,385.00
Hermitage Farm Inc	1	1	3,435.75
Heronwood Farm Inc	1	1	3,348.00
Herridge, G	1	1	4,751.50
Herring, T E	1	2	4,775.00
Hesmonds Stud Ltd	22	34	150,124.35
Hetherton, N	1	1	3,235.50
Hever Castle Stud Farm Ltd	4	8	37,395.45
Heyworth, J	1	1	3,184.00
Hickory Tree Farm	1	1	3,850.00
Hicks, D A And Mrs	3	4	12,339.85
High Point Bloodstock Ltd And Victor Sujanani	1	1	3,590.00
Highclere Stud Ltd	12	19	129,520.75
Highfield Stud Ltd	2	3	11,013.00
Highfield Stud Ltd And P Bradley	1	1	2,532.00
Highfield Stud Ltd And The Glen Andred Stud	1	1	8,019.60
Higson, K	2	2	31,434.00
Hill 'N' Dale Farm	1	1	2,448.00
Hill 'N' Dale Farms And Gainesway Farm	1	1	5,078.40
Hilborough Stud Farm Ltd	1	1	3,392.00
Hillfields Farming Co Ltd	1	1	3,416.80
Hills, Mrs M J	3	6	32,793.85
Hillwood Stud	1	2	55,557.00
Hine, Mrs J R And Miss J Bunting	1	2	7,708.25
Hines, F	1	2	6,637.50
Hintermuller, Hans	1	1	3,523.50
Hislop, Mrs J L	1	2	6,374.25
Hockley Ltd	2	2	8,586.00
Holborn Trust Co	1	2	5,461.00
Holder, J Neville And R J	1	1	3,125.50
Holdsworth, Miss E C	1	2	5,874.00
Holland Martin, T	1	3	9,678.50
Hollyhill Stud	1	2	14,659.00
Hollow Hole Stud	1	1	3,582.00
Home Stud Ltd	2	2	5,305.50
Hopefield Stud Farm	1	1	2,406.00
Hopewell Heritage Farm	1	1	3,497.50
Horgan, Jim	2	4	25,377.00
Horsfield, Mrs E J	1	1	3,548.00
Houghton, John	1	3	10,637.00
Howard de Walden, Lord	12	18	219,291.70
Howland, Marquess & Marchioness Of Tavistock & Lord	2	3	8,513.50
Hue-Williams, Mrs & Exors Of The Late Col F R	2	3	10,482.75
Hue-Williams, Mrs V	1	1	4,581.00
Hughes, Exors Of The Late G C	1	3	9,956.70
Hughes, H B	2	3	16,405.75
Hullin Co N V (International)	1	2	128,343.50
Hundley, Bruce	1	2	7,404.95
Hunt, Des de Vere	1	3	8,724.40
Hunter, Miss Barbara	2	3	46,499.25

	H	W	£
Hurd, J D	2	4	33,212.75
Hutch, L And Mrs	2	3	19,347.75
Hutch, L	1	4	9,968.80
Hyde Stud	1	2	5,524.60
IRIS COMPANY	1	1	3,933.00
Irish Thoroughbred Holdings Ltd	1	1	3,552.75
Islanmore Stud	1	2	5,969.00
Ivory, K T And Partners	1	1	1,970.00
J D WIMPFHEIMER & GILMAN INVESTMENT COMPANY	1	4	36,024.80
J K Bloodstock Ltd	1	1	2,932.50
J L P Investments	1	1	4,199.25
Jackson, Mrs D	1	1	2,927.00
Jafleh, Ali K Al	2	2	8,708.50
Jayeff B Stables	1	1	10,430.00
Jenks, Miss D	1	1	3,015.00
Jeremy Green And Sons	1	2	5,554.00
Jeyes, J N & Mrs	1	1	3,915.00
JJG Partners	1	2	8,685.50
John Redden Farms	1	2	6,056.00
Johnsey, T A	1	2	4,733.80
Johnson, Ann Trimble & Donald T	1	5	22,122.65
Johnson, D & Mrs	1	1	3,844.00
Johnson, Dennis And D Covette	1	1	2,364.00
Johnson, Michael Watt And Miss Jemima	1	2	5,301.00
Johnson, Mr & Mrs Donald	1	1	4,020.50
Johnson, Robert L Spradlin Jnr & Larry Dean	1	1	2,385.00
Joly, Mrs D O	1	2	8,078.50
Jones, B Ned Jones & Bartow	1	1	2,579.00
Jones/Jayeff B Partnership	1	1	4,378.00
Jones, Brereton C	3	3	11,345.25
Jones, Brereton C And Halo Farms	1	1	3,980.00
Jones, H	1	1	2,872.00
Jones, Mrs H T	2	2	7,886.30
Jones, John T Jnr & Barronstown Bloodstock	1	1	3,172.50
Jong, Mrs M de	1	1	3,406.50
Joyce, W H	3	3	10,894.87
JRG Investment Corp	1	1	3,289.50
Juddmonte Farms	38	58	994,853.53
Juddmonte Farms Incorporated	11	14	198,516.92
KALMAN, R	1	3	10,640.50
Karpidas, Mrs P	1	2	7,099.00
Katalpa Farm	1	1	4,935.00
Kaufman, Dr Walter C	1	1	3,523.50
Kavli Ltd	1	3	10,360.50
Kelburn, Dorothea Viscountess	1	4	12,621.00
Kelly, John	1	2	5,630.30
Kelly, Mrs Sean	1	1	4,270.75

	H	W	£
Kendrick, E	1	1	2,243.00
Kennard, Mrs R B	3	4	16,574.50
Kennedy, B	1	1	2,978.50
Kennedy, Capt P W	1	2	5,503.25
Kennedy Patrick	1	3	6,655.80
Kennelot, Carelaine Farm, Riordan, Phillips &	1	1	3,055.50
Kennelot Stables Ltd	1	1	16,570.00
Kent, Edmond And Richard	2	2	7,277.50
Kent, John	2	2	4,985.00
Kent, Michael	1	1	3,261.40
Kentish, M F	3	7	72,652.90
Keogh, R A	2	5	13,890.80
Kerr And Co Ltd	1	2	5,518.00
Keswick, Mrs Henry	1	1	3,611.25
Kettlewell, E W And E A	1	2	5,561.70
Keyes, Edward	1	1	2,259.00
Kidd, Mrs A W	1	1	3,289.50
Kidder, C L Kidder & N L	1	1	5,936.00
Kilmartin, Frank	1	1	2,005.00
Kilroy, W S Farish III And W S	3	6	112,037.05
Kilroy, W S Farish, E J Hudson & W S	1	1	3,552.75
Kiltinan Farms Inc	2	4	9,202.80
King, G J	2	2	6,564.50
King, Hugh G III	1	1	3,026.25
King Ranch Inc	1	1	4,305.00
Kingsbrooke Stud	1	1	2,511.00
Kingwood Stud Ltd	1	1	5,205.00
Kirk, Ronald K	1	1	4,225.50
Kirtlington Stud Ltd	1	1	2,243.00
Klein, A G Smith And M R	1	1	2,761.50
Knight, Landon	2	2	5,453.90
Knockaney Stud	1	2	11,161.00
Knocklong House Stud	1	1	3,687.50
Knowles, Mrs C S	1	1	1,916.90
Knox, T K	1	1	2,243.00
LAHARNA LTD	3	3	15,264.25
Landi, E	1	2	7,721.25
Lane, P J And R M	1	1	4,113.00
Lang, David	1	1	2,070.00
Langham Hall Bloodstock	1	2	15,770.25
Lariston Bloodstock	1	1	5,015.50
Lawson, Mrs H	1	1	2,957.50
Lawson, V Morley	1	1	3,933.00
Lawson-Brown, J And Mrs	1	1	2,412.70
Leach, W B And Mrs F A Veasey	1	1	3,054.20
Leapeau, Mr Roland	1	1	3,640.50
Leigh, Gerald W	6	7	23,187.80
Levasseur, Dr Jaques	1	1	3,465.00
Lewis, Mrs P J	1	5	15,634.30
Lewis, Mrs P	2	2	31,549.00
Lhasa Trading Ltd	1	1	4,709.25
Liam Ward	1	1	3,028.00
Liles, Mrs M	1	1	2,601.40
Limestone Stud	14	20	70,331.45
Lin Pac Containers Ltd	1	1	20,439.00
Lingwood, R T	1	1	3,720.00
Lippert, Cooper Rawls & Clarence C	1	2	10,742.75
Liscannor Stud Ltd	1	1	4,308.00
Little Moreton Stud	1	2	5,023.60
Littleton Stud	8	15	163,676.85
Livock, J	1	1	2,070.00
Llety Stud	5	10	52,487.50

WINNING FLAT RACE BREEDERS IN 1993

	H	W	£
Loch Lea Farm Inc	1	1	3,947.50
Lock, T R	1	2	27,994.50
Loder, E J	7	11	39,789.70
Lodge Park Stud	10	16	112,304.55
London Thoroughbred Services Ltd	4	6	19,360.50
Lonergan, E	3	9	29,437.85
Lonergan, Miss Ruth	1	1	3,501.25
Long, B	1	1	2,511.80
Longdon Stud Ltd	2	3	10,852.40
Longton, Mrs E	1	1	3,933.00
Loradale	1	2	5,908.00
Lordship And Egerton Studs Ltd	1	5	55,861.20
Louise Stud	1	1	2,070.00
Lucey, Frank	1	1	3,004.60
Lumley, W N	1	3	9,671.75
Lusty, Mrs O M	1	2	8,825.00
Luzi S P A	1	3	16,573.65
Lynch, Mrs Lucy	1	1	2,691.60
Lyonstown Stud And Swettenham Stud	1	1	3,435.75
Lyonstown Stud	1	1	2,700.00
M W BLOODSTOCK SHARES LTD	1	1	2,821.10
Mabee, John C & Mrs	2	3	18,697.20
Macauley, Mrs Amanda Skiffington And W	1	3	10,746.00
Macauley, W F	1	1	2,807.00
Maccarthy, M	1	1	2,238.00
Macdee, Jac	1	1	3,913.25
Macgregor, Miss I G And Miss E G	3	6	23,932.55
Macrae, D	1	2	5,046.00
Magnier, D And P	1	2	5,221.50
Magor, R S P Harris And Miss E A M	1	5	29,753.90
Maguire, Tony	1	1	2,924.00
Makin, Mrs J	1	1	3,015.00
Makin, P J	1	2	4,039.50
Malmuth, Marvin	1	1	4,807.00
Mamakos, J	2	2	7,935.50
Manana, Saeed	2	2	11,243.00
Mandysland Farm & Enemy Stable	2	5	44,477.75
Mangan, Dan	1	2	8,202.00
Mareco Ltd	1	1	4,556.75
Marner, Christian	1	1	3,003.00
Marquard, William A	1	3	9,637.60
Marrow, Mrs J	1	1	3,080.00
Marsh, B	1	1	3,080.00
Marten, Lt-Comdr G G	1	1	3,882.50
Martin, Mrs L	1	1	3,262.00
Marystead Farm	4	8	73,218.10
Mascalls Stud Farm	1	1	5,754.00
Mason, C R	2	6	21,314.55
Mason, Sydney	2	6	21,400.90
Masterson, M G	1	1	5,047.25
Matthews, Eugene	1	1	3,348.00
Matthews, Lord Victor	3	5	21,085.50
Maude, E J B	1	1	3,377.25
Maurice And Jeremiah Sheahan	1	1	2,803.00
Mavorah, Elliot	1	1	3,365.00
McAlpine, Lady	1	1	6,664.00
McAlpine, Lord Edwin	2	3	19,654.75
McAlpine, Sir Robin	3	6	153,157.10
McAuley, F D	1	1	4,985.75
McCall, Kim	1	2	9,135.80
McCalmont, M	1	1	3,882.50
McCalmont, P J	1	1	2,579.00
McCarthy, T	1	1	3,521.00
McCausland, M	1	1	2,422.20
McCourt, C And J Sandys And Barbara	1	3	10,429.00
McCreery, L K	2	2	4,535.80
McCreery, Miss S And Stowell Hill Ltd	2	3	28,183.70
McDonagh, T	1	1	3,552.75
McEnery, Martyn J	2	7	19,512.55
McHarg, D W	1	1	4,464.00
McIlveen, S W D	1	1	2,758.20
McInnes, U A	1	1	2,343.00
McKnight, H Turney McKnight & June H	1	1	2,898.80
McLoughlin, A	1	2	5,795.75
McLoughlin, John	1	2	5,523.75
McMahon, Hugh P	1	3	9,348.35
McMahon, Mrs J	2	2	6,845.50
McMahon, Peter J	1	1	5,385.25
McManus, J P	3	3	10,623.00
McMillin Bros	1	1	5,572.00
McNally, Mrs J	1	1	2,821.10
McNamara, John And Mrs	3	7	21,907.30
McQuillan, Mrs P F	1	2	8,375.75
McStay, Mrs M	1	1	6,639.60
Meacock, I Stewart-Brown And M	1	1	3,552.75
Mead, Mrs C F Van Straubenzee And R	2	2	6,337.25
Meadow Grove Farm	1	1	4,542.00
Meehan, Miss Fiona	1	1	6,373.60
Melchester Ltd	1	2	37,282.50
Mellon Stud	2	3	10,253.40
Mellon, Paul	11	16	68,936.05
Meon Valley Stud	9	13	566,561.42
Mercer, K J	2	2	5,874.70
Meredith, Rodney	1	1	3,718.00
Merry, Hugo	1	1	3,523.50
Messinger Stud Ltd	2	4	10,357.80
Mezeray, Haras Du	1	2	45,021.00
Midhurst Farm Inc And Partners	1	1	17,730.00
Mike Channon Bloodstock Ltd	1	1	2,070.00
Mill Ridge Farm Ltd & W Lazy T Ltd	1	2	7,076.25
Miller, Mrs Celia	1	2	5,535.00
Mills, C	1	2	4,038.00
Mills, G W And Sons	3	3	10,187.00
Milltown Stud	1	1	3,131.90
Minahan, Terry	1	2	8,522.00
Minch Bloodstock	1	1	10,029.00
Minty, B	1	2	26,266.00
Mitchell, Fred M And Mrs	1	1	1,828.00
Mitchell, J R	1	2	7,992.50
Mitchell, James William Mitchell And Simon Edward	1	1	3,158.00
Mitchelstown Stud	1	3	7,557.80
Moat View Stud	1	1	2,322.00
Mohammed, Ruffiek A	1	2	8,028.20
Molloy, K	1	2	5,490.40
Moloney, E	3	6	18,533.50
Moloney, Stephen	1	1	3,845.25
Molony, Dr T J	2	2	6,478.00
Monaghan, T J	1	2	178,739.60
Montanari, Marion G	1	1	5,309.00
Moore, John L	2	3	22,129.50
Moran, Donald F	1	1	3,201.75
Morgan, John A Jones	2	4	76,805.00
Morgan-Jones, Rhydian	3	4	28,214.30
Morley, Mrs M	1	2	6,304.60
Morrish, J K And Mrs	1	1	2,490.00
Morrison, C N S Lakin, V Behrens And M	1	2	6,639.55
Morrison, Thomas A	1	1	2,724.00
Morriss, Mr And Mrs H H	1	2	7,878.00
Mount Coote Stud	3	4	20,892.35
Mount Coote Partnership	2	2	8,179.00
Mountain, J A	1	1	3,590.00
Moygaddy Stud	1	1	3,494.25
Mull Enterprizes	2	2	8,146.50
Mumford, Lady Mary	1	2	12,618.00
Murcot Investments Ltd	1	2	5,108.00
Murless, Lady	1	1	3,172.50
Murless, Mrs Beryl	1	2	6,819.95
Murphy, Mrs John	1	2	10,018.50
Mursell, J W	1	2	66,592.50
NAPIER, MRS N	1	2	14,445.00
Nashar, M M	1	3	40,925.00
Nasrullah Holdings	2	2	6,980.00
Navan Stables	1	1	3,285.00
Naver Enterprises Ltd	1	1	3,287.30
Nawara Stud Co Ltd	7	8	159,293.45
Needham, Dr And Mrs Chris Elia And Phil	1	1	5,186.00
Nelson, Mrs M Nabavi, Mrs G Bakhtiar And Mrs M	1	1	2,259.00
Nerses, C C Bromley And Son And A O	1	1	3,640.50
Neville, T Barratt And J	1	1	4,020.50
New Farm Breeding Inc	1	1	3,377.25
New Hope Partnership	1	2	7,029.00
Newall, R F S	1	2	6,164.25
Newgate Stud Ltd	2	4	16,140.10
Newgate Stud Farm Inc	4	8	28,694.35
Newgate Stud Co	9	11	68,134.70
Newlands House Stud	2	5	16,201.55
Newsells Park Stud	1	1	2,787.00
Newsome, T J	1	1	2,406.00
Newton, D	1	1	2,448.00
Newton Stud Farm Inc	1	1	4,965.72
Newton, P And J L	1	2	5,064.00
Newton, William Powell And Bates	1	1	107,464.80
Newtownbarry House Stud	4	4	12,284.50
Newtownbarry House Stud And Miss S Von Schilcher	1	1	3,406.50
Niarchos, S	6	6	27,684.70
Nidd Park Stud	2	2	10,520.00
Nikita Investments	1	1	6,056.00
Nordan, B	2	6	37,444.60

WINNING FLAT RACE BREEDERS IN 1993

	H	W	£
Norfolk, Lavinia Duchess Of	3	5	20,916.30
Normanby Stud Ltd	5	7	24,733.10
North Ridge Farm	1	4	11,867.50
North Ridge Farm Inc	1	1	4,175.00
Northgate Lodge Stud Ltd	2	2	4,906.00
Norton Brookes	1	2	5,682.75
O'BRIEN, A	1	1	2,950.60
O'Brien, G	1	3	22,962.25
O'Brien, Joseph	1	1	3,261.40
O'Brien, Michael G	1	2	7,076.25
O'Callaghan, A F	4	7	21,173.00
O'Callaghan, Gay	7	11	54,735.95
O'Callaghan, Mrs C	1	2	3,082.00
O'Coileain, Leon	1	1	4,435.00
O'Flynn, Mrs Edward Flannery And Christopher	1	1	3,435.75
O'Gorman, E	1	1	5,427.50
O'Gorman, M B	2	4	11,923.50
O'Leary, E.	5	12	34,262.45
O'Loghlen, R	1	1	2,243.00
O'Malley, J F	1	2	13,070.94
O'Neill, J	2	2	5,448.40
O'Regan, J	1	2	6,715.50
O'Regan, W J	1	1	3,984.75
O'Riordan, Mrs S	3	3	23,048.00
O'Toole, M B	1	1	2,448.00
O'Toole, Miss C	1	3	12,558.00
Oak Bloodstock Ltd	1	1	2,269.13
Oak Crest Farm	1	2	5,147.50
Octram Ltd	1	1	3,915.00
Ohrstrom, George L	1	1	5,344.50
Old Meadow Stud	1	2	11,847.55
Old Mill Stud	2	2	6,833.60
Oldtown Stud	2	4	10,469.70
Oldtown Bloodstock Holdings Ltd	1	1	3,825.00
Oppenheim, Baron F Von	1	1	2,812.00
Orbell, J W	1	1	3,209.60
Overbrook Farm	1	1	3,095.00
Overbrook Farm & Henry H FitzGibbon	1	2	18,390.00
Ovidstown Bloodstock Ltd	1	2	8,525.25
Ovidstown Investments Ltd	2	7	52,590.85
Owen-George, Mrs R	1	1	15,962.50
Owens, Robert E	1	3	9,308.80
Oxford Stables	1	2	15,855.00
Oyston, R And Partners	1	3	8,016.65
PAGE, M L	2	2	6,281.00
Paliafito, James L	1	1	9,894.00
Palmer, Mrs M Palmer And G	1	1	1,380.00
Parker, J W	1	1	2,377.40
Parry, Mrs M L And Steele-Mortimer P M	1	2	6,368.50
Patrick Eddery Ltd	1	2	13,259.00
Paul, Mrs Deborah	1	5	17,852.20
Paulson, Allen	1	2	4,497.00
Payson, Mrs Daniel W Evans & Virginia Kraft	1	1	3,049.40
Peacock, Mrs R D	2	3	8,133.00
Peacock, Mrs R D And Swettenham Stud	1	3	11,884.25
Pearce, J L C	4	4	16,953.75
Pearman, Craig	1	3	13,517.50
Pegasus Securities Leasing (Pty) Ltd	2	3	14,536.80
Pendley Farm	6	7	29,368.75
Penser, E	1	2	26,932.00
Percival, Miss S M Rhodes And R G	2	2	5,551.90
Percival, R G	2	3	13,208.00
Peskoff, Stephen D	1	1	4,175.00
Petra Bloodstock Agency Ltd	1	1	2,243.00
Phelan, Seamus	2	3	8,693.40
Philipson, Major C R	1	1	2,788.00
Phillips, Michael Riordan & Jacqueline G	1	2	13,695.75
Phipps, A B	3	4	17,609.50
Pike, D W	2	4	10,586.75
Pilkington, Sir Thomas	1	3	10,448.50
Pillar Stud Inc	3	5	45,438.00
Pillar Stud Inc & Lord Howard de Walden	1	1	3,597.00
Pin Oak Stud	2	3	19,449.50
Pinfold Stud And Farms Ltd	4	6	26,652.20
Pitts Farm Stud	1	1	2,833.00
Player, P D And Mrs	3	7	21,406.05
Plescia, William Plescia & Natalie	1	3	11,417.50
Plumbly, Mrs Helen	1	2	5,917.50
Poland, Michael	2	4	101,408.00
Polinger, H, B Polinger, L Polinger, J Polinger	1	2	8,193.10
Pollard, R J	1	1	1,954.00
Poole, N E And Mrs	1	1	2,932.50
Popely, Mrs L	1	1	3,757.50
Popely, R A And J H	2	2	18,545.00
Popely, Ronald	3	7	45,946.25
Powell, B Mitten And T	1	1	4,240.50
Powell, Brendan And Sheila	3	7	38,956.00
Powell, Brendan	1	1	2,898.80
Powell, Mrs B Skinner And D F	1	1	3,669.75
Powell, R J	1	2	9,664.00
Pratt, Mrs M	1	3	23,261.80
Prendergast, J J	1	2	17,120.00
Prentice, Bryant H III	1	2	7,732.50
Price, Derek R	2	4	16,206.45
Price, J T	1	1	3,816.00
Price, Mrs D	2	5	29,499.90
Pritchard-Gordon, Giles W	2	2	6,943.00
Pritchard-Gordon, Mrs V	1	2	9,121.25
Protheroe-Beynon, Mrs Wilma	1	1	2,847.00
Pryor, C C And Mrs	1	2	5,856.75
QUALITAIR STUD LTD	1	1	2,490.00
Quinn, Mrs Anita	1	2	7,017.50
RAINTREE STUD	1	3	11,296.60
R Powell-Tuck And Partners	1	1	3,444.00
Rand, W Kenan Jnr	1	1	3,523.50
Ranston (Bloodstock) Ltd	1	3	85,541.25
Rash, Warren L King And Mark	1	2	14,945.00
Rathasker Stud	5	7	28,287.30
Rathbone, Mrs L F	1	2	4,660.60
Rathvinden Stud	1	2	5,271.75
Rausing, Miss K	3	4	10,751.30
Ravenstonedale Fold And Bloodstock	2	2	3,973.00
Raylex Stud Farm Co Ltd	1	1	2,070.00
Read, T J G	1	1	2,954.00
Red House Stud	6	10	41,079.30
Red Sox Associates	1	2	6,216.65
Redhead, A D	2	4	12,037.10
Redmond, J A	2	2	8,830.50
Reid, C G	1	3	9,326.75
Resk, Mr Victor	1	1	1,992.50
Reveley, Mrs G R And Partners	1	2	20,830.50
Richmond-Watson, R N	1	2	6,025.85
Riddell-Martin, Mrs A W	1	1	3,183.70
Ridgecourt Stud	4	9	68,429.05
Roan Rocket Partners	1	1	3,078.75
Rochford, Mrs M F	1	1	3,235.50
Rock House Farms Ltd	1	2	7,646.25
Rocklow Stud	3	4	14,131.50
Rogers, Mrs S M	1	1	3,703.50
Rogers, Robert Clay & Trust	1	1	25,003.47
Rokeby Farms	1	1	4,077.50
Roldvale Ltd	5	14	142,873.10
Roncon Ltd And Swettenham Stud	5	9	200,269.70
Roncon Ltd	3	5	24,349.15
Rooker, John W	1	1	9,594.00
Rose, John	1	1	3,289.50
Rose Bank Stud	1	2	6,807.90
Rosemount Stud	1	2	6,189.75
Rosenthal, Mrs George Proskauer & Warren	1	1	29,376.00
Ross Valley Farm	1	1	38,046.20
Rotherwick, Lord	1	1	4,713.25
Rothschild, Exors Of The Late Mrs D M de	3	5	47,511.95
Rowcliffe Stud	1	3	8,030.25
Rowland, D A R Bloodstock Ltd	1	1	3,557.50
Rowland, Mrs V	1	1	2,637.00
Rowlane Investments	1	2	14,006.40
Royle, Dr And Mrs J D	1	2	5,271.30
Rubin, H S	1	1	2,579.00
Rudkin, Mrs D	1	2	7,958.25
Runnymede Farm Inc	1	2	32,670.90
Runnymede Farm Incorporated & Dahar Syndicate	1	1	2,892.60
Russell, A G	2	2	5,245.63
Russell, J B	1	2	19,842.00
Russell, Mrs M	1	1	3,054.00
Rutherford, Mike G	1	1	2,385.00
Ryan, B	2	3	8,311.60
Ryan, J	1	1	7,570.00
Ryan, M	1	1	147,500.00
Ryan, Mrs Frances	1	3	11,834.00
Ryan, Mrs M A	2	2	4,569.30
Ryan, T A	2	3	11,819.25
SADDINGTON, MRS H	1	3	9,099.90

	H	W	£
Saddle Home Farm	1	1	3,816.00
Sagittarius Bloodstock Agency	1	1	3,720.00
Samac Ltd And Potomac Ltd	2	4	13,298.80
Sampson, Mrs N F M	1	1	3,161.40
Samuel, D W	1	1	60,361.20
Sangster, Ben	1	1	2,070.00
Sangster, H Alexander And R E	3	3	9,826.65
Saud, S M	1	2	7,570.00
Saud, T M	2	6	83,340.45
Scarfe, A And M	1	1	3,080.00
Scarteen Stud	3	4	13,358.80
Scott, Hardie	1	2	9,088.80
Scott, Mrs D D	1	2	7,209.90
Scott, Mrs Hardie	1	1	2,898.00
Scott, R M	3	9	35,183.10
Scott-Dunn, Mrs P	1	1	2,243.00
Scully, Robin	1	2	6,520.50
Searle, R	1	1	2,534.20
Sears, R D	2	5	110,001.77
Seend Stud	2	2	6,671.50
Selby, R And Partners	2	3	8,316.00
Seltzer, Edward A	1	1	3,460.00
Sexton, Aidan	1	2	6,250.00
Sexton, C J	1	1	2,553.00
Sexton Enterprises	3	5	14,499.50
Sexton, Vinery, Alec Head, J Sullivan And H	1	1	3,647.25
Seydoux, Mrs Yolande	1	1	3,611.25
Shadwell Farm Inc	7	7	31,813.75
Shadwell Estate Company Limited	20	32	162,528.30
Shadwell Farm Inc & Shadwell Estate Co Ltd	10	12	62,562.75
Shanbally House Stud	2	2	6,928.75
Shannon, Bradley M	1	1	4,371.75
Shannon, R	1	2	6,409.25
Shannon Holdings Ltd	1	2	8,521.25
Shaw, B W Hills And Mrs V	2	3	25,564.00
Shaw, R L	1	1	3,379.00
Sheehan, C	1	2	5,977.40
Shepherd, L M	1	2	7,092.50
Sheriffe, Miss M And A J Tree	1	1	3,817.50
Sherwood, Mrs C Whitwood And N E C	1	1	3,318.75
Shirley, David And Mrs	1	2	6,754.50
Shirley, Mr And Mrs David	1	1	1,548.00
Shutford Stud	4	6	40,932.20
Side Hill Stud	2	2	8,129.00
Sieff, David	1	1	3,850.00
Sigsworth, L C And Mrs A E	2	6	29,835.80
Sigsworth, Mrs A E	2	4	26,938.50
Silverleaf Farm	1	1	3,377.25
Simpson, Alasdair J	1	2	7,715.70
Simpson, James	1	5	15,264.00
Sinanan, Mrs Margaret	2	2	5,907.00
Singh, Maj B	1	3	14,388.00
Skara Glen Stable	1	4	79,354.50
Skirton, B P And Mrs S Camacho	1	1	3,435.75
Slattery, Liam	1	1	3,150.00
Slattery, Patrick McGrath And Liam	1	1	2,549.00
Smalley, R	1	1	2,742.00
Smeaton, A K	1	1	2,778.90
Smith, Arthur E	2	2	15,731.70
Smith, Miss E C Martin	1	1	8,610.00
Smith, Mrs C Martin	1	1	5,526.50
Smith, David	1	1	1,725.00
Smith, R H Cowell And Mrs B R Abel	1	2	5,526.80
Snailwell Stud Co Ltd	3	6	35,443.30
Sneath, Mrs K W	2	2	8,314.25
Snowdrop Stud Co Ltd	1	1	11,647.50
Somerhall Bloodstock Ltd	1	1	2,427.00
Somerville Stud	1	1	3,435.75
Southcourt Stud	3	4	12,250.30
Speelman, A A	1	1	3,348.00
Spendthrift Farm	2	6	53,328.65
Spendthrift Farm, Inc	1	1	3,850.00
Springdale Farms Ltd	1	2	4,606.50
St Simon Foundation	3	5	14,121.95
St George, E G P	1	1	7,096.00
Stack, T And Caradale Trading Co	1	5	15,220.00
Stack, Tommy And Partners	1	1	5,677.50
Stack, T and Sangster, R E	2	2	12,752.80
Stackallan Stud	3	6	18,737.80
Stafford, J B And Mrs N G	1	4	11,939.25
Stafford, Preston Madden & Mrs Florence	1	1	3,231.00
Stallion Development Group	1	2	9,742.25
Stanley Estate And Stud Co	8	12	57,207.75
Staunton, Michael	1	1	3,201.75
Steel, J Goddard And J	1	1	3,525.00
Steele-Mortimer P M	1	2	6,368.50
Steele, Mrs L	1	1	7,044.00
Steinberg, George And Mrs	1	2	6,108.50
Stelcar Stables Inc	2	5	31,133.15
Sterlingbrook Farm	1	1	2,534.20
Stetchworth Park Stud Ltd	8	16	62,609.75
Stevens, C M	1	1	2,070.00
Stevens, J B H	2	4	17,645.30
Stilvi Compania Financiera S A	4	4	15,005.25
Stockwell Ltd	1	1	3,145.00
Stokes, R B	1	1	3,080.00
Stone, C	1	1	2,560.00
Stone, J H	2	8	33,948.20
Stonereath Farms Inc	3	3	14,057.70
Stonereath Farms Inc, Gary Player, Et Al	1	1	3,535.00
Stonethorn Stud Farms Ltd	3	5	19,913.40
Stowell Hill Ltd	3	4	23,396.95
Stowell Hill Ltd And A J Tree	4	10	31,187.35
Strange, Jim	1	2	6,311.10
Stratford Place Stud	4	6	20,674.75
Strawbridge, George Jnr	1	2	7,058.25
Stuart Siegel And Foxfield Thoroughbreds	1	1	3,746.50
Stud-On-The-Chart	5	11	31,700.90
Studcrown Ltd	2	6	56,299.25
Summertree Stud	2	4	26,172.55
Sung, Jerry	1	1	2,637.00
Sunley Stud	3	4	14,530.75
Sutton, Mrs Anne	1	1	3,054.20
Swarraton Stud	1	1	3,640.50
Swettenham Stud	27	37	228,721.97
Swettenham Stud & Mrs Julian G Rogers	1	2	13,483.00
Swiers, J E	1	1	3,236.00
Swire, Miss B	1	1	3,582.00
TABERNER, S	1	1	2,364.00
Tajir, Hadi Al	1	1	5,253.50
Tally-Ho Stud	1	1	1,380.00
Tarry, A	3	7	29,786.55
Tartan Farms Corp	1	2	35,075.00
Tarworth Bloodstock Investments Ltd	1	1	5,469.75
Tateson, C S	1	1	3,262.00
Tauner Dunlap, Jr And Brereton C Jones	1	2	14,195.80
Tavistock, Marquess And Marchioness Of	1	1	3,231.00
Taylor, Mrs Mary	1	2	18,299.50
Tebbutt, N F And Mrs E E	1	1	2,725.70
Tedwood Bloodstock Ltd	1	1	2,952.00
Tellwright, P T	2	2	5,763.00
The Arrow Farm And Stud	1	1	3,210.00
The Aston House Stud	1	1	3,649.00
The Banstead Manor Stud	1	1	2,070.00
The Duke Of Marlborough	1	1	3,183.70
The Duke Of Roxburghe's Stud	1	1	4,449.50
The Lavington Stud	4	5	19,329.00
The National Stud	2	4	16,864.50
The Overbury Stud	10	16	129,476.15
The Sussex Stud	3	5	24,264.75
The Woodhaven Stud	1	4	14,163.06
The Hall Stud Ltd	2	2	6,230.90
Theakston Stud	1	3	7,337.80
Thomas, Peter	1	3	6,942.60
Thomas, Robert J	2	3	11,809.75
Thompson, Mrs B	1	1	2,070.00
Thoroughbred Holdings International	1	1	3,288.00
Thoroughbred Stock Investors Ltd	3	4	12,248.75
Thoroughbreds, Continental	1	2	6,900.50
Throsby, J	1	1	4,503.00
Tierney, A P	1	2	5,744.40
Times Of Wigan Ltd	1	2	5,020.60
Tinkler, Mrs M	1	1	2,070.00
Tomkins, Clive	1	2	6,211.80
Tory, R J And Mrs	1	1	3,184.00
Trafford, Mrs Brian	1	2	6,983.40
Travers, Mrs Mary	1	1	3,036.00
Trotter, Mrs John	3	3	54,113.80
Tsarina Stud	4	9	31,968.35
Tullamaine Castle Stud	1	1	2,717.50
Tullamaine Castle Stud And Partners	1	1	4,435.00
Turner, Edwin	1	1	4,474.50
Turner, R J	2	3	9,905.65
Twelve Oaks Stud Establishment	1	1	3,231.00

	H	W	£
Twomey, D	1	1	10,575.00
Tylden-Wright, D	1	3	11,757.00
Tylor, P A	1	1	2,469.00
UPSDELL, MRS M	1	2	6,766.40
Urquhart, R S A	1	1	2,200.50
V, DENE INVESTMENTS N	1	2	12,267.75
Vanian, Souren	1	1	3,209.60
Vardy, R	1	1	2,242.50
Venner, P And Mrs	2	2	6,793.50
Ventures, Muirfield	1	2	15,530.00
Vesci, Viscount de	1	1	1,679.00
Vestey, Lady	2	2	9,898.25
Vestey, Lord	1	1	1,770.00
Vestey, T R G	1	2	47,876.75
Vickers, A	1	1	4,092.00
Vincent, Mrs A J	1	1	2,070.00
Vintage Services Ltd	1	1	2,826.00
Vonderlohe, Martin W Bach And Chris	1	3	10,323.60
W LAZY T LTD	1	1	5,024.00
Wacker, C III	2	5	19,317.90
Wallace, Exors Of The Late Mrs W	1	1	2,243.00
Wallace Farms (Stud) Ltd	1	1	3,415.00
Walsh, E J Daly And S P	1	1	2,601.40
Walsh, Martin	1	2	6,072.00
Walshe, Louis A	1	1	3,377.25
Walshe, Patrick	1	2	8,418.50
Walwyn, C J Spence And P T	1	3	11,008.00
Walwyn, Michael White And Peter	1	2	7,715.00
Ward, H	2	4	13,598.50
Ward, J	1	2	5,080.40
Ward, L H J	2	5	26,175.70
Ward, T	1	2	4,643.00
Warner, Marvin L	1	1	3,348.00
Warren, B J	1	4	15,474.50
Warren, John	1	1	2,434.00
Warren, R B	2	3	10,543.50
Waters, C A	1	2	5,685.00
Waters, G D	1	1	3,564.00
Wates, M E	3	3	54,208.25
Watkins, A	2	6	66,727.30
Watson, J F	1	1	3,106.00
Watson, R T And Mrs	6	9	38,042.40
Watt, Mrs M	1	1	2,794.00
Waugh, R E And G N Clark	1	1	6,254.50
Waverton Stud Ltd	2	3	13,323.60
Way-Oak Cliff Stable Ltd	1	3	8,254.10
Weber, Francis X	2	2	6,604.50
Weinfeld, J	1	1	2,243.00
Weld, Mrs C L	2	4	21,908.80
Weld, Mrs M F	1	3	17,939.20
Weller-Poley, Mrs J H	1	1	2,238.20
Wellesley, Lady Joanna	2	4	18,141.50
Wertheimer & Frere	1	1	109,537.80
West, Dr & Mrs R, Miller M & Mrs, Et Al	1	2	7,071.25
West, R M	2	3	15,336.40
Wheelersland Stud	2	3	10,139.50
Whent, Mrs G A	2	2	6,625.50
Whitaker, R M	3	4	17,080.50
White, Sir Gordon	1	1	4,077.50
White Lodge Stud Ltd	2	3	15,040.25
Whitechurch Stud	2	2	7,185.00
Whitehead, Mrs A	1	2	4,143.00
Whitewood Stable Inc	1	1	3,640.50
Whitney, Thomas P	2	3	8,329.00
Whitsbury Manor Stud	7	9	50,863.50
Whittingham, Mrs D	3	6	17,483.90
Wick-Dromdiah Investments Ltd	2	5	18,252.45
Wickham, Mrs	3	6	19,561.95
Wigan, James	1	1	3,366.00
Wigan, Mr And Mrs Dare	2	2	7,456.25
Wiggins, C	1	1	4,532.50
Wightman, W G R And Mrs J A Thomson	2	4	17,519.00
Wilkins, M A	2	4	12,616.00
Wilkinson, A And J W Brown	1	1	4,500.00
Wilkinson, R M Whitaker And E	2	4	10,141.40
William Flood	1	1	2,467.00
Williams, R P	4	6	20,537.60
Wills, Sir H D H	4	5	55,935.95
Wilson, F C T	1	1	3,493.00
Wilson, Mrs T	1	1	2,898.80
Wilson, Ralph	1	1	3,687.50
Windfield Farms	1	1	3,339.10
Windfields Farm	3	8	43,054.25
Windflower Overseas	4	5	52,458.20
Winfield, Peter	2	6	32,945.65
Wingfield, S Digby	3	4	41,859.70
Winsome Farm Inc & Star Stable	1	1	3,582.00
Withers, C R And V M	1	2	5,714.40
Wood, D J	1	1	2,924.00
Wooden Horse Inv Inc And Post Time Syndicate	1	2	13,244.00
Woodcote Stud Ltd	1	1	3,377.25
Woodditton Stud Ltd	2	2	8,578.80
Wooden Horse Investments	1	1	4,055.00
Woolford, J L	1	1	3,496.00
Worksop Manor Stud Farm	2	3	10,667.50
Worth, M J	2	3	12,653.50
Wragg, A M	1	1	4,500.00
Wren, J R C And Mrs	1	3	9,639.50
Wretham Stud	2	3	8,917.00
Wright, G	1	1	3,076.50
Wright, Mrs Ann E M	1	1	4,556.75
YARROW, M J	1	4	11,080.50
Yeomanstown Lodge Stud	2	3	16,150.25
Yong, Mrs P L	1	1	3,127.50
Young, H	1	2	9,222.75
Young, Mrs J E	1	1	3,054.20
Young, R Thornhill And J	1	1	2,219.30
ZIW ASSOCIATES	1	1	3,020.80

Leading breeders on the Flat: 1927–93

		Horses	Races Won	Value £
1927	Ld Derby	18	37	41039 10
1928	Ld Derby	20	38	64944 0
1929	Ld Derby	18	43	30644 0
1930	Ld Derby	23	48	35681 0
1931	Ld Dewar	11	18	40837 10
1932	H.H. Aga Khan	15	29	59087 5
1933	Sir Alec Black	17	38	35229 10
1934	H.H. Aga Khan	16	41	57733 10
1935	H.H. Aga Khan	13	23	49285 0
1936	Ld Astor	10	20	38290 0
1937	H.H. Aga Khan	31	51	46252 0
1938	Ld Derby	21	46	31847 0
1939	Ld Rosebery	5	10	37377 10
1940	Mr H E Morriss	5	10	7646 15
1941	Ld Glanely	7	19	8287 15
1942	National Stud	9	17	11990 10
1943	Miss D Paget	11	18	20000 15
1944	Ld Rosebery	9	11	9549 10
1945	Ld Derby	16	34	27763 10
1946	Lt-Col H Boyd-Rochfort	6	14	23059 0
1947	H.H. Aga Khan	18	34	41165 0
1948	H.H. Aga Khan	22	39	38509 0
1949	H.H. Aga Khan	24	50	69976 0
1950	Mr M M Boussac	14	18	59859 0
1951	Mr M M Boussac	16	25	44444 10
1952	H.H. Aga Khan	24	40	90358 9
1953	Mr F Darling	7	11	48099 10
1954	Maj L B Holliday	29	52	45650 14
1955	Someries Stud	7	12	50125 1
1956	Maj L B Holliday	22	47	37333 0
1957	Eve Stud	17	25	53822 0
1958	Mr R Ball	3	6	46652 0
1959	Prince Aly Khan and the late H.H. Aga Khan	7	13	100668 0
1960	Eve Stud Ltd	17	37	96689 0
1961	Eve Stud Ltd	10	19	39653 0
1962	Maj L B Holliday	28	47	72617 0
1963	Mr H F Guggenheim	1	3	66011 0
1964	Bull Run Stud	2	3	98270 0
1965	Mr J Ternynck	1	1	65301 0
1966	Someries Stud	2	3	80153 0
1967	Mr H J Joel	14	22	109882 0
1968	Mill Ridge Farm	1	4	97075 0
1969	Ld Rosebery	17	28	65591 0
1970	Mr E P Taylor	3	7	161302 15
				£ p
1971	Mr P Mellon	8	16	133902·85
1972	Mr J Hislop	4	11	155571·10
1973	Claiborne Farm	3	5	88250·30
1974	Mr N B Hunt	3	5	123702·00
1975	Overbury Stud	7	11	194480·90
1976	Dayton Ltd	5	10	232599·15
1977	Mr E P Taylor	2	4	241120·00
1978	Cragwood Estates Inc	1	3	136012·00
1979	Ballymacoll Stud	6	14	346981·00
1980	Mr P Clarke	2	5	237435·00
1981	H.H. Aga Khan	13	23	445368·00
1982	Someries Stud	4	7	265525·00
1983	White Lodge Stud	8	13	282223·00
1984	Mr E P Taylor	9	14	348693·00
1985	Dalham Stud Farms Ltd	5	10	324214·00
1986	H.H. Aga Khan	27	43	677876·18
1987	Cliveden Stud	6	17	762643·27
1988	H.H. Aga Khan	28	46	636825·18
1989	Hamdan Al-Maktoum	7	12	853780·50
1990	Juddmonte Farms	20	40	615115·30
1991	Barronstown Stud	8	9	674664·55
1992	Swettenham Stud	33	49	759531·80
1993	Juddmonte Farms	38	58	994853·53

Leading Flat race breeders in 1993

	Horses	Races Won	Value £
Juddmonte Farms	38	58	994,854
Meon Valley Stud	9	13	566,561
Baronrath Stud Ltd	2	4	279,381
Dayton Ltd	1	2	273,980
Gainsborough Stud Management Ltd	24	32	272,312
Gainsborough Farm Inc	10	13	254,311
Sheikh Mohammed	32	47	232,860
Swettenham Stud	27	37	228,722
Lord Howard de Walden	12	18	219,292
Roncon Ltd and Swettenham Stud	5	9	200,270

Winning Flat race trainers in 1993

H = Horses; R = Runners; W = Winners; 2 = Seconds; 3 = Thirds; %W-R = Percentage of winners to runners; £WIN = Win money; £W/P = Win and place money

	H	R	W	2	3	%W-R	£WIN	£W/P
Aconley, Mrs V A	13	41	6	2	3	14.6	22,293	25,745
Akehurst, R	58	282	45	36	16	16.0	247,433	331,277
Akehurst, J	13	63	3	4	7	4.8	10,785	21,273
Allan, R	12	57	6	5	8	10.5	27,842	40,366
Allen, C N	10	58	2	6	6	3.4	5,640	14,643
Alston, E J	23	170	18	10	22	10.6	79,253	105,425
Arbuthnot, D W P	19	107	12	8	5	11.2	44,325	58,156
Armstrong, R W	34	142	26	16	14	18.3	115,989	159,365
Bailey, A	33	230	19	21	17	8.3	71,494	117,224
Baker, R J	13	67	2	7	7	3.0	5,801	24,297
Balding, I A	70	338	50	36	38	14.8	383,636	532,864
Balding, J	11	71	6	5	6	8.5	16,028	24,152
Balding, G B	17	80	7	3	6	8.8	24,831	34,977
Banks, J E	13	42	7	4	2	16.7	29,443	35,246
Barker, Mrs P A	10	30	1	0	3	3.3	2,070	3,407
Barker, W L	11	47	1	3	9	2.1	3,377	10,779
Barraclough, M F	6	29	1	0	0	3.4	3,391	3,826
Barron, T D	40	206	17	18	26	8.3	70,506	105,792
Barrow, A	2	7	1	0	0	14.3	2,070	2,070
Barwell, C R	5	14	1	0	0	7.1	3,210	3,210
Bastiman, R	18	95	7	5	8	7.4	21,613	29,717
Beasley, B	20	99	6	13	10	6.1	31,308	58,647
Bell, M	73	351	41	38	31	11.7	163,006	252,086
Bennett, J A	13	63	2	3	3	3.2	6,325	10,185
Bennett, R A	3	25	1	1	1	4.0	3,288	4,557
Benstead, C J	16	86	9	8	8	10.5	30,481	44,101
Bentley, W	5	23	1	1	3	4.3	2,243	5,337
Berry, J	117	772	127	110	93	16.5	540,011	785,520
Bethell, J D	22	121	7	6	14	5.8	56,708	75,839
Bevan, P J	6	21	3	0	2	14.3	7,839	8,957
Blanshard, M	15	118	6	12	12	5.1	26,074	48,767
Bolger, J S	15	25	2	5	2	8.0	54,616	239,000
Booth, C B B	10	52	1	1	4	1.9	3,085	6,605
Bosley, J R	8	34	3	4	3	8.8	8,896	14,126
Boss, R	21	100	9	9	6	9.0	36,294	55,296
Bottomley, J F	12	49	2	5	4	4.1	9,444	16,055
Boutin, F	4	5	1	1	1	20.0	116,335	166,718
Bowring, S R	8	63	4	11	9	6.3	16,620	29,815
Bradley, J M	15	74	6	7	5	8.1	19,110	27,677
Bramall, Mrs S A	3	8	1	0	0	12.5	2,427	2,650
Bravery, G C	15	73	4	8	8	5.5	11,590	28,539
Bridger, J J	12	61	2	0	1	3.3	5,278	6,234
Brisbourne, W M	6	31	2	3	2	6.5	5,594	10,562
Brittain, C E	97	430	34	28	36	7.9	396,693	717,280
Brittain, M	32	195	9	11	16	4.6	27,330	45,709
Broad, C D	8	21	1	1	2	4.8	1,917	3,183
Brooks, C P E	6	17	1	3	1	5.9	12,231	16,894
Brotherton, R	14	34	1	1	1	2.9	1,954	3,554
Burchell, D	17	40	7	5	4	17.5	21,027	29,580
Burgoyne, P	10	37	1	1	2	2.7	3,036	5,064
Burke, K R	17	75	4	3	7	5.3	12,326	17,878
Butler, P	10	59	3	2	4	5.1	7,944	11,419
Bycroft, N	22	125	5	6	9	4.0	16,998	26,202
Callaghan, N A	26	132	9	14	13	6.8	125,704	179,508
Calver, P	14	97	12	6	12	12.4	37,160	50,579
Camacho, M J	22	96	11	9	9	11.5	61,244	90,850
Cambidge, B R	7	35	2	0	2	5.7	4,896	5,835
Campbell, I	13	34	2	0	3	5.9	3,950	5,189
Campion, Mark	11	21	1	2	4	4.8	2,826	6,903

WINNING FLAT RACE TRAINERS IN 1993

	H	R	W	2	3	%W-R	£WIN	£W/P
Candy, H	36	127	6	8	10	4.7	28,628	66,835
Carr, J M	9	45	5	7	9	11.1	11,869	22,866
Casey, T	8	40	1	2	4	2.5	2,238	6,479
Cecil, Mrs J	50	200	28	22	28	14.0	117,709	175,648
Cecil, H R A	108	406	94	63	63	23.2	1,248,318	1,797,621
Chamberlain, N	5	30	1	2	3	3.3	2,960	5,866
Channon, M R	64	388	39	44	36	10.1	168,414	269,698
Chapman, D W	32	178	10	13	13	5.6	29,675	47,098
Chapman, M C	21	97	3	6	12	3.1	9,303	20,310
Chappell, Major D N	3	8	1	0	0	12.5	3,465	3,594
Chapple-Hyam, P W	71	236	52	36	23	22.0	407,059	780,746
Charlton, R	55	185	46	35	15	24.9	374,822	514,950
Cheesbrough, P	2	8	1	1	0	12.5	3,553	4,537
Clay, W	5	13	1	1	0	7.7	1,725	2,662
Cole, P F I	118	467	62	63	80	13.3	318,525	535,139
Collingridge, H J	24	126	7	12	11	5.6	29,556	49,805
Conway, R	3	4	1	0	0	25.0	2,248	2,248
Cosgrove, D J S	11	52	6	2	5	11.5	18,864	24,455
Cottrell, L G	13	81	9	13	10	11.1	36,117	52,284
Craig, T	9	41	2	1	5	4.9	3,999	6,466
Cumani, L M	71	277	39	50	32	14.1	292,610	642,738
Cundell, P D	10	54	7	4	3	13.0	22,904	29,025
Cunningham-Brown, K O	30	124	4	7	3	3.2	14,197	24,440
Curley, B J	5	19	2	1	0	10.5	5,740	7,320
Cyzer, C A	39	217	20	22	23	9.2	99,701	155,312
Dawe, Mrs J C	8	23	1	0	1	4.3	2,700	3,458
Dickin, R	13	65	4	6	4	6.2	27,181	38,764
Dixon, M	12	43	5	1	3	11.6	15,958	18,538
Dods, M	16	114	5	9	9	4.4	18,056	31,958
Donnelly, T W	6	15	1	0	0	6.7	3,202	3,450
Dow, S	39	239	19	18	16	7.9	105,823	146,464
Doyle, Miss Jacqueline S	8	31	2	1	2	6.5	6,604	9,293
Dunlop, J L	115	536	93	73	68	17.4	700,736	1,004,390
Dyer, T	4	11	2	1	0	18.2	4,727	6,271
Easterby, M W	35	209	16	17	13	7.7	66,657	102,041
Easterby, M H	64	389	41	50	52	10.5	148,955	264,600
Eden, G H	11	61	2	2	3	3.3	8,028	16,462
Egerton, C R	5	12	1	1	1	8.3	3,392	5,193
Ellison, B	12	33	1	1	0	3.0	2,070	2,615
Elsey, C W C	17	91	4	6	6	4.4	29,979	48,290
Elsey, C C	13	94	3	2	8	3.2	8,563	18,498
Elsworth, D R C	56	261	31	27	20	11.9	156,448	259,298
Etherington, J	21	128	10	15	18	7.8	30,511	54,445
Eustace, J M P	15	78	6	5	10	7.7	85,373	120,552
Evans, P D	21	91	13	8	9	14.3	37,706	48,112
Eyre, J L	15	83	5	5	13	6.0	27,867	39,518
Fabre, A	12	15	3	4	3	20.0	293,011	439,395
Fahey, R A	3	9	1	0	1	11.1	5,901	6,887
Fairhurst, T	15	124	7	6	14	5.6	15,935	25,793
Fanshawe, J R	59	268	34	42	32	12.7	233,104	363,373
Felgate, P S	13	85	8	6	10	9.4	24,642	36,027
Fetherston-Godley, M J	12	75	7	4	6	9.3	42,208	57,777
Fisher, R F	9	44	5	3	5	11.4	14,393	19,946
FitzGerald, J G	33	160	16	22	15	10.0	55,880	97,166
Flower, R M	5	21	3	2	1	14.3	12,074	14,291
Foster, A G	3	5	1	0	0	20.0	4,092	4,092
Glover, J A	26	112	9	6	14	8.0	36,865	64,041
Gosden, J H M	127	449	109	67	46	24.3	1,018,364	1,421,549
Graham, N A	20	71	5	1	8	7.0	16,757	24,773
Gubby, B	7	27	1	4	2	3.7	2,553	7,151
Guest, R	18	71	9	5	10	12.7	24,475	44,726
Haggas, W J	30	124	12	18	14	9.7	40,165	72,658
Haigh, W W	17	82	8	9	8	9.8	23,039	36,051
Hall, Miss S E	19	93	14	7	7	15.1	55,080	70,186
Hambly, A A	13	54	1	4	3	1.9	2,951	8,047
Hammond, M D	33	154	11	19	15	7.1	32,488	56,838
Hanbury, B	43	221	35	28	35	15.8	196,625	303,958
Hannon, R	203	1179	180	173	146	15.3	1,222,892	1,964,855
Hanson, J	9	29	2	4	2	6.9	6,937	14,312
Harris, J L	30	130	8	9	7	6.2	24,235	37,555
Harris, P W	36	173	19	25	21	11.0	75,229	136,382
Harris, R	6	25	1	0	2	4.0	3,106	3,688
Harrison, A	8	46	1	1	3	2.2	2,243	5,134
Harwood, G	47	203	19	26	29	9.4	81,130	165,003
Haslam, P C	41	213	17	15	21	8.0	49,644	72,971
Haynes, M J	13	65	4	7	7	6.2	15,466	29,338
Head, Mrs C	2	2	2	0	0	100.0	315,245	315,245
Heaton-Ellis, M J	41	211	18	19	14	8.5	69,406	107,013

WINNING FLAT RACE TRAINERS IN 1993

	H	R	W	2	3	%W-R	£WIN	£W/P
Hedger, P R	9	32	1	0	3	3.1	3,641	5,813
Henderson, N J	2	3	1	0	0	33.3	5,299	5,299
Hern, Major W R	44	155	13	24	21	8.4	53,067	113,232
Herries, Lady	18	87	18	11	12	20.7	124,713	175,156
Hetherton, J	14	74	2	8	7	2.7	7,055	17,306
Hide, A	19	87	6	6	13	6.9	21,999	36,634
Hill, C J	20	94	12	6	4	12.8	39,226	47,381
Hills, B W	95	344	37	36	39	10.8	203,495	440,174
Hills, J W	45	232	24	33	21	10.3	126,129	189,857
Hodges, R J	52	292	19	23	27	6.5	128,726	194,502
Hogg, K W	10	69	4	7	3	5.8	12,872	22,810
Hollinshead, R	78	525	34	56	52	6.5	129,191	220,655
Holt, L J	22	152	9	16	7	5.9	47,868	75,128
Horgan, C A	14	87	5	7	9	5.7	24,529	43,712
Houghton, R F Johnson	23	121	7	13	21	5.8	25,799	52,403
Howling, P	30	158	6	4	7	3.8	21,409	35,368
Huntingdon, Lord	65	232	29	32	23	12.5	301,523	435,250
Ingram, R	8	45	5	0	8	11.1	14,698	18,723
Ivory, K T	14	88	2	6	12	2.3	4,733	16,455
James, C	12	62	4	4	1	6.5	28,499	35,346
Jarvis, W	46	182	20	21	13	11.0	205,435	239,885
Jarvis, A P	19	128	7	12	7	5.5	21,146	43,023
Jarvis, M A	31	145	19	22	17	13.1	68,177	114,334
Jenkins, J R	29	130	4	5	10	3.1	13,107	24,872
Johnston, M	67	459	60	78	53	13.1	317,616	494,501
Jones, A P	6	46	3	7	4	6.5	9,858	19,022
Jones, H Thomson	46	182	28	29	24	15.4	122,918	216,783
Jones, T M	6	22	3	2	0	13.6	11,698	13,343
Jones, Bob	18	109	9	15	13	8.3	31,369	83,756
Jones, T Thomson	20	77	5	1	8	6.5	17,731	24,305
Jones, D Haydn	20	116	6	10	8	5.2	16,476	30,012
Jones, A W	5	22	1	1	3	4.5	2,624	4,664
Jordan, F	4	15	1	1	1	6.7	2,679	4,704
Kelleway, Miss Gay	20	89	10	12	11	11.2	27,429	43,707
Kelleway, P A	25	78	6	7	6	7.7	26,654	58,905
Kersey, T	7	29	1	2	0	3.4	3,704	5,873
Kettlewell, S E	10	56	5	3	4	8.9	12,281	17,319
King, Mrs A L M	5	28	1	3	0	3.6	2,669	6,599
King, J S	6	34	2	5	4	5.9	6,457	13,667
Knight, Mrs A	15	47	4	1	3	8.5	12,234	15,082
Laing, D R	17	112	9	5	7	8.0	28,720	37,516
Leach, P	6	16	3	1	1	18.8	8,891	10,665
Lee, F H	34	230	11	18	20	4.8	35,664	74,483
Lee, R	12	48	2	1	5	4.2	4,218	7,942
Leigh, J P	10	27	1	2	1	3.7	3,158	5,622
Lellouche, E	1	2	2	0	0	100.0	273,980	273,980
Lewis, G	47	247	30	13	21	12.1	102,692	143,845
Lines, C V	6	33	2	5	5	6.1	4,733	12,228
Loder, D R	40	185	43	29	27	23.2	193,839	283,040
Macauley, Mrs N	18	96	7	8	9	7.3	19,844	32,600
Mackie, J	10	50	3	3	4	6.0	6,542	9,938
Makin, P J	28	129	10	12	13	7.8	88,351	128,406
Marks, D	8	41	2	1	3	4.9	9,672	12,035
McBride, P J	10	21	1	1	0	4.8	2,601	3,531
McCormack, M	30	136	15	10	17	11.0	65,066	99,171
McGovern, T P	6	28	1	2	1	3.6	2,448	4,376
McMahon, B A	47	240	16	19	20	6.7	74,643	122,564
McMath, B J	11	37	1	4	1	2.7	2,070	6,858
Meehan, B J	32	181	13	14	18	7.2	42,644	69,328
Mellor, S	9	53	4	4	9	7.5	10,530	18,423
Millman, B R	19	120	6	9	9	5.0	15,485	52,901
Mills, T G	23	121	8	18	13	6.6	77,689	130,596
Mitchell, P	15	81	6	6	5	7.4	19,472	31,056
Mitchell, Pat	19	96	4	4	6	4.2	14,807	23,965
Moffatt, D	19	81	3	4	9	3.7	11,723	37,384
Monteith, P	15	61	4	2	3	6.6	10,653	14,065
Moore, G L	32	175	13	10	17	7.4	45,145	77,917
Moore, G M	18	81	6	8	6	7.4	74,085	92,436
Moore, J S	15	72	2	3	3	2.8	5,963	9,954
Moore, A	21	86	6	6	6	7.0	16,697	26,023
Morley, D	27	126	16	15	15	12.7	77,954	108,027
Morris, D	21	116	17	12	13	14.7	91,185	111,082
Muggeridge, M P	14	69	1	5	3	1.4	3,598	9,424
Muir, W R	32	160	8	13	19	5.0	31,840	57,475
Murphy, P G	33	169	12	7	14	7.1	36,956	62,341
Murray, B W	10	44	1	3	2	2.3	2,709	6,044
Murray Smith, D J G	8	40	2	3	5	5.0	10,217	18,348
Musson, W J	27	155	7	18	6	4.5	31,082	58,852

	H	R	W	2	3	%W-R	£WIN	£W/P
Naughton, T J	23	109	15	7	7	13.8	82,367	97,701
Naughton, M P	15	110	4	5	5	3.6	14,183	21,835
Norton, S G	46	277	38	26	31	13.7	123,185	175,515
O'Brien, M V	2	5	1	1	1	20.0	40,645	100,884
O'Donoghue, J	5	28	2	0	4	7.1	6,773	9,196
O'Gorman, W A	17	79	11	14	11	13.9	41,660	59,977
O'Mahony, F J	5	27	1	2	3	3.7	4,221	10,442
O'Neill, J J	9	34	2	4	3	5.9	5,841	10,622
O'Neill, O	7	22	2	2	2	9.1	5,512	8,698
O'Sullivan, R J	24	97	9	4	5	9.3	24,592	32,264
Oldroyd, G R	10	31	2	1	4	6.5	5,073	8,291
Palling, B	26	108	9	9	11	8.3	28,990	47,719
Parker, C	2	8	1	1	0	12.5	2,322	3,094
Parkes, J	9	51	5	9	2	9.8	12,527	23,181
Payne, J W	13	91	11	5	6	12.1	38,221	54,158
Pearce, J	29	159	14	12	14	8.8	37,592	56,515
Perratt, Miss L A	29	157	7	16	17	4.5	24,279	49,469
Phillips, R T	11	36	1	1	0	2.8	3,985	5,230
Piggott, Mrs L	12	68	10	6	5	14.7	32,729	55,171
Pipe, M C	28	97	18	14	13	18.6	95,945	144,810
Prescott, Sir Mark	54	245	50	47	28	20.4	153,138	224,021
Price, R J	8	29	2	2	1	6.9	6,948	9,158
Pritchard-Gordon, G A	32	129	13	6	9	10.1	47,922	69,394
Ramsden, Mrs J R	43	269	30	32	21	11.2	193,341	264,250
Reveley, Mrs M	93	515	82	69	66	15.9	290,295	434,320
Richmond, B	6	29	1	1	3	3.4	3,688	6,535
Rothwell, B S	25	123	4	7	10	3.3	12,685	28,933
Rowe, R	12	34	1	0	1	2.9	2,415	3,108
Ryan, M J	24	177	23	23	11	13.0	77,066	123,500
Sanders, Miss B	11	58	6	4	7	10.3	23,380	32,717
Saunders, M S	4	26	1	2	2	3.8	2,553	6,796
Scargill, Dr J D	24	98	9	12	12	9.2	28,790	57,526
Scott, A A	50	196	20	26	15	10.2	117,241	180,428
Seemar, S	1	2	1	0	0	50.0	5,024	7,845
Shaw, D	8	37	1	0	1	2.7	3,785	5,746
Sherwood, S E	2	5	1	1	0	20.0	8,900	12,520
Siddall, Miss L C	15	109	9	9	15	8.3	28,571	57,978
Simpson, R	18	78	5	10	3	6.4	18,625	35,946
Smart, B	11	44	3	1	2	6.8	7,695	10,331
Smith, A	7	34	3	3	2	8.8	95,284	99,939
Smith, Denys	19	153	12	10	15	7.8	34,701	55,996
Smith, Allan	4	13	1	0	1	7.7	2,070	2,363
Smith, C	10	29	2	2	3	6.9	6,315	8,769
Smith, N A	3	14	1	0	1	7.1	2,832	3,542
Smith, C A	13	50	1	0	1	2.0	2,364	2,764
Spearing, J L	33	159	16	14	11	10.1	76,209	99,652
Spicer, R C	19	73	4	0	5	5.5	14,395	17,573
Stack, T	1	1	1	0	0	100.0	9,681	9,681
Stewart, A C	36	120	11	19	18	9.2	38,953	76,459
Stoute, M R	118	419	65	51	53	15.5	1,071,842	1,529,333
Stringer, A P	9	50	5	2	6	10.0	15,649	21,206
Sutcliffe, J	20	82	4	4	6	4.9	27,912	48,568
Thom, D T	10	67	3	8	6	4.5	9,460	23,277
Thornton, C W	17	97	2	13	15	2.1	10,754	28,850
Tinkler, C	22	103	3	8	10	2.9	7,989	18,858
Tinkler, N	30	123	14	11	15	11.4	81,751	106,025
Toller, J A R	12	41	3	1	4	7.3	47,009	55,297
Tompkins, M H	62	286	27	32	37	9.4	346,068	413,988
Troy, J M	9	21	1	2	1	4.8	3,630	8,081
Tucker, D R	5	18	1	0	2	5.6	2,623	3,310
Turner, W G M	30	122	11	9	18	9.0	31,483	46,321
Twiston-Davies, N A	5	11	1	0	1	9.1	3,417	3,792
Usher, M D I	27	154	11	7	8	7.1	53,744	81,317
Wainwright, J S	16	74	3	5	5	4.1	11,309	25,643
Wall, C F	22	101	13	6	8	12.9	51,071	65,921
Walwyn, P T	37	184	17	20	24	9.2	192,792	255,154
Wane, Martyn	11	68	5	0	11	7.4	18,359	24,724
Waring, Mrs Barbara	11	37	2	3	2	5.4	6,033	10,914
Watts, J W	28	161	17	22	23	10.6	88,806	149,644
Weedon, C	9	38	2	0	4	5.3	4,995	6,695
Weymes, E	17	95	10	13	8	10.5	41,786	65,367
Wharton, J	31	152	14	17	16	9.2	52,255	88,341
Whitaker, R M	48	317	22	33	29	6.9	66,762	117,210
White, J	31	89	10	8	6	11.2	83,321	96,489
Wigham, P	3	13	1	0	0	7.7	3,236	4,058
Wightman, W G R	7	47	4	4	2	8.5	17,519	27,701
Wildman, C P	6	25	2	2	2	8.0	6,843	9,960
Williams, R J R	31	202	15	22	25	7.4	52,538	95,953

	H	R	W	2	3	%W-R	£WIN	£W/P
Williams, M	7	42	5	4	5	11.9	13,272	19,394
Williams, C N	6	38	3	3	3	7.9	8,427	12,801
Wilson, D A	21	176	18	9	14	10.2	64,935	85,709
Wilson, Capt J	11	86	4	7	10	4.7	10,704	22,487
Woods, S P C	21	128	7	8	17	5.5	33,352	73,347
Wragg, G	48	198	35	31	31	17.7	428,417	618,024

Leading trainers on the Flat: 1900–93

		Horses	Races Won	Value £
1900	R Marsh	20	31	43321
1901	J Huggins	16	42	29142
1902	R S Sievier	5	10	23686
1903	G Blackwell	14	24	34135
1904	P P Gilpin	17	44	35694
1905	W T Robinson	26	52	34466
1906	Hon G Lambton	22	46	34068
1907	A Taylor	17	31	24708
1908	C Morton	12	20	26431
1909	A Taylor	25	49	47825
1910	A Taylor	24	47	52364
1911	Hon G Lambton	23	48	49769
1912	Hon G Lambton	29	55	22884
1913	R Wootton	31	66	28284
1914	A Taylor	19	39	52052
1915	P P Gilpin	8	12	15324
1916	R C Dawson	21	32	16386
1917	A Taylor	15	25	17924
1918	A Taylor	14	33	36629
1919	A Taylor	23	41	33208
1920	A Taylor	27	47	35907
1921	A Taylor	28	51	48280
1922	A Taylor	24	55	52059
1923	A Taylor	25	46	49190
1924	R C Dawson	18	26	48857
1925	A Taylor	25	51	56570
1926	F Darling	24	48	63408
1927	Frank Butters	26	54	57468
1928	Frank Butters	27	50	67539
1929	R C Dawson	35	58	74754
1930	H S Persse	26	46	49487
1931	J Lawson	34	69	93899
1932	Frank Butters	34	62	72436
1933	F Darling	32	64	44276
1934	Frank Butters	33	79	88844
1935	Frank Butters	29	48	59687
1936	J Lawson	32	49	61773
1937	C Boyd-Rochfort	26	43	61212
1938	C Boyd-Rochfort	29	44	51350
1939	J L Jarvis	20	34	56219
1940	F Darling	15	25	16166
1941	F Darling	18	37	19025
1942	F Darling	11	20	12843
1943	W Nightingall	18	29	13833
1944	Frank Butters	18	34	17585
1945	W Earl	21	41	29557
1946	Frank Butters	31	60	56140
1947	F Darling	26	56	65313
1948	C F N Murless	33	63	66542
1949	Frank Butters	20	42	71721
1950	C H Semblat (in France)	10	11	57044
1951	J L Jarvis	37	62	56397
1952	M Marsh	15	30	71546
1953	J L Jarvis	39	60	71546
1954	C Boyd-Rochfort	25	39	65326
1955	C Boyd-Rochfort	24	38	74424
1956	C F Elsey	45	83	61621
1957	C F N Murless	32	48	116898
1958	C Boyd-Rochfort	24	37	84186
1959	C F N Murless	32	63	145727
1960	C F N Murless	24	42	118327
1961	C F N Murless	21	36	95972
1962	W Hern	24	39	70206
1963	P Prendergast (in Ireland)	14	19	125294
1964	P Prendergast (in Ireland)	14	17	128102
1965	P Prendergast (in Ireland)	10	11	75323
1966	M V O'Brien (in Ireland)	7	8	123848
1967	C F N Murless	34	60	256899
1968	C F N Murless	30	47	141508
1969	A M Budgett	22	35	105349
1970	C F N Murless	35	53	199524
1971	I Balding	25	45	157488
1972	W Hern	24	42	206767
1973	C F N Murless	21	34	132984
1974	P Walwyn	54	96	206783
1975	P Walwyn	69	121	382527
1976	H Cecil	24	52	261301
1977	M V O'Brien (in Ireland)	13	18	439124
1978	H Cecil	60	109	382301
1979	H Cecil	56	128	683971
1980	W Hern	38	65	831964
1981	M Stoute	53	95	723786
1982	H Cecil	58	111	872614
1983	W Hern	31	57	549598
1984	H Cecil	63	108	551939
1985	H Cecil	67	132	1148189
1986	M Stoute	53	76	1269933
1987	H Cecil	89	180	1882314
1988	H Cecil	72	112	1186083
1989	M Stoute	82	116	1360708
1990	H Cecil	68	111	1519864
1991	P F I Cole	97	67	1256502
1992	R Hannon	198	147	1154201
1993	H Cecil	108	94	1248318

Principal Flat trainers' winning totals: 1977–93

	1977	1978	1979	1980	1981	1982	1983	1984	1985	1986	1987	1988	1989	1990	1991	1992	1993
Akehurst, R	13	15	14	9	1	1	5	2	6	16	27	25	33	34	40	28	45
Armstrong, R	19	30	38	29	45	43	26	23	22	31	25	36	20	22	10	14	26
Balding, I	33	39	39	49	39	58	60	32	59	48	31	43	41	48	53	36	50
Bell, M	—	—	—	—	—	—	—	—	—	—	—	—	18	16	40	39	41
Berry, J	6	20	11	15	19	26	43	30	19	21	32	71	92	118	143	107	127
Brassey, K	—	—	—	—	—	12	19	23	25	17	14	16	13	14	—	—	—
Breasley, A	—	3	19	19	—	—	—	—	—	—	—	—	—	—	—	—	—
Brittain, C	31	52	34	25	54	53	45	33	51	39	38	40	36	41	47	63	34
Brittain, M	—	—	—	—	—	—	—	—	22	24	38	44	25	20	18	7	9
Callaghan, N	24	40	34	14	29	15	9	13	15	25	20	27	29	27	27	19	9
Candy, H	32	35	39	28	30	32	34	10	33	27	33	20	16	23	16	21	6
Cecil, H	74	109	128	84	107	111	92	108	132	115	180	112	117	111	118	109	94
Cecil, Mrs J	—	—	—	—	—	—	—	—	—	—	—	—	—	—	19	28	28
Channon, M	—	—	—	—	—	—	—	—	—	—	—	—	—	16	20	26	39
Chapman, D	2	2	2	5	11	22	21	34	30	14	13	36	27	14	13	12	10
Chapple-Hyam, P.	—	—	—	—	—	—	—	—	—	—	—	—	—	—	27	41	52
Charlton, R	—	—	—	—	—	—	—	—	—	—	—	—	—	36	26	43	46
Cole, P	47	56	61	48	50	39	41	61	54	64	55	43	50	48	67	85	62
Cumani, L	30	53	19	26	30	25	35	50	60	67	83	73	88	108	72	54	39
Dunlop, J	42	73	96	91	67	87	89	89	62	106	61	66	61	74	58	75	93
Durr, F	—	—	38	51	42	13	57	18	22	4	10	2	10	5	—	—	—
Easterby, M H	46	50	74	63	37	43	30	30	29	49	68	64	57	59	58	38	41
Easterby, M W	34	12	31	17	26	18	11	24	31	33	12	25	19	17	14	12	16
Eldin, E	—	—	—	11	11	27	23	15	11	17	6	10	7	6	3	—	—
Elsey, W	21	18	12	26	11	18	10	14	12	7	13	10	10	9	4	9	4
Elsworth, D	—	—	10	12	10	17	24	24	22	31	31	28	35	41	37	31	31
Fairhurst, T	18	34	20	11	13	13	26	17	12	16	8	10	11	10	11	8	7
Fanshawe, J	—	—	—	—	—	—	—	—	—	—	—	—	—	18	22	28	34
FitzGerald, J	15	9	15	13	14	10	24	21	23	17	7	20	18	18	12	7	16
Gosden, J	—	—	—	—	—	—	—	—	—	—	—	—	28	87	84	112	109
Haggas, W	—	—	—	—	—	—	—	—	—	—	17	14	16	21	26	12	12
Hanbury, B	21	18	8	24	21	22	35	34	20	24	31	40	41	35	36	39	35
Hannon, R	37	47	30	37	29	28	49	28	37	56	33	43	53	69	126	147	182
Harwood, G	50	59	48	69	97	120	104	93	84	112	67	73	109	69	55	27	19
Haslam, P	7	10	25	38	35	29	15	25	13	34	23	22	—	—	12	29	17
Hern, W	74	74	61	65	64	44	57	56	53	45	36	30	45	30	23	17	13
Hills, B	76	86	56	61	82	55	58	58	68	55	96	93	73	102	93	61	37
Hindley, J	41	42	41	46	32	39	38	41	42	18	25	—	—	—	—	—	—
Hobbs, B	65	43	42	60	50	42	24	34	24	—	—	—	—	—	—	—	—
Hollinshead, R	49	50	25	26	57	36	43	54	40	28	28	33	30	36	27	55	34
Houghton, R Johnson	54	47	39	42	29	38	29	45	17	34	26	36	24	22	13	10	7
Huffer, G	—	—	23	11	18	22	26	27	30	17	23	12	16	19	—	—	—
Huntingdon, Lord	26	27	27	27	44	22	—	13	15	30	15	31	25	16	34	55	29
Jarvis, A	3	13	5	6	24	34	19	26	15	12	1	—	—	—	1	2	7
Jarvis, M	27	31	39	30	35	31	40	34	21	30	19	31	28	28	24	25	19
Jarvis, W	—	—	—	—	—	—	—	—	12	16	27	26	32	31	28	21	20
Johnston, M	—	—	—	—	—	—	—	—	—	—	1	5	15	28	28	50	60
Jones, H Thomson	15	20	13	40	40	45	42	57	55	43	30	41	37	32	37	27	28
Kelleway, P	6	26	21	23	11	22	25	21	17	18	12	16	13	6	9	16	6
Lewis, G	—	—	—	5	26	19	27	30	29	25	25	32	23	25	41	54	30
Loder, D	—	—	—	—	—	—	—	—	—	—	—	—	—	—	—	2	43
Marshall, W	35	26	16	6	1	3	—	—	—	—	—	—	—	—	—	—	—
McCormack, M	—	—	—	3	3	13	11	16	22	16	7	4	12	5	15	16	15
Mitchell, Philip	3	6	7	12	14	11	13	23	15	9	5	12	14	4	7	4	6
Nelson, C	4	16	16	32	9	22	19	19	18	26	26	22	19	20	9	7	—
Norton, S	2	5	14	14	19	29	41	43	35	21	33	33	11	18	17	25	38
O'Gorman, W	16	32	25	30	25	49	39	44	15	20	10	24	9	36	14	21	11
Prescott, Sir M	26	28	30	34	36	35	33	40	17	39	26	34	40	37	39	49	50
Price, Ryan	73	61	60	48	31	23	—	—	—	—	—	—	—	—	—	—	—
Pritchard-Gordon, G	41	39	58	47	36	43	37	19	38	37	35	20	16	18	14	17	13
Ramsden, Mrs J	—	—	—	—	—	—	—	—	4	—	11	14	32	26	38	24	30
Reveley, Mrs M	—	—	—	—	—	—	4	11	12	6	20	12	15	15	34	68	82
Ryan, M	5	6	23	11	14	22	29	33	23	33	29	22	13	24	19	22	23
Scott, A A	—	—	—	—	—	—	—	—	—	—	—	—	24	29	22	36	20

	1977	1978	1979	1980	1981	1982	1983	1984	1985	1986	1987	1988	1989	1990	1991	1992	1993
Sheather, R	—	6	10	15	13	7	7	16	12	16	12	8	—	—	—	—	—
Smith, Denys	30	28	53	35	29	20	28	17	15	20	16	14	15	7	9	14	12
Smith, Doug	20	12	4	—	—	—	—	—	—	—	—	—	—	—	—	—	—
Stewart, A C	—	—	—	—	—	—	6	13	22	26	37	40	30	40	29	21	11
Stoute, M	62	69	80	101	95	103	89	96	120	76	105	99	116	78	83	74	65
Sutcliffe, Jnr. J	18	24	21	19	24	20	17	22	17	16	13	12	17	16	3	14	4
Swift, B	23	22	24	22	8	14	15	27	—	—	—	—	—	—	—	—	—
Tinkler, C	—	—	—	—	—	—	—	9	20	21	31	24	34	22	14	4	3
Tinkler, N	—	—	—	—	—	7	10	9	14	30	31	24	24	16	13	9	14
Tompkins, M	—	—	—	4	9	12	17	13	17	19	24	16	44	40	41	42	27
Tree, J	17	24	30	30	23	22	35	28	40	35	32	30	29	—	—	—	—
Vigors, N	12	15	13	13	21	12	11	15	14	20	18	15	—	—	—	—	—
Walwyn, P	110	70	44	78	52	48	26	47	42	43	36	30	35	44	24	22	17
Watts, J W	57	50	46	47	51	29	25	28	34	24	32	23	24	24	14	17	17
Weymes, E	17	24	9	19	16	20	10	13	2	5	4	10	6	5	2	12	10
Whitaker, R M	—	—	—	5	4	10	12	15	11	27	33	48	29	35	24	22	22
Williams, R J R ...	—	—	—	—	12	22	14	14	18	25	26	18	17	15	18	14	15
Winter, J	22	23	31	13	19	30	28	32	28	29	23	5	—	—	—	—	—
Wragg, G	—	—	—	—	—	—	27	22	26	32	27	31	25	32	50	44	35
Wragg, H	39	34	30	33	37	30	—	—	—	—	—	—	—	—	—	—	—

[Totals given are for winners trained in Great Britain only]

Winning Flat race jockeys in 1993

	Mounts	1st	2nd	3rd	%W-R	£WIN	£W/P
Adams, N	503	17	27	25	3.4	55,882	106,600
Asmussen, C	43	4	5	5	9.3	221,042	367,260
Avery, C	63	1	2	1	1.6	3,668	6,599
Bardwell, G	344	16	15	15	4.7	46,147	91,270
Biggs, D	344	24	22	25	7.0	94,623	146,995
Birch, M	435	30	50	56	6.9	122,643	240,171
Boeuf, D	1	1	0	0	100.0	79,700	79,700
Bowker, Julie	16	4	1	1	25.0	9,301	10,360
Carlisle, N	325	22	15	22	6.8	123,371	155,197
Carroll, J	619	92	74	74	14.9	412,113	637,956
Carson, W	837	115	93	120	13.7	996,497	1,441,030
Carter, G	306	45	36	34	14.7	207,962	276,071
Charnock, L	348	19	20	25	5.5	94,969	136,293
Clark, A	282	17	18	31	6.0	51,266	90,741
Cochrane, R	724	82	105	83	11.3	634,892	1,094,703
Comber, J	14	1	2	1	7.1	2,873	5,144
Connorton, N	295	30	22	28	10.2	115,206	178,852
Crossley, B	26	2	1	0	7.7	8,321	10,028
Culhane, A	247	17	20	19	6.9	56,445	87,922
Curant, J	9	2	0	1	22.2	5,601	5,931
D'Arcy, P	31	5	7	0	16.1	17,167	24,606
Darley, K	799	137	128	105	17.1	534,935	810,440
Dawson, S	123	1	8	7	0.8	3,417	14,995
Day, N	159	12	20	12	7.5	58,634	107,189
Dettori, L	845	135	114	114	16.0	1,013,158	1,544,262
Duffield, G	753	114	91	98	15.1	453,011	697,580
Dwyer, C	37	1	3	2	2.7	2,951	7,779
Eddery, Paul	596	66	49	62	11.1	306,146	428,143
Eddery, Pat	813	169	131	83	20.8	1,659,078	2,323,297
Elliott, R P	55	1	5	10	1.8	3,558	16,447
Fallon, K	524	59	66	59	11.3	289,998	427,152
Fanning, J	432	19	37	51	4.4	120,572	192,760
Fortune, J	316	25	27	27	7.9	73,497	120,117
Gibson, Dale	322	9	18	29	2.8	32,656	66,305
Greaves, Alex	85	3	5	8	3.5	9,767	19,353
Hills, M	557	73	78	66	13.1	565,969	934,709
Hills, R	441	57	59	51	12.9	251,414	422,935
Hind, G	245	33	26	25	13.5	116,843	170,979
Holland, D	509	62	54	56	12.2	270,884	518,919
Hood, W	46	4	2	2	8.7	12,156	14,537
Johnson, E	76	4	4	3	5.3	11,155	16,736
Kettlewell, Mrs D	5	1	0	0	20.0	1,730	1,730
Kinane, M J	32	4	1	2	12.5	654,226	670,023
Lang, T	10	1	0	0	10.0	3,210	3,210
Lappin, R	63	1	5	4	1.6	3,005	11,062
Lowe, J	523	28	47	33	5.4	202,940	277,347
Lucas, T	131	9	13	10	6.9	38,667	66,273
Mackay, A	427	29	31	28	6.8	114,202	187,871
Marcus, B	31	2	1	0	6.5	13,132	18,308
McGlone, A	381	25	27	27	6.6	108,702	163,459
McKeown, Dean	370	46	50	37	12.4	170,031	258,549
Morris, S	49	2	4	3	4.1	4,786	10,034
Mosse, G	1	1	0	0	100.0	109,538	109,538
Munro, A	666	73	79	68	11.0	363,636	608,582
Newnes, W	517	38	32	44	7.4	131,043	197,359
Nicholls, D	65	4	3	6	6.2	11,308	17,604
O'Gorman, S	103	7	3	6	6.8	24,072	30,828
O'Reilly, J	26	1	0	0	3.8	2,951	3,315
Penza, J	18	1	1	3	5.6	4,878	11,212
Perham, R	172	8	11	9	4.7	27,461	47,952
Perks, S	261	19	24	23	7.3	54,960	101,132
Perrett, M	95	6	5	7	6.3	40,276	55,525
Piggott, L	298	39	27	34	13.1	386,509	636,869
Price, R	201	16	14	15	8.0	54,891	80,858
Quinn, T	813	106	107	89	13.0	600,761	982,791
Quinn, J	619	41	56	57	6.6	158,603	279,706
Raymond, B	453	47	43	53	10.4	186,974	586,922

	Mounts	1st	2nd	3rd	%W-R	£WIN	£W/P
Raymont, S.	109	11	13	4	10.1	61,663	82,997
Reid, J	764	108	108	70	14.1	793,012	1,327,081
Roberts, M	715	114	96	109	15.9	1,326,907	2,097,508
Robinson, P	462	52	46	62	11.3	461,114	581,944
Roche, C	19	1	3	2	5.3	16,570	30,577
Rouse, B	395	33	27	31	8.4	148,236	219,175
Rutter, C	296	13	23	26	4.4	57,051	115,261
Ryan, W	594	87	72	74	14.6	642,174	864,283
Sattar, Abdul	1	1	0	0	100.0	2,248	2,248
Smith, J D	46	6	6	5	13.0	29,374	42,186
Sprake, T	188	17	10	22	9.0	52,813	75,526
Street, R	23	3	0	0	13.0	10,525	10,922
Swinburn, W R	565	92	77	77	16.3	1,232,090	1,782,939
Tebbutt, M	213	17	30	16	8.0	61,723	107,596
Thomas, D	32	3	1	5	9.4	10,385	14,056
Tinkler, Kim	98	3	7	5	3.1	6,228	12,700
Vincent, Lorna	10	1	1	2	10.0	2,758	4,760
Webster, S	188	10	11	25	5.3	41,350	68,446
Whitworth, S	316	20	24	28	6.3	61,256	108,059
Wigham, M	256	10	21	19	3.9	26,707	57,951
Williams, J	563	51	45	47	9.1	258,778	379,885
Williams, T	307	21	34	22	6.8	70,793	118,274
Wood, S	158	8	10	7	5.1	25,673	38,322
Woods, W	290	22	24	31	7.6	90,347	160,871

MISCELLANEOUS

	Mounts	1st	2nd	3rd	%W-R	£WIN	£W/P
Hide, Edward	1	1	0	0	100.0	2,406	2,406
Smith, Bill	1	1	0	0	100.0	0	0
Swinburn, W	1	1	0	0	100.0	2,286	2,286

Champion Flat race jockeys: 1846–1993

Year	Jockey	Wins
1846	E Flatman	81
1847	E Flatman	89
1848	E Flatman	104
1849	E Flatman	94
1850	E Flatman	88
1851	E Flatman	78
1852	E Flatman	92
1853	J Wells	86
1854	J Wells	82
1855	G Fordham	70
1856	G Fordham	108
1857	G Fordham	84
1858	G Fordham	91
1859	G Fordham	118
1860	G Fordham	146
1861	G Fordham	106
1862	G Fordham	166
1863	G Fordham	103
1864	J Grimshaw	164
1865	G. Fordham	142
1866	S Kenyon	123
1867	G Fordham	143
1868	G Fordham	110
1869	G Fordham	95
1870	W Grey	76
	C Maidment	76
1871	G Fordham	86
	C Maidment	86
1872	T Cannon	87
1873	H Constable	110
1874	F Archer	147
1875	F Archer	172
1876	F Archer	207
1877	F Archer	218
1878	F Archer	229
1879	F Archer	197
1880	F Archer	120
1881	R Archer	220
1882	F Archer	210
1883	F Archer	232
1884	F Archer	241
1885	F Archer	246
1886	F Archer	170
1887	C Wood	151
1888	F Barrett	108
1889	T Loates	167
1890	T Loates	147
1891	M Cannon	137
1892	M Cannon	182
1893	T Loates	222
1894	M Cannon	167
1895	M Cannon	184
1896	M Cannon	164
1897	M Cannon	145
1898	O Madden	161
1899	S Loates	160
1900	L Reiff	143
1901	O Madden	130
1902	W Lane	170
1903	O Madden	154
1904	O Madden	161
1905	E Wheatley	124
1906	W Higgs	149
1907	W Higgs	146
1908	D Maher	139
1909	F Wootton	165
1910	F Wootton	137
1911	F Wootton	187
1912	F Wootton	118
1913	D Maher	115
1914	S Donoghue	129
1915	S Donoghue	62
1916	S Donoghue	43
1917	S Donoghue	42
1918	S Donoghue	66
1919	S Donoghue	129
1920	S Donoghue	143
1921	S Donoghue	141
1922	S Donoghue	102
1923	S Donoghue	89
	C Elliott	89
1924	C Elliott	106
1925	G Richards	118
1926	T Weston	95
1927	G Richards	164
1928	G Richards	148
1929	G Richards	135
1930	F Fox	129
1931	G Richards	145
1932	G Richards	190
1933	G Richards	259
1934	G Richards	212
1935	G Richards	217
1936	G Richards	174
1937	G Richards	216
1938	G Richards	206
1939	G Richards	155
1940	G Richards	68
1941	H Wragg	71
1942	G Richards	61
1943	G Richards	65
1944	G Richards	88
1945	G Richards	104
1946	G Richards	212
1947	G Richards	269
1948	G Richards	224
1949	G Richards	261
1950	G Richards	201
1951	G Richards	227
1952	G Richards	231
1953	G Richards	191
1954	D Smith	129
1955	D Smith	168
1956	D Smith	155
1957	A Breasley	173
1958	D Smith	165
1959	D Smith	157
1960	L Piggott	170
1961	A Breasley	171
1962	A Breasley	179
1963	A Breasley	176
1964	L Piggott	140
1965	L Piggott	160
1966	L Piggott	191
1967	L Piggott	117
1968	L Piggott	139
1969	L Piggott	163
1970	L Piggott	162
1971	L Piggott	162
1972	W Carson	132
1973	W Carson	164
1974	Pat Eddery	148
1975	Pat Eddery	164
1976	Pat Eddery	162
1977	Pat Eddery	176
1978	W Carson	182
1979	J Mercer	164
1980	W Carson	166
1981	L Piggott	179
1982	L Piggott	188
1983	W Carson	159
1984	S Cauthen	130
1985	S Cauthen	195
1986	Pat Eddery	176
1987	S Cauthen	197
1988	Pat Eddery	183
1989	Pat Eddery	171
1990	Pat Eddery	209
1991	Pat Eddery	165
1992	M Roberts	206
1993	Pat Eddery	169

Principal Flat jockeys' winning totals: 1977–93

	1977	1978	1979	1980	1981	1982	1983	1984	1985	1986	1987	1988	1989	1990	1991	1992	1993
Barclay, A	—	—	—	—	—	—	6	7	2	—	—	—	—	—	—	—	—
Baxter, G	62	63	64	52	57	52	39	44	37	29	22	19	21	27	21	18	—
Birch, M	62	65	77	71	56	69	51	52	46	53	92	95	91	57	54	39	30
Bleasdale, J	67	90	41	41	18	26	26	16	15	7	13	11	6	7	9	—	—
Bond, A	25	19	16	16	12	9	5	16	7	6	—	1	1	—	—	—	—
Carlisle, N	—	—	1	12	24	16	18	16	21	14	6	9	17	20	25	21	22
Carroll, J	—	—	—	—	—	—	—	1	4	9	24	49	62	50	87	67	92
Carson, W	160	182	142	166	114	145	159	97	125	130	100	130	138	187	155	125	115
Carter, G	—	—	—	—	—	—	1	9	37	34	50	42	45	65	73	68	45
Cauthen, S	—	—	52	61	87	107	102	130	195	149	197	104	164	142	107	107	—
Charnock, L	25	15	25	16	23	25	13	14	32	22	24	18	15	16	17	19	19
Clark, A S	—	—	1	22	28	18	21	29	16	28	18	20	38	22	19	16	17
Cochrane, R	—	—	6	21	22	25	20	47	51	89	111	120	120	109	102	100	82
Connorton, N	—	—	7	24	24	16	22	24	26	27	46	34	21	25	25	29	30
Cook, P	72	90	80	90	84	83	62	43	51	41	36	33	28	—	—	—	—
Curant, R	15	25	31	18	21	22	17	10	9	16	16	5	—	—	—	—	—
Darley, K	11	70	14	19	14	14	37	33	30	30	55	38	68	80	66	91	136
Dettori, L	—	—	—	—	—	—	—	—	—	—	8	22	75	137	94	101	135
Duffield, G	60	75	76	78	94	92	98	86	61	94	64	77	78	62	75	108	114
Durr, F	28	35	—	—	—	—	—	—	—	—	—	—	—	—	—	—	—
Dwyer, C	9	17	20	23	11	12	12	20	13	6	6	3	2	1	2	2	1
Eccleston, C	19	29	4	2	—	—	—	—	—	—	—	—	—	—	—	—	—
Eddery, Paul	—	—	2	17	20	22	23	46	50	49	37	52	44	46	70	72	66
Eddery, Pat	176	148	123	130	109	83	122	107	162	176	195	183	171	209	165	178	169
Eldin, E	49	34	35	—	—	—	—	—	—	—	—	—	—	—	—	—	—
Fallon, K	—	—	—	—	—	—	—	—	—	—	—	31	28	39	29	45	59
Fox, R	29	14	17	26	16	21	23	35	27	9	20	16	11	6	11	2	—
Gray, O	9	11	10	8	10	9	4	7	4	—	—	—	—	—	—	—	—
Hide, E	111	88	53	106	105	65	53	26	10	—	—	—	—	—	—	1	1
Hills, M	—	—	5	13	10	15	39	41	45	40	75	76	77	53	61	82	73
Hills, R	—	—	2	6	12	31	25	39	39	42	46	52	59	53	63	52	57
Holland, D	—	—	—	—	—	—	—	—	—	—	—	—	—	30	79	68	62
Ives, T	41	29	38	53	42	82	71	90	77	72	70	62	30	—	2	—	—
Jago, B	9	11	16	30	19	11	5	2	—	—	—	—	—	—	—	—	—
Johnson, E	72	86	61	48	29	47	27	3	12	—	5	10	4	4	1	2	4
Johnson, I	13	—	3	20	9	14	12	10	13	8	9	20	14	—	—	—	—
Kimberley, A	39	14	27	15	8	4	8	21	18	12	19	12	—	—	—	—	—
Lewis, G	62	44	8	—	—	—	1	—	—	—	—	—	—	—	—	—	—
Lowe, J	86	57	49	54	69	57	52	58	43	38	60	41	36	45	54	33	28
Lynch, J	26	36	65	12	—	—	—	—	—	—	—	—	—	—	—	—	—
Madden, P	10	26	8	8	8	2	1	—	—	—	—	—	—	—	—	—	—
Matthias, J	21	26	23	41	37	40	38	17	29	14	11	7	22	9	—	—	—
McGlone, A	—	—	—	—	15	17	32	26	23	28	9	16	15	25	24	16	25
McKay, D	24	17	23	11	26	20	13	14	12	6	9	5	3	2	—	—	—
McKeown, D	—	—	—	6	13	20	10	2	1	21	20	59	86	87	58	55	46
Marshall, R	30	10	9	1	—	—	—	—	—	—	1	—	—	—	—	—	—
Mercer, J	102	115	164	104	64	58	55	49	43	—	—	—	—	—	—	—	—
Morby, F	18	20	19	19	—	—	1	—	—	—	—	—	—	—	—	—	—
Munro, A	—	—	—	—	—	—	—	—	1	0	6	33	38	90	103	75	73
Murray, A	1	—	2	5	—	22	14	34	39	39	—	—	—	—	—	—	—
Newnes, W	—	7	19	35	28	57	41	—	—	15	48	44	39	47	26	27	38
Nicholls, D	22	8	8	4	7	28	17	47	44	38	33	32	28	24	24	17	4
Perks, S	14	15	8	5	41	26	32	42	30	19	18	18	31	24	20	2	19
Piggott, L	103	97	77	156	179	188	150	100	34	—	—	—	—	3	48	35	39
Quinn, J	—	—	—	—	—	—	—	—	—	12	14	23	19	31	26	42	41
Quinn, T	—	—	—	—	1	21	35	62	47	69	55	46	60	73	86	108	107
Raymond, B	56	48	58	62	73	74	51	63	38	—	45	77	66	70	71	53	47
Reid, J	33	54	72	79	54	63	30	56	53	60	81	79	84	67	78	95	108
Roberts, M	—	25	—	—	—	—	—	—	—	42	74	121	107	128	118	206	114
Robinson, P	—	7	51	59	30	48	52	54	48	40	25	10	—	—	—	52	52
Rogers, T	3	11	16	39	18	19	12	6	2	—	—	—	—	—	5	3	—
Rouse, B	48	60	42	42	65	54	58	67	31	34	50	51	51	33	13	23	33
Ryan, W	—	—	—	—	—	5	27	41	37	56	69	58	49	55	65	96	87
Seagrave, J	43	15	25	24	23	35	27	—	—	—	—	—	—	—	—	—	—
Starkey, G	76	107	98	82	90	103	103	63	81	102	55	48	52	—	—	—	—
Street, R	25	17	13	3	8	9	3	14	10	5	8	6	3	—	2	—	3
Swinburn, W R	—	12	47	49	65	64	62	99	75	83	93	88	93	111	68	82	92
Taylor, B	83	59	56	32	48	53	48	8	—	—	—	—	—	—	—	—	—
Thomas, M L	98	52	48	27	15	24	10	40	26	7	—	7	—	—	—	—	—
Tulk, P	10	2	14	10	8	4	2	1	1	10	—	1	—	—	—	—	—
Waldron, P	44	47	53	53	49	31	31	23	18	31	17	—	—	—	—	—	—
Webster, S	18	23	10	13	12	16	12	17	18	8	3	19	22	19	10	10	10
Wharton, W	18	25	18	15	4	2	1	2	—	3	—	—	1	—	—	—	—
Whitworth, S	—	—	—	—	—	2	7	47	30	28	22	31	24	34	26	20	20
Wigham, M	32	56	25	37	19	16	12	11	18	32	27	23	32	19	9	8	10
Williams, J	—	—	—	—	—	—	—	3	5	14	15	25	35	62	44	49	51
Williams, T	—	—	—	—	—	—	8	51	31	50	53	28	38	27	17	12	21
Young, P	26	13	15	22	33	37	16	6	—	—	—	—	—	—	—	—	—

[Totals given are for winning mounts in Great Britain only]

Winning Flat race apprentices in 1993

	Mounts	1st	2nd	3rd	%W-R	£WIN	£W/P
Adamson, C	32	2	1	2	6.3	6,863	10,664
Armes, Antoinette	64	2	6	1	3.1	7,210	18,541
Aspell, L	36	3	1	5	8.3	7,382	10,022
Baird, M	47	2	2	1	4.3	4,227	7,084
Balding, Claire	111	6	5	12	5.4	16,234	26,668
Bastiman, H	64	5	4	9	7.8	15,711	23,249
Bradley, Michael	14	1	0	1	7.1	2,070	2,363
Carter, L	33	3	2	2	9.1	9,596	12,214
Copp, S	30	6	5	1	20.0	17,598	23,381
Coulter, Ruth	15	1	2	1	6.7	3,132	4,665
Davies, Stephen	212	19	13	29	9.0	71,358	108,365
Denaro, Mark	124	11	17	8	8.9	38,011	61,407
Denaro, Michael	23	2	3	3	8.7	6,957	12,113
Dennis, J	34	2	2	1	5.9	5,795	7,678
Doyle, B	298	30	23	23	10.1	132,745	204,715
Drake, S	4	1	0	0	25.0	2,861	2,861
Drowne, S	155	8	8	11	5.2	36,512	56,130
Dwyer, Martin	8	1	0	0	12.5	2,243	2,243
Edmunds, J	6	1	0	0	16.7	2,070	2,070
Eiffert, S	20	2	1	1	10.0	3,938	4,691
Faulkner, Gina	9	1	1	0	11.1	3,260	4,196
Fenton, M	173	14	16	15	8.1	47,718	76,285
Forster, G	49	3	6	9	6.1	8,396	18,962
Garth, A	175	8	14	16	4.6	37,721	61,272
Geran, A	7	1	0	0	14.3	3,630	4,044
Gibbs, D	55	6	4	4	10.9	29,846	37,508
Gotobed, J	3	1	0	0	33.3	1,725	1,725
Griffiths, D	26	3	5	0	11.5	9,525	14,755
Gwilliams, N	60	1	3	5	1.7	3,184	7,979
Halliday, V	80	7	7	4	8.8	24,769	33,104
Harrison, D	494	39	47	42	7.9	217,733	361,018
Harwood, Gaye	11	3	0	1	27.3	10,477	11,095
Havlin, R	30	3	1	3	10.0	7,753	9,892
Hawksley, C	104	5	3	9	4.8	11,930	22,346
Hodgson, C	140	15	15	9	10.7	86,600	109,487
Houghton, P	7	2	1	0	28.6	5,213	5,677
Humphries, M	67	5	10	5	7.5	27,123	40,457
Husband, E	10	1	0	2	10.0	2,245	3,040
James, S	3	1	0	1	33.3	2,925	3,353
Johnson, P	16	1	2	2	6.3	3,261	5,524
Jones, Wendy	26	3	0	4	11.5	8,190	9,651
Kennedy, N	150	3	10	13	2.0	72,115	110,670
Knott, S	31	5	2	3	16.1	18,876	22,477
Maloney, S	284	27	22	29	9.5	88,035	136,214
Marshall, J	94	10	7	9	10.6	26,331	39,607
McCabe, D	219	19	14	30	8.7	64,709	94,700
McCabe, P	125	15	14	8	12.0	49,389	83,073
McCarthy, S	26	2	3	0	7.7	5,211	7,803
McDonnell, Kim	96	3	3	11	3.1	9,243	18,305
McGrath, G	6	2	0	1	33.3	5,069	5,474
McLaughlin, T G	76	6	7	8	7.9	39,768	51,619
Meredith, D	16	3	1	2	18.8	23,540	26,907
Millard, Sharon	23	1	0	0	4.3	2,534	2,822
Moffatt, Darren	244	21	11	27	8.6	76,367	111,042
Mulvey, S	122	8	11	10	6.6	23,392	41,967
Newton, L	53	6	6	5	11.3	20,037	33,365
Norton, F	278	19	15	20	6.8	79,992	125,474
O'Dwyer, J	17	1	1	1	5.9	2,553	4,051
O'Gorman, Emma	81	7	16	12	8.6	21,211	40,118
O'Neill, D	23	2	4	2	8.7	5,363	9,992
Painter, R	73	12	13	4	16.4	35,365	51,465
Pears, O	266	27	25	31	10.2	90,622	132,163
Plowright, Marie	7	2	0	0	28.6	5,527	5,527
Procter, A	58	4	2	3	6.9	15,804	21,995
Radford-Howes, Sally	17	2	1	0	11.8	6,396	7,270
Roberts, P	48	6	7	5	12.5	17,030	29,588
Rose, P	2	1	0	0	50.0	1,590	1,590

WINNING FLAT RACE APPRENTICES IN 1993

	Mounts	1st	2nd	3rd	%W-R	£WIN	£W/P
Russell, B	107	4	10	3	3.7	10,098	23,760
Rutter, K	108	10	12	6	9.3	29,692	45,033
Sanders, S	57	4	6	6	7.0	16,081	26,657
Scudder, C	5	1	0	0	20.0	8,415	8,658
Slattery, V	23	1	0	2	4.3	2,333	3,195
Strange, G	48	4	8	8	8.3	10,645	20,666
Tate, J	163	18	15	17	11.0	54,255	84,075
Teague, C	55	3	3	6	5.5	8,422	16,121
Thompson, Sarah	29	2	2	6	6.9	5,101	9,182
Toole, D	19	2	2	0	10.5	6,360	7,880
Tucker, A	181	6	5	13	3.3	17,667	33,794
Turner, Elizabeth	8	1	0	1	12.5	2,489	3,231
Varley, N	104	6	10	5	5.8	19,998	33,864
Wands, Iona	19	1	5	1	5.3	3,496	8,080
Weaver, J	357	55	36	35	15.4	270,131	342,397
Whelan, A	29	2	5	3	6.9	6,646	13,235
Williams, S D	135	4	6	6	3.0	11,124	23,597
Wright, D	371	20	23	25	5.4	66,689	125,324
Wynne, S	16	1	2	1	6.3	2,930	5,763

Champion apprentices: 1922–93

Year	Apprentice	Wins
1922	R A Jones	58
1923	E C Elliott	89
1924	E C Elliott	106
1925	C Smirke	70
1926	C Smirke	71
1927	S Wragg	38
1928	G Baines and L Cordell	33
1929	C Adley	35
1930	J Simpson	28
1931	F Rickaby	44
1932	F Rickaby	37
1933	E Smith	52
1934	E Smith	36
1935	E Smith	76
1936	W Wing	37
1937	D Smith	45
1938	G Wells	27
1939	K Mullins	29
1940	G Littlewood	13
1941	K Mullins	9
1942	K Mullins	7
1943	J Sime	5
1944	J Sime	9
1945	F Durr and T Gosling	10
1946	J Sime	40
1947	D Buckle	20
1948	D Buckle	25
1949	W Snaith	31
1950	L Piggott	52
1951	L Piggott	51
1952	J Mercer	26
1953	J Mercer	61
1954	E Hide	53
1955	P Robinson	46
1956	E Hide	75
1957	G Starkey	45
1958	P Boothman	37
1959	R P Elliott	27
1960	R P Elliott	39
1961	B Lee	52
1962	B Raymond	13
1963	D Yates	24
1964	P Cook	46
1965	P Cook	62
1966	A Barclay	71
1967	E Johnson	39
1968	D Coates and R Dicey	40
1969	C Eccleston	41
1970	P Waldron	59
1971	Pat Eddery	71
1972	R Edmondson	45
1973	S Perks	41
1974	A Bond	40
1975	A Bond	66
1976	D Dineley	54
1977	J Bleasdale	67
1978	K Darley	70
1979	P Robinson	51
1980	P Robinson	59
1981	B Crossley	45
1982	W Newnes	57
1983	M Hills	39
1984	T Quinn	62
1985	G Carter and W Ryan	37
1986	G Carter	34
1987	G Bardwell	27
1988	G Bardwell	39
1989	L Dettori	75
1990	J Fortune	46
1991	D Holland	79
1992	D Harrison	52
1993	J Weaver	55

Winning amateur riders on the Flat 1993

	Mounts	1st	2nd	3rd	%W-R	£WIN	£W/P
Arbuthnot, Mrs D	12	2	0	0	16.7	6,571	6,571
Bosley, Mrs S	16	3	2	2	18.8	8,896	11,124
Buckley, Mr M	12	3	2	2	25.0	8,572	10,639
Cowdrey, Mrs M	22	4	3	4	18.2	22,828	26,636
Crossley, Mrs J	9	1	1	0	11.1	2,847	3,607
Cuff, Mr T	18	4	2	0	22.2	9,235	11,189
Deniel, Miss A	6	1	0	0	16.7	2,532	2,532
Eaton, Miss L	7	1	0	0	14.3	1,646	1,646
Elsey, Miss A	6	1	3	0	16.7	2,805	6,907
Farrell, Mrs A	15	2	1	0	13.3	5,332	5,974
Haggas, Mrs M	4	1	0	0	25.0	3,028	3,028
Harwood, Miss A	13	2	1	1	15.4	6,179	7,866
Hide, Miss L	9	1	2	1	11.1	3,236	5,103
Jenkins, Mr M	1	1	0	0	100.0	2,343	2,343
Jones, Miss I Diana W	11	1	3	2	9.1	2,624	8,473
Jones, Miss Diana	19	3	5	2	15.8	7,113	12,062
Kierans, Miss R	1	1	0	0	100.0	3,396	3,396
Lewis, Mr G	4	1	0	0	25.0	2,685	2,685
Marks, Miss K	2	1	0	0	50.0	6,255	6,255
McHale, Mrs D	4	1	0	0	25.0	3,126	3,126
Moore, Mr N	1	1	0	0	100.0	2,070	2,070
Musson, Mrs J	7	1	0	0	14.3	5,127	5,127
Naughton, Mrs J	4	1	1	1	25.0	2,574	3,621
Pearce, Mrs L	34	5	3	4	14.7	11,636	16,432
Perratt, Miss L	4	1	0	0	25.0	2,322	2,322
Pritchard-Gordon, Mr P	5	1	0	0	20.0	2,637	2,637
Southcombe, Miss J	4	1	1	1	25.0	2,560	3,845
Swiers, Mr S	6	1	2	1	16.7	2,646	4,300
Urbano, Mr L A	2	2	0	0	100.0	11,925	11,925

Winning owners: All-weather Flat 1992–93

H = Horses; R = Runners; W = Winners; 2 = Seconds; 3 = Thirds; %W-R = Percentage of winners to runners; £WIN = Win money; £W/P = Win and place money

	H	R	W	2nd	3rd	%W-R	£WIN	£W/P
The Queen	6	15	3	6	2	20.0	6,683	11,178
Adams, Bruce	1	3	1	0	0	33.3	2,448	2,448
Addleshaw, Mrs J	3	19	3	0	3	15.8	7,385	8,330
Ahier, D M	2	5	1	0	1	20.0	2,532	2,850
Allen, David	1	5	2	0	1	40.0	5,190	5,532
Al-Said, K	1	1	1	0	0	100.0	2,406	2,406
A M Packaging Ltd	1	13	2	3	2	15.4	4,413	7,215
Anderson, Mrs David	1	3	1	0	2	33.3	2,427	3,054
Anderton, Colin W	1	12	1	5	2	8.3	2,070	6,192
Baggott, Mrs M	1	7	2	1	0	28.6	4,917	5,559
Baker, I A	1	5	5	0	0	100.0	11,599	11,599
Barratt, Mrs P A	3	16	2	2	1	12.5	4,371	6,006
Berenson, Richard	7	38	10	8	3	26.3	30,407	38,326
Berry, J	4	13	3	3	1	23.1	7,138	9,509
Bigg, J E	1	9	4	1	0	44.4	10,504	11,199
Blumenow, Jack	1	7	3	4	0	42.9	8,313	10,910
Boggis, P F	2	3	1	0	1	33.3	2,734	3,055
Booth, Colin G R	1	5	1	2	0	20.0	2,544	4,119
Brian Yeardley Continental Ltd	1	6	5	1	0	83.3	13,063	13,735
Brodrick, M J	1	3	2	0	0	66.7	8,080	8,080
Brookes, Norton	1	3	1	1	0	33.3	2,343	2,973
Brooks, Mrs M E	1	6	3	0	1	50.0	7,878	8,223
Broughton Thermal Insulation	5	18	4	1	1	22.2	10,474	11,785
Brunton, Sir Gordon	2	5	1	1	0	20.0	2,343	3,003
Burton, Wayne	1	5	1	0	0	20.0	2,427	2,427
Butterfield, G R	2	10	1	2	0	10.0	2,454	3,942
Callaghan, Mrs J	1	6	1	0	1	16.7	2,478	2,849
Capehart, Thomas R	1	7	3	2	0	42.9	7,401	8,703
Cartwright, R T	1	5	1	0	2	20.0	2,385	3,000
Case, B E	1	3	1	0	0	33.3	2,208	2,208
Cayzer, Major H S	1	2	1	0	0	50.0	2,790	3,005
Chapman, David W	6	28	9	4	3	32.1	21,866	25,394
Churm, Mrs P	1	9	1	0	0	11.1	2,343	2,343
Codan Trust Company Limited	1	2	1	0	1	50.0	2,364	2,679
Connors, Terry	1	5	1	1	0	20.0	2,322	3,012
Copyforce Ltd	1	5	1	1	0	20.0	2,820	4,053
Cox, Timothy	1	5	1	1	1	20.0	2,979	4,103
Crawshaw, Lord	1	4	2	2	0	50.0	9,347	10,736
Crowe, Mrs S R	2	3	1	0	1	33.3	3,054	3,369
Cullen, Bob	1	2	1	0	1	50.0	2,856	3,241
Cushing, H A	1	6	1	1	0	16.7	2,070	2,718
David Barron Racing Club	3	8	3	0	1	37.5	7,113	7,731
De Kwiatkowski, Henryk	4	12	4	0	3	33.3	14,821	16,225
Denson, Mrs Louise	1	5	2	0	0	40.0	5,001	5,199
Derby, Lord	2	6	1	2	1	16.7	2,322	3,912
De Walden, Lord Howard	1	4	1	1	1	25.0	2,709	3,915
Doorgachurn, Mrs R J	1	8	2	1	3	25.0	6,566	9,082
Dorji, H E Lhendup	2	9	3	3	1	33.3	6,630	9,541
Doyle, P B	1	7	1	0	2	14.3	2,406	3,033
Eamer, R K	1	3	1	1	1	33.3	2,385	3,405
Elliot, Miss Ruth	1	4	1	0	0	25.0	2,343	2,343
Emmerson, Dr C I	1	3	1	0	0	33.3	2,427	2,427
Facchino, Mrs B	4	24	4	3	4	16.7	11,637	15,060
FitzGerald, J G	3	6	1	0	1	16.7	2,553	2,865
Freeman, Peter G	1	7	1	2	3	14.3	2,406	4,900
Freyne, Garrett J	1	8	1	6	0	12.5	2,301	7,778
Fustok, S	3	8	1	2	1	12.5	2,208	4,538
Gadsden, E J S	1	3	1	0	0	33.3	2,208	2,208
Gibbons, Paul	1	1	1	0	0	100.0	2,070	2,070
Glenton, Ian W	5	13	1	1	1	7.7	2,364	3,252
Golding, Frank W	1	5	2	2	0	40.0	4,770	6,546

	H	R	W	2nd	3rd	%W-R	£WIN	£W/P
Gorrie, Alex	2	3	2	0	1	66.7	5,963	6,413
G R Bailey Ltd (Baileys Horse Feeds)	1	1	1	0	0	100.0	2,070	2,070
Gravy Boys Racing	1	6	2	2	0	33.3	4,388	5,964
Haggas, B.	2	3	2	0	1	66.7	5,867	6,215
Haggas, William	1	1	1	0	0	100.0	2,322	2,322
Haigh, W W	1	3	1	0	0	33.3	2,280	2,280
Hannon, R	1	1	1	0	0	100.0	2,595	2,595
Hardy, N J Forman	1	2	1	1	0	50.0	2,448	3,108
Hawkings, L J	3	14	2	2	1	14.3	4,912	6,607
Hawthorn, Ray	1	1	1	0	0	100.0	2,322	2,322
Hazzard, Don	1	8	1	0	1	12.5	2,574	2,911
Heathcote, Mrs Robert	1	5	1	1	1	20.0	1,292	2,829
Hetherington, D M	1	3	1	0	0	33.3	2,658	2,658
Higson, K.	8	25	3	6	7	12.0	6,717	13,133
Hill, C John	23	93	21	11	10	22.6	52,923	63,833
Hill, A S	1	6	1	1	1	16.7	2,434	3,478
Hills, J W	1	2	1	1	0	50.0	2,364	3,030
Hobbs, David A	1	3	1	1	1	33.3	2,385	3,423
Hobhouse, J S	1	4	1	1	0	25.0	2,208	2,850
Holt, D	1	3	1	1	0	33.3	2,406	3,072
Honour, Fred	1	6	2	0	1	33.3	5,886	6,285
Horgan, Jim	1	1	1	0	0	100.0	2,574	2,574
Hornall, Capt R W	1	7	2	2	2	28.6	5,654	7,870
Hunt, Mrs Judy	1	3	1	1	0	33.3	2,427	3,153
Huntingdon, Lord	2	7	2	1	1	28.6	4,900	5,776
Hyde Sporting Promotions/Saddlehome Farm	1	8	3	1	2	37.5	8,303	10,085
Jacobs, Paul G	1	6	1	2	2	16.7	2,217	4,473
Jannaway, J	1	9	5	1	0	55.6	12,641	13,349
Jenkinson, R.	1	8	3	2	1	37.5	6,735	8,501
Jinks, Richard	2	9	2	1	1	22.2	5,155	6,165
Johnson, Mrs R A	2	8	2	3	1	25.0	4,845	7,266
Jones, Peter	1	7	4	0	0	57.1	10,898	11,262
Kelleway, Mrs G E	2	7	1	1	1	14.3	2,905	3,805
Khan, K F	1	1	1	0	0	100.0	2,385	2,385
Kiernan, R	1	6	1	2	2	16.7	4,092	8,156
Lamb, R	1	6	1	2	0	16.7	2,406	3,931
Lambert, P W	1	4	1	1	1	25.0	2,343	3,312
Lane, Christopher	1	7	1	0	0	14.3	2,489	2,753
Lee, Mrs John	2	4	1	0	1	25.0	2,448	2,805
Lemon, John	1	2	1	0	0	50.0	2,557	2,557
Leonard, P A	2	11	1	1	2	9.1	2,611	4,681
Lunn, N	1	3	1	0	2	33.3	2,208	2,998
Mackie, Mrs J	1	7	2	1	3	28.6	4,707	6,348
Maden, D J	2	9	2	1	1	22.2	4,728	5,664
Makin, Mrs P J	1	7	2	3	0	28.6	4,064	6,656
Mallya, Vijay	1	5	3	0	2	60.0	7,374	8,083
Marchant, R P	1	2	2	0	0	100.0	4,770	4,770
Marchant, Mrs Barbara	1	3	1	1	0	33.3	2,377	3,313
Market Rasen Racing Club	1	7	1	0	0	14.3	2,616	2,616
Marshall, Dave	2	6	1	2	2	16.7	2,427	4,353
Marshall, T C	2	4	1	0	0	25.0	2,208	2,208
Martin, Exors Of The Late Mr J	1	5	1	1	1	20.0	2,385	3,435
Martin Pound Racing Limited	1	7	2	1	1	28.6	4,917	5,858
McCalmont, Harry R D	1	1	1	0	0	100.0	2,322	2,322
McKevitt, Frank	1	9	4	3	1	44.4	9,519	11,772
McManamon, J	2	11	4	1	3	36.4	10,342	13,837
McMullan, L G	1	4	1	1	0	25.0	2,322	3,018
Mills, T G Limited	3	6	1	1	1	16.7	2,427	3,378
Mills, T G	1	2	1	0	1	50.0	3,322	3,631
Mitchell, Mrs Elaine	1	2	1	0	0	50.0	2,208	2,208
Mohan, T	1	3	3	0	0	100.0	7,197	7,197
Monolithic Refractories Ltd	1	9	3	1	2	33.3	7,181	8,615
Moore, G	1	7	1	0	2	14.3	2,832	3,610
Moss, Mrs Jill	1	1	1	0	0	100.0	2,343	2,343
Murley, G P	2	5	1	0	0	20.0	2,700	2,700
Mursell, J W	2	8	1	0	1	12.5	3,231	3,953
Newson, R A	2	6	1	1	1	16.7	2,448	3,557
Nixon, S	1	2	1	1	0	50.0	2,280	2,994
Norton, S G	4	14	3	2	3	21.4	7,470	10,374
Nott, E C	1	5	1	2	2	20.0	2,208	4,027
Oakley, Maurice	1	2	1	0	0	50.0	2,196	2,196
Oberstein, M L	3	6	3	0	1	50.0	7,507	7,948
O'Donnell, Mrs M	2	14	3	1	3	21.4	8,847	10,805
O'Gorman, Curley	1	9	1	4	0	11.1	2,406	5,322
O'Gorman, W A	3	24	3	5	1	12.5	7,020	11,289
Ong, Mrs W K	1	8	1	2	1	12.5	1,182	2,747
Oppenheimer, Sir Philip	2	6	1	1	1	16.7	2,301	3,290
O'Toole, Mattie	4	26	3	6	4	11.5	7,134	12,786
Oxton, Brian	1	6	1	0	2	16.7	2,427	3,076

WINNING OWNERS: ALL WEATHER FLAT 1992–93

	H	R	W	2nd	3rd	%W-R	£WIN	£W/P
Palacegate Corporation Ltd	4	14	1	3	2	7.1	2,385	5,156
Payne, R B	2	5	1	0	1	20.0	2,656	2,959
Peters, John	1	7	1	1	0	14.3	2,427	3,035
Peters, Martin N	1	2	1	0	1	50.0	2,512	2,948
Pfann, Miss Nicola M	1	11	4	2	1	36.4	10,941	12,634
Pickering, D O	2	3	1	1	0	33.3	2,208	3,198
Pollins, Brian	1	12	4	2	2	33.3	10,623	12,556
Popely, R A	1	7	3	1	0	42.9	6,747	7,395
Powell-Tuck, J	1	3	1	1	0	33.3	2,208	2,856
Price, D W	1	8	4	0	1	50.0	10,472	10,781
Price, D A	1	2	1	0	1	50.0	2,238	2,634
Pryce, Mrs Irene	1	10	1	1	0	10.0	2,364	3,018
Purcell, John	6	23	2	4	0	8.7	4,917	8,560
Purdy, P D	5	16	1	2	0	6.3	2,511	4,349
Quinn, M	1	7	1	0	2	14.3	2,280	2,953
Raffel, D G	1	6	2	2	1	33.3	4,833	6,468
Ramsden, Mrs B	2	10	4	1	3	40.0	8,123	9,819
Ratcliffe, J M	1	2	1	0	0	50.0	2,532	2,532
Redman, T S	1	11	5	1	0	45.5	11,842	13,106
Richard Green (Fine Paintings)	1	5	1	3	1	20.0	2,070	5,309
Riley-Smith, T S M S	2	14	5	2	1	35.7	13,526	16,190
Rowbottom, Mrs H	1	5	1	0	0	20.0	2,385	2,385
Russell, R D	1	3	1	1	0	33.3	2,385	3,034
S T A Management Limited	1	3	1	1	0	33.3	2,070	2,808
Sandy Lane Associates	1	1	1	0	0	100.0	3,132	3,132
Saumtally, B M	1	9	3	1	1	33.3	7,602	8,777
Scullion, Daniel	1	8	1	3	2	12.5	3,173	6,657
Sheehan, P J	1	5	3	1	0	60.0	7,279	8,191
Simpson, Mrs Leonard	1	1	1	0	0	100.0	2,208	2,208
Sinclair Developments Limited	2	10	1	3	2	10.0	2,616	5,220
Smeaton, A K	1	5	2	0	1	40.0	5,064	5,370
Smith, Mrs J Murray	2	4	1	0	0	25.0	2,391	2,391
Stable, Red Seven	3	16	4	5	2	25.0	9,518	13,808
Stone, James H	1	2	1	1	0	50.0	2,656	3,358
Sturgis, Keith	2	7	2	2	0	28.6	3,652	4,955
Sturgis, Mrs J	1	2	1	0	0	50.0	2,820	2,820
Sweeney, Noel	2	12	2	2	1	16.7	5,043	6,658
The Entrepreneurs	1	3	2	0	1	66.7	6,137	6,440
The Fairyhouse 1992 Partnership	2	8	3	2	1	37.5	8,989	11,125
The Hammond Partnership	5	10	3	0	0	30.0	7,006	7,006
The Lime Street Racing Syndicate	1	4	1	0	1	25.0	2,616	2,922
The Marketing And Distribution Group	1	9	2	1	0	22.2	4,539	5,406
Thompson, Mrs David	2	3	1	0	2	33.3	2,448	3,598
Thompson, R	1	7	1	0	1	14.3	2,343	2,676
Thompson, Ronald	2	7	1	1	0	14.3	2,070	2,700
Thompson, George S	1	7	1	1	1	14.3	3,493	4,966
Thomson Jones, Mrs Solna	1	6	5	0	0	83.3	13,516	13,516
Times Of Wigan	2	3	1	1	1	33.3	2,385	3,487
Toulson, Miss J E	3	19	2	2	4	10.5	4,896	7,574
Treadwell, Mrs Penny	1	8	4	2	1	50.0	12,792	15,705
Turney, J A	1	3	1	0	0	33.3	2,343	2,343
Voak, B H	2	3	1	1	1	33.3	7,440	8,327
Vogt, Ian A	1	3	2	0	1	66.7	5,884	6,196
Wallace, T S	3	18	2	6	1	11.1	4,959	11,161
Wellard, T W	1	3	1	0	0	33.3	2,490	2,490
Weller, A B	1	1	1	0	0	100.0	2,280	2,280
Wetherby Racing Bureau Plc	2	6	1	1	1	16.7	2,070	3,042
Wheatley, D G	1	7	1	1	0	14.3	2,406	3,060
Whitehills Racing Syndicate	1	2	1	1	0	50.0	2,070	2,640
Whitwood, Mrs Carol	2	4	1	0	0	25.0	2,070	2,070
Whorton, G	1	6	1	2	1	16.7	2,574	4,197
Wilkin, Edward C	1	6	1	0	0	16.7	2,070	2,070
Wilman, John	2	12	1	2	2	8.3	2,532	5,005
Wilson, Capt James	1	4	1	2	0	25.0	2,406	3,816
Wilson, Christopher	1	7	1	1	0	14.3	2,174	3,210
Wilson, D A	1	6	1	1	1	16.7	2,322	3,346
Wiltshire, G	3	4	1	1	0	25.0	2,304	2,946
Wong, Tam	1	4	1	0	1	25.0	2,783	3,132
Woodall, Stephen	1	5	1	0	2	20.0	2,377	3,025
Yeh, Dr Meou Tsen Geoffrey	1	2	1	0	0	50.0	2,301	2,301
York, Mrs S C	1	6	1	1	1	16.7	2,595	3,575

Winning trainers: All-weather Flat 1992–93

H = Horses; R = Runners; W = Winners;
2 = Seconds; 3 = Thirds; %W-R = Percentage of winners to runners;
£WIN = Win money; £W/P = Win and place money

	H	R	W	2nd	3rd	%W-R	£WIN	£W/P
Akehurst, R	9	17	3	1	3	17.6	7,779	9,675
Allen, C N	6	22	2	1	3	9.1	4,833	6,383
Alston, E J	10	31	5	5	2	16.1	11,589	15,402
Arbuthnot, D W P	7	23	5	7	1	21.7	13,876	19,023
Armstrong, R W	4	10	1	0	0	10.0	2,301	2,513
Bailey, A.	10	35	4	3	7	11.4	10,929	15,708
Barron, T D	18	65	13	4	11	20.0	34,247	41,003
Bastiman, R	5	15	1	0	1	6.7	2,343	2,613
Bell, M	6	13	1	4	3	7.7	2,070	6,509
Bennett, J A	9	25	1	2	0	4.0	2,511	4,349
Benstead, C J	3	8	1	2	1	12.5	2,406	4,306
Berry, J	13	45	6	9	5	13.3	14,678	23,223
Bethell, J D	5	7	1	0	1	14.3	2,448	2,805
Blanshard, M	3	10	1	0	2	10.0	2,427	3,076
Booth, C B B	2	9	1	0	0	11.1	2,070	2,070
Boss, R	2	7	1	2	0	14.3	2,208	3,713
Bowring, S R	8	49	4	3	3	8.2	9,078	12,009
Brittain, C E	8	10	1	1	1	10.0	7,440	8,327
Broad, C D	1	3	1	1	0	33.3	2,385	3,034
Burchell, D.	10	28	3	2	2	10.7	7,878	10,074
Burke, K R	4	12	3	1	2	25.0	7,280	8,336
Callaghan, N A	5	15	3	2	1	20.0	7,248	9,395
Campbell, I	3	8	1	1	1	12.5	2,448	3,557
Carter, W	4	7	1	1	1	14.3	2,427	3,378
Cecil, Mrs J	4	10	2	2	1	20.0	5,365	7,273
Channon, M R	15	36	1	4	6	2.8	2,280	8,375
Chapman, D W	18	89	15	10	7	16.9	36,240	46,333
Chapman, M C	13	74	7	11	6	9.5	16,590	26,466
Cole, P F I	7	12	1	1	3	8.3	2,427	4,244
Cottrell, L G	2	6	1	1	0	16.7	2,208	3,169
Dawe, Mrs J C	3	13	1	0	2	7.7	2,574	3,232
Denson, A W	2	12	2	1	1	16.7	5,001	6,387
Dixon, M	4	15	1	2	1	6.7	2,454	4,260
Dow, S	14	35	5	4	8	14.3	12,464	17,884
Elsey, C C	9	39	10	6	3	25.6	30,407	36,827
Elsworth, D R C	7	17	2	0	7	11.8	5,646	8,376
Fairhurst, T	8	21	3	0	3	14.3	7,092	8,161
FitzGerald, J G	6	11	1	1	1	9.1	2,553	3,435
Gosden, J H M	4	12	2	1	2	16.7	4,996	6,668
Graham, N A	2	11	2	4	2	18.2	4,425	8,180
Guest, R	1	5	3	0	2	60.0	7,374	8,083
Haggas, W J	4	5	2	0	1	40.0	4,812	5,160
Haigh, W W	9	26	4	5	3	15.4	9,708	13,827
Hannon, R	14	43	9	4	7	20.9	23,369	29,694
Harris, J L	10	30	1	1	1	3.3	2,070	3,186
Harris, P W	2	8	2	0	3	25.0	6,137	7,301
Harwood, G.	3	16	4	4	2	25.0	12,792	17,683
Heaton-Ellis, M J	4	10	1	2	1	10.0	2,783	4,787
Hedger, P R	2	7	1	2	1	14.3	2,557	4,217
Hill, C J	23	93	21	11	10	22.6	52,923	63,833
Hills, B W	10	15	4	1	4	26.7	9,102	11,504
Hills, J W	7	20	3	8	0	15.0	7,008	13,781
Hodges, R J	12	28	1	1	2	3.6	3,231	5,066
Hollinshead, R.	28	94	13	8	12	13.8	30,916	40,090
Holt, L J	1	1	1	0	0	100.0	2,385	2,385
Howling, P.	11	32	3	1	1	9.4	7,006	7,948
Huntingdon, Lord	21	57	15	14	11	26.3	45,602	58,891
Jarvis, W	2	4	1	0	0	25.0	2,532	2,532
Jarvis, M A	6	11	4	0	3	36.4	9,834	10,767
Johnston, M	15	63	16	15	8	25.4	41,196	55,430
Jones, Bob	4	15	5	1	3	33.3	13,485	15,281

	H	R	W	2nd	3rd	%W-R	£WIN	£W/P
Jones, D Haydn	8	32	3	2	6	9.4	7,181	10,411
Jones, T Thomson	2	10	6	1	0	60.0	15,586	16,270
Jones, A W	4	13	2	1	2	15.4	4,917	6,268
Kelleway, P A	5	17	1	1	2	5.9	2,905	4,093
King, Mrs A L M	1	5	1	1	1	20.0	2,385	3,435
Knight, Mrs A	13	47	2	4	4	4.3	4,912	9,291
Lee, F H	6	10	1	2	0	10.0	2,406	3,984
Loder, D R	3	10	3	3	1	30.0	6,630	9,541
Macauley, Mrs N	9	47	5	3	7	10.6	13,050	17,405
Mackie, J	3	10	2	1	3	20.0	4,707	6,348
Makin, P J	7	22	5	5	1	22.7	11,294	15,454
McEntee, P M	5	7	1	0	0	14.3	2,070	2,070
McMahon, B A	12	51	5	7	6	9.8	14,043	20,927
Mills, T G	1	2	1	0	1	50.0	3,322	3,631
Mitchell, Pat	11	51	4	8	4	7.8	8,994	16,111
Mitchell, P	3	14	4	1	2	28.6	10,511	12,491
Moore, A	17	50	4	10	9	8.0	10,809	22,364
Morris, D	6	17	1	2	3	5.9	2,208	4,631
Muir, W R	7	30	6	4	2	20.0	13,823	17,085
Musson, W J	7	24	4	1	1	16.7	10,474	11,785
Naughton, T J	9	30	4	2	1	13.3	9,051	10,915
Norton, S G	10	28	5	3	5	17.9	15,550	19,908
O'Gorman, W A	18	79	17	20	4	21.5	40,541	57,064
O'Sullivan, R J	9	45	15	4	6	33.3	39,858	46,066
Palling, B	6	8	1	1	0	12.5	3,132	3,750
Peacock, R E	6	25	2	6	1	8.0	4,959	11,161
Pearce, J	10	27	2	3	1	7.4	4,728	7,038
Pickering, J A	3	7	1	1	0	14.3	2,322	3,012
Pipe, M C	3	4	1	1	0	25.0	2,280	2,994
Prescott, Sir Mark	12	30	4	2	7	13.3	10,979	15,157
Richmond, B	5	22	2	2	4	9.1	4,896	7,574
Sanders, Miss B	2	7	1	1	0	14.3	2,820	4,053
Scott, A A	3	9	2	2	1	22.2	5,043	6,683
Shaw, D	2	6	3	1	0	50.0	7,279	8,191
Smith, Denys	3	10	1	2	0	10.0	2,343	3,639
Smith, D J G Murray	2	4	1	0	0	25.0	2,391	2,391
Spearing, J L	7	18	2	4	1	11.1	3,500	6,650
Spicer, R C	12	54	10	7	5	18.5	25,731	35,031
Stewart, A C	1	1	1	0	0	100.0	2,322	2,322
Stringer, A P	2	4	1	0	0	25.0	2,658	2,658
Thom, D T	7	15	1	0	2	6.7	2,070	2,721
Thompson, R	3	10	1	0	1	10.0	2,343	2,676
Thompson, Ronald	4	11	1	1	1	9.1	2,070	3,009
Tinkler, C	8	26	1	5	2	3.8	2,385	6,390
Tinkler, N	12	24	1	1	3	4.2	2,490	4,002
Weedon, C	3	4	1	0	1	25.0	2,512	2,948
Wharton, J	11	26	1	2	2	3.8	2,343	4,266
White, J	8	18	2	2	2	11.1	3,652	5,471
Williams, R J R	4	16	1	8	1	6.3	2,544	8,401
Williams, M	5	9	1	0	1	11.1	2,656	2,959
Wilson, D A	5	25	6	3	2	24.0	15,848	19,536
Wilson, Capt J	7	15	1	3	3	6.7	2,406	5,445
Woods, S P C	4	13	2	3	2	15.4	4,833	7,497
Wragg, G	3	7	1	1	2	14.3	2,301	3,771

Winning jockeys: All-weather Flat 1992–93

	Mounts	1st	2nd	3rd	%W-R	£WIN	£W/P
Adams, N	45	3	1	5	6.7	10,229	14,807
Bardwell, G	171	13	14	12	7.6	31,882	45,494
Biggs, D	123	14	9	16	11.4	37,286	50,380
Birch, M	2	1	0	0	50.0	2,553	2,553
Carroll, J	31	2	4	1	6.5	4,795	8,001
Carter, G	74	6	10	12	8.1	14,925	27,314
Charnock, L	62	4	5	1	6.5	9,948	13,681
Crossley, B	6	1	0	0	16.7	2,301	2,301
Dawson, S	30	1	2	2	3.3	2,490	4,450
Day, N	36	6	4	7	16.7	15,933	21,230
Dettori, L	10	1	2	1	10.0	2,259	4,307
Duffield, G	5	1	0	3	20.0	3,377	4,845
Fanning, J	80	5	4	8	6.3	12,725	18,078
Fortune, J	1	1	0	0	100.0	2,448	2,448
Gibson, Dale	122	6	11	10	4.9	13,834	24,981
Greaves, Alex	68	11	6	12	16.2	28,551	36,917
Hills, M	104	18	23	14	17.3	43,133	67,111
Holland, D	61	12	3	7	19.7	28,777	33,277
Lappin, R	15	1	1	0	6.7	2,406	3,072
Mackay, A	10	3	0	1	30.0	9,632	10,223
McGlone, A	32	3	5	6	9.4	7,828	13,860
McKeown, Dean	140	26	25	17	18.6	65,296	87,231
McLaughlin, J	39	7	7	2	17.9	17,308	25,438
Munro, A	64	9	11	7	14.1	21,507	31,679
Newnes, W	15	2	0	1	13.3	7,692	8,490
Nicholls, D	50	1	6	2	2.0	2,364	7,151
Nutter, C	19	2	2	2	10.5	4,770	6,702
O'Gorman, S	5	1	0	0	20.0	2,554	2,554
Perham, R	25	2	0	5	8.0	5,043	6,689
Quinn, T	104	23	15	15	22.1	64,349	81,873
Quinn, J	244	28	38	19	11.5	70,577	104,504
Reid, J	7	1	1	1	14.3	2,385	3,354
Rouse, B	21	3	4	3	14.3	7,764	11,374
Ryan, W	120	18	19	14	15.0	39,558	59,000
Tebbutt, M	10	1	0	1	10.0	2,532	3,043
Tinkler, Kim	19	1	0	3	5.3	2,490	3,354
Webster, S	54	4	4	4	7.4	9,455	13,157
Williams, T	58	7	5	8	12.1	18,642	25,639
Williams, J	119	10	9	22	8.4	26,237	42,199
Wood, S	114	17	14	6	14.9	41,178	53,943
Woods, W	20	3	4	2	15.0	8,782	12,151

Winning apprentices: All-weather Flat 1992–93

	Mounts	1st	2nd	3rd	%W-R	£WIN	£W/P
Balding, Claire	20	2	0	1	10.0	4,917	5,288
Carson, D	6	3	1	1	50.0	8,014	9,049
Carter, L	12	1	1	1	8.3	2,343	3,285
Davies, Stephen	56	5	7	6	8.9	12,453	19,382
Doyle, B	43	4	3	6	9.3	16,575	21,029
Drowne, S	36	1	0	1	2.8	3,231	3,953
Garth, A	44	3	2	7	6.8	7,764	11,310
Gwilliams, N	12	1	1	1	8.3	2,427	3,379
Halliday, V	10	2	1	1	20.0	4,749	5,706
Harrison, D	41	4	4	2	9.8	9,708	12,956
Howarth, Nicola	3	1	0	0	33.3	2,343	2,343
Humphries, M	39	3	0	7	7.7	6,205	8,750
Husband, E	4	2	0	1	50.0	6,600	6,906
Martinez, A	11	1	2	0	9.1	2,820	4,925
McCabe, D	36	6	5	6	16.7	14,100	19,422
McCarthy, S	17	2	1	4	11.8	4,833	6,497
McDonnell, Kim	50	3	5	6	6.0	5,721	10,918
Mitchell, G	8	1	2	1	12.5	2,448	4,223
Morris, Mrs M	1	1	0	0	100.0	2,553	2,553
Norton, F	56	6	5	7	10.7	15,499	21,450
O'Gorman, Emma	78	16	21	5	20.5	38,520	56,182
Painter, R	4	1	0	0	25.0	2,280	2,280
Pears, O	39	7	7	5	17.9	19,921	26,625
Purdy, Miss A	4	1	1	0	25.0	2,511	3,368
Radford-Howes, Sally	1	1	0	0	100.0	2,322	2,322
Russell, B	36	8	5	2	22.2	20,872	25,568
Rutter, K	17	6	2	1	35.3	14,692	16,648
Tucker, A	44	2	5	7	4.5	4,921	11,100
Weaver, J	10	5	0	0	50.0	13,897	14,095
Williams, S D	51	3	3	4	5.9	7,050	10,608
Wright, D	94	4	8	7	4.3	10,055	18,287
Wynne, S	12	1	0	3	8.3	2,365	3,344

Champion stakes earners on the Flat: 1900–93

		No. of Races	Value £	s
1900	Diamond Jubilee (3 yrs)	5	27985	10
1901	Epsom Lad (4 yrs)	3	18242	0
1902	Sceptre (3 yrs)	6	23195	0
1903	Rock Sand (3 yrs)	5	18425	0
1904	Rock Sand (4 yrs)	5	19719	0
1905	Cherry Lass (3 yrs)	6	13119	0
1906	Keystone II (3 yrs)	5	12837	0
1907	Lally (4 yrs)	3	11555	0
1908	Your Majesty (3 yrs)	4	19286	0
1909	Bayardo (3 yrs)	11	24797	0
1910	Lemberg (3 yrs)	7	28224	0
1911	Stedfast (3 yrs)	8	16079	0
1912	Prince Palatine (4 yrs)	4	20730	0
1913	Jest (3 yrs)	2	11350	0
1914	Black Jester (3 yrs)	5	11008	0
1915	Pommern (3 yrs)	4	11200	0
1916	Cannobie (3 yrs)	3	7829	0
1917	Gay Crusader (3 yrs)	7	10180	0
1918	Gainsborough (3 yrs)	4	13410	0
1919	Tetratema (2 yrs)	5	11494	0
1920	Cinna (3 yrs)	2	8529	0
1921	Craig an Eran (3 yrs)	3	15345	0
1922	Royal Lancer (3 yrs)	5	14522	0
1923	Tranquil (3 yrs)	6	20707	0
1924	Straitlace (3 yrs)	6	17958	0
1925	Saucy Sue (3 yrs)	5	22155	0
1926	Coronach (3 yrs)	5	39624	0
1927	Booklaw (3 yrs)	6	27745	0
1928	Fairway (3 yrs)	4	29707	0
1929	Trigo (3 yrs)	3	23690	0
1930	Rustom Pasha (3 yrs)	3	13933	0
1931	Cameronian (3 yrs)	3	29484	0
1932	Firdaussi (3 yrs)	4	17441	10
1933	Hyperion (3 yrs)	1	23179	10
1934	Windsor Lad (3 yrs)	5	24903	10
1935	Bahram (3 yrs)	4	31328	10
1936	Rhodes Scholar (3 yrs)	2	12466	0
1937	Mid-day Sun (3 yrs)	5	15273	0
1938	Rockfel (3 yrs)	6	22094	0
1939	Blue Peter (3 yrs)	4	31964	0
1940	Pont l'Eveque (3 yrs)	3	6389	15
1941	Owen Tudor (3 yrs)	3	5621	15
1942	Sun Chariot (3 yrs)	4	6470	6
1943	Straight Deal (3 yrs)	3	5358	0
1944	Ocean Swell (3 yrs)	3	6980	5
1945	Sun Stream (3 yrs)	2	13865	0
1946	Airborne (3 yrs)	5	20345	10
1947	Migoli (3 yrs)	6	17215	0

		No. of Races	Value £	s
1948	Black Tarquin (3 yrs)	3	21423	0
1949	Nimbus (3 yrs)	4	320236	0
1950	Palestine (3 yrs)	5	21583	0
1951	Supreme Court (3 yrs)	4	36016	0
1952	Tulyar (3 yrs)	7	75173	14
1953	Pinza (3 yrs)	3	44101	0
1954	Never Say Die (3 yrs)	2	30332	0
1955	Meld (3 yrs)	4	42562	0
1956	Ribot (4 yrs)	1	23727	15
1957	Crepello (3 yrs)	2	32257	0
1958	Ballymoss (4 yrs)	3	38686	0
1959	Petite Etoile (3 yrs)	6	55487	0
1960	St Paddy (3 yrs)	4	71256	0
1961	Sweet Solera (3 yrs)	4	36988	0
1962	Hethersett (3 yrs)	3	38497	0
1963	Ragusa (3 yrs)	3	66011	0
1964	Santa Claus (3 yrs)	1	72067	0
1965	Sea Bird II (3 yrs)	1	65301	0
1966	Charlottown (3 yrs)	2	78075	0
1967	Royal Palace (3 yrs)	2	92998	0
1968	Sir Ivor (3 yrs)	4	97075	0
1969	Blakeney (3 yrs)	1	63108	0
1970	Nijinsky (Can) (3 yrs)	4	159681	0
			£	p
1971	Mill Reef (USA) (3 yrs)	4	121913·00	
1972	Brigadier Gerard (4 yrs)	7	151213·00	
1973	Dahlia (USA) (3 yrs)	1	79230·00	
1974	Dahlia (USA) (4 yrs)	2	120771·00	
1975	Grundy (3 yrs)	4	274175·10	
1976	Wollow (3 yrs)	5	166389·10	
1977	The Minstrel (Can) (3 yrs)	3	201184·00	
1978	Ile de Bourbon (USA) (3 yrs)	3	136012·00	
1979	Troy (3 yrs)	5	310539·00	
1980	Ela-Mana-Mou (4 yrs)	4	236332·00	
1981	Shergar (3 yrs)	4	295644·00	
1982	Kalaglow (4 yrs)	4	242304·00	
1983	Sun Princess (3 yrs)	3	221356·00	
1984	Secreto (3 yrs)	1	227680·00	
1985	Oh So Sharp (3 yrs)	4	311576·00	
1986	Dancing Brave (3 yrs)	5	423601·00	
1987	Reference Point (3 yrs)	5	683028·77	
1988	Mtoto (5 yrs)	4	412002·00	
1989	Nashwan (USA) (3 yrs)	4	772045·50	
1990	In The Groove (3 yrs)	3	459117·00	
1991	Generous (3 yrs)	2	631480·00	
1992	Rodrigo de Triano (3 yrs)	3	494764·00	
1993	Opera House (5 yrs)	3	502097·20	

Leading sires on the Flat 1909–93

Year	Sire	£	s
1909	Cyllene	35550	0
1910	Cyllene	38001	10
1911	Sundridge	33284	0
1912	Persimmon	21993	0
1913	Desmond	30973	10
1914	Polymelus	29607	0
1915	Polymelus	17738	0
1916	Polymelus	16081	0
1917	Bayardo	12337	0
1918	Bayardo	15650	0
1919	The Tetrarch	27976	10
1920	Polymelus	39704	0
1921	Polymelus	34307	0
1922	Lemberg	32988	10
1923	Swynford	37897	0
1924	Son-in-Law	32476	0
1925	Phalaris	41475	0
1926	Hurry On	59109	0
1927	Buchan	45918	0
1928	Phalaris	46393	0
1929	Tetratema	53025	15
1930	Son-in-Law	44754	18
1931	Pharos	43922	1
1932	Gainsborough	34789	11
1933	Gainsborough	38138	16
1934	Blandford	75706	10
1935	Blandford	57538	6
1936	Fairway	57931	10
1937	Solario	52888	15
1938	Blandford	31840	2
1939	Fairway	53441	0
1940	Hyperion	13407	10
1941	Hyperion	22699	15
1942	Hyperion	13801	0
1943	Fairway	12133	18
1944	Fairway	15704	0
1945	Hyperion	39727	5
1946	Hyperion	52960	10
1947	Nearco	42554	0
1948	Big Game	40690	0
1949	Nearco	52545	13
1950	Fair Trial	37887	0
1951	Nasrullah	44664	3

Year	Sire	£	s
1952	Tehran	84177	0
1953	Chanteur II	57164	0
1954	Hyperion	46894	17
1955	Alycidon	54954	0
1956	Court Martial	49238	0
1957	Court Martial	58307	0
1958	Mossborough	66471	0
1959	Petition	75921	0
1960	Aureole	90087	6
1961	Aureole	90898	0
1962	Never Say Die	65901	0
1963	Ribot	121288	0
1964	Chamossaire	136507	0
1965	Court Harwell	114595	0
1966	Psidium	100927	0
1967	Ballymoss	113601	0
1968	Ribot	112635	0
1969	Hethersett	74928	0
1970	Northern Dancer	230540	0

Year	Sire	£ p
1971	Never Bend	125021·85
1972	Queen's Hussar	173592·95
1973	Vaguely Noble	106831·50
1974	Vaguely Noble	140116·30
1975	Great Nephew	291048·70
1976	Wolver Hollow	192362·84
1977	Northern Dancer	349739·75
1978	Mill Reef (USA)	264866·45
1979	Petingo	449512·00
1980	Pitcairn	391651·00
1981	Great Nephew	468253·00
1982	Be My Guest (USA)	392075·00
1983	Habitat	234305·00
1984	Northern Dancer	429232·00
1985	Kris	414630·00
1986	Lyphard (USA)	458697·20
1987	Mill Reef (USA)	947129·87
1988	Busted	450914·00
1989	Blushing Groom (FR)	922163.50
1990	Night Shift (USA)	620416·80
1991	Caerleon (USA)	718300.65
1992	El Gran Senor (USA)	564008·40
1993	Sadler's Wells (USA)	994303·60

Sires 1993 by Andrew Caulfield

THE YEAR OF THE YEN

It wasn't just in the showrooms of our electrical retailers or on the forecourts of our garages that Japan's influence was felt in Britain during 1993.

The British breeding industry also began to see the power of the Yen as a potential problem. While Japanese involvement has been very welcome during the years of recession in Britain, 1993 showed us that such involvement is very much a double-edged sword. And nothing illustrated this better than the magnificent year enjoyed by Dancing Brave, the equine superstar sold to Japan in the autumn of 1991.

By the summer of 1993, The Sporting Life was carrying such comments as "the breeding industry has never made a bigger blunder than it did in exporting Dancing Brave to Japan" - and understandably so.

Even in the face of the tremendous success enjoyed by champion sire Sadler's Wells, there are strong grounds for regarding Dancing Brave as 1993's Stallion of the Year. Despite there being no more than 40 named foals in his third crop, born in 1990, as many as seven of them had gained Group-winner status by the end of 1993, with the Listed race winner Polka Dancer boosting the total of Stakes winners to eight. This would have been bad enough in view of Dancing Brave's sale, but what made the astonishing turn-about in his fortunes even harder to swallow was the fact that there were THREE classic winners among his Group scorers.

White Muzzle set the ball rolling with a five-length success in the Derby Italiano on May 30, with Commander In Chief following up with a similarly impressive victory in the Ever Ready Derby three days later. Hopes of a classic treble in the space of seven days came to naught when Wemyss Bight finished only fifth when favourite for the Oaks, but she promptly turned the table on three of those who had beaten her at Epsom in winning the Kildangan Stud Irish Oaks on July 10.

The ill-fated 1992 Fillies' Mile winner Ivanka was a fourth Group 1 winner from this crop, the other Group winners being Regency (Prix Hocquart and fourth in the Irish Derby), Infrasonic (Queen's Vase) and the Irish filly Rayseka (Royal Whip). For good measure, Dancing Brave's three-year-old sons Advocat, Majority and Revere were placed in Group company. As yet there have been no Group winners from Dancing

Brave's fourth crop, but Tenby's half-brother Bude was third in the Racing Post Trophy, while the French youngsters Brave Note, Cheyenne Dream and Cherokee Rose were all second in Group 3 contests.

This long list of high achievers makes it easy to see why critics were quick to describe Dancing Brave's sale as a major blunder. But these critics weren't nearly as outspoken at the time of his sale, for the good reason that Dancing Brave's early career had all the makings of a major disaster. Consider the facts.

When the shareholders voted on the Japanese offer in October 1991, Dancing Brave's first two crops had won fewer than 20 races in Britain and Ireland, for earnings of little more than £100,000 - less than the cost of one of his nominations at the start of his career. His only Stakes winner at the time was the 1990 Silken Glider Stakes winner Glowing Ardour (another of his daughters, Mohican Girl, was to win a Listed race the following month and his gelded son Zabar was to become a Group winner, but not until the age of five in 1993).

Matters were made worse by the fact that some of Dancing Brave's early progeny were fairly unimpressive individuals, as can be seen from the median price of 58,000 Gns achieved by his five second-crop sale yearlings in 1990. Remember, each of these animals was the result of a £120,000 stud fee.

Two other factors no doubt also told against this brilliant son of Lyphard. Shareholders - especially Khalid Abdulla and Sheikh Mohammed - had invested heavily in him, not only through his £350,000 share price but also through the high-class mares they had sent him in his five years at Dalham Hall Stud. Sadly, his early results suggested strongly that these very expensive mares were at real risk of being devalued.

Another possible contributing factor was the unusually high proportion of fillies among Dancing Brave's offspring. By the time his fifth crop had been born in the spring following his sale, colts accounted for less than 40 per cent of Dancing Brave's output. Such a sex-bias surely told against Dancing Brave at a time when fillies were markedly unpopular at the sales.

All in all, his shareholders could be forgiven for thinking that the Japanese offer of over £3 million was almost too good to be true.

So how do we account for the astonishing reversal of his fortunes? It has to be said that an improvement wasn't totally unexpected - just the scale of it. Robert Acton, the manager of Dalham Hall Stud, told me months before Dancing Brave's sale that the stallion's third crop was easily his best. There are a couple of possible explanations for this. For a start, breeders had had a chance to inspect his first foals by the time they chose which mares to send him in his third season, and therefore had a better idea of what he required.

Probably even more important was the question of Dancing Brave's health. Remember, he had been at death's door during the winter of 1987/88 with Marie's Disease, a once-fatal ailment which results in new bone growth and lameness. It is sparked off by other ailments - in Dancing Brave it was triggered by Avian Tuberculosis, a rare form of bird tuberculosis. The immediate side effect was a temporary fertility scare which resulted in Dancing Brave's second crop being limited to 29 foals.

One has to wonder how much these physical problems - and the drugs required to treat them - contributed to the quiet start made by Dancing Brave's first two crops. He was presumably already suffering from Avian Tuberculosis when he stood his first season and he was very ill before his second. Whereas logic suggests that his genetic influence should have been unaffected, the Racing Post carried an article which argued that Dancing Brave's illness might have caused him to produce "old seed" before his time.

I would also put forward another possible explanation for the improved results achieved by Dancing Brave's offspring in 1993. For much of the year the ground was softer than usual and probably suited quite a number of his offspring, which - like Commander In Chief - showed round actions.

Mention of Commander In Chief brings us back to another reason why the Japanese offer for Dancing Brave was so attractive. If the stallion continued to disappoint, the decision to sell was clearly correct; and if Dancing Brave gave us real cause to regret his departure, wouldn't there be one or two sons worthy of taking his place at stud? Well, there WERE some worthy sons but, sadly, Commander In Chief and White Muzzle have also fallen to Japanese buyers, along with Opera House, their conqueror in the King George VI and Queen Elizabeth II Stakes. The Japanese have succeeded in snapping up several of the leading stallion prospects for the second successive year, following the purchase of Dr Devious and Rodrigo de Triano in 1992. With the brilliant middle-distance performer Old Vic being leased to Japan, and the likes of Shaadi and Shavian being sold, one begins to realise how much we are going to depend on the likes of Sadler's Wells, Caerleon and Rainbow Quest in the second half of the 1990s.

Sadler's Wells, of course, was the stallion who had a prolonged battle with Dancing Brave for the title of 1993's champion sire. The Coolmore stallion had the advantage of roughly twice as many runners in Britain and Ireland, and it was this that proved decisive. When his two-year-old son King's Theatre took the Racing Post Trophy, Sadler's Wells became the first stallion ever to sire the winners of more than £1.6 million in a single season in Britain and Ireland (remember, the figures in Ruff's Guide reflect racing in Britain only). He was also responsible for the previous record mark of £1,514,272, set in 1990, and he has now topped the Anglo-Irish list three times in the last five years, having also headed the 1992 table. Some idea of his dominance of the current scene is given by the fact that he was runner-up in 1989 and 1991 - and his first runners didn't appear until 1988.

Another indication of Sadler's Wells's brilliance is given by the statistics published in the American magazine, Thoroughbred Times. The issue of November 12 showed Sadler's Wells with earnings in North America, Britain, Ireland and France equivalent to 4,939,463 dollars - a total which gave him a handsome lead over his nearest pursuers, the American superstars Danzig and Mr Prospector.

His total reflected the earnings of the Oaks heroine Intrepidity, the champion middle-distance horse Opera House, the Irish 2,000 Guineas winner Barathea and of their fellow British Group winners Sonus and Thawakib. Intrepidity also won two Group 1 races in France, where Fort Wood became a Group 1 winner in the Grand Prix de Paris and where Hunting Hawk and Modhish won Group 2 events. Over in America, Sadler's Wells's ex-European horses Stagecraft, Adam Smith, Kirov Premiere and Johann Quatz all became Graded Stakes winners during 1993. His worldwide total of 1993 Group winners was as high as 14 - and that doesn't include the luckless Royal Ballerina, who was runner-up in both the Oaks and Irish Oaks, or the ill-fated Fatherland, who was second in the Irish 2,000 Guineas.

Such a tally, together with Sadler's Wells's new record earnings, inevitably leads to comparisons with his brilliant sire Northern Dancer, who became the first stallion to sire the winners of over £1 million during a British and Irish season. Suitably enough, that was in 1984, the year Sadler's Wells ranked alongside El Gran Senor, Secreto and the Prix de Diane winner Northern Trick as one of four classic winners from Northern Dancer's 1981 crop. Sadler's Wells has yet to match that extraordinary achievement, but he has already sired as many as six Group 1 winners in a crop of 55 foals. One wonders what he might achieve once his larger crops hit their stride - there are nearly 100 youngsters in his 1992 crop and the latest Return of Mares credits him with having covered 112 mares in 1992.

Two of the exceptional colts which helped make Northern Dancer an international star more than 20 years ago are still making their presence felt. One was the still-active Lyphard, who showed the youngsters a thing or two with his 1993 total of seven Group or Graded Stakes winners which included the British-trained Lyphard's Delta and Tatami, and the very talented but luckless French miler Ski Paradise.

Dancing Brave was just one of five sons of Lyphard to sire a British or Irish Group winner, one of the others being Alzao, a horse bred on similar lines to Dancing Brave. After a disappointingly quiet time with his 1990 crop, Alzao bounced back with the Group-winning two-year-olds Unblest, Relatively Special and Sheridan in his '91 crop - the first sired by him after his move to Coolmore. The Italian filly Alpride is a fourth Group winner from this crop. Lyphard's team was completed by Al Nasr (sire of Prince of Andros), Pharly (Further Flight) and the potentially useful Imperial Frontier (Imperial Bailiwick and Ivory Frontier).

By his own extremely high standards, Nijinsky enjoyed very limited direct success during 1993, his only good British winner being Winged Victory. But Nijinsky's stallion sons more than made amends, with six of them siring British or Irish Group winners, and one grandson, Kahyasi, also got into the act through the Irish 2,000 Guineas third Massyar.

It was Nijinsky's 2,000 Guineas winner Shadeed who sired a second 1,000 Guineas winner in the space of three years when Sayyedati emulated Shadayid, but Shadeed didn't meet with nearly as much success overall as Caerleon or Niniski. Although Tenby ultimately failed to live up to expectations, Caerleon hit the Group 1 target with his progressive daughter Only Royale, the Yorkshire Oaks heroine who finished a fine fifth after being hampered in the Prix de l'Arc de Triomphe.

Niniski also reached the top ten sires in Britain and Ireland despite having considerably fewer runners than many of the other leading sires. Alflora and Assessor led Niniski's domestic team, but his star performer was the Prix du Jockey-Club winner Hernando, who picked up around £125,000 when second to Commander In Chief in the Irish Derby. Other successful Nijinsky stallions were Green Dancer (sire of Takarouna), Vision (sire of Foresee, third in the Irish Derby and St Leger) and the Japan-bound Shahrastani (Cajarian).

Danzig and Storm Bird are two sons of Northern Dancer who generally pass on more speed than stamina, and this was reflected in their contributions to the 1993 season. Danzig himself sired Emperor Jones and Hamas, the latter becoming his third winner of the July Cup. Four of his sons - Chief's Crown, Green Desert, Danzig Connection and Shaadi - also sired Group winners, and all four of these were represented by leading juveniles. Chief's Crown was responsible for the game Dewhurst Stakes winner Grand Lodge, while Danzig Connection came up with Polish Laughter, Green Desert with the Middle Park Stakes runner- up Owington and Shaadi with one of the leading fillies, Velvet Moon.

Storm Bird also sired one of the top juveniles, Stonehatch, plus the Group-winning Irish two-year-old Keraka. Storm Bird's highly successful American-based son Storm Cat supplied the very smart six-and seven-furlong winner Catrail, while the Irish National Stud's Magical Wonder had the Irish Group winners Sea Gazer and Morcote among his total of only 13 runners.

El Gran Senor was another son of Northern Dancer who enjoyed Group success in Ireland, thanks to George Augustus and Chanzi, and his brother Try My Best was ably represented by his stallion son Last Tycoon. This excellent sprinter-miler notched up three Group 1 victories in England through his sons Bigstone (Sussex Stakes and Queen Elizabeth II Stakes) and Ezzoud (Juddmonte International), and Last Tycoon also scored a Group 1 success in France when Lost World took the Grand Criterium.

The combination of Northern Dancer and the great broodmare Fairy Bridge made its presence felt not only through their son Sadler's Wells. Another son, Fairy King, emerged from his older brother's shadow by becoming champion sire of two-year-olds, with help from the Group 1 winners Turtle Island (Phoenix Stakes) and Fairy Heights (Fillies' Mile). A third brother, Tate Gallery, was represented by the Irish Group winner Pernilla. Significantly, thanks to Opera House, Turtle Island and Pernilla, all three brothers sired 1993 Group winners out of mares by High Top. No wonder, then, that High Top proved too strong for Habitat and Roberto at the top of the broodmare sires' table.

Although Nureyev had three Group winners in France, the high-class sprinter Wolfhound was his only British Group winner. However, his American son Theatrical, who supplied the French 1,000 Guineas winner Madeleine's Dream, was also responsible for a couple of very talented Irish fillies in Asema (Desmond Stakes) and Majestic Role.

Other sons of Northern Dancer with 1993 Group winners to their credit were Dixieland Band (Gold Cup hero Drum Taps), Lomond (River North), Shareef Dancer (Spartan Shareef) and The Minstrel (True Hero); and his grandson Salse also played a major role as the sire of the leading juvenile filly Lemon Souffle.

Add all these stallions together and you'll find that 12 sons, 20 grandsons and one great-grandson of Northern Dancer sired Group winners in 1993. Between them they sired the winners of 46 Group races in Britain, consisting of 16 at Group 1 level, 11 at Group 2 and 19 at Group 3. The corresponding Irish figures were five, five and 12, making a total of 22. The combined British and Irish figures of 68 represent exactly half of the 136 Group races contested during the year, which shows that the Northern Dancer line is losing none of its potency. For the record, the 1991 tally was 69 Group victories out of a possible 140 (49.3 per cent), while 1992's score was 63 out of 140 (45 per cent).

It almost goes without saying that none of the rival male lines came anywhere near matching Northern Dancer's extraordinary score, but the male line descending from his broodmare sire, Native Dancer, certainly enjoyed some notable victories. Native Dancer's grandson Mr Prospector enjoyed Group 1 success when his French 2,000 Guineas winner Kingmambo made a successful raid on the St James's Palace Stakes. But it was Mr Prospector's son Gone West who sired Zafonic, the mighty colt who put up the performance of the season in recording his record-breaking victory in the 2,000 Guineas.

Another of Mr Prospector's sons, the American-based Miswaki, made a huge impact on the European season through his Arc-winning daughter Urban Sea and his top Italian son Misil, who went so close to beating Opera House in the Eclipse Stakes. It was a daughter of Miswaki which produced the Prix du Jockey-Club winner Hernando, and it was his son Midyan who was responsible for the very successful Alhijaz, who followed up his Group 2 win at Sandown with several very rewarding efforts in Italy.

Another of Native Dancer's grandsons, Sharpen Up, was also very much to the fore, thanks to his stallion sons Diesis, Kris and Sharpo. The American-based Diesis outshone his older brother Kris, even though Kris sired a Group winner in England and two more in France. Diesis's team included that tremendously effective mudlark Knifebox, the Musidora heroine Marillette, the Diomed Stakes winner Enharmonic and the luckless Sabrehill, who was forced to retire when seemingly on the threshold of an exciting career.

For a stallion whose 1993 fee was only £4,000, Sharpo had a magnificent time. Although that very smart sprinter College Chapel was his only Group winner on the homefront, there was sufficient support from the likes of The Puzzler, Fast Eddy, Splice and Penny Drops to take Sharpo up to eighth place on the British and Irish list. As if that weren't enough, College Chapel, Lavinia Fontana, Penny Drops and Port Lucaya all won Group races in Europe, while Sharp Prod won good prizes in France and Germany. To put the seal on an outstanding year, Sharpo's son Risk Me also reached the top ten sires, with a powerful team headed by those first-rate fillies Niche and Risky.

I have already referred to High Top becoming leading sire of broodmares, an area in which he faced the greatest opposition from Habitat and Roberto, two grandsons of the champion American two-year-old Turn-to. Roberto owed much of his earnings to the Derby and Irish Derby double by Commander In Chief, a son of the excellent Roberto mare Slightly Dangerous. One of Roberto's sons, Bob Back, also got into the classic act, when his bargain son Bob's Return ran out such a decisive winner of the St Leger.

Bob Back was one of three Roberto stallions with a British Group winner to his credit, the others being Robellino, the 1980 Royal Lodge Stakes winner who sired the latest Royal Lodge hero Mister Baileys, and the American-based Silver Hawk, sire of Brigadier Gerard Stakes winner Red Bishop.

Habitat's stallion sons had a pretty wretched record in Europe but it might have been a slightly different story had the top sprinter Double

Form not died young. History repeated itself with Double Form's son Double Schwartz, the leading sprinter who died early in 1993, just before his son Cois Na Tine developed into one of Ireland's best juveniles. Habitat's daughters have, of course, developed into formidable broodmares and in 1993 they added the likes of Barathea, Grand Lodge and Relatively Special to their long list of Group winners.

Turn-to was a son of Royal Charger, whose three-parts-brother Nasrullah ranks as one of the greatest sires this century. Nasrullah's male line is still flourishing, thanks largely to the descendants of his sons Red God and Never Bend.

Red God's main claim to fame is that he sired the brilliant French two-year-old Blushing Groom. Although it was back in 1988 that Blushing Groom underwent surgery for the cancer that was to lead to his death in 1992, he still enjoyed great success worldwide in '93. Gold Splash provided him with what could prove to be his final British Group 1 success when she landed the Coronation Stakes, and we were given further evidence of his great versatility by the victories of Desert Team in the Princess of Wales's Stakes and of Brier Creek in the Henry II Stakes.

Happily, the sense of loss caused by Blushing Groom's early death has been diminished by the emergence of some potential stars among his stallion sons. So far, none has shone so brightly in the Northern Hemisphere as Rainbow Quest, who was represented in England by the 1993 Group winners Armiger, Rainbow Lake and Glatisant. When Armiger finished second in the St Leger, he became the third son of Rainbow Quest to finish runner-up in a 1993 classic – Blue Judge chased home Commander In Chief in the Derby and Bin Ajwaad found only Kingmambo too good in the Poule d'Essai des Poulains. Sadly both colts were unable to race again. Rainbow Quest also sired the Oaks d'Italia heroine Bright Generation and the brothers Raintrap and Sunshack, who won the Prix Royal-Oak and the Criterium de Saint-Cloud to complete a Group 1 double on consecutive Sundays. These brothers represented another triumph for a Roberto mare.

Jalmood was another Blushing Groom stallion with a Group winner to his name, in the shape of Meld Stakes winner Lord of the Field. The French-based Groom Dancer had the French Group winners Le Balafre, Dancienne and Astair among his second crop; the Japanese-based Baillamont sired the Prix Marcel Boussac heroine Sierra Madre; and Nashwan's first crop produced a very promising colt in Golden Nashwan and a good-class filly in Gothic Dream. Expect to hear plenty more of this line in years to come.

Never Bend's immortality hinges on the ability of his sons Mill Reef and Riverman to found successful male lines. Riverman has yet to do so in Europe, although Irish River has proved very effective in the USA. Irish River's daughter Hatoof returned to the scene of her 1992 Guineas success to land another of Newmarket's top events, the Champion Stakes, and another major prize fell to this line when Rousillon's son Vintage Crop took the Irish St Leger, as a prelude to his historic victory in the Melbourne Cup.

Mill Reef has been more effective in founding a male line, thanks almost entirely to his son Shirley Heights. The 1978 Derby winner added three more Group winners to his impressive total, thanks to Zinaad in England, Apogee in France and Know Heights in California. Know Heights took the Grade 2 Carleton F. Burke Handicap the day after Shirley Heights's grandson Kotashaan had taken his 1993 earnings to nearly 2 million dollars with his victory in the Breeders' Cup Turf. Kotashaan is by Shirley Heights's Prix du Jockey-Club winner Darshaan, who also sired the Group-winning English three-year-old fillies Kithanga and Sueboog. Shirley Heights's other classic winner, Slip Anchor, enjoyed Group 1 success via User Friendly in the Grand Prix de Saint-Cloud and also sired the St Leger third Edbaysaan.

Mill Reef's 2,000 Guineas winner Doyoun may also help carry on the line, judging by the impressive National Stakes victory of his son Manntari, a member of his second crop. Manntari's dam is a daughter of the brilliant but short-lived stallion Kalamoun, and so too was the dam of another of the year's Group 1-winning juveniles, the Prix Marcel Boussac heroine Sierra Madre.

Mention of Kalamoun takes us back to another branch of the Nasrullah line – the one descending through Grey Sovereign. This once very effective line had only one 1993 Group success in Britain or Ireland, earned by Kalaglow's son Jeune.

The Bold Ruler branch was also rather quiet, with Persian Bold having just one Group winner in Perfect Imposter (Derrinstown Stud Derby Trial). However, Persian Bold's son Pennine Walk came up with the Irish 1,000 Guineas winner Nicer a year after his exportation to Switzerland. Another branch of the Nasrullah line was ably represented by Petong, whose son Paris House bounced back to the excellent form he'd shown at two.

Another successful branch of the Nearco line is the Derring-Do family. His grandson Primo Dominie has shown many of the qualities for which Derring-Do was valued and he was very ably represented by First Trump, who matched Primo Dominie's feat of three juvenile Group successes. Top Ville, another of Derring-Do's grandsons, sired the King Edward VII Stakes winner Beneficial, who contributed to a notable double achieved by the Green Dancer mare Youthful in Royal Ascot's Group races.

Very few other male lines got a look in. One exception was Ahonoora, who struck with Ruby Tiger and Inchinor. Two of his sons, Don't Forget Me and Indian Ridge, sired two-year-old Group winners in

England. The Ribot line also had its moments, thanks to Alleged's son Muhtarram (Irish Champion Stakes) and grandson Right Win, plus Ardross's son Azzilfi.

Others well deserving a mention are Warning, whose very talented first crop included the Cheveley Park Stakes winner Prophecy; Swing Easy, whose final crop contained the smart Swing Low; the veteran Bustino, sire of Talented; Ela-Mana-Mou, who showed he's still capable of getting such good winners as Anna of Saxony, Snurge and Double Trigger; and the inexpensive sires Lafontaine and Spin Of A Coin, who respectively sired those good stayers Shambo and Roll A Dollar.

Finally, 1993 marked the deaths of several stallions including Nishapour (sire of Prix de Diane winner Shemaka), Music Boy, Dominion, Persian Heights, Double Schwartz, Daring March, K-Battery, Standaan and Sadler's Wells's young brother Classic Music.

Winning stallions on the Flat in 1993

† Denotes first season sire

ABSALOM (1975) by Abwah-Shadow Queen by Darius

	Races Won	Value £	Distances in furlongs
Aberdeen Heather [3] out of Scotch Thistle)	1	5,060.80	10
Absalom's Pillar [3] out of Collapse)	1	4,050.00	11
Absolutely Fayre [2] out of June Fayre)	1	3,348.00	6
Absolution [9] out of Great Grey Niece)	1	2,787.00	5
Billyback [3] out of Petit Secret)	1	2,448.00	10
Claret Bumble [2] out of Mumtaz Mayfly)	2	4,039.50	5 6
Dangerous Shadow [2] out of Golden Decoy)	3	8,832.75	5 6 6
Family Rose [4] out of Greenhill Lass)	1	2,243.00	7
Johnnie The Joker [2] out of Magic Tower)	1	3,158.00	6
Kummel King [5] out of Louise)	1	3,850.00	7
Lucayan Treasure [3] out of Cindys Gold)	2	7,410.60	5 7
Miss Mah-Jong [2] out of Brookfield Miss)	3	7,526.00	5 7 7
Misty View [4] out of Long View)	1	3,076.50	9
Peter Rowley [2] out of Tiszta Sharok)	1	3,444.00	6
Samsolom [5] out of Norfolk Serenade)	5	18,286.25	5 5 6 6 6
Tamar's Brigade [2] out of Girl's Brigade)	2	8,775.90	6 6
	27	88,336.30	

ADONIJAH (1980) by High Line-Shadow Queen by Darius

	Races Won	Value £	Distances in furlongs
Much Sought After [4] out of Lady Clementine)	4	16,165.75	12 11 11 11
Rose Alto [5] out of Rose Music)	2	47,876.75	10 10
	6	64,042.50	

AFFIRMED (USA) (1975) by Exclusive Native (USA)-Won't Tell You by Crafty Admiral

	Races Won	Value £	Distances in furlongs
Decided (Can) [10] out of Expediency (USA))	1	2,448.00	15
Firm Pledge (USA) [3] out of Rutledge Place (USA))	1	5,070.40	7
One Voice (USA) [3] out of Elk's Ellie (USA))	1	2,924.70	12
Seama (USA) [3] out of Isticanna (USA))	2	5,069.00	9 10
	5	15,512.10	

AFLEET (CAN) (1984) by Mr Prospector (USA)-Polite Lady (USA) by Venetian Jester

	Races Won	Value £	Distances in furlongs
Saseedo (USA) [3] out of Barbara's Moment (USA))	1	3,882.50	5
Zuno Star (USA) [2] out of Simplon Pass (USA))	2	7,029.00	6 6
	3	10,911.50	

AHONOORA (1975) by Lorenzaccio-Helen Nichols by Martial

	Races Won	Value £	Distances in furlongs
Arjuzah (Ire) [3] out of Saving Mercy)	2	17,905.00	7 7
Bronze Maquette (Ire) [3] out of Working Model)	1	2,070.00	10
Case Law [6] out of Travesty)	1	3,145.00	5
Cherhill (Ire) [3] out of Battine (USA))	1	2,717.50	5
Dancing Spirit (Ire) [3] out of Instinctive Move (USA))	1	3,201.75	6
Ericolin (Ire) [3] out of Pixie Erin)	1	3,318.75	9
Face The Future [4] out of Chiltern Red)	1	3,366.00	6
Inchinor [3] out of Inchmurrin)	3	68,073.00	7 7 7
Legion Of Honour [5] out of Shehana (USA))	1	4,844.00	11
Post Impressionist (Ire) [4] out of Roblanna)	2	5,708.60	12 16
Purple Splash [3] out of Quay Line)	1	3,523.50	14
Reflecting (Ire) [4] out of Shining Water)	1	3,648.70	9
Ruby Tiger [6] out of Hayati)	1	21,519.00	10
	17	143,040.80	

AJDAL (USA) (1984) by Northern Dancer-Native Partner (USA) by Raise A Native

	Races Won	Value £	Distances in furlongs
Cezanne [4] out of Reprocolor)	1	7,509.60	10
Coureur [4] out of Nihad)	1	3,262.00	8
Garah [4] out of Abha)	1	3,363.00	6
Little Bean [4] out of Sassalya)	1	9,228.60	7
	4	23,363.20	

†AJRAAS (USA) (1986) by Northern Dancer-Shake A Leg (USA) by Raise A Native

	Races Won	Value £	Distances in furlongs
Jasari (Ire) [2] out of Rue Del Peru)	1	4,142.50	6

AKARAD (FR) (1978) by Labus(Fr)-Licata(Fr) by Abdos

	Races Won	Value £	Distances in furlongs
Wakt [3] out of Nasara (Fr))	1	3,287.30	11

†AL HAREB (USA) (1986) by El Gran Senor-Icing by Prince Tenderfoot (USA)

	Races Won	Value £	Distances in furlongs
Bearall (Ire) [2] out of Soxoph)	3	16,573.65	5 8 7

AL NASR (FR) (1978) by Lyphard (USA)-Caretta by Caro

	Races Won	Value £	Distances in furlongs
Aljaz [3] out of Santa Linda (USA))	1	3,348.00	6
Avishayes (USA) [6] out of Rose Goddess)	1	3,687.50	8
Fragrant Belle (USA) [2] out of Zolinana (Fr))	1	4,279.50	8
Modesto (USA) [5] out of Modena (USA))	1	7,310.00	10
Pistols At Dawn (USA) [3] out of Cannon Run (USA))	4	11,867.50	10 11 10 11
Prince Of Andros (USA) [3] out of Her Radiance (USA))	5	49,937.75	12 9 12 12 12
Realize [2] out of Reactress (USA))	1	3,465.00	7
Solomon's Dancer (USA) [3] out of Infinite Wisdom (USA))	2	6,635.75	8 10
	16	90,531.00	

ALLEGED (USA) (1974) by Hoist The Flag (USA)-Princess Pout by Prince John

	Races Won	Value £	Distances in furlongs
Alinova (USA) [3] out of Charmante (USA))	2	8,628.00	13 14
Allegan (USA) [4] out of Artiste)	2	8,239.72	14 16
Colza (USA) [2] out of Dockage (USA))	1	4,305.00	8
Derab (USA) [7] out of Island Charm (USA))	1	8,900.16	12
Icy South (USA) [3] out of Arctic Eclipse (USA))	2	6,520.50	10 9
Long Silence (USA) [4] out of Mystical Mood (USA))	1	3,143.25	14
Maradonna (USA) [4] out of Kiss)	1	4,045.00	11
Muhtarram (USA) [4] out of Ballet de France (USA))	2	15,459.00	8 8
	12	59,240.63	

ALLEGING (USA) (1981) by Alleged (USA)-Sweet Habit by Habitat

	Races Won	Value £	Distances in furlongs
Allesca [3] out of Hitesca)	2	5,225.00	12 11
Allmosa [4] out of Wimosa)	2	5,420.00	11 12
Almost A Princess [5] out of Rabab)	1	3,027.50	12
Inferring [5] out of Be My Darling)	1	2,825.40	9
Just Bob [4] out of Diami)	4	10,578.55	6 5 5 5
Play Hever Golf [3] out of Sweet Rosina)	3	16,924.00	6 5 7
Quick Steel [5] out of Illiney Girl)	1	2,448.00	6
Roberty Lea [5] out of Rosy Lee (Fr))	1	3,629.50	11
Silver Samurai [4] out of Be My Lady)	4	16,607.75	10 10 9 10
	19	66,685.70	

†ALWASMI (USA) (1984) by Northern Dancer-Height of Fashion (Fr) by Bustino

	Races Won	Value £	Distances in furlongs
Khatir (Can) [2] out of Perfect Poppy (USA))	1	2,601.40	9

ALYDAR (USA) (1975) by Raise A Native-Sweet Tooth by On-And-On

	Races Won	Value £	Distances in furlongs
Biljan (USA) [3] out of Best Decision (USA))	1	2,562.00	16
Eaton Row (USA) [3] out of Royal Entrance (USA))	1	3,318.75	11
Kassbaan (USA) [3] out of Ma Biche (USA))	3	14,293.50	7 8 8
	5	20,174.25	

ALYSHEBA (USA) (1984) by Alydar (USA)-Bel Sheba (USA) by Lt Stevens

	Races Won	Value £	Distances in furlongs
Shaiba (USA) [3] out of Stage Luck (USA))	1	9,894.00	14
Shareek (USA) [3] out of All Rainbows (USA))	1	4,077.50	9
	2	13,971.50	

ALZAO (USA) (1980) by Lyphard (USA)-Lady Rebecca by Sir Ivor

	Races Won	Value £	Distances in furlongs
Akkazao (Ire) [5] out of Akka)	1	4,045.00	10
Alzianah [2] out of Ghassanah)	2	13,289.75	5 6
Anusha [3] out of Arita (Fr))	3	8,792.20	8 7 8
Azola (Ire) [3] out of Carnival Dance)	2	5,245.00	8 8
Barossa Valley (Ire) [2] out of Night Of Wind)	1	4,760.00	6
Blaaziing Joe (Ire) [2] out of Beijing (USA))	1	4,175.00	10
Bobzao (Ire) [4] out of Brilleaux)	2	20,604.75	12 10
Cicerao (Ire) [2] out of Massawippi)	1	4,503.00	8
Dancing Diamond (Ire) [3] out of Shay Tien)	2	3,494.20	9 12
Grand Vitesse (Ire) [4] out of Au Revoir)	1	5,526.50	8

	Races Won	Value £	Distances in furlongs
Grey Charmer (Ire) [4] out of Sashi Woo)	2	8,168.00	6 5
Here He Comes [7] out of Nanette)	2	6,419.20	9 10
Mogwai (Ire) [4] out of Maltese Pet)	1	2,742.00	8
Monsieur Dupont (Ire) [3] out of Katie Koo)	1	3,817.50	14
Play With Me (Ire) [3] out of Strike It Rich (Fr))	1	2,792.50	10
Record Lover (Ire) [3] out of Spun Gold)	1	3,882.50	16
Relatively Special [2] out of Someone Special)	2	20,910.25	6 7
Shepton Mallet (Ire) [2] out of Savannah Song (USA))	1	3,840.00	8
Sheridan (Ire) [2] out of Steady The Buffs)	1	4,592.50	8
Slasher Jack (Ire) [2] out of Sherkraine)	1	3,626.00	6
Unblest [2] out of Missed Blessing)	3	46,394.30	6 6 7
	32	181,620.15	

ANITA'S PRINCE (1981) by Stradavinsky-Get Ready by On Your Mark

	Races Won	Value £	Distances in furlongs
Carranita (Ire) [3] out of Take More (Ger))	2	7,017.50	5 6
Princely Favour (Ire) [3] out of Kiss The Bride)	2	6,807.90	6 7
Sporting Heir (Ire) [2] out of Royal Accord)	1	2,070.00	6
	5	15,895.40	

ANOTHER REALM (1978) by Realm-Tiara III by Persian Gulf

	Races Won	Value £	Distances in furlongs
Admirals Realm [4] out of Bedeni)	1	3,877.75	5
Cobblers Hill [4] out of Morning Miss)	1	3,210.00	5
Dead Calm [3] out of Truly Bold)	1	2,243.00	6
Pondering [3] out of Fishpond)	4	10,738.00	12 14 16 12
Regal Chimes [4] out of London Cries (Fr))	2	20,536.70	6 5
	9	40,605.45	

APALACHEE (USA) (1971) by Round Table-Moccasin by Nantallah

	Races Won	Value £	Distances in furlongs
Green's Cassatt (USA) [5] out of Royally Rewarded (USA))	1	2,724.00	11
North Esk (USA) [4] out of Six Dozen (USA))	2	8,947.50	8 8
	3	11,671.50	

ARAGON (1980) by Mummy's Pet-Ica by Great Nephew

	Races Won	Value £	Distances in furlongs
Aradanza [3] out of Divine Fling)	1	28,542.50	6
Aragrove [3] out of Grovehurst)	2	7,708.25	5 5
Beats Working [2] out of Relatively Easy)	2	7,967.00	5 8
Dana Springs (Ire) [3] out of Dance By Night)	4	49,776.40	7 11 12 9
Dance Focus [2] out of Brassy Nell)	1	4,191.00	5
Heart Of Spain [3] out of Hearten)	2	5,809.50	10 10
Knobbleeneeze [3] out of Proud Miss (USA))	1	3,340.00	8
Lucky Noire [5] out of Noire Small (USA))	1	2,954.00	10
Maragon [2] out of Mana (Ger))	1	8,041.00	6
Miss Aragon [5] out of Lavenham Blue)	2	6,139.40	5 6
Mr Butch [3] out of Kittycatoo Katango (USA))	1	4,751.50	7
Mu-Arrik [5] out of Maravilla)	1	2,532.00	6
Quantity Surveyor [4] out of Quaranta)	3	10,660.20	8 8 8
	22	142,412.75	

ARCTIC TERN (USA) (1973) by Sea-Bird II-Bubbling Beauty by Hasty Road

	Races Won	Value £	Distances in furlongs
Arctic Guest (Ire) [3] out of Sojourn)	3	8,225.40	12 14 15
Bay Tern (USA) [7] out of Unbiased (USA))	1	2,913.00	15
Innishowen (USA) [2] out of Skeeb (USA))	2	15,530.00	7 8
Major Yaasi (USA) [3] out of Dimant Rose (USA))	1	4,836.00	9
Ritto [3] out of Melodrama)	1	3,435.75	10
Sun Grebe (Ire) [3] out of Bronzewing)	3	10,448.50	16 16 16
Truben (USA) [4] out of Cadbury Hill (USA))	1	3,460.00	12
Whitechapel (USA) [5] out of Christchurch (Fr))	1	7,505.00	12
	13	56,353.65	

ARDAR (1978) by Relko-Adayra (Fr) by Le Haar

	Races Won	Value £	Distances in furlongs
North Ardar [3] out of Langwaite)	3	9,099.90	7 7 7

ARDROSS (1976) by Run The Gantlet (USA)-Le Melody by Levmoss

	Races Won	Value £	Distances in furlongs
Aahsaylad [7] out of Madam Slaney)	2	61,587.50	20 18
Alderbrook [4] out of Twine)	5	21,873.95	9 10 9 10 10
Alkhafji [4] out of Eljazzi)	1	3,728.25	12
Avro Anson [5] out of Tremellick)	1	3,435.75	17
Azzilfi [3] out of Tanouma (USA))	2	43,381.95	9 13
Duckey Fuzz [5] out of Twine)	3	12,074.25	7 7 7

	Races Won	Value £	Distances in furlongs
Kovalevskia [8] out of Fiordiligi)	1	3,106.00	16
Miss Plum [4] out of Heaven High)	1	7,096.00	18
My Rossini [4] out of My Tootsie)	1	2,794.00	14
Salu [4] out of String Of Beads)	3	9,671.75	12 16 13
St Ninian [7] out of Caergwrle)	1	3,172.50	9
	21	171,921.90	

ASSERT (1979) by Be My Guest (USA)-Irish Bird (USA) by Sea-Bird II

	Races Won	Value £	Distances in furlongs
Tochar Ban (USA) [3] out of Guest Night)	1	4,079.25	10

†ASTRONEF (1984) by Be My Guest (USA)-Mill Princess by Mill Reef (USA)

	Races Won	Value £	Distances in furlongs
Celestial Rumour (Ire) [2] out of Gossip)	1	2,549.00	6
International Star (Ire) [2] out of Brave Ivy)	1	3,231.00	6
Laurel Romeo (Ire) [2] out of Love Me Tight)	1	2,422.20	6
Raven's Return (Ire) [2] out of Passage Falcon)	1	3,435.75	5
	4	11,637.95	

AUCTION RING (USA) (1972) by Bold Bidder-Hooplah by Hillary

	Races Won	Value £	Distances in furlongs
Hopeful Bid (Ire) [4] out of Irish Kick)	1	4,235.00	7
Malcesine (Ire) [4] out of Vain Deb)	1	2,473.50	8
Proud Brigadier (Ire) [5] out of Naughty One Gerard)	2	6,170.80	8 7
Sir Oliver (Ire) [4] out of Eurorose)	1	3,002.00	6
The Auction Bidder [6] out of Stepping Gaily)	1	3,611.25	6
Trianglepoint (Ire) [3] out of Tapestry)	1	2,243.00	8
	7	21,735.55	

BACKCHAT (USA) (1982) by Stage Door Johnny-Dos A Dos (USA) by Advocator

	Races Won	Value £	Distances in furlongs
Big Pat [4] out of Fallonetta)	5	15,634.30	11 12 12 12 11

BAIRN (USA) (1982) by Northern Baby(Can)-Lady Mouse by Sir Ivor

	Races Won	Value £	Distances in furlongs
Batabanoo [4] out of For Instance)	2	5,951.25	11 12
Creche [4] out of Melody Park)	1	2,245.00	7
Danger Baby [3] out of Swordlestown Miss (USA))	1	2,399.80	18
En Attendant (Fr) [5] out of Vizenia)	3	53,954.00	7 7 7
Gipsy Fiddler [5] out of Miss Cindy)	1	2,301.00	5
Harvest Rose [4] out of Ragtime Rose)	1	2,553.00	8
Kinoko [5] out of Octavia)	2	6,667.00	14 12
Lawnswood Junior [6] out of Easymede)	3	10,153.50	8 8 8
Merry Mermaid [3] out of Manna Green)	1	7,044.00	11
Passion Sunday [2] out of Holy Day)	1	2,164.00	7
Premier Dance [6] out of Gigiolina)	1	1,770.00	12
Primula Bairn [3] out of Miss Primula)	3	10,360.50	5 5 5
Stapleford Lass [3] out of Idabella (Fr))	1	2,534.20	10
Young Valentine [4] out of Spinner)	1	2,941.00	7
	22	113,038.25	

BALIDAR (1966) by Will Somers-Violet Bank by The Phoenix

	Races Won	Value £	Distances in furlongs
Baligay [8] out of Gaygo Lady)	1	5,287.50	5
Francis Ann [5] out of Supper Party)	1	2,898.80	6
	2	8,186.30	

BALLACASHTAL (CAN) (1977) by Vice Regent(Can)-Swiss Roll by Counterpoint

	Races Won	Value £	Distances in furlongs
Ballasecret [5] out of Soft Secret)	3	23,540.00	6 6 6
Batchworth Bound [4] out of Treasurebound)	2	5,959.90	5 5
Mentalasanythin [4] out of Lafrowda)	2	7,463.50	8 8
Threepenny-Bridge [2] out of Super Style)	1	2,070.00	6
Wild Strawberry [4] out of Pts Fairway)	2	5,484.00	8 8
	10	44,517.40	

BALLAD ROCK (1974) by Bold Lad(Ire)-True Rocket by Roan Rocket

	Races Won	Value £	Distances in furlongs
Ballad Dancer [8] out of Manx Image)	3	8,764.25	7 5 6
Ballard Ring (Ire) [2] out of Miss Victoria)	1	5,952.00	7
Chilly Breeze [3] out of Chicobin (USA))	1	2,355.00	6
Darren Boy (Ire) [2] out of Trojan Relation)	2	6,936.80	6 6
Exclusion [4] out of Great Exception)	1	3,078.75	8
Green's Stubbs [6] out of Aventina)	1	2,070.00	8
Heavy Rock (Ire) [4] out of Asian Princess)	1	3,052.00	9
Jahangir (Ire) [4] out of Marsh Benham)	1	3,183.70	7
Plainsong [2] out of No Jargon)	1	2,540.10	5
Poetic Form (Ire) [3] out of Bobs)	1	2,924.70	14

	Races Won	Value £	Distances in furlongs
Rafferty's Rules (Ire) [2] out of River Maiden (Fr))	2	12,827.00	6 6
Stack Rock [6] out of One Better)	4	33,590.96	5 6 5 6
Two Moves In Front (Ire) [3] out of Kentucky Wildcat)	1	3,114.00	5
	20	90,389.26	

BALLIOL (1969) by Will Somers-Violet Bank by The Phoenix

	Races Won	Value £	Distances in furlongs
Va Utu [5] out of Flame)	1	3,209.60	11

BATES MOTEL (USA) (1979) by Sir Ivor-Sunday Purchase by T V Lark

	Races Won	Value £	Distances in furlongs
Case For The Crown (USA) [6] out of Crown The Queen (USA))	1	2,847.00	9

BAY EXPRESS (1971) by Polyfoto-Pal Sinna by Palestine

	Races Won	Value £	Distances in furlongs
Express Gift [4] out of Annes Gift)	2	9,222.75	8 10
Sakharov [4] out of Supreme Kingdom)	4	10,700.60	5 5 6 6
	6	19,923.35	

BE MY GUEST (USA) (1974) by Northern Dancer(Can)-What A Treat by Tudor Minstrel

	Races Won	Value £	Distances in furlongs
Ajalan (Ire) [3] out of Intensive (USA))	1	3,465.00	9
Barik (Ire) [3] out of Smoo)	1	4,045.00	8
Be Exciting (Ire) [2] out of Exciting)	1	3,782.00	8
Belmoredean [8] out of Hanna Alta (Fr))	1	3,235.50	7
Captain's Guest (Ire) [3] out of Watership (USA))	1	3,523.50	10
Eightandahalf (Ire) [4] out of Nancy Chere (USA))	2	5,694.00	12 14
Lucky Guest [6] out of Gay Fantasy)	1	12,792.00	10
May Hills Legacy (Ire) [4] out of May Hill)	2	7,104.80	10 10
Moon Carnival [3] out of Castle Moon)	2	5,581.30	12 11
My Patriarch [3] out of Early Rising (USA))	5	29,743.90	14 14 14 16 16
Pampered Guest (Ire) [2] out of Miss Garuda)	1	3,377.25	8
Soba Guest (Ire) [4] out of Brazilian Princess)	1	1,882.50	6
Sobering Thoughts [7] out of Soba)	4	24,786.60	5 6 6 6
Special Dawn (Ire) [3] out of Dawn Star)	1	3,106.00	8
Wisham (USA) [3] out of Massorah (Fr))	1	3,435.75	7
Yildiz [4] out of Yldizlar)	1	12,817.50	11
	26	128,372.60	

BE MY NATIVE (USA) (1979) by Our Native (USA)-Witchy Woman (USA) by Strate Stuff

	Races Won	Value £	Distances in furlongs
Beaumont (Ire) [3] out of Say Yes)	1	2,162.60	9
Red Indian [7] out of Martialette)	1	2,950.60	9
	2	5,113.20	

BELFORT (FR) (1977) by Tyrant (USA)-Belle de Retz by Gilles de Retz

	Races Won	Value £	Distances in furlongs
Echo-Logical [4] out of North Pine)	1	5,775.00	7
Grey Toppa [2] out of Gallic Law)	2	5,977.40	5 5
Jade City [3] out of Dear Glenda)	1	3,720.00	5
Larn Fort [3] out of Larnem)	1	3,287.30	5
Lightning Belle [2] out of Louisianalightning)	1	2,950.60	5
Magic Pearl [3] out of Oyster Gray)	2	8,689.50	5 5
Milbank Challenger [3] out of Princess Sharpenup)	2	5,488.00	5 5
Miss Crusty [5] out of Blue Empress)	1	2,959.00	8
Nigel's Lucky Girl [5] out of Haiti Mill)	1	3,106.00	6
Our Mica [3] out of Aristata)	1	3,106.00	5
Press The Bell [3] out of Northern Empress)	4	12,130.40	5 5 5 5
	17	57,189.20	

BELLYPHA (1976) by Lyphard (USA)-Belga by Le Fabuleux

	Races Won	Value £	Distances in furlongs
Mahaasin [5] out of Dame Ashfield)	1	3,078.75	12
Remany [4] out of Moonscape)	1	3,265.50	11
Tenayestelign [5] out of Opale)	1	3,416.80	10
	3	9,761.05	

BERING (1983) by Arctic Tern (USA)-Beaune (Fr) by Lyphard (USA)

	Races Won	Value £	Distances in furlongs
Amber Valley (USA) [2] out of Olatha (USA))	1	3,647.25	6
Bayrak (USA) [3] out of Phydilla (Fr))	1	2,364.00	12
Chummy's Pal (USA) [3] out of Miss Vestment (USA))	1	2,511.00	11
Lord High Admiral (Can) [5] out of Baltic Sea (Can))	3	14,687.75	5 5 5
Marco Magnifico (USA) [3] out of Viscosity (USA))	1	5,481.00	14

	Races Won	Value £	Distances in furlongs
Peter Davies (USA) [5] out of French Flick (USA))	2	17,380.80	8 8
Rasayel (USA) [3] out of Reham)	1	2,742.00	14
Roveredo (USA) [3] out of Holy Tobin (USA))	1	3,084.75	12
Sharaar (USA) [3] out of Trasimeno)	2	5,673.00	10 10
Wainwright (USA) [4] out of Crystal Bright)	2	18,602.50	8 8
	15	76,174.05	

BET TWICE (USA) (1984) by Sportin' Life (USA)-Golden Dust (USA) by Dusty Canyon

	Races Won	Value £	Distances in furlongs
Promise Fulfilled (USA) [2] out of Kind Prospect (USA))	2	7,497.60	5 6

BEVELED (USA) (1982) by Sharpen Up-Sans Arc (USA) by High Echelon

	Races Won	Value £	Distances in furlongs
Another Jade [3] out of Zamindara)	3	9,639.50	6 5 6
Beveled Edge [4] out of Best Offer)	1	2,812.00	6
Brave Edge [2] out of Daring Ditty)	1	4,240.50	5
Evening Falls [2] out of Encore L'amour (USA))	2	7,578.00	5 5
Loch Patrick [3] out of Daisy Loch)	2	20,632.25	6 5
Lord Alfie [4] out of Fair Nic)	2	7,475.50	7 6
Margaret's Gift [3] out of Persiandale)	2	18,635.00	6 6
Master Beveled [3] out of Miss Anniversary)	1	4,500.00	9
Moon Over Miami [3] out of Run Amber Run)	2	20,330.50	7 7
Patsy Grimes [3] out of Blue Angel)	1	3,598.10	6
Sabre Rattler [3] out of Casbah Girl)	2	13,227.00	5 5
Saifan [4] out of Superfrost)	3	40,925.00	8 8 8
Sharp Gazelle [3] out of Shadha)	2	4,994.70	6 7
	24	158,588.05	

BLAKENEY (1966) by Hethersett-Windmill Girl by Hornbeam

	Races Won	Value £	Distances in furlongs
Crazy For You [2] out of Flopsy)	1	5,205.00	7
Guestwick [3] out of Barsham)	1	2,243.00	15
Our Aisling [5] out of Mrs Cullumbine)	1	2,778.90	15
Regalsett [3] out of Sleepline Princess)	1	2,749.00	9
Santana Lady (Ire) [4] out of Santalina)	1	3,131.90	10
Yes [5] out of Arrapata)	1	2,259.00	6
	6	18,366.80	

BLAZING SADDLES (AUS) (1974) by Todman-Lady Simone by Wilkes

	Races Won	Value £	Distances in furlongs
Goody Four Shoes [5] out of Bronzamer)	1	3,235.50	5

BLUEBIRD (USA) (1984) by Storm Bird(Can)-Ivory Dawn (USA) by Sir Ivor

	Races Won	Value £	Distances in furlongs
Big Blue [4] out of Cassina)	1	3,882.50	8
Birchwood Sun [3] out of Shapely Test (USA))	1	2,601.40	6
Blue Blazer [3] out of View)	1	2,269.13	8
Blue Siren [2] out of Manx Millenium)	2	7,711.25	5 5
Bluegrass Prince (Ire) [2] out of Amata (USA))	2	9,644.80	5 6
Jucea [4] out of Appleby Park)	1	2,301.00	5
Majestic Eagle (Ire) [2] out of Majestic Nurse)	1	4,464.00	6
	9	32,874.08	

BLUSHING GROOM (FR) (1974) by Red God-Runaway Bride by Wild Risk

	Races Won	Value £	Distances in furlongs
Badie (USA) [4] out of Desirable)	1	3,201.75	10
Brier Creek (USA) [4] out of Savannah Dancer (USA))	3	46,626.56	12 13 16
Desert Team (USA) [3] out of Bemiss Heights (USA))	1	38,046.20	12
Gold Splash (USA) [3] out of Riviere D'Or (USA))	1	109,537.80	8
Hillzah (USA) [5] out of Glamour Girl (Arg))	2	8,193.10	12 10
Mithi Al Gamar (USA) [3] out of Raahia (Can))	1	3,640.50	7
Modest Hope (USA) [6] out of Key Dancer (USA))	1	3,687.50	10
Scarlet Tunic (USA) [3] out of Highclere)	1	2,742.00	14
	11	215,675.41	

† BLUSHING JOHN (USA) (1985) by Blushing Groom (Fr)-La Griffe (USA) by Prince John

	Races Won	Value £	Distances in furlongs
Al Battar (USA) [2] out of Golden Way (USA))	1	3,289.50	5

BLUSHING SCRIBE (USA) (1981) by Blushing Groom(Fr)-Takealetter by Monitor

	Races Won	Value £	Distances in furlongs
Forever Blushing [2] out of Rheinza)	1	2,070.00	6
My Ruby Ring [6] out of Bells Of St Martin)	3	9,184.90	6 6 6
	4	11,254.90	

	Races Won	Value £	Distances in furlongs

BOB BACK (USA) (1981) by Roberto (USA)-Toter Back (USA) by Carry Back

	Races Won	Value £	Distances in furlongs
Ann Hill (Ire) [3] out of Yuma (USA))	2	4,497.00	12 10
Bob's Return (Ire) [3] out of Quality Of Life)	3	275,271.10	11 11 14
Robingo (Ire) [4] out of Mill's Girl)	2	17,120.00	16 16
Waterlord (Ire) [3] out of Ringtail)	1	2,286.00	7
	8	299,174.10	

BOLD ARRANGEMENT (1983) by Persian Bold-Arrangement by Floribunda

	Races Won	Value £	Distances in furlongs
Bold Aristocrat (Ire) [2] out of Wyn Mipet)	1	2,444.60	5
Summer Wind (Ire) [3] out of Eurynome)	4	13,003.00	12 14 16 14
Twice In Bundoran (Ire) [2] out of Asturiana)	1	2,820.00	5
	6	18,267.60	

BOLD FORT (1979) by Auction Ring (USA)-Via Mala by Pall Mall

	Races Won	Value £	Distances in furlongs
Inderaputeri [3] out of Hello Cuddles)	1	2,243.00	6
Samson-Agonistes [7] out of Hello Cuddles)	3	7,118.00	5 5 5
	4	9,361.00	

BOLD OWL (1976) by Bold Lad(Ire)-Tawny Owl by Faberge II

	Races Won	Value £	Distances in furlongs
Amron [6] out of Sweet Minuet)	3	26,321.00	5 6 5
Atlantic Way [5] out of Overseas)	2	6,368.50	11 12
Ballyranter [4] out of Whipalash)	2	10,607.00	8 8
Henry's Luck [2] out of Rahesh)	2	3,795.00	6 8
Kathanna [2] out of Moon Charter)	1	2,742.00	5
Rocky Bay [4] out of Overseas)	1	2,679.00	8
	11	52,512.50	

BROKEN HEARTED (1984) by Dara Monarch-Smash by Busted

	Races Won	Value £	Distances in furlongs
Footsteps (Ire) [2] out of Remoosh)	2	8,288.20	6 7
Kaitak (Ire) [2] out of Klairelle)	1	2,005.00	6
Key To My Heart (Ire) [3] out of Originality)	1	6,373.60	11
Starlight Rose (Ire) [3] out of Star Province)	1	3,158.00	8
	5	19,824.80	

BRUSTOLON (1978) by Sharpen Up-Berthe Manet by Crepello

	Races Won	Value £	Distances in furlongs
Mister Beat [2] out of Miss May (Fr))	1	2,534.20	6

BURSLEM (1980) by Nebbiolo-Spice Road (USA) by Gallant Man

	Races Won	Value £	Distances in furlongs
Bo Knows Best (Ire) [4] out of Do We Know)	1	8,237.50	12
Ho-Joe (Ire) [3] out of Walkyria)	2	4,003.80	11 13
Slumber Thyme (Ire) [4] out of Chive)	1	2,763.00	8
	4	15,004.30	

BUSTED (1963) by Crepello-Sans Le Sou by Vimy

	Races Won	Value £	Distances in furlongs
Dr Zeva [7] out of Dance In Rome)	2	7,152.00	16 11

BUSTINO (1971) by Busted-Ship Yard by Doutelle

	Races Won	Value £	Distances in furlongs
Bulaxie [2] out of Galaxie Dust (USA))	1	7,995.00	7
Gone For A Burton (Ire) [3] out of Crimbourne)	1	2,061.20	10
Heart Broken [3] out of Touch My Heart)	1	2,217.00	6
Mysilv [3] out of Miss By Miles)	2	6,723.35	8 9
Romola Nijinsky [5] out of Verchinina)	3	8,646.10	8 9 9
Salda [4] out of Martinova)	1	2,880.00	8
Talented [3] out of Triple Reef)	2	39,068.70	10 10
	11	69,591.35	

BUZZARDS BAY (1978) by Joshua-Grande Merci by Gratitude

	Races Won	Value £	Distances in furlongs
Buzzards Bellbuoy [4] out of Bella Travaille)	1	4,793.75	8

†CADEAUX GENEREUX (1985) by Young Generation-Smarten Up by Sharpen Up

	Races Won	Value £	Distances in furlongs
Cajun Cadet [2] out of Petty Purse)	1	5,439.00	6
Carmot [2] out of Rainbow's End)	2	8,622.80	6 7
Extra Bonus [2] out of Haitienne (Fr))	2	5,426.70	7 7
French Gift [2] out of Soba)	1	3,377.25	6
Million Lights (Ire) [2] out of Fire Flash)	1	3,933.00	7
Ultimo Imperatore [2] out of Norpella)	1	8,357.50	6
	8	35,156.25	

CAERLEON (USA) (1980) by Nijinsky(Can)-Foreseer (USA) by Round Table

	Races Won	Value £	Distances in furlongs
Alaflak (Ire) [2] out of Safe Haven)	1	3,420.00	7
Arc Lamp [7] out of Dazzling Light)	1	3,002.40	5

	Races Won	Value £	Distances in furlongs
Chief Of Staff [4] out of Fanny's Cove)	1	1,730.00	6
Del Deya (Ire) [3] out of Point Of Honour)	2	7,595.00	10 10
Dragon's Teeth (Ire) [3] out of Scots Lass)	1	3,143.25	9
Dreams Are Free (Ire) [3] out of Keep The Thought (USA))	1	3,882.50	9
Ghost Tree (Ire) [3] out of Embla)	1	3,523.50	6
Kassab [3] out of Red Comes Up (USA))	3	11,867.95	12 13 14
Noble Rose (Ire) [2] out of Noble Lily (USA))	1	5,343.00	7
Only Royale (Ire) [4] out of Etoile de Paris)	1	78,598.00	11
Overbury (Ire) [2] out of Overcall)	2	10,628.10	7 8
Pencader (Ire) [2] out of Jackie Berry)	1	5,052.50	7
Samain (USA) [6] out of Samarta Dancer (USA))	1	4,175.00	16
Sherman (Ire) [2] out of Aghsan)	1	4,987.50	8
Stoney Valley [3] out of Startino)	2	17,785.00	10 10
Tajdid (Ire) [3] out of Tarib)	1	3,106.00	7
Tap On Air [3] out of Rappa Tap Tap (Fr))	2	18,485.37	10 10
Tenby [3] out of Shining Water)	2	72,927.00	10 10
Tender Moment (Ire) [5] out of Cannon Boy (USA))	2	24,115.75	7 7
Usk The Way [3] out of One Way Street)	1	2,489.40	16
Welsh Mill (Ire) [4] out of Gay Milly (Fr))	1	11,998.80	12
	29	297,856.02	

CAERWENT (1985) by Caerleon (USA)-Marwell by Habitat

	Races Won	Value £	Distances in furlongs
Westray (Fr) [3] out of Mindena (Fr))	1	1,992.50	14

CANNONADE (USA) (1971) by Bold Bidder-Queen Sucree by Ribot

	Races Won	Value £	Distances in furlongs
Rival Bid (USA) [5] out of Love Triangle (USA))	1	3,348.00	10

CARMELITE HOUSE (USA) (1985) by Diesis-Sancta by So Blessed

	Races Won	Value £	Distances in furlongs
Press Gallery [3] out of Mixed Applause (USA))	2	8,127.35	6 6
Try N' Fly (Ire) [3] out of Gruntled)	1	2,660.00	12
Vilamar (Ire) [3] out of Tacheo)	1	2,467.00	7
White Shoot (Ire) [2] out of Irish Kick)	1	3,465.00	6
	5	16,719.35	

CARO (1967) by Fortino II-Chambord by Chamossaire

	Races Won	Value £	Distances in furlongs
Bayin (USA) [4] out of Regatela (USA))	3	10,524.75	5 6 5
Daru (USA) [4] out of Frau Daruma (Arg))	1	3,172.50	12
Sovereign Page (USA) [4] out of Tashinsky (USA))	3	9,678.50	10 10 10
	7	23,375.75	

CASTLE KEEP (1977) by Kalamoun-Fotheringay by Right Royal V

	Races Won	Value £	Distances in furlongs
Castle Courageous [6] out of Peteona)	2	12,618.00	14 14

CELESTIAL STORM (USA) (1983) by Roberto (USA)-Tobira Celeste (USA) by Ribot

	Races Won	Value £	Distances in furlongs
Continuity [4] out of Tamassos)	2	5,911.50	14 15
Madam Gymcrak [3] out of Finlandaise (Fr))	1	2,243.00	10
Tyrone Flyer [4] out of Dance A Jig)	1	3,406.50	7
	4	11,561.00	

CHIEF SINGER (1981) by Ballad Rock-Principia (Fr) by Le Fabuleux

	Races Won	Value £	Distances in furlongs
Bag Of Tricks (Ire) [3] out of Bag Lady)	1	3,054.00	10
Casting Shadows [4] out of Six Ashes)	1	3,786.75	7
Cavatina [3] out of Pennycuick)	1	3,201.75	7
Choir Practice [6] out of Good Try)	2	8,252.50	5 5
Cotteir Chief (Ire) [2] out of Hasty Key (USA))	3	9,956.70	6 7 7
Election Special [2] out of Electo)	1	3,465.00	6
Gone Troppo [3] out of Tanagrea)	1	3,377.25	9
Honey Seeker [4] out of Honey Thief)	1	3,339.10	6
Let's Get Lost [4] out of Lost In France)	1	3,027.50	8
Northern Chief [3] out of Pacific Gull (USA))	2	6,205.40	7 7
Oubeck Blue [2] out of Blue Brocade)	1	3,622.50	7
Principal Player (USA) [3] out of Harp Strings (Fr))	1	3,095.00	5
Sawtid [2] out of Bourgeonette)	2	5,883.50	6 6
Singer On The Roof [3] out of On The Tiles)	1	2,795.20	8
Singers Image [4] out of Little White Lies)	1	3,582.00	8
Waffle On [3] out of Humble Pie)	1	3,492.50	6
	21	70,136.65	

CHIEF'S CROWN (USA) (1982) by Danzig (USA)-Six Crowns (USA) by Secretariat (USA)

	Races Won	Value £	Distances in furlongs
Erhaab (USA) [2] out of Histoire (Fr))	2	7,495.25	7 7

	Races Won	Value £	Distances in furlongs
Grand Lodge (USA) [2] out of La Papagena)	3	138,708.00	6 7 7
Indian Flash (Ire) [3] out of Sovereign Flash (Fr))	3	9,019.50	11 10 11
Moscow Sea (USA) [3] out of How High The Moon (USA))	2	12,299.25	10 10
Summer Pageant [3] out of Troyanos)	3	10,509.65	11 12 11
Susquehanna Days (USA) [3] out of Gliding By (USA))	2	5,678.75	8 8
	15	183,710.40	

CHILIBANG (1984) by Formidable (USA)-Chili Girl by Skymaster

	Races Won	Value £	Distances in furlongs
Bellsabanging [3] out of Bells Of St Martin)	2	5,754.80	5 5
Bev's Folly [2] out of Demerger)	1	2,070.00	5
Burishki [3] out of Hunza Water)	1	2,768.00	6
Chili Heights [3] out of Highest Tender)	1	6,165.00	7
Corona Gold [3] out of Miss Alkie)	2	5,305.50	8 7
Cracker Jack [3] out of Friendly Jester)	1	1,520.00	5
Flair Lady [2] out of Flair Park)	1	2,070.00	6
Hot Off The Press [3] out of Printafoil)	2	4,812.00	7 8
Kingston Brown [3] out of Smooth Siren (USA))	2	4,264.00	7 7
Newbury Coat [3] out of Deanta In Eirinn)	1	3,525.00	5
Window Display [2] out of Stubble)	1	2,070.00	5
	15	40,324.30	

CHUKAROO (1972) by Kibenka-Wild Word by Galivanter

	Races Won	Value £	Distances in furlongs
Chucklestone [10] out of Czar's Diamond)	1	3,080.00	17

CLANTIME (1981) by Music Boy-Penny Pincher by Constable

	Races Won	Value £	Distances in furlongs
Calamanco [3] out of Laena)	1	3,094.20	5
Cape Merino [2] out of Laena)	2	92,189.50	5 6
Caspian Gold [2] out of Parijoun)	1	2,259.00	5
Join The Clan [4] out of Joint Reward)	2	6,056.00	6 5
Parfait Amour [4] out of Chablisse)	2	5,470.00	7 8
Perfect Passion [3] out of Charming View)	1	2,872.00	5
Saint Express [3] out of Redgrave Design)	1	5,452.00	5
Super Rocky [4] out of Starproof)	1	2,232.00	5
The Fed [3] out of Hyde Princess)	1	3,084.75	5
Tuscan Dawn [3] out of Excavator Lady)	2	6,637.50	5 5
	14	129,346.95	

†CLASSIC SECRET (USA)(1986) by Northern Dancer-Betty's Secret (USA) by Secretariat (USA)

	Races Won	Value £	Distances in furlongs
Northern Celadon (Ire) [2] out of Exemplary)	1	3,675.80	7
Secret Serenade [2] out of Norfolk Serenade)	1	3,028.30	6
Up The Mariners (Ire) [2] out of Tuft Hill)	1	1,380.00	6
	3	8,084.10	

CLAUDE MONET (USA) (1981) by Affirmed (USA)-Madelia (Fr) by Caro

	Races Won	Value £	Distances in furlongs
Artistic Reef [4] out of Kellys Reef)	2	8,028.20	5 5
Claudia Miss [6] out of Palace Travel)	2	5,023.60	6 6
Sweet Revival [5] out of Semperflorens)	1	3,262.00	10
	5	16,313.80	

CLEVER TRICK (USA) (1976) by Icecapade (USA)-Kankakee Miss (USA) by Better Bee

	Races Won	Value £	Distances in furlongs
Clever Minstrel (USA) [3] out of Toor A Lay (USA))	1	2,534.20	7
Talent (USA) [5] out of Contralto)	1	3,687.50	9
	2	6,221.70	

COMMANCHE RUN (1981) by Run The Gantlet (USA)-Volley by Ratification

	Races Won	Value £	Distances in furlongs
Comanche Companion [3] out of Constant Companion)	3	13,853.50	8 8 8
Funny Choice (Ire) [3] out of Best Of Fun)	3	7,557.80	12 15 13
Indian Slave (Ire) [5] out of Commanche Belle)	1	4,110.00	7
No Reservations (Ire) [3] out of Light Link)	1	5,897.50	7
Scalp 'em (Ire) [5] out of Supremely Royal)	1	2,668.60	14
Usaidit [4] out of Smurfiusa (USA))	5	53,039.00	10 10 10 12 10
	14	87,126.40	

COMMON GROUNDS (1985) by Kris-Sweetly(Fr) by Lyphard (USA)

	Races Won	Value £	Distances in furlongs
Common Law (Ire) [3] out of Children's Hour)	1	3,377.25	6
Final Frontier (Ire) [3] out of Last Gunboat)	2	9,316.50	7 7
Gweek (Ire) [3] out of Do We Know)	1	3,002.00	11
Heathcliff (Ire) [2] out of Catherine Linton (USA))	1	4,776.00	7
Just You Dare (Ire) [3] out of Eulalie)	4	16,562.00	8 8 8 8

	Races Won	Value £	Distances in furlongs
Maastricht [3] out of Awatef)	1	2,385.00	8
Pixton (Ire) [3] out of Sallywell)	1	3,552.75	7
Public Way (Ire) [3] out of Kilpeacon)	1	2,959.80	8
Shepherd Market (Ire) [2] out of Dame Solitaire (Can))	1	4,306.50	5
Sweet Decision (Ire) [2] out of Final Decision)	1	2,595.00	5
	14	52,832.80	

CONCORDE HERO (USA) (1980) by Super Concorde (USA)-Method Actress by Round Table

	Races Won	Value £	Distances in furlongs
Air Command (Bar) [3] out of Hubbardair)	1	2,406.00	5

†CONQUERING HERO (USA)(1983) by Storm Bird (Can)-Wave In Glory (USA) by Hoist The Flag (USA)

	Races Won	Value £	Distances in furlongs
Indefence (Ire) [2] out of Cathryn's Song)	2	6,003.00	7 7

CONQUISTADOR CIELO (USA) (1979) by Mr Prospector (USA)-K D Princess (USA) by Bold Commander (USA)

	Races Won	Value £	Distances in furlongs
Contract Court (USA) [3] out of Moth (USA))	1	3,523.50	10

COQUELIN (USA) (1979) by Blushing Groom (Fr)-Topolly (USA) by Turn-to

	Races Won	Value £	Distances in furlongs
Rock The Barney (Ire) [4] out of Lady Loire)	1	3,036.00	9
Swift Romance (Ire) [5] out of Douschkina)	1	1,957.30	12
	2	4,993.30	

COZZENE (USA) (1980) by Caro-Ride The Trails (USA) by Prince John

	Races Won	Value £	Distances in furlongs
Hasten To Add (USA) [3] out of Beau Cougar (USA))	2	9,140.75	12 13

CREE SONG (1976) by Song-Gentle Gael by Celtic Ash

	Races Won	Value £	Distances in furlongs
Rocky Two [2] out of Holloway Wonder)	1	2,219.30	5

CROFTER (USA) (1977) by Habitat-Marie Curie by Exbury

	Races Won	Value £	Distances in furlongs
Farmer Jock [11] out of Some Dame)	1	2,898.80	5

CROFTHALL (1977) by Native Bazaar-Woodland Promise by Philemon

	Races Won	Value £	Distances in furlongs
Craigie Boy [3] out of Lady Carol)	2	6,211.80	6 6
Croft Valley [6] out of Sannavally)	3	23,261.80	7 7 7
First Bid [6] out of Redgrave Design)	2	8,687.50	12 12
Ooh Ah Cantona [2] out of Chablisse)	2	4,671.40	7 7
Rambo's Hall [8] out of Murton Crags)	2	12,387.50	10 8
Snipe Hall [2] out of Geopelia)	4	24,314.10	5 5 5 6
	15	79,534.10	

CRYSTAL GLITTERS (USA) (1980) by Blushing Groom(Fr)-Tales To Tell (USA) by Donut King

	Races Won	Value £	Distances in furlongs
Gant Bleu (Fr) [6] out of Gold Honey)	1	3,209.60	7

CUTLASS (USA) (1970) by Damascus (USA)-Aphonia by Dunce

	Races Won	Value £	Distances in furlongs
Plunder Bay (USA) [2] out of La Ninouchka (USA))	1	5,309.00	7

CYRANO DE BERGERAC (1983) by Bold Lad(Ire)-Miss St Cyr by Brigadier Gerard

	Races Won	Value £	Distances in furlongs
Ann's Pearl (Ire) [2] out of Pariscene)	1	2,243.00	5
Bet A Plan (Ire) [2] out of Thornbeam)	1	2,259.00	6
Cyarna Quinn (Ire) [2] out of Lisdoonvarna)	2	6,250.00	5 6
Elton Ledger (Ire) [4] out of Princess Of Nashua)	1	2,769.30	6
General John (Ire) [4] out of Hill's Realm (USA))	1	4,893.00	6
Morocco (Ire) [4] out of Lightning Laser)	1	6,056.00	7
Mr Bergerac (Ire) [2] out of Makalu)	2	6,699.50	5 5
My Bonus [3] out of Dress In Spring)	1	3,655.00	5
Pommes Frites (Ire) [2] out of Shannon Lady)	1	3,622.50	5
Post Mistress (Ire) [2] out of Postie)	1	2,243.00	5
Roca Murada (Ire) [4] out of Keppols)	3	10,637.00	6 7 7
Roxanian (Ire) [2] out of Sassanian)	3	11,587.80	5 5 6
Wordsmith (Ire) [3] out of Cordon)	1	4,110.00	8
Yo-Cando (Ire) [2] out of Young Grace)	1	3,845.25	6
	20	70,870.35	

DAHAR (USA) (1981) by Lyphard (USA)-Dahlia (USA) by Vaguely Noble

	Races Won	Value £	Distances in furlongs
Utrillo (USA) [4] out of Waltz Me Sue (USA))	1	2,892.60	11

DAMISTER (USA) (1982) by Mr Prospector (USA)-Batucada (USA) by Roman Line

	Races Won	Value £	Distances in furlongs
Bay Queen [3] out of Be My Queen)	4	15,474.50	11 9 9 9

	Races Won	Value £	Distances in furlongs
Chakalak [5] out of Wig And Gown)	1	3,114.00	16
Dam Certain (Ire) [4] out of Certain Story)	1	2,686.00	8
Dance Turn [2] out of Spin Turn)	1	4,932.00	7
Danny Boy [3] out of Irish Isle)	2	5,875.00	8 8
Miss Fascination [3] out of Tantalizing Song (Can))	1	4,737.00	8
Miss Gorgeous (Ire) [3] out of Rocket Alert)	2	7,320.00	7 6
Reason To Dance [2] out of La Nureyeva (USA))	2	8,078.50	5 5
Sparkling Lyric [2] out of Tantalizing Song (Can))	1	2,243.00	7
Velvet Heart (Ire) [3] out of Bottom Line)	1	2,637.00	10
Welsh Mist [2] out of Welwyn)	2	6,766.40	5 5
	18	63,863.40	

DANCE BID (USA) (1978) by Northern Dancer-Highest Trump (USA) by Bold Bidder

	Races Won	Value £	Distances in furlongs
Debsy Do (USA) [4] out of Diablesse (USA))	3	10,623.75	5 6 6

DANCE OF LIFE (USA) (1983) by Nijinsky(Can)-Spring Is Here (USA) by In Reality

	Races Won	Value £	Distances in furlongs
Chickawicka (Ire) [2] out of Shabby Doll)	1	2,982.00	6
Dancing Beau (Ire) [4] out of Kentucky Belle)	1	2,821.10	7
Jafeica (Ire) [2] out of Moretta)	1	4,807.00	8
Mexican Dancer [4] out of Mexican Two Step)	1	1,912.00	8
Night Clubbing (Ire) [4] out of Tigeen)	4	25,023.05	10 12 12 12
Ragsat Al Omor (Ire) [2] out of Brilleaux)	1	3,494.25	8
Trendy Dancer (Ire) [2] out of Ideas And Trends (USA))	1	2,070.00	5
	10	43,109.40	

DANCING BRAVE (USA) (1983) by Lyphard (USA)-Navajo Princess by Drone

	Races Won	Value £	Distances in furlongs
Ballerina (Ire) [2] out of Dancing Shadow)	1	4,110.00	7
Bude [2] out of Shining Water)	1	4,084.50	7
Cambara [3] out of Cambretta (USA))	3	34,940.00	8 8 8
Commander In Chief [3] out of Slightly Dangerous (USA))	4	461,241.25	10 12 10 12
Dancing Tralthee (Ire) [3] out of Tralthee (USA))	1	3,054.20	12
Dover Patrol (Ire) [3] out of Britannia's Rule)	2	6,802.00	13 14
Hunting Ground [5] out of Ack's Secret (USA))	5	15,481.40	15 15 16 15 17
Imaginary (Ire) [3] out of Bold Fantasy)	1	4,012.50	10
Infrasonic [3] out of Infra Green)	1	34,639.80	16
Lowawatha [5] out of Shorthouse)	2	10,518.75	10 10
Majority (Ire) [3] out of Majoritat (Ger))	1	3,494.25	10
Polka Dancer [3] out of Pretty Pol)	2	20,476.40	8 8
White Muzzle [3] out of Fair Of The Furze)	4	20,640.00	10 12 11 12
Winged Victory (Ire) [3] out of Mighty Fly)	2	7,136.25	7 7
	30	630,631.30	

†DANCING DISSIDENT (USA) (1986) by Nureyev (USA)-Absentia (USA) by Raise A Cup (USA)

	Races Won	Value £	Distances in furlongs
Allwight Then (Ire) [2] out of Abergwrle)	2	6,819.95	5 5
Star Jazz (Ire) [2] out of Sterna Regina)	1	4,110.00	7
	3	10,929.95	

†DANEHILL (USA) (1986) by Danzig (USA)-Razyana (USA) by His Majesty (USA)

	Races Won	Value £	Distances in furlongs
Crazy Paving (Ire) [2] out of Clunk Click)	1	5,385.00	6
Danger Point [2] out of Red Comes Up (USA))	1	3,509.00	8
Delta One (Ire) [2] out of Seminar)	1	4,306.50	6
En Cachette (Ire) [2] out of Clandestina (USA))	1	3,913.25	6
Kissing Cousin (Ire) [2] out of First Kiss)	2	7,224.50	6 7
North Reef (Ire) [2] out of Loreef)	1	4,342.25	5
Wafayt (Ire) [2] out of Diamond Field (USA))	2	9,576.25	6 6
	9	38,256.75	

DANZIG (USA) (1977) by Northern Dancer-Pas de Nom (USA) by Admiral's Voyage

	Races Won	Value £	Distances in furlongs
Ajdayt (USA) [3] out of Barely Even (USA))	3	11,506.25	8 8 8
Dagny Juel (USA) [3] out of Puget Sound)	1	3,465.00	7
Danish Fort [3] out of I Want To Be (USA))	2	7,337.75	10 11
Dumaani (USA) [2] out of Desirable)	1	6,570.00	7
Emperor Jones (USA) [3] out of Qui Royalty (USA))	1	23,135.70	8
Hamas (Ire) [4] out of Fall Aspen (USA))	2	128,343.50	6 6

	Races Won	Value £	Distances in furlongs
Maroof (USA) [3] out of Dish Dash)	1	5,057.00	8
Mecklenburg (Ire) [3] out of Forli's Treat (USA))	2	7,712.75	10 10
Miss Shagra (USA) [3] out of Dusty Dollar)	2	7,211.00	10 10
Muhayaa (USA) [4] out of La Basque (USA))	4	36,024.80	10 10 10 12
Zarani Sidi Anna (USA) [3] out of Emmaline (USA))	1	3,055.50	6
	20	239,419.25	

DANZIG CONNECTION (USA) (1983) by Danzig (USA)-Gdynia (USA) by Sir Ivor

	Races Won	Value £	Distances in furlongs
Ocara (USA) [3] out of Relevant (USA))	1	2,794.00	8
Polish Laughter (USA) [2] out of Chuckle (USA))	2	32,670.90	6 6
Riszard (USA) [4] out of Tendresse (USA))	1	16,570.00	22
	4	52,034.90	

DARA MONARCH (1979) by Realm-Sardara by Alcide

	Races Won	Value £	Distances in furlongs
King William [8] out of Norman Delight (USA))	1	3,340.00	16
Royal Roller (Ire) [3] out of Tumble Dale)	1	2,601.40	8
	2	5,941.40	

DARING MARCH (1974) by Derring-Do-March Spray by March Past

	Races Won	Value £	Distances in furlongs
Caleman [4] out of Lillemor)	2	13,156.50	6 7
Daring Destiny [2] out of Raunchy Rita)	1	4,556.75	6
Daring Past [3] out of Better Buy Baileys)	1	2,846.00	10
How's Yer Father [7] out of Dawn Ditty)	2	16,277.50	6 6
Marchman [8] out of Saltation)	1	3,377.25	10
Queen Warrior [4] out of Princess Zenobia)	3	11,008.00	8 7 8
Sir Thomas Beecham [3] out of Balinese)	3	7,353.30	13 12 16
Sunderland Echo [4] out of Incarnadine)	3	8,704.00	12 12 12
Walking The Plank [4] out of Pirate Maid)	2	7,715.00	8 10
	18	74,994.30	

DARSHAAN (1981) by Shirley Heights-Delsy (Fr) by Abdos

	Races Won	Value £	Distances in furlongs
Baladiya [6] out of Bayazida)	2	5,359.40	12 11
Cairo Prince (Ire) [3] out of Sphinx (Ger))	1	3,752.50	11
Darnay [2] out of Flawless Image (USA))	1	5,595.00	7
Daronne [2] out of Pipina (USA))	1	4,306.50	8
Darrery [3] out of Flamenco (USA))	2	8,485.80	10 12
Kithanga (Ire) [3] out of Kalata)	3	39,605.00	12 11 12
Sueboog (Ire) [3] out of Nordica)	1	23,463.00	7
	11	90,567.20	

DAYEEM (USA) (1982) by The Minstrel(Can)-Flight Dancer (USA) by Misty Flight

	Races Won	Value £	Distances in furlongs
Prince Rooney (Ire) [5] out of Fourth Degree)	2	5,874.00	7 7

DEPUTY MINISTER (CAN) (1979) by Vice Regent(Can)-Mint Copy by Bunty's Flight

	Races Won	Value £	Distances in furlongs
Jadirah (USA) [3] out of Sharmila (Fr))	1	3,131.90	7
Labudd (USA) [3] out of Delightful Vie (USA))	1	3,582.00	8
	2	6,713.90	

DERRYLIN (1975) by Derring-Do-Antigua by Hyperion

	Races Won	Value £	Distances in furlongs
Hill Farm Katie [2] out of Kate Brook)	1	2,448.00	5

DESERT OF WIND (USA) (1983) by Lyphard (USA)-Polynesienne (Fr) by Relko

	Races Won	Value £	Distances in furlongs
Desert Laughter (Ire) [3] out of Tickled To Bits)	1	2,924.00	12

DESERT WINE (USA) (1980) by Damascus (USA)-Anne Campbell by Never Bend

	Races Won	Value £	Distances in furlongs
Big Squeeze (USA) [2] out of Davie's Lamb (USA))	1	3,377.25	6

DIAMOND SHOAL (1979) by Mill Reef (USA)-Crown Treasure (USA) by Graustark

	Races Won	Value £	Distances in furlongs
Tiger Claw (USA) [7] out of Tiger Scout (USA))	1	2,889.00	9

DIESIS (1980) by Sharpen Up-Double Sure by Reliance II

	Races Won	Value £	Distances in furlongs
Barahin (Ire) [4] out of Red Comes Up (USA))	3	5,641.40	10 8 10
Bold Sixteen (USA) [2] out of Go For Bold (USA))	1	4,449.50	7
Darecliff (USA) [3] out of Come On Sunshine (USA))	2	10,807.50	10 12

	Races Won	Value £	Distances in furlongs
Diesan (USA) [2] out of Bold Courtesan (USA))	3	12,375.00	6 7 7
Enharmonic (USA) [6] out of Contralto)	1	21,843.00	8
Frogmarch (USA) [3] out of La Francaise (USA))	1	5,380.00	7
Gisarne (USA) [3] out of Fair Sousanne)	2	17,755.00	10 10
Gneiss (USA) [2] out of Rangoon Ruby)	1	4,225.50	6
Ice Pool (USA) [3] out of Skating)	1	4,503.00	10
Keylock (USA) [3] out of Sure Locked (USA))	1	3,597.00	14
Knifebox (USA) [5] out of Matoki (USA))	2	42,486.75	10 10
Knock To Enter (USA) [5] out of Privy (USA))	2	5,549.60	8 6
Kutbeya (USA) [2] out of Antartica (Fr))	1	4,464.00	6
Marillette (USA) [3] out of Stormette (USA))	1	25,003.47	10
Mashair (USA) [3] out of Lucky Lucky Lucky (USA))	1	3,882.50	9
Nizaal (USA) [2] out of Shicklah (USA))	1	4,270.75	6
Sabrehill (USA) [3] out of Gypsy Talk (USA))	1	4,893.00	10
Shujan (USA) [4] out of Linda's Magic (USA))	5	16,301.00	12 12 12 14 14
Stella Mystika (USA) [3] out of Share The Fantasy (USA))	2	7,071.25	7 8
Tawafij (USA) [4] out of Dancing Brownie (USA))	2	15,855.00	7 7
Teshami (USA) [3] out of Carotene (Can))	2	10,212.00	8 8
Winter Forest (USA) [3] out of Stark Winter (USA))	2	4,020.75	8 10
	38	234,586.97	

DIGAMIST (USA) (1985) by Blushing Groom(Fr)-Disconiz (USA) by Northern Dancer

	Races Won	Value £	Distances in furlongs
Hazard A Guess (Ire) [3] out of Guess Who)	3	10,057.60	9 11 11
Heathyards Crusade (Ire) [2] out of Theda)	1	2,243.00	6
Lime Street Blues (Ire) [2] out of Royal Daughter)	2	9,316.25	6 6
No Mean City (Ire) [2] out of Gothic Lady)	2	11,380.00	6 5
Old Hook (Ire) [2] out of Day Dress)	1	2,070.00	5
Second Chance (Ire) [3] out of Flash Donna (USA))	2	7,076.25	7 8
The Multiyorker (Ire) [2] out of Lough Graney)	1	3,523.50	7
Tony's Mist [3] out of Tinas Image)	3	9,334.15	8 8 8
Top Show (Ire) [2] out of Acquire)	2	6,204.50	5 6
	17	61,205.25	

DIXIELAND BAND (USA) (1980) by Northern Dancer-Mississippi Mud (USA) by Delta Judge

	Races Won	Value £	Distances in furlongs
American Swinger (USA) [3] out of Cassowary (USA))	2	9,181.50	9 10
Dixieland Melody (USA) [3] out of Celebration Song (USA))	1	6,709.20	8
Drum Taps (USA) [7] out of Lavendula Rose)	1	107,464.80	20
Ima Red Neck (USA) [4] out of Bright Reply (USA))	1	2,322.00	12
	5	125,677.50	

DOMINION (1972) by Derring-Do-Picture Palace by Princely Gift

	Races Won	Value £	Distances in furlongs
Admiralella [2] out of Mrs Kaydagawn)	1	2,713.40	6
Allegation [3] out of Pageantry)	1	2,070.00	10
Benfleet [2] out of Penultimate)	2	7,118.50	7 8
Coltrane [5] out of Rainbow's End)	2	5,100.50	9 9
Diplomatist [3] out of Dame Julian)	1	1,548.00	12
Domicksky [5] out of Mumruffin)	3	14,389.00	6 6 5
Dominuet [8] out of Stepping Gaily)	1	14,114.40	6
Domulla [3] out of Ulla Laing)	1	3,622.50	6
Essex Girl [3] out of Valiancy)	2	6,101.00	8 8
Mahrajan [9] out of Dame Julian)	2	6,754.50	12 11
Make The Break [2] out of Souadah (USA))	1	3,046.25	5
Mindomica [4] out of Nordica)	1	3,287.30	7
Missed Flight [3] out of Loveskate (USA))	2	10,440.75	8 8
Monticino (Ire) [2] out of Fantoccini)	1	4,985.75	5
Moorish [3] out of Remoosh)	1	20,387.50	8
Pinkerton's Pal [2] out of White Domino)	1	5,390.00	6
Rich Pickings [4] out of Miss By Miles)	1	2,623.00	18
	24	113,692.35	

DOMINION ROYALE (1984) by Dominion-Bahamas Princess by Sharpen Up

	Races Won	Value £	Distances in furlongs
Contract Elite (Ire) [3] out of Salote (USA))	1	7,570.00	12
Dominion King [2] out of Elsocko)	1	3,379.00	5
High Domain (Ire) [2] out of Recline)	2	8,521.25	5 5
Hillsdown Boy (Ire) [3] out of Lady Mary)	1	2,574.00	10
Multi National [2] out of Travel Far)	1	4,337.50	5
Red Grit (Ire) [2] out of Abishag)	1	2,924.70	5

	Races Won	Value £	Distances in furlongs
Royale Figurine (Ire) [2] out of Cree's Figurine)	3	13,517.50	5 5 5
	10	42,823.95	

DOMYNSKY (1980) by Dominion-My Therape by Jimmy Reppin

	Races Won	Value £	Distances in furlongs
Carapelle [2] out of Soosjoy)	1	2,070.00	7
Nordan Raider [5] out of Vikris)	3	11,559.40	6 6 6
Ovideo [2] out of One Last Glimpse)	1	2,807.00	7
Parkside Lady [2] out of Hunslet)	1	2,601.40	5
	6	19,037.80	

DON'T FORGET ME (1984) by Ahonoora-African Doll by African Sky

	Races Won	Value £	Distances in furlongs
A Smooth One (Ire) [2] out of Inner Pearl)	2	26,249.00	5 6
Amnesia (Ire) [2] out of Amboselli)	1	3,564.00	8
Call To Mind (Ire) [2] out of Pharjoy (Fr))	2	15,912.00	7 6
Don't Forget Marie (Ire) [3] out of My My Marie)	1	2,406.00	9
Dontforget Insight (Ire) [2] out of Starlust)	1	4,737.00	7
Early To Rise [3] out of Foreno)	1	2,011.40	12
Eastern Memories (Ire) [3] out of East River (Fr))	3	21,267.00	8 8 8
Forgotten Dancer (Ire) [2] out of Dancing Diana)	1	2,495.00	6
Forgotten Lady (Ire) [2] out of Lady Vivienne)	1	4,378.00	7
Knight Of Shalot (Ire) [3] out of Lady Of Shalott)	1	3,201.75	7
Premier League (Ire) [3] out of Kilmara (USA))	2	7,630.25	9 8
Southern Memories (Ire) [3] out of Our Pet)	1	4,110.00	5
Stylish Rose (Ire) [3] out of Cottage Style)	1	3,552.75	8
War Requiem (Ire) [3] out of Ladiz)	2	5,434.40	9 10
White Creek (Ire) [3] out of Zanskar)	4	9,968.80	8 7 6 6
	24	116,917.35	

DOUBLE SCHWARTZ (1981) by Double Form-Cassy's Pet by Sing Sing

	Races Won	Value £	Distances in furlongs
Elevator Shaft (Ire) [2] out of Silk Trade)	2	5,001.00	6 5
Highborn (Ire) [4] out of High State)	4	10,831.65	7 7 6 6
Jake The Pake (Ire) [3] out of Traminer)	1	1,380.00	7
Lida's Delight (Ire) [3] out of Villars)	1	3,106.00	5

	Races Won	Value £	Distances in furlongs
Storiths (Ire) [3] out of Atlantic Dream (USA))	2	13,070.94	6 6
Takadou (Ire) [2] out of Taka)	1	3,318.75	5
Unification (Ire) [4] out of Hydro Princess)	1	3,600.00	7
	12	40,308.34	

DOULAB (USA) (1982) by Topsider (USA)-Passerine (USA) by Dr Fager

	Races Won	Value £	Distances in furlongs
Absolute Magic [3] out of Trickster)	1	3,640.50	7
Belfry Green (Ire) [3] out of Checkers)	1	3,406.50	7
Chiappucci (Ire) [3] out of Jenny's Child)	1	2,691.60	12
Dream Carrier (Ire) [5] out of Dream Trader)	1	5,047.25	7
Dutosky [3] out of Butosky)	2	8,757.50	10 10
Greenson (Ire) [2] out of Sheba's Princess)	1	2,595.00	5
Nichodoula [3] out of Nicholas Grey)	2	5,452.60	7 7
Shadow Jury [3] out of Texita)	3	9,116.70	5 5 5
Sir Harry Hardman [5] out of Song Grove)	1	6,291.60	6
Sudden Spin [3] out of Lightning Legacy (USA))	1	3,210.00	6
	14	50,209.25	

DOWSING (USA) (1984) by Riverman (USA)-Prospector's Fire (USA) by Mr Prospector (USA)

	Races Won	Value £	Distances in furlongs
Floating Trial [2] out of Miquette (Fr))	2	5,046.00	6 5
Garnock Valley [3] out of Sunley Sinner)	2	8,015.00	6 6
Kismetim [3] out of Naufrage)	1	3,669.75	10
Mary Hinge [2] out of Jeanne Avril)	3	10,746.00	6 5 5
Mister Bloy [2] out of Casbah Girl)	1	3,178.75	5
Putout [3] out of Putupon)	1	3,231.00	5
Siganca [2] out of Gipping)	1	2,511.80	5
Soaking [3] out of Moaning Low)	1	3,131.90	7
Spring Sixpence [3] out of Little Change)	1	2,243.00	6
Water Gypsy [3] out of Fortune Teller)	1	3,080.00	8
	14	44,853.20	

DOYOUN (1985) by Mill Reef (USA)-Dumka(Fr) by Kashmir II

	Races Won	Value £	Distances in furlongs
Canaska Star [3] out of North Telstar)	1	3,590.00	7
Mountain Willow [3] out of Mountain Lodge)	1	2,758.00	15
	2	6,348.00	

DREAMS TO REALITY (USA) (1982) by Lyphard (USA)-d'Arqueangel (USA) by Raise A Native

	Races Won	Value £	Distances in furlongs
Close To Reality [2] out of Edraianthus)	1	3,640.50	6

DRUMALIS (1980) by Tumble Wind (USA)-Virna (USA) by Coursing

	Races Won	Value £	Distances in furlongs
Drumdonna (Ire) [3] out of Decoy Duck)	1	1,548.00	8
Palacegate Episode (Ire) [3] out of Pasadena Lady)	1	8,090.00	5
Palacegate Jo (Ire) [2] out of Welsh Rhyme)	3	9,865.00	5 6 6
Qualitair Rhythm (Ire) [5] out of Abbe's Realm)	1	2,898.80	14
	6	22,401.80	

DUNBEATH (USA) (1980) by Grey Dawn II-Priceless Fame by Irish Castle (USA)

	Races Won	Value £	Distances in furlongs
Cheveux Mitchell [6] out of Hide Out)	1	5,089.50	7
Dundeelin [2] out of Iron Lass)	1	2,070.00	5
Molly Splash [6] out of Nelly Do Da)	1	2,924.70	7
Ragtime Song [4] out of Kelowna (USA))	2	4,329.00	11 16
Shoofk [2] out of River Reem (USA))	1	3,753.50	8
Tinker Osmaston [2] out of Miss Primula)	2	5,601.00	5 5
Two D'S [2] out of Deloraine)	1	2,448.00	6
	9	26,215.70	

EFISIO (1982) by Formidable (USA)-Eldoret by High Top

	Races Won	Value £	Distances in furlongs
Abbey's Gal [3] out of Outward's Gal)	3	23,302.35	6 7 7
Al Moulouki [3] out of Prejudice)	5	18,383.30	7 8 7 7 7
Ashgore [3] out of Fair Atlanta)	2	6,035.35	6 6
Barbaroja [2] out of Bias)	3	20,434.00	7 8 8
Blackpatch Hill [4] out of Myrtlegrove)	3	9,301.55	12 12 12
Casteddu [4] out of Bias)	1	6,504.50	6
Castlerea Lad [4] out of Halo)	3	28,452.75	6 6 6
Chantry Bellini [4] out of Lifestyle)	1	3,184.00	6
Duke Of Dreams [3] out of Tame Duchess)	1	2,821.10	7
Efizia [3] out of Millie Grey)	5	15,851.95	10 10 10 9 9
Efra [4] out of Ra Ra)	2	7,272.50	6 6
Hello Mister [2] out of Ginnies Petong)	1	4,240.50	5
Hever Golf Rose [2] out of Sweet Rosina)	2	23,602.25	7 6
Nakita [2] out of Ra Ra)	1	2,534.20	6
No Extras (Ire) [3] out of Parkland Rose)	3	10,834.50	6 5 5
Oggi [2] out of Dolly Bevan)	1	4,092.00	6
Pips Pride [3] out of Elkie Brooks)	1	15,140.00	6
Sartigila [4] out of Ichnusa)	2	7,721.25	6 8
Sixpees [2] out of Joyce's Best)	1	3,757.50	6
Sunday's Hill [4] out of Elkie Brooks)	1	3,405.00	8
Young Ern [3] out of Stardyn)	2	57,480.45	7 7
Zanzara (Ire) [2] out of Slick Chick)	1	3,501.25	6
	45	277,852.25	

EL GRAN SENOR (USA) (1981) by Northern Dancer-Sex Appeal by Buckpasser

	Races Won	Value £	Distances in furlongs
Barraak [3] out of Rosia Bay)	1	2,243.00	14
Colonel Collins (USA) [2] out of Kanmary (Fr))	2	13,483.00	7 7
El Duco (USA) [3] out of Most Honourable (USA))	2	6,842.25	7 7
Elatis (USA) [3] out of Summer Review (USA))	1	3,728.25	12
Gran Senorum (USA) [3] out of Sanctum Sanctorum (USA))	2	6,432.75	6 8
John Balliol (USA) [5] out of Cecelia (USA))	1	9,354.00	10
Manhattan Sunset (USA) [2] out of Mezimica (USA))	1	20,225.00	7
Riz Biz (USA) [3] out of Dictina (Fr))	1	5,020.00	12
Stoller (USA) [2] out of Caroglen Jo (Can))	1	4,807.00	7
Toledo Queen (Ire) [3] out of Grey Dream)	2	11,675.02	8 7
Woodwardia (USA) [3] out of Chain Fern (USA))	1	3,552.75	7
Young Senor (USA) [4] out of Liturgism (USA))	1	4,396.00	10
	16	91,759.02	

ELA-MANA-MOU (1976) by Pitcairn-Rose Bertin by High Hat

	Races Won	Value £	Distances in furlongs
Anna Of Saxony [4] out of Anna Matrushka)	3	31,661.40	11 11 14
Armenian Coffee (Ire) [3] out of Streamertail)	2	5,509.20	9 9
Aude La Belle (Fr) [5] out of Arjona (Ger))	1	3,582.00	16
Ballet Shoes (Ire) [3] out of River Dancer)	2	6,842.25	5 5
Black Dragon (Ire) [3] out of Indian Lily)	1	3,746.50	10
Bold Ambition [6] out of Queen Of The Dance)	1	3,703.50	13
Carelaman [3] out of Caro's Niece (USA))	1	3,260.25	7
Double Trigger (Ire) [2] out of Solac (Fr))	2	12,267.75	9 10

	Races Won	Value £	Distances in furlongs
Ela Billante [3] out of Billante (USA))	1	2,846.00	14
Elburg (Ire) [3] out of Iosifa)	1	2,243.00	15
Grace Card [7] out of Val de Grace (Fr))	1	3,106.00	21
Haddaaj (Ire) [3] out of Sweet Pleasure)	3	9,689.50	12 14 14
Lomas (Ire) [2] out of Bold Miss)	2	7,929.45	7 7
Mardood [8] out of Tigeen)	3	8,891.00	15 17 18
Minatina (Ire) [3] out of Autumn Tint (USA))	1	3,817.50	10
Mougins (Ire) [4] out of Western Goddess)	1	3,363.00	8
Mystic Memory [4] out of Mountain Memory)	1	2,385.00	13
Spin Doctor (Ire) [3] out of Pig Tail)	1	3,435.75	10
Zajira (Ire) [3] out of Awsaaf (USA))	2	7,632.00	8 12
	30	125,911.05	

ELECTRIC (1979) by Blakeney-Christiana by Double Jump

	Races Won	Value £	Distances in furlongs
Bold Elect [5] out of Famous Band (USA))	1	3,235.50	13
Cara's Pride [3] out of Caraquenga (USA))	1	3,318.75	14
Crackling [4] out of Birch Creek)	1	6,255.00	12
Doctor Roy [5] out of Pushkar)	1	3,290.00	10
Electrolyte [3] out of This Sensation)	1	2,997.00	14
Moidart [3] out of Marypark)	2	7,582.75	11 16
Sparky's Song [3] out of Daring Ditty)	1	2,385.00	10
	8	29,064.00	

ELEGANT AIR (1981) by Shirley Heights-Elegant Tern (USA) by Sea-Bird II

	Races Won	Value £	Distances in furlongs
Brandonhurst [3] out of Wolverina)	1	5,550.00	9
Briggsmaid [5] out of Merry Yarn)	1	3,494.50	16
Clouded Elegance [3] out of Clouded Vision)	1	3,552.75	8
Euphonic [3] out of Monalda (Fr))	1	2,511.00	11
Norfolk Hero [3] out of Caviar Blini)	1	6,664.00	7
Scorched Air [3] out of Misfire)	2	6,511.60	8 11
Smart Daisy [3] out of Michaelmas)	1	2,713.40	10
Wings Cove [3] out of Bel Esprit)	1	3,870.00	14
	9	34,867.25	

†EMARATI (USA) (1986) by Danzig (USA)-Bold Example (USA) by Bold Lad (USA)

	Races Won	Value £	Distances in furlongs
Little Emmeline [2] out of Hyacine)	1	2,490.00	5
Lord Sky [2] out of Summer Sky)	1	2,691.00	5
Strumpet City [2] out of Double Touch (Fr))	1	2,721.00	5
	3	7,902.00	

ENCHANTMENT (1977) by Habitat-Lady Of Chalon (USA) by Young Emperor

	Races Won	Value £	Distances in furlongs
Charmed Knave [8] out of Peerless Princess)	2	6,029.00	6 7
Meeson Times [5] out of National Time (USA))	1	2,898.80	5
	3	8,927.80	

ENTIITLED (1984) by Mill Reef (USA)-Lady Capulet (USA) by Sir Ivor

	Races Won	Value £	Distances in furlongs
Don't Jump (Ire) [3] out of Ruby River)	2	6,453.25	8 8
Workingforpeanuts (Ire) [3] out of Tracy's Sundown)	1	2,364.00	7
	3	8,817.25	

ESKIMO (USA) (1980) by Northern Dancer-Dr Mary Lou (USA) by Dr Fager

	Races Won	Value £	Distances in furlongs
Harpoon Louie (USA) [3] out of Twelfth Pleasure (USA))	1	4,012.50	8
Ice Strike (USA) [4] out of Gama Tres (USA))	1	2,070.00	12
	2	6,082.50	

EXACTLY SHARP (USA) (1985) by Sharpen Up-Exactly So by Caro

	Races Won	Value £	Distances in furlongs
Blurred Image (Ire) [2] out of Bear's Affair)	2	5,245.40	6 6

EXHIBITIONER (1982) by Thatching-Miss Pudge by Green God

	Races Won	Value £	Distances in furlongs
Bandon Castle (Ire) [2] out of Gay Pariso)	1	3,687.50	5
Exhibit Air (Ire) [3] out of Airy Queen (USA))	2	6,736.45	9 8
Knowth (Ire) [4] out of Grain Of Sand)	1	5,385.25	9
Shining Jewel [6] out of Vaguely Jade)	3	8,218.00	8 8 7
Show Faith (Ire) [3] out of Keep The Faith)	2	26,285.00	8 8
Sporting Warrior (Ire) [2] out of Clodianus)	1	2,780.60	5
	10	53,092.80	

EXPLODENT (USA) (1969) by Nearctic-Venomous by Mel Hash

	Races Won	Value £	Distances in furlongs
Rue Rembrandt (USA) [3] out of Fu Fu La Rue (USA))	2	6,772.50	8 7

	Races Won	Value £	Distances in furlongs

FAIRY KING (USA) (1982) by Northern Dancer-Fairy Bridge (USA) by Bold Reason (USA)

	Races Won	Value £	Distances in furlongs
Brockton Dancer [3] out of Susie's Baby)	1	3,231.00	6
Eurolink Thunder [3] out of Prosperous Lady)	3	34,865.40	8 7 7
Fairy Heights (Ire) [2] out of Commanche Belle)	3	106,929.00	7 7 8
Fairy Wisher (Ire) [4] out of Valediction)	1	3,390.90	12
Fiveofive (Ire) [3] out of North Hut)	1	3,287.30	7
Lord Oberon (Ire) [5] out of Vaguely Jade)	1	5,380.50	8
Marjorie's Memory (Ire) [2] out of Burnished Gold)	1	2,406.00	5
Pharaoh's Dancer [6] out of Marie Louise)	1	3,339.10	6
Prince Babar [2] out of Bell Toll)	1	4,175.00	5
Princess Oberon (Ire) [3] out of Flash Of Gold)	1	5,427.50	5
Strephon (Ire) [3] out of Madame Fair)	2	5,108.00	13 14
Titania's Dance (Ire) [2] out of Camden Dancer)	1	2,668.60	5
Turtle Island (Ire) [2] out of Sisania)	3	84,426.10	5 5 6
Ya Malak [2] out of La Tuerta)	2	7,437.80	5 5
	22	272,072.20	

FALIRAKI (1973) by Prince Tenderfoot (USA)-Super Flower by Super Sam

	Races Won	Value £	Distances in furlongs
Dancing Sensation (USA) [6] out of Sweet Satina (USA))	3	10,323.60	6 7 7

FAPPIANO (USA) (1977) by Mr Prospector (USA)-Killaloe (USA) by Dr Fager

	Races Won	Value £	Distances in furlongs
Mutakallam (USA) [3] out of Stark Drama (USA))	1	2,950.00	8
Trippiano [3] out of Hence (USA))	1	3,172.50	8
	2	6,122.50	

FAR NORTH (CAN) (1973) by Northern Dancer-Fleur by Victoria Park

	Races Won	Value £	Distances in furlongs
Northern Trial (USA) [5] out of Make An Attempt (USA))	1	3,465.00	7

FAST TOPAZE (USA) (1983) by Far North(Can)-Pink Topaze by Djakao

	Races Won	Value £	Distances in furlongs
Blue Topaze [5] out of Forever Mary)	2	5,557.60	6 5
Shalabia [4] out of Mangala (USA))	1	2,322.00	6
	3	7,879.60	

FAUSTUS (USA) (1983) by Robellino (USA)-B F's Sailingal by Sail On-Sail On

	Races Won	Value £	Distances in furlongs
Alcove [2] out of Cubby Hole)	1	3,176.25	8
Brackenthwaite [3] out of Cosset)	1	3,106.00	8
Cragganmore [2] out of Special Guest)	1	3,003.00	5
Devilry [3] out of Ancestry)	1	5,469.75	10
Tom Morgan [2] out of Pirate Maid)	1	0.00	7
	5	14,755.00	

FAYRUZ (1983) by Song-Friendly Jester by Be Friendly

	Races Won	Value £	Distances in furlongs
Allinson's Mate (Ire) [5] out of Piney Pass)	1	3,548.00	7
Dayjuz (Ire) [3] out of Moira My Girl)	1	3,002.00	5
Face North (Ire) [5] out of Pink Fondant)	2	5,795.75	6 6
Fay's Song (Ire) [5] out of Harp)	1	3,183.70	6
Friendly Champ (Ire) [2] out of Carriglegan Girl)	3	11,834.00	6 6 7
Frisky Miss (Ire) [2] out of Moira My Girl)	1	2,905.00	6
Jimmy The Skunk (Ire) [2] out of Very Seldom)	6	15,901.30	5 5 6 5 5 6
Million At Dawn (Ire) [2] out of Morning Stroll)	1	3,377.25	5
Miss Whittingham (Ire) [3] out of Windini)	5	14,838.10	5 6 5 6 6
Mister Piste (Ire) [2] out of Gluhwein)	1	3,236.00	5
Mr Rough [2] out of Rheinbloom)	1	2,721.00	8
Nordoora (Ire) [4] out of African Cousin)	2	6,072.00	5 5
	25	76,414.10	

FERDINAND (USA) (1983) by Nijinsky (CAN)-Banja Luka (USA) by Double Jay

	Races Won	Value £	Distances in furlongs
Baron Ferdinand [3] out of In Perpetuity)	2	37,635.25	10 10
King Of Naples (USA) [2] out of Processional (USA))	1	5,435.50	8
	3	43,070.75	

FIGHTING FIT (USA) (1979) by Full Pocket (USA)-Napalm by Nilo

	Races Won	Value £	Distances in furlongs
Criminal Record (USA) [3] out of Charlie's Angel (USA))	1	2,070.00	12

†FIJAR TANGO (FR) (1985) by In Fijar (USA)-Last Tango (Fr) by Luthier

	Races Won	Value £	Distances in furlongs
Dockyard Dora [2] out of Gleeful)	1	2,179.50	5

FINAL STRAW (1977) by Thatch (USA)-Last Call by Klairon

	Races Won	Value £	Distances in furlongs
Courting Newmarket [5] out of Warm Wind)	2	5,526.80	6 7
Rapid Mover [6] out of Larive)	1	1,646.00	11
Welshman [7] out of Joie de Galles)	3	17,486.70	15 16 15
	6	24,659.50	

FLASH OF STEEL (1983) by Kris-Spark Of Fire by Run The Gantlet (USA)

	Races Won	Value £	Distances in furlongs
Backstabber [3] out of Guest List)	1	3,054.20	8
Gallant Jack (Ire) [4] out of Milveagh)	1	3,054.20	8
Mulled Ale (Ire) [3] out of Bru Ri (Fr))	2	5,442.00	8 9
Sylvan Sabre (Ire) [4] out of Flute (Fr))	3	9,342.00	8 8 10
	7	20,892.40	

FOOLS HOLME (USA) (1982) by Noholme II-Fancifool (USA) by Vaguely Noble

	Races Won	Value £	Distances in furlongs
Fawlty Towers (Ire) [2] out of Queen Of The Brush)	1	2,243.00	7
High Holme [2] out of Corn Seed)	1	3,882.50	5
Shalholme [3] out of Shalati (Fr))	1	1,380.00	10
Suaad (Ire) [2] out of Tootle)	1	4,308.00	7
	4	11,813.50	

FORMIDABLE (USA) (1975) by Forli(Arg)-Native Partner (USA) by Raise A Native

	Races Won	Value £	Distances in furlongs
Affordable [5] out of Ophrys)	1	3,158.00	6
Awesome Venture [3] out of Pine Ridge)	1	3,494.25	7
Formaestre (Ire) [3] out of Maestrette)	1	2,243.00	7
Formidable Liz [3] out of Areej)	2	7,570.00	6 6
Fromage [2] out of Collage)	1	3,129.00	6
Hard Task [3] out of Myth)	1	3,840.00	12
Just Jamie [3] out of La Serenata)	1	3,027.50	6
Kensworth Lady [3] out of Icefern)	1	3,172.50	5
Kinnegad Kid [4] out of Revaimer)	1	3,183.70	6
Queens Contractor [3] out of Salazie)	1	2,070.00	11
Quinsigimond [3] out of Quillotern (USA))	4	11,593.00	6 5 6 6
Silky Siren [4] out of Smooth Siren (USA))	3	10,237.90	8 7 6
Tickerty's Gift [3] out of Handy Dancer)	1	4,542.00	10
Vanroy [9] out of Princess Tavi)	1	2,364.00	10
	20	63,624.85	

FORTY-NINER (USA) (1985) by Mr Prospector (USA)-File (USA) by Tom Rolfe

	Races Won	Value £	Distances in furlongs
Luhuk (USA) [2] out of Royal Stance (USA))	1	4,110.50	7

FORZANDO (1981) by Formidable (USA)-Princely Maid by King's Troop

	Races Won	Value £	Distances in furlongs
Abalene [4] out of Riva Renald)	1	2,574.00	12
Flowing Ocean [3] out of Boswellia)	1	3,201.75	8
Great Deeds [2] out of Deed)	2	21,928.70	6 5
High Premium [5] out of High Halo)	1	48,412.50	8
Mill Force [2] out of Milinetta)	1	3,718.00	8
Miriam [2] out of Song Of Hope)	1	3,377.25	5
Philidor [4] out of Philgwyn)	1	65,422.50	8
Resonant [2] out of Madam Cody)	2	6,983.40	5 5
Serious Hurry [5] out of Lady Bequick)	1	3,183.70	5
Times Zando [2] out of Times)	2	5,020.60	7 8
	13	163,822.40	

FREE STATE (1973) by Hotfoot-Born Free by Alycidon

	Races Won	Value £	Distances in furlongs
Cee-Jay-Ay [6] out of Raffinrula)	2	26,266.00	8 7

FULL EXTENT (USA) (1979) by Full Out (USA)-Mary Biz (USA) by T V Lark

	Races Won	Value £	Distances in furlongs
Bold Alex [2] out of Gunner Girl)	1	4,020.50	5
Lucky Parkes [3] out of Summerhill Spruce)	6	23,601.90	5 5 5 5 5 5
	7	27,622.40	

GABITAT (1978) by Arch Sculptor-Golden Hostess by Kythnos

	Races Won	Value £	Distances in furlongs
Glenfield Greta [5] out of Glenfield Portion)	1	3,365.00	7

†GALLIC LEAGUE (1985) by Welsh Saint-Red Rose Bowl by Dragonara Palace (USA)

	Races Won	Value £	Distances in furlongs
Gallant Spirit (Ire) [2] out of So Valiant)	1	3,340.00	6
Major Success (Ire) [2] out of Estivalia)	4	13,254.60	7 5 5 5
Miss Amy Lou (Ire) [2] out of Six Penny Express)	1	3,406.50	5
Vercingetorix (Ire) [2] out of Noble Nancy)	2	9,753.50	5 6
	8	29,754.60	

GEIGER COUNTER (USA) (1982) by Mr Prospector (USA)-Thong by Nantallah

	Races Won	Value £	Distances in furlongs
Geisway (Can) [3] out of Broadway Beauty (USA))	1	21,540.00	10

GLENSTAL (USA) (1980) by Northern Dancer-Cloonlara (USA) by Sir Ivor

	Races Won	Value £	Distances in furlongs
Dancing Days [7] out of Royal Agnes)	2	3,654.00	16 15
Deb's Ball [7] out of De'b Old Fruit)	1	3,106.00	12
Fletcher's Bounty (Ire) [4] out of Maimiti)	1	3,071.80	8
Pavaka [2] out of Fire Risk)	1	2,070.00	7
Shamshom Al Arab (Ire) [5] out of Love Locket)	3	8,724.40	12 11 13
Steadfast Elite (Ire) [2] out of Etching)	2	5,841.10	5 6
	10	26,467.30	

GLINT OF GOLD (1978) by Mill Reef (USA)-Crown Treasure by Graustark

	Races Won	Value £	Distances in furlongs
Forever Shineing [3] out of Patosky)	1	2,243.00	12
Joellise [3] out of Carolside)	1	2,301.00	5
Love Legend [8] out of Sweet Emma)	1	5,049.00	5
Marros Mill [3] out of Springwell)	2	7,715.70	12 12
Rosie's Gold [3] out of New Central)	1	2,460.30	12
Spinning [6] out of Strathspey)	1	4,464.20	11
The Where Withal [3] out of Bourgeonette)	5	14,139.90	11 12 13 12 14
Yaakum [4] out of Nawadder)	1	3,002.40	16
	13	41,375.50	

GLOW (USA) (1983) by Northern Dancer-Glisk by Buckpasser

	Races Won	Value £	Distances in furlongs
Double Echo (Ire) [5] out of Piculet)	1	10,672.50	8
Mazeeka (Ire) [2] out of Saluti Tutti)	2	5,930.50	5 6
	3	16,603.00	

GODSWALK (USA) (1974) by Dancer's Image (USA)-Kate's Intent by Intentionally

	Races Won	Value £	Distances in furlongs
Lookingforarainbow (Ire) [5] out of Bridget Folly)	2	6,216.65	11 14
Misty Goddess (Ire) [5] out of Silent Sail)	2	5,744.40	9 10
	4	11,961.05	

GOLDEN ACT (USA) (1976) by Gummo (USA)-Golden Shore by Windy Sands

	Races Won	Value £	Distances in furlongs
Bardolph (USA) [6] out of Love To Barbara (USA))	1	5,572.00	16

GOLDEN HEIGHTS (1983) by Shirley Heights-Yelney by Blakeney

	Races Won	Value £	Distances in furlongs
Stormy Heights [3] out of Brown Taw)	1	3,610.00	5

GONE WEST (USA) (1984) by Mr Prospector (USA)-Secrettame (USA) by Secretariat (USA)

	Races Won	Value £	Distances in furlongs
Gold Land (USA) [2] out of Lajna)	3	14,216.10	5 6 6
Grotto Pool (USA) [2] out of Ballet de France (USA))	1	3,874.50	5
Link River (USA) [3] out of Connecting Link (USA))	1	4,127.75	8
Pembroke (USA) [3] out of College Bold (USA))	1	3,262.00	7
Solar Wagon (USA) [2] out of Solartic (Can))	1	4,485.25	6
West Quest (Can) [2] out of Veridian (USA))	1	3,231.00	5
Western Cape (USA) [3] out of Blue Bell Pearl (Fr))	2	45,021.00	8 10
Zafonic (USA) [3] out of Zaifon (USA))	1	110,871.20	8
	11	189,088.80	

GOOD TIMES (ITY) (1976) by Great Nephew-Never Angel by Never Say Die

	Races Won	Value £	Distances in furlongs
Forever Diamonds [6] out of Mel Mira)	2	19,842.00	8 7

GORYTUS (USA) (1980) by Nijinsky(Can)-Glad Rags by High Hat

	Races Won	Value £	Distances in furlongs
Full Quiver [8] out of Much Pleasure)	1	2,511.80	14
Gorinsky (Ire) [5] out of Grapette)	4	26,841.50	6 6 5 5
Ibsen [5] out of State Of Mind)	1	2,070.00	12
Lexus (Ire) [5] out of Pepi Image (USA))	2	4,749.00	8 10
	8	36,172.30	

GOVERNOR GENERAL (1983) by Dominion-Law And Impulse by Roan Rocket

	Races Won	Value £	Distances in furlongs
Heathyards Gem [3] out of Quenlyn)	1	2,950.60	6
Knyaz [3] out of Aleda Rose)	1	3,076.50	7
Left Stranded [2] out of Miss Serlby)	4	12,927.00	5 5 5 5
Queen Of The Quorn [3] out of Alumia)	2	4,822.00	6 7
Rankaidade [2] out of Keep Cool (Fr))	1	3,002.40	5
	9	26,778.50	

GREEN DANCER (USA) (1972) by Nijinsky(Can)-Green Valley(Fr) by Val de Loir

	Races Won	Value £	Distances in furlongs
Darkwood Bay (USA) [2] out of Unyielding (USA))	1	4,020.50	7

	Races Won	Value £	Distances in furlongs
Eden's Close [4] out of Royal Agreement (USA))	1	5,015.50	13
Escarpment (USA) [2] out of Revidere (USA))	2	9,396.00	7 7
Green Golightly (USA) [2] out of Polly Daniels (USA))	1	3,757.50	6
Lindon Lime (USA) [3] out of White Reason (USA))	1	15,593.00	10
	6	37,782.50	

GREEN DESERT (USA) (1983) by Danzig (USA)-Foreign Courier by Sir Ivor

	Races Won	Value £	Distances in furlongs
Aquado [4] out of Meliora)	1	3,582.00	5
Ardkinglass [3] out of Reuval)	1	40,432.20	7
Arid [3] out of Fabulous Luba)	2	6,900.75	7 7
Canaska Dancer (Ire) [2] out of Gay France (Fr))	2	9,547.25	6 6
Collier Bay [3] out of Cockatoo Island)	1	3,494.25	14
Count Of Flanders (Ire) [3] out of Marie de Flandre (Fr))	1	3,669.75	9
Desert Green (Fr) [4] out of Green Leaf (USA))	1	3,523.50	6
Desert Lore [2] out of Chinese Justice (USA))	1	3,699.00	5
Desert Nomad [3] out of Pale Gold (Fr))	2	5,633.90	6 6
Desert Power [4] out of Rivers Maid)	1	3,494.25	10
Desert Shot [3] out of Out Of Shot)	1	4,501.75	8
Desert Splendour [5] out of Lost Splendour (USA))	1	2,427.00	7
Dune River [4] out of River Spey)	2	9,443.00	7 6
El Gahar [3] out of Dafinah (USA))	1	3,699.00	8
Etosha [3] out of Sassalya)	2	6,980.25	7 7
Everglades (Ire) [5] out of Glowing With Pride)	3	18,738.80	6 6 6
Ewald (Ire) [5] out of Popular Win)	2	8,525.25	5 5
Fawz (Ire) [4] out of Stay Sharpe (USA))	1	4,978.00	7
Finger Of Light [2] out of Circus Ring)	1	4,737.00	6
Gabr [3] out of Ardassine)	2	17,295.00	8 8
Green Crusader [2] out of Hysterical)	1	4,521.00	7
Green Green Desert (Fr) [2] out of Green Leaf (USA))	1	4,581.00	6
High Summer [3] out of Beacon Hill)	2	6,169.30	14 12
Ishtiyak [2] out of Stay Sharpe (USA))	1	3,260.25	5
Khubza [3] out of Breadcrumb)	1	4,581.00	7
Midhish [3] out of Swanilda (Fr))	1	3,348.00	6
Owington [2] out of Old Domesday Book)	1	7,505.00	6
Set The Fashion [4] out of Prelude)	5	17,774.50	7 8 8 8 7
Siwaayib [3] out of Ma Petite Cherie (USA))	2	8,026.50	6 6
Sun Of Spring [3] out of Unsuspected)	4	19,365.45	9 12 14 12
Thourios [4] out of Graecia Magna (USA))	2	14,068.00	7 7
Tricorne [2] out of Turban)	1	4,342.25	6
	51	262,844.15	

GREEN FOREST (USA) (1979) by Shecky Greene (USA)-Tell Meno Lies (USA) by The Axe II

	Races Won	Value £	Distances in furlongs
Forest Gazelle (USA) [2] out of Nimble Feet (USA))	2	7,852.50	6 6
Forest Star (USA) [4] out of Al Madina (USA))	1	3,300.50	10
Jura Forest [3] out of Kabiyla)	1	5,300.75	8
Miss Siham (Ire) [4] out of Miss Derby (USA))	2	4,564.50	5 5
New Capricorn (USA) [3] out of Size Six (USA))	1	5,360.20	8
Tissisat (USA) [4] out of Expansive)	1	17,993.75	8
	8	44,372.20	

GREEN RUBY (USA) (1981) by Shecky Greene (USA)-Ruby Tuesday (USA) by T V Lark

	Races Won	Value £	Distances in furlongs
Ned's Bonanza [4] out of Miss Display)	1	4,464.00	5

GREINTON (1981) by Green Dancer (USA)-Crystal Queen by High Top

	Races Won	Value £	Distances in furlongs
Green Lane (USA) [5] out of Memory Lane (USA))	2	7,992.50	17 17
Lord Nitrogen (USA) [3] out of Jibber Jabber (USA))	1	3,483.00	12
	3	11,475.50	

GREY DAWN II (1962) by Herbager-Polamia by Mahmoud

	Races Won	Value £	Distances in furlongs
Redoubtable (USA) [2] out of Seattle Rockette (USA))	2	13,244.00	5 5

GREY DESIRE (1980) by Habat-Noddy Time by Gratitude

	Races Won	Value £	Distances in furlongs
Desirable Miss [3] out of Miss Realm)	1	2,560.00	7
Gold Desire [3] out of Glory Gold)	1	2,346.00	8
Heaven-Liegh-Grey [5] out of North Pine)	2	11,511.50	5 5

	Races Won	Value £	Distances in furlongs
My Desire [5] out of Another Move)	2	7,181.75	16 16
Pride Of Pendle [4] out of Pendle's Secret)	5	15,264.00	8 8 7 8 8
Surprise Breeze [2] out of Conrara)	1	2,243.00	5
	12	41,106.25	

GROOM DANCER (USA) (1984) by Blushing Groom(Fr)-Featherhill(Fr) by Lyphard (USA)

	Races Won	Value £	Distances in furlongs
Athens Belle (Ire) [3] out of Greektown)	1	10,690.00	10
Rani (Ire) [3] out of Arab Heritage)	1	3,357.00	11
	2	14,047.00	

GROOVY (USA) (1983) by Norcliffe (Can)-Tinnitus (USA) by Restless Wind

	Races Won	Value £	Distances in furlongs
Keyway (USA) [3] out of Maui Manor (USA))	1	3,026.25	6

GRUB (USA) (1983) by Mr Prospector (USA)-Maimiti (USA) by Never Bend

	Races Won	Value £	Distances in furlongs
Mistress Bee (USA) [4] out of Golden Regent (Can))	1	2,660.00	16

GULCH (USA) (1984) by Mr Prospector (USA)-Jameela (USA) by Rambunctious

	Races Won	Value £	Distances in furlongs
Braari (USA) [2] out of So Cozy (USA))	3	26,315.30	6 6 6
Fayrooz (USA) [2] out of Solar (Can))	1	4,152.00	6
Katiba (USA) [3] out of Schematic (USA))	1	3,512.50	7
Palana (USA) [2] out of Cor Anglais (USA))	2	7,058.25	6 5
	7	41,038.05	

GUNNER B (1973) by Royal Gunner (USA)-Sweet Councillor by Privy Councillor

	Races Won	Value £	Distances in furlongs
Bronze Runner [9] out of Petingalyn)	2	4,570.00	9 11
Gilderdale [11] out of Mertola)	1	3,289.50	10
Sky Burst [3] out of Sky Bonnet)	1	3,015.00	10
	4	10,874.50	

HABITAT (1966) by Sir Gaylord-Little Hut by Occupy

	Races Won	Value £	Distances in furlongs
Arabat [6] out of Kalamac (Fr))	2	6,683.80	6 7
Habeta (USA) [7] out of Prise)	1	3,850.00	8
	3	10,533.80	

HADEER (1982) by General Assembly (USA)-Glinting by Crepello

	Races Won	Value £	Distances in furlongs
Court Minstrel [4] out of Sheer Bliss)	1	3,757.50	6
General Mouktar [3] out of Fly The Coop)	3	19,085.00	10 12 12
Hadeer's Dance [3] out of Harvest Dance)	1	3,406.50	7
Media Messenger [4] out of Willow Court (USA))	1	2,556.60	9
My Abbey [4] out of Rose Barton)	1	3,435.75	5
Sea-Deer [4] out of Hi-Tech Girl)	2	7,797.50	5 5
Turtle Rock [2] out of Light de Light (USA))	1	2,377.40	6
	10	42,416.25	

HALLGATE (1983) by Vaigly Great-Beloved Mistress by Rarity

	Races Won	Value £	Distances in furlongs
Deevee [4] out of Lady Woodpecker)	5	17,852.20	7 7 8 7 8
Great Hall [4] out of Lily Of France)	4	12,621.00	5 5 5 6
Hallorina [3] out of Diorina)	2	5,783.50	5 5
Karukera [3] out of Water Folly)	1	2,761.50	5
Our Rita [4] out of Ma Pierrette)	2	9,614.60	6 6
Thornton Gate [4] out of Lola Black (Fr))	2	6,311.10	7 7
Trinity Hall [3] out of Trigamy)	1	2,684.50	6
	17	57,628.40	

HALO (USA) (1969) by Hail To Reason-Cosmah by Cosmic Bomb

	Races Won	Value £	Distances in furlongs
East Liberty (USA) [3] out of Pennsylvania (USA))	1	4,077.50	8
Solartica (USA) [3] out of Telescopica (Arg))	1	4,269.00	14
	2	8,346.50	

†HANDSOME SAILOR (1983) by Some Hand-Found At Sea (USA) by Pieces of Eight

	Races Won	Value £	Distances in furlongs
In Like Flynn [2] out of Thevetia)	3	15,175.15	7 7 7

HARD FOUGHT (1977) by Habitat-Ambrosia by Alcide

	Races Won	Value £	Distances in furlongs
Highfield Lad [2] out of Jendor)	1	1,553.00	7

HATIM (USA) (1981) by Exclusive Native (USA)-Sunday Purchase (USA) by T V Lark

	Races Won	Value £	Distances in furlongs
Talented Ting (Ire) [4] out of An Tig Gaelige)	3	9,141.80	8 9 8

HEAD FOR HEIGHTS (1981) by Shirley Heights-Vivante by Bold Lad(Ire)

	Races Won	Value £	Distances in furlongs
Mulciber [5] out of Quisissanno)	1	2,678.40	7

	Races Won	Value £	Distances in furlongs
Silky Heights (Ire) [3] out of Silk Trade)	2	6,263.80	11 12
	3	8,942.20	

HELLO GORGEOUS (USA) (1977) by Mr Prospector (USA)-Bonny Jet by Jet Jewel

	Races Won	Value £	Distances in furlongs
Super Benz [7] out of Investiture)	1	2,595.80	7

HERALDISTE (USA) (1982) by Lyphard (USA)-Heiress by Habitat

	Races Won	Value £	Distances in furlongs
Haroldon (Ire) [4] out of Cordon)	1	3,054.20	9
Look Who's Here (Ire) [3] out of House Call)	2	14,659.00	6 6
Phoneaholic (Ire) [2] out of Clonross Lady)	1	1,907.20	6
	4	19,620.40	

†HIGH ESTATE (1986) by Shirley Heights-Regal Beauty (USA) by Princely Native (USA)

	Races Won	Value £	Distances in furlongs
Majestic Heights (Ire) [2] out of Lisa's Favourite)	1	3,699.00	7
State Crystal (Ire) [2] out of Crystal Spray)	1	4,202.75	7
	2	7,901.75	

HIGH LINE (1966) by High Hat-Time Call by Chanteur II

	Races Won	Value £	Distances in furlongs
Always Friendly [5] out of Wise Speculation (USA))	1	4,761.40	12
Dime Bag [4] out of Blue Guitar)	1	7,327.20	14
	2	12,088.60	

HIGH TOP (1969) by Derring-Do-Camenae by Vimy

	Races Won	Value £	Distances in furlongs
Prince Hannibal [6] out of Fluctuate)	2	6,726.75	12 12
Supertop [5] out of Myth)	2	8,205.60	9 9
	4	14,932.35	

HIS MAJESTY (USA) (1968) by Ribot-Flower Bowl by Alibhai

	Races Won	Value £	Distances in furlongs
Rapporteur (USA) [7] out of Sweet Rapport (USA))	2	5,379.00	11 11

HOLD YOUR PEACE (USA) (1969) by Speak John-Blue Moon by Eight Thirty

	Races Won	Value £	Distances in furlongs
Peacefull Reply (USA) [3] out of Drone Answer (USA))	1	2,385.00	6

HOMEBOY (1973) by King's Troop-Reita by Gilles de Retz

	Races Won	Value £	Distances in furlongs
Homemaker [3] out of Ganadora)	1	3,675.80	7

†HOMEBUILDER (USA) (1984) by Mr Prospector (USA)-Smart Heiress (USA) by Vaguely Noble

	Races Won	Value £	Distances in furlongs
Smart Family (USA) [2] out of Enceinte (USA))	1	3,699.00	7

HOMING (1975) by Habitat-Heavenly Thought by St Paddy

	Races Won	Value £	Distances in furlongs
Self Expression [5] out of Subtlety)	3	20,120.50	9 8 8
Trioming [7] out of Third Generation)	2	5,682.75	5 5
	5	25,803.25	

HONEST PLEASURE (USA) (1973) by What A Pleasure (USA)-Tularia by Tulyar

	Races Won	Value £	Distances in furlongs
Sir Joey (USA) [4] out of Sougoli)	3	11,417.50	6 6 5

HORAGE (1980) by Tumble Wind (USA)-Musicienne by Sicambre

	Races Won	Value £	Distances in furlongs
Azureus (Ire) [5] out of Effortless)	3	9,598.70	12 10 12
Carrolls Marc (Ire) [5] out of Rare Find)	2	4,968.00	12 14
Cliburnel News (Ire) [3] out of Dublin Millennium)	3	7,580.20	10 11 12
Ochos Rios (Ire) [2] out of Morgiana)	2	5,503.25	5 6
Sizzling Saga (Ire) [5] out of Alsazia (Fr))	2	4,779.00	7 7
	12	32,429.15	

HOSTAGE (USA) (1979) by Nijinsky(Can)-Entente by Val de Loir

	Races Won	Value £	Distances in furlongs
Camden's Ransom (USA) [6] out of Camden Court (USA))	1	5,186.00	10
Quick Ransom [5] out of Run Amber Run)	2	31,082.40	13 12
	3	36,268.40	

HOTFOOT (1966) by Firestreak-Pitter Patter by Kingstone

	Races Won	Value £	Distances in furlongs
Quiet Riot [11] out of Tuyenu)	1	2,343.00	17
Sloe Brandy [3] out of Emblazon)	1	2,721.00	9
Western Dynasty [7] out of Northern Dynasty)	2	6,233.20	13 14
	4	11,297.20	

†HUBBLY BUBBLY (USA) (1985) by Mr Prospector (USA)-Din (USA) by Drone

	Races Won	Value £	Distances in furlongs
Champagne Ateaster [2] out of Eastern Ember)	1	3,260.25	6

	Races Won	Value £	Distances in furlongs

HUNTINGDALE (1983) by Double Form-Abbeydale by Huntercombe

	Races Won	Value £	Distances in furlongs
Pie Hatch (Ire) [4] out of Small Is Beautiful)	1	2,070.00	11

ILE DE BOURBON (USA) (1975) by Nijinsky(Can)-Roseliere(Fr) by Misti IV

	Races Won	Value £	Distances in furlongs
Anatroccolo [6] out of Art Deco)	1	3,288.00	7

IMP SOCIETY (USA) (1981) by Barrera (USA)-Trotta Sue by Promised Land

	Races Won	Value £	Distances in furlongs
Mr Eubanks (USA) [2] out of Whitesburg Lass (USA))	1	3,720.00	7

IMPERIAL FALCON (CAN) (1983) by Northern Dancer-Ballade (USA) by Herbager

	Races Won	Value £	Distances in furlongs
Awestrike (USA) [3] out of Awe (USA))	1	3,640.50	8
Ikhtiraa (USA) [3] out of True Native (USA))	1	3,582.00	8
	2	7,222.50	

IMPERIAL FRONTIER (USA) (1984) by Lyphard (USA)-Hartebeest (USA) by Vaguely Noble

	Races Won	Value £	Distances in furlongs
Imperial Bailiwick (Ire) [2] out of Syndikos (USA))	3	31,269.25	5 5 5
Iva's Flyer (Ire) [2] out of Salt)	1	3,913.25	5
Medland (Ire) [3] out of Miami Dancer)	1	2,758.20	6
Trentesimo (Ire) [3] out of Be Nimble)	4	9,273.40	6 5 6 6
	9	47,214.10	

IN FIJAR (USA) (1977) by Bold Commander (USA)-Apache Queen by Marshal At Arms

	Races Won	Value £	Distances in furlongs
Dulford Lad [2] out of Highsplasher (USA))	1	2,070.00	7

INDIAN KING (USA) (1978) by Raja Baba (USA)-Protest by Rash Prince

	Races Won	Value £	Distances in furlongs
Macs Maharanee [6] out of High State)	2	8,375.75	6 6
Sharquin [6] out of Lady Of The Land)	1	3,366.00	9
Tiger Shoot [6] out of Grand Occasion)	1	2,243.00	12
	4	13,984.75	

†INDIAN RIDGE (1985) by Ahonoora-Hillbrow by Swing Easy (USA)

	Races Won	Value £	Distances in furlongs
Fumo Di Londra (Ire) [2] out of Fettle)	1	26,796.50	7
Indiahra [2] out of Mavahra)	2	5,899.35	5 5
Island Magic [2] out of Rum Cay (USA))	2	26,688.30	5 7
Kangra Valley [2] out of Thorner Lane)	1	3,699.00	5
Moving Arrow [2] out of Another Move)	1	3,289.50	7
My Lifetime Lady (Ire) [2] out of Liffey Reef)	2	5,490.40	5 5
Silver Slipper [2] out of Irish Isle)	2	5,491.00	7 7
Southern Ridge [2] out of Southern Sky)	1	4,500.00	6
Straight Arrow [2] out of Harmonical (USA))	1	3,523.50	5
	13	85,377.55	

INFANTRY (1982) by Northfields (USA)-Princess Tiara by Crowned Prince (USA)

	Races Won	Value £	Distances in furlongs
Infantry Glen [3] out of Rage Glen)	1	2,511.00	10
Patong Beach [3] out of Winter Resort)	1	2,406.00	10
	2	4,917.00	

INTERREX (CAN) (1984) by Vice Regent(Can)-Betty's Secret(Can) by Secretariat (USA)

	Races Won	Value £	Distances in furlongs
Double Bounce [3] out of Double Gift)	1	2,243.00	6
Kimbolton Korker [3] out of One Sharper)	1	2,725.70	5
Lying Eyes [2] out of Lysithea)	1	2,691.60	5
Northern Bird [3] out of Partridge Brook)	1	7,245.00	7
Ok Bertie [3] out of Rockery)	2	8,825.00	7 6
Royal Interval [3] out of Sister Rosarii (USA))	2	7,835.65	7 8
Super Symphonic [2] out of Super Melody)	1	2,448.00	7
Walk The Beat [3] out of Plaits)	1	3,080.00	6
	10	37,093.95	

IRISH RIVER (FR) (1976) by Riverman (USA)-Irish Star by Klairon

	Races Won	Value £	Distances in furlongs
Colway Rock (USA) [3] out of Petite Diable (USA))	1	9,594.00	8
Hatoof (USA) [4] out of Cadeaux D'Amie (USA))	1	205,707.00	10
Hatta River (USA) [3] out of Fallacieuse)	1	2,950.60	12
River Boyne (USA) [3] out of Bethamane (USA))	2	6,631.50	9 10
River Life [3] out of Exclusive Life (USA))	1	3,720.00	7
Tapis Rouge (Ire) [4] out of Marie Noelle (Fr))	1	4,965.72	10
Tumbling (USA) [5] out of Trephine (Fr))	1	3,276.00	7
	8	236,844.82	

IRISH TOWER (USA) (1977) by Irish Castle (USA)-Royal Loom (USA) by Loom

	Races Won	Value £	Distances in furlongs
Monsignor Pat (USA) [3] out of Song To Remember)	1	3,465.00	8

JALMOOD (USA) (1979) by Blushing Groom(Fr)-Fast Ride(Fr) by Sicambre

	Races Won	Value £	Distances in furlongs
Ball Gown [3] out of Relatively Smart)	1	2,490.00	10
Beneficiary [2] out of Bequeath (USA))	4	11,170.25	6 6 7 7
Castoret [7] out of Blaskette)	1	15,962.50	13
Eiras Mood [4] out of Pure Perfection)	1	3,668.00	10
Harlestone Brook [3] out of Harlestone Lake)	2	6,824.25	12 12
Jalcanto [3] out of Bella Canto)	1	2,511.80	8
Jalore [4] out of Lorelene (Fr))	3	5,770.00	14 12 16
Merry Nutkin [7] out of Merry Cindy)	2	6,164.25	12 13
	15	54,561.05	

JAMESMEAD (1981) by Import-Cathy Jane by Lauso

	Races Won	Value £	Distances in furlongs
She Knew The Rules (Ire) [3] out of Falls Of Lora)	1	2,070.00	16

JAREER (USA) (1983) by Northern Dancer-Fabuleux Jane (USA) by Le Fabuleux

	Races Won	Value £	Distances in furlongs
Amoret (Ire) [2] out of Gentle Freedom)	2	7,848.50	6 7
Balandra Bay (Ire) [2] out of Ballyewry)	2	8,309.70	5 6
Candi Das (Ire) [2] out of Indigo Queen)	1	3,261.40	6
Classic Sky (Ire) [2] out of Nawadder)	2	10,930.30	5 7
Colfax Classic [3] out of Hitopah)	1	3,494.25	7
Devils Den (Ire) [3] out of Whispered Wishes)	2	8,202.00	8 10
Dollar Gamble (Ire) [2] out of Have A Flutter)	2	6,917.50	5 5
Follingworth Girl (Ire) [3] out of Coshlea)	4	11,427.25	14 15 16 15
Home From The Hill (Ire) [3] out of Hill's Realm (USA))	1	3,132.00	11
Queens Cottage (Ire) [2] out of Drora)	1	3,984.75	5
	18	67,507.65	

JAVA GOLD (USA) (1984) by Key to the Mint (USA)-Javamine (USA) by Nijinsky (Can)

	Races Won	Value £	Distances in furlongs
Java Queen (USA) [3] out of Two For The Show (USA))	1	3,545.00	8

JESTER (1979) by Song-Trickster by Major Portion

	Races Won	Value £	Distances in furlongs
Royal Comedian [4] out of Royal Huntress)	1	2,709.00	7
Trevorsninepoints [3] out of Miss Merlin)	3	6,942.60	5 5 5
	4	9,651.60	

†JOLIGENERATION (1984) by Young Generation-Jolisu by Welsh Abbot

	Races Won	Value £	Distances in furlongs
Folly Finnesse [2] out of Magic Milly)	2	5,714.40	6 6

JUNIUS (USA) (1976) by Raja Baba (USA)-Solid Thought by Solidarity

	Races Won	Value £	Distances in furlongs
Catherines Well [10] out of Restless Lady)	2	9,664.00	5 6

JUPITER ISLAND (1979) by St Paddy-Mrs Moss by Reform

	Races Won	Value £	Distances in furlongs
Fuchu [3] out of Dalchroy)	2	7,992.50	7 7
Island Knight (Ire) [4] out of Florence Street)	1	2,821.10	7
Moonlight Eclipse [3] out of Moonlight Bay)	1	2,742.00	16
Silver Standard [3] out of One Half Silver (Can))	1	1,826.00	7
Tudor Island [4] out of Catherine Howard)	1	3,850.00	11
	6	19,231.60	

K-BATTERY (1981) by Gunner B-Kajetana(Fr) by Caro

	Races Won	Value £	Distances in furlongs
Philgun [4] out of Andalucia)	2	6,304.60	13 14

KABOUR (1978) by Habitat-Kermiya by Vienna

	Races Won	Value £	Distances in furlongs
Kabcast [8] out of Final Cast)	1	3,817.50	5
Kalar [4] out of Wind And Reign)	2	5,856.75	5 5
	3	9,674.25	

KAFU (1980) by African Sky-Pampered Dancer by Pampered King

	Races Won	Value £	Distances in furlongs
Call To The Bar (Ire) [4] out of Papun (USA))	1	3,435.75	5
Natural Lad [8] out of Natural Sunshine)	1	2,070.00	9
Royal Girl [6] out of Royal Aunt)	4	12,396.50	7 7 7 7
Teanarco (Ire) [5] out of Lady Kasbah)	1	3,236.00	7
Veloce (Ire) [5] out of Joanns Goddess)	3	12,558.00	8 7 7
	10	33,696.25	

KALA SHIKARI (1973) by Huntercombe-Vigour by Vilmorin

	Races Won	Value £	Distances in furlongs
Failand [6] out of What A Mint)	1	1,954.00	8

	Races Won	Value £	Distances in furlongs
Jess Rebec [5] out of Laleston)	1	2,950.00	5
Macfarlane [5] out of Tarvie)	2	19,049.00	5 5
Shikari's Son [6] out of Have Form)	1	3,995.87	6
	5	27,948.87	

KALAGLOW (1978) by Kalamoun-Rossitor by Pall Mall

	Races Won	Value £	Distances in furlongs
Dorazine [3] out of Doree Moisson (Fr))	3	12,372.00	10 10 8
Eurolink Chieftain [2] out of Allander Girl)	1	3,624.00	8
Glowing Jade [3] out of Precious Jade)	1	3,493.00	7
Glowing Path [3] out of Top Tina)	2	5,081.00	8 8
Jeune [4] out of Youthful (Fr))	1	56,700.00	12
Meavy [3] out of Feather Flower)	1	2,954.00	12
Miss Pin Up [4] out of Allander Girl)	2	8,415.00	12 14
Quick Silver Boy [3] out of Safidar)	2	6,340.00	8 8
	13	98,979.00	

KAMPALA (1976) by Kalamoun-State Pension by Only For Life

	Races Won	Value £	Distances in furlongs
Good For The Roses [7] out of Alleyn)	1	3,915.00	7
Lady Lacey [6] out of Cecily)	2	6,807.00	9 10
	3	10,722.00	

KAYTU (1981) by High Top-Arawak by Seminole II

	Races Won	Value £	Distances in furlongs
Kayartis [4] out of Polyartis)	1	3,184.00	16

†KEFAAH (USA) (1985) by Blushing Groom (Fr)-Tertiary (USA) by Vaguely Noble

	Races Won	Value £	Distances in furlongs
Cazzuto (Ire) [2] out of Hay Knot)	1	3,289.50	7
Violet Crown (Ire) [2] out of Supreme Crown (USA))	1	4,485.25	8
	2	7,774.75	

KENMARE (FR) (1975) by Kalamoun-Belle of Ireland by Milesian

	Races Won	Value £	Distances in furlongs
Laune (Aus) [2] out of Artistic Princess (Aus))	1	4,127.75	5

KEY TO THE KINGDOM (USA) (1970) by Bold Ruler-Key Bridge by Princequillo

	Races Won	Value £	Distances in furlongs
He's A King (USA) [3] out of She's A Jay (USA))	2	7,732.50	8 8
Lock Tight (USA) [3] out of Parissaul)	1	2,243.00	9
	3	9,975.50	

KEY TO THE MINT (USA) (1969) by Graustark-Key Bridge by Princequillo

	Races Won	Value £	Distances in furlongs
Wonderful Years (USA) [3] out of Velvet Storm (USA))	1	2,070.00	10

KIND OF HUSH (1978) by Welsh Pageant-Sauceboat by Connaught

	Races Won	Value £	Distances in furlongs
Coalisland [3] out of Hit The Line)	1	2,976.50	5
Munday Dean [5] out of Nancy Brig)	1	3,054.20	11
My Minnie [3] out of Miami Mouse)	1	2,847.00	8
	3	8,877.70	

KING OF CLUBS (1981) by Mill Reef (USA)-Queen Pot (USA) by Buckpasser

	Races Won	Value £	Distances in furlongs
King Paris (Ire) [3] out of Alkis (USA))	2	7,099.00	8 8
King Rat (Ire) [2] out of Mrs Tittlemouse)	2	4,497.00	5 5
	4	11,596.00	

KING OF SPAIN (1976) by Philip of Spain-Sovereign Sails by Sovereign Path

	Races Won	Value £	Distances in furlongs
City Rocket [3] out of Hat Hill)	1	3,199.50	7
Coconut Johnny [3] out of Gentle Gypsy)	1	3,348.00	5
Prince Rodney [4] out of Dancing Diana)	1	3,153.50	7
Spanish Verdict [6] out of Counsel's Verdict)	2	5,524.60	8 7
The Right Time [8] out of Noddy Time)	2	5,502.20	5 5
	7	20,727.80	

KINGS LAKE (USA) (1978) by Nijinsky(Can)-Fish-Bar by Baldric II

	Races Won	Value £	Distances in furlongs
Albert [6] out of Darine)	3	9,105.20	10 9 9
Jack Button (Ire) [4] out of Tallantire (USA))	2	10,688.75	16 16
Land O'Lakes (Ire) [3] out of Amboselli)	1	2,243.00	8
Princess Evita (Fr) [4] out of Very Bissy (Brz))	1	2,579.30	12
	7	24,616.25	

KNOWN FACT (USA) (1977) by In Reality (USA)-Tamerett by Tim Tam

	Races Won	Value £	Distances in furlongs
Arz (USA) [2] out of Last Request)	1	4,815.00	8

	Races Won	Value £	Distances in furlongs
Averti (USA) [2] out of Safe Play (USA))	1	5,390.00	7
Fact Or Fiction [7] out of Noble Wac (USA))	1	3,084.75	12
Factual (USA) [3] out of Mofida)	1	4,012.50	6
Guesstimation (USA) [4] out of Best Guess (USA))	2	5,147.50	7 8
Magnasonic (USA) [2] out of Itsamazing (USA))	1	5,572.00	6
So Factual (USA) [3] out of Sookera (USA))	1	18,034.50	7
Specified (USA) [3] out of Scierpan (USA))	2	12,440.80	6 6
	10	58,497.05	

†KOMAITE (USA) (1983) by Nureyev (USA)-Brown Berry by Mount Marcy

	Races Won	Value £	Distances in furlongs
Beautete [2] out of New Central)	1	3,582.00	6
Komplicity [2] out of City To City)	1	2,057.50	7
Lady-Bo-K [2] out of Lady Keyser)	1	3,390.90	6
Mokaite [2] out of Manhunt)	2	4,629.70	7 7
Springhead [2] out of Khadino)	1	2,451.00	6
	6	16,111.10	

KRAYYAN (1980) by Tower Walk-Mrs Moss by Reform

	Races Won	Value £	Distances in furlongs
Across The Bay [6] out of Siofra Beag)	1	2,549.00	7
Devious Dancer [3] out of Shabby Doll)	1	2,534.20	7
Metal Boys [6] out of Idle Gossip)	2	8,418.50	5 5
	4	13,501.70	

KRIS (1976) by Sharpen Up-Doubly Sure by Reliance II

	Races Won	Value £	Distances in furlongs
Aneesati [3] out of Dabaweyaa)	1	3,728.25	8
Hawajiss [2] out of Canadian Mill (USA))	2	21,677.60	7 8
Kamikaze [3] out of Infamy)	1	3,435.75	14
Livonian [3] out of Air Distingue (USA))	1	3,210.00	9
Mack The Knife [4] out of The Dancer (Fr))	2	12,597.50	12 12
Moonshine Lake [3] out of Lady Moon)	1	3,523.50	12
Nawafell [2] out of Try To Catch Me (USA))	1	2,623.80	7
Oh So Risky [6] out of Expediency (USA))	1	7,015.40	14
Peter Quince [3] out of Our Reverie (USA))	1	11,053.00	10
Princess Kris [3] out of As You Desire Me)	1	3,582.00	8
Reine de Neige [3] out of Don't Rush (USA))	1	3,933.00	8
Tajannab [2] out of Miss Fancy That (USA))	1	3,551.50	7
Tempering [7] out of Mixed Applause (USA))	1	2,691.00	12
Thinking Twice (USA) [4] out of Good Thinking (USA))	1	5,299.00	12
Yaqthan (Ire) [3] out of Al Sylah)	2	8,248.00	7 7
	18	96,169.30	

L'EMIGRANT (USA) (1980) by The Minstrel(Can)-Suprina by Vaguely Noble

	Races Won	Value £	Distances in furlongs
Mysterious Maid (USA) [6] out of Body Heat (USA))	1	2,385.00	14
Shoofe (USA) [5] out of Bid For Manners (USA))	1	3,365.00	15
	2	5,750.00	

LABUS (FR) (1971) by Busted-Cordovilla by Pharis II

	Races Won	Value £	Distances in furlongs
Balasani (Fr) [7] out of Baykara)	2	23,847.00	14 20

LAFONTAINE (USA) (1977) by Sham (USA)-Valya by Vandale II

	Races Won	Value £	Distances in furlongs
Shambo [6] out of Lucky Appeal)	2	37,983.00	12 13

LAST TYCOON (1983) by Try My Best (USA)-Mill Princess by Mill Reef (USA)

	Races Won	Value £	Distances in furlongs
Bigstone (Ire) [3] out of Batave)	2	273,980.00	8 8
Celia Brady [5] out of Lucayan Princess)	1	4,556.75	8
Ezzoud (Ire) [4] out of Royal Sister II)	2	178,739.60	9 10
First Fling (Ire) [4] out of Flamme D'Amour)	1	2,070.00	12
La Spezia [3] out of Helenetta)	1	3,260.25	10
Spring Loaded [2] out of Time For Romance)	1	3,416.80	6
Taalif [3] out of Imperial Jade)	1	3,348.00	6
Tychonic [3] out of Metair)	1	5,481.00	7
	10	474,852.40	

LATE ACT (USA) (1979) by Stage Door Johnny-Dunce Cap by Tom Fool

	Races Won	Value £	Distances in furlongs
Johns Act (USA) [3] out of Deluxe Type (USA))	1	3,172.50	10

LATEST MODEL (1974) by Reform-Cover Girl II by Edellic

	Races Won	Value £	Distances in furlongs
Mister Jolson [4] out of Impromptu)	2	7,209.90	5 5

LAW SOCIETY (USA) (1982) by Alleged (USA)-Bold Bikini (USA) by Boldnesian

	Races Won	Value £	Distances in furlongs
Abury (Ire) [3] out of Bay Shade (USA))	1	23,815.00	11
Civil Law (Ire) [3] out of Senane)	3	7,599.00	11 12 12
Lord Advocate [5] out of Kereolle)	2	4,730.00	15 15
Mrs Snuggs (Ire) [3] out of Inanna)	1	2,243.00	12
Newton's Law (Ire) [3] out of Catopetl (USA))	2	9,637.00	9 11
Overact (Ire) [2] out of Melodramatic)	2	6,520.50	7 7
Polar Storm (Ire) [3] out of Arctic Winter (Can))	2	11,120.00	6 8
Right Win (Ire) [3] out of Popular Win)	2	34,196.50	8 12
Savoy Truffle (Fr) [3] out of Light Of Hope (USA))	1	3,435.75	10
Scots Law [6] out of Tweedling (USA))	2	5,523.75	7 5
Top Rank [3] out of On The Top)	1	3,260.25	11
Zind (Ire) [3] out of Rose Red (USA))	1	3,265.50	13
	20	115,346.25	

LEAD ON TIME (USA) (1983) by Nureyev (USA)-Alathea by Lorenzaccio

	Races Won	Value £	Distances in furlongs
Cameo Kirby (Fr) [3] out of Nofret (Fr))	2	5,253.00	7 7
Cool Jazz [2] out of Amber Fizz (USA))	1	5,580.00	6
Desert Invader (Ire) [2] out of Aljood)	1	3,687.50	6
Fraam [4] out of Majestic Kahala (USA))	2	28,703.08	8 7
	6	43,223.58	

LEAR FAN (USA) (1981) by Roberto (USA)-Wac (USA) by Lt Stevens

	Races Won	Value £	Distances in furlongs
Bidweaya (USA) [6] out of Sweet Snow (USA))	1	3,080.10	7
Blowing (USA) [3] out of Sleek Lassie (USA))	1	4,016.00	7
Fanatical (USA) [7] out of Gal A Tic (USA))	1	2,511.00	13
King Curan (USA) [2] out of Runaway Lady (USA))	2	8,577.50	7 8
Learmont (USA) [3] out of Wistoral (USA))	2	23,120.00	10 12
	7	41,304.60	

LEGEND OF FRANCE (USA) (1980) by Lyphard (USA)-Lupe by Primera

	Races Won	Value £	Distances in furlongs
Eire Leath-Sceal [6] out of Killarney Belle (USA))	3	10,852.50	11 11 12
Francia [3] out of Relicia)	1	2,739.00	7
Legend Dulac (Ire) [4] out of Westerlake)	1	3,377.25	7
	5	16,968.75	

LEMHI GOLD (USA) (1978) by Vaguely Noble-Belle Marie (USA) by Candy Spots

	Races Won	Value £	Distances in furlongs
Leif The Lucky (USA) [4] out of Corvine (USA))	2	10,742.75	8 7

LIDHAME (1982) by Nureyev (USA)-Red Berry by Great Nephew

	Races Won	Value £	Distances in furlongs
Bichette [3] out of Freely Given)	1	2,243.00	6
Juliasdarkinvader [3] out of Una Donna (Ger))	1	2,660.00	10
Purbeck Centenary [3] out of Double Stitch)	1	3,122.80	5
Sir Tasker [5] out of Susie's Baby)	1	2,976.50	5
	4	11,002.30	

LINKAGE (USA) (1979) by Hoist The Flag (USA)-Unity Hall by Cyane

	Races Won	Value £	Distances in furlongs
Pride Of Britain (Can) [4] out of Witches Alibhai (USA))	1	11,963.00	16
Tilty (USA) [3] out of En Tiempo (USA))	2	6,801.80	15 16
	3	18,764.80	

LITTLE MISSOURI (USA) (1982) by Cox's Ridge (USA)-Win Nona (USA) by Jacinto

	Races Won	Value £	Distances in furlongs
Five To Seven (USA) [4] out of French Galaxy (USA))	3	9,637.60	13 16 16

LITTLE WOLF (1978) by Grundy-Hiding Place by Doutelle

	Races Won	Value £	Distances in furlongs
Popsi's Legacy [6] out of Popsi's Poppet)	1	3,933.00	14

LOCAL SUITOR (USA) (1982) by Blushing Groom(Fr)-Home Love (USA) by Vaguely Noble

	Races Won	Value £	Distances in furlongs
Affa [4] out of Pine)	1	3,753.50	8
Agwa [4] out of Meissarah (USA))	2	7,137.30	6 6
Girl Next Door [3] out of Tight Spin)	1	2,950.60	6
Junction Twentytwo [3] out of Pollinella)	1	1,916.90	10
Marina Park [3] out of Mary Martin)	1	6,750.00	5
Mull House [6] out of Foudre)	1	4,221.00	14
Sweet Romeo [3] out of Ladoucette)	1	3,026.25	6
	8	29,755.55	

†LOCAL TALENT (USA) (1986) by Northern Dancer-Home Love (USA) by Vaguely Noble

	Races Won	Value £	Distances in furlongs
Star Talent (USA) [2] out of Sedra)	2	11,156.25	6 6

LOCHNAGER (1972) by Dumbarnie-Miss Barbara by Le Dieu d'Or

	Races Won	Value £	Distances in furlongs
Aegaen Lady [4] out of Gamma (Ger))	3	8,056.80	9 11 9
Bold Angel [6] out of Lobela)	1	4,500.00	7
Delpiombo [7] out of Precious Petra)	2	4,606.50	8 8
Eager Deva [6] out of Deva Rose)	2	7,850.00	5 5
Fort Erie [2] out of Olibanum)	1	2,399.80	5
Killy's Filly [3] out of May Kells)	2	5,678.00	5 5
Penny Hasset [5] out of Bad Payer)	2	7,292.00	5 5
Slades Hill [6] out of Mephisto Waltz)	3	10,897.65	6 5 6
Thisonesforalice [5] out of Bamdoro)	1	2,242.50	7
	17	53,523.25	

LOMOND (USA) (1980) by Northern Dancer-My Charmer (USA) by Poker

	Races Won	Value £	Distances in furlongs
Balnaha [3] out of On Show)	1	3,611.25	7
Blue Lion [3] out of Percy's Lass)	2	7,992.50	8 10
Bonny Bride (Ire) [2] out of Blue Wedding (USA))	1	4,435.00	8
Clarinda (Ire) [2] out of Warm Welcome)	1	3,201.75	5
Croire (Ire) [3] out of Fighting Run)	1	4,435.00	7
Fluvial (Ire) [3] out of Riverstreak (USA))	1	6,316.00	8
Highland Dress [4] out of Colorspin (Fr))	1	3,348.00	11
Jalib (Ire) [3] out of Crown Godiva)	1	2,976.50	6
Jetbeeah (Ire) [3] out of Welsh Fantasy)	1	4,272.50	8
Oakmead (Ire) [3] out of Amazer (USA))	2	13,905.00	12 11
Queen's View (Fr) [3] out of Mill Path)	1	3,231.00	7
Rising Tempo (Ire) [5] out of May Hill)	1	1,725.00	11
River North (Ire) [3] out of Petillante (USA))	5	55,861.20	9 10 10 10 10
Scottish Peak (Ire) [3] out of Road To The Top)	1	4,448.60	11
Wahem (Ire) [3] out of Pro Patria)	1	3,080.10	7
Wali (USA) [3] out of Magic Slipper)	1	3,492.50	7
Yunus Emre (Ire) [3] out of Thrifty Trio (USA))	2	5,819.10	7 7
	24	132,151.00	

LONGLEAT (USA) (1979) by The Minstrel(Can)-Fair Arrow by Turn-to

	Races Won	Value £	Distances in furlongs
Montendre [6] out of La Lutine)	1	10,464.00	6

LUCKY WEDNESDAY (1973) by Roi Soleil-Pavlova by Fidalgo

	Races Won	Value £	Distances in furlongs
MCA Below The Line [5] out of Delayed Action)	1	3,377.25	7

LYPHARD (USA) (1969) by Northern Dancer-Goofed by Court Martial

	Races Won	Value £	Distances in furlongs
Bagalino (USA) [3] out of Bag Of Tunes (USA))	1	3,492.50	11
Fawaakeh (USA) [2] out of Dish Dash)	1	4,628.25	6
Instant Affair (USA) [3] out of Asiram (USA))	2	7,656.00	10 10
Linney Head (USA) [2] out of Royalivor (USA))	1	4,371.75	7
Lyphard's Delta (USA) [3] out of Proud Delta (USA))	4	79,354.50	8 10 10 10
Smuggler's Point (USA) [3] out of Smuggly (USA))	1	3,231.00	13
Star Manager (USA) [3] out of Angel Clare (Fr))	1	3,850.00	8
Tatami (USA) [2] out of Tash (USA))	3	35,081.75	7 6 7
Um Algowain (USA) [3] out of Moonlight Serenade (Fr))	2	6,315.75	10 10
Witness Box (USA) [6] out of Excellent Alibi (USA))	1	5,078.40	13
	17	153,059.90	

LYPHARD'S SPECIAL (USA) (1980) by Lyphard (USA)-My Bupers by Bupers

	Races Won	Value £	Distances in furlongs
James Is Special (Ire) [5] out of High Explosive)	1	4,878.25	14
Obsidian Grey [6] out of Marcrest)	3	7,234.20	5 7 6
	4	12,112.45	

LYPHARD'S WISH (FR) (1976) by Lyphard (USA)-Sally's Wish (USA) by Sensitivo

	Races Won	Value £	Distances in furlongs
Caromish (USA) [6] out of Carom (USA))	1	2,929.50	6
Lady Donoghue (USA) [4] out of It's High Time)	1	2,889.00	8
Wishing (USA) [2] out of Vivre Libre (USA))	1	5,936.00	8
	3	11,754.50	

M DOUBLE M (USA) (1981) by Nodouble (USA)-Mazda's Miracle by New Policy

	Races Won	Value £	Distances in furlongs
Asian Punter (Ire) [4] out of Centenary Year)	2	9,190.50	14 16

	Races Won	Value £	Distances in furlongs
Golden Chip (Ire) [5] out of Kimangao)	3	10,429.00	7 10 8
Merryhill Maid (Ire) [5] out of Piazza Navona)	1	3,150.00	6
Murray's Mazda (Ire) [4] out of Lamya)	3	6,655.80	6 6 6
	9	29,425.30	

MACMILLION (1979) by So Blessed-Salsafy by Tudor Melody

	Races Won	Value £	Distances in furlongs
Smilingatstrangers [5] out of My Charade)	1	3,521.00	17

MAGIC MIRROR (1982) by Nureyev (USA)-Turkish Treasure (USA) by Sir Ivor

	Races Won	Value £	Distances in furlongs
Shannon Express [6] out of Tatisha)	2	6,237.70	8 8

MAGICAL WONDER (USA) (1983) by Storm Bird(Can)-Flama Ardiente (USA) by Crimson Satan

	Races Won	Value £	Distances in furlongs
Inherent Magic (Ire) [4] out of Flo Kelly)	1	6,639.60	5
Sea Gazer (Ire) [3] out of Apapa Port)	1	10,575.00	5
	2	17,214.60	

MAIN REEF (1976) by Mill Reef (USA)-Lovely Light by Henry the Seventh

	Races Won	Value £	Distances in furlongs
Bondaid [9] out of Regency Gold)	1	2,595.00	9

MAJESTIC LIGHT (USA) (1973) by Majestic Prince-Irradiate by Ribot

	Races Won	Value £	Distances in furlongs
Dayflower (USA) [3] out of Equate (USA))	1	5,024.00	10

MAJESTIC SHORE (USA) (1981) by Majestic Prince-Golden Shore by Windy Sands

	Races Won	Value £	Distances in furlongs
Noeprob (USA) [3] out of Heat Haze (USA))	1	2,070.00	6

†MANASTASH RIDGE (USA) (1986) by Seattle Slew (USA)-Summertide (USA) by Crewman

	Races Won	Value £	Distances in furlongs
Wayfarers Way (USA) [2] out of Miss Daytona (USA))	1	4,055.00	8

MANILA (USA) (1983) by Lyphard (USA)-Dona Ysidra by Le Fabuleux

	Races Won	Value £	Distances in furlongs
Darmstadt (USA) [3] out of Frau Daruma (Arg))	3	18,129.70	11 10 12
Lakab (USA) [3] out of River Lullaby (USA))	1	2,143.70	7
Manila Bay (USA) [3] out of Betty Money (USA))	1	3,465.00	10
	5	23,738.40	

MANSINGH (USA) (1969) by Jaipur-Tutasi by Native Dancer

	Races Won	Value £	Distances in furlongs
Gondo [6] out of Secret Valentine)	2	6,336.25	5 5

MARCHING ON (1974) by Tudor Melody-Procession by Sovereign Path

	Races Won	Value £	Distances in furlongs
Harry's Coming [9] out of Elegant Star)	2	4,775.00	5 5

MARFA (USA) (1980) by Foolish Pleasure (USA)-Gray Matter (USA) by Stratmat

	Races Won	Value £	Distances in furlongs
Flight Lieutenant (USA) [4] out of Lt Golden Girl (USA))	1	21,500.00	14

MARTINMAS (1969) by Silly Season-Calvine by Prince Chevalier

	Races Won	Value £	Distances in furlongs
Martinosky [7] out of Bewitched)	1	3,287.30	6

MASTER WILLIE (1977) by High Line-Fair Winter by Set Fair

	Races Won	Value £	Distances in furlongs
Athar (Ire) [4] out of Walladah (USA))	1	3,289.50	10
Karinska [3] out of Kaiserchronik (Ger))	3	10,413.00	8 6 6
Kiawah [3] out of Polly Packer)	2	5,064.00	9 11
Make A Stand [2] out of Make A Signal)	1	9,325.00	8
Master Charlie [3] out of Maryland Cookie (USA))	1	3,915.00	12
Princess Of Orange [4] out of Outward's Gal)	1	2,870.20	8
Rosietoes (USA) [5] out of Desrose)	1	2,952.00	8
Umbria [4] out of Gay Shadow)	1	2,957.50	5
Will Of Steel [4] out of Collapse)	1	7,438.56	7
Winning Line [2] out of Buckhurst)	1	3,036.00	7
	13	51,260.76	

MAZAAD (1983) by Auction Ring (USA)-Sweet Relations by Skymaster

	Races Won	Value £	Distances in furlongs
Kierchem (Ire) [2] out of Smashing Gale)	1	3,172.50	5
Mazentre Forward (Ire) [2] out of Nation's Game)	2	7,820.50	6 6
Northern Conqueror (Ire) [5] out of Gaylom)	3	7,883.70	9 10 8
Preston Guild (Ire) [3] out of Dying Craft)	3	9,348.35	12 10 10
The Happy Loon (Ire) [2] out of Skimmer)	1	3,158.00	7
	10	31,383.05	

†MAZILIER (USA) (1984) by Lyphard (USA)-Marie Curie by Exbury

	Races Won	Value £	Distances in furlongs
Crystal Magic [2] out of Thulium)	2	7,573.25	5 5

	Races Won	Value £	Distances in furlongs
Eleuthera [2] out of So It Goes)	1	2,872.90	5
	3	10,446.15	

MEADOWLAKE (USA) (1983) by Hold Your Peace (USA)-Suspicious Native by Raise A Native

	Races Won	Value £	Distances in furlongs
Meadow Pipit (Can) [4] out of Delta Slew (USA))	4	25,135.50	8 7 10 10

MELDRUM (1966) by Hard Sauce-Ruffino by Como

	Races Won	Value £	Distances in furlongs
Mellottie [8] out of Lottie Lehmann)	2	20,830.50	8 8

MELYNO (1979) by Nonoalco (USA)-Comely(Fr) by Boran

	Races Won	Value £	Distances in furlongs
Mizyan (Ire) [5] out of Maid Of Erin (USA))	1	2,601.40	14
No Submission (USA) [7] out of Creeping Kate (USA))	1	3,757.50	8
	2	6,358.90	

†MERDON MELODY (1983) by Mummy's Pet-Singing by Petingo

	Races Won	Value £	Distances in furlongs
Kerrie-Jo [2] out of Whipalash)	1	2,820.00	6
Link Miles [2] out of Donna Pavlova)	2	8,944.50	7 7
	3	11,764.50	

MIDYAN (USA) (1984) by Miswaki (USA)-Country Dream (USA) by Ribot

	Races Won	Value £	Distances in furlongs
Alhijaz [4] out of Nawara)	1	35,325.00	8
Amidst [2] out of Aspark)	2	8,092.50	6 6
Baliana [3] out of Okosan (USA))	1	3,084.75	6
Barley Cake [3] out of Fancy Flight (Fr))	2	4,060.70	9 10
Beauchamp Hero [3] out of Buss)	2	26,932.00	8 8
Forthwith [3] out of Top Society)	2	17,814.00	10 10
Fourforfun [3] out of Jennyjo)	5	28,140.25	6 7 7 8 8
Indian Dreamer [2] out of Cool Combination)	2	6,932.70	5 5
Midnight Magpie (Ire) [2] out of Mirabiliary (USA))	1	2,406.00	6
Midyan Blue (Ire) [3] out of Jarretiere)	2	10,066.50	10 12
Saihat (Ire) [2] out of Lone Bidder)	2	7,100.50	6 7
Sheriff [2] out of Daisy Warwick (USA))	1	2,900.00	7
Southern Power (Ire) [2] out of Tap The Line)	1	4,199.25	7
Stelloso [2] out of Follow The Stars)	1	4,092.00	6

	Races Won	Value £	Distances in furlongs
Tioman Island [3] out of Catch The Sun)	3	17,767.50	10 12 14
	28	178,913.65	

MILLFONTAINE (1980) by Mill Reef (USA)-Mortefontaine by Polic

	Races Won	Value £	Distances in furlongs
Millsolin (Ire) [5] out of Isolin)	1	4,709.25	6
The Ordinary Girl (Ire) [3] out of Saulonika)	1	2,238.00	5
	2	6,947.25	

MISTER MAJESTIC (1984) by Tumble Wind (USA)-Our Village by Ballymore

	Races Won	Value £	Distances in furlongs
I'm A Dreamer (Ire) [3] out of Lady Wise)	2	5,659.80	10 10
Volunteer Point (Ire) [3] out of Lola Sharp)	1	2,427.00	12
	3	8,086.80	

MISWAKI (USA) (1978) by Mr Prospector (USA)-Hopespringseternal (USA) by Buckpasser

	Races Won	Value £	Distances in furlongs
Daswaki (Can) [5] out of Nice Manners (Can))	2	8,685.50	8 7
Knave's Ash (USA) [2] out of Quiet Rendezvous (USA))	1	4,163.50	6
Potsclose [2] out of Starr Danias (USA))	1	4,449.50	6
Waki Gold (USA) [6] out of Sainte Croix (USA))	1	2,469.00	9
	5	19,767.50	

MOMENT OF HOPE (USA) (1983) by Timeless Moment (USA)-Careless Moment (USA) by Baffle

	Races Won	Value £	Distances in furlongs
In A Moment (USA) [2] out of Teenage Fling (USA))	1	3,231.00	6

MONTELIMAR (USA) (1981) by Alleged (USA)-L'Extravagante by Le Fabuleux

	Races Won	Value £	Distances in furlongs
Westfield Moves (Ire) [5] out of Rathcoffey Daisy)	1	3,348.00	9

†MOST WELCOME (1984) by Be My Guest (USA)-Topsy by Habitat

	Races Won	Value £	Distances in furlongs
Comeonup [2] out of Scarlet Veil)	1	2,579.00	6
Primost [2] out of Primulette)	1	2,469.00	5
Response [2] out of Knavesmire)	1	3,054.20	9
Sandmoor Chambray [2] out of Valadon)	1	3,947.50	7
Tzu'mu [2] out of Sassalya)	1	5,708.50	6
	5	17,758.20	

MOVE OFF (1973) by Farm Walk-Darling Do by Derring-Do

	Races Won	Value £	Distances in furlongs
Browned Off [4] out of Jenifer Browning)	1	3,236.00	7
Hob Green [4] out of Prejudice)	1	11,452.50	6
	2	14,688.50	

MR PROSPECTOR (USA) (1970) by Raise A Native-Gold Digger by Nashua

	Races Won	Value £	Distances in furlongs
Bashayer (USA) [3] out of Height Of Fashion (Fr))	1	5,346.40	7
Felawnah (USA) [3] out of Ambassador Of Luck (USA))	1	4,084.50	10
Half Term (USA) [3] out of Six Months Long (USA))	2	9,225.00	6 7
Kingmambo (USA) [3] out of Miesque (USA))	1	116,334.60	8
Mujaazafah (USA) [3] out of Cope Of Flowers (USA))	1	3,728.25	8
Placerville (USA) [3] out of Classy Cathy (USA))	2	67,147.80	9 10
Princess Haifa (USA) [3] out of South Sea Dancer (USA))	1	3,552.75	8
Simaat (USA) [3] out of Satiety (USA))	1	3,435.75	8
	10	212,855.05	

MTOTO (1983) by Busted-Amazer by Mincio

	Races Won	Value £	Distances in furlongs
Aljazzaf [3] out of Ibtisamm (USA))	2	12,673.25	10 11
Beaming [2] out of Glancing)	1	4,342.25	5
Fabulous Mtoto [3] out of El Fabulous (Fr))	1	3,590.00	10
Nahlati (Ire) [3] out of Formido)	1	2,243.00	9
Rispoto [3] out of River Spey)	1	2,444.60	12
Sehailah [3] out of Fabulous Rina (Fr))	1	3,289.50	7
Serotina (Ire) [3] out of Northshiel)	1	2,556.60	9
Sumoto [3] out of Soemba)	1	3,406.50	7
Tahdid [3] out of Yaqut (USA))	3	14,365.25	8 7 7
	12	48,910.95	

MUMMY'S GAME (1979) by Mummy's Pet-Final Game by Pardao

	Races Won	Value £	Distances in furlongs
Calisar [3] out of Maycrest)	2	4,729.50	7 6
Nellie's Gamble [3] out of Harmonious Sound)	2	5,219.50	7 8
Oubeck [3] out of School Road)	1	3,406.50	6
Side Bar [3] out of Joli's Girl)	1	2,057.50	14
Sonderise [4] out of Demderise)	1	3,816.00	5
Spectacle Jim [4] out of Welsh Blossom)	1	2,532.00	5
	8	21,761.00	

MUSCATITE (1980) by Habitat-Takette by Takawalk II

	Races Won	Value £	Distances in furlongs
Sinclair Lad (Ire) [5] out of Kitty Frisk)	1	2,658.00	10

MUSIC BOY (1973) by Jukebox-Veronique by Matador

	Races Won	Value £	Distances in furlongs
Antonia's Folly [2] out of Royal Agnes)	1	3,915.00	5
Daily Star [2] out of Kala Rosa)	1	2,070.00	6
Eighteen Twelve [2] out of Glowing Report)	1	2,967.40	5
Food Of Love [5] out of Shortbread)	1	2,238.20	5
Fylde Flyer [4] out of Djimbaran Bay)	1	4,980.80	6
Glen Miller [3] out of Blakeney Sound)	2	5,265.00	7 7
Hannah's Music [2] out of Pink Mex)	2	7,764.20	5 5
Monkey Music [2] out of Low Dalby)	1	3,523.50	5
Music Dancer [4] out of Stepping Gaily)	1	2,847.00	7
Purple Fling [2] out of Divine Fling)	1	3,006.50	5
Rhythmic Dancer [5] out of Stepping Gaily)	1	3,260.25	5
Saddam The Log [2] out of Sallytude)	1	2,880.00	5
Scored Again [3] out of Thorner Lane)	1	2,434.00	5
Stephensons Rocket [2] out of Martian Princess)	1	2,851.25	5
	16	50,003.10	

MY DAD TOM (USA) (1979) by My Dad George (USA)-His Lady Fair by Tom Fool

	Races Won	Value £	Distances in furlongs
Head Turner [5] out of Top Tina)	2	6,842.50	13 14
Izitallworthit [4] out of Torlonia)	1	1,725.00	11
	3	8,567.50	

MY GENERATION (1983) by Young Generation-High Finale by High Line

	Races Won	Value £	Distances in furlongs
Mr M-E-N (Ire) [2] out of Mallabee)	3	15,641.00	5 6 6

MYJINSKI (USA) (1982) by Nijinsky(Can)-English Silver by Mongo

	Races Won	Value £	Distances in furlongs
Ballerina Bay [5] out of Lady Seville)	1	3,318.75	7

	Races Won	Value £	Distances in furlongs
Bells Of Longwick [4] out of Bells Of St Martin)	1	4,622.25	5
	2	7,941.00	

NAEVUS (USA) (1980) by Mr Prospector (USA)-Mudville (USA) by Bold Lad (USA)

	Races Won	Value £	Distances in furlongs
Hilary Gerrard (USA) [3] out of Firm Lady (USA))	1	3,377.25	7

NASHAMAA (1983) by Ahonoora-Balidaress by Balidar

	Races Won	Value £	Distances in furlongs
Kingswell Prince (Ire) [2] out of Amtico)	1	3,054.20	6
Nonios (Ire) [2] out of Bosquet)	2	6,763.60	6 6
Norling (Ire) [3] out of Now Then)	2	4,143.00	5 5
	5	13,960.80	

†NASHWAN (USA) (1986) by Blushing Groom (Fr)-Height of Fashion (Fr) by Bustino

	Races Won	Value £	Distances in furlongs
Golden Nashwan (Ire) [2] out of Music And Dance (USA))	1	4,932.00	7
Muwafik [2] out of Ashayer (USA))	1	4,698.00	10
Uncle Oswald [2] out of Riviere Bleue)	1	4,435.00	8
	3	14,065.00	

NATROUN (FR) (1984) by Akarad(Fr)-Niece Divine by Great Nephew

	Races Won	Value £	Distances in furlongs
Amaze [4] out of Entrancing)	1	4,962.75	8

†NESHAD (USA) (1984) by Sharpen Up-Nasseem (Fr) by Zeddaan

	Races Won	Value £	Distances in furlongs
Palacegate Jack (Ire) [2] out of Pasadena Lady)	3	21,001.00	5 5 6

NEVER SO BOLD (1980) by Bold Lad(Ire)-Never Never Land by Habitat

	Races Won	Value £	Distances in furlongs
Big Sky [3] out of Messaria)	1	4,347.00	6
Bold Acre [3] out of Nicola Wynn)	1	3,622.50	8
Bold Lez [6] out of Classy Nancy (USA))	2	8,712.90	6 5
Bold Melody [4] out of Broken Melody)	1	1,051.00	9
Bold Seven (Ire) [3] out of First Blush)	1	2,489.40	6
Bold Timing [2] out of Brilliant Timing (USA))	1	4,125.40	6
Born To Be [4] out of Beryl's Jewel)	1	5,435.50	5
Braveboy [5] out of Relkina (Fr))	1	7,564.00	7
Brown Carpet [6] out of Geopelia)	1	2,232.50	8
Certificate-X [2] out of Screenable (USA))	2	5,318.00	5 5
Ever So Lyrical [3] out of Lyra)	1	3,933.00	8
Lamsonetti [3] out of Orient)	1	2,739.00	7
Pluck [3] out of Tahilla)	1	3,882.50	6
So Intrepid (Ire) [3] out of Double River (USA))	1	3,687.50	6
	16	59,140.20	

NICHOLAS BILL (1975) by High Line-Centro by Vienna

	Races Won	Value £	Distances in furlongs
Bilberry [4] out of Snow Tribe)	1	3,235.50	14
Biloela [3] out of Maple Syrup)	1	3,348.00	10
Just Bill [2] out of Petiller)	1	2,200.50	7
Stay With Me Baby [3] out of Uranus)	1	3,366.00	8
Will Soon [4] out of Henceforth)	1	2,860.75	7
	5	15,010.75	

NIGHT SHIFT (USA) (1980) by Northern Dancer-Ciboulette by Chop Chop

	Races Won	Value £	Distances in furlongs
Azhar [3] out of Aunt Jemima)	4	27,289.50	12 11 12 12
Barboukh [3] out of Turban)	2	16,154.70	8 8
Baskerville [2] out of Bay Bay)	1	3,557.50	5
Broughtons Formula [3] out of Forward Rally)	1	3,366.00	10
Duty Time [2] out of Moorish Idol)	2	10,583.50	7 8
Glimpse [2] out of Lovers Light)	1	4,464.00	6
Here Comes A Star [5] out of Rapidus)	1	3,080.00	5
Jaazim [3] out of Mesmerize)	1	2,595.00	6
Jacob Bogdani [2] out of Green's Collection)	1	4,378.00	5
Just Happy (USA) [2] out of Mesmerize)	1	3,551.50	6
Master Planner [4] out of Shaky Puddin)	2	20,099.20	6 6
Midnight Legend [2] out of Myth)	1	4,092.00	8
Moon Spin [4] out of Hors Serie (USA))	4	14,498.95	9 8 8 8
Mujawab [3] out of False Front)	2	7,472.50	10 11
Nessun Dorma [3] out of Scala Di Seta)	2	7,878.00	7 10
News And Echo (USA) [2] out of Assisi)	1	7,700.70	7
Nicolotte [2] out of Nicoletta)	2	9,102.75	7 7
Night Edition [3] out of New Chant (Can))	2	4,706.50	10 12
Night Melody (Ire) [3] out of Quaver)	3	12,337.25	5 6 7

	Races Won	Value £	Distances in furlongs
Nightitude [2] out of Rectitude)	1	5,253.50	5
Oare Sparrow [3] out of Portvasco)	1	3,611.25	7
Ricky's Tornado (Ire) [4] out of Fodens Eve)	1	3,370.50	5
Themaam [4] out of Polly's Pear (USA))	1	3,131.90	8
	38	182,274.70	

NIJINSKY (CAN) (1967) by Northern Dancer-Flaming Page by Bull Page

	Races Won	Value £	Distances in furlongs
Arkaan (USA) [3] out of It's In The Air (USA))	1	4,793.75	10
Cascassi (USA) [3] out of Cacti (USA))	1	3,523.50	9
Haunted Wood (USA) [3] out of Fairy Footsteps)	1	3,348.00	12
Mashaallah (USA) [5] out of Homespun (USA))	1	7,270.00	11
Nimphidia (USA) [2] out of Absentia (USA))	1	3,406.50	6
Palace Pageant (USA) [3] out of Crown Treasure (USA))	1	3,318.75	8
Princess Borghese (USA) [3] out of Molly Moon (Fr))	1	3,915.00	10
Sharjah (USA) [3] out of Office Wife (USA))	1	9,472.20	10
Vratislav (USA) [4] out of Mizima (USA))	1	2,814.00	10
Winged Victory (USA) [3] out of Wedding Picture (USA))	1	10,308.75	11
	10	52,170.45	

NINISKI (USA) (1976) by Nijinsky(Can)-Virginia Hills by Tom Rolfe

	Races Won	Value £	Distances in furlongs
Alflora (Ire) [4] out of Adrana)	2	57,818.95	7 8
Assessor (Ire) [4] out of Dingle Bay)	2	69,399.00	13 18
Coigach [2] out of Rynechra)	1	4,485.25	8
Discord [7] out of Apple Peel)	2	11,161.00	14 13
Faugeron [4] out of Miss Longchamp)	1	4,815.00	12
Hoosie [3] out of Hooked Bid (Can))	1	2,847.00	14
Mondragon [3] out of La Lutine)	2	5,540.00	16 13
Pembridge Place [2] out of Rose D'Amour (USA))	1	5,253.50	7
Snow Board [4] out of Troja)	1	6,400.00	18
	13	167,719.70	

NISHAPOUR (FR) (1975) by Zeddaan-Alama by Aureole

	Races Won	Value £	Distances in furlongs
Karachi [3] out of Lady Dacre)	2	6,374.25	10 11

	Races Won	Value £	Distances in furlongs
Moonlight Quest [5] out of Arabian Rose (USA))	3	11,296.60	12 12 12
Mr Vincent [3] out of Brush Away)	2	5,854.25	6 8
Shynon [3] out of Sunset Ray)	3	10,640.50	12 13 14
	10	34,165.60	

NO PASS NO SALE (1982) by Northfields (USA)-No Disgrace by Djakao

	Races Won	Value £	Distances in furlongs
Imperial Bid (Fr) [5] out of Tzaritsa (USA))	3	8,055.50	9 10 11

NOALTO (1978) by Nonoalco (USA)-Lyrical by Gratitude

	Races Won	Value £	Distances in furlongs
Bunty Boo [4] out of Klairove)	1	3,720.00	5
Rise Up Singing [5] out of Incarnadine)	2	9,659.50	7 7
	3	13,379.50	

NODOUBLE (USA) (1965) by Noholme II-Abla-Jay by Double Jay

	Races Won	Value £	Distances in furlongs
Rodeo Star (USA) [7] out of Roundup Rose (USA))	2	35,075.00	16 18

NOMINATION (1983) by Dominion-Rivers Maid by Rarity

	Races Won	Value £	Distances in furlongs
Admiring [2] out of Adriya)	1	2,259.00	6
Charisma Girl [2] out of My Ginny)	1	2,070.00	5
Culsyth Flyer [2] out of Polly Worth)	2	4,644.00	5 6
Gadge [2] out of Queenstyle)	1	11,647.50	6
Gone Savage [5] out of Trwyn Cilan)	1	2,843.00	5
Lucky Fourteen [2] out of Lucky Saran)	1	2,365.10	5
Magication [3] out of Gundreda)	1	2,684.50	6
Plum First [3] out of Plum Bold)	1	5,117.00	5
Star Speeder (Ire) [2] out of M Twenty Five)	2	6,039.00	5 7
	11	39,669.10	

NORDANCE (USA) (1982) by Danzig (USA)-Sister Shu (USA) by Nashua

	Races Won	Value £	Distances in furlongs
Nobby Barnes [4] out of Loving Doll)	2	8,522.00	8 8
Northern Bailiwick (Ire) [2] out of Alpine Dance (USA))	1	1,725.00	7
Orange Place (Ire) [2] out of Little Red Hut)	2	5,271.75	7 7
	5	15,518.75	

NORDICO (USA) (1981) by Northern Dancer-Kennelot by Gallant Man

	Races Won	Value £	Distances in furlongs
Alpine Skier (Ire) [2] out of Heather Lil)	1	5,663.00	7

	Races Won	Value £	Distances in furlongs
Bentico [4] out of Bentinck Hotel)	3	9,326.50	10 10 10
Lochore [3] out of Hound Song)	1	2,269.13	8
Love Of The North (Ire) [2] out of Avec L'amour)	1	2,070.00	7
Moving Image (Ire) [3] out of Aunty Eileen)	1	2,950.60	5
Nordico Princess [2] out of Try Vickers (USA))	1	4,092.00	6
Rooftop Flyer (Ire) [2] out of Audenhove (Ger))	1	4,378.00	6
Rose Flyer (Ire) [3] out of String Of Straw)	1	1,548.00	7
Velasco (Ire) [3] out of Donnarella)	2	6,627.40	8 8
	12	38,924.63	

†NORTHERN FLAGSHIP (USA) (1986) by Northern Dancer-Native Partner (USA) by Raise A Native

	Races Won	Value £	Distances in furlongs
Make A Note (USA) [2] out of Deep Powder (USA))	2	7,404.95	7 8

NORTHERN FLING (USA) (1970) by Northern Dancer-Impetuous Lady by Hasty Road

	Races Won	Value £	Distances in furlongs
Dramanice (USA) [3] out of Almost Pure (USA))	1	3,523.50	8

NORTHERN JOVE (CAN) (1968) by Northern Dancer-Junonia by Sun Again

	Races Won	Value £	Distances in furlongs
Star Goddess (USA) [4] out of Sonseri)	1	3,201.75	7

NORTHERN STATE (USA) (1985) by Northern Dancer-South Ocean(Can) by New Providence

	Races Won	Value £	Distances in furlongs
Alaskan Heir [2] out of Royal Meeting)	1	3,552.75	7
Warm Spell [3] out of Warm Wind)	3	9,381.25	10 12 12
	4	12,934.00	

NORTHERN TEMPEST (USA) (1981) by Northern Jove(Can)-Extreme Turbulence by Swaps

	Races Won	Value £	Distances in furlongs
Tommy Tempest [4] out of Silently Yours (USA))	1	2,924.00	5

NORTHFIELDS (USA) (1968) by Northern Dancer-Little Hut by Occupy

	Races Won	Value £	Distances in furlongs
Aitch N'bee [10] out of Hot Case)	1	3,028.00	7

NORTHIAM (USA) (1981) by Northern Dancer-Lady Rebecca by Sir Ivor

	Races Won	Value £	Distances in furlongs
Lady Phyl [2] out of Phyl)	1	3,720.00	6

	Races Won	Value £	Distances in furlongs
Leap Of Faith (Ire) [2] out of Greek Music)	2	3,082.00	5 5
Selhurstpark Flyer (Ire) [2] out of Wisdom To Know)	4	23,249.00	5 5 5 5
Syabas (Ire) [2] out of Song Of The Glens)	1	3,183.70	7
	8	33,234.70	

NORTHJET (1977) by Northfields (USA)-Jellatina by Fortino II

	Races Won	Value £	Distances in furlongs
Good Hand (USA) [7] out of Ribonette (USA))	2	14,195.80	16 16

NORTHROP (USA) (1979) by Northern Dancer-Sand Buggy by Warfare

	Races Won	Value £	Distances in furlongs
Northern Graduate (USA) [4] out of Lady Blackfoot)	5	22,122.65	12 9 12 13 12

NORWICK (USA) (1979) by Far North(Can)-Shay Sheery by A Dragon Killer

	Races Won	Value £	Distances in furlongs
Charlie Bigtime [3] out of Sea Aura)	1	3,084.75	8
Miss Vaxette [4] out of Langton Herring)	3	16,998.50	5 5 5
Neither Nor [4] out of Leap In Time)	3	11,757.00	6 7 6
Norstock [6] out of Millingdale)	1	2,611.00	16
	8	34,451.25	

NUREYEV (USA) (1977) by Northern Dancer-Special (USA) by Forli(Arg)

	Races Won	Value £	Distances in furlongs
Concordial (USA) [2] out of Louisville (Fr))	2	17,764.00	7 6
King's Signet (USA) [4] out of Sigy (Fr))	3	71,050.00	5 6 5
Mehthaaf (USA) [2] out of Elle Seule (USA))	1	4,110.50	6
Nafuth (USA) [3] out of Costly Array (USA))	1	3,172.50	7
Shalbourne (USA) [2] out of Copperama (Aus))	1	4,175.00	7
Wild Planet (USA) [2] out of Ivory Wings (USA))	1	4,464.00	6
Wolfhound (USA) [4] out of Lassie Dear (USA))	1	81,701.00	6
	10	186,437.00	

OATS (1973) by Northfields (USA)-Arctic Lace by Arctic Chevalier

	Races Won	Value £	Distances in furlongs
Flakey Dove [7] out of Shadey Dove)	1	3,816.00	14

ORCHESTRA (1974) by Tudor Music-Golden Moss by Sheshoon

	Races Won	Value £	Distances in furlongs
Jokist [10] out of What A Picture)	1	3,015.00	6

	Races Won	Value £	Distances in furlongs
Lombard Ships [6] out of Tina's Star)	2	5,080.40	8 8
	3	8,095.40	

PANCHO VILLA (USA) (1982) by Secretariat (USA)-Crimson Saint by Crimson Satan

	Races Won	Value £	Distances in furlongs
Panchellita (USA) [4] out of Counselor's Pride (USA))	3	9,308.80	7 7 6

PENNINE WALK (1982) by Persian Bold-Tifrums by Thatch (USA)

	Races Won	Value £	Distances in furlongs
Halham Tarn (Ire) [3] out of Nouniya)	2	5,685.00	10 12
Nicer (Ire) [3] out of Everything Nice)	1	9,662.50	8
Penny Banger (Ire) [3] out of High Explosive)	5	14,235.80	7 7 7 7 7
	8	29,583.30	

PERSIAN BOLD (1975) by Bold Lad(Ire)-Relkarunner by Relko

	Races Won	Value £	Distances in furlongs
American Hero [5] out of American Winter (USA))	1	4,077.50	12
Bold Stroke [4] out of Fariha)	1	7,985.20	9
Boloardo [4] out of Northshiel)	1	4,747.40	8
Caspian Beluga [5] out of Miss Thames)	1	3,652.00	9
Elaine Tully (Ire) [5] out of Hanna Alta (Fr))	1	3,260.25	13
Fairy Story (Ire) [3] out of Certain Story)	2	12,465.25	7 7
Jazilah (Fr) [5] out of Muznah)	2	7,980.00	9 10
Lijaam (Ire) [3] out of Etoile de Nuit)	1	3,406.50	12
Matila (Ire) [3] out of Peace Girl)	1	3,655.00	6
Olicana (Ire) [3] out of Maniusha)	1	2,579.00	8
Persiansky (Ire) [3] out of Astra Adastra)	4	13,292.85	7 8 8 8
Stash The Cash (Ire) [2] out of Noble Girl)	1	3,810.00	8
Thundering [8] out of Am Stretchin' (USA))	1	2,623.80	8
	18	73,534.75	

PERSIAN HEIGHTS (1985) by Persian Bold-Ready And Willing by Reliance II

	Races Won	Value £	Distances in furlongs
Bumaan (Ire) [2] out of Hufoof)8	1	4,413.75	7
Kezio Rufo (Ire) [2] out of Kashapour)	1	3,285.00	7
Lake Poopo (Ire) [3] out of Bolivia (Ger))	2	7,618.75	13 15
Midnight Heights [3] out of Midnight Music)	3	11,884.25	8 8 10
Pearly Mist (Ire) [3] out of Silent Movie)	1	3,611.25	10
Persian Affair (Ire) [2] out of Lady Chesterfield (USA))	1	3,676.00	7
Persian Brave (Ire) [3] out of Commanche Belle)	2	11,510.40	10 10
Persian Elite (Ire) [2] out of Late Sally)	1	3,465.00	7
Soba Up [3] out of Soba)	1	4,630.00	10
	13	54,094.40	

PETONG (1980) by Mansingh (USA)-Iridium by Linacre

	Races Won	Value £	Distances in furlongs
Barbezieux [6] out of Merchantmens Girl)	2	6,108.50	5 5
Best Kept Secret [2] out of Glenfield Portion)	3	9,326.75	5 5 5
Brookhead Lady [2] out of Lewista)	3	7,337.80	5 6 6
Diwali Dancer [3] out of Dawn Dance (USA))	1	2,929.50	7
Educated Pet [4] out of School Road)	2	7,606.50	5 6
Indian Crystal [2] out of Gentle Gypsy)	1	3,027.50	5
Jade Pet [2] out of Pea Green)	2	7,019.25	5 5
Kingchip Boy [4] out of Silk St James)	3	11,573.00	8 7 8
Norman Warrior [4] out of Petulengra)	1	2,965.00	8
Palacegate Touch [3] out of Dancing Chimes)	4	14,163.06	6 6 6 7
Paris House [4] out of Foudroyer)	2	55,557.00	5 5
Petardia [3] out of What A Pet)	1	8,019.60	7
Petonellajill [3] out of Crackerjill)	1	3,980.00	7
Petula [2] out of Daffodil Fields)	2	12,747.80	5 5
Rain Splash [3] out of Bargouzine)	1	3,752.50	6
Smart Pet [2] out of Petriece)	2	10,965.00	5 5
Sweet Whisper [2] out of Softly Spoken)	1	2,243.00	5
Ttyfran [3] out of So It Goes)	1	2,679.00	12
Tutu Sixtysix [2] out of Odilese)	2	6,765.75	5 5
	35	178,766.51	

PETORIUS (1981) by Mummy's Pet-The Stork by Club House

	Races Won	Value £	Distances in furlongs
Amazing Feat (Ire) [4] out of Mountain Chase)	2	11,847.55	7 7
Battle Colours (Ire) [4] out of Streamertail)	2	6,128.10	8 8
Co Pilot (Ire) [2] out of Turbo Rose)	1	3,626.00	6
Corals Dream (Ire) [4] out of Walkyria)	3	17,939.20	7 7 7
Gold Surprise (Ire) [4] out of Gold Piece)	1	1,702.00	11
Jade Vale [4] out of Deja Vu (Fr))	3	14,388.00	8 8 8

	Races Won	Value £	Distances in furlongs
Once More For Luck (Ire) [2] out of Mrs Lucky)	2	5,518.00	5 8
Pete Afrique (Ire) [2] out of Noir Afrique)	2	9,135.80	6 5
Petraco (Ire) [5] out of Merrie Moira)	1	2,831.50	6
Segala (Ire) [2] out of Cerosia)	1	2,005.00	6
Storm Ship (Ire) [2] out of Selham)	1	4,142.50	6
	19	79,263.65	

PETOSKI (1982) by Niniski (USA)-Sushila by Petingo

	Races Won	Value £	Distances in furlongs
Buckski Echo [3] out of Echoing)	1	2,427.00	6
Gloriette [2] out of Reflected Glory (Swe))	1	3,049.40	7
New Inn [2] out of Pitroyal)	1	2,406.00	7
Peto [4] out of Rimosa's Pet)	1	3,294.00	8
Pickles [5] out of Kashmiri Snow)	1	1,770.00	12
Rafter-J [2] out of Coming Out)	1	2,905.00	6
	6	15,851.40	

PHARLY (FR) (1974) by Lyphard (USA)-Comely(Fr) by Boran

	Races Won	Value £	Distances in furlongs
Cast The Line [3] out of Off The Reel (USA))	1	1,380.00	12
Crime Ofthecentury [3] out of Crime Of Passion)	2	5,957.65	5 5
Eurythmic [3] out of Amalancher (USA))	1	3,272.50	11
Further Flight [7] out of Flying Nelly)	2	31,690.00	15 16
Milngavie (Ire) [3] out of Wig And Gown)	2	6,189.20	8 11
Monarda [6] out of Emaline (Fr))	3	11,296.10	16 14 16
Pharamineux [7] out of Miss Longchamp)	1	4,455.00	14
Pharly Dancer [4] out of Martin-Lavell Mail)	1	2,769.30	12
Pharoah's Guest [6] out of Exuberine (Fr))	1	3,416.80	14
Shuttlecock [2] out of Upper Sister)	1	1,605.50	7
Taroudant [6] out of Melbourne Miss)	4	12,815.50	16 16 14 16
White River [7] out of Regain)	1	3,366.00	14
	20	88,213.55	

PHONE TRICK (USA) (1982) by Clever Trick (USA)-Over The Phone (USA) by Finnegan

	Races Won	Value £	Distances in furlongs
Lucky Message (USA) [2] out of How Fortunate (USA))	1	2,898.00	5

POLISH NAVY (USA) (1984) by Danzig (USA)-Navsup (USA) by Tatan (Arg)

	Races Won	Value £	Distances in furlongs
Astern (USA) [3] out of Casual (USA))	1	3,523.50	8
Blaze Away (USA) [2] out of Battle Drum (USA))	2	8,794.75	7 8
	3	12,318.25	

†POLISH PRECEDENT (USA) (1986) by Danzig (USA)-Past Example (USA) by Buckpasser

	Races Won	Value £	Distances in furlongs
Convoy Point (Ire) [2] out of Mahabba (USA))	1	4,270.75	8
Highly Fashionable (Ire) [2] out of Circulate)	1	3,201.75	7
Waiting [2] out of Just You Wait)	1	4,175.00	7
	3	11,647.50	

PORT ETIENNE (FR) (1983) by Mill Reef (USA)-Sierra Morena(Ity) by Canisbay

	Races Won	Value £	Distances in furlongs
Kadastrof (Fr) [3] out of Kadastra (Fr))	1	3,640.50	14

†POSEN (USA) (1985) by Danzig (USA)-Michelle Mon Amour (USA) by Best Turn (USA)

	Races Won	Value £	Distances in furlongs
Imposing Groom (Ire) [2] out of Beechwood (USA))	1	2,782.50	7

POSSE (USA) (1977) by Forli(Arg)-In Hot Pursuit by Bold Ruler

	Races Won	Value £	Distances in furlongs
Linpac West [7] out of North Page (Fr))	1	20,439.00	12

PRECOCIOUS (1981) by Mummy's Pet-Mrs Moss by Reform

	Races Won	Value £	Distances in furlongs
Allthruthenight (Ire) [4] out of Time For Pleasure)	1	4,624.75	5
Elbio [6] out of Maganyos (Hun))	1	60,361.20	5
Essayeffsee [4] out of Floreal)	2	4,660.60	10 10
Euro Festival [4] out of Quisissanno)	1	3,728.25	7
Jobie [3] out of Lingering)	1	3,395.00	6
Prenonamoss [5] out of Nonabella)	1	6,258.00	8
Simmie's Special [5] out of Zalatia)	1	6,254.50	5
Tahitian [4] out of Pacificus (USA))	1	3,080.00	10
Willshe Gan [3] out of Quisissanno)	1	3,420.00	7
	10	95,782.30	

PRESIDIUM (1982) by General Assembly (USA)-Doubly Sure by Reliance II

	Races Won	Value £	Distances in furlongs
Kildee Lad [3] out of National Time (USA))	1	4,175.00	5

	Races Won	Value £	Distances in furlongs
Knayton Lass [2] out of Sister Hannah)	1	3,377.25	5
Madame Gregoire [2] out of Laleston)	1	2,924.70	5
Mighty Forum [2] out of Mighty Flash)	1	3,184.00	7
Moscow Road [2] out of Missish)	3	9,137.25	5 5 5
True Precision [3] out of Madam Muffin)	2	27,994.50	5 6
	9	50,792.70	

PRIMITIVE RISING (USA) (1984) by Raise A Man (USA)-Periquito (USA) by Olden Times

	Races Won	Value £	Distances in furlongs
Nutty Brown [3] out of Nuthill)	1	2,412.70	8
Pat's Splendour [2] out of Northern Venture)	1	2,243.00	6
	2	4,655.70	

PRIMO DOMINIE (1982) by Dominion-Swan Ann by My Swanee

	Races Won	Value £	Distances in furlongs
Awestruck [3] out of Magic Kingdom)	1	3,172.50	8
Battling Blue [2] out of Ethel Knight)	1	3,415.00	5
Bid For Blue [2] out of Single Bid)	2	13,991.25	5 5
Dancing Domino [3] out of Waltz)	5	13,122.50	7 7 8 8 8
Domino Queen (Ire) [2] out of The Queen Of Soul)	1	3,285.00	5
El Arz [3] out of Zinzi)	1	3,850.00	5
Eternal Flame [5] out of Cameroun)	1	3,004.60	7
Fighter Squadron [4] out of Formidable Dancer)	1	4,793.75	7
First Option [3] out of Merrywren)	2	5,589.50	5 5
First Play [3] out of School Concert)	1	3,172.50	6
First Trump [2] out of Valika)	5	145,395.95	6 6 6 6 6
First Veil [3] out of Valika)	1	3,707.50	7
Hyde's Happy Hour [3] out of Ixia)	1	2,736.00	10
Jolis Absent [3] out of Jolimo)	1	2,511.80	11
Magic Orb [3] out of Tricky)	3	15,144.75	5 5 5
One On One [2] out of Number One Lady)	2	5,663.60	6 6
Pay Homage [5] out of Embraceable Slew (USA))	3	39,790.00	8 8 8
Powerful Edge [4] out of Sharp Castan)	2	7,256.50	7 6
Prairie Grove [3] out of Fairy Fans)	2	5,535.00	6 7
Prima Silk [2] out of Silk St James)	2	5,985.00	5 6
Primo Stampari [2] out of Balatina)	1	4,556.75	5
Sense Of Priority [4] out of Sense Of Pride)	1	2,490.00	5
Smiles Ahead [5] out of Baby's Smile)	1	2,070.00	12
Supreme Master [3] out of French Surprise)	3	13,977.00	12 12 12
Winsome Wooster [2] out of Bertrade)	1	3,454.00	5
	45	317,670.45	

PRINCE RAGUSA (1981) by English Prince-Trapani by Ragusa

	Races Won	Value £	Distances in furlongs
Kagram Queen [5] out of Arodstown Alice)	2	5,561.70	10 11

PRINCE RUPERT (FR) (1984) by Prince Tenderfoot (USA)-Carrozzella (USA) by Vaguely Noble

	Races Won	Value £	Distances in furlongs
Raggerty (Ire) [3] out of Princess Martina)	2	4,643.00	8 10

PRINCE SABO (1982) by Young Generation-Jubilee Song by Song

	Races Won	Value £	Distances in furlongs
Asterix [5] out of Gentle Gael)	2	6,005.50	6 6
Bodari [4] out of City Link Rose)	2	8,578.75	5 5
Carrie Kool [2] out of Loredana)	1	3,054.20	5
Dokkha Oyston (Ire) [5] out of I Don't Mind)	3	8,016.65	6 6 5
Lady Sabo [4] out of Nice Lady)	1	2,243.00	6
Little Beaut [2] out of Ceramic (USA))	1	3,590.00	6
Little Saboteur [4] out of Shoot To Win (Fr))	1	2,880.50	5
Lyndon's Linnet [5] out of Miss Rossi)	1	3,582.50	5
Prince Songline [3] out of Question Mark)	1	3,557.50	6
Royal Insignia [2] out of Stinging Nettle)	2	18,299.50	5 6
Sabo The Hero [3] out of Daima)	2	4,809.50	5 5
Storm Regent [2] out of Bread 'n Honey)	1	3,566.25	6
	18	68,183.85	

†PRIVATE TERMS (USA) (1985) by Private Account (USA)-Laughter (USA) by Bold Ruler

	Races Won	Value £	Distances in furlongs
Venta de Possa (USA) [2] out of Steady Wind (USA))	1	3,746.50	7

PROCIDA (USA) (1981) by Mr Prospector (USA)-With Distinction by Distinctive

	Races Won	Value £	Distances in furlongs
Mr Geneaology (USA) [3] out of Que Mona (USA))	3	8,254.10	12 11 13
Tanagome (USA) [3] out of Tasha Two (USA))	1	3,201.75	6
	4	11,455.85	

RABDAN (1977) by Bold Lad(Ire)-Bualim by Khalkis

	Races Won	Value £	Distances in furlongs
Little Hooligan [2] out of Nutwood Emma)	1	2,243.00	6

	Races Won	Value £	Distances in furlongs

RAFT (USA) (1981) by Nodouble (USA)-Gangster of Love (USA) by Round Table

Dee Raft (USA) [3] out of Pharlette (Fr))	2	7,570.00	10 10

RAGA NAVARRO (ITY) (1972) by Reform-Nooky(Fr) by Neptunus

Navaresque [8] out of Esquinade)	1	2,560.00	7

RAINBOW QUEST (USA) (1981) by Blushing Groom(Fr)-I Will Follow (USA) by Herbager

Armiger [3] out of Armeria (USA))	1	33,526.20	12
Beauman [3] out of Gliding)	1	6,157.50	8
Blackdown [6] out of Cider Princess)	1	1,813.60	13
Chatoyant [3] out of Ouija)	3	20,210.50	8 10 10
Circus Colours [3] out of Circus Plume)	2	9,914.95	10 12
Dreams End [5] out of Be Easy)	1	3,669.75	14
Glatisant [2] out of Dancing Rocks)	2	27,261.00	6 7
Golden Guest [3] out of Intimate Guest)	1	4,581.00	8
Northern Rainbow [5] out of Safe House)	1	1,051.00	9
Old Provence [3] out of Orange Hill)	2	6,205.50	11 12
Rainbow Heights [2] out of Height Of Passion)	1	3,582.00	7
Rainbow Lake [3] out of Rockfest (USA))	3	33,712.50	11 10 11
Requested [6] out of Melody Hour)	1	5,677.50	14
Seek The Pearl [3] out of Made Of Pearl (USA))	2	6,606.50	9 9
Seren Quest [3] out of Serenesse)	1	3,494.25	9
Source Of Light [4] out of De Stael (USA))	2	25,924.70	12 12
Star Quest [6] out of Sarah Siddons (Fr))	1	4,889.50	16
Star Selection [2] out of Selection Board)	1	4,204.25	8
Urgent Request (Ire) [3] out of Oscura (USA))	1	3,318.75	11
Wagon Master (Fr) [3] out of Sunny Flower (Fr))	2	9,731.60	8 8
	30	215,532.55	

RAMBLING RIVER (1977) by Forlorn River-Who-Done-It by Lucero

Beckyhannah [3] out of Munequita)	1	3,003.00	6

†RAMBO DANCER (CAN) (1984) by Northern Dancer-Fair Arabella (USA) by Chateaugay

Arctic Diamond [2] out of Falaka)	1	3,522.00	7
Cabcharge Princess (Ire) [2] out of Eiswave)	1	2,859.50	5
Lambent [2] out of Nafla (Fr))	2	6,371.50	5 7
Prizefighter [2] out of Jaisalmer)	1	2,932.50	7
Rambold [2] out of Boldie)	2	9,270.50	6 6
	7	24,956.00	

RAMPAGE (USA) (1983) by Northern Baby (Can)-Noble Bethenny (USA) by Vaguely Noble

One Off The Rail (USA) [3] out of Catty Queen (USA))	4	11,778.00	10 10 12 12

REACH (1982) by Kris-Gift Wrapped by Wolver Hollow

Reach For Glory [4] out of Carlton Glory)	1	2,377.00	15
Sarah-Clare [5] out of Northern Dynasty)	3	8,939.25	10 7 9
Sea Paddy [5] out of Sea Thyme)	1	2,406.00	11
	5	13,722.25	

REASONABLE (FR) (1982) by Formidable (USA)-Reno (USA) by Pronto

Call Me I'm Blue (Ire) [3] out of Bluebutton)	5	29,753.90	5 5 5 5 5
Mr B Reasonable (Ire) [2] out of Dunbally)	1	3,435.75	5
	6	33,189.65	

RED SUNSET (1979) by Red God-Centre Piece by Tompion

Captain Scarlet (Ire) [2] out of Shangara)	1	5,047.25	8
Corinthian God (Ire) [4] out of Rathcoffey Duchy)	1	2,821.10	11
Hiltons Travel (Ire) [2] out of Free Rein)	1	2,444.60	5
La Reine Rouge (Ire) [5] out of Free Rein)	1	3,055.50	12
Perdition (Ire) [3] out of Free Rein)	1	2,489.40	6
Randonneur (Ire) [2] out of Kentucky Wildcat)	4	13,087.55	5 5 6 6
Rose Ciel (Ire) [2] out of Great Leighs)	1	3,321.10	7
Sandmoor Denim [6] out of Holernzaye)	2	10,989.50	7 8
The Fernhill Flyer (Ire) [2] out of Stradey Lynn)	3	8,567.50	5 6 5
	15	51,823.50	

REESH (1981) by Lochnager-Songs Jest by Song

Bettykimvic [2] out of Palace Pet)	1	3,548.00	5

	Races Won	Value £	Distances in furlongs
Tocco Jewel [3] out of Blackpool Belle)	1	2,679.00	8
Truthful Image [4] out of Token Of Truth)	3	9,233.25	5 5 6
	5	15,460.25	

REFERENCE POINT (1984) by Mill Reef (USA)-Home on the Range by Habitat

	Races Won	Value £	Distances in furlongs
Dusty Point (Ire) [3] out of Noble Dust (USA))	5	18,394.35	11 12 12 13 14
Hello Ireland [2] out of Select Sale)	1	4,542.00	7
Number One Spot [3] out of One In A Million)	1	3,582.00	7
Rahil (Ire) [3] out of Al Khazaama (USA))	3	7,597.10	11 11 10
Refugio [3] out of Fatah Flare (USA))	1	3,205.00	10
	11	37,320.45	

†REPRIMAND (1985) by Mummy's Pet-Just You Wait by Nonoalco (USA)

	Races Won	Value £	Distances in furlongs
Distinctive Air [2] out of Dastina)	1	2,932.50	6
Hobart [2] out of Constant Companion)	1	3,011.00	7
Mild Rebuke [2] out of Mary Bankes (USA))	3	10,773.05	5 5 5
Reprehend [2] out of Lake Ormond)	1	4,077.50	6
Serious Option (Ire) [2] out of Top Bloom)	2	6,639.00	5 6
Sinners Reprieve [2] out of Sunley Sinner)	1	3,435.75	5
Strapped [2] out of Marista)	1	3,248.00	6
	10	34,116.80	

RISEN STAR (USA) (1985) by Secretariat (USA)-Ribbon (USA) by His Majesty

	Races Won	Value £	Distances in furlongs
Areciba (USA) [2] out of Eloquent Minister (USA))	1	4,305.00	6
Planetary Aspect (USA) [3] out of Santiki)	1	4,175.00	8
	2	8,480.00	

RISK ME (FR) (1984) by Sharpo-Run The Risk by Run The Gantlet (USA)

	Races Won	Value £	Distances in furlongs
Always Risky [3] out of Minabella)	2	6,244.80	8 8
Branston Abby (Ire) [4] out of Tuxford Hideaway)	4	29,308.66	5 6 6 6
Daily Sport Don [3] out of Donrae)	2	6,055.45	7 7
Dailysportdutch [3] out of Gold Duchess)	2	3,688.00	6 6
Dances With Risk [2] out of Dancing Belle)	3	9,118.65	5 5 5
En-Cee-Tee [2] out of Kentucky Tears (USA))	1	2,070.00	5
Heavenly Risk [3] out of Halo)	1	4,760.00	5
Legatee [2] out of Legal Sound)	1	3,054.20	5
Lunar Risk [3] out of Moonlight Princess)	2	7,282.50	12 12
Niche [3] out of Cubby Hole)	2	60,444.90	7 8
Noriski'maringer [2] out of Bare Spectacle)	2	5,952.00	6 6
Risk Master [4] out of Trigamy)	1	13,047.20	7
Riskie Things [2] out of Foolish Things)	1	3,640.50	5
Risky [2] out of Dona Krista)	5	114,171.70	5 5 5 5 5
Windrush Lady [3] out of Pusey Street)	1	3,720.00	8
	30	272,558.56	

RIVERMAN (USA) (1969) by Never Bend-River Lady (USA) by Prince John

	Races Won	Value £	Distances in furlongs
Ferryman (USA) [2] out of Go Leasing)	1	2,623.80	6
Kerkura (USA) [3] out of Kenanga)	1	4,402.50	12
Moussahim (USA) [3] out of Abeesh (USA))	1	3,158.00	12
Rafif (USA) [3] out of Reves Celestes (USA))	1	3,434.50	10
Ribhi (USA) [3] out of Antartica (Fr))	3	30,607.00	8 8 10
Sculler (USA) [3] out of Nimble Folly (USA))	1	7,205.00	10
Underwater (USA) [4] out of Itsamazing (USA))	1	3,362.50	7
Watani (USA) [2] out of Azayim)	2	13,052.50	6 6
	11	67,845.80	

ROARING RIVA (1983) by Music Boy-Elton Abbess by Tamerlane

	Races Won	Value £	Distances in furlongs
Cockerham Ranger [3] out of Miss Shegas)	1	2,070.00	5
Mad About Men [2] out of Old Silver)	1	1,903.00	5
	2	3,973.00	

ROBELLINO (USA) (1978) by Roberto (USA)-Isobelline by Pronto

	Races Won	Value £	Distances in furlongs
Adamparis [3] out of Mrs Darling)	2	5,679.00	7 7
Arndilly [2] out of Upper Caen)	1	3,392.00	6
Brigante Di Cielo [3] out of Follow The Stars)	1	7,570.00	10
Champagne Girl [2] out of Babycham Sparkle)	1	3,406.50	5
Ham N'eggs [2] out of Rose And The Ring)	2	7,163.00	7 7
Holly Golightly [3] out of Rengaine (Fr))	1	3,465.00	7

	Races Won	Value £	Distances in furlongs
Ice Rebel [3] out of Ice Chocolate (USA))	1	2,243.00	9
Lobilio (USA) [4] out of Nabila (USA))	2	7,759.00	11 12
Mister Baileys [2] out of Thimblerigger)	3	85,541.25	6 7 8
Nera [2] out of Sunfleet)	1	3,161.40	5
Prime Painter [3] out of Sharp Lady)	2	4,844.40	12 12
Prosequendo (USA) [6] out of Allegedly (USA))	1	2,898.80	16
Rajmapata [2] out of Alipura)	1	17,730.00	6
Robellion [2] out of Tickled Trout)	1	2,833.00	5
Robleu [3] out of Blue Flower (Fr))	1	3,406.50	7
	21	161,092.85	

ROBERTO (USA) (1969) by Hail to Reason-Bramalea by Nashua

	Races Won	Value £	Distances in furlongs
Crystal Cross (USA) [4] out of Crystal Cup (USA))	2	13,789.60	14 11

†ROI DANZIG (USA) (1986) by Danzig (USA)-Gdynia (USA) by Sir Ivor

	Races Won	Value £	Distances in furlongs
Mheanmetoo [2] out of Spinster)	1	3,297.00	7
Nsx [2] out of Salilia)	1	3,231.00	5
Polish Admiral [2] out of Strapless)	1	3,158.00	6
	3	9,686.00	

ROUSILLON (USA) (1981) by Riverman (USA)-Belle Dorine (USA) by Marshua's Dancer (USA)

	Races Won	Value £	Distances in furlongs
Castel Rosselo [3] out of On The House (Fr))	1	3,318.75	7
Charity Crusader [2] out of Height Of Folly)	2	10,372.25	7 8
Crossillion [5] out of Croda Rossa (Ity))	1	5,340.00	8
Fieldridge [4] out of Final Thought)	1	12,230.80	10
Formal Affair [3] out of Muznah)	2	5,193.00	9 8
Free Mover (Ire) [4] out of Free Dance (Fr))	1	4,713.25	14
Gold Blade [4] out of Sharp Girl (Fr))	2	6,822.25	10 9
Hali (Ire) [2] out of Hocus)	1	2,399.80	5
Languedoc [6] out of Can Can Girl)	1	5,427.50	5
Latvian [6] out of Lorelene (Fr))	2	5,430.00	11 12
Little Rousillon [5] out of Carolside)	1	4,878.25	7
Lugano [2] out of Arita (Fr))	1	3,106.00	6
Miliyel [4] out of Amalee)	1	2,884.00	17
Prince Azzaan (Ire) [2] out of Victory Kingdom (Can))	2	5,978.90	5 5
Provence [6] out of Premier Rose)	2	8,830.50	17 18
Rosina Mae [4] out of Dame Ashfield)	1	5,435.50	16
Rousitto [5] out of Helenetta)	1	3,236.00	11
Routing [5] out of Tura)	1	3,062.50	8
	24	98,659.25	

RUNAWAY GROOM (CAN) (1979) by Blushing Groom (Fr)-Yonnie Girl by Call the Witness

	Races Won	Value £	Distances in furlongs
Runaway Pete (USA) [3] out of Pete's Damas (USA))	3	11,672.80	11 12 11

RUNNETT (1977) by Mummy's Pet-Rennet by King's Bench

	Races Won	Value £	Distances in furlongs
Running Glimpse (Ire) [5] out of One Last Glimpse)	1	5,803.00	6

SADLER'S WELLS (USA) (1981) by Northern Dancer-Fairy Bridge by Bold Reason (USA)

	Races Won	Value £	Distances in furlongs
Alyakkh (Ire) [3] out of Al Bahathri (USA))	1	3,377.25	7
Arvola [3] out of Park Appeal)	1	3,494.25	8
Baby Loves [2] out of Millerette)	1	11,326.00	7
Ballet Prince (Ire) [3] out of Sun Princess)	2	7,927.50	11 12
Bella Ballerina [3] out of Bella Colora)	1	3,582.00	9
Campana (Ire) [3] out of Two Rings (USA))	2	7,366.50	8 9
Dance To The Top [2] out of Aim For The Top (USA))	2	8,653.90	7 7
Imperial Ballet (Ire) [4] out of Amaranda (USA))	2	46,039.75	8 8
Intrepidity [3] out of Intrepid Lady (USA))	1	147,500.00	12
King's Theatre (Ire) [2] out of Regal Beauty (USA))	3	97,205.25	8 8 8
Lacotte (Ire) [3] out of La Dame Du Lac (USA))	1	4,305.00	7
Licorne [3] out of Catawba)	3	16,637.40	10 11 10
Lille Hammer [3] out of Smeralda (Ger))	1	10,203.00	14
Nassma (Ire) [3] out of Pretoria)	2	17,516.40	10 13
Opera House [5] out of Colorspin (Fr))	3	502,097.20	12 10 12
Raneen Alwatar [3] out of Samya's Flame)	1	4,012.50	12
Saint Keyne [3] out of Sancta)	1	3,752.50	14
Sonus (Ire) [4] out of Sound Of Success (USA))	2	36,794.00	11 16
Thawakib (Ire) [3] out of Tobira Celeste (USA))	1	59,407.20	12
Viardot (Ire) [4] out of Vive La Reine)	1	3,106.00	12
	32	994,303.60	

SAINT ESTEPHE (FR) (1982) by Top Ville-Une Tornade (Fr) by Traffic

	Races Won	Value £	Distances in furlongs
Call The Guv'nor [4] out of Gay Charlotte)	1	3,655.00	11

SALLUST (1969) by Pall Mall-Bandarilla by Matador

	Races Won	Value £	Distances in furlongs
Top One [8] out of Light Diamond)	1	2,243.00	6

SALMON LEAP (USA) (1980) by Northern Dancer-Fish-Bar by Baldric II

	Races Won	Value £	Distances in furlongs
Reel Of Tulloch (Ire) [4] out of Miss Sandman)	1	2,623.40	15

SALSE (USA) (1985) by Topsider (USA)-Carnival Princess (USA) by Prince John

	Races Won	Value £	Distances in furlongs
Crackling Sike [2] out of Santa Linda (USA))	1	4,664.00	7
Double Down [2] out of Timely Raise (USA))	1	3,746.50	5
Girl From Ipanema [2] out of Honey Pot)	1	4,232.00	7
Lemon Souffle [2] out of Melodrama)	3	24,989.55	5 6 6
Mamara Reef [3] out of Fanny's Cove)	1	2,892.60	14
Recaptured Days (Ire) [2] out of Idrak)	1	4,378.00	6
Vistec Express (Ire) [3] out of Kriswick)	1	3,947.50	9
	9	48,850.15	

SALT DOME (USA) (1983) by Blushing Groom(Fr)-Buda Lady (USA) by Crimson Satan

	Races Won	Value £	Distances in furlongs
Ashkernazy (Ire) [2] out of Eskaroon)	1	3,318.75	5
Bransby Road (Ire) [3] out of Ivory Smooth (USA))	1	2,898.80	15
Fortis Pavior (Ire) [3] out of Heather Lil)	2	6,032.00	5 5
Gingerbird (Ire) [2] out of Vibrant Hue (USA))	1	2,735.80	7
Mohican Brave (Ire) [3] out of Mrs Tittlemouse)	2	4,954.90	8 8
	7	19,940.25	

SANDHURST PRINCE (1979) by Pampapaul-Blue Shark by Silver Shark

	Races Won	Value £	Distances in furlongs
Persian Soldier [6] out of Persian Case)	2	7,646.25	12 12

SARAB (1981) by Prince Tenderfoot (USA)-Carnival Dance by Welsh Pageant

	Races Won	Value £	Distances in furlongs
Missy-S (Ire) [4] out of Monaco Lady)	2	4,048.70	8 8
Palacegate Gold (Ire) [4] out of Habilite)	2	5,833.90	5 6
	4	9,882.60	

†SATCO (FR) (1983) by Blakeney-Satwa by Nonoalco (USA)

	Races Won	Value £	Distances in furlongs
Roche Abbey (Ire) [2] out of Lyphalla)	1	2,322.00	5

SAYF EL ARAB (USA) (1980) by Drone-Make Plans by Go Marching (USA)

	Races Won	Value £	Distances in furlongs
El Yasaf (Ire) [5] out of Winsong Melody)	1	12,277.20	5
Golden Grand [2] out of Lavenham Blue)	2	4,313.00	5 7
Goodbye Millie [3] out of Leprechaun Lady)	5	11,322.60	12 13 13 12 12
Mount Leinster [2] out of Kilttaley)	1	3,125.50	5
Saafend [5] out of Gilt Star)	1	4,474.50	8
Superensis [3] out of Superlife (USA))	1	2,070.00	7
Sword Master [4] out of Swordlestown Miss (USA))	2	6,615.00	11 17
Tinsashe (Ire) [3] out of Rheinbloom)	2	6,548.00	9 10
Unveiled [5] out of Collegian)	2	5,504.40	5 6
	17	56,250.20	

SAYYAF (1977) by Habitat-Pavello by Crepello

	Races Won	Value £	Distances in furlongs
Quinta Royale [6] out of Royal Holly)	1	3,235.50	7

SCORPIO (FR) (1976) by Sir Gaylord-Zambara by Mossborough

	Races Won	Value £	Distances in furlongs
Just Flamenco [2] out of Suzannah's Song)	1	3,262.00	6
Stoproveritate [4] out of Luscinia)	2	5,271.30	7 8
	3	8,533.30	

SCOTTISH REEL (1982) by Northfields (USA)-Dance All Night by Double-U-Jay

	Races Won	Value £	Distances in furlongs
Clyde Goddess (Ire) [2] out of Clymene)	1	4,542.00	7
General Chase [3] out of Make A Signal)	2	6,011.40	9 9
Miss Haggis [4] out of Bambolona)	1	3,201.75	6
Misty Silks [3] out of Silk St James)	4	17,625.10	8 8 8 8
Nitouche [3] out of Loredana)	1	3,779.40	7
Scoffera [3] out of Single Bid)	2	3,984.50	10 8
Scottish Bambi [5] out of Bambolona)	2	8,285.00	10 9
Scottish Wedding [3] out of Pearl Wedding)	1	2,821.10	16
The Little Ferret [3] out of Third Movement)	1	2,243.00	7
	15	52,493.25	

SCRIPT OHIO (USA) (1982) by Roberto-Grandma Lind by Never Bend

	Races Won	Value £	Distances in furlongs
Badawi (Fr) [3] out of Beautiful Bedouin (USA))	1	3,106.00	12

SEATTLE DANCER (USA) (1984) by Nijinsky(Can)-My Charmer (USA) by Poker

	Races Won	Value £	Distances in furlongs
Puget Dancer (USA) [3] out of Basin (USA))	1	3,236.00	11
Salatin (USA) [3] out of Ivory Wings (USA))	1	4,690.40	10
Spot Prize (USA) [2] out of Lucky Brook (USA))	1	3,497.50	5
State Performer (USA) [2] out of Din (USA))	3	37,439.50	6 6 6
	6	48,863.40	

SECRETARIAT (USA) (1970) by Bold Ruler-Somethingroyal by Princequillo

	Races Won	Value £	Distances in furlongs
Tinners Way (USA) [3] out of Devon Diva (USA))	2	23,295.00	6 8

SECRETO (USA) (1981) by Northern Dancer-Betty's Secret by Secretariat (USA)

	Races Won	Value £	Distances in furlongs
Cretoes Dancer (USA) [4] out of Mary Read (USA))	1	2,553.00	10
Declassified (USA) [3] out of Misty Gallore (USA))	1	5,190.00	10
Governor George (USA) [2] out of Sheena Native (USA))	2	14,945.00	5 6
Privy Council (USA) [2] out of Mythical Assembly)	1	4,199.25	7
Truckhaven Secret [2] out of Veronica)	1	3,377.25	8
	6	30,264.50	

†SEEKING THE GOLD (USA) (1985) by Mr Prospector (USA)-Con Game (USA) by Buckpasser

	Races Won	Value £	Distances in furlongs
Mutakddim (USA) [2] out of Oscillate (USA))	1	10,464.00	7

SEYMOUR HICKS (FR) (1980) by Ballymore-Sarah Siddons(Fr) by Le Levanstell

	Races Won	Value £	Distances in furlongs
Drummer Hicks [4] out of Musical Princess)	2	14,445.00	10 8

†SHAADI (USA) (1986) by Danzig (USA)-Unfurled (USA) by Hoist The Flag (USA)

	Races Won	Value £	Distances in furlongs
Luana [2] out of Lucayan Princess)	1	5,663.00	6
Velvet Moon (Ire) [2] out of Park Special)	3	46,891.00	6 5 6
Wizard King [2] out of Broomstick Cottage)	1	3,340.00	6
	5	55,894.00	

SHADEED (USA) (1982) by Nijinsky(Can)-Continual (USA) by Damascus (USA)

	Races Won	Value £	Distances in furlongs
Cyprian Dancer (USA) [3] out of Springtime Fantasy (USA))	1	3,114.00	7
Our Shadee (USA) [3] out of Nuppence)	1	2,490.00	5
Sayyedati [3] out of Dubian)	1	107,063.50	8
Shamam (USA) [3] out of Goodbye Shelley (Fr))	1	6,160.00	8
Taghareed (USA) [2] out of Alghuzaylah)	1	3,200.00	6
	5	122,027.50	

SHAHRASTANI (USA) (1983) by Nijinsky(Can)-Shademah by Thatch (USA)

	Races Won	Value £	Distances in furlongs
Marastani (USA) [3] out of Marianna's Girl (USA))	1	2,880.00	8

SHARDARI (1982) by Top Ville-Sharmada(Fr) by Zeddaan

	Races Won	Value £	Distances in furlongs
Bold Resolution (Ire) [5] out of Valmarine (Fr))	3	22,962.25	16 16 16
Midnight Jazz (Ire) [3] out of Round Midnight)	1	3,289.50	8
	4	26,251.75	

SHAREEF DANCER (USA) (1980) by Northern Dancer-Sweet Alliance (USA) by Sir Ivor

	Races Won	Value £	Distances in furlongs
Cromarty [3] out of Forres)	1	3,435.75	12
Dodgy Dancer [3] out of Fluctuate)	3	8,256.80	14 9 9
Ertlon [3] out of Sharpina)	1	5,253.50	7
Graegos (Ire) [3] out of Trikymia)	1	3,640.50	10
Massiba (Ire) [4] out of Massorah (Fr))	1	5,131.75	6
Scenic Dancer [5] out of Bridestones)	1	3,236.00	12
Spartan Shareef (Ire) [4] out of Spartan Helen)	2	37,282.50	10 11
Spring To Action [3] out of Light Duty)	2	13,249.00	14 14
Surrey Dancer [5] out of Juliette Marny)	2	6,388.00	10 10
Tansy [2] out of Topsy)	1	4,270.75	6
	15	90,144.55	

SHARP SHOT (1981) by Sharpen Up-First Round by Primera

	Races Won	Value £	Distances in furlongs
Son Of Sharp Shot (Ire) [3] out of Gay Fantasy)	1	3,379.00	10

SHARPO (1977) by Sharpen Up-Moiety Bird by Falcon

	Races Won	Value £	Distances in furlongs
Brigade [4] out of Matoa (USA))	1	3,401.00	7
College Chapel [3] out of Scarcely Blessed)	1	40,645.20	6
Cynic [3] out of Cynomis)	1	3,143.25	5
Fast Eddy [2] out of Miller's Creek (USA))	1	3,915.00	6
Fox Sparrow [3] out of Wryneck)	1	3,817.50	10
Hunters Of Brora (Ire) [3] out of Nihad)	2	11,503.00	7 7
Isabella Sharp [2] out of Vivienda)	2	7,480.50	5 5
Mockingbird [2] out of Mountain Bluebird (USA))	1	2,070.00	6
Penny Drops [4] out of Darine)	3	74,235.25	8 8 9
Persuasive [6] out of Queen's Eyot)	2	10,114.00	11 14
Port Lucaya [3] out of Sister Sophie (USA))	1	4,658.00	8
Poyle George [8] out of Hithermoor Lass)	1	4,532.50	5
Sagebrush Roller [5] out of Sunita)	2	8,548.00	6 7
Sharp Prospect [3] out of Sabatina (USA))	1	3,201.75	5
Sharpening [2] out of False Lift)	1	2,243.00	6
Slmaat [2] out of Wasslaweyeh (USA))	1	4,955.00	7
Splice [4] out of Soluce)	2	19,379.40	6 6
Stimulant [2] out of Anodyne)	2	9,984.50	5 5
	26	217,826.85	

SHARROOD (USA) (1983) by Caro-Angel Island (USA) by Cougar(Chi)

	Races Won	Value £	Distances in furlongs
Aroom [3] out of Babycham Sparkle)	1	2,898.00	5
Askern [2] out of Silk Stocking)	1	3,289.50	7
Brierley [2] out of Crystallize)	1	2,700.00	6
Cumbrian Rhapsody [3] out of Bustellina)	4	16,378.55	12 10 14 12
Empire Pool [3] out of Reflection)	1	3,217.50	9
Farmer's Pet [4] out of Rectitude)	3	9,479.25	14 16 14
Galejade [3] out of Sans Blague (USA))	1	2,434.00	11
Grecian Garden [2] out of Greek Goddess)	1	2,070.00	5
Herr Trigger [2] out of Four-Legged Friend)	1	2,532.00	8
Lap Of Luxury [4] out of Lap Of Honour)	2	15,770.25	8 8
Mosaic Gold [2] out of The Yellow Girl)	1	3,523.50	6
Mr Copyforce [3] out of Cappuccilli)	2	9,591.50	11 12
Mrs Dawson [3] out of Faraway Grey)	1	2,803.00	8
Silverlocks [3] out of Philgwyn)	3	11,382.50	8 7 9
The Flying Phantom [2] out of Miss Flossa (Fr))	1	4,113.00	7
Wandering Angel [2] out of Angel Drummer)	2	5,301.00	5 6
	26	97,483.55	

SHERNAZAR (1981) by Busted-Sharmeen(Fr) by Val de Loir

	Races Won	Value £	Distances in furlongs
Brandon Prince (Ire) [5] out of Chanson de Paris (USA))	3	19,011.75	16 15 15
Clairification (Ire) [3] out of St Clair Star)	1	3,652.00	8
Delve (Ire) [4] out of Safe Haven)	1	4,182.10	9
Enfant Du Paradis (Ire) [5] out of Fille de L'orne (Fr))	1	3,339.10	14
Golden Memories (Ire) [2] out of Buz Kashi)	1	5,673.00	8
Princess Ermyn [4] out of Trois Vallees)	2	5,907.00	12 11
Savings Bank [3] out of Yen (Aus))	1	3,260.25	8
The Deep (Ire) [2] out of Duende)	1	5,127.00	8
	11	50,152.20	

SHIRLEY HEIGHTS (1975) by Mill Reef (USA)-Hardiemma by Hardicanute

	Races Won	Value £	Distances in furlongs
Bal Harbour [2] out of Balabina (USA))	1	9,189.60	7
Day Of History (Ire) [4] out of Smeralda (Ger))	2	8,526.75	11 12
El Jubail (Ire) [3] out of Abha)	1	3,611.25	10
Encore Une Fois (Ire) [4] out of Guest Performer)	1	4,836.00	16
Fair Shirley (Ire) [3] out of Fairy Dancer (USA))	1	3,435.75	10
Highflying [7] out of Nomadic Pleasure)	3	65,914.50	11 12 16
Hill Of Dreams [3] out of Forest Flower (USA))	1	3,143.25	13
Kosata (Ire) [3] out of Godzilla)	1	3,435.75	7
League Leader (Ire) [3] out of Happy Kin (USA))	3	68,498.70	12 11 12
Misbelief [3] out of Misguided)	3	10,986.80	9 9 12
Miss Rinjani [2] out of Miss Kuta Beach)	1	4,306.50	7
Nawahil [3] out of Lora's Guest)	1	3,055.50	14
Pursuit Of Glory [2] out of Propensity)	1	1,830.00	6
Shirley Rose [3] out of Corley Moor)	6	18,465.90	9 11 10 11 10 11
Top Cees [3] out of Sing Softly)	1	3,523.50	8
Trammel [3] out of Trampship)	1	3,816.00	12
Tree Of Life [3] out of Cape Chestnut)	1	3,348.00	12
Wannabe [3] out of Propensity)	1	3,845.25	8
Zinaad [4] out of Time Charter)	1	33,794.00	12
	31	257,563.00	

	Races Won	Value £	Distances in furlongs
SHY GROOM (USA) (1979) by Blushing Groom(Fr)-Aspara by Dancer's Image (USA)			
Atherton Green (Ire) [3] out of Primacara)	1	3,915.00	10
Fascination Waltz [6] out of Cuckoo Weir)	1	3,785.00	5
Non Vintage (Ire) [2] out of Great Alexandra)	1	4,435.00	8
Silver Groom (Ire) [3] out of Rustic Lawn)	2	5,461.00	8 8
	5	17,596.00	
SIBERIAN EXPRESS (USA) (1981) by Caro-Indian Call (USA) by Warfare			
Alasib [3] out of Fahrenheit)	2	8,093.50	6 6
Amazon Express [4] out of Thalestria (Fr))	1	3,622.50	12
Bookcase [6] out of Colourful (Fr))	2	8,177.50	12 10
Common Council [4] out of Old Domesday Book)	2	4,475.00	10 12
Cosmic Star [3] out of Miss Bunty)	1	2,070.00	10
Fanfold (Ire) [3] out of Broken Melody)	1	2,243.00	6
Featherstone Lane [2] out of Try Gloria)	1	2,490.00	5
Good Fetch [2] out of Exceptional Beauty)	1	3,080.00	5
Sareen Express (Ire) [5] out of Three Waves)	1	2,700.00	6
Silent Expression [3] out of Silent Sun)	3	15,185.00	7 8 6
Soviet Express [3] out of Our Shirley)	1	1,604.00	7
The Premier Expres [3] out of Home And Away)	1	2,243.00	8
	17	55,983.50	
SICYOS (USA) (1981) by Lyphard (USA)-Sigy(Fr) by Habitat			
Brown's (Fr) [3] out of Charlata (Fr))	2	10,452.30	8 8
SILLY PRICES (1977) by Silly Season-Galosh by Pandofell			
Densben [9] out of Eliza de Rich)	1	3,468.75	6
SILVER HAWK (USA) (1979) by Roberto (USA)-Gris Vitesse by Amerigo			
Fawran (USA) [2] out of By Land By Sea (USA))	1	4,378.00	6
Hawker Hunter (USA) [2] out of Glorious Natalie (USA))	1	3,980.00	7
Ionio (USA) [2] out of Private View (USA))	1	10,052.00	7
Lower Egypt (USA) [3] out of Naughty Nile (USA))	2	7,295.50	7 8
Lt Welsh (USA) [3] out of Lake Ivor (USA))	1	2,579.00	9
Pearl Kite (USA) [2] out of Spur Wing (USA))	1	4,308.00	7
Red Bishop (USA) [5] out of La Rouquine)	2	30,057.00	10 10
Silver Hut (USA) [2] out of Ice House)	1	5,253.50	7
Silver Maple (USA) [3] out of Dead Letter (USA))	1	4,503.00	10
Silver Wedge (USA) [2] out of Wedge Musical)	1	4,182.00	7
Silverdale (USA) [3] out of Norene's Nemesis (Can))	1	3,947.50	12
Tablah (USA) [2] out of Halholah (USA))	1	10,233.60	6
	14	90,769.10	
SIMPLY GREAT (FR) (1979) by Mill Reef (USA)-Seneca by Chaparral			
Angelica Park [7] out of Rosana Park)	1	2,070.00	16
Argyle Cavalier (Ire) [3] out of Fete Champetre)	1	3,825.00	11
Master Foodbroker (Ire) [5] out of Silver Mantle)	1	4,878.25	16
Pistol River (Ire) [3] out of Pampala)	1	4,751.50	12
Simply Finesse [3] out of Spring In Rome (USA))	1	3,557.50	7
Smarginato (Ire) [3] out of Aldern Stream)	4	61,067.50	8 8 7 10
	9	80,149.75	
SIR IVOR (1965) by Sir Gaylord-Attica by Mr Trouble			
Abbraak (USA) [3] out of Happiness (USA))	1	3,231.00	8
Dynamic Deluxe (USA) [2] out of Shanameg (USA))	1	4,807.00	8
Ivory Palm (USA) [3] out of Sunerta (USA))	1	3,143.25	12
Magical Retreat (USA) [3] out of Known Charter)	2	16,468.00	10 10
	5	27,649.25	
SIR WIMBORNE (USA) (1973) by Sir Ivor-Cap and Bells by Tom Fool			
Pondicherry (USA) [3] out of Perceptive Lady (USA))	1	3,201.75	7
SIT IN THE CORNER (USA) (1968) by Hail To Reason-Dunce Cap II by Tom Fool			
Mr Woodcock [8] out of Grey Bird)	1	2,469.00	15

SIZZLING MELODY (1984) by Song-Mrs Bacon by Balliol

	Races Won	Value £	Distances in furlongs
Breakfast Boogie [3] out of Bonne de Berry)	1	2,794.00	5
Covent Garden Girl [3] out of Azelly)	2	5,917.50	5 5
Guv'nors Gift [3] out of La Reine D'Espagne)	2	5,600.00	8 8
Hotaria [3] out of Fair Eleanor)	1	3,669.75	6
Melodic Drive [3] out of Gleneagle)	1	2,070.00	6
Perusal [2] out of High Climber)	2	9,121.25	6 7
Wave Hill [4] out of Trikymia)	1	3,640.50	8
	10	32,813.00	

SKYLINER (1975) by African Sky-Keep Going by Hard Sauce

	Races Won	Value £	Distances in furlongs
Blyton Lad [7] out of Ballinacurra)	2	14,099.40	5 6
Celestine [4] out of Stellaris)	1	3,444.00	7
Monkey's Wedding [2] out of Munequita)	3	9,034.10	6 6 5
Nagida [4] out of Kept In Style)	1	39,640.00	6
Palacegate Sunset [3] out of Grey Morley)	1	2,243.00	9
	8	68,460.50	

SKYWALKER (USA) (1982) by Relaunch (USA)-Bold Captive (USA) by Boldnesian

	Races Won	Value £	Distances in furlongs
Saint Ciel (USA) [5] out of Holy Tobin (USA))	1	2,679.00	10

SLEW O' GOLD (USA) (1980) by Seattle Slew (USA)-Alluvial (USA) by Buckpasser

	Races Won	Value £	Distances in furlongs
Safir (USA) [3] out of Icing)	1	3,114.00	10

SLIP ANCHOR (1982) by Shirley Heights-Sayonara(Ger) by Birkhahn

	Races Won	Value £	Distances in furlongs
Acanthus (Ire) [3] out of Green Lucia)	3	13,129.40	11 14 14
Edbaysaan (Ire) [3] out of Legend Of Arabia)	2	16,692.75	12 13
Fathom Five (Ire) [4] out of Sheer Luck)	1	2,658.00	5
Impeccable Taste [3] out of Spring Triple (USA))	1	2,243.00	11
Kaiser Wilhelm [4] out of Kaisersage (Fr))	2	8,465.40	11 17
Killick [5] out of Enthralment (USA))	1	7,148.00	12
Northern Bound (Ire) [3] out of North Cliff (Fr))	1	3,611.25	11
Safety In Numbers [3] out of Winter Queen)	4	27,671.85	14 16 14 14
Sarawat [5] out of Eljazzi)	1	66,185.00	13
Weigh Anchor [2] out of Argon Laser)	1	5,936.00	8
	17	153,740.65	

SMACKOVER (1975) by Pontifex (USA)-Atanya by Atan

	Races Won	Value £	Distances in furlongs
Manor Adventure [3] out of Klairove)	1	3,125.50	5

SMARTEN (USA) (1976) by Cyane-Smartaire by Quibu

	Races Won	Value £	Distances in furlongs
Smart Teacher (USA) [3] out of Finality (USA))	1	3,377.25	8

SOLFORD (USA) (1980) by Nijinsky(Can)-Fairness by Cavan

	Races Won	Value £	Distances in furlongs
Malenoir (USA) [5] out of Viewed (USA))	1	3,106.00	14

SON OF SHAKA (1976) by Tribal Chief-Pink Garter by Henry the Seventh

	Races Won	Value £	Distances in furlongs
Leigh Crofter [4] out of Ganadora)	2	7,332.00	6 6

SONG (1966) by Sing Sing-Intent by Vilmorin

	Races Won	Value £	Distances in furlongs
Beatle Song [5] out of Betyle (Fr))	1	3,210.00	6
Lochsong [5] out of Peckitts Well)	3	122,648.80	5 5 5
	4	125,858.80	

SORT (USA) (1983) by Nijinsky(Can)-Special (USA) by Forli(Arg)

	Races Won	Value £	Distances in furlongs
Rapid Success (USA) [3] out of Golden Rhyme)	1	4,542.00	8

SOUGHAAN (USA) (1983) by Riverman (USA)-Beaconaire by Vaguely Noble

	Races Won	Value £	Distances in furlongs
Sie Amato (Ire) [4] out of Wolviston)	1	3,209.60	8

SOVIET STAR (USA) (1984) by Nureyev (USA)-Veruschka (Fr) by Venture VII

	Races Won	Value £	Distances in furlongs
Ehtfaal (Ire) [2] out of Bashush (USA))	2	12,726.00	5 6
Ihtiraz [3] out of Azyaa)	3	22,830.40	7 7 7
Majhola (Ire) [3] out of Satinette)	1	3,494.25	9
Mytilene (Ire) [2] out of Dancing Meg (USA))	1	4,050.00	7
Red Cotton [3] out of Cocotte)	1	3,131.90	8
Scorpius [3] out of Sally Brown)	1	3,465.00	11
Soviet Line (Ire) [3] out of Shore Line)	2	7,251.75	8 9

	Races Won	Value £	Distances in furlongs
Trapezium [3] out of Glancing)	1	3,114.00	5
Yeltsin [3] out of Mill On The Floss)	1	3,465.00	10
	13	63,528.30	

SPARKLING BOY (1977) by Comedy Star (USA)-Tinsel by Right Boy

Followmegirls [4] out of Haddon Anna)	1	2,668.60	5

SPECTACULAR BID (USA) (1976) by Bold Bidder-Spectacular (USA) by Promised Land

Spectacular Dawn [4] out of Early Rising (USA))	1	3,201.75	17

SPIN OF A COIN (1978) by Boreen(Fr)-Lovely Linan by Ballylinan

Roll A Dollar [7] out of Handy Dancer)	1	26,892.00	16

†SQUILL (USA) (1985) by Stop The Music (USA)-River Rose (Fr) by Riverman (USA)

Demi-Plie [2] out of Inveraven)	3	6,978.00	6 7 7
Stradishall [2] out of Zilda (Fr))	1	3,757.50	9
	4	10,735.50	

STALKER (1983) by Kala Shikari-Tarvie by Swing Easy (USA)

Highland Magic (Ire) [5] out of Magic Picture)	1	6,264.00	6
Sillars Stalker (Ire) [5] out of Mittens)	1	3,611.25	16
	2	9,875.25	

STALWART (USA) (1979) by Hoist The Flag-Yes Dear Maggy by Iron Ruler (USA)

Glide Path (USA) [4] out of Jolly Polka (USA))	3	26,647.00	12 11 11

STANFORD (1976) by Red God-Sweet Almond by Busted

Chickcharnie [3] out of Lucky Angel)	1	3,406.50	7

STAR APPEAL (1970) by Appiani II-Sterna by Neckar

Young Jason [10] out of Smarten Up)	1	2,924.70	8

STAR DE NASKRA (USA) (1975) by Naskra (USA)-Candle Star (USA) by Clandestine

Celestial Key (USA) [3] out of Casa Key (USA))	1	10,380.00	7

STARCH REDUCED (1970) by Lucky Sovereign-Pont des Fleur by Rope Bridge

Diet [7] out of Highland Rossie)	3	8,030.25	5 6 6

STATELY DON (USA) (1984) by Nureyev (USA)-Dona Ysidra by Le Fabuleux

Pater Noster (USA) [4] out of Sainera (USA))	1	3,260.25	7
Without A Flag (USA) [3] out of Northerly Cheer (USA))	1	3,087.00	10
	2	6,347.25	

STORM BIRD (CAN) (1978) by Northern Dancer-South Ocean(Can) by New Providence

Balanchine (USA) [2] out of Morning Devotion (USA))	2	11,903.20	6 7
Cape Pigeon (USA) [8] out of Someway Somehow (USA))	2	5,856.75	6 7
Full Feather (USA) [3] out of Carolina Moon (USA))	1	3,348.00	7
Highland Legend (USA) [2] out of Santella (USA))	2	6,900.50	7 8
Naif (USA) [3] out of Benguela (USA))	2	7,076.25	8 8
Stonehatch (USA) [2] out of Lively Living (USA))	2	32,783.40	6 6
Storm Canyon (Ire) [3] out of Diamond Field (USA))	3	13,040.00	6 6 6
Storm Free (USA) [7] out of No Designs (USA))	1	2,556.60	10
Vishnu (USA) [3] out of Vachti (Fr))	1	3,757.50	12
Wharf (USA) [3] out of Dockage (USA))	1	10,116.00	9
	17	97,338.20	

STORM CAT (USA) (1983) by Storm Bird(Can)-Terlingua (USA) by Secretariat (USA)

Catrail (USA) [3] out of Tough As Nails (USA))	5	98,341.80	7 6 6 6 7
Elrafa Ah (USA) [2] out of Bubbles Darlene (USA))	2	13,695.75	5 5
In Case (USA) [3] out of In Essence (USA))	2	19,837.50	5 5
Mistle Cat (USA) [3] out of Mistle Toe (USA))	2	18,390.00	8 8
Tabkir (USA) [3] out of Taruma (USA))	1	3,523.50	6
Tajdif (USA) [3] out of Hankow Willow (USA))	1	4,012.50	7
	13	157,801.05	

STREET KAFU (1985) by Kafu-Drora by Busted

	Races Won	Value £	Distances in furlongs
Alllegsnobrain [2] out of Spark Out)	2	4,921.50	6 5

STRIKE GOLD (USA) (1980) by Mr Prospector (USA)-Newchance Lady by Roi Dagobert

	Races Won	Value £	Distances in furlongs
Moon Strike (Fr) [3] out of Lady Lamia (USA))	2	10,528.00	5 6

SULAAFAH (USA) (1982) by Riverman (USA)-Celerity by Dancer's Image (USA)

	Races Won	Value £	Distances in furlongs
Sylvan Breeze [5] out of Langton Herring)	1	3,054.20	6

SUNLEY BUILDS (1978) by Patch-Dance Mistress by Javelot

	Races Won	Value £	Distances in furlongs
Googly [4] out of Cheri Berry)	2	11,735.50	9 10

SUPERLATIVE (1981) by Nebbiolo-Clariden by Hook Money

	Races Won	Value £	Distances in furlongs
Creselly [6] out of Gwiffina)	1	2,479.00	7
Greatest [2] out of Pillowing)	1	4,950.00	7
Harpo's Special [2] out of Sideloader Special)	1	2,553.00	5
Hasta La Vista [3] out of Falcon Berry (Fr))	2	5,848.80	12 12
So Superb [4] out of Top And Tail (USA))	2	6,687.50	5 5
Superlativemaximus (Ire) [5] out of Samra)	2	6,324.50	5 5
Superoo [7] out of Shirleen)	1	3,552.75	7
Supreme Boy [4] out of Rose And The Ring)	1	2,976.50	6
Surprise Offer [3] out of Vexed Voter)	1	6,508.80	5
Susanna's Secret [6] out of Queens Welcome)	1	2,788.00	7
Tandia [2] out of Helluva Time)	1	4,270.75	8
	14	48,939.60	

†SUPERPOWER (1986) by Superlative-Champ d'Avril by Northfields (USA)

	Races Won	Value £	Distances in furlongs
Broctune Gold [2] out of Golden Sunlight)	2	5,184.50	5 6
Mr Devious [2] out of Marton Maid)	1	3,127.50	6
Salvezza (Ire) [2] out of Damezao)	1	3,435.75	6
	4	11,747.75	

SURE BLADE (USA) (1983) by Kris-Double Lock by Home Guard (USA)

	Races Won	Value £	Distances in furlongs
Certain Way (Ire) [3] out of Ruffling Point)	2	5,745.80	8 8
Cut The Red Tape (Ire) [2] out of Russian Ribbon (USA))	1	3,020.80	7
Dashing Fellow (Ire) [5] out of Belle Viking (Fr))	4	13,886.20	12 10 10 12
Iron Baron (Ire) [4] out of Riverine (Fr))	1	2,927.00	12
Island Blade (Ire) [4] out of Queen's Eyot)	1	3,209.60	15
Mustahil (Ire) [4] out of Zumurrudah (USA))	1	3,289.50	8
Paradise News [2] out of Monaiya)	1	1,534.00	5
Qamoos (Ire) [3] out of Zumurrudah (USA))	1	1,630.00	7
Rimouski [5] out of Rimosa's Pet)	1	2,469.00	12
Suntara (Ire) [3] out of First Act)	1	3,435.75	6
Sure Lord (Ire) [4] out of Lady Graustark (USA))	1	5,089.50	6
Tomos [3] out of Princess Genista)	1	3,552.75	12
	16	49,789.90	

SWING EASY (USA) (1968) by Delta Judge-Free Flowing by Polynesian

	Races Won	Value £	Distances in furlongs
Causley [8] out of Four Lawns)	2	7,092.50	7 8
Swing Low [4] out of Ballaquine)	4	107,221.17	7 8 8 8
	6	114,313.67	

SYLVAN EXPRESS (1983) by Baptism-Folle Remont by Prince Tenderfoot (USA)

	Races Won	Value £	Distances in furlongs
Sylvan Starlight [3] out of Kakisa)	2	5,504.40	5 6

TAP ON WOOD (1976) by Sallust-Cat O'Mountaine by Ragusa

	Races Won	Value £	Distances in furlongs
Knock Knock [8] out of Ruby River)	2	9,085.00	10 11

TASSO (USA) (1983) by Fappiano (USA)-Ecstacism (USA) by What A Pleasure (USA)

	Races Won	Value £	Distances in furlongs
Tasset (Can) [3] out of While I'm Away (USA))	1	3,465.00	11

TATE GALLERY (USA) (1983) by Northern Dancer-Fairy Bridge by Bold Reason (USA)

	Races Won	Value £	Distances in furlongs
Art Tatum (Ire) [2] out of Rose Chanelle)	2	6,639.55	8 8
Cubist (Ire) [3] out of Finalist)	1	2,574.00	7
Duveen (Ire) [3] out of Wish You Were Here (USA))	5	15,220.00	10 9 10 9 10
Embankment (Ire) [3] out of Great Leighs)	2	9,133.00	8 8

	Races Won	Value £	Distances in furlongs
Gallery Artist (Ire) [5] out of Avec L'amour)	1	1,679.00	7
Legal Artist (Ire) [3] out of Dowdstown Miss)	2	5,221.50	10 10
Lyric Fantasy (Ire) [3] out of Flying Melody)	1	10,029.00	6
Mr Cube (Ire) [3] out of Truly Thankful (Can))	1	2,700.00	8
Mr Tate (Ire) [4] out of Free Wheeler)	4	14,642.00	10 10 10 10
My Gallery (Ire) [2] out of Sententious)	1	3,494.25	5
Port Sunlight (Ire) [5] out of Nana's Girl)	1	2,851.25	10
Princess Tateum (Ire) [3] out of Church Mountain)	2	5,183.00	8 10
Sister Susan [2] out of Dream Chaser)	2	4,733.80	6 6
Strip Cartoon (Ire) [5] out of Reveal)	2	5,630.30	5 5
Sugar Town (Ire) [2] out of Skhiza)	1	4,342.25	7
Wakil (Ire) [4] out of Arena)	1	4,207.50	8
	29	98,280.40	

TAUFAN (USA) (1977) by Stop The Music (USA)-Stolen Date (USA) by Sadair

	Races Won	Value £	Distances in furlongs
Benzoe (Ire) [3] out of Saintly Guest)	1	13,500.00	6
Captain Horatius (Ire) [4] out of One Last Glimpse)	2	19,761.00	10 12
Circle Of Friends (Ire) [2] out of Pitlessie)	1	8,610.00	6
Glen Echo (Ire) [3] out of Addabub)	1	3,640.50	8
Golden Torque [6] out of Brightelmstone)	1	2,880.00	10
Hoochiecoochie Man (Ire) [3] out of Regal Entrance)	2	5,969.00	10 10
Lady Sheriff [2] out of Midaan)	2	5,554.00	5 5
Love Returned [6] out of Miss Loving)	2	10,765.25	5 5
Montaya [2] out of Kellys Reef)	1	3,629.50	5
Petersford Girl (Ire) [3] out of Engage)	1	3,699.00	6
Pine Ridge Lad (Ire) [3] out of Rosserk)	1	3,720.00	6
Raging Thunder [3] out of Nasty Niece (Can))	2	5,819.80	7 8
Red Fan (Ire) [3] out of The Woman In Red)	1	1,576.00	6
Sir Edward Henry (Ire) [3] out of Finessing)	1	3,004.60	11
Storm Venture (Ire) [3] out of Crimson Crest)	1	2,950.00	10
Suris (Ire) [2] out of Thank One's Stars)	1	3,080.00	6
Taufan Blu (Ire) [4] out of Engage)	1	15,400.00	7
Taunting (Ire) [5] out of Dancing Decoy)	1	2,010.00	10
Teetotaller (Ire) [2] out of Mainly Dry)	1	3,980.00	5

	Races Won	Value £	Distances in furlongs
Walnut Burl (Ire) [3] out of Hay Knot)	1	3,348.00	7
With Gusto [6] out of Finesse)	2	4,106.00	12 11
	27	127,002.65	

TEENOSO (USA) (1980) by Youth (USA)-Furioso by Ballymoss

	Races Won	Value £	Distances in furlongs
Lavender Cottage [3] out of Broomstick Cottage)	1	3,260.25	10
O So Neet [3] out of Lydia Rose)	1	2,637.00	8
Paper Days [3] out of April Days)	1	3,261.40	14
So Saucy [3] out of Saucy Bird)	3	8,361.70	9 10 17
Teen Jay [3] out of Spoilt Again)	1	1,953.40	10
Young Buster (Ire) [5] out of Bustara)	2	11,804.25	10 10
Young Tess [3] out of Bundu (Fr))	1	2,780.60	12
	10	34,058.60	

TEJANO (USA) (1985) by Caro-Infantes by Exclusive Native

	Races Won	Value £	Distances in furlongs
Ballah Shack (USA) [2] out of Granny's Portait (USA))	2	5,908.00	7 5
Tej Singh (USA) [3] out of Deep River Woman (USA))	2	6,666.75	8 9
	4	12,574.75	

TELSMOSS (1976) by Levmoss-Elakonee Wind by Restless Wind

	Races Won	Value £	Distances in furlongs
Hard To Figure [7] out of Count On Me)	2	66,592.50	6 6

TEMPERENCE HILL (USA) (1977) by Stop The Music (USA)-Sister Shannon by Etonian

	Races Won	Value £	Distances in furlongs
Must Be Magical (USA) [5] out of Hon-orine (USA))	1	2,243.00	14

TENDER KING (1979) by Prince Tenderfoot (USA)-Cider Princess by Alcide

	Races Won	Value £	Distances in furlongs
Broughton's Tango (Ire) [4] out of Topless Dancer)	2	7,958.25	12 12
Leave It To Lib [6] out of Nuit de Vin)	2	6,068.50	8 8
Royal Acclaim [8] out of Glimmer)	1	2,070.00	8
Tendresse (Ire) [5] out of Velinowski)	2	6,715.50	10 10
Yonge Tender [6] out of St Clair Star)	1	2,826.00	8
	8	25,638.25	

THATCHING (1975) by Thatch (USA)-Abella by Premonition or Abernant

	Races Won	Value £	Distances in furlongs
Asking For Aces [2] out of Wizardry)	1	2,821.10	6

	Races Won	Value £	Distances in furlongs
Blue Grit [7] out of Northern Wisdom)	1	3,980.00	6
Dawning Street (Ire) [5] out of Dawn Star)	2	33,181.20	8 7
Easy Access (Ire) [3] out of Savannah Song (USA))	1	5,692.00	7
Finjan [6] out of Capriconia)	2	6,247.45	6 6
Go South [9] out of Run To The Sun)	1	2,243.00	16
Harvest Mouse [2] out of Top Mouse)	1	4,597.50	6
Lacerta (Ire) [3] out of Cup Defender (USA))	1	3,494.25	7
Loki (Ire) [5] out of Sigym)	1	7,310.00	10
Olifantsfontein [5] out of Taplow)	1	6,164.00	5
Peerage Prince [4] out of Belle Viking (Fr))	1	3,260.25	5
Summer Hail (Ire) [2] out of Crystal Fountain)	1	4,985.75	6
Thatcherella [2] out of Ella Mon Amour)	1	2,691.00	5
Thousla Rock (Ire) [4] out of Resooka)	1	3,143.25	7
Thunder River (Ire) [3] out of In For More)	1	2,880.00	7
	17	92,690.75	

THE MINSTREL (CAN) (1974) by Northern Dancer-Fleur by Victoria Park

	Races Won	Value £	Distances in furlongs
Colin Muset [3] out of First Kiss)	1	3,289.50	7
Florid (USA) [2] out of Kenanga)	1	4,464.00	8
Mingus (USA) [6] out of Sylph (USA))	2	6,376.50	15 15
Nemea (USA) [3] out of Donna Inez (USA))	1	3,049.40	9
Quaver (USA) [3] out of Que Sympatica)	1	3,493.00	7
Singing Reply (USA) [5] out of Bright Reply (USA))	1	3,131.90	14
Song Of Sixpence (USA) [9] out of Gliding By (USA))	1	8,415.00	10
Sulitelma (USA) [2] out of Sharmila (Fr))	1	2,040.00	5
True Hero (USA) [3] out of Badge Of Courage (USA))	1	29,376.00	10
	10	63,635.30	

THE NOBLE PLAYER (USA) (1980) by The Minstrel(Can)-Noble Mark by On Your Mark

	Races Won	Value £	Distances in furlongs
Lord Olivier (Ire) [3] out of Burkina)	1	3,201.75	5
Mr Nevermind (Ire) [3] out of Salacia)	2	7,739.40	6 7
Precious Caroline (Ire) [5] out of What A Breeze)	1	2,950.60	10
Private Fixture (Ire) [2] out of Pennyala)	1	2,803.00	5
The Noble Oak (Ire) [5] out of Sea Palace)	2	6,189.75	5 5
	7	22,884.50	

THEATRICAL (1982) by Nureyev (USA)-Tree of Knowledge by Sassafras(Fr)

	Races Won	Value £	Distances in furlongs
Broadway Flyer (USA) [2] out of Serena (Saf))	1	3,535.00	8
Redstella (USA) [4] out of Orange Squash)	1	3,816.00	8
Riviere Actor (USA) [3] out of Riviere Salee (Fr))	1	3,525.00	16
	3	10,876.00	

THEN AGAIN (1983) by Jaazeiro (USA)-New Light by Reform

	Races Won	Value £	Distances in furlongs
Down D Islands [2] out of Down The Valley)	2	6,409.25	6 8
Duplicate [3] out of Josilu)	1	2,534.20	12
For The Present [3] out of Axe Valley)	2	8,621.00	6 6
Shotley Again [3] out of Sweet Candice)	1	2,379.00	7
So So [3] out of Swinging Gold)	1	7,440.00	8
Time Again [3] out of Vaula)	1	3,172.50	7
	8	30,555.95	

†THOWRA (FR) (1986) by Sadler's Wells (USA)-Vague Bubble (USA) by Vaguely Noble

	Races Won	Value £	Distances in furlongs
Dancing Lawyer [2] out of Miss Lawsuit)	1	2,826.00	5

TILT UP (USA) (1975) by Olden Times-Unity by Tudor Melody

	Races Won	Value £	Distances in furlongs
Fair Flyer (Ire) [4] out of Fair Siobahn)	1	3,557.50	12

TIME FOR A CHANGE (USA) (1981) by Damascus (USA)-Resolver by Reviewer (USA)

	Races Won	Value £	Distances in furlongs
Time Honored (USA) [3] out of La Paqueline (Fr))	1	3,390.90	7

TIMELESS MOMENT (USA) (1970) by Damascus (USA)-Hour of Parting by Native Dancer

	Races Won	Value £	Distances in furlongs
Appealing Times (USA) [4] out of Appealing One (USA))	1	2,070.00	6
Second Colours (USA) [3] out of Ruffled Silk (USA))	1	2,950.60	5
Tik Fa (USA) [4] out of How Fortunate (USA))	2	9,088.80	8 7
	4	14,109.40	

TIMELESS NATIVE (USA) (1980) by Timeless Moment (USA)-Head Off (USA) by Executioner (USA)

	Races Won	Value £	Distances in furlongs
Umbubuzi (USA) [3] out of Making Rounds (USA))	1	2,243.00	7

TINA'S PET (1978) by Mummy's Pet-Merry Weather by Will Somers

	Races Won	Value £	Distances in furlongs
Ahjay [3] out of City Link Rose)	1	3,231.00	6
Another Lane [6] out of Spinner)	1	2,623.80	5
Bella Parkes [2] out of Summerhill Spruce)	3	10,074.75	6 6 6
Blue Bomber [2] out of Warm Wind)	2	7,471.75	5 6
Cicerone [3] out of Emma Royale)	2	5,814.50	7 7
Feather Face [3] out of Don't Loiter)	1	3,590.00	7
Martina [5] out of Tin Tessa)	4	11,080.50	5 5 5 5
Pageboy [4] out of Edwins' Princess)	1	1,970.00	5
Sweet Mignonette [5] out of Ixia)	5	14,905.95	8 8 9 8 8
	20	60,762.25	

TODAY AND TOMORROW (1981) by African Sky-Super Girl by Super Sam

	Races Won	Value £	Distances in furlongs
High Romance [3] out of Nahawand)	1	2,243.00	5

TOP VILLE (1976) by High Top-Sega Ville(Fr) by Charlottesville

	Races Won	Value £	Distances in furlongs
Beneficial [3] out of Youthful (Fr))	3	86,542.15	9 10 12
Dress Sense (Ire) [4] out of Smarten Up)	1	6,212.00	7
Dukrame [3] out of Durun)	1	4,045.00	10
George Dillingham [3] out of Premier Rose)	1	3,640.50	10
In The Money (Ire) [4] out of Rensaler (USA))	2	14,454.90	12 12
Kelimutu [4] out of Soemba)	4	10,532.50	9 9 10 12
Le Temeraire [7] out of La Mirande (Fr))	1	2,243.00	9
Nijo [2] out of Nibabu (Fr))	1	3,649.00	7
Vallance [5] out of Kindjal)	1	4,709.25	10
	15	136,028.30	

TOPSIDER (USA) (1974) by Northern Dancer-Drumtop (USA) by Round Table

	Races Won	Value £	Distances in furlongs
Jazeel (USA) [2] out of Secretarial Queen (USA))	1	4,396.50	7
Moccasin Run (USA) [2] out of Regal Heights (USA))	1	10,430.00	6
	2	14,826.50	

†TOUCH OF GREY (1983) by Blakeney-Belle (Den) by Comedy Star (USA)

	Races Won	Value £	Distances in furlongs
Gipsy Kid [2] out of Mistress Will (USA))	2	4,038.00	5 6

TOUCHING WOOD (USA) (1979) by Roberto (USA)-Mandera (USA) by Vaguely Noble

	Races Won	Value £	Distances in furlongs
Addicted To Love [4] out of Fleur Rouge)	1	5,754.00	14
Touch Above [7] out of B A Poundstretcher)	2	5,812.20	9 9
Touching Times [5] out of Pagan Deity)	1	2,415.00	16
White Willow [4] out of Dimant Blanche (USA))	2	8,214.75	13 11
	6	22,195.95	

TOWN AND COUNTRY (1974) by Town Crier-First Huntress by Primera

	Races Won	Value £	Distances in furlongs
Rural Lad [4] out of French Plait)	2	8,442.25	7 8

TREASURE KAY (1983) by Mummy's Pet-Welsh Blossom by Welsh Saint

	Races Won	Value £	Distances in furlongs
Bright Paragon (Ire) [4] out of Shining Bright (USA))	1	2,978.50	5
Charity Express (Ire) [3] out of Arminiya)	3	7,735.00	5 5 5
Elle Shaped (Ire) [3] out of Mamie's Joy)	1	7,492.20	5
Gussie Fink-Nottle (Ire) [3] out of Bright Cecilia)	1	2,847.00	5
Treasure Time (Ire) [4] out of Dowcester)	1	2,301.00	5
Wixi (Ire) [2] out of Traminer)	1	3,435.75	5
	8	26,789.45	

TREMPOLINO (USA) (1984) by Sharpen Up-Trephine(Fr) by Viceregal(Can)

	Races Won	Value £	Distances in furlongs
Alderney Prince (USA) [3] out of Princess Of Man)	1	2,976.50	9
Balzino (USA) [4] out of Royal Procession (USA))	1	2,162.50	14
Kissininthebackrow (USA) [2] out of Moviegoer)	1	3,728.25	5
Tremolando (USA) [3] out of Alia)	1	3,611.25	10
Twin Falls (Ire) [2] out of Twice A Fool (USA))	1	4,306.50	8
	5	16,785.00	

TROJAN FEN (1981) by Troy-Fenella by Thatch (USA)

	Races Won	Value £	Distances in furlongs
Blazon Of Troy [4] out of Mullet)	1	3,557.50	12

TRY MY BEST (USA) (1970) by Northern Dancer-Sex Appeal (USA) by Buckpasser

	Races Won	Value £	Distances in furlongs
Best Appearance (Ire) [3] out of Reliable Rosie)	2	5,997.35	9 9
Clifton Chase [4] out of Mrs Cullumbine)	1	2,950.60	11

	Races Won	Value £	Distances in furlongs
Dance Of The Swans (Ire) [2] out of Arrapata)	2	6,057.00	5 5
Don't Be Koi (Ire) [2] out of Saltoki)	1	2,448.40	5
Kimberley Park [5] out of Georgina Park)	1	5,816.00	7
My Best Valentine [3] out of Pas de Calais)	3	13,248.15	7 7 7
Overpower [9] out of Just A Shadow)	3	6,138.00	10 10 9
Pallium (Ire) [5] out of Jungle Gardenia)	1	4,175.00	5
	14	46,830.50	

TYRNAVOS (1977) by Blakeney-Stilvi by Derring-Do

	Races Won	Value £	Distances in furlongs
Tanoda [7] out of Anoda (Fr))	2	6,025.85	10 11

UNCLE POKEY (1974) by Great Nephew-Fallen Star by Busted

	Races Won	Value £	Distances in furlongs
Master Pokey [9] out of September Fire)	1	3,261.40	5

VAGUELY NOBLE (1965) by Vienna-Noble Lassie by Nearco

	Races Won	Value £	Distances in furlongs
Ambiguously Regal (USA) [4] out of Kazatska (USA))	1	5,344.50	11
Jubran (USA) [7] out of La Vue (USA))	1	4,305.00	10
Rose Noble (USA) [3] out of La Papagena)	1	2,924.70	11
	3	12,574.20	

VAIGLY GREAT (1975) by Great Nephew-Dervaig by Derring-Do

	Races Won	Value £	Distances in furlongs
Can Can Charlie [3] out of Norton Princess)	1	3,496.00	7
Champagne Grandy [3] out of Monstrosa)	4	11,939.25	5 5 7 5
Edge Of Darkness [4] out of Atoka)	1	2,070.00	16
Pusey Street Boy [6] out of Pusey Street)	3	8,896.00	8 7 8
The Executor [3] out of Fee)	2	6,319.20	8 8
	11	32,720.45	

VALIYAR (1979) by Red God-Val Divine(Fr) by Val de Loir

	Races Won	Value £	Distances in furlongs
Bobbysoxer [3] out of Beveridge (USA))	3	10,328.50	12 10 12
Hi Nod [3] out of Vikris)	3	25,885.20	7 6 7
My Godson [3] out of Blessit)	1	3,054.00	5
Valiant Man [2] out of Redcross Miss)	1	3,289.50	5
Western Valley [3] out of Another Western)	1	2,780.60	6
	9	45,337.80	

VICTORIOUS (USA) (1980) by Explodent-Paris Breeze by Majestic Prince

	Races Won	Value £	Distances in furlongs
On Y Va (USA) [6] out of Golden Moony)	2	5,001.00	7 7

VIKING (USA) (1977) by Northern Dancer-Paddy's Song by Chanteur II

	Races Won	Value £	Distances in furlongs
Laurel Queen (Ire) [5] out of Prima Bella)	6	18,666.75	7 7 7 6 7 7

VISION (USA) (1981) by Nijinsky(Can)-Foreseer by Round Table

	Races Won	Value £	Distances in furlongs
Bit On The Side (Ire) [4] out of Mistress (USA))	2	9,742.25	10 10
Braille (Ire) [2] out of Winning Feature)	2	5,523.75	6 6
Captain Starlight (Ire) [2] out of Belitis)	1	2,601.40	9
Famous Beauty [6] out of Relfo)	1	2,364.00	12
Field Of Vision (Ire) [3] out of Bold Meadows)	3	14,207.25	7 7 7
Mad Militant (Ire) [4] out of Ullapool)	1	5,374.00	12
Second Sight (Ire) [2] out of Maellen)	1	3,325.00	6
	11	43,137.65	

WAAJIB (1983) by Try My Best (USA)-Coryana by Sassafras(Fr)

	Races Won	Value £	Distances in furlongs
Bitter's End (Ire) [3] out of Annsfield Lady)	1	4,230.00	7
Blair Castle (Ire) [2] out of Caimanite)	1	3,590.00	8
Comet Whirlpool (Ire) [3] out of Remember Mulvilla)	1	3,131.90	5
Connect (Ire) [2] out of My My Marie)	1	2,872.90	5
Monis (Ire) [2] out of Gratify)	1	3,949.00	5
My-O-My (Ire) [3] out of Maimiti)	1	9,681.00	5
Rohita (Ire) [2] out of Ruby River)	2	7,764.80	5 6
Wajiba Riva (Ire) [2] out of Yellow Creek)	2	10,018.50	5 5
	10	45,238.10	

†WARNING (1985) by Known Fact (USA)-Slightly Dangerous (USA) by Roberto (USA)

	Races Won	Value £	Distances in furlongs
Averti (Ire) [2] out of Imperial Jade)	2	9,966.25	6 5
Electrify (USA) [2] out of Dokki (USA))	1	5,162.50	6
Indhar [2] out of Clarista (USA))	2	13,259.00	7 7
Piccolo [2] out of Woodwind (Fr))	1	4,191.00	6
Prophecy (Ire) [2] out of Andaleeb (USA))	3	83,905.12	5 6 6
Queenbird [2] out of Song Test (USA))	3	12,813.40	5 6 6

	Races Won	Value £	Distances in furlongs
Threatening [2] out of Pato)	2	10,085.00	6 7
Torch Rouge [2] out of Sistabelle)	1	3,318.75	5
Tufa [2] out of Emerald (USA))	1	3,991.50	7
	16	146,692.52	

WASSL (1980) by Mill Reef (USA)-Hayloft by Tudor Melody

	Races Won	Value £	Distances in furlongs
Sooty Tern [6] out of High Tern)	3	11,034.00	8 8 8
Tyrian Purple (Ire) [5] out of Sabrine)	1	2,406.00	7
Wassl This Then (Ire) [4] out of Dancing Decoy)	2	6,294.00	10 10
Who's The Best (Ire) [3] out of Rip Roaring)	2	6,045.00	8 10
	8	25,779.00	

WATTLEFIELD (1979) by Red God-Short Commons by Hard Tack

	Races Won	Value £	Distances in furlongs
Never In The Red [5] out of Swing Gently)	1	3,080.00	5

WELSH CAPTAIN (1974) by Welsh Saint-Capua by Darius

	Races Won	Value £	Distances in furlongs
Cool Enough [12] out of Sundrive)	1	3,287.30	7
Super Blues [6] out of Pitskelly Blues)	2	6,419.20	12 12
	3	9,706.50	

WESTHEIMER (USA) (1981) by Blushing Groom (Fr)-Countess North by Northern Dancer

	Races Won	Value £	Distances in furlongs
Western Fleet (USA) [2] out of Fleetwood Fancy)	1	2,668.00	7

WOLF POWER (SAF) (1978) by Flirting Around (USA)-Pandora (Saf) by Casabianca

	Races Won	Value £	Distances in furlongs
Grey Power [6] out of Periquito (USA))	4	12,843.60	16 14 12 12

WOLVERLIFE (1973) by Wolver Hollow-Miralife by Miralgo

	Races Won	Value £	Distances in furlongs
Majed (Ire) [5] out of Martin Place)	2	14,006.40	10 10

WOODMAN (USA) (1983) by Mr Prospector (USA)-Playmate by Buckpasser

	Races Won	Value £	Distances in furlongs
Ajfan (USA) [3] out of Misinskie (USA))	2	7,798.75	8 8
Andromaque (USA) [3] out of Heaven's Mine (USA))	4	25,879.65	8 8 8 8
Moshaajir (USA) [3] out of Hidden Trail (USA))	1	4,935.00	11
Rawya (USA) [2] out of Dance It (USA))	1	3,435.75	7
Sawlajan (USA) [2] out of Crafty Satin (USA))	1	3,377.25	7
Wajih (USA) [3] out of Cokebutton)	1	3,844.00	10
Woodhaunter (USA) [3] out of Naughtiness (USA))	1	2,248.00	8
Xylem (USA) [2] out of Careful (USA))	1	3,532.00	7
	12	55,050.40	

WORLD APPEAL (USA) (1980) by Valid Appeal (USA)-Go Go Windy by Restless Wind

	Races Won	Value £	Distances in furlongs
World Without End (USA) [4] out of Mardie's Bid (USA))	2	6,446.00	17 17

YUKON (USA) (1979) by Northern Dancer-Gold Digger by Nashua

	Races Won	Value £	Distances in furlongs
Merlins Wish (USA) [4] out of Dear Guinevere (USA))	1	1,828.00	8

†ZILZAL (USA) (1986) by Nureyev (USA)-French Charmer (USA) by Le Fabuleux

	Races Won	Value £	Distances in furlongs
Arzina (USA) [2] out of Agri Dagi (USA))	1	3,845.25	5
Monaassabaat (USA) [2] out of It's In The Air (USA))	1	4,378.00	6
Rameau (USA) [2] out of Image Of Reality (USA))	1	4,776.00	7
Zama (USA) [2] out of Mizima (USA))	1	5,127.00	7
	4	18,126.25	

Sires of dams of winners on the Flat in 1993

For winning distances see 'Winning stallions on the Flat'. For example, under Above Suspicion to find the distance over which Sun of Spring won, refer to Green Desert.

ABOVE SUSPICION (1956) by Court Martial

Dam: Winner and Sire	Races Won	Value £
Unsuspected: Sun Of Spring by Green Desert (USA)	4	19,365.45
	4	19,365.45

ABSALOM (1975) by Abwah

Dam: Winner and Sire	Races Won	Value £
Abergwrle: Allwight Then (Ire) by Dancing Dissident (USA)	2	6,819.95
Brazilian Princess: Soba Guest (Ire) by Be My Guest (USA)	1	1,882.50
Faraway Grey: Mrs Dawson by Sharrood (USA)	1	2,803.00
	4	11,505.45

ACK ACK (USA) (1966) by Battle Joined

Dam: Winner and Sire	Races Won	Value £
Ack's Secret (USA): Hunting Ground by Dancing Brave (USA)	5	15,481.40
	5	15,481.40

AFFIRMED (USA) (1975) by Exclusive Native (USA)

Dam: Winner and Sire	Races Won	Value £
Emmaline (USA): Zarani Sidi Anna (USA) by Danzig (USA)	1	3,055.50
Morning Devotion (USA): Balanchine (USA) by Storm Bird (Can)	2	11,903.20
Springtime Fantasy (USA): Cyprian Dancer (USA) by Shadeed (USA)	1	3,114.00
	4	18,072.70

AFRICAN SKY (1970) by Sing Sing

Dam: Winner and Sire	Races Won	Value £
Bewitched: Martinosky by Martinmas	1	3,287.30
Burkina: Lord Olivier (Ire) by The Noble Player (USA)	1	3,201.75
Cameroun: Eternal Flame by Primo Dominie	1	3,004.60
Noir Afrique: Pete Afrique (Ire) by Petorius	2	9,135.80
Sweet Candice: Shotley Again by Then Again	1	2,379.00
	6	21,008.45

AGGRESSOR (1955) by Combat

Dam: Winner and Sire	Races Won	Value £
Merry Yarn: Briggsmaid by Elegant Air	1	3,494.50
	1	3,494.50

AGLOJO (1964) by Skymaster

Dam: Winner and Sire	Races Won	Value £
Silent Sail: Misty Goddess (Ire) by Godswalk (USA)	2	5,744.40
	2	5,744.40

AHONOORA (1975) by Lorenzaccio

Dam: Winner and Sire	Races Won	Value £
Ardassine: Gabr by Green Desert (USA)	2	17,295.00
Aunty Eileen: Moving Image (Ire) by Nordico (USA)	1	2,950.60
Brush Away: Mr Vincent by Nishapour (Fr)	2	5,854.25
Park Appeal: Arvola by Sadler's Wells (USA)	1	3,494.25
Sheba's Princess: Greenson (Ire) by Doulab (USA)	1	2,595.00
	7	32,189.10

AIR TROOPER (1973) by King's Troop

Dam: Winner and Sire	Races Won	Value £
Cheri Berry: Googly by Sunley Builds	2	11,735.50
	2	11,735.50

ALCIDE (1955) by Alycidon

Dam: Winner and Sire	Races Won	Value £
Alleyn: Good For The Roses by Kampala	1	3,915.00
Cider Princess: Blackdown by Rainbow Quest (USA)	1	1,813.60
	2	5,728.60

ALIAS SMITH (USA) (1973) by Al Hattab(USA)

Dam: Winner and Sire	Races Won	Value £
Inveraven: Demi-Plie by Squill (USA)	3	6,978.00
Moonlight Princess: Lunar Risk by Risk Me (Fr)	2	7,282.50
	5	14,260.50

ALLEGED (USA) (1974) by Hoist The Flag(USA)

Dam: Winner and Sire	Races Won	Value £
Amalancher (USA): Eurythmic by Pharly (Fr)	1	3,272.50
Don't Rush (USA): Reine de Neige by Kris	1	3,933.00
Gypsy Talk (USA): Sabrehill (USA) by Diesis	1	4,893.00

Dam Winner and Sire	Races Won	Value £
Nihad: Hunters Of Brora (Ire) by Sharpo	2	11,503.00
Nihad: Coureur by Ajdal (USA)	1	3,262.00
Sylph (USA): Mingus (USA) by The Minstrel (Can)	2	6,376.50
	8	33,240.00

ALPENKONIG (Ger) (1967) by Tamerlane

Dam Winner and Sire	Races Won	Value £
Sphinx (Ger): Cairo Prince (Ire) by Darshaan	1	3,752.50
	1	3,752.50

ALYDAR (USA) (1975) by Raise A Native

Dam Winner and Sire	Races Won	Value £
Al Khazaama (USA): Rahil (Ire) by Reference Point	3	7,597.10
Battle Drum (USA): Blaze Away (USA) by Polish Navy (USA)	2	8,794.75
Charmante (USA): Alinova (USA) by Alleged (USA)	2	8,628.00
Fatah Flare (USA): Refugio by Reference Point	1	3,205.00
Green Leaf (USA): Desert Green (Fr) by Green Desert (USA)	1	3,523.50
Green Leaf (USA): Green Green Desert (Fr) by Green Desert (USA)	1	4,581.00
Happiness (USA): Abbraak (USA) by Sir Ivor	1	3,231.00
Viewed (USA): Malenoir (USA) by Solford (USA)	1	3,106.00
	12	42,666.35

ALZAO (USA) (1980) by Lyphard(USA)

Dam Winner and Sire	Races Won	Value £
Damezao: Salvezza (Ire) by Superpower	1	3,435.75
Thank One's Stars: Suris (Ire) by Taufan (USA)	1	3,080.00
	2	6,515.75

AMBER RAMA (USA) (1967) by Jaipur

Dam Winner and Sire	Races Won	Value £
Anoda (Fr): Tanoda by Tyrnavos	2	6,025.85
	2	6,025.85

AMBIORIX II (1946) by Tourbillon

Dam Winner and Sire	Races Won	Value £
Am Stretchin' (USA): Thundering by Persian Bold	1	2,623.80
	1	2,623.80

APALACHEE (USA) (1971) by Round Table

Dam Winner and Sire	Races Won	Value £
Alpine Dance (USA): Northern Bailiwick (Ire) by Nordance (USA)	1	1,725.00
Best Guess (USA): Guesstimation (USA) by Known Fact (USA)	2	5,147.50
Swordlestown Miss (USA): Sword Master by Sayf El Arab (USA)	2	6,615.00
Swordlestown Miss (USA): Danger Baby by Bairn (USA)	1	2,399.80
	6	15,887.30

ARAGON (1980) by Mummy's Pet

Dam Winner and Sire	Races Won	Value £
Four-Legged Friend: Herr Trigger by Sharrood (USA)	1	2,532.00
Moorish Idol: Duty Time by Night Shift (USA)	2	10,583.50
	3	13,115.50

ARCTIC TERN (USA) (1973) by Sea-Bird II

Dam Winner and Sire	Races Won	Value £
Antartica (Fr): Ribhi (USA) by Riverman (USA)	3	30,607.00
Antartica (Fr): Kutbeya (USA) by Diesis	1	4,464.00
East River (Fr): Eastern Memories (Ire) by Don't Forget Me	3	21,267.00
Fancy Flight (Fr): Barley Cake by Midyan (USA)	2	4,060.70
Finlandaise (Fr): Madam Gymcrak by Celestial Storm (USA)	1	2,243.00
Nafla (Fr): Lambent by Rambo Dancer (Can)	2	6,371.50
Quillotern (USA): Quinsigimond by Formidable (USA)	4	11,593.00
	16	80,606.20

ARTAIUS (USA) (1974) by Round Table

Dam Winner and Sire	Races Won	Value £
Art Deco: Anatroccolo by Ile de Bourbon (USA)	1	3,288.00
Artiste: Allegan (USA) by Alleged (USA)	2	8,239.72
Eljazzi: Sarawat by Slip Anchor	1	66,185.00
Eljazzi: Alkhafji by Ardross	1	3,728.25
Eskaroon: Ashkernazy (Ire) by Salt Dome (USA)	1	3,318.75
Foudroyer: Paris House by Petong	2	55,557.00
Gold Honey: Gant Bleu (Fr) by Crystal Glitters (USA)	1	3,209.60
House Call: Look Who's Here (Ire) by Heraldiste (USA)	2	14,659.00
May Kells: Killy's Filly by Lochnager	2	5,678.00
Miss Rossi: Lyndon's Linnet by Prince Sabo	1	3,582.50
Moretta: Jafeica (Ire) by Dance Of Life (USA)	1	4,807.00
My My Marie: Don't Forget Marie (Ire) by Don't Forget Me	1	2,406.00
My My Marie: Connect (Ire) by Waajib	1	2,872.90
Polyartis: Kayartis by Kaytu	1	3,184.00
Samya's Flame: Raneen Alwatar by Sadler's Wells (USA)	1	4,012.50
Super Style: Threepenny-Bridge by Ballacashtal (Can)	1	2,070.00
	20	186,798.22

ASHMORE (Fr) (1971) by Luthier

Dam Winner and Sire	Races Won	Value £
Day Dress: Old Hook (Ire) by Digamist (USA)	1	2,070.00
Outward's Gal: Princess Of Orange by Master Willie	1	2,870.20

Dam Winner and Sire	Races Won	Value £
Outward's Gal: Abbey's Gal by Efisio	3	23,302.35
	5	28,242.55

ASSAGAI (1963) by Warfare

Dam Winner and Sire	Races Won	Value £
Gal A Tic (USA): Fanatical (USA) by Lear Fan (USA)	1	2,511.00
	1	2,511.00

ASSERT (1979) by Be My Guest(USA)

Dam Winner and Sire	Races Won	Value £
Kalata: Kithanga (Ire) by Darshaan	3	39,605.00
Stormette (USA): Marillette (USA) by Diesis	1	25,003.47
	4	64,608.47

AUCTION RING (USA) (1972) by Bold Bidder

Dam Winner and Sire	Races Won	Value £
Dream Trader: Dream Carrier (Ire) by Doulab (USA)	1	5,047.25
Etching: Steadfast Elite (Ire) by Glenstal (USA)	2	5,841.10
Flying Melody: Lyric Fantasy (Ire) by Tate Gallery (USA)	1	10,029.00
Grey Dream: Toledo Queen (Ire) by El Gran Senor (USA)	2	11,675.02
Harmonious Sound: Nellie's Gamble by Mummy's Game	2	5,219.50
Have A Flutter: Dollar Gamble (Ire) by Jareer (USA)	2	6,917.50
Lone Bidder: Saihat (Ire) by Midyan (USA)	2	7,100.50
Miss Victoria: Ballard Ring (Ire) by Ballad Rock	1	5,952.00
Pirate Maid: Walking The Plank by Daring March	2	7,715.00
Pirate Maid: Tom Morgan by Faustus (USA)	1	0.00
Quality Of Life: Bob's Return (Ire) by Bob Back (USA)	3	275,271.10
Ringtail: Waterlord (Ire) by Bob Back (USA)	1	2,286.00
Select Sale: Hello Ireland by Reference Point	1	4,542.00
Silk Trade: Silky Heights (Ire) by Head For Heights	2	6,263.80
Silk Trade: Elevator Shaft (Ire) by Double Schwartz	2	5,001.00
Single Bid: Scoffera by Scottish Reel	2	3,984.50
Single Bid: Bid For Blue by Primo Dominie	2	13,991.25
	29	376,836.52

AVEROF (1971) by Sing Sing

Dam Winner and Sire	Races Won	Value £
Aventina: Green's Stubbs by Ballad Rock	1	2,070.00
Klairove: Bunty Boo by Noalto	1	3,720.00
Klairove: Manor Adventure by Smackover	1	3,125.50
Peerless Princess: Charmed Knave by Enchantment	2	6,029.00
Queen Of The Brush: Fawlty Towers (Ire) by Fools Holme (USA)	1	2,243.00
	6	17,187.50

BALIDAR (1966) by Will Somers

Dam Winner and Sire	Races Won	Value £
Balatina: Primo Stampari by Primo Dominie	1	4,556.75
Balinese: Sir Thomas Beecham by Daring March	3	7,353.30
Conrara: Surprise Breeze by Grey Desire	1	2,243.00
Steady The Buffs: Sheridan (Ire) by Alzao (USA)	1	4,592.50
Stubble: Window Display by Chilibang	1	2,070.00
Susie's Baby: Sir Tasker by Lidhame	1	2,976.50
Susie's Baby: Brockton Dancer by Fairy King (USA)	1	3,231.00
This Sensation: Electrolyte by Electric	1	2,997.00
	10	30,020.05

BALLAD ROCK (1974) by Bold Lad(Ire)

Dam Winner and Sire	Races Won	Value £
Phyl: Lady Phyl by Northiam (USA)	1	3,720.00
Remember Mulvilla: Comet Whirlpool (Ire) by Waajib	1	3,131.90
Saltoki: Don't Be Koi (Ire) by Try My Best (USA)	1	2,448.40
	3	9,300.30

BALLYMORE (1969) by Ragusa

Dam Winner and Sire	Races Won	Value £
Heather Lil: Fortis Pavior (Ire) by Salt Dome (USA)	2	6,032.00
Heather Lil: Alpine Skier (Ire) by Nordico (USA)	1	5,663.00
	3	11,695.00

BALLYMOSS (1954) by Mossborough

Dam Winner and Sire	Races Won	Value £
Au Revoir: Grand Vitesse (Ire) by Alzao (USA)	1	5,526.50
Gluhwein: Mister Piste (Ire) by Fayruz	1	3,236.00
	2	8,762.50

BANDERILLA (USA) (1968) by Native Dancer

Dam Winner and Sire	Races Won	Value £
Famous Band (USA): Bold Elect by Electric	1	3,235.50
	1	3,235.50

BARACHOIS (Can) (1969) by Northern Dancer

Dam Winner and Sire	Races Won	Value £
Nice Manners (Can): Daswaki (Can) by Miswaki (USA)	2	8,685.50
	2	8,685.50

BARRERA (USA) (1973) by Raise A Native

Dam Winner and Sire	Races Won	Value £
Almost Pure (USA): Dramanice (USA) by Northern Fling (USA)	1	3,523.50
	1	3,523.50

Dam Winner and Sire	Races Won	Value £

BAY EXPRESS (1971) by Polyfoto

Dam Winner and Sire	Races Won	Value £
Appleby Park: Jucea by Bluebird (USA)	1	2,301.00
Bay Bay: Baskerville by Night Shift (USA)	1	3,557.50
Clodianus: Sporting Warrior (Ire) by Exhibitioner	1	2,780.60
Ichnusa: Sartigila by Efisio	2	7,721.25
Orient: Lamsonetti by Never So Bold	1	2,739.00
Six Penny Express: Miss Amy Lou (Ire) by Gallic League	1	3,406.50
Wisdom To Know: Selhurstpark Flyer (Ire) by Northiam (USA)	4	23,249.00
	11	45,754.85

BE FRIENDLY (1964) by Skymaster

Dam Winner and Sire	Races Won	Value £
Be Easy: Dreams End by Rainbow Quest (USA)	1	3,669.75
Friendly Jester: Cracker Jack by Chilibang	1	1,520.00
Noble Girl: Stash The Cash (Ire) by Persian Bold	1	3,810.00
	3	8,999.75

BE MY GUEST (USA) (1974) by Northern Dancer

Dam Winner and Sire	Races Won	Value £
Azayim: Watani (USA) by Riverman (USA)	2	13,052.50
Bag Lady: Bag Of Tricks (Ire) by Chief Singer	1	3,054.00
Barsham: Guestwick by Blakeney	1	2,243.00
Be My Lady: Silver Samurai by Alleging (USA)	4	16,607.75
Be My Queen: Bay Queen by Damister (USA)	4	15,474.50
Cokebutton: Wajih (USA) by Woodman (USA)	1	3,844.00
Deja Vu (Fr): Jade Vale by Petorius	3	14,388.00
Eurynome: Summer Wind (Ire) by Bold Arrangement	4	13,003.00
Exuberine (Fr): Pharoah's Guest by Pharly (Fr)	1	3,416.80
Guess Who: Hazard A Guess (Ire) by Digamist (USA)	3	10,057.60
Guest List: Backstabber by Flash Of Steel	1	3,054.20
Guest Performer: Encore Une Fois (Ire) by Shirley Heights	1	4,836.00
Intimate Guest: Golden Guest by Rainbow Quest (USA)	1	4,581.00
Kentucky Wildcat: Two Moves In Front (Ire) by Ballad Rock	1	3,114.00
Kentucky Wildcat: Randonneur (Ire) by Red Sunset	4	13,087.55
Lajna: Gold Land (USA) by Gone West (USA)	3	14,216.10
Lora's Guest: Nawahil by Shirley Heights	1	3,055.50
Mary Martin: Marina Park by Local Suitor (USA)	1	6,750.00
On The House (Fr): Castel Rosselo by Rousillon (USA)	1	3,318.75
Plum Bold: Plum First by Nomination	1	5,117.00
Quisissanno: Mulciber by Head For Heights	1	2,678.40
Quisissanno: Euro Festival by Precocious	1	3,728.25
Quisissanno: Willshe Gan by Precocious	1	3,420.00
Regal Entrance: Hoochiecoochie Man (Ire) by Taufan (USA)	2	5,969.00
Santiki: Planetary Aspect (USA) by Risen Star (USA)	1	4,175.00
Sojourn: Arctic Guest (Ire) by Arctic Tern (USA)	3	8,225.40
Special Guest: Cragganmore by Faustus (USA)	1	3,003.00
	49	187,470.30

BE MY NATIVE (USA) (1979) by Our Native(USA)

Dam Winner and Sire	Races Won	Value £
Massawippi: Cicerao (Ire) by Alzao (USA)	1	4,503.00
	1	4,503.00

BELDALE FLUTTER (USA) (1978) by Accipiter(USA)

Dam Winner and Sire	Races Won	Value £
Bronzewing: Sun Grebe (Ire) by Arctic Tern (USA)	3	10,448.50
Crystal Spray: State Crystal (Ire) by High Estate	1	4,202.75
Thornbeam: Bet A Plan (Ire) by Cyrano de Bergerac	1	2,259.00
Treasurebound: Batchworth Bound by Ballacashtal (Can)	2	5,959.90
	7	22,870.15

BELIEVE IT (USA) (1975) by In Reality

Dam Winner and Sire	Races Won	Value £
Dance It (USA): Rawya (USA) by Woodman (USA)	1	3,435.75
	1	3,435.75

BELLMAN (Fr) (1978) by Riverman(USA)

Dam Winner and Sire	Races Won	Value £
London Cries (Fr): Regal Chimes by Another Realm	2	20,536.70
Mindena (Fr): Westray (Fr) by Caerwent	1	1,992.50
	3	22,529.20

BELLYPHA (1976) by Lyphard(USA)

Dam Winner and Sire	Races Won	Value £
Bella Colora: Bella Ballerina by Sadler's Wells (USA)	1	3,582.00
Sistabelle: Torch Rouge by Warning	1	3,318.75
	2	6,900.75

BEST TURN (USA) (1966) by Turn-to

Dam Winner and Sire	Races Won	Value £
Best Decision (USA): Biljan (USA) by Alydar (USA)	1	2,562.00
	1	2,562.00

BING II (1961) by Botticelli

Dam Winner and Sire	Races Won	Value £
Precious Petra: Delpiombo by Lochnager	2	4,606.50
	2	4,606.50

BIRDBROOK (1961) by Mossborough

Dam Winner and Sire	Races Won	Value £
Partridge Brook: Northern Bird by Interrex (Can)	1	7,245.00
	1	7,245.00

BISCAY (Aus) (1965) by Star Kingdom

Dam Winner and Sire	Races Won	Value £
Yen (Aus): Savings Bank by Shernazar	1	3,260.25
	1	3,260.25

BLAKENEY (1966) by Hethersett

Dam Winner and Sire	Races Won	Value £
Best Of Fun: Funny Choice (Ire) by Commanche Run	3	7,557.80
Blakeney Sound: Glen Miller by Music Boy	2	5,265.00
Britannia's Rule: Dover Patrol (Ire) by Dancing Brave (USA)	2	6,802.00
Carlton Glory: Reach For Glory by Reach	1	2,377.00
Dame Julian: Mahrajan by Dominion	2	6,754.50
Dame Julian: Diplomatist by Dominion	1	1,548.00
Juliette Marny: Surrey Dancer by Shareef Dancer (USA)	2	6,388.00
Larive: Rapid Mover by Final Straw	1	1,646.00
Lyra: Ever So Lyrical by Never So Bold	1	3,933.00
Mountain Lodge: Mountain Willow by Doyoun	1	2,758.00
Norfolk Serenade: Samsolom by Absalom	5	18,286.25
Norfolk Serenade: Secret Serenade by Classic Secret (USA)	1	3,028.30
Percy's Lass: Blue Lion by Lomond (USA)	2	7,992.50
Rynechra: Coigach by Niniski (USA)	1	4,485.25
Safe Haven: Delve (Ire) by Shernazar	1	4,182.10
Safe Haven: Alaflak (Ire) by Caerleon (USA)	1	3,420.00
Sharmila (Fr): Jadirah (USA) by Deputy Minister (Can)	1	3,131.90
Sharmila (Fr): Sulitelma (USA) by The Minstrel (Can)	1	2,040.00
Silent Sun: Silent Expression by Siberian Express (USA)	3	15,185.00
Taka: Takadou (Ire) by Double Schwartz	1	3,318.75
Tanagrea: Gone Troppo by Chief Singer	1	3,377.25
Westerlake: Legend Dulac (Ire) by Legend Of France (USA)	1	3,377.25
	35	116,853.85

BLAST (1957) by Djebe

Dam Winner and Sire	Races Won	Value £
Blaskette: Castoret by Jalmood (USA)	1	15,962.50
	1	15,962.50

BLUE CASHMERE (1970) by Kashmir II

Dam Winner and Sire	Races Won	Value £
Blue Empress: Miss Crusty by Belfort (Fr)	1	2,959.00
Bluebutton: Call Me I'm Blue (Ire) by Reasonable (Fr)	5	29,753.90
Spinner: Another Lane by Tina's Pet	1	2,623.80
Spinner: Young Valentine by Bairn (USA)	1	2,941.00
	8	38,277.70

BLUSHING GROOM (Fr) (1974) by Red God

Dam Winner and Sire	Races Won	Value £
Al Bahathri (USA): Alyakkh (Ire) by Sadler's Wells (USA)	1	3,377.25
Beechwood (USA): Imposing Groom (Ire) by Posen (USA)	1	2,782.50
Chain Fern (USA): Woodwardia (USA) by El Gran Senor (USA)	1	3,552.75
Fu Fu La Rue (USA): Rue Rembrandt (USA) by Explodent (USA)	2	6,772.50
Galaxie Dust (USA): Bulaxie by Bustino	1	7,995.00
Honorine (USA): Must Be Magical (USA) by Temperence Hill (USA)	1	2,243.00
Red Comes Up (USA): Kassab by Caerleon (USA)	3	11,867.95
Red Comes Up (USA): Barahin (Ire) by Diesis	3	5,641.40
Red Comes Up (USA): Danger Point by Danehill (USA)	1	3,509.00
Wedding Picture (USA): Winged Victory (USA) by Nijinsky (Can)	1	10,308.75
	15	58,050.10

BOLD BIDDER (1962) by Bold Ruler

Dam Winner and Sire	Races Won	Value £
Bold Courtesan (USA): Diesan (USA) by Diesis	3	12,375.00
Shining Bright (USA): Bright Paragon (Ire) by Treasure Kay	1	2,978.50
	4	15,353.50

BOLD FORBES (USA) (1973) by Irish Castle(USA)

Dam Winner and Sire	Races Won	Value £
Go For Bold (USA): Bold Sixteen (USA) by Diesis	1	4,449.50
Royally Rewarded (USA): Green's Cassatt (USA) by Apalachee (USA)	1	2,724.00
	2	7,173.50

BOLD HITTER (USA) (1966) by Bold Native (USA)

Dam Winner and Sire	Races Won	Value £
Happy Kin (USA): League Leader (Ire) by Shirley Heights	3	68,498.70
	3	68,498.70

BOLD HOUR (1964) by Bold Ruler

Dam Winner and Sire	Races Won	Value £
All Rainbows (USA): Shareek (USA) by Alysheba (USA)	1	4,077.50
En Tiempo (USA): Tilty (USA) by Linkage (USA)	2	6,801.80
Maryland Cookie (USA): Master Charlie by Master Willie	1	3,915.00
	4	14,794.30

BOLD LAD (Ire) (1964) by Bold Ruler

Dam: Winner and Sire	Races Won	Value £
Adrana: Alflora (Ire) by Niniski (USA)	2	57,818.95
Amaranda (USA): Imperial Ballet (Ire) by Sadler's Wells (USA)	2	46,039.75
Bold Fantasy: Imaginary (Ire) by Dancing Brave (USA)	1	4,012.50
Bold Miss: Lomas (Ire) by Ela-Mana-Mou	2	7,929.45
Boldie: Rambold by Rambo Dancer (Can)	2	9,270.50
Buz Kashi: Golden Memories (Ire) by Shernazar	1	5,673.00
Crystal Bright: Wainwright (USA) by Bering	2	18,602.50
Merrie Moira: Petraco (Ire) by Petorius	1	2,831.50
Miss Kuta Beach: Miss Rinjani by Shirley Heights	1	4,306.50
Old Silver: Mad About Men by Roaring Riva	1	1,903.00
Pampala: Pistol River (Ire) by Simply Great (Fr)	1	4,751.50
Truly Bold: Dead Calm by Another Realm	1	2,243.00
	17	165,382.15

BOLD RULER (1954) by Nasrullah

Dam: Winner and Sire	Races Won	Value £
Intrepid Lady (USA): Intrepidity by Sadler's Wells (USA)	1	147,500.00
	1	147,500.00

BOLDNESIAN (1963) by Bold Ruler

Dam: Winner and Sire	Races Won	Value £
College Bold (USA): Pembroke (USA) by Gone West (USA)	1	3,262.00
	1	3,262.00

BOLKONSKI (1972) by Balidar

Dam: Winner and Sire	Races Won	Value £
Alsazia (Fr): Sizzling Saga (Ire) by Horage	2	4,779.00
	2	4,779.00

BOMBAY DUCK (USA) (1972) by Nashua

Dam: Winner and Sire	Races Won	Value £
La Ninouchka (USA): Plunder Bay (USA) by Cutlass (USA)	1	5,309.00
	1	5,309.00

BREEDERS DREAM (1968) by Tudor Melody

Dam: Winner and Sire	Races Won	Value £
Northern Dynasty: Western Dynasty by Hotfoot	2	6,233.20
Northern Dynasty: Sarah-Clare by Reach	3	8,939.25
	5	15,172.45

BRETON (1967) by Relko

Dam: Winner and Sire	Races Won	Value £
Burnished Gold: Marjorie's Memory (Ire) by Fairy King (USA)	1	2,406.00
	1	2,406.00

BRIARTIC (Can) (1968) by Nearctic

Dam: Winner and Sire	Races Won	Value £
Arctic Winter (Can): Polar Storm (Ire) by Law Society (USA)	2	11,120.00
Solartic (Can): Solar Wagon (USA) by Gone West (USA)	1	4,485.25
	3	15,605.25

BRIGADIER GERARD (1968) by Queen's Hussar

Dam: Winner and Sire	Races Won	Value £
Girl's Brigade: Tamar's Brigade by Absalom	2	8,775.90
Marie Noelle (Fr): Tapis Rouge (Ire) by Irish River (Fr)	1	4,965.72
Nancy Brig: Munday Dean by Kind Of Hush	1	3,054.20
Naughty One Gerard: Proud Brigadier (Ire) by Auction Ring (USA)	2	6,170.80
Pagan Deity: Touching Times by Touching Wood (USA)	1	2,415.00
Raunchy Rita: Daring Destiny by Daring March	1	4,556.75
	8	29,938.37

BRUNI (1972) by Sea Hawk II

Dam: Winner and Sire	Races Won	Value £
Six Ashes: Casting Shadows by Chief Singer	1	3,786.75
	1	3,786.75

BUCKPASSER (1963) by Tom Fool

Dam: Winner and Sire	Races Won	Value £
Lassie Dear (USA): Wolfhound (USA) by Nureyev (USA)	1	81,701.00
Simplon Pass (USA): Zuno Star (USA) by Afleet (Can)	2	7,029.00
While I'm Away (USA): Tasset (Can) by Tasso (USA)	1	3,465.00
	4	92,195.00

BURGLAR (1966) by Crocket

Dam: Winner and Sire	Races Won	Value £
Acquire: Top Show (Ire) by Digamist (USA)	2	6,204.50
Honey Thief: Honey Seeker by Chief Singer	1	3,339.10
Moaning Low: Soaking by Dowsing (USA)	1	3,131.90
	4	12,675.50

BUSTED (1963) by Crepello

Dam: Winner and Sire	Races Won	Value £
Aunt Jemima: Azhar by Night Shift (USA)	4	27,289.50
Broken Melody: Bold Melody by Never So Bold	1	1,051.00
Broken Melody: Fanfold (Ire) by Siberian Express (USA)	1	2,243.00
Buss: Beauchamp Hero by Midyan (USA)	2	26,932.00
Bustara: Young Buster (Ire) by Teenoso (USA)	2	11,804.25
Bustellina: Cumbrian Rhapsody by Sharrood (USA)	4	16,378.55
Butosky: Dutosky by Doulab (USA)	2	8,757.50

Dam Winner and Sire	Races Won	Value £
Collapse: Will Of Steel by Master Willie	1	7,438.56
Collapse: Absalom's Pillar by Absalom	1	4,050.00
Contralto: Enharmonic (USA) by Diesis	1	21,843.00
Contralto: Talent (USA) by Clever Trick (USA)	1	3,687.50
Drora: Queens Cottage (Ire) by Jareer (USA)	1	3,984.75
Eurorose: Sir Oliver (Ire) by Auction Ring (USA)	1	3,002.00
Fair Sousanne: Gisarne (USA) by Diesis	2	17,755.00
For Instance: Batabanoo by Bairn (USA)	2	5,951.25
Hanna Alta (Fr): Belmoredean by Be My Guest (USA)	1	3,235.50
Hanna Alta (Fr): Elaine Tully (Ire) by Persian Bold	1	3,260.25
Kabiyla: Jura Forest by Green Forest (USA)	1	5,300.75
Melodrama: Ritto by Arctic Tern (USA)	1	3,435.75
Melodrama: Lemon Souffle by Salse (USA)	3	24,989.55
Nicoletta: Nicolotte by Night Shift (USA)	2	9,102.75
Opale: Tenayestelign by Bellypha	1	3,416.80
Prise: Habeta (USA) by Habitat	1	3,850.00
Sovereign Flash (Fr): Indian Flash (Ire) by Chief's Crown (USA)	3	9,019.50
	40	227,778.71

BUSTINO (1971) by Busted

Dam Winner and Sire	Races Won	Value £
Bambolona: Scottish Bambi by Scottish Reel	2	8,285.00
Bambolona: Miss Haggis by Scottish Reel	1	3,201.75
Bayazida: Baladiya by Darshaan	2	5,359.40
Beacon Hill: High Summer by Green Desert (USA)	2	6,169.30
Cape Chestnut: Tree Of Life by Shirley Heights	1	3,348.00
Dish Dash: Maroof (USA) by Danzig (USA)	1	5,057.00
Dish Dash: Fawaakeh (USA) by Lyphard (USA)	1	4,628.25
Falcon Berry (Fr): Hasta La Vista by Superlative	2	5,848.80
False Front: Mujawab by Night Shift (USA)	2	7,472.50
Fire Flash: Million Lights (Ire) by Cadeaux Genereux	1	3,933.00
Height Of Fashion (Fr): Bashayer (USA) by Mr Prospector (USA)	1	5,346.40
Hitopah: Colfax Classic by Jareer (USA)	1	3,494.25
Ladoucette: Sweet Romeo by Local Suitor (USA)	1	3,026.25
Manna Green: Merry Mermaid by Bairn (USA)	1	7,044.00
Overcall: Overbury (Ire) by Caerleon (USA)	2	10,628.10
Silver Mantle: Master Foodbroker (Ire) by Simply Great (Fr)	1	4,878.25
Startino: Stoney Valley by Caerleon (USA)	2	17,785.00
Strapless: Polish Admiral by Roi Danzig (USA)	1	3,158.00
	25	108,663.25

CAERLEON (USA) (1980) by Nijinsky(Can)

Dam Winner and Sire	Races Won	Value £
Size Six (USA): New Capricorn (USA) by Green Forest (USA)	1	5,360.20
	1	5,360.20

CALIBAN (1966) by Ragusa

Dam Winner and Sire	Races Won	Value £
Josilu: Duplicate by Then Again	1	2,534.20
	1	2,534.20

CAMDEN TOWN (1975) by Derring-Do

Dam Winner and Sire	Races Won	Value £
Camden Dancer: Titania's Dance (Ire) by Fairy King (USA)	1	2,668.60
	1	2,668.60

CANNONADE (USA) (1971) by Bold Bidder

Dam Winner and Sire	Races Won	Value £
Cannon Run (USA): Pistols At Dawn (USA) by Al Nasr (Fr)	4	11,867.50
	4	11,867.50

CANONERO II (USA) (1968) by Pretendre

Dam Winner and Sire	Races Won	Value £
Cannon Boy (USA): Tender Moment (Ire) by Caerleon (USA)	2	24,115.75
	2	24,115.75

CAPTAIN JAMES (1974) by Captain's Gig(USA)

Dam Winner and Sire	Races Won	Value £
Pasadena Lady: Palacegate Episode (Ire) by Drumalis	1	8,090.00
Pasadena Lady: Palacegate Jack (Ire) by Neshad (USA)	3	21,001.00
	4	29,091.00

CARO (1967) by Fortino II

Dam Winner and Sire	Races Won	Value £
Bashush (USA): Ehtfaal (Ire) by Soviet Star (USA)	2	12,726.00
Caro's Niece (USA): Carelaman by Ela-Mana-Mou	1	3,260.25
Carom (USA): Caromish (USA) by Lyphard's Wish (Fr)	1	2,929.50
Casual (USA): Astern (USA) by Polish Navy (USA)	1	3,523.50
Kilmara (USA): Premier League (Ire) by Don't Forget Me	2	7,630.25
Ma Petite Cherie (USA): Siwaayib by Green Desert (USA)	2	8,026.50
Oscura (USA): Urgent Request (Ire) by Rainbow Quest (USA)	1	3,318.75
Rutledge Place (USA): Firm Pledge (USA) by Affirmed (USA)	1	5,070.40
Smuggly (USA): Smuggler's Point (USA) by Lyphard (USA)	1	3,231.00
Yuma (USA): Ann Hill (Ire) by Bob Back (USA)	2	4,497.00
	14	54,213.15

CARWHITE (1974) by Caro

Dam Winner and Sire	Races Won	Value £
Birch Creek: Crackling by Electric	1	6,255.00
Blue Flower (Fr): Robleu by Robellino (USA)	1	3,406.50
Idabella (Fr): Stapleford Lass by Bairn (USA)	1	2,534.20
	3	12,195.70

CASTLE KEEP (1977) by Kalamoun

Dam: Winner and Sire	Races Won	Value £
Jaisalmer: Prizefighter by Rambo Dancer (Can)	1	2,932.50
Kept In Style: Nagida by Skyliner	1	39,640.00
	2	42,572.50

CAUCASUS (USA) (1972) by Nijinsky(Can)

Dam: Winner and Sire	Races Won	Value £
Ibtisamm (USA): Aljazzaf by Mtoto	2	12,673.25
Runaway Lady (USA): King Curan (USA) by Lear Fan (USA)	2	8,577.50
	4	21,250.75

CAVO DORO (1970) by Sir Ivor

Dam: Winner and Sire	Races Won	Value £
Bamdoro: Thisonesforalice by Lochnager	1	2,242.50
Musical Princess: Drummer Hicks by Seymour Hicks (Fr)	2	14,445.00
	3	16,687.50

CAWSTON'S CLOWN (1974) by Comedy Star(USA)

Dam: Winner and Sire	Races Won	Value £
Ma Pierrette: Our Rita by Hallgate	2	9,614.60
My Charade: Smilingatstrangers by Macmillion	1	3,521.00
Tuxford Hideaway: Branston Abby (Ire) by Risk Me (Fr)	4	29,308.66
	7	42,444.26

CELTIC ASH (1957) by Sicambre

Dam: Winner and Sire	Races Won	Value £
Gentle Gael: Asterix by Prince Sabo	2	6,005.50
Pennycuick: Cavatina by Chief Singer	1	3,201.75
	3	9,207.25

CHAPARRAL (Fr) (1966) by Val de Loir

Dam: Winner and Sire	Races Won	Value £
Melbourne Miss: Taroudant by Pharly (Fr)	4	12,815.50
	4	12,815.50

CHARLOTTOWN (1963) by Charlottesville

Dam: Winner and Sire	Races Won	Value £
Aleda Rose: Knyaz by Governor General	1	3,076.50
Gay Charlotte: Call The Guv'nor by Saint Estephe (Fr)	1	3,655.00
Maple Syrup: Biloela by Nicholas Bill	1	3,348.00
Marypark: Moidart by Electric	2	7,582.75
Pollinella: Junction Twentytwo by Local Suitor (USA)	1	1,916.90
	6	19,579.15

CHESTERGATE (1959) by Buisson Ardent

Dam: Winner and Sire	Races Won	Value £
Deva Rose: Eager Deva by Lochnager	2	7,850.00
	2	7,850.00

CHIEF SINGER (1981) by Ballad Rock

Dam: Winner and Sire	Races Won	Value £
Song Of Hope: Miriam by Forzando	1	3,377.25
The Queen Of Soul: Domino Queen (Ire) by Primo Dominie	1	3,285.00
	2	6,662.25

CHIEFTAIN II (1961) by Bold Ruler

Dam: Winner and Sire	Races Won	Value £
Lucky Lucky Lucky (USA): Mashair (USA) by Diesis	1	3,882.50
	1	3,882.50

CHOMPION (USA) (1965) by Tompion(USA)

Dam: Winner and Sire	Races Won	Value £
Broadway Beauty (USA): Geisway (Can) by Geiger Counter (USA)	1	21,540.00
	1	21,540.00

CLAUDE (1964) by Hornbeam

Dam: Winner and Sire	Races Won	Value £
Monalda (Fr): Euphonic by Elegant Air	1	2,511.00
Royal Sister II: Ezzoud (Ire) by Last Tycoon	2	178,739.60
	3	181,250.60

CLEVER TRICK (USA) (1976) by Icecapade(USA)

Dam: Winner and Sire	Races Won	Value £
Mountain Bluebird (USA): Mockingbird by Sharpo	1	2,070.00
Polly Daniels (USA): Green Golightly (USA) by Green Dancer (USA)	1	3,757.50
	2	5,827.50

COASTAL (USA) (1976) by Majestic Prince

Dam: Winner and Sire	Races Won	Value £
Santella (USA): Highland Legend (USA) by Storm Bird (Can)	2	6,900.50
	2	6,900.50

COMEDY STAR (USA) (1968) by Tom Fool

Dam: Winner and Sire	Races Won	Value £
Cosset: Brackenthwaite by Faustus (USA)	1	3,106.00
Hunslet: Parkside Lady by Domynsky	1	2,601.40
Mighty Fly: Winged Victory (Ire) by Dancing Brave (USA)	2	7,136.25
Southern Sky: Southern Ridge by Indian Ridge	1	4,500.00
Starproof: Super Rocky by Clantime	1	2,232.00
	6	19,575.65

COMERAM (Fr) (1973) by Amber Rama (USA)

Dam: Winner and Sire	Races Won	Value £
Copperama (Aus): Shalbourne (USA) by Nureyev (USA)	1	4,175.00
	1	4,175.00

CONDORCET (Fr) (1972) by Luthier

Dam: Winner and Sire	Races Won	Value £
Jendor: Highfield Lad by Hard Fought	1	1,553.00
Small Is Beautiful: Pie Hatch (Ire) by Huntingdale	1	2,070.00
	2	3,623.00

CONNAUGHT (1965) by St Paddy

Dam: Winner and Sire	Races Won	Value £
Doree Moisson (Fr): Dorazine by Kalaglow	3	12,372.00
Jackie Berry: Pencader (Ire) by Caerleon (USA)	1	5,052.50
Lillemor: Caleman by Daring March	2	13,156.50
Nice Lady: Lady Sabo by Prince Sabo	1	2,243.00
	7	32,824.00

CORMORANT (USA) (1974) by His Majesty (USA)

Dam: Winner and Sire	Races Won	Value £
Cassowary (USA): American Swinger (USA) by Dixieland Band (USA)	2	9,181.50
	2	9,181.50

CORTEZ (Ger) (1965) by Orsini

Dam: Winner and Sire	Races Won	Value £
Kaiserchronik (Ger): Karinska by Master Willie	3	10,413.00
	3	10,413.00

CORVARO (USA) (1977) by Vaguely Noble

Dam: Winner and Sire	Races Won	Value £
Vaguely Jade: Shining Jewel by Exhibitioner	3	8,218.00
Vaguely Jade: Lord Oberon (Ire) by Fairy King (USA)	1	5,380.50
	4	13,598.50

COUGAR (Chi) (1966) by Tale of two Cities

Dam: Winner and Sire	Races Won	Value £
Beau Cougar (USA): Hasten To Add (USA) by Cozzene (USA)	2	9,140.75
Kentucky Tears (USA): En-Cee-Tee by Risk Me (Fr)	1	2,070.00
Tasha Two (USA): Tanagome (USA) by Procida (USA)	1	3,201.75
	4	14,412.50

COX'S RIDGE (USA) (1974) by Best Turn(USA)

Dam: Winner and Sire	Races Won	Value £
Naughtiness (USA): Woodhaunter (USA) by Woodman (USA)	1	2,248.00
	1	2,248.00

CRASH COURSE (1971) by Busted

Dam: Winner and Sire	Races Won	Value £
Jenny's Child: Chiappucci (Ire) by Doulab (USA)	1	2,691.60
	1	2,691.60

CREDO (1960) by Crepello

Dam: Winner and Sire	Races Won	Value £
Shangara: Captain Scarlet (Ire) by Red Sunset	1	5,047.25
	1	5,047.25

CREETOWN (1972) by Tower Walk

Dam: Winner and Sire	Races Won	Value £
Cree's Figurine: Royale Figurine (Ire) by Dominion Royale	3	13,517.50
	3	13,517.50

CREPELLO (1954) by Donatello II

Dam: Winner and Sire	Races Won	Value £
Best Offer: Beveled Edge by Beveled (USA)	1	2,812.00
Caergwrle: St Ninian by Ardross	1	3,172.50
	2	5,984.50

CRIMSON BEAU (1975) by High Line

Dam: Winner and Sire	Races Won	Value £
Lafrowda: Mentalasanythin by Balacashtal (Can)	2	7,463.50
	2	7,463.50

CRIMSON SATAN (1959) by Spy Song

Dam: Winner and Sire	Races Won	Value £
Crafty Satin (USA): Sawlajan (USA) by Woodman (USA)	1	3,377.25
Sweet Satina (USA): Dancing Sensation (USA) by Faliraki	3	10,323.60
	4	13,700.85

CRISP AND EVEN (1963) by Saint Crespin III

Dam: Winner and Sire	Races Won	Value £
Shortbread: Food Of Love by Music Boy	1	2,238.20
	1	2,238.20

CROFTER (USA) (1977) by Habitat

Dam: Winner and Sire	Races Won	Value £
Zamindara: Another Jade by Beveled (USA)	3	9,639.50
	3	9,639.50

CROONER (1966) by Sammy Davis

Dam: Winner and Sire	Races Won	Value £
Bella Canto: Jalcanto by Jalmood (USA)	1	2,511.80
	1	2,511.80

CROW (Fr) (1973) by Exbury

Dam: Winner and Sire	Races Won	Value £
Corvine (USA): Leif The Lucky (USA) by Lemhi Gold (USA)	2	10,742.75
Mirabiliary (USA): Midnight Magpie (Ire) by Midyan (USA)	1	2,406.00
	3	13,148.75

Dam	Winner and Sire	Races Won	Value £

CROWNED PRINCE (USA) (1969) by Raise A Native

Dam: Winner and Sire	Races Won	Value £
Etoile de Paris: Only Royale (Ire) by Caerleon (USA)	1	78,598.00
Meliora: Aquado by Green Desert (USA)	1	3,582.00
Princess Of Nashua: Elton Ledger (Ire) by Cyrano de Bergerac	1	2,769.30
Supremely Royal: Scalp 'em (Ire) by Commanche Run	1	2,668.60
	4	87,617.90

CRYSTAL PALACE (Fr) (1974) by Caro

Dam: Winner and Sire	Races Won	Value £
Marie de Flandre (Fr): Count Of Flanders (Ire) by Green Desert (USA)	1	3,669.75
Vachti (Fr): Vishnu (USA) by Storm Bird (Can)	1	3,757.50
	2	7,427.25

CURE THE BLUES (USA) (1978) by Stop The Music(USA)

Dam: Winner and Sire	Races Won	Value £
Blue Guitar: Dime Bag by High Line	1	7,327.20
Martian Princess: Stephensons Rocket by Music Boy	1	2,851.25
Three Waves: Sareen Express (Ire) by Siberian Express (USA)	1	2,700.00
Time For Romance: Spring Loaded by Last Tycoon	1	3,416.80
	4	16,295.25

CUTLASS (USA) (1970) by Damascus(USA)

Dam: Winner and Sire	Races Won	Value £
Classy Nancy (USA): Bold Lez by Never So Bold	2	8,712.90
Pete's Damas (USA): Runaway Pete (USA) by Runaway Groom (Can)	3	11,672.80
	5	20,385.70

CYANE (1959) by Turn-to

Dam: Winner and Sire	Races Won	Value £
Caraquenga (USA): Cara's Pride by Electric	1	3,318.75
Nimble Folly (USA): Sculler (USA) by Riverman (USA)	1	7,205.00
	2	10,523.75

DAMASCUS (USA) (1964) by Sword Dancer (USA)

Dam: Winner and Sire	Races Won	Value £
Mistress (USA): Bit On The Side (Ire) by Vision (USA)	2	9,742.25
Mizima (USA): Vratislav (USA) by Nijinsky (Can)	1	2,814.00
Mizima (USA): Zama (USA) by Zilzal (USA)	1	5,127.00
Perceptive Lady (USA): Pondicherry (USA) by Sir Wimborne (USA)	1	3,201.75
Wasslaweyeh (USA): Slmaat by Sharpo	1	4,955.00
	6	25,840.00

DANCE IN TIME (Can) (1974) by Northern Dancer

Dam: Winner and Sire	Races Won	Value £
Angel Drummer: Wandering Angel by Sharrood (USA)	2	5,301.00
Dance A Jig: Tyrone Flyer by Celestial Storm (USA)	1	3,406.50
Dance In Rome: Dr Zeva by Busted	2	7,152.00
Dancing Belle: Dances With Risk by Risk Me (Fr)	3	9,118.65
Leap In Time: Neither Nor by Norwick (USA)	3	11,757.00
Minabella: Always Risky by Risk Me (Fr)	2	6,244.80
Tamassos: Continuity by Celestial Storm (USA)	2	5,911.50
	15	48,891.45

DANCE SPELL (USA) (1973) by Northern Dancer

Dam: Winner and Sire	Races Won	Value £
Flamenco (USA): Darrery by Darshaan	2	8,485.80
	2	8,485.80

DANCER'S IMAGE (USA) (1965) by Native Dancer

Dam: Winner and Sire	Races Won	Value £
Dancing Shadow: Ballerina (Ire) by Dancing Brave (USA)	1	4,110.00
Last Request: Arz (USA) by Known Fact (USA)	1	4,815.00
Manx Image: Ballad Dancer by Ballad Rock	3	8,764.25
Mephisto Waltz: Slades Hill by Lochnager	3	10,897.65
Queen Of The Dance: Bold Ambition by Ela-Mana-Mou	1	3,703.50
	9	32,290.40

DANZIG (USA) (1977) by Northern Dancer

Dam: Winner and Sire	Races Won	Value £
Nimble Feet (USA): Forest Gazelle (USA) by Green Forest (USA)	2	7,852.50
	2	7,852.50

DARA MONARCH (1979) by Realm

Dam: Winner and Sire	Races Won	Value £
Royal Meeting: Alaskan Heir by Northern State (USA)	1	3,552.75
	1	3,552.75

DARING DISPLAY (USA) (1969) by Bold Lad(Ire)

Dam: Winner and Sire	Races Won	Value £
Shirleen: Superoo by Superlative	1	3,552.75
	1	3,552.75

DARING MARCH (1974) by Derring-Do

Dam: Winner and Sire	Races Won	Value £
Daring Ditty: Sparky's Song by Electric	1	2,385.00

Dam Winner and Sire	Races Won	Value £
Daring Ditty: Brave Edge by Beveled (USA)	1	4,240.50
Jenifer Browning: Browned Off by Move Off	1	3,236.00
	3	9,861.50

DEADLY NIGHTSHADE (1966) by Floribunda

Dam Winner and Sire	Races Won	Value £
Shadey Dove: Flakey Dove by Oats	1	3,816.00
	1	3,816.00

DECOY BOY (1967) by Tin Whistle

Dam Winner and Sire	Races Won	Value £
Brave Ivy: International Star (Ire) by Astronef	1	3,231.00
Decoy Duck: Drumdonna (Ire) by Drumalis	1	1,548.00
Golden Decoy: Dangerous Shadow by Absalom	3	8,832.75
Third Generation: Trioming by Homing	2	5,682.75
	7	19,294.50

DEEP DIVER (1969) by Gulf Pearl

Dam Winner and Sire	Races Won	Value £
Magic Picture: Highland Magic (Ire) by Stalker	1	6,264.00
	1	6,264.00

DELTA JUDGE (1960) by Traffic Judge

Dam Winner and Sire	Races Won	Value £
Proud Delta (USA): Lyphard's Delta (USA) by Lyphard (USA)	4	79,354.50
	4	79,354.50

DERRING-DO (1961) by Darius

Dam Winner and Sire	Races Won	Value £
Dastina: Distinctive Air by Reprimand	1	2,932.50
Deed: Great Deeds by Forzando	2	21,928.70
Nelly Do Da: Molly Splash by Dunbeath (USA)	1	2,924.70
Selham: Storm Ship (Ire) by Petorius	1	4,142.50
	5	31,928.40

DERRYLIN (1975) by Derring-Do

Dam Winner and Sire	Races Won	Value £
Do We Know: Bo Knows Best (Ire) by Burslem	1	8,237.50
Do We Know: Gweek (Ire) by Common Grounds	1	3,002.00
Nuthill: Nutty Brown by Primitive Rising (USA)	1	2,412.70
Stradey Lynn: The Fernhill Flyer (Ire) by Red Sunset	3	8,567.50
	6	22,219.70

DEWAN (USA) (1965) by Bold Ruler

Dam Winner and Sire	Races Won	Value £
Diablesse (USA): Debsy Do (USA) by Dance Bid (USA)	3	10,623.75
Marianna's Girl (USA): Marastani (USA) by Shahrastani (USA)	1	2,880.00
Mezimica (USA): Manhattan Sunset (USA) by El Gran Senor (USA)	1	20,225.00
	5	33,728.75

DICTUS (Fr) (1967) by Sanctus II

Dam Winner and Sire	Races Won	Value £
Dictina (Fr): Riz Biz (USA) by El Gran Senor (USA)	1	5,020.00
Moonlight Serenade (Fr): Um Algowain (USA) by Lyphard (USA)	2	6,315.75
	3	11,335.75

DIESIS (1980) by Sharpen Up

Dam Winner and Sire	Races Won	Value £
Chinese Justice (USA): Desert Lore by Green Desert (USA)	1	3,699.00
	1	3,699.00

DIKE (USA) (1966) by Herbager

Dam Winner and Sire	Races Won	Value £
Fodens Eve: Ricky's Tornado (Ire) by Night Shift (USA)	1	3,370.50
	1	3,370.50

DIPLOMAT WAY (1964) by Nashua

Dam Winner and Sire	Races Won	Value £
Golden Way (USA): Al Battar (USA) by Blushing John (USA)	1	3,289.50
	1	3,289.50

DOM RACINE (Fr) (1975) by Kalamoun

Dam Winner and Sire	Races Won	Value £
Donnarella: Velasco (Ire) by Nordico (USA)	2	6,627.40
Sunny Flower (Fr): Wagon Master (Fr) by Rainbow Quest (USA)	2	9,731.60
	4	16,359.00

DOMINION (1972) by Derring-Do

Dam Winner and Sire	Races Won	Value £
Anodyne: Stimulant by Sharpo	2	9,984.50
Daima: Sabo The Hero by Prince Sabo	2	4,809.50
Demerger: Bev's Folly by Chilibang	1	2,070.00
Embla: Ghost Tree (Ire) by Caerleon (USA)	1	3,523.50
Last Gunboat: Final Frontier (Ire) by Common Grounds	2	9,316.50
Martin-Lavell Mail: Pharly Dancer by Pharly (Fr)	1	2,769.30
Miss Primula: Primula Bairn by Bairn (USA)	3	10,360.50
Miss Primula: Tinker Osmaston by Dunbeath (USA)	2	5,601.00
Peace Girl: Matila (Ire) by Persian Bold	1	3,655.00
Star Province: Starlight Rose (Ire) by Broken Hearted	1	3,158.00
Ullapool: Mad Militant (Ire) by Vision (USA)	1	5,374.00
	17	60,621.80

DON (1974) by Yellow God

Dam: Winner and Sire	Races Won	Value £
Carriglegan Girl: Friendly Champ (Ire) by Fayruz	3	11,834.00
In For More: Thunder River (Ire) by Thatching	1	2,880.00
Semperflorens: Sweet Revival by Claude Monet (USA)	1	3,262.00
	5	17,976.00

DON (Ity) (1966) by Grey Sovereign

Dam: Winner and Sire	Races Won	Value £
Donna Pavlova: Link Miles by Merdon Melody	2	8,944.50
Donrae: Daily Sport Don by Risk Me (Fr)	2	6,055.45
Seminar: Delta One (Ire) by Danehill (USA)	1	4,306.50
	5	19,306.45

DOUBLE JUMP (1962) by Rustam

Dam: Winner and Sire	Races Won	Value £
Bottom Line: Velvet Heart (Ire) by Damister (USA)	1	2,637.00
Cuckoo Weir: Fascination Waltz by Shy Groom (USA)	1	3,785.00
	2	6,422.00

DR BLUM (USA) (1977) by Dr Fager

Dam: Winner and Sire	Races Won	Value £
Making Rounds (USA): Umbubuzi (USA) by Timeless Native (USA)	1	2,243.00
	1	2,243.00

DR FAGER (1964) by Rough 'n Tumble

Dam: Winner and Sire	Races Won	Value £
Regatela (USA): Bayin (USA) by Caro	3	10,524.75
Royal Stance (USA): Luhuk (USA) by Forty-Niner (USA)	1	4,110.50
	4	14,635.25

DRAGONARA PALACE (USA) (1971) by Young Emperor

Dam: Winner and Sire	Races Won	Value £
Crime Of Passion: Crime Ofthecentury by Pharly (Fr)	2	5,957.65
Haddon Anna: Followmegirls by Sparkling Boy	1	2,668.60
Maltese Pet: Mogwai (Ire) by Alzao (USA)	1	2,742.00
Marsh Benham: Jahangir (Ire) by Ballad Rock	1	3,183.70
Palace Pet: Bettykimvic by Reesh	1	3,548.00
Pariscene: Ann's Pearl (Ire) by Cyrano de Bergerac	1	2,243.00
	7	20,342.95

DRONE (1966) by Sir Gaylord

Dam: Winner and Sire	Races Won	Value £
Din (USA): State Performer (USA) by Seattle Dancer (USA)	3	37,439.50
Drone Answer (USA): Peacefull Reply (USA) by Hold Your Peace (USA)	1	2,385.00
Moth (USA): Contract Court (USA) by Conquistador Cielo (USA)	1	3,523.50
	5	43,348.00

DSCHINGIS KHAN (1961) by Tamerlane

Dam: Winner and Sire	Races Won	Value £
Smeralda (Ger): Day Of History (Ire) by Shirley Heights	2	8,526.75
Smeralda (Ger): Lille Hammer by Sadler's Wells (USA)	1	10,203.00
	3	18,729.75

DUBASSOFF (USA) (1969) by Sea-Bird II

Dam: Winner and Sire	Races Won	Value £
Douschkina: Swift Romance (Ire) by Coquelin (USA)	1	1,957.30
	1	1,957.30

DUBLIN TAXI (1974) by Sharpen Up

Dam: Winner and Sire	Races Won	Value £
One Sharper: Kimbolton Korker by Interrex (Can)	1	2,725.70
	1	2,725.70

DUNPHY (1978) by Riverman(USA)

Dam: Winner and Sire	Races Won	Value £
Dunbally: Mr B Reasonable (Ire) by Reasonable (Fr)	1	3,435.75
	1	3,435.75

DUST COMMANDER (USA) (1967) by Bold Commander

Dam: Winner and Sire	Races Won	Value £
Noble Dust (USA): Dusty Point (Ire) by Reference Point	5	18,394.35
	5	18,394.35

EASTERN VENTURE (1950) by Marsyas II

Dam: Winner and Sire	Races Won	Value £
Grey Bird: Mr Woodcock by Sit In The Corner (USA)	1	2,469.00
	1	2,469.00

EFFERVESCING (USA) (1973) by Le Fabuleux

Dam: Winner and Sire	Races Won	Value £
Amber Fizz (USA): Cool Jazz by Lead On Time (USA)	1	5,580.00
Sister Sophie (USA): Port Lucaya by Sharpo	1	4,658.00
	2	10,238.00

EL PITIRRE (USA) (1972) by Gallant Romeo (USA)

Dam: Winner and Sire	Races Won	Value £
Gama Tres (USA): Ice Strike (USA) by Eskimo (USA)	1	2,070.00
	1	2,070.00

ELA-MANA-MOU (1976) by Pitcairn

Dam: Winner and Sire	Races Won	Value £
Awatef: Maastricht by Common Grounds	1	2,385.00
Collage: Fromage by Formidable (USA)	1	3,129.00
Ella Mon Amour: Thatcherella by Thatching	1	2,691.00
Fair Of The Furze: White Muzzle by Dancing Brave (USA)	4	20,640.00
First Blush: Bold Seven (Ire) by Never So Bold	1	2,489.40
Greektown: Athens Belle (Ire) by Groom Dancer (USA)	1	10,690.00
	9	42,024.40

ELOCUTIONIST (USA) (1973) by Gallant Romeo(USA)

Dam: Winner and Sire	Races Won	Value £
Mahabba (USA): Convoy Point (Ire) by Polish Precedent (USA)	1	4,270.75
Noire Small (USA): Lucky Noire by Aragon	1	2,954.00
Shapely Test (USA): Birchwood Sun by Bluebird (USA)	1	2,601.40
	3	9,826.15

EMPERY (USA) (1973) by Vaguely Noble

Dam: Winner and Sire	Races Won	Value £
Emaline (Fr): Monarda by Pharly (Fr)	3	11,296.10
	3	11,296.10

ENGLISH PRINCE (1971) by Petingo

Dam: Winner and Sire	Races Won	Value £
Princess Martina: Raggerty (Ire) by Prince Rupert (Fr)	2	4,643.00
Sun Princess: Ballet Prince (Ire) by Sadler's Wells (USA)	2	7,927.50
	4	12,570.50

ENNIS (1954) by Golden Cloud

Dam: Winner and Sire	Races Won	Value £
Harp: Fay's Song (Ire) by Fayruz	1	3,183.70
	1	3,183.70

EXBURY (1959) by Le Haar

Dam: Winner and Sire	Races Won	Value £
Expansive: Tissisat (USA) by Green Forest (USA)	1	17,993.75
Kaisersage (Fr): Kaiser Wilhelm by Slip Anchor	2	8,465.40
	3	26,459.15

EXCELLER (USA) (1973) by Vaguely Noble

Dam: Winner and Sire	Races Won	Value £
Excellent Alibi (USA): Witness Box (USA) by Lyphard (USA)	1	5,078.40
Wistoral (USA): Learmont (USA) by Lear Fan (USA)	2	23,120.00
	3	28,198.40

EXCLUSIVE NATIVE (USA) (1965) by Raise A Native

Dam: Winner and Sire	Races Won	Value £
Elle Seule (USA): Mehthaaf (USA) by Nureyev (USA)	1	4,110.50
Exclusive Life (USA): River Life by Irish River (Fr)	1	3,720.00
Most Honourable (USA): El Duco (USA) by El Gran Senor (USA)	2	6,842.25
Share The Fantasy (USA): Stella Mystika (USA) by Diesis	2	7,071.25
Vibrant Hue (USA): Gingerbird (Ire) by Salt Dome (USA)	1	2,735.80
	7	24,479.80

FABERGE II (1961) by Princely Gift

Dam: Winner and Sire	Races Won	Value £
Rathcoffey Duchy: Corinthian God (Ire) by Red Sunset	1	2,821.10
	1	2,821.10

FABULOUS DANCER (USA) (1976) by Northern Dancer

Dam: Winner and Sire	Races Won	Value £
El Fabulous (Fr): Fabulous Mtoto by Mtoto	1	3,590.00
Fabulous Rina (Fr): Sehailah by Mtoto	1	3,289.50
Miquette (Fr): Floating Trial by Dowsing (USA)	2	5,046.00
	4	11,925.50

FAIR SEASON (1974) by Silly Season

Dam: Winner and Sire	Races Won	Value £
Coming Out: Rafter-J by Petoski	1	2,905.00
	1	2,905.00

FALCON (1964) by Milesian

Dam: Winner and Sire	Races Won	Value £
Passage Falcon: Raven's Return (Ire) by Astronef	1	3,435.75
	1	3,435.75

FAMILY DOCTOR (USA) (1973) by Dr Fager

Dam: Winner and Sire	Races Won	Value £
Granny's Portait (USA): Ballah Shack (USA) by Tejano (USA)	2	5,908.00
	2	5,908.00

FAPPIANO (USA) (1977) by Mr Prospector(USA)

Dam: Winner and Sire	Races Won	Value £
Twelfth Pleasure (USA): Harpoon Louie (USA) by Eskimo (USA)	1	4,012.50
	1	4,012.50

FAR NORTH (Can) (1973) by Northern Dancer

Dam: Winner and Sire	Races Won	Value £
Isticanna (USA): Seama (USA) by Affirmed (USA)	2	5,069.00

Dam Winner and Sire	Races Won	Value £
Linda's Magic (USA): Shujan (USA) by Diesis	5	16,301.00
	7	21,370.00

FAR OUT EAST (USA) (1977) by Raja Baba(USA)

Dam Winner and Sire	Races Won	Value £
Okosan (USA): Baliana by Midyan (USA)	1	3,084.75
	1	3,084.75

FARM WALK (1962) by Kribi

Dam Winner and Sire	Races Won	Value £
Another Move: My Desire by Grey Desire	2	7,181.75
Another Move: Moving Arrow by Indian Ridge	1	3,289.50
	3	10,471.25

FEARLESS KNIGHT (1963) by Round Table

Dam Winner and Sire	Races Won	Value £
Dear Guinevere (USA): Merlins Wish (USA) by Yukon (USA)	1	1,828.00
	1	1,828.00

FINAL STRAW (1977) by Thatch(USA)

Dam Winner and Sire	Races Won	Value £
Breadcrumb: Khubza by Green Desert (USA)	1	4,581.00
Final Thought: Fieldridge by Rousillon (USA)	1	12,230.80
Florence Street: Island Knight (Ire) by Jupiter Island	1	2,821.10
Lap Of Honour: Lap Of Luxury by Sharrood (USA)	2	15,770.25
Mrs Kaydagawn: Admiralella by Dominion	1	2,713.40
Penultimate: Benfleet by Dominion	2	7,118.50
Pretty Pol: Polka Dancer by Dancing Brave (USA)	2	20,476.40
Trikymia: Wave Hill by Sizzling Melody	1	3,640.50
Trikymia: Graegos (Ire) by Shareef Dancer (USA)	1	3,640.50
	12	72,992.45

FIRESTREAK (1956) by Pardal

Dam Winner and Sire	Races Won	Value £
Counsel's Verdict: Spanish Verdict by King Of Spain	2	5,524.60
Flame: Va Utu by Balliol	1	3,209.60
September Fire: Master Pokey by Uncle Pokey	1	3,261.40
	4	11,995.60

FLORESCENCE (1964) by Floribunda

Dam Winner and Sire	Races Won	Value £
Flo Kelly: Inherent Magic (Ire) by Magical Wonder (USA)	1	6,639.60
Kilpeacon: Public Way (Ire) by Common Grounds	1	2,959.80
Light Diamond: Top One by Sallust	1	2,243.00
	3	11,842.40

FLUORESCENT LIGHT (USA) (1974) by Herbager

Dam Winner and Sire	Races Won	Value £
Light de Light (USA): Turtle Rock by Hadeer	1	2,377.40
	1	2,377.40

FOOLISH PLEASURE (USA) (1972) by What A Pleasure(USA)

Dam Winner and Sire	Races Won	Value £
Nabila (USA): Lobilio (USA) by Robellino (USA)	2	7,759.00
Twice A Fool (USA): Twin Falls (Ire) by Trempolino (USA)	1	4,306.50
Unbiased (USA): Bay Tern (USA) by Arctic Tern (USA)	1	2,913.00
Watership (USA): Captain's Guest (Ire) by Be My Guest (USA)	1	3,523.50
	5	18,502.00

FORLI (Arg) (1963) by Aristophanes

Dam Winner and Sire	Races Won	Value £
Enceinte (USA): Smart Family (USA) by Homebuilder (USA)	1	3,699.00
Forli's Treat (USA): Mecklenburg (Ire) by Danzig (USA)	2	7,712.75
Regal Heights (USA): Moccasin Run (USA) by Topsider (USA)	1	10,430.00
Salote (USA): Contract Elite (Ire) by Dominion Royale	1	7,570.00
Spring In Rome (USA): Simply Finesse by Simply Great (Fr)	1	3,557.50
	6	32,969.25

FORLORN RIVER (1962) by Fighting Don

Dam Winner and Sire	Races Won	Value £
Four Lawns: Causley by Swing Easy (USA)	2	7,092.50
Kakisa: Sylvan Starlight by Sylvan Express	2	5,504.40
	4	12,596.90

FORMIDABLE (USA) (1975) by Forli(Arg)

Dam Winner and Sire	Races Won	Value £
Echoing: Buckski Echo by Petoski	1	2,427.00
Floreal: Essayeffsee by Precocious	2	4,660.60
Foreno: Early To Rise by Don't Forget Me	1	2,011.40
Formidable Dancer: Fighter Squadron by Primo Dominie	1	4,793.75
Formido: Nahlati (Ire) by Mtoto	1	2,243.00
Forward Rally: Broughtons Formula by Night Shift (USA)	1	3,366.00
	7	19,501.75

FORTISSIMO (1964) by Fortino II

Dam Winner and Sire	Races Won	Value £
Jolimo: Jolis Absent by Primo Dominie	1	2,511.80
	1	2,511.80

FRANKINCENSE (1964) by Princely Gift

Dam Winner and Sire	Races Won	Value £
Boswellia: Flowing Ocean by Forzando	1	3,201.75

Dam Winner and Sire	Races Won	Value £
Olibanum: Fort Erie by Lochnager	1	2,399.80
	2	5,601.55

FRARI (Arg) (1970) by Aristophanes

Dam Winner and Sire	Races Won	Value £
Frau Daruma (Arg): Daru (USA) by Caro	1	3,172.50
Frau Daruma (Arg): Darmstadt (USA) by Manila (USA)	3	18,129.70
	4	21,302.20

FREE STATE (1973) by Hotfoot

Dam Winner and Sire	Races Won	Value £
Haiti Mill: Nigel's Lucky Girl by Belfort (Fr)	1	3,106.00
High State: Macs Maharanee by Indian King (USA)	2	8,375.75
High State: Highborn (Ire) by Double Schwartz	4	10,831.65
So It Goes: Ttyfran by Petong	1	2,679.00
So It Goes: Eleuthera by Mazilier (USA)	1	2,872.90
	9	27,865.30

FRONTAL (1964) by Le Haar

Dam Winner and Sire	Races Won	Value £
Take More (Ger): Carranita (Ire) by Anita's Prince	2	7,017.50
	2	7,017.50

FULL OF HOPE (1970) by Great Nephew

Dam Winner and Sire	Races Won	Value £
Henceforth: Will Soon by Nicholas Bill	1	2,860.75
	1	2,860.75

FURRY GLEN (1971) by Wolver Hollow

Dam Winner and Sire	Races Won	Value £
Church Mountain: Princess Tateum (Ire) by Tate Gallery (USA)	2	5,183.00
Keep The Faith: Show Faith (Ire) by Exhibitioner	2	26,285.00
Keppols: Roca Murada (Ire) by Cyrano de Bergerac	3	10,637.00
	7	42,105.00

GALIVANTER (1956) by Golden Cloud

Dam Winner and Sire	Races Won	Value £
Gallic Law: Grey Toppa by Belfort (Fr)	2	5,977.40
	2	5,977.40

GALLANT MAN (1954) by Migoli

Dam Winner and Sire	Races Won	Value £
Nancy Chere (USA): Eightandahalf (Ire) by Be My Guest (USA)	2	5,694.00
	2	5,694.00

GARDA'S REVENGE (USA) (1973) by Dancer's Image(USA)

Dam Winner and Sire	Races Won	Value £
Kimangao: Golden Chip (Ire) by M Double M (USA)	3	10,429.00
	3	10,429.00

GAY FANDANGO (USA) (1972) by Forli(Arg)

Dam Winner and Sire	Races Won	Value £
Bear's Affair: Blurred Image (Ire) by Exactly Sharp (USA)	2	5,245.40
Can Can Girl: Languedoc by Rousillon (USA)	1	5,427.50
Gaygo Lady: Baligay by Balidar	1	5,287.50
Mexican Two Step: Mexican Dancer by Dance Of Life (USA)	1	1,912.00
Stepping Gaily: Dominuet by Dominion	1	14,114.40
Stepping Gaily: Rhythmic Dancer by Music Boy	1	3,260.25
Stepping Gaily: The Auction Bidder by Auction Ring (USA)	1	3,611.25
Stepping Gaily: Music Dancer by Music Boy	1	2,847.00
Vain Deb: Malcesine (Ire) by Auction Ring (USA)	1	2,473.50
	10	44,178.80

GAY LUSSAC (Ity) (1969) by Faberge II

Dam Winner and Sire	Races Won	Value £
Solac (Fr): Double Trigger (Ire) by Ela-Mana-Mou	2	12,267.75
	2	12,267.75

GAY MECENE (USA) (1975) by Vaguely Noble

Dam Winner and Sire	Races Won	Value £
Colourful (Fr): Bookcase by Siberian Express (USA)	2	8,177.50
	2	8,177.50

GENERAL ASSEMBLY (USA) (1976) by Secretariat(USA)

Dam Winner and Sire	Races Won	Value £
Mythical Assembly: Privy Council (USA) by Secreto (USA)	1	4,199.25
Soemba: Kelimutu by Top Ville	4	10,532.50
Soemba: Sumoto by Mtoto	1	3,406.50
Warm Welcome: Clarinda (Ire) by Lomond (USA)	1	3,201.75
	7	21,340.00

GENERAL HOLME (USA) (1979) by Noholme II

Dam Winner and Sire	Races Won	Value £
Souadah (USA): Make The Break by Dominion	1	3,046.25
	1	3,046.25

GIFT CARD (Fr) (1969) by Dan Cupid

Dam Winner and Sire	Races Won	Value £
Flamme D'Amour: First Fling (Ire) by Last Tycoon	1	2,070.00
	1	2,070.00

GLEAMING (USA) (1968) by Herbager

Dam Winner and Sire	Races Won	Value £
Bright Reply (USA): Singing Reply (USA) by The Minstrel (Can)	1	3,131.90

Dam Winner and Sire	Races Won	Value £
Bright Reply (USA): Ima Red Neck (USA) by Dixieland Band (USA)	1	2,322.00
Hidden Trail (USA): Moshaajir (USA) by Woodman (USA)	1	4,935.00
	3	10,388.90

GLINT OF GOLD (1978) by Mill Reef(USA)

Dam Winner and Sire	Races Won	Value £
Kentucky Belle: Dancing Beau (Ire) by Dance Of Life (USA)	1	2,821.10
Remoosh: Moorish by Dominion	1	20,387.50
Remoosh: Footsteps (Ire) by Broken Hearted	2	8,288.20
Turban: Barboukh by Night Shift (USA)	2	16,154.70
Turban: Tricorne by Green Desert (USA)	1	4,342.25
	7	51,993.75

GODSWALK (USA) (1974) by Dancer's Image(USA)

Dam Winner and Sire	Races Won	Value £
Aldern Stream: Smarginato (Ire) by Simply Great (Fr)	4	61,067.50
Crown Godiva: Jalib (Ire) by Lomond (USA)	1	2,976.50
Desrose: Rosietoes (USA) by Master Willie	1	2,952.00
Gothic Lady: No Mean City (Ire) by Digamist (USA)	2	11,380.00
Halo: Castlerea Lad by Efisio	3	28,452.75
Halo: Heavenly Risk by Risk Me (Fr)	1	4,760.00
Joanns Goddess: Veloce (Ire) by Kafu	3	12,558.00
Loving Doll: Nobby Barnes by Nordance (USA)	2	8,522.00
Makalu: Mr Bergerac (Ire) by Cyrano de Bergerac	2	6,699.50
Morgiana: Ochos Rios (Ire) by Horage	2	5,503.25
Originality: Key To My Heart (Ire) by Broken Hearted	1	6,373.60
Resooka: Thousla Rock (Ire) by Thatching	1	3,143.25
Zanskar: White Creek (Ire) by Don't Forget Me	4	9,968.80
	27	164,357.15

GOLD SONG (1975) by Song

Dam Winner and Sire	Races Won	Value £
Dear Glenda: Jade City by Belfort (Fr)	1	3,720.00
	1	3,720.00

GOLDEN DIPPER (1964) by Gratitude

Dam Winner and Sire	Races Won	Value £
Morning Miss: Cobblers Hill by Another Realm	1	3,210.00
	1	3,210.00

GOLDEN FLEECE (USA) (1979) by Nijinsky(Can)

Dam Winner and Sire	Races Won	Value £
Gold Piece: Gold Surprise (Ire) by Petorius	1	1,702.00

Dam Winner and Sire	Races Won	Value £
Lady Vivienne: Forgotten Lady (Ire) by Don't Forget Me	1	4,378.00
Pixie Erin: Ericolin (Ire) by Ahonoora	1	3,318.75
	3	9,398.75

GOLDHILL (1961) by Le Dieu d'Or

Dam Winner and Sire	Races Won	Value £
Lottie Lehmann: Mellottie by Meldrum	2	20,830.50
Maimiti: Fletcher's Bounty (Ire) by Glenstal (USA)	1	3,071.80
Maimiti: My-O-My (Ire) by Waajib	1	9,681.00
	4	33,583.30

GOLDHILLS PRIDE (1974) by Goldhill

Dam Winner and Sire	Races Won	Value £
Bread 'n Honey: Storm Regent by Prince Sabo	1	3,566.25
	1	3,566.25

GOOD BOND (1968) by Majority Blue

Dam Winner and Sire	Races Won	Value £
Good Try: Choir Practice by Chief Singer	2	8,252.50
	2	8,252.50

GOOD TIMES (Ity) (1976) by Great Nephew

Dam Winner and Sire	Races Won	Value £
Ganadora: Leigh Crofter by Son Of Shaka	2	7,332.00
Ganadora: Homemaker by Homeboy	1	3,675.80
Pillowing: Greatest by Superlative	1	4,950.00
	4	15,957.80

GORYTUS (USA) (1980) by Nijinsky(Can)

Dam Winner and Sire	Races Won	Value £
Lisa's Favourite: Majestic Heights (Ire) by High Estate	1	3,699.00
Ruffling Point: Certain Way (Ire) by Sure Blade (USA)	2	5,745.80
	3	9,444.80

GRANGE MELODY (1972) by Le Levanstell

Dam Winner and Sire	Races Won	Value £
Loredana: Nitouche by Scottish Reel	1	3,779.40
Loredana: Carrie Kool by Prince Sabo	1	3,054.20
	2	6,833.60

GRATITUDE (1953) by Golden Cloud

Dam Winner and Sire	Races Won	Value £
Noddy Time: The Right Time by King Of Spain	2	5,502.20
	2	5,502.20

GRAUSTARK (1963) by Ribot

Dam Winner and Sire	Races Won	Value £
Billante (USA): Ela Billante by Ela-Mana-Mou	1	2,846.00
Crown Treasure (USA): Palace Pageant (USA) by Nijinsky (Can)	1	3,318.75
Dafinah (USA): El Gahar by Green Desert (USA)	1	3,699.00
Heaven's Mine (USA): Andromaque (USA) by Woodman (USA)	4	25,879.65
Lady Graustark (USA): Sure Lord (Ire) by Sure Blade (USA)	1	5,089.50
Mary Read (USA): Cretoes Dancer (USA) by Secreto (USA)	1	2,553.00
Stark Drama (USA): Mutakallam (USA) by Fappiano (USA)	1	2,950.00
Stark Winter (USA): Winter Forest (USA) by Diesis	2	4,020.75
Summer Review (USA): Elatis (USA) by El Gran Senor (USA)	1	3,728.25
Truly Thankful (Can): Mr Cube (Ire) by Tate Gallery (USA)	1	2,700.00
	14	56,784.90

GREAT NEPHEW (1963) by Honeyway

Dam Winner and Sire	Races Won	Value £
Alumia: Queen Of The Quorn by Governor General	2	4,822.00
Arab Heritage: Rani (Ire) by Groom Dancer (USA)	1	3,357.00
Carotene (Can): Teshami (USA) by Diesis	2	10,212.00
Crystal Fountain: Summer Hail (Ire) by Thatching	1	4,985.75
Grand Occasion: Tiger Shoot by Indian King (USA)	1	2,243.00
Great Grey Niece: Absolution by Absalom	1	2,787.00
In Perpetuity: Baron Ferdinand by Ferdinand (USA)	2	37,635.25
Legend Of Arabia: Edbaysaan (Ire) by Slip Anchor	2	16,692.75
Nasty Niece (Can): Raging Thunder by Taufan (USA)	2	5,819.80
Relatively Smart: Ball Gown by Jalmood (USA)	1	2,490.00
School Road: Educated Pet by Petong	2	7,606.50
School Road: Oubeck by Mummy's Game	1	3,406.50
Snow Tribe: Bilberry by Nicholas Bill	1	3,235.50
	19	105,293.05

GREEN DANCER (USA) (1972) by Nijinsky(Can)

Dam Winner and Sire	Races Won	Value £
Dancing Rocks: Glatisant by Rainbow Quest (USA)	2	27,261.00
Free Dance (Fr): Free Mover (Ire) by Rousillon (USA)	1	4,713.25
Green Lucia: Acanthus (Ire) by Slip Anchor	3	13,129.40
Haitienne (Fr): Extra Bonus by Cadeaux Genereux	2	5,426.70
North Cliff (Fr): Northern Bound (Ire) by Slip Anchor	1	3,611.25
The Dancer (Fr): Mack The Knife by Kris	2	12,597.50
Veridian (USA): West Quest (Can) by Gone West (USA)	1	3,231.00
Youthful (Fr): Jeune by Kalaglow	1	56,700.00
Youthful (Fr): Beneficial by Top Ville	3	86,542.15
	16	213,212.25

GREEN FOREST (USA) (1979) by Shecky Greene(USA)

Dam Winner and Sire	Races Won	Value £
Forest Flower (USA): Hill Of Dreams by Shirley Heights	1	3,143.25
	1	3,143.25

GREEN GOD (1968) by Red God

Dam Winner and Sire	Races Won	Value £
Handy Dancer: Roll A Dollar by Spin Of A Coin	1	26,892.00
Handy Dancer: Tickerty's Gift by Formidable (USA)	1	4,542.00
Princess Of Man: Alderney Prince (USA) by Trempolino (USA)	1	2,976.50
	3	34,410.50

GREY DAWN II (1962) by Herbager

Dam Winner and Sire	Races Won	Value £
Carolina Moon (USA): Full Feather (USA) by Storm Bird (Can)	1	3,348.00
Dawn Dance (USA): Diwali Dancer by Petong	1	2,929.50
Early Rising (USA): Spectacular Dawn by Spectacular Bid (USA)	1	3,201.75
Early Rising (USA): My Patriarch by Be My Guest (USA)	5	29,743.90
Firm Lady (USA): Hilary Gerrard (USA) by Naevus (USA)	1	3,377.25
	9	42,600.40

GREY GHOST (1972) by Yellow God

Dam Winner and Sire	Races Won	Value £
Millie Grey: Efizia by Efisio	5	15,851.95
	5	15,851.95

GREY MIRAGE (1969) by Double-U-Jay

Dam Winner and Sire	Races Won	Value £
Rage Glen: Infantry Glen by Infantry	1	2,511.00
	1	2,511.00

GREY SOVEREIGN (1948) by Nasrullah

Dam Winner and Sire	Races Won	Value £
Croda Rossa (Ity): Crossillion by Rousillon (USA)	1	5,340.00
	1	5,340.00

GROTON (1962) by Nashua

Dam Winner and Sire	Races Won	Value £
Thrifty Trio (USA): Yunus Emre (Ire) by Lomond (USA)	2	5,819.10
	2	5,819.10

GRUNDY (1972) by Great Nephew

Dam Winner and Sire	Races Won	Value £
Dame Ashfield: Mahaasin by Bellypha	1	3,078.75
Dame Ashfield: Rosina Mae by Rousillon (USA)	1	5,435.50
False Lift: Sharpening by Sharpo	1	2,243.00
Glancing: Trapezium by Soviet Star (USA)	1	3,114.00

Dam Winner and Sire	Races Won	Value £
Glancing: Beaming by Mtoto	1	4,342.25
Gratify: Monis (Ire) by Waajib	1	3,949.00
Great Exception: Exclusion by Ballad Rock	1	3,078.75
Gruntled: Try N' Fly (Ire) by Carmelite House (USA)	1	2,660.00
Little Change: Spring Sixpence by Dowsing (USA)	1	2,243.00
Lovers Light: Glimpse by Night Shift (USA)	1	4,464.00
Queen's Eyot: Persuasive by Sharpo	2	10,114.00
Queen's Eyot: Island Blade (Ire) by Sure Blade (USA)	1	3,209.60
Spinster: Mheanmetoo by Roi Danzig (USA)	1	3,297.00
Subtlety: Self Expression by Homing	3	20,120.50
Tuft Hill: Up The Mariners (Ire) by Classic Secret (USA)	1	1,380.00
Valiancy: Essex Girl by Dominion	2	6,101.00
	20	78,830.35

GULF PEARL (1962) by Persian Gulf

Dam Winner and Sire	Races Won	Value £
Buckhurst: Winning Line by Master Willie	1	3,036.00
Inner Pearl: A Smooth One (Ire) by Don't Forget Me	2	26,249.00
Pearl Wedding: Scottish Wedding by Scottish Reel	1	2,821.10
	4	32,106.10

GUMMO (USA) (1962) by Fleet Nasrullah

Dam Winner and Sire	Races Won	Value £
Dimant Blanche (USA): White Willow by Touching Wood (USA)	2	8,214.75
	2	8,214.75

GUNNER B (1973) by Royal Gunner(USA)

Dam Winner and Sire	Races Won	Value £
Gundreda: Magication by Nomination	1	2,684.50
Gunner Girl: Bold Alex by Full Extent (USA)	1	4,020.50
Misfire: Scorched Air by Elegant Air	2	6,511.60
Shay Tien: Dancing Diamond (Ire) by Alzao (USA)	2	3,494.20
	6	16,710.80

GYR (USA) (1967) by Sea-Bird II

Dam Winner and Sire	Races Won	Value £
Godzilla: Kosata (Ire) by Shirley Heights	1	3,435.75
	1	3,435.75

HABAT (1971) by Habitat

Dam Winner and Sire	Races Won	Value £
Checkers: Belfry Green (Ire) by Doulab (USA)	1	3,406.50
Printafoil: Hot Off The Press by Chilibang	2	4,812.00
Serenesse: Seren Quest by Rainbow Quest (USA)	1	3,494.25
	4	11,712.75

HABITAT (1966) by Sir Gaylord

Dam Winner and Sire	Races Won	Value £
Alghuzaylah: Taghareed (USA) by Shadeed (USA)	1	3,200.00
Aristata: Our Mica by Belfort (Fr)	1	3,106.00
Assisi: News And Echo (USA) by Night Shift (USA)	1	7,700.70
Bonne de Berry: Breakfast Boogie by Sizzling Melody	1	2,794.00
Broomstick Cottage: Lavender Cottage by Teenoso (USA)	1	3,260.25
Broomstick Cottage: Wizard King by Shaadi (USA)	1	3,340.00
Bundu (Fr): Young Tess by Teenoso (USA)	1	2,780.60
Cassina: Big Blue by Bluebird (USA)	1	3,882.50
Corley Moor: Shirley Rose by Shirley Heights	6	18,465.90
Dowcester: Treasure Time (Ire) by Treasure Kay	1	2,301.00
Fallacieuse: Hatta River (USA) by Irish River (Fr)	1	2,950.60
Habilite: Palacegate Gold (Ire) by Sarab	2	5,833.90
Hide Out: Cheveux Mitchell by Dunbeath (USA)	1	5,089.50
Kiss: Maradonna (USA) by Alleged (USA)	1	4,045.00
La Papagena: Rose Noble (USA) by Vaguely Noble	1	2,924.70
La Papagena: Grand Lodge (USA) by Chief's Crown (USA)	3	138,708.00
Little Red Hut: Orange Place (Ire) by Nordance (USA)	2	5,271.75
Magic Slipper: Wali (USA) by Lomond (USA)	1	3,492.50
Manx Millenium: Blue Siren by Bluebird (USA)	2	7,711.25
Massorah (Fr): Massiba (Ire) by Shareef Dancer (USA)	1	5,131.75
Massorah (Fr): Wisham (USA) by Be My Guest (USA)	1	3,435.75
Nomadic Pleasure: Highflying by Shirley Heights	3	65,914.50
One Way Street: Usk The Way by Caerleon (USA)	1	2,489.40
Pig Tail: Spin Doctor (Ire) by Ela-Mana-Mou	1	3,435.75
Pretoria: Nassma (Ire) by Sadler's Wells (USA)	2	17,516.40
Propensity: Wannabe by Shirley Heights	1	3,845.25
Propensity: Pursuit Of Glory by Shirley Heights	1	1,830.00
Shorthouse: Lowawatha by Dancing Brave (USA)	2	10,518.75
Sigy (Fr): King's Signet (USA) by Nureyev (USA)	3	71,050.00
Someone Special: Relatively Special by Alzao (USA)	2	20,910.25
Swanilda (Fr): Midhish by Green Desert (USA)	1	3,348.00
Tarib: Tajdid (Ire) by Caerleon (USA)	1	3,106.00
Tatisha: Shannon Express by Magic Mirror	2	6,237.70
Tigeen: Mardood by Ela-Mana-Mou	3	8,891.00
Tigeen: Night Clubbing (Ire) by Dance Of Life (USA)	4	25,023.05
Topsy: Tansy by Shareef Dancer (USA)	1	4,270.75
	59	483,812.45

HAIL TO REASON (1958) by Turn-to

Dam Winner and Sire	Races Won	Value £
Matoki (USA): Knifebox (USA) by Diesis	2	42,486.75

Dam	Winner and Sire	Races Won	Value £
White Reason (USA): Lindon Lime (USA) by Green Dancer (USA)		1	15,593.00
		3	58,079.75

HALO (USA) (1969) by Hail To Reason

Dam: Winner and Sire	Races Won	Value £
Charlie's Angel (USA): Criminal Record (USA) by Fighting Fit (USA)	1	2,070.00
Dame Solitaire (Can): Shepherd Market (Ire) by Common Grounds	1	4,306.50
Her Radiance (USA): Prince Of Andros (USA) by Al Nasr (Fr)	5	49,937.75
Misty Gallore (USA): Declassified (USA) by Secreto (USA)	1	5,190.00
Solar (Can): Fayrooz (USA) by Gulch (USA)	1	4,152.00
	9	65,656.25

HARDICANUTE (1962) by Hard Ridden

Dam: Winner and Sire	Races Won	Value £
Betyle (Fr): Beatle Song by Song	1	3,210.00
	1	3,210.00

HARKEN (Uru) (1972) by Heathen

Dam: Winner and Sire	Races Won	Value £
Very Bissy (Brz): Princess Evita (Fr) by Kings Lake (USA)	1	2,579.30
	1	2,579.30

HAWAII (1964) by Utrillo

Dam: Winner and Sire	Races Won	Value £
Island Charm (USA): Derab (USA) by Alleged (USA)	1	8,900.16
Maui Manor (USA): Keyway (USA) by Groovy (USA)	1	3,026.25
	2	11,926.41

HE LOVES ME (1974) by Sovereign Path

Dam: Winner and Sire	Races Won	Value £
Hello Cuddles: Samson-Agonistes by Bold Fort	3	7,118.00
Hello Cuddles: Inderaputeri by Bold Fort	1	2,243.00
Lady Clementine: Much Sought After by Adonijah	4	16,165.75
Supper Party: Francis Ann by Balidar	1	2,898.80
Tinas Image: Tony's Mist by Digamist (USA)	3	9,334.15
	12	37,759.70

HELLO GORGEOUS (USA) (1977) by Mr Prospector(USA)

Dam: Winner and Sire	Races Won	Value £
French Surprise: Supreme Master by Primo Dominie	3	13,977.00
	3	13,977.00

HENBIT (USA) (1977) by Hawaii

Dam: Winner and Sire	Races Won	Value £
Moira My Girl: Dayjuz (Ire) by Fayruz	1	3,002.00
Moira My Girl: Frisky Miss (Ire) by Fayruz	1	2,905.00
Nutwood Emma: Little Hooligan by Rabdan	1	2,243.00
Saucy Bird: So Saucy by Teenoso (USA)	3	8,361.70
Vaula: Time Again by Then Again	1	3,172.50
	7	19,684.20

HERBAGER (1956) by Vandale II

Dam: Winner and Sire	Races Won	Value £
Bag Of Tunes (USA): Bagalino (USA) by Lyphard (USA)	1	3,492.50
Bemiss Heights (USA): Desert Team (USA) by Blushing Groom (Fr)	1	38,046.20
Donna Inez (USA): Nemea (USA) by The Minstrel (Can)	1	3,049.40
	3	44,588.10

HIGH ECHELON (1967) by Native Charger

Dam: Winner and Sire	Races Won	Value £
Catherine Linton (USA): Heathcliff (Ire) by Common Grounds	1	4,776.00
	1	4,776.00

HIGH HAT (1957) by Hyperion

Dam: Winner and Sire	Races Won	Value £
Prima Bella: Laurel Queen (Ire) by Viking (USA)	6	18,666.75
	6	18,666.75

HIGH LINE (1966) by High Hat

Dam: Winner and Sire	Races Won	Value £
Bell Toll: Prince Babar by Fairy King (USA)	1	4,175.00
Dawn Star: Dawning Street (Ire) by Thatching	2	33,181.20
Dawn Star: Special Dawn (Ire) by Be My Guest (USA)	1	3,106.00
Dubian: Sayyedati by Shadeed (USA)	1	107,063.50
Heaven High: Miss Plum by Ardross	1	7,096.00
High Tern: Sooty Tern by Wassl	3	11,034.00
Hyacine: Little Emmeline by Emarati (USA)	1	2,490.00
It's High Time: Lady Donoghue (USA) by Lyphard's Wish (Fr)	1	2,889.00
Lucayan Princess: Celia Brady by Last Tycoon	1	4,556.75
Lucayan Princess: Luana by Shaadi (USA)	1	5,663.00
Quay Line: Purple Splash by Ahonoora	1	3,523.50
Question Mark: Prince Songline by Prince Sabo	1	3,557.50
Shalati (Fr): Shalholme by Fools Holme (USA)	1	1,380.00
Shore Line: Soviet Line (Ire) by Soviet Star (USA)	2	7,251.75
Trampship: Trammel by Shirley Heights	1	3,816.00
Valadon: Sandmoor Chambray by Most Welcome	1	3,947.50
	20	204,730.70

HIGH TOP (1969) by Derring-Do

Dam Winner and Sire	Races Won	Value £
Circulate: Highly Fashionable (Ire) by Polish Precedent (USA)	1	3,201.75
Circus Plume: Circus Colours by Rainbow Quest (USA)	2	9,914.95
Circus Ring: Finger Of Light by Green Desert (USA)	1	4,737.00
Cockatoo Island: Collier Bay by Green Desert (USA)	1	3,494.25
Colorspin (Fr): Opera House by Sadler's Wells (USA)	3	502,097.20
Colorspin (Fr): Highland Dress by Lomond (USA)	1	3,348.00
Duende: The Deep (Ire) by Shernazar	1	5,127.00
Green's Collection: Jacob Bogdani by Night Shift (USA)	1	4,378.00
High Halo: High Premium by Forzando	1	48,412.50
Hocus: Hali (Ire) by Rousillon (USA)	1	2,399.80
Hysterical: Green Crusader by Green Desert (USA)	1	4,521.00
Mountain Memory: Mystic Memory by Ela-Mana-Mou	1	2,385.00
Nahawand: High Romance by Today And Tomorrow	1	2,243.00
Old Domesday Book: Common Council by Siberian Express (USA)	2	4,475.00
Old Domesday Book: Owington by Green Desert (USA)	1	7,505.00
On The Top: Top Rank by Law Society (USA)	1	3,260.25
Orange Hill: Old Provence by Rainbow Quest (USA)	2	6,205.50
Palace Travel: Claudia Miss by Claude Monet (USA)	2	5,023.60
Pato: Threatening by Warning	2	10,085.00
Pine Ridge: Awesome Venture by Formidable (USA)	1	3,494.25
Puget Sound: Dagny Juel (USA) by Danzig (USA)	1	3,465.00
Rosia Bay: Barraak by El Gran Senor (USA)	1	2,243.00
Royal Daughter: Lime Street Blues (Ire) by Digamist (USA)	2	9,316.25
Sisania: Turtle Island (Ire) by Fairy King (USA)	3	84,426.10
Tight Spin: Girl Next Door by Local Suitor (USA)	1	2,950.60
Top Mouse: Harvest Mouse by Thatching	1	4,597.50
Top Society: Forthwith by Midyan (USA)	2	17,814.00
Top Tina: Head Turner by My Dad Tom (USA)	2	6,842.50
Top Tina: Glowing Path by Kalaglow	2	5,081.00
Upper Caen: Arndilly by Robellino (USA)	1	3,392.00
Whispered Wishes: Devils Den (Ire) by Jareer (USA)	2	8,202.00
	45	784,638.00

HILL CLOWN (USA) (1963) by Hillary

Dam Winner and Sire	Races Won	Value £
May Hill: Rising Tempo (Ire) by Lomond (USA)	1	1,725.00
May Hill: May Hills Legacy (Ire) by Be My Guest (USA)	2	7,104.80
Popsi's Poppet: Popsi's Legacy by Little Wolf	1	3,933.00
	4	12,762.80

HITTITE GLORY (1973) by Habitat

Dam Winner and Sire	Races Won	Value £
Glory Gold: Gold Desire by Grey Desire	1	2,346.00
Hearten: Heart Of Spain by Aragon	2	5,809.50
Lamya: Murray's Mazda (Ire) by M Double M (USA)	3	6,655.80
	6	14,811.30

HOLD YOUR PEACE (USA) (1969) by Speak John

Dam Winner and Sire	Races Won	Value £
Relevant (USA): Ocara (USA) by Danzig Connection (USA)	1	2,794.00
	1	2,794.00

HOME GUARD (USA) (1969) by Forli(Arg)

Dam Winner and Sire	Races Won	Value £
Goodbye Shelley (Fr): Shamam (USA) by Shadeed (USA)	1	6,160.00
Home And Away: The Premier Expres by Siberian Express (USA)	1	2,243.00
Nasara (Fr): Wakt by Akarad (Fr)	1	3,287.30
Villars: Lida's Delight (Ire) by Double Schwartz	1	3,106.00
	4	14,796.30

HOMEBOY (1973) by King's Troop

Dam Winner and Sire	Races Won	Value £
Bertrade: Winsome Wooster by Primo Dominie	1	3,454.00
Hi-Tech Girl: Sea-Deer by Hadeer	2	7,797.50
	3	11,251.50

HOMING (1975) by Habitat

Dam Winner and Sire	Races Won	Value £
Fishpond: Pondering by Another Realm	4	10,738.00
Grovehurst: Aragrove by Aragon	2	7,708.25
Misguided: Misbelief by Shirley Heights	3	10,986.80
Spin Turn: Dance Turn by Damister (USA)	1	4,932.00
	10	34,365.05

HONEST PLEASURE (USA) (1973) by What A Pleasure(USA)

Dam Winner and Sire	Races Won	Value £
Vivre Libre (USA): Wishing (USA) by Lyphard's Wish (Fr)	1	5,936.00
	1	5,936.00

HONEY JAY (USA) (1968) by Double Jay

Dam Winner and Sire	Races Won	Value £
She's A Jay (USA): He's A King (USA) by Key To The Kingdom (USA)	2	7,732.50
	2	7,732.50

HOOK MONEY (1951) by Bernborough

Dam Winner and Sire	Races Won	Value £
Pitlessie: Circle Of Friends (Ire) by Taufan (USA)	1	8,610.00
	1	8,610.00

Dam Winner and Sire	Races Won	Value £

HORAGE (1980) by Tumble Wind(USA)

Song Of The Glens: Syabas (Ire) by Northiam (USA)	1	3,183.70
	1	3,183.70

HOT SPARK (1972) by Habitat

Glimmer: Royal Acclaim by Tender King	1	2,070.00
Incarnadine: Rise Up Singing by Noalto	2	9,659.50
Incarnadine: Sunderland Echo by Daring March	3	8,704.00
La Tuerta: Ya Malak by Fairy King (USA)	2	7,437.80
Madam Cody: Resonant by Forzando	2	6,983.40
	10	34,854.70

HOTFOOT (1966) by Firestreak

Bargouzine: Rain Splash by Petong	1	3,752.50
Dalchroy: Fuchu by Jupiter Island	2	7,992.50
Hayati: Ruby Tiger by Ahonoora	1	21,519.00
Honey Pot: Girl From Ipanema by Salse (USA)	1	4,232.00
Quaranta: Quantity Surveyor by Aragon	3	10,660.20
Soxoph: Bearall (Ire) by Al Hareb (USA)	3	16,573.65
Sunset Ray: Shynon by Nishapour (Fr)	3	10,640.50
	14	75,370.35

HUNTERCOMBE (1967) by Derring-Do

Sea Palace: The Noble Oak (Ire) by The Noble Player (USA)	2	6,189.75
	2	6,189.75

I SAY (1962) by Sayajirao

Ixia: Sweet Mignonette by Tina's Pet	5	14,905.95
Ixia: Hyde's Happy Hour by Primo Dominie	1	2,736.00
	6	17,641.95

ICECAPADE (USA) (1969) by Nearctic

Ice Chocolate (USA): Ice Rebel by Robellino (USA)	1	2,243.00
Tallantire (USA): Jack Button (Ire) by Kings Lake (USA)	2	10,688.75
	3	12,931.75

ILE DE BOURBON (USA) (1975) by Nijinsky(Can)

Glowing With Pride: Everglades (Ire) by Green Desert (USA)	3	18,738.80
Golden Sunlight: Broctune Gold by Superpower	2	5,184.50
Messaria: Big Sky by Never So Bold	1	4,347.00
Princess Genista: Tomos by Sure Blade (USA)	1	3,552.75
Salazie: Queens Contractor by Formidable (USA)	1	2,070.00
String Of Beads: Salu by Ardross	3	9,671.75
Trois Vallees: Princess Ermyn by Shernazar	2	5,907.00
Working Model: Bronze Maquette (Ire) by Ahonoora	1	2,070.00
	14	51,541.80

IMPERIAL FLING (USA) (1976) by Northern Dancer

Divine Fling: Aradanza by Aragon	1	28,542.50
Divine Fling: Purple Fling by Music Boy	1	3,006.50
Lysithea: Lying Eyes by Interrex (Can)	1	2,691.60
Maycrest: Calisar by Mummy's Game	2	4,729.50
	5	38,970.10

IMPORT (1971) by Porto Bello

North Pine: Heaven-Liegh-Grey by Grey Desire	2	11,511.50
North Pine: Echo-Logical by Belfort (Fr)	1	5,775.00
Trwyn Cilan: Gone Savage by Nomination	1	2,843.00
	4	20,129.50

IN REALITY (1964) by Intentionally

Finality (USA): Smart Teacher (USA) by Smarten (USA)	1	3,377.25
Image Of Reality (USA): Rameau (USA) by Zilzal (USA)	1	4,776.00
In Essence (USA): In Case (USA) by Storm Cat (USA)	2	19,837.50
Lady Chesterfield (USA): Persian Affair (Ire) by Persian Heights	1	3,676.00
Taruma (USA): Tabkir (USA) by Storm Cat (USA)	1	3,523.50
	6	35,190.25

INDIAN KING (USA) (1978) by Raja Baba(USA)

Cool Combination: Indian Dreamer by Midyan (USA)	2	6,932.70
Eastern Ember: Champagne Ateaster by Hubbly Bubbly (USA)	1	3,260.25
Finessing: Sir Edward Henry (Ire) by Taufan (USA)	1	3,004.60
Indian Lily: Black Dragon (Ire) by Ela-Mana-Mou	1	3,746.50
Indigo Queen: Candi Das (Ire) by Jareer (USA)	1	3,261.40
	6	20,205.45

IRISH CASTLE (USA) (1967) by Bold Ruler

Killarney Belle (USA): Eire Leath-Sceal by Legend Of France (USA)	3	10,852.50
	3	10,852.50

IRISH RIVER (Fr) (1976) by Riverman(USA)

Dam Winner and Sire	Races Won	Value £
Aim For The Top (USA): Dance To The Top by Sadler's Wells (USA)	2	8,653.90
Blue Wedding (USA): Bonny Bride (Ire) by Lomond (USA)	1	4,435.00
Double River (USA): So Intrepid (Ire) by Never So Bold	1	3,687.50
Maid Of Erin (USA): Mizyan (Ire) by Melyno	1	2,601.40
River Dancer: Ballet Shoes (Ire) by Ela-Mana-Mou	2	6,842.25
River Reem (USA): Shoofk by Dunbeath (USA)	1	3,753.50
Riverstreak (USA): Fluvial (Ire) by Lomond (USA)	1	6,316.00
	9	36,289.55

J O TOBIN (USA) (1974) by Never Bend

Dam Winner and Sire	Races Won	Value £
Celebration Song (USA): Dixieland Melody (USA) by Dixieland Band (USA)	1	6,709.20
Chicobin (USA): Chilly Breeze by Ballad Rock	1	2,355.00
Holy Tobin (USA): Saint Ciel (USA) by Skywalker (USA)	1	2,679.00
Holy Tobin (USA): Roveredo (USA) by Bering	1	3,084.75
Our Reverie (USA): Peter Quince by Kris	1	11,053.00
	5	25,880.95

JACINTO (1962) by Bold Ruler

Dam Winner and Sire	Races Won	Value £
Jibber Jabber (USA): Lord Nitrogen (USA) by Greinton	1	3,483.00
	1	3,483.00

JALMOOD (USA) (1979) by Blushing Groom(Fr)

Dam Winner and Sire	Races Won	Value £
M Twenty Five: Star Speeder (Ire) by Nomination	2	6,039.00
	2	6,039.00

JAN EKELS (1969) by Derring-Do

Dam Winner and Sire	Races Won	Value £
Bridestones: Scenic Dancer by Shareef Dancer (USA)	1	3,236.00
Serena (Saf): Broadway Flyer (USA) by Theatrical	1	3,535.00
	2	6,771.00

JEAN-PIERRE (1964) by Prince John

Dam Winner and Sire	Races Won	Value £
La Basque (USA): Muhayaa (USA) by Danzig (USA)	4	36,024.80
	4	36,024.80

JIM FRENCH (USA) (1968) by Graustark

Dam Winner and Sire	Races Won	Value £
Fille de L'orne (Fr): Enfant Du Paradis (Ire) by Shernazar	1	3,339.10
La Francaise (USA): Frogmarch (USA) by Diesis	1	5,380.00
	2	8,719.10

JIMMY REPPIN (1965) by Midsummer Night II

Dam Winner and Sire	Races Won	Value £
Lifestyle: Chantry Bellini by Efisio	1	3,184.00
Reprocolor: Cezanne by Ajdal (USA)	1	7,509.60
Strathspey: Spinning by Glint Of Gold	1	4,464.20
Waltz: Dancing Domino by Primo Dominie	5	13,122.50
	8	28,280.30

JOLLY JET (1963) by Jet Action

Dam Winner and Sire	Races Won	Value £
Delayed Action: MCA Below The Line by Lucky Wednesday	1	3,377.25
	1	3,377.25

JUKEBOX (1966) by Sing Sing

Dam Winner and Sire	Races Won	Value £
Hound Song: Lochore by Nordico (USA)	1	2,269.13
	1	2,269.13

JULIO MARINER (1975) by Blakeney

Dam Winner and Sire	Races Won	Value £
Asturiana: Twice In Bundoran (Ire) by Bold Arrangement	1	2,820.00
Electo: Election Special by Chief Singer	1	3,465.00
Merrywren: First Option by Primo Dominie	2	5,589.50
	4	11,874.50

JUNGLE SAVAGE (USA) (1966) by Indian Hemp

Dam Winner and Sire	Races Won	Value £
Heat Haze (USA): Noeprob (USA) by Majestic Shore (USA)	1	2,070.00
	1	2,070.00

JUNIUS (USA) (1976) by Raja Baba(USA)

Dam Winner and Sire	Races Won	Value £
Gentle Gypsy: Coconut Johnny by King Of Spain	1	3,348.00
Gentle Gypsy: Indian Crystal by Petong	1	3,027.50
Laleston: Jess Rebec by Kala Shikari	1	2,950.00
Laleston: Madame Gregoire by Presidium	1	2,924.70
Say Yes: Beaumont (Ire) by Be My Native (USA)	1	2,162.60
Soluce: Splice by Sharpo	2	19,379.40
Times: Times Zando by Forzando	2	5,020.60
	9	38,812.80

KALAGLOW (1978) by Kalamoun

Dam Winner and Sire	Races Won	Value £
Catch The Sun: Tioman Island by Midyan (USA)	3	17,767.50

Dam Winner and Sire	Races Won	Value £
Glowing Report: Eighteen Twelve by Music Boy	1	2,967.40
Kala Rosa: Daily Star by Music Boy	1	2,070.00
Shining Water: Tenby by Caerleon (USA)	2	72,927.00
Shining Water: Reflecting (Ire) by Ahonoora	1	3,648.70
Shining Water: Bude by Dancing Brave (USA)	1	4,084.50
	9	103,465.10

KALAMOUN (1970) by Zeddaan

Dam Winner and Sire	Races Won	Value £
As You Desire Me: Princess Kris by Kris	1	3,582.00
Castle Moon: Moon Carnival by Be My Guest (USA)	2	5,581.30
Kalamac (Fr): Arabat by Habitat	2	6,683.80
Molly Moon (Fr): Princess Borghese (USA) by Nijinsky (Can)	1	3,915.00
	6	19,762.10

KAMPALA (1976) by Kalamoun

Dam Winner and Sire	Races Won	Value £
African Cousin: Nordoora (Ire) by Fayruz	2	6,072.00
Down The Valley: Down D Islands by Then Again	2	6,409.25
	4	12,481.25

KAUTOKEINO (Fr) (1967) by Relko

Dam Winner and Sire	Races Won	Value £
Sententious: My Gallery (Ire) by Tate Gallery (USA)	1	3,494.25
	1	3,494.25

KENMARE (Fr) (1975) by Kalamoun

Dam Winner and Sire	Races Won	Value £
Kanmary (Fr): Colonel Collins (USA) by El Gran Senor (USA)	2	13,483.00
	2	13,483.00

KEY TO THE KINGDOM (USA) (1970) by Bold Ruler

Dam Winner and Sire	Races Won	Value £
Hill's Realm (USA): General John (Ire) by Cyrano de Bergerac	1	4,893.00
Hill's Realm (USA): Home From The Hill (Ire) by Jareer (USA)	1	3,132.00
Ma Biche (USA): Kassbaan (USA) by Alydar (USA)	3	14,293.50
	5	22,318.50

KEY TO THE MINT (USA) (1969) by Graustark

Dam Winner and Sire	Races Won	Value £
Hasty Key (USA): Cotteir Chief (Ire) by Chief Singer	3	9,956.70
Lively Living (USA): Stonehatch (USA) by Storm Bird (Can)	2	32,783.40
	5	42,740.10

KIND OF HUSH (1978) by Welsh Pageant

Dam Winner and Sire	Races Won	Value £
Lingering: Jobie by Precocious	1	3,395.00
	1	3,395.00

KING EMPEROR (USA) (1966) by Bold Ruler

Dam Winner and Sire	Races Won	Value £
Gigiolina: Premier Dance by Bairn (USA)	1	1,770.00
Marie Louise: Pharaoh's Dancer by Fairy King (USA)	1	3,339.10
Norene's Nemesis (Can): Silverdale (USA) by Silver Hawk (USA)	1	3,947.50
	3	9,056.60

KING OF SPAIN (1976) by Philip of Spain

Dam Winner and Sire	Races Won	Value £
Dona Krista: Risky by Risk Me (Fr)	5	114,171.70
La Reine D'Espagne: Guv'nors Gift by Sizzling Melody	2	5,600.00
Royal Accord: Sporting Heir (Ire) by Anita's Prince	1	2,070.00
	8	121,841.70

KING'S TROOP (1957) by Princely Gift

Dam Winner and Sire	Races Won	Value £
Ballinacurra: Blyton Lad by Skyliner	2	14,099.40
	2	14,099.40

KINGS LAKE (USA) (1978) by Nijinsky(Can)

Dam Winner and Sire	Races Won	Value £
Lady Of Shalott: Knight Of Shalot (Ire) by Don't Forget Me	1	3,201.75
Lake Ormond: Reprehend by Reprimand	1	4,077.50
Magic Kingdom: Awestruck by Primo Dominie	1	3,172.50
Trasimeno: Sharaar (USA) by Bering	2	5,673.00
	5	16,124.75

KIRTLING (1978) by Grundy

Dam Winner and Sire	Races Won	Value £
Dead Letter (USA): Silver Maple (USA) by Silver Hawk (USA)	1	4,503.00
	1	4,503.00

KLAIRON (1952) by Clarion III

Dam Winner and Sire	Races Won	Value £
Klairelle: Kaitak (Ire) by Broken Hearted	1	2,005.00
Merchantmens Girl: Barbezieux by Petong	2	6,108.50
	3	8,113.50

KNOWN FACT (USA) (1977) by In Reality(USA)

Dam Winner and Sire	Races Won	Value £
Certain Story: Fairy Story (Ire) by Persian Bold	2	12,465.25
Certain Story: Dam Certain (Ire) by Damister (USA)	1	2,686.00
Hufoof: Bumaan (Ire) by Persian Heights	1	4,413.75
Humble Pie: Waffle On by Chief Singer	1	3,492.50

Dam Winner and Sire	Races Won	Value £
Known Charter: Magical Retreat (USA) by Sir Ivor	2	16,468.00
Vivienda: Isabella Sharp by Sharpo	2	7,480.50
	9	47,006.00

KONIGSSTUHL (Ger) (1976) by Dschingis Khan

Dam Winner and Sire	Races Won	Value £
Majoritat (Ger): Majority (Ire) by Dancing Brave (USA)	1	3,494.25
	1	3,494.25

KRIS (1976) by Sharpen Up

Dam Winner and Sire	Races Won	Value £
Aljood: Desert Invader (Ire) by Lead On Time (USA)	1	3,687.50
Argon Laser: Weigh Anchor by Slip Anchor	1	5,936.00
Azyaa: Ihtiraz by Soviet Star (USA)	3	22,830.40
Dusty Dollar: Miss Shagra (USA) by Danzig (USA)	2	7,211.00
First Kiss: Colin Muset by The Minstrel (Can)	1	3,289.50
First Kiss: Kissing Cousin (Ire) by Danehill (USA)	2	7,224.50
Fly The Coop: General Mouktar by Hadeer	3	19,085.00
Kenanga: Florid (USA) by The Minstrel (Can)	1	4,464.00
Kenanga: Kerkura (USA) by Riverman (USA)	1	4,402.50
Kindjal: Vallance by Top Ville	1	4,709.25
Kriswick: Vistec Express (Ire) by Salse (USA)	1	3,947.50
Nawadder: Yaakum by Glint Of Gold	1	3,002.40
Nawadder: Classic Sky (Ire) by Jareer (USA)	2	10,930.30
Point Of Honour: Del Deya (Ire) by Caerleon (USA)	2	7,595.00
Smoo: Barik (Ire) by Be My Guest (USA)	1	4,045.00
	23	112,359.85

KRONZEUGE (1961) by Neckar

Dam Winner and Sire	Races Won	Value £
Arita (Fr): Anusha by Alzao (USA)	3	8,792.20
Arita (Fr): Lugano by Rousillon (USA)	1	3,106.00
	4	11,898.20

LASER LIGHT (1966) by Aureole

Dam Winner and Sire	Races Won	Value £
B A Poundstretcher: Touch Above by Touching Wood (USA)	2	5,812.20
Infra Green: Infrasonic by Dancing Brave (USA)	1	34,639.80
Just A Shadow: Overpower by Try My Best (USA)	3	6,138.00
Metair: Tychonic by Last Tycoon	1	5,481.00
	7	52,071.00

LE FABULEUX (1961) by Wild Risk

Dam Winner and Sire	Races Won	Value £
Awe (USA): Awestrike (USA) by Imperial Falcon (Can)	1	3,640.50
Deep Powder (USA): Make A Note (USA) by Northern Flagship (USA)	2	7,404.95
La Mirande (Fr): Le Temeraire by Top Ville	1	2,243.00
	4	13,288.45

LE HAAR (1954) by Vieux Manoir

Dam Winner and Sire	Races Won	Value £
Rosy Lee (Fr): Roberty Lea by Alleging (USA)	1	3,629.50
	1	3,629.50

LE JOHNSTAN (1968) by El Gallo

Dam Winner and Sire	Races Won	Value £
Lady Keyser: Lady-Bo-K by Komaite (USA)	1	3,390.90
Pendle's Secret: Pride Of Pendle by Grey Desire	5	15,264.00
	6	18,654.90

LE LEVANSTELL (1957) by Le Lavandou

Dam Winner and Sire	Races Won	Value £
Djimbaran Bay: Fylde Flyer by Music Boy	1	4,980.80
Lavendula Rose: Drum Taps (USA) by Dixieland Band (USA)	1	107,464.80
Mill's Girl: Robingo (Ire) by Bob Back (USA)	2	17,120.00
Sarah Siddons (Fr): Star Quest by Rainbow Quest (USA)	1	4,889.50
	5	134,455.10

LEGAL EAGLE (1972) by Manacle

Dam Winner and Sire	Races Won	Value £
Legal Sound: Legatee by Risk Me (Fr)	1	3,054.20
	1	3,054.20

LEVMOSS (1965) by Le Levanstell

Dam Winner and Sire	Races Won	Value £
De'b Old Fruit: Deb's Ball by Glenstal (USA)	1	3,106.00
Love Locket: Shamshom Al Arab (Ire) by Glenstal (USA)	3	8,724.40
	4	11,830.40

LINACRE (1960) by Rockefella

Dam Winner and Sire	Races Won	Value £
Rue Del Peru: Jasari (Ire) by Ajraas (USA)	1	4,142.50
	1	4,142.50

LINES OF POWER (USA) (1977) by Raise A Native

Dam Winner and Sire	Races Won	Value £
Rose D'Amour (USA): Pembridge Place by Niniski (USA)	1	5,253.50
	1	5,253.50

LITTLE CURRENT (USA) (1971) by Sea-Bird II

Dam Winner and Sire	Races Won	Value £
Benguela (USA): Naif (USA) by Storm Bird (Can)	2	7,076.25

Dam Winner and Sire	Races Won	Value £
Willow Court (USA): Media Messenger by Hadeer	1	2,556.60
	3	9,632.85

LOCHNAGER (1972) by Dumbarnie

Dam Winner and Sire	Races Won	Value £
City Link Rose: Bodari by Prince Sabo	2	8,578.75
City Link Rose: Ahjay by Tina's Pet	1	3,231.00
Daisy Loch: Loch Patrick by Beveled (USA)	2	20,632.25
Illiney Girl: Quick Steel by Alleging (USA)	1	2,448.00
Imperial Jade: Taalif by Last Tycoon	1	3,348.00
Imperial Jade: Averti (Ire) by Warning	2	9,966.25
Peckitts Well: Lochsong by Song	3	122,648.80
Princess Sharpenup: Milbank Challenger by Belfort (Fr)	2	5,488.00
	14	176,341.05

LOMOND (USA) (1980) by Northern Dancer

Dam Winner and Sire	Races Won	Value £
Inchmurrin: Inchinor by Ahonoora	3	68,073.00
	3	68,073.00

LONDON BELLS (Can) (1977) by Nijinsky(Can)

Dam Winner and Sire	Races Won	Value £
Dancing Chimes: Palacegate Touch by Petong	4	14,163.06
	4	14,163.06

LONGLEAT (USA) (1979) by The Minstrel(Can)

Dam Winner and Sire	Races Won	Value £
Low Dalby: Monkey Music by Music Boy	1	3,523.50
	1	3,523.50

LORD AVIE (USA) (1978) by Lord Gaylord

Dam Winner and Sire	Races Won	Value £
National Time (USA): Meeson Times by Enchantment	1	2,898.80
National Time (USA): Kildee Lad by Presidium	1	4,175.00
	2	7,073.80

LORD GAYLE (USA) (1965) by Sir Gaylord

Dam Winner and Sire	Races Won	Value £
Blue Angel: Patsy Grimes by Beveled (USA)	1	3,598.10
Desirable: Badie (USA) by Blushing Groom (Fr)	1	3,201.75
Desirable: Dumaani (USA) by Danzig (USA)	1	6,570.00
Gaylom: Northern Conqueror (Ire) by Mazaad	3	7,883.70
Lady Carol: Craigie Boy by Crofthall	2	6,211.80
Lady Kasbah: Teanarco (Ire) by Kafu	1	3,236.00
Lady Wise: I'm A Dreamer (Ire) by Mister Majestic	2	5,659.80
Ra Ra: Efra by Efisio	2	7,272.50
Ra Ra: Nakita by Efisio	1	2,534.20
Saving Mercy: Arjuzah (Ire) by Ahonoora	2	17,905.00
Sigym: Loki (Ire) by Thatching	1	7,310.00
Smashing Gale: Kierchem (Ire) by Mazaad	1	3,172.50
Walkyria: Corals Dream (Ire) by Petorius	3	17,939.20
Walkyria: Ho-Joe (Ire) by Burslem	2	4,003.80
	23	96,498.35

LORENZACCIO (1965) by Klairon

Dam Winner and Sire	Races Won	Value £
Cappuccilli: Mr Copyforce by Sharrood (USA)	2	9,591.50
Lobela: Bold Angel by Lochnager	1	4,500.00
Lorelene (Fr): Latvian by Rousillon (USA)	2	5,430.00
Lorelene (Fr): Jalore by Jalmood (USA)	3	5,770.00
Popular Win: Ewald (Ire) by Green Desert (USA)	2	8,525.25
Popular Win: Right Win (Ire) by Law Society (USA)	2	34,196.50
	12	68,013.25

LT STEVENS (1961) by Nantallah

Dam Winner and Sire	Races Won	Value £
Lt Golden Girl (USA): Flight Lieutenant (USA) by Marfa (USA)	1	21,500.00
	1	21,500.00

LUCKY WEDNESDAY (1973) by Roi Soleil

Dam Winner and Sire	Races Won	Value £
Lucky Angel: Chickcharnie by Stanford	1	3,406.50
Lucky Saran: Lucky Fourteen by Nomination	1	2,365.10
	2	5,771.60

LUSKIN STAR (Aus) (1974) by Kaoru Star

Dam Winner and Sire	Races Won	Value £
Artistic Princess (Aus): Laune (Aus) by Kenmare (Fr)	1	4,127.75
	1	4,127.75

LUTHIER (1965) by Klairon

Dam Winner and Sire	Races Won	Value £
Fabulous Luba: Arid by Green Desert (USA)	2	6,900.75
Flute (Fr): Sylvan Sabre (Ire) by Flash Of Steel	3	9,342.00
Harp Strings (Fr): Principal Player (USA) by Chief Singer	1	3,095.00
Riviere Salee (Fr): Riviere Actor (USA) by Theatrical	1	3,525.00
Rose Music: Rose Alto by Adonijah	2	47,876.75
Sing Softly: Top Cees by Shirley Heights	1	3,523.50
	10	74,263.00

Dam	Winner and Sire	Races Won	Value £

LYPHARD (USA) (1969) by Northern Dancer

Dam: Winner and Sire	Races Won	Value £
American Winter (USA): American Hero by Persian Bold	1	4,077.50
Andaleeb (USA): Prophecy (Ire) by Warning	3	83,905.12
Arabian Rose (USA): Moonlight Quest by Nishapour (Fr)	3	11,296.60
Bequeath (USA): Beneficiary by Jalmood (USA)	4	11,170.25
Cadeaux D'Amie (USA): Hatoof (USA) by Irish River (Fr)	1	205,707.00
Light Of Hope (USA): Savoy Truffle (Fr) by Law Society (USA)	1	3,435.75
Phydilla (Fr): Bayrak (USA) by Bering	1	2,364.00
Reves Celestes (USA): Rafif (USA) by Riverman (USA)	1	3,434.50
Riviere D'Or (USA): Gold Splash (USA) by Blushing Groom (Fr)	1	109,537.80
Royal Procession (USA): Balzino (USA) by Trempolino (USA)	1	2,162.50
Safe House: Northern Rainbow by Rainbow Quest (USA)	1	1,051.00
So Cozy (USA): Braari (USA) by Gulch (USA)	3	26,315.30
Sure Locked (USA): Keylock (USA) by Diesis	1	3,597.00
Sweet Snow (USA): Bidweaya (USA) by Lear Fan (USA)	1	3,080.10
	23	471,134.42

LYPHARD'S WISH (Fr) (1976) by Lyphard(USA)

Dam: Winner and Sire	Races Won	Value £
Harmonical (USA): Straight Arrow by Indian Ridge	1	3,523.50
	1	3,523.50

MAIN REEF (1976) by Mill Reef(USA)

Dam: Winner and Sire	Races Won	Value £
Hay Knot: Walnut Burl (Ire) by Taufan (USA)	1	3,348.00
Hay Knot: Cazzuto (Ire) by Kefaah (USA)	1	3,289.50
Liffey Reef: My Lifetime Lady (Ire) by Indian Ridge	2	5,490.40
Loreef: North Reef (Ire) by Danehill (USA)	1	4,342.25
Naufrage: Kismetim by Dowsing (USA)	1	3,669.75
Tootle: Suaad (Ire) by Fools Holme (USA)	1	4,308.00
	7	24,447.90

MAJESTIC LIGHT (USA) (1973) by Majestic Prince

Dam: Winner and Sire	Races Won	Value £
French Galaxy (USA): Five To Seven (USA) by Little Missouri (USA)	3	9,637.60
How High The Moon (USA): Moscow Sea (USA) by Chief's Crown (USA)	2	12,299.25
Tough As Nails (USA): Catrail (USA) by Storm Cat (USA)	5	98,341.80
	10	120,278.65

MAJESTIC PRINCE (1966) by Raise A Native

Dam: Winner and Sire	Races Won	Value £
Majestic Kahala (USA): Fraam by Lead On Time (USA)	2	28,703.08
	2	28,703.08

MAJOR PORTION (1955) by Court Martial

Dam: Winner and Sire	Races Won	Value £
Trickster: Absolute Magic by Doulab (USA)	1	3,640.50
	1	3,640.50

MALACATE (USA) (1973) by Lucky Debonair

Dam: Winner and Sire	Races Won	Value £
Akka: Akkazao (Ire) by Alzao (USA)	1	4,045.00
	1	4,045.00

MALINOWSKI (USA) (1973) by Sir Ivor

Dam: Winner and Sire	Races Won	Value £
Centenary Year: Asian Punter (Ire) by M Double M (USA)	2	9,190.50
Velinowski: Tendresse (Ire) by Tender King	2	6,715.50
	4	15,906.00

MANACLE (1964) by Sing Sing

Dam: Winner and Sire	Races Won	Value £
Diorina: Hallorina by Hallgate	2	5,783.50
Miss Merlin: Trevorsninepoints by Jester	3	6,942.60
Miss Sandman: Reel Of Tulloch (Ire) by Salmon Leap (USA)	1	2,623.40
Uranus: Stay With Me Baby by Nicholas Bill	1	3,366.00
	7	18,715.50

MANADO (1973) by Captain's Gig(USA)

Dam: Winner and Sire	Races Won	Value £
Addabub: Glen Echo (Ire) by Taufan (USA)	1	3,640.50
Brilleaux: Bobzao (Ire) by Alzao (USA)	2	20,604.75
Brilleaux: Ragsat Al Omor (Ire) by Dance Of Life (USA)	1	3,494.25
Maestrette: Formaestre (Ire) by Formidable (USA)	1	2,243.00
Monaco Lady: Missy-S (Ire) by Sarab	2	4,048.70
Natural Sunshine: Natural Lad by Kafu	1	2,070.00
Parijoun: Caspian Gold by Clantime	1	2,259.00
Sallywell: Pixton (Ire) by Common Grounds	1	3,552.75
	10	41,912.95

MANDAMUS (1960) by Petition

Dam: Winner and Sire	Races Won	Value £
Fee: The Executor by Vaigly Great	2	6,319.20

Dam Winner and Sire	Races Won	Value £
Wig And Gown: Chakalak by Damister (USA)	1	3,114.00
Wig And Gown: Milngavie (Ire) by Pharly (Fr)	2	6,189.20
	5	15,622.40

MANDRAKE MAJOR (1974) by On Your Mark

Dam Winner and Sire	Races Won	Value £
High Climber: Perusal by Sizzling Melody	2	9,121.25
Lewista: Brookhead Lady by Petong	3	7,337.80
Maravilla: Mu-Arrik by Aragon	1	2,532.00
	6	18,991.05

MANSINGH (USA) (1969) by Jaipur

Dam Winner and Sire	Races Won	Value £
Joli's Girl: Side Bar by Mummy's Game	1	2,057.50
Marista: Strapped by Reprimand	1	3,248.00
Miss Cindy: Gipsy Fiddler by Bairn (USA)	1	2,301.00
Thulium: Crystal Magic by Mazilier (USA)	2	7,573.25
	5	15,179.75

MARCH PAST (1950) by Petition

Dam Winner and Sire	Races Won	Value £
Atoka: Edge Of Darkness by Vaigly Great	1	2,070.00
	1	2,070.00

MARCHING ON (1974) by Tudor Melody

Dam Winner and Sire	Races Won	Value £
Munequita: Monkey's Wedding by Skyliner	3	9,034.10
	3	9,034.10

MARDUK (Ger) (1971) by Orsini

Dam Winner and Sire	Races Won	Value £
Audenhove (Ger): Rooftop Flyer (Ire) by Nordico (USA)	1	4,378.00
	1	4,378.00

MARIBEAU (1962) by Ribot

Dam Winner and Sire	Races Won	Value £
Mistle Toe (USA): Mistle Cat (USA) by Storm Cat (USA)	2	18,390.00
	2	18,390.00

MARSHUA'S DANCER (USA) (1968) by Raise A Native

Dam Winner and Sire	Races Won	Value £
Dancing Meg (USA): Mytilene (Ire) by Soviet Star (USA)	1	4,050.00
Samarta Dancer (USA): Samain (USA) by Caerleon (USA)	1	4,175.00
	2	8,225.00

MARTINMAS (1969) by Silly Season

Dam Winner and Sire	Races Won	Value £
Ballaquine: Swing Low by Swing Easy (USA)	4	107,221.17
Bells Of St Martin: My Ruby Ring by Blushing Scribe (USA)	3	9,184.90
Bells Of St Martin: Bells Of Longwick by Myjinski (USA)	1	4,622.25
Bells Of St Martin: Bellsabanging by Chilibang	2	5,754.80
Jennyjo: Fourforfun by Midyan (USA)	5	28,140.25
Martin Place: Majed (Ire) by Wolverlife	2	14,006.40
Martinova: Salda by Bustino	1	2,880.00
Royal Aunt: Royal Girl by Kafu	4	12,396.50
Tin Tessa: Martina by Tina's Pet	4	11,080.50
	26	195,286.77

MASTER DERBY (USA) (1972) by Dust Commander (USA)

Dam Winner and Sire	Races Won	Value £
Kelowna (USA): Ragtime Song by Dunbeath (USA)	2	4,329.00
Miss Derby (USA): Miss Siham (Ire) by Green Forest (USA)	2	4,564.50
	4	8,893.50

MEADOW MINT (USA) (1969) by Herbager

Dam Winner and Sire	Races Won	Value £
What A Mint: Failand by Kala Shikari	1	1,954.00
	1	1,954.00

MEAUTRY (Fr) (1970) by Lionel

Dam Winner and Sire	Races Won	Value £
Nofret (Fr): Cameo Kirby (Fr) by Lead On Time (USA)	2	5,253.00
	2	5,253.00

MELDRUM (1966) by Hard Sauce

Dam Winner and Sire	Races Won	Value £
Larnem: Larn Fort by Belfort (Fr)	1	3,287.30
	1	3,287.30

MIAMI SPRINGS (1976) by Northfields(USA)

Dam Winner and Sire	Races Won	Value £
Lisdoonvarna: Cyarna Quinn (Ire) by Cyrano de Bergerac	2	6,250.00
Miami Dancer: Medland (Ire) by Imperial Frontier (USA)	1	2,758.20
Miami Mouse: My Minnie by Kind Of Hush	1	2,847.00
Springwell: Marros Mill by Glint Of Gold	2	7,715.70
Winter Resort: Patong Beach by Infantry	1	2,406.00
	7	21,976.90

MIDSUMMER NIGHT II (1957) by Djeddah

Dam Winner and Sire	Races Won	Value £
Midnight Music: Midnight Heights by Persian Heights	3	11,884.25
	3	11,884.25

Dam Winner and Sire	Races Won	Value £

MILESIAN (1953) by My Babu

Milveagh: Gallant Jack (Ire) by Flash Of Steel	1	3,054.20
Miss By Miles: Rich Pickings by Dominion	1	2,623.00
Miss By Miles: Mysilv by Bustino	2	6,723.35
	4	12,400.55

MILFORD (1976) by Mill Reef(USA)

Milinetta: Mill Force by Forzando	1	3,718.00
Philgwyn: Philidor by Forzando	1	65,422.50
Philgwyn: Silverlocks by Sharrood (USA)	3	11,382.50
	5	80,523.00

MILL REEF (USA) (1968) by Never Bend

Angel Clare (Fr): Star Manager (USA) by Lyphard (USA)	1	3,850.00
Anna Matrushka: Anna Of Saxony by Ela-Mana-Mou	3	31,661.40
Canadian Mill (USA): Hawajiss by Kris	2	21,677.60
Catawba: Licorne by Sadler's Wells (USA)	3	16,637.40
Exciting: Be Exciting (Ire) by Be My Guest (USA)	1	3,782.00
Fairy Footsteps: Haunted Wood (USA) by Nijinsky (Can)	1	3,348.00
Fanny's Cove: Chief Of Staff by Caerleon (USA)	1	1,730.00
Fanny's Cove: Mamara Reef by Salse (USA)	1	2,892.60
Gay Milly (Fr): Welsh Mill (Ire) by Caerleon (USA)	1	11,998.80
Harvest Dance: Hadeer's Dance by Hadeer	1	3,406.50
Lady Moon: Moonshine Lake by Kris	1	3,523.50
Mesmerize: Jaazim by Night Shift (USA)	1	2,595.00
Mesmerize: Just Happy (USA) by Night Shift (USA)	1	3,551.50
Mill On The Floss: Yeltsin by Soviet Star (USA)	1	3,465.00
Mill Path: Queen's View (Fr) by Lomond (USA)	1	3,231.00
Millerette: Baby Loves by Sadler's Wells (USA)	1	11,326.00
Reflection: Empire Pool by Sharrood (USA)	1	3,217.50
Reham: Rasayel (USA) by Bering	1	2,742.00
River Spey: Dune River by Green Desert (USA)	2	9,443.00
River Spey: Rispoto by Mtoto	1	2,444.60
Skating: Ice Pool (USA) by Diesis	1	4,503.00
State Of Mind: Ibsen by Gorytus (USA)	1	2,070.00
Thalestria (Fr): Amazon Express by Siberian Express (USA)	1	3,622.50
Triple Reef: Talented by Bustino	2	39,068.70
	31	195,787.60

MINNESOTA MAC (1964) by Rough 'n Tumble

Roundup Rose (USA): Rodeo Star (USA) by Nodouble (USA)	2	35,075.00
	2	35,075.00

MIRALGO (1959) by Aureole

Allander Girl: Miss Pin Up by Kalaglow	2	8,415.00
Allander Girl: Eurolink Chieftain by Kalaglow	1	3,624.00
Finesse: With Gusto by Taufan (USA)	2	4,106.00
	5	16,145.00

MISWAKI (USA) (1978) by Mr Prospector(USA)

Deep River Woman (USA): Tej Singh (USA) by Tejano (USA)	2	6,666.75
Olatha (USA): Amber Valley (USA) by Bering	1	3,647.25
Tanouma (USA): Azzilfi by Ardross	2	43,381.95
	5	53,695.95

MONSANTO (Fr) (1972) by Breton

Lily Of France: Great Hall by Hallgate	4	12,621.00
Monstrosa: Champagne Grandy by Vaigly Great	4	11,939.25
Petiller: Just Bill by Nicholas Bill	1	2,200.50
Shannon Lady: Pommes Frites (Ire) by Cyrano de Bergerac	1	3,622.50
	10	30,383.25

MONSEIGNEUR (USA) (1974) by Graustark

Lightning Laser: Morocco (Ire) by Cyrano de Bergerac	1	6,056.00
Madame Fair: Strephon (Ire) by Fairy King (USA)	2	5,108.00
Sister Hannah: Knayton Lass by Presidium	1	3,377.25
Travel Far: Multi National by Dominion Royale	1	4,337.50
	5	18,878.75

MONTEVERDI (1977) by Lyphard(USA)

Encore L'amour (USA): Evening Falls by Beveled (USA)	2	7,578.00
	2	7,578.00

MOORESTYLE (1977) by Manacle

Icefern: Kensworth Lady by Formidable (USA)	1	3,172.50
Queenstyle: Gadge by Nomination	1	11,647.50
Tahilla: Pluck by Never So Bold	1	3,882.50
	3	18,702.50

MORSTON (Fr) (1970) by Ragusa

Cordon: Haroldon (Ire) by Heraldiste (USA)	1	3,054.20
Cordon: Wordsmith (Ire) by Cyrano de Bergerac	1	4,110.00

Dam Winner and Sire	Races Won	Value £
Much Pleasure: Full Quiver by Gorytus (USA)	1	2,511.80
Piculet: Double Echo (Ire) by Glow (USA)	1	10,672.50
	4	20,348.50

MOSSBOROUGH (1947) by Nearco

Dam Winner and Sire	Races Won	Value £
Wimosa: Allmosa by Alleging (USA)	2	5,420.00
	2	5,420.00

MOST SECRET (1968) by Crocket

Dam Winner and Sire	Races Won	Value £
Excavator Lady: Tuscan Dawn by Clantime	2	6,637.50
Soba: Sobering Thoughts by Be My Guest (USA)	4	24,786.60
Soba: French Gift by Cadeaux Genereux	1	3,377.25
Soba: Soba Up by Persian Heights	1	4,630.00
Soft Secret: Ballasecret by Ballacashtal (Can)	3	23,540.00
	11	62,971.35

MOUNT HAGEN (Fr) (1971) by Bold Bidder

Dam Winner and Sire	Races Won	Value £
Astra Adastra: Persiansky (Ire) by Persian Bold	4	13,292.85
Fahrenheit: Alasib by Siberian Express (USA)	2	8,093.50
High Explosive: James Is Special (Ire) by Lyphard's Special (USA)	1	4,878.25
High Explosive: Penny Banger (Ire) by Pennine Walk	5	14,235.80
Mountain Chase: Amazing Feat (Ire) by Petorius	2	11,847.55
Papun (USA): Call To The Bar (Ire) by Kafu	1	3,435.75
Sabrine: Tyrian Purple (Ire) by Wassl	1	2,406.00
	16	58,189.70

MR PROSPECTOR (USA) (1970) by Raise A Native

Dam Winner and Sire	Races Won	Value £
Diamond Field (USA): Storm Canyon (Ire) by Storm Bird (Can)	3	13,040.00
Diamond Field (USA): Wafayt (Ire) by Danehill (USA)	2	9,576.25
Hence (USA): Trippiano by Fappiano (USA)	1	3,172.50
It's In The Air (USA): Arkaan (USA) by Nijinsky (Can)	1	4,793.75
It's In The Air (USA): Monaassabaat (USA) by Zilzal (USA)	1	4,378.00
Kind Prospect (USA): Promise Fulfilled (USA) by Bet Twice (USA)	2	7,497.60
Private View (USA): Ionio (USA) by Silver Hawk (USA)	1	10,052.00
Wise Speculation (USA): Always Friendly by High Line	1	4,761.40
	12	57,271.50

MUMMY'S GAME (1979) by Mummy's Pet

Dam Winner and Sire	Races Won	Value £
Nation's Game: Mazentre Forward (Ire) by Mazaad	2	7,820.50
	2	7,820.50

MUMMY'S PET (1968) by Sing Sing

Dam Winner and Sire	Races Won	Value £
Bourgeonette: The Where Withal by Glint Of Gold	5	14,139.90
Bourgeonette: Sawtid by Chief Singer	2	5,883.50
Children's Hour: Common Law (Ire) by Common Grounds	1	3,377.25
Crimbourne: Gone For A Burton (Ire) by Bustino	1	2,061.20
Fariha: Bold Stroke by Persian Bold	1	7,985.20
Glenfield Portion: Glenfield Greta by Gabitat	1	3,365.00
Glenfield Portion: Best Kept Secret by Petong	3	9,326.75
Lydia Rose: O So Neet by Teenoso (USA)	1	2,637.00
Mavahra: Indiahra by Indian Ridge	2	5,899.35
Missish: Moscow Road by Presidium	3	9,137.25
Mrs Darling: Adamparis by Robellino (USA)	2	5,679.00
Mumruffin: Domicksky by Dominion	3	14,389.00
Odilese: Tutu Sixtysix by Petong	2	6,765.75
Our Pet: Southern Memories (Ire) by Don't Forget Me	1	4,110.00
Petriece: Smart Pet by Petong	2	10,965.00
Petulengra: Norman Warrior by Petong	1	2,965.00
Primulette: Primost by Most Welcome	1	2,469.00
Putupon: Putout by Dowsing (USA)	1	3,231.00
Softly Spoken: Sweet Whisper by Petong	1	2,243.00
Spoilt Again: Teen Jay by Teenoso (USA)	1	1,953.40
Theda: Heathyards Crusade (Ire) by Digamist (USA)	1	2,243.00
Thevetia: In Like Flynn by Handsome Sailor	3	15,175.15
Tremellick: Avro Anson by Ardross	1	3,435.75
Ulla Laing: Domulla by Dominion	1	3,622.50
What A Pet: Petardia by Petong	1	8,019.60
	42	151,078.55

MUSIC BOY (1973) by Jukebox

Dam Winner and Sire	Races Won	Value £
Jeanne Avril: Mary Hinge by Dowsing (USA)	3	10,746.00
Louisianalightning: Lightning Belle by Belfort (Fr)	1	2,950.60
Melody Park: Creche by Bairn (USA)	1	2,245.00
Rengaine (Fr): Holly Golightly by Robellino (USA)	1	3,465.00
Rosana Park: Angelica Park by Simply Great (Fr)	1	2,070.00
School Concert: First Play by Primo Dominie	1	3,172.50
Third Movement: The Little Ferret by Scottish Reel	1	2,243.00
Zalatia: Simmie's Special by Precocious	1	6,254.50
	10	33,146.60

MUSIC MAESTRO (1975) by Song

Dam Winner and Sire	Races Won	Value £
Carolside: Little Rousillon by Rousillon (USA)	1	4,878.25
Carolside: Joellise by Glint Of Gold	1	2,301.00
Winsong Melody: El Yasaf (Ire) by Sayf El Arab (USA)	1	12,277.20
	3	19,456.45

Dam	Winner and Sire	Races Won	Value £

MY SWALLOW (1968) by Le Levanstell

	Races Won	Value £
La Lutine: Montendre by Longleat (USA)	1	10,464.00
La Lutine: Mondragon by Niniski (USA)	2	5,540.00
Rainbow's End: Coltrane by Dominion	2	5,100.50
Rainbow's End: Carmot by Cadeaux Genereux	2	8,622.80
	7	29,727.30

MY SWANEE (1963) by Petition

	Races Won	Value £
Apapa Port: Sea Gazer (Ire) by Magical Wonder (USA)	1	10,575.00
Impromptu: Mister Jolson by Latest Model	2	7,209.90
What A Picture: Jokist by Orchestra	1	3,015.00
	4	20,799.90

MYSOLO (1967) by Sing Sing

	Races Won	Value £
Glamour Girl (Arg): Hillzah (USA) by Blushing Groom (Fr)	2	8,193.10
	2	8,193.10

NASHUA (1952) by Nasrullah

	Races Won	Value £
Make An Attempt (USA): Northern Trial (USA) by Far North (Can)	1	3,465.00
Miss Daytona (USA): Wayfarers Way (USA) by Manastash Ridge (USA)	1	4,055.00
Syndikos (USA): Imperial Bailiwick (Ire) by Imperial Frontier (USA)	3	31,269.25
	5	38,789.25

NATIONAL (1961) by Nashua

	Races Won	Value £
Pepi Image (USA): Lexus (Ire) by Gorytus (USA)	2	4,749.00
	2	4,749.00

NATIVE BAZAAR (1968) by Indigenous

	Races Won	Value £
Casbah Girl: Sabre Rattler by Beveled (USA)	2	13,227.00
Casbah Girl: Mister Bloy by Dowsing (USA)	1	3,178.75
Pusey Street: Pusey Street Boy by Vaigly Great	3	8,896.00
Pusey Street: Windrush Lady by Risk Me (Fr)	1	3,720.00
	7	29,021.75

NATIVE CHARGER (1962) by Native Dancer

	Races Won	Value £
Liturgism (USA): Young Senor (USA) by El Gran Senor (USA)	1	4,396.00
	1	4,396.00

NATIVE PRINCE (1964) by Native Dancer

	Races Won	Value £
Asian Princess: Heavy Rock (Ire) by Ballad Rock	1	3,052.00
	1	3,052.00

NATIVE ROYALTY (USA) (1967) by Raise A Native

	Races Won	Value £
Qui Royalty (USA): Emperor Jones (USA) by Danzig (USA)	1	23,135.70
	1	23,135.70

NEARLY A HAND (1974) by Busted

	Races Won	Value £
Langton Herring: Sylvan Breeze by Sulaafah (USA)	1	3,054.20
Langton Herring: Miss Vaxette by Norwick (USA)	3	16,998.50
	4	20,052.70

NEBBIOLO (1974) by Yellow God

	Races Won	Value £
Grapette: Gorinsky (Ire) by Gorytus (USA)	4	26,841.50
Nuit de Vin: Leave It To Lib by Tender King	2	6,068.50
One Better: Stack Rock by Ballad Rock	4	33,590.96
Redgrave Design: First Bid by Crofthall	2	8,687.50
Redgrave Design: Saint Express by Clantime	1	5,452.00
Sedra: Star Talent (USA) by Local Talent (USA)	2	11,156.25
	15	91,796.71

NELCIUS (1963) by Tenareze

	Races Won	Value £
Flying Nelly: Further Flight by Pharly (Fr)	2	31,690.00
	2	31,690.00

NELTINO (1978) by Bustino

	Races Won	Value £
Miss Lawsuit: Dancing Lawyer by Thowra (Fr)	1	2,826.00
	1	2,826.00

NETHERKELLY (1970) by Le Levanstell

	Races Won	Value £
Joint Reward: Join The Clan by Clantime	2	6,056.00
	2	6,056.00

NEVER BEND (1960) by Nasrullah

	Races Won	Value £
Memory Lane (USA): Green Lane (USA) by Greinton	2	7,992.50
Tash (USA): Tatami (USA) by Lyphard (USA)	3	35,081.75

Dam	Winner and Sire	Races Won	Value £
Unyielding (USA): Darkwood Bay (USA) by Green Dancer (USA)		1	4,020.50
		6	47,094.75

NEW CHAPTER (1966) by Crepello

Pale Gold (Fr): Desert Nomad by Green Desert (USA)	2	5,633.90
	2	5,633.90

NEW PROVIDENCE (1956) by Bull Page

New Chant (Can): Night Edition by Night Shift (USA)	2	4,706.50
	2	4,706.50

NICE DANCER (Can) (1969) by Northern Dancer

Jolly Polka (USA): Glide Path (USA) by Stalwart (USA)	3	26,647.00
	3	26,647.00

NICHOLAS BILL (1975) by High Line

Corn Seed: High Holme by Fools Holme (USA)	1	3,882.50
Kate Brook: Hill Farm Katie by Derrylin	1	2,448.00
Nicola Wynn: Bold Acre by Never So Bold	1	3,622.50
	3	9,953.00

NIJINSKY (Can) (1967) by Northern Dancer

Abeesh (USA): Moussahim (USA) by Riverman (USA)	1	3,158.00
Balabina (USA): Bal Harbour by Shirley Heights	1	9,189.60
Cor Anglais (USA): Palana (USA) by Gulch (USA)	2	7,058.25
Crystal Cup (USA): Crystal Cross (USA) by Roberto (USA)	2	13,789.60
Dancing Brownie (USA): Tawafij (USA) by Diesis	2	15,855.00
De Stael (USA): Source Of Light by Rainbow Quest (USA)	2	25,924.70
Fairy Dancer (USA): Fair Shirley (Ire) by Shirley Heights	1	3,435.75
Instinctive Move (USA): Dancing Spirit (Ire) by Ahonoora	1	3,201.75
Kazatska (USA): Ambiguously Regal (USA) by Vaguely Noble	1	5,344.50
Key Dancer (USA): Modest Hope (USA) by Blushing Groom (Fr)	1	3,687.50
Misinskie (USA): Ajfan (USA) by Woodman (USA)	2	7,798.75
Mixed Applause (USA): Tempering by Kris	1	2,691.00
Mixed Applause (USA): Press Gallery by Carmelite House (USA)	2	8,127.35
Russian Ribbon (USA): Cut The Red Tape (Ire) by Sure Blade (USA)	1	3,020.80
Sainte Croix (USA): Waki Gold (USA) by Miswaki (USA)	1	2,469.00

Dam	Winner and Sire	Races Won	Value £
Tashinsky (USA): Sovereign Page (USA) by Caro		3	9,678.50
		24	124,430.05

NINISKI (USA) (1976) by Nijinsky(Can)

Wryneck: Fox Sparrow by Sharpo	1	3,817.50
	1	3,817.50

NISHAPOUR (Fr) (1975) by Zeddaan

Kashapour: Kezio Rufo (Ire) by Persian Heights	1	3,285.00
Nibabu (Fr): Nijo by Top Ville	1	3,649.00
Salilia: Nsx by Roi Danzig (USA)	1	3,231.00
	3	10,165.00

NO ARGUMENT (1960) by Narrator

Murton Crags: Rambo's Hall by Crofthall	2	12,387.50
	2	12,387.50

NO MERCY (1968) by Fortino II

Count On Me: Hard To Figure by Telsmoss	2	66,592.50
	2	66,592.50

NO ROBBERY (1960) by Swaps

Hankow Willow (USA): Tajdif (USA) by Storm Cat (USA)	1	4,012.50
	1	4,012.50

NOALCOHOLIC (Fr) (1977) by Nonoalco(USA)

Miss Alkie: Corona Gold by Chilibang	2	5,305.50
	2	5,305.50

NODOUBLE (USA) (1965) by Noholme II

Amata (USA): Bluegrass Prince (Ire) by Bluebird (USA)	2	9,644.80
Love Triangle (USA): Rival Bid (USA) by Cannonade (USA)	1	3,348.00
	3	12,992.80

NONOALCO (USA) (1971) by Nearctic

Darine: Albert by Kings Lake (USA)	3	9,105.20
Darine: Penny Drops by Sharpo	3	74,235.25
Double Touch (Fr): Strumpet City by Emarati (USA)	1	2,721.00
Jungle Gardenia: Pallium (Ire) by Try My Best (USA)	1	4,175.00

Dam Winner and Sire	Races Won	Value £
Just You Wait: Waiting by Polish Precedent (USA)	1	4,175.00
Mrs Tittlemouse: Mohican Brave (Ire) by Salt Dome (USA)	2	4,954.90
Mrs Tittlemouse: King Rat (Ire) by King Of Clubs	2	4,497.00
No Jargon: Plainsong by Ballad Rock	1	2,540.10
Nonabella: Prenonamoss by Precocious	1	6,258.00
Ophrys: Affordable by Formidable (USA)	1	3,158.00
	16	115,819.45

NORTHERN BABY (Can) (1976) by Northern Dancer

Dam Winner and Sire	Races Won	Value £
Cadbury Hill (USA): Truben (USA) by Arctic Tern (USA)	1	3,460.00
Mary Bankes (USA): Mild Rebuke by Reprimand	3	10,773.05
	4	14,233.05

NORTHERN DANCER (1961) by Nearctic

Dam Winner and Sire	Races Won	Value £
Arctic Eclipse (USA): Icy South (USA) by Alleged (USA)	2	6,520.50
Armeria (USA): Armiger by Rainbow Quest (USA)	1	33,526.20
Ballet de France (USA): Muhtarram (USA) by Alleged (USA)	2	15,459.00
Ballet de France (USA): Grotto Pool (USA) by Gone West (USA)	1	3,874.50
Catopetl (USA): Newton's Law (Ire) by Law Society (USA)	2	9,637.00
Dokki (USA): Electrify (USA) by Warning	1	5,162.50
Music And Dance (USA): Golden Nashwan (Ire) by Nashwan (USA)	1	4,932.00
Pacificus (USA): Tahitian by Precocious	1	3,080.00
Rose Red (USA): Zind (Ire) by Law Society (USA)	1	3,265.50
Savannah Dancer (USA): Brier Creek (USA) by Blushing Groom (Fr)	3	46,626.56
Six Months Long (USA): Half Term (USA) by Mr Prospector (USA)	2	9,225.00
South Sea Dancer (USA): Princess Haifa (USA) by Mr Prospector (USA)	1	3,552.75
Walladah (USA): Athar (Ire) by Master Willie	1	3,289.50
Yaqut (USA): Tahdid by Mtoto	3	14,365.25
	22	162,516.26

NORTHERN PROSPECT (USA) (1976) by Mr Prospector(USA)

Dam Winner and Sire	Races Won	Value £
Sleek Lassie (USA): Blowing (USA) by Lear Fan (USA)	1	4,016.00
	1	4,016.00

NORTHERN TREAT (USA) (1976) by Northern Dancer

Dam Winner and Sire	Races Won	Value £
Keep Cool (Fr): Rankaidade by Governor General	1	3,002.40
Miss May (Fr): Mister Beat by Brustolon	1	2,534.20
	2	5,536.60

NORTHFIELDS (USA) (1968) by Northern Dancer

Dam Winner and Sire	Races Won	Value £
Dance By Night: Dana Springs (Ire) by Aragon	4	49,776.40
Dress In Spring: My Bonus by Cyrano de Bergerac	1	3,655.00
Gay Shadow: Umbria by Master Willie	1	2,957.50
Golden Moony: On Y Va (USA) by Victorious (USA)	2	5,001.00
Ice House: Silver Hut (USA) by Silver Hawk (USA)	1	5,253.50
Lost In France: Let's Get Lost by Chief Singer	1	3,027.50
Miss Longchamp: Pharamineux by Pharly (Fr)	1	4,455.00
Miss Longchamp: Faugeron by Niniski (USA)	1	4,815.00
Miss Loving: Love Returned by Taufan (USA)	2	10,765.25
Nordica: Mindomica by Dominion	1	3,287.30
Nordica: Sueboog (Ire) by Darshaan	1	23,463.00
Norpella: Ultimo Imperatore by Cadeaux Genereux	1	8,357.50
North Hut: Fiveofive (Ire) by Fairy King (USA)	1	3,287.30
North Page (Fr): Linpac West by Posse (USA)	1	20,439.00
Northern Empress: Press The Bell by Belfort (Fr)	4	12,130.40
Northern Wisdom: Blue Grit by Thatching	1	3,980.00
Northshiel: Boloardo by Persian Bold	1	4,747.40
Northshiel: Serotina (Ire) by Mtoto	1	2,556.60
Pink Fondant: Face North (Ire) by Fayruz	2	5,795.75
Precious Jade: Glowing Jade by Kalaglow	1	3,493.00
Pushkar: Doctor Roy by Electric	1	3,290.00
Queens Welcome: Susanna's Secret by Superlative	1	2,788.00
Shabby Doll: Chickawicka (Ire) by Dance Of Life (USA)	1	2,982.00
Shabby Doll: Devious Dancer by Krayyan	1	2,534.20
Topless Dancer: Broughton's Tango (Ire) by Tender King	2	7,958.25
Tura: Routing by Rousillon (USA)	1	3,062.50
	36	203,858.35

NORTHJET (1977) by Northfields(USA)

Dam Winner and Sire	Races Won	Value £
Beijing (USA): Blaaziing Joe (Ire) by Alzao (USA)	1	4,175.00
Northerly Cheer (USA): Without A Flag (USA) by Stately Don (USA)	1	3,087.00
Pennsylvania (USA): East Liberty (USA) by Halo (USA)	1	4,077.50
	3	11,339.50

NUREYEV (USA) (1977) by Northern Dancer

Dam Winner and Sire	Races Won	Value £
La Nureyeva (USA): Reason To Dance by Damister (USA)	2	8,078.50

Dam	Winner and Sire	Races Won	Value £
Made Of Pearl (USA): Seek The Pearl by Rainbow Quest (USA)		2	6,606.50
Miesque (USA): Kingmambo (USA) by Mr Prospector (USA)		1	116,334.60
Quiet Rendezvous (USA): Knave's Ash (USA) by Miswaki (USA)		1	4,163.50
		6	135,183.10

OATS (1973) by Northfields(USA)

	Races Won	Value £
Fourth Degree: Prince Rooney (Ire) by Dayeem (USA)	2	5,874.00
	2	5,874.00

OLDEN TIMES (1958) by Relic

	Races Won	Value £
Periquito (USA): Grey Power by Wolf Power (Saf)	4	12,843.60
Waltz Me Sue (USA): Utrillo (USA) by Dahar (USA)	1	2,892.60
	5	15,736.20

ON YOUR MARK (1964) by Restless Wind

	Races Won	Value £
Majestic Nurse: Majestic Eagle (Ire) by Bluebird (USA)	1	4,464.00
Marcrest: Obsidian Grey by Lyphard's Special (USA)	3	7,234.20
	4	11,698.20

ORANGE BAY (1972) by Canisbay

	Races Won	Value £
Lady Seville: Ballerina Bay by Myjinski (USA)	1	3,318.75
	1	3,318.75

OUR HERO (USA) (1972) by Bold Ruler

	Races Won	Value £
Ruffled Silk (USA): Second Colours (USA) by Timeless Moment (USA)	1	2,950.60
	1	2,950.60

OUR NATIVE (USA) (1970) by Exclusive Native(USA)

	Races Won	Value £
Betty Money (USA): Manila Bay (USA) by Manila (USA)	1	3,465.00
Rum Cay (USA): Island Magic by Indian Ridge	2	26,688.30
Satiety (USA): Simaat (USA) by Mr Prospector (USA)	1	3,435.75
	4	33,589.05

OVERSKATE (Can) (1975) by Nodouble(USA)

	Races Won	Value £
Loveskate (USA): Missed Flight by Dominion	2	10,440.75
	2	10,440.75

OWEN DUDLEY (1970) by Tudor Melody

	Races Won	Value £
Edwins' Princess: Pageboy by Tina's Pet	1	1,970.00
Sunita: Sagebrush Roller by Sharpo	2	8,548.00
	3	10,518.00

PABLOND (1971) by Paveh

	Races Won	Value £
Highland Rossie: Diet by Starch Reduced	3	8,030.25
	3	8,030.25

PALESTINE (1947) by Fair Trial

	Races Won	Value £
My Ginny: Charisma Girl by Nomination	1	2,070.00
	1	2,070.00

PALL MALL (1955) by Palestine

	Races Won	Value £
Apple Peel: Discord by Niniski (USA)	2	11,161.00
Mallabee: Mr M-E-N (Ire) by My Generation	3	15,641.00
	5	26,802.00

PALM TRACK (1969) by Track Spare

	Races Won	Value £
Moonlight Bay: Moonlight Eclipse by Jupiter Island	1	2,742.00
	1	2,742.00

PAMPAPAUL (1974) by Yellow God

	Races Won	Value £
Crimson Crest: Storm Venture (Ire) by Taufan (USA)	1	2,950.00
Rathcoffey Daisy: Westfield Moves (Ire) by Montelimar (USA)	1	3,348.00
	2	6,298.00

PARDAO (1958) by Pardal

	Races Won	Value £
Flash Of Gold: Princess Oberon (Ire) by Fairy King (USA)	1	5,427.50
Silk Stocking: Askern by Sharrood (USA)	1	3,289.50
	2	8,717.00

PARTHIA (1956) by Persian Gulf

	Races Won	Value £
Bedeni: Admirals Realm by Another Realm	1	3,877.75
	1	3,877.75

PAS DE SEUL (1979) by Mill Reef(USA)

	Races Won	Value £
Constant Companion: Comanche Companion by Commanche Run	3	13,853.50

Dam Winner and Sire	Races Won	Value £
Constant Companion: Hobart by Reprimand	1	3,011.00
Ghassanah: Alzianah by Alzao (USA)	2	13,289.75
Pas de Calais: My Best Valentine by Try My Best (USA)	3	13,248.15
Rose Barton: My Abbey by Hadeer	1	3,435.75
Silk St James: Kingchip Boy by Petong	3	11,573.00
Silk St James: Misty Silks by Scottish Reel	4	17,625.10
Silk St James: Prima Silk by Primo Dominie	2	5,985.00
	19	82,021.25

PERSEPOLIS (Fr) (1979) by Kalamoun

Dam Winner and Sire	Races Won	Value £
Ancestry: Devilry by Faustus (USA)	1	5,469.75
	1	5,469.75

PERSIAN BOLD (1975) by Bold Lad(Ire)

Dam Winner and Sire	Races Won	Value £
Bold Meadows: Field Of Vision (Ire) by Vision (USA)	3	14,207.25
Estivalia: Major Success (Ire) by Gallic League	4	13,254.60
Inanna: Mrs Snuggs (Ire) by Law Society (USA)	1	2,243.00
Katie Koo: Monsieur Dupont (Ire) by Alzao (USA)	1	3,817.50
Ladiz: War Requiem (Ire) by Don't Forget Me	2	5,434.40
Long View: Misty View by Absalom	1	3,076.50
Miss Garuda: Pampered Guest (Ire) by Be My Guest (USA)	1	3,377.25
Persiandale: Margaret's Gift by Beveled (USA)	2	18,635.00
Piney Pass: Allinson's Mate (Ire) by Fayruz	1	3,548.00
Sea Thyme: Sea Paddy by Reach	1	2,406.00
Veronica: Truckhaven Secret by Secreto (USA)	1	3,377.25
	18	73,376.75

PETINGO (1965) by Petition

Dam Winner and Sire	Races Won	Value £
Dingle Bay: Assessor (Ire) by Niniski (USA)	2	69,399.00
Fair Siobahn: Fair Flyer (Ire) by Tilt Up (USA)	1	3,557.50
Fairy Fans: Prairie Grove by Primo Dominie	2	5,535.00
Foudre: Mull House by Local Suitor (USA)	1	4,221.00
Freely Given: Bichette by Lidhame	1	2,243.00
Petingalyn: Bronze Runner by Gunner B	2	4,570.00
Petit Secret: Billyback by Absalom	1	2,448.00
Petty Purse: Cajun Cadet by Cadeaux Genereux	1	5,439.00
Pro Patria: Wahem (Ire) by Lomond (USA)	1	3,080.10
Rimosa's Pet: Rimouski by Sure Blade (USA)	1	2,469.00
Rimosa's Pet: Peto by Petoski	1	3,294.00
	14	106,255.60

PETONG (1980) by Mansingh(USA)

Dam Winner and Sire	Races Won	Value £
Ginnies Petong: Hello Mister by Efisio	1	4,240.50
	1	4,240.50

PHARLY (Fr) (1974) by Lyphard(USA)

Dam Winner and Sire	Races Won	Value £
Blue Bell Pearl (Fr): Western Cape (USA) by Gone West (USA)	2	45,021.00
Deloraine: Two D'S by Dunbeath (USA)	1	2,448.00
Fleur Rouge: Addicted To Love by Touching Wood (USA)	1	5,754.00
Moviegoer: Kissininthebackrow (USA) by Trempolino (USA)	1	3,728.25
Pharjoy (Fr): Call To Mind (Ire) by Don't Forget Me	2	15,912.00
Pharlette (Fr): Dee Raft (USA) by Raft (USA)	2	7,570.00
	9	80,433.25

PITSKELLY (1970) by Petingo

Dam Winner and Sire	Races Won	Value £
Azelly: Covent Garden Girl by Sizzling Melody	2	5,917.50
Cerosia: Segala (Ire) by Petorius	1	2,005.00
Hydro Princess: Unification (Ire) by Double Schwartz	1	3,600.00
Kellys Reef: Artistic Reef by Claude Monet (USA)	2	8,028.20
Kellys Reef: Montaya by Taufan (USA)	1	3,629.50
Pitroyal: New Inn by Petoski	1	2,406.00
Pitskelly Blues: Super Blues by Welsh Captain	2	6,419.20
Reveal: Strip Cartoon (Ire) by Tate Gallery (USA)	2	5,630.30
	12	37,635.70

PLUGGED NICKLE (USA) (1977) by Key To The Mint(USA)

Dam Winner and Sire	Races Won	Value £
One Half Silver (Can): Silver Standard by Jupiter Island	1	1,826.00
	1	1,826.00

PONGEE (1962) by Shantung

Dam Winner and Sire	Races Won	Value £
Grey Morley: Palacegate Sunset by Skyliner	1	2,243.00
	1	2,243.00

PONTIFEX (USA) (1967) by Jaipur

Dam Winner and Sire	Races Won	Value £
Vexed Voter: Surprise Offer by Superlative	1	6,508.80
	1	6,508.80

POPPY JAY (1956) by Double Jay

Dam Winner and Sire	Races Won	Value £
Perfect Poppy (USA): Khatir (Can) by Alwasmi (USA)	1	2,601.40
	1	2,601.40

POSSE (USA) (1977) by Forli(Arg)

Dam Winner and Sire	Races Won	Value £
Batave: Bigstone (Ire) by Last Tycoon	2	273,980.00
Entrancing: Amaze by Natroun (Fr)	1	4,962.75

Dam Winner and Sire	Races Won	Value £
Manhunt: Mokaite by Komaite (USA)	2	4,629.70
Sally Brown: Scorpius by Soviet Star (USA)	1	3,465.00
	6	287,037.45

PRETENSE (1963) by Endeavour II

Dam Winner and Sire	Races Won	Value £
Fall Aspen (USA): Hamas (Ire) by Danzig (USA)	2	128,343.50
	2	128,343.50

PRINCE REGENT (Fr) (1966) by Right Royal V

Dam Winner and Sire	Races Won	Value £
Brightelmstone: Golden Torque by Taufan (USA)	1	2,880.00
Cecily: Lady Lacey by Kampala	2	6,807.00
Regency Gold: Bondaid by Main Reef	1	2,595.00
	4	12,282.00

PRINCE TENDERFOOT (USA) (1967) by Blue Prince II

Dam Winner and Sire	Races Won	Value £
Ballyewry: Balandra Bay (Ire) by Jareer (USA)	2	8,309.70
Cathryn's Song: Indefence (Ire) by Conquering Hero (USA)	2	6,003.00
Free Wheeler: Mr Tate (Ire) by Tate Gallery (USA)	4	14,642.00
Highest Tender: Chili Heights by Chilibang	1	6,165.00
Icing: Safir (USA) by Slew O' Gold (USA)	1	3,114.00
Kitty Frisk: Sinclair Lad (Ire) by Muscatite	1	2,658.00
Lady Blackfoot: Northern Graduate (USA) by Northrop (USA)	5	22,122.65
Madam Slaney: Aahsaylad by Ardross	2	61,587.50
Mamie's Joy: Elle Shaped (Ire) by Treasure Kay	1	7,492.20
Prosperous Lady: Eurolink Thunder by Fairy King (USA)	3	34,865.40
Sonseri: Star Goddess (USA) by Northern Jove (Can)	1	3,201.75
	23	170,161.20

PRINCELY NATIVE (USA) (1971) by Raise A Native

Dam Winner and Sire	Races Won	Value £
Regal Beauty (USA): King's Theatre (Ire) by Sadler's Wells (USA)	3	97,205.25
	3	97,205.25

PRIVATE ACCOUNT (USA) (1976) by Damascus(USA)

Dam Winner and Sire	Races Won	Value £
Classy Cathy (USA): Placerville (USA) by Mr Prospector (USA)	2	67,147.80
Graecia Magna (USA): Thourios by Green Desert (USA)	2	14,068.00
	4	81,215.80

PROPERANTES (USA) (1973) by Protanto (USA)

Dam Winner and Sire	Races Won	Value £
Sister Rosarii (USA): Royal Interval by Interrex (Can)	2	7,835.65
	2	7,835.65

QUEEN'S HUSSAR (1960) by March Past

Dam Winner and Sire	Races Won	Value £
Bosquet: Nonios (Ire) by Nashamaa	2	6,763.60
Czar's Diamond: Chucklestone by Chukaroo	1	3,080.00
Eulalie: Just You Dare (Ire) by Common Grounds	4	16,562.00
Highclere: Scarlet Tunic (USA) by Blushing Groom (Fr)	1	2,742.00
Lady Dacre: Karachi by Nishapour (Fr)	2	6,374.25
Light Duty: Spring To Action by Shareef Dancer (USA)	2	13,249.00
	12	48,770.85

QUI NATIVE (USA) (1974) by Exclusive Native (USA)

Dam Winner and Sire	Races Won	Value £
Sheena Native (USA): Governor George (USA) by Secreto (USA)	2	14,945.00
	2	14,945.00

RABDAN (1977) by Bold Lad(Ire)

Dam Winner and Sire	Races Won	Value £
Miss Shegas: Cockerham Ranger by Roaring Riva	1	2,070.00
Shoot To Win (Fr): Little Saboteur by Prince Sabo	1	2,880.50
	2	4,950.50

RADETZKY (1973) by Huntercombe

Dam Winner and Sire	Races Won	Value £
Chablisse: Ooh Ah Cantona by Crofthall	2	4,671.40
	2	4,671.40

RAFFINGORA (1965) by Grey Sovereign

Dam Winner and Sire	Races Won	Value £
Geopelia: Brown Carpet by Never So Bold	1	2,232.50
Geopelia: Snipe Hall by Crofthall	4	24,314.10
Raffinrula: Cee-Jay-Ay by Free State	2	26,266.00
Rahesh: Henry's Luck by Bold Owl	2	3,795.00
	9	56,607.60

RAGA NAVARRO (Ity) (1972) by Reform

Dam Winner and Sire	Races Won	Value £
Amboselli: Land O'Lakes (Ire) by Kings Lake (USA)	1	2,243.00
Amboselli: Amnesia (Ire) by Don't Forget Me	1	3,564.00
Dancing Diana: Prince Rodney by King Of Spain	1	3,153.50

Dam Winner and Sire	Races Won	Value £
Dancing Diana: Forgotten Dancer (Ire) by Don't Forget Me	1	2,495.00
	4	11,455.50

RAGSTONE (1970) by Ragusa

Dam Winner and Sire	Races Won	Value £
Ragtime Rose: Harvest Rose by Bairn (USA)	1	2,553.00
Shaky Puddin: Master Planner by Night Shift (USA)	2	20,099.20
	3	22,652.20

RAISE A BID (USA) (1968) by Raise A Native

Dam Winner and Sire	Races Won	Value £
Mardie's Bid (USA): World Without End (USA) by World Appeal (USA)	2	6,446.00
	2	6,446.00

RAISE A CUP (USA) (1971) by Raise A Native

Dam Winner and Sire	Races Won	Value £
Absentia (USA): Nimphidia (USA) by Nijinsky (Can)	1	3,406.50
	1	3,406.50

RAISE A MAN (USA) (1977) by Raise A Native

Dam Winner and Sire	Races Won	Value £
Timely Raise (USA): Double Down by Salse (USA)	1	3,746.50
	1	3,746.50

RAISE A NATIVE (1961) by Native Dancer

Dam Winner and Sire	Races Won	Value £
True Native (USA): Ikhtiraa (USA) by Imperial Falcon (Can)	1	3,582.00
	1	3,582.00

RAJA BABA (USA) (1968) by Bold Ruler

Dam Winner and Sire	Races Won	Value £
Ceramic (USA): Little Beaut by Prince Sabo	1	3,590.00
Equate (USA): Dayflower (USA) by Majestic Light (USA)	1	5,024.00
Good Thinking (USA): Thinking Twice (USA) by Kris	1	5,299.00
	3	13,913.00

RARITY (1967) by Hethersett

Dam Winner and Sire	Races Won	Value £
One In A Million: Number One Spot by Reference Point	1	3,582.00
Rare Find: Carrolls Marc (Ire) by Horage	2	4,968.00
Rivers Maid: Desert Power by Green Desert (USA)	1	3,494.25
Very Seldom: Jimmy The Skunk (Ire) by Fayruz	6	15,901.30
	10	27,945.55

REALM (1967) by Princely Gift

Dam Winner and Sire	Races Won	Value £
Abbe's Realm: Qualitair Rhythm (Ire) by Drumalis	1	2,898.80
Avec L'amour: Gallery Artist (Ire) by Tate Gallery (USA)	1	1,679.00
Avec L'amour: Love Of The North (Ire) by Nordico (USA)	1	2,070.00
Irish Isle: Danny Boy by Damister (USA)	2	5,875.00
Irish Isle: Silver Slipper by Indian Ridge	2	5,491.00
Miss Realm: Desirable Miss by Grey Desire	1	2,560.00
Sougoli: Sir Joey (USA) by Honest Pleasure (USA)	3	11,417.50
	11	31,991.30

RECORD TOKEN (1972) by Jukebox

Dam Winner and Sire	Races Won	Value £
Dream Chaser: Sister Susan by Tate Gallery (USA)	2	4,733.80
Princess Zenobia: Queen Warrior by Daring March	3	11,008.00
Token Of Truth: Truthful Image by Reesh	3	9,233.25
	8	24,975.05

RED ALERT (1971) by Red God

Dam Winner and Sire	Races Won	Value £
Clonross Lady: Phoneaholic (Ire) by Heraldiste (USA)	1	1,907.20
Coshlea: Follingworth Girl (Ire) by Jareer (USA)	4	11,427.25
Forever Mary: Blue Topaze by Fast Topaze (USA)	2	5,557.60
Hithermoor Lass: Poyle George by Sharpo	1	4,532.50
Rocket Alert: Miss Gorgeous (Ire) by Damister (USA)	2	7,320.00
Tickled Trout: Robellion by Robellino (USA)	1	2,833.00
Winning Feature: Braille (Ire) by Vision (USA)	2	5,523.75
	13	39,101.30

RED GOD (1954) by Nasrullah

Dam Winner and Sire	Races Won	Value £
Bentinck Hotel: Bentico by Nordico (USA)	3	9,326.50
Chiltern Red: Face The Future by Ahonoora	1	3,366.00
Orange Squash: Redstella (USA) by Theatrical	1	3,816.00
Ruby River: Knock Knock by Tap On Wood	2	9,085.00
Ruby River: Don't Jump (Ire) by Entitled	2	6,453.25
Ruby River: Rohita (Ire) by Waajib	2	7,764.80
Western Goddess: Mougins (Ire) by Ela-Mana-Mou	1	3,363.00
	12	43,174.55

RED REGENT (1972) by Prince Regent(Fr)

Dam Winner and Sire	Races Won	Value £
The Woman In Red: Red Fan (Ire) by Taufan (USA)	1	1,576.00
	1	1,576.00

Dam Winner and Sire	Races Won	Value £

RED SUNSET (1979) by Red God

Dam Winner and Sire	Races Won	Value £
Deanta In Eirinn: Newbury Coat by Chilibang	1	3,525.00
Sunfleet: Nera by Robellino (USA)	1	3,161.40
Tracy's Sundown: Workingforpeanuts (Ire) by Entitled	1	2,364.00
	3	9,050.40

REFLECTED GLORY (USA) (1964) by Jester

Dam Winner and Sire	Races Won	Value £
Glorious Natalie (USA): Hawker Hunter (USA) by Silver Hawk (USA)	1	3,980.00
	1	3,980.00

REFORM (1964) by Pall Mall

Dam Winner and Sire	Races Won	Value £
Blue Brocade: Oubeck Blue by Chief Singer	1	3,622.50
Nuppence: Our Shadee (USA) by Shadeed (USA)	1	2,490.00
Polly Packer: Kiawah by Master Willie	2	5,064.00
	4	11,176.50

RELIANCE II (1962) by Tantieme

Dam Winner and Sire	Races Won	Value £
Crystallize: Brierley by Sharrood (USA)	1	2,700.00
Travesty: Case Law by Ahonoora	1	3,145.00
	2	5,845.00

RELKINO (1973) by Relko

Dam Winner and Sire	Races Won	Value £
Elkie Brooks: Sunday's Hill by Efisio	1	3,405.00
Elkie Brooks: Pips Pride by Efisio	1	15,140.00
Feather Flower: Meavy by Kalaglow	1	2,954.00
Fettle: Fumo Di Londra (Ire) by Indian Ridge	1	26,796.50
Khadino: Springhead by Komaite (USA)	1	2,451.00
Lola Black (Fr): Thornton Gate by Hallgate	2	6,311.10
Park Special: Velvet Moon (Ire) by Shaadi (USA)	3	46,891.00
Relatively Easy: Beats Working by Aragon	2	7,967.00
Relkina (Fr): Braveboy by Never So Bold	1	7,564.00
	13	119,479.60

RELKO (1960) by Tanerko

Dam Winner and Sire	Races Won	Value £
Hunza Water: Burishki by Chilibang	1	2,768.00
One Last Glimpse: Running Glimpse (Ire) by Runnett	1	5,803.00
One Last Glimpse: Captain Horatius (Ire) by Taufan (USA)	2	19,761.00
One Last Glimpse: Ovideo by Domynsky	1	2,807.00
Reflected Glory (Swe): Gloriette by Petoski	1	3,049.40
Regain: White River by Pharly (Fr)	1	3,366.00
Relfo: Famous Beauty by Vision (USA)	1	2,364.00
Reliable Rosie: Best Appearance (Ire) by Try My Best (USA)	2	5,997.35
Relicia: Francia by Legend Of France (USA)	1	2,739.00
Santalina: Santana Lady (Ire) by Blakeney	1	3,131.90
	12	51,786.65

REMAINDER MAN (1975) by Connaught

Dam Winner and Sire	Races Won	Value £
New Central: Rosie's Gold by Glint Of Gold	1	2,460.30
New Central: Beautete by Komaite (USA)	1	3,582.00
	2	6,042.30

REVIEWER (USA) (1966) by Bold Ruler

Dam Winner and Sire	Races Won	Value £
La Vue (USA): Jubran (USA) by Vaguely Noble	1	4,305.00
Processional (USA): King Of Naples (USA) by Ferdinand (USA)	1	5,435.50
Revidere (USA): Escarpment (USA) by Green Dancer (USA)	2	9,396.00
	4	19,136.50

RHEINGOLD (1969) by Faberge II

Dam Winner and Sire	Races Won	Value £
Andalucia: Philgun by K-Battery	2	6,304.60
Rheinbloom: Tinsashe (Ire) by Sayf El Arab (USA)	2	6,548.00
Rheinbloom: Mr Rough by Fayruz	1	2,721.00
Rheinza: Forever Blushing by Blushing Scribe (USA)	1	2,070.00
Strike It Rich (Fr): Play With Me (Ire) by Alzao (USA)	1	2,792.50
	7	20,436.10

RIBERO (1965) by Ribot

Dam Winner and Sire	Races Won	Value £
Moonscape: Remany by Bellypha	1	3,265.50
	1	3,265.50

RIBOBOY (USA) (1973) by Ribot

Dam Winner and Sire	Races Won	Value £
Harlestone Lake: Harlestone Brook by Jalmood (USA)	2	6,824.25
	2	6,824.25

RIBOT (1952) by Tenerani

Dam Winner and Sire	Races Won	Value £
Daisy Warwick (USA): Sheriff by Midyan (USA)	1	2,900.00
Que Mona (USA): Mr Geneaology (USA) by Procida (USA)	3	8,254.10
Ribonette (USA): Good Hand (USA) by Northjet	2	14,195.80
Tobira Celeste (USA): Thawakib (Ire) by Sadler's Wells (USA)	1	59,407.20
	7	84,757.10

RIGHT TACK (1966) by Hard Tack

Dam Winner and Sire	Races Won	Value £
Mofida: Factual (USA) by Known Fact (USA)	1	4,012.50
	1	4,012.50

RIVA RIDGE (USA) (1969) by First Landing

Dam Winner and Sire	Races Won	Value £
Clarista (USA): Indhar by Warning	2	13,259.00
	2	13,259.00

RIVER BEAUTY (1968) by Le Levanstell

Dam Winner and Sire	Races Won	Value £
Maellen: Second Sight (Ire) by Vision (USA)	1	3,325.00
	1	3,325.00

RIVERMAN (USA) (1969) by Never Bend

Dam Winner and Sire	Races Won	Value £
Belle Viking (Fr): Dashing Fellow (Ire) by Sure Blade (USA)	4	13,886.20
Belle Viking (Fr): Peerage Prince by Thatching	1	3,260.25
Costly Array (USA): Nafuth (USA) by Nureyev (USA)	1	3,172.50
Dockage (USA): Wharf (USA) by Storm Bird (Can)	1	10,116.00
Dockage (USA): Colza (USA) by Alleged (USA)	1	4,305.00
Histoire (Fr): Erhaab (USA) by Chief's Crown (USA)	2	7,495.25
Kereolle: Lord Advocate by Law Society (USA)	2	4,730.00
Petillante (USA): River North (Ire) by Lomond (USA)	5	55,861.20
River Lullaby (USA): Lakab (USA) by Manila (USA)	1	2,143.70
River Maiden (Fr): Rafferty's Rules (Ire) by Ballad Rock	2	12,827.00
Riverine (Fr): Iron Baron (Ire) by Sure Blade (USA)	1	2,927.00
Riviere Bleue: Uncle Oswald by Nashwan (USA)	1	4,435.00
Savannah Song (USA): Easy Access (Ire) by Thatching	1	5,692.00
Savannah Song (USA): Shepton Mallet (Ire) by Alzao (USA)	1	3,840.00
	24	134,691.10

ROAN ROCKET (1961) by Buisson Ardent

Dam Winner and Sire	Races Won	Value £
Arminiya: Charity Express (Ire) by Treasure Kay	3	7,735.00
Hat Hill: City Rocket by King Of Spain	1	3,199.50
Rosserk: Pine Ridge Lad (Ire) by Taufan (USA)	1	3,720.00
Safidar: Quick Silver Boy by Kalaglow	2	6,340.00
	7	20,994.50

ROBERTO (USA) (1969) by Hail To Reason

Dam Winner and Sire	Races Won	Value £
Autumn Tint (USA): Minatina (Ire) by Ela-Mana-Mou	1	3,817.50
Cambretta (USA): Cambara by Dancing Brave (USA)	3	34,940.00
I Want To Be (USA): Danish Fort by Danzig (USA)	2	7,337.75
Modena (USA): Modesto (USA) by Al Nasr (Fr)	1	7,310.00
Mystical Mood (USA): Long Silence (USA) by Alleged (USA)	1	3,143.25
Roblanna: Post Impressionist (Ire) by Ahonoora	2	5,708.60
Slightly Dangerous (USA): Commander In Chief by Dancing Brave (USA)	4	461,241.25
Sookera (USA): So Factual (USA) by Known Fact (USA)	1	18,034.50
Sunerta (USA): Ivory Palm (USA) by Sir Ivor	1	3,143.25
	16	544,676.10

ROI SOLEIL (1967) by Skymaster

Dam Winner and Sire	Races Won	Value £
Mel Mira: Forever Diamonds by Good Times (Ity)	2	19,842.00
Sea Aura: Charlie Bigtime by Norwick (USA)	1	3,084.75
	3	22,926.75

ROLFE (USA) (1973) by Tom Rolfe

Dam Winner and Sire	Races Won	Value £
Mighty Flash: Mighty Forum by Presidium	1	3,184.00
	1	3,184.00

ROMAN WARRIOR (1971) by Porto Bello

Dam Winner and Sire	Races Won	Value £
Laena: Cape Merino by Clantime	2	92,189.50
Laena: Calamanco by Clantime	1	3,094.20
	3	95,283.70

ROMANCERO (1959) by Nearula

Dam Winner and Sire	Races Won	Value £
Fair Nic: Lord Alfie by Beveled (USA)	2	7,475.50
	2	7,475.50

ROUND TABLE (1954) by Princequillo

Dam Winner and Sire	Races Won	Value £
Al Madina (USA): Forest Star (USA) by Green Forest (USA)	1	3,300.50
Homespun (USA): Mashaallah (USA) by Nijinsky (Can)	1	7,270.00
La Dame Du Lac (USA): Lacotte (Ire) by Sadler's Wells (USA)	1	4,305.00
Sweet Rapport (USA): Rapporteur (USA) by His Majesty (USA)	2	5,379.00
Two Rings (USA): Campana (Ire) by Sadler's Wells (USA)	2	7,366.50
	7	27,621.00

ROYAL AND REGAL (USA) (1970) by Vaguely Noble

Dam Winner and Sire	Races Won	Value £
Emma Royale: Cicerone by Tina's Pet	2	5,814.50
Muznah: Jazilah (Fr) by Persian Bold	2	7,980.00
Muznah: Formal Affair by Rousillon (USA)	2	5,193.00
Noble Nancy: Vercingetorix (Ire) by Gallic League	2	9,753.50

Dam	Winner and Sire	Races Won	Value £
Rip Roaring:	Who's The Best (Ire) by Wassl	2	6,045.00
Sterna Regina:	Star Jazz (Ire) by Dancing Dissident (USA)	1	4,110.00
		11	38,896.00

ROYAL AVENUE (1958) by Royal Palm

Dam	Winner and Sire	Races Won	Value £
Royal Huntress:	Royal Comedian by Jester	1	2,709.00
		1	2,709.00

ROYAL BUCK (1957) by Buckhound

Dam	Winner and Sire	Races Won	Value £
Royal Holly:	Quinta Royale by Sayyaf	1	3,235.50
		1	3,235.50

ROYAL GUNNER (USA) (1962) by Royal Charger

Dam	Winner and Sire	Races Won	Value £
Make A Signal:	General Chase by Scottish Reel	2	6,011.40
Make A Signal:	Make A Stand by Master Willie	1	9,325.00
		3	15,336.40

ROYAL LEVEE (USA) (1959) by Royal Charger

Dam	Winner and Sire	Races Won	Value £
Cecelia (USA):	John Balliol (USA) by El Gran Senor (USA)	1	9,354.00
		1	9,354.00

ROYAL MATCH (1971) by Sovereign Path

Dam	Winner and Sire	Races Won	Value £
Mrs Lucky:	Once More For Luck (Ire) by Petorius	2	5,518.00
		2	5,518.00

ROYAL PALACE (1964) by Ballymoss

Dam	Winner and Sire	Races Won	Value £
Louise:	Kummel King by Absalom	1	3,850.00
Royal Agnes:	Dancing Days by Glenstal (USA)	2	3,654.00
Royal Agnes:	Antonia's Folly by Music Boy	1	3,915.00
Sleepline Princess:	Regalsett by Blakeney	1	2,749.00
Torlonia:	Izitallworthit by My Dad Tom (USA)	1	1,725.00
		6	15,893.00

ROYAL PREROGATIVE (1969) by Relko

Dam	Winner and Sire	Races Won	Value £
Bias:	Casteddu by Efisio	1	6,504.50
Bias:	Barbaroja by Efisio	3	20,434.00
		4	26,938.50

ROYBEN (1968) by Takawalk II

Dam	Winner and Sire	Races Won	Value £
Axe Valley:	For The Present by Then Again	2	8,621.00
		2	8,621.00

RUN THE GANTLET (USA) (1968) by Tom Rolfe

Dam	Winner and Sire	Races Won	Value £
Durun:	Dukrame by Top Ville	1	4,045.00
Mittens:	Sillars Stalker (Ire) by Stalker	1	3,611.25
Run Amber Run:	Quick Ransom by Hostage (USA)	2	31,082.40
Run Amber Run:	Moon Over Miami by Beveled (USA)	2	20,330.50
Run To The Sun:	Go South by Thatching	1	2,243.00
		7	61,312.15

RUNNETT (1977) by Mummy's Pet

Dam	Winner and Sire	Races Won	Value £
Fighting Run:	Croire (Ire) by Lomond (USA)	1	4,435.00
Great Alexandra:	Non Vintage (Ire) by Shy Groom (USA)	1	4,435.00
Idle Gossip:	Metal Boys by Krayyan	2	8,418.50
Little White Lies:	Singers Image by Chief Singer	1	3,582.00
Miss Serlby:	Left Stranded by Governor General	4	12,927.00
		9	33,797.50

RUNNYMEDE (1961) by Petition

Dam	Winner and Sire	Races Won	Value £
Easymede:	Lawnswood Junior by Bairn (USA)	3	10,153.50
Knavesmire:	Response by Most Welcome	1	3,054.20
Moon Charter:	Kathanna by Bold Owl	1	2,742.00
Pts Fairway:	Wild Strawberry by Ballacashtal (Can)	2	5,484.00
Rectitude:	Farmer's Pet by Sharrood (USA)	3	9,479.25
Rectitude:	Nightitude by Night Shift (USA)	1	5,253.50
		11	36,166.45

RUSTICARO (Fr) (1975) by Caro

Dam	Winner and Sire	Races Won	Value £
Primacara:	Atherton Green (Ire) by Shy Groom (USA)	1	3,915.00
Rustic Lawn:	Silver Groom (Ire) by Shy Groom (USA)	2	5,461.00
Sashi Woo:	Grey Charmer (Ire) by Alzao (USA)	2	8,168.00
		5	17,544.00

SADAIR (1962) by Petare

Dam	Winner and Sire	Races Won	Value £
Airy Queen (USA):	Exhibit Air (Ire) by Exhibitioner	2	6,736.45
		2	6,736.45

SADLER'S WELLS (USA) (1981) by Northern Dancer

Dam	Winner and Sire	Races Won	Value £
First Act:	Suntara (Ire) by Sure Blade (USA)	1	3,435.75
		1	3,435.75

SAGARO (1971) by Espresso

Dam Winner and Sire	Races Won	Value £
Bel Esprit: Wings Cove by Elegant Air	1	3,870.00
Free Rein: La Reine Rouge (Ire) by Red Sunset	1	3,055.50
Free Rein: Perdition (Ire) by Red Sunset	1	2,489.40
Free Rein: Hiltons Travel (Ire) by Red Sunset	1	2,444.60
June Fayre: Absolutely Fayre by Absalom	1	3,348.00
Sannavally: Croft Valley by Crofthall	3	23,261.80
	8	38,469.30

SAHIB (1966) by Sir Gaylord

Dam Winner and Sire	Races Won	Value £
Arodstown Alice: Kagram Queen by Prince Ragusa	2	5,561.70
	2	5,561.70

SALLUST (1969) by Pall Mall

Dam Winner and Sire	Races Won	Value £
Arena: Wakil (Ire) by Tate Gallery (USA)	1	4,207.50
Exceptional Beauty: Good Fetch by Siberian Express (USA)	1	3,080.00
Holernzaye: Sandmoor Denim by Red Sunset	2	10,989.50
Holy Day: Passion Sunday by Bairn (USA)	1	2,164.00
Lady Mary: Hillsdown Boy (Ire) by Dominion Royale	1	2,574.00
Late Sally: Persian Elite (Ire) by Persian Heights	1	3,465.00
Lough Graney: The Multiyorker (Ire) by Digamist (USA)	1	3,523.50
Maniusha: Olicana (Ire) by Persian Bold	1	2,579.00
Midaan: Lady Sheriff by Taufan (USA)	2	5,554.00
North Telstar: Canaska Star by Doyoun	1	3,590.00
Octavia: Kinoko by Bairn (USA)	2	6,667.00
Rangoon Ruby: Gneiss (USA) by Diesis	1	4,225.50
Salt: Iva's Flyer (Ire) by Imperial Frontier (USA)	1	3,913.25
Saltation: Marchman by Daring March	1	3,377.25
St Clair Star: Yonge Tender by Tender King	1	2,826.00
St Clair Star: Clairification (Ire) by Shernazar	1	3,652.00
Starlust: Dontforget Insight (Ire) by Don't Forget Me	1	4,737.00
Zolinana (Fr): Fragrant Belle (USA) by Al Nasr (Fr)	1	4,279.50
	21	75,404.00

SANDFORD LAD (1970) by St Alphage

Dam Winner and Sire	Races Won	Value £
Grain Of Sand: Knowth (Ire) by Exhibitioner	1	5,385.25
Now Then: Norling (Ire) by Nashamaa	2	4,143.00
Restless Lady: Catherines Well by Junius (USA)	2	9,664.00
	5	19,192.25

SANDY CREEK (1976) by Petingo

Dam Winner and Sire	Races Won	Value £
Yellow Creek: Wajiba Riva (Ire) by Waajib	2	10,018.50
	2	10,018.50

SARITAMER (USA) (1971) by Dancer's Image(USA)

Dam Winner and Sire	Races Won	Value £
Bronzamer: Goody Four Shoes by Blazing Saddles (Aus)	1	3,235.50
Fair Eleanor: Hotaria by Sizzling Melody	1	3,669.75
Tame Duchess: Duke Of Dreams by Efisio	1	2,821.10
Time Charter: Zinaad by Shirley Heights	1	33,794.00
	4	43,520.35

SASSAFRAS (Fr) (1967) by Sheshoon

Dam Winner and Sire	Races Won	Value £
Infinite Wisdom (USA): Solomon's Dancer (USA) by Al Nasr (Fr)	2	6,635.75
La Paqueline (Fr): Time Honored (USA) by Time For A Change (USA)	1	3,390.90
Polly's Pear (USA): Themaam by Night Shift (USA)	1	3,131.90
Rose Goddess: Avishayes (USA) by Al Nasr (Fr)	1	3,687.50
Sassalya: Little Bean by Ajdal (USA)	1	9,228.60
Sassalya: Etosha by Green Desert (USA)	2	6,980.25
Sassalya: Tzu'mu by Most Welcome	1	5,708.50
Sassanian: Roxanian (Ire) by Cyrano de Bergerac	3	11,587.80
Scotch Thistle: Aberdeen Heather by Absalom	1	5,060.80
	13	55,412.00

SAUCE BOAT (USA) (1975) by Key To The Mint(USA)

Dam Winner and Sire	Races Won	Value £
By Land By Sea (USA): Fawran (USA) by Silver Hawk (USA)	1	4,378.00
	1	4,378.00

SAULINGO (1970) by Sing Sing

Dam Winner and Sire	Races Won	Value £
Final Cast: Kabcast by Kabour	1	3,817.50
Hit The Line: Coalisland by Kind Of Hush	1	2,976.50
Isolin: Millsolin (Ire) by Millfontaine	1	4,709.25
Parissaul: Lock Tight (USA) by Key To The Kingdom (USA)	1	2,243.00
Saulonika: The Ordinary Girl (Ire) by Millfontaine	1	2,238.00
	5	15,984.25

SCOTTISH RIFLE (1969) by Sunny Way

Dam Winner and Sire	Races Won	Value £
Falls Of Lora: She Knew The Rules (Ire) by Jamesmead	1	2,070.00
Myrtlegrove: Blackpatch Hill by Efisio	3	9,301.55
	4	11,371.55

SEA HAWK II (1963) by Herbager

Dam Winner and Sire	Races Won	Value £
Merry Cindy: Merry Nutkin by Jalmood (USA)	2	6,164.25
Overseas: Atlantic Way by Bold Owl	2	6,368.50
Overseas: Rocky Bay by Bold Owl	1	2,679.00
Princess Tavi: Vanroy by Formidable (USA)	1	2,364.00
	6	17,575.75

SEA-BIRD II (1962) by Dan Cupid

Dam Winner and Sire	Races Won	Value £
Smooth Siren (USA): Kingston Brown by Chilibang	2	4,264.00
Smooth Siren (USA): Silky Siren by Formidable (USA)	3	10,237.90
Steady Wind (USA): Venta de Possa (USA) by Private Terms (USA)	1	3,746.50
	6	18,248.40

SEAEPIC (USA) (1968) by Sea-Bird II

Dam Winner and Sire	Races Won	Value £
Langwaite: North Ardar by Ardar	3	9,099.90
Salacia: Mr Nevermind (Ire) by The Noble Player (USA)	2	7,739.40
	5	16,839.30

SEATTLE SLEW (USA) (1974) by Bold Reasoning(USA)

Dam Winner and Sire	Races Won	Value £
Delta Slew (USA): Meadow Pipit (Can) by Meadowlake (USA)	4	25,135.50
Embraceable Slew (USA): Pay Homage by Primo Dominie	3	39,790.00
Oscillate (USA): Mutakddim (USA) by Seeking The Gold (USA)	1	10,464.00
Seattle Rockette (USA): Redoubtable (USA) by Grey Dawn II	2	13,244.00
	10	88,633.50

SECRETARIAT (USA) (1970) by Bold Ruler

Dam Winner and Sire	Races Won	Value £
Clandestina (USA): En Cachette (Ire) by Danehill (USA)	1	3,913.25
Golden Rhyme: Rapid Success (USA) by Sort (USA)	1	4,542.00
Office Wife (USA): Sharjah (USA) by Nijinsky (Can)	1	9,472.20
Sanctum Sanctorum (USA): Gran Senorum (USA) by El Gran Senor (USA)	2	6,432.75
Secretarial Queen (USA): Jazeel (USA) by Topsider (USA)	1	4,396.50
Tendresse (USA): Riszard (USA) by Danzig Connection (USA)	1	16,570.00
Wish You Were Here (USA): Duveen (Ire) by Tate Gallery (USA)	5	15,220.00
	12	60,546.70

SECRETO (USA) (1981) by Northern Dancer

Dam Winner and Sire	Races Won	Value £
Lady Lamia (USA): Moon Strike (Fr) by Strike Gold (USA)	2	10,528.00
	2	10,528.00

SEMI-PRO (1959) by Khaled

Dam Winner and Sire	Races Won	Value £
Proud Miss (USA): Knobbleeneeze by Aragon	1	3,340.00
	1	3,340.00

SENSITIVE PRINCE (USA) (1975) by Majestic Prince

Dam Winner and Sire	Races Won	Value £
Starr Danias (USA): Potsclose by Miswaki (USA)	1	4,449.50
	1	4,449.50

SETAY (1956) by Precipitation

Dam Winner and Sire	Races Won	Value £
Sweet Minuet: Amron by Bold Owl	3	26,321.00
	3	26,321.00

SEXTON BLAKE (1975) by Blakeney

Dam Winner and Sire	Races Won	Value £
Soosjoy: Carapelle by Domynsky	1	2,070.00
	1	2,070.00

SHAM (USA) (1970) by Pretense

Dam Winner and Sire	Races Won	Value £
Petite Diable (USA): Colway Rock (USA) by Irish River (Fr)	1	9,594.00
Safe Play (USA): Averti (USA) by Known Fact (USA)	1	5,390.00
	2	14,984.00

SHANTUNG (1956) by Sicambre

Dam Winner and Sire	Races Won	Value £
Scala Di Seta: Nessun Dorma by Night Shift (USA)	2	7,878.00
	2	7,878.00

SHAREEF DANCER (USA) (1980) by Northern Dancer

Dam Winner and Sire	Races Won	Value £
Dabaweyaa: Aneesati by Kris	1	3,728.25
Monaiya: Paradise News by Sure Blade (USA)	1	1,534.00
Try To Catch Me (USA): Nawafell by Kris	1	2,623.80
	3	7,886.05

SHARP EDGE (1970) by Silver Shark

Dam Winner and Sire	Races Won	Value £
Gossip: Celestial Rumour (Ire) by Astronef	1	2,549.00
Premier Rose: Provence by Rousillon (USA)	2	8,830.50
Premier Rose: George Dillingham by Top Ville	1	3,640.50
	4	15,020.00

SHARPEN UP (1969) by Atan

Dam Winner and Sire	Races Won	Value £
Asiram (USA): Instant Affair (USA) by Lyphard (USA)	2	7,656.00

Dam Winner and Sire	Races Won	Value £
Bay Shade (USA): Abury (Ire) by Law Society (USA)	1	23,815.00
Fluctuate: Prince Hannibal by High Top	2	6,726.75
Fluctuate: Dodgy Dancer by Shareef Dancer (USA)	3	8,256.80
Ideas And Trends (USA): Trendy Dancer (Ire) by Dance Of Life (USA)	1	2,070.00
Lady Bequick: Serious Hurry by Forzando	1	3,183.70
Lola Sharp: Volunteer Point (Ire) by Mister Majestic	1	2,427.00
Mangala (USA): Shalabia by Fast Topaze (USA)	1	2,322.00
Rapidus: Here Comes A Star by Night Shift (USA)	1	3,080.00
Reactress (USA): Realize by Al Nasr (Fr)	1	3,465.00
Reuval: Ardkinglass by Green Desert (USA)	1	40,432.20
Scierpan (USA): Specified (USA) by Known Fact (USA)	2	12,440.80
Sharp Castan: Powerful Edge by Primo Dominie	2	7,256.50
Sharp Lady: Prime Painter by Robellino (USA)	2	4,844.40
Sharpina: Ertlon by Shareef Dancer (USA)	1	5,253.50
Smarten Up: Young Jason by Star Appeal	1	2,924.70
Smarten Up: Dress Sense (Ire) by Top Ville	1	6,212.00
Smurfiusa (USA): Usaidit by Commanche Run	5	53,039.00
Stay Sharpe (USA): Fawz (Ire) by Green Desert (USA)	1	4,978.00
Stay Sharpe (USA): Ishtiyak by Green Desert (USA)	1	3,260.25
Stinging Nettle: Royal Insignia by Prince Sabo	2	18,299.50
Thimblerigger: Mister Baileys by Robellino (USA)	3	85,541.25
White Domino: Pinkerton's Pal by Dominion	1	5,390.00
	37	312,874.35

SHARPMAN (1976) by Sharpen Up

Dam Winner and Sire	Races Won	Value £
Sharp Girl (Fr): Gold Blade by Rousillon (USA)	2	6,822.25
	2	6,822.25

SHARPO (1977) by Sharpen Up

Dam Winner and Sire	Races Won	Value £
Better Buy Baileys: Daring Past by Daring March	1	2,846.00
Portvasco: Oare Sparrow by Night Shift (USA)	1	3,611.25
Postie: Post Mistress (Ire) by Cyrano de Bergerac	1	2,243.00
Water Folly: Karukera by Hallgate	1	2,761.50
	4	11,461.75

SHECKY GREENE (USA) (1970) by Noholme II

Dam Winner and Sire	Races Won	Value £
Chuckle (USA): Polish Laughter (USA) by Danzig Connection (USA)	2	32,670.90
	2	32,670.90

SHERGAR (1978) by Great Nephew

Dam Winner and Sire	Races Won	Value £
Cynomis: Cynic by Sharpo	1	3,143.25
Sheer Luck: Fathom Five (Ire) by Slip Anchor	1	2,658.00
Sherkraine: Slasher Jack (Ire) by Alzao (USA)	1	3,626.00
	3	9,427.25

SHERNAZAR (1981) by Busted

Dam Winner and Sire	Races Won	Value £
Number One Lady: One On One by Primo Dominie	2	5,663.60
	2	5,663.60

SHINY TENTH (1967) by Queen's Hussar

Dam Winner and Sire	Races Won	Value £
Slick Chick: Zanzara (Ire) by Efisio	1	3,501.25
	1	3,501.25

SHIRLEY HEIGHTS (1975) by Mill Reef(USA)

Dam Winner and Sire	Races Won	Value £
Baby's Smile: Smiles Ahead by Primo Dominie	1	2,070.00
Commanche Belle: Indian Slave (Ire) by Commanche Run	1	4,110.00
Commanche Belle: Persian Brave (Ire) by Persian Heights	2	11,510.40
Commanche Belle: Fairy Heights (Ire) by Fairy King (USA)	3	106,929.00
Height Of Folly: Charity Crusader by Rousillon (USA)	2	10,372.25
Height Of Passion: Rainbow Heights by Rainbow Quest (USA)	1	3,582.00
Infamy: Kamikaze by Kris	1	3,435.75
Kashmiri Snow: Pickles by Petoski	1	1,770.00
Our Shirley: Soviet Express by Siberian Express (USA)	1	1,604.00
Out Of Shot: Desert Shot by Green Desert (USA)	1	4,501.75
Road To The Top: Scottish Peak (Ire) by Lomond (USA)	1	4,448.60
Satinette: Majhola (Ire) by Soviet Star (USA)	1	3,494.25
Scots Lass: Dragon's Teeth (Ire) by Caerleon (USA)	1	3,143.25
Shadha: Sharp Gazelle by Beveled (USA)	2	4,994.70
Silent Movie: Pearly Mist (Ire) by Persian Heights	1	3,611.25
Streamertail: Battle Colours (Ire) by Petorius	2	6,128.10
Streamertail: Armenian Coffee (Ire) by Ela-Mana-Mou	2	5,509.20
View: Blue Blazer by Bluebird (USA)	1	2,269.13
Wizardry: Asking For Aces by Thatching	1	2,821.10
	26	186,304.73

SILENT SCREEN (USA) (1967) by Prince John

Dam Winner and Sire	Races Won	Value £
French Flick (USA): Peter Davies (USA) by Bering	2	17,380.80
Off The Reel (USA): Cast The Line by Pharly (Fr)	1	1,380.00

Dam Winner and Sire	Races Won	Value £
Screenable (USA): Certificate-X by Never So Bold	2	5,318.00
Silently Yours (USA): Tommy Tempest by Northern Tempest (USA)	1	2,924.00
Tiger Scout (USA): Tiger Claw (USA) by Diamond Shoal	1	2,889.00
	7	29,891.80

SILICONN (1962) by Princely Gift

Dam Winner and Sire	Races Won	Value £
Beryl's Jewel: Born To Be by Never So Bold	1	5,435.50
	1	5,435.50

SILLY SEASON (1962) by Tom Fool

Dam Winner and Sire	Races Won	Value £
April Days: Paper Days by Teenoso (USA)	1	3,261.40
Dazzling Light: Arc Lamp by Caerleon (USA)	1	3,002.40
Esquinade: Navaresque by Raga Navarro (Ity)	1	2,560.00
Georgina Park: Kimberley Park by Try My Best (USA)	1	5,816.00
La Rouquine: Red Bishop (USA) by Silver Hawk (USA)	2	30,057.00
Marton Maid: Mr Devious by Superpower	1	3,127.50
Michaelmas: Smart Daisy by Elegant Air	1	2,713.40
Mrs Cullumbine: Our Aisling by Blakeney	1	2,778.90
Mrs Cullumbine: Clifton Chase by Try My Best (USA)	1	2,950.60
Ouija: Chatoyant by Rainbow Quest (USA)	3	20,210.50
	13	76,477.70

SILVER HAWK (USA) (1979) by Roberto(USA)

Dam Winner and Sire	Races Won	Value £
Meissarah (USA): Agwa by Local Suitor (USA)	2	7,137.30
	2	7,137.30

SIMBIR (1970) by Shantung

Dam Winner and Sire	Races Won	Value £
Tina's Star: Lombard Ships by Orchestra	2	5,080.40
	2	5,080.40

SIMPLY GREAT (Fr) (1979) by Mill Reef(USA)

Dam Winner and Sire	Races Won	Value £
Magic Milly: Folly Finnesse by Joligeneration	2	5,714.40
	2	5,714.40

SING SING (1957) by Tudor Minstrel

Dam Winner and Sire	Races Won	Value £
Luscinia: Stoproveritate by Scorpio (Fr)	2	5,271.30
Melody Hour: Requested by Rainbow Quest (USA)	1	5,677.50
	3	10,948.80

SINGH (USA) (1972) by Bold Ruler

Dam Winner and Sire	Races Won	Value £
Deluxe Type (USA): Johns Act (USA) by Late Act (USA)	1	3,172.50
	1	3,172.50

SIR GAYLORD (1959) by Turn-to

Dam Winner and Sire	Races Won	Value £
Bru Ri (Fr): Mulled Ale (Ire) by Flash Of Steel	2	5,442.00
Gay France (Fr): Canaska Dancer (Ire) by Green Desert (USA)	2	9,547.25
Gay Pariso: Bandon Castle (Ire) by Exhibitioner	1	3,687.50
Pipina (USA): Daronne by Darshaan	1	4,306.50
	6	22,983.25

SIR IVOR (1965) by Sir Gaylord

Dam Winner and Sire	Races Won	Value £
Air Distingue (USA): Livonian by Kris	1	3,210.00
Allegedly (USA): Prosequendo (USA) by Robellino (USA)	1	2,898.80
Body Heat (USA): Mysterious Maid (USA) by L'emigrant (USA)	1	2,385.00
Enthralment (USA): Killick by Slip Anchor	1	7,148.00
Guest Night: Tochar Ban (USA) by Assert	1	4,079.25
Ivory Smooth (USA): Bransby Road (Ire) by Salt Dome (USA)	1	2,898.80
Ivory Wings (USA): Salatin (USA) by Seattle Dancer (USA)	1	4,690.40
Ivory Wings (USA): Wild Planet (USA) by Nureyev (USA)	1	4,464.00
Lake Ivor (USA): Lt Welsh (USA) by Silver Hawk (USA)	1	2,579.00
Royalivor (USA): Linney Head (USA) by Lyphard (USA)	1	4,371.75
Santa Linda (USA): Aljaz by Al Nasr (Fr)	1	3,348.00
Santa Linda (USA): Crackling Sike by Salse (USA)	1	4,664.00
Tweedling (USA): Scots Law by Law Society (USA)	2	5,523.75
Viscosity (USA): Marco Magnifico (USA) by Bering	1	5,481.00
	15	57,741.75

SIR WIGGLE (USA) (1967) by Sadair

Dam Winner and Sire	Races Won	Value £
Intensive (USA): Ajalan (Ire) by Be My Guest (USA)	1	3,465.00
	1	3,465.00

SKY GIPSY (1963) by Skymaster

Dam Winner and Sire	Races Won	Value £
Sky Bonnet: Sky Burst by Gunner B	1	3,015.00
	1	3,015.00

SKYLINER (1975) by African Sky

Dam Winner and Sire	Races Won	Value £
Pennyala: Private Fixture (Ire) by The Noble Player (USA)	1	2,803.00
Summer Sky: Lord Sky by Emarati (USA)	1	2,691.00
	2	5,494.00

Dam	Winner and Sire	Races Won	Value £

SKYMASTER (1958) by Golden Cloud

Dam / Winner and Sire	Races Won	Value £
Patosky: Forever Shineing by Glint Of Gold	1	2,243.00
Skimmer: The Happy Loon (Ire) by Mazaad	1	3,158.00
	2	5,401.00

SO BLESSED (1965) by Princely Gift

Dam / Winner and Sire	Races Won	Value £
Babycham Sparkle: Aroom by Sharrood (USA)	1	2,898.00
Babycham Sparkle: Champagne Girl by Robellino (USA)	1	3,406.50
Blessit: My Godson by Valiyar	1	3,054.00
Christchurch (Fr): Whitechapel (USA) by Arctic Tern (USA)	1	7,505.00
Clouded Vision: Clouded Elegance by Elegant Air	1	3,552.75
Missed Blessing: Unblest by Alzao (USA)	3	46,394.30
Pure Perfection: Eiras Mood by Jalmood (USA)	1	3,668.00
Sancta: Saint Keyne by Sadler's Wells (USA)	1	3,752.50
Scarcely Blessed: College Chapel by Sharpo	1	40,645.20
So Valiant: Gallant Spirit (Ire) by Gallic League	1	3,340.00
	12	118,216.25

SONG (1966) by Sing Sing

Dam / Winner and Sire	Races Won	Value £
Dawn Ditty: How's Yer Father by Daring March	2	16,277.50
Foolish Things: Riskie Things by Risk Me (Fr)	1	3,640.50
Miss Bunty: Cosmic Star by Siberian Express (USA)	1	2,070.00
Quaver: Night Melody (Ire) by Night Shift (USA)	3	12,337.25
Sideloader Special: Harpo's Special by Superlative	1	2,553.00
Song Grove: Sir Harry Hardman by Doulab (USA)	1	6,291.60
Song To Remember: Monsignor Pat (USA) by Irish Tower (USA)	1	3,465.00
Super Melody: Super Symphonic by Interrex (Can)	1	2,448.00
Suzannah's Song: Just Flamenco by Scorpio (Fr)	1	3,262.00
Tiszta Sharok: Peter Rowley by Absalom	1	3,444.00
Tricky: Magic Orb by Primo Dominie	3	15,144.75
Zinzi: El Arz by Primo Dominie	1	3,850.00
	17	74,783.60

SONNEN GOLD (1977) by Home Guard(USA)

Dam / Winner and Sire	Races Won	Value £
Cindys Gold: Lucayan Treasure by Absalom	2	7,410.60
Gold Duchess: Dailysportdutch by Risk Me (Fr)	2	3,688.00
	4	11,098.60

SOVEREIGN LORD (1959) by Grey Sovereign

Dam / Winner and Sire	Races Won	Value £
Exemplary: Northern Celadon (Ire) by Classic Secret (USA)	1	3,675.80
	1	3,675.80

SOVEREIGN PATH (1956) by Grey Sovereign

Dam / Winner and Sire	Races Won	Value £
Everything Nice: Nicer (Ire) by Pennine Walk	1	9,662.50
	1	9,662.50

SPARKLER (1968) by Hard Tack

Dam / Winner and Sire	Races Won	Value £
Aspark: Amidst by Midyan (USA)	2	8,092.50
Crackerjill: Petonellajill by Petong	1	3,980.00
Falaka: Arctic Diamond by Rambo Dancer (Can)	1	3,522.00
Follow The Stars: Brigante Di Cielo by Robellino (USA)	1	7,570.00
Follow The Stars: Stelloso by Midyan (USA)	1	4,092.00
Madam Muffin: True Precision by Presidium	2	27,994.50
Spark Out: Alllegsnobrain by Street Kafu	2	4,921.50
	10	60,172.50

SPECTACULAR BID (USA) (1976) by Bold Bidder

Dam / Winner and Sire	Races Won	Value £
Beveridge (USA): Bobbysoxer by Valiyar	3	10,328.50
Hooked Bid (Can): Hoosie by Niniski (USA)	1	2,847.00
Zumurrudah (USA): Mustahil (Ire) by Sure Blade (USA)	1	3,289.50
Zumurrudah (USA): Qamoos (Ire) by Sure Blade (USA)	1	1,630.00
	6	18,095.00

SPRING DOUBLE (1963) by Double Jay

Dam / Winner and Sire	Races Won	Value £
Spring Triple (USA): Impeccable Taste by Slip Anchor	1	2,243.00
	1	2,243.00

ST ALPHAGE (1963) by Red God

Dam / Winner and Sire	Races Won	Value £
Northern Venture: Pat's Splendour by Primitive Rising (USA)	1	2,243.00
	1	2,243.00

ST CHAD (1964) by St Paddy

Dam / Winner and Sire	Races Won	Value £
Chive: Slumber Thyme (Ire) by Burslem	1	2,763.00
	1	2,763.00

ST PADDY (1957) by Aureole

Dam / Winner and Sire	Races Won	Value £
Sheer Bliss: Court Minstrel by Hadeer	1	3,757.50
	1	3,757.50

STAGE DOOR JOHNNY (1965) by Prince John

Dam / Winner and Sire	Races Won	Value £
Rockfest (USA): Rainbow Lake by Rainbow Quest (USA)	3	33,712.50

Dam Winner and Sire	Races Won	Value £
Stage Luck (USA): Shaiba (USA) by Alysheba (USA)	1	9,894.00
Two For The Show (USA): Java Queen (USA) by Java Gold (USA)	1	3,545.00
	5	47,151.50

STANFORD (1976) by Red God

Dam Winner and Sire	Races Won	Value £
Collegian: Unveiled by Sayf El Arab (USA)	2	5,504.40
	2	5,504.40

STAR APPEAL (1970) by Appiani II

Dam Winner and Sire	Races Won	Value £
Clunk Click: Crazy Paving (Ire) by Danehill (USA)	1	5,385.00
Finalist: Cubist (Ire) by Tate Gallery (USA)	1	2,574.00
Gilt Star: Saafend by Sayf El Arab (USA)	1	4,474.50
Go Leasing: Ferryman (USA) by Riverman (USA)	1	2,623.80
Jarretiere: Midyan Blue (Ire) by Midyan (USA)	2	10,066.50
Lucky Appeal: Shambo by Lafontaine (USA)	2	37,983.00
Mullet: Blazon Of Troy by Trojan Fen	1	3,557.50
Round Midnight: Midnight Jazz (Ire) by Shardari	1	3,289.50
Stardyn: Young Ern by Efisio	2	57,480.45
Stellaris: Celestine by Skyliner	1	3,444.00
Verchinina: Romola Nijinsky by Bustino	3	8,646.10
Yldizlar: Yildiz by Be My Guest (USA)	1	12,817.50
	17	152,341.85

STAR DE NASKRA (USA) (1975) by Naskra(USA)

Dam Winner and Sire	Races Won	Value £
Miller's Creek (USA): Fast Eddy by Sharpo	1	3,915.00
	1	3,915.00

STAR MOSS (1960) by Mossborough

Dam Winner and Sire	Races Won	Value £
Elegant Star: Harry's Coming by Marching On	2	4,775.00
	2	4,775.00

STATUS SEEKER (1970) by Red God

Dam Winner and Sire	Races Won	Value £
Sundrive: Cool Enough by Welsh Captain	1	3,287.30
Traminer: Jake The Pake (Ire) by Double Schwartz	1	1,380.00
Traminer: Wixi (Ire) by Treasure Kay	1	3,435.75
	3	8,103.05

STEEL HEART (1972) by Habitat

Dam Winner and Sire	Races Won	Value £
Siofra Beag: Across The Bay by Krayyan	1	2,549.00
Touch My Heart: Heart Broken by Bustino	1	2,217.00
	2	4,766.00

STEPHEN GEORGE (1963) by Welsh Abbot

Dam Winner and Sire	Races Won	Value £
Whipalash: Ballyranter by Bold Owl	2	10,607.00
Whipalash: Kerrie-Jo by Merdon Melody	1	2,820.00
	3	13,427.00

STEVWARD (1959) by Nashua

Dam Winner and Sire	Races Won	Value £
Love To Barbara (USA): Bardolph (USA) by Golden Act (USA)	1	5,572.00
	1	5,572.00

STOP THE MUSIC (USA) (1970) by Hail To Reason

Dam Winner and Sire	Races Won	Value £
Creeping Kate (USA): No Submission (USA) by Melyno	1	3,757.50
Rensaler (USA): In The Money (Ire) by Top Ville	2	14,454.90
Sainera (USA): Pater Noster (USA) by Stately Don (USA)	1	3,260.25
	4	21,472.65

STORM BIRD (Can) (1978) by Northern Dancer

Dam Winner and Sire	Races Won	Value £
Pacific Gull (USA): Northern Chief by Chief Singer	2	6,205.40
Spur Wing (USA): Pearl Kite (USA) by Silver Hawk (USA)	1	4,308.00
	3	10,513.40

STRADAVINSKY (1975) by Nijinsky(Can)

Dam Winner and Sire	Races Won	Value £
Kadastra (Fr): Kadastrof (Fr) by Port Etienne (Fr)	1	3,640.50
	1	3,640.50

STREETFIGHTER (1962) by Aggressor

Dam Winner and Sire	Races Won	Value £
Lavenham Blue: Miss Aragon by Aragon	2	6,139.40
Lavenham Blue: Golden Grand by Sayf El Arab (USA)	2	4,313.00
	4	10,452.40

SUCCESSOR (1964) by Bold Ruler

Dam Winner and Sire	Races Won	Value £
Sound Of Success (USA): Sonus (Ire) by Sadler's Wells (USA)	2	36,794.00
	2	36,794.00

SUN PRINCE (1969) by Princely Gift

Dam Winner and Sire	Races Won	Value £
Alia: Tremolando (USA) by Trempolino (USA)	1	3,611.25
	1	3,611.25

Dam	Winner and Sire	Races Won	Value £

SUPER CONCORDE (USA) (1975) by Bold Reasoning(USA)

Lightning Legacy (USA): Sudden Spin by Doulab (USA)	1	3,210.00
Superlife (USA): Superensis by Sayf El Arab (USA)	1	2,070.00
	2	5,280.00

SUPER MOMENT (USA) (1977) by Big Spruce(USA)

Barbara's Moment (USA): Saseedo (USA) by Afleet (Can)	1	3,882.50
	1	3,882.50

SUPREME SOVEREIGN (1964) by Sovereign Path

Pine: Affa by Local Suitor (USA)	1	3,753.50
	1	3,753.50

SWAPS (1952) by Khaled

Crown The Queen (USA): Case For The Crown (USA) by Bates Motel (USA)	1	2,847.00
	1	2,847.00

SWEET CANDY (Ven) (1977) by Bold And Brave

Parkland Rose: No Extras (Ire) by Efisio	3	10,834.50
	3	10,834.50

SWEET REVENGE (1967) by Compensation

Kiss The Bride: Princely Favour (Ire) by Anita's Prince	2	6,807.90
Sweet Pleasure: Haddaaj (Ire) by Ela-Mana-Mou	3	9,689.50
Sweet Rosina: Play Hever Golf by Alleging (USA)	3	16,924.00
Sweet Rosina: Hever Golf Rose by Efisio	2	23,602.25
Tickled To Bits: Desert Laughter (Ire) by Desert Of Wind (USA)	1	2,924.00
	11	59,947.65

SWING EASY (USA) (1968) by Delta Judge

Diami: Just Bob by Alleging (USA)	4	10,578.55
Elsocko: Dominion King by Dominion Royale	1	3,379.00
Gleneagle: Melodic Drive by Sizzling Melody	1	2,070.00
Holloway Wonder: Rocky Two by Cree Song	1	2,219.30
I Don't Mind: Dokkha Oyston (Ire) by Prince Sabo	3	8,016.65
Swing Gently: Never In The Red by Wattlefield	1	3,080.00
Swinging Gold: So So by Then Again	1	7,440.00
Tarvie: Macfarlane by Kala Shikari	2	19,049.00
	14	55,832.50

T V LARK (1957) by Indian Hemp

Come On Sunshine (USA): Darecliff (USA) by Diesis	2	10,807.50
	2	10,807.50

TACHYPOUS (1974) by Hotfoot

Fair Atlanta: Ashgore by Efisio	2	6,035.35
Fallonetta: Big Pat by Backchat (USA)	5	15,634.30
Greek Music: Leap Of Faith (Ire) by Northiam (USA)	2	3,082.00
Miss Anniversary: Master Beveled by Beveled (USA)	1	4,500.00
Tacheo: Vilamar (Ire) by Carmelite House (USA)	1	2,467.00
	11	31,718.65

TAKE A REEF (1971) by Right Tack

Supreme Kingdom: Sakharov by Bay Express	4	10,700.60
	4	10,700.60

TANFIRION (1974) by Habitat

Bad Payer: Penny Hasset by Lochnager	2	7,292.00
Oyster Gray: Magic Pearl by Belfort (Fr)	2	8,689.50
	4	15,981.50

TAP ON WOOD (1976) by Sallust

Caimanite: Blair Castle (Ire) by Waajib	1	3,590.00
Final Decision: Sweet Decision (Ire) by Common Grounds	1	2,595.00
Lady Woodpecker: Deevee by Hallgate	5	17,852.20
Mumtaz Mayfly: Claret Bumble by Absalom	2	4,039.50
My Tootsie: My Rossini by Ardross	1	2,794.00
Rappa Tap Tap (Fr): Tap On Air by Caerleon (USA)	2	18,485.37
Tap The Line: Southern Power (Ire) by Midyan (USA)	1	4,199.25
Tapestry: Trianglepoint (Ire) by Auction Ring (USA)	1	2,243.00
Taplow: Olifantsfontein by Thatching	1	6,164.00
	15	61,962.32

TARGOWICE (USA) (1970) by Round Table

Skhiza: Sugar Town (Ire) by Tate Gallery (USA)	1	4,342.25
	1	4,342.25

TAUFAN (USA) (1977) by Stop The Music(USA)

Dam: Winner and Sire	Races Won	Value £
Fantoccini: Monticino (Ire) by Dominion	1	4,985.75
Fleetwood Fancy: Western Fleet (USA) by Westheimer (USA)	1	2,668.00
Turbo Rose: Co Pilot (Ire) by Petorius	1	3,626.00
	3	11,279.75

TESCO BOY (1963) by Princely Gift

Dam: Winner and Sire	Races Won	Value £
Hitesca: Allesca by Alleging (USA)	2	5,225.00
	2	5,225.00

THATCH (USA) (1970) by Forli(Arg)

Dam: Winner and Sire	Races Won	Value £
An Tig Gaelige: Talented Ting (Ire) by Hatim (USA)	3	9,141.80
Cottage Style: Stylish Rose (Ire) by Don't Forget Me	1	3,552.75
Ethel Knight: Battling Blue by Primo Dominie	1	3,415.00
Fire Risk: Pavaka by Glenstal (USA)	1	2,070.00
Forres: Cromarty by Shareef Dancer (USA)	1	3,435.75
Iron Lass: Dundeelin by Dunbeath (USA)	1	2,070.00
On The Tiles: Singer On The Roof by Chief Singer	1	2,795.20
Spun Gold: Record Lover (Ire) by Alzao (USA)	1	3,882.50
Top Bloom: Serious Option (Ire) by Reprimand	2	6,639.00
	12	37,002.00

THATCHING (1975) by Thatch(USA)

Dam: Winner and Sire	Races Won	Value £
Abha: Garah by Ajdal (USA)	1	3,363.00
Abha: El Jubail (Ire) by Shirley Heights	1	3,611.25
Arrapata: Yes by Blakeney	1	2,259.00
Arrapata: Dance Of The Swans (Ire) by Try My Best (USA)	2	6,057.00
Dying Craft: Preston Guild (Ire) by Mazaad	3	9,348.35
French Plait: Rural Lad by Town And Country	2	8,442.25
Plaits: Walk The Beat by Interrex (Can)	1	3,080.00
Rabab: Almost A Princess by Alleging (USA)	1	3,027.50
String Of Straw: Rose Flyer (Ire) by Nordico (USA)	1	1,548.00
Twine: Duckey Fuzz by Ardross	3	12,074.25
Twine: Alderbrook by Ardross	5	21,873.95
	21	74,684.55

THE BRIANSTAN (1967) by King's Leap

Dam: Winner and Sire	Races Won	Value £
Blackpool Belle: Tocco Jewel by Reesh	1	2,679.00
Mainly Dry: Teetotaller (Ire) by Taufan (USA)	1	3,980.00
	2	6,659.00

THE MINSTREL (Can) (1974) by Northern Dancer

Dam: Winner and Sire	Races Won	Value £
Brilliant Timing (USA): Bold Timing by Never So Bold	1	4,125.40
Chanson de Paris (USA): Brandon Prince (Ire) by Shernazar	3	19,011.75
Devon Diva (USA): Tinners Way (USA) by Secretariat (USA)	2	23,295.00
Flawless Image (USA): Darnay by Darshaan	1	5,595.00
Itsamazing (USA): Underwater (USA) by Riverman (USA)	1	3,362.50
Itsamazing (USA): Magnasonic (USA) by Known Fact (USA)	1	5,572.00
Miss Fancy That (USA): Tajannab by Kris	1	3,551.50
Sans Blague (USA): Galejade by Sharrood (USA)	1	2,434.00
Shehana (USA): Legion Of Honour by Ahonoora	1	4,844.00
Shicklah (USA): Nizaal (USA) by Diesis	1	4,270.75
Song Test (USA): Queenbird by Warning	3	12,813.40
Tantalizing Song (Can): Miss Fascination by Damister (USA)	1	4,737.00
Tantalizing Song (Can): Sparkling Lyric by Damister (USA)	1	2,243.00
Toor A Lay (USA): Clever Minstrel (USA) by Clever Trick (USA)	1	2,534.20
Zaifon (USA): Zafonic (USA) by Gone West (USA)	1	110,871.20
	20	209,260.70

TICKLED PINK (1969) by Red God

Dam: Winner and Sire	Races Won	Value £
Pink Mex: Hannah's Music by Music Boy	2	7,764.20
Superfrost: Saifan by Beveled (USA)	3	40,925.00
	5	48,689.20

TILT UP (USA) (1975) by Olden Times

Dam: Winner and Sire	Races Won	Value £
Top And Tail (USA): So Superb by Superlative	2	6,687.50
	2	6,687.50

TIM TAM (1955) by Tom Fool

Dam: Winner and Sire	Races Won	Value £
Royal Entrance (USA): Eaton Row (USA) by Alydar (USA)	1	3,318.75
	1	3,318.75

TIN WHISTLE (1957) by Whistler

Dam: Winner and Sire	Races Won	Value £
Nana's Girl: Port Sunlight (Ire) by Tate Gallery (USA)	1	2,851.25
	1	2,851.25

TINA'S PET (1978) by Mummy's Pet

Dam: Winner and Sire	Races Won	Value £
Thorner Lane: Scored Again by Music Boy	1	2,434.00
Thorner Lane: Kangra Valley by Indian Ridge	1	3,699.00
	2	6,133.00

TISAB (USA) (1971) by Loom

Dam: Winner and Sire	Races Won	Value £
Privy (USA): Knock To Enter (USA) by Diesis	2	5,549.60
	2	5,549.60

TOM CAT (1960) by Tom Fool

Dam Winner and Sire	Races Won	Value £
Catty Queen (USA): One Off The Rail (USA) by Rampage (USA)	4	11,778.00
	4	11,778.00

TOM ROLFE (1962) by Ribot

Dam Winner and Sire	Races Won	Value £
Basin (USA): Puget Dancer (USA) by Seattle Dancer (USA)	1	3,236.00
Cacti (USA): Cascassi (USA) by Nijinsky (Can)	1	3,523.50
Cope Of Flowers (USA): Mujaazafah (USA) by Mr Prospector (USA)	1	3,728.25
Gliding By (USA): Song Of Sixpence (USA) by The Minstrel (Can)	1	8,415.00
Gliding By (USA): Susquehanna Days (USA) by Chief's Crown (USA)	2	5,678.75
Matoa (USA): Brigade by Sharpo	1	3,401.00
	7	27,982.50

TOP VILLE (1976) by High Top

Dam Winner and Sire	Races Won	Value £
Iosifa: Elburg (Ire) by Ela-Mana-Mou	1	2,243.00
	1	2,243.00

TOPSIDER (USA) (1974) by Northern Dancer

Dam Winner and Sire	Races Won	Value £
Battine (USA): Cherhill (Ire) by Ahonoora	1	2,717.50
Cup Defender (USA): Lacerta (Ire) by Thatching	1	3,494.25
Skeeb (USA): Innishowen (USA) by Arctic Tern (USA)	2	15,530.00
	4	21,741.75

TOUCH PAPER (1969) by Roan Rocket

Dam Winner and Sire	Races Won	Value £
Hyde Princess: The Fed by Clantime	1	3,084.75
Miss Display: Ned's Bonanza by Green Ruby (USA)	1	4,464.00
	2	7,548.75

TOWER WALK (1966) by High Treason

Dam Winner and Sire	Races Won	Value £
Catherine Howard: Tudor Island by Jupiter Island	1	3,850.00
Kilttaley: Mount Leinster by Sayf El Arab (USA)	1	3,125.50
Magic Tower: Johnnie The Joker by Absalom	1	3,158.00
Miss Thames: Caspian Beluga by Persian Bold	1	3,652.00
Morning Stroll: Million At Dawn (Ire) by Fayruz	1	3,377.25
Redcross Miss: Valiant Man by Valiyar	1	3,289.50
Time For Pleasure: Allthruthenight (Ire) by Precocious	1	4,624.75
	7	25,077.00

TOWN AND COUNTRY (1974) by Town Crier

Dam Winner and Sire	Races Won	Value £
Cubby Hole: Niche by Risk Me (Fr)	2	60,444.90
Cubby Hole: Alcove by Faustus (USA)	1	3,176.25
Don't Loiter: Feather Face by Tina's Pet	1	3,590.00
Hubbardair: Air Command (Bar) by Concorde Hero (USA)	1	2,406.00
	5	69,617.15

TOWN CRIER (1965) by Sovereign Path

Dam Winner and Sire	Races Won	Value £
Valediction: Fairy Wisher (Ire) by Fairy King (USA)	1	3,390.90
	1	3,390.90

TRACK SPARE (1963) by Sound Track

Dam Winner and Sire	Races Won	Value £
Nicholas Grey: Nichodoula by Doulab (USA)	2	5,452.60
Rockery: Ok Bertie by Interrex (Can)	2	8,825.00
	4	14,277.60

TRIBAL CHIEF (1967) by Princely Gift

Dam Winner and Sire	Races Won	Value £
Mertola: Gilderdale by Gunner B	1	3,289.50
Trigamy: Risk Master by Risk Me (Fr)	1	13,047.20
Trigamy: Trinity Hall by Hallgate	1	2,684.50
	3	19,021.20

TROJAN FEN (1981) by Troy

Dam Winner and Sire	Races Won	Value £
Saluti Tutti: Mazeeka (Ire) by Glow (USA)	2	5,930.50
Trojan Relation: Darren Boy (Ire) by Ballad Rock	2	6,936.80
	4	12,867.30

TROMOS (1976) by Busted

Dam Winner and Sire	Races Won	Value £
Dimant Rose (USA): Major Yaasi (USA) by Arctic Tern (USA)	1	4,836.00
Tralthee (USA): Dancing Tralthee (Ire) by Dancing Brave (USA)	1	3,054.20
	2	7,890.20

TROY (1976) by Petingo

Dam Winner and Sire	Races Won	Value £
Amalee: Miliyel by Rousillon (USA)	1	2,884.00
Cocotte: Red Cotton by Soviet Star (USA)	1	3,131.90
Dancing Decoy: Taunting (Ire) by Taufan (USA)	1	2,010.00
Dancing Decoy: Wassl This Then (Ire) by Wassl	2	6,294.00
Etoile de Nuit: Lijaam (Ire) by Persian Bold	1	3,406.50
Fortune Teller: Water Gypsy by Dowsing (USA)	1	3,080.00
Gay Fantasy: Lucky Guest by Be My Guest (USA)	1	12,792.00
Gay Fantasy: Son Of Sharp Shot (Ire) by Sharp Shot	1	3,379.00
Helenetta: Rousitto by Rousillon (USA)	1	3,236.00

Dam Winner and Sire	Races Won	Value £
Helenetta: La Spezia by Last Tycoon	1	3,260.25
Myth: Supertop by High Top	2	8,205.60
Myth: Hard Task by Formidable (USA)	1	3,840.00
Myth: Midnight Legend by Night Shift (USA)	1	4,092.00
Prelude: Set The Fashion by Green Desert (USA)	5	17,774.50
Spartan Helen: Spartan Shareef (Ire) by Shareef Dancer (USA)	2	37,282.50
Troja: Snow Board by Niniski (USA)	1	6,400.00
Troyanos: Summer Pageant by Chief's Crown (USA)	3	10,509.65
	26	131,577.90

TRY MY BEST (USA) (1975) by Northern Dancer

Dam Winner and Sire	Races Won	Value £
Capriconia: Finjan by Thatching	2	6,247.45
Daffodil Fields: Petula by Petong	2	12,747.80
Effortless: Azureus (Ire) by Horage	3	9,598.70
Pea Green: Jade Pet by Petong	2	7,019.25
Riva Renald: Abalene by Forzando	1	2,574.00
Sunley Sinner: Garnock Valley by Dowsing (USA)	2	8,015.00
Sunley Sinner: Sinners Reprieve by Reprimand	1	3,435.75
Try Gloria: Featherstone Lane by Siberian Express (USA)	1	2,490.00
	14	52,127.95

TUDOR MELODY (1956) by Tudor Minstrel

Dam Winner and Sire	Races Won	Value £
Belitis: Captain Starlight (Ire) by Vision (USA)	1	2,601.40
Fiordiligi: Kovalevskia by Ardross	1	3,106.00
Gliding: Beauman by Rainbow Quest (USA)	1	6,157.50
Melodramatic: Overact (Ire) by Law Society (USA)	2	6,520.50
	5	18,385.40

TUDOR MUSIC (1966) by Tudor Melody

Dam Winner and Sire	Races Won	Value £
Light Link: No Reservations (Ire) by Commanche Run	1	5,897.50
Sallytude: Saddam The Log by Music Boy	1	2,880.00
	2	8,777.50

TUMBLE WIND (USA) (1964) by Restless Wind

Dam Winner and Sire	Races Won	Value £
Millingdale: Norstock by Norwick (USA)	1	2,611.00
Night Of Wind: Barossa Valley (Ire) by Alzao (USA)	1	4,760.00
Tumble Dale: Royal Roller (Ire) by Dara Monarch	1	2,601.40
Warm Wind: Courting Newmarket by Final Straw	2	5,526.80
Warm Wind: Warm Spell by Northern State (USA)	3	9,381.25
Warm Wind: Blue Bomber by Tina's Pet	2	7,471.75
Wind And Reign: Kalar by Kabour	2	5,856.75
	12	38,208.95

TYRANT (USA) (1966) by Bold Ruler

Dam Winner and Sire	Races Won	Value £
Love Me Tight: Laurel Romeo (Ire) by Astronef	1	2,422.20
	1	2,422.20

TYRNAVOS (1977) by Blakeney

Dam Winner and Sire	Races Won	Value £
Scarlet Veil: Comeonup by Most Welcome	1	2,579.00
	1	2,579.00

UPPER CASE (USA) (1969) by Round Table

Dam Winner and Sire	Races Won	Value £
Greenhill Lass: Family Rose by Absalom	1	2,243.00
Hot Case: Aitch N'bee by Northfields (USA)	1	3,028.00
Persian Case: Persian Soldier by Sandhurst Prince	2	7,646.25
Piazza Navona: Merryhill Maid (Ire) by M Double M (USA)	1	3,150.00
Upper Sister: Shuttlecock by Pharly (Fr)	1	1,605.50
	6	17,672.75

UPPER NILE (USA) (1974) by Nijinsky(Can)

Dam Winner and Sire	Races Won	Value £
Naughty Nile (USA): Lower Egypt (USA) by Silver Hawk (USA)	2	7,295.50
Schematic (USA): Katiba (USA) by Gulch (USA)	1	3,512.50
	3	10,808.00

VAGUELY NOBLE (1965) by Vienna

Dam Winner and Sire	Races Won	Value £
Amazer (USA): Oakmead (Ire) by Lomond (USA)	2	13,905.00
Elk's Ellie (USA): One Voice (USA) by Affirmed (USA)	1	2,924.70
Expediency (USA): Decided (Can) by Affirmed (USA)	1	2,448.00
Expediency (USA): Oh So Risky by Kris	1	7,015.40
Hors Serie (USA): Moon Spin by Night Shift (USA)	4	14,498.95
Lost Splendour (USA): Desert Splendour by Green Desert (USA)	1	2,427.00
No Designs (USA): Storm Free (USA) by Storm Bird (Can)	1	2,556.60
Noble Lily (USA): Noble Rose (Ire) by Caerleon (USA)	1	5,343.00
Noble Wac (USA): Fact Or Fiction by Known Fact (USA)	1	3,084.75
Royal Agreement (USA): Eden's Close by Green Dancer (USA)	1	5,015.50
	14	59,218.90

VAIGLY GREAT (1975) by Great Nephew

Dam Winner and Sire	Races Won	Value £
Demderise: Sonderise by Mummy's Game	1	3,816.00
Great Leighs: Embankment (Ire) by Tate Gallery (USA)	2	9,133.00

Dam Winner and Sire	Races Won	Value £
Great Leighs: Rose Ciel (Ire) by Red Sunset	1	3,321.10
	4	16,270.10

VAL DE L'ORNE (Fr) (1972) by Val de Loir

Dam Winner and Sire	Races Won	Value £
Louisville (Fr): Concordial (USA) by Nureyev (USA)	2	17,764.00
Norman Delight (USA): King William by Dara Monarch	1	3,340.00
	3	21,104.00

VAL DE LOIR (1959) by Vieux Manoir

Dam Winner and Sire	Races Won	Value £
Val de Grace (Fr): Grace Card by Ela-Mana-Mou	1	3,106.00
Valmarine (Fr): Bold Resolution (Ire) by Shardari	3	22,962.25
	4	26,068.25

VALDEZ (USA) (1976) by Exclusive Native(USA)

Dam Winner and Sire	Races Won	Value £
Keep The Thought (USA): Dreams Are Free (Ire) by Caerleon (USA)	1	3,882.50
	1	3,882.50

VALIYAR (1979) by Red God

Dam Winner and Sire	Races Won	Value £
Valika: First Veil by Primo Dominie	1	3,707.50
Valika: First Trump by Primo Dominie	5	145,395.95
	6	149,103.45

VAYRANN (1978) by Brigadier Gerard

Dam Winner and Sire	Races Won	Value £
Adriya: Admiring by Nomination	1	2,259.00
Nouniya: Halham Tarn (Ire) by Pennine Walk	2	5,685.00
	3	7,944.00

VERBATIM (USA) (1965) by Speak John

Dam Winner and Sire	Races Won	Value £
Kittycatoo Katango (USA): Mr Butch by Aragon	1	4,751.50
Sabatina (USA): Sharp Prospect by Sharpo	1	3,201.75
	2	7,953.25

VICE REGENT (Can) (1967) by Northern Dancer

Dam Winner and Sire	Races Won	Value £
Golden Regent (Can): Mistress Bee (USA) by Grub (USA)	1	2,660.00
Raahia (Can): Mithi Al Gamar (USA) by Blushing Groom (Fr)	1	3,640.50
	2	6,300.50

VICEREGAL (Can) (1966) by Northern Dancer

Dam Winner and Sire	Races Won	Value £
Trephine (Fr): Tumbling (USA) by Irish River (Fr)	1	3,276.00
Victory Kingdom (Can): Prince Azzaan (Ire) by Rousillon (USA)	2	5,978.90
	3	9,254.90

VICTORIA PARK (1957) by Chop Chop

Dam Winner and Sire	Races Won	Value £
Caroglen Jo (Can): Stoller (USA) by El Gran Senor (USA)	1	4,807.00
	1	4,807.00

VIENNA (1957) by Aureole

Dam Winner and Sire	Races Won	Value £
Vive La Reine: Viardot (Ire) by Sadler's Wells (USA)	1	3,106.00
	1	3,106.00

VIKING (USA) (1977) by Northern Dancer

Dam Winner and Sire	Races Won	Value £
Vikris: Nordan Raider by Domynsky	3	11,559.40
Vikris: Hi Nod by Valiyar	3	25,885.20
	6	37,444.60

VISION (USA) (1981) by Nijinsky(Can)

Dam Winner and Sire	Races Won	Value £
Gipping: Siganca by Dowsing (USA)	1	2,511.80
	1	2,511.80

VITIGES (Fr) (1973) by Phaeton

Dam Winner and Sire	Races Won	Value £
Clymene: Clyde Goddess (Ire) by Scottish Reel	1	4,542.00
Senane: Civil Law (Ire) by Law Society (USA)	3	7,599.00
Vizenia: En Attendant (Fr) by Bairn (USA)	3	53,954.00
	7	66,095.00

WAJIMA (USA) (1972) by Bold Ruler

Dam Winner and Sire	Races Won	Value £
Bethamane (USA): River Boyne (USA) by Irish River (Fr)	2	6,631.50
Velvet Storm (USA): Wonderful Years (USA) by Key To The Mint (USA)	1	2,070.00
	3	8,701.50

WARPATH (1969) by Sovereign Path

Dam Winner and Sire	Races Won	Value £
Bobs: Poetic Form (Ire) by Ballad Rock	1	2,924.70
	1	2,924.70

Dam	Winner and Sire	Races Won	Value £

WELL DECORATED (USA) (1978) by Raja Baba(USA)

	Races Won	Value £
Badge Of Courage (USA): True Hero (USA) by The Minstrel (Can)	1	29,376.00
Flash Donna (USA): Second Chance (Ire) by Digamist (USA)	2	7,076.25
	3	36,452.25

WELSH PAGEANT (1966) by Tudor Melody

	Races Won	Value £
Bare Spectacle: Noriski'maringer by Risk Me (Fr)	2	5,952.00
Brookfield Miss: Miss Mah-Jong by Absalom	3	7,526.00
Carnival Dance: Azola (Ire) by Alzao (USA)	2	5,245.00
Eiswave: Cabcharge Princess (Ire) by Rambo Dancer (Can)	1	2,859.50
Fete Champetre: Argyle Cavalier (Ire) by Simply Great (Fr)	1	3,825.00
Flopsy: Crazy For You by Blakeney	1	5,205.00
Investiture: Super Benz by Hello Gorgeous (USA)	1	2,595.80
Joie de Galles: Welshman by Final Straw	3	17,486.70
La Serenata: Just Jamie by Formidable (USA)	1	3,027.50
Nawara: Alhijaz by Midyan (USA)	1	35,325.00
On Show: Balnaha by Lomond (USA)	1	3,611.25
Pageantry: Allegation by Dominion	1	2,070.00
Quenlyn: Heathyards Gem by Governor General	1	2,950.60
Rose And The Ring: Supreme Boy by Superlative	1	2,976.50
Rose And The Ring: Ham N'eggs by Robellino (USA)	2	7,163.00
Rose Chanelle: Art Tatum (Ire) by Tate Gallery (USA)	2	6,639.55
Selection Board: Star Selection by Rainbow Quest (USA)	1	4,204.25
Sense Of Pride: Sense Of Priority by Primo Dominie	1	2,490.00
Tuyenu: Quiet Riot by Hotfoot	1	2,343.00
Welsh Fantasy: Jetbeeah (Ire) by Lomond (USA)	1	4,272.50
Winter Queen: Safety In Numbers by Slip Anchor	4	27,671.85
	32	155,440.00

WELSH SAINT (1966) by St Paddy

	Races Won	Value £
Bright Cecilia: Gussie Fink-Nottle (Ire) by Treasure Kay	1	2,847.00
Gwiffina: Creselly by Superlative	1	2,479.00
Martialette: Red Indian by Be My Native (USA)	1	2,950.60
Peteona: Castle Courageous by Castle Keep	2	12,618.00
Samra: Superlativemaximus (Ire) by Superlative	2	6,324.50
Sweet Emma: Love Legend by Glint Of Gold	1	5,049.00
Welsh Blossom: Spectacle Jim by Mummy's Game	1	2,532.00
Welwyn: Welsh Mist by Damister (USA)	2	6,766.40
Wyn Mipet: Bold Aristocrat (Ire) by Bold Arrangement	1	2,444.60
	12	44,011.10

WHAT A GUEST (1979) by Be My Guest(USA)

	Races Won	Value £
Caviar Blini: Norfolk Hero by Elegant Air	1	6,664.00
Saintly Guest: Benzoe (Ire) by Taufan (USA)	1	13,500.00
Wedge Musical: Silver Wedge (USA) by Silver Hawk (USA)	1	4,182.00
	3	24,346.00

WHAT A PLEASURE (USA) (1965) by Bold Ruler

	Races Won	Value £
Six Dozen (USA): North Esk (USA) by Apalachee (USA)	2	8,947.50
	2	8,947.50

WHAT LUCK (USA) (1967) by Bold Ruler

	Races Won	Value £
Ambassador Of Luck (USA): Felawnah (USA) by Mr Prospector (USA)	1	4,084.50
How Fortunate (USA): Tik Fa (USA) by Timeless Moment (USA)	2	9,088.80
How Fortunate (USA): Lucky Message (USA) by Phone Trick (USA)	1	2,898.00
Lucky Brook (USA): Spot Prize (USA) by Seattle Dancer (USA)	1	3,497.50
Someway Somehow (USA): Cape Pigeon (USA) by Storm Bird (Can)	2	5,856.75
	7	25,425.55

WHISTLING WIND (1960) by Whistler

	Races Won	Value £
Engage: Taufan Blu (Ire) by Taufan (USA)	1	15,400.00
Engage: Petersford Girl (Ire) by Taufan (USA)	1	3,699.00
What A Breeze: Precious Caroline (Ire) by The Noble Player (USA)	1	2,950.60
Woodwind (Fr): Piccolo by Warning	1	4,191.00
	4	26,240.60

WHITESBURG (USA) (1969) by Crimson Satan

	Races Won	Value £
Whitesburg Lass (USA): Mr Eubanks (USA) by Imp Society (USA)	1	3,720.00
	1	3,720.00

WILL SOMERS (1955) by Tudor Minstrel

	Races Won	Value £
Some Dame: Farmer Jock by Crofter (USA)	1	2,898.80
	1	2,898.80

Dam Winner and Sire	Races Won	Value £

WINDJAMMER (USA) (1969) by Restless Wind

Be My Darling: Inferring by Alleging (USA)	1	2,825.40
City To City: Komplicity by Komaite (USA)	1	2,057.50
Edraianthus: Close To Reality by Dreams To Reality (USA)	1	3,640.50
Irish Kick: Hopeful Bid (Ire) by Auction Ring (USA)	1	4,235.00
Irish Kick: White Shoot (Ire) by Carmelite House (USA)	1	3,465.00
Summerhill Spruce: Lucky Parkes by Full Extent (USA)	6	23,601.90
Summerhill Spruce: Bella Parkes by Tina's Pet	3	10,074.75
Windini: Miss Whittingham (Ire) by Fayruz	5	14,838.10
	19	64,738.15

WINDWURF (Ger) (1972) by Kaiseradler

Bolivia (Ger): Lake Poopo (Ire) by Persian Heights	2	7,618.75
Mana (Ger): Maragon by Aragon	1	8,041.00
Una Donna (Ger): Juliasdarkinvader by Lidhame	1	2,660.00
	4	18,319.75

WOLLOW (1973) by Wolver Hollow

Lady Of The Land: Sharquin by Indian King (USA)	1	3,366.00
Recline: High Domain (Ire) by Dominion Royale	2	8,521.25
Secret Valentine: Gondo by Mansingh (USA)	2	6,336.25
	5	18,223.50

WOLVER HOLLOW (1964) by Sovereign Path

Double Stitch: Purbeck Centenary by Lidhame	1	3,122.80
Dowdstown Miss: Legal Artist (Ire) by Tate Gallery (USA)	2	5,221.50
Emblazon: Sloe Brandy by Hotfoot	1	2,721.00
Gentle Freedom: Amoret (Ire) by Jareer (USA)	2	7,848.50
Norton Princess: Can Can Charlie by Vaigly Great	1	3,496.00
Polly Worth: Culsyth Flyer by Nomination	2	4,644.00
Wolverina: Brandonhurst by Elegant Air	1	5,550.00
	10	32,603.80

WOLVERLIFE (1973) by Wolver Hollow

Lady Loire: Rock The Barney (Ire) by Coquelin (USA)	1	3,036.00
Wolviston: Sie Amato (Ire) by Soughaan (USA)	1	3,209.60
	2	6,245.60

WORDEN II (1949) by Wild Risk

Nanette: Here He Comes by Alzao (USA)	2	6,419.20
	2	6,419.20

WORKBOY (1969) by Firestreak

Bella Travaille: Buzzards Bellbuoy by Buzzards Bay	1	4,793.75
Charming View: Perfect Passion by Clantime	1	2,872.00
	2	7,665.75

YELLOW GOD (1967) by Red God

The Yellow Girl: Mosaic Gold by Sharrood (USA)	1	3,523.50
	1	3,523.50

YOUNG EMPEROR (1963) by Grey Sovereign

Tzaritsa (USA): Imperial Bid (Fr) by No Pass No Sale	3	8,055.50
Young Grace: Yo-Cando (Ire) by Cyrano de Bergerac	1	3,845.25
	4	11,900.75

YOUNG GENERATION (1976) by Balidar

Greek Goddess: Grecian Garden by Sharrood (USA)	1	2,070.00
Helluva Time: Tandia by Superlative	1	4,270.75
Idrak: Recaptured Days (Ire) by Salse (USA)	1	4,378.00
Prejudice: Hob Green by Move Off	1	11,452.50
Prejudice: Al Moulouki by Efisio	5	18,383.30
Que Sympatica: Quaver (USA) by The Minstrel (Can)	1	3,493.00
Texita: Shadow Jury by Doulab (USA)	3	9,116.70
	13	53,164.25

YOUR ALIBHAI (1958) by Alibhai

Witches Alibhai (USA): Pride Of Britain (Can) by Linkage (USA)	1	11,963.00
	1	11,963.00

ZANK (1961) by Neckar

Gamma (Ger): Aegaen Lady by Lochnager	3	8,056.80
	3	8,056.80

ZINO (1979) by Welsh Pageant

Zilda (Fr): Stradishall by Squill (USA)	1	3,757.50
	1	3,757.50

Licensed trainers 1993

The following received licences (valid until January 31, 1994) to train under Rule 50(i)

FLAT RACES AND FOR STEEPLE CHASES, HURDLE RACES AND NATIONAL HUNT FLAT RACES

Aconley, Mrs Vivien Ann
Akehurst, Jonathan
Akehurst, Reginald Peter John
Allan, Adam Richard
Allen, Conrad Norman
Alston, Eric James
Arbuthnot, David William Patrick
Armstrong, Robert Walter
Austin, Mrs Sheila Marion
Avison, Maurice

Bailey, Alan
Bailey, Kim Charles
Baker, Rodney John
Balding, Gerald Barnard
Balding, Ian Anthony
Balding, John
Banks, John Edward
Barker, Mrs Patricia Anne
Barker, William Lindsay
Barr, Ronald Edward,
Barraclough, Melvyn Frederick
Barratt, Lowther James
Barron, Thomas David
Barrow, Arthur Kendall
Barwell, Charles Robin
Bastiman, Robin
Beasley, Benjamin James
Beaumont, Peter
Beever, Charles Richard
Bell, Michael Leopold Wentworth
Bennett, James Anthony
*Bennett, Mrs Muriel Janet
=Bennett, Reginald Anthony
Benstead, Christopher John
Bentley, Walter
Berry, Jack
Bevan, Peter John
Bill, Tom Trivett
Bishop, Kevin Shaun
Blanshard, Michael Thomas William
Bolton, Michael John
Booth, Charles Benjamin Brodie
Bosley, John Read
Boss, Ronald
Bostock, John Raymond
Bottomley, John Frederick
Bower, Miss Lindsay Jane
Bowring, Sidney Roy
Bradburne, Mrs Susan
Bradley, John Milton
Bradstock, Mark Fitzherbert
Bramall, Mrs Susan Angela
Bravery, Giles Colin
Brazington, Robert George
Brennan, Owen
Bridger, John James
Bridgwater, Kenneth Stanley
Brisbourne, William Mark
Brittain, Clive Edward
Brittain, Melvyn Anthony
Broad, Christopher David
Brooks, Charles Patrick Evelyn
Brotherton, Roy
Buckley, Edward Thomas
Burchell, Walter David
Burgoyne, Paul Victor John
Burke, Karl Richard
Butler, Patrick
Bycroft, Neville

Caldwell, Terence Harvey
Callaghan, Neville Anthony
Calver, Peter
Camacho, Maurice James Christopher
Cambidge, Burnup Roy
Campbell, Ian
Campion, Andrew Mark
Candy, Henry Derrick Nicholas Bourne
Carr, John Michael
Casey, William Terence
Cecil, Mrs Julia
Chamberlain, Adrian John
Chamberlain, Norman
Champion, Robert
Channon, Michael Roger
Chapman, David William
Chapman, Michael Christopher
Chappell, Major David Nigel
Chapple-Hyam, Peter William
Charles, Martin John
Charles-Jones, Gareth Francis Hugh
Charlton, John Irving Alistair
*Cheesbrough, Peter Ralph
Christian, Simon Peter Livingstone
Clay, William
†Codd, Liam Joseph
Cole, Paul Frederick Irvine
Collingridge, Hugh John
Cosgrove, David Joseph Simon
Cottrell, Leslie Gerald
Craig, Thomas
Cundell, Peter David
Cunningham, William Scott
Cunningham-Brown Kenneth Owen
Curley, Barney Joseph
Curtis Roger
Cuthbert, Thomas Alexander Keir
Cyzer, Charles Alan

Dalton, Paul Thomas
†Dawe, Mrs Jacqueline Constance
†Denson, Andrew William
Dickin, Robin
Dixon, Mark
Dods, Michael Joseph Keil
Donnelly, Terence William
Dooler, James
Dow, Simon Langley
Doyle, Miss Jacqueline Sophie
Dyer, Thomas Hamilton

†Earnshaw, Robert
Easterby, Michael William
Easterby, Miles Henry
Eckley, Malcolm Willis
Eden, Grant Howard
Edwards, John Andrew Child
Egerton, Charles Ralph
Ellerby, Michael William
Ellison, Brian
Elsey, Charles Clare
Elsey, Charles William Carlton
Elsworth, David Raymond Cecil
Enright, Gerard Patrick
Etherington, James
Evans, Paul David
Eyre, John Leslie

Fahey, Richard Aiden
Fairhurst, Christopher
†Fairhurst, Thomas
Fanshawe, James Robert
Feilden, Peter Jonathan
Felgate, Paul Stanley
Fetherston-Godley, Martin John
Ffitch-Heyes, John Ronald
Fisher, Roger Frederick
FitzGerald, James Gerard
†Fleming, Gordon
Flower, Richard Mark
Forbes, Anthony Leslie
Forsey, Brian
Forster, Captain Timothy Arthur
Forte, Andrew Michael
Foster, Alexander George
†Franks, David Russell
Frost, Richard George

†Gallie, Miss Sarah Louise
Gandolfo, David Rostron
Gaselee, Nicholas Auriol Digby Charles
George, Joshua Thomas
Gifford, Joshua Thomas
Glover, Jeremy Anton
Graham, Neil Anthony
Gubby, Brian

Haggas, William John
Haigh, William Wilson
Haine, Mrs Diana Elizabeth Solna
Haldane, John Swanson
Hall, Miss Sarah Elizabeth
Hallett, Trevor Bertram
Ham, Gerald Antony
Hambly, Albert Adrian
Hammond, Michael David
Hannon, Richard Michael
Hanson, John
Harris, James Lawrence
Harris, Peter Woodstock
Harris, Roger
Harrison, Robert Alan
Harwood, Guy
Haslam, Patrick Charles
Haynes, Michael John
Hayward, Peter Alfred
Heaton-Ellis, Michael James Brabazon
Hedger, Peter Ronald
Henderson, Nicholas John
Hern, Major William Richard
Herries, Lady Anne Elizabeth
Hetherton, James
Hide, Anthony Gatehouse
Hills, Barrington William
Hills, John William
Hoad, Roger Peter Charles
Hobbs, Philip John
Hodges, Ronald James
Hollinshead, Reginald
Holmes, Gordon
Horgan, Cornelius Augustus
Howe, Harry Stuart
Howling, Paul

Ingram, Roger
Ivory, Kenneth Thomas

Jackson, Colin Frederick Charles
James, Anthony Paul
James, Charles John
Jarvis, Alan Peter
Jarvis, Michael Andrew
Jarvis, William
Jefferson, Joseph Malcolm
Jenkins, John Renfield
=Jermy, David Charles
Johnson, John Howard
Johnson Houghton, Richard Fulke
Johnston, Mark Steven

Jones, Anthony Paul
Jones, Arthur Whitfield
†Jones, Christopher Harry
Jones, Derek Haydn
Jones, George Haimer
Jones, Harry Thomson
Jones, Peter John
Jones, Robert Walter
Jones, Thomas Michael
Jones, Timothy Thomson
Jordan, Frank Thomas James
Jordan, Mrs Joan
Juckes, Roderick Thomas

Kelleway, Miss Gay Marie
Kelleway, Paul Anthony
Kelly, Gerald Patrick
Kemp, William Thomas
Kersey, Trevor
Kettlewell, Steven Edward
King, Mrs Anabel Louise Moss
King, Jeffrey Steven
Knight, Mrs Angela Jane
Knight, Miss Henrietta Catherine

Laing, Douglas Raymond
Lamb, Reginald Ridley
Leach, Paul Stephen
Leadbetter, Stephen John
†Lee, Adrian Norris
Lee, Francis Henry
Lee, Richard Anthony
Leight, James Patrick
Lines, Clifford Victor
Long, John Edward
Lungo, Leonard

Macauley, Mrs Norma Jacqueline
Mackie, William John Wilkinson
Madgwick, Michael John
Makin, Peter James
Mann, Charles James
Manning, Robert James
Marks, Douglas
Marvin, Richard Frank
McCain, Donald
McConnochie, John Calvin
McCormack, Matthew
*McCourt, Mrs Mary Elizabeth
=McCourt, Matthew
McEntee, Philip Mathew
McGovern, Thomas Patrick
McKie, Mrs Victoria Jane
McMahon, Bryan Arthur
McMath, Brian James
Meade, Christopher Martyn
Meagher, Michael Gerard
Meehan, Brian John

Mellor, Stanley Thomas Edward
Millman, Brian Roderick
Mills, Terence George
Mitchell, Norman Richard
Mitchell, Patrick Kenneth
Mitchell, Philip
Moffatt, Dudley
Monteith, Peter
Mooney, James William
Moore, Arthur
Moore, Gary Lee
Moore, George Mervin
Moore, James Stanley
Morgan, Barry Clive
Morgan, Kevin Alan
Morley, Michael Frederick David
Morris, David
Muggeridge, Menin Patrick
Muir, William Robert
Murphy, Ferdinand
Murphy, Patrick Gerard
Murray, Brendan William
Murray-Smith, David John George
Musson, William James

Nash, Christopher Thomas
Naughton, Michael Paul
Naughton, Thomas Joseph
Nicholls, Paul Frank
Nicholson, David
Nolan, Dolan Alphonsos
Norton, John
Norton, Stephen Geoffrey

O'Donoghue, Jack
O'Leary, Ronald Martin
O'Mahony, Finbarr Jeremiagh
O'Neill, John Joseph
O'Neill, Owen
O'Shea, John Gerard Martin
O'Sullivan, Roland Jeffrey
Old, James Andrew Bertram
Oldroyd, Geoffrey Reginald
Owen, Jun, Edward Hollister

Palling, Brynley
Parker, Colin
Parkes, John Edwin
Parrott, Mrs Hilary Kay
Payne, John William
Payne, Stanley George
Peacock, John Harris
Peacock, Raymond Eric
Pearce, Jeffrey
Perratt, Miss Linda Agnes
Phillips, Richard Timothy
Pickering, John Alan
Piggott, Mrs Susan Elna

Pipe, Martin Charles
Pitman, Mrs Jennifer Susan
Popham, Christopher Leslie
Potts, Anthony William
Preece, William George
Prescott, Sir Mark
Price, Richard John
Pritchard, Peter Anthony
Pritchard-Gordon, Gavin Alexander

Ramsden, Mrs Lynda Elaine
†Reid, Andrew Stephen
Retter, Mrs Jacqueline Gay
Reveley, Mrs Mary Christiana
Richards, Gordon Waugh
Richmond, Basil Armstrong
Roe, Colin Graeme Algernon Maitland
Rothwell, Brian Samuel
Rowe, Richard
Ryan, Michael John

Sanders, Miss Brooke Virginia Jane
Saunders, Malcolm Sydney
Scargill, Dr Jon David
Scott, Alexander Archibald
†Shaw, Derek
Sherwood, Oliver Martin Carwardine
Sherwood, Simon Edward Harlakenden
Siddall, Miss Lynn Christina
Simpson, Rodney
Smart, Bryan
Smith, Alfred
Smith, Charles
Smith, Craig Anthony
Smith, Denys
Smith, John Peter
Smith, Nigel Alan
Smith, Mrs Susan Jane
Spearing, John Lionel
Spicer, Roger Charles
Stevens, Barry
Storey, Wilfred Luke
Stoute, Michael Ronald
Stringer, Andrew Paul
†Sutcliffe, John Robert Earnshaw
Swinbank, Mrs Ann

Tate, Frederick Martin
Tate, Thomas Patrick
Thom, David Trenchard
Thompson, Ronald
Thompson, Ronald
Thompson, Victor
Thorner, Graham Edward
Thornton, Christopher William

Tinkler, Colin Harwin
Tinkler, Nigel Delfosse
Tompkins, Mark Harding
Trietline, Christopher Charles
Tucker, David Richard
Turnell, Andrew
Turner, William George
Turner, William George Michael
Twiston-Davies, Nigel Anthony

Upson, John Ralph
Usher, Mark Donald Ian

Voorspuy, Rufus

Wainwright, John Stanley
Wall, Christian Frederick
Walwyn, Peter Tyndall
Wane, Martyn
Waring, Mrs Barbara
Watson, Frederick
Weaver, Redvers John
Webber, John Huyshe
Weedon, Colin Victor
Weynes, Ernest
Wharton, John Raymond
†Wheeler, Eric Archibald
Whitaker, Richard Mawson
White, John Raymond
White, Kenneth Brian
Whitfield, Miss Avery Joan
†Wightman, William Gilbert Rowell
Wildman, Christopher Philip
Wilkinson, Benjamin Edwin
Wilkinson, Mark John
Williams, Colin Noel
Williams, David Lyndon
Williams, Michael
Williams, Robert James Royston
Wilson, Andrew James
Wilson, David Adam
Wilson, Captain James Hume
Wilton, Miss Susan Jayne
Wingrove, Kenneth George
Wintle, David John
Woodhouse, Robert Dickson Edgar
Woodman, Stephen
Woods, Sean Peter Charles

Yardley, Francis John
Yardley, George Henry

* Temporary
† Relinquished
= Deceased

RESTRICTED FOR FLAT RACES

Bethell, James David William

Cecil, Henry Richard Amherst
Charlton, Roger John
Cumani, Luca Matteo

†Douglass, George William
Dunlop, John Leeper

Eustace, James Maurice Percy

Gosden, John Harry Martin
Guest, Rae

Hanbury, Benjamin
Hill, Courtney John
Holt, Leonard John
Huntingdon, Lord William Edward Robin Hood

Incisa, Don Enrico

Leach, Melvyn Rawson
Lewis, Geoffrey
Loder, David Richard

McBride, Philip James

O'Gorman, William Andrew

Stewart, Alexander Christie

Toller, James Arthur Richard
Troy, John Martin

Watts, John William
Wigham, Percival
Wragg, Geoffrey
Wright, Nigel Camplyon

† Relinquished

RESTRICTED FOR STEEPLE CHASES, HURDLE RACES AND NATIONAL HUNT FLAT RACES

Alner, Robert Henry
Armytage, Roderick Charles
Ayliffe, Nicholas George

Babbage, Norman Mark
Barclay, James
Barnes, Maurice Allen
Barnett, George William
Barons, David Hawken
Baugh, Brian Philip John
Bell, David John
Birkett, John James
Buckler, Robert Hamilton
†Buckley, Edward Thomas

†Callow, Raymond
Campion, Stephen William
Caroe, Miss Clarissa Janet Elizabeth
Carr, Timothy Julian
Chugg, John
Clarke, Peter Cedric
Coathup, Steven
Coatsworth, Geoffrey Michael Redhead
Cole, Sydney Newman
Colston, Jim
Coogan, Alan Brian

†Cosgrave, James
Cowley, Colin
Davies, Gerald Walter James
De Haan, Benjamin
Drewe, Christopher James
Dunn, Allan John Keith

Eckley, Richard Jones
Eddy, Donald
Esden, Darren
Etherington, Timothy James

Fierro, Giuseppe
†Forte, Andrew Michael
Fowler, Anthony

Garraton, Derek Thomas
†Gillen, John Casey
Goldie, Robert Howie
Goulding, John Lennox
Green, Miss Zoe Ann
Grissell, Delagarde Michael

Hall, Miss Pauline Jane
Hellens, John Alan
Hewitt, Mrs Shirley Anne
Hickman, Mrs Virginia Seaburne

†Honeyball, John
Humphrey, Glen Lawrence
Jewell, Mrs Linda Christine
Jones, Christopher Harry
Jones, Mrs Merrita Anne
Joynes, Mrs Pamela May

Lee, Donald
Llewellyn, Bernard John
Long, Mrs Monica Elizabet

MacTaggart, Alexander Bruce
Mann, Wilmer George
McCune, David
McDonald, Robert
McNeill, Michael Patrick
Mullins, James William

†Nolan, Donal Alphonsus

Oliver, James Kenneth Murray

†Peacock, John Harris
Poulton, Julian Charles
Price, William James

Reed, William George
Renfree-Barons, Mrs Jenifer Rose
Richards, Mrs Lydia
Ritchens, Paul Cyril
Rodford, Patrick Reginald

Scudamore, Michael John
Sharpe, Mrs Nicola Susan Aileen
Sly, Mrs Pamela Marigold

Tate, Robin
Taylor, Mrs Susan
Thomson, Mrs Dorothy
Thomson, Neil Barrett

†Vernon, Miller, Charles John

†Walwyn, Mrs Catherine
Williams, Mrs Sarah Daphne
†Willis, Henry
Wonnacott, Mrs Joan

† Relinquished

Permit trainers: hurdles and chases

Permits to train for steeplechases, hurdle races and National Hunt Flat races for the season 1993-94 under Rule 50(ii) of the Rules of Racing

Adam, James Raleigh
Alder, Derek Stanley
Alexander, Hamish Harold Ferguson
Allen, John Scot
Allison, Miss Kimberly Susan
Andrews, Jack
Avery, Steven Bryan
Aylett, Alan Robert

Banks, Michael Charles
Barber, George Harrison
Baring, Peter
Barton, Frank Marshall
Barton, Roger Ben
Bassett, David Francis
Bell, Charles Henry Pearson
Berry, Miss Nicky
Bishop, Vivian Roger
Bissill, William Henry
Black, Mrs Charmian Jennifer
Blackmore, Alan Grenville
Bloom, Mrs Beryl Marguerite
Bloomfield, David Earnest Frank
Bousfield, Bryan
Bowlby, Lady Anne Lavinia Maud
Bradley, Paul
Brewis, Robert
Brooks, Mrs Elizabeth Mary
Brown, David Henry
Brown, Reginald Leslie
Browning, Denis Walter
Brunt, Mrs Barbara

Caine, Edward Malcolm
Callow, Raymond
Cantillon, Donald Edward
Carey, Derek Norman
Carr Evans, Mrs Jeanette Ann
Carroll, Edward Patrick
Chadwick, Stephen George
Chesney, Dr David
Churches, Maxwell Robert
Clutterbuck, Kenneth Frank
†Coathup, Steven
Cole, Henry Toogood
Collins, Richard
Coton, Frank
Cottrell, Anthony Jesse
Cresswell, John Kenneth Silvers
Criddle, Jason Vaughan
Curtis, John William Parker

Dean, Richard
Dennis, Paul Jeffrey
Dennis, Walter William
Dixon, John Edward
Dowson, Mrs Pauline Angela
Dun, Thomas Dixon Connochie
Dutfield, Mrs Pauline Nerys

Eckley, Brian John
Edwards, Gordon Francis
†Emery, Richard William
England, Miss Evelyn Mary Victoria
Evans, Richard Rhys

Farr, Mrs Shan Margaret
Fletcher, Desmond Edward

George, Miss Karen Mary
Gibson, Thomas Metclafe
Giddings, Gordon Wilfrid
Gledson, James Lewis
Goldie, James Sloan
Gollings, Stephen
Goodfellow, Mrs Anne Cicely Dawn
Graham, George Robert
Gray, Frederick
Griffiths, Sirrell George

Hamilton, Mrs Ann
Harriman, John
Haynes, Hedley Edward
Haynes, Jonathan Charles
Henderson, Mrs Rosemary Gillian
Hiatt, Peter William
Hope, John Wallace
Horler, Miss Carol Jane
Hubbuck, John Sidney

Jeffrey, Terence Edward
Jenks, William Percival
Johnsey, Miss Clair
Johnson, Robert William
Johnson, Mrs Susan Mary
Jones, Daniel Gethin
Jones, Gruffydd Elwyn
Jones, Ivor Reginald
Joseph, Jack

Kavanagh, Henry Michael
Kendall, Mrs Margaret Ann
Kinsey, Thomas Richard
Kirby, John

Lamb, Mrs Kathleen Margaret
Lamyman, Mrs Susan
Laxton, Trevor
Le Blond, Alan James
Ledger, Roger Roy
Linton, Kenneth Alexander
Llewellyn, William Brinley
Lloyd, Frank
Lloyd, Melvin Anthony
MacTaggart, Alan Harry
Manners, Herbert John
Mason, Norman Beresford
Mathew, Robert Knox
Mays-Smith, Lady Elizabeth Maria
McInnes Skinner, Mrs Caroline Ann Patricia
McKenzie-Coles, William George
McMillan, Malcolm Douglas
Middleton, Mrs Charmain Winifred
Miller, Norman
Minty, Desmond John
Mitchell, Colin Walter
Morton, Thomas
Moscrop, Mrs Edna

Neaves, Albert Stanley
Needham, John Lees
Nelson, Walter Maxwell

O'Brien, Daniel Christopher
O'Neill, John Gerard

Panvert, John Francis
Park, Ian
Patman, Miss Rebecca Jane
Pilkington, Mrs Jane St Clare
Pilkington, John
Pincombe, Roy William
Pinney, Charles William
Pitman, Miss Susan
Pittendrigh, Stewart Ian
Plater, Ms Linda Christine
Plowright, Mrs Gillian Susan
Price, Mrs Ann
Price, George Michael
Price, Trevor John
Prince, Oswald Roy
Pritchard, Dr Philip Leslie James
Pugh, Roger Charles

Rae, Miss Jacqueline Louise
Raw, William
Reed, William John
Rich, Paul Michael
Richards, Graham
Robertson, David
Roe, Graham Leonard
Russell, Mrs Ailsa
Ryall, Bertram John Miller

Salmon, Peter
Sawyer, Harry
Scott, Mrs Elizabeth Beryl
Scriven, Bernard Anthony Victor
Scrivens, Mrs Janet
Shaw, Bernard
Sheridan, Felix
Slack, Mrs Doris Evelyn
Smith, Francis Godwin
Smith, Malcolm James
Smith, Samuel George
Smith, William James Frederick
Spottiswood, Philip
Stickland, Gordon William
Stirk, Mrs Maxine Katrina
Stone, Richard Frank
Storey, Frederick Stalker
Stronge, Robert Maynard
Swiers, Joseph Edward
Swindlehurst, Derek Gordon

Taylor, Alan John
Taylor, Mrs Lavinia Clare
Temple, Bruce Michael
Tetley, Mrs Pamela Ann
Thomson, Alexander Moffat
Threadgall, Francis John
Tinning, William Hodge
Tomkinson, Mrs Antoinette
Tuck, John Colin
Tucker, Donald Charles
Tucker, Frederick George
Turner, Dennis Terence
Turner, James Richard

Wade, John
Waggott, Norman
Waley-Cohen, Robert Bernard
Walton, Frank Teasdale
Walton, Mrs Kathleen
Ward, Mrs Valerie Claire
Wareham, George Albert
Waterman, Miss Susan Elizabeth
Webb, Henry John Montague
Wellicombe, Derek Roy
Welsh, David Daniel George
Whillans, Alistair Charles
Whillans, Donald Wilson
White, George Francis
Whyte, John William
Williams, David Gwyn
Williams, Mrs Frances Ann Wilson
Winkworth, Peter Leslie
Wood, Robert Stuart
Wordingham, Leonard Walter

Young, Basil Roger James

† Relinquished

Licensed Flat race jockeys and weights 1993

The following received licences (valid until March 17th, 1994) to ride in flat races under Rule 60(i)

Adams, Nicolas Mark 7 7
Avery, Christopher Manuel 7 8

Ballantine, Harry 7 7
Bardwell, Gary Stephen 7 7
Baxter, Geoffrey Edward 8 2
Berry, Raymond John 8 3
Biggs, Darren Derek 7 10
Birch, Mark 8 3
Bowker, Miss Julie 7 7

Carlisle, Nicholas Anthony 7 8
Carroll, John 8 2
Carson, William Fisher Hunter 7 10
†Carter, Gary Alan 7 13
Charnock, Lindsay 7 9
Clark, Anthony Stephen 8 2
Cochrane, Raymond 8 6
Comber, James 8 4
Connorton, Nicholas Brian 8 0
Crossley, Bryn 7 13
Culhane, Patrick Anthony 8 2
Curant, John Arthur 7 13

D'arcy, Paul William 8 2
Darley, Kevin Paul 8 0
Dawson, Steven 7 9
Day, Nigel Patrick 8 2
Dettori, Lanfranco 8 5
Dicks, Andrew Craig 8 4
Duffield, George Peter 8 0
Dwyer, Christopher Ambrose 8 7

Eddery, Patrick James John 8 4
Eddery, Paul Anthony 8 0
Elliott, Robert Peter 8 0

Fallon, Keiran Francis 8 2
Fanning, Joseph Kevin 7 8
Fortune, James Joseph 8 2

Geran, Anthony John 7 9
Gibson, Dale 7 9
Greaves, Miss Alex Ann 8 1

†Hillis, Ronald Patrick 8 3
Hills, Michael Patrick 8 0
Hills, Richard John 8 0
Hind, Gary Edward Patrick 8 0
Holland, Darryll Paul 8 0
Hood, Walter 8 4
Houston, Miss Jacqueline 7 7

†Johnson, Ernest 7 7

†Kelleway, Miss Gay Marie 8 2
Kent, Terence John 10 0

Lang, Thomas Luke 8 2
Lappin, Rodney Thomas 8 0
Lowe, John Joseph 7 8
Lucas, Terry George 8 5

MacKay, Allan 7 9
McDonnell, Miss Kim Susan 7 7
McGlone, Anthony David 7 12
McKeown, Dean Russell 8 2
†McLaughlin, John Fletcher Stephen 8 7
Morris, Allan 8 0
Morris, Mrs Candida Louise 8 0
Morris, Stuart David 8 0
Munro, Alan Keith 7 12
Murray, John Gerard 8 3

Newnes, William Anthony Paul 8 3
†Nicholls, David 8 7
Nutter, Colin 8 0

O'Gorman, Seamus Mark 7 10
O'Reilly, James Francis Patrick 6 13

Perham, Richard Andrew 8 2
Perks, Stephen James 8 6
Perrett, Mark Edward 9 0
Piggott, Lester Keith 8 6
Price, Russell Wayne 7 12
Procter, Brian Thomas 8 3
Proud, Alan 7 10

Quinn, James Anthony 7 7
Quinn, Thomas Richard 8 2

Raymond, Bruce Hunter 8 5
Raymont, Stephen John 7 13
Reid, John Andrew 8 6
Roberts, Michael Leonard 8 0
Robinson, Philip Peter 8 2
Rogers, Trevor 8 6
Rouse, Brian Albert 8 3
Rutter, Christopher Louis Peter 7 10
Ryan, William 8 2

Shoults, Adam Francis 8 0
Slattery, John Vincent 8 7
Smith, Vince 10 0
Sprake, Timothy Joseph 7 11
Stokell, Miss Ann 9 7
Street, Robert 7 7
Swinburn, Walter Robert John 8 6

Tebbutt, Michael John 8 5
Tinkler, Mrs Kim Ann 7 7
Tucker, Andrew Patrick 7 10

Vincent, Miss Lorna Jayne 9 0

Wall, Trevor Richard 9 0
Webster, Stuart Graham 8 3
Wernham, Roger Alan 8 5
Whitworth, Simon John 8 0
Wigham, Michael 8 4
Wilkinson, David 9 7
Williams, John Albert Norman 8 3
Williams, Stephen David 8 4
Williams, Tyrone Leonard 7 9
Williamson, Kevin 8 0
Wilson, Timothy George Albert 7 7
Wood, Michael 8 0
Wood, Stephen 7 7
Woods, Eric Wendyll Joseph 8 2

† Relinquished

Flat race apprentices with masters 1993

The following received licences (valid until March 17th, 1994) to ride for flat races under Rule 60(iii)

†Adams, Robert Nicholas (Mr Michael Bell) 7 12
Adamson, Corey Neil (Mr P C Haslam) 7 0
Ahern, Miss Kate Emma (Mr J L Dunlop) 7 7
Allen, Stuart James (Mr M H Tompkins) 7 10
Armes, Miss Antoinette Carol (Mr Henry Candy) 7 0
Ashley, Thomas Lawton (Mr R Akehurst) 7 10
Aspell, Leighton (Mr R Hollinshead) 7 4

Baird, Mark James (Mr M J Ryan) 7 0
Balding, Miss Claire (Mr John Balding) 7 2
Bastiman, Harvey James (Mr Robin Bastiman) 8 5
Beaver, Thomas Harry (Mr M J Ryan) 8 0
†Berry, Ross Keith (Mr D R C Elsworth) 8 0
Biggs, Miss Debra Delores Marie (Mr Paul Howling) 8 0
Bowe, Paul David Patrick (Mr D J S Cosgrove) 7 12
Bradley, Michael (Mr J M Bradley) 7 8
Bramhill, John Alexander (Mr B A McMahon) 7 3
Branton, Grant John (Mr G Harwood) 8 4
Bream, Miss Rebecca (Mr R J Weaver) 7 6
Bridger, Miss Rachel Jane (Mr J J Bridger) 8 7
†Brookwood, Paul John (Mr R J Manning) 7 9
Byrnes, Miss Clare Samantha (Mr J D Bethell) 9 0

Cairns, Alexander (Mr James Fanshawe) 8 0
†Carson, Derek Alexander (Mr R Hollinshead) 8 3
Carter, Lee Anthony (Mr R Akehurst) 7 10
Cook, Miss Aimee Virginia (Mr P F I Cole) 7 10
Copp, Shane Lee (Mrs M Reveley) 8 0
Coulter, Miss Ruth Elizabeth (Mr J Berry) 7 2
Curran, Sean (Miss Jacqueline S Doyle) 9 7

Daly, Alan Thomas (Mr P F I Cole) 7 0
Davies, Stephen Glyn (Mr P W Chapple-Hyam) 7 12
Davison, Miss Carol Ann (Mrs A Swinbank) 7 7
Denaro, Mark (Mr R Hannon) 7 13
Denaro, Michael Joseph (Mr L M Cumani) 8 2
Denby, Derek James (Mr R Hollinshead) 7 2
Dennis, Jonathan Paul (Mr R Hollinshead) 7 7
Devlin, Paul (Mr J A R Toller) 7 10
Dovey, Miss Kate (Mr P W Chapple-Hyam) 7 8
Doyle, Brett (Mr C E Brittain) 7 9
Drake, Stephen Tony (Mr Henry Candy) 7 10
Drowne, Steven John (Mr R J Hodges) 7 11
Dwyer, Martin Joseph (Mr I A Balding) 7 0
Dykes, Craig (Mr A C Stewart) 7 7

East, Brett Garry (Mr L J Holt) 7 10
Eblet, Glyn Gary (Mr Jeff Pearce) 7 7
Eddery, Allan Mark (Mr R Hollinshead) 7 4
Edmunds, Jason Paul (Mr John Balding) 7 12
Eiffert, Scott (Mr Rae Guest) 8 0

Faulkner, Gavin (Mr W J Musson) 8 4
†Faulkner, Miss Gina (Mr M McCormack) 7 7
Fenton, Michael (Mr Michael Bell) 7 12
Fessey, Paul John (Mr J Berry) 6 8
Fitchett, Miss Karron Louise (Mr Henry Candy) 8 0
Forster, Gary (Mr C N Allen) 7 12
Fuggle, Timothy James (Mr John R White) 7 12

Gallimore, Miss Angela (Mr A Bailey) 7 0
Garth, Anthony Raymond (Mr R Hollinshead) 7 7
Gent, Miss Rhona Jane (Mr R J Charlton) 7 0
†Gibbons, Miss Adelle Louise (Capt James Wilson) 7 2
Gibbs, Daniel (Mr R Hannon) 7 12
Giles, Simon Mark (Mr William Haggas) 8 8
†Goggin, Declan (Mr P F I Cole) 7 6
Gotobed, Jamie Lee (Mr M H Tompkins) 7 11
Gracey, Jason Gerard (Mr P C Haslam) 8 0
Grantham, Ian (Mr A Harrison) 7 4
Greehy, Enda Patrick (Mr R Hannon) 7 0
Griffiths, David Charles (Mr I A Balding) 7 9
Gwilliams, Neil Lee (Mr T G Mills) 7 7

Halliday, Vincent (Mr T D Barron) 7 9
Handley, Mark John (Mr Henry Candy) 8 0
Harris, Michael Patrick (Mr A A Hambly) 8 3
Harrison, David Paul (Lord Huntingdon) 7 10
Hart, Miss Kimberley (Mr T D Barron) 7 5
Harwood, Miss Gaye Michelle (Mr G Harwood) 8 0
Havlin, Robert (Miss L A Perratt) 7 7
Hawksley, Carl Leonard (Mr H J Collingridge) 7 3
Hawksley, Wayne Andrew (Mr A Bailey) 7 6
Henry, Matthew Philip (Mr J W Hills) 7 2
Hodgson, Carl Andrew (Mr L M Cumani) 8 2
Holland, Miss Sarah (Mr Henry Candy) 7 13
Hollick, William John (Mr A Bailey) 7 13
Houghton, Philip (Mr G Harwood) 8 7
Howarth, Miss Nicola (Mr P C Haslam) 7 7
Hughes, Ian Michael (Mr D R Loder) 8 0
Humphries, Mark Brian (Mr R Hollinshead) 7 7
Hunnam, Miss Jo (Mr L M Cumani) 7 6
Hunt, Michael (Mr C A Cyzer) 7 12
†Hunter, Jason John (Mr D R C Elsworth) 9 0
Husband, Eugene Llewellyn (Mr N Tinkler) 9 7

Jacobs, Miss Lisa Ann (Mr H T Jones) 7 10
James, Shaun Patrick (Mr C A Cyzer) 7 10
†Jardine, Iain James (Mr M P Naughton) 8 0
Jermy, Matthew (Mr T J Naughton) 7 12
Johnson, Paul Andrew (Mr M W Easterby) 9 7
Jones, Shane Anthony (Mr William Jarvis) 7 7
Jones, Miss Wendy Jayne (Mr R Hannon) 7 0

Kennedy, Neil Armstrong (Mr F H Lee) 7 7
Kinnon, Neil (Mrs S C Bradburne) 7 4
Knott, Stephen Thomas (Mr E J Alston) 8 2

Lakeman, Andrew (Mr B J Meehan) 7 10
†Lanigan, Stuart (Mr Bill Turner) 7 4
Liggins, Andrew (Mr S P C Woods) 7 5
†Llewellyn, Carl (Mr David W Chapman) 7 10

Maloney, Stephen James (Mr M H Easterby) 7 10
Marsden, Tony (Mr S G Norton) 8 1
Marshall, Jeffrey (Mr M D Hammond) 7 10
Martinez, Antonio Luis (Mr S Dow) 7 10
McCabe David Robert (Mr W J Musson) 7 8
McCabe, Patrick Antony (Mr M J Ryan) 7 7
McCarthy, Sean Bernard (Mr B W Hills) 7 3
McCord, Tony (Mr R J Charlton) 7 12
McGann, Barry Thomas (Mr J J O'Neill) 7 12
McGrath, George Joseph (Mr A P Jarvis) 9 7
McLaughlin, Thomas Gary (Mr P F I Cole) 7 12

FLAT RACE APPRENTICES WITH MASTER 1993

Meredith, Dylan (Mr Robin Dickin) 9 5
Millard, Miss Sharon Camilla (Mr D A Wilson) 7 0
Milligan, Gary Edward Hunter (Mrs Lester Piggott) 7 6
Milligan, Miss Hazel (Mr A A Scott) 7 4
Mills, Garry (Mr C W Thornton) 7 0
†Mitchell, Gary Carlton (Mr Ian Campbell) 7 9
Moffatt, Darren (Mrs M Reveley) 7 0
Mulvey, Sean (Mr M H Tompkins) 7 11
Munday, Colin Joseph Arthur (Mr M W Easterby) 7 11

Newton, Lee (Mr D J S Cosgrove) 7 7
Norton, Francis (Mr G Wragg) 7 7

O'Dwyer, John Joseph (Mr Michael Bell) 7 10
O'Gorman, Miss Emma Samantha (Mr W A O'Gorman) 8 4
O'Neill, Dane William (Mr R Hannon) 7 7

Painter, Richard Bentley (Mr M Channon) 8 2
Parkin, Gyles (Mr R M Whitaker) 7 13
†Pattinson, Kenneth (Mr M R Stoute) 8 1
†Payne, Matthew (Mr G Lewis) 8 7
Pears, Oliver John (Mr S G Norton) 8 0
Plowright, Miss Marie (Mrs Angela Knight) 7 9
Procter, Anthony Richard (Mr Charles Egerton) 8 9
Proctor, Michael Paul (Mr S E Kettlewell) 7 7
Purseglove, Miss Tracey Nicolle (Mr D R C Elsworth) 8 7

Radford-Howes, Miss Sally (Mr W Haggas) 7 0
Roberts, Paul Brian (Mr J Berry) 7 9
Rose, Patrick Desmond (Mr K O Cunningham-Brown) 8 0
Rothwell, Garry (Mr Rod Simpson) 7 4
Russell, Brian James (Mr R Akehurst) 7 9
Rutter, Keith (Mr M A Jarvis) 8 0

Salt, Danny (Lord Huntingdon) 7 10
Sanders, Sebastian (Mr B A McMahon) 7 9
Savage, Finnbarr Michael (Mr R Hollinshead) 7 0
Scally, Christopher (Mr K T Ivory) 8 5
Scudder, Christopher (Mr I A Balding) 8 0
Senior, Miss Sarah Louise (Mr J A Glover) 8 3
Sked, Keith Philip (Mr J D Bethell) 7 2
Smith, Joesph Damian (Mr C A Cyzer) 7 10
Smith, Miss Madeleine Joy (Mrs N Macauley) 7 7
Strange, Graham (Mr S R Bowring) 7 13
Suthern, Lee (Mr J Spearing) 7 7

Tate, Jason Darran (Mr A A Scott) 7 9
Teague, Colin (Mr Denys Smith) 7 0
Thomas, Byron (Mr B Palling) 8 0
Thomas, Darren (Mrs J R Ramsden) 8 2
Thomas, Miss Michelle (Mr Robin Dickin) 7 7
†Thomas, Troy Nathan (Mr C A Cyzer) 7 0
Thompson, Miss Sarah Elizabeth (Mr R J R Williams) 8 0
Toole, Dominic John (Mr M J Haynes) 7 2
Turner, Miss Elizabeth Marie (Mr Jeff Pearce) 7 7

Varley, Neil Gareth (Mr J Fanshawe) 7 5

Wall, Miss Sally Elizabeth (Mr J R Jenkins) 7 7
Wands, Miss Iona Jane Claire (Mr L J Holt) 7 7
†Waterfield, Robert John (Mr P G Murphy) 7 7
Weaver, Jason Charles (Mr L M Cumani) 7 13
†Webb, Charles (Mr P J Makin) 7 12
West, Miss Claire Christine (Mr R R Lamb) 7 7
Whelan, Anthony William Emanuel (Mr R Hannon) 7 5
Wilkinson, Jason (Lord Huntingdon) 7 0
Williams, John Alan (Mr R Bastiman) 7 10
Wright, Daniel Thomas (Mr A Bailey) 7 0
Wynne, Stephen (Mr R Hollinshead) 9 0

† Relinquished

Licensed jockeys: hurdles and chases

Licensed to ride in steeplechases and hurdle races for the season 1993–94 under Rule 60(ii) of the Rules of Racing

Ahern, Maurice John 10 0
Akehurst, James Charles 10 2
Armytage, Miss Gaye 9 7

Beggan, Ronald John 10 2
Bellamy, Robert John 10 0
Bosley, Martin Read 10 3
Bradley, Graham John 10 2
Brennan, Martin Joseph 10 0
Bridgwater, David George 9 9
Burchell, David John 10 0
Burrough, Simon Charles 10 1
Byrne, Derek Cyril 10 0
Byrne, Edmond Martin 10 0

Caldwell, Patrick Andrew 10 2
Caldwell, Peter Harvey 10 2
Callaghan, Jason Glen 10 0
Campbell, Ross 10 1
Carroll, Anthony William 10 0
Charlton, Anthony 10 0
Clay, Miss Diane Lorna 10 0
Clifford, Brian Martin 9 7
Coogan, Alan Brian 10 7
Corkell, Jeremy Dexter 10 1
Crosse, Matthew Joseph 10 1

Dalton, Bernard Patrick 10 0
Davies Hywel James 10 3
Dawe, Nicholas John 10 0
Dennis, Christopher Peter 10 0
Doughty, David Neale 10 6
Duggan, James Daniel 10 4
Dunwoody, Thomas Richard 10 1
Dwyer, Mark Peter 10 3

Earle, Simon Alexander 10 0
Elderfield, William Gerald 10 0

Fitzgerald, Michael Anthony 10 0
Foster, Martin Robin 10 0
Frost, James Douglas 10 4

Gallagher, Dean Thomas 10 0
Garritty, Russell John 10 1
Grant Christopher 10 0
Grantham, Thomas O'Dell 10 0
Guest, Richard Charles 10 1

Harker, Geoffrey Alan 10 0
Harley, Paul Martin 10 0
Harris, John Arthur 10 0
Harvey, Lucien John 10 0
Hawke, Nigel John 10 0
Hawkins, Colin 10 0
Hoad, Mark Richard 10 1
Hobbs, Peter David 10 0
Hodge, Robert James 9 10
Hodgson, Simon Paul 10 0
Holley, Paul Stephen 9 10
Humphreys, William George 10 0

Irvine, Wallace Samuel 9 7

Jarvis, Timothy Owen 10 0
Jenkins, Howard, Lyndon 10 0
Johnson, Kenneth 10 0
Jones, Alan Edward 10 0
Jones, Kevin 10 2

Kavanagh, John Robert 9 7
Keightley, Shaun Leonard 10 0
Kent, Terence John 10 0
Kersey, Miss Susan 9 10
Knox, Wayne David Robert 10 10

Lawrence, Ian Russell 9 7
Leech, Jonathan Peter 10 0
Leech, Patrick Joseph 10 0
Llewellyn, Carl 10 0
Long, Miss Leesa Georgina 9 7
Lower, Jonothan Amnest 10 0
Lyons, Gary 10 0

Mackey, Seamus Christopher 10 0
Maguire, Adrian 10 0
Mann, Nicholas James William 10 0
Marley, Roger John 10 0
Maude, Christopher George 10 0
McCabe, Alan Joseph 9 7
McCourt, Graham Matthew 10 5
McDermott, Peter Simon 10 0
McFarland, William John 10 0
McKeown, Dale Walter Edward 9 12
McKinley, Eamon Mathew 9 9
McNeill, Simon Robert Onslow 10 0
Merrigan, Alan Tyrone Anthony 10 0
Moloney, Michael John 10 0
Morgan, Gary Paul 9 7
Morris, Derrick 10 0
Mulholland, Anthony Bernard 10 0
Murphy, Declan Joseph 10 0
Murphy, Eamon Robert 10 0

Niven, Peter David 10 2

O'Hagan, Anthony Trevor 10 0
O'Hara, Liam Stuart 10 0
Oliver, Miss Jacqueline 10 0
Orkney, Robert Andrew 10 0
Osborne, James Anthony 10 0

Perrett, Mark Edward 9 0
†Pitman, Mark Andrew 10 5
Powell, Brendan Gerard 9 7

Railton, James Andrew 10 2
Ranger, Mark 10 0
Reed, William Timothy 10 3
Richards, Mark Robert 9 12
Robinson, Michael Ian 10 0
Rowe, Geoffrey Thomas 10 0
Rowell, Roger 10 3
Ryan, John Barry 10 0

Sharratt, Mark Raymond 10 0
Shoemark, Ian William 10 0
Skyrme, David Vaughan 10 0
Smith, Adrian Stewart 10 0
Smith, Charles Nicholas 10 0
Smith, Vince 10 0
Smith Eccles, Stephen 10 4
Stokell, Miss Ann 9 7
Storey, Brian 10 0
Supple, Robert John 10 0

Telfer, David Mark 10 2
Tory, Anthony Stewart 10 0
Turner, Stuart 10 0
Turner, Miss Tracy Jean 9 7

Upton, Guy 10 1

Vincent, Miss Lorna Jayne 9 0

Wall, Trevor Richard 9 0
†Webb, Allen 10 0
Wilkinson, David 9 7
Williams, Stephen David 8 4
Williamson, Norman 10 0
Worthington, William Martin 10 0
Wright, Barrie John 10 10
Wyer, Lorcan Andrew 10 0

† Relinquished

Conditional jockeys

Licensed to ride in steeplechases, hurdle races and National Hunt Flat races for the season 1993–94 under Rule 60(iv) of the Rules of Racing

Bates, Aaron (Mr P A Kelleway) 9 9
Bentley, David Branwell (Mr M D Hammond) 9 9
Bentley, Nicholas Andrew (Mr G M Moore) 9 11
Berry, Martin (Mr C P E Brooks) 10 2
†Bohan, David Joseph (Mrs J Pitman) 9 7
Bond, Justin Matthew (Mr J H Peacock) 9 5
Braybrook, Miss Tanya Jane (Mr A M Forte) 9 7
Brown, Kevin (Mr A J Wilson) 9 7
Burke, John Henry (Mrs S A Bramwell) 10 2
Burnett-Wells, Charles Peregrine (Mr R Rowe) 9 10

Cahill, Gearoid Patrick (Mr B Rothwell) 9 7
Carey, Philip Denis (Mr R Alner) 9 7
Carr, Paul Anderson (Mr R Collins) 9 7
Clarke, Jonathan (Mr A Moore) 9 10
Comerford, Kenneth Christopher (Mr J R White) 10 0
Crone, Gary Steven (Mr R Curtis) 9 0
Curran, John Martin (rides as Sean) (Miss J S Doyle) 9 7
Cuthbert, Miss Carol (Mr T A K Cuthbert) 9 0

Dace, Luke Adam (Mr R Rowe) 9 7
Darke, Edward Ross (Mr R G Frost) 10 0
Dascombe, Thomas Geoffrey (Mr M C Pipe) 9 7
Davies, John Joseph (Mrs M Reveley) 9 10
Davies, Miss Judith Anne (Mr M J Charles) 9 7
Davies, Keith (Mr R O'Leary) 9 7
Davis, Miss Katherine Jane (Mr C James) 9 7
Davis, Richard John (Mr G B Balding) 9 10
Dicken, Anthony Robert (Mr S Dow) 9 12
Dobbin, Anthony Gerald (Mr M Barnes) 9 11
Downs, Nicholas Harleigh (Mr C L Popham) 9 7
Doyle, Mark Anthony (Mr F Jordan) 9 7
Driscoll, John Paul (Mr M W Easterby) 9 10
Dwan, William Joseph (Mr J G FitzGerald) 10 0

Edwards, Richard (Mr D McCain) 9 7
Eldredge, Miss Leanne Carol (Mr R Lee) 9 7
Eley, Timothy James (Mr T Forbes) 9 9

Farrant, Rodney Alan (Capt T A Forster) 9 9
Fitzgerald, Michael Paul (Mr M Bradstock) 9 7
Flannigan, Alexander Moor (Mr C D Broad) 9 7
Fortt, Daniel Lloyd (Mr A Turnell) 10 0
Fry, William Stanley (Mr T P Tate) 9 7

Goble, Karl Rowan (Mr A Moore) 9 7
Greene, Roderick Joseph (Mr P Nicholls) 10 0

Harding, Brian Patrick (Mr G Richards) 9 7
Haworth, Steven Michael (Mr J Berry) 9 7
Herrington, Michael (Mrs M Reveley) 9 7
Hide, Philip Edward (Mr J T Gifford) 9 11
Hobbs, David Mark (Mr P Nicholls) 9 4
Hourigan, Michael Patrick (Mr P J Hobbs) 9 7
Huggan, Colin Henry (Mrs Diana Haine) 9 10
Hunter, Jason John (Mr D R C Elsworth) 9 0
Husband, Eugene Llewellyn (Mr N Tinkler) 9 7

James, James Llewellyn Davies (Mr J R Upson) 9 2
Jenks, Tom Percival (Mr N A Twiston-Davies) 9 9
Johnson, Paul Andrew (Mr M W Easterby) 9 7
Juckes, Neil Roderick (Mr K R Burke) 9 7

Larnach, Andrew Alexander (Mr J A Hellens) 9 11
Leach, Neil Richard (Mr G Richards) 9 7
Leahy, Denis (Mr S Christian) 9 9
Leahy, Finbarr Timothy (Mr J G FitzGerald) 9 7
Linton, Alan (Mr T Dyer) 9 7
Lycett, Shaun (Mr G Fierro) 9 7
Lyons, Shane Christopher (Mr M D Hammond) 9 10

Maddock, Patrick James (Mr O O'Neill) 9 7
Marston, Warren John (Mr David Nicholson) 9 7
Mason, Scott Thomas (Mrs M Reveley) 9 7
Massey, Robert Ian (Mr David Nicholson) 9 7
Matthews, David Donald (Mr P G Murphy) 9 12
McCarthy, James Andrew (Mr O M C Sherwood) 9 9
McDougall, Stephen James (Mr W T Kemp) 9 7
McGrath, George Joseph (Mr A P Jarvis) 9 7
McLoughlin, Patrick Joseph (Mr J R White) 9 7
Meade, Dermot Nessan (Mr T Thomson Jones) 9 7
Melia, Paul Christopher (Mr S Christian) 9 7
Meredith, Dylan (Mr Robin Dickin) 9 5
Midgley, Paul Thomas (Mr J S Wainwright) 10 5
Moffatt, Dudley James (Mr D Moffatt) 9 10
Moore, Peter Andrew (Mr J S Moore) 9 7
Moore, Robert William (Mr O Brennan) 9 9
Munday, Marc Darren (Mr N J Henderson) 9 7
Murphy, Barry John (Mr F Murphy) 10 0
Murphy, Paul Thomas James (Mr F Murphy) 9 7
Murphy, Thomas Cyril (Mr Bill Turner) 9 7

Naughton, Paul John (Mr A P Jarvis) 9 10
Neaves, John Paul (Mr N B Thomson) 9 7

O'Hare, Lee Noel Paul (Mrs J Pitman) 9 7
O'Sullivan, Darren Kenneth (Mr R J O'Sullivan) 10 4

Parker, Neal (Mr P J Hobbs) 9 7
Perratt, William Fraser (Mr L Lungo) 9 7
Procter, Anthony Richard (Mr C Egerton) 8 9

Reynolds, Leslie Richard (Mr M C Pipe) 9 7
Rice, John Anthoney (Miss Sue Wilton) 10 0
Richmond, David Sean (Mr M C Pipe) 9 7
Roberts, Mark Anthony (Mr S E Kettlewell) 9 7
Robertson, Gregory Neil (Mr B A McMahon) 9 7
Ryan, Diarmuid Anthony (Mrs M Reveley) 9 7
Ryan, Shane (Mr R Akehurst) 9 7

Salter, Darren Geoffrey (Mr B R Millman) 9 7
Sellars, Miss Kate (Mr M D Hammond) 9 7
Shakespeare, Adam Lee (Mr N A Twiston-Davies) 9 0
Slattery, John Vincent (Mr Owen O'Neill) 8 7
Smith-Eccles, Paul (Mr M H Tompkins) 10 0
Stevens, Mark (Mr Barry Stevens) 10 0
Stocks, Neil Andrew (Mr G M Moore) 10 0

Supple, John Anthony (Mr N B Mason) 9 7

Taylor, Scott Duncan (Mr W Bentley) 9 7

Thompson, Patrick Aiden (Mr N J Henderson) 9 7

Thompson, Timothy Peter (Mr R J Hodges) 9 7

Thornton, Andrew Robert (Mr K C Bailey) 10 0

Tormey, Glenn Eugene (Mr J G FitzGerald) 9 7

Towler, Damian Lee (Mrs S Smith) 9 7

Waggott, Peter (Mr Denys Smith) 9 9

Walsh, David John (Mr D McCain) 9 7

Ward, Peter Daniel (Mr Mark Wilkinson) 9 7

Wilkinson, Richard David James (Mrs S Smith) 9 7

Williams, Paul David (Mrs S C Bradburne) 10 0

Woodall, Christopher (Mrs V A Aconley) 9 9

Wynne, Stephen (Mr R Hollinshead) 9 0

† Relinquished

Restricted conditional jockeys

Restricted to Conditional jockey races and National Hunt Flat races for the season 1993–94.

Appleby, Michael (Mrs V S Hickman) 9 7

Becton, Toby James (Mr Bill Turner) 9 7

Brand, Miss Lorna Elizabeth (Mrs P Sly) 8 12

Burrows, Owen James (Mr M C Pipe) 9 7

Carey, Declan Martin (Mr Glenn Humphrey) 9 7

Collum, Niall Christopher (Mr G B Balding) 9 7

Currie, Wayne Alexander (Mr N A Gaselee) 9 7

Dowling, Andrew Geared (Mr D R Gandolfo) 9 7

Edwards, Robert Matthew (Mr S Sherwood) 10 0

Hogg, Stephen Robert (Mr M D Hammond) 9 10

Keighley, Martin Holmes (Mr David Nicholson) 9 7

Lane, Mark Anthony Phillip (Mr N J Henderson) 9 7

Large, Adam William (Mr K A Morgan) 9 7

Lucas, Andrew Keith (Mr J A Bennett) 9 5

†Lycett, Shaun (Mr G Fierro) 9 7

McEntee, Paul Leon Patrick (Mr P M McEntee) 10 7

Melrose, Stephen (Mr R Allan) 9 10

†Murphy, Thomas Cyril (Mr Bill Turner) 9 7

†Shakespeare, Adam Lee (Mr N A Twiston-Davies) 9 0

Watt, Andrew Robert (Mrs S C Bradburne) 8 7

Webb, Christopher Lee (rides as Christopher) (Mr Stan Mellor) 9 7

Willmington, Nathan Scott (Mr R H Buckler) 9 7

† Relinquished

Amateur riders 1993–94

Riders who have been granted permits to ride in Flat races, steeplechases and hurdle races and National Hunt Flat races. Valid from July 1, 1993 to June 30, 1994 under Rule 60(v).

CATEGORY "A"

Allison, Miss Jane Karen 9 7
Armitage, Miss Annabelle Sophie Jane 8 7

Balding, Miss Clare Victoria 10 6
Barnes, Miss Fiona Alison 10 0
Barrett, Raymond Ernest 8 13
Binnington, Miss Kate Louise Frances 9 8
†Bosley, Mrs Sarah Jane 8 7
Brackenbury, Miss Jane 9 12
Brown, Gary 9 7
Busby, Mrs Melanie Alison 8 0

Cartner, John Wightman 10 7
Clark, Miss Ruth Amanda 9 7
Close, Peter Leslie 8 12

Deniel, Miss Alyson Jodi 8 10
Dixon, William George 10 6
Dods, Mrs Carole Elizabeth 8 10
Donnelly, Lorcan Laurence 9 7
Duckett, Miss Sally Jane 9 7
Durrant, David Peter 10 0
Dyer, Robert Hamilton 10 0

Farrant, Miss Sarah Anne 8 12
Frith, Matthew Giles 9 7

Gollings, Mrs Jayne Marie 8 12

Haigh, Michael Philip 9 7
Haigh, Miss Victoria 9 7
Haynes, Miss Fiona Alexandra 9 7
Haynes, Miss Yvonne 9 0
Hirst, Mrs Corrina 9 0
Horsey, Miss Laura Jayne 8 7

†James, Edward Daniel Luke John 9 12
Jones, Miss Kim 9 7
Judge, Miss Sarah Louise 8 7

Killick, Paul Ronald 10 4

Lake, Miss Catherine Jane 9 7
Lawther, John Rory 10 10
Loads, Keith Frederick John 10 7

Manners, Anthony John 9 7
Mannish, Michael 9 7
Marshall, Miss Victoria Ruth 8 5
McHale, Mrs Denise Alison 8 8
McLaughlin, William John 9 8
Mehmet, Yucel Tasgin 9 7
Metcalfe, Miss Claire 9 7
Millingan, Miss Mary Kate 9 10
Mitchell, Andrew Francis 10 0

Naughton, Mrs Joanne Clare 8 12
Newton, Michael Joseph 9 7
Nicholas, Miss Clare Juliet 8 2

Oldman, Barry Kenneth 10 3

Pickering, Mrs Wendy 8 7
Price, Mrs Carolyn Jane 9 0
Puddy, Daryl Brian 10 5
Purdy, Miss Alison Jane 9 7

Rodda, Mark Geoffrey 10 0
Rowe, Miss Susie 7 10

Sandes, Miss Sally Jane 8 4

Tolhurst, Edward James 9 2

Wallin, Miss Samantha Louise 9 0
Webb, David Christopher 9 7
Wilkinson, Mrs Diane Shirley 8 0
Williams, Mrs Sarah Daphne 9 0

Yardley, Miss Sarah Elizabeth 8 0

Restricted to Steeple Chases and Hurdle Races

Apiafi, Joshua 10 10

Baines, Graham 8 7
Baker, Louis Mark 9 7
Barlow, John Ronald 11 0
Beckingham, Miss Yvonne 8 4
Bevan, Miss Helen Louise 9 10
Bevis, Richard Norman 10 0
Boswell, Miss Louise 9 7
Burton, Gerald Edward 11 2

Charles-Jones, Alexander Skeel 10 0
Cobden, Miss Sally Ann 10 0
Copper, Miss Caroline Louise 9 7
Culloty, James Hugh 9 7

De Burgh, Simon Rufus 9 7
Dixon, Ben 10 4

Gribbin, Anthony David 10 0
Gudgeon, Andrew Lindsey 10 0

Henderson, James Harold 11 7

Johnson, Stephen John 10 0

Kent, John Nicholas 10 4

Milne, Michael Kenneth 12 0

Newey, Adam Stuart 9 7

Ponsonby, Rupert Charles 12 0

Sheridan, Damian Noel 10 4

Thatcher, John Gerald 10 9
Trietline, Charles Jeremy 10 7

Restricted to Flat races

Ager, Miss Tracey Allison Patricia 7 7
Appleby, Charles Edward James 9 0
Arbuthnot, Mrs Diane 8 7
Ayres, Michael Patrick 9 7

Bailey, Tristan Ward 10 0
Barclay, Mrs Stella Elizabeth 10 1
Bedford, Steven John 9 7
Boggis, Mrs Jane Elizabeth 8 8
Bond, Miss Judith Anne 7 13
Boston, Miss Sue Jane, 8 7
Bridger, Miss Madeline Dinah 9 1
Burke, Miss Fiona 9 0
Bycroft, Miss Amanda Susan 8 7

Carson, Miss Melanie 8 0
Chapple-Hyam, Mrs Jane Fiona 9 0
Chittenden, Miss Sara Jane Elizabeth 8 7
Clark, Miss Mary-Ann Victoria 8 9
Craven, Miss Briony 9 3
Crossley, Mrs Jennie 8 7
Cuff, Timothy Stephen 9 0
Cumani, Mrs Sara Doon 9 0
Curley, Charles 10 0

Davies, Miss Susan Philippa 9 0
Denne, Thomas James 10 2
Dunwoody, Mrs Carol 8 7

Easterby, Mrs Sarah Jane 9 7
Eden, Mrs Stephanie Jane 8 10
Edwards, Stephen John 9 12
Elsey, Miss Annie Francesca 8 10
Evans, Glyn 9 7

Feilden, Miss Julia Diane 9 0
Folkes, Miss Emma 9 4
Foustok, Miss Ikbal 8 2
Froggitt, Miss Claudine Ann 9 0

Gatehouse, Miss Elizabeth Bridget 9 0
Greaney, Miss Kim Elizabeth 8 0
Green, Richard Dale 9 7

Haggas, Mrs Maureen 9 0
Hannon, Miss Katherine Anne 9 7
Hide, Miss Lucinda Jane 8 7
Horsfall, Miss Michelle Rosalind 8 12

Jakeway, Miss Sarah 9 0
Jarvis, Mrs Gabrielle Amy Stephanie 9 4
Jenkins, Michael Charles 11 4
Johnson Houghton, Miss Eve Annette 9 7
Jones, Miss Alexandra Whitfield 10 0
Jones, Miss Diana Jane 9 0

Keller, James Alfred 10 4
Kelleway, Miss Sarah Gillian 8 0
Kettlewell, Mrs Deborah Jane 9 0
King, Miss Jayne Claire 9 4

Lawson, Mrs Lucy Rose 8 7
Lukaniuk, Victor Casimir 9 0

Manzi, Miss Karen Francesca 9 4
Marshall, Daniel George 10 0
Martindale, Miss Kerry Angela 8 2
Mills, Miss Elaine Linda 9 0
Moore, Mrs Jayne 8 0
Moore, Mrs Sara Jane 8 0
Morris, Mrs Linda 8 10
Musson, Mrs Judy Angela 8 7

Noonan, Mrs Hazel Margaret 9 12

Peacock, Mrs Carmen Gaye Geraldine 9 4
Pearce, Mrs Lydia Susan 8 0
Perratt, Miss Linda Agnes 9 0
Pritchard-Gordon, Patrick 9 10

Robertson, Miss Leona 9 0
Ross, Robin Lee 10 8
Russell, Miss Joanna Mary 9 5

Sandercock, Miss Mary-Ann 8 0
Sanders, Miss Amanda Kay 8 0
Santana, Kenneth 9 4
Snowdon, Miss Victoria Fray 8 7
Southall, Miss Elizabeth Jane 7 12
Storey, Miss Stella 9 0
Stubbings, Miss Helen 9 0
Sullivan, Christopher 10 7

Tork, Kevin 11 6
Turnell, Mrs Louise 8 9
Turner, Mrs Anna 9 7

Vollaro, Miss Lucy 8 7

Waters, Terry 9 7
Watkins, Miss Sally 8 0
Webster, Miss Heather Jane 8 7
Whittle, Miss Rosalyn Jayne 8 7
Wilkinson, Mrs Clare Denise 9 2
Wray, Mrs Suzanne Caroline 8 7

CATEGORY "B"

*Adkin, Mrs Georgina 9 10
*Armson, Richard John 10 5
*%Armytage, Marcus David 10 4
*Astaire, Steven 11 3

*Bailey, Mrs Tracey Louise 8 7
Barfoot-Saunt, Geoffrey Charles 10 7
*Barlow, Thomas David Bradwall 11 2
*Barraclough, Miss Susannah Mary 9 3
*Baxter, Miss Stephanie Elizabeth 8 9
*%Beardsall, Jonathan Hegue 10 0
Bell, Simon Bernard 9 7
*Billot, Miss Sally Anne 9 0
*Blackwell, Stephen Christopher 10 0
Bonner, Christopher Colin Malcolm 9 7
*Bosley, Mrs Sarah Jane 8 7
*Bowlby, Anthony Adrian 10 12
*Bracegirdle, Miss Tanya 9 4
*%Bradburne, John Gordon 10 4
Bradley, Noel Andrew 9 7
*Brisby, Simon William 10 5
*Brown, Hilary Stephen Leigh (rides as Larry) 11 0
*Brunt, Roger Charles 10 10
Buckley, Mark Alexander 9 9
Burgess, Miss Carol-Ann 9 0
Burnell, Wayne Martin 9 7
Burrows, Mark William 10 0
*%Bush, Stephen 10 8
*Butler, Miss Jayne 9 10
Byrne, Thomas 10 4

*%Cambidge, Jonathan Roy 10 2
Campbell, Charles William 10 0
*Chapman, Mark 10 0
Cosgrove, Guy Desmond 10 0
*Cowdrey, Mrs Maxine 8 10
*%Craggs, Peter Foxton 10 7
*Cregan, Michael Joseph 10 0

*%Dun, John Michael 11 0
Dunlop, Harry James Leeper 10 7
*%Durkan, John Patrick Peter 10 4

*Eaton, Miss Lisa Victoria 9 0
*Ellis, Miss Katie Jane 8 7
*Ellwood, Major Oliver Charles Beauclerk 10 0
*Embiricos, Miss Alexandra Eugenie 10 6
*Ewart, Colin James 10 0

Farrant, Ashley James 10 12
*%Farrell, Mrs Anthea Louise 8 7
*Ford, Richard 10 12
*%Fowler, Anthony 11 10

*Gandolfo, Miss Elizabeth Ann 10 0
Gingell, Matthew James 10 10
*Gladders, Miss Sarah Gillian 9 0
*Glen, Miss Harriet 8 7
*Gordon, Christopher Eugene 10 7
*Greed, Tom Richard 10 9
*Green, Kevin Andrew 10 0
*Green, Roger William 10 0
Griffiths, George Roderick Tudor 10 0

Haine, George William Victor 9 7
%Hale, Richard Andrew 9 11
*%Hambly, Albert Adrian 10 0
*Hamer, Michael Paul 10 7
*%Harding-Jones, Perry 10 5
*Harris, Neil John 9 7
Harvey, Alexander Henry 10 7
Harwood, Miss Amanda Jill 9 0
*Henderson, William John 10 2
Higgins, Miss Stefanie Alice 9 0
*Hills, Mrs Katherine Mary 9 7
*Hobbs, Mrs Sarah Louise 9 0
*Hollowell, Kerry Brian 10 0

*Jackson, Mark Joseph 10 2
James, Edward Daniel Luke John 9 12
Jefford, Leslie David Battershill 9 12
†%Jenks, Tom Percival 9 9
*%Johnson, Peter 11 0
*%Johnson Houghton, Gordon Fulke 9 12
*%Jones, Miss Isobel Diana Whitfield 9 6
Jones, Matthew John 10 8
*Jones, Timothy Lloyd 10 12
Joynes, Scott 9 7
*Judge, Miss Rachel Mary 9 7

*%Kendall, Mrs Margaret Ann 9 7
*King, Neil Bernard 10 5

Lamb, Miss Sarah Kathleen 9 0
*%Lay, Anthony Lawrence 11 0
*Leavy, Barry David 9 9
*%Ledger, Mrs Cynthia (rides as Nicky) 9 7
%Lewis, Guy Miles 9 7
%Llewellyn, John Lewis 9 7
*Love, Dr. Sandy 10 10

*%Mactaggart, David Clive 10 3
*%MacEwan, Andrew George Patrick Burrell 10 11
*Marks, Miss Ann Kelly 9 0
%McCain, Donald Richard 10 0
McCarthy, Timothy Daniel 10 0
*McCaull, Miss Heather 10 0
*McMahon, Edward Sydney Arthur 10 7
*McPherson, Adrian Stewart 10 0
*Mellor, Mrs Mary Elain 8 7
*Miles, Nigel 10 0
*Mills, Robin Cameron 10 9
Mitchell, Nicholas Richard 11 2
Mitchell, Miss Sophie Jane 8 7
Moore, Nicholas Pethick 9 7
*Morgan, William Giles Newberry 11 0
*Morris, Mrs Margaret Ann 9 0
*Morrison, Thomas 9 12
*Mulhall, Clive Anthony 10 4
*Mulligan, Martin 10 0

%Nash, Mrs Philippa Lindy 9 0
*%Needham, Mrs Fiona Emma 9 4
Nichol, Miss Susan Ann 8 7

O'Brien, Julian Louis Chad 9 7

Parker, Andrew 10 0
Parker, David 9 7
Payne, Ryan James 10 10
Pewter, Guy Rupert 9 3
Phillips, Alan John 9 10
*Pickering, Adair William 10 4
Pittendrigh, Stewart Ian 10 10
Pollock, Benjamin Nicholas 9 12
*Poulton, Julian Charles 10 7
Price, Andrew Raymond 10 12
*Pritchard, Julian Michael 10 10
*%Pritchard, Dr Philip Leslie James 9 12

*Rebori, Anthony Dominic 11 0
*%Rees, Mrs Geraldine Sarah 9 0
*Rees, James 9 7
Rimell, Mark Guy 10 0
*Robson, Andrew William 11 0
*Robson, Miss Pauline 9 7
Rowsell, Hamish Giles Morley 10 7

*Sayer, Mrs Heather Dianne 10 0
Shenkin, Gordon Richman 9 7
*Smyth-Osbourne, Julian George 10 7
*Southcombe, Miss Jane Alison 9 0
Spearing, Miss Caroline Mary-Anne 8 10
Spearing, Miss Teresa Sally 8 12
*Stephenson, Timothy Michael 10 5
*%Stickland, Stephen George 10 12
*%Swiers, Stephen James 10 7
*%Swindlehurst, David James 10 4

*Taiano, Paul George 10 10
*Teal, Roger Alan 10 10
*Thomas, Miss Candy Jane 9 0
*%Thurlow, Miss Jacqueline 9 0
*Turner, Miss Amanda Jane 10 0

*Verco, David Ian 10 2
Vigors, Charles Stewart Cliffe 9 13

*%Waggott, Miss Tracy 10 0
*Walton, Ashley Edward 9 0
*Weatherby, Jonathan Roger 11 0
*Welsh, Adam 10 7

Weymes, John Robert 10 4
*Wheeler, Major Gerald Felix 10 9
*Whitaker, Simon Richard 11 7
*White, George Francis 10 7
*White, Raymond 10 0
White, Richard Hocken 10 0
Whiting, Kevin Paul 9 7
*Wilding, Michael William 10 7
*Wilkinson, Mrs Jane Vivienne 9 0
Williams, Richard Evan Rhys 10 2
*Wilson, Christopher Ralph 10 7
*Wingfield Digby, James Hugo 10 2
*Winter, Miss Joanna Dawn 8 10
*Wonnacott, Mrs Claire Louise 10 0

*Yardley, Miss Alison Jayne 8 0
Young, Miss Susan Elizabeth Marie 10 7

† Relinquished
* Indicates over 25 years of age at the time the Permit was granted — Rule 109(iii)(a)
%Indicates over 75 rides against professional jockeys under Rules of Racing at the time the Permit was granted

Winners of big races

Part I: Flat, Great Britain

(The figures in parentheses indicate the number of starters)

LINCOLNSHIRE H'CAP

(1 mile)

(First run 1853)

1900 Sir Geoffrey 5y 8st 6lb (25)
1901 Little Eva 6y 7st 5lb (28)
1902 St Maclou 4y 7st 12lb (23)
1903 Over Norton 6y 7st 6lb (20)
1904 Uninsured 4y 7st 10lb (23)
1905 Sansovino 4y 7st 6lb (18)
1906 Ob 5y 8st (24)
1907 Ob 6y 8st 10lb (24)
1908 Kaffir Chief 6y 7st 11lb (20)
1909 Duke of Sparta 5y 6st 11lb (23)
1910 Cinderello 5y 7st 2lb (27)
1911 Mercutio 6y 8st 4lb (32)
1912 Long Set 5y 8st 2lb (17)
1913 Berrildon 4y 7st 4lb (22)
1914 Outram 5y 7st 1lb (22)
1915 View Law 4y 6st 1lb (23)
1916†Clap Gate 5y 7st (22)
1917–18 No race
1919 Royal Bucks 6y 7st 5lb (15)
1920 Furious 4y 7st 4lb (29)
1921 Soranus 4y 8st 4lb (30)
1922 Granely 4y 7st 9lb (32)
1923 White Bud 6y 6st 5lb (30)
1924 Sir Gallahad III 4y 8st 5lb (27)
1925 Tapin 4y 8st 7lb (26)
1926 King of Clubs 6y 6st 2lb (26)
1927 Priory Park 5y 7st 7lb (30)
1928 Dark Warrior 4y 8st 2lb (26)
1929 Elton 4y 7st 2lb (35)
1930 Leonidas II 5y 8st (31)
1931 Knight Error 5y 7st 7lb (35)
1932 Jerome Fandor 4y 6st 13lb (36)
1933 Dorigen 4y 9st 1lb (28)
1934 Play On 4y 7st 8lb (26)
1935 Flamenco 4y 9st (34)
1936 Over Coat 5y 7st 12lb (34)
1937 Marmaduke Jinks 5y 8st (32)
1938 Phakos 4y 8st 3lb (27)
1939 Squadron Castle 6y 7st 7lb (38)
1940 Quartier-Maitre 5y 8st 1lb (21)
1941 Gloaming 4y 7st 4lb (19)
1942*Cuerdley 4y 8st 7lb (20)
1943*Lady Electra 4y 8st 10lb (17)
1944*Blackbite 5y 7st 8lb (24)
1945*Double Harness 4y 6st 10lb (25)
1946 Langton Abbot 4y 8st 2lb (37)
1947 Jockey Treble 5y 6st (46)
1948 Commissar 8y 8st 9lb (58)
1949 Fair Judgement 4y 7st 10lb (43)
1950 Dramatic 5yh 8st 13lb (40)
1951 Barnes Park 5y 8st (35)
1952 Phariza 5y 6st 12lb (40)
1953 Sailing Light 4y 7st 11lb (41)
1954 Nahar 7y 8st (32)
1955 Military Court 5y 8st 2lb (29)
1956 Three Star II 8y 6st 13lb (41)
1957 Babur 4y 7st 13lb (32)
1958 Babur 5y 9st (37)
1959 Marshal Pil 5y 7st 13lb (32)
1960 Mustavon 5y 6st 13lb (31)
1961 Johns Court 6y 7st 7lb (37)
1962 Hill Royal 4y 7st 9lb (40)
1963 Monawin 8y 7st 9lb (40)
1964 Mighty Gurkha 5y 7st 8lb (45)

Run at Lincoln from 1853 to 1964
*Run at Pontefract
†Run at Lingfield

WILLIAM HILL LINCOLN H'CAP (Doncaster)

(1 mile)

1965 Old Tom 6y 8st 6lb (38)
1966 Riot Act 4y 8st 3lb (49)
1967 Ben Novus 5y 7st 10lb (24)
1968 Frankincense 4y 9st 5lb (31)
1969 Foggy Bell 4y 7st 11lb (25)
1970 New Chapter 4y 8st 1lb (23)
1971 Double Cream 4y 8st 9lb (26)
1972 Sovereign Bill 6y 8st 12lb (21)
1973 Bronze Hill 4y 7st 9lb (26)
1974 Quizair 6y 7st 13lb (26)
1975 Southwark Star 4y 7st 3lb (24)
1976 The Hertford 5y 8st 6lb (26)
1977 Blustery 5y 7st 11lb (26)
1978 Captain's Wings 5y 7st 10lb (25)
1979 Fair Season 5y 8st 10lb (23)
1980 King's Ride 4y 8st 12lb (18)
1981 Saher 5y 8st 12lb (19)
1982 King's Glory 4y 8st 3lb (26)
1983 Mighty Fly 4y 8st 4lb (26)
1984 Saving Mercy 4y 8st 9lb (26)
1985 Cataldi 4y 9st 10lb (26)
1986 K-Battery 4y 8st 4lb (25)
1987 Star of a Gunner 7y 8st 8lb (25)
1988 Cuvee Charlie 4y 8st 1lb (25)
1989 Fact Finder 5y 7st 9lb (25)
1990 Evichstar 6y 7st 12lb (24)
1991 Amenable 6y 8st 1lb (25)
1992 High Low (USA) 4y 8st (24)
1993 High Premium 5y 8st 8lb (24)

CRAVEN STAKES (Newmarket)

(1 mile)

For three year olds
(First run 1878)

1900 Headpiece 8st 7lb (7)
1901 Rigo 9st (12)
1902 Port Blair 9st 6lb (12)
1903 Countermark 8st 13lb (9)
1904 Airlie 9st 3lb (10)
1905 St Oswald 8st 5lb (10)
1906 His Eminence 8st 13lb (5)
1907 Slieve Gallion 9st 6lb (12)
1908 No race
1909 Howick 8st 10lb (9)
1910 Neil Gow 9st 6lb (6)
1911 Irish King 9st 3lb (5)
1912 Jingling Geordie 9st 6lb (12)
1913 Sanquhar 9st 6lb (9)
1914 Kennymore 9st 6lb (8)
1915 Rossendale 8st 5lb (7)
1916*Sir Dighton 8st 5lb
*Roi d'Ecosse 9st 3lb (6)
1917 Dansellon 9st 6lb (9)
1918 Benevente 9st 3lb (8)
1919 Buchan 9st 6lb (8)
1920 Daylight Patrol 8st 5lb (11)
1921 No race
1922 Collaborator 9st 6lb (19)
1923 Light Hand 8st 5lb (11)
1924 St Germnans 8st 5lb (12)
1925 Picaroon 9st 6lb (6)
1926 Harpagon 9st 3lb (11)
1927 Tattoo 8st 3lb (15)
1928 Royal Minstrel 8st 4lb (10)
1929 Cragadour 8st 3lb (13)
1930 Writ 8st 3lb (13)
1931 Philae 8st 3lb (12)
1932 Loaningdale 8st 6lb (7)
1933 Lochiel 8st 5lb (8)
1934 Colombo 9st 8lb (7)
1935 Buckleigh 8st 5lb (16)
1936 Monument 8st 5lb (13)
1937 Snowfall 8st 6lb (14)
1938 Challenge 8st 5lb (6)
1939 Signal Light 9st (13)
1940 Prince Tetra 9st 1lb (14)
1941 Morogoro 9st 4lb (16)
1942–45 No race
1946 Gulf Stream 9st 4lb (8)
1947 Migoli 9st 4lb (6)
1948 My Babu 9st 4lb (9)
1949 Moondust 8st 5lb (8)
1950 Rising Flame 9st (6)
1951 Claudius 8st 6lb (13)
1952 Kara Tepe 8st 5lb (11)
1953 Oleandrin 8st 10lb (7)
1954 Ambler II 8st 5lb (8)
1955 True Cavalier 8st 10lb (9)
1956 Pirate King 8st 5lb (15)
1957 Shearwater 8st 5lb (7)
1958 Bald Eagle 9st 4lb (6)
1959 Pindari 9st 4lb (7)
1960 Tudorich 8st 10lb (13)
1961 Aurelius 8st 6lb (6)
1962 High Noon 8st 10lb (7)
1963 Crocket 9st 6lb (5)
1964 Young Christopher 8st 12lb (12)
1965 Corifi 8st 7lb (7)
1966 Salvo 8st 7lb (11)
1967 Sloop 8st 7lb (11)
1968 Petingo 9st 6lb (4)
1969 Paddy's Progress 8st 7lb (8)
1970 Tamil 8st 12lb (9)
1971 Levanter 9st 2lb (6)
1972 Leicester 8st 5lb (5)
1973 My Drifter 8st 5lb (14)

1974 Numa 8st 10lb (12)
1975 No Alimony 8st 10lb (10)
1976 Malinowski (USA) 8st 10lb (7)
1977 Limone 8st 10lb (9)
1978 Admiral's Launch 8st 10lb (10)
1979 Lyphard's Wish (Fr) 8st 7lb (3)
1980 Tyrnavos 8st 7lb (9)
1981 Kind Of Hush 8st 7lb (9)
1982 Silver hawk (USA) 8st 7lb (9)
1983 Muscatite 8st 7lb (5)
1984 Lear Fan (USA) 8st 12lb (5)
1985 Shadeed (USA) 8st 7lb (6)
1986 Dancing Brave (USA) 8st 7lb (11)
1987 Ajdal (USA) 9st (6)
1988 Doyoun 8st 9lb (5)
1989 Shaadi 8st 9lb (5)
1990 Tirol 8st 12lb (6)
1991 Marju 8st 9lb (8)
1992 Alnasr Alwasheek 8st 9lb (8)
1993 Emperor Jones (USA) 8st 9lb (9)

*Dead-heat

EUROPEAN FREE H'CAP (Newmarket)

(7 fur)

For three year olds

1929 Sir Cosmo 9st (24)
1930 Quothquan 7st 4lb (32)
1931 Zanoff 7st 5lb (26)
1932 Rolling Rock 9st (19)
1933 Cotoneaster 6st 13lb (30)
1934 Phaleron Bay 7st 7lb (25)
1935 Knighted 8st 12lb (25)
1936 Pay Up 8st 2lb (19)
1937 Mid-day Sun 7st 2lb (19)
1938 Lapel 7st (13)
1939 Solar Cloud 7st 6lb (29)
1940*Salt Spring 8st 12lb (20)
1941*Orthodox 8st 3lb (19)
1942–43 No race
1944*Roadhouse 7st 12lb (12)
1945*Grandmaster 8st 13lb (21)
1946 Cama 8st 5lb (17)
1947 Benedictine 8st 7lb (15)
1948 Rear Admiral 8st 11lb (18)
1949 Spy Legend 8st (19)
1950 The Moke 7st 2lb (17)
1951 Wilwyn 7st 12lb (19)
1952 Caerlaverock 7st 12lb (21)
1953 Good Brandy 8st 5lb (12)
1954 Sun Festival 8st 2lb (21)
1955 Counsel 8st 11lb (19)
1956 Honeylight 8st 7lb (18)
1957 Quorum 8st 7lb (13)
1958 Faultless Speech 8st 4lb (14)
1959 Petite Etoile 9st (10)
1960 Running Blue 8st 4lb (20)
1961 Erudite 8st 6lb (19)
1962 Privy Councillor 8st 4lb (18)
1963 Ros Rock 8st 1lb (16)
1964 Port Merion 8st 9lb (23)
1965 Short Commons 8st 4lb (11)
1966 Kibenka 8st 4lb (16)
1967 Supreme Sovereign 8st 1lb (15)
1968 Panpiper 7st 13lb (13)
1969 Welsh Pageant 8st 10lb (15)
1970 Shiny Tenth 8st 3lb (18)
1971 No Mercy 8st 5lb (16)
1972 Panama Canal 7st 11lb (16)
1973 Pitskelly 8st 5lb (16)
1974 Charlie Bubbles 8st 3lb (14)
1975 Green Belt 8st 9lb (15)
1976 Man of Harlech 8st 4lb (19)
1977 Mrs McArdy 8st (19)
1978 Remainder Man 7st 10lb (12)
1979 Lyric Dance 8st 10lb (14)
1980 Moorestyle 8st 10lb (13)
1981 Motavato 8st 13lb (13)
1982 Match Winner (Fr) 9st 4lb (13)
1983 Boom Town Charlie (USA) 8st 11lb (8)
1984 Cutting Wind 8st 8lb (17)
1985 Over The Ocean (USA) 8st 11lb (11)
1986 Green Desert (USA) 9st 7lb (8)
1987 Noble Minstrel (USA) 9st 7lb (11)
1988 Lapierre 9st 1lb (9)
1989 Danehill (USA) 9st 1lb (9)
1990 Anshan 9st 7lb (10)
1991 Mystiko (USA) 9st 2lb (11)
1992 Pursuit of Love 9st 1lb (9)
1993 So Factual 9st 6lb (7)

*Run on July Course

SINGER & FRIEDLANDER GREENHAM STAKES (Newbury)

For three year olds
(First run 1906)

(7 fur)

1935 Theft 9st 4lb (10)
1936 Noble King 8st 5lb (20)
1937 Fairford 8st 5lb (18)
1938 Mirza II 9st 4lb (7)
1939 Fairstone 8st 5lb (22)
1940 Tant Mieux 9st 4lb (16)
1941–48 No race
1949 Star King 9st 4lb (10)
1950 Port o'Light 8st 5lb (12)
1951 No race
1952 Serpenyoe 9st (10)
1953 March Past 9st 4lb (14)
1954 Infatuation 9st 4lb (13)
1955 Counsel 9st (11)
1956 Ratification 9st 4lb (10)
1957 Pipe of Peace 9st 4lb (10)
1958 Paresa 8st 5lb (12)
1959 Masham 9st 4lb (8)
1960 Filipepi 8st 5lb (10)
1961 Primus 8st 10lb (8)
1962 Romulus 9st (12)
1963 Fighting Ship 9st 3lb (9)
1964 Excel 8st 5lb (10)
1965 Silly Season 9st 3lb (11)
1966 No race
1967 Play High 8st 10lb (8)
1968 Heathen 8st 10lb (8)
1969 Tower Walk 8st 10lb (8)
1970 Gold Rod 8st 10lb (6)
1971 Mill Reef (USA) 9st 1lb (7)
1972 Martinmas 8st 10lb (7)
1973 Boldboy 8st 10lb (5)
1974 Glen Strae 8st 10lb (8)
1975 Mark Anthony 9st 1lb (9)
1976 Wollow 9st 1lb (10)
1977 He Loves Me 8st 10lb (11)
1978 Derrylin 8st 10lb (11)
1979 Kris 9st (9)
1980 Final Straw 9st (9)
1981 Another Realm 9st (6)
1982 Cajun 9st (5)
1983 Wassl 9st (5)
1984 Creag-an-Sgor 9st (8)
1985 Bairn (USA) 9st (6)
1986 Faustus (USA) 9st (9)
1987 Risk Me (Fr) 9st (8)
1988 Zelphi 9st (7)
1989 Zayyani 9st (12)
1990 Rock City 9st (6)
1991 Bog Trotter (USA) 9st (7)
1992 Lion Cavern (USA) 9st (8)
1993 Inchinor 9st (7)

LANES END JOHN PORTER E.B.F. STAKES (Newbury)

(1 mile 4 fur 5 yds)

1928 Ox and Ass 3y 9st 1lb (5)
1929 Silver Hussar 4y 8st 13lb (3)
1930 Wedding Favour 3y 7st 11lb (3)
1931 Birthday Book 3y 9st (8)
1932 Corn Belt 4y 8st 10lb (4)
1933 Sarum 4y 8st 7lb (4)
1934 Felicitation 4y 9st 10lb (6)
1935 Night Owl 3y 7st 9lob (6)
1936 St Botolph 4y 8st 1lb (6)
1937 Haulfryn 46y 9st 7lb (3)
1938 Fair Copy 4y 9st 10lb (4)
1939 and 1940 No race
1941 Ruscus 3y 8st 13lb (14)
1942–48 No race
1949 Solar Slipper 4y 9st 1lb (9)
1950 Native heath 5y 9st 5lb (12)
1951 No race
1952 Neron 4y 9st 1lb (4)
1953 Wilwyn 5y 9st 5lb (7)
1954 Harwin 4y 9st 1lb (9)
1955 Entente Cordiale 4y 8st 5lb (9)
1956 Acropolis 4y 9st 1lb (6)
1957 China Rock 4y 9st 1lb (10)
1958 Doutelle 4y 9st 1lb (4)
1959 Cutter 4y 8st 12lb (3)
1960 Aggressor 5y 9st 5lb (12)
1961 High Perch 5y 9st 5lb (8)
1962 Hot Brandy 4y 9st 1lb (9)
1963 Peter Jones 4y 8st 5lb (11)
1964 Royal Avenue 6y 9st 5lb (12)
1965 Soderini 4y 9st 1lb (7)
1966 No race
1967 Charlottown 4y 9st 1lb (8)
1968 Fortissimo 4y 8st 5lb (9)
1969 Crozier 6y 9st 5lb (7)
1970 Torpid 5y 9st 5lb (8)
1971 Meadowville 4y 9st 1lb (12)
1972 Rock Roi 5y 9st 5lb (5)
1973 Rheingold 4y 9st 1lb (15)
1974 Freefoot 4y 8st 6lb (12)
1975 Salado (Ity) 4y 8st 10lb (13)
1976 Quiet Fling (USA) 4y 9st (11)
1977 Decent Fellow 4y 8st 9lb (11)
1978 Orchestra 4y 9st (10)
1979 Icelandic 4y 8st 11lb (12)
1980 Niniski 4y 9st (16)
1981 Pelerin (Fr) 4y 8st 8lb (9)
1982 Glint of Gold 4y 9st (11)
1983 Diamond Shoal 4y 8st 8lb (8)
1984 Gay Lemur 4y 8st 8lb (13)
1985 Jupiter Island 6y 8st 8lb (14)

1986 Lemhill 4y 8st 8lb (8)
1987 Rakaposhi King 5y 8st 10lb (12)
1988 Alwasmi 4y 8st 10lb (8)
1989 Unfuwain (USA) 4y 8st 13lb (7)
1990 Brush Aside (USA) 4y 8st 10lb (11)
1991 Rock Hopper 4y 8st 10lb (10)
1992 Saddlers' Hall 4y 8st 13lb (11)
1993 Linpac West 7y 8st 12lb (7)

Run over 1 mile 5 fur from 1928 to 1935, over 1¼ miles from 1936 to 1938, and over 1 mile 5 fur as the John Porter H'cap in 1941

THRESHER CLASSIC TRIAL (Sandown)

(1 mile 2 fur 7 yds)
For three year olds

1971 L'Apache 8st 7lb (10)
1972 Pentland Firth 8st 12lb (13)
1973 Ksar 8st 12lb (6)
1974 Bustino 8st 9lb (9)
1975 Consol 9st (9)
1976 Riboboy (USA) 9st (7)
1977 Artaius (USA) 8st 9lb (5)
1978 Whitstead 8st 11lb (8)
1979 Troy 8st 7lb (5)
1980 Henbit (USA) 8st 7lb (6)
1981 Shergar 8st 7lb (9)
1982 Peacetime (USA) 8st 7lb (11)
1983 Gordian 8st 7lb (7)
1984 Alphabatim 9st (8)
1985 Damister (USA) 8st 7lb (4)
1986 Shahrastani (USA) 8st 7lb (4)
1987 Gulf King 8st 12lb (8)
1988 Galitzin 8st 7lb (5)
1989 Old Vic 8st 8lb (3)
1990 Defensive Play (USA) 8st 11lb (6)
1991 Hailsham (CAN) 8st 11lb (5)
1992 Pollen Count (USA) 8st 11lb (10)
1993 True Hero (USA) 8st 11lb (6)

TWO THOUSAND GUINEAS (Newmarket—1 mile)

For three year olds

	Starters	Jockeys
1809 Mr C. Wilsons's ch c Wizard, by Sorcerer	8 ...	W. Clift
1810 Lord Grosvenor's b c Hephestion, by Alexander	9 ...	F. Buckle
1811 Mr Andrew's bl c Trophonius, by Sorcerer	11 ...	S. Barnard
1812 Lord Darlington's br c Cwrw, by Dick Andrews	7 ...	S. Chifney jun.
1813 Sir C. Bunbury's bl c Smolensko, by Sorcerer	12 ...	H. Miller
1814 Mr Wyndham's b c Olive, by Sir Oliver	14 ...	W. Arnull
1815 Lord Rous's ch c Tigris, by Quiz	10 ...	W. Arnull
1816 Lord G. H. Cavendish's b c Nectar, by Walton	12 ...	W. Arnull
1817 Mr W. Stonehewer's b c Manfred, by Election	8 ...	W. Wheatley
1818 Lord Foley's b c Interpreter, by Soothsayer	9 ...	W. Clift
1819 Sir J. Shelley's b c Antar, by Haphazard	6 ...	E. Edwards
1820 Duke of Grafton's b c Pindarrie, by Phantom	5 ...	F. Buckle
1821 Duke of Grafton's br c Reginald, by Haphazard	4 ...	F. Buckle
1822 Duke of Grafton's b f Pastille, by Rubens	3 ...	F. Buckle
1823 Mr Roger's ch c Nicolo, by Selim	7 ...	W. Wheatley
1824 Mr Haffenden's b c Schahriar, by Shuttle Pope	7 ...	W. Wheatley
1825 Lord Exeter's ch c Enamel, by Phantom	6 ...	J. Robinson
1826 Duke of Grafton's b c Dervise, by Merlin	7 ...	J. B. Day
1827 Duke of Grafton's b c Turcoman, by Selim	5 ...	F. Buckle
1828 Duke of Rutland's br c Cadland, by Andrew	5 ...	J. Robinson
1829 Lord Exeter's ch c Patron, by Partisan	2 ...	F. Boyce
1830 Lord Exeter's ch c Augustus, by Sultan	2 ...	P. Conolly
1831 Lord Jersey's ch c Riddlesworth, by Emilius	6 ...	J. Robinson
1832 Colonel Peel's b c Archibald, by Paulowitz	7 ...	A. Pavis
1833 Lord Orford's gr c Clearwell, by Jerry	6 ...	J. Robinson
1834 Lord Jersey's ch c Glencoe, by Sultan	7 ...	J. Robinson
1835 Lord Jersey's br c Ibrahim, by Sultan	4 ...	J. Robinson
1836 Lord Jersey's b c Bay Middleton, by Sultan	6 ...	J. Robinson
1837 Lord Jersey's b c Achmet, by Sultan	8 ...	E. Edwards
1838 Lord G. Bentinck's gr c Grey Momus, by Comus	6 ...	J. B. Day
1839 Lord Lichfield's bl c The Corsair, by Sir Hercules	3 ...	W. Wakefield
1840 Lord G. Bentinck's b f Crucifix, by Priam	6 ...	J. B. Day
1841 Lord Albemarle's ch c Ralph, by Dr. Syntax	8 ...	J. B. Day
1842 Mr J. Bowes's ch c Meteor, by Velocipede	8 ...	W. Scott
1843 Mr J. Bowes's b c Cotherstone, by Touchstone	3 ...	W. Scott
1844 Mr J. Day's b c The Ugly Buck, by Venison	7 ...	J. Day, jun
1845 Lord Stradbroke's b c Idas, by Liverpool	5 ...	E. Flatman
1846 Mr W. Scott's b c Sir Tatton Sykes, by Melbourne	6 ...	W. Scott
1847 Sir R. Pigot's b c Conyngham, by Slane	10 ...	J. Robinson
1848 Mr B. Green's b c Flatcatcher, by Touchstone	5 ...	J. Robinson
1849 Mr A. Nichol's bl c Nunnykirk, by Touchstone	8 ...	F. Butler
1850 Mr H. Hill's ch c Pitsford, by Epirus	5 ...	A. Day
1851 lord Enfield's br c Hernandez by Pantaloon	10 ...	E. Flatman
1852 Lord Exeter's ch c Stockwell, by The Baron	9 ...	J. Norman
1853 Mr J. Bowes's b c West Australian, by Melbourne	7 ...	F. Butler
1854 Mr J. Gully's b c The Hermit, by Bay Middleton	9 ...	A. Day
1855 Mr J. Merry's b c Lord of the Isles, by Touchstone	9 ...	J. Aldcroft
1856 Lord Derby's br c Fazzoletto, by Orlando	10 ...	E. Flatman
1857 Lord Zetland's br c Vedette, by Voltigeur	12 ...	J. Osborne
1858 Sir J. Hawley's ch c Fitz-Roland, by Orlando	14 ...	J. Wells
1859 Mr W. Day's br c The Promised Land, by Jericho	9 ...	A. Day
1860 Mr A. Nichol's b c The Wizard, by West Australian	15 ...	T. Ashmall
1861 Lord Stamford's ch c Diophantus, by Orlando	16 ...	A. Edwards

TWO THOUSAND GUINEAS—continued

	Starters	Jockeys
1862 Mr S. Hawke's b c The Marquis, by Stockwell	17 ...	T. Ashmall
1863 Mr R. Naylor's b c Macaroni, by Sweetmeat	9 ...	T. Challoner
1864 Lord Glasgow's b c General Peel, by Y. Melbourne	13 ...	T. Aldcroft
1865 Count de Lagrange's b c Gladiateur, by Monarque	18 ...	H. Grimshaw
1866 Mr R. Sutton's b c Lord Lyon, by Stockwell	15 ...	H. Thomas
1867 Duke of Beaufort's br c Vauban, by Muscovite	18 ...	G. Fordham
1868*Mr W. S. Crawford's br c Moslem, by Knight of St. Patrick		T. Challoner
*Mr G. Jones's ch f Formosa, by Buccaneer	14 ...	J. Osborne
1869 Mr J. Johnstone's br c Pretender, by Adventurer	19 ...	J. Osborne
1870 M. J. Merry's b c Macgregor, by Macaroni	10 ...	J. Daley
1871 Mr J. Johnstone's br c Bothwell, by Stockwell	13 ...	J. Osborne
1872 Mr Jos Dawson's ch c Prince Charlie, by Blair Athol	14 ...	J. Osborne
1873 Mr W. S. Crawford's ch c Gang Forward, by Stockwell	10 ...	T. Challoner
1874 Lord Falmouth's ch c Atlantic, by Thormanby	12 ...	F. Archer
1875 Mr H. C. Vyner's b c Camballo, by Cambuscan	13 ...	J. Osborne
1876 Lord Dupplin's b c Petrarch, by Lord Clifden	14 ...	H. Luke
1877 Count de Lagrange's b c Chamant, by Mortemer	11 ...	J. Goater
1878 Lord Londsdale's ch f Pilgrimage, by The Earl of The Palmer	10 ...	T. Cannon
1879 Lord Falmouth's ch c Charibert, by Thormanby	15 ...	F. Archer
1880 Duke of Beaufort's bl or br c Petronel, by Musket	17 ...	G. Fordham
1881 Hon. R. Grosvenor's b c Peregrine, by Pero Gomez	14 ...	F. Webb
1882 Duke of Westminster's ch f Shotover, by Hermit	18 ...	T. Cannon
1883 Lord Falmouth's br c Galliard, by Galopin	14 ...	F. Archer
1884 Mr J. Foy's br c Scot Free, by Macgregor	10 ...	W. Platt
1885 Mr W. Broderick-Cloete's b c Paradox, by Sterling	7 ...	F. Archer
1886 Duke of Westminster's b c Ormonde, by Bend Or	6 ...	F. G. Barrett
1887 Mr Douglas Baird's ch c Enterprise, by Sterling	8 ...	T. Cannon
1888 Duke of Portland's b c Ayrshire, by Hampton	6 ...	J. Osborne
1889 Mr Douglas Baird's ch c Enterprise, by Sterling	9 ...	T. Cannon
1890 Mr A. W. Merry's b c Surefoot, by Wisdom	9 ...	J. Liddiard
1891 Lord Alington's br c Common, by Isonomy	9 ...	G. Barrett
1892 Mr C. Rose's ch c Bonavista, by Bend Or	14 ...	W. Robinson
1893 Mr H. McCalmont's b c Isinglass, by Isonomy	10 ...	T. Loates
1894 Lord Rosebery's b c Ladas, by Hampton	8 ...	J. Watts
1895 Sir J. B. Maple's b c Kirkconnel, by Royal Hampton	8 ...	J. Watts
1896 Mr leopold de Rothschild's br c St. Frusquin, by St. Simon	7 ...	T. Loates
1897 Mr J. Gubbins's b c Galtee More, by Kendal	8 ...	C. Wood
1898 Mr Wallace Johnstone's b c Disraeli, by Galopin	14 ...	S. Loates
1899 Duke of Westminster' b c Flying Fox, by Orme	8 ...	M. Cannon

1900 H.R.H. The Prince of Wales's Diamond Jubilee, by St. Simon ....H Jones 11–4
Sir E Cassel's Bonarosa ....L Reiff 50–1
Ld Cadogan's Sidus ....T Loates 100–1
4 lengths, $^{3}/_{4}$ length, 1m 41$^{4}/_{5}$s. 10 ran R Marsh

1901 Sir E. Cassel's Handicapper, by Matchmaker ....W Halsey 33–1
Mr Lepold de Rothschild's Coricles ....K Cannon 4–1
Ld Wolverton's Osbech ....H Jones 40–1
2 lengths, neck, 1m 43s. 17 ran F W Day

1902 Mr R. S. Sievier's Sceptre, by Persimmon ....H Randall 4–1
Sir E Vincent's Pistol ....J H Martin 50–1
Mr J Gubbin's Ard Patrick ....K Cannon 9–2
2 lengths, 3 lengths, 1m 39s. 14 ran Owner

1903 Sir J. Miller's Rock Sand, by Sainfoin ....J H Martin 6–4
Sir Daniel Cooper's Flotsam ...D Maher 7–1
Mr Arthur James's Rabelais ...K Cannon 8–1
1$^{1}/_{2}$lengths, 2 lengths, 1m 42s. 11 ran G Blackwell

1904 Mr C. de Rothschild's St. Amant, by St. Frusquin ....K Cannon 11–4
Sir J Thursby's John o'Gaunt ....Mr G Thursby 10–1
Mr J Musker's Henry the First O Madden 8–1
4 lengths, 2 lengths, 1m 38$^{4}/_{5}$s. 14 ran A Hayhoe

1905 Mr F. de Wend-Fenton's Vedas, by Florizel II ....H Jones 11–2
Chev E Ginistrelli's Signorino ..B Dillon 25–1
Mr L Neumann's Llangibby ..O Madden 4–1
2 lengths, head, 1m 41$^{1}/_{5}$s. 13 ran W Robinson

1906 Mr Arthur James's Gorgos, by Ladas ....H Jones 20–1
Mr W Bass's Saucy ....O Madden 100–8
Ld Dalmeny's Ramrod ....W Higgs 100–7
Head, neck, 1m 43$^{4}/_{5}$s. 12 ran R Marsh

1907 Capt J. Greer's Slieve Gallion, by Gallinule ....W Higgs 4–11
Ld Roseberry's Bezonian ......D Maher 100–9
Mr Wm Clark's Linacre ....W Halsey 100–6
3 lengths, $^{3}/_{4}$ length, 1m 41$^{4}/_{5}$s. 10 ran S Darling

1908 Mr A. Belmont's Norman III, by Octagon ....O Madden 25–1
Mr A F Basset's Sir Archibald ....Mr G Thursby 5–1
Mr W Hall Walker's White Eagle ....L Hewitt 100–7
3 lengths, $^{3}/_{4}$length, 1m 44$^{3}/_{5}$s. 17 ran J Watson

1909 His Majesty's Minoru, by Cyllene ....H Jones 4–1
D of Portland's Phaleron ....W Earl 33–1
Mr W Raphael's Louviers ....G Stern 100–7
2 lengths, 1$^{1}/_{2}$ lengths, 1m 37$^{4}/_{5}$s. 11 ran R Marsh

1910 Lord Rosebery's Neil Gow, by Marco ....D Maher 2–1
Mr "Fairie's" Lemberg ....B Dillon 7–2
Mr H P Whitney's Whisk Broom ....J H Martin 100–7
Short head, 2 lengths, 1m 40$^{2}/_{5}$s. 13 ran P Peck

1911 Mr J. B. Joel's Sunstar, by Sundridge ....G Stern 5–1
Ld Derby's Stedfast ....F Wootton 100–9
Mr J B Joel's Lycaon ....E Shaw 50–1
2 lengths, $^{1}/_{2}$ length, 1m 37$^{3}/_{5}$s. 14 ran C Morton

1912 Mr H. B. Duryea's Sweeper II, by Broomstick ....D Maher 6–1
Mr L Neumann's Jaegar ...Walter Griggs 100–1
Mr C Bower Ismay's Hall Cross .... W Saxby 9–2
1 length, $^{1}/_{2}$ length, 1m 38$^{2}/_{5}$s. 14 ran H S Perse

1913 Mr W. Raphael's Louvois, by Isinglass ....J Reiff 25–1
Mr C Bower Ismay's Craganour ....W Saxby 3–1

Mr H P Whitney's Meeting House ....F O'Neill 50–1
Head, 2 lengths, 1m 38⁴/5s. 15 ran D Waugh
1914 Sir J. Thursby's Kennymore, by John o'Gaunt ....G Stern 2–1
Ld Londonderry's Corcyra .... F O'Neill 7–2
Mr J B Joel's Black Jester .....H Randall 20–1
Short head, 2 lengths, 1m 38s. 18 ran Alec Taylor
1915 Mr S. Joel's Pommern, by Polymelus ....S Donoghue 2–1
Mr L Neuman's Tournament .....Walter Griggs 100–6
Ld Carnarvon's The Vizier ....F Bullock 25–1
3 lengths, head, 1m 43²/5s. 16 ran C Peck
1916 Lord Falmouth's Clarissimus, by Radium ....J Clark 100–7
Mr "Fairie's" Kwang-Su ..F Templeman 10–1
Mr J Sandford's Nassovian .....N Spear 20–1
¾length, ½length, 1m 39³/5s. 17 ran W Waugh
1917 Mr "Fairie's" Gay Crusader, by Bayardo ....S Donoghue 9–4
Maj W Astor's Magpie ......O Madden 6–1
Mr J Buchanan's Athdara ....J Evans 25–1
Head, 3 lengths, 1m 40⁴/5s. 14 ran Alec Taylor
1918 Lady James Douglas's Gainsborough, by Bayardo ....J Childs 4–1
Mr C T Garlans's Somme Kiss ....J H Martin 8–1
Maj W Astor's Blink ....R Colling 100–6
1½lengths, 6 lengths, 1m 44³/5s. 13 ran Alec Taylor
1919 Sir A. Black's The Panther, by Tracery ....R Cooper 10–1
Maj W Astor's Buchan ....V Smyth 100–8
Ld Glanely's Dominion ....A Smith 100–6
Neck, ¾ length, 1m 44²/5s. 12 ran G Manser
1920 Major D. McCalmont's Tetratema, by The Tetrarch ....B Carslake 2–1
Mr W Raphael's Allenby ....F Slade 100–7
Sir Ernest Paget's Paragon ......A Smith 8–1
½ length, 3 lengths, 1m 43¹/5s. 17 ran H S Persse
1921 Lord Astor's Craig an Eran, by Sunstar ....J Brennan 100–6
Mr Joseph Watson's Lemonora ..J Childs 100–7
Mr J B Joel's Humorist .....S Donoghue 3–1
¾ length, same, 1m 41³/5s. 26 ran Alec Taylor
1922 Lord Queensborough's St. Louis, by Louvois ....G Archibald 6–1
Mr S Joel's Pondoland ....F O'Neill 5–1
Ld Woolavington's Captain Cuttle ....V Smyth 4–1
3 lengths, 4 lengths, 1m 43³/5s. 22 ran P P Gilpin
1923 Lord Rosebery's Ellengowan, by Lemberg ....E C. Elliott 7–1
Ld Woolavington's Knockando ....G Archibald 25–1
Mrs S Whitburn's D'Orsay ...R A Jones 50–1
Head, ½ length, 1m 37⁴/5s. 18 ran J L Jarvis
1924 H.H. Agar Khan's Diophon, by Grand Parade ....G Hulme 11–2
Ld Astor's Bright Knight .....F Bullock 100–9
Mr J B Joel's Green Fire ....S Donoghue 100–8
Head, neck, 1m 39s. 20 ran R Dawson
1925 Mr H. E. Morriss's Manna, by Phalaris ....S Donoghue 100–8
Sir G Bullough St Becan .....E C Elliott 9–1
Sir E Hulton's Oojah ....C Smirke 10–1
2 lengths, 4 lengths, 1m 39²/5s. 13 ran F Darling
1926 Lord Derby's Colorado, by Phalaris ....T Weston 100–8
Ld Woolavington's Coronach ...J Childs 5–4
Mr J P Hornung's Apple Sammy H Jelliss 10–1
5 lengths, 3 lengths, 1m 43³/5s. 19 ran Hon G Lambton
1927 Mr C. W. Whitburn's Adam's Apple, by Pommern ....J Leach 20–1
Mr F Curzon's Call Boy .....E C Elliott 5–2
Ld Derby's Sickle ....T Weston 10–1
Short head, ½ length, 1m 38¹/5s. 23 ran H L Cottrill
1928 Sir L. Philipp's Flamingo, by Flamboyant ....E C. Elliott 5–1
Capt G P Gough's Royal Minstrel ....H Beasley 7–2
Mr D Sullivan's O'Curry .....P Beasley 33–1
Head, 1½ lengths, 1m 38⁴/5s. 17 ran J L Jarvis
1929 Major D. McCalmont's Mr Jinks, by Tetratema ....H Beasley 5–1
Ld Astor's Cragadour ....H Jelliss 4–1
Sir Victor Sassoon's Gay Day ....S Donoghue 20–1
Head, 1½ lengths, 1m 39⁴/5s. 22 ran H S Perse
1930 Sir Hugo Hirst's Diolite, by Diophon ....F Fox 10–1
Mr W Cazalwt's Paradine ...R Perryman 33–1
Maj J Courtauld's Silver Flare E C Elliott
2 lengths, 1 length, 1m 42²/5s. 28 ran F Templeman
1931 Mr J. A. Dewar's Cameronian, by Pharos ....J Childs 100–8
M M Boussac's Goyescas ....E C Elliott 8–1
Sir J Rutherford's Orpen ......R A Jones 18–1
2 lengths, 3 lengths, 1m 39²/5s. 24 ran F Darling
1932 Mr W. M. G. Singer's Orwell, by Gainsborough ....R A Jones Evens
H.H. Aga Khan's Dastur ......M Beary 10–1
M M Boussac's Hesperus ....E C Elliott 25–1
2 lengths, 1½ lengths, 1m 42²/5s. 11 ran J Lawson
1933 Princess de Faucigny-Lucinge's Rodosto, by Epinard ....R Brethes 9–1
Sir H Cunliffe-Owen's King Salmon ....H Wragg 25–1
H.H. Aga Khan's Gino ......E C Elliott 100–6
1 length, ¾ length, 1m 40²/5s. 27 ran H Count, in France
1934 Lord Glanely's Colombo, by Manna ....W Johnstone 2–7
Mr R Strassburger's Easton ...C Semblat 20–1
H.H. Aga Khan's Badruddin ......F Fox 50–1
1 length, 1½ lengths, 1m 40s. 12 ran T Hogg
1935 H.H. Agar Khan's Baharm, by Blandford ....F Fox 7–2
H.H. Aga Khan's Theft .....G Richards 11–2
Mr C W Gordon's Sea Bequest E Smith 100–7
1½ lengths, 2 lengths, 1m 41²/5s. 16 ran Frank Butters
1936 Lord Astor's Pay Up, by Fairway R Dick 11–2
H.H. Aga Khan's Mahmoud ....S Donoghue 100–8
Mrs J Shand's Thankerton ......T Burns 40–1
Short head, 3 lengths, 1m 39³/5s. 19 ran J Lawson
1937 M. de St. Alary's Le Ksar, by Ksar ....C Semblat 20–1
M Boussac's Goya II ....E C Elliott 7–1
Mrs G B Miller's Mid-day Sun T Lowrey 25–1
4 lengths, ½ length, 1m 44³/5s. 18 ran F Carter, in France
1938 Mr H. E. Morriss's Pasch, by Blandford ....G Richards 5–2
Mr James V Rank's Scottish Union ....B Carslake 9–1
H.H. Aga Khan's Mirza II .....H Wragg 7–1
2 lengths' 1½ lengths, 1m 38⁴/5s. 18 ran F Darling
1939 Lord Rosebery's Blue Peter, by Fairway ....E Smith 5–1
Sir J Jarvis's Admiral Walk ....H Wragg 100–7
Sir Abe Bailey's Fairstone ......M Beary 13–2
½ length, ¾ length, 1m 39²/5s. 25 ran J L Jarvis
1940†M. M. Boussac's Djebel, by Tourbillon ....E C Elliott 9–4
H.H. Aga Khan's Stardust .....H Wragg 100–9
H.H. Maharaja of Kolhapur's Tant Mieux ....G Richards 13–2
2 lengths, head, 1m 43s. 21 ran A Swann, in France
1941†Duke of Westminster's Lambert Simnel, by Fair Trial ....E C Elliott 10–1
H.H. Senior Maharani Saheb of Kohaptur's Morogoro ....H Wragg 100–30
Ld Portal's Sun Castle ....P Beasley 100–7
2 lengths, 1½ lengths, 1m 43¹/5s. 19 ran F Templeman
1942†His Majesty's Big Game, by Bahram ....G Richards 8–11
Ld Derby's Watling Street ....S Ellis 13–2

Mr H A Jelliss's Gold Nib . . . . R A Jones 100–7
4 lengths, 2 lengths, 1m 41s. 14 ran F Darling
1943†Mr A. E. Saunders's Kingsway, by Fairway . . . . S Wragg 18–1
Capt A Gillson's Pink Flower T Lowery 100–9
Lord Astor's Way In . . . . C Richards 100–9
Short head, head, 1m 372/5s. 19 ran J Lawson
1944†Lord Derby's Garden Path, by Fairway . . . . H Wragg 5–1
Mal D H Wills's Growing Confidence . . . . K Mullins 20–1
Prince Aly Khan's Tehran . . . . P Gomez 50–1
Head, 11/2 lengths, 1m 394/5s. 26 ran W Earl
1945†Lord Astor's Court Martial, by Fair Trial . . . . C Richards 13–2
Sir E Ohlson's Dante . . . . W Nevett Evens
Sir J Jarvis's Royal Charger . . . R A Jones 40–1
Neck, 2 lengths, 1m 404/5s. 20 ran J Lawson
1946 Sir W. Cooke's Happy Knight, by Colombo . . . . T Weston 28–1
H.H. Aga Khan's Khaled . . . . R A Jones 100–30
Mr T Lilley's Radiotherapy . . T H Carey 100–6
4 lengths, head, 1m 381/5s. 13 ran H Jelliss
1947 Mr J. A. Dewar's Tudor Minstrel, by Owen Tudor . . . . G Richards 11–8
Princess Aly Khan's Saravan E C Elliott 25–1
H.H. Maharaja of Baroda's Sayajirao . . . . E Britt 33–1
8 lengths, short head, 1m 374/5s. 15 ran F Darling
1948 H.H. Maharaja of Baroda's My Babu, by Djebel . . . . C Smirke 2–1
Lt-Col Giles Loder's The Cobbler . . . . G Richards 100–30
Mr H J joel's Pride of india . . . . E Britt 20–1
Head, 4 lengths, 1m 354/5s. 18 ran F Armstrong
1949 Mrs M. Glenister's Nimbus, by Nearco . . . . E C Elliott 10–1
Major R Macdonald-Buchanan's Abenant . . . . G Richards 5–4
Mr H Lane's Barnes Park . . . . W Cook 100–1
Short head, 4 lengths, 1m 38s. 13 ran G S Colling
1950 H.H. Agar Khan's Palestine, by Fair Trial . . . . C Smirke 4–1
Mr W Woodward's Prince Simon . . . . W H Carr 3–1
Mr E Wanless's Masked Light . . D Smith 7–2
Short head, 5 lengths, 1m 364/5s. 19 ran M Marsh
1951 Mr Ley On's Ki Ming, by Ballyogan . . . . A Beasley 100–8
Sir Victor Sassoon's Stokes . . G Younger 33–1
Mr H E Elvin's Malka's Boy . . . W Cook 40–1
11/2 lengths, short head, 1m 42s. 27 ran M Beary
1952 M. E. Constant's Thunderhead II, by Merry Boy . . . . R Poincelet 100–7
Mr A J Tompsett's King's Bench . . . . T Gosling 22–1
M M Boussac's Argur . . . . E C Elliott 8–1
5 lengths, 1/2 length, 1m 422/5s. 26 ran E Pollett, in France
1953 Mr W. Humble's Nearula, by Nasrullah . . . . E Britt 2–1
Mr. J S Gerber's Bebe Grande W Snaith 10–1
Mr S Niarchos's Oleandrin . . R Faawdon 20–1
4 lengths, 3 lengths, 1m 381/5s. 16 ran C F Elsey
1954 Sir P. Lorrain's Darius, by Dante . . . . E Mercer 8–1
Comte de Chambure's Ferriol . . . . W Johnstone 100–9
H.H. Aga Khan's Poona . . . . C Smirke 40–1
1 length, 5 lengths, 1m 392/5s. 19 ran H Wragg
1955 Mr D. Robinson's Our Babu, by My Babu . . . . D Smith 13–2
Lord Porchester's Tamerlane A Breasley 5–1
M M Fabiani's Klairon . . . . J Deforge 28–1
Neck, short head, 1m 384/5s. 23 ran G T Brooke
1956 Mr A. G. Samuel's Gilles de Retz, by Royal Charger . . . . F Barlow 50–1
Mrs E Foster's Chantelsey . . . . E Britt 10–1
H.H. Aga Khan's Buisson Ardent . . . . R Poincelet 20–1
1 length, 11/2 lengths, 1m 384/5s. 19 ran C Jerdein
1957 Sir Victor Sassoon's Crepello, by Donatello II . . . . L Piggott 7–2
Mr T H Farr's Quorum . . . . A Russell 100–8
Mr. S Niarcho's Pipe of Peace A Breasley 100–30
1/2 length, head, 1m 381/5s. 15 ran C F N Murless
1958 Her Majesty's Pall Mall, by Palestine . . . . D Smith 20–1
Mr H J Joel's Major Portion . . . . E Smith 5–1
Mrs A Plesch's Nagami . . . . J Mercer 8–1
1/2 length, 3 lengths, 1m 392/5s. 14 ran C Boyd-Rochfort
1959 Prince Aly Khan's Taboun, by Tabriz . . . . G Moore 5–2
Mr A R Ellis's Masham . . . . D Smith 9–2
Lt-Col Giles Loder's Carnoustie . . . . L Piggott 11–2
3 lengths, neck, 1m 422/5s. 13 ran A Head, in France
1960 Mr R. N. Webster's Martial, by Hill Gail . . . . R Hutchinson 18–1
Prince Aly Khan's Venture II . . G Moore 6–4
Mr A Kennedy's Auroy . . . . T Gosling 40–1
Head, 4 lengths, 1m 382/5s. 17 ran P J Prendergast, in Ireland
1961 Mr T. C. Yuill's Rockavon, by Rockefella . . . . N Stirk 66–1
Mr J W Weston Evan's Prince Tudor . . . . W Rickaby 66–1
Mr J McGrath's Time Greine . . . . W Williamson 25–1
2 lengths, short head, 1m 392/5s. 22 ran G Boyd
1962 Maj G. Glover's Privy Councillor, by Counsel . . . . W Rickaby 100–6
Mr C W Engelhard's Romulus . . . . W Swinburn 8–1
Lady Sassoon's Prince Poppa . . W H Carr 100–8
3 lengths, 2 lengths, 1m 384/5s. 19 ran T Waugh
1963 Miss M. Sheriffe's Only for Life, by Chanteur II . . . . J Lindley 33–1
Mrs A B Biddle's Ionian . . . . L Ward 18–1
Mr R F Scully's Corpora . . . . A G Mulley 100–6
Short head, 3 lengths, 1m 45s. 21 ran A J Tree
1964 Mrs H. E. Jackson's Baldric II, by Round Table . . . . W Pyers 20–1
Mr N H Wachman's Feberge II J Mercer 28–1
Mr R B Moller's Balustrade . . . . W Williamson 28–1
2 lengths, 1 length, 1m 382/5s. 27 ran E Fellows, in France
1965 Mr W. Harvey's Niksar, by Le Haar . . . . D Keith 100–8
Mr P Mellon's Silly Season . . . . G Lewis 13–2
Comte L de Kerouara's Present II . . . . M Depalmas 100–7
1 length, same, 1m 432/5s. 22 ran W Nightingall
1966 Mr P. Butler's Kashmir II, by Tudor Melody . . . . J Lindley 7–1
Mr J P Philipp's Great Nephew . . . . W Rickaby 66–1
Mr Max Rayne's Celtic Song . . . . D Lake 100–6
Short head, 21/2 lengths, 1m 403/5s. 25 ran C Bartholomew Jun., in France
1967 Mr H. J. Joel's Royal Palace, by Ballymoss . . . . G Moore 100–30
Mme G Courtois's Taj Dewan . . . F Head 4–1
Mr Raymond R Guest's Missile . . L Ward 40–1
Short Head, 11/2 lengths, 1m 392/5s. 18 ran C F N Murless
1968 Mr Raymond R. Guest's Sir Ivor, by Sir Gaylord . . . . L Piggott 11–8
Capt M D Lemos's Petingo . . . J Mercer 9–4
Mrs Sidney Bates's Jimmy Reppin . . . . G Lewis 28–1
11/2 lengths, 21/2 lengths, 1m 391/5s. 10 ran M V O'Brien, in Ireland
1969 Mr J. R. Brown's Right Tack, by Hard Tack . . . . G Lewis 15–2
Mr V W Hardy's Tower Walk . . . . M L Thomas 8–1
Mr H J Joel's Welsh Pageant . . A Barclay 13–2

2½ lengths, head, 1m 41⅗s. 13 ran J Sutcliffe jun.

1970 Mr C. W. Engelhard's Nijinsky (Can), by Northern Dancer ....L Piggott 4–7
Mr D Robinson's Yellow God ....W Williamson 100–6
Mrs W H D Riley-Smith's Roi Soleil ....F Head 25–1
2½lengths, same, 1m 41⅗s. 14 ran M V O'Brien in Ireland

1971 Mrs J. Hislop's Brigadier Gerard, by Queen's Hussar ....J Mercer 11–2
Mr P Mellon's Mill Reef (USA) G Lewis 6–4
Mr D Robinson's My Swallow ...F Durr 2–1
3 lengths, ¾ length,1m 39⅕s. 6 ran W Hern

1972 Sir J. Thorn's High Top, by Derring-Do ....W Carson 85–40
Mr J Galbreath's Roberto (USA) ....W Williamson 7–2
Sir M Sobell's Sun Prince ......J Mercer 60–1
½ length, 6 lengths, 1m 40⅘s. 12 ran B van Cutsem

1973 Mrs B. Davis's Mon Fils, by Sheshoon ....F Durr 50–1
Mr N B Hunt's Noble Decree (USA) ....W Carson 18–1
Mr J J Astor's Sharp Edge ......J Mercer 45–1
Head, 3 lengths, 1m 43s. 18 ran R Hannon

1974 Mme M. Berger's Nonoalco (USA), by Nearctic ....Y Saint-Martin 19–2
Mr C A B St George's Giacometti ....A Murray 12–1
Mr J A Mulcahy's Apalachee (USA) ....L Piggott 4–9
1½ lengths, 1 length, 1m 39⅗s. 12 ran F Boutin in France

1975 Sig. C. d'Alessio's Bolkonski, by Balidar ....G Dettori 33–1
Dr C Vittadini's Grundy .....Pat Eddery 7–2
Col P L M Wright's Dominion I Johnson 33–1
½ length, 3 lengths, 1m 39⅖s. 24 ran H Cecil

1976 Sig. C. d'Alessio's Wollow, by Wolver Hollow ....G Dettori Evens
Mrs M Laloum's Vitiges (Fr) ..G Rivases 10–1
Mrs D Goldstein's Thieving Demon ....F Durr 66–1
1½ lengths, 2 lengths, 1m 38⅕s. 17 ran H Cecil

1977 Mr N. Schibbye's Nebbiolo, by Yellow God ....G Curran 20–1
Mr G Cambanis's Tachypous ...G Lewis 12–1
Mr R Sangster's The Minstrel L Piggott 6–5
1 length, same, 1m 38⅗s. 18 ran K Prendergast in Ireland

1978 Mr J. Hayter's Roland Gardens, by Derring-Do ....F Durr 28–1
Mrs D Jardine's Remainder Man ..T Ives 14–1
Mr E Alkhalifa's Weth Nan ....B Taylor 20–1
1½ lengths, head, 1m 47⅖s. 19 ran D Sasse

1979 Mr A. Shead's Tap on Wood, by Sallust ....S Cauthen 20–1
Lord Howard de Walden's Kris J Mercer 15–8
Mr A Ward's Young Generation ....G Starkey 13–2
½ length, short head, 1m 43⅗s. 20 ran B Hills

1980 Mr K. Abdulla's Known Fact (USA), by In Reality ....W Carson 14–1
Mr O Mills Phipps Posse (USA) ....Pat Eddery 12–1
Mr R E Sangster's Night Alert (USA) ....L Piggott 8–1
Neck, ¾ length, 1m 40⅗s. 14 ran A J Tree
Nureyev (USA) came in first but was disqualified.

1981 Mrs A. Muinos's To-Agori-Mou, by Tudor Music ....G Starkey 5–2
Mr R Tikkoo's Mattaboy ....J Reid 50–1
Mr K Abdulla's Bel Bolide (USA) ....Pat Eddery 14–1
Neck, 1½ lengths, 1m 41⅖s. 19 ran G Harwood

1982 Mr G Oldham's Zino, by Welsh Pageant ....F Head 8–1
Mr R Cyzer's Wind And Wuthering ....S Cauthen 8–1
Esal Commodities Ltd's Tender King ....Y Saint-Martin 11–1
Head, 2 lengths, 1m 37⅕s. 26 ran F Boutin, in France

1983 Mr R. Sangster's Lomond (USA), by Northern Dancer ....Pat Eddery 9–1
Mr C D'Alessio's Tolomeo ....G Dettori 16–1
Kais Al-Said's Muscatite ....B Taylor 12–1
2 length, ¾ length, 1m 43⅘s. 16 ran M V O'Brien, in Ireland

1984 Mr R. Sangster's El Gran Senor (USA), by Northern Dancer ....Pat Eddery 15–8
Mr J C Smith's Chief Singer R Cochrane 20–1
Mr A Salman's Lear Fan ....B Rouse 7–2
2½ lengths, 4 lengths, 1m 37⅖s. 9 ran M V O'Brien, in Ireland

1985 Maktoum Al-Maktoum's Shadeed (USA), by Nijinsky (Can) ....L Piggott 4–5
Sheikh Mohammed's Bairn (USA) ....W Carson 13–2
Capt M Lemos's Supreme Leader ....P Robinson 50–1
Head, 1½ lengths, 1m 37⅖s. 14 ran M Stoute

1986 Mr K. Abdulla's Dancing Brave (USA), by Lyphard ....G Starkey 15–8
Maktoum-Al-Maktoum's Green Desert (USA) ....W R Swinburn 12–1
Mrs P J Threlfall's Huntingdale ..M Hills 6–1
3 lengths, 1½ lengths, 1m 40s. 15 ran G Harwood

1987 Mr Jim Horgan's Don't Forget Me, by Ahonoora ....W Carson 9–1
Mr K Abdulla's Bellotto (USA) ....Pat Eddery 7–1
Prince A A Faisal's Midyan (USA) ....S Cauthen 12–1
Neck, 1 length, 1m 36⅘s. 13 ran R Hannon
Most Welcome finished third but was disqualified

1988 H.H. Aga Khan's Doyoun by Mill Reef (USA) ....W R Swinburn 4–5
Lady Beaverbrook's Charmer W Carson 10–1
Mr E Evans's Bellefella (USA) ....Paul Eddery 100–1
½ length; 2 lengths, 1m 41⅘s. 9 ran M Stoute

1989 Hamdan Al-Maktoum's Nashwan (USA), by Blushing Groom ....W Carson 3–1
Mr K Abdulla's Exbourne (USA) ....C Asmussen 10–1
Mr K Abdulla's Danehill (USA) ....Pat Eddery 9–1
1 length, ½ length, 1m 36⅖s. 14 ran W Hern

1990 Mr J Horgan's Tirol by Thatching ....M Kinane 9–1
Mr S Niarchos's Machiavellian (USA) ....F Head 6–4
Sheikh Mohammed's Anshan ....W R Swinburn 6–1
2 lengths, 2 lengths, 1m 35⅘s. 14 ran R. Hannon

1991 Lady Beaverbrook's Mystiko (USA) by Secreto (USA) ....M Roberts 13–2
Sheikh Mohammed's Lycius (USA) ....S Cauthen 16–1
Mr A E Paulson's Ganges (USA) F Head 16–1
Head, 6 lengths, 1m 37⅘s. 14 ran C Brittain

1992 Mr R E Sangster's Rodrigo de Triano (USA) by El Gran Senor .....L Piggott 6–1
Mr G Howard-Spink's Lucky Lindy ....M J Kinane 50–1
Ld Howard de Walden's Pursuit of Love ....M Roberts 9–2
1½ lengths, ½ length, 1m 38⅖s. 16 ran P W Chapple-Hyam

1993 Mr K Abdulla's Zafonic (USA) by Gone West (USA) ....Pat Eddery 5–6
Sheikh Mohammed's Barathea ....M Roberts 10–1
Mr A Merza's Bin Ajwaad ..B Raymond, 66–1
3½ lengths, 3 lengths, 1m 35⅖s. 14 ran A Fabre, in France

†New Two Thousand Guineas on July Course
*Dead Heat

MADAGANS ONE THOUSAND GUINEAS (Newmarket—1 mile)

For three year old fillies

		Starters	Jockeys
1814	Mr C. Wilson's b f Charlotte, by Orville	5	W. Clift
1815	Lord Foley's br f by Selim, dam by Cesario	4	W. Clift
1816	Duke of Rutland's b Rhoda, by Asparagus	6	S. Barnard
1817	Mr G. Watson's b Neva, by Cervantes	10	W. Arnull
1818	Mr J. Udny's br Corinne, by Waxy	8	F. Buckle
1819	Duke of Grafton's b Catgut, by Comus or Juniper	7	Unknown
1820	Duke of Grafton's ch Rowena, by Haphazard	6	F. Buckle
1821	Duke of Grafton's br Zeal, by Partisan	6	F. Buckle
1822	Duke of Grafton's ch Whizgig, by Rubens	4	F. Buckle
1823	Duke of Grafton's br Zinc, by Woful	5	F. Buckle
1824	Lord Jersey's b Cobweb, by Phantom	4	J. Robinson
1825	Duke of Grafton's ch Tontine, by Election	w.o.	Unknown
1826	Duke of Grafton's ch Problem, by Merlin	5	J. B. Day
1827	Duke of Grafton's br Arab, by Woful	7	F. Buckle
1828	Mr A. Moloney's b Zoe, by Orville	7	J. Robinson
1829	Lord G. H. Cavendish's b by Godolphin—Mouse	4	J. Arnull
1830	Lord Jersey's ch Charlotte West, by Tramp	7	J. Robinson
1831	Sir M. Wood's b Galantine, by Revelier	8	P. Conolly
1832	Lord Exeter's br Galata, by Sultan	4	J. Arnull
1833	Mr T. Cooke's ch Tarantella, by Tramp	10	E. Wright
1834	Lord Berners's ch May Day, by Lamplighter	7	J. B. Day
1835	Mr C. Greville's ch Preserve, by Emilius	3	E. Flatman
1836	Mr T. Houldsworth's ch Destiny, by Sultan	7	J. B. Day
1837	Lord G. Bentinck's b Chapeau d'Espagne, by Dr. Syntax	5	J. B. Day
1838	Lord Albemarle's br Barcarolle, by Emilius	6	E. Edwards
1839	Mr R. Watt's b Cara, by Belshazzar	5	G. Edwards
1840	Lord G. Bentinck's b Crucifix, by Priam	4	J. B. Day
1841	Mr S. Batson's ch Potentia, by Plenipotentiary	5	J. Robinson
1842	Lord G. Bentinck's ch Firebrand, by lamplighter	7	S. Rogers
1843	Mr T. Thornhill's b Extempore, by Emilius	9	S. Chifney jun.
1844	Mr G. Osbaldeston's ch Sorella, by The Saddler	9	J. Robinson
1845	Duke of Richmond's b Pic-nic, by Glaucus	8	W. Abdale
1846	Mr J. Gully's br Mendicant, by Touchstone	7	S. Day
1847	Mr G. Payne's b Clementina, by Venison	5	E. Flatman
1848	Lord Stanley's br Canezou, by Melbourne	9	F. Butler
1849	Mr F. Clarke's b Flea, by Coronation	10	A. Day
1850	Lord Orford's ch by Slane—Exotic	5	F. Butler
1851	Sir J. Hawley's br Aphrodite, by Bay Middleton	6	J. Marson
1852	Mr Sargent's b Kate, by Auckland	6	A. Day
1853	Baron de Rothschild's b Mentmore Lass, by Melbourne	11	J. Charlton
1854	Mr Howard's ch Virago, by Pyrrhus the First	3	J. Wells
1855	Duke of Beford's ch Habena, by Irish Birdcatcher	11	S. Rogers
1856	Mr W. H. Brooke's ch Manganese, by Irish Birdcatcher	5	J. Osborne
1857	Mr J. Scott's b Imperieuse, by Orlando	8	E. Flatman
1858	Mr W. Gratwicke's ch Governess, by Chatham	9	T. Ashmall
1859	Mr W. S. Crawfurd's by Mayonaise, by Teddington	4	G. Fordham
1860	Lord Derby's b Sagitta, by Longbow	13	T. Aldcroft
1861	Mr G. Fleming's b Nemesis, by Newminster	9	G. Fordham
1862	Lord Falmouth's b Hurricane, by Wild Dayrell	11	T. Ashmall
1863	Lord Stamford's ch Lady Augusta, by Stockwell	10	A. Edwards
1864	Baron de Rothschild's b Tomato, by King Tom	15	J. Wells
1865	Duke of Beaufort's br Siberia, by Muscovite	11	G. Fordham
1866	Marquis of Hasting's b Repulse, by Stockwell	9	T. Cannon
1867	Col Pearson's br Achievement, by Stockwell	7	H. Custance
1868	Mr G. Jones's ch Formosa, by Buccaneer	8	G. Fordham
1869	Duke of Beaufort's ch Scottish Queen, by Blair Athol	9	G. Fordham
1870	Mr Jos. Dawson's b Hester, by Thromanby	10	J. Grimshaw
1871	Baron de Rothschild's b Hannah, by King Tom	7	C. Maidment
1872	Mr C. Lefevre's b Reine, by Monarque	11	H. Parry
1873	Lord Falmouth's b Cecilia, by Blair Athol	14	J. Morris
1874	Mr Launde's ch Apology, by Adventurer	9	J. Osborne
1875	Lord Falmouth's b Spinaway, by Macaroni	6	F. Archer
1876	Count de Lagrange's ch Camelia, by Macaroni	13	T. Glover
1877	Lord Hartington's b Belphoebe, by Toxophilite	19	H. Jeffery
1878	Lord Lonsdale's ch Pilgrimage, by The Earl or The Palmer	9	T. Cannon
1879	Lord Falmouth's b Wheel of Fortune, by Adventurer	8	F. Archer
1880	Mr T. E. Walker's b or br f Elizabeth, by Statesman	10	C. Wood
1881	Mr W. S. Crawfurd's ch f Thebais, by Hermit	13	G. Fordham
1882	Mr W. S. Crawfurd's ch f St. Marguerite, by Hermit	6	C. Wood
1883	Mr C. J. Lefevre's b f hauteur, by Rosicrucian	9	G. Fordham
1884	Mr Abington's b f Busybody, by Petrarch	6	T. Cannon
1885	Duke of Westminster's ch f Farewell, by Doncaster	16	G. Barrett
1886	Duke of Hamilton's b f Miss Jummy, by Petrarch	10	J. Watts
1887	Duke of Beaufort's ch f Reve d'Or, by Hampton	12	C. Wood
1888	Mr Douglas Baird's b f Briar-root, by Springfield	14	W. Warne

MADAGANS ONE THOUSAND GUINEAS—continued

		Starters	Jockeys
1889	Mr R. Vyner's b f Minthe, by Camballo	14	J. Woodburn
1890	Duke of Portland's b f Semolina, by St. Simon	10	J. Watts
1891	Mr Noel Fenwick's b f Mimi, by Barcaldine	12	F. Rickaby
1892	Baron de Hirsch's br f La Fleche, by St. Simon	7	G. Barrett
1893	Sir J. B. Maple's ch f Siffleuse, by Saraband	11	T. Loates
1894	Duke of Portland's b f Amiable, by St. Simon	13	W. Bradford
1895	Mr "Fairie's" b or br f Galeottia, by Galophin	15	F. Pratt
1896	H.R.H. The Prince of Wales's br f Thais, by St. Serf	19	J. Watts
1897	Lord Rosebery's b f Chelandry, by Goldfinch	9	J. Watts
1898	Sir J. B. Maple's b f Nun Nicer, by Common	15	S. Loates
1899	Lord W. Beresford's b f Sibola, by Sailor Prince	14	J. F. Sloan

1900 Mr L Brassey's Winifreda, by St Simon
..........S Loates 11–2
Ld Ellesmere's Inquisitive ......J F Sloan 100–7
Sir R Waldie Griffith's Vain Duchess
..........J H Martin 4–1
¾ length, 2 lengths, 1m 46s. 10 ran T Jennings, Jun.

1901 Sir J Miller's Aida, by Galopin D Maher 13–8
Sir E Cassel's Fleur d'Ete .....W Halsey 10–1
Ld Derby's Santa Brigida ....J Reiff 10–1
Neck, 2 lengths, 1m 44⅗s. 15 ran G Blackwell

1902 Mr R S Sievier's Sceptre, by Persimmon
..........H Randall 1–2
Col E W Baird's St Windeline ...W Lane 100–7
Mr L Brassey's Black Fancy .....J Childs 33–1
1½ lengths, 4 lengths, 1m 40⅕s. 15 ran Owner

1903 Ld Falmouth's Quintessence, by St Frusquin ....H Randall 4–1
Prince Soltykoff's Sun-Rose ...W Halsey 20–1
Mr W Raphael's Skyscraper ....D Maher 9–4
1½ lengths, 2 lengths, 1m 48s. 12 ran J Chandler

1904 Maj Eustace Loder's Pretty Polly, by Gallinule ....W Lane 1–4
Mr D Baird's Leucadia ....H Aylin 33–1
Ld Stanley's Flamma ....D Maher 100–1
3 lengths, 4 lengths, 1m 40s. 7 ran P P Gilpin

1905 Mr W Hall Walker's Cherry Lass, by Isinglass ....G McCall 5–4
Ld Ellesmere's Koorhaan ....B Dillon 33–1
Ld Carnarvon's Jongleuse ....H Pipe 33–1
1 length, 3 lengths, 1m 43⅖s. 19 ran W Robinson

1906 Sir Daniel Cooper's Flair, by St Frusquin
..........B Dillon 10–11
Mr W M G Singer's Lischana ..W Higgs 20–1
D of Portland's Paid Up ......H Randall 20–1
3 lengths, ¾ length, 1m 40⅗s. 12 ran P P Gilpin

1907 Mr W Hall Walker's Witch Elm, by Orme
..........B Lynham 4–1
Ld Falmouth's Frugality ......G McCall 20–1
Mr Arthur James's Sixty ......W Halsey 20–1
3 lengths, 1½ lengths, 1m 42⅗s. 17 ran W Robinson

1908 Mr R Croker's Rhodora, by St Frusquin
..........L Lyne 100–8
Capt F Forester's Bracelet ....B Lynham 5–1
Mr J H Houldsworth's Ardentive
..........W Halsey 100–6
2 lengths, neck, 1m 43⅘s. 19 ran G Allen

1909 Mr L Neumann's Electra, by Eager
..........B Dillon 9–1
His Majesty's Princesse de Galles H Jones 5–2
Mr W C Cooper's Perola ....F Wootton 3–1
1 length, 4 lengths, 1m 40⅖s. 10 ran P P Gilpin

1910 Mr W Astor's Winkipop, by William the Third ....B Lynham 5–2
Sir W Bass's Maid of Corinth ....J Jones 100–8
Sir W Bass's Rosedrop ....C Trigg 20–1
1½ lengths, head, 1m 41s. 13 ran W Waugh

1911 Mr J A de Rothschild's Atmah, by Galeazzo ....F Fox 7–1
Mr J B Joel's Radiancy ......J H Martin 25–1
Maj Eustace Loder's Knockfeerna
..........F O'Neill 100–8
Short head, 2 lengths, 1m 38⅖s. 16 ran F Pratt

1912 Mr W Raphael's Tagalie, by Cyllene
..........L Hewitt 20–1
Baron G Springer's Alope ....B Carslake 20–1
Ld Falmouth's Belleisle ....J Jones 7–4
1½ lengths, ¾ length, 1m 39⅗s. 13 ran D Waugh

1913 Mr J B Joel's Jest, by Sundridge
..........F Rickaby Jun. 9–1
D of Devonshire's Taslett ...E Wheatley 6–1
Ld Roseberry's Prue ....D Maher 9–1
Head, ½ length, 1m 40⅘s. 22 ran C Morton

1914 Mr J B Joel's Princess Dorrie, by Your Majesty ....W Huxley 100–9
Ld Derby's Glorvina .....F Rickaby Jun. 100–7
Sir J Thursby's Torchlight ......G Stern Evens
¾ length, neck, 1m 42s. 13 ran C Morton

1915 Ld Rosebery's Vaucluse, by Dark Ronald
..........F Rickaby Jun. 5–2
Mr E Hulton's Silver Tag ...S Donoghue 4–1
Mr J B Joel's Bright ....F Fox 10–1
¾ length, 1½ lengths, 1m 40⅘s. 15 ran F Hartigan

1916 Ld Derby's Canyon, by Chaucer
..........F Rickaby Jun. 9–4
Mr E Hutton's Fifenella ....J Childs 11–10
Mr L Neumann's Salamandra A Whalley 10–1
¾ length, 3 lengths, 1m 40s. 14 ran Hon G Lambton

1917 Ld D'Abernon's Diadem, by Orby
..........R Rickaby Jun. 6–4
Maj W Astor's Sunny Jane ....R Cooper 25–1
Ld Falmouth's Nonpareil .....A Whalley 25–1
½ length, 4 lengths, 1m 43s. 14 ran Hon G Lambton

1918 Ld Derby's Ferry, by Swynford
..........B Carslake 50–1
Mr A W Cox's My Dear ...S Donoghue 6–4
Mr Donald Fraser's Herself ....F Fox 20–1
2 lengths, 3 lengths, 1m 46⅖s. 8 ran Hon G Lambton

1919 Sir E Hulton's Roseway, by Stornoway
..........A Whalley 2–1
Mr L Brassey's Brittania ....F Fox 6–1
Ld Derby's Glaciale ....G Colling 20–1
6 lengths, 1½ lengths, 1m 47⅗s. 15 ran F Hartigan

1920 Sir R W B Jardine's Cinna, by Polymelus
..........Wm Griggs 4–1
Baron E de Rothschild's Cicerole J Childs 100–8
Ld Rosebery's Valescure ....O Preece 25–1
3 lengths, 1 length, 1m 40⅖s. 21 ran T Waugh

1921 Mr W Raphael's Bettina, by Swynford
..........G Bellhouse 33–1
Mr Wm Clark's Petrea ....B Carslake 33–1
Ld Astor's Pompadour ....J Brennan 7–1
1½ lengths, ¾ length, 1m 44⅗s. 24 ran P Linton

1922 Mr B W Parr's Silver Urn, by Juggernaut
..........B Carslake 10–1
Sir E Hulton's Soubriquet .....V Smyth 100–12
Mr Marshall Field's Golden Corn
..........S Donoghue 7–4
2 lengths, ¾ length, 1m 40s. 20 ran H S Perse

1923 Ld Derby's Tranquil, by Swynford
..........E Gardner 5–2
H H Aga Khan's Cos ....G Hulme 10–1
Sir E Hulton;s Shrove .....W McLachlan 100–6
1½ lengths, 1 length, 1m 39s. 16 ran Hon G Lambton

1924 Ld Rosebery's Plack, by Hurry On
..........E C Elliott 8–1
H H Aga Khan's Mumtaz Mahal
..........G Hulme 6–5

Sir E Hulton's Straiglace ......F O'Neill 7–2
1/2 length, same, 1m 393/5s. 16 ran J L Jarvis
1925 Ld Astor's Saucy Sue, by Swynford ....F Bullock 1–4
Ld Astor's Miss Gadabout ....J Brennan 20–1
H H Aga Khan's Firouze Mahal ....B Carslake 7–1
6 lengths, 2 lengths, 1m 422/5s. 11 ran Alec Taylor
1926 Mr A de Rothschild's Pillion, by Chaucer ....R Perryman 25–1
Ld Durham's Trilogy ....F Lane 8–1
Ld Astor's Short Story ....J Brennan 20–1
1 length, 1/2 length, 1m 42s. 29 ran J Watson
1927 Lt-Col G Loder's Cresta Run, by Hurry On ....A Balding 10–1
Ld Astor's Book Law ....H Jeliss 13–2†
Ld Lonsdale's Endowment ......J Childs 3–1†
2 lengths, dead-heat, 1m 38s. 28 ran P P Gilpin
1928 His Majesty's Scuttle, by Captain Cuttle ....J Childs 15–8
Ld Dewar's Jurisdiction ......G Richards 100–8
Ld Derby's Toboggan ....T Weston 11–2
1 length, 6 lengths, 1m 441/5s. 14 ran W Jarvis
1929 M Simon Guthmann's Taj Mah, by Lemberg ....W Sibbritt 33–1
Lt-Col G Loder's Sister Anne ...J Childs 5–2
Sir G Bullough's Ellanvale ...E C Elliott 20–1
3/4 length, short head, 1m 402/5s. 19 ran J Torterolo, in France
1930 Ld Derby's Fair Isle, by Phalaris ....T Weston 7–4
Mr A de Rothschild's Torchere ....R Perryman 10–1
Mr C Wadia's Sister Clover .....J Sirrett 10–1
Short head, neck, 1m 42s. 19 ran Frank Butters
1931 Ld Ellesmere's Four Course, by Tetratema ....E C Elliott 100–9
Mr M H Benson's Lady Marjorie .....G Richards 4–1
Lady H McCalmont's Lindos Ojos ....H Beasley 10–1
Head, 1 length, 1m 394/5s. 20 ran Fred Darling
1932 M E de St Alary's Kandy, by Alcantara II ....E C Elliott 33–1
Mr S Tattersall's Thorndean ..R A Jones 20–1
Ld Woolavington;s Safe Return ....G Richards 100–6
1 length, same, 1m 44s. 19 ran F Carter, in France
1933 Mr W Woodward's Brown Betty, by Friar Marcus ....J Childs 9–1
Mr W M G Singer's Fur Tor ..R A Jones 100–6
Ld Lonsdale's Myrobella .....G Richards 5–1
1/2 length, 3/4 length, 1m 392/5s. 22 ran C Boyd-Rochfort
1934 Sir G Bullough's Campanula, by Blandford ....H Wragg 2–1
Ld Durham's Light Brocade ..B Carslake 100–6
Sir A Butt's Spend a Penny R Perryman 100–9
1 length, 6 lengths, 1m 39s. 10 ran J L Jarvis
1935 M Pierre Wertheimer's Mesa, by Kircubbin ....W Johnstone 8–1
Mr J Shand's Hyndford Bridge H Wragg 20–1
Ld Londsdale Caretta ....G Richards 9–4
3 lengths, 11/2 lengths, 1m 43s. 22 ran M P Corbiere, in France
1936 Ld Derby's Tide-way, by Fairway ....R Perryman 100–39
Ld Derby's Feola ....F Fox 28–1
Mr R F Watson's Ferrybridge G Richards 11–4
11/2 lengths, neck, 1m 42s. 22 ran C Leader
1937 Sir Victor Sassoon's Exhibitionist, by Solario ....S Donoghue 10–1
Maj H Cayzer's Spray ....P Beasley 100–6
Sir J Jarvis's Gainsborough Lass E Smith 10–11
1/2 length, head, 1m 434/5s. 20 ran J Lawson
1938 Sir H Cunliffe-Owen's Rockfel, by Felstead ....S Wragg 8–1
Mr D Crossman's Laughing Water ....W Stephenson 20–1
Sir A Butt's Solar Flower ...R Perryman 20–1
11/2 lengths, 3 lengths, 1m 38s. 20 ran O Bell
1939 Mr R S Clark's Galatea II, by Dark Legend ....R A Jones 6–1
Ld Derby's Aurora ....R Perryman 7–1
Ld Glanely's Olein ....T Lowrey 9–2
3 lengths, 1/2 length, 1m 383/5s. 18 ran J Lawson
1940★Ld Rothermere's Godiva by Hyperion ....D Marks 10–1
Ld Astor's Golden Penny ....G Richards 8–11
Sir M McAlpine's Allure ....M Beary 10–1
5 lengths, 4 lengths, 1m 404/5s. 11 ran W Jarvis
1941★Ld Glanely's Dancing Time by Columbo ....R Perryman 100–8
Mrs A James's Beausite ....H Wragg 7–1
Mr P Beatty's Keystone .....G Richards 11–2
1 length, 2 lengths, 1m 412/5s. 13 ran J Lawson
1942★His Majesty's Sun Chariot by Hyperion ....G Richards Evens
Ld Glanely's Perfect Peace ....R A Jones 5–1
Lady Derby's Light of Day ....S Ellis 25–1
4 lengths, 2 lengths, 1m 393/5s. 18 ran Fred Darling
1943★Ld Derby's Herringbone by King Salmon ....H Wragg 15–2
Ld Rosebery's Ribbon ....E Smith 6–4
Ld Durham's Cincture ....W Nevett 100–7
Neck, 11/2 lengths, 1m 414/5s. 12 ran W Earl
1944★Mr H J Joel's Picture Play by Donatello II ....E C Elliott 15–2
Mr J S Gerber's Grande Corniche ....P Evans 100–6
Mr James V Rank's Superior ..T Weston 100–9
4 lengths, 2 lengths, 1m 403/5s. 11 ran J Watts
1945★Ld Derby's Sun Stream by Hyperion ....H Wragg 5–2
Ld Rosebery's Blue Smoke .....E Smith 25–1
Miss D Paget's Mrs Feather ....A Wragg 4–1
3 lengths, 2 lengths, 1m 452/5s. 14 ran W Earl
1946 His Majesty's Hypericum, by Hyperion ....D Smith 100–6
Mr J A Dewar's Neolight ....G Richards 4–6
Ld Roseberry's Iona ....E Smith 9–1
11/2 lengths, 3/4 length, 1m 413/5s. 13 ran C Boyd-Rochfort
1947 Mme P Corbiere's Imprudence, by Canot ....W Johnstone 4–1
Mme L L Lawrence's Rose O'Lynn ....S Smith 100–6
Mr S Joel's Wild Child ....T Lowrey 20–1
Neck, head, 1m 46s. 20 ran J Lieux, in France
1948 Sir P Loraine's Queenpot, by Big Game ....G Richards 6–1
Mrs C M Woodbridge's Ariostar ....J Marshall 100–6
Lady Zia Wernher's Duplicity W Nevett 33–1
Head, 11/2 lengths, 1m 414/5s. 22 ran C F N Murless
1949 Mr N P Donaldson's Musidora, by Nasrullah ....E Britt 100–8
Mr D H Wills's Unknown Quantity ....W Rickaby 7–2
Mr P Beatty's Solar Myth ....T Gosling 100–8
11/2 lengths, 2 lengths, 1m 40s. 18 ran C F Elsey
1950 M J Ternynck's Camaree, by Maurepas ....W Johnstone 10–1
Mr N P Donaldson's Catchit ....G Littlewood 50–1†
H H Aga Khan's Tambara ...G Richards 10–1†
3 lengths, dead-heat, 1m 37s. 17 ran A Lieux, in France
1951 Mr H S Tufton's Belle of All, by Nasrullah ....G Richards 4–1
Mr H D H Wills's Subtle Difference ....W Rickaby 100–8
Mr J E Ferguson's Bob Run ...K Gethin 50–1
Neck, 2 lengths, 1m 444/5s. 18 ran N Bertie
1952 Sir Malcolm Mc Alpine's Zabara, by Persian Gulf ....K Gethin 7–1
M M Hennessy's La Mirambule ....R Poincelet 2–1
Mr J A Dewar's Refreshed ...G Richards 100–8
1/2 length, 5 lengths, 1m 41s. 20 ran V Smyth

1953 Mr H D H Will's Happy Laughter, by Royal Charger ....E Mercer 10–1
Sir Adrian Jarvis's Tessa Gillian ....W Rickaby 9–2
Mr J S Gerber's Bebe Grande ..W Snaith 4–1
2 lengths, 5 lengths, 1m 45s. 14 ran J L Jarvis
1954 Mr J A Dewar's Festoon, by Fair Trial ....A Beasley 9–2
Maj-Gen J F B Combe's Big Berry ....L Piggott 20–1
Miss P Vaughan's Welsh Fairy ...F Durr 20–1
2 lengths, 1 length, 1m 39s. 12 ran N Cannon
1955 Lady Zia Wernher's Meld, by Alycidon ....W Carr 11–4
Ld Rosebery's Aberlady ....E Mercer 100–7
Mr S Wingfield Digby's Feria A Beasley 6–1
2 lengths, 1 1/2 lengths, 1m 42 1/5s. 12 ran C Boyd-Rochfort
1956 Sir Victor Sassoon's Honeylight, by Honeyway ....E Britt 100–6
M Pierre Werthelimer's Midget II ....R Poincelet 100–30
Mr Phil Bull's Arietta ....E Hide 33–1
2 lengths, 3 lengths, 1m 39 1/5s. 19 ran C F Elsey
1957 H.H Aga Khan's Rose Royale II, by Prince Bio ....C Smirke 6–1
Prince Aly Khan's Sensualita ..J Massard 33–1
Lady Honor Svejdar's Angelet ...E Hide 4–1
1 length, 2 lengths, 1m 39 1/5s. 20 ran A Head, in France
1958 M F Dupre's Bella Paola, by Ticino ....S Boullenger 8–1
Prince Aly Khan's Amante ....J Massard 9–1
Ld Milford's Alpine Bloom ....E Mercer 100–7
1 1/2 lengths, 5 lengths, 1m 38 4/5s. 11 ran F Mathet, in France
1959 Prince Aly Khan's Petite Etoile, by Petition ....D Smith 8–1
Mr J J Astor's Rosalba ....J Mercer 9–4
Prince Aly Khan's Paraguana ...G Moore 5–2
1 length, 4 lengths, 1m 40 2/5s. 14 ran C F N Murless
1960 Mrs H E Jackson's Never Too Late II, by Never Say Die ....R Poincelet 8–11
Mr A R B Owen's Lady in Trouble ....A Breasley 25–1
Mr J P Phillipps's Running Blue E Larkin 100–7
2 lengths, 1/2 length, 1m 39 4/5s. 14 ran E Pollett, in France
1961 Mrs S M Castello's Sweet Solera, by Solonaway ....W Rickaby 4–1
Sir P Loraine's Ambergris .....J Lindley 10–1
Mr F N Shane's Indian Melody ....A Breasley 100–6
1 1/2 lengths, 6 lengths, 1m 38 1/5s. 14 ran Reg Day
1962 Mr R More O'Ferrall's Abermaid, by Abernant ....W Williamson 100–6
Beatrice Lady Granard's Display ....G Bougoure 5–2
Mr H J Joel's West Side Story ...E Smith 5–1
1/2 length, 3/4 length, 1m 39 2/5s. 14 ran H Wragg
1963 Mr P A B Widener's Hula Dancer, by Native Dancer ....R Poincelet 1–2
Mr J G Morrison's Spree ......J Lindley 100–8
Mr W F C Guest's Royal Cypher ....A Breasley 28–1
1 length, same, 1m 42 2/5s. 12 ran E Pollet, in France
1964 Beatrice Lady Granard's Pourparler, by Hugh Lupus ....G Bougoure 11–2
Ld Rosebery's Gwen ....P Robinson 100–9
Maj G Glover's Petite Gina ...R P Elliott 50–1†
Mr G McGrath's Royal Danseuse J Rose 20–1†
1 length, 1 1/2 lengths, dead-heat, 1m 38 4/5s. 18 ran P J Prendergast, in Ireland
1965 Maj L B Holliday's Night Off, by Narrator ....W Williamson 9–2
Mr D A Jackson's Yami ....J Desaint 9–1
Mr S P Williams's Mabel ..R Hutchinson 22–1
Neck, 3 lengths, 1m 45 2/5s. 16 ran W Wharton
1966 Mr J P Mills's Glad Rags, by High Hat ....P Cook 100–6
Mr P Mellon's Berkeley Springs G Lewis 100–8
M F Dupre's Miliza II ...Y Saint-Martin 10–11
Neck, 2 lengths, 1m 40 2/5s. 21 ran M V O'Brien, in Ireland
1967 Mr R C Boucher's Fleet by Immortality ....G Moore 11–2
Mr Stanhope Joel's St Pauli Girl ....B Raymond 66–1
Mr R B Moller's Lacquer R Hutchinson 22–1
1/2 length, head, 1m 44 4/5s. 16 ran C F N Murless
1968 Mrs Noel Murless's Caergwrle, by Crepello ....A Barclay 4–1
Mr H J Joel's Photo Flash ......J Lindley 7–1
Mr R B Moller's Sovereign R Hutchinson 5–1
1 length, short head, 1m 40 2/5s. 14 ran C F N Murless
1969 Mr R B Moller's Full Dress II, by Shantung ....R Hutchinson 7–1
Mrs W H D Riley-Smith's Hecuba ....L Piggott 100–7
Mr J R Brown's Motionless ....G Lewis 100–7
1 1/2 lengths, 1 length, 1m 44 3/5s. 13 ran H Wragg
1970 Lady Ashcombe's Humble Duty, by Sovereign Path ....L Piggott 3–1
Mrs P Wertheimer's Gleam (Fr) ..F Head 100–7
Mr W L Rynolds's Black Satin ....R Hutchinson 100–7
7 lengths, 2 lengths, 1m 42 1/5s. 12 ran P Walwyn
1971 Mr F R Hue-Williams's Altesse Royale by Saint Crespin III ....Y Saint-Martin 25–1
Mrs M Slade's Super Honey ...L Piggott 8–1
Mr T F Blackwell's Catherine Wheel ....J Gorton 12–1
1 1/2 lengths, 3/4 length, 1m 41s. 10 ran C F N Murless
1972 Mrs R Stanley's Waterloo, by Bold Lad (Ire) ....E Hide 8–1
Mrs M F Berger's Marisela ....A Barclay 14–1
Mr H J Joel's Rose Dubarry ...A Murray 5–2
2 lengths, neck, 1m 39 3/5s. 18 ran J W Watts
1973 Mr G Pope Jnr's Mysterious, by Crepello ....G Lewis 11–1
Lady Butt's Jacinth ....J Gorton 4–5
Mr N Robinson's Shellshock ....G Cadwaladr 66–1
3 lengths, 2 lengths, 1m 42 1/5s. 14 ran C F N Murless
1974 Her Majesty's Highclere, by Queen's Hussar ....J Mercer 12–1
Mr L Freedman's Polygamy ..Pat Eddery 4–1
Mr T F Blackwell's Mrs Tiggywinkle ....J Gorton 11–1
Short head, 4 lengths, 1m 40 2/5s. 15 ran W Hern
1975 Mrs D O'Kelly's Nocturnal Spree, by Supreme Sovereign ....J Roe 14–1
Mr D Molin's Girl Friend ....J P Lefevre 13–1
Her Majesty's Joking Apart ....J Mercer 25–1
Short head, 1 length, 1m 41 3/5s. 16 ran H V S Murless, in Ireland
1976 Mr D Wildenstein's Flying Water (Fr), by Habitat ....Y Saint-Martin 2–1
Sig L Gatto-Roissard's Konafa (Can) ....G Dettori 66–1
Mr R Tikkoo's Kesar Queen (USA) ....F Head 14–1
1 length, neck, 1m 37 4/5s. 25 ran A Penna, in France
1977 Mrs E Kettlewell's Mrs McArdy, by Tribal Chief ....E Hide 16–1
Sig L Gatto-Roissard's Freeze the Secret (USA) ....G Dettori 11–2
M G Sammana's Sanedtki ....A Lequeux 12–1
2 lengths, 1 length, 1m 40s. 18 ran M W Easterby
1978 Mr R Bonnycastle's Enstone Spark, by Sparkler ....E Johnson 35–1
Mr S Hanson's Fair Salinia ....G Starkey 25–1
Mrs V Hue-Williams's Seraphima ....Pat Eddery 5–1
1 length, 2 1/2 lengths, 1m 41 3/5s. 16 ran B Hills
1979 Helena Springfield Ltd's One in a Million, by Rarity ....J Mercer Evens
Mrs A Sutton's Abbeydale ....J Lowe 25–1
Col R Poole's Yanuka ....F Morby 33–1

1½ lengths, head, 1m 43s. 17 ran H Cecil

1980 Mr O Mills Phipp's Quick As Lightning (USA), by Buckpasser ....B Rouse 12–1
Mr A Philipps's Our Home ...G Starkey 8–1
Mr E N Kronfeld's Mrs Penny (USA) ....J Matthias 8–1
Neck, ½ length, 1m 41⅘s. 23 ran J Dunlop

1981 Mr H J Joel's Fairy Footsteps, by Mill Reef (USA) ....L Piggott 6–4
Mr G Cambanis's Tolmi ....E Hide 11–2
Mr W Norton's Go Leasing ...G Starkey 13–1
Neck, neck, 1m 40⅖s. 14 ran H Cecil

1982 Sir P Oppenheimer's On The House (Fr), by Be My Guest (USA) ....J Reid 33–1
Mr R Barnett's Time Charter W Newnes 11–1
Mr D Prenn's Dione ....J Mercer 25–1
2½ lengths, 2 lengths, 1m 40⅖s. 15 ran H Wragg

1983 Maktoum Al Maktoum's Ma Biche (USA) by Key to the Kingdom F Head 5–2
Mr E B Moller's Favoridge (USA) ....Pat Eddery 7–2
Mr M Mutawa's Habibti .....W Carson 10–1
1½ lengths, head, 1m 41⅘s. 18 ran Mme C Head, in France

1984 Capt M Lemos's Pebbles by Sharpen Up ....P Robinson 8–1
Mr B Choucair's Meis El-Reem ....A Lequeux 25–1
Mrs J M Corbett's Desirable ..S Cauthen 8–1
3 lengths, neck, 1m 38⅕s. 15 ran C Brittain

1985 Sheikh Mohammed's Oh So Sharp by Kris ....S Cauthen 2–1
Hamdan Al Maktoum's Al Bahathri ....A Murray 11–1
Helena Springfield Ltd's Bella Colora ....L Piggott 7–1
Short head, short head, 1m 36⅘s. 17 ran H Cecil

1986 Mr H H Rainier's Midway Lady by Alleged ....R Cochrane 10–1
Maktoum Al Maktoum's Maysoon ....Y Saint Martin 15–2
Sheikh Mohammed's Sonic Lady (USA) ....W R Swinburn 6–4
¾ length, short head, 1m 41⅗s. 15 ran B Hanbury

1987 Mr S S Niarchos's Miesque (USA), by Nureyev ....F Head 15–8
Helena Springfield Ltd's Milligram ....W R Swinburn 13–2
Mr K Abdulla's Interval .....Pat Eddery 11–2
1½ lengths, head, 1m 38⅖s. 14 ran F Boutin, in France

1988 Ecurie Aland's Ravinella (USA) by Mr Prospector (USA) ....G Moore 4–5
Mohammed Obaida's Dabaweyaa ....W R Swinburn 14–1
Sheikh Mohammed's Diminuendo (USA) ....S Cauthen 6–1
1½ lengths, 1½ lengths, 1m 40⅘s. 12 ran Mrs C Head, in France

1989 Sheikh Mohammed's Musical Bliss (USA) by The Minstrel ....W R Swinburn 7–2
Sheikh Mohammed's Kerrera Pat Eddery 9–1
Rhodabourne Ltd's Aldbourne ....P Hamblett 20–1
¾ length, 1 length, 1m 42⅗s. 7 ran M R Stoute

1990 Hamdan Al-Maktoum's Salsabil by Sadler's Wells ....W Carson 6–4
Mr J Mabee's Heart of Joy (USA) ....W R Swinburn 4–1
Mrs J Corbett's Negligent ...Pat Eddery 11–2
¾ length, 5 lengths, 1m 38s. 10 ran J Dunlop

1991 Hamdan Al-Maktoum's Shadayid (USA) by Shadeed ....W Carson 4–6
Mr M C Throsby's Kooyonga L Piggott 14–1
Mrs A L Chapman's Crystal Gazing (USA) ....L Dettori 6–1
2 lengths, 1 length, 1m 38⅕s. 14 ran J Dunlop

1992 Maktoum Al Maktoum's Hatoof (USA) by Irish River ....W R Swinburn 5–1
Mr E J Loder's Marling ......S Cauthen 5–1
Mr T Wada's Kenbu (FR) ....F Head 11–1
Head, ¾ length, 1m 39⅖s. 14 ran Mrs C Head, in France

1993 Mr Mohamed Obaida's Sayyedati by Shadeed ....W R Swinburn 4–1
Lord Carnarvon's Niche ......L Piggott 6–1
Hamdan Al-Maktoum's Ajfan (USA) ....R Hills 33–1
½ length, head, 1m 37⅖s. 12 ran C Brittain

*New One Thousand Guineas on July Course
†Dead Heat

JOCKEY CLUB STAKES (Newmarket)

(1½ miles)
(First run 1894)

1900 Disguise 3y 8st 9lb (8)
1901 Pietermaritzburg 3y 8st 10lb (8)
1902 Rising Glass 3y 8st 13lb (11)
1903 Sceptre 4y 10st (5)
1904 Rock Sand 4y 9st 11lb (10)
1905 St. Amant 4y 10st 3lb (6)
1906 Beppo 3y 8st 1lb (5)
1907 Sancy 4y 9st 8lb (6)
1908 Siberia 3y 8st 7lb (10)
1909 Phaleron 3y 8st 13lb (10)
1910 Lemberg 3y 9st 6lb (9)
1911 Stedfast 3y 8st 4lb (5)
1912 Prince Palatine 4y 10st 7lb (9)
1913 Cantilever 3y 8st 1lb (7)
1914 Trois Temps 3y 8st 13lb (11)
1915 Lanius 4y 9st 2lb (11)
1916 Cannobie 3y 8st (12)
1917 No race
1918 Prince Chimay 3y 8st 6lb (7)
1919 No race
1920 Torelore 3y 8st 5lb (6)
1921 Milenko 3y 7st 9lb (8)
1922 Lady Juror 3y 8st (8)
1923 Inkerman 3y 8st 9lb (6)
1924 Teresina 4y 9st 1lb (11)
1925 Tatra 3y 7st 11lb (4)
1926 Foxlaw 4y 9st 4lb (5)
1927 Book Law 3y 8st 9lb (8)
1928 Toboggan 3y 8st 9lb (9)
1929 Cyclonic 4y 9st 7lb (8)
1930 Pyramid 3y 7st 6lb (7)
1931 Shell Transport 3y 8st 12lb (11)
1932 Firdaussi 3y 8st 12lb (7)
1933 Tai-Yang 3y 7st 9lb (7)
1934 Umidwar 3y 8st 9lb (11)
1935 Plassy 3y 8st 6lb (7)
1936 Precipitation 3 y 8st 9lb (7)
1937 Solfo 3y 8st 9lb (6)
1938 Challenge 3y 8st 1lb (8)
1939–44 No race
1945 Black Peter 3y 7st 10lb (4)
1946 Rising Light 4y 8st 11lb (7)
1947 Esprit de France 3y 8st 1lb (5)
1948 Alycidon 3y 8st 4lb (5)
1949 Dust Devil 3y 7st 9lb (4)
1950 Holmbush 3y 7st 9lb (6)
1951 Pardal 4y 9st (4)
1952 Mister Cube 3y 8st 1lb (5)
1953 Buckhound 4y 8st 11lb (7)
1954 Brilliant Green 3y 7st 12lb (5)
1955 Nucleus 3y 8st 8lb (5)
1956 Kurun 4y 9st (7)
1957 Court Harwell 3y 8st 1lb (6)
1958 All Serene 3y 7st 9lb (5)
1959 Court Prince 3y 8st 5lb (5)
1960 Prolific 3y 8st 4lb (2)
1961 St Paddy 4y 9st 6lb (5)
1962 Gaul 3y 8st 6lb (11)
1963 Darling Boy 5y 9st 7lb (7)
1964 Fighting Ship 4y 9st 6lb (6)
1965 Bal Masque 5y 9st 1lb (3)
1966 Alcalde 4y 9st (13)
1967 Acrania 4y 9st (3)
1968 Crozier 5y 9st 10lb (7)
1969 Torpid 4y 9st 6lb (9)
1970 Queen of Twilight 4y 8st 11lb (9)
1971 Meadowville 4y 9st 6lb (3)
1972 Knockroe 4y 8st 13lb (4)
1973 Our Mirage 4y 9st 3lb (9)
1974 Relay Race 4y 8st 9lb (5)
1975 Shebeen 4y 8st 10lb (6)
1976 Orange Bay 4y 9st 8lb (8)
1977 Oats 4y 9st 1lb (11)
1978 Classic Example 4y 9st 5lb (7)
1979 Obraztosvy (USA) 4y 8st 11lb (9)
1980 More Light 4y 8st 11lb (8)
1981 Master Willie 4y 8st 12lb (6)
1982 Ardross 6y 8st 12lb (6)
1983 Electric 4y 8st 10lb (11)
1984 Gay Lemur 4y 8st 7lb (6)
1985 Kirmann 4y 8st 7lb (8)
1986 Phardante (Fr) 4y 8st 7lb (3)
1987 Phardante (Fr) 5y 8st 12lb (7)
1988 Almaarad 5y 8st 10lb (4)
1989 Unfuwain (USA) 4y 8st 10lb (6)
1990 Roseate Tern 4y 8st 9lb (7)
1991 Rock Hopper 4y 8st 7lb (8)
1992 Sapience 6y 8st 12lb (9)
1993 Zinaad 4y 8st 9lb (8)

DALHAM CHESTER VASE

(1½ miles 66 yds)

For three year olds

(First run 1907)

1935 Valerius 4y 8st 9lb (6)
1936 Taj Akbar 3y 8st 3lb (11)
1937 Merry Mathew 3y 8st 5lb (15)
1938 Caye Man 3y 7st 5lb (12)
1939 Heliopolis 3y 8st 2lb (10)
1940–45 No race
1946 Sky High 3y 8st (5)
1947 Edward Tudor 4y 9st 10lb (3)
1948 Valognes 3y 7st 11lb (8)
1949 Swallow Tail 3y 8st (4)
1950 Castle Rock 3y 7st 12lb (6)
1951 Supreme Court 3y 8st 1lb (8)
1952 Summer Rain 3y 7st 13lb (5)
1953 Empire Honey 3y 8st (4)
1954 Blue Rod 3y 7st 4lb (7)
1955 Daemon 3y 7st 13lb (5)
1956 Articulate 3y 7st 6lb (7)
1957 King Babar 3y 7st 6lb (5)
1958 Alcide 3y 8st 1lb (7)
1959 Fidalgo 8st 6lb (9)
1960 Mr Higgins 8st 10lb (6)
1961 Sovrango 8st 10lb (10)
1962 Silver Cloud 8st 6lb (6)
1963 Christmas Island 8st 10lb (7)
1964 Indiana 8st 6lb (8)
1965 Gulf Pearl 8st 10lb (6)
1966 General Gordon 8st 6lb (9)
1967 Great Host 8st 10lb (7)
1968 Remand 8st 10lb (4)
1969 No race
1970 Politico (USA) 8st 12lb (6)
1971 Linden Tree (Fr) 8st 12lb (5)
1972 Ormindo 8st 8lb (6)
1973 Proverb 8st 8lb (7)
1974 Jupiter Pluvius 8st 8lb (8)
1975 Shantallah 8st 12lb (7)
1976 Old Bill 8st 8lb (6)
1977 Hot Grove 8st 12lb (6)
1978 Icelandic 8st 12lb (4)
1979 Cracaval 8st 8lb (6)
1980 Henbit (USA) 8st 12lb (5)
1981 Shergar 8st 12lb (10)
1982 Super Sunrise 8st 12lb (8)
1983 No race
1984 Kaytu 8st 8lb (7)
1985 Law Society (USA) 8st 12lb (5)
1986 Nomrood (USA) 8st 12lb (7)
1987 Dry Rock 8st 11lb (8)
1988 Unfuwaiin 8st 11lb (4)
1989 Old Vic 8st 11lb (5)
1990 Belmez (USA) 8st 11lb (3)
1991 Toulon 8st 11lb (5)
1992 Twist and Turn 8st 11lb (5)
1993 Armiger 8st 11lb (6)

Run at 1½ miles and 50 yds up to 1969

Prior to 1959 the race was for three- and four-year-olds

LADBROKE CHESTER CUP

(First run 1824)

(2¼ miles 117 yds)

1900 Roughside 7y 7st 5lb (14)
1901 David Garrick 4y 8st 10lb (16)
1902 Carabine 4y 7st 5lb (16)
1903 Vendale 4y 6st 6lb (15)
1904 Sandboy 4y 6st 2lb (12)
1905 Imari 4y 7st 4lb (10)
1906 Feather Bed 4y 6st 9lb (15)
1907 Querido 4y 8st (12)
1908 Glacis 4y 7st 8lb (13)
1909 Santo Strato 4y 9st (10)
1910 Elizabetta 4y 6st 11lb (21)
1911 Willonyx 4y 8st 2lb (14)
1912 Rathlea 7y 7st 5lb (12)
1913 The Guller 4y 6st 6lb (19)
1914 Aleppo 5y 8st 4lb (17)
1915 Hare Hill 5y 7st 10lb (10)
1916–18 No race
1919 Tom Pepper 4y 7st 4lb (11)
1920 Our Stephen 4y 7st 1lb (15)
1921 No race
1922 Chivalrous 4y 7st 5lb (22)
1923 Chivalrous 5y 8st 11lb (17)
1924 Rugeley 4y 6st 4lb (13)
1925 Spithead 6y 8st 7lb (20)
1926 Hidennis 5y 7st (10)
1927 Dark Japan 4y 8st 11lb (16)
1928 St Mary's Kirk 5y 7st (17)
1929 First Flight 4y 7st 7lb (22)
1930 Mountain Lad 5y 7st 11lb (18)
1931 Brown Jack 7y 9st 6lb (19)
1932 Bonny Brighteyes 4y 7st 3lb (17)
1933 Dick Turpin 4y 7st 10lb (14)
1934 Blue Vision 7y 7st 11lb (20)
1935 Damascus 4y 7st 1lb (17)
1936 Cho-sen 4y 7st 2lb (13)
1937 Faites vos Jeux 6y 7st 4lb (17)
1938 Mr Grundy 4y 7st 5lb (17)
1939 Winnebar 5y 7st 12lb (18)
1940–45 No race
1946 Retsel 4y 7st 9lb (8)
1947 Asmodee II 4y 9st 1lb (14)
1948 Billett 4y 8st 3lb (12)
1949 John Moore 5y 6st 10lb (16)
1950 Heron Bridge 6y 9st 7lb (15)
1951 Wood Leopard 4y 7st 5lb (19)
1952 Le Tellier 7y 8st 11lb (14)
1953 Eastern Emperor 5y 9st 2lb (13)
1954 Peperium 4y 8st 6lb (16)
1955 Prescription 4y 8st 9lb (23)
1956 Golovine 6y 8st 2lb (18)
1957 Curry 6y 8st (11)
1958 Sandiacre 6y 8st 5lb (15)
1959 Agreement 5y 9st 4lb (14)
1960 Trelawny 4y 7st 11lb (16)
1961 hoy 5y 8st (16)
1962 Golden Fire 4y 7st 9lb (19)
1963 Narratus 5y 7st 5lb (21)
1964 Credo 4y 8st 3lb (13)
1965 Harvest Gold 6y 7st 11lb (10)
1966 Aegean Blue 4y 8st 7lb (22)
1967 Mahbub Aly 6y 8st 1lb (14)
1968 Major Rose 6y 8st 7lb (15)
1969 No race
1970 Altogether 4y 7st 5lb (13)
1971 Random Shot 4y 8st 1lb (21)
1972 Eric 5y 7st (16)
1973 Crisalgo 5y 7st 7lb (10)
1974 Attivo 4y 7st 5lb (7)
1975 Super Nova 5y 7st 7lb (15)
1976 John Cherry (USA) 5y 9st 4lb (15)
1977 Sea Pigeon (USA) 7y 8st 8lb (15)
1978 Sea Pigeon (USA) 8y 9st 7lb (13)
1979 Charlotte's Choice 4y 8st 4lb (13)
1980 Arapahos (Fr) 5y 9st 5lb (10)
1981 Donegal Prince 5y 8st 4lb (15)
1982 Dawn Johnny 5y 8st 8lb (16)
1983 No race
1984 Contester 4y 8st 2lb (19)
1985 Morgans Choice 8y 7st 11lb (16)
1986 Western Dancer 5y 9st (22)
1987 Just David 4y 9st 8lb (12)
1988 Old Hubert 7y 7st 8lb (17)
1989 Grey Salute 6y 8st 7lb (14)
1990 Travelling Light 4y 9st 1lb (16)
1991 Star Player 5y 8st 10lb (16)
1992 Welshman 6y 7st 8lb (16)
1993 Rodeo Star (USA) 7y 7st 13lb (18)

ORMONDE E.B.F. STAKES (Chester)

(Prior to 1936 the race was for two year olds over 5 fur)

(1 mile 5 fur 89 yds)

1936 Quashed 4y 8st 11lb (9)
1937 Young England 4y 8st 11lb (11)
1938 Senor 4y 8st 11lb (5)
1939 Tricameron 3y 7st 2lb (6)
1940–45 No race
1946 high Stakes 4y 8st 7lb (4)
1947 Turkish Tune 4y 8st 8lb (7)
1948 Goyama 5y 9st 3lb (5)
1949 Alycidon 4y 9st (4)
1950 Oleins Grace 4y 8st 11lb (6)
1951 Cagire II 4y 9st (7)
1952 Tulyar 3y 7st 9lb (4)
1953 Wyandank 4y 8st 11lb (5)
1954 Stem King 4y 8st 11lb (5)
1955 North Cone 3y 8st 12lb (9)
1956 Stephanotis 3y 8st 12lb (8)
1957 Hindu Festival 3y 8st 12lb (5)
1958 Doutelle 4y 8st 9lb (6)
1959 Primera 5y 9st (6)
1960 Light Horseman 4y 8st 4lb (4)
1961 Alcaeus 4y 8st 9lb (4)
1962 Sovrango 4y 8st 12lb (6)
1963 Sovrango 5y 9st 3lb (7)
1964 Arctic Vale 5y 9st 3lb (3)
1965 Indiana 4y 8st 12lb (4)
1966 Biomydrin 4y 8st 7lb (8)
1967 David Jack 4y 8st 12lb (4)
1968 Hopeful Venture 4y 8st 12lb (3)
1969 No race
1970 Blakeney 4y 9st 2lb (5)
1971 Quayside 4y 8st 4lb (4)
1972 Selhurst 4y 8st 4lb (7)
1973 Ormindo 4y 8st 12lb (5)
1974 Crazy Rhythm 6y 8st 9lb (5)
1975 Rouser 4y 8st 4lb (7)
1976 Zimbalon 4y 8st 6lb (4)
1977 Oats 4y 9st (8)
1978 Crow (Fr) 5y 9st (7)
1979 Remainder Man 4y 8st 10lb (4)
1980 Niniski (USA) 4y 9st 4lb (10)
1981 Pelerin (Fr) 4y 9st 4lb (5)
1982 Six Mile Bottom 4y 8st 10lb (6)
1983 No race
1984 Teenoso (USA) 4y 9st 4lb (5)
1985 Seismic Wave (USA) 4y 8st 10lb (8)
1986 Brunico 4y 8st 10lb (8)
1987 Rakaposhi King 5y 8st 11lb (5)
1988 Mr Pintips 4y 8st 11lb (6)
1989 Mountain Kingdom 5y 8st 11lb (3)

1990 Braashee 4y 8st 11lb (6)
1991 Per Quod (USA) 6y 8st 11lb (7)
1992 Saddlers' Hall 4y 9st 2lb (7)
1993 Shambo 6y 9st 2lb (5)

Run at 1 mile 5 f 75 yds up to 1969

DEE STAKES (Chester)

For three year olds

(First run 1813)

(1¼ miles 75 yds)

1920 Paladin 8st 7lb (6)
1921 No race
1922 Fred Power 9st (7)
1923 Roger de Busli 9st (4)
1924 Battleship 8st 7lb (6)
1925 Runnymede 9st 10lb (6)
1926 No race
1927 Royal Pom 8st 7lb (7)
1928 Ranjit Singh 9st 6lb (6)
1929 Free Forester 8st 7lb (4)
1930 Master Mint 8st 7lb (7)
1931 Mangosteen 9st (8)
1932 Yellowstone 8st 7lb (6)
1933 Highlander 8st 7lb (6)
1934 Alishah 9st 10lb (5)
1935 Pry II 9st (9)
1936 Noble King 9st 5lb (9)
1937 Sunbather 8st (6)
1938 Pactolus 8st 13lb (5)
1939 Triguero 8st 4lb (10)
1940–45 No race
1946 Neapolitan 8st 7lb (3)
1947 Maray 8st 7lb (5)
1948 King's Acre 8st 2lb (3)
1949 Father Thames 8st 11lb (5)
1950 Khorassan 8st 1lb (3)
1951 Sybil's Nephew 8st 11lb (4)
1952 Torcross 8st 8lb (9)
1953 Victory Roll 8st 11lb (6)
1954 Cloonroughan 8st 2lb (7)
1955 Tippecanoe 8st 11lb (9)
1956 Atlas 8st 4lb (6)
1957 Palor 8st 9lb (6)
1958 Pandor 8st 7lb (6)
1959 Parthia 9st 5lb (5)
1960 Alcaeus 8st 7lb (8)
1961 Oakville 8st 12lb (7)
1962 Persian Wonder 8st 12lb (6)
1963 My Myosotis 8st 12lb (4)
1964 Sweet Moss 8st 12lb (7)
1965 Look Sharp 8st 7lb (5)
1966 Grey Moss 8st 7lb (7)
1967 French Vine 8st 12lb (4)
1968 Laureate 8st 12lb (4)
1969 No race
1970 Golden Monad 8st 12lb (5)
1971 Colum 8st 12lb (4)
1972 Our Mirage 8st 12lb (5)
1973 Natsun 8st 12lb (4)
1974 Averof 8st 12lb (7)
1975 Ravel 8st 8lb (7)
1976 Great Idea 8st 12lb (9)
1977 Royal Plume 8st 12lb (5)
1978 Heir Presumptive 8st 12lb (7)
1979 Two of Diamonds 8st 12lb (3)
1980 Playboy Jubilee 8st 6lb (9)
1981 Kirtling 8st 12lb (7)
1982 Ivano (Can) 8st 12lb (11)
1983 No race
1984 Trial By Error (USA) 8st 12lb (8)
1985 Infantry 8st 8lb (7)
1986 Faraway Dancer (USA) 8st 12lb (5)
1987 Sir Harry Lewis (USA) 8st 12lb (6)
1988 Clifton Chapel 8st 12lb (5)
1989 Free Sweater 8st 8lb (9)
1990 Blue Stag 8st 12lb (5)
1991 Hundra (USA) 8st 8lb (9)
1992 My Memoirs 9st 2lb (7)
1993 Beneficial 8st 10lb (6)

TOTE DANTE STAKES (York)

(1 mile 2 fur 85 yds)
For three year olds

1958 Bald Eagle 9st (7)
1959 Dickens 9st (9)
1960 St Paddy 9st (10)
1961 Gallant Knight 9st (5)
1962 Lucky Brief 9st (5)
1963 Merchant Venturer 9st (6)
1964 Sweet Moss 9st (9)
1965 Ballymarais 9st (11)
1966 Hermes 9st (9)
1967 Gay Garland 9st (5)
1968 Lucky Finish 9st (10)
1969 Activator 9st (15)
1970 Approval 9st (8)
1971 Fair World 9st (8)
1972 Rheingold 9st (9)
1973 Owen Dudley 9st (10)
1974 Honoured Guest 9st (6)
1975 Hobnob (Fr) 9st (12)
1976 Trasi's Son 9st (11)
1977 Lucky Sovereign (USA) 9st (15)
1978 Shirley Heights 9st (9)
1979 Lyphard's Wish (Fr) 9st (14)
1980 Hello Gorgeous (USA) 9st (8)
1981 Beldale Flutter (USA) 9st (6)
1982 Simplky Great 9st (6)
1983 Hot Touch 9st (9)
1984 Claude Monet (USA) 9st (15)
1985 Damister (USA) 9st (5)
1986 Shahrastani (USA) 9st (7)
1987 Reference Point 9st (8)
1988 Red Glow 9st (7)
1989 Torjoun 9st (7)
1990 Sanglamore (USA) 9st (7)
1991 Environment Friend 9st (8)
1992 Alnasr Alwasheek 9st (7)
1993 Tenby 9st (5)

POLO MINTS YORKSHIRE CUP (York)

(1 mile 5 fur 194 yds)

1927 Templestowe 5y 7st 7lb (7)
1928 Royal Pom 4y 7st 2lb (12)
1929 The Consul 4y 6st 9lb (9)
1930 The Bastard 4y 8st 4lb (9)
1931 The Scout II 4y 8st 5lb (9)
1932 Trimdon 6y 9st 7lb (7)
1933 Orpen 5y 9st 4lb (12)
1934 Within-the-law 5y 7st 11lb (13)
1935 Felicitation 5y 9st 7lb (8)
1936 Valerius 5y 8st 1lb (10)
1937 Silversol 4y 8st 6lb (11)
1938 Suzerain 5y 8st 13lb (13)
1939 Finis 4y 8st 3lb (11)
1940–44 No race
1945†Kingstone 3y 8st (3)
1946 Stirling Castle 4y 8st 9lb (5)
1947 No Orchids 4y 8st 2lb (7)
1948 Whiteway 4y 8st 9lb (5)
1949 Woodburn 4y 8st 9lb (6)
1950 Miraculous Atom 6y 9st (5)
1951‡Orderly Ann 5y 6st 11lb (6)
1952 Eastern Emperor 4y 8st 9lb (7)
1953 Childe Harold 4y 8st 9lb (5)
1954 Premonition 4y 8st 9lb (9)
1955 By Thunder! 4y 8st 9lb (5)
1956 Romany Air 5y 9st (8)
1957 Souverlone 4y 8st 4lb (11)
1958 Brioche 4y 8st 9lb (4)
1959 Cutter 4y 8st 6lb (5)
1960 Dickens 4y 8st 9lb (9)
1961 Pandofell 4y 8st 9lb (6)
1962 Sagacity 4y 8st 9lb (7)
1963 Honour Bound 5y 8st 4lb (7)
1964 Raise You Ten 4y 8st 9lb (8)
1965 Apprentice 5y 8st 4lb (5)
1966 Aunt Edith 4y 8st 6lb (6)
1967 Salvo 4y 8st 9lb (5)
1968 Sweet Story 6y 9st (9)
1969 Quartette 5y 9st (5)
1970 Rangong 5y 9st (3)
1971 Alto Volante 4y 8st 4lb (6)
1972 Knockroe 4y 8st 8lb (8)
1973 Celtic Cone 6y 8st 10lb (6)
1974 Buoy 4y 8st 13lb (4)
1975 Riboson 4y 8st 5lb (4)
1976 Bruni 4y 9st 1lb (5)
1977 Bright Finish (USA) 4y 8st 10lb (6)
1978 Smuggler 5y 8st 10lb (7)
1979 Pragmatic 4y 8st 7lb (10)
1980 Noble Saint (USA) 4y 9st 1lb (8)
1981 Ardross 5y 8st 12lb (6)
1982 Ardross 6y 9st 1lb (6)
1983 Line Slinger 4y 8st 4lb (10)
1984 Band 4y 8st 10lb (9)
1985 Ilium 4y 8st 7lb (10)
1986 Eastern Music 4y 8st 9lb (7)
1987 Verd-Antique 4y 8st 9lb (7)
1988 Moon Madness 5y 9st (8)
1989 Mountain Kingdom 5y 8st 9lb (6)
1990 Braashee 4y 8st 9lb (6)
1991 Arzanni 4y 8st 9lb (7)
1992 Rock Hopper 5y 8st 13lb (8)
1993 Assessor 4y 9st (8)

†Run as Yorkshire Autumn Cup
‡Run as Yorkshire Stayers H'cap Stakes
Run at 2 miles up to 1965

JUDDMONTE LOCKINGE STAKES (Newbury)

(1 mile)

1958 Pall Mall 3y 8st 6lb (4)
1959 Pall Mall 4y 9st 7lb (5)
1960 Sovereign Path 4y 9st 7lb (5)
1961 Prince Midge 3y 7st 11lb (8)
1962 Superstition 3y 7st 4lb (10)
1963 Queen's Hussar 3y 8st 3lb (10)
1964 The Creditor 4y 9st 4lb (6)
1965 Young Christopher 4y 9st 3lb (10)
1966 Silly Season 4y 9st 5lb (13)

1967 Bluerullah 4y 8st 12lb (5)
1968 Supreme Sovereign 4y 8st 12lb (5)
1969 Habitat 3y 7st 11lb (6)
1970 Welsh Pageant 4y 8st 12lb (6)
1971 Welsh Pageant 5y 9st 2lb (6)
1972 Brigadier Gerard 4y 9st 5lb (5)
1973 Sparkler 5y 8st 12lb (12)
1974 Boldboy 4y 8st 12lb (8)
1975 No race
1976 El Rastro 6y 9st (8)
1977 Relkino 4y 9st (9)
1978 Don 4y 9st 4lb (10)
1979 Young Generation 3y 8st 4lb (10)
1980 Kris 4y 9st 7lb (7)
1981 Belmont Bay 4y 9st (6)
1982 Motavato (USA) 4y 9st (7)
1983 Noalcoholic (Fr) 6y 9st 4lb (10)
1984 Cormorant Wood 4y 9st 5lb (6)
1985 Prismatic 3y 7st 13lb (11)
1986 Scottish Reel 4y 9st 1lb (8)
1987 Then Again 4y 9st 4lb (9)
1988 Broken Hearted 4y 9st 4lb (5)
1989 Most Welcome 5y 9st 1lb (4)
1990 Safawan 4y 9st (6)
1991 Polar Falcon (USA) 4y 9st (4)
1992 Selkirk (USA) 4y 9st 5lb (10)
1993 Swing Low 4y 9st (10)

CHAMPAGNE RUINART OAKS TRIAL STAKES (Lingfield)

(1 mile 3 fur 106 yds)
For three year old fillies

1933 Look Alive 7st 9lb (7)
1934 Shining Cloud 7st 9lb (3)
1935 Milldoria 7st 9lb (7)
1936 Miss Windsor 7st 9lb (8)
1937 Ruby Red 8st 9lb (8)
1938 Night Bird 8st 9lb (11)
1939 Foxcraft 7st 11lb (13)
1940–45 No race
1946 Iona 9st (8)
1947 Solpax 9st (8)
1948 Angelola 9st (6)
1949 Squall 9st (10)
1950 Stella Polaris 9st (4)
1951 Chinese Cracket 9st (10)
1952 Zabara 9st (7)
1953 Nectarine 9st (11)
1954 Angel Bright 9st (7)
1955 Ark Royal 9st (7)
1956 No Pretender 9st (4)
1957 Crotchet 9st (6)
1958 None Nicer 9st (8)
1959 Mirnaya 9st (3)
1960 Running Blue 9st (14)
1961 Impudent 9st (7)
1962 Nortia 9st (13)
1963 Amicable 8st 10lb (70
1964 Beaufront 9st 1lb (10)
1965 Quita II 8st 5lb (6)
1966 Varinia 8st 5lb (5)
1967 Javata 8st 10lb (6)
1968 Our Ruby 8st 10lb (5)
1969 Sleeping Partner 8st 10lb (6)
1970 Pulchra 8st 5lb (5)
1971 Maina 8st 5lb (5)
1972 Ginevra 9st (6)
1973 Syrona 8st 9lb (10)
1974 Riboreen 8st 9lb (7)
1975 Juliette Marny 8st 9lb (7)
1976 Heaven Knows 9st (10)
1977 Lucent 9st (5)
1978 Suni 9st (9)
1979 Reprocolor 9st (7)
1980 Gift Wrapped 9st (7)
1981 Leap Lively (USA) 9st (7)
1982 Tants 9st (9)
1983 Give Thanks 9st (12)
1984 Out of Shot 9st (7)
1985 Kiliniski 8st 9lb (11)
1986 Mill On The Floss 8st 9lb (8)
1987 Port Helene 8st 9lb (8)
1988 Bahamian 8st 9lb (7)
1989 Aliysa 8st 9lb (5)
1990 Rafha 9st 1lb (5)
1991 Ausherra (USA) 8st 9lb (7)
1992 User Friendly 8st 9lb (5)
1993 Oakmead 8st 9lb (6)

Run over 1 1/2 miles until 1989.

ALPINE (DOUBLE GLAZING) DERBY TRIAL STAKES (Lingfield)

(1 mile 3 fur 106 yds)
For three year old colts

1932 April the Fifth 8st 12lb (13)
1933 Myosotis 7st 12lb (13)
1934 Medieval Knight 8st 9lb (5)
1935 Field Trial 7st 9lb (7)
1936 Barrystar 8st 9lb (8)
1937 Mid-day sun 8st 9lb (7)
1938 Blandstar 7st 9lb (13)
1939 Hypnotist 7st 10lb (12)
1940–45 No race
1946 Fast and Fair 9st (9)
1947 Sayajirao 9st (9)
1948 Black Tarquin 9st (4)
1949 Brown Rover 9st (5)
1950 Tramper 9st (10)
1951 North Carolina 9st (8)
1952 Tulyar 9st (12)
1953 Aureole 9st (6)
1954 Rowston Manor 9st (6)
1955 True Cavalier 9st (8)
1956 Induna 9st (8)
1957 Doutelle 9st (10)
1958 Alcide 9st (9)
1959 Parthia 9st (5)
1960 Jet Stream 9st (10)
1961 Pardao 9st (7)
1962 Pindaric 9st (10)
1963 Duplation 9st (11)
1964 Oncidium 9st (16)
1965 Solstice 9st (15)
1966 Black Prince II 9st (12)
1967 Heave Ho 9st (10)
1968 Laureate 9st (9)
1969 The Elk 9st (16)
1970 Meadowville 9st (11)
1971 Homeric 9st (12)
1972 Charling 9st (9)
1973 Ksar 9st (7)
1974 Bustino 9st (7)
1975 Patch 9st (8)
1976 Norfolk Air 9st (8)
1977 Caporello 9st (8)
1978 Whitstead 9st (6)
1979 Milford 9st (8)
1980 Ginistrelli (USA) 9st (10)
1981 Riberetto 9st (8)
1982 Ialmood (USA) 9st (6)
1983 Teenoso (USA) 9st (11)
1984 Alphabatim (USA) 9st (5)
1985 Slip Anchor 9st (8)
1986 Mashkour (USA) 9st (6)
1987 Legal Bid (USA) 9st (8)
1988 Kahyasi 9st (8)
1989 Cacoethes (USA) 9st (7)
1990 Rock Hopper 9st (5)
1991 Corrupt (USA) 9st (8)
1992 Assessor 9st (7)
1993 Bob's Return 9st (8)

Run over 1 1/2 miles until 1989.

EVER READY DERBY (Epsom—1½ miles, 10 yds)

For three year olds

Year	Winner	Starters	Jockeys
	(1 mile)		
1780	Sir C Bunbury's Diomed, by Florizel	9	S. Arnull
1781	Col. D. O'Kelly's Young Eclipse, by Eclipse	15	C. Hindley
1782	Lord Egremont's Assassin, by Sweetbriar	13	S. Arnull
1783	Mr Parker's Saltram, by Eclipse	6	C. Hindley
	(1½ miles)		
1784	Col. D. O'Kelly's Serjeant, by Eclipse	11	J. Arnull
1785	Lord Clermont's Aimwell, by Marc Antony	10	C. Hindley
1786	Mr Panton's Noble, by Highflyer	15	J. White
1787	Lord Derby's Sir Peter Teazie, by Highflyer	17	S. Arnull
1788	Prince of Wales's Sir Thomas, by Pontiac	11	W. South
1789	Duke of Bedford's Skyscraper, by Highflyer	11	S. Chifney, sen.
1790	Lord Grosvenor's Rhadamanthus, by Justice	10	J. Arnull
1791	Duke of Bedford's Eager, by Florizel (ran as Florizel c)	9	F. Stephenson
1792	Lord Grosvenor's John Bull, by Fortitude	7	F. Buckle
1793	Sir F. Poole's Waxy, by Pot-8-os	13	W. Clift
1794	Lord Grosvenor's Daedalus, by Justice	4	F. Buckle
1795	Sir F. Standish's Spread Eagle, by Volunteer	11	A. Wheatley
1796	Sir F. Standish's Didelot, by Trumpator	11	J. Arnull
1797	Duke of Bedford's br c by Fidget—Sister to Pharamond	7	J. Singleton, jun.
1798	Mr J. Cookson's Sir Harry, by Sir Peter Teazle	10	S. Arnull
1799	Sir F. Standish's Archduke, by Sir Peter Teazle	11	J. Arnull
1800	Mr C. Wilson's Champion, by Pot-8-os	13	W. Clift
1801	Sir C. Bunbury's Eleanor, by Whiskey	11	Saunders
1802	Duke of Grafton's Tyrant, by Pot-8-os	9	F. Buckle
1803	Sir H. Williamson's Ditto, by Sir Peter Teazle	6	W. Clift
1804	Lord Egremont's Hannibal, by Driver	8	W. Arnull
1805	Lord Egremont's Cardinal Beaufort, by Gohanna	15	D. Fitzpatrick
1806	Lord Foley's Paris, by Sir Peter Teazle	12	J. Shepherd
1807	Lord Egremont's Election, by Gohanna	13	J. Arnull
1808	Sir H. Williamson's Pan, by St. George	10	F. Collinson
1809	Duke of Grafton's Pope, by Waxy	10	T. Goodison
1810	Duke of Grafton's Whalebone, by Waxy	11	W. Clift
1811	Sir J. Shelley's Phantom, by Walton	16	F. Buckle
1812	Mr R. Ladbroke's Octavius, by Orville	14	W. Arnull
1813	Sir C. Bunbury's Smolensko, by Sorcerer	12	T. Goodison
1814	Lord Stawell's Blucher, by Waxy	14	W. Arnull
1815	Duke of Grafton's Whisker, by Waxy	13	T. Goodison
1816	Duke of York's Prince Leopold, by Hedley	11	W. Wheatley
1817	Mr J. Payne's Azor, by Selim	13	J. Robinson
1818	Mr T. Thronhill's Sam, by Scud	16	S. Chifneym, jun.
1819	Duke of Portland's Tiresias, by Soothsayer	16	W. Clift
1820	Mr T. Thornhill's Sailor, by Scud	15	S. Chifney, jun.
1821	Mr J. Hunter's Gustavus, by Election	13	S. Day
1822	Duke of York's Moses, by Whalebone or Seymour	12	T. Goodison
1823	Mr J. Udney's Emilius, by Orville	11	F. Buckle
1824	Sir J. Shelley's Cedric, by Phantom	17	J. Robinson
1825	Lord Jersey's Middleton, by Phantom	18	J. Robinson
1826	Lord Egremont's Lap-dog, by Whalebone	19	G. Dockeray
1827	Lord Jersey's Mameluke, by Partisan	23	J. Robinson
1828	Duke of Rutland's Cadland, by Andrew	15	J. Robinson
1829	Mr W. Gratwicke's Frederick, by Little John	17	J. Forth
1830	Mr W. Chifney's Priam, by Emilius	23	S. Day
1831	Lord Lowther's Spaniel, by Whalebone	23	W. Wheatley
1832	Mr R. Ridsdale's St. Giles, by Tramp	22	W. Scott
1833	Mr I. Sadler's Dangerous, by Tramp	25	J. Chapple
1834	Mr S. Batson's Plenipotentiary, by Emilius	23	P. Conolly
1835	Mr J. Bowes's Mundig, by Catton	14	W. Scott
1836	Lord Jersey's Bay Middleton, by Sultan	21	J. Robinson
1837	Lord Berners's Phosphorus, by Lamplighter	17	G. Edwards
1838	Sir G. Heathcote's Amato, by Velocipede	23	J. Chapple
1839	Mr W. Ridsdale's Bloomsbury, by Mulatto	21	S. Templeman
1840	Mr D. Robertson's Little Wonder, by Muley	17	W. Macdonald
1841	Mr A. Rawlinson's Coronation, by Sir Hercules	29	P. Connolly
1842	Col. Anson's Attila, by Colwick	24	W. Scott
1843	Mr J. Bowes's Cotherstone, by Touchstone	23	W. Scott
1844	Col. Peel's Orlando, by Touchstone	29	E. Flatman
1845	Mr W. Gratwicke's The Merry Monarch, by Slane	31	F. Bell
1846	Mr J. Gully's Pyrrhus the First, by Epirus	27	S. Day

EVER READY DERBY—continued

		Starters	Jockeys
1847	Mr T. Pedley's The Cossack, by Hetman Platoff	32 ...	S. Templeman
1848	Lord Clifden's Surplice, by Touchstone	17 ...	S. Templeman
1849	Lord Eglinton's The Flying Dutchman, by Bay Middleton	26 ...	C. Marlow
1850	Lord Zetland's Voltigeur, by Voltair	24 ...	J. Marson
1851	Sir J. Hawley's Teddington, by Orlando	33 ...	J. Marson
1852	Mr J. Bowes's Daniel O'Rourke, by Irish Birdcatcher	27 ...	F. Butler
1853	Mr J. Bowes's West Australian, by Melbourne	28 ...	F. Butler
1854	Mr J. Gully's Andover, by Bay Middleton	27 ...	A. Day
1855	Mr F. Popham's Wild Dayrell, by Ion	12 ...	R. Sherwood
1856	Adml. Harcourt's Ellington, by The Flying Dutchman	24 ...	T. Aldcroft
1857	Mr W. I'Anson's Blink Bonny, by Melbourne	30 ...	J. Charlton
1858	Sir J. Hawley's Beadsman, by Weatherbit	23 ...	J. Wells
1859	Sir J. Hawley's Musjid, by Newminster	30 ...	J. Wells
1860	Mr J. Merry's Thormanby, by Melbourne or Windbound	30 ...	H. Custance
1861	Colonel Towneley's Kettledrum, by Rataplan	18 ...	R. Bullock
1862	Mr C. Snewing's Caractacus, by Kingston	34 ...	J. Parsons
1863	Mr R. C. Naylor's Macaroni, by Sweetmeat	31 ...	T. Calloner
1864	Mr W. I'Anson's Blair Athol, by Stockwell	30 ...	J. Snowden
1865	Count de Lagrange's Gladiateur, by Monarque	29 ...	H. Grimshaw
1866	Mr R. Sutton's Lord Lyon, by Stockwell	26 ...	H. Custance
1867	Mr H. Chaplin's Hermit, by Newminster	30 ...	J. Daley
1868	Sir J. Hawley's Blue Gown, by Beadsman	18 ...	J. Wells
1869	Mr J. Johnstone's Pretender, by Adventurer	22 ...	J. Osborne
1870	Lord Falmouth's Kingcraft, by King Tom	15 ...	T. French
	(about 1 1/2 miles)		
1871	Baron de Rothchild's ch c Favonius, by Parmesan	17 ...	T. French
1872	Mr H. Savile's b c Cremorne, by Parmesan	23 ...	C. Maidment
1873	Mr J. Merry's ch c Doncaster, by Stockwell	12 ...	F. Webb
1874	Mr W. Cartwright's ch c George Frederick, by Marsyas	20 ...	H. Custance
1875	Prince Batthyany's b c Galopin, by Vedette	18 ...	J. Morris
1876	Mr A. Baltazzi's b c kisber, by Buccaneer	15 ...	C. Maidment
1877	Lord Falmouth's b c Silvio, by Blair Athol	17 ...	F. Archer
1878	Mr W. S. Crawfurd's b c Sefton, by Speculum	22 ...	H. Constable
1879	Mr Acton's Sir Bevy's, by Favonius	23 ...	G. Fordham
1880	Duke of Westminster's ch c Bend or, by Doncaster	19 ...	F. Archer
1881	Mr P. Lorillard's b c Iroquois, by Leamington	15 ...	F. Archer
1882	Duke of Westminster's ch f Shotover, by Hermit	14 ...	T. Cannon
1883	Sir F. Johnstone's ch c St. Blaise, by Hermit	11 ...	C. Wood
1884†	Mr J. Hammond's b c St. Gatien, by Rotherhill or The Rover		C. Wood
†	Sir J. Willoughby's br c Harvester, by Sterling	15 ...	S. Loates
1885	Lord Hastings's b c Melton, by Master Kildare	12 ...	F. Archer
1886	Duke of Westminster's b c Ormonde, by Bend Or	9 ...	F. Archer
1887	Mr Abington's b c Merry Hampton, by Hampton	11 ...	J. Watts
1888	Duke of Portland's b c Ayrshire, by Hampton	9 ...	F. Barrett
1889	Duke of Portland's b c Donovan, by Galopin	13 ...	T. Loates
1890	Sir James Miller's ch c Sainfoin, by Springfield	8 ...	J. Watts
1891	Sir F. Johnstone's br c Common, by Isonomy	11 ...	G. Barrett
1892	Lord Bradford's ch c Sir Hugo, by Wisdom	13 ...	F. Allsopp
1893	Mr H. McCalmont's b c Isinglass, by Isonomy	11 ...	T. Loates
1894	Lord Rosebery's b c Ladas, by Hampton	7 ...	J. Watts
1895	Lord Rosebery's b c Sir Visto, by Barcaldine	15 ...	S. Loates
1896	H.R.H. the Prince of Wales's b c Persimmon, by St. Simon	11 ...	J. Watts
1897	Mr J. Gubbin's b c Galtee More, by Kendal	11 ...	C. Wood
1898	Mr J. W. Larnach's ch c Jeddah, by Janissary	18 ...	O. Madden
1899	Duke of Westminster's b c Flying Fox, by Orme	12 ...	M. Cannon

1900 H.R.H the Prince of Wales's Diamond Jubilee, by St Simon ....H Jones 6–4
D of Portland's Simon Dale ..M Cannon 100–6
Mr J R Keene's Disguise II .....J F Sloan 8–1
1/2 length, 1 length, 2m 42s. 14 ran R Marsh

1901 Mr W C Whitney's Volodyovski, by Florizel II ....L Reiff 5–2
D of Portland's William the Third ....M Cannon 100–7
Mr D Baird's Veronese ....F Rickaby 40–1
3/4 length, 4 lengths, 2m 40 4/5s. 25 ran J Huggins

1902 Mr J Gubbin's Ard Patrick, by St Florian ....J H Martin 100–14
Col H McCalmont's Rising Glass .....G McCall 40–1
D of Portland's Friar Tuck ...M Cannon 100–7
3 lengths, same, 2m 42 1/5s. 18 ran S Darling

1903 Sir J Miller's Rock Sand, by Sainfoin ....D Maher 4–6
M E Blanc's Vinicius ......G Thompson 11–2
Sir Daniel Cooper's Flotsam ...W Halsey 100–14
2 lengths, same, 2m 42 4/5s. 7 ran G Blackwell

1904 Mr L de Rothschild's St Amant, by St Frusquin ....K Cannon 5–1
Sir J Thursby's John o'Gaunt ....Mr G Thursby 4–1
Mr S B Joel's St Denis ....W Halsey 50–1
3 lengths, 6 lengths, 2m 45 2/5s. 8 ran A Hayhoe

1905 Ld Rosebery's Cicero, by Cyllene ....D Maher 4–11
M E Blanc's Jardy ....G Stern 4–1
Chev E Ginistrelli's Signorino K Cannon 50–1
3/4 length, head, 2m 39 3/5s. 9 ran P P Peck

1906 Major Eustace Loder's Spearmint, by Carbine ....D Maher 6–1
Mr J L Dugdale's Picton Mr G Thursby 18–1
D of Westminster's Troutbeck J H Martin 33–1
1½ lengths, 2 lengths, 2m 36⅘s. 22 ran P Gilpin
1907 Mr R Croker's Orby, by Orme ..J Reiff 100–9
Col E W baird's Wool Winder O Madden 100–9
Capt J Greer's Slieve Gallion ...W Higgs 8–13
2 lengths, ½ length, 2m 44s. 9 ran J Allen, in Ireland
1908 Chev E Ginistrelli's Signorinetta by Chaleureux ....W Bullock 100–1
D of Portland's Primer ....B Dillon 40–1
Mr Barclay Walker's Llangwm D Maher 100–8
2 lengths, neck, 2m 39⅘s. 18 ran Owner
1909 His Majesty's Minoru, by Cyllene ....H Jones 7–2
Mr W Raphael's Louviers ....G Stern 9–1
Ld Michelham's William the Fourth ....W Higgs 20–1
Short head, ½ length, 2m 42⅖s. 15 ran R Marsh
1910 Mr "Fairie's" Lemberg, by Cyllene ....B Dillon 7–4
Ld Villiers's Greenback ....F Templeman 100–8
Mr A P Cunliffe's Charles O'Malley ....S Donoghue 33–1
Neck, 2 lengths, 2m 35⅕s. 15 ran Alec Taylor
1911 Mr J B Joel's Sunstar, by Sundridge ....G Stern 13–8
Ld Derby's Stedfast ....B Lynham 100–8
Capt F Forester's Royal Tender ....S Donoghue 25–1
2 lengths, 4 lengths, 2m 36⅘s. 26 ran C Morton
1912 Mr W Raphael's Tagalie, by Cyllene ....J Reiff 100–8
Mr P Neumann's Jaeger ...Walter Griggs 8–1
Mr Belmont's Tracery ......G Bellhouse 66–1
4 lengths, 2 lengths, 2m 38⅘s. 20 ran D Waugh
1913 Mr A P Cunliffe's Aboyeur, by Desmond ....E Piper 100–1
Mr W Raphael's Louvois ......W Saxby 10–1
Mr W Hall Walker's Great Sport G Stern 20–1
Craganour came in first, beating Aboyeur by a head, but was disqualified Louvois a neck behind 2m 37⅗s. 15 ran T Lewis
1914 Mr H B Duryea's Durbar II, by Rabelais ....M MacGee 20–1
Sir E Cassel's Hapsburg ....C Foy 33–1
Mr H J King's Peter The Hermit ....R Watson 100–1
3 lengths, 1½ lengths, 2m 38⅖s. 30 ran T Murphy
1915*Mr S Joel's Pommern, by Polymelus ....S Donoghue 11–10
Col Hall Walker's Let Fly ....J Childs 10–1
Sir J Thursby's Rossendale ....J Clark 40–1
2 lengths, 3 lengths, 2m 32⅗s. 17 ran C Peck
1916*Mr E Hutton's Fifinella, by Polymelus ....J Childs 11–2
Mr A Cox's Kwang-Su ....F Templeman 3–1
Mr J Sandford's Nassovian ....F O'Neill 11–2
Neck, head, 2m 36⅗s. 10 ran R Dawson
1917*Mr "Fairie's" Gay Crusader, by Bayardo ....S Donoghue 7–4
Sir H Meux's Dansellon ......R Watson 7–1
Sir W Cooke's Dark Legend ....J Childs 100–15
4 lengths, head, 2m 40⅗s. 12 ran Alec Taylor
1918*Lady James Douglas's Gainsborough, by Bayardo ....J Childs 8–13
Maj W Astor's Blink ....R J Colling 100–8
Ld Glanely's Treclare ....W Langford 20–1
1½ lengths, 2 lengths, 2m 33⅕s. 13 ran Alec Taylor
1919 Ld Glaneley's Grand Parade, by Orby ....F Templeman 33–1
Maj J Astor's Buchan ....J Brennan 7–1
Sir W Gilbey's Paper Money S Donoghue 7–1
½ length, 2 lengths, 2m 35⅘s. 13 ran F Barling
1920 Major Giles Loder's Spion Kop, by Spearmint ....F O'Neill 100–6
Ld Derby's Archaic ....G Bellhouse 10–1
Sir H Cunliffe-Owen's Orpheus F Leach 50–1
2 lengths, 1½ lengths, 2m 34⅘s. 19 ran P P Gilpin
1921 Mr J B Joel's Humorist, by Polymelus ....S Donoghue 6–1
Ld Astor's Craig an Eran .....J Brennan 5–1
Mr J Watson's Lemonora ....J Childs 8–1
Neck, 3 lengths, 2m 36⅕s. 23 ran C Morton
1922 Ld Woolavington's Captain Cuttle, by Hurry On ....S Donoghue 10–1
Ld Astor's Tamar ....F Bullock 10–1
Mr B Walker's Craigangower ..M Beary 20–1
4 lengths, 3 lengths, 2m 34⅗s. 30 ran F Darling
1923 Mr B Irish's Papyrus, by Tracery ....S Donoghue 100–15
Ld Derby's Pharos ....E Gardner 6–1
Mr M Goculdas's Perth ....A Walker 33–1
1 length, 1½ lengths, 2m 38s. 19 ran B Jarvis
1924 Ld Derby's Sansovino, by Swynford ....T Weston 9–2
Ld Astor's St Germans ....F Bullock 100–7
Mr S Tattersall's Hurstwood ...V Smyth 20–1
6 lengths, neck, 2m 46⅗s. 27 ran Hon G Lambton
1925 Mr H E Morriss's Manna, by Phalaris ....S Donoghue 9–1
H H Aga Khan's Zionist .....B Carslake 10–1
Mr A K Macomber's The Sirdar A Esling 50–1
8 lengths, 2 lengths, 2m 40⅗s. 27 ran F Darling
1926 Ld Woolavington's Coronach, by Hurry On ....J Childs 11–2
Mr W M G Singer's Lancegaye ....R Perryman 40–1
Ld Derby's Colorado ....T Weston 2–1
5 lengths, short head, 2m 47⅘s. 19 ran F Darling
1927 Mr F Curzon's Call Boy, by Hurry On ....E C Elliott 4–1
Sir Victor Sassoon's Hot Night H Wragg 9–2
Maj Courtauld's Shian Moor .....F Lane 22–1
2 lengths, 8 lengths, 2m 34⅖s. 23 ran J Watts
1928 Sir H Cunliffe-Owen's Felstead, by Spion Kop ....H Wragg 33–1
Sir L Philipp's Flamingo .....E C Elliott 9–2
Mr L Neumann's Black Watch C Smirke 33–1
1½lengths, 6 lengths, 2m 35⅖s. 19 ran O Bell
1929 Mr W Barnett's Trigo, by Blandford ....J Marshall 33–1
Ld Woolavington's Water Gay ....F Fox 100–8
Mr S Tattersall's Brienz ......R A Jones 50–1
1½ lengths, 2 lengths, 2m 36⅖s. 26 ran R Dawson
1930 H.H Aga Khan's Blenheim, by Blandford ....H Wragg 18–1
Mr S Tattersall's Iliad ....R A Jones 25–1
Sir H Girst's Diolite ....C Ray 11–4
1 length, 2 lengths, 2m 38⅕s. 17 ran R Dawson
1931 Mr J A Dewar's Cameronian, by Pharos ....F Fox 7–2
Sir J Rutherford's Orpen ......R A Jones 9–1
Ld Rosebery's Sandwich ......H Wragg 8–1
¾ length, same, 2m 36⅗s. 25 ran F Darling
1932 Mr T Walls's April the Fifth, by Craig an Eran ....F Lane 100–6
H H Aga Khan's Dastur ....M Beary 18–1
Ld Roseberry's Miracle ....H Wragg 100–9
¾ length, short head, 2m 43⅕s. 21 ran Owner
1933 Ld Derby's Hyperion, by Gainsborough ....T Weston 6–1
Sir H Cunliffe-Owen's King Salmon ....H Wragg 7–1
Mr V Emanuel's Statesman ...B Carslake 20–1
4 lengths, 1 length, 2m 34s. 24 ran Hon G Lambton
1934 H.H Maharaja of Rajpipla's Windsor Lad, by Blandford ....C Smirke 15–2
Ld Woolavington's Easton ...G Richards 100–9
Ld Glanely's Colombo .....W Johnstone 11–8
1 length, neck, 2m 34s. 19 ran M Marsh
1935 H.H Aga Khan's Bahram, by Blandford ....F Fox 5–4
Sir Abe Bailey's Robin Goodfellow ....T Weston 50–1
Ld Astor's Field Trial ....R Dick 9–1

2 lengths, 1/2 length, 2m 36s. 16 ran Frank Butters
1936 H H Aga Khan's Mahmoud, by Blenheim
............................C Smirke 100–8
H H Aga Khan's Taj Akbar ..G Richards 6–1
Mrs J Shand's Thankerton ......T Burns 33–1
3 lengths, 3/4 length, 2m 33 4/5s. 22 ran Frank Butters
1937 Mrs G B Miller's Mid-day Sun, by Solario
..............................M Beary 100–7
Mrs F Nagle's Sandsprite ......J Crouch 100–1
H H Aga Khan's Le Grand Duc C Smirke 100–9
1 1/2lengths, same, 2m 37 3/5s. 21 ran Fred Butters
1938 Mr P Beatty's Bois Roussel, by Vatout
.............................E C Elliott 20–1
Mr James V Rank's Scottish Union
..........................B Carslake 8–1
Mr H E Morriss's Pasch .....G Richards 9–4
4 lengths, 2 lengths, 2m 39 1/5s. 22 ran F Darling
1939 Ld Rosebery's Blue Peter, by Fairway
............................E Smith 7–2
Mr E Esmond's Fox Club ...G Richards 100–6
Ld Derby's Heliopolis ......R Perryman 100–9
4 lengths, 3 lengths, 2m 36 4/5s. 27 ran J L Jarvis
1940*Mr F Darling's Pont l'Eveque, by Barneveldt ....S Wragg 10–1
H H Aga Khan's Turkham ....C Smirke 100–7
Ld Derby's Lighthouse II ...R Perryman 85–40
3 lengths, short head, 2m 30 4/5s. 16 ran F Darling
1941*Mrs R Macdonald-Buchanan's Owen Tudor, ... by Hyperion W Nevett 25–1
H H Senior Maharami Saheb of Kilapur's Morogoro ....H Wragg 11–2
Sir W Jury's Firoze Din ...W Stephenson 100–1
1 1/2 lengths, 2 lengths, 2m 32s. 20 ran F Darling
1942*Ld Derby's Watling Street, by Fairway
............................H Wragg 6–1
Ld Rosebery's Hyperides ....E Smith 9–2
Mr A E Allnatt's Ujiji ....C Richards 18–1
Neck, 2 lengths, 2m 39 3/5s. 13 ran W Earl
1943*Miss D Paget's Straight Deal, by Solario
............................T H Carey 100–6
H H Aga Khan's Umiddad ...E C Elliott 100–8
H H Aga Khan's Nasrullah ..G Richards 9–1
Head, 1/2 length, 2m 30 2/5s. 23 ran W Nightingall
1944*Ld Rosebery's Ocean Swell, by Blue Peter
............................W Nevett 28–1
H H Aga Khan's Tehran ....E Smith 8–1
Mr W Hutchinson's Happy Landing
............................R A Jones 22–1
Neck, short head, 2m 31s. 20 ran J L Jarvis
1945*Sir E Ohlson's Dante, by Nearco
............................W Nevett 100–30
Ld Rosebery's Midas ....E Smith 6–1
Ld Astor's Court Martial ....C Richards 100–9
2 lengths, head, 2m 26 3/5s. 27 ran M Peacock
1946 Mr J E Ferguson's Airborne, by Precipitation ....T Lowrey 50–1
Ld Derby's Gulf Stream ....H Wragg 7–1
Mr T Lilley's Radiotherapy ..T H Carey 8–1
1 length, 2 lengths, 2m 44 3/5s. 17 ran R Perryman
1947 Baron G de Waldner's Pearl Diver, by Vatellor ....G Bridgland 40–1
H H Aga Khan's Migoli ....D Smith 20–1
H H Maharaja of Baroda's Sayajirao
..............................E Britt 13–2
4 lengths, 3/4 length, 2m 38 2/5s. 15 ran W Halsey
1948 H.H Aga Khan's My Love, by Vatellor
.........................W Johnstone 100–9
M L Volterra's Royal Drake J Doyasbere 25–1
H H Aga Khan's Noor ....T Weston 22–1
1 1/2 lengths, 4 lengths, 2m 40s. 32 ran R Carver, in France
1949 Mrs M Glenister's Nimbus, by Nearco
..........................E C Elliott 7–1
M L Volterra's Armour Drake
.........................W Johnstone 10–1
Ld Derby's Swallow Tail ......D Smith 100–8
head, same, 2m 42s. 32 ran G S Colling
1950 M.M Boussac's Galcador, by Djebel
.........................W Johnstone 100–9
Mr W Woodward's Prince Simon
..........................W H Carr 2–1
Lady Zia Wernher's Double Eclipse
.............................E Smith 40–1
Head, 4 lengths, 2m 36 4/5s. 25 ran C H Semblat, in France
1951 Mr J McGrath's Arctic Prince, by Prince Chevalier ....C Spares 28–1
Ld Milford's Sybil's Nephew ..E Mercer 50–1
Mr F W Dennis's Signal Box M Molony 20–1
6 lengths, head, 2m 39 2/5s. 33 ran W Stephenson
1952 H.H Aga Khan's Tulyar, by Tehran
............................C Smirke 11–2
Mrs James V Rank's Gay Time L Piggott 25–1
M F Dupre's Faubourg II ...J Doyasbere 100–6
3/4 length, 1 length, 2m 36 2/5s. 33 ran M Marsh
1953 Sir Victor Sassoon's Pinza, by Chanteur
...........................G Richards 5–1
Her Majesty's Aureole ....W H Carr 9–1
Prince Said Toussoun's Pink Horse
.........................W Johnstone 33–1
4 lengths, 1 1/2 lengths, 2m 35 3/5s. 27 ran, N Bertie
1954 Mr R S Clark's Never Say Die, by Nasrullah ....L Piggott 33–1
Mr J E Ferguson's Artabian Night
............................T Gosling 33–1
Sir P Loraine's Darius ....E Mercer 7–18
2 lengths, neck, 2m 35 4/5s. 22 ran J Lawson
1955 Mme L Volterra's Phil Drake, by Admiral Drake ....F Palmer 100–8
Mr J McGrath's Panaslipper ..Jas Eddery 100–1
Alice Lady Derby's Acropolis ...D Smith 11–4
1 1/2 lengths, 3 lengths, 2m 39 4/5s. 23 ran F Mathet, in France
1956 M Pierre Wertheimer's Lavandin, by Verso II ....W Johnstone 7–1
Mr R B Strassburger's Montaval
.............................F Palmer 40–1
Mr J McGrath's Roistar .....Jas Eddery 22–1
Neck, 2 lengths, 2m 36 2/5s. 27 ran, A Head, in France
1957 Sir Victor Sassoon's Crepello, by Donatello II ....L Piggott 6–4
Mr J McShain's Ballymoss .....T Burns 33–1
Mr Stavros Niarchos's Pipe of Peace
...........................A Breasley 100–8
1 1/2 lengths, 1 length, 2m 35 2/5s. 22 ran C F N Murless
1958 Sir Victor Sassoon's Hard Ridden, by Hard Sauce ....C Smirke 18–1
Mr F N Shone's Paddy's Point
.......................G W Robinson 100–1
Mr Apad Plesch's Nagami .....J Mercer 10–1
5 lengths, 1 1/2 lengths, 2m 41 1/5s. 20 ran J Rogers, in Ireland
1959 Sir H de Trafford's Parthia, by Persian Gulf ....W H Carr 10–1
Mr G A Oldham's Fidalgo .....J Mercer 10–1
Baron G de Rothschild's Shantung
............................F Palmer 11–2
1 1/2 lengths, same, 2m 36s. 20 ran C Boyd-Rochfort
1960 Sir Victor Sassoon's St Paddy, by Aureole
.............................L Piggott 7–1
Sir R Brooke's Alcaeus ......A Breasley 10–1
Mr E R More O'Ferrall's Kythnos
.......................R Hutchinson 7–1
3 lengths, 1/2 length, 2m 35 4/5s. 17 ran C F N Murless
1961 Mrs Arpad Plesch's Psidium, by Pardal
..........................R Poincelet 66–1
Mme L Volterra's Dicta Drake M Garcia 100–8
Mrs C O Iselin's Pardao ......W H Carr 13–2
2 lengths, neck, 2m 36 2/5s. 28 ran H Wragg
1962 Mr R R Guest's Larkspur, by Never Say Die ....N Sellwood 22–1
M M Boussac's Arcor ....R Poincelet 40–1
Mme L Volterra's Le Cantilien
.......................Y Saint Martin 8–1
2 lengths, 1/2 length, 2m 37 3/5s. 26 ran M V O'Brien, in Ireland
1963 M F Dupre's Relko, by Tanerko
.......................Y Saint-Martin 5–1

Sir Foster Robinson's Merchant Venturer
............................G Starkey 18–1
Mr J R Mullion's Ragusa ...G Bougoure 25–1
6 lengths, 3 lengths, 2m 39 2/5s. 26 ran F Mathet, in France
1964 Mr J Ismay's Santa Claus, by Chamossaire
............................A Beasley 15–8
Mr C W Engelhard's Indiana ...J Lindley 30–1
Mr L M Gelb's Dilettante II P Matthews 100–1
1 length, 2 lengths, 2m 42s. 17 ran J Rogers, in Ireland
1965 M J Ternynck's Sea-Bird II, by Dan Cupid ....T P Glennon 7–4
Mr G M Bell's Meadow Court L Piggott 10–1
Mr L Freedman's I Say ......R Poincelet 28–1
2 lengths, 1 1/2 lengths, 2m 38 2/5s. 22 ran E Pollet, in France
1966 Lady Zia Wernher's Charlottown, by Charlottesville ....A Breasley 5–1
Mr J A C Lilley's Pretendre .....P Cook 9–2
Mr E B Benjamin's Black Prince II
............................J Lindley 20–1
Neck, 5 lengths, 2m 37 3/5s. 25 ran G Smyth
1967 Mr H J Joel's Royal Palace, by Ballymoss
............................G Moore 7–4
Mr C W Engelhard's Ribocco L Piggott 22–1
Mr M Sobell's Dart Board ...A Breasley 10–1
2 1/2 lengths, 2 lengths, 2m 38 2/5s. 22 ran C F N Murless
1968 Mr R R Guest's Sir Ivor, by Sir Gaylord
............................L Piggott 4–5
Mr H J Joel's Connaught .....A Barclay 100–9
Mr A J Struthers's Mount Athos
............................R Hutchinson 45–1
1 1/2 lengths, 2 1/2 lengths, 2m 38 4/5s. 13 ran M V O'Brien, in Ireland
1969 Mr A M Budgett's Blakeney, by Hethersett ....E Johnson 15–2
Mr P G Goulandris's Shoemaker
............................B Taylor 25–1
Contesse de la Valdene's Prince Regent (Fr) ....J Deforge 13–2
1 length, same, 2m 40 2/5s. 26 ran Owner
1970 Mr C W Engelhard's Nijinsky (Can), by Northern Dancer ....L Piggott 11–8
Mr W F C Guest's Gyr (USA)
............................W Williamson 100–30
Mr G A Oldham's Stintino ..G Thiboeuf 7–1
2 1/2 lengths, 3 lengths, 2m 34 3/5s. 11 ran M V O'Brien, in Ireland
1971 Mr P Mellon's Mill Reef (USA), by Never Bend ....G Lewis 100–30
Mrs D McCalmont's Linden Tree (Fr)
............................D Keith 12–1
Mr E Littler's Irish Ball (Fr) ....A Gibert 25–1
2 lengths, 2 1/2 lengths, 2m 37 1/5s. 21 ran I Balding
1972 Mr J W Galbreath's Roberto (USA), by Hail to Reason ....L Piggott 3–1
Mr H Zeisel's Rheingold .....E Johnson 22–1
Mr V W Hardy's Pentland Firth
............................Pat Eddery 50–1
Short head, 3 lengths, 2m 36s. 22 ran M V O'Brien, in Ireland
1973 Mr A M Budgett's Morston (Fr), by Ragusa ....E Hide 25–1
Capt M D Lemos's Cavo Doro L Piggott 12–1
Mr R B Moller's Freefoot ....Pat Eddery 33–1
1/2 length, 2 1/2 lengths, 2m 36s 25 ran Owner
1974 Mrs N Phillip's Snow Knight, by Firestreak ....B Taylor 50–1
Col F R Hue-Williams's Imperial Prince
............................G Lewis 20–1
Mr C A B St George's Giacometti
............................A Murray 5–2
2 lengths, 1 length, 2m 35s 18 ran P Nelson
1975 Dr C Vittadini's Grundy, by Great Nephew ....Pat Eddery 5–1
Mr N B Hunt's Nobiliary (USA)
............................Y Saint Martin 20–1
Mr R Tikkoo's Hunza Dancer (USA)
............................F Durr 50–1
3 lengths, 4 lengths, 2m 35 2/5s. 18 ran P Walwyn
1976 Mr N B Hunt's Empery (USA), by Vaguely Noble ....L Piggott 10–1
Lady Beaverbrook's Relkino ....J Mercer 25–1
Mr A Aldrey's Oats ....Pat Eddery 10–1
3 lengths, head, 2m 35 3/5s. 23 ran M Zilber in France
1977 Mr R Sangster's The Minstrel (Can), by Northern Dancer ....L Piggott 5–1
Ld Leverhulme's Hot Grove ..W Carson 15–1
H H Aga Khan's Blushing Groom (Fr)
............................H Samani 9–4
Neck, 5 lengths, 2m 35 2/5s. 22 ran M V O'Brien, in Ireland
1978 Ld Halifax's Shirley Heights, by Mill Reef (USA) ....G Starkey 8–1
Mr R Sangster's Hawaiian Sound (USA)
........................W Shoemaker 25–1
Mrs D Jardine's Remainder Man ..T Ives 40–1
Head, 1 1/2 lengths, 2m 35 2/5s. 25 ran J Dunlop
1979 Sir M Sobell's Troy, by Petingo
............................W Carson 6–1
Mme J Binet's Dickens Hill ...A Murray 15–1
Mme A D'Estainville's Northern Baby (Can) ....P Paquet 66–1
7 lengths, 3 lengths, 2m 36 3/5s. 23 ran W Hern
1980 Mrs Arpad Plesch's Henbit (USA), by Hawaii ....W Carson 7–1
Mr W Barnett's Master Willie P Waldron 22–1
Mr R Fennell's Rankin ....G Starkey 14–1
3/4 length, 1 1/2 lengths, 2m 34 4/5s. 24 ran W Hern
1981 H.H Aga Khan's Shergar, by Great Nephew ....W R Swinburn 10–11
Mr P Mellon's Glint of Gold ..J Matthias 13–1
Mr K Dodson's Scintillating Air G Baxter 50–1
10 lengths, 2 lengths, 2m 44 1/5s. 18 ran M Stoute
1982 Mr R Sangster's Golden Fleece (USA), by Nijinsky (Can) ....Pat Eddery 3–1
Maktoum Al Maktoum's Touching Wood (USA) ....P Cook 40–1
Mahmoud Fustok's Silver Hawk (USA)
............................A Murray 14–1
3 lengths, 1 length, 2m 34 1/5s. 18 ran M V O'Brien in Ireland
1983 Mr E B Moller's Teenoso (USA), by Youth (USA) ....L Piggott 9–2
Mr T F Roe's Carlingford Castle
............................M Kinane 14–1
Mr R Sangster's Shearwalk
.......................W R Swinburn 18–1
3 lengths, 3 lengths, 2m 49 4/5s. 21 ran G Wragg
1984 Mr L Miglitti's Secreto (USA), by Northern Dancer ....C Roche 14–1
Mr R Sangster's El Gran Senor (USA)
..........................Pat Eddery 8–11
Mr R J Tory's Mighty Flutter ..B Rouse 66–1
Short head, 3 lengths, 2m 39 1/5s. 17 ran D V O'Brien, in Ireland
1985 Ld Howard de Walden's Slip Anchor by Shirley Heights ....S Cauthen 9–4
Mr S S Niarchos's Law Society (USA)
..........................Pat Eddery 5–1
Mr K Abdulla's Damister (USA)
.......................Y Saint Martin 16–1
7 lengths, 6 lengths, 2m 36 1/5s. 14 ran H Cecil
1986 H.H Aga Khan's Shahrastani (USA), by Nijinsky (Can) ....W R Swinburn 11–2
Mr K Abdulla's Dancing Brave (USA)
..........................G Starkey 2–1
Prince Ahmed Salman's Mashkour (USA)
..........................S Cauthen 12–1
1/2 length, 2 1/2 lengths, 2m 37 1/5s. 17 ran M Stoute
1987 Mr Louis Freedman's Reference Point by Mill Reef ....S Cauthen 6–4
Mr E B Moller's Most Welcome
..........................Paul Eddery 25–1
Mr K Abdulla's Bellotto (USA)
..........................Pat Eddery 11–1
1 1/2 lengths, short head, 2m 34s 19 ran H Cecil
1988 H.H Aga Khan's Kahyasi by Ile de Bourbon ....R Cochrane 11–1

Mr R Sangster's Glacial Storm (USA) ....M Hills 14–1
H H Aga Khan's Doyoun W R Swinburn 9–1
$1^{1}/_{2}$ lengths, $1^{1}/_{2}$ lengths, 2m $33^{4}/_{5}$s. 14 ran L Cumani
1989 Hamdam Al-Maktoum's Nashwan (USA) by Blushing Groom ..W Carson 5–4
Lady Beaverbrook's Terimon M Roberts 500–1
Lady Harrison's Cacoethes (USA) ....G Starkey 3–1
5 lengths, 2 lengths, 2m 35s 12 ran W Hern
1990 Mr K Abdulla's Quest For Fame by Rainbow Quest ....Pat Eddery 7–1
Mr R Sangster's Blue Stag ..C Asmussen 8–1
Hamdan Al-Maktoum's Elmaamul ....W Carson 10–1
3 lengths, $1^{1}/_{2}$ lengths, 2m 37 $^{1}/_{5}$s. 18 ran R Charlton
1991 Mr Fahd Salman's Generous by Caerleon ....A Munro 9–1
Hamdan Al-Maktoum's Marju W Carson 14–1
Mr H DeKwiatkowski's Star of Gdansk ....C Roche 14–1
5 lengths, 7 lengths, 2m 34s 13 ran P Cole
1992 Mr S H Craig's Dr Devious by Ahonoora ....J Reid 8–1
Mrs V Kraft Payson's St Jovite (USA) ....C Roche 14–1
Mrs S Robins's Silver Wisp (USA) ..Paul Eddery 11–1
2 lengths, short head, 2m $36^{1}/_{5}$s 18 ran P W Chapple-Hyam
1993 Mr K Abdulla's Commander in Chief by Dancing Brave ....M J Kinane 15–2
Maktoum Al Maktoum's Blue Judge ....B Raymond 150–1
Mr Wafic Said's Blues Traveller ....D Holland 150–1
$3^{1}/_{2}$ lengths, $2^{1}/_{2}$ lengths, 2m $34^{3}/_{5}$s 16 ran H Cecil

★ Run at Newmarket † Dead heat

EVER READY CORONATION CUP (Epsom)

($1^{1}/_{2}$ miles, 10 yds)
(First run 1902)

1902 Osboch 4y 9st 3lb (6)
1903 Valenza 5y 8st 7lb (6)
1904 Zinfandel 4y 9st 3lb (4)
1905 Pretty Polly 4y 9st (3)
1906 pretty Polly 5y 9st 3lb (3)
1907 The White Knight 4y 9st 3lb (4)
1908 The White Knight 5y 9st 6lb (5)
1909 Dean Swift 8y 9st 3lb (6)
1910 Sir Martin 4y 9st 3lb (9)
1911 Lemberg 4y 9st 3lb (8)
1912 Stedfast 4y 9st 3lb (5)
1913 Prince Palatine 5y 9st 6lb (4)
1914 Blue Stone 4y 8st 7lb (7)
1915†Black Jester 4y 9st 3lb (16)
1916†Pommern 4y 9st 3lb (6)
1917–18 No race
1919 He 4y 8st 7lb (3)
1920 Manilardo 4y 8st 7lb (8)
1921 Silvern 4y 9st 3lb (6)
1922 Franklin 4y 9st 3lb (7)
1923 Condover 4y 8st 7lb (8)
1924 Verdict 4y 9st (7)
1925 St. Germans 4y 9st 3lb (7)
1926 Solario 4y 9st 3lb (5)
1927 Coronach 4y 9st 3lb (3)
1928 Appelle 5y 9st 6lb (4)
1929 Reigh Count 4y 9st 3lb (9)
1930 Plantago 5y 9st 6lb (6)
1931 Parenthesis 4y 9st 3lb (11)
1932 Salmon Leap 5y 9st 6lb (8)
1933 Dastur 4y 9st 3lb (4)
1934 King Salmon 4y 9st 3lb (3)
1935 Windsor Lad 4y 9st 3lb (4)
1936 Plassy 4y 9st 3lb (8)
1937★Cecil 6y 9st 6lb
★His Grace 4y 9st 3lb (8)
1938 Monument 5y 9st 6lb (7)
1939 Scottish Union 4y 9st 3lb (6)
1940 No race
1941†Winterhalter 4y 9st 3lb (6)
1942 No race
1943‡Hyperides 4y 9st (7)
1944‡Persian Gulf 4y 9st (6)
1945‡Borealis 4y 9st (4)
1946 Ardan 5y 9st 3lb (5)
1947 Chanteur II 5y 9st 3lb (5)
1948 Goyama 5y 9st 3lb (5)
1949 Beau Sabreur 4y 9st (3)
1950 Amour Drake 4y 8st 7lb (6)
1951 Tantieme 4y 8st 7lb (5)
1952 Nuccio 4y 8st 7lb (5)
1953 Zucchero 5y 8st 10lb (10)
1954 Aureole 4y 8st 7lb (8)
1955 Narrator 4y 8st 7lb (12)
1956 Tropique 4y 8st 7lb (6)
1957 Fric 5y 8st 10lb (8)
1958 Ballymoss 4y 8st 7lb (5)
1959 Nagami 4y 8st 7lb (3)
1960 Petite Etoile 4y 8st 4lb (3)
1961 Petite Etoile 5y 8st 7lb (5)
1962 Dicta Drake 4y 8st 7lb (7)
1963 Exbury 4y 8st 7lb (9)
1964 Relko 4y 8st 7lb (7)
1965 Oncidium 4y 8st 11lb (10)
1966 I Say 4y 8st 10lb (7)
1967 Charlottown 4y 8st 10lb (7)
1968 Royal Palace 4y 8st 10lb (4)
1969 Park Top 5y 9st (7)
1970 Caliban 4y 9st (4)
1971 lupe 4y 8st 11lb (6)
1972 Mill Reef (USA) 4y 9st (4)
1973 Roberto (USA) 4y 9st (5)
1974 Buoy 4y 9st (5)
1975 Bustino 4y 9st (6)
1976 Quiet Fling (USA) 4y 9st (6)
1977 Excellor (USA) 4y 9st (6)
1978 Crow (Fr) 5y 9st (5)
1979 Ile de Bourbon (USA) 4y 9st (4)
1980 Sea Chimes 4y 9st (4)
1981 Master Willie 4y 9st (8)
1982 Easter Sun 5y 9st (8)
1983 My Native (USA) 4y 9st (6)
1984 Time Charter 5y 8st 11lb (6)
1985 Rainbow Quest (USA) 4y 9st (7)
1986 Saint Estephe (Fr) 4y 9st (10)
1987 Triptych (USA) 5y 8st 11lb (5)
1988 Triptych (USA) 6y 8st 11lb (4)
1989 Sheriff's Star 4y 9st (9)
1990 In The Wings 4y 9st (6)
1991 In The Groove 4y 8st 11lb (7)
1992 Saddlers' Hall 4y 9st (9)
1993 Opera House 5y 9st (8)

★Dead-heat †Run at Newbury
‡Run at Newmarket

ENERGIZER OAKS (Epsom—$1^{1}/_{2}$ miles, 10 yds)

For three year old fillies

	Starters	Jockeys
1779 Lord Derby's Bridget, by Herod	12 ...	R. Goodison
1780 Mr Douglas's Teetotum, by Match'em	11 ...	R. Goodison
1781 Lord Grosvenor's Faith, by Herod	16 ...	R. Goodison
1782 Lord Grosvenor's Ceres, by Sweet William	12 ...	S. Chifney, sen.
1783 Lord Grosvenor's Maid of the Oaks, by Herod	10 ...	S. Chifney, sen.
1784 Mr Burlton's Stella, by Plunder	10 ...	C. Hindley
1785 Lord Clermont's Trifle, by Justice	8 ...	J. Bird
1786 Sir F. Standish's The Yellow Filly, by Tandem	13 ...	J. Edwards
1787 Mr Vernon's Annette, by Eclipse	8 ...	D. Fitzpatrick
1788 Lord Egremont's Nightshade by Pot8os	7 ...	D. Fitzpatrick
1789 Lord Egremont's Tag, by Trentham	7 ...	S. Chifney, sen.
1790 Duke of Bedford's Hippolyta, by Mercury	12 ...	S. Chifney, sen.
1791 Duke of Bedford's Portia, by Volunteer	11 ...	J. Singleton, jun.
1792 Lord Clermont's Volante, by Highflyer	11 ...	C. Hindley

ENERGIZER OAKS—continued

		Starters	Jockeys
1793	Duke of Bedford's Coelia, by Volunteer	10	J. Singleton, jun.
1794	Lord Derby's Hermione, by Sir Peter Teazle	8	S. Arnull
1795	Lord Egremont's Platina, by Mercury	11	D. Fitzpatrick
1796	Sir F. Standish's Parisot, by Sir Peter Teazle	13	J. Arnull
1797	Lord Grosvenor's Nike, by Alexander	5	F. Buckle
1798	Mr J. Durand's Bellissima, by Phenomenon	7	F. Buckle
1799	Lord Grosvenor's Bellina, by Rockingham	4	F. Buckle
1800	Lord Egremont's Ephemera, by Woodpecker	8	D. Fitzpatrick
1801	Sir C. Bunbury's Eleanor, by Whiskey	6	Saunders
1802	Mr J. Wastell's Scotia, by Delpini	6	F. Buckle
1803	Sir T. Gascoigne's Theophania, by Delpini	7	F. Buckle
1804	Duke of Grafton's Pelisse, by Whiskey	8	W. Clift
1805	Lord Grosvenor's Meteora, by Meteor	8	F. Buckle
1806	Mr B. Craven's Bronze, by Buzzard	12	W. Edwards
1807	General Grosvenor's Briseis, by Beningbrough	13	S. Chifney, jun.
1808	Duke of Grafton's Motel, by Sorcerer	10	W. Clift
1809	General Gower's Maid of Orleans, by Sorcerer	11	J. Moss
1810	Sir W. Gerard's Oriana, by Beningbrough	11	W. Peirse
1811	Duke of Rutland's Sorcery, by Sorcerer	12	S. Chifney, jun.
1812	Mr W. Hewett's Manuella, by Dick Andrews	12	W. Peirse
1813	Duke of Grafton's Music, by Waxy	9	T. Goodison
1814	Duke of Rutland's Medora, by Selim	9	S. Barnard
1815	Duke of Grafton's Minuet, by Waxy	11	T. Goodison
1816	General Gower's Landscape, by Rubens	11	S. Chifney, jun.
1817	Mr G. Watson's Neva, by Cervantes	11	F. Buckle
1818	Mr J. Udny's Corinne, by Waxy	10	F. Buckle
1819	Mr T. Thornhill's Shoveler, by Scud	10	S. Chifney, jun.
1820	Lord Egremont's Caroline, by Whalebone	13	H. Edwards
1821	Lord Exeter's Augusta, by Woful	7	J. Robinson
1822	Duke of Grafton's Pastille, by Rubens	10	H. Edwards
1823	Duke of Grafton's Zinc, by Woful	10	F. Buckle
1824	Lord Jersey's Cobweb, by Phantom	13	J. Robinson
1825	General Grosvenor's Wings, by The Flyer	10	S. Chifney, jun.
1826	Mr J. Forth's Lilias (re-named Babel) by Interpreter	15	T. Lye
1827	Duke of Richmond's Gulnare, by Smolensko	19	F. Boyce
1828	Duke of Grafton's Turquoise, by Selim	14	J. B. Day
1829	Lord Exeter's Green Mantle, by Sultan	14	G. Dockeray
1830	Mr W. Stonehewer's Variation, by Bustard	18	G. Edwards
1831	Duke of Grafton's Oxygen, by Emilius	21	J. B. Day
1832	Lord Exeter's Galata, by Sultan	19	P. Conolly
1833	Sir M. Wood's Vespa, by Muley	19	J. Chapple
1834	Mr T. Cosby's Pussy, by Pollio	15	J. B. Day
1835	Mr E. Mostyn's Queen of Trumps, by Velocipede	10	T. Lye
1836	Mr J. Scott's Cyprian, by Partisan	12	W. Scott
1837	Mr T. Powlett's Miss Letty, by Priam	13	J. Holmes
1838	Lord Chesterfield's Industry, by Priam	16	W. Scott
1839	Mr F. Craven's Deception, by Defence	13	J. B. Day
1840	Lord G. Bentinck's Crucifix, by Priam	15	J. B. Day
1841	Lord Westminster's Ghuznee, by Pantaloon	22	W. Scott
1842	Mr G. Dawson's Our Nell, by Bran	16	T. Lye
1843	Mr G. Ford's Poison, by Plenipotentiary	23	F. Butler
1844	Colonel Anson's The Princess, by Slane	25	F. Butler
1845	Duke of Richmond's Refraction, by Glaucus	21	H. Bell
1846	Mr J. Gully's Mendicant, by Touchstone	24	S. Day
1847	Sir J. Hawley's Miami, by Venison	23	S. Templeman
1848	Mr H. Hill's Cymba, by Melbourne	26	S. Templeman
1849	Lord Chesterfield's Lady Evelyn, by Don John	15	F. Butler
1850	Mr G. Hobson's Rhedycina, by Wintonian	15	F. Butler
1851	lord Stanley's Iris, by Ithuriel	15	F. Butler
1852	Mr J. Scott's Songstress, by Irish Birdcatcher	14	F. Butler
1853	Mr J. Wauchope's Catherine Hayes, by Lanercost	17	C. Marlow
1854	Mr W. Cookson's Mincemeat, by Sweetmeat	15	J. Charlton
1855	Mr R. Read's Marchioness, by Melbourne	11	S. Templeman
1856	Mr H. Hill's Mincepie, by Sweetmeat	10	A. Day
1857	Mr W. I'Anson's Blink Bonny, by Melbourne	13	J. Charlton
1858	Mr W. Gratwicke's Governess, by Chatham	13	T. J. Ashmall
1859	Lord Londesborough's Summerside, by West Australian	15	G. Fordham
1860	Mr R. Eastwood's Butterfly, by Turnus	13	J. Snowden
1861	Mr J. Saxon's Brown Duchess, by The Flying Dutchman	17	L. Snowden
1862	Mr R. C. Naylor's Feu de Joie, by Longbow	19	T. Challoner
1863	Lord Falmouth's Queen Bertha, by Kingston	20	T. Aldcroft
1864	Count de Lagrange's Fille de l'Air by Faugh a Ballagh	19	A. Edwards
1865	Mr W. Graham's Regalia, by Stockwell	18	J. Norman
1866	Mr B. Dunbar's Tormentor, by King Tom	17	J. Mann
1867	Baron de Rothschild's Hippia, by King Tom	8	J. Daley
1868	Mr G. Jones's Formosa, by Buccaneer	9	G. Fordham
1869	Sir F. Johnstone's Brigantine, by Buccaneer	15	T. Cannon

ENERGIZER OAKS—continued

Year	Winner	Starters	Jockeys
1870	Mr W. Graham's Gamos, by Saunterer	7	G. Fordham
1871	Baron de Rothschild's Hannah, by King Tom	9	C. Maidment
	(about 1½ miles)		
1872	Mr C Lefevre's Reine, by Monarque	17	G. Fordham
1873	Mr J. Merry's Marie Stuart, by Scottish Chief	18	T. Cannon
1874	Mr Launde's Apology, by Adventurer	11	J. Osborne
1875	Lord Falmouth's Spinaway, by Macaroni	7	F. Archer
1876†	M. Lupin's Enguerrande, by Vermout		
	†Count de Langrange's Camelia, by Macaroni	14	T. Glover
1877	Mr Pulteney's Placida, by Lord Lyon	9	H. Jeffrey
1878	Lord Falmouth's Jannette, by Lord Clifden	8	F. Archer
1879	Lord Falmouth's Wheel of Fortune, by Adventurer	8	F. Archer
1880	Mr C. Perkin's Jenny Howlet, by The Palmer	13	J. Snowden
1881	Mr T. Crawfurd's Thebias, by Hermit	12	G. Fordham
1882	Lord Stamford's b f Geheimniss, by Rosicrucian	5	T. Cannon
1883	Lord Rosebery's b f Bonny Jean, by Macaroni	14	J. Watts
1884	mr Abington's b f Busybody, by Petrarch	9	T. Cannon
1885	Lord Cadogan's b f Lonely, by Hermit	10	F. Archer
1886	Duke of Hamilton's b f Miss Jummy, by Petrarch	12	J. Watts
1887	Duke of Beaufort's ch f Reve d'Or, by Hampton	9	C. Wood
1888	Lord Calthorpe's ch f Seabreeze, by Isonomy	6	W. Robinson
1889	Lord R. Churchill's bl f L'Abbesse de Jouarre, by Trappist	12	J. Woodburn
1890	Duke of Portland's br f Memoir, by St, Simon	7	J. Watts
1891	Mr Noel Fenwick's b f Mimi, by Barcaldine	6	F. Rickaby
1892	Baron de Hirsch's br f La Fleche, by St. Simon	7	G. Barrett
1893	Duke of Portland's b f Mrs Butterwick, by St. Simon	17	J. Watts
1894	Duke of Portland's b f Amiable, by St. Simon	11	W. Bradford
1895	Sir J. Miller's b f la Sagesse, by Wisdom	15	S. Loates
1896	Lord Derby's ch f Canterbury Pilgrim, by Tristan	11	F. Rickaby
1897	Lord Hindlip's ch f Limasol, by Poulet	8	W. Bradford
1898	Mr W. T. Jones's br f Airs and Graces, by Ayrshire	13	W. Bradford
1899	Mr D. Baird's b f Musa, by Martagon	12	O. Madden

1900 Duke of Portland's La Roche, by St Simon ....M Cannon 5–1
Mr W Hall Walker's Merry Gal ....K Cannon 100–7
Mr J Musker's Lady Schomberg J F Sloan 3–1
3 lengths, bad, 2m 45⅕s. 14 ran J Porter

1901 Mr Foxhall Keene's Cap and Bells II, by Domino ....M Henry 9–4
Mr Ellesmere's Sabrinetta ....C Jenkins 50–1
Mr R Crocker's Minnie Dee ....L Reiff 10–1
6 lengths, 2 lengths, 2m 44⅖s. 21 ran S Darling

1902 Mr R S Sievier's Sceptre, by Persimmon ....H Randall 5–2
Col H McCalmont's Glass Jug G McCall 10–1
Ld Cadogan's Elba ....D Maher 25–1
3 lengths, 1½ lengths, 2m 46⅗s. 14 ran Owner

1903 Mr J B Joel's Our Lassie, by Ayrshire ....M Cannon 6–1
Maj Eustace Loder's Hammerkop ....J H Martin 2–1
Mr W Raphael's Skyscraper ....D Maher 100–7
3 lengths, head, 2m 44⅗s. 14 ran C Morton

1904 Major Eustace Loder's Pretty Polly, by Gallinule ....W Lane 8–100
Mr F Alexander's Bitters ....K Cannon 20–1
Ld Falmouth's Fiancee ....J Watts 100–7
3 lengths, bad, 2m 45⅕s. 14 ran P P Gilpin

1905 Mr W Hall Walker's Cherry Lass, by Isinglass ....H Jones 4–5
Mr George Faber's Queen of the Earth ....W Higgs 100–14
Sir J Miller's Amitie ....D Maher 100–6
3 lengths, 6 lengths, 2m 38s 12 ran W Robinson

1906 Ld Derby's Keystone II, by Persimmon ....D Maher 5–2
Mr W Bass's Gold Riach ....O Madden 5–1
Miss Clinton's Snow-Glory ....W Halsey 100–9
3 lengths, 1½ lengths, 2m 38⅗s. 12 ran G Lambton

1907 Mr J B Joel's Glass Doll, by Isinglass ....H Randall 25–1
Mr W M G Singer's Laomedia O Madden 10–1
Mrs Sadlier-Jackson's Lady Hasty ....J Thompson 100–14
½ length, ¾ length, 2m 42s 14 ran C Morton

1908 Chev E Ginistrelli's Signorinetta, by Chaleureux ....W Bullock 3–1
Ld Falmouth's Courtesy ....Wm Griggs 100–7
Mr George Edwardes's Santeve W Higgs 100–7
2 lengths, 2m 42⅖s. 13 ran Owner

1909 Mr W C Cooper's Perola, by Persimmon ....F Wootton 5–1
His Majesty's Princesse de Galles H Jones 11–2
Mr J B Joel's Verne ....Walter Griggs 25–1
2 lengths, same, 2m 39⅘s. 14 ran G Davies

1910 Sir W Bass's Rosedrop, by St Frusquin ....C Trigg 7–1
Mr J Musker's Evolution ....J Thompson 25–1
Mr Reid Walker's Pernelle ....W Higgs 25–1
4 lengths, neck, 2m 38⅕s. 11 ran Alec Taylor

1911 Mr W Brodrick Cloette's Cherimoya, by Cherry Tree ....F Winter 25–1
Capt F Forester's Tootles ....S Donoghue 7–2
Ld Derby's Hair Trigger II ....F Wootton 9–1
3 lengths, 5 lengths, 2m 41⅗s. 21 ran C Marsh

1912 Mr J Prat's Mirska, by St Frusquin ....J Childs 33–1
Mr L de Rothschild's Equitable F O'Neill 33–1
Mr Lionel Robinson's Bill and Coo ....F Wootton 10–1
3 lengths, ¾ length, 2m 43s 14 ran T Jennings

1913 Mr J B Joel's Jest, by Sundridge ....F Rickaby, jun. 8–1
Mr L Neumann's Depeche Walter Griggs 20–1
Mr J P Hornung's Arda ....W Earl 100–8
2 lengths, ½ length, 2m 37⅗s. 12 ran C Morton

1914 Mr J B Joel's Princess Dorrie, by Your Majesty ....W Huxley 11–4
Ld Carnarvon's Wassilissa ....E Huxley 100–6
Sir J Thursby's Torchlight ....G Stern 10–1
2 lengths, 4 lengths, 2m 38⅕s. 21 ran C Morton

1915★Mr L Neumann's Snow Marten, by Martagon ....Walter Griggs 20–1
Mr J B Joel's Bright ....W Huxley 7–1

Mr E Hulton's Silver Tag ..S Donoghue 11–4
4 lengths, head, 2m 36 1/5s. 11 ran P P Gilpin

1916*Mr E Hulton's Fifinella, by Polymelus ....J Childs 8–13
Mr L Neumann's Salamandra A Whalley 8–1
Mr W M G Singer's Market Girl ....S Donoghue 20–1
5 lengths, 1/2 length, 2m 35s 7 ran R Dawson

1917*Major W Astor's Sunny Jane, by Sunstar ....O Madden 4–1
Ld D'Abernon's Diadem ......F Rickaby 7–4
Mr J W Larnach's Moravia ..E Wheatley 100–8
1/2 length, 4 lengths, 2m 43 2/5s. 11 ran Alec Taylor

1918*Mr A W Cox's My Dear, by Beppo ....S Donoghue 3–1
Ld Derby's Ferry ....B Carslake 100–6
Mr W M Cazalet's Silver Bullet ....O Madden 33–1
Stoney Ford came in first by a length but was disqualified dead heat for 3rd place, 2m 34 4/5s. 15 ran Alec Taylor

1919 Lady James Douglas's Bayuda, by Bayardo ....J Childs 100–7
Sir E Hulton's Roseway ....S Donoghue 4–7
Ld Rosebery's Mapledurham ...G Hulme 25–1
1 1/2 lengths, same, 2m 37 1/5s. 10 ran Alec Taylor

1920 Mr A P Cunliffe's Charlebelle, by Charles O'Malley ....A Whalley 7–2
Sir R W B Jardine's Cinna ...Wm Griggs 2–1
Sir E Hulton's Roselet ....V Smyth 25–1
Neck, 4 lengths, 2m 38 1/5s. 17 ran H Braime

1921 Mr J Watson's Love in Idleness, by Bachelor's Double ....J Childs 5–1
Mrs H Nugent's Lady Sleipner P Mason 25–1
Ld Astor's Long Suit ....F Lane 10–1
3 lengths, neck, 2m 38 2/5s. 22 ran Alec Taylor

1922 Ld Astor's Pogrom, by Lemberg ....E Gardner 5–4
Sir E Hulton's Soubriquet ..S Donoghue 7–2
M E de St Alary's Mysia ...G Archibald 100–8
3/4 length, 3 lengths, 2m 36 1/5s. 11 ran Alec Taylor

1923 Vic de Fontarce's Brownhylda, by Stedfast ....V Smyth 10–1
Sir E Hulton's Shrove ....E C Elliott 100–7
H H Aga Khan's Teresina .....G Hulme 8–1
Neck, head, 2m 37s 12 ran R Dawson

1924 Sir E Hulton's Straitlace, by Son-in-Law ....F O'Neill 100–30
Ld Rosebery's Plack ....E C Elliott 11–10
Mrs S Whitburn's Mink ......R A Jones 100–7
1 1/2 lengths, head, 2m 47s 12 ran D Waugh

1925 Ld Astor's Saucy Sue, by Swynford ....F Bullock 100–20
Ld Astor's Miss Gadabout ....J Brennan 100–8
Mr A de Rothschild's Riding Light ....S Donoghue 20–1
8 lengths, same, 2m 38 1/5s. 12 ran Alec Taylor

1926 Ld Astor's Short Story, by Buchan ....R A Jones 5–1
Mr D Sullivan's Resplendent ....T Burns 100–1
Ld Astor's Gay Bird ....J Brennan 100–8
4 lengths, 2 lengths, 2m 43 2/5s. 16 ran Alec Taylor

1927 Ld Durham's Beam, by Galloper Light ....T Weston 4–1
Ld Astor's Book Law ....H Jelliss 5–2
Sir G Bullough's Grande Vitesse ....S Donoghue 25–1
Head, 6 lengths, 2m 34 3/5s. 16 ran Frank Butters

1928 Ld Derby's Toboggan, by Hurry On ....T Weston 100–15
His Majesty's Scuttle ....J Childs Evens
Mr S Tattersall's Flegere ......R A Jones 100–9
4 lengths, 6 lengths, 2m 37 2/5s. 13 ran Frank Butters

1929 Ld Astor's Pennycomequick, by Hurry On ....H Jelliss 11–10
Lt-Col Loder's Golden Silence ....C Ray 20–1
Lt-Col Loder's Sister Anne .....J Childs 7–2
5 lengths, 2 lengths, 2m 35 4/5s. 13 ran J Lawson

1930 Ld Glaneley's Rose of England, by Teddy ....G Richards 7–1
Ld Howard de Walden's Wedding Favour ....M Wing 33–1
Ld Beaverbrook's Micmac ....C Ray 33–1
3 lengths, 2 lengths, 2m 39s 15 ran T Hogg

1931 Lt.-Col C W Birkin's Brulette, by Bruleur ....E C Elliott 7–2
Ld Ellesmere's Four Course ....F Fox 6–1
Mr W M G Singer's Links Tor R A Jones 10–1
1 length, 3/4 length, 2m 39 1/5s. 15 ran F Carter, in France

1932 H.H Aga Khan's Udaipur, by Blandford ....M Beary 10–1
Ld Woolavington's Will o' the Wisp ....G Richards 9–1
Ld Derby's Giudecca ....T Weston 10–1
2 lengths, same, 2m 43 1/5s. 12 ran Frank Butters

1933 Mr E Thornton-Smith's Chatelaine, by Phalaris ....S Wragg 25–1
Miss J B Courtauld's Solfatara ....S Donoghue 20–1
Mr W M G Singer's Fur Tor ..R A Jones 100–8
1 1/2 lengths, 2 lengths, 2m 36 4/5s. 14 ran F Templeman

1934 Ld Durham's Light Brocade, by Galloper Light ....B Carslake 7–4
Mr Z G Michalinos's Zelina S Donoghue 9–4
Ld Astor's Instantaneous ....R Dick 20–1
1 1/2 lengths, 1/2 length, 2m 35 1/5s. 8 ran Frank Butters

1935 Ld Stanley's Quashed, by Obliterate ....H Jelliss 33–1
Mrs G B Miller's Ankaret ....F Fox 100–6
M Pierre Wertheimer's Mesa ....W Johnstone 5–4
Short head, 1 length, 2m 41 2/5s. 17 ran C Leader

1936 Sir A Bailey's Lovely Rosa, by Tolgus ....T Weston 33–1
Sir F Eley's Barrowby Gem ...P Beasley 22–1
Ld Derby's Feola ....F Fox 10–1
3/4 length, 2 lengths, 2m 36s 17 ran H L Cottrill

1937 Sir V Sassoon's Exhibionist, by Solario ....S Donoghue 3–1
Mr F Dennis's Sweet Content W Sibbritt 33–1
Ld Astor's Sculpture ....R A Jones 20–1
3 lengths, head, 2m 37s 13 ran J Lawson

1938 Sir H Cunliffe-Owen's Rockfel, by Felstead ....H Wragg 3–1
Miss D Paget's Radiant ....C Smirke 100–7
Sir A Butt's Solar FFlower ..R Perryman 100–9
4 lengths, 1 1/2 lengths, 2m 37 2/5s. 14 ran O Bell

1939 Mr R S Clark's Galatea II, by Dark Legend ....R A Jones 10–11
Mr E Esmond's White Fox ...E C Elliott 9–1
Duchess of Marlborough's Superbe ....P Beasley 20–1
Head, 3 lengths, 2m 40 2/5s. 21 ran J Lawson

1940*Ld Rothermere's Godiva, by Hyperion ....D Marks 7–4
Mr E Esmond's Silverlace II G Richards 100–8
Mr J A Hirst's Valeraine ......T Weston 33–1
3 lengths, 4 lengths, 2m 30 2/5s. 14 ran W Jarvis

1941*Mr J A Dewar's Commotion by Mieuxce ....H Wragg 8–1
Lt-Col J Robinson's Turkana ....P Evans 100–8
Ld Glanely's Dancing Time R Perryman 4–7
2 lengths, 3/4 length, 2m 37s 12 ran F Darling

1942*His Majesty's Sun Chariot, by Hyperion ....G Richards 1–4
Ld Rosebery's Afterthought ....E Smith 10–1
Ld Glanely's Feberion ....T Carey 20–1
1 length, 1 1/2 lengths, 2m 33 1/5s. 12 ran F Darling

1943*Mr J V Rank's Why Hurry, by Precipitation ....E C Elliott 7–1
Ld Rosebery's Ribbon ....E Smith 5–2
Mrs R Macdonald-Buchanan's Tropical Sun ....G Richards 7–4
Neck, 1 length, 2m 33 1/5s. 13 ran N Cannon

1944*Mr W Woodward's Hycilla, by Hyperion ....G Bridgland 8–1
Mr W F Philips's Monsoon .....P Maher 33–1

Ld Harewood's Kannabis ..A Richardson 18–1
$1^1/2$ lengths, same, 2m $30^2/5$s. 16 ran C Boyd-Rochfort
1945★Ld Derby's Sun Stream, by Hyperion
............................H Wragg 6–4
H H Aga Khan's Naishapur ....D Smith 20–1
Mrs R Macdonald-Buchanan's Solar Princess ....G Richards 20–1
Short head, 3 lengths, 2m 30s 16 ran W Earl
1946 Sir A Butt's Steady Aim, by Felstead
............................H Wragg 7–1
Ld Rosebery's Iona ....E Smith 2–1
Maj L B Holliday's Neila ..... M Beary 7–1
3 lengths, same, 2m 41s 10 ran Frank Butters
1947 Mme P Corbiere's Imprudence, by Canot
........................W Johnstone 7–4
Maj L B Holliday's Netherton Maid
..........................W Rickaby 7–1
Ld Rosebery's Mermaid ....E Smith 6–1
5 lengths, 2 lengths, 2m 40s 11 ran J Lieux, in France
1948 H.H Aga Khan's Masaka, by Nearco
............................W Nevett 7–1
His Majesty's Angelola ....H W Carr 20–1
M M le Baron's Folie II .....J Doyasbere 33–1
6 lengths, 3 lengths, 2m $40^3/5$s. 25 ran Frank Butters
1949 Mr N P Donaldson's Musidora, by Nasrullah ....E Britt 4–1
M M Boussac's Coronation V E C Elliott 6–1
Comte de Chambure's Vice Versa II
........................W Johnstone 5–1
Neck 2 lengths, 2m 40s. 17 ran C F Elsey
1950 M M Boussac's Asmena, by Goya
........................W Johnstone 5–1
M P Lafarge's Plume II ......E C Elliott 10–1
Mr J Musker's Stella Polaris ..M Molony 100–7
1 length, $1^1/2$ lengths, 2m $42^2/5$s. 19 ran C H Semblat, in France
1951 Maj L B Holliday's Neasham Belle, by Nearco ....S Clayton 33–1
Mr H G Blagrave's Chinese Cracker
..........................A Breasley 10–1
Mr H S Tufton's Belle of All E C Eliott 5–1
4 lengths, 2 lengths, 2m $41^1/5$s. 16 ran G T Brooke
1952 Capt A M Keith's Frieze, by Phideas
..............................E Britt 100–7
Sir Malcolm McAlpine's Zabara K Gethin 9–2
Mr W Woodward's Moon Star W H Carr 9–1
3 lengths, $1^1/2$ lengths, 2m $35^4/5$s. 19 ran C F Elsey
1953 Ld Astor's Ambiguity, by Big Game
..............................J Mercer 18–1
H H Aga Khan's Kerkeb .....G Richards 28–1
M P Wertheimer's Noemi .....J Massard 100–8
1 length, same, 2m $36^4/5$s. 21 ran R J Colling
1954 Mme R Forget's Sun Cap, by Sunny Boy
........................W Johnstone 100–8
M M Boussac's Altana ....E Mercer 8–1
M Paul Duboscq's Philante ..J Doyasbere 20–1
6 lengths, 1 length, 2m $39^1/5$s. 21 ran R Carver, in France
1955 Lady Zia Wernher's Meld, by Alycidon
...........................W H Carr 7–4
Mr R D Hollingsworth's Ark Royal
............................E Mercer 8–1
Lt-Col G Fairlie's Reel In ....A Breasley 100–6
6 lengths, 3 lengths, 2m $47^4/5$s. 13 ran C Boyd-Rochfort
1956 Mme L Volterra's Sicarelle, by Sicambre
............................F Palmer 3–1
M M Boussac's Janiari .....S Boullenger 100–8
Prince Aly Khan's Yasmin ....J Massard 25–1
3 lengths, 6 lengths, 2m 42s. 14 ran F Mathet, in France
1957 The Queen's Carrozza, by Dante
............................L Piggott 100–8
Mr J McGrath's Silken Glider ..J Eddery 20–1
H H Aga Khan's Rose Royale II ....J Massard 11–10
Short head, 3 lengths, 2m $37^2/5$s. 11 ran C F N Murless
1958 M F Dupre's Bella Paola, by Ticino
............................M Garcia 6–4
Mr E Littler's Mother Goose ..W H Carr 20–1
Mr R D Hollingsworth's Cutter ...... E Mercer 25–1

3 lengths, same, 2m $40^4/5$s. 17 ran F Mathet, in France
1959 Prince Aly Khan's Petite Etoile, by Petition ....L Piggott 11–2
Mr William Hill's Cantelo ....E Hide 7–4
Mr J R Hindley's Rose of Medina
............................E Smith 100–8
3 lengths, 5 lengths, 2m $35^4/5$s. 11 ran C F N Murless
1960 Mrs H E Jackson's Never Too Late II, by Never Say Die ....R Poincelet 6–5
Mr R B Strassburger's Paimpont
..........................G Thiboeuf 4–1
Baron G de Rothschild's Imberline
.........................J Boullenger 6–1
Head, 2 lengths, 2m $39^1/5$s. 10 ran E Pollet, in France
1961 Mrs S M Castello's Sweet Solera, by Solonaway ....W Rickaby 11–4
The late Sir P Loraine's Ambergris
............................J Lindley 132–
Mr C Clore's Anne la Douce G Thiboeuf 100–6
$1^1/2$ lengths, neck, 2m $39^2/5$s. 12 ran Reg Day
1962 M G P Goulandris's Monade, by Klairon
.......................Y Saint-Martin 7–1
Mr H J Joel's West Side Story ...E Smith 3–1
Mr J F C Bryce's Tender Annie
.......................G Bourgoure 100–6
Short head, $1^1/2$ lengths, 2m $38^1/5$s. 18 ran J Lieux, in France
1963 Mrs J M Olin's Noblesse, by Mossborough ....G Bougoure 4–11
Mr J G Morrison's Spree
............................J Lindley 100–7
Mrs W H D Riley-Smith's Pouponne
...........................A Breasley 33–1
10 lengths, neck, 2m $39^3/5$s. 9 ran P J Prendergast, in Ireland
1964 Sir F Robinson's Homeward Bound, by Alycidon ....G Starkey 100–7
Lt-Col Sir J Darell's Windmill Girl
............................J Mercer 50–1
Baron G de Rothschild's La Bamba
............................J Deforge 10–1
2 lengths, 1 length, 2m $49^2/5$s. 18 ran J Oxley
1965 Mr J Cox Brady's Long Look, by Ribot
............................J Purtell 100–7
Mr G P William's Mabell
............................J Lindley 13–2
Mr E A Holt's Ruby's Princess
......................K Temple-Nidd 33–1
$1^1/2$ lengths, $^3/4$ length, 2m $39^3/5$s. 13 ran M V O'Brien, in Ireland
1966 Mr C Clore's Valoris, by Tiziano
............................L Piggott 11–10
Mr P Mellon's Berkeley Springs G Lewis 6–1
Mr M W Wickham Boynton's Varinia
...........................S Clayton 100–7
$2^1/2$ lengths, 3 lengths, 2m $39^2/5$s. 13 ran M V O'Brien, in Ireland
1967 Countess Margit Batthyany's Pia, by Darius ....E Hide 100–7
Mr Stanhope Joel's St Pauli Girl
...........................B Raymond 7–1
Mr D G Freeman's Ludham ..A Breasley 100–8
$^3/4$ length, 2 lengths, 2m $38^2/5$s. 12 ran W Elsey
1968 M H Berlin's La Lagune, by Val de Loir
..........................G Thiboeuf 11–8
Mr J McShain's Glad One W Williamson 10–1
Maj C H Nathan's Pandora Bay
........................M L Thomas 33–1
5 lengths, short head, 2m $41^3/5$s. 14 ran F Boutin, in France
1969 Ld Rosebery's Sleeping Partner, by Parthia ....J Gorton 10–6
Mr C Spence's Frontier Goddess D Keith 100–7
Mrs P W McGrath's Myastrid L Piggott 28–1
$^3/4$ length, 4 lengths, 2m 40s. 15 ran Doug Smith
1970 Mrs Stanhope Joel's Lupe, by Primera
...........................A Barclay 100–30
Mrs D McCalmont's State Pension
............................D Keith 10–1

Mr J R Mullion's Arctic Wave ...Y Saint Martin 40–1
4 lengths, 1/2 length, 2m 41 2/5s. 16 ran C F N Murless

1971 Mr F R Hue-William's Altesse Royale, by Saint Crespin III ....G Lewis 6–4
Mr H Joel's Maina ....L Piggott 17–2
Marquise du Vivier's La Manille (Fr) ....Y Saint Martin 12–1
3 lengths, 1 1/2 lengths, 2m 37s. 11 ran C F N Murless

1972 Mr C A B St George's Ginevra, by Shantung ....A Murray 8–1
Mr R Scully's Regal Exception (USA) ....M Philipperon 100–1
Mrs C Engelhard's Arkadina (USA) ....L Piggott 6–1
1 1/2 lengths, neck, 2m 39 2/5s. 17 ran H R Price

1973 Mr G Pope jnr's Mysterious, by Crepello ....G Lewis 13–8
Mr A Clore's Where You Lead (USA) ....L Piggott 100–20
Mr P Bull's Aureoletta (Fr) ...W Carson 11–1
4 lengths, 4 lengths, 2m 36 2/5s. 10 ran C F N Murless

1974 Mr L Freedman's Polygamy, by Reform ....Pat Eddery 3–1
Mr R B Moller's Furioso .....A Murray 16–1
Mr N B Hunt's Matuta (USA) W Pyers 16–1
1 lengths, 1/2 length, 2m 39 2/5s. 15 ran P Walwyn

1975 Mr J I Morrison's Juliette Marny, by Blakeney ....L Piggott 12–1
Sir C Clore's Val's Girl (USA) W Carson
Mr H J Joel's Moonlight Night (Fr) ....G Lewis 9–4
4 lengths, 3/4 length, 2m 39 1/5s. 12 ran A J Tree

1976 Mr D Wildenstein's Pawneese (Fr), by Carvin ....Y Saint-Martin 6–5
Mrs J Roger's Roses for the Star (USA) ....W Carson 33–1
Sir P Oppenheimer's African Dancer ....Pat Eddery 15–2
5 lengths, 4 lengths, 2m 35 1/5s. 14 ran A Penna, in France

1977 Her Majesty's Dunfermline, by Royal Palace ....W Carson 6–1
Sig L Gatto-Roissard's Freeze the Secret (USA) ....G Dettori 7–1
Sig L Gatto-Roissard's Vaguely Deb (USA) ....B Raymond 14–1
3/4 length, 3 lengths, 2m 36 3/5s. 13 ran W Hern

1978 Mr S Hanson's Fair Salinia, by Petingo ....G Starkey 8–1
M J Wertheimer's Dancing Maid F Head 2–1
Mr O Waller's Suni ......Y Saint Martin 33–1
Short head, 1 1/2 lengths, 2m 36 4/5s. 15 ran M Stoute

1979 Mr J Morrison's Scintillate, by Sparkler ....Pat Eddery 20–1
Mr A Struther's Bonnie Isle ...W Carson 12–1
Mr L B Holliday's Britannia's Rule ....P Waldron 12–1
3 lengths, 1 length, 2m 43 4/5s. 14 ran J Tree

1980 Mr R D Hollingsworth's Bireme by Grundy ....W Carson 9–2
Mr T Blackwell's Vielle ....G Baxter 9–2
Sir John Astor's The Dancer ..E Johnson 14–1
2 lengths, short head, 2m 34 2/5s. 11 ran W Hern

1981 Mrs B Firestone's Blue Wind by Ld Gayle (USA) ....L Piggott 3–1
Mr G Kaye's Madam Gay ....J Reid 10–1
Mr P Mellon's Leap Lively (USA) ....J Matthias 3–1
7 lengths, 10 lengths, 2m 41s. 12 ran D K Weld, in Ireland

1982 Mr R Barnett's Time Charter, by Saritamer (USA) ....W Newnes 12–1
Mr K Abdulla's Slightly Dangerous (USA) ....P Cook 10–1
Dr M Brosnan's Last Feather (USA) ....S Cauthen 11–2
1 length, 1 1/2 lengths, 2m 34 1/5s. 13 ran H Candy

1983 Sir M Sobell's Sun Princess, by English Prince ....W Carson 6–1
Mr J Hambro's Acclimatise ....G Baxter 20–1
Mr S T Wong's New Coins ....P Young 50–1
12 lengths, 2 1/2 lengths, 2m 41s. 15 ran W Hern

1984 Sir R McAlpine's Circus Plume by High Top ....L Piggott 4–1
Roldvale Ltd's Media Luna ......P Cook 66–1
Mr R A N Bonnycastle's Poquito Queen ....S Cauthen 7–1
Neck, 1 1/2 lengths, 2m 39s. 15 ran J Dunlop (Out Of Shot finished third but was disqualified)

1985 Sheikh Mohammed's Oh So Sharp by Kris ....S Cauthen 6–4
Mr A Clore's Triptych (USA) ..C Roche 15–2
Mr M Obaida's Dubian ......Pat Eddery 5–1
6 lengths, 3/4 length, 2m 41 2/5s. 12 ran H Cecil

1986 Mr H H Ranier's Midway Lady (USA) by Alleged ....R Cochrane 15–8
Mr R H Cowell's Untold ...Paul Eddery 20–1
Maktoum Al Maktoum's Maysoon ....W R Swinburn 12–1
1 length, 3/4 length, 2m 35 3/5s. 15 ran B Hanbury

1987 Sheikh Mohammed's Unite by Kris ....W R Swinburn 11–1
Mr K Abdulla's Bourbon Girl ....C Asmussen 12–1
Sheikh Mohammed's Three Tails ....W Carson 3–1
5 lengths, 3 lengths, 2m 38 1/5s. 11 ran M Stoute

1988 Sheikh Mohammed's Diminuendo by Diesis ....S Cauthen 7–4
Princess Lucy Ruspoli's Sudden Love ....R Cochrane 11–2
Mr J Wertheimer's Animatrice G Moore 20–1
4 lengths, 2 lengths, 2m 35s. 11 ran H Cecil

1989 Mr Saeed Maktoum Al Maktoum's Snow Bride (USA), by Blushing Groom (Fr) ....S Cauthen 13–2
Ld Carnarvon's Roseate Tern W Carson 25–1
Mr A Christodoulou's Mamaluna ....G Starkey 50–1
3 lengths, short head,2m 34 1/5s. 9 ran H Cecil
Aliysa won but on November 20, 1990 was disqualified (prohibited substance, Camphor, in blood)

1990 Hamdan Al-Maktoum's Salsabil, by Sadler's Wells ....W Carson 2–1
Mrs H Phillips's Game Plan ...B Marcus 50–1
Mr F Salman's Knight's Baroness .....T Quinn 16–1
5 lenghts, 1 lenght, 2m 38 4/5s. 8 ran J Dunlop

1991 Maktoum Al Maktoum's Jet Ski Lady (USA), by Vaguely Noble ....C Roche 50–1
Sheikh Mohammed's Shamshir L Dettori 6–1
Hamdan Al-Maktoum's Shadayid (USA) ....W Carson Evens
10 lengths, 3/4 length, 2m 37 2/5s. 9 ran J S Bolger, in Ireland

1992 Mr W J Gredley's User Friendly by Slip Anchor ....G Duffield 5–1
Mr K Abdulla's All At Sea (USA) ....P Eddery 11–10
Mrs B M Fairbarns's Pearl Angel ....L Piggott 33–1
3 1/2, 20 lengths, 2m 39 4/5s 7 ran C E Brittain

1993 Sheikh Mohammed's Intrepidity by Sadler's Wells ....M Roberts 5–1
Mr M Haga's Royal Ballerina ....W J O'Connor 33–1
Mr R E Sangster's Oakmead ...L Dettori 11–1
3/4 length, head, 2m 34 1/5s. 14 ran A Fabre, in France

*Run at Newmarket †Dead-heat

PRINCE OF WALES'S STAKES (Royal Ascot)

(First run 1862)
(1¼ miles)

1920 All Prince 8st 3lb (7)
1921 Polymestor 8st 3lb (4)
1922 Villars 8st 10lb (11)
1923 Eastern Monarch 8st 13lb (7)
1924 Sansovino 9st 5lb (6)
1925 Warminster 9st (5)
1926 Caissor 8st 3lb (9)
1927 Chantrey 8st 3lb (10)
1928 Potocki 8st 13lb (12)
1929 Lyme Regis 8st 4lb (8)
1930 Parenthesis 8st 3lb (11)
1931 Sir Andrew 9st 1lb (15)
1932 Sigiri 8st 3lb (5)
1933 Hyperion 9st 5lb (6)
1934 Achtenan 8st 13lb (11)
1935 Assignation 8st 3lb (10)
1936 Valerian 8st 3lb (13)
1937 Cold Scent 9st 1lb (10)
1938 L'Ouragan III 8st 10lb (14)
1939 Heliopolis 9st 5lb (10)
1940–67 No race
1968 Royal Palace 4y 9st 5lb (2)
1969 Connaught 4y 9st 2lb (5)
1970 Connaught 5y 9st 4lb (4)
1971 Arthur 4y 9st 2lb (4)
1972 Brigadier Gerard 4y 9st 8lb (7)
1973 Gift Card (Fr) 4y 9st 5lb (5)
1974 Admetus (Fr) 4y 9st 5lb (5)
1975 Record Run 4y 9st 2lb (6)
1976 Anne's Pretender (USA) 4y 9st 1lb (7)
1977 Lucky Wednesday 4y 9st 1lb (5)
1978 Gunner B 5y 9st 1lb (7)
1979 Crimson Beau 4y 9st 1lb (7)
1980 Ela-Mana-Mou 4y 9st 4lb (10)
1981 Hard Fought 4y 9st 4lb (9)
1982 Kind of Hush 4y 9st 11lb (7)
1983 Stanerra 5y 8st 12lb (11)
1984 Morcon 4y 9st 1lb (5)
1985 Bob Back (USA) 4y 9st 7lb (4)
1986 English Spring (USA) 4y 8st 12lb (9)
1987 Mtoto 4y 9st 4lb (10)
1988 Mtoto 5y 9st 8lb (4)
1989 Two Timing 3y 8st 4lb (8)
1990 Batshoof 4y 9st 5lb (8)
1991 Stagecraft 4y 9st 3lb (6)
1992 Perpendicular 4y 9st 3lb (11)
1993 Placerville (USA) 3y 8st 4lb (11)

Until 1968 the race was for three year olds only

RIBBLESDALE STAKES (Royal Ascot)

(1½ miles)
For three year old fillies
(First run 1919)

1919 Milton 3y 8st 7lb (3)
1920 Perion 4y 9st 4lb (3)
1921 The Yellow Dwarf 3y 8st 7lb (5)
1922 Dry Toast 3y 8st 7lb (5)
1923 Leighton Tor 4y 9st 1lb (6)
1924 Live Wire 3y 8st 4lb (4)
1925 Glommen 3y 8st (4)
1926 Artist Glow 3y 8st 7lb (5a)
1927 Foliation 4y 9st 9lb (7)
1928 O'Curry 3y 8st 7lb (9)
1929 Sir Cosmo 3y 8st 7lb (6)
1930 Flying Argosy 3y 8st (8)
1931 Doctor Dolittle 3y 8st 12lb (9)
1932 Rose en Soleil 4y 9st 7lb (7)
1933 Versicle 3y 8st 4lb (8)
1934 The Blue Boy 4y 9st 4lb (5)
1935 Easton 4y 9st 12lb (6)
1936 Can-Can 3y 7st 11lb (11)
1937 Rhodes Scholar 4y 9st 12lb (11)
1938 River Prince 3y 8st 5lb (10)
1939 Ombro 3y 8st 4lb (11)
1940–47 No race
1948 Sandastre 8st 9lb (8)
1949 Colonist II 9st 5lb (8)
1950 La Baille 8st 10lb (9)
1951 Chinese Cracker 8st 10lb (9)
1952 Esquilla 8st 10lb (13)
1953 Skye 8st 6lb (12)
1954 Sweet One 8st 10lb (8)
1955 Ark Royal 8st 10lb (11)
1956 Milady 8st 10lb (13)
1957 Almeria 8st 6lb (9)
1958 None Nicer 9st (12)
1959 Cantelo 9st (8)
1960 French Fern 8st 6lb (8)
1961 Futurama 8st 6lb (12)
1962 Tender Annie 8st 6lb (15)
1963 Ostrya 8st 6lb (8)
1964 Windmill Girl 8st 10lb (15)
1965 Bracey Bridge 8st 6lb (9)
1966 Parthian Glance 8st 6lb (13)
1967 Park Top 8st 10lb (12)
1968 Pandora Bay 8st 10lb (9)
1969 Sleeping Partner 9st 4lb (10)
1970 Parmelia 8st 6lb (12)
1971 Fleet Wahine (USA) 8st 10lb (10)
1972 Star Ship 8st 10lb (7)
1973 Miss Petard 8st 10lb (9)
1974 Northern Princess 8st 10lb (8)
1975 Gallina (USA) 8st 10lb (6)
1976 Catalpa 8st 10lb (7)
1977 Nancticious 8st 10lb (9)
1978 Relfo 8st 10lb (12)
1979 Expansive 8st 7lb (7)
1980 Shoot A Line 8st 11lb (9)
1981 Strigida 8st 7lb (9)
1982 Dish Dash 8st 7lb (10)
1983 High Hawk 8st 7lb (14)
1984 Ballinderry 8st 7lb (9)
1985 Sally Brown 8st 7lb (10)
1986 Gull Nook 8st 8lb (12)
1987 Queen Midas 8st 8lb (6)
1988 Miss Boniface 8st 8lb (11)
1989 Alydaress (USA) 8st 8lb (6)
1990 Hellenic 8st 8lb (11)
1991 Third Watch 8st 8lb (14)
1992 Armarama 8st 8lb (8)
1993 Thawakib 8st 8lb (8)

Run over 1 mile for three- and four-year-olds from 1919 to 1939 and over 1½ miles for maiden three-year-olds in 1948 and 1949

COVENTRY STAKES (Royal Ascot)

For two year olds
(First run 1890)
(6 fur)

1900 Good Morning (11)
1901 Sterling Balm (14)
1902 Rock Sand (13)
1903 St Amant (13)
1904 Cicero (7)
1905 Black Arrow (9)
1906 Traquair (7)
1907 Prospector (11)
1908 Louviers (11)
1909 Admiral Hawke (18)
1910 Radiancy (18)
1911 Lady Americus (10)
1912 Shogun (10)
1913 The Tetrarch (8)
1914 Lady Josephine (7)
1915★Marcus (18)
1916★Diadem (12)
1917★Benevente (11)
1918 No race
1919 Sarchedon (8)
1920 Milesius (13)
1921 Pondoland (15)
1922 Drake (16)
1923 Knight of the Garter (10)
1924 Iceberg (9)
1925 Colorado (11)
1926 Knight of the Grail (9)
1927 Fairway (20)
1928 Reflector (14)
1929 Diolite (12)
1930 Lemnarchus (12)
1931 Cockpen (8)
1932 Manitoba (12)
1933 Medieval Knight (9)
1934 Hairan (9)
1935 Black Speck (11)
1936 Early School (18)
1937 Mirza II (11)
1938 Panorama (12)
1939 Turkham (16)
1940 No race
1941★Big Game (5)
1942★Nasrullah (7)
1943★Orestes (11)
1944★Dante (6)
1945 Khaled (8)
1946 Tudor Minstrel (6)
1947 The Cobbler (12)
1948 Royal Forest (14)
1949 Palestine (12)
1950 Big Dipper (11)
1951 King's Bench (11)
1952 Whistler (7)
1953 The Pie King (12)
1954 Noble Chieftain (8)
1955 Ratification (7)
1956 Messmate (17)
1957 Amerigo (10)
1958 Hieroglyph (14)
1959 Martial (13)
1960 Typhoon (9)
1961 Xerxes (17)
1962 Crocket (14)
1963 Showdown (12)
1964 Silly Season (19)
1965 Young Emperor (13)
1966 Bold Lad (Ire) (16)
1967 Mark Royal (16)
1968 Murrayfield (16)
1969 Prince Tenderfoot (USA) (10)
1970 Mill Reef (USA) (5)
1971 Sun Prince (10)
1972 Perdu (7)
1973 Doleswood (12)
1974 Whip It Quick (18)
1975 Galway Bay (Fr) (10)
1976 Cawston's Clown (12)
1977 Solinus (17)
1978 Lake City (USA) (20)
1979 Varingo (18)
1980 Recitation (USA) (13)

1981 Red Sunset (16)
1982 Horage (8)
1983 Chief Singer (14)
1984 Primo Dominie (8)
1985 Sure Blade (USA) (12)
1986 Cutting Blade (19)
1987 Always Fair (USA) 8st 13lb (13)
1988 High Estate 8st 13lb (9)
1989 Rock City 8st 13lb (16)
1990 Mac's Imp 8st 13lb (13)
1991 Dilum (USA) 8st 13lb (14)
1992 Petardia 8st 13lb (12)
1993 Stonehatch (USA) 8st 13lb (6)

*Run at Newmarket

ST. JAMES'S PALACE STAKES (Royal Ascot)

(1 mile)
(First run 1834)

1920 Allenby 9st (5)
1921 Craig an Eran 9st (3)
1922 Captain Cuttle 9st (6)
1923 Ellangowan 9st (7)
1924 Tom Pinch 8st 7lb (8)
1925 Zambo 9st (9)
1926 Coronach 9st (3)
1927 Kincardine 9st (10)
1928 Royal Minstrel 9st (8)
1929 Mr Jinks 9st (8)
1930 Christopher Robin 9st (6)
1931 Cameronian 9st (6)
1932 Andrea 9st (10)
1933 Canon Law 9st (9)
1934 Flamenco 9st (4)
1935 Bahram 9st (5)
1936 Rhodes Scholar 8st 7lb (5)
1937 Goya II 9st (6)
1938 Scottish Union 9st (8)
1939 Admiral's Walk 8st 7lb (6)
1940 No race
1941†Orthodox 9st (7)
1942–42 No race
1946 Khaled 9st (5)
1947 Tudor Minstrel 9st (3)
1948 Black Tarquin 9st (5)
1949 Faux Tirage 9st (8)
1950 Palestine 9st (4)
1951 Turco II 9st (10)
1952 King's Bench 9st (7)
1953 Nearula 9st (6)
1954 Darius 9st (7)
1955 Tamerlane 9st (5)
1956 Pirate King 9st (6)
1957 Chevastrid 8st 7lb (5)
1958 Major Portion 9st (5)
1959 Above Suspicion 8st 7lb (5)
1960 Venture VII 9st (2)
1961 Tudor Treasure 8st 7lb (9)
1962 Court Sentence 8st 7lb (8)
1963 Crockety 9st (10)
1964 Roan Rocket 9st (8)
1965 Silly Season 9st (12)
1966 Track Spare 9st (7)
1967 Reform 9st (5)
1968 Petingo 9st (3)
1969 Right Tack 9st (4)
1970 Saintly Song 9st (6)
1971 Brigadier Gerard 9st (4)
1972 Sun Prince 9st (5)
1973 Thatch (USA) 9st (2)
1974 Averof 9st (7)
1975 Bolkonski 9st (8)
1976 Radetzky 9st (8)
1977 Don 9st (7)
1978 Jaazeiro (USA) 9st (8)
1979 Kris 9st (5)
1980 Posse (USA) 9st (8)
1981 To-Agori-Mou 9st (8)
1982 Dara Monarch 9st (9)
1983 Horage 9st (7)
1984 Chief Singer 9st (8)
1985 Bairn (USA) 9st (8)
1986 Sure Blade 9st (7)
1987 Half A Year (USA) 9st (5)
1988 Persian Heights 9st (7)
1989 Shaadi (USA) 9st (5)
1990 Shavian 9st (8)
1991 Marju 9st (7)
1992 Brief Truce (USA) 9st (8)
1993 Kingmambo (USA) 9st (4)

†Run at Newmarket

QUEEN MARY STAKES (Royal Ascot)

(5 fur)
For two year old fillies
(First run 1921)

1921 Wild Mint (21)
1922 Cos (15)
1923 Mumtaz Mahal (15)
1924 Margeritta (19)
1925 Aloysia (22)
1926 Book Law (29)
1927 Stadacona (18)
1928 Arabella (25)
1929 Wurrat-al-Ain (17)
1930 Atbara (26)
1931 Diamalt (27)
1932 Supervisor (29)
1933 Maureen (24)
1934 Caretta (25)
1935 Fair Ranee 8st 12lb (20)
1936 Night Song 8st 12lb (35)
1937 Queen of Simla 8st 12lb (31)
1938 Belle Travers 8st 12lb (29)
1939 Snowberry 8st 12lb (28)
1940–44 No race
1945 Rivaz 8st 12lb (5)
1946 Apparition 8st 12lb (14)
1947 Masaka 8st 12lb (18)
1948 Coronation V 8st 12lb (28)
1949 Diableretta 8st 12lb (18)
1950 Rose Linnet 8st 12lb (16)
1951 Primavera 8st 12lb (20)
1952 Devon Vintage 8st 12lb (23)
1953 Sybil's Niece 8st 12lb (24)
1954 Bride Elect 8st 12lb (16)
1955 Weeber 8st 12lb (16)
1956 Pharsalia 8st 12lb (19)
1957 Abelia 8st 12lb (14)
1958 A.20 8st 12lb (23)
1959 Paddy's Sister 8st 12lb (21)
1960 Cynara 8st 12lb (17)
1961 My Dream 8st 12lb (11)
1962 Shot Silk 8st 12lb (14)
1963 Lerida 8st 12lb (15)
1964 Brassia 8st 12lb (17)
1965 Visp 8st 12lb (10)
1966 Petite Path 8st 12lb (13)
1967 Sovereign 8st 12lb (12)
1968 Grizel 8st 12lb (13)
1969 Fafalla 8st 12lb (13)
1970 Cawston's Pride 8st 12lb (11)
1971 Waterloo 8st 12lb (11)
1972 Truly Thankful 8st 8lb (14)
1973 Bitty Girl 8st 8lb (13)
1974 Highest Trump (USA) 8st 8lb (10)
1975 Rory's Rocket 8st 8lb (8)
1976 Gramond 8st 8lb (12)
1977 Amaranda (USA) 8st 8lb (13)
1978 Greenland Park 8st 8lb (21)
1979 Abeer (USA) 8st 8lb (14)
1980 Pushy 8st 8lb (17)
1981 Fly Baby 8st 8lb (11)
1982 Widaad 8st 8lb (16)
1983 Night of Wind 8st 8lb 915)
1984 Hi-Tech Girl 8st 8lb (17)
1985 Gwydion (USA) 8st 8lb (14)
1986 Forest Flower 8st 8lb (13)
1987 Princess Athena 8st 8lb (15)
1988 Gloriella 8st 8lb (12)
1989 Dead Certain 8st 8lb (13)
1990 On Tiptoes 8st 8lb (12)
1991 Marling 8st 8lb (14)
1992 Lyric Fantasy 8st 8lb (13)
1993 Risky 8st 8lb (11)

ROYAL HUNT CUP H'CAP (Royal Ascot)

(1 mile)
(First run 1843)

1900 Royal Flush 7y 7st (20)
1901 Stealaway 4y 6st 7lb (22)
1902 Solicitor 4y 7st 4lb (23)
1903 Kunstler 5y 7st 5lb (25)
1904 Csardas 5y 7st 5lb (28)
1905 Andover 4y 8st (25)
1906 Dinneford 4y 7st 7lb (22)
1907 Lally 4y 8st (24)
1908 Billy the Verger 4y 6st 18lb (20)
1909 Dark Ronald 4y 7st 2lb (23)
1910 Bachelor's Double 4y 8st 4lb (20)
1911 Moscato 5y 7st 2lb (18)
1912 Eton Boy 4y 7st 10lb (28)
1913 Long Set 6y 9st 1lb (29)
1914 Lie-a-Bed 3y 6st (25)
1915–18 No race
1919 Irish Elegance 4y 9st 11lb (26)
1920 Square Measure 5y 8st (22)
1921 Illuminator 4y 7st 6lb (22)
1922 Varzy 4y 7st (20)
1923 Weathervane 4y 6st 12lb (25)
1924 Dinkie 4y 6st 10lb (20)
1925 Cockpit 4y 7st 6lb (30)
1926 Cross Bow 4y 9st (31)
1927 Asterus 4y 8st 13lb (29)
1928 Priory Park 6y 8st 12lb (25)
1929 Songe 5y 8st 11lb (29)
1930 The MacNab 4y 7st 8lb (22)
1931 Grand Salute 4y 7st 5lb (18)
1932 Totaig 3y 7st 3lb (31)
1933 Colorado Kid 4y 8st 5lb (28)
1934 Caymanas 4y 8st 4lb (29)
1935 Priok 4y 7st 6lb (37)
1936 Guinea Gap 5y 8st 5lb (31)
1937 Fairplay 4y 8st 3lb (33)
1938 Couvert 5y 7st 12lb (29)
1939 Caerloptic 4y 8st 12lb (24)
1940 No race
1941*Time Step 5y 8st 9lb (11)
1942–44 No race
1945 Battle Hymn 3y 7st 11lb (14)
1946 Friar's Fancy 5y 7st 12lb (16)
1947 Master Vote 4y 7st 6lb (28)
1948 Master Vote 5y 8st 10lb (27)
1949 Sterope 4y 8st 12lb (29)

1950 Hyperbole 5y 8st 8lb (20)
1951 Val d'Assa 4y 8st 8lb (23)
1952 Queen of Sheba 4y 8st 4lb (29)
1953 Choir Boy 4y 7st 8lb (21)
1954 Chivalry 5y 8st 3lb (26)
(1 mile)
1955 Nicholas Nickleby 4y 7st 9lb (22)
1956 Alexander 4y 8st 11lb (27)
1957 Retrial 5y 8st 2lb (18)
1958 Amos 4y 7st 1lb (17)
1959 Faultless Speech 4y 8st 1lb (23)
1960 Small slam 5y 8st 2lb (26)
1961 King's Troop 4y 8st 4lb (39)
1962 Smartie 4y 7st 9lb (31)
1963 Spaniards Close 6y 8st 6lb (38)
1964 Zaleucus 4y 8st 2lb (30)
1965 Casablanca 4y 8st 7lb (26)
1966 Continuation 4y 7st 9lb (15)
1967 Regal Light 4y 7st 6lvb (15)
1968 Golden Mean 5y 8st 4lb (26)
1969 Kamundu 7y 8st 6lb (24)
1970 Calpurnius 45y 7st 13lb (18)
1971 Picture Boy 6y 7st 13lb (18)
1972 Tempest Boy 4y 8st 1lb (20)
1973 Camouflage 5y 7st 9lb (20)
1974 Old Lucky 4y 8st 8lb (30)
1975 Ardoon 5y 8st 3lb (18 ran)
1976 Jumping Hill (USA) 4y 9st 7lb (16)
1977 My Hussar 5y 8st 10lb (15)
1978 Fear Naught 4y 8st (19)
1979 Pipedreamer 4y 8st 5lb (24)
1980 Tender Heart 4y 9st (22)
1981 Teamwork 4y 8st 6lb (20)
1982 Buzzards Bay 4y 8st 12lb (20)
1983 Mighty Fly 4y 9st 3lb (31)
1984 Hawkley 4y 8st 6lb (18)
1985 Come On The Blues 6y 8st 2lb (27)
1986 Patriach 4y 7st 12lb (32)
1987 Vague Shot 4y 9st 5lb (25)
1988 Governorship 4y 9st 6lb (26)
1989 True Panache (USA) 4y 9st 4lb (27)
1990 Pontenuovo 5y 7st 7lb (32)
1991 Eurolink the Lad 4y 8st 9lb (29)
1992 Colour Sergeant 4y 7st 8lb (31)
1993 Imperial Ballet 4y 8st 12lb (30)

*Run at Newbury (7f)

CORONATION STAKES (Royal Ascot)

(1 mile)
For three year old fillies
(First run 1870)

1900*Winifreda
*Sainte Nitouche (9)
1901 Bella Gallina (13)
1902 Doctrine (13)
1903 Oriole (10)
1904 Pretty Polly (8)
1905 Commune (12)
1906 Keystone II (5)
1907 Frugality (11)
1908 Lesbia (8)
1909 Princesse de Galles (7)
1910 Winkipop (10)
1911 Knockfeerna (7)
1912 Polkerris (11)
1913 Prue 8st 10lb (13)
1914 Wassilissa 8st 10lb (16)
1915–18 No race
1919 Flying Spear 8st 10lb (11)
1920 Cinna 9st 3lb (12)
1921 Donna Branca 8st 3lb (9)
1922 Pogrom 9st 3lb (10)
1923 Paola 8st 10lb (7)
1924 Straitlace 9st 3lb (7)
1925 Saucy Sue 9st 10lb (4)
1926 Moti Mahal 8st 10lb (9)
1927 Book Law 8st 10lb (7)
1928 Toboggan 9st 3lb (10)
1929 Daumont 8st 10lb (8)
1930 Wuarrat-al-Ain 8st 10lb (14)
1931 Sunny Devon 8st 4lb (9)
1932 Udaipur 9st 3lb (10)
1933 Betty 8st 10lbn (11)
1934 Foxcroft 8st 4lb (11)
1935 Ankaret 8st 10lb (13)
1936 Traffic Light 8st 10lb (18)
1937 Gainsborough Lass 8st 10lb (17)
1938 Solar Flower 8st 10lb (15)
1939 Olein 8st 11lb (11)
1940–45 No race
1946 Neolight 8st 11lb (7)
1947 Saucy Sal 8st 11lb (9)
1948 Fortuity 8st 4lb (8)
1949 Avila 8st 11lb (15)
1950 Tambara 9st (7)
1951 Belle of All 9st (11)
1952 Zabara 9st (7)
1953 Happy Laughter 9st (7)
1954 Festoon 9st (6)
1955 Meld 9st (5)
1956 Midget II 9st (7)
1957 Toro 9st (11)
1958 St Lucia 9st (8)
1959 Rosalba 9st (8)
1960 Barbaresque 9st (6)
1961 Aiming High 9st (6)
1962 Display 9st (8)
1963 Fiji 9st (7)
1964 Ocean 8st 7lb (6)
1965 Greengage 9st (8)
1966 Haymaking 9st (8)
1967 Fleet 9st (8)
1968 Sovereign 9st (6)
1969 Lucyrowe 9st (10)
1970 Humble Duty 9st (3)
1971 Magic Flute 9st (4)
1972 Calve 9st (7)
1973 Jacinth 9st (9)
1974 Lisadell (USA) 9st (8)
1975 Roussalka 9st (11)
1976 Kesar Queen (USA) 9st (8)
1977 Orchestration 9st (10)
1978 Sutton Place 8st 8lb (14)
1979 One In a Million 9st 4lb (13)
1980 Cairn Rouge 9st 4lb (8)
1981 Tolmi 9st (10)
1982 Chalon 9st (8)
1983 Flame of Tara 9st (6)
1984 Katies 9st 4lb (10)
1985 Al Bahathri (USA) 9st 4lb (7)
1986 Sonic Lady (USA) 9st 4lb (7)
1987 Milligram 9st (6)
1988 Magic of Life 9st (8)
1989 Golden Opinion (USA) 9st (12)
1990 Chimes of Freedom (USA) 9st (7)
1991 Kooyonga 9st (8)
1992 Marling 9st (7)
1993 Gold Splash (USA) 9st (5)

*Dead-Heat

NORFOLK STAKES (Royal Ascot)

(5 fur)
For two year olds
(First run 1843)

1900 Bay Melton 8st 10lb (11)
1901 Duke of Westminster 8st 10lb (10)
1902 Sermon 8st 10lb (13)
1903 Montem 8st 7lb (14)
1904 Llangibby 8st 10lb (9)
1905 Colonia 8st 7lb (7)
1906 Slieve Gallion 8st 10lb (9)
1907 Sir Archibald 8st 10lb (16)
1908 Bayardo 8st 10lb (13)
1909 Lemberg 8st 10lb (12)
1910 Seaforth 9st 3lb (16)
1911 Lomond 8st 10lb (12)
1912 Craganour 8st 10lb (15)
1913 Hapsburg 8st 10lb (17)
1914 Let Fly 8st 10lb (15)
1915–18 No race
1919 Orpheus 8st 10lb (7)
1920 Alan Breck 8st 10lb (16)
1921 Scamp 8st 10lb (11)
1922 Town Guard 8st 10lb (11)
1923 Druid's Orb 9st 6lb (14)
1924 Black Friar 8st 10lb (15)
1925 Buckler 8st 10lb (12)
1926 Damon 8st 10lb (19)
1927 Hakim 8st 10lb (16)
1928 Mr Jinks 8st 10lb (18)
1929 Blenheim 8st 10lb (17)
1930 Lightning Star 8st 10lb (19)
1931 Spenser 8st 10lb (17)
1932 Hyperion 8st 10lb (22)
1933 Colombo 9st 3lb (17)
1934 Eppie Adair c (named Robin Goodfellow) 9st (21)
1935 Bossover c (named Wyndham) 9st (18)
1936 Le Grand Duc 9st (10)
1937 Ramtapa 9st (18)
1938 Meadow 9st (22)
1939 Tant Mieux 9st (13)
1940–45 No race
1946 Petition 9st (10)
1947*Lerins (renamed My Babu) 9st
*Delirium 9st (12)
1948 Makarpura 9st (22)
1949 Master Gunner 9st (12)
1950 Bay Meadows 9st (10)
1951 Bob Major 9st (10)
1952 Blue Lamp 9st (14)
1953 Hydrologist 9st (14)
1954 Tamerlane 9st (9)
1955 Gratitude 9st (7)
1956 Skindles Hotel 9st (15)
1957 Pall Mall 9st (8)
1958 Masham 9st (8)
1959 Sound Track 9st (5)
1960 Floribunda 9st (7)
1961 Abermaid 9st (13)
1962 Daybreak 9st (10)
1963 Ballymacad 9st (8)
1964 No race
1965 Tin King 9st (8)
1966 Falcon 9st (4)
1967 Porto Bello 9st (4)
1968 Song 9st (12)
1969 Tribal Chief 9st (8)
1970 Swing Easy 9st (6)
1971 Phillip of Spain 8st 11lb (5)
1972 Cade's County 8st 11lb (8)
1973 Habat 8st 11lb (11)
1974 Overtown 8st 11lb (12)
1975 Faliraki 8st 11lb (10)
1976 Godswalk (USA) 8st 11lb (5)

1977 Emboss 8st 11lb (5)
1978 Schweppeshire Lad 8st 11lb (8)
1979 Romeo Romani (USA) 8st 11lb (10)
1980 Chummy's Special 8st 11lb (6)
1981 Day Is Done 8st 11lb (8)
1982 Brondesbury 8st 11lb (5)
1983 Precocious 8st 11lb (5)
1984 Magic Mirror 8st 11lb (4)
1985 Marouble 8st 11lb (10)
1986 Sizzlingh Melody 8st 11lb (6)
1987 Colmore Row 8st 13lb (8)
1988 Superpower 8st 13lb (10)
1989 Petillante 8st 8lb (6)
1990 Line Engaged 8st 13lb (9)
1991 Magic Ring 8st 13lb (9)
1992 Niche 8st 8lb (9)
1993 Turtle Island 8st 13lb (8)

Run as New Stakes from 1843 to 1972
*Dead-heat

ASCOT GOLD CUP

(2½ miles)
(First run 1807)

1900 Merman 8y 9st 4lb (6)
1901 Santoi 4y 9st (6)
1902 William the Third 4y 9st (11)
1903 Maximum II 4y 9st 4lb (4)
1904 Throwaway 5y 9st 4lb (4)
1905 Zinfandel 5y 9st 4lb (5)
1906 Bachelor's Button 7y 9st 4lb (5)
1907 The White Knight 4y 9st (9)
1908 The White Knight 5y 9st 4lb (6)
1909 Bomba 3y 7st 7lb (6)
1910 Bayardo 4y 9st (13)
1911 Willonyx 4y 9st (6)
1912 Prince Palatine 4y 9st (7)
1913 Prince Palatine 5y 9st 4lb (8)
1914 Aleppo 5y 9st 4lb (10)
1915–16 No race
1917†Gay Crusader 3y 8st 4lb (3)
1918†Gainsborough 3y 8st 1lb (3)
1919 By Jingo 5y 9st 4lb (4)
1920 Tangiers 4y 9st (6)
1921 Periosteum 4y 9st (7)
1922 Golden Myth 4y 8st (10)
1923 Happy Man 7y 9st 4lb (8)
1924 Massine 4y 9st (11)
1925 Santorb 4y 9st (6)
1926 Solario 4y 9st (6)
1927 Foxlaw 5y 9st 4lb (8)
1928 Invershin 6y 9st 4lb (10)
1929 Invershin 7y 9st 4lb (13)
1930 Bosworth 4y 9st (7)
1931 Trimdon 5y 9st 4lb (10)
1932 Trimdon 6y 9st 4lb (9)
1933 Foxhunter 4y 9st (10)
1934 Felicitation 4y 9st (10)
1935 Tiberius 4y 9st (6)
1936 Quashed 4y 8st 11lb (9)
1937 Precipitation 4y 9st (12)
1938 Flares 5y 9st (10)
1939 Flyon 4y 9st (9)
1940 No race
1941*Finis 6y 9st (7)
1942*owen Tudor 4y 9st (9)
1943*Ujiji 4y 9st (8)
1944*Umiddad 4y 9st (5)
1945 Ocean Swell 4y 9st (10)
1946 Caracall II 4y 9st (7)
1947 Souverain 4y 9st (6)
1948 Arbar 4y 9st (8)
1949 Alycidon 4y 9st (7)
1950 Supertello 4y 9st (13)
1951 Pan II 4y 9st (11)
1952 Aquino II 4y 9st (6)
1953 Souepi 5y 9st (10)
1954 Elpenor 4y 9st (11)
1955 Botticelli 4y 9st (6)
1956 Macip 4y 9st (10)
1957 Zarathustra 6y 9st (9)
1958 Gladness 5y 8st 11lb (8)
1959 Wallaby II 4y 9st (6)
1960 Sheshoon 4y 9st (6)
1961 Pandofell 4y 9st (10)
1962 Balto 4y 9st (7)
1963 Twilight Alley 4y 9st (7)
1964 No race
1965 Fighting Charlie 4y 9st (7)
1966 Fighting Charlie 5y 9st (7)
1967 Parbury 4y 9st (7)
1968 Pardallo II 5y 9st (9)
1969 Levmoss 4y 9st (6)
1970 Precipice Wood 4y 9st (6)
1971 Random Shot 4y 9st (10)
1972 Erimo Hawk 4y 9st (8)
1973 Lassalle (Fr) 4y 9st (7)
1974 Ragstone 4y 9st (6)
1975 Sagaro 4y 9st (9)
1976 Sagaro 5y 9st (7)
1977 Sagaro 6y 9st (6)
1978 Shangamuzo 5y 9st (10)
1979 Le Moss 4y 9st (6)
1980 Le Moss 5y 9st (8)
1981 Ardross 5y 9st (4)
1982 Ardross 6y 9st (5)
1983 Little Wolf 5y 9st (12)
1984 Gildoran 4y 9st (9)
1985 Gildoran 5y 9st (12)
1986 Longboat 5y 9st (11)
1987 Paean 4y 9st (8)
1988 Sadeem 5y 9st (13)
1989 Sadeem 6y 9st (8)
1990 Ashal 4y 9st (11)
1991 Indian Queen 6y 8st 13lb (12)
1992 Drum Taps (USA) 6y 9st 2lb (6)
1993 Drum Taps (USA) 7y 9st 2lb (10)

*Run at Newmarket (2¼ miles)
†Run at Newmarket as Newmarket Gold Cup
Run as The Emperor's Plate from 1845 to 1853

KING EDWARD VII STAKES (Royal Ascot)

(1½ miles)
For three year olds

1926 Finglas 8st 10lb (6)
1927 Buckfast 8st 10lb (16)
1928 Cyclonic 8st 10lb (10)
1929 Horus 8st 10lb (7)
1930 Pinxit 8st 10lb (8)
1931 Sandwich 8st 10lb (3)
1932 Dastur 8st 10lb (6)
1933 Sans Peine 8st 3lb (7)
1934 Berestoi 8st 10lb (8)
1935 Field Trial 8st 10lb (7)
1936 Precipitation 8st 4lb (10)
1937 Solfo 9st 1lb (7)
1938 Foroughi 8st 3lb (11)
1939 Hypnotist 8st 3lb (11)
1940–45 No race
1946 Field Day 8st 3lb (8)
1947 Migoli 8st 10lb (5)
1948 Vic Day 8st 10lb (14)
1949 Swallow Tail 8st 10lb (7)
1950 Babu's Pet 8st 10lb (4)
1951 Supreme Court 9st (9)
1952 Castleton 8st 10lb (10)
1953 Skyraider 8st 10lb (9)
1954 Rashleigh 8st 10lb (8)
1955 Nucleus 8st 10lb (10)
1956 Court Command 8st 6lb (12)
1957 Arctic Explorer 8st 10lb (8)
1958 Restoration 8st 6lb (10)
1959 Pindari 8st 10lb (12)
1960 Atrax 8st 10lb (12)
1961 Aurelius 8st 10lb (10)
1962 Gaul 8st 10lb (9)
1963 Only for Life 8st 10lb (7)
1964 No race
1965 Convamore 8st 10lb (12)
1966 Pretendre 8st 10lb (8)
1967 Mariner 8st 10lb (10)
1968 Connaught 8st 6lb (5)
1969 Vervain 8st 10lb (6)
1970 Great Wall 8st 6lb (5)
1971 Seafriend 8st 10lb (7)
1972 Lord Nelson (Fr) 8st 6lb (6)
1973 Klairvimy 8st 10lb (7)
1974 English Prince 9st (6)
1975 Sea Anchor 8st 10lb (8)
1976 Marquis de Sade 8st 10lb (5)
1977 Classic Example 8st 10lb (10)
1978 Ile de Bourbon (USA) 8st 6lb (10)
1979 Ela-Mana-Mou 8st 5lb (9)
1980 Light Cavalry 8st 6lb (10)
1981 Bustomi 8st 6lb (4)
1982 Open Day 8st 6lb (11)
1983 Shareef Dancer (USA) 8st 6lb (7)
1984 Head For Heights 8st 6lb (10)
1985 Lanfranco 8st 6lb (10)
1986 Bonhomie (USA) 8st 8lb (13)
1987 Love The Groom (USA) 8st 8lb (8)
1988 Sheriff's Star 8st 8lb (8)
1989 Cacoethes (USA) 8st 8lb (6)
1990 Private Tender 8st 8lb (8)
1991 Saddlers' Hall 8st 8lb (9)
1992 Beyton (USA) 8st 8lb (12)
1993 Beneficial 8st 8lb (8)

WOKINGHAM STAKES H'CAP (Royal Ascot)

(6 fur)
(First run 1896)

1900 Bridge 4y 7st 12lb (17)
1901 Rose Tree 5y 7st 9lb (20)
1902 His Lordship 3y 6st 6lb (25)
1903 Glass Jug 4y 7st 9lb (23)
1904 Out o' Sight 5y 8st 5lb (29)
1905 Queen's Holiday 4y 8st 2lb (14)
1906 Golden Gleam 4y 8st (13)
1907 Forerunner II 3y 6st 11lb (23)
1908 Portland Bay 4y 8st 2lb (22)
1909 Portland Bay 5y 8st 2lb (21)
1910 Galleot 6y 8st 4lb (19)
1911 Meleager 3y 7st 6lb (21)
1912 Borrow 4y 8st 2lb (19)
1913 Braxted 5y 8st (22)
1914 Mount William 3y 6st 10lb (24)
1915–18 No race

1919 Scatwell 4y 7st 11lb (11)
1920 Golden Orb 4y 7st 13lb (23)
1921 Santaquest 4y 7st 4lb (9)
1922 Proconsul 4y 8st 3lb (20)
1923 Crowdennis 5y 9st 2lb (16)
1924 Pandarus 5y 7st 3lb (20)
1925 Compiler 5y 8st 1lb (22)
1926 Capture Him 4y 8st 1lb (29)
1927 Nothing Venture 4y 8st 10lb (23)
1928 Hera 4y 7st 8lb (22)
1929 Six Wheeler 4y 7st 4lb (23)
1930 Grandmaster 5y 7st 5lb (17)
1931 Heronslea 4y 8st 7lb (22)
1932 Concerto 4y 8st 6lb (15)
1933 Concerto 5y 9st 3lb (24)
1934 Coroado 4y 8st 9lb (18)
1935 Theio 3y 7st 5lb (23)
1936 Cora Dreans 4y 7st 11lb (26)
1937 Kong 4y 6st 12lb (31)
1938 Bold Ben 4y 8st 9lb (26)
1939 America 4y 8st 12lb (28)
1940–44 No race
1945 Portamara 4y 7st 5lb (10)
1946 The Bug 3y 8st 7lb (21)
1947 Lucky Jordaan 4y 7st 6lb (24)
1948 White Cockade 4y 7st 7lb (32)
1949 The Cobbler 4y 9st 4lb (35)
1950 Blue Book 3y 7st 11lb (24)
1951 Donore 4y 8st 5lb (23)
1952 Malka's Boy 4y 8st 10lb (22)
1953 Jupiter 3y 7st 3lb (22)
1954 March Past 4y 9st (16)
1955 The Plumber's Mate 4y 6st 9lb (19)
1956 Light Harvest 4y 7st 12lb (28)
1957 Dionisio 4y 8st 10lb (8)
1958 Magic Boy 5y 7st 5lb (22)
1959 Golden Leg 4y 7st 1lb (29)
1960 Silver King 4y 7st 11lb (29)
1961 Whistler's Daughter 4y 8st 6lb (28)
1962 Elco 4y 8st 13lb (35)
1963 Marcher 3y 7st 12lb (27)
1964 No race
1965 Nunshoney 3y 7st 2lb (25)
1966 My Audrey 5y 8st 2lb (33)
1967 Spaniards Mount 5y 8st 6lb (19)
1968 Charicles 3y 7st 6lb (21)
1969 Sky Rocket 4y 7st 3lb (21)
1970 Virginia Boy 4y 7st 4lb (28)
1971 Whistling Fool 5y 7st 7lb (21)
1972 Le Johnston 4y 8st 2lb (21)
1973 Plummet 4y 8st 2lb (21)
1974 Ginnies Pet 4y 8st 6lb (22)
1975 Boone's Cabin (USA) 5y 10st (20)
1976 Import 5y 9st 4lb (12)
1977 Calibina 5y 8st 5lb (13)
1978 Equal Opportunity 4y 7st 12lb (24)
1979 Lord Rochford 4y 8st 8lb (28)
1980 Queen's Pride 4y 7st 13lb (29)
1981 Great Eastern 4y 9st 8lb (29)
1982 Battle Hymn 3y 7st 7lb (24)
1983 Melindra 4y 7st 5lb (27)
1984 Petong 4y 9st 6lb (29)
1985 Time Machine 4y 7st 12lb (30)
1986 Touch Of Grey 3y 8st 8lb (28)
1987 Bel Byou 36 8st 3lb (29)
1988 Powder Blue 6y 8st 5lb (30)
1989 Mac's Fighter 4y 9st 12lb (27)
1990 Kinght Of Mercy 4y 8st 6lb (28)
1991 Amigo Menor 5y 8st 7lb (29)
1992 Red Rosein 6y 8st 1lb (29)
1993 Nagida 4y 8st 7lb (30)

HARDWICKE STAKES (Royal Ascot)

(1 1/2 miles)
(First run 1879)

1900 Boniface 4y 8st 4lb (7)
1901 Merry Gal 4y 9st 7lb (5)
1902 Joshua 3y 7st 13lb (11)
1903 Sceptre 4y 9st 7lb (7)
1904 Rock Sand 4y 9st 10lb (4)
1905 Bachelor's Button 6y 9st 10lb (5)
1906 Wombwell 3y 7st 7lb 93)
1907 Beppo 4y 9st 10lb (8)
1908 Bembo 3y 7st 7lb (5)
1909 Primer 4y 8st 4lb (10)
1910 Swynford 3y 7st 7lb (7)
1911 Swynford 4y 90st 10lb (5)
1912 Stedfast 4y 9st 10lb (8)
1913 Lancaster 4y 9st (4)
1914 Peter the Hermit 3y 7st 7lb (10)
1915–18 No race
1919 Sir Douglas 3y 7st 12lb (2)
1920 Black Gauntlet 3y 7st 12lb (10)
1921 Franklin 3y 8st 3lb (12)
1922 Welsh Spear 3y 8st (7)
1923 Chosroes 3y 7st 7lb (6)
1924 Chosroes 4y 9st 10lb (13)
1925 Hurstwood 4y 9st 10lb (7)
1926 Lancegaye 3y 7st 9lb (3)
1927 Coronach 4y 9st 10lb (4)
1928 Foliation 5y 9st 9lb (9)
1929 Posterity 3y 7st 12lb (8)
1930 Alcester 4y 9st 7lb (9)
1931 Orpen 3y 8st 5lb (11)
1932 Goyescas 4y 9st 10lb (12)
1933 Limelight 4y 9st 10lb (8)
1934 Coroneaster 4y 9st 7lb (9)
1935 J. R. Smith 3y 7st 9lb (9)
1936 Corrida 4y 9st 7lb (11)
1937 Mid-day Sun 4y 8st 8lb (5)
1938 Maranta 4y 8st 4lb (7)
1939 Pointis 4y 7st 7lb (11)
1940–45 No race
1946 Priam II 5y 9st 12lb (4)
1947 Nirgal 4y 9st 10lb (5)
1948 Sayajirao 4y 9st 10lb (3)
1949 Helioscope 3y 7st 6lb (8)
1950 Peter Flower 4y 8st 8lb (4)
1951 Saturn 4y 8st 12lb (5)
1952 Dynamiter 4y 9st 1lb (4)
1953 Guersant 4y 9st 1lb (4)
1954 Aureole 4y 9st 1lb (4)
1955 Elopement 4y 9st 1lb (2)
1956 Hugh Lupus 4y 8st 12lb (6)
1957 Fric 5y 9st 1lb (6)
1958 Brioche 4y 9st 4lb (5)
1959 Impatient 4y 8st 8lb (5)
1960 Aggressor 5y 8st 12lb (5)
1961 St Paddy 4y 9st 4lb (4)
1962 Aurelius 4y 9st 4lb (4)
1963 Miralgo 4y 8st 12lb (8)
1964 No race
1965 Soderini 4y 8st 12lb (9)
1966 Prominer 4y 8st 8lb (6)
1967 Salvo 4y 8st 8lb (8)
1968 Hopeful Venture 4y 8st 8lb (6)
1969 Park Top 5y 8st 9lb (4)
1970 Karabas 5y 8st 12lb (5)
1971 Ortis (Ity) 4y 8st 12lb (8)
1972 Selhurst 4y 8st 10lb (5)
1973 Rheingold 4y 9st (4)
1974 Relay Race 4y 8st 10lb (5)
1975 Charlie Bubbles 4y 8st 10lb (11)
1976 Orange Bay 4y 9st (5)
1977 Meneval (USA) 4y 9st (7)
1978 Montcontour (Fr) 4y 8st 12lb (8)
1979 Obraztsovy (USA) 4y 8st 9lb (6)
1980 Scorpio (Fr) 4y 8st 9lb (7)
1981 Pelerin (Fr) 4y 8st 12lb (9)
1982 Critique (USA) 4y 8st 9lb (8)
1983 Stanerra 5y 8st 9lb (10)
1984 Khairpour 5y 8st 12lb (7)
1985 Jupiter Island 6y 8st 9lb (4)
1986 Dihistan 4y 8st 9lb (10)
1987 Orban (USA) 4y 8st 9lb (4)
1988 Almarad 5y 8st 12lb (8)
1989 Assatis (USA) 4y 8st 9lb (4)
1990 Assatis (USA) 5y 9st (7)
1991*Rock Hopper 4y 8st 12lb (9)
1992 Rock Hopper 5y 8st 12lb (5)
1993 Jeune 4y 8st 9lb (5)

* Topanoora finished first in 1991 but was disqualified and placed second.

KING'S STAND STAKES (Royal Ascot)

(5 fur)
(First run 1862)

1920 Diadem 6y 10st 7lb (10)
1921 Tetratema 4y 9st 7lb (7)
1922 King Sol 8y 9st 13lb (6)
1923 Golden Boss 3y 9st 8lb (7)
1924 Golden Boss 4y 10st 7lb (8)
1925 Diomedes 3y 9st 12lb (4)
1926 Highborn II 3y 9st 12lb (5)
1927 Nice Prospect 4y 9st 7lb (8)
1928 Chichester Cross 4y 8st 7lb (18)
1929 Tag End 5y 10st 4lb (11)
1930 Oak Ridge 8y 10st (5)
1931 Stingo 4y 10st 7lb (14)
1932 Lemnarchus 4y 10st 3lb (9)
1933 Gold Bridge 4y 10st 3lb (11)
1934 Gold Bridge 5y 10st 3lb (10)
1935 Shalfleet 4y 9st 7lb (15)
1936 Sweet Polly 4y 9st 4lb (10)
1937 Ticca Gari 3y 7st 11lb (17)
1938 Foray 4y 9st 1lb (8)
1939 Mickey the Greek 5y 9st 9lb (21)
1940–45 No race
1946 Vilmorin 3y 8st (7)
1947 Greek Justice 3y 8st 6lb (10)
1948 Squander Bug 5y 9st 1lb (15)
1949 Abernant 3y 8st 6lb (7)
1950 Tangle 3y 8st (3)
1951 Stephen Paul 3y 8st 6lb (12)
1952 Easter Bride 3y 7st 11lb (5)
1953 Fairy Flax 4y 9st 2lb (13)
1954 Golden Lion 3y 8st 4lb (11)
1955 Pappa Fourway 3y 9st (5)
1956 Palariva 3y 8st 4lb (14)
1957 Right Boy 3y 8st 6lb (8)
1958 Drum Beat 5y 8st 9lb (5)
1959 Chris 3y 8st 10lb (8)
1960 Sound Track 3y 8st 6lb (8)
1961 Silver Tor 3y 8st (8)
1962 Cassarate 3y 7st 11lb (7)
1963 Majority Rule 3y 8st 6lb (9)
1964 No race
1965 Goldhill 4y 9st 1lb (11)
1966 Roughlyn 5y 9st 9lb (10)
1967 Be Friendly 3y 8st 3lb (10)
1968 D'Urberville 3y 8st 3lb (12)
1969 Song 3y 8st 8lb (8)

1970 Amber Rama (USA) 3y 8st 8lb (11)
1971 Swing Easy (USA) 3y 8st 8lb (9)
1972 Sweet Revenge 5y 9st 4lb (7)
1973 Abergwaun 5y 9st 1lb (7)
1974 Bay Express 3y 8st 9lb (10)
1975 Flirting Around (USA) 4y 9st 4lb (12)
1976 Lochnager 4y 9st 3lb (13)
1977 Godswalk (USA) 3y 8st 9lb (11)
1978 Solinus 3y 8st 9lb (8)
1979 Double Form 4y 9st 3lb (13)
1980 African Song 3y 8st 9lb (14)
1981 Marwell 3y 8st 6lb (12)
1982 Fearless Lad 3y 8st 9lb (14)
1983 Sayf El Arab (USA) 3y 8st 9lb (16)
1984 Habibti 4y 9st (11)
1985 Never So Bold 5y 9st 3lb (15)
1986 Last Tycoon 3y 8st 9lb (14)
1987 Bluebird (USA) 3y 8st 9lb (12)
1988 Chilibang 4y 9st 3lb (8)
1989 Indian Ridge 4y 9st 3lb (15)
1990 Dayjur (USA) 3y 8st 10lb (15)
1991 Elbio 4y 9st 3lb (10)
1992 Sheikh Albadou 4y 9st 3lb (10)
1993 Elbio 6y 9st 3lb (8)

NEWCASTLE 'BROWN ALE' NORTHUMBERLAND PLATE H'CAP (Newcastle)

(2 miles 19 yds)
(First run 1833)

1900 Joe Chamberlain 3y 8st 2lb (8)
1901 Reminiscence 5y 6st 1lb (12)
1902 Osbech 7y 9st (10)
1903 Cliftonhall 4y 7st 7lb (8)
1904 Palmy Days 4y 7st 11lb (10)
1905 Princess Florizel 4y 6st 7lb (9)
1906 Outbreak 4y 8st (12)
1907 Killigrew 6y 6st 7lb (11)
1908 Old China 4y 8st 2lb (11)
1909 Sir Harry 4y 8st 7lb (11)
1910 Elizabetta 4y 7st 11lb (11)
1911 Pillo 6y 8st 7lb (10)
1912 Mynora 6y 6st 6lb (9)
1913 The Tylt 4y 7st 13lb (13)
1914 The Guller 5y 8st (9)
1915–45 No race
1919 Trestle 4y 6st 13lb (6)
1920 Irish Lake 4y 7st 7lb (10)
1921 Hunt Law 4y 8st 4lb (12)
1922 Double Hackle 4y 8st 4lb (14)
1923 Carpathus 4y 7st 10lb (11)
1924 Jazz Band 5y 8st 3lb (9)
1925 Obliterate 4y 8st 12lb (10)
1926 Foxlaw 4y 7st 13lb (6)
1927 Border Minstrel 4y 7st 3lb (7)
1928 Primrose League 5y 7st 6lb (14)
1929 Ballynahinch 6y 7st 1lb (13)
1930 Show Girl 4y 8st 4lb (12)
1931 Blue Vision 4y 7st 4lb (8)
1932 Pomarrel 5y 7st 5lb (10)
1933 Leonard 7y 7st 9lb (10)
1934 Whiteplains 4y 7st 1lb (15)
1935 Doreen Jane 5y 7st 8lb (8)
1936 Coup de Roi 4y 7st 13lb (7)
1937 Nectar II 4y 7st 12lb (11)
1938 Union Jack 4y 8st (12)
1939 Oracion 4y 8st (13)
1940–45 No race
1946★Gusty 4y 9st 2lb (5)
1947 Culrain 6y 7st 7lb (9)
1948 Pappatea 5y 9st 5lb (15)
1949 Fol Ami 4y 7st 1lb (13)
1950 Light Cavalry 4y 7st 6lb (8)
1951 Sycomore II 4y 8st 3lb (15)
1952 Souepi 4y 7st 6lb (6)
1953 Nick la Rocca 4y 8st 11lb (14)
1954 Friseur 4y 8st 2lb (20)
1955 Little Cloud 4y 8st 4lb (16)
1956 Jardiniere 4y 8st (12)
1957 Great Rock 4y 7st 8lb (17)
1958 Master of Arts 5y 8st 4lb (21)
1959 Cannebiere 6y 7st 9lb (17)
1960 New Brig 4y 8st 8lb (13)
1961 Utrillo 4y 7st 1lb (20)
1962 Bordone 4y 8st 5lb (13)
1963 Horse Radish 4y 7st 8lb (14)
1964 Peter Piper 4y 7st 9lb (18)
1965 Cagirama 6y 7st 5lb (16)
1966 Sweet Story 4y 8st 4lb (15)
1967 Piaco 4y 9st 1lb (13)
1968 Amateur 4y 7st 9lb (14)
1969 Even Say 4y 7st 11lb (16)
1970 Philoctetes 6y 7st 12lb (16)
1971 Tartar Prince 4y 7st 8lb (18)
1972 Scoria 6y 7st 6lb (13)
1973 Tom Cribb 4y 8st 4lb (11)
1974 Attivo 4y 7st 8lb (11)
1975 Grey God 4y 8st 9lb (12)
1976 Philominsky 5y 8st (11)
1977 Tug of War 4y 8st 7lb (15)
1978 Tug of War 5y 9st 2lb (10)
1979 Totowah 5y 8st 2lb (11)
1980 Mons Beau 5y 7st 7lb (15)
1981 Dawn Johnny (USA) 4y 8st 6lb (18)
1982 No race
1983 Weavers Pin 6y 8st 8lb (14)
1984 Karadar 6y 9st 10lb (19)
1985 Trade Line 4y 7st 10lb (13)
1986 Sneak Preview 6y 8st 12lb (15)
1987 Treasurer Hunter 8y 7st 7lb (20)
1988 Stavordale 5y 9st 2lb (10)
1989 Orpheus (USA) 3y 7st 7lb (12)
1990 Al Maheb (USA) 4y 8st 11lb (12)
1991 Tamarpour (USA) 4y 7st 7lb (14)
1992 Witness Box (USA) 5y 9st 9lb (13)
1993 Highflying 7y 7st 11lb (18)

★Run at Liverpool (2 miles 78 yds)

CORAL-ECLIPSE STAKES (Sandown)

(1 mile 2 fur 7 yds)
(First run 1886)

1900 Diamond Jubilee 3y 9st 4lb (9)
1901 Epsom Lad 4y 9st 13lb (13)
1902 Cheers 3y 8st 8lb (12)
1903 Ard Patrick 4y 10st 2lb (5)
1904 Darley Dale 3y 9st 1lb (7)
1905 Val d'Or 3y 9st 1lb (6)
1906 Llangibby 4y 9st 13lb (9)
1907 Lally 4y 9st 13lb (7)
1908 Your Majesty 3y 8st 13lb (10)
1909 Bayardo 3y 9st 2lb (4)
1910★Lemberg 3y 9st 2lb
★Neil Gow 3y 9st 2lb (6)
1911 Swynford 4y 10st (7)
1912 Prince Palatine 4y 10st (8)
1913 Tracery 4y 10st (7)
1914 Hapsburg 3y 8st 13lb (13)
1915–18 No race
1919 Buchan 3y 8st 6lb (7)
1920 Buchan 4y 9st 10lb (7)
1921 Craig an Eran 3y 8st 12lb (5)
1922 Golden Myth 4y 9st 7lb (12)
1923 Saltash 3y 8st 6lb (9)
1924 Polyphontes 3y 8st 9lb (8)
1925 Polyphontes 4y 9st 10lb (13)
1926 Coronach 3y 8st 12lb (8)
1927 Colorado 4y 9st 10lb (3)
1928 Fairway 3y 8st 9lb (12)
1929 Royal Minstrel 4y 9st 10lb (8)
1930 Rustom Pasha 3y 8st 9lb (11)
1931 Careleon 4y 9st 4lb (11)
1932 Miracle 3y 9st 9lb (13)
1933 Loaningdale 4y 9st 7lb (10)
1934 King Salmon 4y 9st 7lb (10)
1935 Windsor Lad 4y 9st 10lb (5)
1936 Rhodes Scholar 3y 8st 9lb (9)
1937 Boswell 4y 9st 10lb (6)
1938 Pasch 3y 8st 12lb (6)
1939 Blue Peter 3y 8st 12lb (8)
1940–45 No race
1946†Gulf Stream 3y 8st 6lb (5)
1947 Migoli 3y 8st 9lb (5)
1948 Petition 4y 9st 7lb (8)
1949 Djeddah 4y 9st 4lb (7)
1950 Flocon 4y 9st 4lb (6)
1951 Mystery IX 3y 8st 2lb (8)
1952 Tulyar 3y 8st 9lb (7)
1953 Argur 4y 9st (7)
1954 King of the Tudors 4y 9st 7lb (6)
1955 Darius 4y 9st 7lb (7)
1956 Tropique 4y 9st 7lb (8)
1957 Arctic Explorer 3y 8st 9lb (5)
1958 Ballymoss 4y 9st 7lb (7)
1959 Saint Crespin III 3y 8st 9lb (9)
1960 Javelot 4y 9st (9)
1961 St Paddy 4y 9st 7lb (7)
1962 Henry the Seventh 4y 9st (7)
1963 Khalkis 3y 8st 2lb (9)
1964 Ragusa 4y 9st (11)
1965 Canisbay 4y 9st 5lb (8)
1966 Pieces of Eight 3y 8st 7lb (10)
1967 Busted 4y 9st 5lb (9)
1968 Royal Palace 4y 9st 5lb (5)
1969 Wolver Hollow 5y 9st 5lb (7)
1970 Connaught 5y 9st 5lb (3)
1971 Mill Reef (USA) 3y 8st 7lb (6)
1972 Brigadier Gerard 4y 9st 5lb (6)
1973‡Scottish Rifle 4y 9st 5lb (6)
1974 Coup de Feu 5y 9st 5lb (12)
1975 Star Appeal 5y 9st 7lb (16)
1976 Wollow 3y 8st 8lb (9)
1977 Artaius (USA) 3y 8st 8lb (10)
1978 Gunner B 5y 9st 7lb (7)
1979 Dickens Hill 3y 8st 8lb (7)
1980 Ela-Mana-Mou 4y 9st 7lb (6)
1981 Master Willie 4y 9st 7lb (8)
1982 Kalaglow 4y 9st 7lb (9)
1983 Solford (USA) 3y 8st 8lb (9)
1984 Sadler's Wells (USA) 3y 8st 8lb (9)
1985 Pebbles 4y 9st 4lb (4)
1986 Dancing Brave (USA) 3y 8st 8lb (8)
1987 Mtoto 4y 9st 7lb (8)
1988 Mtoto 5y 9st 7lb (8)
1989 Nashwan (USA) 3y 8st 8lb (6)

1990 Elmaamul (USA) 3y 8st 10lb (7)
1991 Environment Friend 3y 8st 10lb (7)
1992 Kooyonga 4y 9st 4lb (12)
1993 Opera House 5y 9st 7lb (8)

*Dead-heat †Run at Ascot
‡Run at Kempton Park

LANCASHIRE OAKS (Haydock)

(1 mile 3 fur 200 yds)
For fillies three year olds and upwards

1939 Cestria 8st 5lb (8)
1940–46 No race
1947 Smoke Screen 8st 7lb (7)
1948 Young Entry 8st 7lb (6)
1949 Eyewash 8st 7lb (7)
1950 Dutch Clover 8st 11lb (9)
1951 Dollarina 8st 4lb (5)
1952 Stream of Light 8st 7lb (4)
1953 Harvest Festival 8st 4lb (8)
1954 Blue Prelude 8st 7lb (5)
1955 Jenny Lind 8st 7lb (8)
1956 Hustle 8st 4lb (10)
1957 Lobelia 8st 4lb (8)
1958 St Lucia 8st 4lb (7)
1959 Noble Lassie 8st 4lb (5)
1960 Chota Hazri 8st 13lb (8)
1961 Irristable 8st 7lb (9)
1962 French Cream 8st 4lb (7)
1963 Red Chorus 8st 5lb (6)
1964 No race
1965 Without Reproach 8st 12lb (6)
1966 Royal Flirt 8st 12lb (7)
1967 The Nun 8st 12lb (6)
1968 Bringley 8st 12lb (8)
1969 Gambola 8st 12lb (2)
1970 Amphora (Fr) 8st 12lb (6)
1971 Maina 8st 12lb (6)
1972 Star Ship 9st (7)
1973 Istiea 8st 6lb (4)
1974 Mil's Bomb 8st 6lb (8)
1975 One Over Part 8st 11lb (5)
1976 Centrocon 8st 11lb (9)
1977 Busaca (Fr) 8st 11lb (5)
1978 Princess Eboli 9st 1lb (9)
1979 Reprocolor 9st 1lb (5)
1980 Vielle 8st 11lb (6)
1981 Rhein Bridge 8st 11lb (7)
1982 Sing Softly 8st 11lb (8)
1983 Give Thanks 9st 1lb (13)
1984 Sandy Island 8st 11lb (9)
1985 Graecia Magna (USA) 8st 11lb (8)
1986 Park Express 8st 11lb (9)
1987 Three Tails 9st 1lb (6)
1988 Andaleeb (USA) 8st 9lb (8)
1989 Roseate Tern 8st 9lb (8)
1990 Pharian (USA) 8st 9lb (4)
1991 Patricia (USA) 3y 8st 4lb (11)
1992 Niodini (USA) 3y 8st 4lb (11)
1993 Rainbow Lake 3y 8st 4lb (8)

Run at Manchester over 1 mile 3 fur from 1939 to 1963

Run as the Lancashire Oaks until 1986 and the Harp Lager Lancashire Oaks in 1987

Until 1990 was for three-year-old fillies only

SBJ GROUP JULY STAKES (Newmarket)

(6 fur)
For two year olds
(First run 1786)

1900*Doricles
1901*Veles (7)
1902 Sceptre (7)
1903 Hammerkop (9)
1904 Montem (8)
1905 Cicero (5)
1906 Gorgos (7)
1907 Traquair (3)
1908 Pearl of the Loch (3)
1909 Battleaxe (5)
1910 Prince Rupert (12)
1911 St Anton (7)
1912 White Star (11)
1913 Rock Flint (10)
1914 Ambassador (11)
1915 Roseland (4)
1916 Figaro (12)
1917 Grand Fleet (6)
1918 No race
1919 Buchan (3)
1920 Sarchedon (4)
1921 Monarch (6)
1922 Lembach (5)
1923 Legality (7)
1924 Diophon (12)
1925 Runnymede (11)
1926 Apple Sammy (6)
1927 The Satrap (7)
1928 Fairway (9)
1929 Mr Jinks (5)
1930 Teacup (4)
1931 Four Course (6)
1932 Riot (6)
1933 Colorow (6)
1934 Alishah (3)
1935 Hilla (2)
1936 Daytona (6)
1937 Foray (7)
1938 Mirza II (4)
1939 Prometheus (4)
1940 Rose of England c (5)
1941 No race
1942 Ujiji (5)
1943–44 No race
1945†Rivaz (3)
1946†Miss Stripes (7)
1947 Masaka (9)
1948 Nimbus (7)
1949 Diableretta (2)
1950 Big Dipper (4)
1951 Bob Major (6)
1952 Empire Honey (5)
1953 Darius (3)
1954 Tamerlane (9)
1955 Edmundo (8)
1956 Earl Marshal *5)
1957 Abelia (4)
1958 Greek Sovereign (4)
1959 Sound Track (2)
1960 Favorita (6)
1961 Burning Thoughts (6)
1962 Romantic (5)
1963 Endless Honey (5)
1964 Ragtime (10)
1965 Sky Gipsy (5)
1966 Golden Horus (3)
1967 Lorenzaccio (5)
1968 Burglar (6)
1969 Huntercombe (3)
1970 Swing Easy (USA) (4)
1971 Deep Diver (8)
1972 Perdu (3)
1973 Dragonara Palace (USA) (4)
1974 Auction Ring (USA) (9)
1975 Super Cavalier (6)
1976 Sky Ship (6)
1977 Royal Harmony (4)
1978 Main Reef (6)
1979 Final Straw (7)
1980 Age Quod Agis (USA) (3)
1981 End of The Line (11)
1982 Horage (7)
1983 Superlative (6)
1984 Primo Dominie (7)
1985 Green Desert (USA) (8)
1986 Mansooj (8)
1987 Sanquirico (7)
1988 Always Valiant (4)
1989 Rock City (4)
1990 Mujtahid (USA) (4)
1991 Showbrook (4)
1992 Wharf (USA) (6)
1993 First Trump (6)

*Dead-heat
†Chesterfield Course (5 fur)
Run over 5 fur. 140yds. until 1960

PRINCESS OF WALES'S STAKES (Newmarket)

(1$^{1}/_{2}$ miles)
(First run 1894)

1900 Merry Gal 3y 7st 13lb (8)
1901 Epsom Lad 4y 9st 2lb (12)
1902 Veles 4y 9st 2lb (6)
1903 Ard Patrick 4y 9st 8lb (9)
1904 Rock Sand 4y 9st 2lb (5)
1905 St Denis 4y 8st 3lb (9)
1906 Dinneford 4y 8st 4lb (6)
1907 Polymelus 5y 9st 7lb (9)
1908 Queen's Advocate 4y 8st 10lb (9)
1909 Dark Ronald 4y 9st 1lb (10)
1910 Ulster King 3y 8st 5lb (9)
1911 Swynford 4y 10st 1lb (5)
1912 Lance Chest 3y 8st 8lb (10)
1913 Lance Chest 4y 9st 12lb (11)
1914 The Curragh 4y 9st 9lb (6)
1915 Rossendale 3y 8st 11lb (6)
1916 Nassovian 3y 7st 10lb (6)
1917 No race
1918 Blink 3y 8st (3)
1919 Buchan 3y 8st 5lb (4)
1920 Attilius 3y 7st 7lb (11)
1921 Orpheus 4y 9st 3lb (7)
1922 Blandford 3y 8st (9)
1923 Triumph 4y 9st 3lb (7)
1924 Salmon-Trout 3y 8st 7lb (6)
1925 Solario 3y 8st 8lb (7)
1926 Tournesol 4y 9st 3lb (7)
1927 Colorado 4y 9st 12lb (5)
1928 Tourist 3y 7st 7lb (11)
1929 Fairway 4y 9st 12lb (4)
1930 Press Gang 3y 8st 5lb (4)
1931*The Recorder 4y 9st 3lb
*Shell Transport 3y 8st 5lb (7)
1932 Jacopo 4y 9st 3lb (8)
1933 Raymond 3y 7st 8lb (11)
1934 Bright Bird 3y 7st 7lb (7)
1935 Fiarbairn 3y 7st 8lb (9)
1936 Taj Akbar 3y 8st 8lb (6)
1937 Flares 4y 9st 6lb (6)
1938 Pound Foolish 3y 8st 5lb (9)
1939 Heliopolis 3y 8st 8lb (8)
1940–44 No race
1945 Stirling Castle 3y 8st (7)

1946 Airborne 3y 8st 10lb (4)
1947 Nirgal 4y 9st 6lb (9)
1948 Alycidon 3y 8st 5lb (5)
1949 Dogger Bank 3y 7st 10lb (6)
1950 Double Eclipse 3y 8st 8lb (6)
1951 Pardal 4y 8st 12lb (5)
1952 Zucchero 4y 9st 6lb (7)
1953 Rawson 4y 9st 6lb (4)
1954 Woodcut 3y 7st 10lb (5)
1955 Cobetto 3y 7st 13lb (8)
1956 Cash and Courage 3y 8st (8)
1957 Wake Up! 3y 7st 11lb (7)
1958 Miner's Lamp 3y 8st 12lb (7)
1959 Primera 5y 9st 6lb (4)
1960 Primera 6y 9st (6)
1961 Apostle 4y 9st 5lb (6)
1962 Silver Cloud 3y 8st 2lb (4)
1963 Trafalgar 3y 8st 2lb (6)
1964 Carrack 3y 7st 7lb (8)
1965 Lommond 5y 9st 2lb (7)
1966 Lomond 6y 9st 5lb (5)
1967 Hopeful Venture 3y 8st 2lb (7)
1968 Mount Athos 3y 8st 2lb (10)
1969 Harmony Hall 3y 7st 11lb (2)
1970 Prince Consort 4y 9st 2lb (6)
1971 Lupe 4y 9st 6lb (4)
1972 Falkland 4y 9st 5lb (8)
1973 Our Mirage 4y 9st 9lb (7)
1974 Buoy 4y 9st 9lb (9)
1975 Libra's Rib (USA) 3y 7st 11lb (10)
1976 Smuggler 3y 7st 11lb (6)
1977 Lord Helpus 4y 9st 2lb (8)
1978 Pollerton 4y 9st 2lb (4)
1979 Milford 3y 8st 2lb (6)
1980 Nicholas Bill 5y 9st 2lb (9)
1981 Light Cavalry 4y 9st 9lb (8)
1982 Height of Fashion (Fr) 3y 7st 11lb (4)
1983 Quilted 3y 8st (11)
1984 Head for Heights 3y 8st 6lb (9)
1985 Petoski 3y 8st (5)
1986 Shardari 4y 9st (6)
1987 Celestial Storm (USA) 4y 9st (9)
1988 Unfuwain (USA) 3y 8st (5)
1989 Carroll House 4y 9st 5lb (5)
1990 Sapience 4y 9st (7)
1991 Rock Hopper 4y 9st 3lb (6)
1992 Saddlers' Hall 4y 9st 5lb (4)
1993 Desert Team (USA) 3y 8st 1lb (7)

⋆Dead-heat

JULY CUP
(Newmarket)

(6 fur)
(First run 1876)

1900 Running Stream 2y 6st (5)
1901 Lord Bobs 3y 9st 5lb (5)
1902 Sundridge 4y 10st 2lb (6)
1903 Sundridge 5y 10st 2lb (2)
1904 Sundridge 6y 10st 2lb (3)
1905 Delaunay 4y 10st 2lb (2)
1906 Thrush 4y 10st 2lb (2)
1907 Dinneford 5y 10st 2lb (5)
1908 Lesbia 3y 9st 2lb (6)
1909 Jack Snipe 4y 10st 2lb (8)
1910 Amore 3y 8st 4lb (3)
1911 Sunder 4y 10st 2lb (3)
1912 Spanish Prince 5y 10st 2lb (4)
1913 Spanish Prince 6y 10st 2lb (3)
1914 Golden Sun 4y 9st 7lb (5)
1915 Volta 3y 9st 5lb (4)
1916 Torloisk 4y 9st 4lb (4)
1917 No race
1918 Irish Elegance 3y 9st 11lb (7)
1919 Diadem 5y 9st 13lb (2)
1920 Diadem 6y 9st 13lb (w.o.)
1921 Tetratema 4y 10st 3lb (3)
1922 Pharmacie 4y 9st 8lb (4)
1923 Golden Corn 4y 9st 2lb (2)
1924 Drake 4y 9st 11lb (5)
1925 Diomedes 3y 9st 5lb (w.o.)
1926⋆Diomedes 4y 10st 3lb
⋆Phalaros 4y 10st 3lb (3)
1927 Highborn II 4y 10st 3lb (4)
1928 Golden Oracle 3y 8st 10lb (4)
1929 Tiffin 3y 9st 2lb (3)
1930 Sir Cosmo 4y 10st 1lb (10)
1931 Xandover 4y 10st 8lb (4)
1932 Concerto 4y 10st 1lb (6)
1933 Myrobella 3y 9st 7lb (4)
1934 Coroado 4y 10st 1lb (7)
1935 Bellacose 3y 9st 10lb (11)
1936 Bellacose 4y 10st 8lb (6)
1937 Mickey the Greek 3y 8st 10lb (6)
1938 Shalfleet 7y 8st 5lb (5)
1939 Portobello 3y 8st 7lb (10
1940 No race
1941 Comatas 4y 8st 8lb (8)
1942–44 No race
1945 Honeyway 4y 9st 6lb (4)
1946 The Bug 3y 8st 4lb (3)
1947 Falls of Clyde 3y 8st 3lb (5)
1948 Palm Vista 3y 7st 10lb (9)
1949 Abernant 3y 8st 10lb (3)
1950 Abernant 4y 9st 8lb (6)
1951 Hard Sauce 3y 8st 10lb (6)
1952 Set Fair 3y 8st 2lb (4)
1953 Devon Vintage 3y 8st 7lb (5)
1954 Vilmoray 4y 8st 8lb (4)
1955 Pappa Fourway 3y 8st 10lb (3)
1956 Matador 3y 8st 10lb (5)
1957 Vigo 4y 9st 8lb (4)
1958 Right Boy 4y 9st 8lb (4)
1959 Right Boy 5y 9st 8lb (6)
1960 Tin Whistle 3y 8st 10lb (w.o.)
1961 Galivanter 5y 9st 8lb (3)
1962 Marsolve 4y 9st 1lb (4)
1963 Secret Step 4y 8st 11lb (8)
1964 Daylight Robbery 3y 8st 2lb (7)
1965 Merry Madcap 3y 7st 13lb (4)
1966 Lucasland 4y 8st 11lb 918)
1967 Forlorn River 5y 9st (9)
1968 So Blessed 3y 8st 2lb (7)
1969 Tudor Music 3y 8st 6lb (3)
1970 Huntercombe 3y 8st 6lb (4)
1971 Realm 4y 9st 3lb (8)
1972 Parsimony 3y 8st 7lb (5)
1973 Thatch (USA) 3y 8st 10lb (6)
1974 Saritamer (USA) 3y 8st 10lb (9)
1975 Lianga (USA) 4y 9st 3lb (13)
1976 Lochnager 4y 9st 6lb (10)
1977 Gentilhombre 4y 9st 6lb (8)
1978 Solinus 3y 9st 11lb (14)
1979 Thatching 4y 8st 6lb (11)
1980 Moorestyle 3y 8st 11lb (14)
1981 Marwell 3y 8st 8lb (14)
1982 Sharpo 5y 9st 6lb (16)
1983 Habibti 3y 8st 8lb (15)
1984 Chief Singer 3y 8st 11lb (9)
1985 Never So Bold 5y 9st 6lb (9)
1986 Green Desert (USA) 3y 8st 11lb (5)
1987 Ajdal (USA) 3y 8st 11lb (11)
1988 Soviet Star (USA) 4y 9st 6lb (9)
1989 Cadeaux Genereux 4y 9st 6lb (11)
1990 Royal Academy (USA) 3y 8st 13lb (9)
1991 Polish Patriot (USA) 3y 8st 13lb (8)
1992 Mr Brooks 5y 9st 6lb (8)
1993 Hamas 4y 9st 6lb (12)

⋆Dead-heat

KING GEORGE VI and QUEEN ELIZABETH DIAMOND STAKES (Ascot—1½ miles)

Year	Winner	Starters	Time	Jockeys
1951	Mrs T Lilley's br c (3y) Supreme Court, by Persian Gulf or Precipitation	19 ...	2 29$\frac{2}{3}$ ...	E C Elliott
1952	H.H. Aga Khan's br c (3y) Tulyar by Tehran	15 ...	2 33$\frac{1}{5}$ ...	C Smirke
1953	Sir Victor Sassoon' b c (3y)Pinza by Chanteur II	13 ...	2 33$\frac{3}{5}$ ...	G Richards
1954	Her Majesty's ch c (4y) Aureole by Hyperion	17 ...	2 44 ...	E Smith
1955	M. Pierre Wertheimer's b c (3y) Vimy by Wild Risk	10 ...	2 33$\frac{3}{5}$ ...	R Poincelet
1956	Marchese Incisa della Rochhetta's ch c (4y) Ribot by Tenerani	9 ...	2 40·24 ...	E Camici
1957	Mr R. B. Strassburger's b c (4y) Montaval by Norseman	12 ...	2 41·02 ...	F Palmer
1958	Mr J. McShain's ch c (4y) Ballymoss by Mossborough	8 ...	2 36·33 ...	A Breasley
1959	Sir H. de Trafford's b c (4y) Alcide by Alycidon	11 ...	2 31·39 ...	W H Carr
1960	Sir H. Wernher's b h (5y) Aggressor by Combat	8 ...	2 35·21 ...	J Lindley
1961	Mme J. Couturie's br c (3y) Right Royal V by Owen Tudor	11 ...	2 32·02 ...	Y Saint-Martin
1962	M. F. Dupre's br c (4y) Match III by Tantieme	11 ...	2 32·02 ...	Y Saint-Martin
1963	Mr J. R. Mullion's b c (3y) Ragusa by Ribor	10 ...	2 33·80 ...	G Bougoure
1964	Mrs H. E. Jackson's b c (4y) Nasram II by Nasrullah	4 ...	2 33·15 ...	W Pyers
1965	Mr G. M. Bell's ch c (3y) Meadow Court by Court Harwell	12 ...	2 33·27 ...	L Piggott
1966	Lt-Col J. Hornung's ch f (4y) Aunt Edith by Primera	5 ...	2 35·06 ...	L Piggott
1967	Mr S. Joel's b c (4y) Busted by Crepello	9 ...	2 33·64 ...	G Moore
1968	Mr H. J. Joel's b c (4y) Royal Palace by Ballymoss	7 ...	2 32·22 ...	A Barclay
1969	Duke of Devonshire's b m (5y) Park Top by Kalydon	9 ...	2 32·46 ...	L Piggott
1970	Mr C. W. Engelhard's b c (3y) Nijinsky (CAN) by Northern Dancer	6 ...	2 36·16 ...	L Piggott
1971	Mr P. Mellon's b c (3y) Mill Reef (USA) by Never Bend	10 ...	2 32·56 ...	G Lewis
1972	Mrs J. Hislop's b c (4y) Brigadier Gerard by Queen's Hussar	9 ...	2 32·91 ...	J Mercer
1973	Mr N. B. Hunt's ch f (3y) Dahlia (USA) by Vaguely Noble	12 ...	2 30·43 ...	W Pyers
1974	Mr N. B. Hunt's ch f (4y) Dahlia (USA) by Vaguely Noble	10 ...	2 33·03 ...	L Piggott
1975	Dr C. Vittadini's ch c (3y) Grundy by Great Newphew	11 ...	2 26·98 ...	Pat Eddery
1976	Mr D. Wildenstein's b f (3y) Pawneese by Carvin	10 ...	2 29·36 ...	Y Saint-Martin
1977	Mr R. Sangster's ch c (3y) The Minstrel (CAN) by Northern Dancer	11 ...	2 30·48 ...	L Piggott
1978	Mr A. D. McCall's b or br (3y) Ile de Bourbon (USA) by Nijinsky (CAN)	14 ...	2 30·53 ...	J Reid
1979	Sir M. Sobell's b c (3y) Troy by Petingo	7 ...	2 33·75 ...	W Carson
1980	Mr S. Weinstock's b c (4y) Ela-Mana-Mou by Pitcairn	10 ...	2 35·39 ...	W Carson
1981	H.H. Aga Khan's b c (3y) Shergar by Great Nephew	7 ...	2 35·40 ...	W R Swinburn
1982	Mr A Ward's gr c (4y) Kalaglow by Kalamoun	9 ...	2 31·88 ...	G Starkey
1983	Mr R. Barnett's b f (4y) Time Charter by Saritamer (USA)	9 ...	2 30·79 ...	J Mercer
1984	Mr E. B. Moller's b c (4y) Teenoso (USA) by Youth (USA)	13 ...	2 27·95 ...	L Piggott
1985	Lady Beaverbrook's b c (3y) Petoski by Niniski (USA)................	12 ...	2 27·61 ...	W Carson
1986	Mr K. Abdulla's b c (3y) Dancing Brave (USA) by Lyphard (USA) ...	9 ...	2 29·49 ...	Pat Eddery
1987	Mr L. Freedman's b c (3y) Reference Point by Mill Reef (USA)	9 ...	2 34·63 ...	S Cauthen
1988	Sheikh Ahmed Al Maktoum's b h (5y) Mtoto by Busted	10 ...	2 37·33 ...	M Roberts
1989	Hamdam Al Maktoum's ch c (3y) Nashwan (USA) by Blushing Groom (FR)..	7 ...	2 32·27 ...	W Carson
1990	Sheikh Mohammed's b c (3y) Belmez (USA) by El Gran Senor (USA)	11 ...	2 30·76 ...	M Kinane
1991	Mr Fahd Salman's ch c (3y) Generous by Caerleon (USA)...........	9 ...	2 28·99 ...	A Munro
1992	Mrs V. Kraft Payson's b c (3y) St Jovite (USA) by Pleasant Colony (USA)...	8 ...	2 30·85 ...	S Craine
1993	Sheikh Mohammed's b h (5y) Opera House by Sadler's Wells (USA) ..	10 ...	2 33·94 ...	M Roberts

JOHN SMITH'S MAGNET CUP (York)

(1 mile 2 fur 85 yds)

1960 Fougalle 3y 7st (14)
1961 Proud Chieftain 4y 8st 10lb (17)
1962 Nortia 3y 8st 4lb (16)
1963 Raccolto 6y 8st 3lb (19)
1964 Space King 5y 8st 9lb (15)
1965 Dark Court 4y 8st 6lb (12)
1966 David Jack 3y 7st 6lb (14)
1967 Copsale 4y 7st 13lb (11)
1968 Farm Walk 6y 8st 13lb (10)
1969 My Swanee 6y 9st 7lb (6)
1970 Timon 4y 7st 4lb (15)
1971 Prominent 4y 8st 8lb (12)
1972 Prominent 5y 9st 4lb (8)
1973 Peleid 3y 7st 9lb (8)
1974 Take A Reef 3y 8st 12lb (13)
1975 Jolly Good 3y 7st 8lb (15)
1976 Bold Pirate (USA) 4y 9st 3lb (9)
1977 Air Trooper 4y 9st 6lb (8)
1978 Town and Country 4y 8st 13lb (9)
1979 Tesoro Mio 4y 8st 3lb (9)
1980 Fine Sun 3y 7st 8lb (12)
1981 Amyndas 3y 8st 5lb (11)
1982 Buzzard's Bay 4y 9st 8lb (6)
1983 Bedtime 3y 7st 9lb (9)
1984 Straight Man 3y 8st 11lb (9)
1985 Chaumiere 4y 9st 7lb (12)
1986 Chaumiere 5y 9st 5lb (11)
1987 ⋆Brave Dancer 3y 8st 8lb (9)
⋆Wolsey 3y 8st 6lb
1988 Bashful Boy 3y 8st 2lb (16)
1989 Icona (USA) 3y 9st 8lb (10)
1990 Eradicate 5y 9st 4lb (19)
1991 Halkopous 5y 7st 3lb (12)
1992 Mr Confusion 4y 8st 3lb (17)
1993 Baron Ferdinand 3y 8st 9lb (13)

⋆Dead-heat

VODAC STEWARDS' CUP (Goodwood)

(6 fur)
(First run 1840)
1900 Royal Flush 7y 7st 13lb (9)
1901 O'Donovan Rossa 4y 7st (28)
1902 Mauvezin 6y 8st 2lb (23)
1903 Dumbarton Castle 3y 7st 4lb (21)
1904 Melayr 3y 6st 9lb (19)
1905 Xeny 4y 7st 9lb (17)
1906 Rocketter 3y 7st 6lb (13)
1907 Romney 3y 6st 3lb (15)
1908 Elmstead 3y 7st (18)
1909 Mediant 3y 7st 13lb (21)
1910 Golden Rod 4y 8st 1lb (21)
1911 Braxted 3y 7st 5lb (19)
1912 Golden Rod 6y 8st 13lb (21)
1913 Lord Annandale 3y 6st 10lb (20)
1914*Golden Sun 4y 8st 12lb
*Lord Annandale 4y 7st 9lb (23)
1915–16 No race
1917†Trojan 3y 6st 13lb (8)
1918 No race
1919 King Sol 5y 7st (14)
1920 Western Wave 4y 8st 7lb (21)
1921 Service Kit 4y 6st 12lb (20)
1922 Tetratema 5y 7st 7lb (30)
1923 Epinard 3y 8st 6lb (14)
1924 Compiler 4y 7st 9lb (24)
1925 Defiance 46y 7st 8lb (24)
1926 Perhaps So 5y 8st 1lb (29)
1927 Priory Park 5y 9st (24)
1928 Navigator 3y 7st 5lb (16)
1929 Fleeting Memory 4y 8st 1lb (19)
1930 Le Phare 4y 8st 1lb (28)
1931 Poor Lad 4y 7st 11lb (15)
1932 Solenoid 3y 7st 10lb (21)
1933 Pharacre 4y 7st 5lb (26)
1934 Figaro 4y 8st 5lb (22)
1935 Greenore 6y 8st 8lb (17)
1936 Solerina 4y 8st 11lb (20)
1937 Firozepore 3y 8st 3lb (30)
1938 Harmachis 5y 7st 6lb (25)
1939 Knight's Caprice 4y 8st 6lb (23)
1940 No race
1941†Valthema 4y 7st 2lb
1942–45 No race
1946 Commissar 6y 7st 12lb (15)
1947 Closeburn 3y 8st 10lb (19)
1948 Dramatic 3y 7st 7lb (16)
1949 The Bite 4y 7st 7lb (21)
1950 First Consul 4y 8st 13lb (21)
1951 Sugar Bowl 4y 7st 12lb (21)
1952 Smokey Eyes 5y 8st 10lb (18)
1953 Palpitate 4y 7st 13lb (22)
1954 Ashurst Wonder 4y 6st 11lb (28)
1955 King Bruce 4y 8st 11lb (26)
1956 Matador 3y 9st 2lb (24)
1957 Arcandy 4y 8st 9lb (16
1958 Epaulette 7y 9st (20)
1959 Tudor Monarch 4y 7st 13lb (21)
1960 Monet 3y 8st 5lb (18)
1961 Skymaster 3y 8st 12lb (22)
1962 Victorina 3y 8st 9lb (26)
1963 Creole 4y 9st 1lb (25)
1964 Dunme 5y 7st 12lb (20)
1965 Potier 3y 8st 5lb (20)
1966 Patient Constable 3y 7st 7lb (25)
1967 Sky Diver 4y 7st 5lb (31)
1968 Sky Diver 5y 7st 6lb (18)
1969 Royal Smoke 3y 7st 9lb (15)
1970 Jukebox 4y 8st 11lb (24)
1971 Apollo Nine 4y 9st 5lb (26)
1972 Touch Paper 3y 8st 2lb (22)
1973 Alphadamus 3y 7st 11lb (27)
1974 Red Alert 3y 9st 2lb (25)
1975 Import 4y 8st (21)
1976 Jimmy the Singer 3y 7st 8lb (17)
1977 Calibina 5y 8st 5lb (24)
1978 Ahonoora 3y 8st (23)
1979 Standaan (Fr) 3y 7st 10lb (16)
1980 Repetitious 3y 7st 2lb (28)
1981 Crews Hill 5y 9st 9lb (30)
1982 Soba 3y 8st 4lb (30)
1983 Autumn Sunset 3y 8st 2lb (23)
1984 Petong 4y 9st 10lb (26)
1985 Al Trui 5y 8st 1lb (28)
1986 Green Ruby (USA) 5y 8st 12lb (24)
1987 Madraco 4y 7st 2lb (30)
1988 Rotherfield Greys 6y 8st 8lb (28)
1989 Very Adjacent 4y 7st 4lb (22)
1990 Knight Of Mercy 4y 9st (30)
1991 Notley 4y 8st 7lb (29)
1992 Lochsong 4y 8st (30)
1993 King's Signet (USA) 4y 9st 10lb (29)

*Dead-heat
†Run at Newmarket as Stewards H'cap

WILLIAM HILL CUP (formerly Chesterfield Cup) (Goodwood)

($1^1/_4$ miles)
(First run 1840)
1900 Spectrum 4y 6st 11lb (9)
1901 Glenapp 3y 6st 1lb (14)
1902 Ypsilanti 4y 7st 12lb (6)
1903 Lady Help 3y 6st 5lb (10)
1904 Union Jack 4y 8st 13lb (9)
1905 Song Thrush 3y 6st 13lb (9)
1906 Gold Riach 3y 7st 12lb (8)
1907 Velocity 5y 9st 10lb (11)
1908 King's Courtship 4y 6st 13lb (12)
1909 Succour 6y 8st 8lb (12)
1910 Land League 7y 8st 3lb (12)
1911 Dean Swift 10y 8st 3lb (8)
1912 Southannan 8y 8st 6lb (10)
1913 Junior 4y 8st 7lb (9)
1914 Kiltoi 4y 7st 1lb (14)
1915–18 No race
1919 Tangiers 3y 7st 9lb (7)
1920 Alasnam 4y 7st 9lb (4)
1921 illuminator 4y 8st 11lb (10)
1922 Statuary 5y 8st 1lb (13)
1923 Evander 5y 8st 11lb (12)
1924 Frater 3y 8st (9)
1925 Warden of the Marches 3y 8st (14)
1926 Warden of the Marches 4y 9st 8lb (11)
1927 Volta's Pride 4y 8st 4lb (9)
1928 Silver Hussar 4y 7st 10lb (4)
1929 Double Life 3y 7st 5lb (13)
1930 The MacNab 4y 8st 11lb (18)
1931 Lord Bill 4y 8st 1lb (10)
1932 Seraph Boy 3y 7st 1lb (14)
1933 Colorado Kid 4y 9st 6lb (15)
1934 Alcazar 3y 7st 9lb (12)
1935 Irongrey 4y 8st 1lb (10)
1936 William of Valence 4y 8st 8lb (20)
1937 Finalist 5y 9st 7lb (14)
1938 Pylon II 5y 8st 1lb (15)
1939 Bacardi 5y 7st 12lb (11)
1940–45 No race
1946 Signalman 3y 8st 4lb (9)
1947 Avignon 4y 7st 13lb (6)
1948 Royal Tara 5y 8st 13lb (10)
1949 Impeccable 5y 9st 12lb (7)
1950 Krakatao 4y 9st 7lb (10)
1951 Grani 5y 7st 11lb (12)
1952 Sunny Brae 4y 8st 5lb (9)
1953 Hilltop 4y 8st 12lb (16)
1954 Prefect 4y 8st 3lb (15)
1955 Royal Maid 4y 7st 3lb (7)
1956 Athenien II 3y 8st 5lb (15)
1957 Rowland Ward 5y 9st (13)
1958 London Cry 4y 8st 12lb (8)
1959 Aggressor 4y 8st 13lb (8)
1960 Rocky Royale 4y 9st 1lb (15)
1961 Stupor Mundi 4y 8st 9lb (13)
1962 Robson's Choice 6y 8st 4lb (11)
1963 St Gulliver 4y 9st 2lb (15)
1964 Early to Rise 4y 8st 7lb (11)
1965 Tarqogan 5y 9st 1lb (11)
1966 Polymint 6y 6st 9lb (10)
1967 Midnight Marauder 5y 8st 3lb (11)
1968 Scottish Sinbad 4y 8st 13lb (11)
1969 Cheval 4y 9st 10lb (10)
1970 Harken 4y 8st 11lb (10)
1971 Tandy 5y 9st 4lb (9)
1972 King Midas 4y 9st 10lb (5)
1973 Prominent 6y 9st 1lb (50
1974 Hail the Pirates (USA) 4y 10st (9)
1975 Edwards Hill 4y 8st 3lb (7)
1976 Blaskette 5y 8st 6lb (7)
1977 Fluellen 4y 10st (6)
1978 Town and Country 4y 9st 13lb (5)
1979 Philodantes 4y 9st 1lb (5)
1980 Borderline 4y 7st 5lb (9)
1981 Commodore Blake 4y 7st 4lb (14)
1982 Criterion 3y 9st 10lb (7)
1983 Morcon 3y 9st (15)
1984 Mailman 5y 8st 10lb (7)
1985 Iroko 3y 8st 13lb (9)
1986 Mailman 7y 8st 8lb (11)
1987 Loud Appeal 4y 8st 11lb (10)
1988 Apache 3y 8st 6lb (7)
1989 Pelorus 4y 10st (10)
1990 Song of Sixpence (USA) 6y 9st 5lb (7)
1991 Ijtihaad (USA) 4y 9st 5lb (10)
1992 Knock Knock 7y 9st (10)
1993 Rose Alto 5y 8st 13lb (13)

SUSSEX STAKES (Goodwood)

(1 Mile)
(First run 1841)
1900 The Raft 8st 4lb (5)
1901 Energetic 8st 3lb (9)
1902 Royal Lancer 8st 13lb (5)
1903 Stephanas 8st 3lb (5)
1904 Mousqueton 8st 10lb (5)
1905 Thrush 8st 13lb (2)
1906 Troubeck 9st 1lb (3)
1907 Wool Winder 9st 1lb (6)

1908 White Eagle 9st 3lb (5)
1909 Minoru 9st 8lb (3)
1910 Winkipop 9st 1lb (5)
1911 Stedfast 9st 1lb (3)
1912 Tracery 9st 1lb (5)
1913 Sun Yat 8st 13lb (5)
1914 Black Jester 9st 1lb (5)
1915–18 No race
1919 Glanmerin 8st 13lb (4)
1920 Braishfield 8st 5lb (6)
1921 Sunblaze 8st 10lb (5)
1922 Diligence 8st 5lb (3)
1923 Hurry Off 9st 1lb (4)
1924 Burslem 8st 5lb (4)
1925 The Monk 8st 7lb (8)
1926 Plimsol 8st 5lb (6)
1927 Rosalia 8st 7lb (7)
1928 Marconigram 8st 13lb (6)
1929 Le Phare 9st 3lb (6)
1930 Paradine 9st 1lb (7)
1931 Inglesant 8st 5lb (6)
1932 Dastur 9st 3lb (2)
1933 The Abbott 8st 13lb (7)
1934 Badruddin 9st 3lb (3)
1935 Harian 8st 12lb (7)
1936 Corpach 8st 2lb (5)
1937 Pascal 9st 3lb (6)
1938 Faroe 9st 1lb (6)
1939 Olein 9st 5lb (7)
1940–45 No race
1946 Radiotherapy 9st 3lb (6)
1947 Combat 9st 3lb (2)
1948 My Babu 9st 8lb (2)
1949 Krakatao 9st 1lb (2)
1950 Palestine 9st 8lb (4)
1951 Le Sage 9st 3lb (7)
1952 Agitator 9st 1lb (5)
1953 King of the Tudors 8st 10lb (4)
1954 Landau 9st 1lb (4)
1955 My Kingdom 8st 9lb (5)
1956 Lucero 9st 1lb (6)
1957 Quorum 9st 1lb (4)
1958 Major Portion 9st 7lb (5)
1959 Petite Etoile 9st 4lb (6)
1960 Venture VII 3y 8st 4lb (6)
1961 Le Levanstelle 4y 8st 10lb (11)
1962 Romulus 3y 8st 4lb (8)
1963 Queen's Hussar 3y 8st 3lb (10)
1964 Roan Rocket 3y 8st 5lb (8)
1965 Carlemont 3y 8st 3lb (11)
1966 Paveh 3y 8st 3lb (7)
1967 Reform 3y 8st 3lb (10)
1968 Petingo 3y 8st 4lb (6)
1969 Jimmy Reppin 4y 9st 4lb (5)
1970 Humble Duty 3y 8st 4lb (5)
1971 Brigadier Gerard 3y 8st 7lb (5)
1972 Sallust 3y 8st 10lb (3)
1973 Thatch (USA) 3y 8st 10lb (7)
1974 Ace of Aces (USA) 4y 9st 7lb (10)
1975 Bolkonski 3y 8st 10lb (9)
1976 Wollow 3y 8st 10lb (9)
1977 Artaius (USA) 3y 8st 10lb (11)
1978 Jaazeiro (USA) 3y 8st 10lb (6)
1979 Kris 3y 8st 10lb (7)
1980 Posse (USA) 3y 8st 10lb (9)
1981 Kings Lake (USA) 3y 8st 10lb (9)
1982 On The House (Fr) 3y 8st 7lb (13)
1983 Noalcoholic (Fr) 6y 9st 7lb (11)
1984 Chief Singer 3y 8st 10lb (5)
1985 Rousillon 4y 9st 7lb (10)
1986 Sonic Lady (USA) 3y 8st 7lb (5)
1987 Soviet Star (USA) 3y 8st 10lb (7)
1988 Warning 3y 8st 10lb (9)
1989 Zilzal (USA) 3y 8st 10lb (8)
1990 Distant Relative 4y 9st 7lb (7)
1991 Second Set 3y 8st 13lb (8)
1992 Marling 3y 8st 10lb (8)
1993 Bigstone 3y 8st 13lb (10)

From 1900 to 1959 the race was for three year olds only and from 1960 to 1974 for three and four year olds only

RICHMOND STAKES (Goodwood)

(6 fur)
For two year olds
(First run 1877)

1900 Handiapper (5)
1901 Duke of Westminster (6)
1902 Mead (7)
1903 Queen's Holiday (6)
1904 Polymelus (7)
1905 Lally (4)
1906 Weathercock (8)
1907 Bolted (9)
1908 Bayardo (4)
1909 Charles O'Malley (5)
1910 Pietri (9)
1911 Sweeper II (6)
1912 Seremond (9)
1913 Black Jester (7)
1914 Pommern (10)
1915–18 No race
1919 Golden Guinea (4)
1920 Sunblaze (4)
1921 Fodder (5)
1922 Bombay Duck (2)
1923 Halcyon (5)
1924 Manna (9)
1925 Pantera (6)
1926 The Satrap (4)
1927 Gang Warily (13)
1928 Rattlin The Reefer (7)
1929 Challenger (9)
1930 Four Course (11)
1931 Spenser (7)
1932 Solar Boy (7)
1933 Colombo (8)
1934 Bobsleigh (11)
1935 Mahmoud (11)
1936 Perifox (12)
1937 Unbreakable (8)
1938 Chancery (13)
1939 Moradabad (8)
1940–45 No race
1946 Petition (4)
1947 Birthday Greetings (10)
1948 Star King (10)
1949 Palestine (3)
1950 Grey Sovereign (7)
1951 Gay Time (4)
1952 Artane (5)
1953 The Pie King (6)
1954 Eubulides (7)
1955 Ratification (4)
1956 Red Gold (5)
1957 Promulgation (7)
1958 Hieroglyph (7)
1959 Dollar Piece (4)
1960 Typhoon (5)
1961 Sovereign Lord (7)
1962 Romantic (5)
1963 Gentle Art (5)
1964 Ragtime (3)
1965 Sky Gipsy (3)
1966 Hambleden (7)
1967 Berber (3)
1968 Tudor Music (3)
1969 Village Boy (5)
1970 Swing Easy (USA) (5)
1971 Sallust (10)
1972 Master Sing (7)
1973 Dragonara Palace (USA) (7)
1974 Legal Eagle (6)
1975 Stand to Reason (9)
1976 J O Tobin (USA) (5)
1977 Persian Bold (5)
1978 Young Generation (5)
1979 Castle Green (USA) (5)
1980 Another Realm (10)
1981 Tender King (7)
1982 Gallant Special (USA) (7)
1983 Godstone (9)
1984 Primo Dominie (6)
1985 Nomination (10)
1986 Rich Charlie (8)
1987 Warning (7)
1988 Heart of Arabia (6)
1989 Contract Law (USA) (5)
1990 Mac's Imp (USA) (7)
1991 Dilum (USA) (4)
1992 Son Pardo (6)
1993 First Trump (5)

TIFFANY GOODWOOD CUP

(2 miles)
(First run 1812)

1900 Mazagan 4y 9st 3lb (8)
1901 Fortunatus 3y 8st (5)
1902 Perseus 3y 7st 1lb (6)
1903 Rabelais 3y 7st 2lb (8)
1904 Saltpetre 4y 7st 10lb (5)
1905 Red Robe 4y 7st 10lb (5)
1906 Plum Tree 3y 7st 12lb (8)
1907 The White Knight 4y 9st 10lb (6)
1908 Radium 5y 9st 2lb (6)
1909 Carrousel 3y 7st 8lb (5)
1910 Magic 3y 7st 2lb (3)
1911 Kilbroney 4y 9st 3lb (5)
1912 Tullibardine 4y 8st 12lb (3)
1913 Catmint 4y 9st 3lb (6)
1914 Son-in-Law 3y 7st 8lb (5)
1915–18 No race
1919 Queen's Square 4y 9st (5)
1920 Mount Royal 3y 7st 7lb (4)
1921 Bucks 3y 7st 8lb (5)
1922 Flamboyant 4y 9st 3lb (5)
1923 Triumph 4y 9st 3lb (3)
1924 Teresina 4y 9st (6)
1925 Cloudbank 4y 9st 3lb (6)
1926 Glommen 4y 9st 3lb (9)
1927 Dark Japan 4y 9st 3lb (3)
1928 Kinchinjunga 4y 9st 3lb (7)
1929 Old Orkney 5y 9st 7lb (6)
1930 Brown Jack 6y 9st 7lb (5)
1931 Salmon Leap 4y 9st 3lb (6)
1932 Brulette 4y 9st 4lb (5)
1933 Sans Peine 3y 7st 11lb (5)
1934 Loosestrife 5y 9st 6lb (4)
1935 Tiberius 4y 9st 7lb (3)
1936 Cecil 5y 9st 6lb (9)
1937 Fearless Fox 4y 9st 2lb (6)
1938 Epigram 5y 9st 6lb (11)
1939 Duvbonnet 4y 8st 1lb (5)
1940–45 No race
1946 Marsyas II 6y 9st 11lb (4)
1947 Monsieur l'Amiral 6y 9st 2lb (4)
1948 Tenerani 4y 8st 12lb (4)
1949 Alycidon 4y 8st 12lb (5)

1950 Val Drake 4y 8st 12lb (4)
1951 Pan II 4y 8st 12lb (4)
1952 Medway 4y 8st 12lb (4)
1953 Souepi 6y 9st (8)
1954 Blarney Stone 5y 9st (5)
1955 Double Bore 4y 9st (8)
1956 Zarathustra 5y 9st (4)
1957 Tenterhooks 3y 7st 10lb (7)
1958 Gladness 5y 8st 11lb (4)
1959 Dickens 3y 7st 10lb (4)
1960 Exar 4y 9st (4)
1961 Predominate 9y 9st (4)
1962 Sagacity 4y 9st (4)
1963 Trelawny 7y 9st (4)
1964 Raise You Ten 4y 9st (5)
1965 Apprentice 5y 9st (5)
1966 Gaulois 3y 7st 10lb (7)
1967 Wrekin Rambler 4y 9st (5)
1968 Ovaltine 4y 9st (7)
1969 Richmond Fair 5y 9st (3)
1970 Parthenon 4y 9st (5)
1971 Rock Roi 4y 9st (5)
1972 Erimo Hawk 4y 9st (4)
1973 Proverb 3y 7st 10lb (4)
1974 Proverb 4y 9st (4)
1975 Girandole 4y 9st (8)
1976 Mr Bigmore 4y 9st (6)
1977 Grey Baron 4y 9st 3lb (8)
1978 Tug of War 5y 9st (5)
1979 Le Moss 4y 9st 7lb (5)
1980 Le Moss 5y 9st 7lb (5)
1981 Ardross 5y 9st 7lb (6)
1982 Heighlin 6y 9st (8)
1983 Little Wolf 5y 9st 7lb (7)
1984 Gildoran 4y 9st 7lb (4)
1985 Valuable Witness (USA) 5y 9st (7)
1986 Longboat 5y 9st 7lb (5)
1987 Sergeyevich 3y 7st 10lb (5)
1988 Sadeem (USA) 5y 9st 7lb (6)
1989 Mazzacano 4y 9st (5)
1990 Lucky Moon 3y 7st 10lb (6)
1991 Further Flight 5y 9st (10)
1992 Further Flight 6y 9st 5lb (11)
1993 Sonus 4y 9st 3lb (9)

Run over 2 miles 5 fur until 1989 and 2½ miles in 1990.
Distance reduced to 2 miles from 1991.

SCHWEPPES GOLDEN MILE HANDICAP (Goodwood)

(1 mile)
(First run 1987)

1987 Waajib 4y 9st 10lb (20)
1988 Strike Force 3y 8st 6lb (21)
1989 Safawan 3y 8st (14)
1990 March Bird 5y 7st 8lb (16)
1991 Sky Cloud 5y 8st 7lb (15)
1992 Little Bean 3y 8st 2lb (21)
1993 Philidor 4y 8st 4lb (19)

GORDON STAKES (Goodwood)

(1½ miles)
For three year olds
In 1902 the race was for three year olds and upwards

1902 Osbech 7y 9st 4lb (3)
1903 Zindanfel 8st 10lb (3)
1904 Delaunay 9st 7lb (3)
1905 Dinneford 8st 7lb (6)
1906 Victorious 9st 4lb (3)
1907 Galvani 9st 7lb (7)
1908 Putchamin 8st 7lb (7)
1909 Moscato 9st 7lb (5)
1910 Cardinal Beaufort 9st (5)
1911 Prince Palatine 9st 7lb (4)
1912 Fantasio 8st 7lb (4)
1913 Augur 8st 4lb (8)
1914 My Prince 9st 7lb (6)
1915–18 No race
1919 Sir Douglas 10st (2)
1920 The Alder 8st (2)
1921 Stanislaus 8st (4)
1922 Tamar 9st (3)
1923 Bold and Bad 9st 1lb (3)
1924 Black Sheep 8st (3)
1925 Kentish Knock 9st 10lb (4)
1926 Thistledown 8st 3lb (4) after a dead-heat with Pantera)
1927 Tiger Hill 8st 3lb (6)
1928 Cyclonic 9st 10lb (10)
1929 Defoe 8st 3lb (7)
1930★Press Gang 9st 10lb
★Ut Majeur 9st (4)
1931 Rose en Soleil 9st 4lb (6)
1932 Firdaussi 9st 3lb (5)
1933 Tavern 8st (4)
1934 Bright Bird 9st 10lb (4)
1935 Bideford Bay 8st 11lb (5)
1936 Magnet 9st (9)
1937 Perifox 9st 4lb (5)
1938 Valedictory 8st 3lb (7)
1939 Wheatland 9st 4lb (4)
1940–45 No race
1946 Fast and Fair 9st 2lb (5)
1947 Merry Quip 9st 2lb (4)
1948 Nathoo 9st 7lb (6)
1949 Royal Forest 9st 2lb (3)
1950 Foxboro 8st 7lb (8)
1951 Prince d'Ouilly 8st 7lb (3)
1952 Gay Time 8st 7lb (3)
1953 Prince Canarina 8st 7lb (4)
1954 Brilliant Green 7st 13lb (9)
1955 Manati 8st 7lb (7)
1956 Dacian 8st 7lb (6)
1957 Pipe of Peace 8st 12lb (6)
1958 Guersillus 8st 12lb (5)
1959 Above Suspicion 8st 12lb (4)
1960 Kipling 8st 12lb (8)
1961 Pardao 8st 12lb (9)
1962 Gay Challenger 8st 7lb (9)
1963 Tiger 8st 12lb (9)
1964 Sweet Moss 8st 12lb (7)
1965 King Log 8st 2lb (6)
1966 Khalekan 8st 2lb (6)
1967 Sun Rock 8st 12lb (7)
1968 Mount Athos 8st 12lb (3)
1969 Harmony Hall 8st 12lb (3)
1970 Rock Roi 8st 7lb (4)
1971 Athens Wood 8st 7lb (5)
1972 Scottish Rifle 8st 10lb (3)
1973 Duke of Ragusa 8st 10lb (4)
1974 Grey Thunder 8st 10lb (8)
1975 Guillaume Tell 8st 10lb (9)
1976 Smuggler 8st 10lb (4)
1977 Pollerton 8st 10lb (4)
1978 Sexton Blake 8st 10lb (5)
1979 More Light 8st 10lb (6)
1980 Prince Bee 8st 10lb (6)
1981 Bustomi 9st 2lb (5)
1982 Electric 8st 13lb (6)
1983 John French 8st 10lb (6)
1984 Commanche Run 8st 10lb (8)
1985 Kazaroun (USA) 8st 10lb (5)
1986 Allez Milord (USA) 9st 2lb (6)
1987 Love The Groom (USA) 9st 2lb (6)
1988 Minster Son 8st 10lb (5)
1989 Warrshan (USA) 8st 10lb (4)
1990 Karinga Bay 8st 10lb (6)
1991 Stylish Senor (USA) 8st 10lb (3)
1992 Bonny Scot 8st 10lb (6)
1993 Right Win 8st 10lb (8)

★Dead-heat

VODAFONE NASSAU STAKES (Goodwood)

(1¼ miles)
(First run 1840)

1920 Most Beautiful 8st 5lb (6)
1921 Pompadour 8st 10lb (6)
1922 Selene 9st 3lb (6)
1923 Concertina 9st 3lb (6)
1924 Straitlace 9st 8lb (3)
1925 Saucy Sue 9st 8lb (3)
1926 Foliation 9st 8lb (6)
1927 Book Law 9st 8lb (6)
1928 La Sologne 8st 5lb (7)
1929 Nuwara Eliya 8st 10lb (7)
1930 Quinine 8st 10lb (8)
1931 Suze 8st 10lb (6)
1932 Ada Dear 9st 1lb (4)
1933 Solfatara 8st 5lb (6)
1934 Zelina 9st 1lb (3)
1935 Coppelia 9st 1lb (11)
1936 Barrowby Gem 8st 10lb (9)
1937 First Flight 9st 1lb (7)
1938 Valedeh 8st 5lb (10)
1939 Olein 9st 8lb (12)
1940–45 No race
1946 Wayward Belle 9st 1lb (7)
1947 Wild Child 8st 10lb (8)
1948 Goblet 9st 8lb (7)
1949 Jet Plane 9st 8lb (6)
1950 Flying Sipper 9st 1lb (8)
1951 Sea Parrot 8st 5lb (7)
1952 Hortentia 8st 10lb (7)
1953 Happy Laughter 9st 8lb (3)
1954 Key 9st 5lb (10)
1955 Reel In 8st 10lb (6)
1956 Dilettante 8st 10lb (9)
1957 Swallowswift 8st 10lb (8)
1958 Darlene 8st 10lb (6)
1959 Crystal Palace 9st 5lb (6)
1960 Desert Beauty 9st 1lb (5)
1961 Rachel 8st 5lb (6)
1962 Nortia 9st 3lb (7)
1963 Spree 8st 5lb (4)
1964 Craker 8st 10lb (6)
1965 Aunt Edith 8st 5lb (6)
1966 Haymaking 9st 3lb (9)
1967 Fair Winter 8st 10lb (5)
1968 Hill Shade 8st (7)
1969 Lucyrowe 8st 9lb (5)
1970 Pulchra 8st 4lb (5)
1971 Catherine Wheel 8st 4lb (5)
1972 Crespinall 8st 8lb (4)
1973 Cheveley Princess 8st 8lb (9)
1974 Mil's Bomb 8st 8lb (4)
1975 Roussalka 3y 8st 8lb (6)
1976 Roussalka 5y 9st 6lbn (10)
1977 Triple First 3y 8st 5lb (8)
1978 Cistus 3y 8st 5lb (7)
1979 Conaught Bridge 3y 8st 5lb (10)
1980 Vielle 3y 8st 5lb (7)
1981 Go Leasing 3y 8st 8lb (11)

1982 Dancing Rocks 3y 8st 5lb (11)
1983 Acclimatise 3y 8st 5lb (60
1984 Optimistic Lass (USA) 3y 8st 8lb (5)
1985 Free Guest 4y 9st 8lb (11)
1986 Park Express 3y 8st 8lb (7)
1987 Nom de Plume (USA) 3y 8st 7lb (5)
1988 Ela Romara 3y 8st 6lb (7)
1989 Mamaluna (USA) 3y 8st 6lb (5)
1990 Kartajana 3y 8st 6lb (6)
1991 Ruby Tiger 4y 9st 4lb (6)
1992 Ruby Tiger 5y 9st 1lb (7)
1993 Lyphard's Delta (USA) 3y 8st 6lb (9)

Until 1975 the race was for three-year-olds only

IBN BEY GEOFFREY FREER STAKES (Newbury)

(1 mile 5 fur 61 yds)

1949 Ridge Wood 9st (4)
1950 Tilloy 8st 11lb (5)
1951 Le Sage 9st (2)
1952 Westinform 8st 11lb (6)
1953 Harwin 9st 2lb (3)
1954 Umberto 9st 2lb (3)
1955 True Cavalier 9st 2lb (4)
1956 Court Command 9st 5lb (7)
1957 Court Harwell 8st 13lb (6)
1958 Owen Glendover 8st 9lb (4)
1959 Kalydon 9st 2lb (4)
1960 High Hat 8st 5lb (6)
1961 Sagacity 3y 8st (4)
1962 Sovrango 4y 9st 3lb (6)
1963 Sovrango 5y 9st 3lb (5)
1964 Sunseeker 3y 8st 3lb (8)
1965 Court Gift 3y 8st 3lb (5)
1966 Charlottown 3y 8st 13lb (40
1967 Hopeful Venture 3y 8st 6lb (6)
1968 Levmoss 3y 8st 4lb (10)
1969 Rangong 4y 9st (5)
1970 High Line 4y 9st 3lb (4)
1971 High Line 5y 9st 5lb (40
1972 Sol'Argent 5y 9st (7)
1973 Attica Meli 4y 9st 5lb (8)
1974 Realistic 5y 9st (7)
1975 Consol 3y 8st 6lb (10)
1976 Swell Fellow 3y 8st 4lb (5)
1977 Valinsky 3y 8st 4lb (5)
1978 Ile de Bourbon (USA) 3y 8st 9lb (7)
1979 Niniski (USA) 3y 8st 1lb (7)
1980 Nicholas Bill 5y 9st 5lb (5)
1981 Ardross 5y 9st 8lb (4)
1982 Ardross 6y 9st 8lb (4)
1983 Khairpour 4y 9st (7)
1984 Baynoun 3y 8st 5lb (5)
1985 Shernazar 4y 8st 3lb (6)
1986 Bakharoff 3y 8st 3lb (6)
1987 Moon Madness 4y 9st 8lb (4)
1988 Top Class 4y 8st 3lb (6)
1989 Ibn Bey 5y 9st 8lb (6)
1990 Charmer 5y 9st 2lb (5)
1991 Drum Taps (USA) 5y 9st 5lb (7)
1992 Shambo 5y 9st 3lb (4)
1993 Azzilfi 3y 8st 5lb (5)

Run as Oxfordshire Stakes from 1949 to 1969 and for three-year-olds only from 1949 to 1960

ASTON UPTHORPE YORKSHIRE OAKS (York)

(1 mile 3 fur 195 yds)
For fillies three year olds and upwards
(First run 1849)

1920 Inflorescence 8st 5lb (5)
1921 Love in Idleness 9st 9lb (9)
1922 Sister in Law 9st 9lb (7)
1923 Splendid Jay 7st 13lb (5)
1924 Blue Ice 7st 12lb (5)
1925 Broderick Bay 7st 12lb (7)
1926 Doushka 9st 3lb (8)
1927 Gloconda 8st 12lb (10)
1928 Rye Water 7st 12lb (9)
1929 Flittemere 7st 12lb (11)
1930 Glorious Devon 7st 12lb (12)
1931 Rackety Lassie 7st 12lb (9)
1932★Nash Light 8st 5lb
★Will o' the Wisp 8st 5lb (6)
1933 Star of England 7st 12lb (7)
1934 Dalmary 7st 12lb (5)
1935 Trigo Verde 7st 12lb (9)
1936 Silversole 9st 1lb (14)
1937 Sculpture 7st 12lb (10)
1938 Joyce W 7st 12lb (12)
1939 Night Shift 7st 12lb (6)
1940–45 No race
1946 Live Letters 8st 10lb (11)
1947 Ladycross 8st 5lb (6)
1948 Angelola 8st 10lb (9)
1949 Unknown Quantity 8st 5lb (6)
1950 Above Board 8st (5)
1951 Sea Parrot 8st 10lb (8)
1952 Frieze 9st 3lb (4)
1953 Kerkeb 8st 5lb (8)
1954 Feevagh 8st 5lb (10)
1955 Ark Royal 9st 3lb (5)
1956 Indian Twilight 8st 5lb (9)
1957 Almeria 9st (7)
1958 None Nicer 9st (8)
1959 Petite Etoile 9st (30
1960 Lynchris 9st (7)
1961 Tenacity 9st (7)
1962 West Side Story 9st (5)
1963 Outcrop 9st (11)
1964 Homeward Bound 9st (7)
1965 Mabel 9st (5)
1966 Parthian Glance 9st (8)
1967 Palatch 9st (6)
1968 Exchange 9st (8)
1969 Frontier Goddess 9st (4)
1970 Lupe 9st (3)
1971 Fleet Wahine (USA) 9st (6)
1972 Attica Meli 9st (6)
1973 Mysterious 9st (50
1974 Dibidale 9st (3)
1975 May Hill 9st (5)
1976 Sarah Siddons (Fr) 9st (13)
1977 Busaca (Fr) 9st (8)
1978 Fair Salinia 9st (10)
1979 Connaught Bridge 9st (5)
1980 Shot A Line 9st (7)
1981 Condessa 9st (11)
1982 Awaasif (Can) 9st (7)
1983 Sun Princess 9st (6)
1984 Circus Plume 9st (5)
1985 Sally Brown 9st (7)
1986 Untold 9st (11)
1987 Bint Pasha (USA) 9st (9)
1988 Diminuendo (USA) 9st (6)
1989 Roseate Tern 9st (5)
1990 Hellenic 9st (6)
1991 Magnificent Star (USA) 3y 8st 11lb (7)
1992 User Friendly 3y 8st 11lb (8)
1993 Only Royale 4y 9st 7lb (8)

★Dead-heat

Until 1990 was for three-year-old fillies only

JUDDMONTE INTERNATIONAL (York)

(1 mile 2 fur 85 yds)

1972 Roberto (USA) 3y 8st 10lb (5)
1973 Moulton 4y 9st 7lb (8)
1974 Dahlia (USA) 4y 9st 4lb (9)
1975 Dahlia (USA) 5y 9st 4lb (6)
1976 Wolow 3y 8st 10lb (7)
1977 Relkino 4y 9st 6lb (8)
1978 Hawaiin Sound (USA) 3y 8st 10lb (10)
1979 Troy 3y 8st 10lb (10)
1980 Master Willie 3y 8st 10lb (12)
1981 Beldale Flutter (USA) 3y 8st 10lb (9)
1982 Assert 3y 8st 10lb (7)
1983 Caerleon (USA) 3y 8st 10lb (9)
1984 Cormorant Wood 4y 9st 3lb (9)
1985 Commanche Run 4y 9st 6lb (6)
1986 Shardari 4y 9st 6lb (12)
1987 Triptych (USA) 5y 9st 3lb (10)
1988 Shady Heights 4y 9st 6lb (6)
1989 Ile de Chypre 4y 9st 6lb (7)
1990 In The Groove 3y 8st 9lb (9)
1991 Terimon 5y 9st 6lb (6)
1992 Rodrigo de Triano (USA) 3y 8st 12lb (12)
1993 Ezzoud 4y 9st 6lb (11)

TOTE-EBOR H'CAP (York)

(1 mile 5 fur 194 yds)
(First run 1843)

1900 Jiffy II 5y 8st 4lb (9)
1901 Gyp 6y 8st 5lb (16)
1902 Wargrave 4y 8st 2lb (17)
1903 McYardley 5y 7st 9lb (13)
1904 War Wolf 5y 7st 9lb (10)
1905 The Page 5y 7st 5lb (12)
1906 Golden Measure 4y 8st 5lb (12)
1907 Wuffy 4y 7st 12lb (9)
1908 Roussay 4y 8st 12lb (4)
1909 Dibs 4y 8st (12)
1910 Claretoi 6y 6st 10lb (14)
1911 Pillo 6y 8st 9lb (19)
1912 Election 5y 7st 4lb (10)
1913 Junior 4y 9st (12)
1914–18 No race
1919 Race Rock 7y 7st (9)
1920 Iron Hand 4y 6st 12lb (11)
1921 March Along 4y 9st 1lb (20)
1922 Flint Jack 5y 8st 9lb (15)
1923 Flint Jack 6y 8st 12lb (8)
1924 Marvex 4y 8st 5lb (20)
1925 Chapeau 5y 7st 6lb (13)
1926 Pons Asinorum 4y 8st 10lb (15)
1927 Cap-a-pie 3y 6st 7lb (16)
1928 Cinq a Sept 4y 8st 4lb (14)
1929 Bonny Boy II 5y 8st 1lb (13)
1930★Gentlemen's Relish 4y 7st 5lb
★Coaster 4y 8st (13)

1931 Brown Jack 7y 9st 5lb (19)
1932 Cat O'Nine Tails 5y 7st 8lb (19)
1933 Dictum 5y 7st 4lb (11)
1934 Alcazar 3y 8st 5lb (14)
1935 Museum 3y 7st 13lb (12)
1936 Penny Royal 3y 7st 9lb (14)
1937 Weathervane 4y 7st 10lb (17)
1938 Foxglove II 3y 8st 1lb (12)
1939 Owenstown 5y 8st 8lb (12)
1940–42 No race
1943†Yorkshire Hussar 4y 8st 8lb (19)
1944†The Kernel 4y 7st 8lb (14)
1945 Wayside Inn 3y 8st 6lb 914)
1946 Foxtrot 3y 7st 13lb (13)
1947 Procne 4y 8st 4lb (11)
1948 Donino 4y 8st 12lb (20)
1949 Miraculous Aron 5y 8st 11lb (16)
1950 Cadzow Oak 4y 7st 12lb (21)
1951 Bob 4y 6st 12lb (25)
1952 Signification 3y 7st 12lb (15)
1953 Norooz 4y 8st 4lb (21)
1954 By Thunder! 3y 6st 12lb (22)
1955 Hyperion Kid 3y 7st 2lb (25)
1956 Donald 3y 7st 10lb 917)
1957 Morecambe 4y 7st 9lb (30)
1958 Gladness 5y 9st 7lb (25)
1959 Primera 5y 9st (21)
1960 Persian Road 5y 8st 4lb (21)
1961 Die Hard 4y 8st 9lb (21)
1962 Sostenuto 4y 8st 10lb (18)
1963 Partholon 3y 7st 8lb (22)
1964 Proper Pride 5y 7st 11lb (20)
1965 Twelfth Man 4y 7st 5lb (25)
1966 Lomond 6y 9st 2lb (23)
1967 Ovaltine 3y 7st (22)
1968 Alignment 3y 7st 8lb (20)
1969 Big Hat 4y 7st 3lb (19)
1970 Tintagel II 5y 8st 5lb (21)
1971 Knotty Pine 5y 8st 7lb (21)
1972 Crazy Rhythm 4y 8st 6lb (21)
1973 Bonne Noel 4y 9st 2lb (20)
1974 Anji 5y 7st 8lb (18)
1975 Dakota 4y 9st 4lb (18)
1976 Sir Montagu 3y 8st (15)
1977 Move Off 4y 8st 1lb (14)
1978 Totowah 4y 8st 1lb (22)
1979 Sea Pigeon (USA) 9y 10st (17)
1980 Shaftesbury 4y 8st 5lb (16)
1981 Protection Racket (USA) 3y 8st 1lb (22)
1982 Another Sam 5y 9st 2lb (15)
1983 Jupiter Island 4y 9st (16)
1984 Crazy (Fr) 3y 8st 13lb (14)
1985 Western Dancer 4y 8st 6lb (19)
1986 Primary (Can) 3y 8st 7lb (22)
1987 Daarkom 4y 9st 3lb (15)
1988 Kneller 3y 8st 1lb (21)
1989 Sapience 3y 8st 4lb (18)
1990 Further Flight 4y 8st 8lb (22)
1991 Deposki 3y 7st 3lb (22)
1992 Quick Ransom 4y 8st 3lb (22)
1993 Sarawat 5y 8st 2lb (21)

*Dead-heat
†Run at Pontefract over 1 1/2 miles

GREAT VOLTIGEUR STAKES (York)

(1 mile 3 fur 195 yds)
For three year olds

1950 Castle Rock 9st 7lb (5)
1951 Border Legend 9st (13)
1952 Childe Harold 9st 3lb (7)
1953 Premonition 9st 7lb (6)
1954 Blue Sail 9st (9)
1955 Acropolis 9st 7lb (5)
1956 Hornbeam 9st 3lb (4)
1957 Brioche 9st (7)
1958 Alcide 9st (5)
1959 Pindari 9st (4)
1960 St Paddy 9st (4)
1961 Just Great 9st (8)
1962 Hethersett 9st (11)
1963 Ragusa 9st (5)
1964 Indiana 9st (6)
1965 Ragazzo 9st (6)
1966 Hermes 9st (8)
1967 Great Host 9st (6)
1968 Connaught 9st (4)
1969 Harmony Hall 9st (6)
1970 Meadowville 9st (4)
1971 Athens Wood 9st (5)
1972 Our Mirage 9st (7)
1973 Buoy 9st (5)
1974 Bustino 9st (3)
1975 Patch 9st (4)
1976 Hawkberry 8st 7lb (7)
1977 Alleged (USA) 8st 11lb (8)
1978 Whitstead 8st 7lb (8)
1979 Noble Saind (USA) 8st 7lb (5)
1980 Prince Bee 8st 7lb (5)
1981 Glint of Gold 9st (6)
1982 Electric 8st 7lb (7)
1983 Seymour Hicks (Fr) 8st 7lb (5)
1984 Rainbow Quest (USA) 8st 7lb (7)
1985 Shardari 8st 7lb (4)
1986 Nisnas 8st 7lb (7)
1987 Reference Point 9st (3)
1988 Sheriff's Star 8st 12lb (4)
1989 Zalazl (USA) 8st 9lb (3)
1990 Belmez (USA) 9st (5)
1991 Corrupt (USA) 8st 9lb (7)
1992 Bonny Scot 8st 9lb (6)
1993 Bob's Return 8st 9lb (9)

Run from 1950 to 1956 as Voltigeur Stakes (for three year old colts)

KEENELAND NUNTHORPE STAKES (York)

(5 fur)

1922 Two Step 3y 8st 5lb (5)
1923 Golden Boss 3y 8st 7lb (4)
1924 Mumtaz Mahal 3y 8st 4lb (5)
1925 Diomedes 3y 8st 7lb (3)
1926 Highborn II 3y 8st 7lb (3)
1927 highborn II 4y 8st 12lb (5)
1928 Tag End 4y 8st 9lb (5)
1929 Tag End 5y 8st 9lb (4)
1930 Tag End 6y 8st 9lb (5)
1931 Portlaw 3y 8st 7lb (5)
1932 Greenore 3y 8st 4lb (6)
1933 Concerto 5y 8st 12lb (3)
1934 Gold Bridge 5y 8st 12lb (6)
1935 Shalfleet 4y 8st 9lb (6)
1936 Bellacose 4y 8st 12lb (9)
1937 Ipsden 4y 8st 9lb (8)
1938 Mickey the Greek 4y 8st 12lb (4)
1939 Portobello 3y 8st 11lb (4)
1940–44 No race
1945 Golden Cloud 4y 9st 5lb (7)
1946 The Bug 3y 9st (4)
1947 Como 5y 9st 5lb (6)
1948 Careless Nora 3y 8st 11lb (6)
1949 Abernant 3y 9st (4)
1950 Abernant 4y 9st 5lb (3)
1951 Royal Serenade 3y 9st (6)
1952 Royal Serenade 4y 9st 5lb (5)
1953 High Treason 2y 7st 3lb (8)
1954 My Beau 2y 7st 3lb (11)
1955 Royal Palm 3y 9st (4)
1956 Ennis 2y 7st 3lb (5)
1957 Gratitude 4y 9st 5lb (5)
1958 Right Boy 4y 9st 5lb (3)
1959 Right Boy 5y 9st 5lb (6)
1960 Bleep-Bleep 4y 9st 5lb (7)
1961 Floribunda 3y 9st (6)
1962 Gay Mairi 3y 8st 11lb (9)
1963 Matatina 3y 8st 11lb (8)
1964 Althrey Don 3y 9st (10)
1965 Polyfoto 3y 9st (8)
1966 Caterina 3y 8st 11lb (11)
1967 Forlorn River 5y 9st 5lb (12)
1968 So Blessed 3y 9st 2lb (5)
1969 Tower Walk 3y 9st 2lb (6)
1970 Huntercombe 3y 9st 2lb (3)
1971 Swing Easy (USA) 3y 9st 2lb (9)
1972 Deep River 3y 9st 2lb (7)
1973 Sandford Lad 3y 9st 2lb (8)
1974 Blue Cashmere 4y 9st 7lb (12)
1975 Bay Express 4y 9st 7lb (10)
1976 Lochnager 4y 9st 6lb (11)
1977 Haveroid 3y 9st 2lb (8)
1978 Solinus 3y 9st 2lb (9)
1979 Ahonoora 4y 9st 6lb (10)
1980 Sharpo 3y 9st 2lb (11)
1981 Sharpo 4y 9st (9)
1982 Sharpo 5y 9st (11)
1983 Habibti 3y 8st 7lb (10)
1984 Committed (USA) 4y 8st 11lb (8)
1985 Never So Bold 5y 9st (8)
1986 Last Tycoon 3y 9st 2lb
1987 Ajdal (USA) 3y 9st 2lb (11)
1988 Handsome Sailor 5y 9st 6lb (12)
1989 Cadeaux Genereux 4y 9st 6lb (11)
1990 Dayjur (USA) 3y 9st 3lb (9)
1991 Sheikh Albadou 3y 9st 3lb (9)
1992 Lyric Fantasy 2y 7st 8lb (11)
1993 Lochsong 5y 9st 3lb (11)

SCOTTISH EQUITABLE GIMCRACK STAKES (York)

(6 fur)
For two year olds
(First run 1846)

1900 Garb Or (13)
1901 Sterling Balm (12)
1902 Chaucer (10)
1903 Barbette (12)
1904 Desiree (14)
1905 Colonia (10)
1906 Polar Star (11)
1907 Royal Realm (11)
1908 Blankey II (13)
1909 Lily Rose (10)
1910 Pietri (9)
1911 Lomond (6)
1912 Flippant (8)
1913 Stornoway (11)
1914–18 No race
1919 Southern (7)
1920 Polemarch (9)
1921 Scamp (12)
1922 Town Guard (8)

1923 Sansovino (7)
1924 Game Shot (7)
1925 Lex (7)
1926 Bold Archer (14)
1927 Black Watch (14)
1928 The Black Abbot (10)
1929 Roral (7)
1930 Four Course (13)
1931 Miracle (7)
1932 Young Lover (7)
1933 Mrs Rustom (10)
1934 Bahram (5)
1935 Paul Beg (8)
1936 Goya II (15)
1937 Golden Sovereign (6)
1938 Cockpit (11)
1939 Tant Mieux (14)
1940–44 No race
1945 Gulf Stream (4)
1946 Petition (5)
1947 Black Tarquin (7)
1948 Star King (12)
1949 Palestine (2)
1950 Cortil (10)
1951 Windy City (10)
1952 Bebe Grande (10)
1953 The Pie King (9)
1954 Precast (11)
1955 Idle Rocks (5)
1956 Eudaemon (7)
1957 Pheidippides (9)
1958 Be Careful (12)
1959 Paddy's Sister (10)
1960 Test Case (7)
1961 Sovereign Lord (11)
1962 Crocket (5)
1963 Talahasse (7)
1964 Double Jump (7)
1965 Young Emperor (8)
1966 Golden Horus (9)
1967 Petingo (9)
1968 Tudor Music (7)
1969 Yellow God (11)
1970 Mill Reef (USA) (8)
1971 Wishing Star (7)
1972 Rapid River (9)
1973 Giacometti (11)
1974 Steel Heart (10)
1975 Music Boy (14)
1976 Nebbiolo (7)
1977 Tumbledownwind (5)
1978 Stanford (11)
1979 Sonnen Gold (7)
1980 Bel Bolide (USA) (9)
1981 Full Extent (USA) (8)
1982 Horage (7)
1983 Precocious (6)
1984 Doulab (USA) (8)
1985 Stalker (6)
1986 Wiganthorpe 9st (11)
1987 Reprimand 9st (6)
1988 Sharp N'Early, 9st (8)
1989 Rock City 9st 3lb (5)
1990 Mujtahid (USA) 9st 3lb (5)
1991 River Falls 9st (5)
1992 Splendent (USA) 9st (8)
1993 Turtle Island 9st 5lb (8)

TRIPLEPRINT CELEBRATION MILE (Goodwood)

(1 mile)

1967 St Chad 3y 8st 3lb (7)
1968 Jimmy Reppin 3y 7st 13lb (6)
1969 Habitat 3y 8st 6lb (6)
1970 Humble Duty 3y 8st 4lb (5)
1971 Brigadier Gerard 3y 8st 6lb (3)
1972 Sallust 3y 8st 13lb (3)
1973 Jacinth 3y 8st 10lb (5)
1974 Pitcairn 3y 8st 8lb (3)
1975 Gay Fandango (USA) 3y 8st 8lb (8)
1976 Free State 3y 8st 3lb (6)
1977 Be My Guest (USA) 3y 8st 7lb (6)
1978 Captain James 4y 8st 13lb (5)
1979†Kris 3y 8st 12lb (8)
1980 Known Fact (USA) 3y 8st 12lb (6)
1981 To-Agori-Mou 3y 8st 12lb (60
1982 Sandhurst Prince 3y 8st 5lb (8)
1983 Montekin 4y 8st 13lb (6)
1984 Rousillon (USA) 3y 8st 6lb (5)
1985 No race
1986 Then Again 3y 8st 7lb
1987 Milligram 3y 8st 7lb (4)
1988 Prince Rupert (Fr) 4y 9st 3lb (6)
1989 Distant Relative 3y 8st 12lb (5)
1990 Shavian 3y 9st (5)
1991 Bold Russian 4y 9st (5)
1992 Selkirk (USA) 4y 9st 3lb (7)
1993 Swing Low 4y 9st 3lb (6)

†Run at Ascot

HAZLEWOOD FOODS SPRINT CUP

(6 fur)

1966 Be Friendly 2y 8st (15)
1967 Be Friendly 3y 9st 4lb (9)
1968 No race
1969 Tudor Music 3y 9st 4lb (11)
1970 Golden Orange 4y 9st 10lb (5)
1971 Green God 3y 9st 6lb (7)
1972 Abergwaun 4y 9st 7lb (10)
1973 The Blues 2y 8st (8)
1974 Princely Son 5y 9st 10lb (11)
1975 Lianga (USA) 4y 9st 7lb (7)
1976 Record Token 4y 9st 8lb (8)
1977 Boldboy 7y 9st 8lb (7)
1978 Absalom 3y 9st 6lb (14)
1979 Double Form 4y 9st 8lb (7)
1980 Moorestyle 3y 8st 12lb (8)
1981 Runnett 4y 9st 3lb (6)
1982 Indian King 4y 9st 3lb (9)
1983 Habibti 3y 8st 9lb (6)
1984 Petong 4y 9st 3lb (9)
1985 Orojoya (USA) 3y 8st 12lb (8)
1986 Green Desert (USA) 3y 8st 12lb (8)
1987 Ajdal (USA) 3y 9st (8)
1988 Dowsing (USA) 4y 9st 2lb (10)
1989 Danehill (USA) 3y 9st 5lb (9)
1990 Dayjur (USA) 3y 9st 6lb (9)
1991 Polar Falcon (USA) 4y 9st 9lb (6)
1992 Sheikh Albadou 4y 9st 9lb (8)
1993 Wolfhound (USA) 4y 9st 9lb (7)

TRIPLEPRINT FLYING CHILDERS STAKES (Doncaster)

(5 fur)

For two year olds

1967 D'Urberville 9st (5)
1968 Tower Walk 9st (6)
1969 Tribal Chief 9st (4)
1970 Mummy's Pet 9st (5)
1971 Rose Dubarry 8st 8lb (5)
1972 Marble Arch (USA) 8st 11lb (8)
1973 Gentle Thoughts (USA) 9st (7)
1974 Hot Spark 9st 4lb (7)
1975 Hittite Glory 9st (5)
1976 Mandrake Major 9st (9)
1977 Music Maestro 9st (8)
1978 Devon Ditty 8st 11lb (7)
1979 Abeer (USA) 8st 11lb (6)
1980 Marwell 8st 11lb (6)
1981 Peterhof (USA) 9st (7)
1982 Kafu 9st (5)
1983 Superlative 9st (10)
1984 Prince Sabo 9st (6)
1985 Green Desert (USA) 9st (8)
1986 Sizzling Melody 9st (6)
1987 Gallic League 8st 11lb (7)
1988 Shuttlecock Corner 8st 11lb (8)
1989 Abandoned
1990 Distinctly North (USA) 8st 11lb (6)
1991 Paris House 8st 11lb (5)
1992 Poker Chip 8st 6lb (7)
1993 Imperial Bailiwick 8st 6lb (8)

LAURENT PERRIER CHAMPAGNE STAKES (Doncaster)

(7 fur)

For two year olds

(First run 1823)

1900 Orchid (6)
1901 Game Chick (7)
1902 Rock Sand (4)
1903 Pretty Polly (5)
1904*Galangal and Vedriana (10)
1905 Achilles (8)
1906 Slieve Gallion (7)
1907 Lesbia (5)
1908 Duke Michael (6)
1909 Neil Gow (4)
1910 Pietri (4)
1911 White Star (7)
1912 Craganour (4)
1913 The Tetrarch (3)
1914 Redfern (6)
1915–18 No race
1919 Tetratema (5)
1920 Lemonora (5)
1921 Golden Corn (7)
1922 Dake (10)
1923 Mumtaz Mahal (5)
1924 Bucellas (6)
1925 Coronach (12)
1926 Damon (8)
1927 Fairway (9)
1928 Arabella (10)
1929 Fair Diana (6)
1930 Portlaw (8)
1931 Orwell (5)
1932 Myrobella (8)
1933 Blazonry (8)

1934 Kingsem (7)
1935 Mahmoud (11)
1936 Foray (10)
1937 Portmarnock (8)
1938 Panorama (7)
1939–40 No race
1941†Big Game (6)
1942–45 No race
1946 Petition (3)
1947 Lerins (renamed My Babu) (4)
1948 Abernant (3)
1949 Palestine (3)
1950 Big Dipper (7)
1951 Orgoglio (7)
1952 Bebe Grande (5)
1953 Darius (6)
1954 Our Babu (9)
1955 Rustam (3)
1956 Eudaemon (4)
1957 Kelly (5)
1958 Be Careful (5)
1959 Paddy' Sister (6)
1960 Ambergis (9)
1961 Clear Sound (8)
1962 King of Babylon (10)
1963 Talahasse (7)
1964 Hardicante (11)
1965 Celtic Song (8)
1966 Bold Lad (Ire) (5)
1967 Chebs Lad (6)
1968 Ribofilio (7)
1969 Saintly Song (6)
1970 Breeders Dream (6)
1971 Crowned Prince (USA) (8)
1972 Otha (USA) (5)
1973 Giacometti (8)
1974 Grundy (10)
1975 Wollow 9st (8)
1976 J O Tobin (USA) (6)
1977 Sexton Blake (7)
1978 R B Chesne (7)
1979 Final Straw (9)
1980 Gielgud (USA) (10)
1981 Achieved (8)
1982 Gorytus (USA) (5)
1983 Lear Fan (USA) (4)
1984 Young Runaway (USA) (5)
1985 Sure Blade (USA) (5)
1986 Don't Forget Me (9)
1987 Warning 9st (4)
1988 Prince of Dance (7)
1989 Abandoned
1990 Bog Trotter (USA) (5)
1991 Rodrigo de Triano (USA) (5)
1992 Petardia (9)
1993 Unblest (4)

⋆Dead-heat
†Run at Newbury

WORTHINGTON BEST BITTER PARK HILL STAKES (Doncaster)

(1 mile 6 fur 132 yds)
For fillies three year olds and upwards
(First run 1839)

1900 Goosander 8st 13lb (8)
1901 St Aldegonde 8st 7lb (9)
1902 Elba 8st 10lb (4)
1903 Quintessence 9st 3lb (6)
1904 Pretty Polly 9st 8lb (5)
1905 Adula 8st 13lb (6)
1906 Demure 8st 10lb (4)
1907 Jubilee 8st 13lb (8)
1908 Siberia 8st 13lb (4)
1909 Electra 9st 3lb 94)
1910 yellow Slave 8st 13lb (4)
1911 Hair Trigger II 8st 13lb (3)
1912 Eufrosina 8st 13lb (5)
1913 Arda 8st 13lb (7)
1914 First Spear 8st 13lb (6)
1915–18 No race
1919 Flying Spear 8st 13lb (5)
1920 Redhead 8st 13lb (5)
1921 Love in Idleness 9st 3lb (5)
1922 Selene 8st 13lb (2)
1923 Brownhylda 9st 3lb (4)
1924 Charley's Mount 8st 7lb (7)
1925 Juldi 8st 6lb (4)
1926 Glasheen 8st 13lb (7)
1927 Cinq a Sept 8st 13lb (7)
1928 Girandola 8st 6lb (8)
1929 Nuwara Eliya 8st 13lb (3)
1930 Glorious Devon 8st 13lb (10)
1931 Volume 8st (8)
1932 Fury 7st 11lb (5)
1933 Typhonic 9st 3lb (7)
1934 Poker 8st 3lb (3)
1935 Fox Lair 8st (6)
1936 Traffic Light 8st 3lb (5)
1937 Nadushka 8st 10lb (11)
1938 Gainly 8st (10)
1939–45 No race
1946 Procne 8st 4lb (4)
1947 Mitrailleuse 8st 8lb (8)
1948 Vertencia 8st 8lb (9)
1949 Sea Idol 8st 4lb (12)
1950 La Baille 9st (14)
1951 Verse 8st 8lb (5)
1952 Moon Star 8st 8lb (14)
1953 Kerkeb 9st (9)
1954 Bara Bibi 9st (14)
1955 Ark Royal 9st (5)
1956 Kyak 8st 4lb (10)
1957 Almeria 9st (8)
1958 Cutter 9st (8)
1959 Collyria 9st (7)
1960 Sunny Cove 9st (6)
1961 Never Say 9st (8)
1962 Almiranta 9st (9)
1963 Outcrop 9st (9)
1964 Cursorial 9st (5)
1965 Bracey Bridge 9st (5)
1966 Parthian Glance 9st (7)
1967⋆Pia 9st
⋆Pink Gem 9st (7)
1968 Bringley 9st (8)
1969 Aggravate 9st (6)
1970 Parmelia 9st (5)
1971 Example 9st (8)
1972 Attica Meli 9st (7)
1973 Reload (Fr) 9st (9)
1974 Mil's Bomb 9st (10)
1975 May Hill 9st (7)
1976 African Dancer 9st (9)
1977 Royal Hive 9st (3)
1978 Idle Waters 9st (10)
1979 Quay Line 9st (5)
1980 Shoot A Line 9st (6)
1981 Alma Ata 9st (13)
1982 Swiftfoot 9st (6)
1983 High Hawk 9st (7)
1984 Borushka 9st (13)
1985 I Want To Be (USA) 9st (7)
1986 Rejuvenate 8st 9lb (12)
1987 Trampship 8st 9lb (5)
1988 Casey 8st 9lb (9)
1989 Lucky Song (USA) 8st 9lb (4)
1990 Madame Dubois 8st 9lb (8)
1991 Patricia (USA) 3y 8st 8lb (11)
1992 Niodini (USA) 3y 8st 5lb (12)
1993 Anna of Saxony 4y 9st 3lb (9)

⋆Dead-heat
Until 1990 was for three-year-old fillies only.

DONCASTER CUP

(2 1/4 miles)
(First run 1801)

1900 King's Courier 3y 8st 4lb (5)
1901⋆Merry Gal 4y 9st 8lb
⋆Sidus 4y 9st 4lb (4)
1902 William the Third 4y 10st (3)
1903 Wavelet's Pride 6y 9st 5lb (8)
1904 Robert le Diable 5y 9st 13lb (3)
1905 Bachelor's Button 6y 9st 12lb (5)
1906 Velocity 4y 9st 4lb (5)
1907 Velocity 5y 10st 11lb (6)
1908 Radium 5y 10st 1lb (7)
1909 Amadis 3y 8st 11lb (6)
1910 Bronzino 3y 8st 4lb (5)
1911 Lemberg 4y 10st (6)
1912 Prince Palatine 4y 10st (2)
1913 Long Set 6y 9st 5lb (2)
1914 Willbrook 3y 8st 4lb (9)
1915–18 No race
1919 Haki 7y 9st 5lb (3)
1920 Buchan 4y 9st 11lb (7)
1921 Flamboyant 3y 8st 4lb (6)
1922 Devizes 5y 9st 12lb (4)
1923 Silurian 4y 9st 11lb (5)
1924 Santorb 3y 8st 4lb (6)
1925 St Germans 4y 9st 11lb (9)
1926 Bongrace 3y 7st 5lb (7)
1927 Bythorne 3y 7st 5lb (4)
1928 Pons Asinorum 6y 9st 4lb (3)
1929 Athford 4y 8st 6lb (4)
1930 Brown Jack 6y 9st 11lb (5)
1931 Singapore 4y 9st 12lb (6)
1932 Foxhunter 3y 7st 8lb (6)
1933 Colorado Kid 4y 8st 6lb (2)
1934 Alcazar 3y 8st 8lb (3)
1935 Black Devil 4y 9st 9lb (5)
1936 Buckleigh 4y 9st 2lb (6)
1937 haulfryn 4y 9st 2lb (6)
1938 Epigram 5y 10st (5)
1939–45 No race
1946 Marsyas II 6y 9st 9lb (4)
1947 Trimbush 7y 9st 6lb (7)
1948 Auralia 5y 9st 6lb (9)
1949 Alycidon 4y 9st 7lb (4)
1950 Aldborough 5y 9st 9lb (8)
1951 Fast Fox 4y 9st 4lb (7)
1952 Aquino II 4y 9st 7lb (7)
1953⋆Souepi 5y 9st 9lb
⋆Nick La Rocca 4y 9st 4lb (7)
1954 Osborne 7y 9st 6lb (9)
1955 Entente Cordiale 4y 9st 4lb (4)
1956 Atlas 3y 8st 3lb (8)
1957 French Beige 4y 9st 4lb (4)
1958 Agreement 4y 9st 4lb (7)
1959 Agreement 5y 9st 9lb (4)
1960 Exar 4y 9st 7lb (2)
1961 Pandofell 4y 9st 7lb (5)
1962 Bonnard 4y 8st 12lb (6)
1963 Raise You Ten 3y 7st 11lb (4)
1964 Grey of Falloden 5y 9st (6)
1965 Prince Hansel 4y 8st 12lb (6)
1966 Piaco 3y 7st 11lb (6)
1967 Crozier 4y 8st 12lb (6)
1968 The Accuser 4y 8st 12lb (4)
1969 Canterbury 4y 8st 12lb (8)
1970 Magna Carta 4y 8st 12lb (4)
1971 Rock Roi 4y 8st 12lb (5)
1972 Biskrah 5y 9st (5)
1973 Attica Meli 4y 8st 11lb (4)
1974 Proverb 4y 9st (3)
1975 Crash Course 4y 9st (3)

1976 Sea Anchor 4y 9st 3lb (4)
1977 Shangamuzo 4y 8st 12lb (5)
1978 Buckskin (Fr) 5y 9st 2lb (6)
1979 Le Moss 4y 9st 2lb (5)
1980 Le Moss 5y 9st 2lb (5)
1981 Protection Racket (USA) 3y 7st 6lb (4)
1982 Ardross 6y 9st 2lb (8)
1983 Karador 5y 8st 5lb (8)
1984 Wagoner 4y 8st 5lb (4)
1985 Spicy Story (USA) 4y 8st 9lb (8)
1986 Longboat 5y 9st 6lb (4)
1987 Buckley 4y 8st 13lb (8)
1988 Kneller 3y 8st 4lb (4)
1989 Weld 3y 8st (3)
1990 Al Maheb (USA) 4y 9st 5lb (10)
1991 Great Marquess 4y 9st 3lb (8)
1992 Further Flight 6y 9st 3lb (5)
1993 Assessor 4y 9st 7lb (5)

*Dead-heat

TOTE PORTLAND H'CAP (Doncaster)

(5 fur 140 yds)
(First run 1855)

1900 Lucknow 5y 7st 4lb (15)
1901 Dieudonne 6y 8st (18)
1902 Gladwin 3y 6st 3lb (23)
1903 Nabot 4y 7st 13lb (22)
1904 Santry 3y 7st 13lb (17)
1905 Xeny 4y 8st 12lb (18)
1906 Nero 3y 6st 5lb (16)
1907 Woolley 5y 6st 7lb (20)
1908 The Welkin 4y 7st 9lb (20)
1909 Americus Girl 4y 8st 13lb (17)
1910 Hallaton 8y 8st 6lb (21)
1911 Stolen Kiss 4y 8st (21)
1912 Wethers Well 4y 9st 1lb (16)
1913 Hornet's Beauty 5y 9st 9lb (11)
1914 Flying Orb 3y 7st 11lb (17)
1915–18 No race
1919 Irish Elegance 4y 10st 2lb (13)
1920 Pelops 3y 7st 12lb (17)
1921 Glanmerin 5y 9st 5lb (14)
1922 Two Step 3y 8st 10lb (14)
1923 Polydipsia 6y 8st 5lb (8)
1924 Heverswood 3y 8st 12lb (14)
1925 Diomedes 3y 9st 2lb (22)
1926 Sunstone 5y 8st (19)
1927 Mayrian 4y 6st 7lb (19)
1928 Tag End 4y 9st (19)
1929 Tag End 5y 9st 5lb (10)
1930 Polar Bear 3y 7st 2lb (18)
1931 Xandover 4y 9st 7lb (11)
1932 Polar Bear 5y 8st 8lb (22)
1933 Valkvrie 4y 7st 5lb (20)
1934 Rosemary's Pet 5y 8st 12lb (16)
1935 Shalfleet 4y 9st 7lb (23)
1936 Shalfleet 5y 9st 2lb (23)
1937*Carissa 3y 8st 3lb (25)
1938 The Drummer 6y 7st 3lb (27)
1939–40 No race
1941†Comatas 4y 8st 11lb (15)
1942–45 No race
1946 The Shah 4y 7st 5lb (14)
1947 Good View 5y 8st (17)
1948 Gold Mist 3y 7st 12lb (18)
1949 Le Lavandou 5y 7st 7lb (28)
1950 Paramount 4y 8st 9lb (19)
1951 Reminiscence 4y 8st 10lb (25)
1952 Stephen Paul 4y 9st 3lb (20)
1953 Reminiscence 6y 8st 8lb (29)
1954 Vilmoray 4y 9st (25)
1955 Princely Gift 4y 9st 4lb (12)
1956 Epaulette 5y 8st 2lb (19)
1957 Refined 3y 8st 10lb (18)
1958 Welsh Abbot 3y 9st 2lb (14)
1959 New World 6y 7st 3lb (11)
1960 Accompanist 5y 7st 6lb (12)
1961 Winna 4y 7st 2lb (16)
1962 Harmon 3y 8st 2lb (18)
1963 Marcher 3y 8st 9lb (20)
1964 Comefast 5y 7st 11lb (17)
1965 Go Shell 3y 8st 7lb (14)
1966 Audrey Joan 3y 7st 3lb (21)
1967 Florescence 3y 8st 13lb (15)
1968 Gold Pollen 3y 7st 7lb (12)
1969 Mountain Call 4y 8st 11lb (20)
1970 Virginia Boy 4y 7st 1lb (15)
1971 Royben 3y 8st 6lb (17)
1972 Privateer 6y 8st 1lb (13)
1973 Supreme Gift 3y 8st 6lb (15)
1974 Matinee 3y 8st 11lb (20)
1975 Walk By 3y 8st 10lb (16)
1976 Hei'land Jamie 5y 7st 13lb (11)
1977 Jon George 3y 7st 12lb (12)
1978 Goldhills Pride 4y 8st 10lb (13)
1979 Oh Simmie 4y 7st (21)
1980 Swelter 4y 8st 2lb (20)
1981 Touch Boy 5y 8st 11lb (21)
1982 Vorvados 5y 8st 13lb (14)
1983 Out of Hand 4y 7st 3lb (15)
1984 Dawn's Delight 6y 7st 8lb (22)
1985 Lochtillum 6y 8st 1lb (17)
1986 Felipe Toro 3y 8st 2lb (23)
1987 Dawn's Delight 9y 8st 13lb (23)
1988 Roman Prose 3y 9st 3lb (22)
1989 Craft Express 3y 8st 9lb (22)
1990 Love Legend 5y 8st 7lb (21)
1991 Sarcita 3y 8st 6lb (21)
1992 Lochsong 4y 8st 12lb (22)
1993 Amron 6y 9st (18)

*Run as Coronation H'cap
†Run over 6 fur at Newmarket

COALITE ST. LEGER (Doncaster—1 mile 6 fur 132 yds)

For three year olds

		Starters	Jockeys
1776	Lord Rockingham's Allabaculla, by Sampson	5 ...	J Singleton jun.
1777	Mr W Sotheron's Bourbon, by Le Sang	10 ...	J Cade
1778	Sir T Gascoigne's Holandaise, by Match'em	8 ...	G Herring
1779	Mr Stapleton's Tommy, by Wildair	10 ...	G Lowrey, sen.
1780	Mr Bethell's Ruler, by Young Marske	7 ...	J Mangles
1781	Colonel Radcliffe's Serina, by Goldfinder	9 ...	R Forster
1782	Mr Pratt's Imperatrix, by Alfred	5 ...	G Searle
1783	Sir J J Kaye's Phenomenon, by Herod	4 ...	A Hall
1784	Mr J Coate's Omphale, by Highflyer	7 ...	J Kearton
1785	Mr Hill's Cowslip, by Highflyer	4 ...	G Searle
1786	Lord A Hamilton's Paragon, by Paymaster	8 ...	J Mangles
1787	Lord A Hamilton's Spadille, by Highflyer	6 ...	J Mangles
1788	Lord A Hamilton's Young Fora, by Highflyer	5 ...	J Mangles
1789	Lord Fitzwilliam's Pewett, by Tandem	6 ...	J Singleton jun.
1790	Mr Dealtry's Ambidexter, by Phenomenon	8 ...	G Searle
1791	Mr J Hutchinson's Y Traveller, by King Fergus	8 ...	J Jackson
1792	Lord A Hamilton's Tartar, by Florizel	11 ...	J Mangles
1793	Mr J Clifton's Ninety-three, by Florizel	8 ...	W Peirse
1794	Mr J Hutchinson's Beningbrough, by King Fergus	8 ...	J Jackson
1795	Sir C Turner's Hambletonian, by King Fergus	5 ...	D Boyes
1796	Mr J Cookson's Ambrosio, by Sir Peter Teazle	7 ...	J Jackson
1797	Mr G Crompton's Lounger, by Drone	8 ...	J Shepherd
1798	Sir T Gascoigne's Symmetry, by Delpini	10 ...	J Jackson
1799	Sir H T Vane's Cockfighter, by Overton	7 ...	T Fields
1800	Mr C Wilson's Champion, by Pot8os	10 ...	F Buckle
1801	Mr G Crompton's Quiz, by Buzzard	8 ...	J Shepherd

COALITE ST. LEGER—continued

Year	Winner	Starters	Jockeys
1802	Lord Fitzwilliam's Orville, by Beningbrough	7	J Singleton, jn.
1803	Lord Strathmore's Remembrancer, by Pipator	8	B Smith
1804	Mr H Mellish's Sancho, by Don Quizote	11	F Buckle
1805	Mr H Mellish's Staveley, by Shuttle	10	J Jackson
1806	Mr J Clifton's Fyldener, by sir Peter Teazle	15	T Carr
1807	Lord Fitzwilliam's Paulina, by Sir Peter Teazle	16	W Clift
1808	Duke of Hamilton's Petronius, by Sir Peter Teazle	12	B Smith
1809	Duke of Hamilton's Ashton, by Walnut	14	B Smith
1810	Duke of Leed's Octasvian, by Stripling	8	W Clift
1811	Mr R Gascoigne's Soothsayer, by Sorcerer	24	B Smith
1812	Mr R Rob's Otterington, by Golumpus	24	R Johnson
1813	Mr R Watt's Altisidora, by Dick Andrews	17	J Jackson
1814	Duke of Hamilton's William, by Governor	12	J Shepherd
1815	Sir W Maxwell's Filho da Puta, by Haphazard	15	J Jackson
1816	Sir B R Graham's The Duchess, by Cardinal York	13	B Smith
1817	Mr H Peirse's Ebor, by Orville	18	R Johnson
1818	Mr H Peirse's Reveller, by Comus	21	R Johnson
1819	Mr J Ferguson's Antonio, by Octavian	14	J Nicholson
1820	Sir E Smith's St Patrick, by Walton	27	R Johnson
1821	Mr T O Powlett's Jack Spigot, by Ardrossan	13	W Scott
1822	Mr E Petre's The Theodore, by Woful	23	T Jackson
1823	Mr R Watt's Barefoot, by Tramp	12	T Goodison
1824	Mr R Gascoigne's Jerry, by Smolensko	23	B Smith
1825	Mr R Watt's Memnon, by Whisker	30	W Scott
1826	Lord Scarborough's Tarrare, by Catton	27	G Nelson
1827	Mr E Petre's Matilda, by Comus	26	J Robinson
1828	Mr E Petre's The Colonel, by Whisker	19	W Scott
1829	Mr E Petre's Rowton, by Oiseau	19	W Scott
1830	Mr Beardsworth's Birmingham, by Filho da Puta	28	P Conolly
1831	Lord Cleveland's Chorister, by Lottery	26	J B Day
1832	Mr J Gully's Margrave, by Muley	17	J Robinson
1833	Mr R Watt's Rockingham, by Humphrey Clinker	20	S Darling
1834	Lord Westminster's Touchstone, by Camel	11	G Calloway
1835	Mr E Mostyn's Queen of Trumps, by Velocipede	11	T Lye
1836	Lord Lichfield's Elis, by Langar	14	J B Day
1837	Mr C Greville's Mango, by Emilius	13	S Day, jun.
1838	Lord Chesterfield's Don John, by Tramp or Waverley	7	W Scott
1839	Major Yarburgh's Charles XII, by Voltaire	24	W Scott
1840	Lord Westminster's Launcelot, by Camel	11	W Scott
1841	Lord Westminster's Satirist, by Pantaloon	11	W Scott
1842	Lord Eglinton's Blue Bonnet, by Touchstone	17	T Lye
1843	Mr S Wrather's Nutwith, by Tomboy	9	J Marson
1844	Mr E H Irwin's Faugh-a-Ballagh, by Sir Hercules	9	H Bell
1845	Mr G Watts's The Baron, by Irish Birdcatcher	15	F Butler
1846	Mr W Scott's Sir Tatton Sykes, by Melbourne	12	W Scott
1847	Lord Eglinton's Van Tromp, by Lanercost	8	J Marson
1848	Lord Clifden's Surplice, by Touchstone	9	E Flatman
1849	Lord Eglinton's The Flying Dutchman, by Bay Middleton	10	C Marlow
1850	Lord Zetland's Voltigeur, by Voltaire	8	J Marson
1851	Mr A Nichol's Newminster, by Touchstone	18	S Templeman
1852	Lord Exeter's Stockwell, by The Baron	6	J Norman
1853	Mr J Bowes's West Australian, by Melbourne	10	F Butler
1854	Mr J Morris's Knight of St George, by Irish Birdcatcher	18	R Basham
1855	Mr T Parr's Saucebox, by St Lawrence	12	J Wells
1856	Mr A Nichol's Warlock, by Irish Birdcatcher	9	E Flatman
1857	Mr J Scott's Imperieuse, by Orlando	11	E Flatman
1858	Mr J Merry's Sunbeam, by Chanticleer	18	L Snowden
1859	Sir C Monck's Gamester, by The Cossack	11	T Aldcroft
1860	Lord Ailesbury's St Albans, by Stockwell	15	L Snowden
1861	Mr W I'Anson's Caller Ou, by Stockwell	18	T Challoner
1862	Mr S Hawke's The Marquis, by Stockwell	15	T Challoner
1863	Lord St Vincent's Lord Clifden, by Newminster	19	J Osborne
1864	Mr W I'Anson's Blair Athol, by Stockwell	10	J Snowden
1865	Count de Lagrange's Gladiateur, by Monarque	14	H Grimshaw
1866	Mr R Sutton's Lord Lyon, by Stockwell	11	H Custance
1867	Colonel Pearson's Ahievement, by Stockwell	12	T Challoner
1868	Mr W Graham's Formosa, by Buccaneer	12	T Challoner
1869	Sir J Hawley's Pero Gomez, by Beadsman	11	J Wells
1870	Mr T V Morgan's Hawthornden, by Lord Clifden	19	J Grimshaw
1871	Baron de Rothschild's Hannah, by King Tom	10	C Maidment
1872	Lord Wilton's Wenlock, by Lord Clifden	17	C Maidment
1873	Mr J Merry's Marie Stuart, by Scottish Chief	8	T Osborne
1874	Mr Launde's Apology, by Adventurer	13	J Osborne
1875	Mr W S Crawford's Craig Millar, by Blair Athol	13	T Challoner
1876	Lord Dupplin's Petrarch, by Lord Clifden	9	J Goater
1877	Lord Falmouth's Silvio, by Blair Athol	14	F Archer
1878	Lord Falmouth's Jannette, by Lord Clifden	14	F Archer

COALITE ST. LEGER—continued

Year	Winner	Starters	Jockeys
1879	Count de Lagrange's Rayon d'Or, by Flageolet	17	J Goater
1880	Mr C Brewer's b c Robert the Devil, by Bertram	12	T Cannon
1881	Mr P Lorillard's br c Iroquois, by Leamington	15	F Archer
1882	Lord Falmouth's br f Dutch Oven, by Dutch Skater	14	F Archer
1883	Duke of Hamilton's b c Ossian, by Salvator	19	J Watts
1884	Mr R C Vyner's b c The Lambkin, by Camballo	13	J Watts
1885	Lord Hasting's b c Melton, by Master Kildare	10	F Archer
1886	Duke of Westminster's Ormonde, by Bend Or	7	F Archer
1887	Lord Rodney's Kilwarlin, by Arbitrator	9	W Robinson
1888	Lord Calthorpe's Seabreeze, by Isonomy	16	W Robinson
1889	Duke of Portland's b c Donovan, by Galopin	12	F Barrett
1890	Duke of Portland's br f Memoir, by St Simon	15	J Watts
1891	Sir F Johnstone's br c Common, by Isonomy	9	G Barrett
1892	Baron de Hirsch's br f La Fleche, by St Simon	11	J Watts
1893	Mr H McCalmont's b c Isinglass, by Isonomy	7	T Loates
1894	Lord Alington's b f Throstle, by Petrarch	8	M Cannon
1895	Lord Rosebery's b c Sir Visto, by Barcaldine	11	S Loates
1896	H R.H the Prince of Wales's Persimmon, by St Simon	7	J Watts
1897	Mr J Gubbins's b c Galtee More, by Kendal	15	C Wood
1898	Capt J Greer's ch c Wildfowler, by Gallinule	12	C Wood
1899	Duke of Westminster's b c Fling Fox, by Orme	16	M Cannon

1900 Prince of Wales's Diamond Jubilee, by St Simon ... H Jones 2–7
Mr W Lowe's Elopement ... M Cannon 100–7
Mr R Walker's Courlan ... J F Sloan 25–1
1 length, 2 lengths, 3m 9 1/5s. 11 ran, R Marsh

1901 Mr L de Rothschild's Doricles, by Florizel II ... K Cannon 40–1
Mr W C Whitney's Volodyovski ... L Reiff 5–6
Mr J Gubbins's Revenue ... H Jones 100–8
Neck, 3 lengths, 3m 8 2/5s. 13 ran, A Hayhoe

1902 Mr R S Sievier's Sceptre, by Persimmon ... F W Hardy 100–3
Col H McCalmont's Rising Glass ... W Halsey 9–1
D of Portland's Friar Tuck .. H Randall 7–1
3 lengths, 2 lengths, 3m 12 2/5s. 12 ran, Owner

1903 Sir J Miller's Rock Sand, by Sainfoin ... D Maher 2–5
Mr J Mustker's William Rufus ... O Madden 100–9
His Majesty's Mead ... M Cannon 7–1
4 lengths, 1/2 length, 3m 9 2/5s. 5 ran, G Blackwell

1904 Maj E Loder's Pretty Polly, by Gallinule ... W Lane 2–5
Mr J Musker's Henry the First ... O Madden 50–1
Ld Harewood's Almscliff ... D Maher 100–6
3 lengths, 6 lengths, 3m 5 4/5s. 6 ran, P P Gilpin

1905 Mr W M G Singer's Challacombe, by St Serf ... O Madden 100–6
Ld Crewe's Polymelus ... M Cannon 10–1
Ld Wavertree's Cherry Lass ... H Jones 4–6
3 lengths, same, 3m 5 2/5s. 8 ran, Alec Taylor

1906 D of Westminster's Troutbeck, by Ladas ... G Stern 5–1
Mr J B Joel's Prince William W Halsey 25–1
Mr J de Rothschild's Beppo .. W Higgs 100–9
Head, same, 3m 4 1/5s. 12 ran, W Waugh

1907 Col E W Baird's Wool Winder, by Martagon ... W Halsey 11–10
Maj E Loder's Baltinglass ... B Dillon 100–8
D of Devonshire's Acclaim ... W Higgs 8–1
6 lengths, 1/2 length, 3m 5 3/5s. 12 ran, H Enoch

1908 Mr J B Joel's Your Majesty, by Persimmon ... Walter Griggs 11–8
Mr W Hall Walker's White Eagle ... D Maher 100–7
Mr L de Rothschild's Santo Strato ... O Madden 100–6
1/2 length, 4 lengths, 3m 6s. 10 ran, C Morton

1909 Mr "Fairie's" Bayardo, by Bay Ronald ... D Maher 10–11
Ld Carnarvon's Valens ... F Wootton 100–8
Mr W Astor's Mirador ... B Dillon 40–1
1 1/2 lengths, 1/2 length, 3m 8 3/5s. 7 ran, Alec Taylor

1910 Ld Derby's Swynford, by John o'Gaunt ... F Wootton 9–2
Mr J de Rothschild's Bronzino ... F Fox 20–1
Mr "Fairie's" Lemberg ... D Maher 4–5
Head, 1 1/2 lengths, 3m 4s. 11 ran, Hon G Lambton

1911 Mr T Pilkington's Prince Palatine, by Persimmon ... F O'Neill 100–30
Mr J B Joel's Lycaon ... G Stern 100–30
Ld Derby's King William ... F Wootton 6–4
6 lengths, 3 lengths, 3m 6s. 8 ran, H Beardsley

1912 Mr A Belmont's Tracery, by Rock Sand ... G Bellhouse 8–1
Mr S Joel's Maiden Erlegh ... G Stern 100–8
Mr J Dugdale's Hector ... A Escott 10–1
5 lengths, 3/4 length, 3m 11 4/5s. 14 ran, J Watson

1913 Col W Hall Walker's Night Hawk, by Gallinule ... E Wheatley 50–1
Mr J B Joel's White Magic .. F Wootton 33–1
Sir B Sheffield's Seremond ... N Spear 33–1
2 lengths, 3 lengths, 3m 3 3/5s. 12 ran, W Robinson

1914 Mr J B Joel's Black Jester, by Polymelus ... Walter Griggs 10–1
Sir J Thursby's Kennymore ... F Templeman 7–2
Sir J Thursby's Cressingham ... H Jeliss 100–1
5 lengths, 3 lengths, 3m 2 3/5s. 18 ran, C Morton

1915*Mr S Joel's Pommern, by Polymelus ... S Donoghue 1–3
Mr L Neumann's Snow Marten ... Walter Griggs 9–1
Mr W M G Singer's Achtol ... C Trigg 25–1
2 lengths, 6 lengths, 2m 55 3/5s. 7 ran, C Peek

1916*Mr J Buchanan's Hurry On, by Marcovil ... C Childs 11–10
Ld Falmouth's Clarissimus ... F Bullock 5–2
Mr E Hulton's Atheling ... J Childs 4–1
3 lengths, 5 lengths, 2m 59 3/5s. 5 ran, F Darling

1917*Mr "Fairie's" Gay Crusader, by Bayardo ... S Donoghue 2–11
Col W Hall Walker's Kingston Black ... T Burns 33–1

Sir H Meux's Dansellon F Rickaby Jun 100–15
6 lengths, bad, 2m 59²/5s. 3 ran, Alec Taylor

1918*Lady James Douglas's Gainsborough by Bayardo .... J Childs 4–11
Mr A W Cox's My Dear S Donoghue 9–1
Mr W Cazalet's Prince Chimay .... O Madden 100–14
3 lengths, 4 lengths, 3m 4s. 5 ran, Alec Taylor

1919 Lord Derby's Keysoe, by Swynford .... B Carslake 100–8
Ld Glanely's Dominion ...... A Smith 7–1
Maj W Astor's Buchan .... J Childs 8–1
6 lengths, 2 lengths, 3m 6⁴/5s. 10 ran, G Lambton

1920 Mr M Goculdas's Caligula, by The Tetrarch .... A Smith 100–6
Sir E Hulton's Silvern ... F Templeman 8–1
Lady Jas Douglas's Manton ..... F Lane 33–1
1/2 length, 3 lengths, 3m 7²/5s. 14 ran, H Leader

1921 Lord Londonderry's Polemarch, by The Tetrarch .... J Childs 50–1
Ld Carnarvon's Franklin .... E Gardner 100–6
Ld Glanely's Westward Ho B Carslake 8–1
1 1/2 lengths, 3 lengths, 3m 6⁴/5s. 9 ran, T Green

1922 Lord Lonsdale's Royal Lancer, by Spearmint .... R A Jones 33–1
Ld Derby's Silurian .... E Gardner 100–8
Sir Abe Bailey's Ceylonese .. F Bullock 25–1
2 lengths, same, 3m 14¹/5s. 24 ran, A D Sadler, jun

1923 Lord Derby's Tranquil, by Swynford .... T Weston 100–9
Mr B Irish's Papyrus ..... S Donoghue 15–8
H H Aga Khan's Teresina ... G Hulme 100–7
2 lengths, 1 1/2 lengths, 3m 5s. 13 ran, C Morton

1924 H H Aga Khan's Salmon-Trout, by The Tetrarch .... B Carslake 6–1
Mr Barclay Walker's Santorb G Hulme 40–1
Mr S Joel's Polyphontes W McLachlan 100–30
2 lengths, 1/2 length, 3m 13¹/5s. 17 ran, R C Dawson

1925 Sir J Rutherford's Solario, by Gainsborough .... J Childs 7–2
H H Aga Khan's Zambo ... B Carslake 6–1
Ld Lonsdale's Warden of the Marches .... W Wells 18–1
3 lengths, same, 3m 4³/5s. 15 ran, R Day

1926 Ld Woolavington's Coronach, by Hurry On .... J Childs 8–15
Ld Derby's Caissot .... B Carslake 100–9
Mr S Tattersall's Foliation ... J Brennan 100–7
2 lengths, 6 lengths, 3m 1³/5s. 12 ran, F Darling

1927 Ld Astor's Book Law, by Buchan .... H Jelliss 7–4
Sir Victor Sassoon's Hot Night .... H Wragg 4–1
Sir A Bailey's Son and Heir B Carslake 25–1
3 lengths, 5 lengths, 3m 14²/5s. 16 ran, Alec Taylor

1928 Ld Derby's Fairway, by Phalaris .... T Weston 7–4
M J Wittouk's Palais Royal II .... M Allemand 100–6
Maj J Courtauld's Cyclonic .. R A Jones 100–15
1 1/2 lengths, 1 length, 3m 3s. 13 ran, Frank Butters

1929 Mr W Barnett's Trigo, by Blandford .... M Beary 5–1
Ld Derby's Bosworth .... T Weston 9–1
Sir L Philipps's Horus ..... E C Elliott 25–1
Short head, 3/4 length, 3m 3²/5s. 14 ran, R C Dawson

1930 Ld Glanely's Singapore, by Gainsborough .... G Richards 4–1
Ld Woolavington's Parenthesis .. F Fox 4–1
H H Aga Khan's Rustom Pasha .... H Wragg 20–1
1 1/2 lengths, 3/4 length, 3m 9¹/5s. 13 ran, T Hogg

1931 Ld Rosebery's Sandwich, by Sansovino .... H Wragg 9–1
Sir J Rutherford's Orpen ...... J Childs 11–2
Mr W Woodward's Sir Andrew .... P Beasley 20–1
4 lengths, 1 length, 3m 11¹/5s. 10 ran, J L Jarvis

1932 H H Aga Khan's Firdaussi, by Pharos .... F Fox 20–1
H H Aga Khan's Dastur ..... M Beary 6–1
Mr C Rich's Silvermere .... R Dick 33–1
Neck, 4 lengths, 3m 4²/5s. 19 ran, Frank Butters

1933 Ld Derby's Hyperion, by Gainsborough .... T Weston 6–4
H H Aga Khan's Felicitation .. M Beary 22–1
Ld Durham's Scarlet Tiger W Carslake 100–8
3 lengths, neck, 3m 6⁴/5s. 14 ran, Hon G Lambton

1934 Mr M H Benson's Windsor Lad, by Blandford................ C Smirke 4–9
Sir Abe Bailey's Tiberius R A Richards 20–1
Mr J A Dewar's Lo Zingaro G Richards 100–9
2 lengths, same, 3m 1³/5s. 10 ran, M Marsh

1935 H H Aga Khan's Bahram, by Blandford C Smirke 4–11
Sir M McAlpine's Solar Ray .... J Sirett 100–6
Ld Glanely's Buckleigh ...... H Wragg 25–1
5 lengths, 3 lengths, 3m 1⁴/5s. 8 ran, Frank Butters

1936 Mr W Woodward's Boswell, by Bosworth .... P Beasley 20–1
Mr A G Smith's Fearless Fox .. E Smith 100–6
H H Aga Khan's Mahmoud C Smirke 5–1
3/4 lengths, 3m 8¹/5s. 13 ran, C Boyd-Rochfort

1937 Ld Glanely's Chulmleigh, by Singapore .... G Richards 18–1
Ld Derby's Fair Copy .... R Perryman 6–1
Mrs G B Miller's Mid-day Sun .... M Beary 3–1
1/2 length, 3/4 length, 3m 7¹/5s. 15 ran, T Hogg

1938 Mr James V Rank's Scottish Union, by Cameronian .... B Carslake 7–1
Sir L Philipps's Challenge ..... E Smith 100–8
Mr H E Morriss's Pasch ... G Richards 6–5
Neck, 4 lengths, 3m 11²/5s. 9 ran, N Cannon

1939 Abandoned owing to outbreak of War

1940†H H Aga Khan's Turkhan, by Bahram .... G Richards 4–1
H H Aga Khan's Stardust .... H Wragg 9–4
Ld Rosebery's Hippius .... E Smith 4–1
3/4 length, same, 3m 32²/5s. 6 ran, Frank Butters

1941‡Ld Portal's Sun Castle, by Hyperion .... G Bridgland 10–1
Mr H E Morris's Chateau Larose .... R A Jones 11–2
Ld Glanely's Dancing Time .. M Beary 25–1
head, 1 length, 3m 4²/5s. 16 ran, C Boyd-Rochfort

1942*His Majesty's Sun Chariot, by Hyperion .... G Richards 9–4
Ld Derby's Watling Street ... H Wragg 2–1
Ld Rosebery's Hyperides ..... E Smith 9–2
3 lengths, 5 lengths, 3m 8¹/5s. 18 ran, F Darling

1943*Lord Derby's Herringbone, by King Salmon .... H Wragg 100–6
Lord Rosebery's Ribbon ...... E Smith 10–1
Miss D Paget's Straight Deal .. T Carey 100–30
Short head, 3/4 length, 3m 5⁴/5s. 12 ran, W Earl

1944*H H Aga Khan's Tehran, by Bois Roussel .... G Richards 9–2
Ld Derby's Borealis .... H Wragg 11–2
Ld Rosebery's Ocean Swell ... E Smith 11–2
1 1/2 lengths, 1 length, 3m 6¹/5s. 17 ran, Frank Butters

1945 Sq-Ldr S Joel's Chamossaire, by Precipitation .... T Lowrey 11–2
His Majesty's Rising Light .... D Smith 9–2
Mr A E Saunders's Stirling Castle .... H Wragg 7–1
2 lengths, 3/4 length, 2m 56³/5s. 10 ran, R Perryman

1946 Mr J E Ferguson's Airborne, by Precipitation .... T Lowrey 3–1
Mr S Joel's Murren .... T Weston 40–1

Ld Astor's Fast and Fair .... G Richards 100–9
1½ lengths, 3 lengths, 3m 10s. 11 ran, R Perryman
1947 H H Maharaja of Baroda's Sayajirao, by Nearco .... E Britt 9–2
M M Boussac's Arbar ..... E C Elliott 5–1
H H Aga Khan's Migoli ... G Richards 9–4
Head, 3 lengths, 3m 7⅘s. 11 ran, F Armstrong
1948 Mr W Woodward's Black Tarquin, by Rhodes Scholar .... E Britt 15–2
Ld Derby's Alycidon .... D Smith 20–1
Mr J McGrath's Solar Slipper E Smith 13–2
1½ lengths, 5 lengths, 3m 8⅗s. 14 ran, C Boyd-Rochfort
1949 Mr G R H Smith's Ridge Wood, by Bois Roussel .... M Beary 100–7
H H Aga Khan's Dust Devil .... W Johnstone 40–1
Mr W Woodward's Lone Eagle .... W H Carr 6–1
2 lengths, ¾ length, 3m 8⅕s. 16 ran, C F N Murless
1950 M M Boussac's Scratch II, by Pharis .... W Johnstone 9–2
Baron G de Rothschild's Vieux Manoir .... J Laumain 7–4
Ld Howard de Walden's Sanlinea .... E Smith 33–1
1 length, 5 lengths, 3m 8⅘s. 15 ran, C H Semblat, in France
1951 M M Boussac's Talma II, by Pharis .... W Johnstone 7–1
H H Begum Aga Khan's Fraise du Bois II .... C Smirke 15–2
M P Bartholomew's Medway D Smith 40–1
10 lengths, 4 lengths, 3m 13⅘s. 18 ran, C H Semblat, in France
1952 H H Aga Khan's Tulyar, by Tehran .... C Smirke 10–11
Mrs L W Smith's Kingsfold ... E Smith 66–1
M M Boussac's Alcinus .... E C Elliott 100–6
3 lengths, 4 lengths, 3m 7⅘s. 12 ran, M Marsh
1953 Brigadier W P Wyatt's Premonition, by Precipitation .... E Smith 10–1
M F Dupre's Northern Light .... G Lequeux 5–2
Her Majesty's Aureole ...... W H Carr 5–4
3 lengths, same, 3m 6⅘s. 11 ran, C Boyd-Rochfort
1954 Mr R S Clark's Never Say Die, by Nasrullah .... C Smirke 100–30
Sir Victor Sassoon's Elopement .... W Nevett 22–1
M M Boussac's Estremadur .. E Mercer 100–6
12 lengths, 4 lengths, 3m 10⅗s. 16 ran, J Lawson
1955 Lady Zia Wernher's Meld, by Alycidon .... W H Carr 10–11
Miss D Paget's Nucleus ..... L Piggott 9–1
M G Wildenstein's Beau Prince .... S Boullenger 4–1
¾ length, 3 lengths, 3m 14⅗s. 8 ran, C Boyd-Rochfort
1956 Mr R B Strassburger's Cambremer, by Chamossaire .... F Palmer 8–1
Ld Astor's Hornbeam .... J Mercer 5–1
Mr R F Dennis's French Beige .... G Littlewood 100–8
¾ length, 1½ lengths, 3m 12⅕s. 13 ran, G Bridgland, in France
1957 Mr J McShain's Ballymoss by Mossborough .... T P Burns 8–1
Mr J R Mullion's Court Harwell .... A Beasley 100–8
Mr W Humble's Brioche ...... E Hide 6–1
1 length, ¾ length, 3m 15⅗s. 16 ran, M V O'Brien, in Ireland
1958 Sir H de Trafford's Alcide, by Alycidon .... W H Carr 4–9
Maj L B Holliday's None Nicer .... S Clayton 10–1
Mr Arpad Plesch's Nagami ... J Mercer 100–8
8 lengths, ¾ length, 3m 6⅖s. 8 ran, C Boyd-Rochfort
1959 Mr William Hill's Cantelo, by Chanteur II .... E Hide 100–7
Mr G A Oldham's Fidalgo ... J Mercer 8–1
Her Majesty's Pindari .... L Piggott 100–6
1½ lengths, 3 lengths, 3m 4⅗s. 11 ran, C J Elsey
1960 Sir Victor Sassoon's St Paddy, by Aureole .... L Piggott 4–6
Mr J McShain's Die Hard G Bougoure 8–1
Sir W Churchill's Vielle .... T Godling 20–1
3 lengths, 1½ lengths, 3m 13⅕s. 9 ran, C F N Murless
1961 Mrs V Lilley's Aurelius, by Aureole .... L Piggott 9–2
Mrs H Leggat's Bounteous ..... J Sime 33–1
Mme L Volterra's Dicta Drake .... M Garcia 6–4
¾ length, same, 3m 6⅗s. 13 ran, C F N Murless
1962 Maj L B Holliday's Hethersett, by Hugh Lupus .... W H Carr 100–8
Mr H Bousher's Monterrico A Beasley 8–1
Mr G Oldham's Miralgo W Williamson 9–1
4 lengths, 1 length, 3m 10⅘s. 15 ran, W Hern
1963 Mr J R Mullion's Ragusa, by Ribot .... G Bougoure 2–5
Maj H R Broughton's Star Moss .... E Smith 8–1
Ld Rosebery's Fighting Ship ... S Smith 28–1
6 lengths, short head, 3m 5⅘s. 7 ran, P Prendergast, in Ireland
1964 Mr C W Engelhard's Indiana, by Sayajirao .... J Lindley 100–7
Lady Granard's Patti .... W Williamson 100–8
Mr L L Lawrence's Soderini .. G Lewis 45–1
Head, 4 lengths, 3m 5s. 15 ran, J F Watts
1965 Mr J J Astor's Provoke, by Aureole .... J Mercer 28–1
Mr G M Bell's Meadow Court .... L Piggott 4–11
Mr C W Engelhard's Solstice .. E Eldin 100–6
10 lengths, 5 lengths, 3m 18⅗s. 11 ran, W Hern
1966 Mr R J Sigtia's Sodium, by Psidium .... F Durr 7–1
Lady Zia Wernher's Charlottown .... J Lindley 11–10
Mr J Fisher's David Jack ..... L Piggott 10–1
Head, 1½ lengths, 3m 9⅘s. 9 ran, G Todd
1967 Mr C W Engelhard's Ribocco by Ribot .... L Piggott 7–2
The Queen's Hopeful Venture G Moore 7–2
Marchese Incisa della Rocchetta's Ruysdael II .... C Ferrari 13–2
1½ lengths, ½ length, 3m 5⅖s. 9 ran, R Johnson Houghton
1968 Mr C W Engelhard's Ribero by Ribot .... L Piggott 100–30
Mr J M Olin's Canterbury .... W Williamson 100–8
Mr C Hetherton's Cold Storage .... H J Greenaway 66–1
Short head, 6 lengths, 3m 19⅘s. 8 ran, R Johnson Houghton
1969 Mr G A Oldham's Intermezzo by Hornbeam .... R Hutchinson 7–1
Mr C W Engelhard's Ribofilio .... L Piggott 11–10
Mr H J Joel's Prince Consort A Barclay 20–1
1½ lengths, 2 lengths, 3m 11⅘s. 11 ran, H Wragg
1970 Mr C W Engelhard's Nijinsky (Can) by Northern Dancer .... L Piggott 2–7
Mr D Robinson's Meadowville .... J Seagrove 20–1
Mrs O Phipps's Politico (USA) .... A Barclay 20–1
1 length, ½ length, 3m 6⅖s. 9 ran, M V O'Brien, in Ireland
1971 Mrs J Rogerson's Athens Wood by Celtic Ash .... L Piggott 5–2
Mr M Sobell's Homeric ...... J Mercer 10–1

Lord Howard de Walden's Falkland .... G Starkey 14–1
Head, neck, 3m 15s. 8 ran, H Thomson Jones
1972 Mr O Phipps's Boucher (USA) by Ribot .... L Piggott 3–1
Mr N Cohen's Our Mirage .. J Lindley 5–1
Mr C A B St George's Ginevra .... A Murray 9–2
1/2 length, 4 lengths, 3m 28 4/5s. 7 ran, M V O'Brien, in Ireland
1973 Col W Behren's Peleid by Derring-Do .... F Durr 28–1
Mr R D Hollingsworth's Buoy .... J Mercer 11–2
Lord Rosebery's Duke of Ragusa .... J Gorton 6–1
2 1/2 lengths, neck, 3m 8 1/5s. 13 ran, W Elsey
1974 Lady Beaverbrook's Bustino, by Busted .... J Mercer 11–10
Mr C A B St George's Giacometti .... L Piggott 11–2
Lady Beaverbrook's Ribbon .. J Lindley 100–1
3 lengths, 4 lengths, 3m 9s. 10 ran, W Hern
1975 Mr C A B St George's Bruni by Sea Hawk II .... A Murray 9–1
Mr J A Mulcahy's King Pellinore (USA) .... L Piggott 2–1
Mrs J Roger's Libra's Rib (USA) .... W Carson 33–1
10 lengths, 1 1/2 lengths, 3m 5 2/5s. 12 ran, H R Price
1976 Mr D Wildenstein's Crow, by Exbury .... Y Saint-Martin 6–1
M J Lagardere's Secret Man (Fr) .... P Paquet 15–2
Mr B Hobb's Scallywag ...... G Lewis 20–1
2 lengths, neck, 3m 13 2/5s. 15 ran, A Penna, in France
1977 Her Majesty's Dunfermline, by Royal Palace .... W Carson 10–1
Mr Fluor's Alleged (USA) ... L Piggott 4–7
Col F Hue-Williams's Classic Example .... Pat Eddery 16–1
1 1/2 lengths, 10 lengths, 3m 5 1/5s. 13 ran, W Hern
1978 Capt M Lemos's Julio Mariner, by Blakeney .... E Hide 28–1
Sig C d'Alessio's Le Moss .... J Mercer 9–1
Essa Alkhalifa's M-Lolshan ... B Taylor 28–1
1 1/2 lengths, head, 3m 5s. 14 ran, C Brittain
1979 Mr A Rolland's Son of Love, by Jefferson .... A Lequeux 20–1
Baron G de Rothschild's Soleil Noir .... Y Saint-Martin 13–1
Lady Beaverbrook's Niniski (USA) .... W Carson 4–1
Short head, 2 1/2 lengths, 3m 9s. 17 ran, R Collett, in France
1980 Mr H J Joel's Light Cavalry, by Brigadier Gerard .... J Mercer 3–1
Lord Rotherwick's Water Mill .... W Carson 11–8
Sig C d'Alessio's World Leader R Guest 25–1
4 lengths, same, 3m 11 2/5s. 7 ran, H Cecil
1981 Sir J Astor's Cut Above, by High Top .... J Mercer 28–1
Mr P Mellon's Glint of Gold J Matthias 4–1
Lady Beaverbrook's Bustomi L Piggott 13–2
2 1/2 lengths, 4 lengths, 3m 11 3/5s. 7 ran, W Hern
1982 Maktoum Al Maktoum's Touching Wood by Roberto (USA) ... P Cook 7–1
Mrs H G Cambanis's Zilos ... G Baxter 40–1
Mr P Mellon's Diamond Shoal .... J Matthias 9–1
1 1/2 lengths, 2 1/2 lengths, 3m 3 3/5s. 15 ran, H Thomson Jones

1983 Sir M Sobell's Sun Princess by English Prince .... W Carson 11–8
Mr R Scully's Esprit Du Nord (USA) .... G More 11–1
Sheikh Mohammed's Carlingford Castle L Piggott 9–2
3/4 length, short head, 3m 16 3/5s. 10 ran, W Hern
1984 Mr I Allan's Commanche Run by Run the Gantlet .... L Piggott 7–4
H H Aga Khan's Baynoun .. S Cauthen 5–2
Mr K Abdulla's Alphabatim G Starkey 7–1
Neck, 1 1/2 lengths, 3m 10s. 11 ran, L Cumani
1985 Sheikh Mohammed's Oh So Sharp by Kris .... S Cauthen 8–11
Mr S Kamel's Phardante (Fr) G Starkey 18–1
Mr C A B St George's Lanfranco .... L Piggott 85–40
3/4 length, head, 3m 7 1/5s. 6 ran, H Cecil
1986 Lavinia, Duchess of Norfolk's Moon Madness by Vitiges ...... Pat Eddery 9–2
Mr Richard L Duchossois's Celestial Storm (USA) .... S Cauthen 6–1
Sheikh Mohammed's Untold .... W R Swinburn 5–2
4 lengths, 2 lengths, 3m 5s. 8 ran, J Dunlop
1987 Mr L Freedman's Reference Point by Mill Reef .... S Cauthen 4–11
Pin Oak Stable's Mountain Kingdom (USA) .... Pat Eddery 9–1
Mr R D Hollingsworth's Dry Dock .... W Carson 11–1
1 1/2 lengths, 8 lengths, 3m 6s. 7 ran, H Cecil
1988 Lady Beaverbrook's Minster Son by Niniski .... W Carson 15–2
Sheikh Mohammed's Diminuendo (USA) .... W R Swinburn 4–7
Duchess of Norfolk's Sheriff's Star .... T Ives 7–2
1 length, 8 lengths, 3m 6 4/5s. 6 ran, N Graham
1989 Mr C A B St George's Michelozzo by Northern Baby .... S Cauthen 6–4
Marquesa de Moratalla's Sapience .... K Fallon 15–1
Lord Carnarvon's Roseate Tern .... W Carson 5–2
8 lengths, 1/2 length, 3m 20 4/5s. 8 ran, H Cecil
1990 Mr M Arbib's Snurge by Ela-Mana-Mou ....T. Quinn 7–2
Lord Weinstock's Hellenic ... W Carson 2–1
Sheikh Mohammed's River God .....S. Cauthen 100–30
3/4 length, 4 lengths, 3m 8 4/5s. 8 ran, P. Cole
1991 Mr K Abdulla's Toulon by Top Ville ....P Eddery 5–2
Lord Weinstock's Saddlers' Hall ..J Reid 13–2
Mr C A B St George's Micheletti (USA) .... L Piggott 6–1
1 1/2 lengths, 15 lengths, 3m 3 1/5s. 10 ran, A Fabre, in France
1992 Mr W J Gredley's User Friendly by Slip Anchor.................. G Duffield 7–4
Sheikh Mohammed's Sonus.. S Cauthen 15–2
Lord Weinstock's Bonny Scot L Dettori 5–2
3 1/2 lengths, neck, 3m 5 3/5s. 7 ran, C. Brittain
1993 Mrs G A E Smith's Bob's Return by Bob Back (USA)............ P Robinson 3–1
Mr K Abdulla's Armiger......P Eddery 4–1
Sheikh Essa Bin Mubarak's Edbaysaan .... W Ryan 25–1
3 1/2 lengths, 1 1/2 lengths, 3m 7 4/5. 9 ran, M H Tompkins

* Run at Newcastle †Run at Thirsk ‡Run at Manchester Run at York 1945 Run at Ayr 1989

ROKEBY FARMS MILL REEF STAKES (Newbury)

(6 fur 8 yds)
For two year olds

1972 Mon Fils 8st 11lb (4)
1973 Habat 9st 4lb (6)
1974 Red Cross 8st 11lb (8)
1975 Royal Boy 8st 11lb (8)
1976 Anax 8st 11lb (6)
1977 Formidable (USA) 8st 11lb (6)
1978 King of Spain 8st 11lb (8)
1979 Lord Seymour 8st 11lb (7)
1980 Sweet Monday 8st 11lb (7)
1981 Hays 8st 11lb (8)
1982 Salieri (USA) 8st 11lb (5)
1983 Vacarme (USA) 8st 11lb (7)
1984 Local Suitor (USA) 8st 11lb (12)
1985 Luqman 8st 11lb (9)
1986 Forest Flower 8st 8lb (9)
1987 Magic of Life (USA) 8st 6lb (5)
1988 Russian Bond (USA) 8st 11lb (4)
1989 Welney 8st 11lb (7)
1990 Time Gentlemen 8st 11lb (7)
1991 Showbrook 9st 1lb (5)
1992 Forest Wind (USA) 8st 11lb (7)
1993 Polish Laughter (USA) 8st 11lb (5)

TOTE AUTUMN CUP (Newbury)

(1 mile 5 fur 61 yds)

1960 The White Knight 3y 7st 11lb (7)
1961 The Page 7y 7st 13lb (9)
1962 Maya 4y 6st 9lb (11)
1963 Bridge of Earn 3y 7st (9)
1964 Admiral Togo III 6y 7st 6lb (9)
1965 Royal Realm 6y 8st 8lb (12)
1966 Balscadden 5y 8st 2lb (7)
1967 Balscadden 6y 8st 7lb (12)
1968–1915 No race
1916 Aboukir 5y 7st 11lb (12)
1917–1918 No race
1919 Silver Bridge 4y 7st 4lb (8)
1920 Aris 5y 7st 7lb (6)
1921 Yutoi 4y 8st 2lb (12)
1922 Norseman 3y 7st 5lb (9)
1923 Ceinturon 5y 8st 7lb (14)
1924 Diapason 3y 6st 12lb (11)
1925 Seradella 3y 6st 9lb (11)
1926 Try Try Again 4y 6st 12lb (8)
1927 Lightning Artist 4y 7st 8lb (12)
1928 Troubadour 3y 7st (8)
1929★Old Orkney 5y 9st
★Show Girl 3y 6st 4lb (9)
1930 Brumeux 5y 7st 13lb (13)
1931 Sandals 4y 7st 3lb (15)
1932 Roi de Paris 4y 7st 9lb (13)
1933 Loosestrife 4y 7st 9lb (13)
1934 Enfield 3y 7st 5lb (16)
1935 Cecil 4y 9st (20)
1936 Coup de Roi 4y 7st 10lb (14)
1937★Dytchley 4y 8st 9lb
★Severino 4y 8st 2lb (19)
1938 Pylon II 5y 8st 3lb (12)
1939–40 No race
1941 Germanicus 5y 8st 5lb (9)
1942–1951 No race
1952 Absolve 4y 8st 8lb (15)
1953 Flighty Frances 5y 8st 10lb (15)
1954 Lepidoptic 4y 9st 7lb (12)
1955 Dragon Fly 4y 7st (11)
1956 Straight Lad 6y 8st 2lb (12)
1957 Maelsheachlainn 4y 9st (10)
1958 No race
1959 Red Dragon 4y 9st 3lb (13)
1960 Tarquinian 5y 7st 9lb (6)
1961 Optimistic 4y 7st 6lb (11)
1962 Rainstorm 5y 7st 6lb (10)
1963 Acrophel 4y 8st 9lb (11)
1964 Ruantallan 3y 8st 5lb (14)
1965 Abletai 7y 8st 4lb (13)
1966 Salvo 3y 7st 4lb (14)
1967 Major Rose 5y 7st 6lb (12)
1968 No race
1969 Knotty Pine 3y 8st 4lb (11)
1970 Golden Love 3y 7st 9lb (16)
1971 Fidel 3y 7st 7lb (9)
1972 Danton 3y 7st 8lb (13)
1973 Sunyboy 3y 7st 13lb (11)
1974 Inventory 6y 8st 8lb (12)
1975 Coed Cochion 3y 8st 2lb (15)
1976 John Cherry (USA) 5y 9st 6lb (4)
1977 Nearly A Hand 3y 8st 4lb (12)
1978 Piccadilly Line 5y 8st 12lb (8)
1979 Greatham House 3y 9st 1lb (13)
1980 Castle Keep 3y 9st 1lb (10)
1981 Telsmoss 5y 8st 4lb (10)
1982 Fitzpatrick 3y 8st 6lb (14)
1983 Jupiter Island 4y 9st 8lb (16)
1984 First Bout 3y 7st 7lb (13)
1985 Eastern Mystic 3y 9st 4lb (16)
1986 Broken Wave 3y 8st 3lb (13)
1987 Aim to Please 3y 8st 2lb (14)
1988 Green Adventure (USA) 3y 9st 10lb (17)
1989 Braashee 3y 9st 5lb (16)
1990 First Victory 4y 9st 6lb (12)
1991 Talos 3y 8st 8lb (14)
1992 Castoret 6y 7st 13lb (18)
1993 Castoret 7y 9st 12lb (20)

★Dead-heat

From 1906 to 1941 run over 2 m 1 fur 1952 to 1978 run over 2 m

LADBROKES AYR GOLD CUP

(6 fur)
(First run 1804)

1935 Grenore 6y 9st 3lb (14)
1936 Marmaduke Jinks 4y 6st 13lb (15)
1937 Daytona 4y 9st (19)
1938 Old Reliance 3y 9st 2lb (13)
1939–45 No race
1946 Royal Charger 4y 9st 7lb (19)
1947 Kilbelin 4y 7st 13lb (12)
1948 Como 6y 8st 9lb (9)
1949 Irish Dance 6y 9st 1lb (16)
1950 First Consul 4y 9st 7lb (17)
1951 Fair Seller 5y 9st 4lb (15)
1952 Vatellus 4y 8st 7lb (13)
1953 Blue Butterfly 4y 8st 9lb (16)
1954 Orthopaedic 3y 8st 1lb (18)
1955 Hook Money 4y 7st 11lb (10)
1956 Precious Heather 4y 7st 7lb (16)
1957 Jacintha 6y 7st 7lb (17)
1958 Rhythmic 3y 8st 5lb (22)
1959 Whistling Victor 3y 7st 8lb (16)
1960 Dawn Watch 5y 7st 2lb (23)
1961 Klondyke Bill 3y 8st 7lb (17)
1962 Janeat 3y 7st 11lb (25)
1963 Egualita 3y 8st (18)
1964 Compensation 5y 8st 10lb (18)
1965 Kamundu 3y 8st 1lb (20)
1966 Milesius 4y 7st 12lb (24)
1967 Be Friendly 3y 8st 9lb (33)
1968 Petite Path 4y 7st 6lb (21)
1969 Brief Star 3y 7st (23)
1970 John Splendid 3y 8st 10lb (19)
1971 Royben 3y 8st 7lb (28)
1972 Swinging Junior 5y 8st 11lb (20)
1973 Blue Cashmere 3y 8st 2lb (19)
1974 Somersway 4y 7st 12lb (23)
1975 Roman Warrior 4y 10lb (23)
1976 Last Tango 5y 7st 5lb (18)
1977 Jon George 3y 8st 4lb (25)
1978 Vaigly Great 3y 9st 6lb (24)
1979 Primula Boy 4y 7st 7lb (22)
1980 Sparkling Boy 3y 9st 2lb (24)
1981 First Movement 3y 7st 10lb (21)
1982 Famous Star 3y 7st 7lb (14)
1983 Polly's Brother 4y 8st 3lb (28)
1984 Able Albert 4y 8st 6lb (29)
1985 Camps Heath 4y 7st 9lb (25)
1986 Green Ruby (USA) 5y 8st 11lb (29)
1987 Not So Silly 3y 7st 10lb (29)
1988 So Careful 5y 7st 7lb (29)
1989 Joveworth 6y 8st 5lb (29)
1990 Final Shot 3y 8st 2lb (29)
1991 Sarcita 3y 8st 10lb (28)
1992 Lochsong 4y 9st (28)
1993 Hard To Figure 7y 9st 6lb (29)

QUEEN ELIZABETH II STAKES (Ascot)

(1 mile)

1955 Hafiz II 3y 8st 4lb (8)
1956 Cigalon 3y 8st 1lb (11)
1957 Midget II 4y 8st 8lb (7)
1958 Major Portion 3y 8st 4lb (4)
1959 Rosalba 3y 8st 2lb (6)
1960★Sovereign Path 4y 8st 11lb (4)
1961 Le levanstell 4y 8st 11lb (6)
1962 Romulus 3y 8st 4lb (7)
1963★The Creditor 3y 8st 4lb (9)
1964 Linacre 4y 8st 11lb (5)
1965 Derring-Do 4y 8st 11lb (6)
1966 Hill Rise 5y 9st 1lb (6)
1967 Reform 3y 8st 8lb (4)
1968 World Cup 3y 8st 4lb (5)
1969 Jimmy Reppin 4y 9st 1lb (6)
1970 Welsh Pageant 4y 9st 11bn (5)
1971 Brigadier Gerard 3y 8st 8lb (3)
1972 Brigadier Gerard 4y 9st 7lb (4)
1973 Jan Ekels 4y 9st (5)
1974 No race
1975 Rose Bowl (USA) 3y 8st 4lb (5)
1976 Rose Bowl (USA) 4y 9st 4lb (8)
1977 Trusted 4y 9st (7)
1978 Homing 3y 8st 7lb (11)
1979 Kris 3y 9st (7)
1980 Known Fact (USA) 3y 9st (7)
1981 To-Agori-Mou 3y 9st (6)
1982 Buzzards Bay 4y 9st (10)
1983 Sackford (USA) 3y 8st 7lb (9)
1984 Teleprompter 4y 9st (6)

1985 Shadeed (USA) 3y 8st 11lb (7)
1986 Sure Blade (USA) 3y 8st 11lb (7)
1987 Milligram 3y 8st 8lb (5)
1988 Warning 3y 8st 11lb (8)
1989 Zilzal (USA) 3y 8st 11lb (5)
1990 Markofdistinction 4y 9st 4lb (10)
1991 Selkirk (USA) 3y 9st (9)
1992 Lahib (USA) 4y 9st 4lb (9)
1993 Bigstone 3y 9st (9)

*Run at Newbury

DIADEM STAKES (Ascot)

(6 fur)
1946 The Bug 3y 9st 2lb (4)
1947 Djelal 3y 8st 11lb (6)
1948 Combined Operations 6y 8st 9lb (3)
1949 Sokonaway 3y 9st 2lb (3)
1950 Abadan 3y 8st 11lb (3)
1951 Ki Ming 3y 9st 2lb (2)
1952 Set Fair 3y 8st 11lb (4)
1953 Rose Coral 3y 8st 8lb (6)
1954 Set Fair 5y 9st 2lb (5)
1955 Pappa Fourway 3y 8st 11lb (2)
1956†King Bruce 5y 9st 7lb (4)
1957 Arcandy 4y 9st 7lb (4)
1958 Jack & Jill 3y 8st 11lb (5)
1959 Jack & Jill 4y 9st 2lb (7)
1960†Zanzibar 5y 9st 2lb (3)
1961 Satan 3y 8st 4lb (5)
1962 La Belle 3y 8st 8lb (13)
1963†Sammy Davis 3y 8st 11lb (6)
1964 Ampney Princess 4y 8st 13lb (13)
1965 Majority Blue 4y 9st 2lb (12)
1966 Lucasland 4y 9st 4lb (13)
1967 Great Bear 3y 9st 2lb (8)
1968 Secret Ray 4y 9st 4lb (4)
1969 Song 3y 9st 2lb (6)
1970 Realm 3y 9st 2lb (4)
1971 Abergwaun 3y 8st 13lb (7)
1972 Home Guard (USA) 3y 9st 2lb (8)
1973 Boldboy 3y 9st 2lb (5)
1974 Saritamer (USA) 3y 9st 2lb (5)
1975 Roman Warrior 4y 9st 7lb (8)
1976 Honeyblest 4y 9st 7lb (7)
1977 Gentilhombre 4y 9st 7lb (6)
1978 Creetown 6y 9st 7lb (14)
1979 Absalom 4y 9st 7lb (6)
1980 Sovereign Rose 3y 9st (9)
1981 Moorestyle 4y 9st 7lb (10)
1982 Indian King (USA) 4y 9st 7lb (12)
1983 Salieri (USA) 3y 9st 3lb (12)
1984 Never So Bold 4y 9st 7lb (9)
1985 Al Sylah 3y 8st 9lb (8)
1986 Hallgate 3y 8st 12lb (12)
1987 Dowsing (USA) 3y 8st 12lb (7)
1988 Cadeaux Genereux 3y 8st 12lb (13)
1989 Chummy's Favourite 4y 9st 2lb (11)
1990 Ron's Victory (USA) 3y 8st 11lb (14)
1991 Shalford 3y 8st 11lb (16)
1992 Wolfhound (USA) 3y 8st 11lb (11)
1993 Catrail (USA) 3y 8st 11lb (9)

†Run at Kempton

ROYAL LODGE STAKES (Ascot)

(1 mile)
For two year olds
1946*Royal Barge 9st 4lb (4)
1947*Black Tarquin 8st 2lb (5)
1948 Swallow Tail 9st (8)
1949 Tabriz 9st (5)
1950 Fraise du Bois II 9st (5)
1951 Khor-Mousa 9st (5)
1952 Neemah 8st 11lb (4)
1953 Infatuation 9st (9)
1954 Solarium 9st (12)
1955 Royal Splendour 9st (4)
1956 Noble Venture 9st (10)
1957 Pinched 9st (6)
1958 Cantelo 8st 11lb (7)
1959 St. Paddy 9st (5)
1960†Bea 8st 11lb (10)
1961 Escort 9st (12)
1962 Star Moss 9st (9)
1963†Casablanca 9st (12)
1964 Prominer 9st (13)
1965 Soft Angels 8st 11lb (11)
1966 Royal Palace 9st (5)
1967 Remand 9st (7)
1968 Dutch Bells 9st (4)
1969 Domineering (USA) 9st (8)
1970 Seafriend 9st (12)
1971 Yaroslav 8st 11lb (7)
1972 Adios 8st 11lb (12)
1973 Straight as a Die (USA) 8st 11lb (13)
1974 No race
1975 Sir Wimborne (USA) 8st 11lb (6)
1976 Gairloch 8st 11lb (6)
1977 Shirley Heights 8st 11lb (8)
1978 Ela-Mana-Mou 8st 11lb (8)
1979 Hello Gorgeous (USA) 8st 11lb (4)
1980 Robellino (USA) 8st 11lb (8)
1981 Norwick (USA) 8st 11lb (9)
1982 Dunbeath (USA) 8st 11lb (9)
1983 Gold And Ivory (USA) 8st 11lb (5)
1984 Reach 8st 11lb (8)
1985 Bonhomie (USA) 8st 11lb (7)
1986 Bengal Fire 8st 11lb (9)
1987 Sanquirico (USA) 8st 13lb (10)
1988 High Estate 8st 13lb (5)
1989 Digression (USA) 8st 10lb (9)
1990 Mujaazif (USA) 8st 10lb (8)
1991 Made of Gold (USA) 8st 10lb (8)
1992 Desert Secret 8st 10lb (10)
1993 Mister Baileys 8st 10lb (9)

*Run over 5 fur
†Run at Newbury

JOCKEY CLUB CUP (Newmarket)

(2 miles)
(First run 1873)
1900 Osbech 5y 8st 12lb (5)
1901 King's Courier 4y 8st 12lb (4)
1902 Black Sand 5y 9st 1lb (3)
1903 Mead 3y 7st 12lb (3)
1904 Zinfandel 4y 8st 12lb (5)
1905 Pretty Polly 4y 8st 9lb (4)
1906 Bachelor's Button 7y 9st 2lb (2)
1907 Radium 4y 8st 12lb (3)
1908 Radium 5y 9st 1lb (2)
1909 Amadis 3y 7st 13lb (2)
1910 Lagos 5y 9st 1lb (5)
1911 Willonyx 4y 8st 12lb (2)
1912 Aleppo 3y 7st 12lb (2)
1913 Aleppo 4y 8st 12lb (3)
1914 Son-in-Law 3y 7st 12lb (2)
1915 Son-in-Law 4y 8st 12lb (5)
1916 Hurry On 3y 8st 4lb (3)
1917 Brown's Prince 3y 7st 12lb (5)
1918 Queen's Square 3y 7st 9lb (3)
1919 Gay Lord 3y 7st 12lb (2)
1920 No race
1921 Nippon 3y 7st 9lb (3)
1922 Bucks Hussar 3y 7st 12lb (5)
1923 Tranquil 3y 7st 9lb (2)
1924 Plack 3y 7st 9lb (3)
1925 Bucellas 3y 7st 12lb (5)
1926 Bongrace 3y 7st 9lb (5)
1927 Mont Bernina 4y 9st (6)
1928 Invershin 6y 9st (2)
1929 Fairway 4y 9st (3)
1930 Brumeux 5y 9st (3)
1931 Noble Star 4y 9st (3)
1932 Brulette 4y 8st 11lb (w.o.)
1933 Nitsichin 5y 8st 11lb (3)
1934 Felicitation 4y 9st (3)
1935 Quashed 3y 7st 11lb (3)
1936 Quashed 4y 8st 11lb (2)
1937 Buckleigh 5y 9st 2lb (4)
1938 Foxglove II 3y 8st 4lb (5)
1939 No race
1940†Atout Maitre 4y 9st 3lb (7)
1941 No race
1942‡Afterthought 3y 8st (12)
1943‡Shahpoor 4y 9st 2lb (6)
1944‡Ocean Swell 3y 8st 3lb (7)
1945 Amber Flash 3y 8st 2lb (4)
1946 Felix II 3y 8st 4lb (4)
1947 Laurentis 4y 9st 2lb (5)
1948 Vic Day 3y 8st 4lb (w.o.)
1949 Vic Day 4y 9st 2lb (4)
1950 Colonist II 4y 9st 2lb (3)
1951 Eastern Emperor 3y 8st 4lb (4)
1952 Blarney Stone 3y 8st 4lb (4)
1953 Ambiguity 3y 8st 1lb (4)
1954 Yorick II 3y 8st 4lb (8)
1955 Romany Air 4y 9st 3lb (5)
1956 Donald 3y 8st 4lb (5)
1957 Flying Flag II 4y 9st 3lb (3)
1958 French Beige 5y 9st 3lb (5)
1959 Vacarme 5y 9st 4lb (6)
1960 Parthia 4y 9st (4)
1961 Apostle 4y 9st (8)
1962 Pardao 4y 9st (7)
1963 Gaul 4y 9st 6lb (3)
1964 Oncidium 3y 8st 7lb (7)
1965 Goupi 3y 8st 7lb (4)
1966 Hermes 3y 8st 7lb (10)
1967 Dancing Moss 3y 8st 1lb (11)
1968 Riboccare 3y 8st 7lb (8)
1969 High Line 3y 8st 4lb (5)
1970 High Line 4y 9st 6lb (5)
1971 High Line 5y 9st 6lb (5)
1972 Irvine 4y 9st 3lb (5)
1973 Parnell 5y 9st 6lb (5)
1974 Petty Officer 4y 9st 3lb (6)
1975 Blood Royal (USA) 4y 9st 6lb (6)
1976 Bright Finish 3y 8st 6lb (6)
1977 Grey Baron 4y 9st 3lb (5)
1978 Buckskin (Fr) 5y 9st 7lb (6)
1979 Nicholas Bill 4y 8st 11lb (8)
1980 Ardross 4y 9st 5lb (5)
1981 Centroline 3y 8st 4lb (9)
1982 Little Wolf 4y 9st 5lb (8)
1983 Karadar 5y 9st 3lb (5)
1984 Old Country 5y 9st 7lb (4)

1985 Tale Quale 3y 8st 4lb (10)
1986‡Valuable Witness (USA) 6y 9st 5lb (4)
1987 Buckley 4y 9st 3lb (11)
1988 Kneller 3y 8st 7lb (5)
1989 Weld 3y 8st 7lb (3)
1990 Great Marquess 3y 8st 3lb (7)
1991 Further Flight 5y 9st 3lb (6)
1992 Further Flight 6y 9st 3lb (4)
1993 Further Flight 7y 9st 3lb (6)

†Run at Nottingham
‡July Course

SUN CHARIOT STAKES (Newmarket)

(1 1/4 miles)
1966 Lucaya 9st (11)
1967 Cranberry Sauce 9st (6)
1968 Hill Shade 9st (6)
1969 Lucyrowe 9st (5)
1970 Popkins 9st (4)
1971 Hill Circus (USA) 8st 8lb (4)
1972 Sleat 8st 10lb (6)
1973 Cheveley Princess 9st 3lb (2)
1974 Sweet Farewell 3y 8st 7lb (6)
1975 Duboff 3y 8st 7lb (11)
1976 Ranimer 3y 8st 7lb (10)
1977 Triple First 3y 9st (7)
1978 Swiss Maid 3y 8st 7lb (9)
1979 Topsy 3y 8st 7lb (8)
1980 Snowy 3y 8st 7lb (7)
1981 Home On The Range 3y 8st 6lb (10)
1982 Time Charter 3y 9st (10)
1983 Cormorant Wood 3y 8st 5lb (9)
1984 Free Guest 3y 8st 4lb (8)
1985 Free Guest 4y 9st 4lb (5)
1986‡Dusty Dollar 3y 8st 7lb (7)
1987 Infamy 3y 8st 7lb (6)
1988 Indian Skimmer (USA) 4y 9st 6lb (6)
1989 Braiswick 3y 8st 7lb (9)
1990 Kartajana 3y 8st 11lb (7)
1991 Ristna 3y 8st 8lb (5)
1992 Red Slippers (USA) 3y 8st 8lb (7)
1993 Talented 3y 8st 8lb (7)

Prior to 1974 the race was for three year old fillies only
‡July Course

WILLIAM HILL CAMBRIDGESHIRE H'CAP (Newmarket)

(1 mile 1 fur)
(First run 1839)
1900 Berrill 4y 7st 9lb (24)
1901 Watershed 3y 7st 7lb (23)
1902 Ballantrae 3y 6st 8lb (24)
1903 Hackler's Pride 3y 6st 10lb (27)
1904 Hackler's Pride 4y 8st 10lb (17)
1905 Velocity 3y 6st 5lb (18)
1906 Polymelus 4y 8st 10lb (20)
1907 Land League 4y 7st 13lb (15)
1908 Marcovil 5y 7st 11lb (23)
1909 Christmas Daisy 4y 7st 2lb (18)
1910 Christmas Daisy 5y 8st 2lb (21)
1911 Long Set 4y 6st 12lb (16)
1912 Adam Bede 4y 7st 12lb (20)
1913 Cantilever 3y 7st 12lb (18)
1914 Honeywood 3y 7st 8lb (17)
1915 Silver Tag 3y 8st 3lb (25)
1916 Eos 3y 7st 6lb (17)
1917 Brown Prince 3y 7st 7lb (14)
1918 Zinovia 3y 8st 7lb (22)
1919 Brigand 5y 6st 10lb (18)
1920 No race
1921 Milenko 3y 7st 1lb (24)
1922 Re-echo 3y 7st 9lb (34)
1923 Verdict 3y 7st 12lb (23)
1924 Twelve Pointer 4y 8st 12lb (27)
1925 Masked Marvel 3y 7st 9lb (24)
1926 Insight II 45y 7st 13lb (32)
1927*Medal 3y 7st 4lb
*Niantic 4y 6st 3lb (21)
1928 Palais Royal II 3y 7st 13lb (27)
1929 double Life 3y 7st 12lb (36)
1930 The Pen 3y 7st 4lb (31)
1931 Disarmament 3y 7st 11lb (24)
1932 Pullover 3y 6st 11lb (33)
1933 Raymond 3y 8st 4lb (26)
1934 Wychwood Abbot 3y 8st 6lb (33)
1935 Commander III 5y 7st 11lb (40)
1936 Dan Bulger 3y 7st 13lb (22)
1937 Artist's Prince 4y 6st 12lb (26)
1938 Helleniqua 5y 6st 12lb (29)
1939‡(Class I) Gyroscope 3y 7st 7lb (27) (Class II) Orichalque 6y 8st 10lb 927)
1940†Caxton 4y 7st 9lb (15)
1941‡Rue de la Paix 5y 8st 13lb (19)
1942–44 No race
1945 Esquire 3y 6st 3lb (28)
1946 Sayani 3y 9st 4lb 934)
1947 Fairey Fulmar 4y 8st 12lb (39)
1948 Sterope 3y 7st 4lb (32)
1949 Sterope 4y 9st 4lb (39)
1950 Kelling 3y 7st 10lb (31)
1951 Fleeting Moment 5y 7st 13lb (45)
1952 Richer 3y 8st (42)
1953 Jupiter 3y 8st 3lb (29)
1954 Minstrel 3y 7st (36)
1955 Retrial 3y 7st 1lb (40)
1956 Loppylugs 4y 7st 8lb (34)
1957 Stephanotis 4y 8st 5lb (38)
1958 London Cry 4y 9st 5lb (33)
1959 Rexequus 3y 8st 7lb (36)
1960 Midsummer Night II 3y 7st 12lb (40)
1961*Violetta II 3y 7st 8lb
*Henry the Seventh 3y 8st 4lb (27)
1962 Hidden Meaning 3y 9st (46)
1963 Commander in Chief 4y 8st (23)
1964 Hasty Cloud 6y 7st 10lb (43)
1965 Tarqogan 5y 9st 3lb (30)
1966 Dites 4y 7st 4lb (34)
1967 Lacquer 3y 8st 6lb (34)
1968 Emerilo 4y 7st 9lb (35)
1969 Prince de Galles 3y 7st 12lb (26)
1970 Prince de Galles 4y 9st 7lb (27)
1971 King Midas 3y 7st 9lb (29)
1972 Negus 5y 9st (35)
1973 Siliciana 4y 8st 5lb (37)
1974 Flyiong Nelly 4y 7st 7lb (39)
1975 Lottogift 4y 8st 2lb (36)
1976 Intermission 3y 8st 6lb (29)
1977 Sin Timon 3y 8st 3lb (27)
1978 Baronet 6y 9st (18)
1979 Smartset 4y 8st 8lb (24)
1980 Baronet 8y 9st 3lb (19)
1981 Braughing 4y 8st 4lb (28)
1982 Century City 3y 9st 6lb (29)
1983 Sagamore 4y 7st 8lb (30)
1984 Leysh 3y 8st 7lb (34)
1985 Tremblant 4y 9st 8lb (31)
1986‡Dallas (USA) 3y 9st 6lb (31)
1987 Balthus 4y 8st 1lb (31)
1988 Quinlan Terry 3y 8st 6lb (29)
1989 Rambo's Hall 4y 8st 6lb (34)
1990 Risen Moon (USA) 3y 8st 9lb (40)
1991 Mellottie 6y 9st 1lb (29)
1992 Rambo's Hall 7y 9st 3lb (30)
1993 Penny Drops 4y 7st 13lb (33)

*Dead-heat
†Run at Nottingham
‡July Course

NEWGATE STUD MIDDLE PARK STAKES (Newmarket)

(6 fur)
For two year old colts
(First run 1866)
1900 Floriform 8st 10lb (10)
1901 Minstead 8st 10lb (9)
1902 Flotsam 9st 3lb (8)
1903 Pretty Polly 9st (7)
1904 Jardy 9st 3lb (9)
1905 Flair 9st (7)
1906 Galvani 9st 3lb (5)
1907 Lesbia 9st (7)
1908 Bayardo 8st 3lb (4)
1909 Lemberg 9st 3lb (8)
1910 Borrow 8st 11lb (5)
1911 Absurd 9st (10)
1912 Craganour 9st 3lb (7)
1913 Corcyra 9st (7)
1914 Friar Marcus 9st 3lb (7)
1915 Argos 8st 10lb (10)
1916 North Star 9st (7)
1917 Benevente 8st 11lb (6)
1918 Stefan the Great 8st 10lb (9)
1919 Tetratema 9st 3lb (5)
1920 Monarch 9st 3lb (8)
1921 Golden Corn 9st (5)
1922 Drake 9st 3lb (7)
1923 Diophorn 9st 3lb (11)
1924 Picaroon 9st 3lb (8)
1925 lex 9st 3lb (3)
1926 Call Boy 9st (12)
1927 Pharamond 8st 10lb (8)
1928 Costaki Pasha 9st 3lb (13)
1929 Press Gang 9st 3lb (4)
1930 Portlaw 9st 3lb (8)
1931 Orwell 9st 3lb (5)
1932 Felicitation 9st (6)
1933 Medieval Knight 9st (11)
1934 Bahram 9st (6)
1935 Abjer 9st (13)
1936 Fair Copy 9st (7)
1937 Scottish Union 9st (5)
1938 Foxborough II 9st (10)
1939†Djebel 9st (20)
1940‡Hyacinthus 9st (7)
1941‡Sun Chariot 8st 11lb (4)
1942‡Ribbon 8st 11lb (8)
1943†Orestes 8st 11lb (8)
1944 Dante 9st (4)
1945 Khaled 9st (6)
1946 Saravan 9st (8)
1947 The Cobbler 9st (4)
1948 Abernant 9st (3)

1949 Masked Light 9st (5)
1950 Big Dipper 9st (5)
1951 King's Bench 9st (8)
1952 Nearula 9st (9)
1953 Royal Challenger 9st (5)
1954 Our Babu 9st (10)
1955 Buisson Ardent 9st (6)
1956 Pipe of Peace 9st (8)
1957 Major Portion 9st (7)
1958 Masham 9st (5)
1959 Venture VII 9st (5)
1960 Skymaster 9st (4)
1961 Gustav 9st (7)
1962 Crocket 9st (4)
1963 Showdown 9st (11)
1964 Spanish Express 9st (4)
1965 Track Spare 9st (9)
1966 Bold Lad 9st (5)
1967 Petingo 9st (3)
1968 Right Track 9st (7)
1969 Huntercombe 9st (7)
1970 Brigadier Gerard 9st (5)
1971 Sharpen Up 8st 11lb (5)
1972 Tudenham 9st (7)
1973 Habat 9st (7)
1974 Steel Heart 9st (8)
1975 Hittite Glory 9st (8)
1976 Tachypous 9st (11)
1977 Formidable (USA) 9st (7)
1978 Junius (USA) 9st (10)
1979 Known Fact (USA) 9st (7)
1980 Mattaboy 9st (9)
1981 Cajun 9st (13)
1982 Diesis 9st (6)
1983 Creag-An-Sgor 9st (9)
1984 Bassenthwaite 9st (8)
1985 Stalker 9st (6)
1986‡Mister Majestic 9st (7)
1987 Gallic League 9st (5)
1988 Mon Tresor 9st (6)
1989 Balla Cove 9st (6)
1990 Lycius (USA) 9st (9)
1991 Rodrigo de Triano (USA) 9st (6)
1992 Zieten (USA) 9st (6)
1993 First Trump 9st (8)

‡July Course
†Run at Nottingham as New Middle Park Stakes

SHADWELL STUD CHEVELEY PARK STAKES (Newmarket)

(6 fur)
For two year old fillies
(First run 1870)

1900 Alruna 9st (6)
1901 Punctilio 9st (14)
1902 Skyscraper 9st (7)
1903 Pretty Polly 9st 3lb (7)
1904 Galantine 9st 3lb (5)
1905 Colonia 9st 3lb (4)
1906 Witch Elm 9st 1lb (6)
1907 Bracelet 9st 1lb (5)
1908 Sceptre f by Cyllene (named Maid of the Mist) 8st 10lb (5)
1909 Maid of Corinth 9st lb (11)
1910 Knockfeerna 9st 6lb (5)
1911 Belleisle 9st 6lb (5)
1912 Merula 8st 10lb (17)
1913 Shake Down 8st 10lb (15)
1914 Lady of Asia 9st 1lb (9)
1915 Fifinella 9st 1lb (4)
1916 Molly Desmond 9st 1lb (8)
1917 Freesia 9st 1lb (5)
1918 Bayuda 8st 10lb (10)
1919 Bright Folly 9st 6lb (9)
1920 Romana 8st 7lb (11)
1921 Selene 9st 7lb (7)
1922 Paola 8st 12lb (12)
1923 Chronometer 8st 7lb (16)
1924 Miss Gadabout 8st 7lb (10)
1925 Karra 8st 7lb (4)
1926 Nipisquit 8st 7lb (22)
1927 Scuttle 9st 3lb (8)
1928 Tiffin 9st 7lb (8)
1929 Merry Wife 8st 12lb (12)
1930 The Leopard 8st 7lb (6)
1931 Concordia 8st 7lb (10)
1932 Brown Betty 9st 7lb (10)
1933 Light Brocade 9st 7lb (8)
1934 Lady Gabriel 8st 7lb (12)
1935 Ferrybridge 8st 7lb (17)
1936 Celestial Way 8st 7lb (12)
1937 Stafaralla 8st 12lb (9)
1938 Seaway 8st 12lb (13)
1939–41 No race
1942 Lady Sybil 8st 12lb (11)
1943 Fair Fame 8st 12lb (9)
1944 Sweet Cygnet 8st 12lb (8)
1945 Neolight 8st 12lb (3)
1946 Djerba 8st 12lb (6)
1947 Ash Blonde 8st 12lb (7)
1948 Pambidian 8st 12lb (7)
1949 Corejada 8st 12lb (3)
1950 Belle of All 8st 12lb (8)
1951 Zabara 8st 12lb (8)
1952 Bebe Grande 8st 12lb (6)
1953 Sixpence 8st 12lb (6)
1954 Gloria Nicky 8st 12lb (10)
1955 Midget II 8st 12lb (8)
1956 Sarcelle 8st 12lb (7)
1957 Rich and Rare 8st 12lb (8)
1958 Lindsay 8st 12lb (15)
1959 Queensberry 8st 12lb (6)
1960 Opaline II 8st 12lb (6)
1961 Display 8st 11lb (10)
1962 My Goodness Me 8st 11lb (10)
1963 Crimea II 8st 11lb (12)
1964 Night Off 8st 11lb (6)
1965 Berkeley Springs 8st 11lb (11)
1966 Fleet 8st 11lb (8)
1967 Lalibela 8st 11lb (18)
1968 Mige 8st 11lb (18)
1969 Humble Duty 8st 11lb (8)
1970 Magic Flute 8st 11lb (11)
1971 Waterloo 8st 8lb (17)
1972 Jacinth 8st 11lb (13)
1973 Gentle Thoughts (USA) 8st 11lb (14)
1974 Cry of Truth 8st 11lb (15)
1975 Pasty 8st 11lb (14)
1976 Durtal 8st 11lb (15)
1977 Sookera (USA) 8st 11lb (10)
1978 Devon Ditty 8st 11lb (7)
1979 Mrs Penny (USA) 8st 11lb (12)
1980 Marwell 8st 11lb (8)
1981 Woodstream (USA) 8st 11lb (13)
1982 Ma Biche (USA) 8st 11lb (9)
1983 Desirable 8st 11lb (12)
1984 Park Appeal 8st 11lb (13)
1985 Embla 8st 11lb (14)
1986‡Minstrella (USA) 8st 11lb (5)
1987 Ravinella (USA) 8st 11lb (8)
1988 Pass The Peace 8st 11lb (7)
1989 Dead Certain 8st 11lb (11)
1990 Capricciosa (IRE) 8st 11lb (11)
1991 Marling 8st 11lb (9)
1992 Sayyedati 8st 11lb (4)
1993 Prophecy 8st 11lb (6)

‡July Course.

DUBAI CHAMPION STAKES (Newmarket)

(1¼ miles)
(First run 1877)

1900 Solitaire 4y 9st (4)
1901 Osbech 3y 8st 5lb (3)
1902 Veles 4y 9st (4)
1903 Sceptre 4y 8st 11lb (3)
1904 Bachelor's Button 4y 9st (4)
1905 Pretty Polly 4y 8st 11lb (2)
1906 Polymelus 4y 9st (2)
1907 Galvani 3y 8st 7lb (6)
1908 Llangwm 3y 8st 7lb (2)
1909 Bayardo 3y 8st 8lb (3)
1910 Lemberg 3y 8st 7lb (2)
1911 Lemberg 4y 9st (w.o.)
1912 Stedfast 4y 9st (3)
1913 Tracery 4y 9st (2)
1914 Hapsburg 3y 8st 7lb (2)
1915 Let Fly 3y 8st 7lb (5)
1916 Clarissimus 3y 8st 7lb (4)
1917 Gay Crusader 3y 8st 7lb (4)
1918 My Dear 3y 8st 4lb (4)
1919 Buchan 3y 8st 7lb (5)
1920 Orpheus 3y 8st 7lb (6)
1921 Orpheus 4y 9st (4)
1922 Franklin 4y 9st (5)
1923 Ellangowan 3y 8st 7lb (4)
1924 Pharos 4y 9st (5)
1925 Picaroon 3y 8st 7lb (2)
1926 Warden of the Marches 4y (4)
1927 Asterus 4y 9st (3)
1928 Fairway 3y 8st 7lb (4)
1929 Fairway 4y 9st (2)
1930 Rustom Pasha 3y 8st 7lb (9)
1931 Goyescas 3y 8st 7lb (5)
1932 Cameronian 4y 9st (6)
1933★Dastur 4y 9st
★Chatelaine 3y 8st 4lb (3)
1934 Umidwar 3y 8st 7lb (9)
1935 Wychwood Abbot 4y 9st (7)
1936 Wychwood Abbot 5y 9st (4)
1937 Flares 4y 9st (4)
1938 Rockfel 3y 8st 5lb (5)
1939 No race
1940†Hippius 3y 8st 8lb (8)
1941†Hippius 4y 9st (5)
1942†Big Game 3y 8st 3lb (50
1943†Nasrullah 3y 8st 6lb (6)
1944†Hycilla 3y 8st 2lb (17)
1945 Court Martial 3y 8st 7lb (4)
1946 Honeyway 5y 9st (8)
1947 Migoli 3y 8st 8lb (4)
1948 Solar Slipper 3y 8st 8lb (7)
1949 Djeddah 4y 9st (5)
1950 Peter Flower 4y 9st (7)
1951 Dynamiter 3y 8st 8lb (19)
1952 Dynamiter 4y 9st (5)
1953 Nearula 3y 8st 7lb (7)
1954 Narrator 3y 8st 7lb (6)
1955 Hafiz II 8st 7lb (5)
1956 Hugh Lupus 4y 9st (11)
1957 Rose Royale II 3y 8st 4lb (7)
1958 Bella Paola 3y 8st 4lb (7)
1959 Petite Etoile 3y 8st 5lb (3)
1960 Marguerite Vernaut 3y 8st 4lb (4)
1961 Bobar II 3y 8st 7lb (8)
1962 Arctic Storm 3y 8st 7lb (7)
1963 Hula Dancer 3y 8st 4lb (11)
1964 Baldric II 3y 8st 7lb (9)
1965 Silly Season 3y 8st 7lb (13)
1966 Pieces of Eight 3y 8st 7lb (8)
1967 Reform 3y 8st 7lb (7)
1968 Sir Ivor 3y 8st 7lb (6)
1969 Flossy (Fr) 3y 8st 4lb (9)
1970 Lorenzaccio 5y 9st (8)
1971 Brigadier Gerard 3y 8st 7lb (10)

1972 Brigadier Gerard 4y 9st 3lb (9)
1973 Hurry Harriet 3y 8st 7lb (16)
1974 Giacometti 3y 8st 10lb (14)
1975 Rose Bowl (USA) 3y 8st 7lb (9)
1976 Vitiges (Fr) 3y 8st 11lb (19)
1977 Flying Water (Fr) 4y 9st (8)
1978 Swiss Maid 3y 8st 7lb (10)
1979 Northern Baby (Can) 3y 8st 10lb (14)
1980 Cairn Rouge 3y 8st 7lb (13)
1981 Vayrann 3y 8st 10lb (16)
1982 Time Charter 3y 8st 7lb (14)
1983 Cormorant Wood 3y 8st 7lb (19)
1984 Palace Music (USA) 3y 8st 10lb (15)
1985 Pebbles 4y 9st (10)
1986†Triptych (USA) 4y 9st (11)
1987 Triptych (USA) 5y 9st (11)
1988 Indian Skimmer (USA) 4y 9st (5)
1989 Legal Case 3y 8st 10lb (11)
1990 In The Groove 3y 8st 9lb (10)
1991 Tel Quel (FR) 3y 8st 12lb (12)
1992 Rodrigo de Triano (USA) 3y 8st 12lb (10)
1993 Hatoof (USA) 4y 9st (12)

★Dead-heat †July Course

TOTE CESAREWITCH H'CAP (Newmarket)

(2¼ miles)
(First run 1839)

1900 Clarehaven 4y 7st 13lb (21)
1901 Balsarroch 3y 6st 5lb (23)
1902 Black Sand 5y 8st 2lb (17)
1903 Grey Tick 7y 6st 9lb (26)
1904 Wargrave 7y 7st 4lb (20)
1905 Hammerkop 5y 8st 9lb (19)
1906 Mintagon 5y 7st (24)
1907 Demure 4y 6st 9lb (13)
1908 Yentoi 4y 7st 10lb (16)
1909 Submit 3y 6st 13lb (17)
1910 Verney 4y 7st 11lb (19)
1911 Willonyx 4y 9st 5lb (16)
1912 Warlingham 3y 6st 12lb (18)
1913 Fiz Yama 4y 7st 7lb (24)
1914 Troubadour 3y 6st 9lb (21)
1915 Son-in-Law 4y 8st 4lb (31)
1916 Sanctum 4y 7st 9lb (19)
1917 Furore 4y 8st 6lb (17)
1918 Air Raid 3y 8st 1lb (24)
1919 Ivanhoe 6y 7st 12lb (19)
1920 Bracket 3y 7st 7lb (32)
1921 Yutoi 4y 8st 5lb (17)
1922 Light Dragoon 4y 7st 3lb (31)
1923 Rose Prince 4y 8st 3lb (29)
1924 Charley's Mount 3y 7st 10lb (34)
1925 Forseti 5y 8st 3lb (33)
1926 Myra Gray 6y 6st 1lb (24)
1927 Eagle's Pride 4y 7st (30)
1928 Arctic Star 4y 8st 2lb (15)
1929 West Wicklow 5y 7st 6lb (35)
1930 Ut Majeur 3y 8st 3lb (28)
1931 Noble Star 4y 8st 12lb (26)
1932 Nitsichin 4y 8st 9lb (26)
1933 Seminole 4y 8st (33)
1934 Enfield 3y 7st 10lb (27)
1935 Near Relation 3y 7st 9lb (29)
1936 Fet 5y 6st 12lb (24)
1937 Punch 4y 7st 11lb (31)
1938 Contrevent 3y 6st 10lb (28)
1939†Cantatrice II 4y 7st 5lb (36)
1940†Hunter's Moon IV 4y 9st 5lb (14)
1941†Filator 3y 7st 12lb (21)
1942–44 No race
1945 Kerry Piper 4y 8st 1lb 926)
1946 Monsieur l'Amiral 5y 8st 5lb (27)
1947 Whiteway 3y 7st 12lb (22)
1948 Woodburn 3y 7st 13lb (32)
1949 Strathspey 4y 7st 11lb (37)
1950 Above Board 3y 7st 10lb (38)
1951 Three Cheers 3y 7st 8lb (30)
1952 Flush Royal 7y 8st 13lb (36)
1953 Chantry 4y 8st 4lb (25)
1954 French Design 7y 8st 3lb (31)
1955 Curry 4y 7st 6lb (21)
1956 Prelone 3y 7st 3lb (19)
1957 Sandiacre 5y 7st 8lb (24)
1958 Morecambe 5y 9st 1lb (30)
1959 Come to Daddy 4y 7st 8lb (17)
1960 Alcove 3y 7st 8lb (20)
1961 Avon's Pride 4y 7st 11lb (27)
1962 Golden Fire 4y 7st 11lb (25)
1963 Utrillo 6y 8st (25)
1964 Grey of Falloden 5y 9st 6lb (26)
1965 Mintmaster 4y 7st 9lb (18)
1966 Persian Lancer 8y 7st 8lb (24)
1967 Bosimoss 3y 7st 1lb (23)
1968 Major Rose 6y 9st 4lb (33)
1969 Floridian 5y 7st 3lb (23)
1970 Scoria 4y 7st (21)
1971 Orosio 4y 8st 2lb (18)
1972 Cider with Rosie 4y 7st 11lb (21)
1973 Flash Imp 4y 7st 8lb (29)
1974 Ocean King 8y 7st 7lb (27)
1975 Shantallah 3y 8st 10lb (17)
1976 John Cherry (USA) 5y 9st 13lb (14)
1977 Assured 4y 8st 4lb (11)
1978 Centurion 3y 9st 8lb (17)
1979 Sir Michael 3y 7st 8lb (11)
1980 Popsi's Joy 4y 8st 6lb (27)
1981 Halsbury 3y 8st 4lb (30)
1982 Mountain Lodge 3y 7st 10lb (28)
1983 Bajan Sunshine 4y 8st 8lb (28)
1984 Tom Sharp 4y 7st 5lb (26)
1985 Kayudee 5y 8st 1lb (21)
1986†Orange Hill 4y 7st 9lb (25)
1987 Private Audition 5y 7st 9lb (28)
1988 Nomadic Way (USA) 3y 7st 9lb (24)
1989 Double Dutch 5y 9st 10lb (22)
1990 Trainglot 3y 7st 12lb (25)
1991 Go South 7y 7st 11lb (22)
1992 Vintage Crop 5y 9st 6lb (24)
1993 Aahsaylad 7y 8st 12lb (31)

†July Course

DEWHURST STAKES (Newmarket)

(7 fur)
For two year olds
(First run 1875)

1900 Lord Bobs 8st 9lb (10)
1901 Game Chick 9st 3lb (10)
1902 Rock Sand 9st 5lb (8)
1903 Henry the First 9st 2lb (9)
1904 Rouge Croix 8st 9lb (9)
1905 Picton 8st 9lb (7)
1906 My Pet II 9st 2lb (5)
1907 Rhodora 8st 7lb (9)
1908 Bayardo 9st 5lb (6)
1909 Lemberg 9st 5lb (2)
1910★King William 8st 9lb
★Phryxus 8st 9lb (7)
1911 White Star 9st 5lb (6)
1912 Louvois 9st 2lb (8)
1913 Kennymore 8st 9lb (7)
1914 Let Floy 9st 5lb (7)
1915 Atheling 8st 13lb (10)
1916 Telephus 8st 9lb (6)
1917 My Dear 8st 7lb (6)
1918 Kinght of Blyth 8st 9lb (6)
1919 Prince Galahad 8st 13lb (7)
1920 No race
1921 Lembach 9st 2lb (4)
1922 Hurry Off 8st 9lb (9)
1923 Salmon-Trout 8st 13lb (6)
1924 Zionist 8st 13lb (6)
1925 Review Order 9st 2lb (6)
1926 Money Maker 9st 2lb (6)
1927 Toboggan 9st (7)
1928 Brienz 9st 2lb (10)
1929 Grace Dalrymple 8st 11lb (7)
1930 Sangre 8st 9lb (8)
1931 Firdaussi 8st 13lb (6)
1932 Hyperion 9st 5lb (6)
1933 Mrs Rustom 9st 3lb (9)
1934 Harian 9st 5lb (5)
1935 Bala Hissar 8st 9lb (12)
1936 Sultan Mohamed 8st 9lb (6)
1937 Manorite 8st 9lb (7)
1938 Casanova 8st 9lb (4)
1939 No race
1940†Fettes 8st 9lb (9)
1941†Canyonero 9st 2lb (5)
1942†Umiddad 8st 9lb (8)
1943†Effervescence 9st 2lb (10)
1944†Paper Weight 9st 2lb (5)
1945 Hypericum 8st 11lb (10)
1946 MNigoli 9st (8)
1947 Pride of India 8st 13lb (11)
1948 Royal Forest 9st 3lb (11)
1949 Emperor II 8st 13lb (7)
1950 Turco II 8st 13lb (6)
1951 Marsyad 8st 9lb (11)
1952 Pinza 8st 13lb (9)
1953 Infatuation 9st 3lb (5)
1954 My Smokey 8st 9lb (9)
1955 Dacian 8st 9lb (10)
1956 Crepello 8st 9lb (4)
1957 Torbella III 8st 6lb (7)
1958 Billum 8st 13lb (8)
1959 Ancient Lights 8st 13lb (7)
1960 Bounteous 8st 13lb (7)
1961 River Chanter 9st 2lb (8)
1962 Follow Suit 8st 12lb (10)
1963 King's Lane 8st 12lb (9)
1964 Silly Seaon 9st 2lb (11)
1965 Pretende 8st 12lb (11)
1966 Dart Board 8st 12lb (13)
1967 Hametus 8st 12lb (7)
1968 Ribofilio 8st 12lb (11)
1969 Nijinsky (Can) 8st 12lb (6)
1970 Mill Reef (USA) 8st 12lb (3)
1971 Crowned Prince (USA) 8st 11lb (11)
1972 Lunchtime 9st (8)
1973 Cellini (USA) 9st (7)
1974 Grundy 9st (8)
1975 Wollow 9st (7)
1976 The Minstrel (Can) 9st (11)
1977 Try My Best (USA) 9st (7)
1978 Tromos 9st (6)
1979 Monteverdi 9st (6)
1980 Storm Bird (Can) 9st (5)
1981 Wind And Wuthering (USA) 9st (9)
1982 Diesis 9st (4)
1983 El Gran Senor (USA) 9st (10)

1984 Kala Dancer 9st (11)
1985 Huntingdale 9st (8)
1986†Ajdal (USA) 9st (5)
1987 No Race abandoned
1988★Prince of Dance 9st
★Scenic 9st (6)
1989 Dashing Blade 9st (7)
1990 Generous (IRE) 9st (8)
1991 Dr. Devious (IRE) 9st (9)
1992 Zafonic (USA) 9st (11)
1993 Grand Lodge (USA) 9st (10)

★Dead-heat
†July Course

RACING POST TROPHY (Doncaster)

(1 mile)
For two year olds

1961 Miralgo 8st 12lb (13)
1962 Noblesse 8st 9lb (12)
1963 Pushful 8st 12lb (10)
1964 Hardicanute 8st 12lb (11)
1965 Pretende 8st 12lb (13)
1966 Ribocco 8st 12lb (11)
1967 Vaguely Noble 8st 12lb (8)
1968 The Elk 8st 12lb (11)
1969 Approval 8st 12lb (9)
1970 Linden Tree (Fr) 8st 12lb (9)
1971 High Top 8st 11lb (13)
1972 Noble Decree (USA) 9st (10)
1973 Apalachee (USA) 9st (10)
1974 Green Dancer (USA) 9st (10)
1975 Take Your Place (USA) 9st (11)
1976 Sporting Yankee (USA) 9st (6)
1977 Dactylographer (USA) 9st (12)
1978 Sandy Creek 9st (11)
1979 Hello Gorgeous (USA) 9st (7)
1980 Beldale Flutter (USA) 9st (7)
1981 Count Pahlen 9st (13)
1982 Dunbeath (USA) 9st (8)
1983 Alphabatim (USA) 9st (9)
1984 lanfranco 9st (10)
1985 Bakharoff 9st (9)
1986 Reference Point 9st (10)
1987 Emmson 9st (5)
1988 Al Hareb (USA) 9st (8)
1989 Be My Chief (USA) 9st (5)
1990 Peter Davies (USA) 9st (4)
1991 Seattle Rhyme (USA) 9st (8)
1992 Armiger 9st (10)
1993 King's Theatre 9st (9)

Run at Newcastle 1989

WILLIAM HILL NOVEMBER H'CAP (Doncaster)

(1½ miles)
(First run 1876)

1900 Lexicon 6y 6st 13lb (18)
1901 Carabine 3y 6st 9lb (22)
1902 St Maclou 4y 9st 4lb 914)
1903 Swith-Cap 3y 6st 6lb (24)
1904 No race
1905 Ferment 3y 6st 2lb (19)
1906 Spate 3y 7st 5lb (17)
1907 Baltinglass 3y 7st 11lb (10)
1908 Old China 4y 7st 11lb (20)
1909 Admiral Togo III 5y 7st 2lb (16)
1910 The Valet 6y 6st 9lb (18)
1911 Ultimus 4y 7st 3lb (17)
1912 Wagstaff 3y 8st 1lb (16)
1913 Dalmatian 6y 7st 8lb (16)
1914 Wardha 3y 6st 5lb (21)
1915 No race
1916 No race
1917 Planet 3y 8st 1lb (17)
1918 No race
1919 King John 4y 8st 6lb (17)
1920 Pomme-de-terre 4y 9st 4lb (12)
1921 Blue Dun 4y 8st 5lb (24)
1922 Torelore 5y 9st (14)
1923 No race
1924 Cloudbank 3y 7st 10lb (17)
1925 No race
1926 No race
1927 Old Orkney 3y 7st 7lb (6)
1928 Saracen 3y 7st 8lb (20)
1929 Promptitude 5y 6st 13lb (19)
1930 Glorious Devon 3y 7st 5lb (28)
1931 North Drift 4y 7st 6lb (42)
1932 Hypostyle 3y 7st 5lb (18)
1933 Jean's Dream 3y 7st 5lb (28)
1934 Pip Emma 3y 7st 9lb (29)
1935 Free Fare 7y 8st 4lb (19)
1936 Newtown Ford 4y 8st 4lb (21)
1937 Solitaire 6y 8st 1lb (31)
1938 Pappageno II 3y 8st 6lb (26)
1939 Tutor 3y 8st 3lb (24)
1940 Beinn Dearg 5y 8st 2lb (20)
1941 Crown Colony 5y 7st 9lb (18)
1942★Golden Boy 4y 8st 11lb (17)
1943★Mad Carew 4y 7st 6lb (21)
1944★Kerry Piper 3y 8st (19)
1945★Oatflake 3y 7st 13lb (23)
1946 Las Vegas 4y 8st 8lb (23)
1947 Regret 4y 6st 3lb (34)
1948 Sports Master 3y 6st 13lb (40)
1949 Fidonia 4y 9st 2lb (41)
1950 Coltbridge 4y 7st 6lb (37)
1951 Good Taste 7y 7st 13lb (31)
1952 Summer Rain 3y 7st 13lb (24)
1953 Torch Singer 4y 6st 5lb (25)
1954 No race
1955 Tearaway 5y 6st 11lb (38)
1956 Trentham Boy 5y 7st 6lb (26)
1957 Chief Barker 4y 6st 5lb (40)
1958 Paul Jones 3y 8st 2lb (30)
1959 Operatic Society 3y 8st 9lb (49)
1960 Dalnamein 5y 7st 10lb (30)
1961 Henry's Choice 4y 8st 2lb (29)
1962 Demredub 5y 8st 1lb 935)
1963 Best Song 4y 9st 6lb (31)
1964 Osier 4y 7st 10lb (28)
1965 Concealdem 6y 8st 10lb (18)
1966 Polish Warrior 3y 7st 3lb (26)
1967 Bugle Boy 4y 7st 8lb (25)
1968 Zardia 4y 7st 8lb (29)
1969 Tintagel II 4y 9st (21)
1970 Saraceno 5y 9st 2lb (21)
1971 Misty Light (USA) 3y 8st 5lb (20)
1972 King Top 3y 7st 11lb (16)
1973 Only for Jo 7st 4lb (22)
1974 Gritti Palace 5y 7st (21)
1975 Mr Bigmore 3y 9st 1lb (12)
1976 Gale Bridge (USA) 3y 8st 12lb (14)
1977 Sailcloth 3y 7st 7lb (20)
1978 Eastern Spring 4y 7st 10lb (21)
1979 Morse Code 4y 8st 3lb (14)
1980 Path of Peace 4y 8st 5lb (22)
1981 Lafontaine (USA) 4y 8st 7lb (20)
1982†Double Shuffle 3y 9st
†Turkoman 3y 8st 7lb (17)
1983 Asir 3y 8st 7lb (25)
1984 Abu Kadra 3y 8st 12lb (23)
1985 Bold Rex (Fr) 3y 8st 7lb (24)
1986 Beijing (USA) 3y 8st 4lb (25)
1987 Swingit Gunner 6y 8st 11lb (25)
1988 Young Benz 4y 8st 4lb (22)
1989 Firelight Fiesta 4y 9st 8lb (19)
1990 Azzaam (USA) 3y 9st 8lb (24)
1991 Hieroglyphic 3y 8st 13lb (22)
1992 Turgenev 3y 9st (25)
1993 Quick Ransom 5y 8st 10lb (25)

†Dead-heat
★Run at Pontefract
Run at Thirsk 1989
Run at Manchester as Manchester November H'cap from 1876 to 1963, then at Doncaster from 1964

Part 2: Overseas

JAMESON IRISH GRAND NATIONAL (Fairyhouse)

(3 miles 5 fur)
(First run 1870)

1900 Mavis of Meath 6y 12st 12lb (5)
1901 Tipperary Boy 7y 12st (9)
1902 Patlander 6y 11st (7)
1903 Kirko 6y 11st 7lb (9)
1904 Ascetic's Silver 7y 11st 7lb (12)
1905 Red Lad 5y 10st 7lb (13)
1906 Brown Bess 5y 10st 11lb (6)
1907 Sweet Cecil 6y 11st 4lb (5)
1908 Lord Rivers 6y 11st 12lb (6)
1909 Little Hack II 10st (9)
1910 Oniche 7y 9st 3lb (8)
1911 Repeater II 10st 6lb (13)
1912 Small Polly 7y 10st 10lb (17)
1913 Little Hack II 10st 10lb (15)
1914 Civil War 5y 10st 7lb (14)
1915 Punch 7y 11st 8lb (19)
1916 All Sorts 6y 11st (11)
1917 Pay Only 7y 12st (14)
1918 Ballyboggan 7y 11st 4lb (14)
1919 No race
1920 Halston 8y 10st 5lb (11)
1921 Bohernore 8y 10st 7lb (11)
1922 Halston 10y 12st 11lb (16)
1923 Be Careful 14y 10st 2lb (11)
1924 Kilbarry 9y 10st 1lb (16)
1925 Dog Fox 11y 10st 2lb (19)
1926 Amberwave 8y 10st (15)
1927 Jerpoint 7y 12st (15)
1928 Don Sancho 8y 12st 1lb (19)
1929 Alike 6y 10st 5lb (11)
1930 Fanmond 7y 9st 8lb (22)
1931 Impudent Barney 9y 10st 3lb (11)
1932 Copper Court 9y 10st 9lb (15)
1933 Red Park 7y 11st 5lb (16)
1934 Poolgowran 4y 9st 11lb (12)
1935 Rathfriland 7y 9st 10lb (9)
1936 Alice Maythorn 6y 10st 1lb (19)
1937 Pontet 7y 10st 2lb (14)
1938 Clare County 7y 11st 3lb (9)
1939 Shaun Peel 7y 9st 7lb (16)
1940 Jack Chaucer 9y 11st 11lb (14)

1941 No race
1942 Prince Regent 7y 12st 7lb (10)
1943 Golden Jack 8y 10st 3lb (8)
1944 Knight's Crest 7y 9st 7lb (13)
1945 Heirdom 13y 9st 7lb (12)
1946 Golden View II 11y 12st 7lb (11)
1947 Revelry 7y 11st 5lb (17)
1948 Hamstar 8y 9st 7lb (17)
1949 Shagreen 8y 10st 10lb (20)
1950 Dominick's Bar 6y 10st 6lb (12)
1951 Icy Calm 8y 10st 3lb (19)
1952 Alberoni 9y 10st 1lb (11)
1953 Overshadow 13y 10st 4lb (15)
1954 Royal Approach 6y 12st (11)
1955 Umm 8y 10st 5lb (16)
1956 Air Prince 12y 10st (19)
1957 Kilballyown 10y 9st 10lb (26)
1958 Gold Legend 8y 9st 7lb (21)
1959 Zonda 8y 10st 6lb (15)
1960 Olympia 6y 9st 11lb (16)
1961 Fortria 9y 12st (14)
1962 Kerforo 8y 10st 3lb (11)
1963 Last Link 7y 9st 7lb (10)
1964 Arkle 7y 12st (7)
1965 Splash 7y 10st 13lb (4)
1966 Flyingbolt 7y 12st 7lb (6)
1967 Vulpine 6y 11st 6lb (12)
1968 Herring Gull 6y 11st 13lb (12)
1969 Sweet Dreams 8y 9st 10lb (18)
1970 Garoupe 6y 9st 9lb (13)
1971 King's Sprite 9y 9st 13lb (12)
1972 Dim Wit 7y 10st 13lb (14)
1973 Tartan Ace 6y 9st 7lb (14)
1974 Colebridge 10y 11st 2lb (10)
1975 Brown Lad 9y 10st 5lb (8)
1976 Brown Lad 10y 12st 2lb (15)
1977 Billycan 7y 10st (20)
1978 Brown Lad 12y 12st 2lb (19)
1979 Tied Cottage 11y 10st 12lb (20)
1980 Daletta 7y 11st 4lb (25)
1981 Luska 7y 9st 9lb (20)
1982 King Spruce 8y 10st 2lb (25)
1983 Bit of a Skite 7y 9st 7lb (27)
1984 Bentom Boy 9y 9st 9lb (29)
1985 Rhyme 'N' Reason 6y 10st 6lb (23)
1986 Insure 8y 9st 11lb (15)
1987 Brittany Boy 8y 10st 10lb (26)
1988 Perris Valley 7y 10st (18)
1989 Maid of Money 7y 11st 6lb (22)
1990 Desert Orchid 11y 12st (14)
1991 Omerta 11y 10st 9lb (22)
1992 Vanton 8y 10st 11lb (23)
1993 Ebony Jane 8y 10st 7lb (27)

DUBAI POULE D'ESSAI DES POULAINS (Longchamp)

(1 mile)
For three year old colts
(First run 1883)

1927 Fiterari (11)
1928 Dark Lantern (14)
1929 Vatout (8)
1930 Xandover (7)
1931 Indus (9)
1932 le Becau (13)
1933 Rodsosto (4)
1934 Brantome (6)
1935 Kant (10)
1936 Davout (8)
1937 Drap d'Or (4)
1938 Gaspillage (6)
1939 MacKann (10)
1940*Djebel (5)
1941 Panipat (9)
1942 Hexton (9)
1943†Dogat (7)
1944**Prince Bio (8)
1945**Mistral (8)
1946 Pactole (6)
1947 Tourment (9)
1948 Rigolo (9)
1949 Amour Drake (5)
1950 Tantieme (6)
1951 Free Man (7)
1952 Guersant (10)
1953 Cobalt (7)
1954 Cote d'Or II (8)
1955 Klairon (9)
1956 Buisson Ardent (10)
1957 Tyrone (8)
1958 Pres du Feu (9)
1959 Thymus (9)
1960 Mincio (7)
1961 Right Royal (5)
1962 Adamastor (9)
1963 Relko (6)
1964 Neptunus (6)
1965 Cambremont (4)
1966 Soleil (12)
1967 Blue Tom (4)
1968 Zeddaan (12)
1969 Don II (9)
1970 Caro (6)
1971 Zug (14)
1972 Riverman (USA) (10)
1973 Kalamoun (10)
1974 Moulines (11)
1975 Green Dancer (USA) (12)
1976 Red Lord (11)
1977 Blushing Groom (6)
1978 Nishapour (14)
1979 Irish River (4)
1980 In Fijar (USA) (13)
1981 Recitation (USA) (10)
1982 Melyno (9)
1983 L'Emigrant (USA) (10)
1984 Siberian Express (14)
1985 No Pass No Sale (9)
1986 Fast Topaze (8)
1987 Soviet Star (USA) (14)
1988 Blushing John (USA) (10)
1989 Kendor (10)
1990 Linamix (FR) (7)
1991 Hector Protector (USA) (6)
1992 Shanghai (USA) (9)
1993 Kingmambo (USA) (10)

*Run at Auteuil
**Run at Maisons-Laffitte
†Run at Le Tremblay

DUBAI POULE D'ESSAI DES POULICHES (Longchamp)

(1 mile)
For three year old fillies
(First run 1883)

1927 Fairy Legend (16)
1928 Roahouga (12)
1929 Poesie (14)
1930 Rose Thé (10)
1931 Pearl Cap (12)
1932 Ligne de Fond (15)
1933 Bipearl (11)
1934 Mary Tudor (7)
1935 The Nile (11)
1936 Blue Bear (10)
1937 Colette Baudoche (6)
1938 Feerie (11)
1939 Yonne (10)
1940 No race
1941 Longthanh (14)
1942 Esmeralda (10)
1943†Caravelle (7)
1944**Palencia (6)
1945**Nikellora (12)
1946 Real (14)
1947 Imprudence (9)
1948 Corteira (16)
1949*Coronation
*Galgala (8)
1950 Corejada (6)
1951 Djelfa (9)
1952 Pomare (7)
1953 Hurnli (10)
1954 Virgule (7)
1955 Dictaway (8)
1956 Apollonia (8)
1957 Toro (15)
1958 Yla (9)
1959 Ginetta (11)
1960 Timandra (12)
1961 Solitude (9)
1962 Le Sega (7)
1963 Altissima (7)
1964 Rajput Princess (10)
1965 La Sarre (7)
1966 Right Away (8)
1967 Gazala (8)
1968 Pola Bella (10)
1969 Koblenza (9)
1970 Pampered Miss (9)
1971 Bold Fascinator (11)
1972 Mata Hari (Ger) (11)
1973 Allez France (USA) (11)
1974 Dumka (9)
1975 Ivanjica (USA) (10)
1976 Riverqueen (11)
1977 Madelia (8)
1978 Dancing Maid (10)
1979 Three Troikas (7)
1980 Aryenne (6)
1981 Ukraine Girl (Ire) (10)
1982 River Lady (9)
1983 L'Attrayante (Fr) (10)
1984 Masarika (11)
1985 Silvermine (10)
1986 Baiser Vole (18)
1987 Miesque (USA) (8)
1988 Ravinella (USA) (8)
1989 Pearl Bracelet (USA) (16)
1990 Houseproud (USA) (14)
1991 Danseuse du Soir (9)
1992 Culture Vulture (USA) (9)
1993 Madeleine's Dream (USA) (8)

*Dead-heat
†Run at le Tremblay
**Run at Maisons-Laffitte

AIRLIE/COOLMORE IRISH 2,000 GUINEAS (Curragh)

(1 mile)
For three year olds

1921 Soldennis 9st 7lb (10)
1922 Spike Island 9st (11)
1923 Soldumeno 9st (9)
1924 Grand Joy 9st 4lb (8)

1925 St Donagh 9st (8)
1926 Embargo 9st 4lb (10)
1927 Fourth Hand 9st 7lb (9)
1928 Baytown 9st (8)
1929 Salisbury 9st (7)
1930 Glannarg 9st (10)
1931 Double Arch 9st (10)
1932 Lindley 9st 4lb (12)
1933 Canteener 9st 4lb (12)
1934 Cariff 9st 4lb (10)
1935 Museum 9st (11)
1936 Hocus Pocus 9st (9)
1937 Phideas 9st 4lb (9)
1938 Nearchus 9st (12)
1939 Cornfield 9st 4lb (16)
1940 Teasel 9st (6)
1941 Khosro 9st (14)
1942 Windsor Slipper 9st (12)
1943 The Phoenix 9st 7lb (12)
1944⋆Slide On 9st
⋆Good Morning 9st (14)
1945 Stalino 9st (20)
1946 Claro 9st (14)
1947 Grand Weather 9st (8)
1948 Beau Sabreur 9st (12)
1949 Solonaway 9st (12)
1950 Might Ocean 9st (10)
1951 Signal Box 9st (16)
1952 D.C.M. 9st (11)
1953 Sea Charger 9st (13)
1954 Arctic Wind 9st (14)
1955 Hugh Lupus 9st (20)
1956 Lucero 9st (13)
1957 Jack Ketch 9st (13)
1958 Hard Ridden 9st (13)
1959 El Toro 9st (15)
1960 Kythnos 9st (14)
1961 Light Year 9st (21)
1962 Arctic Storm 9st (17)
1963 Linacre 9st (14)
1964 Santa Claus 9st (16)
1965 Green Banner 9st (21)
1966 Paveh 9st (15)
1967 Atherstone Wood 9st (19)
1968 Mistigo 9st (15)
1969 Right Tack 9st (15)
1970 Decies 9st (13)
1971 King's Company 9st (14)
1972 Ballymore 9st (14)
1973 Sharp Edge 9st (16)
1974 Furry Glen 9st (10)
1975 Grundy 9st (12)
1976 Northern Treasure 9st (17)
1977 Pampapaul 9st (21)
1978 Jaazeiro (USA) 9st (12)
1979 Dickens Hill 9st (9)
1980 Nikoli 9st (13)
1981 Kings Lake 9st (USA) (13)
1982 Dara Monarch 9st (14)
1983 Wassl 9st (10)
1984 Sadler's Wells 9st (9)
1985 Triptych (USA) 8st 11lb (16)
1986 Flash of Steel 9st (6)
1987 Don't Forget Me 9st (9)
1988 Prince of Birds (USA) 9st (14)
1989 Shaadi (USA) 9st (12)
1990 Tirol 9st (9)
1991 Fourstars Allstar (USA) 9st (12)
1992 Rodrigo de Triano (USA) 9st (6)
1993 Barathea 9st (11)

⋆Dead-heat

I.A.W.S. IRISH 1,000 GUINEAS (Curragh)

(1 mile)
For three year old fillies

1922 Lady Violette 9st (11)
1923 Glenshesk 9st (6)
1924 Voltoi 9st (6)
1925 Flying Dinah 9st (11)
1926 Resplendent 9st (12)
1927 West Indies 9st (9)
1928 Moucheron 9st (13)
1929 Soloptic 9st 7lb (9)
1930 Star of Egypt 9st (9)
1931 Spiral 9st (7)
1932 Petoni 9st (12)
1933 Spy-Ann 9st (17)
1934 Kyloe 9st (6)
1935 Smokeless 9st 4lb (9)
1936 Harvest Star 9st (6)
1937 Sol Speranza 9st (7)
1938 Lapel 9st 4lb (12)
1939 Serpent Star 9st (7)
1940 Gainsworth 9st (12)
1941 Milady Rose 9st (9)
1942 Majideh 9st (13)
1943 Suntop 9st (12)
1944 Annetta 9st (10)
1945 Panastrid 9st 4lb (16)
1946 Ella Retford 9st (13)
1947 Sea Symphony 9st (20)
1948 Morning Wings 9st (16)
1949 Sunlit Ride 9st (18)
1950 Princess Trudy 9st (18)
1951 Queen of Sheba 9st (16)
1952 Nashua 9st (14)
1953 Northern Gleam 9st (15)
1954 Pantomime Queen 9st (16)
1955 Dark Issue 9st (17)
1956 Pederoba 9st (16)
1957 Even Star 9st (15)
1958 Butiaba 9st (15)
1959 Fiorentina 9st (19)
1960 Zenobia 9st (15)
1961 Lady Senator 9st (12)
1962 Shandon Belle 9st (16)
1963 Gazpacho 9st (18)
1964 Royal Danseuse 9st (13)
1965 Ardent Dancer 9st (13)
1966 Valoris 9st (15)
1967 lacquer 9st (15)
1968 Front Row 9st (13)
1969 Wenduyne 9st (13)
1970 Black Satin 9st (13)
1971 Favoletta 9st (17)
1972 Pidget 9st (16)
1973 Cloonagh 9st (12)
1974 Gaily (USA) 9st (17)
1975 Miralla 9st (11)
1976 Sarah Siddons (Fr) 9st (14)
1977 lady Capulet (USA) 9st (14)
1978 More So 9st (17)
1979 Godetia (USA) 9st (12)
1980 Cairn Rouge 9st (18)
1981 Arctique Royale 9st (15)
1982 Prince's Polly 9st (24)
1983 L'Attrayante (Fr) 9st (18)
1984 Katies 9st (23)
1985 Al Bahathri (USA) 9st (15)
1986 Sonic Lady 9st (19)
1987 Forest Flower (USA) 9st (11)
1988 Trusted Partner (USA) 9st (16)
1989 Ensconse (USA) 9st (13)
1990 In The Groove 9st (12)
1991 Kooyonga 9st (12)
1992 Marling 9st (9)
1993 Nicer 9st (14)

PRIX DE DIANE HERMES (Chantilly)

(French Oaks)
(1 mile $2^1/2$ fur)
(First run 1843)

1900 Baron A de Schickler's Semendria (12)
1901 M A Abeille's La Camargo (13)
1902 M de St Alary's Kizil Kourgan (12)
1903 Count de Saint-Phalle's Rose de Mai 914)
1904 M E Blanc's Profane (20)
1905 M E Veil-Picard's Clyde (14)
1906 M L Merino's Flying Star (15)
1907 D de Gramont's Saint Astra (18)
1908 M E Blanc's Medeah (17)
1909 M E Blanc's Union (13)
1910 M E Blanc's Marsa (17)
1911 M A Aumont's Rose Verte (12)
1912 M A Belmont's Qu'elle est Belle II (20)
1913 M M Caillault's Moia (16)
1914 M Olry-Roederer's Alerte IV (12)
1915–18 No race
1919⋆Baron E de Rothschild's Quenouille (13)
1920⋆Baron E de Rothschild's Flowershop (15)
1921 Baron M de Rothschild's Doniazade (21)
1922 M X Balli's Pellsie (14)
1923 M A Sabathier's Quoi (20)
1924 M E Kann's Uganda (23)
1925 Baron R de Rothschild's Aquatinte II (19)
1926 M E Esmond's Dorina (25)
1927 Sir M Davis's Fairy Legend (25)
1928 lady Davis's Mary Legend (22)
1929 Cte de Rivaud's Ukrania (22)
1930 M E Henriquet's Commanderie (21)
1931 Mlle D Esmond's Pearl Cap (17)
1932 Baron E de Rothschild's Perruche Bleue (19)
1933 Baron E de Rothschild's Vendange (15)
1934 M M Boussac's Adargatis (15)
1935 Baron E de Rothschild's Peniche (21)
1936⋆M E Esmond's Mistress Ford (18)
1937 Lady Granard's En Fraude (15)
1938 Baron M de Rothschild's Feerie (12)
1939 M E Martinez de Hoz's Lysistrata (18)
1940 No race
1941⋆M R Mathe-Dumaine's Sapotille II (14)
1942⋆Ctss M A de P de La Rocca's Vigilance (14)
1943†M M Boussac's Caravelle (7)
1944†M R Saint's Pointe a Pitre (9)
1945⋆Mme R Patureau's Nikellora (17)
1946⋆M M Le Baron's Pirette (27)
1947⋆Comte de Chambure's Montenica (19)
1948 M M Boussac's Corteira (22)
1949 Mme R Forget's Bagheera (21)
1950 M H Bletry's Aglae Grace 924)

1951 M Maurice Hennessy's Stratonice (23)
1952 M R B Strassburger's Seria (17)
1953 M P Dubosqc's La Sorellina (18)
1954 Mme J Couturie's Tahiti (14)
1955 M M Goudchaux's Douve (17)
1956 M M Boussac's Apollonia (14)
1957 Baron G de Rothschild's Cerisoles (19)
1958 M F Dupre's Dushka (19)
1959 M R T de la Chaume's Barquette (25)
1960 Baron G de Rothschild's Timandra (19)
1961 Baron G de Rothschild's Hermieres (22)
1962 M F Dupre's La Sega (14)
1963 Mme H Herbaux's La Belle Ferronniere (13)
1964 Mme L Volterra's Belle Sicambre (13)
1965 M G Brun's Blabla (16)
1966 Baron G de Waldner's Fine Pearl (15)
1967 Mr N B Hunt's Gazala (20)
1968 Mme G Bridgland's Roseliere (22)
1969 M M Boussac's Crepellana (16)
1970 Mr S McGrath's Sweet Mimosa (19)
1971 Mme A Head's Pistol Packer (16)
1972 Baron de Rede's Rescousse (21)
1973 M D Wildenstein's Allez France (USA) (25)
1974 Her Majesty's Highclere (22)
1975 No race
1976 M D Wildenstein's Pawneese (11)
1977 M D Wildenstein's Madelia (13)
1978 M J Wertheimer's Reine de Saba (17)
1979 Mme H Love's Dunette (12)
1980 Mr E Kronfeld's Mrs Penny (USA) (14)
1981 Mr G Kaye's Madam Gay (14)
1982 Ecurie Aland's Harbour (14)
1983 Mme J Fellow's Escaline (17)
1984 Mr S Niarchos's Northern Trick (USA) (15)
1985 Mr L T Al Swaidi's Lypharita (Fr) (10)
1986 Mr G Oldham's Lacovia (USA) (14)
1987 Sheikh Mohammed's Indian Skimmer (USA) (14)
1988 Mr J-L Lagardere's Resless Kara (Fr) (16)
1989 Mr M Abdul Karim's Lady In Silver (USA) (14)
1990 Prince A Faisal's Rafha (14)
1991 Mr K Nitta's Caerlina (IRE) (13)
1992 Mr K Abdulla's Jolypha (USA) (12)
1993 H H Aga Khan's Shemaka (14)

*Run at Longchamp
†Run at Le Tremblay

PRIX DU JOCKEY-CLUB LANCIA (Chantilly)

(French Derby)
(1 mile 4 fur)
(First run 1836)

1900 Baron R T Carter's La Moriniere (13)
1901 M E Blanc's Saxon (13)
1902 M Camille Blanc's Retz (14)
1903 Cte H de Portales's Ex Voto (14)
1904 M E Blanc's Ajaz (11)
1905 M M Ephrussi's Finasseur (8)
1906 M W K Vanderbilt's Maintenon (17)
1907 M Michel Ephrussi's Mordant (14)
1908*M W K Vanderbilt's Sea Sick
*M E Deschamps's Quintette (10)
1909 M W K Vanderbilt's Negofol (19)
1910 M Gaston-Dreyfus's Or du Rhin II (17)
1911 Baron de Rothschild's Alcantara II (13)
1912 Prince Murat's Friant II (17)
1913 M E Blanc's Dagor (17)
1914 Baron M de Rothschild's Sardanapale (12)
1915–18 No race
1919‡Mr W Vanderbilt's Tchad (14)
1920‡M J Hennessy's Sourbier (14)
1921 Mme E Blanc's Ksar (19)
1922 M M Boussac's Ramus (15)
1923 M J Desgorce's le Capucin (18)
1924 H H Aga Khan's Pot au Feu (17)
1925 M E Martinez de Hoz's Belfonds (14)
1926 M F de Alzaga-Unzue's Madrigal (14)
1927 M E Martinez de Hoz's Mon Talisman (17)
1928 Cte de Rivaud's Le Correge (20)
1929 M E Esmond's Hotweed (20)
1930 Cte de Rivaud's Chateau Bouscaut (13)
1931 M M Boussac's Tourbillon (16)
1932 M A J Duggan's Strip the Willow (17)
1933 M M Boussac's Thor (12)
1934 M L Volterra's Duplex (14)
1935 M E Esmond's Pearlweed (15)
1936 M E Masurel's Mieuxce (14)
1937 M E Martinez de Hoz's Clarivoyant (12)
1938 M M Boussac's Cillas (15)
1939 M M Boussac's Pharis II (14)
1940§M P Versein's Quicko (8)
1941‡M P Gund's Le Pacha (14)
1942‡Viscomtesse Vigier's Magister (28)
1943†Comte de Chambure's Verso II (11)
1944‡M M Boussac's Ardan (11)
1945‡M M Boussac's Coaraze (12)
1946‡M P Boyriven's Prince Chevalier (15)
1947‡M M Boussac's Sandjar (13)
1948 M Constant Vandamme's Bey (22)
1949 M C Victor-Thomas's Good Luck (7)
1950 M M Boussac's Scratch II (15)
1951 M Jean Stern's Sicambre 914)
1952 M M Boussac's Auriban (13)
1953 M H Letellier's Chamant (20)
1954 M L l Lawrence's Le Petit Prince (19)
1955 Comte F de Ganay's Rapace 915)
1956 M M Boussac's Philius II (16)
1957 Mme A Mariotti's Amber (14)
1958 M R Beamonte's Tamanar (17)
1959 Mme C del Duca's Herbager (16)
1960 H H Aga Khan's Charlottesville (16)
1961 Mme J Couturie's Right Royal (150
1962 Marquise du Vivier's Val de Loir (18)
1963 M J Ternynck's Sanctus (13)
1964 Mme G Weisweiller's Le Fabuleux (14)
1965 M F Dupre's Reliance (9)
1966 M P Dubosqc's Nelcius (13)
1967 Baron L de la Rochette's Astec (13)
1968 M A Plesch's Tapalque (22)
1969 M M Lehmann's Goodly (17)
1970 M A Plesch's Sassafras (15)
1971 Mme F Dupre's Rheffic (14)
1972 M J Kashiyama's Hard to Beat (13)
1973 Mme P Werthelimer's Roi Lear (16)
1974 Mme M-F Berger's Caracolero (USA) (15)
1975 M J Wertheimer's Val de l'Orne (11)
1976 Mr N B Hunt's Youth (USA) (18)
1977 Baron G de Rothschild's Crystal Palace (14)
1978 M M Boussac's Acamas (20)
1979 H H Aga Khan's Top Ville (11)
1980 Mr F Tinsley's Policeman (14)
1981 M J Ouaki's Bikala (Ire) (12)
1982 Mr R Sangster's Assert (14)
1983 Mr R Sangster's Caerleon (USA) (12)
1984 H H Aga Khan's Darshaan (17)
1985 H H Aga Khan's Mouktar (11)
1986 Mme A Head's Bering (13)
1987 H H Aga Khan's Natroun (17)
1988 Marquise de Moratella's Hours After (USA) (16)
1989 Sheikh Mohammed's Old Vic (12)
1990 Mr K Abdulla's Sanglamore (12)
1991 Mr H Chalhoub's Suave Dancer (USA) (7)
1992 Mme B Houillion's Polytain (17)
1993 Mr S Niarchos's Hernando (11)

*Dead-heat
‡Run at Longchamp
†Run at Le Tremblay
§Run at Auteuil

BUDWEISER IRISH DERBY (Curragh)

($1^1/2$ miles)
For three year olds
(First run 1866)

1900 Gallinaria 8st 12lb (12)
1901 Carrigavalla 8st 12lb (9)
1902 St Brendan 9st 5lb (11)
1903 Lord Rossmore 9st 2lb (8)
1904 Royal Arch 8st 2lb (8)
1905 Flax Park 7st 13lb (11)
1906 Killeagh 9st 5lb (9)
1907 Orby 9st 8lb (7)
1908 Wild Bouquet 7st 13lb (8)
1909 Bachelor's Double 9st 5lb (7)
1910 Aviator 9st (9)
1911 Shanballymore 8st 6lb (10)
1912 Civility 8st 12lb (5)
1913 Bachelor's Wedding 9st 1lb (8)
1914 Land of Song 9st 5lb (6)
1915 Ballaghtobin 9st 5lb (12)
1916 Furore 8st 12lb (10)
1917 First Flier 8st 10lb (10)
1918 King John 8st 12lb (7)
1919 Loch Lomond 8st 9lb (8)
1920 He Goes 9st 5lb (8)
1921 Ballyheron 8st 12lb (10)
1922 Spike Island 9st 8lb (12)
1923 Waygood 8st 12lb (15)
1924*Zodiac 8st 12lb
*Haine 9st 2lb (7)
1925 Zionist 9st 5lb (8)
1926 Embargo 9st 5lb (10)
1927 Knight of the Grail 9st 5lb (6)
1928 Baytown 9st 5lb (10)
1929 Kopi 9st 5lb (9)
1930 Rock Star 8st 12lb (12)
1931 Sea Serpent 8st 12lb (6)
1932 Dastur 9st 5lb (10)
1933 Harinero 9st 2lb (8)
1934*Primero 8st 12lb
*Patriot King 8st 2lb (6)
1935 Museum 9st 5lb (8)
1936 Raeburn 9st 2lb (9)
1937 Phideas 9st 5lb (6)
1938 Rosewell 8st 12lb (9)
1939 Mondragon 8st 12lb (9)
1940 Turkhan 9st 5lb (7)
1941 Sol Oriens 8st 12lb (10)
1942 Windsor Slipper 9st 2lb (13)
1943 The Phoenix 9st 5lb (9)
1944 Slide On 8st 2lb (7)
1945 Piccadilly 8st 12lb (8)
1946 Bright news 9st (14)
1947 Sayajirao 9st (11)
1948 Nathoo 9st (12)
1949 Hindostan 9st (12)
1950 Dark Warrior 9st (8)
1951 Fraise du Bois II 9st (16)
1952 Thirteen of Diamonds 9st (10)
1953 Chamier 9st (13)
1954 Zarathustra 9st (11)
1955 Panaslipper 9st (13)
1956 Talgo 9st (10)
1957 Ballymoss 9st (12)
1958 Sindon 9st (12)
1959 Fidalgo 9st (11)
1960 Chamour 9st (7)
1961 Your Highness 9st (18)
1962 Tambourine II 9st (24)
1963 Ragusa 9st (16)
1964 Santa Claus 9st (19)
1965 Meadow Court 9st (21)
1966 Sodium 9st (23)
1967 Ribocco 9st (23)
1968 Ribero 9st (14)
1969 Prince Regent (Fr) 9st (15)
1970 Nijinsky (Can) 9st (13)
1971 Irish Ball (Fr) 9st (15)
1972 Steel Pulse 9st (14)
1973 Weaver's Hall 9st (15)
1974 English Prince 9st (13)
1975 Grundy 9st (13)
1976 Malacate (USA) 9st (17)
1977 The Minstrel (Can) 9st (15)
1978 Shirley Heights 9st (11)
1979 Troy 9st (9)
1980 Tyrnavos 9st (13)
1981 Shergar 9st (12)
1982 Assert 9st (10)
1983 Shareef Dancer (USA) 9st (12)
1984 El Gran Senor (USA) 9st (8)
1985 Law Society (USA) 9st (13)
1986 Shahrastani 9st (11)
1987 Sir Harry Lewis 9st (8)
1988 Kahtyasi 9st (11)
1989 Old Vic 9st (8)
1990 Salsabil 8st 11lb (9)
1991 Generous 9st (6)
1992 St Jovite (USA) 9st (11)
1993 Commander in Chief 9st (11)

*Dead-heat

GRAND PRIX DE PARIS (Longchamp)

For three year olds
(First run 1863)
($1^1/4$ miles)

1900 Baron A de Schickler's Semendria (15)
1901 M M Caillault' Cheri (16)
1902 M E de St Alary's Kizil Kourgan (11)
1903 M E Blanc's Quo Vadis (14)
1904 M E Blanc's Ajax (13)
1905 M M Ephrussi's Finasseur (9)
1906 Major E Loder's Spearmint (13)
1907 Baron E de Rothschild's Sans Souci II (14)
1908 M W K Vanderbilt's Northeast (18)
1909 Baron M de Rothschild's Verdun (11)
1910 Mme N Cherermeteff's Nuage (17)
1911 Marquis de Ganay's As d'Atout (16)
1912 M A Fould's Houli (21)
1913 M E de St Alary's Bruleur 920)
1914 Baron M de Rothschild's Sardanapale (12)
1915–1916 No race
1917‡M W K Vanderbilt's Brumelli (10)
1918‡M J Prat's Montmartin (6)
1919 Mr A de Rothschild's Galloper Light (7)
1920 M E de St Alary's Comrade (15)
1921 Mr J Watson's Lemonora (17)
1922 M N E Ambatielos's Kefalin (15)
1923 M C Ranucci's Filibert de Savoie (18)
1924 M L Mantacheff's Transvaal II (20)
1925 Mr J de Rothschild's Reine Luminere (18)
1926 M J Hennessy's Take My Tip (22)
1927 M M P Moulines's Fiterari (16)
1928 Mr Ogden Mills's Cri de Guerre (18)
1929 M E Esmond's Hotweed (23)
1930 M E Henriquet's Commanderie (21)
1931 Comte de Rivaud's Barneveldt (13)
1932 M A J Duggan's Strip the Willow (20)
1933 Lady Granard's Cappiello (18)
1934 M L Volterra's Admiral Drake (17)
1935 Baron E de Rothschild's Crudite (22)
1936 M E Masurel's Mieuxce (20)
1937 M E Martinez de Hoz's Clairvoyant (24)
1938 M F Tesio's Nearco (18)
1939 M M Boussac's Pharis II (19)
1940*Vicomtesse Vigier's Maurepas (6)
1941 M P Gund's Le Pacha (7)
1942 Victomtesse Vigier's Magister (23)
1943†Mme R de Bonand's Pensbury (16)
1944†M J M Sion's Deux pour Cent (16)
1945 M M Boussac's Caracalla (13)
1946 M F R Schmitt's Souverain (19)
1947 Prince Aly Khan's Avenger (16)
1948 H H Aga Khan's My Love (14)
1949 Mme R Forget's Bagheera (26)
1950 Baron G de Rothschild's Vieux Manoir (18)
1951 M Jean Stern's Sicambre (15)
1952 M E Martinez de Hoz's Orfeo (16)
1953 M F Dupre's Northern Light (22)
1954 M R Thion de la Chaume's Popof (17)
1955 Mme L Volterra's Phil Drake (20)
1956 Mme L Volterra's Vattel (19)
1957 M G Delloye's Altipan (13)
1958 M V Lyon's San Roman (15)
1959 M A Belinguier's Birum (18)
1960 H H Aga Khan's Charlottesville (20)
1961 M Andre Rueff's Balto (18)
1962 M M Goudchaux's Armistice (13)
1963 M J Ternynck's Sanctus (19)
1964 Baron G de Rothschild's White Label (14)
1965 M F Dupre's Reliance (10)
1966 M F Dupre's Danseur (20)
1967 Mme J Stern's Phaeton (13)
1968 Mme G Courtois's Dhaudevi (15)
1969 Mme G Weisweiller's Chaparral (15)
1970 M E A Scheib's Roll of Honour (14)
1971 Mme F Dupre's Rheffic (9)
1972 Baron de Rede's Pleben (12)
1973 M F Burmann's Tennyson (16)
1974 Mr G A Oldham's Sagaro (18)
1975 Mme F Stern's Matahawk (22)
1976 Mr N B Hunt's Exceller (USA) (9)
1977 Mme T J Caralli's Funny Hobby (11)
1978 M A Ben Lassin's Galiani (14)
1979 Baron G de Rothschild's Soleil Noir (7)

1980 Mr A Michel's Valiant Heart (14)
1981 Mr P Mellon's Glint of Gold (11)
1982 Baron G de Rothschild's Le Nain Jaune (11)
1983 Elisha Holding's Yawa (7)
1984 H Al Maktoum's At Talaq (USA) (8)
1985 H H Aga Khan's Sumayr (7)
1986 Mr N Bunker Hunt's Swink (9)

(1¼)

1987 Mr L Norris's Risk Me (9)
1988 Mr M Fustok's Fijar Tango (Fr) (10)
1989 Mr T Wada's Dancehall (USA) (8)
1990 Mr B McNall's Saumarez (8)
1991 Mr O Lecerf's Subotica (9)
1992 Mr P de Moussac's Homme de Loi (10)
1993 Sheikh Mohammed's Fort Wood (USA) (9)

*Run at Auteuil
†Run at le Tremblay
‡Run at Maisons-Laffitte
Run over 1 mile 7 fur until 1986

GRAND PRIX DE SAINT-CLOUD (Saint-Cloud)

(1½ miles)
(First run 1904)

1927 Nino 4y 9st 8lb (12)
1928 Mon Talisman 4y 9st 8lb (9)
1929 Bubbles 4y 9st 8lb (10)
1930 Feb 5y 9st 11lb (11)
1931 Barneveldt 3y 7st (9)
1932 Prince Rose 4y 9st 8lb (15)
1933 Marcaroni 4y 9st 8lb (11)
1934 Assuerus 4y 9st 8lb (12)
1935 Louqsor 3y 8st 7lb (12)
1936 Corrida 4y 9st 5lb (5)
1937 Vatellor 4y 9st 8lb (10)
1938 Victrix 4y 9st 8lb (14)
1939 Genievre 3y 8st 7lb (8)
1940 No race
1941†Maurepas 4y 9st 8lb (5)
1942†Djebel 5y 9st 11lb (8)
1943‡Escamillo 4y 9st 8lb (9)
1944**Un Gaillard 6y 9st 11lb (9)
1945‡Ardan 4y 9st 8lb (60
1946 Coaraze 4y 9st 8lb (3)
1947 Young Lo 4y 9st 8lb (9)
1948 Goyama 5y 9st 11lb (5)
1949 Medium 3y 8st 3lb (10)
1950 Ocarina 3y 8st 7lb (11)
1951 Violoncelle 4y 9st 8lb (9)
1952 Fast Fox 5y 9st 11lb (7)
1953 Magnific 4y 9st 8lb (15)
1954 Banassa 4y 9st 5lb (17)
1955 Chingacgook 3y 8st 7lb (12)
1956*Burgos 4y 9st 8lb
*Oroso 3y 8st 7lb (11)
1957 Tanerko 4y 9st 8lb (13)
1958 Tanerko 5y 9st 11lb (12)
1959 Herbager 3y 8st 7lb (10)
1960 Sheshoon 4y 9st 8lb (9)
1961 Dicta Drake 3y 8st 7lb (17)
1962 Match 4y 9st 8lb (13)
1963 Exbury 4y 9st 8lb (13)
1964 Relko 4y 9st 8lb (10)
1965 Sea-Bird II 3y 8st 7lb (9)
1966 Sea Hawk 3y 8st 7lb (11)
1967 Taneb 4y 9st 8lb (8)
1968 Hopeful Venture 4y 9st 8lb (20)
1969 Felicio 4y 9st 8lb (10)
1970 Gyr (USA) 3y 8st 7lb (8)
1971 Ramsin 4y 9st 8lb (10)
1972 Rheingold 3y 8st 7lb (7)
1973 Rheingold 4y 9st 8lb (9)
1974 Dahlia (USA) 4y 9st 5lb (11)
1975 Un Kopeck 4y 9st 8lb (11)
1976 Riverqueen 4y 8st 6lb (8)
1977 Exceller (USA) 4y 9st 8lb (10)
1978 Guadanini 4y 9st 8lb (9)
1979 Gay Mecene (USA) 4y 9st 8lb (13)
1980*Dunette 4y 9st 5lb (9)
*Shakapour 3y 8st 9lb (9)
1981 Akarad 3y 8st 9lb (10)
1982 Glint of Gold 4y 9st 8lb (9)
1983 Diamond Shoal 4y 9st 8lb (9)
1984 Teenoso (USA) 4y 9st 8lb (11)
1985 Strawberry Road (Aus) 6y 9st 8lb (7)
1986 Acatenango (Ger) 4y 9st 7lb
1987 Moon Madness 4y 9st 8lb (6)
1988 Village Star (Fr) 5y 9st 8lb (10)
1989 Sheriff's Star 4y 9st 8lb (6)
1990 In The Wings 4y 9st 8lb (8)
1991 Epervier Bleu 4y 9st 8lb (12)
1992 Pistolet Bleu 4y 9st 8lb (7)
1993 User Friendly 4y 9st 5lb (8)

*Dead-heat
†Run at Longchamp
‡Run at Maisons-Laffitte
**Run at Le Tremblay

KILDANGAN STUD IRISH OAKS (Curragh)

(1½ miles)
For three year old fillies
(First run 1895)

1900 May Race 8st 10lb (6)
1901 Royal Mantle 8st 3lb (5)
1902 Marievale 8st 10lb (5)
1903 Mary Lester 8st 3lb (5)
1904 Copestone f 9st (5)
1905 Blakestown 9st (3)
1906 Juliet II 10st (6)
1907 Reina 8st 10lb (12)
1908 Queen of Peace 8st 6lb (5)
1909 Fredith 8st 3lb (7)
1910 Blair Royal 8st 3lb (5)
1911 Tullynacree 8st 7lb (6)
1912 Shining Way 9st (6)
1913 Athgreany 8st 10lb (7)
1914 May Edgar 9st 3lb (6)
1915 Latharna 8st 3lb (9)
1916 Captive Princess 9st (6)
1917 Golden Maid 9st 5lb (8)
1918 Judea 8st 13lb (4)
1919 Snow Maiden 9st 5lb (6)
1920 Place Royale 9st (6)
1921 The Kiwi 8st 10lb (7)
1922 Miss Hazelwood 9st (10)
1923 Becka 9st (10)
1924 Amethystine 9st (8)
1925 Ixia 9st 4lb (6)
1926 Resplendent 9st 7lb (7)
1927 Cinq a Sept 9st (7)
1928 Haintonette 9st 4lb (7)
1929 Soloptic 9st 7lb (4)
1930 Theresina 9st 7lb (8)
1931 Nitsichin 9st (9)
1932 Santaria 9st (9)
1933 Salar 9st (14)
1934 Foxcroft 9st 10lb (5)
1935 Smokeless 9st 7lb (8)
1936 Silversol 9st (6)
1937 Sol Speranza 9st 4lb (7)
1938 Conversation Piece 9st 7lb (8)
1939 Superbe 9st 7lb (8)
1940 Queen of Shiraz 9st (11)
1941 Uvira 9st (5)
1942 Majideh 9st 4lb (8)
1943 Suntop 9st 4lb (12)
1944 Avoca 9st (9)
1945 Admirable 9st (14)
1946 Linaria 9st (10)
1947 Desert Drive 9st (14)
1948 Masaka 9st 1lb (10)
1949 Circus Lady 9st (12)
1950 Corejada 9st (16)
1951 Djebellica 9st (13)
1952 Five Spots 9st (13)
1953 Noory 9st (11)
1954 Pantomime Queen 9st (15)
1955 Agar's Plough 9st (12)
1956 Garden State 9st (8)
1957 Silken Gilder 9st (15)
1958 Amante 9st (11)
1959 Discorea 9st (9)
1960 Lynchris 9st (17)
1961 Ambergris 9st (10)
1962 French Cream 9st (12)
1963 Hibernia III 9st (15)
1964 Ancasta 9st (9)
1965 Aurabella 9st (10)
1966 Merry Mate 9st (10)
1967 Pampalina 9st (14)
1968 Celina 9st (12)
1969 Gaia 9st (7)
1970 Santa Tina 9st (14)
1971 Altesse Royale 9st (13)
1972 Regal Exception (USA) 9st (12)
1973 Dahlia (USA) 9st (12)
1974 Dibidale 9st (8)
1975 Juliette Marny 9st (14)
1976 Lagunette (Fr) 9st (18)
1977 Olwyn 9st (8)
1978 Fair Salinia 9st (12)
1979 Godetia (USA) 9st (13)
1980 Shoot A Line 9st (8)
1981 Blue Wind 9st (10)
1982 Swiftfoot 9st (10)
1983 Give Thanks 9st (12)
1984 Princess Pati 9st (11)
1985 Helen Street 9st (9)
1986 Colorspin 9st (8)
1987 Unite 9st (8)
1988*Diminuendo 9st
*Melodist 9st (9)
1989 Alydaress (USA) 9st (5)
1990 Knight's Baroness 9st (10)
1991 Possessive Dancer 9st (10)
1992 User Friendly 9st (9)
1993 Wemyss Bight 9st (11)

*Dead-heat

PRIX ROBERT PAPIN (Maisons-Laffitte)

(5½ fur)
For two year olds
(First run 1901)

1927 Erica 8st 7lb (10)
1928 Necklace 8st 7lb (11)
1929 Chateau Bouscaut 8st 9lb (14)

1930 Pearl Cap 8st 7lb (9)
1931 Coeur de Lion III 8st 9lb (9)
1932 Coque de Noix 8st 7lb (7)
1933 Brantome 8st 9lb (11)
1934 Stratosphere 8st 7lb (7)
1935 Mistress Ford 8st 7lb (5)
1936 Minaudiere 8st 7lb (6)
1937 Gossip 8st 7lb (7)
1938 Bulle de Savon 8st 7lb (5)
1939 Codor 8st 9lb (8)
1940†Longthanh 9st 13lb (9)
1941 Mirko 8st 9lb (10)
1942 Norseman 8st 9lb (5)
1943 Ardan 8st 9lb (7)
1944‡Otero 8st 7lb (9)
1945 Nirgal 8st 9lb (5)
1946 Chesterfield 8st 9lb (40
1947 Primeur 8st 7lb (5)
1948 Coronation 8st 7lb (8)
1949 Emperor 8st 9lb (11)
1950 Pharsale 8st 9lb (13)
1951 Auriban 8st 9lb (12)
1952 Pharel 8st 9lb (6)
1953 Cordova 8st 9lb (9)
1954 Soya 8st 9lb (11)
1955 Fiere 8st 9lb (13)
1956 L'Astrologue 8st 11lb (9)
1957 Neptune II 8st 11lb (13)
1958 Taboun 8st 11lb (11)
1959 Sly Pola 8st 8lb (12)
1960 High Bulk 8st 8lb (11)
1961 Wakamba 8st 8lb (6)
1962 Quiqui 8st 11lb (8)
1963 Djel 8st 11lb (10)
1964 Double Jump 8st 11lb (19)
1965 Kashmir II 8st 11lb (9)
1966 Fin Bon 8st 11lb (12)
1967 Zeddaan 8st 11lb 914)
1968 Folle Rousse 8st 9lb (12)
1969 Ambler Rama (USA) 8st 11lb (18)
1970 My Swallow 8st 11lb (9)
1971 Sun Prince 8st 11lb (9)
1972 Reine du Chant 8st 9lb (12)
1973 Lianga (USA) 8st 9lb (11)
1974 Sky Commander (USA) 8st 11lb (12)
1975 Vitiges 8st 11lb (13)
1976 Blushing Groom 8st 11lb (12)
1977★★Vific 8st 9lb (14)
1978 Pitasia 8st 9lb (8)
1979 Choucri (Can) 8st 11lb (7)
1980 Irish Playboy (USA) 8st 11lb (10)
1981 Maelstrom Lake 8st 11lb (10)
1982 Ma Biche 8st 9lb (9)
1983 Masarika 8st 9lb (5)
1984 Seven Springs 8st 9lb (12)
1985 Baiser Vole 8st 9lb (13)
1986 Balbonella 8st 9lb (7)
1987 Baliwaki 8st 9lb (12)
1988 Philippi 8st 11lb (9)
1989 Ozone Friendly (USA) 8st 9lb (9)
1990 Danseuse du Soir (IRE) 8st 9lb (9)
1991 Arazi (USA) 8st 11lb (6)
1992 Didyme (USA) 8st 11lb (7)
1993 Psychobabble (IRE) 8st 11lb (8)

†Run over 7 fur at Auteuil
‡Run over 5 fur at Longchamp
★★Run over 5½ fur at Evry

PRIX MORNY AGENCE FRANCAISE (Deauville)

(6 fur)
For two year olds
(First run 1902)

1927 Kantar 8st 11lb (12)
1928 Necklace 8st 9lb (15)
1929 Chateau Bouscaut 8st 11lb (11)
1930 Pearl Cap 8st 9lb (12)
1931 Eadhild 8st 9lb (13)
1932 Cecias 8st 11lb (11)
1933 Brantome 8st 11lb (11)
1934 Corrida 8st 9lb (10)
1935 Mistress Fod 8st 9lb (8)
1936 Tizona 8st 9lb (9)
1937 Ad Astra 8st 9lb (8)
1938 Semiramide 8st 9lb (13)
1939 Furane 8st 9lb (9)
1940 No race
1941†Esmeralda 8st 9lb (6)
1942†Fanatique 8st 11lb (6)
1943‡Sampiero 8st 11lb (5)
1944★★Coaraze 8st 11lb (12)
1945‡Nirgal 8st 11lb (8)
1946 Cadir 8st 11lb (8)
1947 Delirium 8st 11lb (10)
1948 Amour Drake 8st 11lb (5)
1949 Ksarinor 8st 11lb (6)
1950 Sanguine 8st 9lb (12)
1951 Auriban 8st 11lb (9)
1952 Bozet 8st 11lb (11)
1953 Cordova 8st 9lb (9)
1954 Chingacgook 8st 11lb (11)
1955 Apollonia 8st 9lb (14)
1956 Mr Pickwick 8st 11lb (14)
1957 Neptune II 8st 11lb (9)
1958 Oceanic 8st 11lb (10)
1959 Pharamond 8st 11lb (12)
1960 Solitude 8st 9lb (15)
1961 Prudent 8st 11lb (11)
1962 Darannour 8st 11lb (10)
1963 Revoquee 8st 8lb (17)
1964 Grey Daawn 8st 11lb (13)
1965 Soleil 8st 11lb (14)
1966 Le Conquerant 8st 11lb (14)
1967 Madina 8st 8lb (14)
1968 Princeline 8st 8lb (13)
1969 Amber Rama (USA) 8st 11lb (9)
1970 My Swallow 8st 11lb (7)
1971 Daring Display 8st 11lb (8)
1972 Filiberto 8st 11lb (17)
1973 Nonoalco (USA) 8st 11lb (7)
1974 Broadway Dancer (USA) 8st 8lb (13)
1975 Vitiges 8st 11lb (13)
1976 Blushing Groom 8st 11lb (11)
1977 Super Concorde (USA) 8st 11lb (10)
1978 Irish River 8st 11lb (11)
1979 Princess Lida (USA) 8st 11lb (10)
1980 Ancient Regime (USA) 8st 8lb (7)
1981 Green Forest (USA) 8st 11lb (5)
1982 Deep Roots 8st 11lb (6)
1983 Siberian Express (USA) 8st 11lb (7)
1984 Seven Springs (USA) 8st 8lb (7)
1985 Regal State 8st 8lb (11)
1986 Sakura Reiko 8st 8lb (8)
1987 First Waltz (Fr) 8st 8lb (8)
1988 Tersa (USA) 8st 8lb (8)
1989 Machiavellian (USA) 8st 11lb (7)
1990 Hector Protector (USA) 8st 11lb (12)
1991 Arazi (USA) 8st 11lb (4)
1992 Zafonic (USA) 8st 11lb (10)
1993 Coup de Genie (USA) 8st 8lb (8)

†Run over 5 fur at Longchamp
‡Run at Maisons-Laffitte
★★Run over 6½ fur at Longchamp

PRIX VERMEILLE ESCADA (Longchamp)

(1½ miles)
For three year old fillies
(First run 1897)

1927 Samphire 9st (13)
1928 Merry Girl 8st 7lb (9)
1929 Calandria 9st (8)
1930 Commanderie 9st (9)
1931 Pearl Cap 9st (3)
1932 Kiddie 8st 7lb (9)
1933 La Circe 8st 7lb (9)
1934 Mary Tudor 9st (9)
1935 Crisa 8st 7lb (9)
1936 Mistress Ford 9st (12)
1937 Tonnelle 8st 7lb (8)
1938 Ma Normandie 8st 7lb (7)
1939 and 1940 No race
1941 Longthanh 9st 2lb (11)
1942 Vigilance 9st 2lb (9)
1943†Folle Nuit 8st 9lb (7)
1944†La Belle du Canay 8st 9lb (12)
1945 Nikellora 9st 2lb (11)
1946 Pirette 9st 2lb (13)
1947 Procureuse 8st 9lb (10)
1948 Corteira 9st 2lb (11)
1949 Bagheera 9st 2lb (11)
1950 Kilette 8st 9lb (10)
1951 Orberose 8st 9lb (12)
1952 La Mirambule 8st 9lb (8)
1953 Radio 8st 7lb (14)
1954 Philante 8st 7lb (13)
1955 Wild MNiss 9st 2lb (14)
1956 Janiari 9st 2lb (9)
1957 Arbencia 9st 2lb (13)
1958 Bella Paola 9st 2lb (5)
1959 Mi Carina 9st 2lb (14)
1960 Lezghinka 9st 2lb (10)
1961★Astola 9st 2lb
★Anne la Douce 9st 2lb (18)
1962 Monade 9st 2lb (11)
1963 Golden Girl 9st 2lb (12)
1964 Astaria 9st 2lb (16)
1965 Aunt Edith 9st 2lb (22)
1966 Haltilala 9st 2lb (16)
1967 Casaque Grise 9st 2lb (19)
1968 Roseliere 9st 2lb (16)
1969 Saraca 9st 2lb (21)
1970 Highest Hopes 9st 2lb (13)
1971 Pistol Packer 9st 2lb (15)
1972★Paysanne 9st 2lb
★San San (USA) 9st 2lb (18)
1973 Allez France (USA) 9st 2lb (13)
1974 Paulista 9st 2lb (15)
1975 Ivanjica (USA) 9st 2lb (13)
1976 Lagunette 9st 2lb (10)
1977 Kamicia 9st 2lb (18)
1978 Dancing Maid 9st 2lb (12)
1979 Three Troikas 9st 2lb (13)
1980 Mrs Penny (USA) 9st 2lb (12)
1981 April Run 9st 2lb (10)
1982 All Along 9st 2lb (13)
1983 Sharaya 9st 2lb (12)
1984 Northern Trick (USA) 9st 2lb (10)

1985 Walensee 9st 2lb (13)
1986 Darara 9st 2lb (8)
1987 Bint Pasha (USA) 9st 2lb (12)
1988 Indian Rose 9st 2lb (8)
1989 Young Mother 9st 2lb (7)
1990 Salsabil 9st 2lb (9)
1991 Magic Night 9st 2lb (14)
1992 Jolypha (USA) 9st 2lb (10)
1993 Intrepidity 9st 2lb (8)

*Dead-heat
†Run at Le Tremblay over 1 mile 3 1/2 fur

JEFFERSON SMURFIT MEMORIAL IRISH ST. LEGER (Curragh)

(1 3/4 miles)

1915 La Poloma 8st 11lb (6)
1916 Captive Princess 8st 11lb (8)
1917 Double Scotch 8st 11lb (5)
1918 Dionysos 9st (7)
1919 Cheap Popularity 8st 11lb (5)
1920 Kirk Alloway 9st (3)
1921 Kircubbin 9st (5)
1922 Royal Lancer 9st 10lb (8)
1923 O'Dempsey 9st (5)
1924 Zodiac 9st 10lb (8)
1925 Spelthorne 9st 7lb (6)
1926 Sunny View 9st 7lb 92)
1927 Ballyvoy 9st (4)
1928 Law Suit 9st 4lb (4)
1929 Trigo 9st 12lb (5)
1930 Sol de Terre 9st (4)
1931 Beaudelaire 9st (2)
1932 Hill Song 9st (4)
1933 Harinero 9st 10lb (6)
1934 Primero 9st 7lb (8)
1935 Museum 9st 10lb (5)
1936 Battle Song 9st (4)
1937 Owenstown 9st 4lb (5)
1938 Ochiltree 9st (7)
1939 Skoiter 9st (6)
1940 Harvest Feast 9st (5)
1941 Etoile de Lyons 9st (6)
1942 Windsor Slipper 9st 7lb (8)
1943 Solferino 9st (4)
1944 Water Street 9st (7)
1945 Spam 8st 11lb (9)
1946 Cassock 9st (9)
1947 Esprit de France 9st (5)
1948 Beau Sabreur 9st (8)
1949 Brown Rover 9st (13)
1950 Morning Madam 8st 11lb (12)
1951 Do Well 9st (10)
1952 Judicate 9st (7)
1953 Sea Charger 9st (10)
1954 Zarathustra 9st (5)
1955 Diamond Slipper 9st (9)
1956 Magnetic North 9st (8)
1957 Ommeyad 9st (11)
1958 Royal Highway 9st (6)
1959 Barclay 9st (7)
1960 Lynchris 8st 11lb (8)
1961 Vimadee 9st (10)
1962 Arctic Vale 9st (9)
1963 Christmas Island 9st (10)
1964 Biscayne 9st (8)
1965 Craighouse 9st (14)
1966 White Gloves 9st (14)
1967 Dan Kano 9st (8)
1968 Giolla Mear 9st (10)
1969 Reindeer 9st (9)
1970 Allangrange 9st (8)
1971 Parnell 9st (8)
1972 Pidget 8st 11lb (7)
1973 Conor Pass 9st (7)
1974 Mistigri 9st (7)
1975 Caucasus (USA) 9st (13)
1976 Meneval (USA) 9st (11)
1977 Transworld (USA) 9st (9)
1978 M-Lolshan 9st (8)
1979 Niniski (USA) 9st (10)
1980 Gonzales (USA) 9st (8)
1981 Protection Racket (USA) 9st (7)
1982 Touching Wood 9st (10)
1983 Mountain Lodge 4y 9st 4lb (10)
1984 Opale 4y 9st 4lb (9)
1985 Leading Counsel (USA) 3y 8st 12lb (12)
1986 Authaal 3y 8st 12lb (6)
1987 Eurobird 3y 8st 9lb (8)
1988 Dark Lomond 3y 8st 9lb (13)
1989 Petite Ile 3y 8st 9lb (10)
1990 Ibn Bey 6y 9st 8lb (12)
1991 Turgeon (USA) 5y 9st 8lb (10)
1992 Mashaallah (USA) 4y 9st 8lb (9)
1993 Vintage Crop 6y 9st 8lb (8)

Up until 1983 for three year olds only

CIGA PRIX DU CADRAN (Longchamp)

(2 1/2 miles)
(First run 1894)

1927 Asteroide 5y 9st 6lb (11)
1928 Nino 5y 9st 6lb (7)
1929 Cacao 4y 9st (9)
1930 Hotweed 4y 9st (8)
1931 Chateau Bouscaut 4y 9st 940
1932 Brulette 4y 8st 10lb (10)
1933 Gris Perle 4y 9st (30
1934 Thor 4y 9st (9)
1935 Brantome 4y 9st (7)
1936 Chaudiere 4y 8st 10lb (7)
1937 Fantastic 4y 9st (9)
1938 Dadji 5y 9st 6lb (7)
1939 Foxlight 4y 9st (12)
1940*Irish Guard 6y 8st 13lb (9)
1941 Maurepas 4y 9st (7)
1942 Nepenthe 4y 9st (10)
1943†Hern the Hunter 4y 9st (7)
1944†Marsyas 4y 9st (8)
1945†Marsyas 5y 9st 6lb (4)
1946 Marsyas 6y 9st 6lb (7)
1947 Marsyas 7y 9st 6lb (7)
1948 Arbar 4y 9st (8)
1949 Turmoil 4y 9st (9)
1950 Ciel Etoile 4y 9st (9)
1951 Ysard 4y 9st (5)
1952 Mat de Cocagne 4y 9st (6)
1953 Feu du Diable 4y 9st (8)
1954 Silex 4y 9st (8)
1955 Elpenor 5y 9st 6lb (8)
1956 Bewitched 4y 9st (10)
1957 Cambremer 4y 9st (10)
1958 Scot 4y 9st (10)
1959 Tello 4y 9st (9)
1960 Le Loup Garou 4y 9st (11)
1961 Puissant Chef 4y 9st (11)
1962 Taine 5y 9st 6lb (6)
1963 Taine 6y 9st 6lb (7)
1964 Azincourt 4y 9st (8)
1965 Waldmeister 4y 9st (60
1966 Fantomas 5y 9st 6lb (7)
1967 Danseur 4y 9st (6)
1968 No race
1969 Levmoss 4y 9st (8)
1970 Le Chouan 4y 9st (11)
1971 Ramsin 4y 9st (9)
1972 Rock Roi 5y 9st 6lb (10)
1973 Lassalle 4y 9st (60
1974 Recupere 4y 9st (13)
1975 Le Bavard 4y 9st (13)
1976 Sagaro 5y 9st 2lb (10)
1977 Buckskin 4y 9st 2lb (5)
1978 Buckskin 5y 9st 2lb (9)
1979 El Badr 4y 9st 2lb (5)
1980 Shafaraz 7y 9st 2lb (6)
1981 Gold River 4y 8st 13lb (6)
1982 El Badr 7y 9st 2lb (5)
1983 Karkour 5y 9st 2lb (6)
1984 Neustrien (Fr) 4y 9st 2lb (6)
1985 Balitou (Fr) 6y 9st 2lb (7)
1986 Air de Cour 4y 9st 2lb (6)
1987 Royal Gait 4y 9st 2lb (9)
1988 Yaka (Fr) 5y 9st 2lb (5)
1989 Trebrook 5y 9st 2lb (3)
1990 Mercalle (FR) 4y 8st 13lb (6)
1991 Victoire Bleue 4y 8st 13lb (7)
1992 Sought Out 4y 8st 13lb (7)
1993 Assessor 4y 9st 2lb (11)

*Run at Auteuil
†Run at Le Tremblay over 2 miles 4 1/2 fur.

CIGA GRAND CRITERIUM (Longchamp)

(1 mile)
For two year olds
(First run 1853)

1927 Kantar 8st 11lb (12)
1928 Amorina 8st 9lb (12)
1929 Godiche 8st 11lb (12)
1930 Indus 8st 11lb (15)
1931 La Bourrasque 8st 9lb (14)
1932 Pantalon 8st 11lb (9)
1933 Brantome 8st 11lb (9)
1934 Pampeiro 8st 11lb (9)
1935 Mistress Ford 8st 9lb (13)
1936 Teleferique 8st 11lb (6)
1937 Gossip 8st 9lb (12)
1938 Turbulent 8st 11lb (12)
1939 No race
1940†*Plaisir de France 9st 2lb
*Longthanh 8st 13lb (7)
1941*Nosca 8st 11lb
*Martia 8st 9lb (7)
1942 Caravelle 8st 9lb (7)
1943 Priam 8st 11lb (7)
1944 Taiaut 8st 11lb (7)
1945 Nirgal 8st 11lb (8)
1946 Clarion 8st 11lb (10)
1947 Rigolo 8st 11lb (9)
1948 Ambiorix 8st 11lb (12)
1949 Tantieme 8st 11lb (13)
1950 Sicambre 8st 11lb (10)
1951 Cosmos 8st 11lb (11)
1952 Dragon Blanc 8st 11lb (12)
1953 Le Geographe 8st 11lb (11)
1954 Beau Prince II 8st 11lb (13)
1955 Apollonia 8st 9lb (8)
1956 Tyrone 8st 11lb (11)
1957 Bella Paola 8st 9lb (12)
1958 Tiepoletto 8st 11lb (11)
1959 Angers 8st 11lb (10)
1960 Right Royal 8st 11lb (7)
1961 Abdos 8st 11lb (5)
1962 Hula Dancer 8st 8lb (10)
1963 Neptunus 8st 11lb (13)

1964 Grey Dawn 8st 12lb (13)
1965 Soleil 8st 12lb (9)
1966 Silver Cloud 8st 8lb (11)
1967 Sir Ivor 8st 12lb (13)
1968 Yelapa 8st 11lb (12)
1969 Breton 8st 11lb (10)
1970 My Swallow 8st 11lb (6)
1971 Hard to Beat 8st 11lb (14)
1972 Satingo 8st 11lb (9)
1973 Mississipian 8st 11lb (8)
1974 Mariacci 8st 11lb (9)
1975 Manado 8st 11lb (11)
1976 Blushing Groom 8st 11lb (10)
1977 Super Concorde (USA) 8st 11lb (13)
1978 Irish River 8st 11lb (12)
1979 Dragon 8st 11lb (8)
1980 Recitation (USA) 8st 11lb (11)
1981 Green Forest (USA) 8st 11lb (10)
1982 Saint Cyrien 8st 11lb (8)
1983 Treizieme 8st 8lb (9)
1984 Alydar's Best (USA) 8st 8lb (6)
1985 Femme Elite (USA) 8st 8lb (11)
1986 Danishkada (Fr) 8st 8lb (8)
1987 Fijar Tango (Fr) 8st 11lb (6)
1988 Kendor (Fr) 8st 11lb (9)
1989 Jade Robbery 8st 11lb (8)
1990 Hector Protector (USA) 8st 11lb (5)
1991 Arazi (USA) 8st 11lb (6)
1992 Tenby 8st 11lb (11)
1993 Lost World 8st 11lb (7)

*Dead-heat
†Run at Auteuil

CIGA PRIX DE L'ARC DE TRIOMPHE (Longchamp)

(1½ miles)

1920 Comrade 3y 8st 9lb (13)
1921 Ksar 3y 8st 9lb (12)
1922 Ksar 4y 9st 6lb (11)
1923 Parth 3y 8st 9lb (13)
1924 Massine 4y 9st 6lb (9)
1925 Priori 3y 8st 9lb (15)
1926 Biribi 3y 8st 9lb (16)
1927 Mon Talisman 3y 8st 9lb (10)
1928 Kantar 3y 8st 10lb (11)
1929 Ortello 3y 8st 9lb (13)
1930 Motrico 5y 9st 6lb (10)
1931 Pearl Cap 3y 8st 7lb (10)
1932 Motrico 7y 9st 6lb (15)
1933 Crapom 3y 8st 10lb (15)
1934 Brantome 3y 8st 10lb (13)
1935 Samos 3y 8st 7lb (12)
1936 Corrida 4y 9st 3lb (10)
1937 Corrida 5y 9st 3lb (12)
1938 Eclair au Chocolat 3y 8st 10lb (10)
1939 and 1940 No race
1941 Le Pacha 3y 8st 10lb (7)
1942 Djebel 5y 9st 6lb (9)
1943*Verso II 3y 8st 10lb (13)
1944*Ardan 3y 8st 10lb (11)
1945 Nikellora 3y 8st 7lb (11)
1946 Caracalla 4y 9st 6lb (9)
1947 Le Paillon 5y 9st 6lb (12)
1948 Migoli 4y 9st 6lb (14)
1949 Coronation 3y 8st 10lb (12)
1950 Tantieme 3y 8st 10lb (12)
1951 Tantieme 4y 9st 6lb (19)
1952 Nuccio 4y 9st 6lb (18)
1953 La Sorellina 3y 8st 7lb (25)
1954 Sica Boy 3y 8st 10lb (21)
1955 Ribot 3y 8st 10lb (23)
1956 Ribot 4y 9st 6lb (20)
1957 Oroso 4y 9st 6lb (24)
1958 Ballymoss 4y 9st 6lb (17)
1959 Saint Crespin 3y 8st 10lb (25)
1960 Puissant Chef 3y 8st 10lb (17)
1961 Molvedo 3y 8st 10lb (19)
1962 Soltikoff 3y 8st 10lb (24)
1963 Exbury 4y 9st 6lb (15)
1964 Prince Royal II 3y 8st 10lb (22)
1965 Sea-Bird II 3y 8st 10lb (20)
1966 Bon Mot 3y 8st 10lb (24)
1967 Topyo 3y 8st 10lb (30)
1968 Vaguely Noble 3y 8st 10lb (17)
1969 Levmoss 4y 9st 6lb (24)
1970 Sassafras 3y 8st 10lb (15)
1971 Mill Reef (USA) 3y 8st 10lb (18)
1972 San San (USA) 3y 8st 7lb (19)
1973 Rheingold 4y 9st 6lb (27)
1974 Allez France (USA) 4y 9st 3lb (20)
1975 Star Appeal 5y 9st 6lb (24)
1976 Ivanjica (USA) 4y 9st 1lb (20)
1977 Alleged (USA) 3y 8st 11lb (26)
1978 Alleged (USA) 4y 9st 4lb (18)
1979 Three Troikas 3y 8st 8lb (22)
1980 Detroit 3y 8st 8lb (20)
1981 Gold River 4y 9st 11lb (24)
1982 Akiyda 3y 8st 8lb (17)
1983 All Along (Fr) 4y 9st 1lb (26)
1984 Sagace (Fr) 4y 9st 4lb (22)
1985 Rainbow Quest (USA) 4y 9st 4lb (15)
1986 Dancing Brave (USA) 3y 8st 11lb (15)
1987 Trempolino (USA) 3y 8st 11lb (11)
1988 Tony Bin 5y 9st 4lb (24)
1989 Carroll House 4y 9st 4lb (19)
1990 Saumarez 3y 8st 11lb (21)
1991 Suave Dancer (USA) 3y 8st 11lb (14)
1992 Subotica 4y 9st 4lb (18)
1993 Urban Sea (USA) 4y 9st 1lb (23)

*Run at Le Tremblay over 1m 3½f

PRIX ROYAL-OAK (Longchamp)

(French St Leger)
(1 mile 7 fur 110 yds)
(First run 1869)

1927 Fiterari (8)
1928 Cacao (9)
1929 Calandria (7)
1930 Taicoun (9)
1931 Deiri (7)
1932 Laeken (8)
1933 Jumbo (7)
1934 Brantome (10)
1935 Bokbul (8)
1936 Fantastic (9)
1937 Victrix (9)
1938 Eclair au Chocolat (8)
1939 and 1940 No race
1941 le Pacha (7)
1942 Tifinar (10)
1943†Verso II (8)
1944†Samaritain (7)
1945 Caracalla (8)
1946 Souverain (8)
1947 Tourment (7)
1948 Spooney (9)
1949 Ciel Etoile (9)
1950 Pan (6)
1951 Stymphale (7)
1952 Feu du Diable (12)
1953 Buisson d'Or (7)
1954 Sica Boy (10)
1955 Macip (12)
1956 Arabian (8)
1957 Scot (12)
1958 Wallaby (10)
1959 Vamour (10)
1960 Puissant Chef (11)
1961 Match (6)
1962 Sicilian Prince (14)
1963 Relko (8)
1964 Barbieri (6)
1965 Reliance (7)
1966 Vasco de Gama (8)
1967 Samos III (9)
1968 Dhaudevi (12)
1969 Le Chouan (6)
1970 Sassafras (8)
1971 Bourbon (7)
1972 Pleben (12)
1973 Lady Berry (11)
1974 Busiris (USA) (11)
1975 Henri le Balafre (16)
1976 Exceller (USA) (7)
1977 Rex Magna (13)
1978 Brave Johnny (8)
1979 Niniski (USA) (9)
1980 Gold River (13)
1981 Ardross (7)
1982 Denel (13)
1983 Old Country (14)
1984 Agent Double (11)
1985 Mersey (12)
1986 El Cuite (10)
1987 Royal Gait (11)
1988 Star Lift (16)
1989 Top Sunrise (9)
1990*Braashee
*Indian Queen (11)
1991 Turgeon (8)
1992 Assessor (12)
1993 Raintrap (8)

* Dead-heat
†Run at le Tremblay over 1 mile 7 fur

LADBROKE H'CAP HURDLE (Leopardstown)

(2 miles)

1969†Normandy 4y 11st 2lb (15)
1970†Persian War 7y 12st (11)
1971 Kelanne 7y 11st 6lb (6)
1972 Captain Christy 6y 11st 6lb (13)
1973 Comedy of Errors 6y 12st (9)
1974 Comedy of Errors 7y 12st (8)
1975 Night Nurse 4y 11st 5lb (9)
1976 Master Monday 6y 10st 2lb (19)
1977 Decent Fellow 4y 11st 4lb (18)
1978 Chinrullah 6y 10st 6lb (12)
1979 Irian (Fr) 5y 10st (20)
1980 Carrig Willy 5y 10st (26)
1981 No race
1982 For Auction 6y 10st 10lb (20)
1983 Fredcoteri 7y 10st (15)
1984 Fredcoteri 8y 10st 4lb (18)
1985 Hansel Rag 5y 10st (20)

1986 Bonalma 6y 10st 13lb (22)
1987 Barnbrook Again 6y 11st 8lb (22)
1988 Roark 6y 11st 1lb (15)
1989 Redundant Pal 6y 10st (7)
1990 Redundant Pal 7y 11st 5lb (27)
1991 The Illiad 10y 10st 13lb (17)
1992 How's The Boss 6y 10st 2lb (20)
1993 Glencloud 5y 10st 13lb (25)

†Run at Fairyhouse

ROTHMANS INTERNATIONAL (Woodbine)

(1½ miles)

1938 Bunty Lawless (T Aimers)
1939 Sir Marlboro (C McTague)
1940 Cerise (H Meynell)
1941 Bunty Lawless (T Aimers)
1942 Shepperton (R Watson)
1943 Shepperton (R Watson)
1944 Be Brief (R Watson)
1945 Tulachmore (P Remillard)
1946 Kingarvie (J Dewhurst)
1947 Brown Hostess (L Stroud)
1948 Canada's Teddy (D Prater)
1949 Arise (D Dodson)
1950 Nephisto (P Remillard)
1951 Bull Page (J Vina)
1952 Beau Dandy (A Licata)
1953 Navy Page (N Shuk)
1954 Resilient (B Green)
1955 Park Dandy (R Ussery)
1956 Eugenia (J Sanchez)
1957 Spinney (J Sanchez)
1958 Jack Ketch (J Sellers)
1959 Martini (C M Clark)
1960 Rocky Royale (J R Adams)
1961 Our Jeep (S Boulmetis)
1962 El Bandido (R Broussard)
1963 The Axe II (J L Rotz)
1964 Will I Rule (R Turcotte)
1965 George Royal (J Longden)
1966 George Royal (I Valenzuela)
1967 He's A Smoothie (S McComb)
1968 Frenetico (R Platts)
1969 Vent du Nord (R Turcotte)
1970 Drumtop (C Baltazar)
1971 One For All (R Turcotte)
1972 Droll Role (B Baeza)
1973 Secretariat (E Maple)
1974 Dahlia (L Piggott)
1975 Snow Knight (J Velasquez)
1976 Youth (S Hawley)
1977 Exceller (A Cordero)
1978 Mac Diarmida (J Cruguet)
1979 Golden Act (S Hawley)
1980 Great Neck (M Venezia)
1981 Open Call (J Velasquez)
1982 Majesty's Prince (E Maple)
1983 All Along (Fr) (W R Swinburn)
1984 Seattle Song (C Asmussen)
1985 Nassipour (USA) (J Samyn)
1986 Southjet (J Santos)
1987 River Memories (USA) (C McCarron)
1988 Infamy (IRE) (R Cochrane)
1989 Hodges Bay (J Cruguet)
1990 French Glory (IRE) (Pat Eddery)
1991 Sky Classic (P Day)
1992 Snurge (IRE) (T Quinn)
1993 Husband (USA) (C Asmussen)

Run at Long Branch from 1938 to 1941, at Dufferin Park from 1942 to 1945, at Long Branch from 1946 to 1955, and at Woodbine from 1956. Run over 1 mile 110 yds from 1938 to 1952, over 1 mile 1 fur in 1953 and 1954, 1 mile 1½ fur in 1955, and 1 mile 5 fur from 1956 to 1986. Run over 1½ miles since 1987.

AMERICAN TRIPLE CROWN

KENTUCKY DERBY (1¼ miles, Churchill Downs, Louisville, Kentucky). First run in 1875.
PREAKNESS STAKES (1 mile 1½ fur, Pimlico, Baltimore, Maryland). First run in 1873.
BELMONT STAKES (1½ miles, Belmont Park, Long Island, New York). First run in 1867.

	Kentucky Derby	**Preakness**	**Belmont**
1920	Paul Jones	Man o'War	Man o'War
1921	Behave Yourself	Broomspun	Grey Lag
1922	Morvich	Pillory	Pillory
1923	Zev	Vigil	Zev
1924	Black Gold	Nellie Morse	Mad Play
1925	Flying Ebony	Coventry	American Flag
1926	Bubbling Over	Display	Crusader
1927	Whiskery	Bostonian	Chance Shot
1928	Reigh Count	Victorian	Vito
1929	Clyde van Dusen	Dr Freeland	Blue Larkspur
1930	★Gallant Fox	Gallant Fox	Gallant Fox
1931	Twenty Grand	Mate	Twenty Grand
1932	Burgoo King	Burgoo King	Faireno
1933	Brokers Tip	Head Play	Hurry Off
1934	Cavalcade	High Quest	Peace Chance
1935	★Omaha	Omaha	Omaha
1936	Bold Venture	Bold Venture	Granville
1937	★War Admiral	War Admiral	War Admiral
1938	Lawrin	Dauber	Pasteurized
1939	Johnstown	Challedon	Johnstown
1940	Gallahadion	Bimelech	Bimelech
1941	★Whirlaway	Whirlaway	Whirlaway
1942	Shut Out	Alsab	Shut Out
1943	★Count Fleet	Count Fleet	Count Fleet
1944	Pensive	Pensive	Bounding Home
1945	Hoop Jr	Polynesian	Pavot
1946	★Assault	Assault	Assault
1947	Jet Pilot	Faultless	Phalanx
1948	★Citation	Citation	Citation
1949	Ponder	Capot	Capot
1950	Middleground	Hill Prince	Middleground
1951	Count Turf	Bold	Counterpoint
1952	Hill Gail	Blue Man	One Count
1953	Dark Star	Native Dancer	Native Dancer
1954	Determine	Hasty Road	High Gun

1955	Swaps	Nashua	Nashua
1956	Needles	Fabius	Needles
1957	Iron Liege	Bold Ruler	Gallant Man
1958	Tim Tam	Tim Tam	Cavan
1959	Tomy Lee	Royal Orbit	Sword Dancer
1960	Venetian Way	Bally Ache	Celtic Ash
1961	Carry Back	Carry Back	Sherluck
1962	Decidedly	Greek Money	Jaipur
1963	Chateaugay	Candy Spots	Chateaugay
1964	Northern Dancer	Northern Dancer	Quadrangle
1965	Lucky Debonair	Tom Rolfe	Hail to All
1966	Kauai King	Kauai King	Amberoid
1967	Proud Clarion	Damascus	Damascus
1968	Dancers Image	Forward Pass	Stage Door Johnny
1969	Majestic Prince	Majestic Prince	Arts and Letters
1970	Dust Commander	Personality	High Echelon
1971	Canonero II	Canonero II	Pass Catcher
1972	Riva Ridge	Bee Bee Bee	Riva Ridge
1973	*Secretariat	Secretariat	Secretariat
1974	Cannonade	Little Current	Little Current
1975	Foolish Pleasure	Master Derby	Avatar
1976	Bold Forbes	Elocutionist	Bold Forbes
1977	*Seattle Slew	Seattle Slew	Seattle Slew
1978	*Affirmed	Affirmed	Affirmed
1979	Spectacular Bid	Spectacular Bid	Coastal
1980	Genuine Risk	Codex	Temperance Hill
1981	Pleasant Colony	Pleasant Colony	Summing
1982	Gato Del Sol	Alamo's Ruler	Conquistador Cielo
1983	Sunny's Halo	Deputed Testamony	Caveat
1984	Swale	Gate Dancer	Swale
1985	Spend A Buck	Tank's Prospect	Creme Fraiche
1986	Ferdinand	Snow Chief	Danzig Connection
1987	Alysheba	Alysheba	Bet Twice
1988	Winning Colors	Risen Star	Risen Star
1989	Sunday Silence	Sunday Silence	Easy Goer
1990	Unbridled	Summer Squall	Go And Go
1991	Strike the Gold	Hansel	Hansel
1992	Lil E Tee	Pine Bluff	A. P. Indy
1993	Sea Hero	Prairie Bayou	Colonial Affair

*Triple Crown winner

WASHINGTON D.C. INTERNATIONAL (Laurel)

(1 mile)

1952 Wilwyn (England), E Mercer
1953 Worden II (France), C Smirke
1954 Fisherman (USA), E Arcaro
1955 El Chama (Venezuela), R Bustamente
1956 Master Boing (France), G Chancelier
1957 Mahah (USA), S Boulmetis
1958 Sailor's Guide (Australia), H Grant (Tudor Era finished first but was disqualified.)
1959 Bald Eagle (USA), M Ycaza
1960 Bald Eagle (USA), M Ycaza
1961 T V Lark (USA), Johnny Longden
1962 Match (France), Y Saint-Martin
1963 Mongo (USA), W Chambers
1964 Kelso (USA), I Valenzuela
1965 Diatome (France), J Deforge
1966 Behistoun (France), J Deforge
1967 Fort Marcy (USA), M Ycaza
1968 Sir Ivor (Ireland), L Piggott
1969 Karabas (England), L Piggott
1970 Fort Marcy (USA), J Velasquez
1971 Run the Gantlet (USA), R Woodhouse
1972 Droll Role (USA), B Baeza
1973 Dahlia (France), W Pyers
1974 Admetus (France), M Philipperon
1975 Nobiliary (USA) (France), S Hawley
1976 Youth (USA) (France), S Hawley
1977 Johnny D (USA), S Cauthen
1978 Mac Diarmida (USA), J Cruguet
1979 Bowl Game, J Velasquez
1980 Argument (France), L Piggott
1981 Providential II, A Lequeux
1982 April Run (France), C Asmussen
1983 All Along (France), W R Swinburn
1984 Seattle Song, C Asmussen
1985 Vanlandingham, D Macbeth
1986 Lieutenant's Lark, R Davis
1987 Le Glorieux, L Pincay
1988 Sunshine Forever, A Cordero
1989 Caltech, R Douglas
1990 Fly Till Dawn, L Pincay
1991 Leariva, E Prado
1992 Zoman (USA) (England), A Munro
1993 Buckhar, J Cruguet

Run over 1½ miles until 1985, then over 1¼ miles until 1992

BREEDERS' CUP SPRINT

(6 fur — dirt)

1984 Eillo 4y 9st (11)
1985 Precisionist 4y 9st (14)
1986 Smile 4y 9st (9)
1987 Very Subtle 3y 8st 9lb (13)
1988 Gulch 4y 9st (13)
1989 Dancing Spree 4y 9st (13)
1990 Safety Kept 4y 8st 11lb (14)
1991 Sheikh Albadou (England), 3y 8st 12lb (11)
1992 Thirty Slews 5y 9st (14)
1993 Cardmania 7y 9st (14)

BREEDERS' CUP MILE

(1 mile — turf)

1984 Royal Heroine 4y 8st 11lb (10)
1985 Cozzene 5y 9st (14)
1986 Last Tycoon (France), 3y 8st 11lb (14)
1987 Miesque (France), 3y 8st 8lb (14)
1988 Miesque (France), 4y 8st 11lb (12)
1989 Steinlen 6y 9st (11)
1990 Royal Academy (Ireland) 3y 8st 10lb (13)

1991 Opening Verse 5y 9st (14)
1992 Lure 3y 8st 10lb (14)
1993 Lure 4y 9st (13)

BREEDERS' CUP JUVENILE

(8½ fur — dirt)
1984 Chief's Crown 8st 10lb (10)
1985 Tasso 8st 10lb (13)
1986 Capote 8st 10lb (13)
1987 Success Express 8st 10lb (13)
1988 Is It True 8st 10lb (10)
1989 Rhythm 8st 10lb (12)
1990 Fly So Free 8st 10lb (11)
1991 Arazi (France) 8st 10lb (14)
1992 Gilded Time 8st 10lb (13)
1993 Brocco 8st 10lb (11)

BREEDERS' CUP JUVENILE FILLIES

(8½ fur — dirt)
1984*Outstandingly 8st 7lb (11)
1985 Twilight Ridge 8st 7lb (12)
1986 Brave Raj 8st 7lb (12)
1987 Epitome 8st 7lb (12)
1988 Open Mind 8st 7lb (12)
1989 Go For Wand 8st 7lb (12)
1990 Meadow Star 8st 7lb (13)
1991 Pleasant Stage 8st 7lb (14)
1992 Eliza 8st 7lb (12)
1993 Phone Chatter 8st 7lb (8)

*In 1984 Fran's Valentine won, but was disqualified.

BREEDERS' CUP DISTAFF

(1 mile 1 fur — dirt)
1984 Princess Rooney 4y 8st 11lb (7)
1985 Life's Magic 4y 8st 11lb (7)
1986 Lady's Secret 4y 8st 11lb (8)
1987 Sacahuista 3y 8st 7lb (6)
1988 Personal Ensign 4y 8st 11lb (9)
1989 Bayakoa 5y 8st 11lb (10)
1990 Bayakoa 6y 8st 11lb (7)
1991 Dance Smartly (Canada), 3y 8st 8lb (13)
1992 Paseana 5y 8st 11lb (14)
1993 Hollywood Wildcat 3y 8st 8lb (8)

BREEDERS' CUP CLASSIC

(1¼ miles — dirt)
1984 Wild Again 4y 9st (8)
1985 Proud Truth 3y 8st 10lb (8)
1986 Skywalker 4y 9st (11)
1987 Ferdinand 4y 9st (12)
1988 Alysheba 4y 9st (9)
1989 Sunday Silence 3y 8st 10lb (8)
1990 Unbridled 3y 8st 9lb (14)
1991 Black Tie Affair 5y 9st (11)
1992 A P Indy 3y 8st 9lb (14)
1993 Arcangues (France) 5y 9st (13)

BREEDERS' CUP TURF

(1½ miles — turf)
1984 Lashkari (France), 3y 8st 10lb (11)
1985 Pebbles (England), 4y 8st 11lb (14)
1986 Manila 3y 8st 10lb (9)
1987 Theatrical 5y 9st (14)
1988 Great Communicator 5y 9st (10)
1989 Prized 3y 8st 10lb (14)
1990 In the Wings (France), 4y 9st (11)
1991 Miss Alleged (France), 4y 8st 11lb (13)
1992 Fraise 4y 9st (10)
1993 Kotashaan 5y 9st (14)

The Breeders' Cup series of races have been held at the following racetracks: 1984 Hollywood Park, 1985 Aqueduct, 1986 Santa Anita, 1987 Hollywood Park, 1988 Churchill Downs, 1989 Gulfstream Park, 1990 Belmont Park, 1991 Churchill Downs, 1992 Gulfstream Park, 1993 Santa Anita. Churchill Downs will host the 1994 running on November 5th.

JAPAN CUP (Tokyo)

(1½ miles)
1981 Mairzy Doates 5y 8st 9lb (15)
1982 Half Iced 5y 8st 9lb (15)
1983 Stanerra (Ireland), 5y 8st 9lb (16)
1984 Katsuragi Ace 4y 9st (14)
1985 Symboli Rudolf 4y 8st 13lb (15)
1986 Jupiter Island (England), 7y 8st 13lb (14)
1987 Le Glorieux (France), 3y 8st 9lb (14)
1988 Pay The Butler 4y 8st 13lb (14)
1989 Horlicks (New Zealand), 6y 8st 9lb (15)
1990 Better Loosen Up (Australia), 5y 8st 13lb (15)
1991 Golden Pheasant (U.S.A.), 5y 8st 13lb (15)
1992 Tokai Teio (Japan), 4y 8st 13lb (14)
1993 Legacy World (Japan), 4y 8st 13lb (16)

Part 3: Hurdles and Chases

TOTE GOLD TROPHY (Newbury)

(2 miles 110 yds)
1963*Rosyth 5y 10st (41)
1964 Rosyth 6y 10st 2lb (24)
1965 Elan 6y 10st 7lb (21)
1966 Le Vermontois 5y 11st 3lb (28)
1967 Hill House 7y 10st 10lb (28)
1968 Persian War 5y 11st 13lb (33)
1969 No race
1970 No race
1971 Cala Mesquida 7y 10st 9lb (23)
1972 Good Review 6y 10st 9lb (26)
1973 Indianapolis 6y 10st 6lb (26)
1974 No race
1975 Tammuz (Fr) 7y 10st 13lb (28)
1976 Irish Fashion 5y 10st 4lb (29)
1977 True Lad 7y 10st 4lb (27)
1978 No race
1979 Within The Law 5y 11st 4lb (28)
1980 Bootlaces 6y 10st 9lb (21)
1981 No race
1982 Dongal Prince 6y 10st 8lb (27)
1983 No race
1984 Ra Nova 5y 10st 6lb (26)
1985 No race
1986 No race
1987 Neblin 8y 10st (21)
1988 Jamesmead 7y 10st (19)
1989 Grey Salute 6y 11st 5lb (10)
1990 Deep Sensation 5y 11st 3lb (17)
1991 No race
1992 Rodeo Star (USA) 6y 10st 10lb (15)
1993 King Credo 8y 10st (16)

*Run at Liverpool over 2 miles 1 fur and a few yards

CORAL WELSH NATIONAL (Chepstow)

(3 miles 5 fur 110 yds)
(First run 1895)
1920 Mark Back 9y 11st 9lb (9)
1921 Mythical 7y 10st 6lb (10)
1922 Simonides 8y 10st 5lb (10)
1923 Clonree 9y 11st 6lb (12)
1924 Dwarf of the Forest 7y 10st 5lb (11)
1925 Vaulx 11y 12st 1lb (16)
1926 Miss Balscadden 7y 9st 9lb (12)
1927 Snipe's Bridge 13y 11st 2lb (12)
1928 Miss Balscadden 9y 9st 7lb (15)
1929 Monduco 7y 10st 2lb (21)
1930 Boomlet 10y 11st 6lb (11)
1931 Wise Don 9y 10st 5lb (15)
1932 Miss Gaynus 6y 11st (10)
1933 Pebble Ridge 8y 10st 11lb (9)
1934 Dream Ship 8y 11st 7lb (10)
1935 Lacatoi 7y 10st 8lb (12)
1936 Sorley Boy 10y 10st 12lb (11)
1937 Lacatoi 9y 10st 5lb (13)
1938 Timber Wolf 10y 11st 3lb (3)
1939 Lacatoi 11y 10st 11lb (11)
1940–47 No race
1948 Bora's Cottage 10y 10st 2lb (16)
1949 Fighting Line 10y 10st 9lb (15)
1950 Gallery 12y 10st 8lb (12)
1951 Skyreholme 8y 10st 13lb (16)
1952 Dinton Lass 10y 10st (16)
1953 Stalbridge Rock 10y 11st 3lb (15)

1954 Blow Horn 10y 10st 6lb (17)
1955 Monaleen 10y 9st 7lb (17)
1956 Crudwell 10y 11st 6lb (16)
1957 Creeola II 9y 10st 5lb (11)
1958 Oscar Wilde 8y 9st 13lb (14)
1959 Limonali 8y 10st 2lb (10)
1960 Clover Bud 10y 10st 10lb (14)
1961 Limonali 10y 11st 12lb (9)
1962 Forty Secrets 8y 10st 11lb (15)
1963 Motel 9y 10st 6lb (10)
1964 Rainbow Battle 8y 10st (11)
1965 Norther 8y 11st (11)
1966 Kilburn 8y 11st 2lb (11)
1967 Happy Spring 11y 10st 4lb (6)
1968 Glenn 7y 10st 4lb (8)
1969 No race
1970 French Excuse 8y 10st 9lb (11)
1971 Royal Toss 9y 10st 12lb (13)
1972 Charlie H 10y 11st 3lb (9)
1973 Deblin's Green 10y 9st 12lb (16)
1974 Pattered 8y 10st 2lb (24)
1975 No race
1976 Rag Trade 10y 11st 2lb (17)
1977 No race
1978 No race
1979 (Feb) No race
1979 (Dec) Peter Scot 8y 10st 2lb (15)
1980 Narvik 7y 10st 10lb (18)
1981 Peaty Sandy 7y 10st 3lb (23)
1982 Corbierre 7y 10st 10lb (10)
1983 Burrough Hill Lad 7y 10st 9lb (18)
1984 Righthand Man 7y 11 st 5lb (18)
1985 Run And Skip 7y 10st 8lb (18)
1986 Stearsby 7y 11st 5lb (17)
1987 Playschool 9y 10st 11lb (13)
1988 Bonanza Boy 7y 10st 1lb (12)
1989 Bonanza Boy 8y 11st 11lb (12)
1990 Cool Ground 8y 10st (14)
1991 Carvill's Hill 9y 11st 12lb (17)
1992 Run For Free 8y 10st 9lb (11)
1993 Riverside Boy 10y 10st (8)

Run over 2½ miles at Cardiff from 1895 to 1898, over 3 miles from 1899 to 1912, over 3 miles 100 yds in 1914, and over 3½ miles from 1920 to 1939. Run over 3 miles 4 fur 150 yds at Newport in 1948

SUNDERLANDS IMPERIAL CUP H'CAP H'DLE (Sandown)

(2 miles 110 yds)
(First run 1907)

1920 Trespasser 4y 12st (9)
1921 Trespasser 5y 12st 7lb (10)
1922 Trespasser 6y 12st 7lb (11)
1923 North Waltham 6y 12st 4lb (11)
1924 Noce d'Argent 4y 11st 2lb (8)
1925 Scotch Pearl 4y 10st 7lb (18)
1926 Peeping Tom 4y 10st 7lb (13)
1927 Zeno 4y 10st 12lb (12)
1928 Royal Falcon 5y 11st 6lb (16)
1929 Hercules 6y 11st 5lb (18)
1930 Rubicon II 4y 11st 3lb (15)
1931 Residue 7y 12st 3lb (14)
1932 Last of the Dandies 5y 11st 4lb (21)
1933 Flaming 6y 11st 4lb (18)
1934 Lion Courage 6y 10st 7lb (13)
1935 Negro 6y 11st 6lb (21)
1936 Negro 7y 11st 3lb (23)
1937 le Maestro 6y 11st (18)
1938 Bimco 5y 10st 12lb (11)
1939 Mange Tout 5y 11st 10lb (20)
1940–46 No race
1947 Tant Pis 5y 10st 9lb (33)
1948 Anglesey 6y 11st 8lb (12)
1949 Secret Service 6y 11st 11lb (17)
1950 Secret Service 7y 11st 10lb (13)
1951 Master Bidar 6y 10st 11lb (21)
1952 High Point 6y 10st 4lb (19)
1953 High Point 7y 10st 7lb (19)
1954 The Pills 6y 10st 5lb (26)
1955 Bon Mot II 6y 10st 11lb (32)
1956 Peggy Jones 6y 10st 10lb (22)
1957 Camugliano 7y 10st 10lb (29)
1958 Flaming East 9y 10st 5lb (23)
1959 Langton Heath 5y 10st 9lb (21)
1960 Farmer's Boy 7y 11st 7lb (20)
1961 Fidus Achates 6y 10st 4lb (23)
1962 Irish Imp 5y 10st 12lb (26)
1963 Antiar 5y 11st 2lb (21)
1964 Invader 6y 11st 4lb (15)
1965 Kildavin 7y 10st 7lb (19)
1966 Royal Sanction 7y 10st 1lb (18)
1967 Sir Thopas 6y 11st 8lb (20)
1968 Persian Empire 5y 11st 4lb (18)
1969 No race
1970 Solomon II 6y 11st 1lb (17)
1971 Churchwood 7y 11st 3lb (12)
1972 Spy Net (Fr) 5y 10st (18)
1973 Lanzarote 5y 12st 4lb (14)
1974 Flash Imp 5y 10st 9lb (17)
1975 No race
1976 Nougat (Fr) 6y 10st 6lb (11)
1977 Acquaint 6y 11st 12lb (20)
1978 Winter Melody 7y 11st 3lb (15)
1979 Flying Diplomat (USA) 8y 10st 6lb (9)
1980 Prayukta 5y 11st (16)
1981 Ekbalco 5y 11st 3lb (14)
1982*Holemoor Star 5y 11st 7lb (7)
1983 Desert Hero 9y 9st 8lb (16)
1984 Dalbury 6y 9st 12lb (13)
1985 Floyd 5y 10st 3lb (16)
1986 Insular 6y 9st 10lb (19)
1987 Inlander 6y 10st 3lb (21)
1988 Sprowstown Boy 5y 10st 11lb (15)
1989 Travel Mystery 6y 10st (8)
1990 Moody Man 5y 10st 13lb (15)
1991 Precious Boy 5y 10st 6lb (13)
1992 King Credo 7y 10st 4lb (10)
1993 Olympian 6y 10st (15)

*Run at Kempton

"SUN ALLIANCE" NOVICE CHASE (Cheltenham)

(3 miles 1 fur)

1964 Buona notte 7y 12st 4lb (16)
1965 Arkloin 6y 11st 7lb (17)
1966 Different Class 6y 11st 12lb (17)
1967 Border Jet 7y 11st (19)
1968 Herring Gull 6y 11st 12lb (16)
1969 Spanish Steps 6y 11st 12lb (22)
1970 Proud Tarquin 7y 11st 12lb (17)
1971 Tantalum 7y 11st 7lb (16)
1972 Clever Scot 7y 11st 7lb (18)
1973 Killiney 7y 11st 3lb (9)
1974 Ten Up 7y 11st (12)
1975 Pengrail 7y 11st (11)
1976 Tied Cottage 8y 11st (15)
1977 Gay Spartan 6y 11st 4lb (15)
1978 Sweet Joe (USA) 6y 11st 4lb (17)
1979 Master Smudge 7y 11st 4lb (17)
1980 Lacson 8y 11st 4lb (17)
1981 Lesley Ann 7y 11st 4lb (17)
1982 Brown Chamberlin 7y 11st 4lb (15)
1983 Canny Danny 7y 11st 4lb (14)
1984 A Kinsman 8y 11st 4lb (18)
1985 Antarctica Bay 8y 11st 4lb (11)
1986 Cross Master 9y 11st 4lb (30)
1987 Kildimo 7y 11st 4lb (18)
1988 The West Awake 7y 11st 4lb (14)
1989 Enropak Token 8y 11st 4lb (15)
1990 Garrison Savannah 7y 11st 4lb (9)
1991 Rolling Ball (FR) 8y 11st 4lb (20)
1992 Miinnehoma 9y 11st 4lb (18)
1993 Young Hustler 6y 11st 4lb (8)

THE QUEEN MOTHER CHAMPION CHASE (Cheltenham)

(2 miles)

1959 Quita Que 10y 12st (9)
1960 Fortria 8y 12st (7)
1961 Fortria 9y 12st (5)
1962 Piperton 8y 12st (7)
1963 Sandy Abbot 8y 12st (5)
1964 Ben Stack 7y 12st (5)
1965 Dunkirk 8y 12st (6)
1966 Flyingbolt 7y 12st (6)
1967 Drinny's Double 9y 12st (8)
1968 Drinny's Double 10y 12st (5)
1969 Muir 10y 12st (11)
1970 Straight Fort 7y 12st (6)
1971 Crisp (Aus) 8y 12st (8)
1972 Royal Relief 8y 12st (5)
1973 Inkslinger (USA) 6y 12st (6)
1974 Royal Relief 10y 12st (6)
1975 Lough Inagh 8y 12st (8)
1976 Skymas 11y 12st (7)
1977 Skymas 12y 12st (8)
1978 Hilly Way 8y 12st (10)
1979 Hilly Way 9y 12st (9)
1980 Another Dolly 10y 12st (7) Chinrullah came in first but was later disqualified
1981 Drumgora 9y 12st (9)
1982 Rathgorman 10y 12st (9)
1983 Badsworth Boy 8y 12st (6)
1984 Badsworth Boy 9y 12st (10)
1985 Badsworth Boy 10y 12st (5)
1986 Buck House 8y 12st (11)
1987 Pearlyman 8y 12st (8)
1988 Pearlyman 9y 12st (8)
1989 Barnbrook Again 8y 12st (8)
1990 Barnbrook Again 9y 12st (9)
1991 Katabatic 8y 12st (7)
1992 Remittance Man 8y 12st (6)
1993 Deep Sensation 8y 12st (9)

DAILY EXPRESS TRIUMPH HURDLE (Cheltenham)

(2 miles 1 fur)
For four year olds

1939 Grey Talk 11st 7lb (15)
1940–49 No race
1950 Abrupto 11st 6lb (19)
1951 Blue Song II 10st 7lb (12)
1952 Hoggar 10st 10lb (15)
1953 Clair Soleil 11st 5lb (13)
1954 Prince Charlemagne 10st 10lb (12)
1955 Kwannin 10st 10lb (12)
1956 Square Dance 10st 12lb (11)
1957 Meritorious 10st 12lb (14)
1958 Pundit 11st 4lb (14)
1959 Amazons Choice 10st 10lb (13)
1960 Turpial 10st 10lb (13)
1961 Cantab 10st 10lb (15)
1962 Beaver II 10st 10lb (11)
1963–64 No race
1965 Blarney Beacon 11st 4lb (7)
1966 Black Ice 11st 4lb (11)
1967 Persian War 11st 8lb (13)
1968 England's Glory 10st 10lb (16)
1969 Coral Diver 11st 4lb (26)
1970 Varma 11st 4lb (31)
1971 Boxer 11st 3lb (18)
1972 Zarib 11st (16)
1973 Moonlight Bay 11st (18)
1974 Attivo 11st (21)
1975 Royal Epic 11st (28)
1976 Peterhof 11st (23)
1977 Meladon 11st (30)
1978 Connaught Ranger 11st (14)
1979 Pollardstown 11st (28)
1980 Heighlin 11st (26)
1981 Baron Blakeney 11st (29)
1982 Shiny Copper 11st (29)
1983 Saxon Farm 11st (30)
1984 Northern Game 11st (30)
1985 First Bout 11st (27)
1986 Solar Cloud 11st (28)
1987 Alone Success 11st (29)
1988 Kribensis 11st (26)
1989 Ikdam 11st (27)
1990 Rare Holiday 11st (30)
1991 Oh So Risky 11st (27)
1992 Duke of Monmouth (USA) 11st (30)
1993 Shawiya 10st 9lb (25)

Run as Triumph Hurdle over 2 miles at Hurst Park from 1939 to 1962

PETROS VICTOR LUDORUM HURDLE (Haydock)

(2 miles)
For four year olds

1962 Pillock's Green 10st 13lb (9)
1963 No race
1964 Makaldar 11st 3lb (11)
1965 Anselmo 11st 3lb (15)
1966 Harwell 11st 3lb (9)
1967 Persian War 11st 3lb (9)
1968 Wing Master 11st 3lb (6)
1969 Coral Diver 11st (11)
1970 No race
1971 Nerak 11st (13)
1972 North Pole 11st (7)
1973 Mythical King (USA) 11st 4lb (13)
1974 Relevant 11st 4lb (15)
1975 Zip Fastener 11st 4lb (11)
1976 Sweet Joe (USA) 11st 9lb
1977 Rathconrath 11st 9lb (12)
1978 Mixed Melody 11st 4lb (13)
1979 Exalted 11st 4lb (13)
1980 Jubilee Saint 11st 4lb (8)
1981 No race
1982 Azaam 11st 4lb (11)
1983 Wollow Will 11st 9lb (8)
1984 Childown (USA) 11st 9lb (11)
1985 Wing And A Prayer 11st 10lb (8)
1986 No race
1987 Cashew King 4y 11st 4lb (6)
1988 Royal Illusion 11st 10lb (13)
1989 Liadett (USA) 11st 10lb (7)
1990 Ninja 11st 4lb (5)
1991 Reve de Valse (USA) 11st 4lb (8)
1992 Snowy Lane 11st 4lb (6)
1993 Bold Boss 11st 10lb (7)

STAKIS SCOTTISH NATIONAL (Ayr)

(4 miles 120 yds)
(First run 1867)

1920 Music Hall 7y 11st 11lb (9)
1921 No race
1922 Sergeant Murphy 12y 11st 7lb (15)
1923 Harrismith 8y 11st 11lb (13)
1924 Royal Chancellor 9y 11st (18)
1925 Gerald L 11y 12st 6lb (11)
1926 Estuna 8y 9st 11lb (18)
1927 Estuna 9y 11st 11lb (12)
1928 Ardeen 11y 11st 1lb (23)
1929 Donzelon 8y 11st 5lb (21)
1930 Drintyre 7y 11st 5lb (15)
1931 Annandale 9y 10st 5lb (10)
1932 Clydesdale 6y 11st 3lb (15)
1933 Libourg 7y 10st 10lb (21)
1934 Southern Hero 9y 11st 5lb (9)
1935 Kellsboro' Jack 9y 11st 10lb (6)
1936 Southern Hero 11y 11st 7lb (10)
1937 Rightun 7y 11st 10lb (14)
1938 Young Mischief 7y 9st 11lb (10)
1939 Southern Hero 14y 12st 3lb (11)
1940–46 No race
1947 Rowland Roy 8y 11st 2lb (15)
1948 Magnetic Fin 9y 10st 5lb (12)
1949 Wot No Sun 7y 11st 5lb (10)
1950 Sanvina 10y 12st 2lb (19)
1951 Court Painter 11y 9st 7lb (13)
1952 Flagrant Mac 8y 11st 12lb (17)
1953 Queen's Taste 7y 10st 2lb (21)
1954 Queen's Taste 8y 10st 9lb (15)
1955 Bar Point 8y 10st 2lb (18)
1956 Queen's Taste 10y 11st (14)
1957 Bremontier 10y 10st 12lb (13)
1958 Game Field 8y 11st 10lb (14)
1959 Merryman II 8y 10st 12lb (18)
1960 Fincham 8y 10st (8)
1961 Kinmont Wullie 7y 10st 7lb (18)
1962 Sham Fight 10y 10st (18)
1963 Pappageno's Cottage 8y 10st 9lb (18)
1964 Popham Down 7y 10st (14)
1965 Brasher 9y 10st 5lb (9)
1966 African Patrol 7y 10st 7lb (17)
1967 The Fossa 10y 9st 12lb (18)
1968 Arcturus 7y 10st 4lb (10)
1969 Playlord 8y 12st (17)
1970 The Spaniard 8y 10st (10)
1971 Young Ash Leaf 7y 10st 2lb (21)
1972 Quick Reply 7y 9st 9lb (17)
1973 Esban 9y 9st 11lb (21)
1974 Red Rum 9y 11st 13lb (17)
1975 Barona 9y 9st 10lb (17)
1976 Barona 10y 10st (23)
1977 Sebastian V 9y 10st 2lb (18)
1978 King Con 9y 9st 13lb (21)
1979 Fighting Fit 7y 10st 10lb (19)
1980 Salkeld 8y 10st (23)
1981 Astral Charmer 8y 9st 10lb (21)
1982 Cockle Strand 9y 9st 11lb (15)
1983 Canton 9y 10st 2lb (22)
1984 Androma 7y 10st (19)
1985 Androma 8y 10st (18)
1986 Hardy Lad 9y 10st (24)
1987 Little Polveir 10y 10st (11)
1988 Mighty Mark 9y 10st 4lb (17)
1989 Roll-A-Joint 11y 10st (11)
1990 Four Trix 9y 10st (28)
1991 Killone Abbey 8y 10st (18)
1992 Captain Dibble 7y 11st (21)
1993 Run For Free 9y 11st 10lb (21)

Run over 3 miles 7 fur at Bogside from 1867 to 1965

WHITBREAD GOLD CUP (Sandown)

(3 miles 5 fur 18 yds)

1957 Much Obliged 9y 10st 12lb (24)
1958 Taxidermist 6y 10st 8lb (31)
1959 Done Up 9y 10st 13lb (23)
1960 Plummers Plain 7y 10st (21)
1961 Pas Seul 8y 12st (23)
1962 Frenchman's Cove 7y 11st 3lb (22)
1963 Hoodwinked 8y 10st 9lb (32)
1964 Dormant 7y 9st 7lb (11)
1965 Arkle 8y 12st 7lb (7)
1966 What A Myth 9y 9st 8lb (8)
1967 Mill House 10y 11st 11lb (13)
1968 Larbawn 9y 10st 9lb (16)
1969 Larbawn 10y 11st 4lb (18)
1970 Royal Toss 8y 10st (17)
1971 Titus Oates 9y 11st 13lb (18)
1972 Grey Sombrero 8y 9st 10lb (28)
1973†Charlie Potheen 8y 12st (21)
1974 The Dikler 11y 11st 13lb (16)
1975 April Seventh 9y 9st 13lb (12)
1976 Otter Way 8y 10st 10lb (14)
1977 Andy Pandy 8y 10st 12lb (15)
1978 Strombolus 7y 10st (15)
1979 Diamond Edge 8y 11st 11lb (14)
1980 Royal Mail (NZ) 10y 11st 5lb (12)
1981 Diamond Edge 10y 11st 7lb (18)
1982 Shady Deal 9y 10st (9)
1983 Drumlargan 9y 10st 10lb (15)
1984 Special Cargo 11y 11st 2lb (13)
1985 By The Way 7y 10st (20)
1986 Plundering 9y 10st 6lb (16)
1987 Lean Ar Aghaidh 10y 9st 10lb (9)
1988 Desert Orchid 9y 11st 11lb (12)

1989 Brown Windsor 7y 10st (18)
1990 Mr Frisk 11y 10st 5lb (13)
1991 Docklands Express 9y 10st 3lb (10)
1992 Topsham Bay 9y 10st 1lb (11)
1993 Topsham Bay 10y 10st 1lb (13)

†Run at Newcastle over 3m 6f

MACKESON GOLD CUP (Cheltenham)

(2½ miles 110 yds)
1960 Fortria 8y 12st (19)
1961 Scottish Memories 7y 10st 12lb (17)
1962 Fortria 10y 12st (25)
1963 Richard of Bordeaux 8y 10st 5lb (20)
1964 Super Flash 9y 10st 5lb (9)
1965 Dunkirk 8y 12st 7lb (8)
1966 Panwbroker 8y 11st 9lb (5)
1967 Charlie Worcester 10y 10st 11lb (13)
1968 Jupiter Boy 7y 10st 3lb (13)
1969 Gay Trip 7y 11st 5lb (14)
1970 Chatham 6y 10st 3lb (17)
1971 Gay Trip 9y 11st 3lb (10
1972 Red Candle 8y 10st (11)
1973 Skymas 8y 10st 5lb (15)
1974 Bruslee 8y 10st 7lb (11)
1975 Clear Cut 11y 10st 9lb (13)
1976★Cancello 7y 11st 1lb (13)
1977 Bachelor's Hall 7y 10st 6lb (16)
1978 Bawnogues 7y 10st 7lb (11)
1979 Man Alive 8y 10st 9lb (11)
1980 Bright Highway 6y 11st 11lb (15)
1981 Henry Kissinger 7y 10st 13lb (11)
1982 Fifty Dollars More 7y 11st (11)
1983 Pounentes 6y 10st 6lb (9)
1984 Half Free 8y 11st 10lb (10)
1985 Half Free 9y 11st 10lb (10)
1986 Very Promising 8y 11st 13lb (11)
1987 Beau Ranger 9y 10st 2lb (14)
1988 Pegwell Bay 7y 11st 2lb (13)
1989 Joint Sovereignty 9y 10st 4lb (15)
1990 Multum In Parvo 7y 10st 2lb (13)
1991 Another Coral 8y 10st 1lb (15)
1992 Tipping Tim 7y 10st 10lb (16)
1993 Bradbury Star 8y 11st 8lb (15)

★Run at Haydock

HENNESSY COGNAC GOLD CUP CHASE (Newbury)

(3¼ miles 110 yds)
1957★Mandarin 6y 11st (19)
1958★Taxidermist 6y 11st 1lb (13)
1959★Kerstin 9y 11st 10lb (26)
1960 Knucklecracker 7y 11st 1lb (20)
1961 Mandarin 10y 11st 5lb (22)
1962 Springbok 8y 10st 8lb (27)
1963 Mill House 6y 12st (10)
1964 Arkle 7y 12st 7lb (8)
1965 Arkle 8y 12st 7lb (8)
1966 Stalbridge Colonist 7y 10st (6)
1967 Rondetto 11y 10st 1lb (13)
1968 Man of the West 7y 10st (11)
1969 Spanish Steps 6y 11st 8lb (15)
1970 Border Mask 8y 11st 1lb (12)
1971 Bighorn 7y 10st 11lb (13)
1972 Charlie Potheen 7y 11st 4lb (13)
1973 Red Candle 9y 10st 4lb (11)
1974 Royal Marshal II 7y 10st (13)
1975 April Seventh 9y 11st 2lb (13)
1976 Zeta's Son 7y 10st 9lb (21)
1977 Bachelor's Hall 7y 10st 10lb (13)
1978 Approaching 7y 10st 6lb (8)
1979 Fighting Fit 7y 11st 7lb (15)
1980 Bright Highway 6y 11st 6lb (14)
1981 Diamond Edge 10y 11st 10lb (14)
1982 Bregawn 8y 11st 10lb (11)
1983 Brown Chamberlain 8y 11st 8lb (12)
1984 Burrough Hill Lad 8y 12st (13)
1985 Galway Blaze 9y 10st (15)
1986 Broadheath 9y 10st 5lb (15)
1987 Playschool 9y 10st 8lb (12)
1988 Strands of Gold 9y 10st (12)
1989 Ghofar 6y 10st 2lb (8)
1990 Arctic Call 7y 11st (13)
1991 Chatam (USA) 7y 10st 6lb (15)
1992 Sibton Abbey 7y 10st (13)
1993 Cogent 9y 10st 1lb (9)

★Run at Cheltenham

TRIPLEPRINT GOLD CUP HANDICAP CHASE (Cheltenham)

(2 miles 5 fur)
1963 Limeking 6y 10st 12lb (14)
1964 Flying Wild 8y 10st 6lb (7)
1965 Flyingbolt 6y 12st 6lb (11)
1966 The Laird 5y 10st 9lb (8)
1967 No race
1968 Tassilo 10y 10st 1lb (14)
1969 Titus Oates 7y 11st 13lb (11)
1970 Simian 8y 11st 8lb (7)
1971 Leap Frog 7y 12st 1lb (12)
1972 Arctic Bow 7y 10st 12lb (11)
1973 Pendil 8y 12st 7lb (8)
1974 Garnishee 10y 10st 6lb (9)
1975 Easby Abbey 8y 11st 10lb (9)
1976 No race
1977 Even Melody 8y 11st 2lb (11)
1978 The Snipe 8y 10st (14)
1979 Father Delaney 7y 10st 10lb (12)
1980 Bueche Giorod 9y 10st (15)
1981 No race
1982 Observe 6y 10st 11lb (15)
1983 Fifty Dollars More 8y 11st 10lb (13)
1984 Beau Ranger 9st 10lb (10)
1985 Combs Ditch 9y 11st 9lb (7)
1986 Oregon Trail 6y 10st 7lb (6)
1987 Bishops Yarn 8y 10st 7lb (5)
1988 Pegwell Bay 7y 10st 13lb (10)
1989 Clever Folly 9y 10st 4lb (6)
1990 No race
1991 Kings Fountain 8y 11st 10lb (8)
1992 Another Coral 9y 11st 4lb (10)
1993 Fragrant Dawn 9y 10st 2lb (11)

KING GEORGE VI TRIPLEPRINT CHASE (Kempton)

(3 miles)
1937 Southern Hero 12y 12st (4)
1938 Airgead Sios 8y 11st 10lb (4)
1939–46 No race
1947 Rowland Roy 8y 11st 13lb (10)
1948 Cottage Rake 9y 12st 6lb (9)
1949 Finnure 8y 11st 10lb (4)
1950 Manicou 5y 11st 8lb (7)
1951 Statecraft 6y 11st 11lb (6)
1952 Halloween 7y 11st 13lb (6)
1953 Galloway Braes 8y 12st 6lb (7)
1954 Halloween 9y 11st 10lb (8)
1955 Limber Hill 8y 11st 13lb (8)
1956 Rose Park 10y 11st 7lb (6)
1957 Mandarin 6y 12st (9)
1958 Lochroe 10y 11st 7lb (7)
1959 Mandarin 8y 11st 5lb (9)
1960 Saffron Tartan 9y 11st 7lb (10)
1961 and 1962 No race
1963 Mill House 6y 12st (3)
1964 Frenchman's Cove 9y 11st 7lb (2)
1965 Arkle 8y 12st (4)
1966 Dormant 9y 11st (7)
1967 and 1968 No race
1969 Titus Oates 7y 11st 10lb (5)
1970 No race
1971 The Dikler 8y 11st 7lb (10)
1972 Pendil 7y 12st (6)
1973 Pendil 8y 12st (4)
1974 Captain Christy 7y 12st (6)
1975 Captain Christy 8y 12st (7)
1976 Royal Marshall II 9y 11st 7lb (10)
1977 Bachelor's Hall 7y 11st 7lb (9)
1978 Gay Spartan 7y 11st 10lb (16)
1979 Silver Buck 7y 11st 10lb (11)
1980 Silver Buck 8y 11st 10lb (8)
1981 No race
1982 Wayward Lad 7y 11st 10lb (6)
1983 Wayward Lad 8y 11st 10lb (5)
1984 Burrough Hill Lad 8y 11st 10lb (3)
1985 Wayward Lad 10y 11st 10lb (5)
1986 Desert Orchid 7y 11st 10lb (9)
1987 Nupsala (FR) 8y 11st 10lb (9)
1988 Desert Orchid 9y 11st 10lb (5)
1989 Desert Orchid 10y 11st 10lb (6)
1990 Desert Orchid 11y 11st 10lb (9)
1991 The Fellow (FR) 6y 11st 10lb (8)
1992 The Fellow (FR) 7y 11st 10lb (8)
1993 Barton Bank 7y 11st 10lb (10)

SMURFIT CHAMPION HURDLE

(2 miles 110 yds) (First run 1927)

1927 Mrs H M Hollins's Blaris b g by Achtoi 6–12–0 .... G Duller 11–10
Mr A H Tennent's Boddam 8–12–0 .... W Speck 7–2
Col A E Jenkins's Harpist 6–12–0 .... F Rees 9–4
8l, 1l. 4m 13 3/5s. 4 ran. W Payne

1928 Maj H A Werner's Brown Jack br g by Jackdaw 4–11–0 .... L Rees 4–1
Maj D Dixon's Peace River 5–11–10 .... T Leader 5–1
Mrs H M Hollins's Blaris 7–12–0 .... G Duller 2–1
1 1/2l, 6l. 4m 5s. 6 ran. Hon A Hastings

1929 Miss Williams-Bulkeley's Royal Falcon ch h by White Eagle 6–12–0 .. F Rees 11–2
Mr T R Rimell's Rolie 8–12–0 W Stott 4–1
Sir John Grey's Clear Cash 4–11–0 .... G Pellerin 7–4
4l, 5l. 4m 1 1/5s. 6 ran. R Gore

1930 Mrs J de Selincourt's Brown Tony br g by Jackdaw 4–11–0 ...... T Cullinan 7–2
Sir John Grey's Clear Cash 5–11–10 .... G Pellerin 6–4
Mr S Wootton's Peertoi 5–11–10 .... S Ingham 7–2
Hd, sht. hd. 4m 20 1/5s. 5 ran. J Anthony

1931 No race

1932 Miss D Paget's Insurance b g by Achtoi 5–11–10 .... T Leader 4–5
Sir H Nugent's Song of Essex 6–12–0 .... W Parvin 5–4
Lord Stalbridge's Jack Drummer 4–11–0 .... T Cullinan 33–1
12l, bad. 4 m 14 1/5s. 3 ran. A Briscoe

1933 Miss D Paget's Insurance b g by Achtoi 6–12–0 .... W Stott 10–11
Mr R Bownass's Windermere Laddie 9–12–0 .... S Ingham 4–1
H.H. Aga Khan's Indian Salmon 4–11–0 .... G Pellerin 100–8
3/4l, 8l. 4m 37 3/5s. 5 ran. A Briscoe

1934 Mr G H Bostwick's Chenago b g by Hapsburg 7–12–0 .... D Morgan 4–9
Mr R Smith's Pompelmoose 4–11–0 .... P Fitzgerald 9–2
Mr G M King's Black Duncan 4–11–0 .... T Cullinan 20–1
5l, 6l. 4m 17s. 5 ran. I Anthony

1935 Mr R Fox-Carlyon's Lion Courage b or br g by Jackdaw 7–12–0 ... G Wilson 100–8
Mrs Crossman's Gay Light 9–12–0 .... S Ingham 9–4
Mr M Pilkington's Hill Song 6–12–0 .... G Pellerin 3–1
1/2l, 3/4l. 4m 0 1/5s. 11 ran. F Brown

1936 Mrs M Stephen's Victor Norman gr g by King Sol 5–11–10 ...... H Nicholson 4–1
Mr B Warner's Free Fare 8–12–0 .... G Pellerin 5–2
Mrs G S L Whitelaw's Cactus II 6–12–020–1
3l, 1 1/2ll. 3m 58 2/5s. 8 ran. M Blair

1937 Mr B Warner's Free Fare ch g by Werwolf 9–12–0 .... G Pellerin 2–1
Mr R Gubbins's Our Hope 8–12–0 .... Capt R Harding 100–8
Miss D Paget's Menton 5–11–10 .... S Ingham 11–2
2l, sht. hd. 4m 19 2/5s. 7 ran. E Gwilt

1938 Mr R Gubbins's Our Hope gr g by Son and Heir 9–12–0 ..... Cap R Harding 5–1
Vicomte de Chambure's Chuchoteur 6–12–0 .... M Plaine 9–2
Mr R Dick's Lobau 6–12–0 .... H Nicholson 100–6
1 1/2l, 10l. 4m 4 4/5s. 5 ran. R Gubbins

1939 Mr H J Brueton's African Sister ch m by Prester John 7–12–0 .... K Piggott 10–1
Mr A F Jack's Vitement 6–12–0 .... E Vinall 20–1
Maj J M J Evans's Apple Peel 9–12–0 .... S Ingham 100–8
3l, 1/2l. 4m 13 3/5s. 13 ran. C Piggott

1940 Miss D Paget's Solford b g by Soldennis 9–12–0 .... S Magee 5–2
Mr H J Brueton's African Sister 8–12–0 .... K Piggott 8–1
Mrs J C Lewis's Carton 5–11–10 .... F Rickaby 3–1
1 1/2l, 4l. 4m 13 2/5s. 8 ran. O Anthony

1941 Sir M McAlpine's Seneca ch c by Caligula 4–11–0 .... R Smyth 7–1
Miss D Paget's Anarchist 4–11–0 .... M Jones 33–1
Mr F Walwyn's Ephorus 5–11–0 .... H Nicholson 8–1
Hd, 2l. 4m 9s. 6 ran. V Smyth

1942 Mr V Smyth's Forestation b g by Felicitation 4–11–0 .... R Smyth 10–1
Miss D Paget's Anarchist 5–11–10 .... T Isaac 100–8
Mr J Barker's Southport 6–12–0 .... F Rickaby 9–2
3l, 3l. 20 ran. V Smyth

1943 and 1944 No race

1945 Mr F Blakeway's Brains Trust ch g by Rhodes Scholar-Easter Bonnet 5–11–10 .... T F Rimell 9–2
Mr A E Saunder's Vidi 4–11–0 .... D Butchers 100–6
Lord Stalbridge's Red April 8–12–0 .... D L Jones 10–1
3/4l, 3/4l. 4m 9 2/5s. 16 ran. Gerald Wilson

1946 Miss D Paget's Distel b g by Rosewell 5–11–10 .... R O'Ryan 4–5
Mr A Gibbes's Carnival Boy 5–11–0 .... T F Rimell 7–2
Mrs J Skinner's Robin O'Chantry 6–12–0 .... J Goodgame 100–6
4l, 1/2l. 4m 5 1/5s. 8 ran. C Rogers, in Ireland

1947 Mr L A Abelson's National Spirit ch g by Scottish Union 6–12–0 D Morgan 7–1
Mme L Aurousseau's Le Paillon 5–11–10 .... A Head 2–1
Lord Bicester's Freddy Fox 8–12–0 .... R Smyth 8–1
1l, 2l. 4m 3 4/5s. 14 ran. V Smyth

1948 Mr L A Abelson's National Spirit ch g by Scottish Union 7–12–0 .. R Smyth 6–4
Lt-Col Philips's DUKW 5–11–10 .... J Maguire 5–1
Lady Latymer's Encoroll 5–11–10 .... M Connors 20–1
2l, 3/4l. 3m 55s. 12 ran. V Smyth

1949 Mrs M H Keogh's Hatton's Grace b g by His Grace 9–12–0 .... A Brabazon 100–7
Mrs V M Pulham's Vatelys 9–12–0 .... R Bates 10–1
Mr F W Chandler's Captain Fox 4–11–0 .... K Mullins 100–9
6l, 1l. 4m 0 3/5s. 14 ran. M V O'Brien in Ireland

1950 Mrs M H Keogh's Hatton's Grace b g by His Grace 10–12–0 ..... A Brabazon 5–2
Mrs E Williams's Harlech 5–11–12 .... M Moloney 9–2

Mrs Z E Lambert's Speciality 5–11–12 .... K Mullins 100–6
$1^1/2$l, 2l, 3m $59^1/5$s. 12 ran. M V O'Brien in Ireland
1951 Mrs M H Keogh's Hatton's Grace b g by His Grace 11–12–0 .... T Molony 4–1
M G Chastenet's Pyrrhus III 8–12–0 .... A Gill 11–2
M G Beauvois's Prince Hindou 5–11–12 .... M Larraun 9–2
5l, $^1/2$l. 4m $10^4/5$s. 8 ran. M V O'Brien in Ireland
1952 Mr M Kingsley's Sir ken b g by Laeken 5–11–12 .... T Molony 4–1
Mr S Wootton's Noholme 5–11–12 .... B Marshall 100–7
Mr L A Abelson's Approval 6–12–0 .... D Dillon 9–1
2l, 4l. 4m $2^3/5$s. 16 ran. W Stephenson
1953 Mr M Kingsley's Sir Ken b g by Laeken 6–12–0 .... T Molony 2–5
Mr J H Griffin's Galatian 6–12–0 .... B Marshall 4–1
Mrs C Magnier's Teapot II 8–12–0 .... P Taaffe 100–9
2l, $1^1/2$l. 3m $55^2/5$s. 7 ran. W. Stephenson
1954 Mr M Kingsley's Sir Ken b g by Laeken 7–12–0 .... T Molony 4–9
Mr S W Everitt's Impney 5–11–12 .... M Pumfrey 9–1
Mr J H Griffin's Galatian 7–12–0 .... P Taaffe 10–1
1l, 3l. 4m $10^4/5$s. 13 ran. W Stephenson
1955 Mr G C Judd's Clair Soleil br g by Maravedis 6–12–0 .... F Winter 5–2
Mr B Hamilton's Stroller 7–12–0 .... T P Burns 7–2
Mrs A C leggatt's Cruachan 7–12–0 .... G Slack 50–1
Hd, 4l. 4m $11^3/5$s. 21 ran. H R Price
1956 Mr C Nicholson's Doornocker ch g by Cacador 8–12–0 .... H Sprague 100–9
Mrs L Brand's Quita Que 7–12–0 .... Mr J R Cox 33–1
Mr M Kingsley's Baby Don 6–12–0 .... T Molony 100–8
$^3/4$l, 4l. 4m 2s. 14 ran. W A Hall
1957 Mr A Jones's Merry Deal b g by Straight Deal 7–12–0 .... G Underwood 28–1
Mrs L Brand's Quita Que 8–12–0 .... Mr J R Cox 15–2
Comte de Monteynard's Tout ou Rien 5–11–12 .... R Emery 100–8
5l, 5l. 4m $6^2/3$s. 16 ran. A Jones
1958 Mrs D Wright's Bandalore b g by Tambourin 7–12–0 .... G Slack 20–1
Mr D Deyong's Tokoroa 7–12–0 .... D V Dick 5–1
Mr Jos Bennett's Retour de Flamme 5–11–12 .... J Lindley 11–2
2l, 3l. 3m 56s. 18 ran. J S Wright
1959 Mr G C Judd's Fare Time b g by Thoroughfare 6–12–0 .... F Winter 13–2
Mr J G Duggan's Ivy Green 9–12–0 .... P Taaffe 40–1
Mrs G R Westmacott's Prudent King 7–12–0 .... T P Burns 13–2
4l, 11l. 4m $7^4/5$s. 14 ran. H R Price
1960 Mr J J Byrne's Another Flash b g by Roi d'Egypte 6–12–0 .... H Beasley 11–4
Mrs C Magnier's Albergo 6–12–0 .... D Page 11–2
Lady Cottenham's Saffron Tartan 9–12–0 .... T P Burns 3–1
2l, 3l, 3m 55s. 12 ran. P Sleator in Ireland
1961 Dr B N Pajgar's Eborneezer b h by Ocean Swell 6–12–0 .... F Winter 4–1
Mrs T O'Brien's Moss Bank 5–11–12 .... J J Rafferty 7–4
Mr A H Birtwhistle's Farmer's Boy 8–12–0 .... D Nicholson 8–1
3l, $1^1/2$l. 4m 10s. 17 ran. H R Price
1962 Sir T Ainsworth's Anzio ro h by Vic Day 5–11–12 .... G W Robinson 11–2
Mrs I R Pitman's Quelle Chance 7–12–0 .... D V Dick 11–2
Mr J J Byrne's Another Flash 8–12–0 .... H Beasley 11–10
3l, $1^1/2$l. 4m $0^1/5$s. 14 ran. F Walwyn
1963 Mr G Spencer's Winning Fair bl or br g by Fun Fair 8–12–0 Mr A Lillingston 100–9
Mrs M E Donnelly's Farrney Fox 8–12–0 .... P Powell 10–1
Mrs I R Pitman's Quelle Chance 8–12–0 .... B Wilkinson 100–7
3l, nk. 4m $15^2/5$s. 21 ran. G Spencer in Ireland
1964 Mr J McGhie's Magic Court br g by Supreme Court 6–12–0 P McCarron 100–6
Mr J J Byrne's Another Flash 10–12–0 .... H Beasley 6–1
Mrs D Beddington's Kirriemuir 4–11–4 .... G W Robinson 100–6
4l, $^3/4$l. 4m 8s. 24 ran. T Robson
1965 Mrs D Beddington's Kirriemuir br g by Tangle 5–11–12 ...... G W Robinson 50–1
Mme P Logut's Spartan General 6–12–0 .... T W Biddlecombe 8–1
Queen Elizabeth's Worcran 7–12–0 .... D Nicholson 8–1
1l, $1^1/2$l. 4m $6^3/5$s. 19 ran. F Walwyn
1966 Mrs J Rogerson's Salmon Spray ch g by Vulgan 8–12–0 .... J Haine 4–1
Lady Aitken's Sempervivum 8–12–0 .... J King 20–1
Mrs T G Williamson's Flyingbolt 7–12–0 .... P Taaffe 15–8
3l, $^3/4$l. 4m $10^1/5$s. 17 ran. R Turnell
1967 Mr K F Alder's Saucy Kit b h by Hard Sauce 6–12–0 .... R Edwards 100–6
Queen Elizabeth's Makaldar 7–12–0 .... D Mould 11–4
Mr M L Healey's Talgo Abbess 8–12–0 .... F Carroll 100–8
Aurelius finished second, beaten 4 lengths, but was disqualified. Makaldar was 1 length further away.
4m. $11^1/5$s. 23 ran. M H Easterby
1968 Mr H S Alper's Persian War b g by Persian Gulf 5–11–12 .... J Uttley 4–1
Lord James Crichton-Stuart's Chorus 7–12–0 .... A Turnell 7–2
Mr R J Cohen's Black Justice 6–12–0 .... B Scott 100–6
4l, 5l. 4m $3^4/5$s. 16 ran. C Davies
1969 Mr H S Alper's Persian War b g by Persian Gulf 6–12–0 .... J Uttley 6–4
Mr I H Stuart Black's Drumikill 8–12–0 .... B Brogan 100–7
Maj G Glover's Privy Seal 5–11–12 .... J Cook 33–1
4l, $2^1/2$l. 4m $41^4/5$s. 17 ran. C Davies
1970 Mr H S Alper's Persian War b g by Persian Gulf 7–12–0 .... J Uttley 5–4
Mr K E Wheldon's Major Rose 8–12–0 .... J Gifford 8–1
Queen Elizabeth's Escalus 5–11–12 .... D Mould 25–1
$1^1/2$l, $1^1/2$l. 4m $13^4/5$s. 14 ran. C Davies
1971 Capt E J Edwards-Heathcote's Bula b g by Raincheck 6–12–0 .... P Kelleway 15–8
Mr H S Alper's Persian War 8–12–0 .... J Uttley 9–2
Mr K E Wheldon's Major Rose 9–12–0 .... T W Biddlecombe 4–1
4l, 1l. 4m $22^1/5$s. 9 ran. F Winter
1972 Capt E J Edwards-Heathcote's Bula b g by Raincheck 7–12–0 .... P Kellaway 8–11

Lord Blakenham's Boxer 5–11–12 .... J Uttley 25–1
Mrs E Swainson's Lyford Cay 8–12–0 .... D Cartwright 66–1
8l, 3l. 4m 25 1/5s. 12 ran. F Winter
1973 Mr E Wheatley's Comedy of Errors br h by Goldhill 6–12–0 .... W Smith 8–1
Mrs W Blow's Easby Abbey 6–12–0 .... R Barry 20–1
Mrs J Samuel's Captain Christy 6–12–0 .... H Beasley 85–40
1 1/2l, 2l. 4m 7 4/5s. 8 ran. T F Rimell
1974 Lord Howard de Walden's Lanzarote br g by Milesian 6–12–0 ...... R Pitman 7–4
Mr E Wheatley's Comedy of Errors 7–12–0 .... W Smith 4–6
Mr D W Samuel's Yenisei (NZ) 7–12–0 .... H Beasley 100–1
3l, 8l. 4m 17·70s. 7 ran F Winter
1975 Mr E Wheatley's Comedy of Errors br h by Goldhill 8–12–0 .... K White 11–8
Mrs O Negus-Fancey's Flash Imp 6–12–0 .... T Stack 12–1
Mrs C Williams's Tree Tangle 6–12–0 .... A Turnell 10–1
8l, hd. 4m 28·50s. 13 ran. T F Rimell
1976 Mr R Spencer's Night Nurse b g by Falcon 5–12–0 .... P Broderick 2–1
Mr I Scott's Birds Nest 6–12–0 .... A Turnell 100–30
Mrs O Negus-Fancey's Flash Imp 7–12–0 .... R Mann 40–1
2 1/2l, 8l. 4m 5·9s. 8 ran. M H Easterby
1977 Mr R Spencer's Night Nurse b g by Falcon 6–12–0 .... P Broderick 15–2
Dr M Mangan's Monksfield 5–12–0 .... T Kinane 15–1
Mr L Thwaite's Dramatist 6–12–0 .... W Smith 6–1
2l, 2l. 4m 24s. 10 ran. M H Easterby
1978 Dr M Mangan's Monksfield b h by Gala Performance 6–12–0 .... T Kinane 11–2
Mr P Muldoon's Sea Pigeon (USA) 8–12–0 .... F Berry 5–1
Mr R Spencer's Night Nurse 7–12–0 .... C Tinkler 3–1
2l, 6l. 4m 12·70s. 13 ran. D McDonogh in Ireland
1979 Mr M Mangan's Monksfield b h by Gala Performance 7–12–0 .... D T Hughes 9–4
Mr P Muldoon's Sea Pigeon (USA) 9–12–0 .... J J O'Neill 6–1
Mr H Joel's Beacon Light 8–12–0 .... J Francome 22–1
3/4l, 15l. 4m 27s. 10 ran. D McDonogh in Ireland
1980 Mr P Muldoon's Sea Pigeon (USA) br g by Sea-Bird II 10–12–0 ... J J O'Neill 13–2
Mr M Mangan's Monksfield 8–12–0 .... D T Hughes 6–5
Mr Scott's Birds Nest 10–12–0 .... A Turnell 11–1
7l, 1 1/2l. 4m 6s. 9 ran. M H Easterby
1981 Mr P Muldoon's Sea Pigeon (USA) br g by Sea-Bird II 11–12–0 ... J Francome 7–4
Mr R Formby's Pollardstown 6–12–0 .... P Blacker 9–1
Mrs H Doyle's Daring Run 6–12–0 .... Mr T Walsh 8–1
1 1/2l, nk. 4m 11o40s. 14 ran. M H Easterby
1982 Mr P Heaslip's For Auction b g by Royal Trip 6–12–0 .... Mr C Magnier 40–1
Lord Northampton's Broadsword 5–12–0 .... P Scudamore 100–30
Tawfuk Fakhouri's Ekbalco 6–12–0 .... D Goulding 7–2
7l, 1 1/2l, 1 1/2l. 4m 12·4s. 14 ran. M Cunningham
1983 Sheikh Ali Abu Khamsin's Gaye Brief b g by Lucky Brief 6–12–0 ... R Linley 7–1
Mr W Lenehan's Boreen Prince 6–12–0 .... N Madden 50–1
Mr F Heaslip's For Auction 7–12–0 .... Mr C Magnier 3–1
3l; 7l. 3m 57·08s. 17 ran. Mrs M Rimell
1984 Mrs C D Hill's Dawn Run b m by Deep Run, 6–11–9 .... J J O'Neill 4–5
Mr R A Padmore's Cima 6–12–0 .... P Scudamore 66–1
Mr R H Mann's Very Promising 6–12–0 .... S Moorshead 16–1
3/4l, 4l. 3m 52·6s 14 ran. P Mullins in Ireland
1985 The Stype Wood Stud Ltd's See You Then br g by Royal Palace, 5–12–0 .... S Smith Eccles 16–1
Mr A Hunt's Robin Wonder 7–12–0 .... J J O'Neill 66–1
Mrs M C Margan's Stans Pride 8–11–9 .... S Moorshead 100–1
7l; 31.3m 51·7s. 14 ran. N J Henderson
1986 The Stype Wood Stud Ltd's See You Then br g by Royal Palace 6–12–0 .... S Smith Eccles 5–6
Sheikh Ali Abu Khamsin's Gaye Brief 9–12–0 .... P Scudamore 14–1
Ulceby Farm Ltd's Nohalmdun 5–12–0 .... J J O'Neill 20–1
7l; 1 1/2l. 3m 53·3s. 23 ran. N J Henderson
1987 The Stype Wood Stud Ltd's See You Then br g by Royal Palace 7–12–0 .... S Smith Eccles 11–10
Mr W L Pape's Flatterer (USA) 8–12–0 .... J Fishback 10–1
Mr M Davies's Barnbrook Again, 6–12–0 .... S Sherwood 14–1
1 1/2l; 1l. 3m 57·3s. 18 ran. N J Henderson
1988 Mr D Horton's Celtic Shot b g by Celtic Cone 6–12–0 .... P Scudamore 7–1
Mr J O'Connell's Classical Charm 5–12–0 .... K Morgan 33–1
Mrs L Sewell's Celtic Chief 5–12–0 .... R Dunwoody 5–2
4l; 3l. 4m 14·4s. 21 ran. F Winter
1989 Mr A Geake's Beech Road ch g by Nearly A Hand 7–12–0 ..... R Guest 50–1
Mrs L Sewell's Celtic Chief 6–12–0 .... G McCourt 6–1
Mr D Horton's Celtic Shot 7–12–0 .... P Scudamore 8–1
2l; 1l. 4m 2·10s. 15 ran. G B Balding
1990 Sheikh Mohammed's Kribensis gr g by Henbit 6–12–0 .... R Dunwoody 95–40
Mr R Sangster's Nomadic Way 5–12–0 ....P Scudamore 8–1
Mr N Hetherton's Past Glories 7–12–0 .... J Quinn 150–1
3l 3/4l. 3m 50.7s. 19 ran. M Stoute
1991 Michael Jackson Bloodstock Ltd's Morley Street ch g by Deep Run 7–12–0 .... J Frost 4–1
Mr. R Sangster's Nomadic Way 6–12–0 .... R Dunwoody 9–1
Mr G D Groarke's Ruling 5–12–0 .... P Niven 50–1
1 1/2l. head, 3m 54.6s. 24 ran. G B Balding
1992 Sheikh Mohammed's Royal Gait b g by Gunner B 9–12–0 .... G McCourt 6–1
Oh So Risky Syndicate's Oh So Risky 5–12–0 .... P Holley 20–1
I MacDonald/J Short's Ruling 6–12–0 .... P Niven 20–1
1/2l, short head. 3m 57.2s. 16 ran. J R Fanshawe
1993 Mr E Scarth's Granville Again ch g by Deep Run 7–12–0 ...... P Scudamore 13–2
Mr M Tabor's Royal Derbi 8–12–0 ....M Perrett 50–1
Mr A Christodoulou's Halkopous 7–12–0 ....A Maguire 9–1
1l, 2 1/2l, 3m 51.6s. 18 ran. M C Pipe

TOTE CHELTENHAM GOLD CUP

(3 miles 2f 110 yds) (First run 1924)

1924 Maj H Wyndham's Red Splash ch g by Copper Ore 5–11–5 .... F Rees 5–1
Maj C Dewhurst's Conjurer II 12–12–0 .... Mr H A Brown 7–1
Maj F J Scott Murray's Gerald L 10–12–0 .... I Morgan 5–1
Hd, nk. 9 ran. F E Withington

1925 M J C Bentley's Ballinode ch m by Machakos 9–12–0 .... T Leader 3–1
Mr W H McAlpine's Alcazar 9–12–0 .... F Rees 8–13
Mr B lemon's Patsey V 11–12–0 .... Mr B Lemon 10–1
5l, bad. 7m 29 3/5s. 4 ran. F Morgan in Ireland

1926 Mr F Barbour's Koko b g by Santoi 8–12–0 .... J Hamey 10–1
Mrs W H Dixon's Old Tay Bridge 12–12–0 .... J Hogan 3–1
Mr W Filmer-Sankey's Ruddyglow 8–12–0 .... Mr W Filmer-Sankey 6–5
4l, 5l. 7m 11s. 8 ran. A Bickley

1927 Lord Stalbridge's Thrown In ch g by Beau Bill 11–12–0 .... Mr H R Grosvenor 10–1
Mr T Ka Laidlaw's Grakle 5–11–5 .... J Moloney 5–1
Mr W H Midwood's Silvo 11–12–0 .... F Rees 13–8
2l, 1 1/2l. 7m 28s. 8 ran. O Anthony

1928 Mr F W Keen's Patron Saint br g by St Girons 5–11–5 .... F Rees 7–2
Col J H Starkey's Vive 13–12–0 .... P Powell 4–5
4l, 2l. 7m 29 3/5s. 7 ran. H Harrison

1929 Mr J H Whitney's Easter Hero ch g by My Prince 9–12–0 .... F Rees 7–4
Capt R F H Norman's Lloydie 7–12–0 .... R McCarthy 100–9
Mr C R Taylor's Grakle 7–12–0 .... K Piggott 11–4
20l, 2l. 6m 57s. 10 ran. J Anthony

1930 Mr J H Whitney's Easter Hero ch g by My Prince 10–12–0 ...... T Cullinan 8–11
Mr C R Taylor's Grakle 8–12–0 .... K Piggott 10–1
Only 2 finished
20l. 7m 6s. 4 ran. J Anthony

1931 No race

1932 Miss D Paget's Golden Miller b g by Goldcourt 5–11–5 .... T Leader 13–2
Lady Lindsay's Inverse 6–12–0 .... R Lyall 8–1
Mr M D Blair's Aruntius 11–12–0 .... D McCann 20–1
4l, bad. 7m 33 2/5s. 6 ran. A Briscoe

1933 Miss D Paget's Golden Miller b g by Goldcourt 6–12–0 .... W Stott 4–7
Mr J H Whitney's Thomond II 7–12–0 .... W Speck 11–4
Mr J B Snow's Delaneige 8–12–0 .... J Moloney 20–1
10l, 5l. 7m 33s. 7 ran. A Briscoe

1934 Miss D Paget's Golden Miller b g by Goldcourt 7–12–0 6–5
Mrs V Mundy's Avenger 5–11–5 .... R Lyall 6–1
Mrs F Ambrose Clark's Kellsboro' Jack 8–12–0 .... D Morgan 10–1
6l, 6l. 7m 4 3/5s. 7 ran. A Briscoe

1935 Miss D Paget's Golden Miller b g by Goldcourt 8–12–0 .... G Wilson 1–2
Mr J H Whitney's Thomond II 9–12–0 .... W Speck 5–2
Mrs F Ambrose Clark's Kellsboro' Jack 9–12–0 .... D Morgan 100–7
3/4l, 5l. 6m 30s. 5 ran. A Briscoe

1936 Miss D Paget's Golden Miller b g by Goldcourt 9–12–0 .... E Williams 21–20
Mr H Lloyd Thomas's Royal Mail 7–12–0 .... Mr F Walwyn 5–1
Mrs F Ambrose Clark's Kellsboro' Jack 10–12–0 .... D Morgan 10–1
12l, 2l. 7m 5 1/5s. 6 ran. O Anthony

1937 No race

1938 Lt-Col D C Part's Morse Code b or ch g by The Pilot 9–12–0 ..... D Morgan 13–2
Miss D Paget's Golden Miller 11–12–0 .... H Nicholson 7–4
Mr H A Steel's Macaulay 7–12–0 .... D Butchers 3–1
2l, 3l. 6m 35 1/5s. 6 ran. I Anthony

1939 Mrs A Smith-Bingham's Brendan's Cottage b h by Cottage 9–12–0 G Owen 8–1
Capt J W Bridge's Morse Code 10–12–0 .... D Morgan 4–7
Mr G S L Whitelaw's Embarrassed 6–12–0 .... Capt P Herbert 25–1
5l, bad. 7m 34 1/5s. 5 ran. G Beeby

1940 Miss D Paget's Roman Hackle b g by Yutoi 7–12–0 .... E Williams Evens
Mrs C Jones's Black Hawk 9–12–0 .... T F Rimell 20–1
Mrs C Evans's Royal Mail 11–12–0 .... D Morgan 100–8
10l, 2l. 6m 46 2/5s. 7 ran. O Anthony

1941 Mr D Sherbooke's Poet Prince ch g by Milton 91–12–0 .... R Burford 7–2
Maj L Montagu's Savon 9–12–0 .... G Archibald 100–30
Lady Sybil Phipp's Red Rower 7–12–0 .... D Morgan 8–1
3l, sht. hd. 15 3/5s. 10 ran. I Anthony

1942 Lord Sefton's Medoc II b g by Van 8–12–0 .... H Nicholson 9–2
Lady Sybil Phipp's Red Rower 8–12–0 .... D Morgan 3–1
Lord Bicester's Asterabad 11–12–0 .... T F Carey 20–1
8l, 4l. 6m 38s. 12 ran. R Hobbs

1943 and 1944 No race

1945 Lord Stalbridge's Red Rower b g by Rameses the Second 11–12–0 .... D L Jones 11–4
Mrs K Cameron's Schubert 11–12–0 .... C Beechener 11–2
Mr R A Holbech's Paladin 11–12–0 .... P Conlon 100–30
3l, 1 1/2l. 6m 16 1/5s. 16 ran. Lord Stalbridge

1946 Mr J V Rank's Prince Regent b g by My Prince 11–12–0 .... T Hyde 4–7
Mrs D Nelson's Poor Flame 8–12–0 .... G Kelly 9–2
5l, 4l. 6m 47 3/5s. 6 ran. T Dreaper in Ireland

1947 Lord Grimthorpe's Fortina ch h by Formor 6–12–0 .... Mr R Black 8–1
Miss D Paget's Happy Holme 8–12–0 .... D L Moore 3–1
Lord Bicester's Prince Blackthorn 9–12–0 .... R Turnell 8–1
10l, 6l. 6m 41 1/5s. 12 ran. H Christie

1948 Mr F L Vickerman's Cottage Rake b or br g by Cottage 9–12–0 A Brabazon 10–1
Miss D Paget's Happy Home 9–12–0 .... M Moloney 6–1

Mr W F Highnam's Coloured School Boy 8–12–0 . . . . E Vinall 10–1
1½l, 10l. 6m 56⅖s. 12 ran. M V O'Brien in Ireland

1949 Mr F L Vickerman's Cottage Rake b or br g by Cottage 10–12–0 A Brabazon 4–6
Maj R Stirling-Stuart's Cool Customer 10–12–0 . . . . P J Murphy 13–2
Mr W F Highnam's Coloured School Boy 9–12–0 . . . . E Vinall 8–1
2l, 6l. 6m 36s. 6 ran. M V O'Brien in Ireland

1950 Mr F L Vickerman's Cottage Rake b or br g by Cottage 11–12–0 A Brabazon 5–6
Lord Bicester's Finnure 9–12–0 . . . . M Moloney 5–4
Marquis de Portago's Garde Toi 9–12–0 . . . . Marquis de Portago 100–1
10l, 8l. 7m 0⅗s. 6 ran. M V O'Brien in Ireland

1951 Lord Bicester's Silver Fame ch g by Werwolf 12–12–0 . . . . M Moloney 6–4
Mr J V Rank's Greenogue 9–12–0 . . . . G Kelly 100–8
Mr L B Chugg's Mighty Fine 9–12–0 . . . . J A Bullock 10–1
Sht. hd, 2l. 6m 23⅖s. 6 ran. G Beeby

1952 Miss D Paget's Mont Tremblant ch g by Gris Perle 6–12–0 . . . . D V Dick 8–1
Mr G Hemsleys Shaef 8–12–0 F Winter 7–1
Lady Orde's Galloway Braes 7–12–0 . . . . R Morrow 66–1
10l, 4l. 7m 2½s. 13 ran. F Walwyn

1953 Mrs M H Keogh's Knock Hard ch g by Domaha 9–12–0 . . . . T Moloney 11–2
Contessa di Sant Elia's Halloween 8–12–0 . . . . F Winter 5–2
Lady Orde's Galloway Braes 8–12–0 . . . . R Morrow 33–1
5l, 2l. 6m 28⅖s. 12 ran. M V O'Brien in Ireland

1954 Mr A Strange's Four Ten b g by Blunderbuss 8–12–0 . . . . T Cusack 100–6
Lord Bicester's Mariner's Log 7–12–0 . . . . P Taaffe 20–1
Contessa di Sant Elia's Halloween 9–12–0 . . . . G Slack 100–6
4l, 4l. 7m 12⅕s. 9 ran. J F Roberts

1955 Mr P J Burt's Gay Donald b g by Gay Light 9–12–0 . . . . A Grantham 33–1
Contessa di Sant Elia's Halloween 10–12–0 . . . . F Winter 7–2
Mr A Strange's Four Ten 9–12–0 . . . . T Cusack 3–1
10l, 8l. 6m 59⅕s. 9 ran. J J Ford

1956 Mr J Davey's Limber Hill ch g by Bassam 9–12–0 . . . . J Power 11–8
Mr A R B Owen's Vigor 8–12–0 . . . . R Emery 50–1
Contessa di Sant Elia's Halloween 11–12–0 . . . . F Winter 100–8
4l, 1½l. 6m 42s. 11 ran. W P Dutton

1957 Mr D Brown's Linwell b g by Rosewell 9–12–0 . . . . M Scudamore 100–9
Mr G H Moore's Kerstin 7–12–0 . . . . G Milburn 6–1
Mr G G Lawrence's Rose Park 11–12–0 . . . . G Nicholls 100–8
1l, 5l. 6m 55⅗s. 13 ran. C Mallon

1958 Mr G H Moore's Kerstin br m by Honor's Choice 8–12–0 . . S Hayhurst 7–1
Mrs P Pleydell-Bouverie's Polar Flight 8–12–0 . . . . G Slack 11–2
Mr P J Burt's Gay Donald 12–12–0 . . . . F Winter 13–2
½l, bad. 6m 55⅗s. 9 ran. C Bewicke

1959 Lord Fingall's Roddy Owen b g by Owenstown 10–12–0 . . . . . . H Beasley 5–1
Mr D Brown's Linwell 11–12–0 . . . . F Winter 11–2
Mrs J Mildmay-White's Lochroe 11–12–0 . . . . A Freeman 100–9
3l, 10l. 7m 28⅖s. 11 ran. D Morgan in Ireland

1960 Mr J Rogerson's Pas Seul b or br g by Erin's Pride 7–12–0 . . . . W Rees 6–1
Mrs J Mildmay-White's Lochroe 12–12–0 . . . . D Mould 25–1
Mrs G St John Nolan's Zonda 9–12–0 . . . . G W Robinson 8–1
1l, 5l. 4m 0s. 12 ran. R Turnell

1961 Col G R Westmacott's Saffron Tartan b or br g by Tartan 10–12–0 . . F Winter 2–1
Mr J Rogerson's Pas Seul 8–12–0 . . . . D V Dick 100–30
Mme K Hennessy's Mandarin 10–12–0 . . . . P Madden 100–7
1½l, 3l. 6m 49⅘s. 11 ran. D Butchers

1962 Mme K Hennessy's Mandarin b g by Deux pour Cent 11–12–0 . . . F Winter 7–2
Mr G Ansley's Fortria 10–12–0 P Taaffe 3–1
Mr W Nodding's Cocky Consort 9–12–0 . . . . C Stobbs 50–1
1l, 10l. 6m 39⅖s. 9 ran. F Walwyn

1963 Mr W H Golling's Mill House b g by King Hal 6–12–0 . . . . . G W Robinson 7–2
Mr G Ansley's Fortria 11–20–0 P Taaffe 4–1
Mr J Tilling's Duke of York 8–12–0 . . . . F Winter 7–1
12l, 4l. 7m 8⅖s. 12 ran. F Walwyn

1964 Anne Duchess of Westminster's Arkle b g by Archive 7–12–0 . . . . P Taaffe 7–4
Mr W H Golling's Mill House 7–12–0 . . . . G W Robinson 8–13
Mr J Rogerson's Pas Seul 11–12–0 . . . . D V Dick 50–1
5l, 25l. 6m 45⅗s. 4 ran. T Dreaper in Ireland

1965 Anne, Duchess of Westminster's Arkle b g by Archive 8–12–0 . . . . P Taaffe 30–100
Mr W H Golling's Mill House 8–12–0 . . . . G W Robinson 100–30
Mr W Roycroft's Stoney Crossing 7–12–0 . . . . Mr W Roycroft 100–1
10l, 30l. 6m 41⅕s. 4 ran. T Dreaper in Ireland

1966 Anne, Duchess of Westminster's Arkle b g by Archive 9–12–0 . . . . . . P Taaffe 1–10
Mrs D M Wells-Kendrew's Dormant 9–12–0 . . . . M Scudamore 20–1
Lord Cadogan's Snaigow 7–12–0 . . . . D Nicholson 100–7
30l, 10l. 6m 54⅕s. 5 ran. T Dreaper in Ireland

1967 Mr H H Collin's Woodland Venture b g by Eastern Venture 7–12–0 . . . . T W Biddlecombe 100–8
Mr R J R Blindell's Stalbridge Colonist 8–12–0 . . . . S Mellor 11–2
Lady Weir's What a Myth 10–12–0 . . . . P Kelleway 3–1
¾l, 2l. 6m 59⅕s. 8 ran. T F Rimell

1968 Col J Thomson's Fort Leney b g by Fortina 10–12–0 . . . . P Taaffe 11–2
Mr H J Joel's The Laird 7–12–0 J King 3–1
Mr R J R Blindell's Stalbridge Colonist 9–12–0 . . . . T W Biddlecombe 7–2
Nk, 1l. 6m 51s. 5 ran. T Dreaper in Ireland

1969 Lady Weir's What a Myth ch g by Coup de Myth 12–12–0 . . . . P Kelleway 8–1
Mr B P Jenks's Domacorn 7–12–0 . . . . T W Biddlecombe 7–2
Mr P Cussin's Playlord 8–12–0 R Barry 4–1
1½l, 20l. 7m 30⅘s. 11 ran. H R Price

1970 Mr R R Guest's L'Escargot ch g by Escart III 7–12–0 . . . . T Carberry 33–1
Mr K Stewart's French Tan 8–12–0 . . . . P Taaffe 8–1
Mr E R Courage's Spanish Steps 7–12–0 . . . . J Cook 9–4
1½l, 10l. 6m 47⅖s. 12 ran. D L Moore in Ireland

1971 Mr R R Guest's L'Escargot ch g by Escart III 8–12–0 . . . . T Carberry 7–2
Mrs R K Mellon's Leap Frog 7–12–0 . . . . V O'Brien 7–2

Mrs D W August's The Dikler 8–12–0 .... B Brogan 15–2
10l, 15l. 8m 03/5s. 8 ran. D L Moore in Ireland
1972 Mr P Doyle's Glencaraig Lady ch m by Fortina 8–12–0 .... F Berry 6–1
Mr H Handel's Royal Toss 10–12–0 .... N Wakley 22–1
Mrs D August's The Dikler 9–12–0 .... B Brogan 11–1
3/4l, hd. 7m 174/5s. 12 ran. F Flood in Ireland
1973 Mrs D August's The Dikler b g by Vulgan 10–12–0 .... R Barry 9–1
Mrs C Swallow's Pendil 8–12–0 .... R Pitman 4–6
Mrs B Heath's Charlie Potheen 8–12–0 .... T W Biddlecombe 9–2
Sht. hd, 6l. 6m 371/5s. 8 ran. F Walwyn
1974 Mrs J M A Samuel's Captain Christy b g by Mon Capitaine 7–12–0 H Beasley 7–1
Mrs D August's The Dikler 11–12–0 .... R Barry 5–1
Queen Elizabeth's Game Spirit 8–12–0 .... T Biddlecombe 20–1
5l, 20l. 7m 5·50s. 7 ran. P Taaffe in Ireland
1975 Anne, Duchess of Westminster's Ten Up b g by Raise You Ten 8–12–0 .... T Carberry 2–1
Mrs M Scott's Soothsayer (USA) 8–12–0 .... R Pitman 28–1
Capt E Edwards-Heathcote's Bula 10–12–0 .... J Francombe 5–1
6l, 1/2l. 7m 51·40s. 8 ran. J Dreaper in Ireland
1976 Sir E Hanmer's Royal Frolic b g by Royal Buck 7–12–0 .... J Burke 14–1
Mrs P Burrell's Brown Lad 10–12–0 .... T Carberry 13–8
Mrs P Burrell's Colebridge 12–12–0 .... F Berry 12–1
5l, 5l. 6m 40·1s. 11 ran. T F Rimell
1977 Mrs J McGowan's Davy Lad, b g by David Jack 7–12–0 ..... D T Hughes 14–1
Mr A Robinson's Tied Cottage 9–12–0 .... T Carberry 20–1
Mr H J Joel's Summerville 11–12–0 .... J King 15–1
6l, 20l. 7m 13·80s. 13 ran. M O'Toole in Ireland
1978 Mrs O Jackson's Midnight Court b g by Twilight Alley 7–12–0 .. J Francombe 5–2
Mrs P E Burrell's Brown Lad 12–12–0 .... T Carberry 8–1
Mrs S Marsh's Master H 9–12–0 .... R Crank 18–1
7l, 1l. 6m 57·30s. 10 ran. F Winter
1979 Snailwell Stud Co's Alverton ch g by Midsummer Night II 9–12–0 .... J J O'Neill 5–1
Mr S Burgess's Royal Mail (NZ) 9–12–0 .... P Blacker 7–1
Mr S Embirico's Aldaniti 9–12–0 .... R Champion 40–1
25l, 20l. 7m 1s. 14 ran. M H Easterby
1980 Mr A Barrow's Master Smudge ch g by Master Stephen 8–12–0 ..... R Hoare 14–1
Miss P Neal's Mac Vidi 15–12–0 .... P Leach 66–1
Major D Wigan's Approaching 9–12–0 .... B R Davies 11–1
8l, 5l, 21/2l. 7m 14·20s. 15 ran. A Barrow
Tied Cottage came in first, but, following a dope test, was later disqualified.
1981 Mr R Wilson's Little Owl b g by Cantab 7–12–0 .... Mr A J Wilson 6–1
Mr R Spencer's Night Nurse 10–12–0 .... A Brown 6–1
Mrs C Feather's Silver Buck 9–12–0 .... T Carmody 7–2
11/2l, 10l. 7m 9·90s. 15 ran. M H Easterby
1982 Mrs C Feather's Silver Buck br g by Silver Cloud 10–12–0 ... R Earnshaw 8–1
Mr M Kennelly's Bregawn 8–12–0 .... G Bradley 18–1
Miss C Hawkey's Sunset Cristo 8–12–0 .... C Grant 100–1
2l, 12l. 7m 11·3s. 22 ran. M Dickinson
1983 Mr J Kennelly's Bregawn ch g by Saint Denys 9–12–0 .... G Bradley 100–30
Mr F Emami's Captain John 9–12–0 .... D Goulding 11–1
Mrs S N Thewlis's Wayward Lad 8–12–0 .... J J O'Neill 6–1
5l; 11/2l. 6m 57·60s. 11 ran. M Dickinson
1984 Mr R S Riley's Burrough Hill Lad b g by Richboy 8–12–0 .... P Tuck 7–2
Mrs B Samuel's Brown Chamberlain 9–12–0 .... J Francombe 5–1
Mr Michael Cuddy's Drumlargan 10–12–0 .... Mr F Codd 16–1
3l, 8l. 6m 41·4s. 12 ran. Mrs J Pitman
1985 T Kilroe and Sons Ltd's Forgive 'N' Forget ch g by Precipice Wood, 8–12–0 .... M Dwyer 7–1
Mrs M M Haggas's Righthand Man 8–12–0 .... G Bradley 15–2
Mr W Hamilton's Earls Brig 10–12–0 .... P Tuck 13–2
11/2l, 21/2l. 6m 48·3s. 15 ran. J Fitzgerald
1986 Mrs C D Hill's Dawn Run b m by Deep Run 8–11–9 .... J J O'Neill 15–8
Mrs S N Thewlis's Wayward lad, 11–12–0 .... G Bradley 8–1
T Kilroe and Sons Ltd's Forgive 'N' Forget 9–12–0 .... M Dwyer 7–2
1l; 21/2l. 6m 35·3s. 11 ran. P Mullins in Ireland
1987 T P M McDonagh Ltd's The Thinker ch g by Cantab 9–12–0 .... R Lamb 13–2
Mr I Bray's Cybrandian 9–12–0 .... C Grant 25–1
Mr H J Joel's Door Latch 9–12–0 .... R Rowe 9–1
11/2l; 21/2l. 6m 56·1s. 12 ran. W A Stephenson
1988 Mrs C Smith's Charter Party br g by Document 10–12–0 .... R Dunwoody 10–1
Mrs J Ollivant's Cavvies Clown 8–12–0 .... S Sherwood 6–1
White Bros. (Taunton) Ltd's Beau Ranger 10–12–0 .... P Scudamore 33–1
6l; 10l. 6m 58·9s. 15 ran. D Nicholson
1989 Mr R Burridge's Desert Orchid gr g by Grey Mirage 10–12–0 ... S Sherwood 5–2
Mr A Parker's Yahoo 8–12–0 .... T Morgan 25–1
Mr C Smith's Charter Party 11–12–0 .... R Dunwoody 14–1
11/2l; 8l. 7m 17·60s. 13 ran. D Elsworth
1990 Mr S Griffiths's Norton's Coin ch g by Mount Cassino 9–12–0 ... G McCourt 100–1
Mrs E Hitchins's Toby Tobias 8–12–0 .... M Pitman 8–1
Mr R Burridge's Desert Orchid 11–12–0 .... R Dunwoody 10–11
3/4l, 4l. 6m 30.9s. 12 ran. S. Griffiths
1991 Autofour Engineering's Garrison Savannah b g by Random Shot 8–12–0 .... M Pitman 16–1
Marquesa de Moratalla's The Fellow (FR) 6–12–0 .... A Kondrat 28–1
Mr R Burridge's Desert Orchid 12–12–0 .... R Dunwoody 4–1
Short head, 15l. 6m 49.8s. 14 ran. Mrs J Pitman
1992 Whitcombe Manor Racing Stables Ltd's Cool Ground ch g Over the River 10–12–0 .... A Maguire 25–1
Marquesa de Moratalla's The Fellow (FR) 7–12–0 .... A Kondrat 7–2

R H Baines's Docklands Express 10–12–0 .... M Perrett 16–1
Short head, 1l. 6m 47.5s. 8 ran. G B Balding
1993 Mr J N Yeadon's Jodami b g by Crash Course 8–12–0 .... M Dwyer 8–1
Hunt & Co (Bournemouth) Ltd's Rushing Wild 8–12–0 .... R Dunwoody 11–1
Messrs G & L Johnson's Royal Athlete 10–12–0 .... B de Haan 66–1
2l, 7l, 6m 34.4s. 16 ran. P Beaumont

MARTELL GRAND NATIONAL H'CAP CHASE

(About 4½ miles) (First run 1837)

1837*The Duke (6)
1838*Sir Henry (10)
1839 Lottery 12st (12)
1840 Jerry 12st (12)
1841 Charity 12st (11)
1842 Gaylad 12st (15)
1843 Vanguard 11st 10lb (16)
1844 Discount 6y 10st 12lb (15)
1845 Cure-All 11st 5lb (15)
1846 Pioneer 6y 11st 12lb (22)
1847 Matthew 10st 6lb (28)
1848 Chandler 11st 12lb (29)
1849 Peter Simple 11st (23)
1850 Abd el Kader 9st 12lb (32)
1851 Abd el Kader 10st 4lb (21)
1852 Miss Mowbray 10st 4lb (24)
1853 Peter Simple 10st 10lb (21)
1854 Bourton 11st 12lb (20)
1855 Wanderer 9st 8lb (20)
1856 The Free-trader 7y 9st 6lb (21)
1857 Emigrant 9st 10lb (28)
1858 Little Charley 12y 10st 7lb (16)
1859 Half-Caste 6y 9st 7lb (16)
1860 Anatis 10y 9st 10lb (19)
1861 Jealousy 7y 9st 12lb (24)
1862 Huntsman 9y 11st (13)
1863 Emblem 7y 10st 10lb (16)
1864 Emblematic 6y 10st 6lb (25)
1865 Alcibiade 5y 11st 4lb (23)
1866 Salamander 7y 10st 7lb (30)
1867 Cortolvin 8y 11st 13lb (23)
1868 The Lamb 6y 10st 7lb (21)
1869 The Colonel 6y 10st 7lb (22)
1870 The Colonel 7y 11st 12lb (23)
1871 The Lamb 9y 11st 5lb (25)
1872 Casse Tete 7y 10st (25)
1873 Disturbance 6y 11st 11lb (28)
1874 Reugny 6y 10st 12lb (22)
1875 Pathfinder 10st 11lb (19)
1876 Regal 5y 11st 3lb (19)
1877 Austerlitz 5y 10st 8lb (16)
1878 Shifnal 9y 10st 12lb (12)
1879 The Liberator 9y 11st 4lb (18)
1880 Empress 5y 10st 7lb (14)
1881 Woodbrook 7y 11st 3lb (13)
1882 Seaman 6y 11st 6lb (12)
1883 Zoedone 6y 11st (10)
1884 Voluptuary 6y 10st 5lb (15)
1885 Roquefort 6y 11st (19)
1886 Old Joe 8y 10st 9lb (23)
1887 Gamecock 8y 11st (16)
1888 Playfair 7y 10st 7lb (20)
1889 Frigate 10y 11st 5lb (20)
1890 Ilex 6y 10st 5lb (16)
1891 Come Away 7y 11st 12lb (21)
1892 Father O'Flynn 7y 10st 5lb (25)
1893 Cloister 9y 12st 7lb (15)
1894 Why Not 13y 11st 13lb (14)
1895 Wild Man From Borneo 7y 10st 11lb (19)
1896 The Soarer 7y 9st 13lb (28)
1897 Manifesto 9y 11st 3lb (28)
1898 Drogheda 6y 10st 12lb (24)
1899 Manifesto 11y 12st 7lb (9)

1900 H.R.H. The Prince of Wales's Ambush II b g by Ben Battle 6–11–3 A Anthony 4–1
Mr C H Brown's Barsac 8–9–12 .... W Halsey 25–1
Mr J G Bulteel's Manifesto 12–12–13 .... G Williamson 6–1
4l, nk. 10m 1s. 16 ran. Trained A Anthon in Ireland
1901 Mr B Bletsoe's Gruden, br h by Old Back 11–10–0 .... A Nightingall 9–1
Mr O J Williams's Drumcree 7–10–0 .... Mr H Nugent 10–1
Mr J E Rogerson's Buffalo Bill 7–9–7 .... H Taylor 33–1
4l, 6l. 9m 47⅕s. 24 ran. Trained J Holland
1902 Mr A Gorham's Shannon Lass b or br m by Butterscotch 7–10–1 ..... D Read 20–1
Mr John Widger's Matthew 6–9–12 .... W Morgan 50–1
Mr J G Bulteel's Manifesto 14–12–8 .... A E Piggott 100–6
3l, same. 10m 3s. 21 ran. Trained J F Hackett
1903 Mr J S Morrison's Drumcree b g by Ascetic 9–11–3 .... P Woodland 13–2fav
Mr White-Heather's Detail 7–19–13 .... A Nightingale 100–14
Mr J G Bulteel's Manifesto 15–12–3 .... G Williamson 25–1
3l, 20l. 10m 9⅔s. 23 ran. Trained Sir Charles Nugent
1904 Mr Spencer Gollan's Moifaa br g by Natator 8–10–7 .... A Birch 25–1
Mr F Bibby's Kirkland 8–10–10 .... F Mason 100–7
Mr John Widger's The Gunner 7–10–4 .... Mr John Widger 25–1
8l, nk. 9m 58⅗s. 26 ran. Trained O'Hickey
1905 Mr F Bibby's Kirkland ch g by Kirkham 9–11–5 .... F Mason 6–1
Capt McLaren's Napper Tandy 8–10–0 .... P Woodland 25–1
Mr P E Speakman's Buckaway II 7–9–11 .... A Newey 100–1
3l, 4l. 9m 48⅘s. 27 ran. Trained E Thomas
1906 Prince Hatzfeldt's Ascetic's Silver ch h by Ascetic 9–10–9 ..... Hon A Hastings 20–1
Mr E M Lucas's Red Lad 6–10–2 .... C Kelly 33–1
Mr B W Parr's Aunt May 10–11–2 .... Mr H Persse 25–1
10l, 2l. 9m 34⅖s. 23 ran. Trained Hon A Hastings
1907 Mr S Howard's Eremon b g by Thurles 7–10–1 .... A Newey 8–1
Mr H Hardy's Tom West 8–9–12 .... H Murphy 100–6
Mr W Nelson's Patlander 11–10–7 .... J Lynn 50–1
6l, bad. 9m 47⅕s. 23 ran. Trained T Couthwaite
1908 Maj F Doublas Pennant's Rubio ch g by Star Ruby 10–10–5 ...... H Bletsoe 66–1
Mr W Cooper's Mattie Macgregor 6–10–6 .... W Bissill 25–1
Mr P Whitaker's The Lawyer III 11–10–13 .... Owner 100–7
10l, 6l. 10m 33⅕s. 24 ran. Trained W Costello
1909 Mr J Hennessy's Lutteur III ch h by St Damien 5–10–11 ...... G Parfrement 100–9co-f

Mr B W Parr's Judas 8–10–10 .... R Chadwick 33–1
Mr F Bibby's Caubeen 8–11–7 .... F Mason 20–1
2l, bad. 9m 53 4/5s. 32 ran. Trained H Escott

1910 Mr S Howard's Jenkinstown b g by Hackler 9–10–5 .... R Chadwick 100–8
Mr C Assheton Smith's Jerry M 7–12–7 .... E Driscoll 6–1fav
Mr R Hall's Odor 9–9–8 .... Owner 100–1
3l, same. 10m 44 1/5s. 25 ran. Trained T Couthwaite

1911 Mr F Bibby's Glenside b g by St Gris 9–10–3 .... Mr J R Anthony 20–1
Mr O H Jones's Rathnally 6–11–0 .... R Chadwick 8–1
Mr P Nelke's Shady Girl 10–10–5 .... G Clancy 33–1
20l, 3l (2nd and 3rd fell but were remounted). 10m 35s. 26 ran. Trained Capt Collis

1912 Sir C Assheton-Smith's Jerry M bg by Walmsgate 9–12–7 .... E Piggott 4–1co–f
Mr C Bower Ismay's Bloodstone 10–11–6 .... F Lyall 40–1
Ld Derby's Axle Pin 8–10–4 I Anthony 20–1
6l, 4l. 10m 13 2/5s. 24 ran. Trained R Gore

1913 Sir C Assheton-Smith's Covertcoat b g by Hackler 7–11–6 ..... P Woodland 100–9
Mr Tyrwhitt Drake's Irish Mail 6–11–4 .... Mr O Anthony 25–1
Mr C H Wildenburg's Carsey 10–12–0 .... Mr H Drake 100–9
Distance, same (3rd fell but was remounted). 10m 19s. 22 ran. Trained R Gore

1914 Mr T Tyler's Sunloch b g by Sundorne 8–9–7 .... W J Smith 100–6
Mr H de Mumm's Trianon III 9–11–9 .... C Hawkins 100–8
Mr J Hennessy's Lutteur III 10–12–6 .... A Carter 10–1
8l, same. 9m 58 4/5s. 20 ran. Trained Owner

1915 Lady Nelson's Ally Sloper br g by Travelling Lad 6–10–5 ... Mr J R Anthony 100–8
Mr C Bower Ismay's Jacobus 8–11–0 .... A Newey 25–1
Lord Suffolk's Father Confessor 6–9–10 .... A Aylin 10–1
2l, 8l. 9m 47 4/5s. 20 ran. Trained Hon A Hastings

1916 Mr P F Heybourn's Vermouth b g by Barcadelle 6–11–10 .... J Reardon 100–8
Mr E Platt's Irish Mail 9–12–5 .... C Hawkins 20–1
Mr H C Davey's Schoolmoney 6–10–2 .... A Saxby 33–1
2l, 6l. 10m 22s. 21 ran. Trained J Bell

†1917 Sir G Bullough's Ballymacad b g by Laveno 10–9–12 .... E Driscoll 100–9
Mr H Trimmer's Chang 7–9–9 .... W Smith 11–2
Lady Nelson's Ally Sloper 8–11–10 .... I Anthony 20–1
8l, 4l. 10m 12 2/5s. 19 ran. Trained Hon A Hastings

†1918 Mrs Hugh Peel's Poethlyn b g by Rydal Head 8–11–6 .... E Piggott 5–1co–f
Mr F R Hunt's Captain Drefuss 10–12–7 .... J Reardon 20–1
Sir G Bullough's Ballymacad 11–11–3 .... I Anthony 7–1
4l, bad. 9m 50 2/5s. 17 ran. Trained H Escott

†Run at Gatwick

1919 Mrs Hugh Peel's Poethlyn b g by Rydal Head 9–12–7 .... E Piggott 11–4fav
Mr E W Hope Johnstone's Ballyboggan 8–11–10 .... W Head 9–1
Mr J L Dugdale's Pollen 10–11–4 .... H Escott 100–7
8l, 6l. 10m 8 2/5s. 22 ran. Trained H Escott

1920 Maj T G C Gerrard's Troytown br g by Zria 7–11–9 .... Mr J R Anthony 6–1
Mr C L Willcox's The Turk II 10–9–7 .... R Burford 66–1
Mr H A Brown's The Bore 9–10–1 .... Owner 28–1
12l, 6l. 10m 20 2/5s. 24 ran. Trained A Anthony in Ireland

1921 Mr T M McAlpine's Shaun Spadah b g by Easter Prize 10–11–7 .... F B Rees 100–9
Mr H A Brown's The Bore 10–11–8 .... Owner 9–1fav
Ld Wavertree's All White 7–10–13 .... R Chadwick 33–1
Distance, same (2nd and 3rd fell but were remounted). 10m 26s. 35 ran. Trained G C Poole

1922 Mr Hugh Kershaw's Music Hall b g by Cliftonhall 9–11–8 .... L B Rees 100–9
Mr Jos. Widger's Drifter 8–10–0 .... W Watkinson 18–1
Mr J C Bulteel's Taffytus 9–11–10 .... T Leader jun 66–1
12l, 6l. 9m 55 4/5s. 32 ran. Trained Owen Anthony

1923 Mr S Sanford's Sergeant Murphy ch g by General Symons 13–11–3 .... Capt G N Bennet 100–6
Sir M McAlpine's Shaun Spadah 12–12–7 .... F B Rees 20–1
Maj C Dewhurst's Conjuror II 11–11–0 .... Mr C P Dewhurst 100–6
3l, 6l. 9m 36s. 28 ran. Trained G Blackwell

1924 Ld Airlie's Master Robert ch g by Moorside II 11–10–5 .... R Trudgill 25–1
Mr T K Laidlaw's Fly Mask 10–10–12 .... J Moylan 100–7
Mr W H Midwood's Silvo 8–12–2 .... G Goswell 100–7
4l, 6l. 9m 40s. 30 ran. Trained Hon A Hastings

1925 Mr D Goold's Double Chance ch g by Roi Herode or Day Comet 9–10–9 .... Maj J P Wilson 100–9
Mrs W H Dixon's Old Tay Bridge 11–11–12 .... J R Anthony 9–1fav
Mr T K Laidlaw's Fly Mask 11–11–11 .... E C Doyle 10–1
4l, 6l. 9m 42 3/5s. 33 ran. Trained F Archer

1926 Mr A C Schwartz's Jack Horner ch g by Cyllius 9–10–5 .... W Watkinson 25–1
Mrs W H Dixon's Old Tay Bridge 12–12–2 .... J R Anthony 8–1
Mr S Sanford's Bright Boy 7–11–8 .... E Doyle 25–1
3l, 1l. 9m 36s. 30 ran. Trained H Leader

1927 Mrs M Partridge's Sprig ch g by Marco 10–12–4 .... T E Leader 8–1fav
Mr G W Pennington's Bovil III 9–10–12 .... Owner 100–1
Mr S Sanford's Bright Boy 8–12–27 .... J R Anthony 100–7
1l, same. 10m 20 1/5s. 37 ran. Trained T Leader

1928 Mr H S Kenyon's Tipperary Tim b g by Cipango 10–10–0 ... Mr W P Dutton 100–1
Mr H Bruce's Billy Barton 10–10–11 .... T Cullinan 33–1
Distance; only two finished. 10m 23 3/5s. 42 ran. Trained J J Dodd

1929 Mrs M A Gemmell's Gregalach ch g by My Prince 7–11–4 .... R Everett 100–1
Mr J H Whitney's Easter Hero 9–12–7 .... J Moloney 9–2fav
Mr R McAlpine's Richmond II 6–10–6 .... W Stott 40–1
6l, bad. 9m 47 3/5s. 66 ran. Trained T R Leader

1930 Mr W H Midwood's Shaun Goilin ch g sire's ped unknown 10–11–7 .... T Cullinan 100–8
Mr W Wilson's Melleray's Belle 11–10–0 .... J Mason 20–1
Mr J H Whitney's Sir Lindsay 9–10–6 .... D Williams 100–7
Nk, 1 1/2l. 9m 40 3/5s. 41 ran. Trained F Hartigan

1931 Mr C R Taylor's Grakle b g by Jackdaw 9–11–7 .... R Lyall 100–6
Mrs M A Gemmell's Gregalach 9–12–0 .... J Moloney 25–1
Lady Glenapp's Annandale 9–10–7 .... T Morgan 100–1
1½l, 10l. 9m 32⁴/₅s. 43 ran. Trained T Coulthwaite

1932 Mr W Parsonage's Forbra br g by Foresight 7–10–7 .... J Hamey 50–1
Mrs Ireland's Egremont 8–10–7 .... Mr E C Paget 33–1
Mr W H Midwood's Shaun Goilin 12–12–4 .... D Williams 40–1
3l, bad. 9m 44³/₅s. 36 ran. Trained T R Rimell

1933 Mrs F Ambrose Clarke's Kellsboro' Jack b g by Jackdaw 7–11–9 .. D Williams 25–1
Maj Noel Furlong's Really True 9–10–12 .... Mr F Furlong 66–1
Mr G S L Whitelaw's Slater 8–10–7 .... Mr M Barry 50–1
3l, nk. 9m 28s. 34 ran. Trained I Anthony

1934 Miss D Paget's Golden Miller b g by Goldcourt 7–12–2 .... G Wilson 8–1
Mr J B Snow's Delaneige 9–11–6 .... J Moloney 100–7
Mr J H Whitney's Thomond II 8–12–4 .... W Speck 18–1
5l, same. 9m 20²/₅s. 30 ran. Trained A Briscoe

1935 Maj N Furlong's Reynoldstown br or bl g by My Prince 8–11–4 Mr F Furlong 22–1
Lady Lindsay's Blue Prince 7–10–7 .... W Parvin 40–1
Mr J H Whitney's Thomond II 9–11–13 .... W Speck 9–2
3l, 8l. 9m 21s. 27 ran. Trained by Owner

1936 Maj N Furlong's Reynoldstown br or bl g by My Prince 9–12–2 .... Mr F Walwyn 10–1
Sir D Llewellyn's Ego 9–10–8 .... Mr H Llewellyn 50–1
Mr James V Rank's Bachelor Prince 9–10–9 .... J Fawcus 66–1
12l, 6l. 9m 37s. 35 ran. Trained by Owner

1937 Mr H Lloyd Thomas's Royal Mail bl g by My Prince 8–11–13 ... E Williams 100–6
Mr James V Rank's Cooleen 9–11–4 .... J Fawcus 33–1
Mr E W W Bailey's Pucka Belle 11–10–7 .... Owner 100–6
3l, 10l. 9m 59³/₅s. 33 ran. Trained I Anthony

1938 Mrs Marion Scott's Battleship ch h by Man o'War 11–11–6 .... B Hobbs 40–1
Mr H C McNally's Royal Danieli 7–11–3 .... D L Moore 18–1
Sir A Maguire's Workman 8–10–2 .... J Brogan 28–1
Hd, bad. 9m 29⁴/₅s. 36 ran. Trained R Hobbs

1939 Sir A Maguire's Workman br g by Cottage 9–10–6 .... T Hyde 100–8
Capt L Scott-Briggs's Mac Moffat 7–10–3 .... I Alder 25–1
Miss D Paget's Kilstar 8–10–3 .... G Archibald 8–1fav
3l, 15l. 9m 42¹/₅s. 37 ran. Trained J Ruttle in Ireland

1940 Ld Stalbridge's Bogskar br g by Werwolf 7–10–4 .... M A Jones 25–1
Capt L Scott-Briggs's Mac Moffat 8–10–10 .... I Alder 8–1
Mr J R Neill's Gold Arrow 8–10–3 .... P Lay 50–1
4l, 6l. 9m 20³/₅s. 30 ran. Trained by Owner

1941–1945 No race

1946 Mr J Morant's Lovely Cottage br g by Cottage 9–10–8 .... Capt R Petre 25–1
Mr L S Elwell's Jack Finlay 7–10–2 .... W Kidney 100–1
Mr James V Rank's Prince Regent 11–12–5 .... T Hyde 3–1fav
4l, 3l. 9m 38¹/₅s. 34 ran. Trained T Rayson

1947 Mr J J McDowell's Caughoo br g by Within-the-Law 8–10–0 .. E Dempsey 100–1
Mrs M Rowe's Lough Conn 11–10–1 .... D McCann 33–1
Sir A Gordon-Smith's Kami 10–10–13 .... Mr J Hislop 33–1
20l, 4l. 10m 3⁴/₅s. 57 ran. Trained H McDowell, in Ireland

1948 Mr J Proctor's Sheila's Cottage b m by Cottage 9–10–7 ..... A P Thompson 50–1
Maj D J Vaughan's First of the Dandies 11–10–4 .... J Brogan 25–1
Ld Mildmay's Cromwell 7–10–11 .... Owner 33–1
1l, 6l. 9m 25²/₅s. 43 ran. Trained N Crump

1949 Mr W F Williamson's Russian Hero b g by Peter the Great 9–10–8 .... L McMorrow 66–1
Ld Bicester's Roimond 8–11–12 .... R Francis 22–1
Mrs M Harvey's Royal Mount 10–10–12 .... Patrick Doyle 18–1
8l, 1l. 9m 24¹/₅s. 43 ran. Trained G Owen

1950 Mrs L Brotherton's Freebooter b g by Steel-point 9–11–11 .... J Power 10–1 co-f
Capt T D Wilson's Wot No Sun 8–11–8(A P Thompson 100–7
Mrs J S Gorman's Acthon Major 10–11–2 .... R O'Ryan 33–1
15l, 10l. 9m 24¹/₅s. 49 ran. Trained R Renton

1951 Mr J Royle's Nickel Coin b m by Pay Up 9–10–1 .... J A Bullock 40–1
Mrs M H Keogh's Royal Tan 7–10–13 .... Mr A O'Brien 22–1
Mr P Digney's Derrinstown 11–10–0 .... A Power 66–1
Won by 6l; Derrinstown fell, was remounted, and finished a bad third. 9m 48⁴/₅s. 36 ran. Trained J O'Donoghue

1952 Mr H Lane's Teal b g by Bimco 10–10–12 .... A P Thompson 100–7
Miss D Paget's Legal Joy 9–10–4 .... M Scudamore 100–6
Capt T D Wilson's Wot No Sun 10–11–7 .... D V Dick 33–1
..... 5l, bad 3rd. 9m 20³/₅s. 47 ran. Trained N Crump

1953 Mr J H Griffin's Early Mist ch g by Brumeux 8–11–12 .... B Marshall 20–1
Miss D Paget's Mont Tremblant 7–12–5 .... D V Dick 18–1
Ld Sefton's Irish Lizard 10–10–6 .... R Turnell 33–1
20l, 4l. 9m 22⁴/₅s. 31 ran. Trained M V O'Brien in Ireland

1954 Mr J H Griffin's Royal Tan ch g by Tarton 10–11–7 .... B Marshall 8–1
Mrs E Truelove's Tudor Line 9–10–17 .... G Slack 10–1
Ld Sefton's Irish Lizard 11–10–5 .... M Scudamore 15–2fav
Nk, 10l. 9m 32⁴/₅s. 29 ran. Trained M V O'Brien in Ireland

1955 Mrs W H E Welman's Quare Times b g by Artist's Son 9–11–0 ..... P Taaffe 100–9
Mrs E Truelove's Tudor Line 10–11–3 .... G Slack 10–1
Mr D J Coughlan's Carey's Cottage 8–10–11 .... T Taaffe 20–1
12l, 4l. 10m 19¹/₅s. 30 ran. Trained M V O'Brien in Ireland

1956 Mrs L Carver's E.S.B. b or br g by Bidar 10–11–3 .... D V Dick 100–7
Mr J J Straker's Gentle Moya 10–10–2 .... G Milburn 22–1
Prince Aly Khan's Royal Tan 12–12–1 .... T Taaffe 28–1
10l, same. 9m 21²/₅s. 29 ran. Trained T F Rimell

1957 Mrs G Kohn's Sundew, ch g by Sun King 11–11–7 .... F Winter 20–1
Miss R M P Wilkinson's Wyndburgh 7–10–7 .... M Batchelor 25–1
Mr E R Courage's Tiberetta 9–10–0 .... A Oughton 66–1
8l, 6l. 9m 42 2/5s. 35 ran. Trained F Hudson

1958 Mr D J Coughlan's Mr What b g by Grand Inquisitor 8–10–6 .. A Freeman 18–1
Mr E R Courage's Tiberetta 10–10–6 .... G Slack 28–1
Ld Cadogan's Green Drill 8–10–10 .... G Milburn 28–1
30l, 15l. 9m 59 4/5s. 31 ran. Trained T J Taaffe in Ireland

1959 Mr J E Bigg's Oxo b g by Bobsleigh 8–10–13 .... M Scudamore 8–1
Mrs J K M Oliver's Wyndburgh 9–10–12 .... T Brookshaw 10–1
Mr D J Coughlan's Mr What 9–11–9 .... T Taaffe 6–1fav
1 1/2l, 8l. 9m 37 4/5s. 34 ran. Trained W Stephenson

1960 Miss W H S Wallace's Merryman II b g by Carnival Boy 9–10–12 .... G Scott 13–2fav
Ld Leverhulme's Badanloch 9–10–9 .... S Mellor 100–7
Mr B Sunley's Clear Profit 10–10–1 .... B Wilkinson 20–1
15l, 2l. 9m 27s. 26 ran. Trained N Crump

1961 Mr C Vaughan's Nicolaus Silver gr g by Nicolaus 9–10–1 .... H Beasley 28–1
Miss W H S Wallace's Merryman II 10–11–12 .... D Ancil 8–1
Mrs S Elliott's O'Malley Point 10–11–4 .... P Farrell 100–6
5l, nk. 9m 22 3/5s. 35 ran. Trained T F Rimell

1962 Mr N Cohen's Kilmore b g by Zalophus 12–10–4 .... F Winter 28–1
Mrs J K M Oliver's Wyndburgh 12–10–9 .... T Barnes 45–1
Mr G V Keeling's Mr What 12–10–9 .... J Lehane 22–1
10l, same. 9m 50s. 32 ran. Trained Ryan Price

1963 Mr P B Raymond's Ayala ch g by Supertello 9–10–0 .... P Buckley 66–1
Mr G Kindersley's Carrickbeg 7–10–3 .... Mr J Lawrence 20–1
Mr W Stephenson's Hawa's Song 10–10–0 .... P Broderick 28–1
3/4l, 5l. 9m 35 4/5s. 47 ran. K Piggott

1964 Mr J K Goodman's Team Spirit b g by Vulgan 12–10–3 ..... G W Robinson 18–1
Mr T Beattie's Purple Silk 9–10–4 .... J Kenneally 100–6
Mrs F Williams's Peacetown 10–10–1 .... R Edwards 40–1
1/2l. 6l. 9m 47s. 33 ran. F Walwyn

1965 Mrs M Stephenson's Jay Trump b g by Tonga Prince 8–11–5 ... Mr C Smith 100–6
Mr R R Tweedie's Freddie 8–11–10 .... P McCarron 7–2fav
Mr C D Collins's Mr Jones 10–11–5 .... Mr C Collins 50–1
1/2l, 20l. 9m 30 3/5s. 47 ran. F T Winter

1966 Mr S Levy's Anglo ch g by Greek Star 8–10–0 .... T Norman 50–1
Mr R R Tweedie's Freddie 9–11–7 .... P McCarron 11–4fav
Mrs D Thompson's Forest Prince 8–10–8 .... G Scott 100–7
20l, 5l. 9m 52 4/5s. 47 ran. F T Winter

1967 Mr C P T Watkins's Foinavon br g by Vulgan 9–10–0 .... J Buckingham 100–1
Mr C Pugh's Honey End 10–10–4 .... J Gifford 15–2fav
Mr J Manners's Red Alligator 8–10–0 .... B Fletcher 50–1
15l, 3l. 9m 49 3/5s. 44 ran. J H Kempton

1968 Mr J Manners's Red Alligator ch g by Magic Red 9–10–0 .... B Fletcher 100–7
Miss P Harrower's Moidore's Token 11–10–8 .... B Brogan 100–6
Mr Gregory Peck's Different Class 8–11–5 .... D Mould 17–2fav
20l, nk. 9m 28 4/5s. 45 ran. Denys Smith

1969 Mr T H McKoy jun's Highland Wedding br g by Question 12–10–4 E P Harty 100–9
Mr J L Drabble's Steel Bridge 11–10–0 .... R Pitman 50–1
Mr A B Mitchell's Rondetto 13–10–6 .... J King 25–1
12l, 1l. 9m 29 4/5s. 30 ran. G Balding

1970 Mr A Chambers's Gay Trip b g by Vulgan 8–11–5 .... P Taaffe 15–1
Gen R K Mellon's Vulture 8–10–0 .... S Barker 15–1
Mrs W Macaulay's Miss Hunter 9–10–0 .... F Shortt 33–1
20l, 1/2l. 9m 38s. 28 ran T F Rimell

1971 Mr F Pontin's Specify br g by Specific 9–10–13 .... J Cook 28–1
Mrs J Watney's Black Secret 7–11–5 .... Mr J Dreaper 20–1
Mr B Jenks's Astbury 8–10–0 J Bourke 33–1
Nk, 2l. 9m 34 1/5s. 38 ran. J E Sutcliffe

1972 Capt T Forster's Well To Do ch g by Phebus 9–10–1 .... G Thorner 14–1
Mr A Chambers's Gay Trip 10–11–9 .... T Biddlecombe 12–1
Mrs J Watney's Black Secret 8–11–2 .... S Barker 14–1
and
Mrs E Newman's General Symons 9–10–0 .... P Kiely 40–1
dead-heated for third place
2l, 3l. 10m 8 2/5s. 42 ran. T Forster

1973 Mr N Le Mare's Red Rum b g by Quorum 8–10–5 .... B Fletcher 9–1co–f
Sir C Manifold's Crisp (Aus) 10–12–0 .... R Pitman 9–1co–f
Mr R Guest's L'Escargot 10–12–0 .... T Carberry 11–1
3/4l, 25l. 9m 1·9s. 38 ran. D McCain

1974 Mr N Le Mare's Red Rum b g by Quorum 9–12–0 .... B Fletcher 11–1
Mr R Guest's L'Escargot 11–11–13 .... T Carberry 17–2
Lt-Col P Bengough's Charles Dickens 10–10–0 .... A Turnell 50–1
7l, sht. hd. 9m 20·50s. 42 ran. D McCain

1975 Mr R Guest's L'Escargot ch g by Escart III 12–11–3 .... T Carberry 13–2
Mr N Le Mare's Red Rum 10–12–0 .... B Fletcher 7–2fav
Mr E Courage's Spanish Steps 12–10–3 .... W Smith 20–1
15l, 8l. 9m 31·10s. 31 ran. D L Moore in Ireland

1976 Mr P B Raymond's Rag Trade ch g by Menelek 10–10–12 .... J Burke 14–1
Mr N Le Mare's Red Rum 11–11–10 .... T Stack 10–1
Mr J Bosley's Eyecatcher 10–10–7 .... B Fletcher 28–1
2l, 8l. 9m 20·90s. 32 ran. T F Rimell

1977 Mr N Le Mare's Red Rum b g by Quorum 12–11–8 .... T Stack 9–1
Mr B Arnold's Churchtown Boy 10–10–0 .... M Blackshaw 20–1
Mr J Bosley's Eyecatcher 11–10–1 .... C Read 18–1
25l, 5l. 9m 30·30s. 42 ran. D McCain

1978 Mrs D Whitaker's Lucius b g by Perhapsburg 9–10–9 .... B R Davies 14–1
Mr R Jeffrey's Sebastian V 10–10–1 .... R Lamb 25–1
Mrs G St John Nolan's Drumroan 10–10–0 .... G Newman 50–1
1/2l, nk. 9m 33·90s. 37 ran. G W Richards

1979 Mr J Douglas's Rubstic br g by I Say 10–10–0 . . . . M Barnes 25–1
Mr D Montagu's Zongalero 9–10–5 . . . . B R Davies 20–1
Mr L Dormer's Rough and Tumble 9–10–7 . . . . J Francombe 14–1
1½l, 5l. 9m 53s. 34 ran. S J Leadbetter

1980 Mr R C Stewart's Ben Nevis ch g by Casmiri 12–10–12 . . . . Mr C Fenwick 40–1
Mr L Dormer's Rough and Tumble 10–10–11 . . . . J Francome a11–1
Mrs G Poole's The Pilgarlic 12–10–4 . . . . R Hyett 33–1
20l, 10l. 10m 17·40s. 30 ran. T Forster

1981 Mr S Embiricos's Aldaniti ch g by Derek H 11–10–13 . . . . R Champion 10–1
Mr M J Thorne's Spartan Missile 9–11–5 . . . . Mr M J Thorne 8–1
Mr John Murray Begg's Royal Mail (NZ) 11–11–7 . . . . P Blacker 16–1
4l, 2l. 9m 47·20s. 39 ran. J Gifford

1982 Mr F Gilman's Grittar b g by Grisaille 9–11–5 . . . . Mr C Saunders 7–1fav
Lady Wates's Hard Outlook 11–10–1 . . . . A Webber 50–1
Mr A Nettley's Loving Words 9–10–11 . . . . R Hoare 16–1
15l, Distance. 9m 12.6s. 39 ran. Owner

1983 Mr B R H Burrough's Corbiere ch g by Harwell 8–11–4 . . . . B de Haan 13–1
Mrs N Todd's Greasepaint 8–10–7 . . . . Mr C Magnier 14–1
Mr N Keane's Yer Man 8–10–0 . . . . T V O'Neill 80–1
¾l, 20l. 9m 47·4s. 41 ran. Mrs J Pitman

1984 Mr Richard Shaw's Hallo Dandy b g by Menelek 10–10–2 . . . . N Doughty 13–1
Mr M W J Smurfit's Greasepaint 9–11–12 . . . . T Carmody 9–1
Mr B R H Burrough's Corbiere 9–12–0 . . . . B de Haan 16–1
4l, 1½l. 9m 21·4s. 40 ran. G W Richards

1985 Anne, Duchess of Westminster's Last Suspect b or br g by Above Suspicion 11–10–5 . . . . H Davies 50–1
Mr A Greenwood's Mr Snugfit 8–10–0 . . . . P Tuck 12–1
Mr B R H Burrough's Corbiere 10–11–10 . . . . P Scudamore 9–1
1½l; 3l. 9m 42·7s. 40 ran. T Forster

1986 Mr P Luff's West Tip b g by Gala Performance 9–10–11 . . R Dunwoody 15–2
Mr J B Russell's Young Driver 9–10–0 . . . . C Grant 66–1
Cheveley Park Stud's Classified 10–10–3 . . . . S Smith Eccles 22–1
2l, 20l, 9m 33s. 40 ran. M Oliver

1987 Mr H J Joel's Maori Venture ch g by St Columbus 11–10–13 . . . . . S C Knight 28–1
Major I C Straker's The Tsarevich 11–10–5 . . . . J White 20–1
Mrs W Tulloch's Lean Ar Aghaidh 10–10–0 . . . . G Landau 14–1
5l, 4l, 9m 19·3s. 40 ran. A Turnell

1988 Miss J Reed's Rhyme 'N' Reason b g by Kemal, 9–11–0 . . . . B Powell 10–1
Mr R Oxley's Durham Edition 10–10–9 . . . . C Grant 20–1
Mr J Meagher's Monanore 11–10–4 . . . . T Taaffe 33–1
4l; 15l. 9m 53·5s. 40 ran. D Elsworth

1989 Mr E Harvey's Little Polveir b g by Cantab, 12–10–3 . . . . J Frost 28–1
Mr P Luff's West Tip 12–10–11 . . . . R Dunwoody 12–1
TPM McDonagh Ltd's The Thinker 11–11–10 . . . . S Sherwood 10–1
7l; ½l. 10m 6·90s. 40 ran. G B Balding

1990 Mrs H Duffey's Mr Frisk ch g by Bivouac 11–10–6 . . . . Mr M Armytage 16–1
Mr R Oxley's Durham Edition 12–10–9 . . . . C Grant 9–1
Mr A Proos's Rinus 9–10–4 N Doughty 13–1
¾l, 20l. 8m 47.8s (record). 38 ran. K Bailey

1991 Sir Eric Parker's Seagram (NZ) ch g by Balak 11–10–6 . . . . N Hawke 12–1
Autofour Engineering's Garrison Savannah 8–11–1 . . . . M Pitman 7–1
Mrs R Wilson's Auntie Dot 10–10–4 . . . . M Dwyer 50–1
5l, 8l, 9m 29.9s. 40 ran. D H Barons

1992 Mrs D Thompson's Party Politics br g by Politico 8–10–7 . . . . . . C Llewellyn 14–1
Mr L J Garrett's Romany King 8–10–3 . . . . R Guest 16–1
Mr J P McManus's Laura's Beau 8–10–0 . . . . C O'Dwyer 12–1
2½l, 15l. 9m 6.3s. 40 ran. N A Gaselee

1993 Race declared void after two false starts.
39 Starters

Riding records in the Classics

Jockey	Year of First Classic Winner	2000Gs	1000Gs	Derby	Oaks	St Leger	Total No. of Winners
L Piggott	1954	5	2	9†	6	8	30
F Buckle	1792	5	6	5	9†	2	27
J Robinson	1817	9†	5	6	2	2	24
F Archer	1874	4	2	5	4	6	21
J Watts	1883	2	4	4	4	5	19
W Scott	1821	3	Nil	4	3	9†	19
J B Day	1826	4	5	Nil	5	2	16
G Fordham	1859	3	7†	1	5	Nil	16
W Carson	1972	4	2	3	4	3	16
J Childs	1912	2	2	3*	4*	4*	15
F Butler	1843	2	2	2	6	2	14
S Donoghue	1915	3	1	6*	2*	2*	14
E C Elliott	1923	5	4‡	3	2‡	Nil	14
G Richards	1930	3‡	3‡	1	2‡	5‡	14
W Clift	1793	2	2	5	2	2	13
T Cannon	1866	4	3	1	4	1	13
H Wragg	1928	1‡	3‡	3‡	4‡	2‡	13
J Osborne	1856	6	2	1	1	2	12
W Johnstone	1934	1	3	3	3	2	12
T Weston	1923	2	1	2	3	3	11
C Smirke	1934	2	1	4	Nil	4	11
E (Nat) Flatman	1835	3	3	1	Nil	3	10
T Challoner	1861	3	Nil	1	1	5	10
C Wood	1880	1	3	3	1	2	10
Pat Eddery	1974	3	Nil	3	2	2	10
S Cauthen	1979	1	1	2	3	3	10
D Maher	1901	2	1	3	1	2	9
S Chifney jun	1807	1	1	2	5	Nil	9
J Wells	1854	1	2	3	Nil	2	8
J Jackson	1791	Nil	Nil	Nil	Nil	8	8
H Jones	1900	4	Nil	2	1	1	8
J Arnull	1784	Nil	2	5	1	Nil	8
J Mercer	1953	1	2	Nil	1	4	8
S Loates	1884	1	2	2	1	1	7
W Arnull	1804	3	1	3	Nil	Nil	7
T Goodison	1809	Nil	Nil	4	2	1	7
E Britt	1947	1	2	Nil	2	2	7
S Templeman	1839	Nil	Nil	3	3	1	7
B Carslake	1919	1	2	Nil	1	3	7
A Day	1849	3	2	1	1	Nil	7
Y Saint-Martin	1962	1	2	1	2	1	7
W R Swinburn	1981	1	3	2	1	Nil	7
B Smith	1803	Nil	Nil	Nil	Nil	6	6
M Cannon	1894	1	Nil	1	2	2	6
C Maidment	1871	Nil	1	2	1	2	6
T Loates	1889	2	1	2	Nil	1	6
J Marson	1843	Nil	1	2	Nil	3	6
P Connolly	1830	1	1	2	1	1	6
T Aldcroft	1855	2	1	1	1	1	6
J Singleton jun	1776	Nil	Nil	1	2	3	6
F Fox	1911	2	1	2	Nil	1	6
E Hide	1959	Nil	2	1	1	2	6
W H Carr	1955	Nil	1	1	1	3	6
O Madden	1898	1	Nil	1	2	1	5
J Mangles	1780	Nil	Nil	Nil	Nil	5	5
D Fitzpatrick	1787	Nil	Nil	1	4	Nil	5
C Hindley	1781	Nil	Nil	3	2	Nil	5
H Custance	1860	Nil	1	3	Nil	1	5
S Chifney senr	1782	Nil	Nil	1	4	Nil	5
T Ashmall	1858	2	2	Nil	1	Nil	5
S Day	1821	Nil	1	3	1	Nil	5
S Arnull	1780	Nil	Nil	4	1	Nil	5
R A Jones	1922	1	1	Nil	2	1	5
R Poincelet	1952	1	2	1	1	Nil	5
W Wheatley	1816	3	Nil	2	Nil	Nil	5
F Rickaby jun	1913	Nil	4	Nil	1	Nil	5
G Lewis	1969	1	1	1	2	Nil	5
G Starkey	1964	2	Nil	1	2	Nil	5

*Includes substitute races run at Newmarket between 1915–1918. †Record for the race.
‡Includes substitute races run at Newmarket 1939–1945.

Double, treble and quadruple winners of Classic races

2000 GUINEAS, 1000 GUINEAS, OAKS and ST LEGER—Formosa* (1868), Sceptre (1902).

2000 GUINEAS, DERBY and ST LEGER—West Australian (1853), Gladiateur (1865), Lord Lyon (1866), Ormonde (1886), Common (1891), Isinglass (1893), Galtee More (1897), Flying Fox (1899), Diamond Jubilee (1900), Rock Sand (1903), Pommern (1915), Gay Crusader (1917), Gainsborough (1918), Bahram (1935), Nijinsky (Can) (1970).

2000 GUINEAS, 1000 GUINEAS and OAKS—Crucifix (1840), Formosa* (1868), Sceptre (1902).

2000 GUINEAS and DERBY—Smolensko (1813), Cadland (1828), Bay Middleton (1836), Cotherstone (1843), West Australian (1853), Macaroni (1863), Gladiateur (1865), Lord Lyon (1866), Pretender (1869), Shotover (1882), Ormonde (1886), Ayrshre (1888), Common (1891), Isinglass (1893), Ladas (1894), Galtee More (1897), Flying Fox (1899), Diamond Jubilee (1900), Rock Sand (1903), St Amant (1904), Minoru (1909), Sunstar (1911), Pommern (1915), Gay Crusader (1917), Gainsborough (1918), Manna (1925), Cameronian (1931), Bahram (1935), Blue Peter (1939), Nimbus (1949), Crepello (1957), Royal Palace (1967), Sir Ivor (1968), Nijinsky (Can) (1970), Nashwan (USA) (1989).

2000 GUINEAS and ST LEGER—Sir Tatton Sykes (1846), Stockwell (1852), West Australian (1853), The Marquis (1862), Gladiateur (1865), Lord Lyon (1866), Formosa* (1868), Petrarch (1876), Ormonde (1886), Common (1891), Isinglass (1893), Galtee More (1897), Flying Fox (1899), Diamond Jubilee (1900), Sceptre (1902), Rock Sand (1903), Pommern (1915), Gay Crusader (1917), Gainsborough (1918), Bahram (1935), Nijinsky (Can) (1970).

2000 GUINEAS, 1000 GUINEAS and ST LEGER—Formosa* (1868), Sceptre (1902).

2000 GUINEAS, OAKS and ST LEGER—Formosa* (1868), Sceptre (1902).

2000 GUINEAS and OAKS—Pastille (1822), Crucifix (1840), Formosa* (1868), Sceptre (1902).

2000 GUINEAS and 1000 GUINEAS—Crucifix (1840), Formosa* (1868), Pilgrimage (1878), Sceptre (1902).

1000 GUINEAS and DERBY—Tagalie (1912).

1000 GUINEAS, OAKS and ST LEGER—Formosa (1868), Hannah (1871), Apology (1874), La Fleche (1892), Sceptre (1902), Pretty Polly (1904), Sun Chariot (1942), Meld (1955), Oh So Sharp (1985).

1000 GUINEAS and OAKS—Neva (1817), Corinne (1818), Zinc (1823), Cobweb (1824), Galata (1832), Crucifix (1840), Mendicant (1846), Governess (1858), Formosa (1868), Hannah (1871), Reine (1872), Apology (1874), Spinaway (1875), Camelia* (1876), Wheel of Fortune (1879), Thebais (1881), Busbybody (1884), Miss Jummy (1886), Reve d'Or (1887), Mimi (1891), La Fleche (1892), Amiable (1894), Sceptre (1902), Pretty Polly (1904), Cherry Lass (1905), Jest (1913), Princess Dorrie (1914), Saucy Sue (1925), Exhibitionist (1937), Rockfel (1938),Galatea II (1939), Godiva (1940), Sun Chariot (1942), Sun Stream (1945), Imprudence (1947), Musidor (1949), Meld (1955), Bella Paola (1958), Petite Etoile (1959), Never Too Late II (1960), Sweet Solera (1961), Altesse Royale (1971), Mysterious (1973), Oh So Sharp (1985), Midway Lady (1986) Salsabil (1990).

1000 GUINEAS and ST LEGER—Imperieuse (1857), Achievement (1867), Formosa (1868), Hannah (1871), Apology (1874), La Fleche (1892), Sceptre (1902), Pretty Polly (1904), Tranquil (1923), Sun Chariot (1924), Herringbone (1943), Meld (1955), Oh So Sharp (1985).

OAKS and ST LEGER—Queen of Trumps (1835), Formosa (1868), Hannah (1871), Marie Stuart (1873), Apology (1874), Jannette (1878), Seabreeze (1888), La Fleche (1892), Sceptre (1902), Pretty Polly (1904), Sun Chariot (1942), Meld (1955), Dunfermline (1977), Sun Princess (1983), Oh So Sharp (1985), User Friendly (1992).

DERBY and OAKS—Eleanor (1801), Blink Bonny (1875), Signorinetta (1908), Fifinella (1916).

DERBY and ST LEGER—Champion (1800), Surplice (1848), The Flying Dutchman (1849), Voltigeur (1850), West Australian (1853), Blair Athol (1864), Gladiateur (1865), Lord Lyon (1866), Silvio (1877), Iroquois (1881), Melton (1885), Ormonde (1886), Donovan (1889), Common (1891), Isinglass (1893), Sir Visto (1895), Persimmon (1896), Galtee More (1897), Flying Fox (1899), Diamond Jubilee (1900), Rock Sand (1903), Pommern (1915), Gay Crusader (1917), Gainsborough (1918), Coronach (1926), Trigo (1929), Hyperion (1933), Windsor Lad (1934), Bahram (1935), Airborne (1946), Tulyar (1952), Never Say Die (1954), St Paddy (1960), Nijinsky (Can) (1970), Reference Point (1987).

*Formosa dead-heated with Moslem for the 2000 Guineas. Camelia dead-heated with Enguerrande for the Oaks.

Royal Ascot statistics: 1993

Owners

	£
S S Niarchos (Kingmambo)	116,335
Exors of the late Sir Robin McAlpine (Beneficial, Jeune)	115,133
R E Sangster (Imperial Ballet, State Performer, Stonehatch, Turtle Island)	114,924
K Abdulla (Infrasonic, Placerville, Source of Light)	112,245
J Wertheimer (Gold Splash)	109,538
Yoshio Asakawa (Drum Taps)	107,465
Brian Brackpool (Elbio)	60,361
Hamdan Al-Maktoum (Thawakib)	59,407
Circlechart Ltd (Alflora)	53,194
Mrs M V O'Brien (College Chapel)	40,645
Sir David Wills (Ardkinglass)	40,432
The late Miss U D Toller (Nagida)	39,640
Roldvale Ltd (Risky)	28,153
I A N Wright (Show Faith)	22,338
M D Smith (Balasani)	20,550
Sheikh Mohammed (Learmont)	19,413
Dubai Racing Syndicate (Great Deeds)	18,745
Henryk De Kwiatkowski (Riszard)	16,570

Trainers

	£
H R A Cecil (Ardkinglass, Imperial Ballet, Placerville)	141,807
F Boutin (Kingmambo)	116,335
G Wragg (Beneficial, Jeune)	115,133
Mrs C Head (Gold Splash)	109,538
Lord Huntingdon (Drum Taps)	107,465
P W Chapple-Hyam (State Performer, Stonehatch, Turtle Island)	70,929
P J Makin (Elbio)	60,361
J L Dunlop (Thawakib)	59,407
C E Brittain (Alflora)	53,194
R Hannon (Risky, Show Faith)	50,491
M V O'Brien (College Chapel)	40,645
J A R Toller (Nagida)	39,640
A Fabre (Infrasonic)	34,640
M C Pipe (Balasani)	20,550
R Charlton (Source of Light)	20,225
J H M Gosden (Learmont)	19,413
M Channon (Great Deeds)	18,745
J S Bolger (Riszard)	16,570

Jockeys

Pat Eddery (Imperial Ballet, Infrasonic, Placerville, Show Faith, Source of Light)	5
J Reid (State Performer, Stonehatch, Turtle Island)	3
W R Swinburn (Elbio, Risky)	2
T Quinn (Great Deeds)	1
C Asmussen (Kingmambo)	1
R Cochrane (Jeune)	1
L Piggott (College Chapel)	1
L Dettori (Drum Taps)	1
W Carson (Thawakib)	1
J Carroll (Learmont)	1
M J Kinane (Alflora)	1
M Hills (Beneficial)	1
G Mosse (Gold Splash)	1
W Ryan (Ardkinglass)	1
J Weaver (Nagida)	1
M Perrett (Balasani)	1
C Roche (Riszard)	1

Breeders

	£
Flaxman Holdings Ltd (Kingmambo)	116,335
Sir Robin McAlpine (Beneficial, Jeune)	115,133
Wertheimer Brothers (Gold Splash)	109,538
Jackie Ward Ramos (Drum Taps)	107,465
Swettenham Stud (Imperial Ballet, Stonehatch)	70,761
D W Samuel (Elbio)	60,361
Barronstown Bloodstock Ltd and Gainesway Thoroughbred Inc (Thawakib)	59,407
E A Cox Jnr. (Placerville)	57,380
Juddmonte Farms (Infrasonic, Source of Light)	54,865
Airlie Stud (Alflora)	53,194
Overbury Stud (College Chapel)	40,645
Sir H D H Wills (Ardkinglass)	40,432
Mrs John Trotter (Nagida)	39,640
Roldvale Ltd (Risky)	28,153
Roncon Ltd and Swettenham Stud (Turtle Island)	24,250
M J Cassidy (Show Faith)	22,338
H H Aga Khan (Balasani)	20,550
Crook Investment Co and Swettenham Stud (State Performer)	19,913
Rhydian Morgan-Jones (Learmont)	19,413
Miss S McCreery and Stowell Hill Ltd (Great Deeds)	18,745
Kennelot Stables Ltd (Riszard)	16,570

Sires

	£
Mr Prospector (USA) (Kingmambo, Placerville)	173,715
Blushing Groom (FR) (Gold Splash)	109,538
Dixieland Band (USA) (Drum Taps)	107,465
Sadler's Wells (USA) (Imperial Ballet, Thawakib)	103,402
Precocious (Elbio)	60,361
Top Ville (Beneficial)	58,433
Kalaglow (Jeune)	56,700
Niniski (USA) (Alflora)	53,194
Sharpo (College Chapel)	40,645
Green Desert (USA) (Ardkinglass)	40,432
Skyliner (Nagida)	39,640
Dancing Brave (USA) (Infrasonic)	34,640
Risk Me (FR) (Risky)	28,153
Storm Bird (CAN) (Stonehatch)	26,766
Fairy King (USA) (Turtle Island)	24,250
Exhibitioner (Show Faith)	22,338
Labus (FR) (Balasani)	20,550
Rainbow Quest (USA) (Source of Light)	20,225
Seattle Dancer (USA) (State Performer)	19,913
Lear Fan (USA) (Learmont)	19,413
Forzando (Great Deeds)	18,745
Danzig Connection (USA) (Riszard)	16,570

Royal Ascot champions: 1977–93

Owners

		£
1977	R E Sangster (2)	24,297
1978	D Schwartz (1)	22,400
1979	R E Sangster (2)	30,709
1980	C d'Alessio (1)	33,498
1981	C St George (1)	39,013
1982	C St George (1)	42,649
1983	F Dunne (2)	44,906
1984	R E Sangster (3)	65,372
1985	Sheikh Mohammed (2)	52,626
1986	Sheikh Mohammed (3)	111,696
1987	Lord Howard de Walden (2)	74,406
1988	H H Prince Yazid Saud (1)	103,869
1989	Sheikh Mohammed (4)	362,911
1990	Hamdan Al Maktoum (3)	155,757
1991	Hamdan Al Maktoum (2)	137,175
1992	Moyglare Stud Farms Ltd (1)	118,188
1993	S S Niarchos (1)	116,335

Trainers

		£
1977	M V O'Brien (3)	48,505
1978	M V O'Brien (2)	37,377
1979	H Cecil (4)	71,891
1980	H Cecil (3)	71,506
1981	H Cecil (4)	79,356
1982	H Cecil (4)	106,834
1983	W Hern (2)	58,906
1984	W Hern (2)	59,876
1985	H Cecil (4)	69,137
1986	J Dunlop (3)	77,052
1987	H Cecil (7)	201,060
1988	J Dunlop (2)	106,305
1989	G Harwood (6)	254,572
1990	H Cecil (4)	293,594
1991	J Dunlop (3)	221,318
1992	R Hannon (4)	154,421
1993	H Cecil (3)	141,807

Jockeys

1977	L Piggott (7)
1978	L Piggott (3)
1979	L Piggott (6)
1980	W Carson (4)
1981	L Piggott (5)
1982	L Piggott (6)
1983	W Carson (5)
1984	W Carson (4)
1985	S Cauthen (4)
1986	Pat Eddery (6)
1987	S Cauthen (7)
1988	Pat Eddery (4)
1989	Pat Eddery (8)
1990	S Cauthen (5)
1991	S Cauthen (4)
1992	Pat Eddery (4)
1993	Pat Eddery (5)

Breeders

		£
1977	P Fuller (1)	19,593
1978	McGrath Trust Co (2)	24,807
1979	The Queen (2)	29,457
1980	McGrath Trust Co (1)	33,498
1981	P J Prendergast (2)	52,679
1982	P J Prendergast (2)	50,414
1983	Moyglare Stud (2)	44,906
1984	H H Aga Khan (2)	43,099
1985	Warner L Jones (3)	50,296
1986	Paul Mellon (2)	62,505
1987	Lord Howard de Walden (2)	74,406
1988	Banstead Manor Stud (1)	103,869
1989	E A Cox Jnr (1)	113,994
1990	Lord Howard de Walden (1)	112,383
1991	Kilcarn Stud (1)	121,905
1992	Moyglare Stud Farm Ltd (1)	118,188
1993	Flaxman Holdings Ltd (1)	116,335

Sires

Year	Sire	£
1977	Dancer's Image (USA) (1)	19,593
1978	Comedy Star (USA) (1)	22,400
1979	Le Levanstell (1)	27,060
1980	Pitcairn (2)	39,666
1981	Habitat (4)	79,740
1982	Run The Gantlet (USA) (1)	42,649
1983	Tumble Wind (2)	45,267
1984	Rheingold (1)	40,334
1985	Bold Lad (IRE) (1)	44,060
1986	Welsh Pageant (2)	55,413
1987	Storm Bird (CAN) (1)	57,724
1988	Persian Bold (1)	103,869
1989	Danzig (USA) (2)	145,294
1990	Kris (1)	112,383
1991	Last Tycoon (1)	121,905
1992	Irish River (FR) (1)	118,188
1993	Mr Prospector (USA) (2)	173,715

The British Horseracing Board 1993

DIRECTORS:

Marquess of Hartington (Chairman)
Sir Nevil Macready (Deputy Chairman)
Michael Darnell
Sir Paul Fox
Peter Jones
David Oldrey
Nicholas Robinson
John Sanderson
Christopher Spence
Lord Swaythling
Marquess of Zetland

Chief Executive — Tristram Ricketts

COMMITTEES OF THE BRITISH HORSERACING BOARD

Finance Committee

Christopher Spence (Chairman)
Michael Arnold
Stanley Jackson
Tristram Ricketts
Lord Swaythling

Race Planning Committee

David Oldrey (Chairman)
Susan Abbott
John Cleverly
Luca Cumani
Peter Cundell
Geoffrey Howard-Spink
Malcolm Kimmins
Major Christo Philipson
Major Michael Wyatt

Racing Development Committee

Marquess of Zetland (Chairman)
Steven Astaire
Deborah Baker
Michael Caulfield
Peter Cundell
Anthony Fairbairn
Morag Gray
Matthew McCloy
Andrew Wates

Industry Committee

Sir Nevil Macready (Chairman)
Bill Adams
Deborah Baker
Michael Caulfield
Michael Darnell
The Hon. Johnny Greenall
Reg Griffin
Guy Harwood
Michael Henriques
Stanley Jackson
Paul Locke
Tim Lyle
Michael MacEwan
Edmond Mahony
James Marshall
Rhydian Morgan-Jones
Lord Swaythling
Justin Wadham

The Jockey Club 1993

PATRONS:

Her Majesty The Queen
Her Majesty Queen Elizabeth the Queen Mother

STEWARDS

Marquess of Hartington (Senior Steward)
A. J. Struthers, Esq. (Deputy Senior Steward)
Capt. W. H. Bulwer-Long C. J. Spence, Esq.
A. D. G. Oldrey, Esq. Marquess of Zetland
A. Mildmay-White, Esq.

MEMBERS:

*His Royal Highness the Prince Philip, Duke of Edinburgh
*His Royal Highness the Prince of Wales
*Her Royal Highness the Princess Royal

Mrs S. J. Abbott
*Prince Khalid bin Abdullah
Marquess of Abergavenny
Viscount Allendale
The Hon. Sir John Astor
Sir John K. Barlow, Bt.
The Hon. Wentworth Beaumont
Col. Sir Piers Bengough
The Rt. Hon. The Lord Benson
R. A. Bethell, Esq.
Gen. Sir Cecil Blacker
P. Blacker, Esq.
D. R. Brotherton, Esq.
Mrs. C.Brudenell-Bruce
A. F. Budge, Esq.
A. M. Budgett,Esq.
Capt. W. H. Bulwer-Long
Major-General Sir George Burns
*Peter Burrell, Esq.
Earl Cadogan
Earl of Carnarvon
Lt.-Col. J.E.S.Chamberlayne
Viscount Chelsea
N. C. Clark, Esq.
S. W. Clarke, Esq.
E. S. M. Collingwood-Cameron, Esq.
C. D. Collins, Esq.
The Hon. Sir Michael Connell
Sir John Cotterell, Bt.
M. E. T. Davies, Esq.
Earl of Derby
Duke of Devonshire
A. S. Dudgeon, Esq.
Sir William S.Dugdale, Bt.
T. E. S. Egerton, Esq.
Mrs S. N. J. Embiricos
Lord Fairhavan
Louis Freedman, Esq.
D. G. J. Gibson, Esq.
Major W. D. Gibson
Miss M. Gordon-Watson
Capt. H. M. Gosling
The Hon. Peter Greenall
Brigadier the Lord Grimthorpe
Earl of Halifax
C. S. Hall, Esq.
Jocelyn Hambro, Esq.
Sir Ernest Harrison
Marquess of Hartington
Brigadier C. B. Harvey
Mrs. P. Hastings
J. R. Henderson, Esq.
M. R. Q. Henriques, Esq.
J. L. Hislop, Esq.
B. R. Hobbs, Esq.
T. D. Holland-Martin, Esq.
L. B. Holliday, Esq.
R. D. Hollingsworth, Esq.
Lord Howard de Walden
B. P. Jenks, Esq.
Mrs. G. T. Johnson-Houghton
M. B. J. Kimmins, Esq.
G. Kindersley, Esq.
Sir Freddie Laker
*Capt. Marcos Lemos
Viscount Leverhulme
Sir Harry Llewellyn
C. L. Loyd, Esq.
R. J. McAlpine, Esq.
Lord McGowan
A. J. Macdonald-Buchanan, Esq.
Capt. J.Macdonald-Buchanan
Capt. the Hon. Gerald Maitland-Carew
*Sheikh Hamdan bin Rashid al Maktoum
*Sheikh Maktoum bin Rashid al Maktoum
*Sheikh Mohammed bin Rashid al Maktoum
Lord Manton
Lord Margadale
J. A. Marshall, Esq.
*Paul Mellon, Esq.
A. Mildmay-White, Esq.
The Hon. James Morrison
J. R. Newton, Esq.
Brigadier F. B. B. Noble
A. D. G. Oldrey, Esq.
Sir Philip Oppenheimer
P. J. O'Sullevan, Esq.
Brigadier A. H. Parker Bowles
G. W. Paul, Esq.
Sir Thomas Pilkington, Bt.
P. D. Player, Esq.
Miss K. Rausing
J. Richmond-Watson, Esq.
R. N. Richmond-Watson, Esq.
J. E. Rose, Esq.
Sir Evelyn de Rothschild
*Prince Fahd Salman
R. E. Sangster, Esq.
C. R. Saunders, Esq.
Earl of Scarbrough
M. G. Sheppard Esq.
The Hon. David Sieff
A. Speelman, Esq.
C. J. Spence, Esq.
C. H. Sporborg, Esq.
Major Ivan Straker
A. J. Struthers, Esq.
J. B. Sumner, Esq.
Duke of Sutherland
Miss J.M.Thompson
Sir John Thomson
R. R. Tweedie, Esq.
Viscount Ullswater
H. B. E. van Cutsem, Esq.
Lord Vestey
R. B. Waley-Cohen, Esq.
J. J. Warr, Esq.
A. T. A. Wates, Esq.
M. E. Wates, Esq.
*C. N. Weatherby, Esq.
*J. H. Weatherby, Esq.
Lord Weinstock
The Hon. G.A.Weir
Lord Westbury
W. H. Whitbread, Esq.
W. T. Whittle, Esq.
M. P. Wiggin, Esq.
P. S. Willett, Esq.
C. M. Wilson, Esq.
Lord Wolverton
M. H. Wrigley, Esq.
Major M. G. Wyatt
Marquess of Zetland

*Honorary Member

EX-OFFICIO MEMBERS

The Queen's Representative at Ascot — Col. Sir Piers Bengough
Queen's Racing Manager—Earl of Carnarvon
The Manager of the Royal Studs — Michael Oswald, Esq.
The Stewards of the Turf Club, Ireland —
Brig. H. J. de W. Waller Michael Osborne, Esq. Dr. M. J. Dargan
J. G. McKinley, Esq.
The Stewards of the Irish National Hunt Steeple Chase Committee —
A. Lillingston, Esq. Mrs. Joan Moore Captain S. H. Walford

THE JOCKEY CLUB 1993

The President of the Societe d'Encouragement et des Steeple Chases de France —
Baron Bertrand du Breuil
The Vice-Presidents — M. Bertrand Belinguier, M. Bernard Le Gentil
and
The Stewards of the Societe —
M. Jacques Bouchara M. Roland Fougedoire M. Robert Fournier Sarloveze
M. Max de Ginestet-Phivert M. Hervé de la Heronniere M. Alain de Kermadec
M. Robert Labouche M. Nicolas Landon M. Serge Landon
M. Philippe Motte Comte. Bertrand de Tarragon
The Chairman of the Jockey Club, New York —
Mr. Ogden Mills Phipps
The Chairman of Committee of the Australian Jockey Club, New South Wales —
R. L. Chavley, Esq.
The Chairman of Committee of the Victoria Racing Club —
David J. Bourke, Esq.
The Chief Steward of the Jockey Club of Canada —
Charles Taylor, Esq.
The President of the New Zealand Racing Conference —
Murray Acklin, Esq.
The Chairman of the Executive Stewards of the Jockey Club of South Africa —
R. S. Napier, Esq.
The Chairman of the Royal Hong Kong Jockey Club —
Sir William Purves

STANDING COMMITTEES OF THE JOCKEY CLUB

Disciplinary Committee
A. Mildmay-White, Esq. (Chairman)
P. D. Player, Esq. (Deputy Chairman)
Miss J. M. Thompson
M. P. Wiggin, Esq.
D. R. Brotherton, Esq.
Sir John Cotterell

Disciplinary Review Committee
A. J. Struthers, Esq. (Chairman)
Lord Fairhaven (Deputy Chairman)
C. L. Loyd, Esq. J. B. Sumner, Esq.
Colonel Sir Piers Bengough Lord Vestey

Licensing Committee
Captain W.H.Bulwer-Long (Chairman)
Lord Wolverton
M. R. Q. Henriques, Esq.
M. G. Sheppard, Esq.

JOCKEY CLUB REPRESENTATIVES ON THE HORSERACE BETTING LEVY BOARD

Sir Paul Fox
R. T. Ricketts, Esq.
P. J. Jones, Esq.

JOCKEY CLUB REPRESENTATIVES ON TATTERSALLS COMMITTEE

T. E. S. Egerton, Esq. (Chairman)
Lord Manton

Index to Rules of Racing

The Rules of Racing

Except where they otherwise provide these Rules apply to all meetings held under the authority of the Jockey Club, and to all races run at such meetings.
These Rules, although subsequently amended from time to time, came into force on January 1st, 1969, upon the amalgamation of the Jockey Club and the National Hunt Committee.

Definitions

In the Rules the following words and phrases shall bear the meaning hereby assigned to them regardless of case.

"All Weather Track" is a track with a racing surface other than turf, which has the approval of the Stewards of the Jockey Club.

"Amateur Rider" is a person who holds a permit to ride as an amateur, which may be restricted to certain types of race, from the Stewards of the Jockey Club.

"Amateur Riders race" is a race in which the only riders permitted to take part are Amateur Riders.

"Approved Pool" is an approved pool within the meaning of and complying with the requirements of Rule 227.

"Arrears" are any sums due from any person by virtue of these Orders and/or Rules and irrespective of whether this term appears in an Order or a Rule i.e. "Arrears" when used in a Rule shall include sums due under the Orders and vice versa.

"Auction Race" on the Flat is a Flat race restricted to two year old maiden horses sold by public auction at specified sales. (Note: Races with auction conditions open to winners shall be defined as "Conditions Stakes").

"Authorised Agent" is an agent or sub-agent duly appointed as such in accordance with the provisions of the Orders except in the case of a Recognised Company when it shall be the registered agent duly appointed by the Company as required in Rule 45.

"Authorised Rider's Agent" is a registered agent duly appointed as such in accordance with the provisions of the Orders.

"Breeder" is the person or entity who owns the dam when the foal is dropped.

"British Horseracing Board" is the British Horseracing Board Limited a company limited by guarantee and incorporated under the Companies Act under registration number 2813358.

"The British Horseracing Board Office" is the office for the time being appointed as the office of the British Horseracing Board. (The present address of the British Horseracing Board is 42 Portman Square, London W1.).

"Claiming race" is a race in which every horse running may be claimed in accordance with Rule 97.

"Conditions Race" is the general description of any Flat race which is not a Handicap, is not restricted to Maidens and is not governed by Selling or Claiming provisions.

"Conditions Stakes" is a Flat race which has not been awarded Pattern or Listed status, is not a Handicap, is not restricted to Maidens, is not governed by Selling or Claiming provisions and is not restricted to Apprentice or Amateur riders if less than £7,500 is added to stakes.

"Cup" is any prize not given in money.

"Day" means twenty-four hours finishing at midnight.

"Declaration of forfeit" is the withdrawal of a horse from a race under the provisions of Order 122.

"Declaration Sheet" the Declaration Sheet(s) is the document in such form as the Stewards of the Jockey Club may from time to time direct which contains such information relating to declarations under Order 124(ii) as the Stewards of the Jockey Club deem appropriate and which is required to be signed under Rule 141(i).

"The Directors" means the directors from time to time of the British Horseracing Board or any one or more of such directors who may be from time to time authorised by the directors of the British Horseracing Board to exercise any function which the Orders and/or Rules may provide shall be performed by the Directors.

"Disqualified Person" is a person who has been declared a disqualified person by the Stewards of the Jockey Club under these Rules, Jockey Club Regulations for Point-to-Point Steeple Chases or Jockey Club Regulations for Arab Horse Racing or who is a disqualified person by virtue of these Rules or those Regulations.

"Evening Meeting" is a meeting where the first race is programmed to start after 4.00 p.m.

"Foal Identity and Vaccination Certificate" is the diagrammatic document of identity issued **by** the Stud Book Authority of Great Britain and Ireland.

"Forfeit List" is a record of arrears published under the authority of the Turf Authority of Great Britain.

"Free handicap" is one in which no liability for stakes or forfeit is incurred until acceptance.

"General Instructions" a) when used in an Order, shall mean instructions issued by

— the Directors of the British Horseracing Board after 1993 through the Chief Executive of the British Horseracing Board; and,

b) when used in the Rules of Racing, shall mean instructions issued by

— the Stewards of the Jockey Club through, prior to July 1st, 1990, the Secretary to the Jockey Club and subsequently the keeper of the Match Book;

— in each case to Managing Executives of Racecourses and Officials and whether relating to a specific racecourse or of general application.

"Great Britain" means England, Scotland and Wales.

"Guaranteed minimum value" is that amount advertised in the conditions of a race which the racecourse undertakes will be given as the total prize money in a sweepstakes even if receipts from entry fees together with the guaranteed prize money do not together amount to that sum.

"Guaranteed prize money" is, for sweepstakes, the minimum published amount contributed towards the stakes by the Racecourse or from other sources, as distinct from additional sums contributed by the Racecourse to meet the guaranteed minimum value of a race and money contributed by the owners of horses engaged. For guaranteed sweepstakes the guaranteed prize money is the amount advertised in the conditions of the race (see definition of guaranteed sweepstakes).

"Guaranteed Sweepstakes" is a race in which the entrance fees, forfeits or other contributions from owners go to the winner or placed horses but in which the Racecourse guarantees that the total prize-money available for distribution in accordance with the requirements of Order 194 shall not be less than a specified amount and where the total entrances, forfeits, etc., exceed that value then the total entrances, forfeits, etc., will be the prize-money.

"Handicap" is a race in which the weights for the horses are allotted by the handicapper for the purpose of equalising their chances of winning.

"Handicapper" means a person appointed by the Directors to be a Handicapper for race meetings.

"Handicap rating" is the number allocated to a horse by the Handicapper on his assessment of that horse's performance.

"Horse" includes mare, gelding, colt, and filly and for the purposes of Rule 35 includes a pony, mule, ass or hinny.

"Horserace" means any race in which any horse runs with any other horse in competition for any prize of any kind or nature whatsoever or for the purposes of deciding the result of any bet or wager and at which more than twenty persons (not including participants in the race) are present save that events at horse shows or gymkhanas, which are restricted to children under 18 years of age, or which involve a substantial element of chance or skill unconnected with horse-riding, shall not be considered horseraces.

"Hunters' Steeple Chase" is a weight-for-age steeple chase confined to horses certified by a Master of Hounds to have been hunted and to amateur riders.

"Jockey" is a person who holds a licence from the Stewards of the Jockey Club to ride for hire and such licences may be limited to Flat races or to Steeple Chases, Hurdle races and National Hunt Flat races.

"Jockey Club Office" is the office for the time being appointed as the office of the Jockey Club. (The present address of the Jockey Club Office is 42, Portman Square, London W1.).

"Limited Stakes" is a Flat Conditions race restricted to horses which have been awarded Handicap ratings at or below a figure specified in the conditions of the race.

"Listed Races" are those Flat races which in any particular year are published in the Pattern Race Book and include races for the period 1980 to 1986 published in the 1987 Pattern Race Book.

"Maiden" for Flat races, is a horse which has never won a flat race other than a National Hunt Flat race in Great Britain, an Arab Horse Race in Great Britain, a match, private sweepstakes or the Newmarket Challenge Cup or Whip, at any recognised meeting in any country, and for Steeple Chases and Hurdle races, is a horse which has never won a Steeple Chase or Hurdle race other than a match or private sweepstakes, a National Hunt Flat race, or a Steeple Chase at a Point-to-Point meeting, at any recognised meeting in any country. **"Maiden"** means a maiden at the time of the start.

"Maiden Handicap" is a Handicap Flat race restricted to Maidens at starting, not open to horses of two years old, which have run at least four times in Flat races in Great Britain.

"Managing Executive" means the person, firm, company or organisation which is responsible for managing a racecourse.

"Match" is a race between horses the property of two different owners on terms agreed by them, and to which no money or other prize is added.

"Median Auction Race" is a Flat race, for maiden horses, restricted to the progeny of stallions which established a median price for the sale of yearlings contemporary with the entrants in the race based on the sale price of one or more animals at specified sales. (Note:— Races with median Auction conditions which are open to winners shall be defined as "Conditions Stakes").

"Medical Officer" is any registered medical practitioner retained by the Stewards of the Jockey Club to give medical advice or attendant at a Race Meeting at the request of the Stewards for medical purposes.

"Month" means a Calendar month.

"National Hunt Flat race" is a race for 4, 5 and 6, years old which at starting have not run under any recognised Rules of Racing except in National Hunt Flat races in Great Britain or in Irish National Hunt Flat races.

"National Jockeys Booking Agency" is an agency appointed by the Stewards of the Jockey Club, in conjunction with the Racing Calendar office, to accept declarations, withdrawals or alterations of riders to horses within appointed times. (The present National Jockeys Booking Agency is based at the offices of The Jockeys Association of Great Britain Ltd., 39 Kingfisher Court, Hambridge Road, Newbury, Berks.)

"Natural Service or Covering" is the physical mounting of a mare by a stallion and which can include the immediate reinforcement of the stallion's service or cover by a portion of the ejaculate produced by that stallion during that service or cover of that same mare.

"Nominator" is the person in whose name a horse is entered for a race.

"Novelty Races" are those races involving a restricted number of runners, other than the numbers determined by the safety Factor and Invitation races, either in regard to horses or riders.

"Novice" for Hurdle Races is a horse which has not won a Hurdle race at the start of the current season and for Steeple Chases is a horse which has not won a Steeple Chase at the start of the current season.

"Nursery handicap" is one confined to two years old horses.

"Offence" save as otherwise specified in these Rules, means a breach of the Rules of Racing.

"Open Maiden Race" is a Flat race restricted to Maidens at starting which is not a Handicap and for which entry is only further restricted by number of starts, or age, or sex, or inclusion in the European Breeders' Fund sponsorship arrangements.

"Order" means an order issued by the Directors of the British Horseracing Board.

"Owner" save as otherwise stated below means the legal not the equitable owner of a horse. In the case of a horse owned by a recognised Stud Company, the word 'Owner' means the nominee of the Company approved and registered in accordance with Rule 43. In the case of a horse owned by a recognised Company the word 'Owner' means the Company. In the case of a horse owned by a recognised Club, the term 'Owner' means the trustees approved and registered in accordance with Rule 41. In the case of a syndicate, the expression 'joint owners' means the members of the syndicate in whom the legal possession of the horse is vested as lessees from the syndicate. In the case of a partnership, the term 'Owner' means all the partners. The term 'Owner' includes' part-owner'. Where a horse is leased the word 'Owner' means the lessee but not the lessor, and the lessor of a horse shall be deemed to have no interest in the horse for the purpose of Rule 47 unless he receives a share of the prize money won by the horse and contributes to the expense of running it.

"Passport" is the approved diagrammatic document of identity of a horse issued by the Stud Book Authority on the authority of the Directors of the British Horseracing Board or otherwise as authorised by the Stewards of the Jockey Club or that of any recognised Turf Authority.

"Pattern Race Book" is the work published on the authority of the British Horseracing Board, the Irish Turf Club, the Société d'Encouragement et des Steeple-Chases de France, the Direktorium fur Vollblutzucht und Rennen and the Jockey Club Italiano.

"Pattern Races" are those Flat races which, in any particular year, appear in the Pattern Race Book, and those Steeple Chases and Hurdle Races which, in any particular year, appear in the list of Pattern Races published in the Programmes of Steeple Chases and Hurdle Races book published by the Authority of the British Horseracing Board. Flat Pattern Races are divided into Groups 1, 2 and 3. Steeple Chase and Hurdle Race Pattern Races are divided into Grades 1, 2 and 3.

'Photograph' is the photograph taken when the horses pass the Winning Post by the race finish camera installed and operated by Racecourse Technical Services Ltd.

"Private sweepstakes" is one to which no money, or other prize is added, and which has not been publicly advertised previous to closing.

"Prohibited Substance" means a substance originating externally whether or not it is endogenous to the horse which falls in any of the categories contained in the List of Prohibited Substances published from time to time in the Racing Calendar. "Substance" includes the metabolites of the substance and the isomers of the substance and metabolites.

'Race' means Cup, Sweepstakes, Guaranteed Sweepstakes, Private Sweepstakes or Match run under these Rules or any race run under the Rules of any recognised Turf Authority but:—

— for calculating penalties, allowances and the qualifications of horses in respect of Flat races "Race" does not include a Steeple Chase, or a Hurdle race run under these Rules or the Rules of any recognised Turf Authority or a National Hunt Flat race run in Great Britain;

— for calculating penalties, allowances and the qualifications of horses in respect of Steeple Chases and Hurdle races "Race" does not include a Flat race or a National Hunt Flat race run under these Rules or a Flat race run under the Rules of any recognised Turf Authority;

— for calculating penalties, allowances and qualification of horses in respect of races for horses that have not won a race, for horses that have not waon a race before a particular date, or for horses that have not won a race of a specified value or distance, wins in a Match, Private Sweepstakes, the Newmarket Challenge Cup or Whip, or a National Hunt Flat race in Great Britain, shall not count;

— shall not include any Arab Horse race in Great Britain or Point to Point Steeple Chase.

NOTE: This definition means that for the calculation of riders' allowances claimed under Rule 109 and also for races confined to Apprentice Jockeys, Conditional Jockeys and Amateur Riders on the Flat all races will count except Arab Horse races or Point to Point Steeple Chases.

"The Racing Calendar" is a work published under that name having the authority of the British Horseracing Board and/or the Jockey Club as the case may be.

"Racing Calendar Office" is the office appointed for the time being as the Racing Calendar Office by the British Horseracing Board. (The present Racing Calendar Office is at Weatherbys, Sanders Road, Wellingborough, Northants.)

"Rated Stakes" is a Handicap Flat race for which the range of weights shall be limited to not more than 14lb.

"Rating Related Maiden Race" is a Flat race, other than a Handicap, restricted to Maidens at starting which have been awarded Handicap ratings at or below a figure specified in the conditions of the race.

"Recognised Club" is a recognised Club within the meaning of and complying with the requirements of Rule 41.

"Recognised Company" is a recognised company within the meaning of and complying with the requirements of Rule 44.

"Recognised meeting" is a meeting authorised by a recognised Turf Authority and in the case of Great Britain which has been authorised by the Stewards of the Jockey Club and granted fixtures by the Directors of the British Horseracing Board.

"The Registered Names of Horses" the **"Non-Thoroughbred Register"** the **Jockey Club Regulations for Point-to-Point Steeple Chases"** and **"Jockey Club Regulations for Arab Horse Racing"** are the works published under those names respectively having the authority of either the British Horseracing Board or the Jockey Club or both as the case may be.

"Recognised Stud Company" is a recognised Stud Company within the meaning of and complying with the requirements of Rule 43.

"Recognised Turf Authority" is any turf Authority included in the list set out in appendix H to these Rules together with other Turf Authorities which the Stewards of the Jockey Club approve as recognised Turf Authorities by exercise of their powers under Rule 1(xvi).

"Registered owner" is an owner whose name has been duly registered under Rule 40.

"Registry Office" is the office for the time being appointed as the Registry Office by the Jockey Club. (The present Registry Office is at the Jockey Club Office, 42 Portman Square, London. W1.)

"Rider" means a jockey licensed by the Stewards of the Jockey Club under the provisions of Rule 60(i), (ii), (iii) or (iv), or an amateur rider permitted by the Stewards of the Jockey Club under the provisions of Rule 60(v) or (vi), or a rider who is the holder of a current licence or permit to ride issued by a recognised Turf Authority under the requirements of Rule 61(i).

"Safety Factor" is that number of horses which the Stewards consider to be the maximum which can be started safely in a particular race.

"Scratching" is the withdrawal of a horse from a race and once received at the Racing Calendar Office cannot be cancelled.

"Season" for the purposes of these Orders and Rules, the Racing Season is for Flat racing from the first day of January until the thirty-first day of December in any year, both dates inclusive, and for Steeple Chasing and Hurdle racing from the first day of Steeple Chasing and Hurdle racing after July 1st in any year until the day before the first day of Steeple Chasing and Hurdle racing after July 1st in the following year.

"Selling race" is a race in which every horse running, if a loser, may be claimed, and, if the winner, must be offered for sale by auction in accordance with the Rules governing Selling races.

"Signed" - means bearing the signature of a person qualified to sign the document concerned. On forms approved or prescribed by the Directors of the British Horseracing Board under the Orders of the British Horseracing Board or by the Stewards of the Jockey Club under the Rules of Racing the signature must be appended at the conclusion.

A Telex message will be deemed to be signed if it bears the name of the qualified person at the conclusion of the message. A document or telex message making an entry, confirmation of entry or declaration to run will only be valid if it is signed and save with the express permission of the Stewards of the Jockey Club includes the security code allotted by the Stewards of the Jockey Club to persons qualified to make such entries, confirmation of entries or declarations.

"Stakeholder" means the person appointed by the Directors to be Stakeholders of all meetings.

"Standard Handicap" is a Handicap Flat race, (other than an Amateur or Apprentice Handicap), not open to horses of two years old for which the lowest possible weight shall be not more than 7st 7lb and the highest not less than 9st 7lb.

"Starter's Orders" - Every horse shall be considered as having come under Starter's Orders which has not been withdrawn from the race when the white flag is raised or the signal given.

"Started" - Every horse shall be considered as having started which has come under Starter's Orders unless it has been declared by the Starter "not to have started" pursuant to Rule 28(xv).

"Stewards" - Wherever the word "Steward" or "Stewards" is used, it means Steward or Stewards of the meeting, or their duly appointed deputy or deputies.

"Stewards of the Jockey Club" includes except for the purposes of Rule 5 a quorum of three Stewards of the Jockey Club duly appointed by the constitution of the Jockey Club or any Standing Committee of the Jockey Club to which the Stewards of the Jockey Club have delegated their duties, powers or functions in accordance with the Rules and Orders of the Jockey Club.

"Stud Book" is the official register of the breeding of thoroughbred horses in their country of origin. **"General Stud Book"** is the official register of the breeding of thoroughbred horses kept by the Stud Book authority of Great Britain and Ireland.

"Sweepstakes" is a race in which the entrance fee, forfeit, subscription, or other contribution of three or more owners go to the winner or placed horses, and any such race is still a sweepstakes when money or other prize is added (subject to the provisions of Order 191).

"Time of Entry" means the time fixed for closing.

"Trainer" is a person who either (a) holds a licence to train horses, which may be limited to either Flat races or Steeple Chases, Hurdle races and National Hunt Flat races, from the Stewards of the Jockey Club, or (b) holds a permit to train horses for Steeple Chases, Hurdle races and National Hunt Flat races, from the Stewards of the Jockey Club or (c), when running horses under these Rules which are trained outside Great Britain, is the duly qualified trainer in the country where the horse is trained.

"Training Agreement" is a written agreement on a prescribed form between owner and trainer which sets out the fees to be charged by the trainer for training each of the owner's horses, the charges for horses owned in partnership being made in proportion to the owner's share in the horse.

"United Kingdom" means England, Scotland, Wales and Northern Ireland.

"V.A.T." means the Value Added Tax for the time being in force.

"Weight-for-age race" is any race which is not a handicap or a selling race.

"Winner" means the winner of a race (see definition of 'race').

"Year" means a Calendar year.

PART 1: DIRECTORS OF THE BRITISH HORSERACING BOARD

Powers of the Directors

1. The Directors have power at their discretion:

(i) (a) To fix the dates on which all meetings shall be held, to cancel such fixtures, to make any alteration in the date of any such Meeting and to supervise and make such alterations as they may think advisable in the programme of, or the conditions of any race at, any Meeting.

(b) To order the transfer of any Race Meeting or race to another licensed racecourse whenever the Directors consider such transfer necessary or expedient in the interests of racing, provided that the two Racecourses concerned have consented to the transfer.

(ii) (a) To authorise Point-to-Point fixtures, to cancel such fixtures, and to make any alterations to them from time to time that they consider necessary.

(b) To authorise Arab horse race fixtures, to cancel such fixtures, and to make alterations to them from time to time that they consider necessary.

(iii) To prohibit the advertisement of any race or meeting in the Racing Calendar, or call upon Managing Executives to alter or expunge any conditions, even after advertisement.

(iv) To authorise the publication in the Racing Calendar and in any newspaper circulating in the United Kingdom and to and through any news agency operating in the United Kingdom (as the Directors shall in their absolute discretion think fit) of their decisions respecting any matter and any person.

(v) To publish in the Racing Calendar from time to time such instructions as they may think fit.

(vi) To exercise any other powers conferred upon them by these Orders or the Rules of Racing and to take such action as they consider necessary for the purpose of carrying out or giving effect to these Orders or the Rules of Racing.

(vii) In cases of emergency or expediency, to modify the Orders or any part thereof, or to suspend any Order or part thereof, for such period or periods as they think fit, without giving previous notice, but should they do so they shall report the fact in the two subsequent consecutive issues of the Racing Calendar.

(viii) To authorise the level of fees, as they shall from time to time determine in relation to these Orders and the Rules of Racing.

(ix) To charge fees in addition to those otherwise provided for in the Rules of Racing if the Directors agree to make exceptional arrangements in respect of the conduct of any race meeting.

(x) To determine the policy in respect of the division of races or elimination of entries under the provisions of Order 125.

PART 1A: STEWARDS OF THE JOCKEY CLUB AND STEWARDS OF MEETINGS

Powers of the Stewards of the Jockey Club

1A. The Stewards of the Jockey Club have power at their discretion:

(i) To grant or to refuse to grant or to renew or refuse to renew licences in respect of Racecourses to the managing executives thereof and to make it a condition of a licence being granted that:

(a) The Managing Executive shall be a member of the association of Racecourses currently approved by the Jockey Club.

(b) Facilities shall be afforded on the Racecourse for the operation of the Totalisator.

(c) Such facilities shall be provided on the racecourses as are reasonably required by any contractor approved by the Stewards of the Jockey Club for the effective provisions of integrity services.

(d) The Managing Executive complies with the General Instructions issued by the Stewards of the Jockey Club whether or not they are published in the Racing Calendar.

(ii) To withdraw licences in respect of Racecourses.

(iii) (a) To order the abandonment of any race or Race Meeting in the care of emergency or expediency.

(iv) (a) To authorise the publication of 'Jockey Club Regulations for Point-to-Point Steeple Chases' and to make any alterations to them from time to time that they consider necessary.

(b) To authorise the publication of "Jockey Club Regulations for Arab Horse Racing" and to make any alterations to them from time to time that they consider necessary.

(c) To authorise the use of a racecourse for an equine event involving the use of the track, provided that the Managing Executive of that racecourse has first given its approval, or to refuse or cancel such authorisation.

(v) (a) To grant or refuse to grant and to renew or to refuse to renew licences to Clerks of the Course, jockeys, trainers and master jockey's valets, and permits to trainers, amateur riders and master valets' assistants. Every application for renewal of any licence or permit shall be treated and regarded in all respects and for all purposes as if it were the first application by the applicant for such a licence or permit.

(b) To grant and withdraw Temporary Licences in the event of the death or injury of a Licensed Trainer and in such other circumstances as the Stewards may deem necessary or convenient. A Temporary Licence holder shall assume all the obligations and responsibilities of a Licenced Trainer and the Licence for which it is substituted shall be of no force or effectiveness and until the Temporary Licence is withdrawn. Unless withdrawn the grant of a Temporary Licence shall remain in force notwithstanding the date for the renewal of the Licence it replaces is due but the Temporary Licensee may at that time apply for an annual licence which application will be treated as in sub-clause (a) above and in the context of the situation as then exists.

(c) To grant or withdraw Certificates of Approval in respect of equine swimming pools.

(vi) To accept or to refuse to accept or to cancel any registration under these Rules, notwithstanding any implication to the contrary whether contained in Rule 31 or elsewhere.

(vii) To allow or to refuse to allow any person to act or continue to act as an Authorised Agent or an Authorised Rider's Agent.

(viii) To make enquiry into and deal with any matter relating to racing whether such matters arise in Great Britain or elsewhere.

For the avoidance of doubt it is hereby declared that this power includes the power to enquire into and adjudicate upon conduct that has already been considered by Stewards of Meetings under Rule 14(iv) or Rule 14(viii) no matter what has been the decision or action of such Stewards and notwithstanding that the matter has not been reported by the Stewards under Rule 15(ii).

(ix) (a) To consider any decision of a Judge under Rule 26(i), and where in their opinion a Judge has made a mistake in determining and announcing the winner or placed horses in a race, which he has failed to correct within the time limit specified in Rule 26(ii), themselves to correct such mistakes and to declare the winner and placed horses: such decision of the Stewards of the Jockey

Club provided it is made within fourteen days of the race shall supercede that of the Judge.

(b) To consider any decision of the Clerk of the Scales under Rule 97(x) and, where in their opinion he has made a mistake, themselves to correct such mistake and to give such instructions as are necessary for the delivery of any horse concerned to its rightful owner. If such correction is made within fourteen days of the race it shall supercede the decision of the Clerk of the Scales.

(x) To entertain and determine appeals from the Stewards of Meetings as provided for by Rules 176-179.

(xi) To entertain and decide objections lodged under Rule 170(v).

(xii) To authorise the publication in the Racing Calendar and to and in any newspaper circulating in the United Kingdom and to and through any news agency operating in the United Kingdom (as the Stewards of the Jockey Club shall in their absolute discretion think fit) of their decisions respecting any matter and any person, and of the decisions and reports of Stewards of Meetings.

(xiii) To publish in the Racing Calendar from time to time such instructions as they may think fit.

(xiv) To exercise any other powers conferred upon them by these Rules or by the Regulations referred to in sub-Rule (iv) of this Rule and to take such action as they consider necessary for the purpose of carrying out or putting into effect these Rules and Regulations.

(xv) In cases of emergency or expediency, to modify the Rules of Racing or Regulations or any part thereof, or to suspend any Rule or Regulation or any part thereof, for such period or periods as they think fit, without giving previous notice, but should they do so they shall report the fact in the two subsequent consecutive issues of the Racing Calendar.

(xvi) To approve at any time the addition of other Turf Authorities to the list of such Authorities set out in Appendix H to these Orders and Rules.

(xvii) To approve or withdraw approval of surfaces for use as All Weather Tracks.

(xviii) To accept or to refuse to accept entries, and in the case of expediency to refuse to allow a horse duly entered to run in any race, in which event the Stewards of the Jockey Club may, at their discretion direct that the entrance money be remitted to the owner.

(xix) To accept or to refuse to accept the declarations, withdrawal, or alteration of riders to horses.

2. (i) When any person subject to the Rules of Racing has committed any breach thereof the Stewards of the Jockey Club have power at their discretion to impose upon such person any one or more of the following penalties, namely:

(a) They may impose any fine not exceeding £27,000.

(b) They may declare him a disqualified person.

Save that where any Rule prescribes a maximum penalty they may not impose any greater penalty or any penalty of some other kind and save that where any Rule prescribes a mandatory penalty they shall impose that penalty. Save as aforesaid the powers given by this Rule are not and are not to be construed as being in any way or in any instance limited or excluded by reason of the fact that some Rules do while others do not prescribe penalties for their breach.

(ii) When any rider has committed a breach of Rule 153 (iii) or 152 (iv) or (v) of the Rules of Racing the Stewards of the Jockey Club have power at their discretion to suspend the rider from riding in any race for such period or periods as they think fit.

(iii) The Stewards of the Jockey Club have power if good cause is shown or when any person has committed any breach of the Rules of Racing to withdraw or suspend his licence or permit.

(iv) The Stewards of the Jockey Club shall have power to exclude or cause or order to be excluded for any period or for an indefinite period from any premises owned, licensed or controlled by them any person whether or not subject to the Rules of Racing

(a) whose conduct they, in their absolute discretion, consider to be such as to make the presence of such person on such premises undesirable in the interest of racing even though such person is not and has not been declared, a disqualified person, or

(b) who has been reported by the Committee of Tattersalls.

(v) (a) When, following an enquiry, the Stewards of the Jockey Club have determined that any person has committed any breach of the Rules of Racing, they shall have power, at their discretion, to order that person to pay such reasonable costs and expenses relating to the enquiry and such reasonable compensation for outlay incurred in connection therewith as they may determine.

(b) On the hearing of an Appeal brought by any person under rules 176–178 hereof, the Stewards of the Jockey Club shall have the power at their discretion, except where they have reversed the decision of the Stewards, to order that person to pay such reasonable costs and expenses relating to the appeal and such reasonable compensation for outlay in connection therewith as they may determine.

(vi) (a) The Stewards of the Jockey Club have power at their discretion, on such occasions and in accordance with such procedures as they consider appropriate, to review any finding by them that a person has committed a breach of these Rules and any penalty, including the withdrawal or suspension of a licence or permit, imposed by them under this or any other Rule, and upon such review, to reverse or otherwise vary any finding of a breach and to rescind, reduce, increase or alter any penalty, including the withdrawal or suspension of a licence or permit; provided that the Stewards of the Jockey Club shall not have the power to review their decision on an appeal brought and heard under Rules 176–179.

(b) The power to review shall include the power to direct a further enquiry. Upon such direction any finding or penalty shall have no effect.

(c) In exercising their powers under this Sub-Rule the Stewards of the Jockey Club shall have power to order that any person who has applied for a Review shall pay such reasonable costs and expenses relating to the Review as they may determine, and to order that when an application for Review is made there shall be lodged a deposit in such sum as they may determine, which may be forfeited in such circumstances as they may determine.

(d) The Stewards of the Jockey Club shall have power to postpone the operation of any penalty imposed by them until there has been a Review under this Sub-Rule.

(e) For the purpose of this Sub-Rule "penalty" shall include disqualification of a horse.

3. (i) The Stewards of the Jockey Club may at their discretion consider any video-recording, transcript, notes of evidence, statements or other material forwarded as required under Rule 153(iv)(b) and may at their discretion cancel any order of suspension made under Rule 153(iv)(a) or reduce the period of the suspension.

(ii) On entertaining any appeal from the decision of the Stewards under Rule 153(iv)(a) or on a full enquiry into the matters the Stewards of the Jockey Club may without prejudice to the powers contained in Rule 2 extend the period of suspension.

(iii) Upon consideration of a matter reported to the Stewards of the Jockey Club under Rule 15(ii)(d) or upon a Review thereafter carried out under Rule 2(vi), the Stewards of the Jockey Club shall have the power to quash or vary any decision of the Stewards to disqualify a horse or alter the placings.

4. The Stewards of the Jockey Club take no cognisance of any disputes or claims with respect to bets, but they have power to give effect to an official report made to them by the Committee of Tattersalls.

5. The Stewards of the Jockey Club have free access to all stands, rooms, enclosures, and other places used for the purposes of racing under these Rules.

6. No person who has been requested by or on behalf of the Stewards of the Jockey Club to attend an enquiry or hearing of an appeal under Rule 178 shall without reasonable cause fail or refuse to do so.

Stewards of Meetings

10. (i) There must be at least four Stewards for every meeting (five if nine or more races are to be run),

including a Chairman, appointed by the Managing Executive and approved by the Stewards of the Jockey Club. Each Steward may appoint a deputy at any time but, in the case of the Chairman, such deputy must have the approval of the Stewards of the Jockey Club, except in an emergency when time does not permit such approval being obtained.

(ii) The powers given by these Rules to the Stewards of Meetings may be exercised by the Chairman and any two other Stewards for the meeting (or their deputies).

(iii) The Stewards of the Jockey Club may at their discretion by Notice to the Racecourse Executive withdraw their approval of a Steward whereupon he, and any deputy appointed by him, shall cease to be empowered to act as a Steward.

11. Should there not be four Stewards or their deputies present, the Clerk of the Course, shall, without delay, see that any vacancy or vacancies are filled, so that there shall be four persons to act, and shall notify conspicuously such appointment.

Powers of the Stewards of Meetings

12. The Stewards have control over, and have free access to, all stands, rooms, enclosures, and other places used for the purposes of the Meeting.

13. The Stewards shall exclude from all stands, rooms, enclosures and other places used for the purposes of the meeting every disqualified person, and all such persons as they may, from time to time, be required by the Stewards of the Jockey Club to exclude.

14. The Stewards of a Meeting have full power:-

(i) to make (and, if necessary, to vary) all such arrangements for the conduct of the meeting or any race run thereat as they think fit, including arrangements for ensuring that races start at the advertised time, and to give all necessary instructions for that purpose.

(ii) Under exceptional circumstances or if the weather or ground be in an unfit state (a) to cancel a parade, or to cancel the requirement that horses should be ridden in front of the Stands before going to the post. (b) at an All Weather Track fixture to cancel the requirement that horses should be brought into the Parade ring prior to the race and to order them to be mounted in the place appointed for saddling. (c) to abandon a day's racing or to abandon any races to postpone any races to the following day or days within the original fixture, provided that all the races originally advertised for any day shall be included in that day's programme. Should the Stewards abandon a day's racing on the grounds specified above a Certificate must be drawn up stating the day and the hour when the decision to abandon was arrived at. The decision to abandon should not normally be taken before 8 a.m. on the day preceding the day's racing in question but in exceptional circumstances where the Stewards are entirely satisfied that no racing can possibly take place, the decision may be taken by noon two days prior to that on which the day's racing has been advertised to take place. The Certificate must be signed by two of the Stewards or by one Steward and the Clerk of the Course and without delay despatched to the Racing Calendar Office.

(iii) To leave out or to alter any (but not more than two) fences or flights of hurdles in the circuit of the course if their retention would necessitate the abandonment of the day's racing, but the original advertised distance of a race must not be decreased.

Should the Stewards authorise the cancellation of either a parade or the requirement that horses should be ridden in front of the Stands or the abandonment or postponement of any races, the deletion of any fences or flights of hurdles or vary in any way the programme as originally advertised they shall without delay report to the Racing Calendar Office their reasons for so doing.

(iv) To determine all questions arising in reference to racing at the meeting whether during the course of or subsequent to the meeting except as otherwise provided in these Rules and subject to appeal under Rule 176.

(v) To call for proof (see Rule 170(i)) that a horse is neither itself disqualified in any respect, nor nominated by, nor the property, wholly or in part, of a disqualified person; and in default of such proof being given to their satisfaction they may declare the horse disqualified. They have power to prevent from running any horse which cannot be shown to be qualified under these Rules or under the conditions of the race.

(vi) At any time to order an examination by such person or persons as they think fit, of any horse entered for a race, or which has run in a race. Where such examination includes the taking of samples for subsequent analysis the samples may be of any body fluid, tissue, excrete, hair or skin scrapings, or of all or any of the same at the discretion of the person conducting the examination and may involve the removal of implants.

(vii) To exclude at their discretion or to eject any person from all stands, rooms, enclosures and other places used for the purposes of the meeting.

(viii) To enquire into, regulate, control, take cognisance of, and adjudicate upon, the conduct of all officials, and of all owners, nominators, trainers, riders, grooms, persons attendant upon horses, and of all persons frequenting the Stands or other places used for the purpose of the Meeting.

(ix) By notices exhibited on the Number Board or elsewhere and by any form of public address system at the Racecourse to state and announce that an objection has been lodged, the subject and nature thereof, and also their decision in respect of such objection, or of any other matter coming within their jurisdiction.

(x) To prohibit a rider from using a particular whip whether or not such whip complies with the specifications approved by the Stewards of the Jockey Club, but, in the event of their so doing they shall without delay submit a report to the Stewards of the Jockey Club.

(xi) On the recommendation of a Medical Officer to order the examination by such officer of any rider declared to ride in a race or who has ridden in a race. Such examination may include at the discretion of the Medical Officer the taking of samples of blood, urine or other body fluid for subsequent analysis.

(xii) At an all weather track fixture to cancel the requirement that horses should be made to stand still for mounting.

15. (i) When in the opinion of the Stewards any person subject to the Rules of Racing has committed any breach thereof they have power at their discretion to impose upon such person a fine not exceeding £1300. Save that where any Rule prescribes a maximum penalty they may not impose any greater penalty or any penalty of some other kind and save that where any Rule prescribes a mandatory penalty they shall impose that penalty. Save as aforesaid the powers given by this Rule are not and are not to be construed as being in any way or in any instance limited or excluded by reason of the fact that some Rules do while others do not prescribe penalties for their breach.

(ii) When in the opinion of the Stewards

(a) there is a reasonable suspicion that any person has committed any breach of the Rules of Racing which in their opinion ought to be considered by the Stewards of the Jockey Club, or

(b) any person has committed any breach of the Rules of Racing and in their opinion some fine or punishment in excess of £1300 ought to be imposed upon such person, or

(c) any person present at the meeting whether or not subject to the Rules of Racing has misconducted himself, or

(d) any rider has committed a breach of Rule 153(iii) or 152(iv) or (v) and in their opinion the rider should either be suspended for a longer period than 14 days, or the breach should be considered by the Stewards of the Jockey Club

they have power at their discretion to report the matter to the Stewards of the Jockey Club.

Upon consideration of the matter the Stewards of the Jockey Club shall not be bound by any finding of the Stewards.

16. in addition to their foregoing powers, the Stewards have the powers of suspension and caution conferred on them in Rule153(iv)(a).
17. The Stewards, as such, shall not entertain any disputes relating to bets.

PART 2: OFFICIALS

General

20. (i) No person shall act as a Clerk of the Course under these Rules, except as provided under Rule 21, unless he has obtained a licence from the Stewards of the Jockey Club which may be issued subject to such restrictions and conditions as they consider necessary.

(ii) A Clerk of the Course shall be appointed for every Meeting by the Managing Executive of that Meeting, subject to the approval of the Stewards of the Jockey Club, and the Managing Executive shall be responsible for any payment for the services of the Clerk of the Course.

(iii) All other officials shall be appointed for every Meeting by the Stewards of the Jockey Club and they shall receive such remuneration from the Jockey Club as is required by the terms of their employment.

(iv) No two offices for the same fixture shall be held by one person, unless by special permission of the Stewards of the Jockey Club.

21. (i) In case of emergency, the Stewards may, during a Meeting, appoint a substitute to fill any office for that Meeting only.

(ii) Every complaint against an official shall be made to the Stewards in writing, signed by the complainant.

Clerk of the Course

22. The Clerk of the Course

(i) shall be the person to whom all General Instructions pertaining to the racecourse and the conduct of racing shall be directed and he shall comply with such General Instructions unless and to the extent that they may have been waived in writing by the Stewards of the Jockey Club or the Directors as the case may be.

(ii) shall be responsible for ensuring that the Managing Executive is made aware of the contents of all General Instructions which affect the responsibilities of the Managing Executive.

(iii) shall carry out such requirements of the General Instructions as are delegated to him by the Managing Executive and such other directions as the Managing Executive considers necessary.

(iv) shall comply with the requirements of these Rules, (particularly Rule 150) and all directions given to him by the Stewards of the Meeting in relation to the conduct of race meetings.

(v) shall have in his possession, for the information of the Stewards, a) the List of persons disqualified or Excluded under the provisions of Rule 2(iv); b) the Lists of trainers and riders reported; and, c) a copy of the latest Forfeit List as specified in Rule 135(i), together with any amendments to this List. He shall not allow any horse the owner or nominator of which is in the Forfeit List or in any amendments to the List, to start for any race.

Clerk of the Scales

23. The Clerk of the Scales shall:-

(i) weigh the riders in accordance with the Rules (see Parts 14 and 16)

(ii) cause to be displayed on the screen or number board any alterations to the following information published in the official race card:

(a) declared horses,

(b) declared riders with allownces claimed if appropriate,

(c) in Flat races the draw,

(d) extra weight or variation of weight or weight allowance,

(e) colours, and,

(f) declarations that horses are wearing a hood, blinkers, visor, eyeshield or eyecover or any combination thereof.

The numbers or changes shall be displayed either continuously or at regular intervals until the horses are started. When the time for declaring runners under Rule 141(i) has elapsed no alteration or addition except as allowed for in Sub-Rule (x) of this Rule and Rule 28 can be made without leave of the Stewards whose reasons for such permission shall be reported to the racing Calendar Office.

(iii) *Deleted.*

(iv) at once display on the number board or screen such alterations as the Stewards shall sanction under Sub-Rule (ii) of this Rule.

(v) should a horse be withdrawn under Rule 28(x) or 28(xii)(e) at once withdraw the number, order a black and white flag to be hoisted, exhibit a notice on the number board or screen stating whether such horse has come under Starter's orders or not, and immediately report to the Stewards that the number is withdrawn by order of the Starter.

(vi) in all cases, except as provided in Rule 160(v), weigh in the riders of the first four horses placed by the Judge, or, in races with prize money allocated under sub-Rules (ii)(c) and (d) of Order 194, the first six horses placed by the Judge, together with other riders as required by the Stewards, and report to the Stewards any rider not presenting himself to be weighed in.

(vii) should an objection be lodged or an enquiry be called for under Rule 171(iii), at once order the appropriate signal to be given on the number board or screen, together with the grounds for objection. Such signals must be displayed continuously until the Stewards' decision on the enquiry is announced.

The appropriate signal shall be:-

All right, Blue flag or light.

Objection and/or enquiry under Rule 171 (iii), Red flag with White E or Red light. This signal must also be given in the event of an enquiry into matters contained in Rule 154.

Enquiry completed, placings unaltered, enquiry signal replaced by White flag or light.

Enquiry completed, placings altered, enquiry signal replaced by Green flag or light.

(viii) at the close of each day's racing send a copy of the card to the Racing Calendar Office with a return of the weights carried in every race and the names of the riders, specifying overweight, if any, and of the horses which failed to complete the course, stating the reasons. A horse may appear on the card in the name of the nominator and the Stewards may, in special circumstances, grant permission for a horse to run in the name of some other person. The Clerk of the Scales shall, in such latter case, send a report to the Racing Calendar Office, stating the grounds upon which the permission was granted.

(ix) make a report to the Racing Calendar Office of the Acting Stewards or any official appointed, of all complaints to and decisions of the Stewards, of any accident during the course of a Flat race or a National Hunt Flat race and the result of the enquiry into the accident, which must be held by the Stewards, of all fines inflicted, and of all horses sold or claimed.

(x) shall not allow a rider to be weighed out for any horse until the entrance fee, additional sums due under the conditions of that race and these Rules or Orders, and any arrears for every horse belonging to the same owner, or standing in his name, the jockey's fee or any fee due in respect of an Amateur Rider, together with any payment due to the Professional Riders Insurance Scheme, any arrears claimed under these Rules and any Value Added Tax payable on or in connection with any of the matters specified in this Sub-Rule, have been paid.

Handicappers

24. Handicappers in making a handicap, shall allot the weights to be carried in accordance with the defini-

tions of a handicap and a handicap rating and the provisions of Orders 94 and 95, together with in Flat races for horses of more than one age a deduction in accordance with the appropriate weight for age allowance as provided under Appendix A to these Orders and Rules. The weights for all handicaps which close more than six days before running shall be published in the Racing Calendar, and those for other handicaps shall be published in the Prestel Service. No alteration shall be made to a weight after publication, except that by express permission of the Directors a weight may be affixed for a horse duly entered, but whose name or weight has been omitted from the handicap, or a correction may be made when, through an error an incorrect weight has been published. Such alterations or additions may only be made up to noon on the Friday before the first declaration of forfeit or, in races for which there is no declaration of forfeit, not later than 2p.m. 48 hours before the afternoon of the day upon which the race is advertised to be run.

Inspector of Courses

25. It shall be the duty of the Inspector of Courses:-

(i) to inspect every Racecourse in respect of which a Racecourse licence has been applied for and to prepare a report thereon for consideration by the Stewards of the Jockey Club.

(ii) to make periodic inspections of Racecourses in respect of which a licence has been granted and to prepare such periodic reports as the Stewards of the Jockey Club might from time to time require.

(iii) to review the provisions of Jockey Club General Instructions and to prepare such amendments and additions thereto as may be considered desirable and to submit the same to the Stewards of the Jockey Club for their approval.

Judge

26. (i) The Judge, or his authorised substituted, must occupy the place designated by the Stewards as the Judge's box at the time when the first horse passes the winning post or the race will be void. He must remain in that place until such time as all the horses which are in a position to complete the course have passed the winning post and his decision in this matter shall be final. No horse which passes the post after the Judge has left the box shall be placed.

(ii) The Judge must announce his decision immediately, or after consulting the photograph, and shall determine the winner according the that part of the horse's head, excluding the ears, which is first past the winning post,the remaining placings being determined in a similar manner, and subject to the powers of the Stewards and the Stewards of the Jockey Club under these Rules to disqualify horses and to alter placings, such decision shall be final, provided that this Rule shall not prevent a Judge at any time within five days of the race from correcting any mistake, and shall be subject to the powers of the Stewards of the Jockey Club under Rule 1 (ix). A correction of a judge shall be subject to confirmation by the Stewards.

(iii) When the Judge has consulted the photograph the degree of enlargement of the print upon which his decision is made is a matter for his discretion. The judge shall certify the print concerned and in the event of the Stewards of the Jockey Club exercising their powers under Rule 1 (ix) that print shall be the main evidence of the result.

(iv) The Judge shall, at the end of each day's racing, sign and send a report of each race to the Racing Calendar Office.

Stakeholder

27. (i) The Stakeholders shall collect all entrance fees and other sums due under the Conditions of Races, arrears and fees due under these Orders and in addition any Value Added Tax payable in connection with those payments.

(ii) The Stakeholders may at their discretion require the above payments to be made in cash.

(iii) The Stakeholders shall at the expiration of fifteen days after the Meeting and subject to Rule 174 credit all stakes, added money, and all sums due in respect of horses sold, bought in or claimed to the persons entitled. Accounts will be rendered and payments made at half-monthly intervals. Except that: (a) where a horse has been the subject of an examination under Rule 14(vi), the stakeholder shall not pay over any money to which any person would (but for this exception) be entitled in respect of the said horse by reason of the race in respect of which such examination was ordered and of any races thereafter in which the said horse has run, until authorised to do so by the Stewards of the Jockey Club or until the trainer of the said horse has been notified that it is not intended to institute disciplinary proceedings. (b) when a horse has been disqualified or its placing altered by or in consequence of a decision by the Stewards of the Jockey Club, and such decision is the subject of an application for Review under Rule 2(vi), the Stakeholder shall not pay over any money to which any person may be entitled by virtue of that decision until the determination or other resolution of the application for Review, or the completion of any further enquiry resulting from the Review.

(iv) The full amount of guaranteed prize money in a sweepstakes together with any additional sum required where a guaranteed minimum value has been advertised or, in a guaranteed sweepstakes, the balance of any guaranteed prize money over and above the owners' entrances, forfeits, etc., and an amount equivalent to the surcharges received under Order 133(ii), must be paid to the Stakeholders within three days of the conclusion of the Meeting.

Starter and Starting

28. (i) The Starter shall obtain a list of runners for each race from the Clerk of the Scales in the Weighing Room.

(ii) (a) Every horse shall be at the Post ready to start at the appointed time.

(b) Horses may not be led on the course on the way to the Start except in a Parade or with the permission of the Stewards, but such permission will not be given for horses ridden by apprentice or conditional jockeys.

(iii) All riders who arrive at the Starting Post must immediately place themselves under the control of the Starter.

(iv) The horses must be started by the Official Starter or his authorised substitute.

(a) All Flat races shall be started from Starting Stalls, or if they are not available, with a flag.

(b) All Steeple Chases, Hurdle races and National Hunt Flat races shall be started by a Starting Gate approved by the Stewards of the Jockey Club unless they have given special permission for a flag to be used.

Except that, in the case of emergency, by permission of the Stewards or the Starter, any race may be started with a flag. When a race is started by flag the advance flagman will raise his tag when the Starter raises his flag and will drop it when the Starter drops his flag to start the race.

(v) The Starter shall check the runners and riders against the list of runners which he has obtained from the Clerk of the Scales and for Flat races assign the horses to the places drawn by lot, all horses taking their place at the Start in the order drawn for them. The rider who has drawn No. 1 must always be placed on the left and other riders must take their places in consecutive numbers from the left.

(vi) The Starter shall give all orders necessary for securing a fair start. In a start from a Starting Gate or with a flag the horses must be started, as far as possible, in a line, but they may be started at such reasonable distance behind the Starting Post as the Starter thinks

necessary. The Starter shall also ensure that a race is not started before the appointed time.
Note: The Time recorded by The Press Association Ltd. shall be taken as the Official time of the start of a race.

(vii) In a start from a Starting Gate or with a Flag, the Starter has full power to remove an unruly horse and, should he do so, he must place it at such a distance to one side of or behind the other runners that it cannot gain any advantage itself or cause danger to, or prejudice the chances of the other horses and riders engaged in the race. Permission may be given by the Starter for a horse to be held or the Starter may himself order an unruly horse to be held, but in all cases the horse must be held behind the other runners at a position to be designated by the Starter. Should an unruly horse cause undue delay it may be "left".

(viii) In a start from Starting Stalls the Starter has full power to remove an unruly horse but no horse shall be permitted to start from outside the Stalls, nor is it permitted, except in an emergency, for a horse to be held in the Stalls. A horse which refuses to enter the stalls, or a horse which enters and through its unruly behaviour damages its stall shall be withdrawn by the Starter.

(ix) The Starter shall order the white flag or signal denoting that the horses are under Starter's orders to be hoisted or given:

(a) for races started from Starting Stalls when he has mounted his rostrum and has raised his hand to indicate to riders that the start is imminent.

(b) for races started from a Starting Gate when he has mounted his rostrum.

(c) for races started by Flag when he has taken up his position to start the race.

(x) Should the Starter consider that through any cause a horse is unable to start (for example, but without imposing any limitation upon the discretion of the Starter, when a horse has broken away before coming under starter's orders and has completed the course) he shall at once notify the Clerk of the Scales that the number must be withdrawn and shall inform him whether the horse came under Starter's orders or not. No horse which has come under Starter's orders shall be withdrawn except under the provisions of Sub-Rules (x), (xii) or (xv) of this Rule.

(xi) Misconduct by a rider at the start is an offence and the Starter shall report to the Stewards any rider whom he considers to have been guilty of such misconduct.

(xii) (a) Should the Starter consider that through any faulty action of the Starting Gate or Starting Stall a fair start has not been effected he shall declare it a false start and order the riders, by means of a recall flag to return to the Post.

(b) Where the recall flag is raised without the orders of the Starter he shall nevertheless declare it a false start.

(c) Unless at least one rider returns to the Starter after the recall flag has been raised for a false start the race shall be void.

(d) Should only one rider return to the Starter and satisfy him as to his having obeyed the recall flag, his horse shall be considered as having walked over for the race. Should more than one return the race shall be started again as soon as the course is clear.

(e) Following the recall flag horses which complete the course in a flat race or which complete a circuit of the course or fall in a steeple chase, hurdle race or National Hunt Flat race shall not be considered as having obeyed the recall flag and shall be withdrawn by the Starter. The riders of such horses shall be regarded as having committed a breach of these Rules.

(f) Runners which do not obey the recall flag shall only be considered as having come under Starter's orders if at the time of the false start the Starter had ordered the white flag to be hoisted or the signal given as required under Sub-Rule (ix) of this Rule to denote that the horses were under Starter's orders.

(g) Should the Starter declare a false start and the recall flag not be raised the race shall be void unless all the horses pull up before completing the course in a flat race or a circuit of the course in a steeple chase, hurdle race or National Hunt flat race, and return to the Starter except that any horse which falls before completing a circuit of the course in a steeple chase, hurdle race or National Hunt flat race shall be regarded as having satisfied the requirements of this sub-Rule but shall be withdrawn by the Starter.

(h) The Starters decision on all matters covered by parts (a) and (d) of this Sub-Rule shall be final.

(xiii) When a race is started in front of the Starting Post or on a wrong course, or before the appointed time it is void (See Rule 154).

(xiv) The Starter shall report to the Stewards, for transmission to the Racing Calendar Office, all cases in which he has dispensed with the Starting Stalls or Starting Gate or made any notification under Sub-Rule (x), and his reasons for doing so, the time at which the race was started, and by whom or by what cause any delay was occasioned.

(xv) The Starter shall forthwith notify the rider and the Clerk of the Scales that a horse will be declared "not to have started" when any of the following circumstances prevail once the horses are under Starter's Orders:—

(a) If in a Steeple Chase, Hurdle Race, National Hunt Flat Race, or a Flat race which is started by Flag,
— the whole body of the horse (with or without its rider) has failed to cross the starting line within a reasonable time determined by the Starter, or,
— the horse has crossed the starting line without its rider.

(b) If in any race and before the remainder of the horses have started:—
— the horse has died or the Starter considers that through any cause a horse is unable to start, or,
— the horse's rider is prevented by accident or illness from riding in the race.

(c) If in a Flat race started from Starting Stalls
— the whole body of the horse fails to leave the Starting Stalls, or,
— the horse leaves the Starting Stalls without its rider.

(xvi) The Starters decision on all matters covered by parts (a) to (c) of Sub-Rule (xv) of this Rule shall be final.

(xvii) (a) Any attempt by the rider to take part in the race once his horse has been declared "not to have started" by the Starter shall be construed as misconduct as laid down in Sub-Rule 28(xi).

(b) Until the Starter declares a horse "not to have started" a rider shall commit an offence unless he makes all reasonable effort to attempt to start in the race.

Stewards' Secretary

29. The Stewards' Secretary shall give to the Stewards such help and advice relating to the conduct of the meeting and the Rules of Racing as they may require.

PART 3: HORSES

Age

30. The age of a horse shall be reckoned as beginning on January 1st in the year in which he is foaled.

Registration of Names

31 (i) A name cannot be registered for a horse before it is a yearling unless the horse is foaled elsewhere than in Great Britain, Ireland or the Channel Islands, or is outside these countries at the date of registration.

(ii) An application for a name must state the colour, sex and age together with the registered name of the sire and dam but if either the sire or dam is not registered such further particulars must be given as will clearly identify the horse from all other horses. Unless the Stewards of the Jockey Club otherwise direct a horse born on or after January 1st, 1974 is not considered to be clearly identified unless it has been:-

1. Accepted for inclusion in the General Stud Book or in one of the Stud Books recognised by the Inter-

national Stud Book Committee and listed in Appendix I to these Orders and Rules, or

2. Accepted for inclusion in the Non-Thoroughbred Register.

(iii) An application for a name may only be registered for a horse by application to the British Horseracing Board at the Racing Calendar Office on the prescribed form signed by or on behalf of the owner or owners of the horse unless otherwise ordered by the Directors.

(iv) Except in the case of a horse which is outside Great Britain, Ireland or the Channel Islands at the time of application, the application must be accompanied by:—

(a) A certificate of age and markings signed by a Veterinary Surgeon who is neither the owner nor the trainer nor a person whose name is included in the Register of Stable Employees as being employed by the trainer of the horse.

If the markings on that certificate are not consistent with those recorded at birth by the Stud Book Authority, or in the case of a horse foaled outside Great Britain, Ireland or the Channel Islands, with the markings contained in the certificate of pedigree (exportation certificate) issued by the Stud Book Authority or Turf Authority of the country of origin and the identity of the horse cannot be verified by a blood test the Directors will not proceed with the application except that where the receipt of a Certificate of Pedigree (exportation certificate) has been delayed the Directors may at their discretion proceed with the application for registration subject to subsequent confirmation.

(b) The passport which has been issued for that horse by the Stud Book Authority unless either the Stewards of the Jockey Club have directed otherwise or the horse was foaled prior to January 1st, 1991.

Note: Horses foaled after December 31st, 1990 will be issued with passports by the Stud Book Authority following acceptance for inclusion in General Stud Book or the Non-Thoroughbred Register. (See Rule 32(i)).

(v) If the name is available within the criteria laid down by the Stewards of the Jockey Club in Appendix E to these Orders and Rules and has not been reserved under Sub-Order (viii) below, the name will be registered and will, from the Monday following the Friday on or before which registration is made, be the horse's name under these Rules; except that in the event of incorrect information being submitted in respect of the requirements of sub-Rules (ii) or sub-Order (iv) above the registration shall thereupon become void.

(vi) A numeral may only be added, when a name is not available, if the horse was foaled in Great Britain, Ireland or the Channel Islands and is not in the General Stud Book.

(vii) When a name is registered for a horse

(a) foaled prior to January 1st, 1988, outside Great Britain, Ireland or the Channel Islands a letter code will be added to denote the country of foaling and this code will form part of the registered name, or

(b) foaled after December 31 st, 1987, outside Great Britain or the Channel Islands a letter code will be added to denote the country of foaling and this code will form part of the registered name.

(viii) A name, if available, may be reserved for a living foal by application made in writing to the Racing Calendar Office stating the sire and dam of the foal. A name so reserved can only be registered in accordance with the preceding paragraphs of this Rule and the registration fee shall be incurred in addition to the reservation fee. A name cannot be reserved for more than twelve months. A reserved name does not identify a horse for the purpose of these Orders and Rules.

(ix) A name may not be changed for any horse:-

(a) whose name has been registered by another recognised Turf Authority except with the permission of that Turf Authority, or

(b) that has run under the Rules of any recognised Turf Authority, or

(c) which was foaled in Great Britain, Ireland or the Channel Islands and the name of which is currently registered when notification of impending publication of the Stud Book is published in the Racing Calendar, or

(d) whose registered name has already been published in the General Stud Book or Non-Thoroughbred Register or the Stud Book or Non-Thoroughbred Register of any recognised Turf Authority.

(x) A change of name must be applied for in the same way as a registration of name and if registered, will, from the Monday following the Friday on or before which registration is made be the horse's name under these Orders and Rules. When such change has been registered the horse will not be qualified to be entered or run in races until the Monday after registration.

(xi) If the same name be simultaneously claimed for two horses, the order of priority shall be determined by lot at the Racing Calendar Office.

(xii) Every provision contained in this Rule or the Orders in this part shall be subject to the power conferred upon the Stewards of the Jockey Club by Rule 1(vi) to accept or to refuse to accept or to cancel any registration under these Rules, notwithstanding any contrary implication which may be contained in any such provision. For the avoidance of doubt it is hereby declared that the Stewards of the Jockey Club will refuse to register the name of any horse unless it and its sire and dam are each the produce of a natural service or covering, and unless a natural gestation took place in and delivery was from the body of the mare in which the foal was conceived, and if a name is registered for a horse produced by other means the registration shall be void.

(xiii) A list of names registered and changes of name shall be published in the Racing Calendar.

(xiv) All naming fees as laid down by the Directors are payable in accodance with the schedule in Appendix M. The fee for a blood test required under sub-Order (iv) is payable by the applicant whether or not the identity of the horse is verified.

(xv) The above requirements regarding the registration of a name or change of name is subject always to the provisions of Rule 31(xii).

(xvi) A registration under these provisions is subject always to the power of cancellation by the Stewards of the Jockey Club exercised under powers contained in Rule 1A.

Passports

32. (i) (a) There must be a passport issued by the British Horseracing Board for named horses foaled prior to January 1st, 1991 which will be issued when they first enter the care of licensed or permitted trainers or otherwise as authorised by the Stewards of the Jockey Club. Except on the instructions of the Stewards of the Jockey Club applications for the issue of Passports for horses foaled in the United Kingdom and the Irish Republic in or after 1977 and prior to January 1st, 1991 must be supported by the Foal Identity and Vaccination Certificate.

(b) Passports issued by the Stud Book Authority for horses foaled after December 31st, 1990 will be revised and re-issued under these Rules when the horse is named or will be issued on the instructions of the Stewards of the Jockey Club.

(c) Passports are returnable on demand and are issued subject to the instructions contained in Appendix G to these Orders and Rules.

(ii) It shall be the responsibility of the trainer to ensure that when any horse trained by him enters property owned, used or controlled by the Managing Executive of a Racecourse its passport is available for inspection at any time while it is on that property.

It is also the responsibility of the trainer of a horse to ensure at all times that vaccinations required under these Rules have been correctly administered and properly endorsed in the passport.

(iii) All fees as laid down by the Directors in connection with the passports are payable in accordance with the schedule in Appendix M.

(iv) When a passport is submitted for endorsement when a horse is to travel abroad the expected date of travel must be given.

Identification Checks

33. (i) When a horse has been declared to run under Rule 141(i) for either.

(a) the first time in Great Britain, or,

(b) when it is trained outside Great Britain

A passport for the horse must be produced and verified by a Veterinary Officer not less than half an hour before the advertised time for the race.

Except that in the case of horses from countries which have not yet adopted passports, the following certificates must be lodged at the Racing Calendar Office or produced for onward transmission to the Racing Calendar Office after verification by a Veterinary Officer not less than half an hour before the advertised time for the race:

1. A certificate of pedigree (exportation certificate) stating the name, pedigree, age, sex, colour and markings of the horse issued and endorsed by a recognised Stud Book Authority or in the absence of a Stud Book Authority by the recognised Turf Authority of the country in which the horse was foaled. This certificate must also be endorsed by a Stud Book Authority or Turf Authority of any further country which the horse has visited prior to importation into Great Britain.

2. A certificate of age and markings signed in Great Britain or Ireland or the Channel Islands by a Veterinary Surgeon who is neither the owner nor the trainer of the horse nor a person whose name is included in the Register of Stable Employees as being employed by the trainer of the horse.

(ii) If the requirements of sub-Rule (i) of this Rule are not satisfied they will apply on every occasion until the documents have been produced and verified.

(iii)A horse may only run for a period of three months following importation, on production of a passport alone. Thereafter a certificate of pedigree (exportation certificate) issued by a recognised Stud Book Authority or Turf Authority must have been lodged at the Racing Calendar Office.

34. (i) Where under Rule 33 certificates of pedigree and age and markings must be lodged at the Racing Calendar Office facsimiles may be sent in lieu of the original documents but the facsimile will not be endorsed for export purposes and the original must be received from the Foreign Stud Book Authority or Turf Authority within two weeks of transmission to the Racing Calendar Office. If the original documents are not received within this time the Stewards of the Jockey Club may at their discretion cancel any registration made or withdraw any passport issued until the original documents are received.

Vaccination

35. (i) No horse shall enter property owned, used or controlled by the Managing Executive of a racecourse unless it is certified by a veterinary surgeon to be correctly vaccinated against equine influenza in accordance with the general requirements of Sub-Rules (ii) and (iii) of this Rule, but this Rule will not apply to horses crossing land used or controlled by the Managing Executive where such land is common ground or is subject to statutory rights for public access for air and exercise, or to any foal which is less than four months old and whose dam was, prior to foaling, vaccinated in accordance with the general requirements of Sub-Rule (ii) of this Rule.

(ii) No horse for which a passport has been issued shall enter property owned, used or controlled by the Managing Executive of a racecourse unless the vaccination section of its passport is endorsed by a veterinary surgeon, who is neither the owner or trainer of the horse, nor a person whose name is included in the Register of Stable Employees as being employed by the trainer of the horse at that time, or by a recognised Turf Authority, that it has received two injections for primary vaccination given no less than 21 days apart and no more than 92 days apart. In addition, where sufficient time has elapsed subsequent to the primary vaccination the passport must be similarly endorsed to show that:-

(a) A horse foaled on or after January 1st, 1980 has received a booster injection given no less than 150 days and no more than 215 days after the second injection of the primary vaccination, and

(b) A horse has received booster injections at intervals Of not more than a year apart (commencing after the second injection of the primary vaccination or the booster injection required under (a) above) or such lesser time as the Stewards of the Jockey Club may, in an emergency, decide, except that for horses foaled before January 1st 1980, the intervals between booster injections given before March 16th, 1981, may have been not more than 14 months.

and that none of these injections has been given within the previous seven days including the day of entry into racecourse property, but excluding the day upon which the injection was given.

N.B. The above are minimum requirements. It is recommended that both primary and first and subsequent booster injections should be given according to the manufacturer's instructions which will automatically fall within the above ruling. In many cases booster injections are recommended at intervals more frequent than 12 months.

(iii) In the case of horses trained in countries where passports are not issued, or in the case of horses for which passports have not been issued and which are brought to a race meeting as companion animals vaccination certificates must be available for inspection and may be accepted,provided that they are in the form of a combined identification certificate correctly identifying the horse and that the certificates have been signed by a Veterinary Surgeon, who is neither the owner or trainer of the horse nor a person whose name is included in the Register of Stable Employees as being employed by the trainer of the horse at that time, stating that it has received the vaccinations required under Sub-Rule (ii) of this Rule and giving the dates of such vaccinations.

36. (i) Except in those cases where Sub-Rule (i) of Rule 35 does not apply, the trainer or the owner of any horse which enters property owned, used or controlled by the Managing Executive of a racecourse when

(a) that horse has not been vaccinated as required under Rule 35, or

(b) the passport is not endorsed as required under Rule 35(ii), or

(c) the passport is not available for inspection as required under Rule 32(ii), or

(d) the combined identification and vaccination certificates are not available for inspection as required under Rule 35

shall be guilty of an offence.

(ii) A passport will not be regarded as being endorsed as required under Rule 35(ii) if on or after January 1st, 1988, any record of vaccination against equine influenza is altered in any way. An incorrect endorsement must be completely deleted and a new endorsement of the whole entry made, signed either by the veterinary surgeon who was responsible for giving the vaccination or by a veterinary surgeon who has received confirmation of the correct date of vaccination either from the veterinary surgeon who gave the vaccination or from the representative of that veterinary surgeon.

(iii) When by reason of a breach of this Rule a horse is not qualified to run and is therefore withdrawn, in imposing any penalty the Stewards shall take account of the fixed penalty consequently imposed under Rule 144.

37. Where in this Part of the Rules of Racing reference is made to the production of passports and/or certificates facsimiles thereof may be produced in substitution provided always that the original documents must be received at the Registry Office within three working days of the facsimile being sent and failure to produce these documents within this time will constitute an offence under the Rules of Racing.

The provisions of Rule 34 are not affected by this Rule.

PART 4: OWNERS, RECOGNISED CLUBS AND COMPANIES, SYNDICATES, PARTNERSHIPS, LEASES, COLOURS

Owners

40. (i) The Stewards of the Jockey Club shall maintain a register of the names of owners of horses. The name of an owner may only be registered by application to the Racing Calendar Office on the prescribed form signed by the owner unless otherwise ordered by the Stewards of the Jockey Club. Except in the case of a recognised Company a fee of £34 (plus V.A.T.) must accompany each application. No company other than a recognised Company may be registered as an owner.

(ii) Registration will be effective on and after the Monday following acceptance of the application. If any registered owner

(a) shall become a disqualified person or

(b) shall have a Bankruptcy Order made against him

his registration shall thereupon become void and if the Stewards of the Jockey Club shall register the name of a person currently disqualified or against whom there is a Bankruptcy Order in force or who is an undischarged bankrupt the registration shall be void. The registration of ownership shall lapse if a registered owner shall not have a horse returned as in training under these Rules for twenty four months.

(iii) The registration of the name of a recognised Company shall become void if the Company ceases to be a recognised Company within the meaning of the Rules.

(iv) In any case where the registration of an Owner has become void and either the disqualification or the Bankruptcy Order has been withdrawn a new application for Registration as an Owner will not be registered until three months have elapsed from the time of withdrawal unless the Stewards of the Jockey Club are satisfied that reasons for voidance disqualification or the issue of a Bankruptcy Order were due to circumstances outside the reasonable control of the Owner.

(v) Except as provided for in Rule 47(xii) no owner shall make use of an assumed name for the purpose of entering or running horses, and any horse entered under an assumed name is liable, on objection, to be disqualified.

(vi) Nothing in these Rules shall prevent the personal representative of a deceased owner running a horse solely under the description 'Executor(s) (or Administrator(s) or Personal Representative) of...deceased". Unless and until called upon by the Stewards to do so, a personal representative need not apply to be put on the register of owners provided that the deceased owner was registered at the time of his death.

Recognised Clubs

41. (i) A "recognised Club" is a Club, whether proprietory or members, which has been approved and registered as a recognised Club' by the Stewards of the Jockey Club.

(ii) A Club may be recognised by the Stewards of the Jockey Club notwithstanding that only a part of its members wish to enter and run a horse provided that in such a case that part of the Club is identifiable and has its own Rules and Regulations, and provided that in such a case every reference to "Club" or "recognised Club" in Sub-Rule (i), paragraphs (b) and (c) of Sub-Rule (iii) and Sub-Rule (v) of this Rule and in Rule 42(iv) shall be deemed to refer both to the Club and to such part of the Club.

(iii) The Stewards of the Jockey Club shall have complete discretion whether to approve and register any Club as a recognised Club or not, save that they shall refuse to approve and register a Club as a recognised Club unless,

(a) they are satisfied that the Club was established for a minimum of two years prior to receipt of the application for registration, for normal social and recreational pursuits and that those pursuits have not and have never had any connection direct or indirect with racehorse ownership anywhere in the world.

(b) they have approved the Rules of the Club and any amendments or additions to or deletions from the Rules required by them have been duly made by the Club:

(c) a list of members of the Club complete as at midnight on the day before lodgement has been lodged at the Registry Office if so required by the Stewards of the Jockey Club.

(iv) A Club shall cease to be a recognised Club upon the decision by the Club, or the Court or by any authorised person, that the Club shall be wound up or dissolved, and its registration shall therefore automatically lapse.

(v) A registration fee shall be paid at the time the application is lodged which will be refunded if the registration thereof is refused.

(vi) Any amendment or addition to or deletion from the Rules of the Club made after the Rules have been approved by the Stewards of the Jockey Club shall be notified to the Stewards of the Jockey Club and the Stewards may at any time require the Club to furnish an up-to-date list of members.

(vii) Without prejudice to the foregoing, the Stewards of the Jockey Club may at their absolute discretion at any time and without assigning any reason therefore withdraw their approval of the Club or such part of the Club as is referred to in Sub-Rule (ii) hereof which thereupon shall cease to be a recognised Club.

(viii) Any unit of Her Majesty's Armed Forces (including any ship's company or any establishment) may at the absolute discretion of the Stewards of the Jockey Club and for so long as they think fit be treated for the purposes of these Rules as a recognised Club. Any unit so treated shall be registered as if it were a recognised Club and the provisions of Sub-Rule(v) hereof and of Rule 42 shall apply to any such unit.

42. (i) A recognised Club may enter and run a horse under its own name provided that the legal ownership of the horse is vested in a body of not more than four trustees on behalf of the Club each of whom has been and is approved by the Stewards of the Jockey Club and each of whose names has been and is registered at the Registry Office. The Stewards of the Jockey Club shall not approve trustees and their names may not be registered unless the Stewards of the Jockey Club have approved any trust deed or other document appointing the trustees and establishing their powers, and unless any amendment or addition to or deletion from the trust deed or other document required by the Stewards of the Jockey Club has been duly made by the Club. Without prejudice to the foregoing the Stewards may at their absolute discretion refuse to approve any trustee without assigning any reason therefor and they may at their absolute discretion at any time and without assigning any reason therefor withdraw the approval of any trustee and cancel the registration of his name.

(ii) The horse shall be entered by one of the trustees or his Authorised Agent but will run under the name of the Club.

(iii) The trustees shall for the purposes of these Rules be treated as though they are joint owners and are subject to all liabilities, duties and privileges of joint ownership.

(iv) The Stewards of the Jockey Club take no cognisance of any disputes arising between the trustees and the members of the Club.

(v) Other than having the privilege of running the horse under the name of the Club no privilege of ownership shall attach to any member of the Club other than the trustees.

Recognised Companies

43. (i) A "recognised Stud Company" means a company incorporated under any statutory enactment and whether with limited or unlimited liability of which the

principal object is to carry on the business of breeding bloodstock and which has been registered at the Registry Office as a "recognised Stud Company".

The Stewards of the Jockey Club shall have complete discretion whether to register a Company as a recognised Stud Company or not save that they shall refuse to register such a Company unless they are satisfied both as to its principal object and that the business of breeding bloodstock is being carried on as a main activity of the Company. The Stewards of the Jockey Club may at their absolute discretion at any time and without assigning any reason therefor cancel the registration of a Company as a recognised Stud Company. A registration fee of £100 (plus V.A.T.) shall be paid at the time the application is lodged, which will be refunded if the registration thereof is refused.

(ii) A recognised Stud Company may enter and run a horse in its ownership through a nominee. Such nominee shall be approved by the Stewards of the Jockey Club who may at their absolute discretion refuse their approval without assigning any reason therefor. They may at their absolute discretion at any time and without assigning any reason therefor withdraw their approval. The name of the nominee when and so long as he is approved by the Stewards of the Jockey Club shall be registered at the Registry Office together with the particulars of the horse concerned. The nominee when registered shall be subject to these Rules in all respects as if he were an owner. A recognised Stud Company may cancel a registration of its nominee only after lodging with the Stewards of the Jockey Club such sum as in the opinion of the Stewards (whose decision shall be final) is sufficient to cover all outstanding liabilities incurred by the nominee in respect of the horse. No horse in the ownership of a recognised Stud Company may fulfil any engagement whilst there is no nominee in respect of it on the Register.

44. (i) This Rule applies to a "recognised Company"' other than a "recognised Stud Company"

(ii) "Recognised Company" means a Company incorporated under any statutory enactment and whether with limited or unlimited liability which has been approved and registered as a "recognised Company" by the Stewards of the Jockey Club.

(iii) A "recognised Company" shall be entitled to apply to the Registry Office, on the prescribed form, for its name to be included on the Register of Owners.

(iv) The Stewards of the Jockey Club shall have complete discretion whether to approve and register any Company as a "recognised Company' or not, save that they shall refuse to approve and register a Company as a "recognised Company" unless:-

(a) they have been provided with a list of the names of the Directors and of the Company Secretary and are satisfied that none of them is a disqualified person.

(b) a copy of each of the following documents has been lodged at the Registry Office if so required by the Stewards of the Jockey Club:-

(i) Memorandum and Articles of Association;
(ii) The Register of Members;
(iii) The latest Annual Report;
(iv) The latest Balance Sheet and Profit and Loss Account

(v) Before giving their approval of any Company as a "recognised Company' the Stewards of the Jockey Club may impose such conditions as they think fit including the provision of guarantees or other security by the Company's Directors or other Officers.

(vi) A registration fee shall be paid at the time the application is lodged which will be refunded if the registration thereof is refused.

(vii) When a Company has been registered as a "recognised Company" the names of any new Directors appointed after registration must be notified to the Registry Office within 21 days of such appointment being made, and any other changes in the Directors or Secretary must also be so notified.

(viii) The Stewards of the Jockey Club may at their absolute discretion at any time and without assigning any reason therefor, withdraw their approval of the Company and cancel its registration as a "recognised Company". Without prejudice to the foregoing, the Stewards of the Jockey Club shall cancel the registration if:-

(a) any Director of the Company is or becomes a disqualified person;

(b) any Officer of the Company fails to furnish to the Stewards of the Jockey Club or the Registry Office such information as they may demand, within a reasonable time;

(c) any registered agent of the Company is or becomes a disqualified person,

any may cancel the registration if:—

(d) the Company shall make any assignment for the benefit of creditors or make any composition with creditors;

(e) any action or proceedings under insolvency or bankruptcy law is taken against the company;

(f) the Company shall be the subject of a voluntary or compulsory liquidation (other than for the purpose of reconstruction or amalgamation);

(g) the Company is made the subject of any administration order or of any proposal under Part 1 of the Insolvency Act 1986 for a composition in satisfaction of its debts.

45. (i) A "recognised Company" shall only be entitled to exercise the powers of an owner through its registered agent.

(ii) A registered agent means a person who is appointed as such by the 'recognised Company", in writing and under due execution either by its Seal or by signature by a director and secretary of the recognised Company, or by two directors of the Company, and expressed to be executed by the Company, and whose appointment has been approved and registered by the Stewards of the Jockey Club at the Registry Office.

(iii) The Stewards of the Jockey Club shall have complete discretion whether to approve and register any person as a registered agent save that they shall not approve and register any person unless they are satisfied that:-

(a) he is not a disqualified person:

(b) he has been duly appointed to act as a registered agent of the "recognised Company".

(iv) If authority to appoint a sub-agent is provided by the document appointing a registered agent any person appointed by the registered agent as sub-agent will be an "Authorised Agent" (see definition section of the Rules) may, unless the appointment of the registered Agent is cancelled, withdrawn or otherwise becomes invalid, make entries, confirmation of entries and declaration for the recognised Company under these Orders and Rules if he has been allotted a security code by the Stewards of the Jockey Club and he may also sign documents as provided under these Orders and Rules on behalf of the recognised Company.

(v) No horse owned by a 'recognised Company" may be entered or fulfil any engagement unless there is in the Register at least one registered agent of that Company.

(vi) The Stewards of the Jockey Club may at their absolute discretion at any time and without assigning any reason therefor, withdraw their approval of any registered agent and cancel his registration. Without prejudice to the foregoing, registration will automatically be cancelled if:-

(a) the registered agent is or becomes a disqualified person;

(b) the registered agent is or becomes bankrupt;

(c) the "recognised Company" ceases, for any reason, to be registered as such.

(d) the payment of the annual fee is in arrear by more than 14 days.

(vii) Registration of a registered agent will be cancelled at the request of the "recognised Company" if, but only if, the request is made in writing and is either under the Company's Seal or is signed by a director and secretary of the Company, or by two directors of the Company, and expressed to be executed by the Company and is accompanied by a copy of a Minute recording the Company's resolution to cancel the said registration.

(viii) A fee in respect of each Registered Agent shall be paid annually

Syndicates

46. (i) A syndicate of not more than 12 persons may share an interest in a horse provided that the legal possession of the horse is vested in not less than three and not more than four members of the syndicate as lessees of the horse from the syndicate.

(ii) The members of the syndicate in whom legal possession of the horse is vested shall be treated and are hereinafter referred to as joint owners and shall be subject to all the liabilities, duties and privileges of joint ownership. Control and management of the horse shall not be exercised by anyone other than members of the syndicate.

(iii) For syndicates registered prior to March 25th 1989 the names of the members of the syndicate and of the joint owners must have been lodged at the Registry Office together with a copy of the agreement between them signed by each member and such further information as the Stewards of the Jockey Club may have required. Subject to the provisions of Sub-Rule (vii) hereof, registration of the agreement will automatically lapse in the event of any change in the membership, shareholding or terms of the syndicate or in the legal possession of the horse.

N.B. On and after 25th March 1989 syndicates will not be accepted for registration.

(iv) The agreement must have included the following details:-

(a) The name and address of each member of the syndicate and the share each member has in the horse.

(b) A statement setting out all financial arrangements agreed between the members and in particular the method of calculating and the timing of payment of any contributions due from members towards training and other expenses.

(c) A declaration that each member has read the Rules of Racing dealing with syndicates and the current Jockey Club instructions relating thereto.

(d) A term imposing upon the joint owners an obligation to keep proper books of account and to send to each member and to the Registry Office a copy of the Annual Accounts duly certified as audited by an Accountant having the qualifications required by Section 389 of the Companies Act, 1985.

(v) Deleted.

(vi) The Stewards of the Jockey Club may order the books of account and the bills, proceeds, vouchers and other documents relating to a syndicate to be examined by such person or persons as they may appoint. If the necessary facilities for such examination are not forthcoming within 14 days of written notice being served on the joint owners, the registration of the syndicate agreement shall automatically lapse. Notice shall be deemed to be served on the joint owners 24 hours after being posted to the last address notified to the Registry Office or, if no address has been notified, then to the address given for them in the agreement.

(vii) No horse in which a syndicate is interested may be entered for any race unless it is the subject of an agreement current at the date of entry. For the purposes of this Sub-Rule an agreement shall be deemed to be current notwithstanding that either:-

(a) a member of the syndicate other than a joint owner has disposed of the whole or part of his share since the agreement was registered provided that no share of any one such member is disposed of more than once in any period of 28 days and provided that notification of each such disposition signed by the transferor and by the transferee and containing a declaration by the transferee that he possesses a copy of the agreement and that he has read the Rules of Racing dealing with syndicates and the current Jockey Club instructions relating thereto is lodged at the Registry Office within 48 hours of the disposition or

(b) a member of the syndicate has died provided that written notification of the death is lodged with the Registry Office within 28 days thereof

unless the Stewards of the Jockey Club by written notice served-in accordance with Sub-Rule (vi) hereof upon the joint owners give notice that at the expiration of 28 days after the date of such notice or such longer period as may be stated in that notice the registration of the agreement previously lodged shall be cancelled and that agreement shall cease to be current within the meaning of this Sub-Rule.

(viii) When a horse in which a syndicate is interested is sold or transferred it shall not be eligible to run until there has been lodged at the Registry Office a memorandum recording the sale and signed by the joint owners. It shall be a breach of the Rules of Racing, unless good cause is shown, for such a memorandum to be submitted more than seven days after the horse is sold or transferred.

(ix) No person may be a member of, or have any interest in, more than 12 syndicates.

(x) The Stewards may at their absolute discretion at any time and without assigning any reason therefor withdraw their approval of any member of a syndicate in which event the registration of the syndicate agreement in respect of that horse will be cancelled.

(xi) A horse in which a syndicate is interested shall not be eligible to be entered for or to run in any race whilst any member of the syndicate is a disqualified person or has a Bankruptcy Order in force against him, or is an undischarged bankrupt and in the event of any such member becoming a disqualified person or having a Bankruptcy Order made against him the registration of any syndicate agreement in respect of that horse shall automatically lapse. This Sub-Rule shall not apply in the case of a Bankruptcy Order or bankruptcy if the syndicate agreement provides for the automatic retirement of a member upon such member having a Bankruptcy Order made against him or becoming bankrupt.

(xii) For the avoidance of any doubt it is hereby expressly declared that nothing in this Rule affects or derogates from the powers of the Stewards of the Jockey Club under Rule 1 (vi).

(xiii) Subject to Rule 112(v) a horse the subject of a Syndicate Agreement may be entered in the name of any of the joint owners.

(xiv) For the purpose of this Rule the expression 'joint owners means the members of the syndicate in whom the legal possession of the horse is vested.

Partnerships, Sales with Contingencies, Leases, etc.

47. The name of the horse must be registered before registration under this Rule can be made and partnerships and leases may only be registered when the partners, of which there shall not be more than twelve, or lessees are registered owners, or are or include recognised Companies or recognised Stud Companies.

(i) When a horse is owned by more than one person or Company other than by syndicates to which the foregoing Rule applies the documents as described hereunder shall be lodged at the Racing Calendar Office or with the Clerk of the Course for transmission to the Racing Calendar Office, whereupon the partnership shall be deemed to be registered unless thereafter the Stewards of the Jockey Club refuse to accept the registration. All partners shall be jointly and severally liable for every stake, forfeit or fee due under these Rules in respect of the horse and shall so remain until a notification of termination has been lodged as described in sub-Rule (ix) of this Rule. No owner shall assign his share, or any part of thereof, in a horse without the consent of his partners.

(ii) The manner of registration and fees payable in respect thereof shall comply with the provisions of Sub-Orders 47(iv) and 47(x).

(iii) A registration under these provisions is subject always to the power of cancellation by the Stewards of the Jockey Club exercised under powers contained in Rule 1A.

(iv) The documents required to be lodged for registration are:-

(a) In the case of a partnership not including a recognised Company or recognised Stud Company, a document stating the name and address of every person having an interest in the horse and the relative proportion of such interest signed by all the partners or their authorised agents;

(b) In the case of a partnership including a recognised company written evidence showing that the company is empowered to enter into partnership, a copy of the partnership agreement duly executed by all the parties thereto; and the names of the registered agents of the company;

(c) In the case of a partnership including a recognised Stud Company written evidence showing that the company is empowered to enter into partnership, a copy of the partnership agreement duly executed by all the parties thereto and the name of the nominee in respect of the horse the subject of the partnership.

(v) Unless the Stewards of the Jockey Club otherwise direct, where a horse is sold with contingencies, leased, or is the subject of any joint arrangement, a document stating the names and addresses of all the parties interested shall be signed and lodged as above and shall state fully the terms of such sale with contingencies, lease, or other arrangement whereupon the sale with contingencies, lease, or other arrangement shall be deemed to be registered unless thereafter the Stewards of the Jockey Club refuse to accept the registration. No party to a lease shall assign his interest in the same without the consent of all other parties to it.

(vi) Where a horse is the property of a partnership, or where it is the subject of any sale with contingencies, lease or arrangement requiring registration under this Rule, registration of the partnership, sale with contingencies, lease or arrangement must have been effected and must not have lapsed before the horse may be entered for any race or run in any race.

(vii) Should a partnership, sale with contingencies, lease or arrangement be entered into after the horse concerned has been entered in a race or races and the horse start for such race or races without the particulars being lodged it shall, on an objection under Rule 170(v) be disqualified, unless it be proved to the satisfaction of the Stewards of the Jockey Club that the omission to lodge the particulars thereof was accidental and unless the Stewards of the Jockey Club certify that they accept the registration thereof, in which case the person responsible for the omission to lodge the particulars shall be fined not less than £95.

(viii) All partnerships, sales with contingencies, leases and other joint arrangements, shall be published in the next available Racing Calendar.

(ix) Upon termination of a partnership for whatever cause there must be lodged at the Racing Calendar Office within 7 days of termination notification of termination signed by at least one of the partners on behalf of the partnership or by the Authorised Agents of all the partners. No horse which was the property of a partnership shall be eligible to run until such notification is lodged. Where there is a change in the membership of a partnership, provided that at least one member of the old partnership continues as a member of the new partnership, registration of the new partnership under this Rule will act as notification of termination of the old partnership.

(x) Registrations under Rule 47 apart from sales with contingencies, are annual, and fees as laid down by the Directors are payable in accordance with the schedule in Appendix M.

(xi) If any partner or lessee ceases to be a registered owner (or where applicable a recognised Company or a recognised Stud Company) any registration effected under this Rule will automatically lapse.

(xii) Subject to Rule 112(v) a horse the property of a partnership may be entered in the name of any of the partners except that, if a partnership name has been registered under Sub-Rule (xiii) of this Rule that partnership name must be given at the time of entry and the horse must run under that name.

(xiii) The Stewards of the Jockey Club shall maintain a register of partnership names. Such names may only be registered by application to the Racing Calendar Office on the prescribed form, signed by all the owners and stating the name(s) of the horse(s) owned by the partnership, unless otherwise ordered by the Stewards of the Jockey Club.

(xiv) A fee must accompany each application and registration will be effective on and after the Monday following acceptance of the application. All partnership names together with the names of the owners in the partnership shall be published in the next available Racing Calendar. In the event of there being any change in the membership of the partnership the registration must be cancelled and a new registration made before any horse owned by the partnership may be entered or run.

Racing Colours

48. (i) Every owner, or part-owner, or partnership in whose name a horse is to run, is required to register colours annually, by application to the British Horseracing Board at the office of the Racing Calendar Office. Colours duly registered shall not be taken by any other person. All disputes as to the right to particular colours shall be settled by the Stewards of the Jockey Club.

(ii) The manner of registration and fees payable in respect thereof shall comply with the provisions of Sub-Order 48(vi).

(iii) A registration under these provisions is subject always to the power of cancellation by the Stewards of the Jockey Club exercised under powers contained in Rule 1A.

(iv) If any owner or partnership runs a horse when colours are not registered for that owner or partnership the Stewards of the Jockey Club will impose a fine of £75 unless the circumstances under which this occurred are acceptable to them.

In the case of horses trained abroad a declaration of colours to the Racing Calendar Office for each race by the time fixed for the closing of entries, or in races closing more than six days before running by the time fixed for confirmation of entries under Order 120(ii) is acceptable in lieu of a registration.

(v) When an owner or partnership has more than one runner in the same race alternative colours may be declared at scale and, where the judge deems it necessary, an owner may be asked to declare alternative colours, but the owner of any horse which otherwise runs in colours other than those registered under these Rules in his name or his partnership name or declared under Sub-Rule(iv) above shall be fined not less than £35 or more than £95 unless the Owner and/or his representative satisfies the Stewards on the day of racing that this is due to circumstances outside their reasonable control.

(iv) Any new registration of racing colours must be made on the form prescribed by the Directors and comply with the instructions contained within except that the Directors may, at their discretion, waive the requirements of those instructions for owners whose colours are registered with a recognised Turf Authority. The annual fee for each registration is as laid down in Appendix M.

Authority to Act

49. The annual fee for each registration of Authority to Act is as laid down in Appendix M. Such fee or any increase or decrease thereof shall be payable on registration and annually thereafter. Registration will remain in force either

(a) until cancelled in writing by the Owner or Authorised Agent or

(b) the payment of the annual fee is in arrear by more than 14 days

(ii) The appointment of an Authorised Agent shall be made by a document signed by the appointor and lodged at the Racing Calendar Office or in urgent cases by telegram, telex or facsimile message. When an Authorised Agent is appointed by telegram, telex or facsimile message the appointment will automatically be cancelled unless a document signed by the appointor confirming such appointment is lodged at the racing Calendar Office within 21 days of receipt of the telegram, telex or facsimile message.

(iii) An Authorised agent shall be permitted to appoint a sub-agent if authority to appoint a sub-agent is provided by the document signed by the appointors appointing the Authorised Agent but such sub-agent will only be qualified to make entries, confirmation of entries and declarations under these Rules if he has been allotted a security code by the Directors. An Authorised Agent appointed by telegram, telex or facsimile message is not authorised to appoint a sub-agent until the confirmation is received including such authority. On a sale with engagements with Authorised Agent of the vendor shall be deemed to be the Authorised Agent of the purchaser but only in respect of all entries already made but not closed at the time of sale.

(iv) The annual fee for each registration of Authority to Act as a Rider's Agent is as laid down in Appendix M. Such fee or any increase or decrease thereof shall be payable on registration and annually thereafter. Registration will remain in force until cancelled in writing by the rider subject to the overriding powers of the Stewards of the Jockey Club under Rule 1A(vii).

(v) The appointment of an Authorised Rider's Agent shall be made by a document signed by the rider and lodged at the Racing Calendar Office or in urgent cases by facsimile message or telex. When an Authorised Rider's Agent is appointed by facsimile message or telex the appointment will be automatically cancelled unless a document signed by the rider confirming such appointment is lodged at the Racing Calendar Office within 21 days of receipt of the facsimile message or telex.

(vi) The manner of registration and fees payable in respect thereof shall comply with the provisions of Sub-Orders 49(i), (ii), (iii), (iv) and (v).

(vii) A registration under these provisions is subject always to the power of cancellation by the Stewards of the Jockey Club exercised under powers contained in Rule 1A.

PART 5: TRAINERS

50. (i) Every trainer in Great Britain of a horse running under these Rules must obtain from the Stewards of the Jockey Club, subject to such restrictions and conditions as they consider necessary, either

(a) a licence, to be applied for annually on the prescribed form which may be granted for any period up to a year, or

(b) a permit, in the case of a person training only those horses for steeple chases, hurdle races or National Hunt Flat races which are the sole property (free of all leases or other joint arrangement, except those between persons for whom he is entitled to train) of himself, his spouse, parents, sons or daughters (or the Executors or Administrators of such persons), to be applied for each season on the prescribed form, which may be granted for any period up to a year,

except that, for the purpose of Hunters' Steeple Chases, the Grand Military Gold Cup and the Royal Artillery Gold Cup, a horse may also be trained privately without licence or permit (subject to the provisions of Rule 186) by the proprietor of the stable from whence the horse was regularly and fairly hunted during the current season, but in that event the owner shall be treated as trainer for all purposes under these Rules. Where the owner is a registered Company the registered Agent appointed in accordance with Rule 45 and who made the entry shall be treated as the trainer.

(ii) The fees (including V.A.T.) to be paid in respect of each licence or permit shall be such as the Stewards of the Jockey Club shall from time to time decide. The sum of £12 from each fee for a licence and £6 from each fee for a permit shall be allocated to the Jockey Club Charities as directed by the Trustees of the Jockey Club Charitable Trust.

(iii) Every trainer will be issued with an Identity Card to enable him to enter racecourse stables, If he is unable to produce that card to gain admission to the stables and the Clerk of the Course issues him with an authorisation to enter the trainer shall be fined not less than £65.

A fee is payable for the replacement of a lost Identity Card.

(iv) A licensed or permitted trainer who is unable to attend a meeting where he has a runner may authorise another trainer, licensed for the same type of races, to enter racecourse stables on his behalf, whether or not that trainer has a horse running at the meeting.

To be admitted to racecourse stables the trainer concerned must produce his own Identity Card together with a letter from the trainer of the horse authorising him to act on his behalf, giving his name, the date, the racecourse and the name of the horse.

51. Every trainer shall conduct his business of training racehorses with reasonable care and skill and with due regard to the interests of his owners and to the safety of his employees and agents and of the horses in his charge.

For the avoidance of any doubt reasonable care and safety under this Rule extends to any horse under the care or control of a trainer whether or not currently in training.

52. (i) The following provisions of this Rule shall apply only where a Training Agreement has been entered into either:—

(a) in the form of Training Agreement Form (TA1), and registered at the racing Calendar Office by the trainer prior to 1st June, 1992, or

(b) in the form of Training Agreement Form (TA3), duly signed by the trainer and owner on and after 1st June, 1992,

and also where it is claimed there are changes to the terms set out in either such form and these have been notified by the trainer to the owner on the prescribed Change of Fee to Training Agreement form TA2 or TA4 respectively. Changes to the terms of an agreement in form TA1 shall only be valid for the purpose of this Rule if they shall have been so notified on form TA2 prior to the 1st June, 1992.

(ii) Any trainer who has not received settlement of an account for training fees and additional charges due from an owner for whom he trains or has trained horses within three months of the date of despatch of the account may, report the matter to the Stewards of the Jockey Club within fifteen months of the expiration of the three months period. Such report shall be in writing, signed by the trainer concerned, giving details of the name and address of the owner, the nature and the amount of the debt, the date upon which the account was rendered together with a copy of the unpaid account(s) which are the subject of the report.

(iii) Provided that the last sub-Rule 52(i) has been complied with and that the account related to training fees and extra charges incurred within the period commencing not more than eighteen months from the date when the account was rendered, the Keeper of the Match Book shall, upon receipt of a complaint, notify the owner concerned that payment should be made or a written explanation sent to the Stewards of the Jockey Club within eight days of the despatch of the notification.

(iv) Should the owner fail to make the payment or should the Stewards of the Jockey Club consider that his explanation is not satisfactory the total amount due, including V.A.T. if appropriate will, after thirty days have elapsed from the date of the despatch of the notification, be considered to be arrears due under these Rules and his name will be added to the Forfeit List.

(v) It shall be a breach of the Rules of Racing for a trainer to submit an unjustified or frivolous report,

(vi) A Training Agreement will lapse if the owner has not had a horse in training for twenty-four months with the trainer with whom he had entered into the Agreement or for twelve months if such trainer has relinquished his licence or it has been revoked or withdrawn.

N.B. 1. On and after 1st June, 1992 Training Agreements will not be accepted for registration at the Racing Calendar Office and (for the purposes of this Rule) the validity of all Training Agreements registered prior to that date will cease on 31st May, 1994.

2. From 1st June, 1992 trainers, who wish to effect changes to those training Agreements (TA1) registered prior to 1st June, 1992, must enter into a new agreement on the prescribed Training Agreement Form (TA3) as opposed to notifying the owner on the Change of Fee Form (TA4).

53. (i) When any horse has been declared to run under Rule 141 (i) and has been the subject of an examination under Rule 14(vi) and the result of an analysis of any sample of its tissue, body fluid or excreta is positive, the stewards of the Jockey Club shall impose a fine upon the trainer of the horse in question and may, at their discretion, withdraw his licence or permit. However, the Stewards of the Jockey Club may waive the fine if the trainer satisfies them that the substance was not administered by him or by any other person whatsoever, whether connected with the trainer or not intentionally and that he had taken all reasonable precautions to avoid a breach of this Rule.

Note. The Rule imposes, and is intended to impose, an absolute and strict liability on the Trainer to ensure that prohibited substances are not administered by anyone whether in any way connected with the Trainer or not. Thus the Rule imposes a mandatory fine on the simple basis of a positive analysis for a prohibited substance.

The second part of Rule 53(i) provides for circumstances where the administration of a prohibited substance is accidental (e.g. theobromine in feed) and where the Trainer has taken all reasonable care. This part of the Rule is to be construed as permitting the Stewards to waive the fine where they are satisfied the substance was not administered intentionally by the Trainer or by any other person whatsoever whether connected with the Trainer or not.

(ii) A result of an analysis of any tissue, excreta or body fluid is positive where the analysis shows the presence in the sample of any Prohibited Substance unless the concentration of such substance is below the threshold level for that substance established from time to time by the Stewards of the Jockey Club.

54. (i) No trainer shall employ any person to work in his stable who has previously been employed in a training stable without referring to the last trainer to employ him and receiving a reply. Any person prevented by this Rule from obtaining or retaining employment shall have the right to appeal to the Stewards of the Jockey Club.

(ii) The Stewards of the Jockey Club shall maintain a Register of the names of Stable Employees. The name of an employee with his employer may only be registered by application to the Registry Office on the prescribed form signed by the trainer, or in his absence from Great Britain, by his Authorised Agent, and the employee and no person may continue to be employed by a trainer unless a duly completed application form is despatched to the Registry Office within 24 hours of the commencement of his employment. This sub-Rule also applies where, with the approval of the Local Education Authority, schoolchildren are employed on a part-time basis.

(iii) Racehorse Attendants' Identity Cards and Validity Passes, which will enable the bearers to enter racecourse stables, will only be issued to persons whose names are duly registered under Sub-Rule (ii) of this Rule. Application for a Racehorse Attendants' Identity Card and Validity Pass must be made on the prescribed form, signed by the trainer, to the Registry Office. Racehorse Attendants' Identity Cards and Validity Passes are the property of the Jockey Club, are returnable on demand and may be granted subject to conditions, refused or cancelled at any time at the absolute discretion of the Stewards of the Jockey Club.

(iv) Fees as laid down by the Directors are payable in accordance with the Schedule in Appendix M for:—

(a) for the initial issue and each renewal of a Racehorse Attendant's Identity Card and Validity Pass:

(b) for the replacement of a Racehorse Attendants' Identity Card and/or Validity Pass which is lost:

(v) Save when they are reasonably required for production to any person entitled to inspect them Racehorse Attendants' Identity Cards and Validity Passes shall be kept in the possession and custody of the trainer but on termination of employment such cards must be returned to the Registry Office immediately.

(vi) Any trainer infringing this Rule shall be reported to the Stewards of the Jockey Club.

(vii) If any employee of a trainer is unable to produce his Racehorse Attendant's Identity Card and Validity Pass to gain admission to racecourse stables the Clerk of the Course may, if he is satisfied as to the employment of the person concerned, issue an authorisation for him to enter stables, but the trainer shall be fined not less than £65.

N.B. For the purposes of this Rule, trainer shall be understood to mean a person holding a licence or permit to train under Rule 50.

55. (i) Every licensed trainer is required to contribute to a pension scheme or arrangement in respect of each employee who is aged 26 or over and who has prior to the annual renewal date of the scheme completed five or more years employment with licensed or permitted trainers since first registration as a stable employee. Such contributions must be at a rate not less than that established by the National Trainer's Federation from time to time. This Order will be satisfied where the contribution is made to the National Trainer's Federation Personal Pension Scheme or the National Trainer's Federation Group Pension Scheme or to a pension plan established either by the employer or by the employee. Where licensed trainers or their employees take out a pension scheme or personal pension plan other than those established by the National Trainer's Federation, the trainer will be required to declare to the Jockey Club that contributions at no less a level than the rate established by the National Trainers' Federation are being and/or will be paid.

(ii) Every licensed and permitted trainer is required to contribute towards the Racing Industry (Accident) Benefit Scheme.

(iii) Payments due for the National Trainers' Federation Personal Pension Scheme or the National Trainers' Federation Group Pension Scheme and the Racing Industry (Accident) Benefit Scheme constitute sums due under these Orders. Payments due from permitted trainers who have entered the National Trainers' Federation Personal Pension Scheme are also due under these Orders.

56. If a trainer becomes a disqualified person his licence or permit is thereby revoked, except that if the disqualification is incurred under Rule 137 his licence or permit shall remain valid for a period of 14 days from the date of publication in the Forfeit List after which it shall be revoked unless the disqualification has been rescinded before that period has elapsed.

57. Every horse sent by a trainer to an equine swimming pool shall be deemed to be in the care of the trainer whilst visiting the pool, whether it is an Approved pool or otherwise, and the trainer will be held responsible for any breach of the Rules committed in relation to the horse whilst so visiting.

58. It shall be the duty of the trainer to check the identity of any horses in his care from the markings shown in the horse's passport as soon as the passport is received. In the case of unnamed horses foaled in the United Kingdom or the Irish Republic it shall be the trainer's duty to check the identity of the horse from the markings shown on the horse's Foal Identity and Vaccination Certificate.

59. (i) Trainers must notify the Racing Calendar Office of the arrival of new horses, or changes in ownership of horses in their care on the prescribed forms before further entries are made or within three days of the horses' arrival in the yard or the change of ownership, whichever is the lesser. Trainers must also correct and return the lists of horses in training sent to them from the Racing Calendar Office at intervals throughout the year.

Note - The prescribed forms are:-
Arrival of new horses - Licensed trainers - Form N1
Arrival of new horses - Permitted trainers - Form N1TP
Changes of ownership - all trainers - Form N2

(ii) When a trainer reports the arrival of a horse from abroad he must:

(a) Obtain details of the horse's racecourse performances and send them to the Racing Calendar Office as required under Order 113(v).

(b) If the horse was foaled outside Great Britain or Ireland complete a naming card and send it with the horse's passport to the Racing Calendar Office having first identified the horse in accordance with Rule 58 and the Instructions contained in the passport. (If the trainer does not receive a passport for such a horse a naming card must still be submitted). The passport will be returned to the trainer after any acceptable amendments to markings have been carried out. The passport must still be produced on the racecourse in accordance with Rule 33 of the Rules of Racing.

PART 6: RIDERS LICENCES AND PERMITS

60. Subject to the provisions of Rule 61 no person shall ride in any race under these Rules unless he has attained the age of sixteen years and he has obtained from the Stewards of the Jockey Club, subject to such restrictions as they consider necessary, a licence or permit as follows:-

(i) A Flat race jockey's licence, to be applied for annually on the prescribed form which may be granted for a period of not more than fifteen months.

(ii) A Steeple Chase and Hurdle race jockey's licence, to be applied for each season on the prescribed form.

(iii) A Flat race apprentice jockey's licence. A joint application for such licences must be made annually by the trainer and the employee on the prescribed form and may be granted for a period of not more than fifteen months. They are only granted in respect of employees who have, of their own free will, and if they are under the age of eighteen with the consent of their parents or guardians, signed an Apprentice Riding Agreement (on the standard agreement form as prescribed by the Stewards of the Jockey Club) with a trainer licensed to train horses for Flat races under these Rules and are over sixteen, but under twenty-five years of age.

On attaining the age of twenty-five no person may ride as an apprentice jockey.

In the event of either:-

the Apprentice Riding Agreement being cancelled by consent, or

the apprentice jockey leaving the trainer's establishment without the trainer's consent, express or implied, or the trainer relinquishing his licence or having it suspended or withdrawn or revoked, or the Apprentice Riding Agreement terminating for any other reason the apprentice jockey's licence shall forthwith be automatically revoked, save that

In the event of the death of the trainer, the apprentice jockey's licence shall remain in force for seven clear days from the date of death and thereafter shall be automatically revoked.

During the seven days' period the apprentice jockey shall be answerable to the Stewards of the Jockey Club in the same manner as he would otherwise have been answerable to the trainer.

(iv) A Steeple Chase and Hurdle Race Conditional Jockey's licence, the holder of which will also be qualified to ride in National Hunt Flat races unless his licence is issued subject to his being restricted to riding in steeplechases and hurdle races. Such licence must be applied for each season jointly by the trainer and the employee on the prescribed form and will only be granted in respect of an employee who has, of his own free will, and if he is under the age of eighteen, with the consent of his parents or guardian, signed a Conditional Jockey's Agreement (on the standard agreement form as prescribed by the Stewards of the Jockey Club) with a trainer licensed or permitted to train horses for Steeple Chases, Hurdle races, and National Hunt Flat races, is over sixteen but under twenty-five years of age and who is entitled to claim an allowance of 7lbs under the provisions of Rule 109(ii)(a).

Should a person holding a Conditional Jockey's licence lose his right to claim an allowance of 7lbs under the provisions for Rule 109(ii)(a), either by reaching the age of 25 years or by having ridden 55 winners, the licence and Conditional Jockey's Agreement shall nevertheless continue in force for three calendar months or until the expiry date whichever is the earlier, unless the Agreement is terminated by either party by giving seven day's written notice to the other.

In the event of either:-

the Conditional Jockey's Agreement being cancelled by consent, or

the Conditional Jockey leaving the trainer's establishment with or without the trainer's consent, or the trainer relinquishing his licence or permit or having it suspended, withdrawn or revoked, or the Conditional Jockey's Agreement terminating for any other reason the Conditional Jockey's licence shall forthwith be automatically revoked, save that

In the event of the death of the trainer, the Conditional Jockey's licence shall remain in force for seven clear days from the date of death and thereafter shall be automatically revoked.

During the seven days period the Conditional jockey shall be answerable to the Stewards of the Jockey Club in the same way as he would otherwise have been answerable to the trainer.

(v) A "Category A" Amateur Rider's Permit, to be applied for on the prescribed form annually each July. Holders of these permits may ride only in any Flat race, Steeple Chase or Hurdle race confined to Amateur Riders.

(vi) A "Category B" Amateur Rider's Permit, to be applied for on the prescribed form annually each July. Holders of these permits may ride in Flat races confined to Amateur Riders, in all Steeple Chases and Hurdle races except those confined to licensed jockeys and in all National Hunt Flat Races.

61. (i) This Rule only applies to riders (including apprentice jockeys) who are the holders of a current licence or permit to ride issued by a recognised Turf Authority, who are not suspended from riding by the Stewards of the Jockey Club or by a recognised Turf Authority and who are not the holders of a licence or permit to ride granted by the Stewards of the Jockey Club.

(Note - Apprentices holding licences from the Irish Turf Club and riding under this Rule may claim riding allowances under Rule 109(i)).

(ii) Subject to Sub-Rule (iii) upon production to the Clerk of the Scales of his current licence or permit, or proof that he holds such licence or permit, together with his Medical Record Book, if he holds a licence or permit from a Turf Authority which issues such documents, and a clearance from his turf Authority if his licence or permit is issued by a Turf Authority of a country not listed in Jockey Club Instruction J2, any rider to whom this Rule applies shall be entitled to ride in any race under these Rules for which his licence or permit would qualify him to ride if it was being run under the Rules of the Turf Authority which issued his licence or permit, subject to such restrictions or conditions as the Stewards of the Jockey Club may consider necessary.

(iii) In their absolute discretion, the Stewards of the Jockey Club may refuse to permit a rider to whom this Rule applies to ride in any or any particular race or races under these Rules and in particular may refuse such permission to any rider who has been resident in Great Britain for more than thirty days.

(iv) It shall be an offence for any rider to whom this Rule applies to ride in any or any particular race or races (as the case may be) under these Rules after he has been duly notified of the decision of the Stewards of the Jockey Club refusing him permission to ride therein.

62. (i) The following persons are not eligible to hold Amateur Rider's permits:

(a) A person who has ever held a professional rider's licence from any recognised Turf Authority except where that person held one or more of the following licences for a period of not more than thirty months from the date of issue of his first licence. (Subject to part (c) of this Sub-Rule.)

1. An Apprentice Jockey's licence.
2. A Conditional Jockey's licence issued under Rule 60(iv) of these Rules.

3. A Steeple Chase and Hurdle Race Jockey's licence issued prior to July 1978.

For the purposes of the exception in this Sub-Rule, the Stewards of the Jockey Club may recognise, at their discretion, an equivalent or similar professional rider's licence issued by a recognised Turf Authority.

(b) A person who has otherwise ever been paid directly or indirectly for riding in a race, with the exception of expenses approved by the Stewards of the Jockey Club as set out in Appendix F to these Orders and Rules and any trophy advertised in the conditions of the race to be given to a rider.

(c) A person whose principal paid occupation is or at any time within the last twelve months has been to ride or groom for a licensed or permitted trainer.

(d) A person who is or who within the last twelve months has been paid as a Huntsman, Kennel Huntsman, or as a Whipper-In.

(ii) It shall be a breach of the Rules of Racing for a jockey during the term of his Licence, or a jockey riding under the provisions of Rule 61, to

(a) Be the owner or part-owner of any horse being entered or run under these Rules or the Rules of any recognised Turf Authority with the exception of horses taking part in Hunter's Steeple Chases only.

(b) (1) bet or instruct any person on his behalf to bet on horseracing.

(2) receive knowingly from any person the proceeds, or any part thereof, of any bet on horseracing.

(These sub-rules apply to any bet regardless of where the bet is placed or horserace is run.)

(c) Receive presents in connection with a race wherever run from persons other than the owner of the horse he rides in that race.

(iii) It shall be a breach of the Rules of Racing for the holder of an amateur rider's permit, or an amateur rider riding under the provision of Rule 61, to

(a) bet or instruct any person on his behalf to bet on any race in which he is riding

(b) receive knowingly from any person the proceeds, or any part thereof, of a bet on any race in which he is riding.

(iv) It shall be a condition of a Jockey's licence and an amateur rider's permit and of riders being entitled to ride under the provisions of Rule 61 that the Jockey or rider shall submit to a medical examination ordered by the Stewards under Rule 14(xi) and shall supply or allow to be taken such samples of blood, urine or other body fluid as are required by the Medical Officer in the course of such examination. It shall be a breach of the Rules of Racing for a jockey or an amateur rider without reasonable cause to refuse to submit to such medical examination or to refuse to supply or allow to be taken samples of blood, urine or other body fluid required by the Medical Officer.

Fees

63. Fees as laid down by the Directors are payable in accordance with the schedule in Appendix M for:—

(i) Flat Race Jockey's licence;

(ii) Steeple Chase and Hurdle Race Jockey's licence;

(iii) Flat Race Apprentice Jockey's licence (to be paid by the trainer);

(iv) Conditional Jockey's licence (to be paid by the trainer);

(v) Category "A- Amateur Rider's Permit;

(vi) Category "B" Amateur Rider's Permit;

and sums subscribed to the Jockey Club Charities shall be allocated as directed by the Trustees of the Jockey Club Charitable Trust.

64. No jockey or amateur rider other than those riding under the provisions of Rule 61 may ride in any race unless he has obtained a Medical Record Book from the Stewards of the Jockey Club. The holder of the Medical Record Book must produce it to the person appointed by the Clerk of the Course before presenting himself to the Clerk of the Scales to be weighed for any race for which he is to ride and if he fails to do so will be fined not less than £30 unless he satisfies the Stewards on the day of racing that this is due to circumstances outside his reasonable control. Medical Record Books are returnable to the Stewards of the Jockey Club on demand and are issued subject to the instructions contained therein. A fee is payable for the replacement of a Medical Record Book.

General

65. Any horse ridden in a race in contravention of Rules 60, 61 or 66 of these Rules shall, on objection, be liable to be disqualified by the Stewards of the Jockey Club.

66. (i) A rider who has been suspended from riding at a racecourse under Rule 153(iii)(a) shall not ride in any race during the period of such suspension.

(ii) An amateur rider or jockey whose permit or licence has been suspended by the Stewards of the Jockey Club shall not ride in any race during the period of his suspension.

(iii) Where an amateur rider or jockey has been suspended from riding by any recognised Turf Authority he shall not ride in any race during the period of his suspension unless the Stewards of the Jockey Club declare that the suspension shall not have effect under these Rules. An application to the Stewards of the Jockey Club for such a declaration may be made by the rider or jockey the subject of suspension provided he has exhausted all procedures for appeal available under the Rules of the recognised Turf Authority. The application must be made in writing to the Registry Office within 48 hours of the final dismissal of appeal under the Rules of the recognised Turf Authority, or, (if there is no procedure for appeal) within 48 hours of the order of suspension. An application received after this time will only be considered if the Stewards of the Jockey Club are satisfied that it has been made at the earliest opportunity and that it was not possible for it to have been made within the time limit.

(iv) A rider who has been declared unfit to ride by a Medical Officer or has been declared unfit to ride under the Jockey Club Regulations for Point-to-Point Steeple Chases may not ride in a race for such period as is specified in the declaration, or, if no period is specified, until he is passed as fit to ride by a Medical Officer.

(v) If an amateur rider or jockey becomes a disqualified person his permit or licence is thereby revoked.

67. A list of amateur riders and licensed jockeys shall be published in the Racing Calendar.

68. Every amateur rider is required to contribute to the Amateur Riders' Insurance Scheme, established by the Amateur Riders Association of Great Britain and the Lady Jockeys' Association of Great Britain Ltd., with the approval of the Jockey Club, and payments due from him in respect of the Scheme constitute sums due under these Rules.

69. (i) No person may act as a Master Jockeys' Valet or a Master Valets' Assistant unless he has obtained the appropriate licence or permit from the Stewards of the Jockey Club, which may be issued subject to such restrictions and conditions as they consider necessary. Licences and permits must be applied for annually on January 1st on the prescribed forms. The annual fee for a Master Valet's licence and the annual fee for a Master Valet's Assistant's permit are as laid down by the Directors in Appendix M and such fees must accompany every application.

(ii) Those holding Master Valet's licences and Master Valet's Assistants' permits will be paid a daily attendance entitlement from the Jockeys' Valets' Attendance Fund on the occasions that they attend and provide their services at race meetings, at a rate to be decided from time to time by the Directors.

(iii) During the term of his licence or permit no Master Jockeys' Valet or Master Valet's Assistant may, at any meeting which he is attending in his capacity as a Master Valet or Master Valet's Assistant,

(a) bet on horseracing or

(b) associate or communicate with bookmakers or their staff on property owned, used or controlled by the Managing Executive of the racecourse,

and any Master Valet or Master Valet's Assistant who may be proved to the satisfaction of the Stewards of the Jockey Club have contravened the requirements of this Sub-Rule is liable to have his licence or permit withdrawn.

(iii) If a Master Valet or a Master Valet's Assistant becomes a disqualified person his licence or permit is thereby revoked.

(iv) A list of Master Valets and Master Valet's Assistants who have received licences or permits shall be published in the Racing Calendar.

PART 7: RIDERS FEES, EXPENSES AND RETAINERS

Fees and Expenses

70. In Flat races the fee to a Jockey, or a Jockey riding under the provisions of Rule 61, shall be £54 (plus V.A.T. where applicable except that in the case of Apprentice Jockeys the fee shall be inclusive of V.A.T. where applicable).

71. In Steeple Chases, Hurdle races and National Hunt Flat races the fee to a Jockey, or a Jockey riding under the provisions of Rule 61, shall be £73.70 (plus V.A.T. where applicable except that in the case of Conditional Jockeys the fee shall be inclusive of V.A.T. where applicable).

72. In Steeple Chases, Hurdle races and National Hunt Flat races other than those restricted to Amateur Riders:
A fee of £73.70 shall be paid to the British Horseracing Board when an Amateur rider, or an Amateur rider riding under the provisions of Rule 61, who has had more than 75 rides in this country in races open to professional riders rides a horse other than those the sole property of himself, his spouse, his mother, or his father.

73. A jockey's fee or fee in respect of an Amateur rider is payable when the rider has weighed out for, and is fit to ride in, a race, except where

(i) by the time fixed for declaration under Rule 141 that race has been abandoned or the declaration under Rule 141(i) withdrawn or

(ii) the horse is prevented from running because the vaccination requirements under Rule 35 have not been satisfied by the time fixed for weighing under Rule 141(vi).

74. Except when a Jockey is riding under the provisions of Rule 61 on each occasion when a jockey's fee becomes payable under Order 70 the owner shall pay a sum the equivalent of 10% of the fee to the Trustees of the Professional Riders Insurance Scheme for application under the Trusts thereof, and on each occasion when a jockey's fee becomes payable under Order 71 or a fee in respect of an Amateur Rider becomes payable under Order 72 the owner shall pay a sum the equivalent of 12 1/2% of the fee to the trustees of the Professional Riders Insurance Scheme, for application under the Trusts thereof.

75. Except when a jockey is riding under the provisions of Rule 61 on each occasion when an apprentice jockey's fee becomes payable under Order 70 the apprentice jockey and his employer shall each pay a sum of 50 pence per ride to the Jockey Club for apprentice training.

PART 8: RACECOURSES AND MEETINGS

Licences and Fixtures

80. (i) Managing Executives of Racecourses must obtain from the Stewards of the Jockey Club a Racecourse licence, to be applied for annually on the prescribed form, which may be granted subject to such restrictions and conditions as the Stewards of the Jockey Club consider necessary or desirable.

(ii) The Managing Executive to whom a Racecourse Licence has been granted shall:

(a) be responsible for the condition of the course and fences and for ensuring that the course is properly measured and marked.

(b) ensure that a Parade Ring is provided.

(c) comply with the requirements of these Rules, Orders and General instructions, as notified to them directly or through the Clerk of the Course, unless and to the extent that they may have been waived in writing by the Stewards of the Jockey Club.

(d) permit the Inspector of Courses to carry out such inspections as he might reasonably require;

(e) give the Stewards of the Jockey Club within a reasonable time such information as they may demand:

(f) take all reasonable steps to ensure that the Clerk of the Course discharges his obligations under the Rules, the Orders and General Instructions or such requirements of the Rules, Orders and General Instructions as are delegated to him by the Managing Executive.

(g) arrange for the publication of a daily official card of the races containing such particulars as the Stewards of the Jockey Club may require.

(h) In the event that the Stewards of the Jockey Club receive a report indicating that the Managing Executive has failed to comply with the provisions of Rule 80 they shall convene an enquiry to be attended by the Managing Executive and any witnesses it may wish to call; if the enquiry concludes that there has been such a failure the Managing Executive shall be liable to a fine and the licence granted for its racecourse may be suspended or withdrawn.

81. No authorised race meeting in Great Britain may be held at any place or on any track which is not licensed by the Stewards of the Jockey Club for that purpose.

82. Managing Executives requiring fixtures for their Racecourse for the following year must send to the British Horseracing Board Office by June 1st of the current year a Statement of accounts for the preceding year made up to December 31st on a form prescribed by the Directors, and obtainable at the offices of the British Horseracing Board. Such statement must be certified by a Chartered or Certified Accountant.

PART 9: PROGRAMMES, HANDICAPS AND SELLING RACES

General Regulations for Programmes

90. (i) The conditions of every race must be published in the Racing Calendar before closing and no alterations can be made in the conditions of any race after such publication except as provided in Sub-Order (v) of this Order. This Order shall not preclude the addition of more money to a race at any time before the start of a race subject to the approval of the Directors.
The advertisement before closing must state:—

- — the dates on which the meeting is to be held;
- — if it is to be held on an All Weather Track;
- — the dates for closing the races;
- — if there is a declaration of forfeit, when the weights for the handicaps will be published;
- — the time from which penalties for winning will be incurred;
  and,
- — the dates for confirmation of entries and declarations to run under Order 120.

It must also state the names of four or more persons as Stewards and the names of the Clerk of the Course, Clerk of the Scales, Judge, Starter, Stewards' Secretaries, Veterinary Officer and Betting Intelligence Officer. If a parade is intended for any race it must be included in the advertisement but in no case shall there be a parade for a race for two year olds.

(ii) A race (other than a Pattern race, Listed race or a race which closes more than six days before running) may be declared void if less than 5 entries are received by the Racing Calendar Office. Only one such race may be declared void at any one race meeting except with the express permission of the Directors.
NOTE: For the purposes of this Order, an entry for a horse which is not qualified at the time of entry shall not count.

(iii) Conditions of races shall provide that:-

(a) The liability at any monetary stage and the total liability for runners shall be in accordance with the scales laid down from time to time by the Directors.

(b) The minimum guaranteed prize money in all races shall be not less than that laid down from time to time by the Directors;

(c) The value of prizes not in money other than those given under the provisions of sub-Order (iv)(c) of this Order must be advertised.

(iv) (a) In Flat races with six prizes and Steeple Chase and Hurdle race Grade 1 Pattern races and other Steeple Chases with guaranteed prize money of £10,000 or more with six prizes the whole stakes may be divided as set out in sub-Orders (ii) (c) or (d) of Order 194. Prizes given specifically to the trainer, rider, breeder or stable in the conditions of the race shall not be included in the calculation.

(b) In other races in which the guaranteed prize money is £4000 or more, all novice steeple chases, or in other races in which by permission of the Directors a fourth prize is given, the whole stakes shall be divided as set out in either Sub-Order (i)(a), (ii)(a), (ii)(b), (iii)(a), or (iv)(a) of Order 194. Prizes given specifically to the trainer, rider, breeder or stable in the conditions of the race shall not be included in the calculation.

(c) In all other races the whole stakes shall be divided as set out in either Sub-Order (i)(b), (iii)(b) or (iv)(b) of Order 194. Prizes given specifically to the trainer, rider, breeder, or stable in the conditions of the race shall not be included in the calculation.

(d) No prize shall be given to persons other than those permitted in Order 194 but with the approval of the Directors, additional prizes may be given to trainers, riders, breeders or stables of the first six horses placed. Such prizes must be included in the conditions of the race.

(v) In the event of any part of the conditions of a race being omitted from the advertisement the Directors shall give such directions as may seem to them in the circumstances to be just.

Regulations for Programmes for Flat Races

91. At every meeting at which Flat races are advertised the following Orders for programmes shall apply for Flat races.

Distribution of Prize Money

(i) One-half at least of the guaranteed prize money shall be apportioned to races of a mile or over for three years old or upwards, and of the sum so apportioned not less than a half shall be for races of a mile and a quarter or upwards but where more than one meeting is held at the same place during the current racing season, the apportionment may be calculated over each meeting or over all the meetings.

Restrictions on Running

(ii) (a) Yearlings shall not run for any race.

(b) There shall be no race of less distance than five furlongs

(c) No horse once it has won a total of three Claiming races in a calendar year shall be qualified to run in a Claiming race until the following calendar year.
NOTE: Wins in Claiming races prior to the start of the 1993 Flat Turf season will not count.

(iii) Except with the permission of the Directors the following restrictions shall apply to two years old races:- Before August 1st there shall not be more than two races confined to two years old in a programme of six races, or more than three such races in a programme of seven races. On and after August 1st there shall not be more than three such races in any programme. In addition, two-year olds shall not run:

(a) before racing on turf commences in any year;

(b) more than five furlongs before the York May Meeting;

(c) more than six furlongs before the Royal Ascot Meeting;

(d) more than seven furlongs before the York August Meeting;

(e) for handicaps before July 1st, nor in handicaps with older horses;

(f) in any race with selling conditions, after having won two such races;

(g) in any race with guaranteed prize money of more than £12,000 before the Epsom Summer Meeting.

General

(iv) (a) There shall not be more than one race per day with selling conditions at any race meeting.

(b) There shall not be more than one claiming race per day at any race meeting unless no selling race is included when there may be two claiming races.

(c) Except with the permission of the Directors there shall be in each day's programme two races of a mile or upwards of the minimum aggregate distance of two miles and a half. These races must differ at least one furlong in the distance. Neither of these shall be open to two years old, and one of them shall be neither a handicap nor a race with selling conditions.

(d) 1. Except with the permission of the Directors or under the provisions contained in (i) below or sub-order 91(v)(a) programmes of races to be run on turf shall consist of at least 6 races including, unless the guaranteed prize money exceeds £60,000 for that day, a minimum of 2 of those races potentially liable to division under Order 125.

2. If the Directors have given permission for a programme of 7 races at least two races which are potentially liable to division must still be programmed but only one shall be permitted to divide at the time for declaration to run under Order 124(ii).

3. Except with the permission of the Directors a maximum of 8 races shall be run on any one day at any meeting. If the number of races potentially liable to division could produce more than 8 races the Directors will nominate an order of precedence for division after those races have closed. Where at the time fixed for declaration under Order 124(ii) the number of horses declared to run in such races exceeds the Safety Factor the races will be divided in the order nominated provided that the maximum of 8 races is not exceeded the remaining races being subject to elimination under Order 125(iii).

(e) Except with the permission of the Directors unless the guaranteed prize money for that particular day exceeds £60,000 the daily programme of races to be run on turf shall:—

1. from the commencement of the season up to the end of the week before the Epsom Summer Meeting, include at least one Open Maiden Race, Median Auction Race or Rating Related Maiden Race race open to three year olds and

2. from the beginning of the week following the Doncaster St Leger Meeting until the end of the season include a race of between six to eight furlongs restricted to maiden two years old and subject to no conditions save only that the race may be an Auction Race, Median Auction Race, Rating Related Maiden Race, be restricted to colts and/or fillies or be horses sired by a stallion whose name is included in the Consolidated Final List of

stallions issued by the European Breeders Fund, or which are eligible under the terms of the Breeders Cup together with a further race which is potentially divisible under the requirements of Order 125.

(f) Except with the permission of the Directors, Flat races shall be sweepstakes with the exception of the following, which may be guaranteed sweepstakes:

(i) races in classes F and G (See Appendix L);

(ii) other Flat races designed to benefit registered charities by permission of the Stewards of the Jockey Club.

(g) Upon all Racecourses having four or more day's racing during the year there shall be at least one race confined to apprentice jockeys for every four days racing except that on All Weather Tracks there shall be at least one race confined to apprentice jockeys for every three days racing.

(h) Matches and private sweepstakes may be sanctioned by the Directors, independent of the above regulations. No prize can be added to private sweepstakes or matches.

(i) An Amateur Riders' race confined to riders of a single sex may only be included in a seven race programme.

(j) No race shall be programmed which restricts entry on the basis of the number of races a horse has won except for Maiden races, Claiming races, and two year old Selling races.

NOTE: Races may however be programmed for horses which have not run more than once or twice.

Handicaps

(v) (a) There shall not be more than four handicaps, including nursery handicaps, in any day's programme and if four handicaps are to be run one of them must be either an apprentice race or a seventh race and if neither is included in the programme there shall not be more than three handicaps.

(b) There shall not be any handicap confined to maidens, or to horses which have not won a race at closing below a minimum value. Such minimum value shall be laid down from time to time by the Directors.

(c) Except by specific permission of the Directors there shall be no handicap with guaranteed prize money of more than £20,000.

(d) In handicaps there shall be no clause permitting an alteration of the weights after publication by the claim of a selling allowance.

Weights

(vi) No horse shall carry less than 7st 7lb in any race unless a riders allowance is claimed as provided in Rule 109, or, in races restricted to apprentice jockeys, as provided in the conditions of the race.

Special Order applicable to Rating Related Maiden Races and Limited Stakes Races

(vii) At every meeting where Rating Related Maiden Races or Limited Stakes races are advertised no horse shall run in such races unless, before the Sunday previous to closing, it has run three times in Flat races in Great Britain other than a match, a private sweepstakes or the Newmarket Challenge Cup or Whip.

Provided always that the handicapper may be prepared to allot a rating to any horse permanently imported into Great Britain from Ireland which is in the care or control of a licensed trainer and which has been previously allotted a handicap rating in Ireland.

Classification of Flat races

(viii) All Flat races run in Great Britain shall be classified in accordance with the criteria set out in Appendix L to these Orders and Rules.

Regulations for Programmes for Steeple Chases and Hurdle Races

92. At every meeting at which Steeple Chases, Hurdle Races or National Hunt Flat races are advertised the following Orders for programmes shall apply to those races:-

Distribution of Prize Money

(i) 55% at least of the guaranteed prize money shall be apportioned to Steeple Chases, but where more than one meeting is held at the same place during the current year, the apportionment may be calculated over each meeting, or all the meetings.

Restrictions on Running

(ii) (a) No horse shall run for a Hurdle race until July 1st of the year in which he is three years old, for a Steeple Chase until July 1st of the year in which he is four years old nor for any race for which certificates from Masters of Hounds are required until February 1st of the year in which he is five years old.

(b) There shall be no Steeple Chase or Hurdle race of less distance than two miles.

(iii) With respect to Hunters' Steeple Chases:-

(a) No such race shall be run before February 1st of the current Steeple Chase and Hurdle race Season, and in all such races the qualification in respect of having been hunted shall be limited to that season.

(b) No horse shall be qualified to be entered or start in such races which

1. has run in a race between November 1st and January 31st (inclusive) of the current Steeple Chase and Hurdle Race season, or

2. has won a Steeple Chase, other than one confined to Amateur Riders, run under the Rules of any recognised Turf Authority during the current season or the two preceding seasons and which has a penalty value of £7,500 or more.

(c) For all such races a Hunters' Certificate upon the form issued by the Stewards of the Jockey Club, in respect of every horse, must be deposited at the Racing Calendar Office with a fee for registration, but such registration cannot be made unless the horse's name has also been registered. A certificate so registered by noon on Wednesday shall qualify the horse concerned to be entered in Hunters' Steeple Chases on and after the Monday following.

(iv) Where a National Hunt Flat race is run on a racecourse having Steeple Chase and Hurdle race courses the programme must consist of at least seven races and the conditions of the National Hunt Flat race shall provide that:-

(a) it shall be a weight for age race of not less than 1 1/2 miles or more than two miles for 4, 5 and 6 years old which at starting have not run under any recognised Rules of Flat racing, Steeple Chasing or Hurdle racing except National Hunt Flat races run under these Rules or Irish National Hunt Flat races.

(b) The horses shall be trained by persons holding licences or permits to train for Steeple Chases, Hurdle Races and National Hunt Flat Races.

(c) The riders shall be conditional jockeys other than those who are restricted to riding in Steeplechases or hurdle races, Amateur Riders holding 'Category B' permits to ride or Amateur Riders riding under the provisions of Rule 61.

(d) a horse shall not be qualified to run if it has previously run in a total of three races, being either

National Hunt Flat races under these Rules or Irish National Hunt Flat races.

General

(v) (a) There shall be in each day's programme at least two Steeple Chases, and from September 15th until the end of the Season one of these must be of three miles or upwards. Prior to that date each meeting with a duration of more than one day must include one Steeple Chase of that distance in the programme for the meeting.

(b) Not more than one selling race per day may be included in the programme.

(c) In the conditions of any race there shall be no restrictions with regard to training stables, nor shall there be any riders' allowances other than those provided by Rule 109 except in Conditional Jockeys' races.

(d) 1. Except with the permission of the Directors, programmes of races shall consist of at least 6 and no more than 7 races.

2. Except with the permission of the Directors, where 6 races have been programmed only one race potentially liable to division shall be permitted to divide, at the time for declaration to run under Order 124(ii).

3. Except with the permission of the Directors, where 7 races have been programmed no race potentially liable to division shall be permitted to divide, at the time for declaration to run under Order 124(ii).

4. Except with the permission of the Directors, a maximum of 7 races shall be run on any one day at any meeting. If the number of races potentially liable to division could produce more than 7 races the Directors will nominate an order of precedence for division after those races have closed. Where at the time for declaration under Order 124(ii) the number of horses declared to run in such races exceeds the Safety Factor and is greater than 17 the races will be divided in the order nominated provided that the maximum of 7 races is not exceeded; the remaining races being subject to elimination under Order 125(iii).

5. Except with the permission of the Directors, no race will be permitted to divide at an evening meeting.

(e) An Amateur Riders' race confined to riders of a single sex may only be included in a seven race programme.

Handicaps

(vi) No handicaps shall be permitted that are confined to horses which are maidens or which have not won a Steeple Chase and/or a Hurdle race at the time of entry.

Weights

(vii) No horse shall carry less than 10st in any race unless a riders allowance is claimed as provided in Rule 109, or, in races restricted to conditional jockeys, as provided in the conditions of the race.

Mixed Meetings

93. At Meetings on All Weather Tracks and at other Meetings where both Flat races and Steeple Chases, Hurdle races or National Hunt Flat races are advertised to be run, the regulations for Programmes contained in Orders 91 and 92 apply as far as possible, but the complete programme shall be subject to approval by the Directors.

Novelty Races, etc.

93A. When a Match, Private Sweepstakes or Novelty race is included in the Programme of any meeting the conditions of the race shall be subject to the approval of the Directors and the special arrangements pertaining thereto shall be subject to the approval of the Stewards of the Jockey Club. Orders 90(iii) and 125 and Rules 126, 141 and 144 will not apply to such races. The conditions and arrangements for Novelty races must be published in the Racing Calendar.

Special Rules Applicable to Handicaps

94. At every Meeting at which Flat races are advertised the following special conditions shall apply for Flat Race handicaps:-

(i) (a) Except as provided in part (b) of this sub-Order no horse shall run in a Handicap unless, before the Sunday previous to closing, or, in races which close more than six days before running, before the Sunday previous to the publication of weights in the Racing Calendar, it has either run three times in Flat Races in Great Britain or four times in Flat races in Great Britain in the case of Maiden Handicaps. In either case, a match, a private sweepstakes or the Newmarket Challenge Cup or Whip do not count. In addition before September 1st no two-year-old shall run in a Handicap, unless, before the Sunday previous to the closing, or in races which close more than six days before running, before the Sunday previous to the publication of weights in the Racing Calendar it has been placed first, second, third or fourth in a race in Great Britain other than a match, a private sweepstakes or the Newmarket Challenge Cup.

Provided always that the handicappers may be prepared to allot a weight to any horse permanently imported into Great Britain from Ireland which is in the care or control of a licensed trainer and which had been previously alloted a handicap rating in Ireland.

(b) A horse aged three-years-old or upwards which has run three times in Flat races in Ireland or a combined total of three times in Flat races in Ireland and Great Britain before the Sunday previous to closing or, in races which close more than six days before running, before the Sunday previous to the publication of weights in the Racing Calendar will be qualified to run in handicaps with guaranteed prize money of £10,000 or over if the Handicapper is prepared to allot a weight. The Handicapper's decision as to whether or not a weight shall be allotted shall be final.

Note: The Handicapper will not be prepared to allot a weight to any horse which in his view would be rated at less than 80 at the time of closing.

(ii) (a) The top weight in Standard Handicaps and Apprentice Handicaps for three years old and in nursery handicaps shall be not less than 9st 7lb and the bottom weight not less than 7st 7lb.

(b) The top weight in Rated Stakes shall be no more than 9st 7lb and the bottom weight not less than 8st 7lb.

(c) In all other races the top weight shall be not less than 10st, or, if a weight is stipulated in the conditions of the race, not less than that weight, and the bottom weight shall be not less than 7st 7lb, or, if a weight is stipulated in the conditions of the race, not less than that weight.

(d) Subject to the provisions of (e) below in all races the Handicapper may frame his handicap down to weights below the permitted bottom weight.

(e) In the case of a Rated Stakes race granted Listed status, no horse will be allocated less weight than equates with a rating of 90.

(iii) (a) In races which closed more than six days before running where the highest original weight remaining engaged at the time fixed for confirmation of entries under Order 124(i) is less than the highest weight stipulated in the conditions of the race, or, where no such weight is stipulated, is less than 9st 7lb in nursery handicaps or races for 3 years old, or less than 9st 10lb in other races, it shall be raised to that weight and all other declared runners equally.

(b) In all races if at the time fixed for declaration under Order 124(ii) the highest weight remaining declared to run, being either an original weight, or if the weights have been raised under part (a) of this Sub-

Order, a weight fixed at the time, is less than the highest weight as set out in the conditions of the race or, where no such weight is stipulated, is less than 9st 7lb in nursery handicaps or races for 3 years old, or less than 9st 10lb in other races, it shall be raised to that weight and all other declared runners equally.

(c) Penalties incurred since the date stated in the conditions of the race shall be added to the final weights fixed under Parts (a) and (b) of this Sub-Order or to the original weights if no increases are necessary.

(d) The weight of any horse whose weight, including any penalties, is then below the lowest weight permitted in the conditions of the race shall be raised to that weight, but when weights are subsequently raised as required under part (b) of this Sub-Order the weights of horses which were originally below the lowest weight permitted shall be re-calculated as though there had been no previous raising of weights.

(e) Penalties incurred after declaration to run under Order 124(ii) shall be similarly calculated on the original weight together with any additional increase under parts (a) and (b) of this Sub-Order.

95. At every Meeting at which Steeple Chases and Hurdle races are advertised the following conditions shall apply for Steeple Chase and Hurdle race handicaps:-

(i) The top weights shall not be less than 12st except in races of three and a half miles or over when it shall be not less than 11st 10lb. The bottom weights shall not be less than 10st, but the Handicapper may frame his handicap down to weights below the permitted bottom weight.

(ii) (a) Weights allotted or based on those allotted under Sub-Order (iii) of this Order shall be disregarded for the purpose of calculating the highest weight remaining declared as required in parts (b) and (c) of this Sub-Order and when weights are raised in accordance with the requirements of those Sub-Orders no weight allotted under Sub-Order (iii) of this Order shall be increased.

(b) In races which closed more than six days before running where the highest original weight remaining engaged at the time fixed for confirmation of entries under Order 124 (i) is less than 11st 7lb in a Steeple Chase of 3½ miles and upwards or 11st 10lb in any other race it shall be raised to that weight and all other declared runners equally subject to part (a) of this Sub-Order.

(c) In all races if at the time fixed for declaration under Order 124(ii) the highest weight remaining declared to run, being either an original weight, or, if the weights have been raised as required under part (b) of this Sub-Order, a weight fixed at that time (excluding penalties and weights allotted under Sub-Order (iii) of this Order), is less than 11st 7lb in a Steeple Chase of 3½ miles and upwards or 11st 10lb in any other race, it shall be raised to that weight and all other declared runners equally, subject to part (a) of this Sub-Order.

(d) Penalties incurred since the date stated in the conditions of the race shall be added to the final weights fixed under parts (a), (b) and (c) of this Sub-Order or to the original weights if no increases are necessary, but no penalty shall increase a horse's weight above 12st in Steeple Chases of 3½ miles and upwards or 12st 7lb in all other races, and no penalties shall be added where the original weight is equal to or above those weights.

(e) The weight of any horse whose weight, including any penalties, is then below the lowest weight permitted in the conditions of the race shall be raised to that weight, but when weights are subsequently raised as required under part (c) of this Sub-Order the weights of horses which were originally below the lowest weight permitted shall be re-calculated as though there had been no previous raising of weights.

(f) Penalties incurred after declaration to run under Order 124(ii) shall be similarly calculated on the original weight together with any additional increase under parts (b) and (c) of this Sub-Order.

(iii) A horse shall be allotted top weight in a handicap unless before the Sunday previous to closing, or in races which close more than six days before running, before the publication of weights in the Racing Calendar, he has either:-

(a) run three times collectively in Steeple Chases or Hurdle races in Great Britain or in Ireland, or

(b) won a Steeple Chase or Hurdle race in Great Britain or in Ireland.

matches and National Hunt Flat Races excepted in all cases, but in exceptional circumstances the Handicapper may allot a weight higher than top weight for such horses and in a handicap for more than one age, three, four, and five-years-old may, at the discretion of the Handicapper, be given the weight-for-age allowance from the top weight of the handicap as provided by Appendix B.

The Handicappers decision as to the weight allotted and whether or not the weight-for-age allowance is given shall be final.

Selling and Claiming Races

96. The following Orders and Rules relating to Selling races apply to all Selling races but in optional Selling races they apply to horses which run as entered to be sold. These Orders and Rules are also subject to Rule 98.

(i) (a) In selling races with guaranteed prize money of up to and including £2000 the selling price shall be £2000.

(b) In selling races with guaranteed prize money of more than £2000 up to an including £3000 the selling price shall be equal to the guaranteed prize money.

(c) In selling races with guaranteed prize money of more than £3000 the selling price shall be at least £3000.

(ii) In all selling races the winner shall be offered for sale by auction immediately after the race except as provided in Rule 98(i).

(iii) In the case of a dead-heat, each of the horses dividing is a winner for the purposes of the Rules relating to claiming and selling, and if a selling race, both shall be put up to auction.

(iv) If a horse walk over (or there be no second horse placed) for a selling race, the winner is still liable to be sold.

(v) No person shall prevent or seek to prevent any other person from bidding for the winner of a selling race, whether by offering any consideration or guarantee or by means of a threat or otherwise, and no person shall accept or offer to accept, any consideration or guarantee or other inducement to refrain from bidding. Any person so offending shall be reported to the Stewards of the Jockey Club.

(vi) If sold, or bought in, the horse shall not leave the place of sale without permission of the auctioneer, and a written order given for his delivery to the actual bidder who alone shall be responsible for the price; and if the horse be not paid for, or the price secured to the satisfaction of the auctioneer within thirty minutes he shall put the horse up a second time, and the purchaser at the first sale shall be responsible for any deficiency arising from the second and shall be treated as a defaulter until it is paid. Whoever issues the delivery order for a horse sold, bought in, or claimed, is responsible for the money and shall pay it over to the Stakeholder for payment in accordance with Rule 27(iv) to the person or persons entitled.

(vii) It shall be a term of any sale by auction of the winner of a selling race that in the event of a cheque or other negotiable instrument tendered in payment being dishonoured on presentation, the Stewards of the Jockey Club shall have the power to declare the sale null and void, and that upon and from the date of such declaration the sale shall be regarded as rescinded without prejudice to any claim or rights in law any person may have against the auctioneer or bidder, or the Stewards of the Jockey Club may exercise their power under Rule 1(xviii) to refuse to accept entries for the horse or to refuse to allow the horse to run in any race until the payment has been honoured.

(viii) No horse, other than the winner, which has run in a selling race shall be offered for sale until after the time set for claiming under Rule 97 (i) for that race has elapsed.

(ix) From the moment the winner has weighed in until the conclusion of the sale, the auctioneer shall give such instructions relating to the control of and showing of the horse being auctioned as he may deem necessary, which may include the order to remove bandages.

(x) Any surplus over the selling price shall be divided equally between the Racecourse and the Owner and in the case of a dead-heat any surplus in either case shall be divided equally between the Racecourse and respective owners.

97. All horses which have come under Starters' Orders in selling and claiming races, apart from the winner of a selling race but including a horse that has walked over in a claiming race must remain on the racecourse property until 35 minutes after the All Right signal has been authorised under Rule 162 and may be claimed at or above the published claiming price subject to the following conditions:-

(i) Every claim must be made in writing on the prescribed form and must sufficiently establish the identity of the horse claimed beyond any reasonable doubt from any other in that particular race. Every claim must also state the amount offered which in a claiming race shall be not less than the claiming price published in the official racecard for the horse concerned and in a selling race shall be not less than the claiming price published in the conditions of the race. Except as provided in sub-Rule (ii) of this Rule:—

(a) The claim must be signed by the person making it and his address must also be given. If any of the details required under this sub-Rule are omitted from the claim particulars of the form, the claim may be void.

(b) Claims made by companies, whether recognised or not, are not acceptable and such claims if made will be void.

(ii) A horse may be claimed in the name of the owner in whose name it ran. For the purposes of this Rule:—

(a) The claim must be signed either by the owner or the trainer of the horse or an employee of the trainer who holds a Racecourse Attendant's Identity Card and Validity Pass who will be regarded as the agents of the owner.

(b) Where the owner is a recognised Company a registered agent of the Company or a person holding a written authorisation signed by such registered agent and available only for the day of the race will also be regarded as agent of the recognised Company.

(iii) The claim shall be sealed and placed in the claims box on the Clerk of the Scales' table not later than ten minutes after the All Right signal has been authorised under Rule 162. Once submitted, a claim may not be withdrawn or altered.

(iv) The horse shall go to the person submitting the highest claim but if there are two or more equal claims for the same horse, the successful claim shall be determined by lot by the Clerk of the Scales. Details of claims other than highest claims shall not be disclosed unless the procedure set out in sub-Rule (vi)(b) of this Rule is followed, when details of the successful claimant shall be disclosed.

(v) The owner of a horse which is claimed shall receive 15% of the surplus above the published claiming price and the racecourse shall receive the balance of the surplus together with, in claiming races, 10% of the published claiming price of any horse claimed.

(vi) The price of every horse claimed must be paid to or secured to the satisfaction of the Clerk of the Scales, or, if present, the Stakeholder's representative within thirty minutes of the All Right signal being authorised under Rule 162, and an order given to him for the delivery of the horse.

If the price be not paid or secured as in this Rule or Order.

(a) The claimant forfeits his right and shall be guilty of an offence and

(b) If there is more than one claimant then the horse shall go to the person submitting a claim of equal value or, if there is no claim of equal value, to the person submitting the next highest claim and the provisions of this Rule shall apply accordingly save that the time within which the price is to be paid or secured to the satisfaction of the Clerk of the Scales shall be extended to forty-five minutes of the All Right signal being authorised under Rule 162.

(vii) The owners in whose names the horses ran shall be entitled to any prize money due under the conditions of the race,

(viii) In the event of a cheque or other negotiable instrument tendered in payment of the claiming price being dishonoured on presentation the Stewards of the Jockey Club shall have the power to declare the claim null and void and that upon and from the date of such declaration the claim shall be regarded as rescinded without prejudice to any claim or rights in law any person may have against the claimant, or the Stewards of the Jockey Club may exercise their power under Rule 1 (xviii) to refuse to accept entries for the horse or to refuse to allow the horse to run in any race until the payment has been honoured.

(ix) No person shall prevent or seek to prevent any other person from claiming a horse in a selling or claiming race, other than the winner of a selling race, whether by offering any consideration or guarantee or by means of a threat or otherwise, and no person shall accept or offer to accept any consideration or guarantee or other inducement to refrain from submitting a claim. Any person so offending shall be reported to the Stewards of the Jockey Club.

(x) Subject to the powers of the Stewards of the Jockey Club under Rule 1(xi), in the event of any dispute the decision of the Clerk of the Scales on matters contained in sub-Rules (i), (ii), (iii), (iv) and (vi) of this Rule shall be final.

(xi) Where a horse is claimed by or on behalf of its owner he is required to pay a sum representing 85% of the surplus above the published claiming price together with, in claiming races, 10% of the published claiming price.

98. The foregoing Orders and Rules relating to selling and claiming races, are subject to the following provisions:-

(i) If an objection be made under Rule 170(iv), and the winner of a selling race is disqualified, or his placing altered, the time for selling and claiming shall be fixed by the Stewards.

(ii) Where an objection is made on any other ground that those mentioned in Rule 170(iv) and sustained or an appeal is lodged under Rule 177 against a decision of the Stewards on an objection under Rule 170(iv) or an enquiry under Rule 171 (iii) and is sustained, the sale of the winner of a selling race, the disposal of the surplus, and any claims under Rule 97 shall not be affected, and in a selling race the horse to whom the race is awarded shall not be offered for sale, nor shall the original winner be liable to be claimed, but in cases where an objection has been lodged on the ground of fraud or substitution, or on the ground that the winner of a selling race or any horse claimed in a selling or claiming race has run at any unrecognised Meeting, and sustained, the Stewards of the Jockey Club may order the sale or claim to be annulled.

(iii) Where the winner of a selling race or any horse claimed has been the subject of an examination under Rule 14(vi) and the result of an analysis of any sample of its tissue, body fluid or excreta is positive the Stewards of the Jockey Club may order the sale or claim to be annulled. For the purposes of this sub-Rule a positive analysis is as defined in Rule 53(ii).

(iv) When a horse is bought or claimed the trainer who ran the horse must lodge its passport with the Clerk of the Scales of the meeting concerned as soon as the sale or claim is confirmed.

(v) When a horse which has been bought or claimed is the subject of an examination under Rule 14(vi) the trainer who ran the horse is responsible for the horse until the examination is completed when he or his representative must hand the horse to its new owner.

99. (i) No horse which is the subject of a lease may be entered or run in a selling or claiming race unless the lessee has written consent from the lessor. If such consent has not been given it will be the responsibility of the lessee to so advise his trainer in writing.

(ii) Any horse which has run in a selling or claiming race in contravention of sub-Rule (i) of this Rule shall, on an objection under Rule 170(v) be disqualified and the

Stewards of the Jockey Club may order the sale, if the horse won the race, or any claim, to be annulled.

PART 10: PENALTIES AND ALLOWANCES

Calculation

100. (i) For the purposes of calculating penalties, allowances and qualifications the winner shall be regarded as having won of the total prize money (excluding supplementary payments which are conditional upon circumstances additional to the performance of the horse in the race and any prize given specifically to the trainer, rider, stable or breeder in the conditions of the race in excess of those provided for in Order 194)

60% in Pattern races with four prizes.

58% in Flat races with six prizes, and Steeple Chases with guaranteed prize money of £10,000 or more with six prizes.

65% in other races with fourth prizes.

70% in all other races.

Where, in a dead-heat, it is necessary to divide the prizes in accordance with Rule 157 the other placed horses shall be regarded as having won of the total prize money (subject to the same exceptions as the winner).

In Pattern races with four prizes:

23% for the second horse.
11.50% for the third horse.
5.50% for the fourth horse.

In Flat races with six prizes, and Steeple Chases with guaranteed prize money of £10,000 or more with six prizes:

22% for the second horse.
11% for the third horse.
5% for the fourth horse.
2.5% for the fifth horse.
1.5% for the sixth horse.

In all other races:

20% for the second horse.
10% for the third horse.
5% for the fourth horse in a race with a fourth prize.

(ii) If a winner has walked over, or no horse has been placed second or in any lower place the percentage of prize money which horses placed second or in any lower place would be regarded as having won under the Order shall be added to the winner's percentage. The value of a race to the winner after deduction of the entrance fee and, in the case of dead-heat, after the prizes have been divided in accordance with Rule 157, shall be published in Raceform Up-to-Date and Chaseform Up-to-Date and this shall be used for the purpose of calculating penalties, allowances and qualifications. For the purposes of this Rule in races with a supplementary entry stage the entrance fee shall be that stated for runners entered at the original closing regardless of the stage at which the horse was entered

(iii) For the purpose of calculating qualifications or allowances 'Pattern Races - includes all races which are regarded as, or are assessed as, the equivalent of Pattern Races under the provisions of Order 103 (ii)

(iv) Where race conditions provide for a penalty to be carried for having won a race such penalty must also be carried when races of superior value or quality have been won, as follows:—

PENALTY FOR WINNING	ALSO INCLUDES THE FOLLOWING
Race(s) of particular value	race(s) of greater value
Listed race	Group races
Group 3 race	Group 1 or 2 races
Group 2 race	Group 1 race

101. For the purpose of calculating the value of races run out of Great Britain and the Channel Islands and the value of horses sold at public auction out of Great Britain and the Channel Islands (exclusive of any tax), the rates of exchange to the £ (Sterling) shown in Appendix C will be used for the relevant year in which the race was run or the horse sold.

These rates may be varied at any time at the discretion of the Directors who may also fix a ratio of "points" to money in respect of races run in countries where points rather than money are used to indicate the importance of a race. In assessing distances of races in kilometres, 200 metres shall be taken to equal one furlong.

102. In the case of a horse trained outside Great Britain and entered

(i) For a race in which there is a declaration of forfeit the trainer must, unless forfeit is declared, forward full details of any racecourse performances outside Great Britain or Ireland by the horse to the Racing Calendar Office by 12 noon on the Tuesday on which the declaration of forfeit is fixed to be made. If a declaration to run under Order 124 is subsequently made for the horse in that race the trainer must forward details of any performances subsequent to the date of declaration of forfeit to the Racing Calendar Office by the time fixed for declaration of runners under Order 124(ii).

(ii) For a race in which there is no declaration of forfeit the trainer must forward full details of any racecourse performances outside Great Britain or Ireland by the horse to the Racing Calendar Office by the time fixed for the closing of entries. If a declaration to run under Order 124 is subsequently made for the horse in that race the trainer must forward details of any subsequent performances by the time fixed for the declaration of runners under Order 124(ii).

102A. In the case of a horse trained outside Great Britain which runs in a race without the details required by Order 102 having been lodged, the trainer shall be fined £275 by the Stewards of the Jockey Club.

Penalties

103. (i) Penalties for winning a fixed sum shall be understood to mean for winning it in one race, unless specified to the contrary.

(ii) For Flat races, penalties for winning a race of a specific class shall be understood to mean the winning of a race as listed in Appendix L to these Orders and Rules.

(iii) For Flat races penalties for winning a Pattern Race a Pattern Race in a specific Group or a Listed Race, shall be understood to mean the winning of a Pattern race or Listed Race as defined.

(iv) If the country in which a race has been won does not have races in the Pattern Race Book or Listed Races and the race took place prior to 1991 the assessments shown below for penalties shall apply.

Value of race to the winner after 1984	Value of race to the winner after 1978	To carry penalty as the winner of a Pattern race in the following Group:
£15,000 and above	£12,000 and above	Group 1
£8750 to £14,999	£7000 to £11,999	Group 2
£5000 to £8749	£4000 to £6999	Group 3

Except in the case of those Graded Stakes races in North America, Belgium, Denmark, Norway, Sweden and Spain which were published in the International Cataloguing Standards Book prior to 1991 and which were run prior to this date, the Grades into which those races were classified will be regarded as the equivalent of the Pattern Race Groups for the purpose of calculating penalties under these Orders. Races run in these countries which were prior to 1991 not graded but in which the value to the winner is more than £15000 will be regarded as the equivalent of Group 3 Pattern races for the purpose of calculating penalties under these Orders. (For qualifications and allowances see Order 100 (iii)).

(v) For races taking place in and after 1991 the assessments shown below for penalties shall apply.

1. In countries which do not have races in the Pattern Race Book the grades of all Graded Stakes races published in the International Cataloguing Standards Book and run in 1991 and thereafter will be regarded as

the equivalent of Pattern Race Groups for the purpose of calculating penalties under these Orders.

2. For Flat race penalties the winning of a Listed Race shall be understood to mean the winning of a Listed Race as defined but, in 1991 and thereafter, all races published in the International Cataloguing Standards Book which are not Graded Races, will be regarded as Listed Races for the purpose of calculating penalties.

(vi) If in the conditions of a race a fixed penalty has to be carried for winning either a race specified by name or a race of a specific class or a Listed race or a race in a Pattern Race Group, horses running a dead-heat for such race shall carry the penalty fixed as if the race had been won outright.

104. Penalties are not cumulative unless so declared by the conditions of the race.

105. (i) Winners of Flat races confined to apprentice jockeys which take place under these Orders or Rules or the Rules of the Irish Turf Club will not incur penalties in any Flat race except in those which are confined to apprentice jockeys and in which the conditions provide for a specific penalty for winners.

(ii) Winners of Opportunity races which took place under the Rules of Racing between July 1st 1970 and June 30th 1982, Opportunity races run under the Irish National Steeple Chase Rules, or of Conditional Jockeys' races will not incur penalties in any Steeple Chase or Hurdle race except Conditional Jockeys' races in which the conditions provide for a specific penalty for winners.

106. (i) A Challenge Cup is not estimated in the value of a race until it is finally won, but when won outright the winner must carry a penalty in respect of the full value of the Cup and money prize.

(ii) Extra weights shall not be incurred in respect of matches or private sweepstakes, or of the Newmarket Challenge Cup or Whip.

(iii) Extra weights shall not be incurred in respect of National Hunt Flat races, except in such races.

(iv) No horse shall carry extra weight for having run second, or in any lower place in a race.

Allowances

107. (i) No horses shall receive allowance of weight, or be relieved from extra weight, for having been beaten in one or more races: provided that this Order shall not prohibit maiden allowances or allowances to horses that have not won within a specified time, or races of a specified value or distance.

(ii) No allowance of weight shall be made to any horse:

(a) for being the produce of a stallion or mare whose produce never won a race;

(b) for being the first produce of a mare;

(c) for being the produce of a stallion covering at, or under, a particular fee;

(d) for being half-bred.

(iii) *Deleted*

(iv) Except with the permission of the Directors in all races, other than Handicaps, for which fillies and mares may be entered, they shall receive the following allowances:

(a) Two years old - 5lb

(b) Three years old and upwards in Flat races other than Pattern races - 5lb

(c) Three-year-olds and upwards in Flat Pattern races - 3lb

(d) Three years old and upwards in Steeple Chases, Hurdle races and National Hunt Flat races - 5lb

(v) In all Flat races, other than handicaps, allowances as shown in Appendix D may be claimed for horses foaled between July 1st and December 31st in the Southern Hemisphere. Such allowances may only be claimed at the time of entry as provided in Order 113(iv).

108. Allowances are cumulative unless otherwise specified.

Riders' Allowances

109. Riders' allowances may be claimed as follows:-

(i) The holders of apprentice jockeys' licences under the provisions of Rule 60(iii) and those apprentices from Ireland riding under the provisions of Rule 61, shall be entitled to claim the following allowances in Flat races:

7lb until they have won 20 races; thereafter
5lb until they have won 50 races; thereafter
3lb until they have won 95 races.

The above allowances can be claimed in the Flat races set out below, with the exception of races confined to apprentice jockeys:-

(1) All handicaps other than those Rated Stakes which are classified as Listed races.

(2) All selling races.

(3) All other races with guaranteed prize money of not more than £8000.

(ii) (a) In Steeple Chases, Hurdle races and National Hunt Flat races open to professional jockeys those riders under the age of 25 years who hold a Conditional jockey's licence or a "Category B" Amateur Rider's permit under these Rules, or who are riding under the provisions of Rule 61 shall be entitled to the following allowances:-

7lb until they have won 15 races, thereafter
5lb until they have won 30 races; thereafter
3lb until they have won 55 races.

The above allowances can be claimed in those Steeple Chases, Hurdle races and National Hunt Flat races that are open to professional jockeys set out below, with the exception of races confined to Conditional Jockeys:-

(1) All handicaps except the Liverpool Grand National Steeple Chase.

(2) All selling races.

(3) All other races with guaranteed prize money of not more than £5000.

(b) In Steeple Chases, Hurdle races and National Hunt Flat races confined to amateur riders, riders shall be entitled to claim the following allowances:-

7lb until they have won 15 races, thereafter
5lb until they have won 30 races; thereafter
3lb until they have won 55 races.

The above allowances can be claimed in those Steeple Chases, Hurdle races and National Hunt Flat races set out below.

(1) All handicaps confined to amateur riders.

(2) All selling races confined to amateur riders.

(3) All other races confined to amateur riders with guaranteed prize money of not more than £5000.

N.B. For calculation of riders' allowances claimed under this Rule and also for races confined to Apprentice Jockeys, Conditional Jockeys and Amateur Riders on the Flat, all races will count except Arab Horse races or Point to Point Steeple Chases.

"Race" means Sweepstakes, Guaranteed Sweepstakes, Private Sweepstakes or Match run under these Rules or any race run under the Rules of a recognised Turf Authority.

(iii) A rider who is duly licensed or permitted under Rules 60(iii), (iv), (v) or (vi) and is entitled to claim a riding allowance under Sub-Rules (i) and (ii) of this Rule shall inform the Racing Calendar Office, within 48 hours of his return to Great Britain, of any winners he has ridden in another country.

(iv) A rider who is the holder of a current licence or permit to ride issued by a recognised Turf Authority outside Great Britain and who is entitled to claim a riding allowance shall provide the Racing Calendar Office with details of the winner(s) he had ridden by 3.30 p.m. on the day fixed for declaration to run under Order 124(ii), or as the Stewards of the Jockey Club shall direct. Failure to comply with the provisions of this Rule shall disentitle the claiming of any riding allowance.

(v) A rider shall be entitled to claim the given riding allowance specified in Sub-Rules (i) and (ii) of this Rule until 2 clear days after the day on which he reaches the maximum number of winners appropriate to the allowance in question.

Note: If, for example, a rider has reached on a Wednesday the maximum number of winners permissible, the allowance can still be claimed on the immediate Thursday and Friday but cannot be claimed on the Saturday.

(vi) For races (other than those covered by the provisions of Sub-Rules (i) and (ii) of this Rule) where riding allowances are specified in the conditions of the race, a rider shall be entitled to claim the riding allowance as specified irrespective of any winners ridden in the period of 2 clear days before the day of the race in question.
Note: If, for example, a rider has ridden the winner of a race on a Wednesday, the allowance, as specified in the conditions of the race, can still be claimed on the immediate Thursday and Friday but cannot be claimed on the Saturday.

(vii) The rider shall be responsible for claiming the correct riding allowance. Failure to claim the correct riding allowance shall constitute a breach of these Rules.

PART 11: ENTRIES, ACCEPTANCES, SUBSCRIPTIONS AND TRANSFERS OF ENGAGEMENTS

Entries and Acceptances

110. Entries and acceptances, subscriptions and transfer of engagements shall be made in accordance with the provisions of the Orders covering such matters and subject to payment of such fees as provided for in the Orders and shall be subject always to the power of the Stewards of the Jockey Club contained in Rule 1A(xviii).

110A. The following provisions shall be subject always to the powers of the Stewards of the Jockey Club contained in Rule 1A(xviii).

110B. (i) No race, with the exception of a sweepstakes with guaranteed prize money of £30,000 or more in a flat race (other than a Rated Stakes), £20,000 or more in a Steeple Chase or £15,000 or more in a Hurdle Race shall close earlier than six days before the day on which it is to be run.

(ii) No race to be run on turf shall close earlier than the February in the year in which the horses concerned are two years old, and except with the permission of the Directors, no Flat race to be run on turf shall close after the last Wednesday in November.

111. (i) Every entry and every acceptance for races closing more than six days before running shall be fixed to close at 12 noon on Wednesdays only, with the exception of supplementary entries which shall close at 12 noon either six or seven days before the race is due to be run or as the Directors shall direct except as provided for in Sub-Order (iii) of this Order. Such entry or acceptance must be made to the Racing Calendar Office and is subject to withdrawal or alteration up to the time of closing.

(ii) Every entry for other races shall be fixed to close at 12 noon either six days or five days before the race is run or as the Directors shall decide except as provided for in Sub-Order (iii) of this Order. Such entry must be made to the Racing Calendar Office and is subject to withdrawal or alteration up to the time of closing.

(iii) (a) Entries may also close to any recognised Turf Authority, if special mention is made in the advertisement of the race in the Racing Calendar;

(b) Entries which close to the Registry Office of the Irish Turf Club may also be made to the Racing Calendar Office by the due time laid down in this Order provided the horse is in the care of and trained by a licensed, permitted or duly qualified trainer in Ireland at the time of entry. Such entries will be subject to a surcharge of £50 per entry charged to the owner of the horse.

(iv) The list of entries shall be closed at the advertised time, and no entry shall be admitted on any ground after the time unless the conditions of the race provide for a supplementary entry stage. Where such provision is made the supplementary list of entries shall be closed at the advertised time and no entry shall be admitted on any ground after that time.

Form of Entry or Nomination

112. (i) (a) Entries and alterations or withdrawals of such entries before the time of closing shall be made by telephone, by the owner of the horse, or his authorised agent, or in writing signed by the owner of the horse or his authorised agent but, save with the express permission of the Directors, in every case such entries or withdrawals will only be accepted if the security code allotted by the Directors to persons qualified to make entries is given. For the purpose of this Order a telegram, telex or facsimile message shall be deemed to be in writing. Entries made by telephone will only be accepted from 2.30 p.m. on the day prior to closing.

(b) A fee is payable for the replacement of a lost security code.

(ii) Entries made under Order 111 (iii) to other recognised Turf Authorities, shall be made in writing signed by the owner of the horse or his authorised agent. For the purpose of this Order a telegram, telex or facsimile message shall be deemed to be in writing. Such entries shall in all respects be subject to these Orders and Rules, except that registrations under Rules 41 to 47, or of Authority to Act, need not be registered in this country provided that in these respects the entry would be valid under the Rules of the Turf Authority of the country where the entry is received.

(iii) Save in the case of a horse trained outside Great Britain at the time of entry, no horse may be entered for any race by or on behalf of any owner or recognised club whose name is not duly registered under Rule 40 or, provided that registration is made in the country in which the horse is trained, any Company which is not duly registered under either Rule 43 or Rule 44 or any syndicate which is not registered under Rule 46, save by leave of the Stewards of the Jockey Club.

(iv) Save in the case of a horse trained outside Great Britain at the time of entry, no entry will be accepted unless the following is complied with:—

— the entry shall be in the name of one person or, where the horse is owned by a recognised Company, in the name of the Company and the name of the owner, together with, where necessary, the registered partnership or club name.

The following information must also be given:—

— the registered name of the horse;
— the name of the Meeting;
— the name of the race;
— the date upon which the race is advertised to be run

except as provided for in Sub-Order (ii) above and Rule 113(iii) together with such other details as may be required by the Directors.

(v) No horse shall be entered in the name of any person as his owner unless that person has a beneficial interest in the horse at least equal to that of each other person with a beneficial interest. This sub-rule does not apply to horses owned on behalf of a recognised Club or by a recognised Stud Company, or the subject of a registered Partnership or a Syndicate Agreement.

(vi) When a horse is the subject of a Partnership or Syndicate Agreement, it may only be entered and run in the name of the same partner or joint owner or registered partnership name in races taking place during any calendar year.

113. (i) Except as permitted under Sub-Rule (iii) of this Rule no horse foaled in Great Britain, Ireland, or the Channel Is- lands shall be entered unless its name has been registered under Rule 31.

(ii) A horse foaled outside Great Britain, Ireland or the Channel Islands may be entered by stating its registered name in the country of foaling together with the country of foaling and such pedigree or description as will identify it.

(iii)No horse shall be entered if its name is not acceptable for registration under Rule 31 and if such an entry is mistakenly or inadvertently accepted the same shall despite such acceptance be void and the horse shall not be qualified to be entered or to start.

(iv) In making an entry to any recognised Turf Authority outside Great Britain or the Channel Islands under Order 111 (iii), the horse shall be considered as identified by giving the name registered for the horse in the country where the entry is made subject to Order 113(v) below.

(v) In making an entry to any recognised Turf Authority outside Great Britain or the Channel Islands under Order 111(iii), no horse shall be entered if its name is not acceptable for registration under Rule 31 and if such an entry is mistakenly or inadvertently accepted the same shall despite such acceptance be void and the horse shall not be qualified to be entered or to start.

(vi) In entries for horses for which an allowance is to be claimed under the provisions of Order 107(v) the name of the horse must be followed by "Southern Hemisphere Allowance" and the amount of the allowance claimed.

(vii) An entry for a horse which has entered training in Great Britain after coming from abroad must be accompanied by full details of any racecourse performances outside Great Britain or Ireland. If the requirements of this Order are satisfied when the horse is first entered they will not apply on future occasions provided that the horse remains in Great Britain during the intervening period. (See Order 59).

114. (i) An acceptance for a free handicap shall be considered as equivalent to an entry, but if the horse be wrongly described the acceptance shall be void.

(ii) Entries shall not become void (except as allowed for in Order 117) on the death of the person in whose name they are made or taken, and all rights, privileges, and liabilities that could have attached to the deceased person had he or she been alive shall attach to his or her personal representative.

(iii) In novice or maiden hurdle races, which are advertised to be divided at entry the number of entries will, where necessary, be reduced to eight times the Safety Factor effective at the time of entry. Where elimination is necessary the entries will be reduced by the elimination of those horses with the highest number of unplaced hurdle race runs up to and including the day prior to closing and where it is necessary to decide which of two or more horses having a similar number of unplaced runs are to be eliminated a ballot will be made.

115. In cases hereinafter mentioned any accidental error, or violation of Orders or Rules effecting entries may be corrected on payment of a fine of not less than £60 provided always that the Stewards are satisfied that there has been no fraud.

(i) Incorrect description of the owner of the horse according to the Orders and Rules of Entry. Correction must be made to the Racing Calendar Office by the time fixed for the declaration of runners under Order 124(ii). Such declaration to run by his owner or duly authorised agent is deemed to be a correction of entry under this Rule. Any notification of correction must be made to the Clerk of the Scales before the rider weighs out for the race concerned.

(ii) Omission to lodge particulars of partnerships, etc, according to Rule 47, provided that the document is lodged and the fine paid before the rider weighs out for the race concerned.

(iii) Omission to give details of performances abroad when the horse has entered training in Great Britain. Correction must be made to the Racing Calendar Office and the details lodged by the time fixed for declaration of runners under Order 124(ii).

If any horse runs without the prescribed correction having been made, the Stewards of the Jockey Club may inflict fines upon, or otherwise deal with, any persons responsible for such errors.

Transfer of Engagements

116. (i) In cases of changes of ownership the engagements can only be transferred to a registered owner and in all such cases the written acknowledgement of both parties, or their authorised agents, that the horse was transferred with engagements, together with details of the engagements transferred, must be lodged at the Racing Calendar Office or with the Clerk of the Course for transmission to the Racing Calendar Office before the horse starts for such engagements. If certain engagements only are specified, those only are sold with the horse. For the purpose of this Order a telegram, telex or facsimile message shall be deemed to be in writing.
A fee is payable for each transfer of engagements lodged.

(ii) If a horse starts for any race without a transfer having been lodged as provided for in Order 116(i), he shall, on objection, be disqualified, unless it be proved to the satisfaction of the Stewards of the Jockey Club that the omission was accidental, in which case the person responsible shall be fined not less than £95.

117. When any engagement is transferred in a race in which there is a declaration of forfeit the transferor cannot strike the horse out of the engagement and the horse may appear in the final programme in the name of its owner instead of the nominator. An engagement in a Private Sweepstakes, or match, cannot be transferred and shall be rendered void on the death of the nominator.

PART 12: DECLARATIONS AND SCRATCHINGS

120. (i) In every race there shall be a declaration of runners on the day before the race or as the Directors shall direct.

(ii) In every race which closes more than six days before running entries must be confirmed either five or six days before the race, or as the Stewards of the Jockey Club shall direct, except that when a supplementary entry is made in accordance with Order 111 (i) it shall be deemed as confirmation of the said entry and all entry fees for the race shall be included in the supplementary entry fee.

121. (i) In races which close six days or less before running there shall be no declaration of forfeit.

(ii) In all other races

(a) a declaration of forfeit maybe fixed for the tuesday not less than eighteen nor more than twenty-four days before running.

(b) an additional declaration of forfeit may be fixed for a handicap on any Tuesday after the publication of weights.

(iii) For Flat races other than handicaps additional declarations of forfeit may be fixed but only on the Tuesday after the Newmarket Craven Meeting and the first Tuesday in July.

122. (i) Declarations of forfeit under Order 121 shall be made to the Racing Calendar Office by 12 noon on the Tuesday fixed in the conditions of the race. Such declarations shall be subject to withdrawal up to the time for declaration of forfeit.

(ii) *Deleted.*

(iii) (a) All declarations or withdrawals of declarations made under this Order which shall state the name of the owner, together with, where necessary the registered partnership or club name, the name of the horse, the name of the Meeting and the name of the race, shall be made by telephone by the owner of the engagement or his authorised agent, or in writing signed by the owner or his authorised agent, but save with the express permission of the Directors, in every case, except those provided for in Part (b) of this sub-Order, such declarations or withdrawals will only be accepted if the security code allotted by the Directors to persons qualified to make entries is given. For the purposes of this Order a telegram, telex or facsimile message shall be deemed to be in writing.

(b) In the case of horses trained outside Great Britain a declaration or withdrawal may be made by the trainer, or, provided that a signed declaration is held by them, by an Official of the Turf Authority under whose Rules the trainer is licensed.

(c) Declarations made by telephone will only be accepted from 2.30 p.m. on the day prior to that on which declarations are due.

123. (i) Scratchings may only be made for horses in races in which there is a declaration of forfeit.

(ii) A scratching shall be made in writing to the Racing Calendar Office by the owner of the engagement or his authorised agent or, in the case of a horse trained outside Great Britain, by the trainer, subject to the Rules relating to sales with engagements. For the purpose of this Order a telegram, telex or facsimile message shall be deemed to be in writing.

(iii) The document scratching a horse out of specific engagements shall state the name of the horse and give details of the engagements, but such document does not constitute a cancellation of a confirmed entry or declared runner under Order 124.

(iv) The notification of the death of a horse to the Racing Calendar Office shall withdraw the horse from all engagements in races.

124. (i) In races which close more than six days before running no horse may run unless a confirmation of entry or supplementary entry has been made to the Racing Calendar Office by noon on the day advertised in the programme of the meeting as required under Order 120(ii). Such confirmation shall be subject to withdrawal up to the time fixed for confirmation.

(ii) (a) Subject to Part (b) of this Order, no horse may run in any race unless a declaration to run (which shall be subject to withdrawal up to the time fixed for declaration) has been made to the Racing Calendar Office by 10 a.m. from Easter Monday until October 31st, inclusive, and 10.15 a.m. from November 1st until Easter Sunday inclusive, on the day before the day on which the race is advertised to run or as the Directors shall decide.

(b) In any race where less than three declarations to run have been received by the Racing Calendar Office by the time(s) for declaration to run the said time(s) for a declaration to be made shall be extended up to 11.00 a.m. on the same day, or such earlier or later time as the Directors shall decide. No declaration to run or otherwise shall be subject to withdrawal once made during this extended time period. (N.B. See Instruction D4 for restrictions and operating procedure.)

(iii) (a) All confirmations declarations and withdrawals made under this Order which shall state the name of the owner, together with, where necessary, the registered partnership or club name, the name of the horse, the name of the Meeting and the name of the race, shall be made by telephone by the owner of the engagement (or the nominator in the case of a withdrawal if the horse has been sold and the engagement not transferred) or by his authorised agent or in writing signed by the owner (or the nominator in the case of a withdrawal if the horse has been sold and the engagement not transferred) or his authorised agent but save with the express permission of the Stewards of the Jockey Club in every case, except those provided for in part (b) of this sub-Order such confirmations, declarations or withdrawals will only be accepted if the security code allotted by the Directors to persons qualified to make entries is given. For the purposes of this Order a telegram, telex or facsimile message shall be deemed to be in writing.

(b) In the case of horses trained outside Great Britain a confirmation, declaration or withdrawal may be made by the trainer, or, provided that a signed declaration is held by them, by an Official of the Turf Authority under whose Rules the trainer is licensed.

(c) Confirmations or declarations made by telephone will only be accepted from 2.30 p.m. on the day prior to that on which they are due.

(iv) *Deleted.*

(v) Trainers are responsible for ensuring that they do not declare horses to run in any races for which they are not qualified under the conditions of the races and these Orders and Rules.

125. If upon expiry of the time fixed for declarations under Order 124(ii) the number of horses in a race exceeds the Safety Factor the race shall be divided or the remaining entries reduced to the number permitted by the Safety Factor, or if at the said time in any Steeple Chase, Hurdle race or National Hunt Flat race the number of horses in a race exceeds the Safety Factor but is less than 18 the entries will be reduced to the number permitted by the Safety Factor, by elimination or ballot, or as the Directors may from time to time instruct as follows:—

(i) (a) In all handicaps (other than the Grand National Steeple Chase), which will be published in handicap weight rating order and random order of horses having the same weights the runners will be reduced by the elimination of horses allotted weights under Order 95(iii) commencing at the top of the list; followed by the elimination of the horses with the lowest weights at the time, commencing at the bottom of the list but disregarding horses which have incurred penalties unless it is necessary to eliminate these horses at their new weights in order to reduce the number of runners to the Safety Factor.

(b) In the Grand National Steeple Chase by the elimination of horses allotted weights under Order 95(iii), unless they have been placed first, second or third in either the Maryland Hunt Cup, the Grand Steeple Chase de Paris or the Velka Pardubicka, commencing at the top of the list; followed by the elimination of the horses with the lowest weights at the time, commencing at the bottom of the list, but disregarding horses which have incurred penalties unless it is necessary to eliminate these horses at their new weights in order to reduce the number of runners to the Safety Factor.

(ii) In all Pattern races other than handicaps the runners will be reduced by the elimination of those horses which in the opinion of the Handicapper have the lowest Handicap Ratings up to and including the day prior to that on which entries closed or, in races which closed more than six days before running, up to and including the day prior to the confirmation of entries.

(iii) Unless the Directors have given their permission for races under this Sub-Order to be divided:-

(a) In all Flat races other than handicaps and Pattern races, in which the guaranteed prize money is greater than £8,500, together with all weight for age selling races run from January 1st until the day prior to the commencement of the Flat Turf season and from the start of the week following the end of the York Spring meeting until December 31st, Limited Stakes races, races run at evening meetings and claiming races run on turf between the beginning of the week following the Doncaster St Leger Meeting and the end of the season, the runners shall be reduced by the elimination of horses by ballot, but unless to do so would mean that the number of horses remaining engaged would be in excess of the Safety Factor, the Directors will endeavour to ensure that no horse shall be eliminated if up to and including the day prior to that on which entries closed or, in races which closed more than six days before running, up to and including the day prior to the confirmation of entries it has:-

1. won a Flat race under the Rules of any recognised Turf Authority
2. previously been eliminated from a Flat race, other than a handicap, under these Orders during the current season.

Where these provisions cannot be fully implemented precedence will be given in the order shown above.

(b) In all National Hunt Flat races the runners shall be reduced by the elimination of horses by ballot but, unless to do so would mean that the horses remaining engaged would be in excess of the Safety Factor, the Directors will endeavour to ensure that no horse shall be eliminated if up to and including the day prior to that on which entries close or, in races which closed more than six days before running, up to and including the day prior to the confirmation of entries it has:—

1. won a National Hunt Flat race or an Irish National Hunt Flat race
2. not run in a National Hunt Flat race or an Irish National Hunt Flat race
3. not run more than once in a National Hunt Flat race

(c) In all novice or maiden hurdle races, in which the guaranteed prize money is greater than £4,500 together with novice selling and claiming Hurdle races with guaranteed prize money of £4,500 or less, other than handicaps and Pattern races, the runners shall be reduced by the elimination of those horses with the highest number of unplaced Hurdle race runs up to an including the day prior to that on which entries close or, in races which closed more than six days before running, up to and including the day prior to the confirmation of entries. Except that at the said time(s) horses which have not won a Hurdle race under the Rules of any recognised Turf authority shall be eliminated before horses which have won a Hurdle race under the Rules of any Recognised Turf authority even though the latter horse(s) may have a greater number of unplaced runs. Where it is necessary to decide which of two or more horses having the same number of unplaced runs are to be eliminated a ballot will be made.

Note: Wins in any National Hunt Flat races do not count as wins for the pruposes of this Sub-Order.

(d) In Hurdle races in which the guaranteed prize money is greater than £4,500 together with selling and claiming Hurdle races with guaranteed prize money of £4,500 or less, but not in either case including those Hurdle races which are handicaps, Pattern races or novice or maiden hurdle races, the runners shall be reduced by the elimination of horses by ballot but unless to do so would mean that the number of horses remaining engaged would be in excess of the Safety Factor the Directors will endeavour to ensure that no horse shall be eliminated if up to and including the day prior to that on which entries closed or, in races which closed more than six days before running, up to and including the day prior to the confirmation of entries it has:

1. won a Hurdle race under the Rules of any recognised Turf Authority.
2. previously been eliminated from a hurdle race other than a handicap or a novice or maiden hurdle race, under these Orders during the current season.

Where these provisions cannot be fully implemented, precedence will be given in the order shown.

(e) In all Steeple Chases other than handicaps and Pattern races, in which the guaranteed prize money is greater than £5,000 together with selling, claiming and Hunters Steeple Chases with guaranteed prize money of £5,000 or less, the runners shall be reduced by the elimination of horses by ballot, but unless to do so would mean that the number of horses remaining engaged would be in excess of the Safety Factor, the Directors will endeavour to ensure that no horse shall be eliminated if up to and including the day prior to that on which entries closed or, in races which closed more than six days before running, up to and including the day prior to the confirmation of entries it has:

1. won a Steeple Chase under the Rules of any recognised Turf Authority
2. never run in a Steeple Chase under the Rules of any recognised Turf Authority
3. previously been eliminated from a Steeple Chase, other than a handicap, under these Orders during the current season
4. been placed second, third or fourth in a Steeple Chase under the Rules of any recognised Turf Authority.

Where these provisions cannot be fully implemented precedence will be given in the order shown above.

(iv) (a) All other flat races shall be divided, subject to the provisions of Order 91(iv), except than when any flat race has to be divided runners in excess of twice the Safety Factor will be eliminated by ballot prior to division being made and the elimination of horses shall be subject to the provisions relating to elimination as set out in Sub-Order (iii)(a) of this Order.

(b) The following Steeple Chase and Hurdle races shall be divided subject to the provisions of Order 92(v) and Sub-Order (iii) of this Order:

1. Novice and Maiden Weight-for-Age Steeple Chases and Hurdle races other than selling and claiming races;

2. Weight-for-Age Steeple Chases and Hurdle races other than selling or claiming races;

except that runners in excess of twice the Safety Factor will be eliminated by ballot prior to division being made and the elimination of horses shall be subject to the provisions relating to elimination as set out in Sub-Orders (iii)(c) (d) and (e) of this Order.

(v) (a) When a horse which should be exempt from elimination under sub-Order (iii) or (iv) of this Order or the conditions of the race is erroneously eliminated from a race, the error may, with the express permission of the Directors, be corrected but only up to 2 p.m. on the day prior to that on which the race is advertised to be run and such correction shall in Flat races be subject to the requirements of Order 127.

(b) Neither the Directors nor anyone acting on their behalf shall be under any liability to any person by reason of the elimination of a horse, notwithstanding that the horse was exempt from elimination under this Order or the conditions of the race.

126. For flat races, subsequent to the operation of Sub-Orders (ii) and (iii) of Order 124 and of Order 125, the draw allotting positions at the start shall then be made at the Racing Calendar Office.

127. (i) Subject to the power of the Stewards contained in Rule 127(ii), once the draw under Order 126 has been made no alteration shall be made except that, by express permission of the Directors, the number of a horse may be added where that horse has been duly entered and declared and not withdrawn or eliminated but has been omitted from the list of runners. Where the addition results in the elimination of another horse the added horse shall take the saddle cloth number and draw position of the eliminated horse but, where no elimination is necessary the original draw for places shall stand and the horse which has been added shall be given the highest number.

(ii) Where the exceptional circumstances detailed in Sub-Order 127(i) above occur on the day of the race the Stewards can effect the same procedures of sub-Order 127(i).

128. (i) In every race for each declared horse there shall be a declaration of rider by 3.30 p.m. on the day fixed for declaration to run under Order 124(ii). The responsibility for compliance with this Order shall lie with the trainer of the horse at the said time where he is the Authorised Agent of the owner but will otherwise lie with the owner of the horse at the said time.

(ii) In races which close six days or less before running the declaration of riders to horses entered will, subject to the provisions of Orders 128(v) and 129, only be accepted.

(a) by the Racing Calendar Office, from 2.30 p.m. on the day before the day on which the race is advertised to close up to 3.30 p.m. on the day fixed for declaration to run under Order 124(ii),

or,

(b) by the National Jockeys Booking Agency, from 2.30 p.m. on the day on which the race is advertised to close up to 3.30 p.m. on the day fixed for declaration to run under Order 124(ii).

(iii) In races which close more than six days before running the declaration of riders to horses entered will, subject to the provisions of Order 128(v) and 129, only be accepted

(a) by the Racing Calendar Office, from 2.30 p.m. on the day before the day on which the entries must be confirmed up to 3.30 p.m. on the day fixed for declaration to run under Order 124(ii).

or

(b) by the National Jockeys Booking Agency, from 2.30 p.m. on the day on which the entries must be confirmed up to 3.30 p.m. on the day fixed for declaration to run under Order 124(ii).

(iv) Declarations of riders to horses may be withdrawn or altered prior to expiry of the time for making such declarations under Sub-Order 128(i). The most recent declaration of rider to horse will automatically replace any previous declaration.

(v) The times specified in this Order shall be subject to such change as the Directors shall decide and in Sub-Orders (ii) and (iii) relate to the overall commencement and closing times for receiving information regarding rider bookings. The specific times within these periods when the Racing Calendar Office and the National Jockeys Booking Agency are open to accept this information are set out in Appendix K to these Orders and Rules.

129. (i) Subject to Sub-Order (iii) of this Order and unless the Stewards of the Jockey Club otherwise permit,

declarations of riders to horses for any race or withdrawals or alterations thereof shall only be made by telephone and only to the Racing Calendar Office or the National Jockeys Booking Agency by:—

(a) the owner of the horse, or

(b) the trainer of the horse, or

(c) an Authorised Agent of the owner or trainer of the horse;

and, in the case of the National Jockeys Booking Agency, also by:—

(d) the intended rider of the horse concerned, or

(e) the Authorised Rider's Agent of the intended rider,

(Note: The use of the answer phone facility will not be available in respect of declarations of riders to horses or withdrawals or alterations thereof).

(ii) Save with the express permission of the Directors, declarations of riders to horses or withdrawals or alterations thereof made by the owner or trainer of the horse, or their respective Authorised Agents, or the intended rider of the horse, or the Authorised Agent thereof will only be accepted if the security code allotted by the Directors to persons qualified to make such declarations is given.

(iii) In the case of horses trained outside Great Britain declarations of riders to horses or withdrawals or alterations thereof will only be accepted by the Racing Calendar Office:—

(a) if made by the owner, trainer, or their respective Authorised Agents, or, provided that a signed declaration is held by them, by an Official of the Turf Authority under whose Rules the trainer is licensed, and,

(b) in addition to telephone, may be made by facsimile message or telex providing such document is signed by one of the persons mentioned in (a) above.

(iv) The Stewards of the Jockey Club shall maintain a register of Authorised Rider's Agents. Such Agents may only be registered by annual application to the Racing Calendar Office on the prescribed form, signed by the Agent. A fee must accompany each application. However, the said fee will be waived where the application is made by:—

(a) a person who is either a spouse, parent, son or daughter of the rider in question and

(b) such person is only acting as an Authorised Rider's Agent for a rider(s) to whom he is so related as stated in (a) above.

PART 13: LIABILITY FOR ENTRANCE MONEY, FORFEITS, ETC.

Liability for Entrances

130. In races for which there is a declaration of forfeit

(i) the nominator as well as every owner of the horse at the time of nomination is liable for the initial entrance fee, which is payable at the time of entry, sums due under Order 133 (i) and (ii) and for any additional sums laid down in the conditions of the race. The amounts due at a forfeit stage are payable at the time fixed for the forfeit and sums due at the time of declaration to run are payable when the race takes place;

(ii) in cases where a transfer of engagements has been lodged under Order 116(i) the transferee is liable for any additional sums payable after the lodgement of the transfer. These amounts are payable at the time laid down in Sub-Order (i) of this Order.

131. In races for which there is no declaration of forfeit

(i) the nominator as well as every owner of the horse at the time of entry is liable for the entrance fee, the sums due under Order 133(i) and (ii) and any surcharge payable under that Order. These sums are payable when the race takes place but if the entry is transferred to any other person the nominator is liable only in case of default by the transferee;

(ii) in cases where a transfer of engagements has been lodged under Order 116(i) the transferee is liable for entrance fee, sums due under Order 133(i) and (ii), and any surcharge payable under that Order and these sums are payable when the race takes place.

132. When a horse has been accidentally entered for a race for which the horse is not qualified the entry may be deleted on payment of a fine of £60 up to the time fixed for confirmation of entries under Order 124(i) or, in races which close six days or less before running, up to 11 a.m. on the day following that upon which entries closed.

133. (i) A fee shall be paid to the British Horseracing Board in respect of each entry received.

(ii) An additional surcharge the amount of which the Directors shall from time to time decide, shall be payable in respect of each entry in the following races:-

(a) Open Maiden, Rating Related Maiden, Median Auction, and auction Flat races with guaranteed prize money of £8,500 or less.

(b) Claiming Flat races with guaranteed prize money of £8,500 or less except those Claiming Flat races run on turf between the beginning of the week following the Doncaster St Leger meeting and the end of the Flat turf season.

(c) Selling Flat races which are not Handicaps with guaranteed prize money of £8,500 or less run between the start of the Flat Turf season up to the end of the week of the York Spring meeting.

(d) All other Conditions Flat races with guaranteed prize money of £8,500 or less except Limited Stakes races.

(e) Weight-for-age Hurdle races in which the guaranteed prize money is £4,500 or less, other than selling or claiming races.

(f) Weight-for-age Steeple Chases in which the guaranteed prize money is £5,000 or less, other than selling or claiming races or Hunters' Steeple Chases.

(g) National Hunt Flat Races.

(iii) A sum of £1.20 shall be paid in respect of each entry to the Trustees of the Animal Health Trust for the benefit of the Equine Research Station.

(iv) Entrance money if so required must be paid at the time of entry together with any arrears.

134. (i) Except as provided for in Sub-Order (iii) of this Order, no entrance money, stake, forfeit or fine is payable either in respect of horses eliminated from a race under the provisions of Order 114(iii) or Order 125 or in respect of horses entered in races which are never run or are void, and all payments made prior to the race shall be returned.

(ii) In a Rating Related Maiden or Limited Stakes Flat race an entry made for a horse shall be invalid if

(a) prior to the time of the closing of the race, the horse does not have a qualifying handicap rating published in the ratings list in the Racing Calendar.

and

(b) the rating subsequently allocated by the Handicapper is outside the rating band specified in the conditions of the race.

All payments made prior to the race in such circumstances shall be returned.

(iii) When a race is divided under the provisions of Order 125 and one or more divisions are not run, provided that at least one division has been run, entrance money is payable in respect of all horses entered for the race except those horses which were declared to run and were allocated to the abandoned division or divisions. The balance of any entrance money remaining after deduction of that allocated to prize money in the divisions which ran shall be paid to the credit of the Race Division Fund.

The Forfeit List

135. (i) The Forfeit List shall be kept at the Racing Calendar Office. A copy of the full Forfeit List shall be published in the first Racing Calendar of the months of January, April, July and October. Amendments to the List will be published in the Racing Calendar at the first practical publication date.

(ii) The Forfeit List shall include all arrears which have been notified by the Stakeholder of any Meeting held under these Rules, or as otherwise provided under these Rules, and shall state the name or names of the persons or Companies from whom, such sums are due. "Arrears" which have been so published must be paid direct to the Racing Calendar Office, and until so paid the name or names of the persons or Companies shall not be removed from the List.

137. (i) So long as the name of a person is in the Forfeit List maintained under the provisions of Rule 135, even though the arrears arose or the Forfeit List was published under the previous Rules of Racing or National Hunt Rules, he is a disqualified person.

(ii) When a person's name appears in the Official Forfeit List published by a recognised Turf Authority he shall be a disqualified person under these Rules until his name ceases to appear in such list unless the Stewards of the Jockey Club declare otherwise. An application for such a declaration must be made to the Stewards of the Jockey Club within seven days of the first publication of the person's name in such list.

(iii) The registration of any recognised Company whose name is in the Forfeit List shall be cancelled.

138. If a horse whose owner's name is in the Forfeit List be entered for any race, the nominator of such horse may be fined a sum not exceeding £180.

V.A.T.

139. Without prejudice to the effect of any Order or Rule specifically imposing liability to V.A.T. it is hereby expressly declared that where a fee or other sum of money is payable under these Orders or Rules the amount of V.A.T. chargeable on the payment shall also be paid by the person or Company making the payment in addition to the fee or other sum of money so payable. For the avoidance of doubt it is hereby expressly declared that nothing in this Order shall in any circumstances be taken as relieving any person or Company from an obligation to pay V.A.T. in addition to any fee or other sum of money payable under these Orders or Rules.

PART 14: WEIGHING OUT, EXHIBITING NUMBERS, ETC.,

The Weighing Room

140. No person shall, without special leave from the Stewards, enter the Weighing Room, except an Official of the Meeting, Directors of the British Horseracing Board, an Official appointed by the Stewards of the Jockey Club, an Official appointed by the Directors of the British Horseracing Board, the owner, trainer, and rider, or other person having the care of a horse engaged in the race, or a licensed master jockey's valet or master valet's assistant. No rider whose licence or permit has been suspended by the Stewards of the Jockey Club under Rule 2(iii) may enter a Weighing Room during the period of his suspension.

No person other than Officials of Meetings of the Jockey Club and of the British Horseracing Board, amateur riders engaged to ride, jockeys and master jockeys' valets and master valets' assistants shall enter Riders' Dressing Rooms with the following exception: For Steeple Chases, Hurdle races and National Hunt Flat races, Trainers or their representatives may enter when, in an emergency, a rider has to be engaged at short notice. Any unauthorised person refusing to leave the Dressing Rooms shall be reported to the Stewards.

Weighing Out

141. (i) No rider shall be weighed out (except as provided below) for any race unless the Declaration Sheet has been duly signed not less than three-quarters of an hour before the time fixed for the race. The signing of the Declaration Sheet shall be a declaration that the horse is to run and that the information contained therein relating to the said horse is correct. The Declaration Sheet may only be signed by the owner, trainer, employee of the trainer on production of his Racehorse Attendant's Identity Card and Validity Pass, or other person on production of a written authorisation by the owner or trainer and valid only for the day of the race. When a horse is owned by a 'recognised Company' declaration may also be made by a registered agent of the Company or by another person on production of a written authorisation signed by such registered agent and valid only for the day of the race. If the information contained in the Declaration Sheet requires alteration, correction should be made at the time of declaration to run. Information on the Declaration Sheet may be corrected without penalty before the time for declaring runners has elapsed. If correction is not made by the said time the person making the declaration, or the trainer, if the declaration was made by his employee, may be fined not less than £45.

(ii) The trainer shall ensure that the horse carries at least the correct weight in accordance with the conditions of the race. The trainer is required to declare the weight his horse will carry or the colours to be worn by the rider if either is different from those appearing on the racecard to the Clerk of the Scales before the rider weighs out. If such declaration is not made the trainer shall be fined not less than £45.

(iii) After 3.30 p.m. on the day fixed for declaration to run under Order 124(ii), or as the Stewards of the Jockey Club shall direct, a substitution of rider shall only be permitted if the Stewards are satisfied that any one of the circumstances below applies:—

(a) illness, or rider declared unfit to ride;

(b) unqualified rider declared;

(c) a meeting on the same day has been abandoned and the rider was declared to ride at the abandoned meeting;

(d) the rider was declared to ride at another meeting on the same day and one of his declared rides is unable to run (See Instruction D2);

(e) the rider was declared to ride another horse in the same race but the horse is unable to run;

(f) some other circumstances acceptable to the Stewards.

In all cases the substitution is subject to the rider being weighed within the times specified in Sub-Rule (vi) of this Rule and to the provisions of Sub-Rule (v) of this Rule.

(N.B. See Instruction D1 for Procedure when Declared Riders are Unable to Ride).

(iv) If a horse has been declared to run under Order 124(ii) and no rider has been declared for the horse as required under Order 128(i) the Stewards may authorise not less than three-quarters of an hour before the time fixed for the race a rider for the horse concerned. Such authorisation shall only be made at the request of the owner, trainer, employee of the trainer on production of his Racehorse Attendant's Identity Card and Validity Pass, or other person on production of a written authorisation by the owner or trainer and available only for the day of the race.

(v) When a rider has been declared to ride under Order 128(i) it shall be an offence if he does not weigh out unless on that day the Stewards are satisfied that this was due to circumstances detailed in Sub-Rule 141(iii). Another rider may, however, with the permission of the Stewards, be substituted provided always that he can be weighed within the times specified in Sub-Rule (vi) of this Rule.

(vi) Every rider must be weighed for a specified horse by the Clerk of the Scales, at the appointed place, not less than a quarter of an hour before the time fixed for the race or where this is not possible due to late running of the preceeding race, not more than five minutes after the Clerk of the Scales has weighed in the winner of that race. In other exceptional cases (for example, but without imposing any limitation on the powers of the Stewards, a sudden change of weather conditions delaying racing) the Stewards may extend the time allowed for declaring runners under this Rule, weighing, declaring weight, and for exhibiting the numbers.

(vii) Riders must acquaint themselves in advance with the correct course over which they are to ride by consulting the plan in the Weighing Room.

142. (i) If a rider intends to carry over-weight, he must declare the amount thereof at the time of weighing out or, if in doubt as to his proper weight, he may declare the weight he intends to carry.

(ii) When weighing out or weighing in, the rider must put into the scale and include in his weight everything that the horse is to carry or has carried except the skull cap, whip, bridle, rings, plates, blinkers, hood, visor, eyeshield, or eyecover and anything worn on the horse's legs. If the rider is to wear spurs during the course of the race they must be correctly worn by the rider when weighing out.

(iii) When weighing out or weighing in, the rider in addition to the items detailed in Sub-Rule (ii) above, will also exclude from the scale any breast plate, breast girth, martingale or neck strap that the horse is to carry or has carried.

(iv) To compensate for their being required to wear body protectors the weight of all riders will be calculated at 1lb less than the weight which is registered on the scale.

143. If a rider after he has been weighed for a specified horse, and before he has come under Starter's Orders, is prevented by accident or illness from riding in the race, another rider may be substituted provided there is no unreasonable delay.

If he fails to ride for any reason other than:—

(a) accident

(b) illness or

(c) withdrawal of the horse by the Starter except when the rider refuses to ride

it shall be an offence unless the rider satisfies the Stewards that his failure to ride was due to circumstances acceptable to them.

Running and Walking Over Non-Runners

144. (i) Every qualified horse which has been declared a runner in a race under Order 124(ii), and in respect of which the declaration has not been withdrawn or the horse eliminated as provided for in Order 125, shall run in that race. If any horse whether qualified or not which has thus been declared a runner does not run in that race the trainer or, if the horse is not in the care of a licensed or permitted trainer, the owner, shall pay a fixed penalty of the amount laid down in Sub-Rule (iv) of this Rule unless either:-

(a) the owner and/or his representative within 48 hours from the time of the race satisfy the Stewards that the failure of the horse to run was caused by circumstances outside the reasonable control of the Owner and/or his representative. In this event the fixed penalty referred to will be waived by order of the Stewards, or

(b) the horse was prevented from running because under Order 27(ii) the rider was not allowed to weigh out when the fixed penalty shall be paid by the Owner, or

(c) the Stewards have reason to believe that the failure of the horse to run took place in circumstances showing a wilful disregard of the interest of racegoers or other reprehensible motive on the part of the Owner and/or his representative. In such event the Stewards may exercise the powers specified in Rule 15 (i) of the Rules of Racing and may in addition (if they see fit) impose the said fixed penalty, or

(d) the Stewards decide to refer the matter to the Stewards of the Jockey Club. In that event the Stewards shall not impose a fixed penalty but the Stewards of the Jockey Club may exercise the powers specified in Rule 2 of the Rules of Racing and may in addition (if they think fit) impose the said fixed penalty.

(ii) Unless the horse runs in both races the Owner and/or his representative shall not leave a horse declared to run after the time fixed for declarations under Order 124(ii) in two or more races on the same day otherwise than as permitted under paragraph (iii) of this rule and the defence afforded by paragraph (i)(a) shall not be available to the Owner and/or his representative in these circumstances. In imposing any penalty for a breach of this sub-Rule the Stewards shall take account of the fixed penalty consequentially imposed under sub-Rule (i) of this Rule.

(iii) The fixed penalty will be waived and no further fine shall be imposed if a horse remains declared to run after the time fixed for declaration under Order 124(ii) in two Steeple Chases or Hurdle races or National Hunt Flat races taking place at different meetings on the same day, provided that the races concerned have guaranteed prize money of over £4,000, that the trainer has advised the Racing Calendar Office by the time fixed for declarations under Order 124(ii) of the meeting at which he would prefer the horse to run and the other meeting at which it is engaged and that the horse either runs at the preferred meeting if it takes place or at the other meeting if the preferred meeting is abandoned.

(iv) The fixed penalty referred to in Sub-Rule (i) shall be 1% of the guaranteed prize money in any race in which the guaranteed prize money is £15,000 or more, or, in other races, £105 in the case of a Flat race and £95 in the case of a Steeple Chase, Hurdle race or a National Hunt Flat race.

(v) Orders made for the imposition and waiver of the fixed penalty provided for under Sub-Rule (i) shall not be published in the Racing Calendar but any other order made under or pursuant to this Rule may be so published.

Equipment

145. (i) The saddle comprises the saddle itself, the girth, the surcingle, the stirrup irons, and the leathers or webs, and the rider is responsible for the fit condition of the saddle which he uses, but in the case of an apprentice or conditional jockey, or where a stable employee rides for the trainer who employs him, the responsibility rests with the trainer.

(ii) Except for methods of attaching reins to bridles which have the approval of the Stewards of the Jockey Club all reins must be stitched to, or fastened by buckle to the bridle and the responsibility for this and all equipment worn by the horse with exception of the saddle, where relevant, rests with the trainer (see sub-Rule (i) of this Rule).

(iii) Trainers are also responsible for ensuring that their horses are properly saddled when they leave the parade ring or at an All Weather Track fixture at which the Stewards have authorised mounting in the place appointed for saddling, when they leave that place.

(iv) If there be any failure of equipment, be it the responsibility of the rider or of the trainer, between leaving the Parade Ring and the start of the race, the rider himself must assume responsibility for carrying out any repair that may be possible with the assistance of such spare tack as may be available at the start. The rider must inspect the spare tack and judge for himself the safety of any repair if he is in doubt he should not start.

146. (i) No rider shall be mounted on a horse when it is on property owned, used or controlled by the Managing Executive of a racecourse nor shall he ride in any race unless he is wearing a correctly fitted and fastened skull cap of a pattern approved by the Stewards of the Jockey Club.

(ii) No rider shall be weighed out for or ride in any race unless he is wearing a body protector of a pattern approved by the Stewards of the Jockey Club.

(iii) The sole responsibility for the wearing and the serviceable condition of the skull cap and the body protector is that of the rider and of no other body or person save as provided by Sub-Rule (iv) hereof.

(iv) In the case of an apprentice or conditional Jockey, or where a stable employee rides for the trainer who employs him, the responsibility for the wearing and serviceable condition of the skull cap and body protector is that of the trainer.

(v) The use of an unserviceable skull cap or body protector shall be regarded as a breach of the Rules of Racing by the rider or, as provided in sub-Rule (iv) above, the trainer, either of whom shall be liable to a fine.

147. (i) (a) If a horse is to run in a hood, blinkers, visor, eyeshield or eyecover a declaration must be made to the Racing Calendar Office by the time fixed for making declarations to run under Order 124(ii) and in the manner laid down for making declarations.

(b) If a horse is to run in a hood fitted with blinkers both must be declared as must any combination of hood, blinkers, visor, eyeshield or eyecover.

Note: for the purpose of this Rule "blinkers" means a garment fitted over a horse's head with holes for the eyes and ears, one or both eyeholes being fitted with cowls cutting out all vision to the rear but permitting full forward vision. "Visor" means a garment similar to blinkers in which one or both cowls have holes cut in them permitting limited side or rear vision. "Hood" means a garment similar to blinkers, incorporating ear covers but without eye cowls. "Eyeshield" means a garment similar to blinkers except that in place of the eye cowls both eyes are covered with a mesh or other transparent material. "Eyecover"means a garment similar to blinkers except that in place of the eye cowls one eye only is completely covered by an opaque cover.

(ii) (a) When a horse has been declared to run in a hood, blinkers, visor, eyeshield or eyecover they must be worn by the horse on the way to the start and during the race and if it is not possible for the horse to wear them he shall not run.

(b) When no declaration of hood, blinkers, visor, eyeshield or eyecover has been made they must not be worn by the horse on the way to the start and during the race and if it is not possible for the horse to race without them he shall not run.

(iii) The use of blinding hoods (except when entering Starting Stalls under the supervision of the Starter) or any form of shutter hood is prohibited nor may any horse run in a race wearing a garment fitted over its head other than a hood, blinkers, visor, eyeshield or eyecover.

148. No horse shall enter the parade ring or run in shoes which have protrusions on the ground surface other than catkins on the hind, limited to 1/4" in height. The use of American type toe-grab plates or those with a sharp flange is forbidden. The trainer is responsible for ensuring that his horses are shod in accordance with the requirements of this Rule.

149. (i) Spurs are not permitted in races confined to apprentice jockeys or conditional jockeys. Spurs which are sharp, fitted with rowels or are angled upward or inward are not permitted in any race.

(ii) No substitute for a whip shall be carried in any race and any whip which is carried must comply with the specifications approved by the Stewards of the Jockey Club. Where the rider is an Apprentice or Conditional jockey failure to comply with the requirements of this Sub-Rule will be regarded as a breach of the Rules of Racing by both the rider and the trainer who employs him.

(iii) Every horse running in a race shall carry a number cloth and the trainer is responsible for ensuring it is worn so that the number is clearly visible.

PART 15: RUNNING, VOID RACES, WALKING OVER AND DEAD-HEATS

Before the Race

150. (i) All horses running at the meeting shall be saddled in the appointed place and brought into the parade ring a reasonable time before the signal to mount is given, unless the Stewards have exercised their powers under Order 14(ii)(b). The attendants shall be provided with badges bearing numbers corresponding with those on the card. In the case of any horse not being brought into the parade ring, or a badge not being exhibited, the trainer shall be reported to the Stewards. No horse shall be admitted to the paddock unless it has been declared to run under Rule 124(ii), or is advertised on the racecard for sale. The parade ring shall be reserved strictly for those horses which are about to run. No person shall, without special leave from the Stewards, enter the parade ring except officials of the meeting and owners, trainers, horse attendants, and riders of horses about to run in the next race. Any person refusing to leave shall be reported to the Stewards.

(ii) The Clerk of the Course shall see that a clean number-cloth, of a pattern approved by the Stewards of the Jockey Club, is provided for every horse for which a rider presents himself to be weighed out.

(iii) Riders must proceed to the Parade Ring (or in the case of an All Weather Track Fixture the place designated for mounting) when so instructed by the Clerk of the Course or his representative.

(iv) No horse is allowed to leave the Parade Ring (or, in the case of an All Weather Track Fixture the place designated for mounting) to proceed to the start before the signal to mount (as laid down in Rule 23(ii)) is given, unless the owner or trainer first obtains the permission of the Stewards. When a horse is unavoidably delayed in the Parade Ring (or, in the case of an All Weather Track Fixture the place designated for mounting) and cannot leave to go to the start in company with the other horses those horses which have not already left for the start shall remain in the Parade Ring until the horse concerned is ready to go to the start with them. This sub-Rule does not prevent Stewards from giving special instructions in cases of emergency.

(v) Unless where at an All Weather Track the Stewards have cancelled the requirement, when the signal to mount is given the horses shall be made to stand still with their heads towards the centre of the Parade Ring. The riders will walk immediately to where their horses are standing and will mount there. If this requirement has been cancelled horses will proceed around the Parade Ring and will be mounted at the walk.

When the rider has mounted he may walk his horse round the Parade Ring in front of those horses which are still standing and he will continue to do this, in the same direction as the horses were walking before they were mounted, until the moment arrives to go down to the start. Horses are not allowed to cross the middle of the Parade Ring.

In the case of an All Weather Track Fixture at which the Stewards have authorised mounting in the place appointed for saddling, when the signal to mount is given horses will be mounted where they are standing. Horses will then proceed direct to the entrance onto the track.

(vi) Subject to the powers of the Stewards under Rule 14 (ii) every horse must be ridden in front of the Stand before going to the post, and the Stewards shall decide the distance to be traversed.

If the requirements of this sub-Rule have not been cancelled and a horse is not ridden in front of the stand the stewards shall hold an enquiry as to whether the rider made reasonable endeavour to comply with this Rule.

(vii) When a parade has been advertised.

(a) The Stewards shall determine the distance and the parade which must include the horses passing the stands, preferably alongside the far rail and, where possible, their cantering to the start past the Stands after they have been released. A plan showing the route of the parade and marking exactly all turning and reference points will be displayed in the Weighing Room.

(b) When the signal is given for the riders to mount in a race for which a parade has been advertised a broadcast announcement must be made to the effect that it is about to take place.

(c) When the riders have mounted all the horses must be led out on to the course by their attendants and must parade in racecard order, except that any horse which is likely to upset the other runners by its behaviour may be placed in such a position in the parade as the Stewards may decide.

(d) The horses will be led by their attendants over the parade route. When they are released at the designated point they will canter to the start by the most direct route.

(e) Except in an emergency no rider may dismount during a parade.

(f) If the Managing Executive wishes the parade may be assisted by outriders at the front and/or rear.

(viii) There shall be no preliminary jump allowed before any race.

151. (i) Every horse which runs in a race shall be run on its merits, whether its owner runs another horse in the race or not.

(ii) The rider of every horse shall take all reasonable and permissible measures throughout the race to ensure that his horse is given a full opportunity to win or of obtaining the best possible placing.

(iii) It shall be the duty of a trainer to ensure that adequate instructions are given to the rider of any horse in his care and no owner, registered agent of a recognised Company, or trainer shall give any instruction to the rider of any horse which if obeyed could or would prevent the horse from winning a race or of obtaining the best possible placing, neither shall they, its rider or any other person prevent or try to prevent in any way any horse from winning a race or of obtaining the best possible placing.

The Race

152. (i) Any horse getting away from its rider in a Steeple Chase or Hurdle race may be remounted, but should it have run out of the course or continued in the race before being caught it shall be brought back to the part of the course where it parted from its rider, and shall continue by jumping all the remaining fences or hurdles. Any rider so losing his horse may be assisted in catching it and remounting it without risk of disqualification.

(ii) If a horse having refused any fence, or hurdle, in a Steeple Chase or Hurdle race, has been led over it by any of the bystanders, or has been given a lead over by any horseman not riding in the race, the horse shall, on an objection under Rule 170(iv), be disqualified.

(iii) If a horse runs the wrong side of a direction post or flag, or misses a fence or hurdle, unless the Stewards have issued instructions to all riders prior to the race that it is to be omitted, his rider shall except as set out in sub-Rule (v) of the Rule, turn back and ride the course correctly from such point, or he shall pull up. He shall not otherwise continue in the race, or his horse shall, on an objection under Rule 170 (iv), be disqualified.

(iv) Where a marker has been inserted in a fence or hurdle to denote that there has been an accident a rider who disregards the marker will be guilty of an offence unless the Stewards are satisfied that he was taking reasonable steps to avoid it. Where cones are deployed to direct runners to the safe end of the obstacle a rider who disregards such cones will be guilty of an offence unless the Stewards are satisfied that he was taking reasonable steps to avoid the unsafe area. If a rider jumps the fence or hurdle within the area denoted by the cones as being unsafe the horse may, on an objection under Rule 170 (iv) be disqualified if the Stewards are satisfied that the result of the race was affected.

(v) Where in an emergency marker cones are deployed right across the front of a fence or hurdle to indicate that it is unsafe to jump riders who have not jumped the obstacle on that or any subsequent circuit of the course must pull up. Any rider who fails without reasonable cause to pull up will be guilty of an offence and the horse shall, in any event, on an objection under Rule 170 (iv), be disqualified.

(vi) Where, because of an accident a fence or hurdle cannot be jumped the race shall be void unless one or more horses have jumped the fence or hurdle prior to cones being deployed to indicate that it is unsafe to jump and have completed the course when the result shall stand subject to Rule 26 and 1 (ix) and the powers of the Stewards or the Stewards of the Jockey Club to disqualify horses or alter placings.

Riding Offences

153. (i) When a horse or its rider has caused interference

(a) By accident in any part of a Flat Race or National Hunt Flat Race or after the penultimate obstacle in a Steeplechase or Hurdle Race, the horse shall, on an objection under Rule 170 (iv), be placed behind the horse or horses with which it has interfered or placed last if the Stewards are satisfied that the interference improved the placing of the horse causing the interference. If they are not so satisfied they shall overrule the objection and order that the placings shall remain unchanged.

(b) By careless riding in any part of a race the horse shall, on an objection under Rule 170 (iv), be placed behind the horse or horses with which it has interfered or placed last except that the Stewards may order that the placings shall remain unchanged if the Judge has placed the horse behind the horse or horses with which it has interfered.

(c) By reckless riding or intentionally in any part of a race the horse shall, on an objection under Rule 170 (iv), be disqualified.

(ii) For the purpose of the application of sub-Rule (i)(a) and (b) the placing of a horse interfered with shall be that decided by the Judge.

(iii) The rider of any horse who, in the opinion of the Stewards of the Meeting or the Stewards of the Jockey Club, has been guilty of reckless, careless or improper riding, or has intentionally caused interference in any part of a race, shall be guilty of an offence.

(iv) (a) When in the opinion of the Stewards any rider has committed any breach of or been guilty of any offence under Sub-Rule (iii) of this Rule or sub-Rules (iv) or (v) of Rule 152 the Stewards in addition to their powers under Rules 14 and 15 have power to suspend him from riding at that racecourse for any period up to fourteen days beginning at the commencement of the ninth day after the day of their decision save that if he shall on that commencement date already be suspended for any other riding offences under these Rules, or suspended by any recognised Turf Authority unless the Stewards of the Jockey Club have declared that such suspension shall not have effect under these Rules, the suspension shall begin at the commencement of the day following the completion of any previous period of suspension. Where in the opinion of the Stewards an apprentice or conditional jockey is guilty of careless or improper riding or has committed any breach of Rule 152 (iv) or (v) and he is both permitted to claim a 7lbs allowance under Rule 109 and has not previously committed any breach of or been guilty of any offence under Sub-Rule (iii) of this Rule the Stewards may in lieu of suspension caution him as to his future conduct in races.

(b) Stewards who have suspended a rider from riding or cautioned an apprentice or conditional jockey under the provisions of Sub-Rule (iv) (a) of this Rule shall, if there is a video recording of the race, forward the video recording forthwith to the Stewards of the Jockey Club, or, if there is no video recording, shall at the request of the Stewards of the Jockey Club forward to them any transcript of evidence, or such notes of evidence, statements or other material as may be required by the Stewards of the Jockey Club for consideration under Rule 3.

Void Races

154. (i) A race shall be void in any of the following circumstances:-

(a) if all the horses have run at the wrong weights;
(b) if all the horses have run over the wrong course;
(c) if it has been started in front of the Starting Post;

(d) if when the recall flag has been raised no horses have returned to the start;

(e) if the starter has declared a false start and the recall flag has not been raised unless all the horses pull up before completing the course in a flat race or a circuit of the course in a Steeple Chase, Hurdle race or National Hunt flat race, and return to the Starter except as provided in Rule 28(xii)(g);

(f) if the Judge is not in the place designated by the Stewards as the Judge's Box at the time when the first horse passes the winning post or is unable to place any horse;

(g) if no horse finishes

(ii) If no qualified horse cover the course in accordance with these Rules the race may be declared void.

Walking Over

155. In walking over for a race, in no case shall it be necessary for a horse to "walk over" the entire course, but if only one horse shall have been declared a runner under Rule 141 that horse shall be ridden past the Judge's box from the correct course, and shall then be deemed the winner.

Dead Heats

156. When horses run a dead-heat, for first or any lower place, the owners shall divide, and the dead-heat shall not be run off, but on a dead-heat for a match, the match is off.

157. When two horses run a dead-heat for first place, all prizes to which each category of persons connected with the first and second horses would have been entitled under Order 194 shall be divided equally between such persons and this principle shall be observed in dividing the prize whatever the number of dead-heaters and whatever the place for which the dead-heat is run. Each horse that divides a race for first place shall be deemed a winner (for penalties, see Orders 100 and 103).

158. (i) When a dead-heat is run for second place, and the winner of the race is subsequently disqualified or its placing altered, the horses which ran the dead-heat shall be deemed to have run a dead-heat for first place. When a dead-heat is run for any lower place and placings are subsequently altered the horses which ran the dead-heat will be deemed to have run that dead-heat for the new placing.

(ii) When under Rule 153(i)(a) or (b) two or more horses are placed last in a race by the Stewards those horses will be regarded as having dead-heated for last place.

159. If the dividing owners cannot agree as to which of them is to have a cup or other prize which cannot be divided, the question shall be determined by lot by the Stewards, who shall decide what sum of money shall be paid by the owner who takes such cup or other indivisible prize, to the other owners or owner.

PART 16: WEIGHING-IN

160. (i) Immediately after pulling up, the riders of the horses placed first, second, and third in each race must ride their horses to the place appointed for unsaddling, and the horses shall remain there until ordered to be taken away by the Clerk of the Scales. The other riders may dismount within a reasonable distance. Every rider must present himself to be weighed by the Clerk of the Scales at once, and, if he fails to complete the course, report the reason. If a rider be prevented from riding back to weigh in by reason of accident or illness, by which he or his horse is disabled, he may walk or be carried to the scales.

(ii) In cases where the Judge, in consulting the photograph,has not announced his decision before the jockeys return to weigh in, they may dismount either inside or within a reasonable distance of the place appointed for unsaddling the winner. In such cases the Clerk of the Scales shall weigh in all jockeys until such time as the Judge's decision is announced.

(iii) It shall be a breach of the Rules of Racing for a rider to dismount before reaching the place appointed for that purpose unless he can satisfy the Stewards that he was justified by extraordinary circumstances.

(iv) If a rider touches, except accidentally, any person or thing other than his own equipment before weighing in, his horse shall, on an objection under Rule 170(iv), be disqualified, unless he can satisfy the Stewards that he was justified by extraordinary circumstances.

(v) If a rider does not present himself to be weighed in his horse, shall, on an objection under Rule 170(iv), be disqualified unless the Stewards are satisfied that he was justified in not doing so by reason of illness, accident or other extraordinary circumstances, that he weighed out at not less than his correct weight and that the proper weight was carried throughout the race.

161. (i) In weighing in, a jockey shall include in his weight everything that the horse has carried in the race, except as provided in Rule 142.

(ii) If a rider weighs in at 2lb or more over the weight at which he weighed out, he shall be reported to the Stewards. The horse shall not be disqualified under this Rule.

(iii) If a rider cannot draw the weight at which he weighed out, the Clerk of the Scales shall allow him 1lb. If he cannot then draw the weight, his horse shall, on an objection under Rule 170(iv), be disqualified.

(iv) If a horse carried less than the weight it should carry in accordance with the conditions of the race and these Rules, it shall on an objection under Rule 170(v), be disqualified by the Stewards of the Jockey Club.

162. (i) When the riders have weighed in to the satisfaction of the Clerk of the Scales, at not less than the weight at which they weighed out, except as under Rule 161(iii), the Stewards shall authorise the All Right signal to be given on the number board or screen. Provided they shall not authorise this until:-

(a) The period allowed for objecting under section (iv) of Rule 170 has elapsed.

(b) Any objection which may have been lodged on grounds mentioned in section (iv) of Rule 170 has been decided.

(c) A decision in any enquiry under Rule 171 (iii) has been made.

(ii) No objection on any grounds other than those mentioned in Rule 170(iv) shall be entertained prior to the giving of the signal.

(iii) After the signal has been given no alteration shall be made to the numbers of the winner or placed horses on the board or screen.

(iv) Trainers or their representatives who have had runners in a race together with the riders who rode the horses must remain on the racecourse until the All Right signal has been authorised.

PART 17: DISPUTES, OBJECTIONS AND APPEALS

Disputes and Objections

170. (i) If an objection to a horse engaged in a race be made not later than half-past ten in the morning of the day of the race, the Stewards may require his qualification to be proved before the race; and in default of such proof being given to their satisfaction they may declare him disqualified.

(ii) An objection to the distance of a course officially designated must be made before a race.

(iii) An objection to any decision of the Clerk of the Scales must be made at once.

(iv) An objection to a horse on the grounds of a cross, jostle, or any act on the part of his rider, or of his not having run the proper course, or of the race having been run on a wrong course, or of any other matter occurring in the race, or before weighing in, or on the grounds that the rider did not present himself to weigh in, or that he could not draw the weight at which he weighed out, must be made within five minutes after the winner has been weighed in or within five minutes of the time the judge has announced his decision on all placings, whichever be later (see also Rule 171 (iii)), or, should the judge revise his original decision before the five minutes have elapsed, within five minutes of the revised decision being given. The Stewards may extend the above period if they are satisfied that it could not have been made within this time. No objection on any other ground than these shall be heard within this time. In the event of the judge revising his original decision after the five minutes have elapsed and within the time limit specified in Rule 26(i) any objection on the grounds set out in this Rule must be made within 48 hours of the revised decision being made. Such objection shall be made in the accordance with the requirements of Rule 171 (i) save that if it shall be made to the Stewards of the Jockey Club at the Registry Office.

(v) An objection on any other ground than those laid down in Rule 170(iv) shall be received within fourteen days of the conclusion of a Meeting. No objection under this paragraph may be heard until the signal has been given in accordance with Rule 162.

(vi) In cases of fraud, or wilful mis-statement, there shall be no limit to the time for objecting provided the Stewards of the Jockey Club are satisfied there has been no unnecessary delay on the part of the objector. Such objection shall not be heard until the signal has been given in accordance with Rule 162.

(vii) Nothing in this Rule shall restrict the operation at any time of Rules 1, 2 and 15.

(viii) Where the Stewards of the Jockey Club correct a mistake of the Judge and declare the winner and placed horses pursuant to their powers under Rule 1 (ix) they may permit an objection on the grounds set out in sub Rule (iv) of this Rule provided it is made within 48 hours of the declaration. Such objection shall be made in accordance with the requirements of Rule 171 (i) save that it shall be made to the Stewards of the Jockey Club at the Registry Office.

171. (i) Every objection shall be in writing, and must be signed by the owner of some horse engaged in the race, his rider, trainer, employee of the trainer on production of his Racehorse Attendant's Identity Card and Validity Pass or other person on production of a written authorisation by the owner or trainer and available only for the day of the race. When a horse is owned by a recognised Company the objection may also be signed by a registered Agent of the Company or by another person on production of a written authorisation signed by such registered Agent and available only for the day of the race.

(a) In cases coming under Sub-Rule (iv) of the Rule 170 it must be made to the Clerk of the Scales.

(b) In all other cases it must be made to the Stewards of the Jockey Club at the Registry Office.

The Objector shall, at the time he makes the objection, sign the objection form and if the objection is subsequently withdrawn or there were no good and reasonable grounds for the objection shall be fined the sum of £50. In the event of the objection being decided to be frivolous or vexatious, it shall be in the power of the Stewards to fine the objector an additional sum not exceeding £220.

(ii) An objection may also be made without deposit by a Steward, Clerk of the Course or official of a Meeting appointed by the Stewards of the Jockey Club in his official capacity or by an official of the Jockey Club. Such objection shall be in writing and signed by the Steward, Clerk of the Course, official of a Meeting or official of the Jockey Club.

(iii) An enquiry called for by the Stewards on any matter contained in Rule 170(iv) within the time prescribed by Rule 170(iv) shall have the force and consequences of an objection and all relevant Rules shall operate as if an objection had been lodged.

(iv) An objection cannot be withdrawn without leave of the Stewards.

172. (i) Every objection made as a consequence of either the Judge revising his original decision after the five minutes after the winner has been weighed-in have elapsed or the Stewards of the Jockey Club having corrected a mistake by the Judge pursuant to their powers under Rule 1(xi) together with cases coming under Sub-Rules (v) or (vi) of Rule 170 shall be decided by the Stewards of the Jockey Club.

(ii) Every other objection shall be decided by three Stewards and their consideration of an objection under Rule 170(iv) shall constitute an enquiry under Rule 171 (iii). Should no decision be given by the Stewards within seven days of the objection being lodged the Clerk of the Course shall report the case to the Stewards of the Jockey Club who may at their discretion decide the matter and if they consider there has been any negligence, order any additional expense arising therefrom to be defrayed out of the funds of the Meeting at which the case occurred.

(iii) All reasonable costs and expenses in relation to determining an objection or conducting an enquiry in relation thereto, and any reasonable compensation for outlay incurred, shall be paid by such person or persons, and in such proportions, as the Stewards of the Jockey Club shall direct, except in the case of objections under Sub-Rule (iv) of Rule 170 determined by the Stewards when they shall be paid as the Stewards shall direct.

173. No horse shall be disqualified on account of any error or violation of any Order or Rule in its entry, which might have been corrected on payment of a fine.

174. Pending the determination of an objection or appeal, any prizes which the horses concerned in the objection or appeal may have won or may win in the race, shall be withheld until the objection or appeal is determined, and any entry fee or forfeit payable by the owner of any other horse shall be paid to and held by the Stakeholder for the person who may be entitled to it. For the purposes of this Rule a report to the Stewards of the Jockey Club under Rule 15(ii)(d) or 153(iv) is to be regarded as an appeal. An objection or appeal (as defined by this Rule), when the subject of an application for Review under Rule 2(vi), is not determined until the application is disposed of, or until any further enquiry resulting from the application has been completed.

175. Where the Stewards or the Stewards of the Jockey Club have disqualified a horse which has won, or been placed in a race, the horse shall be removed from the placings, shall not be entitled to any prize and the other horses shall take positions accordingly. Where the placing of a horse has been changed by the Stewards of the Jockey Club or the Stewards under the provisions of Rule 153(i), including being placed last, the horse concerned will only be entitled to the prize for the position in which it has been placed by the Stewards of the Jockey Club or the Stewards and the other horses shall take positions accordingly.

Appeals

176. Any owner, trainer or rider of a horse in a race the subject of an objection under Rule 170(iv) or enquiry under Rule 171 (iii) who is aggrieved by the Stewards' decision, or any person upon whom any form of penalty has been imposed by the Stewards shall be entitled to appeal to the Stewards of the Jockey Club.

177. The Appellant shall lodge a Notice of Appeal with the Registry Office within seven days except in the case of an Appeal from a decision of the Stewards involving a finding of reckless careless or improper riding or intentionally causing interference under Rule 153 when an Appeal must be lodged within forty eight hours of the decision of the Stewards being announced unless a Saturday, Sunday, Bank Holiday, Good Friday, Christmas Day intervenes when it must be lodged on the first day thereafter that the Registry Office is open for business. On all occasions when an Appeal is lodged a deposit of £220 shall be made at the same time which shall be forfeited unless the Stewards of the Jockey Club shall decide there were good and reasonable grounds for the Appeal.

178. (i) The Notice of Appeal must be signed by the Appellant, his authorised agent or his solicitor and state the grounds of appeal in general terms.

(ii) Where the Appeal is from the imposition of a fine of £250 or less the Notice of Appeal shall also state whether the Appellant wishes:

(a) a personal hearing, or

(b) the Appeal to be decided on a submission of written evidence.

(iii) In the event of an appeal by submission of written evidence the Appellant must within 7 days of the Notice of Appeal being lodged submit to the Registry Office such written evidence and representations as he wishes to be considered by the Stewards of the Jockey Club. The Stewards of the Jockey Club may request the Stewards whose decision is subject to appeal also to submit written evidence. In the event of the Stewards of the Jockey Club requiring further information for the purposes of considering the Appeal they may direct that a written summary of evidence be compiled by such person as is designated by them. The written summary of evidence must be signed by the Appellant. If the Appellant fails to sign the written summary of evidence the Stewards of the Jockey Club will treat the Appeal as one where the Appellant has required a personal hearing.

(iv) The Appeal shall be considered by the Stewards of the Jockey Club. Where the Appeal is from the imposition of a fine of £250 or less and the Appellant has not requested a personal hearing, the Appeal shall be considered in his absence, and the Stewards of the Jockey Club shall communicate their decision to him in writing prior to publication in the Racing Calendar.

(v) The Stewards of the Jockey Club may confirm or reverse or otherwise vary the decision of the Stewards including exercising any of the powers given to them by Rule 2.

(vi) In the event of an appeal against a suspension under Rule 153(iv) being dismissed any suspension imposed will commence either on the date calculated under Rule 153(iv) (a) or in the event of the Appeal not having been concluded by that date on the day following that on which a decision on the Appeal is given.

179. On an appeal the Stewards of the Jockey Club may exercise their powers as to costs in accordance with Rule 2(v)(b).

PART 18: DISQUALIFICATION OF HORSES

180. (i) Any horse which has been the subject of fraudulent practice may, at the discretion of the Stewards of the Jockey Club, be disqualified for such time and for such races as they shall determine.

(ii) Where a horse has been the subject of an examination under Rule 14(vi) and the result of an analysis of any sample of its tissue, body fluid or excreta is positive the horse shall be disqualified for the race in question and may at the discretion of the Stewards of the Jockey Club, be disqualified for such time and for such races subsequent to the race in question as they shall determine. For the purpose of this sub-Rule a positive analysis is as defined in Rule 53(ii).

181. A horse is not qualified to be entered or start for any race:

(i) If he has run at any unrecognised meeting, other than one which has been granted an exemption under Rule 204(ii).

(ii) If and so long as he is in the ownership or part-ownership of a disqualified person, or so long as any disqualified person has any interest in such horse's winnings in such race.

(iii) If and so long as he is in the stable of, or under the care and management of a disqualified person but when such person, other than the owner or part-owner, incurs disqualification under Rule 137 the horse shall be qualified to be entered or run until 14 days have elapsed from the date of publication in the Forfeit List.

(iv) If and so long as he is in the Forfeit List or in the Official Forfeit List published by the recognised Turf Authority of any country.

(v) In any case in which he is by the Orders and these Rules or by the conditions of the race not qualified.

(vi) If he has been declared disqualified by the Stewards of the Jockey Club or has been disqualified or suspended by any recognised Turf Authority, except that entries may be accepted for such horses during the period of disqualification or suspension for races due to run outside that period.

(vii) If, except in the case of a horse trained outside Great Britain coming to Great Britain for the purpose of a particular race, he is the property of either an owner whose name is not duly registered under Rule 40, or a Club which is not duly registered under Rule 41, or a Company which is not duly registered under Rule 43 or Rule 44 provided that if he is trained outside Great Britain such Club or Company is registered by the Turf Authority of the country in which the horse is trained.

(viii) If he is a horse in which a syndicate is interested and if there is no syndicate agreement of which registration is currently in force in accordance with Rule 46 except in the case of a horse trained outside Great Britain coming to Great Britain for the purpose of a particular race and provided that a syndicate agreement is registered by the Turf Authority of the country in which the horse is trained.

(ix) If he is the property of a recognised Company and that Company has no registered agent.

(x) Unless it and its sire and dam are each the produce of a natural service or covering, and unless a natural gestation took place in and delivery was from the body of the mare in which the horse was conceived.

(xi) If its name has been changed, until the Monday after registration.

182. A horse is not qualified to start for a race:

(i) Unless he is duly entered for the same and, in any race which closed more than six days before running, his entry has been confirmed under Order 124(i).

(ii) Unless he has been declared a runner under Order 124(ii).

(iii) If he is qualified to hold a passport and such passport has either not been issued or has not been received by the trainer.

(iv) If he has been tubed on the day of the race.

(v) If he has an implant other than one which is pharmacologically inactive.

(vi) If he has at any time in the fourteen days prior to the race visited an equine swimming pool in Great Britain that is not an approved pool.

(vii) If he has received an injection for vaccination against Equine Influenza within the previous 7 days (including the day of the race).

(viii) If he has not been vaccinated, or, the vaccination details fail to be endorsed into the horse's passport in accordance with the requirements of Rule 35, or, in the case of horses trained in countries where passports are not issued, the details given on vaccination certificates are insufficient to confirm that the horse has been duly vaccinated.

Except that this Sub-Rule shall not be invoked on the first occasion it applies but will be invoked on all future occasions until the requirements of Rule 35 are duly satisfied.

(ix) If he is required to have his identity verified and such verification has not been completed in accordance with the requirements of Rule 33.

(x) If he has been the subject of a neurectomy operation.

(xi) If its rider has not weighed out in accordance with Rule 141.

(xii) If a memorandum of sale or transfer has not been lodged as required under Rule 46(viii).

(xiii) If a termination of partnership has not been lodged as required under Rule 47(ix).

(xiv) If the passport is required for inspection by the Veterinary Officer under Rule 32(ii) and either has not been produced or the trainer has not confirmed in writing that he holds the passport and that the horse is correctly vaccinated by the time fixed for weighing under Rule 141 (vi); but this sub-Rule will not apply if the provisions of Rule 36(i)(c) have been satisfied.

(xv) If he has received a blood transfusion for the purpose of enhancing his performance in that race.
(xvi) If he is trained outside Great Britain and has been in Great Britain.
(a) for more than seven days unless he is under the personal supervision of his trainer.
(b) for more than one calendar month unless he is in the care of a trainer licensed under the Rules of Racing except that in August, September and October in any year the Stewards of the Jockey Club may waive this requirement in respect of horses trained in Australia or New Zealand.

183. If a horse which is not qualified according to Rule 180, 181, 182, or 186 be entered or run for any race, he shall on objection under Rule 170(v) be disqualified by the Stewards of the Jockey Club.

184. A horse is not qualified to start:
(a) for a Flat race unless for the 14 days immediately prior to the race it has been in the care of and trained by persons holding licences to train under these Rules for Flat races or by persons who are duly qualified trainers in the country where the horse has been trained;
(b) for a Steeple Chase, Hurdle race or National Hunt Flat race unless for the 14 days immediately prior to the race it has been in the care of and trained by persons holding licences or permits qualifying them to train under these Rules for the race in question or by persons who are duly qualified trainers in the country where the horse has been trained, except that for a Hunters' Steeple Chase, the Grand Military Gold Cup and the Royal Artillery Gold Cup a horse may have been trained privately by persons without licences or permits under the provisions of Rule 50.

185. If a horse which is not qualified according to Rule 184 run for any race he shall on objection under Rule 170(v) be liable to be disqualified by the Stewards of the Jockey Club.

186. No horse shall be qualified to be entered or start in Hunters' Steeple Chases (or the Grand Military Gold Cup and the Royal Artillery Gold Cup) in any particular Steeple Chase and Hurdle race Season which at any time on or after November 1st of that season, has been stabled with, or trained by, a person holdings permit to train whilst the horse was so stabled or trained, unless the horse was the property of himself, his spouse, parents, sons or daughters, free of all lease or other joint arrangement, except those between such persons.

PART 19: DISTRIBUTION OF PRIZES

191 (i) In sweepstakes the guaranteed prize money, entrances, forfeits, etc., or, if a guaranteed minimum value has been advertised and receipts from these sums do not amount to that sum, the guaranteed minimum value, shall be distributed in accordance with the conditions of the race subject to the provisions of Orders 134 and 194.
(ii) In guaranteed sweepstakes the total entrances, forfeits, etc., or the guaranteed prize money for the race, whichever is the greater, shall be distributed in accordance with the conditions of the race subject to the provisions of Orders 134 and 194.
(iii) Where the conditions for a race provide for a trophy to be given at the option of the winner such trophy if accepted, may be returned to the Managing Executive of the Racecourse concerned within seven days of the race having been run and the prize money increased accordingly.

192. If a winner has walked over, or no horse has been placed second, or in any lower place, the money or prizes to which each category of persons connected with the horse placed second or in any lower place would have been entitled under Order 194 shall be paid to the appropriate category of persons connected with the winner. Prizes given specifically to the trainer, rider, breeder or stable in the conditions of the race for horses placed second or in any lower place shall not be given at all.

193. When a Cup (other than a Challenge Cup) or any guaranteed prize money or guaranteed minimum value is advertised to be run for, it shall be given in the event of a walk-over.

194. The prize money provided by the conditions of races shall be paid over by the Stakeholder as follows:
(i) (a) In all Amateur Riders' races with fourth prizes:-
54.99% to the owner of the winner
17.98% to the owner of the second
8.99% to the owner of the third
4.49% to the owner of the fourth
6.24% to the trainer of the winner
0.97% to the trainer of the second
0.49% to the trainer of the third
0.25% to the trainer of the fourth
3.25% to the stable from which the winner was trained
1.00% to the stable from which the second was trained
0.50% to the stable from which the third was trained
0.25% to the stable from which the fourth was trained
0.60% to apprentice training
(b) In all Amateur Riders' races without fourth prizes:-
59.23% to the owner of the winner
17.98% to the owner of the second
8.99% to the owner of the third
6.74% to the trainer of the winner
0.97% to the trainer of the second
0.49% to the trainer of the third
3.50% to the stable from which the winner was trained
1.00% to the stable from which the second was trained
0.50% to the stable from which the third was trained
0.60% to apprentice training
(ii) (a) In all Flat Pattern Races with four prizes:
46.44% to the owner of the winner
19.22% to the owner of the second
9.56% to the owner of the third
4.60% to the owner of the fourth
5.78% to the trainer of the winner
1.24% to the trainer of the second
0.62% to the trainer of the third
0.31% to the trainer of the fourth
4.06% to the jockey who rode the winner
1.04% to the jockey who rode the second
0.50% to the jockey who rode the third
0.23% to the jockey who rode the fourth
3.00% to the stable fromwhich the winner was trained
1.15% to the stable fromwhich the second was trained
0.57% to the stable fromwhich the third was trained
0.28% to the stable from which the fourth was trained
0.60% to apprentice training
0.20% to the Jockeys' Valets' Attendance Fund
0.60% to the Jockeys' Association Pension Fund.
(b) In all Steeple Chase and Hurdle Pattern Races with four prizes:
44.82 to the owner of the winner
19.22% to the owner of the second
9.56% to the owner of the third
4.60% to the owner of the fourth
5.78% to the trainer of the winner
1.24% to the trainer of the second
0.62% to the trainer of the third
0.31% to the trainer of the fourth
5.64% to the jockey who rode the winner
1.07% to the jockey who rode the second
0.51% to the jockey who rode the third
0.23% to the jockey who rode the fourth
3.00% to the stable from which the winner was trained
1.15% to the stable fromwhich the second was trained
0.57% to the stable fromwhich the third was trained
0.28% to the stable fromwhich the fourth was trained
0.60% to apprentice training
0.20% to the Jockeys' Valets' Attendance Fund
0.60% to the Jockeys' Association Pension Fund.
except in the event of an Amateur Rider being the rider of the winner, second, third or fourth the payments due to the Jockey shall be paid to the British Horseracing Board.
(c) In all Flat Races with six prizes:-
44.89% to the owner of the winner

18.38% to the owner of the second
9.14% to the owner of the third
4.18% to the owner of the fourth
2.02% to the owner of the fifth
1.21% to the owner of the sixth
5.59% to the trainer of the winner
1.19% to the trainer of the second
0.59% to the trainer of the third
0.28% to the trainer of the fourth
0.19% to the trainer of the fifth
0.11% to the trainer of the sixth
3.92% to the jockey of the winner
0.99% to the jockey of the second
0.48% to the jockey of the third
0.21% to the jockey of the fourth
0.14% to the jockey of the fifth
0.09% to the jockey of the sixth
2.90% to the stable from which the winner was trained
1.10% to the stable from which the second was trained
0.55% to the stable from which the third was trained
0.25% to the stable from which the fourth was trained
0.13% to the stable from which the fifth was trained
0.07% to the stable from which the sixth was trained
0.60% to apprentice training
0.20% to the Jockeys' Valets' Attendance Fund
0.60% to the Jockeys' Association Pension Fund.

(d) in all Steeple Chase and Hurdle Race Grade 1 Pattern Races and other Steeple Chases with guaranteed prize money of £10,000 or more with six prizes:-

43.33% to the owner of the winner
18.38% to the owner of the second
9.14% to the owner of the third
4.18% to the owner of the fourth
1.98% to the owner of the fifth
1.19% to the owner of the sixth
5.59% to the trainer of the winner
1.19% to the trainer of the second
0.59% to the trainer of the third
0.28% to the trainer of the fourth
0.19% to the trainer of the fifth
0.11% to the trainer of the sixth
5.45% to the jockey who rode the winner
1.02% to the jockey who rode the second
0.49% to the jockey who rode the third
0.21% to the jockey who rode the fourth
0.18% to the jockey who rode the fifth
0.10% to the jockey who rode the sixth
2.90% to the stable from which the winner was trained
1.10% to the stable from which the second was trained
0.55% to the stable from which the third was trained
0.25% to the stable from which the fourth was trained
0.12% to the stable from which the fifth was trained
0.08% to the stable from which the sixth was trained
0.60% to apprentiice training
0.20% to the Jockeys' Valets' Attendance Fund
0.60% to the Jockeys' Association Pension Fund.

except in the event of an Amateur rider being the rider of the winner, second, third, fourth, fifth or sixth the payments due to the jockey shall be paid to the British Horseracing Board.

(iii) In other Flat Races

(a) with fourth prizes:-

50.11% to the owner of the winner
16.98% to the owner of the second
8.49% to the owner of the third
4.24% to the owner of the fourth
6.24% to the trainer of the winner
0.97% to the trainer of the second
0.49% to the trainer of the third
0.25% to the trainer of the fourth
4.38% to the jockey who rode the winner
0.86% to the jockey who rode the second
0.41% to the jockey who rode the third
0.18% to the jockey who rode the fourth
3.25% to the stable from which the winner was trained
1.00% to the stable from which the second was trained
0.50% to the stable from which the third was trained
0.25% to the stable from which the fourth was trained
0.60% to apprentice training
0.20% to Jockeys' Valets' Attendance Fund
0.60% to the Jockeys' Association Pension Fund.

(b) without fourth prizes:

53.93% to the owner of the winner
16.98% to the owner of the second
8.49% to the owner of the third
6.74% to the trainer of the winner
0.97% to the trainer of the second
0.49% to the trainer of the third
4.76% to the jockey who rode the winner
0.84% to the jockey who rode the second
0.40% to the jockey who rode the third
3.50% to the stable from which the winner was trained
1.00% to the stable from which the second was trained
0.50% to the stable from which the third was trained
0.60% to apprentice training
0.20% to the Jockeys' Valets' Attendance Fund
0.60% to the Jockeys' Association Pension Fund.

(iv) In other Steeple Chases, Hurdle races and National Hunt Flat races.

(a) with fourth prizes:-

48.49% to the owner of the winner
16.98% to the owner of the second
8.49% to the owner of the third
4.24% to the owner of the fourth
6.24% to the trainer of the winner
0.97% to the trainer of the second
0.49% to the trainer of the third
0.25% to the trainer of the fourth
5.97% to the jockey who rode the winner
0.88% to the jockey who rode the second
0.41% to the jockey who rode the third
0.19% to the jockey who rode the fourth
3.25% to the stable from which the winner was trained
1.00% to the stable from which the second was trained
0.50% to the stable from which the third was trained
0.25% to the stable from which the fourth was trained
0.60% to apprentice training
0.20% to the Jockeys' Valets' Attendance Fund
0.60% to the Jockeys' Association Pension Fund.

(b) without fourth prizes:

52.23% to the owner of the winner
16.98% to the owner of the second
8.49% to the owner of the third
6.74% to the trainer of the winner
0.97% to the trainer of the second
0.49% to the trainer of the third
6.43% to the jockey who rode the winner
0.86% to the jockey who rode the second
0.41% to the jockey who rode the third
3.50% to the stable from which the winner was trained
1.00% to the stable from which the second was trained
0.50% to the stable from which the third was trained
0.60% to apprentice training
0.20% to the Jockeys' Valets' Attendance Fund
0.60% to the Jockeys' Association Pension Fund.

except in the event of an Amateur Rider being the rider of the winner, second, third or fourth in any race the payment due to the jockey under sub-paragraphs (a) and (b) above shall be paid to the British Horseracing Board.

(v) Where under this Order a payment is due to a trainer or stable and the horse has been trained either outside Great Britain or privately under Rule 50 the payment shall be made to the owner of the horse except in the case of horses trained in France or Ireland when payment due to a trainer shall be paid to that trainer.

195. Percentages of prize money paid to stables will be sent to the trainers concerned on four occasions in each year and the following conditions will apply:-

(i) Duplicate sheets will be sent with the payment and will include a list of all known current employees of the trainer concerned, with their Stable Employees registration numbers.

(ii) Trainers will be required to complete the return by signing the Recommendation, giving the date upon which payment will be made and adding the amounts that are to be paid to each individual member of staff. If any member of a trainer's staff has been omitted from the list his name must be added and this will also apply in cases where a trainer wishes to make payment to any ex-member of his staff who has left his employment during the period covered by the payment.

(iii) One copy of there turn will be displayed in the Stable Yard in a place where it can be inspected by all employees, and the other must be returned to the Racing Calendar Office within 21 days of the date upon which the sheets were despatched from the Racing Calendar Office.This date will be shown on the sheets.

(iv) Payments may only be made to persons whose names are included in the Register of Stable Employees as being either currently employed by the trainer or employed by him during the period covered by the main payment.

(v) Unless the Stewards of the Jockey Club raise any objection trainers will make payments as shown on the return not less than 10 days and not more than 21 days after signing and returning the sheet.

(vi) No part of the money may be withheld by the trainer for payment at a later date.

Note: this instruction does not preclude employees from asking trainers to hold the money for them but in such cases the Stewards expect trainers to deposit the money with a Building Society or make some other suitable investment so that it may earn interest. Furthermore, any employee leaving must be paid his share of the money held in this way at the time of leaving.

(vii) No deductions may be made from the Percentage Money except those for Income Tax.

The Stewards of the Jockey Club will impose a fine of not less than £40 upon any trainer who fails to comply with the requirements of this Rule unless he can satisfy them that there was good reason for the failure.

196. The breeder of an eligible horse (as recorded in the General Stud Book or the Non-Thoroughbred Register) will be personally qualified to receive a breeders prize payment in respect of relevant races won on and after January 1st, 1993 and subject to acceptance at the Racing Calendar Office of an application signed by the breeder for registration of the horse concerned under the Breeders' Prize Scheme on the prescribed form. Whilst applications received from breeders prior to death or liquidation will validate subsequent successes by any horse, no payments will be made in relation to applications for other horses made by Executors or Personal Representative(s) of deceased or Liquidator(s) even if the breeder could have applied in his lifetime or prior to liquidation.

Such application must certify that the horse concerned was either:

(a) foaled in Great Britain and did not leave Great Britain before July 1st of the year following the year of birth except that in the year of its birth, provided that it returned with its dam before October 1st of that year, it may have accompanied its dam to a stallion outside Great Britain, or

(b) foaled while its dam was visiting a stallion outside Great Britain, provided that it returned with its dam to Great Britain before October 1st of the year of its birth and that it did not again leave Great Britain before July 1st of the following year.

Note: See Instruction J4 for relevant detail concerning the operation of the Breeders' Prize Scheme.

PART 20: PROHIBITED PRACTICES AND DISQUALIFICATIONS OF PERSONS

200. Any person who administers or attempts to administer or allows or causes to be administered or connives at the administration to a horse of a Prohibited Substance with intention to affect the racing performance of that horse in a race or with knowledge that its racing performance in a race could be affected shall be guilty of a breach of the Rules and may be declared a disqualified person or otherwise penalised by the Stewards of the Jockey Club under Rule 2 of these Rules.

201. Any person may be declared a disqualified person or otherwise penalised by the Stewards of the Jockey Club in accordance with their powers under Rule 2 of these Rules who:-

(i) Gives or offers, or promises directly or indirectly, any bribe in any form to any person having official duties in relation to a race or racehorse, or to any trainer, rider, agent or other person having charge of, or access to, any racehorse; or

(ii) Being a person having official duties in relation to a race, or being a trainer, rider, agent or other person having charge of, or access to, any racehorse, accepts or offers to accept any bribe in any form; or

(iii) Wilfully enters or causes to be entered for any race, or causes to start in any race, a horse which he knows or believes to be not qualified; or

(iv) Gives, allows or causes a blood transfusion to be given to a horse for the purpose of enhancing his performance in a race.

(v) *Deleted.*

(vi) Is guilty of or conspires with any other person for the commission of, or connives at any other person being guilty of, any corrupt or fraudulent practice in relation to racing in this or any other country; or

(vii) Is convicted of any criminal offence in relation to racing in this or any other country.

and any such act shall constitute a breach of these Rules.

203. (i) If any person be reported by the Committee of Tattersalls he shall, with effect from the fourteenth day of despatch to him of notice of intended disqualification or exclusion to his last known address, be a disqualified person under these Rules or otherwise excluded under Rule 2(iv) from any premises owned, licensed or controlled by the Stewards of the Jockey Club unless the Stewards of the Jockey Club declare that the disqualification or exclusion should not have effect under these Rules. An application to the Stewards of the Jockey Club for such a declaration may be made by the person affected by this Rule provided that he shall have applied to the Registry Office within seven days of the despatch to him of notice of intended disqualification or exclusion.

(ii) The disqualification or exclusion shall cease immediately upon receipt by the Stewards of the Jockey Club of notification that the report from the Committee of Tattersalls is withdrawn and the person affected shall be so informed at his last known address.

204. (i) (a)Subject to sub-rule (i)(b) of this Rule any person on whom disqualification has been imposed by any recognised Turf Authority is a disqualified person under these Rules so long as the disqualification continues unless the Stewards of the Jockey Club declare that the disqualification shall not have effect under these Rules. An application to the Stewards of the Jockey Club for such a declaration may be made by the person disqualified provided that he has exhausted all procedures for appeal available under the Rules of the recognised Turf Authority. The application must be made in writing to the Registry Office within three days of the final dismissal of appeal under the Rules of the recognised Turf Authority, or, (if there is no procedure for appeal) within three days of the imposition of the disqualification. An application received after this time will only be considered if the Stewards of the Jockey Club are satisfied that it had been made at the earliest opportunity and that it was not possible for it to have been made within the time limit.

(b) Where a person upon whom disqualification has been imposed by a recognised Turf Authority has made an application for a declaration under sub-Rule (i)(a) of this Rule the Stewards of the Jockey Club have power to suspend the disqualification under these Rules pending their decision on the application.

(ii) Any person who owns, trains or rides a horse at an unrecognised meeting in Great Britain or Ireland, or any person who acts in any official capacity in connection with such a meeting, is liable to be declared a disqualified person for a period of twelve months or such a lesser time as the Stewards of the Jockey Club shall think fit, but this Rule shall not apply to:-

(a) Pony races at meetings confined to pony racing, or

(b) Any other specific event comprising or including a horserace or horseraces in respect of which the Stewards of the Jockey Club have granted an exemption from the effect of this Rule, the Stewards of the Jockey Club having the power to impose conditions on the grant of such exemption. No application for exemption will be considered unless it is submitted in writing to the Registry Office at least two months before the event is due to take place.

(iii) Any person who offers or promises any reward, either by way of fee, present, expenses other than those approved by the Stewards of the Jockey Club as set out in Appendix F to these Orders and Rules, or any consideration whatsoever to an Amateur Rider or an Amateur riding under the provisions of Rule 61, for riding in a race or any Amateur Rider or Amateur riding under the provisions of Rule 61 who solicits, accepts or agrees to accept such reward is liable to be made a disqualified person by the Stewards of the Jockey Club, but this Rule shall not prevent the advertisement of a trophy for riders in the conditions of a race, nor the acceptance of a trophy by an Amateur Rider.

(iv) Any licensed jockey, or jockey riding under the provisions of Rule 61, who by advertisement, circular letter, or other means gives or offers to give information concerning horses entered in races under these Rules in return for monetary consideration, other than the receipt of a reasonable fee for giving an interview to the Press or other legitimate news gathering organisation for the purposes of general publication, or any licensed jockey or jockey riding under the provisions of Rule 61 who connives at such practice, is liable to be made a disqualified person by the Stewards of the Jockey Club.

205. A disqualified person, so long as his disqualification lasts, shall not:-

(i) Act as Steward or Official at any recognised Meeting.

(ii) Act as authorised agent under the Orders or these Rules.

(iii) Except as provided by Rule 181 (iii), enter, run, train or ride a horse in any race at any recognised meeting. If any entry made by a disqualified person be mistakenly or inadvertently accepted, the same shall despite such acceptance be void and the horse shall not be qualified to be entered or to start.

(iv) Enter any Racecourse, stands, rooms, enclosures and other places owned or used by the Stewards of any Meeting.

(v) Except with permission of the Stewards of the Jockey Club be employed in any Racing Stable.

(vi) Deal in any capacity with a racehorse (for example, but without imposing any limitation on the absolute prohibition by this Rule, as Manager of or for a syndicate or by selling or placing shares in a horse). Any horse found by the Stewards of the Jockey Club to have been dealt with in contravention of this Rule shall be automatically declared to be disqualified from all future racing until such time as the Stewards are satisfied that the horse has been sold on the open market to a purchaser having no previous connections with the disqualified person concerned, whereupon the disqualification shall be removed.

PART 21: FEES

General

210. (i) Where any Rule of Racing provides for the payment of a fee the amount thereof shall be that sum which is set out in Appendix M against the corresponding Rule number. Any changes to the fee levels from time to time shall be published in the Racing Calendar with the dates on which the changes are to be effective. All persons who are subject to the Rules of Racing acknowledge that the fee levels are set from time to time by the Directors not by the Stewards of the Jockey Club. The Jockey Club requires that all such fees and any arrears due shall be made payable to the British Horseracing Board.

(ii) Where any Order (apart from Part 7) provides for the payment of a fee the amount thereof shall be that which is set out in Appendix M against the corresponding Order number. Any changes to the fee levels from time to time shall be published in the Racing Calendar with the dates on which the changes are to be effective. All such fees and arrears due shall be made payable to the British Horseracing Board.

Fixture Fees

211. On fixtures being granted to a Meeting, fees, the amount of which the Directors shall from time to time decide, will be payable to the British Horseracing Board. when the Fixture takes place together with fees in respect of the receipt of entries. Should the Fixture, or any part of it be abandoned the fees shall nevertheless be paid, unless otherwise ordered by the Directors.

PART 22: MISCELLANEOUS

General

220. (i) No person shall aid or abet the commission of and breach of these Orders or Rules.

(ii) No person shall be guilty of any violent or improper conduct on any land or premises owned, used, licensed or controlled by the Stewards of any Meeting or by the Stewards of the Jockey Club.

(iii) No person shall act in a manner prejudicial to the integrity, proper conduct or good reputation of horseracing in Great Britain whether or not such conduct shall constitute a breach of any of the foregoing Orders or Rules of Racing.

(iv) No person shall without the permission of the Stewards of the Jockey Club associate in connection with horseracing in Great Britain with any person known to be disqualified or known to have acted in a manner prejudicial to the integrity, proper conduct or good reputation of horseracing in Great Britain, whether or not constituting a breach of the Orders or Rules of Racing.

(v) No person shall make or offer to make a bet on horseracing on behalf of a jockey during the term of his licence or on behalf of a jockey riding under the provisions of Rule 61, nor shall he offer a jockey, or a jockey riding under the provisions of Rule 61, the proceeds, or any part thereof, of any bet on horseracing. (This sub-Rule applies to any bet regardless of where the bet is placed or horserace run).

(vi) No person shall make or offer to make a bet on behalf of an amateur rider, or an amateur rider riding under the provisions of Rule 61, on any race in which the rider is riding nor shall he offer such rider the proceeds, or any part thereof, of any bet, on any such race.

(vii) The breach of any under taking given by a licensed person to the Stewards of the Jockey Club or the Directors in relation to the administration of racing shall be an offence.

(viii) It shall be an offence deliberately to mislead or by an overt act endeavour to mislead the Stewards of the Meeting, the Stewards of the Jockey Club or an official of the Jockey Club, official appointed by the Stewards of the Jockey Club or the Directors of the British Horseracing Board or an Official of the British Horseracing Board or a Clerk of the Course either at any enquiry or in connection with the administration or control of racing.

Orders of the British Horseracing Board

221. Every person who is subject to the Rules of Racing is deemed to have knowledge of the Orders

howsoever amended and agrees to observe and at all time to comply with the Orders. Any failure by such a person so to observe the Orders shall be a breach of these Rules. NOTE: This Rule enables the Stewards to consider any failure to comply with the Orders, and to impose penalties in respect thereof pursuant to Rule 2(i) and/or to exercise the power of suspension in Rule 2(iii).

Instructions

221A. Every person shall comply with every instruction of the Directors published in the Racing Calendar from time to time.

221B. (i) Every person shall comply with every instruction of the Stewards of the Jockey Club published in the Racing Calendar from time to time.

(ii) Every person shall comply with the instructions of the Stewards of a Meeting.

New Rules

222. Except in cases where the Stewards of the Jockey Club exercise their powers contained in Rule 1A(xv) notice of any proposed new Rule (in which term is included the repeal or alteration of an existing Rule) shall be sent by the Keeper of the Match Book to the Members of the Jockey Club at least fourteen days before the Meeting at which such Rule is to be proposed. The draft Rule shall also be advertised in the Racing Calendar with the date of the Meeting of the Jockey Club at which it is to be proposed. To be passed the Rule must be approved by a simple majority of the Members of the Jockey Club present at the Meeting, who must also decide the date upon which the new or altered Rule is to come into operation, but the Rule as passed must be published in the Racing Calendar again before that date.

New Orders

222A. Notice of any proposed new Order (in which term is included the repeal or alteration of an existing Order) shall be sent by the Chief Executive of the British Horseracing Board to the Directors before a meeting at which such Order is to be proposed. The proposed Order must be approved by a simple majority of the Directors who must also decide the date upon which the new or altered Order is to come into operation. The Order as approved must be published in the Racing Calendar before that date.

Point-to-Point Steeple Chases

223. Point-to-Point Steeple Chases are held under the sanction of the Jockey Club and under Regulations entitled "Jockey Club Regulations for Point-to-Point Steeple Chases "published from time to time by the Stewards of the Jockey Club and every person taking part in these races shall comply with these Regulations.

Sentences Imposed by the Stewards of the Jockey Club and Stewards of the National Hunt Committee

224. The Stewards of the Jockey Club confirm all current sentences imposed prior to January 1st, 1969, by the Stewards of the Jockey Club or by the Stewards of the National Hunt Committee and all persons warned off prior to January 1st, 1969 are and remain disqualified persons so long as their exclusion continues.

Equine Swimming Pools

227. (i) An "approved pool" means an equine swimming pool in respect of which there is a current Certificate of Approval granted by the Stewards of the Jockey Club.

(ii) A Certificate of Approval shall be applied for annually on the prescribed form.

(iii) The Stewards of the Jockey Club shall have complete discretion whether to grant a Certificate of Approval, save that they shall refuse to grant such a Certificate unless:

(a) they have been provided with:-

(i) the name of the proprietors of the pool;

(ii) if the proprietor is a body corporate, the names of its directors;

(iii) a list of the names of those employed by the proprietors at the pool;

and are satisfied that none of the persons so named is a disqualified person; and

(b) If required by the Stewards of the Jockey Club, the pool has been inspected by their representative.

(iv) The fee (plus V.A.T.) to be paid in respect of each application shall be such as the Directors shall from time to time decide.

(v) Any change of the proprietor of the pool, or, if the proprietor is a body corporate, of its directors and members, or, in the list of those employed by the proprietor at the pool must be notified to the Stewards of the Jockey Club within 14 days of such change taking place.

(vi) The Stewards of the Jockey Club may in their absolute discretion at any time and without assigning any reason therefore withdraw a Certificate of Approval. Without prejudice to the foregoing, the Stewards of the Jockey Club shall withdraw a Certificate of Approval if:-

(a) the proprietor of the pool, or, if the proprietor is a body corporate, any of its directors, or any person employed by the proprietor at the pool is or becomes a disqualified person;

(b) the proprietor of the pool becomes bankrupt, or if the proprietor is a body corporate, the body corporate is being wound up or is in administration or a Receiver has been appointed;

(c) there has been any failure to comply with (v) above.

Starting Stalls Tests

228. When a horse is reported to the Stewards of a Meeting by the Starter for failing to enter starting stalls, or, by its unruly behaviour, damaging the stalls, or for unnecessarily delaying a start from stalls it may not start for a race from stalls until a Starter has passed it satisfactorily through a stalls test. When a horse is presented for testing within 7 days of the original report being made and fails the test the Stewards of the Jockey Club will fine the trainer of the horse £350.

Arab Horse Races

229. Arab Horse Races are held under the sanction of the Jockey Club and under Regulations entitled "Jockey Club Regulations for Arab Horse Racing" published from time to time by the Stewards of the Jockey Club and every person taking part in these races shall comply with these Regulations.

Facsimiles

230. (i) Facsimiles of prescribed forms of application and registration, together with documents required for the registration of leases, partnerships, partnership names, sales with contingencies, Clubs and Stud Companies will be deemed to satisfy the provision for such documents to be in writing provided that the original document in each case is received at the Registry Office or the Racing Calendar Office as appropriate within seven days excluding Bank Holidays of the transmission of such facsimile. If the original documents in each case are not received within this time the Stewards of the

Jockey Club may, in their absolute discretion cancel any registration made or withdraw any licence issued following the receipt of a document by facsimile transmission.

(ii) Facsimiles, other than those provided for in Orders 49, 112, 116, 122, 123 and 124 received at the Registry Office or the Racing Calendar Office between 5p.m. on a Friday and 9 a.m. on the following Monday will be deemed to have been received at 9 a.m. on that Monday.

230A. The conditions and circumstances under which Rule 230 allows for the use of facsimiles shall apply to these Orders.

231. All persons who have agreed to be bound by the Rules of Racing and the overseas owners, riders, trainers and their employees of horses trained outside Great Britain and which are entered to run under these Rules are subject to these Rules and are deemed to have knowledge of them howsoever amended.

1993 Bloodstock Market by Andrew Caulfield

RESCUED FROM THE BRINK

Britain's breeders were preparing for the worst at the end of last year's chapter on the state of the bloodstock market. They were facing potentially lethal attacks on several sides, from such things as the unequal VAT situation, the lengthy recession and the industry's overproduction. Rather like the climax to many an old Western, the breeders had circled their wagons and were vainly fighting off successive attacks.

Their only hope rested with the messenger who had sneaked out under the cover of darkness to alert the troops at the distant cavalry fort. But would the messenger's cries for help be heard in time? In true Hollywood fashion, the cavalry crested the ridge just as disaster seemed inescapable and quickly rescued the beleaguered survivors - the cavalry in this instance being the Government.

I mentioned in last year's notes that three MPs had met the Prime Minister on December 3rd, 1992 to point out the likely consequences of the VAT situation in which the British bloodstock industry was subject to a much higher rate than their counterparts in Ireland and France. It seems that the MPs' cries for assistance helped tip the scales after the breeding industry's long and determined lobbying of Government. By mid-December, the House of Commons Employment Committee had identified VAT registration of owners as the solution to the VAT differentials and the Committee stressed that Customs and Excise must be much more understanding and responsive to the needs of the bloodstock industry. By early January the Sunday Times and Sunday Telegraph were predicting that the forthcoming Budget would allow racehorse owners to register for VAT and that is exactly what happened on March 16th. If anything, the eventual solution is even more satisfactory than the lower rate of VAT that the industry had originally pushed for.

The two-day Two-Year-Olds in Training Sales at Doncaster on March 25th and 26th provided the first opportunity to assess how much difference the VAT breakthrough would make. The answer was that it helped lift the average price from 7,125 Gns to 7,884, while the median rose by 400 Gns. The top price of 40,000 Gns was paid by Cormac McCormack for a colt by Siberian Express, who was one of 12 purchases for Macau. Italian buyers also played a major role, snapping up 39 individuals, but Doncaster director Henry Beeby stressed that British bidders had been very active (if not always successfully). "The whole mood of the sale was totally different", was Beeby's assessment. "People are finally becoming more optimistic".

That optimism surfaced again at Newmarket in mid-April, when Tattersalls held its Breeze-Up Sale. This time the average soared from 4,765 Gns to 8,107, with the median rising from 4,100 to 6,200. And this time the top lot fell to a British buyer, with Mikey Heaton-Ellis going to 41,000 Gns for a Law Society colt later named Fred's Delight. Edmond Mahoney, presiding over his first sale as chairman of Tattersalls, commented that "We have seen the positive side of the Government's decision on the VAT registration of owners reflected in the sale ring this week. It was also very encouraging to see so many bidders from Europe".

So far so good, but how would the yearling market fare once the international circuit got under way at Keeneland in July? After all, it is this section of the industry which has become particularly vulnerable as the studs established by the major Arab owners become increasingly self-sufficient. How many yearlings would these all-conquering owners need to buy when the Maktoum brothers collectively had around 500 home-bred yearlings (with Sheikh Mohammed accounting for more than half that total) and Khalid Abdullah had 109?

The Keeneland July Sale had been cut to just two days as the supply of yearlings worthy of the description Selected becomes ever smaller. Within days of the sale's start, a flurry of speculation arose about whether the Maktoum brothers would be buying. This speculation was apparently fuelled by the cancellation of the hotel reservations for Anthony Stroud and Angus Gold, the men who have customarily done most of the buying for Sheikh Mohammed's Darley Stud Management and Hamdan Al Maktoum's Shadwell Estate Co.

In the end the three eldest Maktoum brothers all made purchases, with Darley buying through trainer John Gosden and agent John Ferguson, while Rick Nichols, manager of the American branch of Shadwell, did the bidding for Hamdan. However, only 13 yearlings fell to Darley, with eight going to Maktoum Al Maktoum's Gainsborough Stud Management and just four to Shadwell. These 25 cost a total of little more than 9 million dollars, compared to the Maktoums' outlay of 14 million in 1992 and of 28 million in '91.

The speculation about the Maktoums' possible absence had a positive knock-on effect in that it spurred American millionaires like Allen Paulson and Aaron Jones into action. Paulson was sitting with veteran breeder John Gaines when Gaines bid a sale-topping 1,050,000 dollars for a colt by Mr Prospector out of the blue-blooded Never Bend mare Reminiscing; and Aaron Jones made the only other seven-figure bid to secure a handsome colt from the first crop by the dazzling Dayjur. The Dayjur colt, out of the Breeders' Cup Juvenile Fillies winner Epitome, headed a very attractive team by the young Shadwell Farm stallion, who ended the sale with an average of 366,363 dollars from 11 yearlings sold. But the sire of the sale was Mr Prospector, who was responsible for ten of the 20 yearlings which fetched 500,000 dollars or more. It must be worrying for American breeders that Mr Prospector will be 24 years old in 1994.

Although the average fell by nearly 9 per cent at Keeneland, the aggregate for the two days rose by 3.6 per cent to nearly 50 million dollars and the general reaction was that the market was now more stable, if far less glamorous than those heady days of the early 1980s when prices went as high as 13.1 million dollars.

Satisfaction was also the reaction to the three-day Saratoga Sale in August, when Shadwell paid the top price of 350,000 dollars for a filly by Dayjur. But would the European circuit prove as satisfactory when it got under way at Deauville later in August?

There had to be some doubts because, for the first time in six years, buyers at the Agence Francaise yearling sale didn't have the added incentive of the very rich Piaget restricted races for Deauville graduates. As things turned out, the end of the Piaget link made no difference: the average for the three most important sessions, on the Saturday, Sunday and Monday, rose by 12 per cent to over 355,000 francs and the median showed a handsome improvement, at 250,000 francs.

The highest price during these select sessions was the 3,200,000 francs paid for a colt by the Coolmore champion Sadler's Wells out of Ameridienne. The colt was reportedly offered to end a foal-sharing arrangement and it transpired that the successful bidder, German International Bloodstock, was acting on behalf of the Coolmore team. The youngster was offered again at Goffs in early October, when his price rose by the equivalent of over 60,000 Gns to 400,000 IR Gns. This time the buyer was the BBA (Ireland).

Four of the other highest prices during the select sessions were also achieved by stallions which stand under the Coolmore banner. Two members of the very large 1992 crop sired by the American-based Woodman proved very popular. Firstly we had the partnership of Patrick Barbe and Morio Sakurai paying 1,600,000 francs for a half-brother to the excellent Epervier Bleu; and then Agence FIPS went to 2,000,000 francs, on behalf of the Marquesa de Moratalla, for a half-sister to the Group-winning Roi de Rome out of a daughter of the top-class Riverqueen.

Sadler's Wells also had two high-priced lots, the other being his filly out of Djallybrook. This 1,950,000-franc purchase by Tim Bulwer-Long is a half-sister to the Group-winning Kanmary, dam of the promising Colonel Collins. Not to be left out, Coolmore's first-crop sire Royal Academy did well with his colt out of the fast Irish mare Bermuda Classic. This half-brother to the smart Irish sprinter Tropical fell to Gainsborough Stud's bid of 2,300,000 francs. Gainsborough also picked up a Nashwan colt for 1,600,000 francs.

Those who left after the select sessions missed one of the main attractions in Lot 320, a filly by Last Tycoon bred by Stavros Niarchos' Haras de Fresnay le Buffard. The filly was already a half-sister to a top winner (Louis Cyphre) by the time the catalogue went to press, but her appeal was then greatly boosted by the emergence of her half-brother Psychobabble as one of the best French juveniles. John Hammond bought her for 1,700,000 francs.

The next stop on the circuit was the St Leger Yearling Sales at Doncaster, where the optimism which had marked the Two-Year-Old in Training Sale was again very much in evidence. The Doncaster team must have been very hopeful of an upturn in trade following the exploits of such as Lyric Fantasy, Turtle Island and Risky, three Royal Ascot two-year-old Group winners who had all been offered at one of the previous two St Leger Sales. Sure enough, the sale produced its best figures since 1990, with the average rising by over 30 per cent from 5,780 Gns to 7,706.

As expected, the star of the show was the full-sister to Risky offered by Elsenham Stud, the home of the filly's sire Risk Me. The filly drew a bid of 56,000 Gns from Danamore, the name used by a Kuwaiti syndicate headed Zaid Al Kulaib. The 1992 top price of 38,000 Gns was also equalled or bettered by four other youngsters - all of them colts. Reprimand, the Mummy's Pet horse whose first crop had already produced a good number of winners, supplied the 41,000-guinea colt from the family of the 1993 Princess Margaret Stakes winner A Smooth One. This purchase by David Morley had cost just 9,400 Gns as a foal. He therefore became one of the numerous yearlings which produced handsome profits for those daring pin-hookers who risked buying foals at the end of a very painful 1992.

Reprimand is based at the National Stud, and so too is Rock City, whose first crop provided one of the three 38,000-guinea purchases. This colt, out of the Italian-bred Silka, had been a 5,000 Gns foal purchase. Also bought for 38,000 Gns was a colt by Aragon out of Davinia, one of several good prices paid by Jack Doyle, and an American-bred youngster by Minshaanshu Amad out of Glorious Quest. The latter fell to the American-based Saudi Arabian, Abdul Aziz Al Saud, who picked up a total of nine yearlings to race in Washington State.

DONCASTER ST LEGER SALES

Year	Sold	Per cent	Aggregate	Average Gns
1984	314	72.6	2,484,850	7,914
1985	338	79.9	2,426,350	7,178
1986	309	86.8	2,387,450	7,726
1987	332	81.8	2,790,200	8,404
1988	390	84.8	3,351,750	8,594
1989	446	92.0	4,367,950	9,794
1990	419	80.7	3,318,750	7,912
1991	378	82.0	2,412,800	6,383
1992	370	85.8	2,138,500	5,780
1993	411	89.9	3,167,350	7,706

More quick-maturing types likely to win at two were on offer at Fairyhouse later in the month, when more than 400 yearlings passed through Tattersalls (Ireland)'s sale ring. Whereas only 79 per cent had found buyers at the 1992 sale, more than 88 per cent were sold in '93, which helps explain why the aggregate rose from 1,409,400 IR Gns to 2,084,950. The average also rose, but not by as much as at Doncaster, the 1993 figure being 5,824 IR Gns.

Three youngsters drew bids of over 30,000 IR Gns, the star of the show being a colt from the first crop by the dual Guineas winner Tirol. This 8,500 IR Gns purchase as a foal became one of the first of several remarkable coups made by Ciaran 'Flash' Conroy's Glenvale Stud at Carrick-on-Suir in Co. Tipperary. With Jack Doyle in the market, Dutch buyer Ed Maas had to go to 42,000 IR Gns to secure the colt who may yet return to Ireland to contest the Tattersalls Breeders' Stakes, the valuable prize restricted to Fairyhouse graduates. Colts by Standaan out of Sleeping Car and by Cadeaux Genereux out of Chevrefeuille were the others to top the 30,000-guinea mark.

Fairyhouse would also have been the scene of the Houghton Yearling Sales had the British Government not yielded on the VAT issue. Happily for Newmarket and Britain, this famous sale once again took place at Park Paddocks and was a much brighter affair than the 1992 debacle, when the Maktoum brothers were conspicuous by their absence.

Too much shouldn't be read into the accompanying ten-year figures achieved in the Tattersalls ring. Remember, the format of the sale has been changed from its Highflyer days, when the aim was to offer only the elite, to a more broadly-based Houghton Sales, in which the minimum price is 5,000 Gns, compared to the Highflyer's 10,000 Gns.

The change in emphasis largely reflects the shortage of high-class youngsters available to the sales companies, now that so many of the best mares are in the hands of non-commercial breeders. However, Tattersalls did well to produce a catalogue which contained 17 yearlings by the all-conquering Sadler's Wells. In the end 14 of these youngsters were offered and 11 were sold, with no fewer than seven of them fetching 200,000 Gns or more - another, the filly out of Mill Princess, was led out unsold at 410,000 Gns.

There was a time when Sadler's Wells's daughters were believed to be considerably inferior, as a group, to their male counterparts. However, the likes of Intrepidity, Royal Ballerina, Spring and Thawakib have shown that the fillies too can develop into top performers. While these fillies' success must have helped Camas Park Stud's filly out of Stavros Niarchos' Whakilyric, the filly hardly needn't any help after the spectacular start Whakilyric has made to her broodmare career. Her first foal, the Sadler's Wells colt Johann Quatz, had won the 1992 Prix Lupin and her second, Hernando, had taken the same Group 1 event on his way to victory in the Prix du Jockey-Club. No wonder Lot 187's price soared to 880,000 Gns as German International Bloodstock, acting on behalf of Baron Georg von Ullman, outlasted Fahd Salman. The filly's price converts to nearly 1,400,000 dollars - a figure considerably higher than any achieved by fillies at the American sales, which points to Sadler's Wells's current status as arguably the world's most fashionable stallion.

That status was again in evidence when Lot 335 entered the ring. This masculine Sadler's Wells colt was the first foal of High Spirited, a mare whose achievements amounted only to victories in handicaps at Yarmouth and Thirsk. However, this daughter of Shirley Heights had the distinction of being a sister to Sheikh Mohammed's tough and high-class High Hawk, a mare whose visits to Sadler's Wells had resulted in the top international performer In The Wings and the 1993 Prix du Jockey-Club third Hunting Hawk. Another Shirley Heights mare had visited Sadler's Wells's brother Fairy King to produce Fairy Heights, winner of the Group 1 Fillies' Mile. It came as no surprise, then, to see the bidding rise to 460,000 Gns before Darley Stud Management emerged victorious.

Mention of Fairy Heights brings us to one of the year's most amazing stories. When her younger sister was offered as a foal at Tattersalls (Ireland)'s December Sale, she fetched just 1,900 IR Gns. Yet when the filly was reoffered just six day's after Fairy Heights' Ascot triumph, the bidding soared to 190,000 Gns, with Charlie Gordon-Watson making the winning bid on behalf of Maktoum Al Maktoum.

The filly was consigned by 'Flash' Conroy's Glenvale Stud, as was another of the sale's most interesting fillies, Lot 272. This filly had several things which would normally have counted seriously against her. For a start she's a daughter of the little-known American stallion Artichoke; then there's the fact that she has a June 25th foaling date; and finally, she was produced by a 23-year-old mare. That mare wasn't any old mare, though, but the highly successful Crimson Saint. By the time Crimson Saint produced the top sprinter-miler Royal Academy, she had already bred the flying American mare Terlingua, the very smart Pancho Villa and the stakes-winning Alydariel. Terlingua is herself responsible for the very successful stallion Storm Cat, while Alydariel is the dam of the Keeneland sale-topper Jeune Homme, a colt who was to do very well in the States towards the end of 1993. The Artichoke filly therefore has considerable potential as a broodmare and this potential had led to her fetching 175,000 dollars at Keeneland in January. This time her price rose to 360,000 Gns, but she appears to have been bought back.

Another who fetched a good deal more than could have been predicted a year earlier was Lot 308, a colt whose sire, Dancing Brave, had salvaged his reputation with a spectacular 1993 season. Bred by a partnership of Ballygallon Stud and Darley Stud Management, the colt is out of Forli's Treat, a winning mare from the family of Be My Guest. Dermot Weld won the day with a bid of 300,000 Gns. This colt was consigned by Timmy Hyde's Camas Park Stud, the establishment also responsible for the sale-topping Sadler's Wells filly and for several other high-priced lots. Among these were the 300,000-guinea Sadler's Wells colt out of Topping Girl (dam of Topanoora and Happy Bride); the 240,000-guinea Royal Academy colt out of Arctic Heroine; and the 230,000-guinea filly by Sadler's Wells out of Passamaquoddy, a sister to the dam of Dancing Brave.

TATTERSALLS HIGHFLYER/HOUGHTON SALES

Year	Sold	Per cent	Aggregate	Average Gns
1984	395	84.2	36,545,600	92,520
1985	383	81.3	30,281,548	79,064
1986	356	88.8	26,852,600	75,428
1987	325	83.3	31,430,900	96,710
1988	320	86.6	27,914,900	88,060
1989	352	100	31,924,000	90,693
1990	280	100	24,047,200	85,882
1991	147	79.9	12,073,500	82,132
1992	229	67.0	10,230,529	44,674
1993	256	85.6	16,198,800	63,276

If the Tattersalls team had every reason to be delighted with the Houghton results, there were some even broader smiles on the faces of the Goffs team by the end of October 5th. That was the occasion of the Orby session of the Irish National Yearling Sale, when buyers were found for 177 of the 185 yearlings offered. Altogether these 177 realised

13,625,500 IR Gns, which represented an astonishing rise of 77 per cent on 1992's aggregate of 7,670,000 IR Gns. The average also bore little resemblance to 1992's figure of 41,461 IR Gns, zooming to 76,980.

The biggest story of all, though, was Goffs' feat of obtaining 1993's highest price for a yearling, with a price of 1,500,000 IR Gns totally eclipsing the best prices achieved in the USA, England and France. The price equates to 1,612,903 Gns at current exchange rates, which is the third highest price ever paid for a yearling in Britain or Ireland, following the Irish St Leger winner Authaal (2,421,875 Gns) and Sadler's Wells's brother Classic Music (2,400,000 Gns).

Once again, the stallion responsible for the sale-topping yearling was Sadler's Wells, who is taking full advantage of the current shortage of proven sires in America with the ability to get top mile-and-a-half performers. But Sadler's Wells certainly can't take all the credit for this very eyecatching youngster. The colt is out of the spectacular broodmare Flame of Tara, whose first five foals include the triple classic winner Salsabil, the Group 1 winner Marju, the 1993 Prix de Psyche heroine Danse Royale and the Group-placed Nearctic Flame. Salsabil, of course, was sired by Sadler's Wells and so too were Nearctic Flame and Flame of Tara's sixth foal, Mokhtar, who topped the 1992 Goffs sale at 560,000 IR Gns.

Hamdan Al Maktoum had succeeded in buying Salsabil and Mokhtar and he made a gallant effort to buy their brother, too. However, a bid of 1,475,000 IR Gns wasn't quite good enough and Billy McDonald made the successful bid on behalf of a syndicate which will place the colt with the legendary Vincent O'Brien.

It was one of O'Brien's former stars, Nijinsky, who supplied the second-best price of the Orby session, when Joss Collins of the BBA outlasted Darley Stud Management for a three-parts-brother to Petoski. Appropriately enough, the winning bid of 625,000 IR Gns was made on behalf of Petoski's owner, the Dowager Lady Beaverbrook, who will have the colt trained by Clive Brittain.

The most popular filly proved to be a chesnut daughter of the 22-year-old Sea-Bird mare Irish Bird. As the filly is by Ela-Mana-Mou, she's a full-sister to the Irish St Leger winner Eurobird and for good measure she's a half-sister to two other classic winners in Bikala and Assert. This is also the family of Last Tycoon, a stallion who enjoyed a memorable 1993. The winning bid of 530,000 IR Gns was paid by Brian Grassick on behalf of German client Mrs Fokker.

Eurobird also enjoyed a memorable sale, through her filly from the first crop by Dayjur. This time the winning bid of 330,000 IR Gns was made on behalf of Hamdan Al Maktoum, who also campaigned Dayjur.

Otherwise it was very much Coolmore's sale. In addition to the sale topper, Sadler's Wells was responsible for the 400,000 IR Gns colt out of Ameridienne, which had topped the Deauville sale, and for the 230,000 IR Gns brother to El Prado out of the Irish 1,000 Guineas heroine Lady Capulet. Sadler's Wells's brother Fairy King also got into the act, with a Japanese bid of 320,000 IR Gns for his filly out of Dr Devious' dam Rose of Jericho. Caerleon did well too, with a 280,000 IR Gns filly out of Lyphard's half-sister Enthraller; and Danehill joined the major league with a 230,000 IR Gns colt out of Negligence, dam of those very smart Ahonoora fillies Negligent and Ala Mahlik.

Addison Racing, which had paid 230,000 Gns for the Sadler's Wells-Passamaquoddy filly at the Highflyer, picked up another high-priced filly at Goffs in the shape of Slip Anchor's 230,000 IR Gns daughter out of Rimosa's Pet. This half-sister to Rock City had cost just 74,000 Gns as a foal.

Other youngsters which fetched 200,000 IR Gns or more at Goffs were an El Gran Senor colt out of Warm the Sauce; a Darshaan colt out of Water Splash; a Royal Academy colt out of Welsh Love; and a Caerleon filly out of Dingle Bay. There was also a distinct improvement in trade at the two-day Orby II session, with the average rising by around 50 per cent to 15,913 IR Gns.

The last major sale in the yearling circuit that takes place is Tattersalls October Sale, which might have been expected to lose some of its better quality youngsters to the broadening scope of the old Highflyer. However, the 1992 October catalogue had already thrown up some smart two-year-olds by the time the '93 sale got under way on October 12th. Among them were the Group-winning Alzao youngsters Unblest, Sheridan and Alpride, so it was only to be expected that demand would be high for Alzao's latest consignment - especially as his team included a sister to Sheridan. In drawing a bid of 100,000 Gns from Brian Grassick, this filly topped the sale, while an Alzao colt out of Beyond Words fetched 68,000 Gns.

The bright showing by Indian Ridge's first crop guaranteed there would be plenty of interest in the yearlings by the Irish National Stud's acquisition. Two of his colts did particularly well, with Yeomanstown Stud receiving 75,000 Gns for a colt out of Summer Fashion which had cost 16,000 Gns as a foal. Kingwood Stud's colt out of Princess Silka Key fetched only 5,000 Gns less, at 70,000. Joining Alzao and Indian Ridge with two high-priced youngsters was Fairy King, who had colts out of Woodland Garden and Daniela Samuel sold for 70,000 and 68,000 Gns.

As the table shows, the final figures were a marked improvement on the 1992 October Sale - the first since the changes in the Highflyer.

NEWMARKET OCTOBER SALES

Year	Sold	Per cent	Aggregate	Average Gns
1984	626	85.4	8,342,040	13,325
1985	678	85.6	9,782,506	14,428
1986	822	88.1	11,656,515	14,180
1987	864	85.5	13,331,662	15,430
1988	887	89.5	12,145,896	15,201
1989	911	88.8	12,937,993	14,201
1990	722	91.4	10,914,700	15,117
1991	749	90.5	12,332,803	16,465
1992	729	86.9	6,064,508	8,318
1993	694	95.1	9,765,731	14,071

After the astonishing profits made by some pin-hookers in 1993, competition seemed likely to be fierce for well-qualified foals at the year-end sales.

'Flash' Conroy ploughed back some of his profits at Goffs in buying a Royal Academy filly out of Soleiade for 75,000 IR Gns, but that price was beaten by a Lyphard filly, which drew a cash bid of 78,000 IR Gns, and a Dancing Dissident colt out Sovereign Dona, which sold for 85,000 IR Gns to Brian Grassick.

Trade was stronger still during the foal sessions at Tattersalls December Sales, when 528 were sold for an average of 13,759 Gns - up from 9,335 Gns in 1992. Competition was especially fierce on the second and third days, during which Ashtown Bloodstock - the name used by the daunting combination of Timmy Hyde and Paul Shanahan - snapped up three of the top lots. The partnership paid 115,000 Gns for a Sadler's Wells filly out of Charming Life; 110,000 Gns for a Caerleon colt out of the smart French filly As You Desire Me; and 105,000 Gns for a colt out of Warning Light, from the first crop by the fast Nureyev horse Polar Falcon. Ashtown Bloodstock was also in contention for the sale's star lot, a colt by Sadler's Wells out of Shady Leaf. However, the final battle for this relative of Saddlers' Hall and Prince of Dance concerned Richard O'Gorman and Jack Doyle, with Doyle paying 230,000 Gns on behalf of the ubiquitous 'Flash' Conroy.

The Mares section of the December Sales catalogue wasn't notably strong, but it contained two distinguished grey fillies in Ruby Tiger and the Irish 1,000 Guineas winner Nicer. Ruby Tiger is bound for Japan after drawing a 220,000 Gns bid from Geoffrey Howson and Nicer is also destined for overseas - the USA in her case - after Fahd Salman bought her for 270,000 Gns. The sale also included a very distinguished draft from Kiltinan Castle Stud, with the mother-and-daughter team of Ivy and Ivyanna selling for 450,000 and 410,000 Gns respectively.

So the auction year ended as it had started - on an upbeat note. At the risk of sounding like one of those dreary people who always find something to complain about, I have to admit that I would have preferred the recovery to have been a bit more gradual. While stallion owners have generally shown admirable restraint in keeping their 1994 stallion fees near the '93 level, I fear that the good sales results will again encourage people to start breeding from mares which simply aren't good enough. We need to cull more of these poorly-qualified mares and fillies if we are to avoid a quick return to overproduction.

Highest priced yearlings 1946–93

This list of the highest priced yearlings sold at public auction in Britain each year since 1946 shows the rise and fall in prices during recent years.

1946	Star of Gujrath (c Nearco—Eleanor Cross) F Armstrong	16,000
1947	Makarpura (c Big Game—Cap d'Or) H.H. Maharaja of Baroda	14,000
1948	Prince's Choice (b c Nearco—Eleanor Cross) H.H. Maharaja of Baroda	17,000
1949	Daneshill (c Dante—Life Hill) Sir Victor Sassoon	18,000
1950	ch c Nasrullah—Painted Vale Jim Ryan	10,000
1951	Prince Christian (c Nasrullah—Church Bell) F W Dennis	14,000
1952	Amora (f Arbar—Temora) Sir Victor Sassoon	13,000
1953	ch c Fair Trial—Respite London Bloodstock Agency	15,000
1954	Mamounia (f Chanteur II—Minaret) London Bloodstock Agency	17,500
1955	Tempest (c Court Martial—Squall) London Bloodstock Agency	13,000
1956	Martial Law (ch c Court Martial—Refreshed) Anglo-Irish Agency	16,500
1957	Sariegail (f Hill Gail-Sarie) J Weston-Evans	17,000
1958	Die Hard (c Never Say Die—Mixed Blessing) M V O'Brien	14,000
1959	Orbit (c Ribot—Eyewash) Jeremy Tree	15,500
1960	Changing Times (c Prince Chevalier—Miss Advertencia) Anglo-Irish Agency	16,000
1961	Shadow (f Alycidon—Sunshade) Duke of Norfolk	17,000
1962	St. George (ch c Saint Crespin III—Discipliner) Curragh Bloodstock Agency	16,500
1963	Donato (c Alycidon—Mamounia) M V O'Brien	15,000
1964	Royal Ransom (c St Paddy—Maurine) Anglo-Irish Agency	27,000
1965	Grecian Sea (c Never Say Die—Marteline) Ron Smyth	27,000
1966	Rodrigo II (c Charlottesville—Rosmerta) Tim Vigors	31,000
1967	Democratie (f Immortality—Review) Tim Vigors	36,000
1968	Entrepreneur (c Ribot—Montea) Anglo-Irish Agency	37,000
1969	La Hague (f Immortality—Review) George Forbes	51,000
1970	Cambrienne (f Sicambre—Torbella III) M V O'Brien	65,000
1971	Princely Review (c Native Prince—Review) Sir Douglas Clague	117,000
1972	L'Ecossaise (f Dancer's Image—Highland Reel) Bertram Firestone	50,000
1973	Hot Spark (c Habitat—Garvey Girl) Ravi Tikkoo	72,000
1974	Relkino (c Relko—Pugnacity) Lady Beaverbrook	58,000
1975	Million (ch c Mill Reef (USA)—Lalibela) British Bloodstock Agency	202,000
1976	Secala (USA) (ch f Secretariat (USA)—Aladancer) T Doyle	160,000
1977	Link (Fr) (b c Lyphard (USA)—Chain (USA)) BBA (Ireland)	250,000
1978	Sand Hawk (ch c Grundy—Parsimony) H Cottrill	264,000
1979	Ghadeer (Fr) (late Sylver (Fr) (b c Lyphard (USA)—Swanilda (Fr)) H Thomson Jones	625,000
1980	Dilligham (Fr) (b c Green Dancer (USA)—Derna II) O Douieb	530,000
1981	South Atlantic (b c Mill Reef (USA)—Arkadina), BBA (Ireland)	640,000
1982	At Tarf (ch c Tap On Wood—Innocent Air), H Thomson Jones	400,000
1983	Hero Worship (ch c Hello Gorgeous (USA)—Centre Piece) British Bloodstock Agency	1,550,000
1984	Authaal (b c Shergar—Galletto (USA), A R G Cherry-Downes	3,100,000
1985	Fusion (b c Mill Reef (USA)—Gift Wrapped) British Bloodstock Agency	600,000
1986	The Soviet (USA) (ch c Nureyev (USA)—Etoile de Paris) Darley Stud Management	600,000
1987	Aldaja (b c Mill Reef (USA)—Lady Constance) British Bloodstock Agency	780,000
1988	Classic Music (b c Northern Dancer—Fairy Bridge) Classic Thoroughbred & Partners	2,400,000
1989	Mellaby (USA) (ch c Nureyev—Hitting Irish) ZHL Associates	700,000
1990	Ines Bloom (b f Sadler's Wells—Welsh Flame) BBA (Ireland)	840,000
1991	Richard of York (b c Rainbow Quest—Triple First) Darley Stud Management	380,000
1992	Mokhtar (b c Sadler's Wells—Flame of Tara) Shadwell Estate Co Ltd	560,000
1993	B c Sadler's Wells–Flame of Tara, William McDonald	1,500,000

Principal sales of bloodstock during 1993

Prices shown are in Guineas and do not include VAT [US sales in $]

1

DONCASTER
Wednesday, January 27th

Property of A F Budge (Equine) Ltd (to be sold without Reserve), from Osberton Hall Stud

Crown Angel (USA) ch m (5yrs) The Minstrel - State Treasure (Secretariat) Covered by Aragon....... (Elsdon Farms) 4,200
Lambarda Style b m (5yrs) Dancing Brave - Santa's Sister (Middle Brother) Covered by Rock City............ (B.B.A.) 9,600
Ruthless Rose (USA) b or br m (8yrs) Conquistador Cielo - Unfurled (Hoist The Flag) Covered by Danehill........ (Cheveley Park Stud) 51,000
Keen Melody (USA) b m (6yrs) Sharpen Up - Sweet Abandon (USA) (Lyphard) Covered by Rock City.................. (Hellwood Farm Stud) 4,300
Chepstow Vale (USA) gr m (11yrs) Key To The Mint - Kushka (First Landing) Covered by Unfuwain (USA)...... (B.B.A.) 32,000
Sister Claire ch m (12yrs) Quayside - Dromos (Cracksman) Covered by Savahra Sound........... (J G FitzGerald) 1,500
b y c Rock City - Chepstow Vale (USA) (Key To The Mint).................. (Cash) 4,800
b y f Rock City - Resonation (CAN) (Coastal) .... (Stratford Homes) 1,000
b y c Night Shift (USA) - Ruthless Rose (USA) (Conquistador Cielo).... (B.B.A.) 20,000
b y f Rock City - Keen Melody (USA) (Sharpen Up)....... (Stratford Homes) 900
b y f Ardross - Sister Claire (Quayside) .... (David Minton Bloodstock) 4,500

2

Property of a Partnership, from Arras Farm & Stud

b y c Dowsing (USA) - State Ball (Dance In Time)............... (M W Easterby) 720

From Barton Stud

b y c Petoski - Farcical (Pharly)............ (Johnny McKeever Bloodstock) 4,100
br y c Double Schwartz - Sahara Breeze (Ela-Mana-Mou).......... (T D Barron) 2,500
ch y f Master Willie - Theanswer Myfriend (USA) (Restless Wind) (M W Easterby) 2,600

To Dissolve a Partnership

ch y c Hadeer - Penny In My Shoe (USA) (Sir Ivor).................. (D Holder) 2,700

Property of a Partnership

b y c Sharrood (USA) - Valiyen (Valiyar) .... (Dandys Farm Stud) 1,900

Property of Mr J S Bell

ch y c Statoblest - Apprila (Bustino) .... (Johnny McKeever Bloodstock) 4,700

From Woodleigh Stud

ch y c Charmer - Celtic Sonata (Music Boy) (J Ttikkirou) 400

Property of Mr W J Wyatt

br y c Satin Wood - Slipperose (Persepolis) (Cash) 1,000
ch y c Faustus (USA) - Loveville (USA) (Assert)...................... (Cash) 1,350
b y f Satin Wood - Haywain (Thatching).... (A Netser) 1,650

3

Property of Helshaw Grange Farms Ltd., from Helshaw Grange Stud

ch y f Good Thyne (USA) - Olympic Course (Crash Course)................ (Cash) 950
br y f Good Thyne (USA) - Padykin (Bustino) .... (M W Easterby) 1,300

Property of Mr D J Christopher, from Upperwood Farm Stud

b c (2yrs) Picea - Edith Piaf (Thatch)....... (J Ttikkirou) 1,500

To Dissolve a Partnership, from Teal Cottage Stud

b y c Rakaposhi King - Pro-Token (Proverb) (M W Easterby) 1,700
ch y f Rakaposhi King - Ancat Girl (Politico) (A Netser) 420
Highmoor Scallyann ch m (7yrs) Scallywag - Ancat Girl (Politico) Covered by Rymer (Mrs A Carter) 950

From Sweeney Stud

Aston Lass b m (9yrs) Headin' Up - Ritzy Dreamer (High Line) Covered by Rakaposhi King........... (L R Smith) 2,200

Property of Mr H McGahon, Co Louth, Ireland

Second Service b m (14yrs) Red Regent - Monte Rosa (Crepello) Covered by Denel........................ (Cash) 680
Amour Libre b m (10yrs) He Loves Me - Carinara (Pitcairn) Covered by Denel... (A Netser) 1,600
All The Girls br f (4yrs) Alzao - Second Service (Red Regent).... (R J Adams) 1,200

4

To Settle An Account

Decent Sort b or br m (9yrs) Decent Fellow - Shanban (Shackleton) Covered by Roscoe Blake............ (I M Lynch) 1,800

Property of Merton Stud, from Merton Stud
Little Token gr m (10yrs) Shack (USA) - Hung Pao (Cumshaw) Covered by Henbit (USA).............. (Mrs A Carter) 950

From Merton Stud
Poco Pierna ch f (3yrs) Ahonoora - Flaunting (Kings Lake)............... (A Netser) 1,000

Property of Mrs J Downing
A Day Late b m (8yrs) Mandalus - Pargio (Parthia)...................... (Cash) 950

To Dissolve a Partnership
Oberon's Daughter b m (6yrs) Fairy King (USA) - Precocious Angel (Persian Bold) Covered by Phountzi.................. (Lady Linda Williams) 1,100

Property of Mr David Osborne, from Catfoss Stud
Cadenette b m (11yrs) Brigadier Gerard - Tremellick (Mummy's Pet) Covered by Daring March, believed NOT to be in foal.................. (Miss T Taylor) 1,200

From Etchingham Stud
Mohibbah (USA) b m (8yrs) Conquistador Cielo (USA) - Gently Dreaming (USA) (Indian Hemp) Covered by Bairn (USA), believed NOT to be in foal. (D Nelson) 2,000

Property of Mrs M Morley, from Stockwell Stud
Pashmina b m (9yrs) Blue Cashmere - Petploy (Faberge II) Covered by Precocious, believed NOT to be in foal.... (F Iqbal) 920

Property of Willow Investments Ltd., from Hedgeholme Stud
Mature b m (14yrs) Welsh Pageant - Material (Song) Covered by Sylvan Express.. (A Netser) 920
My Willow ch m (10yrs) Tap On Wood - Nye (FR) (Sanctus II) Covered by Sylvan Express..................... (F Iqbal) 750

5

Property of W M Promotions Ltd., from Northmore Stud
Pontevecchio Due b m (11yrs) Welsh Pageant - Silvera (Ribero) Covered by Primo Dominie.......... (Angley Stud) 8,400

Property of a Partnership, from Plantation Stud
Superflash ch m (7yrs) Superlative - Photo Flash (Match III) Covered by Keen..... (Johnny McKeever Bloodstock) 5,500

Property of Mr Richard Fahey, from Manor House Stables
It's All Academic b m (5yrs) Mazaad - Princess Of Nashua (Crowned Prince) (P Mitchell) 19,000

From Ticklerton Stud
Choral Sundown b m (7yrs) Night Shift (USA) - Choir (High Top)...... (B.B.A.) 4,800

Property of Mr M Lindsay, from Tupgill Park Stables
Knowing gr m (6yrs) Lochnager - Caroline Lamb (Hotfoot).............. (D Muir) 2,000

Property of A F Budge (Equine) Ltd (to be sold without Reserve), from Cobhall Court Stud
Savahra Sound b h (8yrs) Song - Savahra (Free State)............ (D Chapman) 14,000

From Burtree Stables
Island Set (USA) b h (11yrs) Hawaii - Desk Set (USA) (Tom Rolfe).... (J Ttikkirou) 5,000

6

DONCASTER

Thursday, January 28th

To Settle An Account, from Hanging Hill Stables
ch c (2yrs) Mon Tresor - Northern Amber (Shack).................... (F J Pype) 2,600

To Dissolve A Partnership, from Teal Cottage Stud
ch f (2yrs) Rakaposhi King - Pro-Token (Proverb)...................... (Cash) 1,500

Property of Mr R Wigham
b c (3yrs) Efisio - Snap Tin (Jimmy Reppin) (Cash) 600

From The Racing Stables
Cool Flight ch f (4yrs) Absalom - Fancy Flight (FR) (Arctic Tern)............... (Yair Amsterdamer) 1,050

Property of Miss G Stephenson
Super-Sub b f (4yrs) Formidable (USA) - Charlton Athletic (Bustino)............ (Sagittarius Bloodstock) 1,300

Property of a Partnership, from Westerlands Stud
Zoom Lens ch f (4yrs) Caerleon (USA) - Photo (Blakeney).. (Westerlands Stud) 5,000

From Westhill Stables
Lone Note ch f (4yrs) Song - Cystal's Solo (USA) (Crystal Water)..... (C S Seavill) 1,050

To Settle An Account, from Denton Hall Stables
Sno Serenade b g (7yrs) Song - When The Saints (Bay Express)....... (I Mitchell) 1,400

From Maunby House Stables
Soleil Rayon b g (3yrs) Fayruz - Trust Sally (Sallust)................. (O Sorensen) 1,400
Petered Out br g (3yrs) Nomination - Fading (Pharly).............. (Mr R Lindsey) 1,000

7

Property of Mrs Sharon Sharpstone, from Preston Hill Stables
b g (2yrs) Lighter - Tele Call Lady (The Parson)....................... (Cash) 580

Property of Mr Geoffrey L'Anson & Sons
b c (2yrs) Bairn (USA) - Candle In The Wind (Thatching)... (Out Lane Management) 3,000

From Woodland Stud
b c (3yrs) Kala Shikari - Greenacres Joy (Tycoon II)................ (S B Avery) 800

Property of Rodvic Ltd
Bay Rum b f (3yrs) Green Ruby - Cuba Libre (Rum)....................... (J Tolbol) 1,450
Shaharit b f (3yrs) Shardari - Lady's Flag (USA) (Fifth Marine)....... (D Heaney) 1,650

Property of a Partnership
br c (3yrs) King Of Spain - Lunar Eclipse (Hot Spark)............ (J Carmichael) 850

Property of Mrs J M Findlay
Classic Ring b m (5yrs) Auction Ring (USA) - Classic Choice (Patch) .... (Johnny McKeever Bloodstock) 2,100

To Dissolve a Partnership, from Tupgill Park Stables
Coral Kingdom b g (4yrs) Celestial Storm (USA) - Coral Fury (Mill Reef) .... (P Weinberg) 1,750

From Stonebridge Farm Stables

Emma Victoria b f (5yrs) Dominion - Gwiffina (Welsh Saint).. (R Brotherton) 2,600

To Dissolve A Partnership, from The Grange Stables

Redstella (USA) ch c (4yrs) Theatrical - Orange Squash (Red God).. (N Tinkler) 1,600

8

Property of Mrs Rose Button, from The Grange Stables

Orchid Valley b f (4yrs) Cyrano de Bergerac - Dane Valley (Simbir)..... (J Stewart) 920

Property of Mr B O'Neil

Scottish Ruby b g (4yrs) Scottish Reel - Screenable (USA) (Silent Screen)...... (P Weinberg) 1,350

From Moss Side Racing Stables

Grey Pride gr g (3yrs) Bold Owl - Bri-Ette (Brittany)............... (J Robertson) 1,150

Hills Raceaid ch f (3yrs) Mazaad - Sainthill (St Alphage)............ (S Uppstrom) 5,200

ch f (2yrs) Standaan (FR) - Super Restless (USA) (Restless Wind) .... (Miss H Dunning) 500

From East Everleigh Stables

General Dixie (USA) b g (4yrs) Dixieland Band (USA) - Bold Example (USA) (Bold Lad)......................... (Cash) 4,400

From Osberton Hall Stud (to be sold without Reserve)

Hard Sell ch g (6yrs) Hard Fought - Misoptimist (Blakeney)....... (Miss J Storey) 1,600

Kinclaven b g (6yrs) Comedy Star (USA) - Arachova (High Line).... (P Weinberg) 1,700

Gold Surprise b or br g (4yrs) Petorius - Gold Piece (Golden Fleece)........... (S Kettlewell) 3,800

Property of A F Budge (Equine) Ltd (to be sold without Reserve), from Osberton Hall Stud

Seahawk Retriever ch g (4yrs) Treasure Hunter - Sister Claire (Quayside)...... (J G FitzGerald) 5,600

Muskora b g (4yrs) Muscatite - Singing Wren (Julio Mariner) (G Peter-Hoblyn) 6,400

b g (3yrs) Oats - Mirthful (Will Somers).... (Cash) 11,000

b g (3yrs) Orchestra - Gentle Heiress (Prince Tenderfoot)........ (N Tinkler) 6,400

Corona Gold b g (3yrs) Chilibang - Miss Alkie (Noalcoholic).... (J G FitzGerald) 800

Beverley Knight b g (3yrs) Be My Guest - It's Terrific (Vaguely Noble) (D Murray-Smith) 3,600

Prairie Grove b g (3yrs) Primo Dominie - Fairy Fans (Petingo).......... (B B A) 2,800

La Posada b f (3yrs) Procida (USA) - Chepstow Vale (USA) (Key To The Mint)........................ (B B A) 6,600

Dana Springs b f (3yrs) Aragon - Dance By Night (Northfields)............ (B B A) 3,800

Darshay b f (3yrs) Darshaan - So Gay (Laugh Aloud)............. (F J Pype) 53,000

b c (2yrs) High Estate - Cornelian (Great Nephew)..................... (Cash) 25,000

ch c (2yrs) Woodman (USA) - Resonation (CAN) (Coastal)........... (J Ttikkirou) 5,000

gr f (2yrs) Unfuwain (USA) - Chepstow Vale (USA) (Key To The Mint)...... (B B A) 8,200

b f (2yrs) Polish Precedent (USA) - Ruthless Rose (USA) (Conquistador Cielo)...... (Cash) 28,000

ch f (2yrs) Ardross - Sister Claire (Quayside) .... (J G FitzGerald) 2,500

9

Property of Mr R Lloyd

b f (2yrs) Never So Bold - Neasham Queen (FR) (Roi Dagobert)................ (Yair Amsterdamer) 1,500

Property of Mr D G Mason, from Southburgh Manor Stud

ch c (2yrs) Jester - Finally (Final Straw).... (P Green) 1,400

From Wood Farm Stud

b c (2yrs) Alleging (USA) - Polished Queen (Kings Lake).............. (I Glenton) 1,900

To Dissolve A Partnership, from Ivy House Stables

Fragonard br g (4yrs) Pharly (FR) - Girl On A Swing (High Top).................... (R O'Sheen Bloodstock) 2,000

From Rathmoy Stables

A.A.Bamba b f (4yrs) Slip Anchor - Enchanting Dancer (FR) (Nijinsky)...... (Cash) 3,200

To Dissolve A Partnership, from Serlby Hall Stables

Samsolom b g (5yrs) Absalom - Norfolk Serenade (Blakeney).... (C Hammond) 3,200

Property of Sir Philip Oppenheimer, from Induna Stables

Mrs Jekyll ch f (3yrs) Sure Blade - Grey Walls (Habitat)............. (J Tolbol) 1,600

Property of Grange Bloodstock Ltd., from Abington Place Stables

Convoy gr g (3yrs) Be My Guest (USA) - Be Easy (Be Friendly)........... (W Muir) 9,400

From Phantom House Stables

Elska Dig b f (3yrs) Sayf El Arab (USA) - Galetzky (Radetzky)...... (A Hermans) 1,400

Property of Lord Derby, from Heath House Stables

Diamond Point b f (3yrs) Kalaglow - Diamond Hill (High Top)........ (J Tolbol) 7,200

10

Property of Mr J Carmichael, Co Antrim, Ireland

ch c (2yrs) My Generation - Surreal (Bustino).................. (R W Jaines) 880

Property of Mr H McGahon, Co. Louth, Ireland

Platform One b g (3yrs) Standaan (FR) - Sleeping Car (Scorpio)... (G Flemming) 800

Property of Miss N A Harrod, from Norton Grove Stud

Royal Comedian gr f (4yrs) Jester - Royal Huntress (Royal Avenue)............ (Fir Trading Ltd) 2,700

Property of the exors. of the late Mr J Rhind

Molten Copper ch g (4yrs) Pennine Walk - Danger Signal (Red God)... (F J Pype) 9,200

Property of a Partnership, from Kremlin House Stables

Clifton Chase ch c (4yrs) Try My Best (USA) - Mrs Cullumbine (Silly Season)....... (J L Harris) 12,500

From Seven Springs Stables
Cellito b c (4yrs) Flash Of Steel - Apocalypse (Auction Ring)........ (G Blum) 1,500
Property of a Partnership, from Oak Stables Ltd
Don't Drop Bombs (USA) ch g (4yrs) Fighting Fit - Promised Star (Star de Naskra) (Darren Croft) 7,400
From Spigot Lodge Stables
All Greek To Me b g (5yrs) Trojan Fen - Do We Know (Derrylin)........ (J Parkes) 8,600
Property of Messrs T Fairhurst & C H Newton Jnr Ltd, from Glasgow House Stables
Chilly's Star b g (3yrs) Chilibang - Aquarian Star (Cavo Doro).......... (J Rimmer) 750
Property of Mr D Poole, from Primrose Cottage Stables
Otter Bush b g (4yrs) Daring March - Rhythmical (Swing Easy).... (Harvey Smith) 2,100

11

Property of Mrs Bridget Blum, from Primrose Cottage Stables
Pink 'n' Black b f (4yrs) Double Schwartz - Miss Pinkerton (Above Suspicion) ..... (A Netser) 2,500
Property of a Partnership, from Beverley House Stud
Cappahoosh ch f (4yrs) Salmon Leap - Tagik (Targowice).................. (Cash) 6,200
Property of a Partnership, from Whatcombe Stud
Pistol ch c (3yrs) Glenstal - First Land (Windjammer)............ (C Horgan) 14,000
Titled Girl b f (3yrs) Alzao (USA) - Sweet Goodbye (Petorious)....... (Mrs Wild) 2,900
From Snowdrop Stud Co Ltd
Walstead b c (4yrs) Fairy King (USA) - Tecmessa (Home Guard).... (G Blum) 3,200
To Settle an Account, from Kingsley House Stables
Alphonso b c (4yrs) Forzando - Alice Parry (Kampala).......... (Mrs M Hennessy) 5,800
From Woodlands Stables
Burning Point b g (4yrs) Never So Bold - Billante (USA) (Graustark)...... (Cash) 1,600
Property of M D M Racing (Thoroughbreds) Ltd, from Barton Hall Stables
Long Lane Lady b m (7yrs) Longleat (USA) - Teresa Way (Great White Way) .... (F Iqbal) 1,100
From Whitsbury Stables
Bel Baraka ch g (4yrs) Bering - Typhoon Polly (Lord Gayle)............ (G Blum) 2,500
From Sandy Brow Stables
Persian Fleece ch f (4yrs) Bold Arrangement - Microcosme (Golden Fleece)... (A Netser) 1,950

12

From Racecourse Farm Stables
Ballyanto b g (8yrs) Lepanto (GER) - Balyarctic (Articeelagh)........... (Cash) 4,100
Floodlight b f (3yrs) Exhibitioner - Share The Vision (Vision)................ (G Kaye) 1,200
From Pinewood Stables
Black Boy br g (4yrs) Auction Ring (USA) - Relic Spirit (Relic)............ (Cash) 2,200
To Dissolce a Partnership
gr g (4yrs) Sharrood (USA) - Helcia (Habitat) (D Heaney) 3,600
From Helshaw Gange Stud
br g (4yrs) Lancastrian - Pentoff (Dubasoff) (Cash) 700
To Dissolve a Partnership
br g (4yrs) Treasure Kay - Jenny Dancer (Skyliner)................ (P Clarkson) 3,100
From Radway Stables
ch g (5yrs) Capricorn Line - Fiery Wade (Green God).................. (Cash) 3,400
To Settle An Account
b g (5yrs) Kinglet - Tuletta (Tula Rocket) ... (D Whitehurst) 2,500
From The Beeches Stud, Co Waterford, Ireland
b g (8yrs) Le Moss - Colshaw Lass (Border Chief)................... (P Weinberg) 1,100
b g (6yrs) Le Moss - Pitcoke (Pitpan) ...... (B Woodhouse) 2,800

13

Property of Mr L N Sloan & Mrs A Nore, from Pit Farm Stables
Cleric On Broadway b m (5yrs) The Parson - L O Broadway (Crash Course) .... (Easby Stud) 8,200
Property of Mrs H Whyte, from Greenhill Stables, Co Kildare, Ireland
Ushers Island br g (7yrs) Sandalay - Star Luck (Star Signal)....... (J H Johnson) 12,000
To Dissolve A Partnership
Another March b g (7yrs) Marching On - River Sirene (Another River).... (Cash) 2,100
From Thorndale Stables
Willow Holding br g (8yrs) Some Hand - Catherines April (Fez).... (P Weinberg) 1,500
Property of Mr R A Green, from Douglas Hall Farm Stables
Corby Knowe b g (7yrs) Pragmatic - Easter Noddy (Sir Herbert)..... (Lewis Grant) 1,100
Property of Mr R Williams, from Blackwell Grange Stables
Strike It Right b g (8yrs) Royal Match - Mrs Neddy (Super Song)... (H Rushworth) 2,000
Property of a Lady
Winters Girl b m (7yrs) Beverley Boy - Wintersbrig (New Brig)................ (Mr E Anscombe) 900
Property of Mr N D Tutty
Belarius b g (5yrs) Bellypha - Celebrity (Troy).................. (P Weinberg) 1,500
Property of Mr Tony Clegg, from Castle Farm Stables
Crawn Hawk br g (8yrs) Croghan Hill - Gin An Tonic (Osprey Hawk) .... (Ruth Wollerton) 1,650
To Dissolve a Partnership, from Castle Farm Stables
Passing Thought b g (6yrs) Pollerton - Royal Willow (Royal Buck)..... (P Eckersley) 2,600

14

From Buntree House Stables
Colonial Lord ch g (7yrs) Milford - Miss Fanackapan (Colonist II).... (C Holson) 850

Property of Mrs E Y Hunnisett
Robbie Burns br g (7yrs) Daring March - Gangawayhame (Lochnager).......... (Mrs S Critchley) 2,100
From Great House Stables
Vale Of Secrecy b g (12yrs) The Parson - Arctic Rhapsody (Bargello)............ (Mr J Kirkwood) 1,700
Property of Messrs. A A Penney & I Wardle, from Hamilton Stables
Pondered Bid b g (9yrs) Auction Ring (USA) - Ponca (Jimmy French) (Pat Mitchell) 2,100
Property of Mrs S McGarvie, from New Lodge Racing Stables
Pacific Gem br g (6yrs) Valiyar - Mary Martin (Be My Guest)..... (G Barnett) 1,550
From Star Cottage Stables
Copper Hall ch g (7yrs) Mr Fluorocarbon - Helping Hand (Right Boy)...... (Cash) 1,200
Property of Mr W E Robson
Marnies Refrain b g (7yrs) Blue Refrain - Marnie's Girl (Crooner)............... (M E Sowersby) 3,000
To Dissolve a Partnership
Glenbay b g (8yrs) Hawaiian Return - Scotspree (Lone Star).......... (Cash) 1,400
Property of Mr A Walker, from Tupgill Stables
Reklaw b g (6yrs) Hard Fought - Rubina Park (Ashmore)......... (S Chadwick) 1,500
From Welham Stables
Angel Train ch m (5yrs) Burslem - Senama (FR) (Sanctus II)............... (Cash) 1,300

15

Property of Miss K M George
b c (2yrs) Today And Tomorrow - Blair's Winnie (Ashmore)............. (Cash) 750
b c (2yrs) Today And Tomorrow - Nimble Dancer (Northern Wizard)...... (Cash) 780
Property of Mr R M Smith
ch g (3yrs) Gabitat - Becalmed (Right Tack) (Cash) 750
From Scalibar Farm Stables
Charter Member ch g (7yrs) Posse - Lady Ector (USA) (King Pellinore)........... (Miss Sue Hill) 2,000
To Dissolve a Partnership, from Teal Cottage Stud
The Man From Oman b or br g (10yrs) Decent Fellow - Lady Darnley (Supreme Sovereign) (Miss Tina Gray) 1,000
Property of Mrs P Baldwin
Cherions Brook b g (7yrs) Cherions Rock - Pearl Springs (Silent Spring).... (Cash) 2,600
Property of Miss P Edgar
Aikwood br g (6yrs) Ancient Monro - Straight Sonnet (Boston Two-Step).... (Miss C Raw) 1,800
Property of a Gentleman
Whistling Sam b g (8yrs) Proverb - Windbush (Whistling Wind).... (P Weinberg) 1,200
Property of Mr W H Eastwood
Ice Cold b g (10yrs) Ascertain (USA) - Sally Rowanne (Haris II)......... (J Gurden) 1,500
Property of Mrs J Dodd, from Bonnyhale Stables
Chantry Boy b g (9yrs) Balliol - Glebe (Tacitus).................. (Mrs K Birkett) 1,600

16

Property of Mr B Heyward, from Aiskew Stud
b g (9yrs) Varano - Aileen Aroone (R Fahey) 2,200
Property of Mrs C Ewart
O'Danny Boy b g (7yrs) King Of Diamonds - (hunter Mare)............. (A Ireland) 3,000
Property of Mr J Watson
gr m (10yrs) - .... (A Ireland) 1,200
PRIVATE SALES
From Ridge House Stables
ch g (5yrs) Nicholas Bill - Lingdale Lady (Sandford Lad)....... (Ruth Wollerton) 1,500

17

KILL (Goffs)
Monday, February 8th

Property of Mr Sean Kavanagh
Kavrag b m (12yrs) Raga Navarro (ITY) - Krasny Bor (Parthia) Covered by Castle Keep...................... (I Geddis) 500
Property of a Partnership, from Lough Gowna Lodge
b y c Waajib - Grecian Hill (Ela-Mana-Mou) (Cash) 15,000
Property of Mr James Devereux
Lyster House b m (10yrs) Whistling Deer - Scent Bag (Deep Diver) Covered by Sharp Charter.............. (I Geddis) 600
Property of Mr Barty Roche, from Rockbarton Stud
ch f (5yrs) Cissbury Boy - Clonmel Rose (Indian Ruler).............. (I Geddis) 600
Property of Ms. Gabrielle Berney
br f (4yrs) Good Thyne (USA) - Le Idol (Le Bavard)...................... (Cash) 2,600
From Woodford Stud
Miss Boston (FR) ch m (10yrs) River River (FR) - La Sarre (Prince Taj) Covered by Treasure Kay.... (Mercury Bloodstock) 3,200
Elegant Owl ch m (7yrs) Tumble Wind (USA) - Tawny Owl (Faberge) Covered by Treasure Kay.... (Pascal Crawford) 800
From Rosemount House Stud
ch y c The Noble Player (USA) - Crepe de Paille (Final Straw)............. (Cash) 1,500
b y c Tirol - Sindos (Busted).............. (John Osborne) 2,000
ch y c The Noble Player (USA) - Gentle Rhythm (Ballad Rock)....... (I Geddis) 400

18

Property of Mr T J Culhane
Sahara Red b or br m (9yrs) Saher - Red Lightening (Red God) Covered by Digamist (USA)................ (I Geddis) 800
Leahs Son (IRE) b c (3yrs) Kafu - Sahara Red (Saher)................ (I Geddis) 500
Property of Mr B P McMahon
Montifiore Avenue b g (7yrs) Kings Lake (USA) - Lady Of Cornwall (USA) (Cornish Prince).... (Ro Sheen Bloodstock) 3,500
From Piercetown Stud
Mount Cicero (IRE) b m (4yrs) Wassl - Capital Risk (Bustino) Covered by Common Grounds................ (C B A) 2,800

From Timberlake

Shakiyka (IRE) ch f (4yrs) Shardari - Shanama (Mill Reef) .... (Sagittarius Bloodstock) 1,600

Property of Mr Mark Wright

ch y f Executive Perk - Selkis (Dunbeath) .. (Cash) 750

Property of the Exors of the late Murray McDonell, from Whitechurch Stud

Rosie's Mac (IRE) b c (4yrs) Petorius - Repicado Rose (USA) (Repicado)...... (Kildare Thoroughbred Services) 1,100

From Rathbarry Stud (Agent)

ch y f Buckskin (FR) - Deep Hansel (Deep Run)......................... (Cash) 700

From Brownstown Lodge Stables (Agent)

Divine Saint (IRE) b g (4yrs) Saher - Divine Dilly (Divine Gift)...... (Joseph Dunne) 600

From Friarstown House Stables (A Part Dispersal)

ch g (3yrs) Local Suitor (USA) - Dance Lover's (FR) (Green Dancer).... (C B A) 9,000
ch c (2yrs) Glow (USA) - Camden's Gift (Camden Town)........... (R Hylands) 700
ch f (2yrs) Classic Secret (USA) - Easy On The Eye (Henbit).... (B P Macmahon) 3,800
b f (2yrs) Dahar (USA) - Naxos (USA) (Big Spruce)............... (David Hanley) 5,000
ch c (2yrs) Red Sunset - Jarretiere (Star Appeal)............................ (Browne Bloodstock Enterprises) 1,600
Peace Tribute (IRE) b or br g (4yrs) Nomination - Olderfleet (Steel Heart) .... (Don Kelly Bloodstock) 3,100
Top Wave br g (5yrs) High Top - Sea Fret (Habat).... (David Minton Bloodstock) 7,700

19

Property of a Partnership, from Harrietville Stud

b y c Supreme Leader - Hack Along (Little Buskins).............. (Dudley Taylor) 3,100
b y f Electric - Santa Anita Jet (Grand Conde)............... (Tony Cournane) 460

Property of Mrs C Brosnan, from Harrietville Stud

b y f Executive Perk - Flying Early (Ballyciptic).................. (Tony Broughan) 380

Property of a Partnership, from Harrietville Stud

b y c Electric - Ormskirk Mover (Deep Run) (Cash) 800

Property of Mr John Henry

Barncogue ch m (8yrs) Monseigneur (USA) - Whispering Star (Sound Track) Covered by Jareer believed NOT in foal ... (Cash) 5,400

Property of Mr Ivor Carroll, from South House Stud

ch y c Rontino - Friend's Folly (Sweet Revenge).. (Azienda Agricola Vighome) 4,200

From Oghill House Stud

b g (3yrs) Phardante (FR) - Night Number (Crash Course)........... (Pat Phelan) 900

Property of Mr M C Throsby, from Landscape Stud

Cry In The Dark b m (6yrs) Godswalk (USA) - Embustera (Sparkler) Covered by Classic Music.................. (Cash) 4,400

Property of Brenda Norton

b f (2yrs) Prince Rupert (FR) - Fingers (Lord Gayle)............ (Mr John Geraghty) 1,000

From Milltown Britton Stud

b g (2yrs) Phardante (FR) - Gifted Lady (Divine Gift)......... (Lovestone Stud) 1,200

20

From Treascon Stud (Agent)

br y f Boreen (FR) - Petite Fee (Cut Above) (Alex Boyle) 550
br y f Boreen (FR) - Its All Taboo (Smartset) (W Nolan) 500

From Treascon Stud

br y c Aristocracy - Wilden (Will Somers) .. (R Fahey) 3,500
ch y c Millfontaine - Dynamic Girl (Martinmas)......................... (Cash) 400

From Ardrums House Stud

Hawaiian Peace ch m (9yrs) Henbit (USA) - Quiet Harbour (Mill Reef) Covered by Contract Law (USA)................ (Mercury Bloodstock) 9,500

From Grangemoyle Farm

Lifestyle b m (15yrs) Jimmy Reppin - Cave Girl (Pindari) Covered by Jupiter Island (Ciarain Conroy) 3,600
Fifth Quarter b m (8yrs) Cure The Blues (USA) - Overplay (Bustino) Covered by Fayruz..... (David Minton Bloodstock) 14,000

From Bernard Lodge Stables

Caoimseach (IRE) b g (5yrs) Martin John - La Croisette (Nishapour)....... (Cash) 4,000

From Green Ireland Properties Ltd

Height Of Elegance b m (9yrs) Shirley Heights - Elegida (Habitat)............ (Ms Roisin O'Connor) 3,000

Property of International Thoroughbred Breeders Inc., from Round Hill Stud

Ounavarra ch m (14yrs) Homeric - Montbretia (Aureole) Covered by Nordico (USA)........... (John Sheehan) 2,800
b y f Fools Holme (USA) - War Ballad (FR) (Green Dancer)................ (Cash) 1,900

21

Property of Mrs K Twomey

ch y c Cardinal Flower - Villawood (Quayside)............ (Victor Bowens) 4,200

From Bushy Park Stud

b g (2yrs) Superpower - Cecily (Prince Regent).......... (E Daly Bloodstock) 24,000

Property of Mr Peter O'Gorman, from Old French Furze Stables

Final Favour (IRE) b g (4yrs) Drumalis - Please Oblige (Le Levanstell) .... (Danny Murphy) 6,000

From Green Ireland Properties Ltd

Al Zumurrud ch m (10yrs) Be My Guest (USA) - Mey (Canisbay)...... (P J Foy) 750

From Gaybrooke Estate

b f (4yrs) Celio Rufo - Bella Minna (Chou Chin Chow)........ (Pro-Am & Co Ltd) 1,800
ch f (4yrs) Stalker - Lucie Burslem (Burslem)............ (Pro-Am & Co Ltd) 1,050

b f (4yrs) Sarab - Soudchika (GER) (Dschingis Khan).............. (Cash) 1,050

From Hamwood & Mitchelstown Stud

Future Shock b m (10yrs) Full Out (USA) - Voltigeuse (USA) (Filiberto) Covered by Topanoora.................... (Cash) 1,600

Must Hurry b m (6yrs) Kampala - Precious Gift (Prince Tenderfoot) Covered by Salt Dome (USA).... (Mary O'Connor) 1,600

Secret Heart br m (7yrs) Vision (USA) - Heart 'n' Soul (Bold Lad) Covered by Ballad Rock........... (Sue Lenehan) 1,800

Grange Hollow b m (10yrs) Wolver Hollow - Peg Ahead (USA) (Iron Peg) Covered by Salt Dome (USA).............. (Cash) 900

Reprint b m (11yrs) Kampala - Yellow Pages (Yellow God) Covered by Shernazar....................... (C B A) 3,600

Bel Ria b m (12yrs) Gay Fandango (USA) - Topping Girl (Sea Hawk II) Covered by Law Society (USA)............ (Cash) 3,700

22

From Monread Stud

b y f Taufan (USA) - Duly Elected (Persian Bold)..... (Azienda Agricola Vighome) 3,600

br y c Machiavellian (USA) - Aldhabyih (General Assembly) (Jean-Pierre Deroubaix) 14,500

ch y c Polish Precedent (USA) - Tarib (Habitat).......................... (Cash) 1,900

b y f Master Willie - Dublah (USA) (Private Account)..................... (Cash) 550

Hufoof b m (7yrs) Known Fact (USA) - Al Washl (USA) (The Minstrel) Covered by Persian Heights (Mercury Bloodstock) 3,400

From Fenpark Stables

Coronado br h (5yrs) Rainbow Quest (USA) - Moon Parade (Welsh Pageant)....... (Brian Grassick) 5,200

Property of a Partnership, from Fenpark Stables

Sir Henry Knyvet b g (4yrs) Reference Point - La Mer (NZ) (Copenhagen).......... (Desmond Hughes) 10,000

Property of Mrs Frances Cole

br y c Montelimar (USA) - Semiwild (USA) (Rumbo)...................... (Cash) 1,000

br y f Mandalus - Lenticular (Warpath)..... (Cash) 600

From Glenealy Stud

gr f (3yrs) Strong Gale - Helen's Tower (Dual)................ (John Phelan) 3,700

b f (3yrs) Amazing Bust - Lets Cruise (Deep Run).............. (Ms Andrea Etter) 1,100

23

From Oaklea Stud

Sharply b m (11yrs) Sharpman - Coneenford (Ballymore) Covered by Two Timing (USA) believed NOT in foal........... (Maurice Leamy) 600

From Bolinrush Stud

Enterprisor b m (13yrs) Artaius (USA) - Ceili Mor (Irish Ball) Covered by Sharp Charter............ (Ms Marcella O'Reilly) 1,000

Property of Mr James Devereux

Record Halmony ch m (8yrs) Record Token - Damsel (Pampered King) Covered by Sharp Charter................. (Cash) 850

Property of H H Aga Khan's Studs S.C., from Gilltown Stud

Adarenna (FR) ch m (10yrs) Mill Reef (USA) - Adara (FR) (Le Haar)............... (Jamestown House Stud) 2,000

Altiyna ch m (10yrs) Troy - Alannya (FR) (Relko) Covered by Shernazar......... (Paul Shanahan) 36,000

Badedra b m (6yrs) Kings Lake (USA) - Borushka (Bustino) Covered by Alzao (USA).......... (Mercury Bloodstock) 16,000

Damana (FR) gr m (12yrs) Crystal Palace (FR) - Denia (FR) (Crepello) Covered by Darshaan believed NOT in foal........ (Paul Shanahan) 17,500

Danakala b m (6yrs) Mouktar - Demo (FR) (Abdos) Covered by Kahyasi believed NOT in foal.................. (Cash) 1,600

Dedra (FR) b m (15yrs) Faunus (FR) - Demo (FR) (Abdos) Covered by Shardari believed NOT in foal.......... (Cash) 1,400

Glowing Halo ch m (14yrs) Grundy - Blessed Again (Ballymoss) Covered by Shernazar.......................... (Azienda Agricola Di F Leome) 7,800

Marazika br m (9yrs) Great Nephew - Miss Melody (Tudor Melody) Covered by Kahyasi believed NOT in foal .... (Clem Murphy) 6,000

Nawazish ch m (15yrs) Run The Gantlet (USA) - Nilmeen (Right Royal V) Covered by Akarad (FR) believed NOT in foal......... (Jamestown House Stud) 1,000

Parakara br m (10yrs) Great Nephew - Polana (FR) (Botticelli) Covered by Lashkari .... (James O'Neill) 7,500

Rifada b m (7yrs) Ela-Mana-Mou - Rilasa (FR) (St Paddy) Covered by Kahyasi believed NOT in foal....... (F Trivass) 4,800

Samirza (USA) b m (9yrs) Riverman (USA) - Samata (FR) (Rheffic) Covered by Bikala........................ (Cash) 5,000

Sharata (IRE) b m (5yrs) Darshaan - Shademah (Thatch) Covered by Shardari believed NOT in foal................ (Ashtown House Stud) 7,200

Sharaya (USA) b m (13yrs) Youth (USA) - Shanizadeh (Baldric II) Covered by Doyoun....... (Ashtown House Stud) 45,000

24

From Friarstown House Stud (A Part Dispersal)

Staiconme (USA) ch m (5yrs) Pancho Villa (USA) - Equanimity (USA) (Sir Ivor) Covered by Salt Dome (USA)............ (Northmore Stud) 7,600

Exuberine (FR) b m (12yrs) Be My Guest (USA) - Exuberance (FR) (Val de Loir) Covered by Siberian Express (USA).... (Ashtown House Stud) 27,000

Susan's Angel ch m (8yrs) Lord Gayle (USA) - Lady North (Northfields) Covered by Digamist (USA) .... (Watkins Bloodstock Services Ltd) 13,000

First String (FR) ch m (7yrs) What A Guest - String Along (Crepello).. (Dean Beston) 1,000

Lively Mite b m (6yrs) Elegant Air - Ullapool (Dominion) Covered by Digamist (USA) (Mercury Bloodstock) 3,800

Lypvette (USA) br m (6yrs) Lypheor - Navette (Ashmore)............ (Cash) 820
Loveshine b m (6yrs) Caerleon (USA) - Stapara (Mill Reef) Covered by Ela-Mana-Mou...... (Mercury Bloodstock) 4,600
Sky Lover br m (9yrs) Ela-Mana-Mou - Diamonds In The Sky (African Sky) (Cash) 600
Lomond's Breeze b m (7yrs) Lomond (USA) - Mettle (USA) (Pretendre) Covered by Common Grounds............. (Cash) 5,000
Camden's Gift ch m (9yrs) Camden Town - Crepello Gift (Crepello).. (Mr F Stynes) 1,150
Key Partner b m (6yrs) Law Society (USA) - Roscrea (Ballymore) Covered by Treasure Kay..................... (Cash) 2,600

25

Property of Mrs E Thompson, from Morning Star Stud

br y c Rontino - More Drama (Pragmatic) .. (F M O'Brien) 1,000

Property of Mr James Waldron

Tracy's Sundown b m (9yrs) Red Sunset - Kilpeacon (Florescence) with c f at foot by Posen..... (R O Sheen Bloodstock) 2,600

From Green Ireland Properties Ltd

Snow Maid gr m (15yrs) High Top - Snow Habit (Habitat)................ (Cash) 600

Property of Mr Liam Quirke, from Hymenstown House Stud

br f (4yrs) Supreme Leader - Clerihan Miss (Tarqogan)................... (Cash) 750
br g (4yrs) Royal Fountain - Royal See (Konigssee) (David Minton Bloodstock) 2,000

Property of Abbey Lodge Partnership, from The Irish National Stud

ch y c Ballad Rock - Amanzi (African Sky) .. (David Minton Bloodstock) 3,800

From The Irish National Stud

b y c Dancing Dissident (USA) - Saturne (Bellypha)......... (Whitechurch Stud) 4,600

Property of Abbey Lodge Partnership, from The Irish National Stud

b y c Digamist (USA) - Madelon (Saint Crespin III)....... (B B A (Ireland) Ltd) 3,200

From The Irish National Stud

Phoenesian Pride br m (19yrs) Tyrant (USA) - Daena (Buisson Ardent) Covered by Yashgan..................... (Cash) 700
Ramy's Gayle b m (9yrs) Strong Gale - Secret Top (African Sky) Covered by Yashgan..................... (Cash) 1,500
Saturne b m (11yrs) Bellypha - Shenandoah (URU) (Tapuia)................ (Cash) 760

26

Property of Abbey Lodge Partnership, from The Irish National Stud

Amanzi b m (13yrs) African Sky - Azurn (Klairon) Covered by Petorius (B Snell) 1,350

From Green Ireland Properties Ltd

Sunley Saint b m (10yrs) Artaius (USA) - Lone Bidder (Auction Ring) Covered by High Estate........ (S W D McIlveen) 1,400

Property of Mr P Hanson

Scherzo Impromptu ch f (4yrs) Music Boy - Law And Impulse (Roan Rocket) ...... (Glebe Bloodstock) 7,500

Property of Mrs K Cullen

Miss Goodbody gr m (9yrs) Castle Keep - Grey Autumn (Galivanter) Covered by Mujtahid (USA)................ (Cash) 13,500
Ballysnip b m (15yrs) Ballymore - Into Harbour (Right Tack) Covered by Dancing Dissident (USA)....... (Tally-Ho Stud) 6,000

Property of Suzanne Fairbrother, from Derrymore House

ch y c Noalto - Clann An Oir (IRE) (Tumble Gold).......................... (Cash) 1,000

Property of Mrs T Murphy

b f (3yrs) Mandalus - Ouragh (Ovac)........ (Brendan Williams) 780

From Southwind Bell Of Bar-Lee Stud

ch y c Don't Forget Me - Setif (Habitat).... (M Nolan) 750

Property of Mr James Gordon

ch y c Aylesfield - The Duffery (Hawaiian Return)...................... (Cash) 1,300

From Cloncahir House Stud

Trusted Maiden b m (21yrs) Busted - Merdemain (Tamerlane) (Knocklaney Stud) 500

27

From Rachel Bennett (Agent)

Broadway Royal ch m (15yrs) Royal Match - Goldwyn Princess (Native Prince) ..... (Cash) 2,200

Property of Mr S Armstrong

gr g (5yrs) Sexton Blake - Cuinnaeg (Dusky Boy).......................... (Cash) 900

Property of a Partnership, from Escale House

b m (5yrs) Julio Mariner - Fernez (Fez)..... (Cash) 1,250

28

KILL (Goffs)

Tuesday, February 9th

Property of Mr Barty Roche, from Rockbarton Stud

Miss Duckins b m (12yrs) Simbir - Polly Duckins (Dike) Covered by Bruff Crozier...................... (Cash) 700

Property of Siobhan Connolly, from Hollymount Stud

b y f Venetian Gate - Audio Express (Tanfirion)...................... (M Nolan) 400

Property of Mr John Leigh

br y c Yashgan - Five Swallows (Crash Course)...................... (Cash) 1,000

Property of Mr F Brady

ch y c Pennine Walk - Mrs Lucky (Royal Match)....... (Newlands House Stud) 2,800

From First Flyer Stables

Sway In Tune (IRE) b f (3yrs) Dance Of Life (USA) - Bahrain Vee (CAN) (Blushing Groom)...................... (Cash) 650
b f (3yrs) Dance Of Life (USA) - Bahrain Star (Star Appeal)........... (Elvira Ciacci) 500

From Ballyfair Stud

Matriculation b m (8yrs) Mummy's Pet - Gay Donna (Tudor Jinks) Covered by Maelstrom Lake........ (Elvira Ciacci) 750

From Haresmead

b y f Miner's Lamp - Cora Gold (Goldhill) . . (Cash) 700

Property of Mr Michael Coogan

Joanne's Joy ch m (13yrs) Ballymore - Fiona's Joy (High Top) Covered by Persian Heights. . . . . (Cash) 3,400

Property of Mr Jack Gage

Sandpiper Inn b m (6yrs) Be My Guest (USA) - Wenduyne (Moutiers). . . . . (M Debeusscher) 800

Yuma (USA) gr m (7yrs) Caro - Senator's Choice (USA) (Secretariat) Covered by Roaring Riva. . . . (Mercury Bloodstock) 1,500

Winterlude b m (15yrs) Wollow - Won't Linger (Worden II) Covered by Roaring Riva. . . . . (M Debeusscher) 650

29

Property of Mr Barty Roche, from Rockbarton Stud

Annacotty br m (12yrs) Proverb - Cinema Sally (Whistling Wind) Covered by Bruff Crozier. . . . . (Cash) 600

From Bishopstown Stud

Millers Lodge (IRE) b f (3yrs) Millfontaine - Sajanjal (Dance In Time). . . . . . . (Cash) 450

Property of Mr Leo Caffrey

b y c Balinger - November Bloom (Camden Town). . . . . (Richard Foran) 800

From Kellistown Stud

b y c Baba Karam - Sooner Of Later (Sheshoon). . . . . (Cash) 500

b y c Baba Karam - Timely Thatch (Thatch) (John Cash) 300

From Ballykisteen Stud

ch y c Mansooj - Jarretiere (Star Appeal). . . (I Geddis) 300

From Rosemount House Stud

Kool For Kats b m (11yrs) Malinowski (USA) - Cool Kitten (Frigid Aire) Covered by Bluebird (USA). . . . . . . (Ardenode Stud) 5,500

From Ballylinch Stud

b y c Exactly Sharp (USA) - Settling Down (USA) (Topsider). . . . . (European Bloodstock Agency) 6,400

Gortadoo (USA) b or br m (6yrs) Sharpen Up - Fenny Rough (Home Guard) Covered by Posen (USA). . . . . (Ballyhimikin Stud) 5,000

Property of Miss T Dunne, from Hamwood Stables

Fine Print b m (5yrs) Taufan (USA) - Yellow Pages (Yellow God). . (Edward Lynam) 2,000

30

From Hamwood Stables

Simplistic (IRE) ch f (4yrs) Thatching - Northern Wind (Northfields) . . . . (Michael Halford) 1,100

Property of Miss T Dunne, from Hamwood Stables

Save More (IRE) b f (3yrs) Shy Groom (USA) - Twinkling Toes (Prince Tenderfoot). . . . . (P Kelly) 500

Try Better (IRE) ch f (3yrs) Try My Best (USA) - Sheba's Princess (Ahonoora) . . (Cash) 500

Property of Gainsborough Stud Management, from Woodpark Stud

ch y f Nabeel Dancer (USA) - Rare Roberta (USA) (Roberto). . . . . . (Rathasker Stud) 4,400

From Woodford Stud

Legal Steps (IRE) br f (4yrs) Law Society (USA) - Keep In Step (Dance In Time). . (B.B.A.) 3,000

Miknasa ch m (11yrs) Hot Grove - Minourika (FR) (Zeddaan) Covered by Double Schwartz, believed NOT in foal (Cash) 550

b y f Waajib - Balistic Princess (Lomond) . . (Kerr & Co Ltd) 380

From Little River Stud

Rule The Waves b m (14yrs) Deep Run - Sea Empress (Perhapsburg) Covered by Yashgan. . . . . (Gerard Berkery) 900

From Ballynattin Stud

b y c Satco (FR) - Garden County (Ragapan) (Cash) 2,000

From Ballyward Stud

b f (4yrs) Crash Course - Fugue (Le Prince) (Aidan Nolan) 650

31

From Green Ireland Properties Ltd

Maniusha b m (12yrs) Sallust - Sarir (USA) (Hail To Reason). . . . . (Cash) 500

From Glebe House Stables

Nordic Enigma (IRE) b h (5yrs) Nordico (USA) - Pollination (Pentotal) . . . . (Kelleher Brothers) 1,250

Lyphard Abu (IRE) b f (5yrs) Lyphard's Special (USA) - Ishtar Abu (St Chad) . . . (European Bloodstock Agency) 4,500

Property of Norelands Stud, from Ardenode Stud

Come To Tea (IRE) ch m (5yrs) Be My Guest (USA) - Tea House (Sassafras) Covered by Petorius believed NOT in foal. . . . . (Cash) 5,400

From Ardenode Stud

b g (3yrs) Shernazar - Needlewoman (Moorestyle). . . . . (Cash) 1,100

From Friarstown House Stud (A Part Dispersal)

Balwara (USA) b f (4yrs) Riverman (USA) - Banque Privee (USA) (Private Account) (B.B.A. (Ireland)) 5,000

Wassl's Nanny (IRE) b f (4yrs) Wassl - Granny's Bank (Music Boy). . . . . (Cash) 2,000

Noble Anchor (IRE) b f (4yrs) Slip Anchor - Noble Girl (Be Friendly). . . . . (Cash) 5,000

Dancing Pal (IRE) b f (4yrs) Dance Of Life (USA) - Pitty Pal (USA) (Caracolero). . . . (Cash) 1,200

May We Dance (IRE) b f (4yrs) Dance Of Life (USA) - Sweet Marjorie (FR) (Sir Gaylord). . . . . (J P Kavanagh) 4,300

b y c High Estate - Respectfully (USA) (The Minstrel). . . . . (Timothy E Hyde) 18,500

b y f Bluebird (USA) - Naxos (USA) (Big Spruce). . . . . (Whitechurch Stud) 3,200

b y c Waajib - Camden's Gift (Camden Town). . . . . (Whitechurch Stud) 7,000

ch y c Persian Heights - Dance Lover's (FR) (Green Dancer)................ (Cash) 3,000
b y c High Estate - Exuberine (FR) (Be My Guest)................. (Frank Barry) 30,000
b y c Ela-Mana-Mou - Loveshine (Caerleon) (Cash) 2,000

32

Property of the Exors of the late Countess de Laubespin, from Corbally Stud (Agent)
b y c Pennine Walk - Ishtar Abu (St Chad) (Jimmy Coogan) 2,800
From Springvalley Stud (Agent)
b y c Royal Academy (USA) - Singing Witch (Sing Sing)............... (Frank Barry) 15,000
Property of Mr J Kennedy
Free Rein b m (12yrs) Sagaro - Silk Rein (Shantung) Covered by Red Sunset.... (Sagittarius Bloodstock) 1,300
From Moyglare Stud Farm
Spectacular Rise (USA) ch f (4yrs) Phone Trick - Ready For Action (USA) (Riverman)................ (Dr John Ryan) 6,200
Trade Survivor (IRE) b f (4yrs) Taufan (USA) - Safety Feature (Be My Guest) .... (Kildare Thoroughbred Services) 4,300
From Knocktoran Stud
b y c Al Nasr (FR) - Charara (USA) (Top Command).... (Jean-Pierre Deroubaix) 12,000
b y f Exactly Sharp (USA) - Iswara (USA) (Alleged).......... (David McLoughlin) 500
From Rosemount House Stud
Magic Garter b m (6yrs) Precocious - Magic Flute (Tudor Melody).. (Michael Burke) 600
Sindos b m (12yrs) Busted - Sindo (Derring-Do) Covered by Scenic........ (Cash) 3,400
Cala-Vadella b m (18yrs) Mummy's Pet - Rennet (King's Bench).......... (Cash) 500

33

From Airlie Stud
b y c Glow (USA) - Tante Yvonne (Crowned Prince).................. (P M Berry) 900
b y c King Of Clubs - Habanna (Habitat).... (John Francis Bailey) 1,800
b c (2yrs) Glow (USA) - Sovereign Flash (FR) (Busted).................. (Cash) 650
Property of Mrs A Whitehead, from Owenstown Stud
Tumbleline b m (10yrs) Tumble Wind (USA) - Drag Line (Track Spare) Covered by Nashamaa................ (J E Butler) 1,000
Property of H H Aga Khan's Studs S.C., from Currabeg Stables
Demotika (FR) b f (3yrs) Labus (FR) - Dedra (Faunus).................... (C.B.A.) 9,500
Kalvriya (FR) b f (3yrs) Pampabird - Kallasiya (Busted)................. (Mr Ian Hanamy) 500
Kidamiya (IRE) b f (3yrs) Darshaan - Kimiya (USA) (Sir Ivor).......... (John Malone) 1,100
Nannaka (USA) b or br f (3yrs) Exceller (USA) - Najidiya (Riverman) .... (Patrick Mullins) 2,600
Salamarza (IRE) b f (3yrs) Kahyasi - Samirza (Riverman)...................... (Cash) 1,200

Yallysha (IRE) b f (3yrs) Don't Forget Me - Yalciyna (Nishapour).. (B.B.A. (Ireland)) 1,200
Naiyli (IRE) b c (3yrs) Kahyasi - Naiymat (Troy)............................ (Cash) 2,200

34

From Cassia Lodge
Istiyfa (IRE) gr f (4yrs) Darshaan - Istiara (FR) (Crystal Palace) .... (Sagittarius Bloodstock) 2,500
Property of Mr Des Flanagan, from Meadows Stud
ch y f Fools Holme (USA) - Fickle Femme (Hard Fought)........... (B.B.A. (Italia)) 1,600
Property of Mr Peter McCutcheon
b y c Gallic League - Miel (Pall Mall)....... (Mercury Bloodstock) 1,600
Property of Ballyfree Stud, from Rachel Bennett (Agent)
b f (2yrs) Buckskin (FR) - Head Of The Gang (Pollerton)........... (Gerard Berkery) 1,100
Property of Mr Alan Dargan, from Eyrefield House Stud
Port Princess (IRE) b f (4yrs) Dance Of Life (USA) - Nelly Gail (Mount Hagen)...... (Eddie Ryan) 2,000
From Kildaragh Stud (Agent)
Portenza b f (2yrs) Caerleon (USA) - Mariella (Sir Gaylord)..... (Pipers Hill Stud) 20,000
Cuango (IRE) br c (2yrs) Mtoto - Barinia (Corvaro)..... (Ms. Sarah Hollinshead) 8,700
From Dara Lodge
Simply Beautiful (IRE) b f (5yrs) Simply Great (FR) - Black And Beauty (African Sky) Covered by Common Grounds ... (Cash) 2,000
Property of City And Country Racing Club, from Broguestown Stud
Cardinal Press ch f (4yrs) Sharrood (USA) - Kissin' Cousin (Be Friendly).......... (Sagittarius Bloodstock) 1,350
Chancery Queen (IRE) b f (4yrs) Dara Monarch - Bustina (FR) (Busted)........... (Richard O'Gorman Jnr) 800

35

From Arnstein Stud
ch y f Persian Bold - Kobrin (Bruni)........ (Swordlestown Stud) 1,700
Property of A O'Neill
b y c Executive Perk - Slightly Latin (Ahonoora)..................... (Cash) 850
Lady Limerick (IRE) b m (5yrs) Heraldiste (USA) - Mrs Baggins (English Prince) Covered by Homo Sapien .... (Belinda Fair-Corcoran) 900
Property of Mr Tom Flynn
Liebestraum (IRE) br m (4yrs) Persian Bold - Redwood Hut (Habitat) Covered by Maelstrom Lake (Mercury Bloodstock) 3,600
Property of Mr M Montague, from Straduff Farms
Deer Skin b m (9yrs) Buckskin (FR) - Go Mays (Realm) Covered by Commanche Run........... (Belinda Fair-Corcoran) 680

Small'n Smaller ch m (8yrs) Whistling Deer - Shandon Park (Crash Course) Covered by Regular Guy (Belinda Fair-Corcoran) 580

From Church Hill Stud

Turkish Sultana (IRE) b m (5yrs) Kemal (FR) - Opening Order (Menelek) Covered by Phardante (FR)................ (Cash) 1,700

Property of Mr Niall Healy

b c (2yrs) Don't Forget Me - Justine's Way (USA) (Buffalo Lark)................ (Michael Hourigan) 600

From Willow Stud

b c (2yrs) Taufan (USA) - Scobys Baby (Nishapour)... (R O Sheen Bloodstock) 700

From East Hill Stud

Sahara Goddess ch m (18yrs) Realm - Dorrit (Zucchero) Covered by Seclude (USA)........................ (Cash) 450

Waladah b m (16yrs) Thatch (USA) - Treacle (Hornbeam) Covered by Seclude (USA) (Gerry O'Malley) 700

36

Property of Miss Rita Shah, from Shabra Stables

Shabra Girl b or br m (10yrs) Mandalus - Cheeky Girl (Battle Burn) (Tom Magee) 850

Shabra Princess b or br m (10yrs) Buckskin (FR) - Random View (Random Shot) ... (W B Mullins) 780

Property of Mrs Sheila Treacy

ch f (2yrs) King Luthier - Kylemore Abbey (Junius)...................... (P Kelly) 450

Property of Mr R G Hogan

Deep Rouge b m (7yrs) Deep Run - Lough Street (Milan) Covered by Be My Native (USA)........ (Gerard Berkery) 8,000

Property of Mr John Ryan

ch g (4yrs) Cardinal Flower - Deep Saul (Saulingo)........... (Gerry O'Malley) 6,800

Property of Mrs Ellen Bracken

gr f (2yrs) Roselier (FR) - Newgate Princess (Prince Regent)....... (Michael Scully) 500

Property of Mrs Ellen Bracken, from Newgate House

ch y c Persian Heights - Chive (St Chad)... (Bruno Ditta Grizzetti) 4,600

From Blarney Castle

Shuil Run b m (11yrs) Deep Run - Shuil Dubh (Black Tarquin) Covered by Phardante (FR)................... (C.B.A.) 9,000

From Bushy Park Stud

ch c (2yrs) Northiam (USA) - Brazilian Princess (Absalom)...................... (Edward Daly Bloodstock) 25,000

Property of Mrs V O'Connor

b y c Nashamaa - Caramica (Charlottown).. (Cash) 3,000

37

From Monasteroris House Stud

Noble Call (IRE) b c (3yrs) Darshaan - Noble Girl (Be Friendly)..... (B.B.A. (Ireland)) 900

From Mountarmstrong Stud

Persian Runner b m (7yrs) Pitskelly - Beau Darling (Darling Boy) Covered by Classic Secret (USA).............. (Cash) 5,000

Shooting Party (IRE) b m (4yrs) Phardante (FR) - Shenachie (Sheshoon) Covered by Classic Secret (USA)........ (Cash) 4,800

From Foxbrook Stud

Hossvend b m (12yrs) Malinowski (USA) - Sarah Van Fleet (Cracksman) Covered by Mac's Imp (USA)........... (Cash) 2,000

Lusaka br m (16yrs) Wolver Hollow - Lupulin (Romulus) Covered by Jurado (USA)....................... (Cash) 720

Discerning Lady ch m (10yrs) Le Bavard (FR) - Grangeclare Lady (Menelek) Covered by Orchestra............. (Cash) 3,000

From Friarstown House Stud (A Part Dispersal)

Peace Carrier (IRE) ch f (4yrs) Doulab (USA) - Paradise Bird (Sallust)........ (Cash) 3,500

From Kildare Stud

Pravolo b f (4yrs) Fool's Holme (USA) - Pavello (Crepello)..... (Brian Grassick) 3,200

Property of H H Aga Khan's Stud S C, from Gilltown Stud

Nouktaiya (FR) b f (3yrs) Deep Roots - Noufiyla (Top Ville).... (James O'Neill) 1,000

38

ASCOT
Tuesday, February 16th

Property of Sarl Ewar Stud Farms

(IRE) ch f (2yrs) Bold Arrangement - Malham Tarn (Riverman (USA))........... (Mr Harman) 470

Property of Mr B Minty

Delightful Diane b m (6yrs) Kalaglow - Whip Finish (Be Friendly) Covered by Full Extent (USA)................ (B.B.A.) 1,300

Property of Mr C Wright

California Dreamin b f (4yrs) Slip Anchor - Misguided (Homing)................. (Racing Thoroughbreds Ltd) 625

Property of Mr T S M S Riley-Smith

Trendy Auctioneer (IRE) b g (5yrs) Mazaad - Trendy Princess (Prince Tenderfoot (USA)).................... (L Jewell) 1,650

To Dissolve a Partnership

Red Ballet gr f (3yrs) Siberian Express (USA) - Kabylia (FR) (Dancer's Image).. (B.B.A.) 2,600

Abingdon Flyer (IRE) b g (5yrs) Pennine Walk - Busca (USA) (Mr Prospector (USA))......... (Thorp Perrow Stable) 1,200

Property of Mr P A Hayward

ch c (2yrs) Gabitat - Serious Affair (Valiyar) (P Welch) 675

Madam Intimidator ch f (3yrs) Krayyan - Silver Empress (Octavo (USA))........ (B Badham) 650

Property of the Southcourt Stud

Lady Celestial b f (3yrs) Celestial Storm (USA) - Town Lady (Town Crier)....... (R Barker) 825

Property of Mr J Short

Dancing Boat b g (4yrs) Shareef Dancer (USA) - Sauceboat (Connaught) .... (J L Harris) 2,100

39

Property of Amity Finance Ltd

Freephone (CAN) b g (4yrs) Phone Trick (USA) - Flying Aristocrat (USA) (Prince John)........................(Cash) 575

Property of Mr D McCarthy

Ackers Wood b g (5yrs) Castle Keep - Gloria Maremmana (King Emperor (USA)).... (Cash) 1,200

From Roden House Stables

Saintly Lass b m (9yrs) Derrylin - Saintly Miss (St Paddy)........... (P Cundell) 850

Precious Caroline (IRE) b m (5yrs) The Noble Player (USA) - What A Breeze (Whistling Wind).......... (P Cundell) 650

Property of Mrs S Gay

Mere Chants b f (4yrs) Kings Lake (USA) - Rengaine (FR) (Music Boy) .... (Frank Kavanagh) 825

Property of Newgate Stud Company

Free Crossing br m (8yrs) Super Concorde (USA) - Another Treat (USA) (Cornish Prince)................ (C N Budgett) 1,000

Property of a Partnership

b c (2yrs) Sharpo - Sorayah (Persian Bold).. (Rod Gibson) 750

Property of Woolton House Stud

ch y f Sharpo - Sun Sparkle (USA) (Nureyev (USA))........................ (E Jones) 550

Property of Mrs L Mills

b f (2yrs) Touch Of Grey - Mistress Will (USA) (Master Willie).. (T M Jennings) 2,000

Property of Mrs W Jennings

b c (2yrs) Touch Of Grey - Absurd (Absalom)...................... (Cash) 625

40

Property of Brian Gubby Ltd

Brave Dollar b f (3yrs) Gabitat - Burglars Girl (Burglar)................ (H R T Parry) 675

Queen's Bidder b m (16yrs) Auction Ring (USA) - Stormy Queen (Typhoon)...... (Mr Barrass) 550

Property of Lord Rotherwick, from Kingwood House Stables

Lankridge b c (3yrs) Alzao (USA) - Free Dance (FR) (Green Dancer (USA)) ..... (W R Hern) 8,600

Property of Mr D H Jones

Pooka b m (7yrs) Dominion - Land Of Song (Sing Sing) Covered by Presidium ..... (E E Simmer) 1,450

Aber Cothi b m (8yrs) Dominion - Teye (Mummy's Pet) Covered by Bold Fox.. (Cash) 925

Property of Team Engineering

Market Trader ch f (4yrs) Viking (USA) - Magelka (Relkino)............... (Cash) 625

From Roden House Stables

Gymcrak Fortune (IRE) b g (5yrs) Kafu - Forlorn Chance (Fighting Don).. (Cash) 600

Another Vintage ch g (4yrs) Risk Me (FR) - Meanieminymoe (Star Appeal) .... (P Cundell) 1,550

Emsboy b g (5yrs) Lidhame - Fille de Phaeton (Sun Prince).......... (P Cundell) 1,300

Property of P H Betts (Holdings) Ltd

Black Sapphire ch g (6yrs) Lomond (USA) - Star Of India (General Assembly (USA)) .... (Adrian Clegg) 5,700

41

To Dissolve a Partnership

Belle Soiree ch f (3yrs) Night Shift (USA) - Party Game (Red Alert)... (P McEntee) 3,200

Taciturn (USA) ch f (3yrs) Tasso (USA) - Angling (USA) (Angle Light (USA))..... (Barry Reilly) 1,650

Property of Mrs C P Jamieson

Summer Sands ch m (5yrs) Mummy's Game - Renira (Relkino)................ (Miss N Killick) 1,500

To Dissolve a Partnership

Copper Trader gr f (4yrs) Faustus (USA) - Alicia Markova (Habat) .... (Sagittarius Bloodstock) 1,000

Property of Upper Hatch Farm

Petite Vino b f (3yrs) Petoski - El Vino (Habitat)...................... (Cash) 1,600

b g (3yrs) Pitpan - Hollomoore (Moorstyle) (Cash) 1,400

To Dissolve a Partnership

As Always (IRE) ch m (5yrs) Hatim (USA) - Red Magic (Red God) (Ruth Wollerton) 1,850

Five Clubs (IRE) ch f (3yrs) King Of Clubs - Tristan Du Cunha (Sir Ivor).... (B.B.A.) 900

And Me ch f (5yrs) Don't Forget Me - Nicola Wynn (Nicholas Bill) .... (D N Carey) 1,700

Property of Lord Rotherwick, from Colnbury Park Stud

Crane Hill b g (3yrs) Dancing Brave (USA) - Consolation (Troy).......... (D Jones) 2,700

42

Property of a Lady

Houlston's Will ch f (4yrs) Nicholas Bill - Falcrello (Falcon).............. (B.B.A.) 1,000

Property of Mr M J Johnston

Zagazig b g (10yrs) Chieftain II - I'll Take It (USA) (Royal Levee (USA))............ (Miss T Benham) 825

Property of Mr F J Ellis

Rich Heiress (IRE) b f (4yrs) Last Tycoon - Lamya (USA) (Alydar (USA)) .... (Bob Woodhouse) 1,150

To Settle an Account

C'est La Vie b g (10yrs) Sonnen Gold - Princess Dido (Sayajirao)........ (Cash) 1,000

To Dissolve a Partnership

Flass Vale b g (5yrs) Final Straw - Emblazon (Wolver Hollow).......... (T Fairhurst) 1,250

Property of Mrs R V James

ch f (2yrs) Ballacashtal (CAN) - Miss Worth (Streak).................... (P Smith) 675

Property of Mr V R Bedley

Recit D'Argent b g (3yrs) Legend Of France (USA) - Shiny Penny (Glint Of Gold) ... (A Delaney) 625

Property of Mrs R V James

Samurai Gold (USA) b h (5yrs) Golden Act (USA) - Taipan's Lady (USA) (Bold Hour) .... (Gerry Blum) 4,600

To Dissolve a Partnership
ch g (3yrs) Celtic Cone - Khatti Hawk (Hittite Glory)................. (A Chiney) 520

Property of Coombelands Stables Ltd
Gentle Moment b f (3yrs) Teenoso (USA) - Light O'Battle (Queen's Hussar) (Cash) 1,500
Collaborate (IRE) b g (4yrs) Shareef Dancer (USA) - Royal Saint (USA) (Crimson Satan)................. (Lisa Hannon) 775

43

From South Hatch Stables
Against You b m (6yrs) Auction Ring (USA) - Saranita (Thatch (USA)).. (Gary Mills) 1,750
Devil's Soul b g (5yrs) Faustus (USA) - Ragged Moon (Raga Navarro (ITY)).... (Cash) 2,100
Billy Bunter ch g (4yrs) Nicholas Bill - Cosset (Comedy Star (USA))....... (Cash) 1,400
Fanlight b h (5yrs) Beldale Flutter (USA) - Carib Flash (Mill Reef)...... (A Moore) 3,500

Property of Mr K Smyth
Paddys Gold (IRE) b g (5yrs) Kemal (FR) - Thai Nang (Tap On Wood)...... (Cash) 1,850

Property of Mr E Thorbek
Colonel Fairfax gr g (5yrs) Alias Smith (USA) - Mistress Meryll (Tower Walk) .... (Roger Hoad) 2,200

Property of Mr W Fagan
Badrakhani (FR) b g (7yrs) Akarad (FR) - Burnished Gold (Breton)..... (C Nash) 1,600

From Town Farm Stables
Glowing Prince b g (5yrs) Prince Ragusa - Glowing Spirit (Aglojo) .... (Mary Henderson) 2,700

From Trafford Bridge Stables
Glen Mirage b g (8yrs) Furry Glen - By Mistake (Miralgo).......... (W White) 2,500

Property of The Hon Mrs R G A Whetherly
My Tobias ch g (6yrs) Muscatite - Lady Kimberley (Salvo)....... (J P E Welch) 1,800

44

From Preston Farm Stables
Barton Pride (IRE) b g (4yrs) Phardante (FR) - Ginosa (Kalamoun) .... (David Minton Bloodstock) 1,200
Tells Tower b m (7yrs) Dunbeath (USA) - Gallatin Valley (USA) (Apalachee)...... (Cash) 2,000

Property of Pipe-Scudamore Racing Club
Slavi (FR) ch m (5yrs) Nikos (FR) - Srpkigna (FR) (Sandhedrin (USA)) (C N Budgett) 850

Property of Bankhouse
Shining Art ch g (8yrs) Artaius (USA) - Moonlight Sonata (So Blessed)........ (Mr Eley) 1,000

Property of Mr G S Beccle
West Monkton ch g (7yrs) Croghan Hill - Cora Gold (Goldhill)........... (C Nash) 2,000

To Dissolve a Partnership, from Fowlers Farm
Celery Rise (NZ) b g (9yrs) Palm Beach (FR) - Golden Wedding (NZ) (Sucaryl) .... (Miss A Hill) 1,000

From Ridgeway Paddocks
Hawaiian Bay b g (11yrs) Hawaiian Return (USA) - Baychou (Chou Chin Chow) ... (M Blum) 1,100

Property of Mr A C D Joynson
Fearsome gr g (7yrs) Formidable (USA) - Seriema (Petingo).......... (K Burke) 4,000
Shadeux ch g (7yrs) Valiyar - A Deux (FR) (Crepello)................. (P M Rich) 4,000

Property of W M Smith
Ahlavai ch g (8yrs) Quayside - Play The Part (Deep Run)......... (Judith Di Marte) 1,000

45

Property of Mr N Spreadbury
Viking Venture ch g (8yrs) Viking (USA) - Mattira (FR) (Rheffic).... (John Barrett) 625

Property of Brickhall Farm
br f (4yrs) Lighter - Share (Khalkis) .... (D V Stevens) 700

Property of Roper Bloodstock
ch y c Green Adventure (USA) - Wald Konigin (Kinglet).......... (P Holland) 850

Property of Mr C Parker
b m (5yrs) Meadowbrook - Broadwater (Cawston's Clown)............ (Cash) 1,000

Property of Mr C T Nash
Deep Serenity b m (8yrs) Balinger - Deepness (Deep Run) Covered by Gunner B (not in foal).................. (Cash) 625
Celtic Bizarre b m (5yrs) Celtic Cone - Charity Bazzar (Native Bazaar)......... (R Smedley) 875

Property of The 39 Partnership
Look Lively (USA) b g (8yrs) Smarten (USA) - Danseuse (USA) (Jig Time (USA)) .... (Miss N West) 800

Property of Lt Col Westcott
Courageous Charger (USA) ch g (11yrs) Bold Bidder - Charger's Star (USA) (Pia Star)......................... (Cash) 925

To Dissolve a Partnership
Bifocal b g (6yrs) Vision (USA) - Night Vision (Yellow God).............. (B Baugh) 725
Saunders Lass b m (9yrs) Hillandale - Portella (Porto Bello)........... (P Bevan) 825

46

Property of Saxon House Stables
Wave Breaker ch g (6yrs) Enchantment - Nelski (Skymaster)........... (B.B.A.) 2,300

To Dissolve a Partnership, from Denton Stables
Amber Express b m (6yrs) Lochnager - Belcraig (Foggy Bell)................. (Sagittarius Bloodstock) 700

Property of a Lady, from Preston Farm Stables
Memory Bank b g (6yrs) Palm Track - All Over Yesterdays (Jimsun)...... (Cash) 1,850

Property of Mr Rhys Thomas Williams
Roll A Dance b g (4yrs) Mashhor Dancer (USA) - Sandi's Gold (Godswalk (USA)) (Mr Biddlecombe) 725
Tresilian Owl b g (5yrs) Bold Owl - High Lee (Will Hays (USA))............. (Cash) 725
Double Tricks gr g (10yrs) Peacock (FR) - Mourne Lass (Hereford).. (D M Lloyd) 1,500

Property of Mr F J Yardley
Capallus b g (6yrs) Big Connaught - Chatley's Seedling (Young Nelson) .... (Barbara Falkner) 800

Property of Mr Jonathan Ramsden
Sovereign Niche (IRE) gr g (5yrs) Nishapour (FR) - Sovereign Flash (FR) (Busted) . . . (Arthur Barrow) 900
Property of Hinton Harry Partnership
Hinton Harry (IRE) b g (4yrs) Kafu - Rosy O'Leary (Majetta). . . . . . . (J Ronaldson) 1,200
To Dissolve a Partnership
Pendor Dancer b g (10yrs) Piaffer (USA) - Bounding (Forlorn River). . . . . . . (Cash) 700

47

From Park Head Stables
Maple Thyme b g (7yrs) Palm Track - Greated Nutmeg ((pedigree Unknown)) (Cash) 2,000
Property of Mr P C Clarke
Access Cruise (USA) ch g (6yrs) Wajima (USA) - Lady Of Meadowlane (USA) (Pancho Jay (USA)). . . . . (A Wilson) 800
Property of Mr R Stone
Ma Travers b m (5yrs) Pragmatic - Personality Plus (Master Owen) (Miss J Silk) 675
Property of Mrs A Binks
I'm A Tot br m (5yrs) Jolly Me - Verona Brandy (Hot Brandy) . . . . . (C V Palmer-Jeffrey) 700
Property of Mrs H A Webb
C Sharp ch g (6yrs) Song - Simply Jane (Sharpen Up). . . . . (Jane Tolley) 2,000
Property of Mrs J Downing
Leadalong ch m (9yrs) Leading Man - Upham Reunion (Paridel). . (A Delaney) 675
Property of Miss A Dudley
ch m (6yrs) Balinger - Sheba Queen (Pongee). . . . . (Mrs J Turner) 1,500
Property of Mr F Gray
Merry Matic gr g (10yrs) Pragmatic - Victor's Valley (Deep Run). . . . . (R C Hambleton) 725
Property of Mrs J Thomas
Hand It To Marty ch m (8yrs) Nearly A Hand - Martynia (Simbir). . (Simon Robinson) 2,400
Property of Mr R Craddock
Rintintin ch g (6yrs) Tina's Pet - Countess Down (Roan Rocket). . . . . . , (A Wilson) 1,200

48

Property of Mr S N Burfield
Blue Dun b g (4yrs) Petong - Glyn Rhosyn (Welsh Saint). . . . . (C V Palmer-Jeffrey) 1,350
Property of Avalon Surfacing & Construction Co Ltd
Solemn Melody b g (6yrs) Jalmood (USA) - Garganey (USA) (Quack) (M S Harvey) 775
Property of Mrs J M Rolph
The Tansey Man ch g (7yrs) Millfontaine - Kindle (Firestreak). . . . (Ruth Wollerton) 1,750
Property of Miss E Webber
Quarry Town b g (10yrs) Mandalus - Weary Lil (Tiepolo II). . . . . (A Wintle) 1,500
Property of Mr G Hunt
Merandi Special b g (6yrs) Coquelin (USA) - Mountain Chase (Mount Hagen (FR)) . . (R F Stone) 825

Property of Mrs J Newell
Blue Danube (USA) ch g (9yrs) Riverman (USA) - Wintergrace (USA) (Northern Dancer). . . . . (B Allen) 1,900

49

FAIRYHOUSE
(Tattersalls)
Monday, February 22nd

Property of W J McCay, from White House Stables
b f (2yrs) Aylesfield - Criggan's Lass (IRE) (Orchestra). . . . . (Cash) 620
Property of Annette Doyle
br c (2yrs) Combine Harvester - Classic Loom (Sexton Blake). . . . . (Cash) 400
From Beechlane Stables
b y f Fine Blade (USA) - Fanlight Fanny (Sky Gipsy). . . . . (Cash) 340
Property of Mrs Mary Mulcahy, from The Beeches Stud
b f (3yrs) Lancastrian - Boulta View (Beau Chapeau). (Cash) 640
Property of Mrs Edith Mulcahy, from The Beeches Stud
ch g (4yrs) Buckskin (FR) - Grainne Geal (General Ironside). . . (Maureen Wilson) 2,600
To Dissolve a Partnership
Cimor Hill b g (8yrs) Croghan Hill - Babble (Forlorn River). . . . . (Cash) 620
Property of Mr Brendan Jones
b f (4yrs) Supreme Leader - Redskin Princess (Buckskin). . . . . (Conor Dore) 780
Property of Mr Herbert Rothwell, from The Bullring Stables
b g (4yrs) Niels - Stoney Broke (Pauper) . . . (Cash) 2,000
b g (4yrs) Swan's Rock - Whispering Rose (Le Bavard). . . . . (Cash) 2,200
Property of Mr James Delaney
b f (2yrs) Electric - Nomun Nofun (Creative Plan). . . . . (Cash) 440

50

From Ardrums House Stud
b f (2yrs) Northiam (USA) - Henrietta Maria (USA) (Forli). . . . . (Mercury Bloodstock) 800
b y c Fayruz - Henrietta Maria (USA) (Forli) (Peter Morrow) 460
Property of Mr Colm O'Brennan, from Dunahall Stables
b f (2yrs) Orchestra - Las-Cancellas (Monksfield). . . . . (T Steele) 850
From Clifton Lodge Stud
br m (5yrs) Camden Town - Broccoli (Welsh Saint). . . . . (Cash) 900
To Dissolve a Partnership, from Lismortagh Stables
In The Water ch g (6yrs) Carlingford Castle - Cardamine (Indigenous) . . . . (John Gleeson) 1,800
Property of Mr Christopher Flynn, from Grove Lodge Stud
b g (2yrs) Buckley - Passage To India (FR) (Gay Mecene). . . . . (Cash) 500

From Hamwood & Mitchelstown Studs

b g (3yrs) Coquelin (USA) - Turbina (Tudor Melody)...................... (Cash) 700

From Market Stables

b f (3yrs) Nepotism - Rose Of Leinster (Kaiser)........................ (Cash) 540

Property of P J Farrell

b f (4yrs) Orchestra - Drifting Shadow (Welsh Saint).................. (Cash) 820

Property of Moses McCabe

gr y f Roselier (FR) - River Cabe (Over The River)...................... (H Smith) 450

51

Property of Mr Michael Brennan

ch f (4yrs) Henbit (USA) - Matjup (Simbir) .. (Cash) 900

Property of a Partnership

b g (5yrs) Pollerton - What A Rose (Sir Herbert)...................... (Cash) 2,600

Property of Miss Carol Norton

View To The Future br m (7yrs) Green Shoon - Random View (Random Shot) Covered by Good Thyne (USA) (Cash) 1,300

From Lemongrove House

Corn Kingdom b g (7yrs) Oats - Rosa Ruler (Gambling Debt).............. (Cash) 2,400

Property of Miss Barbara O'Brien

br c (2yrs) Satco (FR) - Seven Hills (FR) (Reform) (Leinster Bloodstock Agency) 1,500

From Punchestown House Stud

b g (2yrs) Le Bavard (FR) - Clonyn (Wolverlife)................... (Cash) 640

Ela Man Hee b m (10yrs) Ela-Mana-Mou - Tante Yvonne (Crowned Prince) Covered by Montelimar (USA) believed NOT in foal......... (Frank Dempsey) 5,000

Clonyn b m (12yrs) Wolverlife - Toranquine (FR) (Right Royal V) Covered by Le Bavard (FR)..... (Aghern House Stud) 600

b y f Torus - Ela Man Hee (Ela-Mana-Mou) (Cash) 680

Property of Clonmill Racing Syndicate

Clonmill ch g (8yrs) Don - Sapristi (Psidium) (David Minton Bloodstock) 4,700

52

Property of Mr V C Eivers

Borestra ch g (6yrs) Orchestra - Boreen Queen (Boreen)...... (R Rattenhuber) 2,100

From Corbal-Lis Stud

b f (4yrs) Hawaiian Return (USA) - Corbal-Lis (Tumble Gold)............. (Cash) 700

From Rahinston Stables

Davy Crockett b g (6yrs) Buckskin (FR) - Branstown Lady (Deep Run).... (Cash) 3,200

Property of Mr Fred Toner

Princess Moy b m (7yrs) Gleason (USA) - Deep Flight (Deep Run) Covered by Celio Rufo................... (Cash) 820

Property of Mr Frank Toole, from Crickstown Stables

b or br g (2yrs) Strong Gale - Let's Compromise (No Argument).. (Rathbarry Stud) 7,600

Property of Mr Pat Crotty, from Bridge Stud

br f (2yrs) Beau Sher - Ballymacarett (Menelek).................... (Victor Reid) 1,400

gr or br y f Roselier (FR) - Bory's Glen (Furry Glen)......................... (Cash) 940

From Aghern House Stud

Gridlock (USA) ch m (11yrs) Winged T (USA) - Negation (USA) (Mongo) Covered by Jolly Jake (NZ)........ (Cash) 740

Come Back Cindy (USA) gr m (13yrs) Jolly Johu (USA) - Evening Scarlet (USA) (Bold Commander) Covered by Jolly Jake (NZ)........... (Peter Corcoran) 880

Property of Mr Edmond Egan, from Abbey Stables

b g (5yrs) Farhaan - Group Problem (Divine Gift)......................... (Cash) 2,600

53

Property of Mr Paddy Byrne, from Abbey Stables

Fairy Blade b m (11yrs) Fine Blade (USA) - Fairy Rath (Indigenous) Covered by Glacial Storm (USA)...... (Peter Wagner) 2,300

From Craheen Stud

ch g (4yrs) Dromod Hill - Bright Point (Shackleton).............. (Pat Flynn) 4,600

Property of Mrs Margaret Dowling, from Tu Va Stables

Gondola Girl b m (6yrs) Deep Run - Time Please (Welsh Saint).................. (Aghern House Stud) 3,400

Property of Mr S Hunt, from Tu Va Stables

The Rum Tum Tugger b g (4yrs) Precocious - Nip In The Air (USA) (Northern Dancer)................ (J Kilpatrick) 880

Property of Mr Patrick Stamp

b y f Welsh Term - Jamie's Lady (Ashmore) .... (S McCully) 600

To Dissolve a Partnership

Gayle Eile ch g (6yrs) Lord Gayle (USA) - Junella (Midsummer Night II) .... (J W Boyers) 5,000

From Thomastown Castle

Rising Waters (IRE) b g (5yrs) Sure Blade (USA) - Over The Waves (Main Reef) .. (Des McDonagh) 7,300

Porphyrine (FR) b m (13yrs) Habitat - Katie May (Busted)............... (T Stack) 4,700

Property of Mrs Ludmilla O'Hanlon, from Craigue House Stud

b g (4yrs) Mandalus - The Tonne (Raise You Ten)......................... (Cash) 1,150

To Dissolve a Partnership, from Lohunda Park Stables

Glindigo (IRE) br g (5yrs) Glow (USA) - Indigo Rose (Petingo) .... (R O Sheen Bloodstock) 3,900

54

From Clongeel Stud

b y c Royal Fountain - Polly Glide (Pollerton) .... (Cash) 2,200

Property of Mr Thomas Horgan

b y c Strong Gale - Lady Brenda (IRE) (Crash Course)............. (P Doyle) 2,600

From Castletown Stud (Agent)

Just Darina br m (21yrs) Three Dons - Atout Noir (Atout Royal) Covered by Glacial Storm (USA).......... (Blanefield Ltd) 800

I've No Idea gr m (9yrs) Nishapour (FR) - Sequoia (Sassafras) Covered by Glacial Storm (USA)........ (Aaron Metcalfe) 3,700

Property of Mr Maurice Byrne, from Glenealy Stud (Agent)

br y f Be My Native (USA) - Cool Amanda (Prince Hansel)............... (Cash) 1,100

ch f (3yrs) Henbit (USA) - Cool Amanda (Prince Hansel)..... (Jorg Von Fmhoff) 1,800

Property of Mr Maurice Byrne, from Glenealy Stud

gr f (2yrs) Executive Perk - Kelly Ryan (On Your Mark)............ (Ciaran Rice) 650

b y c Supreme Leader - Lucky Appeal (Star Appeal)... (Pierre Charles Le Metayer) 4,700

From Ashleigh Stud

br g (4yrs) Bulldozer - Black Pilot (Linacre) (Lady Earle) 4,300

Property of Mr Jerry Rohan

b g (4yrs) Pauper - Pickled Girl (Boreen) ... (Ingrid Lauterbach) 2,200

55

Property of Nicola Rohan

ch g (4yrs) Regular Guy - Merry Cane (Candy Cane)................ (Cash) 1,550

From Coolriver Bloodstock

b y f King's Ride - Enchanted Evening (Warpath).............. (Padge Berry) 720

b y c King's Ride - Six Deep (Deep Run)... (Jeremy Maxwell) 2,200

From Kells Farming Estates

b g (4yrs) Strong Gale - Natasha Ann (Allangrange)................... (Cash) 3,100

From Ballinderry Stud

ch y c Persian Heights - Dianora Dori (Thatch).............. (Frank Keogh) 2,800

b y c Contract Law (USA) - Contrappesatura (Kings Lake).................. (Cash) 2,100

From Brittas House Stud (Agent)

b g (2yrs) Electric - Oakland Leisure (Lucky Brief)................. (D T Hughes) 820

b or br g (2yrs) Buckskin (FR) - Ranamacken (Sexton Blake)..... (Michael Hourigan) 2,200

ch g (2yrs) Electric - Tatec (Carlingford Castle)............... (Peter Tonery) 1,300

Property of P Morrissey

b y f Dominion Royale - Atedaun (Ahonoora).................... (Cash) 360

56

Property of Mr Paul Conway

b y c Strong Gale - Teapot Hall (Royal Buck) .... (Cash) 4,000

From Casletown Stud (Agent)

b g (3yrs) Commanche Run - Star Of Aran (Artaius)....................... (Cash) 910

Property of Mrs Nora Brosnan

b f (2yrs) Royal Fountain - Celtona Peach (Celtic Cone)........... (John Phelan) 400

b f (2yrs) Electric - Flying Early (Ballyciptic) (Cash) 780

Property of Mrs T Murphy, from Park House Stud (Agent)

b y c Mandalus - Ouragh (Ovac).... (Cash) 480

From Park House Stud (Agent)

b y c Strong Gale - Moate Gypsy (Fine Blade)................ (John O'Byrne) 8,000

From Ballywooden House

b g (5yrs) Kafu - Twill (Crocket) .... (P M O'Brien) 1,200

gr g (3yrs) Convinced - Danger Lady (Commando)..................... (Cash) 1,800

b or br f (4yrs) Mandalus - Leah's Luck Penny (Deep Run)............ (Cash) 720

b or br g (4yrs) Denel (FR) - Miss Fanackapan (Colonist II).. (Liam McCarthy) 2,100

57

Property of Mr F J Duffy

No Panic b g (9yrs) Pitpan - Scirea (Cantab) (Cash) 1,000

Property of Mr P J Fortune

b g (4yrs) Good Thyne (USA) - Liscarton (Le Bavard).............. (Eric McNamara) 2,300

Property of a Partnership

b or br y f King's Ride - Serpentine Artiste (Buckskin)..................... (Cash) 1,200

From Galgystown Stud

b f (3yrs) Henbit (USA) - Deep Green (Deep Run)...................... (T Clifford) 960

From Park House Stud

b y c Mandalus - Mistress Sarah (Ashford) (Padge Berry) 4,000

b or br y c Sula Bula - Court Bridge (Mandamus)................ (Padge Berry) 720

br y c Baba Karam - Grand Rose (Grand Roi) .... (B Deegan) 380

Property of Mr P J Doyle

Slap Bang gr m (10yrs) Pitskelly - Slap Up (Gala Performance)........... (Cash) 800

Property of Ms Penny Downes

br f (2yrs) Corvaro (USA) - Merry Servant (Giolla Mear)................ (N Dee) 1,000

From Hamwood & Mitchelstown Studs

Life's Chance (IRE) b m (4yrs) Wolverlife - Persian Palm (Tamerlane) Covered by Topanoora (USA)... (Blackabbey Stud) 1,600

Evocative (IRE) b f (4yrs) Double Schwartz - Rosy Dew (Red Godl)............... (Tony O'Callaghan) 3,200

58

Property of W F Richardson, from Chetwynde Stables

b f (2yrs) Supreme Leader - Two Keo's (Don)................ (William Crowe) 620

From Milltown Britton Stud

ch y f Kambalda - Green Arctic (Green Shoon)......................... (Cash) 1,000

Property of Mr Edward Ryan, from Hilltown Stables

br g (4yrs) Sexton Blake - Show M How (Ashmore)................ (Pat Martin) 2,200

Property of Mr J Mulhall

ch f (2yrs) Orchestra - Money Run (Deep Run).......................... (Cash) 2,100

Property of Mrs Michael Wenteges

br y c Kambalda - Cold War (Lepanto) ..... (D T Hughes) 2,600

Property of Mr Thomas J Bolger, from Clohamon Stud

Bullawn Lady b m (5yrs) Leading Man - Folkland (Auction Ring) Covered by Sharp Charter........... (Jim Bolger) 2,000

Property of Mr David Murphy, from Clohamon Stud

b y f King's Ride - Manhattan Brandy (Frankincense)........... (Robert McCabe) 1,100

Property of a Partnership

Julia Too b m (23yrs) Golden Horus - Blond Star (Tin Whistle) Covered by King's Ride......................... (Cash) 580

Property of T Murphy

b c (2yrs) Step Together (USA) - Reoss (King's Ride).................. (Cash) 700

Property of Mr Paul Timmons, from The Beeches Stud

b y f Buckskin (FR) - Wessex Habit (Monksfield).................. (Cash) 1,380

59

From Avonmore Stud Ltd (a dispersal)

Bavette b m (11yrs) Le Bavard (FR) - Legal Argument (No Argument) Covered by Commanche Run......... (G Cannon) 15,000

Curragh Breeze b or br m (13yrs) Furry Glen - Royal Cup (Politico) Covered by Kings Ride................ (Michael Buckley) 4,200

Property of Mr J Kenneally, from Bishopstown Stud

Lovely Sanara ch m (14yrs) Proverb - Royal Dress (Perspex) Covered by Homo Sapien........................ (Cash) 700

Property of Alice Merrigan

b y f Phardante (FR) - Shining Moon (Deep Run)................. (George Doyle) 1,500

From Boardsmill Stud

b or br y f Carmelite House (USA) - Dance Dress (Ardross)........... (B Deegan) 320

b y f Carmelite House (USA) - Dacice (Tender King)..... (Dermot Montague) 460

Property of Mr E Campbell

ch y f Salluceva - Roriston Queen (Furry Glen)................. (Nancy Cullen) 360

Property of Winscarlet Stud

b y f Satco (FR) - Scarlet Wind (Whistling Wind)........................ (Cash) 600

From Curraghroche Stud

Brickey Gazette br m (12yrs) Fine Blade (USA) - Ladies Gazette (London Gazette) Covered by Dry Dock (believed not in foal)........ (M Doyle) 1,000

From French Furze House Stud

b y c Heavenly Manna - Fida (FR) (Diatome) .... (Cash) 940

60

Property of Mr Gerard Callanan, from Nanallac Stud

b y c King's Ride - Stramillian (Furry Glen) (Cash) 1,000

From Parson Green Stable

Ballyduff Invader b m (11yrs) Brave Invader (USA) - Court Mistress (Harwell) Covered by Rising................. (Cash) 720

Property of Mr Percy Harris, from Athassel House Stud

ch y c Good Thyne (USA) - Whosview (Fine Blade).................. (M O'Rourke) 400

From Donacarney Stud

Lisbawn b m (8yrs) Pitpan - Native Time (Hul A Hul) Covered by Celio Rufo .... (Cash) 1,200

Property of Mr P J Lohan

Side Pride ch m (12yrs) Quayside - Nire's Pride (Beau Tudor) Covered by Coquelin (USA)............... (Cash) 700

Blackhall Lass bl m (6yrs) Black Minstrel - Seamisso (Sea Wolf).. (Eugene Brady) 780

Another Yankee gr m (6yrs) Le Moss - Yankee's Princess (Yankee Gold) ..... (Ml Burke) 900

Comeragh Heather ch m (10yrs) Callernish - Comeragh Vision (Golden Vision) Covered by Beau Sher... (Peter Corcoran) 1,000

Property of Mr Edmund Butler

b or br y c Supreme Leader - Shannon Belle (Pollerton)..................... (Cash) 400

Property of Mr Michael Conroy

b y c Habyom - Toranoda (Torenaga) ...... (F McCormack) 900

61

Property of Mr Con Ryan

Gathering Moss ch m (6yrs) Le Moss - Golden Chestnut (Green Shoon) Covered by Roselier (FR).......... (Cash) 2,600

Property of Mr Eddie Finnegan

ch y f Orchestra - Kathy James (Monksfield).................. (Cash) 560

Property of Mr Patrick Kavanagh

ch y c Be My Native (USA) - Just Clara (Camden Town)............... (Cash) 900

Property of Mr Edward Sexton, from Rathmuc Stud

ch y f Gone Fishin - Flying Jennie (Burslem) .... (Cash) 500

Property of Seaview Stud Ltd

Marietta Meagher (USA) b m (8yrs) Solford (USA) - Hawaiian Island (USA) (Hawaii) (Patrick Kane) 800

Moran's Pet (USA) ch m (5yrs) Naskra (USA) - Vibrant Hue (USA) (Exclusive Native)....................... (Cash) 400

Alice Brackloon (USA) br m (8yrs) Melyno - Arantelle (FR) (Tapioca II)............. (E O'Gorman) 700

b y f Nordico (USA) - Marietta Meagher (USA) (Solford)........ (Tom Brennan) 500

Property of Mr John F Daly

br y f Strong Gale - Shirley Kay (Candy Cane)........................ (Cash) 2,600

Property of Knocklaney Stud

Sharafa b m (8yrs) Ya Zaman (USA) - Sarafan (Rustam) Covered by Camden Town................ (Wilson Faloon) 700

Property of Mr B Gallop

ch m (5yrs) Deep Run - Miss Furlong (Fury Royal).................. (Tim Murray) 1,550

From Harbour Stud (Agent)

Boherash Forest ch m (11yrs) Proverb - In The Forest (Croded Room) Covered by Glacial Storm (USA).. (Peter Corcoran) 620

Whats The Rush b m (10yrs) Pry - Lady Serene (Le Tricolore) Covered by Electric. . . . . (Cash) 580

62

ASCOT
Monday, March 22nd

Property of Miss Zoe F Yates
Nell b m (5yrs) Solent Lad - Miss Babette ((unknown)). . . . . (Cash) 875

Property of a Gentleman
Catcha Thief b g (5yrs) Final Straw - Honey Thief (Burglar). . . . . . (Miss A Blatchley) 1,700

Property of Mr N C Kersey
Lady Linnet br f (4yrs) Nomination - Shiny Kay (Star Appeal). . . . . (Hagas Ltd) 1,750

To Dissolve a Partnership
Charming Gift b m (6yrs) Petorius - Aubretia (USA) (Hatchet Man). . (Edward Lacey) 875

Property of Mr Steve Thompson
Sennon Cove ch f (4yrs) All Systems Go - L'irondelle (On Your Mark). . (D J Line) 875

Property of Mrs L E Lucas
Lime Street Lil b m (5yrs) Precocious - Merchantmens Girl (Klairon) . . . . (Mr Morris) 1,150

Property of Mrs G J C Bingham
Winning Call b m (6yrs) Kinglet - Game Bid (Laurence O). . . . . (Ruth Wollerton) 1,150

Property of Mr R F Johnson-Houghton
Young Sparkie ch c (3yrs) Superlative - Aspark (Sparkler). . . . . (Cash) 550

Property of a Partnership
Sharp Thistle b m (7yrs) Sharpo - Marphousha (FR) (Shirley Heights) . . . . (Garry Mills) 1,300

Property of Mrs V J Hodges
b f (3yrs) Presidium - Sparkling Sovereign (Sparkler). . . . . (A L Ellis) 650

63

Property of Dame Elizabeth and Alexander Csaky
Betty Jane ch m (9yrs) Morston (FR) - Indulgence (Prominer) Covered by Emarati (USA), NOT in foal . . . . (Mr Cooper) 725

Property of Mr M Cran
Derrymore Boy b g (11yrs) Bonne Noel - Sweet Melody (Alcide). . . . . (Cash) 1,300

Property of a Gentleman
b g (3yrs) Governor General - Requiem (Song). . . . . (Jean Povey) 625

Property of The Littleton Stud
gr g (3yrs) Sharrood (USA) - Altana (Grundy) . . . . (Ron Hodges) 1,550

Property of Mr Fahd Salman
Composed b c (3yrs) Sadler's Wells (USA) - Chellita (Habitat). . . . . (E.B.A.) 2,500

Property of Mrs G Merson
b c (2yrs) Vouchsafe - Balilyca (Balidar) . . . . (Mrs A Lucas) 525

Property of Mrs F E Vogt
Champion Reef ch g (2yrs) Hubbly Bubbly (USA) - Meme Chose (USA) (On-And-On). . . . . (B Jones) 650

Property of The Print Finisher Club
Finishing Kind b f (2yrs) Kind Of Hush - Print Finisher (Mandrake Major) . . . . . . (B Jones) 675

To Dissolve a Partnership
gr f (2yrs) Skyliner - Gem-May (Mansingh) (B Jones) 950

Property of Mr R D Sears
b f (2yrs) Minster Son - Superb Lady (Marcus Superbus). . . . . . (Mr Marsella) 550

64

Property of a Gentleman
ch c (2yrs) Northern State (USA) - Mrs Waddilove (Bustino). . . . . . (C M Allen) 675

b c (2yrs) Efisio - Votsala (Tap On Wood) . . (Barry Minting) 850

Property of C & N Bloodstock
b c (2yrs) Cree Song - Passionate (Dragonara Palace) . . . . (Cormack McCormack Bloodstock) 850

b c (2yrs) Reesh - Vent Du Soir (Main Reef) (Cash) 1,350

Property of Danebury Racing Stables Ltd
Home Affair b f (3yrs) Petoski - Miranda Julia (Julio Mariner). . . . . (Miss L Woof) 750

Property of Mrs M E Gibbon
Now Boarding b m (6yrs) Blazing Saddles (AUS) - Strictly Swing (Swing Easy (USA)). . . . . (R Hand) 1,250

Property of Mrs A S Hodges
Emerald Ears ch f (4yrs) Dublin Lad - Impish Ears (Import). . . . . (Racing Thoroughbreds Ltd) 900

Property of Mr J S Jamouneau
Alert The Boys ch g (4yrs) Norwick (USA) - Red Gay (Red Alert). . (Miss B Sinnatt) 825

Property of Mr T S Wallace
Spring Forward b h (9yrs) Double Form - Forward Princess (USA) (Forward Pass (USA)). (Lisa Venn) 950

Property of a Gentleman
Oco Royal b g (4yrs) Tinoco - Queen's Royale (Tobrouk (FR)). . (Mrs C Sturgis) 1,000

65

Property of a Lady
Loviste Bay b f (4yrs) Mummy's Game - Miss Maina (Thatching). . . . . (A L Ellis) 525

Property of a Gentleman
Savalaro b f (4yrs) Tinoco - Miss Shifter (Realm). . . . . (Ruth Wollerton) 1,250

Property of Mr J Short
Wakashan b h (5yrs) Dancing Brave (USA) - Lady Moon (Mill Reef (USA)) . . . . (Terry Cunningham) 2,100

Property of Mr P D Purdy
Over The Cliffs (IRE) b f (3yrs) Bluebird (USA) - Nonnita (Welsh Saint) (J Lamb) 675

Symmetrical ch c (3yrs) Kris - Flawless Image (USA) (The Minstrel (CAN)). . . . . (John Akehurst) 2,400

To Dissolve a Partnership
Falside b g (9yrs) Alias Smith (USA) - High Caraval (High Top) (Meriel Humphreys) 5,800

Property of Mr R Tooth

Alamir (USA) b g (5yrs) Shadeed (USA) - Glamour Girl (Riverman (USA)). . (Cash) 2,400

Property of Mr Tam Wong

Exarch (USA) b c (4yrs) His Majesty (USA) - Velvet (USA) (Sir Ivor). . . . . . . (J Morris) 4,400

Property of a Gentleman

Tulapet gr f (4yrs) Mansingh (USA) - Iridium (Linacre). . . . . (R Sands) 2,700

Property of Mrs C Morgan

Iwan b g (5yrs) Elegant Air - Clouded Vision (So Blessed). . . . . (Joe Lamb) 1,200

66

Property of Mr J E Brown

Sansmoss ch g (8yrs) Le Moss - Coforta (The Parson). . . . . (P McIntyre) 1,150

To Dissolve a Partnership

Bankers Gossip b g (9yrs) Le Bavard (FR) - Gracious View (Sir Herbert). . . . . (Robert Tudor Jones) 4,000

Zest For Life ch g (7yrs) Quayside - Orange Sprite (The Last Hurrah). . . . . (M Weir) 1,600

Property of The Viscount Chelsea

Sound Of Islay b g (8yrs) Deep Run - Sharpaway (Royal Highway) (J Turner) 3,800

Sound Of Jura b g (8yrs) Deep Run - Arctic Chatter (Le Bavard). . . . . (J Turner) 5,400

Property of Mr J W Buxton

The Last Washer (IRE) b g (4yrs) Mazaad - Gigo Jive (Jukebox). . . . (Claire Rogers) 1,850

To Dissolve a Partnership

Jack The Hiker b g (10yrs) Rare One - Royal Dress (Perspex). . . . . (J Bowen) 625

Property of Miss M L Bird

Formation br g (7yrs) Tanfirion - Imagination (FR) (Dancer's Image). . . . . . . (C Taylor) 1,500

Property of Mr N H S New

Cobb Run ch g (7yrs) Deep Run - Inneen Alainn (Prince Hansel). . . . . (Mr. Joppa) 1,050

Property of Mrs Ursula Wainwright

Game Fair b g (6yrs) Lighter - Stagbury (National Trust). . . . . (Cash) 1,600

67

Property of Mr R Williams

Wisebow b g (8yrs) Green Shoon - Lacabeha Lass Vii (Menelek). . (R B Boss) 1,200

Property of a Partnership

Killeshin b g (7yrs) Al Sirat (USA) - Spin Off (Wrekin Rambler). . . . . (Cash) 1,550

Property of Austin-Stroud & Co. Ltd.

Moving Force b g (6yrs) Muscatite - Saint Simbir (Simbir). . . . . (Vicky Bell) 1,200

Property of a Gentleman

Final Top ch g (8yrs) Chaparly (FR) - Peg Top (Star Moss). . . . . (B Watson) 750

To Dissolve a Partnership

Sheiloan br f (4yrs) Cruise Missile - Fair Princess (Quality Fair). . . . . (Fairacre Homes) 1,050

Property of Mrs E Sharp

Sharp As A Needle ch m (5yrs) Saxon Farm - Extramandora (Velvet Prince). . . . . (Mrs S R Phillips) 900

To Dissolve a Partnership

The Cuckoo's Nest b g (5yrs) Precocious - Troy Moon (Troy). . . . (Ruth Wollarton) 1,750

Floodlight (IRE) b f (3yrs) Exhibitioner - Share The Vision (Vision) (K J Palmer) 725

Property of Mr N L Stevens

Jolly Josh ch g (6yrs) Roman Warrior - Jolly Regal (Jolly Good). . . . . (Julie Lee) 1,000

Property of Sally Lock

Nearly Time gr m (10yrs) Nearly A Hand - Half A Minute (Romany Air). . . . (Cash) 150

68

Property of Mr R V Hand

Hinton Mariner b g (6yrs) Julio Mariner - Lavender Rose (Beau Lavender) . . . . . . (P J Chowe) 1,000

To Dissolve a Partnership

Intarsia b g (9yrs) Smartset - London Fancy (London Gazette). . . . . . . (Mr Williams) 1,650

Property of Miss S Thorpe

Summer Rocket ch m (11yrs) Roan Rocket - Summer Love (Silver Cloud) . . . . (R Wollerton) 1,000

Property of Mr P R Saxon

Penygroes br g (10yrs) Welsh Pageant - Wolver Valley (Wolver Hollow) . . . . (Miss P Pickess) 1,300

PRIVATE SALES

Property of Fonthill Stud

b f (2yrs) Superlative - Sequin Lady (Star Appeal). . . . . (G F Muggleston) 300

(Index reference 70 follows)

70

DONCASTER

Thursday, March 25th (Two-year-olds)

Property of Mr John Quinn, from Bellywood Stables

b c (2yrs) Horage - Villars (Home Guard) . . . (Conti Bloodstock) 7,200

From Kirriemuir Stud, Co Kildare, Ireland

b c (2yrs) Petorius - Galatrix (Be My Guest) (C.B.A.) 8,200

Property of a Syndicate, from Manor House Farm Stables

ch c (2yrs) Rich Charlie - Podzola (Royal Prerogative). . . . . (G Barsotti) 4,600

Property of Mr J Haine, from Buona Notte Stud

b c (2yrs) Reprimand - Jenny Splendid (John Splendid). . . . . (J Pattison) 10,000

Property of Mr Dennis Badham, from King's Lodge Stables

b c (2yrs) Dreams To Reality (USA) - Aphabel (Belfort). . (Derby Bloodstock) 1,200

Property of a Partnership, from Ted Voute (Agent)
b c (2yrs) Salt Dome (USA) - Princess Elinor (Captain James). . . . . (J Pearce) 9,800
br c (2yrs) Rambo Dancer (CAN) - Roses Galore (USA) (State Door Johnny) . . . . . (Cormac McCormack Associates) 17,000

Property of Fulling Mill Stud, from Fulling Mill Stud
b c (2yrs) Belfort (FR) - Gavea (African Sky) (P Doyle Bloodstock) 9,800
b c (2yrs) Thowra (FR) - Rota (Reliance II) . . (G Barsotti) 1,700

From Charlestown Stud, Co Westmeath, Ireland
b or br c (2yrs) Hotfoot - Emblazon (Wolver Hollow). . . . . (Derby Bloodstock) 5,600
b c (2yrs) Reasonable (FR) - Almost Heaven (Corvaro). . . . . (P Haslam) 6,200

71

Property of a Syndicate, from East Peterel Field Stables
ch g (2yrs) Chilibang - Deep Lady (Deep Diver) . . . . (Cormac McCormack Associates) 18,000
gr c (2yrs) Bold Owl - Swallow Bay (Penmarric). . . . . (G Barsotti) 8,800

From Bushy Park Stables, Co Kildare, Ireland
b c (2yrs) Jareer (USA) - Carioca (Gala Performance) (R O'Sheen Bloodstock) 12,000

From Torard House Stud, Co Limerick, Ireland
ch c (2yrs) Handsome Sailor - Sobriquet (Roan Rocket). . . . . (R Akehurst) 15,000
ch c (2yrs) Mulhollande (USA) - Lady Portobello (Porto Bello). . . . . (I Baker) 1,500

From Ballinvana House Stud, Co Limerick, Ireland
b c (2yrs) Forzando - Rabuba (Connaught). . (J Tikkirov) 1,400
br c (2yrs) Nashamaa - Bella Lucia (Camden Town). . . . . (Mark Campion) 4,000

From Mocklershill Stables, Co Tipperary, Ireland (Agent)
b c (2yrs) Fayruz - All The Same (Cajun) . . . (Derby Bloodstock) 8,200
ch c (2yrs) Bluebird (USA) - Tecmessa (Home Guard). . . . . (D Murphy) 12,000

From Tally-Ho Stud, Co Westmeath, Ireland
b c (2yrs) Clantime - Miss Spinney (Uncle Pokey). . . . . (B Hills) 8,000
gr c (2yrs) Neshad (USA) - Ishara (Blakeney) . . . . (G Barsotti) 6,000

72

From Lynn Lodge Stud, Co Westmeath, Ireland
b c (2yrs) Heraldiste (USA) - Rosy O'Leary (Majetta). . . . . (C A Smith) 4,400
b c (2yrs) Roaring Riva - Miss Colenca (Petong). . . . . (J Berry) 7,000

From Glenvale Stud, Co Tipperary, Ireland
br c (2yrs) Astronef - Lady Fandet (Gay Fandango). . . . . (N Meade) 17,000

From Yeomanstown Stud, Co Kildare, Ireland
gr c (2yrs) Common Grounds - Zanskar (Godswalk). . . . . (N Jackson) 8,200
b c (2yrs) Sayf El Arab (USA) - Blakeney Heights (Blakeney). . . . . . . (J Akehurst) 5,200

Property of Mr G Cosburn, from High Farm
b c (2yrs) Rich Charlie - Mrs Danvers (Balidar). . . . . (G Barsotti) 3,500

From High Farm Stables
b c (2yrs) Petorius - Tasmania Star (Captain James). . . . . (D Abell) 5,200

Property of Mr Malcolm Bastard
b c (2yrs) Roi Danzig (USA) - Carnival Fugue (High Top) . . . . (Cormac McCormack Associates) 22,000
b c (2yrs) Persian Heights - Charmeuse (Cut Above) . . . . (Richard O'Gorman Bloodstock) 6,400

Property of a Syndicate, from Portlester Stud, Co Meath, Ireland
b c (2yrs) Gallic League - Ex-Imager (Exhibitioner). . . . . (David Minton Bloodstock) 15,000

73

Property of Miss Maggie McGivern, from Portlester Stud, Co Meath, Ireland
b c (2yrs) Mon Tresor - Ribero's Overture (Ribero). . . . . (C A Smith) 4,500

Property of Etchingham Stud, from Etchingham Stud
b c (2yrs) Kala Shikari - Wellington Bear (Dragonara Palace). . . . . (C Shaik) 3,000

From Etchingham Stud
b g (2yrs) Tina's Pet - Anse Chastanet (Cavo Doro). . . . . (M Brittain) 1,900

From Kilminfoyle House Stud, Co Laois, Ireland
b c (2yrs) Al Hareb (USA) - Pam Story (Sallust). . . . . (P Haslam) 7,000

From Beechvale Stud, Co Antrim, Ireland
b c (2yrs) Mazaad - Skimmer (Skymaster) . . (Denys Smith) 16,000

From Mr Dan Barry, Col Cork, Ireland
b c (2yrs) Jareer (USA) - Femme de Fer (USA) (Mr Leader). . . . . (B.B.A.) 6,000

From Malcolm Bastard (Agent)
ch c (2yrs) Bairn (USA) - Sprikng Sunset (Red Sunset). . . . . (G Barsotti) 3,800

From Mocklershill Stables, Co Tipperary, Ireland (Agent)
ch c (2yrs) Glenstal (USA) - Albeni (Great Nephew). . . . . (J Higson) 9,000
b c (2yrs) Petorius - Sinful Secret (Hello Gorgeous). . . . . (Bryan Smart) 3,600

From Tall-Ho Stud, Co Westmeath, Ireland
ch c (2yrs) Precocious - Bacolet (Dominion) (Richard O'Gorman Bloodstock) 18,500

74

From Tally-Ho Stud, Co. Westmeath, Ireland
b f (2yrs) Classic Secret (USA) - Nigel's Star (Ashmore). . . . . (G Barsotti) 1,400

Property of Mr A K Collins, from Carlton Stud
br c (2yrs) Dowsing (USA) - Pyjama Party (Pyjama Hunt). . . . . (B.B.A.) 4,000
b c (2yrs) Belfort (FR) - Tangalooma (Hotfoot). (G Barsotti) 4,000

Property of Mr J Harris, from Carlton Stud
ch c (2yrs) Mazaad - Ziobia (Tribal Chief) . . . (Panetta Bloodstock) 3,200

From Carlton Stud
b c (2yrs) Midyan (USA) - Davill (Record Token).......... (Panetta Bloodstock) 4,000
From Yeomanstown Stud, Co. Kildare, Ireland
b or gr c (2yrs) Siberian Express (USA) - Chrisanthy (So Blessed).............. (Cormac McCormack Associates) 40,000
b c (2yrs) Nomination - Queenstyle (Moorestyle)................. (N Callaghan) 6,400
Property of Mrs D G Mason, from Southburgh Manor Stud
b c (2yrs) Dance Of Life (USA) - Smash (Busted).. (Will Edmeades Bloodstock) 32,000
Property of Mr D G Mason, from Southburgh Manor Stud
ch c (2yrs) Chilibang - Abalone (Abwah).... (C A Smith) 4,600
From Doninga Stud, Co. Kilkenny, Ireland
b c (2yrs) Shirley Heights - Switched On (Known Fact)................ (S Dow) 21,000
ch c (2yrs) Salt Dome (USA) - No Flight (Nonoalco)............... (D Murphy) 10,000

75

Property of Mr W Clarke, Co. Wicklow, Ireland
ch c (2yrs) Fayruz - Instanter (Morston).... (Derby Bloodstock) 8,200
Property of Fulling Mill Stud, from Fulling Mill Stud
b c (2yrs) Komaite (USA) - New Central (Remainder Man)............ (S Dow) 17,000
b c (2yrs) Elegant Air - Wild Moon (USA) (Arctic Tern)..... (Panetta Bloodstock) 5,400
From Suir View Stud, Co Tipperary, Ireland
b c (2yrs) Coquelin (USA) - Turbina (Tudor Melody)...... (R O'Sheen Bloodstock) 5,400
Property of Wellington House Stud, from Mocklershill Stables, Co. Tipperary, Ireland
b f (2yrs) Vision (USA) - Fashion Parade (Mount Hagen).... (J G And V V Hout) 4,200
From Mocklershill Stables, Co Tipperary, Ireland (Agent)
b f (2yrs) Taufan (USA) - Evanna's Pride (Main Reef)................ (J Banks) 6,400
From Tally-Ho Stud, Co. Westmeath, Ireland
b c (2yrs) Belfort (FR) - Hill Of Fare (Brigadier Gerard)............ (J J Bridger) 2,800
ch c (2yrs) Mazaad - Carrick Slaney (Red God)................... (R Akehurst) 7,400
From Lynn Lodge Stud, Co. Westmeath, Ireland
b c (2yrs) Daring March - Bold Event (Persian Bold).......................... (Cormac McCormack Associates) 8,200
br or gr c (2yrs) Merdon Melody - Bri-Ette (Brittany)................. (R Barwell) 3,600

76

From High Farm
gr c (2yrs) Heraldiste (USA) - God's Kiss (Godswalk).............. (C A Smith) 3,700
b c (2yrs) Reasonable (FR) - Dunbally (Dunphy)................. (W J Musson) 7,400
From Torard House Stud, Co. Limerick, Ireland
b c (2yrs) Risk Me (FR) - Sound Type (Upper Case).......... (M Blanshard) 8,400
b c (2yrs) Stalker - Royal Holly (Royal Buck) (J Tikkirou) 2,000
Property of Mr R W Jaines, from R.J.S. Bloodsock
ch c (2yrs) Carmelite House - Salote (USA) (Forli)............ (Derby Bloodstock) 4,000
ch c (2yrs) Sayf El Arab (USA) - Hawali (Gay Fandango)........ (Derby Bloodstock) 3,600
Property of Mr G Hourigan, Co. Tipperary, Ireland
b c (2yrs) Never So Bold - Aligote (Nebbiolo)..................... (R Akehurst) 7,200
ch g (2yrs) The Noble Player (USA) - Free Course (Sandford Lad)...... (K Stone) 9,800
Property of Cobhall Court Stud, from Cobhall Court Stud
b c (2yrs) Damister (USA) - Sainte Joie (FR) (Akarad)................ (G Barsotti) 5,000
b c (2yrs) Mazaad - Avril Blake (Sexton Blake).............. (M Heaton-Ellis) 3,800

77

From Mocklershill Stables, Co. Tipperary, Ireland (Agent)
b c (2yrs) Damister (USA) - Sun Sparkle (USA) (Nureyev).......... (D Murphy) 24,000
From Cross Farm Stables
b c (2yrs) Red Sunset - All Alright (Alzao).. (G Barsotti) 8,200
Property of Dandys Farm, from Dandys Farm
b f (2yrs) Blakeney - Sea Charm (Julio Mariner).................. (J Tikkirou) 9,000
Property of Mrs M T Morgan, from Portlester Stud, Co. Meath, Ireland
b c (2yrs) Ajraas (USA) - Ching A Ling (Pampapaul)............ (N Callaghan) 10,000
Property of Portlester Stud, Co. Meath, Ireland, from Portlester Stud, Co Meath,Ireland
ch f (2yrs) Ballad Rock - Crestia (Prince Tenderfoot).............. (G Barsotti) 2,400
Property of Hanging Hill Stables
b c (2yrs) Fayruz - Pass No Problem (Pas de Seul).............. (Derby Bloodstock) 2,000
From Golden Vale Stud, Co. Limerick, Ireland
b c (2yrs) Colmore Row - Jenny Dancer (Skyliner)................ (G Barsotti) 1,400
b c (2yrs) Gallic League - Minstrel's Shoe (Thatching).............. (T D Barron) 9,400
Property of Manor Farm Stud, from Manor Farm Stud
gr c (2yrs) Heraldiste (USA) - Fine Flame (Le Prince).............. (M Heaton-Ellis) 5,000
b f (2yrs) Hadeer - Starawak (Star Appeal) (N Tinkler) 4,800
From Doninga Stud, Co. Kilkenny, Ireland
b f (2yrs) Waajib - Atlanta Royale (Princes Tenderfoot).............. (G Barsotti) 16,500
From Rudry Park Stud
ch f (2yrs) Dominion - Young May Moon (Hopeful Venture)....... (C R Barwell) 5,600
From Manor Farm Stables
b c (2yrs) Presidium - Full Of Life (Wolverlife)......................... (Gordian Troeller Bloodstock) 5,400

78

DONCASTER
Friday, March 26th
(Two-year-olds)

Property of Swaines Hill Stud, From Swaines Hill Stud

br g (2yrs) Dowsing (USA) - Josephine Gibney (High Top)......... (W R Muir) 3,000

Property of Mr G Hourigan, Co Tipperary, Ireland

b or br c (2yrs) Pennine Walk - Route Royale (Roi Soleil)...... (S R Bowring) 4,500

From Kilnamoragh Stud, Co Kildare, Ireland

b c (2yrs) Maelstrom Lake - Eccentric Lady (London Bells)............... (B.B.A.) 3,400

Property of Mrs Dinah Whittingham

b c (2yrs) Glint Of Gold - Phlox (Floriana)... (J L Harris) 3,800

From Kirriemuir Stud, Co Kildare, Ireland

b c (2yrs) Runnett - Tumbleline (Tumble Wind)............ (Derby Bloodstock) 7,200

br c (2yrs) Pennine Walk - Maura Paul (Bonne Noel)............... (K Stone) 14,000

Property of a Syndicate, from Manor Farm Stables

b c (2yrs) Bold Owl - Misoptimist (Blakeney).................. (C.B.A.) 5,400

b c (2yrs) Governor General - Hurricane Rose (Windjammer)..... (W Williams) 3,000

From Shadowfax Stables

ch c (2yrs) Jareer (USA) - Prodical Daughter (Faraway Son)........... (A M Proos) 1,500

b c (2yrs) Taufan (USA) - Milaire (Tudor Melody)...... (A R G Cherry Downes) 18,000

79

Property of a Syndicate, from Manor House Farm Stables

gr c (2yrs) Grey Desire - Sorrowful (Moorstyle)................(Hallvard Soma) 4,600

ch c (2yrs) Salt Dome (USA) - Winter Harvest (Grundy)........ (Dale McKeown) 8,500

Property of Miss Wendy Carter

b g (2yrs) Nashamaa - On The Road (On Your Mark).............. (D Osmund) 14,000

b c (2yrs) Petorius - Noir Afrique (African Sky)...................... (P D Savill) 12,000

From Sandy Brow Stables

ch c (2yrs) Digamist (USA) - Gothic Lady (Godswalk)............. (A Thomson) 16,000

b f (2yrs) Cyrano de Bergerac - Godwyn (Yellow God)........................ (Cormac McCormack Associates) 8,000

From Bushy Park Stables, Co Kildare, Ireland

ch f (2yrs) Tate Gallery (USA) - Mystery Lady (USA) (Vaguely Noble).......... (J Sutcliffe) 4,200

b c (2yrs) Nashamaa - Park Silver (Beldale Flutter)......................(B.B.A.) 3,000

From Manister House Stud, Co Limerick, Ireland

b c (2yrs) Entitled - Swift Reply (He Loves Me) (Cormac McCormack Associates) 13,000

ch c (2yrs) Persian Heights - Gayla Orchestra (Lord Gayle)......... (E.I.L.) 21,000

80

From Tally-Ho Stud, Co Westmeath, Ireland

b c (2yrs) Bob Back (USA) - Allberry (Alzao) (W R Muir) 5,000

ch f (2yrs) Fayruz - Ferry Lane (Dom Racine) .... (Riston Whins Racing) 4,100

From Lynn Lodge Stud, Co Westmeath, Ireland

ch c (2yrs) Hatim (USA) - Milly Whiteway (Great White Way)......... (P Tseng) 3,200

b or br g (2yrs) Green Ruby (USA) - Girdle Ness (Pitskelly)...................... (Cormac McCormack Associates) 7,400

From Charlestown Stud, Co Westmeath, Ireland

b c (2yrs) Bold Arrangement - Sevens Are Wild (Petorius)............ (P Haslam) 5,600

b c (2yrs) Beveled (USA) - Daisy Topper (Top Ville)......... (Derby Bloodstock) 4,000

From Doninga Stud, Co Kilkenny, Ireland

br c (2yrs) Be My Native - Nishapour's Baby (Nishapour) .... (Cormac McCormack Associates) 38,000

ch f (2yrs) Salt Dome (USA) - Mine At Last (Nishapour)............... (P H Betts) 4,000

From Yeomanstown Stud, Co Kildare, Ireland

b c (2yrs) The Noble Player (USA) - Translation (Fordham).......... (Denys Smith) 9,400

ch c (2yrs) Dominion Royale - Genesee (Viking)............... (G A Hubbard) 4,500

81

Property of Miss Kate Brady, from Portlester Stud, Co Meath, Ireland

gr c (2yrs) Exhibitioner - Hat And Gloves (Wolver Hollow).......... (C B Booth) 20,000

Property of Miss Kate McGivern, from Portlester Stud, Co Meath, Ireland

gr f (2yrs) The Noble Player (USA) - Late Date (Goldhill).......... (S Uppstrom) 1,000

From Kilminfoyle House Stud, Co Laois, Ireland

b c (2yrs) Treasure Kay - Bumpity Bump (Local Suitor)............ (C B Booth) 8,800

From Beechvale Stud, Co Antrim, Ireland

ch c (2yrs) Al Hareb (USA) - Cider Princess (Alcide)......................... (Cash) 3,300

From Suir View Stud, Co Tipperary, Ireland

b c (2yrs) Petorius - Sweet Camden (Camden Town).......... (W Odfuell) 5,000

b c (2yrs) Exhibitioner - Share The Vision (Vision).................. (W Odfuell) 2,300

From Torard House Stud, Co Limerick, Ireland

b c (2yrs) Chilibang - Lune de Miel (Kalamoun).................. (C C Elsey) 10,000

b c (2yrs) Jolly Jake (NZ) - Streaking Sue (USA) (Private Thoughts) .... (J S Wainwright) 3,000

Property of a Partnership, from High Onn Stud

b or br c (2yrs) Belfort (FR) - Peter's Pet Girl (Norwick)............ (Million In Mind) 6,000

ch c (2yrs) Pharly (FR) - Unearthed (Electric) .... (B A McMahon) 7,000

82

Property of a Partnership, from Southburgh Manor Stud

b c (2yrs) Try My Best (USA) - Eloquent Charm (USA) (Private Account)........ (Johnny McKeever Bloodstock) 9,200

Property of Sediment Syndicate, from Southburgh Manor Stud

b c (2yrs) Nomination - Water Pageant (Welsh Pageant)............. (C.B.A.) 3,000

From Mockerlshill Stables, Co Tipperary, Ireland (Agent)

b c (2yrs) Mazaad - Gorgeous Annie (Hello Gorgeous).................... (E.I.L.) 9,200

gr c (2yrs) Standaan (FR) - Mingoon Bell (Ragusa)................ (T C Chiang) 2,000

From Tally-Ho Stud, Co Westmeath, Ireland

b or br c (2yrs) Toca Madera - Magic Picture (Deep Diver) (Peter Doyle Bloodstock) 4,200

From Etchingham Stud

b c (2yrs) Homeboy - Breakfast In Bed (Tickled Pink)......... (Hallvard Soma) 2,200

ch f (2yrs) Indian Ridge - Spring Water (USA) (Effervescing).. (M W Easterby) 5,200

From Manor House Stud

b f (2yrs) Aragon - Maravilla (Mandrake Major).......... (Panetta Bloodstock) 15,000

Property of of a Syndicate, from East Peterel Field Stables

b c (2yrs) Glenstal (USA) - Vaguely Deesse (USA) (Vaguely Noble)............... (Orchard House Stud) 12,500

b c (2yrs) Risk Me (FR) - Sir Tangs Gift (Runnett)............. (J G FitzGerald) 3,800

83

From High Farm

b or br c (2yrs) Classic Secret (USA) - Kitterland (Rheingold) .... (Derby Bloodstock) 4,000

b c (2yrs) Governor General - Nightwood (Sparkler)............... (M Gleeson) 15,000

Property of Mr Malcolm Bastard

ch c (2yrs) Cadeaux Genereux - Storm Riding (USA) (Storm Bird) .... (Cormac McCormack Associates) 15,000

b c (2yrs) Robellino (USA) - Crystal's Solo (USA) (Crystal Water) .... (Cormac McCormack Associates) 33,000

Property of Fulling Mill Stud, from Fulling Mill Stud

ch c (2yrs) Classic Secret (USA) - Tora Tora (Home Guard).......... (J R Jenkins) 5,200

Property of Mr C W Rogers, from Fulling Mill Stud

ch c (2yrs) Interrex (CAN) - Beaute Fatale (Hello Gorgeous)..... (Stanley Moore) 2,000

Property of Fulling Mill Stud, from Fulling Mill Stud

br c (2yrs) Classic Secret (USA) - Soudchika (GER) (Dschingis Khan)............... (Stanley Moore) 2,200

Property of Prosperous Stud, from Portlester Stud, Co. Meath, Ireland

ch c (2yrs) Classic Secret (USA) - Northern Twilight (English Prince)... (C A Smith) 1,800

b c (2yrs) Al Hareb (USA) - Miss Sandman (Manacle)......... (Derby Bloodstock) 2,200

Property of Mr Stefan Uppstrom

b c (2yrs) Common Grounds - Secret Heart (Vision).............. (B A McMahon) 7,000

b c (2yrs) Law Society (USA) - Fair Flutter (Beldale Flutter)............... (E.I.L.) 7,000

ch c (2yrs) Common Grounds - Opening Day (Day Is Done)........ (C C Elsey) 10,000

84

From Beechvale Stud, Co. Antrim, Ireland

br f (2yrs) Astronef - Farrier's Slipper (Prince Tenderfoot)... (M H Tompkins) 3,200

From Beechview Stud, Co. Limerick, Ireland

b c (2yrs) Don't Forget Me - Needy (High Top).................... (A M Proos) 1,300

From Mocklershill Stables, Co. Tipperary, Ireland (Agent)

b c (2yrs) Petorius - Parlais (Pardao)....... (E Alston) 7,400

ch c (2yrs) Red Sunset - Jarretiere (Star Appeal)............................ (Cormac McCormack Associates) 27,000

From Tally-Ho Stud, Co. Westmeath, Ireland

b f (2yrs) Fayruz - Fast Bay (Bay Express).. (Panetta Bloodstock) 3,200

From Torard House Stud, Co. Limerick, Ireland

b c (2yrs) King Of Clubs - Elmar (Lord Gayle)............... (Hallvard Soma) 11,000

b c (2yrs) Exactly Sharp (USA) - Crepe de Paille (Final Straw)............... (E.I.L.) 3,000

From Knockatrina Stud, Co. Laois, Ireland

b or br c (2yrs) Anita's Prince - Mooned (Fair Season).............. (W Haigh) 5,400

br f (2yrs) Mon Tresor - Stifen (Burslem)... (R O'Sheen Bloodstock) 3,600

Property of Mr Liam Wright, from Kilminfoyle House Stud, Co. Laois, Ireland

b c (2yrs) Salt Dome (USA) - Fifty Grand (Ballad Rock)............ (M Haynes) 3,000

85

Property of Mr R Lodge, from Village Farm Stud

gr c (2yrs) Nomination - Vignargenta (Absalom).................... (E.I.L.) 6,600

Property of Mr G Hourigan, Co. Tipperary, Ireland

b c (2yrs) The Noble Player (USA) - Rince Si (Malinowski)............. (M Browne) 15,000

br c (2yrs) Gallic League - Dutch Queen (Ahonoora)......... (Conti Bloodstock) 9,800

Property of Mr V W Jaines, from R.J.S. Bloodstock

gr c (2yrs) Sharrood (USA) - Miss Flossa (FR) (Big John)........... (P H Betts) 5,400

Property of Mr R W Jaines, from R.J.S. Bloodstock

ch c (2yrs) Prince Des Coeurs (USA) - Pink N'perky (Tickled Pink) (Arild Stenbeck) 1,000

Property of Mr Ian W Glenton, from Tall Trees Farm

b c (2yrs) Sayf El Arab (USA) - Guilty Guest (USA) (Be My Guest) (D W Chapman) 5,000

Property of a Partnership, from Ted Voute (Agent)

b c (2yrs) Mill Native (USA) - Hail To You (USA) (Kirtling)...................... (Gordian Troeller Bloodstock) 9,400

b c (2yrs) Tender King - Roundstone Lass (Montekin).................. (T Craig) 5,000

Property of Mr & Mrs John E Wilkinson, from Beaufort Stud

ch f (2yrs) Music Boy - Grove Star (Upper Case)................ (T A Wilkinson) 6,500

b or br f (2yrs) Nomination - Beaufort Star (Great Nephew)......... (C R Barwell) 5,600

86

Property of a Partnership, from Prospect Farm Stables

b c (2yrs) Treasure Kay - Poka Poka (FR) (King Of Macedon)... (M Heaton-Ellis) 4,400

ch c (2yrs) Faustus (USA) - Fall To Pieces (USA) (Forli).............. (B Beasley) 3,200

From Springfield Stud, Co. Clare, Ireland

b c (2yrs) Shardari - Zahiah (So Blessed)... (C A Smith) 4,500

Property of Mr B E Green, from Spa Stud

br c (2yrs) Midyan (USA) - Hot Money (Mummy's Pet)............... (E.I.L.) 15,000

87

DONCASTER
Tuesday, March 30th

Property of Mrs F Tyler, from Riversdale Stud

ch y c Prince Des Coeurs (USA) - Pink N'perky (Tickled Pink).......... (Cash) 480

Property of Mr D Wallis

b y f Sizzling Melody - Broken Silence (Busted)...................... (Cash) 440

Property of Mr & Mrs B T Chambers

b y c Sayf El Arab (USA) - Hot Momma (Free State).................. (Cash) 580

b y c Damister (USA) - Sunningdale Queen (Gay Fandango)............ (P Venner) 1,150

Property of Mr R M West, from Carlton Stud

gr y c Standaan (FR) - Combattente (Reform)................ (T D Barron) 2,700

To Dissolve a Partnership, from Racecourse Farm Stables

b f (2yrs) Sayf El Arab (USA) - Bay Blues (Cure The Blues).............. (Cash) 750

Property of Mr & Mrs D J Deer, from Fawley Stud

b f (2yrs) Reprimand - Haywain (Thatching) (S Kettlewell) 750

Property of Mr John Wills, from Skiddaw Stud

b c (2yrs) Efisio - My Myra (Auction Ring).. (N Callaghan) 3,100

ch f (2yrs) Handsome Sailor - Lady Of Leisure (Record Run) (D W Chapman) 1,500

Property of Mrs J L Wigham, from Underbrow Farm

Touch Of Oriental b f (2yrs) Touch Boy - Shantung Lassie (FR) (Shantung)...... (Miss E L Frew) 580

88

Property of Mr J A Richardson

br or gr c (2yrs) Governor General - Overseas (Sea Hawk II)..... (B P J Baugh) 3,000

Property of Mr F McKevitt

ch g (2yrs) Orchestra - Madame Venard (Red Regent)........... (R W Jaines) 1,000

From Haggswood Stables

b c (2yrs) Entitled - Frighten The Life (King's Lake).................. (S Uppstrom) 1,000

From Wood Farm Stud

b f (2yrs) Primo Dominie - Persian Tapestry (Tap On Wood)....... (Miss E L Frew) 850

From Etchingham Stud

b c (2yrs) Claude Monet (USA) - Sambell (Sammy Davis)....... (D W Chapman) 2,200

From R O Sheen Bloodstock Services

b c (2yrs) Prince Rupert (FR) - Timely Thatch (Thatch)................ (Cash) 980

Property of Mr A H Grant

br c (3yrs) Crofthall - Fidget (Workboy)..... (Mrs J Newnham) 500

Property of Claremont Management Services

b g (2yrs) Bairn (USA) - Be Still (Derring-Do) (J Hutchinson) 650

From Maunby House Stables

Snooty br g (3yrs) Cyrano de Bergerac - Captivate (Mansingh).. (Mrs S Russell) 1,200

Glowing Devil ro g (4yrs) Kalaglow - Romantiki (USA) (Romeo)...... (Cash) 1,600

89

Property of Mrs B Ramsden

Black Jewel b g (10yrs) Welsh Captain - New York Rose (Pieces Of Eight)..... (B J Forber) 1,400

Property of Palacegate Corporation Ltd

Palacegate Girl ch f (3yrs) Music Boy - Long Girl (Longleat)................ (B.B.A.) 1,700

From Seven Springs Stables

Appealing Times (USA) ch g (4yrs) Timeless Moment (USA) - Appealing One (USA) (Valid Appeal)......... (D W Chapman) 2,800

Property of Mr D Richardson

Moodiesburn b f (3yrs) Red Sunset - Acquire (Burglar)....... (M P Maiquer) 1,500

Property of Sir John Astor, from Abington Place Stables

Harquin b c (3yrs) Dancing Brave (USA) - The Dancer (FR) (Green Dancer)...... (L M Bush) 5,100

To Dissolve a Partnership, from Mowbray House Stables

Comiskey Park ch c (4yrs) Caerleon (USA) - Soba (Most Secret)......... (A Smith) 2,000

To Dissolve a Partnership, from Fir Tree Farm Stables

Ace Girl ch f (4yrs) Stanford - Lucky Candy (Lucky Wednesday)........ (T Barratt) 3,500

Property of Mr P Hunter

Ebony Isle gr f (4yrs) Grey Desire - Clairwood (Final Straw)....... (S Bateman) 1,450

Property of Mr R A Moffat

Arak (USA) b h (5yrs) Clever Trick (USA) - Twilight Flight (USA) (Quack)........ (D K Crossland) 4,000

Property of Mr G Brooks

Kadari b f (4yrs) Commanche Run - Thoughtful (Northfields)...... (W Clay) 10,000

90

Property of Mr W Kettlewell

ch f (3yrs) K-Battery - Rock Psalm (Saintly Song)................. (M P Maiquer) 900

Property of Mrs J N Reus

Krakatoa b f (4yrs) Shirley Heights - Konigsalpen (GER) (Priamos)....... (B King) 2,600

From Haggswood Stables

Smoke gr m (7yrs) Rusticaro (FR) - Fire-Screen (Roan Rocket).. (Mary Benson) 2,500

ch c (2yrs) Kirchner - Honest (Relkino)..... (Cash) 680

Property of Mr Robert Lindsay, from Haggswood Stables

Petered Out br g (3yrs) Nomination - Fading (Pharly)........................ (Cash) 1,150

From Barouche Stud

Believe In Me b c (4yrs) Don't Forget Me - Fast Bay (Bay Express)..... (A Smith) 1,900

From Rathmoy Stables

Kaher (USA) b g (6yrs) Our Native (USA) - June Bride (USA) (Riverman).. (C.B.A.) 7,800

Dublin Indemnity b g (4yrs) Alphabatim (USA) - Sailongal (USA) (Sail On Sail On).................. (S Cruikshank) 1,400

From Maddenstown Stables, Co Kildare, Ireland

Distant Drum gr g (7yrs) Warpath - Precipienne (Precipice Wood).... (L Lungo) 5,000

Walkers Point b g (7yrs) Le Moss - Saltee Star (Arapaho)............. (M J Pipe) 6,200

Portstewart ch g (8yrs) Le Bavard (FR) - Gay Countess (Master Buck) .... (M J Pipe) 2,000

91

From Norton Grange Stables

As D'Eboli (FR) b g (6yrs) What A Guest - Ana D'Eboli (FR) (King Of The Castle).. (M Hammond) 1,600

Miss Vagabond b m (5yrs) Scallywag - Once Bitten (Brave Invader).... (Cash) 2,300

Shannon King ch g (5yrs) Boyne Valley - Miss Royal (King's Company) .... (D Yeoman) 6,000

To Dissolve a Partnership, from Norton Grange Stables

Dara Melody b g (4yrs) Dara Monarch - Ascensiontide (Ela-Mana-Mou) .... (S Uppstrom) 4,000

To Dissolve a Partnership, from Racecourse Farm Stables

Sandhurst Park ch g (8yrs) Sandhurst Prince - Sandford Lass (Sandford Lad) (Cash) 2,200

From Racecourse Farm Stables

Doreen's Pride ch m (7yrs) Celtic Cone - Quae Supra (On Your Mark).... (Cash) 1,050

Property of Mr D Tylden-Wright, from Racecourse Farm Stables

Neither Nor ch f (4yrs) Norwick (USA) - Leap In Time (Dance In Time)......... (D Wilson) 3,300

Property of Mrs D Lamb, from Groundhill Stables

Leven Baby br m (6yrs) Blazing Saddles (AUS) - Farababy (FR) (Faraway Son)... (M P Maiquer) 1,300

To Dissolve a Partnership, from Upper Welford House Stables

Judge's Fancy br g (9yrs) Monksfield - Knollwood Court (Le Jean).... (C.B.A.) 20,000

Ghia Gneuiagh br g (7yrs) Monksfield - Kindly (Tarqogan).......... (C.B.A.) 7,400

Mulberry Harbour b g (5yrs) Orchestra - Turbo Lady (Tumble Wind)..... (Cash) 1,500

92

To Dissolve a Partnership, from High Gingerfield Stables

Royal Borough b g (8yrs) Bustino - Lady R B (USA) (Gun Shot).............. (Cash) 920

To Dissolve a Partnership

Portknockie ch m (5yrs) Rymer - Vulpine Lady (Green Shoon)........... (Cash) 2,200

From Hammond Lodge Stables, Co Down, Ireland

Gilbert br g (5yrs) Dalsaan - Pennyala (Skyliner).................... (D N Carey) 700

From Spigot Lodge Stables

Always Royal b g (4yrs) Dara Monarch - Shoshoni (Ballymoss)..... (T Caldwell) 1,650

Toodleoo ch f (4yrs) King's Lake - Boo (Bustino).............. (M P Maiquer) 1,150

From Upper Longdon Stables

Mariner's Legend ch m (7yrs) Julio Mariner - Firs Park (Crozier)........ (S Wilson) 5,000

Klingdon b c (4yrs) Formidable (USA) - Melbourne Miss (Chaparral).... (Cash) 3,500

Property of Mr C Marner

Traders Dream b g (4yrs) Superlative - Divine Thought (Javelot).............. (Mrs K Pickering) 2,500

To Dissolve a Partnership

Another March b g (7yrs) Marching On - River Sirene (Another River).... (Cash) 1,300

Property of Mr G W Turner

Relatively Risky ch f (4yrs) Risk Me (FR) - Skelton (Derrylin).............. (Cash) 1,000

93

From Wadeley Farm

b g (5yrs) Le Moss - Kilclare Lass (Pitpan) (Cash) 1,000

b g (4yrs) Rymer - Pearly Miss (Space King) (A Griffith) 3,000

Property of Mr C Castle, from Eddlethorpe Stables

Cardea Castle b m (5yrs) Fayruz - Yamba (FR) (Amarko)........ (Mrs Cartwright) 1,450

Property of Mrs N Macauley (A Dispersal Sale), from The Sidings Stables

Apres Huit b m (6yrs) Day Is Done - Ma Minti (Mummy's Pet) (Miss E L Frew) 1,000

From R O Sheen Bloodstock Services

Fragonard br g (4yrs) Pharly (FR) - Girl On A Swing (High Top)....... (S Uppstrom) 1,500

Property of Gill and Punter E.T.E.C. Ltd, from Tupgill Park Stables

Burn Bridge (USA) b g (7yrs) Linkage (USA) - Your Nuts (Creme de La Creme)..... (T Caldwell) 1,550

Property of Mr T J Hemmings
Tennis Coach gr g (6yrs) Siberian Express (USA) - Net Call (Song)..... (V Aconley) 3,000
From Welham Stables
Random Warrior b g (9yrs) Random Shot - Regency Cherry (Master Buck)......... (Miss V Jones) 700
Dancing Legend b g (5yrs) Lyphard's Special (USA) - Princess Nabila (King Pellinore)................ (Miss E L Frew) 850
Property of Travail Employment Group Ltd
Travail Temporaire b g (7yrs) Kambalda - Lady Serene (Le Tricolore) (T Caldwell) 2,400

94

From Hammond Lodge Stables, Co Down, Ireland
Silver Bid gr g (5yrs) Scallywag - Melfio Miss (Town Crier)............... (Cash) 2,000
To Dissolve a Partnership
Majestic Form ch m (5yrs) Double Schwartz - Majestic's Gold (Rheingold)..... (G Parrington) 800
Property of Melbourne Hall Stud, from Melbourne Hall Stud
b f (4yrs) Crofthall - Rhythmella (Tudor Rhythm)........................ (Cash) 920
Property of Mr P B Doyle, from Shadowfax Stables
Digger Doyle b g (4yrs) Cragador - Chaconia Girl (Bay Express)........ (L R Duncan) 3,700
From Woodside Farm Stables
Barry Owen b g (7yrs) Owen Anthony - Tacita (Tacitus).......... (S Uppstrom) 1,900
Property of Miss A W Jones, from Pentre David Stables
Lonely Lass b m (7yrs) Headin' Up - Lonely Dawn (USA) (Plenty Old)... (S France) 1,050
Property of Martin Pound Racing Ltd
Baie Petite b f (4yrs) Bay Express - Little Newington (Most Secret) (S Dawson) 1,300
Property of Mr M Graham
Ballad Dancer ch g (8yrs) Ballad Rock - Manx Image (Dancers Image).......... (D Yeoman) 2,100
Miss El Arab ch m (5yrs) Sayf El Arab (USA) - Shining Bright (USA) (Bold Bidder) .... (V Aconley) 1,050
Property of Mrs Eileen Milligan
Carlingford Winter ch g (7yrs) Carlingford Castle - Winter Serenade (Whistling Wind)......................... (Cash) 1,750

95

Property of Mrs Alex Stephenson
Cronksbank ch g (5yrs) Superlative - Rosinante (FR) (Busted)............ (Cash) 1,500
Property of Mr A H Cassells, from Willoughton Stables
Foxy Boy b g (10yrs) Chantro - La Sirene (Pinturischio).............. (A I Aitken) 1,300
Property of Mr C G R Booth, from Willoughton Stables
Just Incredible b g (7yrs) Auction Ring (USA) - Elated (Sparkler).. (Mrs J Kelly) 1,750

Property of Mrs P J Hall
Look Who's Talking b g (5yrs) Daring March - Llanmilo (Realm).............. (Cash) 1,500
Property of a Partnership
Aldington Chappie b g (5yrs) Creetown - Aldington Miss (Legal Eagle).......... (B Preece) 2,600
Aldington Millpond b g (5yrs) Creetown - Dear Catalpa (Dear Gazelle)........... (H Wheeler) 2,100
Aldington Baby Mae ch g (5yrs) Creetown - Mae Mae (Communication)............ (Miss L Townend) 780
Property of Mr George Prodromou
Far Out b g (7yrs) Raga Navarro (ITY) - Spaced Out (Space King).... (E Baker) 1,600
Property of Mrs J Coldicutt, from Arden Park Stables
Never Touched Me b m (6yrs) Belfort (FR) - Realm Gift (Realm).......... (T Dodd) 1,000
From Arden Park Stables
Scu's Lady b f (5yrs) Mazaad - Lydja (Hethersett)................ (D Baird) 1,100

96

Property of Mrs Yvonne Barclay
Eazy Peazy b g (5yrs) Indian King (USA) - Dane Valley (Simbir)...... (D Badham) 1,900
Property of Mr Peter Mee
ch f (2yrs) Ra Nova - Homing Hill (Homing) (Cash) 900
To Dissolve a Partnership
Parisienne King (USA) b g (4yrs) Key To The Kingdom (USA) - Paris Dawn (USA) (Mr Redoy).................. (E Baker) 1,100
Property of Mr J Wardle
Cromaboo b g (5yrs) Starch Reduced - La Belle Epoque (Tachypous) .... (Emma Mills) 2,200
Property of Mrs R E Barr, from Carr House Stables
Happy Cavalier br g (8yrs) King Of Spain - Happy Donna (Huntercombe) .... (J S Cooper) 1,500
From Osberton Stud
Sonic Lord b g (8yrs) Final Straw - Lucent (Irish Ball).................. (A Ireland) 1,450
Property of Mr G M T Foljambe, from Osberton Stud
Neville br g (7yrs) Full Of Hope - Viduli (Firestreak)................ (A Ireland) 2,000
From Burley Hill Stud
b g (5yrs) Son Of Shaka - Home Sweet Home (Royal Palace)...... (P Golding) 920
b c (2yrs) Crowning Honors (CAN) - Wren's Folly (Brigadier Symboli)...... (R Lee) 500
b c (2yrs) Crowning Honors (CAN) - Angie's Darling (Milford)............ (A Laird) 400

97

Property of Mr B McNichol
Doreen's Rhapsody br m (5yrs) Zambrano - Doreen's Darling (Bilsborrow)........ (Ms. L McGowan) 1,150
To Dissolve a Partnership
Granny Mc br m (6yrs) Sparkling Boy - Marcus Miss (Marcus Superbus)...... (H Smith) 2,800

Property of Mrs J A Tinning

Sweet Rose br m (5yrs) Tudor Rhythm - Lund Head Lady (Gracious Melody).... (Miss K Brooks) 1,200

To Dissolve a Partnership

Avec Coeur (USA) b g (11yrs) Cinteelo (USA) - Cadeau de Coeur (USA) (Noblesse Oblige).. (Miss M C Phipps) 900

From Moorwood Farm Stud

Caffre Lily b m (11yrs) Hittite Glory - Calling Low (Reform)............ (D Duxbury) 700

Northern Venture b m (18yrs) St Alphage - Shopping Wise (Floribunda).. (A Laird) 500

RE-OFFERED

Property of Mrs J Newnham

br c (3yrs) Crofthall - Fidget (Workboy)..... (D Duxbury) 820

Property of Mrs L Elliott, from Corner House Stables

Pushmepullyou gr f (3yrs) Nishapour (FR) - Elope (Jimmy Reppin)......... (Cash) 1,000

98

NEWMARKET
Wednesday, April 14th
(Two-year-olds)

Property of a Partnership, from Graham Lodge Stables

b f (2yrs) Forzando - Deed (Derring-Do).... (M Channon) 7,000

Property of Mr T H Morris, from Heath Lodge Stables

b c (2yrs) Jester - Bold Difference (Bold Owl)...................... (R O'Ryan) 3,000

Property of Stetchworth Park Stud Ltd., from Widgham Stables

ch f (2yrs) Hadeer - Baltic Leap (USA) (Northern Dancer) .... (Panetta Bloodstock) 2,200

Property of Carlton Consultants Ltd., from Danebury Stables

b c (2yrs) Formidable (USA) - Distant Relation (Great Nephew).... (M Chapman) 1,500

ch f (2yrs) Glint Of Gold - Irene's Charter (Persian Bold) (K Cunningham-Brown) 15,500

From Shadowfax Stables

br c (2yrs) Forzando - Classical Vintage (Stradavinsky)...... (Conti Bloodstock) 1,500

Property of a Lady, from Shadowfax Stables

b f (2yrs) Rambo Dancer (CAN) - Misty Arch (Starch Reduced)......... (E Stanford) 5,400

Property of a Partnership, from Shronell Stables, Ireland

b g (2yrs) Salt Dome (USA) - Salvationist (Mill Reef (USA))............ (C.B.A.) 7,000

Property of a Partnership, from East Green Bloodstock Ltd

b f (2yrs) Rambo Dancer (CAN) - Be Malicious (Malicious)........ (Mrs C Miller) 1,400

Property of Mr & Mrs J A Duffy, from East Green Bloodstock Ltd

b c (2yrs) Salt Dome (USA) - Ange de Feu (Double Form).. (European Bloodstock) 1,000

99

Property of a Partnership, from College Farm

b f (2yrs) Squill (USA) - Guest Mistress (What A Guest) (R Barnes Bloodstock) 2,000

From Tally-Ho Stud, Ireland

ch c (2yrs) Superpower - Mrs Hooters (Glint Of Gold)......... (Panetta Bloodstock) 16,500

ch g (2yrs) Mazaad - Market Romance (African Sky).......... (Gay Kelleway) 4,800

From Furnace Mill Stud

b c (2yrs) Primo Dominie - Naturally Bold (Bold Lad (IRE)) (New Turf Bloodstock) 25,000

ch c (2yrs) Formidable (USA) - Ryaffi (Affirmed (USA))........... (P Young) 4,000

ch c (2yrs) Blushing John (USA) - Golden Way (USA) (Diplomat Way).......... (Mrs G M Hay) 11,500

Property of Limestone Stud, from Willoughton Stables

Midnight Legend b c (2yrs) Night Shift (USA) - Myth (Troy).... (Mrs G M Hay) 32,000

Property of Tara Stud, Ireland, from Willoughton Stables

b c (2yrs) Kefaah (USA) - Hay Knot (Main Reef)..................... (J Dunlop) 8,200

Property of Mr P Gibbons, from Portlester Stud, Ireland

ch f (2yrs) Entitled - Soyez Sage (FR) (Grundy)......... (Panetta Bloodstock) 1,000

From Barcham Farm Stables

b c (2yrs) Al Hareb (USA) - Gay Surrender (Sir Gaylord)........... (D Brothwell) 13,000

b c (2yrs) Jareer (USA) - Au Revoir (Ballymoss).......... (Conti Bloodstock) 3,800

ch c (2yrs) Indian Ridge - Runabay (Run The Gantlet (USA)).... (Derby Bloodstock) 2,900

100

Property of W H R John and Partners, from Barcham Farm Stables

ch c (2yrs) Mon Tresor - Beaded Bubbles (Simply Great (FR)).... (M Chapman) 4,300

Property of Browne Bloodstock Enterprises, from Mocklershill Stables, Ireland

b c (2yrs) Sutter's Prospect (USA) - Scharade (Lombard (GER)).... (C.B.A.) 7,000

ch c (2yrs) Pharly (FR) - Fanny's Cove (Mill Reef (USA))......................... (Will Edmeades Bloodstock) 16,500

Property of Ballygallon Stud, Ireland, from Heatherwold Stud

ch c (2yrs) Kris - State Treasure (USA) (Secretariat (USA))... (W H Ponsonby) 7,400

From Heatherwold Stud

b f (2yrs) Siberian Express (USA) - Exceptional Beauty (Sallust)........ (C.B.A.) 9,200

From Suir View Stud, Ireland

b c (2yrs) Midyan (USA) - Lola Black (FR) (Relkino)................... (C.B.A.) 16,000

From High Farm

ch c (2yrs) Balidar - Highest Tender (Prince Tenderfoot)........... (I V Matthews) 3,100

From Lynn Lodge Stud, Ireland

b c (2yrs) Lomond (USA) - Miss Allowed (USA) (Alleged (USA)).... (R Whitaker) 20,000

b c (2yrs) Architect (USA) - Tina's Robin (USA) (Robin's Song (USA)).......... (Margaret O'Toole) 1,000

From Tally-Ho Stud, Ireland
b c (2yrs) Mister Majestic - Jazz Tune (FR) (Lyphard (USA)) (European Bloodstock) 5,400
b g (2yrs) Henbit (USA) - I've No Idea (Nishapour (FR))............ (R Curtis) 4,000

101

Property of Mr C N Wright, from Stratford Place Stud
b g (2yrs) Damister (USA) - Cameroun (African Sky)..................... (J Hills) 1,000
Property of a Partnership, from Potters Hill Stables
b c (2yrs) Mazaad - Pocket (Tumble Wind (USA))..................... (J D Abel) 15,000
gr c (2yrs) Cyrano de Bergerac - Cherlinoa (FR) (Crystal Palace (FR)) .... (Panetta Bloodstock) 16,500
ch c (2yrs) Classic Secret (USA) - Yenillik (Rusticaro (FR))........... (M J Haynes) 4,100
From Norton Grange Stables
ch f (2yrs) Digamist (USA) - Amiga Irlande (Whistling Deer).... (Conti Bloodstock) 4,600
Property of a Partnership, from Bloomsbury Stud
Childhood ch f (2yrs) Master Willie - Hilly (Town Crier)............. (J Spearing) 7,200
Morechili gr f (2yrs) Forzando - Meanz Beanz (High Top)............. (J Ince) 1,500
Plinth b c (2yrs) Dowsing (USA) - Pedestal (High Line) (David Minton Bloodstock) 5,600
Property of Browne Bloodstock Enterprises, from Mocklershill Stables, Ireland
b c (2yrs) Astronef - Woo (Stage Door Johnny)....... (New Turf Bloodstock) 40,000
b g (2yrs) Domynsky - North Pine (Import) (D Murphy) 14,500

102

From Suir View Stud, Ireland
b c (2yrs) Glenstal (USA) - Pepilin (Coquelin (USA))....................... (C.B.A.) 15,500
ch c (2yrs) Mazaad - Amber Goddess (Yellow God)...... (Derby Bloodstock) 5,000
From Tally-Ho Stud, Ireland
b g (2yrs) Shy Groom (USA) - Launch The Raft (Home Guard (USA))............ (T Thomson Jones) 7,000
b f (2yrs) Dominion - Mary Mary Mouse (USA) (Valdez (USA))........ (P Doyle) 1,500
From Corner House Stables
ch f (2yrs) Fools Holme (USA) - Medicosma (USA) (The Minstrel (CAN)) .... (D Elsworth) 20,000
From Yeomanstown Stud, Ireland
ch c (2yrs) Common Grounds - Fresh As A Daisy (Stanford)......... (R Akehurst) 8,200
Property of Mr J Carr, from West Hall
ch c (2yrs) Efisio - Tentraco Lady (Gay Fandango (USA))............. (C.B.A.) 2,400

103

NEWMARKET
Thursday, April 15th
(Two-year-olds)

From Pinewood Stables
ch c (2yrs) Absalom - Stolon Time (Good Times (ITY))......................... (Cormac McCormack Associates) 11,000
From Broughton Bloodstock
b c (2yrs) Thatching - Battine (USA) (Topsider (USA))....... (Derby Bloodstock) 7,800
From Knocklong Bloodstock Stud, Ireland (Agent)
ch f (2yrs) Al Hareb (USA) - Angel Divine (Ahonoora)..................... (C B A) 8,600
Property of Mr V O'Donnoghue, from Southburgh Manor Stud
b c (2yrs) Derrylin - Sense Of Occasion (Artaius (USA)).... (Derby Bloodstock) 2,000
Property of Mr P Donworth, from Torard Stud, Ireland
ch c (2yrs) Hatim (USA) - Bright Samovar (Wolverlife)............ (Henri Josse) 1,000
ch c (2yrs) Nordance (USA) - Wolviston (Wolverlife).............. (R Akehurst) 10,000
Property of Aramstone Stud Co., from Yew Tree Stables
gr f (2yrs) Nordico (USA) - May Fox (Healaugh Fox)............. (M Chapman) 6,200
Property of Executive Syndicate, from Shadowfax Stables
b c (2yrs) Risk Me (FR) - Madam de Seul (Pas de Seul)............ (E Stanford) 4,600
b f (2yrs) Scottish Reel - Tina's Melody (Tina's Pet)............ (M Campion) 5,200
b c (2yrs) Jareer (USA) - Daring Choice (Daring Display (USA))............. (Johnny McKeever Bloodstock) 6,200

104

Property of Tara Stud, Ireland, from Willoughton Stables
b f (2yrs) Red Sunset - Plum Fool (Silly Season)......... (Derby Bloodstock) 6,200
Property of Mr H T Pickering, from Willoughton Stables
br f (2yrs) Kind Of Hush - Pickwood Sue (Right Boy).............. (M Channon) 5,000
Property of Tara Stud, Ireland, from Willoughton Stables
b f (2yrs) Heraldiste (USA) - Travel (Saritamer (USA))....... (Henri Josse) 1,000
Property of International Thoroughbred Breeders, Inc., from Round Hill Stud, Ireland
ch c (2yrs) Thatching - Bell Tower (Lyphard's Wish (FR))............... (John Ferguson Bloodstock) 13,000
From Round Hill Stud, Ireland
b c (2yrs) Law Society (USA) - Madame Nureyev (USA) (Nureyev (USA))...... (M Heaton-Ellis) 41,000
From Kilminfoyle House Stud, Ireland
b c (2yrs) Nordance (USA) - Shirleys Princess (Sandhurst Prince). . (D A Wilson) 10,500

b c (2yrs) Never So Bold - Purple Fan (Dalsaan)................. (M Francis) 7,400

From Barcham Farm Stables

ch f (2yrs) Primo Dominie - Be My Honey (Bustino)........... (Mrs Sarah Lakin) 5,200

Property of Mr K Taylor, from Barcham Farm Stables

b f (2yrs) Sizzling Melody - Taylors Pet (Tina's Pet)............... (J A Ward) 2,600

Property of Browne Bloodstock Enterprises, from Mocklershill Stables, Ireland

ch c (2yrs) Mulhollande (USA) - Stomata (USA) (Storm Bird (CAN))............ (Browne Bloodstock) 1,000

105

From Tally-Ho Stud, Ireland

b f (2yrs) Waajib - Sister Eucharia (Oats)... (Johnny McKeever Bloodstock) 10,000

gr f (2yrs) Classic Secret (USA) - African Light (Kalaglow)......... (M Campion) 5,400

Property of Mr M Bastard

ch c (2yrs) Persian Heights - Late Sally (Sallust)..................... (C B A) 15,000

From Hanlons Farm

b c (2yrs) Toca Madera - Botswana (African Sky).................. (M Campion) 1,900

From High Farm

b c (2yrs) Sizzling Melody - Detente (Dominion).............. (J Bleasdale) 14,000

b f (2yrs) Kefaah (USA) - Talking Shop (General Assembly (USA)).. (M Spore) 3,000

From Bridgetown House Stables, Ireland

b c (2yrs) Mister Majestic - Judy O'Grady (Whistler).............. (P K Mitchell) 3,600

ch c (2yrs) Doulab (USA) - Sheba's Princess (Ahonoora)................... (B B A) 9,000

b c (2yrs) Somethingfabulous (USA) - Yours Sincerely (USA) (Stalwart (USA)) ...... (Mrs E Butler) 1,100

Property of Elsdon Farms, from Northmore Stud Farm

b c (2yrs) Tate Gallery (USA) - Nancy Drew (Sexton Blake)............. (J Banks) 9,000

b c (2yrs) Tate Gallery (USA) - Parkeen Princess (He Loves Me).. (E Stanford) 16,500

106

From Greenhill Stables, Ireland

ch c (2yrs) Don't Forget Me - Cloven Dancer (USA) (Hurok (USA)).......... (Conti Bloodstock) 4,000

b c (2yrs) Emarati (USA) - Foiled Again (Bold Lad (IRE))........................... (Cormac McCormack Associates) 18,000

b c (2yrs) Waajib - Travel Away (Tachypous) .... (Dominick Mahony (Agent)) 5,000

From Lynn Lodge Stud, Ireland

b c (2yrs) Classic Secret (USA) - Chenya (Beldale Flutter (USA))............... (Derby Bloodstock) 5,400

From Mocklershill Stables, Ireland (Agent)

b f (2yrs) Alzao (USA) - Vivid Impression (Cure The Blues (USA))......... (B B A) 19,500

From Tally-Ho Stud, Ireland

b f (2yrs) Classic Secret (USA) - Wolverhants (Wolver Hollow)......... (Conti Bloodstock) 4,300

From Tally-Ho Stud, Ireland (Agent)

b f (2yrs) Superpower - Western Goddess (Red God).............. (M Channon) 17,000

From Kilminfoyle House Stud, Ireland

b or br c (2yrs) Fools Holme (USA) - Bit Of A Fiddle (Stradavinsky)............... (Derby Bloodstock) 10,000

b c (2yrs) Dancing Dissident (USA) - Yellow Orchid (On Your Mark).... (J Coogan) 5,500

From Hanlons Farm

ch c (2yrs) Reasonable (FR) - Aha Tina (Ahonoora)................... (B B A) 5,400

ch c (2yrs) Roi Danzig (USA) - Blue Shark (Silver Shark)...... (Conti Bloodstock) 9,500

107

Property of Agence La Taupe, from Portlester Stud, Ireland

ch f (2yrs) Al Hareb (USA) - Lady Bettina (Bustino)............ (W H Ponsonby) 17,500

Property of Mr P J Grady, from Tuddenham Green Stables

b c (2yrs) Superlative - Marchinella (Daring March)................. (Henri Josse) 1,000

Property of Mr Matthew Sharkey, from Graham Lodge Stables

b c (2yrs) Nordance (USA) - Shahrazad (Young Emperor)... (Conti Bloodstock) 5,500

ch c (2yrs) Astronef - Whilst (Dalsaan)..... (S E Kettlewell) 3,300

From Broughton Bloodstock

b f (2yrs) Scottish Reel - Pastrana (King Of Spain)..................... (J Banks) 3,000

Property of a Partnership, from Potters Hill Stables

b c (2yrs) Red Sunset - Crimbourne (Mummy's Pet)......... (J Fanshawe) 23,000

From Hanging Hill Stables

b or br c (2yrs) Law Society (USA) - Strine (USA) (Green Dancer (USA)).......... (Panetta Bloodstock) 10,500

Property of Thurston House Stud, from Village Farm Stud

b f (2yrs) Sizzling Melody - Mimram Melody (Music Boy).................. (B B A) 6,200

Property of a Partnership, from Executive Stud

ch f (2yrs) Beveled (USA) - Recent Events (Stanford)............ (M Heaton-Ellis) 6,400

Property of Mr A Aikin, from Moorwoods Farm Stud

b f (2yrs) Primitive Rising (USA) - Northern Venture (St Alphage)....... (D Morris) 1,500

108

KILL (Goffs)

Monday, April 26th

Property of Bar-Ware Enterprises, from Meadowlands Stud

Promising Run (IRE) b f (5yrs) Commanche Run - Unaria (Prince Tenderfoot) ...... (Lisselan Farms Limited) 1,000

From Corloughan Stud (Part Dispersal)

Belle Aura (IRE) b m (5yrs) Taufan (USA) - Annerbelle (FR) (Aureole)............. (Lisselan Farms Limited) 4,000

Property of Mrs Facchino, from Tu Va Stables
Binns (USA) b g (5yrs) Sportin' Life (USA) - Pleased Miss (USA) (What A Pleasure) (Cash) 1,100
Property of Mrs D Hughes, from Osborne Lodge
Rapid Fire (IRE) ch g (5yrs) Good Thyne (USA) - Princess Pixie (Royal Captive).. (Mr Paddy Brennan) 1,050
From Osborne Lodge
Gathering Time ch g (7yrs) Deep Run - Noble Gathering (Artaius)............... (J H Johnson) 8,000
From Forenaughts Stud
Appealing Bubbles b c (4yrs) Last Tycoon - Bubbling (USA) (Stage Door Johnny)... (European Equine Consultants) 6,900
From Rosewell House Stables
Bart Owen br g (8yrs) Belfalas - Ten Again (Raise You Ten)..... (Peter McCarthy) 2,800
Property of Mr J O'Donnell
Danny Frawley b g (6yrs) Pollerton - Merry Proverb (Proverb).. (T Thomson Jones) 15,000
From Mariner Stud
Carlingford Lakes (IRE) ch m (5yrs) Carlingford Castle - Silver Heights (Even Money)............ (T Thomson Jones) 6,200
From Corloughan Stud (Part Dispersal)
Dublin Saga ch m (8yrs) Sagaro - Dublin Express (Tycoon II)........... (Cash) 3,000

109

Property of Mrs E Joyce, from Greenfield Stables
Calogan br g (6yrs) Callernish - Lady Tarsel (Tarqogan)................. (B Smart) 7,000
From Ballyknockan Stables
Major Cut b g (7yrs) Furry Glen - Quetta's Dual (Dual)..................... (Cash) 2,400
Property of Mr Mervyn Wynne
ch g (5yrs) Carlingford Castle - Last Round (Lucky Guy)..................(D Wolf) 1,800
Property of Mr Pat Pickett
gr g (4yrs) Euphemism - Lucy Grey (Lucifer) .... (Cash) 10,000
Property of Mrs Eleanor Lane
b f (4yrs) Supreme Leader - Flying Early (Ballycipctic)...................... (Cash) 3,000
Property of Gill Browne, from Laurel Lodge Farm
b g (4yrs) Torus - Kinneagh Queen (Le Prince)......................... (Cash) 3,200
From Rockmills Stud
b g (4yrs) Supreme Leader - Nevada Lady (Trimmingham)....... (Thomas Nagle) 3,200
Property of Mr Noel O'Brien
br g (4yrs) Royal Fountain - Mandy Pop (Mandalus)....... (Mr Paddy Brennan) 1,900
Property of Mr John Lordan
br g (4yrs) Dromod Hill - Mistress Anna (Arapaho)...................... (Cash) 4,000
Property of Mr Con Ryan
gr f (4yrs) Roselier (FR) - Golden Seal (Green Shoon)..... (Mrs Diane Haine) 1,200

110

From Clonfad Stud
ch g (4yrs) Le Moss - Slavesville (Charlottesville Flyer)................. (Cash) 2,400

Property of Mr Thomas Corcoran
b or br g (4yrs) Over The River (FR) - Brown Lightning (Continuation)........(Cash) 7,000
From Corbal-Lis Stud
b g (4yrs) Amazing Bust - Grotto Princess (Pollerton)...................(Cash) 2,300
From Curraheen Stud
b g (4yrs) Sheer Grit - Dooney's Daughter (The Parson)........... (C C Trietline) 3,100
Property of Mr Paddy Powell, from Eagle Lodge
b or br g (4yrs) Sandalay - Duskey Lady (Dusky Boy).......................(Cash) 6,000
From Rathturtin Stud
b f (4yrs) Over The River (FR) - Killegney (Reformed Character)................ (Lisselan Farms Limited) 2,300
From Sunnyhill Stud
ch g (4yrs) Good Thyne (USA) - Lady Cromer (Blakeney) (T Thomson Jones) 5,100
From Ashleigh Stud
b f (4yrs) Paean - Truo's Last (Pry)........ (Mrs Diane Haine) 5,200
From Morganstown Stud
b or br f (4yrs) Mandalus - Taylor's Cross (Paddy's Stream)............. (Cash) 6,800
Property of W M Deacon
b g (4yrs) Mandalus - Alfie's Wish (Three Wishes)...................... (Cash) 8,000

111

Property of H H Aga Khan's Studs S.C., from Gilltown Stud
Afghani (IRE) b g (4yrs) Darshaan - Afkaza (FR) (Labus)........... (Tom Mullins) 8,800
Tifasi (IRE) b g (3yrs) Shardari - Tikrara (USA) (Assert)............... (Cash) 5,200
Ranagar (IRE) b g (3yrs) Shernazar - Rasseema (USA) (Youth)....... (Cash) 10,000
Bisstami (IRE) b g (3yrs) Kahyasi - Blissful Evening (Blakeney)........ (Lisselan Farms Limited) 11,000
Kashabi (IRE) b g (3yrs) Shardari - Kaliala (FR) (Pharly)........ (Michael Browne) 7,200
From Rossenarra Stud
b f (3yrs) Supreme Leader - Little Spinner (Tachypous).. (Lisselan Farms Limited) 2,600
Property of Mrs Ann Eustace
br f (3yrs) Callernish - Side Wink (Quayside) ....(R S Carmichael) 1,750
Property of Mr P Moore
b g (3yrs) Good Thyne (USA) - Meadow Rhapsody (Ragusa)............ (Cash) 6,400
Property of a Partnership, from Brooklands Stud
gr g (3yrs) Roselier (FR) - Dame Sue (Mandamus)...................... (Cash) 5,300
Property of M Byrne M.R.C.V.S., from Cappaneale House Stud
b g (3yrs) Commanche Run - Rally (Relko) (Ignatius Geddis) 6,000

112

Property of Mrs F Quinlan, from Church Farm Stables
ch g (3yrs) Tale Quale - Quality Suite (Prince Hansel)................ (Cash) 2,300

Property of Mr D Fitzpatrick
br g (3yrs) Sandalay - Neasham (Nishapour) (David FitzGerald) 1,550
Property of Mr Maurice O'Brien
b g (3yrs) Ragapan - Tangmalangaloo (Laurence O).......... (Ms. Andrea Etter) 2,000
Property of Mr John Ryan
ch g (3yrs) Remainder Man - Mischievous (Le Mesnil).......... (Michael Quigley) 6,600
From Churchland Stud
City Sue (IRE) b f (3yrs) Simply Great (FR) - La Tante (Bold Lad)............ (Cash) 1,100
Property of Mr P Gahan Jnr
b g (3yrs) Remainder Man - Bettons Rose (Roselier)...................... (Cash) 2,400
From Watree Stud
ch g (2yrs) Meneval (USA) - Sky Road (Skyliner)............ (John P Quinlan) 1,400
From Mount Prague Stables
Kings Lord br g (6yrs) King's Ride - Yankee View (Yankee Gold)...... (Sean Egan) 2,700
Northern Ace b g (7yrs) Shareef Dancer (USA) - Monaco Melody (Tudor Melody)................... (Sean Egan) 1,200
Martial Run ch g (6yrs) Deep Run - Lovenos (Golden Love).................. (Cash) 8,500

113

PRIVATE SALES

From Yerville Stables
Gorteera ch g (7yrs) Hello Gorgeous (USA) - Embustera (Sparkler) (Owen Brennan) 2,500
Property of Mr Denis Boland
Sensei ch g (6yrs) Ovac (ITY) - Sweet Gum (USA) (Gummo)......... (Rod Dukes) 2,700
From Carrignaveen Stud
br m (5yrs) Hardboy - Aerial Orchid (Perspex).................. (S G Griffiths) 3,500
Property of Mr E McCormack
b g (4yrs) Torus - Larry's Glen (Laurence O) (Mrs Diane Haine) 5,000
From Ashleigh Stud
br g (3yrs) Denel (FR) - Palhiri (Pall Mall) ... (Cash) 4,300
Property of Mr M J O'Gorman
b g (3yrs) Stetchworth (USA) - Precinda (Le Prince)................ (Jim Brennan) 2,400

(Index reference 115 follows)

115

ASCOT

Tuesday, May 4th

Property of Mr G W Hackling
Kahhal (IRE) gr m (5yrs) Doulab (USA) - Queen's Counsellor (Kalamoun)....... (Mr Bainford) 1,700
Property of Mrs H J Fullerton
Ivinghoe b g (5yrs) Taufan (USA) - Upper Sister (Upper Case (USA)) (Toni Johns) 1,100

Property of Under Orders Racing Syndicate
Sunset Street (IRE) b g (5yrs) Bellypha - Sunset Reef (Mill Reef (USA)) .... (A L Forbes) 1,550
Property of Mr G R Rickman
Aunt Ada ch f (4yrs) Adonijah - Balidilemma (Balidar).............. (Richard Rowe) 750
Property of Mr D Burchell
Argakios b g (6yrs) Busted - Salamina (Welsh Pageant)......... (D M Lloyd) 2,100
Property of Kennet House Stables Ltd
Triple Salko (IRE) br f (3yrs) Tender King - Isolin (Saulingo) .... (Sagittarius Bloodstock) 1,350
Property of Mr Felix Rosenstiels
Venture Prints b g (3yrs) Presidium - Bar Gold (Lucky Brief)......... (S M Cole) 800
Property of a Partnership
Meritre (IRE) ch f (3yrs) Thatching - Dance Of The Nile (Quiet Fling) .... (Sagittarius Bloodstock) 1,650
Property of Mr T G Mills
Al Shany ch m (7yrs) Burslem - Paradise Regained (North Stoke) .... (Johnny McKeever Bloodstock (Ireland)) 1,050
Property of a Partnership
Society Lover (USA) b f (3yrs) Imp Society (USA) - Looks Ten (USA) (Raja Baba) .. (Sagittarius Bloodstock) 1,150
Predestine b g (8yrs) Bold Owl - Combe Grove Lady (Simbir)..... (Mr A Jones) 1,000

116

Property of Stetchworth Park Stud Limited
Maiden Effort br f (2yrs) North Briton - Happy Pollyanna (Caerleon (USA)) ..... (Mr Bainford) 1,000
Mrs Nice Guy b f (3yrs) Hadeer - Way To Go (Troy)..... (Sagittarius Bloodstock) 1,500
Victorian Flower b f (3yrs) Tate Gallery (USA) - Sir Ivor's Sorrow (USA) (Sir Ivor) .... (Johnny McKeever Bloodstock (Ireland)) 1,650
From Woodway Stables
Mr Geneaology (USA) b c (3yrs) Procida (USA) - Que Mona (USA) (Ribot) ...... (John White) 4,100
Property of Woodland Stables
Pass The Key (IRE) b g (4yrs) Treasure Kay - Piney Pass (Persian Bold)...... (Cash) 1,000
To Dissolve a Partnership
First Heiress (IRE) br f (4yrs) Last Tycoon - Age Of Elegance (Troy) .... (Johnny McKeever Bloodstock (Ireland)) 8,600
Property of a Gentleman
Minute Repeater b g (3yrs) Lead On Time (USA) - Gold Maid (FR) (Green Dancer (USA))............. (Mrs M George) 1,300
From West Ilsley Stables
Shirley's Train (USA) b g (4yrs) Malinowski (USA) - Tiger Trap (USA) (Al Hattab (USA)).................. (P J Hobbs) 9,700
Property of Cross-Lorraine Ltd
Bid For Six (USA) b g (4yrs) Saratoga Six (USA) - Savage Bunny (USA) (Never Bend).................. (C Popham) 900

To Dissolve a Partnership (Owing to death of a partner)
Procyon gr g (3yrs) Kalaglow - Sea Fret (Habat)..................... (G West) 1,400

117

To Dissolve a Partnership
Telephonic (USA) b g (3yrs) Phone Trick (USA) - Sound Of Summer (USA) (Drone).................... (A Shetta) 3,000
Property of a Partnership
Serious Action b g (4yrs) Slip Anchor - Silly Woman (Silly Season).......... (Cash) 5,000
Property of Mrs W Tulloch
Kimbers (IRE) b g (5yrs) Lomond (USA) - Take Your Mark (USA) (Round Table) .. (G A Wareham) 2,400
Property of Mr D H Barons
Forward March (NZ) b g (11yrs) March Legend (NZ) - Naughty Marie (NZ) (Wandering Eyes)................ (Cash) 1,000
From Mostyn Hall
Rhewl b g (5yrs) Rymer - Skipton Bridge (Harwell)................. (C Popham) 1,100
From Fowlers Farm Racing Stables
Glen Parish b m (8yrs) Furry Glen - Priestcroft Star (Saintly Song) (J Halford) 1,600
To Dissolve a Partnership, from Teal House Stables
Rushalong ch g (3yrs) Rousillon (USA) - Mosquetade (Moulton)...... (Pat Daly) 6,000
To Settle a Dispute
(IRE) ch c (2yrs) Salt Dome (USA) - Winter Harvest (Grundy)...... (Richard Fahey) 7,000
Property of Miss K George
Spring Forward b h (9yrs) Double Form - Forward Princess (Forward Pass (USA)) .... (B Pearce) 1,200
Property of Mr G Wiltshire
Padiord ch g (6yrs) Caerleon (USA) - Osmunda (Mill Reef (USA))..... (Cash) 1,400
Anderson Rose b m (5yrs) Kind Of Hush - Fille de Bourdon (Ile de Bourbon (USA)) .... (P V Jackson) 1,100

118

Property of The Viscount Chelsea, from Village Farm Stud
Short Leave b g (4yrs) Homeboy - Trysting Day (Black Tarquin)........... (D Taylor) 2,200
Property of Techprint Lettering Systems Ltd
Caspian Prince b g (7yrs) The Brianstan - Bouboulina (Hornbeam) (Martin Black) 1,400
To Dissolve a Partnership
Al Hashimi b g (9yrs) Ile de Bourbon (USA) - Parmesh (Home Guard (USA)) .... (Major A Pearn) 4,400
Property of Mr J W Buxton
The Last Washer (IRE) b g (4yrs) Mazaad - Gigo Jive (Jukebox). .. (Gavin Jackson) 1,300
From Heads Farms Stables
Waldorf T Beagle b g (7yrs) Buckskin (FR) - Arctic Alice (Brave Invader) .... (S A Bowen) 1,050
Property of Eurolink Group PLC
Wave Breaker ch g (6yrs) Enchantment - Nelski (Skymaster)............ (Cash) 1,950

Property of Mr N E C Sherwood
Elmo b m (7yrs) Sunyboy - Elmolyn (St Elmo)......................... (Cash) 1,400
Property of Mr H R Hobson
Doreen's Rhapsody gr m (6yrs) Zambrano - Doreen's Darling (Bilsborrow).......... (J Francis) 1,800
Property of Mrs D Todd
Man Of The West b g (10yrs) Mandalus - Belle Of The West (Royal Buck)....... (James Cooper) 1,450
Property of Lord Cadogan
North Bannister br g (6yrs) Baron Blakeney - Freuchie (Vulgan)..... (David Turner) 2,800

119

Property of Mrs C A Trendell
Shares Of Gold ch f (4yrs) Ore - No Sharing (Young Generation) (Jane Richardson) 1,650
Property of Mrs C Hake
Riverside Moss (IRE) ch g (5yrs) Le Moss - Arctic Chatter (Le Bavard) .... (D C Mason) 1,500
Property of Mrs T North
The Tansey Man ch g (7yrs) Millfontaine - Kindle (Firestreak)........ (C J Austin) 1,750
Property of a Lady
Always Talking b g (12yrs) Bishop Of Orange - Brogeen Lass (Bright As Gold) .... (Cash) 1,000
To Dissolve a Partnership
Toomuch Toosoon (IRE) b g (5yrs) Glenstal (USA) - Star Of India (General Assembly (USA))...... (Jacqueline S Doyle) 1,500
Property of Order of the Sheriff of Gloucestershire
Framlington Court gr h (10yrs) High Top - Princess Runnymede (Runnymede).... (Cash) 1,400
Arraguanie gr h (7yrs) Tolomeo - Princess Runnymede (Runnymede)............ (Kevin Morgan) 3,800
Property of a Lady
Miss Fitness ch f (3yrs) Hallgate - Lady Woodpecker (Tap On Wood).......... (Mrs H Crocker) 975
From West Hill Stables
Crystal Heights ch g (7yrs) Wolver Heights - Crystal's Solo (USA) (Crystal Water (USA)).................... (D Wintle) 1,500
Property of Mr O M C Sherwood
Royal Fool b g (7yrs) Idot's Delight - Royal Celandine (Royal Palace) (Mr Sullivan) 900

120

Property of a Partnership
Mint Master ch g (8yrs) Deep Run - Bold Penny (Beau Chapeau). . (Mrs B Shaw) 2,100
To Dissolve a Partnership
b g (4yrs) Skyliner - Shy Talk (Sharpen Up) (Fiona Lascelles) 1,800
Chinaman b g (4yrs) Noalto - Diorina (Manacle)..................... (W Wightman) 4,800
Property of South Hatch Stables
Sharptino ch c (4yrs) Bustino - Sharper Still (Sharpen Up)................. (Cash) 4,000

Lazy Rhythm (USA) gr g (7yrs) Drone (USA) - Ritual Dance (Godswalk (USA)) ...... (C Hirst) 1,650

Property of Mr R E Morris Adams

Forest Rain b g (10yrs) Paico - Super Money Fan (Super Slip).... (J T Evans) 1,500

To Dissolve a Partnership, from Brightling Park Stables

Breakfast Belle b m (8yrs) Oats - Beau Wonder (Veiled Wonder) .... (Barrie Emerson) 1,350

Property of Mr D Cross

Crossland Leisure b g (8yrs) Torus - Kathleen Beag (Vulgan).. (Euro Horse) 1,300

Property of Mr L Warner

Clonmacogue br g (12yrs) Mandalus - Elusive Dream (Majority Blue) (C J Austin) 750

Emerald Hill br g (8yrs) Wolverlife - Emmerdale (Star Gazer)..... (Mrs L Williams) 1,000

121

To Dissolve a Partnership

Bustonian br g (7yrs) Bustineto - Andonian (Road House II)............ (G K Pink) 2,100

Property of Mr Noel Sweeney

Ferdia (IRE) b c (4yrs) Petorius - Kilvarnet (Furry Glen)................ (J White) 3,400

Property of Lt Col. Sir James Scott

b g (4yrs) Sunley Builds - Warm Up (Hot Brandy).................... (Mr Flint) 2,600

Property of a Lady

Lady Connora b m (7yrs) Connaught - Cousin Nora (Comedy Star).. (J Fraser) 2,000

Property of a Gentleman

Bryansbi b m (9yrs) Golden Passenger - Psidium's Gal (Psidium)... (Sally Lock) 1,000

Capulet b g (10yrs) Henbit (USA) - Lady Juliet (USA) (Gallant Man) .... (Miss L Jones) 1,000

Property of Mr I R Jones

Tonkawa b g (8yrs) Indian King (USA) - Lady Tycoon (No Mercy)............ (Cash) 1,100

Property of Mr L A Snook

Ganoon (USA) ch g (10yrs) Northern Baby (CAN) - Tropical Island (USA) (Raise A Native)................. (C Neneden) 1,050

Property of a Lady

Connaught Cleaners b g (13yrs) Raise You Ten - Bramble Rose (Pals Passage).... (C Neneden) 1,500

Property of Mr A Jessop

Topglow gr g (9yrs) Kalaglow - Lady Gaylass (USA) (Sir Gaylord) .... (Mr Kingdon) 1,150

Jeff Harris b g (9yrs) Tap On Wood - Lady Pamela (Don (ITY))........ (R F Drake) 950

122

Property of The Barnoldby Stud

b f (4yrs) Marching On - What A Popsi (Sagaro)..................... (E Finch) 1,200

Property of Mr George Kidd

Cumbrian Cavalier b g (4yrs) Mansingh (USA) - Lilac Star (Hard Man) .... (J Hurvey) 975

High Mariner ch m (7yrs) Julio Mariner - High Lee (Will Hays (USA)) .... (Mr Bainford) 825

Property of Mrs P Powell

Easy Purchase br g (6yrs) Swing Easy (USA) - Dauphiness (Supreme Sovereign).............. (Kimber Brown) 1,000

Property of Whinholme Stables

Jump gr g (8yrs) General Ironside - Maroon Well (W.Rambler Or Pr.Hansel) .... (C J Austin) 1,600

Property of Mr Paul Waldron

Aldavera ch g (4yrs) Executive Man - Springle (Le Johnstan)... (Mrs Wilson) 1,400

Property of Mr Jerry Widdows

Symmetrical ch c (4yrs) Kris - Flawless Image (USA) (The Minstrel (CAN))..... (A R Aylett) 1,750

Property of Mrs I Abrahams

Ben ch g (7yrs) Seymour Hicks (FR) - Kirin (Tyrant)........... (Miss J Newnham) 825

123

MALVERN
(Russell, Baldwin & Bright)
Thursday, May 6th

Property of Mr R K Sealey

Super Jules (FR) ch g (8yrs) Trio (FR) - Silver Plate (FR) (Son Of Silver) .... (L Wheeler) 1,500

Property of Miss E Duggleby

Tribal Silk gr g (8yrs) Balliol - Ramas Silk (Amber Rama)........... (Mr Kinnear) 1,850

Property of Mr D R Thomas, from The Stud, Laleston

Tell's Tower b m (7yrs) Dunbeath (USA) - Gallatin Valley (USA) (Apalachee (USA)) (Ruth Wollerton) 1,800

Property of Ms. Sarah Ward

Lady Zipper br m (8yrs) Brtianston Zipper - Fortway (Salmonway Spirit).. (J Carter) 1,000

Property of Mr C I Crosthwaite

Mareth Line ch g (10yrs) Royal Palace - Oceania (Aureole)..... (Mr Buchanan) 1,000

Property of Mr T H Lownes, from York Hill Stud

Creggs Boy ch g (9yrs) Buckskin (FR) - My Halo (Be Friendly)............ (R Pike) 1,600

Property of Mrs J Abbot

Fog Light b m (6yrs) Lighter - Mistyacre (Linacre)............... (D Stephens) 850

Property of Mr D A Smith

Gem's Sword b m (8yrs) Broadsword (USA) - Dolben Gem (Mandamus)......... (Mr Nosworthy) 1,450

Property of Mrs C M Brown

Corn Exchange b g (5yrs) Oats - Travellers Cheque (Kibenka)........ (Mr Wellan) 1,000

Property of Hope End Securities Ltd., from hope End Stables

Gen-Tech br g (6yrs) Star Appeal - Targa (GER) (Stani)......... (Dick Chapman) 3,600

124

Property of Mr A Bunn

Kintaro b g (5yrs) Glint Of Gold - Tzarina (USA) (Gallant Romeo (USA)) .... (Sirrell Griffiths) 5,300

Property of Mr J Quigley
Sparkling Shore b g (7yrs) Sparkling Boy - Spring Secret (USA) (Hillary (USA)) .... (K Lewis) 1,300
Property of Mrs J O'Callaghan, from Forest Lodge Stables
Taisie Touch gr g (6yrs) Baron Blakeney - Solhoon (Tycoon II)........ (W Butler) 3,300
Property of Mr R G Russell
Current Attraction b m (7yrs) Paddy's Stream - Chorabelle (Choral Society)... (R Hand) 1,500
Property of Mr J Bowen, from Harewell House Stud
Welsh Clover b m (5yrs) Cruise Missile - National Clover (National Trust) .... (Michael Ings) 4,600
Property of Mr N Connaughton, from Galgystown Stud
Fuzzy Logic (IRE) b g (5yrs) Buckskin (FR) - Sister Cecelia (Trombone) .... (Paul Webber C B A) 9,200
Property of Bacton Stud, from Bacton Stud
ch y f Bairn (USA) - Mylotta (Hotfoot)...... (D Jones) 800
b y c Presidium - Light de Light (USA) (Flurescent Light (USA))........ (Cash) 1,600
b y f Presidium - Francis Furness (Burslem) (Mrs V Allen) 800
b f (2yrs) Presidium - Tell'em Nowt (Anax) (B Temple) 800
ch f (2yrs) Presidium - Miss Skindles (Taufan (USA))............ (M & O Lloyd) 950

125

Property of Middle Hill Farmn and Stud, from Middle Hill Farm and Stud
b y c Bold Fox - Royal Wren (Blast) .... (D Powell) 800
b f (2yrs) Bold Owl - Royal Wren (Blast) ... (A Brewer) 850
Property of Mrs L M Tong, from Butt Oak Farm
ch y f Hasty Word - Knocksharry (Palm Track)..................... (A Bruner) 500
Property of Mrs C W Middleton
b y c Ikdam - Wayward Kate (Cornuto) ..... (Cash) 1,050
Property of Mrs Annabelle Meller, from Leese Hill Stables
b g (2yrs) Alleging (USA) - Miss Monte Carlo (Reform).............. (K White) 2,300
Property of Mr M T Bicknell
b f (2yrs) Gabitat - Springs To Mind (Miami Springs)...................... (N Smith) 1,250
Property of Mr G E Amey, from The Bridge Stud
br f (3yrs) Idiot's Delight - Tropical Swing (Swing Easy (USA))....... (Mrs Briers-Morton) 1,400
ch c (3yrs) Gunner B - Craftsmans Made (Jimsun)................ (Mr Bromley) 3,500
b c (3yrs) Pragmatic - Craftsmans Oats (Oats)..................... (D Gandolfo) 2,500
Property of Mrs B K Johnson, from Bog Hall
ch g (3yrs) Clearly Bust - Cobra Queen (Dawn Review).......... (Mr Johnson) 1,400

126

Property of The Exors of Mr T F M Corrie, from Leightoin Hall Stud
br g (3yrs) Reesh - Wigeon (Divine Gift) .... (R Watkins & Son) 1,500
Property of Mr and Mrs A R Dimmock, from Moor Cottage
ch g (3yrs) Kabour - Penny Pink (Spartan General).............. (Mrs T Spilman) 3,000
Property of Mrs E N Wilson, from Pool Farm
ch g (3yrs) Arkan - Classic Page (London Gazette)..................... (A Stirk) 1,800
From Woodleigh Stud
b g (4yrs) Don't Forget Me - Sweet Eliane (Birdbrook)..... (Mrs Addington-Smith) 3,000
Property of Mr R W Stephenson, from Middle Farm
Poly Trout b m (5yrs) Politico (USA) - Elf Trout (Elf-Arrow)............ (J Carter) 1,800
Property of R & G Berry, from Glebe Farm
b g (3yrs) Pragmatic - Rosa Ruler (Gambling Debt).................... (Mr Allsop) 5,800
Property of Mrs J Redvers, from Tweenhills Farm
No Show (IRE) ch g (3yrs) Shy Groom (USA) - Captive Audience (Bold Lad (IRE))........................ (Cash) 2,000
Property of Mr David J Redvers, from Tweenhills Farm
b g (3yrs) Faustus (USA) - Tin Tessa (Martinmas).................... (K Lewis) 2,300
Property of Messrs. P and D James, from Aston Court Farm
gr g (4yrs) Belfort (FR) - Caique (Ballad Rock).................. (Mrs J Slough) 1,800
bl or br g (3yrs) Roselier (FR) - Clodagh Lady (Boreen (FR))..... (Hilary Parrott) 8,000

127

From White Lodge Farm Stud
b f (3yrs) Saxon Farm - Menel Arctic (Menelek)..................... (J Hoskins) 3,000
Property of Mrs Gill Jones, from Whitefield Court
br f (4yrs) Callernish - Rose Money (Roselier (FR))............... (Mr Trietline) 2,100
Property of Mr S Biddlecombe, from Lower House Farm
Roll-A-Dance b g (4yrs) Mashhor Dancer (USA) - Sandi's Gold (Godswalk (USA)) (Nigel Smith) 2,200
Property of Mr J F F White
b f (4yrs) Town And Country - Hot 'n Scopey (Hot Brandy)..... (D Gandolfo) 1,700
ch m (5yrs) New Member - Spiritus Miss (Master Spiritus).......... (R Buckler) 4,000
Property of Mr T J Houlbrooke, from Bickerton Court Stables
Roman Bride ch f (4yrs) Roman Warrior - Amber Palace (Sallust) .... (Mrs P Aldersey) 2,700
Property of Mr Charles Cope
b g (4yrs) Buzzards Bay - Mizpah (Lochnager).............. (A Brewer) 2,300
Property of Mrs R Todaro-Bowen
br g (4yrs) War Hero - Lansdowne Lady (Orange Bay)............. (D Hughes) 4,000

Property of Mr Richard Evans, from Oxstalls Farm

b g (4yrs) Kaytu - Charlotte Mary (Lauso) .. (Paul Webber) 4,000

Property of Mr A W Jenkinson & Mr J Norris

Fifth In Line (IRE) b g (5yrs) The Parson - Money Spinner (Even Money) .... (Tom George) 9,500

128

Property of Mr J Bowen, from Hardwicke Court Stud

b f (2yrs) Escapism (USA) - Come On Clover (Oats)............ (J Bannister) 1,700

Property of Mr J Bowen, from Batch Farm

Miss Clare b m (5yrs) Cruise Missile - Claredel (Saucy Kit)......... (D Jones) 1,200

Property of Mr J Bowen

b g (3yrs) Rolfe (USA) - National Clover (National Trust)............ (V Gethin) 4,600

b g (4yrs) Celtic Cone - National Clover (National Trust)............. (K Lewis) 4,000

Property of a Lady, from Berkeley House Stables

Primrose Reppin ch f (4yrs) Ra Nova - Laura Reppin (Jimmy Reppin).... (J Marriott) 2,200

Property of Mr James Fenlon, from New House Farm

ch f (4yrs) True Song - Seeker's Sister (Ashmore (FR))............. (N Jones) 2,100

Property of A E Hughes Esq., from The Rock Stables

ch m (5yrs) Soldier Rose - Wicked Pansy (Marine Corps)... (H Howard-Chappell) 950

Property of Mr J P R Deans, from Ingleston Farm

b f (4yrs) Seymour Hicks (FR) - Easterly Gael (Tudor Music)...... (Nigel Smith) 1,500

Property of Mrs C M Brown

b f (4yrs) Oats - Song Of Grace (Articulate) (Cash) 1,900

Property of Mrs J Dunn and Mr & Mrs E Hemmings, from Haylane Farm

Model Mill b g (3yrs) Latest Model - Moore Mill (Majestic Maharaj).. (D Stephens) 1,700

129

Property of Mr J Bowen, from Hardwicke Court Stud

National Clover b m (18yrs) National Trust - Clover Bud (Phebus) Covered by Scottish Reel.............. (Michael Ings) 4,000

Property of Bacton Stud, from Bacton Stud

Border Mouse br m (21yrs) Border Chief - Dunedela (Dumbarnie) sold with bay colt by PRESIDIUM at foot..... (Cash) 1,400

Light de Light (USA) b m (11yrs) Fluorescent Light (USA) - Fastnet Light (CAN) (Connaught) sold in foal to PRESIDIUM .... (D Duxbury) 1,300

Property of Mr D N Carey, from Golf View Stables

And Me ch f (4yrs) Don't Forget Me - Nicola Wynn (Nicholas Bill) (D Tucker) 1,900

Property of Mrs A J Calvert, from Basford Stud

b g (2yrs) Lighter - Precious Sue (Malicious) .... (Mr Snell) 2,600

Property of Mr T J Parrott

Chatanooga Choochoo b g (10yrs) London Gazette - Pet Jackdaw (Vulgan) (Cash) 2,900

Capeli Cone b g (11yrs) Celtic Cone - Capelena (Mon Fetiche) (D Stephens) 1,000

From Creevy Lodge Stables

Course Sweeper ch g (6yrs) Rare One - Olympic Course (Crash Course)....... (Miss Y Coleman) 1,000

Property of Mr Bill Woodward, from Butt Oak Farm

Mighty Chance b g (8yrs) Furry Glen - Cant Pet (Cantab)................. (J King) 1,600

130

CRAWLEAS
(Doncaster Bloodstock Sales)
Monday, May 10th

Property of The Partnership "W A Stephenson & Son"

b g (4yrs) Callernish - Just Reward (Choral Society).................. (O Cooper) 4,800

Luger b g (5yrs) Farhaan - Divine Wonder (Divine Gift)....... (W S Cunningham) 2,600

Green Sheen ch g (5yrs) Green Shoon - Hill Sixtyh (Slippered)......... (E Fenwick) 2,000

Property of Mr J Wade

Cock-A-Doodle-Do b g (7yrs) Petorius - Bertida (Porto Bello)............ (K Clark) 750

Property of The Partnership "W A Stephenson & Son" & Mr P Piller

Military Secret ch g (7yrs) Tug Of War - Leeann (Pitpan).......... (G Moscrop) 3,200

Property of The Partnership "W A Stephenson & Son"

Golden Banker ch g (5yrs) Sandalay - Stylistic (Bargello)............... (J Wade) 5,400

Forest Feather b g (5yrs) Arapahos (FR) - Mistress Boreen (Boreen) (C Weedon) 12,000

Scottish Laird b g (6yrs) Callernish - Serene River (Over The River) .... (Mrs A B Earton) 5,000

Engaging b g (6yrs) Black Minstrel - Ko Mear (Giolla Mear)....... (A J Lappin) 2,000

b g (4yrs) Dromod Hill - Red Gimmy Vii (Believed To Be Out Of) Glentoran Valley...................... (J McGrath) 3,100

Mr Royal b g (7yrs) Royal Match - Bel Ria (Gay Fandango)........ (M Hammond) 14,000

131

Property of The Partnership "W A Stephenson & Son" & Mr J Wilson Walker

Stepfaster gr m (8yrs) Step Together (USA) - Pollyfaster (Polyfoto)...... (N Tinkler) 10,500

Property of The Partnership "W A Stephenson & Son"

Ghost Dancer ch g (8yrs) Rontino - Bartlemy Fair (Town Crier)....... (B Lee) 1,800

Property of Mr P McDonagh

Canbrack b g (4yrs) Glenstal (USA) - Cottage Style (Thatch)......... (R Stone) 2,200

Property of The Partnership "W A Stephenson & Son"
Dark Seam b g (6yrs) Miner's Lamp - Dusky Stream (Paddy's Stream)..... (E Price) 2,400
Property of The Morley Stud
b g (4yrs) Silly Prices - Miniature Miss (Move Off)............... (O Brennan) 2,000
Property of The Partnership "W A Stephenson & Son"
Marchwood ch g (6yrs) Black Minstrel - Lisnagrough (Golden Love)..... (Cash) 5,200
Property of The Partnership "W A Stephenson & Son" & Mr P Piller
Well Briefed br g (6yrs) Miner's Lamp - In Brief (Lucky Brief)......... (R Buckler) 4,400
Property of Mr P Piller
Star Mover ch f (4yrs) Move Off - Start Attention (Northfields) (W G M Turner) 1,400
Bad Trade ch g (11yrs) Over The River (FR) - Churchtown Lass (Master Owen)...... (Cash) 3,900
Property of The Partnership "W A Stephenson & Son"
Bandley Beck ch g (7yrs) Over The River (FR) - Ballinarose (Arctic Slave) (Cash) 2,000
See What I Mean ch g (6yrs) Le Bavard (FR) - Proximity (Gulf Pearl) (R Collins) 4,100

132

Property of Mr P Piller
b y f Imperial Fling (USA) - Line Of Reason (High Line)...... (Pro-Am Bloodstock) 6,000
Property of The Partnership "W A Stephenson & Son"
Fenwick b g (6yrs) Magnolia Lad - Isobel's Choice (Green God)........... (Cash) 3,100
Anchor Bay ch g (6yrs) Tug Of War - Leeann (Pitpan)............... (R Tate) 3,000
Father O'Brien b g (6yrs) The Parson - Tanala (Tanavar)..... (Mrs G Hickman) 7,400
Count Surveyor ch g (6yrs) Corawice - Miss Magello (Bargello)....... (G W Turner) 8,000
b g (4yrs) Supreme Leader - Roebuck Lass (Little Buskins)........... (O Brennan) 6,000
Property of Mr C Leader
Royal Mile b g (8yrs) Tyrnavos - Royal Rib (Sovereign Path)........ (F A Jackson) 2,500
Property of The Partnership "W A Stephenson & Son" & Mr P Piller
Chief Raider br g (5yrs) Strong Gale - Lochadoo (Lochnager)....... (J Wade) 18,000
Property of Miss Sue Hunter
Callroe b g (7yrs) Callernish - Coolroe Aga (Laurence O)............... (I Naylor) 2,400
Property of Mr J Wade
Notarius (FR) b g (5yrs) Deep Roots (FR) - Lady Ring (Tachypous)... (A J Barnett) 3,600

133

Property of The Partnership "W A Stephenson & Son"
Grange Chief b g (5yrs) Lafontaine (USA) - Lisaniskey Lady (Varano)...... (C B A) 27,000
Time Piece b g (5yrs) Quayside - Clockonocra (Shall We Dance)......... (N B Mason) 10,000
Glamorous Guy ch g (6yrs) Orchestra - Glamorous Night (Sir Herbert).. (Cash) 3,700
Ariadler b g (5yrs) Mister Lord (USA) - Arianrhod (L'homme Arme).... (Cash) 4,800
Kilcolgan ch g (6yrs) Le Bavard (FR) - Katula (Khalkis)...................... (Cash) 8,200
Celtic Fountain br g (5yrs) Royal Fountain - Celtic Serenity (Proverb).... (R Collins) 4,700
Coming Alive gr g (6yrs) Saher - Misty Light (Bustino)............... (N B Mason) 13,000
Property of The Partnership "W A Stephenson & Son" & Mr P Piller
Forward Glen br g (6yrs) Sexton Blake - Daring Glen (Furry Glen)....... (Cash) 14,500
Johnny's Slipper br g (8yrs) Slippered - Mudinuri (Little Buskins) (N B Mason) 9,000
Property of The Partnership "W A Stephenson & Son"
Parson's Way b g (6yrs) The Parson - Daithis Coleen (Carnival Night)........ (A A King) 6,600
b g (5yrs) Miner's Lamp - Lady Abednego Vii (Said To Be Abednego) (H Johnson) 17,000
Royal Surprise b g (6yrs) Royal Fountain - Miss Craigie (New Brig)..... (J Walby) 4,400
Val de Rama b g (4yrs) Lafontaine (USA) - Port Magee (Royal Highway).......... (Denys Smith) 8,100
Tighter Budget (USA) br g (6yrs) Desert Wind (USA) - Silver Ice (USA) (Icecapade)................... (R Harrop) 4,100
Hurricane Andrew ch g (5yrs) Hawaiian Return (USA) - Viable (Nagami)........ (J A Moore) 3,800
Willy Waffles ch g (5yrs) Orchestra - Gayles Approach (Strong Gale)..... (R Collins) 2,600
Modest Lady gr m (7yrs) Fujiwara - Cullen Castle (Dear Gazelle)......... (A Day) 3,000

134

Property of The Partnership "W A Stephenson & Son" & Mrs A L Brown
Break The Chain br g (8yrs) Callernish - Lovely Daisy (Menelek) .... (Johnnie McKeever Bloodstock) 27,000
Property of The Partnership "W A Stephenson & Son"
Punter's Overhead b g (5yrs) Black Minstrel - Boyne Saint (Saint Crespin III)........ (J N Hutchinson) 7,200
Property of The Partnership "W A Stephenson & Son" & Mr P Cheesbrough
River House ch g (11yrs) Over The River (FR) - Kinsella's Choice (Middle Temple)......................... (J White) 5,000
Property of The Partnership "W A Stephenson & Son"
ch g (4yrs) Good Thyne (USA) - Rather Grand (Will Somers)........... (C B A) 28,000
Property of Mr P Piller
Wrekin Hill b g (11yrs) Duky - Cummin Hill (Wrekin Rambler)............... (J White) 9,000
Property of The Partnership "W A Stephenson & Son"
b g (4yrs) Henbit (USA) - Press Luncheon (Be Friendly)............... (G Richards) 17,000
Irish Gent br g (7yrs) Andretti - Seana Sheo (Seana Sgeal)........... (F T Scotto) 12,500

br g (4yrs) Callernish - Claddagh Pride (Bargello).................... (Cash) 4,200

Property of Mr J Wade

Sweep ch g (6yrs) - .... (The Zetland Hunt) 4,800

Property of The Partnership "W A Stephenson & Son"

b g (5yrs) Kemal (FR) - Mad For Her Beer (Proverb).................... (Cash) 8,700

135

Property of The Partnership "W A Stephenson & Son" & Mr P Piller

Spree Cross b g (7yrs) Kemal (FR) - Danger Lady (Commando)................... (David Minton Bloodstock) 15,000

Property of The Partnership "W A Stephenson & Son"

Lingerawhile ch g (10yrs) London Gazette - Easter Vigil (Arctic Slave)............. (Mrs N C Ordidge) 2,300

b g (5yrs) Royal Fountain - Payne's Lady (Lock Diamond)............ (R Shiels) 3,200

Shy Duck ch g (7yrs) Shy Groom (USA) - Quack Shot (USA) (Quack).. (L Tindale) 1,600

Property of Mr J Wade

Overstep ch g (7yrs) Over The River (FR) - Madam Exbury (Homeric).... (J Wade) 1,600

Property of Miss Gill Richardson & Miss Jean Manners

br g (4yrs) Over The River (FR) - Money Buck (Mast Buck)............ (C B A) 6,600

Property of The Partnership "W A Stephenson & Son"

Fine Argument b g (5yrs) Fine Blade (USA) - Just Had It (No Argument) (E Fenwick) 5,100

b g (6yrs) Anita's Prince - Musical Puss (Orchestra).............. (J R Adams) 6,100

Property of Miss J Turner

Palm Reader b g (9yrs) Palm Track - Carbia (Escart III).. (David Minton Bloodstock) 24,000

Property of The Partnership "W A Stephenson & Son"

If You Say So ch g (7yrs) Say Primula - Vinovia (Ribston)........... (J L Eyre) 6,000

Mary ch m (9yrs) - .... (J Hickman) 4,200

Deep Dawn br g (10yrs) Deep Run - Sharp-away (Royal Highway).. (N Hammond) 6,200

What A Miss ch m (6yrs) Move Off - Vinovia (Ribston)......... (A Jackson) 3,400

George Moss b g (6yrs) Le Moss - Georgette (Neron).................. (Aynsley Ridley Bloodstock) 4,000

b g (5yrs) Miner's Lamp - Down By The River (Over The River).. (M Hammond) 5,000

Over The Tyne b g (7yrs) Over The River (FR) - Drop In (Master Owen)......... (Jayne Webber) 2,100

Majority Major b g (4yrs) Cheval - La Perla (Majority Blue)................ (Cash) 8,800

136

Property of Mr P Pillar

Captain Mor b g (11yrs) Welsh Captain - Oona More (Straight Deal).. (J L Eyre) 5,800

Property of The Partnership "W A Stephenson & Son"

Ben Rhydding ch g (6yrs) Gladden - Raheen Lady (Candy Cane)....... (W T Kemp) 2,000

Property of The Morley Stud

b g (3yrs) Petoski - Palace Tor (Dominion).. (H Atkinson) 4,800

Property of The Partnership "W A Stephenson & Son"

Winning Over ch g (7yrs) Over The River (FR) - Winnie Owen (Master Owen) ... (M J Simon) 1,500

Fool Of Fortune b g (7yrs) Deroulede - Lady Spiraho (Arapaho)...... (J M Shotton) 1,300

br g (5yrs) Kemal (FR) - Lady Girand (Raise You Ten)................... (T Tate) 6,500

Daring Walk b g (8yrs) Derring Rose - Shuil Comeragh (Laurence O).............. (R M Whitaker) 2,100

Double Standards br g (5yrs) Entre Nous - Miss Minstrel VI (Beau Tudor) .... (Raymond A Green) 13,000

Property of The Partnership "W A Stephenson & Son" & Mr R Causer

Bishopdale ch g (12yrs) Proverb - Garryduff Lady (Deep Run)........ (S Chadwick) 2,500

Property of The Partnership "W A Stephenson & Son"

Dunster Manor b g (7yrs) Carlingford Castle - Daraheen Gate (Arcticeelagh)........ (S Bacon) 1,800

137

Property of Mr P Pillar

Ardelle Grey gr m (6yrs) Ardross - Fair Eleanor (Saritamer) Covered by Cyrano de Bergerac (Sold with a f f by Brush Aside at foot).......... (J Hutchinson) 10,000

Star Attention br m (19yrs) Northfields (USA) - Star Relation (Star Gazer) Sold with a ch f foal by Over The River (FR) at foot................. (J Smethurst) 1,500

Property of The Partnership "W A Stephenson & Son"

Award Winner b g (6yrs) Magnolia Lad - Golden Jewel (Aureole).. (H Patterson) 450

Property of Mr P Pillar

Buckra Mellisuga b g (9yrs) Tumble Wind (USA) - Bedouin Dancer (Lorenzaccio) (J Hellens) 3,600

Jaunty Gig b g (7yrs) Dunphy - Hazel Gig (Captain's Gig)........... (K Thomas) 2,600

Property of T P M McDonagh Ltd

Sailor's Delight b g (9yrs) Idiot's Delight - Sarasail (Hitting Away).. (P M Joynes) 5,800

Property of Mr P Piller

ch c (2yrs) Chief Singer - Star Attention (Northfields)..... (Pro-Am Bloodstock) 4,000

Stay On Tracks gr g (11yrs) Roselier (FR) - Bee In Bonnet (Track Spare).. (N King) 13,000

Property of The Partnership "W A Stephenson & Son"

Castle King b g (6yrs) Crash Course - Caherelly Cross (Royal Buck) .... (A O'Dwyer) 62,000

I'm A Miss ch m (7yrs) Le Coq D'Or - Star Attention (Northfields).... (A Jackson) 2,400

138

Property of Mr M Hodgson

Mrs Murphy b m (11yrs) - .... (Mrs L Sutherland) 1,500

Property of The Partnership "W A Stephenson & Son" & Mr P Piller
Spanish Fair b g (5yrs) Spanish Place (USA) - Bonne Fair (Bonne Noel).......... (Sue Bramall) 72,000
Property of The Partnership "W A Stephenson & Son"
Parson's Quest ch g (7yrs) The Parson - Gortroe Queen (Simbir) .... (Miss Y Beckingham) 4,200
Property of The Partnership "W A Stephenson & Son" & Mr P Piller
Over The Deel ch g (7yrs) Over The River (FR) - Cahernane Girl (Bargello)........ (H Johnson) 18,000
Property of The Partnership "W A Stephenson & Son"
b g (4yrs) Balboa - Ditschla (GER) (Le Mas Marvent).................. (R Collins) 3,600
Mallastang b g (5yrs) Kemal (FR) - Eva's Charm (Carlburg) (Pro-Am Bloodstock) 13,000
Property of The Partnership "W A Stephenson & Son" & Mr P Piller
Blazing Walker ch g (9yrs) Imperial Fling (USA) - Princess Kofiyah (High Line) ... (Pro-Am Bloodstock) 40,000
Property of The Partnership "W A Stephenson & Son"
Fox Tower ch g (7yrs) Smooth Stepper - Dangan View (Bargello)... (W T Reed) 2,200
Heddon Haugh br g (5yrs) Seclude (USA) - Miss Kambalda (Kambalda)..... (Cash) 15,500
Property of The Partnership "W A Stephenson & Son" & Mr P Piller
Hurricane Horace br g (6yrs) Strong Gale - Arctic Tack (Arctic Slave).............. (Denys Smith) 52,000

139

Property of The Partnership "W A Stephenson & Son"
Dunmain Buck b g (6yrs) Buckskin (FR) - Dunmain Stream (Paddy's Stream) .... (Aynsley Ridley Bloodstock) 6,200
Property of Mr David R Thornton
The Laughing Lord b g (7yrs) Lord Ha Ha - Celtic Serenity (Proverb).... (N Tinkler) 17,000
Property of The Partnership "W A Stephenson & Son"
Island River ch g (5yrs) Over The River (FR) - Diana's Flyer (Charlottesvilles Flyer) .. (J Goulding) 6,200
Property of The Partnership "W A Stephenson & Son" & Mr P Piller
One Man gr g (5yrs) Remainder Man - Steal On (General Ironside).... (G Richards) 68,000
Property of The Partnership "W A Stephenson & Son"
Prince Rossini br g (5yrs) Roselier (FR) - Auragne (FR) (Crowned Prince) .... (L Lungo) 12,500
Buckwheat Lad br g (5yrs) Over The River (FR) - Buckwheat Lass (Master Buck).. (Cash) 8,200
b g (5yrs) Lafontaine (USA) - Key To The Door (Patch)............ (A J Lapping) 3,800
Property of Mr P Piller
Lynch Law br g (5yrs) Law Society (USA) - Hogan's Sister (USA) (Speak John) .... (F Farrant) 40,000

Property of The Partnership "W A Stephenson & Son"
Tough Deal b g (5yrs) Sheer Grit - Ballyeel (Girandole)................ (P Bradley) 2,500
Property of The Partnership "W A Stephenson & Son" & Mr P Piller
Strong Views b g (6yrs) Remainder Man - Gokatiego (Huntercombe)... (J White) 33,000

140

Property of The Partnership "W A Stephenson & Son"
ch g (7yrs) Carlingford Castle - Sue Bell (Random Shot).......... (E A Elliott) 2,200
Plum Duff ch g (6yrs) Invited (USA) - Blue Lilly (Mon Capitaine)........... (Cash) 5,800
ch g (4yrs) Duky - Rainy Weather (Menelek) .... (J Upson) 3,600
Hidden Island br g (6yrs) Derring Rose - Monavalla (Kabale).. (Miss L Robinson) 3,200
b g (6yrs) Slippered - Nevada Run (Deep Run).................... (A J Lapping) 2,400
b g (5yrs) Over The River (FR) - Queen Menelek (Menelek)...... (A Johnson) 5,900
Bosco's Dance b g (8yrs) Pimpernel's Tune - Kab Rock (Kabale).... (S J Robinson) 2,900
Property of Mr P Piller
Shelton Abbey br g (7yrs) The Parson - Herald Holidolly (New Member)....... (J Hellens) 16,000
Property of The Partnership "W A Stephenson & Son"
br g (4yrs) Dromod Hill - Rossmire (Smartset)...................... (Cash) 2,000
Property of Mr J Wade
Brushford b g (9yrs) Dublin Taxi - Polymart (Polyfoto)............. (Sue Bramall) 2,100
Property of The Partnership "W A Stephenson & Son"
b g (5yrs) King's Ride - Candy Slam (Candy Cane)...................... (C B A) 19,000

141

DONCASTER
Monday, May 17th

Property of Mr R F G Barlow, from Benhams Stud
ch g (4yrs) Sunley Builds - Damascus Star (Mandamus) .... (David Minton Bloodstock) 3,500
b f (4yrs) Sunley Builds - Coin All (All Tan) (Conjem Ltd) 6,600
Property of Mrs L Lloyd, from Shernal Green
Millie Minx bl or br f (4yrs) Macmillion - Chayze (Seaepic)..... (Mrs R Jackson) 2,600
Property of Mr Alan Townend, from Lockwoods Farm
ch f (4yrs) Rabdan - Miss Quay (Quayside) (M Pipe) 3,000
Property of Messrs R P & M Berrow, from Peasebrook Stud
b g (3yrs) Oats - Ruby's Vision (Balinger) .. (N Gaselee) 10,500

From Willoughton Stables

Tortula ch f (4yrs) Good Times (ITY) - Bristle Moss (Brigadier Gerard).... (T Laxton) 1,600

To Dissolve a Partnership, from Watermill Stud

Omar (USA) ch g (4yrs) Lyphard (USA) - Agretta (USA) (Graustark)...... (Cash) 1,800

Property of Mr P N Dyke, from Park Farm Stud

b g (4yrs) King Of Spain - Second Generation (Decoy Boy)........... (K Lewis) 1,750

Property of Mr H M Rees

b g (4yrs) Steady Eddie - Fair Sara (McIndoe).................... (A R Trotter) 1,500

Property of Fulling Mill Stud, from Fulling Mill Stud

b g (3yrs) Destroyer - Fidessa (Fine Blade) (S Moore) 3,000

b g (4yrs) Pitpan - Again Kathleen (Status Seeker)...................... (Cash) 1,000

142

Property of Miss J Scruton & Mr S Stubbings

b g (4yrs) Lochnager - Mountain Child (Mountain Call)........ (M H Easterby) 6,600

Property of Mrs Caroline Berry, from Firth Stud

gr f (4yrs) Nicholas Bill - Abrasive (Absalom) .... (R Fisher) 2,100

Property of Mr C J Drewe, from Lower Cross Farm

b g (4yrs) Reesh - Abalone (Abwah)....... (A Turnell) 10,000

Property of Mr John Hindmarch

Primitive Faith b or gr g (4yrs) Bellypha - Periquito (USA) (Olden Times)........ (F Doumen) 6,800

Property of Mr P Seagrave, from Copeland Stables

b f (4yrs) Pitpan - Dark Trix (Peacock)...... (R Fisher) 2,100

Property of Messrs P & D H Cockcroft, from Goosemoor Stud

b g (3yrs) Uncle Pokey - Young Romance (King's Troop)................ (C B A) 20,000

Property of Kinneston Farmers

b g (4yrs) Le Bavard (FR) - Betty Sue (Menelek).......... (Mrs A J Bowlby) 7,000

Property of a Partnership, from Hutton Stud

b g (4yrs) Burslem - Living Rough (Wolverlife)................... (Cash) 3,000

Property of Mrs M A Hall, from Springfield Farm Stud

Springfield Baron b g (4yrs) Baron Blakeney - Viceroy Lass (Certingo).. (F Ransom) 3,600

Property of a Partnership, from New Close Farm

Fishermans Lodge ch g (4yrs) Nicholas Bill - Emerald Eagle (Sandy Creek)......... (N Callaghan) 5,000

143

From Needwood Stud

ch g (4yrs) Rymer - Arctic Lion (Arctic Slave).................. (S Campbell) 2,700

Property of C J Hutchings Esq, From Tyre Hill Farm

br g (4yrs) Strong Gale - Hester Ann (Proverb)........................ (C B A) 40,000

From Viander Stables, Co. Antrim, Ireland

b f (4yrs) Fidel - Welsh Symphony (Welsh Saint)...................... (K Bailey) 1,200

Property of Mr M McInnes Skinner, from Primrose Farm Stud

b g (4yrs) Idiot's Delight - Casa's Star (Top Star)..................... (K Bailey) 15,000

To Dissolve a Partnership, from Maizey Manor Farm

br g (4yrs) Royal Fountain - Royal See (Konigssee)............. (R T Dennis) 2,300

ch g (3yrs) King Luthier - Urdite (FR) (Concertino)................ (F Doumen) 9,800

b g (3yrs) Strong Gale - Rambling Gold (Little Buskins)........... (M Francis) 22,000

From Lismortagh Stud, Co. Tipperary, Ireland

b g (4yrs) Supreme Leader - Donegal Queen (Quayside).......... (A Kaplin) 13,000

b g (4yrs) Lancastrian - Infanta Helena (Pollerton)...................... (Cash) 2,000

From Ashtown House Stud, Co. Waterford, Ireland

b g (4yrs) Royal Fountain - Rockholm Rosie (Tudor Rocket) .... (David Minton Bloodstock) 15,000

b g (4yrs) Good Thyne (USA) - Callula (Crash Course).............. (M Pipe) 15,000

144

From Rannfields Stud Farm, Co, Down, Ireland

b or br f (4yrs) Supreme Leader - Jayneymoo (Deep Run)......... (B Lusk) 3,000

b f (3yrs) Corvaro (USA) - Our Cherry (Targogan).................... (C B A) 20,000

From Sleedagh Farm Stud, Co, Wexford, Ireland

b g (4yrs) Mandalus - Hurricane Hattie (Strong Gale)................ (J Old) 5,200

ch g (4yrs) Cardinal Flower - Milworth (Stetchworth)........ (M W Easterby) 6,400

From Suir View Stud, Co, Tipperary, Ireland

ch g (4yrs) Henbit (USA) - Hell's Mistress (Skymaster)....... (N Twiston-Davies) 10,000

b g (4yrs) Buckskin (FR) - Lucky House (Pollerton)............ (John McGrath) 2,600

Property of Mr & Mrs James Hales, from Claxby St Andrew

b g (4yrs) The Parson - Swanee Mistress (My Swanee) .... (David Minton Bloodstock) 30,000

b g (3yrs) Mandalus - Miss Cuckoo (Never Slip).................... (J T Doyle) 6,000

Property of Little Lodge Farm

b f (4yrs) Torus - Right Chimes (Even Money)............. (Anthea Farrell) 4,000

b or br g (4yrs) Sunyboy - Scotch Princess (Murrayfield).................. (Cash) 5,000

b f (4yrs) Mandalus - Lucy's Princess (Lucifer).................... (B Lusk) 16,000

145

From Mocklershill Stables, Co. Tipperary, Ireland

Blooming Spring br f (4yrs) Strong Gale - Ask The Boss (Gulf Pearl).... (M Pipe) 4,700

Property of E H Crow & Son, from Hardwicke Stud

b g (4yrs) Supreme Leader - Dishcloth (Fury Royal)................. (G B Balding) 15,000

Property of Mrs T F Rimell
b g (4yrs) Tremblant - Bird's Custard (Birdbrook)..... (David Minton Bloodstock) 7,800
Property of Cobhall Court Stud, from Cobhall Court Stud
b g (4yrs) Buckley - Petal Princess (Floribunda) .... (Cormac McCormack Associates) 20,000
Property of Peter Scudamore Bloodstock Ltd, from Hoarwithy Farm
ch g (4yrs) Relkino - Metaxa (Khalkis)...... (N Twiston-Davies) 12,000
Property of Mr Charles Scott, from Paradise Stables
ch g (4yrs) Le Moss - Moyne Gael (Lord Gayle)................ (M W Easterby) 1,800
Property of Mr Nigel Dunn, from the Woodram Stud
b g (4yrs) Relkino - Royal Snip (Royal Highway)...................... (T Forster) 4,000
From Crohane Stud, Co. Tipperary, Ireland
b g (4yrs) The Parson - Little Credit (Little Buskins).................... (C B A) 17,000
br g (4yrs) Lighter - In My Dreams (Belfalas) .... (K Bailey) 9,000
From Glenpark Stud, Co. Antrim, Ireland
b g (4yrs) Strong Gale - Arctic Verb (Proverb).................. (O Brennan) 10,000

146

From Field House Stud
ch g (4yrs) Scorpio (FR) - Embuscade (Random Shot).......... (Weston Holdings) 16,000
b g (4yrs) Cataldi - Galloping Santa (Santa Claus)...................... (K Bailey) 16,000
Property of Mrs J Willis, from Goldford Stud
br f (4yrs) The Parson - Irish Hill Lass (Prominer).............................. (Travail Employment Group Ltd) 5,000
ch f (4yrs) Orchestra - Rush Lady (Royal And Regal)................ (C Whitely) 4,200
From Goldford Stud
b g (4yrs) Orchestra - Arctic Vista (Deep Run)....... (David Minton Bloodstock) 15,000
b g (4yrs) Miner's Lamp - Vita Veritas (Linacre)...................... (C B A) 22,000
ch g (4yrs) Orchestra - Sapristi (Psidium)... (D McNeilly) 35,000
Property of Alswick Hall Farms Ltd, from Goldford Stud
br g (4yrs) Strong Gale - Stay As You Are (Buckskin)............. (C R Weedon) 8,600
Property of Mrs C Gowing, from Goldford Stud
b g (4yrs) Ardross - Rhein Symphony (Rheingold) (David Minton Bloodstock) 8,800
From Goldford Stud
b g (4yrs) Strong Gale - Lady Rag (Ragapan) .... (A Mullins) 24,000

147

From Camas Park Stud, Co. Tipperary, Ireland
b g (4yrs) Strong Gale - Desert Maid (Proverb)............. (Weston Holdings) 48,000
br g (4yrs) Phardante (FR) - Avransha (Random Shot)................ (N Meade) 15,500
Property of Mr D Whelan, Co. Cork, Ireland
ch g (4yrs) Roselier (FR) - One Way Only (Le Bavard)................. (B Lusk) 8,000
From Queenford Stud Ltd
ch g (4yrs) Le Moss - Kassina (Laurence O) (C T Nash) 8,000
b g (4yrs) Mandalus - Lucy's Pal (Random Shot)...................... (C Brooks) 7,600
Property of Capt Charles Radclyffe
br g (4yrs) King's Ride - Tranquil Love (Ardoon)..................... (M Pipe) 11,000
Property of Fulling Mill Stud, from Fulling Mill Stud
b g (4yrs) Pitpan - Platinum Blond (Warpath) .... (J Chugg) 8,200
From Piers Field Stud, Ireland
b g (4yrs) Rymer - Dear Jem (Dragonara Palace)........... (T Thomson Jones) 8,200
Property of Breener Fabrications Ltd, from Furnace Mill Stud
br f (3yrs) Strong Gale - First Things First (The Parson)................. (C B A) 17,500
From Furnace Mill Stud
b g (4yrs) Mandalus - Foxy Jane (Pollerton) (G B Barlow) 9,900

148

Property of Woodhaven Stud, from Woodhaven Stud
gr f (4yrs) Pragmatic - Achiever (Tarqogan) (J Wade) 1,100
Property of Tyrnog Stud, from Tyrnog Stud
br g (4yrs) Mandalus - Joy Travel (Ete Indien)..................... (P Hobbs) 8,200
Property of Mr S D Hemstock, from Barton Close Stables
b f (4yrs) Idiot's Delight - Pal Alley (Pals Passage).............. (G McDonagh) 1,000
Property of Tythrop Park Stables, from Tythrop Park Stables
ch g (4yrs) Ovac (ITY) - Iamstopped (Furry Glen)..................... (W Clarke) 8,000
b or br g (3yrs) Roselier (FR) - Woodville Grove (Harwell)............. (J Adam) 9,200
Property of Mrs G B Fairbairn, from Hallington Hall
gr g (3yrs) Alias Smith (USA) - Straight Sonnet (Boston Two Step).. (M Hogg) 3,800
Property of Mrs Elizabeth J Deans, from Ingleston Farm
b or br g (4yrs) Sonnen Gold - Inglebrig (New Brig).............. (Ann Robson) 2,600
Property of Miss Jenny Seaborn
ch g (3yrs) Jester - Raise The Dawn (Rymer)........................ (J Old) 2,800
Property of Mr Patrick Fitzherbert, Co, Waterford, Ireland
gr g (5yrs) Sandalay - Fort Etna (Be Friendly) .... (John White) 6,000
Property of Miss Sandra Hamilton, from Ballylee Stables, Co. Antrim, Ireland
b g (4yrs) Black Minstrel - Collective (Pragmatic)................... (C Trietline) 4,400

149

From Killyfaddy Stables, Co. Londonderry, Ireland
Jarlmar br g (6yrs) Callernish - Billie Gibb (Cavo Doro)............. (O Brennan) 3,600

From High House Farm
b g (5yrs) Strong Gale - Ballyreidy Star (Mon Capitaine)................... (Cash) 6,400
Property of Miss S Reed
gr g (4yrs) Superlative - Caraquenga (USA) (Cyane).......... (Mrs Pauline Argyle) 2,200
Property of Mr F D A Snowden
Pardibarle b g (5yrs) Pardigras - Money Penny (Even Money).. (Miss C Tabbs) 1,700
Property of Mrs Lucy Jebb
b g (5yrs) King Of Spain - Wayleave (Blakeney)............... (G H Dook) 3,000
PRIVATE SALES
From Fifehead Farms
ch g (4yrs) Oats - Le Tequila (Lear Jet) .... (J Campbell) 3,000
Property of Miss H Day, from Pyleigh Court Farm
b g (4yrs) Idiot's Delight - Waterside (Shackleton)............. (O Brennan) 7,000
From Glenville House, Co. Wexford, Ireland
ch g (4yrs) Orange Reef - Miss Hganavak (Abednego)................ (S Moore) 1,500
gr g (3yrs) Sandalay - Nesford (Walshford) (D Barry) 2,000
From Suir View Stud, Co. Tipperary, Ireland
b g (4yrs) Buckskin (FR) - Lucky House (Pollerton).............. (W A Crozier) 2,200
Property of Mr & Mrs James Hales, from Claxby St Andrews
b g (4yrs) Orchestra - Brave Polly (Brave Invader).................. (O Brennan) 15,000
Property of Mr & Mrs Edward Hide, from Huttons Ambo Stud
br f (4yrs) Lochnager - Fountain (Reform) .. (T Laxton) 3,000

RE-SUBMITTED

Property of Mr John Hindmarsh
Babarani ch f (4yrs) Bold Arrangement - Lasani (FR) (Appiani II)......... (Cash) 1,600

150

DONCASTER
Tuesday, May 18th

Property of Mrs A Wilkinson
Shudyman b g (4yrs) Mansingh (USA) - Funny-Do (Derring-Do)......... (Cash) 1,200
Property of Mr P D Purdy
Fiery Perdita b m (5yrs) Sula Bula - Wayward Cottage (Cornuto) .... (T Cunningham) 1,050
Property of Miss H Mitchell
Mr Bumpy b g (7yrs) Bay Express - Balidium (Psidium)............ (R Waind) 1,850
Property of Mr N Stewart
b f (3yrs) Waajib - Careless Whisper (USA) (Broadway Forli)............. (C.B.A.) 3,200
Property of Miss P Edgar
br f (4yrs) Majestic Streak - Hansel's Meadow Vii (Hansel's Nephew)....... (Mrs S Cuthbert) 2,300
Property of Mr R Hancox, from Goodrest Lodge Stables
Chuck The Brief b g (8yrs) Legal Eagle - Golden Amaryllis (Klondyke Bill)....... (Mrs A Webb) 900

Property of Mr P and B Stonehouse, from Hedley North Farm Stables
Hed Nor Tail ch g (5yrs) Import - Expressly Yours (Bay Express).... (J R Winfield) 1,900
Property of Mr T Tayler, from Racecourse Farm Stables
Gaye Rosie gr f (3yrs) Faustus (USA) - Wild Rosie (Warpath)........ (Mrs R Slack) 1,600
Property of Semi-Chem Bargain Centres, from Little Stanneylands Stables
Lavender Glen b c (4yrs) Glenstal (USA) - Lady Aladdin (Persian Bold)........... (Mrs A Walley) 1,200
Property of Mrs R Ball
Dictate (FR) ch g (4yrs) Fast Topaze - First Appeal (Star Appeal)................ (Miss Lorna McGowan) 1,700

151

Property of Capt B E Fanshawe
ch g (6yrs) True Song - Ginger Fury (Fury Royal)................... (J D Hind) 2,800
Property of The Exors of the late Major V McCalmont, Co Kilkenny, Ireland
Lion Rock ch g (5yrs) Quayside - Magar's Pride (No Time)............... (C.B.A.) 5,600
Property of Ulceby Farms Ltd, from Ulceby Vale Stud
ch g (5yrs) Nicholas Bill - Halmsgiving (Free State)..................... (J Curtis) 5,400
To Dissolve A Partnership, from Upper Coombe Farm
Leeming b g (5yrs) Scallywag - Silverstone (Derrylin).................. (B Lusk) 9,000
Property of Mr J Berry, from Moss Side Racing Stables
b g (3yrs) Today And Tomorrow - Rhythm Maker (Song)............. (J L Harris) 2,000
Property of Mrs R F Johnson Houghton, from Woodway Stud
Do Lets b f (4yrs) Pragmatic - Acushla Macree (Mansingh)....... (M Francis) 2,000
b g (3yrs) Broadsword (USA) - Acushla Macree (Mansingh)... (Mrs J Skelton) 1,500
Property of The Snailwell Stud Company Ltd., from Partridge Close Stud
b g (3yrs) Slip Anchor - Great Tom (Great Nephew)........... (Mrs M Reveley) 15,000
To Dissolve a Partnership, from Church Farm Stables
Benbeath b g (3yrs) Dunbeath (USA) - Steelock (Lochnager)... (M Hammond) 1,900
Property of Mr W M & Mrs A Comerford, from Highfield Lodge Stud
b g (4yrs) Buckley - Maladiction (Sunyboy) (Elmhurst Bloodstock) 6,200

152

Property of Mrs A E Goodwin, from Clatford Farm
b g (4yrs) Crash Course - Noelbonne Femme (Bonne Noel)...... (A Mullins) 22,000
b g (4yrs) Buckley - Wing On (Quayside)... (A Turnell) 2,800
Property of Mr Roy Edwards, from Blakeley Stud
ch g (3yrs) Scallywag - Saucy Eater (Saucy Kit).................... (M Roberts) 4,000

Property of a Partnership, from Oaks Farm Stables
br g (3yrs) Ovac (ITY) - Silken Turn (Kemal) (R Fahey) 5,500
Property of Mrs S F Marston, from Muirhead Stud
b g (3yrs) Buckley - La Margarite (Bonne Noel)................ (G J Phillips) 2,500
Property of Mr D Morgan
b g (3yrs) Good Thyne (USA) - Slave's Bangle (Prince Rheingold) (C Thornton) 4,200
Property of Mrs Nerys Dutfield, from Crabhayne Farm Stud
b g (3yrs) Strong Gale - Festive Season (Silly Season)................ (Cash) 16,500
Property of Springhill Bloodstock, from Mount Annan Stables
gr g (4yrs) Al Sikeen (USA) - Knot Too Bad (Quayside)................ (B Lusk) 8,000
b g (3yrs) Kambalda - Wren's Lass (Wren's Hill)................(O Brennan) 5,100
b g (4yrs) Roselier (FR) - Decent Debbie (Decent Fellow).............. (C.B.A.) 16,000

153

Property of Mr & Mrs N A Riddell
b g (4yrs) Scorpio (FR) - Combattente (Reform).................... (B Lusk) 4,000
b g (3yrs) Mandalus - Colleen Donn (Le Moss)......................... (Cash) 12,500
Property of a Partnership, from Rolleston Stud
ch g (3yrs) Broadsword (USA) - Pearl Bride (Spartan General)........... (K Lewis) 1,700
Property of Tythrop Park Stables, from Tythrop Park Stables
b g (3yrs) King's Ride - Atlantic Hope (Brave Invader).................. (P Hobbs) 5,800
ch g (3yrs) Parliament - Frisky Matron (On Your Mark)............... (M Barnes) 5,200
Property of Mrs S M Carter
b f (4yrs) Idiot's Delight - Skipton Bridge (Harwell)..............................
(Johnny McKeever Bloodstock) 3,500
Property of Mr F J Haggas, from Southburgh Manor Stud
b or br f (4yrs) Strong Gale - Drom Lady (Royalty).............. (Mrs D Haine) 9,600
Property of a Partnership, from Southburgh Manor Stud
b f (3yrs) Pollerton - Fumarole (USA) (Sensitive Prince).. (White Lodge Farm Stud) 1,700
Property of Mr Samuel Oliver, from Stoneybrig Stud
b f (3yrs) Salluceva - Patsarann (Pitpan).... (Cash) 1,600
Property of Mr S Collins, Co Down, Ireland
b or br g (4yrs) King's Ride - Matchless Maid (Lucifer)............... (B Lusk) 13,000

154

Property of Mr Peter Murphy, from Bridge Hill Farm, Co Down, Ireland
br g (3yrs) Dromod Hill - Stop Don Ceol (Junius).............. (Miss M Smith) 2,100
From Ballywooden House Stud, Co Down, Ireland
b g (3yrs) Convinced - A Nice Alert (Red Alert)...................... (M Pipe) 2,800

Property of Mr John McNeill, from Goragh Stables, Co Down, Ireland
br g (3yrs) King's Ride - Vale Of Peace (Wolver Hollow)........ (M Jefferson) 16,000
Property of Temple Farming, from Temple Farm Stud
br g (4yrs) King's Ride - Church Brae (The Parson).................. (R Barber) 18,000
b g (4yrs) Strong Gale - Deep Khaletta (Deep Run) (David Minton Bloodstock) 33,000
br g (4yrs) Sunyboy - Chancer's Last (Foggy Bell)........................ (C.B.A.) 28,000
Property of Mrs J A Broad, from Emral Stud
b f (4yrs) Scorpio (FR) - Leading Line (Leading Man)............. (Mrs A Hewitt) 8,000
From Queenford Stud Ltd
b g (4yrs) King's Ride - Golden Robe (Yankee Gold)............ (C Egerton) 14,000
From Camas Park Stud, Co Tipperary, Ireland
b g (4yrs) Sexton Blake - Subiacco (Yellow River).................. (J T Gifford) 30,000
b g (4yrs) The Parson - Alexandra (Song)... (J T Doyle) 15,000
b g (4yrs) Oats - Super Princess (Falcon)... (Johnny McKeever Bloodstock) 15,000

155

From Glenvale Stud, Co Tipperary, Ireland
b g (3yrs) Henbit (USA) - Lilardia (Taufan) .. (C.B.A.) 6,800
b g (3yrs) Electric - Muffet's Gold (Cavo Doro)..................... (D McCain) 1,700
Property of Mr T G Barry, from Rathbarry Stud, Co Cork, Ireland
ch g (4yrs) Phardante (FR) - Richest (Richboy)............................ (C.B.A.) 28,000
From Castle Farm Stud Ltd
b g (3yrs) Buckley - Releta (Relkino)....... (J Glover) 7,400
From Forbes Arms Stud
b g (4yrs) Royal Match - Saucy Sprite (Balliol).................. (P Nicholls) 5,000
From Goldford Stud
b g (3yrs) Buckskin (FR) - Frying Pan (Pitpan)............. (G W Richards) 10,500
Property of Messrs E Stuart Knape & W D Hockenhull, from Goldford Stud
ch g (3yrs) Gunner B - Final Melody (Final Straw)........................ (K Bailey) 6,200
Property of Mrs C Gowing, from Goldford Stud
ch g (3yrs) Scottish Reel - Sun Goddess (FR) (Deep Roots) ....
(David Minton Bloodstock) 27,000
From Goldford Stud
ch g (4yrs) Roselier (FR) - Vaguely Vulgan (Vulgan)......... (T Stopford Sackville) 5,500
ch f (4yrs) Celtic Cone - Graeme's Gem (Pry)........................ (L Lungo) 3,800
ch g (4yrs) Orchestra - Fair Corina (Menelek).................... (J McGrath) 2,700

156

Property of Mr R L Burton, from Goldford Stud
br g (4yrs) Idiot's Delight - Merry Cherry (Deep Run)................ (R Barber) 20,000

Property of High House Farm, from Furnace Mill Stud

ch g (4yrs) Sheer Grit - Deep Toi (Deep Run)........................ (J Adam) 8,000

To Dissolve a Partnership, from Furnace Mill Stud

ch g (4yrs) The Parson - Fisalmar Isle VI (Duky)............... (J Maconnachie) 4,800

From Glenpark Stud, Co Antrim, Ireland

b f (4yrs) Amazing Bust - French Note (Eton Rambler)............ (Jackie Bellamy) 6,200

From Dunadry Stud, Co Antrim, Ireland

br g (4yrs) The Parson - Kenodon (Menelek) .... (R Lee) 14,000

Duke Of Dunadry br g (4yrs) Duky (FR) - Giolla's Trip (Giolla Mear)............. (Mrs S Baker) 5,100

Property of Mr D B Bamber, Co Aintrim, Ireland

br g (3yrs) Strong Statement - Hi Cal (Callernish)....................... (L Lungo) 3,200

Property of Mrs V M Tricks, from Trickledown Stud

b f (3yrs) Idiot's Delight - Rose Mulholland (Lombard).......... (Temple Farming) 4,300

From Trickledown Stud

ch g (4yrs) Norwick (USA) - Dusty Bluebell (Sky Gipsy)................... (Cash) 2,300

b g (4yrs) Scottish Reel - Rhinestone (Never Say Die)... (David Minton Bloodstock) 24,000

157

Property of Mr Derek Weld, from Ballynattin House, Co Wicklow, Ireland

b g (3yrs) The Parson - Tumble Ria (Tumble Wind).................. (P Nicholls) 25,000

Property of Mr Hugh McConnell, from Meadowhead Stables

gr g (3yrs) Alias Smith (USA) - Fernez (Fez) (Mrs A Hewitt) 6,400

b g (3yrs) Meadowbrook - Faskin (Fez) .... (P Diggle) 2,000

Property of Viscount Portman, from Bacton Stud

Cobbs Cross ch g (3yrs) Bairn (USA) - Trapani (Ragusa)....... (T H Caldwell) 4,000

Property of Starleap Bloodstock Ltd., from Burns Farm Stud

b g (3yrs) Dowsing (USA) - Fallen Angel (Quiet Fling)........... (T H Caldwell) 5,200

Property of Mr G G A Gregson, from Beech Tree Stud

b f (3yrs) Rymer - Doddycross (Deep Run) (Harvey Smith) 1,600

Property of Mr M J Stannard

b g (3yrs) Uncle Pokey - Hazeldean (St Paddy).................. (J Penney) 4,500

From Silver Stables

ch f (3yrs) Celtic Cone - Pal Alley (Pals Passage).................. (R Hoad) 3,000

Property of Mrs M Hutcheson

b f (3yrs) Feelings (FR) - Dawns Ballad (Balidar)................. (R A Barker) 1,650

Property of Mr Stanley J Retter, from Home Farm Stud

b g (3yrs) Revlow - Miss Burgundy (Gambling Debt)...... (T Stopford Sackville) 3,000

gr g (3yrs) Revlow - Flying Free (Gambling Debt)....................... (Cash) 2,800

158

Property of Mrs H J Ellerby, from Westgate Carr Farm

b g (3yrs) Doc Marten - Cape Farewell (Record Run)............. (M Barnes) 1,800

PRIVATE SALES

Property of Mr D Goldie

Constant Amusement b m (5yrs) Funny Man - Common City (Comandeer)..... (R Waind) 1,800

Property of Mr Peter A Hume, from Sambirch Stud

b g (4yrs) Gay Meadow - Lady Ace (Space King)...................... (J Glover) 2,300

Property of Mrs B K Broad

Pokolotive b m (5yrs) Uncle Pokey - My Abigail (Long Till)........ (A M Evans) 2,000

From Glenpark Stud, Co Antrim, Ireland

ch g (3yrs) Good Thyne (USA) - Vanda (Florescence).............. (J Durkan) 5,500

159

DONCASTER
Wednesday, May 19th

To Dissolve a Partnership

Dancing Chief b g (5yrs) Lidhame - Darlinga (Derring-Do)................. (Cash) 1,550

Property of Applied Signs Ltd

Applied Signs b m (8yrs) Tycoon II - Arctic Lion (Arctic Slave)....... (R Lightfoot) 850

Property of Mr D Eluidge

Dublin Indemnity b g (4yrs) Alphabatim (USA) - Sailongal (USA) (Sail On Sail On).................. (H M Dunning) 1,400

Property of Mr D Sundin, from Manor Stables

Mister Cumbers b g (6yrs) Bulldozer - Baltic Star (Ballyciptic)........ (P C Browne) 1,900

Property of Mrs Barbara Ramsden

Blue Disc br g (8yrs) Disc Jockey - Kaotesse (Djakao)........ (A L Forbes) 2,200

Property of Kirklees Rock Asphalt Ltd

Kirklees Rock br m (7yrs) Kala Shikari - Lady Farrier (Sheshoon)........ (N Gardner) 1,300

To Dissolve a Partnership

Apache Brave gr g (8yrs) Warpath - Et Tu (Marcus Brutus)........... (T Kersey) 820

From Pinewood Stables

Ivy Benson b f (3yrs) Midyan (USA) - Angel Drummer (Dance In Time)........... (Sagittarius Bloodstock) 950

From Racecourse farm Stables

Somerby br g (6yrs) Tudorville - Nautique (Windjammer)....... (C J Cottingham) 1,800

Another Kingdom gr g (3yrs) Another Realm - Chiquitita (Reliance II) .... (P Howling) 2,100

160

Property of Burntwood Sports Ltd, from Longsides Stables

Niteowlady br f (3yrs) Dreams To Reality (USA) - Palace Pet (Dragonara Palace) (Sagittarius Bloodstock) 2,000

Property of Mr David Young, from Breckenbrough House Stables

Body Language ch f (3yrs) Petoski - Whipp's Cross (Kris).. (Miss A Ritchie) 2,100

Property of Mr B David, from Broomhill Stud

Kiwi Lake (NZ) b g (8yrs) Balkan Knight (NZ) - Tempest True (NZ) (Tempest Boy) ... (Maj W N Sample) 2,000

Property of a Partnership, from Red House Stables

Harry The Cab ch c (4yrs) Hadeer - Hilly (Town Crier)................ (Cash) 6,400

From Yew Tree Stables

Mr Poppleton ch c (4yrs) Ballacashtal (CAN) - Greenstead Lady (Great Nephew).... (Cash) 7,300

Property of Mr J Buzzeo, from Tupgill Park Stables

Chiparopai b m (5yrs) Commanche Run - Violino (USA) (Hawaii).......... (Cash) 2,200

Property of Mr J P Langran

Diamond In The Dark (USA) b h (5yrs) Diamond Prospect (USA) - Implicit (Grundy)...................... (Cash) 2,600

To Dissolve a Partnership

Barry Owen b g (7yrs) Owen Anthony - Tacita (Tacitus)................ (Cash) 1,050

Property of Mr E J Watt

Wensleydale William b g (7yrs) Tudorville - Kingsfold Flash (Warpath).. (W Jeffrey) 1,750

Property of a Partnership, from Tupgill Park Stables

Easby Hopes b g (7yrs) Full Of Hope - Linden Dolly (Gulf Pearl).............. (D Greenwood) 4,600

161

Property of Mrs S A Clarke & Mr W Clarke, from Pit Farm Stables

Eddie Walshe b g (8yrs) Smackover - Ashmore Lady (Ashmore) (Mrs J G Retter) 2,800

Property of Mr & Mrs M Williams, from Groundhill Stables

Dunraven Bay gr g (7yrs) Bay Express - Lydiate (Tower Walk) .... (David Minton Bloodstock) 5,200

To Dissolve a Partnership, from White Lea Stables

Mister Moody (FR) ch g (8yrs) Master Thatch - Moonly (FR) (Lionel) .... (B Baugh) 5,600

Chief Mole (USA) gr g (8yrs) Caro - Head Spy (USA) (Chieftain)...... (D McCain) 1,400

Ginger Pink b g (7yrs) Strong Gale - Zita's Toi (Chinatown)..... (C J Cottingham) 5,400

Property of a Partnership, from Hall Farm Stables

Kind A Smart ch g (8yrs) Kind Of Hush - Treasure Seeker (Deep Diver)......... (K A Morgan) 7,000

Property of Major H R M Porter, from Alscot Park Stables

Fling In Spring b g (7yrs) Last Fandango - Lovely Season (Silly Season) (D Smyly) 3,000

Property of a Partnership, from Alscot Park Stables

Time Slot (USA) ch g (6yrs) Secreto (USA) - Ebbing Tide (USA) (His Majesty) ...... (T Kersey) 1,650

Property of Mrs Brenda Bill, from Riston Whins Stables

Master Salesman b g (10yrs) Torenaga - Madam Milan (Milan) (Miss S Hinkley) 4,000

Property of Mrs Brenda Bill, from Rise Park Stables

Bruce's Castle b g (7yrs) Beau Charmeur (FR) - Maid In The Mist (Pry).......... (M Walsh) 3,200

162

Property of Mr M J Gosse, from Riston Whins Stables

Rhoman Coin br g (5yrs) Rhoman Rule (USA) - Kylemore Abbey (Junius)...... (M Carver) 8,200

Property of a Partnership, from Grange Stables

One For The Chief br g (5yrs) Chief Singer - Action Belle (Auction Ring)..... (Cash) 4,600

To Dissolve a Partnership, from Pollardstown Stables

Skittle Alley b g (7yrs) Adonijah - Skittish (USA) (Far North)............ (W Clay) 1,750

From Woodlands Stables

Cashtal Dazzler b g (6yrs) Ballacashtal (CAN) - Miss Meg (John Splendid) .... (Cash) 1,500

Richmond ch g (5yrs) Hatim (USA) - On The Road (On Your Mark) .... (Mrs Sheila Austin) 1,100

Silence Will Speak b g (5yrs) Taufan (USA) - Shopping (FR) (Sheshoon)........... (Mrs J Musgrove) 1,300

Badenoch Burner b g (3yrs) King Of Spain - Nocturnal Bliss (Pyjama Hunt).. (Cash) 1,250

Property of a Partnership, from Hassendean Bank Stables

Chickabiddy br m (5yrs) Henbit (USA) - Shoshoni (Ballymoss).... (G F Edward) 1,900

Property of Wyre Forresters, from Furnace Mill Stud

Kinlet Vision b m (5yrs) Vision (USA) - Verandah (Jaazeiro)...... (W P Jenks) 1,750

Property of Mr W G Barker, from Brecongill Stables

Czar Nicholas ch g (4yrs) Nicholas Bill - Cateryne (Ballymoss)... (M Hammond) 9,000

163

Property of Linpac Group Ltd (a dispersal sale), from Highfield House Stables

Linpac West b h (7yrs) Posse (USA) - North Page (FR) (Northfields)............ (Group 1 Racing) 47,000

Linpac Press b g (3yrs) Formidable (USA) - North Page (FR) (Northfields)......... (R Thompson) 2,500

ch c (2yrs) Never So Bold - North Page (FR) (Northfields).............. (D Moffat) 6,000

To Dissolve a Partnership, from Shalfleet Stables

Corrin Hill b g (6yrs) Petorius - Pete's Money (USA) (Caucasus)...... (B B A) 9,400

Property of Sir David Wills, from Phantom House Stables

River Lossie b g (4yrs) Bustino - Forres (Thatch)..................... (C B A) 24,000

From Norton Grange Stables

Cavolerie b g (6yrs) Ovac (ITY) - Where's Vallee (Skymaster)...... (Mrs E Verity) 3,200

Property of Mrs Ann Swinbank, from Thorndale Stables

Form-Er-Self ch g (6yrs) Hello Handsome - Waterbeck (Weathercock)...... (Cash) 1,300

From Thorndale Stables

Stone Warrior b g (6yrs) Claude Money (USA) - My Haven (Godswalk) .... (A Ireland) 1,900

Orienteer b g (4yrs) Reference Point - Optimistic Lass (USA) (Mr Prospector) (L Jones) 1,250

Indian Maestro b g (7yrs) Music Maestro - Indian Wells (Reliance II) (G F Edward) 1,000

164

From Everardsgrange Stables, Co. Tipperary, Ireland

No Joker b g (5yrs) Jester - Canta Lair (The Parson)...................... (Cash) 2,200

Property of Darley Stud Management Co Ltd, from Summerdown Stables

Duke Of Monmouth (USA) b g (5yrs) Secreto (USA) - Queen For The Day (USA) (King Emperor) .... (Johnny McKeever Bloodstock) 22,000

Property of Darley Stud Management Co Ltd, from Uplands Stables

Olanthe (USA) ch g (4yrs) Blushing Groom (FR) - Olamic (USA) (Nijinsky) .... (Johnny McKeever Bloodstock) 8,200

Property of Darley Stud Management Co Ltd, from Rhonehurst Stables

Dissimulateur (FR) b c (4yrs) Legend Of France (USA) - Dartana (FR) (Roi Dagobert)........................... (Johnny McKeever Bloodstock) 18,000

Property of Darley Stud Management Co Ltd, from Pond House Stables

Viardot b c (4yrs) Sadlers Wells (USA) - Vive La Reine (Vienna).... (Mrs M Reveley) 18,000

Property of Darley Stud Management Co Ltd, from Seven Barrows

Home Counties ch g (4yrs) Ela-Mana-Mou - Safe Home (Home Guard).. (D Moffat) 12,000

Property of Darley Stud Management Co Ltd, from Heads Farm Stables

Daphnis (USA) b c (4yrs) Lead On Time (USA) - Dancing Vaguely (USA) (Vaguely Noble)...... (G McGuinness) 8,400

Property of Darley Stud Management Co Ltd, from Dereens Stables, Co. Kildare, Ireland

Kalanski gr g (7yrs) Niniski (USA) - Kalazero (Kalamoun)................ (C Egerton) 9,600

From Dereens Stables, Co. Kildare, Ireland

In The Navy b g (7yrs) King's Ride - Fairy Run (Deep Run).............. (M Pipe) 14,000

Property of Mrs G S Rees, from Cross Farm Stables

Lazzaretto b g (5yrs) Ballacashtal (CAN) - Florence Mary (Mandamus)........... (A R Thomas) 2,000

165

Property of a Partnership, from Habton Grange Stables

Antinous ch g (9yrs) Hello Gorgeous (USA) - Marthe Meynet (Welsh Pageant)...... (J H Johnson) 2,600

From Habton Grange Stables

Paperwork Boy ch g (8yrs) Buckskin (FR) - Orinda Way (Deep Run)........ (Cash) 1,150

Property of a Partnership, from Habton Grange Stables

Elder Prince ch g (7yrs) Final Straw - Particular Miss (Luthier).... (R Thompson) 4,100

From Habton Grange Stables

Sheriff's Band ch g (6yrs) Posse (USA) - Willis (FR) (Lyphard)........... (Cash) 4,100

Property of Mr A G Forty, from Burythorpe House

Troodos b g (7yrs) Worlingworth - My Polyanna (Polyfoto)....... (Miss M Austin) 11,500

From Upper Longdon Stables

Lawnswood Sun b g (7yrs) Broadsword (USA) - Lawnswood Miss (Grey Mirage)................... (C Casey) 7,200

From The Croft Stables

Troubador Boy b g (7yrs) Rymer - Sweet Linda (Saucy Kit)........... (C Morris) 2,600

From High Gingerfield Stables

Celtic Breeze b g (10yrs) Celtic Cone - Sipped (Ballyciptic)............ (Cash) 3,800

From Lisaleen Stables, Co. Limerick, Ireland

Frenchman's Buck b g (8yrs) Buckskin (FR) - Miss Symbol (Symbol)..... (C Mann) 3,900

Property of a Partnership, from Bell House Stables

Damer's Cavalry b g (10yrs) Stanford - Margery (FR) (Cadmus) .... (Tanya Shrigley) 2,600

166

Property of Mr A Brown, from Bell House Stables

Arrastra b m (5yrs) Bustino - Island Mill (Mill Reef)...................... (B B A) 6,200

From Norton Grange Stables

Solo Cornet br g (8yrs) Furry Glen - Royal Willow (Royal Buck)....... (P Bradley) 2,800

Learner Driver b g (6yrs) Crash Course - Broken Mirror (Push On)....... (Cash) 2,700

Property of Mrs Ann Swinbank, from Thorndale Stables

Lillah Darak (USA) ch g (5yrs) Shadeed (USA) - Foreign Courier (USA) (Sir Ivor) (V Jones) 1,300

Property of Mr D J Soley, from Thorndale Stables

Bullaford Fair b g (5yrs) Sergeant Drummer (USA) - Clifton Fair (Vimadee) .... (P J & B E Miller) 1,600

Property of Mr John Wright, from Thorndale Stables

Mubaaris ch g (10yrs) Hello Georgeous (USA) - Aloft (High Top).... (E Maggs) 1,600

Property of Mrs Claire Smith, from Jackdaws Castle

Clurican ch g (4yrs) Dara Monarch - Jane Bond (Good Bond)......... (N Tinkler) 15,000

Property of The Million In Mind Partnership (2), from Jackdaws Castle

Beauchamp Grace b f (4yrs) Ardross - Buss (Busted)........................ (Cash) 28,000

Thinking Twice (USA) ch c (4yrs) Kris - Good Thinking (USA) (Raja Baba)...... (N Henderson) 32,000

From Seven Barrows Stables

Whatever You Like b g (9yrs) Deep Run - Garravogue (Giolla Mear).. (P Nicholls) 12,500

167

From Spigot Lodge Stables

Herbalist b g (4yrs) Mandrake Major - Mohican (Great Nephew)....... (J Hellens) 20,000

Hold Your Hat On ch g (4yrs) Celestial Storm (USA) - Thatched Grove (Thatching)....................... (B Pocock) 10,000

From Crackhill Stables

Jolly Roger br g (6yrs) Swan's Rock - Treasure Ship (Sovereign Lord) .... (David Minton Bloodstock) 4,600

Sandy Beau ch g (7yrs) Beau Charmeur (FR) - Straight Sprite (Three Wishes)... (Mrs V Ramm) 7,100

On The Tear br g (7yrs) The Parson - Queen Menelek (Menelek) .... (David Minton Bloodstock) 8,400

Harristown b g (5yrs) Orchestra - Maynooth Belle (Busted)............... (K Bailey) 28,000

Property of Mr J Hanson, from Crackhill Stables

Spanish Blaze b g (5yrs) Spanish Place (USA) - The Blazing Star (Proverb)..... (David Minton Bloodstock) 17,000

Hurdy ch g (6yrs) Arapahos (FR) - Demelza Carne (Woodville II)........... (Cash) 50,000

Property of Mrs M Curtis

Deep Chance b g (7yrs) Deep Run - Sweet Slievenamon (Arctic Slave)..... (Cash) 6,500

Property of Mrs T W Nicholson, Co Tipperary, Ireland

State Lady b f (4yrs) Strong Statement - Ladies Gazette (London Gazette)...... (D Moffat) 5,500

168

Property of Equiname Ltd

Nodform Wonder b g (6yrs) Cut Above - Wonder (Tekoah)....... (J H Johnson) 10,500

Ring Corbitts b g (5yrs) Politico (USA) - Penny Pink (Spartan General) .... (M Roberts) 10,000

Nodforms Inferno b g (4yrs) Idiot's Delight - River Linnet (Forlorn River) .... (David Minton Bloodstock) 8,000

From Greystoke Stables

Real Class b g (10yrs) Deep Run - Our Cherry (Tarqogan) .... (David Minton Bloodstock) 8,000

Mister Tuftie b g (8yrs) Black Minstrel - Articinna (Arctic Slave)... (N Bannister) 13,000

Property of Springhill Bloodstock, from Greystoke Stables

Tartan Turf b g (6yrs) Le Moss - El Scarsdale (Furry Glen)... (I Carmichael) 2,800

From Greystoke Stables

The Tartan Dyer b g (6yrs) Kambalda - Moongello (Bargello).... (W A Bethell) 10,000

Tartan Tornado b g (7yrs) Strong Gale - Frankford Run (Deep Run) (J McGrath) 5,000

Bin Lid b m (4yrs) Henbit - Our Ena (Tower Walk)................ (G W Richards) 5,400

Toaster Crumpet b g (4yrs) Seymour Hicks (FR) - Lady Letitia (Le Bavard).. (Cash) 1,700

169

Property of Mr J Halley, from Suir View Stables, Co Tipperary, Ireland

Ned The Hall br g (5yrs) Callernish - Dream Daisy (Choral Society)....... (K Bailey) 27,000

Property of Mr J O'Donnaghue, Co Dublin, Ireland

Quality Time br m (6yrs) Buckskin (FR) - Miss Rambler (Wrekin Rambler) ...... (B Lusk) 21,000

To Dissolve A Partnership, from Mellon Stud, Co Limerick, Ireland

The Bird O'Donnell b g (7yrs) Monksfield - Sheila's Flame (Reformed Character) .. (Johnny McKeever Bloodstock) 1,700

From Rathcannon Stables, Co Limerick, Ireland

Dashing Brook b g (6yrs) Over The River (FR) - Salty Sea (Sir Herbert) (L Lungo) 4,400

Dromin ch g (5yrs) Over The River (FR) - My Puttens (David Jack).... (J Wright) 5,400

Property of Mr T Radley, Co Waterford, Ireland

Ballylemon b g (5yrs) Royal Fountain - Lohunda Park (Malinowski) .... (T Thomson Jones) 19,500

From Mocklershill Stables, Co Tipperary, Ireland

Highway Five ch g (5yrs) Carlingford Castle - Final Triumph (Laurence O)......... (J W Thompson) 3,600

I'm In Charge ch g (4yrs) Glad Dancer - Little Grannie Vii (Pedigree Unregistered)...................... (Cash) 10,000

Property of Mr J P Berry, M.R.C.V.S., Co Wexford, Ireland

What About That ch g (5yrs) Sandalay - Knockarone Star (Paddy's Stream)..... (Mrs M A Puddick) 6,400

From Glenville House Stables, Co Wexford, Ireland

Caman br g (6yrs) Callernish - Chilly For June (Menelek)........ (R J Manning) 11,000

170

From Walshesten Stud, Co Wexford, Ireland

Royal Irish ch g (9yrs) Le Bavard (FR) - Leuze (Vimy)............ (G B Balding) 20,000

Sunny Boreen b g (6yrs) Boreen Beag - Boreen Fada (Boreen)... (G B Balding) 12,000

Property of Mrs C Magill, from Ballywooden House, Co Down, Ireland

Avostar ch g (6yrs) Buckskin (FR) - Star Cat (Avocat) .... (Cormac McCormack Associates) 30,000

Property of Mr R Duke, Co Down, Ireland

Ballydougan ch g (5yrs) The Parson - Get My Pint (Menelek)................... (David Minton Bloodstock) 12,500

From Mount Davy's Stables, Co Antrim, Ireland
Brockish Bay ch g (6yrs) Le Bavard (FR) - Almanac (London Gazette). . (R Baxter) 6,000
From Suir View Stud, Co Tipperary, Ireland
Logical Fun b g (5yrs) Nishapour (FR) - Thimblerigger (Sharpen Up). . (R Crank) 3,000
Property of Mrs W D Sykes
Pont de Paix b g (7yrs) Cheval - Mattie B (Sea Moss). . . . . (Miss S Hinckley) 16,000
Property of Mr R Burton, from Longner Hall Stables
Blaster Bins b g (5yrs) Vision (USA) - Trail (Thatch). . . . . (J H Johnson) 15,000
Property of Mr R L Burton
Twelth Man b g (6yrs) Remainder Man - Merry Cherry (Deep Run). . . . . (W D Francis) 20,000
Property of Mr W P Jenks, from Glazeley Manor Stables
Once A Knight ch g (7yrs) Duky - Noctiluca (FR) (Dark Tiger). . . . . (A Ireland) 1,400

171

Property of Mr G King
Tsunami b g (5yrs) Niniski (USA) - Seasurf (Seaepic). . . . . (Cash) 10,500
From Ballyhannon Stables, Co Clare, Ireland
Computer Pickings b m (6yrs) Taufan (USA) - Ricciola (USA) (Stage Door Johnny) . . (J Wright) 2,000
Flotation b g (6yrs) Salmon Leap (USA) - Bold Miss (Bold Lad). . . . . (P G Tingey) 1,700
Property of Mr J J McInerney, Co Clare, Ireland
Last Refuge b g (4yrs) Lancastrian - Newland's Bloom (Lucifer). . . . . . (R Dalton) 5,600
From Mount Brown Stud
Kinesiology br g (5yrs) Boreen (FR) - Ardellis Lady (Pollerton). . . . . (Cash) 12,000
From Mount Brown Stud, Co Galway, Ireland
Time Won't Wait b g (4yrs) Bulldozer - Time Will Wait (Milan). (Johnny McKeever Bloodstock) 10,000
Property of Mr Peter Sherry, Co Meath, Ireland
Little Martina b m (5yrs) The Parson - Little Welly (Little Buskins). . . . . (C B A) 8,800
Property of Mr Keith Pearce
Press For Action b g (8yrs) Croghan Hill - Ballynavin Money (Even Money) . . . . . . (Cash) 5,200
Property of Springhill Bloodstock Ltd., from Mount Annan Stables
Springhill Spirit b f (7yrs) The Parson - Please Mum (Kabale). . . . . (Cash) 7,000
Property of Mrs Nerys Dutfield, from Crabhayne Farm Stables
Raglan Road b g (9yrs) Furry Glen - Princess Concorde (Great Heron) . . . . (David Minton Bloodstock) 15,500
Proud Point b m (8yrs) Over The River (FR) - Hightown Jackie (David Jack) (Cash) 5,000

172

Property of Northwest Bloodstock, Co Derry, Ireland
Smart Dresser b g (8yrs) Buckskin (FR) - Cinderwood (Laurence O) (N Pomfret) 2,600
Property of a Partnership, from Ballywee Stables, Co Antrim, Ireland
Fresh'n Minty b m (5yrs) Torus - Golden Value (Northern Value). . . . . (Cash) 7,500
Property of Mrs C S McKeever, from Ballywee Stables, Co Antrim, Ireland
Scotch 'n Irish ch g (4yrs) Torus - Burrenreagh Lass (Vitiges) (Harvey Smith) 5,200
Property of Her Grace Anne Duchess of Westminster
After Four gr g (9yrs) Roselier (FR) - Caherelly Cross (Royal Buck) . . . . (N Cooper) 4,200
Master Tim ch g (9yrs) Timolin (FR) - Straight Beauty (Straight Lad). . . . . (D Smyly) 4,000
From Willoughton Stables
On Your Way b g (11yrs) Ragapan - Fourteen Carat (Sterling Bay) (Linda Jewell) 3,400
Musical Phone b g (3yrs) Music Boy - Kaleidophone (Kalaglow) (C L Popham) 1,700
Property of Riston Whins Racing Ltd, from Riston Whins Stables
Bavanter ch g (7yrs) Le Bavard (FR) - My Lily (Levanter). . . . . (P Davis) 1,600
Property of Mrs J D Goodfellow, from Leadervale Stables
Naval Raid b m (6yrs) Julio Mariner - London Blitz (Home Guard) (S Moule) 2,000
Celtic Bunnie b m (8yrs) Celtic Cone - Charlotte's Festival (Gala Performance) (Cash) 2,300

173

Property of Mr W R Williams, from Potsclose Stables
Red Scorpion b g (9yrs) Furry Glen - Glamorous Night (Sir Herbert) (L E Newey) 3,200
Property of Mr C H P Bell, from Burton Fleming Hall Stables
Lothian Admiral b g (11yrs) Roscoe Blake - Lothian Lady (New Brig). . . . . (Miss V Williams) 1,750
Doxford Hut b g (9yrs) Class Distinction - Tillside Brig (New Brig). . . . . (Cash) 2,200
Property of Mr J Quinn, from Springfield Stud, Co Clare, Ireland
General Giggs br g (5yrs) Sandalay - Cold Sea (Arctic Slave). . . (Lord Yarborough) 11,500
Property of Mrs Barbara McConvey, Co Down, Ireland
Golden Dunsford b g (7yrs) Golden Love - Fragrant Blossom (Straight Deal) . . . . . . (Cormac McCormack Associates) 2,100
Property of Mr A T Lapping
Who's In Charge b g (9yrs) Proverb - I'm Grannie (Perspex). . . . . (G Coatsworth) 1,450
Property of Mrs J A Beighton
Polo Prince gr g (10yrs) Nishapour (FR) - Tiepoless (Tiepolo II). . . . . . (N Gardner) 3,000
Property of Mr A Bealby
Le Toad ch g (8yrs) Le Moss - Regal Sound (Royal Palace). . . . . (S B Clark) 3,000
Property of Mrs E Anderson, from Norwood Stables
North View b g (7yrs) Point North - Jolie Courtisane (Owen Dudley). . . . . (Mrs H Calzini) 2,000

Property of Gamston Equine, from Ropsley Estates Stables
Friendly Banker (AUS) b g (9yrs) Old Crony (USA) - Doubly Bold (AUS) (Home Guard)........... (Miss V Markowiak) 1,800

174

PRIVATE SALES
Property of Mr Victor Semple, Co Antrim, Ireland
ch g (4yrs) Orchestra - Heather-Can (Cantab)........................... (C B A) 20,000
Property of Northwest Bloodstock, Co Derry, Ireland
ch g (5yrs) Fidel - Athen Glen (Athenius)... (Cash) 3,250
Property of Maj H R M Porter, from Alscot Park Stables
Fling In Spring b g (7yrs) Last Fandango - Lovely Season (Silly Season) (D Smyly) 1,500
Property of Mr D F Spence
Via Cavour (USA) gr g (4yrs) Green Dancer (USA) - Princess Verna (USA) (Al Hattab)........................ (W Amos) 5,000
From Glenville House Stables, Co Wexford, Ireland
Caman br g (6yrs) Callernish - Chilly For June (Menelek)............... (Cash) 9,000
Property of Mr G King
Tsunami b g (5yrs) Niniski (USA) - Seasurf (Seaepic)... (David Minton Bloodstock) 10,000

175

ASCOT
Tuesday, June 1st

Property of Mr D F Sansome
Proud Bishop b g (14yrs) The Parson - Maximum Bonus (Wrekin Rambler).... (A Cannel) 1,800
Property of Mr R C Watchorn
Baffinland ch g (12yrs) Pauper - Clody Miss (Gilles de Retz)................ (Cash) 1,500
Property of Mr S J Thorogood
Lions Gate b g (9yrs) Golden Fleece (USA) - Prudent Miss (FR) (Prudent II) .... (Linda Smith) 1,375
Property of Racing Thoroughbreds Plc
Sheer Ecstasy b g (3yrs) Sure Blade (USA) - Height Ofl Passion (Shirley Heights)... (Mark Wellings) 900
Property of Mr D B Clark
Miller's Moll b f (3yrs) Miller's Mate - Bewitched (African Sky).............. (Roger Lightfoot) 725
Property of Mrs N Myers
Allegro Con Brio b g (5yrs) Alleging (USA) - Diami (Swing Easy)............ (Cash) 950
Property of Mr Arishan Ali, from La Grange Stables
Cosmic Future gr c (4yrs) Siberian Express (USA) - Bourgeonette (Mummy's Pet) (Cash) 550
Property of Mr S P Tindall, from Trillium Place
Newton Point b g (4yrs) Blakeney - Assertive (USA) (Assert).................... (David Minton Bloodstock) 6,800

From South Bank Stables
Touch Silver ch g (3yrs) Local Suitor (USA) - Octavia Girl (Octavo (USA))..... (Cash) 1,350
Property of Austin Stroud & Co, from Pollardstown Racing Stables
Bee Beat ch g (5yrs) Bairn (USA) - Thorny Rose (Tap On Wood).......... (Cash) 950

176

To Dissolve a Partnership, from Pollardstown Stables
Anaruka (USA) b or br g (5yrs) Roberto (USA) - Tea And Roses (USA) (Fleet Nasrullah).............. (M R C Price) 1,050
Property of Faal Racing Ltd
Zilfi (USA) b c (3yrs) Lyphard (USA) - Over Your Shoulder (USA) (Graustark) .... (C Popham) 1,700
To Dissolve a Partnership
Slipperton b g (6yrs) Pollerton - June's Slipper (No Argument) (William Bryan) 3,400
Property of Mr R Anderson
Judge And Jury br g (4yrs) Law Society (USA) - Full Of Reason (USA) (Bold Reason)...................... (Cash) 2,000
To Dissolve a Partnership
Fortune Star (IRE) b c (4yrs) Glow (USA) - Lucky For Me (Appiani II) (R J Bridger) 900
Property of The Hon Mrs J Berry, from Park House Racing Stables
Calicon ch g (7yrs) Connaught - Calgary (Run The Gantlet (USA)).... (D James) 1,100
Property of Mr I A Balding, from Park House Racing Stables
Reffolds ch g (10yrs) Green Shoon - Penthouse Pet (Deep Run) (Mrs M Boggis) 1,250
Property of Mr P Mellon, from Park House Stables
Fight To Win (USA) br g (5yrs) Fit To Fight (USA) - Spark Of Life (USA) (Key To The Mint (USA))....... (Bob Manning) 12,000
To Dissolve a Partnership, from Downs House
Beam Me Up Scotty (IRE) br g (4yrs) Orchestra - Bright Path (He Loves Me) (Les Kennard) 3,400
To Dissolve a Partnership
Just A Memory b g (7yrs) Kafu - Souveniers (Relko)............ (Miss E Hepworth) 950

177

From Seven Barrows Racing Stables (Dispersal & Dissolution of a Syndicate)
Brown Sauce (NZ) b g (7yrs) Wolverton - Gold Leaf (NZ) (Princely Note) .... (P Powell) 1,800
Grey Hussar (NZ) gr g (7yrs) War Hawk II - Poi (NZ) (Native Turn (NZ)) .... (B Thormlin) 2,200
Property of The Royal Studs, from Seven Barrows Racing Stables
Dalliston (NZ) b g (7yrs) March Legend (NZ) - Auklyn (NZ) (Auk)........ (Mrs P Sly) 3,400
Property of Mr R Tooth, from Seven Barrows Racing Stables
Vicompt de Valmont b g (8yrs) Beau Charmeur (FR) - Wish Again (Three Wishes).............. (Paul Nicholls) 12,000

Property of Mr G E Amey, from The Bridge Stud

ch f (3yrs) Gunner B - Deep Coach (Deep Run)........................ (Cash) 1,350

b g (4yrs) Pragmatic - Craftsmans Made (Jimsun)................ (P Hobbs) 3,000

Property of a Gentleman, from Grove Farm

(IRE) gr g (2yrs) Saxon Farm - Great Chance (General Ironside)............. (Cash) 4,000

ch g (3yrs) Executive Man - Badsworth Girl (Arch Sculptor).............. (F Gray) 2,500

Property of Miss C Metcalfe

ch g (4yrs) Fairbairn - Celestial Drive (Dublin Taxi)...... (Mick Lambert Bloodstock) 5,800

Property of Mrs F Walwyn, from Saxon House Stables (a Dispersal Sale)

Candle Glow ch m (5yrs) Capitano - Fused Light (Fury Royal)...... (P Hutchinson) 3,400

Capital Punishment ch g (7yrs) Capitano - Loophole (London Gazette)........... (David Minton Bloodstock) 9,200

Roy's Hill b g (7yrs) Royben - Magic Sky (Alto Volante).......... (Ben de Haan) 4,400

The Pursewarden br g (10yrs) Down The Hatch - Miss Sonnet (Master Owen).. (Cash) 1,700

178

Property of Mr Nicholas Blair, from Saxon House Stables (a Dispersal Sale)

Rope br g (7yrs) Rolfe (USA) - Mountain Rescue (Mountain Call)... (A L Forbes) 5,000

Property of a Lady, from Woodcote Stud

Celtic Bhoy b g (7yrs) Red Sunset - Nighty Night (Sassafras)....... (Miss L Fortt) 1,700

To Dissolve a Partnership, from Pond House Stables

Takemethere b g (9yrs) Decent Fellow - Mandaloch (Mandamus)....... (Cash) 8,000

Porto Heli b g (6yrs) Precocious - Coral Heights (Shirley Heights)............ (Gerry Austin) 950

Elegant Touch b f (4yrs) Elegant Air - Teye (Mummy's Pet)............... (Cash) 3,300

Myverygoodfriend b g (6yrs) Swing Easy (USA) - Darymoss (Ballymoss)........ (Mrs Trigg) 1,950

Faithful Star b g (8yrs) Tilden - Star Relation (Star Gazer).................. (Cash) 9,200

Boogie Bopper (IRE) b g (4yrs) Taufan (USA) - Mey (Canisbay)........ (Cash) 3,300

Kings Rank br g (7yrs) Tender King - Jhansi Ki Rani (USA) (Far North (CAN)) (Cash) 8,200

To Dissolve a Partnership

ch g (5yrs) Nearly A Hand - Kiki Star (Some Hand).................... (R Barker) 3,300

Dancing Oats ch g (7yrs) Oats - October Fair (Will Somers).. (Miss E Hepworth) 1,650

179

Property of Mrs J M Corbett

Nathan Blake gr g (8yrs) Sexton Blake - Nana (Forlorn River).......... (C.B.A.) 11,500

Property of Mr D H Barons, from Hendham Farm

Kaharoa (NZ) gr g (7yrs) Ironclad (NZ) - In Haste (NZ) (In The Purple (FR))........ (G J Davies) 1,650

Property of Lord Clinton, from Hendham Farm

Mayoran (NZ) b g (9yrs) Mayo Mellay (NZ) - Bundoran (NZ) (Sally Royal) (P Hobbs) 10,000

Property of Mr D H Barons, from Hendham Farm Stables

Cock A Leekie (NZ) b g (10yrs) Mayo Mellay (NZ) - Summermayo (NZ) (Summer Magic)........... (John Greenhill) 700

Property of Mr V Adams, from West Lockinge Stables

Kildowney Hill b g (7yrs) Kemal (FR) - Nadine's Pride (Double-U-Jay)......... (Jonjo O'Neill) 5,800

Property of Lord Vestey, from West Lockinge Stables

Manders Way b g (8yrs) Furry Glen - Art Mistress (Master Owen)....... (Cash) 16,000

To Dissolve a Partnership, from West Lockinge Stables

Camelot Knight br g (7yrs) Kings Ride - Jeanette Marie (Fighting Don) (C.B.A.) 35,000

Property of Richard Green (Fine Paintings), from West Lockinge Stables

Primitive Singer b g (5yrs) Chief Singer - Periquito (USA) (Olden Times) .... (N de Cort) 800

From Lodge Farm Stud

b g (3yrs) Phardante (FR) - Mellie (Impecunious).... (Mick Lambert Bloodstock) 10,000

Bold Star b g (3yrs) Persian Bold - Star Arrangement (Star Appeal) .... (Sarah Hollinshead) 6,000

b g (3yrs) Town And Country - Cloister Rose (Track Spare)............ (Cash) 6,200

180

From Vinnells Farm

Policeman's Pride bl g (4yrs) Policeman (FR) - Proud Pet (Petingo) .... (Mr Madgwick) 4,000

From Caradoc Court Stables

Pronounced b g (6yrs) Deep Run - Lovely Bio (Double-U-Jay)..... (David Turner) 4,200

Idiom b g (6yrs) Idiot's Delight - Squiffy (Articulate)............ (Jackie Retter) 6,000

Union Castle b g (7yrs) Carlingford Castle - Fair Invader (Brave Invader)........... (David Smyly) 8,000

Cairneymount b g (7yrs) Croghan Hill - Glentoran Valley (Little Buskins)....... (Colin Reader) 3,300

Trusty Friend b g (11yrs) True Song - Princess Camilla (Prince Barle) (C Popham) 4,000

Honest Fred br g (7yrs) Mandalus - Quayside Fairy (Quayside) (Mr Turner) 2,800

Property of Mrs J K Peutherer, from Caradoc Court Stables

Razoo b g (6yrs) Decent Fellow - Alice Johnston (Majetta) (O Vaughan-Jones) 4,200

Don't Light Up b g (7yrs) Lighter - Hannah's Bar (Babu)............. (Paul Nicholls) 9,700

Rufus ch g (7yrs) Cheval - Perdeal (Perspex) .... (B Smart) 20,000

Ross Venture b g (8yrs) Monksfield - Fitz's Buck (Master Buck)........ (L Lungo) 11,500

Red Rondo ch g (9yrs) Rontino - Ivy Hill (Cantab)... (David Minton Bloodstock) 7,500

181

Property of Mrs J K Peutherer, from West Lockinge Farm

Royal Saxon b g (7yrs) Mandalus - La Campesina (Arctic Slave) .... (David Minton Bloodstock) 10,000

To Dissolve a Partnership, from Glenfall Stables

Ferens Hall b g (6yrs) Pollerton - String-Of-Pearls (Pall Mall).......... (M Roberts) 8,200

Black Joker br g (7yrs) Lord Ha Ha - Edwina Marie (Sir Herbert).................... (William & Mandy Bryan) 6,600

Property of Pell-Mell Partners, from Orchard Stables

Fenton Bridge b g (9yrs) Gleason (USA) - Divine Drapes (Divine Gift) .... (H B Geddes) 6,200

Property of Mr W E Gale, from The Downs Racing Stables

Rydal Pride b g (8yrs) Pry - Will Preach (Will Somers)............. (Trevor Painter) 1,700

Property of Mr G T Radmore, from The Downs Racing Stables

Beau Pari br g (9yrs) Beau Charmeur (FR) - Raised-In-Paris (Raise You Ten) .... (Mrs S Maxse) 2,500

Property of Hadrians Bloodstock

Idling By b g (7yrs) Carlingford Castle - Hanslein (Prince Hansel)....... (Cash) 2,700

Property of The Lord Vestey (Stowell Park Stud)

Uncle Mogy ch g (7yrs) Monsanto (FR) - Primrolla (Relko).......... (P J Hobbs) 3,000

Property of Brigadier C B Harvey, from Ford Farm Racing Stables

Fast Study b g (8yrs) Crash Course - Mary May (Little Buskins) (Simon Robinson) 3,200

From Goldford Stud

Technics b g (10yrs) Orchestra - Cashelgarran (Never Say Die).................. (Mrs I McGuinness) 2,400

Down The Mine b g (7yrs) Le Moss - Zauditu (Menelek).... (R T Bainbridge) 2,000

The Artful Rascal br g (9yrs) Scallywag - Quick Exit (David Jack)..... (C Coxen) 7,000

Happy Higgins b g (9yrs) Strong Gale - Quayville (Quayside)................ (David Minton Bloodstock) 4,200

182

Property of Sir John Barlow, from Goldford Stud

Rhu Na Haven b g (9yrs) Le Bavard (FR) - Shuil Dubh (Black Tarquin) (J K Buckle) 6,000

Property of Mr G M Briscoe, from Goldford Stud

Ryme And Run b m (7yrs) Rymer - Altaghaderry Run (Deep Run).......... (P Venner) 2,600

Property of Mr R L Burton, from Goldford Stud

(IRE) br g (4yrs) Phardante (FR) - Kanturk Lady (Tarqogan)......... (Keith Lewis) 1,800

Property of Alswick Hall Farms Ltd, from Goldford Stud

(IRE) b g (4yrs) The Parson - Shanban (Shackleton)....... (Michael Johnson) 3,200

From Goldford Stud

(IRE) b g (4yrs) Phardante (FR) - Merry Miss (Deep Run)............. (Keith Lewis) 2,500

(IRE) b g (4yrs) Phardante (FR) - Speedy Lady (Carlburg).......... (N G Ayliffe) 3,100

Property of The Hon J E Greenall

Alpha One ch g (8yrs) Belfalas - Clonaslee Foam (Quayside) .... (David Minton Bloodstock) 10,000

Property of Mrs A Trigg, from Hazelhurst Farm

(IRE) ch g (3yrs) Treasure Hunter - Clare's Sheen (Choral Society) (Mick Lambert) 3,000

Property of Mr M Kerr-Dineen, from Whitcombe Manor Racing Stables

That's The Business br g (10yrs) Milan - Laragh (Fray Bentos).......... (Cash) 2,400

Property of His Grace The Duke of Atholl, from Whitcombe Manor Racing Stables

Ask Moss ch g (8yrs) Le Moss - Triple Fire (Deep Run).................... (Cash) 1,200

183

Property of Lord Chetwode, from Whitcombe Manor Racing Stables

Farm Week gr g (11yrs) General Ironside - Newsletter (London Gazette) .... (Mick Lambert) 5,000

Property of Park Farm Thoroughbreds

Second Call ch f (4yrs) Kind Of Hush - Matinata (Dike (USA)).... (Tim Forster) 13,000

From Whitsbury Manor Racing Stables

Our Nobby b g (11yrs) McIndoe - Fair Arctic (Bally Russe)...................... (David Minton Bloodstock) 1,600

Wild And Loose b g (5yrs) Precocious - Regain (Relko)......... (Les Kennard) 3,200

Property of Whitcombe Manor Racing Stables

Raging Bull (IRE) b g (3yrs) Bluebird (USA) - Sabrine (Mount Hagen (FR)) .... (Mrs J Miller) 950

Gone's Girl ch m (7yrs) Green Shoon - Gone (Whistling Wind).......... (Cash) 750

Property of a Partnership

Olveston (NZ) b g (9yrs) Sea Anchor - Statira (NZ) (Imperial March (CAN)) .... (David Redvers) 1,600

Property of Mr D Page

River Orchid b f (4yrs) Mashhor Dancer (USA) - Summer Sky (Skyliner) .... (Meriel Humphreys) 2,500

Property of Mr G Solman

Key Dear (FR) ch g (6yrs) Darly (FR) - Keep Happy (FR) (Red Vagabonde) .... (Rod Juckes) 4,200

Property of Mrs L Goulding

b g (5yrs) Son Of Shaka - Home Sweet Home (Royal Palace)....... (M Sibley) 1,200

184

Property of Mrs E K Thorneycroft

(IRE) b f (4yrs) Ovac (ITY) - Swan Girl (My Swanee)................ (M R Clarke) 1,400

Property of a Gentleman

Canadian Boy (IRE) b g (4yrs) Commanche Run - Canadian Guest (Be My Guest (USA)).......... (South Bucks Racing) 1,000

Castle Warrior b g (6yrs) Castle Keep - Christine's Lady (Roman Warrior) ..... (Cash) 625

Property of Mr S Joynes

Pat Cullen b g (8yrs) The Parson - Duhallow Hazel (Major Point)............ (Cash) 1,300

PRIVATE SALES

To Dissolve a Partnership, from Teal House

Boskenna ch m (5yrs) Nearly A Hand - Chuckles Hansel (Prince Hansel) ...... (Ruth Woollerton) 2,000

From Fowlers Farm Racing Stables

Singing Spear gr g (8yrs) Abednego - Royal Banquet (Royal Buck) .... (David Minton Bloodstock) 3,500

From Harcourt Stud (Ireland)

Really An Angel gr m (6yrs) Baron Blakeney - Busy Quay (Quayside) .... (Sally Mullins Bloodstock) 3,750

Property of Spaceage Plastics Limited, from Upper Herdswick Stables

Castlebay Lad bl g (10yrs) Crozier - Carbery Star (Kemal)................ (Mr Farr) 1,500

185

ASCOT

Wednesday, June 2nd

Property of Mr K Walker

Assembly b g (10yrs) General Assembly (USA) - Avocet (Crowned Prince (USA)) (R Wilson) 1,400

Property of Mrs M P McNeill, from Harris Farm Stables

Facts And Figures b m (8yrs) Barley Hill - Statement Of Facts Vii (Quality Fair)... (Sarah Clarke) 1,500

Property of Mr A Shenston

Lady Of Stratton b m (6yrs) Enchantment - Disco Diamond (Le Coq D'Or).. (Cash) 1,300

Property of Mr C C Elsey

All Electric b g (8yrs) Electric - Miss Tweedie (Aberdeen)...... (C Popham) 1,250

Property of Mr J McCarthy, from Folly House Stables

Toccatella b f (3yrs) Chief Singer - Woodwind (FR) (Whistling Wind) .... (R Lightfoot) 775

Property of Mr Frederick Gray

Drewitts Dancer b g (6yrs) Balboa - Vermillon (FR) (Aureole)..... (A Hawkins) 850

Property of Mr P D Purdy

Ringyboy b g (8yrs) Runnett - Graunuaile (Proud Chieftain).......... (R Aungier) 1,150

Property of Mr S Ellerbeck

Dilkush b g (4yrs) Dunbeath (USA) - Good Try (Good Bond).......... (S C Wells) 1,050

Property of Mr A A Penney, from Hamilton Stables

Pondered Bid b g (9yrs) Auction Ring (USA) - Ponca (Jim French)........... (Cash) 675

Property of Mr S H Marriage

Spring Sale b or br m (7yrs) Royal Fountain - Super Valu (Golden Love) .... (R Phizacklea) 2,500

186

Property of a Gentleman

Attic Wit (FR) b g (7yrs) Shirley Heights - Laughing Matter (Lochnager) .... (J Cooper) 800

Property of Mr A T A Wates

Killarney Man br g (7yrs) Pragmatic - Lilly Of Killarney (Sunny Way)..... (V H Smith) 1,800

Bayram (FR) br g (11yrs) Blakeney - Zarin (GER) (Arjon (GER))........ (J Cooper) 950

Property of Mr T D B Barlow

Red Is The Rose b m (6yrs) Bustineto - Red Rose (Saint Denys)....... (J W Elliott) 2,600

Property of Mr A P Payne

Grondola b m (6yrs) Indian King (USA) - Trysting Place (He Loves Me)......... (P McCarthy) 1,050

Property of Mr T G Brooks

Pims Gunner (IRE) b g (5yrs) Montelimar (USA) - My Sweetie (Bleep Bleep)..... (David Minton Bloodstock) 10,000

Property of Brian Gubby Ltd

Gabhadera ch f (3yrs) Gabitat - Hadera (Northfields)................. (Cash) 750

Property of Mrs B Johnson

River Sunset (IRE) ch g (5yrs) Over The River (FR) - Sunset Princess (Prince Hansel)............. (Mrs M C Holt) 1,750

Property of Mr C Johnson and Mr J Johnson

(IRE) b g (3yrs) Lancastrian - More Chat (Torenaga).................... (Cash) 1,500

Property of Miss K George

Elfie's Son b g (9yrs) Sonnen Gold - Elf Trout (Elf Arrow)............. (Cash) 2,000

187

Property of Mr J Gay

Saint Ruby (IRE) ch g (4yrs) Hard Fought - Maquillage (Manado).... (Carol Jones) 1,000

To Dissolve a Partnership

Shared Fortune (IRE) br g (5yrs) Strong Gale - Reaper's Run (Deep Run) ...... (A Gibbs) 1,550

Property of J Joseph Bloodstock

Roger Rabbit (FR) b g (4yrs) Rusticaro (FR) - Bustelda (FR) (Busted)......... (Cash) 1,100

Dragon Spirit gr g (4yrs) Absalom - Fair Eleanor (Saritamer (USA)) .... (Ms Alyson Roberts) 1,300

Property of J Joseph

Brora Rose (IRE) br m (5yrs) Drumalis - Run Swift (Run The Gantlet) (P R Rodford) 5,000

Our Nikki gr f (3yrs) Absalom - Whisper Gently (Pitskelly)........ (P R Rodford) 1,350

Winter Hazel b m (5yrs) Thatching - Walkyria (Lord Gayle (USA)).. (P McCarthy) 1,600

Property of Mr C P E Brooks, from Uplands Racing Stables

Hello Grandad b g (9yrs) Hello Gorgeous (USA) - Emerin (King Emperor).. (Cash) 850

Property of Mr P D Ryland

Formal b g (7yrs) Cidrax (FR) - Late Challange (Tekoah)............. (R Owen) 3,000

Property of Mr R C & Mrs A J Long

Phelioff ch g (9yrs) Dubassoff (USA) - Darymoss (Ballymoss)......... (Cash) 4,000

188

To Dissolve a Partnership, from Preston Farm Stables

Barton Royal (IRE) b g (3yrs) Petorius - Royal Sensation (Prince Regent (FR)) .. (P Ritchens) 3,000

Property of Mr A J Morley

Royal Warden b g (12yrs) Sexton Blake - Lady Sykes (Sovereign Lord)........ (J N Hutchinson) 3,000

Property of Mr Patrick Burling

Poteasy ch g (7yrs) Deep Run - Scalped (Tomahawk IV).......... (B Thornley) 650

Property of Mr D A Smith

Kingswell b g (10yrs) Space King - Calm Ship (Fighting Ship)............ (Cash) 725

Property of Manor House Farm Stables

b c (2yrs) High Kicker (USA) - Lady Songe (Anax)...................... (J Small) 550

Property of Woodland Stables (To Dissolve a Partnership)

Starlight Flyer b g (6yrs) In Fijar (USA) - Nareen (USA) (The Minstrel).......... (T Waters) 1,550

Property of Mrs S Burgess

Remember Mac b g (5yrs) My Dad Tom (USA) - Sur Les Roches (Sea Break) ... (J Trice-Rolph) 1,050

To Dissolve a Partnership

Hatherden Tomboy (IRE) ch g (5yrs) Carlingford Castle - Queen Hadrian (Golden Love)............. (R Parker) 3,000

Property of Mrs C Bailey

Jaaez b g (9yrs) Ela-Mana-Mou - Almagest (Dike).................. (J de Gilen) 1,200

To Dissolve a Partnership

Barton Bendish b g (8yrs) Cut Above - Athry (Be Friendly) .... (David Minton Bloodstock) 2,000

189

From Windy Hill Stud

Foolish Fantasy b g (5yrs) Idiot's Delight - In A Dream (Caruso)......... (J Taylor) 2,400

Stormhill Banker ch g (4yrs) Broadsword (USA) - Bank House Lodge (Funny Man)................ (Mrs D Grissell) 3,000

Property of Queenford Studs Ltd

(IRE) b g (5yrs) Strong Gale - Belle Bavard (Le Bavard)............... (C T Nash) 4,600

Property of The Hon. Mrs B S L Trafford

b g (3yrs) King Of Spain - Stately Gala (Gala Performance)................. (Cash) 1,600

Property of Mrs F Morris

Storm The Fortress b g (4yrs) Fort Nayef - Tel Brig (New Brig)...... (N Benstead) 3,000

Property of Mr C Dawson, from Nunstainton Stables

Jigger ch g (6yrs) Miramar Reef - Visiting (Vitiges (FR)) .... (David Minton Bloodstock) 7,000

Property of Mrs Simon Tindall

Senegalais (FR) b g (9yrs) Quart de Vin (FR) - Divonne (FR) (Vieux Chateau)........ (J Frost) 3,000

Property of Mr S R Hope

Whatagale br m (6yrs) Strong Gale - Gardez Le Reste (Even Money) .... (David Minton Bloodtock) 10,000

Property of Miss Sue Hunter

Pennine Pride ch g (6yrs) Over The River (FR) - Pats'y Girl (Dadda Bert)......... (T Cunningham) 15,000

Property of Mr W Brown

Top Row b g (10yrs) Beldale Flutter (USA) - Connaught Nymph (Connaught)....... (C Twist) 975

190

Property of Mr Ian Brown

Elusive Diana b m (11yrs) Viking Chief - Elusive Butterfly (Fly Over)..... (Cash) 800

King Cap ch g (8yrs) Kinglet - Mandycap (Mandamus).................. (Cash) 1,650

Property of Mr D Curtis

Please Explain gr g (12yrs) General Ironside - Newsletter (London Gazette) .... (David Minton Bloodstock) 2,200

From Rest Hill Farm

ch f (4yrs) Afzal - Secret Stolen (USA) (Sassafras (FR))......... (N Trevithick) 1,100

ch g (4yrs) Lancastrian - Minor Furlong (Native Bazaar).......... (C Weedon) 1,800

Property of Mrs R E Hambro

b g (4yrs) Idiot's Delight - Drink Time (Forlorn River)................. (J Retter) 9,000

From Manor Farm Stables

b g (3yrs) Belfort (FR) - Morlolly (Morston) (Mr Wilson) 900

From Witney Stud Farm

(IRE) ch g (5yrs) Stalker - Bellinor (Le Levanstell)..................... (Cash) 5,600

Property of Mrs Nicola Turner

ch m (5yrs) Sunyboy - Sirenia (Biskrah) .... (M Wells) 1,500

Property of Mr David Fulton

Frozen Minstrel b g (9yrs) Black Minstrel - Arctic Sue (Arctic Slave)...... (Cash) 3,600

191

Property of a Partnership

Maytown ch g (7yrs) Town And Country - Mayotte (Little Buskins)..... (R Nolan) 2,100

Property of Mrs S J Popham, from Bashford Stables

Frans Girl b m (10yrs) Take-A-Reef - March Maid (Marmaduke).......... (R Page) 1,400

Property of Terry Warner Sports

Warner For Pleasure b g (7yrs) Lighter - Gay Park (Pardigras).... (G W Briscoe) 1,650

To Dissolve a Partnership

Double The Black ch m (8yrs) Black Minstrel - Oweena Jay (Double-U-Jay) .... (J Frost) 1,800

Wristwatch gr g (4yrs) Alias Smith (USA) - Time-Table (Mansingh (USA))........ (South Bucks Racing) 2,500

Property of Mrs C M Marles

No Boundaries b g (7yrs) Pitskelly - Santa Chiara (Astec)........ (Thomas Smith) 2,500

Property of Mr G G A Gregson, from Howson Stables

Irish Velvet b g (7yrs) Ballacashtal (CAN) - Normandy Velvet (Normandy).......... (T Saunders) 3,000

Property of Mrs R Morris, from High Onn Stud
b f (12yrs) Seymour Hicks (FR) - Dolly Dickens (Double U Jay) .... (Catherine Gower) 750
Property of Manor Farm Stud
Beggars Point (IRE) b g (5yrs) Shirley Heights - Lady's Bridge (USA) (Sir Ivor) (M Weir) 1,400
Property of Mr T G Lewis
ch c (2yrs) Prince Des Coeurs (USA) - Jealous Sandy (Test Piece)..... (Cash) 400

192

Property of Mr Hugh B Hodge
The Braughingbaron b g (8yrs) Sunyboy - Pelante Barle (Prince Barle)........... (P Gaywood) 1,350
Property of a Lady
(IRE) b m (5yrs) Carlingford Castle - Flying Early (Ballyciptic) (South Bucks Racing) 2,300
Property of Mrs M Howell
Mondino br g (8yrs) Soudno - Ozy Lass (Ozymandias)............ (Mr Gardner) 1,000
Property of a Gentleman
C Sharp ch g (6yrs) Song - Simply Jane (Sharpen Up)..... (South Bucks Racing) 1,800
PRIVATE SALES
Property of Miss S Pilkington
Synonymous ch m (10yrs) New Member - Squiffy (Articulate)............. (Cash) 1,250
Property of Mr John Rose, from Kilvington Stud
Some Pleasure b g (5yrs) Bustino - First Pleasure (Dominion)...... (Mr Christie) 5,500
Property of Mr Rae Edward Eckley
That's Justit b g (7yrs) Le Bavard (FR) - Dereen (Boreen)............. (T Smith) 2,500
Property of Mrs S Cartridge
Jhal Frezi b g (5yrs) Netherkelly - Warham Trout (Barolo).............. (A Barrow) 3,500

193

MALVERN
(Russell, Baldwin & Bright)
Tuesday, June 22nd

Property of Mr A J Turner
Derring Bud br g (9yrs) Derring Rose - Tarune (Tarqogan).................... (Lady Susan Brooke) 2,000
Property of Mr G Brown
Swing Free bl g (11yrs) Swing Easy (USA) - Failing Light (Ballymoss)..... (J Young) 650
Property of Mrs M Wall
Aquamoor b g (12yrs) Java Sea - Skittles (Watergate).............. (M Wanless) 780
To Dissolve A Partnership, from Ness Strange Stables
Weekend Girl b f (4yrs) Vorvados - Mrs Scattercash (Northfields (USA)) .... (Mr Kneath) 1,300
Property of Mrs Carol Lawrence
Sportsnews b g (11yrs) New Member - Dicopin (Deauville II).................. (Midland Bloodstock) 2,000

Property of Unity Farm Holiday Centre Ltd., from Halsey Cross Farm
Badihar (USA) ch g (9yrs) Nijinsky - Nofida (Right Tack)........... (Mrs M Vicary) 3,200
Property of Mr R D Griffiths, from Uppertown Stables
Mount Falcon b g (11yrs) Paico - Lady Mell (Milan)................... (C Morgan) 1,500
Property of Mr G Davies, from Home Farm
Deristone b g (8yrs) Rustingo - Deriside (Saucy Kit)................. (K Archer) 1,300
Property of Mr M W Davies, from Home Farm
Sea Dragon ch m (5yrs) Librate - La Chica (El Cid)................... (H Buckard) 900
Property of Mr Bernard Heffernan
Tranquil Waters (USA) ch g (7yrs) Diesis - Ebbing Tide (USA) (His Majesty (USA)) (P Blockley) 4,500
Golden Acre b g (11yrs) Los Cerrillos (ARG) - Pharaoh's Bride (Pharaoh Hophra).... (Mr Black) 1,500
Garden Centre Boy ch g (9yrs) Riboboy (USA) - Miss Topaz (Pitcairn).......... (P Blockley) 4,200
Honey's Fortune gr g (6yrs) Magic Mirror - Close To You (Nebbiolo)... (G Dibello) 1,500
Garbally Park b g (10yrs) Cut Above - Godwyn (Yellow God) (Mr Doyne-Ditmas) 1,100
Green Secret b g (12yrs) Most Secret - Greenfield Girl (Pendragon)..... (Cash) 650
Brynhill Alert ch g (7yrs) Croghan Hill - Brynhurst Court (Red Alert) (R Beever) 4,500
Ellferandem b g (13yrs) Giolla Mear - Peppardstown (Javelot)........... (Cash) 1,000
Come On Lucky ch m (10yrs) Some Hand - Pharaoh's Bride (Pharaoh Hophra)..... (Cash) 600

194

Property of Miss H L Hall
Anshegee bl m (8yrs) Strong Gale - Fairy Queen (Prefairy)........... (J Bowen) 2,300
Property of Mr J A T de Giles, from Holy Oak Hill Farm
Forged Punt b g (6yrs) Paddy's Stream - Used Notes (New Brig).... (P Funnell) 2,400
From Glebe Farm
The Blue Boy (IRE) ch g (5yrs) Tate Gallery (USA) - Blue Lookout (Cure The Blues (USA))..................... (P Bowen) 4,400
Property of Mr Leslie Law, from Coldcroft Farm Stables
Colonel Bilston b g (8yrs) Mansingh (USA) - Forlorn Leap (Forlorn River). . (J Carter) 1,800
Property of Mr F Appleton, from Coldcroft Farm Stables
Pasonate b g (7yrs) Pas de Seul - Detonate (Derring-Do)............. (Mr Kinnear) 1,600
Property of Mr P Heywood
Shinkansen ch m (6yrs) Remainder Man - Provanhill Girl (Gentilhombre)......... (J Bullock) 1,200
From Bankhouse Stables
Snippetoff b g (5yrs) Dubassoff (USA) - Snippet (Ragstone).......... (P Lucy) 1,700
Golden Croft ch g (10yrs) Crofter (USA) - Rossian (Silent Spring)..... (J Cradley) 1,000

Shamaaly Baby (USA) ch g (5yrs) Northern Baby (CAN) - Shining Skin (USA) (Fappiano (USA))............. (Mr Clothier) 1,600

To Dissolve A Partnership, from Bache Hill Stables

Little Rise b g (11yrs) Starch Reduced - Dido's Hill (Sharpen Up)... (D Tuckley) 850

195

To Dissolve A Partnership, from Little London Farm

Andrelot b g (6yrs) Caerleon (USA) - Seminar (Don (ITY))............ (A Thorpe) 5,000

Property of Mr Bernard Heffernan

Yahoo b g (12yrs) Trombone - Coolroe Aga (Laurence O)............... (R Jones) 10,000

Arthurs Stone ch g (7yrs) Kings Lake (USA) - Two Rock (Mill Reef (USA)) .... (R Beever) 2,100

Fellow's Night ch g (10yrs) Deep Run - Chihuahua (Mustang)...... (A Brooks) 650

Get Stepping ch g (7yrs) Posse (USA) - Thanks Edith (Gratitude).. (W Whitley) 7,000

Whittaborough Miss gr f (3yrs) Homeboy - Firm Conviction (Scottish Rifle)........ (L Wakeham) 620

Only For Love b g (14yrs) Golden Love - Proud Wednesday (Raincheck)......... (D Kelly) 900

Dunphys Handful b g (7yrs) Dunphy - Royal Handful (Some Hand)....... (K Dance) 1,150

Another Bolus gr g (11yrs) Yankee Gold - Pretty Candy (Candy Cane) .... (J Edwards) 2,800

Seal King ch g (8yrs) Royal Match - Seal Flower (Gelert)............ (R Williams) 2,000

196

Property of Mr W Chinn, from Walford Court

Maid Of Onions b or br m (6yrs) Oats - Chin Tu (Shackleton)....... (Mr Woolerton) 1,800

Property of Messrs. Court, Robert and Hill, from Trefeinon Farm

Robcourt Hill br g (8yrs) Callernish - Cooney Island (Distinctly (USA))........ (Cash) 1,600

Property of Mr David Redvers, from Tweenhills Farm

Olveston (NZ) b g (9yrs) Sea Anchor - Statira (NZ) (Imperial Match (CAN)).... (P Hayward) 2,800

Property of Mr P Bowen

Parkbhride b g (7yrs) Wolver Hollow - Gulistan (Sharpen Up)... (W Raymond) 10,000

To Dissolve A Partnership, from Scarifour Stables

Moon Reef ch m (7yrs) Main Reef - Malmsey (Jukebox)............ (C Rogers) 1,800

Property of Mrs P Gibson

Kyme Warrior b g (12yrs) Privy Seal - Dessert Moon (Nulli Secundus) (J Lomas) 1,800

Property of Miss B L Moore, from Hillside Stud

Knockcairn ch g (6yrs) Le Moss - Coforta (The Parson)............... (J Carter) 2,000

Property of Mr David Williams, from Hillside Stud

See More Of It (IRE) b g (5yrs) Seymour Hicks (FR) - Sagrada (Shantung)....... (R Barber) 2,000

Property of Mr C M Gee, from Conduit Farm Stud

Chevalogan b g (9yrs) Cheval - Wrekenogan (Tarqogan)......... (Miss J Duplessis) 2,900

From Locketts Farm

Gunner's Flight ch m (9yrs) Celtic Cone - Lady Lucy (Hardraw Scar) .... (E.M.C. Ltd (Wetherby)) 10,000

197

Property of Mrs G B Walford, from Cornborough Manor Stables

All Or Nothing ch m (5yrs) Scorpio (FR) - Kelton Lass (Lord Nelson (FR))........ (Mrs J Jeffrey) 2,600

Property of Mrs P A Russell

Hot Prospect b f (4yrs) Damister (USA) - Smelter (Prominer)..... (Ms. A Perks) 1,900

Property of Mrs M K Stirk

Fair Rowanna b m (5yrs) Prince Of Peace - Miss Tidy (Gang Warily)..... (C Leech) 1,800

Property of Mr R B Francis, from Cliff Bank Stables

Tara Boy b g (8yrs) Rusticaro (FR) - Flosshilde (Rheingold)............... (J Ferguson Bloodstock) 5,800

Property of a Lady, from Guy's Cliffe Stables

Aston Warrior ch m (6yrs) Roman Warrior - Steeple Delight Vii ((unknown))........ (Mr Buchanan) 1,500

From Clonard Farm

Kamadora ch g (6yrs) Kambalda - Icydora (Arctic Slave)............ (J Robinson) 3,000

Furry Day b g (7yrs) Furry Glen - Bright Company (King's Company) .... (Mr Farrell) 4,000

Property of Mrs C Ratcliff & Miss C Redfern

Orange King ch g (9yrs) Kings Lake (USA) - Jaffa (Right Royal V)....... (G Morley) 3,400

From Hesketh Grange Stables

Thompson Flyer b g (6yrs) Swing Easy (USA) - Off The Mark (On Your Mark) (D Clapham) 2,500

b g (2yrs) Jester - Donnacelli (Don Carlos) (Mr Sharland) 800

b g (4yrs) Green Ruby (USA) - Dancing Clara (Billion (USA))......... (H Pym) 1,300

198

Property of Mr W M Wanless, from Lartington Hall Stables

Fine Fine b g (7yrs) Liberated - Goldness Bing (Bing II)............ (Mr Burson) 1,500

Property of Mrs Sally Gill, from Chastleton Hill Stables

Admiral Oliver ch g (8yrs) New Member - Sea Gal (Sea Hawk II)....... (N Allen) 5,900

Property of Mr W R Denson, from Ashley Stables

San Francisco Joe (USA) br g (9yrs) Plum Bold (USA) - Destacion (USA) (Decimator (USA))............. (P Hutchinson) 3,100

From Picton House Stables

Major Cut b g (7yrs) Furry Glen - Quetta's Dual (Dual).............. (J Gregson) 3,500

Property of Mrs S Siviter, from Elliotte House Farm Stables

Mister Jolly b g (7yrs) Le Moss - Santimwen (Cassim)............ (Mrs Bubb) 2,000

Property of Mrs J Nicholson, from Annettes Field Farm Stables

ch g (3yrs) Buckley - Do Something (Pardao)........................ (T Tate) 2,300

b m (6yrs) Celtic Cone - Little Buskinbelle (Little Buskins)............. (J Carter) 1,750

Property of Mr Robert Reddaway, from Middleton Farm

ch g (4yrs) Blakeney Point - Rambling Rolls (Silver Cloud).......... (Ms. J Arnold) 3,600

Property of Mr W R Lewis, from Silver Birch Stables

b g (4yrs) Push On - Shylyn (Hay Chas).... (F Hollis) 2,400

From Toldrum Farm

Not Another Store (IRE) b g (5yrs) Italic (FR) - Caratasca (FR) (Stratege (USA))...... (B Hensworth) 2,000

b g (3yrs) Little Wolf - Pickled Tink (Tickled Pink)........................ (T Tate) 2,500

199

Property of Mrs J A Sharp

ch g (5yrs) New Member - Tantaliser II (Tenterhooks)................ (K Kay) 3,300

Property of Mr & Mrs D G du Plessis, from Higher Pill Farm

b f (3yrs) Derring Rose - Orange Spice (Orange Bay)........... (Mrs Nelmes) 850

Property of Miss J Smith, from Poplar Lodge Stud

ch m (5yrs) Doctor Wall - Ty-Pren (Precipice Wood)................... (M Wood) 2,200

Property of Mr W I Owens, from Woodhouse Farm

b f (3yrs) Derring Rose - Space Kate (Space King)..................... (B James) 2,100

Property of Mrs P Avison

b f (3yrs) State Diplomacy (USA) - Burntwood Lady (Royal Buck)... (G Andrew) 1,400

Property of Mr P Banks, from Banley Farm

ch f (4yrs) Nearly A Hand - Royal Rushes (Royal Palace)............ (W Morgan) 1,800

Property of Mrs P A Hemmings, from Haylane Farm

ch f (3yrs) Newski (USA) - Caswell Bay (Coronash).............. (Mr Homer) 1,250

ch g (3yrs) Monsanto (FR) - Caswell Bay (Coronash)................ (J Fussell) 900

Property of Mr W R Jones

gr g (3yrs) Scallywag - Pear Drop (Bustino) (A Treckell) 2,100

Property of Mr W Price

ch g (4yrs) Riberetto - Petite Cone (Celtic Cone)................ (Mrs Nelmes) 1,100

200

Property of Mr L J Righton

b f (4yrs) Idiot's Delight - March Maid (Marmaduke)........... (Mrs S Eeley) 1,200

Property of Mrs A Lee Warner

b f (4yrs) Welsh Captain - Sugaran (Hardiran)..................... (D Morley) 1,250

Property of Mr D T Owens, from Luntley Farm

b m (5yrs) Sonnen Gold - Captive Maiden (Manacle)................. (J Payne) 1,250

Property of Mr K C G Edwards

Scally Hicks ch f (2yrs) Seymour Hicks (FR) - Scally Jenks (Scallywag) .... (Sir A Brooke) 950

Property of Mrs M Ree

Late Night Session ch g (4yrs) Cisto (FR) - Belize (Tom Noddy).......... (J King) 2,400

Property of Mr G W Lewis, from Rhydale Farm

b g (3yrs) Ascendant - Hurricane Lizzie (Kalimnos)......... (Miss J Duplessis) 2,500

Property of Llety Farms, from Llety Stud

b y c Bold Owl - Sodina (Saulingo) .... (L Bowen) 1,000

Property of Mrs M H Brown, from Dan-Y-Graig Farm

Brass Fortune b g (3yrs) Motivate - Brass Lady (Bold As Brass).... (G Coombes) 1,600

Property of Mr R Richardson

ch g (2yrs) Mansingh (USA) - Sallusteno (Sallust)................. (Mr Moore) 1,350

Property of Mr D Sherriff

b g (2yrs) Amboise - Image Of War (Warpath)...................... (C Drew) 950

201

From Picton House Stables

ch f (3yrs) Deep River - Native Love (Native Prince)................. (Mr Kneath) 875

Spinayab b f (4yrs) King Of Spain - Pallomere (Blue Cashmere) (R Fanshawe) 1,800

Property of Mr J A C Edwards, from Caradoc Court

Afaristoun (FR) b g (9yrs) Top Ville - Afrique (FR) (Exbury)............. (H Morris) 1,800

Property of Dr J O'Connor

Ora Pronobis b g (7yrs) Kambalda - Let's Compromise (No Argument).......... (R Hancox) 1,400

Property of Viscountess Boyne

Green Goddess b m (7yrs) The Parson - Erins Treasure (Brave Invader (USA)) .. (J Collett) 2,200

202

FAIRYHOUSE (Tattersalls)

Thursday, June 24th

Property of Mr C Maye, from Lake Farm Stud

b g (4yrs) The Parson - Stringfellows (Laurence O)..................... (Cash) 15,000

Property of Mr Laurence King

b g (4yrs) Rising - Brave Dorney (Brave Invader)...................... (Cash) 5,000

Property of Mr Charles Moore

ch g (4yrs) Le Bavard (FR) - Brown Forest (Brave Invader)................ (Cash) 6,000

From Glenarriff Stud

b g (3yrs) Wylfa - Fallen Glass (Shack)..... (J Gorman) 7,000

Property of Mr J Moclair
br or gr g (3yrs) Roselier (FR) - Dame Of St John (Counsel)......... (Tom Mullins) 5,000
From Dunsany Stud
b g (4yrs) Heraldiste (USA) - Calcine (Roan Rocket)........................ (Cash) 3,300
From Oak Lodge Stud
Made Of Steel (IRE) b g (4yrs) Flash Of Steel - Kew Gift (Faraway Son)........ (B Barry) 5,000
From Glenview Farm
b g (3yrs) The Parson - Shores Of Tripoli (Islam)........................ (Cash) 6,600
ch g (3yrs) Glenstal (USA) - Lady Broke (Busted)................ (Frank Barry) 9,200
Property of Mr Patrick Dunford
b f (3yrs) Supreme Leader - Giolla Donn (Giolla Mear)............ (John Upson) 2,100

203

From Park House (Ratoath)
br g (4yrs) Orchestra - Mother Cluck (Energist).................. (John Fowler) 9,000
From Rowanstown Stud
b or br g (4yrs) Henbit (USA) - Kekova (Kythnos)..................... (Cash) 2,000
From Pier House Stud (Agent)
b g (4yrs) Strong Gale - Rosenanti (Three Dons)........................ (Cash) 5,800
Property of T Kilroe & Partners, from Copper Beeches Farm
br g (3yrs) Strong Gale - Dream House (Varano)........................ (Cash) 10,000
From Brook Lodge
ch g (4yrs) Long Pond - The Cardy (Chou Chin Chow)....... (Seamus O'Farrell) 2,000
Property of Mr Martin Cullinane. from Mount Brown Stables
b g (3yrs) Celio Rufo - Ballyholland Star (Laurence O)......... (John McGrath) 3,000
From Longmore Stud
b g (4yrs) Drumalis - Bradawn (Brave Invader)........................ (Cash) 7,600
Property of Miss Olive Taaffe
b f (3yrs) Henbit (USA) - Hazy Belle (Pitpan) (J Jackson) 5,500
Property of Mr Martin Curran
ch f (3yrs) Bulldozer - Gorgeous Gael (Atan) (M Kiernan) 4,000
Property of Mr Noel Lane
b g (4yrs) Orchestra - Susan McCann (Furry Glen)........................ (C.B.A.) 13,500

204

Property of Mr B Kennedy, from Meadowlands Stud
b f (3yrs) Callernish - Lovely Pine (Woodville).................. (E O'Sullivan) 4,000
Property of Mrs Yvonne Glynn, from Knockaderry House Stud
b g (3yrs) Carlingford Castle - Hill Invader (Brave Invader)............. (J Byrne) 5,400
Property of Lombard Bros, from Rahard Stud
br g (3yrs) Saronicos - Shanaway (Moss Court)..................... (D Quinn) 4,000

From Clifton Lodge Stud
b or br g (3yrs) Henbit (USA) - Polar Bee (Gunner B)............. (Al O'Connell) 12,500
From Galgystown Stud
b g (4yrs) Denel (FR) - Garden Of Roses (London Bells)............. (K Bailey) 9,200
Property of Miss M O'Donnell, from Ballynolan Stud
b f (4yrs) Royal Fountain - Hill Lane (Pollerton).................... (O Brennan) 2,100
Property of Mr Garrett Ducey
b or br g (3yrs) Over The River (FR) - Juverna Lass (Chinatown)... (J Quinn) 5,200
ch g (4yrs) Phardante (FR) - Mad For Her Beer (Proverb)............. (C.B.A.) 5,800
From Blackrock Stud (Agent)
br g (4yrs) Roselier (FR) - Eleika (Camden Town)............... (Patrick Evans) 10,500
ch g (3yrs) Roselier (FR) - Coolcanute (Hardicanute)........................ (Cash) 3,800

205

Property of Mrs C J Power, from Spybank Stud
b g (3yrs) Strong Gale - Merry Miss (Deep Run)...................... (J Gifford) 14,000
Property of Mr Sean Gavin, from Redpender Stud
b g (3yrs) Mandalus - Deep Serenade (Deep Run)...................... (W Kane) 2,700
Property of Messrs Liam & Pat Gavin, from Redpender Stud
b g (3yrs) King's Ride - Steel Fort (Giolla Mear)................ (Brickhill Stud) 6,600
Property of Mr William Brannigan, from Ballymacarney Stud
b g (3yrs) Cataldi - Silver Doll (Sovereign Gleam)........................ (Cash) 5,600
Property of Mr Edward Ryan, from Boderan Farm
b or br f (4yrs) Strong Gale - Pampered Run (Deep Run)............. (V A Secker) 7,600
From Sunnyhill Stud
br g (4yrs) Good Thyne (USA) - Mia's Girl (Faberge II).................. (Cash) 9,200
b g (4yrs) Good Thyne (USA) - Current Call (Electrify)..................... (Cash) 30,000
Property of Mr & Mrs C B Poots
gr g (4yrs) Roselier (FR) - Lovely Stranger (Le Bavard).................... (Cash) 8,400
From Leachestown Stud
ch g (4yrs) Sandalay - Golden Goose (Prince Hansel)............ (James McNicoll) 4,800
ch g (4yrs) Decent Fellow - Eadestown (Kinglet).................. (G Balding) 5,000

206

Property of Mrs Mary O'connor, from Lough-Na-Sollis Stud
ch f (4yrs) Le Moss - Ursula's Choice (Cracksman).......... (Crohane Stud) 6,400
Property of Mr D Hynes
ch g (3yrs) Phardante (FR) - Rent A Card (Raise You Ten)......... (P McCreery) 12,500
From Pine Tree Stud
b g (4yrs) Henbit (USA) - St Moritz (Linacre) (Cash) 10,000

b g (4yrs) Buckskin (FR) - Cherry Branch (Menelek). . . . . (Ian Ferguson) 13,000

Property of R R Clarke, from Drumrainey Stud

b g (3yrs) Le Bavard (FR) - Clairellen (Ashmore). . . . . (Fulling Mill Stud) 3,000

From Whitemoor Stud

br g (3yrs) Lafontaine (USA) - Villa Lucia Vii (Ballinvella Boy). . . . . (Frank Barry) 7,200

From Glenvale Stud (Agent)

b g (4yrs) Remainder Man - Stormy Waters (Typhoon). . . . . (Cash) 8,600

b g (4yrs) Teofane - Carraigaloe (Little Buskins). . . . . (Lisselan Farms) 6,400

Property of Mr Michael McKeever, from Glenvale Stud

gr g (4yrs) Celio Rufo - Dinsdale (Menelek) (Frank Barry) 10,000

Property of Mr John Sheehan, from Coolnagour House Stud

ch g (3yrs) Orchestra - Warsaw (Salvo) . . . . (Francois Doumen) 10,000

207

Property of Miss Riona Heffernan

ch g (3yrs) Buckskin (FR) - Kassina (Laurence O). . . . . (John Hellens) 6,000

From Bishopstown Stud

b or br g (4yrs) The Parson - Gemelek (Menelek). . . . . (C.B.A.) 13,500

From Crampscastle Stud

b or br g (3yrs) Strong Gale - Her Name Was Lola (Pitskelly). . . . . (D Forster) 19,500

b g (3yrs) Roselier (FR) - Coolentallagh (Perhapsburg). . . . . (John McGrath) 14,000

From Queenford Stud Ltd

ch g (4yrs) Callernish - Mystical Moonshine (Proverb). (C.B.A.) 11,000

br g (4yrs) King's Ride - Atlantic Hope (Brave Invader). . . . . (K Bailey) 5,600

Property of M & R Bloodstock

b g (4yrs) Strong Gale - Sirrahdis (Bally Joy) (Castlemartin Stud) 21,000

From Little Lodge Farm

b g (3yrs) Strong Gale - Laurello (Bargello) (Cash) 16,000

b g (3yrs) Derring Rose - Always Shining (Tug Of War). . . . . (Cash) 6,100

Property of Mr Brian Bamber

b g (4yrs) Sheer Grit - Welsh Escort (Welsh Captain). . . . . (Mrs J M Mullins) 5,300

br g (4yrs) Miner's Lamp - Abbey Lodge (Master Owen). . . . . (J H Johnson) 5,800

208

Property of Mr Neville J Tector, from Coolbawn Stud

ch g (3yrs) Orange Reef - Judy Cullen (Wrekin Rambler). . . . . (Cash) 5,200

Property of Mr Denis McDonnell

b or br g (4yrs) Celio Rufo - Mugra (Mugatpura). . . . . (M Halford) 7,600

Property of Mrs M Brophy

b g (4yrs) Strong Gale - Orlinda (Levanter) (J A O'Connell) 12,500

Property of Miss E J Sanford, from Augherskea Stables

b g (4yrs) Bishop Of Orange - Dara's Last (March Parade). . . . . (Cash) 7,000

Property of Park Stud

b g (3yrs) Phardante (FR) - Quayville (Quayside) (David Minton Bloodstock) 7,600

From Rathbarry Stud (Agent)

b g (3yrs) Good Thyne (USA) - Just A Maid (Rarity). . . . . (David Minton Bloodstock) 12,000

b or br f (4yrs) Phardante (FR) - Tou Wan (Grand Roi) (David Minton Bloodstock) 16,500

From Bellfield Stud

br g (3yrs) Strong Gale - Ballybrowney Gold (Goldhill). . . . . (Robert Ogden) 25,000

b g (3yrs) Phardante (FR) - Soul Lucy (Lucifer). . . . . (Michael Flynn) 22,000

From Rachel Bennett (Agent)

b or br f (3yrs) Supreme Leader - Rambling Love (Golden Love) . . . . (John C Shearman) 4,800

209

Property of Mr High Williams, from Knockaney Stud

b f (3yrs) The Parson - Etrenne (Happy New Year). . . . . (K Neville) 14,000

Property of Mr David Mitchell

ch g (4yrs) Orchestra - Fiona's Blue (Crash Course). . . . . (K Bailey) 25,500

Property of Fidelma White

br f (4yrs) Buckskin (FR) - Wrekenogan (Tarqogan). . . . . (Cash) 5,400

From Barnore Stud

b g (3yrs) Corvaro (USA) - Welsh Tan (Welsh Saint). . . . . . (Francois Doumen) 6,800

From The Borotown Stud

br g (4yrs) Aristocracy - Shining Green (Green Shoon). . . . . (J F C Maxwell) 17,000

Property of Marshall Parkhill

br g (3yrs) Roselier (FR) - Fly Fuss (Little Buskins). . . . . (D T Hughes) 5,200

br g (3yrs) Roselier (FR) - Queenie Kelly (The Parson). . . . . (Cash) 8,000

b g (3yrs) Idiot's Delight - Joca (Rarity) . . . . (Cash) 15,500

b g (3yrs) King's Ride - Random What (Random Shot). . . . . (Cash) 8,000

br f (4yrs) Strong Gale - Miss Miller (Laurence O). (C.B.A.) 15,000

210

From Cregg Stud

b or br g (3yrs) Roselier (FR) - Deep Link (Deep Run). . . . . (Cash) 5,000

b g (3yrs) Henbit (USA) - Bedouin Dancer (Lorenzaccio). . . . . (Cash) 8,000

Property of Mr D P O'Brien, from Derrygrath Stud

b or br g (4yrs) Roselier (FR) - Sugarstown (Sassafras). . . . . (Seamus O'Ferrall) 5,000

gr g (4yrs) Roselier (FR) - Private Affair (Julion Mariner). . . . . (J FitzGerald) 12,000

b g (4yrs) The Parson - Miss Lucille (Fine Blade). . . . . (C.B.A.) 15,000

b g (4yrs) The Parson - Bright Record (Royal Record II). . . . . (John Upson) 30,000

From Grangegodden Stud

b g (4yrs) Le Bavard (FR) - Credit Card (Current Coin). . . . . (Declan Weld) 24,000

Property of Quarryfield Stud
br g (4yrs) Strong Gale - Super Cailin (Brave Invader).... (David Minton Bloodstock) 20,000
From Quarryfield Stud
b g (3yrs) Mandalus - Milan Pride (Northern Guest)................ (Francis Flood) 15,000
b g (3yrs) Callernish - Lady Albron (Royal Match)........................ (Cash) 7,500

211

From Mellon Stud
Belvoir (FR) b g (4yrs) Quart de Vin (FR) - Herenice (FR) (Laniste).. (Mr Rohaunt) 14,000
Property of Mr P Conway
b g (4yrs) Buckskin (FR) - More Chat (Torenaga)............ (Jim Dreaper) 11,000
Property of Mr R Eustace
b g (3yrs) Roselier (FR) - Suny Salome (Sunyboy).. (David Minton Bloodstock) 7,800
From Tally-Ho Stud
b g (3yrs) Lafontaine (USA) - Garland Song (My Swanee)........... (Peter Doyle) 5,200
ch g (4yrs) Orchestra - Another Bless (Random Shot)............. (D T Hughes) 10,000
Property of Mr Johnnie Browne, from Tourtane House
ch g (4yrs) Fresh Breeze (USA) - Castleblagh (General Ironside)........... (James Trigg) 2,600
b g (4yrs) Supreme Leader - Sapphire Red (Red Alert)........... (Paul Shanahan) 15,500
Property of Mr Michael Fagan
b g (4yrs) Strong Gale - Rathara (Furry Glen) .... (Cash) 12,000
br g (4yrs) Orchestra - Bramble Rose (Pal's Passage)................ (J Charlton) 15,000
Property of Mr & Mrs R A St Geoerge
ch g (3yrs) Callernish - Er In Doors (General Ironside)............. (Paul Shanahan) 20,000

212

From Cloneymeath Farm
ch g (3yrs) Orchestra - Bunkilla (Arctic Slave)........................ (C.B.A.) 11,000
Property of Mrs A S O'Brien, from Landscape Stud
br g (4yrs) Strong Gale - Gamonda (Gala Performance)................. (Cash) 10,000
From Marshalstown House Stud
b f (3yrs) King's Ride - Knockarctic (Quayside)........... (Peter McCreery) 5,000
Property of Mr W Maher
b or br g (4yrs) Mandalus - Russell's Touch (Deep Run)........... (J H Johnson) 10,000
Property of Mr Brian O'Mahoney, from Abbey Stables
ch g (3yrs) Roselier (FR) - Vaguely Vulgan (Vulgan).............. (John Kennedy) 15,500
Property of Mr Michael Byrne, from Abbey Stables
b f (3yrs) Roselier (FR) - Suil Na Gale (Strong Gale)........... (Noel Treacy) 5,600
From The Beeches Stud
br f (3yrs) Buckskin (FR) - Maestra Gama (Master Buck)................. (Cash) 10,000

From Monatrim Stud
br g (4yrs) Strong Gale - Double Wrapped (Double-U-Jay).......... (Mickey Flynn) 20,000
From Lismortagh Stables
b or br g (3yrs) Phardante (FR) - Natural Shine (Indigenous)........... (T Hyde) 12,500
b g (4yrs) Strong Gale - Joint Master (Master Owen)........ (Dessie McDonagh) 16,000
b g (4yrs) Supreme Leader - Panel Pin (Menelek).. (David Minton Bloodstock) 26,000

213

Property of Mr Declan Dower, from Creggs House Stud
br g (4yrs) Strong Gale - Careless Biddy (Laurence O)................. (Cash) 7,800
From Tally-Ho Stud
b g (4yrs) King's Ride - Sea Cygnet (Menelek)................. (Jimmy Byrne) 5,000
From Claremount Stables
br g (4yrs) King's Ride - Glamorous Night (Sir Herbert).......... (J F C Maxwell) 18,000
Property of Claremount Stables
b g (4yrs) Lancastrian - Pitcoke (Pitpan).... (Cash) 3,200
Property of Mr Paul Giles
b g (4yrs) King's Ride Or Radical - Shule Doe (Royal Buck)......... (J Charlton) 3,000
b g (3yrs) Tremblant - My Maizey (Buckskin)................... (P Shanahan) 10,000
Property of Mr Donal Casey, from Leefield Stud
b or br f (3yrs) Phardante (FR) - Donegal Lady (Indigenous)..... (Austin Fenton) 7,300
Property of Mr Jeremy Hill, from Monksgrange Stud
b g (3yrs) Strong Gale - Boro Penny (Normandy).............. (Aidan Murphy) 15,000
Property of Mr Jeremiah Sloane
b or br f (3yrs) Phardante (FR) - Be A Devil (Arctic Slave)......... (Robert Chugg) 7,200
Property of Mr Michael Lysaght, from Abbey Stables
b f (3yrs) Strong Gale - Arctic Verb (Proverb) .... (Cash) 11,500

214

Property of Mr Brian O'Mahoney, from Abbey Stables
ch g (3yrs) Good Thyne (USA) - Cappagh Lady (Al Sirat)........... (T Easterby) 2,600
From Ballywooden House
br g (3yrs) Strong Gale - Dusty Hall (Deep Run)...................... (Tom Barry) 15,500
b or br g (3yrs) Convinced - Goldend (Goldhill)........................... (Cash) 2,500
From Kenilworth House Stud
br g (3yrs) Dromod Hill - Farina (Raise You Ten)...................(Tom Mullins) 10,500
Property of Messrs Robert and Peter Roe
br f (3yrs) Strong Gale - Dual Venture (Deep Run)....................... (T Easterby) 4,400
Property of Mr A Hales
b g (3yrs) Phardante (FR) - Buskins Reward (Little Buskins)........ (Liam Cashman) 5,600
Property of a Partnership
ch g (3yrs) Roselier (FR) - Licifer's Way (Lucifer)..................... (Cash) 6,000

215

FAIRYHOUSE (Tattersalls)

Friday, June 25th

From Kingsfurze House

br g (3yrs) Sheer Grit - Raise The Bells (Belfalas)...................... (Cash) 15,000

Property of Mr P Coghlan

b g (3yrs) Bulldozer - Lucky Favour (Ballyciptic)...................... (Cash) 6,700

br g (3yrs) Over The River (FR) - Patrice Princess (Lucifer).............. (Cash) 7,600

Property of Mr S J Dixon, from Mount Top Stud

br f (3yrs) Strong Gale - Rocky's Gal (Oats) (M Kiernan) 6,100

Property of Mr Michael O'Connor

b g (3yrs) Spanish Place (USA) - Deep Sent (Deep Run)............ (Tom Mullins) 4,000

Property of Mr Tom McGrath

b or br f (3yrs) Tremblant - Knollwood Court (Le Jean)........ (Patrick G McGillion) 3,900

From Ballycrighaun Stud

ch g (4yrs) Phardante (FR) - Maravo (Octavo)...................... (Cash) 3,200

Property of Mrs N Doyle

ch g (3yrs) Burslem - Jackson Miss (Condorcet)...................... (Cash) 6,000

From Monanore Stables

b or br g (4yrs) King's Ride - Alkouri (Al Sirat)...................... (E Crow) 8,400

Property of Mr Raymond Nolan

b g (3yrs) Torus - Peaceful Girl (Keep The Peace)................... (Tom Tate) 8,600

216

Property of Mr John McEnery, from Rossenarra Stud

ch g (3yrs) Le Bavard (FR) - Pencil (Crash Course)...................... (Cash) 6,000

Property of D Newman

br g (4yrs) Sexton Blake - Wild Deer (Royal Buck)............... (Lisselan Farms) 6,200

From Briar Hill Stud

br g (4yrs) Dromod Hill - Fotopan (Polyfoto) (Patrick Flynn) 7,800

From Bal Stables

b g (4yrs) King's Ride - Julio Too (Golden House).... (David Minton Bloodstock) 5,000

From Willow Stud

b g (4yrs) Cataldi - Beeston (Our Babu) .... (Cash) 11,500

From Moortown House

b g (4yrs) Strong Gale - My Only Hope (Brave Invader).......... (Rd Duneen) 2,000

Property of Mrs Kathleen Flood

b or br g (4yrs) Pauper - Lady Abednego Vii ((said To Be) Abednego).. (Tom Kemp) 4,000

b g (4yrs) Asir - Clonroche Floods (Pauper) (Pat Flynn) 3,700

Property of Mr Ivor Dulohery

ch f (4yrs) Over The River (FR) - Honey Come Back (Master Owen)........... (Lisselan Farms) 6,000

Property of Mr Hugh McMahon, from Riversfield Stud

b g (4yrs) Supreme Leader - Inagh's Image (Menelek).................. (C B A) 14,000

217

Property of Miss R Tonson Rye, from Rye Court Stud

b g (3yrs) Clearly Bust - Keep Dancing (Lord Gayle)................. (Tom Mullins) 8,600

From Grange Hill Stud

b g (3yrs) Buckskin (FR) - Loverly Tartan (Push On)............. (Dr D B A Silk) 4,600

Property of Mr Peter McCutcheon

b g (4yrs) Supreme Leader - Muckridge Lady (Deep Run).............. (Cash) 4,400

Property of Mrs A Kitchin

gr g (4yrs) Sexton Blake - Biddy Spatters (Raise You Ten)..... (Eric McNamara) 4,200

From Ballymoney Park Stud

b f (3yrs) Supreme Leader - Cauriedator (Laurence O).................. (Cash) 3,400

Property of Annaclaire Bloodstock Ltd, from Ballymoney Park Stud

br g (3yrs) Strong Gale - Babybush (Boreen) .... (R A Green) 20,000

Property of Anna McDonnell, from Ballymoney Park Stud

br f (3yrs) Lancastrian - Lean Over (Over The River).. (David Minton Bloodstock) 7,200

From Mooreshill Farm

b g (3yrs) Mandalus - Apicat (Buckskin).... (F Doumen) 5,800

ch g (3yrs) Buckskin (FR) - Shining Moon (Deep Run)............ (W Edmonds) 6,000

Property of Mr Leo Doyle

b g (4yrs) Kambalda - Five Ally (Walshford) (T Easterby) 3,400

218

From Craheen Stud

gr g (4yrs) Sexton Blake - Merry Proverb (Proverb)... (David Minton Bloodstock) 9,500

Property of Mr Jack Dwan

br g (4yrs) Strong Gale - Verenda (Roman Gift)......................... (Cash) 8,000

br g (3yrs) Strong Gale - Brown Forest (Brave Invader)....................... (David Minton Bloodstock) 15,000

Property of M Hickey

b g (3yrs) The Parson - Little Welly (Little Buskins)........... (Galgystown Stud) 6,900

Property of Mr Patrick O'Meara, from Abbey Stables

br g (3yrs) Mandalus - Rostrevor Lady (Kemal).............. (Michael Gillow) 11,500

ch f (3yrs) Over The River (FR) - Derrella (Derrylin)................. (F Doumen) 6,200

Property of Mr Michael Crean, from Market Hill Stud

b g (4yrs) Orchestra - Rovral Flo (Whistling Deer)............. (Margaret O'Toole) 13,000

Property of Mr Robert Guiry, from Peppardstown Stud

b f (3yrs) Tremblant - Pepsi Star (Raise You Ten)......................... (Cash) 7,200 br f (3yrs) Good Thyne (USA) - Peppardstown Lady (Gleason).................. (Mrs H J Ponsonby) 5,000

Property of Mr Neville J Tector, from Coolbawn Stud

ch g (4yrs) Orange Reef - Judy Cullen (Wrekin Rambler).............. (Cash) 5,400

219

From Castletown Quarry Stud

b g (3yrs) Celtic Cone - Once Bitten (Brave Invader)........................ (Cash) 7,200

From Ellen Lodge Stables

ch g (4yrs) Orchestra - Good Loss (Ardoon) (Cash) 10,000

Property of Mr Richard E Rohan

gr g (3yrs) Alias Smith (USA) - Saleander (Leander).............. (Arthur Moore) 8,200

Property of Mr Jerry Rohan

b or br g (3yrs) Supreme Leader - Healys Pass (Laurence O)................ (Cash) 5,000

Property of Mr R C A Latta

br g (4yrs) Callernish - Tawney Rose (Tarqogan).............. (Thomond O'Mara) 3,600

b f (4yrs) Callernish - Sally Slave (Paddy's Stream)................ (Martin Lynch) 7,600

From Cregg Stud

br g (3yrs) Celtic Cone - That's Show Biz (The Parson)................... (Cash) 5,600

Property of Ms Dolores Keating

b or br g (4yrs) Pollerton - What A Rose (Sir Herbert)... (David Minton Bloodstock) 4,000

Property of Phena Keating

b or br f (3yrs) Callernish - Flashey Blond (Buckskin).............. (David Harvey) 7,800

Property of Mr John Ward

b g (4yrs) Good Thyne (USA) - Cute Play (Salluceva)............ (J F C Maxwell) 7,400

220

From Morganstown Stud

b g (3yrs) Relkino - Sizzle (High Line)...... (Cormac McCormack Associates) 10,000

b or br f (3yrs) Mandalus - Liffey's Choice (Little Buskins)............... (R Alner) 15,500

To Dissolve a Partnership

b or br g (3yrs) The Parson - Lucie Fort (Lucifer)................. (P Shanahan) 33,000

Property of D Ilk

br g (3yrs) Strong Gale - Wrekenogan (Tarqogan)................ (Mrs J Pitman) 19,000

b g (3yrs) Strong Statement (USA) - Meneleks Daughter (Menelek).......... (John White) 7,200

From Sandy Lane Stables

ch g (4yrs) Crash Course - Flight Of Fashion (Little Buskins)...... (Nora Wycherley) 12,500

Property of Mr James J O'Keeffe, from Harveystown Stud

b or br g (3yrs) Supreme Leader - Safe Run (Deep Run).............. (P Shanahan) 15,000

ch g (3yrs) Callernish - Pennyland (Le Bavard)......................... (T Hyde) 9,000

From Coolanure Stud

b g (4yrs) The Parson - Scotch News (London Gazette).................. (Grangecon North West Syndicate (P/s)) 10,500

b g (3yrs) The Parson - Irish Hill Lass (Prominer).................... (Cash) 10,000

221

Property of Ms Mary Stafford

ch g (3yrs) Sheer Grit - Rising Dipper (Golden Dipper)...... (Seamus Burns) 7,000

From Shamrock Stud

b g (3yrs) Step Together (USA) - Jane Eyre (Master Buck).............. (J Mullins) 9,200

From Ballyhampshire Stud

br g (3yrs) Strong Gale - Gala Noon (Gala Performance)........... (J H Johnson) 13,000

Property of Hilltown Stables

b g (3yrs) Bustineto - Diana Harwell (Harwell)........................ (R Fahey) 4,600

From Mount Eaton Stud

b or br g (3yrs) Strong Gale - Paula's Fancy (Lucky Guy).................... (Cash) 15,500

From Culmullin Stud

b g (3yrs) Phardante (FR) - Hansel Money (Prince Hansel)........... (F Doumen) 31,000

From See Side Stables

br g (4yrs) Mandalus - Money No Object (Goldhill)....................... (Cash) 3,700

From Island Stud

b g (4yrs) Mandalus - Sparkling Stream (Paddy's Stream)............... (Cash) 3,700

From Brandane Stud

b g (3yrs) Celio Rufo - Countess Spray (Even Say)........... (Liam Cashman) 6,400

From Knightsbrook

b or br g (4yrs) Phardante (FR) - Light Whisper (Idiot's Delight)....... (Cash) 6,000

b g (4yrs) The Parson - My Duchess (Duky) (David Minton Bloodstock) 18,000

b g (3yrs) Strong Gale - Golden Tears (Rheingold).............. (T Easterby) 9,000

b g (4yrs) Lancastrian - Chake-Chake (Goldhill)........................ (T Easterby) 8,000

222

Property of Mr Patrick J O'Connor

br g (3yrs) Phardante (FR) - Blajina (Bold Lad).................... (F Doumen) 12,500

b g (3yrs) Strong Gale - Arctic Snow Cat (Raise You Ten)...... (J F C Maxwell) 30,000

ch g (3yrs) The Parson - Sno-Cat (Arctic Slave)........................ (T Hyde) 23,000

ch g (3yrs) Buckskin (FR) - Autumn Queen (Menelek)........................ (Cash) 4,500

b g (3yrs) Strong Gale - Woodford Princess (Menelek)................... (T Hyde) 8,000

From Springmount Stud

br g (4yrs) Mandalus - Shady Lucia (Pollerton).......................... (Cash) 12,000

b or br g (4yrs) Mandalus - Hills Approach (Over The River).............. (Cash) 5,000

br f (4yrs) Strong Gale - Shady Doornocker (Mon Capitaine)................ (Cash) 6,200

Property of Mr B J Ryan, from The Nursery Stud

b g (3yrs) Strong Gale - Little Credit (Little Buskins)....................... (Cash) 14,000

ch g (3yrs) The Parson - People (Al Sirat) .. (T Hyde) 16,000

223

Property of Mr J P Berry, from Clonard Stud

b g (3yrs) Buckskin (FR) - Try Another (Deep Run)............... (D Hughes) 10,000

br g (4yrs) Strong Gale - Gala Noon (Gala Performance)................. (Cash) 20,000

Property of Mr M Berry

br f (4yrs) Strong Gale - Bit Of Fashion (Master Owen)....... (J A O'Connell) 10,000

Property of Mr Thomas Steele, from Beechfield House

gr g (4yrs) Le Moss - Debbie's Friend (General Ironside)....... (Matt Roche) 3,500

From The Borotown Stud

b g (4yrs) Phardante (FR) - Khalketta (Khalkis).............. (D McDonogh) 21,000

b g (4yrs) Buckskin (FR) - Tudor Gello (Bargello).............. (Tom Mullins) 4,900

From Boardsmill Stud

br g (3yrs) Corvaro (USA) - Lysanders Lady (Saulingo)............. (T H Caldwell) 6,000

Property of M W Doran

b g (3yrs) Strong Gale - Bargara (Bargello) (M Morris) 34,000

From Parkville Stud

b g (3yrs) Roselier (FR) - Knock Off (Arctic Slave)...................... (F Flood) 14,000

Property of Marie T Doran

b f (3yrs) Strong Gale - Decent Slave (Decent Fellow).............. (Cash) 15,500

224

Property of a Partnership, from Castledillon Stud

b g (4yrs) Le Bavard (FR) - Colour Clown (Random Shot)........... (M Browne) 8,000

From Coolamurry Stud

ch g (3yrs) Lord Ha Ha - Harbour Shuil (Proverb).................... (Cash) 3,100

br f (3yrs) Mandalus - Green Apple (Green Shoon)................ (Jim Brennan) 4,700

gr g (3yrs) Roselier (FR) - Ramble Bramble (Random Shot)...................... (David Minton Bloodstock) 32,500

b g (3yrs) Mandalus - Lucylet (Kinglet)..... (Mrs M Reveley) 12,000

Property of Mr A Murphy, from Ballycurragh Stud

b or br g (4yrs) Sandalay - Cushla (Zabeg).. (R A Greene) 6,000

ch g (4yrs) Kambalda - Zoom Zoom (Bargello).................... (T J O'Meara) 3,800

Property of Mr W D O'Brien

b g (3yrs) Paean - Gentle Maggie (Tarqogan)...................... (Cash) 10,000

b g (3yrs) Over The River (FR) - Aran Tour (Arapaho)...................... (Cash) 5,200

Property of Mr J McCarthy

b g (3yrs) Strong Gale - Our Gale (Dusky Boy).................. (Mederic Ltd) 20,000

225

Property of Mr E Cashin

ch g (3yrs) Montekin - Lady Of Eilat (Cut Above)................. (Kim Bailey) 5,200

Property of Tanners Investment Co, From The Glebe

b g (4yrs) The Parson - Dream Toi (Carlburg) .... (Cash) 25,000

Property of Dr T A O'Brien, from Ballyegan Stables

b f (3yrs) Be My Native (USA) - Dedham Vale (Dike).................... (Cash) 11,500

Property of Mr John Quinn, from Rhyne Stud

b g (4yrs) Supreme Leader - Arabian Sands (Pollerton).................... (Cash) 7,500

From Bishopstown Stud

b f (3yrs) Buckskin (FR) - Left Hand Woman (Energist).............. (W Edmunds) 7,000

Property of J Coleman & A Heskin, from Bishopstown Stud

b f (3yrs) Buckskin (FR) - Aillwee Dawn (Deep Run)........ (Castlemartin Stud) 15,000

From Rathmore Stud (Agent)

b or br g (3yrs) Strong Gale - Taggs Castle (Levmoss).. (David Minton Bloodstock) 30,000

From Slieveardagh Stud

ch g (4yrs) Le Bavard (FR) - Blackrath Girl (Bargello)..................... (Cash) 7,600

b g (4yrs) Mister Lord (USA) - Glenadore (Furry Glen)................... (Cash) 8,000

Property of Mr Redmond Carroll, from Slieveardagh Stud

ch g (3yrs) King Persian - Alto Mira (Patch) (Cash) 4,200

226

Property of Glenvale Stud

b g (4yrs) Strong Gale - Lough Sholin (Kemal)........................ (Cash) 19,000

b g (4yrs) Supreme Leader - Wraparound Sue (Touch Paper)....... (W A Farrell) 12,000

Property of Mr John Molloy, from Glenvale Stud

b g (3yrs) Henbit (USA) - Sally's Wish (Proverb)...................... (Cash) 4,600

From Cherrystown Stud

b or br g (3yrs) Buckskin (FR) - Moppets Last (Pitpan).................. (Cash) 6,000

b f (3yrs) Buckskin (FR) - Keeping Company (King's Company).......... (J Mallow) 4,500

From Mellon Stud

b g (4yrs) Cataldi - Dunderry Class (Dusky Boy)...................... (J Dreaper) 15,500

Property of Mr John P Quinlan, from Moyneard Stud

br g (3yrs) Maculata - Cool As Ice (Prefairy) (J Fowler) 3,000

From Grove House Stud

br g (3yrs) Royal Fountain - Lace Cap (Jaazeiro)....................... (Cash) 8,600

b g (3yrs) Royal Fountain - Little Finch (Milan)....................... (Cash) 7,000

From Hill View Stud

ch g (4yrs) Callernish - Clashdermot Lady (Shackleton)................ (C B A) 13,500

227

Property of Mr Jim McLoughlin

b g (4yrs) Supreme Leader - Tarmar (Sayfar) .... (P Fahy) 6,000

Property of Mr Daniel Shirley, from Garnaman House
b r g (3yrs) Buckskin (FR) - Rose Of Allendale (Green Shoon)..... (W Edmonds) 5,600
From Lakefield Farm (Agent)
b g (3yrs) The Parson - Calyx Pit (Pitpan)... (J A O'Connell) 8,000
From Lingstown Stud
br g (4yrs) Supreme Leader - Royal Escort (Royal Highway)................ (Cash) 8,000
From Knockaney Stud
b g (4yrs) The Parson - Splendid Run (Deep Run)............... (O'Donoghue Bros) 23,000
From Ballymagarvey Stud
b g (4yrs) King's Ride - Beautiful Noise (Jukebox)........... (A J McNamara) 7,800
ch g (4yrs) Orchestra - Gail Borden (Blue Chariot)............... (Adrian Taylor) 16,000
From Ballymorris & Caherass Studs
b g (3yrs) Henbit (USA) - Thai Nang (Tap On Wood)........................ (Cash) 5,000
Property of Mr D Doran
b g (3yrs) Amazing Bust - Perpetue (Proverb).................. (Wm Harney) 7,000
Property of Mr Gerry Cosgrave, from Shanrod Stables
b g (4yrs) Rontino - Speckled Leinster (Prefairy)............ (T Thompson Jones) 5,500
b g (4yrs) Roselier (FR) - Divine Dibs (Raise You Ten)..................... (Cash) 5,800

228

From Shanrod Stables
b or br g (3yrs) Bulldozer - Coloressa's Pet (Halsafari)..................... (Cash) 3,000
Property of Mr Michael Finn
b g (4yrs) Good Thyne (USA) - Highland Party (Deep Run).......... (Kim Bailey) 18,000
Property of Mr P M O'Roarke
b g (4yrs) Good Thyne (USA) - Watch The Birdie (Polyfoto)....... (Tom McCourt) 13,000
Property of Mr Aidan Furlong
b f (4yrs) Crash Course - La Flamenca (Brave Invader)......... (John Fowler) 4,700
Property of Mr Anthony Cameron
b g (4yrs) Torus - Queen's Prize (Random Shot).................... (S Barkley) 5,000
Property of Miss H Rothwell
b f (3yrs) Mandalus - Daisy Owen (Master Owen).................. (C McKeever) 2,700
From Oyster Farm
b g (3yrs) Phardante (FR) - Shallow Run (Deep Run)................ (Liam Cashman) 28,000
From Rathbritt Stud
b f (3yrs) Henbit (USA) - Right Performance (Gala Performance)............ (Cash) 4,000
Property of Mr Mervyn Wynne
b g (4yrs) Supreme Leader - Last Round (Lucky Guy)................... (Cash) 3,800
From Bryanstown Stud
ch g (3yrs) Le Bavard (FR) - Levi's Star (Levmoss)............ (Sean O'Farrell) 4,000

229

Property of Mrs I P Browne
b f (4yrs) Mandalus - Early Start (Wrekin Rambler)..................... (Cash) 4,800
Property of Mr Jack Manning, from Grefort Stud
b or br g (3yrs) Strong Gale - Sweet Tulip (Beau Chapeau)............... (Cash) 12,000
Property of Mr Eugene Laffan
b g (4yrs) Le Moss - Sunny Sunset (Sunny Walk)........................ (Cash) 6,300
From Riverside Stud
ch g (4yrs) Cardinal Flower - Ross Lady (Master Buck)...................... (David Minton Bloodstock) 6,200

230

ASCOT
Monday, June 28th

Property of Mr E A Johnson
La Perricholi (FR) b m (13yrs) Targowice (USA) - Belle Margot (Counsel) (Cash) 875
Property of Mrs E Ludlow
Kingswood Kitchens b g (13yrs) General Ironside - Tyrone Typhoon (Typhoon) .. (R S Bruce) 1,500
Property of a Lady
Maria b m (6yrs) - Breeding unknown ..... (Cash) 1,050
Property of Miss A J Chandler
My Pilot b g (9yrs) Al Sirat (USA) - Dandyville (Vulgan)................. (Cash) 1,200
Property of Mr M J Hill
Colin's Fancy ch m (9yrs) Take A Reef - Iseult (Songedor)........... (G C Fox) 1,000
Property of Mr T Austin
ch f (4yrs) Lord Ballina (AUS) - Cheyenne (Sovereign Path).............. (Cash) 675
ch f (4yrs) Jalmood (USA) - Lipreader (USA) (Mr Leader)................... (Cash) 950
To Dissolve a Partnership
b y c Efisio - Wimosa (Mossborough)...... (P Thormen) 1,150
Mister Virtuous b c (2yrs) Risk Me (FR) - Very Special Lady (Mummy's Game) .. (M McCormack) 1,750
Property of a Gentleman
Top Gunner (IRE) b g (3yrs) Lomond (USA) - Top Mouse (High Top)..... (B Pearce) 825
Dotty's Walker (FR) b f (3yrs) Double Bed (FR) - Lady Tycoon (No Mercy)........ (Ms J Walker) 825

231

Property of Lawrence Plc
Agil's Pet b f (3yrs) Tina's Pet - High Voltage (Electrify)........... (G Kaye) 1,025
To Dissolve a Partnership, from South Bank Stables
Summer Flower b f (3yrs) Nomination - Hedda Garbler (Stradavinsky) .... (A L Forbes) 1,150
Property of Mr T P Roberts-Hindles
Berry's Sky Lark ch m (6yrs) Crested Lark - Quick Walk (Farm Walk) (Mr Gardner) 825
Property of Mr J T Pickering
Lissadell Lady gr f (4yrs) Sharrood (USA) - Clouded Vision (So Blessed) (D Pope) 1,400

Property of Mrs N Dalgren

Skylarkin ch g (7yrs) Karlinsky (USA) - Rose Cottage (Rose Knight).... (F R Brown) 1,100

Property of Six Furlong Racing

ch c (2yrs) Clantime - Lightning Gem (FR) (African Song)........... (Mr Cooper) 425

b f (2yrs) Crofthall - Cornflower Blue (Tyrnavos).................. (J M Bowen) 750

Property of Mr Ray Hawthorn

Aryan Vesper br g (3yrs) Mansingh (USA) - Lilac Star (Hard Man)........... (Cash) 1,200

Property of Mr R Richards, from Whitsbury Manor Racing Stables

Bold Visit (IRE) ch g (3yrs) Bold Arrangement - Visiting (Vitiges (FR)) (H J Pym) 1,200

Property of Mrs F R Watts

Rubidian ch c (3yrs) Primo Dominie - Red Tapsi (Tap On Wood)..... (P J Hobbs) 5,000

232

Property of Mrs J Woolford

Zorro's Mark b g (6yrs) My Rough Diamond - Hawksbill (Tomahawk IV) .... (Julie Purdie) 6,000

Property of Sally Mullins Bloodstock

Onawing Andaprayer b m (6yrs) Energist - Mary's Double (Majetta)..... (J Porter) 2,300

Property of Mr F J Mills

Baman Powerhouse b g (5yrs) Bold Owl - Bella Abzug (Karabas)........... (Cash) 1,500

Property of Mr Guy Opperman

Paradise Beach b g (8yrs) Skyliner - Looks A Million (Wollow)... (Mr Dangerfield) 2,400

Property of Darley Stud Management Co Ltd, from Rockingham Yard

Red Whirlwind b c (3yrs) Shadeed (USA) - Red Red Rose (USA) (Blushing Groom) (B McMath) 7,800

Property of Mrs B Facchino

Iron Baron (IRE) b g (4yrs) Sure Blade (USA) - Riverrine (FR) (Riverman) (D Yeoman) 6,200

Property of Dickins Ltd

Dickins b c (3yrs) Green Ruby (USA) - Rosie Dickins (Blue Cashmere) .... (Racing Thoroughbreds) 1,250

Call Me Dickins gr g (4yrs) Rusticaro (FR) - Bad Start (USA) (Bold Bidder).......... (Mr Fellows) 1,500

From Greenfield Stables (Co Wexford)

Holy Awl b or br g (8yrs) Buckskin (FR) - Saint Audrey (Cracksman) (C E Sherry) 1,900

ch g (6yrs) Le Moss - Suir Lady (Push On) (Mr Rockmill) 975

(IRE) br c (3yrs) Decent Fellow - Naturally Enough (Aglojo).............(M Hoad) 725

Let's Harmonise ch g (6yrs) Orchestra - Can't Agree (Merrymount)............ (P C Geering) 1,150

Drumbane's Pet ch g (4yrs) Tina's Pet - Confetti Copse (Town And Country)... (Cash) 1,150

233

To Dissolve a Partnership

Holly Martin's (IRE) ch g (5yrs) Buckskin (FR) - Dungourney Lady (Tarqogan)..... (S Spratt) 3,200

Property of Mrs S Piggott

Sensei ch g (6yrs) Ovac (ITY) - Sweet Gum (USA) (Gummo)............ (V Bizley) 1,800

Property of Mrs A Juckes

(IRE) ch g (5yrs) Sylvan Barbarosa - Scaddy Girl (Saulingo)................. (K Kay) 2,500

Property of Mrs S Piggott

Andrea's Pride gr g (10yrs) Camden Town - Funny Friend (FR) (Caro) .... (Alyson Roberts) 925

To Dissolve a Partnership

Tom Parker b g (3yrs) Today And Tomorrow - Winding Street (Pitskelly).. (H J Pym) 1,350

Property of Mr S Whiting

Mallypha (FR) b g (9yrs) Bellypha - Marzala (USA) (Honest Pleasure (USA))........ (M L Weller) 1,200

To Dissolve a Partnership

Buck In Time ch m (6yrs) Buckskin (FR) - Summerville Lass (Deep Run).......... (G Hanmer) 5,400

Bengal Way br g (8yrs) Boreen - Santal Air (Ballyciptic).............. (G Hanmer) 2,100

Property of Mr D R Greig

Moat Legend b g (8yrs) Red Regent - Natflat (Barron's Court) (B Bainbridge) 2,800

Property of Mr R R Strawbridge

Magnus Pym b g (8yrs) Al Nasr (FR) - Full Of Reason (USA) (Bold Reason)....... (N Millard) 2,000

234

Property of Mr R W Emery

Dare Dago b g (9yrs) Homeboy - Tallishire Beverley (The Go Between) .... (G Waters) 875

Dr Jekyll b g (8yrs) Karlinsky - Woodbank Jewel (Fidel)............. (S A Wilson) 1,200

From Harcourt Stud (Ireland)

Deep Certainty b g (7yrs) Deep Run - Arctic Chatter (Le Bavard) .... (A Howard-Chappell) 1,900

To Dissolve a Partnership

Algaihabane (USA) b g (7yrs) Roberto (USA) - Sassabunda (Sassafras (FR))......... (J Barnard) 1,300

Property of Mr J N Hinchliffe

Paperwork Boy ch g (8yrs) Buckskin (FR) - Orinda Way (Deep Run).. (S A Wilson) 1,100

Property of Mr C C Bennett, from Fowlers Farm Racing Stables

Aherlow b g (13yrs) Brave Invader (USA) - Cant Pet (Cantab)........... (P Legge) 1,100

Property of Mr G M Spencer

Grand Value ch g (10yrs) Kambalda - Candy Slam (Candy Cane)..... (S A Dawson) 1,800

Property of Mr Peter Pittendrigh, from Bradley Hall Farm

Vantario b c (3yrs) Van Der Linden (FR) - Salica (ITY) (Hogarth (ITY)) (D Yeoman) 1,600

Acrolight b f (4yrs) Blakelight - Acrolunar (Luna River)............. (S Mullins) 1,800

The Lady's Partner br g (11yrs) Fine Blade (USA) - Owenette (Master Owen)..... (Mr Evans) 2,700

That's Not Gossip ch g (7yrs) Deep Run - Swinging Sovereign (Swing Easy)..... (Cash) 2,000

235

Property of Mr A Green
Colonel Fairfax gr g (5yrs) Alias Smith (USA) - Mistress Meryll (Tower Walk)........ (Mrs N Matthews) 1,600
Property of Mrs N Hicks
Classical Quartet b g (8yrs) Relkino - Daughter Of Song (Song).. (V Meakin) 1,850
Property of Mr T Maycock
Caribbean Prince ch g (5yrs) Dara Monarch - My Ginny (Palestine)................ (Sarah Hollinshead) 4,000
Property of Mr F J Carter
Dark Vision br f (4yrs) Noalto - Valeur (Val de Loir).............. (Ruth Wollerton) 1,500
Property of Mr R Juckes
b g (2yrs) St Columbus - Decipher (Broxted) .... (Linda Millar) 700
Property of Mr R H Barlow
b f (3yrs) Afzal - Rayne Park (Julio Mariner) (T Rockhill) 525
b f (2yrs) Interrex (CAN) - Supper Party (He Loves Me).............. (Mrs F Karle) 850
Property of Mr P D Purdy
Fiery Perdita b m (5yrs) Sula Bula - Wayward Cottage (Cornuto)...... (J Serpill) 1,650
Property of Mrs M Edwards
Prince Vulgan b g (6yrs) Royal Vulcan - Camus Margaret (Peacock)..... (Cash) 2,500
Property of Mr E T D Leadbetter
Whybrows b g (7yrs) Star Appeal - Haida (Astec)................... (H Texner) 1,400

236

Property of Needwood Racing Ltd
ch g (7yrs) Rymer - Arctic Lion (Arctic Slave)............... (Claire Creasey) 2,800
b g (4yrs) Full Extent (USA) - The Doe (Alcide)............. (Brocks Liveries) 1,300
Property of a Lady
Home Affair b f (3yrs) Petoski - Miranda Julia (Julio Mariner)...... (Maxine King) 950
Property of Mr A K Mason
ch g (2yrs) Hubbly Bubbly (USA) - New Top (New Brig).................... (Cash) 1,600
Property of Bluegates Farm
b g (3yrs) Nearly A Hand - Royal Rushes (Royal Palace)............. (H George) 950
ch g (4yrs) Nearly A Hand - Solhoon (Tycoon II)................ (D Turner) 2,000
Property of Miss Clare Bosley
Andy Jack ch g (4yrs) Risk Me (FR) - Gemma Kaye (Cure The Fields) (Cash) 1,400
Property of Mrs S A Chapple, from Westbridge Park Stud
Jessica's Gold ch f (4yrs) Silly Answer - Jessica Bay Vii Pedigree unregistered. (Mr Hulbert) 2,900
Property of Mr K Chapman
Daves Chance ch g (3yrs) Hotfoot - Persian Express (Persian Bold)...... (J Myers) 1,000
Property of Mr Nigel Dunn, from The Woodram Stud
b f (3yrs) Idiot's Delight - Blakesware Gift (Dominion)............. (Julie Purdie) 1,400

237

Property of A E Juggins & Son
b m (5yrs) Broadsword (USA) - Huntless (Songedor)................. (J Porter) 3,100
Landsker Oats b m (7yrs) Oats - Gemmerley Jane (Bally Russe)............ (Mr Gardner) 1,000
Property of Mr J D Downes
Great King Salts ch g (6yrs) Morston (FR) - Miss Shifter (Realm)...... (A Howard-Chappell) 1,350
Property of Mrs A Mutch
Diddums-Do b f (3yrs) Oats - Red Ragusa (Homeric)............ (Saskia Struyck) 800
Property of Avondale Construction Ltd
Call Avondale br g (5yrs) Homeboy - Collectors Girl (Mr Bigmore)......... (Cash) 2,300
Property of D G & Miss C M Wright
Tulip Time b f (3yrs) Hopton Lane - Still Marching (Riboboy (USA)) (N R Taylor) 1,150
PRIVATE SALES
Property of Mrs S Goodman
Missy S (IRE) b f (4yrs) Sarab - Monaco Lady (Manado)................ (Cash) 1,800
From Blackwell Grange Stables
Tharif b g (5yrs) Green Desert (USA) - Mrs Bacon (Balliol)............... (K Dare) 2,000
Property of Miss K George
C Sharp ch g (6yrs) Song - Simply Jane (Sharpen Up)............ (S M Tubbs) 1,800
Property of Mr J C Simmons
Sperrin View ch m (7yrs) Fidel - Baroness Vimy (Barrons Court).... (M F Loggin) 1,850

238

DONCASTER
Tuesday, June 29th

Property of a Partnership
Noble Scamp b m (9yrs) Scallywag - Gouly Duff (Party Mink) With a ch f f at foot by Palm Track................ (Cash) 1,600
Property of Mr William G Young, from Overton Stables
ch f (2yrs) Respect - Night Profit (Carnival Night).................. (K S Dillon) 1,400
Property of Mr J Pinder, from Stockwell Stud
ch f (2yrs) Hard Fought - Mrs Hubbard (Silly Season)................ (K S Dillon) 1,500
Property of Mr P Dowson
ch f (3yrs) Northern State (USA) - Mischievous Miss (Niniski).. (G Parrington) 1,800
Property of Mrs A W Turner
Follow The Sea b h (7yrs) Tumble Wind (USA) - Seapoint (Major Point) .... (M Kirkman) 1,100
To Dissolve a Partnership
Chelsea Player ch g (2yrs) The Noble Player (USA) - Crecora (Royal Captive) .... (P A Smith) 950
Nine Pipes b g (2yrs) Sure Blade (USA) - Winning Look (Relko).. (Mrs K Birkett) 1,100
Property of Heath Racing Stables
Rustus ch f (2yrs) Faustus (USA) - Redhead (Hotfoot)................. (A Smith) 820

Property of Mr T & Mrs H Derbyshire

Cannon's Vision ch g (5yrs) Fingora - Ribble Reed (Bullrush)............... (Cash) 1,900

Property of Mr R Johnson

Newbrano gr m (6yrs) Zambruno - Fanny Adams (Sweet Ration) .... (Ruth Wollerton) 2,000

239

Property of Mr R G Park

br g (5yrs) Politico (USA) - Friday Cottage (Past Petition)......... (G T Thornton) 3,000

Property of Miss J A Douglas

br f (4yrs) Belfort (FR) - Allez Stanwick (Goldhill).......... (Bruce Mactaggart) 1,600

From Spa Stud

b g (3yrs) Alleging (USA) - Bright Stream (Cure The Blues)............... (Cash) 1,600

Property of Miss C Balding, from Spa Stud

Champagne Blush gr f (3yrs) Le Solaret (FR) - French Touch (Dieu Soleil) ...... (K S Dillon) 1,800

Property of Mrs J Trentham, from Spa Stud

Millibee b f (2yrs) Macmillion - Let Me Bee (Taste Of Honey).......... (K S Dillon) 880

Property of Etchingham Stud, from Etchingham Stud

b f (2yrs) Kirchner - Little Whipper (Song) .. (Alan Flack) 1,000

Property of Mr B Brandon

Bantel Bedouin ch g (3yrs) Blushing Scribe (USA) - Bantel Bouquet (Red Regent) .. (K Kay) 1,600

From Moor Farm Stables

b g (3yrs) Teenoso (USA) - Serenata (Larrinaga)........................ (Cash) 1,200

To Resolve a Dispute

ch c (2yrs) Salse (USA) - High Quail (USA) (Blushing Groom)..... (W B Immeson) 850

From Haggswood Stables

Salt N Vinegar ch g (3yrs) Salt Dome (USA) - Karissima (Kalamoun)......... (Cash) 880

240

Property of Mr P F Ellis

b c (2yrs) Mandrake Major - Conjure The Wind (Kala Shikari).... (Miss S Walsh) 780

ch f (2yrs) Valiyar - Lyptosol Gold (Lepanto) (Cash) 520

Property of Mr I Booth, from Northgate Lodge Stables

Matthew David ch c (3yrs) Indian Forest (USA) - Mazurkanova (Song) .... (S Bowring) 780

From Northgate Lodge Stables

Northgate Fireman b c (3yrs) Dowsing (USA) - Vestal Flame (Habitat).. (Cash) 700

To Settle a Dispute

b g (2yrs) Tina's Pet - Anse Chastanet (Cavo Doro)................ (J Harvie) 1,000

From Maunby House Stables

Heber Spring br g (3yrs) Cyrano de Bergerac - Naval Artiste (Captain's Gig) (Alan Flack) 1,350

Moorfield Duchess b f (3yrs) Viking (USA) - Lady Martina (Martinmas) (K Ashcroft) 1,200

As You Do b f (2yrs) Absalom - Jacoletta (Artaius).............. (Mrs L Leeson) 1,200

Cease To Be ch f (2yrs) Sharpo - Lapse (Bold Lad)................ (F Mather) 820

From Musley Bank Stables

Irish Roots b g (3yrs) Caerleon (USA) - Gracious Miss (FR) (Gay Macene) ..... (Cash) 3,300

Paajib b g (3yrs) Waajib - Parkeen Princess (He Loves Me)................ (Cash) 1,300

Chicago gr c (3yrs) Standaan (FR) - Ruling Pride (Bold Lad)............... (Cash) 1,400

Rum Tempest b g (3yrs) Northern Tempest (USA) - Rum Year (Quorum).... (Cash) 1,400

241

From Barsbridge Stables

Lord Vivienne b g (4yrs) Don't Forget Me - Lady Vivienne (Golden Fleece) .... (Mrs P Barker) 3,000

Aragon King b g (3yrs) Aragon - Cadasi (Persian Bold).............. (A Potts) 2,100

Property of Northern Bloodstock Racing Annual Dispersal, from Highfield House Stables

Pesidanamich b g (5yrs) Mummy's Treasure - Bay Supreme (Martinmas) ...... (K Nicholls) 3,500

From Pinewood Stables

Wabwom b g (4yrs) Dunbeath (USA) - Lunar Shamal-Gal (Tumble Wind)...... (S Kettlewell) 1,800

Property of Worksop Manor Stud, from Worksop Manor Stud

Tinstone b f (3yrs) Nishpour (FR) - Tino-Ella (Bustino)................ (S Kettlewell) 1,400

Property of Mr A B Atkins, from Moss Side Racing Stables

Tom Piper b g (3yrs) Music Boy - Run For Love (Runnett)................. (Cash) 2,100

Property of Mr J Berry, from Moss Side Racing Stables

Se Vende b g (2yrs) Maelstrom Lake - Giddy Lyn (USA) (Relko)... (L Abdulla) 1,000

Property of Mr B Smith

Bargee (USA) b g (4yrs) Riverman (USA) - North Mist (USA) (Far North) (S Joyce) 1,700

Property of Mr P Savill, from Woodlands Stables

Broad Agenda b c (2yrs) Petong - Hat Hill (Roan Rocket)................. (Cash) 1,100

From Crackhill Stables

Olicana ch g (3yrs) Persian Bold - Maniusha (Sallust).... (David Minton Bloodstock) 2,200

Wanza b g (3yrs) Petoski - Lovers Light (Grundy)... (David Minton Bloodstock) 17,500

242

From East Everleigh Stables

Folly Vision b f (3yrs) Vision (USA) - Folle Remont (Prince Tenderfoot) .... (B Meehan) 2,700

Property of The Duke of Sutherland, from Hurgill Lodge Stables

Tricycle b g (4yrs) Phardante (FR) - Push Bike (Ballad Rock).......... (P Bradley) 6,600

To Dissolve a Partnership, from St. Gatien Stables
Zastoi ch g (3yrs) Sayf El Arab (USA) - Temple Wood (Sweet Revenge) ...... (T Dodd) 1,100
From Freemason Lodge Stables
Negd (USA) ch c (3yrs) Woodman (USA) - Strait Lake (Sallust)..... (S Kettlewell) 6,400
Property of Mr Fahd Salman, from Whatcombe Stables
Crest b g (3yrs) Dominion - High And Bright (Shirley Heights).............. (Cash) 1,700
To Dissolve a Partnership, from South Bank Stables
Quelque Chose b c (3yrs) Governor General - Ragtime Rose (Ragstone) .... (B Meehan) 2,800
Property of Mr W A Sellers, from Welham Stables
Devil's Soul b g (5yrs) Faustus (USA) - Ragged Moon (Raga Navarro)......... (K Linton) 1,700
Property of Mr T D Smith
Eastern Phoebe ch f (4yrs) Pharly (FR) - Damiya (FR) (Direct Flight)............ (A Buchanan) 1,350
Property of Mr David Swindlehurst, from Lynefoot Farm Stables
Kentucky Chicken (USA) b f (4yrs) Secreto (USA) - Stark Ice (USA) (Icecapade).... (J Byrne) 1,400
Property of Mrs M A Swindlehurst, from Lynefoot Farm Stables
br g (3yrs) Germont - Karena III (Rubor).... (Cash) 2,700

243

From Somerville Lodge Stables
Shamsaan ch c (3yrs) Local Suitor (USA) - Wasslaweyeh (USA) (Damascus)...... (Cash) 1,050
From Little Stanneylands Stables
Paragon Jones ch c (3yrs) Superlative - Summer Posy (Posse)..... (J Douglas) 1,000
From Maunby House Stables
Orient Air b m (5yrs) Prince Sabo - Chinese Falcon (Skymaster)......... (H J Pym) 1,700
Roxkelly Blues ch g (7yrs) Cree Song - Pitskelly Blues (Pitskelly) .... (Martin Wanless) 1,500
Property of Mrs S Hodgkiss, from Rydal Mount Racing Stables Ltd
Acquisition b g (6yrs) Petorius - Steady The Buffs (Balidar)........... (B Forrester) 1,000
Property of Mrs J Clark, from Rydal Mount Racing Stables Ltd
Mister Joe gr g (6yrs) Warpath - Misty Twist (Foggy Bell)..... (F L Matthews) 1,200
From Barton Hall Stables
Red Jam Jar ch g (8yrs) Windjammer (USA) - Macaw (Narrator)............ (H Bell) 2,000
Property of Mr H T Pickering, from Willoughton Stables
Beckingham Ben gr g (9yrs) Workboy - Pickwood Sue (Right Boy)...... (Cash) 1,400
Morpick ro g (6yrs) Morston (FR) - Pickwood Sue (Right Boy)......... (Cash) 1,600

To Dissolve a Partnership
Zinger b g (5yrs) Lucky Wednesday - Starkist (So Blessed)............... (Cash) 1,050

244

Property of Mr J R Wilmington, from Groundhill Stables
De Jordaan br g (6yrs) Callernish - Gorge (Mount Hagen).... (W S Cunningham) 5,000
To Dissolve a Partnership, from Groundhill Stables
Grey Power gr m (6yrs) Wolf Power (SAF) - Periquito (USA) (Olden Times) .... (A Frame) 23,000
Property of Mr A Shelton, from Groundhill Stables
Crestwood Lad (USA) ch g (4yrs) Palace Music - Sweet Ellen (Vitriolic)... (Cash) 1,600
From Whitebog Stables
Captain Teach b g (7yrs) Relkino - Pirate's Cottage (Pirate King).... (S Chadwick) 2,200
From Hammond Lodge Stables, Co. Down, Ireland
Top Prize b g (5yrs) High Top - Raffle (Balidar)...................... (Cash) 1,100
From Rufford Stud
Will gr g (6yrs) Tender King - Fine Flame (Le Prince)........................ (K Kay) 2,500
To Dissolve a Partnership
Bandley Beck ch g (7yrs) Over The River (FR) - Ballinarose (Arctic Slave) (Cash) 2,400
Property of Mrs C J Platts
Scarlet Brave b g (8yrs) Buckskin (FR) - Cherrywood (Vulgan)........ (S Joyce) 1,000
From Kirby Grange Stables
Riseupwilliereilly ch g (7yrs) Deep Run - Sinarga (Even Money)......... (Cash) 1,400
Property of Mr Malcolm Brereton
Miss Enrico b m (7yrs) Don Enrico (USA) - Mill Miss (Typhoon)........ (J Wilson) 3,000

245

To Settle an Account
Gentle Lad b g (9yrs) Bulldozer - Ballincanty (Le Prince)...... (Midland Bloodstock) 1,800
Property of Mr H Morton, from Strelley Lodge Farm
Jimmyshea ch g (5yrs) Tremblant - Another Western (Good Times).......... (K Kay) 2,400
Property of Mrs C Trayes
Blade Of Fortune b g (5yrs) Beldale Flutter (USA) - Foil 'em (USA) (Blade) .... (W H Eastwood) 1,800
Property of Mrs Jane New
Deep Delight b m (6yrs) Idiot's Delight - Browne's Return (Deep Run) .... (R Dalton) 2,000
Property of Mr Robert Evans
Bachelor's Pet b g (7yrs) Petorius - Smile For Me Diane (Sweet Revenge)....... (D K Crossland) 1,200
Property of Mr J Rowsell
Adanac b g (10yrs) Buckskin (FR) - Rosslea (Klairon).............. (D K Crossland) 2,000
Property of a Partnership, from South View Stables
Patrusika b m (7yrs) Full Of Hope - Vulrusika (Vulgan)........... (S Kettlewell) 5,000

Property of Mr D Waggott

Wotusay gr m (6yrs) Lighter - Pannier's Premier (Pannier)..... (Johan Bekaert) 3,600

Property of Mrs E J Wood

Portite Jane b f (4yrs) Grey Desire - Fire Mountain (Dragonara Palace) .... (A Buchanan) 1,350

Property of Miss K A Adams

ch g (4yrs) Eugano - Remaining pedigree unknown................. (L Abdulla) 2,600

246

NEWMARKET
Wednesday, July 7th

From Ballylinch Stud, Ireland (Agent)

Citissima ch m (15yrs) Simbir - Airgead Beo (Hook Money) Covered by Keen ...... (C.B.A.) 4,400

Kentucky Belle b m (9yrs) Glint Of Gold - Baltimore Belle (Bold Lad (IRE)) Covered by Keen................. (C.B.A.) 3,200

Night Starker (USA) ch m (7yrs) Northrop (USA) - Starkling (USA) (Graustark) Covered by Keen................ (C.B.A.) 2,100

From Glebe Stud

Moulin Rapide (USA) b m (10yrs) Roberto (USA) - Fenney Mill (Levmoss) Covered by Chilibang................. (B.B.A.) 2,200

Property of a Partnership, from Bloomsbury Stud

Beanshoot ch or gr m (3yrs) Precocious - Meanz Beanz (High Top) Covered by Phountzi (USA)...... (M McCausland) 1,000

To Dissolve a Partnership, from Watermill Stud Farm

Premier Lady b m (6yrs) Red Sunset - Be A Dancer (Be Friendly) Covered by Touch of Grey................. (L C Morris) 500

Property of Agridale Enterprises Ltd., from Ballyhimikin Stud, Ireland

Taplow b m (9yrs) Tap On Wood - Fighting (Aggressor) Covered by Fairy King (USA).............. (Michael Andree) 31,000

Property of Mr N Bryce-Smith, from Britton House Stud

Ration Of Passion b m (8yrs) Camden Town - Bellagold (Rheingold) Covered by Emarati (USA)....... (J M Gollings) 880

Property of Tarworth Bloodstock Investments Ltd., from Genesis Green Stud

Onika b m (9yrs) Great Nephew - Be Faithful (Vale de Loir) Covered by Terimon.. (J M Gollings) 820

Property of Mr J V Phillips, from Brook Stud

La Pirouette (USA) ch m (14yrs) Kennedy Road (CAN) - Nedancer (USA) (Nearctic) Covered by Statoblest .... (M C Collins) 1,500

247

Property of Brook Stud Ltd., from Brook Stud

b or gr y f Statoblest - Innerglow (Kalaglow) .... (Cash) 620

Property of Mr J V Phillips, from Brook Stud

b y f Sayf El Arab (USA) - Plie (Superlative) (B.B.A.) 1,400

Property of The Hon Lady McAlpine, from Brackenhill Stud

br y f Night Shift (USA) - Gertrude Lawrence (Ballymore)............. (Cash) 3,400

From First Flyer Stables, Ireland

Golden Target (USA) b f (3yrs) Gold Crest (USA) - Freshet (USA) (Believe It (USA)) .... (Mrs S T Shally) 650

Smouldering (IRE) br f (3yrs) Caerleon (USA) - Spark Of Fire (Run The Gantlet (USA))........... (Amanda Skiffington) 20,000

b c (2yrs) Far North (CAN) - Flying Cloud (USA) (Roberto (USA)).. (Lady Herries) 2,400

ch c (2yrs) Dominion - Hot Chocolate (Chief Singer)........... (C & N Bloodstock) 1,500

ch c (2yrs) Rousillon (USA) - Night Starker (USA) (Northrop (USA))........ (Cash) 2,000

b f (2yrs) Dance Of Life (USA) - Arburie (Exbury)................... (G Blum) 2,100

ch f (2yrs) Ogygian (USA) - Battere (USA) (Forli (ARG))............. (L C Morris) 920

gr f (2yrs) Dance Of Life (USA) - Lulubo (USA) (Native Charger)..... (B Hellier) 3,000

248

Property of a Partnership, from Chestnut Tree Stables

Sassamouse b f (3yrs) Bairn (USA) - Westminster Waltz (Dance In Time (CAN)).. (G Blum) 1,150

From Ballyhimikin Stud, Ireland

gr c (2yrs) Jareer (USA) - Covey's Quick Step (Godswalk (USA))............... (Johnny McKeever Bloodstock) 1,000

Property of Property of Mr. Ali K. Al Jafleh

Sabeel ch f (3yrs) Local Suitor (USA) - River Reem (USA) (Irish River (FR)) .... (David Minton Bloodstock) 2,600

Property of Darley Stud Management Co. Ltd, from Eve Lodge Stables

Sehailah b f (3yrs) Mtoto - Fabulous Rina (FR) (Fabulous Dancer (USA)) .... (Johnny McKeever Bloodstock) 12,000

Property of Mr Ali K Al Jafleh, from High Havens Stables.

Shoofe (USA) ch g (5yrs) L'emigrant (USA) - Bid For Manners (USA) (Raise A Bid (USA))................... (K Morgan) 6,400

Property of Mrs David Thompson, from Heath House Stables

Wintering (IRE) ch c (3yrs) Sharpo - Winter Lady (Bonne Noel).................. (Cormack McCormack Associates) 6,000

Property of a Partnership, from Heath House Stables

Serious Delight b f (3yrs) Lomond (USA) - Grey Goddess (Godswalk (USA)) ...... (Ballymorris Stud) 6,000

Property of Darley Stud Management Co. Ltd, from Kremlin House Stables

Dancing Seer br f (3yrs) Lead On Time (USA) - Iie de Danse (Iie de Bourbon (USA)).............. (John McGrath) 1,000

Property of a Partnership, from Kremlin House Stables

Country Girl (IRE) b f (3yrs) Prince Rupert (FR) - Faiblesse (Welsh Saint)......... (Jane Kennedy) 880

from Kremlin House Stables

Dusty's Darling b f (3yrs) Doyoun - Proserpina (FR) (Shafaraz (FR))............ (L T Foster Livestock) 1,100

249

Property of Darley Stud Management Co. Ltd, from Someries Stud

Leaping Water ch f (3yrs) Sure Blade (USA) - Flamenco Wave (Desert Wine (USA)) (Cash) 3,200

Property of Mr P A Leonard, from Breckenbrough House Stables

Laburnum (GR) gr g (5yrs) Glint Of Gold - Lorelene (FR) (Lorenzaccio)............ (John Ferguson Bloodstock) 9,000

Property of a Partnership (partial dispersal of the Exors. of the late Mr K E Wheldon)

Tahitian b g (4yrs) Precocious - Pacificus (USA) (Northern Dancer).... (N Tinkler) 18,000

Safety In Numbers b g (3yrs) Slip Anchor - Winter Queen (Welsh Pageant) .... (Lady Herries) 27,000

Property of Broughton Thermal Insulation

Everset (FR) b g (5yrs) Green Desert (USA) - Eversince (USA) (Foolish Pleasure (USA))............. (David Cosgrove) 1,000

Property of Mr Christopher Wright, from Hill House Stables

Goodnight Girl (IRE) b f (3yrs) Alzao (USA) - I Want My Say (USA) (Tilt Up (USA)) .. (P J Trivass) 1,100

Property of 21st Century Racing Ltd, from Felstead Court Stables

Kissavos ch g (7yrs) Cure The Blue (USA) - Hairbrush (USA) (Sir Gaylord) (C Elsey) 7,400

Serious Hurry ch g (5yrs) Forzando - Lady Bequick (Sharpen Up)....... (C Elsey) 3,500

Absolutely Fact (USA) ch g (3yrs) Known Fact (USA) - Chilly Welcome (General Assembly (USA)) .... (Belgian Brokers B.V.B.A.) 5,400

To Dissolve a Partnership, from Harper Lodge Stables

Diamonds 'n Pearls b g (3yrs) Presidium - Cascabel (Matahawk) .... (Lorna McGowan) 900

250

Property of Mrs J H Weller-Poley, from Boxted Hall Stud

North Call b f (3yrs) Northern State (USA) - Calling High (USA) (Mountain Call)..... (Susannah Garratt) 900

Property of Eclipse Management (Newmarket) Ltd, from Executive Stud

gr f (2yrs) Rousillon (USA) Zodative (FR) (Zeddaan)............... (E A Porter) 400

Property of Mr Jack Gage

gr c (2yrs) Bob Back (USA) - Yuma (USA) (Caro)................ (Gay Kelleway) 4,100

Property of Mrs Rosalie Hawes, from Hackness Villa Stables

Safe Arrival (USA) gr m (5yrs) Shadeed (USA) - Flyingtrip (USA) (Vaguely Noble) .... (P D Evans) 2,300

Property of Shadwell Estate Co. Ltd, from The Croft Stables

Arfrey (IRE) b c (4yrs) Burslem - Last Gunboat (Dominion)... (T Thomson Jones) 1,400

Property of a Partnership, from Induna Stables

Todden b g (3yrs) Aragon - Margurite Gerard (Rheingold)........ (J Hellens) 1,750

Property of a Partnership, from Fitzroy House Stables

Carojango b c (3yrs) Legend Of France (USA) - Lucky Petina (Mummy's Pet) .. (B.B.A.) 1,300

From Fitzroy House Stables

Go Flightline (IRE) ch f (3yrs) Common Grounds - Whilst (Dalsaan) .... (T S M S Riley-Smith) 9,200

Property of Gainsborough Stud Management Ltd, from Glebe House Stables, Ireland

Green Life b or br f (3yrs) Green Desert (USA) - Viceroy Princess (Godswalk (USA)).......... (Ballymorris Stud) 1,200

Zaineh (USA) b f (3yrs) Alleged (USA) - Touching Love (Touching Wood (USA)) (Will Edmeades Bloodstock) 4,200

251

Property of Shadwell Estate Co. Ltd, from Rossmore Lodge Stables, Ireland

Arzaaq (USA) b g (3yrs) Shadeed (USA) - Naqiyah (USA) (In Reality)........... (Cormack McCormack) 9,600

From Rossmore Lodge Stables, Ireland

Haanem b f (3yrs) Mtoto - Nobly Born (USA) (The Minstrel (CAN))... (F Barry) 2,000

Property of Shadwell Estate Co. Ltd, from Rosewell House Stables, Ireland

Bayyinat b c (3yrs) Woodman (USA) - Turn Of Joy (Lomond (USA)) .... (John McGrath) 1,200

Property of Darley Stud Management Co. Ltd, from Currabeg Stables, Ireland

Atacama b f (3yrs) Green Desert (USA) - Pretty Lady (High Top) (Gay Kelleway) 4,100

Property of Darley Stud Management Co. Ltd, from Conyngham Lodge Stables, Ireland

Maxixie (IRE) b or br c (3yrs) Local Suitor (USA) - Maiyaasah (Kris).... (J Norton) 1,200

From Oak Stables Ltd

Fly To The End (USA) b c (3yrs) Gulch (USA) - Bold Flora (USA) (Bold Favourite (USA))................... (Cash) 1,000

Moshaajir (USA) ch c (3yrs) Woodman (USA) - Hidden Trail (USA) (Gleaming (USA))............. (Charles Smith) 9,400

Munnasib (FR) ch c (3yrs) Highest Honor (FR) - Parole Et Musique (USA) (Nureyev (USA))....... (Gay Kelleway) 3,800

Tashreef b g (3yrs) Shareef Dancer (USA) - Lune de Minuit (USA) (Caro) (K Birkett) 820

Property of Shadwell Estate Co Ltd., from Green Lodge Stables

Mumayyaz (IRE) b c (3yrs) Alzao (USA) - Thatcherite (Final Straw) .... (Belgian Brokers B.V.B.A.) 3,600

Jizyah b f (3yrs) Green Desert (USA) - Kawkeb (USA) (Vaguely Noble)........ (B Hellier) 3,600

252

Property of Shadwell Estate Co Ltd., from St Gatien Stables

Genseric (FR) b c (3yrs) Groom Dancer (USA) - Green Rosy (USA) (Green Dancer (USA))............. (T P Tate) 7,400

Property of Shadwell Estate Co Ltd., from Castle Stables

Jihaad (USA) b c (3yrs) Chief's Crown (USA) - Desirable (Lord Gayle (USA))... (D Barron) 9,200

Muhtashim (IRE) b c (3yrs) Caerleon (USA) - Baccalaureate (Crowned Prince (USA)) (D Barron) 11,000

Property of Shadwell Estate Co Ltd., from Windsor House Stables

Kawasir (CAN) b or br c (3yrs) Gulch (USA) - Madame Treasurer (CAN) (Key To The Mint (USA))....... (C & N Bloodstock) 5,600

Property of Lady Howard de Walden, from Windsor House Stables

Warspite b c (3yrs) Slip Anchor - Valkyrie (Bold Lad (IRE))........... (J Joseph) 8,500

Property of Darley Stud Management Co Ltd., from Park House Stables

Handmaiden gr f (3yrs) Shardan - Flyaway Bride (USA) (Blushing Groom (FR)) .... (R Fenwick-Gibson) 6,600

Property of Darley Stud Management Co Ltd., from Bedford House Stables

Tor b or br c (3yrs) Reference Point - Devon Defender (Home Guard (USA)).. (Cash) 3,000

Property of Darley Stud Management Co Ltd., from Rockingham Stud

Rurik (USA) b h (5yrs) Alydar (USA) - Rukann (USA) (Ruken)........ (B.B.A.) 2,600

Farandole b c (3yrs) Shareef Dancer (USA) - Greenhill Lass (Upper Case (USA)) .... (L Stubbs) 1,500

Isle Of Pearls (USA) b c (3yrs) Theatrical - Margaritaville (USA) (Tom Rolfe) ...... (Lady Herries) 13,500

253

Property of Mrs C Miller, from Carlburg Stables

Big Blue b g (4yrs) Bluebird (USA) - Cassina (Habitat)............... (John O'Kelly) 14,000

Property of Eddy Grimstead Honda Ltd, from Carlburg Stables

Grand Honda (IRE) b g (4yrs) Lomond (USA) - Braneakins (Sallust)................. (Belgian Brokers B.V.B.A.) 2,600

Property of Gainsborough Stud Management Ltd, from Carlburg Stables

Al Jawwal ch c (3yrs) Lead On Time (USA) - Littlefield (Bay Express)...... (G King) 2,100

Property of a Partnership, from Clarehaven Stables

Eurythmic gr f (3yrs) Pharly (FR) - Amalancher (USA) (Alleged (USA)).... (Cyril Shack) 7,200

Tanera Mhor b f (3yrs) Shareef Dancer (USA) - Snub (Steel Heart)............ (John Shally) 1,200

Property of Shadwell Estate Co Ltd, from Clarehaven Stables

Bayrak (USA) b c (3yrs) Bering - Phydilla (FR) (Lyphyard (USA))......... (C.B.A.) 17,500

Jaziyah (IRE) br f (3yrs) Lead On Time (USA) - Wabarah (Shirley Heights)..... (Gay Kelleway) 1,600

Property of a Partnership, from Thirty Acre Barn Stables

Mr Vincent ch g (3yrs) Nishapour (FR) - Brush Away (Ahonoora)... (K Morgan) 21,000

From Thirty Acre Barn Stables

Raging Thunder b g (3yrs) Taufan (USA) - Nasty Niece (CAN) (Great Nephew) ... (J Hellens) 15,000

From Seven Springs Stables

Pacific Hero ch c (2yrs) Forzando - On To Glory (Welsh Pageant) (John McGrath) 1,150

254

From Marriott Stables

Dominant Partner b c (2yrs) Dominion - Trila Love (Lomond (USA))......... (B.B.A.) 3,100

Property of Darley Stud Management Co Ltd, from Yew Tree Stables

Tarrock ch g (3yrs) Arctic Tern (USA) - In The Habit (USA) (Lyphard (USA)) ...... (Merrita Jones) 1,250

To Dissolve a Partnership, from Warwick House Stables

Charioteer b g (4yrs) Formidable (USA) - Aunt Charlotte (Charlottown)......... (C & N Bloodstock) 1,200

From Warwick House Stables

Cry Of The Dolphin b or gr f (2yrs) Mazilier (USA) - Ashbocking (Dragonara Palace (USA))............ (Stefan Uppstrom) 2,000

Property of a Partnership, from Charlcombe Lodge Stables

St Alzina (IRE) b c (3yrs) Alzao (USA) - St Padina (St Paddy)................... (Cormac McCormack Associates) 2,600

Property of Mr T J Wall, from Kirtling Stables

Shaurni Girl ch m (5yrs) Precocious - Crockfords Green (Roan Rocket) ...... (Tony Wall) 6,600

255

NEWMARKET

Thursday, July 8th

Property of a Gentleman, from Sackville House Stables

Post Impressionist (IRE) b f (4yrs) Ahonoora - Roblanna (Roberto (USA)) .... (David A Cahal) 6,200

Property of Gainsborough Stud Management Ltd, from Pegasus Stables

Yfool b f (3yrs) Persian Bold - Raiwand (Tap On Wood)..................... (B.B.A.) 5,200

Property of Darley Stud Management Co Ltd, from Pegasus Stables

Shadowplay (FR) b c (3yrs) Shareef Dancer (USA) - Sunset Dawn (USA) (Alleged (USA)).................. (M Naughton) 4,200

From Little Stanneylands Racing Stables

Sir Norman Holt (IRE) b c (4yrs) Ela-Mana-Mou - Ploy (Posse (USA)) .... (A A J Peirce) 4,200

Property of a Partnership, from Somerville Lodge Stables

Le Couteau br g (3yrs) Dowsing (USA) - Razor Blade (Sharp Edge) .... (Cormac McCormack Associates) 3,000

From Somerville Lodge Stables

Premium Bond br c (2yrs) Primo Dominie - Fee (Mandamus)..... (Miss B Couper) 700

From Flint Cottage Stables

Ballymoneyboy ch g (4yrs) Ballacashtal - Honeybuzzard (Sea Hawk II) .... (Lorna McGowan) 1,200

Mrs Snuggs (IRE) gr f (3yrs) Law Society (USA) - Inanna (Persian Bold) .... (Peter Doyle Bloodstock) 5,000

Titch On Time ch f (2yrs) Absalom - Fast Asleep (Hotfoot).......... (Bent Olsen) 1,100

Property of Mr Giles W Pritchard-Gordon, from Trillium Place Stables

Burishki gr f (3yrs) Chilibang - Hunza Water (Relko)............... (Gay Kelleway) 5,600

Texas Cowgirl (IRE) ch f (3yrs) Salt Dome (USA) - Cloven Dancer (Hurok (USA)) .. (European Equine Consultants) 2,600

256

Property of a Partnership, from Kingstone Warren Stables

Sharp Silk b f (3yrs) Sharpo - Temple Row (Ardross)........... (Grovewood Stud) 3,000

From Hurgill Lodge Stables

Red Fan (IRE) b g (3yrs) Taufan (USA) - The Woman In Red (Red Regent) .... (Michael Dods) 8,800

Property of Darley Stud Management Co Ltd, from Someries Stud

Anna Of Kiev ch f (3yrs) Salse (USA) - Anna Matrushka (Mill Reef (USA)).... (Cash) 1,800

Domovoy b f (3yrs) Shareef Dancer (USA) - Heavenly Abode (Habitat) .... (Grovewood Stud) 1,750

Milada (FR) b f (3yrs) Miller's Mate - Baheejah (Northfields (USA))....... (G Blum) 1,400

Samriah (IRE) b f (3yrs) Wassl - Top Treat (USA) (Topsider (USA))......... (Cash) 2,400

Scotch Pebble (IRE) b f (3yrs) Lomond (USA) - L'anno D'Oro (Habitat) .... (Cormac McCormack Associates) 9,400

Westry ch f (3yrs) Gone West (USA) - Sylvan's Girl (Restless Native) .... (William Johnston) 2,300

Property of Darley Stud Management Co Ltd, from Coombelands Stables Ltd

Ravenspur (IRE) b c (3yrs) Reference Point - Royal Nugget (USA) (Mr Prospector (USA)).............. (Jamestown Stud) 2,300

From Coombelands Stables Ltd

Debacle (USA) b or br c (4yrs) Raft (USA) - Kuala (USA) (Hawaii).... (B J McMath) 7,600

Burnt Imp (USA) ch g (3yrs) Imp Society (USA) - Flaming Reason (USA) (Limit To Reason (USA))........ (Susan Moore) 8,400

257

From Freemason Lodge

Ajzem (USA) b c (4yrs) Blushing Groom (FR) - Nobiliare (USA) (Vaguely Noble) (Miss Verkerk) 2,300

Greek Gold (IRE) b g (4yrs) Rainbow Quest (USA) - Gay Hellene (Ela-Mana-Mou)... (J Glover) 7,000

Logan's Luck (USA) b or br c (3yrs) Believe It (USA) - Fancy Wings (Wing Out (USA))...................... (G Blum) 1,600

Moujeeb (USA) b c (3yrs) Riverman (USA) - Capricorn Belle (Nonoalco (USA))...... (P K Mitchell) 4,500

Naawy b c (3yrs) Reference Point - Strike Home (Be My Guest (USA)) .... (Charles Smith) 4,200

Mislemani (IRE) b g (3yrs) Kris - Meis El-Reem (Auction Ring (USA)) .... (Maxine Cowdrey) 7,000

Property of Darley Stud Management Co Ltd, from Freemason Lodge

Al Shaati (FR) b f (3yrs) Lead On Time (USA) - With You All (Free Round (USA)).................. (A A J Peirce) 4,000

Property of Darley Stud Management Co Ltd, from Abington Place Stables

Rising Wolf b c (3yrs) Shirley Heights - Bustara (Busted)...... (R J O'Sullivan) 5,200

Smocking ch f (3yrs) Night Shift - Sue Grundy (Grundy)........... (J Pearce) 4,000

Property of Darley Stud Management Co Ltd, from South Bank Stables

Sierra Madrona ch f (3yrs) Woodman (USA) - Senorita Poquita (Connaught)........ (Thorndale Bloodstock) 2,000

258

Property of Mr F Salman, from Whatcombe Stables

Alderney Prince (USA) ch c (3yrs) Trempolino (USA) - Princess Of Man (Green God)...................... (P Leach) 21,000

Czar's Witness b c (3yrs) Law Society (USA) - Czar's Bride (USA) (Northern Dancer)....... (Thorndale Bloodstock) 4,500

Property of Newgate Stud Company, from Whatcombe Stables

Clear Look b f (3yrs) Green Desert (USA) - Avoid (USA) (Buckpasser) .... (Henry Ponsonby) 10,500

On Golden Pond (IRE) b f (3yrs) Bluebird (USA) - Art Age (Artaius (USA))........ (Susan Moore) 8,500

Property of Mr F Salman, from Whatcombe Stables

Desert Man b g (2yrs) Green Desert (USA) - Grayfoot (Grundy).............. (Cash) 1,200

Property of Mrs P Blacker, from Whatcombe Stables

Bronze Maquette (IRE) b f (3yrs) Ahonoora - Working Model (Ile de Bourbon (USA)) (B J McMath) 7,200

Property of Juddmonte Farms

Storm Falcon (USA) ch c (3yrs) Storm Bird (CAN) - Noble Natisha (USA) (Noble Commander (USA)) .... (David Minton Bloodstock) 7,800

Property of Darley Stud Management Co Ltd, from Diomed Stables

Yoshaarik (IRE) b c (3yrs) Niniski (USA) - Shereeka (Shergar)...... (A C Forbes) 1,700

From Diomed Stables

Lahoob (USA) b c (4yrs) Miswaki (USA) - Sure Locked (Lyphard (USA)) .... (Ian Campbell) 3,400

Wajeeb (USA) b c (4yrs) Majestic Light (USA) - Reham (Mill Reef (USA)) ...... (R Elliott) 1,200

Invisible Luck (IRE) b c (3yrs) Jareer (USA) - Noble Nancy (Royal And Regal (USA)) (A K Collins) 1,800

Marow ch c (3yrs) Formidable (USA) - Clicquot (Bold Lad (IRE))......... (Cash) 1,300

Mohaya (USA) b c (3yrs) Cox's Ridge (USA) - Mazyoun (USA) (Blushing Groom (FR)) .... (Albury Racing Ltd) 2,200

Matrouse (IRE) b f (3yrs) Kris - Princess Matilda (Habitat)............. (Cash) 5,800

Miss Pimpernel b f (3yrs) Blakeney - New Edition (Great Nephew)..... (K Birkett) 2,900

Tribat b f (3yrs) Rousillon (USA) - Shorthouse (Habitat)........ (Mrs L Morris) 1,500

259

Property of Mr F Salman, from Phantom House Stables

Doctoor (USA) ch c (3yrs) Cozzene (USA) - To The Top (USA) (Bold Hour) .... (A A J Peirce) 2,700

From Phantom House Stables

Curtelace ch c (3yrs) Nishapour (FR) - Khandjar (Kris)..... (Maxine Cowdrey) 13,000

Latin Leader b c (3yrs) Primo Dominie - Ravaro (Raga Navarro (ITY))... (C.B.A.) 8,600

Scusi ch c (3yrs) Kris - Dance Quest (FR) (Green Dancer (USA)) .... (R O'Gorman Bloodstock) 10,000

Duart Point ch c (2yrs) Kris - Highland Light (Home Guard (USA))..... (J E Parkes) 5,000

From Southgate Stables

Ponds b f (3yrs) Slip Anchor - Pomade (Luthier)............. (Denise Olsson) 1,000

Property of a Partnership, from Eastwell Hall Stables

Merryhill Madam b f (4yrs) Prince Sabo - Western Line (High Line)............. (Paul Bradley) 2,700

Property of Mrs H Levy, from Delamere Cottage Stables

Convoy gr g (3yrs) Be My Guest (USA) - Be Easy (Be Friendly)..... (Charlie Mann) 7,000

Property of Pendley Farm, from Church Farm Stables

Magic Fan (IRE) b g (3yrs) Taufan (USA) - Magic Gold (Sallust) .... (Thorndale Bloodstock) 1,400

Property of Mr T S M S Riley-Smith, from Cedar Point Racing Stables

Barbezieux b h (6yrs) Petong - Merchantmens Girl (Klairon)... (Michael Dodds) 3,600

260

Property of Mrs V Papkins, from Loder Stables

Easy Does It b f (4yrs) Swing Easy (USA) - Pearl Pet (Mummy's Pet)...... (Cash) 1,250

Quiet Miss b f (4yrs) Kind Of Hush - Miss Acrow (Comedy Star).......... (Cash) 1,100

Witches Coven gr f (4yrs) Sharrood (USA) - Tricky (Song).......... (Elsdon Farms) 1,300

To Dissolve a Partnership, from Corner House Stables

b f (2yrs) Dreams To Reality (USA) - Tawnais (Artaius (USA))......... (G Blum) 1,600

From Yeomanstown Stud, Ireland

b g (2yrs) Common Grounds - Northern Wind (Northfields (USA)) .... (David Cosgrove) 5,000

b g (2yrs) Try My Best (USA) - Pistol Petal (Pitskelly)..................... (Cash) 7,400

261

KEENELAND
Monday, July 19th
(Yearlings)

From Eaton-Williams, Agent for Wooden Horse Investments, Inc

b y c Seattle Slew - Tomorrow's Child (Al Nasr (FR))............ (John A Toffan) 175,000

From Waterwild Farm, Agent

b or br y f Chief's Crown - Willowy Mood (Will Win).............. (Max L Polin) 35,000

From Glenmore Farm, Inc. (L Clay Camp), Agent 1

b y c Risen Star - Yettajet (Tri Jet) .... (Jack G Mondel) 40,000

From Taylor Made Sales Agency, Agent for Richard R Kennedy

ch y f Afleet - Adarling (Alleged) .... (John & M Jane Mulholland) 30,000

From Three Chimneys Farm, Agent

b y f Seattle Slew - Alydar's Promise (Alydar)...... (Rollin W Baugh (Agent)) 175,000

From Gainesway Farm, Agent for F A Genter Stable, Inc, Dispersal

b y c Cryptoclearance - Amo (Hold Your Peace)................. (Tartan Farm) 125,000

From Walnut Green (Jones Bros), Agent

b y f Mr Prospector - Annoconnor (Nureyev) .... (Philip Teinowitz) 325,000

From Lane's End, Agent

b y c Cox's Ridge - Anything For Love (Seattle Slew)....... (B B A (England)) 145,000

Property of Stone Farm and Way Oak Cliff Stable

b y c Halo - Bambina Linda (ARG) (Liloy (FR))....... (J Nerud Revocable Trust) 70,000

Property of David's Farm

b y f Storm Bird - Blushing Redhead (Blushing Groom (FR))...... (J L Gladwell III) 90,000

262

Property of Patchen Wilkes Farm (Warren W Rosenthal)

b y c Nijinsky II - Brave Raj (Rajab)........ (The Adam Corp/group) 225,000

From Eaton-Williams, Agent for Stanley I. Joselson and Louie J. Roussel III

b y c Risen Star - Dinky Pink (What A Pleasure).......... (Stanley Joselson) 45,000

From Three Chimneys Farm, Agent
b or br y f Diesis - Disconiz (Northern Dancer)...... (Walter Bindner (Agent)) 55,000

From Taylor Made Sales Agency, Agent for Pollock Farms/R Coker
Southern Fancy ch y f Silver Hawk - Eastern Prancer (Northern Dancer)........ (Eddie Olczyk) 30,000

Property of Iron County Farms, Inc
ch y c Storm Bird - Electric Fanny (Full Out) (Dogwood Stables, Inc) 180,000

From Jonabell Farm, Inc., Agent
b y c Dayjur - Epitome (Summing)........ (Aaron Jones) 1,000,000

From Gainesway Farm, Agent for Gainesway Thoroughbreds Ltd
b y c Dayjur - Fabuleux Jane (Le Fabuleux) (Harkham & Highes) 400,000

Property of Mare Haven Farm (Dr William O Reed)
ch y f Criminal Type - Gene's Lady (What A Pleasure)..... (The Adam Corp/group) 60,000

Property of Offutt-Cole Farm (To Dissolve a Partnership)
b y c Alysheba - Golden Dust (Dusty Canyon)............... (Crossroad Farm) 110,000

From Hugh C Motley, Agent for Carolyn L Nicewonder
b y c Gone West - Gonfalon (Francis S).... (C Gordon-Watson (Agent)) 150,000

263

Property of Katalpa Farm (Lonnie R Owens) and Oakwind Farm (Verne H Winchell)
gr y c Forty Niner - Hattab Gal (Al Hattab).. (Ron McAnally (Agent)) 160,000

From Pegasus Stud (Melinda A Smith), Agent I
ch y f Woodman - Hushi (Riverman)........ (Pegasus Bloodstock International) 90,000

From Pegasus Stud (Melinda A Smith), Agent III
b y f Sovereign Dancer - Inca Princess (Big Spruce)............. (Ken Ellenberg) 45,000

From Eaton-Williams, Agent
b y c Danzig - Infantes (Exclusive Native) .. (Starstruck Farm) 335,000

From Lane's End, Agent
b or br y c Gulch - Island Escape (Slew O' Gold)............. (Lavin Bloodstock) 155,000
ch y f Java Gold - Jardin de Nuit (Raja Baba) .... (M Sakurai) 130,000

From Trackside Farm (Tom Evans), Agent for Foxfield
b y f Gulch - Key Flyer (Nijinsky II) .... (W Bruce Lunsford) 195,000

From Three Chimneys Farm, Agent
b or br y f Gone West - Lady Ice (Vice Regent)... (Darley Stud Management) 150,000

From Lane's End, Agent
ch y c Mr Prospector - Lisaleen (Northern Dancer).............. (Gainsborough) 800,000

From Walmac Int'l, Agent
b y c Nureyev - Maxencia (FR) (Tennyson) (B B A (England)) 225,000

264

Property of Windfields Farm
b y f Halo - Mesappiano (Fappiano)........ (Edward J Kelly Jr) 125,000

From Waterford Farm (Dr nd Mrs R Smiser West), Agent I
b or br y c Wild Again - Milkshake (Quadratic)................... (Horse France) 80,000

Property of Lockhart Spears (Stoneleigh Farm)
b y f Eastern Echo - Miss Baja (Mr Leader) (Robert Masterson) 60,000

From Three Chimneys Farm, Agent
ch y f Riverman - Nijinska Street (Nijinsky II) .... (Darley Stud Management) 450,000

From Lane's End, Agent
ch y f Rahy - North Of Sunset (Northern Baby)........... (Nick Sacco (Agent)) 35,000

From Taylor Made Sales Agency, Agent for Wycombe House Stud
Quick Silver Dream gr y f Topsider - On To Royalty (On To Glory)............... (The Adam Corp/group) 120,000

Property of Stone Farm
b y f Topsider - Pailleron (Majestic Light) .. (Starstruck Farm) 65,000

From Camas Park Stud (Tim Hyde), Agent
ch y c Nureyev - Pasadoble (Prove Out) ... (Allen Paulson) 600,000

From Taylor Made Sales Agency, Agent for Triple C Thorostock
b or br y f Dayjur - Peacefully (Jacinto) .... (John Ferguson Bloodstock) 175,000

From Brereton C Jones, Agent
b y f Silver Hawk - Picture Tube (T V Commercial)............... (C Vogel) 150,000

265

From Lane's End, Agent
ch y c Riverman - Rare Mint (Key To The Mint)............... (B B A (England)) 290,000

From Eaton-Williams, Agent for Mr and Mrs L E Wolfson and et al
b y c Mr Prospector - Reminiscing (Never Bend)..... (John R Gaines (Agent)) 1,050,000

From Lane's End, Agent
ch y c Easy Goer - Scuff (Forli) .... (Rollin W Baugh (Agent)) 195,000

From Brereton C Jones, Agent
b y c Slew City Slew - Set The Style (Quadrangle)........................ (Pegasus Bloodstock International) 60,000

From Camas Park Stud (Tim Hyde), Agent
ch y f Nureyev - Sex Appeal (Buckpasser) (Harkham & Hughes) 460,000

Property of Fares Farm, Inc
ch y c Blushing John - Sheesham (Sham).. (B B E (England)) 60,000

Property of Mike G Rutherford (Manchester Farm)
ch y c Chief's Crown - She Won't Tell (Exclusive Native) .... (Hartley/de Renzo (Agent)) 45,000

From Eaton-Williams, Agent for Brushwood Stable
b y f Danzig - So She Sleeps (Seattle Slew) (Darley Stud Management) 475,000

Property of Walmac Int'l, Agent
b y f Rahy - Suavite (Alleged)............ (Gainsborough) 135,000

From Matagorda Farm, Inc., Agent
b y f Danzig - Sudden Love (FR) (Kris) ..... (Nicoma Bloodstock (Agent)) 400,000

266

From Three Chimneys Farm, Agent
b y c Mr Prospector - Super Bowl Girl (Far North).......... (Narvick International) 725,000
From Robert E Courtney/Crestfield Farm, Agent for Jaime S Carrion
b y f Sovereign Dancer - Suspicious Native (Raise A Native)....... (Ken Ellenberg) 80,000
From Three Chimneys Farm, Agent
ch y f Forty Niner - Two For The Show (Stage Door Johnny) .... (Nicom Bloodstock (Agent)) 150,000
From Trackside Farm (Tom Evans), Agent for Foxfield
b y f Dayjur - Water Lily (FR) (Riverman) . . . (W S Farish) 250,000
From Eaton-Williams, Agent for Robert L Quinichett & Calogo Bloodstock A G
b y c Sadler's Wells - Wilamae (Tentam) . . . (Heatherway Inc, (Agent)) 250,000
Property of Fares Farms, Inc.
b y c Dayjur - Agretta (Graustark) .... (John A Toffan) 165,000
From King Ranch Farm, Agent
b y f Danzig - Althea (Alydar) .... (Narvick International) 800,000
From Bridlewood Farm, Agent
b or br y c Dayjur - Angel Island (Cougar II) (Dogwood Stable, Inc) 200,000
From Taylor Made Sales Agency, Agent for Gallagher's Stud
b y c Nijinsky II - Asiram (Sharpen Up)..... (Darley Stud Management) 150,000
Property of Fares Farms, Inc.
b or br y c Dayjur - Capades (Overskate) . . . (Gainsborough) 260,000

267

From Walmac Int'l, Agent
b y c Houston - Cassock Of Pearls (Czaravich).. (Robert & Beverly Lewis) 325,000
From Lane's End, Agent.
ch y f Woodman - Chapel Of Dreams (Northern Dancer)........ (F Stronach) 175,000
From Trackside Farm (Tom Evans), Agent for Foxfield.
b y f Nijinsky II - Dovie Lee (Drone) .... (Harold Harrison) 100,000
From Waterford Farm (Dr and Mrs R Smiser West), Agent
b y f Danzig - Egyptian Rose (Sir Ivor) ..... (Pegasus Bloodstock International) 70,000
Property of Glennwood Farm, Inc.
b or br y c Gone West - Elegant Champagne (Alleged) .... (C Gordon-Watson (Agent)) 180,000
From Eaton-Williams, Agent Eaton & Red Bull, Wooden Horse and Manganaro Stb
b y c Danzig - Embellished (Seattle Slew) . . (Allen Paulson) 325,000
From Three Chimneys Farm, Agent
b y f Storm Bird - Fabulous Salt (Le Fabuleux)......... (The Adam Corp/group) 70,000
From Eaton-Williams, Agent for Overbrook Farm.
b y c Easy Goer - Fair To All (Al Nasr (FR)) (Condren & Cornacchia) 105,000

From Westover Ridge, Agent for John W Rooker.
b or br y c Gone West - Fleur de Mont (Graustark)............... (The Oaks) 180,000
Property of Fares Farms, Inc.
b y f Deputy Minister - Gaily Gaily (IRE) (Cure The Blues) .... (G Watts Humphrey Jr) 200,000

268

From Gainesway Farm, Agent for F A Genter Stable, Inc., Dispersal.
ch y f Alysheba - Gana Facil (Le Fabuleux) (Wertheimer Et Frere) 350,000
Property of Mare Haven Farm (Dr William O Reed).
b y c Danzig - Golden Highlights (Secretariat)........... (Nick Sacco (Agent)) 410,000
From Camas Park Stud (Tim Hyde), Agent
ch y c Woodman - Golden Oriole (Northern Dancer)........... (Alexandra Scrope) 450,000
From Highclere (Jeffry Morris), Agent for Cable Farm.
b y c Deputy Minister - Golden Petal (Mr Prospector)........... (John A Toffan) 150,000
From Eaton-Williams, Agent for Wooden Horse Investments, Inc.
b y f Seattle Slew - Highest Glory (Damascus)... (The Adam Corp/group) 200,000
From Fred Seitz, Agent for McMakin's Longue Vue Farm.
b or br y c Gone West - Icy Time (Icecapade).......... (W Bruce Lunsford) 130,000
Property of Stone Farm.
b or br y c Nijinsky II - Infinidad (CHI) (Mr Long)....... (Robert & Beverly Lewis) 335,000
Property of Darby Dan Farm.
ch y c Woodman - Lady Donna (Graustark) (Jim Tafel) 65,000
From Three Chimneys Farm, Agent.
b y f Nijinsky II - Laura's Star (Key To The Kingdom).... (Rollin W Baugh (Agent)) 200,000
From Seahorse Farm, Agent.
ch y c Gone West - Long Legend (Reviewer).... (Condren & Cornacchia) 185,000

269

From Lane's End, Agent.
b y f Zilzal - Meringue Pie (Silent Screen) . . (Equine Brokers) 125,000
From Gainesway Farm, Agent for Gainesway Thoroughbreds Ltd.
b y f Seattle Slew - Mesabi (Minnesota Mac)............. (Edward J Kelly Jr) 350,000
From Taylor Made Sales Agency, Agent.
b y c Danzig - Mint Cooler (Key To The Mint)............... (Aaron U Jones) 125,000
Property of Ashview Farm (Mr and Mrs Wayne G Lyster III).
b or br y c Riverman - Mlle. Liebe (Bupers) (Palides Investments, N V) 125,000
From King Ranch Farm, Agent.
ch y c Easy Goer - Namaqua (Storm Bird) . . (Jeanne G Vance) 400,000
Property of David's Farm.
b y f Gulch - Nastique (Naskra) .... (Mike Ryan (Agent)) 75,000

Property of Fares Farms, Inc.
ch y c Woodman - No. One Bundles (Vice Regent)............. (John A Toffan) 200,000
From Pegasus Stud (Melinda A Smith), Agent V.
b y c Known Fact - Noraa (Maribeau)...... (Lazy Lanes Farms (Agent)) 75,000
Property of Mike G Rutherford (Manchester Farm).
b y c Seattle Slew - Northern Fable (Northern Dancer)..... (Gainsborough) 200,000
From Three Chimneys Farm, Agent.
ch y f Nureyev - Office Wife (Secretariat).. (B B A (England)) 360,000

270

From Taylor Made Sales Agency, Agent II.
b y c Nijinsky II - Past Example (Buckpasser).......... (Dogwood Stable Inc) 160,000
From Eaton-Williams, Agent for Brushwood Stable.
ch y c Forty Niner - Relasure (Relaunch)... (Gainsborough) 150,000
From Waterford Farm (Dr and Mrs R Smiser West), Agent.
ch y c Miswaki - Rose O'Riley (Nijinsky II) (John Ferguson Bloodstock) 160,000
From Eaton-Williams, Agent for Edward a Cox Jnr.
b y f Seeking The Gold - Royal Stance (Dr Fager)................ (Mike Pegram) 130,000
Property of Mare Haven Farm (Dr William O Reed).
b y f Dayjur - Safely Home (Winning Hit)... (Robert & Beverley Lewis) 350,000
Property of Fares Farms, Inc.
ch y c Bering - Santiki (Be My Guest)..... (Don Grego) 35,000
From Lane's End, Agent.
ch y c Woodman - Secret Obsession (Secretariat)........... (Centennial Farms) 135,000
From Walmac Int'l, Agent.
b y f Rahy - Shelia Dacre (Nureyev)....... (Harold Harrison) 60,000
From Lane's End, Agent.
ch y c Gulch - Sulemeif (Northern Dancer) (Columbine Stable) 175,000
From Walmac Int'l, Agent.
b y f Wild Again - Sunshine Linda (Giboulee) .... (Craig Singer) 70,000
From Robert E Courtney/Crestfield Farm, Agent for Jaime S Carrion.
b y c Storm Bird - Suspicious Toosome (Secretariat).............. (C Gordon-Watson (Agent)) 150,000

271

KEENELAND
Tuesday, July 20th (Yearlings)

From Walmac Int'l, Agent.
b y c Topsider - Viva Aviva (Secretariat).... (Mike Ryan) 80,000
Property of Fares Farms, Inc.
ch y c Riverman - Wedge Musical (IRE) (What A Guest)...................... (Darley Stud Management) 150,000
From Taylor Made Sales Agency, Agent for Prestonwood Farm, Inc.
b y c Storm Bird - Abidjan (Sir Ivor)........ (Rokeby Farms) 185,000
From King Ranch Farm, Agent.
b y c Dayjur - Aishah (Alydar)............ (Shadwell Estate Co Ltd) 650,000
Property of Silver Oaks Farm (Brenda Jones).
b or br y f Storm Cat - Amyark (Caro (IRE)) (D Wayne Lukas) 115,000
From Taylor Made Sales Agency, Agent V.
b or br y f Deputy Minister - Cagey Exuberance (Exuberant)....... (Will Wolford) 200,000
From Glencoe Farm, Agent for North Central Bloodstock.
gr y c Relaunch - Circular (What A Pleasure) .... (Starstruck Farm) 135,000
Property of Pegasus Stud (Melinda A Smith).
b y f Clever Trick - Corvine (Crow (FR)).... (Mark Stanley) 115,000
From Three Chimneys Farm, Agent.
b y f Mr Prospector - Dancing Tribute (Nureyev) (John Ferguson Bloodstock) 500,000
From Taylor Made Sales Agency, Agent VI.
b y c Relaunch - Dominant Dancer (Moscow Ballet)..................... (Winter Quarter Farm, Agent) 110,000

272

From Lane's End, Agent.
b y f Danzig - Doubles Partner (Damascus) (Turf Company, Ltd., Agent) 800,000
From Waterford Farm (Dr and Mrs R Smiser West), Agent.
b or br y c Strawberry Road (AUS) - Dynamite (Dynastic)... (W Bruce Lunsford) 175,000
From Eaton-Williams, Agent for Ross Valley Farm.
b y f Private Account - Faneuil Girl (Bolinas Boy).............. (Lavin Bloodstock) 250,000
From Eaton-Williams, Agent for Edward A Cox Jnr.
b y c Cox's Ridge - Girlfriend (Tom Rolfe).. (Clint C Goodrich, Agent) 95,000
From Brereton C Jones, Agent.
ch y c Naevus - Glorious Natalie (Reflected Glory)................ (E K Gaylord II) 90,000
From Gainesway Farm, Agent for F A Genter Stable Inc, Dispersal.
b y f Private Account - Gold Mine (Raise A Native).......................... (Pegasus Bloodstock International) 125,000
From Eaton-Williams, Agent for Summerplace Farm.
ch y c Topsider - Good Thinking (Raja Baba) .... (Shadwell Estate Co Ltd) 125,000
From Eaton-Williams, Agent.
b y c Slew O'Gold - Gueniviere (Prince John).............. (Hartley/de Renzo) 45,000
Property of David's Farm.
ch y f Mt Livermore - Heaven's Nook (Great Above)............ (Alexandra Scrope) 40,000
From Three Chimneys Farm, Agent.
b y f Dayjur - Icing (IRE) (Prince Tenderfoot) .... (Rollin W Baugh, Agent) 280,000

273

From Robert E Courtney/Crestfield Farm, Agent for Jaime S Carrion.

b y f Meadowlake - Inreality Star (In Reality) .... (John A Toffan) 200,000

From Eaton-Williams, Agent for Overbrook Farm.

b y f Gone West - Island Kitty (Hawaii) .... (Michael J Carpenter, Agent) 150,000

From Denali Stud (Craig Bandoroff), Agent I.

b y f Sadler's Wells - Ivory Lane (Sir Ivor) .. (John A Toffan) 375,000

From Glenmore Farm, Inc (L Clay Camp), Agent for Rock Hall Stud.

ch y c Phone Trick - Kalimera (FR) (Le Haar) (Don Robinson) 75,000

From Lane's End, Agent.

b y c Gulch - Killaloe (Dr Fager) .... (Darley Stud Management) 375,000

b y f Woodman - Lea Lucinda (Secreto) ... (Mike Ryan) 110,000

From Eaton-Williams, Agent for Manganaro Stables Ltd.

b y c Woodman - Leo's Lucky Lady (Seattle Slew) .... (Pegasus Bloodstock International) 230,000

From Three Chimneys Farm, Agent.

b or br y c Danzig - Love For Life (Forli) ... (The Oaks) 450,000

Property of Darby Dan Farm.

b y f Sunshine Forever - Love You By Heart (Nijinsky II).......................... (Turf Company, Ltd., Agent) 170,000

Property of Echo Valley Horse Farm Inc.

ro y c With Approval - Matriarch (Wavering Monarch)......... (Centennial Farms) 180,000

274

From Camas Park Stud.

b or br y c Nureyev - Memories (Hail The Pirates)... (Brian Grassick Bloodstock) 285,000

From Lane's End, Agent.

b y c Danzig - Miss Brio (CHI) (Semenenko) (Gainsborough Stud) 300,000

From Eaton-Williams, Agent for Angus Glen Farm Ltd.

b y c Lyphard - Most Likely (Fappiano)..... (Horse France) 160,000

From Taylor-Made Sales Agency, Agent for Richard R Kennedy.

ch y c Afleet - My Lovely (Graustark)...... (W C Freeman, Agent) 40,000

Property of Stone Farm and Wendell Rawls Jnr.

b or br y f Devil's Bag - My Room (Bold Lad)................. (John A Toffan) 180,000

From Bridlewood Farm, Agent.

b or br y c Seattle Slew - North Of Eden (IRE) (Northfields).................... (Lazy Lane Farms, Agent) 400,000

From Three Chimneys Farm, Agent.

b or br y f Seattle Slew - Personable Lady (No Robbery)........ (Harry A Proctor) 600,000

From Westover Ridge, Agent for John W Rooker.

b or br y f Mining - Petite Diable (Sham)... (Seth W Hancock, Agent) 210,000

From Gainesway Farm, Agent for Gainesway Thoroughbreds Ltd.

ch y c Mr Prospector - Polite Lady (Venetian Jester)...... (Shadwell Farm, Inc) 600,000

From Brereton C Jones, Agent.

b y c Silver Hawk - Private Dish (Private Account)....... (Tim McMurry, Agent) 100,000

275

From Winter Quarter Farm, Agent for Maverick Productions Ltd.

b y f El Gran Senor - Refill (Mill Reef) ..... (John Ferguson Bloodstock) 200,000

From Eaton-Williams, Agent for Manhasset Stable.

b or br y f Storm Bird - Ride Sally (Raja Baba)....... (Robert & Beverly Lewis) 335,000

From Waterford Farm (Dr and Mrs R Smiser West), Agent.

b y c Crafty Prospector - Saucy Deb (Mr Leader)....... (H James Bond, Agent) 130,000

From Walnut Green (Jones Bros), Agent.

b or br y f Lyphard - Silent Account (Private Account).......... (Arthur I Appleton) 150,000

From Trackside Farm (Tom Evans), Agent for Foxfield.

ch y f Deputy Minister - Silver Valley (Mr Prospector)......... (Starstruck Farm) 250,000

From Walmac Int'l, Agent.

b y c Nureyev - Smart Angle (Quadrangle) (Gainsborough Stud) 900,000

From Lane's End, Agent.

b y f Nureyev - Squan Song (Exceller) ..... (B.B.A.) 295,000

Property of Fares Farms, Inc.

b or br y f Silver Hawk - Storm And Sunshine (Star de Naskra) .... (Temple Webber) 125,000

Property of Nuckols Farm (Charles Nuckols Jnr and Sons).

gr y f Forty Niner - Summer Pudding (Rich Cream).................. (Jim Tafel) 80,000

From Gainesway Farm, Agent for F A Genter Stable Inc, Dispersal.

ch y f Easy Goer - Tappiano (Fappiano) .... (Seth W Hancock, Agent) 450,000

276

From Gainesway Farm, Agent for Gainesway Thoroughbreds Ltd.

b y c Riverman - The Way We Were (Avatar)............. (Herb Kushner) 175,000

From Lane's End, Agent.

b y f Wild Again - Tis Juliet (Alydar) (I.T.C.) 300,000

b y c Seeking The Gold - Under Oath (Deputed Testamony) .... (Temple Webber) 275,000

From Gainesway Farm, Agent for Tatterstall Farms.

Thisis Mylifestyle ch y f Halo - Wishing Well (Understanding)................ (Shadi Farm (Japan)) 200,000

From Three Chimneys Farm, Agent.

b or br y f Woodman - Youthful Lady (Youth)...................... (I.T.C.) 150,000

Property of Mike G Rutherford (Manchester Farm).
b y c Blushing John - Alyfable (Alydar)..... (Tom St Denis Sr.) 20,000
From Denali Stud (Craig Bandoroff), Agent Jayeff Stables,Crystal Springs Fm
b y f Dayjur - Ambassador Of Luck (What Luck)........ (Cheveley Park Stud Ltd) 300,000
From Highclere (Jeffry Morris), Agent for Tri-Star Stable.
Bencher Q.C ch y c Affirmed - Au Printemps (Dancing Champ) .... (Darley Stud Management) 400,000
From Taylor Made Sales Agency, Agent for Richard R Kennedy.
ch y c Afleet - Avowal (L'enjoleur) .... (F Stronach) 65,000
From Eaton-Williams, Agent.
b y f Forty Niner - Bought Twice (In Reality) (H James Bond, Agent) 335,000

277

Property of Bel-Mar Farm.
ch y c Time For A Change - Casino Babe (Golden Act)... (Bryon Vickory, Agent) 300,000
Property of Echo Valley Horse Farm Inc.
ch y f Nijinsky II - Doubling Time (Timeless Moment)...................... (B.S.I.) 220,000
From John J Greely III (Wintergreen Farm), Agent.
ch y c Woodman - Fall Aspen (Pretense) .. (D Wayne Lukas) 500,000
From Trackside Farm (Tom Evans), Agent for Foxfield.
b y c Deputy Minister - Far Flying (Far North)........... (Centennial Farms) 200,000
From Taylor Made Sales Agency, Agent VIII.
ch y f Deputy Minister - Female Star (Johnny Appleseed)... (John A Toffan) 250,000
From Lane's End, Agent.
b y f Gulch - Flying Rumour (Alydar)........ (M Sakurai) 225,000
From Pegasus Stud (Melinda A Smith), Agent VI.
ch y c Woodman - Foresight Princess (Reviewer)................. (Albatroz) 50,000
From Camas Park Stud (Tim Hyde), Agent.
b y c Sadler's Wells - Forlene (IRE) (Forli) .. (I.T.C.) 250,000
b y c Gulch - Full Card (Damascus)........ (Shadwell Estate Co Ltd) 185,000
From Lane's End, Agent.
ch y f Woodman - Gallanta (FR) (Nureyev) (B.B.A.) 350,000

278

From Robert E Courtney/Crestfield Farm, Agent Jaime S Carrion.
b y c Private Account - Guadery (Golden Act)................ (Starstruck Farm) 235,000
From Lane's End, Agent.
b y c Danzig - Hidden Garden (Mr Prospector)............... (Lavin Bloodstock) 385,000
From Claiborne Farm, Agent.
ch y c Forty Niner - Honest Joy (Honest Pleasure)........... (Starstruck Farm) 325,000

From Bridlewood Farm, Agent.
b y f Rahy - Imagining (Northfields)........ (Robert & Beverly Lewis) 150,000
From Three Chimneys Farm, Agent.
b y c Mr Prospector - Jeanne Jones (Nijinsky II)........ (Centennial Farms) 900,000
From Parrish Hill Farm, Agent for Landon Knight.
b y c Rahy - Lady Of The Light (The Minstrel)......... (B.B.A. (Ireland) Ltd) 410,000
Property of Fares Farms, Inc.
gr y f Mr Prospector - Lady's Secret (Secretariat)................... (M Sakurai) 700,000
From Walmac Int'l, Agent for Wimborne Farm and Wimborne Farm Inc.
b or br y c Wild Again - Lady Winborne (Secretariat)............ (F Stronach) 290,000
From Walmac Int'l, Agent.
ch y c Cox's Ridge - Let It Fly (Hatchet Man)............... (D & B Ventures) 65,000
From Lane's End, Agent.
ch y c Gulch - Line Of Thunder (Storm Bird) (Ken Ellenberg) 40,000

279

From Three Chimneys Farm, Agent.
b y f Mr Prospector - Lypatia (FR) (Lyphard) (Darley Stud Management) 500,000
From Brereton C Jones, Agent.
b y f Gone West - Made In America (Explodent).. (Pharamond Bloodstock, Agent) 110,000
From King Ranch Farm, Agent.
ch y f Forty Niner - Maidee (Roberto)...... (Tom & Maxine Nichols) 150,000
From Eaton-Williams, Agent for Overbrook Farm.
b or br y c Storm Cat - Matoki (Hail To Reason)............. (Rokeby Farms) 510,000
Property of Windfields Farm.
b or br y c Gone West - Minstrelsy (The Minstrel)........ (Gainsborough Stud) 475,000
From Eaton-Williams, Agent for Edward A Cox Jnr.
b y c Seeking The Gold - Ms. Margi (Private Account).......... (B.B.A. (Ireland) Ltd) 210,000
From Waterwild Farm, Agent.
ch y f Silver Hawk - My Turbulent Beau (Beau's Eagle)... (Judy & Phillip Maas) 110,000
From Glenmore Farm Inc (L Clay Camp), Agent II.
ch y c Woodman - Never Scheme (Never Bend)...... (Darley Stud Management) 150,000
Property of Miller Thoroughbred Farm.
ch y f Gone West - Norette (IRE) (Northfields)............ (C Gordon-Watson) 100,000
From Lane's End, Agent.
ch y c Forty Niner - Princess Accord (D'Accord).......... (Manuden Farm) 120,000

280

From Waterford Farm (Dr and Mrs R Smiser West), Agent.
b y c Sovereign Dancer - Printing Press (In Reality).................. (Mike Ryan) 210,000
From Longfield Farm, Agent.
b y f Danzig - Queens And Aces (Fappiano) (Harold Harrison) 160,000

Property of Fares Farms, Inc.
b y c Topsider - Rascal Lass (Ack Ack)..... (Everest Group Inc) 75,000
Property of Mare Haven Farm (Dr William O Reed).
ch y c Forty Niner - Safe At The Plate (Double Zeus)........................ (Clint C Goodrich, Agent) 80,000
From Eaton-Williams, Agent for Overbrook Farm.
b y f Mr Prospector - Seaside Attraction (Seattle Slew)...................... (Cheveley Park Stud Ltd) 750,000
From Walnut Green (Jones Bros), Agent.
b y c Mr Prospector - Sense Of Unity (Northern Dancer)................. (Darley Stud Management) 650,000
From Three Chimneys Farm, Agent.
b y f Sadler's Wells - Shanizadeh (IRE) (Baldric).............. (Patrick Barbe) 200,000
From Eaton-Williams, Agent.
gr y c Seattle Slew - Small Virtue (Al Hattab)........... (William J Condren) 90,000
From Eaton-Williams, Agent for L E Wolfson, E D Jacobs & Manganaro Stables.
b y f Danzig - So Endearing (Raise A Native) .... (Glen Hill Farm) 500,000
From Brereton C Jones, Agent.
b y c Silver Hawk - Speaking Of Sweets (Elocutionist)........................ (Yazel Equine Service, Agent) 220,000

281

From Walmac Int'l, Agent.
ch y f Nureyev - Special Key (Key To The Mint)..... (John Ferguson Bloodstock) 325,000
Property of David's Farm.
b y f Wild Again - Stage Flite (Lord Durham) .... (Sam Speer) 35,000
Property of Darby Dan Farm.
b or br y f Nureyev - Steal A Kiss (Graustark)................ (M Sakurai) 275,000
From Fred Seitz, Agent for Foxfield.
b or br y f Deputy Minister - Sticky Prospect (Mr Prospector)..... (F Stronach) 150,000
Property of Lockhart Spears (Stoneleigh Farm).
b y c Topsider - Stoneleigh's Hope (Damascus)............. (Mike Ryan) 55,000
From Eaton-Williams, Agent for Edward A Cox Jnr.
ch y f Forty Niner - Sum (Spectacular Bid) (John Ferguson Bloodstock) 400,000
Property of Fares Farms, Inc.
b y f Easy Goer - Summer Mood (Raja Baba)............... (Harold Harrison) 115,000

282

ASCOT
Monday, July 26th

From Hyde Stud
b y c Then Again - Bloffa (Derrylin).. (Cash) 675
br y g Daring March - Fille de Phaeton (Sun Prince)...................... (Cash) 1,650
Property of Mr M Simmonds
The Orphan Girl b f (3yrs) Legend Of France (USA) - Damiya (FR) (Direct Flight).................. (J C Boher) 750
Property of Mrs P Flowers
ch g (4yrs) Flying Tyke - Sunshine State (Roi Soleil)............... (D James) 750
Property of Miss Samantha Pepperall
Munjarid ch h (8yrs) Habitat - Connaught Bridge (Connaught)............ (Cash) 800
To Dissolve a Partnership
La Foudre gr g (5yrs) Show-A-Leg - Land Of Ginger (Young Man)........... (Cash) 1,450
Property of Mr John Sillett
Bystrouska br m (7yrs) Gorytus (USA) - Labista (Crowned Prince (USA)) Covered by Bold Arrangement (L Kennard) 1,650
Property of Clarendon Park Stud
Admirable b m (12yrs) Welsh Pageant - Affirmative (Derring-Do) Covered by Salse................ (A L Courtnay) 825
Lady Farrier ch m (15yrs) Sheshoon - Minor Chord (Major Portion).......... (Cash) 600
Property of Mrs V M Hollington
Gt Hayes Pommard b g (3yrs) Trampler - Great Hayes Bene (Night Thought).... (Darren Howells) 725

283

Property of Mr M B Small
b f (3yrs) Sulaafah (USA) - Teevano (Blakeney)........... (R D Matthews) 1,000
Property of Mr David Murray Smith
Fendale b f (2yrs) Northern State (USA) - Lexia (Sharpo)....... (Al-Otaibi Dhawi) 675
Property of Mr H Yardley
Princess Jestina (IRE) b m (5yrs) Jester - Royal Aunt (Martinmas).............. (T Cunningham) 875
Property of a Gentleman
St Athans Girl b m (10yrs) Record Run - Greasby Girl (John Splendid).......... (Pandora Berney-Smith) 1,200
Property of a Partnership
Boldrullah b g (4yrs) Auction Ring (USA) - La Neva (FR) (Arctic Tern (USA)) ...... (P S Payne) 675
To Dissolve a Partnership
Amethystine (USA) ch m (7yrs) Barachoise (CAN) - Amathus (Song).............. (Mark Reeves) 5,000
Property of The Forum Bloodstock Ltd
Planet Forum b g (3yrs) Dowsing (USA) - Bertida (Porto Bello).... (Roger Curtis) 950
Property of a Lady
Sharptino ch c (4yrs) Bustino - Sharper Still (Sharpen Up).............. (K Marks) 1,600
Property of a Partnership
b f (2yrs) Reprimand - Haywain (Thatching) (Al-Otaibi Dhawi) 775
Boy Martin ch g (4yrs) Local Suitor (USA) - Mary Martin (Be My Guest)....... (Al-Otaibi Dhawi) 2,100

284

Property of JBS Malling Services Ltd
Premier Major (IRE) b g (4yrs) Bluebird (USA) - Calvino (Relkino)... (P Rodford) 2,300

Property of Mr A G Hide

Blue Trumpet b g (3yrs) Respect - Sans Blague (Above Suspicion) .... (W D Burchell) 2,500

From Castle Stables

Amrah b f (3yrs) Midyan (USA) - Ranyah (USA) (Our Native (USA)) .... (Mrs V Manning) 900

To Dissolve a Partnership, from South Bank Stables

M'bebe gr c (3yrs) Mtoto - Canton Silk (Runnymede)............... (A Moore) 1,500

From Southgate Stables

Bitran gr c (3yrs) Midyan (USA) - Bishah (USA) (Balzac (USA))... (Kevin Morgan) 4,200

Property of a Partnership

Leigh Crofter ch g (4yrs) Son Of Shaka - Ganadora (Good Times (ITY)) .... (P Cundell) 2,400

From Whitcliffe Grange

Guylain b c (2yrs) Fairy King (USA) - Karonga (Main Reef) (Al-Otaibi Dhawi) 1,100

To Dissolve a Partnership

Stockforce ch g (3yrs) Infantry - Stockline (Capricorn Line)...... (Al-Otaibi Dhawi) 950

Sportsguides Girl b f (2yrs) Dowsing (USA) - Naufrage (Main Reef).... (Mr Cooper) 900

Property of Her Majesty the Queen

Love In The Mist (USA) ch f (3yrs) Primo Dominie - Sleeping Beauty (Mill Reef (USA))................... (L Kennard) 5,400

285

Property of Mr J C Smith

Flashfeet b c (3yrs) Rousillon (USA) - Miellita (King Emperor (USA))... (Cash) 6,000

Property of Llety Farms

La Serenata br m (10yrs) Welsh Pageant - Krafty Kate (Klairon) Covered by Merdon Melody........... (R G McRody) 1,050

Property of Messrs Charles & David Hodge, from Llety Farms

Marwick gr m (10yrs) Roan Rocket - Mathilde (Whistler) Covered by Merdon Melody...................... (Cash) 875

Property of Llety Farms

Sodina b m (15yrs) Saulingo - Red Rag (Ragusa) Covered by Bold Owl (Cash) 575

Property of Mr B Haggas

Cheat (USA) ch c (3yrs) Star de Naskra (USA) - Classic Ambition (USA) (Cyane (USA))............... (Al-Otaibi Dhawi) 3,200

Property of Darley Stud Management Co Ltd, from Rockingham Yard

Shansi (IRE) b c (2yrs) Shaadi (USA) - Chic Belle (USA) (Mr Prospector (USA)) .... (Mark Usher) 5,800

Property of Messrs Mark & David Holt

Coven Moon ch f (3yrs) Crofthall - Mayspark (Stanford)........... (P Hedger) 2,200

Property of G H R & F Ward

Melody Dancer b c (2yrs) Rambo Dancer (CAN) - Secret Song (Tudor Melody)... (Cash) 1,200

Property of Mr T M Jones

Buckski Echo b g (3yrs) Petoski - Echoing (Formidable (USA))..... (W D Burchell) 5,200

Property of a Lady

b f (3yrs) Nomination - Sonbere (Electric) .. (Cash) 1,000

286

To Dissolve a Partnership

Alta Victoria (IRE) b f (3yrs) Fairy King (USA) - Sunland Park (Baragoi)............. (M W Stephenson) 7,600

Property of a Lady

Saddlehome (USA) br g (4yrs) Aragon - Kesarini (USA) (Singh)......... (Cash) 3,500

A Badge Too Far (IRE) b f (3yrs) Heraldiste (USA) - Travel (Saritamer).............. (David Minton Bloodstock) 3,200

To Dissolve a Partnership

Burning Cost b f (3yrs) Lochnager - Sophie Avenue (Guillaume Tell (USA)) .... (David Minton Bloodstock) 2,000

The Spive b g (2yrs) Tina's Pet - Emperor Star (King Emperor (USA))............ (Mary Waterfall) 875

Property of Upper Hatch Farm

b f (4yrs) Native Bazaar - Hot Tramp (Country Retreat)................ (D Dunger) 1,350

Property of International Racing

ch f (2yrs) Bustino - Before Long (Longleat (USA))................ (Peter Wright) 850

Property of Lord Leverhulme

Melody's Daughter b f (3yrs) Sizzling Melody - Dancing Daughter (Dance In Time (CAN))........ (Sagittarius Bloodstock) 2,000

Property of Mr C W C Elsey

Grenoble (IRE) gr f (3yrs) The Noble Player (USA) - Douala (GER) (Pentathlon) ..... (J C Boher) 900

Property of Lord Mostyn

Grogfryn ch f (3yrs) Nicholas Bill - Connaught's Trump (Connaught).......... (C Popham) 1,700

287

Property of Monkey Racing Club Ltd

Monkey Money (IRE) b f (2yrs) Classic Secret (USA) - Mystery Bid (Auction Ring)......................... (Cash) 1,300

Property of M H G Systems Ltd

Moss House (IRE) ch c (2yrs) Persian Heights - Golden Temple (Golden Fleece (USA))................. (Cash) 1,300

Property of Mr M A Humphreys

b f (4yrs) Kabour - Princess Nora (Ahonoora) .... (B F Webb) 850

b m (5yrs) Kabour - King's Fillet (King's Bench)................. (Sarah Biron) 1,400

br g (3yrs) Backchat (USA) - High Venture (High Award)........ (Andrew Moore) 1,000

b m (6yrs) Sparkling Boy - English Princess (English Prince)....... (D Newnham) 1,550

b g (4yrs) Kabour - English Princess (English Prince).................... (Pat Daly) 2,900

ch m (5yrs) Kabour - Proclaimer (Town Crier)................. (Sarah Biron) 1,100

gr f (4yrs) Kabour - Proclaimer (Town Crier) (Cash) 1,800

Property of Miss A L Wright
Buckingham Band (USA) ch g (5yrs) Palace Music (USA) - Intensive (USA) (Sir Wiggle (USA)).................... (Cash) 1,750

288

Property of Mr T Kerr
Derry Gowan ch g (11yrs) Avocat - Es-Na-Laragh (Ballyciptic)... (Lisa Crossman) 1,850
Property of Mr Andrew Hale
Knockavon b g (5yrs) Belfort (FR) - Miss Merlin (Manacle).......... (L Kennard) 2,400
From Caradoc Court Stables
Sheer Motion b g (6yrs) Sheer Grit - Motion Potion (Vulgan's Air)........... (Cash) 2,600
Property of a Gentleman
b c (2yrs) Nordance (USA) - Miami Blues (Palm Track)............. (Mrs Taylor) 725
From Hollins Stables
Live And Let Fly gr g (4yrs) Import - Glendyne (Precipice Wood)......... (Cash) 2,800
Property of Woods Folly Stud
Padiord ch g (6yrs) Carleon (USA) - Osmunda (Mill Reef (USA))........... (Mrs R Luke) 3,200
From South Hatch Stables
Wagon Load ch g (8yrs) Bustino - Noble Girl (Be Friendly).................. (Cash) 1,050
Top Song br f (4yrs) Noalto - Pounelta (Tachypous).................. (Cash) 875
Property of Mr & Mrs R H J Martin
Mappowder Court b f (3yrs) Town And Country - Tim's Brief (Avocat)......... (D Davies) 1,500
Property of a Lady, from South View Stables
Patrusika b m (7yrs) Full Of Hope - Vulrusika (Vulgan)........... (A J Taylor) 2,600

289

Property of Mr R Croker
ch g (4yrs) Nearly A Hand - Tuletta (Tula Rocket)...................... (Cash) 2,300
Property of Mr M C Banks
Danish Ditty ch g (4yrs) Viking (USA) - Irish Limerick (Try My Best)......... (Cash) 2,600
Property of The Exors of M P Murdoch (Deceased)
Palmo Days b g (7yrs) Flower Robe - Lucifer's Dream (Lucifer)............. (D W Browning) 4,200
Property of Lady F Sutton
br g (3yrs) Norwick (USA) - Welsh Flower (Welsh Saint)............. (Tim Tebb) 800
Property of Bluegates Farm
Doordalus (IRE) b or br g (5yrs) Mandalus - Door Key (Fidel)............... (Cash) 1,900
Property of Miss Ellen Ryan
Great Faith (IRE) b m (5yrs) Ahonoora - Princess Seal (Prince Tenderfoot)..... (R Taylor) 3,000
Property of Plum Tree Cottage Stables
Waldorf T Beagle b g (7yrs) Buckskin (FR) - Arctic Alice (Brave Invader).. (F Coton) 2,800
Property of Mrs J Z Munday
Dear Course b g (10yrs) Crash Course - Dellasville (Trouville) (Mrs V Manning) 1,700

Property of Mrs D Knight
Liam's Pride ch g (10yrs) Mart Lane - Miss Manhattan (Bally Joy)...... (T Denton) 1,500
Property of Goatacre Farm
Pimpernel King b g (7yrs) Pimpernell's Tune - Katie's Princess (Prince Hansel)...... (Julian Victor Edge) 1,700

290

Property of Mr W M Lidsey
Wolf Wood ch m (5yrs) Little Wolf - Nightwood (Sparkler)......... (S A Wilson) 1,700
Property of Mr M Sturgis
Serious Result b f (3yrs) Jester - Little Revenge (Runnymede).........(Cash) 900
Property of Kennet House Stables
General Fairfax (IRE) ch g (2yrs) Al Hareb (USA) - Free Reserve (USA) (Tom Rolfe)............. (Andrew Jenkins) 1,050
Property of Mrs A Mutch
Reapers Reward b m (5yrs) Oats - Red Ragusa (Homeric).......... (R Barton) 1,600
To Dissolve a Partnership
Osgathorpe ch g (6yrs) Dunbeath (USA) - Darlingka (Darling Boy)............... (David Minton Bloodstock) 2,000
Man Of Kashmir (IRE) b g (2yrs) Mansooj - Dame Brisene (FR) (Kashmir II) (Cash) 750

291

DONCASTER
Monday, August 9th

Property of Miss S L Judge
The Metropole ch g (4yrs) Where To Dance (USA) - Mother Flutter (Gulf Pearl)..... (Cash) 1,700
Property of Mra A Chambers-Bondi
Spartacus Maximus b c (2yrs) Dreams To Reality (USA) - Starchy (Crisp And Even)..................... (L Morris) 680
Property of Mr A R M Galbraith
Creagmohr gr g (3yrs) Cragador - Cawston's Prejudice (Cawston's Clown)............... (B J Llewellyn) 1,700
Property of Miss E Cooper
Restless Walter b g (3yrs) Belfort (FR) - Morlolly (Morston).... (Lisa McAlpine) 1,250
From Manor Stables
Aragon King b g (3yrs) Aragon - Cadasi (Persian Bold)...................... (Andrew John Ferguson) 850
Property of Mr R S G Jones
Last Typhoon b f (3yrs) Dowsing (USA) - Song Grove (Song)............ (Cash) 1,600
Property of a Syndicate, from Boyden End Stables
Danger Baby ch g (3yrs) Bairn (USA) - Swordlestown Miss (USA) (Apalachee) (Robin Dickin) 3,600
To Dissolve a Partnership
b c (2yrs) Entitled - Frighten The Life (King's Lake).............. (Mrs J Dennison) 1,200
Property of Messrs Frank Sharp & Robert Earnshaw, from High Warren Farm
Fusion b g (9yrs) Mill Reef - Gift Wrapped (Wolver Hollow).......... (J J O'Neill) 1,300

Dear Do b g (6yrs) Swinging Rebel - Earlsgift (Dusky Boy)..................... (David Minton Bloodstock) 8,600
Wyndom Earle b g (3yrs) Good Times (ITY) - Georgian Melody (Hello Gorgeous)... (S Powell) 1,050

292

From Northgate Lodge Stables
Quick Victory b f (3yrs) Sharpo - In Triumph (USA) (Hoist The Flag).......... (Cash) 1,100
From Wold House Stables
Just Bill ch c (2yrs) Nicholas Bill - Petiller (Monsanto).................. (G Blum) 3,600
To Dissolve a Partnership, from Haggswood Stables
Kentucky Dreams b g (3yrs) Dreams To Reality (USA) - Kentucky Tears (USA) (Cougar)............... (Miss S Evans) 1,500
From Whitewall Stables
Norbeck b g (2yrs) Cyrano de Bergerac - Glorino (Bustino)............... (Cash) 750
Lady Lawn ch f (3yrs) Gabitat - Joara (FR) (Radetzky).................... (Cash) 900
Property of Mr A Tikkirou, from Barrow Stables
Makroy b c (2yrs) Stalker - Royal Holly (Royal Buck)................... (Cash) 1,050
Property of Mr W Taylor
Hawaymyson b g (3yrs) Mazaad - Northern Amber (Shack)........... (A Stringer) 2,400
Property of Mr A G Greenwood
Snugfit Annie b f (2yrs) Midyan (USA) - Great Aim (Great Nephew)............ (Tom Shally) 1,000
From Yew Tree Stables
Cheeky Tune b g (4yrs) Precocious - Miami Melody (Miami Springs).. (N.R.L. Burd) 720
Property of Mrs D E Kain
Samantha's Joy b f (3yrs) Marching On - Sister Racine (Dom Racine)........... (A W Potts) 1,150

293

From High Onn Stud
Rosie Dickins b m (11yrs) Blue Cashmere - Deva Rose (Chestergate) Covered by Safawan with f foal at foot by Tina's Pet........................... (Cash) 3,400
ch c (11yrs) Alfie Dickins - Time Of Your Life (Mount Hagen)............ (Cash) 1,450
ch g (2yrs) Alfie Dickins - Time Of Your Life (Mount Hagen)................ (Cash) 500
Property of the Exors of the late Lt-Cmdr W H Crawford
Lothian Lightning ch m (12yrs) Lighter - Lothian Lady (New Brig) Covered by K-Battery with a ch c foal at foot by Ovac (ITY).................. (Mrs Wood) 6,000
Lothian Commander ch y c Alias Smith (USA) - Lothian Lightning (Lighter)..... (R Bellamy) 2,200
Property of Mr P Balding, from Spa Stud
Susie Hall gr m (18yrs) Gold Rod - Cawston Tower (Maharaj Kumar) Covered by Bold Arrangement with a b f foal at foot by Green Ruby (USA)............ (Julie Porter) 850
Aleda Rose b m (16yrs) Charlottown - Urugano (Buisson Ardent) Covered by Lugana Beach with b c foal at foot by Governor General (Silfield Bloodstock) 2,500
Hitravelscene b m (14yrs) Mansingh (USA) - Kassiope (Sir Gaylor) Covered by Lugana Beach with b c foal at foot by Governor General........... (J Hogan) 1,600
Miss Serlby b m (10yrs) Runnet - Sarasingh (Mansingh) Covered by Absalom with a b c foal at foot by Lugana Beach...... (Cash) 6,000
Sabonis (USA) b m (6yrs) The Minstrel (CAN) - Journey (USA) (What A Pleasure) Covered by Absalom with a ch f foal at foot by Master Willie .... (David Minton Bloodstock) 6,200
b y f Green Ruby (USA) - Sabonis (USA) (The Minstrel)........... (T H Caldwell) 2,100

294

Property of Mr G T Revitt, from Blythe Park Stud
Maestroes Beauty bl m (8yrs) Music Maestro - Brazilian Beauty (Busted) Covered by Tina's Pet....... (S Warr) 1,500
Princess Poquito ch m (7yrs) Hard Fought - Poquito (Major Portion) Covered by Nomination with a ch c foal at foot by Savahra Sound................ (Cash) 3,200
Pugilistic b m (8yrs) Hard Fought - Joey (Salvo) Covered by Gunner B... (Cash) 2,900
Property of Mr G T Revitt
ch y f Gunner B - Barston Lady (Mr Fluorocarbon)....................... (Cash) 720
Property of Mr F T Scotto, from The Morley Stud
b y f Primitive Rising - Miniature Miss (Move Off).................. (J Biggin) 750
Property of a Partnership, from Wood Farm Stud
Faw ch m (5yrs) Absalom - Vivchar (Huntercombe) Covered by Safawan... (Cash) 1,500
From Glenmore Stud, Co Tyrone, Ireland
Tickled To Bits b m (19yrs) Sweet Revenge - Anagram (Vilmoray) Covered by Roaring Riva....................... (Cash) 950
Glenvalley Mist br m (14yrs) Pitpan - Silogue (No Argument) Covered by Secret Appeal.................. (P F Quinn) 1,150
Silky Miss b m (8yrs) Torus - Arctic Silk (Arctic Slave) Covered by Roaring Riva (Cash) 950
Glenmore Princess b m (3yrs) Anita's Prince - Tumble One (Tumble Wind) Covered by Roaring Riva....... (Cash) 1,500

295

Property of Mr R Wilkie
Persian Melody b m (3yrs) Persian Heights - Whist Awhile (Caerleon) Covered by Feelings (FR)................. (Cash) 1,500
Property of Mr C David Harrison
Penny Rose b m (12yrs) Whistlefield - Gambling Rose (Game Rights) Covered by Mango Express.... (Mrs L Sutherland) 1,000

Property of Dandy's Farm. from Dandy's Farm
b y c Sharrood (USA) - Valiyen (Valiyar) .... (J And A Young (Leics) Ltd) 2,400
Property of Mrs A Richardson (a dispersal sale)
Gilzie Bank b m (18yrs) New Brig - Pinch A Kiss (Pinhurst) Covered by Arctic Lord with a c foal at foot by Lord Bud ...... (S Kettlewell) 2,600
Danny D'Albi b m (13yrs) Wrens Hill - Annie Babu (Little Buskins) Covered by Arctic Lord with a c foal at foot by Lord Bud (R Dalton) 2,300
b y f Gildoran - Danny D'Albi (Wrens Hill) .. (E Stenton) 1,600
b g (2yrs) Pitpan - Gilzie Bank (New Brig) .. (R McDonald) 1,200
Property of Dr W T Lin, from Brockton House
I Do Care ch c (3yrs) Absalom - Oxide (USA) (Our Native).................. (Northern Racing School) 1,350
Dream Start b c (3yrs) Dreams To Reality (USA) - Bad Start (USA) (Bold Bidder).. (Harvey Smith) 1,100
Property of Mr T F Harrington, from Burley Heyes Stables
Tommy Trungle b g (3yrs) Jalmood (USA) - Lossiewells (Bustino) .... (Northern Racing School) 2,400

296

Property of a Partnership, from Breckenbrough House Stables
Wonderful Years (USA) ch g (3yrs) Key To The Mint - Velvet Storm (Wajima) ..... (B.B.A.) 6,300
Property of L C & A F Sigsworth, from Breckenbrough House Stables
Forenza ch f (3yrs) Formidable (USA) - Rexana (Relko)................ (Cash) 1,000
Property of a Partnership, from Pinewood Stables
Emperor Alexander br g (5yrs) Tender King - Persian Apple (USA) (No Robbery) ... (N Alexander) 1,900
From Longsides Stables
Susanna's Secret b c (6yrs) Superlative - Queens Welcome (Northfields) .... (J L Harris) 3,000
Property of a Partnership, from Longsides Stables
Astrac Trio ro g (3yrs) Timeless Moment (USA) - Fairway Flag (USA) (Fairway Phantom)............... (P Monteith) 7,500
Property of R O'Sheen Bloodstock Services, Co Kilkenny, Ireland
Glen Gloy Again br c (4yrs) Our Native (USA) - Majestic Julie (Majestic Prince) (Cash) 1,550
b g (3yrs) Adonijah - Twist And Shout (Cure The Blues).................... (Cash) 3,500
Spectacular Native br g (3yrs) Timeless Native (USA) - Spectacular Fact (USA) (Spectacular Bid).... (Mrs K Johnston) 1,300
Pacific Hero ch c (2yrs) Forzando - On To Flory (Welsh Pageant)................ (S Biddlecombe) 1,200
From Norton Grange Stables
Best Appearance b g (3yrs) Try My Best (USA) - Reliable Rosie (Relko)......... (J McGrath) 12,000

297

From Ivy House Stables
Montifiore Avenue b g (7yrs) Kings Lake (USA) - Lady Of Cornwall (USA) (Cornish Prince).............. (J J O'Neill) 6,000
Property of a Partnership, from Tupgill Park Stables
Easby Roc b g (5yrs) Bulldozer - Lady Mell (Milan)........................ (Cash) 3,700
From Mowbray House Stables
Vale Of York gr g (5yrs) Kabour - Amber Vale (Warpath).......... (D Chapman) 2,500
Acidosis ch g (4yrs) Kabour - Tang Dancer (Junius)..... (Northern Racing School) 1,900
Property of · Dissolve a Partnership
Top Villain b g (7yrs) Top Ville - Swan Ann (My Swanee)............ (C.H.P. Bell) 2,000
To Dissolve a Partnership
Hutner b g (8yrs) Henbit (USA) - Fountain (Reform)..................... (Cash) 6,800
Property of Mr P Stoner, from Park Leys Stables
Mr Fudge gr g (6yrs) Broadsword (USA) - Blades (Supreme Sovereign).......... (M.E. Sowersby) 9,600
Property of The Pessimists Syndicate
Babcock Boy b g (8yrs) Prince Bee - Gail Borden (Blue Chariot).......... (Cash) 950
To Dissolve a Partnership
Trojan Lancer b h (7yrs) Trojan Fen - Dunster's Cream (Sharpen Up).. (I Bennett) 820
To Dissolve a Partnership, from Flaxton Stables
Auburn Castle b g (4yrs) Good Times (ITY) - Glorious Jane (Hittite Glory)... (C.B.A.) 14,000

298

Property of Mrs Basil Samuel, from Rhonehurst Stables
Springaleak br m (8yrs) Lafontaine (USA) - Union Rules (Workboy)....... (C.B.A.) 15,500
Property of Mr D Chapman & Mrs C Wells, from Seven Barrows Stables
Holy Mackerel ch g (6yrs) The Parson - Shallow Run (Deep Run) (John Porter) 6,600
Property of the Exors of the Late Lt-Cmdr W H Crawford
Glen Morvern ch m (7yrs) Carlingford Castle - Why Ask (Deep Run)...... (Cash) 1,000
Lothian Rose b m (7yrs) Roscoe Blake - Lothian Lady (New Brig)...... (C.B.A.) 4,000
From Rathmore Stud, Co Limerick, Ireland
I'd Say Hardly ch g (6yrs) Deep Run - Merry Madam (Merrymount)... (S Chadwick) 3,100
Property of Mr F Sheehy, from Hazelwood Stables, Co Kildare, Ireland
Ealing Court ch g (4yrs) Blazing Saddles (AUS) - Fille de General (Brigadier Gerard).................. (B O'Ryan) 17,000
From Stablemate Racing Plc, Co Kildare, Ireland
Gnome's Tycoon br g (7yrs) Strong Gale - Fairgoi (Baragoi) .... (Johnny McKeever Bloodstock) 29,000
Property of Mr C McCarthy. from Woodtown House Stables, Co Meath, Ireland
Straight Talk b g (6yrs) Ovac (ITY) - Golden Tipp (Golden Love)......... (R Barber) 15,000

From Toranfield House Stud, Co Wicklow, Ireland

Fraber Glen br g (9yrs) Furry Glen - Lauch Berg (Faberge II)............... (Cash) 1,100

Prince Amanda ch g (7yrs) Deep Run - Cool Amanda (Prince Hansel) (N.R.L. Burd) 850

299

Property of Mr C Rice, Co Limerick, Ireland

House Of Roses b g (5yrs) Spanish Place (USA) - Spanish Gem (Pyrenean) ...... (P Nicholls) 9,000

Property of Mr J Halley, M R C V S, from Suir View Stables, Co Tipperary, Ireland

Judge Roger ch g (7yrs) Decent Fellow - Carnation Cruise (Dual)................ (Johnny McKeever Bloodstock) 18,000

To Dissolve a Partnership, from Moattown Stud, Co Meath, Ireland

I Suppose b g (8yrs) Torenaga - Some Dual (Dual).................. (W Coleman) 1,800

Property of Mr Ivor Dulohery, Co Cork, Ireland

Finnow Quay ch g (4yrs) Quayside - Sheipeil Bawn (Laurence O) .... (David Minton Bloodstock) 7,800

From Dunadry Stud, Co Antrim, Ireland

Making Time gr m (6yrs) Furry Glen - Arctic Border (Arctic Slave) .... (David Minton Bloodstock) 3,800

For Fame br g (5yrs) Remainder Man - Dusky's Lady (Dusky Boy)............ (David Minton Bloodstock) 8,000

Property of Mr W Tudor

The Weather Man b g (5yrs) Official - Deep Depression (Weathercock). . (G Moore) 3,000

Property of a Partnership

Yabbadabbadoo b g (7yrs) Royal Fountain - Annie Buskins (Little Buskins)......... (David Minton Bloodstock) 2,700

Property of Mrs M E Curtis

Clonmill ch g (8yrs) Don - Sapristi (Psidium) (David Minton Bloodstock) 6,800

Alias Silver gr g (6yrs) Alias Smith (USA) - Duresme (Starry Halo).... (John Allen) 8,000

300

Property of Mr A S Corner

Great Pokey br g (8yrs) Uncle Pokey - Mekhala (Menelek)......... (J Wilson) 9,600

Property of Col R N Crossley, from Westfield Farms

Silver Guru gr g (8yrs) Remainder Man - Eastern Promise (Eastern Lyric)....... (David Minton Bloodstock) 3,200

From Creevy Lodge Stud, Co Down, Ireland

Verajo b g (6yrs) Hays - Roque Nublo (Nebbiolo).................... (C Bennett) 2,000

Property of Mrs Patricia Mackean, from Sweet Wall Stables, Co Antrim, Ireland

Clady Water gr g (8yrs) Belfalas - Wensum (Pal's Passage).......... (S Chadwick) 2,500

Property of Mr C S McKeever, from Ballywee Stables, Co Antrim, Ireland

Truly Unique b g (7yrs) Lafontaine (USA) - Musical Rock (Sandy Creek).......... (B W Talbot) 2,000

Property of Mr W Bryan

Guiting Gray gr g (6yrs) Carlingford Castle - Very Pleased (USA) (Al Hattab) (Cash) 3,500

Property of Mrs P Morris

Spartan Flapjack ch g (7yrs) Oats - Miss Spartan (Spartan General)...... (Cash) 4,000

Property of Mrs F Moore, from Kimberley Home Stables

Ovac Star ch g (7yrs) Ovac (ITY) - Dora's Pryde (Pry).............. (S Shefras) 4,400

Property of Mrs G B Walford

All Or Nothing ch m (5yrs) Scorpio (FR) - Kelton Lass (Lord Nelson). . (D C Craig) 3,100

To Dissolve a Partnership

Polaris gr g (7yrs) Move Off - Toadpool (Pongee)................. (E Maggas) 2,200

301

Property of Mr Christopher McCarthy, Co Clare, Ireland

Oriental Sands b g (6yrs) Le Moss - Cherrydawn (Pollerton)............ (C.B.A.) 14,000

Property of Mr D O'Riordan, Co Cork, Ireland

This Ill Do Us ch g (5yrs) Boyne Valley - Swater Girl (Blue Cashmere).......... (A Morley) 7,000

Property of Mr M J McDonagh, from Brickhill Stud, Co Clare, Ireland

Spanish Light b g (4yrs) Spanish Place (USA) - Arconist (Welsh Pageant) ..... (David Minton Bloodstock) 13,500

From Knockderry House Stud, Co Clare, Ireland

Kingofspancilhill b g (6yrs) King's Ride - Cappahard (Record Run).... (R Glynn) 4,800

Property of Mr W Dennison, Co Antrim, Ireland

Millbay br g (5yrs) Pollerton - Night Course (Crash Course)....... (Michael Bloom) 7,800

Longford br g (5yrs) Pragmatic - Tender Soul (Prince Tenderfoot)............. (Michael Bloom) 8,400

From Blackwell Grange Stables

Mists Of Time gr g (10yrs) Grey Dawn II - Hyroglyph (USA) (Northern Dancer).... (J And P Wormall) 2,300

Sir Noddy ch g (10yrs) Tom Noddy - Pinzarose (Pinza)....... (G W Briscoe) 4,800

Property of Mr N E H Hargreave

Wenceslas b g (11yrs) Sovereign King - Wintersbrig (New Brig)............... (Miss F J Hitchings) 1,000

Property of Mr & Mrs R H M Hargreave

Owd Henry b g (10yrs) Rymer - Jo Marie (Master Buck)................. (Cash) 4,600

302

From Whispering Trees Racing Stables

Hannah Millie Nick b m (8yrs) Balinger - Saucy Eater (Saucy Kit)............... (Mrs J Laidlaw) 900

Property of Mr M J R Bannister

Jack Dwyer b g (10yrs) My Fordette - Daraheen Gate (Arcticeelagh)........ (J J Coates) 3,300

It's A Pry b g (12yrs) Pry - Clogga Girl (Levanter)........... (Harold Charlton) 2,000

Property of a Partnership

Rampallion b g (10yrs) Riboboy (USA) - Rampage (Busted)......... (M J Wall) 1,450

To Dissolve a Partnership

Iorwerth b g (7yrs) Rymer - Wicker Basket (Pamroy).............. (Yvonne Frost) 2,000

Property of Mr W Murdoch

Glenmullen b g (9yrs) Furry Glen - Caddy Girl (Avocat)............ (Mrs P Laws) 1,600

Property of Mr D Austin, from Billesdon Lodge Stables

Killelan Lad br g (11yrs) Kambalda - Dusky Glory (Dusky Boy)............. (Cash) 1,400

PRIVATE SALES

To Dissolve a Partnership, from Wold House Stables

Capiche b g (4yrs) Phardante (FR) - Sainthill (St Alphage)........... (G.H.R. Ward) 14,000

Property of Mr C McCarthy, from Woodtown House Stables, Co Meath, Ireland

Bells Hill Lad ch g (6yrs) Buckskin (FR) - Laiton Peni (Laurence O) (N Alexander) 8,000

Property of Mrs B M Lockey, from Kimberley Home Stables

Abitbizarre ch g (7yrs) Sunyboy - Minor Furlong (Native Bazaar)... (P J Russell) 4,400

RE-SUBMITTED

Property of Mr P G Freeman, from Woodside Stables

Homile b g (5yrs) Homing - Rocas (Ile de Bourbon)............. (P G Freeman) 1,700

303

DONCASTER

Tuesday, August 10th

To Dissolve a Partnership

American Hero ch g (5yrs) Persian Bold - American Winter (USA) (Lyphard) ..... (Johnnie McKeever Bloodstock) 24,000

Property of Mrs D R Burkett

Nino Azul b g (4yrs) Today And Tomorrow - Jill Somers (Will Somers)...... (Cash) 820

From Bretby Park Stables

Linpac Express b g (4yrs) Siberian Express (USA) - North Page (FR) (Northfields) .. (Norbert Sauer) 2,100

Property of a Partnership

Naval Raid b m (6yrs) Julio Mariner - London Blitz (Home Guard).. (N Foley) 2,000

Property of Mrs M Bolton

Miss Provision b m (5yrs) Daring March - The Silver Darling (John Splendid)..... (Cash) 1,500

Property of Mr Roger Spencer

King Of Normandy ch g (4yrs) King Of Clubs - Miss Deauville (Sovereign Path) .... (S G Chadwick) 1,700

Property of Mr W McIntosh

Baitin Time b g (7yrs) Sweet Monday - Mashin Time (Palm Track)............ (Mrs D Mason) 1,000

Property of Miss J Storey, from Low Coppice Farm

Hard Sell ch g (6yrs) Hard Fought - Misoptimist (Blakeney)........ (D Greenway) 1,100

Property of Riston Whins Racing Ltd, from Riston Whins Stables

Sum Mede b g (6yrs) King Persian - Brun's Toy (FR) (Bruni)........... (Ann Cane) 750

Property of Mr R Dalton

Dynavon b m (7yrs) Dynastic - Avon Melody (Bilsborrow).......... (N R L Burd) 650

304

Property of Mrs R Parkin

Vaigly Maid ch m (5yrs) Vaigly Great - Normanby Lass (Bustino)............. (P J S Russell) 1,050

Property of Mrs J Everitt & Mrs P Balding, from Spa Stud

Green Ruby (USA) b h (12yrs) Shecky Greene (USA) - Ruby Tuesday (USA) (T V Lark)...................... (Cash) 6,000

Property of a Partnership, from Spa Stud

Ruled By Fashion b f (2yrs) Governor General - Fashion Lover (Shiny Tenth)..... (L Morris) 700

O.K. Guv gr g (3yrs) Governor General - Debbie Do (Absalom)... (C G Graham) 2,500

Property of Mr P Balding, from Spa Stud

gr g (2yrs) Absalom - Frozen Flower (USA) (Arctic Tern)............... (R Smith) 780

Property of Mr G H Leggott, from Greenbury Grange Stables

Dardanelle ch f (3yrs) Stanford - Tarte Aux Pommes (Song)...... (Norbert Sauer) 1,000

Property of Mr R O Manners

Shut Up b f (4yrs) Kind Of Hush - Creetown Lady (Creetown)..... (J W Thompson) 3,000

Property of Mr Robert Gibbons, from Manor House Stables

Dancing North b or br g (8yrs) Shareef Dancer (USA) - Icena (Jimmy Reppin).. (Mrs J Wilson) 920

From Manor House Stables

Future Fame (USA) b c (4yrs) Stately Don (USA) - Hooplah (USA) (Hillary)........ (Mrs S M Austin) 4,300

Property of Mrs Lorraine Hunt, from Manor House Stables

Brooklands Express gr g (3yrs) Absalom - Lucy's Melody (On Your Mark)........ (J C Boher) 1,350

305

From Great Head House Stables

Paint The Wind b f (3yrs) Fayruz - Pink Fondant (Northfields).......... (Cash) 1,300

Goldmire b f (3yrs) Norwick (USA) - Orange Parade (Dara Monarch).. (W H Tinning) 4,200

King Acrylic b c (2yrs) King Of Clubs - Maynooth Belle (Busted)....... (Cash) 1,050

Property of Mr W T Robinson

Morell Bridge ch g (4yrs) Ballad Rock - Laharden (Mount Hagen)....... (Cash) 920

From Barn House Racing Stables

Be The Best b g (5yrs) Rousillon (USA) - Shadywood (Habitat).... (John Whyte) 1,200

From Phantom House Stables

Mr Bean b g (3yrs) Salse (USA) - Goody Blake (Blakeney)............ (K Burke) 5,700

From Nidd Park Stud

Tribal Affair gr g (3yrs) Siberian Express - Tribal Pageant (Welsh Pageant) (Cash) 2,100

From Thirty Acre Barn Stables

Regal Rambler (CAN) ch c (2yrs) Regal Classic - Rushing Rachel (Breezing On) (L J Barrett) 800

From Whitsbury Manor Stables

Ricky's Tornado ch g (4yrs) Night Shift (USA) - Foden's Eve (Dike).. (J Parkes) 2,700

From Whitcliffe Grange Stables

Royal Garden ch g (4yrs) Royal Vulcan - Park Covert (On Your Mark) .... (G B Balding) 11,000

306

Property of Mr M Woods, Co Louth, Ireland

Pennine Pass br g (4yrs) Pennine Walk - Red Realm (Realm)............ (Cash) 4,000

Property of Mr E O'Connor, Co Cork, Ireland

T'int br m (5yrs) Camden Town - Rue Del Peru (Linacre)............. (S Burley) 1,000

Property of Mr Dennis Badham, from King's Lodge Stables

Illogical br m (6yrs) Ile de Bourbon (USA) - Modern Romance (Dance In Time) .... (Mrs P Grainger) 2,600

Property of Shadwell Estate Co Ltd, from The Croft Stables

Azrag b c (3yrs) Bluebird (USA) - Red Val (Red God)........... (Norbert Sauer) 1,600

To Dissolve a Partnership, from Diomed Stables

Little Bid b f (2yrs) Spectacular Bid (USA) - Littlemisstrouble (USA) (My Gallant) ... (Cash) 850

From Moss Side Racing Stables

Tino Tere ch g (4yrs) Clantime - Blueit (FR) (Bold Lad)............. (John Balding) 4,000

Mr Blobby ch g (2yrs) Phardante (FR) - Gay Parthia (Gay Fandango)........ (Cash) 1,100

Me Neither b f (2yrs) Risk Me (FR) - I Don't Mind (Swing Easy)....... (D Dunston) 1,400

Property of Mr Fahd Salman

River Life b c (3yrs) Irish River (FR) - Exclusive Life (Exclusive Native) ...... (Norbert Sauer) 2,800

Property of a Partnership, from Holdforth Stables

Direct Interest ch g (10yrs) Al Sirat (USA) - Honey Come Home (Timobriol) .... (M J Brown) 4,700

307

Property of Mr J Craig, from Cree Lodge Stables

Jimmy Mac Jimmy b g (6yrs) Carriage Way - Tuthill Bello (Porto Bello) (W Lisburn) 5,500

From Dereens Stables, Co Kildare, Ireland

That's The Life ch g (8yrs) Wolverlife - Culleenamore (Northfields) .... (Johnnie McKeever Bloodstock) 10,500

Vavasir b g (7yrs) Carlingford Castle - Decently (Jukebox)......... (P Hobbs) 8,000

Good For A Laugh b g (9yrs) Idiot's Delight - Mekhala (Menelek).... (Sue Bramall) 17,000

Property of the Exors of the late Mr K E Wheldon, from Breckenbrough House Stables

Doc Cottrill b g (3yrs) Absalom - Bridal Wave (Julio Mariner).......... (C B A) 18,000

Will Of Steel ch g (4yrs) Master Willie - Collapse (Busted)..... (Norbert Sauer) 9,000

Chief Minister br g (4yrs) Rainbow Quest (USA) - Riverlily (FR) (Green Dancer)... (T Dyer) 18,000

From Rathmoy Stables

Aquado b g (4yrs) Green Desert (USA) - Meliora (Crowned Prince) .... (Keith Nicolls) 4,400

Blue Point b f (4yrs) On Your Mark (USA) - Littoral (Crash Course)....... (R Kent) 1,500

From Maddenstown Stables, Co Kildare, Ireland

Bluejacket ch g (5yrs) Thatching - Gitane Blue (Cure The Blues)...... (P Byrne) 3,400

Buffet ch g (4yrs) Jalmood - Grub (Be My Guest)................ (J F Williams) 1,800

Smart Debutante b f (4yrs) Glenstal (USA) - Cecily (Prince Regent)..... (J Poynton) 1,700

308

Property of Mr Michael J Bergin, from Ballyheshall House Stables, Co Offaly, Ireland

Cleevaun ch g (5yrs) Orchestra - Valary (Roman Warrior).................... (David Minton Bloodstock) 12,500

From Melitta Lodge Stables, Co Kildare, Ireland

Cloghans Bay b g (4yrs) Dance Of Life - Ringawoody (Auction Ring) .... (S Williams) 33,000

Property of Mr Harry Morrison, from The Glebe House, Co Down, Ireland

No Sir Rom b g (7yrs) Ragapan - Lady Hansel (Prince Hansel)...... (R Dickin) 2,600

Property of Mr P R Chambers, from The Glebe House, Co Down, Ireland

Fly By North (USA) b g (5yrs) Northern Horizon (USA) - Lazy E (CAN) (Meadow Court)...... (David Minton Bloodstock) 2,000

Property of Mr J Hanson, from Crackhill Stables

King Creole b g (4yrs) King's Ride - Lugnagullagh (Pitpan).................. (Johnnie McKeever Bloodstock) 15,500

Dusky Rover ch g (4yrs) Denel (FR) - Dream Away (Dusky Boy) .... (David Minton Bloodstock) 11,500

Tara Rambler ch g (4yrs) Arapahos - Tarabelle (Tarqogan)........... (C Platts) 7,200

Desert Run ch g (5yrs) Deep Run - Another Duchess (Master Buck)... (P Nicholls) 40,000

Property of a Partnership, from Brecongill Stud

Coney Road b g (4yrs) Grey Desire - Miss Diaward (Supreme Sovereign) .... (D Elsworth) 20,000

Property of Mr W O'Gorman, from Hartshill Stud

Fragrant Dawn br g (9yrs) Strong Gale - Aridje (Mummy's Pet)......... (Cash) 25,000

Rocket Launcher b g (7yrs) Strong Gale - Adell (Fordham) .... (Johnnie McKeever Bloodstock) 20,000

309

Property of Mr P O'Donoghue, Co Wexford, Ireland
Grand Rapids (USA) b g (6yrs) Riverman (USA) - Moralisme (Sir Ivor)........... (Sue Wilton) 4,400
Property of Mr J O'Donnaghue, Co Dublin, Ireland
Major Mac b g (6yrs) Mandalus - Ullard Lady (Official)............ (D Williams) 22,000
From Craigue Farm Stud, Co Wexford, Ireland
Staigue Fort b g (5yrs) Torus - Lady Beecham (Laurence O) (Denys Smith) 8,400
From Mocklershill Stables, Co Tipperary, Ireland (Agent)
Trim The Web br g (6yrs) Trimmingham - Snap Cobwebs (Silver Shark).......... (Mrs B A Ledger) 5,600
Property of Mr A O'Connor, Co Clare, Ireland
Par Bar gr m (5yrs) The Parson - Baranee (My Swanee)............ (M J Cringell) 7,600
br m (5yrs) Kemal (FR) - Fort Sunset (Beau Chapeau)...................... (Cash) 1,900
Property of Mr E O'Connor, Co Cork, Ireland
Killula Lass gr m (8yrs) Pragmatic - Lisduff (The Parson)....... (Mrs T M Gibson) 1,800
From Lennymore Stud, Co Antrim, Ireland
Mary Og b m (6yrs) Sayyaf - Maryfield (Hul A Hul).................. (G Hanmer) 3,200
From Dereens Stables, Co Kildare, Ireland
Flashy Buck b g (9yrs) Buckskin (FR) - Flashy Money (Even Money).......... (Cormac McCormack Associates) 7,800
Genista b g (8yrs) Furry Glen - Rossaleigh (Menelek)............... (J Cornwall) 2,500
El Bae b g (7yrs) Lord Ha Ha - Shanaway (Moss Court)................. (Cash) 6,600

310

Property of Mr John Gleason, Co Tipperary, Ireland
Clean Sweep br g (6yrs) Deep Run - The Charwoman (Menelek)...... (R Hand) 3,600
Property of Mr D L O'Byrne, M.R.C.V.S., Co Tipperary, Ireland
Unguided Missile b g (5yrs) Deep Run - Legaun (Levanter)..... (G W Richards) 27,000
Carinci b g (6yrs) Bishop Of Orange - Prairie Stream (Paddy's Stream).... (K Lewis) 3,800
From Moorestown Lodge Stud, Co Tipperary, Ireland
Mystic Micky b g (6yrs) Decent Fellow - Chipmunk (Apollo Eight)............. (David Minton Bloodstock) 10,500
From Coolagh Stud, Co Dublin, Ireland
Mr Grey Fellow gr g (5yrs) Sexton Blake - Wild Lucy (Lucifer).................. (David Minton Bloodstock) 5,300
From Waterloo Lodge, Co Tipperary, Ireland
Fabulous Francy ch g (5yrs) Remainder Man - Francie's Treble (Quayside)..... (David Minton Bloodstock) 9,600
Yes Man b g (4yrs) Remainder Man - Gleness (Deep Run)................. (David Minton Bloodstock) 15,500
Property of Mr T Barr, from Greystoke Stables
Bee Dee Boy b g (5yrs) Julio Mariner - H & K Gambler (Rheingold)........ (B B A) 8,000
Property of Mr R B Hamilton, from Ballynoe Stables, Co Down, Ireland
The Dark Walk br m (6yrs) Kemal (FR) - Bonnetys Bridge (Avocat)........... (J W P Curtis) 7,000
Property of Mr D Minnis, from Ballynoe Stables, Co Down, Ireland
Scrabo View ch g (5yrs) Denel (FR) - Patricia's Choice (Laurence O)........ (David Minton Bloodstock) 7,200

311

Property of Mr David Minnis, Co Down, Ireland
Faughan Lodge b g (6yrs) Kemal (FR) - Patricia's Choice (Laurence O)........ (W Clay) 3,000
Property of Mr W R Stone
Ring Sam b g (7yrs) Ring Bidder - Auto Sam (Even Say).......... (Penny Grainger) 3,800
b m (6yrs) Castle Keep - Asteria (Tycoon II) (B Ellison) 2,200
Property of Mr D Banks
Long Melford ch g (6yrs) Sunyboy - Saucy Eater (Saucy Kit).................... (David Minton Bloodstock) 3,900
Property of Mr P Murphy, from Bridge Hill Farms, Co Down, Ireland
Mini Fete (FR) b or br f (4yrs) Un Desperado (FR) - Minifa (FR) (Pharly) (K Burke) 3,000
Property of Mr R W & Mrs J R Fidler
Colonial Kelly ch g (5yrs) Netherkelly - Nepal (Indian Ruler)........... (C B A) 9,500
Property of Mrf R Robinson, from Distillery Stables
Brookfield Boy b g (6yrs) Roscoe Blake - Forget's Image (Florescence)......... (C E Sherry) 1,700
Property of Mr Jack Peckitt
Pavers Good Shoes b m (5yrs) Good Times (ITY) - Windy Sea (Sea Hawk II)....... (Mrs C W Forman) 2,000
Property of Mr E J Watt
Stormseal Boy b g (7yrs) Tyrnavos - Firente (Firestreak)............. (Mrs H Trigg) 3,800
From Merrivale Trading Company
Lordy ch g (8yrs) Celtic Cone - Onaea (Prince de Galles)............ (C B A) 3,900

312

Property of Mrs S A Minns
The Point Is ch g (6yrs) Major Point - Babble (Forlorn River)................ (David Minton Bloodstock) 7,400
Property of Mr Martin Kemp, from Burnhill Green Farm Stables
b m (5yrs) Buckskin (FR) - Foxborough Lady (Crash Course)............. (C Banks) 2,600
From Deanlands Farm Stud
Major Policy br g (6yrs) Politico (USA) - Misty Doric (Weathercock)... (A Reid) 3,800
Scotch Missile br g (6yrs) Cruise Missile - Scotch Dawn (Jock Scot)... (R Wilcox) 2,500
Property of Mrs Y Barclay
Alice Springs b m (6yrs) Town And Country - Commander Alice (Spartan General).. (Mrs H C Johnson) 2,000

From Rectory Farm Stud
ch g (5yrs) Deep Run - Miss Du Fosse (Eastern Venture).... (Mrs S Williams) 7,400
Property of Mr T A Holliday
Dancing Lord gr g (7yrs) Modern Dancer - Lady Hawkins (Wishing Star)... (Cash) 3,000
Property of Mrs A Lee
b g (5yrs) Import - Flopsy Mopsy (Full Of Hope)................ (Mrs S Skelton) 4,000
Property of Mrs D G Mason, from Southburgh Manor Stud
Riverside Moss ch g (5yrs) Le Moss - Arctic Chatter (Le Bavard)..... (P Wegmann) 3,600
Property of Messrs A W Jenkinson & J Norris
Sixth In Line ch g (5yrs) Deep Run - Yellow Lotus (Majority Blue)...... (B Dehaan) 5,000

313

Property of Springhill Bloodstock, from Mount Annan Stables
ch g (5yrs) Ragapan - Deep Toi (Deep Run) (Cash) 5,700
Property of Edgcote Estate, from Edgcote Estate
b g (5yrs) Sunyboy - Toumanova (High Line) .... (E J Watt) 1,800
From Philpotstown Stud, Co Meath, Ireland
gr g (5yrs) Pragmatic - Woodland Furbelow (Fury Royal).............. (J Chugg) 8,200
Property of Mrs Michele Mary Saul
b g (5yrs) Henbit (USA) - Simmay (Simbir) (Cash) 2,600
Property of Mr C W Foulkes
b g (5yrs) Kinglet - River Valley (Apollonius) (D Waggott) 2,500
Property of Mr W R Stone
b g (5yrs) Jupiter Island - Preobrajenska (Double Form)........... (J Connolly) 3,200
b g (5yrs) Sonnen Gold - Lennoxlove (Lear Jet)......................... (L Lungo) 2,500
Property of a Gentleman
Callroe b g (7yrs) Callernish - Coolroe Aga (Laurence O)............. (C Aitchison) 1,700
Property of Mrs D J Tellwright
ch m (5yrs) Rymer - Funny Ha Ha (Funny Man)........................ (P Morris) 2,100
Property of Mr John Gleeson, Co Tipperary, Ireland
br g (2yrs) Yashgan - Windy Run (Deep Run)......................... (Cash) 3,700

314

Property of Merton Stud, from Merton Stud
b f (2yrs) Gildoran - Sunny Cottage (Sunyboy)...................... (E Stenton) 1,900
Property of The Exors of the late Lt-Cmdr W H Crawford
Summer Island b f (2yrs) King's Badge - Gorgeous Gertie (Harwell).. (A Seavill) 800
Property of Mr W G Barker, from Tancred Stud
gr g (2yrs) Minster Son - Tree Mist (Bruni) (M Wanless) 1,500
b f (2yrs) Northern State (USA) - Mischievous Miss (Niniski)... (Miss S Hall) 2,300
Property of Mr K Hays, Co Wexford, Ireland
bl g (5yrs) Clover Hill - 1/2-Bred Irish Mare (J E Foster) 2,500

Property of Mr John A Owen, from Tyrnog Stud
Night Flight ch g (14yrs) Eborneezer - Weatherwynne (Weathercock)........ (D Barnell) 1,350
Property of Miss P Woodthorpe
Brandon Bay Girl b m (11yrs) - .... (D Greenway) 1,800
PRIVATE SALES
Property of Mr J Craig, from Cree Lodge Stables
Jimmy Mac Jimmy b g (6yrs) Carriage Way - Tuthill Bello (Porto Bello)............ (David Minton Bloodstock) 4,500
From Maddenstown Stables, Co Kildare, Ireland
Morceli gr g (5yrs) Mouktar - Safiak (FR) (St Paddy)................ (J H Johnson) 25,000
From Glenville House House, Co Wexford, Ireland
Betteville b g (6yrs) Sandalay - Kylenora (Dusky Boy)............... (C Broad) 4,500
From Dereens Stables, Co Kildare, Ireland
Genista b g (8yrs) Furry Glen - Rossaleigh (Menelek).............. (N R L Burd) 1,800

(Index reference 316 follows)

316

DONCASTER

Wednesday, August 11th

Property of Mr M Cornthwaite
Derwent Lad b g (4yrs) Lidhame - Swifter Justice (King's Bench) .... (Maurice Barnes) 2,500
Property of Mrs E Tarling
ch g (4yrs) Crofthall - Keep Believing (Sweet Revenge).............. (Cash) 1,300
Property of Mr C David Harrison
b g (3yrs) Faustus (USA) - Our Mable (Posse)................. (D Waggott) 1,600
Property of Mr R Dalton
ch g (5yrs) Alfie Dickins - Society Kate (Choral Society)............... (Cash) 1,000
gr f (4yrs) Alfie Dickins - Waminda (Native Prince)................... (J C Boher) 1,500
Property of S D Williams
Kitley Belle br f (4yrs) Senang Hati - Linney Lawn (Newski).................. (Cash) 1,800
Property of Mrs I Rowcliffe
ch g (4yrs) Import - El Chaperall (Scottish Rifle)........................ (P B Hall) 3,000
Property of Mr C H Bell, from Burton Fleming Hall
b g (4yrs) Meadowbrook - Emerald Valley (Ercolano).............. (L McAlpine) 850
Property of Mr C H P Bell, from Burton Fleming Hall
gr g (4yrs) Alias Smith (USA) - Snare (Poaching).................. (R Fahey) 1,500
Property of The Exors of the late Lt-Cmdr W H Crawford
Lothian Lily ch f (4yrs) Alias Smith - Lothian Lightning (Lighter)............. (Cash) 1,900

Lothian Commodore gr g (3yrs) Alias Smith (USA) - Lothian Lightning (Lighter)..... (T E Hyde) 8,000

317

Property of Mr Alf Watson, from Southfield Farm Stud

Sammy Hick ch g (4yrs) Venturesome - Our Maidie (Jolly Jet).............. (Cash) 1,000

Property of Mr S Dalton

b f (3yrs) Exorbitant - Laharna Girl (Star Appeal)................... (C Seavill) 1,000

Property of Mrs Audrey M Houlston

b g (3yrs) Primitive Rising - Samba Lass (Roan Rocket)................ (Cash) 2,700

Property of Mr M McMullen, from Lower House Farm Stables

Mick's Filly ch f (3yrs) Kamehameha (USA) - Blackwater Stream (Paddyh's Stream) (Cash) 1,300

Property of Mrs J A Elkington

b f (3yrs) Royal Vulcan - What A Popsi (Sagaro)................. (J McGrath) 1,100

Property of Mrs P E W Nicholson, from Oldstead Stud

br f (4yrs) Rymer - Tax Haven (Quayside) .. (F Laird-Portch) 1,700

Property of Miss Joan Wood

Karena's Royal Lass b f (4yrs) Royal Vulcan - Karena Park (Hot Spark)............ (Miss M Buchanan) 2,000

Property of Mrs P M Teare

b f (4yrs) Tuam - Golden Apple (Athens Wood)................... (J A Cole) 1,200

From Mowbray House Stables

b g (4yrs) Kabour - Belhill (Beldale Flutter) (Cash) 1,450

From Common Stud

ch g (4yrs) Grey Desire - Barefoot Contessa (Homeric)......... (Miss M C Phipps) 620

318

Property of Mr & Mrs C Wilson, from Pitts Farm Stud

b g (4yrs) Pablond - Annie Louise (Parthia) (David Minton Bloodstock) 5,000

Property of Mrs Z S Clark, from Scotswood Stud

b g (4yrs) Vital Season - Last Alliance (Honour Bound)................. (J Chugg) 14,000

From Aston House Stud

b f (3yrs) Niniski (USA) - Another Packet (Main Reef)............... (F Forrest) 800

From Hollins Stables

Invisible Luck b c (3yrs) Jareer (USA) - Noble Nancy (Royal And Regal) .... (J J O'Neill) 6,000

From Great Head House Stables

Gleaston Castle b g (5yrs) Fine Blade (USA) - Reformed Lady (Reformed Character) (E Tuer) 2,200

ch g (4yrs) Orchestra - Boyne Bridge (Brave Invader)................ (W D Oakes) 1,700

b g (3yrs) Decent Fellow - Hare Path (Private Walk)............... (G Balding) 3,600

Property of Mr John Needham

b f (4yrs) True Song - Most (Our Mirage) .. (Cash) 1,300

ch f (4yrs) Rymer - Rathmill Syke (True Song)...................... (R Hand) 1,000

Property of Mrs G D Morrissey, from Greenbury Grange Stables

Hollow Thoughts b g (4yrs) Hard Fought - Wolveriana (Wolver Hollow).... (Cash) 2,700

319

Property of Mrs J I Sheedy

br g (4yrs) Idiot's Delight - Spartan's Girl (Spartan General).... (Penny Grainger) 4,900

br f (3yrs) Bold Owl - Spartan's Girl (Spartan General).................... (C.B.A.) 5,000

Property of Mr G T Revitt (part of a dispersal sale)

ch g (3yrs) Gunner B - Barston Lady (Mr Fluorocarbon)............. (T Kersey) 1,800

From Windy Hill Stud

Stormhill Pilgrim b g (4yrs) Politico (USA) - In A Dream (Caruso) .... (David Minton Bloodstock) 5,500

Property of Travail Employment Group Ltd

b or br f (4yrs) The Parson - Irish Hill Lass (Prominer)................. (T Kersey) 2,500

Property of Mrs I P Brown, from Tara Lodge Farm, Co Antrim, Ireland

b g (4yrs) Marktingo - Mystery Women (Tula Rocket)............... (J Castle) 4,800

From Mount Davy's Stables, Co Antrim, Ireland

Dendieu ch g (4yrs) Denel (FR) - Three Dieu (Three Dons)........... (J McNicholl) 9,000

Property of Mr C B Hyslop, from Annanhill Stud

b g (4yrs) Gypsy Castle - Ladyville (Lord Nelson)............. (Tim Easterby) 5,000

From Carlton Stud (Malton)

b g (3yrs) Today And Tomorrow - Rhythm Maker (Song)................. (Cash) 950

Property of a Partnership, from Carseriggan House Stables

b or br g (3yrs) Bob Back (USA) - Angmering (Raga Navarro)...... (Mrs M Stirk) 4,000

320

Property of P & B Stonehouse, from Hedley North Farm Stables

b g (4yrs) Noalto - Condec (Swing Easy) ... (Johnny McKeever Bloodstock) 1,600

Property of Messrs R L Green & Sons, from Heckley High House Stables

b g (4yrs) Politico (USA) - Heckley Surprise (Foggy Bell)................ (R Hand) 7,000

From Manor Farm Stud (Dorset)

Saffron Glory ch g (4yrs) Duky (FR) - Boreen's Glory (Boreen).............. (Johnny McKeever Bloodstock) 3,000

Property of Mr R H Mason, from Wold Newton Stud

b or br g (4yrs) State Diplomacy (USA) - Hoar Frost (Doubtless II)....... (Cash) 4,200

Property of Mr M Cook, from High House Farm

b g (4yrs) Carlingford Castle - Suzanna's Joy (Crozier).................. (Cash) 2,600 b g (4yrs) Lancastrian - Katie Proverb (Proverb)................... (J M Buckley) 3,800

From Mocklershill Stables, Co Tipperary, Ireland (Agent)

ch g (4yrs) Toravich (USA) - Poker Dot (Raise You Ten)..... (Mrs P Brokensha) 3,800

Property of Mr Denis Cleary, from Wellington House Stud, Co Tipperary, Ireland

ch f (4yrs) Orchestra - Quite The Hassle (Deep Run)............... (W Mullins) 2,800

Property of Dr J F Gillespie, Co Armagh, Ireland

b g (4yrs) Abednego - Boogie Woogie (No Argument)................. (J Adam) 9,000

Property of Mr W Dennison, Co Antrim, Ireland

br g (4yrs) Supreme Leader - Cool Amanda (Prince Hansel)........................ (David Minton Bloodstock) 11,000

321

Property of a Partnership, from Sturt Farm Stud

gr f (3yrs) Baron Blakeney - Stella Romana (Roman Warrior)....... (Martin Kemp) 2,000

Property of Michael Jackson Bloodstock Limited, from Higham House Stables

b g (3yrs) Supreme Leader - Carry On Jackie (David Jack).. (Glenview House) 15,000

From Goldford Stud

ch g (4yrs) Sunley Builds - Damascus Star (Mandamus).................. (C.B.A.) 6,000

Gentle Jester br f (4yrs) Reesh - Mirthful (Will Somers)................ (C.B.A.) 6,000

Property of Mr John Gleeson, Co Tipperary, Ireland

b g (4yrs) Supreme Leader - Lishpower (Master Buck)................ (Cash) 4,400

br g (3yrs) Bulldozer - Black Pilot (Linacre) (Michael Browne) 1,200

Property of Mr G L Edwards

b g (4yrs) Seymour Hicks (FR) - Swift Sentence (Paper Cup).......... (Cash) 2,000

Property of NH Bloodstock Ltd., from Merton Place Stud

b g (4yrs) Saxon Farm - Knockeevan Girl (Tarqogan)........... (Colin Weedon) 9,000

Property of Mrs H Trigg

Half 'n Half br f (3yrs) Skyliner - Wharton Manor (Galivanter)......... (J McGrath) 1,750

Property of Mrs R D Hodgson, from Kilmond Wood

gr g (4yrs) Roselier (FR) - Toevarro (Raga Navarro)..................... (C.B.A.) 13,000

322

Property of Mr R L Burton, from Longner Hall Stud

br f (4yrs) Idiot's Delight - Coolek (Menelek) .... (S Clark) 3,000

From Wood Farm Stud

br f (4yrs) Strong Gale - Sharp Vixen (Laurence O).......... (Mrs M Broadhead) 2,800

From Crohane Stud, Co Tipperary, Ireland

ch g (3yrs) Aristocracy - Castle Tyne (Good Thyne)................... (P M Jibson) 3,000

Property of Mr G Cosgrave, from Shanrod Stud, Co Down, Ireland

b g (4yrs) Denel (FR) - Greenpeace (Master Owen)........................ (Cash) 1,500

Property of Mr Michael Berry, Co Wexford, Ireland

b f (3yrs) Mandalus - Monaleigh (Sir Herbert).................. (Tarbrook Stud) 12,000

From Moorestown Lodge, Co Tipperary, Ireland

ch g (4yrs) Remainder Man - First In (Over The River)........ (Sarah Hollinshead) 4,400

Property of Miss M O'Donnell, Co Limerick, Ireland

b f (4yrs) Royal Fountain - Hill Lane (Pollerton)........................ (Cash) 1,500

Property of Mr Eamonn McCormack, from Ballybeg Stables, Co Offaly, Ireland

b g (4yrs) Torus - Larry's Glen (Laurence O) (David Minton Bloodstock) 6,000

Property of Miss Sandra Hamilton, from Ballywee Stables, Co Antrim, Ireland

br g (4yrs) Good Thyne (USA) - Brenda Girl (Tarboosh)........... (Trevor Bishop) 4,000

From Ardsallagh Stud, Co Meath, Ireland

ch g (4yrs) Nepotism - Le Agio (Le Bavard) (David Minton Bloodstock) 3,600

323

Property of Mr Gary Simpson, from Rathmolyon House Stud, Co Meath, Ireland

Foolish Mischief ch g (3yrs) Remezzo - Fools Thought Vii (Unknown) .... (C Seavill) 1,350

From Shepponhill Stables

b g (5yrs) Pragmatic - Corniche Rose (Punchinello)................... (Cash) 5,200

Waspey Rose ch f (4yrs) Royal Vulcan - Rose Beetle (Carlsburg)......... (Cash) 1,800

Property of Mrs A E Holland, from Drennanstown Stud, Co Antrim, Ireland

b g (4yrs) Florida Son - Ashley's Sister (Fidel)........................... (Cash) 2,500

Property of Mr D T Owens, from Luntley Court Farm Stud

b g (4yrs) Buckley - Captive Maiden (Manacle)........................... (Cash) 3,600

Property of Miss Helen King

Binney Boy b g (4yrs) Broadsword (USA) - Binney Brook (Roman Warrior).. (Cash) 2,600

Property of Mr C F Spence

b g (5yrs) Scorpio (FR) - Cute Smokey (My Smokey)...................... (Cash) 1,500

Property of Mr P Jarvis

ch f (3yrs) Little Wolf - Always A Star (Mummy's Game)........... (F Forrest) 850

Property of Mr & Mrs L V & J M Marshall, from Grove Farm

ch g (3yrs) Crofthall - Last Secret (Most Secret)........................ (Cash) 1,000

Property of Mrs R Robson

b f (3yrs) Silver Season - Angelic Frolic (Cherubino).................... (Cash) 1,650

324

Property of Mr G Llewellyn, from Bouts Farm Stud

ch g (3yrs) Henbit (USA) - Friendly Cherry (Bargello).................... (P Berry) 3,500

To Settle An Account, from Wainbody Estates

ch g (4yrs) Lord Ha Ha - Lanahrone Princess (Saulingo)................ (Cash) 1,200

Property of Capt & Mrs Brian Fanshawe
ch f (3yrs) Balinger - Ginger Fury (Fury Royal)........................ (Cash) 2,500
Property of Mr R J Manning, from Kendleshire Farm Stables
Tarsula b f (4yrs) Sula Bula - Tarbella (Tarqogan)............... (Lisa McAlpine) 2,200
Property of Mr Brian Rothwell, from Rise Park Stables
b f (4yrs) Mandalus - Head Away (Regular Guy).................... (L C Oakes) 4,100
Property of Paul Caddick Holdings Plc, from Burns Farm Stud
Moss Pageant b g (3yrs) Then Again - Water Pageant (Welsh Pageant) ...... (J B Walton) 3,800
From Tyrnog Stud
b f (4yrs) Kaytu - Gadabout (Galivanter) .... (Mrs R Boulton) 1,900
Property of Mrs A C Wakeham, from Wothersome Grange Stud
b f (4yrs) Prince Of Peace - My Always (Kalimnos) .... (Johnny McKeever Bloodstock) 3,900
Property of Mr T H Vickers
Gold Ringer b g (4yrs) Ring Bidder - Divadore (Ivotino)............. (Cash) 3,400
Property of Mrs S Nixon & Mrs J Purdham, from Oakwood Stables
b f (4yrs) Bold Fort - Ishka (Tribal Chief) ... (Cash) 1,400
Property of Mr R & Mrs S Nixon
ch g (4yrs) Germont - (a Hunter Mare)..... (S Cruickshank) 1,850

325

PRIVATE SALES
From Aston House Stud
b g (4yrs) Niniski (USA) - Banda Sea (Balidar)...................... (W Amos) 4,100
Property of Mr & Mrs C T Bletsoe
ch g (4yrs) Superlative - Golden Slade (Octavo) .... (Johnny McKeever Bloodstock) 2,000
Property of E H Crow & Son
ch f (4yrs) Little Wolf - Coumenole (Beau Chapeau)................. (F Forrest) 800
Property of McNeill Estates, from Carseriggan House Stables
b g (4yrs) Celtic Cone - Moonduster (Sparkler)................. (Mr McTaggart) 2,400
Property of Mrs R M Wood (Melgund Glen Stud), from Goldford Stud
ch g (3yrs) Gunner B - Olympian Princess (Master Owen).......... (J Townson) 2,500
Property of Mr C S McKeever, from Ballywee Stables, Co Antrim, Ireland
b f (3yrs) Mandalus - Daisy Owen (Master Owen).................. (H Brennan) 3,500
From Ardsallagh Stud, Co Meath, Ireland
b g (4yrs) Montelimar (USA) - Ingrid Volley (ITY) (Romolo Augusto) .... (David Minton Bloodstock) 5,000
b g (3yrs) Le Bavard (FR) - Tassel Tip (Linacre).............. (H C Johnson) 6,000

326

FAIRYHOUSE (Tattersalls)

Thursday, August 12th

Property of Bridget Murphy
b f (2yrs) Miner's Lamp - Paddy's Dancer (Paddy's Stream)........ (James Gault) 850
Property of Mr John Maguire
b g (4yrs) New Express - Agher Glebe (Apollo Eight).................. (Cash) 1,700
Property of Mr B O'Driscoll
Muskerry Miss (IRE) b m (5yrs) Bishop Of Orange - Muskerry Mary (Mon Capitaine)............... (Richard Mathias) 1,500
Property of a Syndicate, from South Park Farm
b g (4yrs) Stetchworth (USA) - Fine Performance (Gala Performance)..... (Cash) 4,600
From Beechmount Stud
br g (3yrs) Phardante (FR) - Fond Memory (Nishapour)................... (Cash) 580
Property of Torard Stud
Allerton Barge (IRE) b m (5yrs) The Parson - Barge Royal (Bargello)......... (Cash) 840
Property of Mr & Mrs C Dougan
gr g (3yrs) Fat-Taak - Bean Fhionn (Virginia Boy)........................ (Cash) 1,200
From Coolmoreen Stables
Morgantwo b g (7yrs) Montekin - Heure de Pointe (Le Fabuleux)........... (Cash) 1,300
Property of Mr R Colthurst, from Turret Farm Stud
br g (3yrs) Henbit (USA) - Driven Snow (Deep Run).................. (Cash) 3,000
Property of Mr Padraig Keane
ch g (3yrs) Henbit (USA) - Miss Greenhills (Tug Of War)................ (Cash) 3,000

327

Property of Mr David O'Sullivan
b f (3yrs) Strong Gale - Lohunda Lady (Ballymore)........... (Sean Gordon) 1,250
From Glidawn Stud
ch f (3yrs) Over The River (FR) - Vermont Angel (Lucifer)............... (Cash) 1,300
Property of Mr Patrick J Maden
b g (3yrs) Miner's Lamp - Canverb (Proverb) .... (Cash) 820
Property of Mr Patrick J Madden
b f (3yrs) Miner's Lamp - Gillogue (Royal Orbit)........................ (Cash) 800
ch f (3yrs) Amoristic (USA) - Golden Hansel (Prince Hansel)............... (Cash) 450
Property of Mr Michael Cosgrave
b g (4yrs) Torus - Bouise (Royal Buck) ..... (Cash) 1,500
From Ballinacourty Stud
ch g (4yrs) Black Minstrel - Lady Perrin (Merrymount)................ (Cash) 500
From Newry Road Stud
ch g (4yrs) Caribo - French Miss (Golden Love)......................... (Cash) 650
Property of Mr Edmond Walsh
Churchfield Lad ch g (6yrs) Tug Of War - Franzieflyer (Charlottesvilles Flyer)..... (Cash) 1,900

Property of Executors of the late Major V McCalmont, from Norelands Stud

School Lab (IRE) b g (3yrs) Doulab (USA) - Trinity Term (FR) (Primera)...... (Cash) 1,700

328

Property of Mr R Rothwell

b f (4yrs) Swan's Rock - Top Rilggin (Jupiter Pluvius)................. (Patrick Kelly) 1,400

Property of Mrs Margaret Barron

ch g (3yrs) Sandalay - Happy Hereford (Bonne Noel).................. (Cash) 1,100

From Rathbarry Stud (Agent)

b g (4yrs) Phardante (FR) - Evas Charm (Carlburg)............................ (Coombe Heights Racing Syndicate) 9,000

Property of Mrs Margaret Walsh, from Centenary Stables

ch g (4yrs) The Parson - Yellow Canary (Miner's Lamp)................. (Cash) 1,500

Property of Mr Robert Kenny Jnr, from Ballingarry House Stud

Diana Moss (IRE) b f (4yrs) Le Moss - El Diana (Tarboosh).. (Mrs Sarah Skelton) 4,000

Property of High Trees Stud, from Ballywooden House

ch g (3yrs) Phardante (FR) - Cherry Glory (Final Straw).......... (Vincent Murray) 480

b g (4yrs) Buckskin (FR) - Stolen Gold (Tycoon II)................. (D Wintle) 8,000

From Strawhall House Stables

Writer's Quay ch g (10yrs) Quayside - Chapter Four (Shackleton)............ (John Jones) 2,700

Pylon Sparks b g (8yrs) Electric - Fancy Work (Sparkler)................ (Cash) 2,800

Property of Haras Sonoita III, from Tu Va Stables

Speaking Tour (USA) b or br g (5yrs) Verbatim (USA) - Tour Verte (FR) (Green Dancer)............ (David O'Connor) 1,800

329

Property of Miss Mary Ryan

br f (4yrs) Mandalus - Sugar Shaker (Quisling).................... (Patrick Lynch) 1,500

From Ballinvarosig House Stud

gr g (3yrs) King's Ride - Chicchick (Smartset)........................ (Cash) 4,000

Property of Mr Bernard McAnarney

b g (4yrs) Treasure Hunter - Young's Express (Laurence O)... (D T Hughes) 6,200

Property of Mr Tony Farrell, from Newtown Farm

b f (3yrs) Torus - General Rain (General Ironside)............... (Colin Andrews) 540

Property of Penny Downes

ch f (3yrs) Radical - Another Bless (Random Shot).......................... (Cash) 2,500

b f (3yrs) Orchestra - Merry Servant (Giolla Mear).............. (Vincent Duignan) 3,500

Property of V Patterson

b f (4yrs) Bulldozer - Burren Orchid (Will Hays).............. (Robert Downes) 3,700

Property of Mrs Peter Prior-Wandesforde, from Well Farm Bloodstock

b f (4yrs) Southern Music - Burl's Sister (Burlington II).................. (Cash) 2,000

Property of The Executors of the late Major McCalmont, from Bullstown

Wave The Wand (IRE) b c (2yrs) Fairy King (USA) - Blasted Heath (Thatching)...... (John McGrath) 6,900

From Glidawn Stud

b f (3yrs) Lancastrian - Last Serenade (Little Buskins)........................ (Cash) 5,400

330

From Rathleigh Stud

br g (4yrs) Radical - Rossaleigh (Menelek).. (Cash) 7,100

Property of Mr John O'Keeffe, from Rathmeehan Stables

b g (4yrs) Mister Lord (USA) - Any Wonder (Hardboy)............ (Gerry Murphy) 3,000

Property of Mr Hugh Fleming

ch g (3yrs) Import - Mancha Lady (Milan) .. (Jim Brennan) 1,700

Property of Mr Thomas Walsh

b g (3yrs) Torus - Indian Isle (Warpath) .... (Cash) 2,700

Property of Mr T O'Meara

b g (3yrs) Roselier (FR) - Bold And True (Sir Herbert)....... (Ashtown House Stud) 6,700

Property of Mrs J Leahy, from Bishopstown Stud

b g (3yrs) Gunner B - The Furniture Maker (Mandalus)................... (Cash) 500

Property of Mr A Heskin, from Bishopstown Stud

ch g (4yrs) Saxon Farm - Edwina's Law (Ercolano).................... (Cash) 920

Property of Mr William Hodgins, from Barnagrotty Hse Stud

b f (4yrs) Farhaan - Emma James (Captain James)........................ (Cash) 1,900

Property of Mr John Halliday, from Oak Lodge Stable

b f (4yrs) Marktingo - Lavenham Lady (Precipice Wood)................. (Cash) 950

From Coolemoyne Farm

ch g (4yrs) Tale Quale - Reynoldstown Rose (Caribo).............. (Adrian Murray) 4,300

331

Property of Mr P Byrne, from Rathbarry Stud

ch g (4yrs) Phardante (FR) - Boule de Soie (The Parson).................. (Cash) 9,000

From Rathbarry Stud (Agent)

b g (3yrs) Phardante (FR) - Cannon's Dream (Le Bavard).... (Ashtown House Stud) 9,200

ch g (4yrs) Be My Native (USA) - Chelsea Charmer (Ballymore).. (J F C Maxwell) 14,500

From Rathbritt Stud

b f (3yrs) Henbit (USA) - Right Performance (Gala Performance).... (David Harvey) 2,500

Property of a Partnership, from Rathmore Stud (Agent)

b g (4yrs) Phardante (FR) - Elite Lady (Prince Hansel)....................... (David Minton Bloodstock) 6,800

From Castledillon Stud

b or br g (3yrs) Good Thyne (USA) - Sun Chimes (Roi Soleil).......... (M Flynn) 8,000

Property of Mr P Kinsella, from Beechbrook Stud

ch g (3yrs) Good Thyne (USA) - Romantic Rhapsody (Ovac).............. (Cash) 2,000

Property of Mr Sean Twomey, from Hawthorn Villa Stud

b g (3yrs) Lancastrian - Southern Dandy (Menelek).................... (Cash) 2,000

From Grangegodden Stud

b g (4yrs) Lancastrian - Gales Chariot (Strong Gale)..... (Annette McMahon) 5,000

Bingo (FR) b g (4yrs) Rahotep - Paglioni (Bamako III)........ (B.B. Racing Club) 2,100

b g (3yrs) Henbit (USA) - Kitty Cullen (Pollerton)........................ (Cash) 1,100

332

From Ballyburn Farm

b g (4yrs) Idiot's Delight - Tropical Swing (Swing Easy).................. (Cash) 6,000

Property of Ballymagarvey Stud

ch f (3yrs) Buckskin (FR) - Windara (Double-U-Jay)......................... (Cash) 6,200

b f (3yrs) Lancastrian - Moneyforusall (Northern Guest)...... (Peter Whelan) 1,250

From Shaneen Stud

b or br f (4yrs) Strong Gale - Woodcliffe (Harwell)..................... (Cash) 2,100

Property of a Partnership, from Spybank Stud

b g (3yrs) Orchestra - Maid Of Moyode (Giolla Mear)...................... (Cash) 4,800

From Springmount Stud

b f (4yrs) Strong Gale - She's Approaching (Ragapan)................. (V Murray) 1,200

From Wraymount Stud

Sylvaner (IRE) b f (4yrs) Montelimar (USA) - Alisazia (FR) (Bolkonski) .... (Seamus O'Farrell) 1,250

Property of Mr George T Williams, from Carrignaveen Stud

b g (3yrs) Hardboy - Spritestown (Bowsprit) .... (Cash) 3,700

From Ballywooden Stud

b g (3yrs) Convinced - Twelve Steps (Tumble Wind)........................ (Cash) 1,800

Property of Mr W I Mackensie

b f (4yrs) Pollerton - Highland Express (London Gazette).............. (Cash) 1,350

333

Property of Mrs P Kelly

ch g (3yrs) Bustomi - Paddys Flyer (Paddy's Stream)....................... (Cash) 1,100

b m (5yrs) Nepotism - Paddys Flyer (Paddy's Stream) (O'Donoghue Bros.) 660

Property of Mr William Drew

b f (3yrs) Salluceva - Fast And Clever (Clever Fella)........... (James Gault) 620

Property of Mr Liam Buckley, from Killadoran Stud

b f (4yrs) Torus - Castle Treasure (Perspex) (Cash) 900

Property of Gainsborough Stud Management Ltd., from Glebe House Stables

Leading Time (FR) b c (4yrs) Lead On Time (USA) - Copy Cat (FR) (King Of Macedon).................. (D T Hughes) 1,000

334

FAIRYHOUSE (Tattersalls)

Friday, August 13th

Property of Miss Catherine O'Brien

b g (3yrs) Torus - Pamrina (Pamroy)....... (Wm O'Neill) 4,800

Property of Mr Owen Clarke

b f (3yrs) Amazing Bust - Christingle (Santa Claus)................ (Eilish Donohoe) 400

Property of Mr M Walsh

b g (2yrs) Venetian Gate - Furryblue (Furry Glen).......................... (Cash) 400

b f (2yrs) Tremblant - Sally Stanford (Daring Display)................. (Pro-Am Ltd) 1,000

Property of M & G Curran

b g (3yrs) Buckskin (FR) - Ballyadam Rose (Roselier).................... (E Crow) 3,900

Property of Mr Patrick Devereux

b f (3yrs) Carlingford Castle - Miss Tarbow (Tarqogan)............... (S Hamilton) 900

b g (4yrs) Carlingford Castle - Secret Romance (Gala Performance)... (Cash) 1,650

b f (4yrs) Carlingford Castle - Miss Tarbow (Tarqogan).................... (Cash) 700

From The Red City Stud

ch g (4yrs) Hard Fought - Twice Regal (Royal Prerogative)...... (Tom Moran) 760

Property of Mr P Powell

ch g (3yrs) Kambalda - No Notice (Mandalus).................. (E O'Sullivan) 3,700

335

Property of a Partnership

ch g (3yrs) Thatching - Home Bird (Ragusa) (Cash) 4,100

Property of Mr Francis M Lyons

b f (3yrs) King's Ride - Lugnagullagh (Pitpan).......................... (Cash) 3,000

From Charlestown Stud

ch g (4yrs) Lancastrian - Lovenos (Golden Love)......................... (Cash) 1,500

Property of Mr & Mrs G J King, from Riverdene Stud

ch f (4yrs) Over The River (FR) - Judy Loe (Red Alert)....... (Rd O'Gorman, Jnr) 1,000

From Grangeduff Stud

b g (3yrs) Roselier (FR) - Velindre (Giolla Mear)........................ (Cash) 3,500

Property of Mr Brendan O'Meara

b g (4yrs) Bustineto - Annan (Maculata).... (Cash) 4,000

Property of a Partnership

b g (3yrs) Roselier (FR) - Buck's Fairy (Master Buck)............... (L Cashman) 4,600

Property of Mr Dan Redmond, from Rosemount House Stud

b or br f (4yrs) Callernish - Mandius Girl Vii (Ozymandias).................. (Cash) 800

Property of Mrs M Brophy

ch g (3yrs) Phardante (FR) - Stay As You Are (Buckskin)................ (Cash) 2,600

Property of Mrs M McDonnell

gr g (4yrs) Lafontaine (USA) - Byron Bay (Habat)........................ (Cash) 1,500

336

From Argle House Stud

b g (3yrs) Buckley - Cherry Opal (St Denys) (Cash) 2,200

Property of Mr W Fogarty, from Argle House Stud

b g (3yrs) Tale Quale - Give Us A Breeze (Brave Invader)................(Cash) 3,100

Property of a Partnership

b g (4yrs) Strong Statement (USA) - Shenton Park (Indigenous)..........(Cash) 1,700

Property of F F McGuiness, from Blackwater Stud

br g (3yrs) Seclude (USA) - Ballykeenan Lady (London Gazette) (John Watson) 4,200

Property of Mr William Sullivan, from Abbey Stables

ch g (4yrs) Denel (FR) - Coldwater Morning (Laurence O)..........(Barney Nolan) 3,000

Property of Mr Michael Byrne, from Abbey Stables

b f (4yrs) Roselier (FR) - Shuil Na Gale (Strong Gale)..................(Cash) 1,250

Property of Mr J Gillespie

ch f (4yrs) Le Bavard (FR) - Five Cherries (Cantab)........................(Cash) 1,500

Property of Mr Gerald McPolin

b g (4yrs) Denel (FR) - Barred-In-Action (Bargello)................(D Harvey) 7,400

Property of Mr Michael Harty

ch g (3yrs) Long Pond - Shining Brightly (Giolla Mear)..............(P Osborne) 6,800

From Limefield Stud

b g (4yrs) Stetchworth (USA) - Poor Elsie (Crash Course)................(Cash) 1,550

ch f (4yrs) Good Thyne (USA) - Fair Freda (Proverb).....................(Cash) 3,000

337

Property of Mr Maurice Bamber

b g (3yrs) Castle Keep - Galloping Gold Vii (Golden Love)..................(Cash) 5,700

Property of Mr Christy Maye, from Lake Farm Stud

gr g (4yrs) Celio Rufo - Reformed Rule (Reformed Character)..........(Cash) 3,300

Property of Mr Donald King, from Ballywooden House

b g (4yrs) The Parson - Run Madam (Deep Run)..................(R H Macnabb) 8,000

Property of Mr Stephen Sinclair

b g (4yrs) Lancastrian - Beau Jo (Joshua) .. (Cash) 1,900

Property of Marie T Doran

b f (3yrs) Mandalus - Four Shares (The Parson)...........(Patrick Hennessy) 4,000

br f (3yrs) Roselier (FR) - Una's Run (Deep Run).........................(Pro-Am) 2,350

Property of Mr John McNamara

ch g (3yrs) Lancastrian - Rev Up (Menelek) (Cash) 1,800

From Phillip McCarten (Agent)

b f (3yrs) Over The River (FR) - Great Desire (Pitpan)................(James Gault) 650

Property of a Gentleman, from Milton House

b g (4yrs) Supreme Leader - Mislay (Henbit) ....(E Crow) 5,200

From The Borotown Stud (Agent)

ch g (4yrs) Tumble Gold - Breda's Choice (Random Shot).................(Cash) 4,800

338

From Morganstown Stud

b g (3yrs) Strong Statement (USA) - Sallstown (Salluceva)..............(Cash) 5,800

b g (4yrs) Torus - Liffey's Choice (Little Buskins)........................(Cash) 6,000

Property of Frm Russelstown Stud

b f (4yrs) King's Ride - Mrs Sauga (Derrylin) (Cash) 3,800

Property of Mr Dermot Maguire, from Farnagh Stud

b g (4yrs) Pollerton - China Blake (Private Walk)...............(Peter Newman) 2,300

From Coolnagour House Stud

b or br f (4yrs) Over The River (FR) - Rugged Lady (Rugged Man) .... (Danny O'Connell) 1,800

Property of Mrs Marie Banville, from Cloughultagh Stud

ch f (4yrs) Buckskin (FR) - Mistic Breeze (Master Owen)..... (Michael O'Brien) 6,000

Property of Mr Martin Cullinane

br g (3yrs) Ovac (ITY) - Moate Gypsy (Fine Blade).........................(Cash) 1,300

gr g (3yrs) Step Together (USA) - Peek-A-Boo (Bustino)..............(Cash) 3,500

Property of Mr Matthew Tynan

b f (3yrs) Carlingford Castle - Larkins Damsel (Menelek)...... (Gerry Moran) 550

b f (4yrs) Lancastrian - Slippery Princess Vii ((said To Be Slippered))........ (Cash) 920

339

Property of Mr William Hubbert

b f (4yrs) Mandalus - Cora Gold (Goldhill) .. (L Woods) 900

Property of Misses A M & J R Baker

ch g (3yrs) Over The River (FR) - Queen Flyer (Charlottesvilles Flyer).... (Cash) 1,000

From Ballyboher Stud

b g (4yrs) Mummy's Treasure - Oileann Carrig (Pitcairn)..................(Cash) 850

From Dollanstown Stud (Agent)

ch f (3yrs) Henbit (USA) - Cool Amanda (Prince Hansel)...... (Charles Byrnes) 1,650

Property of Mr Francis Woods

ch c (4yrs) Abednego - Miss Alex (No Argument).............. (Mrs A Kerr) 2,200

From Island View Farm

b f (3yrs) Le Bavard (FR) - Derring Lass (Derring Rose)............ (D Buckley) 840

Property of Mr Dan Rohan

ch f (3yrs) Sheer Grit - Morning Carl VI (Carlburg).......................(Cash) 1,200

From Mullyloughran Stud

b f (4yrs) Strong Gale - May's Pride (Le Tricolore)............. (Tom Conroy) 2,650

b f (4yrs) Lancastrian - Pure Spec (Fine Blade)..................(E O'Sullivan) 2,100

From Leefield Stud

ch g (3yrs) Camden Town - Cailin Og (Al Sirat)...................... (J T Doyle) 8,600

340

Property of Mr Jack Cowan

br g (5yrs) Cataldi - Light Foot (Little Buskins).................. (Ian Ferguson) 9,200

Property of Mr G Coppola

ch f (3yrs) Dominion Royale - Winterlude (Wollow)............ (Michael Mullins) 620

Property of James Boyd & Major F B Boyd

ch g (4yrs) Strong Statement (USA) - Glare's Hansel (Prince Hansel).. (Cash) 1,200

Property of Mr P J Whelan

ch f (3yrs) Salluceva - Siobhan's Treasure (Boreen)........... (Finbarr O'Connor) 700

b f (3yrs) Corvaro (USA) - Siobhan's Gold (Barrons Court)....... (Colin Magnier) 1,800

From Liatris Stud (Agent)

Queen Of Firs ch m (14yrs) Touch Paper - Suburb's Queen (Levanter) Covered by Trigon............ (Sean McGuinness) 550

Property of Nora Kelly, from Grove House

ch g (3yrs) Le Bavard (FR) - Don's Song (Don)................. (Jeremy Cairns) 2,400

Property of Mrs E P Wilson

br f (3yrs) Amazing Bust - Pointlane (Wolverlife)............... (P Caridia) 1,300

Property of Margaret Barry

br g (4yrs) Strong Gale - Hardy Colleen (Hardboy)............... (L Cashman) 6,700

From Ballywilliam Stud

b y g Le Moss - Greenpeace (Master Owen).............. (Penny Granger) 1,300

Property of Mr Ralph O'Brien

b m (5yrs) The Parson - Zozimus (Rarity)... (Noel Meade) 5,600

(Index reference 342 follows)

342

KILL (Goffs)
Monday, August 16th

Property of Mr Thomas V O'Shaughnessy, from Kilcash Stud

ch g (5yrs) Gladden - Divinitess (Divine Gift) .... (Cash) 800

Property of Mr N Sullivan

ch f (4yrs) Ovac (ITY) - Coolentallagh (Perhapsburg).................... (Cash) 1,000

To Dissolve a Partnership, from St Gatien Stables

Quattro b c (3yrs) Robellino (USA) - Load Line (High Line)............... (Cash) 400

Property of Mr John Flanagan (Jnr)

b g (3yrs) Ovac (ITY) - Sweet Gum (USA) (Gummo)...................... (Cash) 2,000

From Conyngham Lodge Stables

Fantante (IRE) b g (4yrs) Taufan (USA) - La Tante (Bold Lad)..................... (European Equine Consultants) 1,400

Torch Singer b f (3yrs) Bluebird (USA) - Ode (Ancestral)........... (William Treacy) 2,800

Skerries Bell b f (3yrs) Taufan (USA) - Selvi (Mummy's Pet) .... (European Equine Consultants) 5,500

Arrogant Lady b f (3yrs) Aragon - Choire Mhor (Dominion).............. (Cash) 2,000

From Orchard House Syndicate

St Elmo's Fire (NZ) b g (8yrs) Grosvenor (NZ) - Star Quality (NZ) (Bismark II).... (Cash) 2,000

Super Tom (NZ) b g (8yrs) Toms Shu (USA) - Lady Palatine (NZ) (Don Palatine) .... (Christopher Kerrigan) 850

343

From Corloughan Stud (Part Dispersal)

Beglawella b m (6yrs) Crash Course - Prime Mistress (Skymaster).......... (Cash) 3,500

Daylight Lady ch m (6yrs) Deep Run - First Gal (General Ironside).......... (Cash) 800

Property of Mrs Teresa Finn, from Bridge House Stud

b f (4yrs) Trimmingham - Beagle Bay (Deep Run)................... (D T Hughes) 2,100

Property of Beaumont Racing Club

Olde Crescent br g (7yrs) Kambalda - Bush Mistress (Will Somers).. (D T Hughes) 3,000

Property of Mr Michael Ryan

b f (4yrs) Bustineto - Northern Gift (Northern Guest).............. (Cash) 500

From Colestown Stud

b g (4yrs) Balboa - Willabelle (Will Somers) (Cash) 5,000

Property of Mr John O'Brien

b f (4yrs) Broadsword (USA) - Running Game (Run The Gantlet) .... (Rathbarry Stud) 2,200

Property of Mr James J Nolan

ch f (3yrs) Good Thyne (USA) - Highland Party (Deep Run)...... (Eamonn Finn) 5,600

Property of Miss Eva Dodd

b g (4yrs) Salluceva - Sprightly's Last (Random Shot)................. (Cash) 2,300

b g (4yrs) Salluceva - Ross Maid (Random Shot)............... (Paddy Mooney) 2,300

344

Property of Mrs E Bennett, from Miltown Stud

b g (3yrs) Duky - Down The Aisle (Godswalk)......................... (Cash) 2,600

ch f (3yrs) Duky - Injection (On Your Mark) (Oliver Brady) 2,000

From Mocklershill Stables (Agent)

ch f (3yrs) Camden Town - Ask The Boss (Gulf Pearl).................. (Cash) 800

Property of Breda McDonald, from Ferry Inn

gr g (4yrs) Roselier (FR) - Winawalk (Private Walk)....................... (Cash) 6,000

Property of Mrs Maria Mulhern

ch g (3yrs) Creative Plan (USA) - Lordee Lordy (Blue Refrain)........... (Cash) 950

Property of Mrs James Hannon, from Curraheen Stud

b f (4yrs) Sheer Grit - Laurmar Brae (Brave Invader)...................... (Cash) 950

Property of Miss Mary McCarthy

Popeye The Guy (IRE) b g (4yrs) Regular Guy - Debonair Dolly (Cidrax) .... (Patrick Brennan) 3,100

Property of Miss Anne E Thompson
gr f (3yrs) Ore - Distant Thoughts (General Ironside)........................ (Cash) 850
Property of Mr John McCartan
b or br g (3yrs) Buckskin (FR) - Another Side (Bold Lad)........................ (Cash) 4,200
br g (3yrs) Tanfirion - Fitz's Buck (Master Buck)........................ (P Owens) 9,200

345

Property of Mr James P Browne, from Laurel Lodge Farm
ch g (4yrs) Orchestra - Pargio (Parthia)..... (Cash) 6,600
From Martinstown Farm
ch f (4yrs) Le Moss - Gleann Oge (Proverb) (John Bleahen) 2,200
Property of Mr Tom Carrigan
b g (4yrs) Sheer Grit - Animalean (Beau Chapeau)........................ (Cash) 1,800
From Wellwood Stud
b g (3yrs) Mister Majestic - Barely Alive (Wolverlife)........................ (Cash) 2,200
Property of Mr Laurence King
b g (4yrs) Rising - Brave Dorney (Brave Invader)............ (Jimmy Mangan) 3,500
Property of Mrs Mary B O'Donovan
b g (3yrs) Dock Leaf - Dayh Of Rest (Parole) .... (David Nugent) 4,600
From Rockmills Stud
b g (4yrs) Lord Ha Ha - Fanny Brave (Brave Invader).............. (John McGrath) 1,300
Property of Mrs M Fardy
b g (3yrs) Over The River (FR) - Flutter Bug (Lord Gayle)........................ (Cash) 9,500
Property of Mr Liam Quirke, from Hymenstown House Stud
b f (4yrs) Lancastrian - Gragara Rose Vii (Laurence O)..... (Eugene O'Sullivan) 2,400
From Rock Stud
b g (3yrs) Lancastrian - Aberdeen King (Merrymount)....... (Richard Mathias) 1,650

346

From Bishopstown Stud
b g (4yrs) Supreme Leader - Saint Malva (Welsh Pageant).............. (Cash) 1,800
ch f (4yrs) Carlingford Castle - Cash Discount (Deep Run)............. (Cash) 1,600
Property of Tanya Sherrard, from Bishopstown Stud
ch g (3yrs) Torus - Philly Athletic (Sit In The Corner)........................ (Cash) 450
To Dissolve a Partnership, from Abbey Stables
b g (4yrs) Amazing Bust - Ever Mine (Mount Hagen)................. (Cash) 2,750
Property of Mr Noel P Quinlan, from Church Farm Stables
b g (4yrs) Royal Match - Gemini Stone (Le Bavard)........................ (Cash) 1,600
From Boardsmill Stud
ch f (3yrs) Carmelite House (USA) - Mullaghroe (Tarboosh)........... (Cash) 1,900
From Moortown House Stud
ch g (4yrs) Sheer Grit - Merry Mirth (Menelek)........................ (Cash) 14,000

Property of Mr James T Williams, from Carrignaveen Stud
b f (4yrs) Invited (USA) - Star Mill (Milan) .. (Daniel O'Connell) 2,000
Property of Mr Mervyn Wynne
b g (4yrs) Supreme Leader - Last Round (Lucky Guy)........................ (Cash) 2,500
From Garryrichard Stud
ch f (4yrs) Callernish - Well Over (Over The River)........................ (Cash) 2,300

347

Property of Mrs E Joyce
ch f (4yrs) Callernish - Strawberry River (Over The River).............. (Cash) 550
Property of Mrs Nora Prendergast
gr f (4yrs) Roselier (FR) - Sailatel (Golden Love).............. (Danny O'Connell) 1,200
Property of Mr Denis Deegan
gr f (4yrs) Ovac (ITY) - Toberbeg Lady (Le Bavard)........................ (Cash) 1,000
Property of Mr Gerry Murphy
ch f (3yrs) Energist - C.P.V. Lady (Le Moss) (Cash) 1,250
Property of Mrs J O'Regan, from Castle Ivers
br f (3yrs) Phardante (FR) - Siba Vione (Dusky Boy)............ (W Edmonds) 500
Property of Mr M Treacy
b g (3yrs) Aristocracy - Agher Hill Hope (Paico)............ (Derek McConnell) 3,000
From Rahan Stud
Tor b or br c (3yrs) Reference Point - Devon Defender (Home Guard)....... (Cash) 8,000
From Hawthorn Villa Stud
ch g (3yrs) Carlingford Castle - Sweet Annabelle (Deep Run)......... (Cash) 1,800
Property of Miss D Balding
br g (3yrs) Miner's Lamp - Palatine Lady (Pauper)............. (John Bleahen) 2,700
Property of Mr Martin Timlin, from Hilden
b g (2yrs) Lancastrian - London Anne (London Bells)................ (Cash) 3,200

348

Property of Miss Siobhan Connolly, from Hollymount Stud
ch f (3yrs) Decent Fellow - Moment Of Weakness (Pieces Of Eight).... (Cash) 520
From Esker House
ch g (5yrs) Stalker - Lengua Franca (St Chad)........................ (Cash) 1,700
Property of Mrs A J Taylor
ch y f Torus - Caphill (Prince Bee)......... (Sean Quinn) 500
Property of Mr Patrick Abbey
b y g Kambalda - Lisgarvan Highway (Dusky Boy)................ (Ms. P Granger) 1,900
From Liatris Stud
b g (2yrs) Denel (FR) - Fairytale Ending (Sweet Story)........ (Thomas Farrell) 1,000
Property of Mr Eugene Ryan
b f (2yrs) Soughaan (USA) - Grave Error (Northern Treat)......... (Sean Quinn) 750
From Grange Lodge Stables
Clara Bridge b m (6yrs) Le Bavard (FR) - Brickeen's Pet (Fine Blade)..... (Cash) 850

349

ASCOT
Tuesday, August 31st

Property of a Gentleman

Lucksin b g (11yrs) Lucky Wednesday - Galivanter Girl (Galivanter) (Mr Cooper) 800

Property of Miss E C Dowling

Miss Precious b m (5yrs) Precocious - Hissy Missy (Bold Lad)..... (R Harper) 1,000

To Dissolve a Partnership

Legal Conquest gr f (2yrs) Absalom - Rosy Diamond (Jalmood)............ (Cash) 825

Sui Generis (IRE) ch f (3yrs) Doulab (USA) - Markon (On Your Mark).... (T Morris) 800

Property of Ascom Tele Nova Ltd

Ascom Pager (IRE) b f (3yrs) Colmore Row - Milveagh (Milesian)...... (J C Boher) 650

Property of East Green Bloodstock Ltd

Brightandbeautiful ch m (6yrs) Sallust - Shopping (FR) (Sheshoon) (H J Jarvis) 925

Turbo Sprout b m (5yrs) Star Appeal - Censella (Frankincense)............. (The Russian Horse Society) 775

Property of Freedom Farm Stud

Strictly Ballroom b f (2yrs) Rambo Dancer (CAN) - Be Malicious (Malicious)...... (The Russian Horse Society) 875

Property of Manor House Farm Stud

Elegant Ellie b f (3yrs) Alleging (USA) - Highly Polished (High Top)........... (The Russian Horse Society) 1,350

Property of H J Collins

Brown Filly br f (3yrs) Baron Blakeney - Trip To Heaven (Tower Walk)... (R Berker) 950

350

Property of The Team Engineering Company

Mick's Filly (IRE) ch f (3yrs) Kamehameha (USA) - Blackwater Stream (Paddy's Stream)........... (Rowena Fuszard) 1,000

Property of Ray Taylor

Salmonid ch g (7yrs) Salmon Leap (USA) - Persian Polly (Persian Bold) (R Barber) 1,600

To Dissolve a Partnership

Indian Castle (IRE) ch g (2yrs) Nashamaa - Tuckers Witch (Junius (USA))........ (Simon Whitworth) 675

Property of D M Ahier

Wasaya b f (3yrs) Wassl - Wurud (USA) (Green Dancer (USA))............... (The Russian Horse Society) 1,150

To Dissolve a Partnership

Osgathorpe ch g (6yrs) Dunbeath (USA) - Darlingka (Darling Boy)......... (Cash) 1,800

Property of a Gentleman

Araliya ch f (2yrs) Dominion - Character Builder (African Sky)................ (The Russian Horse Society) 850

Pocono Knight gr g (3yrs) Petong - Avahra (Sahib).................. (C H Jones) 1,100

Property of Fulling Mill Stud

Christian Spirit gr g (3yrs) Petong - Hidden Asset (Hello Gorgeous)..... (L Vollaro) 1,300

Property of Sir Peter Cazalet

Jackarew Boy ch c (3yrs) Brotherly (USA) - Lady Peggy (Young Nelson).... (Cash) 750

To Dissolve a Partnership

Doctor-J (IRE) ch c (3yrs) Jareer (USA) - Velvet Breeze (Windjammer (USA)).... (James Morris) 3,000

351

Property of Count K Goess-Saurau

Malzeta (IRE) b f (3yrs) Alzao (USA) - Place Of Honour (Be My Guest (USA))...... (James Morris) 3,400

Property of Darley Stud Management Co Ltd

Passamezzo (IRE) b c (3yrs) Alzao (USA) - Pastel Shade (USA) (Affirmed (USA)).. (Cash) 3,300

Property of Outline Management Ltd

Warning Board b g (2yrs) Bairn (USA) - Candle In The Wind (Thatching)....... (S A Turner) 1,200

Property of a Gentleman

b c (2yrs) Mister Majestic - Jazz Tune (FR) (Lyphard (USA))..................... (The Russian Horse Society) 500

Property of P D Purdy

Almostautomatic (IRE) ch c (4yrs) Mansooj - Juju (Dragonara Palace (USA))....... (D J & C B Clapham) 850

Property of T W Nichols

Eve's Treasure ch f (3yrs) Bustino - Before Long (Longleat (USA)) (S W Campion) 1,400

Property of Mrs L Thompson

Montana D'Or b f (3yrs) Crooner - Ijazah (Touching Wood (USA))..... (T I Fane) 1,100

Property of G Whitaker

Dandy Desire ch g (4yrs) Grey Desire - Karsavina (Silly Season)... (D Morgan) 1,250

We're All Game b f (4yrs) Mummy's Game - Swynford's Pride (Rapid River)....... (R H Thomas) 1,100

Property of Steel Plate & Sections Ltd

True Steel b g (7yrs) Deep Run - Aran Tour (Arapaho)............ (J Trice-Rolph) 2,100

352

To Dissolve a Partnership

Delay No More gr g (3yrs) Nishapour (FR) - Maple Rock (Music Boy).. (J C Boher) 1,500

From West Ilsley Stables

Criminal Record (USA) b c (3yrs) Fighting Fit (USA) - Charlie's Angel (USA) (Halo) (Bill Clay) 9,200

Property of Miss Elizabeth Aldous

Pie Hatch (IRE) b f (4yrs) Huntingdale - Small Is Beautiful (Condorcet (FR)).... (Brian McMath) 11,200

Property of Maj-Gen Sir George Burns

Scottish Ball b f (4yrs) Ardross - Dance In Rome (Dance In Time (CAN)) (F Gray) 5,000

Property of Her Majesty The Queen

Pandrop b f (2yrs) Sharrood (USA) - Trying For Gold (Northern Baby (CAN))....... (Patricia Whitmore) 950

Property of G Smart

Moran Brig ch g (3yrs) Bustino - Aunt Judy (Great Nephew).......... (M Humby) 2,700

Property of G A Farndon, from Teal House Stables

Crackley Lane b g (2yrs) Dreams To Reality - Tyrian Princess (Comedy Star) (Cash) 800

Property of M J K Dods
Cyril Henry (IRE) b g (4yrs) Mister Majestic - Stamina (Star Appeal) (P Winkworth) 3,500

Property of A G Watson
Great Service ch g (6yrs) Vaigly Great - Janlarmar (Habat)............. (Cash) 1,600

To Dissolve a Partnership
Smith N'allan b g (3yrs) Tina's Pet - Mertola (Tribal Chief)................. (Cash) 1,400

353

Property of a Gentleman
Frenchman's Buck b g (8yrs) Buckskin (FR) - Miss Symbol (Symbol)..... (W Pugh) 1,800

To Dissolve a Partnership
Flash Of Straw (IRE) ch g (4yrs) Thatching - Hanna Alta (FR) (Busted)... (R Barber) 2,500

Property of Heyfleet Partnership, from Weathercock House
Run To Form b g (8yrs) Deep Run - Let The Hare Sit (Politico).............. (Cash) 6,800

Property of John Naughton, from Lisaleen Stables (Co Limerick)
Nordic Beat (IRE) b c (4yrs) Nordico (USA) - Pollination (Pentotal)......... (Bill Clay) 1,900

Property of John Keaney, from Lisaleen Stables (Co Limerick)
Somerset Dancer b or br g (6yrs) Green Dancer (USA) - Distant Song (FR) (Faraway Son)................. (M O'Neil) 3,200

Property of Anne Wall, from Lisaleen Stables (Co Limerick)
Chiparopai (IRE) b m (5yrs) Commanche Run - Violino (USA) (Hawaii).... (Cash) 1,500

To Dissolve a Partnership
Glitterbird b m (6yrs) Glint Of Gold - Dovetail (Brigadier Gerard)........... (Mrs C Chadney) 3,400

Property of Couture Marketing Ltd
Couture Innovators b g (6yrs) Music Boy - Miss Couture (Tamerlane)........... (Stanley Pugh Farms) 700

From Barton Hall Stables
Chimes Of The Dawn ch g (9yrs) Tower Walk - Neptia's Word (Great Nephew) (John Griffin) 950

Property of Mrs Helen MacFarlane, from Barton Hall Stables
Sun Ballad b g (8yrs) Ballad Rock - Sunny Eyes (Reliance II)........ (S D Notley) 1,500

354

Property of J Whelan, from Peaked Croft Farm
Scottish Express b g (8yrs) Celtic Cone - Travellers Cheque (Kibenka).......... (R Spencer) 1,500
Welsh Singer ch g (7yrs) Celtic Cone - Madam Butterfly (Deep Run)......... (K Rogers) 8,000
Golden Summer ch m (10yrs) Balinger - Miss Fanackapan (Colonist II)... (Cash) 800

From Courthill Stables
Hello Grandad b g (9yrs) Hello Gorgeous - Emerin (King Emperor)... (J H Forbes) 1,100

Property of Miss M Staples
Young Pitt (IRE) b g (5yrs) Pitskelly - Magloire (FR) (Sir Gaylord)..... (Cash) 3,000

Property of Midland Markets Ltd
Rockridge b g (6yrs) Chief Singer - Croda Rossa (ITY) (Grey Sovereign)... (Cash) 1,250
Wrets b g (4yrs) Kalaglow - Hayley Warren (Habitat)................ (R J Baker) 4,700

Property of Mrs Carol Allen
Bold Street Blues b g (6yrs) Bold Owl - Basin Street (Tudor Melody)......... (J Bennett) 5,000

Property of A A King
Master Beveled b g (3yrs) Beveled - Miss Anniversary (Tachypous) (J F Williams) 5,000

To Dissolve a Partnership
Gotageton b m (6yrs) Oats - Palace Pet (Dragonara Palace)....... (D Clapham) 2,000

355

Property of C H Shankland, from Fowlers Farm Racing Stables
Game Fair b g (6yrs) Lighter - Stagbury (National Trust)............ (G Burton) 1,250

Property of K Pritchard
Work To Win ch g (8yrs) That's Swanee - Lady Cherry (Bargello)......... (Cash) 800

Property of Ray Craggs
Rahif b g (5yrs) Shirley Heights - Vaguely (Bold Lad (IRE)) (Outline Management) 2,300

To Dissolve a Partnership
Velvet Peak ch f (5yrs) Superlative - Velvet Pigeon (Homing).............. (Cash) 2,000

Property of a Partnership
El Persa (USA) gr g (5yrs) Persepolis (FR) - A Realgirl (USA) (In Reality).......... (Mark Usher) 3,300

Property of a Lady
Blue Aeroplane ch g (5yrs) Reach - Shelton Song (Song)............. (Ray Collier) 1,650

To Dissolve a Partnership
Frozen Minstrel b g (9yrs) Black Minstrel - Arctic Sue (Arctic Slave)............. (Mr & Mrs R M Billing) 2,500

Property of B L Lay, from Rest Hill Stud
Autumn Leaf b m (5yrs) Afzal - Autumn Ballet (Averof)........... (Gerald West) 1,500

Property of Miss D Pacey
b f (4yrs) Afzal - Westerlands Finis (Owen Anthony)...................... (Cash) 2,800

Property of Noel Finnegan
b f (3yrs) Rhoman Rule (USA) - Solarina (Solinus)................... (V Sutton) 700

356

Property of Philip Madgwick, from Vinnells Farm
Ukam's Boy b g (3yrs) Risk Me (FR) - Wayward Polly (Lochnager).......... (Mrs M S Harvey) 950

Property of A S Neaves
Do Or Bust b m (6yrs) Posse (USA) - Fardella (ITY) (Molvedo) (Jean French) 1,400
Certain Look b g (6yrs) Yawa - Best Lady (Try My Best (USA)).... (E Wonnacott) 1,300

Property of Joseph Heler
Miss Parkes ch f (4yrs) Mummy's Game - Bonne Baiser (Most Secret).......... (P C Clarke) 1,450

Property of Miss G Gibson
ch g (4yrs) Nearly A Hand - Lady Whitefoot (Martinmas)............... (P Russell) 1,300
Property of G Hamilton
Ray Of Fortune b f (3yrs) Le Solaret (FR) - Green Gypsy (Creetown)............. (Louise McMahon) 1,050
Property of a Lady
Time For Akktion b g (5yrs) Son Of Charm - Ariel (El Brillo).................. (Cash) 2,700
To Dissolve a Partnership
Handy Jenny ch m (8yrs) Nearly A Hand - Polo Pam (Tiepolo II)........... (Cash) 1,400
Property of E Wonnacott
Tonkawa b g (8yrs) Indian King (USA) - Lady Tycoon (No Mercy)............ (Cash) 850
Property of T P MacDonald
Timothy's Quay gr g (5yrs) Scallywag - Miss Quay (Quayside)................ (Miss A Blatchley) 2,100
Property of Mrs C Morgan
Go Grafton b g (9yrs) Churchillian - Second Thoughts (Calpurnius) (Mrs M Phillips) 1,000
Property of Miss P Schofield
River Lad b g (14yrs) -............. (Cash) 700

357

MALVERN
(Russell, Baldwin & Bright)
Friday, September 3rd

Property of P Vaughan
Drumkeeran b g (7yrs) Tanfirion - Sephine (Karabas)................... (G Turner) 2,000
Property of Mrs J M Snape
Flash Of Joy b f (3yrs) Lightning Dealer - Joytime (John de Coombe) (Mr White) 620
Property of a Gentleman
Walkers Point b g (7yrs) Le Moss - Saltee Star (Arapaho)........ (Mrs R Patman) 1,900
Property of S Piggott, from Worsley Racing Stables
Not Gordons b g (4yrs) All Systems Go - Lady Abernant (Abwah)... (K C Lewis) 1,600
Property of Steve Lilley Racing
Trivet ch g (10yrs) Thatching - Borana (Aureole)................ (Mr D Paget) 800
Property of R C F Faiers, from Holme Farm Stables
Sergeant Silver gr g (8yrs) General Ironside - Coolentallagh (Perhapsburg)......... (Mr B Goode) 3,500
Property of A Barrow, from Marsh Mills Racing Stables
Latin Mass ch m (5yrs) Music Boy - Omnia (Hill Clown (USA))........ (B Bramley) 1,500
Property of James O'Connor, from Greenfields Stables, Ireland
Getagrip ch m (6yrs) Lucifer (USA) - Apace (Tarboosh (USA))......... (L Edwards) 1,300
From South Bank Stables To Dissolve a Partnership
Never So Lost ch c (3yrs) Never So Bold - Lost In France (Northfields (USA))..... (P Hiatt) 600
From Picton House Stud
Moyas Charm b g (10yrs) Beau Charmeur (FR) - Casadonna (London Scottish).... (P Hiatt) 850

358

From Suir View Stud, Co Tipperary
Johno'thelodge (IRE) b g (5yrs) Torus - Leapy Lady (Bargello)........ (A Reid) 680
The Fun Of It ch g (8yrs) Ballymore - Aughalion (Pals Passage).. (D Redvers) 2,400
From Little Manor Farm To Dissolve a Partnership
Sang de Fleur (FR) b g (6yrs) Zino - Calamine (Hotfoot)............ (G Turner) 1,600
From Castle Farm Stables
Red Russe b g (7yrs) Sunyboy - Royal Russe (Bally Ruse)....... (Mr A Leigh) 1,200
From Ballyginty Stud
br g (3yrs) Bulldozer - Black Pilot (Linacre) (Mr A Leigh) 2,500
Genista b g (8yrs) Furry Glen - Rossaleigh (Menelek).................. (G Turner) 1,700
Property of John Hindmarsh, from Little London Stables
Chloes Diamond (IRE) ch m (5yrs) Heraldiste (USA) - Salique (Sallust)........ (S Piggott) 600
Property of Mrs B Spry, from Worston Mill Farm
Yealm Lady br f (3yrs) Old Jocus - Henricus (Honorus) (David Morley Team Group) 850
Property of A P Power
Handfull Of Oats br m (5yrs) Oats - Louise Jessica (King's Equity)... (Mr Kinnear) 1,800
Property of Mrs A Taylor, from Park Farm Stud
b m (5yrs) Barley Hill - Border Wedding (Border Chief)............. (Mr Bates) 1,900

359

Property of Mrs K Cumiskey, from Yew Tree Farm
br g (5yrs) Oats - Kayella (Fine Blade (USA)) (H Johnson) 3,300
Property of D G Howard
b g (5yrs) Foolish Ways - Avalanche (Mountain Call)...................... (Cash) 2,000
Property of Mrs J I Pritchard
Out Country ch g (5yrs) Country Retreat - Past Hope (Past Petition)............. (Frank Cornes) 3,100
From Mill Bank Farm
ch g (4yrs) Celtic Cone - Foxwell (Healaugh Fox)..................... (G Turner) 4,500
Property of A Ball, from Sambirch Stud
ch g (3yrs) Starch Reduced - Secret Ingredient (Most Secret)..... (Mr Tredwell) 1,500
Property of Horton Hall Farm Partnership, from Horton Hall Farm
ch g (5yrs) Tremblant - Super Jennie (Stephen George)........ (J Richards) 3,600
Property of Mrs J M Sewell
Follow The Cross (IRE) gr or br f (4yrs) Roselier (FR) - Holy Cross (Arcticeelagh).............. (J Collett) 1,350

Property of J T Bailey, from Gibralter Farm

True Fred ch g (4yrs) True Song - Silver Spartan (Spartan General) .... (R Brotherton) 3,000

Proud Tom b g (4yrs) St Columbus - Adams Pride (Proud Aly).. (Severn Bloodstock) 3,000

From Little Lodge Farm

b f (4yrs) Le Moss - Lady Bluebird (Arapaho).................... (T Rogers) 3,000

360

Property of Mrs Mercy Rimell

ch f (4yrs) Tremblant - Trust Ann (Capistrano).................. (T Rogers) 2,700

Property of Roper Bloodstock, from J M Roper

b f (3yrs) War Hero - Fast Lady (Push On) (David Smyly Bloodstock) 900

Property of a Partnership, from Blackwell Grange Stud

b g (3yrs) Baron Blakeney - Miss Topem (Mossberry)........... (Mr Norwood) 1,500

Property of J W Orbell

b g (3yrs) Good Times (ITY) - Flame (Firestreak)................. (H Kavanagh) 2,000

Property of T J Mansell

gr g (3yrs) Another Realm - Dancing Kathleen (Green God).... (H Johnson) 3,000

Property of Mrs Carol Mole, from Pressland Farm

br f (3yrs) Pragmatic - Gopak (Garda's Revenge (USA))........... (Mr White) 550

Property of Miss A Clift

Regal Penny b f (4yrs) Majestic Maharaj - Casha (Castlenik)............... (Cash) 900

b g (3yrs) Sweet Monday - Teminny (Grey Love)............ (Severn Bloodstock) 1,500

Property of a Partnership, from Glazeley Stud

b g (3yrs) Rakaposhi King - Pro-Token (Proverb)................... (Mr Norwood) 2,100

From Shade Oak Stud

gr f (3yrs) Rakaposhi King - Moll (Rugantino) .... (G Williams) 1,250

b g (3yrs) Full Extent (USA) - Dunoon Court (Dunoon Star).............. (T Wells) 720

b f (3yrs) Rakaposhi King - Sheer Drop (Precipice Wood).......... (J Slough) 1,000

b y c Derrylin - Quelles Amours (Spartan General).................. (M Bent) 500

361

Property of J B Mulcahy, from Home Farm

Silvers Delight gr g (3yrs) Idiot's Delight - Silvers Pride (Owen Anthony)......... (A Verden-Jones) 1,200

Property of W T Robinson

b f (2yrs) Governor General - Pallomere (Blue Cashmere)............ (Mr Burn) 700

Property of Mrs A C Wakeham

ch f (3yrs) Southern Music - My New Way (Newski (USA))............ (R Rogers) 1,500

Property of Mrs J Bastard, from Kitley Stud

Kitley Cruise b f (3yrs) Cruise Missile - Linney Lawn (Newski (USA)).. (C Way) 2,900

Property of Mrs L J Williams, from Cudlic Farm

ch g (3yrs) Old Lucky - Cudlic Cream (No Evil)......................... (Mr White) 700

Property of Mrs M D Williams, from Greenway Farm

b g (3yrs) Escapism (USA) - Nulli's Maid (Nulli Secundus)... (Mrs Guest-Albert) 2,000

From Carlton Stud

ch g (3yrs) Today And Tomorrow - Rhythm Maker (Song)............ (S Harrison) 700

Property of Mrs P A Hemmings, from Haylane Farm

ch g (3yrs) Telsmoss - Swell Surprise (Lombard (GER))................ (G Jones) 750

Property of Mrs S E Wilsdon, from Glyn Common Farm

b f (3yrs) Arkan - Miss May (Marine Corps) (Mr White) 450

ch f (2yrs) Presidium - Title (Brigadier Gerard).................... (Mr Mills) 450

362

Property of W I Owens, from Woodhouse Farm

b f (2yrs) Roman Warrior - Petite Cone (Celtic Cone)................ (B James) 2,000

Property of Vallen Stud, from H M James

ch c (2yrs) High Season - Frogmore Sweet (Morston (FR))............ (S Piggott) 900

Property of Mrs Susan Davies

ch y f So Careful - Clifford's Dove (Rustingo)......................... (Cash) 1,500

From Orwell Lodge Stud

br or gr y f Roselier (FR) - Pacific Ocean (Optimistic Pirate).......... (J Slough) 1,300

Property of W T Lin, from Brockton House

b y f Scottish Reel - Talking Straight (Hasty Word)................... (C A Evans) 420

Jenny Regrets b m (10yrs) Piaffer (USA) - Lady Poppy (Sahib)....... (Mr Barlow) 1,200

From Cobhall Court Stud

Gentle Star br m (14yrs) Comedy Star (USA) - Super Princess (Falcon) .... (V Palmer) 880

363

NEWMARKET
Friday, September 3rd

Property of LEI (Bloodstock), from Ladyswood Racing Stables

Riverillon ch g (5yrs) Rousillon (USA) - Dancer Lover's (FR) (Green Dancer (USA))............................ (Cash) 700

From Jamesfield Place Stables To Dissolve a Partnership

Restless Minstrel (USA) b g (4yrs) The Minstrel (CAN) - Dismasted (USA) (Restless Native)............. (Cash) 700

Property of a Partnership, from Coronation Stables

Imagery b f (3yrs) Vision (USA) - Petty Purse (Petingo)........... (R J Baker) 4,000

Property of Miss K Rausing, from Chestnut Tree Stables

Gloriette br f (2yrs) Petoski - Reflected Glory (SWE) (Relko)........ (R Guest) 2,600

Property of a Partnership, from Fitzroy House Stables

Danseuse Francaise (IRE) b f (3yrs) Sicyos (USA) - Ninette de Valois (FR) (Gay Mecene (USA))............. (N Gilpin) 1,000

Property of a Gentleman, from Upshire Farm Stables

Swiss Mountain b or br f (3yrs) Formidable (USA) - Helvetique (FR) (Val de Loir) . . . (A L Forbes) 2,000

Property of Mrs Marie Hobeika, from Ecurie Georges Mikhalides, France

Bretteville (USA) b f (4yrs) Bering - Bashi (FR) (Stupendous). . . . . . (G Mikhalides) 7,800

Property of a Partnership, from Little Stanneylands Racing Stables

Argyle Cavalier (IRE) b c (3yrs) Simply Great (FR) - Fete Champetre (Welsh Pageant) . . . . (P Thomas) 10,000

From Warwick House Stables

Bold Line br f (3yrs) Never So Bold - Known Line (Known Fact (USA)). . . . . (Bba) 1,100

From Kremlin House Stables

Chiappucci (IRE) b g (3yrs) Doulab (USA) - Jenny's Child (Crash Course) . . . . (John White) 16,000

Doyville (IRE) b or br g (2yrs) Doyoun - Mannevillette (USA) (Foolish Pleasure (USA)). . . . . (Rachel Bridger) 840

364

From Oak Stables Ltd

Moubeed (USA) ch c (3yrs) Secretariat (USA) - Hanoof (USA) (Northern Dancer). . . . . (R J Batemen) 1,350

Property of Shadwell Estate Co Ltd, from Oak Stables

Ijab (CAN) b c (3yrs) Ascot Knight (CAN) - Renounce (USA) (Buckpasser) . . . . (J E Parkes) 9,000

Property of Shadwell Estate Co Ltd, from South Bank Stables

Taahhub (IRE) b c (3yrs) Nordico (USA) - Undiscovered (Tap On Wood). . . . . (J Joseph) 7,000

From South Bank Stables

Imperial Tokay (USA) gr c (3yrs) Caro - Chaudennay (USA) (Assert) . . . . (A L Forbes) 1,100

From Diomed Stables

Dame Prospect br f (2yrs) Damister (USA) - View (Shirley Heights) . . . . (Claremont Management Services) 1,600

Property of D R Stoddart, from High Havens Stables

Mistress Bee (USA) b f (4yrs) Grub (USA) - Golden Regent (CAN) (Vice Regent (CAN)). . . . . (S Coathup) 4,200

Property of a Partnership, from Heath House

Sylvan Serenity ch f (2yrs) Sylvan Express - Miss Kimmy (Tower Walk) . . . . (Sir Mark Prescott) 780

Property of F Salman, from Whatcombe Stables

Biljan (USA) b c (3yrs) Alydar (USA) - Best Decision (USA) (Best Turn (USA)) . . . . . (P Donnelly) 11,000

Prevene (IRE) b c (3yrs) Alzao (USA) - Assya (Double Form). . . . . (J Hanley) 2,800

Property of Lord Howard de Walden, from Warren Place Stables

Anchor Stone b c (3yrs) Slip Anchor - Doumayna (Kouban (FR)). . . . . (Lambert Bloodstock) 1,700

365

From Rosewell House Stables, Ireland

Atlantic Adios ch c (3yrs) Don't Forget Me - Les Enfants (Try My Best (USA)) . . . . . . (G Blum) 4,200

Rich Strike (IRE) ch g (2yrs) Thatching - Impressive Lady (Mr Fluorocarbon) . . . . (Mrs M S Harvey) 600

Sound Man Jimack (IRE) ch c (2yrs) Lomond (USA) - Bawnanell (Viking (USA)). . . . . (Rachel Bridger) 650

From South Hatch Stables

Rutland Water (USA) ch g (6yrs) Sharpen Up - Hemlock (USA) (Big Spruce (USA)) . . . . (D A Cahal) 6,500

Face North (IRE) b g (5yrs) Fayruz - Pink Fondant (Northfields (USA)). . . . . (R Akehurst) 12,000

From Coomberlands Stables Ltd

Regal Aura (IRE) ch g (3yrs) Glow (USA) - Dignified Air (FR) (Wolver Hollow) . . . . . (George Moore) 7,600

Property of Darley Management Co Ltd, from Rockingham Yard

Aird Point b c (3yrs) Reference Point - Singletta (USA) (Nodouble (USA)) . . . . . (G Mills) 640

Modaayin b c (3yrs) Doyoun - Summer Impressions (Lyphard (USA)). . . . . (Elspeth Squirrell) 940

Zermatt (IRE) b c (3yrs) Sadler's Wells - Chamonis (USA) (Affirmed (USA)) . . . . . (M Usher) 1,800

Property of Darley Management Co Ltd, from Kingwood House Stables

Latheron (IRE) b c (3yrs) Reference Point - La Romance (USA) (Lyphard (USA)) . . . (S Aitken) 5,600

366

Property of Darley Management Co Ltd, from Freemason Lodge

Colorful Ambition b c (3yrs) Slip Anchor - Reprocolor (Jimmy Reppin) . . . . (Thorndale Bloodstock) 12,500

Property of P A Leonard, from Breckenbrough House Stables

High Premium b g (5yrs) Forzando - High Halo (High Top). . . . . (C B A) 28,000

Property of a Partnership, from Breckenbrough House Stables

Wordsmith (IRE) b g (3yrs) Cyrano de Bergerac - Cordon (Morston (FR)) . . . . . (D Burchell) 22,000

Property of a Partnership, from Harraton Court Stables

March Of Time b g (2yrs) Dowsing (USA) - Triple Bar (Jimmy Reppin). . (J Hanley) 5,200

Property of Mrsw A M Thom, from Harraton Court Stables

Cuddly Date b f (3yrs) Nomination - Persane (FR) (Persepolis (FR)). . . . . (T W Cunningham) 850

Property of Darley Stud Management Co Ltd, from Clarehaven Stables

Perfay (USA) ch h (5yrs) Nodouble (USA) - Perfect Example (USA) (Far North (CAN)). . . . . (J Joseph) 5,800

From Clarehaven Stables

Vayello b c (2yrs) Mtoto - Khalkeva (FR) (Vayrann).............(Charles Smith) 1,000

Betty Kenwood ch f (3yrs) Dominion - Doogali (Doon)..... (C Maxted-Massey) 650

Property of T S M Riley-Smith, from Cedar Point Racing Stables

Go Flightline (IRE) ch f (3yrs) Common Grounds - Whilst (Dalsaan).... (B B A) 5,000

From Cedar Point Racing Stables

Alnasric Pete (USA) b g (7yrs) Al Nasr (FR) - Stylish Pleasure (USA) (What A Pleasure (USA))..................(Cash) 550

367

From Park Lodge Stables

Export Mondial b g (3yrs) Night Shift (USA) - Star Face (African Sky)............... (Lambert Bloodstock) 5,200

Property of Buckland Thoroughbred, from Ginge Stables

Jake The Pake (IRE) b g (3yrs) Double Schwartz - Traminer (Staus Seeker) ... (G Bravery) 950

To Dissolve a Partnership, from La Grange Racing Stables

Honey Guide b c (3yrs) Hadeer - Diana's Bow (Great Nephew)...... (R J Baker) 720

From La Grange Racing Stables

Cosmic Star gr f (3yrs) Siberian Express (USA) - Miss Bunty (Song).. (G Jones) 5,200

Eastern Glow ch f (3yrs) Hadeer - Turtle Dove (Gyr (USA))..............(B B A) 2,700

To Dissolve a Partnership, from La Grange Racing Stables

Omidjoy (IRE) ch f (3yrs) Nishapour (FR) - Fancy Finish (Final Straw).... (T Long) 2,000

Property of David Allan, from Induna Stables

b f (2yrs) Reprimand - Fire And Ice (FR) (Reliance II).... (Thorndale Bloodstock) 640

Property of Thorncliffe Stud

b c (2yrs) Mashhor Dancer (USA) - Celtic Sonata (Music Boy).... (Carole Wright) 500

Property of Mike Read (The Forum Ltd), from Folly House Stables

Mister Forum b g (3yrs) Damister (USA) - Ballad Island (Ballad Rock)........... (Mrs N Watts) 750

368

DONCASTER
Tuesday, September 7th (Yearlings)

Property of Mr & Mrs A Rhodes

ch y c Clantime - Busted Love (Busted) ... (Johnny McKeever Bloodstock) 2,000

Property of Bellmor Stud, from Bellmor Stud

ch y c Hubbly Bubbly (USA) - Empress Valley (Gay Fandango).. (M P Roberts) 1,000

Property of Miss M Carrington-Smith from Walnut Stud

ch y g Absalom - More Fun (Malicious) .... (David Minton Bloodstock) 2,600

Property of Mr J Bird from Manor Farm Stables

b y f Petong - Westone Paperchase (Accipiter)...................... (Sam Berry) 2,000

Property of Michael Edward Broughton from Broughton Bloodstock

ch y c Bairn (USA) - Bushti Music (Bustino) (G Lewis) 12,000

Property of M Broughton from Broughton Bloodstock

ch y c Fearless Action (USA) - Royal Form (Formidable)...............(Ron Boss) 2,600

Property of Mr R A Cameron from Whitehall Stables

gr y c Grey Desire - Clairwood (Final Straw) (B Gubby Ltd) 3,000

Property of Miss J A Rawding from Manor House Farm Stud

b y f Petong - Dame Corley (L'enjoleur).... (J Arnold) 5,000

Property of Taplin Lee & Cain Ltd. from Witney College

br y c Tina's Pet - Maestroes Beauty (Music Maestro) .... (Johnny McKeever Bloodstock) 2,900

Property of Mrs V H Withers, from Southill Stud

b or br y c Forzando - Lamees (USA) (Lomond).................. (G Lewis) 5,000

369

Property of Mrs V M Withers, from Southill Stud

b y c Warrshan (USA) - Sweet Home (Home Guard)... (R Payne Bloodstock) 5,800

Property of Mr K Pennington

b y f Clantime - Lady Pennington (Blue Cashmere)..................... (Cash) 3,500

Property of Mrs P A Clark from Tregavethan Manor Stud

ch y c Be My Chief (USA) - Rather Romantic (CAN) (Verbatim).... (D McDowell) 1,000

b y c Taufan (USA) - Broadway Rosie (Absalom)................. (G Lewis) 12,500

Trehane b y f Rock City - Trelissick (Electric) .... (M McCormack) 1,500

Property of Mrs J E Morton

ch y c Handsome Sailor - Gitee (FR) (Carwhite)...................... (B.B.A.) 5,800

Property of a partnership, from Meadow Farm Stud

ch y f Beveled (USA) - She Said Yes (Local Suitor)............ (Lord Huntingdon) 7,400

b y f Efisio - Joyce's Best (Tolomeo) ...... (Abaziz Al Saud) 4,200

b y c Emarati (USA) - Double Touch (FR) (Nonoalco)................. (G Lewis) 12,000

Property of Fernedge Bloodstock Ltd. from Chadwell Farm Stud

b y f Dominion - Mrs Musgrove (Jalmood) (J Berry) 5,600

370

Property of Alan Aikin from Moorwoods Farm Stud

b y f Lugana Beach - Bonny Bright Eyes (Rarity)....................... (Cash) 5,000

Property of M.W. & B.A. Littlewort from the National Stud

b y c Blakeney - Relatively Smart (Great Nephew)............... (T H Caldwell) 4,800

From Three Gates Stud

b y c Risk Me (FR) - Sunday Sport's Pet (Mummy's Pet).......... (Peter Harris) 6,200

ch y c Risk Me (FR) - Merry Kate (Shirley Heights)...................... (Cash) 2,200

From Peterwood Stud

b y c Rambo Dancer (CAN) - Beautiful Orchid (Hays)............. (S Norton) 4,600

Property of Dandy's Farm from Dandy's Farm

b y c Siberian Express (USA) - Exceptional Beauty (Sallust)............... (C.B.A.) 5,200

Property of a partnership from Blakeley Stud

ch y c Bairn (USA) - Lady St Clair (Young Generation).......... (Fulling Mill Stud) 4,400

Property of Mr T. Jarvis from Mill Farm Stud

b y c Skyliner - Ma Famille (Welsh Saint) .. (R H S Syn) 3,400

b y c Dunbeath (USA) - Calafuria (Chief Singer)............. (Fulling Mill Stud) 2,000

Property of Mr B. Minty

ch y c Beveled (USA) - Sylvan Song (Song) (M McCormack) 2,200

b y c Full Extent (USA) - Princess Lucianne (Stanford).................. (J Berry) 5,600

371

Property of Mr T. Dodd

b y c Weldnaas (USA) - High Elegance (Elegant Air)............... (Ron Boss) 1,800

Property of Mr Simon Wingfield-Digby, TD DL from Sandley Stud

b y c Never So Bold - Tina Rosa (Bustino) (Abaziz Al Saud) 5,000

Property of a parnertship from Sandley Stud

b or br y f Nomination - Patridge Brook (Birdbrook)................. (G Lewis) 6,600

Property of Mrs F A Veasey from Cinder Farm Stud

ch y c Aragon - Little Egret (Carwhite)..... (L J Upex) 2,800

Property of Shaunlara Pinhooking Syndicate from Shaunlara Stud

ch y c Astronef - Numidia (Sallust) .... (R Payne Bloodstock) 3,300

Property of Shaunlara Stud from Shaunlara Stud

ch y c Precocious - Restless Star (Star Appeal)...................... (Cash) 2,100

Property of R M Eggo from Easter Cruicksfield

gr y c Belfort (FR) - Grand Occasion (Great Nephew)..................... (C Hill) 3,100

Property of Mrs Annabel Meller

b or br y f Belfort (FR) - Eastern Romance (Sahib)....................... (Cash) 1,700

Property of Mr D P Martin from Southburgh Manor Stud

b y f Exodal (USA) - Carlton Glory (Blakeney).............. (R Whitaker) 2,000

Property of Milton Park Stud from Milton Park Stud

b y c Deploy - Waveguide (Double Form) .. (E Baker) 5,600

372

Property of Mrs Y M Neville from Winderton Hill Stud

b y f Statoblest - Jay Gee Ell (Vaigly Great) (J Berry) 7,000

Property of Theobalds Stud from Theobalds Stud

b y c Ti King (FR) - Midnight Owl (FR) (Ardross)..................... (Cash) 4,400

Property of Mr M Sharkey from Milford Stud, Co. Carlow, Ireland

ch y f Ballad Rock - Sweetsider (USA) (Topsider).................... (Cash) 4,200

b y f Waajib - Treeline (High Top) (G Lewis) 12,000

Property of Mr B S Adamson, from Hunsley House Stud

b y g Rambo Dancer (CAN) - Heemee (On Your Mark)..... (Riston Whins Racing) 4,000

Property of Mark Houlston from Hunsley House Stud

b y c Rambo Dancer (CAN) - Falcrello (Falcon)................ (M Channon) 5,200

Property of Mrs M A Rae-Smith from Hunsley House Stud

b y c Rambo Dancer (CAN) - Tea-Pot (Ragstone) (David Minton Bloodstock) 5,400

Property of Messrs P & A G Venner from Petches Farm

b y f Most Welcome - Council Rock (General Assembly)............ (Jim Short) 1,800

Property of Wheerlersland Stud

b y c Be My Chief (USA) - Princess Rosananti (Shareef Dancer)... (C Thornton) 4,800

b y f Indian Ridge - Moonlight Serenade (Crooner)........... (D Murray Smith) 5,400

373

Property of a partnership, from The Elms Stud

b y f Thowra (FR) - Still Laughing (Jester) .. (C.B.A.) 4,200

From Woodlands Stables, Co. Tipperary, Ireland

b y c Magical Strike (USA) - Philigree (Moulton)................... (C.B.A.) 4,000

From Charlestown Stud, Co. Westmeath, Ireland

ch y c Chilibang - Vernair (Super Concorde) (B.B.A.) 5,000

b y c Classic Secret (USA) - Dame Brisene (FR) (Kashmir II) .... (David Minton Bloodstock) 3,800

Property of Messinger Stud Ltd from Nuthurst Farm Stud

b y c Scenic - Rockeater (Roan Rocket).... (Cash) 8,000

b y c Rock City - Prudence (Grundy)....... (R Hollinshead) 14,000

Property of Rodvic Ltd from Nuthurst Farm Stud

b y f Cyrano de Bergerac - Makalu (Godswalk).................. (D Cosgrove) 8,200

From Wingfield Stud

b y c Sharpo - Flambera (FR) (Akarad) ..... (Abaziz Al Saud) 15,000

From Honeypig Stud, Co. Tyrone, Ireland

b y c Salt Dome (USA) - Havana Moon (Ela Mana Mou)..... (R Payne Bloodstock) 3,200

Property of Ian Bryant from Spa Stud

b y c Astronef - Stapelea (FR) (Faraway Son)........ (Peter Doyle Bloodstock) 2,700

b y c Chief Singer - Ravens Peak (High Top) .... (R Thompson) 1,050

374

Property of R B Warren from Nancherrow Stud

gr y f Weldnaas (USA) - Shakana (Grundy) (B Smart) 9,400

Property of A H Warren (Coombe Farm) Ltd from Downclose Stud

b y f Formidable (USA) - Pleasure Island (Dalsaan)............... (M Campion) 1,700

b or gr y f Siberian Express (USA) - Girl's Brigade (Brigadier Gerard)..... (P Cook) 4,800

Property of T K Know from Whitworth Stud

b y c Skyliner - Miss Colenca (Petong)...... (T Easterby) 4,200

From Hever Castle Stud

b y c Efisio - Truly Bold (Bold Lad) .... (Hever Racing Club) 18,000

ch y c Efisio - Sweet Rosina (Sweet Revenge)........ (Hever Racing Club) 33,000

Property of Ham Cross Farming Co. from Ham Cross Farm

br y c Tragic Role - Sideloader Special (Song)..................... (C Thornton) 4,200

Property of Palehouse Farm (P V & J P Jackson) from Trickledown Stud

ch y f Bairn (USA) - Lady Chaser (Posse) .. (B Dumming) 1,000

Property of a partnership from Trickledown Stud

b y f Aragon - Incarnadine (Hot Spark) ..... (Britton House Stud) 2,800

From Trickledown Stud

ch y c Nashamaa - Choral Park (Music Boy) (Mr Bycroft) 3,600

375

Property of R L Cox from Trickledown Stud

b y c Statoblest - My Precious Daisy (Sharpo)...................... (J Berry) 7,800

Property of Major R P Thorman, MC from Vilmoray Lodge Stud

b y c Faustus (USA) - Express Edition (Comedy Star)................ (Cash) 4,400

Property of Hon. Mrs M Christian

b y c Dowsing (USA) - Warning Bell (Bustino)........................... (C.B.A.) 4,000

Property of Mr & Mrs B T Chambers

b y c Chief Singer - To Oneiro (Absalom) .. (G Lewis) 7,000

Property of Mrs E McKee from Melbourne Hall Stud

ch y c Clantime - Dayana (Burglar) .... (J Balding) 5,200

Property of Mrs E C York from Hutton Stud

ch y c Domynsky - Close The Deal (Nicholas Bill).................... (J M Naouki) 2,900

Property of Mrs M J Dandy

b y f Salt Dome (USA) - Sunderland (Dancer's Image)................ (E.I.L.) 5,000

b y f Hallgate - North Pine (Import) (Cash) 5,400

Property of Mr J Hamilton from Etchingham Stud

b y f Faustus (USA) - Kissimmee (Petingo) (Cash) 5,800

Property of Llety Farms from Llety Farms

ch y c Bold Owl - Whirtlygigger (Taufan)... (Riston Whins Racing) 2,500

376

Property of Mrs J Banks from Aike Grange Stud

b y f Belfort (FR) - Torville Gold (Aragon)... (J Spearing) 2,100

Property of Mr & Mrs L T Foster from Stockwell Stud

ch y c Indian Ridge - Lovely Lagoon (Mill Reef)......................... (Cash) 13,500

b y f Efisio - Hicklam Millie (Absalom) ..... (Bozzi Marco) 4,000

From Lostford Manor Stud

ch y f Handsome Sailor - Brave Squaw (High Top).......... (Stratford Homes) 2,500

b y f Puissance - Tyrian Princess (Comedy Star)................... (Rumer Stud) 3,100

Property of Mr & Mrs G Stafford from Britton House Stud

b y c Lugana Beach - Dewberry (Bay Express)............ (Roger Heaton) 9,000

Property of Britton House Stud from Britton House Stud

ch y f Emarati (USA) - Indian Summer (Young Generation)............ (E.I.L.) 2,800

Property of Mr B M Small from Britton House Stud

b y f Statoblest - Safety First (Wassl)...... (C Dingwall) 1,200

Property of Carlton Stud from Carlton Stud (Malton)

b y f Puissance - I Don't Mind (Swing Easy) (J Berry) 10,000

Property of High Onn Stud

b y f Precocious - Sovereign Love (He Loves Me)............. (Ian Balding) 9,000

377

Property of Mr S M & Mrs K Phillips from High Onn Stud

b y f Precocious - Our Ginger (Le Johnstan) (R Thompson) 2,800

From Shinglis Stud, Co. Weathmeath, Ireland

ch y f Accordion - Northern Amber (Shack) (Johnny McKeever Bloodstock) 1,500

From Benham Stud

ch y c Ballacashtal (CAN) - Seymour Ann (Krayyan)..... (Broughton Bloodstock) 3,500

From Catridge Farm Stud

ch y c Master Willie - Mumtaz Mayfly (Tap On Wood)............... (P J Makin) 4,000

Property of Mr R Taylor from Catridge Farm Stud

ch y f Sayf El Arab (USA) - Alanood (Northfields).................. (M Johnston) 2,200

Property of Mr D S W Blacker from Catridge Farm Stud

b y f Formidable (USA) - Tudor Pilgrim (Welsh Pageant)............. (E.I.L.) 8,800

From Catridge Farm Stud

ch y c Indian Ridge - Shy Dolly (Cajun)..... (Johnny McKeever Bloodstock) 5,000

Property of Mascalls Stud from Catridge Farm Stud

b y c Midyan (USA) - Amathus Glory (Mummy's Pet).......... (J J O'Neill) 6,000

From Catridge Farm Stud

b y c Prince Sabo - Final Call (Town Crier) (Simon Dow) 9,600

Property of R J Vines

b y f Absalom - Play For Time (Comedy Star)................. (T J Naughton) 2,600

378

From Elsenham Stud

br y c Risk Me (FR) - Hot Sunday Sport (Star Appeal).................. (Cash) 3,200

ch y c Risk Me (FR) - Minabella (Dance In Time)...................... (B Gubby) 6,200

ch y f Risk Me (FR) - Sunday Sport Star (Star Appeal)................. (A Pitt) 11,500

Property of Mr C W Rogers from Fulling Mill Stud

ch y c Beveled (USA) - Dulcidene (Behistoun).................. (John Quinn) 2,600

ch y f Interrex (CAN) - Jenny's Rocket (Roan Rocket)............. (S Moore) 2,200

Property of Floors Farming from Floors Stud

gr y f Sharrood (USA) - Arita (Never So Bold).................... (Sally Hall) 8,000

Property of Normanby Stud from Floors Stud

br y f Primo Dominie - Rectitude (Runnymede)... (Sandmoor Textile Co Ltd) 6,400

From Commanstown Stud, Co. Kildare, Ireland

b y c Cyrano de Bergerac - Maria Renata (Jaazeiro)............ (M McCormack) 10,000

From Rathberry Stud, Co. Cork, Ireland

b y f Taufan (USA) - Ana Gabriella (USA) (Master Derby)........... (J T Doyle) 10,000

From Rathberry Stud

b or br y f Cyrano de Bergerac - Blackpool Belle (The Brianstan)................. (David Minton Bloodstock) 6,200

379

Property of Rathbarry Stud from Rathbarry Stud

ch y f Kefaah (USA) - Supreme Crown (USA) (Chief's Crown).... (T D Barron) 5,500

From Lynn Lodge Stud. Co. Westmeath, Ireland

b y c Contract Law (USA) - My Covey (Taufan).................... (C Allen) 2,800

From Yeomanstown Stud, Co. Kildare, Ireland

b y c Contract Law (USA) - Brigadina (Brigadier Gerard).......... (D N Chappell) 3,750

b y c Efisio - Miss Vaigly Blue (Vaigly Great) .... (M McCormack) 4,600

b y f Common Grounds - Red Magic (Red God)..................... (Reg Payne) 4,500

From Tally-Ho Stud, Co. Westmeath, Ireland

b y c Gallic League - Alsazia (FR) (Bolkonski) .... (Browne Bloodstock) 4,000

b y c Gallic League - Alsazia (FR) (Bolkonski) .... (E.I.L. & Johnny McKeever Bloodstock) 15,000

ch y c Maelstrom Lake - Gluewein (Ballymoss).............. (Colin Williams) 4,800

From Furnace Mill Stud

b y c Clantime - On The Record (Record Token)..................... (J Berry) 10,500

Property of Mr A H Bennett from Furnace Mill Stud

ch y c Bairn (USA) - Gentle Gain (Final Straw)............... (Mary Reveley) 9,500

380

From Furnace Mill Stud

b y f Chilibang - Princess Diana (Huntercombe)...................... (Cash) 1,000

b y f Aragon - Songstead (Song) .... (Ernie Weymes) 4,200

b y c Dancing Dissident (USA) - Velia (Welsh Saint)........ (Manfred Hofer) 2,600

Property of Messinger Stud Ltd from Furnace Mill Stud

b y f Welsh Captain - Miss Nelski (Most Secret)................ (R Thompson) 3,000

From Hunsley House Stud

b y c Rambo Dancer (CAN) - Having Fun (Hard Fought).... (Browne Bloodstock) 6,000

b y f Rambo Dancer (CAN) - Llanddona (Royal Palace)........... (M Campion) 2,000

Property of Mr W H R John & Partners

br or gr y c Doulab (USA) - Rich Lass (Broxted)........... (M W Easterby) 6,000

Property of Mr D H Jones & P H Davies from Tyrnest Stud

b y f Aragon - Kumzar (Hotfoot).... (E.I.L.) 5,000

From Burns Farm Stud

b y c Astronef - Pharly's Myth (Pharly)..... (B.B.A.) 5,200

Property of Mr T Threlfall from Sunnyside Stables

b y c Prince Sabo - So Kind (Kind Of Hush) (Michael Bell) 16,000

381

Property of Mr D Wosskow from Peterwood Stud

b y c Rambo Dancer (CAN) - Vindictive Lady (USA) (Foolish Pleasure)....... (Cash) 1,300

Property of Mr A Vickers from Peterwood Stud

b y c Pharly (FR) - Try Vickers (USA) (Fuzzbuster) .... (Johnny McKeever Bloodstock) 7,000

Property of Mr M H Wrigley from Low House Stud

ch y c Rock City - Moonwalker (Night Shift) (Lady Herries) 8,000

Property of Mr D B Lamplough from Melbourne Hall Stud

ch y f Persian Heights - Militia Girl (Rarity) (C.B.A.) 4,000

Property of Mr K G Bridges from Limestone Stud

b y c Komaite (USA) - Khadino (Relkino) ... (David Minton Bloodstock) 7,200

Property of Limestone Stud from Limestone Stud

b y f Nomination - Stranger To Fear (Never So Bold)............ (Patrick Haslam) 5,400

Property of Mr J Stevens and Mrs D Roche from Limestone Stud
b y c Komaite (USA) - Khadine (Astec)..... (D Roche) 4,600
Property of Mr Peter C Bourke from Limestone Stud
b y f Komaite (USA) - Senorina Francesca (The Brianstan).......... (T Easterby) 1,000
Property of Swaines Hill Stud from Swaines Hill Stud
br y c Chief Singer - Crystal Gael (Sparkler) (S Moore) 4,600
Property of Fares Stables Ltd from Fares Stables
b y c Highest Honor (FR) - Baino Charm (USA) (Diesis)... (R Payne Bloodstock) 5,000
b y f Never So Bold - Baino Clinic (USA) (Sovereign Dancer)................ (Johnny McKeever Bloodstock) 6,800

382

From Golden Vale Stud, Co. Limerick, Ireland
b y f Gallic League - Frensham Manor (Le Johnstan)................. (G Lewis) 4,600
b y c Gallic League - Slow Hands (Piskelly) (D Cosgrove) 4,000
Property of Lady Legard and Mrs J Jenyns from Burton Agnes Stud
br y c Midyan (USA) - Midnight's Reward (Night Shift)............... (R Hannon) 7,000
Property of Mrs S Hood from Old Mill Stud
ch y c Prince Sabo - No Sharps Or Flats (USA) (Sharpen Up)................ (Johnny McKeever Bloodstock) 3,300
Property of Havenwood Construction Ltd from Havenwood Construction Ltd
br y c Hotfoot - Gunnard (Gunner B)....... (Lambert Bloodstock) 1,800
From Woodlands Stables, Co. Tipperary, Ireland
b y c Magical Strike (USA) - Veldt (High Top)................. (Brian Meehan) 3,600
b y c Glenstal (USA) - Pocket (Tumble Wind)........................ (J Balding) 4,600
Property of Mr E A Badger & Mr P Balding from Spa Stud
b y c Governor General - Calibina (Caliban) (B.B.A.) 5,300
Property of Snowdrop Stud Company Limited from Sandley Stud
b y c Fools Holme (USA) - Madam Bold (Never So Bold).......... (M Channon) 5,200
Property of Mr & Mrs C T Bletsoe from The Elms Stud
br y c Celestial Storm (USA) - Regal Wonder (Stupendous).............. (Cash) 2,200

383

From Three Gates Stud
b y c Rich Charlie - Princess Wendy (Captain James).................. (B.B.A.) 2,500
gr y f Risk Me (FR) - Petite Angel (Burslem) (Cash) 1,000
Property of Mrs G C Stanley
b or br y f Primo Dominie - Shamasiya (FR) (Vayrann).................... (C.B.A.) 6,000

PRIVATE SALES
Property of Ballyearl Stud, from Ballyearl Stud, Co Antrim, Ireland
br y c Skyliner - Shantung Lassie (FR) (Shantung)............... (R O'Shea) 2,000
Property of Scorrier Stud, from Britton House Stud
b y c Charmer - Killifreth (Jimmy Reppin) .. (Cash) 1,000
Property of Mr P C Whales, from Rix Farm Stud
ch y c Kalaglow - Madison Girl (Last Fandango)......... (Commonstown Stud) 2,500

384

DONCASTER
Wednesday, September 8th (Yearlings)

Property of Mr P C Whales from Rix Farm Stud
ch or gr y c Chilibang - Press Corps (Realm) .... (W Muir) 5,000
Property of Samuel Oliver from Honeypig Stud, Co. Tyrone, Ireland
ch y c Common Grounds - Elysium (Ela-Mana-Mou)................... (E.I.L./ McKeever Bloodstock) 3,000
Property of Mr & Mrs G Steinberg from Lavington Stud
b y c Warrshan (USA) - Free On Board (Free State)................ (M McCormack) 7,400
From Ballymorris & Caherass Studs, Co. Clare, Ireland
b y c Cyrano de Bergerac - Hit For Six (Tap On Wood).................... (E.I.L./ mckeever Bloodstock) 5,000
b y c Rock City - Runelia (Runnett)........ (Patrick Haslam) 16,000
From Golden Vale Stud, Co. Limerick, Ireland
br y f Gallic League - Presentable (Sharpen Up)................ (David Cosgrove) 6,600
ch y c Al Hareb (USA) - Time For Pleasure (Tower Walk)................ (J Holt) 7,200
Property of Mrs T Hinde from Trickledown Stud
ch y f Music Boy - Tufty Lady (Riboboy) ... (C C Elsey) 2,800
Property of Benham Stud from Benham Stud
b y c Beveled (USA) - Bar Gold (Lucky Brief) .... (C James) 3,600
b y c Presidium - To The Point (Sharpen Up) .... (P W Harris) 4,400

385

Property of Auldyn Stud Ltd from High Onn Stud
ch y c Forzando - Sharp Celine (Sharpo) ... (R Whitaker) 5,000
b y c Then Again - Pepeke (Mummy's Pet) (I V Matthews) 4,200
Property of Mr D Macrae from Stradishall Manor
b y c Petorius - Comhail (USA) (Nodouble) (G Moore) 7,400
From Rathbarry Stud (Agent)
b y c Taufan (USA) - Bouffant (High Top) .. (David Morley) 15,000

From Partridge Close Stud

b y c Scenic - Swordlestown Miss (USA) (Apalachee)......... (James Bethell) 8,200
b y f Deploy - Quissisanno (Be My Guest) (K McAuliffe) 6,200
b y c Superlative - Aunt Jemima (Busted).. (D Arbuthnot) 10,000

Property of Silfield Bloodstock from Southburgh Manor Stud

b y f Taufan (USA) - Lady Donaro (Ardoon) (M W Easterby) 4,000

Property of a partnership from Southburgh Manor Stud

b y f Nomination - Blue Rhythm (Blue Cashmere)............. (J J O'Neill) 7,000
ch y c Rock City - Sunfleet (Red Sunset)... (G Moore) 13,000

386

From Elsenham Stud

ch y c Risk Me (FR) - Egnoussa (Swing Easy)........................ (Cash) 4,800
ch y f Risk Me (FR) - Bocas Rose (Jalmood) .... (J Bethell) 4,400
b y c Risk Me (FR) - Wayward Polly (Lochnager)............... (M Hofer) 3,800
ch y c Risk Me (FR) - Princess Lily (Blakeney)........... (M McCormack) 9,000

Property of a partnership from Burn House Stud

b y c Reprimand - Ring Of Pearl (Auction Ring)................. (David Morley) 41,000

Property of Bishop Wilton Stud from Bishop Wilton Stud

b y c Fools Holme (USA) - Two's Company (Sheshoon).................. (C.B.A.) 6,400
br y f Rock City - Miss Alkie (Noalcoholic).. (Michael Bell) 8,000

From Forest Stud

ch y c Digamist (USA) - Marine Life (Deep Diver)................. (Noel Meade) 8,600
b y c Statoblest - Valadon (High Line)...... (M Channon) 16,000

Property of Mr T Wybrew from Britton House Stud

gr y c Absalom - Fumarole (USA) (Sensitive Prince).......... (The Winning Team) 7,000

387

Property of Miss J Chaplin from Blisbury Farm

b y c Nomination - Rosy Diamond (Jalmood)................... (Cash) 5,200
b y c Petoski - Folle Idee (Foolish Pleasure) (Peter Doyle Bloodstock) 4,200

Property of Rockhouse Farms Ltd from Bearstone Stud

b y f Puissance - Persian Case (Upper Case) .... (R Whitaker) 7,100

Property of Simon Plumbly from Briery Farm Stud

ch y c Interrex (CAN) - Satin Box (Jukebox) (G Moore) 3,600
b y f Prince Sabo - Bloom Of Youth (Last Tycoon)............ (Equine Services) 6,800

Property of Carlton Stud from Carlton Stud (Malton)

b y c Nordance (USA) - Danova (FR) (Dan Cupid).................... (J Berry) 7,800

Property of Whitsbury Manor Stud from Whitsbury Manor Stud

b y c Distant Relative - Thimblerigger (Sharpen Up).............. (M Hofer) 12,000
b y f Distant Relative - Miller's Melody (Chief Singer)............... (M Hofer) 12,000

Property of a partnership from Stowell Hill Stud

b y c Forzando - Everdene (Bustino)....... (David Abell) 35,000

From Glenvale Stud, Co. Tipperary, Ireland

br y f Fairy King (USA) - Danger Ahead (Mill Reef)............... (Abaziz Al Saud) 26,000

388

From Ashtown House Stud, Co. Waterford Ireland

b or br y c Gallic League - Never Home (Home Guard)...................... (David Minton Bloodstock) 23,000

From Camas Park Stud, Co. Tipperary, Ireland

ch y c Thatching - Whist Awhile (Caerleon) (Abaziz Al Saud) 25,000
b y c Danehill (USA) - Music Of The Night (USA) (Blushing Groom)............. (Peter Doyle Bloodstock) 17,000

From Furnace Mill Stud

b y c My Generation - Mallabee (Pall Mall) (J Berry) 10,000

Property of Courtleigh Stud from Furnace Mill Stud

b y f Aragon - Moaning Low (Burglar) ..... (G Moore) 6,200

Property of Furnace Mill Bloodstock Ltd from Furnace Mill Stud

ch y f Rock City - Shillay (Lomond)........ (Stanley Moore) 3,200

Property of a partnership from Furnace Mill Stud

b y c Dowsing (USA) - Shortning Bread (Blakeney)................ (G Moore) 6,600

Property of W P Jenks from Furnace Mill Stud

b y f Scottish Reel - Mavahra (Mummy's Pet)......... (Peter Doyle Bloodstock) 6,400

From Furnace Mill Stud

b y f Midyan (USA) - Lotte Lenta (Gorytus) (E.I.L./McKeever Bloodstock) 5,200

Property of a partnership from Furnace Mill Stud

b y c Beveled (USA) - Lizzie Bee (Kind Of Hush)...................... (J Berry) 27,000

389

Property of of Mrs P Grubb from Big Acre Stud, Co. Tipperary, Ireland

b y f Cyrano de Bergerac - Hedwige (African Sky).................... (C J Hill) 6,100

Property of Mrs P Grubb from Big Acre Stud, Co. Tipperary, Ireland

b y f Jareer (USA) - King's Chase (King's Leap)................ (M W Easterby) 3,600

Property of Mr J Heelan from Ballinvana House Stud, Co. Limerick, Ireland

b y c Ajraas (USA) - Lamya (Hittite Glory) .. (R O'Ryan) 3,000

From Yeomanstown Stud, Co. Kildare, Ireland

b y c Persian Heights - Altara (GER) (Tarim) (G Mazza) 8,000

b y c Lugana Beach - Fashion Lover (Shiny Tenth)............... (Abaziz Al Saud) 8,000

br y c Tirol - Trusted Maiden (Busted)..... (T Stack) 11,000

b y c Glenstal (USA) - Regiura (High Top).. (Equine Investment Consultants) 23,000

br y c Bluebird (USA) - Royal Wolff (Prince Tenderfoot)............... (D Woods) 13,500

From Ballyhane Stud, Co. Carlow, Ireland

b y c Danzatore (CAN) - Raised By Nuts (USA) (Raised Socially)....... (T Stack) 6,600

From Lynn Lodge Stud, Co. Westmeath, Ireland

ch y c Prince Sabo - Orien (Goldhill) (E.I.L./ McKeever Bloodstock) 12,000

gr y c Contract Law (USA) - Katysue (King's Leap).................. (B McMahon) 6,600

390

From Tally-Ho Stud, Co. Westmeath, Ireland

b y c Classic Secret (USA) - Bally (Balidar) (J Akehurst) 10,000

From Red House Stud

b y c Cyrano de Bergerac - Captivate (Mansingh) (Johnny McKeever Bloodstock) 4,600

b y c Mazilier (USA) - Adana (FR) (Green Dancer).. (E.I.L./mckeever Bloodstock) 3,200

Property of Highfield Stud Ltd from Glen Andred Stud

b y f Petong - Toccata (USA) (Mr Leader).. (M Fetherston-Godley) 8,800

Property of Old Mill Stud from Old Mill Stud

br y c Deploy - Karatachi (Smile).......... (Peter Doyle Bloodstock) 2,000

Property of Mrs S Wood from Old Mill Stud

b y c Statoblest - Ackcontent (USA) (Key To Content).................. (J T Doyle) 15,000

Property of Llety Farms from Llety Farms

b y c Merdon Melody - Donna Pavlova (Don II)............... (The Winning Team) 8,800

b y f Merdon Melody - Royal Scots Greys (Blazing Saddles).......... (W Haigh) 3,600

From Burns Farm Stud

b y c Petong - Velvet Pigeon (Homing).... (J FitzGerald) 2,300

Property of a partnership from Burns Farm Stud

ch y f Music Boy - City Link Rose (Lochnager).......... (M McCormack) 8,000

391

Property of Mr R C Lloyd

ch y c Chilibang - Chacewater (Electric).... (J T Doyle) 3,500

Property of Mr D L C Hodges from Dodford Stud

b y c Primo Dominie - So Bold (Never So Bold)..................... (G Moore) 7,000

br y g Prince Sabo - Sparkling Sovereign (Sparkler)................ (L Mullany) 1,300

From Redpender Stud, Co. Kilkenny, Ireland

b y c Aragon - Davinia (Gold Form)........ (J T Doyle) 38,000

Property of a partnership from Burton Agnes Stud

ch y c Zalazl (USA) - Mrs Danvers (Balidar) (M Campion) 2,000

Property of Bridge End Bloodstock from Sledmere Stud

ch y c Superpower - Shiny Kay (Star Appeal).................. (M Hofer) 5,600

Property of a partnership, from Elmhurst Stud

ch y f Persian Bold - Miss Merlin (Manacle) (David Minton Bloodstock) 15,000

Property of Mr John Needham, from Elmhurst Stud

b y f Sharrood (USA) - Lurking (Formidable) (J M Ranson) 5,400

from Woodcote Stud

b y c Puissance - Safidar (Roan Rocket).... (G Lewis) 12,000

Property of Mr C J Pennick, from Woodcote Stud

b y c Reprimand - Kina (USA) (Bering)..... (G Moore) 4,800

392

DONCASTER
Thursday, September 9th (Yearlings)

Property of Limestone Stud, from Limestone Stud

b y c Nomination - Legendary Dancer (Shareef Dancer)............ (B.B.A.) 13,000

b y c Pharly (FR) - Hay Reef (Mill Reef).... (Ian Balding) 15,000

Property of Bylon Farmers & E R Thomas, from Bylon Farms

b y c Handsome Sailor - Snake Song (Mansingh)............... (John Wharton) 4,400

Property of Bylon Farms, from Bylon Farms

b y c Petong - Boa (Mandrake Major)...... (John Wharton) 11,500

Property of Sexton Enterprises, from Ham Cross Farm

b y c Sizzling Melody - Hellene (Dominion) (M McCormack) 5,200

Property of I & E Macgregor Partnership, from Pinkerton Stud

b y c Dunbeath (USA) - Bustellina (Busted) (M H Easterby) 2,600

b y f Shareef Dancer (USA) - Holy Day (Sallust).................. (G Douglas) 8,000

Property of Clarendon Park Stud, from Ted Voute (agent)

b y c Reprimand - Affirmative (Derring-Do) (Tim Easterby) 5,800

b y c Most Welcome - Affirmation (Tina's Pet)..................... (A Stringer) 5,000

Property of Tarworth Bloodstock Investments Ltd, from Genesis Green Stud

b or br y c Dominion - Onika (Great Nephew).................. (G Lewis) 11,000

393

from Genesis Green Stud

ch y c Timeless Native (USA) - Seeing Stars (USA) (Unconscious)......... (B.B.A.) 19,000

Property of Mr & Mrs R T Watson, from Manor Farm Stud
ch y c Handsome Sailor - Thorner Lane (Tina's Pet).. (Peter Doyle Bloodstock) 15,000
Property of Mr G Harris, from Manor Farm Stud
b y c Mazilier (USA) - Another Lane (Tina's Pet)....... (David Minton Bloodstock) 5,200
Property of Mr & Mrs R T Watson, from Manor Farm Stud
b y f Indian Ridge - Blues Indigo (Music Boy).................. (W Wharton) 28,000
From Rathasker Stud
ch y c Red Sunset - Carcajou (High Top)... (Abaziz Al Alsaud) 8,800
b y c Try My Best (USA) - Tracy's Sundown (Red Sunset).......... (T H Caldwell) 4,800
ch y c Red Sunset - Local Belle (Ballymore) (R O'Sheen Bloodstock) 2,700
Property of Mr J L & Mrs B Skinner, from Helescane Stud
b y f Deploy - Serration (Kris)............. (Tedwood Bloodstock) 3,400
from Catridge Farm Stud
ch y f Indian Ridge - Malibasta (Auction Ring)... (E.I.L., McKeever Bloodstock) 9,000
b y f Midyan (USA) - Fair Eleanor (Saritamer)................. (B.B.A.) 16,000
b y f Indian Ridge - Tiszta Sharok (Song)... (Peter Doyle Bloodstock) 13,500
b y c Absalom - Swift Return (Double Form) .... (G Howson Bloodstock) 20,000

394

from Lodge Park Stud
b y c Tirol - Vain Deb (Gay Fandango) ..... (John Mackie) 10,000
b y f Gallic League - Ruby River (Red God) (Rae Guest) 14,000
Property of Rockhouse Farms Ltd, from Bearstone Stud
b y c Puissance - Jaisalmer (Castle Keep).. (T H Caldwell) 16,800
Property of Bearstone Stud, from Bearstone Stud
b y f Puissance - Waltz (Jimmy Reppin) ... (Jack Berry) 5,000
Property of Mr W H Joyce, from Pantaquesta Stud
ch y c Most Welcome - Stripanoora (Ahonoora)..... (M Fetherston-Godley) 8,600
Property of Mr Simon Plumbly, from Briery Farm Stud
b y f Formidable (USA) - Norfolk Serenade (Blakeney)......... (Jimmy FitzGerald) 14,500
ch y f Absalom - Kinkajoo (Precocious) .... (David Minton Bloodstock) 3,000
ch y c Beveled (USA) - Lustrous (Golden Act).................. (Tim Easterby) 3,200
From Partridge Close Stud
ch y c Jareer (USA) - Avidal Park (Horage) (Jimmy FitzGerald) 6,000
b y c The Noble Player (USA) - Daybreaker (Thatching).. (Peter Doyle Bloodstock) 5,600

395

From Kilminfoyle House Stud
b y c Reprimand - African Dash (African Sky)......... (Peter Doyle Bloodstock) 11,500

Property of Mr J Heelan, from Ballinvana House Stud
b y c Lochnager - Soltago (Touching Wood) (R Whittaker) 5,000
Property of Miss Elizabeth Aldous, from Southburgh Manor Stud
b y c Nomination - Summer Ever (Hotfoot) (Denys Smith) 4,600
Property of Mr D G Mason, from Southburgh Manor Stud
ch y c Salt Dome (USA) - China Blue (Ahonoora)............... (G Bravery) 3,800
ch y f Fayruz - Gandoorah (Record Token) (C J Hill) 4,000
From Camas Park Stud
ch y c Thatching - Joanne's Joy (Ballymore) .... (Frank Barry) 8,000
b y c Common Grounds - Disco Girl (FR) (Green Dancer)...................... (Peter Doyle Bloodstock) 27,000
Property of Mrs P Grubb, from Big Acre Stud
b y c Exactly Sharp - Cape Of Storms (Fordham)............. (B McMahon) 4,500
Property of a Partnership, from Furnace Mill Stud
ch y c Statoblest - Kuwait Night (Morston) (Darley Stud Management) 23,000
Property of The Cricketers Syndicate, from Furnace Mill Stud
ch y c Risk Me (FR) - Nannie Annie (Persian Bold).................. (Ian Balding) 16,500

396

Property of a Partnership, from Furnace Mill Stud
b y c Sizzling Melody - Martin-Lavell Post (Tina's Pet)........... (Roger Fisher) 5,000
Property of The Cricketers Syndicate, from Furnace Mill Stud
ch y f Absalom - Mrs Kaydagawn (Final Straw)......... (Elmhurst Bloodstock) 10,000
From Furnace Mill Stud
b y c Superlative - Mana (GER) (Windwurf) (R J R Williams) 8,600
b y c Reprimand - Cartooness (USA) (Achieved)............. (Nigel Tinkler) 18,000
ch y c Salt Dome (USA) - Mrs Tittlemouse (Nonoalco)................. (C.B.A.) 5,800
From Newtown Stud
br y c Sizzling Melody - Oriental Splendour (Runnett).... (Peter Doyle Bloodstock) 10,500
From Ashtown House Stud
b y c Minshaanshu Amad (USA) - Glorious Quest (USA) (Hawaii) .... (Abaziz Al Alsaud) 38,000
From Glenvale Stud
ch y c Al Hareb (USA) - Spindle Berry (Dance In Time)......... (Jack Doyle) 20,000
Property of Biddestone Stud, from Biddestone Stud
b y c Charmer - Lutine Royal (Formidable) (James Eustace) 4,100
b y c Rock City - Kalandariya (Kris) .... (Peter Doyle Bloodstock) 17,500

397

Property of Cobhall Court Stud, from Cobhall Court Stud

ch y c Rock City - Silka (ITY) (Lypheor) .... (John Wharton) 38,000

From Hunsley House Stud

b y c Rambo Dancer (CAN) - Fast Line (Klairon)............... (Roger Fisher) 4,000

b y f Rambo Dancer (CAN) - Petiller (Monsanto)................. (Denys Smith) 10,500

From Manor House Farm Stables

gr y c Absalom - Agreloui (Tower Walk) ... (Jack Berry) 9,200

Property of a Partnership, from Manor House Farm Stables

ch y f Efisio - La Crima (Runnymede)...... (Cash) 4,200

Property of Mr J Coombes, from Croft House Stud

b y f Risk Me (FR) - Inca Girl (Tribal Chief) (T H Caldwell) 6,000

Property of High Onn Stud, from High Onn Stud

b y c Tina's Pet - Sequoia (Sassafras)...... (A G Greenwood) 8,200

Property of Mr H Hatfield, from High Onn Stud

ch y c Hadeer - By Surprise (Young Generation)..................... (B McMahon) 2,500

From Ballyelm Stud

b y c Superpower - Najat (Tender King).... (M H Easterby) 4,000

ch y c Clantime - Puff Pastry (Reform)..... (M W Easterby) 5,800

398

Property of Miss B Tierney, from Mooreside Stud

gr y f Cyrano de Bergerac - Sweet Class (Rusticaro)......... (Robert Earnshaw) 5,200

Property of Kilboy Estates, from Lynn Lodge Stud

b y c Contract Law (USA) - Kilboy Concorde (African Sky)........................ (David Minton Bloodstock) 35,000

From Lynn Lodge Stud

ch y c Doulab (USA) - Princess Reema (USA) (Affirmed)......... (Peter Savill) 10,000

br y c Garthorn (USA) - Crossover Dreams (USA) (Buckaroo)................... (G Howson Bloodstock) 23,000

From Glen Andred Stud

b y c Mazilier (USA) - Glint Of Silver (Sallust)........... (G Howson Bloodstock) 5,000

From Red House Stud

br y c Petong - Ruthenia (Taufan) .... (John Balding) 6,000

From Glen Andred Stud

ch y f Mazilier (USA) - Mary Miller (Sharpo) (P Diamond) 2,000

From Yeomanstown Stud

b y c Superpower - Marton Maid (Silly Season)............. (John Benstead) 17,000

b y c Fayruz - Red Note (Rusticaro) .... (David Abell) 27,000

b y c Try My Best (USA) - Amiga Irlande (Whistling Deer)...................... (John Ferguson Bloodstock) 12,000

ch y c Common Grounds - Doon Belle (Ardoon)..... (Jack Doyle Bloodstock) 30,000

399

From Tally-Ho Stud

b y c Contract Law (USA) - Valediction (Town Crier) (J McKeever Bloodstock) 7,000

b y f Contract Law (USA) - Racey Naskra (USA) (Star de Naskra)................ (Peter Doyle Bloodstock) 21,000

b y c Cyrano de Bergerac - Princess Raisa (Indian King) ...... (Martin Fetherston-Godley) 6,200

From Manister House Stud

b y c Try My Best (USA) - Sententious (Kauto Keino)............. (G Conroy) 5,000

b y f Gallic League - Trubbach (Vitiges) .... (Brian Meehan) 2,900

Property of Mr Dan Barry

b y c Magical Strike (USA) - Atlantic Passage (USA) (Buckfinder)............... (R O'Sheen Bloodstock) 2,000

From Eaton House Stud

ch y f Prince Sabo - Piccadilly Etta (Floribunda)............... (Ron Thompson) 2,000

From Elsenham Stud

ch y c Risk Me (FR) - Farras (Song) .... (Peter Doyle Bloodstock) 13,000

ch y f Risk Me (FR) - Genna Kaye (Cure The Fields).................. (B J McMath) 1,000

ch y c Risk Me (FR) - Yukosan (Absalom) .. (G Lewis) 7,400

gr y f Risk Me (FR) - Sir Tangs Gift (Runnet) .... (Cash) 1,000

400

Property of Springfield Thoroughbred Syndicate, from Ardenode Stud

ch y c Aragon - Rest (Dance In Time)...... (E.I.L, McKeever Bloodstock) 10,500

Property of a Partnership, from Farmers Hill Stud

b y f Danehill (USA) - Gaucherie (USA) (Sharpen Up)......... (Michael Jarvis) 12,000

PRIVATE SALES

Property of Mr David Barry

b y f Cyrano de Bergerac - Robin Red Breast (Red Alert)......... (Bill Watts) 1,750

From Hall Farm Stud

b y f Domynsky - Actress (Known Fact).... (Mark Johnston) 1,800

401

DONCASTER
Friday, September 10th
(Yearlings)

Property of Mr M J McEnery, from Rossenarra Stud

ch y c Fayruz - Opening Day (Day Is Done) (Eil, McKeever Bloodstock) 7,800 ch y c Classic Secret (USA) - Very Seldom (Rarity).............. (Peter Easterby) 8,600

Property of Mr R Brewis, from Chester Hill Stud

ch y f Precocious - Maple Syrup (Charlottown).................... (Jack Berry) 9,000

From Hunsley House Stud

b y f Rambo Dancer (CAN) - Ozra (Red Alert)............... (Patrick Haslam) 5,100

Property of Heathavon Stables Ltd, from Three Gates Stud

gr y f Absalom - Valldemosa (Music Boy) .. (John Spearing) 14,000

From Lostford Manor Stud

br y f Efisio - Tame Duchess (Saritamer)... (Abaziz Alsaud) 12,000

Property of Mr A C Birkle, from Dungehill Farm Stud

b y c Belfort (FR) - Grafton Ways (Comedy Star).............. (Bryan McMahon) 2,000

gr y f Belfort (FR) - Gentle Gypsy (Junius).. (Abaziz Alsaud) 7,200

Property of Mrs P M Sly, from Singlecote Stud

b y f Salt Dome (USA) - Frill (Henbit) (Cash) 4,000

br y f Prince Sabo - Mehtab (Touching Wood)....................... (Cash) 2,700

402

From Church Farm Stud

ch y c Roi Danzig (USA) - Teresa Deevey (Runnett)............ (Peter Easterby) 18,000

Property of a Partnership, from Wood Farm Stud

b y f Persian Heights - Edraianthus (Windjammer)... (David Minton Bloodstock) 17,000

ch y f Bairn (USA) - Tawnais (Artaius)...... (Rupert Arnold) 3,000

Property of Mr & Mrs G H Peter-Hoblyn, from Maizey Manor Farm

b y c Then Again - Zahiah (So Blessed).... (Jack Doyle) 10,500

ch y c Ballad Rock - Amanzi (African Sky).. (David Minton Bloodstock) 13,000

b y c Salse (USA) - Karonga (Main Reef)... (Eil, McKeever Bloodstock) 5,000

Property of Mr & Mrs Richard Bowers, from Elms Stud

b y c Statoblest - Placid Pet (Mummy's Pet) .... (Jack Berry) 9,000

Property of New England Stud Farm Ltd, from New England Stud Farm

b y c Midyan (USA) - Saint Cynthia (Welsh Saint)........................ (Cash) 6,400

Property of Campbell Stud, from Campbell Stud

b y f Shaadi (USA) - Echoing (Formidable).. (Charles Booth) 10,500

Property of Mr Dan Barry

b y c Runnett - Sallail (Sallust).. (G Mazza) 4,400

403

From Manister House Stud

b y c Taufan (USA) - Jamie's Girl (Captain James)............ (Gymcrak Racing) 2,000

From Aston Park Stud

ch y c Weldnaas (USA) - Shift Over (USA) (Night Shift)............ (Geoff Lewis) 12,000

Property of a Partnership, from Ballyhampshire Stud

b y c Taufan (USA) - Shannon Lady (Monsanto)..... (David Minton Bloodstock) 13,000

ch y c Mulhollande (USA) - Escape Path (Wolver Hollow)........ (M P Roberts) 4,800

Property of Mr John Rose, from Kilvington Stud

b y c Efisio - Mandrian (Mandamus)....... (James Hetherton) 6,600

From The Zetland Stud

b y c Dominion - High Quail (USA) (Blushing Groom)................ (B J McMath) 5,000

b y c Belfort (FR) - Moushka (Song) (Cash) 3,800

From Glenvale Stud

br y c Scenic - Diamond Lake (King's Lake) (J Pearce) 15,000

Property of Mr Thomas Doherty

b y f Taufan (USA) - Blue Bell Lady (Dunphy)................... (Jack Berry) 2,700

Property of Mr David Barry

b y c Magical Strike (USA) - Theda (Mummy's Pet).............. (B.B.A.) 6,200

404

From Shinglis Stud

b y c Prince Rupert (FR) - Calash (Indian King)....................... (C J Hill) 3,900

Property of Branston Stud, from Branston Stud

b y c Risk Me (FR) - Softly Spoken (Mummy's Pet)...... (Mark Johnston) 9,400

b y f Hallgate - Rose Meadow (Mummy's Game)................. (Nigel Tinkler) 3,000

From Old Meadow Stud

gr y c Standaan (FR) - Right Cash (Right Tack).. (Johnny McKeever Bloodstock) 5,000

Property of Hesmonds Stud

b y c Forzando - Foreseen (Reform)....... (James Eustace) 3,400

br y c Dowsing (USA) - Duboff (So Blessed) .... (Robert Aird) 10,500

b y c Doulab (USA) - Hi There (High Top) .. (Lynn Siddall) 3,600

Property of Rannerdale Trust Ltd, from Genesis Green Stud

ch y c Primo Dominie - Jade Ring (Auction Ring)............ (Miss Gay Kelleway) 15,000

Property of Genesis Green Stud Ltd, from Genesis Green Stud

b or br y f Prince Sabo - Battle Of Flowers (Shernazar).............. (Jack Doyle) 7,400

From Tally-Ho Stud

b y c Fayruz - Timiya (High Top) .... (Jack Doyle) 14,000

b y c Classic Secret (USA) - Hinari Disk Deck (Indian King) .... (Riston Whins Racing Ltd) 5,000

405

From Seaborough Manor Stud

b y f Then Again - Axe Valley (Royben) .... (Neville Bycroft) 7,400

b y f Then Again - Starawak (Star Appeal).. (C.B.A.) 5,000

b y f Then Again - Summer Sky (Skyliner).. (C J Hill) 3,400

From Etchingham Stud
b y c Weldnaas (USA) - Coca (Levmoss)... (M Bastard) 6,200
From Elsenham Stud
br y f Risk Me (FR) - Dona Krista (King Of Spain)............ (Danamore Kuwait) 56,000
ch y f Risk Me (FR) - Dancing Belle (Dance In Time).................. (J Spearing) 16,000
ch y c Risk Me (FR) - Always On A Sunday (Star Appeal) (J McKeever Bloodstock) 10,500
ch y c Risk Me (FR) - High Cairn (FR) (Ela-Mana-Mou).............. (B Meehan) 23,000
Property of a Partnership, from the Aramstone Stud
b y c Persian Heights - Dominion Fayre (Dominion)................ (Jack Berry) 9,000
Property of The Aramstone Stud, from the Aramstone Stud
b y f Squill (USA) - June Fayre (Sagaro).... (J Balding) 3,000

406

From Pinfold Stud
b y c Rambo Dancer (CAN) - Northern Venture (St Alphage)....... (J Pearce) 7,400
Property of Minster Enterprises Ltd, from Minster Stud
ch y f Doulab (USA) - Sovereign Rose (Sharpen Up)........... (J Wainwright) 2,000
Property of Carlton Stud, from Carlton Stud
ch y c Clantime - Hollia (Touch Boy)...... (J McKeever Bloodstock) 14,000
From Furnace Mill Stud
b y c Dowsing (USA) - Gwiffina (Welsh Saint)................... (Roger Fisher) 5,000
Property of Messinger Stud Ltd, from Furnace Mill Stud
gr y f Absalom - Miss Cindy (Mansingh) ... (Eil, McKeever Bloodstock) 10,000
From Furnace Mill Stud
ch y c Statoblest - Miss Petella (Dunphy) .. (J McKeever Bloodstock) 3,800
I, Claudius gr y c Never So Bold - Firelighter (Kalaglow)............. (Mrs V Haigh) 3,400
Property of Messinger Stud Ltd, from Furnace Mill Stud
b y f Bairn (USA) - Cindy's Gold (Sonnen Gold)....................... (T Cooper) 4,000
From Furnace Mill Stud
b y c Presidium - Light de Light (USA) (Fluorescent Light).......... (C J Hill) 6,000
Property of Messinger Stud Ltd, from Furnace Mill Stud
b y f Presidium - Glow Again (The Brianstan).................. (C J Hill) 5,600

407

From Glen Andred Stud
b y c Petong - Lovescene (Carwhite)...... (C.B.A.) 5,000
Property of Mrs Rosemary Bowers & Glen Andred Stud, from Glen Andred Stud
br y f Rock City - Lap Of Honour (Final Straw)...................... (B.B.A.) 10,000
From Glen Andred Stud
gr y f Petong - Jans Contessa (Rabdan).... (J Byrne) 5,000
Property of Mr G Martin, from Glen Andred Stud
b y f Mazilier (USA) - Pattis Pet (Mummy's Pet).......................... (Cash) 3,600
Property of Mr E A Fitzpatrick, from Kilminfoyle House Stud
b y c Merdon Melody - Hsian (Shantung) .. (Jack Doyle Bloodstock) 30,000
Property of Mr Liam Wright, from Kilminfoyle House Stud
b y c Fools Holme (USA) - Oak Queen (King Of Clubs)... (Riston Whins Racing Ltd) 3,100
Property of Carlton Stud, from Carlton Stud
b y f Dominion - Vitry (Vitiges)............ (David Minton Bloodstock) 4,800
From Kirriemuir Stud
b y c Contract Law (USA) - Star Heading (Upper Case)..... (The Winning Team) 9,600
Property of Mr R H Mason, from Wold Newton Stud
b y c Superpower - Song's Best (Never So Bold).......................... (A Jarvis) 20,000
ch y c Superpower - Swinging Baby (Swing Easy)............. (Derby Bloodstock) 7,800

408

Property of I & E Macgregor Partnership, from Pinkerton Stud
b y c Warrshan (USA) - Rattle Along (Tap On Wood) (Eil, McKeever Bloodstock) 9,800
Property of Mr & Mrs J K S Cresswell, from Stoneydale Stud
b y c Puissance - Silvers Era (Balidar)...... (Cash) 3,800
b y f Distant Relative - Stoneydale (Tickled Pink)........... (Greenmeadow Stud) 6,800
Property of Mr G Dudfield
gr y f Petong - Karens Pet (Mummy's Pet) (Danamore Kuwait) 9,600
From Hellwood Stud
b y c Primo Dominie - Spinner (Blue Cashmere)....... (Peter Doyle Bloodstock) 17,000
ch y f Insan (USA) - Hyde Princess (Touch Paper)...... (Peter Doyle Bloodstock) 2,000
From Lilliemore Stud
ch y c Statoblest - Our Mother (Bold Lad).. (Jack Doyle Bloodstock) 18,000
Property of Mrs D Whittingham, from Old Mill Stud
ch y c Handsome Sailor - Scottish Legend (Legend Of France)... (James Bethell) 4,200
Property of a Partnership, from Old Mill Stud
b y f Prince Sabo - Deanta In Eirinn (Red Sunset)............ (M McCormack) 7,200
From Collin Stud
gr y f Primo Dominie - Tabeeba (Diesis) ... (R Whitaker) 9,600
Property of Fluorocarbon Bloodstock, from Chippenham Lodge Stud
gr or ro y c Absalom - Western Line (High Line)......................... (C.B.A.) 4,800
ch y c Absalom - Western Singer (Chief Singer)....................... (Cash) 7,000

409

KILL (Goffs)
Monday, September 20th
(Yearlings)

From Castletown Stud (Agent)
ch y f Double Schwartz - Jenny Diver (USA) (Hatchet Man)........................ (Lisselan Farms Limited) 500

Property of Mr & Mrs G J King from Riverdene Stud
b y c Be My Native (USA) - Judy Loe (Red Alert).............. (Edward O'Grady) 9,000

Property of Danny Halford from Hawkfield Stables
b y f Fayruz - June Lady (Junius).......... (Jack Berry) 3,000

From Beech Farm
b y c Ajraas (USA) - Knapping (Busted) .... (Cash) 2,700

From Clonfert Stud
b y c Jareer (USA) - Ko Samat (On Your Mark)...... (David Minton Bloodstock) 3,600

From Trimblestown Stud
ch y c Carmelite House (USA) - La Cita (Le Levanstell).................... (Cash) 1,500

From Golden View Stud
b y f Fayruz - Lady Bidder (Auction Ring) .. (K McAuliffe) 6,200

Property of Mrs Aisling Smith from Woodhouse Estate Stud
b y c Persian Heights - Lady Danjar (FR) (Nadjar).......... (Brown Bloodstock) 3,500

From Hillcrest Stables
ch y c Simply Great (FR) - Lady Moorfield (Sallust)............ (Mr Frank Barry) 7,400

From Ballysheehan Stud
b y f Fairy King (USA) - Lady Omega (Precocious).. (Lisselan Farms Limited) 5,000

410

From Coolnagour House Stud
b y f Simply Great (FR) - Lady Roberta (USA) (Roberto)............... (Cash) 2,800

From Knockatrina Stud
b y c Ajraas (USA) - Ladyship (Windjammer) .... (David Cosgrove) 3,200

From Beech Farm
ch y c Conquering Hero (USA) - Liqueur (FR) (Vitiges).................. (Cash) 4,200

From Clonfert Stud
br y c Carmelite House (USA) - Little Club (King Of Clubs)....................... (Leinster Bloodstock Agency) 1,000

From Golden Vale Stud
br y f Gallic League - Little Wild Duck (Great Heron)....................... (Cash) 4,000

From Kellistown Stud (Agent)
ch y f Be My Guest (USA) - Lough Graney (Sallust)............ (Mark Johnston) 5,000

From Golden Vale Stud
b y f Gallic League - Lune de Miel (Kalamoun)......................... (Cash) 4,000

Property of Robert Kyle from Knockalavalla Stud
b or br y c Vision (USA) - Madame Fair (Monseigneur)....... (Patrick J Flynn) 6,600

b y f Persian Bold - Maiden Fair (Monseigneur)................ (Patrick J Flynn) 5,000

Property of Michael O'Brien from Golden View Stud
b y f Cyrano de Bergerac - Make Your Bid (Auction Ring).... (Brown Bloodstock) 1,200

411

Property of Robert Ryan
b y f Cyrano de Bergerac - Make Your Mark (On Your Mark)... (Brown Bloodstock) 1,700

From Catherinestown Farm
b y f Waajib - Manela Lady (Ela-Mana-Mou) (M Robinson) 6,200

Property of John Nolan
b y c Mister Majestic - Margo's Mink (FR) (Margouillat)........ (P J Prendergast) 8,000

Property of ABF b.v.b.a. from Waterside Stud Ire.
ch y c Glenstal (USA) - Mattira (FR) (Rheffic) .... (O.V.I.M.) 9,800

Property of Mrs C Lucey from Coolcower Stud
b y f Cyrano de Bergerac - Milzao (Alzao) .. (Lisselan Farms Limited) 1,200

From Oldtown Stud
b y f Nordico (USA) - Miss Kelly (Pitskelly) (T H Caldwell) 4,100

Property of Miss D Flanagan
ch y f Nashamaa - Miss Portal (St Paddy) .. (William Gibbon) 500

From Knockatrina Stud
b y c Common Grounds - Miss Tehran (Manacle)........ (Triolo Alessandro) 1,600

Property of Mrs Margaret Sinanan from Rathmuck Stables
b y f Fayruz - Moira My Girl (Henbit) ...... (Jack Berry) 2,700

From Glidawn Stud
b y c Gallic League - Moss Agate (Alias Smith)......................... (Cash) 4,400

412

Property of Salnic AB from Templerainey House Stud
br y f Kahyasi - Nizamiya (Darshaan)....... (Peter J Doyle) 1,600

Property of Declan McCormick
ch y c Nashamaa - Our Galadrial (Salmon Leap)............. (Mark H Tompkins) 4,200

Property of ABF b.v.b.a. from Waterside Stud Ire
b y f Cyrano de Bergerac - Overstay (Be My Guest).......... (John Francis Bailey) 2,000

From Kildarah Stud
b y c Taufan (USA) - Please Kenneh (Golden Fleece)......... (Browne Bloodstock) 6,200

Property of Anthony J Lowry from Bachelors Lodge Stud
ch y f Jareer (USA) - Polisteppin (Jimmy Reppin)....... (Don Kelly Bloodstock) 500

From Kilnamoragh Stud
ch y c Digamist (USA) - Port-O-Call (Import) (Lisselan Farms Limited) 7,800

From Tara Stud
b y c Kefaah (USA) - Primacara (Rusticaro) (Leinster Bloodstock Agency) 1,100

From Moorfield Stud
b y f Thatching - Quai Des Brumes (USA) (Little Current)................ (Cash) 1,500
From Airlie Stud
b y f Ela-Mana-Mou - Queen Of The Dance (Dancer's Image).... (Brendan Powell) 6,000
Property of James Coogan
b y f Waajib - Red Line Fever (Bay Express) (Cash) 6,000

413

From Kellistown Stud
b y f Posen (USA) - Reet Petite (Thatching) (Lisselan Farms Limited) 3,400
Property of Rowland Blennerhassett from Croom House Stud
b y f Glenstal (USA) - Regent Star (Prince Regent)............... (Peter J Doyle) 5,000
Property of Tim Owens
b y c Red Sunset - Rekolette (Relko) ...... (John Halley M.R.C.V.S.) 2,500
Property of a partnership from Drumconrath Stud
b y f Don't Forget Me - Ribot Ann (Kampala)........................... (Cash) 500
From Ballykisteen Stud Ltd
gr y f Kefaah (USA) - Roof (Thatch)......... (J T Doyle) 1,000
Property of Rathduff Stud
b y f Runnett - Rosa Van Fleet (Sallust).... (Nigel Tinkler) 4,600
From Solohead Stables
b y f Kefaah (USA) - Roscrea (Ballymore) .. (S Bjorling) 1,500
Property of Mr M Morrin
b y c Be My Chief (USA) - Royal Agreement (USA) (Vaguely Noble).......... (Cash) 1,200
Property of a partnership from Drumconrath Stud
b y c Don't Forget Me - Running Feud (Prince Tenderfoot)............ (Cash) 6,000
Property of Des Vere Hunt Farm Co. from Garraun Stud
b y c Mulhollande (USA) - Saintly Angel (So Blessed)............... (Peter J Doyle) 20,000

414

From Golden View Stud
ch y f Imperial Frontier (USA) - Salt (Sallust) (S Bjorling) 2,800
From The Willows Stud
b y c Pennine Walk - Sciambola (Great Nephew).............. (Habton Farms) 3,100
From Piercetown Stud
b y f Pennine Walk - Secret Touch (USA) (Nijinsky's Secret)............. (Cash) 500
From Limefield Stud
b y f Gallic League - Serriyya (Tap On Wood)................ (Peter J Doyle) 500
From Taghadoe Stud, Maynooth
ch y f Pennine Walk - Share The Vision (Vision)........................... (Cash) 1,500
From Milltown Stud
b y f Dance Of Life (USA) - Sheer Innocence (Shirley Heights)........ (Cash) 800

From Eyrefield House Stud
b or br y f Ballad Rock - Shikari Rose (Kala Shikari).............. (J S Wainwright) 2,500
Property of Mr Liam Ormsby from Keyhouse Stud
br y c Kahyasi - Shiyra (Darshaan)......... (Danny Murphy) 9,600
Property of of a partnership from Tipper House Stud
b y c Tirol - Sindos (Busted).... (P D Savill) 5,400
Property of Mrs D Hutch from Ardoon Stud
b y f Try My Best (USA) - Skiskette (Malinowski).......... (Browne Bloodstock) 5,000

415

From Trimblestown Stud
ch y c Carmelite House (USA) - Snap Decision (Bay Express).... (Habton Farms) 1,100
Property of Mr & Mrs Leo Collins from Ennistown Stud
b or br y c Treasure Kay - Social Butterfly (USA) (Sir Ivor).......... (James Ryan) 6,200
Property of Mr T Enright
b y f Scenic - Spun Gold (Thatch) (T Stack) 8,200
From Kellistown Stud (Agent)
b y c Rhoman Rule (USA) - Star Of Dulargy (Burslem)......................... (Cash) 850
Property of Mr John O'Dwyer from Ballyclerigan House Stud
b y f Cyrano de Bergerac - Stony Ground (Relko)........................ (Cash) 4,700
From Knockatrina Stud
b or br y c Fools Holme (USA) - Streamertail (Shirley Heights)................... (European Equine Consultants) 11,500
Property of Mr Liam Ormsby from Keyhouse Stud
b y f Common Grounds - Sussita (On Your Mark)...........(Ms. M Reuterschold) 1,700
From Trimblesdown Stud
ch y c Carmelite House (USA) - Tacheo (Tachypous).......... (Jimmy Coogan) 2,600
From Corbally Stud
b y f Law Society (USA) - Talina (General Assembly)....... (Eamonn Fitzpatrick) 4,500
Property of Mr Arthur T Robinson from Such Moor Stud
b y c Posen (USA) - Tameen (FR) (Pharly).. (Cash) 12,500

416

Property of Mr David Browne from Marsh Farm
ch y f Doulab (USA) - Tappen Zee (Sandhurst Prince)......... (J S Wainwright) 2,800
Property of R J Cullen from October Lodge Stud
b y c Damister (USA) - Thanaa (Wassl) .... (Leinster Bloodstock Agency) 2,800
Property of Mrs D Rudkin from Carrigbeg Stud
ch y f Common Grounds - Topless Dancer (Northfields)................ (C Bjorling) 1,800
Property of Mrs P Grubb from Big Acre Stud
b y c Executive Perk - Track Down (Take A Reef)...................... (Noel Meade) 7,000
From Kellistown Stud (Agent)
b y c Rhoman Rule (USA) - Trojan Honey (Trojan Fen)........... (Danny Murphy) 1,100

From Ballyvolane Stud
b y f Cyrano de Bergerac - Trysting Place (He Loves Me) .... (Lisselan Farms Limited) 3,800
Property of Des Vere Hunt Farm Co from Garraun Stud
b y c Glenstal (USA) - Une Parisienne (FR) (Bolkonski)................... (Cash) 5,200
Property of Mr & Mrs A Faeste from Tourgar House Stud
b y f Soughaan (USA) - Vesperale (Rarity) .. (Pro-Am) 500
From Swordlestown Stud
b y c Exhibitioner - Welsh Rhyme (Welsh Term).................... (Jack Berry) 4,000
From Ballymorris Stud
b y c Contract Law (USA) - Whilst (Dalsaan) .... (Cash) 1,500

417

From Woodview Stud
ch y c Coquelin (USA) - Woolton Hill (Blakeney) .... (Leinster Bloodstock Agency) 1,800
From Kilmannock House
br y c Exactly Sharp (USA) - Alicia Markova (Habat)...... (Lisselan Farms Limited) 4,600
Property of Mr Michawl Sweeney from Abbeyleix Stud
b y c Phardante (FR) - Amendola (FR) (Amen).............. (Jimmy Coogan) 4,600
From Corbal-Lis-Stud
b y c Vision (USA) - Angevin (English Prince).. (Leinster Bloodstock Agency) 4,100
From Mr Raymond A Keogh from Irish National Stud
b y f Dancing Dissident (USA) - An Tig Gaelige (Thatch)........ (Des Hughes) 9,600
From Ballykisteen Stud Ltd.
b y f Superpower - Apocalypse (Auction Ring)................... (Frank Barry) 5,400
From Croom House Stud
b y c Jareer (USA) - Arctic Dark (Arctic Tern) .... (Brian Meehan) 6,700
Property of Mr Brian McDonald from Hollymount House Stud
ch y c Carmelite House (USA) - Base Camp (Derring-Do).................. (Cash) 3,400
From Navan Stables
b y f Tirol - Battine (USA) (Topsider)....... (S Bjorling) 1,500
From Ballymorris Stud
ch y f Al Hareb (USA) - Belle-Cote (Coquelin)................... (Cash) 1,000

418

From Catherinestown Farm
b y f Thatching - Biddy Mulligan (Ballad Rock).......... (B.B.A. (Ireland) Ltd) 4,500
From Ballysheehan Stud
b y f Prince Rupert (FR) - Bluebutton (Blue Cashmere)............... (C Bjorling) 4,000
From Long Acre Stud
ch y c Emmson - Blue Racer (IRE) (Pennine Walk)...................... (Cash) 2,200

From Croom House Stud
ch y c Thatching - Bonny's Niece (FR) (Great Nephew).... (Gerard Hourigan) 4,400
Property of Mr & Mrs Leo Collins from Ennistown Stud
ch y c Shy Groom (USA) - Bradan (Salmon Leap)................ (Frank Barry) 3,100
From Kilnamoragh Stud
ch y c Maelstrom Lake - Bridget O'Bird (USA) (Storm Bird)....... (Frank Barry) 2,500
From Rachel Bennett (Agent)
b y c Roi Danzig (USA) - Broadway Royal (Royal Match)...... (Gerard Hourigan) 7,000
From Kilnamoragh Stud
ch y f Conquering Hero (USA) - Cape Race (USA) (Northern Dancer) .... (Derek Southey) 2,700
From Solohead Stables
b y f Vision (USA) - Caralia (Caracolero) .... (T H Caldwell) 1,000
Property of Mr Anthony J Lowry from Bachelors Lodge Stud
b y f Cyrano de Bergerac - Catherine Clare (Sallust)................ (John Cann) 3,400

419

Property of Mr Eugene Doyle from Beeches Stud
b y f Digamist (USA) - Cathryn's Song (Prince Tenderfoot)............ (Cash) 500
Property of Mr Daniel Twomey from Rathbarry Stud
b y c Mazaad - Ceann-Na-Bann (Doulab) ... (Peter J Doyle) 2,500
From Acorn Stud
b y f Red Sunset - Chase Paperchase (Malinowski).............. (C Bjorling) 3,200
From Liffeyside Stud
b y c Exhibitioner - Cheerleader (Floribunda) .... (J S Wainwright) 3,600
Property of Mr William P Fogarty
b y f Gallic League - Columbian Sand (IRE) (Salmon Leap)................ (Cash) 3,100
From Oak Lodge Stud
b y f Runnett - Countess Kildare (Dominion) .... (Andes Yau) 1,400
From Sunnyhill Stud (Agent)
b y c Conquering Hero (USA) - Currnavaca (Condorcet)........... (Milltown Stud) 1,100
Property of Noel Finegan
b y c Glow (USA) - Daidis (Welsh Pageant) (Torard Stud) 1,200
Property of Salnic AB from Templerainey House Stud
br y f Petorius - Ela Minnie Mou (Ela-Mana-Mou)......................... (Cash) 1,000
Property of Mr Richard A Evans from Coppice Farm
ch y c Waajib - Elle Va Bon (Tanfirion) ..... (J T Doyle) 8,000

420

From Newlands House Stud
b y c Scenic - Embroidery (Lords) .... (Equine Investment Consultants) 8,500

From Rangers Lodge
b y c Prince Rupert (FR) - Eyes On The Prize (Lomond)........................ (Leinster Bloodstock Agency) 1,100

From Ballysheehan Stud
b y c Astronef - Fais Vite (USA) (Sharpen Up).................. (Milltown Stud) 7,200

Property of The Rathduff Stud
b or br y f Sharp Victor (USA) - Fine Flame (Le Prince)................ (C Bjorling) 3,200

Property of Mrs C Lucey from Coolcower Stud
ch y f Phardante (FR) - Finessing (Indian King).. (European Equine Consultants) 1,400

From Rathasker Stud
ch y f Carmelite House (USA) - Fleur-De-Luce (Tumble Wind) .... (Messrs. M & J McEnery) 1,500

Property of Mr Mark Clarke
ch y f Carmelite House (USA) - Flower Petals (Busted)...... (Jimmy Coogan) 1,500

Property of Mrs D Norton from Eyrefield House Stud
b y c Law Society (USA) - Flying Diva (Chief Singer)............. (Gerard Hourigan) 7,000

Property of a partnership from Lakefield Farm
b y c Fairy King (USA) - Gloire de Dijon (Blakeney).............. (K McAuliffe) 4,200

Property of Mr Des Mulhall
b y f Cyrano de Bergerac - Golden Room (African Sky).......... (Kerr & Co Ltd) 2,000

421

From Newlands House Stud
ch y f Ballad Rock - Green Memory (USA) (Forli).. (European Equine Consultants) 4,200

From Cedarwood Stud
b y c Shy Groom (USA) - Griqualand (Connaught)...................... (Cash) 1,000

From Confey Stud (Agent)
ch y c Broken Hearted - Hasten (Northfields)... (Curragh Bloodstock Agency) 5,400

Property of Mr John Hayes from Hillbrook Stud
b y c Salt Dome (USA) - Heather Hut (Shack)................ (John R Parkin) 1,800

From Glidawn Stud
b y f Gallic League - Helcia (Habitat)....... (T H Caldwell) 8,600

From Swordlestown Stud
b y c Prince Rupert (FR) - Hill Of Tara (Royal Palace)......................... (Cash) 5,300

Property of Mr Kennett Hall from Ballynattin House
b y f Jareer (USA) - Holt (Mummy's Pet)... (Cash) 1,300

Property of Mr T J Healy from Nanallac Stud
b or br y c Glenstal (USA) - Indian Honey (Indian King).... (Ms. M Reuterschold) 1,200

Property of Mr William Fogarty
b y f Glenstal (USA) - Indian Sand (Indian King).............. (Donal Cummins) 500

From Loughbrown Stud & Martinstown Farm
b y f Belmez (USA) - In High Spirits (Head For Heights)........... (Frank Barry) 6,600

422

Property of The Five Star Syndicate from Swordlestown Stud
b y f Mulhollande (USA) - Ishara (Blakeney) (European Equine Consultants) 500

From Dara Lodge
b y c Pennine Walk - Ishtar Abu (St Chad) (J T Doyle) 18,000

From Swordlestown Stud
b or br y f Vision (USA) - Island Morn (USA) (Our Native).................. (Cash) 1,100

From Carrick Stables
b y c Glow (USA) - Ivory Smooth (USA) (Sir Ivor)........................... (Cash) 1,600

Property of Mr & Mrs John Collins
b y c Broken Hearted - Khatiynza (Nishapour)................... (Cash) 2,400

Property of Mr John Malone from Oak Lodge Stud
ch y c Pennine Walk - Peace Princess (On Your Mark)............ (T H Caldwell) 1,200
b y f Pennine Walk - Fraudulent (Sexton Blake)........... (Peadar Matthews) 800

423

FAIRYHOUSE (Tattersalls)

Tuesday, September 21st (Yearlings)

From Mount Coote Stud
ch y f Shernazar - Jassamy Hall (Crowned Prince) (Johnny McKeever Bloodstock) 2,000

From Scarteem Stud
b y c Petorius - Jubilant (Welsh Pageant) .. (John Quinn) 1,800

Property of Helen Cosgrove
b y f Al Hareb (USA) - June Goddess (Junius).................. (W Schutz) 2,600

From Kildaragh Stud
b y f Carmelite House (USA) - Kabbaala (Brigadier Gerard)................... (German International Bloodstock) 2,000

From Slievardagh Stud
ch y c Deploy - Kai (Kalamoun) (C A Smith) 1,000

From Carrigbeg Stud
b y c Nordico (USA) - Kalonji (Red Alert) ... (C Gordon-Watson Bloodstock) 7,600

From Bewlands House Stud
b y f Petorius - Kentucky Wildcat (Be My Guest)............. (Ernie Weymes) 13,500

Property of Mr David Cornwall, from Morganstown Stud
b y c Broken Hearted - Killyhevlin (Green God)......................... (Cash) 4,500

Property of the late Mr Alan A Alcorn
b y f Cyrano de Bergerac - Konigin Kate (GER) (Authi) .... (C Gordon-Watson Bloodstock) 10,000

From Longfield Stud (Agent)
b y c Tirol - La Patruschka (Ballad Rock) ... (Lisselan Farms Ltd) 3,000

424

Property of Mr John McCartan
ch y f Al Hareb (USA) - Lady Betting (Bustino)................ (Frank Barry) 1,100

Property of Helen Cosgrove
b y c Gallic League - Lady Portobello (Porto Bello)............... (Pat Donworth) 1,400

Property of Mr Kevin Twomey, from Rathbarry Stud (Agent)
ch y c Gadabout (USA) - Leaping Salmon (Salmon Leap)........ (John McGrath) 1,000
From Carrigbeg Stud
gr y c Common Grounds - Legs And Things (Three Legs).................. (C B A) 10,000
From Scarteen Stud
b y f Last Tycoon - Little Me (Connaught).. (Michael Cunningham) 4,900
Property of Aghern House Stud
b y c Fairy King (USA) - Look Of Love (General Assembly)................. (Brown Bloodstock) 5,000
Property of Catherine O'Malley, from Golden Hills Stud
ch y f Simply Great (FR) - Magic Gold (Sallust)............. (Ward O'Malley) 1,100
From Belmont Stud
b y f Simply Great (FR) - Majesty's Nurse (Indian King).............. (R Berneyl) 2,400
Property of Mr Kevin J Molloy, from Dolland House Stud
gr y f Don't Forget Me - Maraquiba (FR) (Kenmare)............... (D Triquart) 6,200
Property of a Partnership, from Herbertstown Stables
b y c Maelstrom Lake - Middle Verde (USA) (Sham)................. (Frank Barry) 6,200

425

Property of Mr Denis Hackett
b y c Grey Desire - Minizen Lass (Hittite Glory)...................... (Ml Hill) 4,700
From Airlie Stud
b y c Reprimand - Minnie Tudor (Tudor Melody)........................... (J Doyle For The Winning Team) 25,000
Property of Mr Seamus Phelan, from Weyland Studs
ch y f Primo Dominie - Miss Suntan (Bruni) (Lord Huntingdon) 13,500
From Knocklong House Stud (Agent)
b y f Law Society - Missing You (Ahonoora) .... (Conrad Allen) 5,800
From Lynn Lodge Stud
br y c Gallic League - Mixed Feelings (Junius)............................. (European Equine Consultants) 3,600
From Tally-Ho Stud
gr y c Classic Secret - Monrovia (FR) (Dancer's Image) (Lisselan Farms Ltd) 14,000
Property of Mr Michael Looby
ro or gr y c Shy Groom (USA) - More Magnanimous (King Persian).......... (Riston Whins Racing Ltd) 2,000
Property of Cyril Humpris Esq, from Islanmore Stud
ch y f Scottish Reel - Mother Courage (Busted).................... (C B A) 3,600
From Slievardagh Stud
ch y c Deploy - Musical Charm (USA) (The Minstrel)............ (Jimmy Coogan) 2,200
From Ballylinch Stud (Agent)
ch y f Keen - Nememsha (Roberto) .... (Sir Mark Prescott) 6,600

426

From Knocklong House Stud (Agent)
b y f High Estate - Nora Yo Ya (Ahonoora) (C Gordon-Watson Bloodstock) 9,000
From Rossenarra Stud (Agent)
ch y c Fayruz - Nous (Le Johnstan)........ (Tom Mullins) 8,800
Property of Mr Nicholas Galvin
b y c Anita's Prince - Ottavia Abu (Octavo) (Cash) 5,900
From Islanmore Stud
b y c Pennine Walk - Oystons Propweekly (Swing Easy)............ (Frank Barry) 19,000
Property of Mrs J Murphy
b y c Pennine Walk - Pampered Rose (Saulingo).... (Roger Allez Bloodstock) 2,750
From Longfield Stud (Agent)
b y f Scenic - Pansoverina (Sovereign Path) (Peter Doyle Bloodstock) 3,800
Property of Mr J R Mitchell, from Beechgrove Stud
b y c Indian Ridge - Patchinia (Patch)...... (C Gordon-Watson Bloodstock) 10,500
From Airlie Stud
ch y c Salt Dome (USA) - Penny Habit (Habitat)................ (Jack Doyle) 5,800
Property of Mr Ted Coonan, from Springfield Farm
b y c Prince Rupert (FR) - Persian Mistress (IRE) (Persian Bold)............ (Cash) 3,100
From Dunmore Stud
gr y f Scenic - Pete's Money (USA) (Caucasus).............. (Joanna Morgan) 9,200

427

Property of Mr John Hutchinson
ch y f Fayruz - Picnic Basket (Pharly)...... (W Schutz) 1,400
Property of Mr P J O'Hagan
b y f Classic Secret (USA) - Plunket's Choice (Home Guard)................ (Lisselan Farms Ltd) 5,000
From Slievardagh Stud
ch y c Belmez (USA) - Poplina (USA) (Roberto)........................... (Axel Donnerstag Bloodstock) 7,200
From Ballyhampshire Stud
b y c Cyrano de Bergerac - Postie (Sharpo) (Sir Mark Prescott) 21,000
Property of Mr John McLoughlin
b y f Pennine Walk - Pounding Beat (Ya Zaman).................... (C Elsey) 3,200
Property of Mr H Lecky, from Carrick Stables
gr y c Standaan (FR) - Prairie Saint (Welsh Saint).............. (Oak Lodge Stud) 5,000
From Ballylinch Stud (Agent)
b y c Groom Dancer (USA) - Preoccupy (Habitat).............. (R Hollinshead) 2,000
From Yeomanstown Stud
b y f Common Grounds - Princess Nabila (USA) (King Pellinore)................ (David Minton Bloodstock) 10,000
From Ballyburn Stud
ch y f Red Sunset - Purple Princess (Right Tack).................. (Con Collins) 3,000
From Yeomanstown Stud
ch y c Imperial Frontier (USA) - Push Bike (Ballad Rock)......................... (German International Bloodstock) 15,000

428

From Ballymorris & Caherass Studs

b y c Midyan (USA) - Queen Of Aragon (Aragon)............ (Brian J Meehan) 6,600

Property of Mr Michael Morrin

b y c Gallic League - Rashana (Sharpen Up) (R O'Ryan) 4,600

Property of Kathleen Reynolds, from Rathbawn House

ch y c Simply Great (FR) - Rathbawn Realm (Doulab)............... (E A M Maas) 16,000

From Windsor Stud

ch y f Classic Secret (USA) - Reasonably French (Reasonable).................. (Axel Donnerstag Bloodstock) 2,400

Property of Travers Bros

b y c Nashamaa - Reelin Elly (Pitskelly).... (Tim Easterby) 3,400

From Staffordstown

b or br y f Nishapour (FR) - Reflected Glory (SWE) (Relko)........... (Mrs Spitzer) 1,800

From Dollanstown Stud (Agent)

b y f Anita's Prince - Regal Charmer (Royal And Regal)........ (Julian Lloyd) 3,100

From Islanmore Stud

br y c Exactly Sharp (USA) - Regal Entrance (Be My Guest)......... (E A M Maas) 8,200

From Killossera House Stud

b y c The Noble Player (USA) - Regal Step (Ribero)................... (Cash) 1,100

Property of International Thoroughbred Breeders Inc, from Round Hill Stud

b y f Scenic - Regal Twin (USA) (Majestic Prince).. (Leinster Bloodstock Agency) 6,800

429

From Scarteen Stud

b y f Cyrano de Bergerac - Ring Dem Bells (Simply Great)...................... (David Minton Bloodstock) 1,800

Property of Mr David Bourke

b or br y f Contract Law (USA) - Rockalong Rosie (Martinmas).... (Brian Meehan) 2,000

Property of Mr James McMullin, from Rathasker Stud

b y f Double Schwartz - Romanovna (Mummy's Pet)....... (Brian Meehan) 2,500

From Moneycooley Stud

b y c Prince Rupert (FR) - Rosa Bengala (Balidar)................................ (German International Bloodstock) 6,800

From Rathbarry Stud (Agent)

b y c Fools Holme (USA) - Royal Cloak (Hardicanute)......... (Ger Hourigan) 6,200

Property of Mr Denis McDonnell

b y f Reprimand - Royal Custody (Reform) (Tim Easterby) 1,100

From Mount Coote Stud

b y f Fools Holme (USA) - Royal Respect (Kings Lake)......................... (German International Bloodstock) 3,400

Property of Clody E Norton, from Newtownbarry House Stud

br y f Gallic League - Run Bonnie (Runnett) (Cormac McCormack Associates) 8,000

b y f Tirol - Run My Beauty (Runnett)...... (C E Brittain) 8,500

From Tally-Ho Stud

b y f Gallic League - Sassalin (Sassafras)... (Charlie Elsey) 3,500

430

From Shambo Stud

b or br y c Scenic - Saybya (Sallust)....... (Pro Am) 23,000

From Waterside Stud (Tara)

ch y c Hatim (USA) - Scottish Welcome (Be My Guest)......................... (Cormac McCormack Bloodstock) 4,800

From Ballymorris & Caherass Studs

b y f Ballad Rock - Secret Heart (Vision) ... (E A M Maas) 6,600

From Grangegodden Stud

b y f Nordico (USA) - Sharp Ego (USA) (Sharpen Up)........ (B B A (England)) 21,000

From Ballylinch Stud (Agent)

b y c Dance Of Life (USA) - Sharp Dresser (USA) (Sharpen Up).................. (German International Bloodstock) 6,200

Property of Mrs C O'Sullivan, from The Rath Farm

b y f Taufan (USA) - Shirotae (Florescence) (Cormac McCormack Associates) 8,800

From Slievardagh Stud

b y c Gallic League - Shy Jinks (Shy Groom) .... (M Thwaites) 14,500

Property of Mr Kevin J Molloy, from Dolland House Stud

b y f Scenic - Sloane Ranger (Sharpen Up) (B B A (Italia)) 8,200

From Windsor Stud

b y f Hatim (USA) - Space Mark (On Your Mark)................ (T O'Mara) 1,000

Property of Annemarie O'Brien

b y f Fayruz - Splendid Yankee (Yankee Gold)............ (Paddy Prendergast) 5,000

431

Property of International Thoroughbred Breeders Inc, from Round Hill Stud

b y c Nordico (USA) - Spring Snow (Reliance II)............ (B B A (England)) 4,500

From Newlands House Stud

b y c Red Sunset - Stradey Lynn (Derrylin) (Mark Johnston) 9,400

From Slievardagh Stud

b y f Slip Anchor - Star Of Dance (Sadler's Wells)................. (R Whittaker) 1,200

From Lodge Park Stud

ch y f Don't Forget Me - Stomata (USA) (Storm Bird)........ (B B A (England)) 2,700

From Airlie Stud

b y c Shernazar - Sun Bed (Habitat) .... (German International Bloodstock) 7,200

b y c Petorius - Surfing (Grundy).......... (C E Brittain) 26,000

From Moneycooley Stud

b y f Simply Great (FR) - Tanimara (Sassafras)............ (M Bannens) 2,600

Property of Mr Michael Morrin

ch y c Simply Great (FR) - Thalssa (Rusticaro)........ (Peter Doyle Bloodstock) 5,000

From Yeomanstown Stud
b y c King Luthier - The Saltings (FR) (Morston)................ (Frank Barry) 11,000
From Rathbarry Stud (Agent)
b or br y f Jareer (USA) - Timinala (Mansingh)................ (E A M Maaas) 6,800

432

From Tally-Ho Stud
b y c Contract Law (USA) - Tora Tora (Home Guard)........................ (Peter Doyle Bloodstock) 13,500
From Airlie Stud
b y f Ela-Mana-Mou - Torriglia (USA) (Nijinsky)........... (Rossenarra Stud) 3,000
From Longfield Stud (Agent)
ch y f Caerleon (USA) - Tremulous (Gregorian)....................... (Cash) 7,000
Property of Owen Bourke
b y f Digamist (USA) - Trust Sally (Sallust) (R Berney) 3,000
From Airlie Stud
b y f Ballad Rock - Walliser (Niniski)....... (Frank Barry) 15,000
Property of R J McKenna
b y c Exhibitioner - Whatawoman (Tumble Wind).................. (George Hill) 13,000
Property of Nesbeitt Bros, from Carrick Stables
b y c Homo Sapien - Wolviston (Wolverlife) (German International Bloodstock) 3,000
From Slievardagh Stud
b y c Top Ville - Woolpack (Golden Fleece) (Mark Johnston) 4,200
From Rathasker Stud
b y f Scenic - Yellow Orchid (On Your Mark) .... (R O Sheen Bloodstock) 1,000
Property of J McEnery, from Rossenarra Stud
ch y f Roi Danzig (USA) - Yellow Pages (Yellow God)....... (Axel Donnerstag) 4,600

433

Property of Martin Kennelly, from Mylerstown Stud
ch y c Pennine Walk - Abrika (Dominion)... (G Hourigan) 5,000
From Slievardagh Stud
ch y c Ballad Rock - Ajuga (USA) (The Minstrel).............. (E A M Maas) 19,000
From Staffordstown
b y f Nishapour (FR) - Allegra (Niniski)..... (Equine Services) 6,000
From Slievardagh Stud
b y f Bluebird (USA) - Amata (USA) (Nodouble)............. (Margaret O'Toole) 19,000
From Mount Coote Stud
b y f Fools Holme (USA) - Amber Lightning (On Your Mark)....... (R M Whitaker) 6,000
Property of Paul Hardy, from Rathasker Stud
b y f Cyrano de Bergerac - Another Match (Sovereign Path)..................... (German International Bloodstock) 2,200
From Craddockstown Lodge Stud
b y c Fayruz - Arwa (Hot Spark)........... (Camas Park Stud) 10,500
From Ballyhane Stud
b y c Thatching - Ascensiontide (Ela-Mana-Mou)................ (Sheena Collins) 6,000

From Belmont Stud
b y c Runnett - Ashkatina (Ashford)....... (John Quinn) 2,500
Property of John McLoughlin
ch y f Fayruz - Ashley Springs (Ballymore) (Con Collins) 1,500

434

From Knocktoran Stud
ch y c Common Grounds - Astral Fields (FR) (Northfields).................. (C B A) 6,000
Property of Aghern House Stud
b y c Jolly Jake (NZ) - Bases Loaded (USA) (Northern Dancer)..... (Liam Browne) 8,000
Property of Patrick F Toole, from Curkeen House
ch y f Magical Strike (USA) - Bel Ria (Gay Fandango)............... (C A Smith) 1,000
From Tsarina Stud
b y c Prince Rupert (FR) - Belle Viking (FR) (Riverman)... (Peter Doyle Bloodstock) 9,000
From Moneycooley Stud
b y f Prince Rupert (FR) - Beloved Mistress (Rarity)............ (Henry Ponsonby) 3,400
From Long Hill Stud
b y c Dancing Dissident (USA) - Betty Bun (St Chad)............ (R M Whittaker) 8,300
Property of a Partnership, from Rathbarry Stud
ch y f Roi Danzig - Bilander (High Line).... (Malcolm Thwaites) 5,800
Property of Seamus Phelan, from Weylands Stud
b y f Sizzling Melody - Bold Duchess (Persian Bold).................... (Cash) 3,600
From Kildaragh Stud
b y f Posen (USA) - Brave Ivy (Decoy Boy) (William R Muir) 3,200
Property of Martin Kennelly, from Mylerstown Stud
br y f Pennine Walk - Brigadier's Nurse (Brigadier Gerard)..................... (European Equine Consultants) 5,100

435

Property of Lee Donald Taicher, from The Irish National Stud Co Ltd
ch y c Digamist (USA) - California Roll (USA) (Key To Content).......... (W Schutz) 3,200
Property of Sean Scully
ch y f Be My Native (USA) - Chance Match (Royal Match).................. (Cash) 2,000
From Hilltown Stables
ch y f Zalazl (USA) - Choral Dancer (USA) (Night Shift)........... (Charlie Elsey) 2,400
Property of Southfork Investments, from Corballis
ch y c Dominion Royale - Ciarain's Choice (Young Emperor).. (Malcolm Thwaites) 5,000
From Carrick Stables
b y c Digamist (USA) - Clifton Beach (Auction Ring)............. (Mick Roberts) 3,500
Property of Seamus Phelan, from Weylands Stud
b y f Gallic League - Clogher Head (Sandford Lad)................ (Jack Berry) 11,000

Property of E A Fitzpatrick, from Kilminfoyle House Stud
b y c Ajraas (USA) - Clubhouse Turn (USA) (King Of Clubs)....... (Danny Murphy) 7,300
Property of Helen Smith
b y f Classic Secret (USA) - Coral Cave (Ashmore)................ (N Jurgen) 2,000
Property of John Hennessy
gr y c Magical Strike (USA) - Covey's Quick (Godswalk)......................... (Leinster Bloodstock Agency) 2,100
From Plunkett Lodge
ch y f Digamist (USA) - Crecora (Royal Captive).................... (O Brady) 3,400

436

From Ardmayle House Stud (Agent)
ch y c The Noble Player (USA) - Crepe de Paille (Final Straw)....... (G Hourigan) 4,000
From Craddockstown Lodge
b y c Keen - Crimson Robes (Artaius)...... (Richard McCormick) 8,400
Property of Dr Frank Healy
ch y f Simply Great - Dance Or Bust (Try My Best)................ (G Hourigan) 1,500
Property of Mrs Clody E Norton, from Newtownbarry House Stud
ch y f Absalom - Dancing Line (High Line) (Jack Berry) 7,700
Property of Anthony Cahill
b y f Waajib - Davill (Record Token) (Cash) 4,200
From Sion House Stud (Agent)
ch y c Waajib - Divine Apsara (Godswalk).. (P Savill) 18,000
From Mellon Stud
b y f Nordico (USA) - Donnarella (Dom Racine).................. (R Hannon) 9,000
From Ballylinch Stud
b or br y f Bob Back (USA) - Doonanore (Ahonoora).................. (W Kane) 1,500
Property of St Simon Foundation, from Ballysax Manor Stud
b y c Treasure Kay - Dublin Millennium (Dalsaan)..................... (Cash) 5,000
From Jigginstown House Stud
b y f Pennine Walk - Eimkar (Junius) ...... (European Equine Consultants) 4,600

437

From Tally-Ho Stud
gr y f Classic Secret (USA) - Eternal Optimist (Relko)..... (Leinster Bloodstock) 2,600
From Knocktoran Stud
b y c In The Wings - Evening Kiss (Kris)... (D Walker) 4,000
From Lupin Stud
b y f Classic Secret (USA) - Exotic Dancer (Posse)............... (T Alessandro) 1,200
From Lynn Lodge Stud
b y c Petorius - Farnacliffe (Taufan)........ (M P Roberts) 2,100
Property of Mr John Bowdren
b y f Al Hareb (USA) - Femme de Fer (USA) (Mr Leader).................. (Cash) 1,000

From Mellon Stud
b y c Sure Blade (USA) - Fencing (Viking).. (Cash) 5,000
From Leinster Stud
b y c Ajraas (USA) - Fifty Grand (Ballad Rock)...................... (C Allen) 1,000
Property of Mr J R Mitchell, from Beechgrove Stud
ch y c Blow The Whistle - Final Game (Pardao)............ (Mark Tompkins) 2,600
From Tally-Ho Stud
b y c Mazaad - Finely Feathered (Prince Tenderfoot).......... (B B A (Ireland)) 7,000
From Windsor Stud
b y c Classic Secret (USA) - Finlarrig (Thatching)............ (B B A (Italia)) 8,400

438

From Dollanstown Stud (Agent)
b y c Anita's Prince - First Wind (Windjammer)......................... (Cash) 2,900
From Larch Hill Stud
b y c Classic Secret (USA) - Flaming Katie (Blue Refrain)........ (Edward Lynam) 2,200
From Lodge Park Stud
b y f Persian Heights - Folle Remont (Prince Tenderfoot).......... (Mark Johnston) 4,000
Property of the Exors of the Late Major V McCalmont, from Norelands Stud
b y f Petorius - Forest Of Arden (Tap On Wood)...................... (Julie Cecil) 15,000
Property of Round Hill Stud
b y c Exactly Sharp (USA) - Frans Cap (Captain James)........ (Tom Mullins) 5,800
From Waterside Stud (Tara)
b y c Red Sunset - Free Rein (Sagaro)..... (J G FitzGerald) 8,000
Property of Mr Gerald Carey, from Athgarvan Farm
b y c Dancing Dissident (USA) - Friendly Sound (Be Friendly).... (John Banens) 6,800
From Hamwood & Mitchelstown Stud
b y c Taufan (USA) - Future Shock (Full Out) .... (Mark Tompkins) 6,000
From Islanmore Stud
br y f Don't Forget Me - Gaelic Jewel (Scottish Rifle).......... (H Ponsonby) 7,200
From Ballymorris & Caherass Studs
b y c Nashamaa - Giddy Lyn (USA) (Relko) (Peter Doyle Bloodstock) 6,000

439

Property of Stonethorn Stud Farms, from Carrowdore Castle Stud
b y c Magical Strike (USA) - Golden Pheasant (Henbit).... (Browne Bloodstock) 7,000
From Moorfield Stud
ch y c Salt Dome (USA) - Good Behaviour (Artaius)................... (W Schutz) 2,800
Property of Ms C O'Brien
ch y f Al Hareb (USA) - Gorgeous Twist (Hello Gorgeous)........ (M Thwaites) 1,000

From Newlands House Stud
b y c Runnett - Grace de Bois (Tap On Wood)................ (M Thwaites) 7,000
From Killeenlea Stud
b y c Anita's Prince - Grave Error (Northern Treat).................. (Andes Yan) 2,100
From Longfield Stud (Agent)
b y f Persian Heights - Hana Marie (Formidable)... (C Gordon-Watson Bloodstock) 11,000
Property of Mr T J Hurley, from Rathbarry Stud
b y c Roi Danzig (USA) - Hear Me (Simply Great)................ (C J Wheeler) 5,000
Property of Mr G J Cullinan, from Horse Park Stud
b y f Pennine Walk - Heather Lil (Ballymore) .... (Peter Doyle Bloodstock) 3,000
Property of Newberry Stud Farm Ltd
b y c Vision (USA) - Ho Han Wai (Sassafras) .... (German International Bloodstock) 3,000
From Rathbarry Stud
ch y f Roi Danzig (USA) - Honagh Lee (Main Reef)............... (David Cosgrove) 1,000

440

Property of Cortown Stud
b y f Classic Secret (USA) - Houwara (IRE) (Darshaan).................... (Cash) 1,700
Property of Mr Gary Simpson, from Rathmolyon House Stud
b y c Nashamaa - How Gorgeous (Frimley Park)............................. (German International Bloodstock) 5,300
From Staffordstown
b y f Ela-Mana-Mou - Ibtihaj (USA) (Raja Baba)............................. (Cormac McCormack Associates) 29,000
Property of Mr Patrick J Walshe, from Foxhall Stud
b or br y c Magical Strike (USA) - Idle Gossip (Runnett)...... (R Hollinshead) 10,000
Property of Mr M J McEnery, from Rossenarra Stud
gr y c Fayruz - Ikala (Lashkari)...... (Cash) 3,500
Property of The Irish National Stud Co Ltd
ch y f Magical Strike (USA) - Inis Ealga (Sallust)............. (Edward Lynam) 12,000
Property of Mr D McAuley, from Ballylinch Stud
b y f Posen (USA) - Innate (Be My Native) (John McLaughlin) 2,000
From Killeenlea Stud
ch y c Salt Dome (USA) - Insight (Ballad Rock).... (John Ferguson Bloodstock) 2,200
From Charlestown Stud
ch y c Jester - Intellect (Frimley Park)..... (Peter Doyle Bloodstock) 2,000
From Larch Hill Stud
b y c Doulab (USA) - Irish Bride (Track Spare).............. (Edward Lynam) 2,600
From Lynn Lodge Stud
b y c Never So Bold - Irish Impulse (USA) (Irish River)................ (R O'Ryan) 4,800
Property of Helen Smith
b y f Classic Secret (USA) - Island Adventure (Touching Wood)...... (L Caffrey) 1,500

441

FAIRYHOUSE (Tattersalls)
Wednesday, September 22nd (Yearlings)

Property of Mr J G Patterson, from Richmond Lodge Stud
ch y f Pennine Walk - Jazirah (Main Reef).. (Geraldine Rees) 4,000
From Mellon Stud
b y f Fools Holme (USA) - Just Fabulous (FR) (Fabulous Dancer)... (Con Collins) 6,500
From Staffordstown
b y f Be My Chief (USA) - Kalaya (Tanerko) (Julie Cecil) 10,000
b y f Nishapour (FR) - Kamada (USA) (Blushing Groom)............ (B.B.A. (Italia)) 13,500
From Longfield Stud (Agent)
b y f Alzao (USA) - Kasala (USA) (Blushing Groom)............... (B.B.A. (Italia)) 5,800
Property of Mr Owen Bourke
b y f Contract Law (USA) - Keen Note (Sharpo)............... (Conrad Allen) 3,000
From Dunsany Stud
b y c Mon Tresor - Kelly's Risc (Pitskelly).. (Peter Doyle Bloodstock) 5,800
From Tara Stud (As Agent)
b y c Petorius - Kilvarnet (Furry Glen)...... (R Hollinshead) 5,000
From Corduff Stud
ch y c Salt Dome (USA) - La Duse (Junius) (C.B.A.) 5,600
From Ballylinch Stud (Agent)
b y f Dance Of Life (USA) - La Francaise (USA) (Jim French)..... (B.B.A. (Italia)) 4,500

442

From Glenvale Stud (Agent)
b y c Simply Great (FR) - La Tanque (USA) (Last Raise)......................... (Equine Investment Consultants) 10,000
From Riverside Stud
ch y f Waajib - Lady Fandet (Gay Fandango) .... (H Ponsonby) 5,500
From Ardrums House Stud
b y c Astronef - Lady Heather (Manado) ... (German International Bloodsdtock) 10,000
From Redpender Stud
b y f Fairy King (USA) - Laureon (Caerleon) (Mick Channon) 10,000
From Glenvale Stud (Agent)
b y f Scenic - Layer Cake (Levmoss) ...... (German International Bloodstock) 4,600
From Sweep Lane Stud
b y c Maelstrom Lake - Lisdoonvarna (Miami Springs) .... (Peter Doyle Bloodstock) 4,600
From Wraymount Stud
b y f Ballad Rock - Little Cynthia (Wolver Hollow)........... (John Wainwright) 1,000
Property of Mr P J Doyle
b y c Salt Dome (USA) - Little Honey (Prince Bee).............. (R Berneyl) 1,000

From Graigueshoneen Stud
b y f Common Grounds - Little Sega (FR) (Bellypha)................. (U Muller) 2,400
From Dollandstown Stud (Agent)
ch y f Weldnaas (USA) - Littleton Song (Song).................... (J Harley) 5,000

443

From Sagamore Stud
b y f Prince Rupert (FR) - Llanelli (Welsh Saint)..... (John Ferguson Bloodstock) 1,400
From Meadow Lane Farm
b y f Satco (FR) - Lucky Fountain (IRE) (Lafontaine)............................ (German International Bloodstock) 1,000
Property of Mr Mark Bourke
b y f Contract Law (USA) - Maid Of Mourne (Fairy King).......... (Mark Johnston) 2,100
Property of Mr Peter Loughran
b y c Sovereign Water (FR) - Marchesana (March Past)........................ (German International Bloodstock) 1,000
Property of Mr Jeremiah Daly, from Kilcaskin Stud
ch y c Don't Forget Me - Maypole Hie (Bold Lad)........................ (Cash) 2,000
From Woodlands Stables
ch y c Rhoman Rule (USA) - Meadow Air (Coquelin)................. (W Schutz) 1,550
From Yeomanstown Stud
b y c Ela-Mana-Mou - Merry Twinkle (Martinmas).................. (Jack Berry) 16,500
Property of Stonethorn Stud Farms Limited, from Carrowdore Castle Stud
b y c Simply Great (FR) - Mey (Canisbay) .. (T Alessandro) 1,000
Property of Mr Tom Radley, from Claramount Stud
b y c Pennine Walk - Micro Mover (Artaius) (Peter Doyle Bloodstock) 6,600
Property of Ballyboher Stud
gr y f Runnett - Mine At Last (Nishapour) .. (W Schutz) 2,600

444

Property of Mr Owen O'Leary
b y f Taufan (USA) - Miss Bagatelle (Mummy's Pet)........... (C Gordon-Watson Bloodstock) 5,000
From Killarkin Stud
ch y c Formidable (USA) - Misty Lady (Habitat).................. (C Gordon-Watson Bloodstock) 24,000
From Sweep Lane Stud
b y c Cyrano de Bergerac - Mitsubishi Art (Cure The Blues)....... (John McGrath) 2,200
From Lynn Lodge Stud
b y f Imperial Frontier (USA) - Morning Stroll (Tower Walk).......... (C Elsey) 6,400
From Corduff Stud
b y c Waki River (FR) - Mrs Feathers (Pyjama Hunt)........... (Frank Barry) 15,500
Property of Mr Patrick Brady
ch y c Pennine Walk - Mrs Lucky (Royal Match).................... (J Harley) 5,000

Property of a Syndicate, from Ballymoney Park
b y c Pharly (FR) - Mums (Mummy's Pet) .. (David Cosgrove) 7,500
From Tara Stud
ch y c Kefaah (USA) - Musical Horn (Music Boy)............... (Rd. McCormack) 7,000
From Killarkin Stud
b y c Mister Majestic - My Louise (Manado) .... (Jack Berry) 13,000
From Egmont Stud
b y c Astronef - My Natalie (Rheingold)..... (J Banens) 4,200

445

From Rock Abbey Stud (Agent)
b y f Nordico (USA) - Nephrite (Godswalk) (Henry Ponsonby) 3,000
From Ballylinch Stud (Agent)
ch y f Keen - Night Starker (USA) (Northrop) ...... (European Equine Investments) 1,000
Property of Mrs A Whitehead, from Broadfield Stud
ch y c Exhibitioner - On The Road (On Your Mark) .... (German International Bloodstock) 3,000
From Rathbarry Stud
b y f Petorius - Overseas Wealth (USA) (Forli)............................... (German International Bloodstock) 1,000
From Egmont Stud
b y f Hatim (USA) - Passage Falcon (Falcon) .... (Axel Donnerstag) 1,000
Property of Mr John Malone
b y f Petorius - Peace Mission (Dunbeath) (Johnny McKeever Bloodstock) 4,000
From Coppice Farm
b y f Scenic - Peaches And Cream (FR) (Rusticaro)................... (Cash) 1,300
From Ardmayne Stud
b or br y c Montekin - Peggy Dell (Sovereign Gleam)............ (Frank Carr) 3,600
Property of Mr J M Lyons
b y c Glenstal (USA) - Perfect Choice (Bold Lad)......................... (Cash) 1,500
Property of Mr Liam Ormsby, from Keyhouse Stud
gr y f Mon Tresor - Perlesse (Bold Lad).... (Axel Donnerstag) 1,400

446

From Killarkin Stud
ch y c Glow (USA) - Persian Myth (Persian Bold).................. (R McCormick) 10,000
Property of a Partnership, from Gurteenard Stud
ch y f Astronef - Pharjoy (FR) (Pharly)..... (Peter Doyle Bloodstock) 6,800
From Coolnagour House Stud
b y f Pennine Walk - Place Dauphine (Sea Hawk II)............... (B.B.A. (Italia)) 1,000
From Ballylinch Stud (Agent)
b y f King Of Clubs - Preservationist (Sadler's Wells)........ (B.B.A. (Italia)) 1,500
From Tally-Ho Stud
b y f Contract Law (USA) - Prissy Miss (Free State).... (Riston Whins Racing) 3,600

From Yeomanstown Stud
b y c Common Grounds - Quack Shot (USA) (Quack)... (Brian Grassick Bloodstock) 8,800
From Tally-Ho Stud
b y c Al Hareb (USA) - Raga Rine (Raga Navarro).......... (Malcolm Thwaites) 11,000
Property of a Partnership, from Castletown Stud (Agent)
bl y c Gallic League - Red Roman (Solinus) (Sundrive Azzurra) 7,400
Property of Mr Patrick Clarke
gr y f Runnett - Redecorate (USA) (Hatchet Man).................... (J S Moore) 1,600
Property of Springfield Thoroughbred Syndicate, from Ardenode Stud
b y c Astronef - Redwood Hut (Habitat).... (Mick Channon) 10,000

447

Property of Mrs A Whitehead, from Owenstown Stud
b y f Doulab (USA) - Regal Promise (Pitskelly).................... (B.B.A.) 8,500
Property of Mrs Loretta Murphy, from Barrettstown Farm & Stud
ch y c Astronef - Relko's Belle (FR) (Relko) (Cash) 5,600
From Silverfort Stud
b y f Shardari - Reprint (Kampala).. (E.B.A.) 1,000
From Ballymorris & Caherass Studs
b y c Roi Danzig (USA) - Requena (Dom Racine).................... (L Walsh) 3,500
From Glenvale Stud
b y c Tirol - Resiusa (ITY) (Niniski)......... (E.A.M. Maas) 42,000
From Laureldean Stud
b y c Astronef - Royal Sensation (Prince Regent) .... (German International Bloodstock) 6,000
From Rthasker Stud
b y f Red Sunset - Rubina Park (Ashmore) (Jack Berry) 6,000
From Riverside Stud
ch y c Magical Strike (USA) - Saint Simbir (Simbir)............ (Henry Ponsonby) 7,000
Property of Mr Martin O'Malley, from Rosemount House Stud
b y c The Noble Player (USA) - Saintly Game (Welsh Saint)... (Canice Farrell) 1,900
From Gerradstown Stud
b y c Roi Danzig (USA) - Salustrina (Sallust) (M Tompkins) 8,200

448

Property of M B J Dolan, from Ashdown House Stud
ch y f Imperial Frontier (USA) - Sassess (Sassafras).................... (Cash) 1,100
Property of Mr Peter Quinn
b y f Jareer (USA) - Sauntry (Ballad Rock).. (Cormac McCormack Associates) 1,700
Property of a Gentleman, from Lordship and Egerton Studs
b y c Nordico (USA) - Scarlet Slipper (Gay Mercene) .... (C Gordon-Watson Bloodstock) 10,000

From Oak Lodge Stud
ch y f Fayruz - Seapoint (Major Point)...... (N McGrath) 2,000
From Ballylinch Stud (Agent)
b y c Dance Of Life (USA) - Sharp Flash (Kris)......................... (B.B.A.) 3,200
Property of a Partnership, from Ballymoney Park
b y c Fayruz - Shay Tien (Gunner B) .... (Declan Gillespie) 8,800
Property of Mr Patrick McCarthy, from Hawthorn Villa Stud
b y f Cyrano de Bergerac - Shuckran Habibi (Thatching).......... (David Cosgrove) 1,000
From Tara Stud
ch y c Double Schwartz - Silk Trade (Auction Ring).. (David Minton Bloodstock) 6,400
From Rathasker Stud
b y f Red Sunset - Simbella (Simbir)....... (B.B.A.) 2,200
Property of Newtownbarry Hse Stud & Stephanie Von Schilcher, from Newtownbarry Hse Stud
b y f Runnett - Sixpenny Express (Bay Express)................ (Jack Berry) 7,400

449

From Yeomanstown Stud
gr y c Standaan (FR) - Sleeping Car (Scorpio)...... (John Ferguson Bloodstock) 32,000
Property of Mrs Clody E Norton, from Newtownbarry House Stud
b y f Petorius - Small Is Beautiful (Condorcet)..... (David Minton Bloodstock) 7,800
Property of Green Ireland Properties Ltd
b y f Thatching - Snow Maid (High Top) ... (Peter Savill) 6,800
From Tally-Ho Stud
b y c Classic Secret (USA) - Soudchika (GER) (Dschingis Khan).............. (Francis Brenaff) 1,900
Property of Mr J R Mitchell, from Beechgrove Stud
b y f Indian Ridge - Sound Of The Sea (Windjammer) .... (C Gordon-Watson Bloodstock) 10,000
From Rathbarry Stud
ch y f Roi Danzig (USA) - Special Meeting (Persian Bold)........... (M Thwaites) 5,200
From Dollanstown Stud (Agent)
b y c Baba Karam - Spring About (Hard Fought).................. (S Tiernan) 1,000
Property of Mr N W Creighton
b y c Cyrano de Bergerac - Spy Girl (Tanfirion).................... (J S Moore) 3,500
From Cooliney Stud
ch y c Try My Best (USA) - Sronica (Midsummer Night II)................. (European Consultants Investments) 9,800
From Rocklow Stud
gr y f Mazaad - Standing Ovation (Godswalk)............................... (Cormac McCormack Associates) 7,600

450

From Rathbarry Stud (Agent)
b y c Jareer (USA) - Sun Gift (Guillaume Tell).................... (Frank Carr) 2,300

From Tally-Ho Stud
b y c Nordico (USA) - Sunley Saint (Artaius) (John Ferguson Bloodstock) 3,000
From Waterside Stud (Tara)
ch y c Superlative - Superlife (USA) (Super Concorde)... (Peter Doyle Bloodstock) 27,000
From Whitechurch Stud
ch y c Fayruz - Susan's Blues (Cure The Blues)................ (Con Collins) 6,000
From Dollandstown Stud (Agent)
b y f Cyrano de Bergerac - Sweet Finale (Sallust).................. (G Baker) 1,100
Property of Mr Sean Twomey, from Hawthorn Villa Stud
ch y f Sharpo - Sympathy (Precocious)..... (Sheena Collins) 8,000
From Carrickhill Stud
b y c Mazaad - Tamara's Reef (Main Reef) (Cash) 2,300
From Lynn Cottage Stables
br y f Contract Law (USA) - Tender Encounter (Prince Tenderfoot) .... (Michael Robinson) 2,100
Property of a Partnership, from Dollanstown Stud
ch y f Magical Strike (USA) - Tinktura (Pampapaul)........................ (Cash) 1,200
From Mountown Farm Stud
b y c Treasure Kay - Traminer (Status Seeker)..... (Peter Doyle Bloodstock) 17,000

451

Property of Mr P Butler, from Rosemount House Stud
b y c Dominion Royale - Translation (Fordham)................ (T Alessandro) 3,000
From Rosemount House Stud
b y c Persian Heights - Tres Bien (Pitskelly) (Browne Bloodstock) 5,300
Property of a Gentleman
b y f Hatim (USA) - Trompe D'Oeil (Longleat)........... (Riston Whins Racing) 3,500
From Milltown Stud
b y c Roi Danzig (USA) - Une Venitienne (FR) (Green Dancer)........... (B.B.A.) 8,800
Property of Mr James G Roche
b y c Cyrano de Bergerac - Velvet Breeze (Windjammer)...................... (German International Bloodstock) 1,500
Property of Mr Tom O'Leary
b y c Contract Law (USA) - Velvet Vixen (Condorcet)........ (Axel Donnerstag) 2,200
Property of Mr Peter Murphy, from Bridge Hill Farm
ch y c Simply Great (FR) - Viva Ronda (Kampala)........................... (Johnny McKeever Bloodstock) 8,000
Property of Clody E Norton & Cyril Humphries, from Newtownbarry House Stud
b y c Law Society (USA) - Warning Sound (Red Alert).......... (Mark Johnston) 10,500
Property of Dr D S Comer & R D Fraser, from Gormanstown Stud
ch y c Doulab (USA) - We've Just Begun (USA) (Huguenot).. (John Wainwright) 2,000
From Carrickhill Stud
b y c Law Society (USA) - What A Candy (USA) (Key To The Mint) .... (B.B.A. (Italia)) 11,000

452

From Lynn Lodge Stud
ch y f Fayruz - Windini (Windjammer)...... (Jack Berry) 13,000
From Ballymorris & Caherass Studs
b y c Shaadi (USA) - Winning Look (Relko) (Mick Channon) 7,300
From Ardmayne Stud
ch y c Montekin - Wurli (Wolver Hollow)... (John McEnery) 2,800
From Gurteenard Stud
gr y c Al Hareb (USA) - Zanskar (Godswalk) (M P Roberts) 4,000
Property of Mr Tom O'Leary
b y c Common Grounds - Zazu (Cure The Blues).............. (D Gillespie) 4,200
From Glenvale Stud (Agent)
ch y c Be My Native (USA) - All The Same (Cajun)................ (M J Grassick) 4,000
From Dollanstown Stud
gr y f Standaan (FR) - Anna Pavlova (USA) (Lyphard)......................... (Cash) 1,000
From Cooliney Stud
b y c Glacial Storm (USA) - April Rhapsody (Main Reef).................. (Cash) 2,800
Property of D & R Dunne, from Whitechurch Stud
b y c Digamist (USA) - Arabian Princess (Taufan)............... (I Lauterbach) 4,200
From Rocklow Stud
b y c Mazaad - Arena (Sallust) .... (M J Grassick) 8,200

453

Property of Mr Richard Black, from Newtownbarry House Stud
b y f Treasure Kay - Arminiya (Roan Rocket) .... (D Cosgrove) 5,600
Property of Mrs Paul Roels, from Urrahill Stables
b y c Phardante (FR) - Avise La Fin (Scottish Rifle).................. (J FitzGerald) 3,000
Property of Shandrum Lodge Stud
b y c Jareer (USA) - Baghio (Ballymore).... (Cash) 4,000
Property of Balaine Partnership
b y c Astronef - Balaine (GER) (Balidar) .... (Frank Carr) 2,500
From Lynn Cottage Stables
b y f Prince Rupert (FR) - Battle Queen (Kind Of Hush)......... (R Hollinshead) 2,800
Property of Rose O'Reilly
b y f Red Sunset - Bay Supreme (Martinmas)........................... (European Equine Consultants) 2,800
From Rock Abbey Stud (Agent)
ch y c Bob Back (USA) - Be My Dame (Be My Guest)...... (Browne Bloodstock) 3,500
From Corduff Stud
b y f Contract Law (USA) - Behroz (Relko) (E Wilson) 2,500
From Oak Farm
ch y c Jareer (USA) - Blue Czarina (Sandhurst Prince)............ (Frank Barry) 7,500
From Dollandstown Stud (Agent)
ch y f Sharp Victor (USA) - Blue Elver (King's Lake).................. (Cash) 1,000

454

Property of Mr & Mrs Leo Collins, from Ennistown Stud

b y c Shy Groom (USA) - Bold Display (USA) (Green Dancer).. (Browne Bloodstock) 2,800

Property of Miss G Field, from Pier House Stud

br y c Glow (USA) - Buzzing Around (Prince Bee) .... (German International Bloodstock) 5,200

Property of E J Kelly

b y c Be My Native (USA) - Cambridge Lodge (Tower Walk) .... (German International Bloodstock) 6,000

Property of Mr John J Ryan, from Donaghmore Farm

b y f Treasure Kay - Carange (Known Fact) (Jack Berry) 4,500

Property of Mrs C A Moore, from Bearforest Stud

b y f Astronef - Carioca (Gala Performance) (Equine Investment Consultants) 1,600

From Oak Lodge Stud

b y f Dancing Dissident (USA) - Carlyle Suite (USA) (Icecapade) .... (R Hollinshead) 3,200

Property of Mrs A Whitehead, from Broadfield Stud

b y c Prince Rupert (FR) - Chepstow House (USA) (Northern Baby)......... (C.B.A.) 1,500

From Lynn Lodge Stud

b y c Cadeaux Genereux - Chevrefeuille (Ile de Bourbon) .... (C Gordon-Watson Bloodstock) 32,000

From Tally-Ho Stud

b y f Contract Law (USA) - Chiarella (Relkino)............... (D Cosgrove) 1,100

Property of Mr Peter Loughran

b y c Pennine Walk - Chimela (Ela-Mana-Mou)................. (Arthur Moore) 3,000

455

Property of Green Ireland Properties Ltd

(USA) ch y f Chromite (USA) - Christi Dawn (USA) (Grey Dawn)............ (Cash) 1,000

From Tally-Ho Stud

b y c Contract Law (USA) - Claire's Thatch (Thatch)........... (Axel Donnerstag) 2,000

From Rock Abbey Stud (Agent)

ch y f Bob Back (USA) - Claremont Girl (Will Hays)........................ (Cash) 4,100

From Rathasker Stud

b y g Red Sunset - Coffee Bean (Doulab) .. (J G FitzGerald) 6,000

From Kilnamoragh Stud

b y f Doubletour (USA) - Country Niece (Great Nephew)........... (P J Flynn) 5,800

Property of Mr David Gordon

b y c Homo Sapien - Cova Kestrel (Ovac) .. (German International Bloodstock) 2,000

From Whitechurch Stud (Agent)

ch y f Classic Secret (USA) - Crimson Crest (Pampapaul).................. (Cash) 1,100

From Mount Prospect Stud

b y c Astronef - Dacani (Polyfoto) .... (German International Bloodstock) 7,200

From Ardmayne Stud

b y c Anita's Prince - Damastown's Lady (Rarity)...................... (Cash) 3,100

From Knocktoran Stud

b y c Exactly Sharp (USA) - Dancing Melba (Gay Fandango) .... (Johnny McKeever Bloodstock) 5,500

456

Property of a Partnership, from Castletown Stud (Agent)

b y f Taufan (USA) - Doobie Do (Derring-Do) .... (Malcolm Thwaites) 9,500

Property of Mr John Malone

b y c Glenstal (USA) - Easy On The Eye (Henbit).......... (Malcolm Thwaites) 7,300

From Gerrardstown Stud

b or br y f Petorius - Eeduff (Auction Ring) (Axel Donnerstag) 1,400

From Riverside Stud

b y f Astronef - Estivalia (Persian Bold) .... (Delta Bloodstock Management) 4,200

Property of Ballyboher Stud

ch y f Magical Strike (USA) - Eurynome (Be My Guest)............. (Jim Gorman) 2,200

Property of Mr & Mrs Leo Collins, from Ennistown Stud

gr or br y c Treasure Kay - Excelling Miss (USA) (Exceller)..... (Kevin McAuliffe) 5,000

From Glenvale Stud

b y f Fairy King (USA) - Faiblesse (Welsh Saint).............. (Charles O'Brien) 15,000

From Graigueshoneen Stud

b y c Don't Forget Me - Fall Of The Hammer (IRE) (Auction Ring) (T Stack) 15,000

From Oak Lodge Stud

ch y f Nordance (USA) - Fantasise (FR) (General Assembly)........... (Cash) 6,800

From Rosemount House Stud

ch y c The Noble Player (USA) - Felicitas (Mr Fluorocarbon)...... (T Alessandro) 3,200

457

Property of Mr Ian Bryant, from Spa Stud

b y c Faustus (USA) - Foudre (Petingo) .... (German International Bloodstock) 4,200

From Burgage Stud

gr y c Dominion Royale - Galaxy Scorpio (Saritamer)............. (John Quinn) 3,000

Property of Rose O'Reilly

b y f Scenic - Gay Reign (Lord Gayle)...... (T Stack) 5,400

From Castletown Stud (Agent)

b y c Al Hareb (USA) - Gay Surrender (Sir Gaylord)........... (Axel Donnerstag) 6,000

Property of Mr John M O'Connor, from Rock Abbey Stud

b y f Superpower - Golden Sunlight (Ile de Bourbon)............ (Jimmy Coogan) 5,000

From Silverfort Stud

ch y f Salt Dome (USA) - Grand Duchy (Prince Tenderfoot)...... (R Simankova) 1,050

Property of Mr P J Doyle

b y c Cyrano de Bergerac - Grecian Sky (African Sky)...... (Charlestown Stud) 2,800

From Tara Stud

b or br y c Petorius - Hay Knot (Main Reef) (Delta Bloodstock) 10,500

From Waterside Stud (Tara)
gr y f Standaan (FR) - Hazy Lady (Habitat).. (T Storme) 10,500
Property of J and A McDonnell
ch y c Be My Native (USA) - Just Clara (Camden Town).......... (J FitzGerald) 4,000

458

From Jigginstown House Stud
ch y f Exhibitioner - Little Town Flirt (Quiet Fling)........................ (Pro Am) 1,000
From Woodlands Stables
ch y c Classic Secret (USA) - Makheeleh (Ahonoora)........... (Michael English) 1,550
From Shambo Stud
ch y f Try My Best (USA) - Peace Please (Stanford)................. (B Connolly) 400
Property of The Irish National Stud Co Ltd
b y c Alzao (USA) - Preening (Persian Bold) (Peter Doyle Bloodstock) 1,500
Property of Mr Ian Bryant, from Spa Stud
b y c Siberian Express (USA) - Rhein Jewel (Sandhurst Prince)........ (W Schutz) 1,250
Property of Mr M Gaffney
ch y f Classic Secret (USA) - Royal Laragon (Welsh Saint)........ (M McCormack) 2,000
Property of Mr L P Ryan
ch y f Don't Forget Me - Siofra Beag (Steel Heart)............................ (Cash) 900
Property of Mrs Blake, from Rosetown Farm
ch y c Jareer (USA) - Snappy Dresser (Nishapour)................ (A Macchi) 3,000
Property of Mr John McLean, from Rockhill
b y f Pennine Walk - Appiana (Prince Ippi) (Pro Am) 4,100
From Cornacrew Stud
b y c Sure Blade (USA) - Dreaming Spires (Saddler's Wells)............ (Pro Am) 1,150

459

From Gurteenard Stud
b y f Jareer (USA) - Dunbally (Dunphy)..... (Cash) 300
Property of Mr Pat Purcell, from Red Pender Stud
b y f Gadabout (USA) - Excruciating (CAN) (Bold Forbes).......... (John McGrath) 2,600
Property of Mr John Lennon, from Loch Cuan Stud
b y c Milk Of The Barley - Fotostar (Polyfoto).................... (C Triouart) 1,200
Property of M McEnery, from Rossenarra Stud
b y f Mon Tresor - Goggle Box (Song)..... (Peter Doyle Bloodstock) 300
Property of Aghern House Stud
b y f Jolly Jake (NZ) - Highlands Babe (USA) (Pappa Steve)................. (Cash) 600

460

DONCASTER

Thursday, September 23rd

Property of By order of the Sheriff of Lancashire
Protected (FR) b m (10yrs) Blakeney - Endymion (Sir Gaylord)...... (Mrs G Frost) 750
ch f (4yrs) High Line - Bridoon (Brigadier Gerard)................... (B Forsey) 900
b f (2yrs) said to be River Mist - said to be Alciyra (FR) (Akarad).. (Mrs C Roberts) 420
Property of J K Dancer, from Spa Stud
Dancing Clara b m (11yrs) Billion - Clary (Royal Record II) Covered by K-Battery (Mrs C Moore) 1,600
Property of Minizen Ltd
ch g (2yrs) Kind Of Hush - Minizen Melody (Hello Gorgeous)..... (Mrs C Roberts) 940
Property of H Frew
Touch Of Oriental b f (2yrs) Touch Boy - Shantung Lassie (FR) (Shantung)....... (Cash) 480
Persian Beauty b f (2yrs) Primo Dominie - Persian Tapestry (Tap On Wood)...... (A C Chapman) 560
Property of J W C Coxon, from Park Place Stud
ch f (2yrs) High Kicker (USA) - Faldwyn (Mr Fluorocarbon)................. (Cash) 400
b f (2yrs) High Kicker (USA) - Avenita Lady (Free State)........... (A C Chapman) 420
Property of Mrs D Cooper
Dramatic Pass ch g (4yrs) Coquelin (USA) - Miss Flirt (Welsh Pageant) (E Dunlop) 1,700

461

Property of Mrs P Churm, from Cherry Court Stables
Company Cash ch c (5yrs) Chief Singer - I'll Try (Try My Best)............ (A Bell) 1,300
Property of Mrs P Flowers
State Tacoma ch f (3yrs) Flying Tyke - Sunshine State (Roi Soleil)..... (Cash) 650
From Priory Stables To Settle An Account
ch c (2yrs) Hadeer - Verchinina (Star Appeal).................. (Janet Savill) 2,100
From Northgate Lodge Stables
ch f (2yrs) Absalom - Real Party (Realm)... (Derrick Dunstan) 420
To Dissolve a Partnership
Ten Times Tango ch f (2yrs) Grey Desire - Tango Lady (Gorytus).......... (Cash) 700
Property of Mrs J M Davenport
Important Decision b g (4yrs) Import - Three Terns (Seapic) (Ruth Wollerton) 1,800
Property of Mrs H J Ellerby
Vital Voltage ch g (4yrs) Soughaan (USA) - Damariscotta (Ahonoora)....... (Cash) 800
Property of M Gleason, from Warwick Lodge Stables
Steanard Boy b c (2yrs) Dreams To Reality (USA) - Orange Silk (Moulton).. (Cash) 720
From Warwick Lodge Stables
Time To Dance b c (2yrs) Hard Fought - Lavender Tiger (Mansingh) .... (Miss S Roberts) 850
Property of J Buzzeo, from Tupgill Park Stables
Olicana ch g (3yrs) Persian Bold - Maniusha (Sallust)....................... (Cash) 920

462

From Tupgill Park Stables
Mokaite b f (2yrs) Komaite (USA) - Manhunt (Posse)............... (David Barron) 1,800

From Maunby House Stables

Kerria b f (3yrs) Celestial Storm (USA) - Tree Mallow (Malicious).............. (Mark Bateman) 550

Icanspell b g (2yrs) Petoski - Bewitched (African Sky)........... (David Barron) 5,400

Property of I Dowell

Watersmeet b f (3yrs) Sizzling Melody - Marble Moon (Le Moss).. (J A Gibson) 900

From Arundel House Stables

Song In Your Heart b g (3yrs) Sizzling Melody - Honeybuzzard (FR) (Sea Hawk II)............................ (Cash) 950

To Dissolve a Partnership

Simply Superb ch g (3yrs) Superlative - Coral Princess (Imperial Fling)......... (E Dunlop) 2,800

Property of A M Wragg

Alberstan b g (3yrs) Stanford - Afrabela (African Sky).................. (Cash) 1,350

Property of Seashore Bloodstock, from Warwick House Stables

Velvet Heart b f (3yrs) Damister (USA) - Bottom Line (Double Jump).......... (Angela Knight) 2,200

Property of F H Lee, from Little Stanneylands Stables

Double The Stake (USA) b g (4yrs) Raise A Man (USA) - Je'da Qua (USA) (Fleet Nasrullah)............. (W D Burchell) 3,000

From Longsides Stables

Hellaby b c (2yrs) Jester - Yahalom (USA) (Diamond Prospect)...... (A Hermans) 1,000

463

From Chips Farm Stud

Jimmy Pip b g (6yrs) Creetown - Beth Of Houndhill (Filiberto)... (D E Townsend) 1,500

Kickcashtal b g (4yrs) Ballacashtal (CAN) - Teenager (Never Say Die)...... (Cash) 1,100

Property of Billy Morgan, from Kingsley House Stables

Educated Pet gr g (4yrs) Petong - School Road (Great Nephew)... (J F Williams) 8,000

From King's Ride Stables

Jordywrath b g (3yrs) Efisio - Hedonist (Mandamus)........ (David Chapman) 1,100

From Racecourse Farm Stables

Seldom In ch g (7yrs) Mummy's Game - Pinzamber (Pinicola)........ (R Foster) 1,500

Walid's Princess b f (3yrs) Waajib - Glomach (USA) (Majestic Light)....... (Mrs G Frost) 2,000

ch f (3yrs) Dominion - Judy's Dowry (Dragonara Palace)............ (D Badham) 880

Property of a Partnership, from Felstead Court Stables

Ghostly Glow gr g (4yrs) Kalaglow - Amerella (Welsh Pageant) (S Coathup) 950

From Glasgow House Stables

Cracker Jack ch g (3yrs) Chilibang - Friendly Jester (Be Friendly).... (Stephen Holt) 1,000

To Dissolve a Partnership, from Moss Side Racing Stables

Convenient Moment ch f (3yrs) Clantime - Panay (Arch Sculptor).......... (Cash) 1,400

464

From Moss Side Racing Stables

Our Mica gr g (3yrs) Belfort (FR) - Aristata (Habitat)................. (L J Barratt) 1,200

Property of N Jackson, from Moss Side Racing Stables

Paris Symphony gr c (2yrs) Common Ground - Zanskar (Godswalk)... (Cash) 1,000

From Moss Side Racing Stables

Monkey Face gr f (2yrs) Clantime - Charming View (Workboy)... (Herbert Jones) 900

Property of Skyline Racing Ltd., from Moss Side Racing Stables

Caponata b f (2yrs) Cyrano de Bergerac - Shining Bright (USA) (Bold Bidder)..... (A Hermans) 1,000

To Dissolve a Partnership, from Moss Side Racing Stables

Nosmo King b c (2yrs) Nordico (USA) - Selenis (Huntercombe)............ (Mrs M A Kendall) 1,200

Property of W Stephenson

Magic Fan b g (3yrs) Taufan (USA) - Magic Gold (Sallust).......... (Stephen Holt) 650

Property of P Asquith

Bluebella ch f (3yrs) Mummy's Game - La Bleu (Blue Cashmere).......... (Cash) 800

From Phantom House Stables

Poor Willie b g (2yrs) Rich Charlie - Julia Mawe (Dominion).............. (Cash) 800

From Brecongill Stables

Matt's Boy b g (5yrs) Runnett - Thatchville (Thatch)...................... (Cash) 2,200

Make Mine A Double ch g (3yrs) Sharpo - My Fair Orchid (Roan Rocket)......... (D Nicholls) 800

Sky Wish b g (3yrs) Skyliner - On The Record (Record Token)..... (B Ellison) 1,500

465

Property of Messrs A U Gauna & M F Barraclough, from Arden Park Stables

Henbury Hall gr g (5yrs) Bellypha - Rustic Stile (Rusticaro)... (Mrs J Clutterbuck) 2,500

Property of R A Moffat, from Pit Farm Stables

State Lady b f (4yrs) Strong Statement - Ladies Gazette (London Gazette)...... (A Barrow) 5,500

To Dissolve a Partnership

Blue Disc br g (8yrs) Disc Jockey - Kaotesse (Djakao)............ (Cash) 1,300

From Hill House Farm

Sunset Street b g (5yrs) Bellypha - Sunset Reef (Mill Reef).... (Miss N Mortimer) 450

To Dissolve A Partnership, from Maunby House Stables

Slades Hill br g (6yrs) Lochnager - Mephisto Waltz (Dancer's Image) (David Barron) 4,600

From Maunby House Stables

Missed The Boat b g (3yrs) Cyrano de Bergerac - Lady Portobello (Porto Bello) .... (Sue Wilton) 4,800

From Whitcliffe Grange Stables

Restraint b f (3yrs) Bustino - Queen's Message (Town Crier).......... (J Barnes) 1,800

Olliver Duckett b g (4yrs) Bustino - Tatiana (Habitat)................. (W Swiers) 2,600

From Mowbray House Stud
ch m (5yrs) Kabour - Tolly's Best (Hittite Glory)........................ (Cash) 1,100
Property of J M Chapman, from Mount Pleasant Farm
ch f (5yrs) Kabour - Underbarrow Rose (Andrea Mantegna)....... (H Charlton) 1,400

466

Property of Mrs J Evans
Shudyman b g (4yrs) Mansingh (USA) - Funny-Do (Derring-Do).......... (Cash) 1,300
Property of D W Macdonald, from Bonny Hill Farm Stables
Miss Avon b f (4yrs) Majestic Streak - Avon Melody (Bilsborrow)....... (R Bewely) 2,400
Property of C Wilson
b f (4yrs) Scallywag - Roadway Mistress (Mandamus).................. (Cash) 2,000
Property of Gledhill House Stud Ltd
b g (4yrs) Supreme Leader - Liberty Calling (Caliban)................ (Sue Wilton) 1,900
From Ballywoden House Stud, Co Down, Ireland
b f (4yrs) Strong Gale - She's Approaching (Ragapan).................. (W Clay) 2,700
Property of High Trees Stud, from Ballywooden Stud, Co Down, Ireland
b g (3yrs) Le Moss - Dandy Lady (Arapaho) (Allan And Caroline Trayes) 950
Property of a Partnership
ch g (3yrs) Phardante (FR) - Cherry Glory (Final Straw).................. (Cash) 850
From Tupgill Park Stables
Routing b g (5yrs) Rousillon (USA) - Tura (Northfields)............... (D Jones) 3,000
Scottish Park ch f (4yrs) Scottish Reel - Moss Agate (Alias Smith).... (J Hams) 2,000
From The Grange Stables
Breeze Away b f (4yrs) Prince Sabo - Ballad Island (Ballad Rock)........ (R Turner) 2,500

467

Property of R Lee
Double Sherry ch f (4yrs) Crofthall - Two's Up (Double Jump).......... (R Turner) 1,100
Property of Mrs C A Wyatt, from The Grange Stables
Sison b g (3yrs) Vacarme (USA) - Silent Sail (Aglojo).................. (D G Mason) 2,100
Property of Mrs D Joly, from The Grange Stables
Glimpse Of Heaven b f (3yrs) Vision (USA) - Adriya (Vayraan)............... (Cash) 1,300
Property of D Powell, from The Grange Stables
Mazina b f (2yrs) Mazilier (USA) - Najd (St Chad)........................ (Cash) 800
Property of A S Reid, from Park End Farm Stables
Sailor Boy b g (7yrs) Main Reef - Main Sail (Blakeney)..................... (Cash) 1,200
Applianceofscience b g (6yrs) Bairn - Moonlight Serenade (Crooner)... (J E Evans) 3,000
To Dissolve a Partnership
Abeloni ch g (4yrs) Absalom - Agreloui (Tower Walk)........... (S Coathup) 7,600

Property of Mrs H J Ellerby
Super Charge b g (4yrs) Superlative - Daisy Warwick (USA) (Ribot/sir Gaylord)..... (C Hawkins) 1,400
Property of Stepaside Stables, Co Kildare, Ireland
Granville Grill b g (8yrs) Furry Glen - Glamorous Night (Sir Herbert).. (J Deutsch) 7,400
Property of Mr & Mrs J J Byrne, from Ballynure Stables, Co Wicklow, Ireland
Dig Deeper b g (6yrs) Seymour Hicks (FR) - Deep Foliage (Deep Run).............. (Jonjo O'Neill) 7,200

468

Property of Mrs H McParland, from Ballynure Stables, Co Wicklow, Ireland
Kilgariff ch g (7yrs) Le Bavard (FR) - Negrada (Nelcius)...... (Jonjo O'Neill) 6,000
Property of Mrs Margaret O'Neill, Co Dublin, Ireland
Test Match ch g (6yrs) Glenstal (USA) - Reprint (Kampala)............ (Bill Clay) 9,000
From Ballywooden House Stables, Co Down, Ireland
Fury Star b g (5yrs) Smackover - Derwent Lass (High Table).............. (Cash) 1,550
From Hammond Lodge Stud, Co Down, Ireland
Muninnane Quiz b m (9yrs) Salluceva - Welsh Quiz (Quisling).......... (Cash) 1,200
Daylight Lady ch m (6yrs) Deep Run - First Gal (General Ironside)........ (S Warr) 1,900
Allerton Barge b m (5yrs) The Parson - Barge Royal (Bargello).... (Sue Wilton) 2,300
Property of John Carr, from Killeaney Stables, Co Kildare, Ireland
Boreen Bridge gr g (8yrs) Boreen (FR) - Lady Peacock (Peacock)... (R Tranter) 1,400
Property of Mrs O Brennan, from Sloswicks Farm Stables
Rapid Fire ch g (5yrs) Good Thyne (USA) - Princess Pixie (Royal Captive)......... (Mr Ruscoe) 3,100
Jarlmar br g (6yrs) Callernish - Billie Gibb (Cavo Doro).................... (Cash) 3,500
From Sloswicks Farm Stables
Floral Bouquet ch f (4yrs) Never So Bold - My Fair Orchid (Roan Rocket).......... (J Barnes) 1,550

469

Property of N Hetherton, from Highfield House Stables
Bilberry b m (4yrs) Nicholas Bill - Snow Tribe (Great Nephew)................ (Stephen Coathup) 5,300
From Barn House Racing Stables
Marandisa ch m (6yrs) Pharly (FR) - Marissiya (Nishapour)..... (T R Darlington) 750
Property of J A Wynn-Williams, from Denton Hall Stables
Young George b g (6yrs) Camden Town - Young Grace (Young Emperor)......... (Harvey Smith) 4,600
Property of D McCune
Vimchase ch g (7yrs) Slim Jim - Vimys Pet (Lord Nelson).................. (Cash) 1,800

From Castle Farm Stables
Catakil (FR) b g (4yrs) Bikala - Catacomb (USA) (Halo).................. (Cash) 2,100
Property of J E Abbey
Leacroft b g (9yrs) Domitor (USA) - Whitmarsh (Hessonite)....... (N A Parker) 850
Property of Mrs S S Langton
Beechmount Lad b g (9yrs) Gleason (USA) - Only Derry (Anthony).......... (A Lee) 1,200
Property of W Boon, from Saverley House Racing Stables
Hannah Bee gr m (6yrs) Humdoleila - Heron's Mirage (Grey Mirage) .... (Stephen Holt) 1,050
From Ladykirk Stables
Public Appeal b g (4yrs) Law Society (USA) - Vacherin (USA) (Green Dancer) .... (T R Darlington) 1,450
To Dissolve a Partnership
ch g (4yrs) Crofthall - Keep Believing (Sweet Revenge)............... (Cash) 1,450

470

Property of B G Riley & Son Ltd
gr or ro f (4yrs) Roaring Riva - Nothing Happened (General Ironside) (J Hogg) 1,850
Property of P Foran
b g (4yrs) Royben - Rest And Welcome (Town And Country)........... (Cash) 1,500
To Dissolve a Partnership
ch g (4yrs) Le Moss - Moyne Gael (Lord Gayle).............. (Ruth Wollerton) 800
Property of Mrs G M Lovell
b g (4yrs) Pitpan - Again Kathleen (Status Seeker)............. (S W Campion) 1,950
Property of Miss C Broughton
Champagne Break ch g (4yrs) Flying Tyke - Horann (Horage)........ (Askew Stud) 1,150
To Dissolve a Partnership, from Burythorpe House Stables
Sanfoyt (USA) br g (4yrs) Foyt (USA) - Kiku San (USA) (Bushido)........... (Cash) 1,550
Property of Scotnorth Racing Ltd, from Burythorpe House Stables
Cougar ch g (7yrs) Song - Flying Milly (Mill Reef)..................... (J Bulman) 1,200
Property of Miss S Rettie
Hobby's Girl br m (8yrs) Straight Knight - Owen's Hobby (Owen Anthony) ...... (Mrs Clow) 1,100
From Elms Farm Stud
Rufus Boy ch g (7yrs) Politico - The Lathkill (Clear River).......... (P J & B Miller) 700
From Park Leys Stables
Loxley Range ch g (5yrs) Hatim - Chantal (Charlottesville)............... (Cash) 1,250

471

To Dissolve a Partnership, from Beacon Hill Stables
Makeminemusic ch g (4yrs) Music Boy - Ultra Vires (High Line).. (J W Mooney) 2,000
To Dissolve a Partnership, from Craiglands Farm Racing Stables
Almost Blue ch g (7yrs) Ballacashtal (CAN) - Blue Garter (Targowice)........ (Cash) 750
From Craiglands Farm Racing Stables
Granny Mc br m (6yrs) Sparkling Boy - Marcus Miss (Marcus Superbus)...... (Cash) 880
Property of Messrs D Bushell & W H Green, from Craiglands Farm Racing Stables
Cantgetout b m (7yrs) Furry Glen - Brave Light (Brave Invader).... (C W Pinney) 2,400
Property of Mrs J Downing
Duke La Farge b g (5yrs) Van Der Linden (FR) - An-Go-Look (Don't Look) (Cash) 5,000
Quarndon ch g (8yrs) Deep Run - Dame Lucy (Prince Hansel)...... (B Watson) 950
Property of Mrs S S Langton
None Too Dear (USA) gr g (11yrs) Caro - Service Compris (USA) (Real Value) ... (I R Bennett) 820
Property of Mrs S Kavanagh
Furry Loch b g (7yrs) Furry Glen - Loreto Lady (Brave Invader)..... (R E Parker) 800
Property of Mrs Carol Reed
Imperial Rain ch m (10yrs) Imperial Fling (USA) - El Chaperall (Scottish Rifle).... (Mrs J Wilson) 800
Property of J Lee, from Keepers Cottage Stables
Smithy's Choice b g (11yrs) Bonne Noel - Passage Falcon (Falcon).............. (Mrs S M Richardson) 950

472

Property of G Winstanley
Jimmy River br g (10yrs) Young Man (FR) - Mary Fox (Mummy's Pet) .... (Burntwood Sports Ltd) 10,000
Property of Miss J Cambidge
Wide Receiver ch g (8yrs) Posse - Red Partridge (Solinus)...... (B Cubberley) 800
Property of H Frew
b m (5yrs) - .... (Cash) 1,200
PRIVATE SALES
Property of A S Reid, from Park End Farm Stables
Mabthul (USA) b g (5yrs) Northern Baby (CAN) - Persuadable (USA) (What A Pleasure)................ (S J Castell) 3,000
Property of Mrs Margaret O'Neill, Co Dublin, Ireland
Background Music ch g (8yrs) Orchestra - Wind Swift (Whistling Wind).......... (Robin Greenwood) 2,250
Property of Mrs D Bowie
Hugo b g (9yrs) Stone Fox - Sharon's Pride (Osimandus/proud Day).... (A Ireland) 2,000

473

ASCOT
Tuesday, September 28th

Property of a Partnership
Miss Suntan gr m (14yrs) Bruni - Miss Sunblest (Whistler) Covered by Faustus .... (J W Parker) 1,050
Property of Mr Stephen Shears
Angel's Wing ch f (4yrs) Precocious - Razor Blade (Sharp Edge)............ (Cash) 1,100

Property of a Lady
ch y f Midyan (USA) - Alipura (Anfield)..... (P Hipwood) 680
Property of Mr S Demanuele
b y c Prince Sabo - Song To Singo (Master Sing)............. (Mrs M Simmonite) 3,000
b y c Petoski - Bunnyloch (Lochnager)..... (S Young) 550
Property of a Lady, from Bonita Racing Stables
b y c Forzando - Jealous Lover (Alias Smith) .... (Mr Panniccia) 400
Property of a Partnership, from Benson Stud
b y c Exodal (USA) - What A Challenge (Sallust)................. (Terry Mills) 2,000
Property of T G & B B Mills
Petite Louie gr f (3yrs) Chilibang - Sisola (USA) (Coastal (USA)).......... (Cash) 1,750
Petite June (IRE) b f (3yrs) Pennine Walk - La Duse (Junius (USA)).. (Adrian Kirby) 1,400
Property of Messrs A & R Saphir
Almonty (IRE) b c (3yrs) Mazaad - Nordic Maid (Vent Du Nord)..... (A L Forbes) 1,150

474

Property of Mr Barry Minty, from Holly Bush Farm
Little Madam ch m (13yrs) Habat - Obedience (Reliance II) Covered by Full Extent (USA)............ (J W Parker) 800
Property of Clear Height Racing, to Dissolve a Partnership
Charisma Girl b f (2yrs) Nomination - My Ginny (Palestine)....... (Roger Curtis) 1,200
Bien Cuit b f (2yrs) Good Times (ITY) - Me Spede (Valiyar)............... (E Diaz) 675
Lucky Helen b f (2yrs) Faustus (USA) - Lismore (Relkino)..... (R D Matthews) 700
Property of Mr J A Redmond
Dodgy b g (6yrs) Homing - Beryl's Jewel (Siliconn)................. (A Knight) 925
Property of Mr R Gray
Kalooki (IRE) ch g (2yrs) Dominion Royale - I Love Lucy (He Loves Me)........... (R Dawlatshahi) 1,000
Property of Mr Alan Spargo
Nick The Biscuit b c (2yrs) Nicholas Bill - Maryland Cookie (USA) (Bold Hour).... (Mark Usher) 1,600
Property of Mr R J Fairlea
Elwazir (USA) b or br g (4yrs) The Minstrel (CAN) - Romeo's Coquette (USA) (Gallant Romeo (USA)).......... (R John) 1,250
To Dissolve a Partnership
Bird Trouble (IRE) b g (3yrs) Bluebird (USA) - La Troublerie (Will Somers).......... (Caroline Walden) 800
Alphonso b g (4yrs) Forzando - Alice Parry (Kampala)................. (Ann Bird) 1,050

475

Property of IRC Limited
Lady Governess b f (2yrs) Governor General - Lochmar (Lochnager) .... (Mrs F Morris) 1,050
Property of Merthyr Tydfil Car Auctions Ltd
Monday At Three ch g (3yrs) Absalom - Angel's Sing (Mansingh) .... (M J Bateman) 850
To Dissolve a Partnership
Ever So Artistic ch g (6yrs) Claude Monet (USA) - Ever So (Mummy's Pet)....... (Mr Cooper) 700
Property of Broughton Thermal Insulation
Broughton Blues (IRE) ch g (5yrs) Tender King - Princess Galicia (Welsh Pageant) (D Morley) 1,700
To Dissolve a Partnership
Who's Tom (IRE) b g (3yrs) Tate Gallery (USA) - Clover Princess (Right Tack)... (Mr Smail) 1,000
Property of Mrs M Smith
Roly Wallace b g (4yrs) Primo Dominie - Ethel Knight (Thatch (USA))........... (A L Forbes) 1,900
To Dissolve a Partnership
Old Comrades ch g (6yrs) Music Boy - Miss Candine (King Emperor (USA)).. (Cash) 1,600
Karib b f (3yrs) K-Battery - Bonny's Pet (Mummy's Pet)........... (K Tipping) 1,050
Property of Mr G H Jones
Cipriani Queen (IRE) b f (3yrs) Seattle Dancer (USA) - Justsayno (USA) (Dr Blum (USA))........... (D F Pengelly) 2,200
Onewithwhitepaw ch g (3yrs) Vaigly Great - Aunt Blue (Blue Refrain) (Adrian Kirby) 1,600

476

Property of a Gentleman, from Upshire Farm Stables
Jafetica gr f (3yrs) Kalaglow - Rashah (Blakeney).................... (Cash) 1,350
From West Ilsley Stables
Pipers Reel ch f (3yrs) Palace Music (USA) - Fair Country (Town And Country)...... (James Williams) 1,000
Steppe Closer gr f (3yrs) Nishapour (FR) - Red Shoes (Dance In Time)........... (C Westmeads) 3,200
Property of Mr L G Lichfield
Bowland Girl (IRE) b f (4yrs) Supreme Leader - El Marcia (Buckskin (FR))..... (Cash) 2,000
Property of Mr H E Yates
Gay Ming b f (4yrs) Gay Meadow - Miss Admington (Double Jump) (K George) 1,350
Property of a Gentleman
Wiltoski b g (5yrs) Petoski - Cojean (USA) (Prince John).............. (R Ledger) 3,200
To Dissolve a Partnership
Raqs Assayf b g (3yrs) Sayf El Arab (USA) - Spin Me Round (High Top).. (Sue Teal) 1,550
Property of a Lady
Mels Rose ch g (8yrs) Anfield - Ragtime Rose (Ragstone)............ (R York) 1,600
Queen Of Dreams ch m (5yrs) Ti King (FR) - Humeur de Reve (USA) (Lord Avie (USA))........................ (Cash) 1,400
Property of a Partnership
Westray b g (3yrs) Caerwent - Mindena (FR) (Bellman)....... (D R Wellicome) 950

477

Property of Bankhouse Stables
Shamaaly Baby (USA) ch g (5yrs) Northern Baby (CAN) - Shining Skin (USA) (Fappiano (USA))........... (Lisa Bentley) 1,100

Sicily Oak b f (3yrs) Ballacashtal (CAN) - Martydom (USA) (Excellor)..... (Cash) 1,600

To Dissolve a Partnership

Abbreviation b g (10yrs) Torus - Wordling (Linacre)........................ (Cash) 1,100

Property of Mr S B Glazer

Dunraven Royal b g (10yrs) Le Bavard (FR) - Vulstar (Vulgan)....... (Mr McDonour) 975

Property of Mr C F Colquhoun

Oh So Handy b g (5yrs) Nearly A Hand - Geordie Lass (Bleep Bleep)........... (Roger Curtis) 2,000

Property of Mrs Kate Curtis

Planet Forum b g (3yrs) Dowsing (USA) - Bertida (Porto Bello)...... (Mr Darnell) 1,000

Property of Mr W A Sellers

Our Survivor b g (9yrs) Trimmingham - Lougharue (Deep Run) (T Underwood) 900

Property of Mrs J Gill

Magsood ch g (8yrs) Mill Reef (USA) - Shark Song (Song)......... (D J Line) 1,700

Property of Mr A P Boden

Belafonte b g (6yrs) Derrylin - Ulla Laing (Mummy's Pet)........... (K George) 3,600

From Weathercock House Stables

Kalakate gr g (8yrs) Kalaglow - Old Kate (Busted).................. (B O'Neill) 2,600

Manzoor Sayadan (USA) b g (5yrs) Shahrastani (USA) - Icing (Prince Tenderfoot (USA))..... (Mrs A B Appleyard) 2,500

478

To Disolve a Partnership

Copper Beach Lady b m (7yrs) Andretti - Mon Chapeau (High Hat)....... (Cash) 950

Property of Mr W H Dore

Sunley Sparkle b m (5yrs) Sunley Builds - Royal Darwin (Royal Palm).... (B.B.A.) 1,200

Property of Mr G Jones

Turbo Minstrel b g (6yrs) Roselier (FR) - Magic Minstrel (Pitpan) .... (David Barnard) 4,400

Property of Mr D J Caro

Time Star (NZ) br g (9yrs) Drums Of Time (USA) - Crescent Star (NZ) (Persian Garden)................ (B Champion) 3,000

Property of Mr David Smith

Charmers Wish b m (9yrs) Beau Charmeur - Velvet's Wish (Three Wishes)......... (R Barber) 2,400

To Dissolve a Partnership

Into The Future b g (6yrs) Mummy's Game - Valley Farm (Red God) (Mrs A Porter) 850

Property of Mr A Roxburgh

Greenhill Go On b or br m (8yrs) Oats - Ballylaneen (Master Buck)............ (Brills Racing) 1,850

Property of Mr R T Macauley, from Ballyward Stud (Co Wicklow)

Cheeky Mouse (IRE) b m (5yrs) Torus - Stormy Breeze (Little Buskins)........ (Morris Avison) 3,100

Dunloughan ch g (8yrs) Torus - Polrevagh (Bargello)............... (Lisa Wallis) 2,100

Sorrel Hill b g (6yrs) Mandalus - Lamb's Head (Laser Light).... (Shirley Vickery) 3,400

479

Property of Mr R J Hodges

Vermont Magic b g (5yrs) Elegant Air - Jove's Voodoo (USA) (Northern Jove (CAN))...................... (G Heal) 850

Property of the Exors of the late Mrs P J Palmer

b g (5yrs) Hyrossi - Hello Luna (The Bo'sun) .... (Cash) 1,300

ch m (6yrs) Hyrossi - Hello Luna (The Bo'sun)................... (Mr Talbot) 1,050

Property of Mr O W King

b g (4yrs) Capricorn Line - Polygon (Tarboosh (USA))............ (C Cornish) 2,500

Property of Countrywide Classic Ltd

Countrywide Boy br g (3yrs) Jalmood (USA) - Embroglio (USA) (Empery (USA))..... (Mr Smail) 1,300

Property of Mrs J Lees

Sharptino ch g (4yrs) Bustino - Sharper Still (Sharpen Up)............. (B Hughes) 1,500

Property of Ballyaden Horses

(IRE) b m (5yrs) Hard Fought - Arista (FR) (Thatching)............ (G Rosevear) 1,550

Property of Mr & Mrs C Wilson

b g (4yrs) Lepanto (GER) - Joyful's Girl (White Prince).......... (R K P Jones) 1,600

Property of The Forum Bloodstock Ltd

Al Forum (IRE) b c (3yrs) Common Grounds - Grange Hollow (Wolver Hollow)...... (O Neill) 950

Property of a Gentleman

Clean Sweep b g (6yrs) Deep Run - The Charwoman (Menelek) .... (Janet Menzies) 4,000

480

To Disolve a Partnership

London Express ch m (9yrs) True Song - Loophole (London Gazette)........... (P R Pullen) 850

Property of Mr E R Bowman

Bartryn b m (8yrs) Barley Hill - Tarylin (Military).............. (Mrs A Jones) 2,000

Property of Mr A A King

Kings Hatch ch g (7yrs) Down The Hatch - Lady Hapsburg (Perhapsburg)......... (Mr Mills) 1,200

Property of Mr C J James

Miss Igloo ch f (2yrs) Beveled (USA) - Northern Scene (Habitat)............. (Antony Fanshawe) 1,100

Property of Mr A L C Figg

Shedarbo ch g (8yrs) Sagaro - Song Of Grace (Articulate).................... (David Smyly Bloodstock) 2,500

Property of Mrs V McKie

Bouley Bay b g (5yrs) Lightning Dealer - Cathedine Flyer (Green Shoon)........ (Mrs J L Raymond) 2,600

Property of Mr B Matthews

Lincoln Lieder ch g (6yrs) Balinger - Metaxa (Khalkis)................. (P R Pullen) 750

Property of Mr P F Henderson

Tomalley b g (9yrs) Reformed Character - High Jean (Arrigle Valley)... (R Barber) 1,300

Daybrook Verb ch g (11yrs) Proverb - Daybrook Lass (Daybrook Lad).. (Cash) 575

Property of Mr T R R Farr

Castlebay Lad br g (10yrs) Crozier - Carbery Star (Kemal)..................... (Cash) 2,700

481

Property of Mr Alan Godrich

Fiction Writer ch g (9yrs) Quayside - Chapter Four (Shackleton)...... (B A Wells) 700

Property of Mr Malcolm Long

Ronocco ch g (11yrs) Baptism - Kilteelagh Lady (King's Leap)............. (Cash) 850

RE-OFFERED

Property of a Partnership

Yabbadabbadoo b g (7yrs) Royal Fountain - Annie Buskins (Little Buskins)......... (Lena Bedford) 2,400

Property of Mr D J E Sherry

Valiant Star b g (7yrs) Noalto - Duns Tew (Mandamus)............. (J Di Marte) 2,500

Property of Mr R J Hodges

Edge Of The Glen b g (5yrs) Alleging (USA) - Scotch Bonnet (Supreme Sovereign) (Mrs P M Bristol) 1,200

Nova Champ ch g (5yrs) Nearly-A-Hand - Laval (Cheval)........ (Rodney Lucas) 1,300

Bare Highlander b g (7yrs) Kambalda - Banross (Allangrange).......... (Cash) 900

Property of Mrs R V James

Annette's Venture ch g (11yrs) Kemal (FR) - Boon Adventure (London Gazette)..... (T Morris) 500

482

NEWMARKET

Wednesday, September 29th (Yearlings)

Property of Grange Hill Stud (UK)

b y f Night Shift (USA) - Jouvencelle (Rusticaro (FR)) (Darley Stud Management) 26,000

Property of Mr and Mrs Jim Strange, from Launceston Stud

ch y f Cadeaux Genereux - Jubilee Song (Song).................. (Rae Guest) 36,000

Property of P D Player, from Whatton Manor Stud

ch y c Night Shift (USA) - Jungle Rose (Shirley Heights)...... (Jack Ramsden) 33,000

From Fares Stables

b y c Nashwan (USA) - Just Class (Dominion)................ (Demmy O'Byrne) 24,000

From Mary James (Cotswold Stud Farms)

b y c Green Desert (USA) - Kereolle (Riverman (USA))......... (Shadwell Estate) 42,000

Property of a Partnership, from Heatherwold Stud

(USA) ch y f Woodman (USA) - Key Tothe Minstrel (USA) (The Minstrel (CAN))... (B.B.A. (Italia)) 36,000

Property of Minster Enterprises Ltd, from Minster Stud

gr y c Caerleon (USA) - Kilmara (USA) (Caro) .... (John Ferguson Bloodstock) 90,000

From Cedar Tree Stud

ch y c Be My Guest (USA) - Konbola (Superlative)................ (B.B.A.) 23,000

Property of Major and Mrs R B Kennard, from Kirtlington Stud

b y c Dominion - La Cabrilla (Carwhite) .... (Rae Guest) 20,000

b y c Green Desert (USA) - La Tuerta (Hot Spark)............................ (Gainsborough Stud Management) 120,000

483

From Cheveley Park Stud

b y c Slip Anchor - Lady Barrister (Law Society (USA))..... (Derby Bloodstock) 25,000

Property of Brick Kiln Stud & Partners, from Brick Kiln Stud

b y c Lear Fan (USA) - Lady Blackfoot (Prince Tenderfoot (USA)) .... (Gainsborough Stud Management) 100,000

Property of Fares Stables Ltd, from Fares Stables

b y f Distant Relative - Lady Lamia (USA) (Secreto (USA))........ (Ben Hanbury) 14,500

From Camas Park Stud, Ireland

b y c Alzao (USA) - Leyete Gulf (Slip Anchor)..................... (B.B.A.) 56,000

Property of Fares Stables Ltd, from Fares Stables

b y f Warning - Litani River (USA) (Irish River (FR))................... (C.B.A.) 34,000

Property of P D Player, from Whatton Manor Stud

b y c Green Desert (USA) - Little Loch (Reform)................ (Rae Guest) 30,000

Property of P V and Mrs J P Jackson, from Trickledown Stud

b y f Beldale Flutter (USA) - Little White Star (Mill Reef (CAN)).. (Reg Akehurst) 35,000

Property of C Bothway, from West Stow Stud

Miss Trouble b y f Lear Fan (USA) - Littlemisstrouble (USA) (My Gallant (USA))..... (David Minton Bloodstock) 19,000

Property of Limestone Stud

ch y f Night Shift (USA) - Loreef (Main Reef)..... (John Ferguson Bloodstock) 36,000

From Floors Stud

ch y c Cadeaux Genereux - Loucoum (FR) (Iron Duke (FR)) .... (Gainsborough Stud Management) 60,000

484

From Tullamaine Castle Stud Ireland, Agent

b y f Sadler's Wells (USA) - Loveliest (USA) (Tibaldo)............... (B.B.A. (Italia)) 90,000

From Ballyhampshire Stud, Ireland

b or br y f Thatching - Lover's Rose (King Emperor (USA))............... (C.B.A.) 38,000

Property of a Partnership, from Newtownbarry House Stud, Ireland

ch y f Bluebird (USA) - Lucky For Me (Appiani II)............ (Corbally Stud) 11,000

From Haras du Quesnay, France
(USA) ch y c Bering - Madame Alydar (USA) (Alydar (USA)) .... (Ben Hanbury & C Gordon-Watson) 25,000
From Cheveley Park Stud
br y c Nashwan (USA) - Made Of Pearl (USA) (Nureyev (USA)) .... (B.B.A. (Ireland)) 125,000
From Mount Coote Stud, Ireland
b y c Bluebird (USA) - Maellen (River Beauty)............. (B.B.A. (Ireland)) 27,000
From Green Ireland Properties Ltd
(USA) ch y c Woodman (USA) - Maria Roberta (Roberto (USA))...... (C.B.A.) 65,000
Property of of Tsarina Stud, from Overbury Stud
b y c Green Desert (USA) - Marie D'Argonne (Jefferson) .... (German International Bloodstock) 100,000
From Mary James (Cotswold Stud Farms)
b y c Warning - Marseillaise (Artaius (USA)) (Conti Bloodstock Services) 31,000
From Corbally Stud, Ireland
b y c Darshaan - Maryinsky (USA) (Northern Dancer)........... (Demmy O'Byrne) 78,000

485

From Landscape Stud, Ireland, Agent
b y f Danehill (USA) - Massawippi (Be My Native (USA)) .... (David Minton Bloodstock) 46,000
Property of Ridgecourt Stud, from Woodcote Stud
(FR) b y c Saumarez - Merry Sharp (Sharpen Up).................. (John Dunlop) 33,000
From Barronstown Stud, Ireland
b y f Sadler's Wells (USA) - Mill Princess (Mill Reef (USA))... (Demmy O'Byrne) 410,000
From Camas Park Stud, Ireland
b y c Persian Bold - Miss Siddons (Cure The Blues) .... (German International Bloodstock) 120,000
From Red House Stud
b y c Be My Chief (USA) - Miss Top Ville (FR) (Top Ville)............... (B.B.A.) 17,000
Property of Minster Enterprises Ltd, from Minster Stud
ch y f Unfuwain (USA) - Model Bride (USA) (Blushing Groom (FR)) ..... (C Gordon-Watson Bloodstock) 28,000
Property of M L Page, from Westerlands Stud
b y c Midyan (USA) - Modica (Persian Bold) (Will Edmeades Bloodstock) 25,000
From Pinfold Stud
b y c Night Shift (USA) - Moonscape (Ribero).... (John Warren Bloodstock) 34,000
Property of a Partnership, from Cobhall Court Stud
ch y c Rock City - More Rizz (Morston (FR)) (Peter Doyle Bloodstock) 30,000
Property of Highclere Stud Ltd
b y c Slip Anchor - Mountain Bluebird (USA) (Clever Trick (USA)).... (B.B.A. (Italia)) 20,000

486

Property of Hesmonds Stud
b y f Green Desert (USA) - Mountain Memory (High Top)...... (Shadwell Estate) 26,000
Property of a Partnership of Meon Valley Stud, from Meon Valley Stud
b y c Elmaamul (USA) - Moviegoer (Pharly (FR)).................. (James Toller) 25,000
Property of J M Greetham, from Gazeley Stud
b y c Warning - Much Too Risky (Bustino) (Michael Stoute) 25,000
From Cornbury Park Stud
b y f Mtoto - Neatfoot (Anfield) .... (Edward Dunlop) 8,500
From Mary James (Cotswold Stud Farms)
(USA) ch y f Arctic Tern - Nether Poppleton (USA) (Deputy Minister (CAN)) .... (Ian Balding) 15,000
Property of a Partnership, from Manor House Stud
ch y f Royal Academy (USA) - Nice Point (Sharpen Up).......... (Dermot Weld) 75,000
Property of Hesmonds Stud
gr y f Mtoto - Nicholas Grey (Track Spare) (John Dunlop) 32,000
Property of a Partnership, from Batsford Stud
ch y f Thatching - Nikitina (Nijinsky (CAN)) (Darley Stud Management) 60,000
Property of Kiltinan Farms Inc, Ireland
b y f Danehill (USA) - Noblanna (USA) (Vaguely Noble)........ (B.B.A. (Italia)) 18,000
From Corbally Stud, Ireland
b y c Danehill (USA) - Noble Dust (USA) (Dust Commander (USA)) .... (Ben Hanbury) 46,000

487

Property of Grange Stud (UK)
b y f Rainbow Quest (USA) - Northshiel (Northfields (USA))........... (B.B.A.) 45,000
From Red House Stud
ch y f Most Welcome - Odile (Green Dancer (USA))......... (B.B.A. (Italia)) 6,500
Property of Sir Eric Parker, from Crimbourne Stud
b or br y c Law Society (USA) - One Life (USA) (L'emigrant (USA))....... (Cash) 24,000
Property of a Partnership, from Partridge Close Stud
b y c Dancing Brave (USA) - One Way Street (Habitat)...................... (Darley Stud Management) 160,000
From Partridge Close Stud
b y c Shirley Heights - Opale (Busted) ..... (Anglia Bloodstock) 50,000
From Haras du Quesnay, France
Passionnee (USA) b y f Woodman (USA) - Pallanza (USA) (Lyphard (USA))........ (London Thoroughbred Services) 160,000
Property of Childwick Bury Stud Management Ltd, from Childwick Bury Stud
ch or gr y c Night Shift (USA) - Pamela Peach (Habitat).... (Derby Bloodstock) 27,000
From Camas Park Stud, Ireland
b y f Sadler's Wells (USA) - Passamaquoddy (USA) (Drone) ... (Tim Bulwer-Long) 230,000
From Haras d'Etreham, France
(USA) ch y c Groom Dancer (USA) - Perle Fine (USA) (Devil's Bag (USA)) .... (D Woods) 62,000

Property of Blue Blood Investments, from Woodcote Stud
b y c Waajib - Phantom Row (Adonijah).... (Demmy O'Byrne) 35,000

488

Property of Corkrose Ltd, from Charlton Down Stud
gr y c Law Society (USA) - Pharland (FR) (Bellypha)............ (Gay Kelleway) 5,500
Property of a Partnership of Meon Valley Stud, from Meon Valley Stud
b y f Slip Anchor - Pick Of The Pops (High Top)........ (R O'Gorman Bloodstock) 94,000
Property of a Partnership, from Bloomsbury Stud
Open Space ch y c Green Dancer (USA) - Picnicing (Good Times (ITY)).......... (Peter Wragg Bloodstock) 35,000
Property of Biddestone Stud
b y c Last Tycoon - Pizziri (Artaius (USA)) .. (Brian Grassick Bloodstock) 120,000
Property of Kiltinan Farms Inc, Ireland
br y c Machiavellian (USA) - Place Of Honour (Be My Guest (USA))............ (Gainsborough Stud Management) 70,000
From Side Hill Stud
b y c Shaadi (USA) - Pluvial (Habat)........ (Sheikh Ahmed Al Sabah) 26,000
From Tullamaine Castle Stud, Ireland, Agent
b y c Sadler's Wells (USA) - Porphyrine (FR) (Habitat)............ (Shadwell Estate) 200,000
Property of F C T Wilson, from The Elms Stud
b y c Slip Anchor - Precious Jade (Northfields (USA))........... (B.B.A. (Italia)) 41,000

489

NEWMARKET
Thursday, September 30th (Yearlings)

Property of Mr and Mrs D A Hicks, from Buckhurst Stud
br y f Be My Chief (USA) - Premiere Cuvee (Formidable (USA)).................... (John Warren Bloodstock) 42,000
From Catridge Farm Stud
ch y c Cadeaux Genereux - Princess Athena (Ahonoora)............ (Ray Richards) 68,000
Property of Haresfoot Stud, from Whitsbury Manor Stud
ch y f Cadeaux Genereux - Princess Eboli (Brigadier Gerard)............ (Conti Bloodstock Services) 24,000
Property of Northmore Stud Farm
(USA) b y f Arctic Tern (USA) - Princess Toy (Prince Tenderfoot (USA)) .... (Clive Brittain) 17,000
Property of Fares Stables Ltd, from Fares Stables
b y f Mtoto - Prospector's Star (USA) (Mr Prospector (USA))...... (B.B.A. (Italia)) 7,800
From Barronstown Stud, Ireland
b y f Sadler's Wells (USA) - Proud Pattie (USA) (Noble Commander (USA))...... (Conti Bloodstock Serviceds) 78,000

Property of Moygaddy Stud, Ireland
b y f Last Tycoon - Pu Yi (Habitat)........ (Clive Brittain) 16,000
Property of Haras du Quesnay, France
(FR) b y f Saumarez - Racing Connection (USA) (Sharpen Up)............ (Cash) 28,000
From Furnace Mill Stud
b y f Indian Ridge - Radiant (USA) (Foolish Pleasure (USA))........ (Andrew Mead International Bloodstock) 30,000
Property of Fares Stables Ltd, from Fares Stables
b y f Warning - Rally For Justice (Dominion) .... (Mark Johnston) 28,000

490

Property of a Partnership of Meon Valley Stud, from Meon Valley Stud
ch y f In The Wings - Rappa Tap Tap (FR) (Tap On Wood).... (Castlemartin Stud) 62,000
From Cheveley Park Stud
b y c Never So Bold - Ravaro (Raga Navarro (ITY)).................... (B.B.A.) 30,000
Property of Readycare Ltd, from Coomb Hill Farm
(USA) ch y c Gulch (USA) - Realisatrice (USA) (Raja Baba (USA))............... (Cormac McCormack Associates) 105,000
Property of Sion House Stud, Ireland (Agent)
ch y c Ballad Rock - Recamier (Reform) ... (Ivan Allan (Hong Kong)) 54,000
Property of P V and Mrs J P Jackson, from Trickledown Stud
ch y f Sharpo - Red Gloves (Red God)..... (R F Kilby) 36,000
From Northmore Stud Farm
b y c Aragon - Red Rose Garden (Electric) (Darley Stud Management) 56,000
From Batsford Stud
b y c Slip Anchor - Res Nova (USA) (Blushing Groom (FR)).......... (Barry Hills) 5,000
Property of a Partnership, from Manor House Stud
b y f Shareef Dancer (USA) - Rexana (Relko) .... (Frank Barry) 18,000
Property of Grange Stud (UK)
ch y f Polish Precedent (USA) - Riviere Bleue (Riverman (USA))........... (Peter Wragg Bloodstock) 15,000
Property of Lordship and Egerton Studs Ltd, from Lordship and Egerton Studs
b y f Woodman (USA) - Rose de Thai (USA) (Lear Fan (USA)).............. (Lillingston Bloodstock) 42,000

491

Property of Kirtlington Stud
ch y c Shadeed (USA) - Rosie Potts (Shareef Dancer (USA)) .... (Mark Johnston) 28,000
Property of a Partnership, from Bloomsbury Stud
b y c Green Desert (USA) - Roussalka (Habitat).. (Shadwell Estate Company) 105,000
Property of Marston Stud & Grange Nominees, from Marston Stud
b y f Nordico (USA) - Royal Climber (Kings Lake (USA)).............. (Darley Stud Management) 33,000

Property of P D Player, from Whatton Manor Stud

ch y c Old Vic - Royal Loft (Homing)....... (B.B.A.) 25,000

From Hilltown Stud, Ireland

b or gr y c Shaadi (USA) - Rustic Lawn (Rusticaro (FR)).......... (Frank Barry) 11,000

From Lodge Park Stud, Ireland

b y c Night Shift (USA) - Sail Loft (Shirley Heights)............ (Dwayne Woods) 42,000

From Tullamaine Castle Stud Ireland, Agent

gr y c Caerleon (USA) - Sandstream (Sandford Lad)............. (Tommy Stack) 23,000

From Furnace Mill Stud

b y f Last Tycoon - Santa Roseanna (Caracol (FR))............. (Dermot Weld) 24,000

Property of Ridgecourt Stud, from Woodcote Stud

b y c Kahyasi - Sarah Georgina (Persian Bold).................. (Mrs Thomas) 50,000

Property of Springfield Thoroughbred Syndicate, from Ardenode Stud, Ireland

b y c Cadeaux Genereux - Sauceboat (Connaught).......... (Gainsborough Stud) 42,000

492

Property of Hesmonds Stud

b y f Distant Relative - Sculpture Bleue (Claude Monet (USA))..... (Barry Hills) 28,000

From Camas Park Stud, Ireland

ch y f Royal Academy (USA) - Seminar (Don (ITY))..... (Brian Grassick Bloodstock) 70,000

Property of Mrs C F van Straubenzee and Partners, from Heatherwold Stud

ch y f Be My Chief (USA) - Settlement (USA) (Irish River (FR))...... (K Fisher) 16,000

From Camas Park Stud, Ireland

b y c Sadler's Wells (USA) - Sharp Castan (Sharpen Up).......... (Patrick Barbe) 215,000

From Mount Coote Stud, Ireland

b y c Roi Danzig (USA) - Sheer Audacity (Troy)................ (B.B.A. (Ireland)) 57,000

From Tullamaine Castle Stud, Ireland, Agent

ch y f Machiavellian (USA) - Shirley Reef (Shirley Heights)..................... (Darley Stud Management) 45,000

From Cheveley Park Stud

b y c Soviet Star (USA) - Shore Line (High Line)........................ (B.B.A.) 25,000

From Mary James (Cotswold Stud Farms)

Ragera (IRE) b y f Rainbow Quest (USA) - Smageta (High Top)................. (Conti Bloodstock Services) 30,000

From Mount Coote and Tsarina Studs, Ireland

b y c Night Shift (USA) - Smeralda (GER) (Dschingis Khan) .... (Conti Bloodstock Services) 44,000

Property of a Partnership, from Landscape Stud, Ireland

ch y f Be My Guest (USA) - Smoo (Kris) ... (Charles O'Brien) 30,000

493

Property of a Partnership of Meon Valley Stud, from Meon Valley Stud

b y f Night Shift (USA) - Someone Special (Habitat).... (R O'Gorman Bloodstock) 260,000

From Landscape Stud, Ireland, Agent

b y f Alzao (USA) - Spring Reel (Mill Reef (USA))............................ (Gainsborough Stud Management) 41,000

From Floors Stud

b y c Persian Bold - Starr Danias (USA) (Sensitive Prince (USA)).............. (Darley Stud Management) 70,000

Property of Fluorocarbon Bloodstock Ltd, from Chippenham Lodge Stud

b y c Polish Precedent (USA) - Startino (Bustino).................... (C.B.A.) 22,000

From Mount Coote Stud, Ireland

b y f Sadler's Wells (USA) - Steel Habit (Habitat).. (Shadwell Estate Company) 180,000

Property of Mrs Mary Taylor, from Kirtlington Stud

b or br y f Prince Sabo - Stinging Nettle (Sharpen Up)................ (B.B.A.) 25,000

From Haras d'Etreham, France

(USA) b y c El Gran Senor (USA) - Stricly (ARG) (Dancing Moss) .... (Shadwell Estate Company) 70,000

Property of Mr C Bothway, from West Stow Stud

(USA) b y f Lomond (USA) - Suprematie (FR) (Gay Mecene (USA))............. (Henry Candy) 16,000

Property of Mary James (Cotswold Stud Farms)

b y f Last Tycoon - Sweeping (Indian King (USA)).... (John Ferguson Bloodstock) 25,000

From Cheveley Park Stud

ch y c Mr Prospector (USA) - Sweet Slew (USA) (Seattle Slew (USA)) .... (John Ferguson Bloodstock) 150,000

494

Property of a Partnership, from Mary James (Cotswold Stud Farms)

Takeshi (IRE) b y f Cadeaux Genereux - Taplow (Tap On Wood) .... (Gainsborough Stud Management) 52,000

Property of Mr T D Holland-Martin and Mr J Haverhals, from Overbury Stud

ch y c Kris - Tashinsky (USA) (Nijinsky (USA))................... (Barry Hills) 40,000

Property of Mr C Ford, from Whatton Manor Stud

b y c Shirley Heights - Tea Rose (Moorestyle)............................. (Gainsborough Stud Management) 50,000

Property of Bryanstown House Stud, Ireland

b y c Royal Academy (USA) - Tendermark (Prince Tenderfoot (USA)) .... (Panetta Bloodstock) 28,000

Property of Sarl Ewar Stud Farms, from Haras de la Pomme, France

Soldier's Leap (FR) b y c Warning - Thalestria (FR) (Mill Reef (USA))....... (Clive Brittain) 42,000

Property of a Partnership, from Landscape Stud, Ireland

gr y f Royal Academy (USA) - Thistlewood (Kalamoun) (David Minton Bloodstock) 52,000

Property of Mr T D Holland-MNartin, from Overbury Stud

b y f Slip Anchor - Throw Away Line (USA) (Assert).............. (B.B.A. (Italia)) 33,000

From Hollyhill Stud, Ireland
b y c Danehill (USA) - To The Limit (Junius (USA)).............. (William Haggas) 32,000

From Barronstown Stud, Ireland
b y c Royal Academy (USA) - Tobira Celeste (USA) (Ribot)........... (Noel Meade) 22,000

Property of a Partnership, from Milton Park Stud
b y f Elmaamul (USA) - Tolstoya (Northfields (USA))..............(C Gordon-Watson Bloodstock) 19,000

495

From Camas Park Stud, Ireland
b y c Sadler's Wells (USA) - Topping Girl (Sea Hawk II)...... (Demmy O'Byrne) 310,000

From Green Ireland Properties Ltd
(USA) b y c Simply Majestic (USA) - Total Chic (USA) (Far North (CAN)) .... (Dwayne Woods) 32,000

Property of Hesmonds Stud
b y f Zalazl (USA) - Triple Reef (Mill Reef (USA)).................... (J Dunlop) 26,000

From Mary James (Cotswold Stud Farms)
(USA) br y c Lyphard (USA) - Triple Tipple (USA) (Raise A Cup (USA)) .... (John Warren Bloodstock) 86,000

From Cheveley Park Stud
b y c In The Wings - Troyanos (Troy) ...... (Sheikh Ahmed Al Sabah) 48,000

Property of Stowell Hill Ltd
ch y f Night Shift (USA) - Turban (Glint Of Gold).. (Geoffrey Howson Bloodstock) 96,000

Property of Branston Stud
ch y c Risk Me (FR) - Tuxford Hideaway (Cawston's Clown).... (Mrs B Haggas) 24,000

Property of a Partnership, from Whatton Manor Stud
ch y c Polish Precedent (USA) - Upend (Main Reef)................. (C.B.A.) 40,000

Property of a Partnership of Meon Valley Stud, from Meon Valley Stud
b y f Fairy King (USA) - Upper Circle (Shirley Heights).... (R O'Gorman Bloodstock) 66,000

Property of a Partnership, from Cheveley Park Stud
b y c Prince Sabo - Valika (Valiyar)......... (Cormac McCormack Associates) 150,000

496

Property of Landscape Stud, Ireland
ch y c Roi Danzig (USA) - Warm December (He Loves Me)....... (B.B.A. (Ireland)) 40,000

From Barronstown Stud, Ireland
b y c Danehill (USA) - Wedgewood Blue (USA) (Sir Ivor)............ (M Bastard) 9,000

Property of Mr P D Player, from Whatton Manor Stud
ch or gr y f Unfuwain (USA) - Well Off (Welsh Pageant)..... (Mark Johnston) 7,000

Property of Camas Park Stud, Ireland
(FR) b y f Sadler's Wells (USA) - Whakilyric (USA) (Miswaki (USA)) .... (German International Bloodstock) 880,000

Property of Barrettstown Stud Farms Ltd, from Whitsbury Manor Stud
ch y c Kris - What A Pity (Blakeney) .... (Horse France) 33,000

From Lyonstown Stud, Ireland (Agent)
(USA) b y c Shirley Heights - Woodstream (USA) (Northern Dancer) (Frank Barry) 5,000

Property of Fares Stables Ltd, from Fares Stables
b y f Warrshan (USA) - Ymirkhan (FR) (Kashmir II) .... (Brian Grassick Bloodstock) 8,000

From Ashtown House Stud, Ireland
(USA) b y c Thorn Dance (USA) - Zummerudd (Habitat)............. (B.B.A.) 70,000

From Camas Park Stud, Ireland
b y f Royal Academy (USA) - Aces Full (USA) (Round Table).......... (B.B.A.) 58,000

From Hilborough Stud Farm
br y f Caerleon (USA) - Aghsan (Lord Gayle (USA))......... (Amanda Skiffington) 82,000

497

Property of Exors of the late Sir Robin McAlpine, from Wyck Hall Stud
b y c Rainbow Quest (USA) - Aigue (High Top)................ (William Haggas) 35,000

Property of Fares Stables Ltd, from Fares Stables
b y c Rainbow Quest (USA) - Aldbourne (Alzao (USA))........................ (Shadwell Estate Company) 100,000

Property of a Partnership, from Farmers Hill Stud
gr y f Don't Forget Me - Aldem Stream (Godswalk (USA)).. (James Fanshawe) 28,000

Property of Hesmonds Stud
(USA) b y c Trempolino (USA) - All For Hope (USA) (Sensitive Prince (USA)) .... (John Gosden) 48,000

From Hilltown Stud, Ireland
(USA) ch y c Elmaamul (USA) - Allesheny (Be My Guest (USA)) .... (Shadwell Estate Company) 48,000

Property of a Partnership, from Mary James (Cotswold Stud Farms)
b y f Royal Academy (USA) - Alys (Blakeney) .... (German International Bloodstock) 210,000

From Crimbourne Stud
ch y f Rainbow Quest (USA) - An Empress (USA) (Affirmed (USA))....... (B.B.A.) 42,000

Property of Mr N W L Abbott, from Britton House Stud
gr y c Reprimand - Anneli Rose (Superlative)..... (Shadwell Estate Company) 52,000

From Red House Stud
b y f Most Welcome - Aonia (Mummy's Pet)... (Johnny McKeever Bloodstock) 9,400

Property of a division of General Agricultural Services Ltd, from Ted Voute, Agent
(USA) b y c Alleged (USA) - Arctic Eclipse (USA) (Northern Dancer) ... (C Gordon-Watson Bloodstock) 33,000

498

From Camas Park Stud, Ireland
ch y c Royal Academy (USA) - Arctic Heroine (USA) (Arctic Tern (USA)) .... (C Gordon-Watson Bloodstock) 240,000

Property of Lordship and Egerton Studs Ltd, from Lordship and Egerton Studs
b y c Law Society (USA) - Arctic Winter (CAN) (Briartic (CAN))..... (Barry Hills) 35,000
Property of The Exors of the late Mrs V Hue-Williams, from Woolton House Stud
gr y c Sadler's Wells (USA) - As You Desire Me (Kalamoun).............. (B.B.A.) 105,000
Property of Fares Stables Ltd, from Fares Stables
b y c Rainbow Quest (USA) - Baddi Baddi (USA) (Sharpen Up).... (Ben Hanbury) 46,000
Property of Hockley Ltd, from Hockley House Stud
b y c Robellino (USA) - Ballerine (USA) (Lyphard's Wish (FR)) .... (Demmy O'Byrne) 24,000
Property of Earl of Halifax, from Side Hill Stud
b y c Soviet Star (USA) - Banket (Glint Of Gold)............. (James Fanshawe) 30,000
From Camas Park Stud, Ireland
ch y c Woodman (USA) - Ruby Setting (Gorytus (USA)) .... (R O'Gorman Bloodstock) 105,000

499

NEWMARKET
Friday, October 1st
(Yearlings)

From Airlike Stud, Ireland
ch y f Polish Precedent (USA) - Bay Empress (Empery (USA)) (D Elsworth) 23,000
from Camas Park Stud, Ireland
b y c Green Desert (USA) - Bay Shade (USA) (Sharpen Up).................. (Shadwell Estate Co) 100,000
From Collin Stud
b y f Warning - Beautiful Dawn (USA) (Grey Dawn II)............ (David Elsworth) 23,000
Property of Biddlestone Stud
(FR) b y c Royal Academy (USA) - Belle Arrivee (Bustino) .... (Gainsborough Stud Management) 120,000
Property of Earl of Halifax from Side Hill Stud
b y c Nashwan (USA) - Bempton (Blakeney) .... (Shadwell Estate Co) 150,000
From West Stow Stud
b y c Reference Point - Bex (USA) (Explodent (USA)).................. (T Stack) 13,000
Property of Fares Stables Ltd, from Fares Stable
gr y c Highest Honor (FR) - Bint Secreto (USA) (Secreto (USA))................ (Gainsborough Stud Management) 56,000
Property of Mr P D Player, from Whatton Manor Stud
ch y c Elmaamul (USA) - Blink Naskra (USA) (Naskra (USA))... (Panetta Bloodstock) 13,000
Property of Mr Alan Gibson, from Warren Park Stud
b y c Old Vic - Blue Brocade (Reform)..... (J Dunlop) 20,000
From Hever Castle Stud
b y c Efisio - Blue Jane (Blue Cashmere) ... (Darley Stud Management) 78,000

500

Property of a Partnership, from Bloomsbury Stud
Social Register ch y c Unfuwain (USA) - Bluebook (USA) (Secretariat (USA)).... (Shadwell Estate Co) 30,000
From Kirtlington Stud
b y f Diesis - Bonne Ile (Ile de Bourbon (USA))...................... (B B A) 28,000
From Northmore Stud Farm
(USA) ch y c Elmaamul (USA) - Both Sides Now (USA) (Topsider (USA)).......... (David Minton Bloodstock) 22,000
From Mary James (Cotswold Stud Farms)
b y f Shirley Heights - Bourbon And Honey (USA) (Key To Content (USA)) (B B A) 41,000
From Patridge Close Stud
b y c Night Shift (USA) - Briar Creek (Busted)... (David Minton Bloodstock) 23,000
From Batsford Stud
b y c Royal Academy (USA) - Brosna (USA) (Irish River (FR))... (Derby Bloodstock) 54,000
Property of a Partnership, from Milton Park Stud
ch y f Night Shift (USA) - Bundled Up (USA) (Sharpen Up) .... (C Gordon-Watson Bloodstock) 52,000
Property of Normanby Stud Ltd, from Floors Stud
b y f Slip Anchor - Canna (Caerleon (USA)) (Hugo Lascelles Bloodstock) 28,000
Property of Whitsbury Manor Stud
b or gr y c Cadeaux Genereux - Catch The Sun (Kalaglow) .... (Brian Grassick Bloodstock) 105,000
From Partridge Close Stud
b y c Be My Guest (USA) - Cavurina (Cavo Doro)................. (B B A (Italia)) 14,000

501

From Green Island Properties Ltd
(USA) ch y c Miswaki (USA) - Cedilla (USA) (Caro)...................... (B B A) 74,000
From Corbally Stud, Ireland
ch y f Persian Bold - Celestial Melody (USA) (The Minstrel (CAN)).. (B B A (Irealnd)) 48,000
From Ashtown House Stud, Ireland
(USA) ch y c El Gran Senor (USA) - Chalfont Place (USA) (Little Current (USA)) ..... (R Sangster) 160,000
From Camas Park Stud, Ireland
b y c Sadler's Wells (USA) - Chamonis (USA) (Affirmed (USA)).............. (B B A (Ireland)) 78,000
Property of Highclere Stud Ltd
ch y c Cadeaux Genereux - Chasing Moonbeams (Final Straw).......... (B Hills) 32,000
Property of Hesmonds Stud
b y c Shardari - Chicobin (USA) (J O Tobin (USA))............ (Sir Mark Prescott) 22,000
From Floors Stud
(FR) b y f Belmez (USA) - Chief's Quest (USA) (Chief's Crown (USA)).......... (Will Edmeades Bloodstock) 25,000
Property of Mr P D Player, from Whatton Manor Stud
b y c Last Tycoon - Choire Mhor (Dominion) .... (Fathi Kalla) 65,000

From Lyonstown Stud, Ireland (Agent)
ch y f Nashwan (USA) - Christabelle (USA) (Northern Dancer)........... (B B A) 190,000
From Mount Coote Stud, Ireland
b y c In The Wings - Circulate (High Top) .. (B B A (Italia)) 39,000

502

From Floors Stud
b y c Salse (USA) - Circus Act (Shirley Heights)..................... (H Cecil) 36,000
From Rathbarry Stud, Ireland (Agent)
b y f Alzao (USA) - Clanjingle (Tumble Wind (USA))......................... (D Weld) 75,000
Property of a Partnership, from Manor House Stud
b y c Shareef Dancer (USA) - Classic Design (Busted)............. (F Barry) 5,000
Property of a Partnership, from Westerlands Stud
b y f Green Desert (USA) - Clunk Click (Star Appeal).................. (B Hanbury) 46,000
Property of a Partnership, from Stowell Hill Ltd.
br y c Polish Precedent (USA) - Cockade (Derring-Do)................. (B B A) 160,000
Property of a Partnership of Meon Valley Stud, from Meon Valley Stud
b y f Warning - Colorvista (Shirley Heights) (Darley Stud Management) 75,000
From Cheveley Park Stud
b y c Reference Point - Comic Talent (Pharly (FR))........................ (Conti Bloodstock Services) 27,000
Property of Mrs B Long, from New England Stud
ch y f Unfuwain (USA) - Cominna (Dominion)......................... (B B A) 31,000
From Glenvale Stud, Ireland
b y f Fairy King (USA) - Commanche Belle (Shirley Heights) .... (C Gordon-Watson Bloodstock) 190,000
From Cornbury Park Stud
b y c Rainbow Quest (USA) - Consolation (Troy)....................... (B B A) 22,000

503

From Airlie Stud, Ireland
b y f In The Wings - Countess Candy (Great Nephew)................ (C Gordon-Watson Bloodstock) 22,000
Property of Wickfield Stud Ltd, from Wickfield Stud
b y c Persian Heights - Cremets (Mummy's Pet)...................... (J Dunlop) 35,000
From Glenvale Stud, Ireland
(USA) b y f Artichoke (USA) - Crimson Saint (USA) (Crimson Satan) (Guy Armengol) 360,000
From Green Ireland Properties Ltd
(USA) ch y c Danzig Connection (USA) - Crystal Cup (USA) (Nijinsky (CAN)) .... (Gainsborough Stud Management) 75,000
Property of Highclere Stud Ltd
b y c Persian Bold - Cubby Hole (Town And Country)........... (Lord Carnarvon) 70,000
Property of Mrs C F van Straubenzee and Partners, from Heatherwold Stud
b y c Thatching - Cut No Ice (Great Nephew) (John Ferguson Bloodstock) 46,000

Property of Laharna Ltd, from Greenland Park Stud
ch y f Rainbow Quest (USA) - Dame Ashfield (Grundy) .... (Darley Stud Management) 62,000
From Woodcote Stud
br y c Caerleon (USA) - Dance By Night (Northfields (USA)).... (T Bulwer-Long) 150,000
Property of Mr & Mrs D J Deer, from Fawley Stud
b y f Machiavellian (USA) - Dance Card (Be My Guest (USA)) .... (Gainsborough Stud Management) 46,000
From Barronstown Stud, Ireland
b y c High Estate - Dance Date (IRE) (Sadler's Wells (USA))........ (B Hills) 42,000

504

Property of Heatherwold Stud
b y c Polish Precedent (USA) - Dancing Crystal (Kris) .... (Darley Stud Management) 46,000
Property of a Partnership, from Genesis Green Stud
b y c Night Shift (USA) - Dazzling Heights (Shirley Heights).................... (David Minton Bloodstock) 24,000
From Fulling Mill Stud
b y f Thatching - Dazzlingly Radiant (Try My Best (USA))............... (R Hannon) 16,000
Property of Kessly Bloodstock Ltd, from Heatherwold Stud
b y f Mtoto - Diamond House (Habitat) .... (M Bell) 12,500
Property of Mrs P D Rossdale, from Cheveley Park Stud
b y f Belmez (USA) - Double Finesse (Double Jump) (Darley Stud Management) 94,000
From Camas Park Stud, Ireland
(USA) ch y f Woodman (USA) - Dry Fly (FR) (Mill Reef (USA))........ (Alex Scrope) 60,000
From Floors Stud
b y f Last Tycoon - Eastern Shore (Sun Prince).... (Darley Stud Management) 24,000
From Hever Castle Stud
b y c Efisio - Elkie Brooks (Relkino)........ (Shadwell Estate Co) 100,000
From Cheveley Park Stud
ch y c Rainbow Quest (USA) - Endless Joy (Law Society (USA)) .... (Gainsborough Stud Management) 150,000
From Ashtown House Stud, Ireland
b y c Scenic - Evangola (Persian Bold) ..... (B B A (Ireland)) 75,000

505

From Hever Castle Stud
b y f Efisio - Explosiva (USA) (Explodent (USA))........................ (B B A) 18,000
From Ashtown House Stud, Ireland
b y c High Estate - Exuberine (FR) (Be My Guest (USA))............ (D Southey) 90,000
Property of Overbury Stud
b y f Shirley Heights - Fairy Feet (Sadler's Wells (USA))............... (C Gordon-Watson Bloodstock) 34,000

From Patridge Close Stud
ch y c Irish River (FR) - Fateful Princess (USA) (Vaguely Noble)................ (Shadwell Estate Co) 65,000

Property of a Partnership, from Burningfold Manor Stud
b y f Unfuwain (USA) - Favorable Exchange (USA) (Exceller (USA))..... (C Brittain) 18,000

From Airlie Stud, Ireland
b y c Slip Anchor - Fenney Mill (Levmoss) (Dwayne Woods) 50,000

Property of a Partnership, from Batsford Stud
b y f Danehill (USA) - Festive Season (USA) (Lypheor)......... (Sir Mark Prescott) 26,000

Property of Miss C M H Wills, from Whatton Manor Stud
b y c Warning - Fetlar (Pharly (FR))........ (J Fanshawe) 22,000

From Lodge Park Stud, Ireland
b y f Waajib - Fettle (Relkino) (Jack Doyle) 45,000

Property of Heatherwold Stud
b y c Nashwan (USA) - Fiesta Fun (Welsh Pageant)............................ (Johnnie McKeever Bloodstock) 100,000

506

From Tullamaine Castle Stud, Ireland
b y f Last Tycoon - Fighting Run (Runnett) (John Warren Bloodstock) 50,000

From Lyonstown Stud, Ireland (Agent)
b y c Sadler's Wells (USA) - Fleur Royale (Mill Reef (USA))............ (D Weld) 220,000

Property of Sir Eric Parker. from Crimbourne Stud
gr y c Royal Academy (USA) - Flo Russell (USA) (Round Table)......... (D Weld) 60,000

From Ashtown House Stud, Ireland
b y c Danehill (USA) - Flyaway Bride (USA) (Blushing Groom (FR))........ (B Hills) 60,000

From Camas Park Stud, Ireland
b y c Dancing Brave (USA) - Forli's Treat (USA) (Forli (ARG)).......... (D Weld) 300,000

From Mary James (Cotswold Stud Farms)
Faldberg b y c Last Tycoon - Formosanta (USA) (Believe It (USA)).............. (Peter Doyle Bloodstock) 12,000

From Cornbury Park Stud
b y c Alzao (USA) - Freesia (Shirley Heights) .... (Sarah Lakin) 22,000

From Tullamaine Castle Stud, Ireland, Agent
b y c Sadler's Wells (USA) - Fruition (Rheingold)................ (T Stack) 150,000

From Camas Park Stud, Ireland.
b y c Night Shift (USA) - Gathering Place (USA) (Hawaii)....... (T Bulwer-Long) 54,000

Property of a Partnership, from Angley Stud
b y f Shaadi (USA) - Gibraltar Heights (High Top)................... (Jack Doyle) 110,000

507

Property of Bryanstown House Stud, Ireland
b y f Tirol - Glendora (Glenstal (USA))...... (Darley Stud Management) 31,000

Property of Sarl Ewar Stud Farms, from Haras de la Pomme, France
Lady Kate (USA) ch y f Trempolino (USA) - Glitter (FR) (Reliance II).... (C Brittain) 41,000

Property of a Partnership, from Mary James (Cotswold Stud Farms)
b y f Royal Academy (USA) - Glory Of Hera (Formidable (USA)) (Demmy O'Byrne) 32,000

Property of Mrs Hugh McCalmont, from Yeomanstown Lodge Stud, Ireland
b y c Alzao (USA) - Gracieuse Majeste (FR) (Saint Cyrien (FR)).................. (Conti Bloodstock Services) 40,000

Property of Stonethorn Stud Farms Ltd, from Carrowdore Castle Stud
ch y c Kris - Green Lucia (Green Dancer (USA))................... (B H Voak) 84,000

Property of Earl of Halifax, from Side Hill Stud
b y c Be My Guest (USA) - Gull Nook (Mill Reef (USA))........................ (John Ferguson Bloodstock) 54,000

From Ashtown House Stud, Ireland
(USA) b or br y c El Gran Senor (USA) - Hail The Lady (USA) (Hail The Pirates (USA)) .... (Demmy O'Byrne) 74,000

Property of Scarteen Stud, Ireland
b y c Tirol - Hajjar (Valiyar)....... (D Weld) 82,000

From Mount Coote Stud, Ireland
b y c Try My Best (USA) - Happy Landing (FR) (Homing).......... (B B A (Italia)) 26,000

From Patridge Close Stud
b y c Slip Anchor - Hayati (Hotfoot)........ (Cormac McCormack Associates) 16,000

508

From Greenville House Stud, Ireland, Agent
b y c Roi Danzig (USA) - Hazy Bird (Ballymore)..... (John Warren Bloodstock) 19,000

Property of a Partnership, from Mellon Stud, Ireland
b y c Polish Precedent (USA) - Heigh Of Passion (Shirley Heights)............ (Anthony Penfold Bloodstock) 105,000

Property of Fluorocarbon Bloodstock Ltd, from Chippenham Lodge Stud
b y c Darshaan - Helens Dreamgirl (Caerleon (USA)).............. (B Hills) 15,000

Property of a Partnership, from Cheveley Park Stud
ch y f Old Vic - Hello Cuddles (He Loves Me).......... (Broughton Homes Ltd) 10,000

From Camas Park Stud, Ireland
(FR) b y c Caerleon (USA) - Helpless Haze (USA) (Vaguely Noble) (Aemon Cleary) 16,000

Property of Mrs E M Burke, from Airlie Stud, Ireland
b y c Sadler's Wells (USA) - High Spirited (Shirley Heights).................... (Darley Stud Management) 460,000

Property of Landscape Stud, Ireland
b y c Danehill (USA) - Hogan's Sister (USA) (Speak John)....................... (Gainsborough Stud Management) 74,000

Property of Russ Ison, from Campbell Stud
b y c Unfuwain (USA) - Honourable Sheba (USA) (Roberto (USA))............... (Shadwell Estate Co) 30,000

From Mary James (Cotswold Stud Farms)
ch y c Midyan (USA) - House Call (Artaius (USA))................. (B Hanbury) 56,000

Property of Mr and Mrs D J Deer, from Fawley Stud
b y c Royal Academy (USA) - Imperial Jade (Lochnager)..... (Shadwell Estate Co) 68,000

509

From Mount Coote Stud, Ireland
ch y c Old Vic - Impudent Miss (Persian Bold)................ (M Heaton-Ellis) 20,000
Property of Mr R H Cowell, from Bottisham Heath Stud
b y c Night Shift (USA) - Infanta Real (Formidable (USA))................... (Darley Stud Management) 36,000
Property of Hon Pearl Lawson-Johnston, from The Elms Stud
gr y f Old Vic - Integrity (Reform) .... (Gay Kelleway) 30,000
From Red House Stud
gr y c Statoblest - Iridium (Linacre) .... (C Gordon-Watson) 27,000
Property of a Partnership, from Minster Stud
b y f Royal Academy (USA) - It's Terrific (Vaguely Noble).............. (C B A) 31,000
Property of Mr H Key, from Beechgrove Stud
b y f Warning - Ivoronica (Targowice (USA)) (Darley Stud Management) 80,000
From Glenvale Stud, Agent
br y f Shirley Heights - Ivory Gull (USA) (Storm Bird (CAN))................... (Mercury Bloodstock) 98,000
Property of Kiltinan Farms Inc., Ireland
br y f Last Tycoon - Ivy (USA) (Sir Ivor) .... (B B A (Ireland)) 185,000

510

KILL (Goffs)
Tuesday, October 5th
(Yearlings)

From Camas Park Stud
b y c Woodman (USA) - Jardiniere (Nijinsky) .... (German International Bloodstock Agency) 30,000
From Oak Lodge Stud
b y c Waajib - June Maid (Junuis) .... (Danny Murphy) 18,000
Property of Doverlodge Stud, from Rathbarry Stud
b y c Salse (USA) - Kentfield (Busted) ..... (Hugo Lascelles) 80,000
From Islanmore Stud
br y c Thatching - Kilarney Ring (Scorpio) ... (Derby Bloodstock) 33,000
Property of Stonethorn Stud Farms, from Carrowdore Castle Stud
b y f Storm Bird (CAN) - Klarifi (Habitat).... (Darley Stud Management) 50,000
From Churchtown House Stud
b y c Thatching - Kurri Kurri (USA) (Vague Image)................. (Frank Barry) 20,000
From Newtown Stud
b or br y c Persian Bold - Lady Bennington (Hot Grove)............... (C Gordon-Watson Bloodstock) 28,000
From Lyonstown Stud (Agent)
b y c Sadler's Wells (USA) - Lady Capulet (USA) (Sir Ivor) .... (Newgate Stud Company) 230,000
From Eyrefield House Stud
b y c Thatching - Lady Nessa (USA) (Al Nasr)...... (Darley Stud Management) 35,000
From Camas Park Stud
b y c Royal Academy (USA) - Last Ball (IRE) (Last Tycoon).......... (Danny Murphy) 22,000
b y f Sadler's Wells (USA) - Le Melody (Levmoss).. (David Minton Bloodstock) 175,000

511

From Monread Stud
b y f Shaadi (USA) - Light Bee (USA) (Majestic Light)...................... (Equine Investment Consultants) 9,000
From Ashtown House Stud
ch y c Woodman (USA) - Lily Lily Rose (USA) (Lypheor).......... (F Stronach) 26,000
From Rowanstown Stud
ch y f Persian Heights - Lycia (Targowice) (John Warren Bloodstock) 22,000
From Airlie Stud
b y c Northern Baby (CAN) - Mabira (Habitat)....... (Darley Stud Management) 130,000
From Pier House Stud
ch y f Royal Academy - Maculatus (USA) (Sharpen Up)......... (B B A (Ireland)) 26,000
From Churchtown House Stud
b y c Be My Guest (USA) - Magic Spell (FR) (Dancer's Image)........... (T Stack) 16,000
From Monread Stud
ch y c Polish Precedent (USA) - Mahabba (USA) (Elocutionist)........ (C Gordon-Watson Bloodstock) 30,000
From Mellon Stud
br y c Ela-Mana-Mou - Majestic's Gold (Rheingold) .... (C Gordon-Watson Bloodstock) 20,000
From Staffordshire
b y c Slip Anchor - Maria Waleska (Filiberto) .... (Sallyview Estates) 33,000
From Rathasker Stud
b y c Royal Academy (USA) - Miss Audimar (USA) (Mr Leader).... (Mark Johnston) 26,000

512

Property of D P O'Brien, from Derrygarth Stud
b y c Fairy King (USA) - Mrs Foodbroker (Home Guard)............. (P Wragg) 85,000
From Tullamaine Castle Stud (Agent)
b y f Danehill (USA) - My Sister Ellen (Lyphard)........ (Panetta Bloodstock) 10,000
From Mellon Stud
ch y c Elmaamul (USA) - Nabila (USA) (Foolish Pleasure).... (M A B Agency) 20,000
From Barronstown Stud
b y c Waajib - Nawara (Welsh Pageant).... (Peter Doyle Bloodstock) 28,000
From Loughbrown Stud & Martinstown Farm
b y f Law Society (USA) - Near The End (Shirley Heights)........ (B B A (Italia)) 18,000
Property of Mrs A Whitehead, from Owenstown Stud
b y c Danehill (USA) - Negligence (Roan Rocket)... (Brian Grassick Bloodstock) 230,000
From Manister House Stud
b y c Alzao (USA) - Night Roofer (Thatching) .... (John Warren Bloodstock) 54,000

From Staffordstown
ch y c Bering - Nijana (USA) (Nijinsky) ..... (C B A) 125,000
From Ballysheehan Stud
b y c Don't Forget Me - Norse Lady (Viking) .... (John Warren Bloodstock) 26,000
From Yeomanstown Stud
b y c Common Grounds - Nothing Personal (Horage)................. (D K Weld) 72,000

513

From Abbeville & Meadow Court Studs (Agent)
b y c Thatching - Notre Histoire (Habitat) .. (Panetta Bloodstock) 14,000
Property of Tyrwhitt Stud, from Tara Stud
b y c Tirol - Olderfleet (Steel Heart) .... (Darley Stud Management) 80,000
From Tullamaine Castle Stud (Agent)
b y f Darshaan - Orangerie (FR) (Gay Mecene)..................... (Cash) 9,000
From Yeomanstown Stud
b y c Tirol - Ounavarra (Homeric).......... (J T Doyle) 18,000
From Abbeville & Meadow Court Studs (Agent)
b y f Ballad Rock - Our Village (Ballymore) (B B A (Ireland)) 32,000
Property of Andrew Bradley, from Broguestown Stud
b y f High Estate - Pampala (Bold Lad)..... (Brendan Powell) 14,000
From Yeomanstown Stud
ch y f Common Grounds - Paradise Bird (Sallust)........................ (Cash) 18,000
From Manister House Stud
gr y f Danehill (USA) - Patchwork (USA) (Diesis)..................... (T Stack) 14,000
From Bellestown Farm Stud
b y c Salse (USA) - Pato (High Top) .... (Ivan Allan) 85,000
From Croom House Stud
b y c Slip Anchor - Peinture (FR) (Valiyar) .. (Frank Barry) 10,000

514

From Camas Park Stud
b y c High Brite (USA) - Petcoke (USA) (Giboulee)....... (Shadwell Estate Co) 50,000
Property of Lynaire Ltd, from Dunmurry Stud
b y c Alzao (USA) - Phoenix Forli (USA) (Forli)...................... (C B A) 36,000
Property of Lord Harrington, from Greenmount House Stud
b y c Fools Holme (USA) - Piffle (Shirley Heights)........ (Shadwell Estate Co) 62,000
From Camus Park Stud
b y f Woodman (USA) - Pirouette (Sadler's Wells)..... (Darley Stud Management) 77,000
From Redpender Stud
b y c Statoblest - Plum Bold (Be My Guest) (Alexander Scott) 52,000
Property of Rockwell Bloodstock, from Genesis Green Stud
b y c Green Desert (USA) - Possessive (Front Row)......................... (Rathbarry Bloodstock Services) 90,000

From Forenaghts Stud (Agent)
b y c Be My Guest (USA) - Prima Ballerina (FR) (Nonoalco).......... (J S Bolger) 14,500
From Ballysheehan Stud
b y c Fairy King (USA) - Queen Cake (Sandhurst Prince).................. (Gainsborough Stud Management) 24,000
From Corduff Stud
ch y c Old Vic - Quiet Harbour (Mill Reef) .. (Danny Murphy) 32,000
Property of Kilcarn Stud
b y c High Estate - Rained Off (Welsh Pageant) .... (German International Bloodstock Agency) 75,000

515

From Lynn Lodge Stud
b y c Bluebird (USA) - Really Sharp (Sharpen Up)................. (C B A) 34,000
From Ballyhane Stud (Agent)
b y c High Estate - Richly Deserved (IRE) (Kings Lake)... (Horse France (Ireland)) 19,000
From Loughbrown Stud & Martinstown Farm
b y f Slip Anchor - Rimosa's Pet (Petingo) (Addison Racing (C B A Agent)) 230,000
From Eyrefield Lodge
b y c Royal Academy (USA) - Ringtail (Auction Ring)....... (Shadwell Estate Co) 85,000
From Ballysheehan Stud
b y f Fairy King (USA) - Rose Of Jericho (USA) (Alleged)....... (Silk Green Inc) 320,000
From Mellon Stud
b y c Slip Anchor - Roxy Hart (High Top)... (C Gordon-Watson Bloodstock) 110,000
From Tullamiane Castle Stud (Agent)
b or br y f Shirley Heights - Sadler's Star (Sadler's Wells)........ (B B A (Italia)) 15,000
From Lisieux Stud
b y c Royal Academy (USA) - Safe Haven (Blakeney)................ (D K Weld) 90,000
From Mooretown Stud
b y f Law Society (USA) - Salette (Sallust) (Dr Alberto Panetta) 10,000
From Ardmayle House Stud (Agent)
b y c Ballad Rock - Salvationist (Mill Reef) (Shadwell Estate Co) 45,000

516

Property of a Partnership, from Genesis Green Stud
b y f Night Shift (USA) - Sangala (FR) (Jim French)........... (Castlemartin Stud) 29,000
From Ballysheehan Stud
b y f Sadler's Wells (USA) - Savannah Song (USA) (Riverman)............ (T Stack) 30,000
From Forenaghts Stud
b y c Green Desert (USA) - Sealy (Filiberto) (Gainsborough Stud Management) 140,000
From Forenaghts Stud (Agent)
ch y c Zilzal (USA) - Sedulous (Tap On Wood)............................ (Gainsborough Stud Management) 100,000
From Staffordstown
b y c Storm Bird (CAN) - Sharmila (FR) (Blakeney) .... (Addison Racing (C B A Agent)) 85,000

From Mellon Stud
b y c Nordico (USA) - Simply Gorgeous (Hello Gorgeous)............. (B B A) 28,000
Property of Kilboy Estate, from Lynn Lodge Stud
ch y c Royal Academy (USA) - Societe Royale (Milford)............ (P Wragg) 48,000
Property of Mrs G W Bronfman, from Lisieux Stud
b y c Last Tycoon - So Directed (Homing).. (D L O'Byrne) 26,000
From Rathbarry Stud (Agent)
b y f Bustino - So Long Boys (FR) (Beldale Flutter)........................ (Cash) 9,500
From Swordlestown Stud
b y c Dance Of Life (USA) - Steady (USA) (Damascus)............ (James Ryan) 17,000

517

From Pipers Hill Stud
b y c Thatching - Style Of Life (USA) (The Minstrel).. (John Ferguson Bloodstock) 80,000
From Eyrefield House Stud
b y c Law Society (USA) - Sun Screen (Caerleon)................ (Noel Meade) 24,000
From Staffordstown
b y c Nijinsky II - Sushila (Petingo) (B B A) 625,000
From Barronstown Stud
b y c Royal Academy (USA) - Take Your Mark (USA) (Round Table).. (C Brittain) 25,000
Property of a Syndicate, from Whitechurch Stud
b y f Ela-Mana-Mou - Taking Steps (Gay Fandango).... (Peter Doyle Bloodstock) 44,000
From Yeomans Stud
b y c Common Grounds - Tap The Line (Tap On Wood)........... (B B A (Ireland)) 50,000
From Bellewstown Farm Stud
b y c Warrshan (USA) - Tartique Twist (USA) (Arctic Tern)................... (John Warren Bloodstock) 32,000
From Ballysheehan Stud
ch y c Woodman (USA) - Thorough (Thatch) .... (C B A) 100,000
From Rathbarry Stud (Agent)
b or br y c Caerleon (USA) - Thread Of Gold (Huntercombe)....... (B B A (Ireland)) 90,000
Property of Mrs T V Ryan, from Kilcoran House Stud
b y c Groom Dancer (USA) - Tiavanita (USA) (J O Tobin) (Darley Stud Management) 60,000

518

From Killarkin Stud
ch y c Ballad Rock - Tigeen (Habitat) ...... (C B A) 18,000
From Corbally Stud
b y c Danehill (USA) - Tony Award (USA) (Kirtling)................. (P W Harris) 16,000
From Pipers Hill Stud
b y f In The Wings - Too Phar (Pharly)..... (F Stronach) 48,000
From Yeomanstown Stud
b y c Waajib - Trail (Thatch)............... (B B A (Ireland)) 60,000

Property of Doverlodge Stud, from Rathbarry Stud
b y c Thatching - Unheard Melody (Lomond).................. (T G Mills) 40,000
From Freedom Farm Stud
b y f Slip Anchor - Valkyrie (Bold Lad) ..... (B B A (Italia)) 16,000
From Yeomanstown Stud
b y c Fairy King (USA) - Vestal Flame (Habitat)..... (Peter Doyle Bloodstock) 26,000
From Highclere (USA) (Jeffry Morris) Agent
b y c Conquistador Cielo - Vivre Libre (USA) (Honest Pleasure)..... (Liam Browne) 17,000
From Ashtown House Stud
ch y c El Gran Senor (USA) - Warm The Sauce (USA) (Sauce Boat) (D K Weld) 225,000
Property of C S Johnson, from Ash Hill Stud
b y c Darshaan - Water Splash (USA) (Little Current)........................... (Gainsborough Stud Management) 200,000

519

From Glenvale Stud
b y c Alzao (USA) - Welsh Fantasy (Welsh Pageant)........ (Shadwell Estate Co) 110,000
From Forenaughts Stud (Agent)
ch y f Zilzal (USA) - Welsh Garden (Welsh Saint) .... (Gainsborough Stud Management) 100,000
Property of Kilcarn Stud
b y c Royal Academy (USA) - Welsh Love (Ela-Mana-Mou).. (Shadwell Estate Co) 200,000
From Airlie Stud
b y f Deputy Minister (CAN) - Whitethroat (Artaius).............. (W McDonald) 28,000
From Camas Park Stud
ch y c Theatrical - Wings Of Wishes (USA) (Alydar)................. (F Stronach) 90,000
From Lyonstown Stud (Agent)
b y c Royal Academy (USA) - Wood Violet (USA) (Riverman)..... (Danny Murphy) 20,000
From Glenvale Stud
ch y c Elmaamul (USA) - Wrap It Up (Mount Hagen)..... (Anthony Penfold (Agent)) 70,000
Property of D P O'Brien, from Derrygarth Stud
b y c Royal Academy (USA) - Zenga (Try My Best)...... (Darley Stud Management) 70,000
From Airlie Stud
b y f Nordico (USA) - Adrana (Bold Lad)..... (Frank Barry) 19,000
From Tullamaine Castle Stud (Agent)
b y c Last Tycoon - Alidiva (Chief Singer) .. (J Dunlop) 36,000

520

From Yeoman Stud
b y c Dancing Dissident (USA) - Allberry (Alzao).............. (B B A (Ireland)) 30,000
From Corbally Stud
b y c Alzao (USA) - Alligatrix (USA) (Alleged) .... (German International Bloodstock Agency) 65,000
From Shadwell Estate Co Ltd
b y c Green Desert (USA) - Almarai (USA) (Vaguely Noble)......... (Peter Harris) 30,000

From Kildaragh Stud
b y f Bluebird (USA) - Angelus Chimes (Northfields).................. (B B A) 30,000
From Corbally Stud
b y f Persian Bold - Anjuli (Northfields) .... (Shadwell Estate Co) 130,000
From Corduff Stud
b y c Alzao (USA) - Arbour (USA) (Graustark) .... (Guy Harwood) 15,000
Property of Brownstown Stud, from Abbeville & Meadow Court Studs
ch y c Dominion - Astra Adastra (Mount Hagen)............ (Hugo Lascelles) 22,000
From Camas Park Stud
b y c Bering - Ballerina Princess (USA) (Mr Prospector)............... (C Gordon-Watson Bloodstock) 175,000
Property of Brownstown Stud, from Abbeville & Meadow Court Studs
b y f Danehill (USA) - Be Discreet (Junius) (Brownstown Stud) 5,000
From Mooretown Stud
gr y c Persian Heights - Bella Pulchella (Lomond)................. (P Wragg) 20,000

521

From Mount Coote Stud (Agent)
b y f Sadler's Wells - Bersid (USA) (Cool Moon)................... (B Hanbury) 42,000
From Grangemore Stud
b y f Danehill (USA) - Best Gal (FR) (Bonne Noel)............... (James G Burns) 15,000
From Corbally Stud
b y f Royal Academy (USA) - Bold Meadows (Persian Bold).. (J S Bolger) 30,000
Property of William Brannigan, from Ballymacarney Stud
b y f Sadler's Wells (USA) - Braneakins (Sallust) .... (German International Bloodstock Agency) 28,000
From Mount Coote Stud
b y c Law Society (USA) - Bristle (Thatch).. (B B A (Italia)) 16,000
From Islanmore Stud
b y c Polish Precedent (USA) - Britannia's Rule (Blakeney).. (Panetta Bloodstock) 9,000
Property of Lord Harrington, from Greenmount House Stud
br y c Doyoun - Calaloo Sioux (USA) (Our Native)................. (Con Collins) 95,000
Property of a Syndicate, from Whitechurch Stud
gr y c Persian Bold - Caranina (USA) (Caro) (Peter Harris) 13,000
From Mellon Stud
b y c Fools Holme - Carhue Lady (Tap On Wood).. (Newturf Bloodstock Agency) 20,000
Property of a Partnership, from Partridge Close Stud
gr y c Night Shift (USA) - Casual (USA) (Caro).................. (C A Horgan) 28,000

522

From Mount Coote Stud
b y c Persian Bold - Catalonda (African Sky) (C Gordon-Watson Bloodstock) 26,000

From Tullamaine Castle Stud (Agent)
b y c Bluebird (USA) - Cat Girl (USA) (Grey Dawn II)..... (Peter Doyle Bloodstock) 15,000
From Corduff Stud
ch y c Dominion - Caymana (FR) (Bellypha) (John Ferguson Bloodstock) 130,000
Property of R Strudwick, from Ballygallon Stud
b y f Caerleon (USA) - Cheese Soup (USA) (Spectacular Bid).......... (J Dunlop) 22,000
From Ballyhane Stud (Agent)
b y c Alleged (USA) - Chilly Welcome (General Assembly).................. (Johnnie McKeever Bloodstock) 24,000
Property of Lord Harrington, from Greenmount House Stud
b y f Nordico (USA) - Church Light (Caerleon).............. (B B A (Italia)) 26,000
From Landscape Stud (Agent)
b y c Danehill (USA) - Cistus (Sun Prince) .. (John Hills) 11,000
From Croom House Stud
ch y f Ballad Rock - Classic Opera (Lomond) .... (D L O'Byrne) 38,000
Property of Addison Racing Inc, from Whitsbury Manor Stud
b y c Distant Relative - Come On Rosi (Valiyar)............................. (Rathbarry Bloodstock Services) 35,000
Property of Mrs A Whitehead, from Owenstown Stud
b y f Tirol - Croglin Water (Monsanto) ..... (D K Weld) 85,000

523

From Kildaragh Stud
b y c Warning - Dancing Place (FR) (Green Dancer)..................... (C B A) 45,000
From Pipers Hill Stud
b y f Shernazar - Danzig Lass (USA) (Danzig).............. (Horse France) 25,000
From Camas Park Stud
b y c Royal Academy (USA) - Dawning Beauty (USA) (Well Decorated)........ (Alberto Chiaverini) 12,000
From Abbeville & Meadow Court Studs (Agent)
ch y c In The Wings - Dawn Is Breaking (Import)......... (Shadwell Estate Co) 100,000
From Ashtown House Stud
ch y c Caerleon (USA) - Demia (FR) (Abdos) (Silky Green Inc) 95,000
Property of Kilboy Estate, from Lynn Lodge Stud
ch y f Royal Academy (USA) - Diamond Field (USA) (Mr Prospector)........... (B B A (Ireland)) 85,000
From Corbally Stud
b y c Persian Bold - Diamond Shine (Kings Lake).................. (B B A (Italia)) 32,000
Property of C A Waters Bloodstock Trading
b y f Sadler's Wells - Diamond Spring (USA) (Vaguely Noble).......... (F Stronach) 75,000
From Airlie Stud
b y f Caerleon (USA) - Dingle Bay (Petingo) (Silky Green Inc) 200,000
Property of Lowquest Ltd, from Westerlands Stud
ch y c Caerleon (USA) - Dwell (USA) (Habitat)..................... (F Stronach) 40,000

524

Property of Mrs Max Morris, from Iverk House Stud

b or br y c Lear Fan (USA) - Easy Romance (USA) (Northern Jove)........ (B B A) 95,000

From Ballyhimikin Stud

ch y f Be My Guest (USA) - Elevate (Ela-Mana-Mou).......... (Silky Green Inc) 190,000

From Barronstown Stud

b y c Caerleon (USA) - Enthraller (USA) (Bold Forbes).......... (W McDonald) 280,000

From Corbally Stud

b y c Bluebird (USA) - Entracte (Henbit).... (Darley Stud Management) 44,000

Property of Stonethorn Stud Farms, from Carrowdore Castle Stud

b y f Dayjur (USA) - Eurbird (Ela-Mana-Mou) .... (Shadwell Estate Co) 330,000

From Redpender Stud

b y c Bluebird (USA) - Everything Nice (Sovereign Path)...................... (Peter Doyle Bloodstock) 66,000

From Tullamaine Castle Stud (Agent)

b y c Alzao (USA) - Fandangerina (Grey Dawn II)........ (Shadwell Estate Co) 60,000

Property of Kilcarn Stud

b y c Law Society - Fiscal Folly (USA) (Foolish Pleasure)................... (German International Bloodstock Agency) 65,000

b y c Sadler's Wells (USA) - Flame Of Tara (Artaius)............ (W McDonald) 1,500,000

From Highclere (USA) (Jeffry Morris) Agent

b y c Imp Society (USA) - Flaming Reason (USA) (Limit To Reason).................. (Anthony Penfold (Agent)) 52,000

525

From Forenaghts Stud

ch y f Royal Academy (USA) - Foolish Passion (USA) (Secretariat)............ (F Stronach) 28,000

From Oldtown Stud

b y f Royal Academy (USA) - Fremanche (FR) (Jim French)......... (B Hanbury) 155,000

Property of Lynaire Ltd, from Dunmurry Stud

ch y c Mt Livermore - Future Past (USA) (Super Concorde).................... (Brian Grassick Bloodstock) 25,000

From Ashtown House Stud

b y c Alzao (USA) - Gaychimes (Steel Heart) .... (Leinster Bloodstock Agency) 75,000

From Tsarina Stud

b y f Alzao (USA) - Gay France (FR) (Sir Gaylord)............ (Brendan Caffrey) 31,000

From Ballysheehan Stud

ch y f Royal Academy (USA) - Gemaasheh (Habitat)............. (B B A (Ireland)) 140,000

From Airlie Stud

b y f Royal Academy (USA) - Glim (USA) (Damascus)............ (Bill Hawkins) 36,000

From Ballysheehan Stud

b y f Danehill (USA) - Godzilla (Gyr)......... (Shadwell Estate Co) 55,000

From Camas Park Stud

b y c Sadler's Wells (USA) - Gwydion (USA) (Raise A Cup)................ (B B A) 180,000

Property of International Thoroughbred Breeders Inc, from Round Hill Stud

b or br y c Royal Academy (USA) - Habituee (Habitat)............................. (Gainsborough Stud Management) 120,000

526

From Staffordstown

b y f Northern Baby (CAN) - Happy Bride (Royal Match)......... (W McDonald) 36,000

From Eyrefield Lodge

b y c Pharly (FR) - Hastening (Shirley Heights)........................ (H Cecil) 26,000

Property of Kilcarn Stud

b y c Last Tycoon - Hi Bettina (Henbit)..... (B B A (Italia)) 38,000

From Whitsbury Manor Stud

b y c Midyan (USA) - High Quinta (High Line).......................... (B B A) 16,000

From Kirtlington Stud

b y f Royal Academy (USA) - Hi Lass (Shirley Heights)...... (B B A (Ireland)) 105,000

Property of Mrs A Whitehead, from Broadfield Stud

b y c Tirol - Hillbrow (Swing Easy)......... (Clem Murphy) 15,000

From Barronstown Stud

b y c Nureyev (USA) - Hitting Irish (USA) (Irish Ruler).............. (F Stronach) 100,000

Property of Kilboy Estate, from Lynn Lodge Stud

br or gr y c Danehill (USA) - Inanna (Persian Bold)................... (Ivan Allan) 65,000

Property of Paul Radley, from Claramount Stud

b y f Gallic League - Inner Pearl (Gulf Pearl) (M F D Morley) 8,500

From Ballyhimikin Stud

b y c Danehill (USA) - In Unison (Bellypha) (German International Bloodstock Agency) 42,000

527

From Airlie Stud

ch y f Ela-Mana-Mou - Irish Bird (USA) (Sea-Bird II).... (Brian Grassick Bloodstock) 530,000

From Tullamaine Castle Stud (Agent)

b y f High Estate - Itching (IRE) (Thatching) (Brian Grassick Bloodstock) 9,000

From Ashtown House Stud

b y c Last Tycoon - Ardmelody (Law Society)............... (Horse France) 21,000

From Camas Park Stud

b y c Sadler's Wells (USA) - Ameridienne (FR) (Targowice)...... (B B A (Ireland)) 400,000

ch y f Woodman (USA) - Crowning Ambition (USA) (Chief's Crown)........... (Leinster Stud) 85,000

528

MALVERN
(Russell, Baldwin & Bright)
Tuesday, October 5th

Property of Robert King

Snaan ch g (9yrs) Kris - She's The One (FR) (Sword Dancer (USA))....... (D Mills) 500

Property of East Withy Stud Ltd., from East Withy Stud

Last Of Mohicans b g (5yrs) Warpath - Gemima Tenderfoot (Prince Tenderfoot (USA)).......................... (Cash) 1,500

Property of Miss Zoe Lewis

Deer Fencer b g (11yrs) Mandalus - Boolaben (Arctic Slave).. (Mr Guilding) 1,400

Property of Mr and Mrs E R Hemmings, from Haylane Farm

Ragged Illusion ch g (8yrs) Ashford (USA) - Raglan Lane (Allangrange)...... (Cash) 900

Property of Mrs M Olden, from Moor Hall Stables

Lady Gail ch f (3yrs) Sharrood (USA) - Martian Princess (Cure The Blues (USA)).......................... (Cash) 850

Property of C E Lewis

Location b g (6yrs) Blakeney - Green Teable (FR) (Green Dancer (USA))... (F Down) 1,450

Lycian Moon b f (4yrs) Norwick (USA) - Brigannie Moon (Brigadier Gerard)..... (P Gardner) 900

Property of K G Godwin

Bairn Free gr m (5yrs) Bairn (USA) - Rustling (Rusticaro (FR))............ (Cash) 1,100

Property of R Fellows

Call Me Dickins gr g (4yrs) Rusticaro (FR) - Bad Start (USA) (Bold Bidder)... (Cash) 3,050

Property of J W Evans

Bronze Effigy ch g (11yrs) Vaigly Great - Sea Fern (Klondyke Bill) .... (Mrs L Campbell) 2,100

529

Property of Mrs Mary Tyner

Coolmoreen (IRE) ch g (5yrs) Carlingford Castle - Sirrahdis (Bally Joy) .... (Mrs L Campbell) 1,500

From Ridgeway Paddocks

ch g (5yrs) Over The River (FR) - Side Wink (Quayside) (David Minton Bloodstock) 2,000

Property of J A T de Giles, from Holy Oak Hill Farms

Jaaez b g (9yrs) Ela-Mana-Mou - Almagest (Dike (USA))........... (J Trice-Rolph) 2,000

To Dissolve a Partnership

Drag Artist br g (8yrs) Artaius (USA) - Drag Line (Track Spare)........... (G Snell) 600

Property of P Towell, Co Meath

Grange Prize ch g (7yrs) Le Bavard (FR) - Queen's Prize (Random Shot)......... (R Greenway) 3,700

Property of Austin-Stroud & Co Ltd

Moving Force b g (6yrs) Muscatite - Saint Simbir (Simbir).......... (Mr Williams) 900

Property of Mrs B M Lockey, from Kimberley Home Farm Stables

Abitbizarre ch g (7yrs) Sunyboy - Minor Furlong (Native Bazaar)....... (S Hiatt) 2,300

From Home Stables

Allegro Con Brio b g (5yrs) Alleging (USA) - Diami (Swing Easy (USA)) .... (Mrs A Slatter) 1,650

Property of Mr G Paul, from Knights Farm

Alcoholic Haze b g (10yrs) Foggy Bell - More Brandy (Hot Brandy)............ (Mr Livingstone) 1,300

Property of W M Smith, from Kelanne Stud

b g (5yrs) Ilium - Waikato River (Native Bazaar).............. (David Redvers) 1,500

ch m (6yrs) Sunley Builds - Waikato River (Native Bazaar)............ (D Davies) 1,300

530

From Suir View Stud, Co Tipperary

Bulgaden Castle b g (5yrs) Castle Keep - Zerbinetta (Henry The Seventh)....... (David Minton Bloodstock) 3,600

Abdul Emir b g (6yrs) Ovac (ITY) - Azul (Majority Blue) .... (David Minton Bloodstock) 2,400

Property of a Partnership, from Ashleigh House Stables

Far Run b g (6yrs) Farhaan - Ballynavin Run (Deep Run).......... (Paul Heywood) 4,400

Property of G O'Regan

Kil Kil Gale br g (7yrs) Strong Gale - Miss Pooh (Deep Run).......... (R Parker) 1,700

Property of J Mason, from Foulrice Farm

Potiphar br g (7yrs) Warpath - Zulaika Hopwood (Royalty)...... (Mr Worthington) 750

Property of Paul C N Heywood, from Penrose Stables

Electress ch m (7yrs) Baron Blakeney - Elect (New Member)........ (D Mills) 350

From Nunstainton Stud

ch g (5yrs) Le Bavard (FR) - Miss Feacle (Bargello).................. (H Muis) 3,600

Property of Mrs S Siviter, from Elliotte House Farm Stables

Mister Jolly b g (7yrs) Le Moss - Shantimwen (Cassim).......... (Beryl Baxter) 1,900

Property of C R Saunders

Pinfold b m (5yrs) Balliol - Changan (Touch Paper)...................... (Cash) 3,800

Property of P Rogers

Two Way Mirror (IRE) ch g (5yrs) Double Schwartz - Alice Kyteler (Crepello)..... (C Menaditch) 700

531

From Little London Farm

Rise Over ch m (7yrs) Smackover - Stewart's Rise (Good Bond)...... (P Atkins) 900

To Dissolve a Partnership

Sly Prospect (USA) ch g (5yrs) Barachois (CAN) - Miss Sly (USA) (Diamond Prospect (USA))................... (Cash) 1,100

Property of Sir Mark Palmer, from Mill Hill Farm

b g (3yrs) Kinglet - Molinello (Balinger)..... (P Gardner) 900

Property of Robin Mathew Q.C.

Mahafel b g (9yrs) Kris - Royal Meath (Realm)............ (East Withy Stud) 1,000

Property of Mrs S E Minton

Smithson ro or gr g (5yrs) Alias Smith (USA) - Endango (Gay Fandango (USA))...... (Cash) 2,350

To Dissolve a Partnership, from Upper Welford House Stables

On The Jar (IRE) gr g (5yrs) Entre Nous - Hot Canary (Tepukei).......... (Cash) 1,550

Sky Venture ch g (9yrs) Paddy's Stream - Mijette (Pauper)........... (R Parker) 2,500

Property of D Kirkland, from Worsley Racing Stables

Hataal (IRE) ch f (4yrs) Hatim (USA) - Tenoria (Mansingh (USA)) (Mr Livingstone) 700

To Dissolve a Partnership, from Blackwater Stud

One For The Cross (IRE) ch g (5yrs) The Parson - Dora-Elliven (Sweet Revenge) (L Wickett) 1,800

Property of Patrick Healy, from Blackwater Stud

Cregg Boreen ch g (6yrs) Boreen (FR) - Denys Eyre (Saint Denys) (A Geering) 1,500

532

Property of W F Reid

br g (4yrs) Adonijah - Lady Lynx (USA) (Stop The Music (USA))...... (Mrs J Arnold) 2,400

Property of W Price, from Cholstrey Stables

House Warming ch g (6yrs) Habitat - Be Sweet (Reform).......... (R B Davies) 2,400

Property of G R Turnbull

Te Aroha b g (3yrs) Welsh Captain - Henny Penny (Le Coq D'Or)...... (Mr James) 2,300

Jolly Holly b f (4yrs) Cruise Missile - Henny Penny (Le Coq D'Or)....... (F Cronin) 2,750

Property of J Horan

ch f (2yrs) Gildoran - Crimson Flag (Kinglet) (Mrs J Starkey) 750

Property of J F Weldhen, from Trekennine Farm Stables

Mummy's Toy Boy br g (7yrs) Mansingh (USA) - Easterly Gael (Tudor Music) ... (Cash) 1,750

PRIVATE SALES

From Castle Farm Stud

Churchfield Lad ch g (6yrs) Tug Of War - Franzieflyer (Charlottesvilles Flyer)..... (Star Construction Ltd) 2,800

533

KILL (Goffs)
Wednesday, October 6th
(Yearlings)

Property of Springwood Stables, from Highclere USA (Jeffry Morris) Agent

(USA) b y c Seattle Song (USA) - Jane Austen (USA) (Arts And Letters) ...... (Sallyview Estates) 25,000

From Rosemount House Stud

b y c Waajib - Jendeal (Troy)....... (Cash) 21,000

From Golden Vale Stud

b y f Waajib - Judy's Pinch (Ballymore) .... (M R Channon) 9,000

From Camas Park Stud (Agent)

b y c Alzao (USA) - Justsayno (USA) (Dr Blum)..... (Conti Bloodstock Services) 30,000

From Barronstown Stud

b y f Alzao (USA) - Katie Koo (Persian Bold) (W McDonald) 28,000

From Ballysheehan Stud

b y f Thatching - Keep The Thought (USA) (Valdez)................................ (Equine Investment Consultants) 14,000

Property of Mr Peter Kelly, from Rathasker Stud

b y f Petorius - Kirsova (Absalom).......... (C Gordon-Watson Bloodstock) 11,000

Property of Kitty's Sister Syndicate, from Tara Stud (Agent)

ch y c Kefaah (USA) - Kitty's Sister (Bustino)...................... (Monofiber) 2,000

Property of Miss Wendy Hyde

ch y c Elmaamul (USA) - Kraemey (USA) (Vaguely Noble)........... (C Gordon-Watson Bloodstock) 15,000

Property of Mr T M Ward

b y f Nabeel Dancer (USA) - Lady Anna Livia (Ahonoora)...... (Panetta Bloodstock) 5,000

534

From Kellistown Stud

b y f Alzao (USA) - Lady Pavlova (Ballymore) .... (John Ferguson Bloodstock) 7,000

From Lynn Lodge Stud

br y c Astronef - Lady Penzance (IRE) (Pennine Walk)............... (B B A) 12,000

Property of R J Powell, from Wellingtown House Stud

b y f Alzao (USA) - Lady Rider (Pitskelly) ... (B B A (Italia)) 28,000

From Triermore Stud

b y c Tirol - Lady Vivienne (Golden Fleece) (P Cole) 16,000

Property of Belmont Stud

b y f Shernazar - Lagolette (Green God) ... (Frank Barry) 7,500

From Ashtown House Stud

b y c Fairy King (USA) - Lassalia (Sallust)... (Darley Stud Management) 64,000

From Tally-Ho Stud

b y f Contract Law (USA) - Late Summer (Habitat)............. (Horse France) 9,500

Property of Mr B Kennedy, from Meadowland's Stud

b y c Taufan (USA) - Laura Margaret (Persian Bold)........ (The Winning Team) 7,500

From Rathbarry Stud

gr y f Nishapour (FR) - La Vosgienne (Ashmore)......... (Lillingston Bloodstock) 9,000

Property of Miss Audrey F Thompson, from Kilmore Stud

b y f Taufan (USA) - Les Saintes (Kris)..... (C Gordon-Watson Bloodstock) 13,500

535

Property of Mr J B Clarke

br y c Simply Great (FR) - Lockwood Girl (Prince Tenderfoot) (Derby Bloodstock) 23,000

From Islandmore Stud

b y f Darshaan - Maiden Eileen (Stradavinsky)....... (Hugo Lascelles) 26,000

Property of Mr Dan Daly, from Brownrath Stud

b y c Cyrano de Bergerac - Mamie's Joy (Prince Tenderfoot).................. (The Winning Team) 9,500

From Green Ireland Properties Ltd
b y c Persian Heights - Maniusha (Sallust) (German International Bloodstock Agency) 18,000
From Pipers Hill Stud
ch y c Magical Strike (USA) - Marble Run (Run The Gantlet)....................(German International Bloodstock Agency) 8,500
From Rathbarry Stud
b y f Warrshan (USA) - Marie de Sologne (Lashkari).................. (R Collet) 13,000
Property of Mr & Mrs Leo Collins, from Ennistown Stud
b y c Simply Great (FR) - Mariposa (Cure The Blues).......... (Declan Gillespie) 6,000
Property of St Simon Foundation, from Ballysax Manor Stud
b y f Double Schwartz - Marqueterie (USA) (Well Decorated)...... (M G Sc Bucci) 6,000
Property of Mr W G McKinley, from Woodridge Stud
ch y c Simply Great (FR) - Martintide (Bustino)............... (Mr Van Frausum) 12,000
Property of Hamish Alexander, from Partridge Close Stud
b y c Shirley Heights - Mary Sunley (Known Fact).................... (J McGrath) 17,000

536

From Glenvale Stud
b y c Statoblest - Million Heiress (Auction Ring)................... (M Channon) 43,000
From Orchardstown Stud Farm
b y f Jareer (USA) - Mira Adonde (USA) (Sharpen Up).... (Shadwell Estate Co) 12,000
From Rathasker Stud
ch y c Red Sunset - Mirabiliary (USA) (Crow)............. (Brian Gubby Ltd) 10,500
From Ashtown House Stud
b y c Kahyasi - Miranisa (Habitat) .... (L Cumani) 16,000
From Abbeyleix Stud Farm
b y c Petorius - Miss Bojangles (Gay Fandango)................ (Sheehy Bros) 9,800
From Ebbeville & Meadow Court Studs (Agent)
b y f Danehill (USA) - Miss Pudge (Green God)..................... (J Hassett) 24,000
Property of Mr W P Fogarty
b y f Waajib - Miss Sandman (Manacles) .. (Sheehy Bros) 12,000
Property of a Partnership, from Genesis Green Stud
b y c Nordico (USA) - Miss Tatting (USA) (Miswaki)..................... (C B A) 47,000
From Victor Stud (Agent)
b y c Fools Holme (USA) - Miss Victoria (Auction Ring)....................... (Johnny McKeever Bloodstock) 22,000
Property of a Gentleman, from Genesis Green Stud
b y f Cadeaux Genereux - Monaiya (Shareef Dancer).................. (C Brittain) 29,000

537

From Highclere USA (Jeffry Morris) Agent
(USA) b y c Imperial Falcon (USA) - Moon O'Gold (USA) (Slew O'Gold)... (B B A) 66,000
From Newborough Stud
b y c Nordico (USA) - Moonsilk (Solinus)... (A Moore) 10,000
From Rowanstown Stud
b y f Shardari - Mo Pheata (Petorius) ...... (Hore France (Ireland) Ltd) 18,000
Property of Mr Pat Dillon, from Abbeyleix Stud Farm
b y c Roi Danzig (USA) - Morning Kiss (Kings Lake)............... (R Collet) 21,000
Property of Mr Gerard Canavan
b y f Nordico (USA) - Mystery Lady (USA) (Vaguely Noble) .... (Stonehall Paddocks Ltd) 2,000
From Kildaragh Stud
b y f Ela-Mana-Mou - Namatanga (USA) (Foolish Pleasure).................... (Southern Bloodstock) 7,200
Property of Mr J G O'Brien, from Ballycummin Castle
b y c Kahyasi - Nasseem (FR) (Zeddaan)... (M Johnston) 6,600
Property of Mr J M O'Connor, from Rock Abbey Stud
b y c Posen (USA) - Naughty Lass (Run The Gantlet).............. (Bobby O'Ryan) 5,000
From Islandmore Stud
b or br y f Darshaan - Nazanin (Sharpo).... (J Dunlop) 6,000
Property of Mr Sean Twomey, from Hawthorn Villa Stud
b y f Shernazar - Neelam (USA) (Arctic Tern) .... (J McLoughlin) 7,200

538

From Glenvale Stud (Agent)
b y f Try My Best (USA) - Never So Free (Never So Bold)....... (Horse France) 8,500
From Oghill House Stud
ch y c Maelstrom Lake - Nielsine (Czaravich)................ (A Moore) 6,500
From Tara Stud
ch y c Kefaah (USA) - Night Of Gaiety (What A Guest) (German International Bloodstock Agency) 12,000
From Corbally Stud
b y f Persian Bold - Night Of Stars (Sadler's Wells)..................... (Suprina) 22,000
From Triermore Stud
b or br y c Tirol - Non Casual (Nonoalco)... (J S Bolger) 33,000
From Cregg Stud
b y c Cyrano de Bergerac - Nonnita (Welsh Saint)........... (Shadwell Estate Co) 33,000
From Home Farm
b y c Prince Rupert (FR) - Norme (FR) (Dark Tiger)....... (Peter Doyle Bloodstock) 6,500
From Ardenode Stud
b y c Simply Great (FR) - No Time To Dance (Shareef Dancer) .... (Johnny McKeever Bloodstock) 8,000
From Redpender Stud
b y c Taufan (USA) - Not Mistaken (USA) (Mill Reef)............. (B B A (Italia)) 16,000
From Mooretown Stud
b y c Scenic - Often (Ballymore) .... (B B A (Italia)) 13,000

539

From Tally-Ho Stud
b y f Law Society (USA) - Organdy (Blakeney)............... (D Elsworth) 8,000
From Airlie Stud
b y c Ela-Mana-Mou - Orillia (Red God) .... (Brian Grassick Bloodstock) 26,000
From Eyrefield Lodge
b y f Roi Danzig (USA) - Overcall (Bustino) (C Gordon-Watson Bloodstock) 43,000
Property of Mr R J Cullen, from October Lodge Stud
b y c Damister (USA) - Over The Rocks (Salmon Leap)........... (Frank Barry) 7,500
From Lodge Park Stud
b y f Dancing Dissident (USA) - Park Elect (Ahonoora).............. (M Channon) 19,000
From Ballysheehan Stud
b y c Thatching - Pas Du Tout (Pas de Seul) (Browne Bloodstock) 7,000
From Corbally Stud
b y c Petorius - Pennine Drive (IRE) (Pennine Walk) (David Minton Bloodstock) 11,500
From Larch Hill Stud
b y c Vision (USA) - Persian Royale (Persian Bold).................. (W McDonald) 26,000
Property of Mr John P Mangan
b y c Kefaah (USA) - Persian's Glory (Prince Tenderfoot) (David Minton Bloodstock) 17,000
From Corduff Stud
br y c Contract Law (USA) - Persian Susan (USA) (Herbager).............. (Cash) 8,000

540

From Ashtown House Stud
b y c Waajib - Petite Liqueurelle (IRE) (Shernazar)........... (R J O'Gorman) 18,000
From Ballysheehan Stud
b y c Don't Forget Me - Petite Realm (Realm)................... (D H Jones) 33,000
From Pipers Hill Stud
gr y c Dance Of Life (USA) - Phazania (Tap On Wood)........... (Danny Murphy) 22,000
From Killeenlea Stud
b y c Waajib - Pitty Pal (USA) (Caracolero) (Danny Murphy) 10,500
From Abbeville & Meadow Court Studs (Agent)
b y c Salt Dome (USA) - Place D'Etoile (Kythnos)...................... (S Okada) 60,000
From Ballylinch Stud
ch y f Shernazar - Pleasant Review (USA) (The Minstrel)... (Southern Bloodstock) 5,000
From Grangemore Stud (Agent)
b y f Keen - Pot Of Gold (Rainbow Quest) (B B A (Italia)) 2,000
From Islanmore Stud
b y f Thatching - Pursue (Auction Ring) .... (Panetta Bloodstock) 11,000
From Irish National Stud
b y f Digamist (USA) - Rahwah (Northern Baby)................ (Ms Natalie Cecil) 7,000
Property of Leamore Stud, from Carribeg Stud
br y c Petorius - Randolina (Wolver Hollow) (Peter Doyle Bloodstock) 16,000

541

From Rathasker Stud
ch y f Nabeel Dancer (USA) - Rare Roberta (USA) (Roberto)................ (Cash) 2,200
Property of J G O'Brien, from Ballycummin Castle
b y f Kahyasi - Raysiya (Cure The Blues) ... (Brian Grassick Bloodstock) 26,000
From Wraymount Stud
b y c Law Society (USA) - Reality (Known Fact).................... (M Channon) 15,500
From Egmont Stud
b y f Tirol - Repicado Rose (USA) (Repicado) .... (M Johnston) 10,500
Property of R Strudwick, from Ballygallon Stud
b y f Bluebird (USA) - Rep's Retton (USA) (J.O.Tobin)................ (C O'Brien) 14,000
From Moygaddy Stud
b y f Alzao (USA) - Ring Of Light (Auction Ring)....... (John Warren Bloodstock) 44,000
From Ballylinch Stud
b y f Posen (USA) - Riva D'Oro (USA) (Riva Ridge)......................... (C B A) 10,000
Property of Olive Thewissen, from Rockwood Stud
b y c Be My Native (USA) - River Low (IRE) (Lafontaine)................... (Cash) 15,500
From Ballylinch Stud (Agent)
b or br y c Posen (USA) - Robinia (USA) (Roberto)............ (K Prendergast) 6,500
From Swordlestown Stud
b or br y f Damister (USA) - Rocket Alert (Red Alert).............. (D H Jones) 11,000

542

Property of Mr David Browne, from Marsh Farm
br y f Ballad Rock - Rossaldene (Mummy's Pet).................... (B B A (Italia)) 8,000
From Kildaragh Stud
b y f Nordico (USA) - Rousinette (Rousillon) (Ms Natalie Cecil) 15,000
From Grangemore Stud (Agent)
b y f Dance Of Life (USA) - Royal Custom (His Majesty).......... (B B A (Italia)) 9,000
Property of Mr M Morrin
b y c Last Tycoon - Royaleffort (Dunphy) .. (Cash) 23,000
From Eyrefield House Stud
b or br y c Law Society (USA) - Ruffling Point (Gorytus) .... (Brian Grassick Bloodstock) 10,000
Property of Mr Renaud Waegenaere-Francois, from Irish National Stud
ch y c Ballad Rock - Rusti La Russe (Rusticaro).................. (Marco Bozzi) 7,000
From Eyrefield House Stud
b y c Taufan (USA) - Sable Coated (Caerleon)................ (C Gordon-Watson Bloodstock) 30,000
b y c Try My Best (USA) - Sable Royale (USA) (Real Value) .... (Shadwell Estate Co) 29,000
From Oak Lodge Stud
ch y f Imperial Frontier (USA) - Sajanjal (Dance In Time).............. (B B A) 12,000

Property of Mr R Corridan, from Rathbarry Stud
b or br y c Petorius - Salacia (Seapic)....... (C B A) 14,000

543

From Corbally Stud
br y c Law Society (USA) - Sammy Joe (Junius)......... (Panetta Bloodstock) 11,500

Property of a Partnership, from Whitechurch Stud
b y c Dancing Dissident (USA) - Saturne (Bellypha)........................... (Rathbarry Bloodstock Services) 14,000

From Oldtown Stud
ch y f Shernazar - Sea Port (Averof)....... (M Tompkins) 8,600

Property of Mr & Mrs Leo Collins, from Ennistown Stud
b y f Bluebird (USA) - Sexy Lady (FR) (Saint Cyrien).............. (M A B Agency) 16,000

From Partridge Close Stud
b y c Persian Bold - Shejrah (USA) (Northjet) .... (J W Hills) 20,000

From Mellon Stud
b y f Doyoun - Sidama (FR) (Top Ville)..... (B B A) 38,000

From Lodge Park Stud
b y c Shaadi (USA) - Silent Hill (USA) (Temperence Hill)..................... (Peter Doyle Bloodstock) 36,000

From Foxbrook Stud
b y f Scenic - Silly Song (Silly Season)..... (European Bloodstock Agency) 3,800

From Tara Stud
b y c Simply Great (FR) - Sistina (Charlottown)....................... (C B A) 6,000
b y c Petorius - Siva (FR) (Bellypha)....... (Jean Lesbordes) 9,400

544

Property of the Exors of the late Major V McCalmont, from Norelands Stud
b y f Taufan (USA) - Sixpenny (English Prince).... (Brian Grassick Bloodstock) 9,000

Property of R Strudwick, from Ballygallon Stud
b y c Ela-Mana-Mou - Solac (FR) (Gay Lussac)................ (R W Huggins) 17,500

From Oak Lodge Stud (Agent)
ch y f Persian Heights - Soleiade (Posse).. (Timothy E Hyde) 75,000

Property of Oldtown Bloodstock Holdings, from Tara Stud
ch y c Magical Strike (USA) - So Stylish (Great Nephew).......... (B Hanbury) 12,000

From Highclere (USA) (Jeffry Morris) Agent
Sir Silver Sox (USA) gr y c Corwyn Bay - Sox In The Box (USA) (Cresta Rider)... (T Stack) 25,000

From Wraymount Stud
b y c Bluebird (USA) - Soxoph (Hotfoot)... (Peter Doyle Bloodstock) 19,000

From Rowanstown Stud
b y f Try My Best (USA) - Spanish Tiara (Coquelin)....... (Panetta Bloodstock) 2,000

From Mocklertown House Stud
b y f Tirol - Spear Dance (Gay Fandango).. (Cash) 9,200

From Churchtown House Stud
ch y f Don't Forget Me - Star Cream (Star Appeal)...................... (B B A) 12,000

From Forenaghts Stud (Agent)
b y f Dancing Dissident (USA) - Star Of Victoria (What A Guest).. (J G Murphy) 7,000

545

Property of Mr John Burns, from Rye Court Stud
b y c Gallic League - Stella Ann (Ahonoora) (C Gordon-Watson Bloodstock) 33,000

From Ardmayle House Stud (Agent)
b y c Double Schwartz - Sterna Star (Corvaro).................. (Horse France) 10,500

From Irish National Stud
b y c Dancing Dissident (USA) - Still River (King's Lake)........................ (Johnny McKeever Bloodstock) 22,000

From Tally-Ho Stud
b y c Indian Ridge - Strapless (Bustino).... (David Minton Bloodstock) 22,000

Property of Mr John P Mangan
ch y f Be My Guest (USA) - Stylish Girl (USA) (Star de Naskra).............. (Ms Natalie Cecil) 12,000

Property of Leamore Stud, from Carribeg Stud
br y c Bob Back (USA) - Summit Talk (Head For Heights)......... (B B A (Ireland)) 50,000

From Highclere (USA) (Jeffry Morris) Agent
ch y c Imp Society (USA) - Super L.B. (USA) (Bold L.B.)......................... (Rathbarry Bloodstock Services) 26,000

Property of Mr J Hayes, from Rathbarry Stud
b y f Law Society (USA) - Sweet Alma (Alzao)................. (J S Bolger) 8,000

From Airlie Stud
b y f Last Tycoon - Sweetbird (Ela-Mana-Mou)............ (Lloyd International) 11,000

From Corbally Stud
b or br y c Vision (USA) - Sweet Marjorie (FR) (Sir Gaylord)....... (Noel Meade) 10,500

546

From Eyrefield House Stud
b y c Ballad Rock - Takastroll (Hello Gorgeous)........... (W McDonald) 72,000

From Tally-Ho Stud
ch y c Ballad Rock - Take My Pledge (IRE) (Ahonoora)............ (Horse France) 8,500

From Catherinestown Farm
b y f Ela-Mana-Mou - Taken By Force (Persian Bold).............. (P Keogh) 12,000

From Irish National Stud
b y c Roi Danzig (USA) - Takhiyra (Vayrann) (B Hanbury) 20,000

Property of Mr Bo Helander
gr y c Kahyasi - Talama (FR) (Shakapour)... (Darley Stud Management) 52,000

From Camas Park Stud
b y c Scenic - Taniokey (Grundy).......... (Darley Stud Management) 55,000

Property of Mr Tom Radley, from Clara Mount Stud
b y c Roi Danzig (USA) - Tarop (USA) (Dr Fager)... (Newturf Bloodstock Agency) 12,000

Property of the Exors of the late Major V McCalmont, from Norelands Stud
b y f Roi Danzig (USA) - Tea House (Sassafras)........... (B B A (Ireland)) 50,000
From Ballysheehan Stud
b y c Fairy King (USA) - Tecmessa (Home Guard)............ (Derby Bloodstock) 13,500
Property of Mrs A Whitehead, from Broadfield Stud
b y c Petorius - Tender Pearl (Prince Tenderfoot).............. (R J McCormack) 16,500

547

Property of Mrs Phyllis MacFerran, from Rathasker Stud
b y f Taufan (USA) - Tender Time (Tender King)..................... (J W Hills) 8,000
Property of Mr Arthur T Robinson, from Such Moor Stud
b y c Persian Heights - Texly (FR) (Lyphard) (Cash) 3,500
From Ashtown House Stud
b y c Scenic - Thank You Note (What A Guest)............. (B B A (Ireland)) 39,000
From Rathbarry Stud
ch y f Roi Danzig (USA) - Thatcherite (Final Straw)............ (Derby Bloodstock) 12,000
From Kellistown Stud
b y c Alzao (USA) - Timbale D'Argent (Petingo).. (Conti Bloodstock Services) 48,000
From Eyrefield House Stud
b y f Petorius - Tiptoe (Dance In Time).... (J R Collins) 11,000

548

KILL (Goffs)
Thursday, October 7th (Yearlings)

From Irish National Stud
b y f Magical Strike (USA) - Tir-An-Oir (IRE) (Law Society).......... (Horse France) 6,700
From Newborough Stud
b y c Thatching - Tootle (Main Reef)....... (B B A (Ireland)) 40,000
From Newlands House Stud
b y f Taufan (USA) - Trace (USA) (Round Table)................. (B B A (Italia)) 13,500
From Carrigbeg Stud
ch y f Fools Holme (USA) - Traumerei (GER) (Surumu).............. (Bo Helander) 3,000
Property of The Executors of the late Major V McCalmont, from Norelands Stud
b y f Danehill (USA) - Tribal Rite (Be My Native)................ (A C Stewart) 12,500
From Highclere (USA) (Jeffry Morris) Agent
b y c Danzatore (CAN) - Trillionaire (USA) (Vaguely Noble).... (Sallyview Estates) 21,000
Property of Mr D P O'Brien, from Derrygrath Stud
b y f Fairy King (USA) - Tripoli (Great Heron) .... (C Gordon-Watson Bloodstock) 10,000
Property of Mr J Hayes, from Rathbarry Stud
b or br y c Cyrano de Bergerac - Trojan Relation (Trojan Fen)..... (M Kauntze) 23,000
From Tara Stud
b y c Petorius - Trojan Tale (USA) (Critque) (Leinster Bloodstock) 7,800
Property of Mrs A Whitehead, from Owenstown Stud
ch y c Simply Great (FR) - Tumbleline (Tumble Wind).............. (T Stack) 9,000

549

Property of Mrs P Grubb, from Big Acre Stud
br y f Gallic League - Unaria (Prince Tenderfoot)...... (Brian Grassick Bloodstock) 10,500
From Airlie Stud
ch y c King Of Clubs - Vaison La Romaine (Arctic Tern).......... (M A B Agency) 5,500
Property of Mr John J Breslin, from Irish National Stud
b y c Magical Wonder (USA) - Ventry (Stanford)............ (Panetta Bloodstock) 4,200
From Rowanstown Stud
b y c Bold Arrangement - Verthumna (Indian King)..... (Panetta Bloodstock) 6,600
From Tally-Ho Stud
b y c Contract Law (USA) - Veruschka (Lorenzaccio)................. (Cash) 6,300
From Longfield Farm
b y c Bluebird (USA) - Very Sophisticated (USA) (Affirmed)...................... (Brian Grassick Bloodstock) 15,000
From Airlie Stud
b y c Ela-Mana-Mou - Virna (USA) (Coursing)...................... (J Coogan) 27,000
Property of Mr R Hodgins
b or br y c Dancing Dissident (USA) - Wavetree (Realm) .... (Brian Grassick Bloodstock) 18,000
Property of Mrs A Whitehead, from Owenstown Stud
b y f Prince Rupert (FR) - Webbiana (African Sky).................... (P P Keogh) 4,600
From Tally-Ho Stud
b y c Ela-Mana-Mou - Windy Cheyenne (USA) (Tumble Wind).... (M Channon) 17,000

550

Property of Mr Arthur T Robinson, from Such Moor Stud
ch y f Sharrood (USA) - Winter Tern (USA) (Arctic Tern)............................. (David Minton Bloodstock) 4,400
From Landscape Stud (Agent)
b y c Pennine Walk - Wintina (Tumble Wind).................. (M Johnston) 4,000
From Ardmayle House Stud (Agent)
b y c Lead On Time (USA) - Wishiah (Persian Bold)................ (C B A) 22,000
From Maryville Stud
b y f Zalazl (USA) - Wuthering Falls (Wind And Wuthering)..... (R J McCormack) 8,000
From Graigueshoneen Stud
b y f Kahyasi - Yashina (FR) (Tennyson).... (J G Murphy) 7,000
From Rathasker Stud
b y c Red Sunset - Yukon Baby (USA) (Northern Dancer)........... (C B A) 16,000

From Tara Stud
b y c Dancing Dissident (USA) - Zany (Junius)............ (R J McCormack) 9,500
Property of a Partnership, from Curragh Stud
b y f Dancing Dissident (USA) - Abergwrle (Absalom)............... (Frank Barry) 17,500
Property of J G O'Brien, from Ballycummin Castle
gr y c Nishapour (FR) - Afeefa (Lyphard) ... (M Kauntze) 15,000
From Tally-Ho Stud
b y f Contract Law (USA) - African Light (Kalaglow).............. (Lynn Lodge) 5,500

551

From Bellewstown Farm Stud
b y c Scenic - All Pink (Hello Gorgeous).... (Panetta Bloodstock) 20,000
From Tally-Ho Stud
b y c Midyan (USA) - Almadaniyah (Dunbeath)................. (B B A (Italia)) 23,000
Property of Olive Thewissen, from Rockwood Stud
b y f Al Hareb (USA) - Alpine Dance (USA) (Apalachee)................... (Cash) 5,000
From Ryrefield House Stud
b y f Be My Guest - Alrayhah (Habitat) .... (B B A (Italia)) 12,000
Property of Mr William Brannigan, from Ballymacarney Stud
br y f High Estate - Alriyaah (Shareef Dancer) ....(C Gordon-Watson Bloodstock) 10,000
From Glidawn Stud
b y f Nordico (USA) - Amalee (Troy) .... (Peter Doyle Bloodstock) 8,000
From Kellistown Stud
ch y f Persian Bold - Ampersand (USA) (Stop The Music)..... (B B A (Ireland)) 13,000
From Staunton Lodge Stud
ch y f Al Hareb (USA) - Annabella (Habitat) (Peter Doyle Bloodstock) 10,000
From Ballyvolane Stud
b y c Taufan (USA) - Apple Rings (Godswalk).............. (M H Tompkins) 8,200
Property of Mr Raymond A Keogh, from Irish National Stud
b y c Danehill (USA) - Art Age (Artaius) .... (J Ferguson) 21,000

552

Property of Ballintyre Stud
b y c Double Schwartz - Ashbourne Lass (Ashmore)..................... (Cash) 25,000
From Cooliney Stud
b y f Law Society (USA) - Atlanta Royaled (Prince Tenderfoot) .... (Bruno Ditta Grizzetti) 9,000
Property of a Partnership, from O K Stud
b y f Scenic - A Toute Vitesse (USA) (Riverman)................... (B B A) 12,000
From Oak Lodge Stud (Agent)
b y c Waajib - Avebury Ring (Auction Ring) (E Cleary) 10,000
From Rathbarry Stud (Agent)
b y f Waajib - Balela (African Sky) .... (Peter Doyle Bloodstock) 23,000

From Great Connell Farms
b y f Kahyasi - Banasiya (Mill Reef) (Cash) 8,000
Property of Mrs T V Ryan, from Kilcoran House Stud
b y c Gallic League - Barbara Ann (Nebbiolo) .... (Derby Bloodstock) 17,500
From Shadwell Estate Company Ltd
b y c In The Wings - Bashush (USA) (Caro) (Sallyview Estates) 21,000
Property of Mr John McGarry, from Mountain View Stud
ch y f Indian Ridge - Bazaar Promise (Native Bazaar)................... (C Gordon-Watson Bloodstock) 20,000
From Green Ireland Properties Ltd
ch y c Mining (USA) - Beautiful Secret (USA) (Secreto)...................... (Leinster Bloodstock Agency) 3,000

553

From Swordlestown Stud
b y f Persian Bold - Bebe Altesse (GER) (Alpenkonig)............ (M Johnston) 3,500
From Croom House Stud
b y f Alzao (USA) - Belle Origine (USA) (Exclusive Native)........ (J S Bolger) 48,000
Property of a Partnership, from Lisieux Stud
b y c Warning - Bequeath (USA) (Lyphard) (J Gosden) 55,000
From Round Hill Stud
b y f High Estate - Bit Of A Fiddle (Stradavinsky).............. (J Hayden) 7,000
From Mellon Stud
b y f Fools Holme (USA) - Black Crow (Sea Hawk II)................ (B B A (Italia)) 11,000
Property of Mr John J Breslin, from Irish National Stud
b y c Magical Strike (USA) - Blue Bell Girl (Blakeney).............. (R Hollinshead) 8,000
From Eyresfield Lodge
b y f Danehill (USA) - Blue Wedding (USA) (Irish River)...... (Panetta Bloodstock) 4,500
From Rathbarry Stud
ch y f Glow (USA) - Bold Miss (Bold Lad) .. (Lillingston Bloodstock) 3,500
Property of Mr P J O'Hagan
b y f Bluebird (USA) - Bonnie Isle (Pitcairn) (I Allan) 18,000
From Tara Stud
ch y f Kefaah (USA) - Bright Landing (Sun Prince)........ (Lillingston Bloodstock) 7,500

554

From Tsarina Stud
gr y c Persian Bold - Brillante (FR) (Green Dancer)..................... (J Ryan) 10,500
From Killeenlea Stud
b y f Taufan (USA) - Bumble-Bee (High Line)................. (D R Elsworth) 6,000
From Eyrefield House Stud
b y c Thatching - Call Me Miss (Hello Gorgeous).. (David Minton Bloodstock) 8,000
Property of a Partnership, from Clonhea Stud
b y f Fairy King (USA) - Canton Lighting (Rheingold)............. (K McAuliffe) 26,000

From Eyrefield Lodge
b y f Alzao (USA) - Carnival Dance (Welsh Pageant)....... (Bruno Ditta Grizzetti) 7,000
From Carrigbeg Stud
b y c Common Grounds - Cartier Bijoux (Ahonoora)........................... (Brian Grassick Bloodstock) 26,000
Property of The Executors of the late Major V McCalmont, from Norelands Stud
ch y f Ballad Rock - Casla (Lomond)........ (J Lloyd) 38,000
From Rathbarry Stud (Agent)
b y f Simply Great (FR) - Chalfont Mo (Mummy's Pet) .... (Lillingston Bloodstock) 7,000
From Islanmore Stud
ch y c Al Hareb (USA) - Cheating Heart (King Of Clubs)........... (L Browne) 9,000
Property of Mr & Mrs G J King, from Riverdene Stud
b y f Petorius - Checkers (Habat).......... (C A Horgan) 9,200

555

From Moygaddy Stud
b y f Taufan (USA) - Chilblains (Hotfoot) ... (D Gillespie) 13,000
b y f Dancing Dissident (USA) - Come True (FR) (Nasram II).......... (D Gillespie) 7,000
From Cooliney Stud
b y f Fairy King (USA) - Cooliney Princess (Bruni).................... (T Stack) 29,000
From Triermore Stud
b y f Last Tycoon - Crown Class (USA) (Chief's Crown)........... (Finaco Srl) 3,500
Property of R J Powell, M.R.C.V.S., from Wellington House Stud
gr y c Ballad Rock - Cumbrian Melody (Petong).... (Newmarket International) 27,000
From Rathbarry Stud
b y f Law Society (USA) - Curie Abu (Crofter)........... (Lillingston Bloodstock) 12,000
From Corbally Stud
b or br y f Persian Bold - Daisy Dobson (Gorytus) .... (Equine Investment Consultant) 8,000
Property of Mrs Chris Harrington
b y c Indian Ridge - Daniella Drive (USA) (Shelter Half).................. (Cash) 24,000
Property of Mr M Morrin
b y c Prince Sabo - Danzig Harbour (USA) (Private Account) .... (Equine Investment Consultants) 8,000
Property of Deln Ltd & Mr H Kaskel, from Eyrefield House Stud
b y c Nordico (USA) - Debbie's Next (USA) (Arctic Tern)........................... (Johnny McKeever Bloodstock) 19,000

556

From Islanmore Stud
b y f Persian Bold - Deer Emily (Alzao)..... (Brian Grassick Bloodstock) 60,000
From Eyrefield House Stud
b or br y c Tirol - Delightful Time (Manado) (M O'Toole) 30,000
From Irish National Stud
b y f Dancing Dissident (USA) - Diva Encore (Star Appeal)................. (B B A) 12,000
From Rathasker Stud
b y f Bluebird (USA) - Dominia (Derring-Do) (Garibold Giacimo) 9,700
Property of Mr Maurice McAuley
b y c Ela-Mana-Mou - Dorado Llave (USA) (Well Deocrated)......... (M O'Toole) 8,500
From Tullamaine Castle Stud (Agent)
b y f Be My Guest (USA) - Dove Cottage (USA) (Alleged)................ (T Stack) 5,800
From Knocktoran Stud
ch y f Astronef - Drama (USA) (Sir Ivor).... (Cash) 4,400
From Triermore Stud
b or br y f Bluebird (USA) - Dusky Diana (Dara Monarch)........ (Horse France) 6,500
Property of Mrs A S O'Brien, from Landscape Stud
b y f High Estate - El Pina (Be My Guest).. (N Meade) 20,000
Property of Mr R Hodgins
b y f Simply Great (FR) - English Lily (Runnett).......... (Pat Fitsimons (Agent)) 2,500

557

Property of Mrs R B Kennedy, from Mountain View Stud
b or br y f Dancing Dissident (USA) - Eskaroon (Artaius) .... (Newturf Bloodstock Agency) 17,000
Property of Stonethorn Stud Farms, from Carrowdore Castle Stud
b y c Roi Danzig (USA) - Eurorose (Busted) (R J McCormack) 7,000
From Milltown Stud
b y c Dominion Royale - Explorelka (Relko) (C B A) 14,000
From Croom House Stud
gr y f Last Tycoon - Faakirah (Dragonara Palace) (C Gordon-Watson Bloodstock) 30,000
From Tally-Ho Stud
b y f Contract Law - Faapette (Runnett) ... (Johnny McKeever Bloodstock) 8,000
From Swordlestown Stud
b y c Ballad Rock - Fair Siobahn (Petingo).. (M Johnston) 9,000
From Oaklawn Stud
b y f Shernazar - Fanellan (Try My Best) ... (Cash) 3,500
From Pipers Hill Stud
b y c Salt Dome (USA) - Feather Glen (Glenstal)................ (J T Doyle) 16,000
From Deerpark Stud
b y f Petorius - Final Decision (Tap On Wood).................... (C Collins) 7,500
Property of Mrs G W Bronfman, from Landscape Stud
b y f Taufan (USA) - Final Veil (USA) (Sadler's Wells)..... (M A B Agency) 24,000

558

From Dunderry Stud
b y c Danehill (USA) - Fire Flash (Bustino).. (P Harris) 21,000

From Airlie Stud
ch y f Ballad Rock - First Blush (Ela-Mana-Mou).............. (J S Wainwright) 9,500
From Oldtown Stud
b y f Nordico (USA) - Fleeting (USA) (Lear Fan)...................... (F Berry) 21,000
From Ballylinch Stud (Agent)
ch y c Keen - Flying Anna (Roan Rocket)... (Brian Grassick Bloodstock) 15,000
Property of Mrs P Grubb, from Big Acre Stud
ch y f Astronef - Folly Gale (Strong Gale).. (M Young) 4,000
Property of Mrs A Whitehead, from Owenstown Stud
b y f Petorius - Footway (Sovereign Path).. (Cash) 8,000
b y c Runnett - Foston Bridge (Relkino).... (J Gorman) 9,000
Property of Mr J Crisp, from Ardenode Stud
br y c Formidable (USA) - Four-Legged Friend (Aragon)...................... (Lillingston Bloodstock) 13,500
From Ballysheehan Stud
b y f Fairy King (USA) - Foxrock (Ribero)... (Bruno Ditta Grizzetti) 10,000
From Rathbarry Stud (Agent)
b y f Persian Bold - Fundraiser (Welsh Saint)............. (Derby Bloodstock) 16,500

559

From Kildaragh Stud
b y f Shaadi (USA) - Future Treasure (Habitat)................... (Bo Helander) 7,000
From Tara Stud
ch y f Kefaah (USA) - Galka (Deep Diver)... (J T Doyle) 10,000
From Carrigbeg Stud
b or br y c Posen (USA) - Geraldville (Lord Gayle)...................... (F Barry) 13,500
From Shadwell Estate Company Ltd
b y f Soviet Star (USA) - Ghaadah (USA) (Linkage) .... (Newturf Bloodstock Agency) 5,500
b y f Reference Point - Ghanayim (USA) (Sharpen Up)...... (Sallyview Estates) 23,000
From Ballysheehan Stud
b y c Fairy King (USA) - Glenveagh (USA) (Seattle Slew).......... (B B A (Italia)) 20,000
From Oak Lodge Stud
b y f Taufan (USA) - Global Princess (Transworld).................... (W Elliot) 8,000
From Corbally Stud
b y f Bluebird (USA) - Golden Grundy (Grundy)........................(Cash) 13,500
From Rathbarry Stud (Agent)
ch y c Waajib - Gratify (Grundy).. (P Harris) 12,000
From Ballysheehan Stud
ch y c Persian Bold - Guest Performer (Be My Guest)............ (M Johnston) 11,000

560

From Golden Vale Stud
br y f Lugana Beach - Havana Blade (USA) (Blade)......... (Mercury Bloodstock) 2,700
From Highclere USA (Jeffry Morris) Agent
b y c Greinton - Heather Bee (USA) (Drone) (Margaret O'Toole) 34,000
From Rowanstown Stud
b y c Don't Forget Me - Heavenward (USA) (Conquistador Cielo) .... (Peter Doyle Bloodstock) 18,000
From Churchtown House Stud
b y f Reference Point - Heracleia (FR) (Kenmare)................... (Cash) 3,700
From Tally-Ho Stud
b y f Tirol - Highland Girl (USA) (Sir Ivor)... (M Channon) 12,500
Property of Mr Gerard Canavan
ch y f Fools Holme (USA) - Honorine (USA) (Blushing Groom).... (Sn Fabio Nassi) 11,000
Property of Belmont Stud
b y f Shernazar - Hostess (Be My Guest).. (Cash) 11,000
From Corbally Stud
b y c Persian Bold - Hot Curry (USA) (Sharpen Up)........... (M A Jarvis) 15,500
From Swordlestown Stud
b or br y f Scenic - Hot Pad (Hotfoot)...... (Cash) 6,500
From Ballysheehan Stud
ch y c Ballad Rock - House Tie (Be Friendly) .... (B B A) 27,000

561

Property of Mrs O M E McKeever, from Greenfields
ch y f Glenstal (USA) - Huntress (Huntercombe).......... (Brownstown Stud) 2,500
Property of J G O'Brien, from Ballycummin Castle
b y c Kahyasi - Ibadiyya (Tap On Wood).... (Panetta Bloodstock) 7,000
From Ballylinch Stud
ch y c Keen - Immediate Impact (Caerleon) (Johnny McKeever Bloodstock) 25,000
From Barronstown Stud
b y f Darshaan - Instinctive Move (USA) (Nijinsky)................ (J T Doyle) 12,000
From Tally-Ho Stud
b y c Dancing Dissident (USA) - In The Clover (Meadow Mint) .... (E I L Bloodstock) 9,000
Property of Mr Tom Shirley, from Garnaman House
b y f Fayruz - Isa (Dance In Time) .... (Sarah Hollinshead) 6,200
From Corbally Stud
ch y f Ballad Rock - Isla Bonita (Kings Lake) (Panetta Bloodstock) 5,600
PRIVATE SALES
From Mount Coote Stud
b y f Thatching - Pertinent (Persepolis) .... (B B A) 20,000
Property of Mr & Mrs Leo Collins, from Ennistown Stud
b y f Petorius - Miss Java (Persian Bold)... (M Johnston) 4,500

(Index reference 581 follows)

581

NEWMARKET
Tuesday, October 12th (Yearlings)

From Kilnamoragh Stud, Ireland
b y c Conquering Hero (USA) - Jem Jen (Great Nephew) .... (David Minton Bloodstock) 6,800
Property of a Partnership, from Dornvalley Stud
b y c Risk Me (FR) - Jobiska (Dunbeath (USA)).......... (Browne Bloodstock) 4,700
Property of Mr W Beasley, from Greenvale Farm
b y f Most Welcome - Jump The Road (CAN) (Darby Creek Road (USA)) ...... (P J McBride) 2,100
Property of a Gentleman, from Woolmer Cottage Stables
b y c Hadeer - Kalorama (FR) (Bold Lad (IRE)).................(B B A (Ireland)) 1,600
Property of Mr G Sheehan, from Westley Hall Stables
b y c Deploy - Kirby's Princess (Indian King (USA)).............................. (German International Bloodstock) 10,000
Property of Michael Broughton, from Broughton Bloodstock
b y c Dowsing (USA) - Knees Up (USA) (Dancing Champ (USA))....... (B B A) 3,500
Property of Stud-On-The-Chart
b y f Chief Singer - La Reine de France (Queen's Hussar).......... (M Ayers) 3,000
Property of His Grace the Duke of Marlborough, from Blenheim Stud
b y c Sizzling Melody - Lady Bequick (Sharpen Up)............... (P Makin) 10,500
Property of Southcourt Stud
gr y f Absalom - Larive (Blakeney).......... (Mick Easterby) 7,000
Property of Worksop Manor Stud
b y c Reprimand - Latakia (Morston (FR)) .. (R O'Gorman Bloodstock) 4,600

582

From Three Gates Stud
ch y f Risk Me (FR) - Lightning Legend (Lord Gayle (USA)).................. (German International Bloodstock) 3,200
From Ted Voute, Agent
b y f Statoblest - Load Line (High Line) .... (Will Edmeades Bloodstock) 24,000
Property of Messrs. I Stewart-Brown & M Meacock, from Longstones Stud
b y f Damister (USA) - Loch Spey (Formidable (USA)).. (R O'Gorman Bloodstock) 1,100
Property of Fares Stables Ltd, from Fares Stables
gr y c Highest Honor (FR) - Lovely Noor (USA) (Fappiano (USA))..... (J Dunlop) 8,400
Property of Mrs A Stacey, from Old Mill Stud
b y c Bustino - Lucky Fingers (Hotfoot) .... (T Walsh) 4,000
Property of a Partnership, from Uplands Park
b y f Hadeer - Lucky Omen (Queen's Hussar)..................... (P Howling) 5,200
Property of Messrs J Strange & N E Poole, from Lauceston & Paradise Farm Stud
b y c Faustus (USA) - Lucky Orphan (Derrylin)........................(T Walsh) 6,000
Property of Mr Simon Wingfield Digby TD.,DL., from Sandley Stud
b y f Robellino (USA) - Madame Bovary (Ile de Bourbon (USA)).................. (David Minton Bloodstock) 2,400
Property of The Exors. of the late Mrs V Hue-Williams, from Woolton House Stud
br y c Midyan (USA) - Magic Vision (Shergar) (German International Bloodstock) 8,400
Property of a Partnership, from New England Stud
b y c Sharpo - Magical Spirit (Top Ville) .... (J Fanshawe) 17,000

583

Property of Wyards Stud
b y f Never So Bold - Makeshift (Night Shift (USA))..................... (G Oxley) 7,000
Property of Mr P T Dyke, from Park Farm Stud
ch y c Komaite (USA) - Manhunt (Posse (USA)) (Geoffrey Howson Bloodstock) 3,000
Property of Mr Rex Comyn Boucher, from Norton Court Stud
b y f Northern State (USA) - Marie Galante (Shirley Heights) ..... (Gavin Pritchard-Gordon) 2,000
From Hilltown Stud, Irelandyorton Court Stud
b y f Nordico (USA) - Marietta Meagher (USA) (Solford (USA)) .... (German International Bloodstock) 12,000
Property of Stud-On-The-Chart
b y c Prince Sabo - Martin-Lavell (Dominion) .... (D Woods) 6,000
From Tally-Ho Stud, Ireland
b y c Classic Secret (USA) - Melting Snows (High Top).. (David Minton Bloodstock) 39,000
From Crichel Stud
ch y c Indian Ridge - Meritsu (IRE) (Lyphard's Special (USA)).............. (Derby Bloodstock) 16,000
Property of Miss E Aldous, from Southburgh Manor Stud
b y c Reprimand - Miami Melody (Miami Springs)................. (R O'Ryan) 3,800
Property of Stud-On-The-Chart
b y c Prince Sabo - Midnight Imperial (Night Shift (USA)).............. (M Halford) 6,000
Property of Mr & Mrs R J Tory, from Trickledown Stud
b y f Indian Ridge - Mighty Flash (Rolfe (USA))................. (D Elsworth) 26,000

584

Property of Milton Park Stud
b y c Be My Chief (USA) - Mill Hill (USA) (Riva Ridge (USA))........... (B B A) 21,000
Property of Mr L Elliott, from Little Peverel
b y c Distant Relative - Misdevious (USA) (Alleged (USA))......... (D Cosgrove) 18,000
From Elsenham Stud
b y f Risk Me (FR) - Miss Mischievous (Star Appeal)................ (P Kelleway) 3,800

Property of Mr & Mrs R Heathcote, from Heathavon Stud
ch y f Risk Me (FR) - Mistral's Dancer (Shareef Dancer (USA))...... (W Muir) 3,800
Property of Mrs G Fane, from Longstones Stud
ch y c Charmer - Mollified (Lombard (GER)) (T Walsh) 3,000
From Charlestown Stud, Ireland
br y c Nashamaa - Mombones (Lord Gayle (USA)).................. (M Channon) 11,000
From Glebe Stud
b y f Scenic - Money Supply (Brigadier Gerard)...................... (C B A) 21,000
From Summetree Stud
b y c Ballacashtal (CAN) - Moreton's Martha (Derrylin)... (David Minton Bloodstock) 2,800
Property of Mr C L Loyd, from Lockinge Stud
b y f Mazilier (USA) - Mosso (Ercolano (USA)).................. (Mrs V Haigh) 1,800
Property of R E A Bott (Wigmore St) Ltd, from Meddler Stud
b y f Never So Bold - Mount Ida (USA) (Conquistador Cielo (USA))..... (Cash) 1,000

585

Property of Henry Cecil Bloodstock Ltd., from Cliff Stud
b y f Faustus (USA) - My Tootsie (Tap On Wood).................. (I Campbell) 1,200
From Cedar Tree Stud
Proliferous (FR) b y c Most Welcome - Nadema (Artaius (USA)).............. (German International Bloodstock) 7,400
Property of Mr Simon Wingfield Digby TD., DL., from Sandley Stud
gr y c Distant Relative - Nelly Do Da (Derring-Do)...................... (B B A) 25,000
Property of Mr M Morrin
ch y c Ballad Rock - One Better (Nebbiolo) (J Berry) 38,000
Property of Mr & Mrs R T Watson, from Manor Farm Stud, Rutland
b y c Salse (USA) - Orient (Bay Express)... (W Haggas) 16,500
Property of Mr L Phelan
b y f Gallic League - Paradise Regained (North Stoke)............ (R Williams) 4,000
Property of Addison Racing Ltd Inc., from Whitsbury Manor Stud
b y c Distant Relative - Pay The Bank (High Top)............. (Brown Bloodstock) 12,000
Property of Southcourt Stud
b y c Rock City - Pearl Cove (Town And Country)... (German Axel Donnerstag) 12,000
Property of Farmers Hill Stud
b y c Distant Relative - Peep Of Day (USA) (Lypheor)................. (R Durant) 7,200
Property of Mr J Jones Morgan
b y f Distant Relative - Philgwyn (Milford).. (T Fairhurst) 10,500

586

Property of Mr K Mercer, from Old Mill Stud
b y c Damister (USA) - Positive Attitude (Red Sunset).............. (T Mullins) 8,600
Property of Mr C Wiggins, from Trickledown Stud
b y c Sharpo - Poyle Princess (Valiyar)..... (P Doyle) 7,000
Property of a Partnership, from Milton Park Stud
ch y f Never So Bold - Prima Domina (Dominion)................. (D Barron) 22,000
Property of Barrettstown Stud Farms Ltd, from Whitsbury Manor Stud
b y f Dowsing (USA) - Princess Matilda (Habitat)...................... (Cash) 1,800
Property of Mr & Mrs R N Khan, from Uplands Park
b y f Charmer - Pringipoula (Dominion).... (B B A) 2,600
Property of Woodhaven Stud
b y c Roi Danzig (USA) - Provocation (Kings Lake (USA))....... (Derby Bloodstock) 14,000
Property of Mr R W Hipkin & Mr R A Speight, from National Stud
ch y f Primo Dominie - Purple Fan (Dalsaan) .... (D Cosgrove) 7,200
Property of Whitsbury Manor Stud
b y f Distant Relative - Pushkar (Northfields (USA))....................... (B B A) 20,000
Property of Barton Stud
b y c Charmer - Quaranta (Hotfoot) (B B A) 4,500
Property of Lofts Hall Stud
b y f Aragon - Queens Welcome (Northfields (USA)) (R O'Gorman Bloodstock) 5,800

587

From Golden Vale Stud, Ireland
ch y f Al Hareb (USA) - Red Red Rose (USA) (Blushing Groom (FR))......... (D Cosgrove) 5,000
Property of a Partnership, from Sussex Stud
ch y c Woodman (USA) - Repercutionist (USA) (Beaudelaire (USA)).. (J Jenkins) 28,000
Property of Summertree Stud
ch y f Master Willie - Ritsurin (Mount Hagen (FR))......................... (German International Bloodstock) 1,700
Property of Major General Sir George Burns, GCVO,CB,IDSO,MC, from Longstones Stud
ch y c Sharpo - River's Rising (FR) (Mendez (FR))................. (J Delahooke) 21,000
From Deerfield Farm
b or br y c Most Welcome - Round Midnight (Star Appeal)... (Agence F I P S) 7,000
Property of Miss E Drax, from Trickledown Stud
b y f Roi Danzig (USA) - Sacred Mountain (St Paddy).......... (R J McCormick) 6,400
Property of Hamilton Bloodstock (UK) Ltd.,lk from Barnwood Stud
b y f Salse (USA) - Salilia (Nishapour (FR)).. (D Morris) 2,600
From Woodditton Stud
ch y f Superlative - Salinity (NZ) (Stgandaan (FR))....... (R O'Gorman Bloodstock) 2,100
Property of Mr R P Williams, from Scorrier House Stud
ch y f Weldnaas (USA) - Sallytude (Tudor Music)...................... (R Lamb) 9,200
Property of Mr L Phelan
b y f Red Sunset - Salonniere (FR) (Bikala) (Cash) 6,200

588

From Theobalds Stud
ch y c Roi Danzig (USA) - Sayulita (Habitat) (C Allen) 14,000

Property of Mr R D Hollinsworth, from Arches Hall Stud
b y c Salse (USA) - Sea Pageant (Welsh Pageant)..................... (B Hills) 3,600

Property of Mr & Mrs L T Foster, from Cliff Stud
b y c Unfuwain (USA) - Seven Seas (FR) (Riverman (USA)).... (L T & M Foster) 9,800

Property of a Partnership, from The Elms Stud
ch y c Deploy - Shannon Princess (Connaught)............................ (Geoffrey Howson Bloodstock) 15,000

Property of a Partnership, from The New England Stud
b y c Celestial Storm (USA) - Sharanella (Shareef Dancer (USA)).............. (F Johnson Houghton) 9,500

Property of Mrs J Langmead, from Stoughton Stud
br y f Tragic Role (USA) - Sharper Still (Sharpen Up)............... (J Dunlop) 8,500

Property of Sussex Stud Ltd., from Sussex Stud
b y c Rock City - Shemsa (Habitat) .... (Horse France (Ireland) Ltd) 14,000

From Cedar Tree Stud
b y f Fijar Tango (FR) - Silver Ore (FR) (Silver Hawk (USA))................. (R Boss) 4,200

Property of Miss J Chaplin, from Blisbury Farm
ch y f Absalom - Sixslip (USA) (Diesis)..... (D Morley) 13,500

Property of Mr R P Williams, from Scorrier House Stud
b y f Zalazl (USA) - Song Grove (Song)..... (N Graham) 5,000

589

Property of Heathavon Stables Ltd., from Heathavon Stud
gr y c Absalom - Star Of Jupiter (Jupiter Island)..................... (I Campbell) 1,000

Property of Worksop Manor Stud
b y f Never So Bold - Stara (Star Appeal) .. (J Shack) 5,200

Property of Mr A J Struthers, from Lofts Hall Stud
b y c Statoblest - Sule Skerry (Scottish Rifle).. (Johnny McKeever Bloodstock) 7,800

Property of a Partnership, from Glen Andred Stud
b y f Petong - Sunley Stars (Sallust) .... (B Meehan) 5,200

Property of Mr G S Shropshire, from West Dereham Abbey Stud
ch y f Ballad Rock - Swift Pursuit (Posse (USA))....... (Peter Doyle Bloodstock) 18,000

Property of Whitsbury Manor Stud
b y f Be My Chief (USA) - Take Heart (Electric)............. (Susan Scargill) 9,400

Property of Heathavon Stables Ltd, from Heathavon Stud
b y f Risk Me (FR) - The High Dancer (High Line).................. (S Uppstrom) 1,600

Property of Fonthill Farms, from Fonthill Stud
ch y f Primo Dominie - Thundercloud (Electric)........................... (J Hill) 14,500

Property of a Partnership, from Toat Farm
b y c Puissance - Tribal Lady (Absalom)........ (J A Parker) 5,400

Property of R E A Bott (Wigmore St) Ltd., from Meddler Stud
ch y c Most Welcome - True Nora (Ahonoora)... (Giles Pritchard Gordon) 9,200

590

Property of a Partnership, from Stud-On-The-Chart
b y c Reprimand - Trull (Lomond (USA)) .... (Lord Huntingdon) 15,500

Property of a Partnership, from Ham Cross Farm
b y f Dowsing (USA) - Try The Duchess (Try My Best)............. (Susan Scargill) 4,000

From Glebe Stud
b y c Colmore Row - Tura (Northfields (USA))............................ (German International Bloodstock) 20,000

Property of His Grace the Duke of Marlborough, from Blenheim Stud
b y c Common Grounds - Tweedling (USA) (Sir Ivor).......... (Sir Mark Prescott) 31,000

From Tally-Ho Stud, Ireland
b y c Contract Law (USA) - Ultra (Stanford) (R O'Gorman Bloodstock) 12,000

Property of Mr K Powter, from Old Mill Stud
ch or gr y f Absalom - Uranus (Manacle)... (A R Fawcett) 9,000

From Charlestown Stud, Ireland
b y c Phardante (FR) - Wallpark Princess (Balidar)............. (J R Parkin) 2,500

Property of Mrs K E Collie, from Skeffington Vale Stud
b y c Risk Me (FR) - Warm Wind (Tumble Wind (USA))..... (Browne Bloodstock) 12,500

Property of Mr R D Hollingsworth, from Arches Hall Stud
b y c Chief Singer - Wave Dancer (Dance In Time (CAN))............ (T M Jones) 3,300

Property of Messrs E & G Bosley, from Dornvalley Stud
ch y f Rich Charlie - Woolcana (Some Hand) .... (Cash) 1,200

591

Property of Devonia Stud
b y c Statoblest - Young Tearaway (Young Generation)............... (P Howling) 10,000
b y c Pennine Walk - Alencon (Northfields (USA))........................... (German International Bloodstock) 7,500

From Hilltown Stud, Ireland
b y c Tirol - Allegheny River (USA) (Lear Fan (USA))........................ (B B A) 15,000

Property of Mr T H Rossiter, from The Elms Stud
b y c Statoblest - Alo Ez (Alzao (USA)) ..... (R Guest) 24,000

Property of The Exors of the late Mrs V Hue-Williams, from Woolton House Stud
b or gr y c Damister (USA) - Amalancher (USA) (Alleged (USA))...... (J Mullins) 4,800

From Barton Stud
ch y f Bluebird (USA) - Ariadne (Bustino)... (B B A) 6,000
Property of Mrs Susan Feddern, from Allan Perry, Agent
b y c Northern State (USA) - Arita (FR) (Kronzeuge)........................ (Cormack McCormack Associates) 6,800
Property of Worksop Manor Stud
b y c Warning - Arfminda (Blakeney) ...... (Brown Bloodstock) 20,000
Property of a Gentleman, from Old Mill Stud
ch y f Pharly (FR) - As Blessed (So Blessed) .... (Peter Doyle Bloodstock) 11,500
Property of Southcourt Stud
b y c Indian Ridge - Aspark (Sparkler)...... (T Mills) 29,000

592

Property of Heathavon Stables Ltd., from Heathavon Stud
ch y f Risk Me (FR) - Astral Suite (On Your Mark).................. (J Spearing) 1,900
Property of Mrs C A Trendell, from Village Farm Stud
b y c Law Society (USA) - Avahra (Sahib) .. (P Thorman) 5,000
Property of a Partnership, from Crockfords Stud
b y f Bustino - B A Poundstretcher (Laser Light) .... (German International Bloodstock) 6,200
From Knocklong House Stud, Ireland (Agent)
b y f Alzao (USA) - Bag Lady (Be My Guest (USA))......... (F Johnson Houghton) 13,000
From Kilnamoragh Stud, Ireland
b y c Ajraas (USA) - Baliana (CAN) (Riverman (USA))... (Giles Pritchard Gordon) 13,000
Property of Mr F C T Wilson, from The Elms Stud
b y f Damister (USA) - Ballad Island (Ballad Rock)........................ (Cash) 6,800
Property of Mr R S A Urquhart, from Hunsley House Stud
b y f Rambo Dancer (CAN) - Barrie Baby (Import)........... (D Ffrench-Davis) 2,500
Property of Mr & Mrs J A Duffy, from Orchard Close Stud
br y c Rock City - Be My Honey (Bustino).. (B T Eastick) 7,200
Property of Mr C W Rogers, from Collin Stud
ch y c Superlative - Beaute Fatale (Hello Gorgeous (USA)) .... (Peter Doyle Bloodstock) 7,800
From Craddoxtown Lodge Stud, Ireland
ch y c Simply Great (FR) - Bellinzona (Northfields (USA))... (Lillingston Bloodstock) 11,000

593

Property of Fluorocarbon Bloodstock Ltd., from Chippenham Lodge Stud
b y c Shavian - Billante (USA) (Graustark) .. (Brown Bloodstock) 8,000
Property of Whitsbury Manor Stud
br or gr y f Midyan (USA) - Bishah (USA) (Balzac (USA))... (Mme Bollack Badel) 2,800
Property of Landi Thoroughbreds Ltd., from Southburgh Manor Stud
b y f Law Society (USA) - Bold Apple (Bold Lad (IRE)).... (Gavin Pritchard Gordon) 3,100
Property of W H R John and Partners
b y c Ballad Rock - Bombshell (Le Levanstell)........... (Brian Meehan) 10,000
From Tally-Ho Stud, Ireland
b y c Contract Law (USA) - Bridal Blush (Coquelin (USA))........ (Simon Dow) 7,000
Property of Mr Simon Wingfield Digby TD., DL., from Sandley Stud
gr y f Pharly (FR) - Bustling Nelly (Bustino) (B B A) 21,000
From Knocklong House Stud, Ireland (Agent)
b y c Bluebird (USA) - Caro Lady (Rusticaro (FR))...... (Horse France (Ireland) Ltd) 22,000
From Batsford Stud
b y c Robellino (USA) - Catkin (USA) (Sir Ivor)...................... (I Balding) 8,600
From Tally-Ho Stud, Ireland
ch y c Weldnaas (USA) - Caviar Bini (What A Guest)........... (D Murray Smith) 16,000
From Barton Stud
b y f Shavian - Choke Cherry (Connaught).. (T Easterby) 7,000

594

Property of a Partnership, from The Elms Stud
b y f Kefaah (USA) - Circe (Main Reef)..... (R Fahey) 2,200
Property of Mr M Morrin
b or br y c Scenic - Circus Lady (High Top) (J Delahooke) 24,000
Property of Mrs P Hastings & Mr S Hastings-Bass, from Collin Stud
b y c Reprimand - Clarandal (Young Generation)........ (Peter Doyle Bloodstock) 17,000
Property of High Canfold Stud
ch y c Kefaah (USA) - Come To Tea (IRE) (Be My Guest (USA)) .... (Johnny McKeever Bloodstock) 9,200
From Tally-Ho Stud, Ireland
b y f Fayruz - Comfrey Glen (Glenstal (USA)) .... (A Scott) 14,000
Property of W H R John and Partners
b y c Sharpo - Constant Delight (Never So Bold)..................... (Sally Hall) 10,500
Property of Highfield Stud Ltd., from Glen Andred Stud
gr y f Petong - Cow Pastures (Homing).... (Jack Doyle) 21,000
Property of Mr R W Hipkin & Mr R A Speight, from National Stud
b y f Reference Point - Cut Loose (High Top)...................... (W Jarvis) 16,500
Property of Llety Farms
b y f Bold Owl - Cymbal (Ribero).......... (Giles Pritchard Gordons) 4,200
Property of Freedom Farm
ch y f Indian Ridge - Dabble (Ballad Rock).. (R Durant) 3,800

595

From Chevington Stud
ch y c Persian Heights - Dance Lover's (FR) (Green Dancer (USA))................ (German International Bloodstock) 12,000

Property of Mr P J Burke, from Hanlons Farm, Ireland
b y c Waajib - Dance On Lady (Grundy).... (B B A) 7,500
Property of Woodhaven Stud
b y f Colmore Row - Dancing Chimes (London Bells (CAN))........ (J Berry) 6,800
Property of Stratford Place Stud
b y c Salse (USA) - Debbie Harry (USA) (Alleged (USA)).............. (P Cole) 7,500
Property of Hockley Ltd., from Hockley House Stud
ch y c Cadeaux Genereux - Diamond Shoes (USA) (Diamond Shoal)............... (Cormac McCormack Associates) 11,500
From Batsford Stud
b y c Dowsing (USA) - Discomatic (USA) (Roberto (USA)) .... (Lillingston Bloodstock) 9,000
Property of Mrs J Langmead, from Stoughton Stud
b y f Warrshan (USA) - Dolly Bea Sweet (USA) (Super Concorde (USA))........ (M Tompkins) 5,000
Property of Witney Stud Farm
b y c Midyan (USA) - Don't Tell Daddy (Song)...... (R O'Gorman Bloodstock) 7,200
Property of a Partnership, from Crockfords Stud
br y c Charmer - Dora's Rocket (Roan Rocket)..................... (B B A) 1,000
From Barton Stud
b y c Danehill (USA) - Dubai Lady (Kris).... (H Michael) 31,000

596

Property of Mr C L Loyd, from Lockinge Stud
b y c Faustus (USA) - Duck Soup (Decoy Boy).................... (A R Fawcett) 7,400
From Theobalds Stud
b y c Sylvan Express - Edwins' Princess (Owen Dudley).............. (P Savill) 11,500
From Cornbury Park Stud
b y c Last Tycoon - Eider (Niniski (USA))... (R O'Ryan) 9,400
Property of Mr G S Shropshire, from West Dereham Abbey Stud
ch y c Ballad Rock - Elabella (Ela-Mana-Mou)......... (Lillingston Bloodstock) 28,000
Property of Michael Broughton, from Broughton Bloodstock
ch y c Fools Holme (USA) - Eloquent Charm (USA) (Private Account (USA)) .... (Peter Doyle Bloodstock) 6,200
From Three Gates Stud
b y c Risk Me (FR) - Estefan (Taufan (USA)) (B.B.A. Italia) 4,000
Property of Michael Broughton, from Broughton Bloodstock
ch y c Charmer - Fairfields (Sharpen Up)... (Tony Hide) 4,200
Property of Whitsbury Manor Stud
b y c Distant Relative - Fairy Ballerina (Fairy King (USA))...... (Richard McCormick) 10,500
Property of Freedom Farm
ch y c Vague Shot - Fairy Fans (Petingo)... (Clive Brittain) 5,600
From Waymount Stud, Ireland
ch y f Ballad Rock - Far From Home (Habitat).............. (James Fanshawe) 4,600

597

Property of Mr and Mrs R G Percival, from Glen Andred Stud
b y c Mazilier (USA) - Feast-Rite (Reform).. (Tom Mullins) 7,000
Property of Sussex Stud Ltd., from Sussex Stud
ch y c Sure Blade (USA) - Field Day (Northfields (USA))......... (Danny Murphy) 8,200
From Carlton Stud
b y f Distant Relative - Final Rush (Final Straw) (European Equine Consultants) 7,000
Property of Miss J Chaplin, from Blisbury Farm
ch y f Rock City - Finlandaise (FR) (Arctic Tern (USA))................... (B.B.A.) 12,500
Property of Mr & Mrs R T Watson, from Manor Farm Stud, Rutland
b y c Emarati (USA) - Flitteriss Park (Beldale Flutter (USA)).......... (John Dunlop) 18,500
Property of Mrs T C Loyd, from Lockinge Stud
b y c Midyan (USA) - Freely Given (Petingo) (Charles Elsey) 4,200
From Hever Castle Stud
b y c Efisio - Gay Hostess (FR) (Direct Flight)............... (Peter Easterby) 34,000
Property of Freedom Farm
b y c Posen - Generals Daughter (USA) (General Holme (USA)).... (R O'Ryan) 6,600
From Three Gates Stud
b y c Risk Me (FR) - Give Me A Day (Lucky Wednesday)....... (Andrea Pecoraro) 5,200
Property of Mr F C T Wilson, from The Elms Stud
b y c Jupiter Island - Glen Dancer (Furry Glen).................. (D F Spence) 7,500

598

Property of Mr A Walder, from Toat Farm and Stud
b y c Formidable (USA) - Glorietta (USA) (Shadeed (USA)).... (Declan Gillespie) 12,000
Property of Worksop Manor Stud
ch y c Kalaglow - Good Try (Good Bond)... (German International Bloodstock) 2,000
From Cornbury Park Stud
b y f Night Shift (USA) - Grayfoot (Grundy) (David Elsworth) 26,000
From Killeenlea Stud, Ireland
b y f Taufan (USA) - Green Bonnet (FR) (Green Dancer (USA)).. (B.B.A. Ireland) 9,200
Property of Marston Stud
b y c Deploy - Guest List (Be My Guest (USA))............ (Sir Mark Prescott) 18,000
From Dunsany Stud, Ireland
b y f Posen (FR) - Gulistan (Sharpen Up)... (Liam Browne) 4,000
Property of Minster Enterprises Ltd., from Minster Stud
b y f Scenic - Haboobti (Habitat) .... (Mme Bollack-Badel) 10,500
From Cornbury Park Stud
b y f Dancing Brave (USA) - Harefoot (Rainbow Quest (USA))....... (B.B.A. Italia) 11,000
Property of G W Mills and Sons, from Highfield Lodge Stud
gr y f Petong - Harmony Park (Music Boy) (C.B.A.) 13,000

Property of Mr Simon Wingfield Digby TD., DL., from Sandley Stud
ch y c Zalazl (USA) - Hedda Garbler (Stradavinsky)............. (R Durant) 6,800

599

From Portlester Stud, Ireland
b y c Petoski - Helvetique (FR) (Val de Loir) (John Dunlop) 9,000
Property of Mr R S A Urquhart, from Hunsley House Stud
b y f Rambo Dancer (CAN) - Hi-Hunsley (Swing Easy (USA))... (Ernie Weymes) 3,000
Property of Mr M M Allen, from Old Mill Stud
b y f Dominion - High Run (HOL) (Runnymede)............... (Ron Popely) 7,600
Property of Mr L Elliott, from Little Peverels
b y c Risk Me (FR) - Highly Polished (High Top)...................... (John Hill) 3,200
From Tally-Ho Stud, Ireland
b y c Cyrano de Bergerac - Holiday Regrets (Silly Season).............. (John Hill) 3,800
From Batsford Stud
(FR) b y c Dowsing (USA) - Honeymooning (USA) (Blushing Groom (FR)).......... (Hannah Ward) 7,600
Property of a Partnership, from Tilstone Lodge Stud
b y f Risk Me (FR) - Hot Stone (Hotfoot)... (Paul Cole) 16,000
Property of Mr T C Whitaker, from Hellwood Farm Stud
b y c Superpower - House Maid (Habitat).. (Alex Scott) 15,000
From Charlestown Stud, Ireland
b y c Ela-Mana-Mou - Irena (Bold Lad (IRE)) (Sir Mark Prescott) 25,000

600

NEWMARKET
Wednesday, October 13th (Yearlings)

Property of Lavington Stud
b y f Warrshan (USA) - Jalopy (Jalmood (USA))......... (Mmme Bollack Badel) 6,200
From Tallyh-Ho Stud, Ireland
b y c Rock City - Jeanne Avril (Music Boy) (Peter Doyle Bloodstock) 27,000
From Kildaragh Stud, Ireland
b y f Petorius - Jet Set Bunny (USA) (Northjet).......................... (B B A) 11,500
Property of Whitsbury Manor Stud
b y f Distant Relative - Jhansi Ki Rani (USA) (Far North (CAN))...... (Mary Hambro) 15,000
Property of Swaines Hill Stud
br y f Charmer - Josephine Gibney (High Top)... (Geoffrey Howson Bloodstock) 1,600
Property of Stud-On-The-Chart
ch y f Never So Bold - Klewraye (Lord Gayle (USA))......................... (Cash) 5,200
From Brownstown Lodge Stud, Ireland
b y f Tirol - Krismas River (Kris)... (P Cole) 10,000

Property of Mr Henry Marsh, from Furnace Mill Stud
b y c Salse (USA) - Kukri (Kris)........... (John Warren Bloodstock) 36,000
From Graigueshoneen Stud, Ireland
b y c Robellino (USA) - Labista (Crowned Prince (USA))................ (B B A) 19,000
From Ashtown House Stud, Ireland
b y c Thatching - Lady Donna (Dominion).. (Cormac McCormack Associates) 27,000

601

From Mary James (Cotswold Stud Farms)
ch y f Cadeaux Genereux - Lady Of The Land (Wollow)....... (R J R Williams) 10,500
Property of Mr and Mrs I W T Loftus, from Bookham Stud
br y f Tirol - Lago Real (Kings Lake (USA)) (D F Powell) 3,600
From Kildaragh Stud, Ireland
gr y c Pharly (FR) - Lammastide (Martinmas).......................... (German International Bloodstock) 10,000
Property of Wickfield Stud Ltd., from Wickfield Stud
b y c Robellino (USA) - Lets Fall In Love (USA) (Northern Baby (CAN)).......... (Hugo Lascelles Bloodstock) 30,000
Property of a Partnership, from Glen Andred Stud
gr y f Petong - Lucky Flinders (Free State) (R Lamb) 9,000
From Northmore Stud Farm
b y c Waajib - Maiacourt (Malacate (USA)) (Tote Cherry-Downes) 15,500
Property of Courtleigh Stud, from Furnace Mill Stud
b y f Petorius - Mainly Sunset (Red Sunset) (J Berry) 14,500
From Cobhall Court Stud
b y c Fairy King (USA) - Maracuja (USA) (Riverman (USA))......... (B Hanbury) 31,000
From Side Hill Stud
(FR) b y c Chief Singer - Marcotte (Nebos (GER))............ (C & N Bloodstock) 9,200
Property of Hesmonds Stud
b y f Belmez (USA) - Margamania (CAN) (Riverman (USA)).... (Stilvi Compania) 5,200

602

From Rathbarry Stud, Ireland (Agent)
b or br y c Assert - Marie de Beaujeu (FR) (Kenmare (FR)).............. (F Barry) 10,500
Property of a Partnership, from Newtownbarry House Stud, Ireland
b y f Nordico (USA) - Martinova (Martinmas) .... (Derby Bloodstock) 10,500
From Ted Voute, Agent
ch y c Master Willie - Maryland Cookie (USA) (Bold Hour)........ (D Elsworth) 16,000
From Collin Stud
b y f Damister (USA) - Mayroni (Bustino) .. (B B A) 2,500
Property of Jeremy Green & Sons, from Bickmarsh Stud
b y f Rock City - Meanieminymoe (Star Appeal)............................ (Cormac McCormack Associates) 21,000

From Yeomanstown Stud, Ireland
ch y c Common Grounds - Mia Gigi (Hard Fought)............. (Bassetlaw Stud) 15,000

Property of Mrs M J Hills, from Burton Agnes Stud
b y f Statoblest - Mild Wind (Porto Bello) .. (M Usher) 6,000

From Tullamaine Castle Stud Ireland, Agent
b y f Danehill (USA) - Mille Fleurs (USA) (Jacinto).................... (H Cecil) 15,500

Property of Mr Ian Wills
b y c Statoblest - Miller's Gait (Mill Reef (USA)).................. (M Channon) 13,000

From Rathbarry Stud, Ireland (Agent)
b or br y f Taufan (USA) - Mini Look (FR) (In Fijar (USA))................... (B B A) 5,200

603

Property of Allan Bloodlines (Agent), from Aston Park Stud
b y c Bluebird (USA) - Miss Willow Bend (USA) (Willow Hour (USA)) (G Gordon-Watson Bloodstock) 26,000

Property of Bishop's Down Farm
b y c Reprimand - Mists Of Avalon (USA) (Nureyev (USA))........... (T Easterby) 12,500

Property of Aston Park Stud
gr y c Dominion - Moments Peace (Adonijah)............... (Allan Bloodlines) 13,500

From Mary James (Cotswold Stud Farms)
b y f Mtoto - Monashee (USA) (Sovereign Dancer (USA)).................. (B B A) 2,600

From Bearstone Stud
b y c Puissance - More Or Less (Morston (FR))................. (B McMahon) 8,800

Property of a Partnership, from Burton Agnes Stud
b y c Deploy - Mrs Darling (Mummy's Pet) (B B A) 4,400

Property of Bolton Grange Stud, from Dullingham House Stud
b y c Distant Relative - Musianica (Music Boy)...................... (C Thornton) 8,200

From The Zetland Stud
b y f Never So Bold - Musical Sally (USA) (The Minstrel (CAN))... (Gay Kelleway) 10,000

From Tally-Ho Stud, Ireland
ch y c Efisio - My Little Bird (Glenstal (USA)).................. (M Blanshard) 6,800

From Catridge Farm Stud
b y f Unfuwain (USA) - Mystery Ship (Decoy Boy)................... (B B A) 7,400

604

Property of Mrs W H Gibson-Fleming, from Furnace Mill Stud
b y c Rock City - Nastassia (FR) (Noble Decree (USA))... (Shadwell Estate Co) 40,000

Property of Jeremy Green & Sons, from Bickmarsh Stud
br y f Reprimand - Nasty Niece (CAN) (Great Nephew).......... (J Spearing) 9,000

Property of Mr G S Shropshire, from West Dereham Abbey Stud
b y c Unfuwain (USA) - Naturally Fresh (Thatching)............................ (Geoffrey Howson Bloodstock) 7,000

From Deerpark Stud, Ireland
ch y c Forzando - Nigel's Dream (Pyjama Hunt)....................... (J Eustace) 32,000

From Mary James (Cotswold Stud Farms)
ch y f Caerleon (USA) - Night Of Wind (Tumble Wind (USA)) .... (John Ferguson Bloodstock) 60,000

Property of Stud-On-The-Chart
b y c Law Society (USA) - No Sugar Baby (FR) (Crystal Glitters (USA)) .... (German International Bloodstock) 17,000

Property of a Partnership, from Furnace Mill Stud
b y f Zalazl (USA) - Noble Haven (Indian King (USA)).......... (Agence F I P S) 17,000

Property of Mr David Allan, from Aston Park Stud
br y f Reprimand - Noble Lustre (USA) (Lyphard's Wish (FR)) (M Bryce-Smith) 14,000

Property of Whitsbury Manor Stud
b y c Robellino (USA) - Norpella (Northfields (USA))........................ (C B A) 23,000

From Tally-Ho Stud, Ireland
b y f Contract Law (USA) - North Hut (Northfields (USA))...... (M Channon) 6,000

605

From Northmore Stud Farm
ch y c Sharpo - Number One Lady (Shernazar) .... (German International Bloodstock) 35,000

From Ted Voute, Agent
b y c Kalaglow - Oatfield (Great Nephew) .. (Shadwell Estate Co) 42,000

From Rathbarry Stud, Ireland
b y c Jareer (USA) - Onthecomet (Chief Singer) .... (Richard O'Gorman Bloodstock) 23,000

Property of Shutford Stud, from Mary James (Cotswold Stud Farms)
b y f Tirol - Pale Gold (FR) (New Chapter) .. (Mr & Mrs B Shaw) 7,500

Property of Furnace Mill Bloodstock Ltd., from Furnace Mill Stud
b y f Never So Bold - Palmella (USA) (Grundy)................. (I Balding) 12,000

Property of Tullamaine Castle Stud, Ireland
ch y f Bluebird (USA) - Palmyra (GER) (Arratos (FR))... (F Johnson-Houghton) 9,000

Property of Jeremy Green & Sons and Mrs A D Fanshawe, from Bickmarsh Stud
b y c Warrshan (USA) - Panama Princess (Indian King (USA))....... (B Meehan) 9,500

From Side Hill Stud
ch y c Persian Heights - Pencarreg (Caerleon (USA))....... (R McCormick) 8,000

From Yeomanstown Stud, Ireland
b y c Forzando - Persian Air (Persian Bold) (David Minton Bloodstock) 18,000

Property of Kingwood Bloodstock Ltd, from Kingwood Stud
ch y c Absalom - Persian Express (Persian Bold)...................... (P Cole) 21,000

606

Property of a Partnership, from Burningfold Manor Stud
b y f Pharly (FR) - Persian Grey (Persepolis (FR))...................... (D Morris) 1,650

From Tullamaine Castle Stud Ireland, Agent
ch y f Royal Academy (USA) - Persian Polly (Persian Bold) .... (John Warren Bloodstock) 33,000
From Bearstone Stud
b or br y f Primo Dominie - Play The Game (Mummy's Game)......... (T Easterby) 14,000
Property of L A C International SA, from Genesis Green Stud
Libero (IRE) b y c Law Society (USA) - Porto Alegre (Habitat) .... (Gallopptrainingsbetrieb) 5,000
From Catridge Farm Stud
ch y f Formidable (USA) - Pretty Thing (Star Appeal)............................... (German International Bloodstock) 9,000
Property of Hon Mrs Cunliffe-Lister, from Burton Agnes Stud
b y f Chief Singer - Primulette (Mummy's Pet)......................... (R Boss) 9,200
From Newtownbarry House Stud, Ireland (Agent)
ch y c Kefaah (USA) - Prosodie (FR) (Relko) (Amanda Skiffington) 35,000
Property of Mrs P J Fairbarns, from Wickfield Stud
ch y c Aragon - Queen Angel (Anfield)..... (L Browne) 9,200
Property of Highfield Stud Ltd, from Glen Andred Stud
b y c Mazilier (USA) - Quick Profit (Formidable (USA)).............. (T Foreman) 21,000
Property of Tibthorpe Stud
b y c Statoblest - Real Party (Realm) ...... (R McCormick) 16,000

607

Property of Mrs M Chaworth-Musters, from Felley Priory Stud
b y f Mazilier (USA) - Renira (Relkino)..... (J Akehurst) 4,000
From Ashtown House Stud, Ireland
b y c High Estate - Respectfully (USA) (The Minstrel (CAN))........ (Tony Nerses) 42,000
Property of Bolton Grange Stud, from Trickledown Stud
ch y c Al Hareb (USA) - Rivulet (USA) (Irish River (FR))...... (Shadwell Estate Co) 26,000
From Rathbarry Stud, Ireland
b y c Cyrano de Bergerac - Roberts Pride (Roberto (USA))....... (Mrs N Myers) 35,000
From Ballyhimikin Stud, Ireland
b y c Magical Strike (USA) - Roundstone Lass (Montekin) .... (Browne Bloodstock Enterprise) 6,400
From Three Gates Stud
ch y c Risk Me (FR) - Royal Clover (Mansingh (USA))........... (M Robinson) 7,600
From Lynn Lodge Stud, Ireland
ch y c Pennine Walk - Royal Liberty (Lord Gayle (USA)) .... (German International Bloodstock) 11,000
Property of Aston Park Stud
b y c Weldnaas (USA) - Run Little Lady (USA) (J O Tobin (USA))... (J J O'Neill) 8,800
b y c Be My Chief (USA) - Safe House (Lyphard (USA))............ (J Banks) 12,000

Property of Lostford Manor Stud
b y f Music Boy - Salacious (Sallust)....... (D Morris) 9,800

608

Property of Stand House Stud, Ireland, from Rathbarry Stud, Ireland (Agent)
ch y c Roi Danzig (USA) - Sally Chase (Sallust)..................... (B B A) 22,000
From Tally-Ho Stud, Ireland
b y f Contract Law (USA) - Sandhurst Goddess (Sandhurst Prince) .... (Richard O'Gorman Bloodstock) 5,600
From Side Hill Stud
ch y f Belmez (USA) - Santa Linda (USA) (Sir Ivor).............. (Horse France) 8,000
From Catridge Farm Stud
b y c Deploy - Santa Magdalena (Hard Fought)................... (S Moore) 3,000
Property of Mr Henry Marsh, from Furnace Mill Stud
b y c Puissance - Sara Sprint (Formidable (USA))................ (N McGrath) 7,000
To Dissolve a Partnership, from Furnace Mill Stud
ch y f Ballad Rock - Savahra (Free State)... (G Steinberg) 16,500
From Collin Stud
b y c Fayruz - Scotch Rocket (Roan Rocket) (P Savill) 9,200
Property of a Partnership, from Kingwood Stud
gr y f Weldnaas (USA) - Sea Kestrel (Sea Hawk II)........... (Aston Park Stud) 5,400
Property of Stud-On-The-Chart
b y f Slip Anchor - Shaiyneen (Kalamoun) .. (Brian Grassick Bloodstock) 10,000
Property of Mr & Mrs S W Dawson, from Mottram St Andrew Stud
b y f Zalazl (USA) - Shapely Test (USA) (Elocutionist (USA))......... (M Dods) 7,400

609

From Ballymorris and Caherass Suds, Ireland
b y c Music Boy - Single Bid (Auction Ring (USA))...................... (B Hills) 29,000
Property of a Partnership, from Burn House Stud
ch y c Never So Bold - Sister Sophie (USA) (Effervescing (USA)) .... (German International Bloodstock) 34,000
From Deerpark Stud, Ireland
b y c Robellino (USA) - Son Et Lumiere (Rainbow Quest (USA))..... (E Lynam) 14,000
From Three Gates Stud
b y f Risk Me (FR) - Sophisticated Lady (FR) (Habitat)................. (T Mullins) 1,500
Property of Al Dahlawi Stud Co Ltd, from Kingwood Stud
b y f Never So Bold - Souadah (USA) (General Holme (USA)).. (H Ponsonby) 10,500
From Kellistown Stud, Ireland (Agent)
b y c Glenstal (USA) - Sound Pet (Runnett) (S Dow) 7,500
From Ballyhampshire Stud, Ireland
b or br y c Cyrano de Bergerac - Souveniers (Relko).......... (Amanda Skiffington) 17,500

From Catridge Farm Stud
ch y f Be My Chief (USA) - Strawberry Song (Final Straw)................ (I Balding) 13,500
Property of Beech Park Bloodstock Ltd, from Mickleham Stud Farm
b y c Music Boy - Summer Posy (Posse (USA)).................... (P Howling) 6,000
Property of Jeremy Green & Sons, from Bickmarsh Stud
b y f Petorius - Sunita (Owen Dudley) ..... (D Arbuthnot) 7,000

610

From Rathbarry Stud, Ireland
b or br y f Taufan (USA) - Sweet Goodbye (Petorius).................. (R O'Ryan) 16,000
From Ted Voute, Agent
b y c Master Willie - Sweet Snow (USA) (Lyphard (USA))............... (C B A) 20,000
From Yeomanstown Stud, Ireland
ch y c Polish Precedent (USA) - Tarib (Habitat)...................... (G Steinberg) 10,500
Property of Rocklow Stud, Ireland, from Raffin Stud
b y f High Estate - The Queen Of Soul (Chief Singer) .... (Brian Grassick Bloodstock) 27,000
From Rathbarry Stud, Ireland
b y f Jareer (USA) - The Woman In Red (Red Regent)................. (Cash) 6,200
Property of a Partnership, from Genesis Green Stud
b y c Shareef Dancer (USA) - Three Piece (Jaazeiro (USA))........ (H Ponsonby) 30,000
From Red House Stud
b y c Mazilier (USA) - Thulium (Mansingh (USA))................ (Guy Armengol) 23,000
From Ashtown House Stud, Ireland
b y c Waajib - Tissue Paper (Touch Paper) (I Balding) 21,000
From Tally-Ho Stud, Ireland
b y f Classic Secret (USA) - Treberth (Gay Fandango (USA)).......... (J Eustace) 5,600
From Elsenham Stud
ch y c Risk Me (FR) - Trip The Daisey (Touching Wood (USA)).. (M Johnston) 7,000

611

From Kellistown Stud, Ireland (Agent)
b y c Persian Heights - Undiscovered (Tap On Wood)........................ (B B A) 6,000
From Rathbarry Stud, Ireland (Agent)
b or br y c Synefos (USA) - Val Lady (FR) (Valdingran (FR))..................... (Peter Doyle Bloodstock) 4,000
Property of Mrs M Chaworth-Musters, from Felley Priory Stud
b y f Dowsing (USA) - Vaula (Henbit (USA)) (D Marks) 4,000
Property of Haresfoot Stud, from Whitsbury Manor Stud
b y f Persian Bold - Vielle (Ribero).......... (P de Vere Hunt) 7,400
From Ashtown House Stud, Ireland
b y c Alzao (USA) - Vivid Impression (Cure The Blues (USA)).......... (N Meade) 16,000

Property of Mascalls Stud, from Cartridge Farm Stud
b y c Deploy - Willowbed (Wollow)........ (C Thornton) 6,600
Property of Mr R Young, from Lavington Stud
b y c Lear Fan (USA) - Windmill Princess (Gorytus (USA)) .... (C Gordon-Watson Bloodstock) 20,000
Property of Bolton Grange Stud, from Trickledown Stud
b y f Zalazl (USA) - Wolverina (Wolver Hollow)................................ (B B A) 5,200
Property of a Partnership, from Burningfold Manor Stud
br y c Rock City - Zalatia (Music Boy)...... (German International Bloodstock) 32,000
From Catridge Farm Stud
b y c Warning - Zalfa (Luthier).. (I Balding) 22,000

612

Property of Mr G R Rickman, from Lavington Stud
b y f Formidable (USA) - Able Mabel (Absalom)................ (P Haslam) 12,000
From Tally-Ho Stud, Ireland
b y c Gallic League - Adivara (Tyrnavos).... (R O'Gorman Bloodstock) 5,000
Property of a Partnership, from Burn House Stud
b y c Don't Forget Me - Alaroos (IRE) (Persian Bold) .... (John Ferguson Bloodstock) 31,000
Property of Mr H Reed, from Collin Stud
b y c Siberian Express (USA) - Alkion (Fordham (USA)).................. (B B A) 4,000
Property of a Partnership, from Furnace Mill Stud
b y f High Estate - Alpine Symphony (Northern Dancer)........ (P Barclay) 5,800
Property of Tarworth Bloodstock Investments Ltd, from Genesis Green Stud
b y f Taufan (USA) - Ancestry (Persepolis (FR))........................ (B B A) 13,000
Property of Bishop's Down Farm
ch y c Sharpo - Anchor Inn (Be My Guest (USA))...... (John Warren Bloodstock) 12,000
Property of a Partnership, from Newtownbarry House Stud, Ireland
ch y f Simply Great (FR) - Annais Nin (Dominion)................ (M Haynes) 2,000
Property of Stand House Stud, Ireland, from Rathbarry Stud, Ireland (Agent)
ch y c Jareer (USA) - Apapa Port (My Swanee)................ (Miss S Hall) 17,000
Property of a Partnership, from Glen Andred Stud
b y f Be My Chief (USA) - Artistic Licence (High Top) .... (Geoffrey Howson Bloodstock) 8,500

613

Property of Lostford Manor Stud
b y c Puissance - Aryaf (CAN) (Vice Regent (CAN))........................ (J Berry) 18,000
From Ballymorris and Caherass Studs, Ireland
gr y c Petong - Ashbocking (Dragonara Palace (USA)) .... (John Warren Bloodstock) 28,000

From Elsenham Stud

b y f Risk Me (FR) - Astrid Gilberto (Runnett)........ (Peter Doyle Bloodstock) 10,000

From Tullamaine Castle Stud, Ireland (Agent)

b y f Scenic - Avra (FR) (Mendez (FR))..... (J Hills) 10,500

From Yeomanstown Stud, Ireland

b y c Alzao (USA) - Awatef (Ela-Mana-Mou) (T Mills) 52,000

From Rathasker Stud, Ireland

b y f Red Sunset - Baby's Smile (Shirley Heights)...................... (B B A) 11,000

From Red House Stud

b y f Forzando - Basenite (Mansingh (USA)) (P J McBride) 7,000

From Elsenham Stud

ch y c Risk Me (FR) - Beauvoir (Artaius (USA))................... (P Diamond) 4,000

From Tullamaine Castle Stud, Ireland (Agent)

b y c Danehill (USA) - Beijing (USA) (Northjet)......................... (P Cole) 32,000

Property of The Hon Lady McAlpine, from Mary James (Cotswold Stud Farms)

b y c Danehill (USA) - Belle Enfant (Beldale Flutter (USA))........ (M W Easterby) 15,000

614

Property of Mrs Clody E Norton, from Newtownbarry House Stud, Ireland

b y f Petorius - Best Niece (Vaigly Great) .. (Allan Bloodlines) 8,000

Property of Hesmonds Stud

b y c Be My Guest (USA) - Between Time (Elegant Air)............. (M Haynes) 2,200

From Rathbarry Stud, Ireland (Agent)

b or br y c Alzao (USA) - Beyond Words (Ballad Rock)........... (M Tompkins) 68,000

From Oak Farm, Ireland

ch y c Digamist (USA) - Blue Vista (IRE) (Pennine Walk)........ (R McCormick) 10,500

From Yeomanstown Stud, Ireland

b y f Common Grounds - Boldabsa (Persian Bold)...................... (B Hills) 15,000

From Ballymorris and Caherass Studs, Ireland

b y f Cyrano de Bergerac - Bosquet (Queen's Hussar).................. (Geoffrey Howson Bloodstock) 9,400

Property of Stud-On-The-Chart

b y f Shavian - Bourgeonette (Mummy's Pet)......................... (B B A) 10,000

From Ballyhimikin Stud, Ireland

gr y c Chilibang - Brittle Grove (Bustino) ... (B B A (Ireland)) 20,000

Property of Sunley Stud Ltd, from Lavington Stud

b y c Warrshan (USA) - Brown Velvet (Mansingh (USA))....... (M Channon) 6,200

From Northmore Stud Farm

ch y f Pharly (FR) - Brown's Cay (Formidable (USA)).................. (A Scott) 9,000

615

Property of a Partnership, from Burningfold Manor Stud

b y c Slip Anchor - Burnished (Formidable (USA)).................. (L Browne) 8,200

From Ballyhimikin Stud, Ireland

b y f Tirol - Busker (Bustino)............. (M W Easterby) 10,500

Property of Lt Col & Mrs D E Coker

ch y c Superlative - Busted Harmony (Busted)..... (Peter Doyle Bloodstock) 8,800

From The Forest Stud

br y c Red Sunset - Buz Kashi (Bold Lad (IRE))..................... (P Haslam) 14,500

From Rathasker Stud, Ireland

b y c Red Sunset - Cafe Society (Sharpen Up)... (Browne Bloodstock Enterprise) 5,000

From Lynn Lodge Stud, Ireland

b y f Contract Law (USA) - Caimanite (Tap On Wood).............. (K McAuliffe) 2,000

Property of Stud-On-The-Chart

b y c Blakeney - Camomilla (Targowice (USA))....... (Peter Doyle Bloodstock) 7,800

b y c Prince Sabo - Canoodle (Warpath) ... (C B A) 11,500

Property of Jeremy Green & Sons and Mrs A D Fanshawe, from Bickmarsh Stud

b y f Tirol - Carillon Miss (USA) (The Minstrel (CAN))........... (Agence F I P S) 10,000

Property of Mr P Hatton, from Mottram St Andrew Stud

b y f Statoblest - Carmen Maria (Bold Lad (IRE))................... (J Spearing) 3,000

616

Property of Mr Gerald W Leigh, from Ted Voute, Agent

b y c Bering - Casey (Caerleon (USA)) ..... (T Mills) 38,000

Property of Rockhouse Farms Ltd, from Bearstone Stud

b y c Puissance - Cassiar (Connaught)..... (P Haslam) 9,000

From Tally-Ho Stud, Ireland

ch y c Classic Secret (USA) - Celeritas (Dominion)......................... (German International Bloodstock) 8,000

From Catridge Farm Stud

b y c Nomination - Clare Celeste (Coquelin (USA))............... (B B A (Ireland)) 25,000

From Furnace Mill Stud

b y c Waajib - Connaught Lace (Connaught) (G Hourigan) 9,600

Property of Aston Park Stud

b y c Beveled (USA) - Crystal Sprite (Crystal Glitters (USA))............... (J Holt) 4,500

Property of Messrs Darley and Townsend, from Daleside Stud

b y c Superpower - Daleside Ladybird (Tolomeo)............... (B Meehan) 5,200

From Tullamaine Castle Stud, Ireland, Agent

b y f Tirol - Damia (Vision (USA))......... (Stilvi Compania) 20,000

From Mary James (Cotswold Stud Farms)

b y f Taufan (USA) - Dancing Berry (Sadler's Wells (USA))............... (W Jarvis) 17,500

Property of Mr and Mrs S W Dawson, from Mottram St Andrew Stud

b y f Don't Forget Me - Dear Heart (Blakeney)................. (P Keogh) 1,000

617

Property of Mrs P Lewis, from Lavington Stud

b y c Aragon - Divine Fling (Imperial Fling (USA)) (C Gordon-Watson Bloodstock) 22,000

Property of L Muller, from Lavington Stud

b y f Midyan (USA) - Double Dutch (Nicholas Bill)............ (Brooke Sanders) 10,000

From The Zetland Stud

b or br y c Primo Dominie - Dovetail (Brigadier Gerard)........ (Axel Donnerstag) 9,000

Property of Hesmonds Stud

b y c Night Shift (USA) - Dreamawhile (Known Fact (USA)) .... (C Gordon-Watson Bloodstock) 14,000

From Ballyhimikin Stud, Ireland

b y f Brush Aside (USA) - Drowsy Maggie (Tumble Wind (USA))..... (I Campbell) 1,200

From Ballymorris and Caherass Studs, Ireland

ch y c Midyan (USA) - Early Call (Kind Of Hush)...................... (P Cole) 10,000

Property of Lostford Manor Stud

b y c Primo Dominie - Eastern Ember (Indian King (USA))................... (David Minton Bloodstock) 14,500

From Northmore Stud Farm

ch y c Bering - Egalite (FR) (Luthier)....... (Stefan Uppstrom) 4,000

Property of Stand House Stud, Ireland, from Rathbarry Stud, Ireland (Agent)

b y c High Estate - Eight Mile Rock (Dominion).......... (Horse France (Ireland)) 17,000

Property of Barrettstown Stud Farms Ltd, from Whitsbury Manor Stud

b y c Cadeaux Genereux - Excelent Alibi (USA) (Exceller (USA))...... (T Nerses) 11,500

618

From Tally-Ho Stud, Ireland

b or br y c Reprimand - Executive Lady (Night Shift (USA)).................... (Peter Doyle Bloodstock) 22,000

Property of Mr N Wallace & Mr D Wallace, from Ted Voute, Agent

b y c Dancing Dissident (USA) - Fair Flutter (Beldale Flutter (USA)).... (W Haggas) 7,400

Property of Stud-On-The-Chart

b y c Persian Heights - Fallen Angel (Quiet Fling (USA))............... (G Hourigan) 7,400

From Yeomanstown Stud, Ireland

b y c Petoski - Farcical (Pharly (FR)) .... (Peter Doyle Bloodstock) 12,000

Property of Whitsbury Manor Stud

b y c Distant Relative - Fast Car (FR) (Carwhite).... (Giles Pritchard-Gorodn) 8,400

From Helescane Stud

br y f Be My Chief (USA) - Feather-In-Her-Cap (Primo Dominie)... (R McCormick) 66,000

Property of Lady Juliet de Chair, from Genesis Green Stud

b y f Glenstal (USA) - Femme Formidable (Formidable (USA))........... (B B A) 7,200

From Oak Farm, Ireland

ch y f Digamist (USA) - Flash Donna (USA) (Well Decorated (USA)).... (P Haslam) 7,000

From Bearstone Stud

b y f Puissance - Flicker Toa Flame (USA) (Empery (USA)).... (Sarah Hollinshead) 2,000

Property of Rockhouse Farms Ltd, from Bearstone Stud

ch y f Cadeaux Genereux - Florentynna Bay (Aragon)........................... (Johnny McKeever Bloodstock) 17,500

619

Property of Whitsbury Manor Stud

b y f Aragon - Follow The Stars (Sparkler).. (D F Powell) 16,000

Property of Messry Darley & Townsend, from Daleside Stud

ch y c Ballad Rock - Forest Blaze (USA) (Green Forest (USA)).................. (Cormac McCormack Associates) 13,000

Property of Hesmonds Stud

b y c Be My Chief (USA) - Forgotten Dreams (FR) (Shoemaker)............ (B B A (Italia)) 15,000

Property of Bishop's Down Farm

b y f Never So Bold - Frasquita (Song)..... (B B A) 4,600

Property of a Partnership, from Burton Agnes Stud

br y c Scottish Reel - French Surprise (Hello Gorgeous (USA))........ (C Thornton) 7,400

From Raffin Stud

b y c Faustus (USA) - Frighten The Life (Kings Lake (USA))................... (Shadwell Estate Co) 16,000

Property of Sir Ernest Harrison, from Burton Agnes Stud

b y f Glenstal (USA) - Gaygo Lady (Gay Fandango (USA))............ (T Stack) 6,200

From Rathbarry Stud, Ireland (Agent)

b y f Taufan (USA) - Gentle Guest (IRE) (Be My Guest (USA))..... (R J R Williams) 15,500

Property of Angley Stud

gr y c Siberian Express (USA) - Glen Na Smole (Ballymore)................... (German International Bloodstock) 16,000

Property of Mr & Mrs R G Percival, from Glen Andred Stud

ch y f Mazilier (USA) - Good Game (Mummy's Game) .... (John Ferguson Bloodstock) 11,000

620

From Brownstown Lodge Stud

b y c Don't Forget Me - Gothic Lady (Godswalk (USA))........... (B B A) 40,000

From Mary James (Cotswold Stud Farms)

b or br y f Robellino (USA) - Granny's Bank (Music Boy)........ (Lord Huntingdon) 6,800

Property of Messrs Darley & Townsend, from Daleside Stud

b y c Statoblest - Great Aim (Great Nephew)........ (Amanda Skiffington) 15,000

From Rathasker Stud, Ireland

b y c Red Sunset - Great Land (USA) (Friend's Choice (USA)).... (Bill Smith) 14,500

From Northmore Stud Farm

b y c Simply Great (FR) - Great Tom (Great Nephew) .... (Browne Bloodstock Enerprise) 3,000

From Cobhall Court Stud
b y c Aragon - Grovette (Derring-Do) ...... (Peter Doyle Blodstock) 14,000
From Oak Farm, Ireland
ch y f Digamist (USA) - Gulf Craft (IRE) (Petorius)............. (Susan Scargill) 5,400
From Genesis Green Stud
b y f Celestial Storm (USA) - Hablitzia (Habitat).. (Conti Bloodstock Services) 5,400
Property of Bishop's Down Farm
b y f Tirol - Haitienne (FR) (Green Dancer (USA))...................... (S Burns) 44,000
From Yeomanstown Stud, Ireland
ch y c Aragon - Hard To Stop (Hard Fought) (Seymour Bloodstock) 7,600

621

From Catridge Farm Stud
b y f Rock City - Hearten (Hittite Glory).... (Cormac McCormack Associates) 16,000
Property of Tibthorpe Stud
ch y f Indian Ridge - Heavely Note (Chief Singer) (C Gordon-Watson Bloodstock) 10,000
From Ballyhimikin Stud, Ireland
b y c Dancing Dissident (USA) - Helen's Dynasty (Habitat) (Amanda Skiffington) 18,500
Property of Wickfield Stud Ltd, from Wickfield Stud
b y f Midyan (USA) - Hemline (Sharpo) .... (C G Adams) 4,400
Property of Angley Stud
b y c Salse (USA) - Hi-Li (High Top) .... (J Naughton) 14,500
Property of Earl Of Halifax, from Side Hill Stud
ch y f Sure Blade (USA) - Hocus (High Top) (Susan Scargill) 7,500
From Catridge Stud
b y f Rock City - Hollow Heart (Wolver Hollow)...................... (Alex Scott) 32,000
From Lynn Lodge Stud, Ireland
b y c Classic Secret (USA) - Holly Bird (Runnett)........ (Shadwell Estate Co) 32,000
Property of a Partnership, from Trickledown Stud
b y c Forzando - Hot Money (Mummy's Pet)... (Geoffrey Howson Bloodstock) 12,000
From The Forest Stud
ch y c Bluebird (USA) - In For More (Don).. (Danny Murphy) 24,000
From Rathbarry Stud, Ireland (Agent)
b y c Common Grounds - Indian Swallow (Indian King (USA))...... (N Callaghan) 37,000
From Oak Farm, Ireland
ch y f Magical Strike (USA) - Indigo Queen (Indian King (USA)).................. (Cormac McCormack Associates) 5,500
From Ballyjimikin Stud, Ireland
Saatchmo b y c Forzando - Into The Fire (Dominion).............. (J Eustace) 24,000
From Red House Stud
b y f Mazilier (USA) - Irenic (Mummy's Pet) (P Makin) 10,500

622

NEWMARKET
Thursday, October 14th
(Yearlings)

Property of a Partnership, from Whatton Manor Stud
b y f Prince Sabo - Jandell (NZ) (Shifnal) ... (W Jarvis) 7,200
From Ballymorris and Caherass Studs, Ireland
br y c Be My Chief (USA) - Julia Flyte (Drone)............ (Anthony Penfold) 40,000
From Mary James (Cotswold Stud Farms)
b y f Caerleon (USA) - Kayrava (Irish River (FR)).......................... (B B A) 24,000
From Corduff Stud, Ireland
b or br y c Lapierre - Kayu (Tap On Wood) (Peter Doyle Bloodstock) 11,000
From Stetchworth Park Stud
ch y c Hadeer - Kick The Habit (Habitat) ... (P Makin) 13,000
From Ballymorris and Caheras Studs, Ireland
b y f Jareer (USA) - Kilfenora (Tribal Chief) (M Channon) 6,200
From Theakston Stud
ch y f Magical Strike (USA) - Kind Thoughts (Kashmir II).................. (B B A) 2,500
From Corduff Stud, Ireland
b y c Dancing Dissident (USA) - Lady Bodmin (IRE) (Law Society (USA)) .... (B B A (Italia)) 12,500
Property of Waverton Stud, from Mary James (Cotswold Stud Farms)
b y c Rambo Dancer (CAN) - Lifestyle (Jimmy Reppin).......... (W Haggas) 11,500
Property of Langton Stud
b y f Salse (USA) - Little Bittern (USA) (Riva Ridge (USA)).............. (P Cole) 11,000

623

Property of Mr E Crow, from Hardwicke Stud
b y c Puissance - Lucky Penny (Bustino)... (Campbell Stud) 13,000
Property of Scarteen Stud, Ireland
ch y c Roi Danzig (USA) - Lundylux (Grundy) .... (Shadwell Estate Co) 17,000
From Ashtown House Stud, Ireland
b y c Don't Forget Me - Lunulae (Tumble Wind (USA))............... (M Dods) 7,200
Property of a Partnership, from Mellon Stud, Ireland
b y f Nordico (USA) - Magia (USA) (Vaguely Noble).... (Conti Bloodstock Services) 5,000
From Camas Park Stud, Ireland
(FR) b y c Fairy King (USA) - Maid Of Erin (USA) (Irish River (FR)) .... (John Ferguson Bloodstock) 42,000
Property of a Partnership, from West Stow Stud
b y f Rock City - Mainmast (Bustino) ...... (T Easterby) 3,400
From Tally-Ho Stud, Ireland
b y f Classic Secret (USA) - Mary Mary Mouse (USA) (Valdez (USA)).......... (John Ferguson Bloodstock) 3,200

Property of Overbury Stud
b y f Night Shift (USA) - Misguided (Homing)..................... (B B A) 7,000
b y c Formidable (USA) - Missed Blessing (So Blessed)......................... (Newmarket International) 54,000
Property of Mr M J Worth, from Whatton Manor Stud
b y c Be My Chief (USA) - Morrish Idol (Aragon)...................... (B B A) 25,000

624

From Riverside Stud, Ireland
b y c Persian Heights - My My Marie (Artaius (USA))........... (Sarah Lakin) 17,000
From Ballymorris and Caherass Studs, Ireland
gr y c Petong - Mycenae Cherry (Troy)..... (B B A) 7,800
From Tally-Ho Stud, Ireland
b y c Contract Law (USA) - Natuschka (Authi).......... (Cheveley Park Stud) 40,000
Property of a Partnership, from Whitechurch Stud, Ireland
b y f Bluebird (USA) - Naxos (USA) (Big Spruce (USA))........... (M Channon) 10,000
From Mary James (Cotswold Stud Farms)
b y f Last Tycoon - Never So Fair (Never So Bold)........... (Shadwell Estate Co) 45,000
Property of Mr W R Jones, from Partridge Close Stud
b y c Faustus (USA) - Never Walk Alone (Anfield)............... (B B A (Italia)) 7,200
Property of Heatherwold Stud
b y c Midyan (USA) - Neverdown (Never So Bold).. (Johnny McKeever Bloodstock) 10,500
From Tally-Ho Stud, Ireland
b y f Fayruz - Nigel's Star (Ashmore (FR)).. (Derby Bloodstock) 4,500
Property of Shutford Stud, from Mary James (Cotswold Stud Farms)
(FR) b y c Dowsing (USA) - Nordica (Northfields (USA))............. (R Charlton) 16,000
From Riverside Stud, Ireland
ch y c Al Hareb (USA) - Norfolk Bonnet (Morston (FR)).... (C & N Bloodstock) 8,500

625

Property of Mr M L Page, from Westerlands Stud
b y f Alzao (USA) - North Telstar (Sallust).. (M Johnston) 14,500
From Ballymorris and Caherass Studs, Ireland
b y c Be My Chief (USA) - Orphys (Nonoalco (USA)).................. (B B A) 16,000
Property of Langton Stud
gr y c Kalaglow - Palama (USA) (Blushing Groom (FR))... (Lillingston Bloodstock) 33,000
From Riverside Stud, Ireland
b y f Bluebird (USA) - Parkeen Princess (He Loves Me)..................... (Cash) 5,500
From Yeomanstown Stud, Ireland
b y c Pennine Walk - Polaregina (FR) (Rex Magna (FR))............ (J FitzGerald) 9,800
From Corduff Stud, Ireland
ch y c Ballad Rock - Priddy Blue (Blue Cashmere)............... (J Eustace) 27,000

Property of Lord Vestey (Stowell Park Stud), from Mary James (Cotswold Stud Farms)
b y c Thatching - Primrolla (Relko) (C B A) 16,000
From Mount Coote Stud, Ireland
ch y c Astronef - Princess Biddy (Sun Prince)................... (N McGrath) 11,000
Property of Aldridge Racing Ltd, from Kingwood Stud
ch y c Indian Ridge - Princess Silca Key (Grundy)................. (C Gordon-Watson Bloodstock) 70,000
Property of Mr P D Player, from Whatton Manor Stud
b y f Reprimand - Queen Ranavalona (Sure Blade (USA))................... (Cash) 6,000

626

From Yeomanstown Stud, Ireland
b y c Taufan (USA) - Queen's Share (Main Reef)........... (Shadwell Estate Co) 35,000
Property of Overbury Stud
b y c Chief Singer - Raffle (Balidar) (B B A) 14,000
From Camas Park Stud, Ireland
b y c Statoblest - Raintree Venture (Good Times (ITY))..... (Shadwell Estate Co) 52,000
Property of Kilboy Estate, Ireland, from Lynn Lodge Stud, Ireland
ch y f Classic Secret (USA) - Ring The Changes (Auction Ring (USA))........ (Peter Doyle Bloodstock) 20,000
Property of Islanmore Stud, Ireland
b y c Bluebird (USA) - Risk All (Run The Gantlet (USA))............... (C B A) 10,000
From Mount Coote Stud, Ireland
b or br y c Tirol - Riverlily (FR) (Green Dancer (USA)).......... (B B A (Italia)) 9,000
Property of Langton Stud
br y c Rock City - Run To The Sun (Run The Gantlet (USA)).......................... (Peter Doyle Bloodstock) 15,500
From Lodge Park Stud, Ireland
b y f Scenic - Sallymiss (Tanfirion) (F Barry) 12,500
b y c High Estate - Saneena (Kris) (B B A) 8,000
Property of Scarteen Stud, Ireland
gr y c Ballad Rock - Sashi Woo (Rusticaro (FR)).................... (N Jackson) 14,500

627

From Mary James (Cotswold Stud Farms)
b y c Belmez (USA) - Sea Fairy (Wollow)... (Darley Stud Management) 21,000
From Lynn Lodge Stud Stud, Ireland
b y c Try My Best (USA) - Secret Hideaway (USA) (Key To The Mint (USA))......... (Shadwell Estate Co) 25,000
From Cobhall Court Stud
b y c Thatching - Senane (Vitiges (FR))..... (Peter Doyle Bloodstock) 27,000
From Corduff Stud, Ireland
b y c Weldnaas (USA) - Shadha (Shirley Heights)........................ (B B A) 15,000
From Ballymorris and Caherass Studs, Ireland
b y c Fairy King (USA) - Shopping (FR) (Sheshoon).......... (B B A (Ireland)) 22,000
From Mount Coote Stud, Ireland
b y c Cricket Ball (USA) - Sine Labe (USA) (Vaguely Noble).............. (M Bell) 19,000

Property of R F Johnson-Houghton, from Overbury Stud
br y c Siberian Express (USA) - Sirnelta (FR) (Sir Tor)...... (Giles Pritchard-Gordon) 12,000
Property of a Partnership of Meon Valley Stud, from Meon Valley Stud
b y c Midyan (USA) - Sistabelle (Bellypha).. (Anthony Penfold) 10,000
From Mellon Stud, Ireland
ch y c Persian Heights - Smart As Paint (USA) (Caerleon (USA))............... (Peter Doyle Bloodstock) 9,000
From Yeomanstown Stud, Ireland
b y f Common Grounds - Song Of The Glens (Horage)........... (C O'Brien) 30,000

628

Property of Islanmore Stud, Ireland
b y f Taufan (USA) - Splendid Chance (Random Shot)...................... (John Warren Bloodstock) 16,500
Property of Mrs J D Trotter, from East Layton Stud
b y f Most Welcome - Star Face (African Sky)........... (Wingfield Stud Farm) 9,000
From Ashtown House Stud, Ireland
ch y c Persian Heights - Starlust (Sallust) .. (T Mullins) 19,000
From Mary James (Cotswold Stud Farms)
b y f Alzao (USA) - Steady The Buffs (Balidar)... (Brian Grassick Bloodstock) 100,000
From Islanmore Stud, Ireland (Agent)
b y c Astronef - Straw Boater (Thatch (USA))............... (Willie Browne) 9,600
Property of M L Page, from Westerlands Stud
b y f Thatching - Sugar Plum Fairy (Sadler's Wells (USA))...... (C Gordon-Watson) 32,000
From Yeomanstown Stud, Ireland
b y c Indian Ridge - Summer Fashion (Moorestyle)............... (D Weld) 75,000
Property of T R Lock, from Kingwood Stud
b y c Dominion - Surf Bird (Shareef Dancer (USA))............ (James Delahooke) 28,000
From Yeomanstown Stud, Ireland
b y c Common Grounds - Tasskeen (FR) (Lyphard (USA)).............. (B B A) 40,000
Property of Mrs C F van Straubenzee and Partners, from Hatherwold Stud
b y c Distant Relative - Top Heights (High Top)................ (Sir M Prescott) 11,000

629

Property of a Partnership of Meon Valley Stud, from Meon Valley Stud
b y c Petoski - Top Of The League (High Top).................... (Con Collins) 17,000
From Corduff Stud, Ireland
ch y c Digamist (USA) - Tunguska (Busted) (Peter Doyle Bloodstock) 5,200
Property of Overbury Stud
b y c Dominion - Valiancy (Grundy) (B B A) 15,000
From Tally-Ho Stud, Ireland
b y c Contract Law (USA) - White Caps (Shirley Heights)... (Derby Bloodstock) 10,500
From Park Lodge Stud, Ireland
b y f Red Sunset - Wilderness (Martinmass) .... (D Allen) 7,400
Property of Langton Stud
b y c Cyrano de Bergerac - Win For Me (Bonne Noel)....................... (R O'Gorman Bloodstock) 10,500
Property of Normanby Stud, from Floors Stud
b y f Be My Chief (USA) - Wizardry (Shirley Heights)...................... (B B A) 5,400
Property of E Crow & D Pugh, from Hardwicke Stud
gr y c Chilibang - Abalone (Abwah)........ (N McGrath) 4,000
From Mellon Stud
b y c Waajib - Achafalaya (USA) (Apalachee (USA))...................... (J Hills) 11,500
From Yeomanstown Stud, Ireland
b y c Law Society (USA) - Ahonita (Ahonoora).......... (J S Wainwright) 10,000

630

Property of Mr M Ervine
b y c Tirol - Annsfield Lady (Red Sunset)... (Cormac McCormack Associates) 33,000
Property of Heatherwold Stud
b y c Unfuwain (USA) - Antilla (Averof) .... (C Thornton) 7,400
Property of Kingwood Bloodstock Ltd, from Kingwood Stud
b or br y c Cyrano de Bergerac - Aunt Eileen (Creative Plan (USA)) .... (H Ponsonby) 7,000
From Mount Coote Stud, Ireland
b y c Taufan (USA) - Aunt Hester (IRE) (Caerleon (USA))........... (N Tinkler) 14,000
Property of Kingwood Bloodstock Ltd, from Kingwood Stud
b y c Dance Of Life (USA) - Bahrain Vee (CAN) (Blushing Groom (FR)).. (B B A) 6,600
From Mount Coote Stud, Ireland
b y c Double Schwartz - Baracuda (FR) (Zeddaan).......................... (Hugo Lascelles Bloodstock) 15,000
From Kirtlington Stud
b y c Rock City - Barsham (Be My Guest (USA)) (C Gordon-Watson Bloodstock) 22,000
Property of Bishop Wilton Stud, from Bishop Wilton Stud
ch y c Be My Chief (USA) - Beacon (High Top)...................... (J Dunlop) 27,000
From Corduff Stud, Ireland
b y c Warrshan (USA) - Bell Toll (High Line) (J Dunlop) 24,000
Property of International Thoroughbred Breeders,Inc, from Round Hill Stud, Ireland
b y f Tirol - Bell Tower (Lyphard's Wish (FR))...... (Brian Grassick Bloodstock) 26,000

631

Property of Overbury Stud
b y c Darshaan - Bercheba (Bellypha)...... (Anthony Penfold) 36,000
Property of Snailwell Stud Co Ltd, from Partridge Close Stud
b y f Warning - Blade Of Grass (Kris)...... (B Hills) 14,000
From Kirtlington Stud
b y f Nomination - Bodham (Bustino)...... (J Wilson) 12,500

From Tally-Ho Stud, Ireland
b y c Contract Law (USA) - Burkina (African Sky)........................ (J Berry) 12,000
From Corduff Stud, Ireland
b y c Waajib - Camden's Gift (Camden Town)............ (James Delahooke) 21,000
From Theakston Stud
ch y f Formidable (USA) - Careful Dancer (Gorytus (USA))......... (C Thornton) 11,000
From Ballymorris and Caherass Studs, Ireland
b y f Be My Chief (USA) - Carmelina (Habitat) .... (Geoffrey Howson Bloodstock) 6,000
Property of Normanby Stud, from Floors Stud
bl y c Persian Bold - Carolside (Music Maestro).......... (Derby Bloodstock) 21,000
From Tally-Ho Stud, Ireland
b y f Contract Law (USA) - Castleforbes (Thatching)................... (S Dow) 7,000
Property of Mr W R Jones, from Patridge Close Stud
ch y c Deploy - Cat's Claw (USA) (Sharpen Up).... (Geoffrey Howson Bloodstock) 17,500

632

From Yeomanstown Stud, Ireland
b y c Common Grounds - Charbatte (FR) (In Fijar (USA))................ (M Dods) 9,500
From Mount Coote Stud, Ireland
b y f Mtoto - Chrism (Baptism).... (B B A) 9,000
Property of Langton Stud
b y c Forzando - Clouded Vision (So Blessed)................... (D Weld) 38,000
From Patridge Close Stud
ro y f Elmaamul (USA) - Comicus (USA) (Northern Jove (CAN))........ (P Cole) 10,000
From Mellon Stud, Ireland
b y c Fools Holme (USA) - Crimson Glen (Glenstal (USA))......... (M Tompkins) 27,000
From Ashtown House Stud, Ireland
b y c High Estate - Crown Godiva (Godswalk (USA))......... (D Murray-Smith) 21,000
From Yeomanstown Stud, Ireland
b y c Dashing Blade - Dara's Bird (Dara Monarch)................... (P Makin) 19,000
From Ashtown House Stud, Ireland
b y c Petong - Deep Blue Sea (Gulf Pearl) (Demmy O'Byrne) 19,000
Property of Islanmore Stud, Ireland
b y f Nordico (USA) - Dewan's Niece (USA) (Dewany (USA))...... (D Lucie Smith) 10,000
From Tally-Ho Stud, Ireland
ch y c Digamist (USA) - Eiswave (Welsh Pageant).......... (C & N Bloodstock) 10,000

633

Property of The Hon Lady McAlpine, from Mary James (Cotswold Stud Farms)
b y f Squill (USA) - Embroideress (Stanford) (D Morley) 10,000
Property of Mrs J D Trotter, from East Layton Stud
b y c Warrshan (USA) - Empty Purse (Pennine Walk)............ (R McCormick) 10,500
Property of Mr Joseph O'Regan, from Rathcannon House Stud, Ireland
b y f Tirol - Etage (Ile de Bourbon (USA)) .. (R J R Williams) 10,500
Property of a Partnership, from Tullamaine Castle Stud, Ireland
b y c Tirol - European Passer (USA) (Caucasus (USA))................ (F Barry) 13,000
Property of Overbury Stud
ch y c Unfuwain (USA) - Eversince (USA) (Foolish Pleasure (USA)).............. (Sir M Prescott) 7,400
Property of Tsarina Stud, from Overbury Stud
b y f Cadeaux Genereux - Fabulous Rina (FR) (Fabulous Dancer (USA))......... (C Gordon-Watson Bloodstock) 10,000
From Mount Coote Stud, Ireland
b y c Nordico (USA) - Fear Naught (Connaught).................... (R Fahey) 10,500
From Corduff Stud, Ireland
b y c Contract Law (USA) - Fiery Song (Ballad Rock)....................... (Will Edmeades Bloodstock) 14,500
Property of Islanmore Stud, Ireland
gr y c Taufan (USA) - Fillette Lalo (FR) (Huntercombe)................... (Peter Doyle Bloodstock) 31,000
Property of Mrs J D Trotter, from East Layton Stud
ch y f Night Shift (USA) - Final Thought (Final Straw)................. (C B A) 16,000
br y f Dowsing (USA) - Flaming Rose (USA) (Upper Nile (USA))........ (D Russell) 16,000

634

From Mount Coote Stud, Ireland
b y c Fools Holme (USA) - Finging Star (USA) (Northern Fling (USA)).......... (M Tompkins) 9,400
From Yeomanstown Stud, Ireland
b y c Primo Dominie - French Plait (Thatching)..................... (N Callaghan) 35,000
Property of H Steckmest, from Whatton Manor Stud
br or gr y c Be My Chief (USA) - Friendly Thoughts (USA) (Al Hattab (USA)) ..... (Tote Cherry Downes) 11,000
Property of Tullamaine Castle Stud and Partners, from Tullamaine Castle Stud, Ireland
b or br y c High Estate - Greatest Pleasure (Be My Guest (USA)) .... (Shadwell Estate Co) 20,000
Property of Round Hill Stud, Ireland
gr y f Danehill (USA) - Grey Dream (Auction Ring (USA)) .... (German International Bloodstock) 30,000
Property of Langton Stud
br y f Damister (USA) - Habutai (Habitat)... (Cash) 5,500
From Stetchworth Park Stud
b y c Hadeer - Harvest Dance (Mill Reef (USA))...................... (L Comer) 3,400
Property of P D Player, from Whatton Manor Stud
b y f Distant Relative - Hens Grove (Alias Smith (USA))............ (T Easterby) 1,800
From Islanmore Stud, Ireland (Agent)
ch y c Bold Arrangement - Hooray Lady (Ahonoora)............................ (International Racing Club Ltd) 11,000
Property of Overbury Stud
ch y f Sharpo - Humble Pie (Known Fact (USA)).... (John Ferguson Bloodstock) 50,000

Property of a Partnership, from Kingwood Stud
b y f Warning - Ice Chocolate (USA) (Ice-capade (USA)) .... (Hugo Lascelles Bloodstock) 42,000

Property of P D Player, from Whatton Manor Stud
gr y c Be My Chief (USA) - Inveraren (Alias Smith (USA)).... (Shadwell Estate Co) 26,000

Property of Langton Stud
b y f Sizzling Melody - Island Mead (Pharly (FR)).................. (D French-Davis) 7,000

From Lynn Lodge Stud, Ireland
b y c Simply Great (FR) - Islet Time (Burslem)............ (C & N Bloodstock) 14,000

635

NEWMARKET
Friday, October 15th
(Yearlings)

Property of Brook Stud Ltd from Brook Stud
b y f Kalaglow - Jacinth (Red God) .... (Guy Reed) 16,500

From Cheveley Park Stud, Agent
b y f Never So Bold - Kala Rosa (Kalaglow) (Cash) 5,600

From Yeomanstown Stud, Ireland
b y c Primo Dominie - Lady Leman (Pitskelly)... (Newmarket International) 62,000

From Three Gates Stud
b y f Risk Me (FR) - La Graciosa (Comedy Star (USA))........ (Matt McCormack) 1,500

Property of Brick Kiln Stud & Lariston Apartments Ltd from Brick Kiln Stud
b y f Formidable (USA) - Lariston Gale (Pas de Seul)............ (Equine Services) 16,000

Property of Mrs D Blackwell from Woodcote Stud
b y f Midyan (USA) - Little Mercy (No Mercy)..... (David Minton Bloodstock) 6,400

From Elsenham Stud
ch y f Risk Me (FR) - Lompoa (Lomond (USA)).................. (E Connolly) 1,000

Property of a partnership from Britton House Stud
b y f Salse (USA) - Madam Cody (Hot Spark).............. (John Benstead) 6,000

Property of Carlton Colsutants Ltd from Home Stud
b y c Nishapour (FR) - Madiyla (Darshaan).. (E M Washington) 3,300

Property of M B Small from Britton House Stud
ch y f Indian Ridge - Maiyaasah (Kris)...... (Browne Bloodstock Enterprise) 4,000

636

Property of Manor House Stud
b y f Nomination - Maravilla (Mandrake Major).................. (Pat Haslam) 7,000

Property of C J R Trotter, from C J R Trotter
b y f Forzando - Matinata (Dike (USA))..... (Henry Candy) 4,800

Property of Brook Stud Ltd, from Brook Stud
b y f Kalaglow - Mevlevi (Shareef Dancer (USA)).................. (T Lightbown) 4,500

Property of a gentleman, from Old Mill Stud
ch y c Prince Sabo - Milne's Way (The Noble Player (USA))..... (M Jameson) 17,000

Property of Mr & Mrs J B Stafford, from Britton House Stud
b y f Emarati (USA) - Minne Love (Homeric) .... (Mrs D La Trobe) 4,200

Property of Glenvale Stud, Ireland
ch y c Glenstal (USA) - Miss Kate (FR) (Nonoalco (USA))... (Rigby Bloodstock) 44,000

Property of Mrs Hugh McCalmont, from Yeomanstown Lodge Stud, Ireland
b y f Thatching - Miss Loving (Northfields (USA))...... (John Warren Bloodstock) 39,000

Property of Mrs R J Nash, from Britton House Stud
ch y f Statoblest - Miss Pisces (Salmon Leap (USA))......... (General Broker) 2,200

Property of Manor House Stud
b y f Damister (USA) - Miss Primula (Dominion)........... (Colin Williams) 7,000

Property of a partnership, from Britton House Stud
b y c Forzando - Moments Joy (Adonijah).. (Shadwell Estate Co) 21,000

637

From Ashtown House Stud, Ireland
b y c Thatching - More Candy (Ballad Rock) (F Carr) 46,000

Property of D MacRae, from Stradishall Manor
ch y c Prince Sabo - Mrs Leader (USA) (Mr Leader (USA)) .... (Peter Doyle Bloodstock) 14,000

From Lynn Lodge Stud, Ireland
b y c Classic Secret (USA) - Mystery Bid (Auction Ring (USA)) .... (David Minton Bloodstock) 12,500

Property of Limestone Stud
ch y c Be My Chief (USA) - Myth (Troy) ... (German International Bloodstock) 13,000

Property of Mrs Hugh McCalmont, from Yeomanstown Lodge Stud, Ireland
b y c Fairy King (USA) - Native Melody (Tudor Music) .... (Brian Grassick Bloodstock) 29,000

From Woodditton Stud
b y c Superlative - Nell Of The North (USA) (Canadian Gil (CAN))... (Paul Howling) 10,500

Property of Brick Kiln Stud & Partners, from Brick Kiln Stud
ch y c Imp Society (USA) - No Chili (Glint Of Gold)..... (Brian Grassick Bloodstock) 37,000

Property of M Soames, from Old Mill Stud
b y f Zalazl (USA) - No Jazz (Jaazeiro (USA)) (B.B.A.) 6,000

Property of Wayland Stud, from Woodcote Stud
b y c Warrshan (USA) - Now In Session (USA) (Diesis) .... (Cormac McCormack Associates) 4,200

From Yeomanstown Stud, Ireland
b y c Indian Ridge - Number Eleven (Local Suitor (USA)) .... (C Gordon-Watson Bloodstock) 40,000

638

From Red House Stud
b y c Sizzling Melody - Odilese (Mummy's Pet)................(Equine Services) 5,600
Property of Manor House Stud
b y c Sizzling Melody - Old Mother Shipton (Bay Express).......... (Horse France) 16,000
Property of Lord Swaythling, from Bloomsbury Stud
Cupronickel (IRE) b y f Distant Relative - One Half Silver (CAN) (Plugged Nickle (USA))..... (David Minton Bloodstock) 10,500
Property of Mrs C Proctor, from Brick Kiln Stud
b y c Komaite (USA) - Orange Silk (Moulton) .... (Pat Haslam) 11,000
Property of a partnership, from Manor House Stud
b y c Bustino - Orlaith (Final Straw) (B.B.A.) 8,200
Property of Redpender Stud, Ireland
b y c Contract Law (USA) - Our Investment (Crofter (USA))........ (B.B.A. (Ireland)) 14,000
Property of a partnership, from Bloomsbury Stud
Endowment (USA) ch y c Cadeaux Genereux - Palm Springs (Top Ville)......... (Shadwell Estate Co) 31,000
Property of Home Stud Ltd
b y c Colmore Row - Perfect Double (Double Form)........................... (Cormac McCormack Associates) 4,400
Property of N W L Abbott, from Britton House Stud
b y c Dominion - Perpignan (Rousillon (USA))..... (David Minton Bloodstock) 13,000
Property of Britton House Stud
b y f Emarati (USA) - Petrol (Troy)......... (Mick Easterby) 5,800

639

From Yeomanstown Stud, Ireland
b y c Tirol - Piney Pass (Persian Bold)..... (Jack Berry) 33,000
Property of Clanville Lodge Stud
b y c Aragon - Plain Tree (Wolver Hollow).. (Sir Mark Prescott) 22,000
Property of A J Simpson, from Old Mill Stud
b y f Sharpo - Plaything (High Top)........ (Lillingston Bloodstock) 11,000
Property of a partnership, from Boxted Hall Stud
b y c Night Shift (USA) - Pomade (Luthier) (Paretta Bloodstock) 8,500
Property of Brook Stud Ltd, from Brook Stud
b y f Shavian - Pride Of Paris (Troy)....... (Tim Easterby) 4,200
Property of a partnership, from Bloomsbury Stud
Pushover (FR) b y c Dowsing (USA) - Pushoff (USA) (Sauce Boat (USA))......... (Clive Brittain) 12,000
From Yeomanstown Stud, Ireland
b y c Statoblest - Queen And Country (Town And Country)...... (Jack Berry) 30,000
From Elsenham Stud
ch y f Risk Me (FR) - Queen's Lake (Kings Lake (USA))........................... (E P Lynam Properties Ltd) 3,200

From Cheveley Park Stud
ch y c Chromite (USA) - Queen's Visit (Top Command (USA))..................... (European Equine Consultants) 13,500
Property of Lt. Col. and Mrs R Bromley Gardner, from Britton House Stud
b y f Dowsing (USA) - Ragged Moon (Raga Navarro (ITY))........... (M Blanshard) 5,200

640

Property of Clanville Lodge Stud
b y c Most Welcome - Red Berry (Great Nephew)............. (David Morris) 3,000
Property of Tetrarch Bloodstock Co., from Gazeley Stud
ch y c Most Welcome - Red Formation (Formidable (USA))................... (German International Bloodstock) 4,600
From Ashtown House Stud, Ireland
b y c Royal Academy (USA) - Red Letter Day (Crepello)...... (Demmy O'Byrne) 50,000
From Wheelersland Stud
ch y f Sharpo - Rose And The Ring (Welsh Pageant)............ (Mark Johnston) 8,000
Property of a partnership, from Britton House Stud
b y c Dominion - Rose Chanelle (Welsh Pageant)..................(Tony Lakin) 10,500
Property of Old Mill Stud
b y f Salse (USA) - Rustic Stile (Rusticaro (FR))... (Geoffrey Howson Bloodstock) 1,900
From Redpender Stud, Ireland
b y f Fairy King (USA) - Sable Lake (Thatching)..................(Neville Callaghan) 40,000
Property of Mrs Hugh McCalmont, from Yeomanstown Lodge Stud, Ireland
b y f Ballad Rock - Salabella (Sallust)...... (Shadwell Estate Co) 30,000
Property of E Gregory, from Woodcote Stud
b y c Far North (CAN) - Sans Dot (Busted) (Mark Johnston) 12,500
From Yeomanstown Stud, Ireland
b y f Common Grounds - Sarah Siddons (Reform)..................... (Cash) 6,300

641

Property of Woodcote Stud Ltd., from Woodcote Stud
b y f Unfuwain (USA) - Sawaki (Song)..... (Johnny McKeever Bloodstock) 9,000
From Cheveley park Stud
ch y c Prince Sabo - School Concert (Music Boy).................... (Jack Berry) 20,000
Property of Mrs Hugh McCalmont, from Yeomanstown Lodge Stud
b y c Petorius - Sea Mistress (Habitat)..... (Dermot Weld) 54,000
Property of D MacRae from Stradishall Manor
ch y c Salse (USA) - Sharmood (USA) (Sharpen Up)............. (C Gordon-Watson Bloodstock) 24,000
Property of a partnership, from Woodcote Stud
b y c Gadabout (USA) - Shirzad (Sherger).. (Richard McCormick) 10,000
Property of Home Stud Ltd
ch y f Dashing Blade - Sly Wink (Song).... (Susan Scargill) 5,000

b y f Distant Relative - Smagiada (Young Generation)....... (Matt McCormack) 2,000

From Ashtown House Stud, Ireland

b y c Roi Danzig (USA) - Snoozy Time (Cavo Doro)..... (John Ferguson Bloodstock) 45,000

Property of Britton House Stud

b y f Robellino (USA) - Song Of Hope (Chief Singer)......... (Wingfield Stud Farm) 40,000

Property of Springfield Thoroughbred Syndicate, from Ardenode Stud, Ireland

b y c Law Society (USA) - Sphinx (GER) (Alpenkonig (GER))..... (B.B.A. (Italia)) 27,000

642

Property of a partnership, from Stowell Hill Stud

b y f Unfuwain (USA) - Spin (High Top) .... (J & T Long) 25,000

From Castletown Stud, Ireland (Agent)

b y f Scenic - Sun On The Spey (Glint Of Gold).... (Hugo Lascelles Bloodstock) 22,000

Property of Stanley Estate and Stud Co., from Woodland Stud

Sandy Hollow ch y f Unfuwain (USA) - Sunshine Coast (Posse (USA)) .... (Gerry Blum) 2,200

From Fawley Stud

b y c Pharly (FR) - Teacher's Game (Mummy's Game) .... (R O'Gorman Bloodstock) 5,000

From Patridge Close Stud

b y c Glacial Storm (USA) - Tina's Melody (Tina's Pet).................. (Cash) 4,200

Property of Mrs R J Nash, from Britton House Stud

b y f Try My Best (USA) - Tomard (Thatching).................... (Pat Haslam) 14,000

Property of Clanville Lodge Stud

b y f Prince Sabo - Top Berry (High Top)... (Susan Scargill) 5,000

From Yeomanstown Stud, Ireland

b y c Midyan (USA) - Top Society (High Top) .... (Neville Callaghan) 20,000

Property of Woodcote Stud Ltd., from Woodcote Stud

ch y c Elmaamul (USA) - Tour D'Argent (USA) (Halo (USA))... (Richard Milburn) 1,000

From Lynn Lodge Stud, Ireland

ch y c Risk Me (FR) - Troyes (Troy)........ (John Dunlop) 31,000

643

From Elsenham Stud

b y c Risk Me (FR) - Vaisigano (USA) (Vaguely Noble).... (Matt McCormack) 4,200

From Patridge Close Stud

b y c Bluebird (USA) - Voltigeuse (USA) (Filiberto (USA))... (James Delahooke) 16,500

Property of Lord and Lady Bolton, from Manor House Stud

br y f Dowsing (USA) - Vynz Girl (Tower Walk)................. (Peter Burrell) 4,000

From Stetchworth Park Stud

b y f Salse (USA) - Wassl's Sister (Troy) ... (Barry Hills) 22,000

Property of Tullamaine Castle Stud, Ireland and Partners, from Tullamaine Castle Stud

b y c Fairy King (USA) - Woodland Garden (Godswalk (USA))....... (Julian Lloyd) 70,000

Property of Stanley Estate and Stud Co., from Woodland Stud

ch y f Pharly (FR) - Woodwind (FR) (Whistling Wind)........................ (Delta Bloodstock Management) 13,000

Property of Wayland Stud, from Woodcote Stud

b y c Warrshan (USA) - Zilda (FR) (Zino) ... (B.B.A.) 8,000

From Red House Stud

br y c Petong - Akka (Malacate (USA)) ..... (Brian Meehan) 8,600

Property of Brook Stud Ltd, from Brook Stud

b y f Statoblest - Allander Girl (Miralgo).... (John Hills) 6,000

Property of K Power, from Old Mill Stud

b y f Statoblest - Alpine Sunset (Auction Ring (USA)).................. (B.B.A.) 20,000

644

Property of C J R Trotter, from Attington Stud

b or br y f Emarati (USA) - Anhaar (Ela-Mana-Mou).................. (B.B.A.) 1,000

From Ashtown House Stud, Ireland

b or br y c Minshaanshu Amad (USA) - Appeal The Rule (USA) (Valid Appeal (USA)).................. (Jack Berry) 31,000

Property of A Gibson, from Warren Park Stud

ch y c Prince Sabo - Ashdown (Pharly (FR)) (Michael Jarvis) 8,000

Property of maristow Farms Ltd, from Blackdown Stud

b y f Reprimand - Astolat (Rusticaro (FR)).. (Will Edmeades Bloodstock) 12,000

From Stetchworth Park Stud

gr y f Absalom - Aunt Blue (Blue Refrain).. (Chris Thornton) 4,000

Property of N W L Abbott, from Britton House Stud

b y f Thatching - Avant-Garde (Pas de Seul) (Geoffrey Howson Bloodstock) 5,600

From Cheveley Park Stud

b y c Primo Dominie - Bambolona (Bustino) (Peter Wragg Bloodstock) 44,000

Property of R H James, from Limestone Stud

b y c Rambo Dancer (USA) - Be Royal (Royal Palm).............. (Ron Boss) 5,200

From Woodditton Stud

ch y f Superlative - Believe The Chick (USA) (Believe It (USA))....... (Neil Graham) 10,000

Property of Mr and Mrs D J Deer, from Fawley Stud

b y c Royal Academy (USA) - Belifontaine (FR) (Bellypha) .... (John Warren Bloodstock) 46,000

645

From Partridge Close Stud

b y c Warrshan (USA) - Black Ivor (USA) (Sir Ivor)................ (William Haggas) 16,000

From Fawley Stud

b y f Taufan (USA) - Bonnie Banks (Lomond (USA)).............. (Mark Tompkins) 2,000

Property of Manor House Stud
b y c Petong - Brigado (Brigadier Gerard) .. (Shadwell Estate Co) 29,000
From Glenvale Stud, Ireland
b y c Fairy King (USA) - Camden Dancer (Camdown Town)............ (C.B.A.) 12,000
From Yeomanstown Stud, Ireland
gr y c Common Grounds - Catherine Linton (USA) (High Echelon (USA))........... (David Cosgrove) 12,500
Property of Mrs J H Weller-Poley, from Boxted Hall Stud
b y c Doulab (USA) - Celestial Air (Rheingold) .... (Cormac McCormack Associates) 6,000
From Woodcote Stud Ltd., From Woodcote Stud
b y f Exodal (USA) - Childish Prank (Teenoso (USA)).............. (B T Eastick) 2,500
From Ashtown House Stud, Ireland
b y c Scenic - Church Mountain (Furry Glen) .... (Peter Doyle Bloodstock) 29,000
Property of Mrs S Joint, from Britton House Stud
br y f Forzando - Classic Vintage (Stradavinsky)................ (Cash) 3,000
Property of Mr & Mrs D A Hicks, from Buckhurst Stud
b y f Tirol - Clicquot (Bold Lad (IRE)).......(Geoffrey Howson Bloodstock) 7,200

646

Property of Brook Stud Ltd., from Brook Stud
b y c Never So Bold - Cornelian (Great Nephew) .... (Andrew Mead International Bloodstock) 37,000
gr y f Chief Singer - Couleur de Rose (Kalaglow)................ (Paul Cole) 5,200
Property of Red House Stud
gr y c Petong - Daffodil Fields (Try My Best (USA)) (C Gordon-Watson Bloodstock) 56,000
Property of Moygaddy Stud, Ireland
b y c Fairy King (USA) - Daniela Samuel (USA) (No Robbery) (Demmy O'Byrne) 68,000
Property of a Partnership, from Stowell Hill Stud
ch y f Forzando - Deed (Derring-Do)........ (Mick Channon) 14,500
From Yeomanstown Stud, Ireland
ch y c Common Grounds - Domino's Nurse (Dom Racine (FR))......... (Paul Cole) 27,000
Property of Blue Blood Investments, from Woodcote Stud
b y c Mtoto - Exotic (Jaazeiro (USA)) ...... (German International Bloodstock) 18,500
From Woodditton Stud
b y f Superlative - False Look (USA) (Alleged (USA)).......................... (R O'Gorman Bloodstock) 6,500
Property of Brook Stud Ltd., from Brook Stud
b y f Kalaglow - Feather Flower (Relkino) .. (Roger Curtis) 3,600
Property of Springfield Thoroughbred Syndicate, from Ardenode Stud, Ireland
ch y c Cadeaux Genereux - Figini (Glint Of Gold)....... (R O'Gorman Bloodstock) 21,000

647

From Stetchworth Park Stud
b y f Nomination - Flamberge (Kris) .... (General Broker) 4,500
Property of F B & Dr S F Barnes Bloodstock Services, from Brick Kiln Stud
b y f Elmaamul (USA) - Fleetwood Fancy (Taufan (USA)) (Lillingston Bloodstock) 7,000
Property of Mr and Mrs D A Hicks, from Buckhurse Stud
b y f Statoblest - Fleur Du Val (Valiyar)..... (C Gordon-Watson Bloodstock) 5,500
Property of a Gentleman, from Old Mill Stud
ch y f Aragon - Forest Blossom (USA) (Green Forest (USA))................ (David Arbuthnot) 7,800
From Stetchworth Park Stud
ch y f Dancing Spree (USA) - Girette (USA) (General Assembly (USA))........... (David Adams) 10,000
Property of Home Stud Ltd
ch y c Emarati (USA) - Good Natured (Troy) (B.B.A.) 1,500
Property of Grange Stud (U.K.)
b y c Dominion - Grain Lady (USA) (Greinton)................... (Henry Candy) 12,000
Property of Tullamaine Castle Stud, Ireland and Partners, from Tullamaine Castle Stud
ch y c Be My Guest (USA) - Haskeir (Final Straw)................... (Frank Barry) 6,200
Property of Brook Stud Ltd., from Brook Stud
b y f Kalaglow - Headrest (Habitat)........ (Geoffrey Howson Bloodstock) 1,700
Property of Manor House Stud
b y f Aragon - Helewise (Dance In Time (CAN))............... (Colin Williams) 7,000

648

Property of J M Greetham, from Gazeley Stud
b y f Most Welcome - Historical Fact (Reform)............ (James Bethell) 3,000
Property of Moygaddy Stud, Ireland
b y c Jareer (USA) - How True (Known Fact (USA))................ (Roger Curtis) 6,800
From Cheveley Park Stud
ch y c Never So Bold - I'll Try (Try My Best (USA))....... (Peter Doyle Bloodstock) 35,000
Property of Mr and Mr D J Deer, from Fawley Stud
b y f Tirol - Icecapped (Caerleon (USA)).... (German International Bloodstock) 8,200
Property of Mr and Mrs D A Hicks, from Buckhurst Stud
b y c Superpower - Ideal Home (Home Guard (USA))....... (Axel Donnerstag) 13,000
Property of Stanley Estate and Stud Co., from Woodland Stud
ch y f Sharpo - Idle Days (Hittite Glory) .... (Darley Stud Management) 27,000
Property of Brook Stud Ltd., from Brook Stud
b y c Statoblest - Intoxication (Great Nephew)........ (Amanda Skiffington) 20,000
Property of Carlton Consultants Ltd., from Home Stud
ch y c Master Willie - Irene's Charter (Persian Bold).................. (C.B.A.) 15,000

Property of Mr & Mrs D J Deer, from Fawley Stud

ch y c Be My Guest (USA) - Ivor's Honey (Sir Ivor)..................... (B.B.A.) 12,500

649

ASCOT
Tuesday, October 19th

To Dissolve a Partnership

Roy's Hill b g (7yrs) Royben - Magic Sky (Alto Volante).......... (Mrs J Starkey) 2,000

Property of Mr H Raby

Fala D'Or br m (7yrs) Le Coq D'Or - Fala Kalima (Sousa)................ (Cash) 1,550

Property of a Gentleman

Flash Of Amber b f (3yrs) Electric - Orange Silk (Moulton)................. (Cash) 600

To Dissolve a Partnership

Apollo de Oriente b g (3yrs) Siberian Express (USA) - Marie Galante (Shirley Heights)...................... (Cash) 750

Property of Fluorocarbon Bloodstock Ltd

Kimmy's Princess ch f (3yrs) Prince Sabo - Miss Kimmy (Tower Walk)..... (Cash) 850

Property of Wyards Stud

b y f Prince Sabo - Cloudless Sky (He Loves Me)....................... (G West) 925

ch y f Jalmood (USA) - Stedham (Jaazeiro (USA))................... (D G Mason) 1,750

Property of Mr M Webb

Dancing Miss (IRE) ch f (4yrs) Heraldiste (USA) - Tasmania Star (Captain James) (Cash) 400

Property of Mrs Livingstone

Foremma b f (2yrs) Formidable (USA) - Great Dilemma (Vaigly Great) .... (G Keene) 600

Property of Lowquest Ltd

Ten Times Tango ch f (2yrs) Grey Desire - Tango Lady (Gorytus)........... (Cash) 725

King Acrylic (IRE) b c (2yrs) King Of Clubs - Maynooth Belle (Busted)....... (Cash) 650

650

Property of Mr D McFarland

Sweet Intent b f (4yrs) Doctor Wall - Honiara (Pitcairn)........... (H Jarvis) 1,150

Property of Mrs M A Craven

Chloes Diamond (IRE) ch m (5yrs) Heraldiste (USA) - Salique (Sallust) (P Halt) 625

General Brooks (IRE) b g (3yrs) Governor General - Choral Park (Music Boy)..... (M J Bateman) 800

Property of Mr B Hine

Above Dispute b m (7yrs) Cut Above - Dare Me (Derring-Do)......... (T G Tarrant) 775

Property of Mr John Rose, from Kilvington Stud

b y f Governor General - Lady Of The Lodge (Absalom).... (Racing Thoroughbreds) 400

To Dissolve a Partnership

General Link b g (3yrs) Governor General - City Link Lass (Double Jump)......... (G M Mutton) 1,250

Property of Miss Julie Self

Rhazya b m (5yrs) Rousillon (USA) - Destina (USA) (Youth (USA))..... (Rick Murray) 650

To Dissolve a Partnership

Sharada b f (2yrs) Shareef Dancer (USA) - Casa Rosada (Known Fact (USA)) ..... (R Atkins) 900

Property of Mr P Burgoyne

Bell Lad (IRE) ch g (3yrs) Common Grounds - Quack Shot (USA) (Quack) .... (Mrs M West) 775

Property of a Partnership

Vaddallian gr g (3yrs) Petong - Rekindle (Relkino)..................... (Cash) 480

651

To Dissolve a Partnership

Abacusam b g (2yrs) Sayf El Arab (USA) - Blakeney Heights (Blakeney).......... (Ms. Russell) 400

Property of Mr V Harrison

Loudest Whisper b g (5yrs) Reach - Dancela (Ela-Mana-Mou)........ (M West) 550

Property of Mr F H Lee

I Remember You (IRE) ch c (3yrs) Don't Forget Me - Non Casual (Nonoalco (USA))..................... (F H Lee) 1,750

Belmont Lodge (IRE) b f (3yrs) Thatching - Belmont Blue (Kashmir II)... (F H Lee) 825

Property of Mr A D Spence

Barrish b h (7yrs) Wassl - Rowa (Great Nephew)................ (D C Potter) 975

Property of Fulling Mill Stud

Mr Mystical (IRE) br c (2yrs) Classic Secret (USA) - Soudchika (GER) (Dschingis Khan).................. (Mrs Y West) 1,500

To Dissolve a Partnership

Ambivalentattitude b g (3yrs) North Briton - Bestena (Bustino)............. (Cash) 1,050

Property of Mr K L Dare

Tharif b g (5yrs) Green Desert (USA) - Mrs Bacon (Balliol)............. (B Walker) 1,350

Property of Mrs S Gay

Eserie de Cores (USA) b c (3yrs) Gold Crest (USA) - April Blues (Cure The Blues)... (R J Burrow) 425

Property of Darley Stud Management Co Ltd, from Stanley House Stables

Livonian b c (3yrs) Kris - Air Distingue (USA) (Sir Ivor).................... (C.B.A.) 15,500

652

To Dissolve a Partnership

Early Star b g (4yrs) Precocious - Staritsa (USA) (Alleged)................ (Cash) 1,800

Pandy b g (7yrs) Thatching - Hot Stone (Hotfoot)........... (Graham Thorner) 4,200

Property of Alleron Racing Club

Barton Pride (IRE) b g (4yrs) Phardante (FR) - Ginosa (Kalamoun).. (Mrs S Maciver) 750

Property of Mr A E Ford

The Leggett b g (10yrs) Faraway Times (USA) - Mrs McNicholas (Tudor Music) (G Jessop) 7,000

Property of Outline Management Ltd

Rahif b g (5yrs) Shirley Heights - Vaguely (Bold Lad (IRE))............... (Cash) 1,000

To Dissolve a Partnership, from Fowlers Farm Racing Stables

River Orchid b f (4yrs) Mashhor Dancer (USA) - Summer Sky (Syliner)......... (M J Bateman) 1,200

To Dissolve a Partnership

Graig Le Moss (IRE) b m (5yrs) Le Moss - Eadestown (Kinglet)...... (M J Foster) 1,250

Proud Drifter br g (6yrs) Crash Course - Purlane (FR) (Kashmir II)....... (Cash) 1,000

Property of Mr I G M Dalgleish

Great Heights b g (6yrs) Shirley Heights - As You Desire Me (Kalamoun)......... (H J Manners) 1,600

To Dissolve a Partnership

Wednesdays Auction (IRE) b g (5yrs) Mazaad - Happy Always (Lucky Wednesday)............. (D C Potter) 2,500

653

Property of Mr John Skull

Sharpridge ch g (9yrs) Nearly A Hand - Maria's Piece (Rose Knight).... (Cash) 2,700

Property of High Buildings Farm

Dual Capacity (USA) b g (9yrs) Coastal (USA) - Fenney Mill (Levmoss)........ (R Chelton) 1,800

Property of Mr F Bayliss

Cairneymount b g (7yrs) Croghan Hill - Glentoran Valley (Little Buskins) (Cash) 3,300

To Dissolve a Partnership

Extra High (USA) ch g (5yrs) Nepal (USA) - Evening Scarlet (USA) (Bold Commander)............... (A K Garside) 1,200

Aisholt ch m (8yrs) Avocat - Bryophila (FR) (Breakspear II)................ (Cash) 1,000

Property of Mr R B Boss

Wisebow b g (8yrs) Green Shoon - Lacabeha Lass Vii (Menelek)............ (Christine Elliott) 1,900

Property of Mrs B Taylor

Eddie Walshe b g (8yrs) Smackover - Ashmore Lady (Ashmore)......... (G Bull) 2,500

Property of a Partnership

Steel Dance b g (5yrs) Mashtor Dancer (USA) - Damaska (USA) (Damascus (USA))............... (Gerald Burton) 1,350

Property of Mr E A Hayward

Arctic Line b g (5yrs) Green Ruby (USA) - Sall Ann III (Port Corsair).. (S R Freen) 1,050

Property of a Partnership

Times Are Changing b m (6yrs) Cruise Missile - Sparella (Spartan General).... (K Podger) 1,550

654

Property of Mr T T Weller

Alto Princess b f (4yrs) Noalto - Queen Of The Hills (Connaught)..... (C H Jones) 1,500

Property of Mr S C Jones

Crosula br g (5yrs) Sula Bula - Crosa (Crozier)....... (Bisgrove Partnership) 3,800

To Dissolve a Partnership

Millie Belle ch m (7yrs) Milford - Charter Belle (Runnymede)........ (A P Gent) 1,500

Property of Mrs H J Manners

Pearly White b f (4yrs) Petong - White's Pet (Mummy's Pet)........ (Dai Williams) 2,000

Property of Mr R H York

Galatea Pearl b m (6yrs) Rabdan - Bridal Wave (Julio Mariner)...... (R Willcox) 750

Property of Mr C M Gee

Royal Fireworks ch g (6yrs) Royal Vulcan - Bengal Lady (Celtic Cone)............ (Dai Williams) 3,000

Property of a Partnership

West End Girl b f (3yrs) Absalom - City Ditty (Camden Town)...... (K George) 900

Property of Mr G W Lugg

Knighton Coombe (NZ) ch g (7yrs) The Expatriate - Sashay (Showoff)........ (S A Bowen) 1,000

Property of Mrs J Lees

Thinking Cap ch g (12yrs) Bargello - Grangeclare Lady (Menelek).... (Cash) 1,300

Property of Mrs J Downing

Laser Track b m (6yrs) Palm Track - Lazerette (Welsh Saint) (Dai Williams) 1,200

655

Property of Mr Charles Ellingworth

Nimrod br g (7yrs) Cisto (FR) - Josephine Vii (Lovella Luciano).............. (Cash) 1,800

Property of Mrs P C Bowles

The Princeling ch g (3yrs) Kinglet - Regal Nod (Tom Noddy)............. (Cash) 1,250

Property of a Gentleman

br g (7yrs) Dalsaan - Thimothea (FR) (Timmy My Boy)....... (Mrs Roberts) 1,800

Property of Mr L V Wadge

Swingtime Belle b m (6yrs) Swing Easy (USA) - Betbellof (Averof)... (B Byford) 875

Rogevic Belle ch g (5yrs) Swing Easy (USA) - Betbellof (Averof)............ (Cash) 1,350

To Dissolve a Partnership

Dynavour House ch f (3yrs) Bairn (USA) - Good Natured (Troy).. (Saskia Struyek) 800

PRIVATE SALES

Property of Miss A L Wright

Persian Haze (IRE) ch g (4yrs) Bold Arrangement - Crufty Wood (Sweet Revenge) (Cash) 4,000

Property of Lady S Palmer

Steels Rock ch g (7yrs) Soudno - Escarita (Escart III).............. (N J Pewter) 5,000

656

DONCASTER

Wednesday, October 20th

Property of Mr A C Batey, from East Ridley Farm Stables

Cormac's gr g (7yrs) Superlative - Tahoume (FR) (Faristan)............. (S House) 620

Taurian Prince b g (4yrs) Petoski - Pitroyal (Pitskelly)............. (Miss S Shaw) 520

b g (3yrs) Derring Rose - La Verite (Vitiges) (Ruth Wollerton) 1,050

Property of Mr E W Fenwick, from Scalla Moor Farm

Mr Beaujolais b g (4yrs) Mister Majestic - Bonvin (Taufan)...... (Ruth Wollerton) 1,250

From Bellwood Stables

Swynford Flyer b f (4yrs) Valiyar - Qualitairess (Kampala)................ (R A M Racecourses) 1,000

Property of Mr R Patrick

Benoso b c (3yrs) Glebe Place (USA) - Fallonette (Tachypous) (Carrie Humble) 450

Cassandra Place b f (3yrs) Glebe Place (USA) - Out To Lunch (Anax)... (Cash) 400

From Tupgill Park Stables

Red Rhapsody b f (4yrs) Sizzling Melody - The Firebird (Busted).... (Miss D Hall) 900

To Settle a Dispute, from Tupgill Park Stables

ch c (2yrs) Astronef - Whilst (Dalsaan)..... (Cash) 720

From Hanging Hill Stables

Strangersinthenite ch g (4yrs) Legend Of France (USA) - Angail (Northfields) .... (Mrs L Copley) 680

Snug Surprise b f (3yrs) Elegant Air - Persevering (Blakeney).......... (F Iqbal) 620

657

Property of Mr R Scott, from Hetlandhill Stables

Good Spirits ch f (2yrs) Good Times (ITY) - Inca Girl (Tribal Chief)....... (L Lungo) 700

Property of Miss C Edgar

Braemoss br f (2yrs) Ovac (ITY) - Brave 'N' Easy (Brave Invader).... (Mrs J Taylor) 920

To Dissolve a Partnership

Ashgrove Cherry b m (5yrs) Creetown - Aldington Cherry (Legal Eagle).. (Cash) 1,650

Property of Mr P Yond

Final Oak b f (3yrs) Nicholas Bill - Final Rush (Final Straw).................. (B B A) 2,000

Property of Martin Pound Racing Ltd, from Pentre David Stables

Last Straw b g (5yrs) Blushing Scribe (USA) - Straw Reef (Final Straw) .... (Victoria Jones) 1,500

From Hendersyde Stables

Sainted Sue ch f (3yrs) Aragon - Nosey (Nebbiolo)........... (Mrs H L Siddall) 620

Property of Mrs I Bray, from Habton Grange Stables

Fair Swop b f (2yrs) Cyrano de Bergerac - Eight Mile Rock (Dominion)... (F Iqbal) 550

Property of Mr A G Black, from Musley Bank Stables

Kiltroum gr g (4yrs) Courtroom (FR) - Kiltie (Habat).................... (R Wylie) 1,700

From Musley Bank Stables

Impressive ch g (2yrs) Formidable (USA) - Ritsurin (Mount Hagen).... (R O'Ryan) 800

Property of Mr P Caplan, from Groundhill Stables

Try N'fly b g (3yrs) Carmelite House - Gruntled (Grundy).. (Stefan Uppstrom) 2,800

658

To Dissolve a Partnership, from Groundhill Stables

Mr Abbot b g (3yrs) Midyan (USA) - Abbotswood (Ahonoora)....... (Cash) 1,300

Lettermore b f (3yrs) Elegant Air - Midnight's Reward (Night Shift)... (B B A) 1,500

Five And Up Five b f (2yrs) Reprimand - Five Farthings (Busted).... (C J Rose) 820

From Harness Grove Stud

Chickcharnie ch g (3yrs) Stanford - Lucky Angel (Lucky Wednesday)............ (C M Meade) 2,000

Property of a Partnership, from Beverley House Stables

Dance On Sixpence b g (5yrs) Lidhame - Burning Ambition (Troy)......... (Cash) 1,500

To Dissolve a Partnership, from Jamesfield Place Stables

Waders Dream b g (4yrs) Doulab (USA) - Sea Mistress (Habitat).... (P Mitchell) 2,900

Tisa Wasiteen b f (2yrs) Taufan (USA) - Evanna's Pride (Main Reef)... (F Iqbal) 820

From Maunby House Stables

Harlosh ch g (3yrs) Marching On - Cottagers Lane (Farm Walk)....... (Cash) 1,100

Master Of Hounds b g (7yrs) Kind Of Hush - Jambalaya (Amboise)... (J Sisterson) 550

From Woodland Stables

Neventer (FR) b g (4yrs) Lead On Time (USA) - Tysfjord (FR) (Silly Season) .... (D Green) 600

659

Property of Northern Bloodstock Racing Annual Dispersal, from Highfield House Stables

Pesidanamich b g (5yrs) Mummy's Treasure - Bay Supreme (Martinmas)...... (A Whillans) 2,400

From Sackville Stables

Pop To Stans b g (4yrs) Gold Crest (USA) - Lady Of Camelot (FR) (Bolkonski) ..... (J Pearce) 650

Property of Burton Park Country Club, from Sackville House Stables

Big Pat b c (4yrs) Back Chat (USA) - Fallonetta (Tachypous)....... (J Spearing) 15,000

To Settle an Account

Dramatic Pass ch g (4yrs) Coquelin (USA) - Miss Flirt (Welsh Pageant)............ (M C Chapman) 1,500

Simply Superb ch g (3yrs) Superlative - Coral Princess (Imperial Fling) (W Clay) 1,400

From Warwick House Stables

Invisible Armour gr g (4yrs) Precocious - Haunting (Lord Gayle)................ (Stefan Uppstrom) 5,600

Ballacascade b g (3yrs) Ballacashtal (CAN) - Pasha's Dream (Tarboosh)............ (Mrs K Bandilla) 1,400

From Thorndale Stables

Alamir (USA) b g (5yrs) Shadeed (USA) - Glamour Girl (FR) (Riverman).......... (S O'Neill) 1,000

Property of Mrs Val Rapkins, from Rathmoy Stables

May Square ch g (5yrs) Nicholas Bill - Casa Rosada (Known Fact).......... (Cash) 650

Property of Mr G D Jackman

Final Dream b m (5yrs) Wassl - Pale Ivory (Silver Shark)................ (F Iqbal) 1,200

660

From Arundel House Stables

Skolern b g (9yrs) Lochnager - Piethorne (Fine Blade)................... (Cash) 550

Property of Mr A Clarke

b g (5yrs) Relkino - Mindblowing (Pongee) (Cash) 3,500

From Great House Stables

br g (3yrs) Blakeney Point - Menhaden (Menelek)...................... (Cash) 1,400

Good Secret ch g (6yrs) Good Thyne (USA) - Etta Girl (Bay Express)........ (Cash) 820

From Denton Stables

Royal Invader b g (9yrs) Silly Prices - Fishermans Lass (Articulate).......... (Cash) 450

From Flaxton Stables

Blue Rosette b g (4yrs) Lucky Wednesday - Cadenette (Brigadier Gerard).......... (David Minton Bloodstock) 3,600

From Habton Grange Stables To Dissolve a Partnership

Secret Castle b g (5yrs) Castle Keep - Excavator Lady (Most Secret).......... (B Baugh) 5,800

Property of Mrs S Easterby, from Habton Grange Stables

Patience Please br f (4yrs) King Of Spain - Navarino Bay (Averof)....... (L Dodds) 2,300

Property of Mr W D McClennon

Coat Of Dreams b g (4yrs) Ballacashtal (CAN) - Montelimar (Wolver Hollow).... (Cormac McCormack Associates) 2,300

Property of Mr C H P Bell, from Burton Fleming Hall Stables

b f (4yrs) Reesh - Starchy (Crisp And Even) (Ruth Wollerton) 1,150

661

Property of The Exors of the late Mr J J G Wrathall

Country Tarragen b g (4yrs) Town And Country - Sweet Spice (Native Bazaar) (B B A) 1,800

From Castle Farm Stud

b g (4yrs) Salluceva - Sprightly's Last (Random Shot)..................... (Cash) 3,000

Property of Mr G Mason

b f (4yrs) State Diplomacy (USA) - Dellassera (Donibristle)....... (R Smith) 1,050

Property of Mrs E Kettlewell, from Groundhill Stables

Kagram Queen b m (5yrs) Prince Ragusa - Arodstown Alice (Sahib).... (D Leech) 2,300

Property of Mr B Harland, from Star Cottage Stables

Spanish Performer br f (4yrs) King Of Spain - Dauphiness (Supreme)....... (F Iqbal) 1,600

Property of Fawley Stud

Knowing gr m (6yrs) Lochnager - Caroline Lamb (Hotfoot)............... (Cash) 2,300

Property of Mr J Cornwall

Vimchase ch g (7yrs) Slim Jim - Vimys Pet (Lord Nelson)............. (B G Duke) 2,400

Property of Mrs Helen Whyte, Co Tipperary, Ireland

St Elmo's Fire (NZ) b g (8yrs) Grosvenor (NZ) - Star Quality (NZ) (Bismark II).... (Miss L Russell) 1,700

Property of Mr A O'Connor, Co Clare, Ireland

Par Bar gr m (5yrs) The Parson - Buranee (My Swanee)................. (Cash) 4,300

From Stepaside Stables, Co Kildare, Ireland

Jacks Army b g (7yrs) Riot Helmet - Eva Dodd (Orchardist).......... (J T Doyle) 10,000

662

Property of Mr George Halford, from Hawkfield Stables, Co Kildare

Gayloire b g (4yrs) Vision (USA) - Magloire (FR) (Sir Gaylord)............... (C B A) 19,000

From Bell House Stables

Classic Statement ch g (7yrs) Mill Reef (USA) - Lady Graustark (USA) (Graustark)............... (J Sisterson) 950

Property of Mr M Murphy, Co Tipperary, Ireland

McCarthy's Hotel ch g (10yrs) Torus - Cantagrena (Cantab)........... (B O'Ryan) 1,000

From Camas Stables, Co Tippeary, Ireland

Castlelake Cross ch g (5yrs) Carlingford Castle - Goose Loose (Dual).......... (J J O'Neill) 5,000

Property of a Partnership

Ballyanto b g (8yrs) Lepanto (GER) - Ballyarctic (Arcticeelagh)........ (J Dixon) 850

From Pit Farm Stud

Wolver Run b g (8yrs) Furry Glen - Roselita (Deep Run)............ (A J Dampier) 600

Property of Mr T Charlesworth

Saoirse br m (5yrs) Horage - Teletype (Guillaume Tell)..............(W Clark) 1,100

From Quarryfield Stud, Co Wexford, Ireland

Billy Bligh b g (8yrs) Buckskin (FR) - Swiftly Belle (Deep Run)................ (Mrs Howard Johnson) 2,800

Sunset Run b g (7yrs) Deep Run - Sunset Queen (Arctic Slave)................ (David Minton Bloodstock) 5,000

Property of Mr Ian Mason

Prospecting br g (5yrs) Damister (USA) - Copt Hall Royale (Right Tack)......... (J Spearing) 8,400

663

Property of Springhill Bloodstock, from Greystoke Stables

Tartan Turf b g (6yrs) Le Moss - El Scarsdale (Furry Glen).......... (Cash) 950

From Thorndale Stables

Queen's Chaplain b g (9yrs) The Parson - Reginasway (Flair Path)........ (Cash) 8,200

Property of Mrs J L Woolford

Spanish Accent b g (7yrs) King Of Spain - Broken Accent (Busted) (Mrs S Soley) 2,300

Property of Mr David Jones

Ponentino b g (7yrs) Strong Gale - Milan United (Milan)....................... (Cormac McCormack Associates) 880

Property of Mr D S Alder, from Locker Mill Stables

Findoglen b g (7yrs) Furry Glen - Pastina's Lass (Bargello).......... (Mrs A Page) 2,000

Property of Mr A J Allright, from Russell Farm Stables

Valassy b g (10yrs) Northern Value (USA) - Plum Sassy (Prince Tenderfoot)....... (Mrs Wendy Muir) 2,000

From Hendersyde Stables
Equator ch g (10yrs) Nijinsky (CAN) - Sound Of Success (USA) (Successor) .... (Ann Lee) 2,000
Dubalea b g (10yrs) Dubassoff (USA) - Thirkleby Kate Vii (Bivouac)..... (Cash) 2,400
Meigle Street b m (8yrs) Balgaddy - Golden Owen (Master Owen).... (G R Taylor) 1,600

Property of Mrs June Taylor, from Globe Farm Stables
Carefree Times b g (6yrs) Good Times (ITY) - Danaka (FR) (Val de Loir)............ (Roger Burgess Ltd) 2,500

664

Property of Mr K Johnson, from Tupgill Stables
Hamanaka (USA) b f (4yrs) Conquistador Cielo (USA) - Tastefully (USA) (Hail To Reason).................... (J Love) 5,300

Property of Mr S G Chadwick, from Eskrigg Stables
Progress Mister gr g (9yrs) Stetchworth (USA) - Suir (Palestine)......... (Cash) 1,000

Property of Mr R G Watson
Certain Beat b g (8yrs) Ascertain (USA) - Jungle Rhythm (Drumbeg) (J Ibbotson) 3,100

Property of Mr J D Ibbotson
Master Evan gr g (7yrs) Entre Nous - Wide Spread (Sparkler).... (Miss B Davison) 720

Property of Mr F Kirby
Underway (FR) b g (7yrs) Djarvis (FR) - Jamaica II (FR) (Tryptic).... (B G Duke) 1,750

Property of Mr J Cornforth
Carryduff ch g (12yrs) Lucifer (USA) - Greenhall Mistress (Master Buck)..... (J Flint) 1,200

Property of Mrs M Cooper
Highland Mourne b f (4yrs) Sunyboy - Highland Chance (Bronze Hill)............. (Equine Services) 1,700
Quite A Madam b m (9yrs) Park Row - Belle Tarquin (Saucy Kit)... (Miss J Costello) 650

Property of Miss K E Lane, from Ashdown Stables
Rose Lillian b m (8yrs) Nemorino (USA) - Mishabo (Royalty).... (Carrie Humble) 450

Property of Mr Bryan Thornley
ch g (5yrs) Deep Run - Miss Du Fosse (Eastern Venture)......... (P Bradley) 2,500

665

Property of Miss Jill Smith-Jones
Charlie Fox ro g (7yrs) - ... (K J Lamacroft) 1,000

Property of Mrs A R Page, from West Farm
Camelot ch g (9yrs) S.T.B. Sovereign King - Unknown...................... (Cash) 620

Property of J R Buckley (Agriculture)
Ravendale Ringer b g (5yrs) Reformed Character - Fair Corriander Vii (Kadir Cup)................ (Mrs V Kellard) 1,000
Ravendale Exasperated ch f (2yrs) Exorbitant - Violet Elizabeth (Richie)......... (M Wharmby) 500

Property of Mr J Cassidy
Taramvid Diamond ch m (6yrs) Knave Of Hearts - Deerpark Lulu (Blackwater Lad)................. (Mrs S France) 650

Property of Mrs D Welsh
Limerick ch g (6yrs) - ..... (K J Lamacroft) 900

PRIVATE SALES

Property of Messrs J & M Douglas Engineering, from Black Pitts Stables
Major Risk ch g (4yrs) Risk Me (FR) - Brampton Grace (Tachypous) .... (R A M Racecourses) 1,300

From Maunby House Stables
Gussie Fink Nottle br g (3yrs) Treasure Kay - Bright Cecilia (Welsh Saint).. (B B A) 2,000

Property of Springhill Bloodstock, from Mount Anna Stables
b g (5yrs) Feelings (FR) - Meg's Mantle (New Brig)................... (Cash) 2,500

To Dissolve a Partnership
Mr Wideawake ch g (6yrs) Royal Match - Dorriba (Ribero)........... (A R Pain) 2,750

Property of Mrs M Ronan, Co Tipperary, Ireland
Ozone Lass ch m (5yrs) Decent Fellow - Arctic Mistress (Quayside)..... (Cash) 2,000

Property of Mr A J Barnett, from Glen Aln Stables
Cannon Lad b g (11yrs) Rajen - Miss Sovereign (Lucky Sovereign)....... (Cash) 1,600

Property of Miss Lucinda V Russell, from Arlary House Stables
Gazzymaz ch g (7yrs) Longleat (USA) - Vaguely Hopeful (Fortino II)........... (G R Taylor) 800

Property of Miss E Spouse
Timaroo p g (9yrs) - .... (Cash) 1,700

Property of Mr D Sandiford
Columbus ch g (8yrs) - .... (R Dalton) 1,900

666

DONCASTER

Thursday, October 21st

Property of Messrs P E & M J Hawkins, from Warren Farm
b g (3yrs) Sergeant Drummer (USA) - Elders Lady (Bold As Brass).......... (Cash) 920

Property of Mr R P Dineen
Pacific Spirit b f (3yrs) Governor General - Mossberry Fair (Mossberry).. (W Haig) 1,700

From Thorndale Stables
b f (2yrs) Reprimand - Fire And Ice (FR) (Reliance II).................. (Cash) 550

Property of Mr B Norman, from Warwick Lodge Stables
Westcoast b g (2yrs) Handsome Sailor - Pichon (Formidable)......... (M Tate) 1,450

From Northgate Lodge Stables
ch c (3yrs) Grey Desire - Barefoot Contessa (Homeric).................. (F Iqbal) 600
b f (3yrs) Grey Desire - Kamaress (Kampala) .... (Miss S Fox) 600

From Edges Farm Racing Stables
Jotra ch g (3yrs) Clantime - Branston Express (Bay Express)......... (Cash) 760

Property of Mr J D Norbury & S T Chapple Gill, from Riston Whins Stables
Sharp Summit b f (2yrs) Exactly Sharp (USA) - Yashville (Top Ville)..... (Cash) 560

Property of Keith Brown Properties Ltd, from Riston Whins Stables
Tenpin Prophet ch f (2yrs) Salt Dome (USA) - Finesse (Miralgo).......... (M Tate) 600

From Hanging Hill Stables
Young Medic b g (2yrs) Doc Marten - Petrinella (Mummy's Pet)...... (Cash) 580
Free Tyson b g (2yrs) Sizzling Melody - Lizarra (High Top)......... (P Keane) 500
Minibar ch f (2yrs) Dominion - Barsham (Be My Guest).................... (Cash) 600

667

From Mowbray House Stables To Dissolve a Partnership
Lucky Fourteen b c (2yrs) Nomination - Lucky Saran (Lucky Wednesday)...... (D W Chapman) 3,200
Cheeky Chappy b c (2yrs) Sayf El Arab (USA) - Guilty Guest (USA) (Be My Guest)............. (D W Chapman) 1,450
Property of a Partnership, from Red House Stables
Lookin' Rosie b f (2yrs) Mazilier (USA) - Shadow Play (Busted).......... (Cash) 700
Property of Mr P Caplan, from Eastwell Hall Stables
Willwin gr f (2yrs) Belfort - Harem Queen (Prince Regent).... (Galoppens Venner) 1,100
From Maunby House Stables
Sectary b g (2yrs) Dancing Dissident (USA) - My Fair Orchid (Roan Rocket) .... (S House) 400
From Sackville House Stables To Dissolve a Partnership
Un Parfum de Femme b c (2yrs) Mill Native (USA) - Hail To You (USA) (Kirtling) .... (Delta Bloodstock) 2,700
From Longsides Stables To Dissolve a Partnership
Captain Keystone b g (2yrs) Welsh Captain - Combe Grove Lady (Simbir)... (Cash) 1,050
Property of Mrs S Allen, from Serlby Hall Stable
Magication b f (3yrs) Nomination - Gundreda (Gunner B)........ (C Allan) 2,800
Property of Mr R Parker
Tobilam b g (2yrs) Tobin Lad (USA) - Esilam (Miss R Samuel) 580
Property of Mr B Nordan
Young Nod ch g (2yrs) Valiyar - Miss Racine (Dom Racine).............. (S Powell) 820

668

Property of a Partnership, from Breckenbrough House Stables
Creek Valley ch g (2yrs) Valiyar - Russell Creek (Sandy Creek)......... (J Tolbol) 950
From Kingsley House Stables To Dissolve a Partnership
Caspian Gold ch g (2yrs) Clantime - Parijoun (Manado)........................ (C Allen) 1,750
Property of Mr S P Page, from Kingsley House Stables
Roche Abbey b f (2yrs) Satco (FR) - Lyphalla (Lyphards Special).............. (Cash) 2,200
Property of Mrs R A Johnson, from Kingsley House Stables
Stardust Express b g (3yrs) Sylvan Express - Sancilia (Dalsaan).................. (Cormac McCormack) 3,100

From Kingsley House Stables To Dissolve a Partnership
Press Onward ch f (3yrs) Presidium - Ondine (Ballacashtal)... (M Wharmby) 1,100
Property of The Fairyhouse 1992 Partnership, from Kingsley House Stables
Take Your Partner b f (3yrs) Dance Of Life (USA) - Kentucky Belle (Glint Of Gold) (T Mattinson) 2,300
From Upper Longdon Stables
Garth gr g (5yrs) Petong - Doppio (Dublin Taxi)........................ (A P James) 1,450
From Upper Longdon Stables To Dissolve a Partnership
Cloudy Reef b f (3yrs) Cragador - Kellys Reef (Pitskelly).... (Sarah Hollinshead) 950
From Upper Longdon Stables
Raven's Return br c (2yrs) Astronef - Passage Falcon (Falcon).... (Sigyn Dysell) 4,300
From Manor House Stables (Butterwick)
Kaydaraj b f (2yrs) Domynsky - Uptown Girl (Caruso)........... (Zborojuka Vsetin) 1,100

669

From Trillium Place Stables
Sweet Disorder b f (3yrs) Never So Bold - Mists Of Avalon (USA) (Nureyev)...... (Johnny McKeever Bloodstock) 4,800
To Dissolve a Partnership
Jeldaire br m (10yrs) Radetsky - Jeldi (Tribal Chief) Covered by Gypsy Castle......... (F Iqbal) 1,100
Property of Mrs C T Pogson, from Allamoor Farm
Parsoness b m (9yrs) The Parson - Pautalia (Pardal) Covered by Dutch Treat ...... (A Dimock) 1,150
Property of Glenmore Stud, from Glenmore Stud, Co Tyrone, Ireland
Golden Verb ch m (8yrs) Proverb - Golden Hansel (Prince Hansel) Covered by Roaring Riva............... (C Lawson) 620
From Glenmore Stud, Co Tyrone, Ireland
Tickled To Bits b m (19yrs) Sweet Revenge - Anagram (Vilmoray) Covered by Roaring Riva................ (M Warmby) 500
Property of Glenmore Stud, from Glenmore Stud, Co Tyrone, Ireland
White Guest ch m (4yrs) Be My Guest (USA) - Lady Blanche (FR) (Sir Gaylord) Covered by Roaring Riva....... (Cash) 500
Glenmore Pride ch m (4yrs) Horage - Knocksoxan (Red Alert) Covered by Roaring Riva................ (F Iqbal) 500
Cherry Bob ch m (4yrs) Adonijah - Cherry Picking (Queen's Hussar) Covered by Roaring Riva........................ (Cash) 500
Property of a Partnership, from Easthorpe Hall Stud
Baroness Gymcrak b m (6yrs) Pharly (FR) - My Therape (Jimmy Reppin) Covered by Reprimand................. (C B A) 2,100
From Springfield House Stud
Gem Of Gold gr m (10yrs) Jellaby - Gold Ribbon (Blast) Covered by Timeless Times..................... (P Calver) 2,000

670

Property of Lord Howard de Walden, from Phantom House Stables

Alacrity b f (2yrs) Alzao (USA) - Hastening (Shirley Heights).......... (J T Doyle) 8,000

From Stormfield Stables, Co Kildare, Ireland

Quick Recovery b f (3yrs) Sharpo - In Triumph (USA) (Hoist The Flag)... (Cash) 950

Younger Days b g (2yrs) My Generation - Schlarigna (Kings Lake)..... (M Wane) 950

Property of a Partnership, from Moss Side Racing Stables

Sober Lad gr g (3yrs) Cyrano de Bergerac - Renzola (Dragonara) .... (Cormac McCormack Associates) 5,000

From Moss Side Racing Stables

Mad About Men b f (2yrs) Roarign Riva - Old Silver (Bold Lad) .... (Zborojuka Vsetin) 1,800

Olympic Bid gr f (2yrs) Absalom - Seven Seas (FR) (Riverman)........ (C Allen) 1,650

Property of Monkey Racing Club Ltd, from Moss Side Racing Stables

Monkey Boy b g (2yrs) Mazaad - Zareeta (Free State)................ (M Wane) 800

Bold Time Monkey ch f (2yrs) Bold Owl - Play For Time (Comedy Star) (M Tate) 1,350

Jersey Monkey b f (2yrs) Nordico (USA) - Quaver (Song).............. (J Tolbol) 900

Property of Exors of the late Mr Charles Carlow, from Cree Lodge Stables

Forrest Master b c (2yrs) Runnett - Fine Form (USA) (Fachendon).... (J Tolbol) 2,600

671

Property of a Partnership, from Somerville Lodge Stables

Moorland Dancer b f (2yrs) Common Grounds - Dance A Jig (Dance In Time) (E B A) 2,100

From Norton Grange Stables

Canny Lad b g (3yrs) Green Ruby (USA) - Young Whip (Bold Owl)........ (Cash) 2,300

Risky Gift b c (2yrs) Risk Me (FR) - Sir Tangs Gift (Runnett)...... (J McGrath) 580

Captain Taffy b c (2yrs) Welsh Captain - Miss Nelski (Most Secret)...... (Cash) 3,500

From Low House Stud

Carnea b f (3yrs) Belfort (FR) - Touch Of Luck (FR) (Tap On Wood)...... (Cash) 1,000

From Ashgill Stables

Oubeck Blue b f (2yrs) Chief Singer - Blue Brocade (Reform)... (Zborojuka Vsetin) 3,200

From Wold House Stables

Spray Of Orchids ch f (4yrs) Pennine Walk - Mana (GER) (Windwurf)..... (R Fahey) 2,000

From Northgate Lodge Stables

Saltpetre ch c (2yrs) Salt Dome (USA) - Kristar (Kris).................. (Cash) 520

Dockyard Dora b f (2yrs) Fijar Tango (FR) - Gleeful (Sayf El Arab)....... (J Tolbol) 2,500

Jarzela ch f (2yrs) Jareer (USA) - Soie Gentille (Shantung)........ (P Melton) 680

672

From Whitcliffe Grange Stables

Pride Of Pendle gr f (4yrs) Grey Desire - Pendle's Secret (Le Johnstan) .... (T Miller) 15,000

Digger Bates br c (2yrs) Roi Danzig (USA) - Chilblains (Hotfoot)............ (Cash) 1,200

From Diomed Stables

Persiansky b g (3yrs) Persian Bold - Astra Adastra (Mount Hagen).... (N Tinkler) 22,000

From Phoenix Lodge Stables

Daring Past b g (3yrs) Daring March - Better Buy Baileys (Sharpo)................ (David Minton Bloodstock) 10,000

From Sandy Brow Stables

Hod-Mod b c (3yrs) Digamist (USA) - Sallymiss (Tanfirion)...... (Miss Z Green) 1,900

Caldervale b g (3yrs) Midyan (USA) - Linguistic (Porto Bello)............ (Cash) 1,200

No Mean City ch g (2yrs) Digamist (USA) - Gothic Lady (Godswalk)... (J McGrath) 18,000

Hesfinmentalto b g (2yrs) Never So Bold - Nativity (USA) (Native Royalty) .... (P Matthiassen) 1,700

Saddam The Log ch f (2yrs) Music Boy - Sallytude (Tudor Music) (Sigyn Dysell) 2,100

Strangersardangers b f (2yrs) Classic Secret (USA) - Bally (Balidar)...... (P Melton) 800

Maz b f (2yrs) Cyrano de Bergerac - Godwyn (Yellow God).......... (A Bailey) 3,600

Mentalasanythin b g (4yrs) Ballacashtal (CAN) - Lafrowda (Crimson Beau) ..... (A Bailey) 12,500

673

Property of the Exors of the late Mrs James De Rothschild, from Beckhampton Stables

Kardelle b or gr f (3yrs) Kalaglow - Arderelle (FR) (Pharly)........................ (Group One Racing 1993 Ltd) 13,000

Property of the Second Kingsley House Partnership, from Kinglsey House Stables

Don't Be Koi ch f (2yrs) Try My Best - Saltoki (Ballad Rock)........... (Cash) 4,000

Property of the Fairyhouse 1992 Partnership, from Kingsley House Stables

Sweet Romeo ch g (3yrs) Local Suitor (USA) - Ladoucette (Bustino).......... (Cormac McCormack Associates) 6,200

Bold County b f (3yrs) Never So Bold - Hants (Exbury) .... (David Minton Bloodstock) 10,500

Arctic Guest ch f (3yrs) Arctic Tern (USA) - Sojourn (Be My Guest)... (R Johnston) 6,400

Property of the Second Kingsley House Partnership, from Kingsley House Stables

Certificate-X b f (2yrs) Never So Bold - Screenable (USA) (Screen).... (C B A) 9,000

Property of the Mariners Partnership

Up The Mariners ch f (2yrs) Classic Secret (USA) - Tuft Hill (Grundy) (S Robinson) 2,100

Property of Mr John G Brearley & Mrs Elizabeth Berry, from Glasgow House Stables

Blue Radiance b f (3yrs) Skyliner - Stellaris (Star Appeal).... (R A M Racecourses) 2,400

Property of Mr J A Turney, from Glasgow House Stables

Bright Gem b f (3yrs) Heraldiste (USA) - Spring Bride (Auction Ring)... (D Fifer) 1,550

Property of Miss N A Harrod

Gold Ford gr g (3yrs) Belfort (FR) - Hunting Gold (Sonnen Gold)........ (A P Pain) 1,100

674

Property of Mr G Parker, from Whispering Trees Racing Stables

Patchouli's Pet b m (10yrs) Mummy's Pet - Primage (Primera)............ (Cash) 1,050

From Fitzroy House Stables

Waiter's Eye ch c (2yrs) The Minstrel (CAN) - Regal Heiress (English Prince)....... (Karen Ensen) 1,300

(YEARLINGS)

Property of Mr David Morton, from the Gables Stud

b y c Chief Singer - Lomond Ring (Lomond) (T M Jones) 1,000

Property of Mrs Valerie Knight, from Welland Paddocks

gr y c Faustus (USA) - Kenmara (FR) (Kenmare).................. (J McGrath) 2,400

Property of Lance Bell & Partners

b or gr y c Most Welcome - Blue Flower (FR) (Carwhite).......... (W T Kemp) 580

gr y c Satin Wood - Slipperose (Persepolis) (Newbridge Stables Ltd) 1,100

Property of Mr Peter Dowson, from Norton Grove Stud

b y c Marching On - La Pepper (Workboy) (P Haslam) 1,050

Property of Mr P Storey

b y f Sulaafah (USA) - Dominance (Dominion)................. (A W Robinson) 700

From Old Hall Stables

b c (2yrs) Lochnager - Ramas Silk (Amber Rama)................. (K A Lynam) 4,000

Property of Mr William Johnstone, from Thorntoun Estate Stables

b y g Durgam (USA) - Glen Maddie (Reasonable)........... (M Johnston) 3,500

b y c Durgam (USA) - Monaco Ville (Rheingold) .... (Johnny McKeever Bloodstock) 4,000

ch y c Durgam (USA) - Miromaid (Simply Great)......................... (Cash) 4,500

675

Property of Miss Elizabeth Streatfield, from Glyme Bank Stud

ch y c King Among Kings - Market Blues (Porto Bello).............. (T W Kemp) 2,000

Property of a Partnership, from Glyme Bank Stud

b y c King Among Kings - Jacinda (Thatching)............ (Browne Bloodstock) 600

Property of Miss Elizabeth Streatfield, from Glyme Bank Stud

b y c King Among Kings - Santo Star (Monsanto).............. (J McGrath) 600

Property of Mrs G Murton

b y c Vouchsafe - Baliliyca (Balidar) (T Lee) 400

Property of Mrs V O'Brien, from Knowles Bank Stud

b y c Today And Tomorrow - Alexzena (Upper Case)............. (A Galbraith) 400

b y f Today And Tomorrow - Targow Girl (Targowice)............ (Linda Perratt) 700

b y c Today And Tomorrow - Sum Star (Comedy Star).. (Elmhurst Bloodstock) 700

b y f Today And Tomorrow - Rectory Maid (Tina's Pet)............. (R McKellar) 450

b y f Today And Tomorrow - Capel Lass (The Brianstan)............... (T Lee) 400

Property of Shade Oak Stud, from Goldford Stud

ch y c Gunner B - Kirsheda (Busted) (Cash) 920

b y f Derrylin - Emerin (King Emperor)..... (P Cundell) 2,700

676

Property of Mrs Jackie Murray, from Moss Side Stables

b y c Ardross - Harmoney Jane (Hardboy).. (Cash) 4,000

Property of Mr John Bury, from Primrose Ghyll Farm

b y c Insan (USA) - Linda's Design (Persian Bold).. (Johnny McKeever Bloodstock) 6,600

Property of Messrs Colin & Ellis Plumb

ch y c Mr Fluorocarbon - Sweet Rosa (Absalom).................. (A Smith) 700

Property of a Partnership

gr y f Sizzling Melody - Pale Glow (Kalaglow)................ (P Downes) 1,000

Property of Mr Alf Watson, from Southfield Stables

b y f Clantime - Ascot Lass (Touching Wood).................. (D Arbuthnot) 2,100

Property of Rodvic Ltd, from Nuthurst Farm Stud

b y f Macmillion - Safe Passage (Charlottown)..................... (J Pearce) 5,000

Property of Mr E G A Smith

b y f Sulaafah (USA) - Freedom Line (Absalom).............. (C B Molson) 450

Property of Lance Bell & Partners

b y f Beveled (USA) - Ballafort (Ballacashtal) .... (J N Ranson) 2,100

b y f Lochnager - Sky Mariner (Julio Mariner).................... (W L Barker) 1,000

b y f Emarati (USA) - Gas Only (Northfields) (M Ellerby) 600

677

Property of Ian Redford Ltd

b y f Rambo Dancer (CAN) - Errol Emerald (Dom Racine).................. (Cash) 1,200

Property of Carrier House Stables

ro or gr y c Hallgate - Pineapple's Pride (John de Coombe)......... (P Cundell) 2,800

Property of Mr H Young

b y c Primative Rising (USA) - Anne's Gift (Ballymoss)........... (Mary Reveley) 9,000

Property of Mr T C Small, from Lower Farm

b y f Fearless Action (USA) - Drynachan (Teenoso)................. (S Powell) 400

b y f Fearless Action (USA) - Lady Jewel (Kibenka)....................... (Cash) 400

Property of Mrs M Leonard & Mrs E Ward

ch y f Kabour - Boom Shanty (Dragonara Palace).................... (G West) 650

Property of Mr & Mrs A R Dimmock, from Moor Cottage Farm

b y f Kabour - Final Cast (Saulingo)........ (Galoppens Venner) 1,200

Property of Miss C J Butroid

b y f Sirgame - Cherry Volante (Alto Volante)...................... (S Powell) 420

Property of Mr W Gott

b y c Rambling River - Hands Off (Nearly A Hand)......................... (Cash) 750

Property of Mr W Gott & Mrs I Bird

b y c Sylvan Express - Addison's Jubilee (Sparkler)..................... (Cash) 10,000

678

From North Allerton Farm

b y c Durgam (USA) - Canty's Gold (Sonnen Gold)....... (J McKeever Bloodstock) 3,000

Property of Messrs James C McGee & Gordon Pollock, from North Allerton Farm

ch y f Good Times (ITY) - Romany Home (Gabitat).................. (J Byrne) 3,000

Property of Mr George N Perratt, from North Allerton Farm

b y f Precocious - Squawbil (Nicholas Bill).. (J McKeever Bloodstock) 4,000

Property of Melbourne Hall Stud, from Melbourne Hall Stud

b y f Crofthall - Rhythmella (Tudor Rhythm) (A Smith) 1,000

Property of Mrs E Stringer, from Melbourne Hall Stud

b y c Domynsky - Blushing Rose (Coquelin) (David Minton Bloodstock) 2,800

PRIVATE SALES

Property of Moor Top Farm Stables

b g (2yrs) Kala Shikari - So Gifted (Niniski) (D Morley) 900

RE-SUBMITTED

Property of J M Roy

Thistle Loch br f (4yrs) Lochnager - Jane Roy (Royalty)................. (Cash) 1,800

Property of Riston Whins Racing Ltd

Blundell's Boy b g (3yrs) Mansingh (USA) - Cala Galera (Mummy's Pet) (H Young) 590

679

DONCASTER
Friday, October 22nd
(Yearlings)

To Dissolve a Partnership

b y f Gallic League - Misniniski (Niniski).... (S Norton) 6,400

Property of Jeremy Green & Sons, from Bickmarsh Stud

b y c Taufan (USA) - Merry Rous (Rousillon) .... (B.B.A.) 7,600

Property of The Mathieson Partnership, from Melbourne Hall Stud

Twice Purple b y c Then Again - Tyrian Belle (Enchantment).. (A C Mathieson) 4,000

Property of Melbourne Hall Stud, from Melbourne Hall Stud

b y f Clantime - Casbar Lady (Native Bazaar) .... (N Bycroft) 2,200

Property of Mr & Mrs D J Allen

b y f Petong - Ra Ra Girl (Shack).......... (B McMahon) 2,100

Property of Mr J H H Benbow

ch y f Cree Song - Dalby Girl (Young Man) (B McMahon) 420

From Tronton Stud

b y f Don't Forget Me - Vera Musica (Stop The Music)............... (D Brown) 2,400

From Fen Farm Barns

b y f Superlative - Fatal Fascination (Imperial Fling)...................... (Cash) 3,000

Property of Mr W G H Barrons, from Moyrath Stud

b y c Mulhollande (USA) - Nurse Tyra (USA) (Dr Blum).... (Peter Doyle Bloodstock) 4,200

From Northgate Lodge Stud

ch y c Indian Forest (USA) - Warthill Lady (Hittite Glory)........... (Mel Brittain) 2,000

b y f Grey Desire - Barefoot Contessa (Homeric).................. (G West) 1,050

680

Property of Mr W G Barker, from Tancred Stud

b y f Sylvan Express - Willow Walk (Farm Walk)..................... (S Powell) 400

ch y c Clantime - Mischievous Miss (Niniski)............. (Mrs M Reveley) 5,400

Property of Mrs S E Wilsdon, from Glyn Common Farm

gr or ro y f Belfort (FR) - Maria Da Gloria (St Chad)............. (Stefan Uppstrom) 2,500

Property of Mrs R Lucas, from Ferry Fields Stables

b y c Handsome Sailor - Ebony Park (Local Suitor)....................... (Cash) 6,400

Property of Messrs G & J Brown, from Castle Farm Stud

gr y f Rambo Dancer (CAN) - Mrs Gray (Red Sunset)........... (Stefan Uppstrom) 3,800

Property of Mr & Mrs J B Walker, from Ravendale Top Farm Stud

ch y f Grey Desire - Pour Moi (Bay Express) ....(D Haydn-Jones) 2,300

b y f Nomination - Beretta (Moorestyle) ... (J McKeever Bloodstock) 1,600

Property of Mr B C Allen, from Rudry Park Stud

ch y f Rich Charlie - Ackabarrow (Laser Light)..................... (D Moffatt) 4,600

Property of Mr Gino P Bernacchi, from Eat Caplaw Stud

b y c Skyliner - Sveltissima (Dunphy) ...... (G J Harris) 2,600

Property of Mrs V O'Brien, from Knowles Bank Stud

b y c Today And Tomorrow - Too Familiar (Oats).......... (Elmhurst Bloodstock) 700

b y f Today And Tomorrow - Schula (Kala Shikari)........ (Elmhurst Bloodstock) 400

b y c Today And Tomorrow - Hamrahi (Final Straw)......... (Elmhurst Bloodstock) 500

681

From Golden Vale Stud, Co Limerick, Ireland

br y f Hatim (USA) - Jenny Dancer (Skyliner) .... (Cash) 1,500

Property of Mr R C Lloyd
b y c Celestial Storm (USA) - Hot Tan (Hotfoot).... (J McKeever Bloodstock) 4,800
Property of Mrs P E Bell, from Warth Beck Stables
b y f Dunbeath (USA) - Spanish Bold (Tower Walk)..................... (S Powell) 600
Property of a Partnership, from Waltonfields Stud
b y f Domynsky - Cornflower Blue (Tyrnavos).......... (Clairtex (Gwent) Ltd) 1,700
Property of Mr W Taylor
b y f Never So Bold - Convivial (Nordance) (G J Harris) 900
b y f Dowsing (USA) - Unearthed (Electric) (Don Lee) 650
Property of White Lodge Farm Stud, from White Lodge Farm Stud
b y g Lugana Beach - Two Friendly (Be Friendly).................. (N Bycroft) 1,400
Property of Mr M J Rozenbroek
b y f Doon Lad - Responder (Vitiges) ...... (S Powell) 720
Property of Mr & Mrs B T Chambers
b y c Damister (USA) - Smelter (Prominer) (Ettore Pistoletti) 5,300
Property of Mr D D Brown, from High Close Stables
b or br y f Lugana Beach - Not So Shy (Star Appeal)......... (Clairtex (Gwent) Ltd) 850

682

Property of Mr & Mrs T K Knox, from Whitworth Stud
ch y c Good Times (ITY) - Drumley Dawn (Red Sunset)........ (Ettore Pistoletti) 5,300
Property of Mrs G J Rowe, from Rowecliffe Stud
b y f Tina's Pet - Highland Rossie (Pablond) (C Wildman) 1,350
Property of a Partnership, from Hunsley House Stud
b y f Rambo Dancer (CAN) - Under The Wing (Aragon)........... (Sigyn Dysell) 1,600
b y f Rambo Dancer (CAN) - Skarberg (FR) (Noir Et Or)................. (R Dixon) 1,100
Property of Norton Grove Stud Ltd., from Norton Grove Stud
gr y c Jester - Royal Huntress (Royal Avenue).......................... (Cash) 1,200
b y f Jester - Hill Of Fare (Brigadier Gerard) (Alf Smith) 500
Property of Mr R T Lingwood, from Norton Grove Stud
b y f Kind Of Hush - Dear Glenda (Gold Song).................. (B M Murray) 720
Property of Mrs G C Stanley, from Firle Stud
b y f Scottish Reel - Ballyreef (Ballymore).. (S Hatfield) 580
Property of Crisps Farm Stud, from Crisps Farm Stud
b y c Cree Song - Mimika (Lorenzaccio) ... (Alf Smith) 3,100
b y f Cree Song - La Balconne (Taj Dewan) (Alf Smith) 750

683

Property of Mr C Blades, from Thornbush Farm Stables
ch y c Clantime - Cool Number (Swing Easy)....... (J McKeever Bloodstock) 3,700
Property of Mrs D R Schreiber, from Hall Park Farm
ch y g Domynsky - Linanhot (Hot Spark) ... (Southburgh Manor Stud) 2,500
Property of Mr P R John, from Park Farm
br y c Adbaas (USA) - Keep Silent (Balidar) (B Palling) 2,000
Property of Mrs M Woolgar, from Primrose Ghyll Farm
b y c Governor General - Lismore (Relkino) (T Easterby) 4,300
Property of Mrs S Weinstein, from Spa Stud
gr y f Green Ruby (USA) - True Liberty (Indian King)......... (Gerald Spencer) 2,000
Property of Mrs J Mackie
b y c Crowning Honors (CAN) - Silicon Lady (Mummy's Game)............ (B.B.A.) 2,400
Property of Mrs J Mackie, from Barton Hall
b y c Efisio - Miss Nanna (Vayrann) .... (T Easterby) 4,400
From Thornby Stud
b y c Zalazl (USA) - Impala Lass (Kampala) (B McMahon) 7,000
b or br y f Efisio - Power And Red (Skyliner) .... (Rae Guest) 1,000
Property of Mr Patrick J Lombard, from Killatty Stud, Co Cork, Ireland
b or br y c Gallic League - Tiefland (Right Tack)........ (Peter Doyle Bloodstock) 5,000

684

Property of Mr R C Lloyd
gr y c Zalazl (USA) - Wild Rosie (Warpath) (B.B.A.) 3,600
Property of Bearstone Stud
ch y f Mon Tresor - Tamango Lady (Shack) (C Thornton) 900
From Killeenlea Stud, Co Kildare, Ireland
b y c Fayruz - Ellen's Luck (Tap On Wood) (G Troeller) 7,800
ch y c Rhoman Rule (USA) - Chocolate Baby (Kashiwa)..... (Peter Diamond) 1,900
From Golden Vale Stud, Co Limerick, Ireland
b y f Gallic League - Lune de Miel (Kalamoun)............... (Ettore Pistoletti) 2,100
b y c Gallic League - Asturiana (Julio Mariner)........... (Sagittarius Bloodstock) 3,000
Property of a Partnership, from Manor House Farm Stables (Butterwick)
ch y f Efisio - La Crima (Runnymede)...... (D Haydn-Jones) 6,000
Property of Mr D Read, from Manor House Farm Stables
b y f Aragon - Hala (Persian Bold) (R Fahey) 900
Property of Mr D D Brown, from High Close Stables
br or b y f Skyliner - Oratava Valley (Mansingh) .... (Cormac McCormack Associates) 3,800
Property of Mr G W Westgarth
ch y c Sylvan Express - Lottie Rose (Blakeney)........... (W G M Turner) 2,000

685

Property of Mr & Mrs B T Chambers
b y f Reprimand - Emmylou (Arctic Tern) .. (E Weymes) 2,000

Property of Llety Farms, from Llety Farms
b y f Merdon Melody - Silvery Moon (Lorenzaccio)........ (Ettore Pistoletti) 2,000
b y f Merdon Melody - Piccadilly Rose (Reform)............... (Jack Berry) 2,400

Property of a Partnership, from Park Farm
b y c Simply Great (FR) - Now Then (Sandford Lad).................. (B Palling) 4,000

Property of Mr & Mrs G R Davies, from Earlsfield Stud
b y c Merdon Melody - Earlsfield (Wolverlife).. (Peter Doyle Bloodstock) 2,000

Property of Mr & Mrs T K Knox, from Whitworth Stud
ch y c Faustus (USA) - Green Pool (Whistlefield).................. (R O'Ryan) 5,200

Property of Mr S Hatfield, from High Onn Stud
ch y c Hadeer - By Surprise (Young Generation)......................... (Cash) 4,200

Property of Mr T Jarvis, from Mill Farm Stud
ch y c Interrex (CAN) - Harmony Heights (Music Boy)....... (Stefan Uppstrom) 4,500

Property of Crisps Farm Stud, from Crisps Farm Stud
b y f Cree Song - Klairove (Averof) .... (R F Davis) 3,000

From Shinglis Stud, Co Westmeath, Ireland
ch y c Glenstal (USA) - Height Of Elegance (Shirley Heights).................... (Cormac McCormack Associates) 4,600

686

Property of Mr David Barry, Co Limerick, Ireland
b y f Phardante (FR) - Brandywell (Skyliner) (Mr Stringer) 800

Property of Ian Flockton Developments Ltd, from Legbourne Abbey Farm
b y c Reprimand - Tree Mallow (Malicious) (J Delahooke) 27,000

Property of Bylon Farmers, from Bylon Farmers
b y c Handsome Sailor - Fire Sprite (Mummy's Game)........ (Jack Berry) 6,000

Property of Newmarket Thoroughbred Breeders (PLC), from Meddler Stud
ch y c Hadeer - Dead End (Bold Lad) ...... (B.B.A.) 600

Property of R E A Bott (Wigmore St) Ltd, from Meddler Stud
ch y f Old Vic - Tuppy (USA) (Sharpen Up) (Ettore Pistoletti) 2,100

Property of a Partnership, from Burton Agnes Stud
b y c Beveled (USA) - The Ranee (Royal Palace).................... (J Glover) 3,400

Property of Mr T Newsome, from Burton Agnes Stud
b y c Kind Of Hush - Winter Resort (Miami Springs)................ (J McGrath) 2,500

Property of Messrs P & A G Venner, from Petches Farm
b y f Petong - Water Pageant (Welsh Pageant).................. (B J McMath) 8,000

Property of Branston Stud, from Branston Stud
b y f Hallgate - Bare Spectacle (Welsh Pageant).................... (Cash) 2,400

Property of I & E Macgregor Partnership, from Pinkerton Stud
gr y c Bairn (USA) - Real Silver (Silly Season)........ (J McKeever Bloodstock) 3,200

687

Property of James Thom & Sons, from Hall Farm Stud
ch y c Handsome Sailor - Bellanoora (Ahonoora).. (J McKeever Bloodstock) 9,600

From Hailthorpe Farm
b y c Anita's Prince - Royal Accord (King Of Spain).......... (Clairtex (Gwent) Ltd) 3,300

From Furnace Mill Stud
ch y c Double Schwartz - Silk Trade (Auction Ring)............... (P Haslam) 15,000
b y c Contract Law (USA) - Brave Juliet (Sexton Blake) .... (Cormack McCormac Associates) 7,800
ch y c My Generation - Secret Lightning (USA) (Secretariat)......... (Jack Berry) 10,000
b y c Astronef - Stapelea (FR) (Faraway Son)..................... (E Weymes) 7,600

From Southburgh Manor Stud
gr or ro y c Absalom - Western Line (High Line)................ (J Delahooke) 20,000

Property of Mr Michael English, from Southburgh Manor Stud
b y c Mazaad - Miss Spencer (Imperial Fling)...................... (B.B.A.) 5,400

Property of Mr G Dudfield
b y f Primo Dominie - Mature (Welsh Pageant)............... (Ettore Pistoletti) 2,100

Property of Mr John Kent, from Ballyhampshire Stud, Co Cork, Ireland
ch y f Absalom - Steffi (Precocious) .... (J McKeever Bloodstock) 4,200

688

From Meadowlands Stud, Co Tipperary, Ireland
b y c Fairy King (USA) - Look Of Love (General Assembly).................. (Peter Doyle Bloodstock) 5,000

Property of Mr Samuel Oliver, from Honeypig Stud
ch y c Accordion - Erck (Sun Prince) (Cash) 1,800

Property of Mr D B Lamplough, from Melbourne Hall Stud
b y c Superpower - Malindi (Mansingh) .... (J McKeever Bloodstock) 4,400

Property of Mr P Russell, from Wood Farm Stud
ch y f Scottish Reel - Wigeon (Divine Gift) (David Nicholls) 5,200

Property of a Partnership, from Wood Farm Stud
b y f Tina's Pet - Faw (Absalom) .... (Clairtex (Gwent) Ltd) 1,000

Property of Dandy's Farm, from Dandy's Farm
b y c Presidium - Phamilla (Bellypha) (Cash) 2,500

Property of Mr Peter Baugh, from Woodlands Farm
gr y f Lochnager - Olibanum (Frankincense) (J Quinn) 6,000

Property of Mr R Kilcran, from Carlton Stud
br y f Cyrano de Bergerac - Zareeta (Free State)........ (Cormac McCormack Associates) 4,800
Property of a Partnership, from Hedgeholme Stud
ch y c Prince Sabo - This Sensation (Balidar) .... (G Troeller) 2,800
From Hunsley House Stud
b y f Rambo Dancer (CAN) - Strathclair (Klairon)........ (P T Dalton) 1,550

689

Property of Mr R Vardy
b y c Hallgate - Bamdoro (Cavo Doro)..... (J McKeever Bloodstock) 4,000
Property of Mr E J B Maude, from Etchingham Stud
b y c Dunbeath (USA) - Hannie Caulder (Workboy)........ (J Delahooke) 4,200
Property of Mr T Dodd, from Bonnyhale Stables
b y c Handsome Sailor - Kopjes (Bay Express)........ (Clairtex (Gwent) Ltd) 5,000
Property of Norton Grove Stud Ltd, from Norton Grove Stud
gr y f Kind Of Hush - Misty Rocket (Roan Rocket)........ (D Ford) 900
Property of Mrs G C Stanley, from Firle Stud
b y f Dunbeath (USA) - Rillandel (Wolver Hollow)........ (P Calver) 850
From Golden Vale Stud, Co Limerick, Ireland
br y f Gallic League - Little Wild Duck (Great Heron)........ (W G M Turner) 2,300
Property of Mrs C Humphrey, from Orchard Rise
b y c Beveled (USA) - Miss Monte Carlo (Reform).... (J McKeever Bloodstock) 4,900
Property of a Partnership, from Brickfield Stud
b y f Conquering Hero (USA) - Darine (Nonoalco)........ (C Thornton) 10,000
Property of Mr R M Eggo, from Easter Cruicksfield Stud
ch y f Gildoran - Mac's Sister (Krayyan).... (J Hamilton) 1,200
Property of Crisps Farm Stud, from Crisps Farm Stud
b y c Cree Song - Little Tich (Great Nephew)........ (M Crossland) 400
ch y f Cree Song - Elsocko (Swing Easy)... (M Harris) 400

690

Property of Mr J Bird, from Manor Farm Stables
b y f Chilibang - Vent Du Soir (Main Reef) (Cash) 1,200
Property of Lord Crawshaw, from Whatton House Stables (Loughborough)
ch y c Domynsky - Armour Of Light (Hot Spark)........ (E.I.L. Bloodstock) 3,000
PRIVATE SALES
Property of Mrs L Wright
ch y c Faustus (USA) - Loveville (USA) (Assert)........ (A Stringer) 1,600
From Redpender Stud, Co Kilkenny, Ireland
gr y c Fayruz - Ikala (Lashkari)...... (Cash) 2,000
From Honeypig Stud
ch y c Jareer (USA) - Godhood (Green God) (P Bamford) 2,300
From Hunsley House Stud
b y c Then Again - Fancy Flight (FR) (Arctic Tern)........ (M Channon) 2,000
From Golden Vale Stud, Co Limerick, Ireland
ch y f Al Hareb (USA) - Yavarro (Raga Navarro)........ (C Allen) 3,250
Property of M F Bloodstock Services Ltd, from Brickfield Stud
b y c Hallgate - Orange Parade (Dara Monarch)........ (Cash) 4,000

691

DONCASTER
Saturday, October 23rd (Yearlings)

Property of Miss K Higgs
b y f Hallgate - Jussoli (Don)........ (A Brandsbury) 1,500
Property of Mrs K Walton
b y c Clantime - Chikala (Pitskelly)........ (R Ormsby) 2,400
Property of a Partnership, from New England Stud
b y f Distant Relative - Haunting (Lord Gayle).. (Johnny McKeever Bloodtock) 12,500
Property of a Partnership
b y f Puissance - Kind Of Shy (Kind Of Hush)........ (J Berry) 4,000
Property of Rockhouse Farms Ltd
b y f Puissance - Sincerely Yours (Kind Of Hush) (Johnny McKeever Bloodstock) 2,000
Property of Messrs J Forsyth & W Cully
b y f Puissance - Regal Salute (Dara Monarch)........ (E O'Leary) 900
Property of Mr G Platt, from Bearstone Stud
gr y f Puissance - Rage Glen (Grey Mirage) (J Berry) 5,600
Property of Mrs M Tyreman
ch y f Move Off - Lehmans Lot (Oats)..... (Cash) 500
Property of Mrs N Stephen, from Sporting House Stud
b y c Runton - Lady Ever-So-Sure (Malicious)........ (J Berry) 1,800
Property of Gymcrak Thoroughbred Breeding, from Howldale Stables
b y f Domynsky - Gymcrak Lovebird (Taufan)........ (T Easterby) 2,200

692

Property of Mr L T Roberts, from The Greenfield Farm Stables
b y f Kind Of Hush - Lady Carol (Lord Gayle) .... (N Bycroft) 1,800
To Dissolve a Partnership
b y c K-Battery - Bonny's Pet (Mummy's Pet)........ (W Elsey) 1,400
Property of Upperwood Farm Stud, from Upperwood Farm Stud
b y f Picea - Mey Madam (Song)........ (Johnny McKeever Bloodstock) 650

Property of Mr A R Peirce, from Upperwood Farm Stud
b y f Mazilier (USA) - English Mint (Jalmood)................. (J Cloake) 2,000

Property of Miss Helen Monteith, from Aynho Stud
b y g Lugana Beach - Fara (Castle Keep)... (S Powell) 700
b y f Governor General - Saltina (Bustino).. (S Powell) 900

Property of Mr E Gregory, from Woodcote Stud
br y f Jalmood (USA) - Cool Combination (Indian King)............... (B Palling) 1,350

Property of Messrs F Steele & C Barnfather, from Crawsknowe Stud
b y f Singing Steven - Miss Drummond (The Brianstan).......... (R Voorspuy) 3,000

Property of Mrs F A Veasey, from Cinder Farm Stud
ch y f Beveled (USA) - Salinas (Bay Express).............. (M W Ellerby) 800

Property of Mr D Woods, from Trowel Stud
ch y c Komaite (USA) - Silently Yours (USA) (Silent Screen) .... (Cormac McCormack Associates) 3,800

693

Property of Mrs Michael McNeil, from Carseriggan House Stables
b y f Bluebird (USA) - Miss Display (Touch Paper)................. (Conjem Ltd) 5,000

Property of a Partnership
b y f Superpower - Ile de Reine (Ile de Bourbon)................... (D Riley) 1,000

Property of Mr J Armstrong, from Etchingham Stud
ch y f Superpower - Rustilly (Busted)...... (Cash) 600

Property of Melbourne Hall Stud, from Melbourne Hall Stud
ch y f Crofthall - Firdale Flyer (The Go-Between).................. (D Riley) 750

Property of Mr A L Robinson, from Melbourne Hall Stud
ch y f Clantime - Moorhill (Vaigly Great) ... (J Berry) 3,300

Property of Mr B Minty
b y g Full Extent (USA) - Delightful Diane (Kalaglow).................. (J Berry) 2,000

Property of Viscount Leverhulme, from Thornton Manor Stud
b y f Jupiter Island - Harifa (Local Suitor)... (Mrs M Reveley) 1,000

Property of By Order of The Sheriff of Lancashire
b y c Deploy - Protected (FR) (Blakeney)... (W L Barker) 1,900
b y f Puissance - Bridoon (Brigadier Gerard) (Cash) 900

Property of Mrs J Trentham, from Spa Stud
b y g Green Ruby (USA) - Let Me Bee (Taste Of Honey).......... (S Powell) 550

694

Property of Mr R Parker, from Spa Stud
b y g Green Ruby (USA) - Esilam (Frimley Park)......................... (Cash) 1,400

Property of Merton Stud, from Merton Stud
gr y c Presidium - Little Token (Shack)..... (Johnny McKeever Bloodstock) 4,000

Property of Mr J R Mitchell, from Beechgrove Stud
br y f Statoblest - Indian Wells (Reliance II) (D Haydn-Jones) 4,000
b y f Blow The Whistle - Whispering Sea (Bustino).............. (Hefin Jones) 520

Property of a Partnership, from Boulstone Stud
b y c Robellino (USA) - Tizona (Pharly)..... (D Baron) 1,250

Property of Mr T Umpleby, from Ye Olde Mill House Stud
b y c Grey Desire - Richesse (FR) (Faraway Son)......................... (S Powell) 620
ch y c Hallgate - Petite Elite (Anfield)...... (N Bycroft) 900

Property of Miss S Previte, from Lemans Barn Farm
ch y c Weldnaas (USA) - Sunny Annie (Sunley Builds).......... (J McRobert) 650

Property of Highclere Stud Ltd
b y f Sharrood (USA) - Greek Goddess (Young Generation)................. (Peter Doyle Bloodstock) 4,600

From Highclere Stud
b y f Robellino (USA) - Lady Tap (Red Sunset).................. (L T Winks) 700

695

Property of Highclere Stud Ltd
b y f Sharrood (USA) - Waitingformargaret (Kris)........ (Peter Doyle Bloodstock) 9,000

Property of a Partnership, from Eaton House Stud
ch y c Risk Me (FR) - Late Idea (Tumble Wind)...................... (D Riley) 1,000

From Bruns Farm Stud
ch y f Mazilier (USA) - La Bleu (Blue Cashmere).................. (T Marshall) 500

Property of Mr R B Warren, from Nancherrow Stud
ch y c Forzando - Lafrowda (Crimson Beau) (E I L Bloodstock) 3,800
b y f Warrshan (USA) - Divissima (Music Boy).................... (C Wildman) 2,300

Property of Havenwood Construction Ltd, from Lodge Farm
ch y c Dunbeath (USA) - Mrs Mills (Ballad Rock)..................... (C Tinkler) 2,100

RE-SUBMITTED

From Harness Grove Stud
b y c Komaite (USA) - Starkist (So Blessed) (R W Jaines) 1,400

696

NEWMARKET
Monday, October 25th

Property of a Partnership, from Folly House Stables
Calibrate b g (3yrs) Blakeney - Vernair (USA) (Super Concorde (USA))..... (C Dysell) 800

Connect (IRE) b g (2yrs) Waajib - My My Marie (Artaius (USA)).... (D H Barons) 2,100

To Dissolve a Paretnership, from Corner House Stables

Redgrave ch c (2yrs) Hotfoot - Dame Du Moulin (Shiny Tenth)... (S A Edwards) 800

Property of Mr Daniel Couper, from Cree Lodge Stables

Persian Charmer (IRE) b g (3yrs) Persian Heights - Merlins Charm (USA) (Bold Bidder)........................ (B B A) 10,000

Merlinsrisk (IRE) b c (2yrs) Kris - Merlins Charm (USA) (Bold Bidder) .... (Johnny McKeever Bloodstock) 4,800

Property of a Partnership, from Cree Lodge Stables

Mister Piste (IRE) b c (2yrs) Fayruz - Gluhwein (Ballymoss)........ (M Thwaites) 16,000

Property of Mr D Munnisett, from Lewes Racing Stables

Apache Prince gr g (6yrs) Red Sunset - Maxi Girl (My Swanee)...... (C Mann) 4,000

Property of Mr J W Biswell, from Chestnut Tree Stables

Gloriette br f (2yrs) Petoski - Reflected Glory (SWE) (Relko)...... (J McGrath) 1,300

Property of a Partnership, from Revida Place Stables

Strike-A-Pose ch f (3yrs) Blushing Scribe (USA) - My Bushbaby (Hul A Hul) ...... (B J Llewellyn) 3,000

Tee Gee Jay b f (3yrs) Northern Tempest (USA) - Immaculate Girl (Habat) .... (C Williams) 1,450

697

From Musley Bank Stables

Certain Way (IRE) ch c (3yrs) Sure Blade (USA) - Ruffling Point (Gorytus (USA)) (D Kent) 4,000

Gallic Gent b g (2yrs) Gallic League - Gentalyn (Henbit (USA))........... (Cash) 600

Property of a Partnership

Newbury Coat b g (3yrs) Chilibang - Deanta In Eirinn (Red Sunset)......... (B B A) 6,000

Property of Sporting Partners, from Foxhill Stables

Sporting Story (IRE) b f (2yrs) Classic Secret (USA) - Coral Cave (Ashmore (FR))......................... (F Iqbal) 1,150

Sporting Start b g (2yrs) Mansingh (USA) - Boa (Mandrake Major)....... (H Ripel) 3,200

Sporting Script (IRE) b g (2yrs) Script Ohio (USA) - Coconut Grove (What A Guest) (B B A) 1,000

Sporting Heir (IRE) b or br g (2yrs) Anita's Prince - Royal Accord (King Of Spain).. (C P Wildman) 3,000

Property of Mr F H Lee, from Little Stanneylands Racing Stables

Bold Seven (IRE) ch f (3yrs) Never So Bold - First Blush (Ela-Mana-Mou) .... (Abdi Aziz M Al Saud) 6,200

Property of a Partnership, from Little Stanneylands Racing Stables

Crystal Jack (FR) b g (5yrs) Crystal Glitters (USA) - Cackle (USA) (Crow (FR))...... (Johnny McKeever Bloodstock) 3,000

Danzig Island (IRE) b c (2yrs) Roi Danzig (USA) - Island Morn (USA) (Our Native (USA))........................ (B B A) 9,200

698

Property of Mr F H Lee, from Little Stanneylands Racing Stables

Move Smartly (IRE) b c (3yrs) Smarten (USA) - Key Maneuver (USA) (Key To Content (USA))................ (B B A) 2,200

Property of a Partnership, from Little Stanneylands Racing Stables

Peacefull Reply (USA) b c (3yrs) Hold Your Peace (USA) - Drone Answer (USA) (Drone)...................... (B B A) 4,000

Sir Harry Hardman b h (5yrs) Doulab (USA) - Song Grove (Song) .... (Abdi Aziz M Al Saud) 26,000

Property of Mr F H Lee, from Little Stanneylands Racing Stables

Umbubuzi (USA) ch c (3yrs) Timeless Native (USA) - Making Rounds (USA) (Dr Blum (USA))........... (C Boutin) 6,000

Property of Crestsmart Ltd, from Cedar Lodge Stables

Coconut Johnny br c (3yrs) King Of Spain - Gentle Gypsy (Jubnius (USA))......... (R Durant) 5,000

Property of Mr M Quinn, from Cedar Lodge Stables

Cyarna Quinn (IRE) b f (2yrs) Cyrano de Bergerac - Lisdoonvarna (Miami Springs)............. (C P Wildman) 7,000

Property of Mrs P Lewis, from Cedar Lodge Stables

Gigue ch f (2yrs) Squill (USA) - Rengaine (FR) (Music Boy)........... (V Palaty) 4,600

Property of Mr M Channon, from Cedar Lodge Stables

Henry's Luck b c (2yrs) Bold Owl - Rahesh (Raffingora)....... (Mr Charalambides) 7,200

From Cedar Lodge Stables

Keys Of Silca b c (2yrs) Hallgate - Princess Silca Key (Grundy)............ (B B A) 5,800

Property of Mr A Kinghorn, from Cedar Lodge Stables

Little Hooligan b or br c (2yrs) Rabdan - Nutwood Emma (Henbit (USA)) .... (J McGrath) 800

699

From Wellbottom Lodge Stables

Granville Corner ch g (3yrs) Formidable (USA) - Zilda (FR) (Zino) (B J McMath) 900

Property of His Grace the Duke of Devonshire, from Wellbottom Lodge Stables

Lord Of The Field b h (6yrs) Jalmood (USA) - Star Face (African Sky).............. (Rainbow Ride Ranch) 60,000

From Wellbottom Lodge Stables

Turret Gates ch c (4yrs) Ahonoora - Cape Race (USA) (Northern Dancer) .... (Angel Babic) 1,500

Wellington Rock (USA) ch g (4yrs) Lyphard's Wish (FR) - Cuz's Star (USA) (Galaxy Libra)................ (C B A) 18,000

From South Hatch Stables

Belle Soiree ch f (3yrs) Night Shift (USA) - Party Game (Red Alert) (Hbaru Iszard) 1,100

Final Frontier (IRE) b g (3yrs) Common Grounds - Last Gunboat (Dominion) ... (Derby Bloodstock) 12,000

Misty Jenni (IRE) b f (3yrs) Night Shift (USA) - Mousil (Moulton) .... (David Minton Bloodstock) 1,350

Requested b g (6yrs) Rainbow Quest (USA) - Melody Hour (Sing Sing) .... (P Burgoyne) 2,400

Property of Sir Eric Parker, from Crimbourne Stud

Digpast (IRE) ch c (3yrs) Digamist (USA) - Starlit Way (Pall Mall).... (R Akehurst) 6,800

Property of Stetchworth Park Stud Ltd, from Widgham Stables

Environmentalist (IRE) b c (2yrs) Sure Blade (USA) - Vielle (Ribero)..... (R Dawson) 7,000

Green Energy ch f (2yrs) Hadeer - Preobrajenska (Double Form)...... (M C Pipe) 1,500

700

Property of Mr & Mrs R N Khan, from Widgham Stables

Mighty Mountain b c (2yrs) Chilibang - Busted Love (Busted)......... (B B A) 1,100

Property of Stetchworth Park Stud Ltd, from Widgham Stables

Perhaps gr c (2yrs) Hadeer - April Wind (Windjammer (USA))........... (B B A) 3,200

Sans Ecocide b c (2yrs) Hadeer - Tithing (USA) (Nureyev (USA)) (Andrew Mead International Bloodstock) 13,500

From Stetchworth Park Stud

Unbelievable b c (2yrs) Warning - Grafitti Gal (USA) (Pronto)............ (B B A) 2,100

Property of a Partnership, from Pegasus Stables

Kiawah ch f (3yrs) Master Willie - Polly Packer (Reform).......... (C C Elsey) 4,300

Property of Dubai Bloodstock, from Pegasus Stables

Major Yaasi (USA) b c (3yrs) Arctic Tern (USA) - Dimant Rose (USA) (Tromos) .. (J Fanshawe) 11,000

Property of Mrs I Phillips, from Pegasus Stables

Milairous (IRE) b c (2yrs) Taufan (USA) - Milaire (Tudor Melody) .... (Roxanne Bryant) 1,000

Property of Gainsborough Stud Management Ltd, from Pegasus Stables

Zaaheyah (USA) ch f (3yrs) Irish River (FR) - Shoag (USA) (Affirmed (USA))......... (David Minton Bloodstock) 2,600

Property of Darley Stud Management Co. Ltd, from Pegasus Stables

Fatalist b c (2yrs) Shareef Dancer (USA) - Just Never Know (USA) (Riverman (USA))........................ (B B A) 2,700

Glossary b f (2yrs) Reference Point - Lustre (USA) (Halo (USA)).......... (A Perry) 3,500

701

From Thomastown Castle Stud, Ireland

Turner Prize (IRE) b c (3yrs) Tate Gallery (USA) - Pansoverina (Sovereign Path) .. (B B A) 6,600

From Oak Stables Ltd

Camro Kirby (FR) b c (3yrs) Lead On Time (USA) - Nofret (FR) (Meautry (FR))..... (D Cosgrove) 5,200

Jawaal ch c (3yrs) Soviet Star (USA) - Pencil Sharpener (USA) (Sharpen Up)........ (Lady Herries) 5,000

Mahool (USA) b c (4yrs) Alydar (USA) - Tax Dodge (USA) (Seattle Slew (USA))..... (C Tinkler Jnr) 6,200

Nawaaya (USA) b f (3yrs) Fappiano (USA) - Skeeb (USA) (Topsider (USA))......... (Cheveley Park Stud Ltd) 13,000

Yaareem b f (2yrs) Shirley Heights - Shining Eyes (USA) (Mr Prospector (USA))..... (F Iqbal) 740

Young Pilot b c (2yrs) Polish Precedent (USA) - Pencil Sharpener (USA) (Sharpen Up).......... (Lady Herries) 2,300

Property of Darley Stud Management Co Ltd, from Oak Stables

Manaarah (USA) ch f (3yrs) Slew O'Gold (USA) - Edgewater (USA) (Verbatim (USA))................. (Pat Mitchell) 5,400

Property of Heathavon Stables Ltd, from Upper Longdon Stables

The Auction Bidder b h (6yrs) Auction Ring (USA) - Stepping Gaily (Gay Fandango (USA))............................. (Kildare Thoroughbred Services) 2,300

Property of Dissolve a Partnership, from Norton Grange Stables

Hasty Bank b c (2yrs) Dowsing (USA) - Pyjama Party (Pyjama Hunt) .... (G Heymans) 6,600

702

From Pond House Stables

Pharly Story b g (5yrs) Pharly (FR) - Certain Story (Known Fact (USA)) .... (Scuderia Elvira Ciacci) 600

Property of Hammy Racing, from The Paddocks

Dulford Lad b c (2yrs) In Fijar (USA) - Highsplasher (USA) (Buckpasser)...... (Cash) 9,600

Property of Mr Alex Smith, from The Paddocks

Karukera ch f (3yrs) Hallgate - Water Folly (Sharpo)............... (Team Group) 740

Property of a Partnership, from The Paddocks

Swift Romance (IRE) ch g (5yrs) Coquelin (USA) - Douschkina (Dubassoff (USA)) (G Barnett) 6,800

Property of Carroll Bloodstock, from Warren Park Stud

b f (2yrs) Never So Bold - Alteza Real (Mansingh (USA)).................... (Emerald Bloodstock) 3,200

Property of Mr Raymond Tooth, from Kingwood Stud

Dents Du Midi (USA) ch f (3yrs) Midyan (USA) - Beverly Hills (FR) (Blakeney)... (F Iqbal) 1,250

Property of Broughton Thermal Insulation, from Saville House Stables

Broughtons Turmoil b g (4yrs) Petorius - Rustic Stile (Rusticaro (FR))........... (Denys Smith) 6,000

Property of Seven Seas Racing, from Lethornes Stables

See My Guest (FR) ch f (2yrs) Be My Guest (USA) - Grammene (Grey Dawn II) .... (Angel Babic) 1,900

To Dissolve a Partnership

Celestial Dance b f (2yrs) Scottish Reel - Celeste (Sing Sing)........... (G Blum) 2,500

Property of a Partnership, from Yew Tree Stables

Elevator Shaft (IRE) b g (2yrs) Double Schwartz - Silk Trade (Auction Ring (USA)) (J McGrath) 11,000

703

Property of a Syndicate, from Yew Tree Stables

Fly For Gold (IRE) b f (4yrs) Simply Great (FR) - Golden Pheasant (Henbit (USA)) (Ran Zeev) 1,000

Property of Mr W G R Wightman, from Ower Farm Stables

Googly ch f (4yrs) Sunley Builds - Cheri Berry (Air Trooper)........... (J White) 23,000

Property of a Partnership, from Ower Farm Stables

Hallorina b f (3yrs) Hallgate - Diorina (Manacle)........................ (A B Aziz) 7,000

Property of Mr T R Mountain, from Ower Farm Stables

Catherine Ofaragon ch f (3yrs) Aragon - Edna (Shiny Tenth).......... (G Blum) 17,500

Property of Cheveley Park Stud, from East Everleigh Stables

Baton Bleu b c (2yrs) Music Boy - Fair Eleanor (Saritamer (USA)) .... (C Hammond) 5,000

Battling Blue b c (2yrs) Primo Dominie - Ethel Knight (Thatch (USA))........... (M Thwaites) 13,500

To Dissolve a Partnership, from East Everleigh Stables

Bonar Bridge (USA) b or br g (3yrs) Quadratic (USA) - Merririver (USA) (Taylor's Falls (USA)).................. (K Burke) 5,200

Brigg Fair b c (3yrs) Aragon - Brig Of Ayr (Brigadier Gerard)..................... (Cormac McCormack Associates) 20,000

Property of Miss L Vickers, from East Everleigh Stables

Boys Of Summer ch c (2yrs) Emarati (USA) - Sion Hill (The Go-Between).. (B B A) 1,000

To Dissolve a Partnership, from East Everleigh Stables

Come Go b f (2yrs) Efisio - Red Jay (Redundant)..................(Tomas Satrh) 2,000

Comeonup b g (2yrs) Most Welcome - Scarlet Veil (Tyrnavos)..... (M Carver) 8,000

704

Property of Mr T Bucknall, from East Everleigh Stables

Courageous Knight gr g (4yrs) Midyan (USA) - Little Mercy (No Mercy)........ (J M Bradley) 13,500

Property of a Partnership, from Diomed Stables

Iron Gent (USA) b c (2yrs) Greinton - Carrot Top (High Hat).... (Derby Bloodstock) 15,500

Jahangir (IRE) ch g (4yrs) Ballad Rock - Marsh Benham (Dragonara Palace (USA)).................. (Pat Mitchell) 11,500

From Diomed Stables

Rasayel (USA) b f (3yrs) Bering - Reham (Mill Reef (USA))......... (P D Evans) 4,500

Wisham (USA) ch c (3yrs) Be My Guest (USA) - Massorah (FR) (Habitat) .... (Scuderia Elvira Ciacci) 600

Property of Mr A C L Sturge, from Downs House Stables

Chouette b f (3yrs) Try My Best (USA) - Bugle Sound (Bustino) .... (Johnny McKeever Bloodstock) 3,800

Property of Mrs R A Johnson, from Downs House Stables

Sylvan Breeze b g (5yrs) Sulaafah (USA) - Langton Herring (Nearly A Hand) ...... (Johnny McKeever Bloodstock) 900

From Rosewell House Stables, Ireland

Nordicolini (IRE) b f (3yrs) Nordico (USA) - Tuyenu (Welsh Pageant) .... (Kildare Thoroughbred Services) 3,000

Paugim (IRE) b c (2yrs) Danehill (USA) - Etty (Relko)..................... (P Martin) 10,000

Somerton Boy (IRE) b c (3yrs) Thatching - Bonnie Bess (Ardoon)............... (David Minton Bloodstock) 6,400

Tigersong (USA) b or br c (3yrs) Seattle Song (USA) - Tovalop (USA) (Northern Dancer)...................... (B B A) 17,500

Viney (USA) b g (3yrs) Trempolino (USA) - Fille Du Nord (FR) (Northern Treat (USA))................... (C Weedon) 2,100

705

Property of Shadwell Estate Co Ltd, from Rosewell House Stables, Ireland

Imad (USA) b or br c (3yrs) Al Nasr (FR) - Blue Grass Field (Top Ville).. (J White) 13,500

Muraafq (IRE) b c (2yrs) Dominion - Wurud (USA) (Green Dancer (USA))... (B B A) 2,300

Ukud (USA) b f (3yrs) Woodman (USA) - Inspire (USA) (Tell (USA))............. (Emerald Bloodstock) 4,000

Tahthab (IRE) b c (2yrs) Common Grounds - Tasskeen (FR) (Lyphard (USA))........ (D Murphy) 28,000

Property of Mrs C E Brittain, from Carlburg Stables

Bellatrix b m (5yrs) Persian Bold - Sorebelle (Prince Tenderfoot (USA)) .... (David Minton Bloodstock) 1,200

Property of Dayspring Company, from Carlburg Stables

Bestello (IRE) b c (3yrs) Waajib - Travel Away (Tachypous).. (Norwood & Sons) 900

Efharisto b c (4yrs) Dominion - Excellent Alibi (USA) (Exceller (USA)) .... (N Callaghan) 31,000

Erckule b c (3yrs) Petoski - Mytinia (Bustino)......................... (B B A) 13,000

Host (IRE) b g (4yrs) Be My Guest (USA) - Take Your Mark (USA) (Round Table) .. (B B A) 11,000

Lobilio (USA) b c (4yrs) Robellino (USA) - Nabila (USA) (Foolish Pleasure (USA)).. (D Burchell) 16,500

Ribbold b c (3yrs) Bustino - Water Woo (USA) (Tom Rolfe)...... (Denys Smith) 9,000
Robenko (USA) b or br c (4yrs) Roberto (USA) - Kendra Road (USA) (Kennedy Road (CAN))............. (R Sharpe) 6,400

706

Property of Mr C E Brittain, from Carlburg Stables

Royal Executive (IRE) b g (3yrs) Waajib - Royal Episode (Royal Match).......... (K Bridgwater) 1,600
Rully ch g (4yrs) Rousillon (USA) - Hysterical (High Top).......... (M Chapman) 1,800

Property of Dayspring Company, from Carlburg Stables

Suivez b c (3yrs) Persian Bold - Butterfly Kiss (Beldale Flutter (USA))........... (Cormac McCormack Associates) 17,000
Virilis b c (3yrs) Niniski (USA) - Valiant Cry (Town Crier)........ (Equine Services) 5,200

Property of Darley Stud Management Co Ltd, from Carlburg Stables

Rousay b c (2yrs) Reference Point - Russian Countess (USA) (Nureyev (USA))...... (European Equine Consultants) 7,400

Property of Mr Khalifa Dasmal, from Carlburg Stables

Nahlati (IRE) b f (3yrs) Mtoto - Formido (Formidable (USA)) (R Fenwick-Gibson) 3,500

Property of Darley Stud Management, from Carlburg Stables

Imperia br f (2yrs) Simply Great (FR) - Hopeful Search (USA) (Vaguely Noble) (D Ali) 1,100
Ericolin (IRE) ch c (3yrs) Ahonoora - Pixie Erin (Golden Fleece (USA)) (N Tinkler) 10,000

Property of a Partnership, from Machell Place Stables

Asian Punter (IRE) ch g (4yrs) M Double M (USA) - Centenary Year (Malinowski (USA)).... (Will Edmeades Bloodstock) 1,800

Property of Mrs J Sutcliffe, from Woodruffe House Stables

Alqairawaan b g (4yrs) Ajdal (USA) - Clare Island (Connaught)...... (G Harwood) 15,000

707

To Dissolve a Partnership, from Woodruffe House Stables

Lets Go Bo (IRE) b g (2yrs) Classic Secret (USA) - Meadow Air (Coquelin (USA)).. (Elizabeth Gomes) 1,000
Superoo b g (7yrs) Superlative - Shirleen (Daring Display (USA))...... (Pam Sly) 2,900

Property of Mr J S Ruddy, from Marriott Stables

Erris Boy gr c (2yrs) Sharrood (USA) - Lady Tap (Red Sunset).......... (Ballering) 2,600

From Marriott Stables

Forever Shineing b f (3yrs) Glint Of Gold - Patosky (Skymaster)................. (David Minton Bloodstock) 4,000

Property of a Partnership, from Marriott Stables

Golden Grand b c (2yrs) Sayf El Arab (USA) - Lavenham Blue (Streetfighter)....... (C B A) 10,000

Property of Mr Colin G R Booth, from Marriott Stables

Imperial Forte b f (3yrs) Midyan (USA) - Sunfleet (Red Sunset)...... (S N Cole) 600

Property of a Partnership, from Marriott Stables

Moment Of Glory (IRE) ch c (2yrs) Harp Islet (USA) - No Distractions (Tap On Wood)..... (David Minton Bloodstock) 5,000

From Marriott Stables

Pretty Baby b f (3yrs) Celestial Storm (USA) - Pretty Thing (Star Appeal)........... (M S Saunders) 3,800
Sahah ch c (2yrs) Kefaah (USA) - Lotte Lenta (Gorytus (USA))... (R Campbell) 1,200

Property of Pendley Farm, from Pendley Farm Racing Stables

Bold Thatcher b c (3yrs) Thatching - Bold Apple (Bold Lad (IRE))................ (Scuderia Emmegi) 8,000
Combellino br c (3yrs) Robellino (USA) - Honeycomb (Valiyar)................. (David Minton Bloodstock) 8,000
Edithmead (IRE) b f (3yrs) Shardari - Bless The Match (So Blessed).............. (Million In Mind (3)) 15,000
Emma Woodford ch f (3yrs) Master Willie - Kindjal (Kris)............... (D Delius) 1,200
Vallance b h (5yrs) Top Ville - Kindjal (Kris) (B B A) 14,500

708

From Clarehaven Stables

Barnet Fayre (IRE) b f (3yrs) Waajib - Kurri Kurri (USA) (Vague Image (USA))...... (B B A) 1,000
Miss Paramount b f (2yrs) Dominion - Glebehill (Northfields (USA)) (M Wane) 1,000

Property of a Partnership, from Clarehaven Stables

Wacky (IRE) b or br f (2yrs) Petorius - Zany (Junius (USA)).......... (R Bastiman) 8,000

Property of Shadwell Estate Co Ltd, from Clarehaven Stables

Alkamar (USA) b c (2yrs) Ogygian (USA) - Peggy Slew (USA) (Seattle Slew (USA)) .... (B B A) 1,500
Adib (USA) b c (3yrs) Alleged (USA) - Santa's Sister (USA) (Middle Brother).. (G Moore) 7,500
Fill ch f (3yrs) Soviet Star (USA) - Aldhabyih (General Assembly (USA))........... (Kildare Thoroughbred Services) 1,000
Rafiq (IRE) b c (2yrs) Jareer (USA) - Trendy Princess (Prince Tenderfoot (USA)).... (Norwood & Sons) 2,000

Property of Darley Stud Management Co Ltd, from Clarehaven Stables

Ya Mai br f (3yrs) Mtoto - Glory Of Hera (Formidable (USA))...... (M Chapman) 1,400

To Dissolve a Partnership, from East Everleigh Stables

Danny Boy b or br c (3yrs) Damister (USA) - Irish Isle (Realm)............ (G Blum) 15,000
Grand Vitesse (IRE) b c (4yrs) Alzao (USA) - Au Revoir (Ballymoss) (A D Bastiman) 12,000

709

Property of Highclere Tholroughbred Racing, from East Everleigh Stables

Greenfinch (CAN) b g (2yrs) Green Dancer (USA) - Princess Verna (USA) (Al Hattab (USA))................ (M P Naughton) 5,000

Property of Mr P F Boggis, from East Everleigh Stables

Heretical Miss br f (3yrs) Sayf El Arab (USA) - Silent Prayer (Queen's Hussar) .... (B B A) 3,800

Property of N T C Racing Ltd, from East Everleigh Stables

Jackpot Star ch c (3yrs) Pharly (FR) - Claironcita (Don Carlos) (J P de Gaste) 32,000

Property of Mr L Razzak, from East Everleigh Stables

M A El-Sahn b c (3yrs) Presidium - Hoonah (FR) (Luthier)............ (Julie Roark) 900

Property of Mr and Mrs T C Blackwell, from Phantom House Stables

Clapping b f (2yrs) Elegant Air - Lap Of Honour (Final Straw).......... (B B A) 3,200

From Phantom House Stables

Courtenay Bee b c (4yrs) Absalom - Broken Accent (Busted)........... (T George) 3,000

Property of a Partnership, from Phantom House Stables

Pagoda gr f (2yrs) Petong - Priors Dean (Monsanto (FR))........ (Angel Babic) 600

Storm Venture (IRE) b g (3yrs) Taufan (USA) - Crimson Crest (Pampapaul).. (C B A) 20,000

Property of Mr B Haggas, from Somerville Lodge Stables

High Low (USA) b g (5yrs) Clever Trick (USA) - En Tiempo (USA) (Bold Hour).. (P C Haslam) 12,000

Property of a Partnership, from Somerville Lodge Stables

Let's Get Lost ch c (4yrs) Chief Singer - Lost In France (Northfields (USA))........ (C B A) 12,500

710

Property of Million In Mind Partnership 2, from Somerville Lodge Stables

Millionetta (IRE) b f (2yrs) Danehill (USA) - Ash Ridge (USA) (Bold Reason) .... (Conti Bloodstock Services) 3,400

Property of Mr B Haggas, from Somerville Lodge Stables

Rafters b g (4yrs) Celestial Storm (USA) - Echoing (Formidable (USA)) (M Carver) 13,500

From Somerville Lodge Stables

Supercool ch c (2yrs) Superlative - Florentynna Bay (Aragon) .... (Miss Sarah Hollinshead) 4,800

Property of a Parttnership, from Fitzroy House Stables

Ablest Son b g (2yrs) Absalom - Moaning Low (Burglar)......... (Gay Kelleway) 820

Allez Hombre b or br c (2yrs) Cadeaux Genereux - Aphrosina (Known Fact (USA)).................... (F Watson) 1,300

From Fitzroy House Stables

Bali Warrior (IRE) ch g (2yrs) Persian Bold - Miss Bali (Crepello)........ (Ballering) 10,500

Dancing Rebel (IRE) b c (2yrs) Dancing Dissident (USA) - Soucaro (Rusticaro (FR))........................ (B B A) 4,100

Duveen (IRE) b g (3yrs) Tate Gallery (USA) - Wish You Were Here (USA) (Secretariat (USA))....... (N Twiston-Davies) 25,000

Green's Fair (IRE) b g (3yrs) Carmelite House (USA) - Lockwood Girl (Prince Tenderfoot (USA))........ (N G Ahier) 7,400

Green's Impression b f (2yrs) Alzao (USA) - Vivid Impression (Cure The Blues (USA))........................ (B B A) 1,600

King Paris (IRE) ch g (3yrs) King Of Clubs - Alkis (USA) (Roberto (USA))........... (P Wetermans) 11,000

Manila Bay (USA) b c (3yrs) Manila (USA) - Betty Money (USA) (Our Native (USA)) (J S King) 18,500

711

Property of a Partnership, from Fitzroy House Stables

Misty Wise b f (2yrs) Rambo Dancer (CAN) - Gigiolina (King Emperor (USA))....... (T Wassenaar) 1,000

From Fitzroy House Stables

Night Snow b f (2yrs) Night Shift (USA) - Snowdonia (SAF) (Caerdeon).......... (Abdi Aziz M Al Saud) 7,800

Noyan ch c (3yrs) Northern Baby (CAN) - Istiska (FR) (Irish River (FR)) (L Lungo) 14,000

Property of a Partnership, from Fitzroy House Stables

Premier Star ch g (3yrs) Precocious - Grove Star (Upper Case (USA)).... (M Dods) 12,000

From Fitzroy House Stables

Royal Insignia b c (2yrs) Prince Sabo - Stinging Nettle (Sharpen Up).......... (Abdi Aziz M Al Saud) 34,000

Soul Emperor b or br c (3yrs) Our Native (USA) - Dance Empress (USA) (Empery (USA))..................... (L Comer) 1,300

Property of a Partnership, from Fitzroy House Stables

Totally Unique (USA) b c (3yrs) Al Nasr (FR) - Heavenly Halo (USA) (Halo (USA)).... (B B A) 2,000

From Fitzroy House Stables

Yunus Emre (IRE) ch c (3yrs) Lomond (USA) - Thrifty Trio (USA) (Groton)..... (R Arnold) 7,000

From Southgate Stables

Intention (USA) b c (3yrs) Shahrastani (USA) - Mimi Baker (USA) (What Luck (USA)) (R Campbell) 1,100

Million In Mind (IRE) ch f (4yrs) Lomond (USA) - Klairlone (Klairon).... (J White) 29,000

Nera b f (2yrs) Robellino (USA) - Sunfleet (Red Sunset).......... (C P Wildman) 6,800

Night In A Million b g (2yrs) Night Shift (USA) - Ridalia (Ridan (USA))......... (Tote Cherry-Downes) 8,200

Pixton (IRE) b c (3yrs) Common Grounds - Sallywell (Manado).................. (Kildare Thoroughbred Services) 3,600

Press Gallery ch c (3yrs) Carmelite House (USA) - Mixed Applause (USA) (Nijinsky (CAN))............ (Scuderia Emmegi) 8,400

Saihat (IRE) b c (2yrs) Midyan (USA) - Lone Bidder (Auction Ring (USA)) .... (B B A (Ireland)) 20,000

Bandmaster (USA) b c (4yrs) Dixieland Band (USA) - Queen's Bid (USA) (Hoist The Flag (USA)).......... (A Gorrie) 2,200

712

Property of Darley Stud Manageent Co. Ltd., from Southgate Stables

Tillaook b c (3yrs) Shadeed (USA) - Till You (USA) (Exclusive Native (USA))........ (J McGrath) 2,000

Property of J Jannaway, from Linkslade Stables

Anorak (USA) b c (3yrs) Storm Bird (CAN) - Someway Somehow (USA) (What Luck (USA)).............................. (Cormac McCormack Associates) 10,000

Property of a Partnership, from Linkslade Stables

Lunar Risk b c (3yrs) Risk Me (FR) - Moonlight Princess (Alias Smith (USA)) ..... (B Sanders) 9,500

Property of J Jannaway, from Linkslade Stables

Not For Joe br g (2yrs) Dowsing (USA) - Josephine Gibney (High Top) .... (G Heymans) 5,000

Property of a Partnership, from Linkslade Stables

Only A Mirage b c (3yrs) Damister (USA) - Magic Vision (Shergar) (R Wetemans) 1,600

Property of R Haim, from Linkslade Stables

Robby (IRE) b c (2yrs) Bob Back (USA) - Allberry (Alzao (USA)) .... (Kildare Thoroughbred Services) 3,800

Property of A Patrick, from Linkslade Stables

Superensis ch g (3yrs) Sayf El Arab (USA) - Superlife (USA) (Super Concorde (USA)).................. (J Le Brocq) 4,000

Property of a Partership, from Linkslade Stables

Sure Lord (IRE) ch c (4yrs) Sure Blade (USA) - Lady Graustark (USA) (Graustark).................... (B B A) 2,200

Property of a Gentleman, from Summerdown Stables

Rue Rembrandt (USA) b c (3yrs) Explodent (USA) - Fu Fu La Rue (USA) (Blushing Groom (FR)).................. (C B A) 20,000

Property of R Fahey, from Manor House Farm Stables

Ok Bertie b g (3yrs) Interrex (CAN) - Rockery (Track Spare)........... (Ballering) 21,000

Property of Dozen Dreamers Partnership, from Hall Place Stables

Dozens Divine b c (2yrs) Superlative - Divine Thought (Javelot)............. (Carmine Cocca) 2,000

Oyston's Life b g (4yrs) Be My Guest (USA) - I Don't Mind (Swing Easy (USA))..... (T Bandilla) 1,200

Radiant Dancer b f (3yrs) Mazilier (USA) - Adana (FR) (Green Dancer (USA)) ..... (R Phillips) 1,700

713

NEWMARKET
Tuesday, October 26th

From Park Lodge Stables

Bold Greek b c (2yrs) Never So Bold - Thessaloniki (Julio Mariner)... (B.B.A.) 5,200

Briggsmaid b m (5yrs) Elegant Air - Merry Yarn (Aggressor) .... (Will Edmeades Bloodstock) 6,500

Expo Mondial (IRE) b c (3yrs) Last Tycoon - Hamada (FR) (Habitat)... (M Thwaites) 4,800

Judge Dread b g (2yrs) Cyrano de Bergerac - Sarong (Taj Dewan) (J Groenenboom) 1,700

Property of T C Marshall Ltd., from Felstead Court Stables

Dazzling Fire (IRE) b f (4yrs) Bluebird (USA) - Fire Flash (Bustino)........ (J Clarke) 4,200

Ritzy gr f (3yrs) Sharrood (USA) - Ritsurin (Mount Hagen (FR)).... (T A Johnsey) 3,100

Turtle Beach ch g (4yrs) Primo Dominie - Double Finesse (Double Jump) .... (C C Elsey) 2,600

To Dissolve a Partnership, from East Everleigh Stables

Merlin's Field (IRE) b c (2yrs) Common Grounds - Red Magic (Red God) ...... (Wilming Yeo) 7,200

Property of Million In Mind Syndicate, from East Everleigh Stables

Million Lights (IRE) ch f (2yrs) Cadeaux Genereux - Fire Flash (Bustino) .... (C.B.A.) 24,000

Property of Roldvale Ltd, from East Everleigh Stables

Miss Risky b f (2yrs) Risk Me (FR) - Merle (Gunner B)............... (J L Harris) 600

714

Property of Theobalds Stud Ltd., from East Everleigh Stables

Mr Devious b c (2yrs) Superpower - Marton Maid (Silly Season)..... (Conrad Allen) 7,000

Property of Winning Team Racing, from East Everleigh Stables

Jasari (IRE) b g (2yrs) Ajraas (USA) - Rue Del Peru (Linacre) ..... (Andrew Mead International Bloodstock) 7,000

Link Miles b c (2yrs) Merdon Melody - Donna Pavlova (Don (ITY)).... (B.B.A.) 33,000

Perusal b c (2yrs) Sizzling Melody - High Climber (Mandrake Major)........... (Cormac McCormack Associates) 27,000

Shareoftheaction gr g (2yrs) Sharrod (USA) - Action Belle (Auction Ring (USA)) ..... (Peter Doyle Bloodstock) 2,600

Slasher Jack (IRE) b g (2yrs) Alzao (USA) - Sherkraine (Shergar)..... (P Teasdale) 7,500

Property of Juddmonte Farms Ltd

Azilian (IRE) b or br c (3yrs) Top Ville - D'Azy (Persian Bold) .... (Cormac McCormack Associates) 16,500

Ballet Royal (USA) b c (4yrs) Nureyev (USA) - Crystal Queen (High Top) .... (Margaret O'Toole) 11,000

Property of Juddmonte Farms Inc.
Autumnis (USA) ch c (3yrs) Diesis - Autumn Glory (USA) (Graustark) .... (Kildare Thoroughbred Services) 6,500
Property of Juddmonte Farms Ltd.
Balnibarbi b c (4yrs) Rainbow Quest (USA) - Balabine (USA) (Nijinsky (CAN)) .... (Thomas Dyer) 25,000
Corrouge (USA) b c (4yrs) Alleged (USA) - Lake Country (CAN) (Caucasus (USA)) (C.B.A.) 52,000
Ecologist b h (5yrs) Rainbow Quest (USA) - Infra Green (Laser Light) .... (M.A.B. Agency) 25,000

715

Property of Juddmonte Farms Inc.
El Duco (USA) b c (3yrs) El Gran Senor (USA) - Most Honourable (USA) (Exclusive Native (USA)) .... (R O'Gorman Bloodstock) 135,000
Property of Juddmonte Farms Ltd.
In Case (USA) b c (3yrs) Storm Cat (USA) - In Essence (USA) (In Reality) .... (Cheveley Park Stud) 70,000
Lake District (USA) b c (3yrs) Mr Prospector (USA) - Lake Country (CAN) (Caucasus (USA)).......... (Abdi Aziz M Al Saud) 10,500
Property of Juddmonte Farms Inc.
Sculler (USA) b c (3yrs) Riverman (USA) - Nimble Folly (USA) (Cyane) .... (Tote Cherry-Downes) 42,000
Property of Juddmonte Farms Ltd.
Trammel b c (3yrs) Shirley Heights - Trampship (High Line).......... (M Thwaites) 34,000
Tremoldando (USA) ch c (3yrs) Trempolino (USA) - Alia (Sun Prince).............. (Rainbow Ridge Ranch) 92,000
Urgent Request (IRE) br or gr c (3yrs) Rainbow Quest (USA) - Oscura (USA) (Caro)................ (Stewart Aitken) 32,000
Western Cape (USA) b c (3yrs) Gone West (USA) - Blue Bell Pearl (FR) (Pharly (FR)) ..... (Cormac McCormack Associates) 86,000
From Beckhampton House Stables
Frontier Flight (USA) b c (3yrs) Flying Paster (USA) - Sly Charmer (USA) (Valdez (USA))...................... (C.B.A.) 12,000
Jareef's Way (IRE) b c (2yrs) Jareer (USA) - Honagh Lee (Main Reef) .... (Tony Nerses) 26,000
Monticino (IRE) ch c (2yrs) Dominion - Fantoccini (Taufan (USA)).............. (Abdi Aziz M Al Saud) 12,500
Pridwell b g (3yrs) Sadler's Wells (USA) - Glowing With Pride (Ild de Bourbon (USA))..................... (M C Pipe) 8,500
Prime Of Life (IRE) b g (3yrs) Midyan (USA) - Ominous (Dominion)................. (James Eustace) 12,000
Strumpet City b f (2yrs) Emarati (USA) - Double Touch (FR) (Nonoalco (USA))... (Stewart Aitken) 9,500

716

From Castle Stables
Acanthus (IRE) b c (3yrs) Slip Anchor - Green Lucia (Green Dancer (USA)) .... (Sue Wilton) 7,500
Armenian Coffee (IRE) b c (3yrs) Ela-Mana-Mou - Streamertail (Shirley Heights) ... (B.B.A.) 30,000
Bitter Eloe b g (4yrs) Green Desert (USA) - Sometime Lucky (Levmoss) .... (Guy Harwood) 11,000
Property of a Partnership, from Castle Stables
Bold Stroke br g (4yrs) Persian Bold - Fariha (Mummy's Pet)........... (M C Pipe) 36,000
From Castle Stables
Cadenabbia (USA) ch f (2yrs) Ferdinand (USA) - Blink Naskra (USA) (Naskra (USA))..................... (C C Elsey) 6,200
Property of a Gentleman, from Castle Stables
Carelaman b c (3yrs) Ela-Mana-Mou - Caro's Niece (USA) (Caro) .... (Abdi Aziz M Al Saud) 36,000
Cretan Gift ch c (2yrs) Cadeaux Genereux - Caro's Niece (USA) (Caro).... (D Kent) 1,350
From Castle Stables
Chiligray gr c (2yrs) Formidable (USA) - Chili Girl (Skymaster).............. (B.B.A.) 5,200
Property of a Partnership, from Castle Stables
Circus Colours b c (3yrs) Rainbow Quest (USA) - Circus Plume (High Top) ...... (D Kent) 21,000
Corcovado b c (2yrs) Formidable (USA) - High Halo (High Top)......... (B.B.A.) 2,800

717

From Castle Stables
Don Tocino b c (3yrs) Dominion - Mrs Bacon (Balliol)........... (John White) 15,000
Duty Time b c (2yrs) Night Shift (USA) - Moorish Idol (Aragon) .... (Cormac McCormack Associates) 35,000
Ecu de France (IRE) ch c (3yrs) Groom Dancer (USA) - Racing Connection (USA) (Sharpen Up)........ (D Knight) 14,000
Property of a Partnership, from Castle Stables
Guestwick b c (3yrs) Blakeney - Barsham (Be My Guest (USA)).. (Gerry Cusack) 15,000
Property of Shadwell Estate Co. Ltd, from Castle Stables
Falah (USA) ch c (3yrs) Topsider (USA) - Secretarial Queen (USA) (Secretariat (USA))............... (Danny Murphy) 4,600
Wufud (USA) b or br c (3yrs) Woodman (USA) - Olden Damoiselle (USA) (Olden Times)..................... (C.B.A.) 24,000
Property of S Crown, from Whatcombe Stables
Clear Look b f (3yrs) Green Desert (USA) - Avoid (USA) (Buckpasser) .... (David Minton Bloodstock) 5,800
Diamond Crown (IRE) ch g (2yrs) Kris - State Treasure (USA) (Secretariat (USA)).................. (M Wane) 600
Property of Richard Green (Fine Paintings), from Whatcombe Stables
Green's Bid gr c (3yrs) Siberian Express (USA) - Arianna Aldini (Habitat)........ (D W Chapman) 5,800
Property of S Crown, from Whatcombe Stables
Lord Sky b g (2yrs) Emarati (USA) - Summer Sky (Skyliner)......... (C Gordon-Watson Bloodstock) 6,800
Red Leader (IRE) b c (3yrs) Vision (USA) - Try My Rosie (Try My Best (USA)) .... (G Charles-Jones) 3,000

718

Property of T S Liang, from Whatcombe Stables

Tejano Gold (USA) ch c (3yrs) Tejano (USA) - Nelli Forli (USA) (Broadway Forli (USA))................ (Paul Bradley) 4,800

Property of F Salman, from Whatcombe Stables

Gran Senorum (USA) ch c (3yrs) El Gran Senor (USA) - Sanctum Sanctorum (USA) (Secretariat (USA))............. (B.B.A. (Ireland)) 25,000

Moorish b c (3yrs) Dominion - Remoosh (Glint Of Gold).......... (John White) 31,000

Old Red (IRE) ch c (3yrs) Ela-Mana-Mou - Sea Port (Averof)..... (Richard Fahey) 18,500

From Bonita Racing Stables

Champagne Girl b f (2yrs) Robellino (USA) - Babycham Sparkle (So Blessed)....... (Peter Doyle Bloodstock) 5,200

Property of A W Schiff, from Bonita Racing Stables

Chili Lady ch f (3yrs) Chilibang - Barbary Court (Grundy).............. (W Clay) 1,100

Property of a Partnership, fro Bonita Racing Stables

Jade Green b f (4yrs) Midyan (USA) - Pilley Green (Porto Bello).................. (Conti Bloodstock Services) 10,000

Property of A W Schiff, from Bonita Racing Stables

Noble Pet gr g (4yrs) Petong - Barbary Court (Grundy)....... (Fahad Al Shatti) 9,200

Property of Hesmonds Stud, from Upshire Farm Stables

Fromage b f (2yrs) Formidable (USA) - Collage (Ele-Mana-Mou)................ (Abdi Aziz M Al Saud) 10,500

Property of a Partnership, from Maunby House Stables

Brackenthwaite ch g (3yrs) Faustus (USA) - Cosset (Comedy Star (USA))... (Cash) 8,600

719

Property of Mrs M Day, from Tattenham Corner Stables

Vanborough Lad b g (4yrs) Precocious - Lustrous (Golden Act (USA)).......... (Mrs S P Elphick) 4,800

Property of Gentleman, from Frankland Lodge Stables

Divine Rain b g (3yrs) Dowsing (USA) - Le Reine de France (Queens Hussar)..... (Charlotte Bathe) 1,050

Property of Roldvale Ltd

b g (2yrs) Risk Me (FR) - Spinney Hill (Dominion)........ (Albury Racing Ltd) 1,100

Sunday Risk ch c (2yrs) Risk Me (FR) - Always On A Sunday (Star Appeal).... (B.B.A.) 2,000

Property of R M Cyzer, from Elliots

Keep Safe b f (3yrs) Superlative - Jem Jen (Great Nephew)........ (J Clutterbuck) 820

Secret Assignment (USA) ch g (3yrs) Naevus (USA) - Swedish Ivy (USA) (Northjet).......................... (Geoffrey Howson Bloodstock) 1,800

Property of Mr R M Cyzer, from Elliotts

Sleeptite (FR) gr g (3yrs) Double Bed (FR) - Rajan Grey (Absalom) (Mrs V A Ward) 1,600

Property of a Partnership, from Elliotts

Temple Knight b g (4yrs) Never So Bold - Nelly Do Da (Derring-Do)............ (T A Johnsey) 7,000

Property of Mr R M Cyzer, from Elliotts

Tip Me Up b f (3yrs) Governor General - Single Gal (Mansingh (USA)).. (B.B.A.) 1,000

Tropical Jungle (USA) b g (3yrs) Majestic Shore (USA) - Diamond Oyster (Formidable (USA)).............. (P J Makin) 5,000

Without A Flag (USA) ch g (3yrs) Stately Don (USA) - Northerly Cheer (USA) (Northjet)............... (John White) 15,000

720

Property of Swettenham Stud, from Manton House Stables

Bunderburg (USA) br c (3yrs) Nureyev (USA) - Hortensia (FR) (Luthier) .... (J Joseph) 11,000

Knight Of Shalot (IRE) b g (3yrs) Don't Forget Me - Lady Of Shalott (Kings Lake (USA)).. (Mohammed Al-Qatami) 5,200

Sarangani Bay (USA) b c (3yrs) Manila (USA) - Homespun (USA) (Round Table) .... (D Chang) 10,000

Property of Mr M R Charlton, from Breckenbrough House Stables

Beats Working b g (2yrs) Aragon - Relatively Easy (Relkino).................. (Lillingston Bloodstock) 47,000

Property of Mr J Swiers, from Breckenbrough House Stables

Browned Off br g (4yrs) Move Off - Jenifer Browning (Daring Match)..... (C.B.A.) 9,500

Property of a Partnership, from Breckenbrough House Stables

Close To Reality b g (2yrs) Dreams To Reality (USA) - Edraianthus (Windjammer (USA)).................. (W Muir) 23,000

Property of Mr A P Leonard, from Breckenbrough House Stables

Doc Cottrill b g (3yrs) Absalom - Bridal Wave (Julio Mariner).......... (C.B.A.) 15,000

Property of Mr R C Moody, from Breckenbrough House Stables

Harpo's Special b g (2yrs) Superlative - Sideloader Special (Song)..... (B.B.A.) 4,800

Property of Mr M R Charlton, from Breckenbrough House Stables

Hill Reef (FR) b g (2yrs) Danehill (USA) - Green Reef (Mill Reef (USA)) .... (Andrew Mead International Bloodstock) 26,000

In Demand b g (2yrs) Nomination - Romantic Saga (Prince Tenderfoot (USA)) .... (J R Ramsden) 1,200

Midnight Magpie (IRE) b g (2yrs) Midyan (USA) - Mirabiliary (USA) (Crow (FR)) .. (B.B.A.) 5,000

721

Property of a Partnerhip, from Breckenbrough House Stables

Nickname b g (3yrs) Nicholas Bill - Linpac North Moor (Moorestyle)..... (B.B.A.) 1,200

From Stanley House Stables Ltd

Collier Bay b c (3yrs) Green Desert (USA) - Cockatoo Island (High Top).... (C.B.A.) 46,000

King Athelstan (USA) b h (5yrs) Sovereign Dancer (USA) - Wimbledon Star (USA) (Hoist The Flag (USA))..... (K Morgan) 9,400

Strictly Personal (USA) b g (3yrs) Secreto (USA) - Tash (USA) (Never Bend)....... (Racing 2000) 14,500

Property of Shadwell Estate Co Ltd, from Stanley House Stables

Tajhiz (USA) b c (3yrs) Woodman (USA) - Princess Ivor (USA) (Sir Ivor).......... (M Thwaites) 17,000

Property of Darley Stud Management Co Ltd, from Stanley House Stables

Admiral's Well (IRE) b c (3yrs) Sadler's Wells - Exotic Bride (USA) (Blushing Groom (FR)).............. (R Akehurst) 18,000

Amaam Amaam b c (3yrs) Last Tycoon - What A Pity (Blakeney)..... (T G Mills) 8,600

Bezique (USA) gr c (3yrs) Caro - Card Player (USA) (Lyphard (USA))................ (Kildare Thoroughbred Services) 6,400

Caledonian Bay (USA) gr c (3yrs) Pleasant Colony (USA) - Future Bright (Lyphard's Wish (FR))........... (Doreen Wilson) 6,000

Flintlock (IRE) ch c (3yrs) Kris - Foolish Lady (USA) (Foolish Pleasure (USA))........ (David Minton Bloodstock) 5,200

Kingdom Of Shades (USA) ch c (3yrs) Risen Star (USA) - Dancers Countess (USA) (Northern Dancer).......... (R Ogden) 26,000

Majboor Yafooz (USA) b c (3yrs) Silver Hawk (USA) - Forced To Fly (USA) (Accipiter (USA)) (Miss J M Bodycote) 7,000

Minus One (USA) b or br c (3yrs) Al Nasr (FR) - Drop The Mark (USA) (No Robbery)........ (David Minton Bloodstock) 4,000

Saxon King (IRE) ch c (3yrs) Ahonoora - My Therape (Jimmy Reppin) (Mark Usher) 7,800

Zajko (USA) b c (3yrs) Nureyev (USA) - Hope For All (USA) (Secretariat (USA)) (Lady Herries) 6,000

722

Property of Shadwell Estate Co Ltd, from Green Lodge Stables

Ajnas (IRE) b or br f (2yrs) Doyoun - Narjis (USA) (Blushing Groom (FR)).......... (Ran Zeev) 2,200

Alsryeh b f (2yrs) Shaadi (USA) - Tarib (Habitat)........ (Abdi Aziz M Al Saud) 5,000

Dalalah br f (3yrs) Doyoun - Balqis (USA) (Advocator).................. (B.B.A.) 12,000

Mitraas (USA) br c (3yrs) Chief's Crown (USA) - Khwlah (USA) (Best Turn (USA)) .... (Abdi Aziz M Al Saud) 19,000

Samah ch c (3yrs) Pennine Walk - Ghanayim (USA) (Sharpen Up) .... (Stewart Aitken) 21,000

Wazin (USA) b c (2yrs) Afleet (CAN) - On To Royalty (USA) (On To Glory (USA)) .... (B.B.A.) 11,500

Property of Grange Bloodstock Ltd, from Abington Place Stables

Castel Rosselo b or br c (3yrs) Rousillon (USA) - On The House (Be My Guest (USA))................ (Ron Dawson) 3,400

To Dissolve a Partnership, from Abington Place Stables

Deduce b g (4yrs) Ardross - Miss Maud (Tennyson (FR))......... (John White) 17,000

Property of Mr and Mrs H H Morris, from Abington Place Stables

Nessun Dorma b c (3yrs) Night Shift (USA) - Scala de Seta (Shantung)................ (J P de Gaste) 45,000

Property of Grange Bloodstock Ltd, from Abington Place Stables

Praxitiles b c (2yrs) Sure Blade (USA) - Guest Artiste (Be My Guest (USA)).... (B Hobbs) 3,400

723

Property of Mr J L C Pearce, from Abington Place Stables

Toujours Riviera ch c (3yrs) Rainbow Quest (USA) - Miss Beaulieu (Northfields (USA))...................... (J Pearce) 24,000

Property of Darley Stud Management Co Ltd, from Abington Place Stables

Mount Fuji gr c (3yrs) Kalaglow - Cherry Ridge (Riva Ridge (USA)) .... (Abdi Aziz M Al Saud) 8,500

Property of Kingstone Warren Partners, from Kingstone Warren Stables

Elara ch f (2yrs) Nicholas Bill - Lunar Queen (Queen's Hussar)........ (Angel Babic) 1,700

Property of Mr T A F Frost, from Kingstone Warren Stables

Exclusion ch c (4yrs) Ballad Rock - Great Exception (Grundy)................ (Cormac McCormack Associates) 10,500

Property of Kingstone Warren Partners, from Kingston Warren Stables

Ground Nut (IRE) ch g (3yrs) Fools Holme - Corn Seed (Nicholas Bill)............ (David Minton Bloodstock) 22,000

Property of Mr F Salman, from Kingstone Warren Stables

High Five (IRE) b g (3yrs) High Line - Finger Lake (Kings Lake (USA)) (Henry Candy) 1,800

Outset (IRE) ch g (3yrs) Persian Bold - It's Now Or Never (High Line)........... (Michael Hammond) 6,200

Property of Mr H Candy, from Kingstone Warren Stables

Primocelle br f (3yrs) Primo Dominie - Jouvencelle (Rusticaro (FR)) (O W Garrard) 1,100

Property of Hesmonds Stud, from Kingstone Warren Stables

Run With Joy (IRE) b g (2yrs) Sharrood (USA) - Durun (Run The Gantlet (USA)) (David Minton Bloodstock) 8,400

Property of a Gentleman, from Kingstone Warren Stables

Sea Siren gr f (3yrs) Slip Anchor - Seriema (Petingo).... (R O'Gorman Bloodstock) 16,000

724

Property of Kingstone Warren Partners, from Kingstone Warren Stables

Season's Star b f (3yrs) Nomination - Tosara (Main Reef)..... (R T Edwards) 1,600

Property of a Partnership, from Kingstone Warren Stables

Will Soon ch g (4yrs) Nicholas Bill - Henceforth (Full Of Hope)................ (Will Edmeades Bloodstock) 11,500

From Kingsclere Stables

Dynamic Deluxe (USA) ch c (2yrs) Sir Ivor - Shanameg (USA) (Rise Jim (USA))..... (C.B.A.) 32,000

Lady Tetrus b f (2yrs) Music Boy - Belaka (Beldale Flutter (USA)) .... (Abdi Aziz M Al Saud) 4,000

Major Clinton b c (2yrs) Robellino (USA) - Patraana (Nishapour (FR))..... (B.B.A.) 5,600

Powerful Edge ch g (4yrs) Primo Dominie - Sharp Castan (Sharpen Up) .... (R O'Gorman Bloodstock) 48,000

Property of Her Majesty The Queen, from Kingsclere Stables

Scarlet Diva ch f (2yrs) Soviet Star (USA) - Soprano (Kris)........ (Delta Bloodstock) 10,500

From Kingsclere Stables

Sophisticated Air b f (3yrs) Elegant Air - Blubella (Balidar)..................... (David Minton Bloodstock) 10,000

The Lone Dancer b c (2yrs) Mashhor Dancer (USA) - Solo Vacation (Pas de Seul)....................... (G Baker) 10,000

Tingle Factor b c (2yrs) Robellino (USA) - Bracey Brook (Gay Fandango (USA))... (Cormac McCormack Associates) 6,800

725

Property of Her Majesty The Queen, from Kingsclere Stables

Tissisat (USA) ch g (4yrs) Green Forest (USA) - Expansive (Exbury) .... (R Sheather) 42,000

From Freemason Lodge

Doubling Dice b c (2yrs) Jalmood (USA) - Much Too Risky (Bustino).... (R Allan) 5,200

Handsome Star (IRE) ch c (3yrs) El Gran Senor (USA) - Irish Valley (USA) (Irish River (FR))................... (B.B.A.) 3,600

Lyphantastic (USA) b c (4yrs) Lyphard's Wish (FR) - Tango Five Juliet (USA) (Fappiano (USA))....... (Charlie Mann) 9,800

Miswaki Dancer (USA) b c (3yrs) Miswaki (USA) - Simply Divine (USA) (Danzig (USA)).................. (Lady Herries) 8,200

Property of Darley Stud Management Co Ltd, from Freemason Lodge

Almamzar (USA) b c (3yrs) Theatrical - Promising Risk (USA) (Exclusive Native (USA))....... (Peter Doyle Bloodstock) 27,000

Colnbrook (USA) b c (3yrs) Irish River (FR) - Colophon (USA) (Nijinsky (CAN)) ...... (C.B.A.) 4,100

Home Park (IRE) ch c (3yrs) Shernazar - Home Address (Habitat).............. (Danny Murphy) 4,700

Map Of Stars (USA) b c (3yrs) Danzig (USA) - Luminaire (USA) (Al Hattab (USA)) ... (C.B.A.) 25,000

Property of P D Savill, from Maunby House Stables

Across The Bay ch g (6yrs) Krayyan - Siofra Beag (Steel Heart)..... (David Barron) 2,800

Diamond Panther ch c (2yrs) Cadeaux Genereux - Bessie Wallis (Prince de Galles) (20th Century Racing) 6,800

Minnesota Viking b g (2yrs) Northern State (USA) - Miskin (Star Appeal) .... (Lady Herries) 5,500

Parisian Lover br g (2yrs) Gallic League - Dear Heart (Blakeney)........ (B.B.A.) 1,100

726

Property of P D Savill, from Groundhill Farm

Amazing Feat (IRE) b g (4yrs) Petorius - Mountain Chase (Mount Hagen (FR)) .. (Scuderia Allegria) 80,000

Northern Graduate (USA) b g (4yrs) Northrop (USA) - Lady Blackfoot (Prince Tenderfoot (USA)).. (Million In Mind 3) 25,000

Property of P D Savill, from Habton Grange Stables

Celestial Rumour (IRE) b g (2yrs) Astronef - Gossip (Sharp Edge).... (Wilming Yeo) 10,000

Dancing Domino ch g (3yrs) Primo Dominie - Waltz (Jimmy Reppin) .... (Mohamed Kaled) 20,000

Passion Sunday ch g (2yrs) Bairn (USA) - Holy Day (Sallust)..... (David Nicholls) 6,200

Property of P D Savill, from Maunby Stables

Sea Gazer (IRE) ch c (3yrs) Magical Wonder (USA) - Apapa Port (My Swanee)....... (James Delahooke) 62,000

Property of P D Savill, from Longsides Stables

Turtle Rock b c (2yrs) Hadeer - Light de Light (USA) (Fluorescent Light (USA)).. (B.B.A. (Ireland)) 20,000

Property of P D Savill, from Lodge Farm Stables

Daytona Beach (IRE) ch g (3yrs) Bluebird (USA) - Water Spirit (USA) (Riverman (USA))......... (Lambert Bloodstock) 6,000

Property of P D Savill, from East Everleigh Stables

Echo-Logical gr c (4yrs) Belfort (FR) - North Pine (Import)............. (P J Martin) 42,000

Property of Mr P D Savill, from East Everleigh Stables

Night Melody (IRE) br c (3yrs) Night Shift (USA) - Quaver (Song)................ (Abdi Aziz M Al Saud) 105,000

Sweet Whisper gr f (2yrs) Petong - Softly Spoken (Mummy's Pet) .... (Kevin McAuliffe) 7,000

727

Property of Mr P D Savill, from The Croft Stables

Honey Seeker b c (4yrs) Chief Singer - Honey Thief (Burglar) .... (Robert Wetemans) 8,000

Wolf Power (IRE) b g (3yrs) Taufan (USA) - Heather Lark (Red Alert) .... (Mrs M Reveley) 8,000

From Castle Stables

Haddiah b f (2yrs) Persian Bold - Ashshama (USA) (Arctic Tern (USA)).. (L Browne) 7,400

Hinakia (IRE) b f (2yrs) Dowsing (USA) - Ranyah (USA) (Our Native (USA))...... (Mr Kozel) 1,000

Property of a Partnership, from Castle Stables
Imposing Groom (IRE) b c (2yrs) Posen (USA) - Beechwood (USA) (Blushing Groom (FR)).................. (B.B.A.) 9,000
Lady Silk ch f (2yrs) Prince Sabo - Adduce (USA) (Alleged (USA)).................. (James Hetherton) 4,400

From Castle Stables
Little Munchkin (IRE) ch c (3yrs) Nordance (USA) - Margo's Mink (FR) (Margouillat (FR)).................. (J P de Gaste) 90,000
Ma Bella Luna b f (4yrs) Jalmood (USA) - Macarte (FR) (Gift Card (FR)).......... (Stanley Moore) 4,800
Prince Hannibal b h (6yrs) High Top - Fluctuate (Sharpen Up).................. (Conti Bloodstock Services) 22,000
Riviere Actor (USA) b c (3yrs) Theatrical - Riviere Salee (Luthier).................. (Mohamed Kaled) 26,000

728

Property of a Partnership, from Castle Stables
Queen's Trust b f (2yrs) High Estate - Settlement (USA) (Irish River (FR)) .... (Cormac McCormack Associates) 14,000
Sangare (IRE) b f (2yrs) Shaadi (USA) - Light Bee (USA) (Majestic Light (USA))...... (Kildare Thoroughbred Services) 5,000

From Castle Stables
Subsonic (IRE) b h (5yrs) Be My Guest (USA) - Broken Wide (Busted) .... (M Wane) 7,400
Swagger Lady b f (2yrs) Tate Gallery (USA) - Live Ammo (Home Guard (USA))..... (David Nicholls) 4,800

From Bedford House Stables
Coneybury (IRE) b c (3yrs) Last Tycoon - Jackie Berry (Connaught)............ (German International Bloodstock) 56,000
Dragon's Teeth (IRE) b c (3yrs) Caerleon (USA) - Scots Lass (Shirley Heights) ... (Geoffrey Howson Bloodstock) 23,000
Fortensky (USA) b c (3yrs) Blushing Groom (FR) - Casey (Caerleon (USA))......... (C Gordon-Watson Bloodstock) 8,000

Property of Highclere Thoroughbred Racing, from Bedford House Stables
Masai Man (USA) ch c (2yrs) Riverman (USA) - Green Oasis (FR) (Green Dancer (USA))........................ (John Warren Bloodstock) 6,800

From Bedford House Stables
Northern Bred (IRE) b c (3yrs) Alzao (USA) - Good Relations (Be My Guest (USA)).. (R O'Gorman Bloodstock) 12,000
Olivadi (IRE) b c (3yrs) Prince Rupert (FR) - So Stylish (Great Nephew)............ (Rupert Arnold) 5,600
Run To Au Bon (IRE) b c (3yrs) Commanche Run - Donna Sabina (Nonoalco (USA)) (B.B.A. (Italia)) 9,200
Spiffer (IRE) b c (2yrs) Posen (USA) - Namatanga (USA) (Foolish Pleasure (USA)).......................... (B.B.A.) 900

729

Property of Darley Stud Management Co Ltd & Gerald W Leigh, from Bedford House Stables
Kamikaze gr c (3yrs) Kris - Infamy (Shirley Heights)................ (John White) 44,000

Property of Darley Stud Management Co Ltd, from Bedford House Stables
Mount Rose ch c (3yrs) Blushing Groom (FR) - Outstandingly (USA) (Exclusive Native (USA))........... (David Sasse) 5,600
Nahla b f (3yrs) Wassl - Bassita (Bustino) .. (Jacqueline Doyle) 2,600

Property of Roldvale Ltd, from Thirty Acre Barn Stables
Awfull Risky b f (2yrs) Risk Me (FR) - Gemma Kaye (Cure The Blues (USA)).. (P D Evans) 1,000
Dances With Risk ch f (2yrs) Risk Me (FR) - Dancing Belle (Dance In Time Can).... (Mohamed Kaled) 6,500

Property of Laurel (Leisure) Ltd, from Thirty Acre Barn Stables
Martina b m (5yrs) Tina's Pet - Tin Tessa (Martinmas)......................... (Johnny McKeever Bloodstock) 4,200

Property of Roldvale Ltd, from Thirty Acre Barn Stables
Richard's Error ch c (2yrs) Risk Me (FR) - Bocas Rose (Jalmood (USA)) .... (Gerd Smottebraten) 1,700
Risk Of Fire br or gr c (2yrs) Risk Me (FR) - Grey Twig (Godswalk (USA)).......... (G Heymans) 4,000

From Warwick House Stables
Amoret (IRE) b f (2yrs) Jareer (USA) - Gentle Freedom (Wolver Hollow)...... (B.B.A.) 21,000

To Dissolve a Partnership, from Warwick House Stables
Festin br g (3yrs) General Assembly (USA) - Roses Galore (USA) (Stage Door Johnny)........................... (Kildare Thoroughbred Services) 4,000

730

Property of Viscount Scarsdale, from Warwick House Stables
General John (IRE) br g (4yrs) Cyrano de Bergerac - Hill's Realm (USA) (Key To The Kingdom (USA)) (Bjorn Bjorkman) 3,000

From Warwick House Stables
Reel Of Tulloch (IRE) b g (4yrs) Salmon Leap (USA) - Miss Sandman (Manacle) (Paolo Santini) 3,200

To Dissolve a Partnership, from Warwick House Stables
Red Admiral ch g (3yrs) Formidable (USA) - Dancing Meg (USA) (Marshua's Dancer (USA))......... (C And N Bloodstock) 11,500

Property of Viscount Scarsdale, from Warwick House Stables
Shuttlecock ch g (2yrs) Pharly (FR) - Upper Sister (Upper Case (USA))........... (Johnny McKeever Bloodstock) 5,200

To Dissolve a Partnership, from Warwick House Stables
Warwick Warrior (IRE) b g (2yrs) Reasonable (FR) - Almost Heaven (Corvaro (USA))......... (C And N Bloodstock) 5,400

Property of Mr C Murray, from Calder Park Stables

Kawasir (CAN) b or br g (3yrs) Gulch (USA) - Madame Treasurer (CAN) (Key To The Mint (USA)) .... (Cormac McCormack Associates) 2,000

731

NEWMARKET
Wednesday, October 27th

Property of Roldvale Ltd, from Charnwood Stables

Sport Racing Club b f (2yrs) Taufan (USA) - Razor Blade (Sharp Edge) .... (Lambert Bloodstock) 1,350

Property of Mr F J Sainsbury, from Barbury Castle Stables

Elaine Tully (IRE) b m (5yrs) Persian Bold - Hanna Alta (FR) (Busted) .... (Mrs P G Wilkin) 10,000

Mallam Waters (IRE) b f (2yrs) Mister Majestic - Petty Session (Blakeney) ... (Equine Services) 1,100

Property of a Partnership, from Barbury Castle Stables

Murphy's Hope (IRE) b c (3yrs) Common Grounds - Legs And Things (Three Legs)................. (Cedric Boutin) 2,600

Property of Mr P G Lowe, from Barbury Castle Stables

Queens Contractor b g (3yrs) Formidable (USA) - Salazie (Ile de Bourbon (USA)) (David Minton Bloodstock) 2,000

Property of Watership Down Racing, from Barbury Castle Stables

Visimotion (USA) ch g (3yrs) Imp Society (USA) - Ditdad (USA) (Tudor Grey)..... (Tote Cherry-Downes) 7,000

Property of a Partnership, from Coronation Stables

Free Mover (IRE) br g (4yrs) Rousillon (USA) - Free Dance (FR) (Green Dancer (USA))....... (Peter Doyle Bloodstock) 16,500

Property of Mr J Shack, from Groundhill Farm

Eurythmic gr f (3yrs) Pharly (FR) - Amalancher (USA) (Alleged (USA))..... (Cyril Shack) 6,000

Property of Mr E F Parsons, from Harper Lodge Stables

Heathcliff (IRE) gr c (2yrs) Common Grounds - Catherine Linton (USA) (High Echelon (USA))............... (C B A) 10,000

Property of S Corman Ltd, from Harper Lodge Stables

Toton Lad b c (2yrs) Chilibang - Corman-Style (Ahonoora)............. (B B A) 3,400

732

Property of a Partnership, from Longsides Stables

Affordable b g (5yrs) Formidable (USA) - Ophrys (Nonoalco (USA))..... (W Clay) 6,000

Anar (IRE) ch c (4yrs) Sharpo - Only A Dream (FR) (Green Dancer (USA)) ..... (L C Maultby) 5,000

Property of Five To Seven Partnership, from Longsides Stables

Five To Seven (USA) b g (4yrs) Little Missouri (USA) - French Galaxy (USA) (Majestic Light (USA)) (Chris Thornton) 41,000

Property of a Partnership, from Longsides Stables

Formaestre (IRE) b f (3yrs) Formidable (USA) - Maestrette (Manado) .... (David Minton Bloodstock) 4,000

Property of Mr J Lawson-Brown, from Longsides Stables

Nutty Brown b g (3yrs) Primitive Rising (USA) - Nuthill (Derrylin).... (J Joseph) 12,000

Property of a Partnership, from Longsides Stables

Shamshom Al Arab (IRE) gr h (5yrs) Glenstal (USA) - Love Locket (Levmoss) ..... (Victoria Haigh) 8,800

Property of Mrs A M Norton, from Longsides Stables

World Without End (USA) ch g (4yrs) World Appeal (USA) - Mardie's Bid (USA) (Raise A Bid (USA))........... (W Clay) 30,000

Property of a Partnership, from Rathmoy Stables

Chief Executive b c (2yrs) Unfuwain (USA) - Two Worlds (USA) (Diesis)... (W Muir) 8,200

Lugano b c (2yrs) Rousillon (USA) - Arita (FR) (Kronzeuge).................... (Kildare Thoroughbred Services) 15,000

Property of Roldvale Ltd, from Rathmoy Stables

Stready Risk ch g (2yrs) Risk Me (FR) - Greenstead Lass (Double-U-Jay) ...... (Rachel Bridger) 600

733

Property of Mr G Mazza, from Shalfleet Stables

Iommelli (IRE) ch c (3yrs) Don't Forget Me - Inner Pearl (Gulf Pearl)........ (B B A) 30,000

Property of Roldvale Ltd, from Shalfleet Stables

Mr Eubanks (USA) ch c (2yrs) Imp Society (USA) - Whitesburg Lass (USA) (Whitesburg (USA))................. (B B A) 24,000

Opus Magnum (USA) ch c (2yrs) Bering - Erin On Your Toes (USA) (Irish River (FR))........................ (B B A) 1,800

To Dissolve a Partnership, from Shalfleet Stables

Rita's Captain (IRE) ch f (2yrs) Thatching - Forest Of Arden (Tap On Wood) ...... (Equine Services) 1,400

From Coombelands Stables Ltd

Bonaigua (IRE) ch c (2yrs) Lomond (USA) - Watership (USA) (Foolish Pleasure (USA))........... (Pro-Am & Co Ltd) 26,000

Lear King (USA) b c (3yrs) Lear Fan (USA) - Our Tina Marie (USA) (Nijinsky (CAN)) (C B A) 21,000

Lucky Noire b m (5yrs) Aragon - Noire Small (USA) (Elocutionist (USA)) .... (Luke Comer) 2,400

Marastani (USA) ch g (3yrs) Shahrastani (USA) - Marianna's Girl (USA) (Dewan (USA))......... (Tote Cherry-Downes) 43,000

Mato b c (2yrs) Mtoto - Compton Lady (USA) (Sovereign Dancer (USA))....... (J Groenenboom) 6,400

Thaleros b c (3yrs) Green Desert (USA) - Graecia Magna (USA) (Private Account (USA))........................ (G Moore) 20,000
Trooping (IRE) b c (4yrs) Auction Ring (USA) - Tunguska (Busted) .... (M R J Bloodstock) 17,000
Young Freeman (USA) b c (4yrs) Nijinsky (CAN) - Committed (USA) (Hagley (USA))........................ (B B A) 24,000

734

Property of Darley Stud Management Co Ltd, from Coombelands Stables Ltd

Scots Pine (USA) ch c (2yrs) Woodman (USA) - Dowry (USA) (Damascus (USA)) .... (B B A (Italia)) 2,500

Property of a Partnership, from South Bank Stables

Abbots Daughter ch f (2yrs) Absalom - Blakesware Saint (Welsh Saint) .... (Stephen Uppstrom) 2,400
Carbon Steel (IRE) b c (3yrs) Sure Blade (USA) - Alligatrix (USA) (Alleged (USA)) (Wilming Yeo) 10,500
Chief's Song b g (3yrs) Chief Singer - Tizzy (Formidable (USA))........... (S Dow) 18,000
Chummy's Pal (USA) b c (3yrs) Bering - Miss Vestment (USA) (Magesterial (USA))............. (J Groenenboom) 18,000
Chummy's Saga ch c (3yrs) Caerleon (USA) - Sagar (Habitat)........... (Len Lungo) 8,400
Cyrus The Bold (IRE) b g (3yrs) Persian Bold - Etoile Des Galles (Busted)........... (Kildare Thoroughbred Services) 5,000

From South Bank Stables

Dee Raft (USA) b c (3yrs) Raft (USA) - Pharlette (FR) (Pharly (FR)).... (C B A) 20,000
Gaiete ch f (2yrs) Risk Me (FR) - Stepping Gaily (Gay Fandango (USA)) (P Young) 1,050

Property of a Partnership, from South Bank Stables

Kimberley Boy b c (3yrs) Mtoto - Diamond House (Habitat)........... (R Sharpe) 16,000
King Bruce b c (2yrs) Clantime - Miss Spinney (Uncle Pokey) .... (R O'Gorman Bloodstock) 3,700
Major Success (IRE) br c (2yrs) Gallic League - Estivalia (Persian Bold) ...... (Wilming Yeo) 21,000
Mint A Million (IRE) b g (2yrs) Thatching - Often (Ballymore)...... (M Blanshard) 3,100
Miss Snozzle (IRE) b f (2yrs) Cyrano de Bergerac - Shuckran Habibi (Thatching) (B B A) 1,050
Queens Stroller (IRE) b f (2yrs) Pennine Walk - Mount Isa (Miami Springs) ..... (C C Elsey) 6,600

735

From South Bank Stables

Risque-Tout ch f (2yrs) Risk Me (FR) - Valldemosa (Music Boy).. (T P Young) 1,800

Property of a Partnership, from South Bank Stables

Royal Cape ch c (2yrs) Efisio - Tame Duchess (Saritamer (USA)).... (B B A) 3,000
Snow Board gr g (4yrs) Niniski (USA) - Troja (Troy)................. (J Delahooke) 22,000

From South Bank Stables

Sozzled gr c (2yrs) Absalom - The High Dancer (High Line)........... (B Hills) 13,500

Property of a Partnership, from South Bank Stables

The Seer b c (3yrs) Robellino (USA) - Serration (Kris).......................... (B B A) 11,500
Talos (IRE) b g (5yrs) Taufan (USA) - Jovial Josie (USA) (Sea Bird II).. (W Bentley) 6,000

From South Bank Stables

Water Skier b c (3yrs) Nishapour (FR) - Wave Dancer (Dance In Time (CAN)) .. (M Chapman) 6,000
Wynberg b c (2yrs) Robellino (USA) - Pellinora (USA) (King Pellinore (USA)) ..... (B Hobbs) 3,500

Property of Shadwell Estate Co Ltd, from South Bank Stables

Ghadyah (IRE) b f (2yrs) Nordico (USA) - Tristan Du Cunha (USA) (Sir Ivor)..... (Barrett Watson) 650

Property of Hon Mrs Henry Keswick, from Windsor House Stables

China Robin ch f (2yrs) Night Shift (USA) - Portvasco (Sharpo)....... (P D Evans) 3,200

736

Property of Hesmonds Stud Ltd, from Windsor House Stables

Devotee b f (2yrs) Superlative - Gallant Believer (Gallant Romeo (USA)) .... (David Minton Bloodstock) 13,500
Golden Fern ch f (2yrs) Glint Of Gold - Icefern (Moorestyle) .... (Pro-Am & Co Ltd) 6,800

Property of a Partnership, from Windsor House Stables

Walking The Plank b g (4yrs) Daring March - Pirate Maid (Auction Ring (USA)) ...... (N Tinkler) 20,000

Property of Shadwell Estate Co Ltd, from Windsor House Stables

Dyab (USA) b c (3yrs) Diesis - Petrava (NZ) (Imposing (AUS))......... (C Williams) 14,000
Mawayed (USA) b c (3yrs) Blushing Groom (FR) - Thaidah (CAN) (Vice Regent (CAN))................ (Cedric Boutin) 6,200
Wali (USA) b c (3yrs) Lomond (USA) - Magic Slipper (Habitat).. (B J McMath) 5,200

Property of Heathavon Stables Ltd, from Moss Side Racing Stables

Royal Music ch g (3yrs) Music Boy - Astral Suite (On Your Mark).......... (Cash) 1,000

Property of Mr B R Allen, from Moss Side Racing Stables

Trentisimo (IRE) ch g (3yrs) Imperial Frontier (USA) - Be Nimble (Wattlefield).... (Tote Cherry-Downes) 10,000

Property of Mr W Grubmuller, from Induna Stables

Cool Harry (USA) b or br c (2yrs) Sir Harry Lewis (USA) - No Chili (Glint Of Gold).. (R M Botterill) 3,200

Property of Mrs Coral E Hamson, from Induna Stables

Corals Dream (IRE) b c (4yrs) Petorius - Walkyria (Lord Gayle (USA)) .... (R O'Gorman Bloodstock) 30,000

737

Property of Mr C J A Hughes, from Induna Stables

Countercheck (IRE) b g (4yrs) Try My Best (USA) - Swift Reply (He Loves Me).... (D McCain) 2,000

Property of a Partnership, from Induna Stables

Elanmatina (IRE) ch f (4yrs) Burslem - Sally St Clair (Sallust) (Emerald Bloodstock) 4,800

Property of a Gentleman, from Induna Stables

Hardliner b or br c (4yrs) Sizzling Melody - Miss Trilli (Ardoon)...... (Luke Comer) 800

Property of a Partnership, from Induna Stables

Lola Wants b f (3yrs) Lidhame - Plain Tree (Wolver Hollow).......... (T Bandilla) 1,150

Property of Mr Jack Fisher, from Induna Stables

Mysilv ch f (3yrs) Bustino - Miss By Miles (Milesian)......... (Million In Mind (3)) 27,000

Property of a Partnership, from Induna Stables

Sylvan (IRE) b or br f (4yrs) Taufan (USA) - Unspoiled (Tina's Pet).... (W Bentley) 3,400

Thatched (IRE) b c (3yrs) Thatching - Shadia (USA) (Naskra (USA))....... (R E Barr) 2,600

From Durdans Stables

Play Hever Golf b g (3yrs) Alleging (USA) - Sweet Rosina (Sweet Revenge)....... (M Thwaites) 38,000

Property of Sheikh Abdullah Al Quassimi, from Eve Lodge Stables

Shatan b c (2yrs) Taufan (USA) - Mawaal Habeebee (Northfields (USA))......... (Kildare Thoroughbred Services) 3,000

Property of Mr & Mrs T Painting

Olifantsfontein b g (5yrs) Thatching - Taplow (Tap On Wood).................. (David Minton Bloodstock) 6,000

738

Property of Mr S Hinton, from Lethornes Stables

Sunday's Hill b c (4yrs) Efisio - Elkie Brooks (Relkino)................ (M Thwaites) 36,000

Property of a Partnership, from Cadland House Stables

Island Knight (IRE) b g (4yrs) Jupiter Island - Florence Street (Final Straw).......... (Equine Services) 2,000

From Cadland House Stables

Roca Murada (IRE) br g (4yrs) Cyrano de Bergerac - Keppols (Furry Glen)....... (David Minton Bloodstock) 15,000

Property of Darley Stud Management Co Ltd, from Ecurie A Fabre, France

Canadia Shield (IRE) b c (3yrs) Slip Anchor - Tundra Goose (Habitat)............... (Cormac McCormack Associates) 38,000

Cherkassy b c (3yrs) Soviet Star (USA) - Chalon (Habitat)........ (B B A (Italia)) 5,000

Western Roll (USA) b or br c (2yrs) Storm Cat (USA) - Western Adventure (Double Form).............. (B B A (Italia)) 6,000

Property of Darley Stud Management Co Ltd, from Rockingham Yard

Desert Challenger (IRE) b g (3yrs) Sadler's Wells (USA) - Verily (Known Fact (USA)) .... (J R Jenkins) 6,800

Darzee b c (3yrs) Darshaan - Royal Lorna (USA) (Val de L'orne (FR)) .... (P R Hedger) 5,400

Dakar Rally b c (3yrs) Green Desert (USA) - Overdrive (Shirley Heights) .... (Bettina Keller) 6,400

Nebaal (USA) ch g (3yrs) Storm Cat (USA) - Primevere (USA) (Irish River (FR)) ..... (G Thorner) 1,700

Tasset (CAN) ch c (3yrs) Tasso (USA) - While I'm Away (Buckpasser)......... (Luke Comer) 3,000

Zeretelli (USA) b c (3yrs) Nureyev (USA) - Elect (USA) (Vaguely Noble) .... (John Warren Bloodstock) 6,200

739

Property of Darley Stud Management Co Ltd, from Currabeg Stables, Ireland

Birthplace (IRE) b or br c (3yrs) Top Ville - Birthday Party (FR) (Windwurf (GER)).. (J Mackie) 10,500

Jebi (USA) b c (3yrs) Phone Tick (USA) - Smokey Legend (USA) (Hawaii) .... (David Minton Bloodstock) 10,000

National Flag (FR) b c (3yrs) Sure Blade (USA) - On The Staff (USA) (Master Willie).................. (Karl Burke) 3,200

Sumy b c (3yrs) Never So Bold - Sumara (USA) (Nureyev (USA)).. (D Arbuthnot) 6,600

Property of Darley Stud Management Co Ltd, from Someries Stud

Alzia (IRE) b f (3yrs) Alzao (USA) - Special Meeting (Persian Bold).............. (Peter Doyle Bloodstock) 1,400

Celesta (IRE) b f (3yrs) Celestial Storm (USA) - Strident Note (The Minstrel (CAN)).................. (D Campbell) 850

Property of Heathavon Stables, from East Everleigh Stables

Noble Risk b c (3yrs) Risk Me (FR) - Nativity (USA) (Native Royalty (USA)).......... (B de Haan) 8,000

Property of Roldvale Ltd, from East Everleigh Stables

Obvious Risk b c (2yrs) Risk Me (FR) - Gymnopedie (Jaazeiro (USA)) .... (D Woods) 16,000

Property of N T C Racing Ltd, from East Everleigh Stables

Son Pardo b c (3yrs) Petong - Flitteriss Park (Beldale Flutter (USA)) .... (Shadwell Estate Co) 46,000

To Dissolve a Partnership, from East Everleigh Stables

Swing Low ch c (4yrs) Swing Easy (USA) - Ballaquine (Martinmas).. (Roldvale Ltd) 145,000

Venture Capitalist ch g (4yrs) Never So Bold - Brave Advance (USA) (Bold Laddie (USA))....... (Peter Doyle Bloodstock) 23,000

Well Suited b g (3yrs) Elegant Air - Gay Appeal (Star Appeal).... (B J McMath) 7,800

740

Property of a Partnership, from West Ilsley Stables

Blue Flag (USA) b g (4yrs) Dixieland Band (USA) - Stuttsman County (USA) (Damascus (USA))........ (G Thorner) 4,500

From West Ilsley Stables

Colour Sergeant b g (5yrs) Green Desert (USA) - Tartan Pimpernel (Blakeney)... (John Warren Bloodstock) 16,000

Property of a Partnership, from West Ilsley Stables

Coltrane b g (5yrs) Dominion - Rainbow's End (My Swallow).......... (M C Pipe) 22,000

From West Ilsley Stables

Green Kilt b c (3yrs) Green Desert (USA) - Kilinski (Niniski (USA)).................. (J Groenenboom) 18,000

Hierarch (USA) ch c (4yrs) Diesis - Highclere (Queen's Hussar)...... (D Sasse) 13,000

High Summer b g (3yrs) Green Desert (USA) - Beacon Hill (Bustino).......... (T Thomson Jones) 37,000

Property of a Partnership, from West Ilsley Stables

Straight Arrow ch c (2yrs) Indian Ridge - Harmonical (USA) (Lyphard's Wish (FR)).................. (Ettore Pistoetti) 80,000

From West Ilsley Stables

Talent (USA) b g (5yrs) Clever Trick (USA) - Contralto (Busted)............. (C B A) 28,000

Top Register (USA) b c (4yrs) Dixieland Band (USA) - Contralto (Busted)....... (Fahad Sa Shatti) 8,500

To Dissolve a Partnership, from St Gatien Stables

Shujan (USA) b c (4yrs) Diesis - Linda's Magic (USA) (Far North (CAN))........ (R Akehurst) 36,000

741

Property of Shadwell Estate Co Ltd, from St Gatien Stables

Ikhtiraa (USA) b c (3yrs) Imperial Falcon (CAN) - True Native (USA) (Raise A Native)............ (Equine Services) 7,000

Dawalib (USA) ch c (3yrs) Danzig Connection (USA) - Centavos (USA) (Scout Leader (USA))........... (D H Jones) 6,200

Property of a Partnership, from Woodway Stables

Colne Valley b f (2yrs) Mazillier (USA) - Mary Miller (Sharpo) .... (Hungarian Zsoke Club) 2,500

From Woodway Stables

Kedge b c (3yrs) Slip Anchor - Bercheba (Bellypha).................. (W Clay) 6,600

Property of a Partnership, from Woodway Stables

Mogwai (IRE) b c (4yrs) Alzao (USA) - Maltese Pet (Draganora Palace (USA)) (S Dow) 7,400

From Warren Place Stables

Alkhafji b c (4yrs) Ardross - Eljazzi (Artaius (USA)).................. (C Macmillan) 5,200

Barratry ch c (3yrs) Caerleon (USA) - Tolmi (Great Nephew)...... (B B A (Ireland)) 18,000

Gingerbird (IRE) ch f (2yrs) Salt Dome (USA) - Vibrant Hue (USA) (Exclusive Native (USA))........... (G Heymans) 9,600

Kinchenjunga b f (3yrs) Darshaan - Konigsalpen (GER) (Priamos (GER)) (W Muir) 5,400

Nile Delta (IRE) b c (4yrs) Green Desert (USA) - Tolmi (Great Nephew) .... (D Campbell) 5,400

Vishnu (USA) b c (3yrs) Storm Bird (CAN) - Vachti (FR) (Crystal Palace (FR))....... (C Barker) 10,000

742

Property of Darley Stud Management Co Ltd, from Warren Place Stables

Fire In Winter (IRE) b c (2yrs) Polish Precedent (USA) - Fatah Flare (USA) (Alydar (USA)).................. (Lady Herries) 7,000

Jagged Sword ch c (2yrs) Kris - Cherry Hinton (USA) (Nijinsky (CAN))......... (Marco Bozzani) 3,800

Yeltsin ch c (3yrs) Soviet Star (USA) - Mill On The Floss (Mill Reef (USA))........ (Brian Wilson) 76,000

Property of Darley Stud Management Co Ltd, from Kingwood House Stables

Jelabna b f (2yrs) Jalmood (USA) - Labwa (USA) (Lyphard (USA)).. (M Blanshard) 2,100

Leewa (IRE) b c (3yrs) Caerleon (USA) - Princess Nawaal (USA) (Seattle Slew (USA))...................... (W Muir) 7,800

Sentiment b f (2yrs) Dancing Brave (USA) - Sweet Habit (Habitat).... (P R Hedger) 15,000

Tammuz b or br c (2yrs) Reference Point - Pretty Lady (High Top).. (Lady Herries) 7,000

Yahmi (IRE) b c (3yrs) Law Society (USA) - Hogan's Sister (USA) (Speak John) .... (C B A) 10,000

Property of Shadwell Estate Co Ltd, from Kingwood House Stables

Faez b c (3yrs) Mtoto - Ghanimah (Caerleon (USA)).................... (R Arnold) 6,500

Glorious Peak (USA) ch c (3yrs) Topsider (USA) - Brilliant Future (USA) (Forli (ARG)).................... (M Wane) 950

743

Property of Million in Mind Partnership 2, from Hurgill Lodge Stables

A Million Watts b or br g (2yrs) Belfort (FR) - Peters Pet Girl (Norwick (USA))...... (Lady Herries) 4,800

From Hurgill Lodge Stables

Blue Grotto (IRE) ch c (3yrs) Bluebird (USA) - Ganna (ITY) (Molvedo) (M Tompkins) 16,000

Faetal Shock b f (3yrs) Electric - Mortal Sin (USA) (Green Forest (USA))........... (R J Bateman) 1,000

Ovideo b f (2yrs) Domynsky - One Last Glimpse (Relko)...... (David Elsworth) 6,500

Silver Standard b g (3yrs) Jupiter Island - One Half Silver (CAN) (Plugged Nickle (USA)).................. (B Hobbs) 7,800

From Kremlin House Stables

Monazite b c (3yrs) Damister (USA) - Princely Maid (King's Troop) (A Wilkinson) 6,200

Property of Darley Stud Management Co Ltd, from Kremlin House Stables

Dubai Summer b c (3yrs) Green Desert (USA) - Gesedeh (Ela-Mana-Mou) ..... (Mohamed Kaled) 14,500

Maashai Lawm (IRE) b g (3yrs) Lomond (USA) - Gay Apparel (CAN) (Up Spirits) (R Durant) 4,000

Property of Mr R Lamb, from The Limes Stables
Tadora (IRE) b or br g (4yrs) Tate Gallery (USA) - Silbadora (Don (ITY))... (B B A) 4,200

Property of Shadwell Estate Co Ltd, from The Limes Stables
Jalib (IRE) b c (3yrs) Lomond (USA) - Crown Godiva (Godswalk (USA)) (R W Hipkin) 4,000
Tartib (IRE) b c (3yrs) Fayruz - June Lady (Junius)........ (Kjell-Aule Tonnessen) 4,600

744

Property of Darley Stud Management Co Ltd, from Heath House Stables
Callabonna b f (2yrs) Cadeaux Genereux - A Lyph (USA) (Lypheor)..... (J Fretheim) 3,600

Property of Mr F Salman, from Heath House Stables
Donia (USA) ch f (4yrs) Graustark - Katrinka (USA) (Sovereign Dancer (USA))....... (J L Harris) 5,200

Property of Mr J B Haggas, from Heath House Stables
Keyway (USA) ch c (3yrs) Groovy (USA) - Maui Manor (USA) (Hawaii)........... (Tote Cherry-Downes) 21,000

Property of a Partnership, from Heath House Stables
Post Mistress (IRE) b or br f (2yrs) Cyrano de Bergerac - Postie (Sharpo) (N Greig) 17,000

Property of Lady Fairhaven, from Heath House Stables
Quantity Surveyor b c (4yrs) Aragon - Quaranta (Hotfoot)....... (R Akehurst) 10,500

Property of a Partnership, from Heath House Stables
Quinsigimond ch f (3yrs) Formidable (USA) - Quillotern (USA) (Arctic Tern (USA)) .. (R O'Gorman Bloodstock) 28,000

Property of Cheveley Park Stud, from Heath House Stables
Red Bouquet b f (2yrs) Reference Point - Cerise Bouquet (Mummy's Pet)....... (B B A) 5,400

Property of Mr F Salman, from Heath House Stables
Seama (USA) ch f (3yrs) Affirmed (USA) - Isticanna (USA) (Far North (CAN))....... (Mohamed Kaled) 10,000

Property of a Partnership, from Heath House Stables
Sure Haven (IRE) b g (4yrs) Sure Blade (USA) - Tea House (Sassafras (FR)).... (Ron Hodges) 26,000
Swordsmanship b g (2yrs) Sure Blade (USA) - Tashinsky (USA) (Nijinsky (CAN))................. (G Heymans) 7,400
Sylvan Starlight b or br f (3yrs) Sylvan Express - Kakisa (Forlorn River)....... (J M Bradley) 2,600
The Where Withal b c (3yrs) Glint Of Gold - Bourgeonette (Mummy's Pet)........ (Geoffrey Howson Bloodstock) 49,000

745

Property of Pinnacle Racing Stable, from Heath House Stables
Time Honored (USA) b c (3yrs) Time For A Change (USA) - La Paqueline (FR) (Sassafras (FR))....... (Soren Jensen) 4,000

Property of a Partnership, from Heath House Stables
Velasco (IRE) b g (3yrs) Nordico (USA) - Donnarella (Dom Racine (FR)).. (C B A) 25,000

Property of Mr Giles W Pritchard-Gordon, from Trillium Place Stables
Candi Das (IRE) b f (2yrs) Jareer (USA) - Indigo Queen (Indian King (USA))...... (B B A) 6,600
Forest Loch ch f (2yrs) Lomond (USA) - Arbour (USA) (Graustark)............. (Jill Lamb Bloodstock) 4,200

Property of Million in Mind Partnership, from Trillium Place Stables
Million At Dawn (IRE) b f (2yrs) Fayruz - Morning Stroll (Tower Walk).......... (E O'Leary) 7,800

From Whitsbury Manor Stables
Aberdeen Heather b g (3yrs) Absalom - Scotch Thistle (Sassafras (FR))........ (Abdi Aziz M Al Saud) 10,500
Bixby (USA) b c (3yrs) Seattle Dancer (USA) - Golden Secretariat (USA) (Secretariat (USA))..................... (A Bathe) 2,300
Gift Box (IRE) b f (2yrs) Jareer (USA) - Mira Adonde (USA) (Sharpen Up)... (B B A) 750
Mind The Roof (IRE) b f (3yrs) Thatching - Thunderflash (Runnett)............... (David Minton Bloodstock) 2,400
Young Max b g (4yrs) Nomination - Hollow Heart (Wolver Hollow)........ (B Wall) 800

746

Property of Darley Stud Management Co Ltd, from Whitsbury Manor Stables
Aghar (IRE) ch c (3yrs) Ahonoora - Foliage (Thatching)....... (Robert Wetemans) 4,200
Fasht Eldebl b c (2yrs) Sadler's Wells (USA) - Tralthee (USA) (Tromos)..... (B B A) 7,200

Property of Earl of Halifax, from High Havens Stables
Tree Of Heaven b f (2yrs) Robellino (USA) - Cape Chestnut (Bustino)...... (B B A) 16,000

Property of Shadwell Estate Co Ltd, from High Havens Stables
Mutawali (IRE) ch c (3yrs) Exactly Sharp (USA) - Ludovica (Bustino) (R J Baker) 5,200
Qaffal (USA) b c (3yrs) Seattle Dancer (USA) - Samalex (Ela-Mana-Mou)...... (Richard Phillips) 6,000
Tajdif (USA) br c (3yrs) Storm Cat (USA) - Hankow Willow (USA) (No Robbery)... (Lillingston Bloodstock) 8,500
Wakt b f (3yrs) Akarad (FR) - Nasara (FR) (Home Guard (USA))........ (J White) 9,500

Property of a Partnership, from Flint Cottage Stables
Badger's Bend b f (2yrs) North Briton - Sunset Ray (Hotfoot)................ (Hungarian Zsoke Club) 2,600
Ellaruth (IRE) b f (2yrs) Kefaah (USA) - Gaelic Jewel (Scottish Rifle)......... (Mulder Behar B V) 3,500
Feliz (IRE) ch f (2yrs) Roi Danzig (USA) - Onthecomet (Chief Singer)........... (C P R Rowe) 600

747

From Flint Cottage Stables

Gweek (IRE) ch f (3yrs) Common Grounds - Do We Know (Derrylin) (Ahmed Kaled) 10,000

Salt Stone (IRE) ch f (2yrs) Salt Dome (USA) - Petrina (Petingo).. (Pro Am & Co Ltd) 2,600

Property of a Partnership, from Flint Cottage Stables

Snowdon Slights b f (2yrs) Aragon - Folle Idee (USA) (Foolish Pleasure (USA)) ... (Petrovitch Bell) 1,300

Solo Charter b c (3yrs) Chief Singer - Royal Agreement (USA) (Vaguely Noble)..... (G J M Bloodstock) 6,200

Space-Peril (IRE) br f (2yrs) Astronef - Farriers Slipper (Prince Tenderfoot (USA)) (Equine Services) 1,700

From Flint Cottage Stables

Super Symphonic ch c (2yrs) Interrex (CAN) - Super Melody (Song)......... (B B A) 3,000

Property of a Partnership, from Flint Cottage Stables

Ume River (IRE) b g (3yrs) Nordance (USA) - So Delighted (Main Reef) .... (Barrett Watson) 1,600

Waddle (IRE) ch g (2yrs) Fayruz - All Time High (Sandhurst Prince)........ (B B A) 2,400

From Cedar Point Racing Stables

Bodari b c (4yrs) Prince Sabo - City Link Rose (Lochnager)...... (B B A (Italia)) 9,000

Property of Mr Christopher Wright, from Hill House Stables

Complete Madness ch g (3yrs) Irish River (FR) - Candle In The Wind (Thatching) (Lars Sward) 12,500

Pelican Island b g (2yrs) Damister (USA) - Cameroun (African Sky)............. (Carmine Cocca) 600

748

To Dissolve a Syndicate, from La Grange Racing Stables

Northern Storm (IRE) b c (2yrs) Fayruz - Beautiful (Aragon)...... (Sean Woods) 1,400

From La Grange Racing Stables

Stapleford Lass b f (3yrs) Bairn (USA) - Idabella (FR) (Carwhite).. (Luke Comer) 1,800

Property of a Partnership, from Calder Park Stables

Royal Roller (IRE) b g (3yrs) Dara Monarch - Tumble Dale (Tumble Wind (USA)) .... (Alan Smith) 15,000

Property of a Partnership, from Loretta Lodge Stables

Just Greenwich gr f (2yrs) Chilibang - What A Challenge (Sallust)...... (P D Evans) 2,000

749

NEWMARKET
Thursday, October 28th
(Yearlings)

From Northgate Lodge Stud

b or br y c Grey Desire - Jalstar (Jalmood (USA))....... (Peter Doyle Bloodstock) 4,000

Property of Mrs N Madsen, from Albany Stud

b y f Emarati (USA) - Kinz (Great Nephew) (W Haggas) 1,800

Property of Shaunlara Pinhooking Syndicate, from Shaunlara Stud

b y c Zalazl (USA) - Knavesmire (Runnymede)............. (M P Roberts) 3,900

Property of J P & A J Hall, from Badger Hill Stud

ch y c Ballacashtal (CAN) - Lady Brave (IRE) (Commanche Run)........... (B B A) 1,400

Property of Collectors Investments Ltd, from Ednaston Lodge Stud

ch y f High Kicker (USA) - Lady Songe (Anax)................. (Petrovich Bell) 1,000

Property of Mrs D Paul, from Huntingfield Stud

gr y c Pittacus (USA) - Lady Woodpecker (Tap On Wood)............ (R Durant) 3,000

Property of Mr S Uppstrom

b y c Astronef - Lautremont (Auction Ring (USA)).................. (L Casey) 3,800

Property of Collectors Investments Ltd, from Ednaston Lodge Stud

ch y f Crowning Honors (CAN) - Lilac Lady (Fair Turn)..................... (B B A) 500

Property of a Gentleman, from Stud-On-The-Chart

b y c Deploy - Loveskate (USA) (Overskate (CAN))................... (J Glover) 7,000

Property of Mr Allan Perry

ch y f Dunbeath (USA) - Lucy Manette (Final Straw).......... (Susan Piggott) 4,500

750

Property of Stud-On-The-Chart

b y f High Estate - Martin-Lavell News (Song)................... (W Haggas) 5,200

From Northgate Lodge Stud

gr y c Grey Desire - Mazurkanova (Song) .. (J McKeever Bloodstock) 4,100

Property of Mr & Mrs P J Sands, from Grovewood Stud

b or br y c Sayf El Arab (USA) - Mia Fillia (Formidable (USA)).... (Susan Scargill) 2,000

Property of Collectors Investments Ltd, from Ednaston Lodge Stud

b y f Crowning Honors (CAN) - Mio Mementa (Streak)......(David Nicholls) 3,100

ch y c High Kicker (USA) - Miss Poll Finders (Swing Easy (USA)).. (Equine Services) 1,800

Property of Etchingham Stud

b y f Midyan (USA) - Mohibbah (USA) (Conquistador Cielo (USA)) .... (A J Young) 3,600

Property of Mr L A J Lodge, from Little Stud Farm

b y f Sayf El Arab (USA) - Moment In Time (Without Fear (FR))......... (J Pearce) 4,000

From Three Gates Stud

b y f Risk Me (FR) - Moonlight Princess (Alias Smith (USA))........... (B B A) 3,200

Property of Witney Stud Farm

b y c Satin Wood - Mrs Bizz (Status Seeker) .... (Richard Phillips) 3,000

Property of Chantry Farm

ch y c Risk Me (FR) - Mrs Scattercash (Northfields (USA))..... (B B A (Italia)) 1,600

751

Property of Stud-On-The-Chart
b y f Pharly (FR) - National Dress (Welsh Pageant)................ (W J Payne) 2,000
Property of Mr G S Shropshire, from West Dereham Abbey Stud
b y f Prince Sabo - Naturally Bold (Bold Lad (IRE))............... (M Bryce-Smith) 5,800
Property of Mr M J Paver
gr y f Rock City - Normanby Lass (Bustino) (M Brittain) 3,500
From Elsenham Stud
ch y f Risk Me (FR) - Our Lucy (Porto Bello) (R O'Ryan) 2,000
Property of a Partnership, from Trickledown Stud
b y f Puissance - Pearl Pet (Mummy's Pet) (Alan Smith) 3,300
Property of J P & A J Hall, from Badger Hill Stud
b y f Chaparly (FR) - Pen Bal Queen (Record Run)................. (Petrovich Bell) 450
Property of Sexton Enterprises, from Ham Cross Farm
b y f Nomination - Persian Tapestry (Tap On Wood)................ (Mrs E Butler) 700
Property of Freedom Farm
ch y c Vague Shot - Plum Blossom (USA) (Gallant Romeo (USA)) .... (Pro-Am & Co Ltd) 5,000
Property of The Hon J G Lambton, from Longholes Stud
ch y c Minster Son - Preziosa (Homing).... (B B A) 5,000
Property of Mr J G Charlton
b y f Aragon - Primrose Way (Young Generation).................. (Pat Mitchell) 3,600

752

Property of Mr P J Hunt, from Manston Farm Stables
b y c Emarati (USA) - Princess Charybdis (Ballymoss).. (J McKeever Bloodstock) 4,000
Property of Witney Stud Farm
b y f Satin Wood - Ra Ra (Lord Gayle (USA)) .... (Cash) 2,600
Property of a Partnership, from Executive Stud
ch y c Executive Man - Recent Events (Stanford)................ (A Stringer) 850
From West Stow Stud
ch y f Prince Sabo - Red Tapsi (Tap On Wood).................. (Ron Boss) 2,400
Property of Witney Stud Farm
b y c Superlative - Rheinbloom (Rheingold) (Lambert Bloodstock) 4,000
Property of Mrs D Onions, from Witney Stud Farm
ch y c Faustus (USA) - Rueful Lady (Streetfighter)...... (Peter Doyle Bloodstock) 3,200
From Silver Ley Stables
b y f Thowra (FR) - Run For Rosemary (Petorius).................... (B B A) 500
Property of W & R Barnett Ltd, from Ted Voute, Agent
b y f Cadeaux Genereux - Sarajill (High Line) .... (Cash) 2,700
Property of L J & A P Roberts, from Shaunlara Stud
b y g Arctic Lord - Save It Lass (Nicholas Bill)................ (Richard Phillips) 620
Property of J P & A J Hall, from Badger Hill Stud
ch y c Beveled (USA) - Scenic Villa (Top Ville)........ (Peter Doyle Bloodstock) 5,200

753

Property of Mr C W Rogers, from Collin Stud
ch y c Ballacashtal (CAN) - Screen Goddess (Caliban)........ (Lambert Bloodstock) 4,400
Property of Raylex Co Ltd, from Old Mill Stud
ch y f Chief Singer - Smitten (Run The Gantlet (USA))............... (B B A) 1,750
Property of a Partnership, from Barcham Farm Stud
ch y f Prince Sabo - So Rewarding (Never So Bold)............ (Charles Smith) 1,700
Property of Mr M G Williams, from Barcham Farm Stud
b y f Merdon Melody - Spare Wheel (Track Spare).................... (A G Hide) 2,500
To Dissolve a Partnership
b y f Dashing Blade - Spinney Hill (Dominion).................... (R Sheather) 3,000
From Elsenham Stud
b y f Risk Me (FR) - Sporting Lass (Blakeney).................. (B B A) 1,600
b y f Risk Me (FR) - Sundaysport Splash (Lord Gayle (USA)).. (Jacqueline Doyle) 4,000
From Woodditton Stud
b y c Sayf El Arab (USA) - Supergreen (Superlative) (R O'Gorman Bloodstock) 15,500
From Three Gates Stud
ch y f Rich Charlie - Sweet And Sour (Sharpen Up)........................ (R O'Gorman Bloodstock) 3,000
Property of Stud-On-The-Chart
ch y f Charmer - Sweet Relief (Sweet Revenge)................. (M Ayers) 2,100

754

From Three Gates Stud
ch y c Risk Me (FR) - Thinkluckybelucky (Maystreak)......... (Fiona Needham) 4,200
Property of Worksop Manor Stud
b y c Distant Relative - Tino-Ella (Bustino).. (R Hollinshead) 1,700
Property of Mr J Wilson, from Grove Farm Stud
b y f Most Welcome - Tolomette (Tolomeo) .... (David Redvers) 2,400
Property of a Partnership, from Executive Stud
gr y c Executive Man - Tria Romantica (Another Realm)......... (F Sheridan) 800
Property of Mr J M Ratcliffe, from Manor Farm Stud
b y c Prince Sabo - Turnabout (Tyrnavos) .. (B B A) 3,600
From Barcham Farm Stud
ch y c Prince Daniel (USA) - Virginia Creeper (Hard Fought)... (E Campbell) 550
Property of K T Ivory Farms, from Houndswood Stud
b y f Never So Bold - Vogos Angel (Song) (M Pratt) 2,400

From Stetchworth Park Stud
b y f Hadeer - Way To Go (Troy) .... (Equine Services) 1,600
Property of J P & A J Hall, from Badger Hill Stud
ch y c Chaparly (FR) - Wolver Top (Wolver Heights)............... (J Frankham) 650
Property of Carroll Bloodstock, from Warren Park Stud
ch y c Precocious - Amazing Journey (USA) (Spectacular Bid (USA))..... (J Pearce) 4,600

755

Property of Mr R H James, from Limestone Stud
b y c Rambo Dancer (CAN) - Be Malicious (Malicious)............. (Pat Mitchell) 5,200
Property of Mr J G Charlton
ch y f Interrex (CAN) - Bedelia (Mr Fluorocarbon)................ (M Sharkey) 1,900
Property of Snowdrop Stud Co Ltd, from Sandley Stud
b y f Tragic Role (USA) - Bourbon Queen (Ile de Bourbon (USA)) .... (Derby Bloodstock) 2,200
Property of Witney Stud Farm
ch y f Presidium - Cardinal Palace (Royal Palace).............. (Richard Phillips) 3,000
Property of Mrs Celia Emery
ch or ro y f Weldnaas (USA) - Catulle (Roan Rocket)..................... (B B A) 1,000
Property of Mr J T Robson, from North Munstead Stud
b y c Prince Daniel (USA) - Chaconia Girl (Bay Express)... (Lambert Bloodstock) 8,000
Property of Mr B J Warren, from Lofts Hall Stud
b y c Petoski - Challanging (Mill Reef (USA)) ....(M Bell) 9,400
Property of Sunley Stud Ltd, from Sunley Stud
b y f Dowsing (USA) - Charlton Athletic (Bustino)............. (David Nicholls) 1,700
Property of a Partnershijp, from Southburgh Manor Stud
ch y c Salt Dome (USA) - China Blue (Ahonoora)........................... (Cormac McCormack Associates) 7,400
Property of Mrs D Onions, from Witney Stud Farm
b y f Faustus (USA) - Chinese Princess (Sunny Way)............ (P J McBride) 1,550

756

Property of Mrs W M Ward, from Blackthorne Stables
b y f Wuzo (USA) - Coumarine (FR) (Nonoalco (USA))........... (P J McBride) 1,300
Property of Mr J W Orbell, from Glebe Cottage
b y f Hotfoot - Crabtree (King Of Spain).... (James Hetherton) 1,600
Property of Worksop Manor Stud
b y f Reprimand - Dalmally (Sharpen Up)... (P Kelleway) 1,900
Property of Mrs N Madsen, from Albany Stud
b y f Emarati (USA) - Djanila (Fabulous Dancer (USA))..... (Derby Bloodstock) 1,700

From Woodditton Stud
b y f Damister (USA) - Double Society (USA) (Nodouble (USA))....... (B B A) 2,100
Property of Shaunlara Pinhooking Syndicate, from Shaunlara Stud
b y c Presidium - Dragusa (Dara Monarch) (Cormac McCormack Associates) 7,200
Property of Mr L A J Lodge, from Little Stud Farm
b y c Cyrano de Bergerac - Dress In Spring (Northfields (USA))................... (Peter Doyle Bloodstock) 3,000
From Northgate Lodge Stud
ch y f Indian Forest (USA) - Dunesian (Dunbeath (USA))......... (M Brittain) 1,500
Property of Oak Bloodstock Ltd, from Lofts Hall Stud
b y f Scenic - El Vino (Habitat) .... (Pro-Am & Co Ltd) 1,600
From Stetchworth Park Stud
ch y c Hadeer - Emeraude (Kris) (L Harris) 4,000

757

Property of Worksop Manor Stud
ch y c Celestial Storm (USA) - Enchanting Melody (Chief Singer)............... (Ettore Pistolatti) 6,200
Property of Collectors Investments Ltd, from Ednaston Lodge Stud
gr y f Le Solaret (FR) - Enthusiasm (Abwah) (Petrovich Bell) 800
From Stetchworth Park Stud
ch y c Hadeer - Ever Welcome (Be My Guest (USA))........................ (R O'Gorman Bloodstock) 5,200
From Northgate Lodge Stud
b y c Crowning Honors (CAN) - Fine A Leau (USA) (Youth (USA))..... (M Campion) 2,000
Property of Ewar Stud Farms
b y f Shavian - Flower Arrangement (Lomond (USA))... (Derby Bloodstock) 7,800
Property of Sunley Stud Ltd, from Sunley Stud
b y f Dowsing (USA) - Fortune Teller (Troy) (Cormac McCormack Associates) 2,800
Property of W and R Barnett Ltd, from Ted Voute, Agent
ch y f Master Willie - Fresh Thoughts (Young Generation)........... (B B A) 2,600
From Theobalds Stud
ch y f Carmelite House (USA) - God Speed Her (Pas de Seul)..... (Johnny Drews) 1,800
Property of Collectors Investments Ltd, from Ednaston Stud
b y f Le Solaret (FR) - Godara (Bustino)..... (B B A) 400
Property of Mr Richard Withers, from Southill Stud
br y c Then Again - Golden October (Young Generation)............... (A Stringer) 2,000
Property of Freedom Farm
ch y c Vague Shot - Golden Panda (Music Boy)............................ (B B A) 4,800
From Theobalds Stud
b y f Sharpo - Imperatrice (USA) (Kings Lake (USA))......... (David Cosgrove) 4,600
Property of a Partnership, from College Farm Stud
gr y f Statoblest - Innerglow (Kalaglow).... (J Sheehan) 2,800

Property of The Hon J G Lambton, from Longholes Stud
b y c Minster Son - Ixia (I Say)............ (Mrs M Reveley) 8,200

758

KILL (Goffs)
Friday, October 29th

Property of Miss Claire Murphy
Teddys Treasure (IRE) b g (5yrs) Le Johnstan - Ballycastle (Ballyciptic)..... (Cash) 800

Property of Mr Tom Walsh, from Kilburn Stables
Tajanama (IRE) b m (5yrs) Gorytus (USA) - Tafaana (FR) (Top Ville)........ (Cash) 1,500

Property of Miss Marian Cullinane, from Carna Lodge Stud
All The Gods (IRE) gr f (3yrs) Standaan (FR) - Godhood (Green God)........ (Cash) 500

From Carhue Stables
Bob The Yank (IRE) b g (3yrs) Bar Dexter (USA) - Jambrel (USA) (Tropic King II).. (Cash) 400

To Dissolve a Partnership, from Ballyroe House Stud
Darimoon br g (11yrs) Vividari - Moonraker VI (Giolla Mear).............. (Cash) 1,700
Deep Tarbow b g (6yrs) Deep Run - Miss Tarbow (Tarqogan)............ (Cash) 1,100

To Dissolve a Partnership, from Seven Springs Stables
Desert Waltz (IRE) ch g (4yrs) Gorytus (USA) - Desert Pet (Petingo).... (Cash) 800

Property of The Ratoath Hockey Club
Nunivak (USA) ch m (5yrs) Bering - Snow The Judge (USA) (Court Recess)...... (F Ennis) 3,200

From Hamwood Stables
Fancy Boots (IRE) ch f (2yrs) Salt Dome (USA) - Jolly Widow (Busted)......... (European Bloodstock Agency) 3,000

Property of Mr R N R Auld, from Ghost Lodge Stud
ch g (2yrs) Stalker - Killraga (Raga Navarro) (Cash) 1,500

759

To Dissolve a Partnership, from Brownstown House Stables
Allegro Simply (IRE) b g (2yrs) Simply Great (FR) - Waves Of Tory (Thatching)...... (Inger Sundloef) 400

From Deer Park House Stud
Sound Performance b f (4yrs) Ahonoora - Tough Battle (Captain James)......... (Lodge Park Stud) 6,700

Property of Armon Syndicate
Crowded House (IRE) b g (5yrs) Mazaad - Standing Ovation (Godswalk)......... (G McArdle) 15,000

Property of Mr John Keaney
Collector General (IRE) b g (2yrs) Treasure Kay - Door To Door (USA) (Nureyev)... (Barry V Kelly) 1,600

From First Flyer Stables
b c (2yrs) Harp Islet (USA) - Bahrain Star (Star Appeal)............ (D Chawke) 400
b f (2yrs) Dance Of Life (USA) - Blue Lookout (Cure The Blues) (Tom Flynn) 500
Can't Recall (USA) ch f (3yrs) Cure The Blues (USA) - Sworn Statement (USA) (Believe It).................. (J Ryan) 1,000
Tribal Memories (IRE) ch f (3yrs) Commanche Run - Museum Ball (USA) (Danzig)...................... (Cash) 400

From Landfall Paddocks, Curragh
Northern Latitude (IRE) b f (2yrs) Northern State (USA) - Shalati (FR) (High Line) .. (C B A) 400
Euroflower (IRE) b or br f (2yrs) King Of Clubs - Eurorose (Busted)..... (C B A) 1,000
Megadrive (IRE) b c (2yrs) Dominion Royale - Riveress (Dunphy)... (H Markwalder) 500
Final Reminder (IRE) ch c (2yrs) Don't Forget Me - Pleasant Review (USA) (The Minstrel).. (Brian Grassick Bloodstock) 5,200
Astro Reef (IRE) ch g (2yrs) Astronef - Ceann-Na-Bann (Doulab)..... (J Coyle) 400
Arnaga (IRE) br f (2yrs) Cyrano de Bergerac - Good Relations (Be My Guest)...... (Ms Annette Hirt) 1,500
Overall Majority (IRE) b f (2yrs) Cyrano de Bergerac - Glamorous Ways (Valiyar) .. (European Equine Consutltants) 3,200

760

From Maddenstown Lodge Stables
Appian Glorious (IRE) ch f (2yrs) Sharp Victor (USA) - Revelette (Runnett)..... (Ms Radka Simankova) 500
Evictress (IRE) ch f (2yrs) Sharp Victor (USA) - Nurse Jo (USA) (J O Tobin).... (B B A (Ireland)) 3,200
Sender Victorious (IRE) ch f (2yrs) Sharp Victor (USA) - Al-Nadda (Be My Guest) (Ms Alice Reeves Smith) 3,000

Property of Mr A Redmond, from Mountjoy Lodge
Wanovowers (IRE) b g (5yrs) Reasonable (FR) - Sisterhood (Malinowski).. (Cash) 10,000

Property of Mr H B Eastwood, from Mountjoy Lodge
Iceflow (FR) b f (3yrs) Siberian Express (USA) - Yarzah (USA) (Silver Hawk).... (Jim Cash) 700

Property of Miss M T Murphy, from Mountjoy Lodge
Son Of Tempo (IRE) b g (4yrs) Sandhurst Prince - Top Love (USA) (Topsider) .... (J Carr) 550

From Fenpark Stables (The Curragh)
Winter's Over b f (2yrs) Persian Bold - American Winter (USA) (Lyphard) ..... (European Bloodstock Agency) 4,200

Property of Kerr Technology Ltd, from Tu Va Stables
Aran Exile br f (3yrs) Ahonoora - Gallic Pride (USA) (Key To The Kingdom).......... (R McDonnell) 3,000

From First Flyer Stables
Inauguration (IRE) b g (4yrs) Ela-Mana-Mou - Crimson Robes (Artaius) .... (Declan Gillespie) 2,400

Gold Vision (IRE) b c (3yrs) Darshaan - Hilo Girl (USA) (Pago Pago) .... (Jim McInerney) 5,000
Proud Moment (IRE) br c (3yrs) Rainbow Quest (USA) - Preoccupy (Habitat)..... (S FitzGerald) 400
Red Glitter (USA) gr g (3yrs) Time For A Change (USA) - Glittering Heights (USA) (Golden Fleece)......... (Cash) 500
Urban Dancing (USA) ch g (4yrs) Nureyev (USA) - Afifa (USA) (Dewan) (A Moore) 9,000

761

From Landfall Paddocks, Curragh

Orange Pleasure (USA) b or br f (2yrs) Foolish Pleasure (USA) - Orange Grove (USA) (Sharpen Up)....... (J C Harley) 4,000
Libran Rock (IRE) b g (3yrs) Ballad Rock - Saint Cynthia (Welsh Saint)........... (Bobby O'Ryan) 3,600
Running Guest (IRE) br f (3yrs) Runnett - Guest House (What A Guest)........... (Christer Ljung) 2,200
Roundwood Rose (IRE) b f (3yrs) Doulab (USA) - Romfaea (USA) (Alleged)...... (Cash) 1,100
Putty Road (IRE) ch g (3yrs) Bob Back (USA) - Mill's Girl (Le Levanstell)...... (Cash) 6,100
Curragh Ranger (IRE) b g (3yrs) Colmore Row - Derrinturn (Touch Paper)....... (E J Counihan) 1,200
Butternut (IRE) b f (3yrs) Alzao (USA) - Ampersand (USA) (Stop The Music)... (P Curran) 600

Property of Narrow Water Syndicate

Donmir Lovebird b f (3yrs) Magical Wonder (USA) - Waadi Hatta (USA) (Upper Nile) (G Swift) 500

Property of Mr John Houghton

Keppols Harrier (IRE) b or br g (3yrs) Phardante (FR) - Keppols (Furry Glen)...... (L McMahon) 6,000

From Mountarmstrong Stud

b g (2yrs) Classic Secret (USA) - Elite Exhibition (Exhibitioner)... (D Chawke) 500
b f (2yrs) Classic Secret (USA) - Miss Ming (Tender King) (Peter Doyle Bloodstock) 2,000
Respondtochallenge (IRE) ch g (3yrs) Exhibitioner - Persian Runner (Pitskelly) .... (J Coyle) 1,350

762

From Tu Va Stables

Coq Hardi Smokey (IRE) gr g (5yrs) Celio Rufo - Bella Minna (Chou Chin Chow) (K C Bailey) 8,600

From Ballydoyle and Ridge Manor Stables

Britannia Bay (IRE) ch c (3yrs) Waajib - Red Line Fever (Bay Express).............. (B B A (Ireland)) 16,000
Station House (IRE) b g (3yrs) Prince Rupert - Webbiana (African Sky).... (O Brady) 4,500
Cross Swords (USA) b g (2yrs) Sword Dance (USA) - Falabella (Steel Heart).. (Alfonso Ballestero) 5,400
Piper Zero (IRE) ch g (2yrs) Tate Gallery (USA) - Truly Thankful (CAN) (Graustark).................. (Cash) 2,600
Platinum Empire (USA) b g (3yrs) Nijinsky (CAN) - Kelley's Day (USA) (Graustark) (M O'Toole) 26,000

Property of Darley Stud Management Co Ltd., from Kildangan Stud

Plains Indians b f (2yrs) Dancing Brave (USA) - Prairie Venus (GER) (Surumu).. (Emerald Bloodstock) 3,000
Fluted Rock (IRE) b c (2yrs) Reference Point - Flut D'Oa (Kalamoun).......... (B B A (Ireland)) 3,600

From Bullstown

Miss Twin Peaks (IRE) b f (3yrs) Persian Heights - Monterana (Sallust)... (Cash) 700

Property of Darley Stud Management Co Ltd., from Bullstown

Home From Home b c (2yrs) General Holme (USA) - Dancing Home (Shareef Dancer)............ (Inger Sundloef) 500
Devil's Holiday (USA) b g (3yrs) Devil's Bag (USA) - Mizima (USA) (Damascus)..... (M Kauntze) 10,500

763

From Bullstown

Quiet Confidence (IRE) b f (3yrs) Pennine Walk - Northern Wisdom (Northfields) (G J M Bloodstock) 1,900

From Moyglare Stud Farm

Renewed Dynasty (USA) ch c (3yrs) Arctic Tern (USA) - Sweetened Offer (General Assembly)............ (E McNamara) 3,100
Sheer Opulance (IRE) b c (3yrs) Shernazar - Specially Packaged (USA) (Blushing Groom)...................... (Cash) 6,000
Upward Surge (IRE) ch c (3yrs) Kris - Sizes Vary (Be My Guest)....... (K C Bailey) 6,000
Sharp Review (IRE) b g (5yrs) Sharpen Up - Pleasant Review (USA) (The Minstrel) (Peter Doyle Bloodstock) 10,000
Overseas Transfer (IRE) gr c (2yrs) Mtoto - Offshore Boom (Be My Guest)....... (B B A (Ireland)) 8,000
Tackling Reality (IRE) b c (2yrs) Soviet Star (USA) - Trusted Partner (USA) (Affirmed)................... (Cash) 2,200
Special Issue (IRE) b c (2yrs) Caerleon (USA) - Speciality Package (USA) (Blushing Groom).......... (M Burke) 10,000
Confidence Boost (USA) ch f (2yrs) Trempolino (USA) - Bubinka (USA) (Nashua) (Oldtown Stud) 15,000

Property of H H Aga Khan Studs S.C., from Currabeg Stables

Adjalari (IRE) b c (2yrs) Al Nasr (FR) - Adjanada (Nishapour)..... (M O'Toole) 7,000
Tadjik (USA) ch g (3yrs) Arctic Tern (USA) - Taysha (Habitat)...... (B B A (Ireland)) 29,000
Kharasar (IRE) b c (3yrs) Standaan (FR) - Khatima (Relko)........ (Tony Mullins) 5,000

764

Property of Darley Stud Management Co Ltd., from Currabeg Stables

Cypriot ch c (2yrs) Sure Blade (USA) - Lady Of The Sea (Mill Reef).. (James Cash) 3,200

Anlace b f (4yrs) Sure Blade (USA) - Ascot Strike (USA) (Mr Prospector).......... (B B A (Ireland)) 7,000

From Warren Place Stables

Kaiser Wilhelm b c (4yrs) Slip Anchor - Kaisersage (FR) (Exbury)...... (C B A) 30,000

From Conyngham Lodge Stables

Foolish Flight (IRE) ch f (2yrs) Fools Holme (USA) - Black Crow (Sea Hawk II) ..... (D Magnier) 6,200

Rose Bunch ch c (2yrs) Never So Bold - Frasquita (Song)..... (M L Bloodstock) 3,000

Honours Degree (FR) ch g (2yrs) Entitled - Fahrenheit (Mount Hagen)............ (Margrit Markwalder) 1,700

Sleet (IRE) b f (3yrs) Flash Of Steel - Gentle Rain (Tower Walk)...... (James Cash) 800

Caravelle Lad (IRE) b or br g (3yrs) Cyrano de Bergerac - Ziobia (Tribal Chief) ..... (James Cash) 1,050

Baeza ch g (3yrs) Arctic Tern (USA) - Tashinsky (USA) (Nijinsky)......... (Cash) 1,000

Property of Connections of Racing Syndicate, from New Rathbride Stables

Uster (IRE) b f (2yrs) Waajib - Kangaroo (Kampala)............ (J O'Callaghan) 650

765

Property of Knockduff Racing Syndiate, from New Rathbride Stables

Bold Molly (IRE) b or br f (4yrs) Treasure Kay - Ice Baby (Grundy)..... (J Harley) 1,600

Property of Dr Tony O'Reilly, from Castlemartin Abbey House Stables

Vladimir's Way (IRE) b c (4yrs) Don't Forget Me - Susan's Way (Red God)... (Cash) 1,100

Gold And Blue (IRE) b f (3yrs) Bluebird (USA) - Golden Grundy (Grundy) (Cash) 1,000

From Milltown Stud

Brugatti (IRE) b f (2yrs) Astronef - Fota Island (Indian King) .... (European Bloodstock Agency) 4,800

Property of Mrs H D McCalmont, from Yeomanstown Lodge Stud

Touching Moment (IRE) b g (3yrs) Pennine Walk - Sea Mistress (Habitat)......... (A L Moore) 1,300

(YEARLINGS)

Property of Mr Charles Elkin, from Carrick Stables

ch y c Salt Dome (USA) - Jadhringa (Petingo)................. (J Coogan) 700

From Garrick Stables

b y c Simply Great (FR) - Lola Sharp (Sharpen Up)............ (M O'Toole) 10,000

Property of Mrs A Cassidy

ch y f Common Grounds - Luan Causca (Pampapaul).... (Mercury Bloodstock) 1,100

From Ballysax Manor Stud (Argent)

ch y f Double Schwartz - Mon Mistal (Kemal)...................... (Cash) 650

From Trimblestown Stud

ch y f Carmelite House (USA) - Mullaghroe (Tarboosh).................... (Cash) 800

766

Property of Mr Thomas Downey

b y f Red Sunset - Park Silver (Beldale Flutter)............ (Lovestone Stud) 500

From Errigal Stud

b y c Digamist (USA) - Persian Flirt (Persian Bold)........... (Mercury Bloodstock) 2,200

From Trimblestown Stud

b y g Carmelite House (USA) - Somethingrare (Rarity).............. (Cash) 600

b y f Broken Hearted - Theatral (Orchestra) (Cash) 650

From Rathbarry Stud

b y f Jareer (USA) - Tigora (Ahonoora) ..... (Tony Watkins) 1,100

Property of Mr & Mrs D Veitch

b y f Fijar Tango (FR) - Ukraine's Affair (USA) (The Minstrel)..... (P Timmons) 2,500

From Kilshannig Stud

b y f Bold Arrangement - Ward Of Court (IRE) (Law Society)............ (Cash) 3,000

Property of Mr Robert O'Brien

b y c Be My Native (USA) - Zalazula (Lord Gayle)........................ (Cash) 3,800

Property of Mr G Bourke, from Silogue Stud

b y c Magical Strike (USA) - African Bloom (African Sky)........ (Joanna Morgan) 5,200

Property of Mr Seamus Mitten

ch y f Salt Dome (USA) - Blessed Persian (Persian Bold).......... (James Cash) 1,050

767

From Newtown Lodge Stud

gr or ch y f Gadabout (USA) - Cimerosa (IRE) (Lomond)............ (J Malone) 2,350

Property of Mr E Ryan, from Lisieux Stud

b y f Hatim (USA) - Dame Pattie (Wolverlife) .... (Cash) 1,100

Property of Mr D C Cullen

gr y f High Estate - Fairway Lady (Miami Springs)......... (Browne Bloodstock) 5,300

From Trimblestown Stud

b y f Orchestra - Haut Lafite (Tamerlane) .. (Cash) 800

From Carrick Stables

ch y c Kefaah (USA) - Highland Culture (Lomond).............. (M Robinson) 4,500

Property of Mr John Culleton

ch y f Classic Secret (USA) - Hurricane Hazel (Lorenzaccio)......... (J Feane) 4,000

To Dissolve a Partnership, from Hillview Farm

b y f Classic Secret (USA) - Island Adventure (Touching Wood) (Christer Ljung) 1,200

From French Furze Stables

Top State (IRE) b or br f (2yrs) High Estate - Shikari Rose (Kala Shikari)...... (Cash) 2,500

Property of Mr M Tunney, from Tu Va Stables

Rufo's Coup gr g (6yrs) Celio Rufo - Wadowice (Targowice).............. (Peter D McCreery) 2,100

Property of Mr John P Moore, from Tu Va Stables

Sinergia (IRE) b g (3yrs) Thatching - El Pina (Be My Guest)................ (Cash) 1,500

768

From Maddenstown Lodge Stables

Victor Emmanuel (IRE) ch c (2yrs) Sharp Victor (USA) - Elea (GER) (Dschingis Khan)......... (Ms Radka Simankova) 1,850

Norse Victor (IRE) ch c (2yrs) Sharp Victor (USA) - Nordic Dance (USA) (Graustark) .... (M Tierney) 800

Property of The Albany Syndicate, from Ballingara Stables

Brazen Angel (IRE) b f (3yrs) Nordico (USA) - Angel Passing (Kind Of Hush) (Cash) 4,000

From Thomastown Castle

Oroville b f (3yrs) Sizzling Melody - Pollyworth (Wolver Hollow) (James Cash) 1,100

Splendid King (IRE) b c (3yrs) Fairy King (USA) - Irish Splendour (Guillaume Tell) (B B A (Ireland)) 1,400

Pharuzal b or br f (3yrs) Pharly (FR) - Lightning Gem (FR) (African Song) (G Swift) 500

PRIVATE SALES

From Landfall Paddocks Curragh

Last Emperor (USA) b g (6yrs) Forli (ARG) - Image Intensifier (USA) (Dancer's Image).................. (P J Tynan) 950

Property of Mr Steven Gilmore

b y f Waajib - Lady Lane (Tanfirion)........ (P Donworth) 2,700

From Triermore Stud

ch y f Emmson - Neshoma (Realm) .... (J Heelan) 800

769

FAIRYHOUSE (Tattersalls)

Wednesday, November 3rd

To Dissolve a Partnership

Cahills Hill b g (6yrs) Callernish - Pampin (Pam[illegible])

Property of Mr Michael Hughes

br f (3yrs) King's Ride - Regency Shot (Random Shot)..... (Vincent Leonard) 2,200

Property of Mr Seamus Durkan

b g (3yrs) Sanchi Steeple - Lovely Venture (He Loves Me)..... (Seamus O'Farrell) 1,550

Property of Mrs L Roche

b g (3yrs) Strong Statement (USA) - Levitstown Lady (Paddy's Stream).......... (Jorg Von Jmhoff) 2,700

Property of Mrs L Griffin

gr g (3yrs) Roselier (FR) - Private Affair (Julio Mariner)........... (J Crowley) 1,750

Property of Mr John F Hadden

b g (4yrs) Buckskin (FR) - Lara's Teddy (Goldhill).................. (A Sadik) 1,160

Property of Mrs Bernadette Kenny

Tullykyne Bells gr g (4yrs) Le Solaret (FR) - Cowbells (Mountain Call) (Joe Magee) 1,500

Property of R J Hetherington, from Woodlands Farm Stud

b g (3yrs) Abednego - Miss Alex (No Argument)........................ (Cash) 1,900

Property of A Bannon

Curraghtown b m (6yrs) The Parson - Deep Down (Deep Run)...... (Gerry Mullen) 2,000

Property of Mrs B McCormack, from Palace Farm

ch f (3yrs) Shy Groom (USA) - Angela's Gem (My Swallow)......... (P Casey) 3,600

770

From Cherryvalley Stud

Fingerhill (IRE) b g (4yrs) Boyne Valley - Diamond Glow (Kalaglow)............ (David Minton Bloodstock) 6,000

Wayuphill b m (6yrs) Furry Glen - Queen Weasel (Gulf Pearl).... (Vincent Ward) 2,800

Property of J & S Davidson

ch f (3yrs) Over The River (FR) - Princess Isabella (Divine Gift)..... (Paddy Reilly) 1,900

Property of Mr Paddy McDermott

b f (3yrs) Delamain (USA) - Crag Mo Chroi (Duky)................ (Andrew Baird) 850

From Killowen House Stables

br f (3yrs) Strong Gale - Magic Minstrel (Pitpan)...................... (C B A) 5,000

From Rangers Lodge Stables

Red Micks Wife (IRE) b f (3yrs) Red Sunset - Irish Bride (Track Spare)............ (Paul Nicholls) 1,000

Property of Michael & Eileen McNamara

ch f (3yrs) Phardante (FR) - Miss Good Night (Buckskin)........ (John Smyth) 700

From Skryne Stables

Look Nonchalant (IRE) ch f (4yrs) Fayruz - Gobolino (Don)......... (Tom Gillson) 950

Property of Ann Smurfit Bloodstock

ch f (3yrs) Roselier (FR) - Island Dream (Lucifer).................. (F Feeney) 820

From Templeigh Stud

b f (3yrs) Torus - Beech Glen (Furry Glen).. (B Hallahan) 2,350

771

Property of Jay Bowe

ch g (4yrs) Torus - Uzonkopru (Status Seeker)...................... (Cash) 5,200

From Rinville Meadows Stud

b f (4yrs) Callernish - Cacador's Point (Pitpan).................... (John Smyth) 800

Property of E Cosgrave, from Shanrod Stud

b or br g (3yrs) Mister Lord (USA) - Penny Buskins (Little Buskins)........ (Cash) 4,700

Property of Mr J Buckley

b g (3yrs) The Parson - Corun Girl (Apollo Eight)......................... (K Purcell) 5,900

From Lakefield Farm (Agent)

br g (3yrs) Miner's Lamp - Palatine Lady (Pauper)............. (A J McNamara) 10,000

Property of Martin Conheady

br f (4yrs) Over The River (FR) - Rich Belle (Goldhill)......... (Commonstown Stud) 4,100

From Longmore Stud

b g (3yrs) Remainder Man - Ilawn (Simbir) (Cash) 8,000

Property of Mr James Slevin

b f (4yrs) Lancastrian - Shannon Belle (Pollerton)....................... (L Ryan) 1,200

Property of Mrs M McGearty, from Rathnally Farm

ch g (4yrs) Over The River (FR) - Celtic Chariot (Derring Rose)......... (Cash) 1,900

To Dissolve a Partnership

Offaly Rose (IRE) b m (5yrs) The Parson - Somer's Jewel (Will Somers)......... (A Moore) 3,000

772

Property of Mrs Ann Roche
b f (3yrs) Strong Gale - Mad Rodger (Royal Match).............. (Mrs J A Walsh) 2,000
Property of Mr Robert McLean, from Ballyrickard House
b g (4yrs) Pollerton - Merton Lass (Super Slip)......................... (Cash) 2,000
Property of Mr Michael Ryan
b f (4yrs) Bustineto - North Rose Vii (Northern Guest)..... (R Rattenhuber) 1,350
From Alexander Stud
b g (3yrs) Hardboy - Spritestown (Bowsprit) .... (Martin Lynch) 4,000
Property of Ms Mary Ryan
ch f (3yrs) Orchestra - Sandyela (Sandy Creek)........................ (Cash) 1,800
ch f (3yrs) Exhibitioner - Run-A-Line (Deep Run).................... (Ian Geddis) 700
Property of Jean Splaine
ch g (4yrs) Phardante (FR) - My Halo (Be Friendly)............ (Michael Halford) 7,600
b or br g (4yrs) Kambalda - Star Luck (Star Signal)................. (John Turner) 4,600
Property of Mr F F O'Neill
ch f (3yrs) Strong Statement (USA) - Barbara Brook (Over The River).... (Cash) 900
ch f (3yrs) Strong Statement (USA) - Beggs Meadow (Quayside)........... (Cash) 700

773

Property of Mr P Anglin, from Kilmullen House
b g (3yrs) Castle Keep - Sure Magic (Gleason)..................... (Cash) 1,200
Property of Mr Sean Prendergast, from Burgatia Stud
b f (3yrs) Strong Gale - Housewife (Sunyboy)........................ (Cash) 750
Property of Miss Stella Falkner, from Ballinapierce
b g (3yrs) Erin's Hope - Golden Rapid (Over The River)........... (Maurice Curran) 2,700
From Cherryvalley Stud
b g (3yrs) Corvaro (USA) - Diamond Glow (Kalaglow).................... (Cash) 2,100
From Conna Stud
ch g (4yrs) Fresh Breeze (USA) - Castleblagh (General Ironside)..... (Cash) 2,000
From Corraun Stables
gr g (4yrs) Sexton Blake - Sheila's Flame (Reformed Character).. (J A O'Connell) 8,000
Property of Mrs D Lambert
b f (3yrs) Strong Gale - Brave Ruby (Proverb).................. (Joe Molloy) 3,200
From Bryanstown Stud (Agent)
b f (3yrs) Torus - Raheen Princess (Raise You Ten)........... (Peter McCreery) 2,000
Property of Mr Martin Liddy
b g (3yrs) Convinced - Vulace (Vulgan)..... (T O'Brien) 2,800
From Hilltop Stables
b f (3yrs) Mandalus - Bramble Girl (Ovac) .. (John McCormack) 1,000

774

From Rathbarry Stud (Agent)
ch g (4yrs) Le Moss - Niatpac (Royal Highway)..................... (C Kinane) 4,200
b g (3yrs) Sheer Grit - November Bloom (Camden Town)............... (Cash) 1,900
b f (3yrs) Phardante (FR) - Lady's Wager (Girandole)...................... (Cash) 2,800
Property of Mrs B D Byrne, from Slieveardagh Stud
br g (3yrs) Phardante (FR) - Flying Silver (Master Buck)................... (David Minton Bloodstock) 5,000
Property of Mr Oliver Maguire
b f (3yrs) Cataldi - Firhouse Fancy (Brave Invader)........... (John McLoughlin) 2,300
Property of Mr Noel P Quinlan, from Church Farm Stables
b f (4yrs) Roselier (FR) - Ashford House (Brave Invader)......... (Paddy Reilly) 2,000
Property of Mr P Coupland, from Mocklers Hill Stables (Agent)
ch g (3yrs) Sexton Blake - Six Deep (Deep Run).......... (Burrem Park Prop. Ltd) 4,000
Property of M Walsh
ch f (4yrs) Le Moss - Arctic Arrian (Apollo Eight)...................... (M Ahern) 1,700
Property of Lingstown Stud
b g (3yrs) Asir - Churchlands Madam (Proverb)................ (Mrs P Granger) 4,100
From Ballinaglouck Stud
b g (4yrs) Delamain (USA) - Divine Wonder (Divine Gift).................. (Cash) 2,500

775

Property of Dick Ferguson, from Mulgannon House
b g (3yrs) Le Bavard (FR) - Johns County (Crash Course)................ (Cash) 5,400
Property of Lt Col & Mrs J A Dene, from Kilteelagh Stud
b g (3yrs) Lafontaine (USA) - Maltese Queen (Queen's Hussar)....... (Cash) 4,300
From Streamstown House Stud
b g (4yrs) Radical - Court Dame (Court Fool) .... (Suzy Barkley) 4,600
From Kilcaskin Stud
b g (3yrs) Trimmingham - Maypole Hie (Bold Lad).................... (Cash) 1,250
Property of Sillogue Stud
br g (4yrs) Roselier (FR) - Buckybrill (Buckskin)........................... (Cash) 5,000
Property of M J Blake from Castle Wood House
ch c (3yrs) Phardante (FR) - Foredefine (Bonne Noel)............ (Jn. Dineen) 2,000
b g (3yrs) Sheer Grit - Highland Worker (Giolla Mear).................. (Cash) 3,000
Property of Mrs Frank Warren
b g (4yrs) Strong Statement (USA) - Dream Daisy (Choral Society).......... (Cash) 5,600
Property of Marie T Doran
b f (3yrs) Phardante (FR) - Orient Conquest (Dual)................. (D O'Connell) 2,700
From Kilbridge Stud (Agent)
ch g (3yrs) Black Minstrel - Marital Trial (Deep Run).................. (Cash) 780

776

From Cregg Stud
b f (3yrs) Carlingford Castle - Mrs Hill (Strong Gale)........ (George Stewart) 1,600

Property of Alan Cloney

b f (3yrs) Erin's Hope - Tops O'Crush (Menelek)........... (Burrey Hill Prop. Ltd) 1,700

Property of Brian Kennedy, from Mewadowlands Stud

b f (3yrs) Callernish - Lovely Pine (Woodville).......................... (Cash) 3,600

Property of D Ilk

b g (3yrs) Phardante (FR) - Ring Road (Giolla Mear)....................... (Cash) 5,600

Property of William R Deacon

b f (4yrs) Mandalus - Flynn's Field (The Parson).... (Jimmy Byrne Bloodstock) 7,500

Property of Donal O'Brien

b f (3yrs) Lancastrian - Pitalina (Pitpan)..... (Mrs Valerie Cooper) 6,000

Property of Patrick M Sinnott

b g (4yrs) Phardante (FR) - Mount St Helen (Mount Hagen).... (Michael Bartmann) 3,100

Property of James G Kehoe

b g (3yrs) Cardinal Flower - Sasscombe (Sahib)................ (Ronald Duke) 2,900

Property of Hugh J Holohan, from Grangeduff Stud

b g (3yrs) Castle Keep - Advantage (Perspex)................ (Kieran McGinn) 20,000

Property of Harold McGahern

b g (3yrs) Roselier (FR) - Molly Coddle (Belfalas)...................... (Cash) 2,900

777

From Culmullin Stud

b f (4yrs) Strong Gale - Mention Of Money (Le Bavard).............. (J C Harley) 2,600

Property of W I MacKenzie

b g (4yrs) Le Bavard (FR) - Northern Push (Push On)..................... (Cash) 4,200

Property of Marshall Parkhill

ch f (3yrs) Orchestra - Rule The Waves (Deep Run)..................... (Cash) 1,000

From Culworth Stud

br g (3yrs) Strong Gale - Distant Castle (Deep Run)................ (I Geddis) 10,000

From Coolamurry Stud

b f (3yrs) Meneval (USA) - Kasam (General Ironside)....... (Commonstown Stud) 4,700

Property of Neville J Tector, from Coolbawn Stud

b or br f (4yrs) Callernish - Spindle Tree (Laurence O)................... (Cash) 3,000

Property of Laurence Curran

b f (4yrs) Mandalus - Game As A Pebble (Skyliner)........... (R Rattenhuber) 2,700

Property of John O'Keeffe

b f (3yrs) Remainder Man - Clockonocra (Shall We Dance)......... (John Smith) 700

Property of Moy Stud

ch g (4yrs) Duky - Vixen's Red (Bargello)... (Cash) 1,650

Property of Mrs Gill Browne, from Laurel Lodge Farm

b f (4yrs) Roselier (FR) - Capital Katie (Distinctly)...................... (Cash) 1,900

778

Property of Joseph J Fisher

ch f (3yrs) Le Bavard (FR) - Arctic Mistress (Quayside)................ (T O'Mara) 1,500

Property of Mrs M Wentges

b g (3yrs) Tremblant - Jollidee (Jolly Good) (Cash) 2,000

Property of M Purcell

b or br g (3yrs) Gunner B - Great Aunt Emily (Traditionalist)............ (J McGrath) 2,500

Property of M Ryan

b or br g (3yrs) Mandalus - Sunrise Highway Vii (Master Owen)............. (Cash) 1,000

Property of J L Rothwell

ch g (4yrs) Swan's Rock - Pollys Crash (Crash Course)............... (Cash) 2,700

Property of Roland Rothwell

ch g (4yrs) Swan's Rock - Wish Again (Three Wishes)............... (Cash) 4,200

Property of Donal Turner

b g (3yrs) Black Minstrel - Delia Murphy (Golden Love)................. (Cash) 2,600

Property of Ms F Roycroft

b g (3yrs) Mandalus - Fiancee (Royal Match) (Cash) 9,000

Property of J Manning, from Grey Fort Stud

b g (3yrs) Mandalus - Laois Story (Royal Match).......... (Andrew McNamara) 4,800

ch f (4yrs) Le Bavard (FR) - Good Credentials (Take A Reef)............ (Cash) 850

779

From The Flat House Stud

b g (4yrs) Teofane - Lovely Daisy (Menelek) .... (Cash) 8,500

Property of Mrs S Brennan, from Farnagh Stud

b f (3yrs) Bulldozer - Random View (Random Shot)................... (Cash) 750

b f (3yrs) King's Ride - Ironclad Alibi (General Ironside)............ (F Kiernan) 950

Property of Frank McClure

b f (3yrs) Castle Keep - Gowran Lady (Raise You Ten)..................... (Cash) 1,000

Property of Crahaan Stud

b f (4yrs) Good Thyne (USA) - Carry On Polly (Pollerton)............... (Cash) 2,100

From Lennymore Stud

br f (4yrs) Supreme Leader - Fiorafy (Electrify)....................... (Cash) 1,700

From Keelogues Farm

gr g (4yrs) Roselier (FR) - Miss Reindeer (Reindeer)........... (Eric McNamara) 4,600

Property of Thomas Brady, from Robinstown Stud

b f (4yrs) Supreme Leader - Just Darina (Three Dons)................... (Cash) 8,800

Property of C J Smyth, from Milton House

ch f (2yrs) Le Bavard (FR) - Lonely Wind (Tumble Wind).............. (J Smyth) 600

Property of Mrs C Van C Anthony, from Stonebrook Stud

b f (2yrs) Satco (FR) - Linbel (Linacre)...... (Declan Weld) 2,800

780

Property of Holly Lodge Stud

b f (2yrs) King's Ride - Crest Bavard (Le Bavard)...................... (Cash) 850

Property of Hugh McCann

ch f (2yrs) Executive Perk - Deep Captain (Deep Run)................... (Cash) 1,750

Property of Miss Avril Campbell, from Ballywooden House Stud
ch g (2yrs) Convinced - Miss Billie (Nicholas Bill).......... (Andrew Younghusband) 700
Property of Jennifer Clarke, from Ballywooden House
b g (2yrs) Convinced - Sweeten Your Step (Frigid Aire)............. (Brian Byrne) 400
Property of Danny O'Sullivan, from The Beeches Stud
ch g (2yrs) Le Moss - Fixed Addition (Mr Fordette)........... (David FitzGerald) 1,000
From Mountain View Stud
b f (2yrs) Roselier (FR) - Connah's Quay (FR) (Mummy's Pet)........(Jn. Smith) 520
Property of James Kelly, from Raheen Stables
b g (2yrs) Hollow Hand - Golden Moth (Ballad Rock)................ (Cash) 2,250
PRIVATE SALES
Property of Mr Robert Guiry, from Peppardstown Stud
b g (3yrs) Torus - Paldamask (Native Prince) .... (G Stewart) 2,900
Property of Mr James J Nolan
b g (4yrs) Good Thyne (USA) - Bowerina (Daring Display)............... (Cash) 2,900
Property of Mr Richard Hennessy
gr g (3yrs) Roselier (FR) - Quincy Bay (Buckskin).................. (Mrs Dutfield) 5,000
From Knightsbridge
br g (4yrs) Lancastrian - Chake-Chake (Goldhill).......................... (Cash) 11,000

781

FAIRYHOUSE (Tattersalls)
Thursday, November 4th (Yearlings)

Property of Michael Hughes
ch y f Orchestra - Gypsy Major (Deep Run) (Edward Fitzpatrick) 1,000
Property of Nickie Flavin
b y f Supreme Leader - Deep Adventure (Deep Run).................. (Cash) 1,600
Property of Alec Noonan, from Dromin Lodge
b y g Strange Love (FR) - Castleview Lady (Sandford Lad)........... (Mrs Carroll) 300
Property of S McKitterick
ch y g Zaffaran (USA) - Clearing Mist (Double Jump).................. (F Lloyd) 1,000
Property of Seamus Killen, from Kirkistown Stud
b y g Merrymount - Scirea (Cantab) .... (M Bamber) 300
Property of M O'Brien
b y c Black Minstrel - Repetitive (USA) (Tell) .... (Anne Marie Willis) 1,500
Property of Paddy Byrne, from Abbey Stables
b y g Glacial Storm (USA) - Little Slip (Super Slip)................... (Col Cramsie) 2,000
Property of Tom O'Connor, from Coolflugh House Stables
br y g Mandalus - Fiancee (Royal Match) .. (Cash) 3,200

Property of John McNamee
br y c Be My Native (USA) - Star With A Glimer (Montekin)... (Joanna Morgan) 2,000
Property of James Ward
ch y c Phardante (FR) - Jock's Fancy (Patch) .... (David Minton Bloodstock) 2,200

782

Property of Mrs Margaret Walsh from Centenary Stables
b y g Yashgan - Yellow Canary (Miner's Lamp).................. (R Mathias) 1,550
Property of Ann Stack, from Coolagown Stud
b y f Rock Chanteur - Progressive Girl (Kafu)..................... (P Gillen) 400
From Abbeville & Meadow Court Studs (Agent)
b y g Over The River (FR) - Clogrecon Lass (Raise You Ten).......... (M O'Reilly) 5,500
Property of J G Fletcher, from Glascar Hill Stud
gr y g Over The River (FR) - Fortina's General (General Ironside)...... (Cash) 2,900
From Shade Oak Stud
b y f Derrylin - Sheer Drop (Precipice Wood) .... (Mrs Sally Grantham) 600
b y f Gunner B - Thevicarsdaughter (The Parson)..................... (Cash) 500
ch y f Gunner B - Domtony (Martinmas) ... (A Johnston) 750
Property of Joseph R Lalor
ch y g Noalto - People (Al Sirat).... (Cash) 3,500
Property of Michael Aherne
b y g Roselier (FR) - Shanagale Vii (Strong Gale)..................... (T Steele) 850
Property of C Geelan, from Rinnview Stable
b y f Persian Mews - Fifth Gear (Red Sunset)..................... (Cash) 1,000

783

From Rathbarry Stud (Agent)
b y g Brush Aside (USA) - Baranee (My Swanee).................... (Cash) 3,200
From Rathbarry Stud
b y g Strong Gale - Scotch News (London Gazette)............. (Wickfield Farm) 13,500
b y g Good Thyne (USA) - Night Blade (Fine Blade)..... (David Minton Bloodstock) 7,000
Property of Ms Irene Gowen, from Rathbarry Stud
b y f Strong Gale - Toi Figures (Deep Run) (P J Conroy) 7,800
Property of Mrs Eleanor McCormack, from Broguestown Stud
b y f King's Ride - Paddy's Team (Ballymore)............. (P McCutcheon) 600
From Blackabbey Stud
b y f Wood Chanter - Lucky Cooper (General Ironside)....... (Loughtown Stud) 400
From Sprinvalley Stud (agent)
b y g Strong Gale - Deep Kitty (IRE) (Deep Run)............. (Ms R Tonson-Rye) 10,000
Property of Danny O'Sullivan, from The Beeches Stud
ch y g Buckskin (FR) - Fixed Addition (Mr Fordette)..................... (Cash) 1,000
Property of Dunmahon Stud
ch y g Ore - Better Again (Deep Run) ..... (Cash) 1,400

From Corbal-Lis Stud
b or br y g Asir - Miss Cali (Young Man) ... (J P Berry) 5,800

784

Property of Ms Jessica Riordan, from Rathbarry Stud
ch y g Rising - Bawnard Lady (Ragapan) ... (J McNeill) 4,500
From Rathbarry Stud (Agent)
b y f Strong Gale - Twilight Dawn (Deep Run)........................ (Cash) 7,600
Property of Louis Vambeck
b y c King's Ride - Tipperary Moss (Le Moss)........................ (Cash) 1,000
Property of Mark Delaney, from Kilmullen House
b y g Executive Perk - Lady Penthony (Ramdom Shot)........ (R H McNabb) 900
Property of John Hussey, from Augherskea Stables
ch y g Be My Native (USA) - Planet Star (Jupiter Pluvius)................ (Cash) 1,650
From Pallas Stud (agent)
b y g Brush Aside (USA) - Ballybree (Buckskin).................... (C Thornton) 5,000
b y f Be My Native (USA) - Dorrha Daisy (Buckskin)................. (M Dibbs) 2,500
Property of Declan Dower, from Creggs House Stud
b y g Executive Perk - Proverbial Biddy (Proverb).................... (Cash) 5,000
Property of David J Motherway
ch y g Phardante (FR) - Present Tense (Proverb)................ (B O'Meara) 2,300
Property of a Partnership, from Claramount Stud
b y g Brush Aside (USA) - Blooming Rose (Proverb).................... (C B A) 16,500

785

Property of Patrick J Connor
b y g Strong Gale - Woodford Princess (Menelek).............. (Padge Berry) 8,400
Property of James Ryan
ch y g Doubletour (USA) - Well Chaperoned (Sallust)................... (J Byrne) 4,300
Property of Nicolas Lambert
b or br y g Buckskin (FR) - Brighter Outlook (London Gazette).................. (Cash) 5,400
From Oldtown House Stud
b y g Altountash - Paico Lane (Paico)...... (P Gillen) 600
Property of Henry Fairweather
ch y g Over The River (FR) - Woodside Run (IRE) (Deep Run).............. (Cash) 2,600
Property of Mrs Phil Heskin, from Bishopstown Stud
b y g King's Ride - Mum's Girl (Deep Run) (Cash) 4,000
From Cregg Stud
b y g Henbit (USA) - Brownstown Lady (Charlottesvilles Flyer)................ (Rathmore Stud) 3,800
br y g Electric - Turvey (Royal Buck)....... (C B A) 4,700

b y f Royal Fountain - Unacceptable (Le Moss)................... (L Fennessy) 1,200
From Rathvin Stud
b y g Be My Native (USA) - Shake Up (Paico)................ (Paula Connon) 5,600
br y g Mandalus - Nicky's Dilemma (Kambalda)...................... (J Harty) 7,000

786

From Cloneymeath Farm
b or br y g Over The River (FR) - Galeshula (Strong Gale).................. (David Minton Bloodstock) 8,000
From Modreeny Stud
b or br y g Mandalus - Swanny Jane (Bargello)................ (L Fitzpatrick) 4,500
Property of Patrick J O'Connor
br y g Brush Aside (USA) - Flash Parade (Boreen)......................... (Cash) 4,600
Property of Mrs A S O'Brien, from Landscape Stud
b y g Royal Fountain - Dancing Princess (Prince Regent)................. (Cash) 1,500
b y g Strong Gale - Moate Gypsy (Fine Blade).............. (Derrygrath Stud) 15,500
b or br y g Strong Gale - Another Miller (Gala Performance) .... (Ghost Lodge Stud) 19,000
Property of Mrs C Kenneally from Bishopstown Stud
b or br y g King's Ride - Solar Jet (Mandalus).................. (P Johnson) 4,100
From Bishopstown Stud
b or br y g Brush Aside (USA) - Great Aunt Emily (Traditionalist)........... (Cash) 2,100
br y f Phardante (FR) - The Furniture Maker (Mandalus)....... (Bishopstown Stud) 2,600
Property of R N R Auld, from Ghost Lodge Stud
b or br y g Mandalus - Royal Reliance (Rymer)..................... (Cash) 6,000
b or br y g Be My Native (USA) - Wild Justice (Sweet Revenge).. (J O'Byrne) 8,200
b or br y g Strong Gale - Chantecler (Sayyaf) .... (J Berry) 9,000

787

Property of John O'Byrne, from Lodge Stud
b y f Strong Gale - Lady Buck (Pollerton)... (Anna Lane) 3,600
From Rathmore Stud
ch y g Saxon Farm - Milworth (Stetchworth) .... (Cash) 4,000
Property of Noel J Tector
ch y g Over The River (FR) - Morning Susan (Status Seeker)...... (Wickfield Farm) 4,500
Property of Richard T H Morrow
br y g Strong Gale - Glenbury Lady (Kemal) (Cash) 7,500
Property of Messrs Paul & Graham Morrow
br y g Air Display (USA) - Shining Green (Green Shoon)........... (M Murphy) 7,000
From Suir View Stud
br y g Be My Native (USA) - April Shade (Harwell).................. (P Johnson) 3,200
b or br y g Supreme Leader - Announcement (Laurence O) .... (Millbank Syndicate) 4,000

Property of Philip Dennison, from Dunadry Stud
b y g Brush Aside (USA) - Lovely Sanara (Proverb)........................ (Cash) 1,750
Property of P Dennison, from Dunadry Stud
ch y g Over The River (FR) - Aganish (IRE) (Callernish).................... (Cash) 1,100
b y g Denel (FR) - Sometimes Lucky (Levmoss)..... (David Minton Bloodstock) 7,200

788

Property of Navan Stables
b y g Strong Gale - Misty Venture (Foggy Bell)...................... (B O'Brien) 10,500
Property of Mrs S Brennan, from Farnagh Stud
b y f Tidaro (USA) - Random View (Random Shot).......................... (Cash) 700
b y g Boreen (FR) - Holly Grove Lass (Le Moss)........................ (Cash) 1,050
b y g King's Ride - Girseach (Furry Glen)... (G Stewart) 8,000
b y g King's Ride - Golden Cherry (IRE) (Le Moss).................... (J Quinlan) 2,300
b y f King's Ride - Dawn Blade (Fine Blade) (Paddy McDermott) 500
Property of P J King, from Ballywooden House Stud
ch or b y g Buckskin (FR) - Mollamoss (Le Moss)........................ (Cash) 3,000
b or br y g Arokar (FR) - Carrownfreagh (Jester).................. (J Dineen) 500
Property of a Partnership, from Castledillon Stud
b y g Tremblant - Rossnagran (Ardross).... (J O'Byrne) 5,400
From Carrickhill Stud
b y g Lafontaine (USA) - Dollyacker (General Ironside).................... (Cash) 4,800

789

Property of Jerry Murphy, from Spital Stud
br y g Black Minstrel - Royal Bonnet (Beau Chapeau).. (David Minton Bloodstock) 5,800
Property of M A Doyle
br y g Lord Americo - Badsworth Madam (Over The River)............... (D Ilk) 6,200
Property of Michael G Sinclair, from Rathbarry Stud
b y g Brush Aside (USA) - Happy Party (Invited)................ (Pat Furlong) 2,000
From Rathbarry Stud (Agent)
b y g Phardante (FR) - Extra Chance (Pollerton)................. (Pauline Cogan) 1,700
b y g Brush Aside (USA) - Gales Money (Strong Gale)..................(C B A) 3,300
b y g Brush Aside (USA) - Light The Lamp (Miner's Lamp)..................... (David Minton Bloodstock) 6,200
Property of Mrs Mary Teresa Ward
b y f Boreen (FR) - Ashville Lady (IRE) (Le Bavard)................. (T J R Walls) 1,650
From Ashleigh Stud
br y g Royal Fountain - Door Rapper (IRE) (Mandalus)........ (Charlestown Stud) 4,600
b y g Carlingford Castle - Hal's Pauper (Official)................. (Ml Quinn) 1,300

From Grange Stud
br or gr y g Electric - I've No Idea (Nishapour).................. (Cash) 9,800

790

From Grange Stud (Agent)
b y g Supreme Leader - Honeymoon Miss (FR) (Arctic Tern)............. (Cash) 2,000
From Grange Stud
b y g Supreme Leader - Silent Run (Deep Run)....... (David Minton Bloodstock) 5,800
b y g Arokar (FR) - Double Wrapped (Double-U-Jay)................ (M Flynn) 8,800
Property of P Dennison, from Dunadry Stud
br y g Supreme Leader - Nights Crack (Callernish).............. (M Downey) 2,800
From Island View Farm
br y g Montelimar (USA) - Derring Lass (Derring Rose)............ (R Haggas) 9,400
Property of Miss Josephine McClements, from Fortview Stables
b or br y g Electric - Culkeern (Master Buck) .... (M Quinn) 500
Property of Mrs Sarah C Sands
ch y g Torus - Gueranne (Green God)...... (M Quinn) 500
Property of Mrs B D Byrne, from Slieveardagh Stud
br y f Brush Aside (USA) - Flying Silver (Master Buck)........ (Mr P Johnson) 500
Property of D T Maxwell, from Carrick Stables
b y c Bustineto - Sunland Park (Baragoi) ... (B O'Meara) 1,400
Property of Jim Hewitt, from Blossom Hill
b y c Satco (FR) - Persian Caprice (Persian Bold).................. (Declan Weld) 1,500

791

Property of Sean Prendergast, from Burgatia Stud
ch y g Lancastrian - Glandore Run (Deep Run)......................... (Cash) 380
Property of Miss M P Canavan
b y g Strong Gale - Buskalinda (Little Buskins).................... (M Haggas) 8,200
From Abalon Stables
gr y c Standaan (FR) - Prairie Saint (Welsh Saint)........................ (Cash) 1,500
Property of Roger Ryan
ch y c Good Thyne (USA) - Dis Fiove (Le Bavard)...................... (Cash) 4,800
Property of James Cottrell, from The Island Stud
b y g Electric - Right Then (No Argument) (David Minton Bloodstock) 7,200
Property of P Ryan
b y f Be My Native (USA) - Castle Stream (Paddy's Stream)........ (C Thornton) 1,100
Property of E Kirtland
b y g Kambalda - Diamond Daw (Lock Diamond)................(Joe Hearn) 3,700
Property of Martin Dunne
b y g Le Bavard (FR) - Monk's Rambler (Monksfield)................. (J Egan) 2,100
b y g Le Bavard (FR) - Allured (Decoy Boy) (Ms Ellen M Hodgson) 5,800

Property of Thomas Walsh

br or gr y f General Ironside - Merillion (Touch Paper).......... (Leo McGrath) 450

PRIVATE SALES

Property of Mr Donal King, from Ballywooden House Stud

b y g Lancastrian - Cousin Flo (True Song) (Mrs H Silk) 1,900

Property of P Dennison, from Dunadry Stud

b y g Cardinal Flower - Miss Monksfield (Monksfield).................... (Cash) 2,500

Property of Ann Byrne

br y g Satco (FR) - Illinois Belle (Le Bavard) (Cash) 2,000

Property of Mr Patrick Hickey

b y f Lafontaine (USA) - Red Donna (Don).. (Cash) 2,600

792

FAIRYHOUSE (Tattersalls)

Friday, November 5th (Yearlings)

Property of Victoria Heslop, from Tooracurragh Stud

b y c Noalto - Tendale (Raise You Ten).... (Cash) 1,600

Property of J J Harty

br y c Phardante (FR) - Loughaderra (IRE) (Strong Gale).......... (J G FitzGerald) 7,200

Property of John Fletcher, from Liffey View Stud

b y g Lafontaine (USA) - Bumps-A-Daisy (Windjammer)......... (John Sheehan) 2,400

Property of a Partnership

b y c Torus - Bel Slipper (Belfalas) .... (Paul Grimes) 440

Property of Elizabeth McGuinness, from Oakley Park Stud

b y c Orchestra - Lyngard (Balliol)... (Cash) 1,000

From Shade Oak Stud

b y f Derrylin - Upham Reunion (Paridel) ... (Cash) 450

Property of J Thompson, from Shade Oak Stud

ch y f Rakaposhi King - Early Run (Deep Run)........................ (Cash) 1,150

From Shade Oak Stud

b y f Derrylin - Little Oats (Oats).... (Cash) 380

From Brownstone Stud

b or br y g Mandalus - Hyde's Pride (Proverb).......................... (Cash) 3,000

Property of Major F B & James Boyd, from Hillburn House

b y g Tremblant - Queen's Tricks (Le Bavard)............... (Edward Ryan) 4,000

793

Property of Miss J R Baker

b y f Torus - Yankee Pedlar (Yankee Gold) (Cash) 1,000

From Killossery Stud

b y c Orchestra - Vaghe Stelle (ITY) (Looking For)...................... (Cash) 3,500

Property of S Wilson

ch y f Yashgan - Kilbricken Glen (Furry Glen)................... (Fred Doyle) 2,000

Property of J Perrot, from Riverview House Stud

br y g Iron Duke (FR) - Miyana (FR) (Sanctus II)............................ (D Ilk) 2,500

Property of John J Gahan

b y g Supreme Leader - Polly's Slipper (Pollerton)............... (D Magnier) 3,100

Property of Brian O'Neill, from Milton House

b y c Le Bavard (FR) - Vultellobar (Bargello) (Penny Grainger) 2,000

Property of Lt Col & Mrs J A Dene, from Kilteelagh Stud

b y g Lafontaine (USA) - Sanctify (Joshua) (Cash) 3,000

From Chaelstown Stud

b y g Dromod Hill - Strong Willed (Strong Gale).......................... (Cash) 4,300

Property of Eileen, Countess of Mount Charles

ch y g Orchestra - Permanent Lady (The Parson).................. (Ml Haggas) 3,500

b y f Orchestra - Fiery Fosse (Furry Glen) .. (Cash) 300

794

From Riversfield Stud

b y g Tale Quale - Loobagh Bridge (River Beauty).............. (Mrs M Carroll) 700

b y f Tale Quale - Awbeg Lady (The Parson) .... (Cash) 300

Property of Eugene McDermott, from Kenny Court Stud Farm

b y f Strong Gale - Kemchee (Kemal)...... (Cash) 3,350

From Clonpriest Stud

b y f Brush Aside (USA) - Deep Cailin (Deep Run)........................ (Cash) 840

Property of Denis W Macauley

ch y f Phardante (FR) - Rozifer (Lucifer).... (Cash) 300

Property of Hugh McCann

b y f Mandalus - Pollerton Park (Pollerton) (Cash) 860

ch y f Bowling Pin - Clare Dawn (Prince Hansel)................ (Niall Blehan) 1,600

Property of Noel Murphy, from Ballinteskin Stud

b y f Strong Gale - Court Session (Seymour Hicks)............... (Tommy Steele) 2,800

Property of Mrs C Magill, from Ballywooden House Stud

b y g Electric - Ballykilleen (The Parson) ... (W Deacon) 1,900

b y g Buckskin (FR) - Black Tulip (Pals Passage)..................... (Cash) 3,000

795

Property of High Trees Stud, from Ballywooden House Stud

ch y g Buckskin (FR) - Mad House (Kabour) (Cash) 1,500

From Liatris Stud (Agent)

b y g Homo Sapien - Dream Away (Dusky Boy)............... (David O'Connor) 2,900

From Liatris Stud
ch y g Denel (FR) - Coldwater Morning (Laurence O)............ (Joe Magee) 2,000
From Liatris Stud (Agent)
b y g Homo Sapien - Ever Mine (Mount Hagen)........................ (Cash) 2,800
Property of Robert Kenny Jnr, from Ballingarry House Stud
b or br y g Lafontaine (USA) - Mandavard (IRE) (Mandalus)............... (Cash) 1,900
Property of Mr & Mrs J Harold-Barry
b y g Dry Dock - Popular View (Torus)..... (Cash) 3,000
b y g Tale Quale - Cherish (Bargello) (Cash) 6,400
Property of Penny Downes
ch y g Persian Mews - Kindly (Tarqogan)... (Derrygrath Stud) 11,000
b y f Montelimar (USA) - Many Views (Bargello)........................ (Cash) 2,500
From Brittas House Stud (Agent)
b y g Lapierre - Merenda's Sister (Pauper) (F Barry) 1,900

796

Property of Mr G Lane, from Rathbarry Stud
ch y g Over The River (FR) - Carnowen (Deep Run)............ (Ivor Dulohery) 1,800
From Rathbarry Stud (Agent)
b y g Brush Aside (USA) - Lady's Wager (Girandole)........... (Chris Thornton) 2,400
Property of Mr John Quane
b or br y g Be My Native (USA) - Dream Toi (Carlburg).............. (John Nallen) 12,500
b y g King's Ride - Chatty Actress (Le Bavard)...................... (Cash) 3,600
Property of Bansha House Stud Farm, from Bansha House
b y g Strong Gale - Miss Le Bavard (Le Bavard)...................... (Cash) 10,500
b y g Brush Aside (USA) - Mary O'Malley (Patch)........................ (Cash) 14,000
Property of Mr Michael Lysaght, from Ardmayle Stud
b y g King's Ride - Cassaurina (IRE) (Le Moss)............. (Mr Edward Ryan) 3,500
b y g Over The River (FR) - Country Seat (Paddy's Stream).............. (Cash) 14,000
Property of Mr Peter Kehoe
ch y g Treasure Hunter - Realma (Realm).. (Cash) 3,000
From The Rath Farm
b y g Strong Gale - Ethel's Daughter (Deep Run)........................ (Cash) 19,500

797

From Commonstown Stud
b or br y f Be My Native (USA) - Spin A Coin (Torus).......... (Derek Rothwell) 14,000
From Orwell Lodge Stud (Agent)
ch y g Be My Native (USA) - Shuil Ard (Quayside).............. (J R Weston) 3,800
Property of Mr Patrick Cashman
b y g Supreme Leader - Miss Lacemore (Red Alert) (David Minton Bloodstock) 7,000
From Lough-Na-Sollis Stud
b or br y g Phardante (FR) - Borecca (Boreen)...................... (Cash) 2,700

b y g Satco (FR) - Arabian Sands (Pollerton) (Cash) 2,700
Property of Mr R Colthurst, from Turret Farm Stud
b y g Henbit (USA) - Shuil Run (Deep Run) (David Minton Bloodstock) 7,100
From Boardsmill Stud
ch y g Orchestra - Clarrie (Ballyciptic)...... (Cash) 3,000
Property of a Partnership, from Claramount Stud
b y g Strong Gale - Pallastown Run (Deep Run)............... (James Brislane) 13,000
Property of Mr Kenneth Sherrard & Dr Seamus O'Donoghue, from Bishopstown Stud
b y g King's Ride - Summerfield Gold (Cracksman).............. (J P Berry) 2,700
From Bishopstown Stud
b y g Buckskin (FR) - Left Hand Woman (Energist)..................... (Cash) 9,200

798

From Glenvale Stud (Agent)
b y g Simply Great (FR) - Melarka (Dara Monarch)........................ (Cash) 8,000
From Glenvale Stud Agent for Ghost Lodge Stud
b y g Be My Native (USA) - Due Consideration (Sir Herbert).............. (Cash) 13,000
Property of Mr R N R Auld, from Ghost Lodge Stud
b y g Carlingford Castle - Good Sailing (Scorpio)...................... (Cash) 3,900
Property of Round Hill Stud
br y c Be My Native (USA) - Terrama Sioux (Relkino)... (David Minton Bloodstock) 12,500
From Grange Stud
b y f Supreme Leader - Everdancing (Dance In Time)..................... (Cash) 2,600
Property of Mr B D Darrer, from Suir View Stud
b or br y g Lafontaine (USA) - Iron Mermaid (General Ironside).............. (Cash) 3,500
b or br y g Brush Aside (USA) - Sea Skin (Buckskin).................... (Cash) 8,000
From Rathbarry Stud (Agent)
br y g Strong Gale - Rent A Card (Raise You Ten)......................... (Cash) 15,000
b y g Good Thyne (USA) - Shady Lady (Proverb)............... (Mrs E Martin) 2,400
From Rathbarry Stud
b y g Be My Native (USA) - Smart Cookie (Lord Gayle)............ (Mederic Ltd) 11,000
b y g Brush Aside (USA) - La Grande Dame (Niniski)....................... (Cash) 9,000

799

From Rathbarry Stud (Agent)
b or br y f Strong Gale - Frosty Face (Fine Blade)......................... (Cash) 1,000
Property of a Partnership, from Helshaw Grange Stud
br y g Strong Gale - Sister Delaney (Deep Run)....................... (Rita Lett) 18,000
From Market Hill Stud
b y f Executive Perk - Amber Ballad (Ballad Rock)................... (J Crowley) 1,100

From Meadowbank Stud
b y g Strong Gale - Ariannrun (Deep Run).. (Ml Haggas) 20,000
br y g Phardante (FR) - Fane Bridge (Random Shot)............ (Mrs V Cooper) 7,000
Property of M McGearty, from Rathnally Farm
br y g Mandalus - Mum's Chariot (Callernish)....... (David Minton Bloodstock) 7,600
From The Beeches Stud
gr y g Lancastrian - Moll Of Kintire (Politico) .... (Cash) 1,500
b y g Buckskin (FR) - Give Me A Name (Pollerton).................... (Cash) 3,800
Property of Mr Nicholas Phelan, from Knockouse Stud
gr y g Roselier (FR) - Honey Dream (Orchestra).................(J Dunlop) 3,400
From Redpender Stud
br y g Strong Gale - Baybush (Boreen)..... (Cash) 14,000

800

From Morganstown Stud
b y c Electric - Celtic Bombshell (Celtic Cone)......................... (Cash) 3,000
Property of Ms Jill Finegan
b y g Montelimar (USA) - Fontaine Royale (Lafontaine)...........(J A O'Connell) 5,800
From Grangemore Stud
b y c Tremblant - In My Time (Levmoss)... (Cash) 5,000
From Morganstown Stud
b or br y c Strong Gale - Sizzle (High Line) (Cash) 12,000
Property of Templerainey House Stud, from Rachel Bennett (Agent)
ch y g Buckskin (FR) - Tiny O'Day (FR) (Johnny O'Day)............... (Cash) 720
Property of Mr Karl Strecker, from Rachel Bennett (Agent)
b y f Buckskin (FR) - Sallstown (Salluceva) (Cash) 1,800
From Rachel Bennett (Agent)
b y g Arokar (FR) - Mourne Trix (Golden Love)......................... (Cash) 2,000
Property of S W D McIlveen, from Monkstown House Stud
ch y g Orchestra - Torview (Tug Of War) .. (Cash) 4,800
Property of Mr Denis Barry, from Bartlemy Stud
b y g Rising - What's The Point (Major Point)......................... (Cash) 800
Property of Mr Michael Garrigan, from Sunnyhill Stud
b y f Montelimar (USA) - Always Smiling (Prominer)................. (F Doyle) 3,100

801

From Ballintober Stud
b y g The Bart (USA) - Katebeaujolais (Politico).................... (E Dowley) 2,200
Property of Mr B Corscadden & Capt D Foster
br y f Strong Gale - Jane Bond (Good Bond) .... (David Minton Bloodstock) 10,000
Property of Mr Joe Dwyer, from Crickstown Stable
b y g Lancastrian - Please Oblige (Le Levanstell)....... (Philpotstown Stud) 2,000

Property of Mr Cyril B Maguire
gr y c Celio Rufo - Taketheblameagain (Deep Run)......... (David O'Connor) 1,000
b y c Cataldi - Fine Cut (Salluceva)......... (Tim Anthony) 1,400
Property of Mr Joseph Murphy
b y c Satco (FR) - Carmel's Castle (Deep Run)............................. (Cash) 5,000
Property of Miss Mary Hanafin, from Ballinakill Stud
ch y g Buckskin (FR) - Courreges (Manado) (Pk Lohan) 1,700
Property of Mr John F Daly
b or br y f Strong Gale - Shirley Kay (Candy Cane)........................ (Jn Bleahan) 2,500
Property of Ann Smurfit Bloodstock
b y c Be My Native (USA) - Island Dream (Lucifer)............ (Penny Granger) 4,600
From Donacarney Stud
gr y g Peacock (FR) - Aunty Babs (Sexton Blake)........................ (Cash) 1,800

802

From Keyhouse Stud
b y c Tidaro (USA) - Spendapromise (Goldhill)............... (Joseph Crowley) 700
b y f Mandalus - Carn Countess (The Parson)......................... (Cash) 400
Property of Anne B McDonnell
b y g Brush Aside (USA) - Gentle Madam (Camden Town) .... (David Minton Bloodstock) 10,000
Property of Bernie Hennessy
b y g Be My Native (USA) - Polly's Cottage (Pollerton)................. (J Dunlop) 5,000
Property of Mr Seamus Spillane, from The Beeches Stud
b y g Lancastrian - Kilclare Lass (Pitpan) ... (Niall Bleahen) 1,500
Property of Mr James Kelly, from Raheen Stables
ch y c Executive Perk - Cara Alanna (Dalsaan)................. (Tom Anthony) 700
PRIVATE SALES
To Dissolve a Partnership
Cahills Hill b g (6yrs) Callernish - Pampin (Pamroy)............. (Liam Lennon) 800
Property of Mr P B Scott, from Barnfield House
Quayfield b m (7yrs) Monksfield - Quayside Charm (Quayside)....... (C McKeever) 1,400
From Templeigh Stud
ch f (4yrs) Le Bavard (FR) - Fine Artiste (Fine Blade)........... (Paul Nicholls) 3,500
Property of Ms Anne Sammon
b g (3yrs) Treasure Hunter - Bell Of St Mark (Belfalas).................. (L Lennon) 500

803

PRIVATE SALES
Property of Mrs Monica Byrne
ch g (3yrs) Sheer Grit - Rising Dipper (Golden Dipper)....... (Peter Dyggan) 5,000
Property of Mr Leo Feely, from Ennel Lodge Stud
b f (2yrs) Buckskin (FR) - Ballygriffin (Deep Run)......................... (Cash) 4,000

Property of a Gentleman
b y g Strong Gale - Dunleer Duchess (Our Mirage)................... (M Parkhill) 5,000
From Aghern House Stud
b y f Jolly Jake (NZ) - Half Smashed (Belfalas)................. (D O'Brien) 700
From Minnview Stable
b y f Noalto - Clonmeen Official (Official) .. (Tom Hamilton) 600
From Bishopstown Stud
br y f Phardante (FR) - The Furniture Maker (Mandalus)................ (R Chugg) 2,600
Property of Mr Noel James
b y g Carlingford Castle - Jillie James (The Parson).................. (Joe Heron) 1,900
Property of Mr Richard Hennessy, from Abbey Stables
b y f Executive Perk - Quincy Bay (Buckskin)......................... (Cash) 1,500
From Bansha House Stud Farm
b y g Brush Aside (USA) - Nelly Gleason (Gleason)............ (Mrs C L Shaw) 3,500
Property of Mr Neville J Tector, from Coolbawn Stud
b y f Lord Americo - Coolbawn Lady (Laurence O)............ (Drumdeel Stud) 2,250
Property of Matthew P Collins
br y g Executive Perk - Tanarpa (Dusky Boy) .... (Cash) 3,250

804

FAIRYHOUSE (Tattersalls) Monday, November 8th (Foals)

Property of Mrs Ann Power
b c f Dry Dock - Poor Elsie (Crash Course) (Cash) 800
Property of Mr Michael Sinnott, from Bramble Farm
ch f f Torus - Monalma (IRE) (Montekin) ... (Eilish Donohoe) 420
Property of Mrs Teresa Bergin
b c f Good Thyne (USA) - Surely Madam (Torenaga)............. (Ron O'Leary) 2,000
From Herbertstown House Stud
ch f f Moscow Society (USA) - Devon Pixie (Hardboy)...... (Commonstown Stud) 400
Property of Mr J McCartan, from Glenfarm Stable
ch c f Denel (FR) - Tactique (FR) (Annes Pretender)............... (Paul Duffy) 950
Property of S MacKinnon, from Brentford Stud (Agent)
b c f Brush Aside (USA) - Random Arrow (Random Shot)........ (Peter Holmes) 2,800
Property of Mr A J Keating
b c f Homo Sapien - Fountain's Glory (IRE) (Royal Fountain)................ (Cash) 850
From Shade Oak Stud
ch f f Rakaposhi King - Paper Dice (Le Dauphin)...................... (Cash) 200
Property of Mr J Thompson, from Shade Oak Stud
ch f f Rakaposhi King - Dawn Encounter (Rymer)..................... (Cash) 200

From Shade Oak Stud
b f f Rakaposhi King - Herald The Dawn (Dubussoff)................. (Cash) 200

805

Property of Mr J Thompson, from Shade Oak Stud
b f f Derrylin - Donna Farina (Little Buskins) (Cash) 2,600
Property of Mr Joseph D Molloy, from Raheen Park
b c f Yashgan - Sweet Run (Deep Run).... (Cash) 3,400
Property of A Partnership, from Kellsboro House Stud (Agent)
b c f King's Ride - Lady Siobhan (Laurence O)................... (The Yearlings) 4,800
Property of Mr Martin W Hennessy
b c f Phardante (FR) - I'm Grannie (Perspex) .... (Tythorp Park) 3,600
Property of Mary Hennessy
ch f f Good Thyne (USA) - Owen's Toi (Master Owen).......... (Jn. Cahalan) 1,000
Property of William W Hatton
b c f Mandalus - Tempestuous Girl (Tumble Wind)........................ (Cash) 980
Property of Mr N Sullivan, from Knockhouse Stud
b f f Beau Sher - Coolentallagh (Perhapsburg).................... (Cash) 500
From Ballyward Stud
b f f Capitano - Gold Bank (Over The River) (Cash) 740
Property of Miss Josephine McClements, from Fortview Stables
ch c f Classic Memory - Culkeern (Master Buck)................. (Pat Greene) 420
From Longsea Stud
ch f f Yashgan - Joanoora (Ahonoora) ..... (Cash) 320

806

From Longlea Stud
b c f Aylesfield - Seryona (Seymour Hicks) (W T Bourke) 300
b f f Yashgan - Shesadream (Green Shoon) (J Watson) 1,100
Property of Mrs C Ross
b or br c f Jurado (USA) - Home In The Glen (Furry Glen)............... (M Carroll) 1,650
b f f Jurado (USA) - Callifyecan (Callernish) (Cash) 540
Property of Mr Alan Ross
ch c f Orchestra - Rush For Gold (Mugatpura)......................... (Cash) 4,200
Property of Mr Michael O'Donoghue, from Rathbarry Stud
b c f Brush Aside (USA) - Mad For Her Beer (Proverb)..................... (Cash) 1,550
From Park House Stud (Agent)
b c f Arctic Lord - Panning (Pitpan).. (Cash) 250
b f f War Hero - Panhandler (Pitpan) (Cash) 200
b f f Arctic Lord - Happy Patter (Pitpan).... (Colin Bravery) 360
Property of Miss Avril Campbell, from Ballywooden House
b c f Lafontaine (USA) - Kerry's Castle (Deep Run)....... (O'Donoghue Bros) 1,500

807

From Brittas House Stud

b f f Be My Native (USA) - Pisa (IRE) (Carlingford Castle).......... (R Irvine) 900
ch f f Be My Native (USA) - Knockananna (Torus).............. (Thomas Steele) 900
b f f Supreme Leader - Gales Chariot (Strong Gale)..... (Andrew Kavanagh) 1,100

Property of Mr Colm O'Brennan

ch f f Tremblant - Paldamask (Native Prince) .... (Cash) 600
b f f Mandalus - Les-Cancellas (Monksfield) (Cash) 1,000

Property of Mrs Emila Corrigan, from Liscolman House

b c f Mandalus - Cash Discount (Deep Run) (Cash) 700

Property of Mrs C W L Woollard

b f f Welsh Term - Cherry Ogue (Le Bavard) .... (Cash) 280

Property of Mill Bridge Farm

b c f Strong Gale - Thousand Flowers (Take A Reef)........................ (Rathbarry Bloodstock Services) 7,200

Property of Mr Diarmuid Horgan

b c f Royal Fountain - Kerrie's Pearl (Proverb).................. (Ivor Dulohery) 3,600
b f f King's Ride - Kerries Black (Black Minstrel)............. (Pat Hennessy) 400

808

From Gortnacloona Stud

br f f Eurobus - Swift Trip (IRE) (Duky)..... (Cash) 200

From Bryanstown Stud

b c f Phardante (FR) - Levi's Star (Levmoss) ...... (Rathbarry Bloodstock Services) 10,000

Property of Mr Paddy Cronin

ch c f Montelimar (USA) - Liberties (Don) .. (Eugene McDermott) 2,200

Property of Mrs Mary Cronin

b c f Supreme Leader - Florenanti (Floriferous)....................... (Cash) 2,000

Property of Mr T F Duggan, from Carrignaveen Stud

ch c f Good Thyne (USA) - Deep Black (Deep Run)........ (Bernard Maguire) 2,000
b c f King's Ride - Euroville Lady (Light Brigade).................... (P Keane) 2,200

Property of Mr George T Williams, from Carrignaveen Stud

b f f Torenaga - Unsinkable Suzie (IRE) (Invited)...................... (Cash) 300

From Killymaddy Stables

b c f Be My Native (USA) - Tickenor Wood (Le Bavard).................. (Cash) 5,400

Property of Lady Melissa Brooke, from Glenbevan Stud

b c f Brush Aside (USA) - Patrice Princess (Lucifer)........... (Queensford Stud) 2,600

Property of Mr Jack Hamilton, from Cunningburn Stud

b c f Yashgan - Jaflora (Welsh Captain).... (Cash) 300

809

Property of H O C Byrne, from Blakefield

b c f Satco (FR) - Fandia (Saher).... (Cash) 700

Property of Ann Byrne

br c f Satco (FR) - Illinois Belle (Le Bavard) (Thomas Steele) 1,800

Property of Anngrove Stud

b f f Welsh Term - Sunk Island (Nicholas Bill)......................... (Cash) 200
b f f Welsh Term - Black Crash (Crash Chourse)............ (Pat Hennessy) 320

Property of Mr J A Slattery

br f f Mandalus - Minnie's Dipper (Royal Captive)............ (Jenny Seaborn) 1,200
br f f Supreme Leader - Henry Woman (IRE) (Mandalus)......... (John Watson) 1,400
b or br c f Torus - Moppit-Up (Pitpan)...... (Cash) 3,700

Property of Navan Stables

ch c f Be My Native (USA) - Christy's Best (IRE) (The Parson)............ (Cash) 1,500
b f f Be My Native (USA) - La Christyana (IRE) (The Parson)......... (G Williams) 600

From Park House Stud (Agent)

b f f Mandalus - Mares Eat Oats (IRE) (Ovac)........................ (Cash) 450

810

From Bulmer Stud

ch c f Orchestra - Booly Bay (Le Prince) ... (Cash) 2,000
b c f Homo Sapien - Pearl Of The Bay (He Loves Me).................. (Cash) 2,400

Property of Mr Maurice Healy

b c f Phardante (FR) - Daffydown Lady (Menelek)................... (Cash) 1,900
b f f Supreme Leader - Daffydown Dolly (IRE) (The Parson)............. (Cash) 600

Property of Mr P J Prendergast, from Melitta Stud

b c f Montelimar (USA) - Princess Seal (Prince Tenderfoot)... (Seamus Smith) 4,000
b c f Montelimar (USA) - Scaravie (IRE) (Drumalis).................... (Cash) 6,200

Property of Mr George Roberts, from Rachel Bennett (Agent)

b c f Montelimar (USA) - Lucky Bride (Lucifer)............ (Queenford Stud) 4,100

From Grange Stud

b c f Glacial Storm (USA) - Castleblagh (General Ironside)...... (E McDermott) 4,200

From Brittas House Stud

b c f Supreme Leader - Gentle Madam (Camden Town)......... (Frank Keogh) 2,800

From Park House Stud (Agent)

br f f Mandalus - Cherry Dancer (Monksfield)........... (Declan Weld) 1,100

811

From Barrowford Stables

b or br c f Be My Native (USA) - Sketch Plan (Stetchworth)............ (Cash) 3,400

From Hill View Stud

b c f Strong Gale - Lady Rag (Ragapan).... (Cash) 14,000

Property of Mr Clement Fenton, from Hill View Stud

b c f King's Ride - Kylogue's Delight (Strong Gale).................. (Tythorp Park) 6,000

From Cregg Stud
ch c f Be My Native (USA) - Hi'upham (Deep Run).................. (C B A) 5,400
From Riverstown Stud
ch c f Boreen (FR) - Lady Leona (Leander) (David Minton Bloodstock) 5,000
Property of Mr John Hennessy
b or br c f Royal Fountain - No Tigers (Strong Gale)................ (Cash) 4,000
Property of Mr Richard J Hennessy
b or br f f King's Ride - More Than Words (Proverb)............. (Alan Stennett) 1,600
Property of Mr John Hennessy, from Knockeevan Farm
b f f Camden Town - Vaguely Decent (Decent Fellow)...............(Cash) 400
b f f Castle Keep - Daddy's Folly (Le Moss) (Cash) 200
Property of Messrs Diarmuid & Michael O'Connor, from Shamrock Lodge
b or br f f Strong Gale - Brown Forest (Brave Invader)........ (George Doyle) 5,000

812

From Abbeville & Meadow Court Studs
b c f Be My Native (USA) - Lady Helga (Aristocracy)...... (Broguestown Stud) 6,200
From Abbeville & Meadow Court Studs (Agent)
b c f Lafontaine (USA) - Clogrecon Lass (Raise You Ten)............... (Cash) 3,400
Property of M Doran
br f f Royal Fountain - Strong Slave (IRE) (Strong Gale)............ (P J Smyth) 1,050
gr f f Roselier (FR) - Una's Polly (Pollerton) (Donal Strain) 550
b f f Brush Aside (USA) - Four Shares (The Parson).................. (B Maguire) 3,200
From The Beeches Stud
b f f Commanche Run - Princess Andromeda (Corvaro).......... (Cash) 530
ch f f Buckskin (FR) - Superville (IRE) (Supreme Leader)... (Jimmy Mangan) 620
Property of Mr Seamus Spillane, from The Beeches Stud
b c f Commanche Run (FR) - Kilclare Lass (Pitpan)...................... (Cash) 3,200
From Liatris Stud
ch c f General Ironside - Leadhill Lady (Parva Stella)............ (Joe Magee) 500
From Cois Na Habhna Stud
b c f Phardante (FR) - Rather Grand (Will Somers)...................... (Cash) 3,800

813

Property of Miss Diana Turner, from Graigue Little
b f f Lafontaine (USA) - Whisht Lassie (Menelek)............. (Vivian Noone) 900
Property of Mr & Mrs J Lonergan, from Graigue Little
b c f Lafontaine (USA) - Black Again (Strong Gale)............. (O'Donoghue Bros) 1,200
b f f Be My Native (USA) - Menebeans (IRE) (Duky).................. (Cash) 1,000
Property of Mr Oliver Burke
br c f Be My Native (USA) - Verbana (Boreen)...................... (Cash) 7,200

Property of Angela Bracken
b c f Torus - Bonne Bouch (Bonne Noel)... (O'Donoghue Bros) 1,200
From Brittas House Stud
b c f Glacial Storm (USA) - Deep Captain (Deep Run).................. (Cash) 1,800
b c f Montelimar (USA) - Riverhead (Quayside).................... (Cash) 9,000
Property of Navan Stables
b c f Glacial Storm (USA) - Misty Venture (Foggy Bell).................. (Cash) 1,500
b c f Be My Native (USA) - Panel Pin (Menelek)................... (Cash) 3,100
b f f Lafontaine (USA) - French Class (The Parson)...................... (Cash) 2,650

814

From Carrigdownane Stud (Agent)
b f f Be My Native (USA) - Marsha's Daughter (Merrymount)............. (Marian Higgins) 1,100
From Carrigdownane Stud
br f f King's Ride - What's The Story (Homeboy).......... (Marian Higgins) 850
Property of Messrs John & Sean Hussey, from Augherskea Stables
b f f Mandalus - Crinkle Lady (Buckskin)... (Cash) 2,500
b f f Commanche Run - Planet Star (Jupiter Pluvius)...................... (Cash) 360
To Dissolve a Partnership, from Four Piers Stables
b f f Roselier (FR) - Spicy Lady (Decent Fellow)................ (Pat Greene) 520
Property of Mr Alec Gilchrist, from Pyleigh Court Farm es
ch c f Phardante (FR) - Shuil Run (Deep Run)................. (Alan Stennett) 6,800
Property of Ms June Finegan
b f f King's Ride - Jacquelines Glen (Furry Glen)................ (The Yearlings) 1,700
Property of M J McEnery, from Rossenarra Stud
b f f Montelimar (USA) - Instanter (Morston) .... (C B A) 3,500
Property of Mrs B D Byrne, from Slieveardagh Stud
b or br f f Brush Aside (USA) - Flying Silver (Master Buck)................. (Cash) 540
To Dissolve a Partnership
br c f Jolly Jake (NZ) - Pendarron (Green Shoon)................ (Tom Curran) 2,000

815

From Aghern House Stud
b f f Jolly Jake (NZ) - Earnrun (Deep Run).. (Maria Mulcahy) 800
b f f Supreme Leader - Ladylemoss (Le Moss)........... (Brendan Bashford) 1,000
Property of Mr G J McCartney
b c f Young Man - Patrician Maid (Milan) .. (Tom Curran) 3,000
Property of Mr B Butler
b f f Phardante (FR) - Cherry Allen (Giolla Mear)....................... (Cash) 1,600

Property of Mr Patrick J O'Connor
ch c f Executive Perk - Twinkle Sunset (Deep Run)................... (Cash) 2,500
Property of Miss Betty Sykes
b f f Macmillion - Feodora (Songedor) ...... (Cash) 420
b c f Escapism (USA) - Khotso (Alcide)..... (Cash) 850
From Ballybrennan Stud
ch c f The Bart (USA) - Bridgetown Girl (Al Sirat)................ (David O'Connor) 660
b c f Lord Americo - Leallen (Le Bavard)... (Sean Twomey) 500
Property of Miss Sharon Kiely, from Ballinree Stud
b c f Be My Native (USA) - Sugar Lady (Dalsaan)....................... (Cash) 1,100

816

Property of Miss Frances Boyle, from Ballinree Stud
ch f f Glacial Storm (USA) - China Doe (Buckskin)..................... (Cash) 240
Property of Mr Eamonn Garrett, from Coolyhenan Stud
br c f Good Thyne (USA) - Rendezvous (Lorenzaccio)........ (Queenford Stud) 2,400
Property of Mr J R McLoughlin
b f f Strong Gale - Dedham Vale (Dike) .... (O'Donoghue Bros) 6,200
PRIVATE SALES
Property of Mr D Canavan
b c f Mazaad - Lady Sipash (Erin's Hope) .. (Cash) 300
Property of Mr Franic M Lyons
b c f Celio Rufo - Star Of Monroe (Derring Rose)......................... (Cash) 1,150
Property of Mrs Emila Corrigan, from Liscolman House
b or br c f Mandalus - Aragon Park (Aragon) (Cash) 800
Property of Mr Anthony Cameron
b c f Good Thyne (USA) - First Prize (IRE) (The Parson)............. (J O'Connor) 1,300
From Park House Stud (Agent)
br f f Mandalus - Away And Gone (Comedy Star)................ (Mrs N Dutfield) 1,500

(Index reference 818 follows)

818

FAIRYHOUSE (Tattersalls)
Tuesday, November 9th (Foals)

Property of Patricia Byrne, from Silver Sand Stud
b c f Mandalus - Inch Tape (Prince Hansel) (Weathersfield Ltd) 7,400
Property of Mr M V Morrissey
b c f Castle Keep - Majority Straight (Majority Blue)................. (P Conway) 1,800
Property of Messrs Daniel C & Patrick J Keating
b c f Brush Aside (USA) - Park Breeze (IRE) (Strong Gale)......... (Johnson Bros) 2,800
Property of Mr Denis Scully
b c f Buckskin (FR) - Yvonne's Dream (Tumble Wind)................ (Cash) 1,550
Property of Mr Matt Murphy
b c f Camden Town - Bann River (Over The River)............ (Philpotstown Stud) 3,500
Property of Mr Tom Healy, from Nanallac Stud
b c f Be My Native (USA) - Angolass (Al Sirat)................... (M A Murphy) 1,800
Property of Mr J Power, from Riverview House Stud
br f f Decent Fellow - Talkative Princess (Prince Regent)............... (Cash) 480
Property of M McGearty, from Rathnally Farm
br or gr c f Roselier (FR) - Deceptive Response (Furry Glen) (James Cleary) 1,100
Property of Mr Patrick Crotty, from Bridge Stud
ch f f Roselier (FR) - Ballymacarett (Menelek).................... (Victor Reid) 600
From Rockmills Stud
br c f Royal Fountain - Mariner's Dash (Master Buck)............... (C.B.A.) 5,400

819

Property of Mr William Drew
b c f Yashgan - Couleurs Volants (Peacock) (Cash) 1,150
Property of Mr P J Maher, from Dromin House Stud
ch c f Be My Native (USA) - Parkroe Lady (IRE) (Deep Run)........... (J Halley) 4,100
b f f Glacial Storm (USA) - Swift Lady (Royal Highway)............. (Ronan Wilson) 2,100
From Ballynattin House
b f f Satco (FR) - Buffs Express (Bay Express).......................... (Cash) 1,050
b f f Satco (FR) - Grandpa's River (Over The River).............. (Knockaney Stud) 520
b f f Un Desperado (FR) - Bilma (IRE) (Glenstal)........................ (Cash) 400
Property of Lynus Fahy, from Ballynattin House
b f f Un Desperado (FR) - Brisbee (Prince Bee)................................ (Cash) 400
From Ballinvarosig House Stud
b c f Homo Sapien - Mullaun (Deep Run) .. (J G Kehoe) 500
b c f King's Ride - Niagara Lad (Prince Hansel)...... (Peter Doyle Bloodstock) 4,600
b c f Homo Sapien - Fair Rullagh (Bluerullah).................... (J Somers) 800
b c f King's Ride - Kim's Choice (Le Bavard) .... (Commonstown Stud) 3,000

820

Property of Mr Jimmy FitzGerald
b c f Glacial Storm (USA) - Glittering Moon (Proverb)...................... (Cash) 3,000
Property of Mr John Hodnett
b or br c f Good Thyne (USA) - Cathy's Girl (Sheer Grit)............... (T Whales) 2,800

Property of Mr Patrick Sheehan, from Castlemartix Stables
b c f Good Thyne (USA) - Lochda (Crash Course)..... (Peter Doyle Bloodstock) 2,600
From Morning Star Stud
ch c f Long Pond - Spanish Flame (IRE) (Spanish Place)................(Cash) 3,000
Property of Mr J H Ramsden (Dispersal Sale), from Kilteelagh Stud
b c f Montelimar (USA) - Tax Code (Workboy)......................... (Cash) 9,400
b c f Montelimar (USA) - Sanctify (Joshua) (Peter Doyle Bloodstock) 3,800
Property of Mrs Mary Teresa Ward
ch c f Good Thyne (USA) - Queen's Prize (Random Shot)................. (Cash) 820
Property of Mr Raymond Burroughs
b c f Mazaad - Chief Dilke (Saulingo) ...... (Commonstown Stud) 650
Property of Mr Hugh A Warnock, from Rockmore Stud
b c f Milk Of The Barley - Super Amber (Yellow God)................ (B.B.A.) 2,000
b c f Milk Of The Barley - Princess Sirene (Prince Tenderfoot)...... (Henry Park) 480

821

From Clonpriest Stud
b c f Brush Aside (USA) - Deep Cailin (Deep Run).......................... (Cash) 6,600
Property of Mr John Smiddy, from Clonpriest Stud (Agent)
b c f Strong Gale - New Talent (The Parson) .... (Cash) 6,200
From Clonpriest Stud (Agent)
b c f Royal Fountain - Eyre Street Lady (Carlingford Castle)............ (Cash) 1,400
Property of Mrs Patricia Mackean, from Sweet Wall Stables
b c f Florida Son - Helen's Birthday (Quisling).......................... (Cash) 1,900
Property of Mrs Mary Sheehan, from Castlematrix Stables
b c f Executive Perk - War Saint (Tug Of War)................(Eric McNamara) 1,400
Property of Mr Eugene McDermott, from Kenny Court Stud Farm
br c f Strong Gale - Kemchee (Kemal) ..... (Philpotstown Stud) 14,000
Property of Mr Gerard Hayes, from Grange Stud
ch c f Glacial Storm (USA) - Miss Shamrock (Saritamer)................... (Cash) 600
Property of Mrs Rory Brown
br c f Orchestra - Coctail Bid (Mandalus)... (P Conway) 1,500
Property of Mr Michael Garrigan, from Sunnyhill Stud
b f f Montelimar (USA) - Always Smiling (Prominer).......................... (Cash) 540
Property of Mr W P Murphy, from Ballycurragh Stud
b or br c f Ardross - First Things First (The Parson)...................... (Cash) 5,800

822

Property of a Partnership, from Russellstown Stud
b c f Persian Mews - Bold Kim (King's Ride) .... (Cash) 1,700
From Russellstown Stud
gr c f Persian Mews - Countess Spray (Even Say)....... (Broguestown Stud) 3,800
b c f Persian Mews - Laurestown Rose (Derring Rose)...... (Edward Cawley) 5,000
ch c f Persian Mews - Back To Bahrain (Mandalus).................... (Cash) 2,000
Property of Mr Edmond Coleman
b c f Supreme Leader - Kitty Cullen (Pollerton)......... (Peter Doyle Bloodstock) 7,600
b f f Homo Sapien - Kassina (Laurence O) (Cash) 880
From Keyhouse Stud
b c f Yashgan - Spendapromise (Goldhill) .. (O'Donoghue Bros) 900
b f f Tidaro (USA) - Carn Countess (The Parson)...................... (Cash) 380
Property of Mr William Hubbert
ch f f Over The River (FR) - Dromoland Lady (Pollerton).................... (Cash) 550
From Market Hill Stud
b f f Glacial Storm (USA) - Amber Ballad (Ballad Rock)........... (Pat Downey) 1,100
b c f Glacial Storm (USA) - Dual Adventure (Deep Run)............. (R B McKay) 1,050

823

Property of Mr William Treacy, from Market Hill Stud
b c f Mister Lord (USA) - Abbey Belle (Kambalda)........ (Eamon O'Connell) 1,000
Property of Mr John Lorden
b or br c f King's Ride - Lispatrick Lass (Kambalda)......... (Redpender Stud) 4,200
Property of Mr Jimmy Mangan, from Conna Stud
b c f Be My Native (USA) - Speedy Debbie (Pollerton)................... (Cash) 6,700
From Rathbarry Stud (Agent)
b c f Brush Aside (USA) - Eimer's Pet (Paddy's Stream) .... (Peter Doyle Bloodstock) 2,900
Property of Mr Dermot O'Byrne, from Rathbarry Stud
b c f Brush Aside (USA) - Shuilernish (Callernish)...................... (Cash) 3,700
ch c f Phardante (FR) - Pedigree Corner (Pollerton)................... (Cash) 7,400
From Rathbarry Stud (Agent)
b c f Strong Gale - Maul More (Deep Run) (Peter Doyle Bloodstock) 16,500
From Brittas House Stud
b f f Supreme Leader - Forward Gal (The Parson)....... (Laurence McGuinness) 620
ch f f Be My Native (USA) - Here She Comes (Deep Run)......... (J Lawlor) 1,700
b f f Lafontaine (USA) - Deep Stream (Deep Run)................... (Paddy King) 1,600

824

Property of Mrs Phil Heskin, from Bishopstown Stud
ch f f Balinger - Buckingham Lady (Buckskin)......................... (Cash) 320

Property of Tanya Sherrard, from Bishopstown Stud
b f f Boreen (FR) - Philly Athletic (Sit In The Corner)........................ (Cash) 540
Property of Mrs C Walsh, from Bishopstown Stud
ch f f Commanche Run - Tipperary Star (Arcticeelagh)................. (Cash) 340
Property of Mr Patrick Crotty, from Bridge Stud
b f f Castle Keep - Divine Dibs (Raise You Ten)................... (J G Kehoe) 1,200
Property of Mr John Bellingham
b c f Persian Mews - La Scala Da Seta (Dalsaan)..................... (Cash) 400
Property of Mr Jonn Bellingham
b c f Supreme Leader - Rathtrim (Strong Gale).............. (Kevin O'Donnell) 4,200
Property of Mr Stephen Eustace
b c f Lord Americo - Narrow Chance (IRE) (Mandalus)..................... (Cash) 2,700
Property of Mrs Roberta Bell, from Park House Stud (Agent)
b or br c f Mandalus - Lone Run (Kemal)... (Cash) 3,700
ch f f Good Thyne (USA) - Deep Pride (Deep Run).................. (Cash) 300
br f f Mandalus - Galway Grey (Gala Performance)....................... (Cash) 600

825

From Park House Stud (Agent)
b c f Mandalus - Some Madam (Some Hand)........................ (Cash) 2,200
gr f f Mandalus - Misty Joy (General Ironside).................. (Liam Gavin) 1,600
br c f Mandalus - Milan Pride (Northern Guest)...................... (Cash) 4,300
Property of Mr Denis McDonnell
b c f King's Ride - Julia Too (Golden Horus) (Cash) 2,700
Property of Mr G Verling
b c f Broadsword (USA) - Four Sport (Swing Easy)............... (Liam McAteer) 16,500
From Ballywilliam Stud
gr c f Celio Rufo - Greenpeace (Master Owen)........................ (Cash) 2,200
Property of Mr & Mrs G A Coppola
ch f f Montelimar (USA) - Subiacco (Yellow River)....................... (Cash) 4,800
Property of Corbally Stud (Co Down)
b f f Buckskin (FR) - Dippers Daughter (Strong Gale)..... (Paddy Prendergast) 7,000
Property of Mr J G Fletcher, from Glascar Hill Stud
b c f Miner's Lamp - Somelli (Candy Cane) (Cash) 1,000
Property of Mrs A Riddle-Martin, from Lisieux Stud
b c f Moscow Society (USA) - Firing (Tarboosh)........... (O'Donoghue Bros) 7,500

826

From Rathbarry Stud (Agent)
ch c f Phardante (FR) - Carminda (Proverb) (M Skinner) 7,200
ch c f Tale Quale - Meandering (Le Moss) (Padge Berry) 1,000
Property of Mrs Mercy Rimell, from Rathbarry Stud
b f f Phardante (FR) - Gaye Memory (Buckskin)........................ (Cash) 17,000
From Park House Stud (Agent)
br c f Mandalus - Flinging (Good Times) ... (Dr D Chesney) 3,600
b c f Mandalus - Dandy Poll (Pollerton) .... (Keith Lewis) 10,500
br c f Mandalus - Nice Little Earner (Warpath).......... (Commonstown Stud) 2,100
Property of Mrs L Eadie
b c f King's Ride - Live Aid (Little Buskins) (David Minton Bloodstock) 10,000
ch f f Orchestra - Coforta (The Parson) .... (Simon Brosnan) 950
Property of Mrs A L Smyth
ro c f Good Thyne (USA) - Lady Barnaby (Young Barnaby)............. (Cash) 1,100
From Orwell Stud
b c f Commanche Run - Myra Gaye (Buckskin)..................... (D Newell) 12,000

827

Property of Pam Sweeney, from Orwell Stud
b c f Castle Keep - Run Of Luck (Lucky Brief)................ (Arthur Moore) 2,600
ch c f Roselier (FR) - Jacob's Creek (IRE) (Buckskin).......... (M G Sheppard) 2,000
From Orwell Stud
br f f Be My Native (USA) - Artist's Jewel (Le Moss).................... (Cash) 4,600
From Orwell Lodge Stud
br c f Roselier (FR) - Bluebell Avenue (Boreen Beag)...... (David O'Connor) 2,200
br c f Roselier (FR) - Hope You're Lucky (Quayside).................... (Cash) 4,000
From Orwell Stud
ch f f Castle Keep - Artist's Design (Precipice Wood)................ (Cash) 14,000
From Orwell Lodge Stud (Agent)
b c f Lord Americo - Shuil Ard (Quayside).. (Cash) 3,100
Property of Mr Jerry Mackey, from Rachel Bennett (Agent)
ch c f Commanche Run - Kind Sir She Said (Decent Fellow)............... (Cash) 540
From Rachel Bennett (Agent)
ch c f Over The River (FR) - Spanish Royale (Royal Buck).......... (M G Sheppard) 3,000
b c f Un Desperado (FR) - Hooch (Warpath) (Dr D Chesney) 4,700

828

Property of Coolruss Stud, from Rachel Bennett (Agent)
ch c f Montelimar (USA) - Eurolink Sea Baby (Deep Run).......... (Mederic) 14,000
Property of Ms B Cunningham
b or br f f Roselier (FR) - Cotton Gale (Strong Gale).................. (Cash) 550
b or br c f Strong Gale - Ballyhoura Lady (Green Shoon)................ (Cash) 11,000

ch c f Phardante (FR) - House Keyes (Le Moss).......................... (Cash) 4,100

Property of Dan and Margaret O'Neill, from Roundhill Stud

b c f Phardante (FR) - Pallastown Run (Deep Run).................. (Cash) 4,100

From Yellowford Farm

gr f f Roselier (FR) - Supreme Glen (IRE) (Supreme Leader).......... (Pat Tobin) 1,000

Property of Mr Oliver Loughlin

b c f Phardante (FR) - Mrs Neill (Proverb) .. (Cash) 3,400

Property of Mrs Norman G Cook

b c f Buckskin (FR) - Geeaway (Gala Performance)................ (Tythrop Park) 7,400

Property of Mr Aidan Furlong

b f f King's Ride - Lady Albron (Royal Match)............ (David Matthews) 620

Property of Mrs Patricia Furlong

b c f King's Ride - Arumah (Arapaho) ...... (Ned Byrne) 5,100

b or br f f Mandalus - Bold Empress (Decent Fellow)........... (D Newell) 1,700

829

Property of Mrs S Sinnott

b f f Roselier (FR) - Catspaw (Laurence O) (Kerr & Co) 950

Property of Portavo Bloodstock, from Liatris Stud (Agent)

ch c f Be My Native (USA) - Pampered Russian (Deep Run)........... (Cash) 12,000

b c f Commanche Run - Bavette (Le Bavard)....................... (Cash) 4,000

From Liatris Stud

b c f General Ironside - Leney Character (Reformed Character) .... (Philpotstown Stud) 2,000

Property of Mr James Hannon, from Curraheen Stud

b c f Balinger - Merry Mirth (Menelek)..... (Tythrop Park) 3,600

ch c f Balinger - Castle Duchess (Abednego)......................... (Cash) 1,000

b f f Balinger - Papa's Pigeon (Lion) .... (Jn Lawless) 230

Property of Mr Sean Twomey, from Hawthorn Villa Stud

b f f Be My Native (USA) - Gina's Love (Golden Love).... (B Bashford (Agent)) 1,500

b c f Brush Aside (USA) - Hawthorn Dandy (Deep Run).. (Peter Doyle Bloodstock) 12,000

From Brittas House Stud

b c f Executive Perk - Banna's Retreat (Vitiges)................. (M Skinner) 4,300

830

From Foxbrook Stud

b c f Montelimar (USA) - Rossaleigh (Menelek)......................... (Cash) 4,000

From The Beeches Stud

gr f f Glacial Storm (USA) - Scally Bell (Scallywag).................... (Cash) 660

b c f Commanche Run - Got To Fly (IRE) (Kemal).............. (Johnson Bros) 2,900

Property of High Trees Stud, from Ballywooden House Stud

b f f Commanche Run - Stolen Gold (Tycoon II)............ (Henry Park) 300

Property of Mr P King, from Ballywooden House Stud

b c f Glacial Storm (USA) - Black Nancy (Monksfield)...... (Charlestown Stud) 1,600

From Rathbarry Stud (Agent)

ch c f Phardante (FR) - Lena's Reign (Quayside)..................... (Cash) 3,000

Property of Mr M O'Donoghue, from Rathbarry Stud

b c f Good Thyne (USA) - Gogginstown (Green Shoon).......... (W P Higgins) 500

Property of Mr & Mrs James Lonergan, from Graigue Little Stud

ch f f Glenstal (USA) - Talk Is Cheap (Le Bavard).................. (Ml Martin) 310

Property of Mrs S L Jackson, from Graigue Little Stud

b c f Commanche Run - Karenda (Kambalda)..................... (Hawthorn Villa) 3,300

Property of Mr & Mrs J Lonergan, from Graigue Little Stud

b or br c f Royal Fountain - Flags Flying (Paico)........................ (Cash) 2,700

831

Property of Mr Noel Murphy, from Ballinteskin Stud

b f f King's Ride - Gortroe Queen (Simbir) (Cash) 3,700

b c f Brush Aside (USA) - Mogen (Adonijah) (Peter Doyle Bloodstock) 11,500

b f f King's Ride - Youthful Capitana (Hardboy)......................... (Cash) 800

Property of a Partnership, from Seskin Lodge

b c f Glacial Storm (USA) - Our Little Lamb (Prince Regent)............... (Cash) 3,500

From Seskin Lodge

b f f Executive Perk - Hopeful Chimes (Reformed Character).......... (Cash) 600

From Tierhogar House

br c f Yashgan - Theme Music (Tudor Music).................. (Ml Murphy) 2,100

Property of Mr John P A Kenny

ch f f Executive Perk - Crash Run (Crash Course)............... (George Allen) 380

br f f Be My Native (USA) - Tuney Doon (Quayside)....... (Nicholas Keogh, Jr) 520

Property of South Park Farm

b c f Lafontaine (USA) - Goose Loose (Dual) .... (Pat Cahalan) 2,300

Property of Mr James F Murdoch

b c f Glacial Storm (USA) - Candora (Cantab) .... (F Somers) 950

832

Property of Miss D L Murdoch

ro f f General Ironside - Lindora (Whistling Top).......................... (Cash) 400

Property of Mrs James F Murdoch

br c f Electric - Door Key (Fidel)..... (Cash) 1,050

Property of Mrs Theresa Abbey, from Crosneen Stables

br f f Mandalus - Fayafi (Top Ville)......... (L McGuinness) 700

Property of Mr Simon Kearney
b c f Mandalus - Mrs Guru (Le Bavard) .... (Broguestown Stud) 3,500
b f f The Bart (USA) - Kilnock Lass (Rymer) (Cash) 420
Property of Mr R T McLoughlin
b f f Brush Aside (USA) - Torus Court (Torus).................... (Cash) 1,650
Property of Mr Cyril B Maguire
b c f Tidaro (USA) - Taketheblameagain (Deep Run).................... (Cash) 280
Property of Mrs M Mulcahy
b f f Buckskin (FR) - Boulta View (Beau Chapeau).................... (Cash) 280
Property of Mr Michael Healy
b or gr c f Supreme Leader - Autumn Spirit (Deep Run).................... (Cash) 1,500
PRIVATE SALES
From Shade Oak Stud
b y f Gunner B - Thevicarsdaughter (The Parson).................... (N Powel) 250
Property of Bernie Stack, from Coolagown Stud
ch y c Rock Chanteur - Winetto (Condorcet) .... (R Herdman) 190
Property of Mr N Sullivan, from Knockhouse Stud
b or br y c Parliament/roselier (FR) - Aria (Saintly Song)........ (Mrs V O'Leary) 1,400
Property of a Lady, from Four Piers Stables
ch y c Noalto - Mainstown Belle (Peacock) (P Greene) 550
Property of Mr John McGuinness
b y f Sexton Blake - King's Reserve (King's Ride).................... (R Herdman) 250
Property of Mr Jerry Mackey, from Rachel Bennett (Agent)
b y c Commanche Run - Esperia (Jalmood) (Cash) 1,500

(Index reference 834 follows)

834

FAIRYHOUSE (Tattersalls)
Wednesday, November 10th (Foals)

Property of Mr Raymond Sheedy
b c f Top Of The World - Lady Gondola (Tug Of War).................... (Cash) 500
Property of Mr Thomas Walsh
b c f Zaffaran (USA) - Merillion (Touch Paper).................... (Cash) 500
Property of Margaret Little, from Ennel Lodge Stud
b f f Executive Perk - Carry On Dreaming (The Parson)............... (M Liddy) 440
ch f f Roselier (FR) - Dontellvi (The Parson) (Cash) 280
b or br c f Executive Perk - Below The Wind (Gala Performance)...... (R B McKay) 1,150
Property of Margaret & Brendan Shanley, from Ennel Lodge Stud
ch f f Aristocracy - Mrs Fantastic (Sexton Blake)............ (Eugene Angland) 220
From Ennel Lodge Stud
br f f Boreen (FR) - All Gone (Giolla Mear) (Robert Kenny, Jnr) 320
Property of Mr Finbarr O'Neill, from Firgrove Stud
b c f Buster King - Rising Sara (IRE) (The Parson)............ (Eugene Angland) 360
Property of Carole Adams, from Courtmacsherry Stables
br c f Royal Fountain - Mini-Pop (Black Minstrel)................ (Walter Kent) 1,750
Property of Mr Alan Cloney
br c f Camden Town - Tops O'Crush (Menelek)............ (Augherskea Stud) 4,300
br f f The Bart (USA) - Shady Jumbo (Callernish)............ (Maurice Keane) 300
b f f The Bart (USA) - Goldvine (Pollerton).. (Vincent Burke) 240

835

From Rosemount House Stud
b f f Asir - Philosophical (Welsh Chanter) .. (Jn. Cuffe) 540
From Aghern House Stud
b f f Jolly Jake (NZ) - Acot Touchseal (NZ) (Mayo Mellay)......... (Vincent Burke) 270
b c f Jolly Jake (NZ) - Chelsea Charmer (Ballymore).............. (S Mangan) 2,300
b f f Jolly Jake (NZ) - Corrie's Duchess (IRE) (Burslem).................... (Cash) 1,200
b f f Jolly Jake (NZ) - Campyard (Deep Run) .... (Cash) 260
Property of Mr William McCarthy
ch or b f f Electric - Afford The Queen (Pitpan)............... (Fiona Kinnear) 2,400
b f f Phardante (FR) - Let's Compromise (No Argument)........... (R B McKay) 1,350
Property of Miss Lileagh Fox, from Oak Lodge Stud
ch c f Electric - Vixen Run (Deep Run)..... (Broguestown Stud) 2,500
Property of Mr P Ryan
ch c f Be My Native (USA) - Castle Stream (Paddy's Stream)............. (Cash) 2,600
Property of Mr Frank Latham, from Blackrath Stud
ch c f Torus - Blackrath Gem (Bargello)..... (Cash) 1,100

836

Property of Mrs Patricia Whelan, from Blackrath Stud
b f f Top Of The World - Rugged Cop (Rugged Man)............... (Cash) 300
Property of Mr Finbarr O'Neill, from Firgrove Stud
b c f Buster King - Merry Damsel (Ovac)... (David O'Connor) 500
Property of Messrs J & M Kidd
b c f Zaffaran (USA) - Niamh's Friend (Laurence O)............. (Hugh Holohan) 1,000

From Rathbarry Stud (Agent)

ch c f Phardante (FR) - Glen Laura (Kambalda)........................ (Cash) 4,100

b f f Brush Aside (USA) - Rare Dreamer (IRE) (Le Moss)..... (Martin O'Malley) 680

Property of Mr Henry Hogan, from Rathcannon Hill

b f f Electric - Candy Smile (Candy Cane) .. (Seamus Marshall) 550

From Rathvin Stud

b f f Be My Native (USA) - Paddy's Team (Ballymore)........ (Seamus Marshall) 540

b f f Be My Native (USA) - Rathshade (Bustineto)............. (John Kirwan) 500

From Blackabbey Stud

b f f Glacial Storm (USA) - Green Gale (Strong Gale)............ (R B McKay) 400

Property of Mr Richard Busher

b c f Tremblant - Supreme Cherry (Buckskin)........................ (Cash) 1,300

837

Property of Messrs Richard & William Nicholson

b c f Millfontaine - No Breeze (Strong Gale) (Commonstown Stud) 400

Property of Mr & Mrs R Coghlan, from Balief Stud

b c f Yashgan - Sounds Symphonic (Orchestra)........ (Charlestown Stud) 2,500

Property of a Partnership, from Balief Stud

b c f Yashgan - Welsh Glen (Furry Glen)... (Cash) 1,300

From Mountain View Stud

br c f Strong Gale - My Lovely Rose (IRE) (Orchestra).......... (Edward Cawley) 9,000

Property of a Partnership

ch c f Glacial Storm (USA) - Barnhill Rose (Lucifer)..................... (Cash) 1,750

b f f Buckskin (FR) - Determined Sara (Yellow River)..... (Seamus Marshall) 380

Property of Portavo Bloodstock, from Liatris Stud (Agent)

b c f Commanche Run - Paupers Spring (Pauper)............... (Tythrop Stud) 6,000

b c f Buckskin (FR) - Shady Miss (Mandamus)................ (Keith Lewis) 8,600

From Farnagh Stud

ch c f Orange Reef - Green Fairy (Green Shoon)............. (Edward Cawley) 750

Property of Mr Hugh McCann

b f f Bowling Pin - Dontlike (Amazon)....... (Cash) 1,000

b f f Mandalus - Slievenanee (Avocat) ..... (Val O'Brien) 1,600

ch f f Roi Guillaume (FR) - Gothic Arch (Gail Star)......................... (Cash) 680

ch c f Executive Perk - Dawn Infidel (IRE) (Fidel)....................... (C B A) 1,500

ch f f Good Thyne (USA) - Emmodee (Bowling Pin)................ (Tony Sutton) 450

838

From Lisfinny Castle

b or br c f Be My Native (USA) - Evergreen Lady (Smartset) .... (David Minton Bloodstock) 4,200

b c f Buckskin (FR) - Torekulu (Torenaga) .. (Cash) 1,150

b c f Buckskin (FR) - Giverahand (Le Moss) (Cash) 3,900

Property of Mr Thomas Foy, from Grangecam Stud

b c f Royal Fountain - Golden Vixen (Goldhill)..................... (Val O'Brien) 5,000

From Lady Rathdonnell

b c f Mandalus - Best Of Kin (Pry) .... (R W McLean) 5,300

Property of Jessica Wilkinson

b c f Buckskin (FR) - Men's Fun (Menelek) (Cash) 4,200

Property of Ann Twomey

b c f Satco (FR) - Tudor Lady (Green Shoon) .... (Cash) 2,200

Property of Mrs F S Miller

b c f Mandalus - Cletic Bombshell (Celtic Cone).......................... (C B A) 6,200

Property of Mr Michael Barron

b c f Homo Sapien - Money Back (Master Buck).................. (Tom Keating) 1,300

Property of Mr Thomas Tormey

ch c f Orchestra - Rambling Ivy (Mandalus) (Cash) 3,000

839

Property of Mr Brian Kennedy, from Meadowlands Stud

ch c f Simply Great (FR) - Sister Duke (Bonne Noel)............... (J Ward) 1,500

From Rathbarry Stud (Agent)

br c f Strong Gale - Pryoress (Pry)......... (Ballyneale House Stud) 6,000

br f f Strong Gale - Billy's Pet (Le Moss)... (Cash) 1,600

From Rathbarry Stud

b c f Brush Aside (USA) - Molten (Ore) .... (Cash) 4,400

From Rathbarry Stud (Agent)

br c f Royal Fountain - Orospring (Tesoro Mio)........................ (Cash) 4,800

Property of Mr & Mrs M Ross

b f f Jurado (USA) - What A Duchess (Bargello) .... (Rathbarry Bloodstock Services) 1,650

Property of Penny Downes

b c f Celio Rufo - In View Lass (Tepukei) .. (Cash) 5,200

b f f Radical - Yankee View (Yankee Gold) (Robert Brabazon) 460

ch c f Montelimar (USA) - Many Views (Bargello).................. (J McNeill) 5,400

From Ballyburn Stud

b f f Buckskin (FR) - Lady Laburnum (Carlingford Castle).. (Aghern House Stud) 1,150

b c f Buckskin (FR) - River Glen (Furry Glen) .... (M G Sheppard) 4,400

b f f Buckskin (FR) - Nordic Fling (Viking) .. (Seamus Marshall) 600

b f f Buckskin (FR) - Narcone (Kambalda) .. (James Cottrell) 840

840

Property of Lyle Buttimer

b c f King's Ride - Ballyoran Princess (The Parson)...................... (Cash) 2,100

Property of Amber Stud, from Rachel Bennett (Agent)

b c f King's Ride - Turbo Run (Deep Run).. (Cash) 1,300

From Rachel Bennett (Agent)

b c f King's Ride - Milan Moss (Le Moss).. (Cash) 600

b c f Glacial Storm (USA) - Killiney Rose (Buckskin)........ (O'Donoghue Bros.) 3,100

br c f Welsh Term - Ballinkillen (Levmoss) (Mark Miller) 1,650

b c f Strong Gale - Comeragh Princess (Le Moss)............................ (Brian Grassick Bloodstock Services) 13,000

Property of Mr Louis Vambeck

br f f Brush Aside (USA) - Random What (Random Shot).......... (Eddie White) 500

b c f Strong Gale - Fairly Deep (Deep Run) (Cash) 11,000

Property of Mr Stephen Vambeck

b f f Yashgan - Coast A While (IRE) (Strong Gale).......................... (Cash) 560

Property of Mr Louis Vambeck

b c f King's Ride - Radical Review (Radical) (Noel Finegan) 2,600

841

Property of Mr Niall Flynn, from Five Naughts Stud

br c f Good Thyne (USA) - Shuil Liss (Deep Run).................. (R W McLean) 7,400

From Derrynagowan Stud

b or br f f Montelimar (USA) - Run For Shelter (Strong Gale)........... (Cash) 3,900

From Boardsmill Stud

b c f Orchestra - Knight's Maid (Giolla Mear)........................ (Cash) 8,400

b c f Orchestra - Madonna Pica (Salluceva) (Cash) 2,000

From The Beeches Stud

b c f Commanche Run - Merenda's Sister (Pauper)............... (Paddy Griffin) 3,000

b f f Mandalus - Technical Merit (Gala Performance)......... (John Lenihan) 1,250

b f f Buckskin (FR) - Carry The Can (Deep Run)................. (Pat McCarthy) 900

ch f f Commanche Run - Drachma (Netherkelly)........................(Cash) 850

From Rochestown Stud

b f f Glenstal (USA) - Primrose Forest (Menelek)..................... (Cash) 1,600

b c f Montelimar (USA) - Golden Privet (IRE) (Kemal)........................ (Cash) 10,000

b c f Glenstal (USA) - Right Then (No Argument)........................ (Cash) 2,000

842

From Commonstown Stud

b c f Montelimar (USA) - Spin A Coin (Torus)............ (Broguestown Stud) 10,000

Property of Mr Godfrey Deacon

b c f Brush Aside (USA) - Deep Dollar (Deep Run)............ (Frank Keogh) 7,800

From Stonepark Stud

b c f Be My Native (USA) - Society News (Law Society)............... (P Berry) 6,800

b c f Be My Native (USA) - Fight For It (Strong Gale)................. (Cash) 10,500

Property of Mr J G Charlton

b c f Good Thyne (USA) - Lady Solstice (Vital Season)............................ (David Minton Bloodstock Services) 5,400

b c f Arctic Lord - Ananda (Majestic Maharaj)................. (P Conway) 3,200

b f f Gildoran - Royal Pam (Pamroy) (Cash) 850

Property of Mr Peter Kehoe

b c f Lafontaine (USA) - Bellalma (Belfalas) (Cash) 2,600

Property of Mr Michael Madden

b c f Montelimar (USA) - Tarrants Cross (Pitpan)................................(Cash) 5,800

From Rathbarry Stud

b f f Phardante (FR) - Relishing (Relkino)... (Cash) 1,100

843

From Rathbarry Stud (Agent)

br c f Phardante (FR) - Johnstown Love (IRE) (Golden Love)............ (Cash) 4,500

From Rathbarry Stud

b c f Strong Gale - Mrs Simpson (Kinglet).. (C B A) 14,500

From Brittas House Stud

br c f Supreme Leader - Rivers Secret (Young Man)....................(Cash) 2,400

br c f Executive Perk - Precipienne (Precipice Wood)........... (Jim Dreaper) 11,000

Property of Mr K Riordan, from Grange Stud

ch c f Be My Native (USA) - Twilight Dawn (Deep Run)............... (John Corry) 7,000

Property of Portavo Bloodstock, from Liatris Stud (Agent)

b c f Buckskin (FR) - Night Trix (IRE) (Spin Of A Coin)........................ (Cash) 4,600

From Boardsmill Stud

ch f f Orchestra - Asinara (Julio Mariner)... (Margaret Foley) 950

b or br f f Jurado (USA) - Lysanders Lady (Saulingo)...................... (Cash) 2,600

From Briar Hill Stud

b f f Good Thyne (USA) - Raise The Bells (Belfalas)............ (John Sweeney) 3,100

b f f Homo Sapien - Merry Love (Golden Love).................. (N O'Mahony) 800

844

Property of Mr P O'Donovan, from Briar Hill Stud

ch c f Glacial Storm (USA) - Sindy's Gale (Strong Gale)......... (Hugh Holohan) 780

Property of a Partnership, from Briar Hill Stud

b c f Euphemism - Hollywood And Vine (Radical)........................ (Cash) 500

From Punchestown House Stud

ch c f Montelimar (USA) - Lousion (Lucifer) (Noel Finegan) 2,500

Property of Mr Denis MacAuley

b or br f f Welsh Term - Miss McNight (Master Buck)................. (Cash) 820

Property of Mr Donal King, from Ballywooden House Stud

b c f Be My Native (USA) - Salufair (Salluceva)................. (James Hales) 4,600

b c f Mandalus - Sister Of Dawn (Owen Anthony)......... (O'Donoghue Bros) 1,450
ch c f Be My Native (USA) - Cousin Flo (True Story).................. (C B A) 4,100
b c f Be My Native (USA) - Greek Gale (Strong Gale)....... (Denis Cummins) 2,000

From Grange Stud

b f f Supreme Leader - Queen's Run (IRE) (Deep Run)...... (Laurence O'Connor) 1,250
b f f Commanche Run - Cauriedator (Laurence O)............. (Dr T O'Brien) 1,000
b f f Glacial Storm (USA) - Roamaway (Gala Performance)................. (Cash) 5,000

845

Property of Mr P J Mulhall

b c f Electric - Lily Gale (IRE) (Strong Gale) (Patrick Hayes) 750

Property of Mr Robert Kenny Jnr, from Ballingarry House Stud

b or br c f Satco (FR) - Tuney Two (Le Bavard)........... (Old Meadow Stud) 1,850
b or br f f Ring Of Ford - Blakes Hollow (IRE) (Sexton Blake).................. (Seamus Marshall) 350
ch c f Montelimar (USA) - Country Melody (IRE) (Orchestra)...... (Johnson Bros) 1,600

From Bruis Farm

b f f Royal Fountain - Noel's Flash (Deep Run)......................... (Cash) 660

From Gartlandstown Stud

b c f Brush Aside (USA) - Prudent Rose (Strong Gale)......... (J A O'Connell) 5,400

Property of Mr Frank Fagan, from Gartlandstown Stud

ch c f Good Thyne (USA) - Reynoldstown Rose (Caribo)................. (Cash) 3,700

Property of Mrs S Brennan, from Farnagh Stud

b c f King's Ride - Dawn Blade (Fine Blade) (Hugh McGahan) 3,300
b f f King's Ride - Jims Monkey (Monksfield).......... (Michael Tallon) 2,100
b f f Tidaro (USA) - Parson's Glen (IRE) (Glen Quaich)........... (E Angland) 250

846

Property of Mr Denis John O'Brien

b c f Yashgan - Golden Robe (Yankee Gold) .... (Cash) 850
b c f Yashgan - Cherry Bright (IRE) (Miner's Lamp)................. (Martin Liddy) 850

Property of Rosemary Coghlan

b c f Royal Fountain - Shannon Foam (Le Bavard)............. (Maurice Byrnes) 5,300

Property of Mr J A Slattery

b c f Torus - Miss Brantridge (Riboboy).... (Cash) 2,100

Property of Mrs Jean Wilson, from Boltown House

b or br c f Jurado (USA) - Kiltarquin (Deep Run).. (Rathbarry Bloodstock Services) 3,700

From Brownstone Stud

br f f Phardante (FR) - Gemelek (Menelek) (C B A) 2,000
br f f Good Thyne (USA) - Random Wind (Random Shot)........ (M Harrington) 2,000

Property of Mr Robert Kenny Jnr, from Ballingarry House Stud

b or br c f Lafontaine (USA) - Proven Right (IRE) (Kemal).......... (Noel Finegan) 1,800
ch c f Be My Native (USA) - Kerry Minstrel (Black Minstrel)............ (W Doran) 3,550
b or br c f Lafontaine (USA) - Country Glen (Furry Glen).................. (Cash) 2,700

847

Property of Mr Thomas P Ward

br f f Strong Gale - Laurie Belle (Boreen) .. (Regina McCarthy) 8,400

From Thomastown Stud

b or br f f Little Bighorn - Mamie's Fun (Lord Gayle).......... (Jimmy Coffey) 320
b or br c f Little Bighorn - Black River Lady (River Beauty).......... (Mandy King) 1,750
b c f Little Bighorn - Pepper Cannister (Lord Gayle)............................. (McLoughlin Madden Partnership) 2,800
b c f Little Bighorn - Our Dorcet (Condorcet) .... (J Lenihan) 2,800
b c f Little Bighorn - Goldfoot (Prince Tenderfoot).................... (J Byrne) 2,400
b f f Little Bighorn - Our Decision (Hawaiian Return)...................... (Cash) 2,100

Property of Gerry Mulvey, from Graigue Little Stud

b c f Supreme Leader - Daring Duchess (Brave Invader).......... (C J Sexton) 2,500

Property of Messrs Bernard & Thomas Murphy

b c f Strong Gale - Astral River (Over The River)....................... (Cash) 15,000

From Skehanagh Stud

b f f Lafontaine (USA) - Serena Bay (Furry Glen)............................. (David Minton Bloodstock Services) 250

848

Property of Mr John Salley

b c f Nearly A Nose (USA) - Sartfield Princess (Le Bavard)...... (J W Lalor) 500

Property of Mr Patrick Dunford

b f f Glacial Storm (USA) - Giolla Donn (Giolla Mear)............. (E Angland) 420

Property of Mr Nigel McCord

b c f Mandalus - Deep Cristina (Deep Run) (Cash) 3,500

Property of Mrs Margaret Norton

b or br c f Camden Town - Ballydonnell Rose (Raise You Ten).......... (Cash) 3,000

From Confey Stud (Agent)

ch f f Montelimar (USA) - Pampered Julie (Le Bavard)....... (David Geoghegan) 300

Property of Mr R Bennett

ch c f Tremblant - Cuban Maiden (Fidel) ... (Ian Ferguson) 780

Property of Mr Michael Coburn

br f f King's Ride - Urroca (Rowlandson) ... (James Cregan) 280
b f f Euphemism - Hawaii's Princess (Hawaiian Return).......... (A Griffin) 250
b f f Little Bighorn - Wolle Princess (Wolverlife)................ (W Carey) 200

From Oak Lodge Stables

br c f Strong Gale - Pamela's Princess (Black Minstrel)................ (Cash) 9,000

849

PRIVATE SALES

From Shade Oak Stud

b y f Gunner B - The Vicarsdaughter (The Parson)..................... (N Powel) 250

Property of Bernie Stack, from Coolagown Stud

ch y c Rock Chanteur - Winetto (Condorcet) .... (R Herdman) 190

Property of Mr N Sullivan, from Knockhouse Stud

b or br y c Parliament/roselier (FR) - Aria (Saintly Song)......... (Mrs V O'Leary) 1,400

Property of a Lady, from Four Piers Stables

ch y c Noalto - Mainstown Belle (Peacock) (P Greene) 550

Property of Mr John McGuinness

b y f Sexton Blake - King's Reserve (King's Ride).................... (R Herdman) 250

Property of T G Cooke

b c f Executive Perk - Our Charm (Goldhill) (Cash) 2,200

Property of James Boyd, from Hillburn House

b c f Mandalus - Queen's Tricks (Le Bavard) .... (M Byrnes) 3,000

Property of J G Fletcher, from Glascar Hill Stud

b c f Miner's Lamp - Somelli (Candy Cane) (Cash) 1,000

Property of Mr Jerry Mackey, from Rachel Bennett (Argent)

b y c Commanche Run - Esperia (Jalmood) (James Hales) 1,500

From The Beeches Stud

b y c Commanche Run - Lancastrian Heights (IRE) (Lancastrian)............ (Johnson Bros) 2,250

From Seskin Lodge

b f f Executive Perk - Daring Glen (Furry Glen).................. (Peter Casey) 1,000

From Oldtown House Stud

br c f Clearly Bust - Pai-Collect (Paico)..... (Robert Roe) 1,450

Property of Miss Catherine Breen

b c f Yashgan - Lanalgo (IRE) (Lancastrian) (P Mulhall) 700

Property of Mr Daniel Breen

b c f Tremblant - Conderlea (Scorpio)...... (R Carmichael) 1,000

850

FAIRYHOUSE (Tattersalls)

Thursday, November 11th

From Skryne Stables

Streets b m (7yrs) Furry Glen - Malone (Politico)................ (M O'Connor) 2,600

Property of Mr John J Judge

Tonto's Girl b m (7yrs) Strong Gale - No Battle (Khalkis) Covered by Phardante (FR)........................... (Cash) 1,500

From Strawhall Stables

Doll Acre b m (17yrs) Linacre - Dolau (King's Bench) Covered by Glacial Storm (USA)............. (E McArdle) 500

Property of Mrs J B Ross, from Mount Top Stud

Samajan gr m (13yrs) Tachypous - Donrae (Don) Covered by White Christmas.... (E McArdle) 500

From Liatris Stud (Agent)

Queen Of The Firs ch m (14yrs) Touch Paper - Suburb's Queen (Levanter) Covered by Trigon....... (E McArdle) 500

Property of Mr J O'Neill, from Kellsboro House Stud (Agent)

Miss Lamb ch m (9yrs) Relkino - Young Lamb (Sea Hawk II) Covered by King's Ride.......................... (Cash) 8,600

Property of a Partnership, from Kellsboro House Stud (Agent)

Melarka b m (8yrs) Dara Monarch - Melka (Relko) Covered by King's Ride .... (Mrs E Eadie) 9,000

Property of Anngrove Stud

Mrs Morse (IRE) ch m (3yrs) Sexton Blake - Ballinkillen (Levmoss) Covered by Treasure Hunter.......... (Denis Hackett) 1,050

From Brittas House Stud

b m (5yrs) Sunyboy - Stanegate (Coliseum) Covered by Executive Perk........... (Pat Cooke) 1,000

Knockananna b m (10yrs) Torus - Scottish Vulgan (Vulgan) Covered by Electric ... (Ballywilliam Stud) 1,100

851

Property of Mr J H Ramsden (Dispersal Sale), from Kilteelagh Stud

Sanctify b m (13yrs) Joshua - Preshine (Specific) Covered by Shardari.. (Cash) 1,600

From Grange Stud

Lohunda Lady b m (15yrs) Ballymore - Marble Clip (Raise You Ten) Sovered by Supreme Leader... (Mrs S Mullins) 550

Raby br m (14yrs) Pongee - Sherry (King's Coup) Covered by Glacial Storm (USA) (Cash) 550

Property of a Partnership, from Balief Stud

Welsh Glen b m (6yrs) Furry Glen - Welsh Tan (Welsh Saint) Covered by Yashgan (Mrs S Coghlan) 1,100

Property of Mr Edward Tynan

Giorradana ch m (11yrs) Lord Ha Ha - Glounanarrig (Dike) Covered by Alphabatim (USA).................. (Cash) 400

Property of The Irish National Stud

Inis Ealga b m (15yrs) Sallust - Mear-Aille (Hard Ridden) Covered by Broken Hearted...................... (Cash) 520

Property of Noelle Walsh, from Knockananig Stables

Legal Puzzler br m (8yrs) Strong Gale - Pardalote (King's Company) Covered by Supreme Leader.............. (Cash) 750

From Ballyburn Stud

Nordic Fling b m (7yrs) Viking (USA) - Stampede Affair (CAN) (Victoria Park) Covered by Be My Native (USA) (Cash) 800

Property of Mr Hugh McCann

Maria Blossom b m (9yrs) Mandalus - Crepitus (Suki Desu) Covered by Be My Native(USA)................. (Cash) 600

Emmodee ch m (7yrs) Bowling Pin - Mariners Leap (King's Leap) Covered by Mandalus.................... (Cash) 960

Straight Shot b m (13yrs) Reformed Character - Honours Bless (Straight Deal) Covered by Mandalus............. (Cash) 2,000

852

To Dissolve a Partnership, from Knockaney Stud

Tell A Tale b m (6yrs) Le Bavard (FR) - Four Shares (The Parson) Covered by Tremblant......................... (Cash) 4,000

From Rathbarry Stud (Agent)

Quayside Romance b m (6yrs) Quayside - Pixielated (Mon Capitaine) Covered by Phardante(FR)................ (Cash) 3,400

Katomi b m (7yrs) Monksfield - Greenane Beauty (Arctic Chevalier) Covered by Montelimar(USA)............. (C B A) 5,800

Moorsville (IRE) b m (3yrs) Phardante (FR) - Semiville (Seminole II) Covered by Good Thyne(USA).... (M B O'Connor) 1,000

From Riversfield Stud

Holiday Blues ch m (8yrs) Cure The Blues - Holiday Regrets (Silly Season) Covered by Brush Aside(USA)..... (E McArdle) 640

Awbeg Lady b m (9yrs) The Parson - Ascot's Vulgan (Vulgan) Covered by Phardante(FR)........... (Ian Geddis) 540

Strong Tide b m (8yrs) Strong Gale - Quadro (Dusky Boy) Covered by Good Thyne(USA).............. (Joe Duffy) 780

From Grange Stud

Noon Performance br m (7yrs) Strong Gale - Gala Noon (Gala Performance) Covered by Supreme Leader........ (Cash) 5,000

Marsharon ch m (10yrs) Deep Run - Marsha (Arctic Slave) Covered by Supreme Leader....................... (Cash) 1,200

Property of A Heskin, from Bishopstown Stud

b m (4yrs) Buckskin (FR) - Glencairn Belle (Golden Love) Covered by Cardinal Flower....................... (Cash) 1,000

853

Property of Mr Hugh McCann

Dawn Infidel (IRE) ch m (3yrs) Fidel - Clare Dawn (Prince Hansel) Covered by Be My Native(USA).... (Park House Stud) 2,000

Tuftarney b m (6yrs) Mandalus - Slievenanee (Avocat) Covered by Bowling Pin....................... (Cash) 400

Slievenanee b m (14yrs) Avocat - Cantangle (Cantab) Covered by Bowling Pin...... (Cash) 800

From Skehanagh Stud

Lady Seeker ch m (10yrs) Royal Match - Gay Seeker (Status Seeker) Covered by Executive Perk................ (Cash) 700

Property of A Partnership, from Skehanagh Stud

Cutty Sark br or br m (8yrs) Strong Gale - Speedy Lady (Carlburg) Covered by Be My Native(USA).......... (C McCann) 1,200

From Skehanagh Stud

Sanguine Sketch (IRE) b m (5yrs) Pollerton - Ten Again (Raise You Ten) Covered by Phardante(FR)....................... (David Minton Bloodstock) 6,000

From Brittas House Stud

It Beat All b m (10yrs) Laurence O - Fleeting Sunshine (Giolla Mear) Covered by Glacial Storm(USA)............ (Cash) 1,150

Milworth b m (9yrs) Stetchworth (USA) - Milan United (Milan) Covered by Glacial Storm(USA)......................... (Jimmy Byrne Bloodstock) 2,000

From Abbeville & Meadow Court Studs (Agent)

Clogrecon Lass b m (16yrs) Raise You Ten - Saucy Slave (Arctic Slave) Covered by Torus................. (T Cassidy) 1,800

Property of Mr D P O'Brien, from Derrygrath Stud

Miss Lucille ch m (11yrs) Fine Blade (USA) - Lucille (Master Owen) Covered by Buckskin(Fr).................. (Cash) 5,500

854

Property of Foster & Allen

Nancy Myles ch m (8yrs) The Parson - Break The Bank (Gala Performance) Covered by Montelimar(USA)......... (James Kiernan) 30,000

From Meadowbank Stud

Just Don't Know br m (8yrs) Buckskin (FR) - My Friend Fashion (Laurence O) Covered by Good Thyne(USA).. (M Dixon) 1,600

Property of Mrs F J Maxwell, from Ballee House Stud

Who Says (IRE) b m (4yrs) Amazing Bust - Xandor (Songedor) Covered by Denel(Fr)............... (Sean Carroll) 1,200

Property of Mr Seamus Larkin, from Wood House Stud

Kyle Aris b m (7yrs) Energist - Gusserane Lark (Napoleon Bonaparte) Covered by Carefree Dancer(USA)......... (Cash) 1,000

Property of a Partnership

Katday (FR) br m (6yrs) Miller's Mate - Kanara (FR) (Hauban)................. (Old Meadow Stud) 1,500

Property of Mr P J Prendergast, from Melitta Stud

Scaravie (IRE) b m (4yrs) Drumalis - Arctic Chimes (Arctic Slave) Covered by Montelimar(USA)............. (D Magnier) 10,500

From Ennel Lodge Stud

Madame Vitesse ch m (11yrs) Le Bavard (FR) - Boreen (Babur) Covered by Boreen(Fr).............. (Jim Martin) 1,200

Property of Mr G M Stokes, from Brownstone Stud

Cameo Class b m (6yrs) Roi Guillaume (FR) - Dunderry Class (Dusky Boy) Covered by Be My Native(USA).............. (Brittas House Stud) 1,000

Property of Mr Patrick Sheehan, from Castlematrix Stables

Roisin's Friend ch m (6yrs) Buckskin (FR) - Niamh's Friend (Laurence O) Covered by Good Thyne (USA)... (Henry Lynch) 820

Property of a Gentleman

Lady Jennifer (IRE) b m (3yrs) Supreme Leader - Breda's Choice (Random Shot) Covered by King's Ride... (E McArdle) 500

855

From Broadsmill Stud

Vaghe Stelle (ITY) br m (8yrs) Looking For - Via Del Tabacco (Ballymoss) Covered by Orchestra.................. (Cash) 1,900

Asinara b m (11yrs) Julio Mariner - Sardinia (Romulus) Covered by Jurado(USA) ... (B Ward) 850

From Grange Stud

Slap Bang gr m (10yrs) Pitskelly - Slap Up (Gala Performance) Covered by Glacial Storm(USA).................. (Cash) 1,550

From Carrigdownane Stud (Agent)

Marsha's Daughter b m (14yrs) Merrymount - Marsha (Arctic Slave) Covered by Alphabatim(USA)...... (E McArdle) 550

Property of Mr Michael Comber

Well Why (IRE) b m (4yrs) The Parson - Winnie Owen (Master Owen) Covered by Alphabatim(USA)........... (Cash) 1,100

From Brittas House Stud

Grin And Bear It b m (7yrs) Deep Run - Boherdeel (Boreen) Covered by Glacial Storm(USA).................. (Cash) 720

Miss Cynthia b m (11yrs) Dawn Review - Kamiros (Prince Hansel) Covered by Supreme Leader.............. (Cash) 1,050

From Glidawn Stud

Bit Of A Chance b m (9yrs) Lord Ha Ha - Romany Miss (Master Owen) Covered by Montelimar(USA)........... (Cash) 4,000

Property of Mr Pat O'Rourke, from Newtown Stud

Nohoval Jane ch m (8yrs) Amoristic - Pulleen Maid (Apollonius) Covered by Hollow Hand.................. (Cash) 500

Kingstown Lass ch m (9yrs) Whistling Deer - Kingstown Girl (Bright Will) Covered by Meneval(USA)........ (O Brennan) 500

856

Property of Mr D Murphy

Pure True ch m (6yrs) Deep Run - Ascot Princess (Prince Hansel)....... (Cash) 1,000

Property of Mr Michael Higgins

Annie Panny b m (15yrs) Take A Reef - Honaria (Honeyway) Covered by King's Ride.......................... (Cash) 500

From Rachel Bennett (Agent)

City Girl (IRE) b m (2yrs) Supreme Leader - Maestra Gama (Master Buck) Covered by Be My Native(USA) (Beeches Stud) 5,000

From Ballinvarosig House Stud

Anti Social (IRE) ch m (5yrs) Cardinal Flower - Miss Taurus (Bullrush) Covered by King's Ride...... (E McArdle) 700

Quelliney ch m (14yrs) High Line - Quelle Pas (Kelling) Covered by King's Ride... (Laura Devitt) 900

Texarkana (IRE) b m (5yrs) Furry Glen - Baby Conway (Martinmass) Covered by Homo Sapien....... (Roland Rothwell) 500

From Culleenamore House and Stables

Poll Curraig ch m (9yrs) The Parson - Kandaya (FR) (Venture Vii) Covered by King Luthier.......... (A D C Cathers) 750

From Rathvin Stud

Rathshade br m (7yrs) Bustineto - April Shade (Harwell) Covered by Executive Perk.................. (Brian Ward) 650

Paddy's Team gr m (12yrs) Ballymore - Ashaireez (Abernant) Covered by Buckskin(Fr)...................... (Cash) 540

From Moortown House Stud

Sunbath ch m (6yrs) Krayyan - Sunshot (Candy Cane) Covered by Strong Gale (Cash) 10,000

857

Property of R S Waterworth

Whackers World ch m (10yrs) Whistling Deer - Perceptive (Ballyciptic) Covered by King Persian...... (Sammy Wilson) 1,000

To Dissolve a Partnership, from Treascon Stud

Millfontaine b h (13yrs) Mill Reef (USA) - Mortefontaine (Polic)........... (Cash) 7,600

PRIVATE SALES

Property of Mrs Breda Brady

b c f Mandalus - Colleen Donn (Le Moss).. (T Clements) 2,100

Property of The Exors of the late Mr Maurice E McAuley, from Winter Lodge Stables

Ruby Lodge b m (10yrs) Peacock (FR) - Winter Lodge (Super Slip) Covered by Yashigan..................... (Cash) 8,000

858

DONCASTER
Monday, November 15th
(Foals)

Property of Mr Phillip Gaunt, from Beulah Farm Stud

b or gr f f Sizzling Melody - Trynova (Tyrnavos)................. (Ralph Lloyd) 420

Property of Mr G R Parkin & Sons, from Hogg Bush Stud

b or ch c f Totem (USA) - Ella's Lullaby (Sexton Blake)........... (C L Turner) 600

Property of Mrs F Tyler, from Riversdale Stud

b f f Prince Des Coeurs (USA) - Pink N'perky (Tickled Pink).... (C L Turner) 450

Property of Mr A Rutter, from Etchingham Stud

b f f Daring March - Vickenda (Giacometti) (M Gielty) 580

Property of Minizen Ltd, from Trowel Stud

b or br c f Kind Of Hush (USA) - Prospect Beach (Grey Desire)...... (C L Turner) 550

ch f f Kind Of Hush - Minizen Melody (Hello Gorgeous)................. (M Plumb) 400

Property of Mr P M Steele-Mortimer & Mrs M L Parry

gr c f Safawan - Swallow Bay (Penmarric) (J McKeever Bloodstock) 8,200

Property of Mrs Susan Miles, from Sainsfoins Stables

ch c f Interrex (CAN) - Super Lady (Averof) (J J O'Neill) 2,200

From Stetchworth Park Stud

br f f North Briton - Fly The Coop (Kris).... (C L Turner) 780

b f f North Briton - Rainbow Ring (Rainbow Quest)............ (Burns Farm Stud) 900

859

Property of Mrs E Cunningham

b f f Kind Of Hush - Musical Note (Sharpo) (Ralph Lloyd) 1,200

From Northgate Lodge Stud

b f f Grey Desire - Tango Lady (Gorytus)... (M Gielty) 700

Property of Mr A Charalambous, from Northgate Lodge Stud

ch c f Indian Forest (USA) - My-Elane (Welsh Saint)....... (Mrs D Schreiber) 680

From Northgate Lodge Stud

b or br f f Grey Desire - Kamaress (Kampala).................. (Paul Gardner) 600

Property of North Cheshire Trading & Storage, from Hedgeholme Stud

br or gr c f Sylvan Express - Grand Espoir (Kenmare).. (David Minton Bloodstock) 1,500

Property of T Kilroe & Partners, from Copper Beeches Farm

ch c f Rakaposhi King - Lebrannagh Lass (Ballad Rock)......... (M W Easterby) 650

Property of Mrs G C Stanley, from Firle Stud

b or br f f Daring March - Ballyreef (Ballymore).................. (P Travers) 400

Property of Mr & Mrs D J Deer, from Fawley Stud

br f f Northern State (USA) - Hot Case (Upper Case)............ (David Ford) 1,250

ch f f Northern State (USA) - Loveville (USA) (Assert).............. (C Stone) 400

b f f Northern State (USA) - Haywain (Thatching).................. (Cash) 400

ch f f Faustus (USA) - Dependable (Formidable)................ (Mrs N Stewart) 620

860

Property of a Partnershikp, from Norton Grove Stud

b c f Warrshan (USA) - Sirenivo (USA) (Sir Ivor)............. (Eddie Brennan Ltd) 4,600

Property of Norton Grove Stud Ltd, from Norton Grove Stud

ch f f Crowning Honors (USA) - Hill Of Fare (Brigadier Gerard)....... (E M Gavain) 500

From Srpingfield House Stud

b c f Rich Charlie - Annie Ra (Ra) .... (C L Turner) 650

To Dissolve a Partnership, from Springfield House Stud

b c f Macmillion - Parijoun (Manado)...... (F Watson) 1,550

Property of Mr P Young, from Three Gates Stud

ch c f Rich Charlie - Miss Mischievous (Star Appeal)...................... (Cash) 500

b f f Risk Me (FR) - Lana's Pet (Tina's Pet) (Cash) 1,400

b f f Rich Charlie - Legal Sound (Legal Eagle)............ (Miss P Sylvester) 1,700

From Ticklerton Stud

b c f Lochnager - Sky Mariner (Julio Mariner).................... (W L Barker) 700

b c f Lochnager - Soudley Lady (Glenstal).. (Paul Gardner) 800

Property of a Partnership

b f f Superpower - Gymcrak Lovebird (Taufan)......................... (Cash) 2,300

ch f f Ron's Victory - Baroness Gymcrak (Pharly)...................... (Cash) 4,100

861

From Bearstone Stud (Agent)

b c f Mon Tresor - Highland Daisy (He Loves Me)......... (Mrs B Chambers) 700

Property of Bearstone Stud, from Bearstone Stud

b f f Keen - Practical (Ballymore).......... (Eddie Brennan Ltd) 1,500

b c f Mon Tresor - Arabian Nymph (Sayf El Arab)........ (Peter Doyle Bloodstock) 5,000

Property of Miss P Westbrook, from Upperwood Farm Stud

b c f Thowra (FR) - Royal Bat (Crowned Prince) .... (Cormac McCormack Associates) 1,800

Property of Upperwood Farm Stud, from Upperwood Farm Stud

b f f Picea - Formula (Reform) (C L Turner) 700

Property of Mrs Cheryl L Owen

ch c f Safawan - Energia (Alias Smith)..... (Peter Doyle Bloodstock) 4,000

Property of Mr P Hurst, from Easthorpe Hall Stud

br f f Rock City - Final Shot (Dalsaan)...... (Miss P Sylvester) 5,400

Property of Mr T H Rossiter, from The Elms Stud

b c f Phountzi (USA) - Alipampa (Glenstal) (D J Brown) 1,200

From The Elms Stud

b f f Jupiter Island - Infanta Maria (King Of Spain).................. (Ian Glenton) 800

Property of Mr J Wills, from Skiddaw Stud

b f f Handsome Sailor - Vico Equense (Absalom)............ (Miss T Liddle) 650

b c f Timeless Times - Skiddaw Bird (Bold Owl) (Cormac McCormack Associates) 2,200

ch c f Domynsky - Whimbrel (Dara Monarch)........ (Peter Doyle Bloodstock) 4,000

ch c f Bustino - Martyrdom (USA) (Exceller) (M R J Bloodstock) 3,200

862

From Sturt Farm Stud

br c f Petong - State Romance (Free State) (Springfield Thoroughbred Syndicate) 6,200

b f f Buzzards Bay - Hi-Hannah (Red Sunset)............. (M R J Bloodstock) 1,700

Property of Mr T P Finch

ch f f Timeless Times (USA) - Kiverton Komet (Precocious).................. (David Minton Bloodstock) 2,700

Property of Barraca Bloodstock

b c f Belfort (FR) - Divine Penny (Divine Gift).................... (Mrs Mason) 1,700

b c f Belfort (FR) - Fishpond (Homing) ..... (Cash) 1,250
b f f Belfort (FR) - Hot Tan (Hotfoot) .... (Ralph Lloyd) 850

Property of Mr R Lightfoot

b c f Superpower - Rekindle (Relkino) ..... (Cash) 2,500

Property of Mr L A C Ashby, from Newhall Estate Farm

b c f Emarati (USA) - Gaelic Air (Ballad Rock) .... (Mrs Hughes) 750

From Britton House Stud

ch f f Emarati (USA) - Spring In Rome (USA) (Forli) .... (Ian Glenton) 1,050

Property of A H Warren (Coombe Farm) Ltd, from Downclose Stud

ch f f Then Again - Nonasalome (Absalom) (Cash) 440
b c f Then Again - Simply Jane (Sharpen Up) .... (P Bamford) 1,900

863

Property of Mr P Young, from Three Gates Stud

b c f Rich Charlie - Princess Wendy (Captain James) .... (C L Turner) 700
ch c f Rich Charlie - Ballagarrow Girl (North Stoke) .... (Miss M Bell) 1,300

From Three Gates Stud

b f f Risk Me (FR) - Deep Lady (Deep Diver) .... (Cash) 1,400

From West Penhill Stud

b f f Common Grounds - Pastrana (King Of Spain) ...... (David Minton Bloodstock) 6,600
b f f Common Grounds - Habitually Dancing (Habitat) .... (Britton House Stud) 2,000

Property of Mr D Gill, from Scarcroft Hall

b c f Clantime - Mrs Meyrick (Owen Dudley) ..... (J McKeever Bloodstock) 3,000
ch c f Clantime - Petroc Concert (Tina's Pet) .... (G Revitt) 2,300

Property of Mr J G & Mrs J M Brearley

b c f Skyliner - Stellaris (Star Appeal) ...... (J Bird) 4,200

Property of Mr B A Winn

ch c f Double Schwartz - Tableaux (Welsh Pageant) .... (Cash) 5,600

Property of Mr P Nash, from Croft House Stud

gr c f Belfort (FR) - Peter's Pet Girl (Norwick) ...... (David Minton Bloodstock) 4,200

864

Property of Mr J Coombes & Mr A J Smith, from Croft House Stud

b c f Superlative - Good Time Girl (Good Times) .... (Cash) 2,400

Property of a Partnership, from Wood Farm Stud

ch c f Persian Heights - Tawnais (Artaius) .. (G O'Callaghan) 8,800
ch f f Safawan - Edraianthus (Windjammer) (Peter Doyle Bloodstock) 4,600
ch f f Safawan - Faw (Absalom) .... (Ralph Lloyd) 1,500

Property of The Exors of the late Mr T F M Corrie, from Wood Farm Stud

ch f f Safawan - Wigeon (Divine Gift) ...... (J McKeever Bloodstock) 540

From Benham Stud

br c f Inca Chief - Noble Soul (Sayf El Arab) (J A Holmes & Son) 450
br f f Inca Chief - To The Point (Sharpen Up) .... (M Crump) 1,500
ch c f Presidium - Missish (Mummy's Pet) (K O'Callaghan) 7,800

From Furnace Mill Stud

b c f Puissance - Miss Petella (Dunphy) .... (David Minton Bloodstock) 6,000

From Low Barns Stud

ch c f Music Boy - Cindy's Princess (Electric) .... (H Alexander) 8,200

865

From Ticklerton Stud

b c f Lochnager - Red Squaw (Tribal Chief) (W L Barker) 1,000
b f f Lochnager - Soltago (Touching Wood) (Cash) 1,000

Property of Mr & Mrs R J Wakelam, from Sainsfoins Stables

ch c f Phountzi (USA) - Mrs Feathers (Pyjama Hunt) ..... (Terence Wybrew) 2,200

Property of Messrs P & A G Venner, from Petches Farm

gr c f Petong - Respray (Rusticaro) .... (A Spalding) 5,200
gr f f Petong - Velvet Pigeon (Homing) .... (P Gardner) 2,000

From Elsenham Stud

b c f Rich Charlie - Sound Type (Upper Case) .... (F Watson) 580
b c f Risk Me (FR) - Very Special Lady (Mummy's Game) .... (T Holdcroft) 1,700
ch f f Risk Me (FR) - Tricky Tracey (Formidable) .... (Cash) 1,050
b c f Rich Charlie - Julia Mawe (Dominion) (M Cornthwaite) 550
b f f Rich Charlie - Sports Delight (Star Appeal) .... (Mrs K Heath) 750

866

From Carlton Stud

b f f Distant Relative - Geoffrey's Bird (Master Willie) .... (J Balding) 5,600

From West Penhill Stud

b c f Common Grounds - Proserpina (FR) (Shafaraz) .... (K O'Callaghan) 5,600
b c f Inca Chief - Sports Post Lady (M Double M) .... (Cash) 8,000
b c f Inca Chief - Easy Match (Royal Match) (Cash) 1,000

Property of Mrs V M Tricks, from Litton Castle Stud

ch f f Indian Ridge - Soon To Be (Hot Spark) .... (D Powell) 7,500

Property of Mr D J Watkins, from The Broadleaf Stud

b c f Colmore Row - Consistent Queen (Queens Hussar) .... (Cash) 4,100

From Helshaw Grange Stud

b f f Lapierre - Isobel's Choice (Green God) (J Balding) 650

Property of Highfield Stud Ltd, from Barleythorpe Stud

ch c f Mazilier (USA) - Deep Blue Sea (Gulf Pearl) .... (Peter Doyle Bloodstock) 8,000 b c f Mazilier (USA) - Entourage (Posse) . . . (T & M A Bibby) 1,900

(MARES)

From Rushbrooke Stud

Spring Sparkle ch m (7yrs) Lord Gayle (USA) - Friendly Ann (Artaius) Covered by Robellino. . . . (Elmhurst Bloodstock) 6,600

867

Property of Mrs M O'Donnell, from Brickfields Stud

Princess Roxanne b m (6yrs) Prince Tenderfoot (USA) - Godwyn (Yellow God) Covered by Statoblest . . . . (Peter Doyle Bloodstock) 7,000

Property of Mr & Mrs D J Deer, from Fawley Stud

Foudre b m (18yrs) Petingo - Lighted Lamp (USA) (Sir Gaylord) Covered by Northern State. . . . . (Cash) 720

Haywain b m (10yrs) Thatching - Contention (Connaught) Covered by Northern State. . . . . (B B A) 1,100

From Britton House Stud

Indian Summer ch m (10yrs) Young Generation - Neeran (Wollow) Covered by Forzando. . . . . (Lostford Manor) 2,100

Property of a Partnership, from Beechgrove Stud

Marble Moon ch m (10yrs) Le Moss - Marble Chip (Raise You Ten) Covered by Blow The Whistle. . . . . (S Johnson) 700

Dunphate br m (8yrs) Dunphy - Consensus (Majority Blue) Covered by Blow The Whistle. . . . . (Fin Kruse) 400

Property of Mrs L Elliot

Greatest Of All ch m (5yrs) Ela-Mana-Mou - Red Jade (Red God) Covered by Risk Me (FR). . . . . (J McKeever Bloodstock) 4,000

Sally Saad gr m (5yrs) Green Desert (USA) - Biding (Habat) Covered by Deploy. . . . . (Sagittarius Bloodstock) 9,000

From Benham Stud

Missish b m (7yrs) Mummy's Pet - Miss Kuta Beach (Bold Lad) Covered by Presidium. . . . . . (Peter Doyle Bloodstock) 4,000

Property of Mr T Haimsworth, from Whitwell House Stud

Miss Abbi b m (6yrs) Jalmood (USA) - The Shrew (Relko). . . . . (A Young) 600

868

Property of Mr T P Finch

Kiveton Komet ch m (6yrs) Precocious - Beaufort Star (Great Nephew) Covered by Rambo Dancer (CAN) (Peter Baugh) 3,800

From West Penhill Stud

Saint Navarro ch m (8yrs) Raga Navarro (ITY) - Saint Motunde (Tyrant) Covered by Common Grounds. . . . (J Hamilton) 5,000

Colombelles ch m (5yrs) Jupiter Island - That's Rich (Hot Spark). . . . . (Cash) 1,300

From Lostford Manor Stud

Tyrian Princess br m (9yrs) Comedy Star (USA) - Chasten (Manacle) Covered by Safawan. . . . . (B Winn) 1,800

Property of Mr A J Smith, from Croft House Stud

Good Time Girl b m (9yrs) Good Times (ITY) - Inca Girl (Tribal Chief) Covered by Superlative. . . . . (J Hamilton) 1,500

Property of T Kilroe & Partners, from Copper Beeches Farm

Lebrannagh Lass ch m (5yrs) Balla Rock - Kenton's Girl (Record Token) Covered by Gunner B. . . . . (B B A) 1,150

Property of Kenton Utilities & Developments Ltd, from Low House Stud

Donalee ch m (8yrs) Don - Tralee Falcon (Falcon) Covered by Superpower. . . . . . (Cash) 1,650

Property of Mr & Mrs T K Knox, from Whitworth Stud

Marock Morley b m (17yrs) Most Secret - Nasca (King's Bench) Covered by Sylvan Express. . . . . (R Lightfoot) 500

Brave Squaw br m (7yrs) High Top - Cheyenne (Sovereign Path) Covered by Sylvan Express. . . . . (B B A) 3,000

Property of Mr M J Rozenbroek

Responder ch m (11yrs) Vitiges (FR) - Clean Canasta (Silly Season) Covered by Totem. . . . . (Cash) 1,500

869

To Dissolve a Partnership

Real Stunner ch m (6yrs) Chief Singer - Real Party (Realm) Covered by Barry's Gamble. . . . . (J McGrath) 2,500

Property of Mr B Nordan

Miss Racine b m (12yrs) Dom Racine - Miss Morgan (Native Prince) Covered by Precocious. . . . . (A A Jones) 920

Property of Mr B Minty

New Street (USA) b m (7yrs) Our Native (USA) - Ten Strike (USA) (Tentam) Covered by Ballacashtal (CAN). . . . . (Cash) 800

Property of Mr J Watts

Valiyma b m (10yrs) Top Ville - Valka (Val de Loir) Covered by Mas Media. . . . . (F Mather) 800

Property of Silfield Bloodstock, from Southburgh Manor Stud

Aleda Rose b m (16yrs) Charlottown - Urugano (Buisson Ardent) Covered by Lugana Beach. . . . . (P J Spradbury) 550

Lady Donaro b m (13yrs) Ardoon - Lady Kasbah (Lord Gayle) Covered by Classic Secret. . . . . (Cash) 2,900

Property of Mr D P Martin, from Southburgh Manor Stud

It's A Romp b m (12yrs) Hotfoot - Tudor Romp (Tudor Melody) Covered by Nomination. . . . . (A J Owen) 3,200

From Elsenham Stud

Tricky Tracey b m (11yrs) Formidable (USA) - Detonate (Derring-Do) Covered by Risk Me (FR). . . . . (M Wallis) 1,200

Julia Mawe b m (8yrs) Dominion - Second Generation (Decoy Boy) Covered by Risk Me (FR). . . . . (J Tollboll) 1,300

From The Elms Stud

Infanta Maria b m (9yrs) King Of Spain - Pearling (Ribero). . . (J & C Bloodstock) 1,100

870

Property of a Partnership
Gymcrak Lovebird b m (6yrs) Taufan - Waadi Hatta (USA) (Upper Nile) Covered by Mazilier.......... (T Easterby) 4,200
Property of Freedom Farm Stud, from Freedom Farm Stud
Miss Derby (USA) ch m (15yrs) Master Derby (USA) - Miss Treasure (USA) (Candy Spots) Covered by Weld ...... (B Minty) 800
From Harness Grove Stud
Lucky Monashka b m (6yrs) Lucky Wednesday - Monashka (Sica Boy) Covered by Komaite............. (Mrs J Stewart) 1,050
Property of Mr P Shorrock
Karla's Star b m (8yrs) Kampala - Naval Artiste (Captain's Gig).... (R Lightfoot) 550
From Crisps Farm Stud
May Bond ch m (18yrs) Good Bond - Izetse (Lavandin) Covered by Cree Song ..... (F Cosgrove & Son) 480
Aldington Cherry b m (15yrs) Legal Eagle - Flowering Trees (Ennis) Covered by Cree Song........... (P J Spradbury) 400
Property of Mr N Stewart
Careless Whisper (USA) b m (10yrs) Broadway Forli (USA) - Overdrawn Lady (USA) (Raja Baba) Covered by Nomination................ (P J & G F Burman) 450
Property of Minizen Ltd, from Trowel Stud
Minizen Melody ch m (7yrs) Hello Gorgeous - Hear My Song (Song) Covered by Timeless Times (USA) (B B A) 950
Prospect Beach br m (4yrs) Grey Desire - Minizen Lass (Hittite Glory) Covered by Timeless Times (USA)......... (Cash) 780
From Manor Farm (Huntingfield)
Just Never Know b m (8yrs) Riverman (USA) - Thoughtless Doll (Unconscious) Covered by Nicholas......... (B Minty) 1,300
PRIVATE SALES
Property of Rockhouse Farms Ltd, from Bearstone Stud
ch f f Mon Tresor - Our Mable (Posse) .... (M W Easterby) 700
Property of Miss C A Mather
b c f Precocious - Bonny Bright Eyes (Rarity)...... (Peter Doyle Bloodstock) 2,000
From Glen Andred Stud
Lovescene b m (5yrs) Carwhite - Mrs Waddilove (Bustino) Covered by Mazilier(USA)... (P R & P J Spradbury) 1,000
Property of Mr & Mrs R W Eaves, from Wilderness Farm
Tilly Topaz gr m (7yrs) Kalaglow - Mums (Mummy's Pet)........... (F Mather) 400

871

DONCASTER
Tuesday, November 16th (Yearlings)

Property of Mr William Oakes
gr y g Absalom - Formidable Task (Formidable)................. (Miss N Stokes) 750
From Plainville Stud
ch y g Weldnaas (USA) - Misfire (Gunner B) .... (N Bycroft) 1,500
ch y g Jareer (USA) - Mallee (Malinowski) (Peter Doyle Bloodstock) 2,800
From Wood Hill Farm Stud
b y g Hallgate - Sum Music (Music Boy) ... (B Murray) 720
Property of Mr N P Williams
b y f Wuzo (USA) - Killarney Belle (USA) (Irish Castle)............... (D Smith) 550
Property of Mr G A Farndon, from Springfield Farm Stud
br y f Ring Bidder - Spider Woman (Touching Wood)...................... (Cash) 400
Property of Mr J Carr
b y f Dancing High - Pegeen Mike (Sharpen Up)........................ (H Tulip) 400
Property of Mr B Nordan
ch y f Hard Fought - Miss Racing (Dom Racine)................. (M Camacho) 400
Property of Mr P Williams, from Northgate Lodge Stud
ch y c Indian Forest (USA) - Small Fee (Blue Cashmere).................. (Cash) 400
From Northgate Lodge Stud
ch y f Indian Forest (USA) - Glory Gold (Hittite Glory)................. (Cash) 720

872

Property of A Partnership, from Northgate Lodge Stud
b y f Grey Desire - Telegraph Callgirl (Northern Tempest)........... (Cash) 2,100
Property of Mr John Harding-Rolls, from Mariusmilton Stud
ch y f Ballacashtal (CAN) - Princess Xenia (USA) (Transworld)...... (M B Cocker) 400
Property of Mrs K P M Bradley
ch y f Good Times (ITY) - Lucy Lovat (Record Token)............... (Cash) 400
Property of Bellmoor Stud, from Bellmoor Stud
b y f Hubbly Bubbly (USA) - Far Dominion (In Fijar)...................... (Cash) 1,500
Property of Mrs J E Morton
ch y c Singing Steven - Waiariki (Condorcet) .... (Mrs M Dunning) 550
Property of Mrs Charlrotte Pople, from Hellwood Stud
Dithery b y f Rambling River - Feathery (Le Coq D'Or)................ (S Powell) 760
Property of J & C Bloodstock
b y f Kala Shikari - Cherrywood Blessin (Good Times)................. (Cash) 400
Property of Mr & Mrs B T Chambers
b y c Rymer - City Sound (On Your Mark).. (P Haslam) 4,600
Property of Normanby Grange Stud, from Normanby Grange Stud
b y f Hallgate - Miss Britain (Tudor Melody) (T D Barron) 880
From Harness Grove Stud
ch y c Komaite (USA) - Hutton Barns (Saintly Song)............ (T M Jones) 2,000

873

Property of Mr D Gill, from Scarcroft Hall
b y c Clantime - Panay (Arch Sculptor)..... (Peter Doyle Bloodstock) 4,600

ch y f Crofthall - Petroc Concert (Tina's Pet) .... (Cash) 750

From Three Gates Stud

ch y c Risk Me (FR) - Ballagarrow Girl (North Stoke)........ (B B A) 5,000

ch y f Rich Charlie - Cabra (Red Sunset) ... (Cash) 600

b y c Rich Charlie - Podzola (Royal Prerogative)........ (J Naouri) 2,000

ch y f Rich Charlie - Maria Whittaker (Cure The Blues)........ (Cash) 650

b y f Risk Me (FR) - Tralee Maiden (Persian Bold)........ (Cash) 1,000

From Asher Stud, Co Down, Ireland

b y f Bob Back (USA) - Near Miracle (Be My Guest)........ (A Lund) 1,400

Property of Mr P A Taylor

gr y c Prince Sabo - Cawston's Prejudice (Cawston's Clown)... (Mrs M Reveley) 4,000

From Pinfold Stud & Farms Ltd

b y f Governor General - Eucharis (Tickled Pink).... (Newmarket Horse Services) 5,200

874

From Southburgh Manor Stud

ch y f Jalmood (USA) - Stedham (Jaazeiro) (Cormac McCormack Associates) 1,600

To Dissolve a Partnership

Sandy Hollow ch y f Unfuwain (USA) - Sunshine Coast (Posse)........ (Cash) 3,600

b y f Reprimand - Mother Brown (Candy Cane)........ (G Blum) 2,600

Property of Mr M J Rozenbroek

b y c Unfuwain (USA) - Supper Time (Shantung)........ (T Fairhurst) 14,500

From Twin Acre Nurseries

b y c Dowsing (USA) - Taiga (Northfields) .. (Cash) 1,700

Property of Mr A Charalambous, from Northgate Lodge Stud

ch y c Indian Forest (USA) - My-Elane (Welsh Saint)........ (Cash) 1,000

From Northgate Lodge Stud

ch or gr y c Grey Desire - Indian Star (Indian King)........ (Cash) 1,100

ch or gr y f Grey Desire - Sinclair Lady (Absalom)........ (Cash) 1,100

To Dissolve a Partnership

ch y c Bering - Egalite (FR) (Luthier)....... (G Mazza) 5,000

From Partridge Close Stud

b y f Cyrano de Bergerac - Robin Red Breast (Red Alert) .... (David Minton Bloodstock) 3,000

875

From West Penhill Stud

b y f Never So Bold - Kala Rosa (Kalaglow) (A Lund) 4,800

Property of Mr Roy Mathews

b y g Pennine Walk - Pro Scania (Niniski) .. (A Lund) 2,100

(HORSES-IN-TRAINING)

From Wold House Stables

Tarnside Banker br g (3yrs) Mansingh (USA) - Iridium (Linacre)..... (R Holdsworth) 600

Molly Brazen ch f (3yrs) Risk Me (FR) - Polly Peachum (Singing Standard).... (Cash) 1,000

To Dissolve a Partnership, from Wold House Stables

Legal Train ch c (2yrs) Siberian Express (USA) - Pushkinia (FR) (Pharly) .... (W Edmeades) 4,600

From Wold House Stables

Bojolly b f (2yrs) Absalom - String Of Beads (Ile de Bourbon)......... (A Hermans) 2,000

From Gravel Pit Farm Stables

Montone b c (3yrs) Pennine Walk - Aztec Princess (Indian King)......... (C B A) 1,500

To Settle an Account, from Gravel Pit Farm Stables

Meesons ch f (3yrs) Salt Dome (USA) - Buzzing Around (Prince Bee)......... (R H Darrel) 650

From Gravel Pit Farm Stables

Baliana b f (3yrs) Midyan (USA) - Okosan (USA) (Far Out East)........... (Cash) 800

Inovar b g (3yrs) Midyan (USA) - Princess Cinders (King Of Spain)........ (Cash) 2,100

876

From Upper Longdon Stables

Gaelic Star b c (2yrs) Gallic League - Derring Dee (Derrylin)......... (J Bethell) 2,000

Property of The Exors of the Late Mr B J Swain, from Upper Longdon Stables

Thee & Me b f (2yrs) Risk Me (FR) - Miss Camellia (Sonnen Gold)........ (Cash) 640

Birchwood Star ch f (2yrs) Niniski (USA) - St Isadora (Lyphard)......... (A Meuser) 1,100

From Phoenix Lodge Stables

Tutu Sixtysix b f (2yrs) Petong - Odilese (Mummy's Pet).... (Don Enrico Incisa) 5,800

Property of a Partnership, from Barbury Castle Stables

Waterlord b g (3yrs) Bob Back (USA) - Ringtail (Auction Ring).... (D Nicholls) 5,000

Property of A Partnership, from Barbury Castle Stables

Florac b f (3yrs) Sayf El Arab (USA) - Marton Maid (Silly Season)....... (J Baldinbg) 2,600

Property of Mr John B Sunley, from Barbury Castle Stables

Water Gypsy b f (3yrs) Dowsing (USA) - Fortune Teller (Troy)..... (G Kelleway) 4,100

Property of Mr A L Sanders, from The Sidings Stables

Express Mariecurie ro f (3yrs) Persian Heights - Sweety Grey (Young Emperor).............. (Elevid S.D.F.) 2,700

From Britton House Stud

La Croisic b f (2yrs) Emarati (USA) - Birch Run (Blakeney)............. (D Smith) 750

Property of Mr G S Thompson, from Yew Tree Stables

Foot Tapper b g (2yrs) Hotfoot - Silver Stone (Derrylin)............... (Cash) 1,000

877

Property of The Northern Partnership, 1993, from Hambleton Lodge Stables

Highland Princess b f (3yrs) Northern State (USA) - Gay Princess (Lord Gayle) ..... (Lakeside Equestrian Services) 650

From Whatcombe Stables

Heathfield (USA) b c (3yrs) Procida (USA) - Mlle. Judy (USA) (Silent Screen) ...... (J Byrne) 2,500

Kellysi br g (2yrs) Primo Dominie - Formidable Dancer (Formidable) .... (Cormac McCormack Associates) 5,100

Kennet Boy b c (2yrs) Nomination - Helewise (Dance In Time).. (J Tollboll) 1,400

Lake Parva ch c (2yrs) Thatching - Laugharne (Known Fact)........... (A Lund) 1,000

Property of Mr F Salman, from Whatcombe Stables

Agadir b c (2yrs) Red Sunset - Milk And Honey (So Blessed) (Equine Services) 3,600

Property of Newgate Stud Company, from Whatcombe Stables

Alaskan Princess b f (3yrs) Prince Rupert (FR) - Ivory North (Sir Ivor).. (B Smart) 4,600

From Rathmoy Stables

Mentmore Lad ch c (2yrs) Persian Heights - Approche (FR) (Sharpman).. (J Tollboll) 1,500

Property of A Partnership, from Heath House Stables

Sylvan Serenity ch f (2yrs) Sylvan Express - Miss Kimmy (Tower Walk)..... (Cash) 1,600

Property of Gainsborough Stud Management, from Pegasus Stables

Desert Time b or br c (3yrs) Green Desert (USA) - Supper Time (Shantung) ...... (Peter Doyle Bloodstock) 13,500

878

Property of Mr A J Asquith, from Longsides Stables

Scottish Wedding b f (3yrs) Scottish Reel - Pearl Wedding (Gulf Pearl)... (W Clay) 5,200

From Longsides Stables

Rosie Valentine ch f (2yrs) Superlative - Coral Princess (Imperial Fling)............ (G Kelleway) 2,300

Property of Elite Racing Club, from Longsides Stables

Beckenham Lady ch f (2yrs) Al Hareb (USA) - Angel Divine (Ahonoora).... (J Smail) 600

Property of Elite Racing Club, from Southgate Stables

Salutation b g (2yrs) Salt Dome (USA) - Salvationist (Mill Reef).. (Colin Tinkler) 3,600

From Southgate Stables

Selkirk Dancer (USA) b c (2yrs) Sovereign Dancer (USA) - Weekend Spree (USA) (Clever Trick)................. (Cash) 900

To Dissolve a Partnership, from Southgate Stables

Ginza Lights b c (2yrs) Tate Gallery (USA) - Parkeen Princess (He Loves Me)...... (E Pick) 4,800

Property of Mr R Aird, Moss Side Racing Stables

Never In The Red b g (5yrs) Wattlefield - Swing Gently (Swing Easy) (P Nicholls) 6,200

Property of Blackpool Evening Gazette & Herald, from Moss Side Racing Stables

Fylde Flyer ch c (4yrs) Music Boy - Djimbaran Bay (Le Levanstell)............. (J McKeever Bloodstock) 24,000

Property of Raymond Kilgour Holdings Ltd., from Moss Side Racing Stables

Killy's Filly b f (3yrs) Lochnager - May Kells (Artaius)................ (J N Bradley) 5,400

Property of Monkey Racing Club Ltd., from Moss Side Racing Stables

Monkey's Wedding b g (2yrs) Skyliner - Munequita (Marching On)...... (Cash) 12,000

Monkey Magic b g (2yrs) Fayruz - Charo (Mariacci)................ (J Bethell) 4,400

Monkey Music ch g (2yrs) Music Boy - Low Dalby (Longleat)....... (A Barendgret) 1,800

Forbidden Monkey br f (2yrs) Gabitat - State Romance (Free State).... (Cash) 700

Monkey Wench b f (2yrs) Taufan (USA) - Northern Valkyrie (Glenstal)........... (The Monkey Racing Club 1994) 5,200

879

Property of Fluorocarbon Bloodstock Ltd., from Chippenham Lodge Stud

Ela Billante ch f (3yrs) Ela Mana Mou - Billante (USA) (Graustark)............. (David Minton Bloodstock) 10,000

Westering b f (3yrs) Auction Ring (USA) - Westerlake (Blakeney).......... (Cash) 4,000

Skiptamaloo b f (2yrs) Northern State (USA) - Pronetta (USA) (Mr Prospector)....... (Don Enrico Incisa) 3,500

Property of Misses I & E MacGregor

Pinkerton's Silver gr g (3yrs) Northern State (USA) - Real Silver (Silly Season) ...... (Ulla Freidesberg) 2,700

Property of Messrs Philip Tseng & E Tong, from Sefton Lodge Stables

Sylvania b c (3yrs) Thatching - Silvationist (Mill Reef).............. (G Kelleway) 2,000

From Huntshaw Racing Stables

Lock Keeper b g (7yrs) Riverman (USA) - Jamila (Sir Gaylord)..... (Elevid S.D.F.) 4,000

From Brecongill Stables

Amerigue gr f (3yrs) Absalom - Caroline Lamb (Hotfoot)............... (Cash) 1,450

From Star Cottage Stables

Prince Palaccio ch g (3yrs) Legend Of France (USA) - Thatchville (Thatch) .... (D Burchell) 2,000

Demon Dancer b c (2yrs) Gallic League - Ex-Imager (Exhibitioner)...... (A Lund) 2,100

Property of Lord Matthews, from Star Cottage Stables

Noragan b c (2yrs) Most Welcome - Tribal Pageant (Welsh Pageant) (P E Hargan) 3,000

880

From Star Cottage Stables

Matabungkay b c (2yrs) Good Times (ITY) - Danaka (FR) (Val de Loir)....... (Cash) 1,250

Property of G B Turnbull Ltd, from Star Cottage Stables

Sharone ch f (2yrs) Sharrood (USA) - Ward One (Mr Fluorocarbon)...... (J Naouri) 500

From Star Cottage Stables

ch f (2yrs) Kind Of Hush - Maybehandy (Some Hand)............ (M Batman) 500

Property of Mr W G Pallister, from Spigot Lodge Stables

Able McCleod gr g (3yrs) Bold Owl - Slap Bang (Pitskelly)........ (Mrs K Walton) 2,000

Property of Mrs J J Kirk-Scott, from Spigot lodge Stables

Chantry Beath ch c (2yrs) Dunbeath (USA) - Sallametti (USA) (Giacometti)... (Cash) 6,800

From Phantom House Stables

Badge Of Courage b f (2yrs) Roi Danzig - Spring Sparkle (Lord Gayle) (D Morris) 1,000

From Oak Stables Ltd

Teguila ch f (2yrs) Salse (USA) - Free Touch (Kris)..................... (Bent Olsen) 680

From Freemason Lodge Stables

China's Pearl b f (2yrs) Shirley Heights - Rapide Pied (USA) (Raise A Native).... (D Cooper) 7,400

To Dissolve a Partnership, from Thirty Acre Barn Stables

Bering Island (USA) b c (3yrs) Bering - Ivanjica (USA) (Sir Ivor)... (W Bentley) 6,400

From East Everleigh Stables

Tony's Mist b g (3yrs) Digamist (USA) - Tina's Image (He Loves Me).......... (J N Bradley) 12,000

881

Property of Mrs G Fane, from Manor House Stables

Spice And Sugar ch f (3yrs) Chilibang - Pretty Miss (So Blessed)............. (M Blockham) 5,800

To Dissolve a Partnership, from Manor House Stables

Russia With Love ro f (3yrs) Siberian Express (USA) - Late Matinee (Red Sunset)................... (J Bethell) 2,300

Property of Deepwood Farm Stud, from Warwick House Stables

Bold Melody b f (4yrs) Never So Bold - Broken Melody (Busted)....... (Cash) 1,700

Property of Viscount Scarsdale, from Warwick House Stables

Bend Sable b g (3yrs) Mtoto - Chrism (Baptism)...................... (Cash) 1,300

To Dissolve a Partnership, from Warwick House Stables

High Chair ch f (3yrs) Precocious - Camp Chair (Ela-Mana-Mou)................ (Mrs Elvira Ciacci) 700

From Warwick House Stables

Little Senor b g (2yrs) Al Hareb (USA) - Pam Story (Sallust)...................... (Newmarket Horse Services) 1,100

Property of a Partnership, from Warwick House Stables

Morojak Moore b g (2yrs) Cyrano de Bergerac - Immunity (Brave Shot)..... (P & B Stonehouse) 1,050

From Warwick House Stables

Claret Bumble ch f (2yrs) Abasalom - Mumtaz Mayfly (Tap On Wood)............ (A Hermans) 7,000

To Dissolve a Partnership, from Warwick House Stables

Deer In The Glen b f (2yrs) Hadeer - Concorde Lady (Hotfoot).... (S R Bowring) 1,700

Property of a Partnership, from Warwick House Stables

Woodland Whisper ch f (2yrs) Most Welcome - Bardling (Welsh Pageant)...... (J Clark) 1,000

882

Property of Laurel Leisure Ltd, from Moss Side Racing Stables

Laurel Romeo b c (2yrs) Astronef - Love Me Tight (Tyrant)... (Stefan Uppstrom) 4,000

Property of Mr D Fish, from Moss Side Racing Stables

Floating Trial b f (2yrs) Dowsing (USA) - Miquette (FR) (Fabulous Dancer)...... (Ian Glenton) 3,500

Property of Skyline Racing Ltd, from Moss Side Racing Stables

El Salvador b c (2yrs) Efisio - San Salvador (GER) (Klairon).......... (Bent Olsen) 900

Property of Mr B Kielany, from Moss Side Racing Stables

Nooran b c (2yrs) Risk Me (FR) - Susie Hall (Gold Rod).................... (Cash) 1,900

From Moss Side Racing Stables

Curie Crusader gr c (2yrs) Belfort (FR) - Katysue (King's Leap)................ (J T Doyle Bloodstock) 3,000

Coventry Kid ch g (2yrs) Clantime - Callace (Royal Palace)............ (R Hollings) 600

Property of Express Newspapers Plc, from Moss Side Racing Stables

Daily Star b or ro f (2yrs) Music Boy - Kala Rosa (Kalaglow)........... (J Bethell) 4,200

Starsport ch g (2yrs) Salt Dome (USA) - Ivory Smooth (USA) (Sir Ivor)......... (B Carson) 4,000

From Windsor House Stables

Takhrij (USA) ch c (2yrs) Riverman - Madame Dancer (Northern Dancer).... (Sagittarius Bloodstock) 800

Property of Lady Howard de Walden, from Windsor House Stables

Gilboa b f (2yrs) Shirley Heights - Grimpola (GER) (Windwurf)............. (Cash) 1,000

883

Property of Mr J Watts

Last Lake b f (3yrs) Kings Lake (USA) - Camden Dancer (Camden Town)...... (Mrs Elvira Ciacci) 650

From Ivy House Stables

Lady Gwen b f (2yrs) Taufan (USA) - Special Meeting (Persian Bold)......... (Cash) 1,100

Property of Mr D H Blackwood, from Cree Lodge Stables

Monsieur Bleu ch g (2yrs) Jalmood (USA) - Misowni (Niniski)........... (J Tollboll) 2,200

From Maunby House Stables

Harlosh ch g (3yrs) Marching On - Cottagers Lane (Farm Walk) (J H Pickard) 2,300

Property of Mr D Gill, from The Grange Stables

Arta ch g (2yrs) Clantime - Petroc Concert (Tina's Pet)................. (A Lund) 1,000

From The Grange Stables

Hotcroft ch f (2yrs) Crofthall - Hyde Princess (Touch Paper)...... (Bent Olsen) 500

Property of Lady Kennard, from Carlburg Stables

Elegant Hussar b c (3yrs) Shareef Dancer (USA) - Brigata (Brigadier Gerard)...... (J R Fenlon) 1,400

From Carlburg Stables

Ballon b f (3yrs) Persian Bold - La Vosgienne (Ashmore).. (Michael Dods) 3,000

Property of Messrs W McGregor & M L Page, from Carlburg Stables

Arecibo b c (2yrs) Salse (USA) - North Telstar (Sallust) (Elmhurst Bloodstock) 6,600

Property of Mrs Sigyn Dysell, from Roadrunner Racing Stables, Stockholm, Sweden

Maja Graddnos b f (3yrs) Glint Of Gold - Tzarina (USA) (Gallant Romeo) .... (J Magee) 550

884

Property of a Partnership, from Little Stanneylands Stables

Sir Arthur Hobbs b g (6yrs) Lyphard's Special (USA) - Song Grove (Song)........ (W Bentley) 1,000

Property of Mr F H Lee, from Little Stanneylands Stables

Quessong gr c (3yrs) Petong - Marquessa D'Howfen (Pitcairn)...... (N B Mason) 1,550

Property of Mr F H Lee & Mr P Asquith, from Little Stanneylands Stables

Dayjuz b g (3yrs) Fayruz - Moira My Girl (Henbit)............... (Michael Dods) 1,500

Property of Mr F H Lee, from Little Stanneylands Stables

Freddie Jack b c (3yrs) Midyan (USA) - Sule Skerry (Scottish Rifle).......... (Cash) 1,200

Property of a Partnership, from Elm Stud

Klondike b g (3yrs) Glint Of Gold - Shannon Princess (Connaught)...... (Mrs P Sly) 3,200

Property of Mr A C Edwards, from Red House Stables

Our Stella b f (2yrs) Petong - Lucky Flinders (Free State).................. (Cash) 400

To Dissolve a Partnership, from Flaxton Stables

Robin's Dreamgirl b f (3yrs) Primo Dominie - Blue Brocade (Reform)....... (Cash) 400

Clover Honey ch f (3yrs) King Of Clubs - Rathvindon (Realm)............ (Cash) 1,000

Arkindale Spirit b g (2yrs) Gallic League - Highland Culture (Lomond)... (G Craig) 580

Lastofthebradfields b f (2yrs) Risk Me (FR) - Crimpsall (Vaigly Great)......... (Cash) 400

885

To Dissolve a Partnership, from Spring Cottage Stables

Mystical Mickey br c (2yrs) Anita's Prince - Mooned (Fair Season)...... (J Tollboll) 1,200

Property of Mr T Hawkins, from Spring Cottage Stables

Sharpish Words b g (2yrs) Reprimand - Tabeeba (Diesis)............ (J Tollboll) 620

Property of Mrs H J Ellerby

Nowt Spoiling b g (2yrs) Hard Fought - Sophie's Star (Noalcoholic)..... (Cash) 400

Property of Mr J K Dancer, from Stonebridge Racing Stables (Colton)

Sarah Heights b f (3yrs) Sayyaf - Temple Heights (Shirley Heights)....... (Cash) 500

Property of Miss N A Harrod, from Hanging Hill Farm

Dauntless Fort gr f (2yrs) Belfort (FR) - Dauntless Flight (Golden Mallard) ..... (B W Murray) 500

From Hanging Hill Farm

b g (2yrs) Jolly Jake (NZ) - Streaking Sue (USA) (Private Thoughts) (Sara Davies) 400

Property of Mr W Beasley, from Greenvale Farm Stud

Jump The Ridge b f (2yrs) Vanlandingham (USA) - Jump The Road (CAN) (Darby Creek Road)............. (P McBride) 650

Property of J & C Bloodstock

Harpham Hero b c (2yrs) Tina's Pet - Siconda (Record Token)............ (Ulla Freidesberg) 1,000

PRIVATE SALES

From Pinfold Stud & Farms Ltd

b y f Lugana Beach - Racemosa (Town Crier)..................... (J Balding) 1,000

Property of James Morris, from Barbury Castle Stables

Malzeta b f (3yrs) Alzao (USA) - Place Of Honour (Be My Guest)......... (Cash) 3,500

From Huntshaw Racing Stables

Eliza Wooding b m (5yrs) Faustus - Red Gloves (Red God)........ (J McGrath) 850

From Brecongill Stables

Young Tess b f (3yrs) Teenoso (USA) - Bundu (FR) (Habitat).... (Mrs A Knight) 3,800

Property of Miss S Miller, from Highfield Stables

Clar Dubh ch f (3yrs) Double Schwartz - Tableaux (FR) (Welsh Pageant) (Cash) 500

886

DONCASTER

Wednesday, November 17th (Yearlings)

Property of Mr M J Barber

b y g Primitive Rising - Changatre (Malinowski)..................... (R Fahey) 900

Property of Mr David Holman, from Crundale House Farm

b y f Broadsword (USA) - Borotown (Treboro)................... (C L Turner) 800

Property of Mr R M Eggo, from Easter Cruicksfield Stud

br y f Super Sunrise - Jennifer Wren (Julio Mariner)................ (C L Turner) 700

From Church Farm Stables

ch y f Executive Man - Fool To Cry (Balidar) (C L Turner) 500

Property of Mrs P R Crawford

b y c Be My Native (USA) - Kakapo (Oats) (E Gillie) 2,000

b y c Arctic Lord - Brave 'n' Easy (Brave Invader).................. (S Powell) 460

From Needwood Stud

b y f Rolfe (USA) - Needwood Fortune (Tycoon II)................ (S Powell) 400

Property of Merton Stud, from Merton Stud
ch y f Buckley - H & K Gambler (Rheingold) (F Murtagh) 660
Property of Mr W M Lidsey, from Hill Farm
b y g Macmillion - Nightwood (Sparkler) . . . (Mr & Mrs J Alford) 2,200
Property of Shade Oak Stud, from Shade Oak Stud
b y f Derrylin - Minim (Rymer) . . . . (Mrs S Ward) 680

887

Property of Mr J Thompson
b y f Rakaposhi King - Dawn Encounter (Rymer). . . . . (R H Darell) 720
b y f Derrylin - Jennie's First (Idiot's Delight). . . . . (E A Brook) 1,000
From Shade Stud
b y f Gunner B - Woodford Lady (Mandalus) . . . . (S Powell) 500
ch y f Derrylin - Sweet Ryme (Rymer) . . . . . (Mr & Mrs J Alford) 500
Property of Normanby Grange Stud, from Normanby Grange Stud
ch y g Lord Bud - Mini Gazette (London Gazette). . . . . (D Alinson) 420
Property of Mr & Mrs B T Chambers
b y c Scottish Reel - Siegerin (Wolver Hollow). . . . . (Bent Olsen) 900
b or ro y c Alias Smith (USA) - Cindy's Princess (Electric). . . . . (C R Saunders) 1,400
From Forke Farm
b y f Arctic Lord - Play It Sam (Mandamus) (S Powell) 400
Property of Mr R Lodge, from Village Farm Stud
b y f Broadsword (USA) - Vignargenta (Absalom). (Cash) 520
Property of Mr V Semple, Co Londonderry, Ireland
ch y f Orchestra - Heather-Can (Cantab) . . . (Cash) 1,500

888

Property of Mr R J Brereton, from Helshaw Grange Stud
gr y f Neltino - True Missile (True Song) . . . (F Murtagh) 700
From Helshaw Grange Stud
b y f Brush Aside (USA) - Our Chrisy (Carlburg). . . . . (Mrs A Goodwyn) 2,300
Property of R F Hayward (Kelton Farms Ltd), from The Elms Stud
b or gr y f Neltino - Broad Ryde (Broadsword). . . . . (Mr & Mrs J Alford) 1,700
Property of Mr & Mrs G H Peter-Hoblyn, from Maizey Manor Farm
b y g Ardross - Leading Line (Leading Man) (Liam Cashman) 14,000
From Dunsany Stud, Co Meath, Ireland
b y f Doubletour (USA) - Calcine (Roan Rocket). . . . . (J Hamilton) 920
From Cobhall Court Stud
b y g Petoski - Tommy's Dream (Le Bavard) . . . . (R K Simmons) 1,200

Property of Normanby Grange Stud, from Normanby Grange Stud
b y f Lord Bud - Sandkit (Saucy Kit) . . . . (M W Easterby) 820
(FOALS)
Property of Mr Richard Bowers, from The Elms Stud
b c f Broadsword (USA) - Saucy Linda (Saucy Kit). . . . . (G Bailey) 1,000
From The Elms Stud
b f f Jupiter Island - Firmiter (Royal Palace) (C L Turner) 720
Property of Mr S Kettlewell
b c f Lord Bud - Gilzie Bank (New Brig) . . . . (T Bill) 400

889

Property of Miss Sara Davies, from Cwm Ban Fawr
b c f Lord Bud - Saint Motunde (Tyrant) . . . (Mrs B T Chambers) 700
Property of Mrs C A Mitchell, from Parkfairn Stud
b c f Derrylin - Lindisfarne Rose (Deep Run) . . . . (A J Geake) 4,400
b f f Teenoso - Dublin Ferry (Celtic Cone) . . (David Minton Bloodstock) 2,000
Property of Peter Scudamore Bloodstock
ch f f Gunner B - Corbitt Coins (Deep Run) (Cash) 420
Property of Conduit Farm Partnership, from Conduit Farm
ch c f Gildoran - Metaxa (Khalkis) . . . . (M Skinner) 3,000
Property of Mr S J N Sweeting and Conduit Farm Partnership, from Conduit Farm
gr c f Neltino - Valiant Vision (Brave Invader) . . . . (A J Geake) 1,800
Property of Conduit Farm Partnership, from Conduit Farm
ch c f Gildoran - Nosey's Daughter (Song) (Merton Stud) 2,300
Property of Mr Michael Cosgrove, from Hedrick Rigg Stud
b c f Rakaposhi King - Own Free Will (Nicholas Bill). . . . . (Conjem Ltd) 2,800
Property of Mr E Stuart Knape, from Park Farm Stud
b c f Rakaposhi King - Raise The Dawn (Rymer). . . . . (Glazeley Manor Stud) 1,300
b f f Rolfe (USA) - Once Bitten (Brave Invader). . . . . (M Waring) 640
b f f Gildoran - Flo Jo (DEN) (Pelton Lad) . . (C Stone) 500
b c f Bustino - Sharp Vixen (Laurence O) . . (M G Sheppard) 2,800

890

Property of Mr E H Vestey
b f f Broadsword (USA) - Foxtrot Pie (Shernazar). . . . . (W A Nave) 700
Property of Court Farms, from Court Farms
b c f Cruise Missile - Shoa (Menelek). . . . . . (Cash) 1,500
b c f Cruise Missile - Dragon Lass (Cheval) (Mrs Milward) 1,750

From Cobhall Court Stud
gr c f Arzanni - Realm Wood (Precipice Wood)..... (David Minton Bloodstock) 2,500
Property of Mrs D Sinclair, from Cobhall Court Stud
b c f Buckley - Native Star (Go Native)..... (D Francis) 1,250
From Cobhall Court Stud
b f f Arzanni - Another Molly (Choral Society)................(M Waring) 1,300
b c f Buckley - Celtic Silk (Celtic Cone) .... (Cash) 1,750
Property of Mr P Byrne, from Park House Stud Co Carlow, Ireland
b f f Mandalus - Spartan Park (Scorpio) .... (Alec Dawson) 500
br f f Mandalus - Only Flower (War Path) .. (Mrs S Welsh) 2,300
b c f Mandalus - Phantom Thistle (Deep Run)................ (Beeches Stud) 940

891

From Forke Farm
b f f Arctic Lord - Royal Snip (Royal Highway)..................... (K Forster) 420
br f f Good Thyne (USA) - Play It Sam (Mandamus).......... (G B Edmonson) 620
b f f Arctic Lord - Burlington Belle (Galivanter)................ (Mrs P Nicholson) 750
Property of Mrs K A Proudman
ch c f Teamster - Cobusino (Bustino)...... (David Minton Bloodstock) 680
Property of Mr & Mrs C Wilson, from Pitts Farm Stud
br c f Lepanto (GER) - Golden Card (FR) (Nice Havrais)................. (Cash) 3,700
b c f Pablond - Cilerna Jet (Lear Jet) ...... (G Baker) 1,500
b f f Lepanto (GER) - Diaphantine (Corvaro) (Cash) 1,200
Property of Chesters Stud, from Chesters Stud
b c f Ovac (ITY) - Sponsorship (Sparkler)... (J L Gledson) 950
b c f Lighter - Saleander (Leander) .... (J L Gledson) 950
Property of Major R P Thorman, M.C., from Vilmoray Lodge Stud
b c f Vital Season - Kate The Shrew (Comedy Star)............. (P J Diamond) 1,200

892

From Trickledown Stud
ch c f Vital Season - Armagnac Messenger (Pony Express)............. (G Bailey) 1,900
Property of Lady Sutton
b c f Vital Season - Welsh Flower (Welsh Saint).................. (C D J Lock) 400
Property of Mr P Byrne, from Park House Stud, Co Carlow, Ireland
b f f Mandalus - Miss Ranova (Giacometti) (Cressward Partnership) 2,000
br c f Mandalus - The Foalicule (Imperial Fling)...... (David Minton Bloodstock) 3,300
b f f Mandalus - Double Talk (Dublin Taxi).. (P Berry) 920

Property of Mr R J Brereton, from Helshaw Grange Stables
b f f Neltino - True Missile (True Song) .... (R D M Sharp) 1,000
Property of Mr D James, from Helshaw Grange Stud
ch c f Remainder Man - Hot Flush (Crimson Beau)................... (J S Haldane) 650
From Helshaw Grange Stud
ch f f Le Moss - Running For Gold (Rymer) (S Wilson) 920
br c f Henbit (USA) - Minor Furlong (Native Bazaar)................... (M Avison) 2,000
Property of Mrs David Jenks, from Hartshill Stud
ch c f Derrylin - Goldaw (Gala Performance) .... (Redenham Park Stud) 800
br c f Derrylin - Levantine Rose (Levanter) (C R Saunders) 600

893

Property of Mr & Mrs D Jenks & Shade Oak Stud, from Shade Oak Stud
b f f Rakaposhi King - Rim Of Pearl (Rymer) (S Wilson) 950
Property of Ulceby Farms Ltd, from Ulceby Vale Stud Ltd
b c f Lord Bud - Halmsgiving (Free State).. (Cash) 1,500
Property of T Kilroe & Partners, from Copper Beeches Farm
ch f f Henbit (USA) - Queen's Darling (Le Moss)................ (J S Haldane) 400
Property of Mr John Bradley, from Stratton Audley Hall Stables
b f f Gildoran - Miss Quick (Longleat)...... (C B A) 400
Property of Mr David Holman, from Crundale House Farm
b c f Arctic Lord - Borotown (Treboro)..... (Linda Bruce) 520
From Cobhall Court Stud
gr c f Buckley - Another Spring (Town Crier) .... (M Avison) 2,200
ch c f Arzanni - Cherry Opal (St Denys).... (Cash) 880
gr c f Arzanni - Chancebeg (Random Shot) (David Minton Bloodstock) 3,500
Property of Mr Roy Edwards, from Blakeley Stud
gr f f Weld - Summer Path (Warpath)...... (I Lynch) 1,400
ch c f Opening Run (USA) - Golfe (Idiot's Delight)...................... (Cash) 900

894

Property of Shade Oak Stud, from Shade Oak Stud
b f f Derrylin - Emerin (King Emperor) ..... (Cash) 840
From Ruletownhead Stud
ch or ro g f Colway Radial - Millstone Star (Lord Nelson)........... (D McGarva) 920
Property of Mr J W McNeill
b f f Bedford (USA) - Aserbaidschan (GER) (Dschingis Khan)......... (D Leggate) 660

Property of Normanby Grange Stud, from Normanby Grange Stud
ch f f Broadsword (USA) - Celtic Burn (Celtic Cone).............. (S Welsh) 1,200
Property of Mrs J C Phillips, from Trehir Uchaf Farm Stud
b c f Bold Fox - Boncath (Welham) (T Bill) 550
Property of Mr T Eryl Phillips, from Trehir Uchaf Farm Stud
b c f Bold Fox - Tory Blues (Final Straw)... (R Saunders) 1,000
gr c f Bold Fox - Annie Bee (Rusticaro).... (Mrs G List) 1,000
Property of Mrs G Guest
ch c f Backchat (USA) - Saila Thims (Alias Smith)...................... (Cash) 1,250
Property of Miss Susan Harrison, from Bradley Grange Stud
ch f f Rakaposhi King - Blakesware Gift (Dominion)................... (Cash) 600
To Dissolve a Partnership, from Hartsoil Farm
b f f Rakaposhi King - Kilglass (Fidel) ...... (R Nixon) 500

895

Property of Mrs A J Dow
ch c f Hatim (USA) - Colly Cone (Celtic Cone).................. (D J Boulton) 480
From Vowchurch Court Stud
b f f Cruise Missile - New Cherry (New Brig)...................... (J Peckitt) 1,150
(MARES)
Property of Design & Planning Consultants Ltd
Caithness Dawn ch m (7yrs) Deep Run - Regal Dawn (Golden Love) Covered by Henbit........................ (Cash) 2,500
Property of Peter Scudamore Bloodstock
Corbitt Coins ch m (12yrs) Deep Run - Kassina (Laurence O) Covered by Henbit........................ (S Powell) 1,000
Property of Mr J Thompson, from Shade Oak Stud
Rare Vermillion b m (3yrs) Rakaposhi King - Red Rambler (Rymer) Covered by Derrylin...................... (J Magee) 620
Property of Mrs Janet Greenway
Lady Lawyer br m (15yrs) Mandamus - Highly Paid (Compensation) Covered by Roscoe Blake............ (D Leggate) 800
Property of Mr E H Vestey
Foxtrot Pie ch m (5yrs) Shernazar - Round Dance (Auction Ring) Covered by Roscoe Blake..... (Mr & Mrs B Toye) 1,200
From The Elms Stud
Firmiter br m (11yrs) Royal Palace - Vikrom (Menelek)......... (Mrs L Sutherland) 1,100
From Woodland Stables
Surf Boat ch m (4yrs) Master Willie - Wave Dancer (Dance In Time) Covered by Lord Bud............... (R Lightfoot) 520
Property of Mr V Semple, Co Londonderry, Ireland
Heather Run ch m (5yrs) Deep Run - Heather-Can (Cantab) Covered by Florida Sun...................... (Cash) 780

896

Property of Mr P A Leonard, from Cobhall Stud
Miss Lawn (FR) ch m (5yrs) Lashkari - Miss Jonquiere (FR) (Dictus) Covered by Arzanni....................... (Cash) 1,150
Property of Mr Michael Cosgrove, from Hedrick Rigg Stud
Macusla b m (11yrs) Lighter - Purcella (Straight Lad) Covered by Minster Son (Jane Micklethwaite) 3,500
From Forke Farm
Windmill Sails b m (8yrs) Pollerton - Rosecon (Typhoon) Covered by Sunley Builds.................. (C J Boland) 680
Property of Mrs J M Antill, from Woodcote Stud
Majestic Melody ch m (5yrs) Crooner - Royal Birthday (St Paddy) Covered by Derrylin.................. (S Powell) 2,500
From Ruletownhead Farm Stud
Cool Kit ch m (17yrs) Saucy Kit - Cool Mrs (Arctic Slave) Covered by Dancing High .... (R Lightfoot) 800
Property of Mr J G O'Neill, from Stratton Audley Hall Stables
Dane-Jor's b m (15yrs) Take A Reef - Red Rose (Saint Denys) Covered by Broadsword.................. (J McGrath) 1,600
Over The Mill b f (8yrs) Milford - Achiever (Tarqogan) Covered by Gildoran....... (E G Ormond) 1,450
Property of Mr K Bruce, from Calaburn Farm
Florin Burn ch m (8yrs) Celtic Cone - Snow Time (Deep Run) Covered by Broadsword...................... (E Gillie) 1,200
Property of The Barton Stallion Partnership
Somerford Glory b m (15yrs) Hittite Glory - Peregrine Peach (Falcon) Covered by Nicholas Bill............. (P J Garner) 400
Kamakaze Girl b m (7yrs) Kampala - Glencara (Sallust) Covered by Nicholas Bill (R O'Sheen Bloodstock) 3,000

897

Property of Mr David Holman, from Crundale House Farm
Borotown b m (9yrs) Treboro - Flaretown (Town Crier) Covered by Sunley Builds (N Kidd) 900
Property of Mr T Tredwell & Son, from Sandpit Farm Stables
Baytino gr m (10yrs) Neltino - Fleet Fen (St Paddy) Covered by Ra Nova .... (D Leggate) 680
Property of Roper Bloodstock
Wald Konigin ch m (7yrs) Kinglet - Nightwood (Sparkler) Covered by Troy Fair.. (Mrs J Taylor) 650
Property of Mr W N Mawle, from Manor Farm Stables
Sunylyn b m (13yrs) Sunyboy - Elmolyn (St Elmo) Covered by Crested Lark .... (C Wilson) 2,700
PRIVATE SALES
Property of Mr & Mrs O Fox-Pitt, from Knowlton Stud
b y g Dragonara (FR) - Sombreuil (Bold Lad) (Cash) 3,750

Property of Mr Michael Cosgrove, from Hedrick Rigg Studd
b c f Primitive Rising (USA) - Tiqueteen (Teenoso)................ (T R Hewitt) 1,950
Property of Mr & Mrs C Wilson, from Pitts Farm Stud
b c f Pablond - Speckyfoureyes (Blue Cashmere)..................... (D Coles) 2,000
ch f f Lepanto (GER) - Glorious Jane (Hittite Glory)................... (W Wilding) 700
From Helshaw Grange Stud
ch f f Henbit (USA) - Mervins (Foggy Bell) (Mrs C A Mitchell) 700
Property of Mrs J A Broad, from Emral Stud
b c f Ardross - Leading Line (Leading Man) (G Peter-Hoblyn) 6,800
Property of Shade Oak Stud, from Shade Oak Stud
b c f Henbit (USA) - Edwina's Dawn (Space King)............... (N H Bloodstock) 3,500

898

DONCASTER

Thursday, November 18th

Property of Mr D Bentley
Almonty b c (3yrs) Mazaad - Nordic Maid (Vent Du Nord)............... (W Webb) 1,000
Property of Mrs D Ventress
Vanda's Creation b m (8yrs) Creative Plan (USA) - Vanda (Floresence)...... (Cash) 400
Property of a Partnership, from Brown Moor Stables
Battuta ch m (4yrs) Ballacashtal (CAN) - Valpolicella (Lorenzaccio)... (D Walker) 1,050
From Lea Farm Stud
b g (3yrs) Troy Fair - Mountainette (Peter Wrekin)............... (K J Lamacroft) 750
Property of Mrs D M Douglas-Pennant, from Quillet Stud
b g (2yrs) Town And Country - Eastern Air (Levanter).............. (D R Tucker) 500
Property of Mr J G O'Neill, from Stratton Audley Hall Stables
b f (2yrs) Lightning Dealer - Lillytip (Tepukei)...................... (Cash) 620
Property of Mrs Carol Reed
b g (2yrs) Respect - Imperial Rain (Imperial Fling)......................... (Cash) 700
Property of Mr H T Pickering
Aitchtee-P gr g (5yrs) Belfort (FR) - Lucky Donation (Lucky Brief).......... (Cash) 2,600
b f (3yrs) Noblissimo (FR) - Lucky Donation (Lucky Brief)............... (W Webb) 750
Property of Mr E Harvey, from Hill-Side Stables
b f (3yrs) Fairy King (USA) - Vieux Carre (Pas de Seul)............. (J McGrath) 1,300

899

Property of Miss C M Parker
b f (4yrs) Celtic Cone - Clear Trade (Menelek)........................ (J Gillam) 1,250
Property of Mr D Montgomerie
Zenouska b f (4yrs) Silver Season - River Bark (Rapid River)........ (M Arundel) 1,300

Property of Mr H C Martin, from Viander Stud, Co Antrim, Ireland
b f (4yrs) Valiyar - Orange Silk (Moulton)... (D R Tucker) 660
From Ballywooden House, Co Down, Ireland
Belle de Seul br m (6yrs) Pas de Seul - Burford Belle (Roman Warrior)........ (R Page) 1,500
From Harness Grove Stud
br g (4yrs) Lucky Wednesday - Relikon (Relkino)............ (Ruth Wollerton) 1,000
Property of Mr John Wynne Morris, from Aberconwy Stud
Sianiski b f (4yrs) Niniski (USA) - Pagan Queen (Vaguely Noble)......... (Cash) 850
Property of Mr J Purcell, from Barsbridge Stables
Broad Appeal ch m (5yrs) Star Appeal - Cinderwench (Crooner)... (R C Spicer) 600
Property of Mr Brian Greenley
Charlottes Billo b g (3yrs) Aragon - Daring Display (Daring March).... (D R Tucker) 560
Property of Mr A Salcamando, from Tupgill Park Stables
Carousel Magic ch g (3yrs) Dunbeath (USA) - Tap The Honey (Tap On Wood)...... (Lisa McAlpine) 2,000
Property of The Challengers, from Spigot Lodge Stables
Challenger Row b g (3yrs) Colmore Row - Tunguska (Busted)............ (Cash) 2,700

900

From Creevy Lodge Stud, Co Down, Ireland
gr f (3yrs) Peacock (FR) - Slippery Bell (No Argument).................. (M Pain) 1,550
Property of a Partnership
b g (3yrs) Colmore Row - Bambag (Goldhill) (Cash) 780
Property of The Exors of the late Mrs D B Gillam, from Tarbrook Stud
b f (3yrs) Mandalus - Monaleigh (Sir Herbert)....................... (P Berry) 7,200
Kingscombe b g (2yrs) Arctic Lord - Queenscombe (Kinglet)........ (Cash) 1,600
Property of R F Hayward (Kelton Farms Ltd), from The Elms Stud
b f (2yrs) Neltino - Celtic Well (Celtic Cone) (P T Dalton) 4,200
From Sandybrow Stables
Mummy's Rocket ch f (4yrs) Mummy's Game - Rockery (FR) (Roan Rocket)... (Mrs L Copley) 600
Lady Broker b f (3yrs) Petorius - Phoenix Rose (Frankincense)................ (Esprit de Corp Racing) 3,000
Property of a Partnership, from Shadowfax Stables
Sean's Scholar (USA) b m (6yrs) Kris S (USA) - Nallee's Scholar (USA) (Nalee's Man)......................... (Cash) 4,100
From Woodland Stables
Operation Wolf ch g (7yrs) Adonijah - Sesta (Artaius)................ (A Bowling) 1,000
Property of Miss M Carson, from Holdforth Stables
Paulinus b g (5yrs) Nomination - New Ribbons (Ribero).......... (Peter Storey) 2,200

901

To Dissolve a Partnership, from Holdforth Stables

Desert Mist gr f (4yrs) Sharrood (USA) - Misty Halo (High Top).. (T H Caldwell) 6,200

Property of Albury Racing Ltd, from Holdforth Stables

Khalloof b g (4yrs) Ballad Rock - Tapiola (Tap On Wood)............... (Cash) 2,000

To Dissolve a Partnership, from Holdforth Stables

Auckland Castle b g (2yrs) Chilibang - Palace Tor (Dominion).... (Mrs S Collins) 4,100

Property of Mr David Cahal, from Eastwell Hall Stables

Merryhill Gold b g (2yrs) Glint Of Gold - Phlox (Floriana)..................... (David Minton Bloodstock) 2,000

To Dissolve a Partnership, from Ingmanthorpe Stables

Lord Vivienne b g (4yrs) Don't Forget Me - Lady Vivienne (Golden Fleece)........ (Mrs H Siddall) 870

From Bleak House Stables

Al-Torfanan b g (9yrs) Taufan (USA) - Powder Box (Faberge II)....... (Cash) 900

Cromers Express ch g (4yrs) Mansingh (USA) - Sallusteno (Sallust) (D Mayes) 900

To Dissolve a Partnership, from Edges Farm Stables

Shannon Express gr g (6yrs) Magic Mirror - Tatisha (Habitat)............... (Cash) 520

Property of Mr E Briggs

City Lighter bl f (3yrs) Lighter - Another City (Scallywag).............. (J Gledson) 1,000

To Dissolve a Partnership

Yaslou ch g (6yrs) Yashgan - Lough Graney (Sallust)..................... (Cash) 750

Miss Kingfisher (USA) b f (4yrs) Temperence Hill (USA) - Glory Street (USA) (The Pruner)............ (W Edwards) 650

902

Property of Highfield Stud Ltd

Dawn Success br h (7yrs) Caerleon (USA) - Dawn Echo (Don)............. (Cash) 1,150

Property of Mrs D E Walker

Melford b m (5yrs) Petoski - Coral Fury (Mill Reef)................ (Lisa McAlpine) 4,400

Property of Mr J Carr, from Killeaney Stables, Co Kildare, Ireland

Orient Melody b g (11yrs) Pitpan - Orient Goddess (Even Money)..... (R Parkin) 900

From Killeaney Stables, Co Kildare, Ireland

Son Of Tempo b g (4yrs) Sandhurst Prince - Top Love (USA) (Topsider)..... (Cash) 1,000

Property of a Partnership (Co Kildare, Ireland)

Rare Order b g (9yrs) Rarity - Caramore Lady (Deep Run) .... (David Minton Bloodstock) 4,700

From Merrycourt Stud, Co Meath, Ireland

Loughlinstown Boy b g (8yrs) Ela-Mana-Mou - Tante Yvonne (Crowned Prince) (J A Riddell) 2,100

Property of Mr Mark Rimell, from Throckmorton Court Stud

Frisco City (CHI) br g (7yrs) Domineau (USA) - Farrerita (CHI) (Crivelli).. (Cash) 6,600

To Dissolve a Partnership

Levy Free ch g (8yrs) Kinglet - Metaxa (Khalkis)...................... (Cash) 1,350

Property of Mr W A Sellers

Drum Sergeant b g (6yrs) Elegant Air - Cala-Vadella (Mummy's Pet)........ (Cash) 1,150

Riseupwilliereilly ch g (7yrs) Deep Run - Sinarga (Even Money)......... (Cash) 1,250

903

Property of Mr J Heyes

Gabish b g (8yrs) Try My Best (USA) - Crannog (Habitat)...... (Mrs R Hewitt) 1,500

Property of Mr G K Gordon

Bill And Coup b m (8yrs) Nicholas Bill - Counter Coup (Busted)........ (Cash) 4,500

From Creevy Lodge Stud, Co Down, Ireland

C'an Botana br g (8yrs) Spin Of A Coin - Cala San Vicente (Gala Performance) .. (G Goodchild) 1,050

Property of "The Yearlings", from Furnace Mill Stud

Ronans Birthday b g (11yrs) Furry Glen - Mountain Sedge (Goldhill)........... (David Minton Bloodstock) 5,000

Property of Mr John Naughton, Co Limerick, Ireland

Darimoon br g (11yrs) Vividari - Moonraker VI (Giolla Mear)......... (F Ransome) 2,000

Property of Mr M Cregan, Co Limerick, Ireland

Deep Tarbow b g (6yrs) Deep Run - Miss Tarbow (Tarqogan)..... (N P Williams) 4,000

From Crohane Stud, Co Tipperary, Ireland

Tipperary Rose gr m (5yrs) Roselier (FR) - Vaguely Vulgan (Vulgan)........ (Cash) 1,800

Property of Mr A R Boyd-Rochfort, from Rhonehurst Stables

Bardesan b g (7yrs) Kambalda - Early Start (Wrekin Rambler)............. (C B A) 4,000

Property of Mr & Mrs V Burgass, from The Papermill Stud

More Laughter b m (7yrs) Oats - Sound Of Laughter (Hasty Word)............... (Ruth Wollerton) 1,500

Property of Design & Planning Consultants Ltd

Portavogie b g (9yrs) Kambalda - Mary's Honour (Honour Brand)...... (I Lynch) 5,000

904

Property of Triple Diamond Racing, from Viander Stables, Co Antrim, Ireland

Khazari (USA) ch g (5yrs) Shahrastani (USA) - Kozana (Kris)............. (S Wilson) 2,300

From Phantom House Stables

Clapping b f (2yrs) Elegant Air - Lap Of Honour (Final Straw)....... (D Wilson) 850

From Glebe House Stables

Forward View b g (7yrs) Crash Course - Burl's Sister (Burlington II)........... (Mrs J A Donner) 1,000

Property of Mrs D Batchelor

Soldier Eve ch m (7yrs) Soldier Rose - Jubilee Eve (Royalty)... (S Bowerman) 1,000

Property of Mrs B K Thomson, from Lambden Stables

Raise A Smile br m (7yrs) Sunyboy - Great Aunt Emily (Traditionalist) .... (Ruth Wollerton) 1,700

To Dissolve a Partnership, from Tupgill Park Club

Master Of The House b g (7yrs) Kind Of Hush - Miss Racine (Dom Racine)..... (Cash) 800

Property of Mr N B Mason

Jim-Joe br g (8yrs) Royal Fountain - Sugar Maple (Sweet Story)........... (Cash) 1,500

From Lea Green Stables

Little Wenlock b g (9yrs) Tycoon II - Oujarater (Adropejo)...... (Mrs T M Gibson) 1,700

Miss Enrico b m (7yrs) Don Enrico (USA) - Mill Miss (Typhoon).... (Miss E Noble) 2,500

b f (3yrs) Looking Glass - Miss Criquette Vii ((unregistered))....... (Lisa McAlpine) 850

905

Property of Palacegate Corporation Ltd

Sire Nantais (FR) br g (9yrs) Meisir (FR) - Farala (FR) (Faunus)............ (Cash) 900

From Ridgeway Paddocks

Muskerry Miss b m (5yrs) Bishop Of Orange - Muskerry Mary (Mon Capitaine)......................... (Cash) 3,000

To Dissolve a Partnership, from Park Leys Stables

Elite Design br g (6yrs) Tender King - Lanata (Charlottown).............. (Cash) 750

Property of Mr B Molloy, from Burley Heyes Stables

Sharp Order ch g (8yrs) Sharpo - Cardinal Palace (Royal Palace).. (Miss A Taylor) 900

Property of Mrs J Hicks

Butler's Pet b g (14yrs) Mummy's Pet - Reluctant Maid (Relko).. (S J Walklan) 600

Property of Mr R G Turvey

Rhewel b g (5yrs) Rymer - Skipton Bridge (Harwell)...................... (Cash) 620

From Knitsley Mill Stables

Lady Daring b f (2yrs) Dunbeath (USA) - Lady Barnett (Daring March).... (Cash) 680

Property of Mrs I H Hadden & Mrs P Lusher

Lady Maskin ch m (6yrs) Nearly A Hand - Miss Maskin (Sikander) .... (Miss D Medlicott) 1,500

Property of Mr D J Smith

Dance Of Gold b g (6yrs) Jalmood (USA) - Prima Ballerina (FR) (Nonoalco)......... (C Watchorn) 2,700

Lord Jester b g (4yrs) Jester - Morlolly (Morston).................. (T Glass) 2,000

906

Property of Mr R M Smith

b f (4yrs) State Diplomacy (USA) - Dellassera (Donibristle)...... (S Jones) 750

Property of Mr S A Blyth, from Lake House Stables

Royal Approval ch g (10yrs) Privy Seal - Delilah Dell (The Dell).. (Mrs R Harvey) 9,600

Property of Mrs S Henderson-Watts

Stardom b g (9yrs) - .... (A K Pilgon) 1,100

From Lucy Cross Stables

Tim b g (7yrs) - .... (P Bandilla) 2,500

Property of Mrs P A McLeod

Patrick b g (4yrs) - .... (R Crank) 1,500

Property of Mrs M Gray

Bellissimo gr m (9yrs) - ..... (A Brewster) 1,950

Tacograf b g (10yrs) - .... (G R Taylor) 1,500

PRIVATE SALES

Property of Mr G W Lewis, from Rhydale Farm

b g (3yrs) Doctor Wall - Mary Mile (Athenius)................. (S L Edwards) 2,000

Property of Chantry Farm, from Chantry Farm

b g (3yrs) Giacometti - Mrs Scattercash (Northfields)........... (D J Simpson) 1,200

Property of R F Hayward (Kelton Farms Ltd), from The Elms Stud

b g (2yrs) Neltino - Rydewells Daughter (Celtic Cone)............. (P T Dalton) 9,000

From Woodland Stables

Lady Buchan b f (4yrs) Elegant Air - Regain (Relko).................. (R G Myram) 1,500

Property of Albury Racing Ltd., from Holdforth Stables

Wearside ch g (5yrs) Noalto - Shela (Sheshoon)............. (M McArthur) 1,900

Property of Mr T Suiter

Whiskey Blues b g (8yrs) Cure The Blues (USA) - Ozone (Auction Ring) .... (M J Kennedy) 2,000

907

KILL (Goffs)
Friday, November 19th
(Yearlings)

From Ballylinch Stud

ch y c Bob Back (USA) - Java Jive (Hotfoot) (David Minton Bloodstock) 10,000

Property of Mrs Anne Coughlan, from Ridge Manor Stud

b y c Polish Patriot (USA) - Joshua's Daughter (Joshua).............. (J T Doyle) 25,000

b y c Contract Law (USA) - Jumana (Windjammer).. (John Ferguson Bloodstock) 4,500

From Greg Magee (Agent)

b y c Scenic - June Ann (IRE) (Try My Best) (Michael O'Brien) 3,200

From Kildaragh Stud

b y c Exactly Sharp (USA) - Kabbaala (Brigadier Gerard)................ (M A B) 3,900

Property of Mr William Johnstone, from Jamestown House Stud

ch y c Durgam (USA) - Kaliala (USA) (Pharly) .... (Cash) 5,000

(FOALS)

Property of Mrs Nora Brosnan

b f f Archway (IRE) - Kangaroo (Kampala) ... (Cash) 1,800

From Navan Stables

br f f Distinctly North (USA) - Kashapour (Nishapour).................. (Cash) 9,000

Property of Mrs K Moeran & Mrs H D McCalmont

b c f Petorius - Kayu (Tap On Wood) (Cash) 1,000

From Ashfield Farm

b c f Distinctly North (USA) - Kaysama (FR) (Kenmare).................. (B B A) 18,000

908

From Friarstown House Stud

b or br f f Treasure Kay - Key Partner (Law Society)........... (Alexander Scott) 2,600

Property of Mrs P Grubb, from Big Acre Stud
b c f Distinctly North (USA) - King's Chase (King's Leap)............. (J T Doyle) 10,000
From New Park Stud
b c f Distinctly North (USA) - Kowalski (USA) (Cyrano de Bergerac)........... (Timothy E Hyde) 13,500
From Airlie Stud
ch c f Salt Dome (USA) - Kristar (Kris)..... (T J Cooper) 5,000
Property of Mr T M Ward
b f f Taufan (USA) - Lady Anna Livia (Ahonoora) (David Minton Bloodstock) 6,200
From Ardrums House Stud
b or br c f Contract Law (USA) - Lady Heather (Manado)................... (Miss Joanna Morgan) 2,400
From Dollanstown Stud (Agent)
b or br c f Anita's Prince - Lady Of Man (So Blessed)............. (Seamus Lynch) 4,200
Property of M J McEnery, from Rossanarra Stud
b f f Fayruz - La Mortola (Bold Lad)....... (Richard Black) 3,900
From Sandville Stud (Agent)
b c f Fairy King (USA) - La Petruschka (Ballad Rock).................. (Cash) 15,000
From Knocktoran Stud
b c f Last Tycoon - Lautreamont (Auction Ring)................. (Elsoon Farms) 8,500

909

Property of Miss Audrey F Thompson, from Kilmore Stud
b f f Fayruz - Les Saintes (Kris)........... (Marco Bozzi) 4,200
Property of Mr J F Moore
b f f Law Society (USA) - Libergold (Rheingold)..... (Scuderia Andy Capp) 4,300
Property of Mr Jack Gage
b f f Roaring Riva - Littleton Song (Song).. (Teresa Phelan) 1,400
Property of Mr J B Clarke
b or br c f Digamist (USA) - Lockwood Girl (Prince Tenderfoot)....... (T O'Leary) 8,200
Property of Mr T McDonald, from Jigginstown House Stud
b f f Bluebird (USA) - Lone Bidder (Auction Ring)..... (John Ferguson Bloodstock) 9,000
From Kellistown Stud (Agent)
b f f Nordico (USA) - Lough Graney (Sallust) .... (Equine Associates) 4,200
From Somerton Stud
ch c f Magical Wonder (USA) - Lowtown (Camden Town)..................... (Equine Investment Consultants) 4,000
From Solohead Stables
b c f Shahrastani (USA) - Lucky Realm (Realm)...................... (Cash) 6,000
From Trimblestown Stud
b f f Petorius - Madam Slaney (Prince Tenderfoot) (David Minton Bloodstock) 4,000
Property of Mr Matthew Carr
b c f Law Society (USA) - Madaraya (USA) (Shahrastani).......... (Peter J Doyle) 10,000

910

Property of Mr Mark Bourke
b c f Mac's Imp (USA) - Maid Of Mourne (Fairy King)......................... (John Ferguson Bloodstock) 8,000
From Belmont Stud
b c f Dancing Dissident (USA) - Majesty's Nurse (Indian King)... (Seamus Burns) 8,200
Property of Noel Finegan
b c f Mac's Imp (USA) - Makheeleh (Ahonoora)......... (Ballymorris Stud) 9,000
From Pipers Hill Stud
b f f Prince Rupert (FR) - Marble Run (Run The Gantlet)............ (Mrs A Enright) 2,400
From Green Ireland Properties Ltd.
b or br f f Lyphard (USA) - Maria Roberta (USA) (Roberto)............... (Cash) 78,000
Property of Gemma Doyle, from Barrettstown Farm House
b c f Be My Guest (USA) - Maricica (Ahonoora)............. (Forest Stud) 13,000
From New Park Stud
ch f f Anshan - Marie de Solesmes (FR) (Sassafras)......... (Agences F I P S) 5,200
From Kilnamoragh Stud
b c f Imperial Frontier (USA) - Markon (On Your Mark)........... (Peter J Doyle) 19,000
From Mount Prospect Stud
b f f Roi Danzig (USA) - Melbourne Miss (Chaparral).................... (Cash) 7,500
From Rooske Lodge Stud
b f f Ballad Rock - Merry Twinkle (Martinmas)....................... (Cash) 5,000

911

Property of Springfield House Stud, from Ardenode Stud Ltd.
b c f Pennine Walk - Merville (Fairy King).. (Declan McCormick) 3,000
Property of Mr John H Orpen, from Kealfoun Farm
ch c f Classic Music (USA) - Midnight Patrol (Ashmore)... (Peter Doyle Bloodstock) 15,000
Property of Mr Edward Doyle, from Mount Prospect Stud
b c f Magical Strike (USA) - Milly Whiteway (Great White Way)... (Danny Murphy) 9,000
Property of Mr Owen O'Leary
b c f Nabeel Dancer (USA) - Miss Bagatelle (Mummy's Pet)........... (J T Doyle) 24,000
From Acorn Stud
b c f Waajib - Miss Galwegian (Sandford Lad).................. (Acorn Farm) 3,200
Property of Mr Peter Clarke, from Cookstown Stud
b c f Prince Rupert (FR) - Mistral Wood (USA) (Far North).... (Michael English) 2,000
From Lisieux Stud
b f f Taufan (USA) - More Candy (Ballad Rock).............. (Dermot Brennan) 7,200
Property of Mr Peter McCutcheon
b or br c f Last Tycoon - Moretta (Artaius) (B B A (Ireland)) 25,000
From Moygaddy Stud
b f f Soviet Lad (USA) - Mrs Dell (USA) (Northjet)......... (Matthew Sharkey) 3,500

Property of A Partnership, from Quarry View Farm
b or br c f Cyrano de Bergerac - Mrs Merryman (Bellypha)..........(B B A) 12,000

912

From Airlie Stud
b c f Glow (USA) - Mrs Tittlemouse (Nonoalco)..........................(Cash) 3,200
From Egmont Stud
b c f Archway (IRE) - My Natalie (Rheingold) ....(Cash) 11,500
Property of Bearforest Stud, from Rathbarry Stud
ch c f Soviet Lad (USA) - Nancy Drew (Sexton Blake)... (Team Punchestown) 12,500
From Sandville Stud (Agent)
ch f f Archway (IRE) - Naomi Joy (Sun Prince)................. (Marco Bozzi) 3,300
Property of A Syndicate, from Ardenode Stud Ltd.
b c f Don't Forget Me - Needlewoman (Moorestyle)...................(Cash) 1,800
From Ballylinch Stud (Agent)
b c f Posen (USA) - Nephrite (Godswalk)... (Equine Associates) 6,400
Property of Miss Audrey F Thompson, from Kilmore Stud
b c f Posen (USA) - New Light (Reform) .... (B B A (Ireland)) 26,000
From Mount Pleasant Farm
b f f Danehill (USA) - Nolnocan (Colum)..... (Lynn Lodge Stud) 8,000
From Cregg Stud
b c f Taufan (USA) - Nonnita (Welsh Saint) (Springfield Thoroughbred Syndicate) 16,000
Property of A Partnership, from North Kildare Lodge
b c f Distinctly North (USA) - North Kildare (USA) (Northjet)..... (Ballymorris Stud) 12,500

913

Property of Mr C S Bird, from Asigh Stud Farm
b f f Taufan (USA) - Not Mistaken (USA) (Mill Reef).......................(Cash) 6,500
Property of Mr Michael J Foley, from Springhill Farm
b f f Scenic - Occupation (Homing).......... (Marco Bozzi) 900
From Grangemore Stud
ch c f Polish Patriot (USA) - Often (Ballymore)........................ (Cash) 9,000
Property of M J McEnery, from Rossenarra Stud
b c f Mac's Imp (USA) - Opening Day (Day Is Done).............. (Peter J Doyle) 10,000
From Grangemore Stud
b c f Thatching - Osmunda (Mill Reef)...... (M A B Agency) 20,000
From Curraghroche Stud
b c f Nordico (USA) - Ounavarra (Homeric) (Meadow Farm Stud) 6,000
From Abbeville & Meadow Court Studs (Agent)
b f f Scenic - Overspent (Busted) .... (Conti Bloodstock Service) 4,000

From Ballyhane Stud (Agent)
ch f f Mac's Imp (USA) - Pasadena Lady (Captain James).... (Jose Hormaeche) 25,000
Property of R J Cotter, from Brook House Stud
b c f Scenic - Petrolea Girl (Connaught)..... (Stockwell Ltd) 14,000
From Airlie Stud
b f f Ballad Rock - Play The Queen (IRE) (King Of Clubs)...............(B B A) 5,000

914

From Green Ireland Properties Ltd.
b c f Classic Music (USA) - Pourboire (Star Appeal).............. (Peter J Doyle) 5,000
From Knocktoran Stud
ch c f Exactly Sharp (USA) - Princely Penny (Prominer)...................(Cash) 1,300
From Ballygodoon Stud
b c f Cyrano de Bergerac - Princess Biddy (Sun Prince)..................(Cash) 5,600
From Ballintyre Stud
b c f Double Schwartz - Princess Fleet (Prince Tenderfoot)............(Cash) 3,800
Property of Mrs K Cullen
b c f Distinctly North (USA) - Princess Raisa (Indian King).............. (T E Hyde) 22,000
Property of Messrs Peter O'Connor & Peter Deane
b f f Scenic - Princesse Smile (Balidar)..... (Denis Brosnan) 5,000
From Grangemore Stud
b c f Royal Academy (USA) - Pudibunda (Bold Lad)............. (Bobby Barry) 38,000
Property of Mr T M Ward
ch f f Mac's Imp (USA) - Quai Des Brumes (USA) (Little Current)..... (W Hamilton) 3,600
From Knocknagat Stud
b c f Classic Music (USA) - Queen Of Wolves (Wolver Hollow)............... (Equine Investment Consultants) 7,500
Property of Gemma Doyle, From Barrettstown Farm House
b c f Posen (USA) - Queen's Share (Main Reef).......... (J T Doyle Bloodstock) 10,500

915

From Dooneen Stud
b c f Soviet Lad (USA) - Que Tranquila (Dominion)......................... (Equine Investment Consultants) 7,200
From French Furze House Stud
b c f Magical Strike (USA) - Rachel Pringle (IRE) (Doulab)... (Miss Joanna Morgan) 2,000
From Ballylinch Stud (Agent)
ch f f Nabeel Dancer (USA) - Raging Storm (Horage)............. (Seamus Burns) 5,800
Property of Regent Bloodstock, from Loughbrown Stud
gr c f Be My Guest (USA) - Rarely Irish (USA) (Irish Tower)........... (Cash) 11,000
From Airlie Stud
b f f Niniski (USA) - Reine Du Chene (IRE) (Dara Monarch)................ (Cash) 3,400
Property of Mr Patrick Heffernan
ch c f Magical Wonder (USA) - Reliable Rosie (Relko)..... (Equine Associates) 6,000

From Oaklawn Stud
b c f Great Commotion (USA) - Rhein Hoeny (Rheingold)......... (T E Hyde) 11,500
Property of J G Patterson, from Rihmond Lodge Stud
br c f Scenic - Richmond Lillie (Fairbairn)... (Cash) 6,800
Property of Mrs B Mooney, from Hazel Drive Farm
b c f Law Society (USA) - Rising Lady (Alzao)..... (Conti Bloodstock Service) 7,800
Property of Mr Arthur S Phelan, from New Park Stud
b c f Jareer (USA) - Riveress (Dunphy)..... (Cash) 3,600

916

From Pier House Stud
b c f Don't Forget Me - River Serenade (USA) (Riverman).............. (Cash) 8,400
From Ballymorrough Stud
ch c f Bluebird (USA) - Rockeater (Roan Rocket).................. (J T Doyle) 8,500
From Swordlestown Stud
ch f f Great Commotion (USA) - Rocket Alert (Red Alert)..... (Agence F I P S) 6,600
From Ballylinch Stud (Agent)
b f f Petorius - Romfaea (USA) (Alleged)... (Ian Bryant) 3,500
From Tullamaine Castle Stud (Agent)
b f f Classic Music (USA) - Rose Garland (USA) (Seattle Slew).... (F I N A C O) 16,000
From Coolagown Stud
gr or b c f Archway (IRE) - Rosserk (Roan Rocket).................. (M English) 4,200
From Rooske Lodge Stud
b f f Prince Rupert (FR) - Route Royale (Roi Soleil)........................ (Cash) 1,400
From Ballylinch Stud (Agent)
ch c f Keen - Royal Custom (His Majesty).. (R J McCormack) 18,000
Property of Mr Thomas Corbett, from St Clerans
ch c f Classic Music (USA) - Royal Daughter (High Top) .... (Equine Investment Consultants) 18,000
From Tullamaine Castle Stud (Agent)
b c f Law Society (USA) - Sadler's Star (Sadler's Wells).............. (Cash) 9,500

917

Property of Abbey Lodge Stud Partnership, from The Irish National Stud
ch c f Be My Guest (USA) - Safe Home (Home Guard)......................... (Brian Grassick Bloodstock) 23,000
From Oak Lodge Stud
ch c f Imperial Frontier (USA) - Safiya (USA) (Riverman)......................... (Cash) 8,000
From Ballybin Stud (Agent)
b c f Petorius - Salagangai (Sallust) (Cash) 14,500
Property of Michael Donnelly, from Honeysuckle Farm
b c f Waajib - Saltoki (Ballad Rock)........ (B B A (Ireland)) 24,000
Property of Gerald Casey, from Athgarvan Farm
b f f Don't Forget Me - Santa Patricia (IRE) (Taufan).... (David Minton Bloodstock) 3,500
From Coolfore House Stud
b c f Danehill (USA) - Sassy Lane (Sassafras)......... (Ballymorris Stud) 8,800
From Glebe Stud
b f f Mac's Imp (USA) - Second Movement (Music Boy)................. (Cash) 11,000
From Dollanstown Stud (Agent)
b c f Waajib - Seldovia (Charlottown)...... (B Morrin) 8,000
From Castletown Stud
b f f Last Tycoon - Shabbaba (USA) (Arctic Tern)................... (N O'Byrne) 5,000
Property of D P O'Brien, from Derrygrath Stud
b f f Bluebird (USA) - Shadia (USA) (Naskra) (Croom House Stud) 8,000

918

From Ballylinch Stud (Agent)
ch c f Be My Guest (USA) - Sharp Flash (Kris)............. (Goodwins Lodge) 10,000
From Rathbarry Stud (Agent)
br c f Cyrano de Bergerac - Shenley Lass (Prince Tenderfoot)........... (Cash) 4,500
From Friarstown House Stud
b f f Digamist (USA) - She's No Laugh Ben (USA) (Alleged)............... (Cash) 1,200
Property of Michael Donnelly, from Honeysuckle Farm
b c f Waajib - Shprinza (Vitiges) (T O'Leary) 5,200
Property of Patrick McCarthy, from Hawthorn Villa Stud
ch c f Al Hareb (USA) - Shuckran Habibi (Thatching).. (Scud. Antares Tavazzani) 3,500
From Kilbarry House Stud
b c f Distinctly North (USA) - Shy Jinks (Shy Groom)............. (B B A (Ireland)) 22,500
Property of Demos Brennan, from Racefield Farms
b c f Digamist (USA) - Siwana (IRE) (Dom Racine)...................... (B B A) 6,000
Property of Mrs D W Hutch, from Ardoon Stud
ch c f Nashamaa - Skiskette (Malinowski).. (Conti Bloodstock Service) 5,500
Property of Peter McCutcheon
ch c f Waajib - Sky Piper (Local Suitor) .... (Cash) 4,700
From Kildaragh Stud
ch c f Persian Heights - Slightly Latin (Ahonoora) (David Minton Bloodstock) 7,000

919

Property of J McAuley
ch c f Jareer (USA) - Snipe Singer (Tyrnavos)...... (Scud. Antares Tavazzani) 1,500
Property of Kilcarn Stud
b f f Scenic - Sodium's Niece (Northfields) (T E Hyde) 9,500
b c f Royal Academy (USA) - Soleiade (Posse)............ (Glenvale Stude) 75,000
From Rathbarry Stud
ch f f Mujtahid (USA) - So Long Boys (FR) (Beldale Flutter)............... (Cash) 3,000

From Loughbrown Stud
b c f Dancing Dissident (USA) - Sovereign Dona (Sovereign Path) .... (Brian Grassick Bloodstock) 85,000
From Sherlockstown Stud
ch f f Imperial Frontier (USA) - Spring About (Hard Fought).................(P J Doyle) 3,400
From Barnane Stud
b c f Soviet Lad (USA) - Stapelea (FR) (Faraway Son)........................(Cash) 9,600
From Castletown Stud
b f f Waajib - Star Of Aran (Artaius) .... (R J McCormick) 4,000
Property of Canice Farrell, from Knockatrina Stud
ch c f Common Grounds - Stifen (Burslem) (Marco Bozzi) 4,500
From Knocktoran Stud
b or br c f Persian Bold - Sulmona (USA) (Miswaki)................. (T E Hyde) 26,000

920

Property of Owen Bourke
b c f Classic Secret (USA) - Susan's Blues (Cure The Blues)...........(L Ormsby) 3,300
Property of Thomas Stacey, from Newtownbarry House Stud
b c f Nashamaa - Swan Upping (Lord Gayle) .... (Cash) 4,500
Property of J Hayes, from Rathbarry Stud
b or br c f Mujtahid (USA) - Sweet Alma (Alzao)...................(P J Doyle) 25,000
From Ballylinch Stud (Agent)
b f f Be My Guest (USA) - Sweet Justice (Law Society) .... (Johnny McKeever Bloodstock) 19,500
From Greenwood Stud
b c f Distinctly North (USA) - Sweet Reprieve (Shirley Heights) (Paul Shanahan) 23,000
From Airlie Stud
ch c f Ballad Rock - Sweetsider (USA) (Topsider).... (Kingswood Bloodstock) 13,000
From Rathasker Stud
ch c f Red Sunset - Sybaris (Crowned Prince)................ (Louis Walshe) 7,000
From Carrigbeg Stud
b c f Fayruz - Tabriya (Nishapour) .... (John Ferguson Bloodstock) 8,500

921

KILL (Goffs)
Saturday, November 20th (Foals)

Property of William Curtin from Rathbarry Stud
b f f Jareer (USA) - Take My Pledge (IRE) (Ahonoora)............................(Cash) 2,600
From Airlie Stud
b c f Glow (USA) - Tanta Yvonne (Crowned Prince)................ (B B A (Italia)) 3,600
Property of R J Powell, from Wellington House Stud
b f f Taufan (USA) - Tapestry (Tap On Wood)........................ (Cash) 5,400
From Carrigbeg Stud
b c f Classic Music (USA) - Taunsa (Nishapour)..... (Team Punchestown) 12,000
Property of Paul J Larkin
br c f Cyrano de Bergerac - That's Easy (Swing Easy)............. (T J Cooper) 9,000
From Clonsast Stud
b c f Fayruz - The Way She Moves (North Stoke)........................... (Cash) 17,000
From Grangemore Stud
gr c f Royal Academy (USA) - Thistlewood (Kalamoun)........ (Hamish Alexander) 36,000
From Killowen House Stables
b c f Soviet Lad (USA) - Thit Kho (Irish Love) .... (Scud Antarez Tavazzani) 7,500
Property of Mrs Chris Harrington, from Ridge Manor Stud
b c f Polish Patriot (USA) - Tinas Image (He Loves Me)............... (J T Doyle) 20,000
From Swordleston Stud
ch c f Great Commotion (USA) - Tinktura (Pampapaul).......... (Peter J Doyle) 14,500

922

From Kellistown Stud
b f f High Estate - Tintomara (IRE) (Niniski) (Knocklong House Stud) 1,800
Property of Mrs P Grubb, from Big Acre Stud
b c f Be My Native (USA) - Track Down (Take A Reef).. (Miss Joanna Morgan) 3,500
Property of Mrs R Leonard, from Moortown
b c f Al Hareb (USA) - Tucker's Witch (Junius)........ (Miss Joanna Morgan) 2,800
From Belmont Stud
b c f Bluebird (USA) - Tudor Loom (Sallust) (Johnny McEever Bloodstock) 4,200
From Airlie Stud
b f f Ballad Rock - Tumble Dale (Tumble Wind)................ (M A B Agency) 4,800
From Rathbarry Stud
b c f Taufan (USA) - Twin Island (IRE) (Standaan).............. (Forest Stud) 11,000
Property of Mr & Mrs D Veitch, from Brackagh Moss Stud
ch c f Common Grounds - Ukraine's Affair (USA) (The Minstrel) .... (Lynn Lodge Stud) 9,000
Property of Mr & Mrs Noel McCaffrey, from Mill House Stud
b c f Simply Great (FR) - Uninvited Guest (Be My Guest)................ (Cash) 3,600
From Egmont Stud
b f f Waajib - Up The Gates (Captain James) .... (Cash) 4,500
From Rathbarry Stud (Agent)
b or br f f Dancing Dissident (USA) - Val Lady (FR) (Valdingran)......... (B B A) 6,200

923

Property of Mr & Mrs Noel McCaffrey, from The Mill House Stud
b c f Kefaah (USA) - Veldt (High Top)...... (B B A) 7,200
Property of James Roche
ch f f Waajib - Velvet Breeze (Windjammer) (Cash) 2,000

From Milltown Stud
b f f Posen (USA) - Viceroy Express (Jalmood)........................ (Cash) 1,000
b c f Roi Danzig (USA) - Viceroy Princess (Godswalk)........................... (John Ferguson Bloodstock) 9,000
Property of Mrs R Leonard, from Moortown
b or br f f Cyrano de Bergerac - Wallpark Princess (Balidar)............... (Cash) 3,600
Property of Castlesize Stud, from Lisieux Stud
ch c f Bluebird (USA) - Warm December (He Loves Me)....... (Danny Murphy) 22,000
From Ballyinch Stud (Agent)
b or br c f Polish Patriot (USA) - What A Summer (USA) (What Luck).......... (Jimmy Coogan) 8,500
From Ballylea Stud (Agent)
b f f Don't Forget Me - Wish You Were Here (USA) (Secretariat) (Bo Helander) 4,200
Property of J B Clarke
br c f Magical Wonder (USA) - Woody's Colours (USA) (Caro).. (M A B Agency) 6,400
Property of Ann Stack, from Coolagown Stud
b f f Kahyasi - Yalciyna (Nishapour)......... (B B A (Italia)) 4,200

924

From Rathasker Stud
ch c f Red Sunset - Yellow Orchid (On Your Mark)......................... (Cash) 3,600
From Ballylinch Stud (Agent)
b f f Darshaan - Yes My Dear (USA) (Affirmed)........................... (Johnny McKeever Bloodstock) 33,000
Property of J Hayes, from Rathbarry Stud
b or br c f Cyrano de Bergerac - Albenita (IRE) (Alzao)........ (Claramount Stud) 4,700
From Acorn Stud
b c f Red Sunset - All Alright (Alzao)....... (M English) 4,200
From Mount Pleasant Farm
b f f Tirol - Allberry (Alzao)................ (Ballymorris Stud) 15,500
From Castletown Stud
ro f f Shernazar - All In White (FR) (Carwhite)................ (Klaus Scholer) 2,800
Property of P Conlan
b c f Glenstal (USA) - Almalat (Darshaan) .. (R J McCormick) 8,200
From Rathbarry Stud (Agent)
b c f Soviet Lad (USA) - Anglo Irish (Busted) .... (Hamish Alexander) 9,000
Property of of a Partnership, from Rathbarry Stud
b c f Cyrano de Bergerac - Any Price (Gunner B)................... (Cash) 6,500
b c f Ajraas (USA) - Arctic Ford (FR) (Arctic Tern).............. (Ballymorris Stud) 4,300

925

From Grangemore Stud
b c f Danehill (USA) - Ardmelody (Law Society)............. (B B A (Ireland)) 21,000
From Killowen House Stables
b c f Jareer (USA) - Arfjah (Taufan)........ (Ms Nicola Cross) 2,000
From Barnane Stud
b c f Fairy King (USA) - Ascensiontide (Ela-Mana-Mou).................. (Cash) 27,000
Property of M Ervine
br c f Last Tycoon - Atral Way (Hotfoot) ... (Cash) 12,000
Property of Thomas E Fitzsimons
b or br c f Don't Forget Me - Avebury Ring (Auction Ring)......... (Peter J Doyle) 15,000
From Airlie Stud
b c f Salt Dome (USA) - Babilla (USA) (Raja Baba).......... (Scuderia Andy Capp) 7,500
Property of Mrs A Riddell-Martin, from Lisieux Stud
b c f Bluebird (USA) - Baby Caroline (Martin John)................ (M A B Agency) 9,000
From Knocktoran Stud
b f f Astronef - Ballybannon (Ballymore) ... (Keyhouse Stud) 1,600
From Airlie Stud
ch f f Salt Dome (USA) - Barely Alive (Wolverlife)........ (Franca Lombardi) 1,500
Property of Jack Gage
b c f Roaring Riva - Barratt Oak (Daring Display)............. (M A B Agency) 4,200

926

From Cregg Stud
ch c f Al Hareb (USA) - Bedouin Dancer (Lorenzaccio)................. (Cash) 4,000
From Grangemore Stud
b or br f f Tirol - Bella Pulchella (Lomond).. (B B A) 8,500
Property of of a Partnership, from Lisieux Stud
b f f Warning - Bequeath (USA) (Lyphard).. (B B A) 25,000
From Oak Lodge Stud
b f f Dancing Dissident (USA) - Black Molly (IRE) (High Top)............... (Cash) 15,000
From Rooske Lodge Stud
b f f Topanoora - Blue Alicia (Wolver Hollow)...... (John Ferguson Bloodstock) 4,400
Property of Joseph Heavey
ch c f Mac's Imp (USA) - Bluemore (Morston)......................... (Cash) 10,500
From Acorn Stud
b c f Fayruz - Blunted (Sharpen Up) .... (Springfield Thoroughbred) 6,400
Property of Roger Ryan, from Glen-Spring Stud
ch c f Classic Music (USA) - Bold Kate (Bold Lad)................ (John I O'Byrne) 19,000
From Brittas House Stud (Agent)
b c f Fairy King (USA) - Bold Starlet (Precocious)... (David Minton Bloodstock) 20,000
Property of of a Partnership, from Dromoland Stud
b f f Common Grounds - Bonny Hollow (Wolver Hollow) .... (Brian Grassick Bloodstock) 6,000

927

Property of Matthew Carr
b c f Bluebird (USA) - Born To Fly (IRE) (Last Tycoon)......... (Peter J Doyle) 10,000
From Rathbarry Stud (Agent)
b c f Polish Patriot (USA) - Bouffant (High Top)............ (Hamish Alexander) 52,000

From Deerpark Stud
b c f Nordico (USA) - Bounayya (USA) (Al Nasr)................... (John Ryan) 13,500
From Kildaragh Stud (Agent)
ch c f Exactly Sharp (USA) - Bridewell Belle (Saulingo).. (David Minton Bloodstock) 3,800
Property of Mr & Mrs D Veitch, from Brackagh Moss Stud
b or br f f Magical Wonder (USA) - Brook's Dilemma (Known Fact)......... (Cash) 1,900
From Airlie Stud
b f f Standaan (FR) - Buzzing Around (Prince Bee)............................ (Cash) 2,500
Property of Frank Lynch, from Green Gates Stables
ch c f Classic Music (USA) - Camanime (Hello Gorgeous).... (R J McCormick) 5,000
From Knocktoran Stud
b c f Mtoto - Caprarola (FR) (Bellypha)..... (W Brannigan) 19,000
From Rathasker Stud
b c f Red Sunset - Carcajou (High Top).... (David Minton Bloodstock) 9,000
From Castle Stud
b c f Cyrano de Bergerac - Catherine Clare (Sallust)............................ (Equine Investment Consultants) 9,000

928

Property of Eugene Doyle, from Beeches Stud
ch f f Scenic - Cathryn's Song (Prince Tenderfoot).......... (Kileenlea Stud) 5,100
From Kildarah Stud
ch c f Ballad Rock - Caymana (FR) (Bellypha)........ (Moortown House Stud) 5,800
From Airlie Stud
b c f Salt Dome (USA) - Ce Soir (Northern Baby)......................... (Cash) 5,200
From Castletown Stud
b c f Warrshan (USA) - Chez Nous (Habitat) (Cash) 5,200
From Commonstown Stud
b c f Be My Native (USA) - Christmas Show (Petorius)..................... (Cash) 5,000
From Lisieux Stud
b c f Danehill (USA) - Circus Maid (IRE) (High Top)............. (Mellon Stud) 24,000
From Oak Lodge Stud
ch c f Digamist (USA) - Classic Choice (Patch)....................... (Cash) 9,900
Property of F Lynch, from Rathbarry Stud
b c f Soviet Lad (USA) - Classic Dilemma (Sandhurst Prince).. (Lynn Lodge Stud) 10,500
From Airlie Stud
b c f Ela-Mana-Mou - Come In (Be My Guest)............... (Peter J Doyle) 13,000
Property of Ms V A Charlton
b c f Distinctly North (USA) - Cool Gales (Lord Gayle)......... (R J McCormick) 7,500

929

From Oak Lodge Stud
ch c f Imperial Frontier (USA) - Countess Kildare (Dominion)................... (David Minton Bloodstock) 5,000

Property of J M O'Connor, from Rock Abbey Stud
b c f Distinctly North (USA) - Crannog (Habitat)........... (Claramount Stud) 15,500
Property of Anthony Cambell, from Tara Stud
ch c f Double Schwartz - Creggan Vale Lass (Simply Great)................ (Cash) 5,200
From Newton Park Stud
b or br c f Astronef - Crimson Sails (Lomond).................. (Ian Bryant) 1,100
From Rathasker Stud
ch c f Fayruz - Crimson Sunset (Red Sunset)............(Emerald Bloodstock) 4,400
Property of P Burke
b c f Distinctly North (USA) - Crossed Line (Thatching).......... (R J McCormick) 8,500
Property of R J Powell, from Wellington House Stud
gr c f Ballad Rock - Cumbrian Melody (Petong)................ (Peter J Doyle) 11,000
Property of J Kelly, from Rosemount House Stud
b c f Fayruz - Cut It Fine (USA) (Big Spruce) (Brendan Morrin) 9,000
Property of Gemma Doyle, from Barrettstown Farm House
ch c f Shavian - Dauntess (Formidable) .... (Tom Newman) 600
Property of David A Burke, from Taghadoe Stud
ch c f Salt Dome (USA) - David's Pleasure (Welsh Saint)....... (Franca Lombardi) 1,600

930

From New Park Stud
b c f Reprimand - Dazzling Maid (IRE) (Tate Gallery)............... (Stockwell Ltd) 14,000
From Coolfore House Stud (Agent)
b c f High Estate - Dear Lorraine (FR) (Nonoalco)...... (Team Punchestown) 25,000
From Rathasker Stud
ch c f Don't Forget Me - Derring Dee (Derrylin)......................... (Cash) 3,400
From Rosemount House Stud
b c f Fayruz - Divine Apsara (Godswalk).... (Equine Investment Consultants) 9,200
From O.K.Stud
b f f Magical Strike (USA) - Dotis Dictio (Ballymore).................. (R Kyle) 2,000
From Mount Prospect Stud
b c f Red Sunset - Douschkina (Dubassoff) (Otto Langels) 4,500
From Brittas House Stud (Agent)
br c f Distinctly North (USA) - Dowdstown Miss (Wolver Hollow).. (Peter J Doyle) 6,000
From Torard House Stud
b c f Astronef - Duck Hands (IRE) (Prince Tenderfoot).................... (Cash) 4,900
Property of Graefin Gabriele Deym, from Fenagh House Farm
b f f Two Timing (USA) - Easter Morning (FR) (Nice Havrais).................. (Tipper House Stud) 4,200
From Ballylinch Stud (Agent)
b c f Keen - Eastern View (IRE) (Persian Bold)................. (Stockwell Ltd) 8,200

931

Property of Peter McCutcheon
b c f Roi Danzig (USA) - Evanna's Pride (Main Reef)................... (Cash) 9,200
From Butlersgrove Stud
b c f Don't Forget Me - Excruciating (CAN) (Bold Forbes)................. (Cash) 6,400
From Lupin Stud
b or br c f Classic Secret (USA) - Exotic Dancer (Posse)........................ (John Ferguson Bloodstock) 3,400
From Milltown Stud (Agent)
b f f Cyrano de Bergerac - Explorelka (Relko).............. (Edward Doody) 3,900
From Grangemore Stud
ch f f Classic Music (USA) - Eyre Square (IRE) (Flash Of Steel).......... (Cash) 4,600
From Kildaragh Stud (Agent)
ch c f Carmelite House (USA) - Fait Dodo (On Your Mark).................. (Cash) 2,400
From Oak Lodge Stud
b c f Cyrano de Bergerac - Fantasise (FR) (General Assembly)............ (Cash) 1,600
From Rosemount House Stud
b c f Bluebird (USA) - Fariha (Mummy's Pet) .... (Kellistown Stud) 8,500
Property of Mrs C Lucey from Coolcower Stud
b c f Soviet Lad (USA) - Finessing (Indian King).................. (John Crosse) 3,800
From Oak Lodge Stud
ch f f Great Commotion (USA) - First Fleet (Artaius)............... (Marco Bozzi) 3,800

932

From Ballylinch Stud (Agent)
b c f Red Sunset - Flying Anna (Roan Rocket)............. (Liam McAteer) 6,000
From Milltown Stud
b c f Roi Danzig (USA) - Follow The Rainbow (Rainbow Quest)... (B B A (Italia)) 3,800
Property of Mrs A Riddell-Martin, from Lisieux Stud
b f f Nabeel Dancer (USA) - Fordes Cross (Ya Zaman) .... (European Bloodstock Agency) 11,000
From Churchtown House Stud
ch c f Archway (IRE) - Forliana (Forli) (Cash) 12,500
Property of John Malone
ch or gr c f Imperial Frontier (USA) - Fraudulent (Sexton Blake)............ (Cash) 4,300
To dissolve a partnership, from Ballyhampshire Stud
b or br c f Cyrano de Bergerac - Gale Force Seven (Strong Gale)........... (Cash) 9,500
Property of Matthew Tynan, from Moyglass Stud
b c f Waajib - Gallic Aire (USA) (Caerleon).. (Stockwell Ltd) 12,500
From Pier House Stud
ch f f Classic Music (USA) - Ganna (ITY) (Molvedo)...... (Scuderia Andy Capp) 5,200
From Green Ireland Properties Ltd
b or br c f Last Tycoon - Gay Bentley (USA) (Riverman)......... (Scuderia Antares) 6,200
From Ballylinch Stud (Agent)
b f f Posen (USA) - General's Daughter (USA) (General Holme).. (Bo Helander) 2,200

933

From Rathbarry Stud (Agent)
b or br c f Polish Patriot (USA) - Girl On A Swing (High Top)..................... (Brian Grassick Bloodstock) 33,000
From Loughbrown Stud
ch f f Great Commotion (USA) - Giselle (USA) (To The Quick)..... (Skara Stud) 11,500
Property of Andrew Bailey, from Broguestown Stud
ch c f Bluebird (USA) - God Speed Her (Pas de Seul)... (Brian Grassick Bloodstock) 15,000
Property of Mrs A Kitchin
b or br f f Posen (USA) - Gortadoo (USA) (Sharpen Up)................. (B B A) 2,200
From Kellistown Stud
ch c f Glenstal (USA) - Grapette (Nebbiolo) (Cash) 3,800
From Rathasker Stud
b c f Red Sunset - Great Land (USA) (Friend's Choice).............. (Cash) 8,800
From Pipers Hill Stud
b f f Great Commotion (USA) - Green Wings (General Assembly) .... (David Minton Bloodstock) 11,800
From Leinster Stud
b c f Mac's Imp (USA) - Halimah (Be My Guest)......................... (Cash) 10,000
From Airlie Stud
ch c f Standaan (FR) - Havana Moon (Ela Mana Mou)........... (John McGrath) 3,200
From Rathbarry Stud (Agent)
b or br c f Soviet Lad (USA) - Hear Me (Simply Great)...................... (Moortown House Stud) 6,500

934

From Churchtown House Stud
ch c f Glenstal (USA) - Helcia (Habitat)..... (Claramount Stud) 5,200
Property of Kilcarn Stud
b f f Priolo (USA) - Hi Bettina (Henbit) ..... (Michael Andree) 37,000
Property of Mrs K Cullen
ch c f Digamist (USA) - Highland Culture (Lomond)......... (Margaret O'Toole) 5,700
From Belmont Stud
b f f Simply Great (FR) - Hostess (Be My Guest)............ (Matthew Sharkey) 7,000
From Moygaddy Stud
b c f Magical Strike (USA) - How True (Known Fact)................. (Cash) 1,800
Property of Mrs O M E McKeever, from Greenfields
ch c f Waajib - Huntress (Huntercombe) ... (Marco Bozzi) 3,600
Property of Mrs M Hayes
b c f Cyrano de Bergerac - Immunity (Brave Shot)................. (Miss J Short) 1,500
From Pier House Stud (Agent)
ch c f Shernazar - Iamstopped (Furry Glen) (Cash) 7,000
Property of D P O'Brien, from Derrygrath Stud
b f f Glenstal (USA) - In Form (Formidable) (Brian Grassick Bloodstock) 2,500
From Loughbrown Stud
b c f Dancing Dissident (USA) - In High Spirits (Head For Heights)........... (Patrick J Flynn) 7,000

935

From Pipers Hill Stud
b c f Salt Dome (USA) - Inisfail (Persian Bold)................... (J T Doyle) 7,200
Property of Michael J Foley, from Springhill Farm
b f f Tirol - In The Clover (Meadow Mint) .. (Seamus Phelan) 7,000
From Airlie Stud
ch c f Glow (USA) - Ivory Smooth (USA) (Sir Ivor)............. (Scuderia Antares) 2,500
From Fortbarrington Stud
b c f Scenic - Eastern Aura (IRE) (Ahonoora) .... (Paul Shanahan) 12,500
b c f Don't Forget Me - Guest House (What A Guest)............................. (Equine Investment Consultants) 5,800
From Ballysax Manor Stud (Agent)
b c f Treasure Kay - Marqueterie (USA) (Well Decorated).............. (Cash) 4,500
Property of James Mulcahy
b c f Tirol - Gay Appeal (Star Appeal) .... (B B A (Ireland)) 28,000
Property of J Finnegan
ch f f Archway (IRE) - Amtico (Bairn) ...... (Chevington Stud) 6,900
Property of Mr William P Fogarty
b c f Tirol - Sunlit Ride (Ahonoora) .... (Frank Keogh) 6,000
From Grange Hill Stud
ch c f Great Commotion - Betsy Baker (Kings Lake)....... (Ballyhimikin Stud) 8,500

936

KILL (Goffs)
Sunday, November 21st
(Mares)

Property of Mrs A Riddell-Martin, from Lisieux Stud
Jambo Jambo (IRE) b m (5yrs) Kafu - Miss Goodbody (Castle Keep) Covered by Polish Patriot (USA)........... (Cash) 21,000
Property of Mrs Gemma Doyle, from Barrettstown Farm House
June Darling b m (10yrs) Junius (USA) - Beau Darling (Darling Boy) Covered by Imperial Frontier (USA).........(Cash) 1,900
Property of H H Aga Khan's Studs S.C., from Gilltown Stud
Kamadara (IRE) b f (2yrs) Kahyasi - Kamanaya (FR) (Mill Reef) .... (John Malone) 1,100
From Winterwell Stud
Kaskazi b m (4yrs) Dancing Brave (USA) - Fly Me (FR) (Luthier) Covered by Taufan (USA)................. (J T Doyle) 28,000
From Ashfield Farm
Kaysama (FR) br m (13yrs) Kenmare (FR) - Karosa (FR) (Caro) Covered by Distinctly North (USA) (Barronstown Stud) 8,500
From Friarstown House Stud
Key Partner b m (6yrs) Law Society (USA) - Roscrea (Ballymore) Covered by Sharp Victor (USA).................. (Cash) 5,000
Property of H H Aga Khan's Studs S.C., from Sheshoon Stud
Kinaliza (IRE) b m (3yrs) Chief Singer - Kinaana (Posse) Covered by Shahrastani (USA).... (Brendan Hayes) 6,000
Koldia br m (6yrs) Darshaan - Koblenza (Hugh Lupus) Covered by Shahrastani (USA)........... (Stonehall Paddocks) 24,000
From Airlie Stud
Kristar (IRE) ch m (11yrs) Kris - Guest Night (Sir Ivor) Covered by Roi Danzig (USA) (Cash) 4,000
From Wraymount Stud
Lady Aladdin bl m (11yrs) Persian Bold - Relic Spirit (Relic) Covered by Law Society (USA)................. (Cash) 3,000

937

From Dollanstown Stud (Agent)
Lady Of Man b or br m (18yrs) So Blessed - Tranquility Base (Roan Rocket) Covered by Anita's Prince...... (Kevin Wallace) 2,000
From Brittas House Stud (Agent)
La Joya (IRE) b m (4yrs) Affirmed (USA) - Watership (USA) (Foolish Pleasure) Covered by Masterclass (USA) (B B A) 5,200
From Winterwell Stud
Lashing (USA) b m (9yrs) Stormbird (CAN) - Rain Wind (USA) (Apalachee) Covered by Kefaah (USA)..................... (Ms Kathleen McElroy) 1,600
From Airlie Stud
Little Money b or br m (8yrs) Prince Bee - Petite Bourguoise (Crowned Prince) Covered by Simply Great (FR)......... (Stud Hjortebo) 1,100
From Friarstown House Stud
Lomond's Breeze b m (7yrs) Lomond (USA) - Mettle (USA) (Pretendre) Covered by Silver Kite (USA)............... (Cash) 10,000
From Winterwell Stud
Lost Splendour (USA) b m (14yrs) Vaguely Noble - Roussalka (Habitat) Covered by Alzao (USA)..... (Emerald Bloodstock) 3,000
From The Irish National Stud
Lucky Pick b m (9yrs) Auction Ring (USA) - La Fortune (Le Haar) Covered by Dancing Dissident (USA)............ (Cash) 4,600
From Ballylinch Stud
Maevella (IRE) ch m (3yrs) Ahonoora - Pleasant Review (USA) (The Minstrel) Covered by Posen (USA) .... (Brian Grassick Bloodstock) 4,000
From Lime Lodge Stud
Maid Of Vision (IRE) b m (4yrs) Vision (USA) - Marks Maid (On Your Mark) Covered by Tirol...................... (Brian Grassick Bloodstock) 6,000
From Belmont Stud
Majesty's Nurse b m (8yrs) Indian King (USA) - Lagolette (Green God) Covered by Shernazar......... (Seamus Burns) 6,000

938

Property of H H Aga Khan's Studs S.C., from Gilltown Stud
Manzala (USA) b f (3yrs) Irish River (FR) - Marazika (Great Nephew) .... (Brian Grassick Bloodstock) 9,500

Property of Mr Kevin J Molloy, from Dolland House Stud

Maraquiba (FR) gr m (13yrs) Kenmare (FR) - Quibala (Crepello) Covered by Bluebird (USA)................ (Kerr & Co Ltd) 2,600

From Fenpark Stables (The Curragh)

Markievicz (IRE) b or br f (3yrs) Doyoun - Bell Tower (Lyphard's Wish).......... (Nikita Investments) 16,000

Property of Gainsborough Stud Management Ltd, from Woodpark Stud

Meissarah (USA) b m (9yrs) Silver Hawk (USA) - Countess Babu (USA) (Bronze Babu) Covered by Marju (IRE)......... (B B A (Italia) 6,500

From Rathbarry Stud

Midaan ch m (12yrs) Sallust - Some Thing (Will Somers) Covered by Cyrano de Bergerac............. (Carlos Reyero) 3,000

Property of H H Aga Khan's Studs S.C., from Sheshoon Stud

Modiyna gr m (11yrs) Nishapour (FR) - Monique (Tanerko) Covered by Akarad (FR).................. (Ballylea Stud) 12,000

From O.K. Stud

Mrs Snuggs (IRE) gr f (3yrs) Law Society (USA) - Inanna (Persian Bold) .... (Patrick J Flynn) 5,000

Must Hurry b m (6yrs) Kampala - Precious Gift (Prince Tenderfoot) Covered by Arcane (USA) .... (Scuderia Andy Capp Srl) 3,500

From Tullamaine Castle Stud (Agent)

My Sister Ellen ch m (6yrs) Lyphard (USA) - Cat Girl (USA) (Grey Dawn) Covered by High Estate (USA).. (Chevington Stud) 17,000

From Moorfield Stud

Naglaa (USA) ch m (10yrs) State Dinner (USA) - Snow Empress (USA) (Young Emperor) Covered by Waajib... (Cash) 5,000

939

Property of a Syndicate, from Ardenode Stud Ltd

Needlewoman b m (10yrs) Moorestyle - Thimblerigger (Sharpen Up) Covered by Maledetto (IRE)............... (Cash) 3,000

From Oghill House Stud

Nielsine ch m (8yrs) Czaravich (USA) - Natuschka (Authi) Covered by Maelstrom Lake............... (Cash) 5,000

From Ballylinch Stud (Agent)

Night Starker (USA) ch m (7yrs) Northrop (USA) - Starkling (USA) (Graustark) Covered by Keen.......... (B B A (Italia)) 12,000

From Redmonstown Stud

Nikitis (USA) b m (3yrs) Cox's Ridge (USA) - Waving (USA) (Nijinsky) Covered by Roi Danzig (USA)..... (Monksgrange Stud) 7,500

Property of a Partnership, from North Kildare Lodge

North Kildare (USA) b m (6yrs) North Jet - Lady Blackfoot (Prince Tenderfoot) Covered by Distinctly North (USA)..... (B B A (Ireland)) 15,000

From Ballysax Manor Stud (Agent)

Ocean Blue (IRE) b f (3yrs) Bluebird (USA) - Miss Allowed (USA) (Alleged)......... (Barrackstown Stud) 4,200

From Winterwell Stud

Olamic (USA) b m (14yrs) Nijinsky (CAN) - Continuation (USA) (Forli) Covered by Kefaah (USA)................ (C B A) 14,000

From Redmondstown Stud

Over Swing (FR) b m (6yrs) Saint Cyrien (FR) - Charlata (FR) (Chaparral) Covered by Roi Danzig (USA)........... (Cash) 2,600

Property of H H Aga Khan's Studs S.C., from Gilltown Stud

Pariyana (IRE) b f (2yrs) Shernazar - Parakara (Great Nephew)................. (Rossenarra Stud) 2,400

From Moyglare Stud Farm

Prime Interest (IRE) b m (4yrs) Kings Lake (USA) - Wise Blood (Kalamoun) Covered by Maelstrom Lake... (Dan Daly) 2,000

940

From Premier Enterprises

Print Press (IRE) b m (4yrs) Taufan (USA) - Yellow Pages (Yellow God) Covered by Masterclass (USA).... (Kevin Wallace) 2,300

From Newberry Stud

Redeem Herself ch m (11yrs) General Assembly (USA) - Redowa (Red God) Covered by Thatching......... (C B A) 9,200

From Ballyvolane Stud

Red Lory br m (12yrs) Bay Express - Powderhall (Murrayfield) Covered by Cyrano de Bergerac.. (Peter G Deane) 1,600

From Friarstown House Stud

Respectfully (USA) ch m (10yrs) The Minstrel (CAN) - Treat Me Nobly (USA) (Vaguely Noble) Covered by High Estate...................... (C B A) 29,000

Property of H H Aga Khan's Studs S.C., from Gilltown Stud

Rifaya (IRE) b f (3yrs) Lashkari - Riyda (Be My Guest)......... (Seamus O'Farrell) 3,200

From Tullamaine Castle Stud (Agent)

Rose Garland (USA) b m (8yrs) Seattle Slew (USA) - Rose Red (USA) (Northern Dancer) Covered by Nigh Shift (USA).. (F.I.N.A.C.O. Srl) 80,000

From Ballylinch Stud (Agent)

Royal Custom b m (8yrs) His Majesty (USA) - Sweet Habit (Habitat) Covered by Bob Back (USA)..... (Mercury Bloodstock) 20,000

From Rathasker Stud

Rubina Park b m (15yrs) Ashmore (FR) - Keep Going (Hard Sauce) Covered by Red Sunset.................. (Cash) 3,300

From Tullamaine Castle Stud (Agent)

Sadler's Star b m (6yrs) Sadler's Wells (USA) - Princesse Timide (USA) (Blushing Groom) Covered by Kenmare (FR) (Hugo Merry) 75,000

From Ashfield Farm

Saga's Humour ch m (14yrs) Bustino - Summer Day (Golden Cloud) Covered by Shalford (IRE)...... (Peter J Doyle) 5,800

941

From Moorfield Stud

Salamarza (IRE) b m (3yrs) Kahyasi - Samirza (USA) (Riverman) Covered by Bluebird (USA) .... (Watkins Bloodstock Services) 8,200

Property of Mr Liam Phelan
Salonniere (FR) b m (8yrs) Bikala - Supine (Supreme Sovereign) Covered by Mujadil (USA)................ (Cash) 6,500
From Newbury Stud
Sans Ceriph (IRE) b m (3yrs) Thatching - No Jargon (Nonoalco) Covered by Ballad Rock... (Watkins Bloodstock Services) 13,500
Property of H H Aga Khan's Studs S.C., from Gilltown Stud
Sarakarta (USA) ch f (3yrs) Trempolino (USA) - Sarshara (Habitat) .... (Paschal Carmody) 3,000
From Knockeen Stud
Seamill (IRE) b m (4yrs) Lafontaine (USA) - Pearl Reef (Main Reef) Covered by Mandalus.................... (Cash) 3,000
From Winterwell Stud
Seattle Siren (USA) b m (12yrs) Seattle Slew (USA) - Miss Ooh La La (USA) (Wallet Lifter) Covered by Ela-Mana-Mou......................... (Cash) 4,200
Property of Mrs Frances Cole
Semiwild (USA) b or br m (7yrs) Rumbo (USA) - African Desert (African Sky) Covered by Ajraas (USA) .... (Franco Giacopelli) 2,500
From Ballylinch Stud
Settling Down (USA) b m (8yrs) Topsider (USA) - Galushka (USA) (Vaguely Noble) Covered by Petorius... (Peter J Doyle) 13,000
Property of a Partnership, from Cleaboy Stud
Sevruga (USA) ch m (4yrs) Czaravich (USA) - Dusty Heart (USA) (Run Dusty Run) Covered by Sharp Victory (USA) (Cash) 6,000
From Milltown Stud
Shaiybaniyda b m (11yrs) He Loves Me - Shaiyra (Relko) Covered by Be My Guest (USA).................. (Cash) 15,000

942

Property of H H Aga Khan's Studs S.C., from Gilltown Stud
Sharakawa (IRE) b f (3yrs) Darshaan - Sharaya (USA) (Youth) .... (Neville O'Byrne) 19,000
From Friarstown House Stud
She's No Laugh Ben (USA) b m (6yrs) Alleged (USA) - Swirlaway (USA) (Sir Ivor) Covered by Masterclass (USA)... (Cash) 6,000
Property of Mr M F Whelan, from Mocklershill Stables (Agent)
Sialia (IRE) b f (3yrs) Bluebird (USA) - Lancette (Double Jump) Covered by River Falls..................... (Tara Stud) 12,000
From Friarstown House Stud
Sky Lover br m (9yrs) Ela-Mana-Mou - Diamonds In The Sky (African Sky) Covered by Imperial Frontier (USA) (Cash) 4,000
From Moyglare Stud Farm
Soviet Choice (IRE) b f (3yrs) Soviet Star (USA) - Miracle Drug (USA) (Seattle Slew)............. (Michael Begley) 15,500
From Hamwood Stud
Special Offer (IRE) b f (3yrs) Shy Groom (USA) - Big Bugs Bomb (Skymaster)... (Dan Daly) 4,200

From Meadowlands Stud
ch m (3yrs) Commanche Run - Spear Dance (Gay Fandango) Covered by Astronef............ (Victor Connolly) 4,000
From Winterwell Stud
Spoilt Again b m (8yrs) Mummy's Pet - Reload (FR) (Relko) Covered by Great Commotion (USA) .... (Hawthorn Villa Stud) 10,500
From Churchtown House Stud
Star Cream b m (10yrs) Star Appeal - Tropical Cream (USA) (Creme de La Creme) Covered by Don't Forget Me .... (J T Doyle) 17,000
From Moyglare Stud Farm
Strategic Timing (IRE) b f (3yrs) Chief Singer - Going Digital (USA) (Northern Baby).............. (Seamus Murphy) 3,000

943

Property of Darley Stud Management, from Ragusa Stud
Sue Grundy b m (10yrs) Grundy - Susanna (USA) (Nijinsky) Covered by Shernazar (Michael Murray) 5,200
Property of Dr John P Ryan, from Ballymorris Stud
Sun Eclipse (IRE) ch m (4yrs) Palace Music (USA) - Sun Breiz (FR) (Boran) Covered by Silver Kite (USA)........... (Cash) 5,000
Property of Mr H O'Shea, from Mocklershill Stables (Agent)
Surprise Move (IRE) b m (3yrs) Simply Great (FR) - Persian Apple (USA) (No Robbery) Covered by River Falls ...... (Forenaghts Stud) 10,500
From Ballylinch Stud (Agent)
Sweet Justice b m (6yrs) Law Society (USA) - Hilo Girl (USA) (Pago Pago) Covered by Bob Back (USA)......... (Croom House Stud) 23,000
To Dissolve a Partnership, from Ballylea Stud (Agent)
Take Your Mark (USA) b m (19yrs) Round Table - Society Column (USA) (Sir Gaylord)...................... (Cash) 4,600
Property of Mr David A Cahill, from Irish National Stud
Testarossa (FR) ch m (9yrs) Kenmare (FR) - Dressed In Red (Red Alert) Covered by Magical Wonder (USA)......... (Cash) 3,600
Property of Shadwell Estate Company Ltd, from Derrinstown Stud
Thubut (USA) b m (6yrs) Tank's Prospect (USA) - Social Lesson (USA) (Forum) Covered by Shareef Dancer (USA)..... (Stonehall Paddocks) 26,000
From Whitsbury Manor Racing Stables
Tochar Ban (USA) b f (3yrs) Assert - Guest Night (Sir Ivor) .... (Brian Grassick Bloodstock) 28,000
From Moyglare Stud Farm
Tough Battle b m (10yrs) Captain James - Lady Aureola (Aureole) Covered by Waajib........................ (Cash) 6,500
From Milltown Stud (Agent)
Une Venitienne (FR) b m (12yrs) Green Dancer (USA) - Greener Pastures (FR) (Rheingold) Covered by Imp Society (USA).................. (John Flavin) 2,000

944

Property of Shadwell Estate Company Ltd, from Derrinstown Stud

Velvet Habit ch m (15yrs) Habitat - Red Velvet (Red God) Covered by Ela-Mana-Mou........ (Jamestown House Stud) 2,200

From Tara Stud

Verusa (IRE) b f (3yrs) Petorius - Night Of Gaiety (What A Guest)... (Acorn Stud) 5,000

From Tullamaine Castle Stud (Agent)

Vineyard Cat (IRE) b m (3yrs) Alzao (USA) - Cat Girl (USA) (Grey Dawn II) Covered by Be My Chief (USA) (Otto Langelis) 16,000

Property of a Partnership, from Cleaboy Stud

Visiting Royalty (USA) br m (5yrs) Riverman (USA) - Noble Lady (USA) (Vaguely Noble) Covered by Sharp Victor (USA) (Cash) 6,500

From Airlie Stud

Wind In The Willow b m (8yrs) Tumble Wind - Montbretia (Aureole) Covered by Salt Dome (USA)..... (Niall Hogan) 2,800

From Newberry Stud

Winter Dreams (IRE) b m (4yrs) Sadler's Wells (USA) - Current Jargon (USA) (Little Current) Covered by Ballad Rock (B B A) 7,000

Property of Stone Thorn Stud Farms, from Carrowdore Castle (At Landfall Paddocks)

Wogogo (IRE) ch f (3yrs) Dominion - Euromill (Shirley Heights)............ (Ballysheehan Stud) 13,000

Property of Mr J Hardiman, from Rathasker Stud

Yellow Princess (IRE) ch f (3yrs) Tate Gallery (USA) - Yellow Orchid (On Your Mark)............... (Brian Acheson) 800

From O.K. Stud

Abaca (USA) b m (4yrs) Manila (USA) - Pert (USA) (Damascus) Covered by Arcane (USA)........................ (Cash) 2,000

From Kilfrush Stud

Ah Ya Zein b m (10yrs) Artaius (USA) - Come True (FR) (Nasram II) Covered by Priolo (USA)............ (Joe O'Flynn) 16,500

945

Property of Gainsborough Stud Management Ltd, from Woodpark Stud

Al Hayoola (IRE) gr m (4yrs) Reference Point - Sheristadar (Shergar) Covered by Jareer (USA)..... (Ennistown Stud) 6,500

From Premier Enterprises

Alice Brackloon (USA) br m (8yrs) Melyno - Arantelle (FR) (Tapioca II) Covered by Shalford (IRE)................. (Cash) 5,000

From Hamwood Stud

All Away (IRE) b m (4yrs) Glow (USA) - All Ours (Northfields) Covered by Topanoora.......... (Mr Michael Buckley) 4,600

Property of P Conlan

Almalat b m (6yrs) Darshaan - Amila (Great Nephew) Covered by Distinctly North (USA).......... (Mercury Bloodstock) 5,400

Property of Darley Stud Management, from Ragusa Stud

Amerindian b m (6yrs) Commanche Run - Supremely Royal (Crowned Prince) Covered by Doyoun.................. (Watkins Bloodstock Services) 18,500

From Athneasy Stud

Angel Street b m (13yrs) Comedy Star (USA) - Diagonale II (Ribot) Covered by Astronef.................... (Cash) 2,000

From Winterwell Stud

Annonay (IRE) b m (4yrs) Rousillon (USA) - Melodiosa (Diamonds Are Trump) Covered by Be My Guest (USA).......... (Scuderia Andy Capp Srl) 12,500

Arab Heritage b m (10yrs) Great Nephew - Our Home (Habitat) Covered by Salt Dome (USA)......... (Paul Shanahan) 7,500

From Barnane Stud

Ascensiontide b m (9yrs) Ela-Mana-Mou - Rose Above (Sir Herbert) Covered by Fairy King (USA).............. (Cash) 13,000

From Airlie Stud

Babilla (USA) b m (11yrs) Raja Baba (USA) - Tender Camilla (Prince Tenderfoot) Covered by Ela-Mana-Mou .... (Cleaboy Stud) 4,000

946

Property of H H Aga Khan's Studs S.C., from Gilltown Stud

Bahnasa (IRE) b f (3yrs) Shardari - Banasiya (Mill Reef)........ (Roemerhof Stud) 4,000

From Ballydoyle and Ridge Manor Stables

Bajan Queen (IRE) b f (3yrs) Fairy King (USA) - Foxrock (Ribero).. (Pat Martin) 6,200

From Kilfrush Stud

Ballybannon b m (17yrs) Ballymore - Arctic Melody (Arctic Slave) .... (Declan McPartlin) 2,200

Property of H H Aga Khan's Studs S.C., from Sheshoon Stud

Banana Peel b m (12yrs) Green Dancer (USA) - Barbra (FR) (Le Fabuleux) Covered by Doyoun.............. (B C A) 20,000

From Cloghran Stud

Barely Alive ch m (9yrs) Wolverlife - Bare Costs (Petition) Covered by Salt Dome (USA)........................ (Cash) 1,550

Property of Dr A J F O'Reilly, from Castlemartin Stud Farm

Bawnanell ch m (7yrs) Viking (USA) - Winning Feature (Red Alert) Covered by Imperial Frontier (USA).............. (John H McLoughlin) 7,200

From The Cottage Stud

Bel Ria b m (12yrs) Gay Fandango (USA) - Topping Girl (Sea Hawk) Covered by Mujadil (USA)........ (Rathasker Stud) 2,700

From Hamwood Stud

Better Goods (IRE) b f (3yrs) Glow (USA) - Bold Miss (Bold Lad).......... (Cash) 1,200

From Moyglare Stud Farm

Biserta (GER) b m (12yrs) Priamos (GER) - Brisbane (GER) (Dhaulagiri) Covered by Shernazar.................... (Cash) 2,800

Property of Darley Stud Management, from Tara Stud
Bosa ch m (5yrs) Kris - Tralthee (USA) (Tromos) Covered by Kefaah (USA)..... (Acorn Stud) 1,600

947

From Moyglare Stud Farm
Brief Merger (IRE) ch f (3yrs) Shernazar - Software (USA) (Lyphard).. (J T Doyle) 3,600
From Juddmonte Farms Ltd
Busca (USA) ch m (11yrs) Mr Prospector (USA) - Bag Of Tunes (USA) (Herbager) Covered by Persian Heights .... (B B A (Italia)) 21,000
From Brittas House Stud (Agent)
Caitanya (USA) b m (16yrs) Roberto (USA) - Fish-Bar (Baldric II) Covered by High Estate.................... (S Connolly) 1,900
Property of Mr T C Butler, from Canadian Stud
Canadian Guest ch m (10yrs) Be My Guest (USA) - Connaught Beach (Connaught) Covered by Law Society (USA) (Cash) 10,000
From Sworlestown Stud
Caranina (USA) gr m (11yrs) Caro - Jojima (USA) (Wajima) Covered by Kenmare (FR)........................... (Cash) 7,500
From Winterwell Stud
Chaika (USA) b m (5yrs) Bering - Red Red Rose (Blushing Groom) Covered by Great Commotion (USA)........ (Cash) 1,600
Chalkey Road b m (14yrs) Relko - Feather Bed (Gratitude) Covered by Taufan (USA)............ (Caesar House Stud) 3,200
Cinnamon Fern (IRE) b m (5yrs) Sadler's Wells (USA) - Osmunda (Mill Reef) Covered by Petorius .... (Watkins Bloodstock Services) 14,000
From Ballylinch Stud (Agent)
Citissima ch m (15yrs) Simbir - Airgead Beo (Hook Money) Covered by Keen ...... (Equine Management Services) 3,800
From Glidawn Stud
Clandestine Affair (IRE) b f (3yrs) Nordico (USA) - Clanjingle (Tumble Wind)...... (John M Weld) 7,500

948

Property of Mr Kevin J Molloy, from Dolland House Stud
Cloven Dancer (USA) ch m (12yrs) Hurok (USA) - Clova (USA) (Gustav) Covered by Shalford (IRE)............... (Cash) 5,000
From Gaybrooke Stud
Collegian ch m (12yrs) Stanford - Arodstown Tan (Atan).... (Ms Rose Dunne) 1,600
From Ballylinch Stud
Corradus (IRE) b m (5yrs) Sure Blade (USA) - Marble Run (Run The Gantlet) Covered by Bob Back (USA)............. (Watkins Bloodstock Services) 5,400
Property of Mr J Kelly, from Rosemount House Stud
Cut It Fine (USA) b m (11yrs) Big Spruce (USA) - Diamond Till (USA) (Model Fool) Covered by Petorius........... (Cash) 3,400

From Abbeville & Meadow Court Studs (Agent)
Dawn Is Breaking b m (15yrs) Import - Brief Chorus (Counsel) Covered by Dancing Dissident (USA)................ (Cash) 18,000
Property of Mr Frank Hardy, from Bluebell Stables
Desert Squaw b m (6yrs) Commanche Run - Top Of The League (High Top)....... (Michael Andree) 7,000
Property of David and Sandra Meredith, from Dromard House
Deverells Walk (IRE) b m (5yrs) Godswalk (USA) - Deverell's Lady (Sterling Bay) Covered by Classic Secret (USA)...... (Rosemount Stud) 3,000
From Rathasker Stud
Dominia b m (16yrs) Derring-Do - Dominant (Behistoun) Covered by Classic Secret (USA)............. (Patrick McCarthy) 2,100
From O.K. Stud
Dotis Dictio ch m (11yrs) Ballymore - Judy Gee (Will Somers) Covered by Arcane (USA)..................... (C Maye) 4,000
Property of Mr J Waldron, from Jigginstown House Stud
Eimkar b m (8yrs) Junius (USA) - Royal Display (Right Royal V) Covered by Red Sunset........... (Peter D McCreery) 4,500

949

From Cleaboy Stud
Elea (GER) br m (10yrs) Dschingis Khan - Envira (FR) (Yoggi) Covered by Sharp Victor (USA)........ (Michael Andree) 10,000
From Moyglare Stud Farm
Elegant Bloom (IRE) b f (3yrs) Be My Guest (USA) - Honey Bend (USA) (Never Bend).................... (Tara Stud) 12,500
Property of Mr Paul Hardy, from Rathasker Stud
Elegida b m (16yrs) Habitat - Merta (USA) (Jaipur) Covered by Tirol....... (Cash) 3,800
Property of Gainsborough Stud Management Ltd, from Woodpark Stud
Etoile de Nuit b m (11yrs) Troy - Melbourne Miss (Chaparral).................... (Ms Kathleen McElroy) 700
From Premier Enterprises
Evening Elsewhere b m (9yrs) Sharpo - Evening Slipper (Above Suspicion) Covered by Shalford (IRE)................ (Rosemount Stud) 3,000
From Tullamane Castle Stud (Agent)
Fandangerina ch m (14yrs) Grey Dawn II - Prima Ballerina (Royal Vale) Covered by Alzao (USA).................... (Cash) 25,000
From Little Well Stud
Farnacliffe b m (9yrs) Taufan (USA) - Bold Tradition (Traditionalist) Covered by Classic Secret (USA)...... (J T Doyle) 10,000
Fifth Quarter b m (8yrs) Cure The Blues - Overplay (Bustino) Covered by Shalford (IRE).................. (Hugo Merry) 45,000
From Strawhall House Stables
Fitzrovia (USA) b m (8yrs) One For All (USA) - Woodsome (Runnymede)......... (Az Agr S Uberto Srl) 7,000

From Moyglare Stud Farm

Florentink (USA) ch m (14yrs) The Minstrel (CAN) - Gala Lil (USA) (Spring Double) Covered by Shernazar................ (Caesar House Stud) 9,700

950

From Milltown Stud

Full Baord (FR) b m (7yrs) Fabulous Dancer (USA) - All Found (USA) (Alleged) ..... (Emerald Bloodstock) 3,200

From Ballylinch Stud (Agent)

Future Tense (USA) b m (20yrs) Pretense (USA) - Flail (USA) (Bagdad) Covered by Bob Back (USA)...... (Owen O'Leary) 2,400

From Loughbrown Stud

Giselle (USA) ch m (11yrs) To The Quick (USA) - Maryinsky (USA) (Northern Dancer) Covered by Law Society (USA) .... (Axel Donnerstag Bloodstock) 7,000

From Glidawn Stud

Goodby Heart (IRE) b m (4yrs) Be My Native (USA) - Lucy Limelight (Hot Spark) Covered by Nordico (USA) ..... (P Burns) 5,000

From Premier Enterprises

Haraabah (USA) ch m (10yrs) Topsider (USA) - Marie de Sarre (FR) (Queen's Hussar) Covered by Masterclass (USA) (Cash) 2,800

Havenwood Princess b m (9yrs) Pitskelly - Tragara (Buisson Ardent) Covered by Masterclass (USA).. (Franco Giacopelli) 2,200

From Moyglare Stud Farm

Honest Attempt (IRE) b f (3yrs) Shernazar - Sally's Wish (USA) (Sensitive)......... (Ballysheehan Stud) 10,000

From Belmont Stud

Hostess b m (14yrs) Be My Guest (USA) - Ginger (Red God) Covered by Bob Back (USA)................ (Peter J Doyle) 7,000

From Piercetown Stud

Houwara (IRE) b m (5yrs) Darshaan - Haughty Manner (High Top) Covered by Mac's Imp (USA)....... (J T Doyle) 7,500

From Friarstown House Stud

Ice The Cake (IRE) ch m (4yrs) Thatching - Queen Cake (Sandhurst Prince) Covered by Imperial Frontier (USA) (Cash) 2,800

951

Property of Dr A J F O'Reilly, from Castlemartin Stud

Impressive Lady b m (8yrs) Mr Fluorocarbon - Concave (Connaught) Covered by Imperial Falcon (USA)....... (C Maye) 2,200

From Ballysheehan Stud

Infanta (USA) ch m (14yrs) Intrepid Hero (USA) - Isobella (Bold Ruler) Covered by Ballad Rock......... (Brendan Morrin) 5,500

From Loughbrown Stud

In High Spirits b m (7yrs) Head For Heights - Sovereign Dona (Sovereign Path) Covered by Lahib (USA) .... (John McLoughlin) 10,000

To Dissolve a Partnership, from Ballylea Stud (Agent)

Instinctive Move (USA) b m (12yrs) Nijinsky (CAN) - Boldc Bikini (USA) (Boldnesian) Covered by Thatching (John O'Connor) 13,000

From Athneasy Stud

Iswara (USA) b m (9yrs) Alleged (USA) - Leaf Fall (FR) (Lyphard) Covered by Astronef................ (Victor Stud) 3,000

From Corbally Stud

Stride On (IRE) b m (4yrs) Pennine Walk - Isla Bonita (Kings Lake) Covered by Prince Rupert (FR)............. (Cash) 2,100

From Oaklawn Stud

Fanellan b m (6yrs) Try My Best (USA) - Scotia Rose (Tap On Wood) Covered by Doyoun (Brian Grassick Bloodstock) 8,500

PRIVATE SALES

From Wraymount Stud

b f f Classic Music (USA) - Lady Aladdin (Persian Bold).......... (J F O'Malley) 6,000

Property of Mr Andrew Bannon

br or gr c f Ballad Rock - Right Cash (Right Tack)................ (Eddie O'Leary) 9,500

From Innismore Stud

b c f Treasure Kay - Finely Feathered (Prince Tenderfoot)............ (Cash) 2,500

Property of H H Aga Khan's Studs S.C., from Gilltown Stud

Shaikala (IRE) b f (3yrs) Doyoun - Shaiyra (Relko)......... (Emerald Bloodstock) 21,000

Property of Mr R J Powell M.R.C.V.S., from Wellington House Stud

Tapestry ch m (8yrs) Tap On Wood - Fear Naught (Connaught) Covered by Polish Patriot (USA).................. (Cash) 12,000

Property of J G Patterson, from Richmond Lodge Stud

ch c f Al Hareb (USA) - Jazirah (Main Reef) (B B A) 6,800

From Baro'g Stud

b c f Sayaarr (USA) - Khaki Campbell (USA) (Quack)............. (Tim O'Connor) 1,500

From Oaktree Lodge

ch f f Digamist (USA) - Royal Cloak (Hardicanute).... (David Minton Bloodstock) 3,200

952

ASCOT
Monday, November 22nd

Property of Mr F Cunliffe

Franklins Boy b y c Clantime - Sky Fighter (Hard Fought)............. (G Rees) 825

Property of Mr R Allen

Angelic Appeal b m (16yrs) Star Appeal - Angel's Hair (Le Haar).......... (Cash) 580

Property of Campbell Stud

Derring Miss ch m (11yrs) Derrylin - Katherina (Frankincense) Covered by Chilibang............. (David Branton) 460

Property of Mr A H Warren (Coombe Farm) Ltd

Pleasure Island ch m (10yrs) Dalsaan - Pleasure Boat (Be Friendly) Covered by Then Again.............. (Mr Mason) 1,050

Nonasalome ch m (11yrs) Absalom - Impromtu (My Swanee) Covered by Then Again................ (B Eccles) 650

Classic Times b m (10yrs) Dominion - Salt Of The Earth (Sterling Bay (SWE)) Covered by Then Again........ (B Eccles) 1,800

Property of Mr S J Moss

b y f Precocious - Dermerger (Dominion) .. (A S Reid) 1,250

Property of Mr & Mrs D A Hicks

b y f Petoski - Fair Atlanta (Tachypous) .... (Mrs N Smith) 1,350

Property of Mrs A Rothschild

b y f Dowsing (USA) - Spring Sparkle (Lord Gayle (USA))................... (Cash) 500

Property of a Partnership, from Vale Bloodstock

b y f Interrex (CAN) - Lappet (Kampala) .... (B Wilkinson) 500

953

Property of Mr C James

b y c Hard Fought - Roses Galore (USA) (Stage Door Johnny)........... (Cash) 900

Property of a Gentleman

b y f Salse (USA) - Peak Squaw (USA) (Icecapade (USA))............. (Cash) 675

Property of Messrs P E & M J Hawkins

b y f Lochnager - Megara (USA) (Thatching) (A Stringer) 1,200

b y g Tinoco - Caven Rock (Ballad Rock) ... (Mrs M L Hewitt) 725

Property of Mrs H George

Saucy Sprite b m (11yrs) Balliol - Sprightly Sprite (Babur) Covered by Ardross .... (Cash) 2,100

b f f Lighter - Saucy Sprite (Balliol) .... (B Eccles) 850

b f (2yrs) Rakaposhi King - Domtony (Martinmas)......................... (Cash) 850

From Berkeley House Stables

New Wood b f (2yrs) Ra Nova - Wood Heath (Heres)................. (Cash) 950

Sprig Muslin br y f Ra Nova - Wood Heath (Heres)......................... (Cash) 450

Property of Holt Manor Farm Partners

b f (2yrs) Pragmatic - Landa's Tipple (Jimsun)......................... (Cash) 1,100

954

To Dissolve a Partnership

Rose Of Medina ch f (3yrs) Hadeer - Red Rose Garden (Electric)... (G J Phillips) 1,300

Property of Mr James Cumiskey

b g (3yrs) Dominion - Elzaahirah (Irish Ball (FR))................... (Equitus Ltd) 1,500

Property of Mr E R Thomas

Salda b g (4yrs) Bustino - Martinova (Martinmas).................. (P J Hobbs) 8,000

Property of Needwood Stud

Moorland Dancer (IRE) b f (2yrs) Common Grounds - Dance A Jig (Dance In Time (CAN))..................... (B Pearson) 1,400

Property of a Partnership, from Whitsbury Manor Stables

White Flash b f (2yrs) Sure Blade (USA) - Princess Matilda (Habitat)...... (Cash) 2,200

Property of a Gentleman

Commanche Star ch g (3yrs) Commanche Run - Lehzen (Posse (USA)) .... (Mr Gilham) 575

Property of Houndswood Stud

Threeofus gr g (3yrs) Robellino (USA) - Teacher's Game (Mummy's Game).... (J Chapman) 1,500

Property of Darley Stud Management Co Ltd, from Marriott Stables

Shiro b c (3yrs) Fabulous Dancer (USA) - Miss Shirley (FR) (Shirley Heights)..... (G Macchi) 8,200

Property of Darley Stud Management Co Ltd, from Summerdown Stables

Teen Jay b c (3yrs) Teenoso (USA) - Spoilt Again (Mummy's Pet)...... (F J Bush) 4,200

Property of Mr Khalifa Dasmal, from Oak Stables

Kefahi (IRE) ch g (2yrs) Kefaah (USA) - Shomoose (Habitat)....... (G Macchi) 9,200

955

Property of Darley Stud Management Co Ltd, from Stanley House Stables

Smuggler's Point (USA) b g (3yrs) Lyphard (USA) - Smuggly (USA) (Caro)......... (Roger Ingram) 14,000

Property of a Gentleman

Silky Magna b f (2yrs) Farajullah - Bella Magna (Mr Fluorocarbon)............. (David Branton) 1,400

Hostile Invader (USA) b g (3yrs) Irish Tower (USA) - August Days (USA) (In Reality) (Sheila Thomas) 1,700

Brave Hero (USA) b g (3yrs) Our Native (USA) - Decision (USA) (Resound) ..... (Helen Taylor) 525

Resist The Force (USA) br g (3yrs) Shadeed (USA) - Countess Tully (Hotfoot) ...... (Geoffrey Howson Bloodstock) 1,400

Property of a Partnership

Sea Prodigy b g (4yrs) Precocious - Aunt Judy (Great Nephew)..... (S Brunson) 1,350

Property of Mr C P Billot

Master Dancer b g (6yrs) Mashhor Dancer - Silent Dancer (Quiet Fling) (Mr Dyson) 5,200

Property of Highclere Stud Ltd

Mockingbird ch f (2yrs) Sharpo - Mountain Bluebird (USA) (Clever Trick (USA)).... (D Wilson) 1,700

Property of a Partnership

Barbary Reef (IRE) b g (5yrs) Sarab - Brown's Cay (Formidable (USA)) ...... (Mr Manners) 1,550

Property of a Gentleman, from Kremlin House Stables

Mr Moriarty (IRE) ch g (2yrs) Tate Gallery (USA) - Bernica (FR) (Caro) .... (A L Forbes) 1,350

Parrot Cage b g (2yrs) Fools Holme (USA) - Blue Parrot (FR) (Lyphard) (C Popham) 575

956

Property of Mr G Lewis

Dancing Diamond (IRE) b f (3yrs) Alzao (USA) - Shay Tien (Gunner B) .... (Brooke Sanders) 4,000

Property of a Gentleman

Great Indy ch f (3yrs) Vaigly Great - Indian Flower (Mansingh (USA))..... (T John) 525

To Dissolve a Partnership

Tyrian Purple (IRE) b h (5yrs) Wassl - Sabrine (Mount Hagen (FR)) .... (T J Naughton) 5,000

Ain'tlifelikethat gr h (6yrs) Godswalk (USA) - Blue Alicia (Wolver Hollow) .... (T J Naughton) 2,000

Property of Mr M Sturgis

Romanian (IRE) ch g (5yrs) Sallust - Cailin D'Oir (Roi Soleil)...... (Rona Knowles) 925

Property of Her Majesty The Queen

Red Point b f (2yrs) Reference Point - Red Shoes (Dance In Time)..... (K Bishop) 5,800

Property of Mr M E Wates

Mischievous Mead b f (2yrs) Reprimand - Island Mead (Pharly (FR)) (Equitus Ltd) 750

Property of a Partnership

Tea Boy b c (2yrs) Doyoun - Tea Rose (Moorestyle)........ (Michael Barden) 500

Concinnity (USA) b c (4yrs) Hello Gorgeous (USA) - Cincinnity (USA) (Shareef Dancer (USA))................. (Cash) 1,500

Nymph Errant b f (3yrs) Be My Guest (USA) - Shirley Superstar (Shirley Heights) ... (George Knight) 775

957

From Bonita Racing Stables

Noted Strain (IRE) b g (5yrs) Gorytus (USA) - Almuadiyeh (Thatching)....... (Cash) 2,100

To Dissolve a Partnership

Only Fools b g (2yrs) Midyan (USA) - Dame Scarlet (Blakeney)..... (M J Bateman) 650

Blowing (USA) b g (3yrs) Lear Fan (USA) - Sleek Lassie (USA) (Northern Prospect (USA)).................. (N Carlisle) 1,250

Property of Mr C David Harrison

Dynamitella b f (3yrs) Sayf El Arab (USA) - Stubble (Balidar) (R D & P A Radmore) 2,600

To Settle a Dispute

Lyph (USA) b g (7yrs) Lypheor - Scottish Lass (Scotland)........ (Mark Reeves) 1,800

To Settle an Account

Blushing Times b g (8yrs) Good Times (ITY) - Cavalier's Blush (King's Troop)....... (S L Pinney) 1,900

Property of Pigeon House Stud

Heavenly Helen ch f (2yrs) Faustus (USA) - Teacher's Game (Mummy's Game).... (Cash) 625

Property of Fayzad Thoroughbred Ltd

Faynaz ch h (7yrs) Tumble Wind (USA) - Ceduna (FR) (Right Tack) .... (Badger Farm) 1,400

Property of Mr Clive Colquhoun

Knox's Corner ch g (8yrs) Green Shoon - Sister Fiona (Tepukei)... (Roger Curtis) 1,250

To Settle an Account

Quail Creek br g (8yrs) Rymer - Casa Estella (Jock Scott)............. (Mr Muston) 1,400

958

To Dissolve a Partnership, from Cedar Point Racing Stables

Cathos (FR) b g (8yrs) Bellman (FR) - Charming Doll (Don (ITY))...... (Cash) 850

Property of Mr A Moore

Summerhill Scoop ch g (5yrs) Castle Keep - New Top (New Brig) (Mrs R J Burrow) 550

Property of Mr Andrew Wilson

Gentleman Angler ch g (10yrs) Julio Mariner - San Salvador (GER) (Klairon) ..... (Stephen Merrick) 1,300

Property of Mr W D Edwards

Robcourt Hill br g (8yrs) Callernish - Cooney Island (Distinctly (USA)) (Richard Read) 2,500

To Dissolve a Partnership

Matawai (NZ) b g (6yrs) Prince Simbir (NZ) - Tudor Maid (NZ) (Monitor).. (D Barons) 8,200

Ramlosa (NZ) b g (9yrs) Uncle Remus (NZ) - Sereniwai (NZ) (Golden Plume)........ (G M Thomson) 2,600

Sharp Prince ch g (4yrs) Sharpo - Jungle Queen (Twilight Alley) (R A B Brassey) 4,600

Property of Mr M J Lee

Nomadic Prince (IRE) b g (4yrs) Fairy King (USA) - Go Anywhere (Grundy)........ (P Smith) 1,150

To Dissolve a Partnership

Fire And Reign (IRE) b g (5yrs) Sandhurst Prince - Fine Form (USA) (Fachendon) (Cash) 2,100

Property of Mrs Patterson

Punky Knave bl g (7yrs) Rough Lad - Prince's Daughter (Black Prince) ...... (John Barnard) 1,700

959

Property of Mr W B Imison

Shannon King (IRE) ch g (5yrs) Boyne Valley - Miss Royal (King's Company)........ (David Smith) 2,300

From West House Farm

Snaefugl ch g (6yrs) Deep Run - Wren's Lass (Wren's Hill)....... (Mr Pearson) 1,350

Selskar Abbey (IRE) b g (4yrs) Lancastrian - Rising Dipper (Golden Dipper).. (Cash) 1,600

See What I Mean ch g (6yrs) Le Bavard (FR) - Proximity (Gulf Pearl)..... (Cash) 1,150

Celtic Fountain (IRE) br g (5yrs) Royal Fountain - Celtic Serenity (Proverb) .... (P W Hiatt) 1,300

Willy Waffles (IRE) ch h (5yrs) Orchestra - Gayles Approach (Strong Gale)........ (C D Lilley) 900

Property of Mr R Dalton

Derwent Mist b m (7yrs) Majestic Streak - Minimist (Bilsborrow).. (Miss S Clarke) 1,150

Property of Mr R Bootle

Sea Search ch g (6yrs) Deep Run - Gift Seeker (Status Seeker)........ (Cash) 1,750

Property of Mr D Bowen

b f (4yrs) Remezzo - Passionate (Dragonara Palace)............ (Patrick Chamings) 2,400

b g (4yrs) Conargo - Office Girl (Official) ... (Cash) 1,750

960

Property of Mr K Lewis

b g (4yrs) King Of Spain - Second Generation (Decoy Boy)...... (Richard Bailey) 1,750

Property of Mrs V O'Brien
Oberons Butterfly b g (6yrs) Full Of Hope - Y I Oyston (Dublin Taxi) (Mr Chapman) 2,500
b f (3yrs) Today And Tomorrow - Alexzena (Upper Case)........... (K Lamacraft) 825
Property of Mr M Stevens
Alpine Trooper ch g (6yrs) Burslem - Alpina (King's Troop)............ (H Hobson) 1,200
Property of Mrs L Seale
High Street Blues b g (6yrs) White Prince (USA) - Crendle Hill (French Beige) .... (J Pullen) 425
Property of a Partnership
Kittinger b g (12yrs) Crash Course - Mandaloch (Mandamus).. (Mrs T Pritchard) 1,200
Property of Miss Ann Flemming
Pilloco b g (7yrs) Rontino - Hardy Lady (Hard Tack).................. (Cash) 1,400
Property of Miss C Walker
Freemount Minstrel (IRE) ch g (5yrs) Black Minstrel - List To Me (Pamroy)........ (J P Rawlins) 1,400
Property of Mr P G F Oliver
Abso b g (5yrs) Absalom - Classical Vintage (Stradavinsky)............. (D Jermy) 800
Property of Mr R Stone
Canbrack (IRE) b g (4yrs) Glenstal (USA) - Cottage Style (Thatch)... (R Simpkins) 650

961

Property of Mr B C Plaistowe
Soneeto br g (7yrs) Teenoso (USA) - Flying Bid (Auction Ring (USA)).... (W Tudor) 1,250
To Dissolve a Partnership
Syd's Brother b g (7yrs) Tachypous - Hollow Creek (Tarqogan).. (John Leyland) 1,000
Property of Mr Nick Duke
Athassel Abbey b g (7yrs) Tender King - Pearl Creek (Gulf Pearl)........ (R Lee) 1,500
Property of Mr L Sopp
b f (4yrs) Green Ruby (USA) - Miss Serlby (Runnett).................. (R Murray) 2,000
Property of Mrs L Sopp
b f (4yrs) Green Ruby (USA) - Fashion Lover (Shiny Tenth)............. (R Murray) 1,600
Property of Mrs A Lee
Scawsby Lees ch m (9yrs) Stanford - Pay Roll (Burglar)........... (J S Rawlins) 2,000
To Dissolve a Partnership
Emerald Ears ch f (4yrs) Dublin Lad - Impish Ears (Import)............... (J Styles) 750
Property of Mr C D Lilley
Miss Hokee Pokee ch m (6yrs) Winden - Deep Depression (Weathercock)...... (J Pullen) 875
To Dissolve a Partnership
b g (6yrs) Cruise Missile - Saucey Violet (Saucey Kit)............... (S Mullins) 1,100
Property of Mr P W Hiatt
Sixash Star ch g (7yrs) Mr Fluorocarbon - Waving Corn (Undulate (USA)) .... (J Styles) 550
Property of a Gentleman
Algaihabane (USA) b g (7yrs) Roberto (USA) - Sassabunda (Sassafras (FR))......... (D C Roberts) 650

962

NEWMARKET
Tuesday, November 23rd (Yearlings)

Property of Mr C J Rowlands, from Yeoland Stud
ch y c Sharpo - Taj Victory (Final Straw).... (N Callaghan) 8,500
Property of Messrs C D Bulmer & G T Gaines, from Valial Trading
ch y c Infantry - Gohar (USA) (Barachois (CAN))...................... (B B A) 1,200
br or gr y c Kalaglow - Rashah (Blakeney).. (B B A) 2,700
Property of Mr M Broughton, from Broughton Bloodstock
b y c Dance Of Life (USA) - Sharp Flash (Kris).................. (B B A (Italia)) 10,000
Property of Baron F C von Oppenheim, from Allan Perry, Agent
b y c Dominion - Eastern Command (USA) (Far Out East (USA))..... (S G Norton) 2,500
Property of Mr & Mrs B T Chambers
b y c Hadeer - Betsy Bay (FR) (Bellypha)... (Cash) 1,300
b y c Sayf El Arab (USA) - Hot Momma (Free State).......... (W G M Turner) 3,200
Property of Bacton Stud
ch y c Bairn (USA) - Abdera (Ahonoora).... (Cormac McCormack Associates) 1,700
ch y f Presidium - Missish (Mummy's Pet) (Delta Bloodstock Management) 7,000
Property of Fluorocarbon Bloodstock Ltd, from Chippenham Lodge Stud
b y c Robellino (USA) - My Greatest Star (Great Nephew).......... (C Williams) 8,400

963

From Glebe Stud
ch y c Master Willie - Moulin Rapide (USA) (Roberto (USA))............. (B B A) 3,200
Property of Mr & Mrs S W Dawson, from Mottram St Andrew Stud
ch y f Persian Heights - Silent Girl (Krayyan) .... (B B A) 3,000
Property of Mr P Locke, from Crimbourne Stud
ch y f Master Willie - Antoinette Jane (Ile de Bourbon (USA)).... (Gay Kelleway) 2,500
From Woodditton Stud
b y f Compliance (USA) - Our Marie (USA) (Our Native (USA)) (Mlle Bollock-Badel) 3,600
Property of Mr & Mrs A B Barraclough, from Sentinels Stud
b y f Puissance - Princess Story (Prince de Galles)... (Will Edmeades Bloodstock) 4,200
Property of Mrs Harrington, from Tim Vigors (Agent)
b y c Indian Ridge - Daniella Drive (USA) (Shelter Half (USA))..... (J Fanshawe) 25,000
From Kilnamoragh Stud, Ireland
ch y c Conquering Hero (USA) - Alitos Choice (Baptism)............................ (Cormac McCormack Associates) 8,400

b y c Conquering Hero (USA) - Doppio Filo (Vision (USA)). . . . . . (Lord Huntingdon) 2,100

Property of Mr & Mrs Leo Collins, from Ennistown Stud, Ireland

b y c Ajraas (USA) - Romantic Love (Sovereign Path). . . . . (J T Doyle) 6,000

Property of Ballykisteen Stud Ltd, Ireland (Agent), from Ballykisteen Stud, Ireland

b y c Superpower - Hanna Alta (FR) (Busted). . . . . (B B A) 2,000

964

Property of Ballykisteen Stud Ltd, Ireland, from Ballykisteen Stud, Ireland

b y f Posen (USA) - Tajniak (USA) (Irish River (FR)) (Brian Grassick Bloodstock) 9,000

Property of Jeremy Green & Sons, from Bickmarsh Stud

b y c Forzando - Chalet Girl (Double Form) (R Voorspuy) 3,600

Property of Jeremy Green & Sons and Mrs A D Fanshawe, from Bickmarsh Stud

b y c Ballad Rock - All Hat (Double Form) . . (Peter Doyle Bloodstock) 23,000

Property of Woodhaven Stud

b y c Roi Danzig (USA) - Noble Flirt (Kings Lake (USA)) . . . . (Conti Bloodstock Services) 9,000

Property of R J Powell, from Wellington House Stud

b y c Taufan (USA) - Tapestry (Tap On Wood). . . . . (B B A) 4,300

Property of a Partnership, from Tilstone Lodge Stud

gr y c Absalom - As Sharp (Sharpo) . . . . (J Berry) 3,100

From Waterside Stud, Ireland

ch y c Glenstal (USA) - Mattira (FR) (Rheffic (FR)). . . . . (Panetta Bloodstock) 8,600

Property of Mr R P Williams, from Scorrier House Stud

b y c Robellino (USA) - Irish Isle (Realm) . . . (Cormac McCormack Associates) 14,000

From Catridge Farm Stud

b y f Mazilier (USA) - Mo Ceri (Kampala) . . . (Cash) 3,200

From Rathasker Stud, Ireland

ch y c Persian Heights - Derring Dee (Derrylin) . . . . (Cormack McCormack Associates) 9,000

b y f Pennine Walk - Eimkar (Junius (USA)) (Lord Huntingdon) 3,800

b y f Petorius - Sybaris (Crowned Prince (USA)). . . . . (P Howling) 10,500

965

Property of Fulling Mill Stud

br y f Prince Sabo - Brassy Nell (Dunbeath (USA)). (S Moore) 6,000

Property of a Partnership, from Glen Andred Stud

b y c Petong - Balearica (Bustino) (J Berry) 6,200

From Golden Vale Stud, Ireland

ch y c Waajib - Regal Rhapsody (Owen Dudley). . . . . (Cash) 5,600

From Killeenlea Stud, Ireland

b y c Magical Strike (USA) - Fortera (FR) (Sanctus II). . . . . (M Bastard) 4,600

From Redpender Stud, Ireland

b y f Persian Bold - Vielle (Ribero). . . . . (Gay Kelleway) 10,000

ch y c Kefaah (USA) - Come To Tea (IRE) (Be My Guest (USA)). . . . . . (Pat Doyle) 10,000

From Stetchworth Park Stud

b y f North Briton - Diana's Bow (Great Nephew). . (Conti Bloodstock Services) 1,000

ch y f Hadeer - Baltic Leap (USA) (Northern Dancer). . . (Conti Bloodstock Services) 3,000

b y c North Briton - Sarah's Love (Caerleon (USA)). . . . . (W R Muir) 2,800

Property of Majors Racing International, from Angley Stud

b y f Dominion - Bugle Sound (Bustino). . . . (B B A) 8,000

966

Property of Mr J M Greetham, from Gazeley Stud

b y f Blakeney - Crusader's Dream (St Paddy). . . . (Conti Bloodstock Services) 2,600

ch y f Most Welcome - Port (Blakeney). . . . (B B A) 1,000

Property of Mr T R Lock, from Kingwood Stud

ch y c Weldnaas (USA) - Polly's Teahouse (Shack (USA)). . . . . (B B A) 3,200

Property of Miss Jean O'Regan, from Rathcannon House Stud, Ireland

ch y c Waajib - Talking Shop (General Assembly (USA)). . . . . (T M Jones) 2,000

Property of Mr Joseph O'Regan, from Rathcannon House Stud, Ireland

ch y f Al Hareb (USA) - Velinowski (Malinowski (USA)). . . . . (B B A) 4,000

Property of Southcourt Stud

b y f Most Welcome - Rosalka (ITY) (Relko) (Conti Bloodstock Services) 1,000

b y c Aragon - San Marguerite (Blakeney) . . (Peter Doyle Bloodstock) 3,200

From Ballyhimikin Stud, Ireland

ch y c Jareer (USA) - Ludovica (Bustino) . . . (B B A (Italia)) 6,400

Property of Mrs Mary Taylor, from Red House Stud

Rosa Bonheur b y f Absalom - Masirah (Dunphy). . . . . (B B A) 7,200

From Rathbarry Stud, Ireland

b y f Alzao (USA) - Festival Of Magic (USA) (Clever Trick (USA)) . . . . (Mrs Amanda Skiffington) 11,500

b or br y c Nishapour (FR) - Kimiya (USA) (Sir Ivor). . (Conti Bloodstock Services) 2,800

967

From Rathbarry Stud, Ireland (Agent)

b y c Jareer (USA) - Yetta (Ragusa) (B B A) 1,600

Property of Fonthill Farms, from Whitsbury Manor Stud

ch y c Sharpo - Sequin Lady (Star Appeal) (Panetta Bloodstock) 28,000

Property of Whitsbury Manor Stud

b y f Distant Relative - Aphrosina (Known Fact (USA)). . . . . (D Chappell) 2,400 b y c Rock City - Tittlemouse (Castle Keep) (D Ffrench-Davis) 1,000

Property of a Partnership, from Whitsbury Manor Stud

b y f Distant Relative - Blue Guitar (Cure The Blues (USA)).............. (B B A) 5,000

Property of Mr G Dickinson, from Britton House Stud

b y c Emarati (USA) - Massawa (FR) (Tennyson (FR)).............. (N Quinlan) 1,400

Property of Bolton Grange Stud, from Trickledown Stud

b y f Fairy King (USA) - Foliage (Thatching) (Gay Kelleway) 4,600

Property of Mr D L C Hodges, from Trickledown Stud

b y f Teenoso (USA) - Miranda Julia (Julio Miranda).. (Conti Bloodstock Services) 3,600

From Trickledown Stud

b y c Efisio - Wimosa (Mossborough)...... (B Palling) 5,000

Property of Lofts Hall Stud

b y f Reprimand - Pussy Foot (Red Sunset) (J Naughton) 4,000

968

Property of Mr Joseph G O'Brien, from Ballycummin Castle Stud, Ireland

b y c Doyoun - Rozmiyn (Caerleon (USA)).. (P C Le Metayer) 4,000

Property of Hamilton Bloodstock (UK) Ltd, from Barnwood Stud

Reborn Star b y f Most Welcome - Broken Wide (Busted)......................... (Conti Bloodstock Services) 4,600

Property of Total Asset Ltd, from Burley Heyes Stud

b y c Try My Best (USA) - Tracy's Sundown (Red Sunset)........... (T A Scothern) 8,200

From Craigueshoneen Stud, Ireland

b y f Exactly Sharp (USA) - Children's Hour (Mummy's Pet)........ (P W Bennett) 3,600

Property of C P Ranson Esq, from Grove Farm Stud

b y f Saint Cyrien (FR) - Sunclad (FR) (Tennyson (FR))............ (N Faulks) 2,700

Property of a Partnership, from Kiltake Stud, Ireland

ch y c Roi Danzig (USA) - Miss Flirt (Welsh Pageant)........... (Axel Donnerstag) 3,000

From Milford Park Stud

b y c High Kicker (USA) - Tafaana (FR) (Top Ville)......................... (B B A) 6,000

Property of Afarn Stud, from Old Mill Stud

b y f Siberian Express (USA) - Glas Y Dorlan (Sexton Blake)............. (B Palling) 3,900

Property of Raylex Co Ltd, Old Mill Stud

b y f Shavian - Rheinza (Rheingold)........ (C Gordon-Watson Bloodstock) 3,800

Property of Uronspare Ltd, from Old Mill Stud

b y f Pharly (FR) - Springwell (Miami Springs).......... (Stuart C Williams) 2,200

969

Property of a Partnership, from Old Mill Stud

b y f Dowsing (USA) - Tsungani (Cure The Blues (USA))............... (R Guest) 1,500

Property of R S Cockerill (Farms) Ltd, from Providence Stud

ch y c Good Times (ITY) - Cateryne (Ballymoss)........................ (B B A) 1,000

From Rosemount House Stud, Ireland

b y c Dominion Royale - Cala-Vadella (Mummy's Pet)...................... (David Minton Bloodstock) 9,000

Property of Mrs Frances Ryan, from Sunnyhill Stud, Ireland

ch y f Fayruz - Carriglegan Girl (Don)...... (E Ryan) 3,700

Property of Swaines Hill Stud

b y c Distant Relative - Drama School (Young Generation)........... (B B A) 1,000

From Glidawn Stud, Ireland

br y f Gallic League - Drora (Busted)....... (G Burke) 3,900

From Theakston Stud

b y f Simply Great (FR) - La Neva (FR) (Arctic Tern (USA))........... (C B A) 1,700

b y c Dancing Dissident (USA) - Princesse Legere (USA) (Alleged (USA))......... (D Ffrench-Davis) 3,100

Property of The Exors of the late Mrs V Hue-Williams, from Woolton House Stud

ch y f Most Welcome - Fabulous Luba (Luthier)................... (R Curtis) 2,700

b y f Tragic Role (USA) - Lady Capilano (Nebbiolo)................... (B B A) 1,000

b y c Law Society (USA) - Reine D'Beaute (Caerleon (USA))..................... (Peter Doyle Bloodstock) 17,000

970

Property of Marston Stud

ch y c Aragon - Bargouzine (Hotfoot)...... (Conti Bloodstock Services) 4,400

Property of Marston Stud & Grange Nomanees, from Marston Stud

b y f Alzao (USA) - Diavolina (USA) (Lear Fan (USA))............ (N A Graham) 14,000

Property of Greenland Park Stud, from Collin Stud

b y c Rock City - Corley Moor (Habitat).... (Gay Kelleway) 15,500

Property of Letts Green Farm, from Collin Stud

b or br y f Prince Daniel (USA) - Granny's Birthday (Young Generation)... (B B A) 1,000

From Collin Stud

ch y f Night Shift (USA) - Judeah (Great Nephew)................ (Julie Cecil) 17,000

b y c Fayruz - Sorrow (Wolver Hollow)..... (Panetta Bloodstock) 1,000

Property of Mr C W Rogers, from Collin Stud

b y f Tirol - Ultimate Dream (Kafu)........ (R Phillips) 1,600

From Collin Stud

b y c Danehill (USA) - Charmina (FR) (Nonoalco (USA))............ (Willie Browne) 12,500

Property of a Partnership, from Batsford Stud

b y f Fairy King (USA) - Purchase Paperchase (Young Generation).. (C Gordon-Watson Bloodstock) 26,000

Property of Tarworth Bloodstock Investments Ltd, from Genesis Green Stud

b y f Danehill (USA) - Flying Fairy (Bustino) (Knut Eng) 5,000

971

Property of Mr A Gibson, from Warren Park Stud

b y c Rock City - Bridestones (Jan Ekels) .. (David Minton Bloodstock) 36,000

From Hilltown Stud, Ireland

b y f Danehill (USA) - Joma Kaanem (Double Form)........... (R J McCormick) 17,000

b y c Dancing Dissident (USA) - Soucaro (Rusticaro (FR))...... (R J McCormick) 5,000

From Side Hill Stud

b y c Kris - Thakhayr (Sadler's Wells (USA)) (J Fanshawe) 25,000

From Haras du Quesnay, France

Kafkaienne (FR) b y f Groom Dancer (USA) - Key Role (Be My Guest (USA))........ (J Dunlop) 5,400

(USA) b y c Bering - Looks Sensational (USA) (Majestic Light (USA)).......... (Conti Bloodstock Services) 6,200

From Barronstown Stud, Ireland

b y f Royal Academy (USA) - Our Duckling (USA) (Quack (USA)) .... (Conti Bloodstock Services) 5,200

Property of a Gentleman, from Warren Park Stud

b y f Sadler's Wells (USA) - Braneakins (Sallust) .... (German International Bloodstock) 12,000

Property of Mr J G Vaughan, from Warren Park Stud

br y f Dowsing (USA) - Thessaloniki (Julio Mariner).................. (K T Ivory) 1,600

From Highclere, U S A Jeffry Morris, (Agent)

(USA) ch y c Imp Society (USA) - Beauty Hour (USA) (Bold Hour) .... (Peter Doyle Bloodstock) 5,800

(USA) b y c Alleged (USA) - Painted Molly (USA) (Painted Wagon (USA)).. (C B A) 32,000

(USA) b y c Imp Society (USA) - Irish Action (USA) (Irish Tower (USA)) .... (Panetta Bloodstock) 13,500

972

Property of Islanmore Stud, Ireland, from Islanmore Stud, Ireland (Agent)

(USA) b y c Arctic Tern (USA) - Blue Dance (FR) (Green Dancer (USA))........... (Roberto Borchia) 10,500

Property of Islanmore Stud, Ireland

b y f In The Wings - I Want My Say (USA) (Tilt Up (USA))............. (J Bethell) 9,000

From Corduff Stud, Ireland

b y c Alzao (USA) - Arbour (USA) (Graustark) .... (C Gordon-Watson) 15,000

(USA) b y c Affirmed (USA) - Eunice Mullis (T.V Lark)........ (Panetta Bloodstock) 20,000

b y f Dancing Dissident (USA) - Lady Tyrrel (Pall Mall).................... (B B A) 4,100

(USA) b y c Green Forest (USA) - Minstrel Guest (Be My Guest (USA)) .... (Derby Bloodstock) 27,000

From Ted Voute, Agent

ch y c Chief's Crown (USA) - Batna (USA) (Cyane)................. (Paul Nataf) 34,000

(USA) gr y f Star de Naskra (USA) - Din (USA) (Drone)........ (B B A (Ireland)) 20,000

Property of Mr Alan Ricketts, from Ted Voute, Agent

b y c Infantry - What A Present (Pharly (FR)) .... (Peter Doyle Bloodstock) 8,400

Property of Highclere Stud Ltd, from Side Hill Stud

b y c Midyan (USA) - Celebrity (Troy) ...... (Peter Doyle Bloodstock) 5,100

973

From Cobhall Court Stud (Agent)

Scottish Ball (FR) b y c Cricket Ball (USA) - Petticoat Lane (FR) (Baldric II)......... (Peter Doyle Bloodstock) 15,000

Polylead (FR) ch y c Lead On Time (USA) - Polyphase (FR) (Bikala)............... (Cormac McCormack Associates) 25,000

From Furnace Mill Stud

b y c Roi Danzig (USA) - Grass Court (Thatch (USA)) .... (Peter Doyle Bloodstock) 11,000

b y c Mon Tresor - Kellys Risc (Pitskelly)... (Cormac McCormack Associates) 8,800

Property of a Partnership, from Furnace Mill Stud

b y f Statoblest - Louise Moillon (Mansingh (USA))...... (Mrs Amanda Skiffington) 6,000

To Dissolve a Partnership, from Furnace Mill Stud

(USA) ch y c Woodman (USA) - Najidiya (USA) (Riverman (USA)) (M Tompkins) 33,000

Property of Mr R L Burton, from Furnace Mill Stud

ch y f Royal Academy (USA) - Tricky Note (Song).................. (W Haggas) 27,000

From Staunton Lodge Stud, County Limerick, Ireland

b y c Cyrano de Bergerac - Perfect Chance (Petorius).................... (C B A) 10,500

From Knocktoran Stud, Ireland

b y c Darshaan - North Forland (FR) (Northfields (USA)) .... (Kildare Thoroughbred Services) 37,000

From Lanwades Stud

b y f Nishapour (FR) - La Commere (USA) (Dr Fager)....... (Panetta Bloodstock) 5,500

974

Property of Round Hill Stud, Ireland

b y c Taufan (USA) - Madame Nureyev (USA) (Nureyev (USA))..... (D Woods) 15,000

From Partridge Close Stud

b y c Fayruz - Scotch Rocket (Roan Rocket) (Lynn Lodge Stud) 2,700

(USA) b or br y c Imperial Falcon (CAN) - Ivory Lady (USA) (Sir Ivor)..... (B B A) 7,200

Property of Overbury Stud

b y c Pharly (FR) - Buzzbomb (Bustino) .... (M A O'Toole) 13,000

Property of Mount Coote Stud, Ireland

(USA) b y c Private Thoughts (USA) - Abyssinie (FR) (Dancer's Image (USA)) (B B A) 8,000

From Glenvale Stud, Ireland

b y c Ela-Mana-Mou - Dorado Llave (USA) (Well Decorated (USA)) (J Delahooke) 15,000

Property of Lordship and Egerton Studs
b y f Royal Academy (USA) - Turn The Key (Home Guard (USA)) .... (Lynn Lodge Stud) 8,000
b y f Law Society (USA) - Gourgandine (Auction Ring (USA)) .... (Cormac McCormack Associates) 32,000
b y c Royal Academy (USA) - Vernonhills (Hard Fought).......... (B B A (Italia)) 8,200

To Dissolve a Partnership, from Neustrian Associates Haras du Buff, France
ch y f Irish River (FR) - Mermaid's Purse (CAN) (Devil's Bag (USA)) .... (Lillingston Bloodstock) 50,000

975

Property of a Partnership, from Mellon Stud, Ireland
(USA) ch y c Arctic Tern (USA) - Alicia's Lady (USA) (Al Nasr (USA)) .... (P Kelleway P L T Partnership) 18,000
b y f Northern Jove (CAN) - Outofthebluebell (USA) (Red Ryder (USA)) (Gay Kelleway) 15,000
(USA) ch y c Bering - Passerine (USA) (Dr Fager). . (P Kelleway P L T Partnership) 10,000

From Mellon Stud, Ireland
(USA) ch y f Beau Genius (CAN) - Time And Tide (USA) (Mr Leader (USA)). . (Cash) 10,500

Property of a Partnership of Meon Valley Stud, from Meon Valley Stud
b y c Chief Singer - Mumtaz Flyer (USA) (Al Hattab (USA))............. (K T Ivory) 4,600

Property of Shadwell Estate Co Ltd, from Derrinstown Stud, Ireland
Albarih ch y c Old Vic - Ostora (USA) (Blushing Groom (FR)) .... (Conti Bloodstock Services) 4,000
Thwaab b y c Dominion - Velvet Habit (Habitat)........... (Ballymorris Stud) 4,600

From Ballysheehan Stud, Ireland
b y c High Estate - Crown Witness (Crowned Prince (USA)) .... (Miss Margaret O'Toole) 9,200

Property of a Partnership, from Ballyhampshire Stud, Ireland
b y f Forzando - Piney Lake (Sassafras (FR)) (Mrs Amanda Skiffington) 4,300

From Ballyhampshire Stud, Ireland
ch y f Thatching - Scuba Diver (Kings Lake (USA))....... (Peter Doyle Bloodstock) 6,000

976

From Leinster Stud, Ireland
b y f Sovereign Water (FR) - Kirmiz (Silver Shark).......................... (B B A) 1,000

Property of Springfield Thoroughbred Syndicate, from Ardenode Stud, Ireland
b y f Dancing Dissident (USA) - Miss St Cyr (Brigadier Gerard).................... (Peter Doyle Bloodstock) 11,000

Property of a Gentleman, from Burn House Stud
b or br y f Primo Dominie - Shamasiya (FR) (Vayrann)........................ (B B A) 2,200

From Churchtown House Stud, Ireland
ch y c Waajib - Mirhar (FR) (Sharpen Up) .. (Peter Doyle Bloodstock) 5,000

From Kildaragh Stud, Ireland
b y c Dominion Royale - Back To Earth (FR) (Vayrann)................ (P C Haslam) 9,800

Property of a Partnership, from Mary James (Cotswold Stud Farms)
b y f Royal Academy (USA) - Glory Of Hera (Formidable (USA)). . (Anthony Penfold) 39,000

Property of Mr P J H Wills, from Mary James (Cotswold Stud Farms)
b y f Simply Great (FR) - Inesdela (Wolver Hollow)..... (Mrs Amanda Skiffington) 5,700

From Mary James (Cotswold Stud Farms)
b y c Last Tycoon - Marquina (FR) (Posse (USA))................ (P C Haslam) 12,000

From Pipers Hill Stud, Ireland
br y c Petorius - Walkyria (Lord Gayle (USA))..................... (J Pearce) 10,000

From Yeomanstown Stud, Ireland
ch y c Statoblest - Apprila (Bustino) .... (Pat Doyle) 8,000
b y c Scenic - Embroidery (Lords (USA)) ... (Cash) 15,500
b y c Pharly (FR) - Mums (Mummy's Pet) .. (N Callaghan) 14,000
ch y f Common Grounds - Paradise Bird (Sallust)...................... (B B A) 15,000

977

Property of a Gentleman, from Lavington Stud
b y c Aragon - Aimee Jane (USA) (Our Native (USA))............. (J Hayden) 7,000
(USA) gr y c Manila (USA) - Casessa (USA) (Caro)............ (Anthony Penfold) 15,500

From Lavington Stud
ch y c Imp Society (USA) - Jenastic (USA) (Dynastic (USA))............. (B B A) 12,500

Property of a Gentleman, from Lavington Stud
(USA) b y f Imperial Falcon (CAN) - One Tough Lady (USA) (Mr Prospector (USA)).................. (P Sheehan) 6,400

Property of Mr M L Page, from Westerlands Stud
b y c Danehill (USA) - Perfect Alibi (Law Society (USA)). . (Elmhurst Bloodstock) 12,500

From Wheelersland Stud
ch y c Be My Chief (USA) - Fair And Wise (High Line)............. (P J L Wright) 6,600

Property of Tibthorpe Stud
b y f Rambo Dancer (CAN) - Djimbaran Bay (Le Levanstell)............ (D Woods) 7,000

Property of Silfield Bloodstock, from Southburg Manor Stud
b y f Thatching - Biddy Mulligan (Ballad Rock)..... (Brian Grassick Bloodstock) 8,400

Property of a Partnership, from Southburg Manor Stud
ch y f Persian Heights - Militia Girl (Rarity) (B B A) 5,600

Property of Messrs Darley & Townsend, from Daleside Stud
ch y c Old Vic - No Restraint (Habitat) ..... (B B A (Italia)) 12,000

978

Property of Sir Gordon Brunton, from North Munstead Stud

b y f Pharly (FR) - Rose Parade (Thatching) (B B A) 2,500

Property of Mr C H Bothway, from Old Hall Farm

b y f Primo Dominie - Amina (Brigadier Gerard)........................ (R Guest) 11,000

From Hill Walk Stud, Ireland

b y c Cyrano de Bergerac - Mind The Beat (Gulf Pearl)................ (Pat Doyle) 8,500

From Old Meadow Stud, Ireland

b y f Waajib - Red Line Fever (Bay Express) (B B A (Italia)) 3,500

From Carrigbeg Stud, Ireland

gr y c Petorius - Mysterious Lady (Melyno) (J Glover) 6,800

ch y c Astronef - Perle's Fashion (Sallust).. (Jacqueline Doyle) 2,800

From West Stow Stud

b y f Shareef Dancer (USA) - Bahamas Princess (Sharpen Up)........ (B B A) 8,600

Property of a Partnership, from Hedgeholme Stud

b y c Daring March - Kept Waiting (Tanfirion)........................ (C B A) 7,200

Property of Willow Investments, from Hedgehome Stud

ch y c Shavian - My Willow (Tap On Wood) (B B A) 2,400

Property of Mr B Stevens, from Pine Ridge Farm Ltd

b y c Sizzling Melody - Contadina (Memling) .... (B B A) 3,000

979

Property of a Partnership, from Pine Ridge Farm Ltd.

b y c Cyrano de Bergerac - Daima (Dominion)........ (Mrs Amanda Skiffington) 10,500

Property of Ewar Stud Farms Ltd, from Ewar Stud Farms

ch y c Bold Arrangement - Thalassa (IRE) (Appiani II)................. (C Brittain) 3,500

Property of Mr E P Jameson, from Sledmere Stud

b y f Insan (USA) - Godly Light (FR) (Vayrann).................... (B B A) 1,000

Property of Benson Stud

b y f Infantry - Phyl (Ballad Rock).. (B B A) 3,200

b y c Prince Daniel (USA) - Rising Star (St Paddy)................. (J Pennick) 2,200

Property of Summertree Stud

b y c Celestial Storm (USA) - Deflowered (Red God).................. (B B A) 1,000

Property of Mr E S Knape, from Park Farm Stud

b y c Bustino - Collage (Ela-Mana-Mou)..... (C Gordon-Watson Bloodstock) 5,500

b y c Be My Chief (USA) - Shalta (FR) (Targowice (USA))........... (J Glover) 5,000

Property of a Gentleman

b y c Double Schwartz - Kasarose (Owen Dudley)..... (Peter Doyle Bloodstock) 10,000

Property of a Gentleman, from Qualitair Stud

gr y c Dominion - Altaia (FR) (Sicyos (USA)) (W Haggas) 12,500

980

Property of Bamberg Bloodstock Holdings Ltd, from High Onn Stud

ch y c Scottish Reel - Sense Of Pride (Welsh Pageant)......... (N D Tinkler) 8,400

Property of a Partnership, from Pinkerton Stud

b y f Shareef Dancer (USA) - Holy Day (Sallust).................. (C Brittain) 8,500

Property of a Partnership, from College Farm

b y c Nomination - Sea Aura (Roi Soleil) ... (B B A) 4,300

b y c Damister (USA) - So Precise (FR) (Balidar).................. (T Robson) 3,800

Property of Mr C R Withers, from Southill Stud

b y f Dominion - Love Street (Mummy's Pet)......... (Peter Doyle Bloodstock) 5,800

Property of Mrs V M Withers

b y c Warrshan (USA) - Sweet Home (Home Guard (USA)).... (Mlle Bollock-Badel) 7,000

Property of Mr R J Turner, from Wards Hill Stud

b y f Beveled (USA) - Sister Rosarii (USA) (Properantes (USA))........... (B B A) 2,000

From Church Farm Stud

b or br y c Rock City - Norska (Northfields (USA))..................... (J Pearce) 13,500

Property of Mrs Mette Campbell-Andenaes, from Andbell Stud

b or br y f Mango Express - Andbell (Trojan Fen)......... (Peter Doyle Bloodstock) 4,800

981

NEWMARKET
Thursday, November 25th
(Foals)

Property of Dandy's Farm Stud

gr c f Petong - Altara (GER) (Tarim)........ (J McKeever Bloodstock) 11,000

b c f Prince Sabo - Royal Agnes (Royal Palace).............. (Richard Fahey) 5,200

From Barcham Farm Stud

b f f Rambo Dancer (CAN) - Lady Eccentric (IRE) (Magical Wonder (USA))......... (John Coupland) 2,300

Property of Mr L Audus

b f f Siberian Express (USA) - Silk St James (Pas de Seul)....... (Equine Services) 5,000

Property of Mrs C Humphrey, from Orchard Rise

ch f f Sayf El Arab (USA) - Princess Zeddera (English Prince)...... (John Coupland) 3,800

Property of Mrs J Langmead, from Stoughton Stud

b c f Warrshan (USA) - Gentle Stream (Sandy Creek)..... (Margaret O'Toole) 4,200

Property of a Partnership

gr f f Petong - Thevetia (Mummy's Pet) ... (M Sharkey) 8,800

Property of Mr J L Acklam, from Thorncliffe Stud

ch c f Petoski - M Kelly (Longleat (USA))... (Laurie Smalley) 1,400

Property of Mr B D Cantle

ch f f Risk Me (FR) - Mummy's Chick (Mummy's Pet)........ (Phillip Young) 2,500

ch c f Risk Me (FR) - Muninga (St Alphage) (Margaret O'Toole) 6,200

982

From Wyards Stud

ro f f Sharrood (USA) - Sheznice (IRE) (Try My Best (USA))..... (David Hammett) 8,200

Property of Mr T Minahan, from Hawkwind Stud

b f f Timeless Times (USA) - Ash Amour (Hotfoot)....... (Elmhurst Bloodstock) 1,400

b f f Keen - Shaieef (IRE) (Shareef Dancer (USA))..................... (K Powter) 5,600

Property of North Cheshire Trading & Storage Ltd, from Hedgeholme Stud

b f f Petong - Bo'babbity (Strong Gale) .... (B B A) 7,600

Property of Mr S C Palmer, from Heath Farm Stud

b or br c f Robellino (USA) - Graved Lax (Home Guard (USA)) .... (Brillbury Hall Farm) 1,900

Property of Lovegroves Stud

br c f Damister (USA) - Superfina (USA) (Fluorescent Light (USA))...... (Cash) 4,800

Property of Mr David Walker, from Boundary Farm Stud

b c f Indian Ridge - No Hard Feelings (IRE) (Alzao (USA)).... (Yeomanstown Stud) 28,000

b f f Indian Ridge - Henpot (IRE) (Alzao (USA))................ (Fittocks Stud) 9,200

Property of Mrs Sheila Walker, from Boundary Farm Stud

ch c f Dominion Royale - Shining Wood (Touching Wood (USA)).... (R O'Ryan) 2,200

Property of Swaines Hill Stud

ch f f Be My Chief (USA) - Josephine Gibney (High Top) .... (Bishop Wilton Stud) 3,000

983

Property of Mr C R Withers, from Southill Stud

ch c f Chilibang - Golden October (Young Generation)................... (Cash) 5,000

b c f Robellino (USA) - Lamees (USA) (Lomond (USA)) .... (Peter Doyle Bloodstock) 9,500

b c f Emarati (USA) - Magic Milly (Simply Great (FR))............... (R O'Ryan) 5,800

Property of Mr A Walder, from Toat Farm and Stud

ch c f Superlative - Glorietta (USA) (Shadeed (USA))......... (J W Parker) 2,200

Property of a Partnership, from Toat Farm and Stud

ch or gr c f Keen - Miss Suntan (Bruni) .... (P A C Bloodstock) 6,500

Property of Llety Farms

b c f Merdon Melody - Lake Superior (Right Tack)............... (Joanna Morgan) 1,500

ch c f Bold Owl - Cymbal (Ribero).......... (G R Butterfield) 2,600

b f f Merdon Melody - Tripolitaine (FR) (Nonoalco (USA))..... (John Coupland) 4,100

Property of a Partnership, from Hunsley House Stud

b c f Rambo Dancer (CAN) - Skarberg (FR) (Noir Et Or)................ (R Dickin) 2,000

Property of Summertree Stud

b c f Anshan - Nosey (Nebbiolo) (D Taylor) 8,800

984

Property of Miss E Aldous, from Southburgh Manor Stud

b c f Reprimand - Fine Asset (Hot Spark) .. (Sarah Lakin) 3,200

b c f Statoblest - Summer Eve (Hotfoot) ... (John Ferguson Bloodstock) 6,600

b c f Statoblest - Miami Melody (Miami Springs)........ (Ashtown Bloodstock) 7,600

Property of Miss D Birkbeck, from Southbury Manor Stud

ch f f Anshan - Miss Trilli (Ardoon) .... (Rodvic Ltd) 4,200

Property of Messrs S Rea & E Watts, from Eggarton Manor Stud

ch c f Safawan - Syaf As Houses (Sayf El Arab (USA)) .... (Ballymorris & Caherass Studs) 9,600

Property of Mr & Mrs N F Tebbutt, from Hollow Farm Stud

ch c f Music Boy - One Sharper (Dublin Taxi)........ (J McKeever Bloodstock) 7,400

Property of Mr P Madelein, from Old Mill Stud

(BEL) br c f Formidable (USA) - Heavy Land (FR) (Recitation (USA)) .... (John Ferguson Bloodstock) 12,000

(BEL) br c f Sayf El Arab (USA) - Two Seasons (Martinmas).. (T J Naughton) 1,100

Property of SARL Ewar Stud Farms Ltd, France, from Ewar Stud Farms

b f f Local Talent (USA) - My Mother's Eyes (FR) (Saint Cyrien (FR))..... (P O'Neill) 6,600

Property of Ewar Stud Farms Ltd, France, from Ewar Stud Farms

ch f f Shavian - Sunset Reef (Mill Reef (USA)).................. (T G Holdcroft) 5,200

985

From Hever Castle Stud

b c f Nomination - Cadi Ha (Welsh Pageant) .... (R A Popely) 2,200

Property of Lockinge Stud

br f f Rock City - Freely Given (Petingo) ... (K D Crabb) 880

b f f Nomination - Mosso (Ercolano (USA)) (David Cosgrove) 2,700

ch c f Charmer - Salt Of The Earth (Sterling Bay (SWE)).. (J McKeever Bloodstock) 3,500

Property of a Partnership, from Oakshott Stud

b c f Sharpo - Scotch Thistle (Sassafras (FR))............... (Aston Park Stud) 6,800

ch c f Sharrood (USA) - Priors Dean (Monsanto (FR))........... (Mrs M Woolgar) 2,700

b f f Salse (USA) - Unsuitable (Local Suitor (USA))........... (Stratford Place Stud) 7,600

b f f Faustus (USA) - Key In The Ring (Pyjama Hunt)...... (Conti Bloodstock) 1,550

Property of Dr Barry Lewis, from Bungeons Farm

ch c f Indian Ridge - Red Riding Hood (FR) (Mummy's Pet)..... (Fiona Needham) 14,000

Property of Coln Valley Stud, from The National Stud

b f f Aragon - Miss Foxtrot (Bustino) ...... (David Minton Bloodstock) 1,700

986

Property of Mrs T F Phillips, from The National Stud

b f f Rock City - Antum (Hittite Glory) ..... (J Williamson) 8,000

Property of The National Stud

b f f Keen - Constant Companion (Pas de Seul).................. (T J Naughton) 6,200

ch f f Chilibang - Emma's Double (Double Form).......... (R Barnes Bloodstock) 1,500

ch f f Keen - Sisola (USA) (Coastal (USA)).. (R J McCormick) 5,600

gr c f Rock City - Vacherin (USA) (Green Dancer (USA))........................ (David Minton Bloodstock) 7,200

ch f f Chilibang - Etreinte (USA) (Nureyev (USA)).......... (The Rathasker Stud) 1,800

Property of a Partnership, from Lilliemore Stud

br f f Shaadi (USA) - Bellagio (Busted)..... (John Ferguson Bloodstock) 14,000

Property of Messrs T H Evans & Sons, from Goldfoot Farm Stud

b c f Puissance - Village Idol (Blakeney).... (S Rendle) 5,200

Property of Coxland Stud

b f f Forzando - Eaves (Thatching)......... (David Minton Bloodstock) 5,800

b c f Nomination - Formidable Dancer (Formidable (USA))....... (Richard Fahey) 4,600

987

Property of Miss D Birkbeck, from Southburgh Manor Stud

b f f Sizzling Melody - Raintree Venture (Good Times (ITY)) (Miss E Streatfield) 3,700

From Southburgh Manor Stud

ch c f Forzando - Finally (Final Straw)...... (John Ferguson Bloodstock) 20,000

Property of Mrs R Chapman, from Southburgh Stud

b c f Dowsing (USA) - Tendency (Ballad Rock).......... (Lostford Manor Stud) 3,000

Property of Mr G Dickinson M.R.C.V.S., from Britton House Stud

b c f Emarati (USA) - White African (Carwhite)...................... (T Jarvis) 2,200

Property of Miss Y Weldon, from Britton House Stud

br c f Emarati (USA) - Spanish Chestnut (Philip Of Spain) (Lostford Manor Stud) 2,500

Property of New Hall Estate Farm (L A C Ashby), from Britton Hosue Stud

ch c f Emarati (USA) - Sandy Looks (Music Boy).............. (Conti Bloodstock) 2,200

Property of Rockhouse Farms Ltd, from Bearstone Stud

b c f Puissance - Florentynna Bay (Aragon) (Jill Lamb Bloodstock) 7,800

Property of Bearstone Stud

b f f Primo Dominie - Femme Formidable (Formidable (USA)).................. (Seymour Bloodstock) 7,500

From Highclere Stud, U.S.A.

(USA) b f f Imp Society (USA) - Precentage (USA) (Vaguely Noble)................ (John Ellis & Son) 8,000

(USA) b f f Imp Society (USA) - Urakawa (USA) (Roberto (USA))... (M Hawkett) 7,200

988

Property of Miss E Drax, from Millbrook Stud

ch c f Rock City - Waveguide (Double Form) .... (Knocklong House Stud) 5,800

b or br f f Anshan - Visible Form (Formidable (USA))........ (Mrs J Langmead) 4,200

ch f f Polar Falcon (USA) - Spirit Of India (Indian King (USA))................... (Cheveley Park Stud) 6,000

b f f Batshoof - Sacred Mountain (St Paddy) .... (Cash) 5,500

Property of Clarendon Park Stud, from Ted Voute, Agent

b c f Most Welcome - Lominda (IRE) (Lomond (USA))............ (R Dickin) 640

ch c f Sayf El Arab (USA) - My Polished Corner (IRE) (Tate Gallery (USA))...... (David Minton Bloodstock) 10,000

Property of Mrs J H Weller-Poley, from Boxted Hall Stud

ch c f Keen - Razor Blade (Sharp Edge)..... (Pengam Investments Ltd) 4,000

b f f Indian Ridge - Pomade (Luthier)...... (C Gordon-Watson Bloodstock) 9,200

Property of a Partnership, from Longstones Stud

b c f Slip Anchor - Nordic Beauty (USA) (Northjet).......... (Conti Bloodstock) 3,500

Property of J B Fenwick & Son, from Longstones Stud

gr c f Siberian Express (USA) - Superior Quality (Star Appeal) ...... (C Gordon-Watson Bloodstock) 4,000

989

Property of Sir Eric Parker, from Crimbourne Stud

b c f Deploy - Morina (USA) (Lyphard (USA)) .... (Emerald Bloodstock) 11,500

Property of Highfield Stud Ltd, from Barleythokrpe Stud

b or br f f Petong - Quick Profit (Formidable (USA))........... (Ketton Ashwell Ltd) 11,000

b c f Petong - Toccata (USA) (Mr Leader (USA))................ (Miss M Green) 9,000

Property of a Partnership, from Glen Andred Stud

b c f Petong - Mrs Waddilove (Bustino).... (Equine Services) 4,600

br f f Petong - What A Pet (Mummy's Pet) (L Cashman) 20,000

Property of Mr John Needham, from Glen Andred Stud

b f f Rock City - Lurking (Formidable (USA)) (Elmhurst Bloodstock) 11,000

Property of Brook Stud Ltd, from Brook Stud
b f f Shavian - Feather Flower (Relkino)..... (Roseland Stables) 5,800
gr f f Kalaglow - Mevlevi (Shareef Dancer (USA))............. (Conti Bloodstock) 2,400

Property of Courtown Stud
b c f Shareef Dancer (USA) - Almitra (Targowice (USA))......... (Dick Morgan) 8,000
b c f Batshoof - Bold Tango (FR) (In Fijar (USA))................... (Dr M Boffa) 17,000
br c f Sharpo - Corr Lady (Lorenzaccio) .... (K D Crabb) 3,000
b or gr c f Deploy - Lady Regent (Wolver Hollow)........................(Cash) 2,200
gr c f Petong - Steffi (Precocious).......... (Dick Morgan) 10,500

990

From Graigueshoneen Stud, Ireland
ch c f Common Grounds - Labista (Crowned Prince (USA))....... (B B A) 19,000
gr c f Petong - Light Thatch (Thatch (USA)) (B B A) 42,000

Property of Mr R M West, from Carlton Stud
b c f Hatim (USA) - My Ginny (Palestine) .. (Cash) 3,600

Property of Mr & Mrs S W Dawson, from Mottram St Andrew Stud
ch f f Classic Music (USA) - Foreno (Formidable (USA))............ (Fittocks Stud) 12,000
b c f Law Society (USA) - Silent Girl (Krayyan).... (Peter Doyle Bloodstock) 10,500

Property of Mr C J R Trotter, from Attington Stud
b c f Anshan - Anhaar (Ela-Mana-Mou)..... (David Minton Bloodstock) 10,000
b f f Midyan (USA) - Spin Dry (High Top)... (Dick Morgan) 7,600

From Rosetown Farm, Ireland
b f f Magical Strike (USA) - Drowsy Maggie (Tumble Wind (USA))... (C J Wheeler) 4,000
ch c f Roi Danzig (USA) - Island Goddess (Godswalk (USA))..................... (Agridale Enterprises) 3,600
ch c f Mac's Imp (USA) - No Dowry (Shy Groom (USA)).. (The Aramstone Stud) 5,600

991

Property of Mrs R Blake, from Rosetown Farm, Ireland
b f f Magical Strike (USA) - Snappy Dresser (Nishapour (FR))...... (John Coupland) 3,000

From Cheveley Park Stud
ch f f Music Boy - Piccadilly Etta (Floribunda)............ (Mrs J Langmead) 6,400
b f f Prince Sabo - Bloom Of Youth (IRE) (Last Tycoon)............ (Ted Voute) 2,800

From Collin Stud
ch f f Sharpo - Angels Are Blue (Stanford) (Collin Stud-Foal Syndicate) 3,600

Property of Mr C W Rogers, from Collin Stud
br c f Sayf El Arab (USA) - Dulcidene (Behistoun)........... (Peter Molony) 2,200
b c f Statoblest - Ultimate Dream (Kafu) ... (Ashtown Bloodstock) 12,500

From Collin Stud
b c f Pharly (FR) - Tabeeba (Diesis)........ (Bylon Farmers) 3,100

Property of Farmers Hill Stud
ch f f Statoblest - Corinthia (USA) (Empery (USA))............................(Cash) 6,000

Property of a Partnership, from Farmers Hill Stud
b f f Alzao (USA) - Insaf (USA) (Raise A Native)......... (Ashtown Bloodstock) 25,000

Property of Farmers Hill Stud
ch f f Statoblest - Kukri (Kris)............. (Geoffrey Howson Bloodstock) 8,200
b c f Puissance - Rambadale (Vaigly Great) (Cash) 6,600
b f f Most Welcome - Ranya's Pet (Busted) (Miss P A Clark) 2,800

992

From Woodditton Stud
b c f Damister (USA) - Believe The Chick (USA) (Believe It (USA)).. (T J Cooper) 3,600
b f f Batshoof - Salinity (NZ) (Standaan (FR)) .... (Taplin Lee & Cain Ltd) 2,000
b c f Sayf El Arab (USA) - Miss Orient (Damister (USA)) .... (Cormac McCormack Associates) 4,700

Property of Mr B Kennedy, from Meadowlands Stud
b f f Kefaah (USA) - Avidal Park (Horage) ... (Barouche Stud) 4,000

Property of Mr C Kennedy, from Meadowlands Stud
ch f f Soviet Lad (USA) - Candy's Sister (Great Nephew) .... (Mrs W H Gibson Fleming) 3,400
ch c f Simply Great - Now Then (Sandford Lad)........................ (Cash) 6,200

Property of Mr B Kennedy, from Meadowlands Stud
b c f Soviet Lad (USA) - Nozet (Nishapour (FR))....... (David Minton Bloodstock) 15,000

Property of Silfield Bloodstock, from Southburgh Manor Stud
b c f Anshan - Norfolk Serenade (Blakeney) (Will Edmeades) 25,000
b c f Governor General - Aleda Rose (Charlottown)........................ (Peter Doyle Bloodstock) 4,000
ch f f Mac's Imp (USA) - Ethel Knight (Thatch (USA)) .... (Springfield Thoroughbred Syndicate) 12,500

993

Property of a Partnership, from Tregavethan Manor Stud
ch c f Forzando - La Belle Princesse (Royal Match)......... (Emerald Bloodstock) 3,500

Property of R B Warren (Nancherrow Stud), from Tregavethan Manor Stud
ch c f Weldnaas (USA) - Divissima (Music Boy)..................... (Ballymorris Stud) 6,400
ch f f Prince Sabo - Lafrowda (Crimson Beau)........................... (Cash) 2,500

Property of Bearstone Stud
b c f Puissance - Flicker Toa Flame (USA) (Empery (USA))............. (C B A) 5,800

Property of a Gentleman, from Warren Park Stud

b c f Reprimand - Ashdown (Pharly (FR))... (Bearstone Stud) 6,200

Property of Stall Steigenberger, from Warren Park Stud

b c f Alzao (USA) - Kijafa (USA) (Chief's Crown (USA))... (Ashtown Bloodstock) 45,000

Property of Mr D L C Hodges, from Trickledown Stud

b c f Reprimand - So Bold (Never So Bold) (R Brunger) 2,500

b c f Beveled (USA) - Sparklingsovereign (Sparkler).... (Peter Doyle Bloodstock) 3,200

Property of Mr C Wiggins, from Trickledown Stud

b c f Reprimand - Hithermoor Lass (Red Alert)............ (Margaret O'Toole) 17,000

b c f Most Welcome - Poyle Princess (Valiyar)..................... (B B A) 6,500

994

Property of a Partnership, from Trickledown Stud

b c f Colmore Row - Into The Fire (Dominion).............. (P A C Bloodstock) 9,200

Property of Mr R L Cox, from Trickledown Stud

b c f Distant Relative - My Precious Daisy (Sharpo)............ (R J McCormick) 8,000

Property of Bristol Bloodstock Ltd., from Trickledown Stud

b c f Emarati (USA) - French Plait (Thatching)......................... (S T S) 8,000

b c f Beveled (USA) - Pink Mex (Tickled Pink)...... (David Minton Bloodstock) 9,000

Property of a Partnership, from Ham Cross Farm

ch f f Cadeaux Genereux - Try The Duchess (Try My Best (USA)) (Whitsbury Farm) 13,000

Property of Sexton Enterprises, from Ham Cross Farm

b c f Colmore Row - Hellene (Dominion)... (Camilla Horn) 1,000

Property of P & A G Venner, from Petches Farm

b c f Formidable (USA) - Baileys By Name (Nomination).................. (Cash) 10,000

b f f Anshan - Council Rock (General Assembly (USA)) .... (J McKeever Bloodstock) 5,500

ch f f Keen - Hasty Key (USA) (Key To The Mint (USA)).... (Jill Lamb Bloodstock) 13,000

b c f Indian Ridge - Valadon (High Line).... (Margaret O'Toole) 8,500

ch c f Most Welcome - Water Pageant (Welsh Pageant)......... (D Redvers) 4,800

995

From Meddler Stud

ch c f Indian Ridge - Billie Blue (Ballad Rock)....................... (B B A) 15,000

From Highclere Stud, U.S.A.

(USA) b c f Imp Society (USA) - Lady Kirtling (USA) (Kirtling).... (I A Balding) 13,500

(USA) ch f f Imp Society (USA) - Lady Limbo (USA) (Dance Spell (USA))...... (Britton House Stud) 8,500

(USA) ch f f Imp Society (USA) - Mrs Magnum (USA) (Nothjet)............ (Ballymorris & Caherass Studs) 9,500

(USA) b f f Imp Society (USA) - Sad Song (USA) (Roberto (USA)).............. (Sir Stephenson Hastings) 10,000

Property of Snowdrop Stud Co Ltd., from Sandley Stud

b c f Distant Relative - Lindfield Belle (IRE) (Fairy King (USA))............ (Cash) 3,000

To Dissolve a Partnership, from Nidd Park Stud

ch f f Kris - Noirmant (Dominion).......... (I V Matthews) 60,000

From Nidd Park Stud

b f f Pharly (FR) - Gwiffina (Welsh Saint)... (John Warren Bloodstock) 5,400

b f f Salse (USA) - Irish Cookie (Try My Best (USA))........... (Emerald Bloodstock) 3,000

b f f Sayf El Arab (USA) - Mana (GER) (Windwurf (GER))................... (Will Edmeades Bloodstock) 7,000

b c f Statoblest - Oriental Splendour (Runnett)... (C Gordon-Watson Bloodstock) 12,000

b f f Warrshan (USA) - Princess Dina (Huntercombe)............... (M Sharkey) 5,000

996

NEWMARKET
Friday, November 26th
(Foals)

Property of Alvecote Stud

b c f Puissance - Alvecote Lady (Touching Wood (USA))............ (D A Collins) 900

b f f Dominion - On The Top (High Top).... (D A Collins) 4,600

b c f Nicholas (USA) - Sawk (Sea Hawk II) (Conti Bloodstock) 1,200

b c f Puissance - Sally Delight (Homing) ... (S Rendle) 2,800

Property of Mr J Purcell

b c f Shareef Dancer (USA) - Possessive Lady (Dara Monarch)....... (J Purcell) 10,500

Property of R D Sears, from Hatchland Stud

ch c f Indian Ridge - Ballaquine (Martinmas) .... (Sarah Lakin) 13,000

Property of a Partnership, from Copgrove Hall Stud

b c f Kris - Siouan (So Blessed) (Guy Reed) 13,000

From Deep Lane Farm Stud

ch f f Primo Dominie - Maria Isabella (Young Generation).................. (Emerald Bloodstock) 7,000

ch c f Polar Falcon (USA) - Farewell Letter (USA) (Arts And Letters)... (S Rendle) 7,600

Property of a Partnership, from Old Mill Stud

b f f Slip Anchor - Positive Attitude (Red Sunset).................. (K Mercer) 4,600

b f f Slip Anchor - Forest Blossom (USA) (Green Forest (USA))...... (D Woods) 18,000

997

From Rathbarry Stud, Ireland

b c f Polish Patriot (USA) - It's Now Or Never (High Line)..... (J P Deroubaix) 10,500

From Rathbarry Stud, Ireland (Agent)
ch c f Classic Music (USA) - Beyond Words (Ballad Rock)........ (R J McCormick) 23,000
From Rathbarry Stud, Ireland
b c f Polish Patriot (USA) - Don't Be Cruel (Persian Bold)... (Amanda Skiffington) 20,000
From Rathbarry Stud, Ireland (Agent)
b c f Ron's Victory (USA) - Saint Cynthia (Welsh Saint).... (Emerald Bloodstock) 5,200
From Rathbarry Stud, Ireland
b or br c f Soviet Lad (USA) - Stop The Cavalry (Relko).. (Partridge Close Stud) 24,000
From Rathbarry Stud, Ireland (Agent)
ch c f Imperial Frontier (USA) - Unspoiled (Tina's Pet) .... (John Ferguson Bloodstock) 10,500
From Stetchworth Park Stud
ch f f Hadeer - Flamberge (Kris)............ (Hartford Bloodstock) 1,000
ch f f Hadeer - Ever Welcome (Be My Guest (USA))........ (G R Butterfield) 2,700
b c f Most Welcome - Girette (USA) (General Assembly (USA)) .... (Will Edmeads Bloodstock) 4,000
b c f Hadeer - Harvest Dance (Mill Reef (USA)) (Johnny McKeever Bloodstock) 3,200
b c f Damister (USA) - Ivory Waltz (USA) (Sir Ivor)........... (Conti Bloodstock) 1,800
b c f Dowsing (USA) - Way To Go (Troy)... (Emerald Bloodstock) 2,200
b c f Hadeer - Swift And Sure (Valdez (USA))............ (Ashton Park Stud) 1,700
ch c f Keen - Diana's Bow (Great Nephew) (Cash) 6,300

998

Property of Brook Stud Ltd, from Brook Stud
b c f Kalaglow - Pride Of Paris (Troy) ...... (M W Easterby) 1,700
b f f Be My Chief (USA) - Sea Fret (Habat) (B B A) 8,200
ch f f Shavian - Spinelle (Great Nephew)... (P Carter) 4,200
Property of R B Warren (Nancherrow Stud), from Tregavethan Manor Stud
ch f f Rock City - Lustrous (Golden Act (USA))........................ (B B A) 13,500
ch f f Weldnaas (USA) - Singalong Lass (Bold Lad (IRE))............. (J C Bird) 3,200
Property of a Partnership, from Tregavethan Manor Stud
b c f Weldnaas (USA) - Alcassa (FR) (Satingo)........................ (B B A) 10,000
Property of Mr and Mrs C Spencer-Phillips, from Doverlodge Stud
b f f Thatching - Kentfield (Busted)........ (Ashtown Bloodstock) 15,000
Property of a Partnership, from Bloomsbury Stud
b f f Dowsing (USA) - Pillowing (Golden Times (ITY)).................. (Cash) 1,800
Property of Mr and Mrs R Craddock, from Bloomsbury Stud
b f f Sharpo - Shadiliya (Red Alert) .... (Brian Grassick Bloodstock) 15,000
Property of a Partnership, from Bloomsbury Stud
Correct Form ch f f Master Willie - Top And Tail (USA) (Tilt Up (USA))...... (B B A) 1,700

999

From Swettenham Stud, Agent
b c f Law Society (USA) - La Toulzanie (Sanctus II)........... (G E M Wates) 10,500
From Mount Coote Stud, Ireland
b f f Nordico (USA) - Royal Respect (Kings Lake (USA)).......................... (David Minton Bloodstock) 5,000
b c f Cadeaux Genereux - Bristle (Thatch (USA))......................... (S T S) 8,000
b f f Thatching - Aunt Hester (IRE) (Caerleon (USA)).................... (John Ferguson Bloodstock) 28,000
b c f Green Desert (USA) - Civility (Shirley Heights)... (Lillington Bloodstock (Ire)) 32,000
Property of Mr and Mrs C Blackwell, from Langham Hall Stud
b c f Danehill (USA) - Artic Mistral (CAN) (Briartic (CAN)).... (Margaret O'Toole) 17,000
Property of Mr and Mrs T C Blackwell, from Langham Hall Stud
ch c f Be My Guest (USA) - Palmella (USA) (Grundy)... (David Minton Bloodstock) 5,800
Property of a Partnership, from Langham Hall Stud
b f f Mtoto - Lap Of Honour (Final Straw).. (K Prowter) 5,000
Property of Mr P V McCalmont, from Tally-Ho Stud, England
ch f f Ron's Victory (USA) - La Troienne (Henbit (USA))............. (S Rendle) 1,800
Property of a Partnership, from Tally-Ho Stud, England
ch f f Lycius (USA) - Vestal Flame (Habitat) (Amanda Skiffington) 14,000
b c f Keen - Jamaican Punch (IRE) (Shareef Dancer (USA))................ (B B A) 28,000
b c f Lycius (USA) - Inshirah (USA) (Caro).. (Darley Stud Management) 52,000

1000

Property of Mr P V McCalmont, from Tally-Ho Stud, England
b c f Danehill (USA) - Blasted Heath (Thatching)......................... (Shadwell Estate Company) 55,000
From Knocktoran Stud, Ireland
b c f Astronef - Angel Street (Comedy Star (USA))...................... (P Asquith) 5,000
ch c f Exactly Sharp (USA) - Bhama (FR) (Habitat)..... (H E Brooks & Sons Ltd) 5,600
b c f Common Grounds - Gale Warning (IRE) (Last Tycoon) (Margaret O'Toole) 26,000
ch c f Be My Guest (USA) - Miss Mulaz (FR) (Luthier) (Peter Doyle Bloodstock) 15,000
b c f Taufan (USA) - Unheard Melody (Lomond (USA)) .... (Will Edmeads Bloodstock) 26,000
Property of a Partnership, from Burton Agnes Stud
b c f Last Tycoon - State Ball (Dance In Time (CAN))......................... (Cormac McCormack Associates) 14,000
b c f Cadeaux Genereux - Tight Spin (High Top)......................... (B B A) 26,000
From Riverside Stud, Ireland
b f f Distinctly North (USA) - Miss Allowed (USA) (Alleged (USA))......... (B B A) 16,500

Property of Mr & Mrs P J Sands, from Grovewood Stud
ch c f Anshan - Angel's Sing (Mansingh (USA)).................... (S Rendle) 2,000
ch c f Lycius (USA) - Melanoura (Imperial Fling (USA)).......................... (David Minton Bloodstock) 32,000
ch f f Belmez (USA) - Ring Of Pearl (Auction Ring (USA))... (Lillingston Bloodstock) 14,000

1001

Property of Ian Glenton Bloodstock, from Grovewood Stud
b or br c f Rambo Dancer (CAN) - Spin Me Round (High Top)...... (Tim Easterby) 2,600
Property of a Partnership, from Grovewood Stud
b or br c f Absalom - Wyns Vision (Vision (USA)).............. (L T & M Foster) 8,400
b f f Batshoof - Agreloui (Tower Walk)..... (Allan Perry) 1,500
Property of Hockley Ltd, from Hockley House Stud
b f f Zalazl - Song Of Gold (Song)......... (J D Ward) 750
Property of a Partnership, from Raffin Stud
b c f Forzando - Ella Mon Amour (Ela-Mana-Mou).......... (Ashtown Bloodstock) 26,000
From Raffin Stud
b c f Scenic - Charmeuse (Cut Above)..... (C Gordon Watson Bloodstock) 5,000
Property of Mr & Mrs P Blacker, from Raffin Stud
b c f Rambo Dancer (CAN) - Aligote (Nebbiolo)..................... (S Rendle) 3,500
Property of M H D Madden and Partners, from Higher Tregawne Stud
b c f Be My Chief (USA) - Travel Magic (Henbit (USA))..... (Margaret O'Toole) 6,200
b f f Shareef Dancer (USA) - Travel Mystery (Godswalk (USA))... (E H Crow & Son) 9,400
b f f Rock City - Travel On (Tachypous).... (Jeremy Green & Sons) 10,500
b f f Reprimand - Travel Storm (Lord Gayle (USA))............. (Equine Services) 4,300

1002

Property of Benson Stud
b c f Prince Sabo - Hidden Asset (Hello Gorgeous (USA)) .... (Johnny McKeever Bloodstock) 5,400
b or br c f Safawan - Lady Leman (Pitskelly) .... (Fiona Needham) 15,000
ch c f Red Sunset - Free Rein (Sagaro) .... (Peter Doyle Bloodstock) 6,200
Property of Lt Col and Mrs R Bromley Gardner, from Kingtscote Park Stud
b c f Forzando - Ragged Moon (Raga Navarro (ITY))................ (B B A) 40,000
Property of Mrs Rita Kennedy, from Brownstown Lodge Stud, Ireland
b c f Thatching - Eskaroon (Artaius (USA)) (Brian Grassick Bloodstock) 27,000
Property of a Partnership, from Baroda Stud, Ireland
b c f Exactly Sharp (USA) - Debach Dust (Indian King (USA))..... (G E M Watts) 3,000
From Baroda Stud, Ireland
ch f f Maelstrom Lake - Woodcote Belle (Connaught)....... (Derby Bloodstock) 1,800
From Heatherwold Stud
b f f Siberian Express (USA) - Exceptional Beauty (Sallust)................ (Cash) 2,600
Property of Heatherwold Stud
b f f Rock City - Lyra (Blakeney) .... (Johnny McKeever Bloodstock) 3,500
Property of Arrow Farm and Stud Partnership (Part of a Dispersal),from Heatherwold Stud
b c f Mtoto - Lightning Legacy (USA) (Super Concorde (USA))............. (B B A) 19,000
b c f Sharrood (USA) - Cache (Bustino) .... (B B A) 7,000

1003

From Genesis Green Stud
ch c f Anshan - Ancona (USA) (Woodman (USA))............. (Michael Downey) 7,000
ch c f Keen - Santa's Queen (USA) (Sovereign Dancer (USA)) (Walton Grange) 3,700
Property of a Partnership, from Genesis Green Stud
b c f Puissance - Seattle Mama (USA) (Seattle Song (USA)) .... (Neil Edmeads Bloodstock) 14,000
Property of Mr Eric Dafydd, from Genesis Green Stud
b c f Governor General - Bright Stream (Cure The Blues (USA)) .... (Michael Downey) 3,200
From Woodditton Stud
ch c f Superlative - Superlife (USA) (Super Concorde (USA)) .... (Messrs Darley & Townsend) 13,500
ch c f Cadeaux Genereux - Penny Mint (Mummy's Game) .... (H E Brooks & Sons) 13,000
b c f Most Welcome - False Look (USA) (Alleged (USA))..................... (Cormac McCormack Associates) 7,200
Property of a Partnership, from Aston Park Stud
ch c f Weldnaas (USA) - Atlantic Line (Capricorn Line).......... (Mrs D B Mulley) 4,000
ch c f Weldnaas (USA) - Atlantic Air (Air Trooper)............... (Bryan Smart) 4,100
From Aston Park Stud
b f f Weldnaas (USA) - Classy Nancy (USA) (Cutlass (USA))..... (Bex Minister Ltd) 3,500
b f f Nicholas (USA) - Easterly Wind (Windjammer (USA))......... (I N A Bryant) 1,300
b c f Weldnaas (USA) - Superb Lady (Marcus Superbus)..... (Bryan Smart) 7,200

1004

Property of a Partnership, from Aston Park Stud
b f f Weldnaas (USA) - Final Attraction (Jalmood (USA))........ (Bryan Smart) 1,500
From Airlie Stud, Ireland
ch c f Double Schwartz - Abbeydale (Huntercombe)..................... (S T S) 8,000
b c f Fairy King (USA) - Cipriani (Habitat) ... (Amanda Skiffington) 36,000

gr f f Standaan (FR) - Frill (Henbit (USA))... (Kingwood Bloodstock) 7,000
b f f Shirley Heights - Summerhill (Habitat) (B B A) 15,500
ch f f Ela-Mana-Mou - Torriglia (USA) (Nijinsky (CAN))........ (M Sharkey) 5,800
b c f Salt Dome (USA) - Walliser (Niniski (USA))............... (P C Le Metayer) 14,000

From Kildaragh Stud, Ireland

ch c f Fayruz - Lightning Laser (Monseigneur (USA))......... (Ballymorris Stud) 9,200
b c f Posen (USA) - Jet Set Bunny (USA) (Northjet)........................ (C B A) 9,600
b c f Great Commotion (USA) - Gracieuse Amie (FR) (Gay Mecene (USA))........ (Margaret O'Toole) 20,000
b c f Priolo (USA) - Rousinette (Rousillon (USA))......... (Ashtown Bloodstock) 25,000
b c f Fayruz - Laughing Matter (Lochnager) (S Rendle) 6,500
b c f In The Wings - Mariella (Sir Gaylord).. (P M Hicks) 13,500

1005

From Cheveley Park Stud

b c f Never So Bold - Hope And Glory (USA) (Well Decorated (USA)) .... (Peter Doyle Bloodstock) 11,000
ch f f Never So Bold - Brilliant Timing (USA) (The Minstrel (CAN))............ (Cash) 6,500
ch c f Never So Bold - Irish Impulse (USA) (Irish River (FR))........... (W Jarvis) 10,500
b or gr c f Prince Sabo - Kala Rosa (Kalaglow).... (Broughton Bloodstock) 7,200
b c f Never So Bold - X-Data (On Your Mark)........... (Bishop Wilton Stud) 3,600

From West Blagdon

b f f Green Desert (USA) - Sweeping (Indian King (USA))......... (Equine Services) 42,000
b c f Marju (IRE) - Blinding (IRE) (High Top) (B B A (Ireland)) 70,000
b f f Sadler's Wells (USA) - Charming Life (Habitat)....... (Ashtown Bloodstock) 115,000

Property of International Thoroughbred Breeders, Inc., from Round Hill Stud, Ireland

b c f Taufan (USA) - Noble Treasure (USA) (Vaguely Noble) .... (P V & J P Jackson Partnership) 20,000
b c f Thatching - Bell Tower (Lyphard's Wish (FR)) (Brian Grassick Bloodstock) 35,000

1006

From Mary James (Cotswold Stud Farms)

ch c f Sharrood (USA) - Suva (USA) (Northjet)...................... (C Olsen Ltd) 2,600
ch c f Thatching - Blue Guitar (Cure The Blues (USA)) .... (Ballymorris & Caheiss Studs) 13,000
br or gr c f Sharrood (USA) - Sea Fairy (Wollow)..................... (J Chambers) 700

Property of Mrs C Van Anthony, from Stonebrook Stud, Ireland

b f f Marju (IRE) - Island Time (USA) (Bold Hour)......................... (S Burns) 9,400

Property of Mr J Martin-Smith, from Stonebrook Stud, Ireland

b c f Taufan (USA) - Silks Princess (Prince Tenderfoot (USA)) .... (Peter Doyle Bloodstock) 20,000
b c f Fairy King (USA) - Lightino (Bustino).. (Margaret O'Toole) 38,000
b c f Persian Bold - Pickety Place (Prince Tenderfoot (USA)) .... (Peter Doyle Bloodstock) 39,000

From Greenville House Stud, Ireland (Agent)

b c f Mac's Imp (USA) - Lady's Turn (Rymer)............................. (B B A) 7,000

From Swettenham Stud, Agent

b c f Tirol - Avra (FR) (Mendez (FR)) .... (Stilvi Compania) 4,600

Property of a Partnership, from West Stow Stud

br f f Reprimand - Artistic Licence (High Top)...................... (P Thorman) 6,200

1007

Property of Mr C Bothway, from Cotton Stud

b c f Shadeed (USA) - Good Thinking (USA) (Raja Baba (USA))................ (Patridge Close Stud) 30,000

From Castletown Stud, Ireland

b c f Soviet Star (USA) - Aldhabyih (General Assembly (USA))...... (J P Deroubaix) 10,500
b c f Don't Forget Me - Double Do (Derring-Do).................... (Forest Stud) 12,000
gr c f Darshaan - Safka (USA) (Irish River (FR))........................ (Cash) 11,000
ch c f Mac's Imp (USA) - Audenhove (GER) (Marduk (GER))............ (G Tana) 24,000
b f f Dancing Dissident (USA) - Sigym (Lord Gayle (USA)).... (Agridale Enterprises) 12,000
b c f Archway (IRE) - Polynesian Charm (USA) (What A Pleasure (USA)) .... (Margaret O'Toole) 14,000

Property of Mr and Mrs D A Hicks, from Buckhurst Stud

b c f Midyan (USA) - Champ D'Avril (Northfields (USA)) .... (London Thoroughbred Services) 30,000
b c f Lycius (USA) - Premiere Cuvee (Formidable (USA))........ (Horse France) 25,000
b or gr c f Dominion - Shot Stopper (Bellypha)...................... (B B A) 15,000

1008

Property of Tasia Ltd, from Norelands Stud

ch c f Royal Academy (USA) - Broadway Rosie (Abasalom)............ (C B A) 23,000

Property of David's Star Partnership, from Norelands Stud

b c f Mujtahid (USA) - David's Star (Welsh Saint)............. (B B A (Ireland)) 30,000

Property of Mr J Crisp, from Norelands Stud, Ireland

b c f Ballad Rock - Four-Legged Friend (Aragon) .... (Ballymorris & Caherass Studs) 25,000

Property of Exors of the late Major McCalmont, from Norelands Stud

b c f Taufan (USA) - Casla (Lomond (USA)) (B B A) 15,000
b c f Two Timing (USA) - Heads We Called (IRE) (Bluebird (USA))....... (C B A) 10,000
b f f Shaadi (USA) - Trinida (Jaazeiro (USA)) (B B A) 10,000

Property of Norelands Bloodstock, from Norelands Stud
b f f Darshaan - Tribal Rite (Be My Native (USA))..... (David Minton Bloodstock) 26,000
From Cheveley Park Stud
b c f Mtoto - Cerise Bouquet (Mummy's Pet)................ (R J McCormick) 16,000
Property of Mr D P Martin, from Cheveley Park Stud
b c f Music Boy - Carlton Glory (Blakeney) (B B A) 12,500
From Cheveley Park Stud
ch c f Polar Falcon (USA) - Hysterical (High Top)........ (Peter Doyle Bloodstock) 62,000

1009

Property of a Partnership, from Cheveley Park Stud
b c f Polish Precedent (USA) - Height Of Passion (Shirley Heights)............. (Broughton Homes Ltd) 38,000
ch f f In The Wings - Known Line (Known Fact (USA))........... (G A Haywood) 15,000
From Cheveley Park Stud
b c f Polar Falcon (USA) - Warning Light (High Top)...... (Ashtown Bloodstock) 105,000
ch c f Primo Dominie - Bambolona (Bustino) .... (Margaret O'Toole) 7,800
From Barronstown Stud, Ireland
b c f High Estate - Alpine Symphony (Northern Dancer) .... (Johnny McKeever Bloodstock) 13,000
b f f Thatching - Instinctive Move (USA) (Nijinsky (CAN)) .... (Brian Grassick Bloodstock) 25,000
b f f Fairy King (USA) - Breyani (Commanche Run)........ (Dr Klaus Rohde) 15,000
Property of Mr N Bryce-Smith, from Britton House Stud
b c f Emarati (USA) - Katie Scarlett (Lochnager)................... (B B A) 7,500
Property of New Hall Estate Farm (L A C Ashby), from Britton House Stud
b f f Forzando - Nice Lady (Connaught) .... (J Johnston) 5,200
Property of Mrs R J Nash, from Britton House Stud
b c f Bustino - Tomard (Thatching) .... (J C S Wilson) 1,500

1010

From Britton House Stud
b c f Forzando - Abbotswood (Ahonoora) .. (R J McCormick) 17,500
Property of a Partnership, from Britton House Stud
b c f Emarati (USA) - Gas Only (Northfields (USA))....... (Peter Doyle Bloodstock) 7,000
Property of Mr J Wynne-Morris, from Britton House Stud
b c f Forzando - Pagan Queen (Vaguely Noble)...................... (B B A) 12,500
Property of Mrs N Sampson, from Britton House Stud
b c f Forzando - Sunfleet (Red Sunset) .... (Will Edmeades Bloodstock) 27,000
Property of Mr M B Small, from Britton House Stud
ch c f Be My Chief (USA) - Maiyaasah (Kris) .... (Partridge Close Stud) 17,000
Property of Miss Lorraine Davies, from Britton House Stud
b c f Emarati (USA) - Hoop La (Final Straw) (David Minton Bloodstock) 6,000
Property of a Partnership, from West Moor Stud
b f f Kris - Fairy Flax (IRE) (Dancing Brave (USA))................. (L Sigsworth) 9,000
From Foxbrook Stud, Ireland
b c f Last Tycoon - Inshad (Indian King (USA))........... (Emerald Bloodstock) 14,000
b c f Mujtahid (USA) - Silly Tune (IRE) (Coquelin (USA)) (Patridge Close Stud) 38,000
Property of Mr P D Player, from Whatton Manor Stud
ch f f Anshan - Mary Bankes (USA) (Northern Baby (CAN)).............. (Geoffrey Howson Bloodstock) 4,200

1011

Property of Mr M J Worth, from Whatton Manor Stud
ch c f Be My Chief - Fire Risk (Thatch (USA))........................ (Cash) 9,000
Property of Mrs J Shipway-Pratt, from Whatton Manor Stud
b or br c f Nomination - Roman Blue (Charlottown)........... (D G Mason) 9,000
Property of Mr C Ford, from Whatton Manor Stud
b c f Alzao (USA) - Tea Rose (Moorestyle) (Conti Bloodstock) 10,000
Property of a Partnership, from Lavington Stud
b c f Green Desert (USA) - Alik (FR) (Targowice (USA))...................... (Brian Grassick Bloodstock) 58,000
Property of Mr J A Haverhals, from Lavington Stud
b c f Aragon - Anzeige (GER) (Soderini) .... (S T S) 6,600
Property of Sunley Stud Ltd, from Lavington Stud
b f f Aragon - Sunley Sinner (Try My Best (USA))............. (Axel Donnerstag) 5,700
Property of a Partnership, from Lavington Stud
b f f Aragon - Jolies Eaux (Shirley Heights) (Peter Doyle Bloodstock) 13,000
Property of Mr R P Williams, from Scorrier House Stud
b c f Anshan - Astolat (Rusticaro (FR)) ..... (John Ferguson Bloodstock) 16,000
b f f Be My Chief (USA) - Million Heiress (Auction Ring (USA)) .... (John Warren Bloodstock) 13,000
b c f Primo Dominie - Runelia (Runnett) ... (S Rendle) 6,000
b c f Indian Ridge - Song Grove (Song) .... (G Tana) 22,000

1012

Property of a Partnership, from Raffin Stud
b c f Danehill (USA) - Lyndonville (IRE) (Top Ville)........... (Ashtown Bloodstock) 47,000

Property of Melton Park & West Lodge Stud, to Dissolve a Partnership, from Raffin Stud

b c f Thatching - Prima Domina (FR) (Dominion)........................ (London Thoroughbred Services) 58,000

From Raffin Stud

b c f Emarati (USA) - Four Love (Pas de Seul)................. (Jack Doyle) 4,500

Property of Heathavon Stables Ltd, from Heathavon Stud

ch c f Risk Me (FR) - Astral Suite (On Your Mark)................. (Jack Doyle) 6,200

b c f Music Boy - Stepping Gaily (Gay Fandango (USA))......... (Jack Doyle) 9,400

ch c f Absalom - The High Dancer (High Line)................ (Bolton Grange) 6,200

Property of Little Peverels

b c f Distant Relative - Highly Polished (High Top).... (Whitsbury Manor Stud) 5,600

Property of mr James Burridge, from Ab Kettleby Stud

ch f f Kind Of Hush - Hodsock Venture (Major Portion)............ (J Zilenski) 1,750

1013

NEWMARKET
Saturday, November 27th
(Foals)

Property of Mr G E Amey, from Chatley Stud

b c f Weldnaas (USA) - Safe House (Lyphard (USA))....... (J E Chambers) 3,200

Property of Mr E J B Maude, from Etchingham Stud

b c f Indian Ridge - Hannie Caulder (Workboy)........................... (B B A) 18,000

Property of Wickfield Stud Ltd, from Wickfield Stud

ch c f Rahy (USA) - Gaijin (Caerleon (USA)) (H Alexander) 60,000

From Knocklong House Stud, Ireland (Agent)

b c f Be My Guest (USA) - Caro Lady (Rusticaro (FR))........................ (Kingwood Bloodstock) 13,000

From Catridge Farm Stud

b c f Efisio - Moharabuiee (Pas de Seul) ... (Amanda Skiffington) 23,000

ch c f Governor General - Sorcha (IRE) (Shernazar)................... (B B A) 2,500

Property of a Partnership, from Catridge Farm Stud

b f f Slip Anchor - Tura (Northfields (USA)) (Geoffrey Howson Bloodstock) 24,000

From Catridge Farm Stud

ch c f Indian Ridge - Alanood (Northfields (USA)) (C Gordon-Watson Bloodstock) 30,000

Property of a Partnership, from Catridge Farm Stud

b c f Formidable (USA) - Great Aim (Great Nephew)...... (Kingwood Bloodstock) 15,000

Property of Commander S Emmet, from Catridge Farm Stud

b f f Governor General - Nuit de Vin (Nebbiolo)...................... (A de Vos) 1,700

1014

Property of Mr D S W Blacker

ch f f Forzando - Hat Hill (Roan Rocket).... (Joseph Johnston) 4,200

Property of Stud-On-The-Chart

b c f Rock City - Lady Warninglid (Ela-Mana-Mou)................ (Bolton Grange) 11,000

ch c f Prince Sabo - Joli's Girl (Mansingh (USA))....... (Peter Doyle Bloodstock) 19,000

ch c f Bluebird (USA) - Riveryev (USA) (Irish River (FR))....... (Panetta Bloodstock) 8,000

Property of a Partnership, from Stud-On-The-Chart

b c f Indian Ridge - Trull (Lomond (USA)) .. (Kingwood Bloodstock) 10,000

Property of Stud-On-The-Chart

b c f Classic Music (USA) - Ultra Vires (High Line)..... (John Ferguson Bloodstock) 8,500

Property of Dunchurch Lodge Stud Co, from Dukes Stud

ch c f Be My Chief (USA) - Collapse (Busted)... (David Minton Bloodstock) 13,000

b c f Shavian - Collide (High Line) .... (Janet Chaplin) 3,600

ch c f Pharly (FR) - Sixslip (USA) (Diesis)... (Yeoland Stud) 2,600

b c f Niniski (USA) - Stedham (Jaazeiro (USA))........................ (Cash) 10,500

b c f Sharpo - Swift Return (Double Form) (Conti Bloodstock) 9,500

1015

To Dissolve a Partnership, from Fawley Stud

ch f f Risk Me (FR) - The Boozy News (USA) (L'emigrant (USA)) .... (David Minton Bloodstock) 3,200

Property of Blue Blood Investments, from Woodcote Stud

b c f Shadeed (USA) - Skidmore Girl (USA) (Vaguely Noble)............. (B B A) 17,000

Property of Bryanstown House Stud, Ireland

ch f f Polish Patriot (USA) - Glendora (Glenstal (USA)).... (Conti Bloodstock) 6,200

b c f Marju (IRE) - Royaleffort (Dunphy).... (Mercury Bloodstock) 5,200

b f f Last Tycoon - Soyata (Bustino) (B B A) 11,500

ch f f Royal Academy (USA) - Tendermark (Prince Tenderfoot (USA))...... (S T S) 21,000

b c f Danehill (USA) - Vernonhills (Hard Fought).... (Darley Stud Management) 66,000

From Stradishall Manor

ch c f Sharpo - Silent Pearl (USA) (Silent Screen (USA))................ (Cash) 20,000

Property of Mr T D Holland-Martin & The Kris Syndicate (Foal Share), from Overbury Stud

b f f Kris - Throw Away Line (USA) (Assert) (London Thoroughbred Serviceds) 50,000

From Swettenham Stud, Agent

b c f Alzao (USA) - Judicial (USA) (Law Society (USA))............ (T G Mills) 30,000

b c f Don't Forget Me - Damia (Vision (USA)).... (David Minton Bloodstock) 10,000

1016

From Tullamaine Castle Stud, Ireland, Agent

b f f Fairy King (USA) - Working Model (Ile de Bourbon (USA))........ (D Woods) 40,000 b f f Alzao (USA) - Lady Vivienne (Golden Fleece (USA)).... (Saverio Brenciaglia) 12,000

Property of Major and Mrs R B Kennard, from Kirtlington Stud

b f f Midyan (USA) - Charming (Glenstal (USA))................ (Alpenford Ltd) 4,800

From Woodland Stud

b f f Bluebird (USA) - Lala (Welsh Saint)... (Conti Bloodstock) 9,400

Property of F B & Dr S F Barnes Bloodstock Services & Ptnrs, from Brick Kiln Stud

b f f Polish Patriot (USA) - Fleetwood Fancy (Taufan (USA)) .... (Will Edmeades Bloodstock) 13,500

Property of Brick Kiln Stud & Partners, from Brick Kiln Stud

b c f Midyan (USA) - Royal Agreement (USA) (Vaguely Noble)................ (John Ferguson Bloodstock) 9,800

Property of Mrs R D Peacock, from Manor House Stud

ch c f Glow (USA) - Lizarra (High Top)..... (David Minton Bloodstock) 3,400

Property of Manor House Stud

b c f Rusticaro (FR) - Lunaire (Try My Best (USA))............................ (Cormac McCormack Associates) 3,600

From Grange Stud (UK)

ch f f Nashwan (USA) - Northshiel (Northfields (USA))................ (B B A) 90,000

Property of Mr P T Tellwright, from Tyrley Castle Stud

b c f Be My Chief (USA) - Rimosa's Pet (Petingo)......................... (London Thoroughbred Services) 68,000

b c f Rock City - Lambada Style (Dancing Brave (USA))...................... (Ballymorris & Caherass Studs) 16,000

b c f Prince Sabo - Shillay (Lomond (USA)) (Peter Doyle Bloodstock) 9,000

1017

Property of Mrs G Peel, from Warren Stud

b f f Anshan - Kinkajoo (Precocious)....... (Peter Doyle Bloodstock) 3,700

Property of New England Stud Farm Ltd, from New England Stud

b c f Ron's Victory (USA) - Camp Chair (Ela-Mana-Mou)........... (Janet Chaplin) 4,800

Property of Mr Rex Comyn Boucher, from New England Stud

b c f Anshan - Marie Galante (Shirley Heights)..................... (S T S) 8,200

Property of Stratford Place Stud

ch c f Pharly (FR) - Candle In The Wind (Thatching).... (Lillingston Bloodstock) 8,400

Property of Mr W R Lewis, from Silver Birch Stables

b c f Mtoto - Eider (Niniski (USA))......... (Margaret O'Toole) 6,400

Property of Mrs Mette Campbell-Andenaes, from Andbell Stud

b f f Midyan (USA) - Nineteenth Of May (Homing)...... (Staunton Lodge Stud) 3,500

b f f Distant Relative - Andbell (Trojan Fen) (P Thorman) 3,000

b f f Midyan (USA) - Bumpkin (Free State) (D Cosgrove) 6,500

From Spring Valley Stud, Ireland (Agent)

ch f f Roi Danzig (USA) - Little Me (Connaught)..... (Peter Doyle Bloodstock) 8,200

Property of Mr and Mrs A B Barraclough, from Sentinels Stud

b or br c f Batshoof - Louise Moillon (Mansingh (USA))................... (Peter Doyle Bloodstock) 23,000

1018

Property of The Exors of the late Mrs V Hue-Williams, from Woolton House Stud

b c f Shareef Dancer (USA) - Amalancher (USA) (Alleged (USA)) (M A B Agency) 7,200

gr c f Shirley Heights - Reine D'Beaute (Caerleon (USA))...... (J P Deroubaix) 43,000

ch c f Formidable (USA) - Seraphima (Reform)........... (E H Crow & Son) 12,000

br c f Caerleon (USA) - As You Desire Me (Kalamoun)..... (Ashtown Bloodstock) 110,000

From Theakston Stud

b f f Dancing Dissident (USA) - Gay Music (FR) (Gay Mecene (USA))............. (Agence F.I.P.S.) 8,200

From Three Gates Stud

ch c f Rich Charlie - Miss Camellia (Sonnen Gold)................. (S L Edwards) 7,200

From Elsenham Stud

ch f f Risk Me (FR) - Nannie Annie (Persian Bold)................. (P A Kelleway) 6,600

ch c f Risk Me (FR) - Farras (Song)........ (John Ferguson Bloodstock) 14,000

b f f Risk Me (FR) - Farrh Nouriya (IRE) (Lomond (USA))............... (Cash) 10,000

ch c f Risk Me (FR) - She's A Sport (Jalmood (USA))......... (J Naughton) 8,000

1019

From Rathasker Stud, Ireland

b c f Taufan (USA) - Crimbourne (Mummy's Pet)....................... (D Taylor) 15,500

b c f Nordico (USA) - Kingston Rose (Tudor Music)...................... (B B A) 10,500

b c f Red Sunset - Little Eileen (Trojan Fen) (D G Mason) 5,500

b c f Posen (USA) - Tracy's Sundown (Red Sunset)......... (Genesis Green Stud) 5,400

b c f Tirol - Yukon Baby (USA) (Northern Dancer)........... (Margaret O'Toole) 25,000

Property of Mr P Kelly, from Rathasker Stud, Ireland

ch c f Be My Guest (USA) - Kirsova (Absalom)......................... (London Thoroughbred Services) 15,500

From Parkway Farm, Ireland

b f f Last Tycoon - Santa Roseanna (Caracol (FR))..... (Will Edmeades Bloodstock) 12,000

Property of Barouche Stud Ltd, Ireland

b f f Midyan (USA) - Ladyfish (Pampapaul) (D Woods) 19,500

b f f Puissance - My Croft (Crofter (USA)).. (B A McMahon) 1,800

b c f Treasure Kay - Tarkhana (IRE) (Dancing Brave (USA))............. (P Gardner) 1,100

1020

Property of Milltown Stud, Ireland

b c f Taufan (USA) - Full Board (FR) (Fabulous Dancer (USA)) .... (Peter Doyle Bloodstock) 1,200
b c f Cyrano de Bergerac - Mitsubishi Fax (King Of Clubs).......... (V Connolly) 7,200
ch c f Miswaki (USA) - Vire En Paix (Nureyev (USA)) .... (John Ferguson Bloodstock) 35,000
b f f Marju (IRE) - Shaiybaniyda (He Loves Me)..................... (K Powter) 11,000
b f f Polish Patriot (USA) - Sheer Innocence (Shirley Heights).............. (Cash) 9,200

From Barronstown Stud, Ireland

b f f Fairy King (USA) - Rivulet (USA) (Irish River (FR))........ (Renato Discepolo) 12,000
b f f Fairy King (USA) - Highland Girl (USA) (Sir Ivor)......... (Scuderia Blueberry) 14,000
b f f Fairy King (USA) - Rising Spirits (Cure The Blues (USA))..... (C Olsen Ltd) 11,000
b c f Alzao (USA) - Exotic Bride (USA) (Blushing Groom (FR)) .... (London Thoroughbred Services) 38,000

Property of Whitsbury Manor Stud

br or gr f f Polar Falcon (USA) - Bishah (USA) (Balzac (USA)) .... (Lillingston Bloodstock) 9,000
ch f f Pharly - Follow The Stars (Sparkler) .. (C Olsen Ltd) 9,000

1021

From Ardenode Stud Ltd, Ireland

b f f Doyoun - Miss Siddons (Cure The Blues (USA))....... (Chevington Stud) 15,000
ch f f Shernazar - Perfect Guest (What A Guest)..................... (P Hardy) 7,800
b c f Danehill (USA) - Welsh Fantasy (Welsh Pageant)................. (J T Doyle) 55,000
b f f Polish Patriot (USA) - Ukraine Girl (Targowice (USA))........... (B B A) 17,000

From St Simon Stud

b c f Kendor (FR) - Ahohoney (Ahonoora) .. (S Rendle) 5,200
b f f Deploy - Wryneck (Niniski (USA)) ..... (Dick Morgan) 7,000

From Pier House Stud, Ireland (Agent)

b f f Alzao (USA) - Bean Siamsa (Solinus) .. (Cash) 13,500
b f f Bluebird (USA) - Petite Liqueurelle (IRE) (Shernazar).............. (Cash) 7,000

Property of Bergh Apton Stud Ltd

b c f Precocious - Aubade (Henbit (USA)) .. (P & H E Ives) 2,200
b f f Efisio - Zebra Grass (Run The Gantlet (USA))............... (Bylon Farmers) 3,400

1022

Property of Mrs J R Hine and Miss J A Bunting MRCVS, from Shelton Stud

b c f Aragon - Grovehurst (Homing) .... (S Rendle) 12,000
b or gr c f Reprimand - Ica (Great Nephew) (H Alexander) 14,000

From Abbeville and Meadow Court Studs, Ireland

b c f Alzao (USA) - Curie Point (USA) (Sharpen Up)....................... (Brian Grassick Bloodstock) 52,000

From Cottage Stud, Ireland (Agent)

b f f Danehill (USA) - Need For Cash (USA) (Raise A Native) .... (Johnny McKeever Bloodstock) 13,000
b c f Polish Patriot (USA) - Swalthee (FR) (Sword Dancer (USA))..... (Joe Foley) 12,000

Property of Mr T J Monaghan, from The Cottage Stud, Ireland

b f f Thatching - Bag Lady (Be My Guest (USA))......... (Ashtown Bloodstock) 13,000
ch c f Polish Patriot (USA) - Etty (Relko) ... (Forthrite Ltd) 9,800

Property of Mr M Doyle, from The Gables Stud, Ireland

b f f Distinctly North (USA) - Church Mountain (Furry Glen)...................... (Ballymorris & Caherass Studs) 12,500
b c f Don't Forget Me - Curie Abu (Crofter (USA))........... (Margaret O'Toole) 11,000
b c f Taufan (USA) - Senane (Vitiges (FR)).. (J H Wall) 6,200
b c f Bluebird (USA) - Sun On The Spey (Glint Of Gold) .... (Peter Doyle Bloodstock) 18,000

1023

Property of Home Stud Ltd

b c f Forzando - Between The Sticks (Pharly (FR))........... (Britton House Stud) 8,400

Property of a Partnership, from Home Stud

b f f Warrshan (USA) - Money Supply (Brigadier Gerard)........ (P Thorman) 4,000

Property of Home Stud Ltd

b c f Robellino (USA) - Queen And Country (Town And Country) .... (London Thoroughbred Services) 9,000
b f f Belmez (USA) - Salazie (Ile de Bourbon (USA))................ (B B A (Italia)) 16,500
gr f f Old Vic - Sandstream (Sandford Lad) (Cash) 5,800

Property of Carlton Consultants Ltd, from Home Stud

b c f Formidable (USA) - Madiyla (Darshaan) .... (John Ferguson Bloodstock) 14,000
ch f f Formidable (USA) - Distant Relation (Great Nephew).......... (M Bastard) 1,700

From Swettenham Stud

b c f Alzao (USA) - Rentina (Adonijah) ..... (Johnny McKeever Bloodstock) 34,000

Property of Mr J A E Hobby, from Hillwood Stud

b c f Petong - Nevis (Connaught) .... (Roger Craddock) 15,500
b c f Thatching - Ower (IRE) (Lomond (USA))........ (Lillingston Bloodstock) 21,000

1024

From Churchtown House Stud, Ireland

b f f Alzao (USA) - Belize Tropical (IRE) (Baillamont (USA)) .... (Ashtown Bloodstock) 62,000

ch c f Archway (IRE) - Inner Pearl (Gulf Pearl)....................(J T Doyle) 18,000
b f f Danehill (USA) - Atyaaf (USA) (Irish River (FR)) (Lordship & Egerton Studs) 36,000
b f f Fairy King (USA) - Elevated (Shirley Heights)..................(C Gordon-Watson Bloodstock) 11,000
b c f Fairy King (USA) - Phantom Row (Adonijah)...... (Ashtown Bloodstock) 42,000
b c f Royal Academy (USA) - Festive Season (USA) (Lypheor) ....(Amanda Skiffington) 37,000
b c f Sadler's Wells (USA) - Shady Leaf (IRE) (Glint Of Gold)....... (J T Doyle) 230,000

From Hilltown Stud, Ireland

b c f Dancing Dissident (USA) - Clonsella Lady (High Top)..... (R J McCormick) 37,000
b c f Bluebird (USA) - Dreamy River (USA) (Bates Motel (USA)) ....(Ballymorris & Caherass Studs) 17,500

Property of a Partnership, from Langton Stud

b c f Batshoof - Quiet Harbour (Mill Reef (USA))........................(S T S) 27,000

1025

From Langton Stud

b c f Emarati (USA) - Carmen Maria (Bold Lad (IRE))................(J T Doyle) 5,000

Property of Dunchurch Lodge Stud Co, from Dukes Stud

b f f Shavian - Frozen Flower (USA) (Arctic Tern (USA))........... (J C S Wilson) 1,200
gr f f Absalom - Sliprail (USA) (Our Native (USA))..................(R W Hipkin) 3,800

Property of a Partnership, from Rosemount House Stud, Ireland

b f f Polish Patriot (USA) - Sepideh (Habitat) ....(D A Shekells) 7,200

Property of Ash Hill Stud, Ireland

b c f Petorius - Ask Samoa (USA) (Naskra (USA))........................(B B A) 4,700
b c f Mujtahid (USA) - Firefly Night (Salmon Leap (USA)) ....(C Gordon-Watson Bloodstock) 50,000
b c f Marju (IRE) - Moon Parade (Welsh Pageant)....... (Partridge Close Stud) 70,000

From Pantaquesta Stud

b f f Generous (IRE) - Sipsi Fach (Prince Sabo)............... (B B A (Ireland)) 45,000

Property of Campbell Stud

b c f Batshoof - Echoing (Formidable (USA)) ....(Dr M Boffa) 20,000
b c f Prince Sabo - Spring Water (USA) (Effervescing (USA)) ....(John Ferguson Bloodstock) 12,000

1026

Property of a Partnership, from Campbell Stud

b c f Dominion - Shih Ching (USA) (Secreto (USA))............................(Cormac McCormack Associates) 16,500

Property of Mr and Mrs N E Poole, from Paradise Farm Stud

b c f Be My Chief (USA) - Prudence (Grundy)......................(S T S) 15,500

Property of Mrs W H Gibson-Fleming, from Paradise Farm Stud

b c f Anshan - Bermuda Lily (Dunbeath (USA))......................(C B A) 14,000

Property of Mr R L Burton, from Furnace Mill Stud

ch c f Elmaamul (USA) - Overdue Reaction (Be My Guest (USA)) ....(Aston Park Stud) 7,000
ch f f Caerleon (USA) - Tricky Note (Song) (Agence F.I.P.S.) 51,000

Property of Mr W Jenks, from Furnace Mill Stud

b f f Safawan - Avahra (Sahib) (W R Milner) 4,000
b c f Polar Falcon (USA) - Savahra (Free State)..... (Brian Grassick Bloodstock) 17,000

From Barronstown Stud, Ireland

b f f Thatching - Smoo (Kris).............(Brian Grassick Bloodstock) 4,000
b c f Thatching - Lady Donna (Dominion) ..(Johnny McKeever Bloodstock) 38,000
b f f Alzao (USA) - Dawning Beauty (USA) (Well Decorated (USA)) ....(B B A (Ireland)) 52,000
ch c f Be My Guest (USA) - Darazina (FR) (Labus (FR)).. (Peter Doyle Bloodstock) 80,000
b c f Fairy King (USA) - Rising Tide (Red Alert)..... (John Ferguson Bloodstock) 62,000
b c f High Estate - Bonnie Isle (Pitcairn) ...(Margaret O'Toole) 9,500
b c f Alzao (USA) - Richly Deserved (IRE) (Kings Lake (USA))... (Agence F.I.P.S.) 68,000
b c f Thatching - Measuring (Moorestyle) ..(Luciano Loreto) 3,000
b f f Royal Academy (USA) - Tobira Celeste (USA) (Ribot).................(B B A) 20,000

1027

Property of a Partnership, from Beechgrove Stud

b f f Efisio - Maestrette (Manado).........(Brian Grassick Bloodstock) 7,000

From Ballyhimikin Stud, Ireland

b c f Marju (IRE) - Busker (Bustino) ....(Kildare Thoroughbred Services) 31,000
b f f Polish Patriot (USA) - Merry Devil (IRE) (Sadler's Wells (USA))...............(Johnny McKeever Bloodstock) 16,000
b f f Danehill (USA) - Taplow (Tap On Wood)...... (Peter Doyle Bloodstock) 15,000
b f f Classic Music (USA) - Trail (Thatch (USA)).... (Lordship & Egerton Studs) 10,000
b or br c f Bob Back (USA) - Toshair Flyer (Ballad Rock)................. (S T S) 11,000

From Fittocks Stud

b f f Polar Falcon (USA) - Lorne Lady (Local Suitor (USA))....... (Conti Bloodstock) 8,000

Property of a Partnership, from Pine Ridge Farm Ltd

b c f Rock City - Global Lady (Balliol) ......(Peter Doyle Bloodstock) 10,000

Property of Mrs F G Allen, from Barton Stud

b c f Shareef Dancer (USA) - Note Book (Mummy's Pet) ....(Brian Grassick Bloodstock) 19,000

Property of The Hon Mrs Christian, from Barton Stud

b c f Warrshan (USA) - Madam Cody (Hot Spark).......... (Genesis Green Stud) 3,600

b c f Dowsing (USA) - Naufrage (Main Reef) .... (J Chambers) 1,500
b f f Rambo Dancer (CAN) - Warning Bell (Bustino)..................... (B B A) 1,500

Property of Lode Moors Farm

b c f Blakeney - Empress Corina (Free State)........................ (B B A) 2,700

From Cornbury Park Stud

b c f Last Tycoon - Harefoot (Rainbow Quest (USA))........... (Horses A.G.) 15,500
b f f Alzao (USA) - Consolation (Troy)...... (David Minton Bloodstock) 26,000
br f f Rock City - Free Dance (FR) (Green Dancer (USA))......... (Janet Chaplin) 6,200

Property of Mr T R G Vestey, from Waltons Stud

ch c f Dominion - Fairy Fortune (Rainbow Quest (USA))......................... (David Minton Bloodstock) 8,600

1028

NEWMARKET
Monday, November 29th (Mares)

Property of Mr P Woodley, from Manor House Farm Stud

Fiction b m (4yrs) Dominion - Sans Blague (USA) (The Minstrel (CAN)) Covered by Absalom....... (Wingfield Stud Farm) 23,000

Property of Mr D O Moon, from The Downs

Floralia b m (5yrs) Auction Ring (USA) - Norpella (Northfields (USA)) Covered by Formidable (USA).................... (Lillingston Bloodstock) 20,000

From Barrackstown Stud, Ireland

Loveskate (USA) b m (9yrs) Overskate (CAN) - Gangster Of Love (USA) (Round Table) Covered by Archway (IRE)........................ (R Morgan) 20,000

Property of Woodhaven Stud

Noble Flirt b m (10yrs) Kings Lake (USA) - Frivolous (Buckpasser) Covered by Efisio........................ (B B A) 1,000
Welcome Break b m (13yrs) Wollow - Intermission (Stage Door Johnny) Covered by Old Vic........................ (Cash) 25,000

From Clonshambo Stud, Ireland

Bridget O'Bird (USA) b m (9yrs) Storm Bird (CAN) - Bridget O'Brick (USA) (Mr Brick) Covered by Maelstrom Lake.... (Mercury Bloodstock) 3,300
Ellafitzetty (IRE) b m (4yrs) Ela-Mana-Mou - Etty (Relko) Covered by Imperial Frontier (USA).............. (B B A (Italia)) 14,000

Property of Abbey Lodge Stud Partnership, from Irish National Stud

Talayra (IRE) gr f (3yrs) Taufan (USA) - Callixena (Kalamoun).......... (B B A) 6,800

Property of Mr & Mrs P H Locke, from Crimbourne Stud

Antionette Jane b m (6yrs) Ile de Bourbon - Hability (Habitat) Covered by Robellino (USA)........ (Jeremy Green & Sons) 13,500

From Northmore Stud Farm

Goodnight Girl (IRE) b f (3yrs) Alzao (USA) - I Want My Say (USA) (Tilt Up (USA)) .. (Rathbarry Bloodstock Services) 2,000

Witches Coven gr f (4yrs) Sharrood (USA) - Tricky (Song)........................ (David Minton Bloodstock) 1,600

1029

Property of Mr J Purcell

Lady St Lawrence (USA) ch m (4yrs) Bering - Lady Norcliffe (USA) (Norcliffe (CAN)) Covered by Ron's Victory (USA)....... (A H Warren (Coombe Farm) Ltd) 10,000

Property of a Partnership, from Farmers Hill Stud

Barlogan b m (5yrs) Dunbeath (USA) - Corinthia (USA) (Empery (USA)) Covered by Bluebird (USA)............. (B B A) 12,000

Property of Mr P T Tellwright, from Tyrley Castle Stud

Lambada Style (IRE) b m (5yrs) Dancing Brave (USA) - Santa's Sister (USA) (Middle Brother) Covered by Be My Chief (USA)............. (J R Collins) 60,000

Property of International Thoroughbred Breeders, Inc. From Round Hill Stud, Ireland

Bell Tower b m (8yrs) Lyphards Wish (FR) - Ring The Changes (Auction Ring (USA)) .... (Brian Grassick Ltd) 38,000

Property of Addison Racing Ltd. Inc. From Barnwood Stud

Jolie Pelouse (USA) b m (10yrs) Riverman (USA) - Social Column (USA) (Vaguely Noble) Covered by Distant Relative.... (Conti Bloodstock) 12,000

Property of Hamilton Bloodstock, from Barnweood Stud

Broken Wide b m (12yrs) Busted - Relkalim (Relko) Covered by Most Welcome.... (M S Brown) 4,400

Property of Fares Stables Ltd, From Fares Stables

Killer Queen (USA) b m (8yrs) Grey Dawn II - Keeper (USA) (Prince John) Covered by Bustino................... (B B A) 6,400
Oakbrook Tern (USA) b m (6yrs) Arctic Tern (USA) - Oakbrook Lady (USA) (Exceller (USA)) Covered by Forzando.......... (Mrs P A Clark) 7,200

From Woodditton Stud

Breakaway b m (8yrs) Song - Catherine Howard (Tower Walk) Covered by Damister (USA)..... (Scorrier Esdates) 10,500
Brown Maid (URU) b m (10yrs) Admirals Launch - Northern Maid (Northfields (USA)) Covered by Most Welcome.... (Peter Wragg Bloodstock) 8,000
Salinity (NZ) ch m (10yrs) Standaan (FR) - Rauriki (NZ) (Persian Garden) Covered by Damister (USA)........... (B B A) 2,600

1030

From Leinster Stud, Ireland

Dagian (USA) b m (13yrs) Vigors (USA) - Amya (FR) (Sanctus II) Covered by Mujtahid (USA).. (Amanda Skiffington) 15,500

Property of Mr M Ervine

Dubai Lady ch m (7yrs) Kris - Amata (USA) (Nodouble (USA)) Covered by Last Tycoon........ (Sir Stephen Hastings) 26,000

From Rathbarry Stud, Ireland (Agent)
Fanfan (IRE) b m (3yrs) Taufan (USA) - Bouffant (High Top) Covered by Polish Patriot (USA) (Peter Doyle Bloodstock) 10,000
Macquarie Ridge (USA) b m (5yrs) Cox's Ridge (USA) - Ocean's Answer (USA) (Northern Answer (CAN)) .... (Horse France) 27,000

Property of Brook Stud Ltd, from Brook Stud
Mevlevi b m (6yrs) Shareef Dancer (USA) - Meliora (Crowned Prince (USA)) Covered by Kalaglow. . (Mansour El Thayi) 8,200
Sea Fret gr m (13yrs) Habat - Fluke (Grey Sovereign) Covered by Statoblest ..... (Scorrier Esdates) 9,000
Betelgeuse b m (4yrs) Kalaglow - Feather Flower (Relkino) Covered by Statoblest (Dick Morgan) 6,700
Spinelle ch m (12yrs) Great Nephew - Jacinth (Red God) Covered by Statoblest. . (Peter Doyle Bloodstock) 5,000

Property of Jeremy Green & Sons, from Bickmarsh Stud
Chalet Girl b m (12yrs) Double Form - Flosshilde (Rheingold) Covered by Reprimand. . . . . (M S Brown) 5,200

Property of Palehouse Farm, (P.V & J.P. Jackson) from Trickledown Stud
Searching Star b m (5yrs) Rainbow Quest (USA) - Little White Star (Mill Reef (USA)) Covered by Primo Dominie. . . . . (Lillingston Bloodstock (Ireland)) 29,000
Guyum br m (5yrs) Rousillon (USA) - Lady Of Chalon (USA) (Young Emperor) Covered by Polish Precedent (USA) . . . . (P B & J B Jackson Partnership) 27,000

1031

Property of Gestut Ittlingen, from Ted Voute, Agent
Crazy Mystery (USA) ch f (2yrs) Chief's Crown (USA) - Confirm (USA) (Proudest Roman (USA)) (Silver Leaf Farms Inc.) 18,000

Property of Clovelly Farms, from Ted Voute, Agent
En Sillage (USA) ch f (3yrs) Bering - Shroud (USA) (Vaguely Noble). . . . . (B B A) 7,000

Property of Mrs G W Bronfman, from Freynestown Stud, Ireland
Final Veil (USA) b m (6yrs) Sadler's Wells (USA) - A Streaker (USA) (Dr Fager) Covered by Priolo (USA) (B B A (Italia)) 44,000

From Hesmonds Stud
Carmen's Joy br m (5yrs) Chief Singer - Bag Lady (Be My Guest (USA)) Covered by Aragon. . . . . (B B A) 15,000
Icefern b m (8yrs) Moorestyle - Ice Galaxie (USA) (Icecapade (USA)) Covered by Polar Falcon (USA). . . . . (Dick Morgan) 17,000

From Stradishall Manor
Ladina br m (10yrs) Taufan (USA) - Wintina (Tumble Wind (USA)) Covered by Elmaamul (USA). . (Silfield Bloodstock) 5,400

Property of Exord of the late Mr D Macrae, from Stradishall Manor
Blyostka (USA) ch m (4yrs) Gone West (USA) - Calypsa (USA) (The Minstrel (CAN)) Covered by Efisio. . . . . . (B B A) 19,000

Property of Exors of the late Mr D Macrae, from Stradishall Manor
Sharmood (USA) ch m (9yrs) Sharpen Up - Dreamsend (USA) (Herbager) Covered by Salse (USA). . . . (Silfield Bloodstock) 9,200

From Stradishall Manor
Czar's Bride (USA) b m (14yrs) Northern Dancer - American Legacy (Hail To Reason) Covered by Alleged (USA) . . . . (B B A) 31,000

Property of Ash Hill Stud, Ireland
Ask Samoa (USA) ch m (10yrs) Naskra (USA) - Pago Dancer (USA) (Pago Pago) Covered by Fools Holme (USA) . . . . . . (Andrew Mead International Bloodstock) 13,000

1032

From Kirtlington Stud
Shernborne ch m (7yrs) Kalaglow - Cley (Exbury) Covered by Prince Sabo. . . . . . (Emerald Bloodstock) 3,800
Ile de Danse b m (10yrs) Ile de Bourbon (USA) - Super Dancer (Taj Dewan) Covered by Primo Dominie. . (B P Hayes) 8,400

Property of Mr C M Budgett, from Kirtlington Stud
Free Crossing (USA) b or br m (8yrs) Super Concorde (USA) - Another Treat (USA) (Cornish Prince) Covered by Kylian (USA). . . . . (Mansieur El Thayi) 1,100

Property of Major and Mrs R B Kennard, from Kirtlington Stud
Charming ch m (6yrs) Glenstal (USA) - Threes A Charm (Nebbiolo) Covered by Keen. . . . . (Hugo Lascelles Bloodstock) 3,000

Property of Major R B Kennard, from Kirtlington Stud
Guanhumara ch f (3yrs) Caerleon (USA) - Smarten Up (Sharpen Up) . . . . (Johnny McKeever Bloodstock) 39,000

Property of Mr Joseph G O'Brien, from Ballycummin Castle Stud, Ireland
Afeefa b m (15yrs) Lyphard (USA) - Afrique (FR) (Exbury) Covered by High Estate. . (Emerald Bloodstock) 14,500
Raysiya ch m (6yrs) Cure The Blues (USA) - Rilasa (FR) (St Paddy) Covered by Be My Guest (USA). (Brian Grassick Bloodstock) 65,000

Property of Heathavon Stables, from Heathavon Stud
The High Dancer b m (13yrs) High Line - Sovereign Help (Sovereign Lord) . . . . . . (David Minton Bloodstock) 2,700

Property of Courtown Stud
Bold Tango (FR) b m (7yrs) In Fijar (USA) - Last Tango (FR) (Luthier) Covered by Sharpo. . . . . (Eurl Du Chene) 30,000
Tetradonna (IRE) br m (5yrs) Teenosa (USA) - Miss Bali Beach (Nonoalco (USA)) Covered by Petong. . . . . (Dick Morgan) 30,000

1033

Property of a Gentleman, from Nidd Park Stud
Careless Whisper b m (10yrs) Homing - Depict (Derring-Do) Covered by Statoblest. . . . . (B B A) 13,000

Lotte Lenta ch m (6yrs) Gorytus (USA) - Jeanie Duff (USA) (Majestic Prince (USA)) Covered by Efisio .... (Margaret O'Toole) 15,000
Princess Dina b m (15yrs) Huntercombe - Russian Princess (Henry The Seventh) Covered by Kalaglow......... (B B A) 3,500
Irish Cookie ch m (11yrs) Try My Best (USA) - Irish Kick (Windjammer (USA)) Covered by Aragon........... (B B A) 1,400
Urry Urry Urry b f (3yrs) Never So Bold - Gwiffina (Welsh Saint) .... (Kildare Thoroughbred Services) 2,000

Property of The Exors of the late Mrs V Hue-Williams, from Woolton House Stud

Amalancher (USA) b or br m (11yrs) Alleged (USA) - Flyingtrip (USA) (Vaguely Noble) Covered by Sharpo .... (Catridge Farm Stud) 9,000
As You Desire Me gr m (16yrs) Kalamoun - Royal Saint (Saint Crespin III) Covered by Generous (IRE).. (Anthony Penfold) 110,000
Fabulous Luba ch m (15yrs) Luthier - Altesse Royale (Saint Crespin III) Covered by Pharly (FR)........... (B B A) 7,800
Reine D'Beaute gr or ch m (7yrs) Caerleon (USA) - As You Desire Me (Kalamoun) Covered by Kris............... (B B A) 135,000
Princess Kris b f (3yrs) Kris - As You Desire Me (Kalamoun)...................... (Hugo Lascelles Bloodstock) 100,000
Golden Guest ch f (3yrs) Rainbow Quest (USA) - Intimate Guest (Be My Guest (USA))................ (Kerr & Co Ltd) 47,000
Desert Delight (IRE) br f (2yrs) Green Desert (USA) - As You Desire Me (Kalamoun)................. (Raffin Stud) 24,000

1034

Property of Pendley Farm

Bless The Match b m (14yrs) So Blessed - Matloch (Matador) Covered by Waajib (Catridge Farm Stud) 8,200

From Cornbury Park Stud

Harefoot br m (6yrs) Rainbow Quest (USA) - Swiftfoot (Run The Gantlet (USA)) Covered by Mtoto............ (B B A) 26,000
Consolation b m (11yrs) Troy - Conciliation (St Paddy) Covered by Suave Dancer (USA)................ (Horse France) 27,000

From Newlands House Stud, Ireland

Tracy's Sundown b m (9yrs) Red Sunset - Kilpeacon (Florescence) Covered by Astronef (Hugo Lascelles Bloodstock) 6,800
Yellow Orchid ch m (8yrs) On Your Mark - Yellow Pages (Yellow God) Covered by Mujadil (USA) .... (Hugo Lascelles Bloodstock) 4,400

From Milltown Stud, Ireland

Arctic Drama b m (11yrs) Northern Baby (CAN) - Melodramatic (Tudor Melody) Covered by Bob Back (USA)......... (Emerald Bloodstock) 2,000

From Milltown Stud, Ireland (Agent)

Mysuma (IRE) ch m (4yrs) Ahonoora - Miralla (Allangrange) Covered by Be My Guest (USA) (R O'Gorman Bloodstock) 35,000

From Milltown Stud, Ireland

Sheer Innocence b or br m (10yrs) Shirley Heights - Varishkina (Derring-Do) Covered by Last Tycoon......... (B B A) 10,000

Property of Milltown Stud, Ireland

Nememsha (USA) b or br m (7yrs) Roberto (USA) - Nasseem (FR) (Zeddaan) Covered by Bluebird (USA).. (Mam S R L) 14,500
Vivre En Paix b m (11yrs) Nureyev (USA) - Veda (FR) (Snob) Covered by Darshaan (R J Flight Bloodstock) 15,000
Hopesville (IRE) b f (3yrs) Top Ville - Shaiybaniyda (He Loves Me).......... (Kerr & Co Ltd) 8,400

1035

Property of Sussex Stud

Baby Brew b m (17yrs) Green God - Carnival Park (Carnival Dancer) Covered by Rock City......................... (Johnny McKeever Bloodstock) 8,000

From Glenvale Stud, Ireland

Darayna (IRE) b m (4yrs) Shernazar - Dafayna (Habitat) Covered by Sadler's Wells (USA)...................... (German International Bloodstock) 340,000
Light The Moon b m (5yrs) Baillamont (USA) - Lighted Glory (USA) (Nijinsky (CAN)) Covered by Caerleon (USA) .... (R J O'Gorman Bloodstock) 90,000
Green Slippers br m (4yrs) Green Dancer (USA) - Our Reverie (USA) (J O Tobin (USA)) Covered by Thatching .... (Augusto Rampa) 20,000

From Swettenham Stud, Agent

Measuring ch m (10yrs) Moorestyle - Devon Night (Midsummer Night II) Covered by Night Shift (USA)........ (Scuderia Andy Capp) 20,000
Louveciennes (USA) b m (10yrs) Super Concorde (USA) - Lupe (Primera) Covered by Kenmare (FR).. (Horse France) 15,000
Majolique (USA) b m (7yrs) Irish River (FR) - Morana (FR) (Val de Loir) Covered by Danehill (USA)........... (J R Collins) 50,000

From Swettenham Stud, Agent, Ireland

Euterpe (IRE) b m (4yrs) Dance Of Life (USA) - Warm December (He Loves Me) Covered by Don't Forget Me ..... (Conti Bloodstock) 19,000

Property of Darley Stud Management Co. Ltd, from Dalham Hall Stud

Chic Belle (USA) b m (13yrs) Mr Prospector (USA) - Sleek Belle (USA) (Vaguely Noble) Covered by Belmez (USA) ..... (C Gordon-Watson) 40,000
Glenarff (USA) ch m (4yrs) Irish River (FR) - Kraemer (USA) (Lyphard (USA)) Covered by Old Vic........ (Dick Morgan) 26,000
Halstead b m (7yrs) Bustino - Romara (Bold Lad (IRE)) Covered by Nordico (USA) .. (Saverio Brenciaglia) 18,000
Helenetta b m (11yrs) Troy - Lauretta (Relko) Covered by Assert and Top Ville .... (Planarrive Ltd) 14,000
In The Habit (USA) b m (9yrs) Lyphard (USA) - Sisterhood (USA) (Exclusive Native (USA)) Covered by Mtoto ...... (Amanda Skiffington) 23,000

Invite b m (7yrs) Be My Guest (USA) - Burghclere (Busted) Covered by Lycius (USA)........................ (B B A) 21,000
Kates Cabin ch m (6yrs) Habitat - Old Kate (Busted) Covered by Cadeaux Genereux............ (Emerald Bloodstock) 6,200
Les Dancelles b m (7yrs) Pas de Seul - Ladoucette (Bustino) Covered by Belmez (USA)................. (B B A) 16,000
Maji b m (4yrs) Shareef Dancer (USA) - Majoritat (GER) (Konigsstuhl (GER)) Covered by Robellino (USA) .... (Dick Morgan) 29,000
Monongelia ch m (13yrs) Welsh Pageant - Bird Of Dawning (USA) (Sea Bird II) Covered by Alzao (USA) (Marco Bozzi) 7,500
Pelangi b m (3yrs) Rainbow Quest (USA) - Cherry Hinton (USA) (Nijinsky (CAN)) Covered by Highest Honor (FR) .... (John Ferguson Bloodstock) 37,000
Prickle b m (12yrs) Sharpen Up - Jungle Queen (Twilight Alley) Covered by Persian Heights and Be My Guest........ (Northmoore Stud Farm) 11,000
Princess Lieven b m (14yrs) Royal Palace - Lady Dacre (Queen's Hussar) Covered by Belmez (USA)...... (Yeoland Stud) 9,000
Oribi b m (4yrs) Top Ville - Regents Fawn (CAN) (Vice Regent (CAN)) Covered by Mtoto.............. (Theobalds Stud) 12,000
She's The Tops b m (5yrs) Shernazar - Troytops (Troy) Covered by Lycius (USA)................ (Dick Morgan) 21,000
State Apartment (USA) b f (3yrs) Shadeed (USA) - Silver Dollar (Shirley Heights) Covered by Never So Bold .... (Hugo Lascalles Bloodstock) 12,000
Sylvatica ch m (9yrs) Thatching - Thistlewood (Kalamoun) Covered by Niniski (USA)....................... (David Minton Bloodstock) 22,000
Tafila ch m (7yrs) Adonijah - Brigata (Brigadier Gerard) Covered by Old Vic...... (Middle Park Stud) 16,000
Till You (USA) b m (12yrs) Exclusive Native (USA) - Hill Shade (Hillary (USA)) Covered by Old Vic........ (P R Solomon) 18,000
Town Flower b m (4yrs) Top Ville - Dance Flower (CAN) (Northern Dancer) Covered by Mtoto... (Emerald Bloodstock) 9,500
Tralthee (USA) ch or br m (10yrs) Tromos - Swalthee (FR) (Sword Dancer (USA)) Covered by Soviet Star (USA)......... (Emerald Bloodstock) 16,000
Unfold ch m (5yrs) Kris - Untold (Final Straw) Covered by Shareef Dancer (USA)............ (Middle Park Stud) 55,000
Villota b m (4yrs) Top Ville - Vilikaia (USA) (Nureyev (USA)) Covered by Lycius (USA).......... (Ashtown Bloodstock) 47,000
Whitecairn b m (3yrs) Sure Blade (USA) - White Star Line (USA) (Northern Dancer) Covered by Bering .... (Ashtown Bloodstock) 38,000
Zarissa (USA) b m (5yrs) Lyphard (USA) - I Want To Be (USA) (Roberto (USA)) Covered by Royal Academy (USA)..... (Johnny McKeever Bloodstock) 45,000

1036

Property of Darley Stud Management Co. Ltd, from Abington Place Stables

Coral Gem b f (3yrs) Be My Guest (USA) - Coral Fury (Mill Reef (USA)) .... (Johnny McKeever Bloodstock) 6,000

Property of Darley Stud Management Co. Ltd, from Bedford House Stables

Dancing Tralthee (IRE) b f (3yrs) Dancing Brave (USA) - Tralthee (USA) (Tromos) (J W Payne) 7,500
Threemilestone (USA) b f (3yrs) Secreto (USA) - Three Tails (Blakeney)......... (Middle Park Stud) 32,000

Property of Darley Stud Management Co. Ltd, from Bullstown Stables, Ireland

June Moon (IRE) b f (2yrs) Sadler's Wells (USA) - Kerrera (Diesis)............... (Blue Blood Investments) 31,000

Property of Darley Stud Management Co. Ltd, from Carlburg Stables

Bajina b f (3yrs) Dancing Brave (USA) - Babita (Habitat)..... (Aston Park Stud) 3,100
Pearly Mist (IRE) b f (3yrs) Persian Heights - Silent Movie (Shirley Heights)......... (Maif Laotaibi) 13,500

Property of Darley Stud Management Co Ltd, from Clarehave Stables

Fattaanah (USA) b or br f (3yrs) Nureyev (USA) - Special Key (USA) (Key To The Mint (USA)) .... (Hugo Lascelles Bloodstock) 34,000

Property of Darley Stud Management Co Ltd, from Creeve Stables

Royal Antelope (FR) b f (3yrs) Top Ville - Regent's Fawn (CAN) (Vice Regent (CAN)).......................... (Cash) 4,000
Saffron Crocus b f (3yrs) Shareef Dancer (USA) - Bright Crocus (USA) (Clev Er Tell (USA)).. (R O'Gorman Bloodstock) 17,500
World's View b f (3yrs) Top Ville - Favorite Prospect (USA) (Mr Prospector (USA)) (Brian Grassick Bloodstock) 7,000

1037

Property of Darley Stud Management Co Ltd, from Hurgill Lodge Stables

Dunnellon b f (3yrs) Shareef Dancer (USA) - Dunoof (Shirley Heights)...... (B B A) 15,500

Property of Darley Stud Management Co Ltd, from Kingwood House Stables

Aabet (USA) b f (3yrs) Alleged (USA) - Reactress (USA) (Sharpen Up) .... (John Warren Bloodstock) 21,000
Snowdrop Tree b f (3yrs) Shirley Heights - Dance Flower (Northern Dancer) .... (Johnny McKeever Bloodstock) 8,000

Property of Darley Stud Management Co Ltd, from Someries Stud

Birthday Dress b f (2yrs) Shareef Dancer (USA) - Birthday Fever (USA) (Master Willie)............. (Conti Bloodstock) 2,000
Clockwatch (USA) b f (4yrs) Alleged (USA) - Clocks Secret (USA) (Apalachee (USA)) (Middle Park Stud) 3,800
Floating Island ch f (3yrs) Risen Star (USA) - Bechamel (USA) (Sauce Boat (USA))... (Lanwades Stud) 3,400

La Fille de Feu b f (3yrs) Never So Bold - Prima Ballerina (FR) (Nonoalco (USA)).. (Bloomsbury Stud) 5,400
Lavender Cottage b f (3yrs) Teensoso (USA) - Broomstick Cottage (Habitat) .. (J Bethell) 3,600
Mazarine Blue (USA) ch f (3yrs) Chief's Crown (USA) - Mis Mazepah (USA) (Nijinsky (CAN))........... (J R Collins) 11,000
Mtoto's Gift b f (3yrs) Mtoto - Token Gift (USA) (Lyphard (USA)).................. (Mercury Bloodstock) 3,000
Mysterious Move ch f (3yrs) Miswaki (USA) - Sweet Mover (USA) (Nijinsky (CAN)) (Emerald Bloodstock) 8,200
Nunatak (USA) ch f (3yrs) Bering - Zolinana (FR) (Sallust)..... (Ashtown Bloodstock) 19,000
Sea Of Clouds b f (3yrs) Soviet Star (USA) - Port Helene (Troy).. (Middle Park Stud) 30,000
Talking Point b f (3yrs) Reference Point - Lustre (USA) (Halo (USA)) .... (Johnny McKeever Bloodstock) 8,000
Tass b f (3yrs) Soviet Star (USA) - Sweet Habit (Habitat)........................... (Peter Doyle Bloodstock) 42,000
Tenakee (USA) b f (3yrs) Diesis - Tennis Partner (USA) (Northern Dancer) ...... (B B A) 21,000
Tinaca (USA) b f (3yrs) Manila (USA) - Immense (USA) (Roberto (USA)) ...... (John Ferguson Bloodstock) 45,000
Winged Island b f (3yrs) Topsider (USA) - Swept Away (Kris)............ (Cash) 13,000
Zemlya b f (3yrs) Rainbow Quest (USA) - Gatchina (Habitat).. (Saverio Breniaglia) 4,500

1038

Property of Darley Stud Management Co Ltd, from South Bank Stables

Landrail (USA) ch f (3yrs) Storm Bird (CAN) - Vaguely Sensitive (USA) (Sensitive Prince (USA)) (Peter Doyle Bloodstock) 4,000
Ringlet (USA) b f (3yrs) Secreto (USA) - Double Lock (Home Guard (USA)) ...... (B B A) 48,000

Property of Darley Stud Management Co Ltd, from Southgate Stables

Foinery b or gr f (3yrs) Reference Point - Fracassina (Rusticaro (FR))............ (P C Le Metayer) 5,200
Iota b or br f (4yrs) Niniski (USA) - Iosifa (Top Ville)................ (J L Harris) 4,100

Property of Darley Stud Management Co Ltd, from Stanley House Stables

Charlotte Dundas b f (3yrs) Master Willie - Boathouse (Habitat)................... (John Warren Bloodstock) 12,000
La Spezia b f (3yrs) Last Tycoon - Helenetta (Troy)......................... (C B A) 18,000
Rixa (USA) b f (3yrs) Polish Navy (USA) - Bambina Linda (ARG) (Liloy (FR)) ...... (B B A) 6,200
Secret b f (3yrs) Rainbow Quest (USA) - Elusive (Little Current (USA)).......... (Silver Leaf Farms Inc.) 6,200
Wazeerah (USA) b f (3yrs) The Minstrel (CAN) - Gramy (FR) (Tapioca II)......... (Silver Leaf Farms Inc.) 17,000

Property of Darley Stud Management Co Ltd, from Ecurie H A Pantall, France

Bodkin b f (3yrs) Reference Point - Prickle (Sharpen Up)............. (K Morgan) 4,800
Kotsina b f (3yrs) Top Ville - Kottna (USA) (Lyphard (USA))....... (Kerr & Co Ltd) 4,600
Litze gr f (3yrs) Rainbow Quest (USA) - Lily Of The Valley (GER) (Pentathlon)...... (Hilal S Al Shahlbani) 7,000

1039

Property of Darley Stud Management Co Ltd, from Ecurie J Hammond, France

Zabeta ch f (3yrs) Diesis - Haidee (FR) (Irish River (FR))..... (Ashtown Bloodstock) 16,000
Zagrafi (IRE) b f (3yrs) Shirley Heights - Zoumorrod (USA) (Al Nasir (FR)) (Cash) 18,000
Suzhou (USA) b c (3yrs) Gren Dancer (USA) - Suavite (USA) (Alleged (USA)) (B B A) 4,000

Property of Darley Stud Management Co Ltd, from Rockingham Yard

Danish Fort b c (3yrs) Danzig (USA) - I Want To Be (USA) (Roberto (USA)).. (B B A) 21,000

Property of Darley Stud Management Co Ltd, from Ecurie A Fabre, France

Wayne County (IRE) b or br c (3yrs) Sadler's Wells (USA) - Detroit (FR) (Riverman (USA)).......... (S Rendle) 23,000

Property of Shadwell Estate Co Ltd, from Castle Stables

Badie (USA) ro c (4yrs) Blushing Groom (FR) - Desirable (Lord Gayle (USA)) .... (Tony Nurses) 22,000

Property of Shadwell Estate Co Ltd, from Shadwell Stud

Sabbaq (USA) b c (3yrs) Theatrical - Cancan Madame (USA) (Mr Prospector (USA)) (P Laniyman) 2,200

From Castle Stables

Casteddu b c (4yrs) Efisio - Bias (Royal Prerogative)....... (Wood Farm Stud) 75,000
Flying Brave b h (5yrs) Persian Bold - Flying Sauce (Sauce Boat (USA)) .... (Dalgety Bloodstock) 35,000
Silvernesian (USA) b or br c (4yrs) Alleged (USA) - Loot (USA) (Boldnesian)...... (R O'Gorman Bloodstock) 57,000

1040

From Stanley House Stables Ltd

Flowing Ocean ch c (3yrs) Forzando - Boswellia (Frankincense)... (J Bethell) 9,500

From Rosewell House Stables, Ireland

Lifewatch Vision b h (6yrs) Vision (USA) - Maellen (River Beauty).............. (Mansieur El Thayi) 1,400
Sleet Skier b h (6yrs) Niniski (USA) - Fleet Girl (Habitat)............ (I M Rashid) 15,000

Property of Winning Team Racing, from East Everleigh Stables

Gay Devil ch c (2yrs) Forzando - Pagan Queen (Vaguely Noble)............... (Lillingston Bloodstock) 8,500
Mazentre Forward (IRE) b c (2yrs) Mazaad - Nation's Game (Mummy's Game)....... (C B A) 34,000

Telephone Tap b c (2yrs) Night Shift (USA) - Prince's Lieven (Royal Palace) .... (Kildare Thoroughbred Services) 2,500

Property of Mr F Salman, from Whatcombe Stables

Frescade (USA) b c (3yrs) Green Dancer (USA) - Breeze Me (USA) (Best Turn (USA)).............. (Agence F I P S) 32,000

Fret (USA) b c (3yrs) Storm Bird (CAN) - Windy And Mild (USA) (Best Turn (USA)).................... (G Moore) 8,000

Jape (USA) b c (4yrs) Alleged (USA) - Northern Blossom (CAN) (Snow Knight) .... (B B A) 30,000

Lindon Lime (USA) br c (3yrs) Green Dancer (USA) - White Reason (USA) (Hail To Reason)..................... (John Ferguson Bloodstock) 52,000

1041

From West Ilsley Stables

Enharmonic (USA) ch h (6yrs) Diesis - Contralto (Busted).. (Jill Lamb Bloodstock) 60,000

Property of Mr R F Scully, from Ted Voute, Agent

Crack Regiment (USA) b h (5yrs) El Gran Senor (USA) - Ancient Regimes (USA) (Olden Times) (Rainbow Ridge Ranch) 62,000

Property of Clovelly Farms, from Ted Voute, Agent

Montauciel (USA) b c (4yrs) Conquistador Cielo (USA) - Likely Split (USA) (Little Current (USA))..... (Conti Bloodstock) 5,200

Rushing Water (USA) ch c (3yrs) Irish River (FR) - Fischer (USA) (Raise A Native) .. (Jonez Nedoy) 1,300

(STALLIONS)

From Three Gates Stud

Rich Charlie ch h (9yrs) Young Generation - Maiden Pool (Sharpen Up)..... (Cash) 2,500

From Hedgeholme Stud

Anvari b h (6yrs) Persian Bold - Anne Stuart (FR) (Bolkonski).............. (B B A) 7,200

1042

NEWMARKET
Tuesday, November 30th
(Mares)

Property of Mr Canice Farrell, from Nocknatrina Stud, Ireland

Spun Gold b m (10yrs) Thatch (USA) - Colourful (Busted) Covered by Common Grounds......... (S V Wilkinson) 14,000

Property of Mr J W (Pip) Payne

Coral Flutter b m (6yrs) Beldale Flutter (USA) - Countess Olivia (Prince Tenderfoot (USA)) Covered by Risk Me (FR).. (Lascelles Bloodstock) 6,000

From Chevington Stud

Dedara b m (6yrs) Head For Heights - Denia (FR) (Crepello) Covered by Last Tycoon (Horse France) 30,000

Property of J B R Leisure Ltd, from Woodruffe House Stables

Saafend b m (5yrs) Sayf El Arab (USA) - Gilt Star (Star Appeal) Covered by Most Welcome.................... (B.B.A.) 10,000

Property of Mr S M Threadwell, from The Elms Stud

Gippeswyck Lady b m (6yrs) Pas de Seul - Estivalia (Persian Bold) Covered by Indian Ridge .... (Hugo Lascettes Bloodstock) 10,000

Property of a Partnership, from Baroda Stud, Ireland

Debach Dust b m (7yrs) India King (USA) - Texly (FR) (Lyphard (USA)) Covered by Shernazar....... (Agridale Enterprises) 7,000

From Hamwood Stud, Ireland

Glowing Style (IRE) b m (3yrs) Glow (USA) - Delmora (USA) (Sir Gaylord) Covered by Topanoora .... (R O'Gorman Bloodstock) 7,400

Happy Bliss (IRE) b m (4yrs) Vision (USA) - Topping Girl (Sea Hawk II) Covered by Tirol.............. (Margaret O'Toole) 20,000

Lifewish ch m (7yrs) Bold Lad (IRE) - Brews Bridge (Thatching) Covered by Topanoora.................. (I M Rashid) 3,200

Party Piece b m (10yrs) Thatch (USA) - Mulvilla (Prince Tenderfoot (USA)) Covered by Fairy King (USA)....... (Cash) 30,000

1043

Property of Mr LLoyd Thompson, from Kilbrennal Stud, Ireland

Alhamiya ch m (9yrs) Taufan (USA) - Riot Girl (Right Boy) Covered by Waajib .... (Hugo Lascelles Bloodstock) 4,500

Property of The Hon Mrs Mary Watt, from Gazeley Stud

Tizzy b m (12yrs) Formidable (USA) - Penny Blessing (So Blessed) Covered by Primo Dominie................ (Cash) 8,500

Property of Mr & Mrs D J Deer, from Fawley Stud

No Can Tell (USA) br or br m (10yrs) Clev Er Tell (USA) - Priddy Blue (Blue Cashmere) Covered by Never So Bold ..... (D F Powell) 5,400

Silken Words (USA) b m (4yrs) Alleged (USA) - Tie A Bow (USA) (Dance Spell (USA)) Covered by Faustus (USA) ..... (Scavi A R L) 17,000

From Ballylinch Stud, Ireland (Agent)

Bold Princess (IRE) b m (5yrs) M Double M (USA) - Excruciating (CAN) (Bold Forbes (USA)) Covered by Keen .... (Horse France) 15,000

Eastern View (IRE) b or br m (4yrs) Persian Bold - Clear Picture (Polyfoto) Covered by Shernazar.... (Mercury Bloodstock) 12,000

Muffitys b m (11yrs) Thatch (USA) - Contrail (Roan Rocket) Covered by Darshaan... (J P de Gaste) 45,000

Classic Beam b m (10yrs) Cut Above - Electric Flash (Crepello) Covered by Last Tycoon................. (B.B.A.) 16,000

Property of Mr R J Powell, from Wellington House Stud, Ireland

Cumbrian Melody gr m (7yrs) Petong - Avahra (Sahib) Covered by Danehill (USA)........... (A B And V J Deane) 30,000

From Kildaragh Stud, Ireland

Namatanga (USA) b m (9yrs) Foolish Pleasure (USA) - Nonoalco (FR) (Nonoalco (USA)) Covered by Lycius (USA)........ (France Turf International) 20,000

Jwaayiz b f (3yrs) Reference Point - Rapide Pied (USA) (Raise A Native)........... (Mercury Bloodstock) 7,000

1044

From Thomastown Castle Stud, Ireland

Les Saintes b m (11yrs) Kris - Tour Des Dames (Nonoalco (USA)) Covered by Fairy King (USA).............. (J Weld) 19,000

Property of Kessly Bloodstock (part of a Dispersal Sale), from Heatherwold Stud

Fraulein Tobin (USA) br m (11yrs) J O Tobin (USA) - Fruhlingstag (FR) (Orsini) Covered by Never So Bold....... (B.B.A.) 15,000

Property of a Partnership (part of a Dispersal Sale), from Heatherwold Stud

Key To The Minstrel (USA) ch m (13yrs) The Minstrel (CAN) - Seven Locks (USA) (Jacinto) Covered by Salse (USA) .... (Cash) 12,000

Quest For The Best b m (4yrs) Rainbow Quest (USA) - Bold Flawless (USA) (Bold Bidder) Covered by Midyan (USA) .... (B.B.A.) 12,000

Property of Kessly Bloodstock (part of a Dispersal Sale), from Heatherwold Stud

Diamond House b m (9yrs) Habitat - Bold Flawless (USA) (Bold Bidder) Covered by Never So Bold.................... (David Minton Bloodstock) 22,000

Property of a Partnership (part of a Dispersal Sale), from Heatherwold Stud

Bold Flawless (USA) b m (15yrs) Bold Bidder - Hardliner (USA) (Buckpasser) Covered by Warning.............. (Cash) 42,000

Allegedly Blue (USA) b m (12yrs) Alleged (USA) - Meadow Blue (USA) (Raise A Native) Covered by Soviet Star (USA).. (David Minton Bloodstock) 52,000

Property of Heatherwold Stud

Neverdown ch m (6yrs) Never So Bold - Bourton Downs (Philip Of Spain) Covered by Indian Ridge.............. (Hugo Lascelles Bloodstock) 9,200

Property of Arrow Farm & Stud Partnership (part of a Dispersal)

Lightning Legacy (USA) ch m (12yrs) Super Concorde (USA) - Leave It To Me (Levmoss) Covered by Lahib (USA)........ (Amanda Skiffington) 12,000

Far Pavilion (IRE) b m (5yrs) Pennine Walk - Fair Abode (Habitat) Covered by Rudimentary (USA)..... (Conti Bloodstock) 10,500

1045

From Side Hill Stud

Roxy Music (IRE) b m (4yrs) Song - Roxy Hart (High Top) Covered by Batshoof.. (B.B.A. (Ireland)) 26,000

Spin Turn b m (11yrs) Homing - The Dancer (FR) (Green Dancer (USA)) Covered by Batshoof................. (D Woods) 12,500

Swift Linnet b m (10yrs) Wolver Hollow - Persian Palm (Tamerlane) Covered by Batshoof .... (Azienda Agriecola Filli Brivio) 5,200

Property of the Earl of Halifax, from Side Hill Stud

Fanny's Cove b m (14yrs) Mill Reef (USA) - Honeypot Lane (Silly Season) Covered by Be My Chief (USA) .... (Cormac McCormack Associates) 13,000

Property of Highclere Stud Ltd, from Side Hill Stud

Celebrity b or br m (11yrs) Troy - Matinee (Zeddaan) Covered by Midyan (USA) .. (Mrs P A Clark) 13,000

From Side Hill Stud

Cubist (IRE) b f (3yrs) Tate Gallery (USA) - Finalist (Star Appeal)................. (A H Warren (Coombe Farm) Ltd) 15,000

Property of Snailwell Stud Co Ltd

Circus Ring b m (14yrs) High Top - Bell Song (Tudor Melody) Covered by Slip Anchor.............. (B.B.A. (Ireland)) 48,000

Clare Island b m (14yrs) Connaught - Island Lore (Court Martial) Covered by Be My Chief (USA)................. (B.B.A.) 18,000

From Abbeville and Meadow Court Studs, Ireland (Agent)

Curie Point (USA) ch m (6yrs) Sharpen Up - Marie Curie (Exbury) Covered by Night Shift (USA).......... (B.B.A. (Ireland)) 85,000

Property of Islanmore Stud, Ireland

Dewan's Niece (USA) b m (10yrs) Dewan (USA) - Gay Niece (USA) (Sir Gaylord) Covered by Polish Patriot (USA)....... (Agricola Ficomontanino S R L) 12,000

Ridge The Times (USA) ch m (12yrs) Riva Ridge (USA) - Oath Of Allegiance (USA) (Olden Times) Covered by Caerleon (USA)............... (B.B.A. (Ireland))210,000

1046

From Swettenham Stud, Agent

Salesca (GER) b m (11yrs) Kronzeuge - Satanella (GER) (Pentathlon) Covered by High Estate......... (B.B.A. (Italia)) 16,500

Nuit de Lune (FR) ch m (10yrs) Crystal Palace (FR) - Skelda (FR) (La Varende) Covered by Pistolet Bleu (IRE) .... (Northmore Stud Farm) 5,400

From Green Ireland Properties Ltd

Broadway Gal (USA) b m (7yrs) Foolish Pleasure (USA) - Royal Suspicion (USA) (Bagdad) Covered by Ballad Rock ..... (Brian Grassick Bloodstock) 4,800

Cedilla (USA) ch m (12yrs) Caro - Mashteen (USA) (Majestic Prince (USA)) Covered by Sadler's Wells (USA)............. (Geoffrey Howson Bloodstock)100,000

Pourboire b m (11yrs) Star Appeal - Primage (Primera) Covered by Classic Music (USA)................. (B.B.A.) 2,200

From Mary James (Cotswold Stud Farms)

Kiri b m (11yrs) Kris - Kereolle (Riverman (USA)) Covered by Exit To Nowhere (USA)................ (Luciano Loreto) 15,000

Monashee (USA) b m (5yrs) Sovereign Dancer (USA) - Empress Express (USA) (Private Account (USA)) Covered by Thatching.................... (B.B.A.) 5,500

Suva (USA) ch m (5yrs) Northjet - Relko (FR) (Targowice (USA)) Covered by Pursuit Of Love.................. (B.B.A.) 22,000
Top The Rest b m (4yrs) Top Ville - No Restraint (Habitat) Covered by Sillery (USA).......... (Mercury Bloodstock) 15,000
Sudah (USA) b or br f (3yrs) Rainbow Quest (USA) - Sledge (Young Generation).... (Brian Grassick Bloodstock) 37,000

1047

Property of Exors of the late Major McCalmont, from Norelands Stud, Ireland

Fernlea (USA) b m (5yrs) Sir Ivor - Pampas (Pampapaul) Covered by Shalford (IRE) (Glebe Stud) 17,000
Heads We Called (IRE) b m (4yrs) Bluebird (USA) - Natuschka (Authi) Covered by Thatching.... (Peter Doyle Bloodstock) 36,000
Kilarney Ring br m (6yrs) Scorpio (FR) - Corbalton (Milesian) Covered by Roi Danzig (USA)......... (Patrick O'Neill) 29,000
Track Twenty Nine (IRE) gr m (4yrs) Standaan (FR) - Sleeping Car (Scorpio (FR)) Covered by Ballad Rock.............. (Lillington Bloodstock (Ire)) 18,000
Danish (IRE) b f (2yrs) Danehill (USA) - Tea House (Sassafras (FR))....... (C.B.A.) 18,000
Cliff Edge (USA) ch f (3yrs) Diesis - Adventurine (Thatching)........... (W Jarvis) 8,500
Gate Lodge (IRE) b f (3yrs) Last Tycoon - Tigeen (Habitat)..................... (John Warren Bloodstock) 28,000
Tin Roof (IRE) ch f (2yrs) Thatching - Sixpenny (English Prince).............. (David Minton Bloodstock) 2,500

Property of a Partnership, from Norelands Stud, Ireland

Teslemi (USA) b m (4yrs) Ogygian (USA) - Martha Queen (USA) (Nijinsky (CAN)) Covered by Danehill (USA).... (B.B.A.) 17,000

Property of a Partnership, from Derrygrath Stud, Ireland

Zenga b m (11yrs) Try My Best (USA) - Dusky Evening (Chamier) Covered by Don't Forget Me............. (B.B.A.) 42,000

1048

From West Stow Stud

Adjusting (IRE) b m (5yrs) Busted - Julip (Track Spare) Covered by Don't Forget Me........ (John Warren Bloodstock) 25,000
Mainmast b m (9yrs) Bustino - Main Sail (Blakeney) Covered by Reprimand..... (Northmore Stud Farm) 7,000

From Kingscote Park Stud (Agent)

Piney River ch m (9yrs) Pharly (FR) - Pluvial (Habat) Covered by Mujtahid (USA).... (B Kline) 32,000

From Cliff Stud

Double Celt ch m (12yrs) Owen Dudley - Bally's Mil (Ballymoss) Covered by Slip Anchor...................... (B.B.A.) 12,000

From Sallins Stud, Ireland (Agent)

Gertrude Lawrence b m (13yrs) Ballymore - Sarah Siddons (FR) (Le Levanstell) Covered by Be My Guest (USA).......... (Northmore Stud Farm) 16,500

Property of a Partnership, from Sallins Stud, Ireland (Agent)

Ilia (USA) b m (6yrs) Shadeed (USA) - Helen Street (Troy) Covered by Tirol......... (Marco Bozzi) 16,000
Ingerence (FR) b f (4yrs) Akarad (FR) - Lady Jeff (FR) (Jefferson)... (Patrick O'Neill) 2,200

Property of Mrs M C Keogh, from Rossenarra Stud, Ireland

Pechina (IRE) br m (4yrs) Persian Bold - Edwinarowe (Blakeney) Covered by Tirol....................... (B.B.A.) 8,000

Property of Mr John Needham, from Westerlands Stud

Lurking b m (6yrs) Formidable (USA) - Hiding (So Blessed) Covered by Primo Dominie....... (Elmhurst Bloodstock) 18,500

Property of Mr M L Page, from Westerlands Stud

Sugar Plum Fairy b m (7yrs) Sadler's Wells (USA) - Epithet (Mill Reef (USA)) Covered by Midyan (USA).. (Dick Morgan) 22,000

1049

From Pinfold Stud

Remany gr m (4yrs) Bellypha - Moonscape (Ribero) Covered by Primo Dominie ... (David Minton Bloodstock) 40,000

Property of Milton Park & West Lodge Studs (to Dissolve a P'ship),from Raffin Lodge Stu

Prima Domina (FR) b m (8yrs) Dominion - Swan Ann (My Swanee) Covered by Suave Dancer (USA).. (Barouche Stud) 76,000

Property of Carlton Consultants Ltd, from Collin Stud

Distant Relation b m (8yrs) Great Nephew - Perchance (Connaught) Covered by Distant Relative.......... (Collin Stud-Foal Syndicate) 3,000
Madiyla gr m (6yrs) Darshaan - Manntika (Kalamoun) Covered by Formidable (USA)............. (Bloomsbury Stud) 41,000
Arrastra b m (5yrs) Bustino - Island Mill (Mill Reef (USA))............. (J Delahook) 8,400

From Rathasker Stud, Ireland

Baby's Smile b m (13yrs) Shirley Heights - Two's Company (Sheshoon) Covered by Mujadil (USA).............. (Cash) 10,500
Little Eileen b m (6yrs) Trojan Fen - Panserina (Sovereign Path) Covered by Mujadil (USA)....................... (Johnny McKeever Bloodstock) 10,000
Rosy Sunset (IRE) b m (4yrs) Red Sunset - Miss Audimar (USA) (Mr Leader (USA)) Covered by Mujadil (USA)........... (Geoffrey Howson Bloodstock) 14,500

Property of C A Waters Bloodstock Trading, from Glebe Stud

Hayati ro or gr m (11yrs) Hotfoot - Silecia (Sky Gipsy) Covered by Green Desert (USA)............... (B.B.A. (Ireland)) 78,000

Property of a Partnership, from Broguestown Stud, Ireland

Invitation Only (IRE) b m (4yrs) Be My Guest (USA) - Persian Susan (USA) (Herbager) Covered by High Estate.... (Cash) 25,000

1050

Property of Wyck Hall Stud

Arctic River (FR) b m (9yrs) Arctic Tern (USA) - Glena (FR) (Riverman (FR)) Covered by Highest Honor (FR)........... (Northmore Stud Farm) 12,000

Bien Melee ch m (10yrs) Kenmare (FR) - Warsaw (Salvo) Covered by Darshaan (Agence F I P S) 17,000

Circus Spot b m (4yrs) Reference Point - Circus Plume (High Top) Covered by Mtoto.............................(Cash) 22,000

Conservatoire ch m (11yrs) Quizair - Conservatory (Major Portion) Covered by Shareef Dancer (USA)............... (David Minton Bloodstock) 4,000

Ecran b m (7yrs) Kings Lake (USA) - High Finale (High Line) Covered by Sillery (USA)........... (Massimo Marchetti) 35,000

Honeybun (FR) ch m (8yrs) Kenmare (FR) - Syrona (Salvo) Covered by Belmez (USA)................. (Nicolo Casini) 14,000

On Air (FR) b or br m (5yrs) Chief Singer - Green Light (FR) (Green Dancer (USA)) Covered by Cadeaux Genereux, believed NOT in foal... (Jerry O'Brien) 4,000

Samite (FR) b or br m (13yrs) Tennyson (FR) - Sybarite (Royal Record) Covered by Sharpo, believed NOT in foal....... (Jerry O'Brien) 9,200

Shangrila (FR) b m (15yrs) Riverman (USA) - Garden Green (Pinturischio) Covered by Kaldoun (FR)......... (Eurl Du Chene) 3,800

Silver Light (FR) ch m (17yrs) Luthier - Silver Zara (Silver Shark) Covered by Lead On Time (USA).. (J P Deroubaix) 5,000

Soulful (FR) b m (6yrs) Zino - Musical Soul (USA) (Youth (USA)) Covered by Shernazar........................... (B.B.A.) 2,200

White-Wash b m (8yrs) Final Straw - Cecilia Bianchi (FR) (Petingo) Covered by Sanglemore (USA), believed NOT in foal... (Mrs A Rothschild) 11,500

1051

From Forenaghts Stud, Ireland

Lady Wishing Well (USA) gr m (6yrs) Hero's Honor (USA) - Ispahan (Rusticaro (FR)) Covered by Darshaan................ (R O'Gorman Bloodstock) 145,000

From Lanwades Stud

Soignee b m (4yrs) Night Shift (USA) - Scala Di Seta (Shantung) Covered by Petong (Emerald Bloodstock) 16,500

Vanudetta (USA) b m (4yrs) Trempolino (USA) - Vaslava (Habitat) Covered by Nishapour (FR)........................ (Brian Grassick Bloodstock) 3,500

Vaslava b m (12yrs) Habitat - Vacances (USA) (Nijinsky (CAN)) Covered by Pursuit Of Love..................... (B.B.A.) 5,000

Beyond The Lace (IRE) b m (5yrs) Lomond (USA) - Rustic Lace (Rusticaro (FR))... (John Ferguson Bloodstock) 46,000

From Churchtown House Stud, Ireland

Shabbaba (USA) ch m (5yrs) Arctic Tern (USA) - Shicklah (USA) (The Minstrel (CAN)) Covered by Law Society (USA) (B.B.A.) 15,000

Toast (IRE) b m (4yrs) Be My Guest (USA) - Princess Tiara (Crowned Prince (USA)) Covered by High Estate.............. (Whitsbury Farm Stud Ltd) 28,000

From Glenvale Stud, Ireland

Final Verdict (IRE) br m (5yrs) Law Society (USA) - Catopetl (USA) (Northern Dancer) Covered by Alzao (USA)...... (Kildare Thoroughbred Services) 29,000

Juniper Berry (IRE) b m (4yrs) Last Tycoon - Jackie Berry (Connaught) Covered by Caerleon (USA)...... (B.B.A. (Ireland)) 150,000

Speedy Beauty b m (4yrs) Rousillon (USA) - Rye Tops (Ile de Bourbon (USA)) Covered by night Shift (USA)...... (Cash) 38,000

1052

Property of Mrs Hugh McCalmont, from Yeomanstown Lodge Stud, Ireland

Miss Loving ch m (11yrs) Northfields (USA) - Sacred Ibis (Red God) Covered by Tirol......... (Whitsbury Farm & Stud) 18,000

From Swettenham Stud, Agent

Page Blanche (USA) gr m (13yrs) Caro - Pixie Tower (Songedor) Covered by Marignan (USA)............... (Cash) 2,600

Watt A Lot (IRE) b m (4yrs) Glow (USA) - Admit (Welsh Pageant) Covered by High Estate.. (Peter Doyle Bloodstock) 14,000

Property of Kiltinan Farms Inc, from Kiltinan Castle Stud, Ireland

Northern Script (USA) b m (13yrs) Arts And Letters - My Nord (USA) (Vent Du Nord) Covered byu Nureyev (USA) .... (B.B.A. (Ireland)) 155,000

Ivyanna (IRE) b or br m (4yrs) Reference Point - Ivy (USA) (Sir Ivor) Covered by Arazi (USA).......... (B.B.A. (Ireland)) 410,000

India Atlanta ch m (7yrs) Ahonoora - Place Of Honour (Be My Guest (USA)) Covered by Persian Heights.............. (Michael Page) 100,000

Place Of Honour ch m (12yrs) Be My Guest (USA) - Sutton Place (Tyrant (USA)) Covered by Mujtahid (USA), believed NOT in foal....... (The Corbally Stud) 14,500

Aminata b m (6yrs) Glenstal (USA) - Belle Epoque (Habitat) Covered by Gulch (USA)............... (B.B.A. (Ireland)) 95,000

Ivy (USA) b m (12yrs) Sir Ivor - Durga (USA) (Tatan (ARG)) Covered by Nureyev (USA)............... (B.B.A. (Ireland)) 450,000

Roblanna b m (10yrs) Roberto (USA) - Noblanna (USA) (Vaguely Noble) Covered by Sharp Victor (USA).... (B.B.A.) 8,000

1053

Property of Juddmonte Farms Ltd, from Juddmonte Farms

Newquay b m (10yrs) Great Nephew - Quay Line (High Line) Covered by Slip Anchor........... (Conti Bloodstock) 9,400

Poplina (USA) ch m (8yrs) Roberto (USA) - Populi (USA) (Star Envoy (USA)) Covered by Primo Dominie .... (Conti Bloodstock) 15,000

Sidara b m (9yrs) Golden Fleece (USA) - Sarah Siddons (FR) (Le Levanstell) Covered by Lycius (USA)...... (A Decrion) 32,000
Star Of Dance b m (6yrs) Sadler's Wells (USA) - Three Stars (Star Appeal) Covered by Persian Bold.......... (B.B.A.) 13,000
Three Stars b or br m (11yrs) Star Appeal - Pirogue (Reliance II) Covered by Unfuwain (USA).. (P And A G Venner) 16,500
Vian (USA) b m (9yrs) Far Out East (USA) - Loveliest (USA) (Tibaldo) Covered by Don't Forget Me.............. (Cash) 15,000

Property of Juddmonte Farms Ltd

From Afar (USA) ch f (3yrs) Riverman (USA) - Meteoric (High Line)............... (Johnny McKeever Bloodstock) 3,800
Godille (USA) b f (3yrs) Riverman (USA) - Go Leasing (Star Appeal)............. (B.B.A. (Italia)) 4,400
Guv's Joy (IRE) b f (3yrs) Thatching - Joanne's Joy (Ballymore)............. (Emerald Bloodstock) 3,000
Intrepid br f (3yrs) Rousillon (USA) - Bold And Beautiful (Bold Lad (IRE))......... (Emerald Bloodstock) 4,000
Istelle (USA) b f (3yrs) Alleged (USA) - Artiste (Artaius (USA))................ (Lamwades Stud) 15,500

1054

Property of Juddmonte Farms Inc

Ivory Palm (USA) b f (3yrs) Sir Ivor - Sunerta (USA) (Roberto (USA)).. (Minster Stud) 83,000

Property of Juddmonte Farms Ltd

Legendra ch f (3yrs) Legend Of France (USA) - Obertura (USA) (Roberto (USA)) .... (R J Holder) 3,000

Property of Juddmonte Farms Inc

Mali (USA) b f (3yrs) Storm Bird (CAN) - Ala Mahlik (Ahonoora)............ (C.B.A.) 15,000

Property of Juddmonte Farms Ltd

Manicala b f (3yrs) Ela-Mana-Mou - Modica (Persian Bold)...................... (John And Susan Davis Bloodstock) 13,000
Nomadic Quest (IRE) b f (3yrs) Rainbow Quest (USA) - Nomadic Pleasure (Habitat)......................... (Cash) 40,000

Property of Juddmonte Farms Inc

Pelagic b f (3yrs) Rainbow Quest (USA) - Fleet Girl (Habitat).. (M de Chambure) 33,000

Property of Juddmonte Farms Ltd

Qena ch f (3yrs) The Minstrel (CAN) - Queens Only (USA) (Marshua's Dancer (USA))...................... (B.B.A.) 31,000
Ranora (IRE) b f (3yrs) Ahonoora - Gold Runner (Runnett).................... (David Minton Bloodstock) 9,200
River Erne (USA) b f (3yrs) Irish River (FR) - Valderna (FR) (Val de Loir)............ (Emerald Bloodstock) 15,000
Secret Guest (IRE) b f (3yrs) Be My Guest (USA) - Ack's Secret (USA) (Ack Ack (USA))...................... (B.B.A.) 16,500
Surf Rider (USA) b f (3yrs) Raft (USA) - Golden Alibi (USA) (Empery (USA)).... (R O'Gorman Bloodstock) 52,000
Vague Pass (USA) b f (3yrs) Vaguely Noble - Flare Pass (USA) (Buckpasser)........ (Silverleaf Farms, Inc) 14,000

Venerate (IRE) b f (3yrs) Ahonoora - Royal Saint (USA) (Crimson Satan).......... (B.B.A. (Italia)) 7,600

1055

Property of Gerecon Italia, from Castle Stables

Atmospheric Blues (IRE) b f (4yrs) Double Schwartz - Saga's Humour (Bustino)... (C.B.A.) 6,600
Legend's Daughter (USA) b f (3yrs) Alleged (USA) - Din (USA) (Drone).... (B Mills) 17,000

Property of a Partnership, from Castle Stables

Cloud Of Dust b f (4yrs) Aragon - Lady Bequick (Sharpen Up).. (J P de Gaste) 88,000

From Castle Stables

Sleepy Lagoon b f (3yrs) Sadler's Wells (USA) - Bempton (Blakeney).......... (J R Collins) 74,000

Property of Mr Peter S Winfield, from Castle Stables

Spetacular Dawn gr f (4yrs) Spectacular Bid (USA) - Early Rising (USA) (Grey Dawn II)........ (Brian Grassick Bloodstock) 21,000

Property of Shadwell Estate Co Ltd, from Castle Stables

Wadia (USA) b f (3yrs) Lyphard (USA) - Histoire (FR) (Riverman (USA))........ (Brian Grassick Bloodstock) 62,000

Property of Mr Paul Mellon KBE, from Park House Stables, Kingsclere

East Liberty (USA) ch f (3yrs) Halo (USA) - Pennsylvania (USA) (Northjet)......... (John Warren Bloodstock) 60,000
Silent Circle (IRE) gr f (3yrs) Reference Point - English Spring (USA) (Grey Dawn II).................. (Winners) 22,000
Susquehanna Daysa (USA) b f (3yrs) Chief's Crown (USA) - Gliding By (USA) (Tom Rolfe)..... (Mr And Mrs J D Cantillon) 16,500

Property of Mr E P Jameson, from Whatcombe Stables

Lee Artiste b m (5yrs) Tate Gallery (USA) - Mirkan Honey (Ballymore)............ (B Burrough) 60,000

1056

From Whatcombe Stables

Ruby Tiger gr m (6yrs) Ahonoora - Hayati (Hotfoot).......... (Geoffrey Howson) 220,000

Property of Shadwell Estate Co Ltd, from Windsor House Stables

Akhlak (IRE) b or br f (3yrs) Soviet Star (USA) - Pilot Bird (Blakeney)... (B.B.A.) 5,200
Ibtikar (USA) b f (3yrs) Private Account (USA) - Anne Campbell (USA) (Never Bend).......... (Amanda Skiffington) 56,000
Mataris b f (3yrs) Shirley Heights - Pyslla (Beldale Flutter (USA))......... (Cash) 8,400

Property of a Parnership, from South Bank Stables

Nicer (IRE) gr f (3yrs) Pennine Walk - Everything Nice (Sovereign Path)........... (Anthony Penfold Bloodstock) 270,000

Property of a Parnership, from Freemason Lodge

Guest Room (IRE) ch f (3yrs) Be My Guest (USA) - Sunny Valley (Val de Loir) ..... (Johnny McKeever Bloodstock) 140,000

Property of a Partnership, from Freemason Lodge

Red Cotton ch f (3yrs) Soviet Star (USA) - Cocotte (Troy)............ (N Alotaibi) 23,000

Property of Swettenham Stud, from Manton House Stables

Cherhill (IRE) b f (3yrs) Ahonoora - Battine (USA) (Topsider (USA))............... (Mercury Bloodstock) 7,500

Lacerta (IRE) b f (3yrs) Thatching - Cup Defender (USA) (Topsider (USA))...... (John Ferguson Bloodstock) 40,000

Lamu Lady (IRE) b f (3yrs) Lomond (USA) - Noble Mark (On Your Mark).......... (B.B.A. (Ireland)) 17,500

1057

Property of a Partnership, from Shadowfax Stables

Toocando (IRE) b f (3yrs) Nordance (USA) - Romantic Air (He Loves Me).......... (E Puerari) 42,000

From Glebe House Stables, Ireland

Jomel Amou (IRE) b f (4yrs) Ela-Mana-Mou - Joma Kaanem (Double Form) (B.B.A.) 16,000

Pernila (IRE) b f (3yrs) Tate Gallery (USA) - Clonsella Lady (High Top)............ (Brian Grassick Bloodstock) 50,000

Property of Invosture Ltd, from Trillium Place Stables

Adamparis b f (3yrs) Robellino (USA) - Mrs Darling (Mummy's Pet).............. (Johnny McKeever Bloodstock) 8,200

Property of David Midwood, from Trillium Place Stables

Farmer's Pet ch f (4yrs) Sharrood (USA) - Rectitude (Runnymede).. (J Naughton) 15,000

Property of Mr S A Meacock, from Trillium Place Stables

Trianglepoint (IRE) b f (3yrs) Auction Ring (USA) - Tapestry (Tap On Wood)...... (Johnny McKeever Bloodstock) 7,000

From Brecongill Stables

Royal Diva ch f (3yrs) Chief Singer - Rustle Of Silk (General Assembly (USA)).... (Kildare Thoroughbred Services) 2,200

From Flint Cottage Stables

Star Family Friend (IRE) ch f (3yrs) Double Schwartz - Jane's Idea (Ballad Rock)..... (Musaed Sa Al-Salem) 35,000

From Thomastown Castle, Ireland

Atsuko (IRE) b f (3yrs) Mtoto - Maresca (Mill Reef (USA)).................... (Brian Grassick Bloodstock) 16,000

Miss Mistletoes (IRE) b f (3yrs) The Minstrel (CAN) - December Blossom (Condorcet (FR))............ (B V Sangster) 58,000

My-O-My (IRE) b f (3yrs) Waajib - Maimiti (Goldhill).......... (Swettenham Stud) 78,000

1058

Property of Mrs S Gibson Fleming, from East Everleigh Stables

Gold Tassel b f (3yrs) Glint Of Gold - Nastassia (FR) (Noble Decree (USA)) .. (J Nedoy) 1,600

Property of Mr J G Davis, from East Everleigh Stables

Reminiscence (IRE) ch f (2yrs) Thatching - Measuring (Moorestyle).............. (Hilal S Al Sahaibani) 5,500

Property of a Partnership, from East Everleigh Stables

Only Dreaming b f (2yrs) Dominion - Welsh Jane (Bold Lad (IRE))... (B.B.A. (Italia)) 7,500

To dissolve a partnership, from Warwick House Stables

Belated b or gr f (4yrs) Bellypha - Enchanted (Song)...... (B.B.A. (Italia)) 7,000

Property of Earl of Halifax, from Pegasus Stables

Shilka b f (3yrs) Soviet Star (USA) - Gull Nook (Mill Reef (USA)).............. (Peter Doyle Bloodstock) 9,600

Property of Mr B E Nielsen, from Pegasus Stables

Funny Hilarious (USA) ch f (3yrs) Sir Ivor - Polestar (Northfields (USA))... (B.B.A.) 23,000

Nemea (USA) b f (3yrs) The Minstrel (CAN) - Donna Inez (USA) (Herbager)........ (Overbury Stud) 31,000

Solartica (USA) b or br f (3yrs) Halo (USA) - Telescopica (ARG) (Table Play) (B.B.A.) 62,000

From Southgate Stables

Cropton b f (3yrs) Flash Of Steel - Crymlyn (Welsh Pageant)..................... (Will Edmeades Bloodstock) 6,000

Property of Mr P D Player, from Sefton Lodge Stables

Mild Rebuke b f (2yrs) Reprimand - Mary Bankes (USA) (Northern Baby (CAN)) .. (Musaed Sa Al-Salem) 30,000

1059

NEWMARKET
Wednesday, December 1st (Mares)

From West Penhill Stud

Sports Post Lady (IRE) ch m (5yrs) M Double M (USA) - Pasadena Lady (Captain James) Covered by Silver Kite(USA)......... (Margaret O'Toole) 24,000

Quatre Femme b m (6yrs) Petorius - Irisk Kick (Windjammer (USA)) Covered by Common Grounds.... (B B A (Ireland)) 9,000

Property of Swaines Hill Stud

Grey Gypsy gr m (7yrs) Absalom - Nyeri (Saint Crespin III) Covered by Chilibang (B B A) 5,200

Josephine Gibney b m (11yrs) High Top - Tagik (Targowice (USA)) Covered by Terimon................ (I M Rachid) 4,000

Property of Mr P Hurst, from Easthorpe Hall Stud

Final Shot br m (6yrs) Dalsaan - Isadora Duncan (Primera) Covered by Reprimand......... (Whitsbury Farm & Stud) 27,000

Property of Mr M Doyle, from The Gables Stud, Ireland

Balistic Princess ch m (7yrs) Lomond (USA) - Drama (USA) (Sir Ivor) Covered by Waajib.................. (Kerr & Co) 9,800

Property of Mr John Shorthouse, from Furnace Mill Stud

Firelighter gr or br m (8yrs) Kalaglow - Belle Reef (Mill Reef (USA)) Covered by Anshan........................ (B B A) 8,000

Property of Mr R L Burton, from Furnace Mill Stud

Overdue Reaction ch m (8yrs) Be My Guest (USA) - Temporary Lull (USA) (Super Concorde (USA)) Covered by Pursuit Of Love........................ (C B A) 30,000

Property of Hockley Ltd (part of a Dispersal), from Hockley House Stud

Ballerine (USA) b m (10yrs) Lyphard's Wish (FR) - Blithe Spirit (FR) (Luthier) Covered by Polar Falcon(USA)............ (Catridge Farm Stud) 45,000

b f (2yrs) Elegant Air - Ballerine (USA) (Lyphard's Wish (FR))......... (B B A) 3,600

1060

From Fittocks Stud

Helietta b m (10yrs) Tyrnavos - Hurgy-Gurdy (Espresso) Covered by Kahyasi (Agridale Enterprises) 6,000

Property of R G Stokes, from Fittocks Stud

Vice Vixen (CAN) b m (9yrs) Vice Regent (CAN) - Super Foxe (USA) (Blood Royal (USA)) Covered by Rainbow Quest(USA)........................ (London Thoroughbred Services) 145,000

Property of Lordship and Egerton Studs Limited, from Lordship and Egerton Studs

Arctic Winter (CAN) b m (11yrs) Briartic (CAN) - Tabola (USA) (Round Table) Covered by Royal Academy(USA) ..... (London Thoroughbred Services) 29,000

Oleari b m (4yrs) Lead On Time (USA) - Princesse Legere (USA) (Alleged (USA)) Covered by Caerleon(USA) .... (Geoffrey Howson Bloodstock) 70,000

Rose de Thai (USA) b m (7yrs) Lear Fan (USA) - Reve de Reine (USA) (Lyphard (USA)) Covered by Green Desert(USA) (Barouche Stud) 160,000

Property of Monsieur Pierre Talvard, from Haras du Cadran, France

Badiane (USA) b m (4yrs) Green Forest (USA) - Bonshamile (Ile de Bourbon) Covered by Saumarez... (C Olsen Ltd) 15,000

From Haras de La Tuilerie, France

Tamaya (IRE) b m (4yrs) Darshaan - Kahara (Habitat) Covered by Saumarez .... (J P Deroubaix) 15,000

Property of Brick Kiln Stud & Partners, from Brick Kiln Stud

Whisper's Shadow b m (4yrs) Northern Baby (CAN) - Sir Ivor's Sorrow (USA) (Sir Ivor) Covered by Imp Society(USA) (R O'Gorman Bloodstock) 12,000

Property of M J Worth, from Whatton Manor Stud

Fire Risk b m (12yrs) Thatch (USA) - Last Call (Klairon) Covered by Nomination .. (Hugo Lascelles Bloodstock) 2,800

Property of Sir David Wills C.B.E., T.D., from Whatton Manor Stud

Portree b m (4yrs) Slip Anchor - Rynechra (Blakeney) Covered by Salse.......... (Lillingston Bloodstock (Ireland)) 13,000

1061

Property of a partnership of Meon Valley Stud, from Meon Valley Stud

Well Ahead b m (4yrs) Last Tycoon - Sistabelle (Bellypha) Covered by Midyan(USA)............ (J R Collins) 45,000

Belladari b m (3yrs) Shardari - Sistabelle (Bellypha) Covered by Petong......... (Raffin Stud) 15,500

From Lyonstown Stud, Ireland

Lake Isle (FR) br m (4yrs) Caerleon (USA) - Inisfree (USA) (Hoist The Flag (USA)) Covered by Classic Music(USA)....... (B B A) 33,000

Property of Whitsbury Manor Stud

Aphrosina br m (10yrs) Known Fact (USA) - Lady Of Chalon (USA) (Young Emperor) Covered by Be My Chief(USA)........ (German International Bloodstock) 11,000

Bishah (USA) gr m (10yrs) Balzac (USA) - Paaora (Sea Hawk II) Covered by Cadeaux Genereux .... (Hugo Lascelles Bloodstock) 9,200

From Genesis Green Stud

Glacial Moon (USA) b m (4yrs) Arctic Tern (USA) - Hortensia (FR) (Luthier) Covered by Royal Academy(USA)......... (Overbury Stud) 82,000

Pravolo b m (4yrs) Fools Holme (USA) - Pavello (Crepello) Covered by Persian Bold.................... (Raffin Stud) 30,000

Qui Suis Je (IRE) b or br m (5yrs) Pennine Walk - Relfo (Relko) Covered by Fairy King(USA).................. (B B A) 31,000

Property of Tarworth Bloodstock Investments Ltd

Neviskia (USA) b f (4yrs) Arctic Tern (USA) - Water Dancer (USA) (Nijinsky (CAN)) .. (B B A) 12,000

Property of a partnership, from Overbury Stud

Waffle On br f (3yrs) Chief Singer - Humble Pie (Known Fact (USA)) .... (Peter Mitchell) 56,000

1062

From Corbally Stud, Ireland

Azurai b m (11yrs) Dance In Time (USA) - Wichuraiana (Worden II) Covered by Law Society(USA) (Saverio Brenciaglia) 7,400

Golden Grundy ch m (12yrs) Grundy - Pale Gold (New Chapter) Covered by Persian Bold .... (Kildare Thoroughbred Services) 7,000

Rienroe (IRE) b m (4yrs) Caerleon (USA) - Flying Bid (Auction Ring (USA)) Covered by Persian Bold.. (B B A (Ireland)) 52,000

Storm Riding (USA) b m (7yrs) Storm Bird (CAN) - Nellie Forbes (USA) (Secretariat (USA)) Covered by Thatching......... (R M Whitaker) 17,000

From Swettenham Stud, agent

Flyaway Bride (USA) gr m (10yrs) Blushing Groom (FR) - Blue Angel's Image (CAN) (Ruritania (USA)) Covered by Danehill(USA)........ (M.A.B. Agency) 36,000

Hasanati (FR) b m (4yrs) Akarad (FR) - Heracleia (FR) (Kenmare (FR)) Covered by Pistolet Bleu(IRE)... (Horse France) 29,000

From Cheveley Park Stud

Constant Delight b m (6yrs) Never So Bold - Lady Constance (Connaught) Covered by Prince Sabo.............. (Will Edmeades Bloodstock) 14,000

Tina's Melody b m (9yrs) Tina's Pet - Green Chartreuse (French Beige) Covered by La Grange Music.............. (Hugo Lascelles Bloodstock) 7,500

Makeshift b m (6yrs) Night Shift (USA) - Fall To Pieces (USA) (Forli (ARG)) covered by Prince Sabo.............. (Peter Doyle Bloodstock) 15,000

Screenable (USA) b m (13yrs) Silent Screen (USA) - Hardliner (USA) (Buckpasser) Covered by La Grange Music.......... (Emerald Bloodstock) 6,500

Queen's Visit b m (10yrs) Top Command (USA) - Par Excellance (CAN) (L'enjoleur (CAN)) Covered by Saddler's Hall(IRE)........... (Jose Hormaeche) 11,000

False Lift ch m (11yrs) Grundy - Gliding (Tudor Melody) Covered by Saddler's Hall(IRE)........... (Woodditton Stud) 23,000

1063

To dissolve a partnership, from Cheveley Park Stud

Trojan Lady (USA) ch m (6yrs) Irish River (FR) - Troyanos (Troy) Covered by Pursuit Of Love............ (Glebe Stud) 24,000

From Cheveley Park Stud

Pellinora (USA) b m (14yrs) King Pellinore (USA) - Frontonian (USA) (Buckpasser) Covered by Rudimentary(USA)........ (Catridge Farm Stud) 9,500

Wishes b m (3yrs) Caerleon (USA) - Talon D'Aiguille (USA) (Big Spruce (USA)) Covered by Prince Sabo.............. (Conti Bloodstock) 18,000

Property of Cliveden Stud Ltd

Queen Midas ch m (9yrs) Glint Of Gold - Star Court (Aureole) Covered by Soviet Star(USA)... (R O'Gorman Bloodstock) 100,000

Property of Lord Howard de Walden, from Plantation Stud

Doumayna b m (14yrs) Kouban (FR) - Delsy (FR) (Abdos) Covered by Slip Anchor .. (Horse France (Ireland)) 8,400

Grimpola (GER) b m (11yrs) Windwurf (GER) - Gondel (GER) (Zank) Covered by Kenmare(FR)..... (K D Ellerbracke) 14,000

Property of Home Stud Ltd

Between The Sticks gr m (6yrs) Pharly (FR) - Sandstream (Sandford Lad) Covered by Robellino(USA).............. (John Ferguson Bloodstock) 15,500

Salazie b m (9yrs) Ile de Bourbon (USA) - Top Call (High Top) Covered by Midyan(USA).............. (Derby Bloodstock) 41,000

Property of Mr & Mrs Leo Collins, from Ennistown Stud, Ireland

Mariposa b m (6yrs) Cure The Blues (USA) - Madelon (Saint Crespin III) Covered by Royal Academy(USA)........ (P Barbe) 50,000

From Haras du Buff, France

Bubble Prospector (USA) b m (9yrs) Miswaki (USA) - Bubble Company (USA) (Lyphard (USA)) Covered by Arctic Tern(USA)............. (B B A (Italia)) 36,000

Hybla (FR) ch m (12yrs) Arctic Tern (USA) - Helvetie (Klairon) Covered by Saumarez .... (C Gordon-Watson Bloodstock) 72,000

1064

Property of Mr Julian Byng, from Wrotham Park

Harold's Girl (FR) b m (14yrs) Northfields (USA) - Naughty Marcia (Connaught) Covered by Sharpo. . (P & A G Venner) 9,000

Troppo Cara b m (11yrs) Sharpman - Igraine (USA) (Round Table) Covered by Kenmare (FR)....... (Emerald Bloodstock) 15,000

River Maiden (USA) ch f (3yrs) Riverman (USA) - Harold's Girl (FR) (Northfields (USA)).......................... (B B A) 6,200

Property of Mr T S M S Riley-Smith, from Meddler Stud

Thimbalina ch m (7yrs) Salmon Leap (USA) - Maestrette (Manado) Covered by Rock Hopper........... (Angley Stud) 8,600

Property of a Lady, from Woodcote Stud

Chandni (IRE) b m (4yrs) Ahonoora - Jardiniere (Nijinsky (CAN)) Covered by Marju(IRE)............ (Raffin Stud) 54,000

Property of Woodcote Stud Ltd, from Woodcote Stud

Sister Sal ch m (6yrs) Bairn (USA) - Mercy Cure (No Mercy) Covered by Aragon .. (Lostford Manor Stud) 6,200

Property of a Partnership, from Bansha House, Ireland

Magic Arts (IRE) ch m (5yrs) Fairy King (USA) - Maura Paul (Bonne Noel)...... (C Olsen Ltd) 5,000

Property of a Gentleman, from Lavington Stud

High Halo b m (10yrs) High Top - Halomata (Hallez (FR)) Covered by Warrshan (USA)......................... (B B A) 7,400

Property of Hyde Sporting Promotions Ltd, from Lavington Stud

Miss Hyde (USA) br m (4yrs) Procida (USA) - Little Niece (Great Nephew) Covered by Warrshan (USA)........... (B B A) 4,400

Property of Sunley Stud Ltd, from Lavington Stud

Sunley Silks b or br m (4yrs) Formidable (USA) - Brown Velvet (Mansingh (USA)) Covered by Aragon. . (Rathasker Stud) 11,000

1065

Property of a Partnership, from Theakston Stud

Butterfly Kiss b m (10yrs) Beldale Flutter (USA) - Ready And Willing (Reliance II) Covered by Alzao (USA)............. (Luciano Loreto) 15,500

From Theakston Stud

Cadisa b or br m (9yrs) Top Ville - Callianire (Sir Gaylord) Covered by Sharpo ...... (Emerald Bloodstock) 16,000

Property of Laharna Ltd, from Greenland Park Stud

Rosina Mae b f (4yrs) Rousillon (USA) - Dame Ashfield (Grundy)....... (C B A) 14,500

Property of Freedom Farm Stud

Debach Daisy b m (6yrs) Ahonoora - Princess Seal (Prince Tenderfoot (USA)) Covered by Anshan........... (Cash) 5,000

Debach Delight b m (9yrs) Great Nephew - Crack Of Light (Salvo) Covered by Lahib (USA)................... (B B A) 10,000

Property of Campbell Stud

Jetty (FR) b m (8yrs) Fabulous Dancer (USA) - Melantha (Roan Rocket) Covered by Doyoun (Chantilly Bloodstock) 13,500

Spring Water (USA) ch m (8yrs) Effervescing (USA) - Sabrine (Mount Hagen (FR)) Covered by Primo Dominie........... (Peter Doyle Bloodstock) 7,200

Property of a Partnership, from Burningfold Manor Stud

Persian Grey gr m (5yrs) Persepolis (FR) - Burnished (Formidable (USA)) Covered by Indian Ridge .... (Peter Wragg Bloodstock) 12,500

From Tullamaine Castle Stud Ireland, Agent

Working Model b m (9yrs) Ile de Bourbon (USA) - Siliciana (Silly Season) Covered by Last Tycoon..................... (London Thoroughbred Services) 14,000

From Ballyhimikin Stud, Ireland

Mory Kante (USA) b m (6yrs) Icecapade (USA) - Mousseline de Soie (FR) (Riverman (USA)) Covered by Waajib (B B A) 18,000

No Dowry ch m (6yrs) Shy Groom (USA) - Collateral (Compensation) Covered by Danehill (USA) .... (Hugo Lascelles Bloodstock) 11,000

1066

Property of Mr and Mrs P Blacker, from Raffin Stud

Aligote br m (13yrs) Nebbiolo - Alexandra (GER) (Ozean) Covered by Rambo Dancer (CAN)............. (C Gordon-Watson Bloodstock) 3,500

Property of Mr and Mrs P Blacker

Taiga b m (12yrs) Northfields (USA) - Question Mark (High Line) Covered by Prince Sabo......................... (Will Edmeades Bloodstock) 6,500

From Glenvale Stud, Ireland

Top Table b m (4yrs) Shirley Heights - Lora's Guest (Be My Guest (USA)) Covered by Alzao (USA) .... (Peter Doyle Bloodstock) 41,000

Swan Heights b m (4yrs) Shirley Heights - Swan Ann (My Swanee) Covered by Sadler's Wells (USA).......... (B B A) 190,000

Zaya (USA) b or br m (5yrs) Riverman (USA) - Percipient (USA) (Topsider (USA)) Covered by Caerleon (USA)........... (Raffin Stud) 75,000

From Mount Coote Stud, Ireland

Aunt Hester (IRE) b m (5yrs) Caerleon (USA) - Lady Hester (Native Prince) Covered by In The Wings .... (Cotswold Stud) 35,000

Civility b m (13yrs) Shirley Heights - Makeacurtsey (USA) (Herbager) Covered by Suave Dancer (USA).......... (C Gordon-Watson Bloodstock) 38,000

Royal Respect b m (9yrs) Kings Lake (USA) - Makeacurtsey (USA) (Herbager) Covered by Roi Danzig (USA)..... (B B A) 5,500

Steel Habit b m (14yrs) Habitat - Ampulla (Crowned Prince (USA)) Covered by Sadler's Wells (USA).. (B B A (Ireland)) 310,000

Property of Mr Gerald W Leigh, from Eydon Hall Farm

Pericolo (IRE) b m (4yrs) Kris - Wild Abandon (USA) (Graustark) Covered by Royal Academy (USA)............... (Dolphin Bloodstock) 37,000

Propensity br m (9yrs) Habitat - Kalamac (FR) (Kalamoun) Covered by Suave Dancer (USA)............. (Winners) 42,000

1067

From Floors Stud

Pelargonia ch m (4yrs) Primo Dominie - Pellinora (USA) (King Pellinore (USA)) Covered by In The Wings .... (Panetta Bloodstock) 35,000

From Airlie Stud, Ireland

Blazing Glory (IRE) b m (4yrs) Glow (USA) - Salvationist (Mill Reef (USA)) Covered by Salt Dome (USA).. (Roundhill Stud) 14,000

Property of a Partnership, from Airlie Stud, Ireland

Chamonis (USA) ro m (9yrs) Affirmed (USA) - Timely Tammy (USA) (Tim Tam) Covered by Danehill (USA)............... (Lillingston Bloodstock (Ireland)) 40,000

From Airlie Stud, Ireland

Countess Candy b m (13yrs) Great Nephew - Zoomie (Pinza) Covered by Mujtahid (USA)............ (Florent Couturier) 20,000

Sun Bed ch m (10yrs) Habitat - Sky's Sunny (USA) (Dewan (USA)) Covered by Don't Forget Me....... (Saverio Brenciaglia) 12,500

From Ardenode Stud, Ireland

Polista (FR) b m (5yrs) Persepolis (FR) - Danesta (USA) (Majestic Prince (USA)) Covered by Caerleon (USA)........... (Milton Park Stud) 70,000

From Swettenham Stud, Agent

Girouette (USA) gr m (9yrs) Nodouble (USA) - Gray Dove (USA) (T V Lark) Covered by Nashwan (USA) .... (Florent Couturier) 45,000

Short Wave (FR) b m (9yrs) Trepan (FR) - Saraca (Shantung) Covered by Last Tycoon............... (Horse France) 14,500

From Woodland Stud

Dance Machine b m (11yrs) Green Dancer (USA) - Never A Lady (Pontifex (USA)) Covered by Kris .... (Geoffrey Howson Bloodstock) 15,000

Likeness ch m (10yrs) Young Generation - Picture (Lorenzaccio) Covered by Sharpo..... (David Minton Bloodstock) 4,000

Cynic ch f (3yrs) Sharpo - Cynomis (Shergar)......................... (B B A) 3,000

1068

Property of Shadwell Estate Co Ltd, from Beech House Stud

Ghanayim (USA) ch m (9yrs) Sharpen Up - Libras Shiningstar (USA) (Libra) Covered by Old Vic .... (Allevamento Del Lagoni) 21,000

Turkish Treasure (USA) gr m (18yrs) Sir Ivor - Turban (USA) (Bagdad) Covered by Mtoto. . . . . (B B A (Ireland)) 11,000

Property of Hadi Al Tajir, from Beech House Stud

Sharpina ch m (13yrs) Sharpen Up - Regal Splendour (Sovereign Path) Covered by Soviet Star (USA). . . . . (Johnny McKeever Bloodstock) 10,000

Wish Of Luck (USA) b m (5yrs) Diesis - Kesar Queen (USA) (Nashua) Covered by Marju (IRE). . . . . . . (Razza Del Sole) 15,000

Light Bee (USA) ch m (10yrs) Majestic Light (USA) - Haneena (Habitat) Covered by Unfuwain (USA) . . . . (Scudaria Andy Capp) 5,500

Property of Shadwell Estate Co Ltd, from Derrinstown Stud, Ireland

Ghaadah (USA) b m (6yrs) Linkage (USA) - Strings Attached (USA) (Tudor Minstrel) Covered by Unfuwain (USA) . . . . (K D Ellerbracke) 28,000

Tarib ch m (10yrs) Habitat - Red Coral (AUS) (Red God) Covered by Ela-Mana-Mou, believed NOT in foal (Lanwades Stud) 11,000

From Monread Stud, Ireland

Tebre (USA) b f (3yrs) Sir Ivor - Ignition (CHI) (Damascus Silver (USA)) . . . . (Middle Park Stud) 16,000

Property of Gainsborough Stud Management Ltd, from Gainsborough Stud

A Kiss In Deed (USA) b m (6yrs) Shadeed (USA) - Passakiss (USA) (Buckpasser) Covered by Bering (Conti Bloodstock) 11,000

Guapa b m (5yrs) Shareef Dancer (USA) - Sauceboat (Connaught) Covered by Lahib (USA). . . . . (M.A.B. Agency) 74,000

Hug Me b m (8yrs) Shareef Dancer (USA) - Loveshine (USA) (Gallant Romeo (USA)) Covered by Mtoto. . . . . (Whitsbury Farm & Stud) 14,500

Jameelapi (USA) ch m (12yrs) Blushikng Groom (FR) - Itsamaza (USA) (Limit To Reason (USA)) Covered by Soviet Star (USA). . . . . (Horses A.G.) 20,000

Magical Veil ch m (5yrs) Majestic Light (USA) - Jameelapi (USA) (Blushing Groom (FR)) Covered by Salse (USA). . . . (P D Player) 19,000

Please Kenneh b m (8yrs) Golden Fleece (USA) - Dancing Meg (USA) (Marshua's Dancer (USA)) Covered by Rock Hopper. . . . . (B B A) 6,200

1069

From International Bloodstock, France

Mary Linoa (USA) b m (7yrs) L'emigrant (USA) - Marie Noelle (FR) (Brigadier Gerard) Covered by Machiavellian (USA)— . . . . (B B A) 220,000

Scene Galante (FR) b m (5yrs) Sicyos (USA) - Lilac Charm (Bustino) Covered by Kendor (FR). . . . . . (Adrian Greenwood) 20,000

Shahlanya (FR) b m (4yrs) Rainbow Quest (USA) - Barbra (FR) (Le Fabuleux) Covered by Royal Academy (USA) . . . . (Kerr & Co) 115,000

Three Terns (USA) b m (7yrs) Arctic Tern (USA) - Three Troikas (FR) (Lyphard (USA)) Covered by Sharpo . . . . (Mrs A Rothschild) 19,000

Property of Stowell Hill Ltd, from Stowell Hill Stud

Lady Zi b m (13yrs) Manado - Exbury Grace (FR) (Exbury) Covered by Priolo (USA) (Mrs A Rothschild) 32,000

Property of Her Majesty The Queen, from The Royal Studs

Etiquette b m (4yrs) Law Society (USA) - Livry (USA) (Lyphard (USA)) Covered by Sharpo. . . . (Brian Grassick Bloodstock) 11,000

Reflection b m (12yrs) Mill Reef (USA) - Joking Apart (Jimmy Reppin) Covered by Selkirk (USA). . . . . (Campbell Stud) 15,000

Silver Dollar b m (11yrs) Shirley Heights - Circlet (Baldric II) Covered by Lear Fan (USA). . . . . (Dick Morgan) 23,000

Varnish ch m (6yrs) Final Straw - Rainbow's End (My Swallow) Covered by Primo Dominie. . . . . (Emerald Bloodstock) 18,000

From Haras de Saint Leonard des Parcs, France

Havinia ch m (6yrs) Habitat - Lavinia (FR) (Run The Gantlet (USA)) Covered by Risen Star (USA). . . . . . (Forthrite Ltd) 16,000

Quemora (FR) b m (13yrs) Riverman (USA) - Moquerie (FR) (Beaugency (FR)) Covered by Dixieland Band (USA). . . . . (London Thoroughbred Services) 36,000

1070

(HORSES-IN-TRAINING)

From International Bloodstock

La Millieme b f (3yrs) Pennine Walk - Lady Zi (Manado). . . . . (Mercury Bloodstock) 5,200

Property of shadwell Estate Co Ltd, from Kingwood House Stables

Ramiya b f (3yrs) Dancing Brave (USA) - Nouvelle Star (AUS) (Luskin Star (AUS)) . . . . (Emerald Bloodstock) 5,000

Property of Mrs M V O'Brien, from Ballydoyle and Ridge Manor Stables

Endsong (USA) b f (3yrs) El Gran Senor (USA) - Mystical River (USA) (Riverman (USA)). . . . . (N Clement) 8,000

Fairy Lore (IRE) b f (3yrs) Fairy King (USA) - Gentle Freedom (Wolver Hollow). . . . . . (David FitzGerald) 7,500

Property of Shadwell Estates Co Ltd, from Green Lodge Stables

Araadh (USA) b f (3yrs) Blushing Groom (FR) - Idle Gossip (USA) (Lyphard (USA)) (C Gordon-Watson Bloodstock) 70,000

Lakab (USA) ch f (3yrs) Manila (USA) - River Lullaby (USA) (Riverman (USA)) . . . . . . (C Gordon-Watson Bloodstock) 38,000

Saja (USA) b f (3yrs) Ferdinand (USA) - Summer Silence (USA) (Stop The Music (USA)). . . . . (R Wilkie) 1,600

Taalif b f (3yrs) Last Tycoon - Imperial Jade (Lochnager). . . . . (B B A) 34,000

To dissolve a partnership, from Abington Place Stables

Croire (IRE) b f (3yrs) Lomond (USA) - Fighting Run (Runnett) (Mrs N Elwes) 10,500

Property of Hascombe & Valiant Studs, from Abington Place Stables

Nuryandra b f (3yrs) Reference Point - Nuryana (Nureyev (USA))...... (B B A) 55,000

1071

Property of Shadwell Estate Co Ltd, from St Gatien Stables

Unnab b f (3yrs) Shareef Dancer (USA) - Index To Forli (USA) (Forli (ARG))...... (D Smith) 2,600

Zajira (IRE) b f (3yrs) Ela-Mana-Mou - Awsaaf (USA) (Naskra (USA)).. (C B A) 14,000

From Warren Place Stables

Cromarty b f (3yrs) Shareef Dancer (USA) - Forres (Thatch (USA)) .... (David Minton Bloodstock) 9,200

Dreams Are Free (IRE) b f (3yrs) Caerleon (USA) - Keep The Thought (USA) (Valdez (USA)).... (Northmore Stud Farm) 8,000

Magique Rond Point (USA) b f (3yrs) Greinton - Petit Rond Point (USA) (Round Table)... (Anthony Penfold Bloodstock) 26,000

Usk The Way b f (3yrs) Caerleon (USA) - One Way Street (Habitat)..... (B B A) 24,000

From First Flyer Stables, Ireland

Forest Concert (IRE) ch f (4yrs) Thatching - Sense Of Rhythm (Cure The Blues (USA)).......................... (C B A) 20,000

Overcast (IRE) ch f (3yrs) Caerleon (USA) - Ask The Wind (Run The Gantlet (USA)) (D A Shekells) 26,000

Property of Shadwell Estate Co Ltd, from Rossmore Lodge Stables, Ireland

Na-Ammah (IRE) b f (3yrs) Ela-Mana-Mou - Adrana (Bold Lad (IRE)) .... (Mercury Bloodstock) 5,200

Property of Shadwell Estate Co Ltd, from Rosewell House Stables, Ireland

Kuddam (IRE) b or br f (3yrs) Doyoun - Forest Lair (Habitat).......... (B B A) 3,200

1072

From West Ilsley Stables

Last Embrace (USA) b f (4yrs) Shernazar - Melodramatic (Tudor Melody)......... (C de Moubray) 21,000

Ricochet Romance (USA) b f (3yrs) Shadeed (USA) - For The Flag (USA) (Forli (ARG))........ (Lord Huntingdon) 11,000

Property of C T Olley & Partners, from Carlburg Stables

Armarama ch f (4yrs) Persian Bold - Rossitor (Pall Mall).............. (E Puerari) 60,000

Property of Mr & Mrs R Crutchley, from Woodway Stables

Heavenly Waters b f (4yrs) Celestial Storm (USA) - Idle Waters (Mill Reef (USA)) .. (Amanda Skiffington) 27,000

To dissolve a partnership, from Shalfleet Stables

Hazy Kay (IRE) gr f (3yrs) Treasure Kay - Hazy Lady (Habitat)..... (R G Percival) 6,000

From Bedford House Stables

Mamara Reef b f (3yrs) Salse (USA) - Fanny's Cove (Mill Reef (USA)) .... (D Smith) 8,000

Wannabe b f (3yrs) Shirley Heights - Propensity (Habitat)..... (Agence F.I.P.S.) 15,000

From Currabeg Stables, Ireland

Oiseau de Feu ch f (3yrs) Nijinsky (CAN) - Fleur Royale (Mill Reef (USA)) .... (E Puerari) 88,000

Sharkashka (IRE) ch f (3yrs) Shardari - Kashka (USA) (The Minstrel (CAN)) .... (C B A) 20,000

Property of Shadwell Estate Co Ltd, from Stanley House Stables

Darajah (USA) ch f (3yrs) Diesis - Whitethroat (Artaius (USA))......... (B B A) 6,500

1073

Property of a partnership, from Beckhampton House Stables

Athens Belle (IRE) b f (3yrs) Groom Dancer (USA) - Greektown (Ele-Mana-Mou) ... (C B A) 100,000

Ballet Shoes (IRE) b f (3yrs) Ela-Mana-Mou - River Dancer (Irish River (FR))......... (Lillingston Bloodstock (Ireland)) 42,000

Property of Lord Howard de Walden, from Phantom House Stables

Keylock (USA) b f (3yrs) Diesis - Sure Locked (USA) (Lyphard (USA)) .... (Lillingston Bloodstock (Ireland)) 52,000

Property of Shadwell Estate Co Ltd, from Clarehaven Stables

Al Katiriyah (IRE) ch f (3yrs) Sure Blade (USA) - Buthayna (Habitat).. (J Nedoy) 1,900

Nawahil b f (3yrs) Shirley Heights - Lora's Guest (Be My Guest (USA))... (B B A) 28,000

Property of R M Cyzer, from Elliotts Stables

Impeccable Taste b f (3yrs) Slip Anchor - Spring Triple (USA) (Spring Double).... (David Redvers) 3,300

Formal Affair b f (3yrs) Rousillon (USA) - Muznah (Royal And Regal (USA))...... (David Minton Bloodstock) 10,000

Molly Splash b m (6yrs) Dunbeath (USA) - Nelly Do Da (Derring-Do) .... (Aston Park Stud) 3,500

Property of a partnership, from Fitzroy House Stables

Ancestral Dancer gr f (3yrs) Siberian Express (USA) - Exuberine (FR) (Be My Guest (USA))........... (B B A (Italia)) 60,000

Home From The Hill (IRE) b f (3yrs) Jareer (USA) - Hill's Realm (USA) (Key To The Kingdom (USA))........... (C Gordon-Watson Bloodstock) 16,000

Isabella Sharp b f (2yrs) Sharpo - Vivienda (Known Fact (USA)).................. (John Warren Bloodstock) 26,000

Puget Dancer (USA) b f (3yrs) Seattle Dancer (USA) - Basin (USA) (Tom Rolfe) .... (F Chapman) 25,000

1074

From Oak Stables Ltd

Nawafell b f (2yrs) Kris - Try To Catch Me (USA) (Shareef Dancer (USA))......... (Conti Bloodstock) 13,000

Property of Mrs B Fairbarns, from Woodditton Stud

Pearl Angel ch f (4yrs) Superlative - More Or Less (Morston (FR))............... (Rainbow Ridge Ranch) 42,000

From Seven Springs Stables

Mindomica b f (4yrs) Dominion - Nordica (Northfields (USA))............ (Cash) 24,000

Property of G Strawbridge, from Ecurie J Pease, France

Style For Life (IRE) b f (3yrs) Law Society (USA) - Style Of Life (USA) (The Minstrel (CAN))......... (Agence F.I.P.S.) 7,000

Property of a partnership, from Ecurie Smaga, France

Prima Voce (IRE) ch f (3yrs) Ela-Mana-Mou - Sea Singer (USA) (Sea Bird II)........ (Brian Grassick Bloodstock) 45,000

Property of a partnership, from Ecurie Hammond, France

Helen's Gamble (IRE) b f (3yrs) Spectacular Bid (USA) - Troyanna (Troy)............ (Brian Grassick Bloodstock) 17,500

Property of a partnership, from Crottanstown Stables, Ireland

Eichtercua (IRE) b f (2yrs) Petorius - Night Of Gaiety (What A Guest)............ (Kildare Thoroughbred Services) 60,000

From Ballingara Stables, Ireland (Agent)

Gorgeous Dancer (IRE) b f (4yrs) Nordico (USA) - Simply Gorgeous (Hello Gorgeous (USA)) (Mercury Bloodstock) 21,000

Property of Dr C E Stelling

Bali House (USA) b f (3yrs) Java Gold (USA) - Ice House (Northfields (USA))........ (Brian Grassick Bloodstock) 5,200

Property of a partnership, from Whitechurch Stables, Ireland

Be My Hope (IRE) b f (4yrs) Be My Native (USA) - Diamond Gig (Pitskelly)........ (B B A (Ireland)) 52,000

1075

Property of F J Sainsbury, from Barbury Castle Stables

Massiba (IRE) b f (4yrs) Shareef Dancer (USA) - Massorah (FR) (Habitat)....... (Hilal S Al Sahaibani) 30,000

Property of R Staels, from Collin Stud

Zero Time br m (6yrs) Alzao (USA) - Queen Of Time (USA) (Roi Dagobert).......... (David Redvers) 2,000

Property of R J Turner, from Sigwells Racing

Yours By Right ch f (3yrs) Entitled - Super Style (Artaius (USA))..... (I M Rachid) 8,500

1076

NEWMARKET
Thursday, December 2nd (Mares)

Property of Countrywide Classic Ltd

Night Gown b m (4yrs) Night Shift (USA) - Mossage (Ballymoss) Covered by Risk Me(FR)... (Hugo Lascelles Bloodstock) 2,700

Pure Green (USA) ch m (6yrs) Green Forest (USA) - Malakya (Artaius (USA)) Covered by Crofthall (Centaur Bloodstock) 3,500

Property of J K Dancer, from Dordale Farm

Not So Shy b m (8yrs) Star Appeal - Nanushka (Lochnager) Covered by Bold Arrangement........................ (Hugo Lascelles Bloodstock) 3,400

Une Emigree (USA) b m (8yrs) L'emigrant (USA) - Cadi Ha (Welsh Pageant) Covered by Rambo Dancer(CAN)......... (Mansour El Thayi) 3,000

Vernair (USA) ch m (12yrs) Super Concorde (USA) - What A Pannie (USA) (What A Pleasure (USA)) Covered by Absalom.. (J A And P Duffy) 2,100

Property of J L Acklam, from Thorncliffe Stud

Celtic Sonata br m (10yrs) Music Boy - Celtic Melody (Tudor Melody) Covered by Sizzling Melody (Mansour El Thayi) 800

Miss Vaigly Blue b m (10yrs) Vaigly Great - La Sinope (FR) (Thatch (USA)) Covered by Sizzling Melody....... (W A Wood) 800

My Little Bird ch m (6yrs) Glenstal (USA) - Myna (Ela-Mana-Mou) Covered by Most Welcome............ (B.B.A.) 2,200

Property of Northgate Lodge Stud Ltd

Jalstar b m (7yrs) Jalmood (USA) - Explosiva (USA) (Explodent (USA)) Covered by Indian Forest(USA)... (B.B.A.) 2,700

Mazurkanova b m (9yrs) Song - Red Lady (Warpath) Covered by Grey Desire.... (T Jennings) 3,200

1077

From Little Peverels

Highly Polished b m (13yrs) High Top - Brilliantine (USA) (Stage Door Johnny) Covered by Deploy............ (Cash) 2,100

Misdevious (USA) b m (11yrs) Alleged (USA) - I'll Be Around (USA) (Isgala) Covered by Chilibang................ (Ridge Barn Farm) 3,400

Property of R J Turner, from Wards Hill Stud

Keyboard br m (13yrs) High Top - Happy Music (Hethersett) Covered by Interrex(CAN).... (Peter Doyle Bloodstock) 5,200

Property of S Corman Ltd, from Houndswood Stud

Corman-Style b or br m (8yrs) Ahonoora - Miss Millicent (Milesian) Covered by Primo Dominie........................ (Johnny McKeever Bloodstock) 5,500

Property of Fernedge Bloodstock Ltd, from Chadwell Farm Stud

Until June (USA) ch m (10yrs) Be My Guest (USA) - Cesarina (Milesian) Covered by Be My Chief(USA)........... (B.B.A.) 6,200

Property of a Lady

Karonga b m (9yrs) Main Reef - Karmala (FR) (Tanerko) Covered by Nicholas(USA)............ (P Thorman) 2,100

Property of Cedar Tree Stud

Nadema b m (10yrs) Artaius (USA) - Nadwa (Tyrant (USA)) Covered by Anshan.... (C.B.A.) 6,500

Property of T Minahan, from Hawkwind Stud

Ash Amour b m (6yrs) Hotfoot - Loving Doll (Godswalk (USA)) Covered by Chilibang .... (Hugo Lascelles Bloodstock) 4,500

Property of a partnership, from Glasgow House
Margs Girl b m (6yrs) Claude Monet (USA) - Aquarian Star (Cavo Doro) Covered by Barrys Gamble. . (Mercury Bloodstock) 4,700
Property of P & A G Venner, from Petches Farm
Council Rock b m (8yrs) General Assembly (USA) - Dancing Rocks (Green Dancer (USA)) Covered by Keen .... (Susan Piggott) 11,000

1078

From Dullingham House Stud
Cov Tel Lady ch m (4yrs) Celestial Storm (USA) - Silette (Siliconn) Covered by Interrex(CAN)........ (Mrs K M Mack) 5,000
Property of a partnership, from Grovewood Stud
Anne de Guise (FR) ch m (11yrs) Pharly (FR) - Adelaide Adams (ITY) (Braccio Da Montone) Covered by Indian Ridge.... (Mrs P de Ferrari) 7,200
Property of Corkrose Ltd, from Charlton Down Stud
Glint Of Victory b m (9yrs) Glint Of Gold - Victory Kingdom (CAN) (Viceregal (CAN)) Covered by Rudimentary(USA) (R Matthews) 3,600
Property of Miss E Aldous, from Southburgh Manor Stud
Miami Melody b m (12yrs) Miami Springs - Melodia (Tudor Melody) Covered by Reprimand................... (Cash) 2,200
Property of a partnership, from Loretta Lodge Stables
What A Challenge ch m (8yrs) Sallust - Glendalough (USA) (High Finance) Covered by Formidable(USA)... (T G Mills) 6,000
Property of Mr & Mrs T G Mills, from Loretta Lodge Stables
Gladeer (IRE) ch f (4yrs) Hadeer - Really Sharp (Sharpen Up)...... (A Spalding) 1,250
Greenwich Bambi b m (5yrs) Music Boy - Coca (Levmoss)............. (B.B.A.) 4,100
Property of Oak Bloodstock Ltd, from Lofts Hall Stud
El Vino b m (8yrs) Habitat - Press Corps (Realm) Covered by Shareef Dancer(USA)................ (B.B.A.) 8,000
Property of a partnership, from Glen Andred Stud
White's Pet b m (9yrs) Mummy's Pet - Miss St Jame's (Sovereign Path) Covered by Petong.............. (B.B.A.) 6,000
Property of Summertree Stud
Nosey b m (12yrs) Nebbiolo - Little Cynthia (Wolver Hollow) Covered by Indian Ridge.................. (R J Turner) 6,200

1079

Property of Stratford Place Stud
Candle In The Wind b m (9yrs) Thatching - Her Grace (Great Nephew) Covered by Aragon................. (Naif Alotaibi) 3,900
From Hever Castle Stud
Cadi Ha b m (14yrs) Welsh Pageant - Super Dancer (Taj Dewan).................. (Peter Doyle Bloodstock) 800
Property of Hyde Stud
Fighting Arethusa (IRE) b m (3yrs) Never So Bold - Ausonia (Beldale Flutter (USA)) Covered by Aragon........... (B.B.A.) 3,500
Prydwen ch m (9yrs) Hard Fought - Favant (Faberge II) Covered by Rock City..... (Cash) 4,700
Property of Stud-On-The-Chart
Lady Warninglid b m (10yrs) Ela-Mana-Mou - Rosy Lee (FR) (Le Haar) Covered by Rock City.................... (Cash) 6,200
Martin-Lavell Post b m (6yrs) Tina's Pet - Stradey Park (Murrayfield) Covered by Keen..... (Hugo Lascelles Bloodstock) 880
Property of a partnership, from Stud-On-The-Chart
Trull b m (6yrs) Lomond (USA) - Bird Point (USA) (Alleged (USA)) Covered by Aragon.................. (D A Shekells) 13,000
Property of Stud-On-The-Chart
Ultra Vires b m (16yrs) High Line - Ultra Violet (Sunny Brae) Covered by Pharly(FR).................. (B.B.A.) 3,200
From Grange Stud
Riverette b f (3yrs) Caerleon (USA) - Riviere Bleue (Riverman (USA)) .... (Johnny McKeever Bloodstock) 5,800
Property of Snowdrop Stud Co Ltd, from Sandley Stud
Dance Move b m (6yrs) Shareef Dancer (USA) - Rapide Pied (USA) (Raise A Native) Covered by Cadeaux Genereux (B.B.A. (Ireland)) 22,000
Madam Bold b m (6yrs) Never So Bold - Sophisticated Lady (FR) (Habitat) Covered by Midyan(USA) .... (Lastford Manor Stud) 8,200
Queenstyle b or br m (8yrs) Moorestyle - Queen's Niece (Great Nephew) Covered by Emarati(USA) .... (Mansour El Thayi) 3,000

1080

Property of Fahd Salman, from Sandley Stud
La Delitzia (USA) ch f (3yrs) Diesis - Hotel Street (USA) (Alleged (USA))......... (Silverleaf Farm, Inc) 4,800
Property of a partnership, from Woodcote Stud
Elmaarrah (CAN) ch m (6yrs) Caro - Play Around Honey (USA) (Exclusive Native (USA)) Covered by Warrshan(USA) .... (B.B.A.) 6,400
Property of E Gregory, from Woodcote Stud
Tinkoo (IRE) b m (3yrs) Heraldiste (USA) - Sistina (Charlottown) Covered by Digamist(USA)...... (Mercury Bloodstock) 4,500
Property of Pigeon House Stud, from Fawley Stud
Bonnie Banks b m (8yrs) Lomond (USA) - Light Link (Tudor Music) Covered by Never So Bold .... (Hugo Lascelles Bloodstock) 3,800
Lady Of Letters ro m (4yrs) Primo Dominion - Teacher's Game (Mummy's Game) Covered by Forzando.......... (Hugo Lascelles Bloodstock) 4,500
Property of Mr I D Muir, from Fawley Stud
The Boozy News (USA) b m (5yrs) L'emigrant (USA) - Zitherplay (USA) (Graustark) Covered by Northern State(USA)......... (Aston Park Stud) 2,000

Property of Courtown Stud
Lady Regent gr m (13yrs) Wolver Hollow - Seriema (Petingo) Covered by Deploy (Cash) 1,200
Property of J Mantz, fro Ridge Farm Ltd
Unhambi b m (3yrs) Dowsing (USA) - Global Lady (Balliol) Covered by Chilibang .... (Hugo Lascelles Bloodstock) 1,700
Property of Mrs Ruth Mason, from Pine Ridge Farm Ltd
Global Lady b m (9yrs) Balliol - Princess Nefertiti (Tutankhamen) Covered by Unfuwain(USA)..................... (David Minton Bloodstock) 5,000
Point Of Law b f (3yrs) Law Society (USA) - Relatively Sharp (Sharpen Up)......... (Silfield Bloodstock) 800

1081

Property of Sir Gordon Brunton, from North Munstead Stud
Rose Parade b m (9yrs) Thatching - Scented Air (Derring-Do) Covered by Lycius(USA)....... (Mrs C S Knowles) 12,000
Tiffany Gem (IRE) ch m (4yrs) Caerleon (USA) - Lady Habitat (Habitat) Covered by Reprimand........ (Patrick O'Neill) 19,000
Property of a Partnership, from Lode Moors Farm
Appealing b m (11yrs) Star Appeal - Mayfell (Rockefella) Covered by Chilibang ..... (D J Simpson) 2,200
Property of a Partnership, from Hunsley House Stud
Skarberg (FR) ch m (10yrs) Noir Et Or - Musken (FR) (Caracolero (USA)) Covered by Rambo Dancer(Can).. (B.B.A.) 1,400
Property of Tyrnest Stud
Kumzar br m (9yrs) Hotfoot - Welsh Jane (Bold Lad (IRE)) Covered by Salse(USA) .... (Miss M E Gibbon) 8,000
Property of Mr T Barr, from National Stud
Bee Dee Dancer ch m (3yrs) Ballacashtal (CAN) - Albion Polka (Dance In Time (CAN)) Covered by Chilibang.......... (Susan Scargill) 1,550
Property of National Stud
Sisola (USA) b m (10yrs) Coastal (USA) - Water Woo (USA) (Tom Rolfe) Covered by Rock City..... (Panetta Bloodstock) 20,000
Vacherin (USA) b m (10yrs) Green Dancer (USA) - She's Decided (USA) (Decidedly) Covered by Chilibang..... (Cash) 2,100
Property of The Hon J G Lambton, from Longholes Stud
Lake Mistassiu b m (6yrs) Tina's Pet - Kakisa (Forlorn River) Covered by Ron's Victory(USA) .... (David Minton Bloodstock) 3,600
Preziosa ch m (8yrs) Homing - Ixia (I Say) Covered by Anshan...... (B A Wallis) 3,800

1082

Property of Whitting Commodities Ltd, from Castle Farm Stud
Kannbaniya gr m (6yrs) Mouktar - Kabbaala (Brigadier Gerard) Covered by Petoski (Mercury Bloodstock) 2,000
Property of Castle Farm Stud
Magnifica ch m (12yrs) Sandy Creek - Tots (Dual) Covered by Aragon .... (Jill Lamb Bloodstock) 2,300
Touraine (FR) ch m (15yrs) Luthier - Tour Nobel (FR) (Habitat) Covered by Never So Bold........ (Jill Lamb Bloodstock) 3,000
From Elsenham Stud
Queen's Lake b m (9yrs) Kings Lake (USA) - Latin Verses (Appiani II) Covered by Risk Me(Fr)................ (K Griffin) 6,200
Property of Benson Stud
Istiyfa (IRE) gr m (4yrs) Darshaan - Istiara (FR) (Crystal Palace (FR)) Covered by Prince Daniel(USA)........... (B.B.A.) 3,000
From Meddler Stud
Nikatino b m (7yrs) Bustino - Latakia (Morston (FR)) Covered by Superlative ..... (Mrs H Raw) 3,500
Property of M H D Madden and Partner, from High Tregawne Stud
Travel Legend b m (12yrs) Tap On Wood - Bananaquit (USA) (Prove It) Covered by Indian Ridge................. (B.B.A.) 3,400
b f (2yrs) Blakeney - Travel Magic (Henbit (USA)).................. (M Madden) 3,500
Property of Limestone Stud
Kaleidophone b m (9yrs) Kalaglow - Plum Bold (Be My Guest (USA)) Covered by Nomination.... (R Barnes Bloodstock) 3,000
Property of a Partnership, from Greens Park, Towcester
Angel Drummer b m (10yrs) Dance In Time (CAN) - First Watch (Primera) Covered by Petong.......... (Scorrier Estates) 9,800

1083

From Stetchworth Park Stud
Willow Court (USA) b m (17yrs) Little Current (USA) - Fleet Treat (Fleet Nasrullah) Covered by Environment Friend.................. (R D Soars) 3,100
Property of Clarendon Park Stud, from Ted Voute, Agent
Wild Moon (USA) b m (8yrs) Arctic Tern (USA) - Wild Lover (USA) (Lyphard (USA)) Covered by Hadeer (R D Soars) 800
From Ted Voute, Agent
High Matinee gr m (13yrs) Shirley Heights - Matinee (Zeddaan) Covered by Robellino(USA)............. (R Birkle) 8,000
Patraana gr m (12yrs) Nishapour (FR) - Polana (FR) (Botticelli) Covered by Sharpo.................... (K Griffin) 1,100
Property of a Partnership, from Trickledown Stud
Anderson Rose b m (5yrs) Kind Of Hush - Fille de Bourbon (Ille de Bourbon (USA)) Covered by Faustus(USA)...... (B.B.A.) 800
Property of Mount Coote Stud, Ireland
Added Attraction (IRE) b m (3yrs) Alzao (USA) - Welcome Addition (Habitat) Covered by Fools Holme(USA)........ (Alle Vamento Del Sei) 2,800
From Mount Coote Stud, Ireland
b f (2yrs) Fairy King (USA) - Civility (Shirley Heights).............. (Cotswold Stud) 13,500

Property of Brook Stud Ltd, from Brook Stud

Inneglow gr m (6yrs) Kalaglow - Intoxication (Great Nephew) Covered by Shavian .. (E Fleming) 7,200

From Elsenham Stud

Wayward Polly br m (13yrs) Lochnager - Trigamy (Tribal Chief) Covered by Risk Me (FR)............. (Naif Alotaibi) 2,500

From Aston Park Stud

Chiming Melody b m (8yrs) Cure The Blues (USA) - Bentinck Hotel (Red God) ..... (Britton House Stud) 1,200

Contadora b m (4yrs) Shardari - Antrona (Royal Palace) Covered by Weldnaas (USA).................. (P D Player) 10,000

Glowing Reference b or br m (4yrs) Reference Point - Select Sale (Auction Ring) Covered by Weldnaas (USA).......... (A Spalding) 5,000

Gold Palatia (USA) b m (4yrs) Miswaki (USA) - Palpitate (USA) (Blushing Groom (FR)) Covered by Weldnaas (USA)................. (J C S Wilson) 1,400

1084

Property of Lord Haddington, from Aston Park Stud

Jove's Voodoo (USA) gr m (12yrs) Northern Jove (CAN) - Doll Dreams (FR) (Reliance II) Covered by Weldnaas (USA) .. (Cash) 3,200

From Aston Park Stud

Loufagh (USA) ch m (5yrs) Bering - Nibabu (FR) (Nishapour (FR)) Covered by Nicholas (USA)...... (Centaur Bloodstock) 5,000

Property of Aston Park Stud

Misfire ch m (12yrs) Gunner B - Brookfield Miss (Welsh Pageant) Covered by Weldnaas (USA)... (Mrs C Humphrey) 2,200

From Fittocks Stud

Eskimo Spring (USA) ch m (7yrs) Riverman (USA) - Wintergrace (USA) (Northern Dancer) Covered by Statoblest........ (Musaed Al-Salem) 13,500

Humanity ch m (5yrs) Ahonoora - Helietta (Tyrnavos) Covered by Warrshan (USA) (Musaed Al-Salem) 8,000

Shining Through ch m (3yrs) Be My Guest (USA) - Brillantissime (USA) (Riverman (USA)) Covered by Statoblest... (Cash) 9,500

Property of P H & J G Locke, Farming and Forestry, from Crimbourne Stud

Dabbiana (CAN) b or br m (10yrs) Fappiano (USA) - Baby Diamonds (Habitat) Covered by Niniski (USA) believed NOT in foal.................. (Planarrive Ltd) 6,500

Property of Home Stud Ltd

Queen And Country b m (12yrs) Town And Country - Polairia (Polic) Covered by Never So Bold........... (P Thorman) 5,500

Selaginella ch m (4yrs) Pharly (FR) - Smagiada (Young Generation) Covered by Emarati (USA)...... (J C S Wilson) 1,400

From Ewar Stud Farms

Flower Arrangement b m (6yrs) Lomond (USA) - Arrangement (Floribunda) Covered by Shavian.. (Manor House Stud) 11,000

1085

(HORSES-IN-TRAINING)

Property of Shadwell Estate Co Ltd, from Shadwell Stud

Hamseh (USA) b f (2yrs) Danzig (USA) - Aghani (USA) (Blushing Groom (FR))... (Mercury Bloodstock) 5,000

Property of Mr J L C Pearce, from Abington Place Stables

Miss Kinabalu b f (3yrs) Shirley Heights - Miss Kuta Beach (Bold Lad (IRE)) ..... (J Pearce) 8,000

From Abington Place Stables

Vinnamera b f (3yrs) Niniski (USA) - Vaslava (Habitat)..................... (Cash) 800

Property of Juddmonte Farms Ltd

Anbo (IRE) ch f (2yrs) Ballad Rock - Tatouma (USA) (The Minstrel (CAN)) ..... (Centaur Bloodstock) 2,600

Andanito (IRE) b c (2yrs) Darshaan - Newquay (Great Nephew)... (Lady Herries) 17,000

Appro b f (2yrs) Rousillon (USA) - Apply (Kings Lake (USA))..... (Mab Agency) 2,800

Banjoist (USA) b c (2yrs) The Minstrel (CAN) - Blue Grass Field (Top Ville).... (C.B.A.) 21,000

Certain Flair b f (2yrs) Danehill (USA) - Welsh Daylight (Welsh Pageant) ...... (D Adams) 9,000

Clinking b g (2yrs) Glint Of Gold - Kai (Kalamoun)............. (Ted Voute) 21,000

County Set b c (2yrs) Mtoto - Countess Olivia (Prince Tenderfoot (USA))....... (Tony Nerses) 44,000

Dee ch f (2yrs) Caerleon (USA) - Riverstreak (USA) (Irish River (FR)).. (Mab Agency) 16,500

Deliver (IRE) b f (2yrs) Rousillon (USA) - Livry (USA) (Lyphard (USA))... (B.B.A.) 9,800

Diary Date (USA) b f (2yrs) Alysheba (USA) - Social Column (USA) (Vaguely Noble).. (Mercury Bloodstock) 38,000

1086

Property of Juddmonte Farms Inc

Ferryman (USA) ch c (2yrs) Riverman (USA) - Go Leasing (Star Appeal)............ (Conti Bloodstock) 8,000

Property of Juddmonte Farms Ltd

Gilbertina (USA) b f (2yrs) Known Fact (USA) - Royal Graustark (USA) (Graustark).................. (B.B.A.) 11,500

Gingerly (USA) b f (2yrs) Ferdinand (USA) - Fruhingstag (FR) (Orsini)............. (Northmore Stud Farm) 8,500

Jangle (IRE) b c (2yrs) Danehill (USA) - Soleiade (Posse (USA)) (Tony Nerses) 22,000

Jet Skiff (USA) b c (2yrs) Lear Fan (USA) - Cox Girl (USA) (Cox's Ridge (USA)).... (N Clement) 17,500

Property of Juddmonte Farms Inc

Marshall Ney (USA) b c (2yrs) Danzig Connection (USA) - Godetia (USA) (Sir Ivor) (Lillingston Bloodstock) 21,000

Property of Juddmonte Farms Ltd

Nightjar (USA) b c (2yrs) Storm Bird (CAN) - Catty (USA) (Never Bend)..... (C.B.A.) 27,000

Pandysia (USA) b f (2yrs) Storm Bird (CAN) - Artiste (Artaius (USA)) .... (Silverleaf Farms, Inc) 20,000
Pazzo b c (2yrs) Danehill (USA) - Sand Grouse (USA) (Arctic Tern (USA))...... (Conti Bloodstock) 10,000
Restate (IRE) b f (2yrs) Soviet Star (USA) - Busca (USA) (Mr Prospector (USA)) ... (D Murray Smith) 11,500
Romancer (IRE) br c (2yrs) Caerleon (USA) - Courtesane (USA) (Majestic Light (USA)). .... (C.B.A.) 13,000
Square Deal (FR) b c (2yrs) Sharpo - River Dove (USA) (Riverman (USA)).......... (Peter Doyle Bloodstock) 4,800
Sunbaked (USA) b f (2yrs) Lyphard (USA) - Island Charm (Hawaii)......... (C.B.A.) 34,000
Tropical Rain b f (2yrs) Rainbow Quest (USA) - Atropa (USA) (Vaguely Noble) .. (Emerald Bloodstock) 4,800
Wry Smile b c (2yrs) Nashwan (USA) - Bourbon Girl (Ile de Bourbon (USA)) ... (J Nedoy) 1,800
Zacaroon b f (2yrs) Last Tycoon - Samaza (USA) (Arctic Tern (USA)).............. (Lord Huntingdon) 8,800

1087

Property of Mr F Salman, from Kingstone Warren Stables

Penny Fan b f (3yrs) Nomination - Trwyn Cilan (Import) .... (Kildare Thoroughbred Services) 8,000

From South Bank Stables

Sword Sail b f (3yrs) Kris - Main Sail (Blakeney).................... (B.B.A.) 2,200
Wavelet ch f (2yrs) Sharrood (USA) - Wave Dancer (Dance In Time (CAN)) .... (Axel Donnerstag) 4,000

From Warren Place Stables

Bewails (IRE) b f (2yrs) Caerleon (USA) - Honey Reef (Mill Reef (USA)).......... (A Walder) 1,200
Piedi Lane (USA) b f (3yrs) Alleged (USA) - Northeastern (USA) (Northern Dancer) (Alle Vam Ento Del Sei) 5,000

From Freemason Lodge

Tokyo b f (3yrs) Mtoto - Rosetta Stone (Guillaume Tell (USA)).................... (Jill Lamb Bloodstock) 5,200

Property of Mr Fahd Salman, from Whatcombe Stables

Eye Witness (IRE) b f (3yrs) Don't Forget Me - Mariakova (USA) (The Minstrel (CAN)). .... (C Gordon-Watson) 7,000
Western Friend (USA) ch f (3yrs) Gone West (USA) - Lajna (Be My Guest (USA)). .... (Cheveley Park Stud) 6,800

From Bedford House Stables

Balmoral Belle b f (3yrs) Shirley Heights - Highland Ball (Bold Lad (IRE)) .... (David Minton Bloodstock) 7,000
La Menorquina (USA) b or br f (3yrs) Woodman (USA) - Hail The Lady (USA) (Hail The Pirates (USA)) .... (Geoffrey Howson Bloodstock) 10,000

1088

From Beckhampton House Stables

Hello Ireland b f (2yrs) Reference Point - Select Sale (Auction Ring (USA)) ...... (Will Edmeades Bloodstock) 12,000

From Stanley House Stables Ltd

Ragamuffin Mandy (USA) b f (2yrs) Manila (USA) - Rascal Rascal (USA) (Ack Ack (USA)). .... (Mercury Bloodstock) 1,800

Property of a Partnership, from Lodge Farm Stables

Famous Beauty b m (6yrs) Vision (USA) - Relfo (Relko)............. (I M Rachid) 7,400

Property of Mrs B Facchino, from Woodside Stables

City Times (IRE) b f (3yrs) Last Tycoon - Sea Harrier (Grundy)...... (Hyde Stud) 3,600

Property of Barouche Stud, from Woodside Stables

Polar Moon b f (3yrs) Damister (USA) - Almitra (Targowice (USA))...... (Cash) 3,400

Property of Mr D J & Mrs S Allen, from Woodside Stables

Virginia Cottage b f (4yrs) Lomond (USA) - Bermuda Classic (Double Form)..... (Mercury Bloodstock) 5,000

Property of Mr R M Cyzer, from Elliotts

Haven Of Love (IRE) b f (3yrs) Waajib - Arena (Sallust) .... (Kildare Thoroughbred Services) 2,000
Chase The Stars b f (3yrs) Riverman (USA) - Burning Issue (Persian Bold).......... (Dolphin Bloodstock) 31,000

Property of a Partnership, from Coronation Stables

Silver Sea (IRE) b f (3yrs) Silver Hawk (USA) - Bonnie Isle (Pitcairn)................ (Mrs S C Thomas) 1,800

From Southgate Stables

Champagne 'n Roses ch f (3yrs) Chief Singer - Pushoff (USA) (Sauce Boat (USA)). .... (Bloomsbury Stud) 4,400
Cut Fine b f (3yrs) Kris - Belle Arrivee (Bustino)............ (Lanwades Stud) 7,000
Shikoku b f (3yrs) Green Desert (USA) - Sandy Island (Mill Reef (USA)) .... (Dolphin Bloodstock) 20,000

1089

From Albert House Stables

Major's Triumph (IRE) ch f (3yrs) Hatim (USA) - Hetty Green (Bay Express) .... (Alan Spargo) 2,200

Property of a Gentleman, from Charnwood Stables

Dailysportdutch b f (3yrs) Risk Me (FR) - Gold Duchess (Sonnen Gold) .... (J Nedoy) 2,000

Property of Mr R Dawson, from Charnwood Stables

Miliyel ch f (4yrs) Rousillon (USA) - Amalee (Troy)...................... (T Shally) 1,260

Property of Thermal Glazing Systems, from Upper Herdswick Farm

Do The Right Thing ch m (5yrs) Busted - Taniokey (Grundy) .... (Mercury Bloodstock) 6,000

Property of Northern Partnership, from Hambleton Lodge Stables
Viking Waters b f (3yrs) Viking (USA) - Melting Snows (High Top) (Finn Kruse) 1,050

(STALLION)

Property of a Partnership, from Hart Hill Stud
Sulaafah (USA) br h (11yrs) Riverman (USA) - Celerity (FR) (Dancer's Image (USA)) (Cormac McCormack Associates) 4,600

1090

FAIRYHOUSE (Tattersalls)

Sunday, December 5th

Property of Mr James Meaney
Tough Character b g (5yrs) Farhaan - In The Limelight (Prince Hansel)............. (Ronnie Kelly) 1,500

Property of Judith Scott
b g (2yrs) Record Run - Familiarity (Gleason) .... (Cash) 800

Property of Miss Constance O'Reill Hyland, from Hollywood House
b f (4yrs) Supreme Leader - True Minstrel (Prince Hansel)....... (John McGrath) 3,500

Property of Mr Brendan Egan
ch f (3yrs) Wolverlife - Follow Gold (Yankee Gold)................ (George Young) 2,000

From Beehive Stables
b c (2yrs) Celio Rufo - Dunmahon Lady (General Ironside)............. (Cash) 800

Property of Mr Thomas Ryan, from Tyone Stables
ch g (3yrs) Salluceva - Moredee (Morston) (Cash) 1,800

Property of E Cosgrove, from Shanrod Stud
ch f (4yrs) Phardante (FR) - Frensham (FR) (Floribunda).............. (C Stringer) 400

From Aghalacca Stud
b f (3yrs) Toca Madera - Interj (Salmon Leap)......................... (Cash) 460
ch f (3yrs) Henbit (USA) - Who's She (Tall Noble)....................... (Cash) 1,600

Property of P Joyce, from Clogher Stables
Rosshill River gr m (6yrs) Over The River (FR) - Annies Owen (Master Owen) ... (Cash) 1,400

1091

Property of Kilbrew Stud
br f (3yrs) Supreme Leader - I'm Tops (Tumble Wind)....... (Joseph Dwyer) 1,300

Property of Mr Michael Fox
b f (3yrs) Bulldozer - Selonati (Selko) ...... (P J Foy) 550
b g (4yrs) Bulldozer - La Mola (FR) (Tarbes) (R Wright) 550

Property of Mr Desmond O'Sullivan
b g (2yrs) Electric - Oakland Leisure (Lucky Brief)........................ (Cash) 500

Property of Mr Jack Dwan
King Girseach (IRE) b g (4yrs) King's Ride - Girseach (Furry Glen).......... (Cash) 11,500

Property of Mr Ned Hannon
ch g (2yrs) John French - Pearl Reef (Main Reef)........................ (Cash) 1,500

Property of Mr Patrick O'Donnell, from Hilltop Stables
b g (3yrs) said to be Roselier (FR) - said to be Pineys D'Lght (Proverb) .... (Pat Greene) 2,200

Property of Mr Bernard Murphy
b f (4yrs) Over The River (FR) - Taragreen (Tarqogan).................. (Cash) 1,500

Property of Mr Hugh Holohan
b f (4yrs) Le Moss - Cherry Token (Prince Hansel)...................... (Cash) 2,000

Property of a Partnership
b f (3yrs) Strong Gale - Housewife (Sunyboy)................ (Stanley Moore) 1,300

1092

Property of Rachel Bennett (Agent)
ch f (2yrs) Stalker - Miss Quotation (Sexton Blake)............... (Coppice Farm) 1,100

Property of a Gentleman
ch f (3yrs) Hatim (USA) - So Serene (Dalsaan)................. (George Doyle) 800
ch g (3yrs) Hatim (USA) - Jumana (Windjammer)...................... (Cash) 5,800

From Boardsmill Stud
ch f (2yrs) Carmelite House (USA) - Asinara (Julio Mariner)............... (Cash) 700

From Hartfield Stud
ch y f Executive Perk - Corrib Agreement (Lucifer).............. (W R Collum) 1,300

Property of Mr J R McLoughlin
b y f Phardante (FR) - Wenvoe (Konigssee) (John McGrath) 1,000

From Ballymagarvey Stud
br y f Executive Perk - The Steel Woman (Steel Heart).......... (George Doyle) 1,300

Property of Mr S Wilson
b y g Yashgan - Quay Wall (Paddy's Stream)............. (Fionna Kinnear) 1,600

Property of Mrs A M Corcoran, from Knockmartin Stud
b y g Tremblant - Wiasma (Ashmore)...... (Patrick Ward) 1,200

Property of Mrs Hazel O'Haire
b y g Tremblant - Star Gold (Bonne Noel) .. (Cash) 1,000

1093

Property of L Lannigan
ch y g Orchestra - Madonna Pica (Salluceva)....................... (Cash) 1,700
ch y g Orchestra - Clarrie (Ballyciptic)...... (Cash) 2,700

From Boardsmill Stud
ch y c Carmelite House (USA) - Asinara (Julio Mariner)........ (George Doyle) 1,500

Property of S McKitterick
b y f Cataldi - Paulines Girl (Hello Gorgeous) .... (George Doyle) 780

Property of Mr Michael Murphy, from Clohamon Stud
ch y c Sharp Charter - Restless Lady (Sandford Lad)................ (J McGrath) 1,300

Property of Mrs R M Boyd, from Lough View House
br y f Executive Perk - Merseyside (Anfield) .... (Cash) 620
Property of Mrs A L McCoubrey
b c f Poet's Dream - Rapid Rhythm (Free State)........................ (Cash) 400
Property of Mr Shane Power
b f f Lafontaine (USA) - Calamaire (Callernish)......................... (Cash) 400
Property of Mr Tim Owens
b f f Montelimar (USA) - Winter Run (Deep Run)......................... (Cash) 1,550
From Ashleigh Stud
br f f Royal Fountain - Right Hand (Oats)... (Cash) 750
br f f Royal Fountain - Door Rapper (IRE) (Mandalus).................. (Cash) 700

1094

Property of Mr Danny Doran
ch c f Broadsword (USA) - In My View (King's Ride).................... (Cash) 2,300
From Aghern House Stud
b f f Jolly Jake (NZ) - Black Betty (Furry Glen)......................... (Cash) 950
Property of Mr Thomas Carey
b f f Broken Hearted - Cool Glen (Furry Glen)......................... (Cash) 1,200
Property of Mr W Hanbidge
b f f Yashgan - Glendee (Boreen)... (Cash) 480
From Sea View Stud (Agent)
b c f Supreme Leader - Sudaf (Welsh Saint) .... (Jimmy Byrne Bloodstock) 1,600
Property of Mr Gerard Hannan
b c f Spanish Place (USA) - Glenair Princess (Tanfirion)............... (J Dreaper) 1,400
Property of a Partnership
Anteamos (IRE) b m (3yrs) Phardante (FR) - Kamiros (Prince Hansel) Covered by Le Bavard (FR)............ (Joe O'Boyle) 2,000
From Castletown Quarry Stud
Foprtysumthin (IRE) b m (4yrs) Forties Field (FR) - Strawberry Mess (Pardal) Covered by Yashgan.... (Mrs P Hourigan) 1,050
Property of Marshall Parkhill
Fly Fuss b m (12yrs) Little Buskins - Black Fuss (Black Rock) Covered by Orchestra.............. (Joe O'Boyle) 660
Property of Mr John Carmichael
Matouba (USA) ch m (6yrs) Riverman (USA) - Indoor (FR) (Caracolero) Covered by Zaffaran (USA)....... (Pat O'Loughlin) 850
Surreal ch m (8yrs) Bustino - Swiftacre (Bay Express) Covered by Zaffaran (USA).... (Pat O'Loughlin) 1,100

1095

From Grove Lodge Stud
Trio Royaal b m (9yrs) King's Ride - Castle Creeper (Royal Buck) Covered by Prince Rupert (FR)..... (John McEvoy) 700
Property of D P Smith
Queen Of Swords b m (10yrs) Reform - Grade Well (Derring-Do) Covered by King Luthier........... (Joe O'Boyle) 860

PRIVATE SALES
Property of Ms P Haselden
Red Barons Lady (IRE) b m (4yrs) Electric - Tour Nobel (FR) (Habitat) .... (Emerald Bloodstock) 2,650
From Ardmore Stud
b g f King's Ride - Judith Shakespeare (Daybrook Lad)........ (John McNeill) 2,500

1096

FAIRYHOUSE (Tattersalls)

Monday, December 6th

Property of T Clarke
Lady Native (IRE) b f (2yrs) Mill Native (USA) - Denise's Tia (USA) (London Company)............ (P Hutchinson) 400
Property of Mr Seamus Fahey
Party Guest ch m (6yrs) What A Guest - Tremiti (Sun Prince).......... (Pat Cox) 2,100
Property of Miss G Finn, from Blackhall Little Stable
Louises Fancy (IRE) ch f (3yrs) Horage - Choclate Baby (Kashiwa) .... (Pat Hutchinson) 400
Property of Darley Stud Management Co Ltd, from Brownstown House Stables
Raincheck b g (2yrs) Mtoto - Lashing (USA) (Storm Bird)............. (Andes Yau) 900
Property of Dr Tony O'Reilly, from Castlemartin Stud Farm
Montego Bay (IRE) b f (2yrs) Be My Guest (USA) - Susan's Way (Red God)....... (Pat Hutchinson) 450
From Glebe House Stables
Europe (USA) b c (3yrs) Lear Fan (USA) - Clara Bow (USA) (Coastal)........... (Peter Doyle Bloodstock) 1,000
Property of Mr Patrick J Foy, from Drummindoo Stud
ch f (2yrs) The Noble Player (USA) - Samosa (Sexton Blake)........ (Cash) 550
Property of Mrs O O'Connor, from Hazelwood Stables
Oranedin b c (2yrs) Squill (USA) - Moments Joy (Adonijah)................. (Cash) 19,000
To Dissolve a Partnership, from Hazelwood Stables
Brigenser (IRE) b g (3yrs) Digamist (USA) - Lady Anna Livia (Ahonoora).... (Cash) 4,000
From First Flyer Stables
b g (2yrs) Dance Of Life (USA) - Future Tense (USA) (Pretense)... (Andes Yau) 2,000

1097

Property of Mr Frank Dunne, from Hamwood Stud
b f (3yrs) Commanche Run - Fiery Song (Ballad Rock)................ (Cash) 650
br f (2yrs) Glow (USA) - Reprint (Kampala) (Cash) 400
Property of Mr Joe Patterson
b f (2yrs) Presidium - Generation Gap (Young Generation)............ (Cash) 400

Property of Mr S Scully

ch f (2yrs) Scottish Reel - Chance Match (Royal Match)................. (Cash) 400

Property of Mr Kevin Kearney

Sunshine Seal ch m (6yrs) Horage - Finely Feathered (Prince Tenderfoot) .... (Seamus Fahey) 2,000

Property of a Partnership, from Lohunda Park Stables

Kar Or br c (3yrs) Doyoun - Cape Race (USA) (Northern Dancer) .... (Kerr & Co Ltd) 15,500

Another Fiddle (IRE) b g (3yrs) Waajib - Elmar (Lord Gayle)....... (Jack Doyle) 5,400

From Castletown Quarry Stud

Wonderful Venture (IRE) gr c (2yrs) Taufan (USA) - Tender And True (USA) (Prove Out).......................... (Cash) 550

From Thomastown Castle

Marketplace (IRE) b c (2yrs) Runnett - Ordinary Fare (USA) (What A Pleasure) .... (Sl Manlova Radka) 1,300

Property of a Partnership, from Rossmore Lodge Stables

Suave Redskin ch c (2yrs) Persian Bold - Richman Sisters (Captain James)...... (Leonard Jarven) 3,000

1098

(YEARLINGS)

From Meeleen Stud

b y c Shernazar - Perfect Guest (What A Guest).......... (Emerald Bloodstock) 4,600

Property of Mr Reobert Kennedy

ch y c Nashamaa - Sweet Camden (Camden Town)............... (Cash) 1,700

Property of Mr Patrick J Kearns

b y f Welsh Term - Labour Of Love (Miami Springs)...................... (Cash) 480

Property of Mrs A M Corcoran, from Knockmartin Stud

b y f Anita's Prince - Malibu Lady (Ragapan) .... (Cash) 620

b y f Anita's Prince - Soft Moss (Santamoss)...................... (Cash) 500

Property of Mr Dermot Finnegan, from Balbray Stud

b y c Doulab (USA) - Stanza Dancer (Stanford)................. (Pat Donworth) 3,000

From Richmond Park Stud

ch y c Doubletour (USA) - Shygate (Shy Groom)............... (Ger Hourigan) 3,000

Property of Mr & Mrs Leo Collins, from Ennistown Stud

b y f Nordico (USA) - Shyoushka (Shy Groom)................ (Kilcarty Stud) 2,600

Property of Mr John H Orpen, from Kealfoun Farm

b y f Mansooj - Jep Chapeau (Viking)...... (Sean McGuinness) 340

From Aghern House Stud

gr y f Bar Dexter (USA) - Sabev (USA) (Saber Thrust)................. (Cash) 380

b y f Architect (USA) - Lady Bountiful (USA) (Strike Gold).................. (Cash) 370

b y f Jolly Jake (NZ) - Her Beads (USA) (Ruken).......... (Sean McGuinness) 340

1099

Property of Mr Conor Crowley, from Dolly's Grove Stud

b y f King Of Clubs - Selham (Derring-Do).. (Pat McCarthy) 1,000

Property of Mr E Farrell

b y c Nashamaa - Opera Guest (Be My Guest)...................... (Cash) 700

From Tally-Ho Stud

ch y f Try My Best (USA) - Song Beam (Song)...................... (Cash) 1,000

Property of Dr Frank Healy

ch y c Horage - Court Ballet (Barrons Court) .... (Cash) 2,000

Property of Mr Brian McGagh, from Lodge House Stud

ch y f Nashamaa - Silver Shoals (USA) (Mill Reef).................. (Alan Clarke) 500

From Ballyhampshire Stud

ch y f Gadabout (USA) - Ginosa (Kalamoun) (M Kerenan) 550

Property of Nora (Ann) Lawlor, from Oak Lodge Stud

b y f Soughaan (USA) - Rocklands Rosie (Muscatite).......... (Thomas Smith) 450

Property of Mr Frank Lynch, from Green Gates Stables

b y f Bluebird (USA) - Borough Counsel (Law Society)............. (S Moore) 5,500

From Gortnacloona Stud

ch y c Exactly Sharp (USA) - Flora Rubra (Red God)................... (Cash) 1,150

(FOALS)

Property of Mrs C Bastable, from Oristown Lodge

b c f Standaan (FR) - Bidwell (Auction Ring) (R Colclough) 1,200

1100

Property of Mr Tim Owens

b f f Maelstrom Lake - Rekolette (Relko)... (Pat McGree) 550

Property of Mr Patrick Ruane

b c f Doubletour (USA) - Princess Lydia (Shack)....... (Newlands House Stud) 750

Property of Mr Michael Markey

b c f Sharp Victor (USA) - Tara View (IRE) (Wassl)....................... (Cash) 4,300

Property of Mr Anthony Ross

ch f f Ajraas (USA) - Penny On The Jack (IRE) (Hatim).................. (Cash) 320

b c f Ajraas (USA) - Kilima (Mount Hagen) (David Minton Bloodstock) 4,400

From Newton Park Stud

b or br f f Standaan (FR) - Lypharden (IRE) (Lyphard's Special).... (Sean Costello) 370

Property of S W D McIlveen, Monkstown House Stud

b c f Sharp Victor (USA) - Vicky's Last (Muscatite).................. (Cash) 2,000

From Williamstown Stud

ch f f Magical Wonder (USA) - Humble Mission (Shack)............... (Cash) 3,400

Property of Mrs F Ferguson

b c f Red Sunset - Golden Empress (Cavo Doro)...................... (D Barry) 2,350 b c f Fayruz - Galapagos (Pitskelly).. (Cash) 6,200

1101

Property of Nora (Ann) Lawlor, from Oak Lodge Stud
ch c f Imperial Frontier (USA) - Rocklands Rosie (Muscatite)............. (Cash) 3,200
Property of Mr Sean Madigan
b c f Simply Great (FR) - Rosy O'Leary (Majetta)..................... (Cash) 5,400
From Aghern House Stud
b f f Jolly Jake (NZ) - Image Of Beauty (USA) (Say Numero Uno)... (Ed Duffy) 450
From Carrickhill Stud
b c f Doubletour (USA) - Tamara's Reef (Main Reef)..................... (Cash) 500
ch f f Soviet Lad (USA) - Shopping (FR) (Sheshoon)........ (Goldenview Stud) 1,850
Property of Mrs M Keating
b c f Syrtos - Tumble On (Tumble Wind)... (Martin Finegan) 1,700
Property of a Partnership, from Rathcannon House Stud
ch c f Eurobus - Rose And Honey (Amber Rama)......................... (Cash) 800
b f f Exactly Sharp (USA) - Summer Bloom (Silly Season)........... (Acorn Farm) 3,600
From Thomastown Stud
ch f f Topanoora - Elegant Miss (Prince Tenderfoot)................... (Cash) 440
From Ballylinch Stud
b c f Bob Back (USA) - Heirloom (Tanfirion) (C B A) 1,650

1102

From Scarteen Stud
b f f Cyrano de Bergerac - Reading Light (IRE) (Thatching)............. (Cash) 1,000
ch f f Be My Native (USA) - Tenoria (Mansingh)........................ (Cash) 1,650
From Gerrardstown Stud
b c f Prince Rupert (FR) - Moutalina (Ela-Mana-Mou)................... (Cash) 1,250
Property of Mr John O'Byrne, from Lodge Stud
b c f Distinctly North (USA) - Lisa's Music (Abwah)...................... (Cash) 4,600
From Kildare Stud
b c f Distinctly North (USA) - Na Suila (Montekin)...................... (Cash) 2,000
From Williamstown Stud
gr f f Broken Hearted - Miss Deauville (Sovereign Path)............... (Cash) 1,500
ch c f Magical Wonder (USA) - Zestino (Shack)......................... (Cash) 3,600
Property of Mr Joseph R Hardy
b c f Cyrano de Bergerac - Reshuffle (Sassafras)............... (Liam Ormsby) 2,800
From Rathturtin Stud
b c f Distinctly North (USA) - Late And Lamented (Dublin Taxi)......... (Cash) 900
Property of Mr Denis McDonnell
b f f Cyrano de Bergerac - Royal Custody (Reform)...................... (Cash) 400

1103

Property of Dr T J Molony
ch c f Prince Rupert (FR) - St Clair Star (Sallust)....................... (Cash) 4,200
Property of Mr Maurice Phelan, from Maplestown Stud
br c f John French - Jib (Welsh Pageant) (Cash) 480
From Castle Stud
b f f Cyrano de Bergerac - Polisteppin (Jimmy Reppin)................ (Cash) 600
Property of Mrs R M Boyd, from Lough View House
b c f My Generation - Merseyside (Anfield) (Cash) 450
From Kildare Stud
b c f Distinctly North (USA) - Be My Million (Taufan).......... (Charlestown Stud) 2,400
Property of Mr P Farrell, from Copperalley Stud
ch c f Classic Secret (USA) - Direct Link (USA) (Super Concorde).............. (David Minton Bloodstock) 1,900
Property of Ivan Freeley
b c f Archway (IRE) - Anita's Princess (Miami Springs)............... (S T S) 5,600
Property of Mr J A Slattery
b c f Brush Aside (USA) - Gifted Lady (Divine Gift).................... (Cash) 3,000
Property of Mr Peter Casey, from Palace Farm
b f f Pennine Walk - Polyester Girl (Ridan) (Cash) 4,100
From Summerseat Stud
ch f f Lanfranco - Seapoint (Major Point)... (Cash) 800

1104

Property of Waterside Stud, from Loughmore Stud
b c f Cyrano de Bergerac - Algonquin Park (High Line)...................... (Cash) 3,200
b f f Kefaah (USA) - Wind Armour (IRE) (Heraldiste)...................... (Cash) 360
From Grove Lodge Stud
b f f Pennine Walk - Sir Elnaas (USA) (Sir Ivor)........................ (Cash) 3,200
Property of Mr Kevin Maginn
b f f Maelstrom Lake - True Colour (FR) (Known Fact)................ (J D Hill) 500
Property of Mr Edward Tynan
b c f Salt Dome (USA) - Trojan Honey (Trojan Fen)........... (Maurice Burns) 1,500
Property of Mr Liam Burke, from Tichglass Stud
b f f Nashamaa - Rosebran Ruby (Orchestra)...................... (Cash) 2,100
Property of Ballintry Stables
b c f Broken Hearted - Windfield Princess (Wolverlife).................. (F Mallon) 400
From Ardoon Stud
b f f Nashamaa - Hard Sweet (Hard Fought) .... (N Stassen) 3,300
Property of a Partnership
b or br c f Mulhollande (USA) - Silojoka (Home Guard)......... (Ger Hourigan) 4,600
(MARES)
From Ballygallon Stud
State Treasure ch m (13yrs) Secretariat (USA) - Diomedia (USA) (Sea Bird II) Covered by Be My Guest (USA)....... (Canice Farrell) 8,000
Reps Retton (USA) b or br m (10yrs) J O Tobin (USA) - Repetitious (Northfields) Covered by Law Society (USA) (Cash) 2,600

Esh Sham (USA) b m (12yrs) Damascus (USA) - Dusky Evening (USA) (Tim Tam) Covered by Ela-Mana-Mou.... (C B A) 10,500

1105

Property of Mrs M Gilmore, from Bernice Stud

Straw Bonnet b m (14yrs) Thatch (USA) - I've A Bee (USA) (Sir Ivor) Covered by Roaring Riva.................. (Cash) 400

Secret Lightning (USA) ch m (13yrs) Secretariat (USA) - Flash Flooding (USA) (Jaipur) Covered by Roaring Riva......... (Aghern House Stud) 720

Property of Waterside Stud, from Loughmore Stud

Rockbourne b m (4yrs) Midyan (USA) - River Music (Riverman).............. (Meath Stud Farm) 5,300

From Carrickhill Stud

Tamara's Reef b m (10yrs) Main Reef - Gay Nipper (Aggressor) Covered by Broken Hearted...................... (Cash) 1,050

From Sommerville

Ciarain's Choice b m (15yrs) Young Emperor - Pretty Patch (Golden Cloud) Covered by Petorius........... (Cash) 1,050

Property of Anthony Ross

Penny On The Jack (IRE) b m (4yrs) Hatim (USA) - Kilima (Mount Hagen) Covered by Kefaah(USA)............... (Cash) 680

Kilima b m (12yrs) Mount Hagen (FR) - Valbelle (Val de Loir) Coveredy by Simple Great(FR)................. (Cash) 1,100

From Leinster Stud

Storm Crest b m (17yrs) Lord Gayle (USA) - Nectareous (Tutan Khamen) Covered by Ajraas(USA)................ (Cash) 750

From Hamwood Stud

Embroidery b m (9yrs) Lords (USA) - Thread Of Gold (Huntercombe) Covered by Treasure Kay......... (Maurice Burns) 1,000

Property of John McLaughlin

Ashley Springs ch m (10yrs) Ballymore - Sarahcee (Prominer) Covered by Broken Hearted.................. (Cash) 860

1106

Property of P J O'Hagan

Plunkets Choice b m (12yrs) Home Guard (USA) - First Draft (USA) (Tom Rolfe) Covered by Mac's Imp......... (Cash) 4,500

From Ballysax Manor Stud (Agent)

Ever So b m (11yrs) Mummy's Pet - Brig Of Ayr (Brigadier Gerard) Covered by Maledetto(IRE).................. (Cash) 1,700

Property of Maurice Phelan, from Maplestown Stud

Simply Reply (IRE) b m (5yrs) Simply Great (FR) - Yes My Dear (USA) (Affirmed) Coveredy by John French...... (Cash) 800

Property of Strand Syndicate

Tahaddi (USA) ch m (6yrs) Northern Baby (CAN) - Nofertiti (FR) (Exbury) Covered by Arcane(USA)............... (Cash) 6,200

From Lodge Stud

Miss Eurolink br m (6yrs) Touching Wood (USA) - Sule Skerry (Scottish Rifle).... (Cash) 2,000

Property of a partnership

b y f Be My Chief (USA) - Countess Olivia (Prince Tenderfoot)... (M E D Francis) 4,600

b y f Dancing Dissident (USA) - Butterfly Kiss (Beldale Flutter).. (Pat Dunworth) 4,100

1107

KILL (Goffs)

Tuesday, December 7th

Property of Mr Edward Keyes

b y f Soviet Lad (USA) - Thornbeam (Beldale Flutter)........... (T Slattery) 5,000

From Kilnamoragh Stud

b y c Sayaarr (USA) - March The Second (Millfontaine)................. (Cash) 6,200

Santa Maria (GER) b m (13yrs) Literat - San Salvador (GER) (Klairon) Covered by Conquering Hero(USA)..... (M Dillon) 400

From Lee Valley Farm

b y c Prince Rupert - Lady Celina (FR) (Crystal Palace)............... (Cash) 900

b y f Kefaah (USA) - Merrie Moment (IRE) (Taufan)............. (Ms Anne Ryder) 800

From Longfield Farm

ch y f Topanoora - Salt (Sallust)........... (Golden View Stud) 2,000

From Loughandys House Stud

b y c Cyrano de Bergerac - Silver Stone (Derrylin).................... (Cash) 500

From Malton Stud

Run To Daddy ch m (9yrs) Ballad Rock - Kalympia (Kalydon) Covered by Contract Law(USA)........ (T H Caldwell) 1,000

b or br y f Contract Law (USA) - Run To Daddy (Ballad Rock).... (T Broughton) 400

b y c Contract Law (USA) - Remember Mulvilla (Ballad Rock)............... (Redpender Stud) 5,400

b y c Contract Law (USA) - Truly Flattering (Hard Fought).............. (P Doyle) 3,000

1108

Property of F D McAuley

b or br y c Broken Hearted - Innate (Be My Native)....................... (Cash) 5,000

Property of Mr Jim McGing

b y f Archway (IRE) - Hollow Candle (Wolver Hollow)............... (Cash) 600

From Mile-Stream Stud

b y f Glenstal (USA) - Dear And Near (Ahonoora).................. (Cash) 400

Alibar's Pet (IRE) ch f (3yrs) Hatim (USA) - Pluvia (USA) (Raise A Native)... (Cash) 4,500

From Mount Pleasant Farm

ch y c Archway (IRE) - Push Bike (Ballad Rock)................(Kileenlea Stud) 5,000

Property of Mr Matther Tynan, from Moyglass Stud

b y f Waajib - Sweet Unison (USA) (One For All)............................ (Cash) 570

Property of Mr Patrick Joseph Murray

b or br y f Camden Town - Mary Morison (Ragusa)..................... (Cash) 1,200

Property of Mr Sean Murphy

b y c Ajraas (USA) - Mine Hostess (IRE) (Shernazar)........................ (Cash) 1,500

Property of Mr Michael T O'Donnell

Gliding Beauty (IRE) b m (5yrs) Muscatite - Caroline's Mark (On Your Mark) Covered by Treasure Kay...... (M Scully) 450

Property of Mr Michael O'Halloran

b or br y c Eve's Error - Manuale Del Utente (Montekin)........................ (Cash) 500

1109

From Oak Lodge Stud

b y f Primo Dominie - Cadasi (Persian Bold) (Kellsboro House Stud) 7,000

b y c Maelstrom Lake - Golden View (Ragusa).................... (J Cash) 580

Property of C & M Bourke, from Oak Lodge Stud

Derrinturn ch m (14yrs) Touch Paper - Lovely Pretense (USA) (Pretense) Conquering Hero(USA)......... (T F Lacy) 700

From Oak Lodge Stud

First Fleet ch m (14yrs) Artaius (USA) - Fleet (Immortality).......... (M Dillon) 520

Property of Mrs John Pollock

b c f Ajraas (USA) - Whichcombe (Huntercombe).... (David Minton Bloodstock) 2,800

From Rathbarry Stud (agent)

ch f f Fayruz - Win For Me (Bonne Noel)... (T Slattery) 7,000

From Rathurtin Stud

Late And Lamented ch m (6yrs) Dublin Taxi - North Hut (Northfields) Covered by River Falls........................ (Cash) 1,000

From Riversfield Stud

Final Bluff (IRE) b m (4yrs) Auction Ring (USA) - Crepe de Paille (Final Straw) Covered by Cyrano De Bergerac ...... (Centaur Bloodstock Agency) 7,200

Nisha Society (IRE) b m (4yrs) Law Society (USA) - Final Moment (Nishapour) Covered by Cyrano De Bergerac.......... (Suzanne O'Neill) 3,000

Vroom Vroom (IRE) ch f (3yrs) Baillamont (USA) - Flushing Meadow (USA) (Raise A Native)...................... (Cash) 600

Fairy Bride (IRE) b f (3yrs) Fairy King (USA) - Swift Linnet (Wolver Hollow) (J Cash) 500

1110

From Rockville House

b or br f f Contract Law (USA) - Souveniers (Relko).................. (T J Cooper) 1,800

From Rosemount House Stud

gr f f Distinctly North (USA) - Caring (Crowned Prince)......... (J M Egan) 12,000

b f f Distinctly North (USA) - Swoon Along (Dunphy)........................ (Cash) 3,700

From Rossenarra Stud

Wicklow Way (IRE) b or br f (3yrs) Pennine Walk - Faraway Places (Flair Path)..... (D McDonogh) 10,500

From Rossmore Lodge

Lydia Mc (IRE) b f (2yrs) Fairy King (USA) - La Petruschka (Ballad Rock) .... (Mercury Bloodstock) 2,000

Haanem b f (3yrs) Mtoto - Noble Born (USA) (The Minstrel).... (Stal P C C O) 4,300

From Rye House Stables

b c f Classic Music (USA) - Atedaun (Ahonoora).................. (Cash) 7,500

Property of Michael Scully

b c f Salt Dome (USA) - Grange Hollow (Wolver Hollow)........ (G Renaghan) 1,600

From Skehanagh Stud

Payne's Grey gr m (6yrs) Godswalk (USA) - Rarest Flower (USA) (Carlemont) Covered by Distinctly North(USA)......... (Ennistown Stud) 3,200

Property of Brendan Smith

b f f Petorius - Magic Green (Magic Mirror) (D Cosgrove) 1,150

1111

From Solohead Stables

b or br c f Cyrano de Bergerac - Scobys Baby (Nishapour).......... (T Slattery) 3,600

From Somerton Staud (agent)

Zertxuna b m (14yrs) Averof - Hannah Darling (Match III) Covered by Digamist(USA)...................... (Cash) 750

From Tara Vale Farm

b f f Posen (USA) - Dame Ross (Raga Navarro)........... (Claramount Stud) 3,000

Property of a partnership, from Tipper House Stud

ch c f Simply Great (FR) - Melarka (Dara Monarch).................... (Cash) 5,700

From Tipper House Stud (agent)

b c f Homo Sapien - Halpin (Yashgan) ..... (A O'Gorman) 500

c f Homo Sapien - Maria Tudor (Sassafras) (Cash) 750

To dissolve a partnership, from Treascon Stud

Asta Madera (IRE) br f (3yrs) Toca Madera - Asta (Captain's Gig)....... (D Palmer) 16,000

Property of T C Butler, from Treascon Stud

Pam Story b m (13yrs) Sallust - Lady Pamela (Don) Covered by Archway(IRE).... (Cash) 2,600

From Trimblestown Stud

b f f Carmelite House (USA) - Cheerful Heart (Petingo)................ (Cash) 450

b f f Carmelite House (USA) - Mousil (Moulton)..................... (Cash) 650

ch f f Carmelite House (USA) - Rheinsparkle (Rheingold).......... (Boston Stables) 800

1112

Property of Paul McEnery, from Vinesgrove Stables

b c f Glenstal (USA) - All Time High (Sandhurst Prince)........... (E Fitzpatrick) 2,200

ch c f Archway (IRE) - Gobolino (Don) ..... (Cash) 5,200

Property of P A Ward

Beachcomber Lass ch m (8yrs) Day Is Done - Polyxo (Polyfoto) Covered by Desperado(FR)................ (Cash) 1,150

From Argle House Stud (agent)

b c f Distinctly North (USA) - Angel Of Music (Burslem).............. (Cash) 3,700

Property of B M J Dolan, from Ashdown House Stud

b c f Contract Law (USA) - Monrovia (FR) (Dancer's Image) .... (Knocklong House Stud) 3,500

From Ashfield Farm

Bap's Miracle b m (13yrs) Track Spare - Bap (Current Coin) Covered by Shalford(FR) (Benson Stud) 4,200

Property of Michael J Holden, from Ballintober Stables

b c f Jurado (USA) - Lusaka (Wolver Hollow) .... (Cash) 1,200

Property of Mrs Gerald Cantrell, from Ballintyre Stud

Princess Fleet b m (10yrs) Prince Tenderfoot (USA) - Parler Mink (Party Mink) Covered by Maledetto...... (M Scully) 400

Property of Angel Frances Kavanagh, from Ballintyre Stud

Record Song b m (6yrs) Indian King (USA) - Turkish Song (Aglojo) Covered by Digamist(USA)............. (Benson Stud) 850

Property of Sean Finnegan, from Ballybee House Stud

ch c f Archway (IRE) - Next Ballet (Ballymore)................. (J Gaughan) 2,100

1113

Property of M R Maguire, from Ballybee House Stud

b f f Nashamaa - Raggy (Smoggy)......... (M Scully) 400

Property of R Maguire, from Ballybee House Stud

ch c f Archway (IRE) - Rebecca's Girl (IRE) (Nashamaa).................. (Cash) 8,300

From Ballycrystal Stud

b f f Accordion - Mandy's Last (Krayyan)... (Cash) 500

Property of John Purfield, from Ballymagarvey Stud

b f f Tirol - Salique (Sallust)............... (B B A (Ireland)) 5,200

Property of Mrs V J Thompson, from Ballyroe Stud

b c f Maelstrom Lake - Village Countess (IRE) (Reasonable).............. (Cash) 500

From Ballysax Manor Stud (Agent)

b c f Double Schwartz - True Vintage (Horage)............ (Miss J Morgan) 2,700

Property of William Tierney, from Ballyvelish Stud

ch c f Exactly Sharp (USA) - Style (Homing) (Cash) 800

From Beech House Stud

b c f Scenic - Knapping (Busted).......... (L Walshe) 10,500

Property of J R & A Bell

Bold And Brief b m (14yrs) Bold Lad (IRE) - Brief Agenda (Levmoss) Covered by Jareer(USA)............. (K Wallace) 2,500

From Belmont Stud

Hat And Gloves gr m (9yrs) Wolver Hollow - Dancing Hat (High Hat) Covered by Shalford(IRE)................. (E B A) 5,500

b f f Dancing Dissident (USA) - Hat And Gloves (Wolver Hollow)....... (E B A) 4,600

b f f Bluebird (USA) - Jody Ann (Prince Tenderfoot).................. (Cash) 2,700

Satinas Best b m (9yrs) Tyrnavos - Satina (Pall Mall)................ (M Scully) 400

b f f Runnett - Satina's Best (Tyrnavos).... (M Kernan) 400

1114

From Bendemeer Stud

Sound The Alarm b m (18yrs) Brigadier Gerard - Melodina (Tudor Melody) Covered by Homo Sapien......... (Cash) 550

Property of Owen Burke

gr c f Magical Strike (USA) - Secret Assignment (Vitiges)................. (Cash) 2,000

Property of Patrick Brady

ch f f Classic Secret (USA) - Mrs Lucky (Royal Match)............. (R Black) 3,400

Property of John Brennan

b c f Broken Hearted - Lady Wise (Lord Gayle).............. (Baletry Stables) 1,800

From Brittas House Stud (agent)

Wavering Flame (USA) ch m (11yrs) Roberto (USA) - Kadesh (USA) (Lucky Mel) Covered by Shalford(IRE)........ (M Bozzi) 8,000

Property of R J Cotter, from Brook House Stud

b f f Tirol - Royal Episode (Royal Match)... (Equine Associates) 1,100

From Bryanstown Stud (agent)

ch f f Red Sunset - Mo Mhuirnin (Miner's Lamp)....................... (Cash) 400

Property of Patrick Purcell, from Butlersgrove Stud

b f f Mazaad - Nikkicola (USA) (Damascus) (Cash) 500

Property of Miss Mary Caesar, from Caesar House Stud

b f f Classic Music (USA) - Paddock Princess (Dragonara Palace)............ (B B A (Ireland)) 5,500

From Cappagh House Stud

Phar Lapa gr m (11yrs) Grundy - Cottage Pie (Kalamoun) Covered by Fools Holme(USA)........... (T H Caldwell) 2,100

ch c f Jareer (USA) - Phar Lapa (Grundy)... (Cash) 2,000

Hit For Six ch m (7yrs) Tap On Wood - Sixpenny (English Prince) Covered by River Falls.................... (Cash) 4,500

ch f f Soviet Lad (USA) - Hit For Six (Tap On Wood).................. (T Slattery) 3,000

1115

Property of Mrs A Cassidy

ch f f Mac's Imp (USA) - Luan Causca (Pampapaul)............... (L Fillitico) 3,400

From Castletown Stud (agent)

All In White (FR) gr m (12yrs) Carwhite (FR) - Concord Hymn (Emerson).......... (Maryville Stud) 1,100

Chez Nous ch m (15yrs) Habitat - Knighton House (Pall Mall)....... (Ms S O'Neill) 900

Star Of Aran b m (8yrs) Artaius (USA) - Pride Of Kilcarn (Klairon) Covered by Waajib.............. (Nanallac Stud) 500

Gay Surrender b m (19yrs) Sir Gaylord - Renounce (Big Game) Covered by Archway(IRE)......... (Maryville Stud) 1,100

Property of J F J Regan, from Church Hill Stud

ch c f Doubletour (USA) - Smurfette (Baptism)............ (Mercury Bloodstock) 600

Property of Dr John A Waldron, from Cloondarome Stud Farm

b f f Fayruz - Cupid Miss (Anita's Prince) .. (Cash) 3,400

Property of Mrs C A Moore, from Clunemore Lodge

Jargonel (IRE) b f (3yrs) Jareer (USA) - Native Flower (Tumble Wind)......... (J J Bolton) 420

From Commonstown Stud

b f f Kefaah (USA) - Arthur's Daughter (Artaius)......................... (Cash) 1,500

ch f f Kefaah (USA) - Elite (Lord Gayle) .... (Ms B Egan) 4,000

1116

Property of James Conroy

b c f Prince Rupert (FR) - Redington Belle (Ahonoora)................. (M Scully) 400

From Coolfore House Stud

b c f Don't Forget Me - Sokolova (Red Regent).......... (Charlestown Stud) 6,800

Property of Cornelius Crowley

ch c f Salt Dome (USA) - Hada Rani (Jaazeiro)................ (Carrick Stables) 2,100

Property of Mrs K Cullen

ch f f Digamist (USA) - My Covey (Taufan) (W Hill) 1,000

From Curragh House

b c f Salt Dome (USA) - Dancing Lass (King Emperor).................. (L Filitico) 1,250

From Deerpark Stud

b f f Distinctly North (USA) - Numidia (Sallust)...................... (T Slattery) 5,600

From Dollanstown Stud (agent)

b f f Anita's Prince - Regal Charmer (Royal And Regal)............ (Rathasker Stud) 1,650

b or br c f Anita's Prince - Kiss The Bride (Sweet Revenge)..... (Carrick Stables) 3,500

Property of Mrs P Mullins, from Doninga Stud

b f f Imperial Frontier (USA) - Dundovail (Dunphy)........ (Hutson Valley I C P) 1,600

b c f Distinctly North (USA) - Whatyawant (Auction Ring).. (Bermuda Associates) 10,500

Property of Jacqueline Donnelly

ch c f Mulhollande (USA) - Charo (Mariacci) (Cash) 2,000

Property of Albert Douglas

b f f Jurado (USA) - Tranacate (Malacate) .. (M Scully) 400

Property of a parternship, from Dromin House Stud

b f f Distinctly North (USA) - Travel Away (Tachypous).................. (Cash) 1,250

1117

KILL (Goffs)
Wednesday, December 8th

Property of A G Moylan, from Earlspark Stud

Sweet Million ch m (13yrs) Sweet Revenge - Cendrillon (Sound Track) Covered by Cyrano De Bergerac........... (Cash) 400

Property of The Elms Stud

ch c f Mulhollande (USA) - Sexton Belle (Sexton Blake).......... (Marco Bozzi) 1,000

Property of Dara Ni Choileain, from Ennistown Stud

b c f Treasure Kay - Door To Door (USA) (Nureyev)......................(Cash) 400

Property of Erindale Stud

b f f Digamist (USA) - Islet Time (Burslem) (Dermot Carty) 2,200

Property of Evergreen Stud

b c f Topanoora - Zazu (Cure The Blues) ... (Cash) 3,000

Property of Adrian Egan, from Farnane House

c f Distinctly North (USA) - Kuwaiti (Home Guard)....................... (Cash) 3,000

Property of Mr E O'Riordan, from Fenpark Stables

Two Magpies ch f (6yrs) Doulab (USA) - Captive Audience (Bold Lad).... (Cash) 1,650

From Fortbarrington Stud

ch f f Archway (IRE) - Why Not Glow (IRE) (Glow)...................... (Cash) 3,700

From Foxbrook Stud

ch f f Mac's Imp (USA) - Hossvend (Malinowski).......... (Golden View Stud) 2,600

Property of Mr Steven Gilmore

b f (2yrs) Mister Majestic - Shirley's Joy (Shirley Heights)......... (Ml Gilmore) 3,400

1118

From Green Hills Stud

b f f Distinctly North (USA) - Achafalaya (USA) (Apalachee)............ (Cash) 900

Property of Mr Hubert Hardiman

b c f Mac's Imp (USA) - Burkina (African Sky)........... (Richard A McDonnell) 15,000

Sassalin ch m (17yrs) Sassafras - Madlin (Sovereign Path) Covered by Mac's Imp(USA)............ (Tally-Ho Stud) 3,200

b c f Distinctly North (USA) - Sassalin (Sassafras)........... (Glenvale Stud) 10,000

From Hawkfield Stables

Jive b m (6yrs) Ahonoora - Rince Si (Malinowski) Covered by Distinctly North(USA)...................(Cash) 6,000

b c f Toca Madera - Erins Rose (Artaius)... (Cash) 400

Property of Mr John Hennessy

b c f Astronef - Covey's Quick Step (Godswalk)..... (David Minton Bloodstock) 4,600

From Herbertstown Stud (Agent)

b c f Distinctly North (USA) - Foulkesmills (Tanfirion).. (David Minton Bloodstock) 4,000

ch c f Al Hareb (USA) - I'll Take Paris (USA) (Vaguely Noble)..........(T J Cooper) 2,600

Property of Mrs Loretta Murphy, from Herbertstown Stud (Agent)

b f f Shahrastani (USA) - Relko's Belle (FR) (Relko)................. (Acorn Stud) 3,000

1119

Property of Lorcan Higgins

b c f Mazaad - Lucky Charm (IRE) (Pennine Walk).......... (Mercury Bloodstock) 2,000

Property of Mrs S Lenehan, from Hollow Farm
b or br f f Ballad Rock - Secret Heart (Vision)................ (Boston Stables) 3,900
Property of Mr Denis Houlihan
b f f Waajib - Hyland Rose (Steel Heart) ... (Cash) 2,500
From Innismore Stud
b f f Classic Music (USA) - Ceral Queen (Oats)........................ (C B A) 2,700
From Ballylea Stud
b c f Thatching - Ski Sailing (USA) (Royal Ski)................ (Ballymorris Stud) 5,500
b c f Fairy King (USA) - Sanedtki (Sallust) .. (Marco Bozzi) 2,100
Property of a Syndicate, from Broguestown Stud
Mister Majestic b h (9yrs) Tumble Wind (USA) - Our Village (Ballymore)........ (Edward Daly) 4,000
Property of Mr Eddie Kavanagh
ch y f Glenstal (USA) - Park Lady (Tap On Wood)........................ (Cash) 5,000
Property of Mr Michael Kindregan
b y f Waajib - Lady Huntingtower (Hard Fought)............ (Damien Maguire) 1,100
From Laureldean Stud
b y c Gallic League - Dane Valley (Simbir).. (Cash) 5,000

1120

Property of Mr Maurice Leamy
b y c Carmelite House (USA) - Maiden's Walk (Tower Walk)............. (Cash) 580
Property of a Gentleman, from Leemark Stud
b y f Pennine Walk - Heather Lil (Ballymore) .... (Old Meadow Stud) 5,000
Property of Mr Patrick Hayes, from Mill House Stud
b y c Dance Of Life (USA) - Hellebore (IRE) (Shernazar)............. (Marco Bozzi) 4,500
Property of Mr Seamus Mitten
br y f Glow (USA) - Athry (Be Friendly) .... (Mercury Bloodstock) 1,100
From Moorfield Stables
b y f Gallic League - Naglaa (USA) (State Dinner)................ (Czech Racing) 1,050
From Newtown House
b y f The Noble Player (USA) - Skevena (Niniski)............ (Mr Bo Helander) 600
From Oak Lodge Stud
b y f Waajib - Balistic Princess (Lomond) .. (Cash) 600
Property of Mr Edward Doyle, from Punchestown House Stud
ch y f Fools Holme (USA) - Milly Daydream (Hard Fought) .... (European Bloodstock Agency) 1,100
From Redmondstown Stud
b y c Fools Holme (USA) - Dream Of Spring (Hello Gorgeous).............. (Cash) 7,500
From Rochestown Stud
b y f Fayruz - Grecian Blue (Majority Blue) (Cash) 2,100

1121

From Rosemount House Stud
ch y c The Noble Player (USA) - Fair Mark (On Your Mark) (Mercury Bloodstock) 1,400
From Rye House Stables
b y f Dominion Royale - Epoch (Wolver Hollow)................ (Denis Lynch) 1,700
Property of Mr T C Butler, from Canadian Stud
b y f Don't Forget Me - Canadian Guest (Be My Guest)...... (Mercury Bloodstock) 3,000
From Acorn Stud
b y f Cyrano de Bergerac - All Alright (Alzao) .... (Cash) 1,000
ch y f Dominion Royale - Miss Galwegian (Sandford Lad)................. (Cash) 1,600
From Aghern House Stud
b y f Jolly Jake (NZ) - Tina's Robin (USA) (Robin's Song)...... (Mr Bo Helander) 400
Property of a Gentleman, from Allenvale Stbles
b y c The Noble Player (USA) - Miss Tan A Dee (Tanfirion)........ (Comino Sech) 650
From Ardmore Stud
b y f Glenstal (USA) - Fourp'ny Rock (Ahonoora)....... (Liam O'Donoghue) 1,000
From Ballagh Stud
b y c Treasure Kay - God Save (USA) (Empery)...................... (Cash) 1,050
ch y f Nashamaa - Royal Gina (Royal Match) .... (Andrew Kinsella) 400

1122

Property of Miss Orla Whelton, from Ballintemple Hill Stables
b y c Skyliner - Dream Academy (Town And Country)........ (Mercury Bloodstock) 3,000
Property of Mr Sean Finnegan,from Ballybee House Stud
ch y c Nashamaa - Next Ballet (Ballymore) (Cash) 1,500
Property of Mr Frank Lacy,from Ballycrystal Stud
b y g Accordion - Mandy's Last (Krayyan).. (Con Marnane) 450
From Belfry Lodge Stud
ch y c Emmson - Mainham (Boreen) ...... (Comini Sech) 1,100
From Bellview Stud
b y c Classic Secret (USA) - Miss Ming (Tender King)........... (Marco Bozzi) 1,100
Property of Templerainey House Stud,from Rachel Bennett (Agent)
ch y c John French - Red Sox (Red Alert).. (Con Marnane) 1,100
Property of D J Sweeney,from Big Acre Stud
b y f Gallic League - Mistress Vyne (Prince Tenderfoot)................ (N C Bell) 2,700
Property of Mr Owen Bourke
b y c Contract Law (USA) - Cordon (Morston)............... (Joseph Crowley) 4,600
b y c Fayruz - Miss Retlaw (Kampala)...... (Mr Michael Scully) 550
Property of Mr John Bowdren
b y f Al Hareb (USA) - Femme de Fer (USA) (Mr Leader)......... (David Cosgrove) 1,600

1123

Property of Mr Matthew Carr
b y f Mister Majestic - Vivungi (USA) (Exburg)...................... (Cash) 440

From Clonfert House
b y c Prince Rupert (FR) - Route Royale (Roi Soleil)................... (T A Regan) 4,000
From Coolnaleen House Stud
ch y c Be My Native (USA) - Nelly Gail (Mount Hagen)..................... (Cash) 8,000
Property of a Partnership,from Dawn House
b y c Carmelite House - Shou Good (Octavo)........ (Mercury Bloodstock) 1,700
From Evans Dier
b y c The Noble Player (USA) - Angmering (Raga Navarro)..... (Donald Redmond) 1,000
From Eyrefield Lodge
b y c Tirol - Coupe D'Hebe (Ile de Bourbon) (Mercury Bloodstock) 12,000
From Greenwood Stud
b y f Cyrano de Bergerac - Sweet Reprieve (Shirley Heights)...... (David Cosgrove) 1,000
Property of Miss J Harnett
ch y c Bold Arrangement - Taree Gold (Tumble Wind)......... (Marco Bozzi) 5,000
From Hawkfield Stables
ch y c Fayruz - Jive (Ahonoora)..... (Cash) 450
From Herbertstown Stud (Agent)
br y f Roi Danzig (USA) - Midnight Child (Manado)................. (T A Regan) 5,600
ch y f Thatching - Rising Tide (Red Alert) .. (Pat Burns) 10,500
b y f Glenstal (USA) - Vaguely Deesse (USA) (Vaguely Noble)... (Marco Bozzi) 750
ch y f Al Hareb (USA) - I'll Take Paris (USA) (Vaguely Noble)..... (Pascal Carmody) 700

1124

Property of Mr R Hodgins
ch y f Glacial Storm - Kew Gift (Faraway Son)..................... (Leo Curtin) 900
Property of Siobhan Connolly,from Hollymount House Stud
b y f Doubletour (USA) - Ice Baby (Grundy) (Mercury Bloodstock) 800
Property of Mrs J Cummins,from Horeswood Stud
b or br y f King Luthier - Racy Lady (Continuation)....... (Mercury Bloodstock) 3,200
Property of Mr Tom Hughes
b y c Al Hareb (USA) - Jeewan (Touching Wood)............. (David Cosgrove) 5,200
b y f Waajib - Walnut Lass (Tap On Wood) (Cash) 400
From Belmount Stud
ch y f Exhibitioner - Jody Ann (Prince Tenderfoot).............. (James Gorman) 500
From Feagh Stud
b or br y c Don't Forget Me - With Diamonds (Shirley Heights)............. (Mercury Bloodstock) 3,700
Property of Olive Thenissen,from Rockwood Stud
b c f Accordion - Anka (GER) (Solo Dancer) (Cash) 1,200
Property of Mr Robert Kearney
Over The Maigue (IRE) b f (2yrs) Glenstal (USA) - Arctic Dark (Arctic Tern) (Cash) 400
From Beckfield Stud
ch y c Krayyan - Emma Louise (Shack) .... (Cash) 1,450

1125

Property of Chris Pearse (Agent)
Stride On (IRE) b m (4yrs) Pennine Walk - Isla Bonita (Kings Lake) Covered by Prince Rupert (FR)............. (Cash) 1,400
Property of A G Moylan, from Earlspark Stud
ch y f Gadabout (USA) - Sweet Million (Sweet Revenge)........ (Donie Hunt) 400
From Solohead Stables
br y f Vision (USA) - Lucky Realm (Realm) (Kevin Wallace) 1,200
From Birdcatcher Stables
Three Musketeers (IRE) b g (4yrs) Taufan (USA) - Catherine Clare (Sallust)....... (Don Kelly Bloodstock) 2,000
To Dissolve a Partnership, from Tullahought Stables
Calamity Cane (IRE) ch m (5yrs) Pollerton - Just Image (Saidam)..... (John Codd) 400
From Clonshambo Stud
Stormy Hero (IRE) b c (2yrs) Conquering Hero (USA) - Doppio Filo (Vision) .... (Mr Martin Treacy) 400
Property of Mr J Hunt, from Tu Va Stables
Takahanada (IRE) b c (3yrs) Al Nasr (FR) - Camarange (FR) (Carmarthen).. (Cash) 650
From Bullstown
Domino's Ring (IRE) b g (4yrs) Auction Ring (USA) - Domino's Nurse (Dom Racine) (R H Buckler) 4,000
Property of a Partnership, from Rathkenty Stables
Naycab ch m (7yrs) Le Moss - Vultang Lady (Le Bavard)................... (Cash) 800
Property of a Partnership, from Moyanna Stables
b g (4yrs) Pollerton - We Might (Furry Glen) (Cash) 520

1126

Property of Mr John P Phelan
ch g (3yrs) Gunner B - Celtic Slave (Celtic Cone)...................... (Cash) 1,600
From Ascon Stables
b f (3yrs) Callernish - Tanfirion Star (Tanfirion).............. (Matthew Maher) 1,100
Property of Mr P Brennan
gr g (3yrs) Celio Rufo - Little Gort (Roselier) (Cash) 4,600
From Forest View Stud
b g (3yrs) Aylesfield - Its All Taboo (Smartset)................. (K Furlong) 1,400
From North Kildare Stud
ch g (3yrs) Parliament - Sabie Star (Hardgreen)......................... (Cash) 4,000
Property of McGrath Bros
br g (3yrs) Dancing Lights (USA) - Weaver's Fool (Weavers Hall)...... (Paul O'Reilly) 3,000
From Hunters Lodge Stud
b g (4yrs) Kambalda - Tip The Gold (Harwell) .... (Cash) 4,800
From Strawhall House Stables
ch f (3yrs) Phardante (FR) - Sacajawea (Tanfirion)............... (Gary Finlay) 4,700
From Woodhouse Estate Stud
b g (3yrs) Lancastrian - Breeze Dancer (Torus)....................... (Cash) 4,000

b or br g (3yrs) Phardante (FR) - Sketch Plan (Stetchworth)................ (Cash) 3,100

1127

Property of Mr John Blake

b g (4yrs) Marktingo - April Glimmer (Slippered)....................... (Cash) 2,000

Property of Mr Des Lalor

b g (5yrs) Spanish Place (USA) - Ilen (Pitskelly).......... (David FitzGerald) 2,400

Property of E Pakenham, from Clongrave Stables

b g (3yrs) Convinced - Marmessie (Martinmas)......................... (Cash) 450

Property of Mr Wilson C Eakins

b f (3yrs) Over The River (FR) - Tawendo (FR) (Tamelo) .... (European Bloodstock Agency) 2,700

b or br f (3yrs) Torus - Half Circle (Tarqogan) .... (Emerald Bloodstock) 1,600

From New Wells Stud

b g (3yrs) Strong Statement (USA) - The Hoggett (Cheval).............. (Cash) 1,200

From Garryrichard Stud

b or br g (4yrs) Whistling Deer - Across The Miles (Honoured Guest)........ (Cash) 2,000

Property of Mr Tom Dorgan

ch g (4yrs) Remainder Man - Aylesbury Lady (Le Bavard).............. (Cash) 2,300

Property of Mr W R Deacon

Ross Tudor (IRE) b g (4yrs) Roselier (FR) - Countess Tudor (Beau Tudor)......... (Patrick Flaherty) 2,000

Property of Mr Seamus Keane, from Russelstown Stud

gr f (4yrs) Roselier (FR) - Lake Road (Boreen).................. (John Carr) 1,150

1128

To Dissolve a Partnership, from Clonshambo Stud

Swiss Tactic (IRE) b g (4yrs) Strong Gale - Julia's Pauper (Pauper).......... (Cash) 1,100

Property of Mr Michael Heskin

b f (4yrs) Strong Gale - Cinderwood (Laurence O)..................... (Cash) 1,100

From Hymenstown House Stud

b or br f (4yrs) Royal Fountain - In The Forest (Crowded Room).............. (G J M Bloodstock) 1,850

From Rockmills Stud

b g (5yrs) Lord Ha Ha - Fanny Brave (Brave Invader)..... (Mr Christopher Dawson) 2,400

Property of Mr William Joyce

b g (3yrs) Millfontaine - How Are You (Brave Invader)................ (Cash) 2,000

To Dissolve A Partnership, from Seaside Stud

ch f (4yrs) Torus - Two Shares (The Parson) (Brian Glavin) 1,000

From Bridge Lawn Stud

b g (3yrs) Good Thyne (USA) - Tina O'Flynn (Martinmas).......... (John R Sullivan) 5,200

From Martinstown Farm

ch g (4yrs) Parliament - Holy Terror (Divine Gift)........................ (Cash) 1,550

From Woodhouse Estate Stud

b or br f (2yrs) Strong Gale - Busy Girl (Bustiki)...................... (Cash) 4,500

b f (2yrs) Clearly Bust - Spyglass (Double Form)....................... (Cash) 500

1129

Property of Mr Robert Kearney

ch g (2yrs) The Noble Player (USA) - Anglesea Market (Sea Hawk II) (Cash) 3,000

From Roriston Stud

b f (2yrs) Corvaro (USA) - Boreen Queen (Boreen)................ (John Lynch) 500

From The Beeches Stud

b f (2yrs) Lancastrian - Merenda's Sister (Pauper).............. (John O'Brien) 2,000

Property of E Pakenham, from Clongrave Stables

b g (2yrs) Deep Society - Riah (Furry Glen) (P Powell) 1,500

Property of Mr Joseph Kruger II, from Rathaldron Stud

ch g (2yrs) Orchestra - Linda Dudley (Owen Dudley)............. (James Flaherty) 500

From Woodhouse Estate Stud

b g (2yrs) Le Moss - Tangaroa (Lord Gayle) (Cash) 1,350

b f (2yrs) Henbit (USA) - Breeze Dancer (Torus)........ (Mr Michael Canleady) 1,000

b f (2yrs) Cyrano de Bergerac - Lodina (Kala Shikari)...................... (Cash) 450

Property of Mr Matthew Carr

b f (2yrs) Yashgan - Quick Dream (Crepello) .... (Mr Vincent O'Toole) 500

Property of Mr G Redford

Sheer Power (IRE) b g (4yrs) Exhibitioner - Quality Blake (Blakeney)... (John Carr) 400

Hollow Vision (IRE) b g (5yrs) Cataldi - Clonderlaw (Kalamoun)..... (R Maars) 850

Tale A Tale (IRE) b g (4yrs) Tale Quale - Go In Time (Saulingo).. (Richard Shannon) 450

1130

PRIVATE SALES

From Lisiuex Stud

b c f Nashamaa - Amaprincess (Burslem) .. (Leonardo Filitico) 1,300

From Newtown House

br c f Topanoora - Skevena (Niniski) .... (Hilltown Stud) 3,000

Property of Mrs Anne Quinn

b c f Cyrano de Bergerac - Simple Love (Simply Great)....... (Rathbarry Stud) 2,500

From Rossenarra Stud (Agent)

b f f Fayruz - Nous (Le Johnstan) .... (Kenwood Bloodstock) 5,000

From Belfry Lodge Stud

ch c f Carefree Dancer (USA) - Mainham (Boreen)............. (Joseph Coates) 400

From Forest View Stud

b c f Millfontaine - Botswana (African Sky) (Eric Atkinson) 1,800

From Fortbarrington Stud

b c f Al Hareb (USA) - Bonvin (Taufan)..... (W Brannigan) 2,500

Property of Mr Hubert Hardiman
ch c f Archway (IRE) - Precision Chop (Hard Fought)........... (Ballymorris Stud) 1,650
From Jamestown House Stud
b f f Pennine Walk - Excitingly (USA) (Val de L'orne)........... (Michael Conaghan) 900
Property of Christina Hindley, from Ballydavid Stables
ch y c Krayyan - Zedosa's Pet (Prince Bee) (Charlestown Stud) 775

1131

PRIVATE SALES
Property of Mr Hubert Hardiman
b y f Gallic League - Damaslin (Camden Town)............... (Pat Donworth) 450
Property of E Pakenham, from Cloncrave Stables
ch f (3yrs) Meneval (USA) - Brave Queen (Brave Invader)........... (John Carr) 425
From Corries Stud
b y g Mummy's Luck - Queen Of Myshal (Majetta)............. (Fergus Hutton) 572
Property of Mr Jack Lett
b y g Phardante (FR) - Willabelle (Will Somers)................. (Liam Ryan) 850
From Clearystown House Stud
b y f Over The River (FR) - Ogan Spa (Tarqogan)....... (Maurice Morrissey) 550
From Corbal-Lis-Stud
b y g Royal Fountain - Noel's Flash (Deep Run)......................... (Cash) 2,500
Property of Mr Alan Dunlop, from Balloo Stables
b y f Buckskin (FR) - Arctic Conditions (Lucifer)............ (Eamonn Garrett) 1,500
Property of Mr Pauric B Goonan P C, from Boherdeel House Stud
b y c Broken Hearted - Karry's Sister (Super Slip)................ (Patrick Beirne) 1,700
From Blackabbey Stud
b y c Riverhead (USA) - Urdite (FR) (Concertino)................... (Lady Earle) 1,000

RE-SUBMITTED

From Tipper House Stud (Agent)
f f Homo Sapien - Bridget Folly (Crofter)... (Mr Michael Scully) 450
From The Elms Stud
ch y c Broken Hearted - Sexton Belle (Sexton Blake)......... (Denis Lynch) 750

1132

KILL (Goffs)
Thursday, December 9th

From Toomevara Stud
b y f Duca Di Busted - Araemo (Northern Guest)......................... (Cash) 1,000
Property of Tim McCarthy
b y c Carlingford Castle - Ilen Valley (Tanfirion)............. (Richard E Rohan) 1,000
Property of Mrs C Lucey, from Coolcower Stud
ch y g Carlingford Castle - Doucha Girl (Sheer Grit).................. (Cash) 13,500
From Greenwood Stud
b y f Executive Perk - Wonder (Tekoah) ... (Cash) 1,300
Property of Denis Murphy, from Ballyroberts Stable
b y g Good Thyne (USA) - Condonstown Rose (Giolla Mear)............ (Cash) 3,700
From Clearystown House Stud
ch y f Over The River (FR) - French Gateaux (Le Bavard)......... (Philip Morrissey) 520
From Corbal-Lis Stud
b y g Royal Fountain - Noel's Flash (Deep Run)................. (Sean Tiernan) 1,800
Property of Mrs M Graham
b y g Homo Sapien - Ivy Holme (Silly Season)............... (Joe Magee) 900
Property of Glenn Turley
b y c Asir - Kindly Lass (Wolver Hollow) ... (Cash) 4,900
From Knockaney Stud
ch y g Phardante (FR) - Go In Peace (The Parson)....................... (Cash) 1,100

1133

From Woodhouse Estate Stud
b y g Strong Gale - Miss Mims (Little Wolf) (David Minton Bloodstock) 4,400
From Lisfinny Castle
b y g Executive Perk - Radalgo (Ballad Rock).............. (Richard E Rohan) 1,500
From Mocklershill Stables (agent)
br y g Celio Rufo - Laurestown Rose (Derring Rose)............. (James Hales) 6,300
Property of P J Molloy, from Boley Farm
b y g Over The River (FR) - June Bug (Welsh Saint)........ (James Delaney) 5,000
b y g Supreme Leader - Whisht A Minute (IRE) (Balbao)........ (James Delaney) 2,500
From Cappmurragh Stud
b y g Balinger - Mustang Pride (Floriferous) (Cash) 800
ch y g Balinger - Nire's Pride (Beau Tudor) (Cash) 1,350
Property of John Mangan
b y c Phardante (FR) - Trendy Princess (Prince Tenderfoot)........... (Cash) 6,200
Property of James Ruane
gr y f Orchestra - Tara Grey (General Ironside)..................... (M Kernan) 600
From Liatris Stud
ch y g General Ironside - Just Killiney (Bargello)............... (Joe Magee) 1,800

1134

Property of The Marquis of Donegal, from Dunbrody Park Estates
ch y f Salluceva - Salt Mills (Proverb) (Cash) 700
From Garryrichard Stud
b y f Miner's Lamp - Romany River (Over The River)............ (Donal Hassett) 2,000
From Rosemount House Stud
b y f Executive Perk - Knight's Row (Le Bavard)............ (Philip Morrissey) 800
From Belmont Stud
b y c Be My Native (USA) - Swift Invader (Brave Invader) (Jeremy F C Maxwell) 6,800

Property of Messrs Michael and Tony O'Brien
b y g Electric - Sapphire Red (Red Alert) . . . (Annette McMahon) 5,200
Property of Mrs M O'Keeffe
b y g Brush Aside (USA) - Fair Vic (Fair Turn). . . . . (Cash) 4,500
Property of Tom Archdeacon
b y f Satco (FR) - Duchess (Electrify) . . . . . . (Jerry Mulvey) 1,500
Property of Charmspire Ltd, from John Sheehan
b y g King's Ride - The Best I Can (Derring Rose). . . . . (Cash) 4,200
b or br y g Pitpan - Thats Irish (Furry Glen) (David McCabe) 2,000
Property of E Mullins
b c f Miner's Lamp - Wind Chimes (The Parson). . . . . (Ms Paula Connon) 2,600

1135

From Jack Lett
b c f Sharp Charter - Willabelle (Will Somers). . . . . (Cash) 720
b c f Meneval (USA) - Rosie Josie (Trombone). (John Black) 650
From Aghern House Stud
b f f Jolly Jake (NZ) - Rosy Dawn (Rushmere). . . . . (E O'Mahony) 400
b c f Jolly Jake (NZ) - Loughrealt (Carlingford Castle). . . . . (Cash) 3,300
Property of Messrs. P & C Murphy
b c f Commanche Run - Slavesville (Charlottesville Flyer). . . . . (Leslie Young) 1,550
Property of Michael Murray, from Clohamon Stud
ch c f Sharp Charter - Lakefield Lady (Over The River). . . . . (Martin Ryan) 800
From Haresmead
b or br f f Lord Americo - Cora Gold (Goldhill). . . . . (Cash) 400
Property of Johanna O'Donovan, from The Colomane Stables
gr f f Roselier (FR) - Indian Idol (Indian Ruler). . . . . (Cash) 820
From Blackabbey Stud
b c f Topanoora - Life's Chance (IRE) (Wolverlife) (David Minton Bloodstock) 1,250
Property of Richard Fortune
gr c f Castle Keep - Sexton Lady (Sexton Blake). (Joe Allen) 950

1136

From Derrymore House
ch f f Roselier (FR) - Derrymore's Mossy (Le Moss). . . . . (Colm Farrell) 700
Property of T C Butler, from Canadian Stud
b c f Supreme Leader - Parveen (FR) (Kouban). . . . . (Cash) 1,900
From Coolnaleen House Stud
b c f Be My Native (USA) - Bellatollah (Bellman) . . . . (Equine Invesment Consultants) 3,200
From Ballynatin House
b f f Satco (FR) - Holy Times (IRE) (The Parson). . . . . (Colm Farrell) 420

From Ballynattin House
b f f Un Desperado (FR) - Sparkling Mary (Kambalda). . . . . (L Lee) 600
From Lisfinny Castle
b f f Buckskin (FR) - Infanta Helena (Pollerton). . . . . (Brittas House Stud) 400
b f f Commanche Run - Castle Leney (Mandalus). . . . . (Ms Catherine McLoughlin) 400
Property of Gary Simpson, from Rathmolyon House Stud
b c f Strong Gale - Donegal Moss (Le Moss). . . . . (Cash) 4,000
b c f Cataldi - Kiri's Return (Hawaiian Return). . . . . (Lady Earle) 1,200
From Rathmolyon House Stud
b c f Strong Gale - Regal Spark (Royal Match). . . . . (Cash) 8,000

1137

From Grange Stud
ch c f Glacial Storm (USA) - Raby (Pongee) (Frank Keogh) 2,900
Property of Mrs M F Magnier, from Grange Stud
b c f Supreme Leader - Rossacurra (Deep Run). . . . . (J T Doyle) 3,000
From Grange Stud
b c f Glacial Storm (USA) - Clontinty Queen (Laurence O). . . . . (Cash) 3,500
From Ballinteskin Stud
b or br f f Buckskin (FR) - Emerson Supreme (IRE) (Supreme Leader) . . . . . (Mark Travers) 1,300
Property of Mr & Mrs J Harold-Barry
ch c f Dry Dock - Popular View (Torus) . . . . (Patrick Beirne) 1,800
From Hillbrow Farm
b c f Tremblant - The Magpie Bush (Jasmine Star). . . . . (Cash) 1,800
Property of M Foster
gr f f Montelimar (USA) - Nancy's Sister (The Parson). . . . . (Louis Vambeck) 1,700
Property of Mrs C Ross
b c f Montelimar (USA) - Time Will Tell (Whistling Deer) . . . . (Equine Investment Consultants) 3,800
Property of Patrick Shanahan
br c f Glacial Storm (USA) - Theos Gin (Teofane). . . . . (John Rye) 900
ch c f Castle Keep - Gin An Tonic (Osprey Hawk). . . . . (John Brennan) 900

1138

From Lisfinny Castle
b c f Commanche Run - Anna Moss (Le Moss). . . . . (Cash) 1,100
b f f Be My Native (USA) - Annes Grove (Raise You Ten). . . . . (Cash) 750
From Ballynattin House
b c f King's Ride - Fern Glen (Furry Glen) . . (William Cribbin) 5,000
From Carrigdownane Stud (agent)
b c f Executive Perk - Wiji Damar (Laurence O). . . . . (Lady Earle) 1,700

b f f Lafontaine (USA) - Stella Romana (Roman Warrior)... (John B O'Connor) 800

Property of John O'Connor, from O.K.Stud

b f f Be My Native (USA) - Miss Gosling (Prince Bee)................. (Cash) 2,600

b c f Be My Native (USA) - Rhein Valley (IRE) (King's Lake).............. (Cash) 5,200

Property of Michael Conroy

b c f Tremblant - Snatchingly (Thatch) ..... (Ms Linda Harney) 1,100

Property of Michael Nurney, from Ardcarn Stud

ch or ro c f Ala Hounak - Elphin Girl (IRE) (Kafu)............... (Tom McGuckian) 1,000

From Rosemount House Stud

b f f Asir - Miss Cali (Young Man).......... (Kim Bye) 500

1139

Property of C J & Mrs C E Hodgins, from Old Fort Farm

b f f Satco (FR) - Rullena (IRE) (Boreen).... (Cash) 750

From Bishopstown Stud

b f f Supreme Leader - Cinderwood (Laurence O)....................... (Cash) 400

From Yellow House Stud

ch c f Over The River (FR) - Orient Moonbeam (Deep Run)..... (Francis Quinn) 1,650

Property of Catherine Conlon, from Ardcarn Stud

ch f f Ala Hounak - Just Louise (Pony Express)....................... (Cash) 1,400

Property of Joseph J Fisher

b f f Torus - Keep The Cut (Tarqogan) ..... (Cash) 1,100

b f f Brush Aside (USA) - Arctic Mistress (Quayside)............. (A McCarren) 1,100

From Barnore Stud

br f f Mandalus - Clerical Artist (IRE) (The Parson)................ (Ms Kim Bye) 500

Property of Ilish Kinsella

b c f Lord Americo - Shreelane (Laurence O)............................. (Cash) 10,000

From Shanco House Stud

br c f Royal Fountain - Arrogant Miss (Kings Ride).................. (Michael Tallon) 1,550

PRIVATE SALES

Property of Brid Bergin & Thomas Maher

b y g Naheez (USA) - Moycarkey (Raise You Ten)..................... (B J Coleman) 1,100

Property of Mr Michael Nurney, from Ardcarn Stud

ch or ro y f Ala Hounak - Elphin Girl (IRE) (Kafu)......................... (Cash) 500

1140

KILL (Goffs)
Friday, December 10th

From Sharavogue Stud

ch f f Montelimar (USA) - Smart Cookie (Lord Gayle)..... (Ms Richella O'Neill) 3,000

Property of Mrs Marie Byrne

b c f Tremblant - Lady Virtue (Oats) (Cash) 750

Property of Mr P J O'Donnell

b or br f f Be My Native (USA) - Sunnyhill Girl (Whistling Deer)........... (Cash) 800

Property of Mr Michael C O'Leary

ch c f Heavenly Manna - Mad Rodger (Royal Match)...... (Michael Browne) 4,200

Property of Peggy Creedon

b c f Commanche Run - Madam's Well (Pitpan)............ (Patrick J Connole) 1,300

Property of Mr R A Ward

b f f Over The River (FR) - Augusta Victoria (Callernish)........... (John M Byrne) 750

ch f f Over The River (FR) - Augusta Eliza (IRE) (Callernish).... (Michael Buckley) 850

Property of Mr T Walsh

b c f Supreme Leader - Lennoxlove (Lear Jet)..................... (John Roche) 1,100

Property of Mr Tim Broderick

ch c f Moscow Society (USA) - Mexican Chant (Solinus).......... (John Roche) 750

Property of Mr W F Richardson, from Chetwynde Stud

b c f Denel (FR) - Two Keo's (Don) (Cash) 1,800

1141

Property of Mr Maurice O'Brien

ch or ro f f Roselier (FR) - Princess Geeno (Cheval)......................... (Cash) 1,000

Property of Mrs Mary B O'Donovan

b c f Regular Guy - Day Of Rest (Parole)... (John Black) 1,300

Property of Mr Michael Phelan

b c f Camden Town - Dunmahon Lady (General Ironside)... (Richard Mathias) 1,350

Property of Mrs Riggs-Miller

b c f Yashgan - Corston Velvet (Bruni)..... (Michael Nolan) 750

From Bolinrush Stud

b f f Sharp Charter - Crook Lady (Croghan Hill)............................ (Cash) 700

ch c f Sharp Charter - Lumax (Maximilian) (John I O'Byrne) 5,000

Property of R J Powell, from Wellington House Stud

b f f Brush Aside (USA) - Her Name Was Lola (Pitskelly)................ (Cash) 1,350

Property of Katherine Costello

b c f Un Desperado (FR) - Strong Willed (Strong Gale)............ (Mrs A Kerr) 1,500

Property of G Berger, from Strawhall House Stables

b f f Montelimar (USA) - Fitzrovia (USA) (One For All)..... (Rathdrishoge Farm) 4,000

From Thomastown Stud

b c f Little Bighorn - Gayable (Gay Fandango)............... (Michael Nolan) 1,000

1142

Property of Emma Finegan, from Thomastown Stud

b f f Little Bighorn - Melissa Claire (Camden Town)......................... (Cash) 450

Property of Miss C Griffin

b or br c f Good Thyne (USA) - Vanhalensdarling (Green Shoon).......... (David Minton Bloodstock) 3,700

From Dromard Stud

b or br c f Homo Sapien - Jane Pitt (Pitpan) (R B McKay) 2,400

Property of Mr John Needham

b c f Lafontaine (USA) - Running Valley (Buckskin).............. (John Ryan) 400

Property of Mr James Hannon, from Curraheen Stud

b c f Balinger - Lisnacoilla (Beau Chapeau) (Cash) 500

From Killough House

b f f Be My Native (USA) - Promising Very Vii (Deep Run)............... (Cash) 1,100

From Farnagh Stud

br c f Tidaro (USA) - Noreen Beag (Thatching).......................... (Cash) 800

From Sunnyhill Stud

b c f Montelimar (USA) - Lady Cromer (Blakeney)................... (Cash) 3,500

From Rachel Bennett (Agent)

b f f Brush Aside (USA) - Dawn Rising (Le Moss)......................... (Cash) 520

Property of Messrs. Patrick, Frank & Colm Hennigan, to Dissolve A Parnership

b c f Good Thyne (USA) - Bornacurra Ella (Bargello)......... (Peter D McCreery) 4,800

1143

From Knockdav House Stud

b f f Yashgan - Pottlerath (Paddy's Stream) (Rathdriseog Farm) 1,800

Property of Mr W P Doyle

b f f Broken Hearted - Why Not Ask (Quayside)............. (John Lynch) 700

From The Beeches Stud

b f f Buckskin (FR) - Picton Lass (Rymer) .. (Cash) 820

ch c f Commanche Run - Blaze Of Hope (IRE) (Le Moss)............... (Cash) 1,150

Property of Mrs S Brennan, from Farnagh Stud

b c f Yashgan - Fatal Hesitation (Torus).... (David Minton Bloodstock) 4,600

Property of Mr James Devereux

b c f Brush Aside (USA) - Diane's Glen (Furry Glen)............ (John I Byrne) 6,200

From Derrygrath Stud

b f f Executive Perk - Derryclare (Pollerton) (T Coughlan) 400

From Monatrim Stud

b c f Commanche Run - That's It (Adropejo) .... (Cash) 1,150

From Boardsmill Stud

ch c f Orchestra - Bernish Lass (Radical)... (David Lawlor) 3,200

ch c f Carmelite House (USA) - Rosmarita (Sallust).............. (Leslie Young) 650

1144

From Russellstown Stud

ch c f Persian Mews - What A Queen (King's Ride).................. (Cash) 3,800

b f f Celio Rufo - Knockaville (Crozier) ..... (Cash) 2,500

Property of Penny Downes

ch c f Persian Mews - Happy View (Royal Buck)............ (Broguestown Stud) 2,350

From Grange Stud (Agent)

ch c f Glacial Storm (USA) - Tou Wan (Grand Roi).................. (Cash) 4,200

Property of Messrs. Michael & Tony O'Brien, from Grange Stud

b f f Glacial Storm (USA) - Sapphire Red (Red Alert)......... (Teddy O'Connor) 6,200

Property of Miss M Hickey

b or br c f Strong Gale - Little Welly (Little Buskins).......... (Peter D McCreery) 5,700

Property of Mr Peter McDowell, from Asigh Stud

ch f f Phardante (FR) - Larry's Peach (Laurence O).......... (William Feighery) 2,400

From Asigh Stud

b f f Brush Aside (USA) - Asigh Glen (Furry Glen)........................ (Cash) 4,600

From Orwell Stud

br or gr f f Roselier (FR) - Leschenault (IRE) (Over The River).............. (Cash) 580

From Orwell Lodge Stud

b f f Roselier (FR) - Brave Mum (Brave Invader)........... (William Feighery) 800

b c f Roselier (FR) - Gaye Le Moss (Le Moss)............... (Robert Ogden) 16,000

1145

From Woodhouse Estate Stud

c f Be My Native (USA) - Island Bridge (Mandalus).......... (John I O'Byrne) 7,600

Property of Mr Frank Latham, from Blackrath Stud

b c f Top Of The World - La 'bavette (Le Bavard)................ (P J Kinney) 1,250

From Rathurtin Stud

b c f Brush Aside (USA) - Fairy Island (Prince Hansel)...... (John I O'Byrne) 5,800

From Whitemoor Stud

gr c f Supreme Leader - Nanny Kehoe (IRE) (Sexton Blake)................ (Cash) 500

Property of Mrs C Farrell, from Kellsboro House Stud (Agent)

b f f Homo Sapien - Tender Toe (Burslem) (Cash) 400

Property of Mr Michael Healy

b c f Executive Perk - Tatec (Carlingford Castle)....................... (Cash) 2,300

Property of Mr Denis Power

ch f f Noalto - Islandkeane Girl (Mon Capitaine)............... (Derek O'Dwyer) 750

From Boardsmill Stud

ch f f Orchestra - Clarrie (Ballyciptic) (Cash) 1,200

b f f Orchestra - Princess Annabelle (English Prince).................. (Cash) 580

gr c f Carmelite House (USA) - Haut Lafite (Tamerlane)......... (Ms Laura Devitt) 1,100

1146

Property of Mr John Stafford

b c f Lord Americo - C.C. Meade (Paddy's Stream).......... (Charlestown Stud) 1,600

Property of Mrs Brenda Stafford

ch c f Over The River (FR) - Silver Gala (Gala Performance)............ (Cash) 2,000

Property of Mr Liam Skehan

b c f Bustineto - Markup (Appiani II) (Cash) 1,500

Property of Mr John Sheppard

b c f Mandalus - Ouragh (Ovac)........... (Ms Marie O'Sullivan) 1,400

Property of Mr Thomas Henry, from Edandale Stables

b c f Persian Mews - Colins Joy (Tumble Gold)........................(Cash) 1,000

Property of Mr T J Hodgins

ch f f Naheez (USA) - Texel Belle (Al Sirat) (P J Glynn) 550

Property of Mrs Hazel O'Haire

b f f Tremblant - Dusky Jo (Dusky Boy).... (Cash) 750

From Taghadoe Stud

br or bl c f Top Of The World - Rareitess (Rarity).................. (Feagh Stud) 850

From Kilnagornan

ch f f Yashgan - Daytona Lass (Dalsaan)... (Oliver Mescall) 400

b f f Broken Hearted - Darlington County (Taufan).............. (William Crowe) 400

1147

Property of Mrs Olive Manley

b c f Lord Americo - April Gold (King's Leap) ....(Cash) 2,800

Property of Siobhain Connolly, from Hollymount House Stud

br m f Point North - Annan (Maculata)..... (Denis Hallington) 750

From Grangemore Stud

Bella Velutina b m (6yrs) Coquelin (USA) - In My Time (Levmoss) Covered by Montelimar(USA).... (Mercury Bloodstock) 3,200

In My Time b m (19yrs) Levmoss - Time To Leave (Khalkis) Covered by Montelimar(USA)..... (Tipper House Stud) 3,800

Property of Mr Maurice Phelan, from Maplestown Stud

Bean Og ch m (6yrs) Sheer Grit - Mon Chapeau (High Hat) Covered by Aylesfield............ (Derek O'Dwyer) 700

From Rachel Bennett (Agent)

Buckalgo (IRE) b m (5yrs) Buckskin (FR) - Caralgo (Miralgo) Covered by Commanche Run................ (J Kemmy) 560

From Harbour Stud

Laurolin b m (17yrs) Laurence O - Muslin (Mustang) Covered by Supreme Leader ....(Cash) 870

From Grange Stud

Honeymoon Miss (FR) ch m (13yrs) Arctic Tern (USA) - Lueur Doree (Le Haar) Covered by Supreme Leader... (Cash) 1,550

Property of Mrs E Corrigan, from Liscolman House

Aragon Park b m (5yrs) Aragon - Faster Still (Giolla Mear) Covered by Mandalus.... (Liam Ryan) 1,200

Cash Discount ch m (12yrs) Deep Run - Dame Lucy (Prince Hansel) Covered by Mandalus..................... (Cash) 1,000

Clonodfoy br m (7yrs) Strong Gale - Moykendu (Tudor Music)...... (Cash) 1,500

1148

Property of Mr Charles Moore

Shannon Minstrel ch m (9yrs) Black Minstrel - Shannon Lek (Menelek) Covered by Alphabatim(USA)........... (Cash) 2,500

Property of Mr Peter McDowell, from Asigh Stud

Larry's Peach ch m (14yrs) Laurence O - Aurora Peach (Anthony) Covered by Brush Aside(USA)......... (G Metcalfe) 6,500

To Dissolve a Partnership, from Asigh Stud

Index Lady br m (9yrs) Decent Fellow - Holy Hills (Welsh Saint) Covered by Satco(Fr)............ (William Crowe) 600

Property of Mrs E E Whelan

Iama Princess gr m (10yrs) Miami Springs - Aughalion (Pals Passage) Covered by Roselier(Fr).......... (Michael Scully) 1,000

Castle Pearl br m (6yrs) Welsh Term - Tarenure (Targowice) Covered by Hollow Hand........... (Roger Lightfoot) 650

From Grange Stud

ch m (6yrs) Deep Run - Yellow Idol (Yellow God) Covered by Supreme Leader .... (N Walsh) 1,800

Lil's Charm b m (13yrs) Free State - Lily Langtry (Prince de Galles) Covered by Glacial Storm(USA)............ (Cash) 650

Property of Ann Hogan, from Rath Stud

Delmonte Serene b m (8yrs) Mandalus - Lady Serene (Le Tricolore) Covered by Alphabatim(USA)............... (Cash) 740

From Coolnaleen House Stud

Emma Clew (IRE) ch m (5yrs) Remainder Man - Supple (Poynton) Covered by Miners Lamp................. (S R McKee) 680

From Ballyward Stud

Gold Bank ch m (11yrs) Over The River (FR) - Golden Highway (Royal Highway) Covered by Capitano... (John Keegan) 2,000

1149

Property of Ms C & M Bourke, from Oak Lodge Stud

Little Peach ch m (16yrs) Ragapan - Lucky Peach (Lucky Guy) Covered by Good Thyne(USA)............. (Martin Ryan) 1,100

Property of Mr C Farrell, from Kellsboro House Stud (Agent)

Tender Toe b m (8yrs) Burslem - Tender Sara (Prince Tenderfoot) Covered by Dry Dock........... (Roger Lightfoot) 520

From Kellsboro House Stud (Agent)

Cereal Queen b m (14yrs) Oats - Bandit Queen (FR) (Jim French) Covered by Dry Dock..................... (Cash) 600

Property of Mr Gary Simpson, from Rathmolyon House Stud

Regal Spark ch m (11yrs) Royal Match - Saffron Hill (Gulf Pearl)... (John Byrne) 2,500

From Grange Stud (Agent)

Chevaux-Vapeur b or br m (6yrs) Le Moss - Tarabelle (Tarqogan) Covered by Supreme Leader...... (Ms Ann Kelly) 600

PRIVATE SALES

Property of John Martin McLoughney

ch y f Venetian Gate - Bluebayeh (Wassl Merbayeh)................. (J Bates) 500

From Mountrice Farm

b y f Yashgan - Desert Gale (Taufan) (Cash) 700

From Forest View Stud

b y c Boreen (FR) - Mossy Bank (IRE) (Le Moss)................ (John Walsh) 1,250

Property of Mr Alan Dunlop, from Ballyhoo Stables

b y f Denel (FR) - Arctic Conditions (Lucifer) .... (Jim Rossiter) 800

Property of Mr James O'Byrne

b y c Royal Fountain - Portane Miss (Salluceva)....................... (Cash) 1,650

From Killough House

b y f Commanche Run - Travelling Maggie (Le Moss)............ (Gerard Hehir) 400

From Farnagh Stud

b y c Tidaro (USA) - Bibi's Girl (Boreen).... (John Carr) 420

Property of Mr Garrett Ducey

b y c Over The River (FR) - Pitpan Lass (Pitpan)................ (R B McKay) 1,500

Property of W G Slattery, from Knockmullen Lodge

b y c Montelimar (USA) - Friar's Pass (Monksfield).......... (John Sheehan) 3,250

From Ash Tree Stud

b y f Lafontaine (USA) - Above Makica (Cut Above).......... (Michael O'Rourke) 400

Index to Sales of Bloodstock 1993

Racing records

PURCHASE PRICES IN ENGLAND

Horses in training

Amount	Horse	Buyer	Vendor	Sale and Date
1,400,000 gs	Ravinella 3-year-old f	Narvick International	Societe Aland	Newmarket Sales November 29, 1988
1,100,000 gs	Roseate Tern 3-year-old f	Horse France	Lord Carnarvon	Newmarket Sales December 5, 1989
1,020,000 gs	Tenea 3-year-old f	British Bloodstock Agency	Mrs H Cambanis	Newmarket Sales, November 30, 1982
1,000,000 gs	Desirable 3-year-old f	Coomore Stud	South Bank Stables	Newmarket Sales, December 5, 1984
760,000 gs	Dark Lomond 3-year-old f	B.B.A. (Ireland)	Swettenham Stud	Newmarket Sales, November 29, 1988
700,000 gs	Magic Slipper 3-year-old f	Shadwell Estate Co	H J Joel	Newmarket Sales, December 2, 1986

Yearlings

Amount	Horse	Buyer	Vendor	Sale and Date
2,400,000 gs	b c Northern Dancer —Fairy Bridge	Classic Thoroughbreds	Lyonstown Stud	Newmarket Sales, September 29, 1988
1,550,000 gs	ch c Hello Gorgeous (USA)—Centre Piece	British Bloodstock Agency	Lodge Park Stud, Ireland	Newmarket Sales, September 27, 1983
1,500,000 gs	ch c Nijinsky (CAN) —Sex Appeal	Darley Stud Management	Lyonstown Stud	Newmarket Sales, September 30, 1988
1,400,000 gs	b c General Assembly (USA)—Sarah Siddons (FR)	J Delahooke	Ardenode Stud, Ireland	Newmarket Sales, September 27, 1983
1,400,000 gs	br c Nureyev (USA) —Alathea	Heron Bloodstock	Haras d'Etreham, France	Newmarket Sales, October 2, 1984

Foals

Amount	Horse	Buyer	Vendor	Sale and Date
538,348 gs	ch f Royal Academy (USA) —Doff The Derby	Michael Otto	Barronstown Stud, Ireland	Newmarket Sales, November 28, 1992
490,000 gs	ch f Golden Fleece (USA) —Chemise	T.A. Vigors	Tullamaine Castle Stud	Newmarket Sales, December 1, 1984
470,000 gs	b c (FR) Shareef Dancer (USA)—Chappelle Blanche (USA)	Derrinstown Stud	Bloodstock Breeders Plc	Newmarket Sales, November 30, 1985
440,000 gs	b c Last Tycoon —Doff The Derby	Timmy Hyde	Barronstown Stud, Ireland	Newmarket Sales, November 29, 1991
350,000 gs	ch f Julio Mariner —La Dolce	Newmarket Bloodstock	Partnership Property	Newmarket Sales, December 1, 1984

Brood mares

Amount	Horse	Buyer	Vendor	Sale and Date
1,600,000 gs	Reine Mathilde	W McDonald	Societe Aland	Newmarket Sales, November 30, 1988
820,000 gs	Dunette (FR)	British Bloodstock Agency	Exors of late Mrs Margaret D Love	Newmarket Sales, November 30, 1983
750,000 gs	Princess Pati	Hesmonds Stud	Ardenode Stud	Newmarket Sales, December 5, 1990
730,000 gs	Greenland Park	Whitsbury Manor Stud	Greenland Park Stud	Newmarket Sales, December 2, 1981
720,000 gs	Fairy Footsteps	British Bloodstock Agency	H J Joel	Newmarket Sales, December 2, 1986
700,000 gs	Tenea	B.B.A. (Ireland)	Swettenham Stud	Newmarket Sales, December 2, 1987
600,000 gs	Lady Moon	Darley Stud Management	H J Joel	Newmarket Sales, December 2, 1986
510,000 gs	Valderna	Areen Ltd	International Bloodstock	Newmarket Sales, December 1, 1982
500,000 gs	Sweet Rhapsody	Mike Ryan	Airlie Stud	Newmarket Sales, December 5, 1984
460,000 gs	Burghclere	British Bloodstock Agency	The Queen	Newmarket Sales, December 2, 1981
460,000 gs	Jardiniere	British Bloodstock Agency	Swettenham Stud	Newmarket Sales, December 3, 1986

Selling Plate winners

Amount	Horse	Buyer	Vendor	Sale and Date
23,000 gs	Bali Sunset	Bought in	J R Featherstone	Leicester, May 30, 1989

The Derby

Record time: 2 min 33 4/5sec (35·06 m.p.h.) by Mahmoud (1936). Best electrically timed: Kahyasi 2m 33·84 (1988).
Record field: Biggest—34 in 1862. Smallest—4 in 1794.
Shortest priced favourite: Ladas (9-2 on), 1894.
Disqualified winners: Running Rein (1844) and Craganour (1913).
Dead-heats: 1828—Cadland beat The Colonen in a run-off.
1884—St Gatien and Havesteer divided the stakes.
Smallest winner: Daniel O'Rourke (1852), 14 hands 3 inches. Little Wonder (1840) stood 14 hands 3 1/2 inches high. Hyperion (1933) measured 15 hands 1 1/2 inches.
Most successful trainer: Robert Robson, John Porter, and Fred Darling: 7 winners each.
Most successful jockey: Lester Piggott: 9 winners.
Most successful owner: Lord Egremont and H.H. Aga Khan: 5 winners each.
Most successful sire: Sir Peter Teazle, Waxy, Cyllene and Blandford: 4 winners each.
First woman owner of winner: Lady James Douglas, Gainsborough (1918). Mrs G Miller, Mid-day Sun (1937), was the first to own the winner of a Derby run at Epsom.
Winning fillies: Eleanor (1801), Blink Bonny (1857), Shotover (1882), Signorinetta (1908), Tagalie (1912), Fifinella (1916).
Oldest winning jockey: John Forth, over 60 years of age when he rode and trained Frederick, the 1829 winner.
Youngest winning jockey: John Parsons, believed to be 16 years old when successful on Caractacus (1862).

The Grand National

Record time: 8m 47.8s Mr Frisk (1990)
Record field: Biggest—66 in 1929. Smallest—10 in 1883.
Shortest priced favourite: Golden Miller (2-1), 1935.
Smallest winner: The Lamb (1868 and 1871), 15 hands 1in. Other small winners are Team Spirit (1964), 15 hands 1 1/2 in; Casse Tete (1872), Regal (1876), Abd el Kader (1850) and 1851) and Why Not (1894), 15 hands 2 in; Battleship (1938), 15 hands 2 1/2 in.
Most successful trainers: Hon. Aubrey Hastings and T F Rimell. 4 winners each.
Most successful jockey: George Stevens, 5 winners.
Most successful owners: Capt J O Machell, Sir Charles Assheton-Smith and Mr N H Le Mare, 3 winners each.
First woman owner of winner: Lady Nelson, Ally Sloper (1915).
First woman trainer of winner: Mrs Jenny Pitman Corbiere (1983).
Winning mares: Charity (1841), Miss Mowbray (1852), Anatis (1860), Jealousy (1861), Emblem (1863), Emblematic (1864), Casse Tete (1872), Empress (1880), Zoedone (1883), Frigate (1889), Shannon Lass (1902), Sheila's Cottage (1948), Nickel Coin (1951).
Youngest winning jockey: Bruce Hobbs was 17 years old when successful on Battleship (1938).
Triple winner: Red Rum (1973, 1974 and 1977).
Dual winners: Peter Simple (1849 and 1853). Abd el Kader (1850 and 1851). The Colonel (1869 and 1870), The Lamb (1868 and 1871), Manifesto (1897 and 1899), Poethlyn (1918 and 1919), Reynoldstown (1935 and 1936).
Void Race: 1993, after two false starts.

Fastest horse

Indigenous, four-year-old by Mustang—Silver Thistle, carried 9st 5lb (L Piggott) and won the Tadworth Handicap Stakes, 5 furlongs, Epsom, June 2, 1960, in 53·60 seconds (hand times), 41·97 m.p.h.

Spark Chief, four-year-old by Chieftain—Heavenly Spark, carried 7st 12lb (W. Carson) and won Vladivar Vodka Trophy Handicap, 5 furlongs, Epsom, August 30, 1983, in 53·7 secs (electric timing) 41·90 m.p.h.

Fastest two-year-olds

Lady Trace (Epsom, June 5, 1931), Scarlet Pimpernel (Lewes, June 8, 1953), Cerise (Epsom, June 4, 1954) and Kerrabee (Epsom, June 3, 1960) all clocked 55 1/5 sec, 40·76 m.p.h. over 5 furlongs.

Oldest horses to win a race

Flat: Marksman 19 years old when winning at Ashord (1826).
Jumps: Sonny Somers 18 years old Southwell (chase) and Lingfield (chase) (1980).

Entries for one race

1001 for the 2000 Gns 1974
920 for the Epsom Derby 1974.
835 for the 1000 gns 1974.

Highest Steeplechase jump

The Open Ditch (Chair fence) at Aintree, the fifteenth jump in the Grand National course, is 5 ft 2 in high, 3 ft 9 in wide, ditch on take-off side 6 ft wide, guard rail in front of ditch 1 ft 6 in high.

Biggest priced winner

Equinoctial 250–1 (Kelso, Nov 21, 1990).

Totalisator dividends

Single, to win, £341 2s 6d. to 2s. stake paid over Coole at Haydock Park. November 30, 1929.

Single, a place, £67·32 to 10p stake paid over Strip Fast at Nottingham, October 31, 1978.

Single to win, £141 14s. 6d. to 4s. stake paid over Adam Gee at Redcar, April 27, 1963. Single, a place, £39 12s. 2d. to 4s stake paid over Peat Moss at Newcastle, December 12, 1959.

Daily Double, £5062 13s. to 10s. stake for Battleship and Barbedeche, Liverpool, March 25, 1938.

Daily Treble—£4307 17s. to 5s. stake paid on Blue Lamp, Castleton and Giuliano, Ascot, June 19, 1952.

Quadpool—£2510 8s to 5s. stake paid on Sky Gipsy, Nunshoney, Soderini and Grey of Falloden, Ascot, June 18, 1965.

Jackpot—£63114 13s. to 5s. stake paid on Top of the Pops, The Knack, Greek Streak, Lomond and Queen Dido (Sixth race winner unbacked), Ascot, June 18, 1966.

Jackpot-Consolation Dividend £8331 17s to 5s. stake paid on Morris Dancer, d'Urberville, Spaniards Mount, Salvo and Alciglide (First five winners), Ascot, June 23, 1967.

Dual Forecast: (4s. stake): £294 4s 0d. for Regal Wine and Ruddy Alf, at Kelso, October 21, 1967.

Dual Forecast (10p stake): £329·98 for Primula Boy and Valeriga, Ayr, September 21, 1979.

Staight Forecast (4s. stake): £142 15s 0d for Bird of Honour and Qebir Kuh, Chester, July 9, 1965.

Staight Forecast (2s. stake): £97 19s. 9d. for Hislet and Another Rake, Towcester, October 23, 1954.

Highest stakes winners over jumps (to end of 1991–92 season)

	Races Won	£ p
Desert Orchid	34	544,238.00
Wayward Lad	28	217,923·50
Burrough Hill Lad	21	195,608·95
Mr Frisk	18	194,312·00

Runners at one Meeting

171 in six races at Manchester, November 12, 1959.
176 in eight races at Newbury, October 26, 1989.
214 in seven Race at Newmarket, June 15, 1915.
216 in twelve races at Warwick, May 3, 1975.
219 in fourteen races at Hereford, May 1, 1975.
229 in eight races at Worcester, January 13, 1965.

Runners in one race

Jumping: 66 started for the Grand National. March 22, 1929.

Flat racing: 58 started for the Lincolnshire Handicap, March 13, 1948.

Races won in one season

	Year	Races Won
Horse: Fisherman	1856	23
Sire: Stockwell	1866	132
Owner: Sheikh Mohammed	1992	185
Breeder: Major L B Holliday	1954	52
Trainer: R Hannon	1993	182
Jockey: G Richards	1947	269
Trainer (jumps): M Pipe	1990–91	230
Jockey (jumps): P Scudamore	1988–89	221

Winners of most races in Britain

Catherina, from 1833–1841, won 79 out of 176 races.
Fisherman, from 1855–1859, won 69 out of 119 races.
The Shadow, from 1838–1847, won 64 out of 114 races.
Isaac, from 1833–1846, won 53 out of 112 races.
Alice Hawthorn, from 1841–1845, won 52 out of 71 races.
Beeswing, from 1835–1842, won 51 out of 64 races.
Lady Flora, from 1840–1849, won 51 out of 137 races.
Crudwell, from 1949–1960, won 50 out of 108 races.
Timeless Times won 16 races as a two-year-old in 1990.
Provideo won 16 races as a two-year-old in 1984.
The Bard won 16 races in succession as a two-year-old in 1885.
Gordon Richards, from 1921–1954, rode 4,870 winners.
Lester Piggott, from 1948–1993 has ridden 4,474 winners.
Willie Carson from 1962–1993 has ridden 3,549 winners.
Pat Eddery from 1969–93 has ridden 3,418 winners.
Doug Smith from 1932–1967 rode 3,111 winners.
Joe Mercer from 1950–85 rode 2,810 winners.
Fred Archer, from 1870–1886, rode 2,748 winners.
Edward Hide, from 1951–1985 rode 2,591 winners.
George Fordham, from 1850–1884, rode 2,587 winners.
Eph Smith, from 1930–1965 rode 2,313 winners.
Scobie Breasley, from 1950–1968 rode 2,161 winners.
Bill Nevett, from 1924–1956 rode 2,067 winners.
Greville Starkey, from 1956–1989 rode 1,886 winners.
Peter Scudamore was the most successful steeplechase jockey with 1,678 winners when he retired a few weeks before the end of the 1992–93 season.
Stan Mellor was the first steeplechase jockey to reach 1000 winners and when he retired at the end of the 1971–72 season Mellor had ridden 1,035 winners.
Miss Dorothy Paget, from 1930–1960, won 1,532 races.
H.H. Aga Khan, from 1922–1957, won 784 races, value £1,025,592.
Stockwell's progeny won 1,153 races between 1858 and 1876.

Consecutive winners by jockeys

Flat: Gordon Richards: 12 consecutive winners, October 1933.

Jumps: Johnny Gilbert: 10 consecutive winners, September 8–30, 1959, Phil Tuck: 10 consecutive winners, Aug 23–Sept 3, 1986.

Most winners in a day

Flat: Pat Eddery: 7 winners on June 26, 1992.
Jumps: M. Dickinson: 12 winners on December 27, 1982.

Consecutive winners by trainers

Jumps: M. C. Pipe: seven consecutive winners August 13–14, 1987, Devon and Exeter and seven consecutive winners August 25–29, 1989, Devon and Exeter (2), Hereford (1), Newton Abbot (4).

Dead-Heats

Quadruple: 1808—Honest Harry, Miss Decoy, Beningborough, and Peteria in a £50 plate, Bogside, June 7.

1851—Defaulter, Squire of Malton, Reindeer, and Pulcherrina in the Omnibus Stakes, The Hoo, April 26.

1855—Overreach, Unexpected, Gamester, and Lady Golightly in a £10 Sweepstakes for two year olds, Newmarket, October 22.

Triple: Glasgow Stakes and Subscription Handicap Plate, Newmarket, October 30, 1845. March Stakes, Goodwood, August 3, 1849. Cesarewitch, Newmarket, October 13, 1857, Craven Plate, Salisbury, April 29, 1858. Abbey Handicap, Shrewsbury, November 16, 1858. Post Stakes: Newmarket, October 10, 1877, Deerhurst Nursery Selling Handicap, Worcester, October 31, 1877, Astley Stakes, Lewes, August 6, 1880, Sandown Derby, Sandown, June 2, 1882. Badminton Plate, York, August 25, 1896, Huntingdon Stakes, Derby, September 2, 1897. Walton Selling Plate, Sandown, April 23, 1915. Royal Borough Handicap, Windsor, September 21, 1923. Long Course Selling Plate, Newmarket, April 23, 1924. Stayers Handicap, Folkestone, September 5, 1925.

Last dead-heat run-off: Last run-off following a dead-heat in Great Britain was in the Berks Selling Handicap, Newbury, June 25, 1930, when Ruby's Love beat Walloon.

AN INTERNATIONAL CLASSIFICATION 1993

For two years old only, which during the current season have run in France, Germany, Great Britain, Ireland or Italy, and are jointly assessed at a rating of 110/7st 12lb or above by the Official Handicappers. Rating differences are calculated in units of 1lb and evaluated up to and including December 31, 1993.
*Has run outside Europe in 1993.

Rating	Weight st. lb.	Horse's Name	Sex	Country Trained	Trainer
120	8 8	Grand Lodge (USA)	C	GB	W. Jarvis
119	8 7	Stonehatch (USA)	C	GB	P W Chapple-Hyam
118	8 6	Lemon Souffle (GB)	F	GB	R Hannon
		Lost World (IRE)	C	FR	E Lellouche
		Nicolette (GB)	C	GB	G Wragg
		Sunshack (GB)	C	FR	A Fabre
		Turtle Island (IRE)	C	GB	P W Chapple-Hyam
117	8 5	*Coup de Genie (USA)	F	FR	F Boutin
		First Trump (GB)	C	GB	G Wragg
116	8 4	King's Theatre (IRE)	C	GB	H R A Cecil
		Owington (GB)	C	GB	G Wragg
		Polish Laughter (USA)	C	GB	B Hanbury
		Signe Divin (USA)	C	FR	A Fabre
115	8 3	Colonel Collins (USA)	C	GB	P W Chapple-Hyam
		Manntari (IRE)	C	IRE	J M Oxx
		Mister Baileys (GB)	C	GB	M Johnston
		Redoubtable (USA)	C	GB	R Hannon
114	8 2	Carmot (GB)	C	GB	P F I Cole
		Concordial (USA)	C	GB	R Charlton
		Las Meninas (IRE)	F	IRE	T Stack
		Overbury (IRE)	C	GB	D R Loder
		Psychobabble (IRE)	C	FR	F Boutin
		Sierra Madre (FR)	F	FR	P Bary
		Velvet Moon (IRE)	F	GB	P F I Cole
		Wessam Prince (GB)	C	FR	C Laffon-Parias
113	8 1	Bonash (GB)	F	FR	A Fabre
		Fadeyev (USA)	C	FR	A Fabre
		Flagbird (USA)	F	FR	A Fabre
		Prophecy (IRE)	F	GB	J H M Gosden
		Torrismondo (USA)	C	GB	P F I Cole
112	8 0	Celtic Arms (FR)	C	FR	P Bary
		Chimes Band (USA)	C	FR	P Bary
		Fumo di Londra (IRE)	C	GB	J L Dunlop
		Mehthaaf (USA)	F	GB	J L Dunlop
		Risky (GB)	F	GB	R Hannon
		Ultimo Imperatore (GB)	C	GB	J L Dunlop
		Unblest (GB)	C	GB	J R Fanshawe
		Zindari (GB)	C	FR	F Boutin
111	7 13	Alanees (GB)	C	GB	C E Brittain
		Fairy Heights (IRE)	F	GB	N A Callaghan
		Gothic Dream (IRE)	F	IRE	J M Oxx
		River Deep (USA)	C	GB	P F I Cole
		State Performer (USA)	C	GB	P W Chapple-Hyam
		Tatami (USA)	C	GB	L M Cumani
		The Deep (IRE)	C	GB	B W Hills
110	7 12	*Devon Port (FR)	C	FR/US	—
		Ensorcelles Moi (USA)	F	FR	A Fabre
		Fast Eddy (GB)	C	GB	D R Loder
		Forest Gazelle (USA)	C	GB	R Charlton
		Foxhound (USA)	C	FR	A Fabre
		Fred Bongusto (IRE)	C	ITY	R Brogi
		Glatisant (GB)	F	GB	G Wragg
		Gunboat Diplomacy (FR)	C	FR	E Lellouche
		Hawajiss (GB)	F	GB	M R Stoute
		Hawker Hunter (USA)	C	GB	P F I Cole
		Innishowen (USA)	C	GB	R Hannon
		Just Happy (USA)	C	GB	M R Stoute
		Key of Luck (USA)	C	FR	Mrs C Head
		Late Parade (IRE)	C	ITY	A Renzoni
		Majestic Role (FR)	F	IRE	M J McC Kauntze
		*Ocean Indien (FR)	C	FR	F Boutin
		Party Season (GB)	C	GB	C A Cyzer
		Prince Babar (GB)	G	GB	G A Pritchard-Gordon
		Sail Storm (USA)	F	FR	Mrs C Head
		Spain Lane (USA)	F	FR	A Fabre
		Three Angels (USA)	F	FR	F Boutin
		Tikkanen (USA)	C	FR	J Pease

AN INTERNATIONAL CLASSIFICATION 1993

For three years old only, which during the current season have run in France, Germany, Great Britain, Ireland or Italy, and are jointly assessed at a rating of 110/7st 12lb or above by the Official Handicappers. Horses racing over different distances will be credited with those performances by inclusion in the appropriate columns.
Rating differences are calculated in units of 1lb and evaluated up to and including December 31, 1993.
*Has run outside Europe in 1993. **Rating achieved on dirt.

Rating	Weight st. lb.	Horse's Name	Sex	Country Trained	5 fur+ 1000m+	7 fur+ 1400m+	9½fur+ 1900m+	11 fur+ 2200m+	14 fur+ 2800m+
130	9 4	Zafonic (USA)	C	FR		130			
127	9 1	Commander In Chief (GB)	C	GB				127	
		*White Muzzle (GB)	C	GB				127	
126	9 0	*Bigstone (IRE)	C	FR		126			
123	8 11	*Barathea (IRE)	C	GB		123			
		*Hernando (FR)	C	FR				123	
		Kingmambo (USA)	C	FR		123			
		Lando (GER)	C	GER				123	
122	8 10	Bob's Return (IRE)	C	GB				122	116
		*Catrail (USA)	C	GB	122				
		*Intrepidity (GB)	F	FR				122	
121	8 9	Monsun (GER)	C	GER				121	
		*Ski Paradise (USA)	F	FR		121			
120	8 8	*Dernier Empereur (USA)	C	FR			120		
		Komado (GB)	C	GER				120	
		*Sayyedati (GB)	F	GB		120			
		Talloires (USA)	C	FR				120	
		*Wemyss Bight (GB)	F	FR				120	
119	8 7	Blue Judge (IRE)	C	IRE				119	
		College Chapel (GB)	C	IRE	119				
		Royal Ballerina (IRE)	F	IRE				119	
118	8 6	Astair (FR)	C	FR		118			
		*Blues Traveller (IRE)	C	GB				118	
		Bright Moon (USA)	F	FR				118	
		Foresee (GB)	C	IRE				118	116
		Fort Wood (USA)	C	FR			118		
		*Inchinor (GB)	C	GB		118			
		Oakmead (IRE)	F	GB				118	
		Sabrehill (USA)	C	GB			118		
		Tenby (GB)	C	GB			118		
117	8 5	Armiger (GB)	C	GB			117		
		Hunting Hawk (IRE)	C	FR				117	
		Madeleine's Dream (USA)	F	FR		117			
		Niche (GB)	F	GB		117			
		Pips Pride (GB)	C	GB	117				
116	8 4	Bin Ajwaad (IRE)	C	GB		116			
		Dolphin Street (FR)	C	FR		116			
		*Newton's Law (IRE)	C	GB				116	
		Placerville (USA)	C	GB			116		
		Shemaka (IRE)	F	FR			116		
115	8 3	Baya (USA)	F	FR		115	115		
		Dancienne (FR)	F	FR				115	
		Gold Splash (USA)	F	FR		115			
		*Husband (USA)	C	FR				115	
		*Jeune Homme (USA)	C	FR		115			
		Komtur (USA)	C	GER			115		
		Le Balafre (FR)	C	FR		115			
		Siam (USA)	C	FR			115		
		Turners Hill (GB)	C	FR				115	
		Ventiquattrofogli (IRE)	C	GB		115			
114	8 2	Ardkinglass (GB)	C	GB		114			
		Desert Team (USA)	C	IRE				114	
		*Elizabeth Bay (USA)	F	FR		114			
		Emperor Jones (USA)	C	GB			114		
		**Golden Klair (GB)	F	GB/US		114			
		Pelder (IRE)	C	ITY		114			
		Port Lucaya (GB)	C	GB			114		
		*Regency	C	FR				114	
		River North (IRE)	G	GB			114	114	
		*Surprise Offer (GB)	G	GB	114				
		*Tinners Way (USA)	C	GB		114			
		Tropical (GB)	F	IRE	114				

Rating	Weight st. lb.	Horse's Name	Sex	Country Trained	5 fur+ 1000m+	7 fur+ 1400m+	91/2fur+ 1900m+	11 fur+ 2200m+	14 fur+ 2800m+
113	8 1	*Ajfan (USA)	F	GB		113			
		Beneficial (GB)	C	GB				113	
		Dana Springs (IRE)	F	GB				113	
		Kithanga (IRE)	F	GB				113	
		Matelot (USA)	C	FR		113			
		Minydoun (IRE)	C	FR			113		
		Mistle Cat (USA)	C	GB		113			
		Nasr Allah (USA)	C	GER		113			
		Petardia (GB)	C	GB		113			
		Quebrada (IRE)	F	GER		113			
		Raintrap (GB)	C	FR					113
		Revelation (IRE)	C	GB		113	113		
		Right Win (IRE)	C	GB			113	113	
		Semillon (GB)	C	FR		113			
		Zieten (USA)	C	FR	113				
112	8 0	Badolato (USA)	C	FR				112	
		*Bright Generation (IRE)	F	GB/US				112	
		*Fastness (IRE)	C	FR/US		112			
		*Fatherland (IRE)	C	IRE		112			
		Marchand de Sable (USA)	C	FR				112	
		*Miami Sands (IRE)	F	IRE/US			112		
		Mr Richard (IRE)	C	ITY				112	
		Needle Gun (IRE)	C	GB		112		112	
		*Nicer (IRE)	F	GB		112			
		Rainbow Lake (GB)	F	GB				112	
		Silver Wizard (USA)	C	GB		112			
		Sternkonig (IRE)	C	GER				112	
		Talented (GB)	F	GB			112		
		Zarani Sidi Anna (USA)	F	GB		112			
111	7 13	Asema (USA)	F	IRE		111			
		Azzilfi (GB)	C	GB				111	
		Cairo Prince (IRE)	C	GB				111	
		Corrazona (USA)	F	FR			111		
		Dankal (USA)	C	FR	111				
		Fresher (GB)	F	US		111			
		*Guide (FR)	C	FR/US		111			
		Infrasonic (GB)	C	FR				111	
		*Sharman (USA)	C	FR		111			
		Shrewd Idea (GB)	C	IRE				111	
		*Wharf (USA)	C	GB		111			
110	7 12	Accommodating (USA)	F	FR			110		
		Andromaque (USA)	F	GB			110		
		Borodislew (USA)	F	FR		110			
		Dancing Bloom (IRE)	F	GB		110	110	110	
		Danse Royale (IRE)	F	IRE			110	110	
		Eurolink Thunder (GB)	C	GB		110			
		Felawnah (USA)	F	GB		110			
		Gabr (GB)	C	GB		110			
		Holly Golightly (GB)	F	GB		110			
		Kadounor (FR)	C	FR		110			
		*Lyphard's Delta (USA)	F	GB			110		
		*Marina Park (GB)	F	GB		110			
		Maroof (USA)	C	GB		110			
		Massyar (IRE)	C	IRE		110			
		Nidd (USA)	F	FR		110			
		Prince of Andros (USA)	C	GB				110	
		*Ranger (FR)	C	FR		110			
		Sharp Prod (USA)	C	GB	110				
		*Smarginato (IRE)	C	GB		110			
		Sueboog	F	GB				110	
		Thawakib (IRE)	F	GB				110	
		Wootton Rivers (USA)	C	GB			110		

AN INTERNATIONAL CLASSIFICATION 1993

For four years old and upwards, which during the current season have run in France, Germany, Great Britain, Ireland or Italy, and are jointly assessed at a rating of 110/7st 12lb or above by the Official Handicappers.

Horses racing over different distances will be credited with those performances by inclusion in the appropriate columns.

Rating differences are calculated in units of 1lb and evaluated up to and including December 31, 1993.

*Has run outside Europe in 1993. **Rating achieved on dirt.

Rating	Weight st. lb.	Horse's Name	Age	Sex	Country Trained	5 fur+ 1000m+	7 fur+ 1400m+	9½fur+ 1900m+	11 fur+ 2200m+	14 fur+ 2800m+
129	9 3	*Opera House (GB)	5	H	GB				129	
128	9 2	**Arcangues (USA)	5	H	FR		123	128		
125	8 13	*Urban Sea (USA)	4	F	FR				125	
		*Wolfhound (USA)	4	C	GB	125				
124	8 12	*Luazur (FR)	4	C	FR/US				124	
		*Platini (GER)	4	C	GER				124	
123	8 11	Lochsong (GB)	5	M	GB	123				
122	8 10	*Hatoof (USA)	4	F	FR			122		
		*Misil (USA)	5	H	ITY				122	
121	8 9	Only Royale (IRE)	4	F	GB				121	
		Vert Amande (FR)	5	H	FR			121		
120	8 8	*Apple Tree (FR)	4	C	FR				120	
		Environment Friend (GB)	5	H	GB				120	
		*Ezzoud (IRE)	4	C	GB			120		
		Hamas (IRE)	4	C	GB	120				
		User Friendly (GB)	4	F	GB				120	
119	8 7	Keen Hunter (USA)	6	H	GB	119				
		*Modhish (IRE)	4	C	FR				119	
		Shanghai (USA)	4	C	FR		119			
		*Verveine (USA)	4	F	FR		119			
		*Vintage Crop (IRE)	6	G	IRE					119
118	8 6	*Drum Taps (USA)	7	H	GB					118
		Knifebox (USA)	5	H	GB			118		
		Paris House (GB)	4	C	GB	118				
117	8 5	*Alflora (IRE)	4	C	GB		117			
		Alhijaz (GB)	4	C	GB		117			
		Assessor (IRE)	4	C	GB					117
		*Dear Doctor (FR)	6	H	FR			117	117	
		Elbio	6	H	GB	117				
		*Swing Low (GB)	4	C	GB		117			
116	8 4	Great Palm (USA)	4	C	GB			116		
		Inner City (IRE)	4	C	GB		116			
		*Marildo (FR)	6	H	FR			116		
		Muhtarram (USA)	4	C	GB			116		
		Petit Loup (USA)	4	C	FR				116	
		Polytain (FR)	4	C	FR			116		
		*Serrant (USA)	5	G	FR/US				116	
		Snurge (IRE)	6	H	GB				116	
115	8 3	Bobzao (IRE)	4	C	GB			115		
		*George Augustus (USA)	5	H	IRE			115	115	
		*Robin des Pins (USA)	5	H	FR/US	115	115			
		*Voleris (FR)	4	C	FR		115			
114	8 2	Dadarissime (FR)	4	C	FR				114	
		*Know Heights (IRE)	4	C	FR/US			114	114	
		*Monde Bleu (GB)	5	H	FR	114				
		Montendre (GB)	6	G	GB	114				
113	8 1	Culture Vulture (USA)	4	F	GB		113			
		Guado d'Annibale (IRE)	4	C	ITY			113	113	
		Hazaam (USA)	4	C	GB		113			
		Karinga Bay (GB)	6	H	GB			113		
		*La Francesa (ARG)	5	M	FR		113			
		*Market Booster (USA)	4	F	IRE			113		
		Northern Crystal (GB)	5	H	FR		113			
		Young Buster (IRE)	5	H	GB				113	

Rating	Weight st. lb.	Horse's Name	Age	Sex	Country Trained	5 fur+ 1000m+	7 fur+ 1400m+	91/2fur+ 1900m+	11 fur+ 2200m+	14 fur+ 2800m+
112	8 0	Blyton Lad (IRE)	7	G	GB	112				
		Dariyoun (USA)	5	H	FR				112	
		Fabriano (GB)	4	C	GER			112		
		Jeune (GB)	4	C	GB				112	
		Mashaallah (USA)	5	H	GB					112
		Prospective Ruler (USA)	5	H	ITY		112			
		Sonus (IRE)	4	C	GB					112
		Spartan Shareef (IRE)	4	C	GB				112	
		Take Risks (FR)	4	C	FR		112			
		Usaidit (GB)	4	C	GB			112		
111	7 13	Big Tobin (ITY)	4	C	ITY			111	111	111
		Carlton (GER)	4	C	GER			111	111	
		Enharmonic (USA)	6	H	GB		111	111		
		Further Flight (GB)	7	G	GB					111
		Green Senor (USA)	5	H	ITY				111	
		Hondo Mondo (IRE)	5	H	ITY			111	111	
		Lavinia Fontana (IRE)	4	F	IRE	111				
		Lord of the Field (GB)	6	H	GB			111		
		Lucky Lindy (IRE)	4	C	GB			111		
		*Mellottie (GB)	8	G	GB		111			
		Pre-Eminent (IRE)	6	G	IRE			111		
		Protektor (GER)	4	C	GER				111	
		Red Bishop (USA)	5	H	GB				111	
		Stack Rock (IRE)	6	M	GB	111				
		*Stubass (IRE)	4	C	GB		111			
		Sugunas (GER)	5	H	GER			111	111	
		Twist And Turn (GB)	4	C	GER			111	111	
		Zinaad (GB)	4	C	GB				111	111
110	7 12	*Acteur Francais (USA)	5	H	FR		110			
		Arranvanna (GB)	5	M	ITY	110				
		Bradawn Breever (IRE)	4	C	IRE	110				
		Captain Horatius (IRE)	4	C	GB				110	
		Dauberval (USA)	4	C	FR	110				
		*Fanmore (USA)	5	G	FR/US		110	110		
		Ruby Tiger (IRE)	6	M	GB			110		
		Sought Out (IRE)	5	M	FR					110
		Vincenzo (GER)	4	C	GER			110		
		Zabar (GB)	5	G	FR		110			

Comparative table of distances

Metres		Furlongs		Miles
200	....	1	....	
1,000	....	5	....	
1,200	....	6	....	3/4
1,400	....	7	....	
1,600	....	8	....	1
1,700	....	8 1/2	....	
1,800	....	9	....	
2,000	....	10	....	1 1/4
2,200	....	11	....	
2,400	....	12	....	1 1/2
2,600	....	13	....	
2,800	....	14	....	1 3/4
3,000	....	15	....	
3,200	....	16	....	2
3,600	....	18	....	2 1/4
4,000	....	20	....	2 1/2
4,800	....	24	....	3

Comparative table of weights

(The English weights are shown to the nearest 1/2 lb.)

Kilograms		Stones/lbs		Pounds
41	....	6 6	....	90
41 1/2	....	6 7 1/2	....	91 1/2
42	....	6 9	....	93
42 1/2	....	6 10	....	94
43	....	6 11	....	95
43 1/2	....	6 12	....	96
44	....	6 13	....	97
44 1/2	....	7 0	....	98
45	....	7 1	....	99
45 1/2	....	7 2	....	100
46	....	7 3	....	101
46 1/2	....	7 4 1/2	....	102 1/2

Kilograms	Stones/lbs	Pounds
47	7 6	104
47½	7 7	105
48	7 8	106
48½	7 9	107
49	7 10	108
49½	7 11	109
50	7 12	110
50½	7 13	111
51	8 0½	112½
51½	8 1½	113½
52	8 3	115
52½	8 4	116
53	8 5	117
53½	8 6	118
54	8 7	119
54½	8 8	120
55	8 9	121
55½	8 10	122
56	8 11½	123½
56½	8 13	125
57	9 0	126
57½	9 1	127
58	9 2	128
58½	9 3	129
59	9 4	130
59½	9 5	131
60	9 6	132
60½	9 7	133
61	9 8½	134½
61½	9 10	136
62	9 11	137
62½	9 12	138
63	9 13	139
63½	10 0	140

The Sporting Life-Coral nap award winners 1961–93

Jumping

		W.	L.	N.R.	Longest seq. W.	Longest seq. L.	Profit £1 level Stakes £ s. d.
1962–63	Western Mail Carlton	10	32	2	2	15	26 18 6
1963–64	Daily Sketch Gimcrack	31	48	4	3	6	36 16 8
1964–65	Irish Times Brown Jack	29	60	4	3	14	33 5 1
1965–66	Irish Press Merlin	23	50	6	4	15	16 8 3
1966–67	Irish Times Brown Jack	26	63	3	3	11	29 4 2
1967–68	Daily Mail Robin Goodfellow	28	44	1	4	4	34 9 1
1968–69	Sporting Life Solon	25	38	6	6	8	32 15 8
1969–70	Sun Templegate	33	62	5	3	8	16 8 8
							£ p
1970–71	Western Mail Carlton	46	57	6	7	8	30.51
1971–72	Daily Mirror Newsboy	44	66	2	5	8	25.53
1972–73	Morning Star Cayton	22	82	4	2	12	25.92½
1973–74	Morning Star Cayton	46	46	12	5	5	29.57½
1974–75	Morning Advertiser Gainsborough	30	53	7	4	5	31.96½
1975–76	Scottish Daily Express Scotia	39	64	4	6	9	16.22½
1976–77	Liverpool Post Argus	20	63	6	3	16	20.96
1977–78	Sporting Life Form	41	48	3	5	9	30.66
1978–79	Western Mail Carlton	16	24	5	3	7	22.64
1979–80	Daily Mail Robin Goodfellow	35	60	5	4	7	23.22
1980–81	Morning Star Cayton	42	56	8	10	11	26.84
1981–82	Northern Echo Capt Day	34	51	6	4	8	29.73
1982–83	Daily Mail Robin Goodfellow	40	58	4	2	5	33.80
1983–84	East Anglian Daily Times	47	47	11	7	4	27.92
1984–85	Sporting Life, Stop Watch	32	47	5	4	5	29.07
1985–86	Sunday Express, Tom Forrest	35	37	3	3	4	38.01
1986–87	Daily Mirror, Newsboy	27	63	8	3	11	42.21
1987–88	The Sporting Life, Nick Deacon	43	49	4	7	7	45.74
1988–89	The Independent, John Karter	34	74	6	4	11	40.15
1989–90	Daily Telegraph, Tony Stafford	41	56	9	4	10	42.20
1990–91	Glasgow Herald, Martin Gale	37	55	10	4	12	42.45
1991–92	Western Daily Press, Bob Watts	50	49	5	6	7	30.13
1992–93	Sun, Templegate	33	70	8	6	9	27.88

Flat

		W.	L.	N.R.	Longest seq. W.	Longest seq. L.	Profit £1 level Stakes £ s. d.
1961	Daily Sketch Gimcrack	56	134	2	6	14	16 14 9
1962	Daily Mail Robin Goodfellow	60	121	5	4	13	19 5 11
1963	Sporting Express Winco	79	102	2	6	7	7 10 6
1964	Daily Express The Scout	48	123	6	4	9	28 9 5
1965	Daily Mail Robin Goodfellow	59	117	3	4	12	32 16 9
1966	Western Mail Carlton	47	131	7	3	14	40 8 9
1967	Sun Templegate	52	125	4	3	8	45 10 5
1968	Daily Mail Robin Goodfellow	55	113	1	3	12	49 5 9
1969	Scottish Daily Express Scotia	64	106	1	5	8	25 18 1
1970	Sheffield Morning Telegraph Fortunatus	61	113	2	5	13	34 12 11
							£ p
1971	Yorkshire Post The Duke	70	111	2	7	8	43.84
1972	Daily Mirror Newsboy	55	126	3	4	13	13.87
1973	Guardian Richard Baerlein	61	119	6	3	7	64.21
1974	Birmingham Post Stable Boy	56	136	4	4	15	26.97½
1975	Daily Mail Robin Goodfellow	57	128	2	5	11	29.33½
1976	Northern Echo Capt Day	69	117	3	5	12	25.64½
1977	Daily Express The Scout	84	104	1	7	6	41.38½
1978	Sheffield Morning Telegraph Fortunatus	71	113	4	5	12	39.55
1979	Daily Mail Robin Goodfellow	63	121	3	6	18	70.07
1980	Yorkshire Post The Duke	52	129	2	4	11	45.06
1981	East Anglian Daily Times Bruce Jackson	59	129	6	4	13	30.19
1982	East Anglian Daily Times Bruce Jackson	69	119	4	7	14	64.27
1983	Western Morning News Quicksight	93	89	9	5	7	65.99
1984	Morning Star, Cayton	61	134	2	5	12	45.50
1985	Daily Record, Garry Owen	73	110	3	8	13	72.94
1986	Sunday Mirror	64	123	8	4	8	46.45
1987	Glasgow Herald, Martin Gale	44	140	9	4	16	108.01
1988	Daily Express, The Scout	71	120	3	6	10	30.90
1989	Sporting Life, Nick Deacon	69	120	10	5	9	39.70
1990	Western Morning News, Jeffrey Ross	72	126	3	5	15	49.96
1991	Daily Post, Roy David	63	129	6	6	12	60.30
1992	Western Morning News, Jeffrey Ross	81	109	10	4	9	52.16
1993	Daily Telegraph, Tony Stafford	61	128	5	6	10	49.69

Addresses and Telephone Numbers

J. A. Allen & Co. Ltd., 1 Lower Grosvenor Place, Buckingham Palace Road, London SW1W 0EL (071–834 5606)
Amateur Riders Association of Great Britain, 5 Bywater Street, London SW3 4XD (071–584 5638)
Animal Health Trust, Balaton Lodge, Snailwell Road, Newmarket, Suffolk CB8 7DW (0638 661111)
Ascot Bloodstock Sales, The Lodge, Flaxton, York YO6 7PZ (090486 240)
Bedfordshire & District Race Club: Ann Atkinson, 17 Dalton Way, Whitwell, Hitchin, Herts.
Betting Office Licensees' Association, Francis House, Francis Street, London SW1P 1DE (071–630 0667)
British Equine Veterinary Association, Hartham Park, Corsham, Wilts. SN13 0BQ (0249 715723)
British Horseracing Board, 42 Portman Square, London W1H 0EN (071–396 0011)
British Racing School (Apprentice training), Snailwell Road, Newmarket, Suffolk CB8 7NU (0638 665103)
British Veterinary Association, 7 Mansfield Street, London W1M 0AT (071–636 6541–4)
Cheltenham and Three Counties Race Club: Ray Hitchin, 6 Wentworth Close, Cheltenham, Glos. (0242 527762).
Doncaster Bloodstock Sales, Auction Mart Offices, Hawick, Roxburghshire TD9 9NN (0450 72222)
Doncaster Race Club: Doncaster Racecourse, Grand Stand, Leger Way, Doncaster (0302 320066)
East Midlands Racing Club: Grenville Davies, 26 Gothic Close, Basford, Nottingham NG6 0NU (0602 791936)
Equine Research Station, Balaton Lodge, Snailwell Road, Newmarket, Suffolk CB8 7DW (0638 661111)
European Breeders' Fund, Stanstead House, The Avenue, Newmarket, Suffolk CB8 9AA (0638 667960)
Fakenham Racecourse Supporters Club: Mr H. Parvin, 17 East Park Street, Chatteris, Cambs. (03543 3229)
Federation of Bloodstock Agents (GB) Ltd., The Old Brewery, Hampton Street, Tetbury, Glos. GL8 8PG (0666 503595)
Federation of British Racing Clubs, 4 Bosley Crescent, Wallingford, Oxon OX10 9AS (0491 32399)
Gaming Board for Great Britain, Berkshire House, High Holborn, London WC1 (071-240 0821)
Goffs Bloodstock Sales, Kildare Paddocks, Kill, Co. Kildare (045 77211)
Horserace Betting Levy Board, 52 Grosvenor Gardens, London SW1W OAU (071–333 0043)
Horserace Totalisator Board, Tote House, 74 Upper Richmond Road, Putney, London SW15 2SU (081–874 6411)
Horserace Writers' and Reporters' Association, 59 Blenheim Road, Horsham, W. Sussex (0403 60831)
Horse Racing Abroad, Golden Key Building, 15 Market Street, Sandwich, Kent CT13 9DA (0304 612424)
Hunters' Improvement and National Light Horse Breeding Society, 96 High Street, Edenbridge, Kent TN8 5AR (0732 866277)
Injured Jockeys' Fund, PO Box 9, Newmarket, Suffolk CB8 8JG (0638 662246)
International Racing Bureau, Alton House, 117 High Street, Newmarket, Suffolk CB8 9AG (0638 668881)
Irish Thoroughbred Breeders' Association, Old Connell House, Newbridge, Co. Kildare (045 31890)
Irish Racecourse Association, Paddock Lodge, Ratoath, Co. Meath, Ireland (Dublin 8256618)
Irish Racehorse Trainers' Association, Leigh House, 4 Moorfield Terrace, Newbridge, Co. Kildare (045 34059)
Irish Racing Writers' Association, 12 Clifden Road, Dublin 10 (Dublin 6265165)
Irish Racing Board, Leopardstown Racecourse, Foxrock, Dublin 18 (Dublin 2892888)
Irish Turf Club, The Curragh, Co. Kildare (045 41599)
Italian Jockey Club, Via Portuense 96/D, 2nd Floor, 00153 Rome, Italy (Rome 395.58330925)
Jockey Club, 42 Portman Square, London W1H 0EN (071–486 4921)
Jockey Club Officials Association, Ash Lane Farm, Seven Sisters Lane, Ollerton, Knutsford, Cheshire WA16 8RQ (0565 54349)
Jockeys' Association of Great Britain, 39 Kingfisher Court, Hambridge Road, Newbury, Berks RG14 5SJ (0635 44102)
Lady Jockeys' Association of Great Britain, 10 Ferncroft Avenue, London NW3 7PH (071–435 1312)
London Racing Club: Colin Wilby, 13 Kinross Avenue, Worcester Park, Surrey KT4 7AJ (081–330 3756)
National Association of Bookmakers Ltd., 298 Ewell Road, Surbiton, Surrey KT6 7AQ (081–390 8222)
National Foaling Bank, Meretown Stud, Newport, Shropshire (0952 811234)
National Head Lads' Association, 196 New Cheveley Road, Newmarket, Suffolk CB8 8BZ (0638 662683)
National Horseracing Museum, 99 High Street, Newmarket, Suffolk CB8 8JL (0638 667333)
National Jockeys' Booking Agency, 39 Kingfisher Court, Hambridge Road, Newbury, Berks RG14 5SJ (0635 580070)
National Sporting League, Francis House, Francis Street, London SW1P 1DE (071–630 0234)
National Stud, Newmarket, Suffolk CB8 0XE (0638 663464)
National Trainers Federation, 42 Portman Square, London W1H 0AP (071–935 2055)
Newmarket Stud Farmers Association, 136 High Street, Newmarket, Suffolk (0638 661221)
North East Race Club: Allan Kelly, 11 Camelot Close, Seaham, Co. Durham SR7 7AN
Northern Racing School, Rossington Hall, Doncaster, S. Yorks DN11 0HN (0302 865462)
North West Racing Club: George Harris, 65 Lower Bank Road, Fulwood, Preston, Lancs. PR2 4NU (0772 716640)
Permit Trainers Association Ltd., 42 Portman Square, London W1H 9FF
Pratt and Co., 11 Boltro Road, Haywards Heath, Sussex RH16 1BP (0444 441111)
Press Association Ltd., 85 Fleet Street, London EC4P 4BE (071–353 7440)
Professional Riders' Insurance Scheme, The Racecourse, Newbury, Berks RG14 7NZ (0635 45707)
Racecourse Association Ltd., Winkfield Road, Ascot, Berkshire SL5 7HX (0344 25912)
Racecourse Holdings Trust Ltd., 42 Portman Square, London W1H 0EN (071–486 4921)
Racecourse Technical Services Ltd., 88 Bushey Road, Raynes Park, London SW20 0JH (081–947 3333)
Raceform, Compton, Newbury, Berks RG16 0NL (0635 578080)
Racegoers Club: c/o Flagstaff Enterprises, Flagstaff House, High Street, Twyford, Berks (0734 341666)
Racehorse Owners' Association, 42 Portman Square, London W1H 9FF (071–486 6977)
Racehorse Transporters Association Ltd., 21 Lisburn Road, Newmarket, Suffolk CB8 8HS (0638 663155)
Racing Club of Ireland Ltd., 1d Brighton Road, Foxrock Village, Dublin 18
Racing Post, 120 Coombe Lane, Raynes Park, London SW20 0BA (081–879 3377)
Racing World Video, 1 Hughes Mews, 143 Chatham Road, London, London SW11 6HJ (071–924 4066)
Satellite Information Services Ltd., 17 Corsham Street, London N1 6DR (071–253 2232)
Scottish Racing Club: Graeme MacDiarmid, 41 Beechwood Drive, Broomhill, Glasgow (041–357 0331)

Societe d'Encouragement et des Steeple-Chases de France, 46 Place Abel Gance, 92100 Boulogne, France (Paris 49.10.20.30)
Society of International Thoroughbred Auctioneers, Toomers Wharf, Newbury, Berks, RG13 1DY (0635 551515)
South West Racing Club: c/o Newton Abbot Racecourse, Kingsteignton Road, Newton Abbot, Devon (0626 53235)
Sporting Life, Orbit House, 1 New Fetter Lane, London EC4A 1AR (071–353 0246)
Stable Lads Association, 4 Dunsmore Way, Midway, Burton-on-Trent, Staffs DE11 7LA (0283 211522)
Stable Lads Welfare Trust, Clifton House, 121 High Street, Newmarket, Suffolk CB8 9AJ (0638 560763)
T & GWU, Transport House, Smith Square, London SW1 (071–828 7788)
Tattersalls Bloodstock Sales, Terrace House, Newmarket, Suffolk CB8 9BT (0638 665931)
Tattersalls (Ireland) Ltd., Fairyhouse, Ratoath, Co. Meath, Ireland (Dublin 8256777)
Tattersalls' Committee PO Box 13, 19 Wilwyne Close, Grosvenor Road, Caversham, Reading RG4 0EP (0734 461757)
Thoroughbred Breeders' Association, Stanstead House, The Avenue, Newmarket, Suffolk CB8 9AA (0638 661321)
Timeform, Timeform House, Northgate, Halifax, W. Yorks HX1 1XE (0422 330330)
Turf Guardian Society, 10 Grange Gardens, Eastbourne, Sussex BN20 7DB (0323 20638)
Turf Newspapers Ltd., 18 Clarges Street, London W1Y 7PG (071–499 4391)
United Racecourses Ltd., The Paddock, Epsom Racecourse, Epsom, Surrey (0372 726311)
Valets Association of G.B., Oxlynch, The Shawl, Leyburn, N. Yorks DL8 5DG (0969 23150)
Weatherbys, Sanders Road, Wellingborough, Northants NN8 4BX (0933 440077)
West Berkshire Racing Club: Ricki Peacock, 4 Bosley Crescent, Wallingford, Oxon OX10 9AS (0491 32399)
West Midlands Racing Club: Chris Pitt, 17 Cross Farm Road, Harborne, Birmingham B17 0NB (021–426 1877)
Yorkshire Racing Club: Ken Barton, 12a Hadleigh Rise, Pontefract, West Yorkshire WF8 4SJ (0977 797600)

RACECOURSE TELEPHONE NUMBERS [BRITAIN]

Ascot—(0344) 22211
Ayr—(0292) 264179
Bangor-on-Dee—(0978) 780323
Bath—(0225) 424609
Beverley—(0482) 867488
(0482) 882645 (race-days)
Brighton—(0273) 682912
(0273) 603580 (race-days)
Carlisle—(0228) 22504
Cartmel—(05395) 36340, 36494 (race-days)
Catterick Bridge—(0748) 811478
Cheltenham—(0242) 513014
Chepstow—(0291) 622260
Chester—(0244) 323170 (race-days)
Doncaster—(0302) 320066 or 320067
Edinburgh—(0292) 264179,
(031) 665 2859 (race-days)
Epsom—(0372) 726311
Exeter—(0392) 832599
Fakenham—(0328) 862388
Folkestone—(0303) 266407, 268449
Fontwell Park (0243) 543335
Goodwood—(Office) (0243) 774107,
(0243) 774838 (race-days)
Hamilton Park—(0698) 283806
Haydock Park—(0942) 725963 and 728017
Hereford—(0432) 273560
Hexham—(0434) 603738 (course),
606881 (office)
Huntingdon—(0480) 453373 or 454610
Kelso—(0573) 224767
Kempton Park—(0932) 782292
Leicester—(0533) 716515
Lingfield Park—(0342) 834800
Liverpool—(051–523) 2600
Ludlow—(058477) 221
Market Rasen—(0673) 843434
Newbury—(0635) 40015
Newcastle—(091) 236 2020
Newmarket—Rowley Mile (0638) 662762, 662524
July course—(0638) 662752, 662759
Westfield House office (0638) 663482
Newton Abbot—(0626) 53235
Nottingham—(0602) 580620
Perth Hunt—(0738) 51597
Plumpton—(0273) 890383
Pontefract—(0977) 703224,
Course 702210, (race-days)
Redcar—(0642) 484068 (Office),
484254 (course)
Ripon—(0765) 602156, or 603696
Salisbury—(0722) 326461/327327
Sandown Park—(0372) 463072/464348
Sedgefield—(0642) 557081, (0740) 20366 (race-days)
Southwell—(0636) 814481
Stratford-on-Avon—(0789) 267949
Taunton—(0823) 337172, 275575 (race-days)
Thirsk—(0845) 522276
Towcester—(0327) 353414
Uttoxeter—(0889) 562561
Warwick—(0926) 491553
Wetherby—(0937) 582035
Wincanton—(0963) 32344
Windsor—(0753) 865234, 864726
Wolverhampton—(0902) 24481
Worcester—(0905) 25364, 23936
Yarmouth—(0493) 842527
York—(0904) 620911

Racecourses closed since 1900

The following list of courses which ceased to race under the Rules of Racing since January 1st, 1900, is not complete and does not contain Hunt fixtures run as Bona Fide meetings.

Aldershot last meeting 1 April, 1939
Alexandra Park last meeting 8 September, 1970
Beaufort last meeting 14 April, 1956
Birmingham last meeting 21 June, 1965 (evening meeting)
Blackpool (Clifton Park) first meeting 1 August, 1911; last meeting 26 April, 1915
Bogside last meeting 10 April, 1965
Bournemouth first meeting 17 April, 1925; last meeting 10 April, 1928
Bridgnorth last meeting 20 May, 1939
Bridgwater last meeting 13 May, 1904
Buckfastleigh last meeting 27 August, 1960
Bungay last meeting 29 May, 1939
Burgh-by-Sands last meeting 16 April, 1900
Cardiff last meeting 27 April, 1939
Carmarthen last meeting 17 April, 1914
Champion Lodge (Maldon) last meeting 29 April, 1903
Chelmsford last meeting 29 April, 1935
Colchester last meeting 4 April, 1904
Colwell Park last meeting 25 May, 1939
Cottenham last meeting 7 May, 1925
Cowbridge last meeting 4 May, 1939
Croxton Park last meeting 2 April, 1914
Dawlish last meeting 20 September, 1900
Derby last meeting 9 August, 1939
Dunbar last meeting 22 March, 1906
Gatwick last meeting 15 June, 1940
Harpenden last meeting 7 May, 1914
Hawthorn Hill last meeting 4 April, 1939
Hethersett first meeting 16 April, 1903; last meeting 4 May, 1939
Hooton Park last meeting 26 December, 1914
Hurst Park last meeting 10 October, 1962
Keele Park last meeting 12 May, 1906
Lanark last meeting 18 October, 1977
Lewes last meeting 14 September, 1964
Lincoln last meeting 21 May, 1964
Maiden Erlegh last meeting 12 April, 1906
Malton last meeting 4 February, 1904
Manchester last meeting 9 November, 1963
Monmouth last meeting 4 May, 1933
Newport last meeting 17 May, 1948
Northampton last meeting 31 March, 1904
Oswestry last meeting 29 April, 1939
Paisley last meeting 10 August, 1906
Pershore last meeting 1 May, 1939
Picton first meeting 19 April, 1909; last meeting 11 April, 1914
Plymouth last meeting 5 September, 1929
Portsmouth Park last meeting 13 April, 1914
Ross-on-Wye last meeting 18 April, 1904
Rothbury last meeting 10 April, 1965
Sheffield last meeting 5 November, 1901
Shincliffe last meeting 6 May, 1914
Shirley Park last meeting 11 March, 1940
Stockton last meeting 16 June, 1981
Tarporley last meeting 26 April, 1939
Tenby last meeting 29 October, 1936
Torquay last meeting 25 March, 1940
Totnes last meeting 1 September, 1938
Wenlock last meeting 5 May, 1939
Woore last meeting 1 June, 1963
Wye last meeting 2 May, 1974

RACING FIXTURES IN 1994

KEY: Flat meetings in bold type
NH meetings in light type
Irish meetings in italic
* denotes evening meeting
† denotes all weather track fixture

JANUARY

1 Saturday Southwell†, Lingfield†, Catterick, Newbury, Nottingham, *Naas*
3 Monday Wolverhampton†, Ayr, Cheltenham, Leicester, Exeter, Windsor, *Fairyhouse, Tramore*
4 Tuesday Lingfield†, Newton Abbot
5 Wednesday Sedgefield, Southwell†, Lingfield, *Punchestown*
6 Thursday Market Rasen, Lingfield†, Worcester, *Thurles*
7 Friday Southwell†, Edinburgh, Towcester
8 Saturday Lingfield†, *Wolverhampton†, Haydock, Sandown, Warwick, *Leopardstown*
10 Monday Wolverhampton†, Lingfield
11 Tuesday Chepstow, Leicester, **Lingfield†**
12 Wednesday Kelso, Plumpton, Southwell†
13 Thursday Lingfield†, Wetherby, Wincanton, *Gowran Park*
14 Friday Southwell†, Ascot, Edinburgh
15 Saturday Lingfield†, Ascot, Warwick, Newcastle, *Punchestown*
16 Sunday *Navan*
17 Monday Wolverhampton†, Carlisle, Fontwell
18 Tuesday Lingfield†, Folkestone
19 Wednesday Ludlow, Southwell†, Windsor, *Fairyhouse*
20 Thursday Ayr, Lingfield†, Taunton, *Tramore*
21 Friday Southwell†, Catterick, Kempton
22 Saturday Lingfield†, *Wolverhampton†, Catterick, Haydock, Kempton, Market Rasen, *Naas*
23 Sunday *Leopardstown*
24 Monday Wolverhampton†, Leicester
25 Tuesday Chepstow, **Lingfield†**, Nottingham
26 Wednesday Lingfield, Sedgefield, Southwell†, *Down Royal*
27 Thursday Lingfield†, Huntingdon, Newton Abbot, *Tramore*
28 Friday Southwell†, Doncaster, Uttoxeter, Wincanton
29 Saturday Lingfield†, Ayr, Cheltenham, Doncaster, *Naas*
31 Monday Wolverhampton†, Plumpton

FEBRUARY

1 Tuesday Lingfield†, Nottingham, Sedgefield
2 Wednesday Leicester, Windsor, Southwell†
3 Thursday Lingfield†, Edinburgh, Towcester, *Clonmel*
4 Friday Southwell†, Lingfield, Kelso
5 Saturday Lingfield†, *Wolverhampton†, Chepstow, Sandown, Stratford, Wetherby, *Navan*
6 Sunday *Leopardstown*
7 Monday Wolverhampton† Fontwell
8 Tuesday Carlisle, **Lingfield†**, Warwick
9 Wednesday Ascot, Ludlow, Southwell†
10 Thursday Lingfield†, Huntingdon, Wincanton, *Thurles*
11 Friday Southwell†, Bangor-on-Dee, Newbury
12 Saturday Lingfield†, Ayr, Catterick, Newbury, Uttoxeter, *Fairyhouse*
14 Monday Wolverhampton†, Hereford, Plumpton
15 Tuesday Lingfield†, Newton Abbot, Towcester
16 Wednesday Folkestone, Sedgefield, Southwell†, Worcester
17 Thursday Lingfield†, Leicester, Sandown, Taunton, *Thurles*
18 Friday Southwell†, Edinburgh, Fakenham, Sandown
19 Saturday Lingfield†, *Wolverhampton†, Chepstow, Newcastle, Nottingham, Windsor, *Gowran Park*
20 Sunday *Punchestown*
21 Monday Wolverhampton†, Fontwell, *Limerick*
22 Tuesday Lingfield†, Huntingdon, Sedgefield
23 Wednesday Doncaster, Folkestone, Southwell†, Warwick
24 Thursday Lingfield†, Catterick, Wincanton, *Tipperary*
25 Friday Southwell†, Haydock, Kempton
26 Saturday Lingfield†, Edinburgh, Haydock, Kempton, Market Rasen, *Naas*
27 Sunday *Fairyhouse*
28 Monday Leicester, Plumpton, **Wolverhampton†**

MARCH

1 Tuesday Nottingham, **Lingfield†**
2 Wednesday Southwell†, Wetherby, Worcester, *Downpatrick*
3 Thursday Ludlow, Warwick, Lingfield†, Taunton, *Clonmel*
4 Friday Southwell†, Kelso, Newbury
5 Saturday Lingfield†, *Wolverhampton†, Doncaster, Hereford, Newbury, Stratford, *Navan*
6 Sunday *Leopardstown*
7 Monday Wolverhampton†, Doncaster, Windsor
8 Tuesday Leicester, Lingfield†, Sedgefield
9 Wednesday Bangor-on-Dee, Catterick, Folkestone, Southwell†, *Tralee*
10 Thursday Carlisle, Towcester, Wincanton, *Wexford*
11 Friday Ayr, Market Rasen, Sandown
12 Saturday Ayr, Chepstow, Sandown, Southwell, *Naas*
14 Monday Plumpton, Taunton
15 Tuesday Cheltenham, Sedgefield
16 Wednesday Cheltenham, Huntingdon, Newton Abbot
17 Thursday Lingfield†, Cheltenham, Hexham, *Leopardstown, Limerick, Down Royal*
18 Friday Fakenham, Lingfield, Southwell
19 Saturday *Wolverhampton†, Chepstow, Lingfield, Newcastle, Uttoxeter, *Navan*
21 Monday Newcastle, Plumpton
22 Tuesday Fontwell, Newcastle, Nottingham
23 Wednesday Exeter, Kelso, Worcester
24 Thursday Doncaster, Stratford, Wincanton, *Thurles*
25 Friday Doncaster, Ludlow, Newbury
26 Saturday Doncaster, Lingfield†, Warwick, Bangor-on-Dee, Newbury, Sedgefield, *Tipperary*
27 Sunday *Naas*
28 Monday Folkestone, Hexham
29 Tuesday Newcastle, Sandown
30 Wednesday Catterick, Ascot, Worcester, *Downpatrick*
31 Thursday Hamilton, Leicester, Brighton

APRIL

2 Saturday Haydock, Kempton, *Wolverhampton†, Carlisle, Towcester, Uttoxeter, Newton Abbot, Plumpton, *Curragh,*

Mallow
4 Monday Newcastle, Nottingham, Warwick, Kempton, Carlisle, Wetherby, Fakenham, Hereford, Huntingdon, Market Rasen, Towcester, Uttoxeter, Chepstow, Newton Abbot, Plumpton, Wincanton, *Mallow, Fairyhouse*
5 Tuesday Newcastle, Chepstow, Wetherby, *Fairyhouse*
6 Wednesday Ripon, Ascot, Ludlow, *Fairyhouse*
7 Thursday Brighton, Leicester, Aintree, *Tipperary*
8 Friday Beverley, Lingfield†, Aintree
9 Saturday Beverley, Aintree, Hereford
10 Sunday *Curragh*
11 Monday Folkestone, Kelso
12 Tuesday Newmarket, Sedgefield
13 Wednesday Newmarket, Pontefract, Worcester, *Down Royal*
14 Thursday Newmarket, Ripon, Ayr, *Clonmel*
15 Friday Newbury, Thirsk, ***Warwick**, Ayr, *Taunton
16 Saturday Newbury, Thirsk, ***Wolverhampton**†, Ayr, Bangor-on-Dee, Stratford, *Leopardstown*
18 Monday Brighton, Nottingham, Edinburgh, *Ballinrobe*
19 Tuesday Folkestone, Pontefract
20 Wednesday Catterick, Cheltenham, Perth, ***Kempton**, *Newton Abbot, *Gowran Park*
21 Thursday Beverley, Perth, Fontwell, *Mallow*
22 Friday Carlisle, Sandown, Perth, *Ludlow, *Taunton
23 Saturday Sandown (mixed), **Leicester, Ripon**, Market Rasen, *Hexham, *Worcester, *Curragh*
25 Monday Pontefract, Southwell†, ***Windsor**, *Hexham, *Sligo*
26 Tuesday Bath, Nottingham, *Ascot, *Punchestown*
27 Wednesday Ascot, Exeter, *Huntingdon, Kelso, *Cheltenham, *Punchestown*
28 Thursday Hamilton, Newmarket, Salisbury, *Punchestown*
29 Friday Hamilton, Newmarket, Newton Abbot, *Bangor-on-Dee, *Sedgefield
30 Saturday Haydock, Newmarket, Thirsk, Hereford, Uttoxeter, *Hexham, *Plumpton, *Naas*

MAY

1 Sunday *Gowran Park*
2 Monday Doncaster, Kempton, Newcastle, Warwick, Exeter, Fontwell, Haydock, Ludlow, Southwell, Towcester, *Navan, Down Royal, Limerick*
3 Tuesday Chester, Newton Abbot
4 Wednesday Chester, Edinburgh, Brighton, *Uttoxeter, *Wetherby
5 Thursday Salisbury, Carlisle, Chester, ***Hamilton**, *Sedgefield, *Tramore*
6 Friday Beverley, Carlisle, Lingfield, *Wincanton, *Market Rasen, *Downpatrick*
7 Saturday Bath, Beverley, Lingfield, Worcester, *Newcastle, *Warwick, *Downpatrick, Leopardstown*
8 Sunday *Killarney*
9 Monday Redcar, Southwell†, ***Windsor**, *Towcester, *Killarney*
10 Tuesday York, Chepstow, *Folkestone, , *Killarney*
11 Wednesday York, Hereford, Southwell, *Huntingdon, *Perth
12 Thursday Brighton, York, Perth, *Tipperary*
13 Friday Newbury, Thirsk, Nottingham, *Newton Abbot, *Stratford
14 Saturday Newbury, Southwell†, **Thirsk**, ***Hamilton**, ***Lingfield**, ***Wolverhampton**†, Bangor-on-Dee, *Navan*
15 Sunday *Curragh*
16 Monday Bath, Edinburgh, *Mallow*
17 Tuesday Beverley, Goodwood, *Cheltenham, *Mallow*
18 Wednesday Goodwood, Worcester, Sedgefield, *Leopardstown*
19 Thursday Newcastle, Goodwood, Exeter, *Uttoxeter, *Perth, *Clonmel*
20 Friday Catterick, Hamilton, Newmarket, *Stratford, *Fakenham, *Dundalk*
21 Saturday Ayr, Catterick, Lingfield, Newmarket, ***Kempton**, *Southwell, *Warwick, *Curragh*
23 Monday Ayr, Leicester, ***Windsor**, *Roscommon*
24 Tuesday Folkestone, Southwell†, *Tramore*
25 Wednesday Brighton, Hamilton, ***Ripon**, ***Newbury**, Cartmel
26 Thursday Brighton, Carlisle, Hereford, *Tipperary*
27 Friday Haydock, Nottingham, Salisbury, ***Pontefract**, *Towcester, *Dundalk*
28 Saturday Doncaster, Haydock, Kempton, ***Lingfield**, ***Warwick**, ***Wolverhampton**†, Cartmel, Hexham, *Fairyhouse*
30 Monday Chepstow, Doncaster, Leicester, Redcar, Sandown, Cartmel, Hereford, Huntingdon, Fontwell, Uttoxeter, Wetherby, *Kilbeggan, *Down Royal*
31 Tuesday Redcar, Leicester, ***Sandown**, *Hexham

JUNE

1 Wednesday Epsom, Yarmouth, ***Beverley**, *Curragh*
2 Thursday Epsom, Beverley, Uttoxeter, *Clonmel, *Ballinrobe*
3 Friday Epsom, Catterick, Southwell†, ***Haydock**, ***Goodwood**, *Stratford, *Wexford*
4 Saturday Epsom, Haydock, Doncaster, ***Chepstow**, Stratford, *Market Rasen, *Curragh*
5 Sunday *Sligo, Tralee*
6 Monday Pontefract, Nottingham, *Tralee, Leopardstown*
7 Tuesday Pontefract, Salisbury
8 Wednesday Beverley, Yarmouth, ***Hamilton**, ***Kempton**, *Leopardstown*
9 Thursday Newbury, Hamilton, *Tipperary*
10 Friday Sandown, Southwell†, **York**, ***Edinburgh**, ***Goodwood**, *Dundalk*
11 Saturday Bath, Sandown, York, ***Lingfield**, ***Leicester**, ***Wolverhampton**†, *Naas*
12 Sunday *Roscommon*
13 Monday Brighton, Edinburgh, ***Nottingham**, ***Windsor**, *Roscommon*
14 Tuesday Royal Ascot, Thirsk, *Clonmel*
15 Wednesday Royal Ascot, Ripon,
16 Thursday Royal Ascot, Ripon, *Naas*
17 Friday Royal Ascot, Ayr, Redcar, ***Goodwood**, ***Newmarket**
18 Saturday Ascot, Ayr, Redcar, ***Lingfield**, ***Southwell**†, ***Warwick**, *Gowran Park*
19 Sunday *Gowran Park*
20 Monday Edinburgh, Pontefract, ***Windsor**, ***Warwick**, *Kilbeggan*
21 Tuesday Brighton, Yarmouth, ***Newbury**
22 Wednesday Carlisle, Salisbury, ***Chester**, ***Kempton**, *Wexford*
23 Thursday Carlisle, Salisbury, Wolverhampton†, *Thurles*
24 Friday Doncaster, Newmarket, Lingfield, ***Bath**, ***Goodwood**, ***Newcastle**
25 Saturday Chepstow, Newcastle, Newmarket, ***Doncaster**, ***Lingfield**, ***Wolverhampton**†, *Curragh*
26 Sunday *Curragh*

27 Monday Nottingham, Wolverhampton†, *Hamilton, *Windsor, **Limerick*
28 Tuesday Chepstow, Folkestone, **Sligo*
29 Wednesday Catterick, Warwick, *Epsom, *Yarmouth, **Gowran Park*
30 Thursday Brighton, Catterick, Yarmouth, *Haydock, **Tipperary*

JULY

1 Friday Haydock, Sandown, Wolverhampton†, *Beverley, *Nottingham, **Wexford*
2 Saturday Bath, Beverley, Haydock, Sandown, *Naas*
4 Monday Edinburgh, Leicester, *Ripon, *Windsor, **Roscommon*
5 Tuesday Newmarket, Pontefract, **Bellewstown*
6 Wednesday Bath, Newmarket, *Kempton, *Redcar, **Bellewstown*
7 Thursday Newmarket, Redcar, *Chepstow, **Bellewstown*
8 Friday Lingfield, Warwick, York, *Ayr, *Chester
9 Saturday Chester, Lingfield, Salisbury, York, *Southwell†, *Wolverhampton†, *Carlisle, *Curragh*
10 Sunday *Dundalk, Tipperary*
11 Monday Edinburgh, Wolverhampton†, *Leicester, *Windsor, **Killarney*
12 Tuesday Edinburgh, Folkestone, **Killarney, *Dundalk*
13 Wednesday Catterick, Southwell†, *Sandown, *Yarmouth, *Down Royal, Killarney*
14 Thursday Catterick, Sandown, *Chepstow, *Hamilton, *Killarney, Down Royal*
15 Friday Newbury, Wolverhampton†, Thirsk, *Hamilton, *Newmarket, **Kilbeggan*
16 Saturday Newbury, Newmarket, Ripon, *Ayr, *Lingfield, *Southwell†, *Leopardstown*
18 Monday Ayr, Bath, *Windsor, *Beverley, **Ballinrobe*
19 Tuesday Beverley, Folkestone, **Wexford*
20 Wednesday Doncaster, Yarmouth, *Redcar, *Sandown, **Naas*
21 Thursday Brighton, Hamilton, Yarmouth, *Doncaster, **Tipperary*
22 Friday Ascot, Carlisle, Chester, *Pontefract
23 Saturday Ayr, Ascot, Newcastle, Southwell†, *Warwick, *Wolverhampton†, *Curragh*
25 Monday Lingfield, Newcastle, *Nottingham, *Windsor, **Galway*
26 Tuesday Beverley, Goodwood, **Galway*
27 Wednesday Catterick, Goodwood, *Epsom, *Leicester, *Galway*
28 Thursday Goodwood, Yarmouth, Southwell†, *Hamilton, *Salisbury, *Galway*
29 Friday Goodwood, Thirsk, *Edinburgh, *Newmarket, Bangor-on-Dee, **Galway*
30 Saturday Goodwood, Newmarket, Thirsk, *Windsor, Newton Abbot, *Market Rasen, *Galway*

AUGUST

1 Monday Ripon, Newton Abbot, *Leopardstown, Tipperary*
2 Tuesday Brighton, Redcar, **Roscommon*
3 Wednesday Brighton, Pontefract, *Kempton, *Nottingham, Exeter, **Fairyhouse*
4 Thursday Bath, Brighton, Pontefract, **Laytown, *Mallow*
5 Friday Redcar, Southwell†, *Haydock, *Newmarket, Plumpton, **Kilbeggan*
6 Saturday Ayr, Haydock, Newmarket, Redcar, *Lingfield, *Wolverhampton†, *Worcester, *Gowran Park*
7 Sunday *Leopardstown*
8 Monday Windsor, *Leicester, *Thirsk, Worcester, **Roscommon*
9 Tuesday Bath, Yarmouth, **Sligo*
10 Wednesday Beverley, Salisbury, *Sandown, Fontwell, *Sligo*
11 Thursday Beverley, Salisbury, Newton Abbot, **Gowran Park*
12 Friday Folkestone, Newbury, Southwell†, *Catterick, *Haydock
13 Saturday Newbury, Ripon, *Lingfield, *Nottingham, Bangor-on-Dee, Stratford, *Curragh*
14 Sunday *Ballinrobe, Tramore*
15 Monday Hamilton, Windsor, **Tramore, *Dundalk*
16 Tuesday Folkestone, York, **Tramore*
17 Wednesday Carlisle, Yarmouth, York, *Kempton, *Hereford, **Tramore*
18 Thursday Ayr, Yarmouth, York, *Salisbury, *Uttoxeter, **Tipperary*
19 Friday Chester, Sandown, Perth, **Wexford*
20 Saturday Chester, Ripon, Sandown, *Wolverhampton†, Perth, *Market Rasen, *Leopardstown*
21 Sunday *Tralee*
22 Monday Nottingham, Hexham, **Tralee*
23 Tuesday Brighton, Pontefract, **Tralee*
24 Wednesday Redcar, Brighton, Exeter, *Tralee*
25 Thursday Edinburgh, Lingfield, Worcester, *Tralee*
26 Friday Goodwood, Newmarket, Thirsk, *Tralee*
27 Saturday Goodwood, Newcastle, Newmarket, *Windsor, Cartmel, *Hereford, *Curragh*
29 Monday Chepstow, Epsom, Newcastle, Ripon, Warwick, Wolverhampton†, Cartmel, Huntingdon, Newton Abbot, Plumpton, Southwell, *Downpatrick, Roscommon*
30 Tuesday Epsom, Ripon
31 Wednesday York, Fontwell, Newton Abbot, *Ballinrobe*

SEPTEMBER

1 Thursday York, Salisbury, Southwell
2 Friday Haydock, Kempton, Sedgefield, *Kilbeggan*
3 Saturday Haydock, Kempton, Thirsk, *Wolverhamßpton†, Stratford, *Fairyhouse*
5 Monday Hamilton, Southwell†, **Galway*
6 Tuesday Leicester, Lingfield, **Galway*
7 Wednesday Doncaster, Exeter, Uttoxeter, *Galway*
8 Thursday Doncaster, Folkestone, Newton Abbot, *Clonmel*
9 Friday Doncaster, Goodwood, Worcester
10 Saturday Chepstow, Doncaster, Goodwood, Bangor-on-Dee, Worcester, *Leopardstown*
11 Sunday *Curragh*
12 Monday Bath, Leicester, Plumpton, *Roscommon*
13 Tuesday Sandown, Yarmouth, Sedgefield
14 Wednesday Beverley, Sandown, Yarmouth, Exeter
15 Thursday Ayr, Beverley, Lingfield, Yarmouth, *Dundalk*
16 Friday Ayr, Newbury, Huntingdon
17 Saturday Ayr, Catterick, Newbury, *Wolverhampton†, Market Rasen, *Curragh, Down Royal*
19 Monday Edinburgh, Folkestone, Nottingham, Pontefract, *Listowel*
20 Tuesday Kempton, Nottingham, *Listowel*
21 Wednesday Brighton, Chester, Perth, *Listowel*
22 Thursday Ascot, Perth, Taunton, *Listowel*
23 Friday Ascot, Haydock, Redcar, *Listowel*
24 Saturday Ascot, Haydock, Redcar, Carlisle, Market

Rasen, Worcester, *Listowel*
25 Sunday *Curragh*
26 Monday Bath, Hamilton, Southwell†, Fontwell
27 Tuesday Brighton, Newcastle, Exeter
28 Wednesday Newmarket, Salisbury, Folkestone, Sedgefield, *Downpatrick*
29 Thursday Newmarket, Lingfield, Cheltenham, *Gowran Park*
30 Friday Newmarket, Goodwood, Hexham

OCTOBER

1 Saturday Goodwood, Newmarket, *Wolverhampton†, Chepstow, Kelso, Uttoxeter, *Fairyhouse*
2 Sunday *Tipperary*
3 Monday Pontefract, Warwick
4 Tuesday Redcar, Warwick, Newton Abbot
5 Wednesday Haydock, York, Towcester, Market Rasen, *Mallow*
6 Thursday Haydock, York, Ludlow, Wincanton, *Punchestown*
7 Friday Ascot, Carlisle, Cheltenham
8 Saturday Ascot, York, Ayr, Bangor-on-Dee, Worcester, *Naas, Down Royal*
10 Monday Leicester, Carlisle, Fontwell, *Roscommon*
11 Tuesday Chepstow, Leicester, Sedgefield
12 Wednesday Exeter, Wetherby, Uttoxeter, *Navan*
13 Thursday Newmarket, Redcar, Hexham, Taunton, *Thurles*
14 Friday Catterick, Newmarket, Ludlow
15 Saturday Catterick, Newmarket, *Wolverhampton†, Kelso, Kempton, Stratford, *Curragh*
16 Sunday *Limerick*
17 Monday Folkestone, Nottingham, Hereford
18 Tuesday Chepstow, Plumpton
19 Wednesday Yarmouth, Exeter, Newcastle, *Gowran Park*
20 Thursday Newbury, Pontefract, Wincanton, *Punchestown*
21 Friday Doncaster, Fakenham, Newbury
22 Saturday Doncaster, Newbury, Huntingdon, Worcester, *Naas, Down Royal*
24 Monday Leicester, Lingfield
25 Tuesday Leicester, Redcar, Newton Abbot
26 Wednesday Yarmouth, Fontwell, Cheltenham, *Navan*
27 Thursday Nottingham, Sedgefield, Stratford, *Tipperary*
28 Friday Newmarket, Bangor-on-Dee, Wetherby
29 Saturday Newmarket, *Wolverhampton†, Ascot, Warwick, Wetherby, *Leopardstown*
30 Sunday *Wexford, Galway*
31 Monday Newcastle, Plumpton, *Galway, Leopardstown*

NOVEMBER

1 Tuesday Redcar, Exeter, *Clonmel*
2 Wednesday Haydock, Kelso, Uttoxeter, Kempton, *Curragh*
3 Thursday Edinburgh, Lingfield†, Uttoxeter, Wincanton, *Gowran Park*
4 Friday Doncaster, Hexham, Market Rasen
5 Saturday Doncaster, Chepstow, Newcastle, Sandown, *Navan*
6 Sunday *Punchestown*
7 Monday Folkestone, Carlisle
8 Tuesday Southwell, Sedgefield, Fontwell
9 Wednesday Lingfield†, Newbury, Worcester, *Downpatrick*
10 Thursday Kelso, Taunton, Towcester, *Clonmel*
11 Friday Lingfield†, Ayr, Cheltenham, Huntingdon
12 Saturday *Wolverhampton†, Ayr, Cheltenham, Nottingham, Windsor, *Naas*
13 Sunday *Leopardstown*
14 Monday Leicester, Plumpton
15 Tuesday Newton Abbot, Warwick, Wetherby
16 Wednesday Southwell, Haydock, Hereford, Kempton, *Fairyhouse*
17 Thursday Haydock, Ludlow, Wincanton, *Tipperary*
18 Friday Ascot, Leicester, Sedgefield
19 Saturday Aintree, Ascot, Catterick, Market Rasen, Towcester, *Navan*
21 Monday Catterick, Folkestone
22 Tuesday Southwell†, Huntingdon, Stratford
23 Wednesday Cheltenham, Hexham, Windsor
24 Thursday Carlisle, Nottingham, Taunton, *Naas*
25 Friday Bangor-on-Dee, Newbury, Southwell
26 Saturday Lingfield†, ***Wolverhampton**†, Newbury, Newcastle, Warwick, *Punchestown*
27 Sunday *Clonmel*
28 Monday Lingfield†, Kelso, Worcester
29 Tuesday Fontwell, Leicester, Newcastle
30 Wednesday Southwell†, Catterick, Huntingdon

DECEMBER

1 Thursday Lingfield†, Uttoxeter, Windsor, *Thurles*
2 Friday Exeter, Hereford, Sandown
3 Saturday Chepstow, Sandown, Towcester, Wetherby, *Fairyhouse*
4 Sunday *Fairyhouse*
5 Monday Edinburgh, Ludlow
6 Tuesday Plumpton, Sedgefield
7 Wednesday Lingfield†, Haydock, Worcester
8 Thursday Fakenham, Haydock, Taunton, *Clonmel*
9 Friday Cheltenham, Doncaster, Hexham
10 Saturday *Wolverhampton†, Cheltenham, Doncaster, Edinburgh, Lingfield, *Punchestown*
12 Monday Warwick, Newton Abbot
13 Tuesday Folkestone, Southwell†
14 Wednesday Lingfield†, Bangor-on-Dee, Exeter
15 Thursday Southwell†, Kelso, Towcester
16 Friday Catterick, Market Rasen, Uttoxeter
17 Saturday Lingfield†, Ascot, Nottingham, Uttoxeter, Catterick, *Navan*
18 Sunday *Navan, Thurles*
19 Monday Edinburgh, Lingfield
20 Tuesday Lingfield†, Hereford
21 Wednesday Hexham, Ludlow, Southwell
26 Monday Ayr, Hereford, Huntingdon, Kempton, Market Rasen, Newton Abbot, Sedgefield, Wetherby, Wincanton, Wolverhampton, *Leopardstown, Limerick, Down Royal*
27 Tuesday Southwell†, Wolverhampton, Chepstow, Kempton, Wetherby, *Leopardstown, Limerick*
28 Wednesday Newcastle, Plumpton, Stratford, *Leopardstown, Limerick*
29 Thursday Carlisle, Fontwell, Taunton, Warwick, *Leopardstown, Limerick*
30 Friday Newbury, Folkestone, Leicester
31 Saturday Lingfield†, ***Wolverhampton**†, Catterick, Nottingham, Newbury, *Punchestown*

INTERNATIONAL BLOODSTOCK SALE DATES 1994

JANUARY

8–9 William Inglis Sydney Festival Yearlings (AUS)
9 Fasig-Tipton Kentucky Winter Mixed (USA)
10–12 Keeneland Horses of All Ages (USA)
14–16 Volvo Magic Millions Yearlings, Gold Coast (AUS)
17–19 Ocala Breeders' Winter Mixed (USA)
24 Barretts Mixed (USA)
24–25 Wrightson Premier Yearlings, Karaka (NZ)
26–27 Doncaster January Mixed (GB)
27–28 Wrightson Anniversary Yearlings, Karaka (NZ)
28 Dalgety Mixed (AUS)
30–31 Wrightson "Magic Millions" Yearlings, Hamilton (NZ)
30–31 TBA of South Africa Goodwood Sales (SA)

FEBRUARY

1 Wrightson Waikato Yearlings, Hamilton, (NZ)
7 OBS Selected 2YO's in Training, Calder (USA)
7–8 Goffs February Mixed (IRE)
11 William Inglis Summer Thoroughbreds (AUS)
14 Wrightson Waikato Summer Mixed, Hamilton (NZ)
21–22 Tattersalls (Ireland) February (IRE)
22 Ascot Horses in & out of Training, Mixed (GB)
27 William Inglis Yearlings (AUS)
28–Mar 1 Fasig-Tipton Selected 2YO's in Training, Fl. (USA)

MARCH

8–9 Barretts Selected 2YO's in Training (USA)
10 Goffs "Breeze-up", Naas (IRE)
12–13 Dalgety Premier Yearlings (AUS)
12–13 Volvo 440 Magic Million Golden Nugget Yearlings (AUS)
19–23 TBA of South Africa National Yearlings (SA)
21 Dalgety Mixed (AUS)
22 Ascot 2YO's in Training Mixed (GB)
22–23 Ocala Breeders' Open 2YO's in Training (USA)
24–25 Doncaster 2YO's in Training (GB)
28 Doncaster Lincoln Handicap Mixed (GB)
30 Doncaster "Breeze-up" Lingfield Park (GB)

APRIL

5–7 William Inglis Easter Yearlings (AUS)
9 Goffs France "Breeze-up", Evry (FR)
10–11 William Inglis Easter Broodmares (AUS)
13–14 Tattersalls "Breeze-up" (GB)
15 William Inglis Easter Thoroughbreds (AUS)
17 Dalgety VOBIS Extra Yearlings (AUS)
18 Dalgety Autumn Yearlings (AUS)
19–20 Keeneland 2YO's in Training (USA)
25 Goffs Punchestown Festival NH (IRE)
25–28 Ocala Spring 2YO's in Training (USA)
29 Goffs France Horses in Training, Saint-Cloud (FR)

MAY

3 Ascot NH & Flat in & out of Training (GB)
9 Dalgety Mixed (AUS)
9–10 Wrightson National Broodmares & Foals, Karaka (NZ)
11 Wrightson Waikato Autumn Mixed, Hamilton (NZ)
16–19 Doncaster Spring Sales (GB)
17 Barretts 2YO's in Training & Mixed (USA)
18 William Inglis Scone Mixed (AUS)
22 William Inglis Scone Yearlings (AUS)
30 Goffs France Horses in Training, Saint-Cloud (FR)
31 Ascot NH Derby Sale (GB)

JUNE

10 Elders Winter Carnival Foals & Thoroughbreds (AUS)
13–14 Ocala Breeders' Open 2YO's & Horses in Training (USA)
19 William Inglis Winter Yearling/Weanlings (AUS)
20 William Inglis Winter Thoroughbreds (AUS)
23–24 Tattersalls (Ireland) Derby Sale (IRE)
27–28 Ascot Premier Mixed (GB)
29 Doncaster Summer Mixed (GB)
30–Jul 1 TBA of South Africa, Natal Yearlings (SA)

JULY

3 Dalgety Foals (AUS)
4 Dalgety Mixed (AUS)
6–7 Tattersalls July Mixed (GB)
7 Goffs France Horses in Training, Longchamp (FR)
18–19 Keeneland July Selected Yearlings (USA)
20 Fasig-Tipton Selected Yearlings, Kentucky (USA)
25 Ascot Mixed (GB)
30 Goffs France Horses in Training, Saint-Cloud (FR)

AUGUST

8–10 Doncaster August National Hunt (GB)
9–11 Fasig-Tipton Saratoga Selected Yearlings NY (USA)
13–14 TBA of South Africa, National 2YO's (SA)
15–16 Goffs National Hunt (IRE)
18 Tattersalls (Ireland) National Hunt (IRE)
mid-Aug Wrightson South Island 2YO's, Christchurch (NZ)
20–25 Agence Francaise Yearlings, Deauville (FR)
22 Ocala Breeders' Selected Yearlings (USA)
23–25 Ocala Breeders' Open Yearlings (USA)
30 Ascot Mixed (GB)

SEPTEMBER

2 Tattersalls September Horses in Training (GB)
3 BBAG Yearlings, Baden-Baden (GER)
6–9 Doncaster St Leger Yearlings (GB)
7 CBS Selected Yearlings, Woodbine (CAN)

9–10	Fasig-Tipton September Yearlings Ky (USA)
12–20	Keeneland September Yearlings (USA)
mid–Sept	Wrightson 2YO's in Training, Karaka (NZ)
17	ANAC Select Yearlings, Settimo Milanese (ITY)
18–19	Goff's Premier Yearlings (IRE)
19–21	Tattersalls (Ireland) September Yearlings (IRE)
22	Doncaster Horses in Training & Mixed (GB)
23	William Inglis Spring Thoroughbreds (AUS)
26	Ascot Flat & NH H-in/out-T & Mixed (GB)
26	Goffs France Horses in Training, Saint-Cloud (FR)
27–28	CBS Open Yearlings & Breeding Stock, Woodbine (CAN)
28–30	Tattersalls Houghton Yearlings (GB)

OCTOBER

1	Goffs France "Arc" Sale, Saint-Cloud (FR)
4–6	Goffs National Yearlings (IRE)
5–7	Tattersalls (Ireland) Non-Thoroughbreds (IRE)
10–14	Ocala Breeders' Sales Fall Mixed (USA)
10–14	Tattersalls October Yearlings (GB)
17	Ascot Yearlings (GB)
17–18	ANAC Qualified Yearlings, Settimo Milanese (ITY)
17–18	Barretts Selected/Open Yearlings (USA)
17–19	Agence Francaise Yearlings, Deauville (FR)
19–22	Doncaster October (GB)
24–29	Tattersalls Horses in Training/Yearlings (GB)
28	Goffs Horses in Training/Yearlings (IRE)
29	BBAG Mixed Sale, Baden-Baden (GER)
31–Nov 12	Tattersalls (Ireland) National Hunt Horses in Training & Breeding Stock (IRE)

NOVEMBER

3–4	Goffs France Autumn Mixed, Longchamp (FR)
4–6	Fasig-Tipton Fall Mixed, Kentucky (USA)
6–13	Keeneland November Breeding Stock (USA)
14–18	Doncaster November (GB)
18–20	Goffs Premier Foal & Breeding Stock (IRE)
21	Tattersalls December Part I—Yearlings (GB)
22	Ascot Mixed (GB)
23–26	Tattersalls December Part II—Foals (GB)
28–Dec 2	Tattersalls December Part III—Mares etc. (GB)

DECEMBER

1	Goffs France Horses in Training, Maisons-Laffitte (FR)
3–5	Agence Francaise Mixed Sales, Deauville (FR)
4–5	Tattersalls (Ireland) Breeding Stock (IRE)
6–7	Goffs December Foal, Yearling & Breeding Stock (IRE)
8–10	Goffs National Hunt Breeding Stock (IRE)
9	William Inglis December Thoroughbreds (AUS)
19–20	Ascot Mixed (GB)

The Sporting Life

FLAT RESULTS 1993

Published 1993 by The Sporting Life
Orbit House, 1 New Fetter Lane, London EC4A 1AR

ISBN 0 901091 69 3

Editorial and Production by Martin Pickering Bloodstock Services
Cover designed by P. W. Reprosharp Ltd, London EC1
Cover printed by Ark Litho Ltd, London SW19
Preliminaries typeset by LBJ Enterprises Ltd, of Chilcompton and Aldermaston
Text printed by Bath Press Ltd, Bath and London

Cover picture
Fairy Heights (nearside) and Alan Munro just beat Taghareed (USA), ridden by Richard Hills, by 1/2 a length in the Listed Columbus Sweet Solera Stakes at Newmarket.
(Photo: Phil Smith, The Sporting Life)

Contents

1993 FLAT AVERAGE TIMES FOR COURSES

(Revised up to and incl. 1992)

SPORTING LIFE Adjusted Average Times represent the theoretical time a top class horse be expected to clock under ideal conditions carrying nine stone. They embrace previous fast times over a course and distance and honed to compensate for the state of the ground, weight carried, calibre of horse and adjusted to nine stone. They provide an accurate and reliable benchmark for each individual trip and track with which we can compare the actual times recorded at a meeting.

ASCOT

5f	1m 0.3s
6f	1m 13.4s
7f	1m 26.3s
1m (St)	1m 39s
1m (Rnd)	1m 39.5s
1m 2f	2m 3.7s
1m 4f	2m 28.2s
2m 45yds	3m 25s
2m 4f	4m 16.5s
2m 6f 34yds	4m 47s

AYR

5f	58.1s
6f	1m 10.9s
7f	1m 24s
1m	1m 37.7s
1m 1f	1m 50.3s
1m 2f	2m 5s
1m 3f (10f 192yds)	2m 14s
1m 5f 13yds	2m 46s
1m 7f 90yds	3m 12.5s
2m 1f 105yds	3m 44s
2m 4f 90yds	4m 26s

BATH

5f 11yds	1m 0.5s
5f 161yds	1m 9.4s
1m 8yds	1m 39s
1m 2f 46yds	2m 6.4s
1m 3f 144yds	2m 27s
1m 5f 22yds	2m 48.3s
2m 1f 34yds	3m 44s

BEVERLEY

5f	1m 1.7s
7f 100yds	1m 30.3s
1m 100yds	1m 42.8s
1m 2f (9f 207yds)	2m 1.4s
1m 4f (11f 216yds)	2m 31s
2m 35yds	3m 29s
2m 3f 100yds	4m 15.5s

BRIGHTON

5f 59yds	1m 0.1s
6f (5f 213yds)	1m 8.4s
7f (6f 209yds)	1m 20s
1m (7f 214yds)	1m 32.4s
1m 2f (9f 209yds)	1m 58.2s
1m 4f (11f 196yds)	2m 27.5s

CARLISLE

5f	1m
6f (5f 207yds)	1m 13s
7f (6f 206yds)	1m 25.4s
1m (7f 214yds)	1m 37.9s
1m 1f 80yds	1m 57s
1m 4f	2m 30s
1m 6f 32yds	2m 57.8s

CATTERICK

5f	57.5s
6f (5f 212yds)	1m 11s
7f	1m 23s
1m 4f 44yds	2m 35s
1m 5f 175yds	2m 55.5s
1m 7f 177yds	3m 21.5s

CHEPSTOW

5f 16yds	57s
6f 16yds	1m 9.5s
7f 16yds	1m 20s
1m 14yds	1m 32.4s
1m 2f 36yds	2m 3.6s
1m 4f 23yds	2m 31.5s
2m 49yds	3m 27s
2m 1f 40yds	3m 41s

CHESTER

5f 16yds	1m 0.3s
6f 18yds	1m 13.5s
7f 2yds	1m 25.4s
7f 122yds	1m 32s
1m 2f 75yds	2m 9.1s
1m 3f 79yds	2m 23.3s
1m 4f 66yds	2m 36.8s
1m 5f 89yds	2m 50s
2m (15f 195yds)	3m 25s
2m 2f 117yds	3m 59.5s

CURRAGH

5f	58.3s
6f	1m 10.5s
6f 63yds	1m 14.5s
7f	1m 23.2s
1m	1m 36.6s
1m 1f	1m 49.5s
1m 2f	2m 2.8s
1m 4f	2m 29.5s
1m 5f	2m 41.3s
1m 6f	2m 55.5s
2m	3m 21.5s

DONCASTER

5f	58.8s
5f 140yds	1m 7.1s
6f	1m 11.4s
6f 110yds	1m 17.4s
7f	1m 23.4s
1m (St)	1m 36.8s
1m (Rnd)	1m 36.7s
1m 2f 60yds	2m 6.7s
1m 4f	2m 30.5s
1m 6f 132yds	3m 4.5s
2m 110yds	3m 30s
2m 2f	3m 52s

EDINBURGH

5f 57.8s
7f 15yds 1m 25.2s
1m 16yds 1m 38.5s
1m 3f 32yds 2m 19.5s
1m 4f 31yds 2m 32.8s
1m 7f 16yds 3m 12s

EPSOM

5f 54.7s
6f 1m 7.9s
7f 1m 20.4s
1m 114yds 1m 42s
1m 2f 18yds 2m 4.3s
1m 4f 10yds 2m 35.5s

FOLKESTONE

5f 58.6s
6f 1m 11s
7f (6f 189yds) 1m 20.9s
1m 2f (9f 149yds) 1m 57.6s
1m 4f 2m 30.5s
1m 7f 92yds 3m 18.5s
2m 93yds 3m 31s

GOODWOOD

5f 56.8s
6f 1m 10.4s
7f 1m 24.6s
1m 1m 37.2s
1m 1f 1m 52s
1m 2f 2m 5.5s
1m 4f 2m 33s
1m 6f 2m 57.3s
2m 3m 24s
2m 4f 4m 14s

HAMILTON

5f 4yds 58.3s
6f 5yds 1m 10.7s
1m 65yds 1m 44s
1m 1f 36yds 1m 54s
1m 3f 16yds 2m 20s
1m 4f 17yds 2m 33s
1m 5f 9yds 2m 46s

HAYDOCK

5f 58.8s
6f 1m 11.6s
7f 30yds 1m 27.2s
1m 30yds 1m 40.6s
1m 2f 120yds 2m 11s
1m 4f (1m 3f 200yds) 2m 29.8s
1m 6f 2m 57.5s
2m 45yds 3m 26s
2m 1f 130yds 3m 47s
2m 3f 4m 3s

KEMPTON

5f 58.2s
6f 1m 10.8s
7f (Rnd) 1m 24.3s
7f (Jubilee) 1m 24.1s
1m (Jubilee) 1m 36.8s
1m (Rnd) 1m 37s
1m 1f (Rnd) 1m 50s
1m 2f (Jubilee) 2m 1.8s
1m 3f 30yds 2m 17.3s
1m 4f 2m 31s
1m 6f 2m 58s
2m 3m 24.5s

LEICESTER

5f 2yds 58.7s
6f (5f 218yds) 1m 10.4s
7f 9yds 1m 21.9s
1m 8yds 1m 35.1s
1m 2f (9f 218yds) 2m 2.9s
1m 4f (11f 183yds) 2m 28.5s

LEOPARDSTOWN

5f 58.7s
6f 1m 11.5s
7f 1m 25.4s
1m 1m 38s
1m 1f 1m 50.5s
1m 2f 2m 4.7s
1m 4f 2m 31s
1m 5f 2m 43s
1m 6f 2m 56s
2m 3m 25s
2m 2f 3m 51s
2m 4f 4m 17s

LINGFIELD (Turf)

5f 56.9s
6f 1m 9s
7f 1m 20.7s
7f 140yds 1m 28.3s
1m 1f 1m 49s
1m 2f 2m 5s
1m 3f 106yds 2m 24.2s
1m 6f 2m 55s
2m 3m 23.5s

LINGFIELD (All-Weather)

5f 58.2s
6f 1m 10.8s
7f 1m 23.4s
1m 1m 36.2s
1m 2f 2m 3.2s
1m 4f 2m 29.3s
1m 5f 2m 43s
2m 3m 22s

NAAS

5f 58s
6f 1m 9.5s
7f 1m 22.6s
1m 1m 35.8s
1m 1f 1m 50s
1m 2f 2m 4s
1m 3f 2m 16.5s
1m 4f 2m 30s
2m 3m 24s

NEWBURY

5f 34yds 1m 0.3s
6f 8yds 1m 11.7s
7f 1m 24.1s
7f 64yds 1m 27.3s
1m (St) 1m 37.1s
1m 7yds (Rnd) 1m 35.8s
1m 1f 1m 49.2s
1m 2f 6yds 2m 3s
1m 3f 6yds 2m 16.2s
1m 4f 5yds 2m 29.6s
1m 5f 61yds 2m 46.2s
2m 3m 26s

NEWCASTLE

5f 58.9s
6f 1m 12s
7f 1m 24s
1m (Rnd) 1m 39s
1m 1f 9yds 1m 52s
1m 2f 32yds 2m 6.5s
1m 4f 93yds 2m 37.7s
2m 19yds 3m 26s

NEWMARKET (Rowley Mile Course)

5f (Rous) 58.6s
6f (Bretby) 1m 11.4s
7f (Dewhurst) 1m 23.5s
1m (Rowley) 1m 37.2s
1m 1f (Cambs) 1m 49.7s
1m 2f 2m 2.7s
1m 4f (Ces) 2m 29.6s
1m 6f (Ces) 2m 56s
2m (Ces) 3m 24s
2m 2f 3m 50s
2m 4f 4m 18s

NEWMARKET (July Course)

5f (Chesterfield) 58.7s
6f (Bunbury) 1m 11.7s
7f (Bunbury) 1m 24.2s
1m (Bunbury) 1m 37.9s
1m 2f (Suffolk) 2m 2.2s
1m 4f (Suffolk) 2m 28.8s
1m 6f 175yds 3m 6s
2m 22yds 3m 23s
2m 4f 4m 18s

NOTTINGHAM

5f 13yds 58.2s
6f 15yds 1m 11.5s
1m 54yds 1m 40s
1m 2f (9f 213yds) 2m 3s
1m 6f 15yds 2m 57.9s
2m 9yds 3m 24.2s
2m 2f 18yds 3m 51.5s

PONTEFRACT

5f 1m 1.2s
6f 1m 14.7s
1m 4yds 1m 42.1s
1m 2f 6yds 2m 8.2s
1m 4f 8yds 2m 35s
2m 1f 22yds 3m 39.5s
2m 2f (17f 216yds) 3m 51.5s
2m 5f 122yds 4m 40s

REDCAR

5f 56.7s
6f 1m 9.7s
7f 1m 21.8s
1m 1m 34.9s
1m 1f 1m 48.5s
1m 2f 2m 1.2s
1m 3f 2m 15.4s
1m 4f 2m 29.5s
1m 5f 135yds 2m 49.9s
1m 6f 19yds 2m 56.5s
2m 4yds 3m 23s
2m 3f 4m 3s

RIPON

5f 58s
6f 1m 10.6s
1m 1m 38.3s
1m 1f 1m 51s
1m 2f 2m 4s
1m 4f 60yds 2m 35s
2m 3m 25s
2m 1f 203yds 3m 51s

SALISBURY

5f 59.8s
6f 1m 12.5s
7f (6f 212yds) 1m 25.6s
1m 1m 39.5s
1m 2f (9f 209yds) 2m 4s
1m 4f 2m 32s
1m 6f 2m 57.7s

SANDOWN

5f 6yds 59.5s
7f 16yds 1m 26.5s
1m 14yds 1m 39.1s
1m 1f 1m 51.2s
1m 2f 7yds 2m 3.9s
1m 3f 91yds 2m 20s
1m 6f 2m 54.3s
2m 78yds 3m 29s

SOUTHWELL (Turf)

6f 1m 14s
7f 1m 27s
1m 3f 2m 21.8s
1m 4f 2m 34s
2m 3m 26s

SOUTHWELL (All-Weather)

5f 57.9s
6f 1m 13.4s
7f 1m 26.1s
1m 1m 39s
1m 3f 2m 21.8s
1m 4f 2m 33.9s
1m 5f 2m 47.3s
1m 6f 3m
2m 3m 26.5s

THIRSK

5f 57.2s
6f 1m 10s
7f (6f 216yds) 1m 22.8s
1m 1m 35.9s
1m 4f 2m 30.2s
2m 3m 24s
2m 1f 3m 38s
2m 2f 3m 51s

WARWICK

5f 58.2s
6f 1m 11.7s
7f 1m 23.8s
1m 1m 36.8s
1m 2f 169yds 2m 12.8s
1m 4f 115yds 2m 37.9s
1m 6f 194yds 3m 8.3s
2m 20yds 3m 25.5s
2m 2f 180yds 4m 3.5s

WINDSOR

5f 10yds 59s
6f (5f 217yds) 1m 10.3s
1m 67yds 1m 41s
1m 2f 7yds 2m 2.5s
1m 3f 135yds 2m 23s

WOLVERHAMPTON

5f 57s
7f 1m 24s
1m 1m 37.8s
1m 200yds 1m 49.3s
1m 3f 2m 15.5s
1m 4f 70yds 2m 32.5s
1m 6f 134yds 3m 5s
2m 201yds 3m 35.5s

YARMOUTH

5f 43yds 1m 0.7s
6f 3yds 1m 11s
7f 2yds 1m 23.2s
1m 3yds 1m 35.8s
1m 2f 21yds 2m 4s
1m 3f 101yds 2m 23.5s
1m 6f 17yds 2m 57s
2m 1f 170yds 3m 56s
2m 2f 51yds 4m 1s

YORK

5f 57.3s
6f 1m 10s
7f (6f 214yds) 1m 21.7s
1m (7f 202yds) 1m 36.3s
1m 1f (1m 205yds) 1m 49.2s
1m 2f 85yds 2m 8s
1m 4f (11f 195yds) 2m 28s
1m 6f (13f 194yds) 2m 55s
2m (15f 195yds) 3m 21s

CHANTILLY

5f (Str) 57.5s
5f 110yds (Str) 1m 3.5s
6f (Str) 1m 9.7s
7f (Str) 1m 22.3s
1m (Rnd) 1m 34.7s
1m 1f 1m 47.5s
1m 2f 2m 0.9s
1m 2f 110yds 2m 6.6s
1m 3f 2m 14s
1m 4f 2m 27s
1m 7f 3m 8s
2m 2f 3m 50s
2m 4f 4m 16s

DEAUVILLE

5f 56s
6f 1m 8.4s
6f 110yds 1m 15s
7f 1m 22s
7f 110yds 1m 27s
1m (Str) 1m 35s
1m (Rnd) 1m 34.7s
1m 2f 2m 1.7s
1m 4f 110yds 2m 36.5s
1m 5f 110yds 2m 49s
1m 7f 3m 9.4s
2m 3m 23.5s
2m 2f 3m 51s

EVRY

5f 59s
5f 110yds 1m 5s
6f 1m 10.3s
6f 110yds 1m 16.4s
7f 1m 25s
7f 110yds (M) 1m 32s
1m (M) 1m 37.4s
1m (G) 1m 38.4s
1m 1f (G) 1m 51.3s
1m 1f (M) 1m 51s
1m 2f (M) 2m 4s
1m 2f (G) 2m 3.5s
1m 2f 110yds (M) 2m 11s
1m 4f (M) 2m 30.8s
1m 4f (G) 2m 30.8s
1m 6f (G) 2m 58s
1m 7f (G) 3m 11s
1m 7f 110yds (G) 3m 18s

LONGCHAMP

(G) Grande
(M) Moyenne
(P) Petite

5f 55.5s
7f 1m 19.5s
1m (M) 1m 36s
1m (G) 1m 37.5s
1m 110yds (P) 1m 44.2s
1m 110yds (M) 1m 42.8s
1m 1f (M) 1m 49s
1m 1f 55yds (G) 1m 52s
1m 1f 110yds (M) 1m 56s
1m 1f 165yds (G) 1m 59s
1m 2f (G) 2m 2.1s
1m 2f (M) 2m 2.3s
1m 2f 110yds (G) 2m 8.8s
1m 2f 110yds (M) 2m 9s
1m 3f (G) 2m 15.2s
1m 3f 110yds (G) 2m 22.3s
1m 4f (G) 2m 29.1s
1m 4f 110yds (G) 2m 35.3s
1m 5f 110yds (P) 2m 50s
1m 7f (G) 3m 10s
1m 7f (M) 3m 9.5s
1m 7f 110yds (G) 3m 16.5s
2m 110yds (G) 3m 31s
2m 4f 4m 14s

MAISONS-LAFFITTE

4f 45.5s
4f 110yds 51.6s
5f 57.5s
5f 110yds 1m 3.7s
6f 1m 9.5s
6f 110yds 1m 15.3s
7f (Str) 1m 22s
7f 1m 22.6s
1m (Str) 1m 34.7s
1m 1m 35.5s
1m (CD) 1m 36.3s
1m 110yds (CD) 1m 42.5s
1m 1f (Str) 1m 48s
1m 1f (CD) 1m 49.3s
1m 2f (Str) 2m 1.4s
1m 2f (CD) 2m 1.6s
1m 2f 110yds 2m 7.7s
1m 2f 110yds 2m 8.4s
1m 3f 2m 14.2s
1m 3f 110yds (CG) 2m 20.8s
1m 3f 110yds 2m 21.2s
1m 4f 2m 28s
1m 4f 110yds 2m 34.5s
1m 4f 110yds 2m 33.4s
1m 5f (CD) 2m 40.2s

1m 7f (CD) 3m 6s
1m 7f 110yds 3m 13s
2m (CD) 3m 20s

SAINT-CLOUD

4f 48.5s
4f 110yds 54.4s
6f 1m 12.5s
6f 110yds 1m 18.7s
7f 1m 25.4s
7f 110yds 1m 31.6s
1m 1m 38.5s
1m 2f 2m 4s
1m 2f 110yds 2m 10.5s
1m 3f 2m 17s
1m 4f 2m 30s
1m 4f 110yds 2m 37s
1m 6f 2m 56s
1m 6f 110yds 3m 1.5s

Draw Advantage

ASCOT	No advantage.
AYR	High numbers best except on soft going when low numbers are favoured, especially in big fields.
BATH	No advantage.
BEVERLEY	High numbers best.
BRIGHTON	Low numbers favoured in sprints except on heavy going.
CARLISLE	High numbers best except on soft going.
CATTERICK	No advantage.
CHEPSTOW	High numbers best except on soft going.
CHESTER	Low numbers best.
DONCASTER	High numbers best on straight course except on soft going. Low best on round course.
EDINBURGH	High best except on soft going when low numbers favoured.
EPSOM	High numbers have an advantage.
FOLKESTONE	Low best in sprints except on soft ground when high numbers have a marked advantage in large fields.
GOODWOOD	High numbers best in sprints except on soft ground.
HAMILTON	High numbers best on soft going.
HAYDOCK	High numbers best on soft going.
KEMPTON	Low best in sprints except on soft going when high numbers have the advantage. High numbers have a marked advantage when stalls on far rail.
LEICESTER	Middle to high numbers best on soft going.
LINGFIELD *(Turf)*	High numbers have a big advantage on straight course.
LINGFIELD *(AW)*	Low numbers best.
NEWBURY	High numbers best in sprints.
NEWCASTLE	Low numbers best on soft going.
NEWMARKET	Depends on prevailing going and where the stalls are placed.
NOTTINGHAM	Advantage with rail nearest stalls.
PONTEFRACT	Low best.
REDCAR	High numbers have a big advantage.
RIPON	Low numbers best in sprints.
SALISBURY	Low best on soft going.
SANDOWN	High numbers best on sprint course when stalls on the far rail.
SOUTHWELL *(AW)*	Low numbers best.
THIRSK	High best on straight course.
WARWICK	No advantage.
WINDSOR	High numbers slightly favoured in sprints.
WOLVERHAMPTON	High numbers slightly favoured.
YARMOUTH	High numbers slightly favoured.
YORK	Low numbers best on sprint course when ground is soft and have a big advantage over seven furlongs on any ground.

Index to Meetings

Abandoned Meetings

Sat	Apr	10	The Curragh	Waterlogged
Mon	Apr	12	Newcastle	Waterlogged
Thurs	June	10	Southwell (after 1st race)	Waterlogged
Sat	June	12	Naas	Waterlogged
Mon	June	14	Southwell	Waterlogged
			Roscommon	Waterlogged
Thurs	Sept	16	Beverley	Waterlogged
Fri	Oct	1	Goodwood	Waterlogged
Sat	Oct	2	Goodwood	Waterlogged
Wed	Oct	6	Haydock (after 2nd race)	Unsafe course
Thurs	Oct	7	Haydock	Unsafe course
Fri	Oct	8	Ascot	Waterlogged
Sat	Oct	9	Ascot	Waterlogged
Mon	Oct	11	Leicester	Waterlogged
Tues	Oct	12	Chepstow	Waterlogged
			Leicester	Waterlogged
Mon	Oct	25	Lingfield (7th race not run)	Security alert
Wed	Oct	27	Yarmouth (7th race not run)	Security alert

Licensed trainers 1993

The following received licences (valid until January 31, 1994) to train under Rule 50(i)

FLAT RACES AND FOR STEEPLE CHASES, HURDLE RACES AND NATIONAL HUNT FLAT RACES

Aconley, Mrs Vivien Ann
Akehurst, Jonathan
Akehurst, Reginald Peter John
Allan, Adam Richard
Allen, Conrad Norman
Alston, Eric James
Arbuthnot, David William Patrick
Armstrong, Robert Walter
Austin, Mrs Sheila Marion
Avison, Maurice

Bailey, Alan
Bailey, Kim Charles
Baker, Rodney John
Balding, Gerald Barnard
Balding, Ian Anthony
Balding, John
Banks, John Edward
Barker, Mrs Patricia Anne
Barker, William Lindsay
Barr, Ronald Edward,
Barraclough, Melvyn Frederick
Barratt, Lowther James
Barron, Thomas David
Barrow, Arthur Kendall
Barwell, Charles Robin
Bastiman, Robin
Beasley, Benjamin James
Beaumont, Peter
Beever, Charles Richard
Bell, Michael Leopold Wentworth
Bennett, James Anthony
*Bennett, Mrs Muriel Janet
=Bennett, Reginald Anthony
Benstead, Christopher John
Bentley, Walter
Berry, Jack
Bevan, Peter John
Bill, Tom Trivett
Bishop, Kevin Shaun
Blanshard, Michael Thomas William
Bolton, Michael John
Booth, Charles Benjamin Brodie
Bosley, John Read
Boss, Ronald
Bostock, John Raymond
Bottomley, John Frederick
Bower, Miss Lindsay Jane
Bowring, Sidney Roy
Bradburne, Mrs Susan
Bradley, John Milton
Bradstock, Mark Fitzherbert
Bramall, Mrs Susan Angela
Bravery, Giles Colin
Brazington, Robert George
Brennan, Owen
Bridger, John James
Bridgwater, Kenneth Stanley
Brisbourne, William Mark
Brittain, Clive Edward
Brittain, Melvyn Anthony
Broad, Christopher David
Brooks, Charles Patrick Evelyn
Brotherton, Roy
Buckley, Edward Thomas
Burchell, Walter David
Burgoyne, Paul Victor John
Burke, Karl Richard
Butler, Patrick
Bycroft, Neville

Caldwell, Terence Harvey
Callaghan, Neville Anthony
Calver, Peter
Camacho, Maurice James Christopher
Cambidge, Burnup Roy
Campbell, Ian
Campion, Andrew Mark
Candy, Henry Derrick Nicholas Bourne
Carr, John Michael
Casey, William Terence
Cecil, Mrs Julia
Chamberlain, Adrian John
Chamberlain, Norman
Champion, Robert
Channon, Michael Roger
Chapman, David William
Chapman, Michael Christopher
Chappell, Major David Nigel
Chapple-Hyam, Peter William
Charles, Martin John
Charles-Jones, Gareth Francis Hugh
Charlton, John Irving Alistair
*Cheesbrough, Peter Ralph
Christian, Simon Peter Livingstone
Clay, William
†Codd, Liam Joseph
Cole, Paul Frederick Irvine
Collingridge, Hugh John
Cosgrove, David Joseph Simon
Cottrell, Leslie Gerald
Craig, Thomas
Cundell, Peter David
Cunningham, William Scott
Cunningham-Brown Kenneth Owen
Curley, Barney Joseph
Curtis Roger
Cuthbert, Thomas Alexander Keir
Cyzer, Charles Alan

Dalton, Paul Thomas
†Dawe, Mrs Jacqueline Constance
†Denson, Andrew William
Dickin, Robin
Dixon, Mark
Dods, Michael Joseph Keil
Donnelly, Terence William
Dooler, James
Dow, Simon Langley
Doyle, Miss Jacqueline Sophie
Dyer, Thomas Hamilton

†Earnshaw, Robert
Easterby, Michael William
Easterby, Miles Henry
Eckley, Malcolm Willis
Eden, Grant Howard
Edwards, John Andrew Child
Egerton, Charles Ralph
Ellerby, Michael William
Ellison, Brian
Elsey, Charles Clare
Elsey, Charles William Carlton
Elsworth, David Raymond Cecil
Enright, Gerard Patrick
Etherington, James
Evans, Paul David
Eyre, John Leslie

Fahey, Richard Aiden
Fairhurst, Thomas
Fanshawe, James Robert
Feilden, Peter Jonathan
Felgate, Paul Stanley
Fetherston-Godley, Martin John
Ffitch-Heyes, John Ronald
Fisher, Roger Frederick
FitzGerald, James Gerard
†Fleming, Gordon
Flower, Richard Mark
Forbes, Anthony Leslie
Forsey, Brian
Forster, Captain Timothy Arthur
Forte, Andrew Michael
Foster, Alexander George
†Franks, David Russell
Frost, Richard George

†Gallie, Miss Sarah Louise
Gandolfo, David Rostron
Gaselee, Nicholas Auriol Digby Charles
George, Joshua Thomas
Gifford, Joshua Thomas
Glover, Jeremy Anton
Graham, Neil Anthony
Gubby, Brian

Haggas, William John
Haigh, William Wilson
Haine, Mrs Diana Elizabeth Solna
Haldane, John Swanson
Hall, Miss Sarah Elizabeth
Hallett, Trevor Bertram
Ham, Gerald Antony
Hambly, Albert Adrian
Hammond, Michael David
Hannon, Richard Michael
Hanson, John
Harris, James Lawrence
Harris, Peter Woodstock
Harris, Roger
Harrison, Robert Alan
Harwood, Guy
Haslam, Patrick Charles
Haynes, Michael John
Hayward, Peter Alfred
Heaton-Ellis, Michael James Brabazon
Hedger, Peter Ronald
Henderson, Nicholas John
Hern, Major William Richard
Herries, Lady Anne Elizabeth
Hetherton, James
Hide, Anthony Gatehouse
Hills, Barrington William
Hills, John William
Hoad, Roger Peter Charles
Hobbs, Philip John
Hodges, Ronald James
Hollinshead, Reginald
Holmes, Gordon
Horgan, Cornelius Augustus
Howe, Harry Stuart
Howling, Paul

Ingram, Roger
Ivory, Kenneth Thomas

Jackson, Colin Frederick Charles
James, Anthony Paul
James, Charles John
Jarvis, Alan Peter
Jarvis, Michael Andrew
Jarvis, William
Jefferson, Joseph Malcolm
Jenkins, John Renfield
Jermy, David Charles
Johnson, John Howard
Johnson Houghton, Richard Fulke
Johnston, Mark Steven
Jones, Anthony Paul

LICENSED TRAINERS 1993

Jones, Arthur Whitfield
†Jones, Christopher Harry
Jones, Derek Haydn
Jones, George Haimer
Jones, Harry Thomson
Jones, Peter John
Jones, Robert Walter
Jones, Thomas Michael
Jones, Timothy Thomson
Jordan, Frank Thomas James
Jordan, Mrs Joan
Juckes, Roderick Thomas

Kelleway, Miss Gay Marie
Kelleway, Paul Anthony
Kelly, Gerald Patrick
Kemp, William Thomas
Kersey, Trevor
Kettlewell, Steven Edward
King, Mrs Anabel Louise Moss
King, Jeffrey Steven
Knight, Mrs Angela Jane
Knight, Miss Henrietta Catherine

Laing, Douglas Raymond
Lamb, Reginald Ridley
Leach, Paul Stephen
Leadbetter, Stephen John
†Lee, Adrian Norris
Lee, Francis Henry
Lee, Richard Anthony
Leight, James Patrick
Lines, Clifford Victor
Long, John Edward
Lungo, Leonard

Macauley, Mrs Norma Jacqueline
Mackie, William John Wilkinson
Madgwick, Michael John
Makin, Peter James
Mann, Charles James
Manning, Robert James
Marks, Douglas
Marvin, Richard Frank
McCain, Donald
McConnochie, John Calvin
McCormack, Matthew
*McCourt, Mrs Mary Elizabeth
=McCourt, Matthew
McEntee, Philip Mathew
McGovern, Thomas Patrick
McKie, Mrs Victoria Jane
McMahon, Bryan Arthur
McMath, Brian James
Meade, Christopher Martyn
Meagher, Michael Gerard
Meehan, Brian John

Mellor, Stanley Thomas Edward
Millman, Brian Roderick
Mills, Terence George
Mitchell, Norman Richard
Mitchell, Patrick Kenneth
Mitchell, Philip
Moffatt, Dudley
Monteith, Peter
Mooney, James William
Moore, Arthur
Moore, Gary Lee
Moore, George Mervin
Moore, James Stanley
Morgan, Barry Clive
Morgan, Kevin Alan
Morley, Michael Frederick David
Morris, David
Muggeridge, Menin Patrick
Muir, William Robert
Murphy, Ferdinand
Murphy, Patrick Gerard
Murray, Brendan William
Murray-Smith, David John George
Musson, William James

Nash, Christopher Thomas
Naughton, Michael Paul
Naughton, Thomas Joseph
Nicholls, Paul Frank
Nicholson, David
Nolan, Dolan Alphonsos
Norton, John
Norton, Stephen Geoffrey

O'Donoghue, Jack
O'Leary, Ronald Martin
O'Mahony, Finbarr Jeremiagh
O'Neill, John Joseph
O'Neill, Owen
O'Shea, John Gerard Martin
O'Sullivan, Roland Jeffrey
Old, James Andrew Bertram
Oldroyd, Geoffrey Reginald
Owen, Jun, Edward Hollister

Palling, Brynley
Parker, Colin
Parkes, John Edwin
Parrott, Mrs Hilary Kay
Payne, John William
Payne, Stanley George
Peacock, John Harris
Peacock, Raymond Eric
Pearce, Jeffrey
Perratt, Miss Linda Agnes
Phillips, Richard Timothy
Pickering, John Alan
Piggott, Mrs Susan Elna

Pipe, Martin Charles
Pitman, Mrs Jennifer Susan
Popham, Christopher Leslie
Potts, Anthony William
Preece, William George
Prescott, Sir Mark
Price, Richard John
Pritchard, Peter Anthony
Pritchard-Gordon, Gavin Alexander

Ramsden, Mrs Lynda Elaine
Reid, Andrew Stephen
Retter, Mrs Jacqueline Gay
Reveley, Mrs Mary Christiana
Richards, Gordon Waugh
Richmond, Basil Armstrong
Roe, Colin Graeme Algernon Maitland
Rothwell, Brian Samuel
Rowe, Richard
Ryan, Michael John

Sanders, Miss Brooke Virginia Jane
Saunders, Malcolm Sydney
Scargill, Dr Jon David
Scott, Alexander Archibald
†Shaw, Derek
Sherwood, Oliver Martin Carwardine
Sherwood, Simon Edward Harlakenden
Siddall, Miss Lynn Christina
†Simpson, Rodney
Smart, Bryan
Smith, Alfred
Smith, Charles
Smith, Craig Anthony
Smith, Denys
Smith, John Peter
Smith, Nigel Alan
Smith, Mrs Susan Jane
Spearing, John Lionel
Spicer, Roger Charles
Stevens, Barry
Storey, Wilfred Luke
Stoute, Michael Ronald
Stringer, Andrew Paul
Sutcliffe, John Robert Earnshaw
Swinbank, Mrs Ann

Tate, Frederick Martin
Tate, Thomas Patrick
Thom, David Trenchard
Thompson, Ronald
Thompson, Ronald
Thompson, Victor
Thorner, Graham Edward
Thornton, Christopher William

Tinkler, Colin Harwin
Tinkler, Nigel Delfosse
Tompkins, Mark Harding
Trietline, Christopher Charles
Tucker, David Richard
Turnell, Andrew
Turner, William George
Turner, William George Michael
Twiston-Davies, Nigel Anthony

Upson, John Ralph
Usher, Mark Donald Ian

Voorspuy, Rufus

Wainwright, John Stanley
Wall, Christian Frederick
Walwyn, Peter Tyndall
Wane, Martyn
Waring, Mrs Barbara
Watson, Frederick
Weaver, Redvers John
Webber, John Huyshe
Weedon, Colin Victor
Weynes, Ernest
Wharton, John Raymond
†Wheeler, Eric Archibald
Whitaker, Richard Mawson
White, John Raymond
White, Kenneth Brian
Whitfield, Miss Avery Joan
†Wightman, William Gilbert Rowell
Wildman, Christopher Philip
Wilkinson, Benjamin Edwin
Wilkinson, Mark John
Williams, Colin Noel
Williams, David Lyndon
Williams, Michael
Williams, Robert James Royston
Wilson, Andrew James
Wilson, David Adam
Wilson, Captain James Hume
Wilton, Miss Susan Jayne
Wingrove, Kenneth George
Wintle, David John
Woodhouse, Robert Dickson Edgar
Woodman, Stephen
Woods, Sean Peter Charles

Yardley, Francis John
Yardley, George Henry

* Temporary
† Relinquished
= Deceased

RESTRICTED FOR FLAT RACES

Bethell, James David William

Cecil, Henry Richard Amherst
Charlton, Roger John
Cumani, Luca Matteo

†Douglass, George William
Dunlop, John Leeper

Eustace, James Maurice Percy

Gosden, John Harry Martin
Guest, Rae

Hanbury, Benjamin
Hill, Courtney John
Holt, Leonard John
Huntingdon, Lord William Edward Robin Hood

Incisa, Don Enrico

Leach, Melvyn Rawson
Lewis, Geoffrey
Loder, David Richard

McBride, Philip James

O'Gorman, William Andrew

Stewart, Alexander Christie

Toller, James Arthur Richard
Troy, John Martin

Watts, John William
Wigham, Percival
Wragg, Geoffrey
Wright, Nigel Camplyon

† Relinquished

RESTRICTED FOR STEEPLE CHASES, HURDLE RACES AND NATIONAL HUNT FLAT RACES

Alner, Robert Henry
Armytage, Roderick Charles
Ayliffe, Nicholas George

Babbage, Norman Mark
Barclay, James
Barnes, Maurice Allen
Barnett, George William
Barons, David Hawken
Baugh, Brian Philip John
Bell, David John
Birkett, John James
Buckler, Robert Hamilton
†Buckley, Edward Thomas

†Callow, Raymond
Campion, Stephen William
Caroe, Miss Clarissa Janet Elizabeth
Carr, Timothy Julian
Chugg, John
Clarke, Peter Cedric
Coathup, Steven
Coatsworth, Geoffrey Michael Redhead
Cole, Sydney Newman
Colston, Jim
Coogan, Alan Brian
†Cosgrave, James

Cowley, Colin

Davies, Gerald Walter James
De Haan, Benjamin
Drewe, Christopher James
Dunn, Allan John Keith

Eckley, Richard Jones
Eddy, Donald
Esden, Darren
Etherington, Timothy James

Fierro, Giuseppe
†Forte, Andrew Michael
Fowler, Anthony

Garraton, Derek Thomas
†Gillen, John Casey
Goldie, Robert Howie
Goulding, John Lennox
Green, Miss Zoe Ann
Grissell, Delagarde Michael

Hall, Miss Pauline Jane
Hellens, John Alan
Hewitt, Mrs Shirley Anne
Hickman, Mrs Virginia Seaburne
†Honeyball, John

Humphrey, Glen Lawrence

Jewell, Mrs Linda Christine
Jones, Christopher Harry
Jones, Mrs Merrita Anne
Joynes, Mrs Pamela May

Lee, Donald
Llewellyn, Bernard John
Long, Mrs Monica Elizabet

MacTaggart, Alexander Bruce
Mann, Wilmer George
McCune, David
McDonald, Robert
McNeill, Michael Patrick
Mullins, James William

†Nolan, Donal Alphonsus

Oliver, James Kenneth Murray

†Peacock, John Harris
Poulton, Julian Charles
Price, William James

Reed, William George

Renfree–Barons, Mrs Jenifer Rose
Richards, Mrs Lydia
Ritchens, Paul Cyril
Rodford, Patrick Reginald

Scudamore, Michael John
Sharpe, Mrs Nicola Susan Aileen
Sly, Mrs Pamela Marigold

Tate, Robin
Taylor, Mrs Susan
Thomson, Mrs Dorothy
Thomson, Neil Barrett

†Vernon, Miller, Charles John

†Walwyn, Mrs Catherine
Williams, Mrs Sarah Daphne
†Willis, Henry
Wonnacott, Mrs Joan

† Relinquished

Licensed Flat race jockeys and weights 1993

The following received licences (valid until March 17th, 1994) to ride in flat races under Rule 60(i)

Adams, Nicolas Mark 7 7
Avery, Christopher Manuel 7 8

Ballantine, Harry 7 7
Bardwell, Gary Stephen 7 7
Baxter, Geoffrey Edward 8 2
Berry, Raymond John 8 3
Biggs, Darren Derek 7 10
Birch, Mark 8 3
Bowker, Miss Julie 7 7

Carlisle, Nicholas Anthony 7 8
Carroll, John 8 2
Carson, William Fisher Hunter 7 10
†Carter, Gary Alan 7 13
Charnock, Lindsay 7 9
Clark, Anthony Stephen 8 2
Cochrane, Raymond 8 6
Comber, James 8 4
Connorton, Nicholas Brian 8 0
Crossley, Bryn 7 13
Culhane, Patrick Anthony 8 2
Curant, John Arthur 7 13

D'arcy, Paul William 8 2
Darley, Kevin Paul 8 0
Dawson, Steven 7 9
Day, Nigel Patrick 8 2
Dettori, Lanfranco 8 5
Dicks, Andrew Craig 8 4
Duffield, George Peter 8 0
Dwyer, Christopher Ambrose 8 7

Eddery, Patrick James John 8 4
Eddery, Paul Anthony 8 0
Elliott, Robert Peter 8 0

Fallon, Keiran Francis 8 2
Fanning, Joseph Kevin 7 8
Fortune, James Joseph 8 2

Geran, Anthony John 7 9
Gibson, Dale 7 9
Greaves, Miss Alex Ann 8 1

†Hillis, Ronald Patrick 8 3
Hills, Michael Patrick 8 0
Hills, Richard John 8 0
Hind, Gary Edward Patrick 8 0
Holland, Darryll Paul 8 0
Hood, Walter 8 4
Houston, Miss Jacqueline 7 7

Johnson, Ernest 7 7

†Kelleway, Miss Gay Marie 8 2
Kent, Terence John 10 0

Lang, Thomas Luke 8 2
Lappin, Rodney Thomas 8 0
Lowe, John Joseph 7 8
Lucas, Terry George 8 5

MacKay, Allan 7 9
McDonnell, Miss Kim Susan 7 7
McGlone, Anthony David 7 12
McKeown, Dean Russell 8 2
†McLaughlin, John Fletcher Stephen 8 7
Morris, Allan 8 0
Morris, Mrs Candida Louise 8 0
Morris, Stuart David 8 0
Munro, Alan Keith 7 12
Murray, John Gerard 8 3

Newnes, William Anthony Paul 8 3
Nicholls, David 8 7
Nutter, Colin 8 0

O'Gorman, Seamus Mark 7 10
O'Reilly, James Francis Patrick 6 13

Perham, Richard Andrew 8 2
Perks, Stephen James 8 6
Perrett, Mark Edward 9 0
Piggott, Lester Keith 8 6
Price, Russell Wayne 7 12
Procter, Brian Thomas 8 3
Proud, Alan 7 10

Quinn, James Anthony 7 7
Quinn, Thomas Richard 8 2

Raymond, Bruce Hunter 8 5
Raymont, Stephen John 7 13
Reid, John Andrew 8 6
Roberts, Michael Leonard 8 0
Robinson, Philip Peter 8 2
Rogers, Trevor 8 6
Rouse, Brian Albert 8 3
Rutter, Christopher Louis Peter 7 10
Ryan, William 8 2

Shoults, Adam Francis 8 0
Slattery, John Vincent 8 7
Smith, Vince 10 0
Sprake, Timothy Joseph 7 11
Stokell, Miss Ann 9 7
Street, Robert 7 7
Swinburn, Walter Robert John 8 6

Tebbutt, Michael John 8 5
Tinkler, Mrs Kim Ann 7 7
Tucker, Andrew Patrick 7 10

Vincent, Miss Lorna Jayne 9 0

Wall, Trevor Richard 9 0
Webster, Stuart Graham 8 3
Wernham, Roger Alan 8 5
Whitworth, Simon John 8 0
Wigham, Michael 8 4
Wilkinson, David 9 7
Williams, John Albert Norman 8 3
Williams, Stephen David 8 4
Williams, Tyrone Leonard 7 9
Williamson, Kevin 8 0
Wilson, Timothy George Albert 7 7
Wood, Michael 8 0
Wood, Stephen 7 7
Woods, Eric Wendyll Joseph 8 2

† Relinquished

Flat race apprentices with masters 1993

The following received licences (valid until March 17th, 1994) to ride for flat races under Rule 60(iii)

†Adams, Robert Nicholas (Mr Michael Bell) 7 12
Adamson, Corey Neil (Mr P C Haslam) 7 0
Ahern, Miss Kate Emma (Mr J L Dunlop) 7 7
Allen, Stuart James (Mr M H Tompkins) 7 10
Armes, Miss Antoinette Carol (Mr Henry Candy) 7 0
Ashley, Thomas Lawton (Mr R Akehurst) 7 10
Aspell, Leighton (Mr R Hollinshead) 7 4

Baird, Mark James (Mr M J Ryan) 7 0
Balding, Miss Claire (Mr John Balding) 7 2
Bastiman, Harvey James (Mr Robin Bastiman) 8 5
Beaver, Thomas Harry (Mr M J Ryan) 8 0
†Berry, Ross Keith (Mr D R C Elsworth) 8 0
Biggs, Miss Debra Delores Marie (Mr Paul Howling) 8 0
Bowe, Paul David Patrick (Mr D J S Cosgrove) 7 12
Bradley, Michael (Mr J M Bradley) 7 8
Bramhill, John Alexander (Mr B A McMahon) 7 3
Branton, Grant John (Mr G Harwood) 8 4
Bream, Miss Rebecca (Mr R J Weaver) 7 6
Bridger, Miss Rachel Jane (Mr J J Bridger) 8 7
†Brookwood, Paul John (Mr R J Manning) 7 9
Byrnes, Miss Clare Samantha (Mr J D Bethell) 9 0

Cairns, Alexander (Mr James Fanshawe) 8 0
†Carson, Derek Alexander (Mr R Hollinshead) 8 3
Carter, Lee Anthony (Mr R Akehurst) 7 10
Cook, Miss Aimee Virginia (Mr P F I Cole) 7 10
Copp, Shane Lee (Mrs M Reveley) 8 0
Coulter, Miss Ruth Elizabeth (Mr J Berry) 7 2
Curran, Sean (Miss Jacqueline S Doyle) 9 7

Daly, Alan Thomas (Mr P F I Cole) 7 0
Davies, Stephen Glyn (Mr P W Chapple-Hyam) 7 12
Davison, Miss Carol Ann (Mrs A Swinbank) 7 7
Denaro, Mark (Mr R Hannon) 7 13
Denaro, Michael Joseph (Mr L M Cumani) 8 2
Denby, Derek James (Mr R Hollinshead) 7 2
Dennis, Jonathan Paul (Mr R Hollinshead) 7 7
Devlin, Paul (Mr J A R Toller) 7 10
Dovey, Miss Kate (Mr P W Chapple-Hyam) 7 8
Doyle, Brett (Mr C E Brittain) 7 9
Drake, Stephen Tony (Mr Henry Candy) 7 10
Drowne, Steven John (Mr R J Hodges) 7 11
Dwyer, Martin Joseph (Mr I A Balding) 7 0
Dykes, Craig (Mr A C Stewart) 7 7

East, Brett Garry (Mr L J Holt) 7 10
Eblet, Glyn Gary (Mr Jeff Pearce) 7 7
Eddery, Allan Mark (Mr R Hollinshead) 7 4
Edmunds, Jason Paul (Mr John Balding) 7 12
Eiffert, Scott (Mr Rae Guest) 8 0

Faulkner, Gavin (Mr W J Musson) 8 4
†Faulkner, Miss Gina (Mr M McCormack) 7 7
Fenton, Michael (Mr Michael Bell) 7 12
Fessey, Paul John (Mr J Berry) 6 8
Fitchett, Miss Karron Louise (Mr Henry Candy) 8 0
Forster, Gary (Mr C N Allen) 7 12
Fuggle, Timothy James (Mr John R White) 7 12

Gallimore, Miss Angela (Mr A Bailey) 7 0
Garth, Anthony Raymond (Mr R Hollinshead) 7 7
Gent, Miss Rhona Jane (Mr R J Charlton) 7 0
†Gibbons, Miss Adelle Louise (Capt James Wilson) 7 2
Gibbs, Daniel (Mr R Hannon) 7 12
Giles, Simon Mark (Mr William Haggas) 8 8
†Goggin, Declan (Mr P F I Cole) 7 6
Gotobed, Jamie Lee (Mr M H Tompkins) 7 11
Gracey, Jason Gerard (Mr P C Haslam) 8 0
Grantham, Ian (Mr A Harrison) 7 4
Greehy, Enda Patrick (Mr R Hannon) 7 0
Griffiths, David Charles (Mr I A Balding) 7 9
Gwilliams, Neil Lee (Mr T G Mills) 7 7

Halliday, Vincent (Mr T D Barron) 7 9
Handley, Mark John (Mr Henry Candy) 8 0
Harris, Michael Patrick (Mr A A Hambly) 8 3
Harrison, David Paul (Lord Huntingdon) 7 10
Hart, Miss Kimberley (Mr T D Barron) 7 5
Harwood, Miss Gaye Michelle (Mr G Harwood) 8 0
Havlin, Robert (Miss L A Perratt) 7 7
Hawksley, Carl Leonard (Mr H J Collingridge) 7 3
Hawksley, Wayne Andrew (Mr A Bailey) 7 6
Henry, Matthew Philip (Mr J W Hills) 7 2
Hodgson, Carl Andrew (Mr L M Cumani) 8 2
Holland, Miss Sarah (Mr Henry Candy) 7 13
Hollick, William John (Mr A Bailey) 7 13
Houghton, Philip (Mr G Harwood) 8 7
Howarth, Miss Nicola (Mr P C Haslam) 7 7
Hughes, Ian Michael (Mr D R Loder) 8 0
Humphries, Mark Brian (Mr R Hollinshead) 7 7
Hunnam, Miss Jo (Mr L M Cumani) 7 6
Hunt, Michael (Mr C A Cyzer) 7 12
†Hunter, Jason John (Mr D R C Elsworth) 9 0
Husband, Eugene Llewellyn (Mr N Tinkler) 9 7

Jacobs, Miss Lisa Ann (Mr H T Jones) 7 10
James, Shaun Patrick (Mr C A Cyzer) 7 10
†Jardine, Iain James (Mr M P Naughton) 8 0
Jermy, Matthew (Mr T J Naughton) 7 12
Johnson, Paul Andrew (Mr M W Easterby) 9 7
Jones, Shane Anthony (Mr William Jarvis) 7 7
Jones, Miss Wendy Jayne (Mr R Hannon) 7 0

Kennedy, Neil Armstrong (Mr F H Lee) 7 7
Kinnon, Neil (Mrs S C Bradburne) 7 4
Knott, Stephen Thomas (Mr E J Alston) 8 2

Lakeman, Andrew (Mr B J Meehan) 7 10
†Lanigan, Stuart (Mr Bill Turner) 7 4
Liggins, Andrew (Mr S P C Woods) 7 5
†Llewellyn, Carl (Mr David W Chapman) 7 10

Maloney, Stephen James (Mr M H Easterby) 7 10
Marsden, Tony (Mr S G Norton) 8 1
Marshall, Jeffrey (Mr M D Hammond) 7 10
Martinez, Antonio Luis (Mr S Dow) 7 10
McCabe David Robert (Mr W J Musson) 7 8
McCabe, Patrick Antony (Mr M J Ryan) 7 7
McCarthy, Sean Bernard (Mr B W Hills) 7 3
McCord, Tony (Mr R J Charlton) 7 12
McGann, Barry Thomas (Mr J J O'Neill) 7 12
McGrath, George Joseph (Mr A P Jarvis) 9 7
McLaughlin, Thomas Gary (Mr P F I Cole) 7 12

Meredith, Dylan (Mr Robin Dickin) 9 5
Millard, Miss Sharon Camilla (Mr D A Wilson) 7 0
Milligan, Gary Edward Hunter (Mrs Lester Piggott) 7 6
Milligan, Miss Hazel (Mr A A Scott) 7 4
Mills, Garry (Mr C W Thornton) 7 0
†Mitchell, Gary Carlton (Mr Ian Campbell) 7 9
Moffatt, Darren (Mrs M Reveley) 7 0
Mulvey, Sean (Mr M H Tompkins) 7 11
Munday, Colin Joseph Arthur (Mr M W Easterby) 7 11

Newton, Lee (Mr D J S Cosgrove) 7 7
Norton, Francis (Mr G Wragg) 7 7

O'Dwyer, John Joseph (Mr Michael Bell) 7 10
O'Gorman, Miss Emma Samantha (Mr W A O'Gorman) 8 4
O'Neill, Dane William (Mr R Hannon) 7 7

Painter, Richard Bentley (Mr M Channon) 8 2
Parkin, Gyles (Mr R M Whitaker) 7 13
†Pattinson, Kenneth (Mr M R Stoute) 8 1
†Payne, Matthew (Mr G Lewis) 8 7
Pears, Oliver John (Mr S G Norton) 8 0
Plowright, Miss Marie (Mrs Angela Knight) 7 9
Procter, Anthony Richard (Mr Charles Egerton) 8 9
Proctor, Michael Paul (Mr S E Kettlewell) 7 7
Purseglove, Miss Tracey Nicolle (Mr D R C Elsworth) 8 7

Radford-Howes, Miss Sally (Mr W Haggas) 7 0
Roberts, Paul Brian (Mr J Berry) 7 9
Rose, Patrick Desmond (Mr K O Cunningham-Brown) 8 0
Rothwell, Garry (Mr Rod Simpson) 7 4
Russell, Brian James (Mr R Akehurst) 7 9
Rutter, Keith (Mr M A Jarvis) 8 0

Salt, Danny (Lord Huntingdon) 7 10
Sanders, Sebastian (Mr B A McMahon) 7 9
Savage, Finnbarr Michael (Mr R Hollinshead) 7 0
Scally, Christopher (Mr K T Ivory) 8 5
Scudder, Christopher (Mr I A Balding) 8 0
Senior, Miss Sarah Louise (Mr J A Glover) 8 3
Sked, Keith Philip (Mr J D Bethell) 7 2
Smith, Joesph Damian (Mr C A Cyzer) 7 10
Smith, Miss Madeleine Joy (Mrs N Macauley) 7 7
Strange, Graham (Mr S R Bowring) 7 13
Suthern, Lee (Mr J Spearing) 7 7

Tate, Jason Darran (Mr A A Scott) 7 9
Teague, Colin (Mr Denys Smith) 7 0
Thomas, Byron (Mr B Palling) 8 0
Thomas, Darren (Mrs J R Ramsden) 8 2
Thomas, Miss Michelle (Mr Robin Dickin) 7 7
†Thomas, Troy Nathan (Mr C A Cyzer) 7 0
Thompson, Miss Sarah Elizabeth (Mr R J R Williams) 8 0
Toole, Dominic John (Mr M J Haynes) 7 2
Turner, Miss Elizabeth Marie (Mr Jeff Pearce) 7 7

Varley, Neil Gareth (Mr J Fanshawe) 7 5

Wall, Miss Sally Elizabeth (Mr J R Jenkins) 7 7
Wands, Miss Iona Jane Claire (Mr L J Holt) 7 7
†Waterfield, Robert John (Mr P G Murphy) 7 7
Weaver, Jason Charles (Mr L M Cumani) 7 13
†Webb, Charles (Mr P J Makin) 7 12
West, Miss Claire Christine (Mr R R Lamb) 7 7
Whelan, Anthony William Emanuel (Mr R Hannon) 7 5
Wilkinson, Jason (Lord Huntingdon) 7 0
Williams, John Alan (Mr R Bastiman) 7 10
Wright, Daniel Thomas (Mr A Bailey) 7 0
Wynne, Stephen (Mr R Hollinshead) 9 0

† Relinquished

Riding records in the Classics

Jockey	Year of First Classic Winner	2000Gs	1000Gs	Derby	Oaks	St Leger	Total No. of Winners
L Piggott	1954	5	2	9†	6	8	30
F Buckle	1792	5	6	5	9†	2	27
J Robinson	1817	9†	5	6	2	2	24
F Archer	1874	4	2	5	4	6	21
J Watts	1883	2	4	4	4	5	19
W Scott	1821	3	Nil	4	3	9†	19
J B Day	1826	4	5	Nil	5	2	16
G Fordham	1859	3	7†	1	5	Nil	16
W Carson	1972	4	2	3	4	3	16
J Childs	1912	2	2	3*	4*	4*	15
F Butler	1843	2	2	2	6	2	14
S Donoghue	1915	3	1	6*	2*	2*	14
E C Elliott	1923	5	4‡	3	2‡	Nil	14
G Richards	1930	3‡	3‡	1	2‡	5‡	14
W Clift	1793	2	2	5	2	2	13
T Cannon	1866	4	3	1	4	1	13
H Wragg	1928	1‡	3‡	3‡	4‡	2‡	13
J Osborne	1856	6	2	1	1	2	12
W Johnstone	1934	1	3	3	3	2	12
T Weston	1923	2	1	2	3	3	11
C Smirke	1934	2	1	4	Nil	4	11
E (Nat) Flatman	1835	3	3	1	Nil	3	10
T Challoner	1861	3	Nil	1	1	5	10
C Wood	1880	1	3	3	1	2	10
Pat Eddery	1974	3	Nil	3	2	2	10
S Cauthen	1979	1	1	2	3	3	10
D Maher	1901	2	1	3	1	2	9
S Chifney jun	1807	1	1	2	5	Nil	9
J Wells	1854	1	2	3	Nil	2	8
J Jackson	1791	Nil	Nil	Nil	Nil	8	8
H Jones	1900	4	Nil	2	1	1	8
J Arnull	1784	Nil	2	5	1	Nil	8
J Mercer	1953	1	2	Nil	1	4	8
S Loates	1884	1	2	2	1	1	7
W Arnull	1804	3	1	3	Nil	Nil	7
T Goodison	1809	Nil	Nil	4	2	1	7
E Britt	1947	1	2	Nil	2	2	7
S Templeman	1839	Nil	Nil	3	3	1	7
B Carslake	1919	1	2	Nil	1	3	7
A Day	1849	3	2	1	1	Nil	7
Y Saint-Martin	1962	1	2	1	2	1	7
W R Swinburn	1981	1	3	2	1	Nil	7
B Smith	1803	Nil	Nil	Nil	Nil	6	6
M Cannon	1894	1	Nil	1	2	2	6
C Maidment	1871	Nil	1	2	1	2	6
T Loates	1889	2	1	2	Nil	1	6
J Marson	1843	Nil	1	2	Nil	3	6
P Connolly	1830	1	1	2	1	1	6
T Aldcroft	1855	2	1	1	1	1	6
J Singleton jun	1776	Nil	Nil	1	2	3	6
F Fox	1911	2	1	2	Nil	1	6
E Hide	1959	Nil	2	1	1	2	6
W H Carr	1955	Nil	1	1	1	3	6
O Madden	1898	1	Nil	1	2	1	5
J Mangles	1780	Nil	Nil	Nil	Nil	5	5
D Fitzpatrick	1787	Nil	Nil	1	4	Nil	5
C Hindley	1781	Nil	Nil	3	2	Nil	5
H Custance	1860	Nil	1	3	Nil	1	5
S Chifney senr	1782	Nil	Nil	1	4	Nil	5
T Ashmall	1858	2	2	Nil	1	Nil	5
S Day	1821	Nil	1	3	1	Nil	5
S Arnull	1780	Nil	Nil	4	1	Nil	5
R A Jones	1922	1	1	Nil	2	1	5
R Poincelet	1952	1	2	1	1	Nil	5
W Wheatley	1816	3	Nil	2	Nil	Nil	5
F Rickaby jun	1913	Nil	4	Nil	1	Nil	5
G Lewis	1969	1	1	1	2	Nil	5
G Starkey	1964	2	Nil	1	2	Nil	5

*Includes substitute races run at Newmarket between 1915–1918. †Record for the race.
‡Includes substitute races run at Newmarket 1939–1945.

Double, treble and quadruple winners of Classic races

2000 GUINEAS, 1000 GUINEAS, OAKS and ST LEGER—Formosa* (1868), Sceptre (1902).

2000 GUINEAS, DERBY and ST LEGER—West Australian (1853), Gladiateur (1865), Lord Lyon (1866), Ormonde (1886), Common (1891), Isinglass (1893), Galtee More (1897), Flying Fox (1899), Diamond Jubilee (1900), Rock Sand (1903), Pommern (1915), Gay Crusader (1917), Gainsborough (1918), Bahram (1935), Nijinsky (Can) (1970).

2000 GUINEAS, 1000 GUINEAS and OAKS—Crucifix (1840), Formosa* (1868), Sceptre (1902).

2000 GUINEAS and DERBY—Smolensko (1813), Cadland (1828), Bay Middleton (1836), Cotherstone (1843), West Australian (1853), Macaroni (1863), Gladiateur (1865), Lord Lyon (1866), Pretender (1869), Shotover (1882), Ormonde (1886), Ayrshre (1888), Common (1891), Isinglass (1893), Ladas (1894), Galtee More (1897), Flying Fox (1899), Diamond Jubilee (1900), Rock Sand (1903), St Amant (1904), Minoru (1909), Sunstar (1911), Pommern (1915), Gay Crusader (1917), Gainsborough (1918), Manna (1925), Cameronian (1931), Bahram (1935), Blue Peter (1939), Nimbus (1949), Crepello (1957), Royal Palace (1967), Sir Ivor (1968), Nijinsky (Can) (1970), Nashwan (USA) (1989).

2000 GUINEAS and ST LEGER—Sir Tatton Sykes (1846), Stockwell (1852), West Australian (1853), The Marquis (1862), Gladiateur (1865), Lord Lyon (1866), Formosa* (1868), Petrarch (1876), Ormonde (1886), Common (1891), Isinglass (1893), Galtee More (1897), Flying Fox (1899), Diamond Jubilee (1900), Sceptre (1902), Rock Sand (1903), Pommern (1915), Gay Crusader (1917), Gainsborough (1918), Bahram (1935), Nijinsky (Can) (1970).

2000 GUINEAS, 1000 GUINEAS and ST LEGER—Formosa* (1868), Sceptre (1902).

2000 GUINEAS, OAKS and ST LEGER—Formosa* (1868), Sceptre (1902).

2000 GUINEAS and OAKS—Pastille (1822), Crucifix (1840), Formosa* (1868), Sceptre (1902).

2000 GUINEAS and 1000 GUINEAS—Crucifix (1840), Formosa* (1868), Pilgrimage (1878), Sceptre (1902).

1000 GUINEAS and DERBY—Tagalie (1912).

1000 GUINEAS, OAKS and ST LEGER—Formosa (1868), Hannah (1871), Apology (1874), La Fleche (1892), Sceptre (1902), Pretty Polly (1904), Sun Chariot (1942), Meld (1955), Oh So Sharp (1985).

1000 GUINEAS and OAKS—Neva (1817), Corinne (1818), Zinc (1823), Cobweb (1824), Galata (1832), Crucifix (1840), Mendicant (1846), Governess (1858), Formosa (1868), Hannah (1871), Reine (1872), Apology (1874), Spinaway (1875), Camelia* (1876), Wheel of Fortune (1879), Thebais (1881), Busbybody (1884), Miss Jummy (1886), Reve d'Or (1887), Mimi (1891), La Fleche (1892), Amiable (1894), Sceptre (1902), Pretty Polly (1904), Cherry Lass (1905), Jest (1913), Princess Dorrie (1914), Saucy Sue (1925), Exhibitionist (1937), Rockfel (1938),Galatea II (1939), Godiva (1940), Sun Chariot (1942), Sun Stream (1945), Imprudence (1947), Musidor (1949), Meld (1955), Bella Paola (1958), Petite Etoile (1959), Never Too Late II (1960), Sweet Solera (1961), Altesse Royale (1971), Mysterious (1973), Oh So Sharp (1985), Midway Lady (1986) Salsabil (1990).

1000 GUINEAS and ST LEGER—Imperieuse (1857), Achievement (1867), Formosa (1868), Hannah (1871), Apology (1874), La Fleche (1892), Sceptre (1902), Pretty Polly (1904), Tranquil (1923), Sun Chariot (1924), Herringbone (1943), Meld (1955), Oh So Sharp (1985).

OAKS and ST LEGER—Queen of Trumps (1835), Formosa (1868), Hannah (1871), Marie Stuart (1873), Apology (1874), Jannette (1878), Seabreeze (1888), La Fleche (1892), Sceptre (1902), Pretty Polly (1904), Sun Chariot (1942), Meld (1955), Dunfermline (1977), Sun Princess (1983), Oh So Sharp (1985), User Friendly (1992).

DERBY and OAKS—Eleanor (1801), Blink Bonny (1875), Signorinetta (1908), Fifinella (1916).

DERBY and ST LEGER—Champion (1800), Surplice (1848), The Flying Dutchman (1849), Voltigeur (1850), West Australian (1853), Blair Athol (1864), Gladiateur (1865), Lord Lyon (1866), Silvio (1877), Iroquois (1881), Melton (1885), Ormonde (1886), Donovan (1889), Common (1891), Isinglass (1893), Sir Visto (1895), Persimmon (1896), Galtee More (1897), Flying Fox (1899), Diamond Jubilee (1900), Rock Sand (1903), Pommern (1915), Gay Crusader (1917), Gainsborough (1918), Coronach (1926), Trigo (1929), Hyperion (1933), Windsor Lad (1934), Bahram (1935), Airborne (1946), Tulyar (1952), Never Say Die (1954), St Paddy (1960), Nijinsky (Can) (1970), Reference Point (1987).

*Formosa dead-heated with Moslem for the 2000 Guineas. Camelia dead-heated with Enguerrande for the Oaks.

Results from 1992 not published in that Annual. 1993 Results start page 28

Flat Race Results 1992

SOUTHWELL (A.W) (std)
Tuesday November 10th

Going Correction: MINUS 0.10 sec. per fur. (races 1,2,3,4,5,6), MINUS 0.20 (7)

4660a Alex Lawrie Claiming Stakes (Div I) CLASS F (3-y-o and up) £2,364 6f ....(12:50)

PRETONIC 4-8-0 T Williams (2) *chsd ldrs, sn rdn alng, hdwy on inner 2 fs out, styd on to ld appr fnl furlong, jst hld on*.......................... (10 to 1 op 7 to 1) 1

AFRICAN CHIMES 5-9-4 (3*) Emma O'Gorman (4) *in tch, gd hdwy 2 fs out, effrt and rdn ins fnl furlong, jst fld*. ....(6 to 4 fav op 2 to 1 tchd 9 to 4) 2

DEBSY DO (USA) 3-8-0 (5*) O Pears (5) *in tch, hdwy 2 fs out, rdn and styd on fnl furlong*. ....(6 to 1 op 5 to 1 tchd 13 to 2 and 7 to 1) 3

PESIDANAMICH (Ire) (bl) 4-8-6 (5*) Stephen Davies (7) *cl up, rdn and ev ch appr fnl furlong, no extr nr finish*. ....(14 to 1 op 10 to 1) 4

SWINGING LADY 4-8-0 J Quinn (6) *led, rdn 2 fs out, hdd and wknd appr fnl furlong*. ....(11 to 1 op 14 to 1 tchd 16 to 1) 5

SWINGING TICH 3-8-3 A Munro (1) *slwly into strd and beh till styd on und pres fnl 2 fs*....... (25 to 1 op 20 to 1) 6

SOBA GUEST (Ire) 3-8-10 J Carroll (9) *chsd ldrs, rdn and ev ch o'r 2 fs out, sn wknd*. (6 to 1 op 9 to 2 tchd 7 to 1) 7

SUPER BENZ 6-8-13 J Fanning (8) *cl up, rdn alng hfwy, sn wknd*..........................(7 to 2 tchd 4 to 1) 8

BETTER STILL (Ire) 3-9-1 Dale Gibson (3) *slwly away, al beh*.........................(50 to 1 op 25 to 1) 9

Dist: Sht-hd, 1½l, nk, 5l, hd, ½l, 2l, 8l. 1m 17.20s. a 3.80s (9 Ran).

SR: -/18/-/1/-/-/ (Brian Yeardley Continental Ltd), M Johnston

4661a Bach Nursery CLASS F (0-75 2-y-o) £2,616 7f.................. (1:20)

MASTER SINCLAIR (Ire) [60] 8-9 (7*) A Garth (9) *hld up and beh, gd hdwy o'r 2 fs out, effrt to ld wl ins fnl furlong cmftbly*..(10 to 1) 1

COMTEC'S LEGEND [51] 8-7 J Quinn (4) *hdwy 2 fs out, led one furlong out, sn rdn, hdd and no extr ins last*. ....(9 to 1 op 7 to 1) 2

SPLASH OF SALT (Ire) [65] 9-7 W Ryan (1) *led, rdn 2 fs out, hdd and one pace one furlong out*. ....(9 to 4 fav op 2 to 1 tchd 5 to 2) 3

ANOTHER KINGDOM [59] 9-1 J Williams (12) *hld up and beh, hdwy on outer 2 fs out, styd on*. (9 to 1 op 8 to 1) 4

JORDYWRATH [58] 8-7 (7*) G Mitchell (8) *in tch, hdwy to chal one and a half fs out, sn rdn and wknd*. ....(3 to 1 op 7 to 2 tchd 4 to 1) 5

GOODBYE MILLIE [62] 8-13 (5*) O Pears (10) *mid-div, effrt 3 fs out, sn rdn and kpt on one pace*. ....(12 to 1 tchd 14 to 1) 6

MAKE IT HAPPEN (Ire) [54] 8-10 J Carroll (7) *cl up till rdn and wknd o'r 2 fs out*................(7 to 1 op 6 to 1) 7

SCOFFERA [58] 9-0 Kim Tinkler (2) *chsd ldr, rdn 3 fs out, sn wknd*...(25 to 1) 8

COLFAX STARLIGHT [61] 9-0 (3*) D Harrison (3) *chsd ldrs, rdn o'r 3 fs out, wknd over 2 furlongs out*.... (20 to 1) 9

BOLD FLASH [62] 9-4 Dale Gibson (5) *sn rdn alng and beh*. ....(14 to 1 op 10 to 1) 10

SOUNDS RISKY [47] (bl) 7-10 (7*) Darren Moffatt (11) *al beh*. .... (33 to 1 op 50 to 1) 11

Dist: ¾l, 5l, 5l, nk, 1½l, 6l, 1½l, 1½l, nk, 10l. 1m 32.10s. a 5.80s (11 Ran).

SR: 5/-/-/-/-/-/ (Sinclair Developments Limited), R Hollinshead

4662a Handel Claiming Stakes CLASS F (3-y-o and up) £2,532 1½m....(1:50)

NOTED STRAIN (Ire) 4-8-5 D Holland (15) *hld up and beh, gd hdwy o'r 4 fs out, effrt 2 furlongs out, styd on und pres fnl furlong to ld nr finish*. .... (9 to 1 op 8 to 1 tchd 10 to 1) 1

MR WISHING WELL (e/s) 6-8-7 J Quinn (6) *mid-div, gd hdwy 5 fs out, led 2 furlongs out, rdn fnl furlong, hdd and no extr nr finish*........... (10 to 1 tchd 14 to 1) 2

BALZINO (USA) 3-8-2 G Baxter (3) *hld up, hdwy 4 fs out, rdn and kpt on fnl 2 furlongs*. .... (11 to 1 op 7 to 1 tchd 12 to 1) 3

BIGHAYIR (bl) 5-9-7 J Reid (4) *hld up, hdwy 4 fs out, rdn and kpt on fnl 2 furlongs*......................(7 to 2 jt-fav op 2 to 1 tchd 4 to 1) 4

CLIFTON CHASE (bl) 3-8-0 A Munro (13) *prmnt, effrt to chal 2 fs out, sn rdn and wknd appr fnl furlong*. ....(14 to 1 tchd 16 to 1) 5

TEMPERING 6-8-11 S Wood (2) *led, rdn o'r 3 fs out, hdd 2 furlongs out, grad wknd*. ....(7 to 2 jt-fav op 3 to 1 tchd 4 to 1) 6

PREMIER DANCE 5-8-4 (5*) N Gwilliams (5) *in tch, hdwy 6 fs out, rdn o'r 3 furlongs out, sn btn*.......... (20 to 1) 7

FREE TRANSFER (Ire) 3-8-8 N Day (12) *hld up and beh, some hdwy fnl 3 fs, nvr dngrs*..... (14 to 1 op 12 to 1) 8

PETITE BELLE 3-7-9[2] N Carlisle (9) *chsd ldr till rdn and wknd 4 fs out*..(25 to 1) 9

FIREFIGHTER 3-8-12 W Ryan (8) *mid-div, hdwy 6 fs out, rdn o'r 3 furlongs out, sn btn*........ (7 to 1 op 6 to 1) 10

LORD ADVOCATE (v) 4-8-2 (3*) D Harrison (10) *chsd ldrs 7 fs, sn wknd*..(14 to 1) 11

PONDERED BID (bl) 8-8-6[4] (3*) S Webster (1) *al rear*. ....(33 to 1) 12

STRATFORD LADY (bl) 3-7-1[1] (7*) D Wright (7) *al rear*. .... (8 to 1 op 10 to 1) 13

LODGING (v) 5-8-6 (5*) S D Williams (14) *nvr a factor*. ....(33 to 1) 14

TEN HIGH (Ire) 3-7-9 J Fanning (11) *chsd ldrs till rdn and wknd 5 fs out*...............................(50 to 1) 15

Dist: ½l, 3l, ½l, 1l, 5l, 5l, ¾l, 5l, 6l, ½l. 2m 42.40s. a 8.50s (15 Ran).

(D M Ahier), P J Makin

4663a Henry Boot Northern Limited Handicap CLASS F (0-70 3-y-o and up) £2,553 1m.................. (2:20)

CRESELLY [49] 5-8-11 M Birch (1) *made all, rdn 2 fs out, ran on strly*.........................(7 to 1 op 12 to 1) 1

ABBEY STRAND (USA) [69] 3-10-0 A Munro (14) *mid-div, gd hdwy o'r 3 fs out, rdn to chal 2 furlongs out, kpt on one pace*...(10 to 1 op 8 to 1) 2

MILITARY EXPERT [50] (bl) 3-8-2 (7*) J Marshall (13) *al prmnt, ev ch o'r 2 fs out, sn rdn and one pace*. ....(7 to 1 op 5 to 1) 3

GOOD FOR THE ROSES [48] 6-8-10 J Reid (2) *mid-div, hdwy 3 fs out, styd on one pace fnl 2 furlongs*. ....(3 to 1 fav tchd 4 to 1) 4

TARA'S DELIGHT [53] 5-8-12 (3*) Emma O'Gorman (7) *slwly into strd, sn chasing ldrs, rdn o'r 3 fs out, one pace*. ....(16 to 1 op 12 to 1) 5

ABELONI [58] (bl) 3-9-3 J Williams (4) *beh, hdwy 3 fs out, styd on fnl 2 furlongs*............. (16 to 1 op 12 to 1) 6

CEE-JAY-AY [63] 5-9-4 (7*) P Roberts (15) *dwlt and beh, hdwy 3 fs out, sn rdn and one pace*. .... (9 to 1 op 8 to 1 tchd 10 to 1) 7

BLACK BOY (Ire) [53] 3-8-7 (5*) S D Williams (16) *beh, hdwy on outer hfwy, sn rdn and wknd 2 fs out*...... (16 to 1) 8

KUMMEL KING [62] 4-9-10 J Quinn (9) *chsd ldrs to hfwy, sn wknd*...(14 to 1) 9

MEDIA MESSENGER [60] 3-9-5 W Ryan (11) *in tch, hdwy o'r 3 fs out, rdn and wknd 2 furlongs out*..... (33 to 1) 10

CANDESCO [63] 6-9-6 (5*) J Weaver (5) *mid-div, effrt and hdwy on outer o'r 2 fs out, sn rdn and one pace*. ....(33 to 1) 11

PLEASURE QUEST [42] 3-7-12 (3*) D Harrison (12) *nvr rchd ldrs*.. (14 to 1) 12

VANART [54] 3-8-13 A Culhane (3) *chsd ldrs till rdn and wknd o'r 3 fs out*................(20 to 1 tchd 25 to 1) 13

QUINZII MARTIN [49] (v) 4-8-11 T Williams (6) *in tch, effrt hfwy, sn rdn and wknd wl o'r 2 fs out*. .... (14 to 1 op 12 to 1) 14

STAIRWAY TO HEAVEN (Ire) [51] (bl) 4-8-6 (7*) V Halliday (8) *slwly away, al beh*..... (7 to 1 op 5 to 1 tchd 8 to 1) 15

SNO SERENADE [66] 6-10-0 S Webster (10) *cl up 3 fs, sn rdn and beh, tld off*.............. (50 to 1 op 33 to 1) 16

Dist: 3l, 2½l, 2l, ½l, nk, 2½l, sht-hd, 6l, hd, nk. 1m 42.40s. a 2.90s (16 Ran).

SR: 42/50/23/18/21/22/22/8/2/ (J G FitzGerald), J G FitzGerald

4664a Alex Lawrie Claiming Stakes (Div II) CLASS F (3-y-o and up) £2,343 6f ....(2:50)

ALLINSON'S MATE (Ire) 4-9-1 Alex Greaves (6) *in tch, effrt and hdwy 2 fs out, rdn and styd on wl ins last to ld nr finish*.......... (3 to 1 jt-fav op 9 to 4 tchd 100 to 30) 1

QUATRE FEMME 5-8-0 T Williams (3) *led, wide strt, rdn fnl fs, wknd and ct nr finish*............ (5 to 1 op 9 to 4) 2

SAMSOLOM 4-8-7 J Williams (1) *al cl up, rdn 2 fs out, ev ch till wknd entering fnl furlong*.... (8 to 1 op 7 to 1) 3

THE DREAM MAKER (Ire) 3-7-12 (7*) M Humphries (5) *beh till styd on fnl 2 fs*...................................(20 to 1) 4

DON'T RUN ME OVER 3-7-11 (7*) S Sanders (7) *cl up, rdn 3 fs out, wknd 2 furlongs out*........(16 to 1 op 14 to 1) 5

STRIP CARTOON (Ire) (bl) 4-8-11 G Baxter (2) *cl up, ev ch o'r 2 fs out, sn rdn and btn*......(100 to 30 op 5 to 1) 6
KINNEGAD KID 3-8-5 A McGlone (4) *slwly away, al rear.* ....(33 to 1) 7
EMPEEKA (USA) (h) 3-8-3 (3*) Emma O'Gorman (9) *chsd ldrs till rdn and wknd wl o'r 2 fs out*............(3 to 1 jt-fav op 7 to 2) 8
MISS BRIGHTSIDE 4-8-0 N Adams (8) *chsd ldrs, rdn hfwy, sn wknd*.......................(33 to 1 op 25 to 1) 9
Dist: 1½l, 2½l, 1½l, 2l, 2½l, ½l, ½l, 3l. 1m 17.40s. a 4.00s (9 Ran).
SR: 9/-/-/-/-/- (Peter Jones), T D Barron

4665a Vivaldi Maiden Stakes CLASS F (2-y-o) £2,427 1m............... (3:20)

I'M A DREAMER (Ire) 9-0 Dale Gibson (7) *chsd ldrs, rdn alng 3 fs out, hdwy on inner 2 furlongs out, led entering fnl furlong, ran on und pres.* (8 to 1 tchd 12 to 1) 1
BUGLET 8-9 N Day (5) *slwly into strd, hdwy hfwy, effrt 2 fs out, sn rdn and styd on fnl furlong.* ....(11 to 4 fav op 6 to 4 tchd 3 to 1) 2
PONDERING (bl,e/s) 9-0 J Quinn (9) *hdwy hfwy, effrt 2 fs out, sn rdn and kpt on*.............(7 to 1 op 6 to 1) 3
BLOWEDIFIKNOW 9-0 J Williams (11) *mid-div, gd hdwy o'r 3 fs out, ev ch 2 furlongs out, sn rdn and wknd entering fnl furlong*................(8 to 1 op 6 to 1) 4
SHARRO 9-0 Gay Kelleway (10) *mid-div, hdwy 3 fs out, sn rdn, kpt on one pace fnl 2 furlongs.* (6 to 1 op 3 to 1) 5
NORTH ARDAR 9-0 R P Elliott (2) *led, rdn 2 fs out, edgd rght and hdd entering fnl furlong, sn wknd.* ....(8 to 1 op 7 to 1) 6
LIDOMA (Ire) 8-9 D Holland (6) *in tch, rdn and wknd o'r 2 fs out*...............................(6 to 1 op 4 to 1) 7
IRISH ROOTS (Ire) (v) 9-0 M Birch (12) *cl up, ev ch 3 fs out, sn rdn and wknd 2 furlongs out*... (20 to 1 op 33 to 1) 8
MISS OFFIE 8-9 W Ryan (8) *al rear*....(8 to 1 op 25 to 1) 9
ANDREA'S GIRL 8-9 J Carroll (3) *cl up till rdn and wknd o'r 2 fs out*..........(14 to 1 op 12 to 1 tchd 16 to 1) 10
ALTONA GOLD 8-9 A Proud (13) *sn beh*.........(33 to 1) 11
TEMPLE HILL 8-9 S Morris (1) *slwly away, al beh.* ....(33 to 1) 12
Dist: 2l, sht-hd, 2½l, hd, 2l, 7l, 8l, ¾l. 1m 44.20s. a 4.70s (12 Ran).
SR: 18/7/11/3/2/-/ (Dave Marshall), W W Haigh

4666a Mozart Handicap CLASS F (0-100 3-y-o and up) £2,532 5f....... (3:50)

LOVE RETURNED [77] 5-8-8² M Tebbutt (9) *chsd ldrs stands side, rdn and hdwy appr fnl furlong, styd on wl to ld ins last*.......... (13 to 2 op 7 to 1 tchd 10 to 1) 1
TINO TERE [73] 3-7-11 (7*) P Roberts (6) *cl up gng wl, led one and a half fs out, sn rdn, hdd and not quicken ins last*..........................(14 to 1 op 12 to 1) 2
PEERAGE PRINCE [66] (bl) 3-7-11² A Munro (8) *chsd ldrs stands side, rdn alng hfwy, styd on and ev ch entering fnl furlong, kpt on*................(10 to 1 op 8 to 1) 3
ABSOLUTION [69] 8-7-11 (3*) D Harrison (2) *cl up far side, ev ch appr fnl furlong, not quicken entering last.* ....(13 to 2 op 5 to 1) 4
VERY DICEY [80] 4-8-11 W Ryan (1) *beh stands side till styd on wl appr fnl furlong, nrst finish.* ....(12 to 1 op 8 to 1) 5
BRANSTON ABBY (Ire) [97] 3-10-0 (7ex) J Reid (11) *cl up far side, rdn 2 fs out, wknd entering fnl furlong.* ....(7 to 4 fav op 11 to 8 tchd 2 to 1) 6
SIZZLING SAGA (Ire) [97] 4-10-0 J Williams (10) *chsd ldrs, rdn 2 fs out, sn one pace*..........(12 to 1 op 10 to 1) 7
ANOTHER EPISODE (Ire) [90] 3-9-7 J Carroll (7) *led, rdn hfwy, hdd and wknd quickly one and a half fs out.* .... (15 to 2 op 4 to 1 tchd 8 to 1) 8
SANDMOOR DENIM [63] 5-7-8¹ J Quinn (12) *chsd ldrs and pushed alng stands side, outpcd hfwy.* ....(12 to 1 op 10 to 1) 9
CRECHE [93] (bl) 3-9-5 (5*) S D Williams (3) *cl up till rdn and wknd quickly 2 fs out*.........(12 to 1 op 16 to 1) 10
SIR TASKER [80] 4-8-11 D Holland (4) *nvr rchd ldrs.* ....(20 to 1) 11
BRISAS [62] (bl) 5-7-7 J Fanning (5) *dwlt, al rear.* (25 to 1) 12
Dist: 1l, nk, 1½l, nk, 1½l, ½l, 1½l, 1½l, nk, hd. 59.20s. a 0.90s (12 Ran).
SR: 56/48/40/37/47/58/56/43/10/ (J M Ratcliffe), W Jarvis

LINGFIELD (A.W) (std)
Wednesday November 11th
Going Correction: MINUS 0.50 sec. per fur.

4667a Medway Claiming Stakes (Div I) CLASS F (3-y-o and up) £2,385 1m ....(12:50)

TRIAL TIMES (USA) 3-8-11 (3*) Emma O'Gorman (3) *led aftr 2 fs, drw wl clr frm 3 out, unchlgd.* (5 to 2 tchd 11 to 4) 1
CRETOES DANCER (USA) (bl) 3-7-7 (7*) Kim McDonnell (5) *beh til ran on o'r 2 out, took second pl ins fnl furlong.* ....(7 to 1 op 4 to 1) 2
DANCING BEAU (Ire) (e/s) 3-8-6 J Reid (9) *sn pushed alng, hdwy aftr 3 fs, outpcd frm three out.* ....(4 to 1 tchd 5 to 1) 3
CHANCE REPORT 4-8-0 R Lappin (2) *ldg grp, rdn and outpcd last 3 fs*..... (16 to 1 op 12 to 1 tchd 20 to 1) 4
SHARP DANCE 3-8-1 Dale Gibson (8) *nvr better than mid-div*................(14 to 1 op 12 to 1 tchd 16 to 1) 5
OSGATHORPE 5-8-9 T Quinn (11) *nvr on terms.* ....(20 to 1 op 14 to 1) 6
PLEASE PLEASE ME (Ire) 4-7-12 N Adams (4) *in tch to hfwy*......................... (20 to 1 op 14 to 1) 7
LORD LEITRIM (Ire) 3-8-0 T Williams (1) *led for 2 fs, wknd quickly bef hfwy, tld off*........(12 to 1 tchd 16 to 1) 8
STING IN THE TAIL (bl) 3-8-0³ D Holland (6) *wth ldrs til lost pl o'r 4 out, tld off*................(50 to 1 op 33 to 1) 9
BRIDGE STREET BOY 3-8-1 A Munro (7) *early pace, lost pl aftr 3 fs, tld off*..................(50 to 1 op 25 to 1) 10
COMMON COUNCIL 3-8-11 (3*) D Harrison (10) *uns rdr sn aftr leaving stalls*............. (13 to 8 fav op 5 to 4) ur
Dist: 6l, 6l, 1½l, 7l, sht-hd, 8l, 25l, 3l, 4l. 1m 37.23s. a 0.33s (11 Ran).
SR: 35/3/-/-/-/-/ (Times Of Wigan), W A O'Gorman

4668a Wye Maiden Stakes CLASS F (2-y-o) £2,385 6f.................... (1:20)

ARAGROVE 9-0 J Reid (1) *made all, rdn and styd on wl ins fnl furlong*......................(3 to 1 op 2 to 1) 1
PIPERS REEL 8-9 A Munro (8) *cld on ldrs 3 out, kpt on one pace ins fnl furlong.* (9 to 4 fav op 2 to 1 tchd 5 to 2) 2
THE ORDINARY GIRL (Ire) 8-9 J Quinn (5) *al handily plcd, rdn and not quicken appr fnl furlong.* ....(5 to 1 op 9 to 2 tchd 6 to 1) 3
WESTERN VALLEY 8-9 D Holland (9) *ldg grp, rdn and no extr o'r one out*.........(3 to 1 op 4 to 1 tchd 5 to 2) 4
GORODENKA BOY 8-7 (7*) Kim McDonnell (2) *pressed ldrs til rdn and wknd ins fnl furlong.* ....(16 to 1 op 20 to 1 tchd 25 to 1) 5
MELOS MODUS (Ire) (e/s) 9-0 J Williams (3) *slwly into strd, wl outpcd in rear til moderate hdwy appr fnl furlong, nvr nrr*.............. (10 to 1 op 4 to 1 tchd 12 to 1) 6
STEVEN'S DREAM (Ire) 8-9 Dale Gibson (7) *outpcd.* ....(16 to 1 op 12 to 1 tchd 20 to 1) 7
LAID BACK BEN 9-0 N Adams (6) *wth ldrs to hfwy, lost pl quickly*........................ (33 to 1 op 25 to 1) 8
BROOKLANDS EXPRESS 9-0 T Quinn (4) *al outpcd.* .... (9 to 1 op 7 to 1 tchd 10 to 1) 9
Dist: 4l, ¾l, 1l, nk, 12l, 1½l, 6l, 2½l. 1m 13.13s. a 2.33s (9 Ran).
(K F Khan), L J Holt

4669a Medway Claiming Stakes (Div II) CLASS F (3-y-o and up) £2,385 1m ....(1:50)

SUPER SUMMIT 3-9-0 G Bardwell (6) *hrd rdn in mid-div hfwy, ran on o'r one out, led nr line.* ....(7 to 2 tchd 9 to 2) 1
SALLY'S SON 6-8-4 (3*) Emma O'Gorman (7) *pressed ldrs, dsptd ld o'r 2 out, not quicken wl ins fnl furlong.* ....(5 to 2 fav op 2 to 1 tchd 11 to 4) 2
KING'S GUEST (Ire) 3-9-0 N Day (1) *led aftr 2 fs til hdd and no extr nr line*.........(11 to 4 op 7 to 4 tchd 3 to 1) 3
LADY SABO 3-7-12 (3*) D Harrison (4) *handily plcd, rdn alng and one pace appr fnl furlong.* ....(8 to 1 op 6 to 1 tchd 9 to 1) 4
CANADIAN CAPERS 3-7-13 J Quinn (9) *led for 2 fs outpcd ins fnl two furlongs*............. (7 to 2 op 5 to 1) 5
CAPTAIN MARMALADE 3-8-8 J Williams (3) *al outpcd.* ....(16 to 1 op 12 to 1) 6
SIMON ELLIS (Ire) 3-7-11² (5*) A Tucker (2) *nvr on terms.* ....(16 to 1 op 14 to 1 tchd 20 to 1) 7
HOT PROSPECT (bl) 3-7-9 J Fanning (8) *ldg grp til rdn alng and lost pl appr hfwy*............(16 to 1 op 14 to 1) 8
LOST MOMENT 8-8-12 V Smith (10) *sn in rear, tld off aftr 3 fs*.......................(33 to 1 tchd 50 to 1) 9
Dist: ¾l, nk, 3½l, 2l, ¾l, ¾l, 1l, dist. 1m 38.67s. a 1.77s (9 Ran).
SR: 13/4/10/-/-/-/ (D J Maden), J Pearce

4670a Arun Handicap CLASS F (0-70 3-y-o and up) £2,490 1¼m.........(2:20)

LOOKINGFORARAINBOW (Ire) [57] 4-10-0 N Day (1) *wl in tch, not much room o'r 4 out, hrd drvn and ran on to ld last hundred yards, all out*.........(9 to 1 op 7 to 1) 1
FLASH OF STRAW (Ire) [41] (bl) 3-8-4 (3*) D Harrison (7) *mid-div, hdwy 3 out, rdn and ran on wl entering fnl furlong, jst fld*......... (8 to 1 op 7 to 1 tchd 10 to 1) 2
KHRISMA [59] 3-9-11 M Hills (2) *wth ldrs, led o'r 3 out, hdd last hundred yards, rallied nr line* ....(4 to 1 op 5 to 2 tchd 5 to 1) 3+
VAGRANCY [56] 3-9-8 D Holland (8) *rdn to cl on ldrs hfwy, styd on wl ins fnl furlong*.......(9 to 4 fav op 7 to 2) 3+
PUSEY STREET BOY [39] 5-8-10 A Munro (4) *ldg grp, ev ch 2 out, one pace appr fnl furlong*.... (7 to 1 op 6 to 1) 5
SAFETY (USA) [51] (bl) 5-9-8 T Quinn (5) *led aftr 2 fs, hdd o'r 3 out, no extr last two furlongs.* .... (14 to 1 op 12 to 1 tchd 16 to 1) 6

DR ZEVA [30] 6-8-1 S Dawson (6) *rdn alng in mid-div o'r 4 out, not rch ldrs*..........(10 to 1 op 8 to 1) 7
CORMORANT BAY [55] 3-9-7 J Reid (12) *led for 2 fs, wknd hfwy*...................(3 to 1 op 4 to 1 tchd 5 to 1) 8
TRENDY AUCTIONEER (Ire) [35] (bl) 4-8-6 D Biggs (10) *al rear div*.............(16 to 1 op 14 to 1 tchd 20 to 1) 9
SILLY HABIT (USA) [51] 6-9-8 V Smith (9) *al beh*.
....................(33 to 1 op 25 to 1 tchd 50 to 1) 10
EMILY ALLAN (Ire) [41] 3-8-7 J Williams (3) *al outpcd in rear*................ (25 to 1 op 20 to 1 tchd 33 to 1) 11
AFFIRMED'S DESTINY (USA) [39] 3-8-5 G Carter (11) *effrt o'r 3 out, wknd over 2 out*.
....................(12 to 1 op 8 to 1 tchd 14 to 1) 12
Dist: Nk, sht-hd, dd-ht, 2l, 12l, 2½l, 7l, 4l, 8l, 6l. 2m 6.88s. a 3.68s (12 Ran).
SR: 27/5/22/19/3/-/ (B M Saumtally), Bob Jones

4671a Stour Apprentice Handicap CLASS F (0-70 3-y-o and up) £2,406 2m ....(2:50)

DIME BAG [71] 3-9-3 (7*,3ex) S McCarthy (2) *ldg grp, led o'r 3 out, sn drw clr*.
.... (11 to 8 on op 5 to 4 on tchd 11 to 10 on) 1
SILKEN WORDS (USA) [52] 3-8-5 Kim McDonnell (7) *wth ldrs, led 7 out till o'r 3 out, sn outpcd*.
....................(12 to 1 op 6 to 1 tchd 14 to 1) 2
PLEASURE AHEAD [37] 5-8-0 A Tucker (5) *hld up towards rear, improved frm hfwy, rdn and ran on 4 out, not rch wnr*..................(10 to 1 op 6 to 1 tchd 12 to 1) 3
CHILD STAR (Fr) [49] 3-8-2 A Garth (9) *hld up in last pl til ran on o'r 4 out, no imprsn on ldrs*.
..........................(7 to 2 op 3 to 1 tchd 4 to 1) 4
TIFFANY GEM (Ire) [55] 3-8-8 D Harrison (4) *rcd in mid-div, no hdwy 5 out*....... (16 to 1 op 12 to 1 tchd 20 to 1) 5
WOTAMONA [30] 4-7-7[3] (3*) M Humphries (10) *hld up in rear, short lived effrt aftr hfwy, no prog last 4 fs*.
..................................(33 to 1 op 20 to 1) 6
THE LAST EMPRESS (Ire) [65] 4-10-0 Stephen Davies (8) *chsd ldrs til wknd o'r 4 out*.
....................(12 to 1 op 7 to 1 tchd 14 to 1) 7
SINGING REPLY (USA) [35] 4-7-9 (3*) Claire Balding (1) *led for 9 fs, wknd 5 out*................(20 to 1 op 12 to 1) 8
I'M CURIOUS [41] 3-7-8[1] J Fanning (3) *ldg grp til wknd 5 out*..................................(50 to 1 op 33 to 1) 9
CAROUSEL MUSIC [50] 5-8-13 F Norton (6) *in tch to hfwy*.
....................(20 to 1 op 12 to 1 tchd 25 to 1) 10
Dist: 12l, hd, 7l, 2½l, 2l, 7l, ½l, 2l, 8l. 3m 24.26s. a 2.26s (10 Ran).
SR: 7/-/-/-/-/-/ (K Al-Said), B W Hills

4672a Rother Handicap CLASS F (0-70 3-y-o and up) £2,364 5f...........(3:20)

INDIAN ENDEAVOUR [52] 3-8-12 M Hills (5) *led for o'r one furlong, cl up, led ag'n over one out, rdn out*.
..................................(10 to 1 op 8 to 1) 1
LITTLE SABOTEUR [63] 3-9-9 J Reid (3) *hld up, rdn alng hfwy, ran on o'r one out, fnshd wl*.
....................(3 to 1 fav op 4 to 1 tchd 5 to 2) 2
SERIOUS HURRY [54] (v) 4-9-0 T Quinn (2) *dsptd ld, rdn and no extr appr fnl furlong*..................(5 to 1) 3
TAUBER [63] 8-9-6 (3*) S O'Gorman (4) *broke fst, led o'r 3 out till over one out, sn btn*..........(9 to 1 op 5 to 1) 4
TOMMY TEMPEST [46] 3-8-6 W Supple (8) *nvr able to chal*.
.... (11 to 2 op 9 to 2 tchd 6 to 1) 5
INSWINGER [40] 6-8-0 G Bardwell (10) *mid-div, rdn alng hfwy, styd on one pace appr fnl furlong*.
..................................(11 to 1 op 7 to 1) 6
HEAVEN-LIEGH-GREY [68] (bl) 4-10-0 A Munro (6) *speed for 3 fs*.....................(9 to 2 op 4 to 1 tchd 5 to 1) 7
PENDOR DANCER [50] (bl) 9-8-10 J Williams (7) *nvr trbld frnt rnk*...............................(12 to 1 op 10 to 1) 8
DOESYOUDOES [60] (v) 3-9-6 D Holland (1) *al outpcd*.
..................................(14 to 1 tchd 16 to 1) 9
EVER SO ARTISTIC [43] (bl) 5-8-3 D Biggs (9) *fst away, outpcd aftr 2 fs, tld off*...........(12 to 1 op 10 to 1) 10
Dist: 2l, 2½l, 1½l, sht-hd, ½l, 1½l, 2l, 3½l, 15l. 58.88s. a 0.38s (10 Ran).
SR: 40/43/24/27/9/1/23/-/-/ (Vijay Mallya), R Guest

4673a Thames Handicap CLASS F (0-75 3-y-o and up) £2,490 7f....... (3:50)

DAM CERTAIN (Ire) [47] 3-8-0 (3*) D Harrison (3) *made virtually all, drvn out fnl furlong*.
.... (9 to 1 op 8 to 1 tchd 10 to 1) 1
COLOSSUS [67] 4-9-11 Dale Gibson (1) *pressed wnr, ev ch one out, not quicken nr line*.........(7 to 1 op 5 to 1) 2
SUPER SERENADE [72] 3-10-0 T Quinn (9) *prog hfwy, rdn alng o'r one out, ran on wl nr line*... (5 to 1 op 6 to 1) 3
GUESSTIMATION (USA) [49] 3-8-5 G Bardwell (14) *outpcd in rear, rdn and ran on o'r 2 out, styd on ins fnl furlong*............... (11 to 2 op 5 to 1 tchd 6 to 1) 4
COURTING NEWMARKET [57] 4-8-9[1] (7*) S Wynne (12) *broke wl, lost pl aftr 2 fs, cld on ldrs o'r two out, no extr over one out*........................ (10 to 1 op 5 to 1) 5
BOY MARTIN [65] 3-9-7 (6ex) Dean McKeown (13) *hdwy o'r 2 out, styd on one pace ins last two fs*.
..................................(4 to 1 fav op 5 to 1) 6

LADY SNOOBLE [36] 5-7-8 N Carlisle (15) *effrt 3 out, no imprsn on frnt rnk last 2 fs*...... (25 to 1 tchd 33 to 1) 7
HARCLIFF [63] 3-9-2 (3*) F Norton (16) *prmsg hdwy frm rear 3 out, btn wl o'r one out*.... (10 to 1 tchd 11 to 1) 8
ALDAHE [37] 7-7-9 N Adams (7) *cl up til lost pl o'r 2 out*.
..................................(14 to 1 tchd 16 to 1) 9
AYR RAIDER [61] 5-9-5 J Williams (5) *mid-div, no extr last 2 fs*..................(9 to 1 op 8 to 1 tchd 10 to 1) 10
ERIK ODIN [43] 5-7-8 (7*) G Milligan (8) *handily plcd for o'r 4 fs, wknd*........................ (20 to 1 op 16 to 1) 11
GEMINI BAY [50] (bl) 3-8-6 S Dawson (4) *wl plcd til wknd 2 out*.............................. (20 to 1 op 16 to 1) 12
POYLE AMBER [49] 3-8-5 G Carter (11) *outpcd*.
.... (20 to 1 op 16 to 1) 13
BLUE DRIFTER (Ire) [45] 3-8-1 A Munro (2) *nvr rchd ldrs*.
..................................(12 to 1) 14
HONEY HEATHER (Ire) [58] 3-9-0 D Biggs (10) *nvr on terms*.
.... (11 to 1 op 10 to 1 tchd 12 to 1) 15
Dist: ¾l, sht-hd, 1½l, 5l, 2½l, nk, ½l, 1½l, ¾l, 1l. 1m 25.03s. a 1.43s (15 Ran).
SR: 15/35/37/9/4/2/ (Mrs Louise Denson), A W Denson

ST-CLOUD (FR) (heavy)
Wednesday November 11th
Going Correction: PLUS 1.60 sec. per fur.

4674a Prix Le Fabuleux (Listed) (3-y-o and up) £12,333 1¼m 110yds......(2:00)

REVIF (Fr) 4-9-0 M Roberts,............................ 1
MICHEL GEORGES 4-9-3 C Le Scrill,.................... 2
BIKASAITE (Fr) 3-8-12 C Asmussen,..................... 3
GRAND FLOTILLA (USA) 5-9-0 D Boeuf,................. 4
Dist: 1½l, 2½l, 1l, 5l, 4l, 5l, 5l, 5l, nk. 2m 29.60s. a 18.60s (10 Ran).
SR: 82/82/72/72/ (S Corman Ltd), A C Stewart

LINGFIELD (A.W) (std)
Saturday November 14th
Going Correction: MINUS 0.30 sec. per fur.

4675a Leviathan Claiming Stakes (Div I) CLASS F (2-y-o) £2,385 1m.. (12:50)

ABSOLUTELY FACT (USA) 8-7 T Quinn (8) *midfield, led 3 out, quickened wl clr, cmftbly*.
....................(13 to 8 fav op 2 to 1 tchd 6 to 4) 1
MISTER BLAKE (bl) 8-4 (3*) Emma O'Gorman (12) *wl plcd, outpcd frm 3 out, styd on one pace fnl furlong*.
....(8 to 1 op 7 to 1) 2
HILLSDOWN BOY (Ire) (bl,e/s) 8-11 D Holland (5) *chsd ldrs, rdn alng and outpcd frm 3 out, kpt on ag'n clsg stages*.
.... (20 to 1 op 16 to 1) 3
HUSH BABY (Ire) (v) 7-13[1] A Munro (6) *beh til ran on ins last 2 fs, fnshd wl*.............. (12 to 1 tchd 14 to 1) 4
TONY'S MIST 8-8 (3*) R Perham (7) *ldg grp, outpcd frm 3 out, no further hdwy*.................(6 to 1 tchd 7 to 1) 5
HOBEY CAT 7-11 (5*) B Doyle (9) *in tch till rdn and no hdwy o'r 3 out*.......... (5 to 1 op 7 to 2 tchd 6 to 1) 6
POLY VISION (Ire) (v) 8-7 J Quinn (2) *led for 5 fs, wknd fnl 2 furlongs*................................(10 to 1 op 8 to 1) 7
CONBRIO STAR 8-7 G Baxter (10) *nvr on terms*.
.... (25 to 1 op 20 to 1 tchd 33 to 1) 8
LADY ARGENT (Ire) 7-5 (7*) D Wright (4) *al beh*.
..................................(33 to 1 op 14 to 1) 9
FRECKENHAM 7-10[1] (3*) F Norton (11) *slwly into strd, al rear div*..............................(33 to 1 op 20 to 1) 10
MRS JEKYLL (Ire) (bl) 8-0 N Carlisle (1) *wl plcd for 3 fs, sn wknd*.................. (9 to 2 op 9 to 4 tchd 5 to 1) 11
RISK PROOF 8-9 G Bardwell (3) *early speed, beh appr hfwy*.............(9 to 1 op 6 to 1 tchd 10 to 1) 12
Dist: 5l, 3l, ½l, 2½l, 2l, hd, ½l, 12l, ¾l, ¾l. 1m 40.70s. a 3.80s (12 Ran).
(Richard Berenson), C C Elsey

4676a EBF Albion Maiden Stakes CLASS F (2-y-o) £2,595 7f..............(1:20)

BICHETTE 8-6 (3*) R Perham (8) *handily plcd, shaken up to ld o'r one out, sn clr*.
.... (2 to 1 fav op 6 to 4 tchd 11 to 4 and 3 to 1) 1
MEDLAND (Ire) 9-0 M Hills (13) *led till hdd o'r one out, not quicken*................(6 to 1 op 8 to 1 tchd 11 to 2) 2
WITHOUT A FLAG (USA) 9-0 G Carter (11) *slwly into strd, improved hfwy, rdn and ran on ins last 2 fs, nrst at line*..........................(10 to 1 op 6 to 1) 3
COVEN MOON 8-9 J Quinn (2) *trkd ldrs, rdn and styd on one pace fnl furlong*.
............(5 to 1 op 8 to 1 tchd 10 to 1 and 4 to 1) 4
RUANO 9-0 W Woods (14) *ldg grp, ev ch 2 out, rdn and no extr o'r one out*................ (33 to 1 op 20 to 1) 5
VILLAVINA (e/s) 8-9 T Quinn (3) *wl plcd, reminders and no extr appr fnl furlong*... (8 to 1 op 7 to 1 tchd 10 to 1) 6
SORAYAH'S PET 9-0 C Nutter (7) *outpcd, rdn alng hfwy, styd on one pace frm 2 out*.........(14 to 1 op 6 to 1) 7
PRECUSSION 9-0 B Crossley (6) *nvr nrr*.
.... (12 to 1 op 7 to 1) 8

DUCHESS DIANNE (Ire) 8-9 J Williams (12) *outpcd most of way*................ (12 to 1 op 10 to 1 tchd 14 to 1) 9
BROUGHTONS FORMULA (e/s) 8-7 (7*) P Bowe (1) *sn beh.* ....(5 to 1 op 9 to 4) 10
TOM PARKER 9-0 N Carlisle (9) *outpcd bef hfwy.* (33 to 1) 11
DOOGAREY 9-0 Dale Gibson (5) *chsd ldrs for o'r 3 fs, sn lost pos*........................(33 to 1 op 25 to 1) 12
EL GRANDO 9-0 G Bardwell (4) *outpcd.* .... (33 to 1 op 16 to 1) 13
YOUNG GENINSKY (bl) 8-2 (7*) A Daly (10) *sn beh.* (33 to 1) 14
Dist: 5l, 2½l, sht-hd, ¾l, 2l, 2l, 1½l, 3½l, 3l, nk. 1m 27.19s. a 3.59s (14 Ran).
SR: 10/-/-/-/-/-/ (R Hannon), G L Moore

4677a Leviathan Claiming Stakes (Div II) CLASS F (2-y-o) £2,364 1m... (1:50)

EXCESS BAGGAGE (Ire) 9-1 D Holland (11) *steady prog o'r 3 out, led ins fnl furlong, pushed out.* ....(13 to 8 on op 11 to 10) 1
MOONSTRUCK BARD 8-3 W Woods (3) *pressed ldrs, rdn and not quicken appr fnl furlong.* ....(14 to 1 tchd 16 to 1) 2
FESTIN (bl) 9-3 Dale Gibson (5) *led til rdn and hdd ins fnl furlong, no extr*.................. (7 to 1 op 5 to 1) 3
PATONG BEACH 8-12 M Hills (7) *cld on ldrs frm hfwy, styd on one pace from 2 fs out*........... (8 to 1 op 5 to 1) 4
MRS DAWSON (v) 7-10[1] (3*) F Norton (1) *slwly into strd, sn wl plcd, lost pos o'r 3 fs out, ran on ag'n over one out.* .... (14 to 1 op 12 to 1 tchd 16 to 1) 5
JULIASDARKINVADER 8-9 Candy Morris (8) *outpcd hfwy, kpt on ag'n appr fnl furlong*..... (33 to 1 op 20 to 1) 6
NANNY MARGARET (Ire) (bl) 7-12 G Bardwell (12) *slwly into strd, sn wth ldrs, rdn and wknd frm 3 fs out.* .... (33 to 1 op 25 to 1) 7
LADY OF SHADOWS (bl,e/s) 8-0 J Quinn (10) *ldg grp til rdn and no prog o'r 2 fs out.* .... (12 to 1 op 8 to 1 tchd 14 to 1) 8
HALHAM TARN (Ire) 9-0 (7*) Ross Berry (9) *slwly into strd, al outpcd*.......................... (16 to 1 op 12 to 1) 9
AMBIVALENTATTITUDE 8-5 S Dawson (2) *cl up for o'r 4 fs, sn btn*...................................(33 to 1) 10
TITLED GIRL (Ire) 8-9 (7*) T G McLaughlin (4) *broke wl, lost pos bef hfwy*......................(4 to 1 tchd 9 to 2) 11
BAY RUM 8-4 G Carter (6) *al wl outpcd, tld off.* .... (33 to 1 op 20 to 1) 12
Dist: 2l, ½l, ½l, 2l, 2l, 2l, 4l, 6l, 2l, 1l. 1m 41.05s. a 4.15s (12 Ran).
SR: 3/-/-/-/-/-/ (Frank W Golding), N A Callaghan

4678a Kritter Brut de Brut Handicap CLASS F (0-70 3-y-o and up) £2,448 1¼m......................... (2:20)

DOUBLE ECHO (Ire) [68] 4-10-0 A Munro (1) *ldg grp, shaken up to ld o'r one furlong out, rdn clr.* .... (11 to 2 op 9 to 2 tchd 6 to 1) 1
AWESOME POWER [64] 6-9-10 M Hills (6) *hld up in mid-div, not clr run 2 out, rdn and ran on fnl furlong, fnshd wl*................................(5 to 2 fav op 3 to 1) 2
DONIA (USA) [67] 3-9-1 (7*) T G McLaughlin (9) *chsd ldr, led o'r 3 out till over one furlong out, sn btn.* .... (10 to 1 op 8 to 1) 3
TWILIGHT SECRET [57] 3-8-12 J Williams (4) *mid-div, effrt o'r 2 out, not quicken appr fnl furlong.* ....(8 to 1 op 6 to 1 tchd 9 to 1) 4
CORRIN HILL [60] 5-9-6 T Quinn (5) *wl plcd, rdn and not quicken 2 out, no extr appr fnl furlong.* .... (12 to 1 op 10 to 1) 5
FAYNAZ [47] 6-8-0 (7*) Kim McDonnell (3) *ldg grp til lost pl ins last 3 fs*.......................(14 to 1 op 10 to 1) 6
CHARIOTEER [55] 3-8-10 Dale Gibson (11) *towards rear most of way*......... (12 to 1 op 10 to 1 tchd 14 to 1) 7
BROUGHTON BLUES (Ire) [34] (e/s) 4-7-8 J Quinn (10) *nvr nr ldrs*..........(16 to 1 op 14 to 1 tchd 20 to 1) 8
REFLECTING (Ire) [68] 3-9-9 D Holland (2) *led til o'r 3 out, eased whn btn ins last 2 fs.* ....(9 to 2 op 4 to 1 tchd 5 to 1) 9
JADE GREEN [65] 3-9-6 G Carter (14) *mid-div, no hdwy fnl 4 fs*............ (12 to 1 op 10 to 1 tchd 14 to 1) 10
EIRAS MOOD [50] 3-8-0 (5*) Stephen Davies (7) *handily plcd til wknd o'r 3 fs out*.......... (12 to 1 op 8 to 1) 11
AL BILLAL [54] (bl) 4-9-0 G Bardwell (8) *al beh*.... (33 to 1) 12
OLD FOX (Fr) [50] 3-8-5 R Price (12) *al in rear grp.* .... (33 to 1 op 25 to 1) 13
GREY BUT ROSY (Ire) [45] (bl) 3-7-11 (3*) D Harrison (13) *hdwy hfwy, wknd quickly o'r 3 fs out, tld off.* .... (25 to 1 op 20 to 1) 14
Dist: 2½l, 2½l, 1½l, 7l, 3½l, 3½l, ¾l, 1l, ¾l, 1l. 2m 6.05s. a 2.85s (14 Ran).
SR: 56/47/40/27/21/1/-/-/6/ (Mrs John Lee), J D Bethell

4679a Eagle Handicap CLASS F (0-90 3-y-o and up) £2,733 1½m.......... (2:50)

THE KARAOKE KING [56] (bl) 3-7-7 Dale Gibson (8) *hld up in rear, hdwy 4 fs out, rdn to ld o'r one out, styd on.* .... (10 to 1 op 8 to 1) 1
CASPIAN BELUGA [62] 4-8-3 (3*) F Norton (6) *trkd ldr, led o'r 3 fs out, hdd und pres over one out, ran on same pace*............ (6 to 1 op 5 to 1 tchd 8 to 1) 2
SNOW BLIZZARD [56] (e/s) 4-8-0 J Quinn (2) *pressed ldrs, rdn and not quicken appr fnl furlong.* ....(7 to 2 op 4 to 1) 3
FIRST FLING (Ire) [60] 3-7-9[1] (3*) D Harrison (10) *steady hdwy frm rear hfwy, shaken up and ran on ins last 2 fs, no imprsn on wnr.* (12 to 1 op 10 to 1 tchd 14 to 1) 4
SLIGHT RISK [61] (e/c) 3-7-12 G Bardwell (1) *led til o'r 3 fs out, wknd 2 out*.................... (5 to 1 op 4 to 1) 5
A A BAMBA [56] 3-7-0 (7*) D Wright (9) *settled towards rear, outpcd frm 5 fs out*..........(20 to 1 op 14 to 1) 6
RAPPORTEUR (USA) [84] 6-10-0 T Quinn (7) *ldg grp til pushed alng 5 fs out, lost pl wl o'r 3 out.* .... (10 to 1 op 6 to 1 tchd 12 to 1) 7
ROYAL VERSE (Fr) [59] 5-8-3[10] R Price (3) *chsd ldrs till wknd hfwy, tld off.* ....(100 to 1 op 33 to 1 tchd 150 to 1) 8
GUECA SOLO [73] 4-9-3 A Munro (5) *mid-div, wknd hfwy, tld off*................ (10 to 1 op 6 to 1 tchd 12 to 1) 9
RESOUNDING SUCCESS (Ire) [68] 3-8-5 D Holland (4) *al beh, tld off*...................... (5 to 2 fav op 7 to 4) 10
Dist: 2½l, 2l, sht-hd, 12l, sht-hd, 3l, 20l, 3l, dist. 2m 31.58s. a 1.88s (10 Ran).
SR: 24/32/22/18/-/-/18/-/-/ (P F Boggis), R Hannon

4680a Bulwark Handicap CLASS F (0-70 3-y-o and up) £2,574 1m..... (3:20)

SAREEN EXPRESS (Ire) [46] 4-8-4 G Bardwell (3) *slwly into strd, improved frm rear o'r 2 fs out, rdn to ld over one out, kpt on*..........................(16 to 1 op 20 to 1) 1
KINGCHIP BOY [52] (v) 3-8-2 (5*) A Tucker (7) *wl plcd, not much room o'r 2 fs out, rdn and ran on ins last.* .... (7 to 2 fav op 4 to 1 tchd 9 to 2 and 5 to 1) 2
DASWAKI (Can) [70] (bl) 4-10-0 B Rouse (2) *led til hdd o'r one furlong out, no extr.* .... (5 to 1 op 4 to 1 tchd 11 to 2) 3
KISSAVOS [58] 6-9-2 T Quinn (4) *ldg grp, not quicken ins last 2 fs*.....(9 to 2 op 4 to 1 tchd 11 to 2 and 6 to 1) 4
DIACO [58] 7-9-2 A Munro (1) *chsd ldrs, no extr frm 2 fs out*.................. (6 to 1 op 4 to 1 tchd 13 to 2) 5
PREDICTABLE [58] 6-9-2 J Quinn (12) *cl up til rdn and wknd o'r one furlong out.* ....(7 to 1 op 5 to 1 tchd 8 to 1) 6
VERNONIA [58] 3-8-13 D Holland (5) *improved into mid-div haflway, sn rdn alng, no imprsn last 2 fs.* .... (12 to 1 op 7 to 1) 7
4673a[8] HARCLIFF [63] (e/s) 3-9-1 (3*) F Norton (9) *chsd ldrs, rdn o'r 3 out, wknd frm 2 fs out.* ....(8 to 1 op 10 to 1 tchd 14 to 1) 8
SPEEDY CLASSIC (USA) [49] 3-8-4 G Carter (6) *pressed ldr til wknd quickly o'r 3 fs out.* ....(16 to 1 op 12 to 1 tchd 20 to 1) 9
DON'T WORRY (Ire) [49] 3-8-4 Dale Gibson (11) *al outpcd in rear*............................(25 to 1 op 14 to 1) 10
GRAND FELLOW (Ire) [52] (v) 3-8-7 M Hills (10) *settled towards rear, effrt hfwy, not rch ldrs last 2 fs.* .... (25 to 1 op 14 to 1) 11
BRIGHTNESS [64] 3-9-5 Gay Kelleway (8) *al outpcd in rear, tld off*..................... (25 to 1 op 20 to 1) 12
Dist: 1½l, 2l, 2l, 3l, nk, 3l, 7l, 4l, 5l, 1½l. 1m 38.61s. a 1.71s (12 Ran).
SR: 28/26/41/23/14/13/1/-/-/ (Don Hazzard), Mrs J C Dawe

4681a Ladbroke All Weather Trophy Handicap Qualifier CLASS E (0-70 3-y-o and up) £3,132 6f............ (3:50)

NOBLE POWER (Ire) [64] 3-9-3 (5*) Stephen Davies (6) *hld up in tch, ran on 2 out, led ins fnl furlong, held on cl hme*............................(7 to 1 tchd 15 to 2) 1
FACE NORTH (Ire) [55] 4-9-0 G Carter (11) *hdwy and not clr run 2 out, str run fnl furlong, jst fld.* ....(2 to 1 fav op 3 to 1) 2
LIFT BOY (USA) [44] 3-7-9 (7*) B Russell (2) *led til hdd ins fnl furlong, kpt on gmely*.........(16 to 1 op 14 to 1) 3
SIRMOOR (Ire) [49] (bl) 3-8-7 A McGlone (14) *mid-div, cld on ldrs o'r 2 out, styd on one pace fnl furlong.* ....(14 to 1 op 12 to 1) 4
AIN'TLIFELIKETHAT [54] 5-8-10 (3*) D Harrison (7) *dwlt, beh til ran on strly appr fnl furlong.* .... (10 to 1 op 8 to 1 tchd 12 to 1) 5
FURIELLA [59] (bl) 4-9-4 Dale Gibson (8) *ldg grp, rdn and wknd o'r one furlong out*......... (7 to 1 tchd 8 to 1) 6
PIGALLE WONDER [43] 4-7-11 (5*) A Tucker (4) *pressed ldr til lost pl 2 fs out*.....(14 to 1 op 16 to 1 tchd 12 to 1) 7
MOGWAI (Ire) [63] (bl) 3-9-7 T Quinn (5) *nvr nrr.* ....(6 to 1 op 7 to 1 tchd 8 to 1) 8
LUCKNAM STYLE [49] (v) 4-8-8 N Howe (10) *outpcd.* ....(50 to 1) 9
CATALANI [47] 7-8-6 D Holland (3) *ldg grp til wknd o'r 3 fs out*.................................(12 to 1 op 8 to 1) 10
KIRRIEMUIR [47] 4-8-6 N Carlisle (9) *outpcd.* .... (10 to 1 op 8 to 1 tchd 12 to 1) 11
LORD NASKRA (USA) [68] 3-9-9 (3*) Emma O'Gorman (13) *slwly into strd, al beh*........................ (20 to 1) 12
Dist: Hd, ½l, 2½l, 2½l, 2½l, 2l, 2½l, 1½l, ½l, 1½l. 1m 12.71s. a 1.91s (12 Ran).

SR: 34/25/11/6/2/-/ (Sandy Lane Associates), B Palling

CAPANNELLE (ITY) (heavy)
Sunday November 15th

4682a **Premio Roma (Group 1) (3-y-o and up) £106,352 1¼m............(2:10)**

MISIL (USA) 4-8-13 L Dettori (4) *pushed alng o'r 5 fs out, 6th strt, hrd rdn to ld one and a half furlongs out, sn clr*........ 1
ALHIJAZ 3-8-12 W Carson (9) *5th strt, hdwy wl o'r 2 fs out, ev ch one and a half furlongs out, one pace*...... 2
GUADO D'ANNIBALE (Ire) 3-8-12 J Freda (3) *al prmnt, second strt, led 3 fs out to one and a half out, one pace*. 3
VASARELLI (Ire) 3-8-12 V Mezzatesta (6) *4th strt, wknd o'r 2 fs out*........ 4
GREEN SENOR (USA) 4-8-13 M Tellini (10) *rear to strt, some prog fnl 2 fs, nvr nrr*........ 5
ERDELISTAN (Fr) 5-8-13 E Botti (5) *nvr a factor*........ 6
RED BISHOP (USA) 4-8-13 Pat Eddery (8) *cl up to hfwy, btn o'r 3 fs out*........ 7
IN A TIFF (Ire) 3-8-12 P Shanahan (1) *led aftr one furlong to 3 out, wknd quickly*........ 8
ASTRO DI LUCE (USA) 3-8-12 D Zarroli (2) *al rear*........ 9
BATEAU ROUGE 5-8-13 F Jovine (7) *led for one furlong, 3rd strt, wknd 3 out*........ 10

Dist: 5½l, ½l, 5l, 2l, ½l, 2l, 3½l, 1 ¾l, 6l. 2m 7.40s. (10 Ran).
(Scuderia Laghi), C Vittorio

LEOPARDSTOWN (IRE) (yielding)
Sunday November 15th
Going Correction: PLUS 1.05 sec. per fur.

4683a **Sutton Race (3-y-o and up) £5,520 1 ¼m........................ (1:30)**

MINING TYCOON (Ire) 3-9-7 K J Manning (5) ... (2 to 1 on) 1
NINJA DANCER (USA) 3-9-7 S Craine (3)..........(6 to 1) 2
BAHI (Ire) (bl) 3-9-7 R J Griffiths (1)................ (5 to 2) 3
TESLEMI (USA) 3-8-0 (8*) P P Murphy (4).........(50 to 1) 4

Dist: 4l, 5l, 1½l. 2m 19.10s. a 14.40s (4 Ran).
SR: 68/60/50/34/ (D H W Dobson), J S Bolger

4684a **Knockaire Stakes (Listed) (3-y-o and up) £8,625 7f.............(2:00)**

DASHING COLOURS (Ire) 3-8-7 W J Supple (6) *hld up, prog 2 fs out, quickened to ld one out, kpt on wl*....(14 to 1) 1
STREET REBEL (Can) (bl) 4-9-7 S Craine (9) *mid-div, prog 2 fs out, swtchd to chal on far side rail ins last, styd on strly*..........(7 to 1) 2
TWO LEFT FEET 5-8-12 W J O'Connor (8) *wl plcd, dsptd ld 2 fs out to one out, kpt on*..........(6 to 1) 3
BEZELLE 3-9-2 P V Gilson (7) *wl plcd, ev ch 2 fs out, wknd ins last*.......... (5 to 4 fav) 4
KAYFA (Ire) 3-8-7 P Carberry (1) *trkd ldr, ev ch 2 fs out, sn rdn and wknd*..........(12 to 1) 5
CHEVIOT AMBLE (Ire) 4-8-9 A Munro (3) *wl plcd, dsptd ld 2 fs out, sn rdn and wknd*.......... (5 to 1) 6
STRIPPED CLEAN 3-8-10 R J Griffiths (5) *mid-div, rdn 3 fs out, kpt on one pace*..........(20 to 1) 7
NORDIC PAGEANT (Ire) 3-9-0 C Roche (2) *led to 2 fs out, sn wknd*..........(5 to 1) 8
FLORA MACLEOD (Ire) (bl) 3-8-10 B Coogan (10) *al rear*. ....(25 to 1) 9
SAND OR STONE (Ire) 4-8-12 A J Nolan (4) *mid-div, rdn and wknd 2 fs out*..........(25 to 1) 10
DSHAMILJA 5-8-9 B P Gowran (11) *slwly away, al rear*. ....(33 to 1) 11

Dist: 1l, sht-hd, 2l, ¾l. 1m 35.30s. a 9.90s (11 Ran).
SR: 55/66/56/54/43/-/ (Duncan McGregor), Daniel J Murphy

4685a **Leopardstown November Handicap (3-y-o and up) £13,000 2m.... (3:00)**

PHARFETCHED [-] 3-7-8 (2*) R M Burke (18)......(12 to 1) 1
TONY'S FEN [-] 3-8-4 W J Supple (20)........... (10 to 1) 2
BITOFABANTER [-] 5-8-5 R Hughes (21) ....(11 to 2 jt-fav) 3
SHANTALLA BAY [-] 5-7-3 (8*) R T Fitzpatrick (7) ... (9 to 1) 4
CROWDED HOUSE (Ire) [-] 4-8-4 A Munro (15)...... (7 to 1) 5
GREEN GLEN (USA) [-] 3-7-5 (6*) J J Behan (23) .. (12 to 1) 6
SHAKANDA (Ire) [-] 3-8-9 (2*) D G O'Shea (5)..... (10 to 1) 7
LOSHIAN (Ire) [-] 3-6-13 (8*) P P Murphy (3).......(25 to 1) 8
SANNDILA (Ire) [-] 4-9-1 (6*) J R Barry (14) .. (11 to 2 jt-fav) 9
FLUSTERED (USA) [-] 6-9-2 (4*) M Fenton (16).... (25 to 1) 10
ST.DONAVINT [-] 5-7-8² (8*) R V Skelly (11)........ (25 to 1) 11
GAMARA (Ire) [-] 4-8-0 Joanna Morgan (12)........(8 to 1) 12
DESERT SQUAW [-] 5-8-6 (4*) W J Smith (10).....(10 to 1) 13
DUHARRA (Ire) [-] (bl) 4-9-1 (8*) D J O'Donohoe (9) (9 to 1) 14
MAID OF VISION (Ire) [-] 3-7-12³ (6*) J A Heffernan (8) ....(20 to 1) 15
MAYFIELD PRINCE (Ire) [-] 3-7-10⁴ (8*) B Bowens (17) ....(25 to 1) 16
ENQELAAB (USA) [-] 4-8-9 C Roche (22)......... (14 to 1) 17
DIRECT LADY (Ire) [-] 3-8-9¹ K J Manning (6)..... (14 to 1) 18
AQUA LILY [-] 4-8-5 J P Deegan (1)..............(33 to 1) 19
MORNING SARGE [-] 4-8-1 N G McCullagh (13) .. (33 to 1) 20
NANARCH (USA) [-] 8-8-5 A J Nolan (19).........(25 to 1) 21
NATIVE HIGH LINE [-] 5-8-4 J Fanning (2)........ (40 to 1) 22

Dist: Sht-hd, sht-hd, 3½l, 3l. 3m 44.30s. a 19.80s (22 Ran).
SR: 52/59/59/47/51/-/ (James Shanahan), Mrs A M O'Brien

4686a **Colibri Gifts Handicap (3-y-o and up) £4,140 1m 1f............. (3:30)**

TONY'S DELIGHT (Ire) [-] 4-8-12 (6*) B J Walsh (15) (10 to 1) 1
THATCH AND GOLD (Ire) [-] 4-9-1 (6*) J R Barry (14) .... (3 to 1 fav) 2
FONTANAYS (Ire) [-] 4-7-10⁹ (6*) J J Behan (8).... (20 to 1) 3
NORDIC SIGN (Ire) [-] 3-7-6¹ (8*) B A Hunter (7) ... (14 to 1) 4
LARNACA [-] 5-9-9 S Craine (13)................. (7 to 1) 5
GDANSK VICTORY (USA) [-] 4-9-8 (6*) J A Heffernan (5) ....(10 to 1) 6
VISTAGE (Ire) [-] 4-8-8 J Deegan (20)............(16 to 1) 7
THE MAN FROM COOKS (Ire) [-] 3-7-10 (4*) M Fenton (16) ....(6 to 1) 8
KASKAZI [-] 3-9-9 (2*) D G O'Shea (4)............(12 to 1) 9
MAY WE DANCE (Ire) [-] (bl) 3-7-13 N G McCullagh (17) ....(14 to 1) 10
CISEAUX (USA) [-] 3-9-0 (10*) W J Walsh (6)...... (20 to 1) 11
CALOUNIA (Ire) [-] 3-9-7 R Hughes (3)..............(7 to 1) 12
ROMAN FORUM (Ire) [-] (bl) 4-9-0 K J Manning (2) (25 to 1) 13
MUGNANO [-] 6-8-2 (4*) W J Smith (11)..........(25 to 1) 14
VLADIMIR'S WAY (Ire) [-] 3-8-4 W J Supple (9).... (10 to 1) 15
OLD TALKA RIVER [-] 5-8-9 (8*) D J O'Donohoe (21) (25 to 1) 16
THE MAIN CHOICE (Ire) [-] (bl) 3-7-8 Joanna Morgan (1) ....(50 to 1) 17
ARLINGTON HEIGHTS (Ire) [-] 3-9-0 R J Griffiths (12) ....(14 to 1) 18

Dist: ¾l, hd, 3½l, 2½l. 2m 6.20s. a 15.70s (18 Ran).
SR: 10/11/-/-/-/-/ (Mrs C Harrington), Kevin Prendergast

SOUTHWELL (A.W) (std)
Tuesday November 17th
Going Correction: NIL

4687a **Trent Navigation Nursery CLASS F (2-y-o) £2,343 6f..............(1:20)**

BRIGHT GEM [48] 7-9 J Fanning (5) *nvr far away, drvn to ld o'r 2 fs out, jst hld on*............ (7 to 1 op 6 to 1) 1
GREENWICH CHALENGE [74] 9-7 A Munro (7) *trkd ldg trio, drvn to draw level last 2 fs, ran on, jst fld*. ....(5 to 1 op 5 to 2) 2
MR CUBE (Ire) [60] 8-0 (7*) T G McLaughlin (8) *drvn up on outsd to joine ldrs hfwy, hrd driven last 2 fs, one pace*. ....(9 to 4 fav op 3 to 1 tchd 4 to 1) 3
COLMAR [48] (v) 7-9¹ J Quinn (9) *sluggish strt, drvn into midfield hfwy, no imprsn last 2 fs*. .... (10 to 1 op 12 to 1 tchd 20 to 1) 4
JOTRA [55] 7-9 (7*) D Wright (1) *last and drvn alng hfwy, styd on last 2 fs, nrst finish*.........(8 to 1 op 20 to 1) 5
MOVING IMAGE (Ire) [68] 9-1 C Dwyer (2) *led early, lost pl aftr one and a half fs, drvn alng, no imprsn*. .... (9 to 1 op 4 to 1 tchd 10 to 1) 6
WALID'S PRINCESS (Ire) [58] 8-5 J Williams (3) *chsd ldg 5, rdn hfwy, sn btn*....... (7 to 1 op 9 to 2 tchd 7 to 2) 7
4661a⁹ COLFAX STARLIGHT [61] (bl) 8-5 (3*) D Harrison (6) *drvn to ld aftr one and a half fs, hdd o'r 2 out, fdd*. .... (14 to 1 op 10 to 1) 8
MY FOXY LADY [52] 7-13 T Williams (4) *sn led, hdd aftr one and a half fs, btn entering strt*..... (15 to 2 op 6 to 1) 9

Dist: Hd, 2½l, 7l, sht-hd, 3l, nk, sht-hd, 10l. 1m 16.70s. a 3.30s (9 Ran).
SR: 15/40/16/-/-/-/ (J A Turney), T Fairhurst

4688a **Humber Claiming Stakes CLASS F (3-y-o and up) £2,364 1¾m....(1:50)**

GHOSTLY GLOW (v) 3-7-13¹ A Munro (1) *nvr far away, drvn to ld o'r one furlong out, styd on wl*. ...(4 to 1 jt-fav op 7 to 2) 1
4662a⁶ TEMPERING 6-8-11 S Wood (7) *led, quickened hfwy, rdn and hdd o'r one furlong out, kpt on same pace*. ....(9 to 2 op 3 to 1) 2
JALORE 3-7-7² (7*) M Humphries (2) *chsd ldrs, improved entering strt, kpt on wl fnl furlong*. (7 to 1 op 10 to 1) 3
REACH FOR GLORY 3-7-12 Dale Gibson (3) *drvn up frm midfield hfwy, feeling pace entering strt, not pace to chal*..........(6 to 1 op 5 to 1) 4
GLENSTAL PRIORY (bl) 5-8-4 T Quinn (6) *bustled alng in midfield hfwy, hdwy last 2 fs, nvr nrr*.......(4 to 1 jt-fav tchd 5 to 1) 5
KILLICK (bl) 4-8-1¹ D Holland (5) *trkd ldr, hrd drvn entering strt, sn lost tch*...(16 to 1 op 14 to 1 tchd 20 to 1) 6
PHARGOLD (Ire) 3-7-12 J Quinn (10) *trkd ldg 4, hrd drvn hfwy, lost tch entering strt*....... (25 to 1 op 14 to 1) 7
SEA PADDY 4-8-10 (7*) H Bastiman (9) *al struggling, tld off*..........(7 to 1 op 6 to 1 tchd 9 to 1) 8
FRANCISCAN 5-8-2 (5*) O Pears (4) *struggling aftr 3 fs, tld off hfwy*.......... (25 to 1 op 20 to 1) 9

UNPAID MEMBER 8-8-11 J Williams (8) *chsd ldg 5, lost grnd hfwy, tld off*..................(7 to 1 op 6 to 1) 10
J'ARRIVE 3-7-11 G Bardwell (11) *chsd ldrs to hfwy, tld off*.
..................................(8 to 1 tchd 9 to 1) 11
Dist: 1½l, 4l, 5l, 10l, 8l, 10l, ½l, 8l, 10l, 7l. 3m 9.80s. a 9.80s (11 Ran).
(Richard Berenson), C C Elsey

4689a Nottingham Life Managers' Circle Handicap CLASS F (0-70 3-y-o and up) £2,700 1½m..............(2:20)

4662a² MR WISHING WELL [48] (e/s) 6-8-7 T Quinn (2) *patiently rdn, hdwy on bit to ld o'r one furlong out, quickened, easily*..............(2 to 1 fav op 3 to 1 tchd 7 to 2) 1
SILVER SAMURAI [67] 3-9-3 (3*) F Norton (7) *wtd wth, hdwy on ins to ld entering strt, hdd o'r one furlong out, kpt on same pace*.... (14 to 1 op 12 to 1 tchd 16 to 1) 2
FALCONS DAWN [54] 5-8-13 G Baxter (10) *settled midfield, improved entering strt, drvn alng last 2 fs, one pace*.
..................................(8 to 1 op 7 to 1) 3
MAPLE BAY (Ire) [64] 3-9-3 A Munro (12) *nvr far away, drvn alng entering strt, not quicken last 2 fs*.
..................................(14 to 1 op 10 to 1) 4
TOUCH ABOVE [51] 6-8-3 (7*) V Halliday (13) *patiently rdn, improved on outsd appr strt, ridden, no imprsn last 2 fs*..............................(14 to 1 op 12 to 1) 5
THUNDERBIRD ONE (USA) [61] 3-9-0 J Carroll (11) *settled midfield, drvn alng appr strt, nvr able to chal*.
..................................(14 to 1 op 10 to 1) 6
SURF BOAT [60] 3-8-13 D Holland (1) *trkd ldrs, hrd drvn entering strt, outpcd last 2 fs*......(4 to 1 tchd 9 to 2) 7
LIZZIE DRIPPIN (Can) [46] 3-7-11¹ (3*) D Harrison (8) *last and drvn alng hfwy, styd on und pres last 2 fs, nvr nrr*.
..................................(25 to 1 op 20 to 1) 8
JAMES IS SPECIAL (Ire) [49] 4-8-8 J Quinn (6) *settled midfield, cld appr strt, fdd 2 fs out*.... (25 to 1 op 16 to 1) 9
PETAVIOUS [69] 7-10-0 N Day (9) *in tch, chsd alng in midfield appr strt, fdd 2 fs out*......(12 to 1 op 9 to 1) 10
TANCRED GRANGE [56] 3-8-4 (5*) O Pears (16) *improved frm midfield to track ldrs appr strt, rdn and btn 2 fs out*..................(12 to 1 op 10 to 1 tchd 14 to 1) 11
BIRTHDAYS' CHILD [51] 4-8-10 M Hills (5) *trkd ldrs, drvn to ld hfwy, hdd entering strt, sn btn*.
..................................(20 to 1 op 14 to 1) 12
LOMBARD OCEAN [45] 3-7-5 (7*) D Wright (3) *reared and rdr lost irons strt, dsptd ld aftr one furlong, lost tch hfwy, tld off*..........................(25 to 1 op 16 to 1) 13
ACHELOUS [60] (v) 5-9-5 Dean McKeown (14) *led to hfwy, lost pl quickly appr strt, tld off*.... (6 to 1 tchd 7 to 1) 14
Dist: 3½l, ¾l, 3½l, 1l, 4l, 2l, sht-hd, 3l, ¾l, 10l. 2m 41.80s. a 7.90s (14 Ran).
SR: 14/20/11/8/-/-/ (S Dow), S Dow

4690a Grand Union Canal Handicap CLASS F (0-70 3-y-o and up) £2,511 7f..............................(2:50)

4673a* DAM CERTAIN (Ire) [50] 3-8-3 (3*,5ex) D Harrison (7) *tucked away in midfield, hrd drvn to improve entering strt, styd on wl to ld ins fnl furlong*.
..................(3 to 1 fav op 4 to 1 tchd 9 to 2) 1
4660a³ DEBSY DO (USA) [66] 3-9-3 (5*) O Pears (11) *patiently rdn, improved entering strt, led briefly ins fnl furlong, one pace*..................................(8 to 1 op 6 to 1) 2
4660a⁴ PESIDANAMICH (Ire) [70] (bl) 4-9-9 (5*) Stephen Davies (8) *led, drvn alng appr strt, hdd ins fnl furlong, no extr*.
..................................(12 to 1 op 10 to 1) 3
EAST BARNS (Ire) [45] (bl) 4-7-10 (7*) V Halliday (15) *drvn alng and plenty to do hfwy, styd on last 2 fs, nrst finish*................(11 to 1 op 12 to 1 tchd 10 to 1) 4
4666a⁹ SANDMOOR DENIM [60] 5-9-4 S Webster (3) *settled, swtchd outsd to improve o'r 2 fs out, styd on, nvr nrr*.
..........................(5 to 1 op 7 to 1 tchd 9 to 2) 5
SPENDER [43] 3-7-10 (3*) F Norton (12) *chsd alng to improve frm midfield entering strt, kpt on, nrst finish*.
..................................(25 to 1 op 12 to 1) 6
HARD SELL [60] 5-9-4 Dean McKeown (9) *trkd ldg 4, drvn alng entering strt, btn 2 fs out*.....(16 to 1 op 10 to 1) 7
4673a AYR RAIDER [61] 5-9-5 J Williams (1) *ran in snatches, last strt, styd on und pres last 2 fs, nvr nrr*.
..................................(20 to 1 op 12 to 1) 8
THE NEW GIRL [48] 3-8-4 D Holland (2) *trkd ldr, drvn alng appr strt, outpcd last 2 fs*.........(16 to 1 op 12 to 1) 9
COMPANY CASH [55] (bl) 4-8-7¹ (7*) H Bastiman (4) *chsd ldg 5, hrd drvn o'r 2 fs out, fdd*.......(25 to 1 op 16 to 1) 10
MAGNETIC POINT (USA) [44] (bl) 3-8-0 A Munro (16) *in tch, drvn up on outsd appr strt, wknd 2 fs out*.
..................(12 to 1 op 10 to 1 tchd 14 to 1) 11
4663a QUINZII MARTIN [49] (v) 4-8-7 T Williams (5) *in tch for o'r 4 fs*..............................(16 to 1 op 12 to 1) 12
DANCING SENSATION (USA) [40] 5-7-12 J Fanning (13) *drvn alng hfwy, struggling entering strt*.......... (16 to 1) 13
WHO'S THAT LADY [58] 3-9-0 J Quinn (14) *chsd alng hfwy, lost tch last 2 fs*.... (12 to 1 op 7 to 1 tchd 14 to 1) 14
ADMIRALS REALM [62] 3-9-4 T Quinn (6) *wth ldrs, lost grnd appr strt, sn btn*.............. (9 to 1 op 6 to 1) 15
GRUBBY [57] 3-8-8 (5*) A Garth (10) *drvn alng hfwy, sn btn*..................(25 to 1 op 20 to 1 tchd 16 to 1) 16

Dist: 1½l, 1½l, nk, 1½l, ¾l, 5l, ½l, 3l, ¾l, sht-hd. 1m 30.30s. a 4.00s (16 Ran).
SR: 32/43/44/18/28/7/11/10/-/ (Mrs Louise Denson), A W Denson

4691a River Idle Maiden Stakes CLASS F (2-y-o) £2,448 7f..............(3:20)

POLEDEN (USA) 9-0 J Fortune (7) *made all, drvn clr last 2 fs, kpt on wl nr finish*. (7 to 1 op 8 to 1 tchd 10 to 1) 1
MAJOR TRIUMPH (Ire) 8-9 M Hills (1) *sluggish strt, drvn to improve on ins entering strt, kpt on wl last 100 yards*.
..................(11 to 2 op 8 to 1 tchd 5 to 1) 2
LAND O'LAKES (Ire) 9-0 C Nutter (11) *nvr far away, drvn alng frm hfwy, styd on und pres ins fnl furlong*.
..............(11 to 8 fav op 11 to 10 on tchd 7 to 4) 3
ANN HILL (Ire) 8-9 A Munro (6) *trkd ldrs, drvn alng o'r 2 fs out, one pace*..........................(16 to 1 op 12 to 1) 4
4676a² MEDLAND (Ire) 8-11 (3*) D Harrison (10) *trkd wnr, hrd drvn entering strt, not quicken last 2 fs*.
..................(11 to 1 op 8 to 1 tchd 12 to 1) 5
NUTTY BROWN 8-11 (3*) F Norton (5) *wth ldrs, feeling pace entering strt, fdd 2 fs out*......(3 to 1 op 9 to 4) 6
STAR RAGE (Ire) 9-0 J Williams (9) *trkd ldg 5, rdn o'r 2 fs out, sn btn*..........................(12 to 1 op 6 to 1) 7
PRINCE OF SOUL 9-0 J McLaughlin (3) *chsd alng in midfield, no imprsn last 2 fs*..........(33 to 1 op 20 to 1) 8
MY BALLYBOY (bl) 8-7 (7*) P Bowe (4) *bustled alng in midfield, no imprsn last 2 fs*.
..................(14 to 1 op 7 to 1 tchd 16 to 1) 9
QUATTRO 9-0 B Crossley (2) *sluggish strt, outpcd*.
..................................(20 to 1 op 8 to 1) 10
HALMANERROR 9-0 J Carroll (8) *sluggish strt, not reco'r*.
..................................(33 to 1 op 14 to 1) 11
Dist: ½l, 1l, 1½l, 3l, 3½l, 1½l, 4l, 3½l, 2½l, 2l. 1m 31.30s. a 5.00s (11 Ran).
SR: 25/18/20/10/6/-/ (N J Forman Hardy), A A Scott

4692a Mersey Canal Handicap CLASS F (0-90 3-y-o and up) £2,385 6f.. (3:50)

4660a* PRETONIC [61] 4-8-4 (7ex) Dean McKeown (1) *dsptd ld till squeezed out bend aftr one furlong, hdwy and not clr run o'r one out, squeezed through to lead last 50 yards*.
..................(4 to 1 fav op 9 to 2 tchd 11 to 2) 1
WELLSY LAD (USA) [56] 5-7-13 S Wood (3) *led early, drvn alng and wide strt, drw level fnl furlong, ran on*.
..................................(7 to 1 tchd 8 to 1) 2
PANIKIN [85] 4-10-0 J Williams (10) *chsd alng to improve last 2 fs, ran on wl last 50 yards*.
..................(12 to 1 tchd 14 to 1 and 11 to 1) 3
4666a⁵ VERY DICEY [80] 4-9-9 D Holland (9) *wth ldr, led o'r 2 fs out till ins last, no extr*.
..................(10 to 1 op 8 to 1 tchd 11 to 1) 4
GYMCRAK TYCOON [75] 3-9-3 J Quinn (2) *drpd out strt, rapid hdwy appr fnl furlong, fnshd wl*.
..........................(6 to 1 op 8 to 1 tchd 9 to 1) 5
APPLEDORN [81] 5-9-3 (7*) S Sanders (5) *chsd ldrs, hrd drvn hfwy, kpt on same pace*.
..................(12 to 1 op 10 to 1 tchd 14 to 1) 6
LOVE LEGEND [75] (bl) 7-9-4 A Munro (12) *chsd alng to improve last 2 fs, nrst finish*......... (7 to 1 op 4 to 1) 7
4666a* LOVE RETURNED [81] 5-9-10 (7ex) M Tebbutt (8) *chsd alng in midfield, hrd drvn hfwy, not rch ldrs*.
..........................(8 to 1 op 4 to 1 tchd 9 to 1) 8
SONDERISE [64] 3-8-6 N Carlisle (4) *struggling hfwy, styd on last 2 fs, nvr nrr*..............(25 to 1 op 14 to 1) 9
GENTLE HERO (USA) [71] 6-9-0 Jaki Houston (11) *speed to hfwy, sn btn*.........(12 to 1 op 11 to 1 tchd 16 to 1) 10
4666a⁴ ABSOLUTION [70] 8-8-13 T Quinn (7) *sn led, set str pace till o'r 2 fs out, fdd*......................(9 to 1 op 7 to 1) 11
GENERAL JOHN (Ire) [76] 3-9-4 Dale Gibson (6) *struggling to hold pl aftr 2 fs, sn beh*.
..................(25 to 1 op 16 to 1 tchd 33 to 1) 12
Dist: Hd, nk, 3½l, ¾l, hd, hd, 1l, nk, 2½l, 1l. 1m 16.00s. a 2.60s (12 Ran).
SR: 38/32/60/41/32/38/31/33/14/ (Brian Yeardley Continental Ltd), M Johnston

EVRY (FR) (soft)
Wednesday November 18th
Going Correction: PLUS 1.30 sec. per fur.

4693a Prix des Chenes (Group 3) (2-y-o) £20,555 1m................(1:40)

DANCIENNE (Fr) 8-8 D Boeuf (2) *hld up, 4th strt, quickened 2 fs out, led one and a half out, hrd rdn and ran on wl*..................................(23 to 10) 1
DERNIER EMPEREUR (USA) 8-11 T Jarnet (6) *rear and last strt, fnshd wl, not rch ldr*..............(11 to 10 fav) 2
RANGER (Fr) 8-11 C Asmussen (5) *led, rdn 2 fs out, hdd one and a half out, kpt on one pace*.........(34 to 10) 3
ACCOMMODATING (USA) 8-8 F Head (1) *prmnt, second strt, effrt 2 fs out, one pace*.................. (78 to 10) 4
DIANA LODGE (Fr) 8-11 O Peslier (4) *trkd ldr, 3rd strt, rdn and unbl to quicken 2 fs out*................. (17 to 1) 5
LIT DE JUSTICE (USA) 8-11 W Mongil (3) *nvr dngrs*.
..................................(91 to 10) 6
Dist: 1l, sht-nk, 2½l, 1l, 1½l. 1m 53.67s. a 15.77s (6 Ran).

SR: 13/13/12/1/1/-/ (C Sarmant), E Lellouche

4694a Prix Belle de Nuit (Listed) (3 & 4-y-o) £12,333 1½m................ (2:35)

EGYPTOWN (Fr) 3-8-9 E Legrix,........................ 1
AFRICAN PEACE (USA) 3-8-9 T Jarnet,.................. 2
ZALLAKA (Ire) 3-8-9 G Guignard,...................... 3
SAQUIACE (USA) 4-8-11 D Boeuf,....................... 4
Dist: 8l, 1½l, 1l, 4l, 8l, 5l, 3l. 2m 50.94s. a 19.94s (8 Ran).
SR: 52/36/33/33/ (J Wertheimer), Mme C Head

SOUTHWELL (A.W) (std)
Wednesday November 18th

Going Correction: NIL (races 1,2,3,4,5), MINUS 0.50 (6,7)

4695a Friar Tuck Claiming Stakes (Div I) CLASS F (2-y-o) £2,385 7f....(12:40)

4665a[8] IRISH ROOTS (Ire) (v) 7-10[1] (3*) F Norton (4) *al prmnt, rdn 2 fs out, styd on to ld entering fnl furlong, hld on wl.* ....(33 to 1 op 25 to 1) 1
4661a* MASTER SINCLAIR (Ire) 8-3 (5*) A Garth (3) *hld up and beh, hdwy hfwy, effrt ins fnl furlong, sn rdn and jst fld.* ....(6 to 4 fav op 13 to 8 tchd 5 to 2) 2
KNOBBLEENEEZE (v) 8-2 G Carter (1) *led, rdn 2 fs out, hdd and wknd entering fnl furlong*...... (7 to 2 op 9 to 4) 3
4665a[6] NORTH ARDAR 8-2 R P Elliott (11) *in tch, effrt and hdwy 3 fs out, rdn and one pace fnl 2 furlongs.* ....(9 to 1 op 11 to 1 tchd 8 to 1) 4
FOREST SONG 7-10[4] (3*) D Harrison (7) *outpcd and beh till styd on fnl 2 fs*.......... (5 to 1 op 3 to 1) 5
MISS DELIVERY 7-9[2] N Carlisle (10) *chsd ldrs, rdn hfwy, sn one pace*..........(50 to 1) 6
HONEY JUICE 7-1[1] (7*) Darren Moffatt (8) *nvr rch ldrs.* ....(50 to 1 op 33 to 1) 7
DONTBETALKING (Ire) 7-13 J Quinn (2) *effrt and hdwy hfwy, sn rdn and wknd o'r 2 fs out*.......... (20 to 1) 8
SUPREME SOVIET 7-12 J Fanning (12) *chsd ldrs, rdn 3 fs out, sn wknd*..........(50 to 1 op 33 to 1) 9
WITCHWAY NORTH 7-13 Dale Gibson (6) *slwly into strd and outpcd*..........(50 to 1 op 33 to 1) 10
BARLEY CAKE 8-1 D Holland (9) *cl up till rdn and wknd o'r 2 fs out*..........(9 to 1 op 10 to 1 tchd 8 to 1) 11
HABEEBITTI NADIA 7-9 G Bardwell (5) *beh frm hfwy.* ....(25 to 1 op 16 to 1) 12
Dist: Sht-hd, 4l, 4l, 1½l, 1½l, 1½l, 1l, 1½l, 5l, 4l. 1m 32.30s. a 6.00s (12 Ran).
SR: -/3/-/-/-/-/ (Mrs H Rowbottom), C Tinkler

4696a Robin Hood Apprentice Handicap CLASS F (0-70 3-y-o and up) £2,490 1m.........................(1:10)

TENDRESSE (Ire) [37] 4-7-11 Stephen Davies (12) *in tch, hdwy o'r 2 fs out, led entering fnl final and sn clr.* ....(6 to 1 op 3 to 1) 1
NO COMEBACKS [55] 4-9-1 A Tucker (8) *slwly away and beh, hdwy on outer 3 fs out, styd on wl fnl furlong.* ....(10 to 1 op 7 to 1) 2
SUGEMAR [57] 6-9-3 S D Williams (16) *chsd ldrs, effrt o'r 2 fs out, rdn to ld appr fnl furlong, hdd entering last and one pace*.......... (16 to 1 tchd 20 to 1) 3
4663a* CRESELLY [54] 5-9-0 (5ex) J Fanning (13) *led 2 fs, cl up, ev ch o'r one furlong out, sn rdn and one pace.* ....(2 to 1 fav op 6 to 4 tchd 9 to 4) 4
CANBRACK (Ire) [40] 3-7-12 N Kennedy (14) *al prmnt, effrt to ld briefly one and a half fs out, sn rdn and wknd entering fnl furlong*..........(20 to 1 op 16 to 1) 5
4673a[5] COURTING NEWMARKET [57] 4-9-3 S Drowne (11) *in tch, rdn o'r 3 fs out, kpt on one pace*... (12 to 1 op 16 to 1) 6
ROYAL ACCLAIM [44] (v) 7-7-11 (7*) Michael Bradley (9) *beh till styd on fnl 3 fs*..........(20 to 1) 7
BELIEVE IN ME (Ire) [55] 3-8-13 S Sanders (6) *mid-div, effrt and hdwy o'r 3 fs out, rdn and one pace 2 furlongs out.* ....(20 to 1 tchd 25 to 1) 8
BIDWEAYA (USA) [40] 5-8-0[1] O Pears (3) *in tch, rdn 3 fs out, no imprsn*..........(10 to 1 op 7 to 1) 9
LORD NEPTUNE [50] 3-8-8 R Perham (2) *cl up, led aftr 2 fs to two furlongs out, sn wknd.* ....(8 to 1 op 20 to 1 tchd 25 to 1) 10
4663a STAIRWAY TO HEAVEN (Ire) [51] (bl) 4-8-11 V Halliday (10) *beh, effrt and rdn 2 fs out, no hdwy.* (12 to 1 op 8 to 1) 11
GOLD BELT (Ire) [42] 3-8-0 M Humphries (7) *al rear.* ....(20 to 1 op 16 to 1) 12
LITTLEWICK (Ire) [59] 3-9-3 F Norton (1) *nvr rch ldrs.* ....(20 to 1 op 10 to 1) 13
4663a SNO SERENADE [66] 6-9-8 (4*) J Marshall (15) *chsd ldrs, rdn hfwy, sn wknd*..........(33 to 1 op 20 to 1) 14
RED INK [52] 3-8-10 D Harrison (4) *chsd ldrs till wknd quickly hfwy, sn beh*..........(14 to 1 op 10 to 1) 15
Dist: 5l, hd, 2½l, 1½l, ½l, 1l, hd, 4l, 3l, sht-hd. 1m 44.80s. a 5.30s (15 Ran).
SR: 4/7/8/-/-/-/ (C John Hill), C J Hill

4697a Friar Tuck Claiming Stakes (Div II) CLASS F (2-y-o) £2,385 7f.....(1:40)

GOLDEN KLAIR 7-9 G Bardwell (8) *mid-div, pushed alng hfwy, gd hdwy o'r 2 fs out, led appr fnl furlong, ran on wl*..........(5 to 1 op 20 to 1 tchd 25 to 1) 1
CERTAIN WAY (Ire) (v) 7-12 J Quinn (3) *chsd ldrs, hdwy and ev ch one and a half fs out, sn rdn and kpt on.* ....(12 to 1 op 8 to 1) 2
MARK'S CLUB (Ire) 7-11 (7*) V Halliday (6) *beh, hdwy 3 fs out, rdn and styd on one pace fnl 2 furlongs.* ....(11 to 2 op 3 to 1 tchd 6 to 1) 3
4661a[6] GOODBYE MILLIE 7-2[2] (7*) D Wright (7) *beh, effrt and hdwy 3 fs out, kpt on one pace fnl 2 furlongs.* ....(7 to 1 tchd 6 to 1) 4
NANCY (Ire) 7-4[4] (7*) Claire Balding (9) *beh till styd on fnl 2 fs*..........(16 to 1 op 8 to 1) 5
4677a[3] FESTIN (bl) 8-4 Dale Gibson (1) *sn led, rdn o'r 2 fs out, soon hdd and wknd.* (5 to 2 fav op 2 to 1 tchd 3 to 1) 6
MAASTRICHT 8-6 Dean McKeown (11) *cl up, ev ch o'r 2 fs out, sn rdn and wknd.* (11 to 2 op 3 to 1 tchd 13 to 2) 7
GENESIS FOUR (bl) 7-11 (3*) F Norton (5) *chsd ldrs till rdn and wknd o'r 3 fs out*..........(33 to 1) 8
SWIFT REVENGE 7-7[3] (5*) B Doyle (2) *in tch to hfwy.* ....(20 to 1) 9
DICKINS 8-8 J Carroll (4) *sn outpcd and beh.* ....(16 to 1 op 14 to 1) 10
ELEGANT ELLIE (e/s) 7-11 S Wood (10) *chsd ldrs 2 fs, sn lost pl and beh frm hfwy*..........(16 to 1) 11
Dist: 2½l, 7l, 1½l, 1l, 2½l, 2½l, 8l, 4l, 1½l, 4l. 1m 29.90s. a 3.60s (11 Ran).
SR: 27/22/7/-/-/-/ (C John Hill), C J Hill

4698a William Stones Handicap CLASS F (0-70 3-y-o and up) £2,448 2m (2:10)

QUALITAIR RHYTHM (Ire) [50] 4-8-10 (7*) G Mitchell (10) *trkd ldrs, gd hdwy 3 fs out, effrt 2 furlongs, rdn to ld ins fnl furlong, ran on wl.* (11 to 8 fav op 6 to 4 tchd 2 to 1) 1
4662a LORD ADVOCATE [42] (v) 4-8-6 (3*) D Harrison (9) *trkd ldrs, hdwy o'r 4 fs out, sn led, rdn clr 2 furlongs out, hdd and no extr ins last*..........(12 to 1 op 20 to 1) 2
MOOT POINT (USA) [61] (bl) 4-10-0 G Baxter (4) *hld up, gd hdwy 6 fs out, rdn 2 furlongs out, kpt on one pace.* ....(13 to 2 op 6 to 1 tchd 7 to 1) 3
SULUK (USA) [42] 7-8-2 (7*) M Humphries (11) *hld up and beh, gd hdwy 4 fs out, rdn and kpt on one pace fnl 2 furlongs*..........(12 to 1 op 8 to 1 tchd 14 to 1) 4
BALAAT (USA) [48] 4-8-10 (5*) S D Williams (5) *hld up, hdwy hfwy, rdn and ev ch 3 fs out, one pace, wknd fnl 2 furlongs*..........(9 to 1 op 16 to 1 tchd 8 to 1) 5
AS ALWAYS (Ire) [38] 4-8-5 S Webster (3) *led till 5 fs out, sn wknd*..........(20 to 1) 6
POST IMPRESSIONIST (Ire) [59] 3-9-3 D Holland (8) *cl up, led 5 fs out, hdd o'r 3 furlongs out, sn rdn and wknd.* ....(7 to 2 op 3 to 1) 7
BLYTON STAR (Ire) [38] 4-8-5 S Wood (2) *trkd ldrs, rdn alng 6 fs out, wknd 3 furlongs out*..........(33 to 1) 8
SPRING FORWARD [29] (v) 8-7-10 J Quinn (6) *lost pl hfwy, sn tld off*..........(33 to 1) 9
Dist: 1l, 5l, 1l, 5l, 2½l, nk, ¾l. 3m 48.50s. a 22.00s (9 Ran).
(R A Newson), I Campbell

4699a Maid Marion Claiming Handicap CLASS F (0-60 3-y-o and up) £2,616 6f.........................(2:40)

KLAIROVER [42] 5-8-11 D Holland (7) *in tch, hdwy o'r 2 fs out, str run to ld ins fnl furlong, ran on.* ....(8 to 1 op 5 to 1 tchd 9 to 1) 1
MISS CALCULATE [58] 4-9-13 J Fanning (5) *hdwy hfwy, led 2 fs out, rdn appr fnl furlong, hdd and no extr ins last*..........(14 to 1) 2
4660a[6] SWINGING TICH [47] 3-8-8 (7*) S Sanders (13) *mid-div, hdwy on outer o'r 2 fs out, sn rdn and ev ch, not quicken entering fnl furlong*...... (8 to 1 op 16 to 1) 3
SAKHAROV [41] 3-8-9 A Munro (3) *in tch on inner whn hmpd aftr one furlong, hdwy 2 fs out, kpt on.* ....(16 to 1 op 12 to 1 tchd 20 to 1) 4
4664a[4] THE DREAM MAKER (Ire) [47] 3-8-8 (7*) M Humphries (6) *beh, hdwy o'r 2 fs out, styd on fnl furlong.* ....(8 to 1 op 5 to 1) 5
4663a[8] BLACK BOY (Ire) [53] 3-9-2 (5*) S D Williams (16) *chsd ldrs, rdn o'r 2 fs out, sn one pace*...... (14 to 1 op 10 to 1) 6
4664a[6] STRIP CARTOON (Ire) [53] (bl) 4-9-1 (7*) M Harris (4) *led till hdd 2 fs out, grad wknd*...... (8 to 1 tchd 9 to 1) 7
4664a[2] QUATRE FEMME [58] 5-9-13 Dean McKeown (10) *cl up till rdn and wknd o'r 2 fs out*..........(8 to 1 op 5 to 1) 8
JUDGEMENT CALL [50] 5-8-12 (7*) T G McLaughlin (2) *chsd ldrs, rdn and one pace fnl 2 fs*.......... (16 to 1) 9
SHANAKEE [49] 5-8-13 (5*) A Tucker (1) *outpcd and beh till styd on fnl 2 fs*.......... (33 to 1) 10
MONSCOMA (Ire) [43] 4-8-12 A McGlone (11) *al rear.* ....(33 to 1) 11
LIFE'S A BREEZE [43] 3-8-11 G Carter (12) *chsd ldrs 3 fs, sn wknd*.......... (8 to 1 op 7 to 1 tchd 9 to 1) 12

NORDOORA (Ire) [40] 3-8-8 A Proud (14) *prmnt to hfwy.* .... (10 to 1 op 7 to 1) 13
MU-ARRIK [48] (v) 4-9-3 S Morris (8) *cl up, effrt and ev ch 2 fs out, sn rdn and wknd appr fnl furlong.* ....(5 to 1 fav op 7 to 1 tchd 8 to 1) 14
SUPER-SUB [41] 3-8-9 J Carroll (9) *al rear*....... (33 to 1) 15
CELLITO (Ire) [51] (bl) 3-9-2 (3*) Emma O'Gorman (15) *al beh.* .... (16 to 1 op 14 to 1 tchd 20 to 1) 16
Dist: 1l, 1l, 1½l, sht-hd, 4l, sht-hd, 1l, 2½l, hd, nk. 1m 17.30s. a 3.90s (16 Ran).
SR: 19/31/15/3/8/-/ (C John Hill), C J Hill

4700a Little John Maiden Stakes CLASS F (2-y-o) £2,616 5f..............(3:10)

TANAGOME (USA) (v) 8-9 (5*) O Pears (12) *rdn alng to chase ldrs stands side, styd on strly to ld ins fnl furlong, cmftbly*...........(9 to 2 op 6 to 1 tchd 7 to 1) 1
BROADSTAIRS BEAUTY (Ire) 8-9 (5*) S D Williams (13) *o'rall ldr stands side, clr 2 fs out, rdn, hdd and no extr ins last*.................(9 to 1 op 16 to 1 tchd 8 to 1) 2
JOCKS JOKER 9-0 G Carter (5) *al prmnt, rdn and not quicken appr fnl furlong.* .... (9 to 1 op 7 to 1 tchd 10 to 1) 3
4668a[5] GORODENKA BOY 8-7 (7*) Kim McDonnell (7) *al prmnt, rdn and one pace appr fnl furlong.* .... (9 to 1 op 7 to 1 tchd 10 to 1) 4
MISS GORGEOUS (Ire) 8-6 (3*) Emma O'Gorman (6) *chsd ldrs, rdn and one pace fnl 2 fs*....... (6 to 1 op 4 to 1) 5
WESSHAUN 8-2 (7*) T G McLaughlin (2) *mid-div, rdn 2 fs out, kpt on*.................................(33 to 1) 6
PALACEGATE GIRL 8-9 J Carroll (4) *gd speed far side for o'r 3 fs*..............(7 to 2 fav op 5 to 2 tchd 9 to 4) 7
MUSICAL TIMES 8-9 Dean McKeown (1) *chsd ldrs far side o'r 3 fs*,.......................... (10 to 1 op 7 to 1) 8
JOELLISE 8-2 (7*) Claire Balding (9) *in tch far side, rdn 2 fs out, one pace*...............................(33 to 1) 9
SAFE BID 8-4[2] (7*) Carl Llewellyn (14) *chsd ldrs centre 3 fs.* ....(14 to 1) 10
PERFECTLY ENTITLED (Ire) 8-9 G Bardwell (15) *prmnt 3 fs.* ....(20 to 1) 11
ROMEO OSCAR 9-0 M Wood (3) *slwly into strd, nvr dngrs*.............................. (9 to 2 op 2 to 1) 12
MANADEL (bl) 8-9 S Webster (11) *al rear*.........(33 to 1) 13
MECONOPSIS 8-9 J Fanning (8) *chsd ldrs to hfwy, sn wknd*...........................(33 to 1 op 20 to 1) 14
ESS-PEE-CEE 8-4 (5*) A Garth (10) *al rear, hng badly lft hfwy, tld off fnl 2 fs*........................ (33 to 1) 15
Dist: 2l, 1½l, 1l, 2l, 1l, 1½l, 2l, sht-hd, 5l, sht-hd. 59.10s. a 0.80s (15 Ran).
SR: 34/26/20/16/3/-/ (S G Norton), S G Norton

4701a Sherwood Forest Handicap CLASS F (0-70 3-y-o and up) £2,532 5f (3:40)

LE CHIC [42] 6-8-2 S Wood (7) *cl up centre, led 2 fs out, quickened clr fnl furlong*.........(14 to 1 op 11 to 1) 1
4666a[3] PEERAGE PRINCE [64] (bl) 3-9-10 A Munro (12) *chsd ldrs stands side, effrt and ev ch appr fnl furlong, sn rdn and not quicken*...............(7 to 2 fav op 5 to 1) 2
4672a[9] DOESYOUDOES [60] (v) 3-8-13 (7*) Kim McDonnell (15) *o'rall ldr stands side, rdn and hdd 2 fs out, kpt on one pace*...(20 to 1) 3
JOE SUGDEN [55] 8-9-1 N Carlisle (10) *beh till styd on fnl 2 fs*....................(9 to 1 op 8 to 1 tchd 10 to 1) 4
SAMMY SLEW (USA) [54] 3-9-0 M Wood (6) *mid-div, rdn and styd on fnl 2 fs*.............. (20 to 1 op 16 to 1) 5
LINCSTONE BOY (Ire) [54] (v) 4-9-0 S Webster (1) *cl up far side till rdn and wknd o'r one furlong out.* ....(8 to 1 op 6 to 1) 6
4664a[5] DON'T RUN ME OVER [46] 3-7-13 (7*) S Sanders (2) *prmnt far side till rdn and wknd o'r one furlong out.* .... (12 to 1 op 10 to 1) 7
STAMSHAW [39] 3-7-6 (7*) J Bramhill (8) *slwly into strd, styd on fnl 2 fs*................... (33 to 1 op 25 to 1) 8
ROCK OPERA (Ire) [58] 4-9-1 (3*) D Harrison (9) *beh till styd on fnl 2 fs*......................... (9 to 1 op 6 to 1) 9
4672a[6] INSWINGER [40] 6-8-0 G Bardwell (4) *nvr rch ldrs.* .... (14 to 1 op 10 to 1) 10
JOHN O'DREAMS [43] (v) 7-8-3 G Carter (11) *nvr a factor.* ....(10 to 1 tchd 12 to 1) 11
IMCO DOUBLE (Ire) [61] 4-9-7 J McLaughlin (14) *nvr dngrs.* ....(16 to 1) 12
HINARI VIDEO [50] 7-8-10 Dean McKeown (16) *cl up stands side 3 fs, sn wknd*....... (4 to 1 op 9 to 2 tchd 6 to 1) 13
SIMMIE'S SPECIAL [57] 4-8-12 (5*) A Garth (3) *cl up far side 3 fs, grad wknd*.................. (14 to 1 op 12 to 1) 14
ALDINGTON PEACH [48] 3-8-8[1] J Carroll (13) *chsd ldrs, rdn hfwy, sn wknd*...................(33 to 1 op 25 to 1) 15
Dist: 3l, ½l, 1½l, ½l, hd, hd, hd, 1l, nk, ¾l. 58.90s. a 0.60s (15 Ran).
SR: 26/36/30/19/16/15/6/-/13/ (John Wilman), D W Chapman

CAPANNELLE (ITY) (heavy)
Sunday November 22nd

4702a Premio Umbria (Group 3) (2-y-o and up) £30,028 6f................(1:45)

SWING LOW (bl) 3-9-7 T Quinn, *rcd in 3rd on rls, took second 2 out, str brst to ld wl ins fnl furlong*.......... 1
ARRANVANA 4-9-3 V Mezzatesta, *rcd in second, led aftr one and a half fs till wl ins last, ran on one pace*..... 2
FLIGHT OF DESTINY 6-9-7 Jacqueline Freda, *mid-div, 3rd 2 out, kpt on one pace*.......... 3
HANTAYO YO (Ity) 6-9-7 A Luongo, *5th 2 fs out, not pace to trble ldrs*.......... 4
RUSVON (Ity) 3-9-7 D Zarroli, *led one and a half fs, grad wknd*.......... 5
CRACK REGIMENT (USA) 4-9-7 M Boutin, *mid-div, 4th 2 fs out, not quicken*.......... 6
SECRET THING (USA) 3-9-7 B Jovine, *al toward rear*..... 7
PIZZA CONNECTION 2-8-4 D Holland, *mid-div, nvr trbld ldrs*.......... 8
PUNCH N'RUN 4-9-7 M Latorre, *al rear*.......... 9
VINTAGE ONLY 4-9-7 A Corniani, *al rear*.......... 10
Dist: 2½l, 3½l, 1l, 2 ¼l, ½l, 2 ¼l, 1 ¾l, 1l, sht-hd. 1m 11.40s. (10 Ran).
(D B Gallop), R Hannon

4703a Premio Guido Berardelli (Group 2) (2-y-o) £34,886 1¼m..........(2:10)

WOOTTON RIVERS (USA) 8-11 D Holland, *11th strt, hdwy on outsd 4 fs out, led wl o'r 2 out, quickened clr*....... 1
MR RICHARD (Ire) 8-11 D Zarroli, *tenth strt, hdwy to chal 3 out, kpt on one pace last 2 fs*.......... 2
MAD MARTIGAN 8-11 Jacqueline Freda, *mid-div, 8th strt, hdwy 4 out, rdn and one pace fnl 2 fs*.......... 3
WISE COMMANCHE (Ity) 8-11 B Jovine, *trkd ldrs, 4th strt, effrt on outsd 3 fs out, hrd rdn and not quicken*....... 4
SABALIMAN (Ity) 8-11 A Luongo, *12th strt, gd hdwy on ins to chal 3 fs out, sn rdn and one pace*.......... 5
CAMPALTO (Ire) 8-11 , *5th strt, effrt 3 fs out, sn one pace.* 6
IMCO ACE (Ity) 8-11 V Mezzatesta, *7th strt on ins, no prog last 3 fs*.......... 7
DARK STREET (Ire) 8-11 M Jerome, *9th strt, nvr a factor.* 8
FRESCADE (USA) 8-11 A Munro, *led to 3 fs out, sn wknd.* 9
FUTURBALLA 8-11 T Quinn, *trkd ldrs, second strt, rdn and wknd wl o'r 2 fs out*.......... 10
BOBBIE DEE 8-8 J Williams, *prmnt, 3rd strt, wknd quickly last 3 fs*.......... 11
MINNESANG (USA) 8-11 , *4th strt, sn btn*.......... 12
Dist: 3½l, 3l, 5l, 1½l, 2½l, 1l, ½l, nk, 8l, 2½l. 2m 10.90s. (12 Ran).
(R E Sangster), P W Chapple-Hyam

TURIN (ITY) (soft)
Sunday November 22nd

4704a Premio Avv. Amedeo Peyron (Listed) (2-y-o) £20,911 1m....... (2:50)

JOHNNY STECCHINO (USA) 8-11 S Soto,.......... 1
ÇAPTAIN LE SAUX (Ire) 8-11 C Bertolini,.......... 2
STEVE CURTIS (Ity) 8-11 S Dettori,.......... 3
CANTON JUDGE (Ire) 8-11 P G Alford,.......... 4
CRESTA TREMENDOUS (USA) 8-11 ,.......... 5
VISCARDO (Ire) 8-11 ,.......... 6
ADMIRAL FROBISHER (USA) 8-11 ,.......... 7
FUTURE STORM (USA) 8-11 ,.......... 8
BESABEL (Ity) 8-11 ,.......... 9
LADY OUNAVARRA (Ire) 8-11 ,.......... 10
BOURBON JACK 8-11 ,.......... 11
Dist: ½l, 3l, nk, 2l, ½l, 2l, 3l, 3½l, 2 ¼l, dist. 1m 41.00s. (11 Ran).
(Scuderia Lady M), L D'Auria

SOUTHWELL (A.W) (std)
Tuesday November 24th
Going Correction: NIL

4705a Groundsmen Handicap CLASS F (0-70 3-y-o and up) £2,595 1m (1:10)

DON'T DROP BOMBS (USA) [35] (v) 3-7-8 Dale Gibson (13) *mid-div, hdwy o'r 3 fs out, rdn to ld entering last, ran on*.......................... (10 to 1 op 16 to 1) 1
4670a* LOOKINGFORARAINBOW (Ire) [59] 4-9-6 N Day (14) *beh, hdwy 3 fs out, effrt 2 out, ev ch entering last, kpt on.* .... (12 to 1 op 6 to 1) 2
HENIU (USA) [55] (v) 3-9-0 A Munro (11) *cl up, led aftr 2 fs, rdn two out, hdd and no extr entering last.* .... (14 to 1 op 10 to 1) 3
LOCK KEEPER (USA) [55] 6-9-2 G Carter (16) *prmnt, rdn 2 fs out, kpt on one pace*........... (14 to 1 op 10 to 1) 4
SALMAN (USA) [42] 6-7-10 (7*) D Wright (10) *mid-div, hdwy 3 fs out, rdn and kpt on one pace frm 2 out.* .... (10 to 1 op 7 to 1) 5
4696a* TENDRESSE (Ire) [37] 4-7-12 D Holland (3) *slwly into strd, hdwy hfwy, rdn and one pace 2 fs out.* ....(6 to 5 fav op 6 to 4 tchd 13 to 8) 6
SOVEREIGN NICHE (Ire) [36] 4-7-11 J Fanning (1) *al mid-div*..........................(8 to 1 tchd 11 to 1) 7
4699a MU-ARRIK [48] 4-8-2 (7*) G Parkin (4) *nvr rch ldrs.* .... (12 to 1 op 10 to 1) 8

4699a SHANAKEE [49] 5-8-5 (5*) A Tucker (12) *nvr rch ldrs.* ....(25 to 1) 9
INDIAN MAESTRO [43] 6-8-4 K Darley (15) *prmnt, rdn 3 fs out, sn wknd*....................(33 to 1) 10
4696a^{8} BELIEVE IN ME (Ire) [55] 3-9-0 T Quinn (2) *al rear.* (25 to 1) 11
GOLD SURPRISE (Ire) [54] 3-8-13 Dean McKeown (8) *chsd ldrs to hfwy, sn wknd.* ....(11 to 1 op 12 to 1 tchd 14 to 1) 12
4689a TANCRED GRANGE [56] 3-8-10 (5*) O Pears (7) *prmnt 3 fs, sn wknd*..........(16 to 1 op 20 to 1 tchd 25 to 1) 13
GLASGOW [51] 3-8-10 J Quinn (9) *sn beh.* ....(20 to 1 op 16 to 1) 14
SHANNON EXPRESS [63] 5-9-10 M Hills (5) *led 2 fs, cl up till rdn and wknd 3 out*.......... (20 to 1 op 25 to 1) 15
4681a LORD NASKRA (USA) [61] 3-9-3 (3*) Emma O'Gorman (6) *al rear*....................(20 to 1 op 16 to 1) 16

Dist: ¾l, 1l, 5l, ½l, 5l, nk, 2½l, 1l, 7l, 3½l. 1m 43.30s. a 3.80s (16 Ran).
SR: 23/47/38/25/10/-/ (Mrs S C York), A A Scott

4706a Bob Lee Claiming Stakes CLASS F (3-y-o and up) £2,448 5f.......(1:40)

4666a CRECHE (bl) 3-9-7 N Day (5) *al prmnt, rdn o'r 2 fs out, led appr last, edgd lft and ran on.* ....(11 to 1 op 8 to 1 tchd 12 to 1) 1
4666a^{8} ANOTHER EPISODE (Ire) 3-9-1 J Carroll (1) *quickly away, led, tacked rght to stands rls aftr one furlong, rdn 2 out, hdd and no extr appr last.* ....(3 to 1 op 5 to 2 tchd 7 to 2) 2
4692a^{4} VERY DICEY (bl) 4-9-1 T Quinn (9) *dwlt, swtchd lft aftr one furlong, hdwy hfwy, sn rdn, kpt on fnl furlong.* ....(5 to 2 fav op 7 to 2) 3
4664a^{3} SAMSOLOM 4-8-7 J Williams (2) *chsd ldrs, rdn and kpt on fnl 2 fs*....................(9 to 1 op 7 to 1) 4
4701a^{3} DOESYOUDOES (v) 3-7-3 (7*) Kim McDonnell (4) *cl up, rdn and wknd appr fnl furlong.* ....(7 to 1 tchd 8 to 1 and 13 to 2) 5
4701a^{8} STAMSHAW 3-7-10 S Wood (11) *dwlt, rdn hfwy, styd on fnl 2 fs*.................... (33 to 1) 6
GOLDEN SICKLE (USA) 3-8-4 (3*) Emma O'Gorman (10) *chsd ldrs to hfwy*.................... (20 to 1 op 16 to 1) 7
BARBARA'S CUTIE (v) 4-7-12 G Bardwell (8) *speed to hfwy.* .... (20 to 1 op 14 to 1) 8
LONELY LASS 6-7-10 J Quinn (7) *al rear*......... (25 to 1) 9
MAID WELCOME (bl) 5-8-8 Dean McKeown (6) *cl up stands rls, rdn 2 fs out, sn wknd*.......... (8 to 1 tchd 10 to 1) 10
4666a SIR TASKER 4-9-1 D Holland (3) *al beh.* ....(11 to 1 op 10 to 1 tchd 12 to 1) 11

Dist: 1½l, hd, 1½l, 1l, 1½l, ¾l, sht-hd, 1l, nk, 3½l. 1m 1.00s. a 2.70s (11 Ran).
SR: 53/41/40/26/11/5/13/3/-/ (Brian Pollins), Mrs N Macauley

4707a Simon Davis Handicap CLASS F (0-70 3-y-o and up) £2,658 1½m ....(2:10)

MODEST HOPE (USA) [49] 5-8-6 (5*) A Garth (1) *al prmnt, chlgd 2 fs out, sn led, styd on wl.* ....(6 to 1 op 7 to 1 tchd 8 to 1) 1
EMPEROR ALEXANDER (Ire) [60] 4-9-8 A Munro (6) *al prmnt, rdn o'r 2 fs out, styd on appr last*......(16 to 1) 2
4688a^{2} TEMPERING [62] 6-9-10 T Quinn (3) *led, rdn 2 fs out, sn hdd and one pace*................ (8 to 1 tchd 10 to 1) 3
EUROTWIST [65] 3-9-7 K Darley (9) *hld up beh, hdwy hfwy, rdn and one pace fnl 2 fs.* ....(9 to 1 op 7 to 1 tchd 10 to 1) 4
4698a* QUALITAIR RHYTHM (Ire) [55] 4-8-10 (7*,5ex) G Mitchell (10) *hld up, hdwy hfwy, rdn o'r 2 fs out, sn btn.* ....(2 to 1 fav tchd 5 to 2) 5
4679a* THE KARAOKE KING [60] (bl) 3-9-2 Dale Gibson (12) *beh, rdn and hdwy 5 fs out, styd on one pace frm 3 out.* ....(7 to 1 op 6 to 1) 6
4670a^{5} PUSEY STREET BOY [37] 5-7-13 J Quinn (7) *mid-div, hdwy hfwy, rdn and one pace 3 fs out.* ....(9 to 1 op 8 to 1 tchd 10 to 1) 7
MALENOIR (USA) [53] 4-9-1 Dean McKeown (8) *cl up, rdn alng 5 fs out, hmpd and lost pl o'r 4 out, no ch aftr.* ....(20 to 1) 8
4662a^{9} PETITE BELLE [37] 3-7-0 (7*) D Wright (5) *beh till some hdwy fnl 3 fs*....................(25 to 1) 9
MEDBOURNE (Ire) [37] 3-7-7 S Wood (13) *beh, hdwy hfwy, sn wknd*....................(33 to 1) 10
GESNERA [32] 4-7-8^{1} N Carlisle (15) *al rear.* ....(16 to 1 tchd 20 to 1) 11
NIPOTINA [37] 6-7-6 (7*) F Savage (16) *al beh*..... (25 to 1) 12
INDIAN TERRITORY [48] 3-7-13 (5*) N Gwilliams (14) *al rear.* ....(9 to 1 op 8 to 1 tchd 10 to 1) 13
4696a^{2} NO COMEBACKS [55] 4-9-3 M Hills (4) *al rear.* ....(8 to 1 op 11 to 2 tchd 9 to 1) 14
4688a^{9} FRANCISCAN [42] 5-8-0^{1} (5*) O Pears (11) *chsd ldrs to hfwy, sn wknd*....................(33 to 1) 15
GREAT ABSALOM [40] 3-7-10 J Fanning (2) *pld hrd, chsd ldrs to hfwy, sn wknd*............(33 to 1 op 25 to 1) 16

Dist: ¾l, 4l, 1½l, 4l, 2l, 1½l, nk, ¾l, 6l, 4l. 2m 40.60s. a 6.70s (16 Ran).
SR: 30/39/33/27/15/10/-/5/-/ (J McManamon), R C Spicer

4708a Les Meredith Nursery CLASS F (0-75 2-y-o) £2,427 6f......... (2:40)

4700a^{2} BROADSTAIRS BEAUTY (Ire) [58] 8-5 (5*) S D Williams (7) *cl up, led aftr 2 fs, clr o'r two out, rdn and ran on fnl furlong*.............. (6 to 1 op 4 to 1 tchd 7 to 1) 1
GUSSIE FINK-NOTTLE (Ire) [61] 8-13 K Darley (11) *hdwy hfwy, rdn 2 fs out, ran on wl, not rch wnr.* ....(9 to 2 fav tchd 5 to 1) 2
HERETICAL MISS [62] (bl) 8-11 (3*) R Perham (3) *beh, hdwy hfwy, sn rdn, styd on fnl furlong.* (7 to 1 tchd 8 to 1) 3
4687a* BRIGHT GEM [55] 8-7 (7ex) J Fanning (13) *chsd ldrs, effrt and ev ch o'r 2 fs out, sn rdn and one pace.* ....(7 to 1 tchd 8 to 1) 4
4700a^{3} JOCKS JOKER [60] 8-12 G Carter (8) *led 2 fs, cl up, rdn o'r two out, wknd*....................(7 to 1 tchd 8 to 1) 5
4661a^{4} ANOTHER KINGDOM [55] 8-7 J Williams (12) *slwly into strd and beh, hdwy hfwy, rdn and styd on fnl 2 fs.* ....(8 to 1 op 7 to 1) 6
ANUSHA [69] 9-7 J Carroll (1) *outpcd till styd on fnl 2 fs.* ....(5 to 1 op 7 to 2) 7
CASHABLE [56] 8-1 (7*) Kim McDonnell (9) *prmnt to hfwy, sn wknd*.............(12 to 1 op 10 to 1) 8
HERSHEBAR [55] 8-7 S Webster (10) *chsd ldrs 2 fs, sn lost pl*.................... (20 to 1) 9
4677a^{8} LADY OF SHADOWS [44] (bl,e/s) 7-10 J Quinn (6) *cl up till rdn and wknd o'r 2 fs out*......... (14 to 1 op 16 to 1) 10
SWIFTLET (Ire) [54] (bl) 8-3 (3*) D Harrison (2) *al rear.* ....(16 to 1) 11
4700a^{8} MUSICAL TIMES [65] 9-3 Dean McKeown (5) *al rear.* .... (16 to 1 op 14 to 1 tchd 20 to 1) 12
MATTHEW DAVID [66] 8-11 (7*) J Marshall (4) *al rear.* .... (16 to 1 op 14 to 1) 13

Dist: 1½l, 6l, ½l, ¾l, 1l, 2l, ¾l, nk, 2l, 1l. 1m 17.40s. a 4.00s (13 Ran).
SR: 16/13/-/-/-/-/ (Mrs Judy Hunt), M C Chapman

4709a Robert Clay Maiden Stakes CLASS F (2-y-o) £2,301 1m...........(3:10)

4676a^{8} PRECUSSION 9-0 B Crossley (4) *slwly into strd, sn pushed alng, hdwy 3 fs out, led ins last, soon clr.* ....(8 to 1 tchd 10 to 1) 1
4691a^{4} ANN HILL (Ire) 8-9 A Munro (1) *outpcd and beh till styd on strly fnl 2 fs*....................(4 to 1 op 7 to 2) 2
4665a^{2} BUGLET 8-9 N Day (8) *in tch, hdwy 3 fs out, chlgd 2 out, sn rdn, ev ch till wknd ins last.* ....(5 to 2 fav tchd 11 to 4) 3
4677a^{7} NANNY MARGARET (Ire) (bl) 8-9 G Bardwell (3) *dsptd ld, led hfwy, hrd rdn 2 fs out, hdd and wknd ins last.* ....(16 to 1 op 14 to 1) 4
4675a^{3} HILLSDOWN BOY (Ire) (bl,e/s) 9-0 T Quinn (7) *dsptd ld to hfwy, cl up, ev ch 2 fs out, sn hrd rdn, wknd entering last*....................(8 to 1 op 6 to 1) 5
JOY OF FREEDOM 8-4 (5*) B Doyle (2) *chsd ldrs, rdn and wknd o'r 3 fs out*..................(10 to 1 op 7 to 1) 6
WORKING TITLE (Ire) 9-0 M Hills (5) *chsd ldrs, rdn and wknd o'r 3 fs out*............(7 to 2 op 3 to 1) 7
STEPPE CLOSER 8-9 Dean McKeown (6) *prmnt, rdn hfwy, sn wknd*....................(9 to 2 op 7 to 2) 8

Dist: 3l, ¾l, sht-hd, 2l, 3l, 10l, 2l. 1m 45.80s. a 6.30s (8 Ran).
SR: 6/-/-/-/-/ (Dr Meou Tsen Geoffrey Yeh), R W Armstrong

4710a Kevin Voce Handicap CLASS F (0-70 3-y-o and up) £2,490 7f....... (3:40)

4690a^{2} DEBSY DO (USA) [66] 3-9-3 (5*) O Pears (10) *chsd ldrs, hdwy 2 fs out, rdn to ld wl ins last, ran on.* ....(9 to 2 op 4 to 1 tchd 7 to 2 and 5 to 1) 1
JOHNSTON'S EXPRESS (Ire) [37] 4-7-9^{1} J Quinn (7) *chsd ldrs, hdwy 3 fs out, led one and a half out, sn rdn, hdd and no extr wl ins last*..............(10 to 1 op 8 to 1) 2
4699a* KLAIROVER [47] 5-8-5 (5ex) D Holland (6) *beh, hdwy 3 fs out, ev ch appr last, sn rdn, kpt on.* ....(4 to 1 fav op 9 to 2 tchd 6 to 1) 3
4690a^{5} SANDMOOR DENIM [59] 5-9-3 S Webster (11) *in tch, hdwy o'r 2 fs out, rdn appr last, kpt on.* ....(9 to 2 op 5 to 1 tchd 6 to 1) 4
4696a^{3} SUGEMAR [57] 6-8-10 (5*) S D Williams (12) *in tch, hdwy 3 fs out, sn rdn and one pace.* ....(7 to 1 op 6 to 1 tchd 8 to 1) 5
4690a^{4} EAST BARNS (Ire) [45] (bl) 4-8-3 K Darley (5) *outpcd, hdwy 3 fs out, sn rdn, kpt on one pace frm 2 out.* ....(9 to 1 op 7 to 1 tchd 10 to 1) 6
4699a^{5} THE DREAM MAKER (Ire) [51] 3-8-0 (7*) M Humphries (2) *beh till styd on fnl 2 fs*..............(14 to 1 tchd 16 to 1) 7
4690a COMPANY CASH [55] (bl) 4-8-13 Dean McKeown (4) *led, rdn 2 fs out, sn hdd and wknd*.....(20 to 1 op 16 to 1) 8
4690a^{7} HARD SELL [60] 5-9-4 J Fanning (8) *nvr rch ldrs.* ....(16 to 1 op 10 to 1) 9
4690a^{3} PESIDANAMICH (Ire) [70] (bl) 4-9-9 (5*) Stephen Davies (9) *chsd ldr, rdn o'r 2 fs out, sn wknd.* (10 to 1 op 8 to 1) 10
4663a^{9} KUMMEL KING [58] 4-9-2 M Hills (3) *cl up, rdn and wknd o'r 3 fs out*..........(12 to 1 op 10 to 1) 11
REZA [37] 4-7-9^{2} G Bardwell (14) *sn outpcd, al rear.* ....(20 to 1 tchd 33 to 1) 12
4678a OLD FOX (Fr) [40] 3-7-10 Dale Gibson (13) *al rear.* .... (33 to 1 op 25 to 1) 13
VERRO (USA) [36] (bl) 5-7-8^{1} N Carlisle (1) *beh hfwy.* ....(12 to 1 op 14 to 1 tchd 10 to 1) 14

Dist: Hd, ½l, hd, 5l, 1½l, ½l, 3l, 1½l, ½l, 4l. 1m 30.40s. a 4.10s (14 Ran).

SR: 47/19/27/38/21/4/6/3/3/ (S G Norton), S G Norton

ST-CLOUD (FR) (heavy)
Tuesday November 24th
Going Correction: PLUS 2.00 sec. per fur.

4711a Prix Fille de l'Air (Group 3) (3-y-o and up) £20,555 1¼m 110yds. .(1:35)

HALESIA (USA) 3-8-9 D Boeuf (11) *mid-div, 4th strt, hdwy wl o'r one and a half fs out, led one and a half out, ran on well*..........(6 to 4 fav) 1
ON CREDIT (Fr) 4-8-11 E Legrix (12) *mid-div, 8 strt, hdwy o'r one furlong out, ran on wl fnl furlong*....(74 to 10) 2
LUPESCU 4-8-11 W R Swinburn (6) *al wl plcd, 5th strt, effrt 2 fs out, ran on well fnl furlong*.........(43 to 10) 3
SECONDE BLEUE 4-8-11 T Jarnet (14) *mid-div, quickened 2 fs out, ran on fnl furlong*..........(14 to 1) 4
IRISH SOURCE 3-8-9 O Peslier (7) *mid-div, led 2 fs out, hdd one and a half out, one pace*............(22 to 1) 5
SALAAM (Spa) 4-8-11 G Guignard (9) *some late hdwy*. ....(48 to 1) 6
LA TIRANA (Fr) 5-8-11 W Mongil (8) *nvr dngrs*...(97 to 10) 7
RIVER NYMPH (USA) 3-9-2 M Boutin (10) *nvr dngrs*. ....(18 to 10) 8
RENASHAAN (Fr) 3-8-9 G Dubroeucq (15) *al beh.* (78 to 10) 9
STOP PRESS (USA) 4-8-11 C Asmussen (3) *led till o'r 2 fs out*..........(18 to 1) 10
JDAAYEL 3-8-9 W Carson (2) *al prmnt, second strt, led briefly o'r 2 fs out till two out, wknd quickly*. (10 to 1) 11
POLYXENA (USA) 3-8-9 O Doleuze (4) *mid-div till wknd strt*..........(78 to 10) 12
CIUDADELLA (Fr) 3-8-9 C Le Scrill (13) *al rear*.... (63 to 1) 13
ALHENA (Fr) 3-8-9 E Saint-Martin (5) *nvr a factor*. (29 to 1) 14
IONIAN SEA 3-8-9 M de Smyter (1) *prmnt till wknd strt*. ....(50 to 1) 15

Dist: 1½l, 1½l, 2l, 2½l, 2½l, ¾l, 2l, ¾l, ¾l. 2m 34.00s. a 23.00s (15 Ran).
SR: 75/74/71/67/60/57/55/56/47/ (D Wildenstein), E Lellouche

EVRY (FR) (heavy)
Wednesday November 25th
Going Correction: PLUS 1.10 sec. per fur.

4712a Prix Contessina (Listed) (2-y-o) £12,333 6f 110yds............ (1:40)

NIGHT JAR 9-4 A Munro,.......... 1
TABAC (USA) 9-7 T Jarnet,.......... 2
SHIVAREE (Fr) 9-7 M Boutin,.......... 3
ISAIAH 9-7 G Guignard,.......... 4

Dist: ½l, 5l, hd, ½l, 1l, sht-hd, sht-nk, 15l. 1m 25.68s. a 9.28s (9 Ran).
SR: 61/62/42/41/ (J T Thomas), Lord Huntingdon

4713a Prix Isonomy (Listed) (2-y-o) £12,333 1m 1f................ (2:35)

SIN KIANG (Fr) 8-9 T Jarnet,.......... 1
NICOTERA (Ire) 8-6 W Mongil,.......... 2
BETAFEU (USA) 8-6 M Boutin,.......... 3
BUZZATI (USA) 8-9 O Doleuze,.......... 4

Dist: 2½l, ½l, sht-nk, 4l. 2m 7.56s. a 16.56s (5 Ran).
(Mme Y Seydoux de Clausonne), A Fabre

SOUTHWELL (A.W) (std)
Friday November 27th
Going Correction: PLUS 0.05 sec. per fur. (races 1,2,3,4,5), MINUS 0.15 (6)

4714a Daffodil Handicap CLASS F (3-y-o and up) £2,280 1¾m.........(12:50)

HIGHLAND FANTASY (USA) [71] (bl) 3-9-1 D Holland (3) *made all, shaken up appr strt, clr o'r one furlong out, styd on wl, eased cl hme.* .... (7 to 4 fav op 2 to 1 tchd 3 to 1 and 13 to 8) 1
FIVE TO SEVEN (USA) [83] 3-9-8 (5*) O Pears (7) *chsd ldrs, improved o'r 3 fs out, sn rdn alng, styd on ins last.* ....(4 to 1 op 9 to 4 tchd 5 to 1) 2
MAAMUR (USA) [71] 4-9-3 (5*) Stephen Davies (1) *trkd ldg pair, pushed alng o'r 5 fs out, one pace entering strt.* ....(5 to 1 op 4 to 1 tchd 6 to 1) 3
4698a^{5} BALAAT (USA) [48] 4-7-13 S Wood (5) *hld up in tch, rdn to improve o'r 4 fs out, not quicken entering strt.* ....(14 to 1 op 12 to 1 tchd 16 to 1) 4
4688a^{3} JALORE [49] 3-7-7^{7} (7*) M Humphries (4) *hld up and beh, hdwy fnl 3 fs, nvr nr to chal*.......(10 to 1 op 8 to 1) 5
SURE HAVEN (Ire) [72] 3-9-2 C Nutter (8) *keen hold, trkd ldr, rdn alng 4 fs out, wknd entering strt.* ....(5 to 1 tchd 4 to 1) 6
HIGH FINANCE [42] 7-7-0 (7*) A Daly (2) *chsd ldrs, sn pushed alng, lost tch hfwy, styd on fnl furlong.* ....(33 to 1 op 20 to 1) 7
4678a^{7} CHARIOTEER [51] 3-7-9 Dale Gibson (6) *in tch, effrt o'r 4 fs out, sn wknd*..........(14 to 1 op 12 to 1) 8
BRIDGE PLAYER [49] 5-8-0 J Quinn (9) *dwlt and beh, struggling hfwy, tld off*........... (10 to 1 op 8 to 1) 9

Dist: ½l, 4l, 3½l, 1l, 8l, 5l, hd, 6l. 3m 10.10s. a 10.10s (9 Ran).
SR: 7/18/5/-/-/-/ (A B Weller), B W Hills

4715a Daisy Claiming Stakes CLASS F (3-y-o and up) £2,490 1½m...... (1:20)

4678a JADE GREEN 3-7-11 S Dawson (4) *settled midfield, hdwy 4 fs out, wide strt, ran on to ld appr last, sn clr.* ....(8 to 1 op 7 to 1 tchd 9 to 1) 1
CONTINUITY 3-7-11 Dale Gibson (11) *beh, rdn to improve 4 fs out, ev ch o'r one out, one pace ins last.* ....(11 to 2 op 5 to 2 tchd 6 to 1) 2
KARAMOJA (bl) 3-9-0 Dean McKeown (1) *chsd ldrs, rdn and ev ch o'r one furlong out, not quicken ins last.* ....(16 to 1 op 10 to 1) 3
MAJESTIC SINCLAIR (Ire) 3-7-12 A Munro (8) *settled mid-field, effrt and rdn o'r 2 fs out, kpt on same pace ins last*..........(8 to 1) 4
4707a^{3} TEMPERING 6-9-3 S Wood (12) *dwlt, sn reco'red to chase ldrs, led entering strt till appr fnl furlong, soon btn.* ....(6 to 1 op 5 to 1) 5
4689a^{2} SILVER SAMURAI 3-8-13 G Baxter (3) *hld up, improved 4 fs out, rdn alng o'r 2 out, wknd last*....(9 to 2 op 6 to 1) 6
4689a* MR WISHING WELL (e/s) 6-8-12 T Quinn (5) *hld up, hdwy 5 fs out, chlgd appr last, wknd quickly.* ....(15 to 8 fav op 5 to 2 tchd 3 to 1) 7
4688a^{4} REACH FOR GLORY 3-8-3 J Fanning (10) *trkd ldrs, cld 6 fs out, rdn alng, wknd appr strt*..... (14 to 1 op 12 to 1) 8
ATLANTIC WAY 4-8-10 G Bardwell (2) *wth ldr, led aftr 2 fs till entering strt, rdn and wknd.* ....(14 to 1 op 12 to 1 tchd 16 to 1) 9
KRONPRINZ (Ire) 4-8-9 (5*) S D Williams (7) *hld up, lost tch hfwy, tld off*..........(33 to 1 op 20 to 1) 10
GREAT NORTH ROAD (e/s) 3-8-7 J McLaughlin (6) *led 2 fs, trkd ldr, drvn alng o'r 6 out, sn wknd, tld off.* ....(50 to 1 op 33 to 1) 11

Dist: 1½l, 1½l, 2½l, 1½l, 1½l, ½l, 6l, ¾l, 25l. 2m 42.20s. a 8.30s (11 Ran).
SR: 6/3/17/-/12/5/3/-/-/ (T W Wellard), P J Makin

4716a Derry Building Services Handicap CLASS F (0-70 3-y-o and up) £2,448 6f.......................... (1:50)

4710a^{2} JOHNSTON'S EXPRESS (Ire) [36] 4-7-12 J Quinn (8) *in tch, hdwy to ld o'r one furlong out, sn clr, easily.* ....(5 to 1 op 4 to 1 tchd 7 to 2) 1
4699a^{3} SWINGING TICH [47] 3-8-8 A Munro (12) *beh, improved entering strt, ran on ins fnl furlong, no ch wth wnr.* ....(8 to 1 op 6 to 1 tchd 9 to 1) 2
4701a^{9} ROCK OPERA (Ire) [58] 4-9-3 (3*) D Harrison (6) *cl up, sn rdn alng and lost pl, styd on o'r one furlong out, nrst finish*..........(9 to 1 op 7 to 1 tchd 10 to 1) 3
4706a^{4} SAMSOLOM [59] 4-9-7 J Williams (9) *hld up, effrt and hdwy o'r 2 fs out, not quicken ins last.* .... (9 to 1 op 11 to 2) 4
4699a^{7} STRIP CARTOON (Ire) [52] (bl) 4-9-0 S Webster (4) *chsd ldr, effrt and rdn entering strt, not quicken o'r one furlong out*.......... (12 to 1 op 10 to 1) 5
4701a JOHN O'DREAMS [43] (v) 7-8-5 G Carter (3) *hld up, drvn to improve entering strt, one pace ins fnl furlong.* ....(10 to 1 op 12 to 1) 6
4692a^{2} WELLSY LAD (USA) [56] 5-9-4 S Wood (10) *in tch, effrt appr strt, wknd fnl 2 fs.* ....(4 to 1 fav op 3 to 1 tchd 5 to 1) 7
FAIR ENCHANTRESS [46] 4-8-8 T Quinn (1) *early pace, sn rdn and lost pl, one pace entering strt.* ....(12 to 1 op 14 to 1 tchd 10 to 1) 8
LYNDON'S LINNET [60] (bl) 4-9-8 A McGlone (2) *sn led and clr, rdn entering strt, hdd o'r one furlong out, fdd.* ....(7 to 1 op 9 to 2) 9
JOVIAL KATE (USA) [63] 5-9-11 M Hills (13) *chsd ldrs, drvn alng hfwy, wknd*.... (12 to 1 op 10 to 1 tchd 14 to 1) 10
4696a^{5} CANBRACK (Ire) [40] 3-7-10 (5*) N Kennedy (7) *sluggish strt, not reco'r*..........(14 to 1) 11
SAVINIEN (Ire) [39] (e/s) 3-8-0 Dale Gibson (5) *slwly into strd, nvr wnt pace, tld off*......... (33 to 1 op 20 to 1) 12

Dist: 5l, 1l, sht-hd, 1l, 1½l, ¾l, 3½l, ½l, 7l, 3½l. 1m 16.30s. a 2.90s (12 Ran).
SR: 32/22/30/30/19/4/14/-/2/ (Frank McKevitt), E J Alston

4717a Tulip Nursery CLASS F (2-y-o) £2,679 1m.................. (2:20)

4697a* GOLDEN KLAIR [49] 7-13 (7ex) G Bardwell (1) *mid-div, drvn alng bef hfwy, hdwy entering strt, ran on to ld one furlong out, sn clr.* (7 to 4 fav tchd 6 to 4 and 9 to 4) 1
4675a* ABSOLUTELY FACT (USA) [66] 9-2 T Quinn (12) *chsd ldrs, led o'r 2 fs out to one out, sn outpcd by wnr.* ....(11 to 2 op 5 to 1 tchd 7 to 1) 2
4697a^{2} CERTAIN WAY (Ire) [52] (v) 8-2 J Quinn (6) *chsd ldrs, effrt and hrd rdn entering strt, one pace fnl 2 fs.* .... (8 to 1 op 10 to 1 tchd 12 to 1) 3

4675a² MISTER BLAKE [56] (bl) 8-3 (3*) Emma O'Gorman (8) *led till o'r 3 fs out, ev ch over 2 out, not quicken.* ....(14 to 1 op 10 to 1) 4
4677a* EXCESS BAGGAGE (Ire) [71] 9-4 (3*) D Harrison (2) *chsd ldrs, effrt entering strt, wknd o'r one furlong out.* ....(7 to 1 op 4 to 1) 5
4697a⁴ GOODBYE MILLIE [59] (v) 8-2 (7*) D Wright (13) *chsd ldrs till rdn and wknd fnl 2 fs*............(20 to 1 op 12 to 1) 6
LOCHORE [58] 8-8 A McGlone (14) *hld up, effrt o'r 3 fs out, no imprsn entering strt.* ....(10 to 1 op 20 to 1 tchd 25 to 1) 7
BRACKENTHWAITE [56] 7-13 (7*) V Halliday (3) *sn beh, drvn alng appr strt, nvr on terms*.........(25 to 1 op 33 to 1) 8
4695a* IRISH ROOTS (Ire) [56] (v) 8-6 (7ex) G Carter (11) *cl up, ev ch o'r 2 fs out, sn wknd*.............(12 to 1 tchd 14 to 1) 9
4665a³ PONDERING [66] (bl,e/s) 8-9 (7*) A Martinez (10) *mid-div, drvn alng hfwy, sn wknd*......... (16 to 1 op 14 to 1) 10
4665a⁵ SHARRO [62] (bl) 8-12 A Munro (5) *wth ldr, led o'r 3 fs out till over 2 out, rdn and sn btn*.....(10 to 1 tchd 8 to 1) 11
4691a⁹ MY BALLYBOY [61] 8-4 (7*) P Bowe (4) *beh, struggling hfwy, tld off*..................(20 to 1 op 16 to 1) 12
4665a⁴ BLOWEDIFIKNOW [62] 8-12 J Williams (9) *mid-div, sn pushed alng, wknd hfwy, tld off*.............(20 to 1) 13
BONNY PRINCESS [49] 7-13 S Dawson (7) *al beh, tld off.* ....(25 to 1 op 20 to 1) 14

Dist: 2l, 5l, ¾l, 5l, 2l, nk, 1l, 1½l, 1½l, 2½l. 1m 44.40s. a 4.90s (14 Ran).
SR: 18/29/-/2/2/-/ (C John Hill), C J Hill

4718a Rose Maiden Stakes CLASS F (2-y-o) £2,364 7f................ (2:50)

SPRING FLYER (Ire) 8-4 (5*) A Tucker (2) *chsd ldg trio, effrt appr strt, hdwy o'r 2 fs out, led over one out, sn clr, eased cl hme*............(9 to 2 op 3 to 1 tchd 5 to 1) 1
4691a³ LAND O'LAKES (Ire) 9-0 C Nutter (5) *sn led, shaken up entering strt, hdd o'r one furlong out, not quicken.* ....(6 to 4 on op Evens tchd 11 to 10) 2
JAMAICA BRIDGE 9-0 J Fanning (6) *trkd ldr, ev ch o'r one furlong out, rdn and one pace ins last.* ....(6 to 1 op 4 to 1) 3
ROSE FLYER (Ire) 8-9 S Webster (4) *cl up, rdn and wknd hfwy*............................ (20 to 1 op 10 to 1) 4
HOTSOCKS 8-9 J McLaughlin (1) *beh, sn pushed alng, nvr able to chal*.........(16 to 1 op 12 to 1 tchd 20 to 1) 5
BALLACASCADE 9-0 Dale Gibson (8) *sluggish strt, sn drvn alng, no imprsn entering strt, tld off.* ....(10 to 1 op 4 to 1) 6
ALTNAHARRA 8-9 Dean McKeown (7) *beh whn pld up aftr 3 fs, dismounted*...........................(5 to 1 op 5 to 2) pu

Dist: 4l, hd, 6l, 7l, 8l. 1m 31.60s. a 5.30s (7 Ran).
SR: 21/14/13/-/ (Codan Trust Company Limited), A Bailey

4719a Iris Handicap CLASS F (3-y-o and up) £2,385 5f.................(3:20)

4701a² PEERAGE PRINCE [67] (bl) 3-9-13 A Munro (7) *dsptd ld, led o'r one furlong out, hld on gmely und pres towards finish*.......................(4 to 1 jt-fav tchd 5 to 1) 1
4672a² LITTLE SABOTEUR [66] 3-9-12 T Quinn (11) *in tch, effrt hfwy, ran on wl ins fnl furlong, jst fld*.......(4 to 1 jt-fav op 3 to 1 tchd 5 to 1) 2
4706a⁵ DOESYOUDOES [54] (v) 3-9-0 J Williams (1) *nvr far away, ev ch ins fnl furlong, no extr towards finish.* ....(10 to 1 op 7 to 1) 3
4660a⁷ SOBA GUEST (Ire) [61] 3-9-0 (7*) A Daly (12) *speed stands side, rdn alng 2 fs out, kpt on ins last.* ....(7 to 1 op 5 to 1) 4
4692a ABSOLUTION [68] 8-9-7 (7*) S Wynne (3) *dsptd ld till rdn and no extr o'r one furlong out*.....(11 to 1 op 9 to 1) 5
MEESON TIMES [65] 4-9-11 M Hills (9) *chsd alng beh ldrs, styd on o'r one furlong out, nvr dngrs.* ....(16 to 1 op 14 to 1) 6
GRAND TIME [60] 3-9-6 G Baxter (13) *sn drvn alng beh ldrs, styd on ins fnl furlong, no imprsn.* ....(12 to 1 op 10 to 1) 7
4701a⁶ LINCSTONE BOY (Ire) [54] (v) 4-9-0 S Webster (10) *in tch, effrt hfwy, kpt on same pace ins fnl furlong.* ....(8 to 1 op 7 to 1) 8
4672a⁵ TOMMY TEMPEST [43] 3-7-10 (7*) D Wright (2) *cl up centre till rdn and wknd o'r one furlong out.* ....(10 to 1 op 9 to 1 tchd 11 to 1) 9
LAST STRAW [36] 4-7-10 J Quinn (4) *trkd ldrs centre, rdn hfwy, sn wknd*..................(16 to 1 op 10 to 1) 10
KALAR [44] (bl) 3-8-4 S Wood (6) *trkd ldrs centre, rdn alng hfwy, wknd*......................(10 to 1 op 6 to 1) 11
4699a NORDOORA (Ire) [40] 3-8-0 A Proud (5) *sn beh and pushed alng, nvr on terms*...............(25 to 1 op 16 to 1) 12
CUMBRIAN CAVALIER [33] 3-7-7 G Bardwell (8) *squeezed out strt, not reco'r*...............(33 to 1 op 16 to 1) 13

Dist: Sht-hd, ½l, 1l, ¾l, ¾l, ½l, 1½l, hd, 1l, 2l. 1m 0.60s. a 2.30s (13 Ran).
SR: 52/50/36/39/43/37/30/18/6/ (David A Hobbs), Pat Mitchell

LINGFIELD (A.W) (std)
Saturday November 28th
Going Correction: MINUS 0.40 sec. per fur.

4720a Abbey Life Maiden Stakes CLASS F (2-y-o) £2,301 5f..............(1:00)

LUCAYAN TREASURE (v) 9-0 T Quinn (4) *chsd ldrs, led appr fnl furlong, ran on strly.* ....(9 to 1 op 6 to 1 tchd 10 to 1) 1
4700a⁵ MISS GORGEOUS (Ire) 8-6 (3*) Emma O'Gorman (5) *chsd ldrs, effrt 2 fs out, ran on wl ins last.* (4 to 1 op 5 to 2) 2
THE INSTITUTE BOY (bl) 9-0 S Webster (8) *cl up, led o'r 3 fs out till appr last, one pace*..........(8 to 1 op 5 to 1) 3
COMET WHIRLPOOL (Ire) (bl) 9-0 A Munro (10) *cl up, wide into strt, sn one pace*..............(12 to 1 op 7 to 1) 4
4668a³ THE ORDINARY GIRL (Ire) (v) 8-9 J Quinn (3) *cl up, led aftr one furlong to o'r 3 out, wknd ins last.* ....(7 to 2 op 5 to 2 tchd 4 to 1) 5
4700a⁶ WESSHAUN 8-2 (7*) T G McLaughlin (1) *cl up till wknd appr fnl furlong*.................. (20 to 1 op 14 to 1) 6
4700a⁴ GORODENKA BOY 8-7 (7*) Kim McDonnell (7) *broke wl, led for one furlong, wth ldrs till wknd o'r one out.* ....(16 to 1 op 7 to 1) 7
M A EL-SAHN 8-11 (3*) R Perham (2) *chsd ldrs, not much room on ins hfwy, sn btn.* ....(9 to 4 fav op 3 to 1 tchd 4 to 1) 8
MOUNTAIN SPRING 8-11 (3*) D Harrison (9) *outpcd.* ....(14 to 1 op 7 to 1) 9
IMSHI 8-9 D Holland (6) *outpcd*...... (25 to 1 op 14 to 1) 10

Dist: 3l, 1½l, 1l, 1½l, 2l, ¾l, 1½l, 5l, sht-hd. 59.84s. a 1.34s (10 Ran).
SR: 33/16/15/11/-/-/ (H E Lhendup Dorji), D R Loder

4721a Vittoria Claiming Stakes CLASS F (3 & 4-y-o) £2,406 1½m......... (1:30)

BREAKDANCER (Ire) 3-8-5¹ T Quinn (1) *hld up beh ldrs, rdn to ld ins fnl furlong, ran on wl.* ....(5 to 1 op 4 to 1 tchd 7 to 1) 1
DISPUTED CALL (USA) 3-9-0 M Hills (9) *keen hold, wth ldr till led 4 fs out, hdd ins last, kpt on und pres.* ....(10 to 1 op 4 to 1) 2
4662a* NOTED STRAIN (Ire) 4-8-13 D Holland (4) *hld up in rear, hdwy o'r 4 fs out, ev ch 2 out, one pace appr last.* ....(11 to 10 fav op 5 to 4 tchd Evens) 3
MENTALASANYTHIN 3-8-8 (7*) D Wright (6) *pld hrd, trkd ldg pair till outpcd 3 fs out, styd on ins last.* ....(10 to 1 op 6 to 1) 4
JOLI'S GREAT 4-8-1 (7*) P McCabe (8) *trkd ldrs, rdn appr 2 fs out, wknd o'r one out*............(5 to 2 op 9 to 4) 5
4680a DON'T WORRY (Ire) 3-8-1 Dale Gibson (3) *hld up in tch, effrt 4 fs out, sn btn.* (20 to 1 op 12 to 1 tchd 25 to 1) 6
4678a AL BILLAL (bl) 4-8-11 G Bardwell (7) *led aftr 2 fs till 4 out, sn wknd*..................(50 to 1 op 33 to 1) 7
LAJADHAL (Fr) 3-8-10 N Carlisle (5) *strted slwly, sn chsd ldrs, pushed alng hfwy, wknd o'r 3 fs out.* ....(50 to 1 op 33 to 1) 8
COOL FLIGHT 3-7-12 J Fanning (2) *led for 2 fs, sn wknd, lost tch 5 out, tld off*............. (50 to 1 op 33 to 1) 9

Dist: Nk, 3l, 5l, 4l, 7l, 2l, 7l, 25l. 2m 31.81s. a 2.11s (9 Ran).
SR: 22/30/23/15/-/-/ (J Jannaway), W R Muir

4722a Badajoz Handicap CLASS F (0-90 3-y-o and up) £2,758 1m...... (2:00)

4680a³ DASWAKI (Can) [70] 4-9-3 B Rouse (6) *cl up, led o'r one furlong out, sn clr, easily*...........(7 to 2 op 5 to 1) 1
4667a* TRIAL TIMES (USA) [71] 3-8-13 (3*) Emma O'Gorman (9) *cl up, led 4 fs out till o'r one out, one pace.* ....(7 to 2 op 9 to 4) 2
4663a² ABBEY STRAND (USA) [70] 3-9-1 A Munro (2) *trkd ldrs, effrt and one pace fnl 2 fs.* ....(100 to 30 fav op 2 to 1 tchd 7 to 2) 3
MULCIBER [64] 4-8-11 M Hills (5) *led till 4 fs out, rdn and wknd o'r one out*.... (16 to 1 op 12 to 1 tchd 20 to 1) 4
SARUM [64] 6-8-11 Dale Gibson (4) *in tch, effrt 3 fs out, nvr on terms*........................(20 to 1 op 10 to 1) 5
4680a* SAREEN EXPRESS (Ire) [51] 4-7-12 G Bardwell (3) *outpcd and sn drvn alng, cld o'r 2 fs out, soon btn.* ....(9 to 2 op 7 to 2) 6
FEN DANCE (Ire) [83] 3-10-0 D Holland (7) *al beh.* ....(12 to 1 op 8 to 1 tchd 14 to 1) 7
4696a⁶ COURTING NEWMARKET [54] 4-8-1 J Quinn (8) *chsd ldrs, rcd wide hfwy, sn btn, tld off.* ....(14 to 1 op 10 to 1 tchd 16 to 1) 8

Dist: 3½l, hd, 7l, 2½l, 3l, 1l, 20l. 1m 36.78s. b 0.12s (8 Ran).
SR: 57/45/43/18/10/-/15/-/ (David Allen), R Hannon

4723a Salamanca Apprentice Handicap CLASS F (0-70 3-y-o and up) £2,343 1¼m......................... (2:30)

4678a⁴ TWILIGHT SECRET [54] 3-8-12 D Harrison (3) *trkd ldr, led o'r 4 fs out, clr over one out, ran on wl*.......(4 to 1 jt-fav op 5 to 1) 1
4678a³ DONIA (USA) [65] 3-9-9 T G McLaughlin (5) *trkd ldrs till crrd back and lost pl 4 fs out, hdwy o'r 2 out, ran on ins last*................................(7 to 1 op 6 to 1) 2

ABSONAL [65] 5-9-13 R Perham (12) *beh, hdwy hfwy, kpt on one pace o'r one furlong out.* ....(9 to 2 op 6 to 1 tchd 8 to 1) 3
LADY LACEY [49] (v) 5-8-4 (7*) Iona Wands (6) *in tch, styd on fnl 2 fs, nrst finish*..........(10 to 1 op 6 to 1) 4
4689a[3] FALCONS DAWN [54] 5-9-2 A Tucker (10) *dwlt, hdwy o'r 2 fs out, one pace*..........(7 to 1 op 5 to 1) 5
TALENTED TING (Ire) [70] 3-10-0 J Fanning (9) *trkd ldrs till wknd o'r one furlong out*..........(4 to 1 jt-fav op 3 to 1 tchd 9 to 2) 6
VA UTU [45] 4-8-2[2] (7*) R Painter (8) *beh, hdwy 5 fs out, wknd o'r one out*..........(20 to 1) 7
4667a[5] SHARP DANCE [40] 3-7-9 (3*) D Wright (2) *al beh.* ....(20 to 1 op 10 to 1) 8
4690a DANCING SENSATION (USA) [36] (bl) 5-7-12 Stephen Davies (7) *trkd ldrs till rdn and wknd o'r 3 fs out.* ....(14 to 1 op 12 to 1) 9
4667a[2] CRETOES DANCER (USA) [51] (bl) 3-8-6 (3*) Kim McDonnell (11) *beh, cld o'r 4 fs out, sn btn*..........(8 to 1 tchd 9 to 1) 10
TULAPET [39] (bl,e/s) 3-7-11[4] (3*) A Martinez (1) *rcd freely, led till o'r 4 fs out, sn wknd and hmpd, tld off.* ....(33 to 1 op 20 to 1) 11
Dist: 2l, ½l, 2l, 1l, sht-hd, hd, 1l, 5l, 2½l, 25l. 2m 5.38s. a 2.18s (11 Ran).
SR: 36/43/46/26/29/40/18/7/-/ (Norton Brookes), J W Hills

4724a Almaraz Nursery CLASS F (2-y-o) £2,790 7f.................... (3:00)

ABERDEEN HEATHER [82] 9-7 J Williams (7) *beh, hdwy 3 fs out, led ins last, ran on wl.* ....(15 to 2 op 5 to 2 tchd 8 to 1) 1
PERSIAN GUSHER (Ire) [67] (e/s) 8-6 T Quinn (8) *trkd ldrs, led appr 2 fs out till ins last, no extr und pres.* ....(12 to 1 tchd 10 to 1) 2
4676a* BICHETTE [68] 8-4 (3*) R Perham (3) *trkd ldrs, one pace und pres frm 2 fs out*..........(4 to 1 op 7 to 2) 3
4687a[2] GREENWICH CHALENGE [79] 9-4 A Munro (10) *beh and pushed alng, hrd rdn 3 fs out, kpt on.* ....(11 to 2 op 5 to 1 tchd 13 to 2) 4
SASEEDO (USA) [77] 8-13 (3*) Emma O'Gorman (11) *missed break, sn reco'red, cl up till wknd appr fnl furlong.* ....(11 to 4 fav op 4 to 1) 5
4695a[5] FOREST SONG [54] (v) 7-7 G Bardwell (6) *chsd ldrs, effrt o'r 2 fs out, no hdwy*..........(12 to 1 op 8 to 1) 6
4677a[4] PATONG BEACH [58] (bl) 7-8 (3*) D Harrison (5) *led till appr 2 fs out, wknd*..........(12 to 1 op 8 to 1) 7
WAR REQUIEM (Ire) [54] 7-0 (7*) D Wright (9) *trkd ldrs till wknd o'r 2 fs out*.....(20 to 1 op 14 to 1 tchd 25 to 1) 8
4697a[6] FESTIN [64] 8-3 Dale Gibson (1) *slwly into strd, outpcd.* ....(12 to 1 op 9 to 1) 9
4676a[7] SORAYAH'S PET [58] 7-11 C Nutter (2) *strted slwly, outpcd*..........(20 to 1 op 14 to 1) 10
4676a BROUGHTONS FORMULA [58] (e/s) 7-11 J Quinn (4) *outpcd*..........(12 to 1 op 7 to 1) 11
Dist: 1½l, 3l, sht-hd, 1½l, ¾l, ¾l, ¾l, hd, hd, ¾l. 1m 25.54s. a 1.94s (11 Ran).
SR: 36/16/8/18/11/-/ (Major H S Cayzer), D R C Elsworth

4725a Ladbroke All Weather Trophy Handicap Qualifier CLASS E (0-75 3-y-o and up) £3,106 7f............. (3:30)

4680a[4] KISSAVOS [55] (v) 6-8-11 T Quinn (6) *trkd ldrs, led o'r 2 fs out, sn clr, ran on wl*....(4 to 1 op 3 to 1 tchd 9 to 2) 1
VELOCE (Ire) [56] 4-8-5 (7*) D Wright (13) *trkd ldrs, chsd wnr frm o'r one furlong out, ran on wl*..........(10 to 1) 2
VUCHTERBACHER [48] 6-7-11 (7*) T Wilson (9) *sn rdn alng in mid-div, hdwy o'r one furlong out, ran on.* ....(16 to 1 op 14 to 1) 3
CORAL FLUTTER [62] (bl) 5-9-4 D Holland (4) *sn led, hdd o'r 4 fs out, one pace*..........(9 to 1 op 8 to 1) 4
BRIGHT PARAGON (Ire) [46] 3-8-0 J Quinn (5) *mid-div, effrt o'r 2 fs out, styd on*..........(16 to 1 op 14 to 1) 5
4681a[9] LUCKNAM STYLE [43] 4-7-13 G Bardwell (12) *cl up till wknd o'r one furlong out*..........(33 to 1 op 20 to 1) 6
THE CUCKOO'S NEST [53] 4-8-9 J Williams (2) *beh, styd on frm o'r one furlong out, nvr on terms*..........(25 to 1) 7
MADAGANS GREY [68] 4-9-7 (3*) R Perham (1) *missed break, hdwy o'r one furlong out, nvr on terms.* ....(33 to 1 op 25 to 1) 8
4669a[2] SALLY'S SON [64] (bl) 6-9-3 (3*) Emma O'Gorman (8) *cl up, led o'r 4 fs out to over 2 out, wknd.* ....(3 to 1 fav op 9 to 2 tchd 5 to 1) 9
TRUTHFUL IMAGE [70] (bl) 3-9-10 A Munro (7) *beh fnl 3 fs.* ....(12 to 1 tchd 14 to 1) 10
SYLVAN BREEZE [66] (bl) 4-9-8 M Hills (14) *chsd ldrs to hfwy*..........(20 to 1 op 16 to 1) 11
JUCEA [54] 3-8-5 (3*) D Harrison (3) *trkd ldrs till wknd appr 3 fs out*..........(12 to 1) 12
4681a[4] SIRMOOR (Ire) [48] (bl) 3-8-2 A McGlone (15) *chsd ldrs till wknd o'r 2 fs out*..........(10 to 1 op 7 to 1) 13
CONISTON LAKE (Ire) [64] (v) 3-9-4 B Rouse (16) *al beh.* ....(10 to 1 op 7 to 1) 14
4673a GEMINI BAY [46] (bl) 3-8-0 S Dawson (10) *beh hfwy.* ....(50 to 1) 15
Dist: 1l, 5l, sht-hd, 2l, nk, ½l, ¾l, hd, 2l, ½l. 1m 25.38s. a 1.78s (15 Ran).
SR: 28/26/3/16/-/-/-/11/6/ (Richard Berenson), C C Elsey

MAISONS LAFFITTE (FR) (heavy)
Saturday November 28th
Going Correction: PLUS 0.95 sec. per fur.

4726a Prix Tantieme (Listed) (3-y-o and up) £12,333 1m.............. (1:25)

BLUE DAISY (USA) 4-8-8 G Dubroeucq, ... 1
4684a[3] TWO LEFT FEET 5-8-11 E Legrix, ... 2
LEARIVA (USA) 5-8-9 F Head, ... 3
UNITED KINGDOM (USA) 3-8-8 J Boisnard, ... 4
DANAGROOM (USA) 3-8-8 O Doleuze, ... 5
ARCHANGE (USA) 3-8-11 T Jarnet, ... 6
SOGNO (Fr) 3-8-11 P Bruneau, ... 7
SEBA LE ROUGE (Fr) 5-8-11 G Guignard, ... 8
SPRING LORENZO (Fr) 4-8-11 O Peslier, ... 9
Dist: 5l, 3l, nk, 4l, 2l, 8l, ½l, 10l. 1m 43.60s. a 8.90s (9 Ran).
SR: 74/62/51/49/37/34/10/8/-/ (Sheikh Mohammed), A Fabre

CAPANNELLE (ITY) (soft)
Sunday November 29th

4727a Premio Roma Vecchia (Group 3) (3-y-o and up) £34,691 1¾m..... (2:10)

SPRING 3-8-5 W Carson (6) *al in tch, 6th strt, hdwy o'r 2 fs out, led one and a half out, ran on wl*.......... 1
ALMANOR 3-8-8 D Zarroli (4) *hdwy 6 fs out, 3rd strt, ev ch o'r one out, kpt on one pace*.......... 2
BIG TOBIN (Ity) 3-8-8 O Fancera (1) *hld up, hdwy fnl 3 fs, nrst finish*.......... 3
STRONG LIFE (Ire) 4-8-13 G Favretto (10) *led 7 fs out till 4 out, kpt on one pace*.......... 4
ONESIXNINE (Ire) 4-8-9 P Shanahan (5) *hld up, some prog fnl 2 fs, nvr nr to chal*.......... 5
SNURGE 5-9-9 T Quinn (11) *al prmnt, 4th strt, dsptd ld o'r 3 fs out till over one out, one pace*.......... 6
DAMA GRANDE 3-8-5 Jacqueline Freda (8) *prmnt, 5th strt, led 4 fs out to one and a half out, wknd ins last*.......... 7
GIROLAMO 3-8-10 G Pucciatti (7) *nvr dngrs*.......... 8
MENANDRO (Ire) 3-8-8 S Soto (3) *prmnt till wknd 3 fs out.* 9
TROPICAL STORM (Arg) 3-8-13 A Herrera (2) *led for 7 fs, second strt, sn wknd*.......... 0
ACYL (USA) 3-8-8 L Ficuciello (9) *al rear*.......... 0
Dist: 1 ¾l, hd, nk, ½l, 1 ¾l, nk, ¾l, 3l, 7l. 3m 0.90s. (11 Ran).
(Lord Halifax), J L Dunlop

TOKYO (JPN) (good)
Sunday November 29th

4728a Japan Cup (Group 1) (3-y-o and up) £739,815 1½m.............. (6:20)

TOKAI TEIO (Jpn) 4-8-13 Y Okabe (14) ....(9 to 1) 1
NATURALISM (NZ) 4-8-13 L Dittman (7) ....(57 to 10) 2
DEAR DOCTOR (Fr) 5-8-13 C Asmussen (9) ....(8 to 1) 3
LEGACY WORLD (Jpn) 3-8-9 H Koyauchi (6) ....(169 to 10) 4
HISHI MASARU (Jpn) 3-8-9 Y Take (13) ....(134 to 10) 5
USER FRIENDLY 3-8-5 G Duffield (1) ....(22 to 10 fav) 6
LET'S ELOPE (NZ) 5-8-9 D Beadman (10) ....(7 to 1) 7
LET'S GO TARQUIN (Jpn) 5-8-13 S Osaki (4) ....(277 to 10) 8
IKUNO DICTUS (Jpn) 5-8-9 Y Muramoto (2) ......(64 to 1) 9
QUEST FOR FAME 5-8-13 Pat Eddery (11) ......(94 to 10) 0
DR DEVIOUS (Ire) 3-8-9 C McCarron (5) ....(109 to 10) 0
VERT AMANDE (Fr) 4-8-13 D Boeuf (3) ....(168 to 10) 0
YAMANIN GLOBAL (Jpn) 5-8-13 H Kawachi (8) (278 to 10) 0
HASHIRU SHOGUN (Jpn) 4-8-9 Y Take (13) ....(449 to 10) 0
Dist: Nk, ½l, 3½l, ¾l, ¾l, 4l, 1 ¾l, nk, nose, nk. 2m 24.60s. (14 Ran).
(M Uchimura), S Matsumoto

HOLLYWOOD (USA) (firm)
Sunday November 29th

4729a The Matriarch (Grade 1) (Turf) (3-y-o and up) £117,021 1m 1f...........

FLAWLESSLY (USA) 4-8-11 C McCarron, ...(14 to 10 fav) 1
SUPER STAFF (USA) 4-8-11 E Delahoussaye, ...(9 to 2) 2
KOSTROMA 6-8-11 K Desormeaux, ...(19 to 10) 3
CAMPAGNARDE (Arg) 5-8-11 P Valenzuela, ...(33 to 1) 4
HYDRO CALIDO (USA) 3-8-8 A Solis, ...(27 to 1) 5
SPORADES (USA) 3-8-8 G Stevens, ...(24 to 1) 6
RE TOSS (Arg) 5-8-11 A Lopez, ...(48 to 1) 7
LADY SHIRL (USA) 5-8-11 L Pincay Jr, ...(91 to 10) 8
LITE NIGHT (USA) 4-8-11 C Nakatani, ...(43 to 1) 9
Dist: 1l, 2l, ½l, ¾l, hd, ½l, 6l, 5l. 1m 46.00s. (9 Ran).
(Harbor View Farm), R Dutrow

LINGFIELD (A.W) (std)

Monday November 30th

Going Correction: MINUS 0.30 sec. per fur.

4730a Gleneagles Maiden Stakes CLASS F (2-y-o) £2,574 7f. . . . . (12:40)

EASTERN MEMORIES (Ire) (bl) 9-0 B Rouse (9) *cl up, led o'r 4 fs out, clr over one out, ran on wl*. . . . .(5 to 2 jt-fav tchd 3 to 1) 1
PATSY GRIMES 8-9 Dean McKeown (13) *al cl up, kpt on one pace o'r one furlong out*. . . . .(7 to 1 op 8 to 1) 2
STRICTLY PERSONAL (USA) 9-0 D Holland (5) *chsd ldrs, shaken up and styd on wl ins fnl furlong*. . . . .(3 to 1 op 7 to 4 tchd 7 to 2) 3
PLAY HEVER GOLF 9-0 G Carter (8) *led till o'r 4 fs out, cl up till wknd ins last*. . . . .(12 to 1) 4
STALLED (Ire) 9-0 A Munro (11) *chsd ldrs, styd on one pace fnl 2 fs*. . . . .(5 to 2 jt-fav op 7 to 4 tchd 3 to 1) 5
CONVOY 8-11 (3*) F Norton (3) *beh and rdn, styd on fnl 2 fs, nvr nrr*. . . . .(10 to 1 op 8 to 1) 6
SPORTING MISSILE (USA) 8-9 M Hills (7) *nvr on terms*. . . . .(5 to 1 op 9 to 4) 7
FREDDIE JACK 9-0 R Lappin (1) *strted slwly, sn reco'red, beh hfwy*. . . . .(14 to 1 op 12 to 1) 8
ALMONTY (Ire) 9-0 T Quinn (4) *chsd ldrs, pushed alng hfwy, wknd o'r 2 fs out*. . . . .(20 to 1) 9
ROSIE'S GOLD 8-4 (5*) Stephen Davies (10) *strted slwly, al beh*. . . . .(11 to 2 op 5 to 1 tchd 6 to 1) 10
GREY WATCH 8-9 J Williams (2) *al beh*. . . . .(12 to 1 op 8 to 1) 11
4691a⁸ PRINCE OF SOUL 9-0 J McLaughlin (12) *in tch till hrd rdn and beh hfwy*. . . . .(20 to 1) 12

Dist: 2l, ½l, 5l, sht-hd, 10l, ¾l, hd, sht-hd, hd, nk. 1m 26.30s. a 2.70s (12 Ran).
SR: 28/17/20/5/4/-/ (Jim Horgan), R Hannon

4731a Walton Heath Claiming Stakes (Div I) CLASS F (3-y-o and up) £2,322 1¼m. . . . . (1:10)

ANNACURRAGH (Ire) 3-8-0 A Munro (4) *trkd ldrs, led 3 fs out, sn clr, edgd rght ins last, cmftbly*. . . . .(5 to 2 op 5 to 4 tchd 11 to 4) 1
CARLOWITZ (USA) (v) 4-7-10 (7*) B Russell (2) *trkd ldrs, kpt on wl o'r one furlong out*. . . . .(20 to 1 tchd 33 to 1) 2
4662a⁵ CLIFTON CHASE (bl) 3-8-5 G Carter (1) *outpcd and beh, styd on wl 3 fs out, nrst finish*. . . . .(7 to 2 op 5 to 1 tchd 6 to 1) 3
4669a* SUPER SUMMIT 3-8-13 G Bardwell (8) *trkd ldrs, chsd wnr 2 fs out, wknd ins last*. . . . .(11 to 8 fav op 6 to 4 tchd 11 to 10) 4
4660a⁹ BETTER STILL (Ire) 3-8-8 Dale Gibson (6) *trkd ldrs till outpcd 4 fs out*. . . . .(33 to 1 op 20 to 1) 5
4669a⁵ CANADIAN CAPERS 3-7-12 J Quinn (7) *led till 3 fs out, wknd*. . . . .(8 to 1 tchd 10 to 1) 6
JUVENARA 6-8-9 D Holland (5) *cl up, sn rdn, wknd 5 fs out, tld off*. . . . .(9 to 1 op 5 to 1 tchd 10 to 1) 7
SOUTARI 4-9-3 J Williams (3) *al beh, tld off*. . . . .(50 to 1 op 33 to 1) 8

Dist: 5l, 7l, ¾l, 10l, 3l, 25l, 3½l. 2m 5.58s. a 2.38s (8 Ran).
SR: 32/25/13/19/-/ (Harry R D McCalmont), A C Stewart

4732a St Andrew's Handicap CLASS F (0-70 3-y-o and up) £2,532 1¼m . . . .(1:40)

COLTRANE [62] (v) 4-9-10 A Munro (4) *made all, rdn ins fnl furlong, ran on wl*. . . (100 to 30 op 2 to 1 tchd 7 to 2) 1
LADY DUNDEE (USA) [60] 3-9-4 D Holland (2) *cl up, hrd rdn o'r 2 fs out, not quicken*. (3 to 1 op 7 to 2 tchd 4 to 1) 2
4723a⁵ FALCONS DAWN [54] 5-9-2 G Baxter (7) *trkd ldrs, hrd rdn 2 fs out, one pace*. . . . .(6 to 1 op 5 to 1) 3
4673a BLUE DRIFTER (Ire) [39] 3-7-11 J Quinn (5) *hld up, cld 4 fs out, hrd rdn 2 out, wknd*. . . . .(20 to 1 op 8 to 1) 4
TOP VILLAIN [35] 6-7-11 J Fanning (1) *pushed alng thrght, trkd ldrs till wknd o'r 3 fs out*. . . . .(5 to 1 tchd 6 to 1) 5
BOUNDER ROWE [37] 5-7-13 Dale Gibson (6) *al beh, lost tch o'r 4 fs out*. . . . .(50 to 1 op 25 to 1) 6
VALIANT WORDS [52] 5-9-0 T Quinn (3) *cl up, pushed alng hfwy, wknd quickly, tld off*. . . . .(15 to 8 fav op 2 to 1) 7

Dist: 3½l, 1l, 4l, 4l, 8l, 15l. 2m 6.33s. a 3.13s (7 Ran).
SR: 49/36/32/5/ (M L Oberstein), Lord Huntingdon

4733a Wentworth Handicap CLASS F (0-70 3-y-o and up) £2,406 1m. . . . . . (2:10)

TADORA (Ire) [46] 3-8-12 T Quinn (11) *beh, hdwy o'r 3 fs out, led one out, ran on wl*. . . . .(20 to 1 op 16 to 1 tchd 25 to 1) 1
SIR NORMAN HOLT (Ire) [53] (bl) 3-9-5 R Lappin (7) *led till appr 3 fs out, rallied und pres ins last*. . . . .(12 to 1 op 10 to 1) 2
PRECIOUS AIR (Ire) [46] 4-9-0 B Rouse (12) *beh, hdwy fnl 2 fs, fnshd wl*. . . . .(7 to 1 op 10 to 1) 3
4725a² VELOCE (Ire) [56] 4-9-10 J Williams (1) *cl up, led appr 3 fs out, hdd one out, one pace*. . . . .(3 to 1 fav op 7 to 2 tchd 11 to 4) 4
4690a* DAM CERTAIN (Ire) [56] 3-9-5 (3*) D Harrison (4) *pushed alng in tch, no hdwy fnl 2 fs*. (9 to 2 op 7 to 2 tchd 13 to 2) 5
4722a⁶ SAREEN EXPRESS (Ire) [51] 4-9-0 (5*) A Tucker (8) *trkd ldrs till wknd o'r 2 fs out*. (8 to 1 op 10 to 1 tchd 12 to 1) 6
4663a⁴ GOOD FOR THE ROSES [46] 6-9-0 A Munro (10) *in tch 3 fs, sn beh*. . . . .(6 to 1 op 4 to 1) 7+
4673a⁴ GUESSTIMATION (USA) [49] 3-9-1 G Bardwell (5) *chsd ldrs, hrd rdn 3 fs out, wknd 2 out*. . . . .(9 to 2 op 3 to 1) 7+
UP THE PUNJAB [61] 3-9-13 Candy Morris (2) *beh frm hfwy*. . . . .(33 to 1 op 25 to 1) 9
SERIOUS ACTION [62] 3-10-0 C Nutter (3) *nvr gng wl, al beh*. . . . .(16 to 1 op 14 to 1) 10
GOLD JUBILEE [50] 3-9-2 D Holland (6) *strted slwly, sn rdn, mid-div whn broke leg 4 fs out, destroyed*. . . . .(12 to 1 op 10 to 1) pu

Dist: ¾l, 1½l, 2l, 5l, sht-hd, 3l, dd-ht, 7l, 2l. 1m 39.39s. a 2.49s (11 Ran).
SR: 25/30/20/24/7/3/ (R Lamb), C J Benstead

4734a Sunningdale Nursery CLASS F (0-75 2-y-o) £2,406 6f. . . . . (2:40)

IOLITE [65] 9-7 M Hills (2) *trkd ldrs gng wl, squeezed through on ins to ld one furlong out, ran on well*. . . . .(2 to 1 fav op 9 to 4) 1
NUT BUSH [64] 9-6 G Carter (5) *led till one furlong out, one pace und pres*. . . . .(9 to 4 op 2 to 1) 2
4687a³ MR CUBE (Ire) [60] 9-2 T Quinn (10) *rdn and hdwy hfwy, one pace appr fnl furlong*. . . . . (5 to 2 op 9 to 4) 3
WEALTHYWOO [53] (bl) 8-9 J Quinn (4) *chsd ldrs, kpt on und pres ins fnl furlong*. . . . .(25 to 1) 4
MARWELL MITZI [52] 8-8 J Williams (8) *outpcd, hdwy und pres o'r one furlong out, kpt on*. . . . .(20 to 1) 5
AIR COMMAND (Bar) [65] 9-4 (3*) R Perham (6) *cl up, ev ch o'r one furlong out, wknd*. . . . . (5 to 1) 6
4687a⁶ MOVING IMAGE (Ire) [64] 9-6 C Dwyer (7) *cl up, wkng whn short of room appr fnl furlong*. . . . .(20 to 1) 7
NIKKI NOO NOO [60] 9-2 D Holland (9) *al beh, tld off*. . . . .(7 to 1 op 6 to 1) 8

Dist: 2l, 4l, ¾l, nk, ½l, 3l, 12l. 1m 13.25s. a 2.45s (8 Ran).
SR: 22/13/-/-/-/ (R P Marchant), M A Jarvis

4735a Walton Heath Claiming Stakes (Div II) CLASS F (3-y-o and up) £2,301 1¼m. . . . . (3:10)

4678a² AWESOME POWER 6-8-13 M Hills (7) *hld up in tch, cld o'r 3 fs out, led one out, quickened clr*. . . . .(13 to 8 fav op 6 to 4 tchd 2 to 1) 1
4667a COMMON COUNCIL 3-8-8 (3*) D Harrison (2) *cl up, led appr 2 fs out till one out, one pace*. . . . .(4 to 1 op 3 to 1 tchd 5 to 2 and 9 to 2) 2
4723a³ ABSONAL 5-8-8 (3*) R Perham (4) *hld up beh, hdwy 4 fs out, ev ch 2 out, one pace appr last*. . . . .(5 to 2 op 2 to 1 tchd 7 to 4) 3
GOLD BLADE (bl) 3-8-3 D Holland (1) *led till 2 fs out, one pace*. . . . .(3 to 1 tchd 9 to 2 and 11 to 4) 4
4723a CRETOES DANCER (USA) (bl) 3-7-8 (7*) Kim McDonnell (8) *trkd ldrs till wknd 3 fs out, styd on ins last*. . . . .(20 to 1 op 12 to 1 tchd 25 to 1) 5
SOL ROUGE (Ire) 3-7-8 J Fanning (5) *cl up till wknd 4 fs out, tld off*. . . . .(50 to 1 op 33 to 1) 6
CHAFF (v) 5-8-2 (5*) Stephen Davies (6) *trkd ldrs till wknd hfwy, tld off*. . . . .(25 to 1 op 16 to 1) 7
CAMEO SHADES 5-9-3 J Williams (3) *strted slwly, al beh, tld off*. . . . . (25 to 1 op 14 to 1 tchd 33 to 1) 8

Dist: 5l, ¾l, 4l, 1½l, 20l, 10l, 15l. 2m 5.56s. a 2.36s (8 Ran).
SR: 45/33/31/15/10/ (Garrett J Freyne), J W Hills

4736a St George's Handicap CLASS F (0-70 3-y-o and up) £2,385 6f. . (3:40)

BANBURY FLYER [47] 4-8-10 A Munro (6) *cl up, led one furlong out, sn clr*. . . . . . .(7 to 2 op 3 to 1 tchd 4 to 1) 1
4681a³ LIFT BOY (USA) [45] 3-8-0 (7*) B Russell (8) *cl up, led o'r 3 fs out till one out, one pace*. . . . .(4 to 1 op 9 to 2) 2
4681a⁷ PIGALLE WONDER [40] (bl) 4-8-3 D Biggs (7) *led till o'r 3 fs out, one pace*. . . . .(20 to 1 op 14 to 1) 3
4701a HINARI VIDEO [47] 7-8-10 Dean McKeown (10) *sn pushed alng to chase ldrs, no hdwy 2 fs out*. . . . .(11 to 2 op 5 to 1 tchd 6 to 1) 4
TOSHIBA COMET [65] (bl) 5-9-7 (7*) T G McLaughlin (2) *outpcd till styd on ins fnl furlong*. (20 to 1 op 14 to 1) 5
LOOTING (USA) [40] 6-8-0 (3*) D Harrison (9) *pushed alng to chase ldrs, nvr on terms*. . . . .(20 to 1 op 14 to 1) 6
4701a⁴ JOE SUGDEN [53] 8-9-2 N Carlisle (3) *trkd ldrs till wknd appr fnl furlong*. . . . .(7 to 1 op 9 to 2) 7
4701a IMCO DOUBLE (Ire) [58] 4-9-7 J McLaughlin (4) *al beh*. . . . .(14 to 1 op 12 to 1 tchd 16 to 1) 8
4701a INSWINGER [38] 6-8-1 G Bardwell (5) *sn outpcd*. . . . .(10 to 1 tchd 12 to 1) 9
4710a³ KLAIROVER [48] 5-8-11 D Holland (1) *al beh*. . . . .(11 to 4 fav op 3 to 1 tchd 9 to 2) 10

Dist: 5l, 2½l, 1l, 1½l, ¾l, 1l, 1l, 1½l, 5l. 1m 11.96s. a 1.16s (10 Ran).
SR: 37/14/-/3/15/-/ (Exors Of The Late Mr J Martin), Mrs A L M King

ST-CLOUD (FR) (heavy)

Monday November 30th
Going Correction: PLUS 1.60 sec. per fur.

4737a Prix Edellic (Listed) (3-y-o and up) £12,333 1¼m 110yds......... (3:00)

MARILDO (Fr) 5-8-12 G Guignard, ... 1
MATARUN (Ire) 4-8-12 N Jeanpierre, ... 2
SAKURA BERING (USA) 3-9-2 E Legrix, ... 3
4711a[7] LA TIRANA (Fr) 5-8-13 W Mongil, ... 4
Dist: 3l, 1½l, ¾l, 2l, 1½l, nk, nose, 6l. 2m 31.10s. a 20.10s (9 Ran).
SR: 65/59/60/55/ (D Smaga), D Smaga

MAISONS LAFFITTE (FR) (heavy)
Tuesday December 1st
Going Correction: PLUS 1.50 sec. per fur.

4738a Prix Herbager (Listed) (2-y-o) £12,333 1m................. (1:40)

MADELEINE'S DREAM (USA) 8-10 F Head, ... 1
SUDAH (USA) 8-10 G Guignard, ... 2
GALLO NERO (Fr) 9-4 P Julien, ... 3
ZIGREEN (Fr) 8-10 W Mongil, ... 4
Dist: ¾l, 2l, 5l, 5l. 1m 53.90s. a 19.20s (5 Ran).
(Allen E Paulson), F Boutin

SOUTHWELL (A.W) (std)
Wednesday December 2nd
Going Correction: MINUS 0.15 sec. per fur.

4739a Julius Caesar Claiming Stakes (Div I) CLASS F (3-y-o and up) £2,427 6f ....(12:10)

4692a[6] APPLEDORN 5-8-6 A Munro (5) *chsd ldrs, effrt and hdwy 2 fs out, led entering fnl furlong, sn clr.* ....(5 to 2 op 11 to 4 tchd 3 to 1 and 7 to 2) 1
4692a* PRETONIC 4-8-1[1] R P Elliott (6) *dsptd ld till led aftr one furlong, rdn 2 out, sn hdd, kpt on.* ....(9 to 4 fav op 5 to 2) 2
ARC LAMP 6-8-5 J Fanning (7) *cl up, effrt and hdwy to ld one and a half fs out, sn rdn, hdd entering fnl furlong, one pace.*..............................(12 to 1 op 7 to 1) 3
BELATED 3-9-2 Dale Gibson (1) *chsd ldrs, effrt and rdn 2 fs out, wknd appr fnl furlong.* ....(9 to 2 op 5 to 2 tchd 5 to 1) 4
4692a GENTLE HERO (USA) 6-8-7 Alex Greaves (8) *mid-div, effrt and hdwy 2 fs out, styd on fnl furlong.* ....(12 to 1 op 10 to 1) 5
EASTLEIGH 3-8-7 W Ryan (4) *dsptd ld for one furlong, cl up, effrt and ev ch 2 out, sn rdn, wknd appr fnl furlong.*..............................(12 to 1 op 7 to 1) 6
4706a MAID WELCOME (bl) 5-8-6 Dean McKeown (11) *in tch, effrt and hdwy on outer 2 fs out, rdn and wknd appr fnl furlong.*..............................(12 to 1 op 8 to 1) 7
INNOCENT GEORGE 3-8-6[1] M Hills (10) *al rear.* ....(20 to 1 op 25 to 1) 8
4705a INDIAN MAESTRO 6-8-11 G Carter (9) *in tch to hfwy, sn drvn alng and wknd.*..............(25 to 1 op 20 to 1) 9
GALLEY GOSSIP 3-8-7[6] J Williams (2) *slwly into strd, al beh.*..............................(33 to 1 op 20 to 1) 10
WOOLAW GIRL 4-7-7 (7*) Claire Balding (3) *outpcd.* ....(33 to 1) 11
Dist: 3l, 1½l, 2l, hd, ½l, 1½l, 1½l, 1½l, 20l, 2½l. 1m 14.90s. a 1.50s (11 Ran).
SR: 44/27/25/28/18/16/9/3/2/ (Mrs B Facchino), B A McMahon

4740a Macbeth Maiden Stakes CLASS F (2-y-o) £2,343 1m........... (12:40)

4668a[2] PIPERS REEL 8-9 A Munro (7) *trkd ldrs, hdwy o'r 3 fs out, effrt and hng lft 2 out, led appr fnl furlong, cmftbly.* ....(11 to 10 fav op 6 to 4 on tchd 5 to 4) 1
4661a[8] SCOFFERA 8-9 L Charnock (8) *led till o'r 3 fs out, sn rdn, led 2 out, hdd and one pace entering fnl furlong.* ....(14 to 1 op 10 to 1) 2
4677a[2] MOONSTRUCK BARD 9-0 W Woods (5) *cl up gng wl, led o'r 3 fs out, rdn and hdd 2 out, sn btn.* ....(7 to 1 op 5 to 2) 3
4691a QUATTRO 9-0 B Crossley (6) *beh and sn rdn, styd on wl fnl 2 fs.*..............(9 to 4 op 7 to 2 tchd 4 to 1) 4
4695a[7] HONEY JUICE 8-9 Dean McKeown (2) *in tch, rdn o'r 3 fs out, sn wknd.*..................................(20 to 1) 5
STREPHON (Ire) 8-7 (7*) S Mulvey (3) *prmnt, rdn and wknd 3 fs out.*..............................(14 to 1 op 10 to 1) 6
4691a[7] STAR RAGE (Ire) 9-0 J Williams (1) *al beh.* ....(14 to 1 op 10 to 1) 7
WHYALLA RAIN 8-9 W Ryan (4) *slwly into strd, al rear.* ....(14 to 1 op 10 to 1 tchd 20 to 1) 8
Dist: 1½l, 5l, 2l, nk, nk, 8l, ¾l. 1m 46.00s. a 6.50s (8 Ran).
(Sir Gordon Brunton), Lord Huntingdon

4741a King Lear Claiming Stakes CLASS F (2-y-o) £2,490 6f.............(1:10)

4661a[3] SPLASH OF SALT (Ire) 7-10 J Quinn (10) *al prmnt, led o'r 2 fs out, hdd one and a half out, sn hrd rdn, rallied to ld wl ins last.*.........(7 to 4 fav op 6 to 4 tchd 9 to 4) 1
GIRL NEXT DOOR 7-7 S Wood (12) *al cl up, effrt and hdwy to ld one and a half fs out, sn rdn, hdd and no extr wl ins fnl furlong.*..............(12 to 1 op 10 to 1) 2
4695a[3] KNOBBLEENEEZE (v) 8-2[1] G Carter (8) *cl up, led 3 fs out till 2 out, sn rdn and one pace.*......(11 to 2 op 7 to 2) 3
4661a[5] JORDYWRATH 7-9 (7*) G Mitchell (1) *chsd ldrs, rdn 2 fs out, styd on.*..............(4 to 1 op 3 to 1 tchd 4 to 1) 4
SOLEIL RAYON (Ire) 7-12 J Fanning (2) *chsd ldrs, rdn 2 fs out, kpt on one pace.*..............(11 to 2 op 4 to 1) 5
4708a[9] HERSHEBAR 7-11[2] (5*) N Kennedy (7) *chsd ldrs, rdn o'r 2 fs out, one pace.*..................................(25 to 1) 6
PAINT THE WIND (Ire) 7-2 (7*) D Wright (4) *mid-div, effrt and some hdwy 2 fs out, nvr dngrs.* ....(9 to 1 op 7 to 1 tchd 10 to 1) 7
PYTCHLEY DAWN 8-0 (5*) Stephen Davies (3) *slwly into strd, some hdwy fnl 2 fs.*..........(20 to 1 op 16 to 1) 8
4697a[8] GENESIS FOUR (bl) 7-5 (7*) Darren Moffatt (13) *nvr rch ldrs.* ....(25 to 1 op 20 to 1) 9
4708a MUSICAL TIMES (bl) 7-8[1] (7*) Madeleine Smith (6) *mid-div, effrt and some hdwy hfwy, sn rdn and wknd.* ....(16 to 1 op 12 to 1) 10
4675a[8] CONBRIO STAR 7-12 G Bardwell (11) *led till 3 fs out, wknd quickly.*..............................(25 to 1 op 20 to 1) 11
4700a MANADEL (bl) 8-7 S Webster (5) *al rear.* ....(33 to 1 op 25 to 1) 12
ASHGROVE PLUM 7-13 A Munro (9) *slwly into strd, al beh.*..............................(20 to 1 op 12 to 1) 13
Dist: Nk, 2½l, 1½l, 2l, ¾l, 2½l, ½l, 2½l, 6l, 3l. 1m 15.90s. a 2.50s (13 Ran).
SR: 14/10/9/3/-/-/ (B Haggas), W J Haggas

4742a Taming Of The Shrew Handicap CLASS F (0-70 3-y-o and up) £2,616 1¾m.......................... (1:40)

ISLAND BLADE (Ire) [48] 3-8-7 G Carter (7) *mid-div, hdwy hfwy, led 6 fs out, wl clr o'r 2 out, eased fnl furlong.* ....(8 to 1 op 5 to 1) 1
4707a[8] MALENOIR (USA) [53] 4-9-5 Dean McKeown (13) *mid-div, hdwy 6 fs out, rdn o'r 2 out, kpt on one pace.* ....(8 to 1 op 10 to 1) 2
MINGUS (USA) [53] 5-9-5 J Fanning (6) *steady hdwy 5 fs out, rdn o'r 2 out, kpt on one pace.* ....(10 to 1 op 8 to 1 tchd 11 to 1) 3
4698a[2] LORD ADVOCATE [44] (v) 4-8-10 D Holland (2) *al prmnt, sn rdn, hdwy 4 fs out, one pace fnl 3 furlongs.* ....(15 to 2 op 6 to 1 tchd 8 to 1) 4
4714a[5] JALORE [42] 3-7-8 (7*) M Humphries (4) *in tch, effrt and hdwy 4 fs out, sn rdn and no imprsn.* (8 to 1 op 6 to 1) 5
ZOOM LENS (Ire) [57] 3-9-2 W Ryan (1) *mid-div, effrt and hdwy 5 fs out, sn rdn and one pace.* ....(17 to 2 op 6 to 1 tchd 9 to 1) 6
LAFKADIO [48] 5-8-9 (5*) S D Williams (15) *prmnt, rdn 6 fs out, sn wknd.*..................................(20 to 1) 7
PEAK DISTRICT [40] 6-8-1 (5*) A Tucker (14) *effrt and some hdwy hfwy, sn btn.*..............(10 to 1 op 6 to 1) 8
4714a[9] BRIDGE PLAYER [49] (v) 5-8-8 (7*) Darren Moffatt (5) *nvr a factor.*..................................(14 to 1) 9
4688a* GHOSTLY GLOW [49] (v) 3-8-8 A Munro (10) *chsd ldrs, rdn hfwy, wknd 4 fs out.* (9 to 4 fav op 9 to 2 tchd 5 to 1) 10
KHOJOHN [48] (bl) 4-8-9 (5*) Stephen Davies (11) *chsd ldr, rdn 4 fs out, wknd.*..................................(25 to 1) 11
4671a[6] WOTAMONA [27] 4-7-5[3] (5*) A Garth (8) *al rear*....(25 to 1) 12
4670a SILLY HABIT (USA) [48] 6-9-0 V Smith (9) *al rear, tld off fnl 3 fs.*..............................(20 to 1 op 16 to 1) 13
IRISH NATIVE (Ire) [58] 4-9-10 R P Elliott (12) *al beh, tld off.* ....(33 to 1) 14
4705a GLASGOW [51] (bl) 3-8-10 J Quinn (16) *mid-div, effrt and hdwy hfwy, sn wknd, tld off.*..... (12 to 1 op 20 to 1) 15
4698a[8] BLYTON STAR (Ire) [32] 4-7-11[4] (5*) N Kennedy (17) *led till 6 fs out, sn wknd, tld off.*..............(33 to 1) 16
Dist: 3½l, ½l, 5l, 2l, 7l, 3l, 1½l, 1½l, 1½l, 3l. 3m 9.30s. a 9.30s (16 Ran).
(The Lime Street Racing Syndicate), R Akehurst

4743a Julius Caesar Claiming Stakes (Div II) CLASS F (3-y-o and up) £2,406 6f ....(2:10)

4660a[2] AFRICAN CHIMES 5-9-0 (3*) Emma O'Gorman (1) *trkd ldrs gng wl, effrt 2 fs out, led appr fnl furlong, quickened clr.*..............................(Evens fav op 6 to 4) 1
KILTROUM (Fr) 3-8-1 L Charnock (2) *chsd ldrs, rdn 2 fs out, kpt on wl fnl furlong.*..........(25 to 1 op 20 to 1) 2
4699a[8] QUATRE FEMME 5-7-10 J Fanning (11) *al prmnt, ev ch 2 fs out, sn rdn and kpt on.*............ (12 to 1 op 7 to 1) 3
4660a[5] SWINGING LADY 4-7-10 J Quinn (6) *cl up, led o'r 2 fs out, rdn and hdd appr fnl furlong, sn wknd.* ....(10 to 1 op 7 to 1) 4
4706a[6] STAMSHAW 3-7-4[1] (7*) J Bramhill (10) *chsd ldrs, rdn 2 fs out, kpt on one pace.*..............................(25 to 1) 5

FIGHTER SQUADRON 3-8-7^{3} (5*) S D Williams (4) *led till o'r 2 fs out, sn rdn and wknd*........(14 to 1 op 10 to 1) 6
4716a JOVIAL KATE (USA) 5-8-6 M Hills (7) *beh, some hdwy 2 fs out, nvr dngrs*.......(10 to 1 op 14 to 1 tchd 16 to 1) 7
4706a* CRECHE (bl) 3-9-7 N Day (5) *cl up, ev ch 2 fs out, sn rdn and wknd*..............(9 to 2 op 5 to 2 tchd 5 to 1) 8
GINA'S DELIGHT 4-7-3 (7*) Darren Moffatt (8) *al rear*. ....(33 to 1) 9
BOLD HABIT 7-8-10 (5*) Stephen Davies (3) *al rear*. ....(4 to 1 op 5 to 2 tchd 9 to 2) 10
GRACELAND LADY (Ire) (bl) 4-7-10 N Carlisle (9) *slwly into strd, rapid hdwy hfwy, rdn and wknd quickly 2 fs out*. ....(33 to 1) 11

Dist: 7l, ¾l, 1½l, 2l, 2l, 3l, 1½l, ½l, 1l, 12l. 1m 15.20s. a 1.80s (11 Ran).
SR: 49/5/-/-/-/-/ (D G Wheatley), W A O'Gorman

4744a King Henry VI Handicap CLASS F (0-80 3-y-o and up) £2,448 1m (2:40)

4710a^{6} EAST BARNS (Ire) [45] (bl) 4-7-10 J Fanning (11) *hdwy hfwy, led o'r 2 fs out, sn clr, rdn fnl furlong, ran on*. ....(12 to 1 op 8 to 1) 1
4705a^{4} LOCK KEEPER (USA) [55] 6-8-6 G Carter (6) *prmnt whn hmpd aftr one furlong and beh, swtchd wide strt, str run fnl 2 fs, not rch wnr*..........(12 to 1 op 10 to 1) 2
RINGLAND (USA) [77] 4-9-7 (7*) Darren Moffatt (5) *beh, hdwy 2 fs out, sn rdn and kpt on*... (12 to 1 op 8 to 1) 3
BALLERINA BAY [59] (v) 4-8-10 J Williams (13) *mid-div, hdwy hfwy, effrt o'r 2 fs out, sn rdn and one pace*. ....(4 to 1 tchd 9 to 2 and 3 to 1) 4
HAWAII STORM (Fr) [68] 4-9-0 (5*) A Tucker (10) *chsd ldrs, effrt 3 fs out, sn rdn and one pace*. ....(10 to 1 tchd 11 to 1) 5
4692a^{5} GYMCRAK TYCOON [74] 3-9-9 J Quinn (3) *dwlt, beh till hdwy on bit o'r 3 fs out, ev ch 2 out, sn rdn and btn*. ....(7 to 2 fav op 9 to 2 tchd 5 to 1) 6
4705a* DON'T DROP BOMBS (USA) [44] (v) 3-7-7 (5ex) G Bardwell (14) *chsd ldrs, ev ch o'r 2 fs out, sn rdn and wknd appr fnl furlong*.........................(8 to 1 op 5 to 1) 7
4696a^{4} CRESELLY [58] 5-8-9 Dean McKeown (12) *chsd ldrs, rdn 3 fs out, sn wknd*........................(12 to 1 op 6 to 1) 8
4707a NO COMEBACKS [56] 4-8-7 S Webster (8) *nvr rch ldrs*. ....(11 to 1 op 9 to 1) 9
BEST EFFORT [61] 6-8-12 A Munro (2) *cl up till rdn and wknd 3 fs out*........................(20 to 1 op 14 to 1) 10
CASHTAL DAZZLER [51] (bl) 5-8-2^{1} L Charnock (7) *led till o'r 2 fs out, sn wknd*.............................(20 to 1) 11
4692a GENERAL JOHN (Ire) [72] 3-9-7 Dale Gibson (9) *cl up, rdn o'r 3 fs out, sn wknd*.........................(25 to 1) 12
SCOTTISH PARK [62] 3-8-6 (5*) Stephen Davies (4) *prmnt till rdn and wknd o'r 3 fs out*. ....(16 to 1 op 14 to 1 tchd 20 to 1) 13
4710a^{5} SUGEMAR [58] 6-8-6^{2} (5*) S D Williams (1) *al rear*. ....(10 to 1 op 8 to 1) 14

Dist: 1l, 2l, hd, 4l, 1l, 3½l, sht-hd, sht-hd, 1½l, 5l. 1m 43.20s. a 3.70s (14 Ran).
SR: 9/16/32/13/10/11/ (Mrs M Baggott), T D Barron

4745a Hamlet Nursery CLASS F (2-y-o) £2,385 7f.................... (3:10)

4717a^{4} MISTER BLAKE [56] 8-3 D Holland (5) *chsd ldrs, effrt 2 fs out, rdn to ld appr fnl furlong, ran on*. ....(9 to 2 op 7 to 2) 1
4691a* POLEDEN (USA) [74] 9-7 M Hills (6) *sn led, rdn 2 fs out, hdd appr fnl furlong, kpt on*...........(7 to 2 op 2 to 1) 2
4708a^{2} GUSSIE FINK-NOTTLE (Ire) [61] 8-8 Alex Greaves (2) *chsd ldr, ev ch 2 fs out, sn rdn and btn*. ....(5 to 4 on op 11 to 8 tchd 6 to 4) 3
THE ATHELING (Ire) [63] 8-3 (7*) S Mulvey (4) *chsd ldrs, rdn hfwy, sn wknd*...................(9 to 1 op 6 to 1) 4
CIZARD (Ire) [46] 7-7 S Wood (1) *chsd ldrs to hfwy, sn wknd*.......................................(33 to 1) 5
FIVE CLUBS (Ire) [50] 7-4 (7*) Kim McDonnell (3) *outpcd*. ....(16 to 1) 6
4665a^{9} MISS OFFIE [54] 7-10 (5*) A Garth (7) *dwlt, outpcd till some hdwy und pres hfwy, sn wknd*...............(12 to 1) 7

Dist: 2l, 10l, 3l, 2l, 5l, 2l. 1m 30.50s. a 4.20s (7 Ran).
SR: 10/22/-/-/ (Red Seven Stable), W A O'Gorman

LINGFIELD (A.W) (std)
Thursday December 3rd
Going Correction: MINUS 0.50 sec. per fur.

4746a Dancing Floor Claiming Stakes (Div I) CLASS F (3-y-o and up) £2,364 1m ....(12:10)

KING PARROT (Ire) 4-7-12 (3*) D Harrison (4) *settled in 3rd pl, shaken up to ld wl ins fnl furlong, ran on*. ....(12 to 1 op 8 to 1 tchd 14 to 1) 1
NELLIE DEAN 3-7-10 Dale Gibson (1) *led til hdd und pres wl ins fnl furlong, kpt on nr line*............(5 to 2 jt-fav op 9 to 4 tchd 7 to 2) 2
ULLADULLA 3-8-9 T Quinn (11) *hdwy o'r 3 out, jnd ldr ins fnl furlong, ev ch, not quicken cl hme*. ....(9 to 1 op 4 to 1 tchd 10 to 1) 3

4733a^{9} UP THE PUNJAB 3-7-8^{7} (7*) B Russell (2) *chsd ldr til o'r 3 out, outpcd appr fnl furlong*. ....(15 to 2 op 7 to 1 tchd 8 to 1) 4
WESSEX MILORD 7-7-8 (7*) Claire Balding (7) *drpd towards rear aftr 2 fs, styd on one pace ins last two furlongs*. ....(66 to 1 op 50 to 1 tchd 100 to 1) 5
TSAR ALEXIS (USA) 4-8-1 A Munro (10) *outpcd in rear til moderate late hdwy*........................(33 to 1) 6
4680a^{6} PREDICTABLE 6-8-5 J Quinn (8) *mid-div, rdn alng 3 out, no imprsn on ldrs*............(5 to 2 jt-fav tchd 2 to 1) 7
JUST CALL ME MADAM (Ire) 3-7-12^{7} (3*) S O'Gorman (3) *chsd frnt rnk, rdn and no prog 2 out*.........(33 to 1) 8
DREAM CARRIER (Ire) 4-8-13 B Rouse (9) *improved frm rear o'r 3 out, rdn and wknd 2 out*. ....(100 to 30 op 3 to 1 tchd 4 to 1) 9
ROCKY BAY 3-7-10^{5} (5*) N Gwilliams (6) *nvr plcd to chal frm hfwy*.....................(33 to 1 op 14 to 1) 10
TRICKY VERA (Ire) 3-7-8 G Bardwell (5) *pld hrd, speed to hfwy, sn wknd*...................(50 to 1 op 20 to 1) 11

Dist: Hd, nk, 10l, ¾l, nk, ¾l, 1½l, 5l, 2l, 3l. 1m 39.58s. a 2.68s (11 Ran).
(Lord Huntingdon), Lord Huntingdon

4747a Three Hostages Maiden Stakes CLASS F (2-y-o) £2,343 6f....(12:40)

TEE-EMM 8-7 (7*) L Carter (2) *made virtually all, rdn clr wl o'r one out*...................(50 to 1 op 33 to 1) 1
SQUIRE YORK 9-0 J Williams (8) *dwlt, improved o'r 3 out, rdn and ran on appr fnl furlong, not rch wnr*. ....(25 to 1 op 14 to 1) 2
RED ADMIRAL 9-0 Dale Gibson (4) *chsd wnr, rdn and outpcd wl o'r one out*. (10 to 1 op 8 to 1 tchd 11 to 1) 3
CHRISTIAN SPIRIT 8-11 (3*) R Perham (7) *cld on ldrs, o'r 3 out, one pace ins last 2 fs*..........(25 to 1 op 14 to 1) 4
PISTOL (Ire) (bl) 9-0 T Quinn (5) *cl up in 3rd pl til rdn and wknd wl o'r one out*. ....(9 to 4 on op 2 to 1 on tchd 7 to 4 on) 5
4720a^{8} M A EL-SAHN 9-0 B Rouse (6) *in tch, rdn and no imprsn ins last 2 fs*.........................(10 to 1 op 6 to 1) 6
4676a^{5} RUANO 9-0 W Woods (3) *al outpcd*. ....(8 to 1 op 6 to 1 tchd 10 to 1) 7
4668a^{4} WESTERN VALLEY 8-9 D Biggs (1) *broke fst, speed to hfwy, grad lost tch*...............(5 to 1 tchd 9 to 2) 8

Dist: 3l, 3l, 1l, sht-hd, 6l, 2l, 8l. 1m 12.91s. a 2.11s (8 Ran).
(The Hammond Partnership), P Howling

4748a Dancing Floor Claiming Stakes (Div II) CLASS F (3-y-o and up) £2,364 1m ....(1:10)

4688a^{6} KILLICK 4-7-10 J Quinn (8) *pressed ldr, led o'r 4 out, pushed clr over 2 out, styd on ins fnl furlong*. ....(16 to 1 op 33 to 1) 1
SUNSET STREET (Ire) 4-8-1 A Munro (3) *slwly into strd, beh til ran on frm 2 out, fnshd wl*. ....(2 to 1 op 9 to 4 tchd 5 to 2) 2
DANCING BOAT (bl) 3-7-12 (3*) D Harrison (5) *ldg grp, rdn and not quicken last 2 fs*. ....(12 to 1 op 10 to 1 tchd 14 to 1) 3
NATIVE CHIEFTAN 3-8-11 B Rouse (11) *wl in tch, rdn and one pace frm 2 out*...........(6 to 4 fav op 6 to 4 on) 4
4678a^{6} FAYNAZ (bl) 6-7-8 (7*) Kim McDonnell (4) *slwly into strd, sn pressing ldrs, wknd appr fnl furlong*. ....(11 to 2 op 6 to 1 tchd 7 to 1) 5
RIO TRUSKY 3-8-1 D Biggs (1) *slwly into strd, nvr nr to chal frm hfwy*...................(33 to 1 op 25 to 1) 6
ITHKURNI (USA) 3-8-4 G Carter (6) *led till hdd o'r 4 out, rdn and wknd over one out*..........(8 to 1 op 5 to 1) 7
4699a LIFE'S A BREEZE 3-8-7 J Williams (2) *sn beh*. ....(12 to 1 op 8 to 1 tchd 14 to 1) 8
PRINCESS EUROLINK 4-7-6^{1} (5*) A Garth (7) *in tch til wknd hfwy*...................................(33 to 1) 9
NUTMEG LASS 3-8-3^{2} G Baxter (10) *al outpcd*. ....(33 to 1 op 25 to 1) 10

Dist: 2l, 4l, 3l, 5l, 6l, 3l, 1½l, 2l, 12l. 1m 38.32s. a 1.42s (10 Ran).
SR: 1/-/-/-/-/-/ (T S Wallace), R E Peacock

4749a Thirty Nine Steps Handicap CLASS F (0-90 3-y-o and up) £2,709 1¼m ....(1:40)

4670a^{3} KHRISMA [59] 3-8-6 W Ryan (1) *made all, stdly drw wl clr frm 3 out*...............(9 to 2 op 7 to 2 tchd 5 to 1) 1
4723a^{6} TALENTED TING (Ire) [70] 3-9-3 Dale Gibson (6) *trkd wnr, rdn and outpcd frm 2 out*. ....(9 to 1 op 5 to 1 tchd 10 to 1) 2
4678a* DOUBLE ECHO (Ire) [73] 4-9-10 A Munro (4) *al racing in 3rd pl, rdn and outpcd o'r 2 out*. ....(13 to 8 fav op 2 to 1 tchd 9 to 4) 3
VINTAGE [77] 7-10-0 J Williams (3) *hld up in rear, pushed alng and outpcd 4 out, styd on ag'n fnl furlong, nrst at finish*.................(12 to 1 op 8 to 1 tchd 14 to 1) 4
PENNY DROPS [67] 3-8-11 (3*) D Harrison (2) *in tch, pushed alng 5 out, wknd o'r 3 out*... (4 to 1 op 2 to 1) 5
SCALES OF JUSTICE [73] 6-9-10 M Hills (5) *in tch til pushed alng and wknd o'r 3 out, tld off*. ....(5 to 1 tchd 11 to 2 and 9 to 2) 6

Dist: 12l, sht-hd, ¾l, 3l, 15l. 2m 5.08s. a 1.88s (6 Ran).
SR: 23/10/16/18/-/-/ (Lord Howard de Walden), Mrs J Cecil

4750a Greenmantle Handicap CLASS F (0-70 3-y-o and up) £2,343 1m 5f ....(2:10)

AMAZON EXPRESS [52] 3-8-11 T Quinn (8) *prog frm rear 7 out, chsd ldr 5 out, led on bridle entering fnl furlong, hrd hld*........(11 to 10 fav op 5 to 4 on tchd 5 to 4) 1
4670a[7] DR ZEVA [28] 6-7-2[2] (7*) D Wright (9) *beh til ran on 3 out, styd on wl ins fnl furlong, not quicken nr line.* ....(16 to 1 op 14 to 1) 2
4679a[2] CASPIAN BELUGA [63] 4-9-7 (7*) T G McLaughlin (3) *led, wl clr aftr 4 fs, hdd entering fnl furlong, no extr.* ....(9 to 2 op 4 to 1 tchd 5 to 1) 3
RIYADH LIGHTS [35] 7-7-12[1] (3*) D Harrison (1) *wl plcd, outpcd 5 out, styd on one pace appr last 2 fs.* (33 to 1) 4
4671a[3] PLEASURE AHEAD [35] 5-8-0 Dale Gibson (4) *sn pushed alng in 4th pl, outpcd o'r four out.* ....(7 to 2 op 4 to 1 tchd 9 to 2) 5
4671a[5] TIFFANY GEM (Ire) [51] (v) 3-8-10 A Munro (2) *wl plcd til wknd last 4 fs*....................(16 to 1 op 12 to 1) 6
LUSTY LAD [42] 7-8-7[1] B Rouse (6) *beh aftr 4 fs.* ....(20 to 1 op 14 to 1) 7
4678a[8] BROUGHTON BLUES (Ire) [30] (e/s) 4-7-9 J Quinn (5) *al rear div*..................(12 to 1 op 10 to 1 tchd 16 to 1) 8
MAGADEER (USA) [64] 3-9-9 G Carter (7) *mid-div til wknd 5 fs out*............................(8 to 1 op 6 to 1) 9
Dist: 3l, 3l, 5l, 10l, 8l, 2l, 1½l, 5l. 2m 45.13s. a 2.13s (9 Ran).
SR: 11/-/16/-/-/-/ (Mrs Jill Moss), R Akehurst

4751a Richard Hannay Handicap CLASS F (0-70 3-y-o and up) £2,301 7f.. (2:40)

4705a[3] HENIU (USA) [55] (v) 3-9-4 A Munro (5) *wth ldr, led 4 out, pushed clr wl o'r one out, not extended.* ....(7 to 4 fav op 9 to 4 tchd 5 to 2) 1
4690a QUINZII MARTIN [45] 4-8-9 J Williams (3) *beh til ran on ins last 2 fs, not rch wnr*... (9 to 1 op 8 to 1 tchd 10 to 1) 2
4690a[6] SPENDER [40] 3-8-3 J Quinn (7) *pressed ldrs, ev ch 2 out, rdn and not quicken o'r one out.* ....(9 to 1 op 10 to 1 tchd 12 to 1) 3
4725a[9] SALLY'S SON [64] 6-9-11 (3*) Emma O'Gorman (1) *ldg grp, one pace und pres appr fnl furlong.* ....(13 to 2 op 4 to 1 tchd 7 to 1) 4
4725a[6] LUCKNAM STYLE [43] 4-8-7 G Bardwell (2) *chsd frnt rnk, not quicken 3 out, styd on one pace appr fnl furlong.* ....(33 to 1 op 16 to 1) 5
NOBBY BARNES [52] 3-9-1 G Carter (8) *slwly into strd, cld on ldrs hfwy, rdn and no extr last 2 fs.* ....(6 to 1 op 4 to 1) 6
JOLTO [47] 3-8-10 D Biggs (4) *led for 3 fs, wknd and eased frm 2 out*..............(7 to 1 op 6 to 1 tchd 8 to 1) 7
4736a[2] LIFT BOY (USA) [45] 3-8-8 B Rouse (6) *wl plcd til wknd o'r 2 out, eased whn btn*.............. (9 to 2 op 3 to 1) 8
4725a SIRMOOR (Ire) [48] (bl) 3-8-11 A McGlone (9) *slwly into strd, al beh, eased whn btn appr last 2 fs, tld off.* ....(16 to 1 op 10 to 1 tchd 20 to 1) 9
Dist: 3l, 1l, 1½l, 1½l, 4l, 6l, sht-hd, 20l. 1m 25.71s. a 2.11s (9 Ran).
SR: 20/2/-/13/-/-/ (Henryk de Kwiatkowski), Lord Huntingdon

4752a Fleurets Handicap CLASS F (0-80 3-y-o and up) £2,499 5f....... (3:10)

4672a* INDIAN ENDEAVOUR [60] 3-8-11 M Hills (2) *cl up, led hfwy, pushed clr wl o'r one out, kpt on strly.* ....(2 to 1 fav tchd 9 to 4 and 7 to 4) 1
4672a[3] SERIOUS HURRY [52] (v) 4-8-3 J Quinn (8) *led to hfwy, one pace appr fnl furlong*.............(4 to 1 tchd 6 to 1) 2
PALEY PRINCE (USA) [74] 6-9-11 A Munro (9) *sn in tch, styd on one pace appr fnl furlong, no imprsn on wnr.* ....(11 to 2 op 5 to 1 tchd 6 to 1) 3
4706a[3] VERY DICEY [77] (bl) 4-10-0 T Quinn (6) *ldg grp, rdn and no extr o'r one out*........ (7 to 2 op 5 to 1 tchd 11 to 2) 4
4672a[8] PENDOR DANCER [47] 9-7-12 D Biggs (7) *chsd ldrs till lost pl hfwy, kpt on ag'n appr fnl furlong.* ....(20 to 1 op 12 to 1) 5
SUMMER EXPRESS [66] 3-8-10 (7*) M Humphries (1) *hmpd and lost pl aftr 100 yards, nvr on terms later stages.* ....(16 to 1 op 12 to 1 tchd 20 to 1) 6
4672a[4] TAUBER [60] 8-8-8 (3*) S O'Gorman (4) *nvr better than mid-div*...............(15 to 2 op 9 to 2 tchd 8 to 1) 7
4706a SIR TASKER [76] 4-9-13 J Williams (10) *speed to hfwy, sn btn*...............(16 to 1 op 10 to 1 tchd 20 to 1) 8
4706a[7] GOLDEN SICKLE (USA) [67] 3-9-1 (3*) Emma O'Gorman (3) *al outpcd in rear*.....(33 to 1 op 12 to 1 tchd 50 to 1) 9
FORT HOPE [45] (bl) 3-7-10 G Bardwell (5) *al beh.* ....(33 to 1 op 25 to 1 tchd 50 to 1) 10
Dist: 5l, ¾l, 2½l, 1l, 2½l, 2½l, ¾l, 5l, 7l. 58.12s. b 0.38s (10 Ran).
SR: 55/27/46/39/5/14/-/11/-/ (Vijay Mallya), R Guest

ST-CLOUD (FR) (heavy)
Saturday December 5th
Going Correction: PLUS 2.00 sec. per fur.

4753a Prix Saraca (Listed) (2-y-o) £12,333 1¼m.......................(1:00)

SAWASDEE (Fr) 9-2 J Boisnard,........................ 1
EMBROS (USA) 8-11 E Saint-Martin,........................ 2
MISS KADROU (Fr) 8-8 M Boutin,........................ 3
ROUMENIEN DANCE (Fr) 8-12 O Poirier,........................ 4
Dist: 4l, 3l, 3l, sht-nk, ½l, 3l. 2m 29.10s. a 24.10s (7 Ran).
SR: 61/48/39/37/ (G Samama), J P Pelat

4754a Prix Denisy (Listed) (3-y-o and up) £12,333 1½m................ (2:00)

LADY OF PERSIA (USA) 5-8-10 E Legrix,........................ 1
ON Y REVIENT 3-9-1 E Saint-Martin,........................ 2
4737a* MARILDO (Fr) 5-9-3 G Guignard,........................ 3
GLORIA MUNDI (Fr) 5-9-0 W Mongil,........................ 4
Dist: Nk, hd, 6l, 4l, 4l, 6l. 2m 57.80s. a 26.80s (7 Ran).
SR: 68/72/73/58/ (Mme C Peters), M A Jarvis

LINGFIELD (A.W) (std)
Wednesday December 9th
Going Correction: MINUS 0.25 sec. per fur.

4755a Art Deco Maiden Stakes (Div I) CLASS F (2-y-o) £2,448 1m.. (12:40)

4747a[4] CHRISTIAN SPIRIT 8-11 (3*) R Perham (2) *led aftr one furlong, hrd rdn appr last, jst hld on.* ....(50 to 1 op 33 to 1) 1
4730a[3] STRICTLY PERSONAL (USA) 9-0 D Holland (8) *hld up, prog hfwy, sn pushed alng, ran on strly ins last, jst fld.* ....(9 to 4 op 6 to 4 tchd 5 to 2) 2
4730a[2] PATSY GRIMES 8-9 Dean McKeown (11) *cl up, jnd wnr o'r 2 fs out, rdn and unbl to quicken ins last.* ....(11 to 2 op 5 to 1 tchd 9 to 2 and 6 to 1) 3
HEART OF SPAIN 9-0 T Quinn (1) *prmnt, rdn hfwy, one pace fnl 2 fs*........................(10 to 1 op 6 to 1) 4
4676a[4] COVEN MOON 8-9 J Quinn (3) *cl up, rdn o'r 2 fs out, sn btn*.................. (20 to 1 op 33 to 1 tchd 50 to 1) 5
4730a ROSIE'S GOLD 8-9 D Biggs (6) *rear, rdn hfwy, nvr on terms*........................(20 to 1 tchd 33 to 1) 6
TACITURN (USA) 8-9 C Nutter (9) *sn last and rdn alng, nvr dngrs*........................(20 to 1 op 12 to 1) 7
4676a DOOGAREY 9-0 Dale Gibson (10) *rdn aftr 3 fs, al beh.* ....(100 to 1 op 33 to 1) 8
4691a[5] MEDLAND (Ire) 9-0 M Hills (5) *wth wnr till rdn and wknd o'r 2 fs out*........................(20 to 1 op 12 to 1) 9
VILLAGE GREEN (Fr) 9-0 A Munro (7) *chsd ldrs, rdn o'r 3 fs out, sn wknd*.......(11 to 8 fav op 5 to 4 tchd 6 to 4) 10
YOUNG SPARKIE 9-0 W Ryan (4) *led one furlong, sn drpd out, tld off frm 2 out*............ (100 to 1 op 50 to 1) 11
Dist: Hd, 1l, 7l, ½l, 2½l, 3l, ¾l, 3½l, 1½l, 15l. 1m 39.87s. a 2.97s (11 Ran).
SR: 25/24/16/-/-/-/ (Bruce Adams), R Hannon

4756a Louis Claiming Stakes CLASS F (3-y-o and up) £2,574 7f......... (1:10)

4735a[3] ABSONAL 5-8-9 A McGlone (13) *rcd wide, prog to join ldrs o'r 2 fs out, hrd rdn and ran on wl to ld cl hme.* ....(3 to 1 fav op 7 to 4) 1
4667a[4] CHANCE REPORT 4-7-10 N Carlisle (3) *wth ldr, led o'r 2 fs out, hrd rdn appr last, hdd cl hme.* (20 to 1 op 14 to 1) 2
4746a[3] ULLADULLA 3-8-11 (3*) R Perham (11) *mid-div, prog to chase ldrs 3 fs out, styd on wl appr last, nvr able to chal*..............(100 to 30 op 3 to 1 tchd 7 to 2) 3
4736a[6] LOOTING (USA) 6-8-1 A Munro (1) *led till o'r 2 fs out, hrd rdn and one pace*................(20 to 1 tchd 25 to 1) 4
SUNLEY SILKS 3-8-13 T Quinn (10) *sn rdn alng, prmnt till one pace fnl 2 fs*........(9 to 2 op 7 to 2 tchd 5 to 1) 5
BEL BARAKA (Ire) 3-8-8 J Williams (14) *wl in rear till ran on appr fnl furlong, nvr nr to chal.* ....(10 to 1 op 6 to 1 tchd 12 to 1) 6
4736a[5] TOSHIBA COMET (bl) 5-8-4 (7*) T G McLaughlin (16) *rcd wide, sn pushed alng in rear, some prog 3 fs out, nvr rchd ldrs*........................(8 to 1 op 7 to 1) 7
4748a[8] LIFE'S A BREEZE 3-8-3 (7*) R Painter (12) *prmnt till wknd 2 fs out, eased whn btn.* ....(33 to 1 op 25 to 1 tchd 50 to 1) 8
LITMORE DANCER 4-7-10 Dale Gibson (9) *nvr bey mid-div*........................(20 to 1 tchd 33 to 1) 9
4735a[6] SOL ROUGE (Ire) 3-7-9 J Fanning (5) *cl up till rdn and wknd 3 fs out*........................ (33 to 1 op 20 to 1) 10
MISTER LAWSON 6-8-1 D Biggs (4) *al wl beh*.... (33 to 1) 11
OFFAS IMAGE 4-7-12[2] (5*) A Tucker (8) *al wl beh.* ....(33 to 1 op 20 to 1) 12
4719a CUMBRIAN CAVALIER 3-8-6 G Bardwell (7) *last away, al wl beh*........................(50 to 1 op 33 to 1) 13
DAL MISS 5-8-2 J Quinn (2) *mid-div till wknd hfwy, sn beh*........................(50 to 1 op 33 to 1) 14
CERTAIN LADY 3-7-8 (5*) A Garth (6) *mid-div, wknd hfwy, sn beh*........................(10 to 1 op 7 to 1) 15
Dist: Nk, 4l, ¾l, 4l, ¾l, 1l, ¾l, 1½l, 2l, 3l. 1m 25.66s. a 2.06s (15 Ran).
SR: 38/24/30/15/15/8/8/5/-/ (Capt R W Hornall), R Hannon

4757a Regency Handicap CLASS F (0-70 3-y-o and up) £2,406 7f........ (1:40)

4733a[2] SIR NORMAN HOLT (Ire) [53] (bl) 3-9-1 R Lappin (5) *made all, hrd rdn appr fnl furlong, hld on wl.* ....(11 to 4 fav op 5 to 2 tchd 3 to 1) 1
ON Y VA (USA) [54] 5-9-3 M Hills (2) *wtd wth, gd prog hfwy, chlgd and ev ch ins fnl furlong, rdn and not quicken cl hme*........(10 to 1 op 7 to 1 tchd 12 to 1) 2
SCOTS LAW [36] 5-7-13 D Biggs (7) *pushed alng to chase wnr, hrd rdn and ev ch appr fnl furlong, not quicken.* ....(16 to 1 op 20 to 1 tchd 33 to 1) 3
4751a[7] JOLTO [47] (v) 3-8-9 T Quinn (3) *prmnt, ev ch 2 fs out, rdn and one pace*........ (14 to 1 op 12 to 1 tchd 16 to 1) 4
ALBERT THE BOLD [66] (e/s) 3-10-0 A Munro (11) *beh, effrt and prog hfwy, nvr rchd ldrs.* .... (11 to 2 op 5 to 1 tchd 13 to 2) 5
4725a[3] VUCHTERBACHER [46] 6-8-2 (7*) T Wilson (1) *sn last and pushed alng, ran on appr fnl furlong, nrst finish.* ....(7 to 2 op 5 to 2 tchd 4 to 1) 6
4725a[7] THE CUCKOO'S NEST [49] 4-8-12 J Williams (9) *beh, effrt o'r 2 fs out, nvr on terms*........ (25 to 1 op 16 to 1) 7
ENTERPRISE LADY (Fr) [40] 5-8-3 S Dawson (6) *al beh.* .... (50 to 1 op 33 to 1) 8
4725a[4] CORAL FLUTTER [60] (bl) 5-9-9 J Quinn (8) *chsd ldrs till rdn and wknd hfwy*............ (5 to 1 tchd 7 to 1) 9
TENDER MOMENT (Ire) [64] 4-9-13 W Ryan (4) *mid-div, lost tch 3 fs out*...........(12 to 1 op 8 to 1 tchd 14 to 1) 10
4723a TULAPET [39] (bl,e/s) 3-8-1[4] D Holland (10) *chsd ldrs till wknd aftr hfwy*................(20 to 1 tchd 14 to 1) 11
Dist: ½l, 3l, 3l, 1l, hd, 2l, 5l, hd, 2½l, 12l. 1m 25.65s. a 2.05s (11 Ran).
SR: 44/44/17/18/34/14/11/-/6/ (D Holt), F H Lee

4758a Adams Handicap CLASS F (0-70 3-y-o and up) £2,595 1m.......... (2:10)

4748a* KILLICK [34] 4-8-0 (5ex) J Quinn (1) *made all, clr o'r 3 fs out, ran on wl appr last.* ....(7 to 4 fav op 5 to 4 tchd 2 to 1) 1
4733a* TADORA (Ire) [51] 3-9-1 (5ex) T Quinn (6) *mid-div, prog to chase wnr 3 fs out, rdn and ran on one pace appr last.* ....(6 to 1 op 5 to 2) 2
4680a[2] KINGCHIP BOY [55] 3-9-5 D Biggs (7) *lost pl and rdn aftr 2 fs, rng on whn not clr run two out, styd on und pres ins last, nrst finish*..................(7 to 2 tchd 4 to 1) 3
4667a[3] DANCING BEAU (Ire) [54] (bl,e/s) 3-9-4 A Munro (10) *rdn alng to chase ldrs, kpt on one pace fnl 2 fs.* .... (14 to 1 op 10 to 1 tchd 16 to 1) 4
BUDDY'S FRIEND (Ire) [55] 4-9-7 M Hills (11) *prog frm mid-div 3 fs out, sn rdn and no imprsn.* .... (10 to 1 op 8 to 1 tchd 12 to 1) 5
4751a[5] LUCKNAM STYLE [39] 4-8-5 S Dawson (2) *chsd wnr to 3 fs out, sn btn*.....................(20 to 1 op 14 to 1) 6
4663a[5] TARA'S DELIGHT [51] 5-9-0 (3*) Emma O'Gorman (5) *strted slwly, beh till effrt o'r 3 fs out, sn no prog.* .... (11 to 2 op 6 to 1 tchd 7 to 1) 7
MAY SQUARE (Ire) [58] 4-9-10 W Ryan (4) *prmnt till wknd o'r 2 fs out*...................... (25 to 1 op 20 to 1) 8
4667a[6] OSGATHORPE [44] 5-8-10 J Williams (3) *al beh.* .... (25 to 1 op 20 to 1) 9
HINTON HARRY (Ire) [38] (bl) 3-8-2[1] D Holland (12) *sn pushed alng in mid-div, no ch fnl 3 fs*........(50 to 1) 10
4706a[8] BARBARA'S CUTIE [40] 4-8-6 G Bardwell (8) *rdn and lost pl aftr a furlong, beh after*..........(20 to 1 op 14 to 1) 11
KATHY FAIR (Ire) [43] 3-8-2 (5*) A Tucker (9) *sn rdn alng, chsd ldrs till wknd hfwy*......... (25 to 1 op 20 to 1) 12
Dist: 4l, 5l, ¾l, sht-hd, 5l, nk, 1½l, nk, ½l, 5l. 1m 38.99s. a 2.09s (12 Ran).
SR: 25/28/17/14/16/-/ (T S Wallace), R E Peacock

4759a Sheraton Apprentice Handicap CLASS F (0-70 3-y-o and up) £2,427 1¼m......................... (2:40)

TAUNTING (Ire) [49] 4-8-11 S McCarthy (6) *chsd ldrs, rdn to ld o'r 2 fs out, ran on wl ins last, jst hld on.* .... (25 to 1 op 20 to 1 tchd 33 to 1) 1
4735a* AWESOME POWER [71] 6-10-5 (5ex) D Gibbs (2) *led for 2 fs, prmnt aftr, chlgd gng wl appr last, hrd rdn and no extr last strds*..........(13 to 8 fav op 6 to 4 tchd 2 to 1) 2
4723a[7] VA UTU [43] 4-7-12 (7*) G Rothwell (8) *rcd wide, beh, lost tch hfwy, styd on wl appr fnl furlong, nvr nrr.* .... (12 to 1 op 10 to 1) 3
4733a[3] PRECIOUS AIR (Ire) [46] 4-8-1 (7*) R Painter (3) *prmnt, ev ch 2 fs out, sn wknd*...................(5 to 1 op 4 to 1) 4
4748a[3] DANCING BOAT [41] (bl) 3-7-13 J Dennis (1) *led aftr 2 fs till o'r two out, sn btn*................(13 to 2 op 9 to 2) 5
SARAH-CLARE [51] 4-8-13 L Carter (9) *prmnt, rdn and ev ch 2 fs out, sn wknd*....(11 to 4 op 2 to 1 tchd 3 to 1) 6
4696a[7] ROYAL ACCLAIM [41] (v) 7-7-10 (7*) Michael Bradley (5) *beh, lost tch hfwy, styd on fnl 2 fs, nvr nrr.* .... (16 to 1 op 14 to 1) 7
4721a[5] JOLI'S GREAT [47] 4-8-2 (7*) T Beaver (4) *chsd ldrs till rdn and wknd aftr hfwy*............. (12 to 1 op 10 to 1) 8
LORICA D'OR [31] 5-7-7 G Milligan (7) *al beh, tld off fnl 3 fs*...................................(66 to 1 op 50 to 1) 9
Dist: Sht-hd, 8l, sht-hd, ½l, 1l, ½l, 6l, 25l. 2m 8.77s. a 5.57s (9 Ran).
SR: 16/37/-/-/-/-/ (Brian Oxton), M Blanshard

4760a Chippendale Handicap CLASS F (0-70 3-y-o and up) £2,448 1½m ....(3:10)

EL VOLADOR [54] 5-9-9 W Ryan (13) *mid-div, steady prog frm hfwy, rdn to ld ins fnl furlong, ran on wl.* ....(7 to 2 fav op 3 to 1) 1
STRAT'S LEGACY [41] 5-8-10 J Quinn (4) *chsd ldrs, prog o'r 3 out, led wl over one furlong out till ins last, ran on one pace*.............(11 to 2 op 5 to 1 tchd 6 to 1) 2
4723a[4] LADY LACEY [48] (v) 5-9-3 J Williams (12) *hld up, prog on outer hfwy, ev ch 3 fs out, sn rdn and not quicken, ran on ag'n ins last*...................(4 to 1 tchd 9 to 2) 3
EL DOMINIO [57] 4-9-12 D Holland (11) *prog hfwy, rdn to ld 2 fs out, sn hdd and one pace*.................(20 to 1) 4
4731a[2] CARLOWITZ (USA) [41] (v) 4-8-10 Candy Morris (1) *rcd freely, led aftr 2 fs till two out, sn btn.* ....(16 to 1 tchd 20 to 1) 5
4750a[5] PLEASURE AHEAD [35] 5-7-13 (5*) A Tucker (6) *prog frm rear 4 fs out, kpt on, nvr rchd ldrs*............ (8 to 1) 6
4670a[6] SAFETY (USA) [46] (bl) 5-9-1 M Hills (14) *mid-div, prog 5 fs out, ev ch o'r 2 out, sn btn*........(20 to 1 op 16 to 1) 7
4721a* BREAKDANCER (Ire) [58] 3-9-7 T Quinn (15) *prog to chase ldrs 5 fs out, no imprsn 2 out, eased whn btn.* ....(7 to 1 tchd 6 to 1) 8
SHARP TOP [42] 4-8-11 D Biggs (3) *sn pushed alng, prmnt till wknd hfwy*........(11 to 2 op 5 to 1 tchd 6 to 1) 9
4699a MONSCOMA (Ire) [38] 4-8-7 A McGlone (9) *led 2 fs, wknd o'r 4 out*.............................. (33 to 1 op 20 to 1) 10
NASEER (USA) [54] (bl) 3-9-3 N Day (10) *keen hold, chsd ldrs till wknd 4 fs out*............ (10 to 1 op 12 to 1) 11
4714a[8] CHARIOTEER [44] (bl) 3-8-7 Dale Gibson (5) *prmnt till wknd aftr hfwy*..................(25 to 1 op 20 to 1) 12
LADY WESTGATE [24] 8-7-4[4] (7*) Iona Wands (8) *drpd last hfwy, beh aftr*..................................(50 to 1) 13
BURRACOPPIN [40] 5-8-9 G Bardwell (7) *al beh.* ....(66 to 1 tchd 100 to 1) 14
Dist: 1½l, 2½l, 2½l, sht-hd, 2l, 2½l, ¾l, 12l, 5l, 1½l. 2m 33.03s. a 3.33s (14 Ran).
SR: 46/30/32/36/19/9/15/19/-/ (I A Baker), R J O'Sullivan

4761a Art Deco Maiden Stakes (Div II) CLASS F (2-y-o) £2,427 1m... (3:40)

4734a[3] MR CUBE (Ire) 9-0 T Quinn (11) *wtd wth, prog to join ldr 3 fs out, led on bit ins last, pushed out.* ....(6 to 4 fav tchd 7 to 4 and 11 to 8) 1
4730a[6] CONVOY (bl) 9-0 M Hills (10) *trkd ldrs, led o'r 3 fs out, rdn and hdd ins last, no ch wth wnr.* ....(9 to 2 op 5 to 2 tchd 5 to 1) 2
ONE OFF THE RAIL (USA) 9-0 Candy Morris (7) *prmnt till outpcd 3 fs out, kpt on*.............. (8 to 1 op 5 to 1) 3
4677a[9] HALHAM TARN (Ire) 9-0 J Williams (6) *beh till styd on wl appr fnl furlong, nvr nr to chal*.....(5 to 1 op 6 to 1) 4
4718a[6] BALLACASCADE 9-0 Dale Gibson (3) *prmnt till rdn and outpcd 3 fs out*................... (20 to 1 op 12 to 1) 5
4730a[8] FREDDIE JACK 9-0 R Lappin (5) *mid-div, rdn o'r 3 fs out, kpt on*.......................... (12 to 1 op 10 to 1) 6
4697a ELEGANT ELLIE (e/s) 8-9 A Munro (1) *mid-div, rdn and no prog hfwy*........................... (25 to 1 op 20 to 1) 7
BEYOND THE LIMIT 8-9 S Dawson (8) *beh, effrt hfwy, sn btn*.................. (11 to 2 op 4 to 1 tchd 13 to 2) 8
PERSIAN STAR (Fr) 8-9 D Biggs (2) *rdn aftr 3 fs, al beh.* .... (25 to 1 op 12 to 1) 9
ONE MORE POUND 8-11 (3*) R Perham (9) *rdn aftr 3 fs, al beh*..(20 to 1 op 12 to 1) 10
MISS PIGLET (Ire) 8-9 A McGlone (4) *led till o'r 3 fs out, wknd rpdly*......................(25 to 1 op 20 to 1) 11
Dist: 2l, 10l, nk, ½l, sht-hd, 6l, ½l, 5l, 1½l, 12l. (Time not taken) (11 Ran).
(Mrs David Anderson), P F I Cole

SOUTHWELL (A.W) (std)

Thursday December 10th

Going Correction: PLUS 0.05 sec. per fur. (races 1,2,3,4,5,6), MINUS 0.25 (7)

4762a Quick Step Nursery CLASS F (2-y-o) £2,322 6f.................. (12:30)

4741a[2] GIRL NEXT DOOR [49] 7-13 S Wood (6) *in tch, gd hdwy 3 fs out, led o'r over one and a half out, sn clr.* ....(3 to 1 fav op 5 to 2 tchd 7 to 2) 1
4720a[4] COMET WHIRLPOOL (Ire) [58] (bl) 8-8 A Munro (9) *chsd ldrs, effrt and rdn 2 fs out, styd on one pace.* .... (17 to 2 op 6 to 1 tchd 9 to 1) 2
MISSED THE BOAT (Ire) [59] 8-9 Alex Greaves (5) *beh, hdwy 2 fs out, sn rdn, kpt on one pace*............. (12 to 1) 3
4734a[2] NUT BUSH [64] 9-0 W Ryan (2) *cl up, sn rdn alng, ev ch 2 fs out, grad wknd*........ (9 to 2 op 5 to 1 tchd 11 to 2) 4
4700a* TANAGOME (USA) [71] (v) 9-0 (7*) D Wright (3) *sn outpcd and rdn alng, hdwy o'r 2 fs out, staying on whn not clr run appr fnl furlong, nvr dngrs.* (100 to 30 op 5 to 2) 5

4700a[9] JOELLISE [47] 7-4 (7*) Claire Balding (8) *in tch till rdn and wknd o'r 2 fs out*.............................. (33 to 1) 6
BAJKA [59] 8-4 (5*) A Garth (4) *chsd ldrs, rdn o'r 2 fs out, sn wknd*..........(12 to 1 op 20 to 1 tchd 25 to 1) 7
4747a* TEE-EMM [58] 8-1 (7*,7ex) L Carter (7) *sn led, rdn wl o'r 2 fs out, hdd over one and a half out, soon wknd*.
....(4 to 1 op 3 to 1) 8
Dist: 6l, sht-hd, hd, 1½l, 1l, 2½l, 3l. 1m 17.10s. a 3.70s (8 Ran).
SR: 11/-/-/-/1/ (Terry Connors), J A Pickering

4763a Rumba Claiming Stakes (Div I) CLASS F (3-y-o and up) £2,343 1½m ....(1:00)

4689a[6] THUNDERBIRD ONE (USA) 3-8-9 Alex Greaves (2) *al prmnt, effrt and hdwy to ld o'r 2 fs out, sn clr, kpt on*.
............(5 to 1 op 9 to 2 tchd 6 to 1 and 7 to 1) 1
SWEET REVIVAL 4-8-5[1] (5*) S D Williams (1) *trkd ldrs, hdwy 3 fs out, rdn 2 out, styd on, not rch wnr*.
....(12 to 1 op 10 to 1) 2
IRON BARON (Ire) 3-8-5 W Ryan (10) *hld up and beh, steady hdwy 5 fs out, ev ch o'r 2 out, sn rdn, hng lft, one pace*.............................(7 to 2 op 2 to 1) 3
4715a[3] KARAMOJA (bl) 3-8-5 Dean McKeown (5) *prmnt, jnd ldr 7 fs out, rdn to ld 2 and a half out, sn hdd and one pace*.
..............................(Evens fav op 5 to 4 on) 4
BY FAR (USA) 6-7-7 (7*) D Wright (9) *slwly away and beh, hdwy 5 fs out, sn rdn, not rch ldrs*.
........(12 to 1 op 16 to 1 tchd 20 to 1 and 25 to 1) 5
PIP'S OPTIMIST 3-7-13 Dale Gibson (6) *sn led, rdn o'r 4 fs out, hdd 2 and a half out, soon wknd*.........(33 to 1) 6
4707a GESNERA (v) 4-8-2 N Carlisle (8) *prmnt to hfwy, sn wknd*.
.....................................(25 to 1 op 20 to 1) 7
ELIZA WOODING 4-8-4 D Biggs (3) *al beh*.
.....................................(14 to 1 op 10 to 1) 8
WHISKEY BLUES 7-8-7 J Quinn (7) *chsd ldr till rdn and wknd hfwy, sn beh*..............................(33 to 1) 9
PROSPECT OF WHITBY 6-8-2 G Bardwell (4) *al rear, rdn hfwy, tld off fnl 3 fs*..............................(33 to 1) 10
Dist: 2l, 5l, ½l, 7l, 3l, 2l, 2l, ½l. 2m 41.90s. a 8.00s (10 Ran).
SR: 21/17/3/2/-/-/ (Miss Ruth Elliot), Denys Smith

4764a Tango Handicap CLASS F (0-70 3-y-o and up) £2,469 1m..........(1:30)

4744a* EAST BARNS (Ire) [50] (bl) 4-9-2 (7ex) Alex Greaves (10) *beh, hdwy hfwy, wide strt, rdn 2 fs out, styd on wl to ld nr finish*..................(9 to 2 op 7 to 2 tchd 5 to 1) 1
CLAUDIA MISS [53] 5-9-5 Dean McKeown (9) *cl up, led 3 and a half fs out, rdn appr fnl furlong, hdd and no extr nr finish*..............(17 to 2 op 7 to 1 tchd 9 to 1) 2
4744a[2] LOCK KEEPER (USA) [53] 6-9-5 G Carter (14) *prmnt, effrt 2 fs out, sn rdn, ev ch till no extr ins fnl furlong*.
.................................(9 to 4 fav tchd 5 to 2) 3
4744a[7] DON'T DROP BOMBS (USA) [40] (v) 3-8-4 Dale Gibson (3) *in tch, effrt and hdwy 3 fs out, rdn and one pace appr fnl furlong*..................(9 to 1 op 8 to 1 tchd 10 to 1) 4
RURAL LAD [62] 3-9-12 M Hills (4) *trkd ldr, effrt and rdn o'r 2 fs out, wknd wl over one out*. (14 to 1 op 12 to 1) 5
4663a CANDESCO [57] 6-9-4 (5*) A Garth (5) *mid-div, rdn and hdwy o'r 3 fs out, kpt on one pace fnl 2*.
.......................(14 to 1 op 12 to 1 tchd 16 to 1) 6
4744a SUGEMAR [56] 6-9-3 (5*) S D Williams (6) *chsd ldrs, rdn and wknd o'r 2 fs out*............(14 to 1 op 12 to 1) 7
4744a CASHTAL DAZZLER [50] 5-9-2 Kim Tinkler (2) *nvr rch ldrs*.
.....................................(25 to 1 op 16 to 1) 8
FRIENDLYPERSUASION (Ire) [55] 4-9-7 W Ryan (8) *beh and sn rdn alng, nvr dngrs*............(12 to 1 op 8 to 1) 9
NORTH FLYER [55] 3-9-5 A Dicks (13) *chsd ldrs to hfwy, sn rdn and wknd*...................(14 to 1 op 10 to 1) 10
4733a SERIOUS ACTION [62] 3-9-12 C Nutter (11) *al rear*.
.....................................(20 to 1 op 14 to 1) 11
CHOICE LOT [45] 5-8-11 C Dwyer (7) *cl up till rdn and wknd 2 and a half fs out*......................(33 to 1) 12
GREEN'S SEAGO (USA) [62] (bl) 4-9-7 (7*) S Wynne (1) *led to hfwy, sn rdn and wknd*............(33 to 1 op 25 to 1) 13
THISONESFORALICE [41] (v) 4-8-7 A Munro (12) *al rear*.
.....................(11 to 1 op 10 to 1 tchd 12 to 1) 14
Dist: Nk, 1l, nk, 3½l, 2l, 5l, 1l, 3½l, 3l, 5l. 1m 44.60s. a 5.10s (14 Ran).
SR: 32/34/31/15/26/17/1/-/-/ (Mrs M Baggott), T D Barron

4765a Fox Trot Handicap CLASS F (0-100 3-y-o and up) £2,364 7f....... (2:00)

4664a* ALLINSON'S MATE (Ire) [76] 4-8-10 Alex Greaves (1) *hld up, hdwy 3 fs out, smooth run on outer to ld ins fnl furlong*.
.................................(7 to 2 jt-fav op 4 to 1) 1
4692a[3] PANIKIN [85] 4-9-5 J Williams (9) *cl up, led 2 and a half fs out, sn rdn, hdd and not quicken ins last*....(7 to 2 jt-fav op 5 to 2) 2
4710a* DEBSY DO (USA) [69] 3-7-9 (7*) D Wright (2) *chsd ldrs, effrt 2 fs out, sn ev ch, rdn and one pace appr fnl furlong*.
.........................(4 to 1 op 7 to 2 tchd 9 to 2) 3
4739a[6] EASTLEIGH [67] 3-8-0[1] A Munro (7) *hld up, hdwy o'r 2 fs out, sn ev ch, rdn and wknd entering fnl furlong*.
.....................................(14 to 1 op 12 to 1) 4
POP TO STANS [77] 3-8-10 G Bardwell (4) *chsd ldrs, sn rdn alng, grad wknd fnl 2 fs*......................(12 to 1) 5
4710a[4] SANDMOOR DENIM [61] 5-7-9[1] J Quinn (6) *hdwy hfwy, ev ch 2 fs out, sn rdn and wknd*........(4 to 1 op 7 to 2) 6
4743a[7] JOVIAL KATE (USA) [60] 5-7-8 S Wood (5) *led, rdn and hdd 2 and a half fs out grad wknd*.
.........(12 to 1 op 14 to 1 tchd 20 to 1 and 25 to 1) 7
AFFAIR OF STATE (Ire) [90] 3-9-9 G Carter (3) *chsd ldrs till lost pl and beh frm hfwy*...............(10 to 1 op 8 to 1) 8
Dist: 1½l, 2½l, nk, 5l, sht-hd, 1½l, 20l. 1m 30.30s. a 4.00s (8 Ran).
SR: 41/45/20/17/12/ (Peter Jones), T D Barron

4766a Jive Maiden Stakes CLASS F (2-y-o) £2,448 7f..................... (2:30)

DANCE TO ORDER (Ire) 9-0 C Nutter (6) *cl up, led aftr one furlong, rdn 2 out, hdd entering fnl furlong, rallied gmely to ld on line*..................(7 to 1 op 3 to 1) 1
4691a[2] MAJOR TRIUMPH (Ire) 8-9 M Hills (4) *chsd ldrs, hdwy hfwy, chlgd 2 fs out, rdn and slight ld entering last furlong, hdd and no extr nr line*.
.....................................(5 to 4 on tchd 6 to 4) 2
4740a[2] SCOFFERA 8-9 Kim Tinkler (11) *chsd ldrs, rdn 2 fs out, kpt on one pace*..........................(10 to 1 op 8 to 1) 3
BADAWI (Fr) 8-7 (7*) G Forster (10) *outpcd and beh, hdwy hfwy, styd on fnl 2 fs, nrst finish*. (10 to 1 op 16 to 1) 4
4747a[7] RUANO 9-0 W Woods (7) *led one furlong, cl up till rdn and wknd 2 fs out*....(11 to 1 op 10 to 1 tchd 12 to 1) 5
NYMPH ERRANT 8-9 W Ryan (2) *prmnt, rdn wl o'r 2 fs out, sn wknd*..............................(6 to 1 op 7 to 1) 6
BUZZ-B-BABE 8-9 (5*) S D Williams (3) *nvr rch ldrs*.
.....................................(25 to 1 op 20 to 1) 7
KEEP BREATHING 8-7 (7*) S Mulvey (5) *outpcd and beh*.
..............................(14 to 1 tchd 16 to 1) 8
PERSONIMUS 9-0 G Carter (9) *al outpcd and beh*.
.....................................(20 to 1 op 33 to 1) 9
GIRTON BELLE 8-9 A Munro (1) *slwly away, al beh*.
....(33 to 1) 10
WOODLANDS ELECTRIC 9-0 J Williams (8) *chsd ldrs to hfwy, sn wknd*..............................(50 to 1) 11
Dist: Sht-hd, 8l, nk, 5l, ½l, hd, 5l, 2l, 3½l, 7l. 1m 30.90s. a 4.60s (11 Ran).
SR: 36/30/6/10/-/-/ (Mrs David Thompson), Sir Mark Prescott

4767a Rumba Claiming Stakes (Div II) CLASS F (3-y-o and up) £2,343 1½m ....(3:00)

4715a[5] TEMPERING 6-8-11 S Wood (9) *sn led and clr, quickened 3 fs out, unchlgd*.....(9 to 4 fav op Evens tchd 5 to 2) 1
4715a[4] MAJESTIC SINCLAIR (Ire) (bl) 3-8-1 A Munro (8) *chsd ldrs, rdn alng 4 fs out, styd on one pace fnl 2 furlongs*.
....(4 to 1 op 11 to 4) 2
4689a[4] MAPLE BAY (Ire) 3-9-1 J Williams (5) *chsd ldr, rdn o'r 3 fs out, sn one paced*..................(5 to 1 tchd 7 to 1) 3
4705a BELIEVE IN ME (Ire) 3-8-9 M Hills (4) *chsd ldr, rdn o'r 4 fs out, one pace*..............(16 to 1 tchd 20 to 1) 4
FAUSTNLUCE LADY 3-7-9[1] J Quinn (3) *nvr rch ldrs*.
....(20 to 1) 5
SWAGMAN (USA) 5-8-9 G Carter (1) *chsd ldrs, rdn 5 fs out, sn wknd*.......................(16 to 1 op 14 to 1) 6
UNASSUMING (bl) 4-8-13[3] D Nicholls (7) *chsd ldrs to hfwy, sn wknd*...........................(20 to 1 op 33 to 1) 7
BASSIO (Bel) 3-8-5 G Bardwell (6) *al rear*.
....(7 to 2 op 5 to 1) 8
COIN GAME (Ire) 4-8-7 S Webster (2) *al beh, tld off fnl 5 fs*.
....(50 to 1) 9
Dist: 10l, 2l, 1½l, 5l, nk, 10l, 1½l. 2m 42.50s. a 8.60s (9 Ran).
SR: 17/-/-/-/-/-/ (David W Chapman), D W Chapman

4768a Viennese Waltz Handicap CLASS F (0-70 3-y-o and up) £2,511 5f.. (3:30)

4752a* INDIAN ENDEAVOUR [68] 3-10-5 (7ex) M Hills (2) *beh far side, rdn alng hfwy, hdd o'r one and a half fs out, styd on to ld nr finish*...............(4 to 1 fav op 5 to 2) 1
4736a[4] HINARI VIDEO [47] 7-8-12 Dean McKeown (8) *cl up centre, effrt and rdn to ld ins fnl furlong, edgd lft, hdd nr finish*..(16 to 1) 2
4739a[3] ARC LAMP [56] 6-9-7 J Fanning (10) *cl up centre, rdn and ev ch entering fnl furlong, no extr nr finish*.
......................(11 to 2 op 8 to 1 tchd 10 to 1) 3
4719a[8] LINCSTONE BOY (Ire) [52] (bl) 4-9-3 S Webster (11) *cl up, ev ch appr fnl furlong, sn rdn and kpt on*.
.....................................(14 to 1 op 20 to 1) 4
4701a* LE CHIC [52] 6-9-3 S Wood (12) *o'rall ldr stands side, hdd and wknd ins fnl furlong*.
.......................(13 to 2 op 6 to 1 tchd 7 to 1) 5
4716a[9] LYNDON'S LINNET [56] 4-9-7 A McGlone (16) *chsd ldr stands side, rdn 2 fs out, styd on fnl furlong*.
.......................(14 to 1 op 12 to 1 tchd 16 to 1) 6
4699a[6] BLACK BOY (Ire) [49] 3-9-0 G Carter (6) *beh, rdn and styd on fnl 2 fs*..........................(33 to 1 op 25 to 1) 7
4710a[7] THE DREAM MAKER (Ire) [47] 3-8-12 N Day (3) *cl up far side till rdn and wknd appr fnl furlong*.
.......................(16 to 1 op 25 to 1 tchd 14 to 1) 8

DRUMMER'S DREAM (Ire) [40] (v) 4-8-5 A Munro (1) *gd speed far side till wknd one and a half fs out.* .... (8 to 1 op 14 to 1 tchd 16 to 1) 9

4719a^{6} MEESON TIMES [63] 4-10-0 W Ryan (14) *sluggish strt and beh, rdn hfwy, styd on fnl furlong.* .... (12 to 1 op 10 to 1 tchd 14 to 1) 10

4719a^{3} DOESYOUDOES [55] (v) 3-9-6 J Williams (15) *chsd ldr stands side, rdn and wknd 2 fs out.*.......... (10 to 1) 11

4736a^{7} JOE SUGDEN [53] 8-9-4 D Nicholls (17) *chsd ldrs stands side, rdn and one pace fnl 2 fs.*..... (10 to 1 op 7 to 1) 12

CAMINO A RONDA [38] 3-7-10 (7*) Kim McDonnell (7) *gd speed centre for 3 fs.*........ (50 to 1) 13

4743a^{6} FIGHTER SQUADRON [57] (v) 3-9-3 (5*) S D Williams (9) *nvr rch ldrs.*........ (14 to 1 op 10 to 1) 14

CALVANNE MISS [49] 6-9-0 D Biggs (13) *nvr a factor.* .... (9 to 1 op 12 to 1 tchd 16 to 1 and 8 to 1) 15

BASSETLAW BELLE [30] 3-7-9 J Quinn (4) *al rear.* (33 to 1) 16

4719a^{7} GRAND TIME [58] 3-9-9 G Bardwell (5) *al rear.* .... (10 to 1 op 7 to 1) 17

Dist: Sht-hd, 1½l, ¾l, sht-hd, hd, ½l, sht-hd, hd, 2½l, 3l. 1m 0.20s. a 1.90s (17 Ran).

SR: 56/34/37/30/29/32/23/20/12/ (Vijay Mallya), R Guest

HOLLYWOOD (USA) (firm)
Sunday December 13th

4769a Hollywood Turf Cup (Grade 1) (3-y-o and up) £146,277 1½m.............

FRAISE (USA) 4-9-0 P Valenzuela,............ (10 to 7 on) 1D

BIEN BIEN (USA) 3-8-10 C McCarron,.......... (46 to 10) 1

TRISHYDE (USA) 3-8-7 A Solis,.............. (66 to 10) 3

REVASSER (USA) 3-8-7 C Nakatani,............ (71 to 10) 4

4729a^{4} CAMPAGNARDE (Arg) 5-8-11 C Black,....... (10 to 7 on) 5

TEL QUEL (Fr) 4-9-0 G Stevens,.............. (44 to 10) 6

Dist: Nose, 1 ¼l, 1 ¾l, nk, 12l. 2m 31.20s. (6 Ran).

(Truely McCaffery), P Gonzalez

SOUTHWELL (A.W) (std)
Tuesday December 15th

Going Correction: PLUS 0.10 sec. per fur. (races 1,2,3,5,7,8), MINUS 0.10 (4,6)

4770a Coverdale Claiming Stakes (Div I) CLASS F (2-y-o) £2,343 7f....(12:00)

4717a* GOLDEN KLAIR 8-7 D Holland (3) *steadied strt, dashed up on outsd hfwy, led appr fnl furlong, ran on strly.* .... (9 to 4 tchd 2 to 1 and 5 to 2) 1

DAANIERA (Ire) 8-4 G Carter (4) *made most till hdd and rdn appr fnl furlong, kpt on same pace.* .... (9 to 1 op 7 to 1 tchd 10 to 1) 2

LARN FORT 8-0 J Fanning (6) *nvr far away, drvn alng whn pace quickend last 2 fs, one pace.* .... (20 to 1 op 16 to 1) 3

4708a^{6} ANOTHER KINGDOM 7-12 J Quinn (5) *trkd ldg quartet, hrd at work o'r 2 fs out, no imprsn.* (10 to 1 op 7 to 1) 4

4717a^{3} CERTAIN WAY (Ire) (v) 7-12 L Charnock (2) *pressed ldg pair, drvn alng whn pace lifted 2 fs out, sn outpcd.* .... (6 to 1 op 7 to 1 tchd 5 to 1) 5

4741a^{8} PYTCHLEY DAWN 7-13^{1} (5*) Stephen Davies (7) *unruly at strt, broke wl to show speed to hfwy, lost pl, styd on ag'n fnl furlong.*.... (20 to 1 op 12 to 1 tchd 25 to 1) 6

4762a* GIRL NEXT DOOR 7-9 S Wood (1) *broke smartly to show speed to hfwy, lost pl and drvn alng one pace last 2 fs.* .... (7 to 4 fav op 13 to 8 tchd 9 to 4) 7

4717a^{7} LOCHORE (bl) 7-7 (5*) A Garth (9) *settled midfield, hrd at work hfwy, outpcd last 2 fs.* .... (14 to 1 op 10 to 1 tchd 20 to 1) 8

STRATAGEM 7-12 D Biggs (8) *sn flt out and struggling, tld off frm hfwy.*........ (25 to 1 op 14 to 1) 9

Dist: 2½l, 4l, 1½l, 1½l, 1½l, sht-hd, 3l, 20l. 1m 31.10s. a 4.80s (9 Ran).

SR: 32/21/5/-/-/-/ (C John Hill), C J Hill

4771a Southwell Amateur Riders Handicap CLASS F (0-80 3-y-o and up) £2,595 1m.................. (12:30)

4751a^{6} NOBBY BARNES [49] 3-10-8 Miss E Bronson (8) *confidently rdn, led on bit jst o'r one furlong out, shaken up, easily.*........ (15 to 2 op 7 to 1) 1

4744a^{5} HAWAII STORM (Fr) [67] 4-11-9 (5*) Mrs F Whitfield (1) *trkd ldg trio, ran wide and lost grnd entering strt, gd hdwy o'r one out, ran on wl.*......... (10 to 1 tchd 14 to 1) 2

PRIME MOVER [63] (bl) 4-11-5 (5*) Mr N Miles (9) *al hndy, effrt and drvn alng last 2 fs, kpt on same pace.* .... (7 to 1 tchd 5 to 1) 3

4767a* TEMPERING [67] 6-11-9 (5*,5ex) Miss R Clark (11) *bolted gng to strt, set gd clip and sn clr, wknd and hdd appr fnl furlong.*........... (15 to 2 op 5 to 1 tchd 8 to 1) 4

BREEZED WELL [57] 6-10-13 (5*) Mrs H Noonan (13) *trkd ldg half dozen, feeling pace hfwy, rallied and not much room fnl furlong, styd on.*... (16 to 1 op 14 to 1) 5

PARKING BAY [63] 5-11-5 (5*) Mr R Pritchard-Gordon (10) *chsd ldg bunch, outpcd hfwy, styd on last 2 fs, nvr nrr.* .... (12 to 1 op 8 to 1 tchd 14 to 1) 6

4764a^{7} SUGEMAR [56] 6-10-12 (5*) Mr M Chapman (2) *chsd ldg quartet, hrd at work hfwy, styd on, nvr nrr.* .... (16 to 1 op 14 to 1) 7

4739a^{9} INDIAN MAESTRO [48] 6-10-4 (5*) Mr Chris Wilson (12) *patiently rdn, steady hdwy on outsd to improve entering strt, not quicken last 2 fs.*............... (33 to 1) 8

BUZZARDS CREST [36] 7-9-6 (5*) Miss Diana J Jones (4) *beh and chsd alng hfwy, gd hdwy o'r one furlong out, nvr nrr.*........ (20 to 1 op 16 to 1) 9

4744a^{4} BALLERINA BAY [57] (v) 4-11-4 Miss I Diana W Jones (7) *tucked away in midfield, feeling pace appr strt, nvr able to chal.*....... (3 to 1 fav op 11 to 4 tchd 4 to 1) 10

BILL MOON [54] 6-11-1 Miss J Feilden (3) *chsd ldg pair, drvn alng entering strt, fdd.*........ (8 to 1 op 5 to 1) 11

CREPT OUT (Ire) [63] 3-11-3 (5*) Mr A Walton (15) *chsd alng to go pace hfwy, nvr a threat.*..... (14 to 1 op 10 to 1) 12

NORTHERN CONQUEROR (Ire) [38] 4-9-8 (5*) Mrs J Naughton (14) *chsd ldg 5, hrd at work hfwy, sn btn.* .... (10 to 1 op 7 to 1) 13

SENNON COVE [35] 3-9-7^{4} (5*) Mr S Joynes (16) *chsd ldg bunch, struggling hfwy, sn lost tch.*......... (50 to 1) 14

Dist: 3l, ¾l, 3l, ¾l, nk, ¾l, 2½l, nk, 1½l, 2½l. 1m 47.10s. a 7.60s (14 Ran).

SR: 20/31/25/20/8/13/4/-/-/ (T S M S Riley-Smith), D A Wilson

4772a Coverdale Claiming Stakes (Div II) CLASS F (2-y-o) £2,322 7f.....(1:00)

4740a^{3} MOONSTRUCK BARD 8-4 W Woods (1) *nvr far away, led o'r one furlong out, drvn out.*..... (14 to 1 op 10 to 1) 1

DIAMOND POINT 8-0 C Nutter (6) *al hndy, led entering strt till o'r one furlong out, rallied gmely.* .... (10 to 1 op 6 to 1) 2

4745a* MISTER BLAKE 8-1 D Holland (2) *last and niggled alng aftr 2 fs, improved frm off the pace last two furlongs, nrst finish.*........ (7 to 4 fav tchd 2 to 1) 3

PETERED OUT 7-12 J Fanning (4) *trkd ldg 5, scrubbed alng hfwy, no imprsn last 2 fs.*.. (12 to 1 tchd 14 to 1) 4

4695a^{2} MASTER SINCLAIR (Ire) 7-13 (5*) A Garth (7) *improved frm midfield hfwy, hrd at work 2 fs out, no extr.* .... (2 to 1 op 7 to 4 tchd 9 to 4) 5

4717a^{9} IRISH ROOTS (Ire) (v) 7-12 J Quinn (3) *wth ldrs, hrd drive o'r 2 fs out, fdd.*........ (9 to 1 op 6 to 1 tchd 10 to 1) 6

4741a^{7} PAINT THE WIND (Ire) (bl) 7-12^{1} L Charnock (5) *made most till hdd entering strt, fdd.*........ (12 to 1 op 10 to 1) 7

4766a^{8} KEEP BREATHING (v) 7-12^{7} (7*) S Mulvey (8) *trkd ldg half dozen, und pres entering strt, nvr dngrs.* .... (20 to 1 tchd 25 to 1) 8

SCHOOL OF SCIENCE 8-7 Alex Greaves (9) *chsd alng to keep up hfwy, nvr a factor.*............ (20 to 1) 9

Dist: Nk, 5l, 3½l, ¾l, 6l, 1½l, 7l, 2l. 1m 30.80s. a 4.50s (9 Ran).

SR: 33/28/14/-/4/-/ (D G Raffel), S P C Woods

4773a Classic Car Weekly Celebration Nursery CLASS F (2-y-o) £2,364 5f ....(1:30)

4734a* IOLITE [73] 9-7 M Hills (2) *al gng wl, led nrly 2 fs out, sprinted clr fnl furlong.* .... (13 to 8 fav op 7 to 4 tchd 6 to 4 and 15 to 8) 1

4762a^{2} COMET WHIRLPOOL (Ire) [58] (bl) 8-6 W Ryan (4) *nvr far away, ev ch and drvn alng o'r one furlong out, not pace of wnr.*........... (11 to 2 op 7 to 2 tchd 6 to 1) 2

4708a^{5} JOCKS JOKER [64] 8-12 G Carter (8) *broke fst to ld for jst o'r 3 fs, rdn and no extr fnl furlong.* .... (11 to 2 op 7 to 1 tchd 8 to 1) 3

4708a^{4} BRIGHT GEM [54] 8-2 J Fanning (9) *al frnt rnk, drvn alng whn pace quickened o'r one furlong out, one pace.* .... (6 to 1 op 9 to 2 tchd 13 to 2) 4

4741a^{6} HERSHEBAR [52] (bl) 8-0 J Quinn (10) *wl-plcd stands side for o'r 3 fs, no extr.*........ (12 to 1 op 10 to 1) 5

WELL TRIED (Ire) [53] 7-10 (5*) A Garth (7) *chsd alng to go pace hfwy, kpt on, nvr nrr.*....... (20 to 1 op 14 to 1) 6

4734a^{8} NIKKI NOO NOO [57] 8-5 G Bardwell (5) *chsd alng to improve frm midfield last 2 fs, nrst finish.* .... (12 to 1 op 8 to 1) 7

BURBLE [45] 7-7 S Wood (1) *unruly gng to post, swrvd badly lft leaving stalls, nvr able to reco'r.*..... (33 to 1) 8

IGNITED [48] 7-10 Dale Gibson (3) *drvn alng to keep up aftr 2 fs, nvr a factor.*..................... (33 to 1) 9

DON'T TELL JEAN [49] 7-11^{2} D Biggs (6) *taken to post early, bustled alng thrght, al outpcd.*......... (33 to 1) 10

PAT POINDESTRES [53] 7-12 (3*) D Holland (11) *drvn alng to go pace aftr 2 fs, tld off.*........ (16 to 1 op 12 to 1) 11

Dist: 4l, ¾l, ½l, 2l, ¾l, nk, 12l, ½l, 2½l, 10l. 1m 0.60s. a 2.30s (11 Ran).

SR: 51/20/23/11/1/-/2/-/-/ (R P Marchant), M A Jarvis

4774a Littondale Claiming Stakes CLASS F (3-y-o and up) £2,406 6f..... (2:00)

4699a^{2} MISS CALCULATE 4-7-12 J Fanning (11) *trkd ldg quartet, improved o'r one furlong out, ran on grimly to ld last strds.*........................ (7 to 1 op 5 to 1) 1

4739a* APPLEDORN 5-8-8 W Ryan (8) *nvr far away, led and quickened 2 fs out, wknd and ct last strds.* ....(11 to 10 on op 5 to 4 tchd 6 to 4) 2
4716a4 SAMSOLOM 4-8-7 G Carter (10) *chsd ldg 5, improved und pres last few fs, styd on same pace.* (11 to 1 op 10 to 1) 3
4743a5 STAMSHAW 3-7-8 S Wood (9) *chsd alng in midfield, improved 2 fs out, nvr able to chal.* (20 to 1 op 14 to 1) 4
4743a4 SWINGING LADY 4-7-10[1] J Quinn (4) *broke wl to dispute ld for o'r 4 fs, fdd*..................(5 to 1 op 3 to 1) 5
4731a7 JUVENARA 6-8-1 G Bardwell (5) *pushed alng to improve frm off the pace last 2 fs, nvr nr to chal.* ....(16 to 1 op 14 to 1 tchd 20 to 1) 6
EWALD (Ire) 4-8-2 R P Elliott (2) *slight ld for 4 fs, fdd und pres o'r one furlong out.* ....(9 to 1 op 14 to 1 tchd 8 to 1) 7
KAYRUZ 4-8-7 Dean McKeown (7) *bustled alng in midfield, nvr able to trble ldrs*.........(16 to 1 op 12 to 1) 8
4756a7 TOSHIBA COMET (bl) 5-8-10[1] D Nicholls (6) *lost pl aftr 2 fs, nvr a factor*......................(14 to 1 op 16 to 1) 9
PINK'N BLACK (Ire) 3-7-7[3] (5*) A Garth (1) *wth ldrs, stumbled and lost grnd aftr 2 fs, not reco'r.* ....(20 to 1 op 16 to 1) 10
MISS BELL RINGER 4-8-0 D Biggs (3) *beh thrght.* (25 to 1) 11
Dist: Hd, 5l, 3½l, nk, 2l, 4l, ¾l, 4l, 2l, 4l. 1m 16.60s. a 3.20s (11 Ran).
SR: 32/41/20/-/-/-/ (Capt James Wilson), Capt J Wilson

4775a Garsdale Handicap CLASS F (0-70 3-y-o and up) £2,427 5f....... (2:30)

4768a9 DRUMMER'S DREAM (Ire) [40] (v) 4-8-0 Dale Gibson (8) *scrubbed alng in midfield, improved o'r one furlong out, ran on grimly to ld cl hme*......(8 to 1 op 7 to 1) 1
4768a5 LE CHIC [52] 6-8-12 S Wood (9) *led or dsptd ld, definite advantage hfwy, wknd fnl furlong, jst ct.* ....(9 to 2 tchd 6 to 1) 2
4768a4 LINCSTONE BOY (Ire) [52] (bl) 4-8-12 S Webster (5) *dsptd ld centre, drvn alng o'r one furlong out, kpt on same pace*.................... (6 to 1 op 9 to 2 tchd 13 to 2) 3
4716a* JOHNSTON'S EXPRESS (Ire) [47] 4-8-7 J Quinn (7) *bustled alng in midfield, improved o'r one furlong out, ran on, nvr nrr*............(7 to 2 fav op 9 to 4 tchd 4 to 1) 4
4719a5 ABSOLUTION [66] 8-9-12 D Holland (2) *broke wl to show gd speed for o'r 3 fs, no extr*.........(6 to 1 op 5 to 1) 5
4768a7 BLACK BOY (Ire) [49] (v) 3-8-4 (5*) S D Williams (3) *reco'red frm sluggish strt to press ldrs for over 3 fs, no extr.* ....(7 to 1 op 10 to 1 tchd 11 to 1) 6
4768a DOESYOUDOES [55] 3-8-8 (7*) Kim McDonnell (10) *drvn alng in chasing grp hfwy, styd on, nvr able to chal.* ....(12 to 1 op 10 to 1) 7
4736a8 IMCO DOUBLE (Ire) [54] 4-9-0 J McLaughlin (4) *chsd ldrs, hrd at work hfwy, nvr able to chal.* ....(12 to 1 op 10 to 1) 8
4768a3 ARC LAMP [62] 6-9-8 Dean McKeown (6) *dsptd ld centre, drvn alng last 2 fs, fdd.* (6 to 1 op 5 to 1 tchd 13 to 2) 9
ORIENTAL SONG [33] (bl) 3-7-0 (7*) D Wright (1) *struggling to keep up hfwy, nvr a threat*..... (33 to 1 op 25 to 1) 10
Dist: Hd, 1l, 1l, 1½l, sht-hd, ½l, 1l, nk, 10l. 1m 0.70s. a 2.40s (10 Ran).
SR: 28/39/35/26/39/21/25/20/27/ (Wayne Burton), Mrs N Macauley

4776a Windermere Handicap CLASS F (0-70 3-y-o and up) £2,427 1¾m ....(3:00)

4705a2 LOOKINGFORARAINBOW (Ire) [62] 4-10-0 N Day (11) *patiently rdn, smooth hdwy to join ldr entering strt, sn led, kpt on wl fnl furlong.* ....(8 to 1 op 11 to 2 tchd 9 to 1) 1
4742a3 MINGUS (USA) [51] 5-9-3 D Nicholls (10) *drpd out strt, steady hdwy to improve on ins entering strt, ev ch o'r one furlong out, kpt on same pace.* (10 to 1 op 8 to 1) 2
SHAKINSKI [63] (v) 3-9-8 D Biggs (2) *nvr far away, drvn through on ins entering strt, styd on one pace fnl furlong*................(9 to 1 op 7 to 1 tchd 10 to 1) 3
KINOKO [43] 4-8-9 J Corrigan (3) *bustled alng in midfield aftr a m, styd on wl last 2 fs, needed race.* ....(9 to 1 op 9 to 2) 4
4742a* ISLAND BLADE (Ire) [56] 3-9-1 G Carter (9) *settled midfield, dashed up to ld appr strt, hdd o'r 2 fs out, sn btn.* ....(7 to 4 on op 5 to 4 on tchd 11 to 10 on) 5
COSMIC DANCER [50] 5-8-9 (7*) A Liggins (8) *settled off the pace, styd on last 2 fs, nvr able to chal.* ....(33 to 1 op 25 to 1) 6
4742a5 JALORE [42] (bl) 3-7-8 (7*) M Humphries (6) *chsd ldg trio for o'r a m, rdn entering strt, no extr.* ....(25 to 1 op 14 to 1 tchd 33 to 1) 7
4767a6 SWAGMAN (USA) [43] 5-8-4 (5*) Stephen Davies (4) *slight ld till hdd and wknd appr strt*....... (25 to 1 op 20 to 1) 8
SPANISH WHISPER [32] 5-7-12 Dale Gibson (7) *struggling to go pace thrght, tld off*........ (25 to 1 op 16 to 1) 9
4760a6 PLEASURE AHEAD [35] 5-8-1[2] D Holland (1) *dsptd ld for a m, tld off entering strt*...........(25 to 1 op 14 to 1) 10
4679a6 A A BAMBA [50] (bl) 3-8-9 W Ryan (5) *pressed ldg pair for o'r a m, tld off*...................(20 to 1 op 14 to 1) 11
Dist: 1½l, 1½l, 4l, ½l, 1l, 3l, 20l, 8l, 2½l, 2½l. 3m 11.40s. a 11.40s (11 Ran).
SR: 14/-/2/-/-/-/ (B M Saumtally), Bob Jones

4777a Levy Board Maiden Stakes CLASS F (3-y-o) £2,301 1m.............(3:30)

TACIT MAC (USA) 9-0 D Holland (1) *patiently rdn, improved o'r one furlong out, swshd tail, kpt on to ld last 50 yards*........................(3 to 1 tchd 4 to 1) 1
4767a4 BELIEVE IN ME (Ire) 9-0 M Hills (4) *wth ldr, led hfwy, rdn and ct last 50 yards*................ (25 to 1 op 20 to 1) 2
4722a3 ABBEY STRAND (USA) 8-9 W Ryan (6) *trkd ldg pair, feeling pace and rdn entering strt, one pace last 2 fs.* ....(6 to 5 on op 6 to 4 on tchd Evens) 3
4735a4 GOLD BLADE (bl) 9-0 Dean McKeown (3) *settled gng wl, effrt and rdn entering strt, no response.* ....(5 to 1 op 5 to 2) 4
OUR MAN IN HAVANA 9-0 D Nicholls (5) *slight ld to hfwy, hrd at work 2 fs out, sn btn*......(20 to 1 tchd 25 to 1) 5
MERRYHILL MADAM 8-9 J Quinn (2) *crossed legs and uns rdr leaving stalls*......(10 to 1 op 8 to 1 tchd 11 to 1) ur
Dist: 1½l, 7l, 1½l, 10l. 1m 43.90s. a 4.40s (6 Ran).
SR: 46/41/15/15/-/-/ (T Mohan), W A O'Gorman

LINGFIELD (A.W) (std)
Wednesday December 16th
Going Correction: MINUS 0.50 sec. per fur.

4778a Grohe Maiden Stakes CLASS F (2-y-o) £2,385 1m..............(12:20)

4755a2 STRICTLY PERSONAL (USA) 9-0 D Holland (9) *cl up, trkd ldr o'r 3 fs out, led appr last, ran on wl.* .... (6 to 5 on op 11 to 8 on tchd 11 to 10 on) 1
4761a3 ONE OFF THE RAIL (USA) 9-0 B Rouse (4) *prmnt, led o'r 5 fs out, rdn and hdd appr last, ran on one pace.* ....(12 to 1 op 14 to 1 tchd 16 to 1) 2
MISS FASCINATION 8-9 M Hills (5) *chsd ldrs, effrt 3 fs out, sn rdn and one pace*................(7 to 4 op 6 to 4) 3
4709a4 NANNY MARGARET (Ire) (bl) 8-9 G Bardwell (8) *prmnt, rdn o'r 3 fs out, sn btn*.....(16 to 1 op 8 to 1 tchd 20 to 1) 4
4677a TITLED GIRL (Ire) 8-9 T Quinn (6) *cl up, rdn 3 fs out, sn wknd*................(14 to 1 op 12 to 1 tchd 16 to 1) 5
PETITE VINO (bl) 8-10[8] (7*) Rachel Bridger (7) *nvr on terms wth ldg grp*.............................(50 to 1 op 33 to 1) 6
DORMSTON BOYO 9-0 Dean McKeown (1) *led for one furlong, sn lost pl and struggling*............. (33 to 1) 7+
4740a4 QUATTRO 9-0 B Crossley (3) *al wl beh.* ....(14 to 1 op 10 to 1 tchd 16 to 1) 7+
KAFIOCA (Ire) 8-6 (3*) R Perham (2) *led aftr one furlong till o'r 5 out, wknd rpdly 3 out.* ....(16 to 1 op 14 to 1 tchd 20 to 1) 9
GENTLE MOMENT 8-2 (7*) Gaye Harwood (10) *rcd wide, wl beh frm hfwy*.......................(16 to 1 op 12 to 1) 10
4730a9 ALMONTY (Ire) 9-0 Dale Gibson (11) *al beh, tld off fnl 3 fs.* ....(33 to 1 op 20 to 1) 11
Dist: 3l, 6l, 8l, 3l, 3l, 5l, dd-ht, 1l, 4l, 30l. 1m 38.85s. a 1.95s (11 Ran).
SR: 11/2/-/-/-/-/ (R K Eamer), J H M Gosden

4779a Toinha Claiming Stakes CLASS F (3-y-o and up) £2,385 5f......(12:50)

4706a2 ANOTHER EPISODE (Ire) 3-9-3 G Carter (3) *trkd ldrs, led o'r one furlong out, rdn and jst hld on cl hme.* ....(7 to 4 fav op 6 to 4 tchd 15 to 8) 1
RESPECTABLE JONES 6-8-6 D Biggs (2) *outpcd in mid-div, prog frm hfwy, ran on strly appr fnl furlong, jst fld*..................................(7 to 2 op 9 to 4) 2
4743a8 CRECHE (bl) 3-9-7 N Day (5) *wth ldr till led o'r 3 fs out, rdn and hdd appr last, ran on one pace.* ....(7 to 2 op 9 to 4) 3
4752a2 SERIOUS HURRY (v) 4-8-1 J Quinn (1) *led for o'r one furlong, prmnt aftr till wknd appr last.* ....(11 to 2 op 4 to 1 tchd 6 to 1) 4
SADDLEHOME (USA) 3-8-9 W Ryan (6) *outpcd in mid-div, nvr nr to chal*.........(10 to 1 op 8 to 1 tchd 12 to 1) 5
4756a CUMBRIAN CAVALIER 3-8-4 R Lappin (4) *sn rdn alng, al beh*..................(66 to 1 op 33 to 1 tchd 100 to 1) 6
4672a EVER SO ARTISTIC 5-8-3[1] (7*) Debbie Biggs (7) *chsd ldg trio for 2 fs, sn rdn and wknd*..... (50 to 1 op 25 to 1) 7
4752a FORT HOPE (bl,e/s) 3-7-13 G Bardwell (8) *sn rdn alng, al beh*..................(50 to 1 op 33 to 1 tchd 66 to 1) 8
Dist: Sht-hd, 3½l, 2½l, 8l, 5l, 1l, 12l. 58.17s. b 0.33s (8 Ran).
SR: 60/48/49/19/-/ (Palacegate Corporation Ltd), J Berry

4780a Neva Consultants PLC Maiden Stakes CLASS F (3-y-o) £2,364 1½m ....(1:20)

4721a2 DISPUTED CALL (USA) 9-0 M Hills (4) *hld up, prog hfwy, led on inner wl o'r one furlong out, sn clr, eased cl hme.* ....(6 to 5 on op 5 to 4 tchd 6 to 4 and 5 to 4 on) 1
ETIQUETTE 8-9 Dean McKeown (3) *led, rdn 2 fs out, sn hdd, ran on one pace*..............(7 to 2 op 5 to 2) 2
BLUE SEA 9-0 W Ryan (9) *prmnt, pushed alng hfwy, rdn and unbl to quicken 3 fs out, kpt on one pace.* ....(3 to 1 op 5 to 4) 3

FUNDEGHE (USA) (bl) 9-0 D Biggs (6) *prmnt, rdn 3 fs out, sn btn*.............. (10 to 1 op 8 to 1 tchd 14 to 1) 4
4721a[8] LAJADHAL (Fr) 9-0 D Holland (2) *prmnt till wknd o'r 4 fs out*................ (50 to 1 op 20 to 1 tchd 66 to 1) 5
RICH HEIRESS (Ire) 8-9 Candy Morris (8) *in tch till lost pl hfwy, struggling aftr*.
.... (50 to 1 op 33 to 1 tchd 66 to 1) 6
EARLY GALES 8-9 G Bardwell (1) *trkd ldrs, hrd rdn 5 fs out, sn wknd*........ (50 to 1 op 25 to 1 tchd 66 to 1) 7
PRINCESS JO 8-9 J Quinn (7) *rdn 5 fs out, al beh*.
.... (40 to 1 op 20 to 1 tchd 66 to 1) 8
KALOKAGATHOS (v) 8-11 (3*) R Perham (5) *al beh, tld off 5 fs out*.............. (50 to 1 op 33 to 1 tchd 66 to 1) 9
Dist: 3½l, 4l, 10l, 5l, ½l, 12l, 1l, dist. 2m 32.79s. a 3.09s (9 Ran).
SR: 9/-/-/-/-/-/ (J W Hills), J W Hills

4781a Dr Frances Handicap CLASS F (0-80 3-y-o and up) £2,432 7f....... (1:50)

4722a* DASWAKI (Can) [78] 4-10-0 B Rouse (4) *set steady pace for 3 fs, led ag'n and quickened 2 out, ran on wl ins last*.
.... (2 to 1 fav op 2 to 1) 1
4725a* KISSAVOS [60] (v) 6-8-10 T Quinn (7) *prmnt, led 4 fs out till 2 out, rdn and not quicken, eased whn btn ins last*.
.... (11 to 4 op 3 to 1 tchd 5 to 2) 2
AMETHYSTINE (USA) [59] 6-8-2 (7*) S Drowne (3) *last and pushed alng hfwy, ran on appr fnl furlong, nvr nrr*.
.... (14 to 1 op 10 to 1) 3
4681a[8] MOGWAI (Ire) [61] (bl) 3-8-10 W Ryan (6) *keen hold, cl up till rdn and not quicken 2 fs out*.
.... (10 to 1 op 6 to 1 tchd 12 to 1) 4
4744a[6] GYMCRAK TYCOON [73] 3-9-8 J Quinn (2) *keen hold, trkd ldrs till unbl to quicken o'r 2 fs out*.
.... (5 to 1 op 7 to 2 tchd 6 to 1) 5
4722a[5] SARUM [61] 6-8-11 Dale Gibson (1) *keen hold, trkd ldrs, rdn 3 fs out, one pace*............. (12 to 1 op 8 to 1) 6
SHARPTINO [70] 3-9-2 (3*) R Perham (5) *prmnt till wknd o'r 2 fs out*........... (12 to 1 op 8 to 1 tchd 14 to 1) 7
Dist: 5l, hd, 1½l, ½l, 1l, 8l. 1m 24.87s. a 1.27s (7 Ran).
SR: 42/9/7/3/13/-/-/ (David Allen), R Hannon

4782a Source Limited Handicap CLASS E (0-100 3-y-o and up) £3,021 1¼m ....(2:20)

4722a[4] MULCIBER [60] 4-8-8 G Carter (2) *al prmnt, rdn 2 fs out, ran on to wl ins last, drvn out*.
.... (20 to 1 op 16 to 1 tchd 25 to 1) 1
4749a* KHRISMA [71] 3-9-2 W Ryan (12) *prmnt, rdn to ld 2 fs out, hdd and no extr wl ins last*.
.... (13 to 8 fav op 6 to 4 tchd 2 to 1) 2
BELMOREDEAN [76] 7-9-10 D Biggs (6) *al cl up, rdn 2 fs out, ran on appr last, nrst finish*.
.... (16 to 1 op 12 to 1 tchd 20 to 1) 3
4749a[6] SCALES OF JUSTICE [70] 6-9-4 M Hills (1) *trkd ldrs gng wl, outpcd o'r 2 fs out, ran on ins last, nvr nrr*.
.... (20 to 1 op 14 to 1) 4
4731a* ANNACURRAGH (Ire) [66] 3-8-6 (5*) Stephen Davies (11) *prmnt, led o'r 3 fs out till 2 out, rdn and one pace*.
.... (5 to 1 op 6 to 1 tchd 8 to 1) 5
BOOKCASE [72] (e/s) 5-8-13 (7*) J Hunter (5) *hld up and beh, effrt whn hmpd o'r 2 fs out, ran on ins last, nrst finish*............... (10 to 1 op 12 to 1 tchd 14 to 1) 6
4679a[7] RAPPORTEUR (USA) [80] 6-10-0 T Quinn (10) *beh, pushed alng to improve on outer hfwy, sn outpcd, styd on ag'n appr fnl furlong*..... (20 to 1 op 12 to 1 tchd 25 to 1) 7
4748a[4] NATIVE CHIEFTAN [71] 3-9-2 B Rouse (3) *led till o'r 3 fs out, sn wknd*............ (12 to 1 op 10 to 1 tchd 14 to 1) 8
4749a[3] DOUBLE ECHO (Ire) [73] 4-9-7 Dean McKeown (7) *prog to join ldrs o'r 3 fs out, sn wknd*.
.... (5 to 1 op 4 to 1 tchd 7 to 2) 9
AKKAZAO (Ire) [75] 4-9-4 (5*) N Gwilliams (9) *trkd ldrs till rdn and wknd 3 fs out*.
.... (20 to 1 op 10 to 1 tchd 25 to 1) 10
4767a[8] BASSIO (Bel) [73] 3-8-11 (7*) G Forster (4) *mid-div, rdn hfwy, sn wknd*...... (33 to 1 op 20 to 1 tchd 50 to 1) 11
4760a[4] EL DOMINIO [57] 4-8-5 D Holland (8) *rcd wide, rdn hfwy, al last*.............................. (5 to 1 op 6 to 1) 12
Dist: 1½l, 2l, 2½l, sht-hd, 2½l, hd, 2½l, nk, ½l, 6l. 2m 5.16s. a 1.96s (12 Ran).
SR: 24/29/33/22/14/18/25/8/12/ (Mrs Penny Treadwell), G Harwood

4783a S.W. Shower Supplies Limited Handicap CLASS F (0-70 3-y-o and up) £2,364 6f.................(2:50)

4736a[3] PIGALLE WONDER [37] (bl) 4-7-11 D Biggs (11) *prmnt, led wl o'r 2 fs out, rdn and hdd over one out, rallied to ld well ins last*........... (11 to 2 op 5 to 1 tchd 6 to 1) 1
4736a* BANBURY FLYER [57] 4-9-3 J Quinn (5) *cl up gng wl, effrt to ld o'r one furlong out, hdd and not quicken well ins last*................ (9 to 4 fav op 2 to 1 tchd 5 to 2) 2
MASTER HYDE (USA) [52] 3-8-12 M Hills (10) *rear, rdn hfwy, ran on strly appr fnl furlong, nvr nrr*.
.... (14 to 1 op 10 to 1) 3
4719a[2] LITTLE SABOTEUR [68] 3-10-0 D Holland (8) *cl up, effrt and rdn 2 fs out, ran on ins last, nrst finish*.
.... (11 to 2 op 4 to 1 tchd 6 to 1) 4

PRECIOUS WONDER [64] 3-9-5 (5*) A Garth (4) *rear, rdn and rng on whn not clr run 2 fs out, styd on ins last, nvr nrr*........................ (12 to 1 op 8 to 1) 5
4719a LAST STRAW [32] (bl) 4-7-1[2] (7*) D Wright (3) *led till wl o'r 2 fs out, rdn and one pace*......... (25 to 1 op 20 to 1) 6
4725a JUCEA [51] (v) 3-8-11 T Quinn (2) *prmnt, hrd rdn hfwy, wknd o'r one furlong out*.
.... (9 to 1 op 10 to 1 tchd 12 to 1) 7
4725a GEMINI BAY [42] (bl) 3-8-2 S Dawson (7) *squeezed out strt, last till styd on o'r one furlong out, nvr dngrs*. (33 to 1) 8
4752a[5] PENDOR DANCER [44] 9-8-1 (3*) R Perham (9) *prmnt, ev ch 2 fs out, wknd appr last*........ (14 to 1 tchd 16 to 1) 9
4756a[4] LOOTING (USA) [36] 6-7-10 Dale Gibson (12) *al rear*.
.... (10 to 1 op 8 to 1 tchd 12 to 1) 10
4768a MEESON TIMES [63] 4-9-9 W Ryan (6) *sn rdn alng, al rear*.
.... (8 to 1 op 5 to 1 tchd 10 to 1) 11
EMERALD EARS [39] (bl) 3-7-13[10] (7*) S Drowne (1) *al beh*.
.... (33 to 1 op 20 to 1) 12
4758a BARBARA'S CUTIE [40] (v) 4-8-0 G Bardwell (13) *beh, drvn alng to improve hfwy, sn wknd*....(33 to 1 op 20 to 1) 13
Dist: ½l, 1½l, hd, 3½l, nk, sht-hd, sht-hd, ¾l, 1½l, 3l. 1m 12.68s. a 1.88s (13 Ran).
SR: -/3/-/7/-/-/ (Miss Nicola M Pfann), R J O'Sullivan

4784a Levy Board Apprentice Handicap CLASS F (0-70 3-y-o and up) £2,280 1 ¼m........................ (3:20)

4759a[3] VA UTU [43] 4-8-10 (5*) R Painter (5) *wtd wth, prog 3 out, led a furlong out, ran on wl*.
.... (6 to 1 op 7 to 1 tchd 8 to 1) 1
4723a* TWILIGHT SECRET [59] 3-10-0 Mark Denaro (8) *prmnt, led wl o'r 3 fs out, hdd one out, unbl to quicken*.
.... (11 to 10 on op 11 to 10 tchd 6 to 5) 2
4759a* TAUNTING (Ire) [54] 4-9-12 (5ex) S McCarthy (4) *prmnt till rdn and ev ch 2 fs out, ran on one pace*.
.... (6 to 1 op 5 to 2 tchd 7 to 1) 3
SHARP THISTLE [43] 6-9-1 D McCabe (1) *wtd wth, prog o'r 3 fs out, hrd rdn and one pace appr last*.
.... (8 to 1 op 12 to 1 tchd 6 to 1) 4
4723a[9] DANCING SENSATION (USA) [32] (bl) 5-8-4 T Wilson (2) *prmnt, led o'r 4 fs till over 3 out, hrd rdn and wknd appr last*.............. (6 to 1 op 14 to 1 tchd 5 to 1) 5
4746a[4] UP THE PUNJAB [53] 3-9-8 M Humphries (3) *led till o'r 4 fs out, wknd rpdly*................ (14 to 1 op 10 to 1) 6
4757a TULAPET [35] (bl,e/s) 3-8-4 A Martinez (7) *al wl beh, tld off fnl 3 fs*.......................... (50 to 1 op 33 to 1) 7
VERMONT MAGIC [55] 4-9-13 C Avery (6) *al beh, tld off fnl 3 fs*.............................. (33 to 1 op 20 to 1) 8
Dist: 1½l, 1l, 1½l, 4l, 15l, 12l, 12l. 2m 7.39s. a 4.19s (8 Ran).
SR: 9/19/15/1/-/ (M Quinn), M R Channon

SOUTHWELL (A.W) (std)
Thursday December 17th
Going Correction: PLUS 0.15 sec. per fur.

4785a Clive Wisdom Claiming Stakes (Div I) CLASS F (3-y-o and up) £2,343 1m ....(12:20)

4764a[3] LOCK KEEPER (USA) 6-8-3 G Carter (8) *pushed alng to improve frm off the pace entering strt, led jst o'r one furlong out, drvn clr, eased*.
.... (15 to 8 op 5 to 2 tchd 3 to 1) 1
4756a* ABSONAL 5-8-9 A McGlone (9) *nvr far away, quickened to ld briefly o'r one furlong out, kpt on same pace fnl furlong*............ (5 to 4 fav op Evens tchd 6 to 4) 2
SIRTELIMAR (Ire) 3-8-5 (5*) A Garth (1) *dictated pace, kicked for hme entering strt, hdd o'r one furlong out, rallied*.......................................(10 to 1) 3
4764a NORTH FLYER 3-8-5[1] A Dicks (3) *al hndy, rdn whn pace quickened last 2 fs, fdd*.................... (14 to 1) 4
AMENABLE 7-9-5 Alex Greaves (4) *settled off the pace, improved entering strt, fdd 2 fs out, needed race*.
.... (9 to 2 op 2 to 1 tchd 5 to 1) 5
4696a SNO SERENADE 6-8-1 L Charnock (5) *trkd ldg pair, feeling pace entering strt, btn 2 fs out*.
.... (16 to 1 tchd 20 to 1) 6
CAL'S BOY 3-9-0 J Quinn (2) *sluggish strt, drvn into midfield hfwy, fdd 2 fs out*....... (33 to 1 op 20 to 1) 7
SOLEMN MELODY (bl) 5-8-0[1] (3*) A Tucker (6) *sluggish strt, nvr able to reco'r*.............................. (50 to 1) 8
ANGEL TRAIN (Ire) 4-7-12 Dale Gibson (7) *broke wl to show early speed, wknd rpdly frm hfwy*. (16 to 1 op 14 to 1) 9
Dist: 4l, sht-hd, 15l, 3½l, 3½l, 4l, 1½l, 4l. 1m 43.50s. a 4.00s (9 Ran).
SR: 47/41/41/-/-/-/ (Mrs J Mackie), J Mackie

4786a Louise Clark Catering Apprentice Handicap CLASS F (0-70 3-y-o and up) £2,196 1m..............(12:50)

4696a GOLD BELT (Ire) [37] 3-8-4 M Humphries (6) *tucked away on ins, led hfwy, shaken up last 2 fs, kpt on strly*.
.... (12 to 1 op 10 to 1) 1

4746a* KING PARROT (Ire) [60] 4-9-9 (5*) J Wilkinson (3) *slight ld to hfwy, pushed alng to chal ag'n o'r one furlong out, kpt on*........... (11 to 10 fav op 7 to 4 on tchd 5 to 4) 2
REKLAW [31] (bl) 5-7-13 S Mulvey (1) *last and detached hfwy, gd hdwy und pres last 2 fs, fnshd wl.*
........................(9 to 2 op 4 to 1 tchd 5 to 1) 3
4759a7 ROYAL ACCLAIM [41] (v) 7-8-4 (5*) Michael Bradley (4) *bustled alng in midfield, improved und pres o'r 2 fs out, hng lft, styd on same pace.*
.... (4 to 1 op 3 to 1 tchd 9 to 2 and 5 to 1) 4
NIGHT CLUB (Ger) [33] 8-8-1 C Avery (5) *rdn to improve frm midfield hfwy, not much room on ins 2 fs out, kpt on one pace*........................ (10 to 1 op 8 to 1) 5
4705a SHANNON EXPRESS [56] 5-9-5 (5*) S Knott (2) *dsptd ld, rdn o'r 2 fs out, not quicken*..... (6 to 1 tchd 13 to 2) 6
Dist: 1l, sht-hd, 3l, nk, 1½l. 1m 46.80s. a 7.30s (6 Ran).
SR: -/20/-/ (Maurice Oakley), R Hollinshead

4787a Clive Wisdom Claiming Stakes (Div II) CLASS F (3-y-o and up) £2,343 1m ....(1:20)

4731a4 SUPER SUMMIT 3-8-10 G Bardwell (6) *trkd ldr, led o'r one furlong out, sprinted clr.*
.... (7 to 4 fav op Evens tchd 2 to 1) 1
4777a MERRYHILL MADAM 3-8-5 J Quinn (4) *drvn up frm midfield to go hndy entering strt, kpt on same pace ins last.*
.... (12 to 1 op 10 to 1) 2
4764a6 CANDESCO 6-7-11 (5*) A Garth (7) *nvr far away, brght wide and ev ch 2 fs out, one pace ins last.*
................................(9 to 2 op 3 to 1) 3
FERDIA (Ire) 3-8-10 W Ryan (8) *sluggish strt, improved frm off the pace entering strt, kpt on, nvr nrr.*
.... (11 to 2 op 4 to 1 tchd 6 to 1) 4
INTREPID FORT (v) 3-8-2 J Fanning (5) *set gd clip, clr hfwy, wknd and hdd o'r one furlong out*........... (33 to 1) 5
NO SUBMISSION (USA) 6-8-7 S Wood (3) *wth ldrs till lost grnd entering strt, rallied last 2 fs.*
........................(6 to 1 op 4 to 1 tchd 7 to 1) 6
CRAFT EXPRESS 6-8-7 R P Elliott (9) *bustled alng to go pace hfwy, tld off last 2 fs*....... (14 to 1 tchd 16 to 1) 7
RED SOMBRERO 3-8-3 N Carlisle (1) *struggling to go pace hfwy, tld off*.......................... (8 to 1 op 12 to 1) 8
MAKEMEASTAR (Ire) 4-9-2 D Biggs (2) *struggling to keep up hfwy, sn tld off*..........................(16 to 1) 9
Dist: 4l, 2l, ½l, nk, 2l, 25l, 15l, 12l. 1m 44.50s. a 5.00s (9 Ran).
SR: 39/22/13/19/10/9/ (D J Maden), J Pearce

4788a Poachers Inn Handicap CLASS F (0-70 3-y-o and up) £2,574 1½m ....(1:50)

4731a3 CLIFTON CHASE [40] (bl) 3-8-4 Dean McKeown (2) *al gng wl, led entering strt, quickened clr o'r one out, drvn out*................................(7 to 1 op 8 to 1) 1
4715a9 ATLANTIC WAY [39] 4-8-8 G Bardwell (12) *settled midfield, improved entering strt, styd on, nvr nrr.*
........................(4 to 1 op 9 to 2 tchd 7 to 2) 2
4707a* MODEST HOPE (USA) [54] 5-9-4 (5*) A Garth (15) *nvr far away, ev ch and drvn alng entering strt, one pace last 2 fs*................................ (6 to 1 tchd 13 to 2) 3
4776a4 KINOKO [43] 4-8-12 J Corrigan (9) *trkd ldr, ev ch and rdn entering strt, not quicken last 2 fs.*
........................(9 to 2 op 7 to 2 tchd 5 to 1) 4
4763a2 SWEET REVIVAL [35] (v) 4-8-4 G Carter (1) *trkd ldrs, effrt and drvn alng entering strt, one pace last 2 fs.*
........................(7 to 2 fav op 5 to 2 tchd 4 to 1) 5
4763a* THUNDERBIRD ONE (USA) [58] 3-9-8 (5ex) Alex Greaves (7) *chsd ldg bunch, feeling pace aftr a m, styd on, nvr nrr.*
.... (10 to 1 op 8 to 1) 6
4742a4 LORD ADVOCATE [43] (v) 4-8-12 D Holland (8) *dictated pace till hdd and wknd entering strt.*
.... (12 to 1 op 10 to 1) 7
DANCING DAYS [40] (bl) 6-8-9 L Charnock (17) *bustled alng to keep up hfwy, some hdwy last 2 fs, no imprsn.*
................................(25 to 1) 8
4707a NIPOTINA [30] 6-7-6 (7*) F Savage (13) *chsd ldg bunch for a m, fdd und pres appr strt*.................. (33 to 1) 9
4764a9 FRIENDLYPERSUASION (Ire) [55] 4-9-10 W Ryan (3) *nvr far away, rdn appr strt, sn btn*....... (16 to 1 op 14 to 1) 10
4707a9 PETITE BELLE [34] 3-7-12 J Fanning (6) *chsd alng in midfield hfwy, struggling aftr a m*............... (25 to 1) 11
4742a IRISH NATIVE (Ire) [53] (bl) 4-9-8 J Quinn (11) *pressed ldrs till lost pl quickly hfwy, eased whn btn*...... (33 to 1) 12
BRIGTINA [43] 4-8-12 D Nicholls (10) *shwd up wl till wknd quickly aftr a m, tld off*.......... (20 to 1 op 25 to 1) 13
DEMOKOS (Fr) [35] 7-8-4 Dale Gibson (16) *struggling to keep in tch aftr a m, tld off*....(16 to 1 op 14 to 1) 14
HASTY SPARK [35] 4-8-4 N Carlisle (4) *trkd ldg bunch, lost grnd quickly aftr a m, tld off*.................. (14 to 1) 15
CHARMED LIFE [59] 3-9-6 (3*) A Tucker (14) *sluggish strt, al beh, tld off*.................................... (25 to 1) 16
Dist: 5l, 2½l, 1½l, sht-hd, 4l, 1½l, 15l, 1½l, ¾l, ½l. 2m 42.40s. a 8.50s (16 Ran).
SR: 23/17/27/13/4/14/1/-/-/ (A K Smeaton), M A Jarvis

4789a Stickney Organisation Handicap CLASS F (0-70 3-y-o and up) £2,385 7f........................(2:20)

4775a4 JOHNSTON'S EXPRESS (Ire) [47] 4-8-6 (5*) Stephen Davies (15) *settled gng wl, led jst o'r one furlong out, drifted lft, ran on*..............(4 to 1 op 3 to 1 tchd 9 to 2) 1
4764a4 DON'T DROP BOMBS (USA) [40] (v) 3-8-3 D Holland (4) *nvr far away, effrt and drvn alng o'r one furlong out, kpt on same pace*..........................(13 to 2 op 6 to 1) 2
4756a9 LITMORE DANCER [41] 4-8-2 (3*) A Tucker (6) *led briefly aftr one furlong, styd hndy and ev ch last 2 fs, ran on same pace*.................................. (25 to 1) 3
4775a6 BLACK BOY (Ire) [49] 3-8-8[1] (5*) S D Williams (12) *sluggish strt, weaved through frm off the pace last 2 fs, fnshd wl*................................(10 to 1 op 8 to 1) 4
4710a8 COMPANY CASH [50] (bl) 4-8-7 (7*) H Bastiman (10) *improved frm midfield hfwy, led entering strt till o'r one furlong out, no extr.*
.... (16 to 1 op 12 to 1 tchd 20 to 1) 5
4725a5 BRIGHT PARAGON (Ire) [43] 3-8-6 J Quinn (8) *trkd ldg 5, effrt and drvn alng last 2 fs, one pace.*
.... (12 to 1 op 10 to 1) 6
4739a5 GENTLE HERO (USA) [64] 6-10-0 Alex Greaves (14) *pushed alng to keep in tch hfwy, styd on last 2 fs, nvr nrr.*
.... (10 to 1 op 12 to 1) 7
4690a WHO'S THAT LADY [54] 3-9-3 G Carter (2) *wth ldrs, rdn entering strt, fdd*.... (16 to 1 op 10 to 1 tchd 20 to 1) 8
4716a2 SWINGING TICH [47] 3-8-10 W Ryan (9) *chsd alng in midfield, no imprsn last 2 fs*............(7 to 1 op 11 to 2) 9
4746a2 NELLIE DEAN [56] (bl) 3-9-5 Dale Gibson (11) *made most till hdd entering strt, btn 2 fs out*......(8 to 1 op 11 to 2) 10
4739a8 INNOCENT GEORGE [54] 3-9-3 L Charnock (5) *broke wl to show speed for o'r 4 fs, fdd*.....................(25 to 1) 11
LONG LANE LADY [43] 6-8-7 S Wood (1) *bustled alng to keep up, nvr a factor*........................ (16 to 1) 12
4764a2 CLAUDIA MISS [53] 5-9-3 Dean McKeown (7) *unruly in stalls, slow away, nvr able to reco'r.*
.... (7 to 2 fav op 9 to 2 tchd 5 to 1 and 11 to 2) 13
4752a9 GOLDEN SICKLE (USA) [60] 3-9-6 (3*) Emma O'Gorman (13) *led briefly early, styd hndy for o'r 4 fs, fdd*....(16 to 1) 14
Dist: 1½l, 2½l, 1l, 1l, 4l, nk, 1½l, ¾l, 5l, ¾l. 1m 31.40s. a 5.10s (14 Ran).
SR: 36/23/17/21/20/-/21/5/-/ (Frank McKevitt), E J Alston

4790a Design Contractors Midlands Limited Nursery CLASS F (0-75 2-y-o) £2,385 7f.................. (2:50)

4772a3 MISTER BLAKE [62] (bl) 8-5 (3*) Emma O'Gorman (2) *co'red up on ins, pld out to improve over one furlong out, shaken up to ld fnl furlong, ran on.*
.... (11 to 2 op 5 to 1 tchd 6 to 1) 1
ERLKING (Ire) [75] 9-7 Dean McKeown (9) *al hndy, led o'r 2 fs out to ins last, rdn and not quicken.*
........................(5 to 1 tchd 11 to 2) 2
4718a* SPRING FLYER (Ire) [65] 8-11 G Carter (8) *al hndy, ev ch and drvn alng 2 fs out, kpt on same pace.*
........................(2 to 1 fav op 5 to 2) 3
4741a5 SOLEIL RAYON (Ire) [58] 8-4 Alex Greaves (4) *settled midfield, hdwy o'r 2 fs out, edgd lft, styd on.*
.... (13 to 2 op 6 to 1 tchd 7 to 1) 4
4755a* CHRISTIAN SPIRIT [58] 8-4 (5ex) A McGlone (7) *dictated pace for o'r 4 fs, fdd*...............(5 to 2 op 11 to 8) 5
4717a8 BRACKENTHWAITE [54] 8-0 J Fanning (1) *last and struggling hfwy, some late hdwy, nvr nrr.*
.... (16 to 1 op 12 to 1) 6
4724a BROUGHTONS FORMULA [54] 8-0 J Quinn (3) *chsd alng to keep up hfwy, nvr a factor*....... (14 to 1 op 12 to 1) 7
THE CUT [47] 7-2[2] (7*) D Wright (6) *bustled alng in midfield hfwy, sn struggling*.........................(33 to 1) 8
Dist: 2l, 1½l, sht-hd, 8l, ½l, 1½l, 4l. 1m 32.30s. a 6.00s (8 Ran).
SR: 20/27/12/4/-/ (Red Seven Stable), W A O'Gorman

4791a Fiona Herbert Maiden Stakes CLASS F (2-y-o) £2,343 6f.....(3:20)

4720a2 MISS GORGEOUS (Ire) 8-6 (3*) Emma O'Gorman (7) *patiently rdn, hdwy on outsd o'r one furlong out, shaken up to ld cl hme.*
........................(6 to 5 fav op 2 to 1 tchd 9 to 4) 1
4730a4 PLAY HEVER GOLF 9-0 G Carter (10) *al hndy, led o'r 2 fs out, hrd rdn fnl furlong, jst ct.*
.... (13 to 2 op 6 to 1 tchd 8 to 1) 2
FRIENDLY SMILE 8-9 C Dwyer (6) *nvr far away, rdn and ev ch o'r one furlong out, not quicken.*
.... (12 to 1 op 10 to 1) 3
APOLLO DE ORIENTE 8-7 (7*) G Parkin (5) *pushed alng to improve frm midfield hfwy, hrd drvn o'r one furlong out, one pace*................................(20 to 1) 4
4747a3 RED ADMIRAL 9-0 Dale Gibson (8) *led aftr one furlong till o'r 2 out, not quicken und pres*..... (10 to 1 op 8 to 1) 5
MUDGEE 8-9 Alex Greaves (11) *sluggish strt, improved into midfield o'r 2 fs out, nrst finish.*
.... (12 to 1 op 6 to 1 tchd 20 to 1) 6
4741a ASHGROVE PLUM 8-9 W Ryan (3) *led for one furlong, styd hndy till fdd 2 fs out*........ (20 to 1 op 16 to 1) 7

4734a[6] AIR COMMAND (Bar) (bl) 8-11 (3*) R Perham (4) *chsd ldg half dozen, rdn o'r 2 fs out, sn btn*... (7 to 1 op 3 to 1) 8
TELEPHONIC (USA) 9-0 C Nutter (9) *sluggish strt, chsd alng to go pace hfwy, nvr dngrs.* .... (16 to 1 op 8 to 1 tchd 20 to 1) 9
GENERAL LINK 9-0 J Quinn (2) *drvn alng to keep up hfwy, nvr a threat*.................. (8 to 1 op 5 to 1) 10
ELSKA DIG 8-9 N Day (1) *chsd alng to go pace, struggling frm hfwy*....................(12 to 1 op 5 to 1) 11
Dist: ¾l, 5l, 1½l, nk, 3½l, nk, 1l, nk, 5l, 5l. 1m 18.50s. a 5.10s (11 Ran).
SR: 11/13/-/-/-/-/ (Thomas R Capehart), W A O'Gorman

HOLLYWOOD (USA) (firm)
Saturday December 19th

4792a Hollywood Starlet Stakes (Grade 1) (2-y-o) £74,162 1m 110yds.........

CREAKING BOARD 8-8 C Nakatani,........... (6 to 4 fav) 1
PASSING VICE (USA) 8-8 G Stevens,........... (72 to 10) 2
MADAME L'ENJOLEUR (USA) 8-8 P Valenzuela,.. (19 to 1) 3
NIJIVISION (USA) 8-8 L Pincay Jr,............. (13 to 1) 4
BLUE MOONLIGHT (USA) 8-8 M Pedroza,....... (44 to 1) 5
TURKSTAND (USA) 8-8 F Alvarado,............ (37 to 10) 6
FIT TO LEAD (USA) 8-8 C Black,................ (49 to 1) 7
ZOONAQUA (USA) 8-8 A Solis,................. (26 to 10) 8
LILY LA BELLE (USA) 8-8 D Flores,............. (40 to 1) 9
Dist: 8l, hd, 1 ¼l, 1 ¾l, ½l, hd, ½l, 11l. 1m 43.06s. (9 Ran).
(A J B P C Stable), P Bary

LINGFIELD (A.W) (std)
Saturday December 19th
Going Correction: MINUS 0.45 sec. per fur.

4793a Northern Racing Services Maiden Claiming Stakes (Div I) CLASS F (3-y-o and up) £1,182 1¼m..... (12:10)

4760a[5] CARLOWITZ (USA) 4-7-10 (7*) B Russell (1) *led aftr 2 fs, rdn and ran on wl o'r one out*........... (5 to 1 op 4 to 1) 1
4759a[5] DANCING BOAT 3-8-2 G Carter (6) *in tch, hrd rdn 3 fs out, styd on ins last, no ch wth wnr*..... (7 to 1 op 4 to 1) 2
4679a[4] FIRST FLING (Ire) (v) 3-8-0 J Quinn (3) *prmnt, chsd wnr o'r 3 fs out, rdn and ev ch 2 out, one pace.* ....(15 to 8 on op 7 to 4 on tchd 2 to 1 on) 3
LYPH (USA) 6-8-3 S Dawson (7) *mid-div, rdn hfwy, styd on one pace fnl 3 fs, nvr dngrs*.....(16 to 1 op 10 to 1) 4
4721a[6] DON'T WORRY (Ire) 3-7-13 G Bardwell (5) *sn chsd alng in mid-div, btn o'r 2 fs out*............ (12 to 1 op 8 to 1) 5
4763a[6] PIP'S OPTIMIST 3-8-0 Dale Gibson (8) *led for 2 fs, wth wnr aftr till wknd rpdly wl o'r 3 out*... (33 to 1 op 20 to 1) 6
VERSAILLESPRINCESS 4-8-0 D Biggs (2) *al beh, tld off fnl 4 fs*.............................. (33 to 1 op 20 to 1) 7
RAPID ROSIE 4-8-4 Dean McKeown (4) *cl up to hfwy, wknd rpdly, tld off fnl 3 fs*......... (50 to 1 op 20 to 1) 8
Dist: 4l, 1½l, 8l, 5l, 20l, 5l, 3l. 2m 5.63s. a 2.43s (8 Ran).
SR: 20/11/6/-/-/ (K Higson), A Moore

4794a Lydia Maiden Stakes CLASS F (2-y-o) £1,245 7f............... (12:40)

4724a[2] PERSIAN GUSHER (Ire) (e/s) 9-0 T Quinn (7) *trkd ldrs gng wl, led well o'r one furlong out, pushed clr cmftbly.* .... (11 to 4 op 5 to 2 tchd 7 to 2) 1
4755a[3] PATSY GRIMES 8-9 Dean McKeown (5) *led till wl o'r one furlong out, ran on one pace*.......(3 to 1 tchd 7 to 2) 2
4766a[2] MAJOR TRIUMPH (Ire) 8-9 W Ryan (2) *wth ldr, rdn o'r 2 fs out, one pace*.................(6 to 4 fav op 2 to 1) 3
4734a[5] MARWELL MITZI 8-9 J Williams (3) *mid-div, rdn to chase ldg trio hfwy, nvr on terms*........(16 to 1 op 12 to 1) 4
ARAWA 8-2 (7*) S McCarthy (6) *mid-div, rdn aftr 3 fs, sn outpcd, kpt on fnl furlong*........ (20 to 1 op 16 to 1) 5
4761a[5] BALLACASCADE 9-0 Dale Gibson (10) *rdn and lost tch hfwy, kpt on one pace fnl furlong*. (33 to 1 op 20 to 1) 6
DIWALI DANCER 9-0 G Carter (8) *dwlt, sn rdn alng and beh, nrst finish*.................. (20 to 1 op 10 to 1) 7
BELLE SOIREE (e/s) 8-9 S Dawson (4) *chsd ldrs till wknd aftr hfwy*......................... (12 to 1 op 7 to 1) 8
UNIVERSAL (Fr) 8-9 D Biggs (9) *al wl beh.* .... (20 to 1 op 14 to 1) 9
4766a GIRTON BELLE 8-9 G Bardwell (1) *al wl beh.* .... (50 to 1 op 33 to 1) 10
Dist: 4l, 2l, 6l, sht-hd, sht-hd, 2½l, 3½l, 6l, nk. 1m 25.56s. a 1.96s (10 Ran).
SR: 23/6/-/-/-/-/ (Gravy Boys Racing), S Dow

4795a Northern Racing Services Maiden Claiming Stakes (Div II) CLASS F (3-y-o and up) £1,182 1¼m...... (1:10)

4735a[5] CRETOES DANCER (USA) (bl) 3-7-7 (7*) Kim McDonnell (1) *made all, clr 4 fs out, ran on wl, unchlgd.* ....(2 to 1 fav op 9 to 4) 1
4669a[7] SIMON ELLIS (Ire) 3-8-6 W Ryan (3) *in tch, rdn to chase wnr ins fnl 2 fs, nvr able to chal*.... (15 to 2 op 9 to 2) 2

4756a[6] BEL BARAKA (Ire) 3-8-8 J Williams (8) *trkd ldrs, wnt second 4 fs out, rdn and one pace o'r 2 out.* ....(9 to 4 op 2 to 1 tchd 5 to 2) 3
KING OF NORMANDY (Ire) 3-8-0 D Biggs (6) *rdn alng and outpcd in mid-div, kpt on appr fnl furlong, no dngr.* ....(7 to 1 op 6 to 1 tchd 8 to 1) 4
4760a MONSCOMA (Ire) (bl) 4-9-1 A McGlone (4) *chsd wnr, rdn hfwy, sn wknd*...........................(20 to 1 op 14 to 1) 5
4746a[6] TSAR ALEXIS (USA) 4-8-3 G Bardwell (7) *rdn thrght and nvr gng pace, nrst finish*.......... (12 to 1 op 8 to 1) 6
LONESOME DOVE (Ire) 4-7-12 Dale Gibson (2) *al beh, tld off fnl 3 fs*.......... (16 to 1 op 14 to 1 tchd 20 to 1) 7
4735a[8] CAMEO SHADES (v) 5-8-5[3] (3*) R Perham (5) *al beh, tld off frm hfwy*........................ (20 to 1 op 12 to 1) 8
Dist: 8l, 8l, 7l, hd, 1½l, 25l, 6l. 2m 6.18s. a 2.98s (8 Ran).
SR: 11/1/-/-/-/ (Mrs W K Ong), W R Muir

4796a Atropos Handicap CLASS F (0-95 3-y-o and up) £2,343 6f....... (1:40)

4765a[2] PANIKIN [86] 4-9-5 (5*) S D Williams (7) *wtd wth, prog gng wl hfwy, str run ins fnl furlong to ld nr finish.* ....(7 to 1 op 4 to 1) 1
INVOCATION [72] 5-8-10 B Rouse (6) *pressed ldr till led o'r one furlong out, rdn and edgd lft ins last, hdd cl hme.* ....(25 to 1 op 14 to 1 tchd 33 to 1) 2
4768a* INDIAN ENDEAVOUR [72] 3-8-10 M Hills (8) *prmnt, rdn o'r 2 fs out, ev ch ins last, unbl to quicken nr finish.* ....(7 to 4 fav op 5 to 4 tchd 9 to 4) 3
4692a[7] LOVE LEGEND [72] (bl) 7-8-10 J Williams (3) *chsd alng beh ldrs, hmpd and swtchd o'r 2 fs out, ran on ins fnl last, nrst finish*.................... (13 to 2 op 6 to 1) 4
4725a TRUTHFUL IMAGE [66] (bl) 3-8-4 D Biggs (4) *cl up on inner, effrt and rdn appr fnl furlong, rng on whn hmpd wl ins last, not reco'r*.................... (9 to 2 op 12 to 1) 5
4752a[4] VERY DICEY [74] 4-8-12 T Quinn (2) *led till o'r one furlong out, hrd rdn and wknd*. (4 to 1 op 5 to 1 tchd 6 to 1) 6
4739a[4] BELATED [80] 3-9-4 Dale Gibson (5) *chsd ldrs, rdn hfwy, wknd appr fnl furlong*.............. (7 to 1 op 5 to 1) 7
BUSTER [85] 4-9-9 G Bardwell (1) *taken dwn early, al wl beh*.............................. (33 to 1 op 20 to 1) 8
4716a SAVINIEN (Ire) [57] 3-7-9[2] J Quinn (9) *al beh.* ....(100 to 1 op 50 to 1) 9
Dist: 1l, sht-hd, 1l, ¾l, 4l, 8l, 7l, 8l. 1m 12.53s. a 1.73s (9 Ran).
SR: 21/3/2/-/-/-/ (P W Lambert), J Wharton

4797a Hotspur Handicap CLASS F (0-85 3-y-o and up) £1,443 2m...... (2:10)

4760a[7] SAFETY (USA) [42] (bl) 5-8-0 Dale Gibson (2) *trkd ldrs, prog gng wl 5 out, led ins fnl 2 fs, rdn out.* ....(9 to 2 op 7 to 1 tchd 4 to 1) 1
4742a[2] MALENOIR (USA) [51] (v) 4-8-9 Dean McKeown (4) *cl up, led 3 out, hdd ins fnl 2 fs, rdn and unbl to quicken.* ....(9 to 4 fav op 2 to 1 tchd 5 to 2) 2
4750a[4] RIYADH LIGHTS [35] 7-7-0 (7*) Kim McDonnell (12) *cl up, chsd alng 4 fs out, ev ch o'r 2 out, one pace.* .... (16 to 1 op 12 to 1) 3
4760a BURRACOPPIN [35] 5-7-7 G Bardwell (10) *prmnt, led hfwy till 3 fs out, sn btn*................(33 to 1 op 25 to 1) 4
SING THE BLUES [35] 8-7-0 (7*) Antoinette Armes (11) *prmnt, led aftr 6 fs till hfwy, btn wl o'r 2 furlongs out.* ....(50 to 1 op 16 to 1 tchd 66 to 1) 5
PERSIAN FLEECE [52] 3-8-3 G Carter (3) *chsd ldrs, hrd rdn and wknd 3 fs out*......(9 to 2 op 4 to 1 tchd 5 to 1) 6
PANATHINAIKOS (USA) [35] 7-7-7[7] (7*) T Wilson (13) *rcd wide, beh till moderate late prog, nvr dngrs.* .... (14 to 1 op 10 to 1) 7
4767a[5] FAUSTNLUCE LADY [42] (bl) 3-7-1[1] (7*) D Wright (1) *al beh, struggling frm hfwy*................(66 to 1 op 25 to 1) 8
4742a SILLY HABIT (USA) [40] 6-7-12 J Quinn (5) *led for 6 fs, wknd aftr hfwy*........................ (25 to 1 op 20 to 1) 9
4671a[7] THE LAST EMPRESS (Ire) [60] 4-8-11 (7*) P McCabe (9) *beh frm hfwy, tld off fnl 3 fs*.......................... (10 to 1) 10+
HUNTING GROUND [62] 4-9-6 W Ryan (8) *al beh, tld off fnl 3 fs*.................(12 to 1 op 10 to 1 tchd 14 to 1) 10+
SMARTIE LEE [53] (bl) 5-8-11 T Quinn (6) *prmnt till wknd hfwy, tld off fnl 4 fs*................ (8 to 1 op 6 to 1) 12
GO SOUTH [70] (bl) 8-10-0 N Day (7) *al last, tld off aftr 6 fs, pld up hfwy*........... (15 to 2 op 6 to 1 tchd 8 to 1) pu
Dist: 2l, 7l, 10l, hd, 3½l, 3l, ¾l, 2½l, 20l, dd-ht. 3m 24.13s. a 2.13s (13 Ran).
(Keith Sturgis), J White

4798a Witch Of Endor Handicap CLASS F (0-70 3-y-o and up) £1,224 1½m ....(2:40)

4760a* EL VOLADOR [60] 5-10-0 W Ryan (4) *al gng wl, trkd ldrs, prog to ld well o'r one furlong out, sn drw clr.* ....(11 to 8 fav op 7 to 4) 1
KEEN VISION (Ire) [40] 4-8-8 M Hills (11) *prog frm midfield 4 out, rdn and ev ch 2 fs out, ran on one pace.* .... (8 to 1 op 6 to 1 tchd 10 to 1) 2
4721a[4] MENTALASANYTHIN [65] 3-9-7 (7*) D Wright (7) *hld up, prog o'r 3 fs out, ev ch 2 out, sn rdn and one pace.* .... (5 to 1 op 10 to 1 tchd 14 to 1) 3

4679a^{8} ROYAL VERSE (Fr) [28] 5-7-10 G Bardwell (3) *prmnt, led o'r 3 fs out till wl over one out, one pace.* .... (25 to 1 op 20 to 1 tchd 33 to 1) 4
4757a^{8} ENTERPRISE LADY (Fr) [35] 5-8-3 S Dawson (6) *hld up, prog 3 fs out, nvr rchd ldrs*.................... (33 to 1) 5
4756a MISTER LAWSON [52] 6-9-6 J Williams (1) *hld up and beh, pushed alng and outpcd 4 fs out, styd on appr last, nvr dngrs*.................................... (33 to 1) 6
4782a EL DOMINIO [56] 4-9-10 D Biggs (8) *ran in snatches, rdn and some prog 4 fs out, sn btn.* .... (12 to 1 op 8 to 1 tchd 14 to 1) 7
AUVILLAR (USA) [49] (v) 4-9-3 Dean McKeown (10) *led aftr a furlong till o'r 3 out, sn wknd.* .... (13 to 2 op 5 to 1 tchd 7 to 1) 8
4715a^{7} MR WISHING WELL [57] (e/s) 6-9-11 T Quinn (2) *mid-div, prog to chase ldrs 3 out, wknd rpdly wl o'r one furlong out*................................(9 to 2 op 3 to 1) 9
4750a^{8} BROUGHTON BLUES (Ire) [27] 4-7-9^{2} J Quinn (9) *mid-div, rdn 5 fs out, sn wknd.* (14 to 1 op 8 to 1 tchd 16 to 1) 10
4731a^{8} SOUTARI [38] 4-8-6^{3} (3*) R Perham (5) *led for one furlong, prmnt till wknd 4 out*......................(33 to 1) 11
Dist: 6l, ¾l, 1l, 10l, ½l, 7l, 5l, 2½l, 2½l, 2l. 2m 31.50s. a 1.80s (11 Ran).
SR: 42/10/28/-/-/-/ (I A Baker), R J O'Sullivan

4799a Ladbroke All Weather Trophy Handicap Qualifier CLASS E (0-70 3-y-o and up) £3,106 1m...........(3:10)

4757a^{3} SCOTS LAW [36] (bl) 5-7-11 D Biggs (12) *made all, rdn 2 fs out, hld on wl ins last*..............(10 to 1 op 8 to 1) 1
4771a* NOBBY BARNES [54] 3-9-0 (5ex) G Carter (11) *in tch, prog 3 fs out, rdn and ran on ins last, not rch wnr.* .... (15 to 2 op 5 to 1 tchd 8 to 1) 2
4758a* KILLICK [46] 4-8-7 J Quinn (7) *cl up, chsd wnr 3 out, hrd rdn appr fnl furlong, ran on one pace.* ....(5 to 2 fav op 2 to 1 tchd 11 to 4) 3
4757a^{6} VUCHTERBACHER [45] 6-8-6 N Day (8) *prmnt, rdn 2 fs out, ran on ins last, nrst finish*.... (14 to 1 op 10 to 1) 4
4758a^{5} BUDDY'S FRIEND (Ire) [52] 4-8-13 M Hills (2) *beh, prog o'r 2 fs out, ran on ins last, nrst finish.* ....(7 to 1 op 8 to 1 tchd 6 to 1) 5
4759a^{4} PRECIOUS AIR (Ire) [46] 4-8-7 B Rouse (5) *pushed alng aftr 2 fs, prog o'r two out, styd on one pace ins last.* .... (14 to 1 op 10 to 1) 6
4751a^{2} QUINZII MARTIN [46] 4-8-7 J Williams (4) *beh till prog o'r 2 fs out, styd on one pace ins last*.... (7 to 1 op 10 to 1) 7
4733a^{4} VELOCE (Ire) [58] 4-8-12 (7*) D Wright (1) *lost pl aftr 2 fs, no dngr after*........................ (10 to 1 op 12 to 1) 8
4758a^{2} TADORA (Ire) [53] 3-8-13 T Quinn (6) *mid-div, effrt o'r 2 fs out, wknd appr last*..... (7 to 1 op 5 to 1 tchd 8 to 1) 9
4732a^{4} BLUE DRIFTER (Ire) [35] (bl) 3-7-9 G Bardwell (9) *chsd wnr till hrd rdn and wknd o'r 3 fs out.* ....(14 to 1 tchd 16 to 1) 10
4748a^{2} SUNSET STREET (Ire) [58] (e/s) 4-9-5 W Ryan (10) *last away, al beh*........................(9 to 1 op 10 to 1) 11
LORD VIVIENNE (Ire) [64] 3-9-10 Dean McKeown (3) *sn chsd alng in tch till hfwy*..............(33 to 1 op 25 to 1) 12
Dist: ¾l, hd, 1l, 2l, ¾l, sht-hd, 4l, 2l, 5l, 7l. 1m 37.52s. a 0.62s (12 Ran).
SR: 20/35/27/23/24/16/15/15/3/ (Mrs R J Doorgachurn), R J O'Sullivan

LINGFIELD (A.W) (std)
Tuesday December 22nd
Going Correction: MINUS 0.30 sec. per fur.

4800a Thin Red Line Maiden Stakes (Div I) CLASS F (2-y-o) £2,322 1m.. (12:00)

I'LLEAVEITOYOU (Ire) (e/s) 9-0 G Carter (9) *nvr far away, hdwy on outsd to ld o'r one furlong out, drvn out.* .... (14 to 1 op 10 to 1) 1
4755a^{4} HEART OF SPAIN 9-0 W Ryan (8) *prmnt, rdn o'r one furlong out, kpt on one pace, took second nr finish.* ....(2 to 1 fav op 3 to 1 tchd 7 to 2) 2
4730a^{5} STALLED (Ire) 9-0 D Biggs (1) *prmnt, led aftr 3 fs to one out, hrd rdn, lost second pl nr finish.* (7 to 2 op 2 to 1) 3
HOOCHIECOOCHIE MAN (Ire) 9-0 T Quinn (7) *chsd ldrs, rdn 2 fs out, ran on one pace.* ....(12 to 1 op 5 to 1 tchd 14 to 1) 4
HIGH SUMMER 9-0 Dean McKeown (4) *beh till hdwy o'r one furlong out, nvr nr to chal.* .... (13 to 2 op 2 to 1 tchd 7 to 1) 5
NIGELS PROSPECT 9-0 J Williams (2) *outpcd.* .... (33 to 1 op 12 to 1) 6
4709a^{3} BUGLET 8-9 N Day (5) *al struggling.* .... (5 to 1 op 7 to 2 tchd 11 to 2) 7
HONORARY GUEST 8-9 T Rogers (10) *led 2 fs, wknd quickly 3 out*........................(16 to 1 op 10 to 1) 8
4745a^{4} THE ATHELING (Ire) 8-7 (7*) S Mulvey (3) *led aftr 2 fs to 5 out, wknd sn after hfwy*................(10 to 1 op 7 to 1) 9
Dist: 2½l, nk, 4l, ¾l, nk, 3l, hd, 6l. 1m 40.04s. a 3.14s (9 Ran).
SR: 17/9/8/-/-/-/ (Ray Hawthorn), S Dow

4801a Thin Red Line Maiden Stakes (Div II) CLASS F (2-y-o) £2,301 1m.. (12:30)

4761a^{2} CONVOY (bl) 9-0 M Hills (4) *nvr far away, rdn 2 fs out, led wl ins last, drvn out.* .... (11 to 8 fav op 6 to 4 tchd 7 to 4 and 5 to 4) 1
4778a^{2} ONE OFF THE RAIL (USA) 9-0 B Rouse (2) *al frnt rnk, led 3 fs out, hrd rdn and hdd wl ins last, rallied, jst fld.* .... (15 to 8 op 2 to 1 tchd 9 to 4) 2
STEVIE'S WONDER (Ire) 8-9 (5*) N Gwilliams (3) *mid-div, hdwy o'r 2 fs out, outpcd last*..... (50 to 1 op 20 to 1) 3
4730a^{7} SPORTING MISSILE (USA) 8-9 D Holland (1) *nvr far away, hdwy o'r 2 fs out, sn rdn and one pace.* ....(7 to 2 op 3 to 1 tchd 5 to 1) 4
ARAGON KING 9-0 Gay Kelleway (10) *outpcd early, hdwy 2 fs out, one pace ins last*.........(20 to 1 op 12 to 1) 5
4755a^{7} TACITURN (USA) 8-9 C Nutter (6) *led one furlong, led 5 out to 3 out, wknd*........................ (14 to 1 op 7 to 1) 6
4778a^{6} PETITE VINO (bl) 8-9^{7} (7*) Rachel Bridger (5) *led aftr one furlong to 5 out, wknd.* ....(50 to 1 op 33 to 1 tchd 66 to 1) 7
4730a GREY WATCH 8-2 (7*) L Carter (8) *slwly away, rdn to cl aftr one furlong, wknd wl o'r 2 out.* .... (20 to 1 op 12 to 1) 8
4761a^{8} BEYOND THE LIMIT 8-9 S Dawson (9) *al beh.* .... (20 to 1 op 12 to 1) 9
4761a ONE MORE POUND 8-11 (3*) R Perham (7) *al beh.* .... (33 to 1 op 14 to 1) 10
Dist: Nk, 5l, 1½l, 2l, 3l, 4l, 1½l, 2l, nk. 1m 39.83s. a 2.93s (10 Ran).
SR: 20/19/4/-/-/-/ (J Jannaway), W R Muir

4802a Levy Board Claiming Stakes CLASS F (3-y-o and up) £2,490 1m....(1:00)

4765a^{4} EASTLEIGH 3-9-1 W Ryan (6) *trkd ldrs, swtchd lft and squeezed through to ld entering fnl furlong, drvn out, jst hld on*........................ (5 to 1 op 7 to 2) 1
4733a^{7} GUESSTIMATION (USA) 3-9-1 G Bardwell (1) *prmnt, led 2 fs out till entering last, rallied wl und pres, jst fld.* .... (12 to 1 op 10 to 1) 2
4758a^{4} DANCING BEAU (Ire) (bl,e/s) 3-8-11 J Williams (5) *slwly into strd, hdwy o'r 2 fs out, kpt on one pace ins last.* .... (9 to 2 op 12 to 1 tchd 14 to 1) 3
4756a^{3} ULLADULLA 3-8-12 (3*) R Perham (12) *mid-div till hdwy 2 fs out, rdn and kpt on one pace.* ....(3 to 1 fav op 7 to 2 tchd 5 to 1) 4
4782a^{8} NATIVE CHIEFTAN (bl) 3-9-7 B Rouse (3) *prmnt, no extr appr fnl furlong*........................(7 to 1 op 7 to 2) 5
4748a^{5} FAYNAZ (bl) 6-7-11 (7*) Kim McDonnell (4) *prmnt, led hfwy to 2 fs out, und pres whn bumped entering last, no ch aftr*.........(25 to 1 op 16 to 1 tchd 33 to 1) 6
4783a EMERALD EARS 3-7-13^{8} (7*) S Drowne (9) *beh till some hdwy o'r 2 fs out, nvr nr to chal.* ....(66 to 1 op 25 to 1 tchd 100 to 1) 7
4756a^{5} SUNLEY SILKS 3-9-0 G Carter (10) *chsd ldrs till wknd 2 fs out*........................(5 to 1 op 4 to 1) 8
4746a^{7} PREDICTABLE (bl) 6-8-10 J Quinn (2) *led to hfwy, sn rdn and wknd*........................(12 to 1 op 8 to 1) 9
4784a^{6} UP THE PUNJAB 3-7-12 Dale Gibson (7) *prmnt till wknd hfwy*........................(8 to 1 tchd 10 to 1) 10
BOLTON FLYER 6-7-13 S Dawson (11) *al beh, tld off.* .... (50 to 1 op 25 to 1) 11
GENUINE LADY 4-7-10 (7*) D Wright (8) *nvr gng wl, virtually pld up hfwy*................(20 to 1 op 12 to 1) 12
Dist: Sht-hd, 2l, 3l, 1½l, ½l, 3½l, 1l, 12l, 2½l, dist. 1m 38.90s. a 2.00s (12 Ran).
SR: 35/34/24/19/20/1/ (J E Bigg), R Hollinshead

4803a Alma Handicap CLASS F (0-90 3-y-o and up) £2,660 7f.............(1:30)

4783a^{3} MASTER HYDE (USA) [52] 3-8-1 D Biggs (7) *tucked in on rail towards rear, hdwy and strly rdn appr fnl furlong, ran on to ld nr finish*....(7 to 1 op 5 to 1 tchd 8 to 1) 1
SPENCER'S REVENGE [68] 3-9-3 Dean McKeown (6) *led 2 fs, led 3 out, clr appr last, wknd and hdd nr finish.* .... (10 to 1 op 9 to 2) 2
4757a^{2} ON Y VA (USA) [57] 5-8-7 M Hills (4) *in tch, wnt second wl o'r one furlong out, no extr fnl stages.* ....(100 to 30 op 11 to 4 tchd 7 to 2) 3
4781a* DASWAKI (Can) [83] 4-10-5 (5ex) B Rouse (8) *sn pushed alng, nvr far away, not pace to chal ins fnl furlong.* ....(6 to 4 fav tchd 13 to 8) 4
4783a LOOTING (USA) [43] 6-7-0 (7*) Kim McDonnell (9) *outpcd to hfwy, kpt on fnl 2 fs, nvr dngrs*....(50 to 1 op 20 to 1) 5
4751a^{4} SALLY'S SON [61] 6-8-8 (3*) Emma O'Gorman (1) *led aftr 2 fs to 3 out, wknd appr last.* .... (13 to 2 op 5 to 1 tchd 8 to 1) 6
4765a^{5} POP TO STANS [73] 3-9-8 G Bardwell (3) *chsd ldrs till wknd 2 fs out*..................(12 to 1 tchd 20 to 1) 7
4783a^{5} PRECIOUS WONDER [64] 3-8-6 (7*) S Drowne (2) *chsd ldrs, no hdwy ins fnl 2 fs*... (12 to 1 op 8 to 1 tchd 14 to 1) 8
MERE CHANTS [53] 3-8-2 J Quinn (5) *slwly away, al struggling*.............(33 to 1 op 25 to 1 tchd 50 to 1) 9
Dist: 1l, ¾l, 1½l, 3½l, 3½l, nk, hd, 12l. 1m 25.08s. a 1.48s (9 Ran).
SR: 33/46/34/55/4/11/21/11/-/ (Hyde Sporting Promotions/Saddlehome Farm), P Mitchell

4804a Light Brigade Claiming Stakes CLASS F (3-y-o and up) £2,280 6f

................................(2:00)

4779a² RESPECTABLE JONES 6-8-10 W Ryan (1) *al frnt rnk, rdn to ld wl ins fnl furlong, all out.* ....(4 to 1 on op 9 to 4 on) 1
4779a³ CRECHE (bl) 3-9-2 N Day (8) *led till wl ins fnl furlong, rallied, jst fld*.......... (4 to 1 op 5 to 2 tchd 9 to 2) 2
4783a⁸ GEMINI BAY (bl) 3-8-8 S Dawson (3) *outpcd early, kpt on fnl 2 fs, no ch wth 1st two*........(20 to 1 tchd 33 to 1) 3
CHERRYWOOD LASS 4-7-13 G Bardwell (7) *chsd ldrs, no ch fnl 2 fs*.......................(50 to 1 op 33 to 1) 4
4696a LORD NEPTUNE 3-8-4 J Quinn (5) *al beh.* ....(20 to 1 tchd 33 to 1) 5
4768a JOE SUGDEN 8-8-8 J Murray (4) *prmnt to hfwy, sn outpcd*............................(25 to 1 op 12 to 1) 6
NIGALS FRIEND 3-8-8 J Williams (6) *outpcd.* ....(25 to 1 op 12 to 1) 7

Dist: Sht-hd, 15l, 1l, 3½l, ½l, 3l. 1m 11.74s. a 0.94s (7 Ran).
SR: 41/46/-/-/ (Mrs B Ramsden), R Hollinshead

4805a Inkerman Nursery CLASS F (0-75 2-y-o) £2,406 7f.............. (2:30)

4717a⁵ EXCESS BAGGAGE (Ire) [71] 9-5 W Ryan (1) *beh, rdn and hdwy o'r 2 fs out, led und str pres cl hme.* ....(4 to 1 tchd 5 to 1) 1
4717a² ABSOLUTELY FACT (USA) [72] 9-6 T Quinn (3) *prmnt, led entering fnl furlong, hrd rdn, ct cl hme.* .... (4 to 1 op 3 to 1 tchd 11 to 4) 2
4724a³ BICHETTE [65] 8-13 B Rouse (12) *led till o'r 4 fs out, led over 2 out, hrd rdn and hdd entering last, no extr.* .... (6 to 1 op 4 to 1 tchd 13 to 2) 3
4741a³ KNOBBLEENEEZE [64] (v) 8-12 G Carter (6) *prmnt, hrd rdn entering fnl furlong, one pace*......(12 to 1 op 7 to 1) 4
4766a⁵ RUANO [48] 7-10 G Bardwell (7) *prmnt on outsd, rdn and no hdwy appr fnl furlong*.........(8 to 1 tchd 14 to 1) 5
4778a⁹ KAFIOCA (Ire) [50] 7-12 Dale Gibson (8) *outpcd, kpt on ins fnl 2 fs*...............(33 to 1 op 25 to 1 tchd 40 to 1) 6
EXPRESS MARIECURIE (Ire) [73] 9-7 N Day (14) *prmnt, led o'r 4 fs out till over 2 out, wknd entering last.* ....(25 to 1 op 20 to 1 tchd 33 to 1) 7
4740a* PIPERS REEL [59] (v) 8-7 Dean McKeown (9) *mid-div, no hdwy fnl 2 fs*.....(100 to 30 fav op 3 to 1 tchd 7 to 2) 8
4724a⁸ WAR REQUIEM (Ire) [50] 7-12 S Dawson (2) *nvr on terms.* ....(16 to 1 op 12 to 1) 9
SILENT PRINCE [50] 7-5 (7*) Kim McDonnell (5) *al beh.* .... (33 to 1 op 20 to 1 tchd 50 to 1) 10
4734a⁷ MOVING IMAGE (Ire) [59] 8-7 C Dwyer (10) *prmnt till wknd ins fnl 2 fs*........... (33 to 1 op 20 to 1 tchd 40 to 1) 11
4734a⁴ WEALTHYWOO [50] (bl) 7-12 J Quinn (4) *chsd ldrs, wknd wl o'r one furlong out*..............(33 to 1 op 14 to 1) 12
HOME AFFAIR [68] 8-13 (3*) R Perham (11) *speed to hfwy, sn rear*.............. (33 to 1 op 25 to 1 tchd 50 to 1) 13

Dist: Sht-hd, 2½l, 1½l, 4l, ¾l, sht-hd, 1½l, 1½l, ¾l, 1½l. 1m 25.98s. a 2.38s (13 Ran).
SR: 38/38/23/17/-/-/11/-/-/ (Frank W Golding), N A Callaghan

4806a Sebastopol Handicap CLASS F (0-80 3-y-o and up) £2,454 1m 5f.... (3:00)

4750a² DR ZEVA [40] 6-7-2² (7*) D Wright (2) *beh, hdwy o'r 2 fs out, styd on to ld ins last*..............(8 to 1 tchd 12 to 1) 1
4749a⁴ VINTAGE [75] 7-10-0 J Williams (5) *wtd wth, hdwy to ld o'r 2 fs out, hdd ins last, one pace.* ....(9 to 4 fav op 7 to 4 tchd 5 to 2) 2
KENYATTA (USA) [45] 3-7-0 (7*) Kim McDonnell (1) *led 2 fs, steadied in mid-div, str brst fnl furlong, not rch 1st two*..................(10 to 1 tchd 7 to 1 and 12 to 1) 3
4707a INDIAN TERRITORY [45] 3-7-1¹ (7*) S McCarthy (6) *chsd ldr, rdn 4 fs out, one pace aftr.* ....(6 to 1 op 5 to 1 tchd 7 to 1) 4
4707a² EMPEROR ALEXANDER (Ire) [64] 4-8-10 (7*) T G McLaughlin (7) *beh, hdwy hfwy, not pace to chal fnl 2 fs.* ....(5 to 2 op 3 to 1 tchd 7 to 2 and 9 to 4) 5
KOVALEVSKIA [40] 7-7-7 G Bardwell (8) *beh, nvr nr to chal*...............................(25 to 1 op 8 to 1) 6
4758a⁸ MAY SQUARE (Ire) [54] 4-8-7 W Ryan (9) *pld hrd, led aftr 2 fs, hdd o'r two out, sn wknd.* .... (25 to 1 op 10 to 1 tchd 33 to 1) 7
4707a⁷ PUSEY STREET BOY [42] 5-7-9² J Quinn (4) *pld hrd, prmnt till wknd o'r 2 fs out*..............(12 to 1 op 8 to 1) 8
WAYWARD SON [50] 3-7-12⁵ D Biggs (3) *al beh, tld off.* ....(25 to 1 op 16 to 1) 9

Dist: 1½l, hd, 5l, sht-hd, 3½l, 2½l, 1½l, 15l. 2m 47.34s. a 4.34s (9 Ran).
SR: -/29/-/-/6/-/ (G R Butterfield), M Dixon

4807a Crimea Handicap CLASS F (0-80 3-y-o and up) £2,656 1¼m.... (3:30)

4732a² LADY DUNDEE (USA) [60] 3-8-9 W Ryan (3) *al prmnt, rdn to ld appr fnl furlong, all out.* .... (11 to 2 op 7 to 2 tchd 6 to 1) 1
4782a* MULCIBER [65] 4-9-3 (5ex) G Carter (1) *nvr far away, hrd rdn entering fnl furlong, ran on wl, jst fld.* ....(9 to 2 op 3 to 1 tchd 5 to 1) 2
4784a* VA UTU [43] 4-7-9 Dale Gibson (5) *rear, rdn 4 fs out, styd on ins fnl 2 furlongs*.........................(7 to 2 jt-fav op 4 to 1 tchd 9 to 2 and 3 to 1) 3
4760a NASEER (USA) [50] (bl) 3-7-6 (7*) D Wright (9) *led aftr 2 fs to 4 out, no imprsn appr last.* .... (20 to 1 op 14 to 1 tchd 33 to 1) 4
NIGHT CLUBBING (Ire) [75] 3-9-7 (3*) R Perham (8) *beh till styd on ins fnl 2 fs, nvr dngrs*................(7 to 2 jt-fav op 4 to 1 tchd 11 to 4) 5
4782a³ BELMOREDEAN [76] 7-10-0 D Biggs (2) *led 2 fs, led 4 out till appr last, no extr*.... (9 to 2 op 6 to 1 tchd 7 to 1) 6
4662a⁷ PREMIER DANCE [41] 5-7-1¹ (7*) S McCarthy (7) *slwly away, hdwy hfwy, no imprsn fnl 2 fs.* ....(25 to 1 op 14 to 1) 7
4758a⁹ OSGATHORPE [43] 5-7-9² J Quinn (6) *prmnt till wknd 2 fs out*..........................(50 to 1 op 33 to 1) 8
4781a³ AMETHYSTINE (USA) [59] 6-8-4 (7*) S Drowne (4) *al rear.* .... (14 to 1 op 10 to 1 tchd 16 to 1) 9
4764a SERIOUS ACTION [54] 3-8-3 C Nutter (10) *slwly away, al struggling*.......................(50 to 1 op 33 to 1) 10

Dist: Sht-hd, 3l, ¾l, ½l, 2l, nk, 4l, 1½l, 8l. 2m 6.09s. a 2.89s (10 Ran).
SR: 36/43/15/17/41/41/5/-/12/ (James H Stone), Mrs J Cecil

SOUTHWELL (A.W) (std)
Monday December 28th
Going Correction: PLUS 0.25 sec. per fur.

4808a Christmas Pudding Handicap CLASS F (0-80 3-y-o and up) £2,385 6f.......................... (12:40)

4739a² PRETONIC [64] 4-8-12 Dean McKeown (6) *chsd ldr, effrt to ld one and a half fs out, ran on wl.* ....(4 to 1 fav op 3 to 1) 1
4710a PESIDANAMICH (Ire) [68] (bl) 4-8-9 (7*) S Mulvey (4) *sn led, rdn 2 fs out, soon hdd, kpt on und pres.* .... (14 to 1 op 12 to 1) 2
4774a⁹ TOSHIBA COMET [53] (e/s) 5-8-1 D Biggs (10) *chsd ldrs, effrt and rdn 2 fs out, styd on*...... (9 to 1 op 14 to 1) 3
4774a⁴ STAMSHAW [45] 3-7-5⁵ (7*) J Bramhill (2) *al prmnt, rdn o'r 2 fs out, kpt on one pace*......................(16 to 1) 4
4774a³ SAMSOLOM [58] 4-8-6 L Charnock (1) *prmnt, ev ch and hrd rdn 2 fs out, wknd fnl furlong.* .... (9 to 2 op 9 to 1 tchd 10 to 1) 5
4752a⁸ SIR TASKER [72] 4-9-1 (5*) S D Williams (9) *beh and sn pushed alng, styd on fnl 3 fs*.................(20 to 1) 6
4775a* DRUMMER'S DREAM (Ire) [47] (v) 4-7-9² Dale Gibson (13) *chsd ldrs, rdn o'r 2 fs out, kpt on one pace.* ....(10 to 1 op 7 to 1) 7
4716a⁷ WELLSY LAD (USA) [56] 5-8-4 S Wood (8) *chsd ldrs, rdn 2 fs out, grad wknd*....... (13 to 2 op 5 to 1 tchd 7 to 1) 8
4781a⁵ GYMCRAK TYCOON [70] (bl) 3-9-4 J Quinn (5) *in tch, effrt and hdwy o'r 2 fs out, sn rdn and wknd.* ....(8 to 1 op 7 to 1) 9
4764a CHOICE LOT [45] 5-7-2² (7*) D Wright (3) *al rear.* .... (33 to 1 op 25 to 1) 10
4775a⁹ ARC LAMP [57] 6-8-5 G Bardwell (7) *sn pushed alng, al rear*..........................(11 to 1 op 8 to 1) 11
4743a BOLD HABIT [80] 7-10-0 W Ryan (12) *al rear.* ....(8 to 1 op 7 to 1) 12
4789a⁵ COMPANY CASH [51] (bl) 4-7-13⁴ S Dawson (11) *al rear.* .... (11 to 1 op 12 to 1) 13

Dist: 2l, ½l, 1l, sht-hd, 3l, 1½l, ¾l, ¾l, 3l, ½l. 1m 17.80s. a 4.40s (13 Ran).
SR: 40/36/19/7/19/21/-/-/7/ (Brian Yeardley Continental Ltd), M Johnston

4809a Christmas Claiming Stakes CLASS F (2-y-o) £2,511 1m........... (1:10)

4772a* MOONSTRUCK BARD 8-4 W Woods (9) *hdwy hfwy, effrt to ld wl o'r one furlong out, rdn and ran on well fnl furlong*........................... (9 to 2 op 3 to 1) 1
4790a* MISTER BLAKE (bl) 8-7 (3*) Emma O'Gorman (8) *chsd ldrs, hdwy 3 fs out, led 2 out, rdn and hdd wl o'r one out, styd on gmely fnl furlong*......... (5 to 1 op 11 to 2) 2
4772a⁵ MASTER SINCLAIR (Ire) 8-1 (5*) A Garth (6) *slwly into strd and beh, hdwy 3 fs out, rdn and styd on one pace frm 2 out*.............................. (13 to 2 op 6 to 1) 3
4772a² DIAMOND POINT 8-2 C Nutter (11) *cl up, led o'r 3 fs out, rdn and hdd 2 out, sn wknd.* ....(6 to 4 fav tchd 13 to 8 and 7 to 4) 4
4718a⁴ ROSE FLYER (Ire) 7-9 S Wood (4) *chsd ldrs, rdn 2 and a half fs out, kpt on one pace*..................(20 to 1) 5
4741a⁹ GENESIS FOUR (bl) 7-12 N Carlisle (10) *cl up till rdn and wknd hfwy*..................... (40 to 1 op 33 to 1) 6
4778a⁵ TITLED GIRL (Ire) 8-1³ (7*) T G McLaughlin (3) *chsd ldrs to hfwy, sn lost pl*...... (9 to 1 op 14 to 1 tchd 16 to 1) 7
BIG-W 8-10 R P Elliott (7) *slwly away, al beh*.... (33 to 1) 8
RED BALLET (bl) 8-1 Dale Gibson (2) *slwly into strd, sn led, hdd and wknd quickly o'r 3 fs out.* .... (9 to 1 op 8 to 1 tchd 10 to 1) 9
PINK CITY 8-6⁷ (7*) J Edmunds (5) *al beh, tld off fnl 3 fs.* .... (50 to 1 op 33 to 1) 10

Dist: ½l, 3½l, 5l, 2l, 8l, 2½l, 5l, 8l, 5l. 1m 46.20s. a 6.70s (10 Ran).
SR: 20/24/9/-/-/-/ (D G Raffel), S P C Woods

4810a National Plant & Transport Handicap CLASS F (0-80 3-y-o and up)

£2,448 7f. .... (1:40)

4789a* JOHNSTON'S EXPRESS (Ire) [53] 4-9-8 J Quinn (14) *trkd ldrs gng wl, hdwy on bit 2 fs out, effrt and edgd lft appr last, quickened to ld ins last, styd on.* ....(4 to 1 fav op 7 to 2 tchd 9 to 2) 1

4774a[6] JUVENARA [37] 6-8-6 G Bardwell (1) *slwly into strd and beh, hdwy o'r 3 fs out and wide strt, effrt 2 out, rdn and ran on fnl furlong*..................(7 to 1 op 12 to 1) 2

TYRONE FLYER [59] 3-9-6 (7*) A Bates (2) *led, quickened clr o'r 2 fs out, rdn appr last, hdd and no extr ins last.* ....(12 to 1 op 10 to 1) 3

4799a[4] VUCHTERBACHER [44] 6-8-6 (7*) T Wilson (5) *chsd ldrs, effrt and rdn 2 fs out, styd on one pace.* ....(9 to 2 op 5 to 1 tchd 6 to 1) 4

4765a[6] SANDMOOR DENIM [59] 5-10-0 S Webster (13) *beh till styd on fnl 2 fs, not rch ldrs*.................... (10 to 1) 5

4789a[8] WHO'S THAT LADY [51] 3-9-5 D Nicholls (12) *cl up, ev ch o'r 2 fs out, sn rdn and wknd*........(25 to 1 op 20 to 1) 6

BALLYRANTER [55] 3-9-9 V Smith (8) *al mid-div.* ....(14 to 1 tchd 16 to 1) 7

FIT THE BILL [44] 4-8-13 L Charnock (11) *nvr rch ldrs.* ....(20 to 1 op 16 to 1) 8

4789a[9] SWINGING TICH [47] 3-9-1 Dale Gibson (3) *slwly into strd, al rear*..........................(12 to 1 op 10 to 1) 9

4789a[4] BLACK BOY (Ire) [47] (v) 3-8-10 (5*) S D Williams (7) *chsd ldrs till rdn and wknd 2 and a half fs out.* ....(11 to 2 op 8 to 1 tchd 5 to 1) 10

4715a KRONPRINZ (Ire) [36] 4-7-12 (7*) Darren Moffatt (10) *nvr a factor*..........................(25 to 1 op 20 to 1) 11

COMISKEY PARK (Ire) [46] 3-9-0 S Wood (9) *nvr rch ldrs.* ....(25 to 1) 12

4787a[2] MERRYHILL MADAM [50] 3-9-4 Dean McKeown (16) *chsd ldr, rdn o'r 2 fs out till wknd*...... (11 to 1 op 10 to 1) 13

4699a CELLITO (Ire) [46] 3-8-11 (3*) Emma O'Gorman (15) *al rear.* ....(20 to 1 op 16 to 1) 14

4787a[5] INTREPID FORT [33] (v) 3-8-1 D Biggs (4) *cl up till rdn and wknd 2 and a half fs out.* ....(11 to 1 op 10 to 1 tchd 12 to 1) 15

4690a GRUBBY [52] 3-9-6 W Ryan (6) *slwly into strd, al rear.* ....(16 to 1) 16

Dist: 2½l, 1l, ¾l, 4l, hd, 4l, nk, ¾l, 2l, ¾l. 1m 31.60s. a 5.30s (16 Ran).
SR: 55/31/49/33/36/26/18/7/7/ (Frank McKevitt), E J Alston

4811a Derry Building Services Nursery CLASS F (0-75 2-y-o) £2,322 1m ....(2:15)

4770a* GOLDEN KLAIR [70] 9-7 J Quinn (3) *hld up, hdwy on bit 3 fs out, led appr last, easily*......(13 to 8 fav op 5 to 4) 1

4665a* I'M A DREAMER (Ire) [64] 9-1 Dean McKeown (4) *cl up, rdn alng and outpcd 3 fs out, styd on and ev ch appr last, sn no chance wth wnr*................(4 to 1 op 7 to 2) 2

4794a[5] ARAWA [47] 7-7[2] (7*) S McCarthy (1) *chsd ldr, led o'r 2 fs out, sn rdn, hdd and wknd appr last.* ....(8 to 1 op 14 to 1 tchd 16 to 1) 3

4791a* MISS GORGEOUS (Ire) [60] 8-8 (3*) Emma O'Gorman (6) *chsd ldrs, rdn 3 fs out, sn btn*..... (5 to 2 tchd 11 to 4) 4

4790a[4] SOLEIL RAYON (Ire) [58] 8-9 Alex Greaves (5) *chsd ldrs, rdn 3 fs out, sn btn*.........(13 to 2 op 7 to 1 tchd 6 to 1) 5

4773a[5] HERSHEBAR [50] 8-1 S Wood (2) *led, hdd o'r 2 fs out, sn wknd*..........................(20 to 1 op 16 to 1) 6

Dist: 2l, 3l, 3l, ¾l, 2½l. 1m 47.00s. a 7.50s (6 Ran).
SR: 25/13/-/ (C John Hill), C J Hill

4812a Turkey Claiming Stakes CLASS F (3-y-o and up) £2,469 1½m. . . . (2:45)

4771a[4] TEMPERING 6-9-1 S Wood (12) *cl up, led aftr 2 fs, sn clr, rdn appr last, jst hld on.* ....(9 to 4 fav op 3 to 1 tchd 7 to 2) 1

CLASSIC ACCOUNT 4-8-9 J McLaughlin (9) *al chasing wnr, rdn 2 fs out, styd on wl fnl furlong.* ....(11 to 1 op 8 to 1) 2

4715a[6] SILVER SAMURAI 3-8-1 (7*) S Mulvey (14) *hld up, hdwy 5 fs out, rdn and wknd one and a half out*............. (6 to 1) 3

4787a[4] FERDIA (Ire) 3-8-6 W Ryan (15) *hld up, hdwy 5 fs out, rdn and wknd 2 out*.....................(8 to 1 tchd 9 to 1) 4

4788a[6] THUNDERBIRD ONE (USA) 3-8-10 Alex Greaves (16) *chsd ldrs, effrt and hdwy 4 fs out, rdn and wknd o'r 2 out.* ....(6 to 1 tchd 7 to 1) 5

4788a[5] SWEET REVIVAL 4-8-2 G Bardwell (6) *mid-div, effrt and hdwy 4 fs out, sn rdn and one pace.* (8 to 1 op 7 to 1) 6

4787a[3] CANDESCO 6-8-4 Dean McKeown (2) *chsd ldrs, effrt 5 fs out, sn rdn and wknd 3 out*.....................(12 to 1) 7

4788a PETITE BELLE 3-7-2[2] (7*) D Wright (5) *nvr rch ldrs.* ....(40 to 1 op 25 to 1) 8

4787a[6] NO SUBMISSION (USA) 6-8-10 J Quinn (11) *nvr a factor.* ....(10 to 1 op 8 to 1) 9

PARISIENNE KING (USA) 3-7-7[2] (7*) M Humphries (7) *al rear*..........................(40 to 1 op 25 to 1) 10

SHARP ISSUE (USA) 4-7-10 (7*) Darren Moffatt (4) *in tch to hfwy, sn wknd*....................(33 to 1 op 25 to 1) 11

4671a[8] SINGING REPLY (USA) 4-7-11 (7*) S McCarthy (3) *nvr rch ldrs*.............................. (20 to 1) 12

THE PRUSSIAN (USA) 6-8-9 Dale Gibson (8) *chsd ldrs till wknd quickly hfwy, tld off*........(10 to 1 op 20 to 1) 13

4779a[6] CUMBRIAN CAVALIER 3-8-4 R Lappin (1) *led 2 fs, prmnt till wknd hfwy, sn tld off*..........(40 to 1 op 25 to 1) 14

4743a[9] GINA'S DELIGHT 4-7-12 N Carlisle (13) *al rear, tld off fnl 5 fs*..............................(40 to 1 op 25 to 1) 15

Dist: ½l, 7l, 6l, 3l, 3l, 7l, nk, sht-hd, ½l, sht-hd. 2m 42.40s. a 8.50s (15 Ran).
SR: 46/39/24/10/8/-/ (David W Chapman), D W Chapman

4813a Mistletoe Handicap CLASS F (0-80 3-y-o and up) £2,490 2m. . . . . (3:15)

4797a[2] MALENOIR (USA) [53] (v) 4-8-3 (5*) A Garth (6) *hld up, hdwy hfwy, effrt to chal 2 fs out, rdn to ld and edgd rght ins last, styd on*........(11 to 4 fav op 7 to 2 tchd 4 to 1) 1

4776a[6] COSMIC DANCER [47] (bl) 5-8-2[4] W Woods (13) *hld up and beh, hdwy 4 fs out, led 2 out and sn hrd rdn, hdd and no extr ins last*........(15 to 2 op 8 to 1 tchd 10 to 1) 2

4788a[2] ATLANTIC WAY [42] 4-7-11 G Bardwell (5) *trkd ldrs gng wl, hdwy 4 fs out, led briefly o'r 2 out, sn rdn and styd on one pace*..............(9 to 2 op 7 to 2) 3

4742a[7] LAFKADIO [43] (bl) 5-7-12 S Wood (8) *chsd ldrs, rdn 3 fs out, styd on one pace.* ....(14 to 1 op 16 to 1 tchd 20 to 1) 4

ANTIGUAN FLYER [76] 3-9-10 J McLaughlin (7) *al prmnt, effrt and ev ch o'r 2 fs out, sn rdn and one pace.* ....(16 to 1 op 14 to 1) 5

4776a[3] SHAKINSKI [62] (v) 3-8-10 D Biggs (4) *hld up, hdwy o'r 4 fs out, rdn and wknd 2 out*............(3 to 1 op 7 to 2) 6

SIR PAGEANT [64] 3-8-7 (5*) S D Williams (9) *cl up, led aftr 7 fs till o'r 2 out, sn wknd*...........(12 to 1 op 10 to 1) 7

4698a[4] SULUK (USA) [39] 7-7-8[7] (7*) M Humphries (1) *hld up and beh, effrt and some hdwy 4 fs out, nvr dngrs.* ....(8 to 1 op 7 to 1) 8

4797a GO SOUTH [60] 8-9-1 N Carlisle (3) *nvr rchd ldrs.* ....(16 to 1 op 12 to 1) 9

RAIN-N-SUN [38] 6-7-2[2] (7*) Darren Moffatt (11) *led 7 fs, cl up till wknd quickly 6 out*....................(33 to 1) 10

CLOS DU BOIS (Fr) [42] 6-7-11 Dale Gibson (2) *chsd ldrs till rdn and wknd o'r 6 fs out*......... (33 to 1 op 25 to 1) 11

4742a[8] PEAK DISTRICT [40] 6-7-2 (7*) D Wright (12) *chsd ldrs, rdn hfwy, sn wknd*....................(14 to 1 op 12 to 1) 12

FRIENDLY COAST [50] 6-8-5 J Quinn (10) *al beh, tld off fnl 6 fs*.............................. (33 to 1 op 20 to 1) 13

Dist: 1l, 4l, 6l, nk, 3½l, 2½l, 7l, 1½l, 12l, nk. 3m 46.20s. a 19.70s (13 Ran).
(John Purcell), R C Spicer

LINGFIELD (A.W) (std)
Thursday December 31st
Going Correction: MINUS 0.30 sec. per fur.

4814a 'Any Port' Maiden Stakes CLASS F (3-y-o) £1,098 1m. . . . . (12:35)

4777a[3] ABBEY STRAND (USA) 8-9 Dean McKeown (1) *made all, quickened clr appr fnl furlong, easily.* ....(2 to 1 on op 7 to 4 on tchd 11 to 8 on) 1

4780a[6] RICH HEIRESS (Ire) 8-9 Candy Morris (4) *cl up, hrd rdn o'r one furlong out, one pace.* ....(50 to 1 op 16 to 1 tchd 66 to 1) 2

SECRET TREATY (Ire) 8-9 W Ryan (5) *beh, shaken up o'r one furlong out, kpt on ins last.* ....(20 to 1 op 8 to 1 tchd 25 to 1) 3

OTHELLO 8-9 (5*) N Gwilliams (3) *cl up, keen hold early, pushed alng 3 fs out, one pace*.......(3 to 1 op 7 to 4) 4

BAYIN (USA) 9-0 J Williams (2) *outpcd, hdwy to track ldg trio aftr hfwy, sn btn.* ....(25 to 1 op 20 to 1 tchd 50 to 1) 5

4780a[4] FUNDEGHE (USA) (bl) 9-0 D Biggs (6) *beh hfwy, tld off.* ....(8 to 1 tchd 12 to 1) 6

Dist: 12l, 1½l, ¾l, ¾l, 12l. 1m 40.13s. a 3.23s (6 Ran).
SR: 11/-/-/ (The Queen), Lord Huntingdon

4815a 'Cold As Charity' Claiming Stakes CLASS F (3-y-o and up) £1,140 6f ....(1:05)

4804a* RESPECTABLE JONES 6-8-12 W Ryan (2) *hld up, keen hold, hdwy o'r one furlong out, led ins last, sn clr.* ....(4 to 1 on op 3 to 1 on tchd 11 to 4 on) 1

4752a[8] SUMMER EXPRESS 3-8-4 Dean McKeown (1) *wtd wth in cl tch, hdwy and ev ch o'r one furlong out, kpt on one pace*..................(9 to 2 op 3 to 1 tchd 5 to 1) 2

SAVALARO 3-7-9 J Quinn (4) *led till ins fnl furlong, one pace*..........................(14 to 1 op 6 to 1) 3

4736a[9] INSWINGER 6-8-7 J Williams (6) *outpcd, sn pushed alng, styd on ins last*................(33 to 1 op 16 to 1) 4

4804a[4] CHERRYWOOD LASS 4-7-9 G Bardwell (3) *cl up, sn rdn alng, wknd o'r one furlong out*.... (50 to 1 op 20 to 1) 5

4774a PINK'N BLACK (Ire) 3-7-6 (5*) A Garth (5) *wth ldr, rdn o'r 2 fs out, wknd over one out.* ....(25 to 1 op 10 to 1 tchd 33 to 1) 6

Dist: 3½l, 2l, 1l, 3l, 3½l. 1m 13.40s. a 2.60s (6 Ran).
SR: 10/-/-/ (Mrs B Ramsden), R Hollinshead

4816a 'All's Fair' Handicap CLASS F (0-80 3-y-o and up) £1,478 7f. . . . . . (1:35)

4783a* PIGALLE WONDER [40] (bl) 4-8-6 D Biggs (6) *cl up, led 3 fs out, sn clr, easily*.................(9 to 4 tchd 11 to 4) 1
4803a5 LOOTING (USA) [37] 6-7-10 (7*) Kim McDonnell (2) *trkd ldr, led 4 fs out to 3 out, one pace.*
..........................(6 to 1 op 5 to 1 tchd 7 to 1) 2
4789a6 BRIGHT PARAGON (Ire) [41] 3-8-6 J Quinn (7) *hld up, cld o'r 2 fs out, kpt on one pace*............(8 to 1 op 6 to 1) 3
4781a2 KISSAVOS [62] (v) 6-10-0 W Ryan (4) *hld up in tch, pld hrd, hdwy 2 fs out, hard rdn o'r one out, one pace.*
.... (6 to 4 fav tchd 7 to 4) 4
PRINCE ROONEY (Ire) [58] 4-9-3 (7*) S Drowne (3) *trkd ldrs till wknd wl o'r one furlong out*... (20 to 1 op 10 to 1) 5
4748a7 ITHKURNI (USA) [60] 3-9-11 J Williams (5) *beh, hdwy o'r one furlong out, nvr on terms.*
.... (33 to 1 op 20 to 1 tchd 50 to 1) 6
FALCON FLIGHT [54] 6-9-3 (3*) A Tucker (1) *led 3 fs, wknd.*
.... (14 to 1 op 12 to 1 tchd 16 to 1) 7
Dist: 6l, ½l, 1l, 3½l, hd, 7l. 1m 26.01s. a 2.41s (7 Ran).
SR: 24/3/4/23/8/8/-/ (Miss Nicola M Pfann), R J O'Sullivan

4817a 'Apple A Day' Handicap CLASS F (0-70 3-y-o and up) £1,318 1¼m ....(2:05)

4807a2 MULCIBER [65] 4-9-11 M Hills (7) *hld up beh ldrs, hdwy o'r 2 fs out, led over one out, ran on wl.*
.................................(5 to 4 fav op 6 to 4) 1
4807a7 PREMIER DANCE [40] 5-7-7 (7*) S McCarthy (11) *strted slwly, hdwy to chase ldrs aftr 3 fs, kpt on wl fnl furlong*................(16 to 1 op 14 to 1 tchd 20 to 1) 2
4795a* CRETOES DANCER (USA) [50] (bl) 3-8-0 (7*) Kim McDonnell (2) *led till o'r one furlong out, one pace.*
.... (10 to 1 op 5 to 1) 3
4678a9 REFLECTING (Ire) [65] 3-9-8 D Holland (12) *beh, rdn alng 3 fs out, styd on one pace frm 2 out*...(10 to 1 op 6 to 1) 4
4802a3 DANCING BEAU (Ire) [51] (bl,e/s) 3-8-8 J Williams (6) *sn chasing ldrs, rdn and one pace fnl 2 fs.*
.................................(6 to 1 tchd 7 to 1) 5
4807a3 VA UTU [47] 4-8-7 W Ryan (9) *beh, hdwy 4 fs out, hng lft o'r one out, not rch ldrs.*
.... (9 to 1 op 6 to 1 tchd 10 to 1) 6
TROVE [70] 3-9-6 (7*) D Wright (13) *dwlt, hdwy to track ldrs o'r 5 fs out, wknd over 2 out*..(50 to 1 op 25 to 1) 7
4793a2 DANCING BOAT [40] (bl) 3-7-11 G Bardwell (10) *sn rdn alng to chase ldrs, hrd ridden 2 fs out, wknd o'r one out.*
.................................(7 to 1 tchd 8 to 1) 8
4798a6 MISTER LAWSON [44] 6-8-4 D Biggs (3) *trkd ldrs 3 fs, sn lost pl*..........................(50 to 1 op 33 to 1) 9
4680a9 SPEEDY CLASSIC (USA) [43] 3-8-0 Dale Gibson (5) *al beh.*
.... (50 to 1 op 20 to 1) 10
MARDIOR [33] 4-7-7 Dana Mellor (4) *sn outpcd.*
.... (33 to 1 op 20 to 1) 11
ROCK BAND (Ire) [61] 3-9-4 Dean McKeown (8) *prmnt till rdn and wknd 4 fs out*............(50 to 1 op 20 to 1) 12
GREATEST OF ALL (Ire) [36] 4-7-10² J Quinn (1) *cl up till wknd o'r 5 fs out*.................(50 to 1 op 33 to 1) 13
Dist: 2l, 1l, 3l, 2l, 4l, 1½l, ½l, 3½l, 2½l, 2½l. 2m 6.08s. a 2.88s (13 Ran).
SR: 52/23/28/37/19/10/27/-/-/ (Mrs Penny Treadwell), G Harwood

4818a 'Bald Coot' Handicap CLASS F (0-70 3-y-o and up) £1,292 5f....... (2:35)

RHYTHMIC DANCER [67] 4-10-0 Dean McKeown (8) *strted slwly, sn tracking ldrs, led appr fnl furlong, easily.*
.... (12 to 1 op 8 to 1 tchd 14 to 1) 1
4719a9 TOMMY TEMPEST [39] (bl) 3-7-7 (7*) D Wright (7) *cl up, led o'r 3 fs out till appr last, one pace.* (9 to 2 op 11 to 4) 2
4779a4 SERIOUS HURRY [52] (v) 4-8-13 J Quinn (5) *cl up, ev ch o'r one furlong out, hrd rdn, one pace.*
.........................(7 to 4 fav op 11 to 4 tchd 3 to 1) 3
4775a7 DOESYOUDOES [51] (v) 3-8-12 J Williams (3) *cl up, led aftr one furlong till o'r 3 out, sn outpcd.*
..................................(5 to 1 tchd 6 to 1) 4
4783a9 PENDOR DANCER [41] (bl) 9-8-2 D Biggs (4) *outpcd hfwy.*
....(12 to 1) 5
RUSHANES [65] 5-9-12 W Ryan (6) *sn outpcd.*
...................................(9 to 1 op 7 to 1) 6
4779a7 EVER SO ARTISTIC [33] 5-7-8 G Bardwell (1) *outpcd.*
..............................(14 to 1 tchd 16 to 1) 7
TREASURE TIME (Ire) [64] 3-9-11 Dale Gibson (2) *led one furlong, sn drpd out*... (11 to 2 op 6 to 1 tchd 8 to 1) 8
Dist: 3l, ¾l, 5l, ¾l, 6l, 1l, 2l. 59.86s. a 1.36s (8 Ran).
SR: 57/17/27/6/-/ (Mrs Robert Heathcote), J L Spearing

4819a 'Gift Horse' Handicap CLASS F (0-70 3-y-o and up) £1,351 1½m.... (3:10)

4798a* EL VOLADOR [65] 5-9-11 W Ryan (4) *chsd ldrs, hdwy o'r 3 fs out, led over one out, drvn out.* (2 to 1 fav op 5 to 2) 1
4760a2 STRAT'S LEGACY [43] 5-8-3 J Quinn (2) *settled beh ldrs, pushed alng o'r 4 fs out, sn cld, ev ch over one out, one pace*........(9 to 2 op 4 to 1 tchd 7 to 2 and 5 to 1) 2
4679a5 SLIGHT RISK [56] (e/c) 3-8-11 G Bardwell (1) *led, clr 4 fs out, hdd o'r one out, no extr*........(12 to 1 op 7 to 1) 3
4806a* DR ZEVA [35] 6-7-2 (7*,5ex) D Wright (9) *beh, styd on frm o'r one furlong out, nrst finish.*
.....................(3 to 1 op 6 to 4 tchd 100 to 30) 4
4797a HUNTING GROUND [55] 4-8-12 (3*) A Tucker (8) *reminders early, beh, styd on fnl furlong, nvr nrr.*
.... (50 to 1 op 33 to 1) 5
4670a2 FLASH OF STRAW (Ire) [45] (bl) 3-8-0 D Biggs (10) *chsd ldrs, outpcd fnl 3 fs*..........(4 to 1 op 6 to 1 tchd 8 to 1) 6
4798a4 ROYAL VERSE (Fr) [36] 5-7-10⁸ (5*) N Gwilliams (7) *nvr better than mid-div.* (33 to 1 op 20 to 1 tchd 50 to 1) 7
4807a4 NASEER (USA) [51] (bl) 3-8-6¹ J Williams (5) *trkd ldr, wknd o'r 3 fs out*..................... (14 to 1 tchd 20 to 1) 8
4788a9 NIPOTINA [33] 6-7-0 (7*) F Savage (3) *al beh.*
.... (40 to 1 op 33 to 1 tchd 50 to 1) 9
4758a HINTON HARRY (Ire) [38] (bl) 3-7-7 Dana Mellor (6) *rcd freely, trkd ldg pair till wknd hfwy, tld off.*
.... (66 to 1 op 50 to 1) 10
Dist: 2l, 3½l, 5l, 2½l, nk, sht-hd, ¾l, 15l, 25l. 2m 31.63s. a 1.93s (10 Ran).
SR: 56/30/31/5/20/4/-/7/-/ (I A Baker), R J O'Sullivan

Flat Race Results 1993

SOUTHWELL (A.W) (std)
Friday January 1st
Going Correction: PLUS 0.30 sec. per fur. (races 1,2,3,4,5), MINUS 0.25 (6)

1 New Year Resolution Apprentice Handicap CLASS F (0-60 3-y-o) £2,364 1m. . . . . . . (1:00)

4790a^{6} BRACKENTHWAITE [50] 9-1 V Halliday (3) *hld up, hdwy 3 fs out, effrt 2 out, sn rdn and hng lft, styd on to ld ins last*. . . . . . (9 to 1 op 8 to 1) 1
4677a^{5} MRS DAWSON [45] (v) 8-10 P McCabe (8) *slwly into strd, hdwy to ld aftr 2 fs and sn clr, rdn o'r one out, hdd ins last, kpt on*. . . . . . (10 to 1 op 7 to 1) 2
SPECIAL RISK (Ire) [56] 9-2 (5*) J O'Dwyer (2) *al prmnt, rdn and styd on one pace fnl 2 fs*. . . . . . (13 to 2 op 4 to 1) 3
4718a^{5} HOTSOCKS [48] 8-13 Kim McDonnell (7) *hld up, hdwy o'r 2 fs out, not rch ldrs*. . . . . . (12 to 1 op 8 to 1) 4
4805a^{6} KAFIOCA (Ire) [44] 8-4 (5*) Mark Denaro (10) *chsd ldrs, effrt and hdwy 3 fs out, rdn and wknd 2 out*. . . . . . (13 to 2 op 7 to 1 tchd 8 to 1) 5
4675a^{4} HUSH BABY (Ire) [43] 8-8 G Forster (11) *in tch, effrt 3 fs out, rdn and wknd 2 out*. . . . . . (13 to 2 op 6 to 1 tchd 5 to 1 and 7 to 1) 6
4770a^{4} ANOTHER KINGDOM [52] 9-3 T Wilson (1) *trkd ldrs, rdn 3 fs out, grad wknd*.. (11 to 4 fav op 7 to 2 tchd 4 to 1) 7
4762a^{7} BAJKA [55] 9-6 M Humphries (5) *in tch till rdn and wknd o'r 2 fs out*. . . . . . (20 to 1 op 25 to 1) 8
4773a DON'T TELL JEAN [40] 8-5 G Parkin (4) *led 2 fs, prmnt till rdn and wknd 3 out*. . . . . . (33 to 1 op 25 to 1) 9
4790a^{7} BROUGHTONS FORMULA [50] 8-10 (5*) D McCabe (6) *al rear*. . . . . (11 to 2 op 14 to 1 tchd 16 to 1 and 5 to 1) 10
4773a^{6} WELL TRIED (Ire) [51] 8-11 (5*) J Dennis (9) *al rear*. . . . . . (14 to 1 tchd 16 to 1) 11

Dist: ½l, 3l, 7l, 1l, 1l, 4l, 1½l, 2l, 4l, 1l. 1m 46.90s. a 7.90s (11 Ran).
SR: 19/12/14/-/-/-/ (David Barron Racing Club), T D Barron

2 Hair Of The Dog Claiming Stakes CLASS F (3-y-o) £2,427 7f. . . . . (1:30)

4724a^{4} GREENWICH CHALENGE (v) 8-1 (5*) N Gwilliams (1) *quickly away, made all, quickened clr 2 and a half fs out, rdn and ran on fnl furlong*. . . . . . (7 to 4 jt-fav tchd 2 to 1) 1
4809a* MOONSTRUCK BARD 8-8 W Woods (4) *hld up in tch, hdwy 3 fs out, effrt and rdn 2 out, styd on, not rch wnr*. . . . . . (7 to 4 jt-fav op 6 to 4 tchd 9 to 4) 2
4809a^{3} MASTER SINCLAIR (Ire) 8-1 (5*) A Garth (2) *dwlt, sn in tch, rdn 2 fs out, styd on fnl furlong*. . . . . . (5 to 1 op 4 to 1 tchd 11 to 2) 3
4697a^{3} MARK'S CLUB (Ire) 8-4 Alex Greaves (5) *chsd wnr, rdn 2 fs out, wknd appr last*. . . . . (9 to 2 op 4 to 1 tchd 5 to 1) 4
4791a^{3} FRIENDLY SMILE 8-7 C Dwyer (3) *chsd wnr, rdn and wknd o'r 2 fs out*. . . . . . (12 to 1 op 8 to 1) 5

Dist: 2½l, 1½l, hd, 2½l. 1m 32.40s. a 6.30s (5 Ran).
SR: 29/23/16/13/8/ (T G Mills Limited), W Carter

3 New Year Handicap CLASS F (0-70 4-y-o and up) £2,490 1½m. . . . . (2:00)

4788a* CLIFTON CHASE [49] (bl) 4-8-5 Dean McKeown (9) *trkd ldrs, hdwy o'r 3 fs out, led over 2 out, sn rdn and ran on wl*. . . . . . (11 to 4 fav tchd 3 to 1 and 5 to 2) 1
WELL AND TRULY [35] 6-7-5^{2} (7*) J Bramhill (4) *in tch, hdwy 4 fs out, ev ch 2 out, sn rdn and kpt on wl*. . . . . . (33 to 1 op 25 to 1) 2
4788a^{3} MODEST HOPE (USA) [54] 6-8-10 (5*) A Garth (7) *mid-div, hdwy 4 fs out, ev ch one and a half out, sn rdn, one pace fnl furlong*. . . . . . (6 to 1 op 5 to 1) 3
4771a^{7} SUGEMAR [53] 7-9-0 S Webster (6) *chsd early ldrs, rdn 3 fs out, kpt on one pace fnl 2 furlongs*. . . . . . (16 to 1 op 20 to 1) 4
4776a^{2} MINGUS (USA) [51] 6-8-12 D Nicholls (10) *hld up, hdwy 4 fs out, effrt on inner 2 out, not much room appr last, one pace*. . . . . . (13 to 2 op 7 to 1 tchd 8 to 1) 5
4715a^{2} CONTINUITY [58] 4-9-0 J Quinn (5) *mid-div, hdwy 4 fs out, effrt 2 out, sn rdn and one pace*... (12 to 1 op 10 to 1) 6
4689a^{5} TOUCH ABOVE [47] 7-8-8 Alex Greaves (12) *beh till hdwy 3 fs out, kpt on, not rch ldrs*. . . . . . (10 to 1 op 7 to 1) 7
4707a^{4} EUROTWIST [64] 4-9-6 J Fanning (16) *beh, some hdwy o'r 2 fs out, nvr dngrs*. . . . . . (10 to 1 tchd 8 to 1) 8
NO MORE THE FOOL [67] 7-9-7 (7*) P Roberts (13) *led, rdn 3 fs out, sn hdd and wknd*. . . . . . (25 to 1 op 20 to 1) 9
4806a^{5} EMPEROR ALEXANDER (Ire) [60] 5-9-0 (7*) T G McLaughlin (14) *cl up, rdn o'r 3 fs out, sn wknd*. (8 to 1 op 10 to 1) 10
4788a IRISH NATIVE (Ire) [45] (bl) 5-8-6 A Proud (8) *al rear*. . . . . . (50 to 1) 11
4662a^{8} FREE TRANSFER (Ire) [48] (bl) 4-8-4 L Charnock (11) *prmnt, rdn 6 fs out, wknd quickly*. . . . . . (20 to 1 tchd 33 to 1) 12
4763a^{3} IRON BARON (Ire) [54] 4-8-10 W Ryan (3) *nvr rch ldrs*. . . . . . (10 to 1 op 8 to 1) 13
SECRET LIASON [35] 7-7-9^{6} (7*) D McCabe (1) *nvr rch ldrs*. . . . . . (25 to 1 op 20 to 1) 14
4771a^{9} BUZZARDS CREST [32] 8-7-3^{3} (7*) D Wright (2) *al beh*. . . . . . (25 to 1 op 20 to 1) 15
NAJEB (USA) [45] 4-8-1 Dale Gibson (17) *al rear, drvn alng hfwy*. . . . . . (25 to 1 op 20 to 1) 16

Dist: ½l, ¾l, 1½l, 1½l, 2½l, 4l, nk, 1½l, 1l, 5l. 2m 42.80s. a 8.90s (16 Ran).
SR: 38/28/45/41/36/33/19/30/35/ (A K Smeaton), M A Jarvis

4 Hung Over Maiden Claiming Stakes CLASS F (4-y-o) £2,070 7f. (2:30)

4789a INNOCENT GEORGE 8-7 L Charnock (1) *dsptd ld 2 fs, cl up till led appr last, sn rdn and ran on wl*. . . . . . (10 to 1 op 7 to 1 tchd 12 to 1) 1
4810a^{9} SWINGING TICH 8-0 J Quinn (2) *dwlt, hdwy 3 fs out, rdn and ev ch appr last, no extr wl ins last*. . . . . . (13 to 8 fav op 7 to 4 tchd 2 to 1) 2
HONEY VISION (bl) 8-3 G Bardwell (3) *dsptd ld till led aftr 2 fs, rdn two out, hdd and wknd appr last*. . . . . . (6 to 1 op 4 to 1) 3
4785a^{4} NORTH FLYER 8-6 A Dicks (5) *chsd ldrs, rdn o'r 2 fs out, sn wknd*. . . . . . (13 to 2 op 5 to 1 tchd 7 to 1) 4
LITTLE NOD 8-7 Dale Gibson (6) *cl up, rdn 2 and a half fs out, sn btn*. . . . . . (2 to 1 op 7 to 4) 5
4768a BASSETLAW BELLE 7-10 S Wood (4) *al rear*. . . . . . (25 to 1 op 20 to 1) 6

Dist: ½l, 3l, 2l, 7l, 7l. 1m 33.40s. a 7.30s (6 Ran).
SR: 15/6/-/ (Edward C Wilkin), C B B Booth

5 New Era Maiden Stakes CLASS F (4-y-o and up) £2,070 1m. . . . . (3:00)

4810a MERRYHILL MADAM 4-8-9 J Quinn (4) *in tch, hdwy 3 fs out, led o'r 2 out and sn clr, easily*... (5 to 2 op 3 to 1) 1
PRINCESS DECHTRA (Ire) 4-8-9 W Ryan (7) *chsd ldrs, effrt and ev ch o'r 2 fs out, sn rdn and kpt on one pace*. . . . . . (11 to 2 op 6 to 1 tchd 13 to 2 and 7 to 1) 2
4777a^{2} BELIEVE IN ME (Ire) 4-9-0 Dean McKeown (6) *cl up, hrd rdn o'r 2 fs out, sn btn*. . . . . . (11 to 10 fav op 5 to 4 on) 3
TIBBS INN 4-9-0 J Carroll (3) *cl up, rdn 3 fs out, sn wknd*. . . . . . (25 to 1 tchd 33 to 1) 4
WHITWELL HILL 4-8-9 L Charnock (2) *led, rdn 3 fs out, sn hdd and wknd*. . . . . . (50 to 1 op 33 to 1) 5
FAIRSPEAR (bl) 4-9-0 Dale Gibson (8) *al rear*. . . . . . (9 to 1 op 10 to 1) 6
THE OLD MITRE 5-8-3 (7*) J Bramhill (5) *chsd ldrs till wknd quickly 2 and a half fs out*. . . . . . (16 to 1 op 12 to 1) 7
KAYMONT 5-8-10 G Bardwell (1) *sn lost pl, wl beh fnl 3 fs*. . . . . . (25 to 1 tchd 33 to 1) 8

Dist: 3l, 6l, 2l, nk, 3l, 6l, 12l. 1m 48.20s. a 9.20s (8 Ran).
(H A Cushing), J L Harris

6 Hogmanay Handicap CLASS F (0-70 4-y-o and up) £2,322 5f. (3:30)

4768a^{2} HINARI VIDEO [50] 8-9-0 Dean McKeown (12) *cl up stands rls, effrt to ld ins fnl furlong, ran on wl*. . . . . . (5 to 2 fav op 4 to 1) 1
4719a^{4} SOBA GUEST (Ire) [60] 4-9-10 J Carroll (11) *al prmnt, hdwy to chal appr fnl furlong, sn rdn and not quicken wl ins last*. . . . . . (9 to 2 op 5 to 1) 2
4775a^{2} LE CHIC [53] 7-9-3 S Wood (8) *led, rdn appr fnl furlong, hdd ins last, no extr*.... (5 to 1 op 9 to 2 tchd 11 to 2) 3
MARTINA [64] 5-9-9 (5*) S Wynne (9) *chsd ldrs, rdn 2 fs out, styd on fnl furlong*. . . . . . (12 to 1 op 10 to 1) 4
4768a^{8} THE DREAM MAKER (Ire) [45] 4-8-9 Dale Gibson (10) *chsd ldrs stands side, rdn and kpt on fnl 2 fs*. . . . . . (12 to 1) 5
4765a^{7} JOVIAL KATE (USA) [56] 6-9-1 (5*) S D Williams (4) *in tch and rdn alng, kpt on one pace fnl 2 fs*. . . . . . (14 to 1 op 12 to 1) 6
4716a^{5} STRIP CARTOON (Ire) [49] (v) 5-8-13 J Quinn (7) *outpcd till styd on fnl 2 fs*. . . . . . (12 to 1) 7
4808a COMPANY CASH [47] (bl) 5-8-6^{2} (7*) H Bastiman (6) *outpcd till some hdwy fnl 2 fs*. . . . . . (20 to 1 op 16 to 1) 8
4808a ARC LAMP [57] 7-9-7 D Nicholls (5) *chsd ldrs, rdn hfwy, wknd o'r one furlong out*. . . . . . (10 to 1 op 8 to 1) 9
4775a^{3} LINCSTONE BOY (Ire) [51] (bl) 5-9-1 S Webster (1) *chsd ldrs, rdn 2 fs out, sn wknd*. . . . . . (8 to 1 op 7 to 1) 10
4768a CAMINO A RONDA [35] 4-7-6 (7*) Kim McDonnell (2) *beh frm hfwy*. . . . . . (33 to 1) 11
SAKOSAN [37] 4-8-1 J Fanning (3) *al rear, beh frm hfwy*. . . . . . (40 to 1) 12

Dist: 1l, nk, 1½l, ½l, 2l, 1l, hd, nk, 1l, 3½l. 1m 0.00s. a 1.70s (12 Ran).
SR: 41/47/39/44/23/26/15/12/21/ (L G McMullan), M Johnston

LINGFIELD (A.W) (std)
Saturday January 2nd
Going Correction: MINUS 0.20 sec. per fur.

7 Santander Handicap CLASS F (0-70 3-y-o) £2,325 5f. .... (12:50)

4720a3 THE INSTITUTE BOY [59] (bl) 8-12 S Webster (7) *led aftr 2 fs, clr wl o'r one out, rdn and wknd ins last, jst hld on.* .... (5 to 1 op 3 to 1 tchd 11 to 2) 1

4741a* SPLASH OF SALT (Ire) [63] 9-2 J Quinn (2) *chsd ldrs, rdn wl o'r one furlong out, styd on well ins last, not rch wnr.* ....(9 to 4 op 2 to 1 tchd 5 to 2) 2

4762a8 TEE-EMM [66] 8-12 (7*) L Carter (3) *led 2 fs, chsd wnr aftr til wknd ins last*...................(10 to 1 op 5 to 1) 3

4773a2 COMET WHIRLPOOL (Ire) [58] (bl) 8-11 W Woods (6) *rear, rdn and styd on fnl 2 fs, nvr able to chal.* ....(4 to 1 op 5 to 2) 4

4805a4 KNOBBLEENEEZE [62] (v) 9-1 T Quinn (1) *sn rdn alng, chsd ldrs till wknd 2 fs out.* ....(85 to 40 fav op 2 to 1 tchd 9 to 4) 5

4805a WEALTHYWOO [62] (bl) 9-1 C Dwyer (4) *outpcd.* .... (33 to 1 op 20 to 1) 6

4805a HOME AFFAIR [68] 9-7 G Bardwell (5) *beh frm hfwy.* .... (50 to 1 op 20 to 1) 7

Dist: ½l, 3l, sht-hd, 6l, 2l, 1l. 1m 0.79s. a 2.59s (7 Ran).

SR: 26/28/19/10/ (Mrs J Addleshaw), K R Burke

8 Vigo Claiming Stakes CLASS F (4-y-o and up) £2,477 1½m. .... (1:20)

4760a8 BREAKDANCER (Ire) 4-8-6 T Quinn (4) *hld up, smooth prog to track ldr o'r 3 fs out, led on bit appr last, rdn out.* ....(13 to 8 fav op 9 to 4) 1

4793a4 LYPH (USA) 7-8-3 S Dawson (10) *prmnt, led 4 fs out, rdn 2 out, hdd appr last, ran on.* ....(10 to 1 op 14 to 1 tchd 16 to 1) 2

4793a3 FIRST FLING (Ire) (v) 4-7-11[4] (7*) P McCabe (2) *in tch, rdn 5 fs out, ran on to chase ldg pair o'r 2 out, not quicken ins last*............. (100 to 30 op 9 to 4 tchd 7 to 2) 3

4795a2 SIMON ELLIS (Ire) 4-7-12 G Bardwell (3) *chsd ldrs, hrd rdn and styd on one pace fnl 4 fs*..... (16 to 1 op 10 to 1) 4

4802a5 NATIVE CHIEFTAN 4-8-5 (7*) Mark Denaro (8) *pressed ldr till wknd o'r 3 fs out*.................. (6 to 1 op 5 to 1) 5

4797a6 PERSIAN FLEECE 4-7-2[2] (7*) D Wright (6) *sn last and rdn alng, nvr a dngr*....... (5 to 1 op 4 to 1 tchd 11 to 2) 6

ANNE'S BANK (Ire) 5-8-2 Candy Morris (9) *beh, shaken up o'r 3 fs out, no prog*............... (33 to 1 op 25 to 1) 7

4780a5 LAJADHAL (Fr) 4-8-8 W Ryan (5) *led 2 fs, losing pl whn hmpd hfwy, beh aftr*.............. (33 to 1 op 25 to 1) 8

4746a ROCKY BAY 4-7-4 (7*) S McCarthy (7) *pld hrd, led aftr 2 fs till 4 out, wknd rpdly*............ (25 to 1 op 16 to 1) 9

4782a BASSIO (Bel) (v) 4-7-12[1] (7*) G Forster (1) *chsd ldrs, hrd rdn 5 fs out, sn wknd*..................(16 to 1 op 12 to 1) 10

Dist: 1½l, 1½l, 10l, 2½l, 6l, 8l, 3½l, ½l, 1½l. 2m 34.75s. a 5.45s (10 Ran).

SR: 14/8/2/-/-/-/ (J Jannaway), W R Muir

9 Santiago Handicap CLASS E (0-90 4-y-o and up) £3,201 1¼m. .... (1:50)

4782a7 RAPPORTEUR (USA) [79] 7-10-0 J Williams (7) *pressed ldr, pushed alng frm hfwy, ran on strly ins last to ld cl hme, gmely*.................(25 to 1 op 14 to 1 tchd 33 to 1) 1

4759a2 AWESOME POWER [75] 7-9-10 M Hills (8) *trkd ldrs gng wl, prog to ld well o'r one furlong out, ran on, hdd cl hme.* ....(11 to 4 co-fav op 7 to 2) 2

4776a* LOOKINGFORARAINBOW (Ire) [65] 5-9-0 N Day (4) *trkd ldrs gng wl, not clr run 2 fs out, ran on well ins last, nrst finish.* (11 to 4 co-fav op 5 to 2 tchd 100 to 30 and 7 to 2) 3

4782a2 KHRISMA [73] 4-9-5 W Ryan (5) *led, rdn 2 fs out, sn hdd, wknd ins last.* (11 to 4 co-fav op 2 to 1 tchd 3 to 1 and 7 to 2) 4

4798a3 MENTALASANYTHIN [60] 4-8-6 G Bardwell (3) *hld up, rdn and not quicken 3 fs out, ran on ins last, nvr nrr.* .... (12 to 1 op 6 to 1) 5

4807a6 BELMOREDEAN [75] 8-9-10 D Biggs (1) *chsd ldrs till rdn and wknd wl o'r 2 fs out*...........(10 to 1 op 8 to 1) 6

MEL'S ROSE [66] 8-8-8 (7*) P McCabe (6) *al beh.* .... (25 to 1 op 14 to 1 tchd 33 to 1) 7

4806a7 MAY SQUARE (Ire) [48] 5-7-11 J Quinn (2) *chsd ldrs till rdn and wknd 3 fs out*....................(8 to 1 op 14 to 1) 8

Dist: ½l, nk, 4l, ¾l, 4l, hd, 1½l. 2m 6.27s. a 3.07s (8 Ran).

SR: 63/58/47/44/29/39/29/8/ (Richard Berenson), C C Elsey

10 Alpine Double Glazing Maiden Stakes CLASS F (4-y-o and up) £2,174 6f. ..... (2:20)

4751a9 SIRMOOR (Ire) (bl) 4-9-0 A McGlone (5) *led aftr 2 fs, drvn out ins last*......................(4 to 1 tchd 5 to 1) 1

4774a7 EWALD (Ire) 5-9-0 T Quinn (7) *led 2 fs, chsd wnr aftr, hrd rdn o'r one out, unbl to quicken.* .... (3 to 1 fav tchd 7 to 2) 2

4705a6 MU-ARRIK 5-9-0 M Hills (6) *outpcd hfwy, ran on appr fnl furlong, nvr able to chal.* ....(7 to 2 op 5 to 2 tchd 4 to 1) 3

GYMCRAK FORTUNE (Ire) 5-9-0 W Woods (2) *outpcd and wl beh till ran on appr fnl furlong, no dngr.* ....(10 to 1 tchd 14 to 1) 4

4804a7 NIGALS FRIEND 4-9-0 J Williams (4) *chsd ldrs till wknd o'r 2 fs out*............... (11 to 2 op 4 to 1 tchd 6 to 1) 5

ANOTHER VINTAGE 4-9-0 W Ryan (3) *al wl beh.* ....(4 to 1 op 7 to 2 tchd 5 to 1) 6

4746a TRICKY VERA (Ire) (bl) 4-8-9 J Quinn (1) *cl up till wknd rpdly hfwy*.......... (16 to 1 op 20 to 1 tchd 25 to 1) 7

Dist: 1½l, 3½l, 2½l, ¾l, 12l, 6l. 1m 14.08s. a 3.28s (7 Ran).

SR: 10/4/-/-/ (Christopher Wilson), R Hannon

11 Lima Handicap CLASS F (0-80 4-y-o and up) £2,820 6f. .... (2:50)

RUNNING GLIMPSE (Ire) [74] 5-9-7 (7*) A Martinez (6) *led aftr 2 fs, made rst, rdn and ran on wl appr last.* .... (14 to 1 op 8 to 1) 1

4818a* RHYTHMIC DANCER [74] 5-10-0 (7ex) J Williams (5) *hld up in tch, chsd wnr o'r 2 fs out, rdn appr last, ran on nr finish*.......................... (11 to 10 fav op 2 to 1) 2

4796a3 INDIAN ENDEAVOUR [73] 4-9-13 M Hills (2) *trkd ldrs, effrt and rdn o'r one furlong out, ran on ins last, nrst finish.* ....(6 to 1 op 4 to 1 tchd 7 to 1) 3

4796a4 LOVE LEGEND [71] (bl) 8-9-11 T Quinn (3) *chsd ldrs, rdn and ev ch 2 fs out, wknd ins last.* ....(4 to 1 op 7 to 2 tchd 6 to 1) 4

4808a3 TOSHIBA COMET [53] (e/s) 6-8-7 D Biggs (8) *beh and rdn alng, prog o'r 2 fs out, not rch ldrs*...(8 to 1 op 5 to 1) 5

4804a3 GEMINI BAY [40] (bl) 4-7-8 G Bardwell (1) *rdn hfwy, al beh.* ....(20 to 1 tchd 33 to 1) 6

HARDLINER [70] 4-9-10 W Ryan (7) *cl up till wknd hfwy.* .... (40 to 1 op 14 to 1) 7

4743a3 QUATRE FEMME [52] 6-8-6 R P Elliott (4) *led 2 fs, wknd two out*.................. (10 to 1 op 5 to 1 tchd 11 to 1) 8

Dist: ½l, ¾l, 3½l, 3½l, 4l, 1½l, 1½l. 1m 12.65s. a 1.85s (8 Ran).

SR: 53/51/47/31/-/ (Copyforce Ltd), Miss B Sanders

12 Ladbroke All Weather Trophy Handicap Qualifier CLASS E (0-75 3-y-o and up) £3,080 1m. .... (3:20)

4785a2 ABSONAL [64] 6-9-5 A McGlone (2) *trkd ldrs, led wl o'r one furlong out, rdn and ran on well ins last.* .... (9 to 1 op 8 to 1 tchd 10 to 1) 1

4805a* EXCESS BAGGAGE (Ire) [75] 3-8-10 W Ryan (6) *prog frm midfield hfwy, rdn and ran on appr fnl furlong, nvr able to chal*.......................... (4 to 1 op 6 to 1) 2

4803a* MASTER HYDE (USA) [56] 4-8-10 D Biggs (7) *beh, rdn and prog o'r 3 fs out, rng on whn hmpd ins last, nvr nrr.* ....(9 to 2 op 7 to 2) 3

4751a* HENIU (USA) [61] (v) 4-9-1 M Hills (4) *set fst pace till hdd wl o'r one furlong out, btn whn edgd rght and hmpd ins last*........... (5 to 2 fav op 3 to 1 tchd 7 to 2) 4

4796a2 INVOCATION [73] 6-9-7 (7*) B Russell (12) *wl beh, rdn 3 fs out, ran on appr last, nvr nrr*..... (12 to 1 op 10 to 1) 5

4799a9 TADORA (Ire) [53] 4-8-7 T Quinn (8) *prmnt, ev ch o'r 2 fs out, sn wknd*.........................(12 to 1 op 8 to 1) 6

4757a5 ALBERT THE BOLD [65] (e/s) 4-9-5 J Williams (5) *wl beh till modest late prog, nvr dngrs*.......(7 to 1 tchd 10 to 1) 7

DIGGER DOYLE [67] 4-9-0 (7*) G Forster (1) *dwlt, rdn alng to chase ldrs, wknd o'r 3 fs out*.... (33 to 1 op 20 to 1) 8

4771a BILL MOON [52] 7-8-0 (7*) Kim McDonnell (10) *prmnt till wknd wl o'r 2 fs out*............... (14 to 1 op 20 to 1) 9

4781a6 SARUM [59] 7-9-0 Dale Gibson (3) *mid-div till wknd wl o'r 3 fs out*..................... (20 to 1 op 12 to 1) 10

MASRUR (USA) [70] 4-9-10 S Dawson (11) *wl beh frm hfwy, fnshd tld off*................(33 to 1 op 20 to 1) 11

EMAURA [55] 4-8-9 G Bardwell (9) *lost pl aftr 2 fs, beh after, fnshd tld off*............... (33 to 1 op 20 to 1) 12

Dist: 2l, ¾l, 3½l, 2½l, 3½l, 6l, sht-hd, sht-hd, 3l, 15l. 1m 38.49s. a 2.29s (12 Ran).

SR: 47/32/30/24/29/-/ (Capt R W Hornall), R Hannon

SOUTHWELL (A.W) (std)
Monday January 4th
Going Correction: PLUS 0.20 sec. per fur.

13 Babes In The Wood Handicap CLASS F (0-80 4-y-o and up) £2,448 1m. .... (1:10)

4777a* TACIT MAC (USA) [69] 4-10-0 D Holland (8) *trkd ldrs, hdwy o'r 3 fs out, quickened to ld ins last, cmftbly.* ....(7 to 1 op 9 to 2 tchd 8 to 1) 1

DIAMOND INTHE DARK (USA) [53] (v) 5-8-13 L Charnock (15) *chsd ldrs, hdwy 4 fs out, effrt 2 out and sn led, rdn, hdd and no extr ins last*.. (16 to 1 op 14 to 1 tchd 20 to 1) 2

4785a* LOCK KEEPER (USA) [63] 7-9-4 (5*) S Wynne (16) *chsd ldrs, hdwy 3 fs out, ev ch o'r one out, sn rdn and one pace.* ....(9 to 2 fav op 5 to 1 tchd 6 to 1) 3

4764a* EAST BARNS (Ire) [55] (bl) 5-9-1 Alex Greaves (5) *chsd ldrs, hdwy 4 fs out, led 2 and a half out, sn rdn, hdd o'r one and a half out, one pace*.......... (5 to 1 op 11 to 2) 4

4785a[3] SIRTELIMAR (Ire) [60] 4-9-0 (5*) A Garth (9) *sn led, rdn and hdd 2 and a half fs out, one pace.* ....(6 to 1 op 5 to 1 tchd 7 to 1) 5
4799a[2] NOBBY BARNES [57] 4-8-11 (5*) S D Williams (13) *in tch, effrt and hdwy 3 fs out, sn rdn and kpt on one pace.* .... (6 to 1 op 5 to 1 tchd 13 to 2) 6
HOT PUNCH [40] 4-7-13 N Carlisle (11) *in tch, effrt and hdwy o'r 2 fs out, sn hrd rdn and one pace.* .... (25 to 1 op 20 to 1) 7
LILY'S LOVER (USA) [49] 7-8-9 A Dicks (1) *chsd ldrs till rdn and wknd 3 fs out*.................(20 to 1 op 16 to 1) 8
4760a CHARIOTEER [39] 4-7-12 Dale Gibson (2) *nvr rch ldrs.* ....(20 to 1 tchd 33 to 1) 9
4744a SCOTTISH PARK [59] 4-8-11 (7*) S Mulvey (7) *dwlt, al rear.* .... (25 to 1 op 20 to 1) 10
4807a SERIOUS ACTION [46] 4-8-5 C Nutter (10) *cl up, rdn o'r 3 fs out, sn wknd*...........................(25 to 1) 11
4802a* EASTLEIGH [64] 4-9-9 W Ryan (14) *chsd ldrs, effrt and hdwy 3 fs out, sn rdn and wknd frm 2 out.* .... (13 to 2 op 11 to 2) 12
4810a COMISKEY PARK (Ire) [46] 4-8-5 S Wood (12) *al rear.* .... (33 to 1 op 25 to 1) 13
ALBERT [38] 6-7-12 G Bardwell (3) *sn outpcd and beh.* .... (16 to 1 op 20 to 1) 14
MELTONBY [66] 4-9-11 J Carroll (4) *cl up till rdn and wknd 3 fs out*...........................(20 to 1) 15
4786a[6] SHANNON EXPRESS [53] 6-8-13 J Quinn (6) *al rear.* .... (25 to 1 op 20 to 1) 16
Dist: 1½l, 3l, 1½l, 2l, sht-hd, 1½l, 2l, sht-hd, sht-hd, hd. 1m 45.30s. a 6.30s (16 Ran).
SR: 44/24/25/12/10/6/ (T Mohan), W A O'Gorman

14 Jack And The Beanstalk Claiming Stakes CLASS F (4-y-o and up) £2,385 1½m...(1:40)

4812a* TEMPERING 7-9-4 S Wood (1) *made all, quickened 4 fs out, sn clr, unchlgd*...........(6 to 4 on op 2 to 1 on) 1
4812a[4] FERDIA (Ire) 4-8-10 W Ryan (2) *trkd ldr, effrt 4 fs out, sn hrd rdn and one pace*... (9 to 2 op 4 to 1 tchd 5 to 1) 2
4812a[3] SILVER SAMURAI 4-8-3 (7*) S Mulvey (4) *trkd ldr, rdn 4 fs out, one pace*...................(4 to 1 tchd 5 to 1) 3
4763a[8] ELIZA WOODING 5-8-2 G Bardwell (5) *in tch, rdn alng hfwy, sn beh*.....................(12 to 1 op 8 to 1) 4
SUMMER SANDS 5-8-0 J Quinn (6) *hld up, hdwy hfwy, sn rdn and wknd o'r 4 fs out*........ (33 to 1 op 16 to 1) 5
DERRY REEF 6-8-4 L Charnock (3) *in tch, rdn 5 fs out, sn wknd and beh*....... (25 to 1 op 16 to 1 tchd 33 to 1) 6
Dist: 7l, 3l, 12l, 10l, hd. 2m 44.80s. a 10.90s (6 Ran).
SR: 19/-/-/ (David W Chapman), D W Chapman

15 Sleeping Beauty Handicap CLASS F (0-70 3-y-o) £2,385 1m.................... (2:10)

1* BRACKENTHWAITE [50] 7-11 (7*) V Halliday (5) *hld up and beh, hdwy and wide strt, rdn one and a half fs out, styd on wl to ld well ins last*..... (9 to 4 fav op 2 to 1) 1
4809a[5] ROSE FLYER (Ire) [50] 8-4 S Wood (3) *led, quickened clr 3 fs out, rdn and hdd wl ins last, no extr.* .... (20 to 1 op 16 to 1) 2
4809a[2] MISTER BLAKE [67] (bl) 9-4 (3*) Emma O'Gorman (1) *hld up, hdwy o'r 3 fs out, rdn 2 out, sn one pace.* ....(5 to 2 op 3 to 1) 3
4766a[3] SCOFFERA [51] 8-5 Kim Tinkler (8) *prmnt, rdn 2 and a half fs out, grad wknd*................. (11 to 2 op 5 to 1) 4
4794a[6] BALLACASCADE [52] 8-6 Dale Gibson (6) *chsd ldr, hrd rdn 3 fs out, sn wknd*.................(14 to 1 op 12 to 1) 5
MUSICAL PHONE [57] 8-4 (7*) S Mulvey (7) *chsd ldr till rdn and wknd 3 fs out*..................(20 to 1 op 16 to 1) 6
4801a* CONVOY [63] (bl) 9-3 M Hills (2) *beh, hrd drvn 3 fs out, nvr a factor*..........................(11 to 4 op 9 to 4) 7
Dist: 1½l, 12l, 5l, 15l, 4l, 2½l. 1m 45.00s. a 6.00s (7 Ran).
SR: 24/19/-/-/ (David Barron Racing Club), T D Barron

16 Aladdin Claiming Stakes CLASS F (3-y-o) £2,364 6f........................... (2:40)

4773a[7] NIKKI NOO NOO 7-9 G Bardwell (9) *chsd ldrs, effrt and rdn o'r 2 fs out, styd on strly to ld ins last, sn clr.* ....(100 to 30 op 6 to 1 tchd 7 to 1 and 3 to 1) 1
4770a[2] DAANIERA (Ire) (v) 8-8 J Carroll (5) *led, quickened clr 2 and a half fs out, rdn o'r one out, hdd and no extr ins last.* ....(2 to 1 fav op 6 to 4 tchd 9 to 4) 2
PINE RIDGE LAD (Ire) 8-2 R P Elliott (6) *al prmnt, rdn o'r 2 fs out, kpt on one pace*..............(7 to 1 tchd 8 to 1) 3
4770a[7] GIRL NEXT DOOR 8-1 S Wood (2) *hdwy 3 fs out, styd on und pres frm 2 out*..................(4 to 1 op 11 to 4) 4
4811a[5] SOLEIL RAYON (Ire) 7-12 J Fanning (4) *chsd ldrs, rdn o'r 2 fs out, sn wknd*...................... (8 to 1 op 7 to 1) 5
4811a[6] HERSHEBAR (v) 8-2 J Quinn (11) *chsd ldr, rdn o'r 2 fs out, sn wknd*........................(12 to 1 tchd 14 to 1) 6
4770a[6] PYTCHLEY DAWN 8-1 D Biggs (7) *nvr rch ldrs.* .... (14 to 1 op 10 to 1) 7
BOULMERKA 7-10 (7*) Darren Moffatt (10) *al rear.* (33 to 1) 8
4791a ELSKA DIG 7-5[3] (5*) A Garth (8) *al rear*............(20 to 1) 9
4809a PINK CITY 8-3 (7*) J Edmunds (1) *beh frm hfwy.* .... (50 to 1 op 33 to 1) 10
Dist: 3l, ¾l, nk, 2l, 7l, 2½l, 4l, 3l, 2½l. 1m 16.70s. a 3.30s (10 Ran).
SR: 39/40/31/29/18/-/ (C John Hill), C J Hill

17 Snow White Handicap CLASS F (0-90 4-y-o and up) £2,259 7f.....................(3:10)

4771a[3] PRIME MOVER [62] (v) 5-8-0 L Charnock (1) *chsd ldrs, hdwy 3 fs out, effrt to ld wl o'r one out, ran on well und pres fnl furlong*........................(12 to 1 op 7 to 1) 1
4789a CLAUDIA MISS [57] 6-7-9 Dale Gibson (7) *chsd ldrs, rdn o'r one furlong out, styd on wl ins last.* (12 to 1 op 8 to 1) 2
4810a* JOHNSTON'S EXPRESS (Ire) [60] 5-7-12 (7ex) J Quinn (6) *trkd ldrs gng wl, hdwy 2 fs out, effrt and ev ch entering last, sn rdn and not quicken nr finish.* ....(15 to 8 fav op 9 to 4 tchd 7 to 4) 3
4765a* ALLINSON'S MATE (Ire) [80] 5-9-4 Alex Greaves (5) *hld up, hdwy 3 fs out, sn rdn and styd on one pace fnl 2 furlongs*...............................(3 to 1 tchd 7 to 2) 4
4808a[2] PESIDANAMICH (Ire) [68] (bl) 5-7-13 (7*) S Mulvey (2) *led, rdn 2 fs out, hdd and wknd wl o'r one out.* ....(7 to 1 tchd 8 to 1) 5
4796a* PANIKIN [90] 5-9-9 (5*) S D Williams (4) *chsd ldrs, rdn o'r 2 fs out, wknd wl over one out.* ....(7 to 1 op 6 to 1 tchd 8 to 1) 6
4808a[8] WELLSY LAD (USA) [56] 6-7-8 S Wood (3) *prmnt till rdn and wknd 2 fs out*...(12 to 1 op 10 to 1 tchd 14 to 1) 7
4785a[5] AMENABLE [87] 8-9-11 W Ryan (8) *hld up, effrt and some hdwy 3 fs out, sn rdn and wknd fnl 2 furlongs.* ....(25 to 1 op 12 to 1 tchd 33 to 1) 8
Dist: Nk, nk, 5l, 1½l, 1l, ½l, 7l. 1m 31.60s. a 5.50s (8 Ran).
SR: 25/19/21/26/9/28/-/2/ (Mrs M E Brooks), D Burchell

18 Cinderella Handicap CLASS F (0-85 4-y-o and up) £2,280 1¾m.................(3:40)

4813a[3] ATLANTIC WAY [42] 5-8-3 G Bardwell (8) *hld up, hdwy 6 fs out, led 2 out, sn clr, easily.* ....(6 to 4 fav op 7 to 4 tchd 2 to 1) 1
MASTER'S CROWN (USA) [40] 5-8-1 D Biggs (7) *mid-div, effrt and hdwy 4 fs out, styd on und pres fnl 2 furlongs, no ch wth wnr*............................(8 to 1 op 6 to 1) 2
4788a[8] DANCING DAYS [32] (bl) 7-7-5[3] (5*) A Garth (2) *hld up and beh, hdwy o'r 4 fs out, rdn and swtchd 2 out, styd on.* ....(25 to 1) 3
4698a[3] MOOT POINT (USA) [57] (bl) 5-9-4 D Nicholls (10) *hld up, hdwy hfwy, rdn and ev ch o'r 2 fs out, sn wknd.* ....(5 to 1 op 7 to 2 tchd 11 to 2) 4
3[9] NO MORE THE FOOL [67] (bl) 7-10-0 J Carroll (4) *in tch, hdwy to ld 6 fs out, rdn 3 out, hdd 2 out and sn wknd.* ....(12 to 1 op 10 to 1) 5
LUKS AKURA [37] 5-7-5 (7*) M Baird (3) *led 6 fs, cl up till lost pl o'r 5 out*.........(7 to 1 op 6 to 1 tchd 15 to 2) 6
4813a[7] SIR PAGEANT [64] 4-9-0 (5*) S D Williams (1) *cl up, led aftr 6 fs till six out, sn lost pl*..............(8 to 1 tchd 10 to 1) 7
INVISIBLE ARMOUR [48] 4-8-3 Dale Gibson (5) *prmnt till wknd 6 fs out, sn beh*..............(10 to 1 op 7 to 1) 8
PORT IN A STORM [52] 4-8-7 Kim Tinkler (6) *chsd ldrs to hfwy, sn beh*...........(15 to 2 op 6 to 1 tchd 8 to 1) 9
BLACKWATER PANTHER (Ire) [46] 4-7-8 (7*) D Wright (9) *mid-div till lost pl and beh fnl 6 fs, tld off*..... (16 to 1) 10
Dist: 2½l, 1l, 10l, 2l, 10l, hd, 6l, ¾l. 3m 11.00s. a 11.00s (10 Ran).
SR: 7/-/-/-/1/-/ (C John Hill), C J Hill

LINGFIELD (A.W) (std)
Thursday January 7th
Going Correction: MINUS 0.25 sec. per fur.

19 Tennyson Claiming Stakes CLASS F (4-y-o and up) £2,347 7f.....................(1:00)

4815a* RESPECTABLE JONES 7-9-3 W Ryan (6) *steadied strt, smooth hdwy frm o'r 2 fs out, led appr fnl furlong, sn clr*............ (7 to 1 op 6 to 1 on tchd 5 to 1 on) 1
FARM STREET 6-7-12 (5*) N Gwilliams (4) *in tch, led 2 and a half fs out, hdd appr fnl furlong, sn outpcd.* ....(33 to 1 op 20 to 1 tchd 50 to 1) 2
4816a[2] LOOTING (USA) 7-7-12 (7*) Kim McDonnell (5) *pressed ldrs, ev ch 2 fs out, sn outpcd.* (7 to 1 op 6 to 1 tchd 8 to 1) 3
10[5] NIGALS FRIEND (v) 4-8-7 J Williams (3) *led 4 fs out, hdd 2 and a half furlongs out, sn btn*....(16 to 1 op 10 to 1) 4
FOUROFUS 4-8-4 (3*) A Tucker (1) *sn beh, nvr dngrs.* .... (50 to 1 op 20 to 1) 5
4699a[9] JUDGEMENT CALL 6-8-6 (7*) L Carter (2) *led till hdd 4 fs out, sn btn*...............(25 to 1 op 10 to 1) 6
Dist: 6l, 6l, 6l, 4l, 1½l. 1m 25.71s. a 2.31s (6 Ran).
SR: 42/10/-/ (Mrs B Ramsden), R Hollinshead

20 Daily Star Challenge Handicap Qualifier CLASS F (0-70 4-y-o and up) £2,611 1¼m ....(1:30)

4817a[4] REFLECTING (Ire) [65] 4-9-6 D Holland (5) *hdwy 4 fs out, styd on to ld jst ins last, drvn out*....(9 to 2 op 3 to 1) 1
4819a[3] SLIGHT RISK [56] (e/c) 4-8-11 G Bardwell (7) *led, rdn alng frm 2 fs out, hdd jst ins last, not quicken.* ....(3 to 1 tchd 4 to 1) 2

4817a^2 PREMIER DANCE [39] 6-7-4 (7*) S McCarthy (3) *hld up, hdwy 4 fs out, shaken up one and a half furlongs out, one pace*.......... (5 to 2 fav op 9 to 4 tchd 11 to 4) 3
SAMURAI GOLD (USA) [55] (v) 5-8-13 Dale Gibson (2) *chsd ldrs till wknd 2 fs out*. .... (33 to 1 op 20 to 1 tchd 50 to 1) 4
4810a^8 FIT THE BILL [44] 5-8-2 L Charnock (6) *beh most of way*. .... (10 to 1 op 8 to 1 tchd 12 to 1) 5
MODESTO (USA) [70] 5-10-0 D Biggs (1) *sn rdn, lost tch aftr 3 fs, tld off 4 furlongs out, tailed off*. .... (12 to 1 op 5 to 1 tchd 14 to 1) 6
4782a^4 SCALES OF JUSTICE [68] 7-9-12 M Hills (4) *trkd ldrs till wknd quickly 5 fs out, tld off*. ....(7 to 2 op 4 to 1 tchd 3 to 1) 7
Dist: 2½l, nk, 10l, 2l, 20l, 10l. 2m 6.29s. a 3.09s (7 Ran).
SR: 50/36/21/17/2/-/-/ (P A Leonard), J H M Gosden

21 Alpine Double Glazing Maiden Stakes CLASS F (3-y-o) £2,208 5f.............(2:00)

4791a^2 PLAY HEVER GOLF 9-0 D Holland (6) *made all, kpt on wl fnl furlong*..........(6 to 4 fav op Evens tchd 13 to 8) 1
PIRATES GOLD (Ire) 9-0 Dale Gibson (3) *al prmnt, kpt on to chase wnr one and a half fs out, no imprsn*. ....(2 to 1 op 7 to 4 tchd 9 to 4) 2
4794a^8 BELLE SOIREE (e/s) 8-9 T Quinn (5) *chsd wnr to one and a half fs out, not quicken*............(5 to 1 tchd 8 to 1) 3
4695a^6 MISS DELIVERY 8-2 (7*) L Carter (7) *nvr rchd ldrs*. .... (50 to 1 op 20 to 1) 4
4794a GIRTON BELLE (bl) 8-9 J Williams (4) *sn outpcd*. .... (50 to 1 op 20 to 1) 5
GREY PRIDE 9-0 J Carroll (2) *prmnt early, sn outpcd*. .... (8 to 1 op 5 to 1 tchd 10 to 1) 6
4801a^7 PETITE VINO (bl) 8-11^9 (7*) Rachel Bridger (1) *al outpcd*. .... (50 to 1 op 33 to 1) 7
Dist: 1l, 2l, 6l, 1l, hd, 5l. 1m 0.90s. a 2.70s (7 Ran).
SR: 21/17/4/-/ (R A Popely), T J Naughton

22 Keats Handicap CLASS F (0-80 3-y-o) £2,716 6f..................................(2:30)

7* THE INSTITUTE BOY [66] (bl) 8-10 (7ex) S Webster (1) *hdwy 3 fs out, drvn to ld ins last, rdn out*. ....(5 to 1 op 3 to 1 tchd 6 to 1) 1
4724a^5 SASEEDO (USA) [74] 9-1 (3*) Emma O'Gorman (4) *dwlt, sn reco'red, pressed ldrs 2 fs out, ev ch appr fnl furlong, no extr*.............................. (7 to 4 tchd 2 to 1) 2
7^4 COMET WHIRLPOOL (Ire) [58] (bl) 8-2 J Quinn (3) *sn led, rdn alng o'r one furlong out, hdd ins last, one pace*. ....(6 to 1 op 4 to 1 tchd 7 to 1) 3
4794a* PERSIAN GUSHER (Ire) [77] (e/s) 9-0 (7*) A Martinez (2) *nvr gng pace of ldrs, lost tch fnl 2 fs*. ....(5 to 4 fav op 6 to 4 tchd 13 to 8) 4
Dist: 2l, 1l, 5l. 1m 13.47s. a 2.67s (4 Ran).
SR: 13/13/-/-/ (Mrs J Addleshaw), K R Burke

23 Wordsworth Claiming Stakes CLASS F (3-y-o) £2,391 1¼m.....................(3:00)

4800a^8 HONORARY GUEST 7-1 (7*) D Wright (3) *beh, pushed alng 3 fs out, hdwy 2 furlongs out, squeezed through to ld wl ins last, sn clr*........................(14 to 1 op 7 to 1) 1
4805a^3 BICHETTE 8-4 T Quinn (7) *chsd ldrs, rdn alng o'r 2 fs out, hdwy, ev ch and swtchd lft ins last, styd on*. ....(11 to 10 on op Evens tchd 5 to 4) 2
4766a^4 BADAWI (Fr) 7-11^1 (7*) G Forster (6) *sn in tch, led o'r one furlong out, rdn, edgd rght and hdd ins last, not rcvr*. .... (3 to 1 tchd 4 to 1 and 11 to 4) 3
BUCKSKI ECHO 8-1 S Dawson (4) *took str hold, chsd ldr till led 3 and a half fs out, hdd o'r one furlong out, styd on same pace*....... (50 to 1 op 20 to 1 tchd 100 to 1) 4
4709a^2 ANN HILL (Ire) 7-7 (5*) A Garth (1) *rdn alng hfwy, nvr dngrs*.................. (7 to 2 op 2 to 1 tchd 4 to 1) 5
LOBELIA (Ire) 8-0 G Bardwell (5) *slwly into strd, nvr rchd ldrs*..............................(33 to 1 op 10 to 1) 6
4761a^7 ELEGANT ELLIE (e/s) 7-12 J Quinn (2) *led till hdd 3 and a half fs out, sn wknd*. ....(50 to 1 op 20 to 1 tchd 100 to 1) 7
Dist: 1½l, sht-hd, 1½l, 2½l, 4l, 2l. 2m 10.75s. a 7.55s (7 Ran).
(Mrs J Murray Smith), D J G Murray Smith

24 Coleridge Handicap CLASS F (0-70 4-y-o and up) £2,432 7f........................(3:30)

4799a^7 QUINZII MARTIN [45] (v) 5-9-0 J Williams (3) *prmnt, chlgd 2 fs out, led o'r one furlong out, rdn out*. ....(6 to 1 op 7 to 1) 1
4816a* PIGALLE WONDER [45] (bl) 5-9-0 (5ex) D Biggs (5) *trkd ldrs, effrt frm o'r 2 fs out, styd on, not pace of wnr*. .... (6 to 4 on op 5 to 4 on tchd 11 to 10 on) 2
4789a^2 DON'T DROP BOMBS (USA) [42] (bl) 4-8-4 (7*) J Tate (6) *prmnt, led 3 and a half fs out, hdd o'r one furlong out, one pace*.......................... (7 to 1 op 4 to 1) 3
4799a^8 VELOCE (Ire) [56] 5-9-4 (7*) D Wright (1) *beh and outpcd, pushed alng o'r one furlong out, styd on ins last*. .... (8 to 1 op 7 to 1 tchd 10 to 1) 4

4810a^3 TYRONE FLYER [59] 4-10-0 T Quinn (7) *led till hdd 3 and a half fs out, wknd wl o'r one furlong out*. .... (10 to 1 op 7 to 1) 5
4758a^6 LUCKNAM STYLE [37] 5-8-6 G Bardwell (2) *rdn alng hfwy, nvr dngrs*........................(14 to 1 op 10 to 1) 6
4817a GREATEST OF ALL (Ire) [34] (bl) 5-8-3 J Quinn (4) *al beh*. ....(66 to 1 op 50 to 1 tchd 100 to 1) 7
Dist: 1l, 1½l, 2l, 3l, 4l, 10l. 1m 26.09s. a 2.69s (7 Ran).
SR: 33/30/22/30/24/-/-/ (Monolithic Refractories Ltd), D Haydn Jones

SOUTHWELL (A.W) (std)
Friday January 8th
Going Correction: PLUS 0.40 sec. per fur.

25 Bolsover & Shirebrook Amateur Riders Handicap CLASS F (0-70 4-y-o and up) £2,553 1¾m..................................(1:20)

BEDOUIN PRINCE (USA) [42] 6-9-3 (5*) Mrs M Morris (11) *chsd ldrs, hdwy hfwy, led 3 and a half fs out, hdd 2 out, rdn to ld appr fnl furlong, ran on wl*..... (33 to 1) 1
3^4 SUGEMAR [53] 7-10-0 (5*) Mr M Chapman (8) *chsd ldrs, effrt to ld 2 fs out, hdd appr fnl furlong, rallied wl und pres ins last*........................ (6 to 1 tchd 7 to 1) 2
COSMIC FUTURE [53] 4-9-8 (5*) Miss L Hide (10) *in tch, hdwy 5 fs out, effrt and rdn o'r 2 out, one paced*. ....(12 to 1 op 10 to 1) 3
MILLY BLACK (Ire) [40] 5-9-1 (5*) Mrs J Gault (12) *hld up, hdwy hfwy, rdn o'r 2 fs out, sn one paced*. ....(9 to 2 op 5 to 2 tchd 5 to 1) 4
3^6 CONTINUITY [58] 4-10-4 Miss I Diana W Jones (9) *in tch, effrt and hdwy 3 fs out, rdn and one pace 2 out*. .... (7 to 1 op 8 to 1 tchd 10 to 1) 5
POSTAGE STAMP [69] 6-11-7 Mrs L Pearce (5) *mid-div, pushed alng hfwy, nvr dngrs*..(2 to 1 fav tchd 5 to 2) 6
CATHOS (Fr) [54] 8-10-6 Miss E Bronson (6) *prmnt till rdn and wknd o'r 2 fs out*....(4 to 1 op 7 to 2 tchd 9 to 2) 7
HONEY DANCER [62] 9-10-9 (5*) Mrs F Whitfield (2) *led till hdd and wknd 3 and a half fs out*. (33 to 1 op 20 to 1) 8
3 IRISH NATIVE (Ire) [45] (v) 5-9-6 (5*) Mrs D Smith (3) *cl up till rdn and wknd wl o'r 2 fs out*.....(20 to 1 tchd 25 to 1) 9
LEGAL WIN (USA) [45] 5-9-6 (5*) Mr G Shenkin (1) *al rear, tld off fnl 4 fs*..........................(33 to 1 op 20 to 1) 10
QUELLE CHEMISE [42] 7-9-3 (5*) Miss A Yardley (7) *al rear, tld off fnl 4 fs*.................................(50 to 1) 11
FAR DARA [34] 7-8-9 (5*) Miss A Bycroft (4) *cl up to hfwy, sn wknd, tld off fnl 4 fs*...................... (100 to 1) 12
Dist: Sht-hd, 7l, ½l, 1l, 2½l, 2½l, 2½l, ¾l. 3m 15.20s. a 15.20s (12 Ran).
SR: 12/22/2/-/4/16/ (Miss J E Toulson), B Richmond

26 Clipston & Thoresby Claiming Stakes CLASS F (3-y-o) £2,322 1m........... (1:50)

4809a^4 DIAMOND POINT 8-3 C Nutter (3) *hld up in tch, hdwy o'r 3 fs out, led 2 out and sn clr*........ (5 to 4 fav op Evens) 1
2^3 MASTER SINCLAIR (Ire) (bl) 8-4 (5*) A Garth (2) *dwlt, sn cl up, effrt to ld 3 fs out, hdd 2 out, soon one paced*. .... (11 to 8 op 11 to 10 tchd 6 to 4) 2
4801a^5 ARAGON KING 9-3 Gay Kelleway (1) *cl up, led briefly hfwy, sn rdn and one paced o'r 2 fs out*. ....(9 to 2 op 4 to 1 tchd 6 to 1) 3
4695a WITCHWAY NORTH 7-10 L Charnock (4) *led to hfwy, sn wknd*.............................(33 to 1 op 20 to 1) 4
Dist: 6l, 2½l, 2l. 1m 48.20s. a 9.20s (4 Ran).
(Lord Derby), Sir Mark Prescott

27 Rufford, Annesley & Silverhill Handicap CLASS F (0-80 4-y-o and up) £2,322 1m (2:20)

4810a^2 JUVENARA [37] 7-7-9 G Bardwell (5) *sn rdn alng in rear, gd hdwy o'r 3 fs out, effrt and styd on to ld appr fnl furlong, ridden and ran on*. .... (Evens fav op 6 to 4 tchd 13 to 8) 1
13^4 EAST BARNS (Ire) [55] (bl) 5-8-6 (7*) V Halliday (2) *hdwy hfwy, effrt and rdn 2 fs out, styd on fnl furlong*. ....(100 to 30 op 5 to 2) 2
BOROCAY [40] 5-7-12 L Charnock (3) *chsd ldr, rdn 2 fs out, kpt on one pace*................... (33 to 1 op 16 to 1) 3
13 SHANNON EXPRESS [53] (bl) 6-8-11 J Quinn (1) *led, quickend clr 3 fs out, rdn 2 out, hdd and wknd appr fnl furlong*..........(25 to 1 op 16 to 1 tchd 33 to 1) 4
MAJAL (Ire) [71] 4-10-0 D Nicholls (4) *in tch, effrt and rdn 3 fs out*.............................. (10 to 1 op 6 to 1) 5
4771a^2 HAWAII STORM (Fr) [67] 5-9-8 (3*) A Tucker (6) *chsd ldr, rdn 2 and a half fs out, sn btn*......(100 to 30 op 11 to 4) 6
Dist: 3l, ½l, 8l, 4l, 1½l. 1m 46.90s. a 7.90s (6 Ran).
SR: 11/20/3/ (C John Hill), C J Hill

28 Welbeck, Harworth & Bilsthorpe Claiming Stakes CLASS F (4-y-o and up) £2,469 6f ....(2:50)

4808a* PRETONIC 5-8-3 T Williams (2) *prmnt, hdwy 3 fs out, led 2 out and sn clr, ran on wl*. .... (5 to 2 op 9 to 4 tchd 11 to 4) 1

4774a* MISS CALCULATE 5-7-13 J Fanning (5) *prmnt, effrt and hdwy 2 fs out, sn rdn, styd on one pace fnl furlong.* .... (11 to 2 op 5 to 1 tchd 6 to 1) 2
4666a² TINO TERE 4-8-5 (7*) P Roberts (1) *cl up, led hfwy, rdn and hdd 2 fs out, wknd appr fnl furlong.* ....(7 to 1 op 6 to 1) 3
6⁵ THE DREAM MAKER (Ire) 4-7-9⁵ (7*) M Humphries (3) *beh till styd on fnl 2 fs*..........................(33 to 1 op 20 to 1) 4
4808a⁶ SIR TASKER 5-8-5 (5*) S D Williams (6) *sn led, hdd hfwy, grad wknd*...........(20 to 1 op 16 to 1 tchd 25 to 1) 5
4774a² APPLEDORN 6-8-7 D Biggs (9) *dwlt, effrt and hdwy hfwy, sn rdn, hng lft and hmpd 2 fs out, soon btn.* ....(2 to 1 fav op 9 to 4 tchd 5 to 2) 6
4673a⁶ BOY MARTIN 4-8-8 S Webster (8) *nvr rch ldrs.* .... (14 to 1 op 12 to 1 tchd 16 to 1) 7
4808a BOLD HABIT 8-8-10 J Carroll (7) *al rear.* ....(12 to 1 tchd 14 to 1) 8
4812a CUMBRIAN CAVALIER 4-8-2 R Lappin (4) *chsd ldrs till rdn and wknd 2 and a half fs out*......(66 to 1 op 33 to 1) 9
Dist: 2l, 1½l, 3½l, nk, sht-hd, 1½l, ½l, 8l. 1m 18.00s. a 4.60s (9 Ran).
SR: 45/33/40/11/23/19/14/14/-/ (Brian Yeardley Continental Ltd), M Johnston

29 Cotgrave & Calverton Handicap CLASS F (0-70 3-y-o) £2,238 7f.................. (3:20)

4811a⁴ MISS GORGEOUS (Ire) [60] 8-11 (3*) Emma O'Gorman (4) *made all, quickened clr 2 fs out, easily.* .... (11 to 4 op 7 to 4 tchd 3 to 1) 1
1³ SPECIAL RISK (Ire) [56] 8-3 (7*) J O'Dwyer (1) *hld up, hdwy o'r 2 fs out, sn rdn and styd on one pace.* ....(2 to 1 fav op 9 to 4) 2
4762a³ MISSED THE BOAT (Ire) [59] 8-13 Alex Greaves (3) *hld up, hdwy 3 fs out, sn rdn, one pace fnl 2 furlongs.* ....(3 to 1 tchd 7 to 2) 3
1⁹ DON'T TELL JEAN [40] 7-8 J Fanning (2) *chsd ldr, rdn o'r 2 fs out, sn wknd*...... (20 to 1 op 25 to 1 tchd 40 to 1) 4
4708a* BROADSTAIRS BEAUTY (Ire) [67] 9-2 (5*) S D Williams (5) *chsd ldr, effrt and hdwy o'r 2 fs out, sn rdn and wknd.* ....(4 to 1 tchd 9 to 2) 5
Dist: 5l, sht-hd, 8l, 10l. 1m 32.60s. a 6.50s (5 Ran).
SR: 45/26/28/-/-/ (Thomas R Capehart), W A O'Gorman

30 Ollerton & Bevercotes Handicap CLASS F (0-70 4-y-o and up) £2,406 1½m....... (3:50)

3² WELL AND TRULY [35] 6-8-8 D Biggs (5) *trkd ldrs, hdwy 4 out, led o'r 2 out, sn clr, easily.* ....(7 to 4 fav op 2 to 1 tchd 9 to 4) 1
4812a⁶ SWEET REVIVAL [38] 5-8-11 Dale Gibson (3) *cl up, led aftr 4 fs, rdn and hdd o'r 2 out, kpt on, no ch wth wnr.* ....(6 to 1 tchd 7 to 1) 2
4705a⁶ TENDRESSE (Ire) [46] 5-9-5 J Quinn (7) *hld up, hdwy 4 fs out, rdn 2 out, sn one paced.* .... (5 to 2 op 2 to 1 tchd 11 to 4) 3
4776a⁸ SWAGMAN (USA) [35] 6-8-8 T Williams (4) *cl up, effrt hfwy, rdn and wknd o'r 3 fs out*......... (10 to 1 op 25 to 1) 4
4784a⁴ SHARP THISTLE [43] 7-8-9 (7*) D McCabe (2) *in tch, rdn 4 fs out, sn btn*...............(7 to 1 op 5 to 1 tchd 8 to 1) 5
LATOUR [51] 5-9-10 D Nicholls (1) *chsd ldrs, rdn hfwy, sn lost pl*.................. (11 to 1 op 8 to 1 tchd 12 to 1) 6
CLEAN SINGER [32] 4-8-0 L Charnock (6) *led 4 fs, cl up till grad wknd frm hfwy*............ (20 to 1 tchd 25 to 1) 7
Dist: 7l, 2½l, 6l, hd, 2½l, 15l. 2m 45.30s. a 11.40s (7 Ran).
SR: 28/17/20/-/4/7/-/ (Peter G Freeman), B A McMahon

LINGFIELD (A.W) (std)
Saturday January 9th
Going Correction: MINUS 0.40 sec. per fur.

31 Bluebell Claiming Stakes CLASS F (3-y-o) £2,304 5f........................... (12:55)

7² SPLASH OF SALT (Ire) 8-2 D Holland (2) *ldg grp, chsd ldr hfwy, shaken up to ld entering fnl furlong, not extended*.....(11 to 4 on op 9 to 4 on tchd 2 to 1 on) 1
7³ TEE-EMM 8-4 (7*) L Carter (4) *led til hdd entering fnl furlong, rdn and one pace*...........(6 to 1 op 7 to 2) 2
PURBECK CENTENARY 8-13 Lorna Vincent (1) *improved hfwy, not quicken wl o'r one out, styd on nr finish.* .... (33 to 1 op 20 to 1 tchd 50 to 1) 3
4791a⁸ AIR COMMAND (Bar) 7-13 D Biggs (5) *chsd ldr to hfwy, wknd o'r one out*........(6 to 1 op 7 to 2 tchd 7 to 1) 4
7⁶ WEALTHYWOO (v) 7-1 (7*) D Wright (3) *al outpcd in rear.* .... (14 to 1 op 10 to 1 tchd 16 to 1) 5
Dist: 2l, hd, 5l, nk. 59.17s. a 0.97s (5 Ran).
SR: 29/30/31/-/-/ (G Wiltshire), T J Naughton

32 Alpine Double Glazing Maiden Stakes CLASS F (3-y-o) £2,208 1¼m..........(1:25)

DIAMOND LUCY 8-6 (3*) Emma O'Gorman (8) *pressed ldrs, led wl o'r 3 out, quickened clr 2 out, easily.* .... (10 to 1 op 7 to 1) 1
4800a⁵ HIGH SUMMER 9-0 M Hills (11) *mid-div, rdn alng frm hfwy, squeezed through and styd on appr fnl furlong.* ....(100 to 30 op 5 to 2 tchd 7 to 2) 2
SALBUS (e/s) 9-0 A McGlone (2) *handily plcd, outpcd 2 out, styd on und pres fnl furlong.* .... (12 to 1 op 10 to 1 tchd 14 to 1) 3
4778a⁴ NANNY MARGARET (Ire) (bl) 8-9 G Bardwell (10) *led aftr 3 fs, hdd wl o'r three out, wknd over one out.* .... (14 to 1 op 10 to 1) 4
4801a⁴ SPORTING MISSILE (USA) 8-9 D Holland (12) *sn in tch, rdn alng frm 4 out, eased whn btn fnl furlong.* ....(9 to 4 fav op 4 to 1) 5
4805a SILENT PRINCE 8-7 (7*) Kim McDonnell (3) *styd on frm rear last 2 fs, nvr nrr*.................................(33 to 1) 6
4800a³ STALLED (Ire) 9-0 D Biggs (1) *led for 3 fs, wknd 2 out.* ....(7 to 2 op 5 to 2 tchd 4 to 1) 7
WESTRAY (Fr) 8-11 (3*) A Tucker (4) *slwly into strd, nvr trbld frnt rnk*..................................(33 to 1) 8
4801a⁸ GREY WATCH 8-9 J Williams (7) *settled towards rear, moderate effrt o'r 2 out, no imprsn*........... (12 to 1) 9
4801a³ STEVIE'S WONDER (Ire) 8-9 (5*) N Gwilliams (6) *al rear grp.* .... (10 to 1 op 7 to 1 tchd 14 to 1) 10
BARSAL (Ire) 9-0 Dale Gibson (5) *slwly into strd, al beh.* .... (20 to 1 op 8 to 1 tchd 25 to 1) 11
4801a⁶ TACITURN (USA) 8-9 C Nutter (9) *ldg grp to hfwy, sn rdn and wknd*........... (14 to 1 op 10 to 1 tchd 20 to 1) 12
ROWLANDSONS GOLD (Ire) 8-9 J Quinn (13) *strted slwly, al beh*.................. (25 to 1 op 12 to 1 tchd 33 to 1) 13
Dist: 4l, hd, 7l, 1½l, 1l, ¾l, ¾l, 3½l, 4l, 2l. 2m 8.90s. a 5.70s (13 Ran).
(S Fustok), W A O'Gorman

33 Daffodil Handicap CLASS E (0-90 4-y-o and up) £3,460 1m........................(1:55)

4799a* SCOTS LAW [45] (bl) 6-7-7 J Quinn (4) *made all, quickened clr appr hfwy, styd on ins fnl furlong.* ....(4 to 1 op 3 to 1) 1
12³ MASTER HYDE (USA) [57] 4-8-4 D Biggs (6) *mid-div, rdn alng o'r 3 out, ran on und pres ins fnl furlong.* ....(6 to 4 fav op 7 to 4 tchd 11 to 8) 2
12 SARUM [57] 7-8-5 Dale Gibson (7) *hld up in last pl till improved hfwy, rdn 3 out, styd on fnl furlong.* .... (12 to 1 op 14 to 1 tchd 16 to 1) 3
12* ABSONAL [70] 6-9-4 A McGlone (2) *chsd wnr til o'r one out, no extr*........... (7 to 4 op 11 to 8 tchd 2 to 1) 4
TRY LEGUARD (Ire) [77] 4-9-7 (3*) A Tucker (5) *chsd ldrs for 5 fs, sn lost tch*........(12 to 1 op 6 to 1 tchd 14 to 1) 5
4796a⁸ BUSTER [80] 5-9-9 (5*) K Rutter (1) *in tch til pushed alng and wknd o'r 4 out, sn lost touch.* (33 to 1 op 25 to 1) 6
4816a⁶ ITHKURNI (USA) [55] 4-8-2 G Bardwell (3) *wl plcd til drpd out o'r 3 out, tld off*.............. (33 to 1 op 25 to 1) 7
Dist: 2½l, 5l, 2½l, 10l, 8l, 10l. 1m 38.82s. a 2.62s (7 Ran).
(Mrs R J Doorgachurn), R J O'Sullivan

34 Violet Handicap CLASS F (0-80 4-y-o and up) £2,820 1m 5f........................... (2:25)

ROMANIAN (Ire) [43] 5-7-10 J Quinn (4) *wl plcd, led 3 out, rdn clr o'r one out*.............. (100 to 30 op 5 to 2) 1
4819a⁴ DR ZEVA [40] 7-7-0 (7*) D Wright (7) *chsd ldr til 4 out, rdn and outpcd o'r 2 out, ran on ag'n ins fnl furlong.* ....(3 to 1 jt-fav op 5 to 2 tchd 100 to 30) 2
SCOTONI [59] 7-8-12 D Biggs (6) *led til 3 out, kpt on same pace appr fnl furlong*..........(3 to 1 jt-fav op 4 to 1) 3
4819a⁵ HUNTING GROUND [51] 5-8-1 (3*) A Tucker (1) *drpd rear aftr 3 fs, styd on ag'n ins last 2 furlongs.* ....(6 to 1 tchd 7 to 1) 4
4806a² VINTAGE [75] 8-10-0 J Williams (3) *hld up towards rear, rdn and effrt o'r 4 out, no imprsn on ldrs last 3 fs.* ....(4 to 1 op 5 to 2) 5
COLERIDGE [68] (v) 5-9-2 (5*) K Rutter (2) *al towards rear, tld off*.......................................(12 to 1 op 6 to 1) 6
ILDERTON ROAD [51] 6-8-4 G Bardwell (5) *chsd ldrs til rdn and wknd o'r 4 out, tld off*.......... (50 to 1 op 25 to 1) 7
Dist: 2½l, sht-hd, 2½l, 3l, 20l, 15l. 2m 46.72s. a 3.72s (7 Ran).
SR: -/-/3/-/8/-/-/ (Mrs J Sturgis), R Akehurst

35 Primrose Apprentice Handicap CLASS F (0-60 4-y-o and up) £2,629 1¼m....... (2:55)

4793a* CARLOWITZ (USA) [47] 5-9-4 B Russell (5) *pressed ldr, led hfwy, rdn clr o'r one out*.............. (9 to 2 op 5 to 1) 1
4817a³ CRETOES DANCER (USA) [49] (bl) 4-9-3 Kim McDonnell (1) *ldg grp, ev ch 2 out, not quicken appr fnl furlong.* ....(6 to 1 op 5 to 1) 2
4784a³ TAUNTING (Ire) [53] 5-9-5 (5*) S McCarthy (11) *ran on frm rear o'r 3 out, styd on ins fnl furlong.* (8 to 1 op 5 to 1) 3
BEAM ME UP SCOTTY (Ire) [46] 4-9-0 N Gwilliams (10) *in tch, rdn alng and not quicken o'r 3 out, styd on one pace clsg stages*.................... (20 to 1 op 10 to 1) 4
9⁵ MENTALASANYTHIN [55] 4-9-9 D Wright (2) *led for 5 fs, wknd o'r 2 out*.................(7 to 2 fav op 4 to 1) 5
STATION EXPRESS (Ire) [30] 5-7-8 (7*) G Rothwell (3) *trkd frnt rnk til found no extr appr last 2 fs.* .... (16 to 1 op 10 to 1) 6
11⁶ GEMINI BAY [36] (bl) 4-8-4 S Drowne (13) *dwlt, effrt 3 out, no imprsn on ldrs*...............................(20 to 1) 7

4819a[6] FLASH OF STRAW (Ire) [44] (bl) 4-8-7 (5*) T Ashley (8) *mid-div, rdn alng appr hfwy, nvr dngrs.* (15 to 2 op 4 to 1) 8
4814a[5] BAYIN (USA) [40] 4-8-8 A Tucker (6) *chsd ldrs til rdn and wknd o'r 4 out*..................(14 to 1 op 25 to 1) 9
5* MERRYHILL MADAM [50] 4-9-4 J Tate (9) *mid-div, rdn alng and no hdwy o'r 3 out*..............(5 to 1 op 9 to 2) 10
4798a BROUGHTON BLUES (Ire) [22] (bl) 5-7-6[4] (5*) D McCabe (7) *al beh*..........................(14 to 1 op 10 to 1) 11
4812a[8] PETITE BELLE [27] (v) 4-7-9 A Garth (4) *ldg grp to hfwy, sn lost pl*..........................(25 to 1 op 14 to 1) 12
LEAH JAY [31] (bl) 6-7-9 (7*) J Wilkinson (12) *al in rear, tld off*..................(20 to 1 op 12 to 1 tchd 25 to 1) 13
Dist: 2½l, 1½l, 5l, 6l, 1l, 1l, 2l, 1l, 2l, 6l. 2m 6.89s. a 3.69s (13 Ran).
SR: 27/21/25/5/2/-/ (K Higson), A Moore

36 Ladbroke All Weather Trophy Handicap Qualifier CLASS F (0-70 3-y-o and up) £2,794 6f.................................(3:25)

13[6] NOBBY BARNES [57] 4-9-9 J Williams (3) *slwly into strd, rear til ran on 2 out, pushed out vigorously to get up last strides*..................(8 to 1 op 6 to 1) 1
10* SIRMOOR (Ire) [52] (bl) 4-9-4 A McGlone (1) *rdn alng to ld sn aftr strt, hdd und pres last strds.* (11 to 2 op 7 to 2) 2
4783a[2] BANBURY FLYER [59] 5-9-11 J Quinn (7) *trkd ldg grp, ev ch frm 2 out, rallied wl cl hme, jst fld.* ....(9 to 4 fav op 7 to 4 tchd 5 to 2) 3
4816a[3] BRIGHT PARAGON (Ire) [40] 4-8-6 Dale Gibson (2) *wth ldrs, rdn and not quicken ins fnl furlong.* (8 to 1 op 5 to 1) 4
4783a MEESON TIMES [60] 5-9-12 M Hills (5) *chsd frnt rnk, pushed alng o'r 3 out, one pace appr fnl furlong.* ....(12 to 1 tchd 14 to 1) 5
11[5] TOSHIBA COMET [51] (e/s) 6-9-3 D Biggs (4) *in tch, rdn alng hfwy, wknd frm 2 out*.........(7 to 2 tchd 9 to 2) 6
4818a[6] RUSHANES [62] 6-9-7 (7*) B Russell (6) *ldg grp til wknd rpdly hfwy, tld off*..................(5 to 1 op 8 to 1) 7
Dist: Nk, sht-hd, 1½l, 2l, 5l, 20l. 1m 13.32s. a 2.52s (7 Ran).
SR: 11/5/11/-/ (T S M S Riley-Smith), D A Wilson

SOUTHWELL (A.W) (std) Monday January 11th

Going Correction: PLUS 0.20 sec. per fur.

37 Fiskerton Claiming Stakes CLASS F (3-y-o) £2,343 6f...........................(1:30)

16[2] DAANIERA (Ire) 8-5 (3*) Emma O'Gorman (4) *trkd ldrs, hdwy on ins 2 fs out, styd on to ld inside last.* ....(17 to 2 op 5 to 1 tchd 9 to 1) 1
2* GREENWICH CHALENGE (v) 8-2 (7*) D McCabe (1) *trkd ldrs, hdwy o'r 2 fs out, rdn to ld appr last, hdd and no extr ins fnl furlong*......(2 to 1 op 7 to 4 tchd 6 to 4) 2
16* NIKKI NOO NOO 7-9 G Bardwell (2) *outpcd, rdn alng and beh, hdwy hfwy, wide strt, styd on und pres fnl 2 fs, nrst finish*..........(11 to 8 fav op 2 to 1 tchd 9 to 4) 3
16[4] GIRL NEXT DOOR 7-4 (7*) D Wright (9) *chsd ldrs, hdwy o'r 2 fs out, sn rdn, one pace*............(7 to 1 op 6 to 1) 4
16[3] PINE RIDGE LAD (Ire) 8-4 R P Elliott (5) *led, rdn and hdd 2 and a half fs out, wknd*..................(12 to 1 op 6 to 1) 5
2[4] MARK'S CLUB (Ire) 8-2 Alex Greaves (8) *trkd ldrs gng wl, led 2 and a half fs out, sn rdn, hng lft, hdd and wknd o'r one out*..................(12 to 1 op 8 to 1) 6
KUTE LUCY 7-9 S Wood (3) *dwlt, sn in tch, rdn and wknd 3 fs out*......................................(33 to 1) 7
4741a[4] JORDYWRATH 7-12 T Williams (6) *cl up, rdn 3 fs out, sn wknd*..............................(12 to 1 op 8 to 1) 8
4695a BARLEY CAKE 7-7 J Fanning (7) *cl up, rdn and wknd quickly 3 fs out, tld off*...........(25 to 1 op 16 to 1) 9
Dist: ¾l, 3½l, nk, sht-hd, hd, 8l, nk, 25l. 1m 18.30s. a 4.90s (9 Ran).
SR: 20/18/-/-/-/ (J Berry), J Berry

38 Mansfield Handicap CLASS F (0-80 4-y-o and up) £2,364 1m......................(2:00)

4812a[9] NO SUBMISSION (USA) [65] 7-8-13 S Wood (9) *made all, quickened 2 fs out, rdn appr fnl furlong, styd on strly.* ....(16 to 1 tchd 20 to 1) 1
4803a[2] SPENCER'S REVENGE [70] 4-9-3 M Hills (4) *trkd ldrs, hdwy to chase wnr 2 fs out, rdn and ev ch appr last, sn one pace*........... (7 to 4 fav op 2 to 1 tchd 9 to 4) 2
13[3] LOCK KEEPER (USA) [63] 7-8-6 (5*) S D Williams (11) *mid-div, hdwy 4 fs out, effrt and rdn 2 furlongs out, sn one pace*..... (100 to 30 op 4 to 1 tchd 9 to 2 and 3 to 1) 3
13[2] DIAMOND INTHE DARK (USA) [53] (v) 5-8-1 L Charnock (2) *cl up, ev ch o'r 2 fs out, sn rdn and wknd.* ....(7 to 2 op 2 to 1 tchd 4 to 1) 4
MARTINI EXECUTIVE [80] (bl) 5-10-0 D Nicholls (8) *hld up beh, rdn alng and hdwy o'r 3 fs out, styd on frm 2 out.* ....(16 to 1 op 12 to 1) 5
BROAD APPEAL [45] 5-7-7 G Bardwell (6) *slwly into strd, hdwy hfwy, rdn and wknd o'r 2 fs out.* ....(16 to 1 op 12 to 1) 6
4696a STAIRWAY TO HEAVEN (Ire) [46] (bl) 5-7-8 J Fanning (10) *chsd ldrs, rdn o'r 3 fs out, sn wknd.* ....(16 to 1 op 12 to 1) 7

4810a KRONPRINZ (Ire) [45] 5-7-1[1] (7*) Darren Moffatt (5) *cl up, rdn 3 fs out, wknd*....................(40 to 1 op 50 to 1) 8
13 MELTONBY [66] 4-8-13 J Quinn (7) *cl up, rdn 3 fs out, sn btn*..................................(33 to 1 op 20 to 1) 9
BALLYMONEYBOY [62] 4-8-2 (7*) S Mulvey (3) *slwly into strd, al rear*..........................(12 to 1 op 7 to 1) 10
8 BASSIO (Bel) [58] 4-7-12 (7*) G Forster (1) *unruly strt, chsd ldrs, rdn alng aftr 3 fs, sn lost pl.* ....(20 to 1 op 33 to 1 tchd 16 to 1) 11
Dist: 2½l, 4l, hd, 4l, 4l, 1½l, nk, 7l, ¾l, 2½l. 1m 44.30s. a 5.30s (11 Ran).
SR: 44/40/22/11/26/-/ (T S Redman), D W Chapman

39 Staythorpe Claiming Stakes CLASS F (4-y-o and up) £2,385 7f....................(2:30)

17[4] ALLINSON'S MATE (Ire) 5-9-3 Alex Greaves (6) *hld up, hdwy 3 fs out, effrt 2 out, styd on wl to ld ins last, sn clr*..................(11 to 10 on op 5 to 4) 1
4810a[6] WHO'S THAT LADY 4-8-4 J Quinn (2) *al cl up, effrt and ev ch appr fnl furlong, sn rdn and one pace.* ....(12 to 1 tchd 14 to 1) 2
28[7] BOY MARTIN 4-8-12 S Webster (8) *hdwy o'r 3 fs out, rdn 2 out, styd on ins last*..................(8 to 1 op 6 to 1) 3
28[8] BOLD HABIT 8-8-9 M Hills (9) *hld up beh, hdwy 3 fs out, rdn 2 out, kpt on*........(9 to 2 op 5 to 1 tchd 7 to 1) 4
13 SCOTTISH PARK 4-8-2 L Charnock (1) *led, rdn 2 fs out, hdd and wknd ins last*............(14 to 1 op 12 to 1) 5
TOP ONE 8-8-7 S Wood (3) *prmnt, rdn 2 and a half fs out, sn one pace*..................(12 to 1 op 10 to 1) 6
4[2] SWINGING TICH (bl) 4-8-0 T Williams (5) *dwlt, sn prmnt, rdn and ev ch 2 fs out, soon edgd lft, wknd o'r one out.* ....(8 to 1 tchd 9 to 1) 7
4803a[7] POP TO STANS 4-9-0 G Bardwell (7) *chsd ldrs, sn rdn alng, beh fnl 3 fs*...... (9 to 1 op 8 to 1 tchd 10 to 1) 8
4748a NUTMEG LASS 4-8-4 D Biggs (4) *prmnt till rdn and wknd quickly o'r 3 fs out*..........................(66 to 1) 9
Dist: 2½l, ¾l, ¾l, sht-hd, 8l, ½l, 2l, 30l. 1m 31.80s. a 5.70s (9 Ran).
SR: 39/18/24/19/11/-/ (Peter Jones), T D Barron

40 Averham Handicap CLASS F (0-70 3-y-o) £2,322 1m..........................(3:00)

1 BROUGHTONS FORMULA [46] (bl) 8-1 J Quinn (6) *hld up, hdwy o'r 3 fs out, effrt 2 out, sn chasing ldr, rdn appr last, styd on wl to ld nr finish.* ....(9 to 1 op 10 to 1 tchd 8 to 1) 1
15[2] ROSE FLYER (Ire) [50] 8-5[1] S Webster (4) *led, hrd rdn o'r one furlong out, hdd and no extr nr finish.* ....(3 to 1 tchd 5 to 2 and 100 to 30) 2
4811a[2] I'M A DREAMER (Ire) [66] 9-2 (5*) S D Williams (7) *prmnt, effrt and ev ch o'r 2 fs out, sn rdn and one pace.* ....(8 to 1 op 7 to 1) 3
26[2] MASTER SINCLAIR (Ire) [59] 8-9 (5*) A Garth (2) *dwlt, beh and rdn alng, hdwy 3 fs out, styd on one pace frm 2 out.* ....(7 to 1 op 6 to 1) 4
2[2] MOONSTRUCK BARD [63] 9-4 W Woods (11) *hld up beh, hdwy 3 fs out, rdn 2 out, sn one pace.* ....(11 to 4 fav op 5 to 2 tchd 7 to 2) 5
1[6] HUSH BABY (Ire) [43] 7-12 G Bardwell (1) *chsd ldrs, rdn o'r 2 fs out, wknd*....................(16 to 1 op 14 to 1) 6
ARCTIC GUEST (Ire) [48] 8-3 R P Elliott (3) *hld up in rear, some hdwy 3 fs out, nvr dngrs*..... (11 to 1 op 9 to 1) 7
4770a[3] LARN FORT [54] 8-9 J Fanning (5) *chsd ldrs, rdn 2 and a half fs out, sn btn*..................(11 to 1 op 8 to 1) 8
FREE DANCER [59] 9-0 T Williams (9) *slwly into strd, sn rdn alng, hdwy 5 fs out, ridden and wknd 3 out.* ....(50 to 1 op 33 to 1) 9
4772a[4] PETERED OUT [44] 7-6 (7*) D Wright (8) *nvr rch ldrs.* ....(11 to 1 op 10 to 1) 10
1[8] BAJKA [51] 8-6 Dale Gibson (12) *prmnt, rdn o'r 3 fs out, wknd*.......................................(25 to 1) 11
GIRL AT THE GATE [63] 8-11 (7*) J O'Dwyer (10) *cl up, rdn and wknd quickly 3 fs out*..........(8 to 1 op 7 to 1) 12
Dist: ¾l, 8l, nk, ¾l, sht-hd, 5l, 4l, 2l, 2l, 5l. 1m 45.40s. a 6.40s (12 Ran).
SR: 15/17/9/1/3/-/ (Broughton Thermal Insulation), W J Musson

41 Morton Handicap CLASS F (0-70 4-y-o and up) £2,343 7f.........................(3:30)

6[8] COMPANY CASH [46] (bl) 5-8-6 M Hills (4) *cl up, led 3 and a half fs out, sn clr, rdn one and a half out, styd on gmely*....................(13 to 2 op 4 to 1 tchd 7 to 1) 1
17[3] JOHNSTON'S EXPRESS (Ire) [60] 5-9-6 J Quinn (1) *chsd ldrs, effrt o'r 2 fs out, sn rdn, kpt on one pace.* .....(11 to 8 on op 5 to 4 on tchd 11 to 10 on and 6 to 4 on) 2
GIRTON DEGREE [44] 4-8-4 D Biggs (7) *chsd ldrs, rdn 3 fs out, sn btn*..................(16 to 1 op 12 to 1) 3
4764a[5] RURAL LAD [61] 4-9-7 J McLaughlin (8) *chsd ldrs, effrt and rdn 3 fs out, sn btn*..................(6 to 1 op 7 to 2) 4
4810a GRUBBY [47] 4-8-2 (5*) A Garth (6) *led one furlong, cl up till rdn and wknd o'r 3 out*....... (20 to 1 op 14 to 1) 5
17[5] PESIDANAMICH (Ire) [68] (bl) 5-9-9 (5*) S D Williams (5) *led aftr one furlong to 3 and a half out, sn wknd.* ....(11 to 2 op 5 to 1 tchd 7 to 1) 6
MANSE KEY GOLD [33] 6-7-1[1] (7*) D Wright (3) *sn beh, tld off 3 fs out*..................................(33 to 1) 7

6 SAKOSAN [33] 4-7-7 J Fanning (2) *sn beh, tld off 3 fs out.* ....(50 to 1 op 40 to 1) 8
Dist: 1½l, 10l, 1½l, 1l, ¾l, 5l, 20l. 1m 33.20s. a 7.10s (8 Ran).
SR: 7/16/-/-/-/ (Mrs P Churm), R Bastiman

42 Ollerton Handicap CLASS F (0-70 4-y-o and up) £2,406 1½m......................(4:00)

3³ MODEST HOPE (USA) [56] 6-9-10 J McLaughlin (2) *made all, rdn 2 fs out, ran on gmely fnl furlong.* ....(6 to 1 tchd 7 to 1) 1
18* ATLANTIC WAY [47] 5-9-1 (5ex) G Bardwell (5) *hld up beh, hdwy 4 fs out, wide strt, effrt 2 out, rdn and ran on wl fnl furlong*..............(4 to 1 op 5 to 2 tchd 9 to 2) 2
25* BEDOUIN PRINCE (USA) [47] 6-9-1 (5ex) T Williams (6) *in tch, hdwy hfwy, effrt 3 fs out, rdn 2 out, ev ch, kpt on one pace appr last*.... (10 to 1 op 8 to 1 tchd 12 to 1) 3
18² MASTER'S CROWN (USA) [40] 5-8-8 S Webster (11) *prmnt, effrt and ev ch 2 fs out, sn rdn, wknd entering last.* .... (12 to 1 op 9 to 1) 4
3* CLIFTON CHASE [53] (bl) 4-9-2 M Hills (8) *trkd ldrs, hdwy 4 fs out, ev ch 2 out, sn rdn, wknd appr last*..(2 to 1 fav) 5
QUALITAIR SOUND (Ire) [56] 5-9-10 L Charnock (10) *chsd ldrs, hdwy 5 fs out, rdn and wknd 2 and a half out.* .... (13 to 2 op 5 to 1 tchd 7 to 1) 6
4705a⁷ SOVEREIGN NICHE (Ire) [32] 5-8-0 D Biggs (7) *nvr rch ldrs.* ....(9 to 1 op 6 to 1) 7
RUPPLES [30] 6-7-5 (7*) Darren Moffatt (4) *mid-div, hdwy 5 fs out, sn rdn and wknd*..........(50 to 1 op 33 to 1) 8
8⁶ PERSIAN FLEECE [38] 4-7-8 (7*) Angela Gallimore (3) *chsd ldrs till rdn and wknd hfwy*.......(16 to 1 op 14 to 1) 9
4802a BOLTON FLYER [25] 7-7-1¹ (7*) D Wright (12) *cl up, rdn and wknd hfwy*...................................(66 to 1) 10
4688a UNPAID MEMBER [47] (v) 9-8-10 (5*) S D Williams (9) *cl up 5 fs, sn lost pl and beh*............(20 to 1 op 16 to 1) 11
Dist: Nk, 3½l, ¾l, 6l, 8l, 3½l, 2½l, 1l, 10l, 15l. 2m 42.60s. a 8.70s (11 Ran).
SR: 47/37/30/21/17/9/ (J McManamon), R C Spicer

LINGFIELD (A.W) (std)
Thursday January 14th
Going Correction: MINUS 0.10 sec. per fur.

43 Hood Apprentice Claiming Stakes CLASS F (4-y-o and up) £2,521 1m............. (1:00)

13 EASTLEIGH 4-8-9¹ (4*) D Carson (6) *pressed ldrs, shaken up to ld fnl furlong, kpt on wl*...... (5 to 1 op 4 to 1) 1
4⁴ NORTH FLYER 4-7-12 (4*) T Wilson (10) *beh til ran on o'r 2 fs out, fnshd strly*....(25 to 1 op 12 to 1 tchd 33 to 1) 2
4782a⁵ ANNACURRAGH (Ire) 4-8-3 A Tucker (4) *wth ldrs, rdn and not quicken o'r one out, styd on nr line.* .... (11 to 8 fav op 5 to 4 on) 3
33⁵ TRY LEGUARD (Ire) 4-8-2 (4*) D Wright (1) *made most of rng till hdd one out, no extr.* ....(5 to 1 op 3 to 1 tchd 11 to 2) 4
4771a NORTHERN CONQUEROR (Ire) 5-8-5 N Gwilliams (2) *beh till styd on last 2 fs, nvr nrr.* ....(16 to 1 op 8 to 1 tchd 20 to 1) 5
4746a⁵ WESSEX MILORD 8-8-3 Kim McDonnell (9) *mid-div, outpcd o'r 3 fs out*....................(66 to 1 op 20 to 1) 6
LAMORE RITORNA 4-7-13 S Drowne (8) *handily plcd till outpcd o'r 3 fs out*.....(10 to 1 op 8 to 1 tchd 16 to 1) 7
12 MASRUR (USA) 4-8-12 (4*) S McCarthy (3) *slwly into strd, effrt frm rear o'r 4 fs out, wknd 3 out.* ....(14 to 1 op 12 to 1) 8
CASTLE GALAH 6-7-12 B Doyle (5) *al towards rear.* ....(50 to 1 op 33 to 1) 9
4814a² RICH HEIRESS (Ire) 4-7-13 B Russell (7) *trkd ldrs till outpcd o'r 3 fs out*......(20 to 1 op 10 to 1 tchd 25 to 1) 10
4756a DAL MISS 6-7-12 (4*) P McCabe (11) *ldg grp to hfwy, drpd rear quickly, tld off*............... (66 to 1 op 33 to 1) 11
Dist: ½l, nk, 1l, 3½l, 2l, 2l, 4l, 2l, 10l, 20l. 1m 40.12s. a 3.92s (11 Ran).
SR: 27/15/15/15/3/-/ (J E Bigg), R Hollinshead

44 Alpine Double Glazing Maiden Stakes CLASS F (3-y-o) £2,208 6f.............(1:30)

KRYPTOS (USA) 8-9 J Williams (3) *slwly into strd, improved appr hfwy, rdn and ran on to ld last 100 yards*..................(5 to 1 op 2 to 1 tchd 11 to 2) 1
21² PIRATES GOLD (Ire) 9-0 Dale Gibson (4) *sn pushed alng, prog o'r 3 fs out, led over one out, hdd and not quicken last 100 yards*......................(5 to 4 on op Evens) 2
21³ BELLE SOIREE (e/s) 8-9 A McGlone (6) *chsd ldrs, rdn and not quicken appr fnl furlong, styd on und pres.* ....(8 to 1 op 6 to 1) 3
4811a³ ARAWA 8-2 (7*) S McCarthy (2) *made most of rng till hdd o'r one furlong out, kpt on same pace.* ....(12 to 1 op 7 to 1) 4
WATERLORD (Ire) 9-0 M Hills (7) *pressed ldr till rdn and btn o'r one furlong out*.................(6 to 1 op 4 to 1) 5
21⁶ GREY PRIDE 8-7 (7*) P Roberts (5) *sn outpcd, rdn alng frm hfwy, nvr on terms*....(14 to 1 op 8 to 1 tchd 16 to 1) 6
4720a⁹ MOUNTAIN SPRING 9-0 T Williams (1) *prmnt till drpd rear hfwy, tld off*.....................(25 to 1 op 16 to 1) 7
Dist: 1l, 3½l, 3l, 1½l, 4l, 30l. 1m 13.75s. a 2.95s (7 Ran).
SR: 24/25/6/-/ (Henryk de Kwiatkowski), Lord Huntingdon

45 Warspite Handicap CLASS F (0-80 3-y-o) £2,872 1¼m........................ (2:00)

4805a² ABSOLUTELY FACT (USA) [76] 9-7 J Williams (5) *hld up, hdwy and edgd lft o'r 5 out, dsptd ld frm 3 out, found extr und pres nr line*... (5 to 2 op 9 to 4 tchd 11 to 4) 1
12² EXCESS BAGGAGE (Ire) [76] 9-7 M Hills (8) *hld up in rear, prog hfwy, led 3 fs out till hdd und pres last strds.* ....(9 to 4 fav op 7 to 4) 2
23⁵ ANN HILL (Ire) [56] 7-8 (7*) M Humphries (2) *wl plcd till hmpd and last pos o'r 5 fs out, not clr run over 4 out, styd on ag'n last 2 furlongs*.........(12 to 1 op 8 to 1) 3
4766a⁷ BUZZ-B-BABE [48] 7-7 S Wood (1) *settled towards rear aftr one furlong, moderate effrt 3 out, no imprsn on frnt rnk*.................................(20 to 1 op 16 to 1) 4
1² MRS DAWSON [50] (v) 7-9 J Quinn (6) *ldg grp, led aftr 4 fs till 3 out, sn wknd.* ....(3 to 1 op 3 to 1 tchd 100 to 30 and 7 to 2) 5
1⁴ HOTSOCKS [48] 7-0 (7*) Kim McDonnell (3) *led for 4 fs, wknd o'r 3 out*.......................(25 to 1 op 16 to 1) 6
23⁴ BUCKSKI ECHO [48] 7-7 G Bardwell (4) *pressed ldrs, dsptd ld aftr 4 fs, wknd four out, tld off*...(10 to 1 op 6 to 1) 7
Dist: Sht-hd, 5l, 6l, 3½l, 6l, 20l. 2m 8.96s. a 5.76s (7 Ran).
SR: 39/38/8/-/ (Richard Berenson), C C Elsey

46 Renown Claiming Stakes CLASS F (4-y-o and up) £2,477 1m 5f................. (2:30)

4819a⁸ NASEER (USA) 4-7-12 T Williams (2) *handily plcd, ran on to ld entering last 2 fs, rdn out and hld on.* .... (9 to 1 op 7 to 1 tchd 10 to 1) 1
8² LYPH (USA) 7-8-5 S Dawson (4) *wl plcd, led o'r 5 fs out till 4 out, dsptd ld frm 2 out, edgd rght nr finish, jst fld.* ....(9 to 2 op 7 to 2 tchd 5 to 1) 2
4776a PLEASURE AHEAD 6-8-0 (7*) Kim McDonnell (10) *dwlt, beh till cld on ldrs o'r 3 out, ev ch ins fnl furlong, not quicken close hme*... .(20 to 1 op 12 to 1 tchd 25 to 1) 3
8* BREAKDANCER (Ire) 4-8-8 J Williams (7) *hld up towards rear, hdwy 3 fs out, chalg whn squeezed for room ins last, no extr*........(5 to 4 on op Evens tchd 11 to 10) 4
3 IRON BARON (Ire) 4-7-13 (5*) A Garth (8) *hld up in rear, ran on appr last 2 fs, styd on nr finish.* .... (9 to 1 op 5 to 1 tchd 10 to 1) 5
MON PETITNAMOUR (Ire) 4-8-11 G Bardwell (5) *ldg grp, led 4 out, hdd entering last 2 fs, sn wknd.* ....(14 to 1 op 12 to 1 tchd 20 to 1) 6
MAGNUS PYM 8-9-7 D Biggs (9) *settled towards rear, improve und pres o'r 3 out, no hdwy last 2 fs.* ....(25 to 1 op 12 to 1) 7
SALIC DANCE 5-8-6¹ A Dicks (6) *settled in 3rd pl till rdn and wknd o'r 4 fs out*............. (50 to 1 op 33 to 1) 8
MAMALAMA 5-8-11¹⁰ (7*) Rachel Bridger (3) *pressed ldr till wknd o'r fs out*................... (33 to 1 op 20 to 1) 9
SONEETO 7-8-8¹ M Hills (1) *led till o'r 5 fs out, sn wknd.* ....(50 to 1 op 33 to 1) 10
Dist: Sht-hd, ¾l, 1½l, ½l, 10l, 5l, ½l, 7l, 5l. 2m 49.15s. a 6.15s (10 Ran).
SR: 10/16/16/14/9/-/ (Mrs J Callaghan), N A Callaghan

47 Repulse Handicap CLASS F (0-70 4-y-o and up) £2,633 6f..........................(3:00)

6² SOBA GUEST (Ire) [61] 4-9-4 (3*) Emma O'Gorman (1) *wl plcd, led o'r 2 fs out, hld on last strds.* ....(2 to 1 fav op 9 to 4) 1
4³ HONEY VISION [53] (bl) 4-8-13 G Bardwell (5) *hdwy frm rear hfwy, rdn to cl on wnr ins fnl furlong, jst fld.* ....(16 to 1 op 12 to 1 tchd 20 to 1) 2
4817a SPEEDY CLASSIC (USA) [35] (bl) 4-7-2 (7*) D Wright (11) *gd hdwy o'r 2 fs out, ran on ins last, fnshd wl.* ....(16 to 1 op 25 to 1 tchd 33 to 1) 3
6⁶ JOVIAL KATE (USA) [53] 6-8-13 S Wood (6) *pressed ldrs, no extr appr fnl furlong.* ....(8 to 1 op 6 to 1 tchd 9 to 1 and 10 to 1) 4
NORTH ESK (USA) [68] 4-10-0 M Tebbutt (10) *ran on frm rear last 2 fs, not rch frnt rnk*..... (33 to 1 op 16 to 1) 5
24⁴ VELOCE (Ire) [56] (bl) 5-9-2 J Quinn (2) *handily plcd, rdn and one pace appr fnl furlong.* ....(7 to 1 op 5 to 1 tchd 8 to 1) 6
ROCKBOURNE [55] 4-9-1 M Hills (7) *hdwy frm rear o'r 2 fs out, one pace appr fnl furlong.* ....(11 to 2 op 4 to 1 tchd 6 to 1) 7
4808a⁵ SAMSOLOM [55] 5-9-1 J Williams (9) *beh till moderate prog ins last 2 fs*.........(7 to 1 op 5 to 1 tchd 8 to 1) 8
4815a⁶ PINK'N BLACK (Ire) [35] 4-7-6² (5*) A Garth (4) *cl up, led o'r 4 fs out till over 2 out, wknd one out.* (33 to 1 op 25 to 1) 9
4815a³ SAVALARO [50] 4-8-10 T Williams (3) *led for o'r one furlong, wknd over 3 out*............ (14 to 1 op 10 to 1) 10
4818a⁸ TREASURE TIME (Ire) [60] (bl) 4-9-6 Dale Gibson (8) *chsd ldrs till lost pl quickly frm hfwy, sn lost tch.* ....(12 to 1 op 8 to 1) 11
Dist: Sht-hd, hd, 3½l, hd, 3l, 1l, 1l, ½l, 8l, 12l. 1m 13.03s. a 2.23s (11 Ran).
SR: 50/41/22/26/40/16/11/7/-/ (Richard Jinks), J Berry

48 Nelson Handicap CLASS F (0-70 4-y-o and up) £2,544 1m........................(3:30)

4799a5 BUDDY'S FRIEND (Ire) [50] 5-9-6 M Hills (2) *hld up, prog 3 fs out, rdn and ran on to ld nr line.* ....(6 to 1 op 7 to 2 tchd 7 to 1) 1
4799a3 KILLICK [47] 5-9-3 J Quinn (8) *made most of rng till hdd und pres nr line*........(11 to 4 op 7 to 2 tchd 4 to 1) 2
33³ SARUM [57] 7-9-13 Dale Gibson (3) *settled in mid-div, rdn and ran on frm 2 fs out, styd on cl hme.* ....(9 to 1 op 5 to 1 tchd 10 to 1 and 12 to 1) 3
4784a5 DANCING SENSATION (USA) [27] (bl) 6-7-11 J Fanning (5) *cl on ldrs o'r 3 out, rdn and ev ch ins fnl furlong, no extr clsg stages*..........(14 to 1 op 10 to 1) 4
4733a6 SAREEN EXPRESS (Ire) [49] 5-9-5 G Bardwell (6) *beh till ran on last 2 fs, nrst finish*..........(10 to 1 tchd 12 to 1) 5
33* SCOTS LAW [45] (bl) 6-9-1 (5ex) D Biggs (4) *slwly into strd, beh till effrt und pres 2 fs out, not rch ldrs fnl furlong.* ....(15 to 8 fav op 5 to 4 tchd 2 to 1) 6
PRECIOUS CAROLINE (Ire) [49] 5-9-5 W Woods (7) *chsd ldrs till wknd 2 fs out*..........(33 to 1) 7
19³ LOOTING (USA) [37] 7-8-0 (7*) Kim McDonnell (9) *trkd ldr till wknd o'r 2 fs out*..........(14 to 1 op 8 to 1) 8
INDIAN MOHAWK (Ire) [28] 5-7-12 T Williams (1) *ldg grp till wknd rpdly hfwy, tld off and virtually pld up last 2 fs.* ....(33 to 1 op 20 to 1) 9

Dist: Hd, hd, 1l, 4l, 1½l, 5l, 1½l, 30l. 1m 40.02s. a 3.82s (9 Ran).
SR: 37/33/42/9/19/10/ (Colin G R Booth), R J R Williams

SOUTHWELL (A.W) (std)
Friday January 15th
Going Correction: PLUS 0.10 sec. per fur.

49 Timothy Claiming Stakes (Div I) CLASS F (4-y-o and up) £2,385 1m..........(12:55)

13⁵ SIRTELIMAR (Ire) 4-8-12 J McLaughlin (8) *al hndy, brght wide to ld appr strt, kpt on*..........(9 to 4 fav op 3 to 1) 1
EXPRESS SERVICE 4-8-13 (3*) Emma O'Gorman (4) *patiently rdn, hdwy on ins o'r 2 fs out, shaken up fnl furlong, not quicken*..........(6 to 1 op 9 to 2) 2
39² WHO'S THAT LADY 4-8-7 J Quinn (9) *trkd ldg quartet, effrt and bustled alng last 2 fs, one pace.* ....(7 to 2 op 5 to 2 tchd 4 to 1) 3
ROUND BY THE RIVER 4-8-11 Dale Gibson (1) *sluggish strt, hdwy last 2 fs, nrst finish*..........(6 to 1 op 5 to 1) 4
4* INNOCENT GEORGE 4-8-12 L Charnock (5) *al hndy, ev ch and drvn alng entering strt, not quicken last twe fs.* ....(11 to 2 op 6 to 1 tchd 5 to 1) 5
38⁹ MELTONBY (v) 4-8-7 M Hills (2) *made most till appr strt, fdd o'r 2 fs out*..........(12 to 1 op 10 to 1) 6
VAGUE NANCY (Ire) 5-8-0 S Wood (7) *bustled alng to go pace, some hdwy last 2 fs, nvr dngrs.* ....(25 to 1 op 20 to 1) 7
4814a6 FUNDEGHE (USA) 4-8-10 N Day (6) *trkd ldg 5, rdn entering strt, fdd*..........(25 to 1 op 16 to 1) 8
MAI PEN RAI 5-8-11 D Biggs (10) *broke wl, sn drvn alng and lost pl*..........(16 to 1 op 12 to 1) 9
EDGE OF THE GLEN 5-8-10 (7*) S Drowne (11) *drvn alng aftr 2 fs, tld off*..........(50 to 1 op 33 to 1) 10
ANGEL'S WING 4-8-1 S Dawson (3) *wth ldrs, rdn o'r 2 fs out, tld off*..........(25 to 1 op 20 to 1) 11

Dist: 1½l, 3l, 3½l, 5l, 2½l, 2l, 1l, 1½l, 15l, 1l. 1m 47.00s. a 8.00s (11 Ran).
(D W Price), R C Spicer

50 Timothy Claiming Stakes (Div II) CLASS F (4-y-o and up) £2,364 1m..........(1:25)

38³ LOCK KEEPER (USA) 7-8-12 J Quinn (5) *nvr far away, led and quickened o'r 2 fs out, styd on strly.* ....(Evens fav tchd 5 to 4 on and 11 to 10) 1
17⁸ AMENABLE 8-9-7 Alex Greaves (2) *patiently rdn, hdwy entering strt, ran on wl, prmsg*..........(7 to 1 op 3 to 1) 2
4736a KLAIROVER 6-8-6 S Wood (1) *tucked away on ins, not clr run and swtchd wide entering strt, kpt on wl fnl furlong*..........(7 to 2 op 3 to 1 tchd 4 to 1) 3
4802a7 EMERALD EARS 4-7-13⁷ (7*) S Drowne (9) *rcd wide, made most till o'r 2 fs out, rdn and no extr.* ....(14 to 1 op 25 to 1 tchd 12 to 1) 4
FELSINA (Ire) 4-7-12 (7*) J Tate (4) *trkd ldg pair, rdn o'r 2 fs out, sn outpcd*..........(12 to 1 op 8 to 1 tchd 14 to 1) 5
CYRILL HENRY (Ire) 4-8-9 S Webster (3) *wth ldrs, drvn alng entering strt, fdd*..........(25 to 1) 6
ELABJER (USA) 4-9-6 M Hills (6) *pressed ldrs, rdn entering strt, sn btn*..........(13 to 2 op 4 to 1) 7
BEIJA FLOR 6-8-4 (7*) D Wright (8) *chsd ldrs, hrd rdn entering strt, tld off*..........(33 to 1) 8
MISS MAC 6-8-2 J Fanning (7) *pressed ldg trio, rdn and lost grnd entering strt, tld off*..........(50 to 1) 9

Dist: 3½l, 3½l, 6l, 2l, 1l, 2l, 20l, 6l. 1m 47.30s. a 8.30s (9 Ran).
(Mrs J Mackie), J Mackie

51 Cowslip Maiden Stakes CLASS F (3-y-o) £2,070 6f..........(1:55)

22³ COMET WHIRLPOOL (Ire) (bl) 9-0 J Quinn (4) *trkd ldg quartet, rdn to draw level 2 fs out, kpt on to ld last 100 yards*..........(4 to 1 tchd 5 to 1 and 7 to 2) 1
16⁶ HERSHEBAR (bl) 9-0 S Webster (1) *co'red up in midfield, hrd drvn and hng lft last 2 fs, kpt on finish.* ....(14 to 1 op 16 to 1) 2
40² ROSE FLYER (Ire) 8-2 (7*) D McCabe (6) *al hndy, led 2 fs out, hdd and not quicken last 100 yards.* ....(9 to 4 fav op 7 to 4) 3
4745a3 GUSSIE FINK-NOTTLE (Ire) 9-0 Alex Greaves (5) *patiently rdn, shaken up to improve last 2 fs, kpt on, no nrr.* ....(5 to 2 op 6 to 4 tchd 3 to 1) 4
4700a7 PALACEGATE GIRL 8-9 L Charnock (2) *broke fst to ld 4 fs, fdd ins last*..........(8 to 1 op 4 to 1) 5
4791a4 APOLLO DE ORIENTE 8-7 (7*) G Parkin (7) *nvr far away, jnd ldg pair 2 fs out, no extr ins last.* ....(14 to 1 op 10 to 1) 6
ROBIX (Ire) 9-0 D Nicholls (3) *last and pushed alng hfwy, nvr a threat*..........(16 to 1 op 14 to 1) 7
BADENOCH BURNER 9-0 Kim Tinkler (8) *wth ldrs, rdn o'r 2 fs out, sn lost tch*..........(25 to 1 op 14 to 1) 8

Dist: 1l, 1½l, 1l, 1½l, 1l, 12l, 25l. 1m 19.90s. a 6.50s (8 Ran).
(Colin W Anderton), Pat Mitchell

52 Yorkshire Fog Claiming Stakes CLASS F (3-y-o) £2,364 7f..........(2:25)

PERSIAN TRAVELLER (Ire) 8-9¹ D Nicholls (2) *made all, quickened hfwy, drvn clr appr fnl furlong.* ....(7 to 1 op 5 to 1) 1
15³ MISTER BLAKE (bl) 8-5 (3*) Emma O'Gorman (3) *trkd wnr, niggled alng 3 fs out, no extr appr last.* ....(7 to 4 op 13 to 8 tchd 6 to 4) 2
26* DIAMOND POINT 8-1 C Nutter (1) *last and hld up, effrt hfwy, styd on one pace last 2 fs.* ....(11 to 8 on tchd 11 to 10 on) 3
PERSIAN NOBLE 8-5 S Wood (4) *pressed ldg pair, feeling pace hfwy, edgd lft o'r 2 fs out, sn btn.* ....(25 to 1 op 20 to 1) 4

Dist: 3l, 2½l, 15l. 1m 32.80s. a 6.70s (4 Ran).
SR: 5/ (Ian W Glenton), T Fairhurst

53 Foxglove Handicap CLASS F (0-80 4-y-o and up) £2,511 2m..........(2:55)

42² ATLANTIC WAY [47] 5-8-6 (5ex) G Bardwell (8) *patiently rdn, cld entering strt, led o'r one furlong out, drvn out.* ....(4 to 1 op 3 to 1 tchd 9 to 2) 1
4813a4 LAFKADIO [40] 6-7-13 S Wood (1) *wl plcd on ins, led o'r 2 fs out till over one out, rallied*..........(8 to 1 tchd 7 to 1) 2
4813a6 SHAKINSKI [50] (v) 4-8-2 D Biggs (5) *led, jnd appr strt, hdd o'r 2 fs out, no extr*..........(7 to 2 op 5 to 1 tchd 3 to 1) 3
4813a* MALENOIR (USA) [57] (v) 5-8-11 (5*) A Garth (7) *nvr far away, rdn appr strt, lost tch last 2 fs.* ....(5 to 2 fav tchd 7 to 2) 4
SIGNOR SASSIE (USA) [60] 5-9-5 L Charnock (4) *trkd ldrs, reminders aftr one m, lost tch appr strt.* ....(12 to 1 tchd 14 to 1) 5
AUDE LA BELLE (Fr) [64] 5-9-2 (7*) S Drowne (6) *trkd ldrs, reminders aftr one m, sn lost tch*..........(5 to 1 op 5 to 2) 6
14⁶ DERRY REEF [37] 6-7-10 J Fanning (2) *trkd ldrs, feeling pace hfwy, tld off appr strt*..........(33 to 1 op 25 to 1) 7
BAHER (USA) [72] 4-9-10 D Nicholls (3) *chsd ldrs, drvn alng hfwy, tld off*..........(20 to 1 op 16 to 1) 8

Dist: 1½l, 8l, 20l, 1l, 12l, 12l, 4l. 3m 45.60s. a 19.10s (8 Ran).
(C John Hill), C J Hill

54 Ryegrass Handicap CLASS F (0-80 4-y-o and up) £2,448 7f..........(3:25)

13* TACIT MAC (USA) [74] 4-10-0 (3*,5ex) Emma O'Gorman (7) *confidently rdn, hdwy to ld o'r one furlong out, easily.* ....(2 to 1 fav tchd 5 to 2) 1
4803a3 ON Y VA (USA) [57] 6-9-0 M Hills (11) *nvr far away, ev ch and drvn alng o'r 2 fs out, kpt on, no chance wth wnr.* ....(7 to 1 op 6 to 1 tchd 8 to 1) 2
28⁴ THE DREAM MAKER (Ire) [44] 4-7-8 (7*) M Humphries (10) *al hndy, ev ch and drvn alng o'r 2 fs out, kpt on same pace*..........(16 to 1 op 12 to 1) 3
4802a9 PREDICTABLE [50] 7-8-7 D Biggs (3) *led, rdn and hdd o'r one furlong out, no extr*..........(16 to 1 tchd 14 to 1) 4
27* JUVENARA [43] 7-8-0 (5ex) G Bardwell (6) *chsd alng, effrt o'r 2 fs out, nvr nrr*..........(4 to 1 op 5 to 2 tchd 9 to 2) 5
36⁶ TOSHIBA COMET [51] (e/s) 6-8-8 Alex Greaves (2) *steadied strt, improved hfwy, effrt o'r 2 fs out, not quicken.* ....(14 to 1 op 10 to 1 tchd 16 to 1) 6
17² CLAUDIA MISS [57] 6-9-0 Dale Gibson (4) *trkd ldg 6, drvn alng o'r 2 fs out, no imprsn.* ....(11 to 2 op 6 to 1 tchd 5 to 1) 7
4808a9 GYMCRAK TYCOON [68] 4-9-11 J Quinn (5) *steadied strt, effrt and niggled alng hfwy, nvr nr to chal*...(12 to 1) 8
27⁵ MAJAL (Ire) [71] 4-10-0 D Nicholls (12) *chsd ldg 5, feeling pace o'r 2 fs out, sn btn*..........(16 to 1 tchd 20 to 1) 9
PREMIER ENVELOPE (Ire) [43] 4-8-0 Kim Tinkler (9) *pressed ldrs for o'r 4 fs, sn btn*..........(50 to 1 op 33 to 1) 10
5² PRINCESS DECHTRA (Ire) [47] 4-7-13 (5*) A Garth (8) *wth ldrs, rdn hfwy, lost tch o'r 2 fs out.* (12 to 1 op 10 to 1) 11

Dist: 5l, 1l, 1½l, nk, 3½l, 8l, ¾l, 1l, 15l. 1m 30.70s. a 4.60s (11 Ran).
SR: 59/27/11/12/4/1/ (T Mohan), W A O'Gorman

55 Brown Jacobson Handicap CLASS F (0-90 4-y-o and up) £2,343 1½m............ (3:55)

25² SUGEMAR [53] 7-8-0 (7*) D McCabe (8) *al gng wl, led o'r one furlong out, drw clr.* ....(5 to 2 fav op 3 to 1 tchd 4 to 1) 1
14* TEMPERING [81] 7-10-7 (7ex) S Wood (7) *led aftr one furlong, hdd and drvn alng o'r one out, kpt on.* ....(7 to 1 op 5 to 1) 2
3⁸ EUROTWIST [60] 4-8-9 Alex Greaves (9) *tucked away in midfield, rdn to join ldrs o'r 2 fs out, one pace appr last.* ....(11 to 2 op 4 to 1 tchd 6 to 1) 3
30* WELL AND TRULY [47] 6-8-1 (7ex) D Biggs (6) *settled midfield, improved to go hndy o'r 2 fs out, sn rdn and no extr*..........(9 to 2 op 7 to 2 tchd 5 to 1) 4
LE TEMERAIRE [69] 7-9-9 Kim Tinkler (5) *patiently rdn, improved o'r 2 fs out, ran on finish.* ....(14 to 1 op 12 to 1) 5
4715a* JADE GREEN [61] 4-8-10 S Dawson (1) *led one furlong, rdn hfwy, sn btn*......(15 to 2 op 5 to 1 tchd 8 to 1) 6
LA REINE ROUGE (Ire) [46] 5-8-0 J Quinn (10) *improved frm midfield to chal aftr one m, wknd und pres o'r 2 fs out.* ....(16 to 1) 7
14² FERDIA (Ire) [66] 4-8-11¹ (5*) S Wynne (2) *co'red up beh ldrs, effrt appr strt, found little*... (20 to 1 op 14 to 1) 8
TIGER CLAW (USA) [45] 7-7-13⁷ (7*) S Drowne (4) *in tch, chsd alng hfwy, sn btn*..........(10 to 1 tchd 11 to 1) 9
18⁵ NO MORE THE FOOL [63] (bl) 7-8-10 (7*) P Roberts (3) *trkd ldrs for o'r one m, fdd entering strt*..........(16 to 1) 10

Dist: 6l, nk, 8l, 3l, ½l, 3½l, 8l, 1l, nk. 2m 40.20s. a 6.30s (10 Ran).
SR: 42/58/31/7/23/9/ (Mattie O'Toole), M C Chapman

LINGFIELD (A.W) (std)
Saturday January 16th
Going Correction: MINUS 0.25 sec. per fur.

56 Antrim Claiming Stakes CLASS F (4-y-o and up) £2,477 6f.......................(1:20)

28⁶ APPLEDORN 6-8-8 M Hills (3) *trkd ldrs, led aftr 2 fs out, pushed alng and sprinted clr.* ....(4 to 1 op 9 to 2 tchd 5 to 1 and 11 to 2) 1
28³ TINO TERE 4-8-4 (7*) P Roberts (4) *strted slwly, sn reco'red, led over 3 fs to aftr 2 out, one pace.* ....(13 to 2 op 4 to 1) 2
19* RESPECTABLE JONES 7-8-13 J Williams (6) *in tch, hdwy o'r 2 fs out, sn rdn and one pace.* ....(7 to 4 fav op 6 to 4 tchd 2 to 1) 3
MAC'S FIGHTER 8-8-8 D Biggs (2) *outpcd, ran on frm o'r one furlong out, nrst finish*.......(6 to 1 tchd 13 to 2) 4
4804a² CRECHE (bl) 4-9-2 N Day (5) *wth ldr til wknd wl o'r one furlong out*..........(3 to 1 op 5 to 2 tchd 7 to 2) 5
4739a⁷ MAID WELCOME (v) 6-7-12 (7*) Madeleine Smith (1) *led til hdd o'r 3 fs out, wknd appr 2 out.* (33 to 1 op 25 to 1) 6

Dist: 5l, sht-hd, 3½l, 5l, 1l. 1m 11.41s. a 0.61s (6 Ran).
SR: 52/35/36/17/5/-/ (Mrs B Facchino), B A McMahon

57 Alpine Double Glazing Maiden Stakes CLASS F (3-y-o) £2,208 7f............(1:50)

BOLD STREET (Ire) 9-0 J Quinn (3) *cl up, led 3 fs out, quickened o'r one out, ran on wl.* ....(15 to 8 fav op 4 to 1) 1
SPANISH REFUGE 9-0 M Hills (5) *strted slwly, beh, hdwy wl o'r one furlong out, kpt on ins last.* ....(3 to 1 op 2 to 1) 2
4791a GENERAL LINK 9-0 W Woods (6) *cl up, ev ch wl o'r one furlong out, kpt on well und pres.* (33 to 1 op 10 to 1) 3
29² SPECIAL RISK (Ire) 8-7 (7*) J O'Dwyer (1) *trkd ldrs, one pace fnl 2 fs*..........(3 to 1 op 9 to 4) 4
2⁵ FRIENDLY SMILE 8-9 C Dwyer (4) *led til hdd 3 fs out, wknd*..........(4 to 1 op 2 to 1 tchd 9 to 2) 5
THATCHED (Ire) 9-0 S Webster (2) *al beh.* ....(8 to 1 op 5 to 1 tchd 10 to 1 and 12 to 1) 6

Dist: 1½l, nk, 2½l, ½l, 2½l. 1m 27.78s. a 4.38s (6 Ran).
SR: 8/3/2/ (B E Case), A Bailey

58 Daily Star Challenge Handicap Qualifier CLASS F (0-70 4-y-o and up) £2,733 1½m ....(2:20)

4819a* EL VOLADOR [70] 6-9-7 (7*) B Russell (3) *hld up tracking ldrs, not much room 3 fs out, hdwy 2 out, ran on to ld last strds*..........(7 to 4 fav op 9 to 4 tchd 5 to 2) 1
4798a⁷ EL DOMINIO [50] 5-8-8 G Bardwell (7) *cl up, led o'r 2 fs out till hdd last strd*..........(8 to 1 tchd 9 to 1) 2
20* REFLECTING (Ire) [69] 4-9-9 M Hills (6) *hld up tracking ldrs, hdwy 2 fs out, ev ch ins last, no extr cl hme.* ....(2 to 1 op 6 to 4) 3
35³ TAUNTING (Ire) [52] 5-8-3 (7*) S McCarthy (2) *wtd wth beh, effrt and hdwy o'r one furlong out, styd on one pace.* ....(6 to 1 op 7 to 1 tchd 8 to 1 and 10 to 1) 4
4798a⁹ MR WISHING WELL [50] (e/s) 7-8-8 A McGlone (5) *wtd wth beh, effrt 2 fs out, not pace to chal.* (12 to 1 op 8 to 1) 5
18⁶ LUKS AKURA [35] (v) 5-7-0 (7*) M Baird (4) *led til hdd o'r 2 fs out, wknd*..........(20 to 1 op 12 to 1) 6
NOTHING DOING (Ire) [42] 4-7-10 Dale Gibson (1) *took keen hold, cl up, rdn alng o'r 3 fs out, sn wknd.* ....(12 to 1 op 7 to 1) 7

Dist: Sht-hd, ¾l, 4l, ½l, 2l, 12l. 2m 35.16s. a 5.86s (7 Ran).
SR: 25/4/17/-/ (I A Baker), R J O'Sullivan

59 Fermanagh Handicap CLASS D (0-95 4-y-o and up) £3,949 1¼m..................(2:50)

4817a* MULCIBER [70] 5-9-1 W Woods (4) *trkd ldrs, led ins fnl furlong, pushed out.* ....(5 to 2 fav op 7 to 4 tchd 11 to 4) 1
9* RAPPORTEUR (USA) [83] 7-10-0 J Williams (6) *beh and sn pushed alng, hdwy o'r 3 fs out, led over 2 out til hdd and one pace ins last*...(13 to 2 op 4 to 1 tchd 7 to 1) 2
LYN'S RETURN (Ire) [57] 4-7-13⁵ (3*) A Tucker (3) *beh, hdwy o'r 3 fs out, kpt on*..........(12 to 1 op 7 to 1) 3
9² AWESOME POWER [78] 7-9-9 M Hills (2) *wtd wth beh, rdn and hdwy o'r 2 fs out, styd on*..... (4 to 1 tchd 9 to 2) 4
4722a⁷ FEN DANCE (Ire) [79] 4-9-7 S Dawson (8) *trkd ldrs, pushed alng 4 fs out, wknd wl o'r one out.* (20 to 1 op 14 to 1) 5
9⁶ BELMOREDEAN [72] 8-9-3 D Biggs (5) *hld up in mid-div, hdwy 5 fs out, led 4 out till hdd and hmpd o'r 2 out, sn wknd*..........(10 to 1 op 8 to 1 tchd 12 to 1) 6
AREMEF (USA) [74] 4-9-2 J Quinn (1) *led aftr one furlong till hdd 4 fs out, wknd*..........(4 to 1 op 5 to 1) 7
20⁶ MODESTO (USA) [60] 5-8-5 G Bardwell (7) *led one furlong, cl up til wknd o'r 3 fs out*..........(7 to 1 op 10 to 1) 8

Dist: 1½l, ¾l, 1½l, 7l, hd, 4l, 10l. 2m 6.31s. a 3.11s (8 Ran).
SR: 45/55/24/45/29/24/15/-/ (Mrs Penny Treadwell), G Harwood

60 Armagh Handicap CLASS F (0-80 3-y-o) £2,820 7f.......................... (3:20)

29* MISS GORGEOUS (Ire) [70] 8-11 (3*) Emma O'Gorman (3) *cl up, led 5 fs out, clr appr last, ran on wl.* ....(Evens fav tchd 5 to 4 on and 5 to 4) 1
STARDUST EXPRESS [61] 8-5 T Williams (2) *beh, rdn and hdwy o'r 3 fs out, one pace frm over one furlong out.* ....(8 to 1 op 6 to 1) 2
4790a² ERLKING (Ire) [77] 9-7 M Hills (5) *strted slwly, sn reco'red, cl up, kpt on one pace frm over one furlong out.* ....(5 to 2 tchd 9 to 4) 3
4755a⁹ MEDLAND (Ire) [58] 8-2 J Quinn (4) *sn pushed alng, nvr on terms*..........(14 to 1 tchd 12 to 1) 4
4805a⁷ EXPRESS MARIECURIE (Ire) [67] (v) 8-11 N Day (1) *led 2 fs, wknd o'r two furlongs out.* ....(5 to 1 op 6 to 1 tchd 7 to 1) 5

Dist: 2½l, hd, 10l, 5l. 1m 26.59s. a 3.19s (5 Ran).
SR: 26/9/24/-/-/ (Thomas R Capehart), W A O'Gorman

61 Londonderry Handicap CLASS F (0-70 4-y-o and up) £2,656 2m...................(3:50)

34⁶ COLERIDGE [62] (bl) 5-9-5 (5*) K Rutter (8) *in tch, cld to track ldrs hfwy, led 5 fs out, shaken up appr last, pushed out*..........(10 to 1) 1
MIZYAN (Ire) [66] 5-10-0 N Day (5) *hdwy to track ldrs hfwy, rdn and kpt on one pace fnl 3 fs*..........(7 to 2) 2
4806a⁶ KOVALEVSKIA [35] 8-7-11⁴ T Williams (7) *wtd wth, hdwy 6 fs out, hrd rdn 3 out, one pace*......(10 to 1 op 8 to 1) 3
4797a* SAFETY (USA) [47] (bl) 6-8-9 Dale Gibson (10) *pld hrd, in tch, cld o'r 4 fs out, styd on*..........(4 to 1 op 11 to 4) 4
4806a³ KENYATTA (USA) [45] 4-7-7 (7*) B Russell (2) *took keen hold, cl up, led aftr 6 fs till hdd six out, wknd.* .....(11 to 4 fav op 3 to 1 tchd 100 to 30 and 5 to 2) 5
4797a⁴ BURRACOPPIN [31] 6-7-7 G Bardwell (9) *strted slwly, sn prmnt, led 6 fs out to 5 out, wknd*..........(20 to 1) 6
8³ FIRST FLING (Ire) [50] (v) 4-8-5 J Quinn (3) *in tch til wknd o'r 4 fs out*..........(9 to 2 op 3 to 1) 7
CLAIR SOLEIL (USA) [57] 4-8-12 Candy Morris (4) *al beh.* ....(20 to 1 op 16 to 1) 8
8⁸ LAJADHAL (Fr) [42] 4-7-9³ (5*) B Doyle (1) *cl up till pushed alng and wknd 6 fs out*..........(33 to 1) 9
4813a CLOS DU BOIS (Fr) [36] 7-7-12² D Biggs (6) *led 6 fs, sn drpd out, tld off whn pld up 7 furlongs out*..........(33 to 1) pu

Dist: 1½l, 6l, 4l, 15l, sht-hd, 2½l, 2l, 7l. 3m 24.99s. a 2.99s (10 Ran).
SR: 40/42/5/13/-/-/ (P J Sheehan), D Shaw

SOUTHWELL (A.W) (std)
Monday January 18th
Going Correction: PLUS 0.10 sec. per fur.

62 Farndon Maiden Stakes CLASS F (3-y-o) £2,070 1m.......................... (1:20)

RECORD LOVER (Ire) 9-0 Dean McKeown (5) *settled gng wl, not much room entering strt, led o'r 2 fs out, ran on strly*..........(9 to 2 op 7 to 2 tchd 5 to 1) 1
4794a⁷ DIWALI DANCER 9-0 J Quinn (1) *sluggish strt, reco'red to go hndy aftr 2 fs, hmpd and lft in ld over two out, kpt on same pace*..........(5 to 2 op 2 to 1 tchd 3 to 1) 2

15[4] SCOFFERA 8-9 Kim Tinkler (8) *patiently rdn, improved to join issue o'r 2 fs out, ridden and one pace fnl furlong.* .... (10 to 1 op 8 to 1) 3

DON'T BE SAKI (Ire) 8-9 L Charnock (10) *drvn up frm midfield hfwy, effrt and rdn o'r 2 fs out, not quicken.* .... (14 to 1 op 12 to 1) 4

32 BARSAL (Ire) 9-0 Alex Greaves (6) *chsd ldg bunch, drvn alng to go pace hfwy, not quicken last 2 fs.* .... (25 to 1 op 16 to 1) 5

4800a[2] HEART OF SPAIN 9-0 M Hills (9) *settled midfield, effrt and drvn alng appr strt, no imprsn.* ....(13 to 8 fav op 7 to 4 tchd 15 to 8) 6

KEATING (Aus) 9-0 D Nicholls (7) *broke wl to dispute ld for o'r 5 fs, fdd*........................(12 to 1 op 8 to 1) 7

BECKY'S GIRL 8-9 T Williams (3) *sluggish strt, drvn up to dispute ld aftr 2 fs, fdd o'r two out.* (33 to 1 op 20 to 1) 8

23[6] LOBELIA (Ire) 8-9 G Bardwell (11) *chsd ldg half-dozen till wknd quickly o'r 2 fs out.* .... (14 to 1 op 14 to 1 tchd 16 to 1) 9

4665a TEMPLE HILL (bl) 8-9 M Wood (2) *missed break, al wl beh.* ....(25 to 1) 10

4766a[9] PERSONIMUS 9-0 J Fanning (4) *made most till shied frm whip and ran out through rls o'r 2 fs out.* ....(25 to 1 op 20 to 1) ro

Dist: 1l, 2l, 5l, ½l, ¾l, 7l, 1½l, 3½l, 2l. 1m 48.10s. a 9.10s (11 Ran).

(M L Oberstein), Lord Huntingdon

63 East Markham Claiming Stakes CLASS F (3-y-o) £2,322 7f........................ (1:50)

37[3] NIKKI NOO NOO 7-11 J Quinn (5) *pressed ldg trio, rdn hfwy, ran on gmely to ld cl hme.* (11 to 8 jt-fav op 7 to 4) 1

37[2] GREENWICH CHALLENGE (v) 8-1 (7*) D McCabe (2) *tried to make all, drvn alng last 2 fs, ran on, jst ct.* (11 to 8 jt-fav op 6 to 5 tchd 6 to 4) 2

40[8] LARN FORT (bl) 8-4 J Fanning (6) *nvr far away, drvn alng last 2 fs, not quicken*................ (14 to 1 op 10 to 1) 3

15[6] MUSICAL PHONE (v) 8-3 L Charnock (3) *trkd ldg pair, feeling pace and drvn alng o'r 2 fs out, no extr.* .... (20 to 1 op 14 to 1) 4

PARIS BY NIGHT (Ire) 7-11 G Bardwell (8) *sluggish strt, ran green thrght, ran on fnl furlong, improve.* .... (9 to 1 op 7 to 1 tchd 25 to 1) 5

40[4] MASTER SINCLAIR (Ire) 8-0 (5*) A Garth (4) *missed break, drvn up and hmpd hfwy, feeling pace o'r 2 fs out, no imprsn*................................(7 to 1 op 5 to 1) 6

MEESON IMPOSSIBLE 8-6[1] M Hills (1) *sluggish strt, dashed up to join issue hfwy, wknd quickly o'r 2 fs out.* .... (16 to 1 op 14 to 1 tchd 20 to 1) 7

Dist: ½l, 5l, 2½l, hd, 5l, 12l. 1m 32.80s. a 6.70s (7 Ran).

SR: -/2/-/-/ (C John Hill), C J Hill

64 Barnby Handicap CLASS F (0-85 4-y-o and up) £2,385 1½m..................... (2:20)

SWORD MASTER [73] 4-9-9 N Day (8) *nvr far away, drvn to nose ahead o'r one furlong out, kpt on ins last.* ....(9 to 2 op 7 to 2 tchd 5 to 1) 1

42[4] MASTER'S CROWN (USA) [39] 5-7-7 S Wood (5) *tried to make all, quickened aftr a m, hdd o'r one out, ran on one pace*..........................(7 to 1 op 12 to 1) 2

42[3] BEDOUIN PRINCE (USA) [46] 6-8-0 T Williams (4) *trkd ldr, rdn appr strt, outpcd last 2 fs.* ....(7 to 2 op 4 to 1 tchd 9 to 2) 3

CHEERFUL TIMES [56] 10-8-10 D Biggs (2) *al wl plcd, feeling pace and drvn alng appr strt, btn 2 fs out.* ....(10 to 1 op 8 to 1 tchd 14 to 1) 4

53* ATLANTIC WAY [52] 5-8-6 (5ex) J Quinn (3) *trkd ldg quartet, niggled alng appr strt, nvr able to chal.* ....(2 to 1 fav op 5 to 4) 5

RIVER ISLAND (USA) [72] 5-9-12 Dean McKeown (7) *chsd ldrs, drvn alng to go pace hfwy, nvr a threat.* ....(8 to 1 op 6 to 1) 6

4786a[3] REKLAW [39] (bl) 6-7-7 J Fanning (1) *trkd ldg bunch, hrd drvn appr strt, sn lost tch*......... (8 to 1 op 14 to 1) 7

CELTIC BOB [54] 13-8-8 S Dawson (6) *sn struggling to go pace, tld off frm hfwy*............(33 to 1 op 20 to 1) 8

Dist: 2l, 10l, 3½l, 4l, 1½l, 8l, 4l. 2m 40.90s. a 7.00s (8 Ran).

SR: 51/17/4/7/-/12/-/-/ (Ian A Vogt), Bob Jones

65 Darlton Claiming Stakes CLASS F (4-y-o and up) £2,427 1½m..................... (2:50)

55[2] TEMPERING 7-9-10 S Wood (2) *set gd pace, drw wl clr hfwy, eased ins fnl furlong*... (9 to 4 on op 2 to 1 on) 1

4788a[7] LORD ADVOCATE (v) 5-8-7 Alex Greaves (5) *drvn up frm midfield hfwy, styd on grimly last 2 fs, no ch wth wnr.* ....(11 to 2 op 4 to 1) 2

RAMBLE (USA) 6-8-11 Dean McKeown (7) *patiently rdn, improved into midfield hfwy, chsd alng last 3 fs, styd on, nvr nrr*........................(20 to 1 op 10 to 1) 3

14[4] ELIZA WOODING 5-8-1 G Bardwell (10) *sluggish strt, improved frm off the pace hfwy, styd on last 2 fs.* .... (12 to 1 op 7 to 1) 4

AMOUR ROYAL 6-9-0 D Nicholls (4) *chsd wnr aftr 2 fs, rdn hfwy, no imprsn last two furlongs.* (14 to 1 op 8 to 1) 5

CARDEA CASTLE (Ire) 5-8-6[3] M Hills (1) *bustled alng in midfield hfwy, nvr rch chalg pos*.. (50 to 1 op 33 to 1) 6

SUMMER CRUISE 4-8-4 J Quinn (12) *drvn alng to go pace hfwy, nvr rchd ldrs*.. (16 to 1 op 14 to 1 tchd 20 to 1) 7

5[5] WHITWELL HILL 4-8-3 L Charnock (8) *trkd ldrs, feeling pace hfwy, fdd appr strt*..............................(50 to 1) 8

4763a[9] WHISKEY BLUES 8-8-8[1] (5*) S D Williams (11) *drvn alng to keep up hfwy, nvr a factor*........ (50 to 1 op 33 to 1) 9

DEHAR BOY 7-8-12 R Lappin (6) *chsd ldrs, rdn hfwy, tld off*..................................(33 to 1 op 25 to 1) 10

4739a WOOLAW GIRL 5-8-9 S Webster (3) *broke wl, lost grnd rpdly hfwy, tld off*........... (100 to 1 op 33 to 1) 11

HAND IN GLOVE 7-8-6 T Williams (9) *wl plcd till pld up 6 fs out, lme*................................(16 to 1 op 14 to 1) pu

Dist: 6l, 1l, ½l, 1l, 12l, 2½l, 1l, 12l, dist, 3l. 2m 44.40s. a 10.50s (12 Ran).

SR: 17/-/-/-/-/-/ (David W Chapman), D W Chapman

66 Askham Handicap CLASS F (0-80 3-y-o) £2,280 6f........................... (3:20)

21* PLAY HEVER GOLF [66] 9-0 M Hills (2) *made all, quickened clr entering strt, styd on gmely fnl furlong.* ....(100 to 30 op 9 to 4) 1

37[5] PINE RIDGE LAD (Ire) [59] 8-7 Dean McKeown (3) *chsd wnr to strt, rdn 2 fs out, rallied fnl furlong.* ....(3 to 1 op 3 to 1 tchd 7 to 2) 2

22[2] SASEEDO (USA) [73] 9-4 (3*) Emma O'Gorman (5) *lost many ls strt, took clr order entering strt, kpt on same pace fnl furlong*..............(2 to 1 fav op 13 to 8 tchd 7 to 4) 3

51* COMET WHIRLPOOL (Ire) [63] (bl) 8-11 (7ex) J Quinn (6) *drvn up to chase wnr entering strt, no extr ins fnl furlong.* ....(4 to 1 op 9 to 2 tchd 5 to 1) 4

37[9] BARLEY CAKE [49] 7-11 J Fanning (1) *chsd ldg trio, feeling pace entering strt, sn btn*..........(25 to 1 op 12 to 1) 5

51[6] APOLLO DE ORIENTE [54] 8-2 L Charnock (4) *struggling to go pace thrght, nvr a factor*.......... (12 to 1 op 20 to 1) 6

Dist: 1½l, 1l, 2½l, 12l, ¾l. 1m 18.30s. a 4.90s (6 Ran).

SR: 14/1/11/ (R A Popely), T J Naughton

67 Southwell Amateur Riders Handicap CLASS F (0-70 4-y-o and up) £2,511 1m....... (3:50)

RIPSNORTER (Ire) [58] 4-11-9 (5*) Miss A Purdy (15) *dashed up frm midfield hfwy, led appr fnl furlong, quickened, kpt on*.............................. (20 to 1 op 16 to 1) 1

13 ALBERT [33] 6-10-4 Miss E Bronson (5) *settled midfield, hrd rdn to improve last 2 fs, fnshd wl.* ....(3 to 1 op 7 to 2 tchd 4 to 1) 2

4756a SOL ROUGE (Ire) [34] 4-9-13 (5*) Mr A Deeprose (14) *settled midfield, improved o'r 2 fs out, styd on one pace.* .... (50 to 1 op 33 to 1) 3

38[4] DIAMOND INTHE DARK (USA) [57] (v) 5-12-0 Miss I D W Jones (1) *wth ldr, hrd drvn 2 fs out, no extr.* .... (13 to 2 op 6 to 1 tchd 7 to 1) 4

24[3] DON'T DROP BOMBS (USA) [42] (bl) 4-10-7 (5*) Miss T Bracegirdle (8) *made most till hdd appr fnl furlong, fdd.* ....(5 to 2 fav op 7 to 2) 5

SILK DYNASTY [30] 7-9-10 (5*) Miss C Carden (13) *beh and pushed alng, styd on last 2 fs, nvr nrr.* .... (33 to 1 op 20 to 1) 6

4785a[7] CAL'S BOY [35] 4-10-0 (5*) Mrs C Dunwoody (6) *pressed ldrs, feeling pace o'r 2 fs out, fdd*............(33 to 1) 7

4802a[2] GUESSTIMATION (USA) [51] 4-11-7 Mrs L Pearce (7) *wth ldrs till wknd and eased last 2 fs.* ....(7 to 2 op 3 to 1 tchd 9 to 2) 8

4771a[5] BREEZED WELL [56] 7-11-8 (5*) Mrs H Noonan (4) *trkd ldg half-dozen, rdn o'r 2 fs out, sn btn.* .... (14 to 1 op 12 to 1 tchd 16 to 1) 9

13 COMISKEY PARK (Ire) [39] (bl) 4-10-4 (5*) Miss R Clark (10) *wth ldrs, pushed alng o'r 2 fs out, fdd appr last.* .... (20 to 1 op 12 to 1) 10

RESISTING (USA) [31] 5-10-2[6] (5*) Mr M Chapman (3) *sluggish strt, nvr a factor*............. (33 to 1 op 20 to 1) 11

HADLEIGHS CHOICE [29] 6-9-9 (5*) Mr D T Robinson (9) *sluggish strt, improved entering strt, nvr a threat.* .... (50 to 1 op 33 to 1) 12

41[7] MANSE KEY GOLD [32] 6-9-12 (5*) Mr D Wilcox (11) *struggling in rear thrght*................................(33 to 1) 13

5[8] KAYMONT [25] 5-9-5 (5*) Miss J Bond (12) *pressed ldrs for o'r 4 fs, fdd*........................ (50 to 1 op 33 to 1) 14

10[4] GYMCRAK FORTUNE (Ire) [52] 5-11-9 Mr C Vigors (16) *chsd alng to go pace hfwy, nvr dngrs*.... (14 to 1 op 8 to 1) 15

SCOTTISH FLING [30] (bl) 9-10-1 Mrs A Farrell (2) *co'red up on ins, feeling pace and drvn alng entering strt, fdd, fnshd lme*..........................(16 to 1 op 14 to 1) 16

Dist: Nk, 7l, 3l, hd, 3l, nk, 1l, ½l, nk, 3½l. 1m 48.00s. a 9.00s (16 Ran).

SR: 19/-/-/-/-/-/ (P D Purdy), J A Bennett

LINGFIELD (A.W) (std)
Tuesday January 19th
Going Correction: MINUS 0.20 sec. per fur.

68 Newport Handicap CLASS F (0-70 4-y-o and up) £2,364 1¼m..................... (1:25)

55[8] FERDIA (Ire) [63] 4-9-2 (5*) S Wynne (7) *hld up in tch, rdn to ld 3 fs out, sn quickened clr, very easily.* ....(9 to 2 op 8 to 1) 1
4777a[4] GOLD BLADE [60] 4-9-4 J Williams (4) *hld up, rapid hdwy 4 fs out, dsptd ld 3 out, kpt on one pace.* (15 to 8 jt-fav op 6 to 4 tchd 2 to 1) 2
DEBACLE (USA) [70] 4-10-0 M Perrett (2) *led till hdd 3 fs out, kpt on one pace aftr.* (15 to 8 jt-fav op 6 to 4 tchd 2 to 1) 3
WITH GUSTO [47] 6-8-1 (7*) B Russell (6) *chsd ldrs, one pace fnl 3 fs*...........(6 to 1 op 7 to 1 tchd 8 to 1) 4
CAL NORMA'S LADY (Ire) [60] 5-9-7 W Woods (1) *chsd ldrs, no hdwy fnl 3 fs*...................(25 to 1 op 20 to 1) 5
4689a[8] LIZZIE DRIPPIN (Can) [40] 4-7-12 J Quinn (3) *al beh.* ....(11 to 1 op 8 to 1 tchd 12 to 1) 6
4748a[6] RIO TRUSKY [38] 4-7-10[2] Dale Gibson (5) *pld hrd, dsptd ld till rdn and wknd 4 fs out, tld off.* (25 to 1 op 20 to 1) 7
Dist: 10l, ¾l, ½l, 2l, 3½l, 10l. 2m 6.82s. a 3.62s (7 Ran).
SR: 51/28/36/15/24/-/-/ (Noel Sweeney), R Hollinshead

69 Cowes Claiming Stakes CLASS F (4-y-o and up) £2,542 1m.......................(1:55)

43* EASTLEIGH 4-8-7[2] (7*) D Carson (5) *pressed ldr, led o'r 4 fs out, clr 3 out, rdn and hld on wl ins last.* ....(7 to 4 fav op 5 to 4 tchd 2 to 1) 1
43[4] TRY LEGUARD (Ire) 4-7-13 (7*) D Wright (8) *in rear, gd hdwy o'r 3 fs out, kpt on wl ins last.* ....(9 to 2 op 7 to 2 tchd 5 to 1) 2
48[5] SAREEN EXPRESS (Ire) 5-8-6 (3*) A Tucker (2) *slwly away, towards rear till hdwy o'r 2 fs out, styd on wl ins last.* ....(5 to 1 op 8 to 1) 3
46[6] MON PETITNAMOUR (Ire) 4-9-1 D Biggs (6) *hdwy hfwy, ev ch 2 fs out, hrd rdn and outpcd entering last.* ....(10 to 1 tchd 14 to 1) 4
APPEALING TIMES (USA) 4-8-11 (3*) Emma O'Gorman (3) *led till hdd o'r 4 fs out, wknd appr fnl furlong.* ....(9 to 2 op 2 to 1 tchd 5 to 1) 5
YONGE TENDER (bl) 6-8-4 J Quinn (4) *chsd ldrs, no hdwy fnl 3 fs*..........................(12 to 1 op 7 to 1) 6
4746a[8] JUST CALL ME MADAM (Ire) 4-7-9[1] (5*) B Doyle (9) *outpcd frm hfwy*.......................... (33 to 1 op 20 to 1) 7
VELLANDRUCHA 4-7-11 Dale Gibson (1) *outpcd frm strt, tld off*..............................(33 to 1 op 20 to 1) 8
ACKERS WOOD (v) 5-8-7 J Williams (7) *pld hrd, trkd ldrs early, wknd hfwy, tld off*........ (33 to 1 op 20 to 1) 9
Dist: Hd, 3l, 1½l, 8l, sht-hd, 7l, 15l, 2½l. 1m 38.79s. a 2.59s (9 Ran).
SR: 35/28/22/23/-/-/ (J E Bigg), R Hollinshead

70 Shanklin Handicap CLASS E (0-90 4-y-o and up) £3,460 6f.......................(2:25)

28* PRETONIC [70] 5-8-9 Dean McKeown (5) *trkd ldr, led on ins appr fnl furlong, all out.* .... (11 to 4 op 5 to 2 tchd 3 to 1) 1
11* RUNNING GLIMPSE (Ire) [77] 5-8-9 (7*) A Martinez (6) *al prmnt, led hfwy, hrd rdn and hdd appr fnl furlong, ran on und pres*............... (5 to 2 jt-fav op 7 to 4) 2
11[2] RHYTHMIC DANCER [75] 5-9-0 J Williams (4) *slwly into strd, sn in tch, ev ch one furlong out, ran on und pres.* ....(5 to 2 jt-fav op 9 to 4) 3
TYRIAN PURPLE (Ire) [66] 5-7-12 (7*) M Humphries (3) *led till hdd hfwy, wknd quickly wl o'r one furlong out.* ....(20 to 1 op 14 to 1) 4
36[2] SIRMOOR (Ire) [54] (bl) 4-7-7 G Bardwell (2) *outpcd frm strt, tld off*.......................(5 to 1 op 4 to 1) 5
Dist: Nk, nk, 12l, 15l. 1m 11.90s. a 1.10s (5 Ran).
SR: 49/55/52/-/-/ (Brian Yeardley Continental Ltd), M Johnston

71 Yarmouth Handicap CLASS F (0-70 3-y-o) £2,409 7f........................... (2:55)

TAKE YOUR PARTNER (Ire) [49] 8-0 T Williams (2) *led for one and a half fs, lost pl, hrd rdn appr fnl furlong, ran on strly to ld cl hme*................ (12 to 1 op 10 to 1) 1
60* MISS GORGEOUS (Ire) [75] 9-9 (3*,5ex) Emma O'Gorman (5) *led aftr one and a half fs, rdn and kpt on, hdd nr finish*.............(11 to 8 fav op 5 to 4 tchd 6 to 4) 2
15[7] CONVOY [62] (bl) 8-13 M Hills (7) *in rear, rdn and hdwy o'r 2 fs out, kpt on ins last*.............(9 to 2 op 7 to 2) 3
44[4] ARAWA [47] 7-5 (7*) S McCarthy (6) *sn chsd ldr, kpt on one pace fnl furlong, lost second pl cl hme.* ....(8 to 1 tchd 12 to 1) 4
31* SPLASH OF SALT (Ire) [66] 9-3 J Quinn (4) *hdwy hfwy, one pace fnl furlong*.......(5 to 2 op 7 to 4 tchd 11 to 4) 5
32 TACITURN (USA) [43] 7-8 G Bardwell (3) *sn rdn alng, al beh*................(12 to 1 op 10 to 1 tchd 14 to 1) 6
40 BAJKA [51] (v) 7-11 (5*) A Garth (1) *al struggling in rear.* .... (33 to 1 op 25 to 1) 7
Dist: ¾l, nk, nk, ¾l, 7l, 5l. 1m 26.68s. a 3.28s (7 Ran).
SR: 16/40/26/10/27/-/-/ (The Fairyhouse 1992 Partnership), M Johnston

72 Alpine Double Glazing Maiden Stakes CLASS F (3-y-o) £2,208 1¼m..........(3:25)

32[2] HIGH SUMMER 9-0 Dean McKeown (2) *led 1st 2 fs, led ag'n 4 out, shaken up and ran on wl fnl furlong.* ....(Evens fav op 5 to 4 tchd 5 to 4 on) 1
40[6] HUSH BABY (Ire) 8-9 G Bardwell (5) *led aftr 2 fs, hdd 4 out, hrd rdn fnl two, no imprsn cl hme.* (14 to 1 op 10 to 1) 2
4761a[4] HALHAM TARN (Ire) (e/s) 9-0 J Williams (3) *rcd in tch on ins, styd on wl inside fnl furlong*........(5 to 1 op 7 to 1) 3
23[3] BADAWI (Fr) (v) 8-7 (7*) G Forster (4) *trkd ldrs, rdn appr fnl furlong, kpt on one pace.* ....(4 to 1 op 3 to 1 tchd 9 to 2) 4
UMHAMBI 8-9 M Hills (1) *mid-div, effrt 2 fs out, rdn appr last, one pace*...................... (7 to 1 op 5 to 2) 5
4761a[9] PERSIAN STAR (Fr) 8-9 D Biggs (7) *beh whn hmpd aftr 3 fs, nvr got into race, tld off*..........(33 to 1 op 25 to 1) 6
26[3] ARAGON KING 9-0 N Day (8) *prmnt on outsd till rdn and wknd o'r 3 fs out, tld off.* ....(10 to 1 op 6 to 1 tchd 12 to 1) 7
4778a[7] DORMSTON BOYO 8-11 (3*) A Tucker (6) *in tch till hrd rdn 5 fs out, sn beh, tld off*............ (33 to 1 op 25 to 1) 8
Dist: 1½l, ¾l, hd, ½l, 15l, 5l, 2½l. 2m 10.38s. a 7.18s (8 Ran).
SR: 8/-/3/2/-/ (The Queen), Lord Huntingdon

73 Ryde Handicap CLASS F (0-70 4-y-o and up) £2,476 1m 5f.......................(3:55)

4819a[2] STRAT'S LEGACY [45] 6-9-0 J Quinn (6) *wtd wth, rdn and hdwy to go second 3 fs out, led wl o'r one out, edgd lft, ran on*.................(7 to 2 op 3 to 1 tchd 9 to 2) 1
34[4] HUNTING GROUND [49] 5-9-1 (3*) A Tucker (7) *led till hfwy, lost pl 4 fs out, styd on ag'n ins fnl 2.* ....(11 to 1 op 8 to 1 tchd 12 to 1) 2
WICK POUND [55] (bl) 7-9-10 J Williams (5) *trkd ldr, led hfwy, hdd o'r 3 fs out, hmpd slightly entering last, one pace aftr*...............(11 to 2 op 7 to 2 tchd 6 to 1) 3
58[2] EL DOMINIO [50] 5-8-12 (7*) B Russell (4) *beh till hdwy o'r 2 fs out, styd on, nvr nr to chal.* ....(7 to 4 fav tchd 2 to 1 and 6 to 4) 4
35[8] FLASH OF STRAW (Ire) [40] 4-8-5 T Williams (1) *in tch, led o'r 3 fs out, hdd wl over one out, wkng whn hmpd sn aftr, one pace*..........(9 to 1 op 8 to 1 tchd 10 to 1) 5
34[2] DR ZEVA [40] 7-8-2 (7*) D Wright (2) *al beh, tld off.* ....(5 to 1 op 4 to 1 tchd 11 to 2) 6
BURSANA [31] 7-8-0 G Bardwell (3) *chsd ldrs till wknd o'r 4 fs out, tld off*......(40 to 1 op 25 to 1 tchd 50 to 1) 7
Dist: 3l, ¾l, 1½l, nk, 12l, 20l. 2m 48.79s. a 5.79s (7 Ran).
SR: 16/14/18/10/ (Jack Blumenow), D W P Arbuthnot

CAGNES-SUR-MER (FR) (good)
Friday January 22nd

74 Prix d'Ajaccio (3-y-o) £8,363 1¼m.....(1:35)

FAY WRAY (Fr) 8-10 G Elorriaga-Santos,................. 1
FABULEUX BRINK (Fr) 9-0 M Cesandri,.................. 2
TELL ME WHY (Fr) 8-10 J Guilloteau,.................... 3
32[3] SALBUS 8-9 J Reid,...................................... 7
Dist: 2l, 2l, 2l, 2½l, 1l, ½l. 2m 7.10s. (16 Ran).
M Pimbonnet

75 Prix du Docteur Gazagnaire (4-y-o and up) £8,363 1¼m........................ (2:05)

PETER BERHEL (Fr) 7-8-5 T Gillet,...................... 1
CHORUS LINE (Fr) 6-8-9 G Elorriaga-Santos,............. 2
VENGADOR (USA) 4-8-9 N Jeanpierre,.................... 3
FLY AWAY SOON (USA) 5-8-8[2] J Reid,.................. 8
Dist: 3l, ½l, ½l, 4l, nk, sht-hd. 2m 5.50s. (15 Ran).
Yves Lalleman

SOUTHWELL (A.W) (std)
Friday January 22nd
Going Correction: PLUS 0.50 sec. per fur.

76 Oyster Claiming Stakes CLASS F (4-y-o and up) £2,448 6f.........................(1:40)

17* PRIME MOVER (v) 5-8-7 L Charnock (11) *nvr far away, quickened ahead o'r one furlong out, kpt on grimly ins last*................................ (6 to 1 op 3 to 1) 1
56* APPLEDORN 6-8-12 D Biggs (9) *patiently rdn, swtchd outsd to chal o'r one furlong out, edgd lft, not quicken.* ....(5 to 4 on op 2 to 1 on tchd 11 to 10) 2
6[4] MARTINA 5-8-8 J Williams (3) *tucked away on ins, ev ch and drvn last 2 fs, outpcd last 100 yards.* ....(4 to 1 op 6 to 1) 3
4810a BLACK BOY (Ire) 4-8-3 T Williams (1) *made most, rdn o'r 2 fs out, hdd and fdd over one out*....(14 to 1 op 8 to 1) 4
4666a BRISAS (bl) 6-8-5 J Fanning (10) *pressed ldg pair, feeling pace and rdn 2 fs out, sn btn*...... (25 to 1 op 16 to 1) 5
BUZBOUR 5-8-9 S Wood (8) *lost many ls strt, improved to chase ldrs hfwy, better for race*....(50 to 1 op 20 to 1) 6
4815a[5] CHERRYWOOD LASS 5-7-10 G Bardwell (5) *trkd ldg bunch, rdn hfwy, wknd quickly.* (33 to 1 tchd 50 to 1) 7
54[5] JUVENARA 7-8-5 J Quinn (4) *beh and drvn alng most of way, nvr a threat*..... (8 to 1 op 10 to 1 tchd 12 to 1) 8
4722a[8] COURTING NEWMARKET 5-8-5 Dean McKeown (2) *led early, continued to dispute ld till wknd 2 fs out.* .... (25 to 1 op 20 to 1) 9

4808a CHOICE LOT 6-7-10 (7*) D Wright (6) *chsd ldg half-dozen for o'r 3 fs, sn btn*.................(50 to 1 op 33 to 1) 10
50[5] FELSINA (Ire) 4-8-4 Alex Greaves (7) *al struggling to keep up, nvr a factor*..................(33 to 1 op 12 to 1) 11
Dist: ¾l, 5l, 3l, 4l, 2½l, ¾l, 1l, 2l, 1½l, ½l. 1m 18.60s. a 5.20s (11 Ran).
SR: 49/51/27/10/-/-/ (Mrs M E Brooks), D Burchell

77 Lobster Handicap CLASS F (0-80 4-y-o and up) £2,301 7f.........................(2:10)

54[4] PREDICTABLE [50] 7-8-8 Alex Greaves (4) *enterprisingly rdn, made all, kicked clr hfwy, unchlgd*. ....(100 to 30 op 5 to 1) 1
49[2] EXPRESS SERVICE [64] 4-9-5 (3*) Emma O'Gorman (7) *patiently rdn, improved on outsd hfwy, edgd lft and crrd head high, not rch wnr*.........(4 to 1 op 9 to 4) 2
35[9] BAYIN (USA) [35] 4-7-1[1] (7*) D Wright (2) *sluggish strt, drvn into midfield hfwy, styd on last 2 fs, nvr nrr*. ....(16 to 1 op 25 to 1 tchd 14 to 1) 3
50[3] KLAIROVER [48] 6-8-6 J Quinn (6) *nvr far away, feeling pace and drvn alng hfwy, kpt on same pace last 2 fs*. ....(6 to 4 fav op 5 to 4 tchd 2 to 1) 4
4807a[9] AMETHYSTINE (USA) [58] 7-8-9 (7*) S Drowne (1) *pressed ldg pair, rdn hfwy, no imprsn last 2 fs*. ....(9 to 1 op 6 to 1) 5
17[7] WELLSY LAD (USA) [54] 6-8-12 S Wood (8) *last and niggled alng hfwy, kpt on last 2 fs, nvr nrr*.. (9 to 1 op 8 to 1) 6
54[9] MAJAL (Ire) [66] 4-9-10 D Nicholls (3) *wth wnr to hfwy, fdd und pres o'r 2 fs out*..............(20 to 1 op 16 to 1) 7
4739a GALLEY GOSSIP [41] 4-7-13[2] T Williams (5) *pressed ldg quartet, rdn hfwy, sn btn*.....................(33 to 1) 8
Dist: 3½l, 2½l, nk, 3½l, 3½l, 1l, 12l. 1m 33.10s. a 7.00s (8 Ran).
SR: 42/45/8/20/19/4/13/-/ (L J Hawkings), Mrs A Knight

78 Crab Handicap CLASS F (0-70 4-y-o and up) £2,616 1½m......................... (2:40)

38[8] KRONPRINZ (Ire) [29] 5-7-11 S Wood (12) *nvr far away, effrt and hrd drvn last 2 fs, kpt on gmely to ld post*. ....(20 to 1) 1
3 EMPEROR ALEXANDER (Ire) [57] (bl) 5-9-8 (3*) S D Williams (16) *led aftr one furlong, quickened hfwy, hrd rdn last 2 fs, jst ct*..............................(8 to 1 op 7 to 1) 2
14[3] SILVER SAMURAI [60] 4-9-3 (7*) S Mulvey (14) *trkd ldrs, improved on outsd to chal o'r one furlong out, kpt on wl*.................................. (8 to 1 op 6 to 1) 3
4819a[7] ROYAL VERSE (Fr) [27] 6-7-9[1] Dale Gibson (2) *settled midfield, improved on ins to chal o'r one furlong out, kpt on same pace last 50 yards*.........(10 to 1 op 7 to 1) 4
20[5] FIT THE BILL [36] 5-8-4 L Charnock (4) *settled midfield, rdn aftr a m, no imprsn last 2 fs*. ....(15 to 2 op 12 to 1 tchd 7 to 1) 5
64[4] CHEERFUL TIMES [56] 10-9-10 D Biggs (13) *chsd ldg trio, feeling pace appr strt, outpcd last 2 fs*. .... (9 to 1 op 12 to 1) 6
13[7] HOT PUNCH [40] 4-8-4 N Carlisle (3) *led one furlong, lost grnd hfwy, rallied entering strt, nrst finish*... (20 to 1) 7
THIN RED LINE [44] (e/s) 9-8-12 J Williams (8) *sluggish strt, bustled into midfield hfwy, kpt on, nvr nrr*....(20 to 1) 8
68[6] LIZZIE DRIPPIN (Can) [40] 4-8-4 W Woods (6) *chsd ldg 5, bustled alng hfwy, outpcd entering strt*.......(25 to 1) 9
12[8] DIGGER DOYLE [60] 4-9-10 Dean McKeown (7) *pressed ldg pair for one m, fdd entering strt*. ....(10 to 1 op 12 to 1 tchd 8 to 1) 10
30[3] TENDRESSE (Ire) [43] 5-8-11 G Bardwell (5) *settled midfield, chsd alng to go pace hfwy, nvr a threat*. ....(6 to 1 fav op 4 to 1) 11
HEIR OF EXCITEMENT [33] 8-8-1 T Williams (15) *chsd ldg bunch, rdn hfwy, sn lost tch*...... (12 to 1 op 16 to 1) 12
BORING (USA) [55] 4-9-5 S Webster (9) *drvn alng to go pace thrght, nvr dngrs*. ....(12 to 1 op 8 to 1 tchd 16 to 1) 13
30[6] LATOUR [47] 5-9-1 D Nicholls (1) *beh and drvn alng thrght, tld off*.....................(14 to 1 op 12 to 1) 14
49[7] VAGUE NANCY (Ire) [26] 5-7-1 (7*) D Wright (11) *al struggling, tld off*.....................(14 to 1 op 12 to 1) 15
55[7] LA REINE ROUGE (Ire) [46] 5-9-0 J Quinn (10) *chsd ldg bunch for a m, sn lost tch, tld off*...(9 to 1 tchd 8 to 1) 16
Dist: Sht-hd, hd, nk, 15l, ¾l, 2l, 3l, 3l, 3l, 2½l. 2m 46.80s. a 12.90s (16 Ran).
SR: 14/41/39/9/-/6/ (Market Rasen Racing Club), M C Chapman

79 Shark Handicap CLASS F (0-90 4-y-o and up) £2,217 1m............................ (3:10)

38* NO SUBMISSION (USA) [72] 7-8-12 (7ex) S Wood (5) *made all, quickened o'r 2 fs out, styd on strly*. ....(11 to 10 on op 11 to 8 on tchd Evens) 1
38[5] MARTINI EXECUTIVE [80] (bl) 5-9-6 J Fanning (4) *sluggish strt, reco'red to join wnr hfwy, rdn and kpt on same pace last 2 fs*......................(7 to 1 op 10 to 1) 2
39[3] BOY MARTIN [68] (bl) 4-8-7 S Webster (1) *pressed ldg pair, feeling pace and drvn alng o'r 2 fs out, no imprsn*. ....(4 to 1 tchd 5 to 1 and 7 to 2) 3
4802a[4] ULLADULLA [63] 4-8-2 J Quinn (3) *shwd up wl to hfwy, feeling pace and rdn o'r 2 fs out, one pace*. ....(10 to 1 op 7 to 1) 4
4743a* AFRICAN CHIMES [88] 6-9-11 (3*) S D Williams (2) *last and hld up, effrt hfwy, rdn o'r 2 fs out, nvr able to chal*. ....(4 to 1 op 3 to 1 tchd 5 to 1) 5
Dist: 3l, 1½l, 2½l, 5l. 1m 47.50s. a 8.50s (5 Ran).
SR: 31/30/12/-/10/ (T S Redman), D W Chapman

80 Halibut Claiming Stakes CLASS F (3-y-o) £2,511 1m............................ (3:40)

DORAZINE 7-9 J Quinn (4) *al hndy, led o'r 2 fs out, quickened clr, eased considerably*. (3 to 1 tchd 6 to 1) 1
52[2] MISTER BLAKE (bl) 8-7 (3*) Emma O'Gorman (9) *nvr far away, effrt and drvn alng entering strt, kpt on same pace fnl furlong*....(13 to 8 fav op 5 to 2 tchd 4 to 1) 2
37[6] MARK'S CLUB (Ire) (bl) 8-4 Alex Greaves (1) *patiently rdn, moved up entering strt, styd on one pace last 2 fs*. ....(9 to 2 op 5 to 1 tchd 6 to 1 and 4 to 1) 3
MRS SNUGGS (Ire) 7-12[8] (7*) S Mulvey (6) *sluggish strt, improved into midfield hfwy, styd on strly fnl furlong*. ....(14 to 1 op 6 to 1) 4
52* PERSIAN TRAVELLER (Ire) 8-12 D Nicholls (2) *tried to make all, hdd and rdn o'r 2 fs out, fdd*.....(9 to 4 op 6 to 4) 5
16[8] BOULMERKA (bl) 7-8 (5*) A Garth (10) *beh and drvn alng hfwy, styd on late, nvr nrr*.................... (33 to 1) 6
4772a[9] SCHOOL OF SCIENCE (bl) 8-1[1] L Charnock (8) *wth ldr for o'r 4 fs, fdd*..............................(20 to 1) 7
HOTEL CALIFORNIA (Ire) 8-3 S Wood (5) *in tch, pushed alng hfwy, nvr plcd to chal*.........(14 to 1 op 8 to 1) 8
MISS IN-A-BIT 8-2 (7*) T G McLaughlin (3) *missed break, nvr able to reco'r*............................(33 to 1) 9
GLOWING PATH 8-4 D Biggs (12) *broke wl to show speed for o'r 4 fs, fdd*..................(12 to 1 op 7 to 1) 10
4745a[5] CIZARD (Ire) 7-13 N Carlisle (7) *struggling to go pace aftr one furlong, nvr a factor*......................(33 to 1) 11
LADY MAGADI 7-7 G Bardwell (11) *pressed ldrs for o'r 4 fs, wknd rpdly*......................(25 to 1 op 16 to 1) 12
Dist: 2l, 2½l, 5l, 3l, 5l, 5l, 5l, 1l, 2½l, 1½l. 1m 48.00s. a 9.00s (12 Ran).
SR: 6/15/1/-/-/-/ (C John Hill), C J Hill

81 Octopus Handicap CLASS F (0-80 4-y-o and up) £2,343 1¾m.....................(4:10)

64[3] BEDOUIN PRINCE (USA) [46] 6-8-0 T Williams (2) *last and scrubbed alng hfwy, relentless prog to ld ins fnl furlong, ran on wl*.......................(8 to 1 op 5 to 1) 1
65* TEMPERING [81] 7-10-7 (7ex) S Wood (7) *rcd keenly in clr ld, began to tire o'r one furlong out, hdd and no extr ins last*.................(5 to 1 op 9 to 2 tchd 6 to 1) 2
55* SUGEMAR [63] 7-8-10 (7*,7ex) D McCabe (1) *pld hrd, chsd ldg pair, styd on ins fnl furlong, nvr nrr*. (7 to 2 jt-fav op 9 to 2) 3
4776a[5] ISLAND BLADE (Ire) [53] 4-8-2 J Quinn (6) *settled midfield, struggling to go pace appr strt, kpt on same pace last 2 fs*...............................(11 to 2 op 7 to 2) 4
53[3] SHAKINSKI [50] (v) 4-7-13 D Biggs (3) *rdn to keep up hfwy, late hdwy, nvr nrr*.................... (9 to 2 op 7 to 2) 5
9[3] LOOKINGFORARAINBOW (Ire) [68] 5-9-8 N Day (5) *chsd clr ldr, effrt and hng lft und pres 2 fs out, fdd*. (7 to 2 jt-fav op 3 to 1 tchd 4 to 1) 6
53[6] AUDE LA BELLE (Fr) [64] 5-9-4 Dean McKeown (4) *struggling to keep in tch hfwy, nvr a dngr*. ....(10 to 1 op 8 to 1 tchd 12 to 1) 7
Dist: 3½l, ¾l, 3l, 2½l, 4l, 2l. 3m 13.10s. a 13.10s (7 Ran).
SR: 25/53/33/12/4/19/11/ (Miss J E Toulson), B Richmond

LINGFIELD (A.W) (std)
Saturday January 23rd
Going Correction: MINUS 0.35 sec. per fur.

82 Alpine Double Glazing Maiden Stakes CLASS F (4-y-o and up) £2,208 1½m. .(12:55)

35[4] BEAM ME UP SCOTTY (Ire) 4-9-0 M Hills (5) *trkd ldrs, led o'r 3 fs out, clr over one out, eased cl hme*. ....(8 to 1 op 6 to 1) 1
DOC'S COAT 8-9-4 Dale Gibson (6) *chsd ldrs, rdn alng 4 fs out, kpt on wl fnl 2 furlongs*.......(50 to 1 op 20 to 1) 2
46[2] LYPH (USA) 7-9-4 S Dawson (11) *chsd ldrs, pushed alng 4 fs out, one pace frm o'r 2 out*.........(7 to 4 op 9 to 4) 3
4780a[2] ETIQUETTE 4-8-9 Dean McKeown (8) *dsptd ld, led 6 fs out till hdd o'r 3 out, one pace*. ....(6 to 4 on op 7 to 4 on tchd 5 to 4 on) 4
43[9] CASTLE GALAH (v) 6-8-8 (5*) B Doyle (3) *trkd ldrs till rdn and one pace fnl 3 fs*............. (50 to 1 op 20 to 1) 5
ST JOHN'S HILL 5-9-4 J Williams (9) *beh, styd on frm o'r one furlong out, nrst finish*. ....(33 to 1 op 20 to 1 tchd 50 to 1) 6
PARISIAN 8-9-1 (3*) A Tucker (7) *in tch, effrt o'r 4 fs out, sn wknd*..................................(33 to 1 op 16 to 1) 7
43 RICH HEIRESS (Ire) 4-8-9 Candy Morris (2) *al beh*. ....(33 to 1 op 16 to 1) 8
GLOSSY 6-9-4 D Biggs (4) *dsptd ld, wkng whn hmpd o'r 4 fs out, sn beh*......... (11 to 1 op 6 to 1 tchd 12 to 1) 9
WRITTEN AGREEMENT 5-9-4 J Quinn (10) *chsd ldrs to hfwy*.............................. (50 to 1 op 20 to 1) 10

DUNMAGLASS 6-8-11 (7*) S Drowne (1) *pld hrd beh ldrs, sn behind, tld off*..................(50 to 1 op 20 to 1) 11

Dist: 4l, 5l, nk, nk, 10l, nk, 8l, 12l, 2½l, 10l. 2m 34.21s. a 4.91s (11 Ran).
SR: 9/5/-/-/-/-/ (Mrs Elaine Mitchell), P Mitchell

83 Harrington Bird Claiming Stakes CLASS F (3-y-o) £2,434 1¼m....................(1:25)

45[3] ANN HILL (Ire) 7-9 (7*) M Humphries (10) *beh, hdwy 5 fs out, led 3 out, pushed out*..............(7 to 4 op 11 to 4) 1
4755a[6] ROSIE'S GOLD 7-12 (5*) Stephen Davies (1) *trkd ldrs, led briefly o'r 3 fs out, kpt on und pres*. ....(14 to 1 op 20 to 1 tchd 33 to 1) 2
32[8] WESTRAY (Fr) 9-7 J Williams (2) *beh, hdwy o'r 4 fs out, one pace appr last*....... (40 to 1 op 16 to 1 tchd 50 to 1) 3
45[4] BUZZ-B-BABE 8-0 (7*) C Munday (6) *chsd ldrs, pushed alng and lost pl o'r 4 fs out, styd on frm over one out*. ....(50 to 1 op 25 to 1) 4
23* HONORARY GUEST 7-7 (7*) D Wright (9) *beh, effrt and hdwy o'r 3 out, styd on one pace*. (6 to 4 fav op 5 to 4) 5
60[5] EXPRESS MARIECURIE (Ire) 8-2 (7*) Madeleine Smith (8) *wth ldr till wknd o'r 2 fs out*.......(12 to 1 op 6 to 1) 6
32[4] NANNY MARGARET (Ire) (bl) 8-4 G Bardwell (7) *led aftr one furlong till hdd o'r 3 fs out, hrd rdn and wknd*. ....(9 to 1 op 8 to 1 tchd 10 to 1) 7
32 ROWLANDSONS GOLD (Ire) 8-2 J Quinn (5) *strted slwly, nvr on terms wth ldrs*............ (33 to 1 op 20 to 1) 8
4794a[9] UNIVERSAL (Fr) 9-2 Dean McKeown (11) *al beh*. .... (40 to 1 op 25 to 1 tchd 50 to 1) 9
4740a[6] STREPHON (Ire) (v) 8-5 D Biggs (4) *led one furlong, trkd ldrs till rdn and wknd o'r 4 fs out*. .... (20 to 1 op 8 to 1 tchd 25 to 1) 10
4778a GENTLE MOMENT 8-0 (7*) Gaye Harwood (3) *al beh, tld off 4 fs out*............ (25 to 1 op 12 to 1 tchd 33 to 1) 11

Dist: 2l, 5l, 6l, 2½l, 2½l, 10l, 2½l, ¾l, 2l, 10l. 2m 9.19s. a 5.99s (11 Ran).
(A S Hill), R Hollinshead

84 Daily Star Challenge Handicap Qualifier CLASS F (0-70 4-y-o and up) £2,905 1¼m....................(1:55)

20[2] SLIGHT RISK [56] (e/c) 4-9-6 G Bardwell (5) *cl up, took keen hold, led 5 fs out, clr 2 out, pushed out nr finish*. ....(3 to 1 tchd 100 to 30 and 11 to 4) 1
PRESENT TIMES [34] 7-7-8 (7*) B Russell (6) *beh, hdwy o'r 4 fs out, styd on wl frm over 2 out*. ....(7 to 1 op 8 to 1 tchd 10 to 1 and 5 to 1) 2
68* FERDIA (Ire) [65] 4-9-10 (5*,5ex) S Wynne (4) *hld up, hdwy o'r 4 fs out, one pace fnl 2 furlongs*. ....(7 to 4 fav op 6 to 4) 3
4817a[6] VA UTU [44] 5-8-6 (5*) B Doyle (2) *trkd ldrs, lost pl o'r 4 fs out, styd on*............(7 to 2 op 3 to 1 tchd 9 to 2) 4
APPLIANCEOFSCIENCE [42] 6-8-2 (7*) P McCabe (7) *trkd ldrs til rdn and wknd o'r 3 fs out*.. (33 to 1 op 16 to 1) 5
38[6] BROAD APPEAL [40] 5-8-7 J Quinn (3) *in tch, cld and ev ch 4 fs out, wknd 3 out*. (16 to 1 op 10 to 1 tchd 20 to 1) 6
59[8] MODESTO (USA) [50] 5-9-3 D Biggs (1) *led til hdd 5 fs out, sn wknd*.............. (9 to 1 op 6 to 1 tchd 10 to 1) 7

Dist: 3l, 2½l, 3l, 5l, 1l, 8l. 2m 8.34s. a 5.14s (7 Ran).
SR: 20/-/18/-/. (Mrs G E Kelleway), P A Kelleway

85 Stubbs Amateur Riders Handicap CLASS E (0-80 4-y-o and up) £3,088 1m.........(2:25)

33[2] MASTER HYDE (USA) [57] 4-11-12 Mr R Teal (3) *trkd ldrs, led o'r 2 fs out, clr over one out, ran on wl*. ....(11 to 4 fav op 9 to 2) 1
67* RIPSNORTER (Ire) [63] 4-11-13 (5*,5ex) Miss A Purdy (4) *beh, hdwy o'r 4 fs out, rdn and styd on wl ins last*. .... (15 to 2 op 6 to 1 tchd 8 to 1) 2
THUNDERING [28] 8-9-12 Miss I Diana W Jones (12) *cl up, led briefly o'r 2 fs out, one pace*....(25 to 1 op 12 to 1) 3
12[9] BILL MOON [47] 7-11-3 Miss J Feilden (7) *in tch, cld hfwy, effrt and one pace fnl 2 fs*............... (8 to 1 op 6 to 1) 4
43[5] NORTHERN CONQUEROR (Ire) [38] 5-10-3 (5*) Mrs J Naughton (2) *beh, styd on frm o'r one furlong out, nvr on terms*.......................... (14 to 1 op 10 to 1) 5
67[9] BREEZED WELL [56] 7-11-7 (5*) Mrs H Noonan (1) *chsd ldrs til wknd 3 fs out*.................. (20 to 1 op 14 to 1) 6
41[4] RURAL LAD [59] 4-11-9 (5*) Miss S Kelleway (9) *led til hdd o'r 2 fs out, wknd*..... (12 to 1 op 8 to 1 tchd 14 to 1) 7
43[2] NORTH FLYER [50] 4-11-0 (5*) Mr N Miles (5) *chsd ldrs till wknd o'r 3 fs out*.................... (4 to 1 op 6 to 1) 8
20[4] SAMURAI GOLD (USA) [50] (v) 5-11-1 (5*) Mr E James (8) *trkd ldrs till wknd wl o'r 2 fs out*.. (25 to 1 op 20 to 1) 9
4806a[9] WAYWARD SON [38] (bl) 4-10-2 (5*) Miss M Bridger (6) *strted slwly, al beh*......................(33 to 1 op 20 to 1) 10
67[2] ALBERT [33] 6-10-3 Miss E Bronson (10) *beh, nvr rch challening pos*..............................(7 to 2 op 7 to 4) 11
4817a MARDIOR [25] 5-9-7[3] (5*) Mr G Kille (11) *cl up 2 fs, sn wknd, tld off*.............................(25 to 1 op 20 to 1) 12

Dist: 2½l, 2½l, 2l, 3½l, nk, 3l, nk, 1l, 2½l, 1½l. 1m 42.46s. a 6.26s (12 Ran).
SR: 4/2/-/-/-/-/ (Hyde Sporting Promotions/Saddlehome Farm), P Mitchell

86 Cecil Aldin Handicap CLASS F (0-70 4-y-o and up) £2,521 5f....................(2:55)

47* SOBA GUEST (Ire) [64] 4-9-7 (3*) Emma O'Gorman (6) *beh, rapid hdwy on outsd o'r one furlong out, led ins last, sn clr*...............(4 to 1 fav op 3 to 1 tchd 9 to 2) 1
4768a[6] LYNDON'S LINNET [55] 5-9-1 A McGlone (2) *sn pushed alng, beh, hdwy on ins o'r one furlong out, kpt on wl*. ....(8 to 1 op 5 to 1) 2
10[2] EWALD (Ire) [50] 5-8-10 Dean McKeown (7) *wth ldr, ev ch appr fnl furlong, kpt on one pace*. ....(10 to 1 op 7 to 1 tchd 11 to 1) 3
6[3] LE CHIC [54] 7-9-0 S Wood (10) *trkd ldrs, ev ch appr fnl furlong, one pace*...................(11 to 2 op 4 to 1) 4
4818a[2] TOMMY TEMPEST [40] (bl) 4-7-7 (7*) T Williams (8) *led til hdd ins fnl furlong, wknd cl hme*. (8 to 1 tchd 12 to 1) 5
4701a SIMMIE'S SPECIAL [52] 5-8-5 (7*) M Humphries (9) *nvr on terms*.......................(16 to 1 op 10 to 1 tchd 20 to 1) 6
28[5] SIR TASKER [68] 5-10-0 J Quinn (1) *sn pushed alng, chsd ldrs till rdn and wknd o'r one furlong out*. ....(5 to 1 tchd 9 to 2 and 11 to 2) 7
4818a[3] SERIOUS HURRY [52] (bl) 5-8-12 J Williams (5) *nvr on terms*...............................(9 to 2 op 7 to 1) 8
36[7] RUSHANES [58] 6-9-4 D Biggs (4) *sn beh*. ....(6 to 1 op 12 to 1) 9
19[5] FOUROFUS [47] 4-8-0 (7*) T G McLaughlin (3) *sn outpcd*. ....(50 to 1 op 33 to 1) 10

Dist: 2½l, ½l, ¾l, 2l, ½l, 5l, 1½l, 2l, nk. 59.14s. a 0.94s (10 Ran).
SR: 56/37/30/31/9/19/15/-/-/ (Richard Jinks), J Berry

87 Ladbroke All Weather Trophy Handicap Qualifier CLASS E (0-70 3-y-o and up) £3,106 7f..................................(3:25)

4816a[4] KISSAVOS [62] (v) 7-9-5 (5*) B Doyle (8) *trkd ldrs, led appr fnl furlong, rdn out*................ (9 to 1 op 5 to 1) 1
48[2] KILLICK [48] 5-8-10 J Quinn (12) *cl up, led 4 fs out till hdd o'r 2 out, kpt on wl*.. (7 to 2 fav op 4 to 1 tchd 5 to 1) 2
48[3] SARUM [57] 7-9-5 Dale Gibson (13) *mid-div, rdn and hdwy 3 fs out, kpt on und pres*...... (7 to 1 op 5 to 1) 3
4725a[8] MADAGANS GREY [65] 5-9-13 M Tebbutt (7) *mid-div, hdwy o'r one furlong out, kpt on und pres ins last, better for race*...............................(5 to 1 op 10 to 1) 4
APOLLO RED [49] 4-8-11 A McGlone (1) *chsd ldrs, rdn and one pace fnl 2 fs*.............................(33 to 1) 5
36[5] MEESON TIMES [57] 5-9-5 M Hills (15) *wth ldr, led o'r 2 fs out till hdd appr last, wknd cl hme*. ....(8 to 1 tchd 10 to 1) 6
36* NOBBY BARNES [60] 4-9-8 J Williams (10) *beh, rdn and hdwy o'r one furlong out, not pace to chal*. .... (11 to 2 op 5 to 1 tchd 6 to 1) 7
24[2] PIGALLE WONDER [52] 5-9-0 D Biggs (4) *led til hdd 4 fs out, rallied und pres o'r one out, wknd ins last*. .... (6 to 1 op 5 to 1 tchd 13 to 2) 8
4789a NELLIE DEAN [54] 4-8-9 (7*) D Wright (6) *al beh*. .... (14 to 1 op 8 to 1 tchd 16 to 1) 9
MUSIC DANCER [59] 4-9-7 J McLaughlin (2) *trkd ldrs to hfwy*.............................. (16 to 1 op 14 to 1) 10
11[7] HARDLINER [63] 4-9-6 (5*) K Rutter (14) *trkd ldrs til wknd o'r 3 fs out*........................ (25 to 1 op 16 to 1) 11
43[8] MASRUR (USA) [59] 4-9-7 S Dawson (3) *strted slwly, al beh*................ (20 to 1 op 14 to 1 tchd 25 to 1) 12
12 EMAURA [47] 4-8-9 Dean McKeown (11) *nvr gng wl, al beh*................ (20 to 1 op 14 to 1 tchd 25 to 1) 13
BELJINSKI [31] 5-7-7 G Bardwell (9) *al beh, tld off*. ....(50 to 1) 14

Dist: 2l, hd, sht-hd, nk, 3½l, sht-hd, ½l, 2l, nk, 5l. 1m 26.49s. a 3.09s (14 Ran).
SR: 27/7/15/22/5/2/4/-/-/ (Richard Berenson), C C Elsey

CAGNES-SUR-MER (FR) (good)
Sunday January 24th

88 Prix des Camelias (c & g) (3-y-o) £5,974 1m.................................(1:50)

BAISER PAPIER VOLE (Fr) 8-11 R Laplanche,............. 1
AFFIRMED MINISTER (USA) 8-11 M Boutin,.............. 2
DEEP WINNER (Ire) 8-11 M de Smyter,................ 3
SOLDIERS BAY 8-11 G Guignard,...................... 4

Dist: 1l, 1l, sht-hd, nk, 2l. 1m 47.70s. (17 Ran).
(B Giraudon), C Maillard

89 Prix Firouzan (fillies) (3-y-o) £5,974 1m (2:15)

SISKEI (Fr) 8-11 C Le Scrill,.......................... 1
MYKERINA (USA) 8-11 R Laplanche,.................... 2
RODERLINDA (Fr) 8-11 L Pascouau,.................... 3
MOUNTAIN WILLOW 8-11 G Guignard,................. 0

Dist: 1l, 3l, 1l, 1l, 1l. 1m 41.70s. (19 Ran).
(Mme R Seibert), Mme R Seibert

90 Prix Henri et Roger Cravoisier (Lady Riders) (4-y-o and up) £4,182 1m 3f.......... (3:10)

MARGANCE (Fr) 5-9-6 Mme J Rossi,..................... 1
REINE KAMI (Fr) 4-8-12 Mlle C Grosse,................. 2
HIERARCH (USA) 4-8-11 Mlle M Fougy,.................. 3

Dist: Dist, 1l, 6½l, ½l. 2m 25.80s. (9 Ran).
(F Di Lorenzo), A Rossio

SOUTHWELL (A.W) (std)
Monday January 25th
Going Correction: PLUS 0.25 sec. per fur.

91 **Mars Apprentice Handicap CLASS F (0-70 4-y-o and up) £2,406 7f. . . . . (1:50)**

4705a LORD NASKRA (USA) [54] (bl) 4-9-5 Emma O'Gorman (13) *al prmnt, wide strt, effrt 2 fs out, rdn and styd on to ld nr finish*. . . . .(14 to 1 op 10 to 1 tchd 16 to 1) 1
54[2] ON Y VA (USA) [59] 6-9-7 (3*) G Mitchell (2) *al prmnt, hdwy on inner to ld 2 fs out, rdn appr last, hdd and no extr nr finish*. . . . .(4 to 1 fav tchd 5 to 1) 2
67[4] DIAMOND INTHE DARK (USA) [53] (v) 5-9-4 O Pears (12) *cl up, ev ch 2 fs out, rdn and one pace appr fnl furlong*. . . . .(6 to 1 tchd 7 to 1) 3
10[3] MU-ARRIK [43] (bl) 5-8-5 (3*) G Parkin (7) *cl up, ev ch 2 fs out, sn rdn and one paced*. . . . .(14 to 1 op 12 to 1) 4
48[4] DANCING SENSATION (USA) [28] (bl) 6-7-4 (3*) D Wright (9) *hdwy hfwy, rdn 2 fs out, styd on fnl furlong*. . . . . (17 to 2 op 6 to 1 tchd 9 to 1) 5
67[3] SOL ROUGE (Ire) [34] 4-7-13 B Russell (1) *cl up, led hfwy, hdd 2 fs out, grad wknd*. . . . .(12 to 1 op 10 to 1) 6
41[3] GIRTON DEGREE [41] 4-8-6 K Rutter (6) *hdwy hfwy, rdn 2 fs out, no imprsn*. . . . .(14 to 1 op 10 to 1) 7
54[3] THE DREAM MAKER (Ire) [45] 4-8-10 M Humphries (10) *prmnt, rdn 2 and a half fs out, sn wknd*. . . . .(6 to 1 op 7 to 1 tchd 8 to 1) 8
4812a PARISIENNE KING (USA) [38] (bl) 4-8-3[12] (5*) T Ashley (11) *sn pushed alng, al rear*. . . . .(50 to 1) 9
54 PREMIER ENVELOPE (Ire) [37] 4-8-2 C Munday (5) *mid-div, rdn hfwy, sn beh*. . . . .(33 to 1) 10
49[5] INNOCENT GEORGE [53] 4-9-4 S D Williams (4) *nvr rch ldrs*. . . . .(14 to 1 op 10 to 1) 11
41* COMPANY CASH [50] (bl) 5-9-1 H Bastiman (3) *dwlt, hdwy to chase ldrs hfwy, sn rdn and wknd*. . . . .(9 to 2 op 4 to 1) 12
41[5] GRUBBY [42] 4-8-2 (5*) J Dennis (8) *led to hfwy, sn wknd*. . . . . (16 to 1 op 20 to 1) 13

Dist: ¾l, 1l, 1½l, 1l, 5l, nk, nk, 12l, 1½l, 1½l. 1m 32.10s. a 6.00s (13 Ran).
SR: 41/44/35/20/2/-/-/2/-/ (Curley O'Gorman), W A O'Gorman

92 **Venus Claiming Stakes CLASS F (4-y-o) £2,238 1½m. . . . . (2:20)**

43[3] ANNACURRAGH (Ire) 8-0 J Quinn (6) *hld up, hdwy 4 fs out, chsd ldr 2 out, sn rdn, styd on wl to ld ins last*. . . . .(6 to 5 on op 5 to 4 on tchd Evens) 1
53[8] BAHER (USA) 8-13 D Nicholls (2) *cl up, led 7 fs out, quickened clr 2 and a half out, rdn wl o'r one out, hdd and no extr ins last*. . . . .(16 to 1 op 12 to 1) 2
4763a[4] KARAMOJA 8-11 Dean McKeown (3) *trkd ldrs, effrt and rdn 3 fs out, sn one paced*. . . . . (6 to 1 op 5 to 1) 3
FUTURES GIFT (Ire) 8-7 S Webster (7) *hld up, hdwy 4 fs out, sn rdn, not rch ldrs*. . . . .(25 to 1 op 16 to 1) 4
VALSEUR (USA) 8-7 J Fanning (5) *led 5 fs, cl up till rdn and wknd 4 out*. . . . .(8 to 1 op 7 to 2) 5
42[9] PERSIAN FLEECE 8-0 L Charnock (1) *prmnt till rdn and wknd o'r 3 fs out*. . . . .(10 to 1 op 8 to 1) 6
46[5] IRON BARON (Ire) 8-9 W Ryan (8) *trkd ldrs, effrt 3 fs out, sn rdn and wknd 2 furlongs out*. . . . . (5 to 1 op 7 to 2) 7
LIVE AND LET FLY 8-11 S Wood (4) *in tch, pushed alng 6 fs out, wknd o'r 4 out, sn tld off*. . . . . (10 to 1 op 16 to 1) 8

Dist: 1½l, 12l, 2½l, 1l, 6l, 5l, 15l. 2m 45.30s. a 11.40s (8 Ran).
SR: 2/12/-/-/-/ (C John Hill), C J Hill

93 **Jupiter Handicap CLASS F (0-75 3-y-o) £2,406 1m. . . . . (2:50)**

40* BROUGHTONS FORMULA [54] (bl) 8-8 (7*) D McCabe (7) *beh, hdwy o'r 3 fs out, str run over one out, led ins last, sn clr*. . . . . (9 to 4 jt-fav tchd 5 to 2) 1
63* NIKKI NOO NOO [61] 9-8 (5ex) J Quinn (1) *mid-div, gd hdwy 3 fs out, led o'r one out, sn rdn, headway and no extr ins last*. . . . .(100 to 30 op 5 to 2 tchd 7 to 2) 2
71[6] TACITURN (USA) [43] (bl) 8-4 G Duffield (3) *led, rdn o'r 2 fs out, hdd and wknd over one out*. . . . .(8 to 1 op 7 to 1) 3
51[7] ROBIX (Ire) [47] (bl) 8-8 S Wood (5) *trkd ldrs, effrt and hdwy 2 and a half fs out, sn rdn, wknd one and a half out*. . . . .(9 to 4 jt-fav op 2 to 1 tchd 11 to 4) 4
62[3] SCOFFERA [47] 8-8 Kim Tinkler (2) *chsd ldr till rdn and wknd 2 and a half fs out*. . . . . (5 to 1 op 7 to 1) 5
SONG IN YOUR HEART [42] 8-3 J Fanning (6) *sn rdn alng and beh, wide strt*. . . . .(25 to 1 op 20 to 1) 6
62[7] KEATING (Aus) [60] 9-7 D Nicholls (4) *mid-div, rdn hfwy, sn wknd and beh*. . . . .(20 to 1) 7

Dist: 3½l, 5l, 1l, ½l, 10l, 25l. 1m 47.30s. a 8.30s (7 Ran).
SR: 6/2/-/-/ (Broughton Thermal Insulation), W J Musson

94 **Saturn Claiming Stakes CLASS F (4-y-o and up) £2,343 2m. . . . .(3:20)**

81[2] TEMPERING 7-9-7 S Wood (10) *hld up, hdwy to ld aftr 6 fs, clr o'r 3 out, unchlgd*. . . . .(6 to 4 on op 3 to 1 on tchd 11 to 8 on) 1
65[5] AMOUR ROYAL 6-9-0 D Nicholls (8) *in tch, rdn o'r 3 fs out, styd on one pace*. . . . . . (9 to 1 op 7 to 1 tchd 10 to 1) 2
CITY LINE 4-8-4 (3*) A Tucker (1) *chsd ldrs, rdn and outpcd 4 fs out, styd on fnl 2 furlongs*. . . . . . (8 to 1 op 6 to 1) 3
65[6] CARDEA CASTLE (Ire) 5-8-5 J Quinn (2) *led 6 fs, chsd wnr, rdn 3 furlongs out, wknd wl o'r one out*. . . . . (40 to 1 op 33 to 1) 4
65[2] LORD ADVOCATE (v) 5-8-11 Alex Greaves (3) *prmnt, rdn 4 fs out, grad wknd*. . . . .(11 to 2 op 6 to 1 tchd 5 to 1) 5
MASTER FOODBROKER (Ire) 5-8-7 (7*) D McCabe (11) *sn beh, styd on fnl 4 fs, not rch ldrs*. . . . .(7 to 1 op 5 to 1 tchd 8 to 1) 6
67 RESISTING (USA) 5-8-13 (3*) S D Williams (4) *nvr a factor*. . . . . (50 to 1 op 33 to 1) 7
CASUAL PASS 10-8-11 J Fanning (7) *mid-div, effrt and hdwy 7 fs out, sn rdn and wknd quickly 4 out*. . . . . (12 to 1 op 33 to 1 tchd 50 to 1) 8
MRSUNVALLEYPEANUTS 7-8-12[3] (5*) S Wynne (5) *chsd ldrs, wknd 6 fs out, sn tld off*. . . . . (50 to 1 op 33 to 1) 9
MOUNTAIN GLOW 6-8-12 T Williams (9) *sn beh, tld off fnl 4 fs*. . . . .(40 to 1 op 33 to 1) 10

Dist: 6l, ¾l, ½l, 3½l, 8l, 8l, 6l, dist, 4l. 3m 52.00s. a 25.50s (10 Ran).
(David W Chapman), D W Chapman

95 **Earth Maiden Stakes CLASS F (3-y-o) £2,070 7f. . . . . (3:50)**

51[3] ROSE FLYER (Ire) 8-2 (7*) D McCabe (3) *made all, quickened clr 2 and a half fs out, rdn o'r one out, unchlgd*. . . . . (2 to 1 fav op 7 to 4 tchd 9 to 4 and 5 to 2) 1
4730a PRINCE OF SOUL 9-0 J McLaughlin (2) *chsd ldrs, rdn alng 3 fs out, kpt on one pace*. . . . . (16 to 1 op 14 to 1) 2
51[4] GUSSIE FINK-NOTTLE (Ire) 9-0 Alex Greaves (5) *chsd wnr, rdn o'r 2 fs out, sn one paced*. . . . .(85 to 40 op 7 to 4 tchd 5 to 2 and 11 to 4) 3
63[5] PARIS BY NIGHT (Ire) 8-9 G Bardwell (7) *mid-div, rdn alng hfwy, styd on fnl 2 fs, nvr dngrs*. . . . .(5 to 1 op 2 to 1) 4
44[6] GREY PRIDE (bl) 9-0 L Charnock (6) *chsd ldrs, rdn wl o'r 2 fs out, sn wknd*. . . . . (10 to 1 op 7 to 1) 5
VADDALLIAN 9-0 W Ryan (1) *slwly into strd, al rear*. . . . .(6 to 1 op 8 to 1) 6
BUDBY PRINCESS 8-9 Dean McKeown (4) *slwly into rear, al beh*. . . . .(7 to 1 op 12 to 1) 7
63[7] MEESON IMPOSSIBLE 9-0 T Williams (8) *al rear*. . . . .(20 to 1 op 16 to 1) 8

Dist: 7l, 1½l, ½l, 15l, 7l, ½l, 2l. 1m 33.40s. a 7.30s (8 Ran).
SR: 12/-/-/-/-/ (A M Packaging Ltd), M C Chapman

96 **Pluto Handicap CLASS F (0-70 4-y-o and up) £2,343 6f. . . . . (4:20)**

6 LINCSTONE BOY (Ire) [51] (bl) 5-9-4 S Webster (7) *made all, quickened clr o'r 2 fs out, rdn and styd on fnl furlong*. . . . . (9 to 1 op 11 to 2) 1
4719a KALAR [40] 4-8-7 S Wood (5) *al chasing ldrs, rdn 2 fs out, kpt on fnl furlong*. . . . .(9 to 1 op 6 to 1) 2
47[8] SAMSOLOM [54] 5-9-7 M Tebbutt (6) *chsd ldrs, rdn 2 fs out, styd on*. . . . .(5 to 1 op 6 to 1 tchd 9 to 2) 3
50[4] EMERALD EARS [36] 4-7-10 (7*) S Drowne (9) *chsd ldrs, effrt and rdn o'r 2 fs out, kpt on one pace fnl furlong*. . . . .(8 to 1 tchd 10 to 1) 4
4774a MISS BELL RINGER [32] 5-7-13 G Bardwell (10) *sn pushed alng, wide strt, hdwy 2 fs out, soon rdn and styd on fnl furlong*. . . . . (8 to 1 op 6 to 1 tchd 9 to 1) 5
6[7] STRIP CARTOON (Ire) [47] 5-9-0 J Quinn (2) *chsd ldrs, rdn o'r 2 fs out, kpt on one pace*. . . . . (11 to 2 op 4 to 1) 6
47[4] JOVIAL KATE (USA) [51] 6-9-4 T Williams (11) *cl up, effrt and rdn o'r 2 fs out, grad wknd*. . (4 to 1 fav op 9 to 2) 7
4775a[8] IMCO DOUBLE (Ire) [50] 5-9-3 J McLaughlin (8) *cl up till rdn and wknd o'r 2 fs out*. . . . .(8 to 1 op 14 to 1) 8
JUST BOB [61] 4-9-7 (7*) M Humphries (3) *dwlt, al rear*. . . . . (20 to 1 op 14 to 1) 9
MANULEADER [53] (bl) 4-9-6 D Nicholls (4) *slwly into strd, al rear*. . . . . (25 to 1 op 14 to 1) 10
WOOD KAY (Ire) [58] 4-9-11 W Ryan (1) *outpcd, al rear*. . . . .(14 to 1 op 10 to 1 tchd 16 to 1 and 20 to 1) 11

Dist: 2l, ¾l, nk, sht-hd, 1l, 1½l, ¾l, ¾l, 5l, 3l. 1m 18.40s. a 5.00s (11 Ran).
SR: 34/15/26/7/2/13/11/7/15/ (Mrs J Addleshaw), S R Bowring

CAGNES-SUR-MER (FR) (good)
Wednesday January 27th

97 **Prix Joseph Collignon (3-y-o) £8,363 1m 110yds. . . . . (2:40)**

WAKRIA (Ire) 8-9 M Boutin, ... 1
BURD KING (Fr) 9-2 W Mongil, ... 2
RESARIO (Fr) 8-9 A Junk, ... 3
4800a* I'LLEAVEITOYOU (Ire) 8-13 O Peslier, ... 5

Dist: 1l, hd, sht-hd, 1½l, sht-hd. 1m 46.60s. (14 Ran).
(Sultan Al Kabeer), R Collet

LINGFIELD (A.W) (std)
Thursday January 28th

Going Correction: MINUS 0.30 sec. per fur.

98 Hungerford Claiming Stakes CLASS F (3-y-o) £2,377 1m.......................... (1:40)

80^3 MARK'S CLUB (Ire) (bl) 8-1 Alex Greaves (3) *in rear early, hdwy to join ldr aftr 3 fs, led o'r 2 out, came wide into strt, ran on wl*..................(4 to 1 tchd 9 to 2) 1
60^3 ERLKING (Ire) 9-1 Dean McKeown (5) *pld hrd, led till hdd o'r 2 fs out, ev ch till rdn and one pace entering last.* ....(9 to 4 on op 6 to 4 on) 2
$4809a^6$ GENESIS FOUR (bl) 7-9[1] (5*) B Doyle (2) *in rear, styd on und pres ins fnl 2 fs.* (50 to 1 op 25 to 1 tchd 100 to 1) 3
21^4 MISS DELIVERY 7-12 J Quinn (4) *chsd ldr for 3 fs, sn rdn, no hdwy fnl three*....(33 to 1 op 14 to 1 tchd 50 to 1) 4
80^4 MRS SNUGGS (Ire) 7-8 Dale Gibson (1) *slwly into strd, lost tch fnl 3 fs*.......................... (4 to 1 op 6 to 1) 5
Dist: 6l, 6l, 3l, 10l. 1m 41.15s. a 4.95s (5 Ran).
(Stephen Woodall), T D Barron

99 Chelsea Handicap CLASS E (0-80 4-y-o and up) £3,231 5f........................ (2:10)

MISTER JOLSON [58] 4-8-2 (7*) S Drowne (4) *nvr far away, rdn and ran on to ld ins fnl furlong.* (10 to 1 op 7 to 1) 1
$4783a^4$ LITTLE SABOTEUR [67] 4-9-4 W Ryan (1) *chsd ldrs, rdn o'r one furlong out, ran on wl to go second cl hme.* .... (10 to 1 op 7 to 1 tchd 12 to 1) 2
86^4 LE CHIC [54] 7-8-5 S Wood (10) *made most on outsd till rdn and hdd wl ins fnl furlong*..... (10 to 1 op 8 to 1) 3
70^3 RHYTHMIC DANCER [75] 5-9-12 J Williams (3) *chsd ldrs, rdn appr fnl furlong, kpt on one pace.* ....(4 to 1 tchd 5 to 1) 4
70^2 RUNNING GLIMPSE (Ire) [77] 5-9-7 (7*) A Martinez (8) *beh till ran on ins fnl furlong*... (5 to 1 op 7 to 2 tchd 6 to 1) 5
56^2 TINO TERE [75] 4-9-5 (7*) P Roberts (9) *wth ldr till wknd o'r one furlong out*...................(7 to 1 op 4 to 1) 6
76^3 MARTINA [63] 5-9-0 J Quinn (5) *prmnt early, rdn hfwy, sn btn*.................. (8 to 1 op 6 to 1 tchd 9 to 1) 7
86^8 SERIOUS HURRY [52] 5-7-12 (5*) B Doyle (6) *al beh.* .... (14 to 1 op 10 to 1 tchd 16 to 1) 8
6* HINARI VIDEO [54] 8-8-5 Dean McKeown (2) *al struggling in rear*............. (7 to 2 fav op 4 to 1 tchd 9 to 2) 9
86^7 SIR TASKER [68] 5-9-2 (3*) S D Williams (7) *al outpcd.* .... (14 to 1 op 12 to 1 tchd 16 to 1) 10
Dist: 1½l, 1½l, hd, hd, 2l, ¾l, ¾l, ¾l, 1l. 59.20s. a 1.00s (10 Ran).
SR: 45/48/29/49/50/40/25/11/10/ (J W Mursell), R J Hodges

100 Alpine Double Glazing Maiden Stakes CLASS F (3-y-o) £2,208 1m......... (2:40)

DEE RAFT (USA) 9-0 Dean McKeown (5) *trkd ldr, led o'r 2 fs out, sn drw clr, easily.* ....(3 to 1 on op 4 to 1 on tchd 11 to 4 on) 1
$4766a^6$ NYMPH ERRANT 8-9 W Ryan (1) *beh till rdn and hdwy 2 fs out, ran on to go second ins last.* ....(8 to 1 op 6 to 1 tchd 9 to 1) 2
60^4 MEDLAND (Ire) 9-0 J Quinn (2) *beh, rdn and hdwy hfwy, chsd wnr 2 fs out till wknd ins last.* (10 to 1 op 12 to 1) 3
ASCOM PAGER TOO 8-9 B Crossley (3) *chsd ldrs early, sn beh.*..................................(33 to 1 op 12 to 1) 4
57^3 GENERAL LINK 9-0 G Bardwell (4) *led, rdn 3 fs out, sn hdd, drpd out quickly*........ (5 to 1 op 9 to 2 tchd 6 to 1) 5
Dist: 4l, 1l, 10l, 1l. 1m 41.16s. a 4.96s (5 Ran).
(D O Pickering), B W Hills

101 Vauxhall Handicap CLASS D (0-80 4-y-o and up) £3,655 7f...................(3:10)

38^2 SPENCER'S REVENGE [73] 4-9-6 Dean McKeown (9) *al prmnt on outsd, led o'r one furlong out, pushed clr ins last*...................................(7 to 2 op 9 to 4) 1
39^4 BOLD HABIT [66] 8-8-8 (5*) Stephen Davies (7) *in rear till gd hdwy 2 fs out, ev ch appr last, rdn and outpcd.* ....(7 to 2 tchd 4 to 1) 2
87^3 SARUM [57] 7-8-4 Dale Gibson (5) *nvr far away, rdn o'r 2 fs out, hdwy appr last, no imprsn on 1st two.* ....(3 to 1 fav op 4 to 1 tchd 9 to 2) 3
76^2 APPLEDORN [81] 6-10-0 D Biggs (3) *slwly away, sn in tch, rdn 2 fs out, styd on ins last*......... (4 to 1 op 5 to 2) 4
12^7 ALBERT THE BOLD [64] (bl,e/s) 4-8-11 J Williams (6) *sn trkd ldr, led hfwy, hdd o'r one furlong out, one pace.* .... (9 to 1 op 7 to 1 tchd 10 to 1) 5
56^4 MAC'S FIGHTER [81] (bl) 8-9-7 (7*) B Russell (4) *trkd ldr early, rdn 2 fs out, wknd appr last.* (7 to 1 tchd 8 to 1) 6
$4781a^4$ MOGWAI (Ire) [59] (bl) 4-8-6 W Ryan (1) *al beh.* ....(16 to 1 op 10 to 1 tchd 20 to 1) 7
33^6 BUSTER [72] 5-9-5 G Bardwell (8) *led till rdn and hdd hfwy, wknd quickly*............. (50 to 1 op 33 to 1) 8
Dist: 3½l, 1l, 1½l, sht-hd, 3l, 8l, 4l. 1m 25.77s. a 2.37s (8 Ran).
SR: 39/21/9/28/10/18/-/-/ (Lord Crawshaw), Lord Huntingdon

102 Westminster Claiming Stakes CLASS F (4-y-o and up) £2,534 1½m............ (3:40)

46^4 BREAKDANCER (Ire) 4-8-9 J Williams (2) *wtd wth in rear, hdwy o'r 4 fs out, led 3 out, sn clr, easily.* ....(5 to 2 on op 7 to 2 on tchd 2 to 1 on) 1
$4723a^8$ SHARP DANCE 4-7-10 J Quinn (1) *led till hdd 3 fs out, kpt on one pace*..........................(11 to 4 op 3 to 1) 2
GONE BUST (Ire) 4-8-6 W Ryan (3) *trkd ldr, rdn o'r 3 fs out, sn btn*..............................(8 to 1 op 3 to 1) 3
46^8 SALIC DANCE 5-8-0 (5*) Stephen Davies (4) *in tch till wknd o'r 4 fs out*.......................... (33 to 1 op 20 to 1) 4
Dist: 12l, 12l, 2½l. 2m 35.28s. a 5.98s (4 Ran).
(J Jannaway), W R Muir

103 Albert Handicap CLASS F (0-70 4-y-o and up) £2,807 1½m...................(4:10)

85 ALBERT [36] 6-7-8[1] J Quinn (6) *hld up, rdn and hdwy o'r 4 fs out, led one and a half out, pushed clr.* ....(3 to 1 fav tchd 4 to 1 and 9 to 2) 1
$4816a^7$ FALCON FLIGHT [49] 7-8-4 (3*) A Tucker (8) *chsd ldrs, rdn and ev ch appr fnl furlong, kpt on one pace.* ....(6 to 1 op 3 to 1 tchd 7 to 1) 2
46* NASEER (USA) [47] 4-8-1 T Williams (3) *beh, pushed alng frm hfwy, hdwy o'r 2 fs out, one pace entering last.* ....(7 to 2 tchd 4 to 1) 3
34^5 VINTAGE [70] 8-10-0 J Williams (5) *mid-div, hdwy to ld o'r 3 fs out, hdd one and a half out, one pace.* ....(5 to 1 op 4 to 1 tchd 11 to 2) 4
BY ARRANGEMENT (Ire) [47] 4-7-10 (5*) B Doyle (9) *slwly away, sn in tch, hdwy to go second 5 out, one pace fnl 3 fs*....................(10 to 1 op 8 to 1 tchd 12 to 1) 5
61^6 BURRACOPPIN [35] 6-7-7 G Bardwell (2) *led till hdd o'r 3 fs out, rdn and wknd over 2 out.* ....(33 to 1 op 20 to 1 tchd 50 to 1) 6
73^5 FLASH OF STRAW (Ire) [40] 4-7-1 (7*) D Wright (4) *al beh, nvr on terms*......................(5 to 1 tchd 7 to 1) 7
68^4 WITH GUSTO [47] 6-8-5 D Biggs (7) *prmnt till wknd 4 fs out*.................... (8 to 1 op 7 to 1 tchd 9 to 1) 8
UP ALL NIGHT [46] 4-8-0 Dale Gibson (1) *chsd ldr till wknd quickly 5 fs out, tld off*...........(20 to 1 op 12 to 1) 9
Dist: 2½l, 4l, 3½l, 2½l, 4l, 2½l, 1½l, 30l. 2m 34.99s. a 5.69s (9 Ran).
(T S M S Riley-Smith), D A Wilson

CAGNES-SUR-MER (FR) (good)
Friday January 29th

104 Prix Robert de Villeneuve-Bargemon (4-y-o and up) £8,961 1m 5f...........(1:25)

$4754a^3$ MARILDO (Fr) 6-8-9 G Guignard,........................ 1
DANAE DE BRULE (Fr) 6-9-1 R Laplanche,............... 2
INDIA DANCER (Fr) 4-8-9 W Mongil,..................... 3
75^8 FLY AWAY SOON (USA) 5-8-9 J Reid,.................... 8
Dist: 1l, 4l, nk, 2½l, hd. 2m 50.30s. (10 Ran).
(D Smaga), D Smaga

105 Prix Renoir (3-y-o) £7,168 1¼m..... (1:50)

VILLAGE STORM (Fr) 9-2 O Peslier,...................... 1
NOBILIUM (Fr) 8-13 R Laplanche,....................... 2
SHARPELA 8-13 M Boutin,............................... 3
74^7 SALBUS 8-9 J Reid,.................................... 5
Dist: Sht-hd, 2½l, 1l, hd, sht-hd. 2m 6.30s. (16 Ran).
(Mrs Janet Salz), A de Moussac

SOUTHWELL (A.W) (std)
Friday January 29th

Going Correction: PLUS 0.30 sec. per fur.

106 Annesley Handicap CLASS F (0-90 3-y-o) £2,259 6f......................... (1:55)

66* PLAY HEVER GOLF [73] 9-8 (7ex) W Ryan (6) *made all, quickened 2 fs out, styd on strly*..... (4 to 1 op 3 to 1) 1
60^2 STARDUST EXPRESS [61] 8-10 Dean McKeown (5) *chsd wnr, rdn 2 fs out, kpt on one pace.* (5 to 1 tchd 9 to 2) 2
66^4 COMET WHIRLPOOL (Ire) [58] (bl) 8-7 J Quinn (4) *chsd ldrs, effrt 2 fs out, sn rdn and one pace.* .... (6 to 1 op 5 to 1 tchd 13 to 2) 3
63^3 LARN FORT [49] (bl) 7-12 J Fanning (1) *beh, hdwy hfwy, sn rdn and no imprsn*..... (13 to 2 op 6 to 1 tchd 7 to 1) 4
29^3 MISSED THE BOAT (Ire) [57] 7-13 (7*) V Halliday (7) *beh, wide strt, sn rdn and no real hdwy*......(7 to 1 tchd 8 to 1) 5
37* DAANIERA (Ire) [72] 9-4 (3*) Emma O'Gorman (3) *hld up in tch, gd hdwy 3 fs out, chalg and ev ch 2 furlongs out, sn rdn, wknd wl o'r one furlong out.* ....(9 to 4 fav op 2 to 1) 6
4708a MATTHEW DAVID [63] 8-5 (7*) J Marshall (2) *chsd ldrs, rdn hfwy, sn wknd*....................(25 to 1 op 20 to 1) 7
Dist: 2l, 1½l, 2½l, 2l, 3½l, 10l. 1m 18.00s. a 4.60s (7 Ran).
SR: 52/32/23/4/4/5/-/ (R A Popely), T J Naughton

107 Danethorpe Maiden Stakes CLASS F (4-y-o and up) £2,070 6f............... (2:25)

76^6 BUZBOUR 5-9-0 S Wood (8) *trkd ldrs, gd hdwy 2 and a half fs out, led appr fnl furlong, kpt on.* ....(6 to 1 tchd 7 to 1) 1

4783a^{6} LAST STRAW 5-8-9 (5*) O Pears (2) *led, rdn 2 fs out, hdd o'r one furlong out, ran on und pres.* ....(10 to 1 op 14 to 1) 2
WEE SARAH 5-8-9 Alex Greaves (5) *beh, styd on wl fnl 2 fs, nrst finish*.......... (8 to 1 op 6 to 1) 3
77^{2} EXPRESS SERVICE (bl) 4-8-11 (3*) Emma O'Gorman (1) *in tch, effrt and hdwy 2 and a half fs out, sn rdn and one pace*..........(2 to 1 fav op 7 to 4 tchd 5 to 2) 4
47^{2} HONEY VISION (bl) 4-8-9 G Bardwell (3) *chsd ldr, rdn o'r 2 fs out, sn btn*..........(9 to 4 tchd 2 to 1 and 5 to 2) 5
77^{3} BAYIN (USA) 4-8-7 (7*) D Wright (4) *nvr rch ldrs.* ....(12 to 1 op 14 to 1) 6
91^{7} GIRTON DEGREE 4-8-9 Dean McKeown (7) *prmnt, effrt o'r 2 fs out, sn rdn and wknd.* ....(9 to 1 op 6 to 1 tchd 10 to 1) 7
LOS ANGELES (Ire) 4-8-9 J Fanning (6) *prmnt 3 fs, sn wknd and beh*..........(7 to 1 op 7 to 2) 8
4756a OFFAS IMAGE 5-9-0 D Biggs (9) *slwly away, al beh.* ....(33 to 1) 9
Dist: ½l, 3½l, 2l, sht-hd, 1½l, ¾l, 6l, 10l. 1m 18.60s. a 5.20s (9 Ran).
SR: 32/30/11/8/2/1/ (David W Chapman), D W Chapman

108 Fackley Claiming Stakes CLASS F (4-y-o and up) £2,469 1m..........(2:55)

79* NO SUBMISSION (USA) 7-9-8 S Wood (3) *made all, quickened o'r 2 fs out, very easily*..........(7 to 4 on op Evens) 1
THEMAAM 4-8-12 Dean McKeown (4) *chsd ldrs, rdn 2 fs out, styd on fnl furlong, no ch wth wnr.* ....(14 to 1 op 8 to 1) 2
78 DIGGER DOYLE 4-8-1 (3*) F Norton (7) *chsd wnr, rdn o'r 2 fs out, kpt on one pace*..........(14 to 1 op 10 to 1) 3
78^{3} SILVER SAMURAI 4-8-5 (7*) S Mulvey (1) *slwly into strd, hdwy o'r 3 fs out, rdn 2 furlongs out, kpt on one pace.* ....(7 to 1 op 6 to 1 tchd 8 to 1) 4
50* LOCK KEEPER (USA) 7-8-6 J Quinn (11) *mid-div, effrt and rdn alng 3 fs out, styd on fnl 2 furlongs, nvr dngrs.* ....(3 to 1 op 2 to 1 tchd 4 to 1) 5
67^{7} CAL'S BOY (bl) 4-8-4 R Lappin (9) *cl up pulling hrd, rdn 3 fs out, sn wknd*..........(66 to 1 op 25 to 1) 6
5^{7} THE OLD MITRE 5-7-0 (7*) D Wright (10) *nvr a factor.* ....(33 to 1 op 25 to 1) 7
19^{4} NIGALS FRIEND (v) 4-8-7 J Williams (8) *al rear.* ....(25 to 1 op 16 to 1) 8
MAHZOOZ 4-8-8 G Bardwell (2) *slwly into strd, al rear.* ....(33 to 1 op 25 to 1) 9
BOLD SPARK 5-8-0 J Fanning (6) *chsd ldrs to hfwy, sn wknd*..........(50 to 1 op 25 to 1) 10
Dist: 1½l, 1½l, sht-hd, 1½l, 12l, 1½l, 10l, 6l, hd. 1m 44.90s. a 5.90s (10 Ran).
SR: 55/40/27/34/23/-/ (T S Redman), D W Chapman

109 Carlton-on-Trent Handicap CLASS F (0-80 3-y-o) £2,343 7f..........(3:25)

4811a* GOLDEN KLAIR [78] 9-7 J Quinn (5) *hld up in tch, hdwy on bit 2 fs out, led wl o'r one furlong out, pushed out.* ....(5 to 4 on op Evens) 1
KINGSTON BROWN [57] 7-12^{1} (3*) F Norton (3) *in tch, effrt 2 fs out, sn rdn, styd on wl fnl furlong.* ....(14 to 1 op 10 to 1 tchd 16 to 1) 2
ASHOVER [70] 8-13 Alex Greaves (1) *in rear and outpcd hfwy, styd on fnl 2 fs, not rch ldrs.* ....(12 to 1 op 10 to 1 tchd 14 to 1) 3
QUICK SILVER BOY [66] 8-9 L Charnock (7) *chsd ldrs, effrt o'r 2 fs out, sn rdn and wknd over one furlong out.* ....(10 to 1 op 6 to 1) 4
57* BOLD STREET (Ire) [70] 8-6 (7*) D Wright (6) *cl up, hdwy to ld 3 fs out, rdn and hdd one and a half furlongs out, wknd quickly*..........(11 to 4 op 2 to 1) 5
4772a^{7} PAINT THE WIND (Ire) [50] 7-7 J Fanning (2) *chsd ldrs, rdn 3 fs out, sn wknd*..........(8 to 1 op 6 to 1) 6
ANDREW'S EXPRESS (Ire) [50] (bl) 7-7 S Wood (4) *led, hdd 3 fs out, sn wknd*..........(25 to 1 op 20 to 1) 7
Dist: 2l, 8l, 2½l, 5l, 2½l, 5l. 1m 32.00s. a 5.90s (7 Ran).
SR: 50/23/12/-/ (C John Hill), C J Hill

110 Eakring Handicap CLASS F (0-70 4-y-o and up) £2,490 1m..........(3:55)

35^{5} MENTALASANYTHIN [50] 4-9-0 Kim Tinkler (8) *al cl up, effrt 2 fs out, sn rdn, styd on to ld ins last.* ....(11 to 2 op 9 to 2 tchd 6 to 1) 1
ADMIRALS SECRET (USA) [64] 4-10-0 S Webster (2) *cl up, led 2 fs out, sn rdn, hdd one furlong out, kpt on wl.* ....(12 to 1 tchd 14 to 1) 2
24* QUINZII MARTIN [50] (v) 5-9-1 J Williams (6) *chsd ldrs, hdwy 2 and a half fs out, rdn to ld one furlong out, sn hdd and no extr nr finish.* ....(11 to 2 op 9 to 2 tchd 6 to 1) 3
4810a^{7} BALLYRANTER [50] 4-9-0 J Quinn (9) *hld up, outpcd 3 fs out, rdn and styd on fnl 2 furlongs.* ....(11 to 1 op 12 to 1 tchd 14 to 1) 4
49* SIRTELIMAR (Ire) [57] 4-9-7 J McLaughlin (5) *led, rdn 2 and a half fs out, sn hdd and grad wknd.* (5 to 1 op 9 to 2) 5
27^{3} BOROCAY [40] 5-8-5 L Charnock (7) *hdwy 3 fs out, effrt and rdn 2 furlongs out, sn one pace.* (10 to 1 op 8 to 1) 6
4786a^{4} ROYAL ACCLAIM [38] (v) 8-8-3 J Fanning (4) *beh, rdn alng hfwy, nvr dngrs*..........(20 to 1 op 16 to 1) 7
91* LORD NASKRA (USA) [54] (v) 4-9-1 (3*) Emma O'Gorman (1) *nvr rch ldrs*..........(2 to 1 fav op 9 to 4 tchd 5 to 2) 8
67^{8} GUESSTIMATION (USA) [51] 4-9-1 G Bardwell (3) *chsd ldrs, rdn o'r 3 fs out, sn btn*..........(12 to 1 op 8 to 1) 9
5^{4} TIBBS INN [34] 4-7-11^{6} (7*) J Tate (10) *prmnt to hfwy, sn lost pl*..........(25 to 1) 10
Dist: 2l, 1l, 2l, 2l, nk, 2l, 10l, 3l, hd. 1m 45.60s. a 6.60s (10 Ran).
SR: 37/45/29/22/23/6/ (Mrs M O'Donnell), N Tinkler

111 Balderton Handicap CLASS F (0-70 4-y-o and up) £2,511 1¾m..........(4:25)

64^{2} MASTER'S CROWN (USA) [38] 5-7-8 (7*) D McCabe (8) *made all, quickened clr o'r 2 fs out, unchlgd.* ....(5 to 2 fav op 3 to 1 tchd 100 to 30) 1
4812a^{2} CLASSIC ACCOUNT [65] 5-9-7 (7*) S Mulvey (4) *al prmnt, chsd wnr frm hfwy, rdn and one pace 2 fs out.* ....(10 to 1 op 9 to 1 tchd 12 to 1) 2
55^{4} WELL AND TRULY [43] 6-8-6 D Biggs (6) *chsd ldrs, effrt and rdn 3 fs out, one pace.* ....(6 to 1 op 9 to 2 tchd 13 to 2) 3
3^{5} MINGUS (USA) [51] 6-9-0 D Nicholls (12) *hld up and beh, steady hdwy 6 fs out, rdn 3 furlongs out, no imprsn.* ....(5 to 1 op 7 to 1) 4
BLUE DISC [33] 8-7-8^{5} (7*) M Humphries (2) *nvr rch ldrs.* ....(33 to 1 op 20 to 1) 5
78^{4} ROYAL VERSE (Fr) [30] 6-7-7 G Bardwell (1) *chsd ldrs, rdn 4 fs out, sn wknd*..........(5 to 1 op 4 to 1 tchd 6 to 1) 6
53^{4} MALENOIR (USA) [56] 5-9-0 (5*) S Wynne (5) *hld up and beh, rdn 6 fs out, no hdwy*..........(7 to 1 op 5 to 1) 7
34* ROMANIAN (Ire) [48] 5-8-11 J Quinn (7) *hld up and beh, effrt and hdwy 6 fs out, rdn 4 furlongs out, sn wknd.* ....(4 to 1 op 7 to 2 tchd 5 to 1) 8
GEE DOUBLE YOU [41] 7-8-4 L Charnock (9) *chsd wnr to hfwy, rdn 5 fs out, grad wknd*..........(33 to 1 op 25 to 1) 9
VANDA'S GIRL [40] 5-7-10 (7*) D Wright (10) *chsd ldrs till wknd quickly 6 fs out, sn tld off*..........(33 to 1) 10
Dist: 6l, 6l, 3½l, 6l, 2½l, 2l, 8l, 10l. 3m 10.60s. a 10.60s (10 Ran).
SR: 23/38/4/5/-/-/ (Mattie O'Toole), M C Chapman

LINGFIELD (A.W) (std)
Saturday January 30th
Going Correction: MINUS 0.10 sec. per fur.

112 Crusader Claiming Stakes CLASS F (4-y-o and up) £2,355 7f..........(1:20)

56^{3} RESPECTABLE JONES 7-8-13 W Ryan (1) *hld up on heels of ldrs, quickened to ld one out, sn clr, easily.* ....(7 to 2 on tchd 10 to 3 on) 1
4815a^{2} SUMMER EXPRESS 4-8-6 Alex Greaves (5) *chsd ldr, rdn and ev ch appr fnl furlong, kpt on one pace.* ....(9 to 2 op 7 to 2) 2
48^{6} SCOTS LAW 6-8-11 D Biggs (4) *led til hdd and outpcd one furlong out*..........(10 to 1 op 4 to 1) 3
4793a^{8} RAPID ROSIE 5-7-13 T Williams (2) *hld up, rdn alng to join ldrs 4 fs out, wknd last 2 furlongs.* ....(66 to 1 tchd 100 to 1) 4
35 LEAH JAY (bl) 6-8-9 J Quinn (3) *sn rdn alng in rear, al outpcd*..........(66 to 1 op 33 to 1 tchd 100 to 1) 5
Dist: 3½l, 2l, 6l, sht-hd. 1m 27.85s. a 4.45s (5 Ran).
SR: 22/4/3/-/-/ (Mrs B Ramsden), R Hollinshead

113 Centurion Apprentice Handicap CLASS F (0-70 4-y-o and up) £2,554 1m..........(1:50)

85* MASTER HYDE (USA) [64] 4-10-0 S O'Gorman (5) *stumbled aftr one furlong, hdwy frm rear 4 fs out, rdn to ld appr fnl furlong, pushed clr*..........(2 to 1 fav tchd 5 to 2) 1
87^{8} PIGALLE WONDER [51] (bl) 5-9-2 B Russell (6) *chsd ldrs, rdn o'r 2 fs out, not quicken over one out, styd on last 100 yards*..........(9 to 2 op 5 to 1 tchd 11 to 2) 2
4817a^{8} DANCING BOAT [35] (bl) 4-7-13 F Norton (8) *wl plcd, rdn alng frm 2 fs out, kpt on ins fnl furlong.* ....(8 to 1 op 7 to 1 tchd 10 to 1) 3
4786a^{2} KING PARROT (Ire) [58] 5-9-1 (8*) D Salt (9) *led til hdd appr fnl furlong, no extr*..........(6 to 1 op 3 to 1) 4
QUEEN OF DREAMS [37] 5-7-11 (5*) P McCabe (2) *str run frm rear o'r 3 fs out, ev ch 2 out, one pace ins fnl furlong*..........(20 to 1 op 14 to 1 tchd 25 to 1) 5
COOL SOCIETY (USA) [58] 4-9-3 (5*) D McCabe (7) *drpd rear aftr 3 fs, nvr dngrs afterwards.* ....(16 to 1 op 10 to 1) 6
69^{3} SAREEN EXPRESS (Ire) [47] 5-8-12 A Tucker (1) *strted slwly, al in rear*..........(11 to 4 op 9 to 4 tchd 3 to 1) 7
4673a^{7} LADY SNOOBLE [34] 6-7-13^{1} S Drowne (4) *sn pushed alng in tch, outpcd frm hfwy.* ....(25 to 1 op 20 to 1 tchd 33 to 1) 8
35^{7} GEMINI BAY [31] (bl) 4-7-9 B Doyle (3) *dwlt, sn wl plcd, rdn and wknd o'r 3 fs out.* ....(20 to 1 op 16 to 1 tchd 25 to 1) 9
Dist: 3l, 1½l, hd, 1½l, 3l, 1l, 2l, 7l. 1m 40.34s. a 4.14s (9 Ran).
SR: 40/19/-/20/-/5/ (Hyde Sporting Promotions/Saddlehome Farm), P Mitchell

114 Daily Star Challenge Handicap Qualifier CLASS F (0-70 4-y-o and up) £2,678 1¼m ....(2:20)

84^3 FERDIA (Ire) [65] 4-9-9 W Ryan (12) *slwly into strd, cld on ldrs o'r 3 fs out, rdn to ld over one out, hld on.* ....(6 to 1 op 5 to 1 tchd 13 to 2) 1
35* CARLOWITZ (USA) [52] 5-8-6 (7*) B Russell (11) *prog o'r 5 fs out, led over 3 out, hdd appr fnl furlong, styd on ag'n nr finish*......................... (3 to 1 fav op 5 to 2) 2
20^3 PREMIER DANCE [41] 6-8-2 D Biggs (6) *rcd in mid-div, cld on ldrs o'r 2 fs out, rdn and one pace fnl furlong.* ....(5 to 1 op 9 to 2) 3
30^5 SHARP THISTLE [37] 7-7-12 Dale Gibson (7) *settled towards rear, ran on 3 fs out, rdn and styd on appr fnl furlong*......................... (12 to 1 op 10 to 1) 4
58^4 TAUNTING (Ire) [51] 5-8-5 (7*) S McCarthy (14) *prog o'r 3 fs out, one pace ins last 2 furlongs.* ....(8 to 1 op 6 to 1 tchd 9 to 1) 5
43^6 WESSEX MILORD [32] 8-7-0 (7*) Kim McDonnell (1) *drpd rear aftr 2 fs, moderate hdwy last two furlongs.* ....(33 to 1 tchd 50 to 1) 6
87 MUSIC DANCER [56] 4-9-0 J McLaughlin (10) *wl plcd, led o'r 5 fs out till over 3 out, sn btn*.............. (20 to 1) 7
4816a^5 PRINCE ROONEY (Ire) [54] 5-8-8 (7*) S Drowne (5) *trkd ldrs til wknd o'r 3 fs out*.............. (12 to 1 op 10 to 1) 8
85^8 NORTH FLYER [47] 4-8-0 (5*) Stephen Davies (2) *ldg grp til lost pl o'r 4 fs out*....................(8 to 1 op 7 to 1) 9
CHESTER TERRACE [32] 9-7-0 (7*) D Wright (3) *beh aftr 4 fs*.. (33 to 1) 10
68^3 DEBACLE (USA) [70] 4-10-0 A McGlone (9) *pressed ldrs til wknd o'r 4 fs out*.................(12 to 1 op 10 to 1) 11
33^7 ITHKURNI (USA) [47] 4-8-5 T Williams (13) *slwly into strd, improved frm rear on outsd 3 fs out, sn rdn, eased whn btn o'r one out*.. (33 to 1) 12
43^7 LAMORE RITORNA [45] 4-8-3 G Bardwell (8) *cl up for o'r 6 fs, wknd quickly*....................(16 to 1 op 14 to 1) 13
87 EMAURA [41] 4-7-13 J Quinn (4) *led for o'r 4 fs, sn lost pl.* ....(16 to 1 op 14 to 1) 14

Dist: 1½l, 3l, 2l, 3l, nk, 2½l, ¾l, ¾l, 7l, 3l. 2m 7.39s. a 4.19s (14 Ran).
SR: 57/44/27/19/27/7/23/22/10/ (Noel Sweeney), R Hollinshead

115 Challenger Handicap CLASS D (0-90 4-y-o and up) £3,841 1½m.................(2:50)

58* EL VOLADOR [74] 6-8-12 (7*) B Russell (6) *hld up towards rear, hdwy 3 fs out, led wl o'r one out, rdn clr.* ....(4 to 1 op 3 to 1) 1
73^4 EL DOMINIO [53] 5-7-12 G Bardwell (5) *pressed ldr, rdn and outpcd wl o'r one furlong out, styd on clsg stages.* ....(8 to 1 op 7 to 1 tchd 10 to 1) 2
59* MULCIBER [73] 5-9-4 W Ryan (7) *hld up, hdwy to ld o'r 2 fs out, hdd and outpcd wl over one out.* ....(7 to 2 op 3 to 1 tchd 4 to 1) 3
59^2 RAPPORTEUR (USA) [83] 7-10-0 J Williams (3) *led aftr 2 fs, hdd 3 out, styd on same pace.* ....(11 to 2 op 5 to 1 tchd 6 to 1) 4
82* BEAM ME UP SCOTTY (Ire) [56] 4-7-11 N Carlisle (4) *settled in mid-div, one pace last 3 fs*.....(10 to 1 tchd 12 to 1) 5
59^3 LYN'S RETURN (Ire) [56] 4-7-9^3 (5*) B Doyle (1) *hld up in rear, rdn alng and outpcd o'r 4 fs out.* ....(3 to 1 fav op 5 to 2) 6
42* MODEST HOPE (USA) [60] 6-8-5 J Quinn (2) *led for 2 fs, led ag'n 3 out, sn hdd, wknd und pres o'r one out.* ....(13 to 2 op 5 to 1) 7

Dist: 7l, ½l, hd, 1½l, sht-hd, hd. 2m 34.13s. a 4.83s (7 Ran).
SR: 45/10/29/38/4/3/10/ (I A Baker), R J O'Sullivan

116 Alpine Double Glazing Maiden Stakes CLASS F (3-y-o) £2,208 6f..........(3:20)

44^2 PIRATES GOLD (Ire) 9-0 Dale Gibson (1) *settled towards rear, rdn and hdwy o'r 3 fs out, hng lft one out, got up last 50 yards*................ (6 to 5 fav op 6 to 4 on) 1
31^3 PURBECK CENTENARY 9-0 Lorna Vincent (6) *slwly into strd, sn tracking ldrs, led o'r one furlong out, hdd and not quicken last 50 yards*...........(2 to 1 op 5 to 2) 2
44^3 BELLE SOIREE (e/s) 8-9 A McGlone (5) *cl up, led o'r 3 out, hdd over one out, no extr.* ....(12 to 1 op 6 to 1 tchd 14 to 1) 3
45^6 HOTSOCKS 8-2 (7*) Kim McDonnell (4) *chsd ldrs til outpcd 3 fs out, ran on ag'n clsg stages*.. (100 to 1 op 20 to 1) 4
51^5 PALACEGATE GIRL (v) 8-9 L Charnock (2) *led 5 fs out til o'r 3 out, wknd last 2 furlongs.* ....(4 to 1 op 7 to 2 tchd 9 to 2) 5
4755a YOUNG SPARKIE 9-0 W Ryan (3) *led for one furlong, sn outpcd and lost tch*.. (33 to 1 op 25 to 1 tchd 50 to 1) 6

Dist: 1l, 3½l, 3½l, 4l, 12l. 1m 14.32s. a 3.52s (6 Ran).
SR: 18/14/-/ (E C Nott), J White

117 Comet Handicap CLASS F (0-70 3-y-o and up) £2,782 6f.......................(3:50)

47^3 SPEEDY CLASSIC (USA) [37] (bl) 4-7-2 (7*) D Wright (4) *chsd ldr, led o'r 3 fs out, pushed out.* ....(11 to 2 op 7 to 2 tchd 6 to 1) 1
4720a* LUCAYAN TREASURE [70] (v) 3-8-12 W Ryan (9) *hld up, ran on und pres ins last 2 fs, styd on nr line.* ....(9 to 4 op 7 to 4 tchd 5 to 2) 2
86* SOBA GUEST (Ire) [71] 4-9-12 (3*) Emma O'Gorman (6) *wl in tch, cld on ldrs hfwy, rdn and one pace appr fnl furlong*................(2 to 1 fav op 5 to 2 tchd 11 to 4) 3
54^6 TOSHIBA COMET [49] (e/s) 6-8-7 J Quinn (7) *beh til styd on last 2 fs, nrst finish*...............(12 to 1 tchd 14 to 1) 4
86^6 SIMMIE'S SPECIAL [49] 5-8-0 (7*) M Humphries (5) *chsd ldrs til outpcd frm hfwy*.. (12 to 1 op 10 to 1 tchd 14 to 1) 5
4815a^4 INSWINGER [35] 7-7-7 G Bardwell (3) *outpcd most of way.* ....(9 to 1 op 12 to 1 tchd 8 to 1) 6
36^4 BRIGHT PARAGON (Ire) [39] 4-7-11 Dale Gibson (1) *outpcd til effrt hfwy, no imprsn on ldrs last 2 fs.* ....(14 to 1 op 8 to 1 tchd 16 to 1) 7
31^2 TEE-EMM [63] 3-7-12 (7*) L Carter (8) *led for o'r 2 fs, wknd two out*..............(10 to 1 op 8 to 1 tchd 12 to 1) 8
7^7 HOME AFFAIR [58] 3-8-0 N Carlisle (2) *al outpcd.* ....(50 to 1 op 25 to 1) 9

Dist: 1½l, 3l, 2½l, ¾l, 3l, ¾l, 7l, 4l. 1m 13.06s. a 2.26s (9 Ran).
SR: 24/35/40/8/5/-/ (Tam Wong), M J Heaton-Ellis

CAGNES-SUR-MER (FR) (good)
Sunday January 31st

118 Prix Charles du Breil (4-y-o and up) £4,182 1m 3f..............................(1:25)

CARESPA (USA) 4-9-11 Mme B Scandella, ... 1
TANSON (Fr) 9-10-1 M C Mosse, ... 2
HISTOIRE VRAI (Fr) 4-10-5 M F Foresi, ... 3
90^3 HIERARCH (USA) 4-10-1 Mlle M Fougy, *al mid-div, nvr nrr.* 12

Dist: 1l, nk, nk, 1l, hd. 2m 25.60s. (18 Ran).

119 Prix de Bastia (3-y-o) £5,974 1¼m...(2:30)

ROCHESSON (Fr) 8-9 S Coffigny, ... 1
OUBLIES MOI (USA) 7-12 M Cesandri, ... 2
AFFIRMED MINI (Fr) 8-9 M Boutin, ... 3
88^4 SOLDIERS BAY 8-9 G Guignard, *ev ch, rdn 3 fs out, kpt on one pace*............... 5

Dist: 1l, ½l, 1l, 1½l, 1l. 2m 4.00s. (20 Ran).
G Philippeau

SOUTHWELL (A.W) (std)
Monday February 1st
Going Correction: PLUS 0.30 sec. per fur.

120 Walnut Handicap CLASS F (0-70 4-y-o and up) £2,343 1m.....................(2:00)

110^5 SIRTELIMAR (Ire) [57] 4-9-11 J McLaughlin (9) *made all, hrd pressed last 2 fs, kpt on grimly last 100 yards.* ....(11 to 2 op 7 to 2 tchd 13 to 2) 1
48* BUDDY'S FRIEND (Ire) [52] 5-9-6 J Quinn (8) *confidently rdn, cruised up to chal last 2 fs, ridden but fld to catch wnr last 100 yards*............(5 to 2 fav tchd 100 to 30) 2
WATCH ME GO (Ire) [46] 4-9-0 N Day (10) *al 1st 3, ev ch and drvn alng o'r one furlong out, styd on same pace.* ....(12 to 1 tchd 14 to 1) 3
27^2 EAST BARNS (Ire) [55] (bl) 5-9-9 Alex Greaves (1) *drpd out strt, broke wide to improve entering strt, styd on, nvr nrr*..........................(4 to 1 op 7 to 2) 4
MILL BURN [48] 4-9-2 N Carlisle (5) *trkd ldg trio, ev ch and drvn alng o'r 2 fs out, one pace*.... (7 to 2 tchd 4 to 1) 5
4804a^5 LORD NEPTUNE [37] (bl) 4-8-0 (5*) B Doyle (2) *sluggish strt, drvn up to press ldg pair, feeling pace o'r 2 fs out, fdd.* ....(25 to 1) 6
4810a^5 SANDMOOR DENIM [58] 6-9-12 S Webster (6) *chsd alng to keep in tch hfwy, nvr able to rch ldrs.* ....(9 to 1 op 7 to 1 tchd 10 to 1) 7
49^9 MAI PEN RAI [37] 5-8-5 G Bardwell (3) *settled strt, drvn in midfield hfwy, nvr a threat*...... (14 to 1 op 12 to 1) 8
92^4 FUTURES GIFT (Ire) [37] 4-8-5 D Biggs (4) *chsd ldg half dozen, feeling pace hfwy, sn btn*.. (16 to 1 op 14 to 1) 9
96 WOOD KAY (Ire) [58] 4-9-12 W Ryan (7) *sn drvn alng to keep up, tld off last 3 fs*.......... (33 to 1 op 20 to 1) 10

Dist: 1½l, nk, 4l, sht-hd, 3l, 3½l, 12l, 3½l, 30l. 1m 45.80s. a 6.80s (10 Ran).
SR: 45/35/28/25/17/-/7/-/-/ (D W Price), R C Spicer

121 Teak Claiming Stakes CLASS F (3-y-o) £2,238 6f..........................(2:30)

66^2 PINE RIDGE LAD (Ire) (bl) 8-7 Dean McKeown (6) *broke fst, made all, shaken up o'r one furlong out, kpt on wl.* ....(11 to 8 fav op 7 to 4 tchd 5 to 4) 1
37^8 JORDYWRATH 7-11^1 (5*) Stephen Davies (2) *nvr far away, drvn alng on ins last 2 fs, kpt on same pace.* ....(7 to 1 op 8 to 1 tchd 10 to 1) 2
106^6 DAANIERA (Ire) 9-0 (3*) Emma O'Gorman (5) *trkd wnr, rdn and put head in air o'r one furlong out, no imprsn.* ....(5 to 2 op 7 to 4) 3

5[12] HERSHEBAR (bl) 8-9 S Webster (4) *chsd ldg trio thrght, rdn o'r 2 out, styd on, nvr nrr.* ....(13 to 2 op 4 to 1 tchd 8 to 1) 4
1 WELL TRIED (Ire) 7-8[1] (7*) M Humphries (7) *scrubbed alng to keep up hfwy, nvr a factor*..... (16 to 1 op 12 to 1) 5
RED EDGE 8-0 L Charnock (1) *chsd alng to go pace aftr 2 fs, nvr a factor*....................(25 to 1 op 20 to 1) 6
Dist: 3l, 2½l, 3½l, 15l, ½l. 1m 18.20s. a 4.80s (6 Ran).
SR: 33/15/21/ (R Jenkinson), M Johnston

122 Pine Handicap CLASS F (0-70 4-y-o and up) £2,322 2m.....................(3:00)

61[3] KOVALEVSKIA [32] 8-7-12 G Bardwell (7) *scrubbed alng in midfield, improved frm off the pace entering strt, led o'r one out, styd on wl*...............(6 to 1 op 7 to 2) 1
82[4] ETIQUETTE [56] 4-9-2 Dean McKeown (9) *trkd ldg pair, led gng wl appr strt, hdd and rdn o'r one out, no extr.* ....(6 to 1 op 4 to 1) 2
18[4] MOOT POINT (USA) [52] (bl) 5-8-13 (5*) B Doyle (3) *nvr far away, lost grnd whn pace quickened appr strt, styd on ag'n fnl furlong*........(6 to 1 op 7 to 1 tchd 11 to 2) 3
ONE FOR THE CHIEF [32] 5-7-5 (7*) D Wright (10) *chsd alng to keep in tch aftr one circuit, styd on und pres last 2 fs, nvr nrr*........................... (25 to 1 op 20 to 1) 4
81[7] AUDE LA BELLE (Fr) [60] 5-9-9 (3*) F Norton (6) *co'red up on ins, effrt and pushed alng last m, styd on same pace last 2 fs*............................(10 to 1 op 8 to 1) 5
94[5] LORD ADVOCATE [37] (v) 5-8-3 Alex Greaves (1) *dictated pace till hdd appr strt, fdd*......... (6 to 1 op 4 to 1) 6
81* BEDOUIN PRINCE (USA) [50] 6-9-2 T Williams (8) *patiently rdn, improved to go hndy hfwy, fdd und pres entering strt*.................(5 to 2 fav op 2 to 1 tchd 11 to 4) 7
94[7] RESISTING (USA) [29] 5-7-2 (7*) Darren Moffatt (5) *trkd ldr, drvn to maintain pos hfwy, lost tch appr strt.* .... (20 to 1 op 14 to 1) 8
ADMINISTER [62] 5-9-7 (7*) W Hollick (2) *chsd ldg quartet, lost grnd whn pace quickened appr strt, sn btn.* .... (33 to 1 op 12 to 1) 9
4776a[7] JALORE [35] 4-7-8[6] (7*) M Humphries (4) *struggling to keep up aftr 4 fs, tld off frm hfwy.* .... (9 to 1 op 16 to 1 tchd 8 to 1) 10
Dist: 3l, 5l, 5l, 3½l, 1½l, 7l, 12l, 10l, ¾l. 3m 38.00s. a 11.50s (10 Ran).
SR: 17/32/29/4/28/3/9/-/-/ (D A Wilson), D A Wilson

123 Oak Claiming Stakes CLASS F (4-y-o and up) £2,406 1m.....................(3:30)

108[3] DIGGER DOYLE 4-8-13 (3*) F Norton (4) *made all, quickened to forge clr o'r 2 fs out, styd on strly.* ....(4 to 1 op 3 to 1 tchd 9 to 2) 1
76[8] JUVENARA 7-8-1 G Bardwell (1) *trkd ldrs, drvn to improve o'r 2 fs out, styd on, nvr nrr.* ....(15 to 8 op 5 to 4 tchd 2 to 1) 2
107* BUZBOUR 5-8-6 J Quinn (9) *patiently rdn, improved gng wl hfwy, drvn alng o'r 2 fs out, fdd.* ....(7 to 4 fav op 2 to 1) 3
LARA'S BABY (Ire) 5-8-11 Kim Tinkler (7) *last and hld up, feeling pace hfwy, some late hdwy, nvr nrr.* .... (12 to 1 op 6 to 1) 4
BATTUTA 4-8-11 Alex Greaves (8) *wth ldrs, hrd at work whn pace lifted o'r 2 fs out, sn outpcd.* .... (14 to 1 op 10 to 1 tchd 16 to 1) 5
4771a CREPT OUT (Ire) 4-8-6 Dean McKeown (2) *chsd alng to go pace hfwy, nvr a factor*.........(10 to 1 tchd 12 to 1) 6
WALLANGRIFF (bl) 5-9-2 W Ryan (6) *wth ldrs, feeling pace and lost grnd entering strt, sn lost tch*....... (20 to 1) 7
49 ANGEL'S WING 4-7-3 (7*) Darren Moffatt (3) *in tch, hrd drvn half way, tld off entering strt.* .... (25 to 1 op 20 to 1) 8
Dist: 6l, 10l, 4l, 2l, 2l, 10l, 20l. 1m 45.80s. a 6.80s (8 Ran).
SR: 36/3/-/-/-/ (P B Doyle), C N Allen

124 Rosewood Handicap CLASS F (0-80 3-y-o) £2,280 7f......................... (4:00)

80* DORAZINE [61] 9-7 D Biggs (1) *trkd ldg trio, quickened ahead 2 fs out, ran on strly.* ....(11 to 10 on op Evens tchd 5 to 4 on) 1
62 PERSONIMUS [35] 7-9 J Fanning (3) *sluggish strt, improved on outsd hfwy, effrt and edgd lft o'r one out, styd on*................ (7 to 1 op 6 to 1 tchd 8 to 1) 2
83[6] EXPRESS MARIECURIE (Ire) [58] (bl) 9-4 Alex Greaves (2) *dictated pace for 5 fs, no extr und pres appr fnl furlong*.................................. (14 to 1 op 8 to 1) 3
95* ROSE FLYER (Ire) [61] 9-0 (7*,5ex) D McCabe (4) *wth ldr, drvn to hold pos hfwy, fdd und pres last 2 fs.* ....(9 to 4 op 2 to 1 tchd 5 to 2) 4
93[3] TACITURN (USA) [39] (bl) 7-13 G Bardwell (5) *chsd ldg pair, hrd at work hfwy, sn lost tch.* ....(8 to 1 op 6 to 1 tchd 9 to 1) 5
4745a[7] MISS OFFIE [47] 8-7 W Ryan (6) *drvn alng to go pace, tld off frm hfwy*.........(33 to 1 op 16 to 1 tchd 40 to 1) 6
Dist: 4l, 1½l, 8l, 5l, 12l. 1m 32.80s. a 6.70s (6 Ran).
SR: 38/-/18/ (C John Hill), C J Hill

125 Cherrywood Handicap CLASS F (0-80 4-y-o and up) £2,364 1½m............. (4:30)

HORIZON (Ire) [54] (bl) 5-8-3 D Biggs (8) *made most, quickened entering strt, drw clr, eased fnl furlong.* ....(7 to 2 tchd 4 to 1) 1
4707a[5] QUALITAIR RHYTHM (Ire) [56] 5-7-12 (7*) G Mitchell (9) *al chasing ldrs, effrt und pres o'r 2 fs out, styd on, no ch wth wnr*.........................(6 to 1 tchd 11 to 2) 2
64* SWORD MASTER [80] 4-9-11 N Day (2) *al hndy, rdn whn pace quickened o'r 2 fs out, no extr.* .... (5 to 2 fav tchd 3 to 1) 3
STEPPEY LANE [72] 8-9-7 Dean McKeown (6) *last and hld up, pushed alng to improve last 3 fs, prmsg.* .... (20 to 1 op 14 to 1) 4
81[3] SUGEMAR [60] 7-8-2 (7*) D McCabe (5) *nvr far away, und pres entering strt, btn 2 fs out*.................(5 to 1) 5
79[4] ULLADULLA [59] 4-8-4 J Quinn (4) *chsd alng in midfield, effrt appr strt, nvr nr to chal*...... (10 to 1 op 7 to 1) 6
55[5] LE TEMERAIRE [64] 7-8-13 Kim Tinkler (1) *broke wl, feeling pace and drpd back quickly hfwy, no further dngr.* .... (14 to 1 op 12 to 1 tchd 16 to 1) 7
NORTHERN NATION [44] 5-7-7 G Bardwell (7) *trkd ldg bunch, struggling to keep up aftr a m, sn btn.* .... (11 to 2 op 4 to 1 tchd 6 to 1) 8
94 MOUNTAIN GLOW [51] 6-8-0[1] T Williams (3) *sn struggling, tld off frm hfwy*..................(50 to 1 op 33 to 1) 9
Dist: 2l, hd, 8l, 2l, 10l, 4l, ½l, 30l. 2m 44.10s. a 10.20s (9 Ran).
SR: 23/21/40/20/4/-/ (Mrs Solna Thomson Jones), T Thomson Jones

LINGFIELD (A.W) (std)
Thursday February 4th
Going Correction: MINUS 0.15 sec. per fur.

126 Hansom Claiming Stakes CLASS F (4-y-o and up) £2,556 1m 5f.............. (1:40)

82[3] LYPH (USA) 7-8-2 (3*) A Tucker (1) *hdwy 3 fs out, rdn to ld wl ins last*...........................(5 to 1 op 4 to 1) 1
102* BREAKDANCER (Ire) 4-8-9 T Quinn (6) *hdwy 6 fs out, led 2 out, rdn and hdd wl ins last.* (13 to 8 fav op 11 to 10) 2
92[7] IRON BARON (Ire) (bl) 4-8-5 W Ryan (7) *beh till hdwy hfwy, ev ch entering last, no extr cl hme.* .... (10 to 1 op 8 to 1 tchd 12 to 1) 3
61[7] FIRST FLING (Ire) 4-7-8 G Bardwell (3) *led 5 fs out, hdd 2 out, wknd ins last*......(3 to 1 op 4 to 1 tchd 9 to 2) 4
SOUL TRADER 4-7-12 (7*) Marie Plowright (2) *prmnt early, beh hfwy, one pace*.............. (50 to 1 op 33 to 1) 5
46[3] PLEASURE AHEAD 6-7-10 (7*) B Russell (4) *prmnt till wknd 4 fs out*......... (5 to 1 op 4 to 1 tchd 11 to 2) 6
82 WRITTEN AGREEMENT 5-8-0 (3*) F Norton (8) *prmnt early.* .... (66 to 1 op 33 to 1) 7
102[2] SHARP DANCE 4-7-10 J Quinn (5) *led to 5 fs out, sn btn.* .... (16 to 1 op 14 to 1) 8
Dist: ¾l, sht-hd, 3½l, 4l, nk, 3½l, 10l. 2m 47.74s. a 4.74s (8 Ran).
SR: 24/26/21/3/6/3/-/-/ (John Lemon), P R Hedger

127 Alpine (Double Glazing) Maiden Stakes CLASS F (4-y-o and up) £2,208 7f....(2:10)

107[4] EXPRESS SERVICE 4-8-11 (3*) Emma O'Gorman (3) *wtd wth, rdn to ld o'r one furlong out, ran on wl.* ....(6 to 4 on op 2 to 1 on) 1
WELL BOUGHT (Ire) 4-8-4 (5*) K Rutter (2) *trkd ldr till outpcd 2 fs out, kpt on one pace to go second nr finish.* ....(7 to 2 op 5 to 2 tchd 9 to 2) 2
91[4] MU-ARRIK (bl) 5-8-7 (7*) G Parkin (4) *led till hdd o'r one furlong out, wknd ins last*..........(7 to 1 op 5 to 1) 3
54 PRINCESS DECHTRA (Ire) 4-8-9 W Ryan (1) *al last, lost tch fnl 2 fs*................................ (5 to 1 op 7 to 2) 4
Dist: 3½l, nk, 5l. 1m 27.41s. a 4.01s (4 Ran).
SR: 24/8/12/-/ (W A O'Gorman), W A O'Gorman

128 Daily Star Challenge Handicap Qualifier CLASS F (0-70 4-y-o and up) £2,684 1¼m ....(2:40)

81[6] LOOKINGFORARAINBOW (Ire) [66] 5-10-0 N Day (1) *al prmnt, in ld o'r 2 fs out, drw clr appr last.* .... (5 to 2 fav tchd 3 to 1) 1
77[7] MAJAL (Ire) [62] 4-9-8 D Nicholls (4) *hdwy fnl 2 fs to go second ins last*.................... (12 to 1 op 8 to 1) 2
84[5] APPLIANCEOFSCIENCE [40] (bl) 6-7-9 (7*) P McCabe (2) *in 3rd 3 fs out, kpt on one pace.* ....(8 to 1 op 10 to 1 tchd 12 to 1) 3
NORDANSK [38] 4-7-12 T Williams (7) *dsptd ld 4 fs out, one pace fnl 2*...........(14 to 1 op 10 to 1 tchd 16 to 1) 4
MERSEYSIDE MAN [52] (v) 7-8-9 (5*) K Rutter (10) *nvr plcd to chal*..............(10 to 1 op 6 to 1 tchd 12 to 1) 5
4788a FRIENDLYPERSUASION (Ire) [49] 5-8-11 W Ryan (8) *al beh.* .... (10 to 1 op 6 to 1) 6
84[2] PRESENT TIMES [36] 7-7-10[5] (7*) B Russell (9) *chsd ldrs, led briefly o'r 4 fs out, wknd wl over one out.* ....(7 to 2 op 9 to 4 tchd 4 to 1) 7

82 DUNMAGLASS [38] 6-8-0[10] (7*) S Drowne (6) *pld hrd early, nvr on terms*......................(33 to 1 op 25 to 1) 8

84[7] MODESTO (USA) [43] 5-8-5 G Bardwell (5) *led till hdd o'r 4 fs out, hrd rdn and sn btn, tld off.* ....(6 to 1 op 8 to 1 tchd 10 to 1) 9

ELIZABETHAN AIR [49] 4-8-9 J Quinn (3) *mid-div to hfwy, tld off*...........(10 to 1 op 8 to 1 tchd 12 to 1) 10

Dist: 4l, ¾l, ¾l, 3l, 2½l, nk, 1l, 10l, 3l. 2m 8.63s. a 5.43s (10 Ran).

SR: 45/31/9/3/13/5/ (B M Saumtally), Bob Jones

129 Landau Handicap CLASS E (0-80 3-y-o) £3,348 1¼m...................... (3:10)

40[7] ARCTIC GUEST (Ire) [45] 7-12 T Williams (4) *wtd wth, hdwy 4 fs out, led o'r 2 furlongs out, rdn out ins.* ....(9 to 1 op 5 to 1 tchd 10 to 1) 1

93* BROUGHTONS FORMULA [59] (bl) 8-12 (5ex) J Quinn (1) *hld up in tch, wnt second 2 fs out, kpt on one pace.* ....(9 to 2 op 3 to 1 tchd 5 to 1) 2

72[5] UMHAMBI [51] 8-4 W Ryan (8) *nvr far away, ev ch 2 fs out, kpt on one pace*.......(9 to 2 op 3 to 1 tchd 11 to 2) 3

72[3] HALHAM TARN (Ire) [58] 8-11 J Williams (3) *in rear till hdwy ins fnl 3 fs, nvr rchd 1st three.* ....(8 to 1 op 7 to 1 tchd 10 to 1) 4

32* DIAMOND LUCY [68] 9-4 (3*) Emma O'Gorman (12) *trkd ldr, led 5 fs out, hdd o'r 2 furlongs out, sn btn.* ....(11 to 4 fav op 5 to 2 tchd 3 to 1) 5

83* ANN HILL (Ire) [56] 8-2 (7*) M Humphries (11) *in tch till wknd o'r 3 fs out*...............(9 to 1 op 6 to 1) 6

40[9] FREE DANCER [53] 8-6 N Adams (7) *rdn hfwy, nvr on terms*......................................(33 to 1) 7

31[4] AIR COMMAND (Bar) [58] (e/s) 8-11 A McGlone (6) *al in rear* ....(16 to 1 op 14 to 1) 8

83[4] BUZZ-B-BABE [42] 7-9 G Bardwell (2) *in tch till wknd sn aftr hfwy*.......................(16 to 1 op 12 to 1) 9

57[4] SPECIAL RISK (Ire) [53] (bl) 8-1 (5*) M Fenton (10) *rdn hfwy, nvr on terms*........................(9 to 1 op 8 to 1) 10

83 GENTLE MOMENT [47] (bl) 8-0[12] (7*) Gaye Harwood (9) *in tch early, tld off frm hfwy.* ....(66 to 1 op 33 to 1 tchd 100 to 1) 11

Dist: 1l, 3½l, 7l, 1½l, 5l, 7l, 3l, 4l, 8l, 12l. 2m 6.96s. a 3.76s (11 Ran).

SR: 31/43/28/21/28/6/ (The Fairyhouse 1992 Partnership), M Johnston

130 Phaeton Apprentice Handicap CLASS F (0-70 4-y-o and up) £2,536 1m....... (3:40)

113[4] KING PARROT (Ire) [58] 5-9-2 (5*) J Wilkinson (5) *led till hdd o'r 4 fs out, rallied wl ins last to ld on line.* ....(11 to 4 tchd 5 to 2 and 3 to 1) 1

101[3] SARUM [57] 7-9-6 A Martinez (3) *al frnt rnk, led o'r 2 fs out, rdn and hdd on line.* ....(2 to 1 fav op 7 to 4 tchd 5 to 2) 2

113[5] QUEEN OF DREAMS [37] 5-8-0 G Milligan (1) *in tch till outpcd 2 fs out, ran on wl ins last.* ....(12 to 1 op 7 to 1 tchd 14 to 1) 3

69* EASTLEIGH [65] 4-10-0 D Carson (4) *trkd ldr, led o'r 4 fs out, hdd over 2 out, one pace ins last.* ....(3 to 1 op 9 to 4 tchd 100 to 30) 4

85[5] NORTHERN CONQUEROR (Ire) [35] 5-7-12[1] M Jermy (2) *sn beh, struggling hfwy, ran on ins fnl furlong.* ....(5 to 1 op 4 to 1 tchd 11 to 2) 5

Dist: Sht-hd, ½l, 1l, 2½l. 1m 40.39s. a 4.19s (5 Ran).

SR: 26/24/2/27/-/ (Lord Huntingdon), Lord Huntingdon

131 Dog Cart Amateur Riders' Handicap CLASS F (0-70 4-y-o and up) £2,669 6f ....(4:10)

87[7] NOBBY BARNES [60] 4-11-4 Miss E Bronson (4) *al prmnt, led entering last, all out.* ....(13 to 2 op 4 to 1 tchd 7 to 1) 1

76[9] COURTING NEWMARKET [49] 5-10-7 Miss S A Billot (11) *nvr far away, ev ch entering fnl furlong, ran on.* ....(14 to 1 op 8 to 1) 2

70[4] TYRIAN PURPLE (Ire) [62] 5-11-6 Mr R Teal (13) *al prmnt, led 2 fs out, hdd entering last, kpt on.* ....(8 to 1 op 10 to 1) 3

47[6] VELOCE (Ire) [54] (bl) 5-10-9[2] (5*) Mr W Dixon (6) *al prmnt, kpt on ins fnl furlong*.............(12 to 1 op 10 to 1) 4

11[4] LOVE LEGEND [70] 8-11-9 (5*) Mrs D Arbuthnot (10) *hdwy o'r 2 fs out, ran on ins last*...........(8 to 1 op 6 to 1) 5

85[4] BILL MOON [45] 7-10-3 Miss J Feilden (1) *al abt same pl, kpt on*.....................(5 to 1 op 5 to 1 tchd 9 to 2) 6

86[9] RUSHANES [55] 6-10-8 (5*) Mrs C Dunwoody (2) *led, hdd 2 fs out, wknd ins last*..............(10 to 1 tchd 14 to 1) 7

96[3] SAMSOLOM [54] 5-10-12 Mrs L Pearce (14) *prmnt till wknd appr fnl furlong*..............(8 to 1 op 4 to 1) 8

86[2] LYNDON'S LINNET [56] 5-10-9 (5*) Mr P Killick (8) *nvr got into race*..................(9 to 2 fav op 6 to 1) 9

85[9] SAMURAI GOLD (USA) [45] (v) 5-10-3[6] (5*) Mr E James (5) *slwly away, al beh*.................(33 to 1 op 20 to 1) 10

96[9] JUST BOB [61] (bl) 4-11-0 (5*) Mrs D Kettlewell (12) *al beh.* ....(20 to 1 op 25 to 1 tchd 33 to 1) 11

112[2] SUMMER EXPRESS [64] 4-11-3 (5*) Miss C Spearing (9) *speed to hfwy*.........(10 to 1 op 8 to 1 tchd 12 to 1) 12

4706a[9] LONELY LASS [37] 7-9-9 Miss I Diana W Jones (7) *al beh.* ....(33 to 1 op 25 to 1) 13

117[6] INSWINGER [35] 7-9-2 (5*) Mr G Kille (3) *broke wl, sn outpcd*..........................(33 to 1 op 25 to 1) 14

Dist: Hd, ½l, ½l, nk, ½l, 2l, ½l, 1l, 1½l, 2½l. 1m 14.48s. a 3.68s (14 Ran).

SR: 40/28/39/29/44/17/19/16/14/ (T S M S Riley-Smith), D A Wilson

CAGNES-SUR-MER (FR) (good)
Friday February 5th

132 Prix des Palmiers (3-y-o) £6,571 1¼m ....(2:35)

74* FAY WRAY (Fr) 8-12 G Elorriaga-Santos, ... 1

97* WAKRIA (Ire) 8-12 M Boutin, ... 2

MICROCLIMAT 8-3 P Courty, ... 3

89 MOUNTAIN WILLOW 8-5 G Guignard, ... 9

Dist: ½l, 12l, sht-hd, 1½l, ½l. 2m 6.90s. (20 Ran).

M Pimbonnet

SOUTHWELL (A.W) (std)
Friday February 5th
Going Correction: PLUS 0.45 sec. per fur.

133 New Balderton Apprentice Claiming Stakes CLASS F (4-y-o and up) £2,322 1m ....(2:10)

FIABA 5-7-12 (3*) Sally Radford-Howes (7) *al hndy, quickened ahead entering strt, sn clr, easily.* ....(6 to 1 op 5 to 1 tchd 8 to 1) 1

114[9] NORTH FLYER 4-7-12 Stephen Davies (6) *tried to make all, hdd entering strt, styd on same pace last 2 fs.* ....(6 to 1 op 4 to 1 tchd 7 to 1) 2

BOWDEN BOY (Ire) (bl) 5-9-6 (3*) E Husband (8) *sluggish strt, bustled alng to improve o'r 2 fs out, kpt on, nvr nrr*.................................(12 to 1 op 4 to 1) 3

39[6] TOP ONE 8-7-12 F Norton (5) *tucked away gng wl, hrd drvn whn pace quickened entering strt, no response.* ....(6 to 5 on op 6 to 4 tchd 2 to 1) 4

91[6] SOL ROUGE (Ire) 4-7-7 (3*) Nicola Howarth (2) *dsptd ld to hfwy, lost grnd o'r 2 fs out, rallied fnl furlong.* ....(8 to 1 op 7 to 1 tchd 10 to 1) 5

SEASIDE MINSTREL 5-8-8 A Tucker (4) *bustled alng thrght, nvr a factor*...............(12 to 1 op 7 to 1) 6

123[6] CREPT OUT (Ire) 4-8-8 S D Williams (3) *patiently rdn, shaken up entering strt, nvr nr to chal.* ....(12 to 1 op 6 to 1) 7

92[8] LIVE AND LET FLY 4-8-10 (3*) S Mulvey (1) *chsd alng to go pace hfwy, nvr a factor*..........................(33 to 1) 8

Dist: 3l, 6l, 2½l, nk, 7l, 2l, 5l. 1m 47.20s. a 8.20s (8 Ran).

SR: 18/6/13/-/-/ (William Haggas), W J Haggas

134 Halam Handicap CLASS F (0-70 4-y-o and up) £2,364 7f......................(2:40)

110[3] QUINZII MARTIN [50] (v) 5-8-12 J Williams (6) *patiently rdn, quickened up to ld jst ins fnl furlong, kpt on wl.* ....(9 to 2 op 4 to 1 tchd 5 to 1) 1

91[2] ON Y VA (USA) [59] 6-9-7 J Quinn (2) *trkd ldg 5, effrt and squeezed for room entering strt, ev ch o'r one out, kpt on*..................(9 to 4 fav op 7 to 2 tchd 2 to 1) 2

91[8] THE DREAM MAKER (Ire) [45] 4-8-0 (7*) M Humphries (10) *co'red up in midfield, swtchd outsd to improve last 2 fs, nrst finish*...........(14 to 1 op 12 to 1 tchd 16 to 1) 3

4742a BLYTON STAR (Ire) [32] 5-7-8 N Adams (7) *nvr far away, squeezed for room entering strt, led o'r 2 out till jst ins fnl furlong, no extr*.............. (25 to 1 op 50 to 1) 4

4818a[4] DOESYOUDOES [48] 4-8-10 T Williams (1) *patiently rdn, steady hdwy frm off the pace last 2 fs, prmsg.* (12 to 1) 5

79[3] BOY MARTIN [66] (bl) 4-9-11 (3*) S D Williams (8) *wth ldrs, hrd at work o'r 2 fs out, sn outpcd.* ....(14 to 1 op 7 to 1 tchd 16 to 1) 6

91[3] DIAMOND INTHE DARK (USA) [53] (v) 5-8-10 (5*) O Pears (5) *dictated pace till hdd and squeezed out entering strt, fdd*...................(11 to 2 op 6 to 1 tchd 5 to 1) 7

96[2] KALAR [40] 4-8-2 S Wood (3) *wl plcd on ins for o'r 4 fs, fdd*.....................(8 to 1 op 6 to 1 tchd 9 to 1) 8

91 COMPANY CASH [50] (bl) 5-8-12 Dean McKeown (9) *reluctant to race, reminders and rapid hdwy to ld entering strt, wnt lft, hdd and btn o'r 2 fs out.* (8 to 1 op 7 to 1) 9

BEATLE SONG [59] 5-9-0 (7*) S Drowne (4) *chsd ldg trio, hrd at work entering strt, sn btn.* ....(14 to 1 op 10 to 1 tchd 16 to 1) 10

Dist: 2l, ¾l, ¾l, 3l, ¾l, 2½l, 2½l, 3l, 8l. 1m 32.90s. a 6.80s (10 Ran).

SR: 43/46/30/15/22/38/17/-/-/ (Monolithic Refractories Ltd), D Haydn Jones

135 Mansfield Handicap CLASS F (0-60 4-y-o and up) £2,658 1½m...............(3:10)

78 HEIR OF EXCITEMENT [30] 8-7-13 (3*) F Norton (7) *tucked away on ins, pushed ahead entering fnl furlong, styd on*..........................(6 to 1 op 8 to 1) 1

MR POPPLETON [50] 4-9-4 W Ryan (5) *trkd ldr, led appr strt, rdn and hdd entering fnl furlong, one pace.* ....(8 to 1 op 6 to 1 tchd 9 to 1) 2

111⁹ GEE DOUBLE YOU [41] 7-8-13 J Williams (12) *improved frm midfield to go hndy hfwy, hrd at work o'r one furlong out, one pace*............(16 to 1) 3
LEXUS (Ire) [41] 5-8-13 J Quinn (6) *chsd alng to improve frm midfield entering strt, ev ch o'r one furlong out, not quicken*............(5 to 1 op 6 to 1) 4
ROCK LEGEND [42] 5-8-9 (5*) K Rutter (2) *trkd ldg 5, feeling pace and drvn alng appr strt, styd on fnl furlong.*............(9 to 2 op 4 to 1 tchd 6 to 1) 5
67 COMISKEY PARK (Ire) [34] 4-8-2 S Wood (4) *in tch, feeling pace and rdn aftr a m, styd on fnl furlong, nvr nrr.*............(16 to 1 op 33 to 1) 6
78* KRONPRINZ (Ire) [33] 5-7-12 (7*) D McCabe (9) *trkd ldg pair, hrd at work entering strt, no imprsn.*............(4 to 1 fav op 11 to 4) 7
108⁶ CAL'S BOY [35] (bl) 4-8-3 R Lappin (11) *pld hrd, wth ldrs for o'r a m, fdd*............(33 to 1) 8
42⁸ RUPPLES [24] 6-7-3 (7*) Darren Moffatt (3) *in tch, improved und pres aftr a m, fdd last 2 fs*.....(14 to 1 op 16 to 1) 9
VERY EVIDENT (Ire) [56] (bl) 4-9-10 D Nicholls (1) *dictated pace till appr strt, fdd*............(16 to 1 op 12 to 1) 10
4814a³ SECRET TREATY (Ire) [45] 4-8-6 (7*) D Wright (10) *chsd alng to keep up hfwy, nvr a factor*............(16 to 1) 11
30⁴ SWAGMAN (USA) [31] 6-7-12 (5*) Stephen Davies (8) *lost tch quickly hfwy, tld off*.... (8 to 1 op 7 to 1 tchd 9 to 1) 12

Dist: 1½l, 1½l, sht-hd, sht-hd, 2l, 5l, 1l, 2l, 15l, 8l. 2m 47.10s. a 13.20s (12 Ran).
SR: 10/23/15/14/14/-/ (D M Hetherington), A P Stringer

136 Old Clipstone Claiming Stakes CLASS F (3-y-o) £2,259 1m....................(3:40)

116⁴ HOTSOCKS 7-3 (7*) Kim McDonnell (2) *nvr far away, led o'r 2 fs out, hld on gmely fnl furlong.*............(10 to 1 op 6 to 1 tchd 11 to 1) 1
93² NIKKI NOO NOO 8-1 G Bardwell (6) *last and niggled alng, squeezed out entering strt, swtchd ins and not clr run o'r 2 out, ev ch inside last, one pace.*............(11 to 4 on op 9 to 4 on tchd 2 to 1 on) 2
37⁷ KUTE LUCY 7-10 S Wood (1) *wth ldr, led hfwy till o'r 2 fs out, not quicken und pres.*............(16 to 1 op 12 to 1 tchd 20 to 1) 3
62⁴ DON'T BE SAKI (Ire) 8-0¹ L Charnock (5) *nvr far away, ev ch and drvn alng last 2 fs, one pace.*............(8 to 1 op 7 to 2 tchd 9 to 1) 4
15⁵ BALLACASCADE 8-4 Dean McKeown (4) *pressed ldg pair, hrd at work o'r 2 fs out, fdd*........ (14 to 1 op 8 to 1) 5
4809a⁸ BIG-W 9-0 R P Elliott (8) *sluggish strt, dashed up on outsd aftr 2 fs, fdd entering strt*......... (50 to 1 op 20 to 1) 6
QUICK VICTORY 7-9³ (7*) J Marshall (3) *slight ld to hfwy, fdd und pres o'r 2 fs out*..........(50 to 1 op 33 to 1) 7
95⁷ BUDBY PRINCESS 8-3 T Williams (7) *chsd ldg quartet till wknd quickly o'r 2 fs out.*............(25 to 1 op 20 to 1 tchd 33 to 1) 8

Dist: ¾l, 5l, 1½l, 5l, 8l, 5l, 7l. 1m 47.80s. a 8.80s (8 Ran).
SR: 4/7/-/-/-/ (The Marketing And Distribution Group), Pat Mitchell

137 Gamston Handicap CLASS F (0-90 4-y-o and up) £2,259 2m..................(4:10)

61* COLERIDGE [67] (bl) 5-9-1 (5*) K Rutter (6) *nvr far away, brght wide to ld appr fnl furlong, styd on wl.*............(6 to 1 op 11 to 2 tchd 7 to 1) 1
122⁷ BEDOUIN PRINCE (USA) [50] (bl) 6-7-12 (5*) Stephen Davies (2) *patiently rdn, quickened ahead o'r 5 fs out, ridden and hdd appr fnl furlong, one pace.*............(6 to 1 op 5 to 1 tchd 13 to 2) 2
111* MASTER'S CROWN (USA) [48] 5-7-8 (7*,5ex) D McCabe (4) *led aftr 2 fs till o'r 5 out, rallied and ev ch appr fnl furlong, one pace*...(7 to 4 fav op 9 to 4 tchd 13 to 8) 3
53² LAFKADIO [43] 6-7-10 S Wood (5) *led for 2 fs, settled into midfield hfwy, effrt and drvn alng o'r two out, styd on.*............(6 to 1 op 5 to 1 tchd 7 to 1) 4
111² CLASSIC ACCOUNT [65] 5-8-11 (7*) S Mulvey (3) *trkd ldg quartet, feeling pace and drvn alng o'r 2 fs out, kpt on same pace*............(5 to 1 op 4 to 1) 5
111⁴ MINGUS (USA) [51] 6-8-4 J Fanning (1) *last and hld up, effrt appr strt, styd on, nvr nrr*.....(12 to 1 op 8 to 1) 6
GREEN LANE (USA) [71] 5-9-10 Dean McKeown (7) *pressed ldg trio, drvn alng whn pace quickened o'r 5 fs out, nvr dngrs*............(10 to 1 op 8 to 1 tchd 11 to 1) 7

Dist: 1½l, ½l, ½l, sht-hd, 3l, 12l. 3m 52.40s. a 25.90s (7 Ran).
(P J Sheehan), D Shaw

138 Langford Handicap CLASS F (0-60 3-y-o and up) £2,553 6f....................(4:40)

107² LAST STRAW [30] 5-7-11 (7*) Claire Balding (5) *dsptd ld, definite advantage o'r 2 fs out, hld on grimly fnl furlong*............(7 to 1 op 9 to 2) 1
76 CHOICE LOT [35] (v) 6-8-2 (7*) D Wright (9) *chsd alng to go pace, swtchd wide to improve last 2 fs, edgd lft, ran on.*............(50 to 1 op 33 to 1) 2
11⁸ QUATRE FEMME [50] 6-9-10 Dean McKeown (14) *slight ld aftr one furlong, hdd o'r 2 fs out, rallied und pres.*............(10 to 1 op 8 to 1) 3
47⁷ ROCKBOURNE [53] 4-9-13 W Ryan (6) *settled midfield, rdn to improve 2 fs out, styd on same pace fnl furlong.*............(10 to 1 op 8 to 1 tchd 11 to 1) 4
96⁶ STRIP CARTOON (Ire) [47] (bl) 5-9-7 N Adams (8) *nvr far away, feeling pace and drvn alng 2 fs out, not quicken.*............(8 to 1 op 6 to 1) 5
117⁴ TOSHIBA COMET [49] (bl) 6-9-9 J Quinn (3) *sluggish strt, steady hdwy frm off the pace last 2 fs, nrst finish.*............(4 to 1 fav op 6 to 1 tchd 7 to 1) 6
96⁴ EMERALD EARS [36] 4-8-3 (7*) S Drowne (15) *pressed ldrs, hrd at work o'r 2 fs out, one pace*.. (12 to 1 op 8 to 1) 7
MORPICK [51] 6-9-6 (5*) Stephen Davies (13) *bustled alng to keep up hfwy, styd on fnl furlong, nvr nrr.*............(12 to 1 op 14 to 1 tchd 16 to 1) 8
HITCHIN A RIDE [34] 6-8-8 J Williams (4) *struggling to keep up hfwy, nvr rch ldrs.*............(16 to 1 op 14 to 1 tchd 20 to 1) 9
6⁹ ARC LAMP [54] 7-9-11 (3*) S D Williams (2) *chsd ldrs, feeling pace hfwy, btn 2 fs out*......(20 to 1 op 8 to 1) 10
96⁷ JOVIAL KATE (USA) [51] 6-9-11 T Williams (7) *trkd ldrs, hrd at work o'r 2 fs out, fdd*............(10 to 1 op 6 to 1) 11
SUPREME DESIRE [51] 5-9-11 S Webster (1) *led for one furlong, lost pl hfwy, nvr able to reco'r.*............(14 to 1 op 12 to 1 tchd 16 to 1) 12
109⁶ PAINT THE WIND (Ire) [50] (bl) 3-8-8 J Fanning (12) *chsd alng to keep up hfwy, nvr a threat*..... (25 to 1 op 16 to 1) 13
96⁵ MISS BELL RINGER [32] 5-8-6 G Bardwell (11) *beh and drvn alng, nvr nr to chal*............(8 to 1 op 9 to 2) 14
LONG LAST [34] 4-8-8 S Wood (10) *sluggish strt, al tld off*............(50 to 1) 15

Dist: ¾l, nk, 1½l, 2l, nk, 4l, nk, sht-hd, nk. 1m 19.20s. a 5.80s (15 Ran).
SR: 28/30/44/41/27/28/-/13/-/ (Martin Pound Racing Ltd), A W Jones

LINGFIELD (A.W) (std)
Saturday February 6th
Going Correction: MINUS 0.35 sec. per fur.

139 Alpine Double Glazing Maiden Stakes CLASS F (4-y-o and up) £2,208 1¼m (1:50)

LOWAWATHA 5-8-11 (5*) Stephen Davies (7) *led aftr one furlong, quickened clr 2 out, pushed out.*............(8 to 1 op 4 to 1) 1
SET THE FASHION (v) 4-9-0 Dean McKeown (8) *chsd wnr frm hfwy, hrd rdn o'r 3 out, outpcd ins last 2 fs.*............(5 to 4 on op 2 to 1 on) 2
82⁵ CASTLE GALAH (v) 6-8-6 (5*) B Doyle (4) *wl plcd, improved into 3rd pl hfwy, rdn and one pace last 3 fs.*............(11 to 1 op 10 to 1 tchd 12 to 1) 3
3 FREE TRANSFER (Ire) (v) 4-9-0 D Nicholls (5) *nvr gng pace of ldrs, lost tch 3 out*............(11 to 4 tchd 5 to 2) 4
MARSH WARBLER 5-9-2 J Williams (1) *sn pushed alng in rear, nvr on terms, lost tch 3 out*....(12 to 1 op 8 to 1) 5
82⁸ RICH HEIRESS (Ire) (bl) 4-8-9 Candy Morris (3) *led for one furlong, chsd ldr til wknd rpdly hfwy, sn lost tch.*............(14 to 1 op 10 to 1) 6

Dist: 5l, 20l, 6l, 2½l, 5l. 2m 5.94s. a 2.74s (6 Ran).
SR: 40/28/-/ (N Lunn), D Morris

140 Cochrane Claiming Stakes CLASS F (4-y-o and up) £2,489 7f....................(2:20)

131⁸ SAMSOLOM 5-8-7 J Quinn (2) *made all, quickened 3 out, rdn out and hld on nr line*.........(12 to 1 op 7 to 1) 1
112* RESPECTABLE JONES 7-9-1 W Ryan (4) *chsd wnr thrght, rdn wl o'r one out, kpt on nr finish.*............(7 to 4 op 6 to 4 tchd 2 to 1) 2
101² BOLD HABIT 8-7-12 (5*) Stephen Davies (3) *steadied leaving stalls, hdwy frm rear, squeezed for room wl o'r one out, ran on last 100 yards*...... (6 to 4 fav tchd 5 to 4) 3
101⁶ MAC'S FIGHTER (bl) 8-8-0 (7*) B Russell (1) *settled in 3rd pl, rdn and not quicken 3 out, styd on ins fnl furlong.*............(3 to 1 op 7 to 2 tchd 4 to 1) 4
108⁹ MAHZOOZ 4-8-7 G Bardwell (5) *steadied leaving stalls, al in rear, tld off last 3 fs.*............(40 to 1 op 33 to 1 tchd 50 to 1) 5

Dist: Nk, ½l, ½l, 20l. 1m 29.72s. a 6.32s (5 Ran).
(The Hammond Partnership), P Howling

141 Collingwood Handicap CLASS F (0-70 4-y-o and up) £2,976 1½m..............(2:50)

115⁷ MODEST HOPE (USA) [60] 6-10-0 J McLaughlin (3) *handily plcd, shaken up o'r one out, quickened to ld ins fnl furlong, styd on strly*...............(8 to 1 op 6 to 1) 1
73* STRAT'S LEGACY [49] 6-9-3 J Quinn (7) *hld up in rear, prog 3 out, ev ch o'r one out, not quicken, kpt on nr line*............(13 to 8 fav op 5 to 4 tchd 7 to 4) 2
115² EL DOMINIO [53] 5-9-7 G Bardwell (5) *al wl plcd, rdn to ld o'r 3 out, hdd and no extr ins fnl furlong.*............(9 to 2 op 3 to 1) 3
73² HUNTING GROUND [49] 5-9-0 (3*) A Tucker (2) *hld up towards rear, rdn and outpcd 5 out, styd on appr fnl furlong*............(11 to 2 op 9 to 2) 4
103³ NASEER (USA) [47] 4-8-11 T Williams (9) *mid-div, rdn to join ldrs 4 out, wknd o'r one out*.....(8 to 1 op 7 to 1) 5

78 LA REINE ROUGE (Ire) [41] 5-8-6 (3*) F Norton (4) *chsd ldr, led o'r 4 out till over 3 out, wknd last 2 fs*......(20 to 1) 6
113^{6} COOL SOCIETY (USA) [57] 4-9-0 (7*) D McCabe (10) *beh most of way*......... (11 to 1 op 10 to 1 tchd 12 to 1) 7
ROGER RABBIT (Fr) [40] 4-8-4 N Adams (8) *hdwy 6 out, rdn and wknd 3 out*......(25 to 1 op 20 to 1 tchd 33 to 1) 8
EASTER TERM [33] 5-8-1^{3} G Carter (1) *al rear grp, outpcd 3 out*..........(20 to 1) 9
68^{5} CAL NORMA'S LADY (Ire) [53] 5-9-7 W Ryan (6) *led til o'r 4 out, sn wknd*..........(8 to 1 op 20 to 1) 10
Dist: 1½l, hd, 5l, 4l, 1½l, 4l, 3l, 12l, 1½l. 2m 35.27s. a 5.97s (10 Ran).
SR: 12/-/1/-/-/-/ (J McManamon), R C Spicer

142 Jervis Handicap CLASS D (0-90 4-y-o and up) £3,806 1m......................(3:20)

39* ALLINSON'S MATE (Ire) [80] 5-9-8 Alex Greaves (5) *hld up, hdwy o'r 3 out, hrd rdn to ld ins fnl furlong, ran on.*..........(7 to 1 op 6 to 1) 1
87^{2} KILLICK [52] 5-7-8^{1} J Quinn (6) *chsd ldr frm hfwy, ev ch entering fnl furlong, kpt on one pace nr line.*..........(9 to 2 op 4 to 1) 2
112^{3} SCOTS LAW [54] (bl) 6-7-10^{2} D Biggs (2) *led til hdd und pres ins fnl furlong, wknd.*..........(9 to 2 op 5 to 2 tchd 5 to 1) 3
50^{2} AMENABLE [72] 8-9-0 J McLaughlin (4) *hld up in rear, rdn alng 3 out, styd on ins fnl furlong, nrst at finish.*..........(7 to 1 op 6 to 1) 4
110^{9} GUESSTIMATION (USA) [51] 4-7-7 G Bardwell (1) *settled towards rear, rdn alng hfwy, nvr trbld frnt rnk.*..........(10 to 1 op 14 to 1) 5
69^{2} TRY LEGUARD (Ire) [59] 4-7-8 (7*) D Wright (7) *slwly into strd, sn in tch, hrd rdn 2 out, wknd fnl furlong.*..........(5 to 2 fav op 3 to 1 tchd 7 to 2) 6
108* NO SUBMISSION (USA) [86] 7-10-0 S Wood (3) *chsd ldr to hfwy, sn rdn and lost pl.* (3 to 1 op 9 to 4 tchd 7 to 2) 7
Dist: 2l, 4l, sht-hd, hd, ½l, 3½l. 1m 37.97s. a 1.77s (7 Ran).
SR: 39/5/-/12/-/-/12/ (Peter Jones), T D Barron

143 Blackwood Handicap CLASS E (0-80 3-y-o) £3,231 1m.......................... (3:50)

71* TAKE YOUR PARTNER (Ire) [54] 7-12 T Williams (4) *wl in tch, led o'r 3 out, drvn out and styd on.*..........(9 to 4 fav op 2 to 1 tchd 3 to 1) 1
80^{2} MISTER BLAKE [65] (bl) 8-6 (3*) Emma O'Gorman (3) *improved frm rear hfwy, pushed alng and ev ch entering fnl furlong, kpt on same pace.* (5 to 1 tchd 11 to 2) 2
44* KRYPTOS (USA) [65] 8-9 Dean McKeown (2) *hld up in tch, squeezed through to chal o'r one out, not quicken last 100 yards*..........(7 to 2 op 3 to 1 tchd 4 to 1) 3
109^{3} ASHOVER [65] 8-9 Alex Greaves (6) *led aftr one furlong till o'r 4 out, lost pl, kpt on ag'n fnl furlong.*..........(16 to 1 op 10 to 1 tchd 20 to 1) 4
22^{4} PERSIAN GUSHER (Ire) [75] (e/s) 8-12 (7*) A Martinez (5) *pld hrd in ldg grp, led o'r 4 out till over 3 out, no extr ins last 2 fs*.......... (8 to 1 op 7 to 1) 5
45* ABSOLUTELY FACT (USA) [77] 9-7 T Quinn (7) *pressed ldrs, rdn o'r 2 out, btn over one out*..... (3 to 1 tchd 7 to 2) 6
98* MARK'S CLUB (Ire) [63] (bl) 8-7 D Biggs (1) *led for one furlong, handily plcd til wknd und pres o'r one out.*..........(8 to 1 op 6 to 1) 7
Dist: 1½l, 2l, 4l, ½l, 1½l, ¾l. 1m 40.03s. a 3.83s (7 Ran).
(The Fairyhouse 1992 Partnership), M Johnston

144 Ladbroke All Weather Trophy Handicap Qualifier CLASS E (0-75 3-y-o and up) £3,002 6f.......................... (4:20)

12^{4} HENIU (USA) [61] (v) 4-9-3 T Quinn (3) *made virtually all, pushed clr o'r one out, not extended.*..........(5 to 1 op 4 to 1 tchd 11 to 2) 1
77^{6} WELLSY LAD (USA) [52] 6-8-8 S Wood (5) *trkd ldrs, ev ch 2 out, not quicken o'r one out, styd on same pace.*..........(12 to 1 op 14 to 1 tchd 16 to 1) 2
12^{5} INVOCATION [72] 6-9-7 (7*) B Russell (6) *cld on ldrs hfwy, rdn alng o'r 2 out, styd on ins fnl furlong.*..........(8 to 1 op 6 to 1 tchd 10 to 1) 3
4803a^{6} SALLY'S SON [59] 7-8-12 (3*) Emma O'Gorman (2) *ldg grp, rdn and ev ch 2 out, no extr appr fnl furlong.*..........(9 to 1 op 10 to 1 tchd 12 to 1) 4
4681a^{5} AIN'TLIFELIKETHAT [52] 6-8-1 (7*) M Jermy (10) *strted slwly, beh til styd on ins last 2 fs, nrst at finish.*..........(14 to 1 op 10 to 1) 5
106* PLAY HEVER GOLF [80] 3-9-6 W Ryan (7) *pressed ldr, rdn and not quicken wl o'r one out, wknd clsg stages.*..........(5 to 1 op 3 to 1) 6
47^{5} NORTH ESK (USA) [68] 4-9-10 M Tebbutt (8) *mid-div til outpcd frm hfwy*..........(10 to 1 op 8 to 1) 7
36^{3} BANBURY FLYER [61] 5-9-3 J Williams (4) *settled in mid-div, rdn and no hdwy ins last 2 fs.*..........(7 to 2 fav op 9 to 2) 8
99^{9} HINARI VIDEO [54] 8-8-10 Dean McKeown (1) *al beh.*..........(6 to 1 op 5 to 1 tchd 13 to 2) 9
ESTHAL (Ire) [73] 3-8-6 (7*) S Drowne (9) *al outpcd.*..........(10 to 1 op 7 to 1) 10

4779a^{5} SADDLEHOME (USA) [68] 4-9-10 N Day (11) *al outpcd, lost tch hfwy*..........(11 to 1 op 8 to 1 tchd 12 to 1) 11
Dist: 3l, nk, ¾l, 3l, sht-hd, nk, ½l, 6l, 2l, ½l. 1m 12.46s. a 1.66s (11 Ran).
SR: 28/7/26/10/-/2/5/-/-/ (Henryk de Kwiatkowski), Lord Huntingdon

CAGNES-SUR-MER (FR) (good)
Sunday February 7th

145 Prix William-Alexandre Ruinat (4-y-o and up) £8,961 1m 5f.................. (1:30)

104^{2} DANAE DE BRULE (Fr) 6-9-0 R Laplanche,.......... 1
CHESNAO (Fr) 4-8-9 O Doleuze,.......... 2
104* MARILDO (Fr) 6-9-4 G Guignard,.......... 3
104^{8} FLY AWAY SOON (USA) 5-8-9 J Reid,.......... 0
Dist: 2l, 7½l, hd, 1l, 5½l. 2m 49.70s. (11 Ran).
(L Seile), A Fabre

SANTA ANITA (USA) (firm)
Sunday February 7th

146 Charles H Strub Stakes (Grade 1) (4-y-o) £182,119 1¼m..........................

SIBERIAN SUMMER (USA) 8-6 C Nakatani,........(16 to 1) 1
BERTRANDO (USA) 8-10 C McCarron,....... (10 to 3 on) 2
MAJOR IMPACT (USA) 8-6 G Stevens,..........(74 to 10) 3
STAR RECRUIT (USA) 8-8 L Pincay Jr,..........(61 to 10) 4
DAROS 8-8 E Delahoussaye,.......... (15 to 1) 5
ZURICH (USA) 8-6 D Flores,..........(49 to 1) 6
AL SABIN (USA) 8-6 A Solis,..........(42 to 10) 7
BRILLIANT BLUE (USA) 8-6 K Skinner,..........(81 to 1) 8
Dist: 1 ¼l, 2l, 3l, ½l, 1l, nose, 19l. 2m 0.78s. (8 Ran).
(Buckram Oak Farm), R McAnally

SOUTHWELL (A.W) (std)
Monday February 8th

Going Correction: PLUS 0.35 sec. per fur.

147 Basil Claiming Stakes CLASS F (4-y-o and up) £2,427 6f......................(1:50)

144^{4} SALLY'S SON 7-8-6 (3*) Emma O'Gorman (14) *chsd ldrs, wide strt, effrt o'r one furlong out, led ins last, kpt on.*..........(13 to 2 op 7 to 2) 1
138^{3} QUATRE FEMME 6-7-9^{1} T Williams (13) *dwlt, sn cl up, wide strt, rdn to ld o'r one and a half fs out, hdd and no extr ins last*..........(2 to 1 fav op 3 to 1) 2
4768a GRAND TIME 4-7-13 G Bardwell (12) *prmnt, effrt 2 fs out, ev ch one furlong out, kpt on und pres.*..........(4 to 1 op 5 to 1 tchd 10 to 1 and 11 to 1) 3
99 SIR TASKER 5-9-5 T Quinn (9) *led, rdn 2 fs out, sn hdd and grad wknd*..........(12 to 1 op 10 to 1 tchd 14 to 1) 4
134^{6} BOY MARTIN (bl) 4-9-5 S Webster (2) *mid-div, pushed alng hfwy, styd on und pres fnl 2 fs*..... (12 to 1 op 8 to 1) 5
SULLY'S CHOICE (USA) 12-8-0 S Wood (8) *mid-div, pushed alng hfwy, styd on fnl 2 fs.* (25 to 1 op 14 to 1) 6
HANSOM LAD 10-8-13 Dean McKeown (11) *mid-div, rdn o'r 2 fs out, not rch ldrs*.......... (33 to 1 op 20 to 1) 7
49^{3} WHO'S THAT LADY 4-8-7 J Quinn (3) *cl up till rdn and wknd 2 and a half fs out*.......... (5 to 1 op 7 to 2) 8
76^{4} BLACK BOY (Ire) (bl) 4-8-4 (3*) F Norton (5) *chsd ldrs, rdn 2 and a half fs out, sn wknd*........ (16 to 1 op 12 to 1) 9
MISS MOODY 7-7-9^{1} N Adams (4) *sn rdn alng, al rear.*..........(33 to 1 op 25 to 1) 10
123^{7} WALLANGRIFF (bl) 5-7-13 (5*) M Fenton (7) *al beh.*..........(33 to 1 op 20 to 1) 11
76^{5} BRISAS (bl) 6-8-9 J Fanning (6) *al rear.*..........(14 to 1 op 10 to 1) 12
MISS EL ARAB (Ire) 5-8-1 (3*) A Tucker (10) *chsd ldrs, rdn and wknd o'r 2 fs out*.......... (20 to 1 op 12 to 1) 13
4796a^{9} SAVINIEN (Ire) 4-7-6 (7*) Kim McDonnell (1) *slwly away and outpcd, sn tld off*..........(100 to 1) 14
Dist: 1½l, ½l, 2½l, nk, 2½l, 1½l, ½l, 2l, 1½l, sht-hd. 1m 18.90s. a 5.50s (14 Ran).
SR: 27/7/9/19/18/-/ (W A O'Gorman), W A O'Gorman

148 Thyme Handicap CLASS F (0-80 4-y-o and up) £2,322 1½m......................(2:20)

125* HORIZON (Ire) [59] (bl) 5-9-5 (5ex) D Biggs (9) *made all, quickened clr 2 and a half fs out, rdn appr fnl furlong, kpt on*..........(13 to 8 on tchd 6 to 4 on) 1
125^{5} SUGEMAR [60] 7-8-13 (7*) D McCabe (6) *hld up, hdwy hfwy, rdn 3 fs out, styd on wl fnl 2 furlongs.*..........(11 to 1 op 7 to 1) 2
81^{4} ISLAND BLADE (Ire) [51] 4-8-7 G Carter (7) *in tch, hdwy 5 fs out, effrt to chase wnr 2 and a half furlongs out, sn rdn and one pace appr fnl furlong*......(9 to 1 op 6 to 1) 3
108^{4} SILVER SAMURAI [63] (bl) 4-8-12 (7*) S Mulvey (10) *chsd ldrs, rdn 3 fs out, grad wknd*...... (12 to 1 op 7 to 1) 4
RED INDIAN [40] 7-8-0 L Charnock (1) *chsd ldrs, rdn 3 fs out, sn wknd*..........(50 to 1) 5

64[5] ATLANTIC WAY [52] 5-8-12 G Bardwell (3) *hld up, hdwy hfwy, rdn 4 fs out, sn btn*..........(11 to 1 op 8 to 1) 6
92[2] BAHER (USA) [66] 4-9-8 D Nicholls (8) *chsd wnr, rdn o'r 3 fs out, sn wknd*..........(12 to 1 tchd 14 to 1) 7
125[7] LE TEMERAIRE [64] 7-9-10 Kim Tinkler (4) *nvr rch ldrs*. ....(33 to 1 op 20 to 1) 8
WESTFIELD MOVES (Ire) [62] 5-9-8 J Quinn (2) *al rear*. ....(16 to 1 op 14 to 1) 9
123[5] BATTUTA [41] 4-7-4 (7*) D Wright (5) *chsd ldrs 4 fs, sn lost pl, tld off fnl 5 furlongs*..........(25 to 1 op 20 to 1) 10
Dist: 1½l, nk, 8l, 2l, 8l, hd, 10l, 2l, 20l. 2m 44.60s. a 10.70s (10 Ran).
SR: 40/38/24/20/-/-/2/-/-/ (Mrs Solna Thomson Jones), T Thomson Jones

149 Parsley Handicap CLASS F (0-80 3-y-o) £2,238 7f.......................... (2:50)

121* PINE RIDGE LAD (Ire) [64] (bl) 9-2 (5ex) Dean McKeown (4) *made all, quickened clr 2 and a half fs out, rdn o'r one furlong out, kpt on wl*..........(9 to 4 op 2 to 1) 1
121[2] JORDYWRATH [55] 8-7 J McLaughlin (2) *trkd ldrs, effrt and hdwy o'r 2 fs out, sn rdn, kpt on*. ....(10 to 1 op 8 to 1) 2
124[4] ROSE FLYER (Ire) [58] 8-3 (7*) D McCabe (5) *in tch, pushed alng, hdwy o'r 2 fs out, kpt on one pace*. ....(9 to 1 op 6 to 1 tchd 10 to 1) 3
109[2] KINGSTON BROWN [62] 8-11 (3*) F Norton (6) *in tch, effrt and rdn 3 fs out, sn one pace*. ....(7 to 4 fav op 6 to 4 tchd 2 to 1 and 9 to 4) 4
124[3] EXPRESS MARIECURIE (Ire) [58] (bl) 8-10 Alex Greaves (3) *cl up, effrt 3 fs out, sn rdn and wknd 2 furlongs out*. ....(9 to 2 op 6 to 1 tchd 4 to 1) 5
80[5] PERSIAN TRAVELLER (Ire) [69] 9-0 (7*) G Parkin (7) *cl up till rdn and wknd 2 fs out*..........(10 to 1 op 7 to 1) 6
Dist: 1½l, 2½l, ¾l, 12l, 15l. 1m 32.00s. a 5.90s (6 Ran).
SR: 50/36/31/33/-/-/ (R Jenkinson), M Johnston

150 Sage Claiming Stakes CLASS F (4-y-o and up) £2,301 7f...................... (3:20)

108[5] LOCK KEEPER (USA) 7-8-4 J Quinn (5) *hld up in tch, hdwy on bit o'r 2 fs out, led over one furlong out, very easily*. ....(9 to 4 on op 7 to 2 on tchd 2 to 1 on) 1
39[8] POP TO STANS 4-8-10 G Bardwell (1) *led and rousted alng, hdd 3 fs out, styd on und pres fnl furlong*. ....(3 to 1 op 9 to 2) 2
4757a[7] THE CUCKOO'S NEST 5-8-8 Dean McKeown (2) *cl up, led 3 fs out, rdn 2 furlongs out, hdd o'r one furlong out, sn wknd*..........(7 to 1 op 8 to 1) 3
108 BOLD SPARK 5-8-0 N Adams (4) *chsd ldrs till rdn and wknd o'r 2 fs out*..........(20 to 1 op 10 to 1) 4
Dist: 3l, nk, 10l. 1m 43.50s. a 17.40s (4 Ran).
(C John Hill), C J Hill

151 Rosemary Maiden Stakes CLASS F (3-y-o) £2,070 6f.......................... (3:50)

ALWAYS BAILEYS 8-9 Dean McKeown (10) *chsd ldrs, hdwy 2 fs out, effrt and rdn to ld appr fnl furlong, kpt on*..........(11 to 8 fav op 7 to 4) 1
121[4] HERSHEBAR (bl) 9-0 S Webster (6) *beh, hdwy o'r 2 fs out, effrt and ev ch entering fnl furlong, not quicken und pres*..........(6 to 1 op 4 to 1) 2
4773a[8] BURBLE 8-9 S Wood (11) *beh, wide strt, gd hdwy 2 fs out, sn rdn, kpt on fnl furlong*..........(25 to 1) 3
63[4] MUSICAL PHONE (bl) 9-0 D Nicholls (9) *al prmnt, effrt to ld 2 fs out, sn rdn, hdd and wknd appr fnl furlong*. ....(11 to 1 op 10 to 1 tchd 12 to 1) 4
66[6] APOLLO DE ORIENTE 8-7 (7*) G Parkin (2) *prmnt, rdn 2 and a half fs out, grad wknd*......(20 to 1 op 16 to 1) 5
VILAMAR (Ire) 8-9 J Quinn (7) *cl up, led hfwy to 2 fs out, grad wknd*..........(16 to 1 op 14 to 1 tchd 20 to 1) 6+
MAGICATION 8-2 (7*) Claire Balding (8) *beh till styd on fnl 2 fs, not rch ldrs*..........(5 to 1 op 4 to 1 tchd 11 to 2) 6+
CRACKER JACK (bl) 9-0 J Fanning (1) *led to hfwy, sn wknd*..........(25 to 1 op 20 to 1) 8
116[5] PALACEGATE GIRL (bl) 8-9 J Carroll (5) *cl up till rdn and wknd o'r 2 fs out*..........(9 to 1 op 7 to 1) 9
GOOD IMAGE 9-0 T Quinn (3) *al rear*. ....(6 to 1 op 4 to 1 tchd 13 to 2) 10
4790a[8] THE CUT 8-9 L Charnock (4) *chsd ldrs to hfwy, sn wknd*. ....(25 to 1 op 20 to 1) 11
Dist: 1l, 3l, 3l, 4l, ½l, dd-ht, 5l, 4l, hd, 5l. 1m 19.30s. a 5.90s (11 Ran).
SR: 19/20/3/-/-/-/ (G R Bailey Ltd (Baileys Horse Feeds)), M Johnston

152 Chive Handicap CLASS F (0-70 4-y-o and up) £2,469 1m...................... (4:20)

120* SIRTELIMAR (Ire) [60] 4-9-8 (5ex) J McLaughlin (2) *made all, clr 2 fs out, sn rdn and kpt on wl*.... (6 to 1 op 5 to 1) 1
110* MENTALASANYTHIN [56] 4-8-11 (7*) D Wright (4) *al prmnt, chsd wnr 2 fs out, sn hrd rdn and kpt on*. ....(5 to 2 fav op 7 to 2 tchd 4 to 1) 2
135[6] COMISKEY PARK (Ire) [34] (bl) 4-7-10 S Wood (12) *mid-div, hdwy o'r 3 fs out, rdn and kpt on fnl 2 furlongs*. ....(25 to 1 op 20 to 1) 3
110[7] ROYAL ACCLAIM [36] (v) 8-7-12 N Adams (5) *beh till styd on und pres fnl 2 fs, nrst finish*....(25 to 1 op 16 to 1) 4
110[2] ADMIRALS SECRET (USA) [65] 4-9-13 S Webster (10) *chsd ldrs, lost pl o'r 2 fs out, styd on fnl furlong*. ....(11 to 2 op 9 to 2) 5
122[8] RESISTING (USA) [31] 5-7-7[7] (7*) Claire Balding (3) *beh till styd on fnl 2 fs, nvr dngrs*..........(50 to 1 op 33 to 1) 6
85[2] RIPSNORTER (Ire) [65] 4-9-13 T Quinn (7) *prmnt, chsd wnr 3 fs out, rdn 2 furlongs out and sn wknd*. ....(4 to 1 op 6 to 1) 7
84[6] BROAD APPEAL [36] (v) 5-7-12 J Quinn (8) *dwlt, nvr rch ldrs*..........(16 to 1 op 14 to 1) 8
MARIETTE LARKIN [46] 4-8-8 J Fanning (9) *mid-div, effrt and some hdwy o'r 2 fs out, sn rdn and wknd*. ....(25 to 1 op 16 to 1) 9
113[7] SAREEN EXPRESS (Ire) [46] 5-8-8 G Bardwell (1) *dwlt, hdwy to chase ldrs hfwy, rdn 3 fs out and sn wknd*. ....(14 to 1 op 10 to 1) 10
120[8] MAI PEN RAI [37] 5-7-13 D Biggs (11) *al rear*. ....(25 to 1 op 14 to 1) 11
123* DIGGER DOYLE [60] 4-9-5 (3*,5ex) F Norton (13) *chsd ldrs, rdn 3 fs out, sn wknd*..........(7 to 1 op 5 to 1) 12
COOL PARADE (USA) [53] 5-9-1 Dean McKeown (6) *al rear*. ....(25 to 1 op 20 to 1) 13
Dist: 1½l, 4l, 3l, 3l, ½l, sht-hd, 1½l, 2½l, hd, 2l. 1m 45.50s. a 6.50s (13 Ran).
SR: 53/44/10/3/23/-/20/-/-/ (D W Price), R C Spicer

CAGNES-SUR-MER (FR) (good)
Wednesday February 10th

153 Prix de la Californie (3-y-o and up) £7,168 6f 110yds.......................... (1:50)

HUNDREDFOLD (USA) 4-9-0 O Doleuze, ... 1
97[5] I'LLEAVEITOYOU (Ire) 3-8-3 O Peslier, ... 2
BOOMING (Fr) 5-9-0 M Boutin, ... 3
Dist: Nk, 1½l, 1½l, 5l, 1l. 1m 22.60s. (11 Ran).
(Henry-Charles Seymour), Mlle I Turc

154 Prix du Logis du Pin (3-y-o) £5,974 1m .... (4:05)

ART SCRIPT (Fr) 8-11 W Mongil, ... 1
105[5] SALBUS 8-11 O Peslier, ... 2
89[2] MYKERINA (USA) 8-7 R Laplanche, ... 3
Dist: 2l, sht-hd, 5½l, ½l, 3½l. 1m 41.20s. (20 Ran).
(J-P Azzoulai), A Tarifa

LINGFIELD (A.W) (std)
Thursday February 11th
Going Correction: MINUS 0.20 sec. per fur.

155 Damson Claiming Stakes CLASS F (4-y-o and up) £2,511 1m.................. (1:50)

142[7] NO SUBMISSION (USA) 7-9-7 S Wood (6) *trkd ldg pair, wnt second 4 fs out, led o'r one out, hrd hld*. ....(2 to 1 op 9 to 4 tchd 5 to 2) 1
130[4] EASTLEIGH 4-8-9 W Ryan (5) *in tch, effrt 3 fs out, ev ch one out, kpt on one pace*..........(6 to 4 fav op 5 to 4) 2
87[9] NELLIE DEAN 4-7-10 Dale Gibson (3) *led one furlong, led ag'n wl o'r 4 out, hdd over one out, one paced*. ....(11 to 2 op 4 to 1 tchd 6 to 1) 3
STORM FREE (USA) 7-8-1 G Bardwell (4) *sn pushed alng in rear, not pace to chal*..........(33 to 1 op 16 to 1) 4
69[5] APPEALING TIMES (USA) 4-8-8 (3*) Emma O'Gorman (1) *led aftr one furlong till hdd wl o'r 4 fs out, wknd*. ....(11 to 2 op 3 to 1) 5
87 MASRUR (USA) 4-8-11 G Carter (2) *missed break, sn tld off*..........(25 to 1 op 20 to 1 tchd 33 to 1) 6
Dist: ¾l, 3½l, 2½l, 1½l, 30l. 1m 38.67s. a 2.47s (6 Ran).
SR: 46/32/8/5/10/-/ (T S Redman), D W Chapman

156 Peach Handicap CLASS F (0-70 3-y-o) £2,586 5f.......................... (2:20)

121[3] DAANIERA (Ire) [69] (bl) 9-7 J Carroll (1) *wnt lft strt, beh, hdwy o'r one furlong out, ran on und pres to ld cl hme*. ....(8 to 1 op 9 to 2) 1
106[3] COMET WHIRLPOOL (Ire) [56] (bl) 8-8 J Quinn (6) *cl up, led o'r one furlong out till hdd close hme*. ....(7 to 2 op 11 to 4 tchd 4 to 1) 2
116[3] BELLE SOIREE [50] (e/s) 8-2[1] A McGlone (5) *cl up, ev ch one furlong out, hrd rdn and not quicken*. ....(6 to 1 op 8 to 1) 3
22* THE INSTITUTE BOY [69] (bl) 9-7 S Webster (3) *in tch, rdn and styd on fnl 2 fs, not pace to chal*. ....(9 to 2 op 11 to 4) 4
117[8] TEE-EMM [59] 8-4 (7*) L Carter (4) *led til rdn and hdd o'r one furlong out, wknd*.. (9 to 2 op 4 to 1 tchd 5 to 1) 5
71[5] SPLASH OF SALT (Ire) [66] 9-4 G Carter (2) *outpcd*. ....(11 to 4 fav tchd 3 to 1) 6
Dist: 1l, 2l, ½l, ½l, 3l. 1m 0.03s. a 1.83s (6 Ran).
SR: 50/33/19/36/24/19/ (J Berry), J Berry

157 Greengage Handicap CLASS E (0-80 4-y-o and up) £3,114 1m..................(2:50)

113² PIGALLE WONDER [52] (bl) 5-9-1 D Biggs (1) *hld up beh, hdwy o'r 2 fs out, led one out, sn clr, cmftbly.* ....(13 to 2 op 4 to 1 tchd 7 to 1) 1
120² BUDDY'S FRIEND (Ire) [52] 5-9-1 M Hills (3) *hld up beh, hdwy 2 fs out, ran on.*...............(3 to 1 op 2 to 1) 2
87⁵ APOLLO RED [49] 4-8-12 A McGlone (2) *trkd ldrs, short of room and lost grnd 2 fs out, swtchd rght o'r one out, ran on und pres ins last*...........(12 to 1 op 7 to 1) 3
4733a⁵ DAM CERTAIN (Ire) [56] 4-9-5 T Quinn (7) *cl up, led appr 2 fs out, hdd one out, one pace.* ....(14 to 1 op 8 to 1 tchd 16 to 1) 4
130² SARUM [56] 7-9-5 Dale Gibson (5) *took keen hold, trkd ldrs, hrd rdn o'r one furlong out, wknd ins last.* ....(11 to 4 fav op 5 to 2 tchd 3 to 1) 5
101⁵ ALBERT THE BOLD [62] (bl,e/s) 4-9-11 L Dettori (6) *trkd ldrs, rdn 2 fs out, wknd o'r one out..* (6 to 1 op 8 to 1) 6
131³ TYRIAN PURPLE (Ire) [62] 5-9-11 G Carter (4) *led, pushed alng 3 fs out, hdd appr 2 out, wknd quickly, tld off.* ....(7 to 2 tchd 4 to 1) 7

Dist: 3l, nk, nk, 1l, 1l, 25l. 1m 39.16s. a 2.96s (7 Ran).
SR: 33/24/20/26/23/26/-/ (Miss Nicola M Pfann), R J O'Sullivan

158 Daily Star Challenge Handicap Qualifier CLASS F (0-70 4-y-o and up) £2,660 1½m ....(3:20)

103* ALBERT [44] 6-9-4 J Quinn (8) *chsd ldrs, cld 3 fs out, led o'r one out, hrd rdn, all out....* (7 to 4 fav tchd 2 to 1) 1
SUPER LUNAR [54] 9-10-0 G Carter (4) *hld up in rear, hdwy appr 3 fs, led wl o'r 2 furlongs out till hdd over one out, rallied, jst fld..*...........(16 to 1 op 12 to 1) 2
TENAYESTELIGN [35] 5-8-9 T Quinn (2) *hld up, hdwy 4 fs out, one pace fnl 2 furlongs......* (20 to 1 op 14 to 1) 3
4806a⁴ INDIAN TERRITORY [42] 4-8-12 T Williams (5) *beh, rdn and hdwy o'r 4 fs out, one paced frm over 2 out.* ....(7 to 1 op 4 to 1) 4
131 SAMURAI GOLD (USA) [44] (v) 5-9-4 Dale Gibson (9) *pld hrd, trkd ldr, ev ch o'r 2 fs out, wknd over one out.* ....(16 to 1 op 14 to 1) 5
103⁸ WITH GUSTO [40] 6-9-0 G Bardwell (3) *trkd ldrs, one pace fnl 3 fs*..............(10 to 1 op 12 to 1 tchd 14 to 1) 6
55 NO MORE THE FOOL [54] (bl) 7-10-0 J Carroll (6) *led til hdd wl o'r 2 fs out, wknd*.............(12 to 1 op 10 to 1) 7
103⁵ BY ARRANGEMENT (Ire) [46] 4-8-11 (5*) B Doyle (7) *beh, hdwy hfwy, sn reminders, wknd.....*(6 to 1 op 4 to 1) 8
35² CRETOES DANCER (USA) [50] (bl) 4-8-13 (7*) Kim McDonnell (1) *trkd ldrs, sn pushed alng, wknd o'r 3 fs out.* ....(3 to 1 op 2 to 1) 9

Dist: Sht-hd, 8l, ¾l, hd, 3l, 3l, 3l, 12l. 2m 34.41s. a 5.11s (9 Ran).
SR: 29/38/3/4/9/-/7/-/-/ (T S M S Riley-Smith), D A Wilson

159 Alpine Double Glazing Maiden Stakes CLASS F (4-y-o and up) £2,208 1¼m (3:50)

68² GOLD BLADE 4-8-12 T Quinn (1) *wtd wth, hdwy 3 fs out, led o'r 2 out, sn clr, eased cl hme.* ....(6 to 4 on op 2 to 1 on) 1
135⁴ LEXUS (Ire) 5-9-0 J Quinn (2) *wtd wth in tch, hdwy on ins o'r 2 fs out, ran on, no ch with wnr..* (5 to 1 op 7 to 2) 2
61⁵ KENYATTA (USA) 4-8-12 Candy Morris (8) *wtd wth, hdwy 6 fs out, ev ch o'r 2 out, one pace.* ....(13 to 2 op 5 to 1 tchd 7 to 1) 3
127⁴ PRINCESS DECHTRA (Ire) 4-8-7 W Ryan (3) *led til hdd o'r 2 fs out, wknd over one out.* ....(10 to 1 op 6 to 1 tchd 12 to 1) 4
76⁷ CHERRYWOOD LASS (bl) 5-8-9 G Bardwell (4) *trkd ldrs, rdn alng 4 fs out, btn whn hmpd o'r 2 out.* ....(33 to 1 op 20 to 1) 5
112⁵ LEAH JAY (bl) 6-8-11 (3*) F Norton (5) *trkd ldrs till wknd 3 fs out..*..........................(33 to 1 op 20 to 1) 6
I RAN LOVELY 4-8-7 T Williams (6) *beh, shrtlvd effrt hfwy.* ....(20 to 1 op 10 to 1) 7
102³ GONE BUST (Ire) 4-8-12 M Hills (7) *trkd ldr, rdn 3 fs out, sn bumped and wknd*....................(12 to 1 op 7 to 1) 8

Dist: 1½l, 2½l, 20l, 3l, 1½l, 10l, 1½l. 2m 8.50s. a 5.30s (8 Ran).
SR: 25/24/17/-/-/ (Richard Berenson), N A Graham

160 Cherry Handicap CLASS F (0-70 3-y-o) £2,562 7f.......................... (4:20)

106² STARDUST EXPRESS [61] 9-7 Dean McKeown (3) *took keen hold, cl up, led o'r 3 fs out, drvn and ran on wl.* ....(6 to 4 fav tchd 11 to 4 and 13 to 8) 1
71⁴ ARAWA [48] 8-8 T Quinn (4) *hld up in cl tch, chsd wnr frm o'r one furlong out, hrd rdn and kpt on.* ....(5 to 1 tchd 7 to 1) 2
16⁷ PYTCHLEY DAWN [46] 8-1 (5*) Stephen Davies (1) *led til hdd o'r 3 fs out, rdn and one pace appr last.* ....(11 to 4 op 6 to 4 tchd 3 to 1) 3
136* HOTSOCKS [45] 7-12 (7*,5ex) Kim McDonnell (2) *sn pushed alng in tch, outpcd o'r 2 fs out.* ....(9 to 4 op 2 to 1 tchd 5 to 2) 4

Dist: 2½l, 3½l, 1l. 1m 27.60s. a 4.20s (4 Ran).
SR: 23/2/-/-/ (Mrs R A Johnson), M Johnston

SOUTHWELL (A.W) (std)
Friday February 12th
Going Correction: PLUS 0.40 sec. per fur.

161 Flying Dragon Maiden Stakes CLASS F (4-y-o and up) £2,070 1m.............(2:15)

108² THEMAAM 4-9-0 Dean McKeown (9) *cl up, led aftr 2 fs, quickened two out, pushed out.* ....(13 to 8 on op 5 to 4 on) 1
MAROWINS 4-9-0 J Quinn (12) *chsd wnr, effrt and ev ch 2 fs out, sn rdn and one pace appr fnl furlong.* ....(20 to 1 op 12 to 1) 2
107³ WEE SARAH 5-8-9 Alex Greaves (1) *mid-div, hdwy 3 fs out, styd on fnl 2 furlongs..*.........(11 to 2 op 9 to 2) 3
SPEED OIL 4-8-8¹ (7*) H Bastiman (5) *beh till styd on fnl 2 fs, nrst finish..*..................(20 to 1 op 10 to 1) 4
50⁷ ELABJER (USA) 4-9-0 Dale Gibson (3) *led 2 fs, cl up till rdn two and a half furlongs out, sn wknd.* ....(10 to 1 op 8 to 1 tchd 12 to 1) 5
SURE SHOT NORMAN 4-8-7 (7*) Darren Moffatt (4) *chsd ldrs till rdn and wknd o'r 3 fs out.*.....(16 to 1 op 8 to 1) 6
SUNKALA SHINE 5-9-0 L Charnock (8) *hld up and beh, some hdwy fnl 3 fs, nvr dngrs.* ....(16 to 1 op 8 to 1 tchd 20 to 1) 7
110 TIBBS INN 4-9-0 S Webster (6) *al rear.* ....(33 to 1 op 20 to 1) 8
ABBEY GREEN 5-9-0 D Biggs (11) *unruly strt and slwly away, rapid hdwy to chase ldrs aftr 2 fs, rdn 3 out, wknd quickly..*..................(33 to 1 op 16 to 1) 9
123⁸ ANGEL'S WING 4-8-2 (7*) Marie Plowright (10) *chsd ldrs till rdn and wknd 3 fs out..*......................(33 to 1) 10
CRIMSON CONSORT (Ire) 4-9-0 Kim Tinkler (7) *mid-div, effrt and some hdwy 3 fs out, sn wknd.* ....(33 to 1 op 20 to 1) 11
RUBY VISION (Ire) 4-8-9 W Ryan (2) *slwly away, al outpcd and tld off..*.......................(33 to 1 op 16 to 1) 12

Dist: 3l, 5l, 2½l, 1½l, 1½l, nk, 8l, 2½l, 2½l, 1½l. 1m 47.00s. a 8.00s (12 Ran).
SR: 28/19/-/-/-/-/ (Wetherby Racing Bureau Plc), T Thomson Jones

162 Peacock Claiming Stakes CLASS F (3-y-o) £2,343 1m......................... (2:45)

136² NIKKI NOO NOO 8-1 J Quinn (5) *hld up, hdwy 3 fs out, led on bit 2 out, rdn one out, kpt on.* (Evens fav tchd 5 to 4) 1
80 GLOWING PATH 8-2 G Bardwell (6) *pld hrd, hld up and beh, gd hdwy 2 fs out, styd on strly fnl furlong.* ....(25 to 1 op 14 to 1 tchd 33 to 1) 2
62⁵ BARSAL (Ire) 9-2 Alex Greaves (8) *beh, hdwy 2 fs out, rdn and styd on wl fnl furlong*.......(33 to 1 op 16 to 1) 3
45⁵ MRS DAWSON (v) 7-7 (7*) P McCabe (2) *dwlt, led aftr one furlong, rdn and hdd 2 out, kpt on one pace.* ....(11 to 4 op 2 to 1) 4
80⁶ BOULMERKA (bl) 7-8 (7*) Darren Moffatt (4) *chsd ldrs till lost pl hfwy, wide strt and ran on fnl 2 fs.* ....(33 to 1 op 20 to 1) 5
136³ KUTE LUCY 8-0 S Wood (3) *unruly strt, led one furlong, cl up and ev ch 2 out, sn rdn and wknd appr fnl furlong..*............(12 to 1 op 6 to 1 tchd 14 to 1) 6
4668a⁶ MELOS MODUS (Ire) (bl,e/s) 8-6 W Ryan (9) *chsd ldrs till rdn and wknd 3 fs out..*...........(12 to 1 op 8 to 1) 7
121⁶ RED EDGE 8-0¹ L Charnock (1) *al rear.* ....(33 to 1 op 20 to 1) 8
80⁸ HOTEL CALIFORNIA (Ire) 8-3 N Adams (7) *chsd ldrs to hfwy, sn wknd.* ....(11 to 2 op 6 to 1 tchd 5 to 1 and 13 to 2) 9

Dist: ½l, nk, ¾l, 1½l, nk, 7l, 8l, 1½l. 1m 49.80s. a 10.80s (9 Ran).
(C John Hill), C J Hill

163 Great Bear Handicap CLASS F (0-70 4-y-o and up) £2,427 7f...................(3:15)

85⁷ RURAL LAD [55] 4-8-13 J McLaughlin (4) *chsd ldrs, hdwy 2 fs out, rdn to ld ins fnl furlong, kpt on.* ....(9 to 1 op 8 to 1) 1
134⁷ DIAMOND INTHE DARK (USA) [53] (v) 5-8-11 Dean McKeown (9) *al cl up, effrt 2 fs out, ev ch ins fnl furlong, no extr nr finish.......* (9 to 1 op 8 to 1 tchd 10 to 1) 2
134⁴ BLYTON STAR (Ire) [36] 5-7-8¹ N Adams (8) *mid-div, hdwy o'r 2 fs out, sn rdn, styd on ins last..* (7 to 1 op 8 to 1) 3
107⁶ BAYIN (USA) [35] 4-7-1¹ (7*) Darren Moffatt (11) *chsd ldrs, hdwy and wide strt, led o'r 2 fs out, sn rdn, hdd and wknd ins fnl furlong*...............(16 to 1 op 14 to 1) 4
138² CHOICE LOT [35] (v) 6-7-0 (7*) D Wright (7) *slwly into strd and beh, hdwy 2 fs out, styd on fnl furlong.* ....(11 to 2 op 5 to 1 tchd 6 to 1) 5
4746a⁹ DREAM CARRIER (Ire) [67] 5-9-11 Alex Greaves (3) *beh, hdwy fnl 2 fs, not rch ldrs*..........(16 to 1 op 10 to 1) 6
110⁸ LORD NASKRA (USA) [57] (bl) 4-8-12 (3*) Emma O'Gorman (5) *beh, hdwy and wide strt, sn rdn and no imprsn.* ....(7 to 2 fav op 9 to 2 tchd 6 to 1) 7
152³ COMISKEY PARK (Ire) [35] (bl) 4-7-7 S Wood (2) *cl up, rdn 2 fs out, grad wknd*................(10 to 1 op 12 to 1) 8

138[8] MORPICK [51] 6-8-4 (5*) Stephen Davies (13) *al mid-div.* ....(16 to 1 op 14 to 1) 9
DESERT SPLENDOUR [62] 5-9-1 (5*) S Wynne (12) *nvr rchd ldrs*....................(16 to 1 op 20 to 1) 10
133* FIABA [70] 5-9-9 (5*) O Pears (1) *led and sn pushed alng, hdd and wknd 2 and a half fs out*... (8 to 1 op 5 to 1) 11
133[4] TOP ONE [45] 8-8-3 J Quinn (6) *chsd ldrs till rdn and wknd 3 fs out*.................... (14 to 1 op 6 to 1) 12
138 MISS BELL RINGER [35] 5-7-7 G Bardwell (10) *chsd ldrs, rdn o'r 3 fs out, sn wknd*......... (16 to 1 op 12 to 1) 13
Dist: 1½l, hd, nk, 2½l, 1½l, 5l, hd, 3l, ½l, 2½l. 1m 32.70s. a 6.60s (13 Ran).
SR: 42/35/17/15/7/34/9/-/-/ (John Purcell), R C Spicer

164 Sea Goat Claiming Stakes CLASS F (4-y-o and up) £2,343 1½m................(3:45)

133[5] SOL ROUGE (Ire) 4-7-6[2] (7*) Nicola Howarth (4) *made all, rdn 2 fs out, ran on wl.* ....(12 to 1 op 8 to 1 tchd 16 to 1) 1
94[2] AMOUR ROYAL 6-9-2 D Nicholls (8) *trkd ldrs, hdwy 5 fs out, effrt o'r 2 furlongs out, sn rdn, kpt on one pace fnl furlong*....................(9 to 2 tchd 5 to 1) 2
READY TO DRAW (Ire) 4-8-6 R P Elliott (5) *al prmnt, hdwy to chase wnr 4 fs out, rdn 2 out, ev ch one out, wknd ins last*....................(7 to 1 op 9 to 2) 3
123[4] LARA'S BABY (Ire) 5-8-3 Kim Tinkler (1) *in tch till lost pl hfwy, hdwy 4 fs out, rdn o'r 2 out, one pace.* ....(7 to 4 fav op 6 to 4 tchd 2 to 1) 4
122[6] LORD ADVOCATE (v) 5-8-5 Alex Greaves (3) *mid-div, effrt o'r 4 fs out, sn rdn and no imprsn.* ....(7 to 2 op 3 to 1 tchd 4 to 1) 5
QUALITAIR IDOL 4-7-11 D Biggs (9) *hld up, hdwy hfwy, rdn and wknd 3 fs out*....................(16 to 1 op 14 to 1) 6
78[9] LIZZIE DRIPPIN (Can) 4-7-0 (7*) D Wright (6) *beh, effrt and some hdwy o'r 4 fs out, sn rdn and wknd.* ....(12 to 1 op 10 to 1 tchd 14 to 1) 7
122[9] ADMINISTER 5-8-2 (7*) W Hollick (2) *prmnt till rdn and wknd o'r 4 fs out*......(8 to 1 op 5 to 1 tchd 10 to 1) 8
MISS CARANGE (Ire) (v) 5-7-11 J Quinn (7) *chsd ldr till wknd quickly o'r 4 fs out*.........(25 to 1 op 20 to 1) 9
Dist: 2l, 3l, 5l, 2½l, ¾l, ½l, 30l. 2m 46.00s. a 12.10s (9 Ran).
SR: 10/25/9/-/-/-/ (R Thompson), R Thompson

165 Milky Way Handicap CLASS F (0-60 4-y-o and up) £2,574 1¾m................(4:15)

148* HORIZON (Ire) [59] (bl) 5-9-13 (5ex) D Biggs (1) *led, rdn 2 fs out, hdd appr fnl furlong, rallied to ld und pres ins last, styd on gmely.* ....(11 to 10 fav op 11 to 8 on tchd 6 to 4 on) 1
111[3] WELL AND TRULY [40] 6-8-8 T Quinn (6) *al prmnt, effrt 2 fs out, rdn to ld appr fnl furlong, hdd and no extr ins last.* ....(10 to 1 op 6 to 1) 2
13 SERIOUS ACTION [40] 4-8-3 G Carter (7) *chsd wnr, rdn 2 fs out, sn wknd*..........(13 to 2 op 7 to 1 tchd 8 to 1) 3
137[2] BEDOUIN PRINCE (USA) [50] (bl) 6-8-13 (5*) Stephen Davies (3) *in tch, effrt 4 fs out, sn rdn and one pace.* ....(10 to 1 op 6 to 1) 4
135* HEIR OF EXCITEMENT [35] 8-8-0 (3*,5ex) F Norton (4) *chsd ldrs, rdn 4 fs out, sn one pace*......(14 to 1 op 8 to 1) 5
65[4] ELIZA WOODING [34] 5-8-2 G Bardwell (9) *beh and rdn alng, kpt on fnl 3 fs, nvr dngrs.* ....(3 to 1 op 10 to 1 tchd 16 to 1) 6
EQUITY CARD (Ire) [60] 5-10-0 W Ryan (10) *wl beh, some hdwy 5 fs out, sn rdn and no imprsn.* ....(33 to 1 op 16 to 1) 7
126[5] SOUL TRADER [39] 4-7-10[1] (7*) Marie Plowright (11) *nvr rchd ldrs*....................(33 to 1 op 20 to 1) 8
135[9] RUPPLES [25] 6-7-1[1] (7*) Darren Moffatt (12) *chsd ldrs 7 fs, sn lost pl*....................(33 to 1 op 25 to 1) 9
135[7] KRONPRINZ (Ire) [33] 5-7-9[1] (7*) D McCabe (8) *chsd ldrs till rdn and wknd o'r 4 fs out*......... (20 to 1 op 14 to 1) 10
94[4] CARDEA CASTLE (Ire) [30] 5-7-12 J Quinn (5) *al rear, tld off fnl 4 fs*....................(25 to 1 op 14 to 1) 11
Dist: 2l, 10l, nk, 10l, ¾l, 1½l, 3l, 3l, 25l, 10l. 3m 11.40s. a 11.40s (11 Ran).
SR: 55/32/7/21/-/-/6/-/-/ (Mrs Solna Thomson Jones), T Thomson Jones

166 North Star Handicap CLASS F (0-90 3-y-o and up) £2,238 6f..................(4:45)

ROSEATE LODGE [80] 7-9-10 G Carter (6) *beh, rapid hdwy o'r 2 fs out, led one out, edgd lft and rdn clr.* ....(11 to 1 op 16 to 1) 1
41[2] JOHNSTON'S EXPRESS (Ire) [62] 5-8-6 J Quinn (7) *trkd ldrs gng wl, smooth hdwy 2 fs out, rdn and ev ch appr fnl furlong, kpt on one pace*..... (4 to 1 jt-fav tchd 9 to 2) 2
147[2] QUATRE FEMME [50] 6-7-8 G Bardwell (4) *led, rdn clr o'r 2 fs out, hdd one furlong out, no extr ins last.* (4 to 1 jt-fav op 3 to 1) 3
101[4] APPLEDORN [80] 6-9-10 T Quinn (5) *beh, hdwy on inner 2 fs out, kpt on one pace fnl furlong*...(7 to 1 op 5 to 1) 4
138[6] TOSHIBA COMET [49] (bl,e/s) 6-7-0 (7*) Kim McDonnell (2) *chsd ldrs, till rdn and wknd 2 fs out.* ....(10 to 1 op 8 to 1) 5
99[6] TINO TERE [72] 4-9-2 J Carroll (3) *dwlt, hdwy to chase ldrs aftr 2 fs, rdn o'r two furlongs out, sn wknd.* ....(13 to 2 op 6 to 1 tchd 7 to 1) 6

96* LINCSTONE BOY (Ire) [60] (bl) 5-8-4[1] S Webster (8) *cl up till rdn and wknd 2 fs out*..............(7 to 1 op 5 to 1) 7
79[5] AFRICAN CHIMES [84] 6-9-11 (3*) S D Williams (1) *al rear.* ....(8 to 1 op 7 to 1) 8
Dist: 2½l, sht-hd, 3½l, 3l, 2½l, 5l, 6l. 1m 18.80s. a 5.40s (8 Ran).
SR: 50/22/9/25/-/ (D A Price), K R Burke

LINGFIELD (A.W) (std)
Saturday February 13th
Going Correction: MINUS 0.25 sec. per fur.

167 Happy Couple Claiming Stakes CLASS F (3-y-o) £2,422 1m....................(1:25)

143[2] MISTER BLAKE (bl) 8-8 (3*) Emma O'Gorman (4) *wl plcd, jnd ldr 2 fs out, led well o'r one out, cleverly.* ....(7 to 4 on op 2 to 1 on tchd 13 to 8 on) 1
160[4] HOTSOCKS 7-5 (7*) Kim McDonnell (8) *led aftr 3 fs, rdn and hdd wl o'r one out, not quicken.* ....(7 to 2 op 5 to 2 tchd 4 to 1) 2
98[3] GENESIS FOUR (bl) 7-9[1] (5*) B Doyle (3) *led 3 fs, rdn and kpt on ins fnl furlong*............ (50 to 1 op 25 to 1) 3
PREMIER BLUES (Fr) 7-10 D Biggs (6) *pushed alng in rear hfwy, ran on o'r 2 fs out, styd on one pace fnl furlong.* ....(14 to 1 op 8 to 1) 4
LITTLE KARLIE (Den) 7-7 (7*) D Wright (1) *steadied strt, nvr rch ldrs*....................(25 to 1 op 20 to 1) 5
31[5] WEALTHYWOO 7-9[1] J Quinn (5) *settled rear, pushed alng hfwy, nvr on terms*................(10 to 1 op 8 to 1) 6
45[7] BUCKSKI ECHO 8-1 N Adams (7) *in tch, rdn and not quicken appr last 2 fs*............ (25 to 1 op 20 to 1) 7
100[5] GENERAL LINK 8-3 G Bardwell (2) *chsd ldrs till wknd o'r 3 fs out*.................... (9 to 1 op 7 to 1 tchd 10 to 1) 8
Dist: 2l, 1½l, 2l, 3l, ½l, ¾l, 6l. 1m 41.00s. a 4.80s (8 Ran).
(Red Seven Stable), W A O'Gorman

168 Alpine Double Glazing Maiden Stakes CLASS F (3-y-o) £2,208 6f...........(2:00)

4747a[2] SQUIRE YORK 9-0 T Quinn (3) *made virtually all, shaken up o'r one furlong out, kpt on nr line.* ....(8 to 1 op 4 to 1 tchd 10 to 1) 1
116[2] PURBECK CENTENARY 9-0 Lorna Vincent (7) *hld up, hdwy hfwy, ev ch one furlong out, no extr last 100 yards*................(11 to 4 op 7 to 4 tchd 3 to 1) 2
QUELQUE CHOSE 9-0 M Hills (4) *chsd ldrs, rdn and one pace appr fnl furlong.* ....(11 to 8 fav op 6 to 4 tchd 7 to 4) 3
151 GOOD IMAGE 9-0 D Nicholls (5) *pressed ldrs, ev ch 2 fs out, wknd o'r one out*............. (14 to 1 op 6 to 1) 4
21[5] GIRTON BELLE (v) 8-2 (7*) D Wright (6) *in tch till outpcd hfwy*.................... (50 to 1 op 25 to 1) 5
98[4] MISS DELIVERY 8-2 (7*) L Carter (1) *wth ldr to hfwy, sn lost pl*.............. (33 to 1 op 20 to 1 tchd 50 to 1) 6
RYDAL WATER 8-9 Dean McKeown (2) *strted slwly, sn rdn alng, al beh*...........(11 to 4 op 7 to 4 tchd 3 to 1) 7
Dist: 1l, 2l, 5l, 8l, 2l, 8l. 1m 13.88s. a 3.08s (7 Ran).
SR: 8/4/-/-/ (J Powell-Tuck), J L Spearing

169 Shirley And Lance Bradnam Handicap CLASS D (0-95 4-y-o and up) £4,503 1¼m ....(2:30)

115[3] MULCIBER [72] 5-9-4 M Hills (7) *mid-div, ran on 4 fs out, led appr last, jst hld on*........ (6 to 1 jt-fav op 5 to 1) 1
142[2] KILLICK [52] 5-7-12 J Quinn (5) *pressed ldrs till outpcd o'r 2 fs out, str brst ins last, jst fld*...............(12 to 1) 2
152[2] MENTALASANYTHIN [56] 4-7-7 (7*) D Wright (6) *mid-div, cld on ldrs frm 2 fs out, not much room entering last, fnshd wl*.................... (10 to 1 op 8 to 1) 3
58[3] REFLECTING (Ire) [71] 4-9-1 W Ryan (3) *hld up in rear, hdwy and not clr run 2 fs out, styd on strly fnl furlong.* .... (13 to 2 op 5 to 1 tchd 7 to 1) 4
4732a* COLTRANE [67] (v) 5-8-13 Dean McKeown (2) *led till appr fnl furlong, rallied und pres.* (6 to 1 jt-fav tchd 13 to 2) 5
128* LOOKINGFORARAINBOW (Ire) [73] 5-9-5 N Day (4) *ldg grp, ev ch wl o'r one furlong out, fdd*.....(7 to 1 op 6 to 1) 6
114[2] CARLOWITZ (USA) [54] 5-7-9[2] (7*) B Russell (8) *sn tracking ldrs, rdn and not quicken ins last 2 fs.* .... (9 to 1 op 8 to 1 tchd 10 to 1) 7
113* MASTER HYDE (USA) [71] 4-8-12 (3*) S O'Gorman (1) *in tch, rdn and no extr o'r one furlong out.* ....(7 to 1 tchd 15 to 2) 8
115[4] RAPPORTEUR (USA) [82] 7-9-9 (5*) B Doyle (12) *effrt frm rear 4 fs out, no imprsn from 2 out.* (12 to 1 op 10 to 1) 9
152[7] RIPSNORTER (Ire) [65] 4-8-9 T Quinn (13) *beh, effrt o'r 2 fs out, sn rdn and btn*.............. (16 to 1 op 14 to 1) 10
MOONLIGHT QUEST [80] 5-9-12 G Baxter (10) *al rear.* ....(20 to 1) 11
158[9] CRETOES DANCER (USA) [50] (bl) 4-7-1 (7*) Kim McDonnell (9) *pressed ldrs 6 fs, wknd quickly.* ....(12 to 1 tchd 16 to 1) 12
Dist: Sht-hd, ¾l, ¾l, sht-hd, ¾l, 1½l, nk, 5l, 2l, 7l. 2m 5.68s. a 2.48s (12 Ran).
SR: 54/33/33/46/43/47/25/39/42/ (Mrs Penny Treadwell), G Harwood

170 Jack And Gill Cole Handicap CLASS E (0-80 4-y-o and up) £3,172 5f........ (3:00)

86³ EWALD (Ire) [50] 5-7-9 (5*) B Doyle (2) *made virtually all, reminders and ran on strly appr fnl furlong.* ....(7 to 2 co-fav op 5 to 2 tchd 4 to 1) 1
99⁸ SERIOUS HURRY [49] 5-7-13 J Quinn (3) *chsd wnr, rdn and kpt on fnl furlong*............(14 to 1 op 10 to 1) 2
ASSIGNMENT [74] 7-9-10 T Williams (1) *in tch, pushed alng hfwy, not quicken frm 2 fs out.* (9 to 1 op 12 to 1) 3
99⁵ RUNNING GLIMPSE (Ire) [78] 5-9-7 (7*) A Martinez (5) *hdwy frm rear o'r one furlong out, fnshd wl.* ....(8 to 1 op 7 to 1) 4
76* PRIME MOVER [68] (v) 5-9-4 L Charnock (4) *outpcd in rear till effrt o'r one furlong out, not rch ldrs.* ....(9 to 2 op 3 to 1) 5
99* MISTER JOLSON [65] 4-8-8 (7*) S Drowne (7) *chsd ldrs for o'r 3 fs, sn btn*..............(7 to 2 co-fav op 11 to 4) 6
117³ SOBA GUEST (Ire) [70] 4-9-6 J Carroll (8) *prmnt on outsd, rdn alng 2 fs out, no extr appr last.* (7 to 2 co-fav op 4 to 1) 7
131⁷ RUSHANES [53] 6-8-0 (3*) F Norton (6) *trkd ldrs till wknd and hmpd o'r one furlong out.* .... (8 to 1 op 10 to 1 tchd 12 to 1) 8

Dist: 1½l, 2½l, nk, 2l, ½l, ½l, 5l. 59.37s. a 1.17s (8 Ran).
SR: 38/31/46/49/31/26/29/-/ (Daniel Scullion), M Johnston

171 Cupid Claiming Stakes CLASS F (4-y-o and up) £2,489 1½m................ (3:30)

126² BREAKDANCER (Ire) 4-8-9 T Quinn (3) *settled in 4th pl, hdwy o'r 3 fs out, led over 2 out, styd on strly.* .... (7 to 2 op 11 to 4) 1
59⁴ AWESOME POWER 7-9-7 M Hills (5) *pld hrd, trkd ldr till lost pl o'r 3 fs out, ran on und pres fnl furlong.* .... (7 to 4 on tchd 6 to 4 on) 2
128⁷ PRESENT TIMES 7-8-7 N Adams (6) *improved frm rear o'r 3 fs out, rdn and no extr wl over one out.* ....(11 to 1 op 10 to 1 tchd 12 to 1) 3
126³ IRON BARON (Ire) (bl) 4-8-5 W Ryan (4) *pld hrd, led o'r 5 fs out till over 2 out, wknd over one out.* .... (11 to 2 op 9 to 2 tchd 6 to 1) 4
GIN AND ORANGE (e/s) 7-8-1 (5*) B Doyle (1) *effrt frm rear 4 fs out, rdn and wknd 2 out*...... (16 to 1 op 12 to 1) 5
PEACH BRANDY 4-8-0 D Biggs (2) *set slow pace early, hdd o'r 5 fs out, sn drpd rear*...... (50 to 1 op 20 to 1) 6

Dist: ½l, 6l, 6l, ½l, ¾l. 2m 43.17s. a 13.87s (6 Ran).
(J Jannaway), W R Muir

172 T.I.M. Thank You For Calling Handicap CLASS E (0-80 3-y-o) £3,321 1m..... (4:00)

32 STEVIE'S WONDER (Ire) [50] 8-8 J Quinn (2) *pressed ldr, led o'r 4 fs out, styd on und pres ins last.* .... (11 to 2 op 5 to 1 tchd 7 to 1) 1
44⁵ WATERLORD (Ire) [63] 9-7 M Hills (4) *led for o'r 3 fs, pressed ldr till no extr last 100 yards*........(4 to 1 op 11 to 4) 2
143* TAKE YOUR PARTNER (Ire) [59] 9-3 Dean McKeown (1) *reared in stalls and lost grnd, sn tracking ldrs, hrd rdn o'r 3 fs out, one pace appr last.* ....(2 to 1 on op 9 to 4 on) 3
109⁴ QUICK SILVER BOY [61] 9-5 L Charnock (3) *settled rear, rdn alng 3 fs out, no imprsn on ldrs frm 2 out.* .... (14 to 1 op 8 to 1 tchd 16 to 1) 4

Dist: 1l, 3l, 5l. 1m 41.23s. a 5.03s (4 Ran).
(T G Mills), T G Mills

CAGNES-SUR-MER (FR) (good)
Sunday February 14th

173 Prix de la Baie Des Anges (3-y-o) £5,974 1m 110yds........................(1:25)

154² SALBUS (bl) 8-5 O Peslier, *trkd ldr, 3rd strt, led appr fnl furlong, ran on wl*.. 1
PRINCE DIANON (Fr) 8-5 M de Smyter, ... 2
97² BURD KING (Fr) 8-5 E Saint-Martin, ... 3

Dist: 1½l, 2l, 2l, ½l, sht-hd. 1m 46.00s. (15 Ran).
(Tudor Travel Ltd), S Dow

174 Prix Des Poms (3-y-o claimer) £4,799 1¼m ....(1:50)

SAUKARA (Fr) 8-1 (7*) S Culin, ... 1
119⁵ SOLDIERS BAY 8-11 G Guignard, *mid-div, 5th strt, ev ch 2 fs out, kpt on*.. 2
STAR HORSE (Fr) 8-5 (5*) G Heurtault, ... 3

Dist: 2l, 2l, sht-hd, 3½l, 1l. 2m 5.30s. (20 Ran).
M Pimbonnet

SOUTHWELL (A.W) (std)
Monday February 15th
Going Correction: PLUS 0.40 sec. per fur. (races 1,2,3,4,5), PLUS 0.10 (6)

175 Ski-ing Handicap CLASS F (0-80 4-y-o and up) £2,364 2m....................(2:10)

137* COLERIDGE [69] (bl) 5-9-3 (5*) K Rutter (10) *al prmnt, led 6 fs out and sn clr, ran on wl fnl 2.* ....(5 to 2 fav op 2 to 1 tchd 3 to 1) 1
165⁴ BEDOUIN PRINCE (USA) [50] (bl) 6-7-12 (5*) Stephen Davies (3) *trkd ldrs, hdwy 6 fs out, chsd wnr 2 out, sn rdn and kpt on*.. (13 to 2 op 5 to 1 tchd 7 to 1) 2
148⁶ ATLANTIC WAY [52] 5-8-5 G Bardwell (2) *chsd ldrs, hdwy 6 fs out, rdn 3 out, sn one paced.* ....(8 to 1 op 5 to 1 tchd 9 to 1) 3
122* KOVALEVSKIA [40] 8-7-7 J Quinn (9) *in tch, rdn alng and outpcd aftr 6 fs, styd on und pres fnl 3.* ....(4 to 1 op 3 to 1 tchd 9 to 2) 4
137⁴ LAFKADIO [42] 6-7-9 S Wood (7) *made most to 6 fs out, sn rdn, wknd o'r 4 out*......(7 to 1 op 6 to 1 tchd 8 to 1) 5
122⁴ ONE FOR THE CHIEF [40] (v) 5-7-0 (7*) D Wright (5) *hld up and beh, rdn alng hfwy, nvr a factor*......... (20 to 1) 6
AS D'EBOLI (Fr) [60] 6-8-13 J Fanning (1) *chsd ldrs, rdn 6 fs out, sn wknd*..........................(14 to 1 op 9 to 1) 7
111⁷ MALENOIR (USA) [54] (v) 5-8-7 J McLaughlin (8) *cl up, rdn alng hfwy, wknd 6 fs out*.......... (5 to 1 tchd 6 to 1) 8
CASTLE SECRET [75] 7-10-0 L Charnock (4) *hld up in rear, rdn alng 6 fs out, sn wl beh*........(20 to 1 op 10 to 1) 9
25 FAR DARA [42] 7-7-9² N Adams (6) *al rear, wl tld off frm hfwy*..............................(100 to 1 op 50 to 1) 10

Dist: 7l, 8l, ½l, 15l, 2l, 3l, 1½l. 3m 48.80s. a 22.30s (10 Ran).
(P J Sheehan), D Shaw

176 Husky Claiming Stakes CLASS F (4-y-o and up) £2,385 7f....................(2:40)

19² FARM STREET 6-7-11 (7*) B Russell (11) *cl up, led o'r 2 fs out, sn rdn, ran on wl fnl furlong.* ....(14 to 1 op 10 to 1 tchd 16 to 1) 1
142⁶ TRY LEGUARD (Ire) 4-8-2 J Quinn (1) *chsd ldrs, effrt 2 fs out, sn rdn and edgd lft, kpt on one pace.* ....(5 to 1 tchd 11 to 2) 2
123² JUVENARA 7-7-13 G Bardwell (7) *beh, wide strt, rdn and styd on fnl 2 fs, nrst finish*......... (12 to 1 op 7 to 1) 3
147* SALLY'S SON 7-8-9 (3*) Emma O'Gorman (10) *prmnt, effrt and rdn 2 fs out, sn one paced.* (7 to 2 jt-fav op 5 to 2) 4
152 DIGGER DOYLE 4-9-3 Dean McKeown (5) *sn led, rdn and hdd o'r 2 fs out, grad wknd.* ....(9 to 1 op 7 to 1 tchd 10 to 1) 5
147⁵ BOY MARTIN (bl) 4-8-9 S Webster (4) *sn beh, rdn hfwy, styd on fnl 2 fs*.......... (4 to 1 op 5 to 1 tchd 6 to 1) 6
147⁶ SULLY'S CHOICE (USA) (bl) 12-7-13 S Wood (2) *beh, hdwy 2 fs out, sn rdn and kpt on one pace.* ....(14 to 1 op 10 to 1 tchd 16 to 1) 7
NEVENTER (Fr) 4-9-10 V Smith (9) *slwly into strd, hdwy to chase ldrs hfwy, sn rdn and wknd.* ....(33 to 1 op 100 to 1) 8
28² MISS CALCULATE 5-8-9 J Fanning (3) *prmnt, rdn 3 fs out, sn wknd*..........(7 to 2 jt-fav op 3 to 1 tchd 4 to 1) 9
THE TONDY (Ire) 5-9-10 D Nicholls (6) *slwly away, hdwy to chase ldrs hfwy, sn rdn and wknd.* ....(33 to 1 op 100 to 1) 10
123³ BUZBOUR 5-9-8 G Carter (8) *chsd ldrs to hfwy, sn wknd, tld off*..............................(33 to 1 op 16 to 1) 11

Dist: 1½l, sht-hd, 1½l, 3l, nk, hd, 5l, 1l, dist. 1m 33.20s. a 7.10s (11 Ran).
SR: 26/19/15/23/19/10/-/9/-/ (R D Russell), C D Broad

177 Ice-Skating Handicap CLASS F (0-70 4-y-o and up) £2,385 7f....................(3:10)

134* QUINZII MARTIN [56] (v) 5-9-8 J Williams (6) *hld up in rear, gd hdwy o'r 2 fs out, led appr fnl furlong, rdn out.* ....(11 to 4 fav tchd 3 to 1 and 5 to 2) 1
163⁷ LORD NASKRA (USA) [57] (bl) 4-9-6 (3*) Emma O'Gorman (7) *chsd ldrs, effrt 2 fs out, rdn and one pace entering fnl furlong*..............................(7 to 1 op 6 to 1) 2
134³ THE DREAM MAKER (Ire) [45] 4-8-4 (7*) M Humphries (5) *mid-div, hdwy 2 fs out, styd on und pres fnl furlong.* ....(7 to 1 op 5 to 1) 3
163⁵ CHOICE LOT [38] (v) 6-7-11 (7*) D Wright (8) *prmnt, smooth hdwy to ld wl o'r 2 fs out, rdn one and a half furlongs out, sn hdd and wknd ins last*.... (6 to 1 tchd 11 to 2) 4
138⁴ ROCKBOURNE [53] 4-9-5 W Ryan (2) *chsd ldrs, effrt and rdn o'r 2 fs out, sn btn.* (3 to 1 op 11 to 4 tchd 4 to 1) 5
144² WELLSY LAD (USA) [54] 6-9-6 S Wood (3) *cl up, rdn and wknd o'r 2 fs out*.......(13 to 2 op 5 to 1 tchd 7 to 1) 6
96 MANULEADER [50] (bl) 4-9-2 D Nicholls (4) *sn led, hdd hfwy, rdn and wknd o'r 2 fs out*... (20 to 1 op 25 to 1) 7
131 JUST BOB [58] 4-9-10 S Webster (1) *cl up, led hfwy to o'r 2 fs out, sn wknd*............ (16 to 1 op 25 to 1) 8

Dist: 2½l, 1l, ½l, 5l, 4l, 5l, 2½l. 1m 33.50s. a 7.40s (8 Ran).
SR: 39/32/17/8/8/ (Monolithic Refractories Ltd), D Haydn Jones

178 Curling Handicap CLASS F (0-70 3-y-o) £2,259 7f.......................... (3:40)

149* PINE RIDGE LAD (Ire) [69] (bl) 9-12 (5ex) Dean McKeown (3) *made all, rdn one and a half fs out, kpt on wl ins last.* ....(Evens fav tchd 5 to 4 on and 11 to 10) 1

160³ PYTCHLEY DAWN [46] 7-13¹ (5*) Stephen Davies (7) *in tch, hdwy 3 fs out, wide strt, gd run 2 out, hng lft appr last, ran on wl und pres, jst fld*.........(13 to 2 op 7 to 1) 2
116* PIRATES GOLD (Ire) [64] 9-7 Dale Gibson (2) *chsd ldrs, hdwy hfwy, effrt and rdn to squeeze through on inner appr fnl furlong, no extr ins last*.....(9 to 1 op 3 to 1) 3
149³ ROSE FLYER (Ire) [56] 8-6 (7*) D McCabe (8) *cl up, chlgd 2 fs out, sn rdn, wkng whn hng lft o'r one furlong out*. ....(11 to 2 op 5 to 1 tchd 13 to 2) 4
143⁴ ASHOVER [62] 9-5 Alex Greaves (4) *outpcd and beh till styd on fnl 2 fs*.................(12 to 1 tchd 16 to 1) 5
151³ BURBLE [42] 7-13 S Wood (1) *unruly strt, cl up, effrt 2 fs out, sn rdn and btn whn hmpd o'r one out*. ....(7 to 1 op 5 to 1) 6
DESIRABLE MISS [45] (bl) 8-2 G Carter (5) *chsd ldrs, wknd 3 fs out*.......................(25 to 1 op 20 to 1) 7

Dist: Sht-hd, 1½l, 8l, 2l, ½l, 15l. 1m 33.80s. a 7.70s (7 Ran).
SR: 39/15/28/-/ (R Jenkinson), M Johnston

179 Toboggan Maiden Stakes CLASS F (4-y-o and up) £2,070 1½m................(4:10)

135² MR POPPLETON 4-9-0 T Quinn (2) *made all, rdn clr 2 fs out, easily*.......................(4 to 1 op 6 to 1) 1
MULAWIH (USA) 5-8-12 (5*) O Pears (1) *trkd ldrs, hdwy 5 fs out, effrt to chase wnr 2 out, sn rdn and kpt on one pace*.............................(25 to 1 op 16 to 1) 2
ALBERTITO (Fr) 6-8-12 (5*) S Wynne (6) *beh, rdn alng 6 fs out, kpt on fnl 2, nvr dngrs*.........(5 to 2 op 11 to 8) 3
122² ETIQUETTE 4-8-9 Dean McKeown (7) *cl up, rdn 3 fs out, sn wknd*............ (6 to 5 on op Evens tchd 5 to 4 on) 4
MISS LAWN (Fr) 5-8-12 L Charnock (3) *chsd ldrs, rdn 6 fs out and sn beh*...............(25 to 1 op 20 to 1) 5
152⁶ RESISTING (USA) 5-9-3 D Nicholls (5) *chsd wnr till rdn and wknd 6 fs out*.................(33 to 1 op 20 to 1) 6
61⁹ LAJADHAL (Fr) (v) 4-9-0 J Carroll (4) *al beh, tld off fnl 4 fourlongs*........................(33 to 1 op 20 to 1) 7
125⁹ MOUNTAIN GLOW 6-8-12 (5*) Stephen Davies (8) *chsd ldrs till rdn and wknd quickly 5 fs out, tld off*..... (50 to 1) 8

Dist: 5l, 5l, ½l, 8l, 8l, dist, 5l. 2m 44.60s. a 10.70s (8 Ran).
SR: 41/34/24/15/2/ (S T A Management Ltd), D W P Arbuthnot

180 Bobsleigh Handicap CLASS F (0-70 3-y-o and up) £2,364 5f..................(4:40)

138* LAST STRAW [37] 5-7-5³ (7*) Claire Balding (5) *cl up, led 2 fs out, rdn and kpt on wl fnl furlong*. ....(11 to 2 op 5 to 1 tchd 6 to 1) 1
138⁵ STRIP CARTOON (Ire) [44] (bl) 5-8-2 J Quinn (4) *chsd ldrs, hdwy 2 fs out, effrt to chal one out, rdn and no extr nr finish*.............................(14 to 1 op 7 to 1) 2
131⁵ LOVE LEGEND [70] 8-10-0 T Quinn (7) *outpcd and beh hfwy, sn rdn, styd on strly fnl furlong*. ....(8 to 1 tchd 10 to 1) 3
166⁷ LINCSTONE BOY (Ire) [59] (bl) 5-9-3 S Webster (9) *led, rdn and hdd 2 fs out, wknd fnl furlong*.. (9 to 1 op 6 to 1) 4
147⁴ SIR TASKER [64] 5-9-3 (5*) B Doyle (10) *cl up, rdn 2 fs out, kpt on one pace*.................. (7 to 1 tchd 8 to 1) 5
4808a⁷ DRUMMER'S DREAM (Ire) [42] (v) 5-8-0 Dale Gibson (6) *prmnt, rdn 2 fs out, kpt on*......... (10 to 1 op 8 to 1) 6
96⁸ IMCO DOUBLE (Ire) [47] (bl) 5-8-5 J McLaughlin (1) *chsd ldrs, rdn and one pace 2 fs out*. ....(14 to 1 op 12 to 1 tchd 16 to 1) 7
99³ LE CHIC [53] 7-8-11 L Dettori (8) *cl up, ev ch 2 fs out, sn rdn and wknd appr fnl furlong*. ....(3 to 1 fav op 5 to 2 tchd 7 to 2) 8
108⁸ NIGALS FRIEND [38] (v) 4-7-10 G Bardwell (2) *pushed alng and beh frm hfwy*................(25 to 1 op 20 to 1) 9
144⁹ HINARI VIDEO [52] 8-8-10 R P Elliott (3) *nvr rch ldrs*. ....(7 to 1 op 5 to 1) 10
138 LONG LAST [36] 4-7-8¹ J Fanning (11) *chsd ldrs 3 fs, sn wknd*...............(40 to 1 op 33 to 1 tchd 50 to 1) 11

Dist: Nk, 2½l, nk, 1l, dd-ht, 2½l, sht-hd, 3l, ¾l, 1l. 1m 1.00s. a 3.10s (11 Ran).
SR: 29/35/51/39/40/18/13/18/-/ (Martin Pound Racing Ltd), A W Jones

CAGNES-SUR-MER (FR) (good)
Thursday February 18th

181 Prix Raoul Fabre (3-y-o) £6,571 1m..(2:50)

88² AFFIRMED MINISTER (USA) 8-7 M Boutin,............... 1
ESCRIVAN (Fr) 8-10 S Culin,............................ 2
MARSEILLAISE (Fr) 8-5 A Faucher,...................... 3
153² I'LLEAVEITOYOU (Ire) 8-11 O Peslier,.................. 6

Dist: 2½l, ½l, 2l, 1½l, 1l, 1l. 1m 42.50s. (11 Ran).
(H Chalhoub), R Collet

LINGFIELD (A.W) (std)
Thursday February 18th
Going Correction: MINUS 0.45 sec. per fur.

182 Bishop's Rock Apprentices' Handicap CLASS F (0-70 4-y-o and up) £2,831 2m ....(1:50)

165³ SERIOUS ACTION [40] 4-8-1 K Rutter (10) *made all, drw clr ins fnl 2 fs*............. (9 to 1 op 7 to 1 tchd 10 to 1) 1
141⁴ HUNTING GROUND [47] 5-9-0 Emma O'Gorman (2) *wtd wth, hdwy aftr 6 fs, pressed ldr six furlongs out till one pace ins fnl 2*...........(9 to 2 op 4 to 1 tchd 5 to 1) 2
141³ EL DOMINIO [53] 5-9-6 D Carson (12) *slwly into strd, settled in rear, hdwy hfwy, styd on fnl 2 fs, nvr nrr*. ....(7 to 1 op 6 to 1) 3
73⁶ DR ZEVA [38] 7-8-5 D Wright (3) *beh till hdwy aftr 7 fs, styd on ins fnl 2*.......(17 to 2 op 8 to 1 tchd 9 to 1) 4
122⁵ AUDE LA BELLE (Fr) [57] 5-9-10 F Norton (1) *hld up, outpcd sn aftr hfwy, styd on ins fnl furlong*. (6 to 1 op 4 to 1) 5
126* LYPH (USA) [47] 7-9-0 A Tucker (6) *mid-div, effrt 4 fs out, one pace fnl 2*.................. (4 to 1 fav op 3 to 1) 6
175⁸ MALENOIR (USA) [54] (v) 5-9-7 M Fenton (9) *in rear whn rdn hfwy, nvr got into race*......(10 to 1 tchd 12 to 1) 7
115⁵ BEAM ME UP SCOTTY (Ire) [53] 4-9-0 B Russell (5) *in rear early, hdwy hfwy, rdn to ld chasing grp o'r 4 fs out, sn wknd*..............................(8 to 1 op 6 to 1) 8
CAROLES CLOWN [31] 7-7-12 D Toole (11) *chsd wnr early, beh fnl 4 fs*...................(16 to 1 op 12 to 1) 9
SAILOR BOY [45] 7-8-12 P McCabe (8) *prmnt to hfwy, sn beh*.......................... (25 to 1 tchd 33 to 1) 10
SPRING TO THE TOP [45] 6-8-12 S Drowne (7) *al beh, tld off fnl 2 fs*.......... (20 to 1 op 16 to 1 tchd 25 to 1) 11
139³ CASTLE GALAH [35] (v) 6-8-2 B Doyle (4) *chsd ldrs till wknd sn aftr hfwy, tld off*......(20 to 1 tchd 25 to 1) 12

Dist: 8l, ½l, 1½l, ¾l, 8l, 5l, 1½l, 1l, 1l, 15l. 3m 24.44s. a 2.44s (12 Ran).
SR: -/-/1/-/1/-/ (G Moore), Sir Mark Prescott

183 Hurst Point Claiming Stakes CLASS F (3-y-o) £2,377 1m.....................(2:20)

143⁷ MARK'S CLUB (Ire) (bl) 8-11 D Biggs (6) *hld up, hdwy 3 fs out, led 2 out, sn clr, easily*. ....(5 to 1 op 4 to 1 tchd 11 to 2) 1
167³ GENESIS FOUR (bl) 8-0 (5*) B Doyle (1) *led till hdd 2 fs out, sn outpcd*.........................(16 to 1 op 12 to 1) 2
CHILTERN HUNDREDS (USA) 8-6 (7*) D McCabe (2) *slwly into strd, styd on ins fnl 2 fs*........(10 to 1 op 7 to 1) 3
167* MISTER BLAKE (bl) 9-0 (3*) Emma O'Gorman (5) *trkd ldrs, shaken up 3 fs out, one pace and no hdwy aftr*. ....(5 to 2 on op 11 to 4 on tchd 9 to 4 on) 4
167⁴ PREMIER BLUES (Fr) 8-2 J Quinn (4) *chsd ldr, rdn 3 fs out, sn btn*.......................... (16 to 1 op 14 to 1) 5
117⁹ HOME AFFAIR 7-12 G Bardwell (3) *beh frm hfwy, tld off ins fnl 2 fs*.......... (33 to 1 op 20 to 1 tchd 50 to 1) 6

Dist: 3l, hd, ¾l, 3l, 15l. 1m 41.36s. a 5.16s (6 Ran).
(Mrs Barbara Marchant), R J O'Sullivan

184 Eddystone Handicap CLASS F (0-70 4-y-o and up) £2,831 1m..................(2:50)

59⁶ BELMOREDEAN [70] 8-9-7 (7*) B Russell (5) *outpcd early, hdwy 2 fs out, squeezed through gap entering strt, led one out, ran on wl*...... (7 to 1 op 6 to 1 tchd 8 to 1) 1
128³ APPLIANCEOFSCIENCE [39] 6-7-9⁵ (7*) P McCabe (6) *towards rear till hdwy o'r one out, ran on*. ....(12 to 1 op 7 to 1) 2
127* EXPRESS SERVICE [61] 4-9-2 (3*) Emma O'Gorman (3) *chsd ldrs, rdn and one pace fnl furlong*. ....(7 to 2 op 3 to 1 tchd 4 to 1) 3
152* SIRTELIMAR (Ire) [66] 4-9-10 (5ex) J McLaughlin (1) *led till hdd entering fnl furlong, no extr*. (2 to 1 jt-fav tchd 9 to 4) 4
87⁴ MADAGANS GREY [65] 5-9-9 L Dettori (4) *trkd ldr, rdn and no extr fnl furlong*. (2 to 1 jt-fav op 9 to 4 tchd 5 to 2) 5
69⁶ YONGE TENDER [40] (bl) 6-7-12 J Quinn (7) *wl beh frm hfwy, tld off*...................(12 to 1 tchd 14 to 1) 6

Dist: 2l, 1½l, nk, hd, 20l. 1m 39.64s. a 3.44s (6 Ran).
SR: 8/-/-/ (Fred Honour), R J O'Sullivan

185 Alpine Double Glazing Maiden Stakes CLASS F (3-y-o) £2,208 1¼m........(3:20)

MARCO MAGNIFICO (USA) 9-0 M Hills (3) *trkd ldr, led o'r 4 fs out, hdd briefly 2 out, shaken up and styd on wl*. ....(3 to 1 on op 4 to 1 on) 1
DARING PAST 9-0 W Ryan (10) *wtd wth, rdn and gd hdwy to ld briefly 2 fs out, ran on one pace und pres*. ....(20 to 1 op 12 to 1) 2
129⁴ HALHAM TARN (Ire) (e/s) 9-0 J Williams (9) *beh till hdwy aftr 4 fs, rdn 2 out, styd on*. ....(10 to 1 op 8 to 1 tchd 12 to 1) 3
57⁶ THATCHED (Ire) 9-0 J McLaughlin (7) *mid-div, hdwy 2 fs out, nvr nr to chal*... (25 to 1 op 20 to 1 tchd 33 to 1) 4
NEDAARAH 8-9 W Newnes (4) *trkd ldrs till rdn and wknd 2 fs out*............................ (33 to 1 op 20 to 1) 5
83⁸ ROWLANDSONS GOLD (Ire) 8-9 J Quinn (6) *nvr on terms*. ....(50 to 1 op 33 to 1) 6
72² HUSH BABY (Ire) 8-9 G Bardwell (2) *led till hdd o'r 4 fs out, sn wknd*............................ (20 to 1 op 10 to 1) 7
BOXBOY 9-0 D Biggs (1) *al beh*......(50 to 1 op 33 to 1) 8
62⁸ BECKY'S GIRL 8-9 T Williams (8) *al in rear*. ....(50 to 1 op 33 to 1) 9

83² ROSIE'S GOLD 8-9 M Tebbutt (5) *in rear whn wknd rpdly 3 fs out. tld off, broke blood vessal*... (7 to 1 op 6 to 1) 10
Dist: 1½l, 1l, 7l, 1l, 10l, 12l, 3l, 10l, dist. 2m 8.48s. a 5.28s (10 Ran).
SR: 2/-/-/-/-/-/ (Mrs Leonard Simpson), B W Hills

186 Dungeness Point Handicap CLASS E (0-80 3-y-o) £3,318 1¼m................ (3:50)

129² BROUGHTONS FORMULA [63] 8-4 J Quinn (4) *hld up, rdn and hdwy o'r 3 fs out, ran on strly to ld wl ins last.* .... (11 to 4 op 2 to 1) 1
100* DEE RAFT (USA) [80] 9-7 M Hills (3) *wtd wth in tch, outpcd 2 fs out, styd on ins last to go second cl hme.* ....(11 to 8 on op Evens) 2
98² ERLKING (Ire) [72] 8-13 Dean McKeown (2) *trkd ldr, led 3 fs out, rdn and hdd wl ins last, no extr.* .... (5 to 1 op 4 to 1 tchd 11 to 2) 3
129⁵ DIAMOND LUCY [64] 8-2 (3*) Emma O'Gorman (1) *sn led, hdd 3 fs out, wknd appr last, eased.* ....(9 to 2 op 4 to 1 tchd 5 to 1) 4
Dist: 2l, hd, 10l. 2m 7.98s. a 4.78s (4 Ran).
SR: -/10/1/-/ (Broughton Thermal Insulation), W J Musson

187 Needles Handicap CLASS F (0-70 3-y-o and up) £2,872 5f.................... (4:20)

170² SERIOUS HURRY [49] 5-9-6 T Quinn (7) *trkd ldr, led hfwy, drvn out fnl furlong*.....(7 to 2 op 3 to 1 tchd 9 to 2) 1
180⁸ LE CHIC [53] 7-9-10 L Dettori (5) *outpcd, hdwy 2 fs out, ran on und pres ins last, pressed wnr to line.* ....(4 to 1 op 3 to 1) 2
170* EWALD (Ire) [57] 5-10-0 (7ex) Dean McKeown (2) *led to hfwy, hrd rdn and ev ch till no extr cl hme.* ....(5 to 2 fav op 6 to 4) 3
156² COMET WHIRLPOOL (Ire) [56] (bl) 3-8-12 J Quinn (4) *in tch, outpcd 2 fs out, rdn and kpt on ins last.* ....(7 to 2 op 3 to 1 tchd 9 to 2) 4
PALACEGATE GOLD (Ire) [45] (bl) 4-8-9 (7*) S Drowne (6) *in tch till rdn and wknd sn aftr hfwy.* ....(20 to 1 op 16 to 1 tchd 25 to 1) 5
170⁸ RUSHANES [53] 6-9-10 J Williams (3) *chsd ldr till outpcd 2 fs out*................(14 to 1 tchd 20 to 1) 6
109⁵ BOLD STREET (Ire) [66] 3-9-8 G Carter (1) *slwly away, sn outpcd, tld off*................(7 to 1 op 8 to 1) 7
Dist: Hd, 1½l, ¾l, 5l, sht-hd, 20l. 59.43s. a 1.23s (7 Ran).
SR: 36/39/37/18/2/9/-/ (Richard Berenson), C C Elsey

SOUTHWELL (A.W) (std)
Friday February 19th
Going Correction: PLUS 0.25 sec. per fur.

188 Maplebeck Claiming Stakes (Div I) CLASS F (4-y-o and up) £2,280 1m.........(1:50)

49⁴ ROUND BY THE RIVER 4-8-5 Dean McKeown (1) *trkd ldrs, hdwy o'r 2 fs out, led one and a half furlongs out, rdn clr*................ (5 to 1 op 4 to 1) 1
150* LOCK KEEPER (USA) 7-8-8 J Quinn (9) *mid-div, rdn 3 fs out, styd on fnl 2 furlongs, not rch wnr.* ....(11 to 10 fav op Evens tchd 5 to 4) 2
163 FIABA 5-7-12 (3*) F Norton (8) *cl up, hdwy to ld 2 and a half fs out, sn rdn, hdd one and a half furlongs out, soon wknd*................ (9 to 2 op 4 to 1 tchd 5 to 1) 3
133³ BOWDEN BOY (Ire) (bl) 5-8-4 W Ryan (3) *chsd ldrs, outpcd 3 fs out, styd on und pres fnl 2 furlongs.* ....(5 to 1 op 4 to 1) 4
152⁹ MARIETTE LARKIN 4-7-11 J Fanning (2) *cl up, led hfwy till 2 and a half fs out, sn rdn and wknd.* ....(12 to 1 tchd 14 to 1) 5
176⁸ NEVENTER (Fr) 4-9-0 V Smith (6) *slwly away, hdwy to chase ldrs aftr 3 fs, sn rdn and wknd three furlongs out*................(16 to 1) 6
140⁵ MAHZOOZ 4-8-8 J McLaughlin (4) *al beh*.........(33 to 1) 7
TIBBY HEAD (Ire) 5-8-5 G Carter (5) *led to hfwy, sn wknd.* ....(20 to 1) 8
NEVER TOUCHED ME 6-7-9² N Adams (7) *beh, effrt and hdwy hfwy, sn rdn and wknd, tld off fnl 2 fs.* (50 to 1) 9
Dist: 4l, 5l, 6l, 3½l, ½l, 2l, 3½l, 12l. 1m 45.50s. a 6.50s (9 Ran).
SR: 24/15/-/-/-/-/ (W W Haigh), W W Haigh

189 Kirkby-In-Ashfield Apprentices' Handicap CLASS F (0-90 4-y-o and up) £2,280 1½m ....(2:20)

148² SUGEMAR [58] 7-9-4 S D Williams (3) *trkd ldrs, gng wl, smooth hdwy 3 fs out, led o'r 2 furlongs out and sn clr, rdn and styd on fnl furlong*...... (5 to 4 fav op Evens) 1
141⁶ LA REINE ROUGE (Ire) [38] 5-7-12¹ F Norton (1) *prmnt, effrt and swtchd wide 2 and a half fs out, rdn to chase wnr appr fnl furlong, sn one pace.* ....(10 to 1 op 8 to 1 tchd 12 to 1) 2
EIRE LEATH-SCEAL [49] 6-8-9 J Marshall (5) *led, rdn 4 fs out, hdd and one pace o'r 2 furlongs out.* ....(12 to 1 op 8 to 1 tchd 14 to 1) 3
KATY'S LAD [63] 6-9-9 S Sanders (4) *cl up, rdn alng 5 fs out, wknd 3 furlongs out*........... (4 to 1 op 3 to 1) 4
L'UOMO CLASSICS [64] 6-9-10 T G McLaughlin (6) *prmnt, hdwy to chal ldr 5 fs out, rdn o'r 3 furlongs out, sn wknd*................ (7 to 2 op 4 to 1 tchd 9 to 2) 5
4714a⁴ BALAAT (USA) [43] 5-8-3 D McCabe (2) *al rear.* ....(14 to 1 op 10 to 1) 6
Dist: 4l, ¾l, 4l, 3½l, 2l. 2m 45.00s. a 11.10s (6 Ran).
SR: 23/-/4/10/4/-/ (Mattie O'Toole), M C Chapman

190 Maplebeck Claiming Stakes (Div II) CLASS F (4-y-o and up) £2,280 1m.........(2:50)

SILKY SIREN (bl) 4-7-9 J Quinn (8) *cl up, led hfwy, quickened clr o'r 2 fs out, easily*..........(5 to 1 op 5 to 2) 1
176³ JUVENARA 7-7-12 G Bardwell (6) *beh, wide strt, hdwy 2 fs out, sn rdn and styd on, not rch wnr.* ....(6 to 4 fav op 5 to 4 tchd 7 to 4) 2
150² POP TO STANS (bl) 4-8-10 L Dettori (1) *trkd ldrs, effrt to chase wnr 2 fs out, sn rdn and one pace.* ....(7 to 2 op 5 to 2) 3
107⁷ GIRTON DEGREE 4-7-13¹ (7*) S Sanders (2) *al prmnt, rdn o'r 2 fs out, sn wknd*.............. (10 to 1 op 7 to 1) 4
35 MERRYHILL MADAM 4-8-0 (5*) B Doyle (5) *prmnt to hfwy, sn lost pl*................ (9 to 2 tchd 5 to 1) 5
120 WOOD KAY (Ire) 4-7-13 N Adams (3) *nvr dngrs.* ....(25 to 1 op 16 to 1) 6
65 DEHAR BOY (bl) 7-8-0⁵ (5*) Stephen Davies (7) *chsd ldrs o'r 4 fs, sn wknd*....... (25 to 1 op 14 to 1 tchd 33 to 1) 7
KACHINA MAID 8-7-11² D Biggs (4) *led to hfwy, sn rdn and wknd*................ (33 to 1 op 25 to 1) 8
Dist: 4l, 1½l, 6l, 10l, 4l, 3l, 12l. 1m 46.20s. a 7.20s (8 Ran).
SR: 3/-/1/-/-/ (S Nixon), M C Pipe

191 Girton Handicap CLASS F (0-100 3-y-o) £2,259 6f......................... (3:20)

117² LUCAYAN TREASURE [72] (v) 9-1 L Dettori (4) *trkd ldrs, gng wl, smooth hdwy 3 fs out, led o'r 2 furlongs out and sn clr, unchlgd*................(3 to 1 op 6 to 4) 1
178* PINE RIDGE LAD (Ire) [71] (bl) 9-0 (7ex) Dean McKeown (2) *chsd ldr, rdn o'r 2 fs out, kpt on one pace.* ....(9 to 4 fav op 6 to 4 tchd 5 to 2) 2
63² GREENWICH CHALENGE [73] 9-2 T Quinn (3) *chsd ldrs, effrt and hdwy 3 fs out, rdn and wknd 2 furlongs out.* ....(3 to 1 tchd 4 to 1) 3
144⁶ PLAY HEVER GOLF [78] 9-7 M Hills (1) *led, rdn and hdd o'r 2 fs out, wknd quickly*...(5 to 2 op 3 to 1 tchd 7 to 2) 4
Dist: 5l, 8l, hd. 1m 19.00s. a 5.60s (4 Ran).
SR: 19/ (H E Lhendup Dorji), D R Loder

192 Hardwick Claiming Stakes CLASS F (4-y-o) £2,217 2m................... (3:50)

92³ KARAMOJA 8-7 T Quinn (3) *hld up, gd hdwy 7 fs out, led 5 furlongs out, clr 3 furlongs out, rdn and kpt on wl fnl furlong*..........(13 to 8 fav op 5 to 4 tchd 7 to 4) 1
165⁸ SOUL TRADER 7-12 D Biggs (1) *trkd ldrs, pushed alng 6 fs out, effrt to chase wnr 2 furlongs out, edgd lft and no extr fnl furlong*................(10 to 1 tchd 14 to 1) 2
KLINGON (Ire) 8-13 W Ryan (4) *led, hdd 5 fs out, one pace 3 furlongs out*.......... (9 to 4 op 2 to 1 tchd 5 to 2) 3
WITCHES COVEN 8-1 (3*) F Norton (2) *trkd ldr, pulling hrd, ev ch 5 fs out, sn rdn, wknd 3 furlongs out, eased.* ....(5 to 2 op 7 to 4 tchd 3 to 1) 4
Dist: 1½l, 7l, 15l. 3m 57.30s. a 30.80s (4 Ran).
(Paul G Jacobs), N A Graham

193 New Houghton Maiden Stakes CLASS F (3-y-o) £2,070 7f...................... (4:20)

136⁴ DON'T BE SAKI (Ire) 8-4 (5*) O Pears (1) *made virtually all, rdn 2 fs out, hld on gmely und pres fnl furlong.* .... (9 to 1 op 10 to 1 tchd 7 to 1) 1
GREEN'S FAIR (Ire) 8-9 (5*) M Fenton (4) *in tch, effrt 2 fs out, rdn to chal appr fnl furlong, edgd lft and ev ch ins last, no extr*................(3 to 1 op 2 to 1) 2
95² PRINCE OF SOUL 9-0 J McLaughlin (5) *outpcd and beh hfwy, styd on und pres appr fnl furlong.* ....(6 to 1 op 5 to 1 tchd 8 to 1) 3
4800a⁴ HOOCHIECOOCHIE MAN (Ire) 9-0 T Quinn (3) *prmnt, effrt and ev ch 2 fs out, sn rdn and wknd o'r one furlong out.* ....(2 to 1 fav op 6 to 4) 4
151⁶ MAGICATION (bl) 8-2 (7*) Claire Balding (2) *cl up till rdn and wknd o'r 2 fs out*....(3 to 1 op 3 to 1 tchd 7 to 2) 5
Dist: Nk, 15l, nk, 2l. 1m 33.60s. a 7.50s (5 Ran).
SR: 9/13/ (Ronald Thompson), Ronald Thompson

194 Laxton Handicap CLASS F (0-70 4-y-o and up) £2,238 6f......................(4:50)

166² JOHNSTON'S EXPRESS (Ire) [62] 5-9-8 (5*) Stephen Davies (6) *in tch, gd hdwy hfwy, led one and a half fs out, cmftbly*........... (11 to 10 fav op 11 to 8 tchd 6 to 4) 1
177⁴ CHOICE LOT [38] (v) 6-7-10 (7*) D Wright (4) *beh, gd hdwy 2 fs out, rdn and styd on fnl furlong*.. (6 to 1 op 9 to 2) 2
166³ QUATRE FEMME [52] 6-9-3 D Biggs (5) *cl up, led 2 and a half fs out till hdd one and a half furlongs out, sn btn.* ....(9 to 2 op 3 to 1) 3

147^{7} HANSOM LAD [63] 10-10-0 Dean McKeown (7) *cl up, effrt and ev ch 2 fs out, sn rdn, edgd lft and wknd.* .... (25 to 1 op 16 to 1) 4
134^{5} DOESYOUDOES [46] 4-8-11 L Dettori (1) *prmnt till rdn and wknd o'r 2 fs out*....... (11 to 2 op 7 to 2 tchd 6 to 1) 5
91 GRUBBY [39] 4-7-11 (7*) M Humphries (2) *cl up till rdn and wknd o'r 2 fs out*.............. (33 to 1 op 20 to 1) 6
138 ARC LAMP [52] 7-9-3 D Nicholls (3) *led to 2 and a half fs out, sn wknd*.......... (9 to 1 op 8 to 1 tchd 14 to 1) 7
Dist: 1½l, 5l, 5l, 3l, 1½l, 3l. 1m 17.80s. a 4.40s (7 Ran).
SR: 55/25/19/10/ (Frank McKevitt), E J Alston

LINGFIELD (A.W) (fast)
Saturday February 20th
Going Correction: MINUS 0.45 sec. per fur.

195 Palacegate Racing Claiming Stakes CLASS F (4-y-o and up) £2,489 5f....(2:20)

99^{2} LITTLE SABOTEUR 4-8-5 W Ryan (1) *sn pushed alng, cl up, led ins fnl furlong, pushed out.* .... (11 to 8 fav op 6 to 4) 1
4779a* ANOTHER EPISODE (Ire) 4-9-8 J Carroll (3) *led till hdd ins fnl furlong, ran on*..... (11 to 4 op 9 to 4 tchd 3 to 1) 2
56^{5} CRECHE (bl) 4-9-2 N Day (5) *cl up, rdn and outpcd appr fnl furlong*.......... (3 to 1 op 2 to 1) 3
SAVAHRA SOUND 8-9-8 D Nicholls (6) *trkd ldg trio, pushed alng hfwy, not pace to chal.* (12 to 1 op 8 to 1) 4
147^{3} GRAND TIME 4-7-12 G Bardwell (4) *sn outpcd.* .... (14 to 1 op 8 to 1 tchd 16 to 1) 5
BLAZING SENSATION 5-8-12 D Biggs (2) *slwly into strd, nvr gng pace*.......... (33 to 1 op 25 to 1) 6
Dist: ¾l, 6l, 4l, 7l, 4l. 58.10s. b 0.10s (6 Ran).
SR: 48/62/32/22/-/-/ (Mrs P J Makin), P J Makin

196 Alpine Double Glazing Claiming Stakes CLASS F (3-y-o) £2,208 6f...........(2:50)

156* DAANIERA (Ire) (bl) 8-13 J Carroll (1) *trkd ldr, led wl o'r 3 fs out, not extended.* .... (9 to 4 on op 5 to 2 on tchd 2 to 1 on) 1
168^{2} PURBECK CENTENARY 8-10 Lorna Vincent (2) *missed break, cld and ev ch o'r 2 fs out, outpcd frm over one out*.......... (9 to 4 op 2 to 1 tchd 5 to 2) 2
FOREST FLYER 7-12 G Bardwell (3) *led till hdd wl o'r 3 fs out, sn wknd, tld off*.. (10 to 1 op 7 to 1 tchd 12 to 1) 3
Dist: 3½l, 20l. 1m 12.95s. a 2.15s (3 Ran).
SR: 2/-/-/ (J Berry), J Berry

197 Evelyn Anthony Handicap CLASS D (0-90 4-y-o and up) £4,092 7f............. (3:20)

144^{3} INVOCATION [73] 6-9-7 N Adams (12) *made all, hrd rdn appr fnl furlong, ran on gmely*..... (10 to 1 op 8 to 1) 1
163* RURAL LAD [60] 4-8-8 J McLaughlin (4) *cl up, outpcd appr fnl furlong, kpt on wl ins last.* .... (7 to 1 op 6 to 1 tchd 8 to 1) 2
131^{2} COURTING NEWMARKET [51] 5-7-12^{2} (3*) F Norton (11) *cl up, pushed alng o'r 3 fs out, kpt on one pace.* .... (9 to 1 op 8 to 1) 3
140^{4} MAC'S FIGHTER [76] (bl) 8-9-3 (7*) B Russell (1) *mid-div, hdwy und pres wl o'r one furlong out, ran on ins last.* .... (15 to 2 op 9 to 1 tchd 7 to 1) 4
134^{2} ON Y VA (USA) [60] 6-8-8 J Williams (2) *hld up beh, rdn and hdwy o'r one furlong out, nrst finish.* .... (9 to 2 op 6 to 1) 5
87* KISSAVOS [67] (v) 7-8-10 (5*) B Doyle (3) *rdn alng thrght, chsd ldrs, no hdwy fnl 2 fs*....... (4 to 1 fav op 7 to 2) 6
140* SAMSOLOM [60] 5-8-8 J Quinn (5) *mid-div, no hdwy fnl 3 fs*.......... (8 to 1 op 6 to 1) 7
170^{4} RUNNING GLIMPSE (Ire) [77] 5-9-4 (7*) A Martinez (9) *prmnt till wknd o'r 2 fs out*..... (7 to 1 op 5 to 1 tchd 8 to 1) 8
MASNUN (USA) [80] 8-10-0 D Biggs (6) *nvr better than mid-div*.......... (20 to 1 op 16 to 1 tchd 25 to 1) 9
140^{2} RESPECTABLE JONES [80] 7-10-0 W Ryan (7) *al beh.* .... (8 to 1 op 7 to 1 tchd 9 to 1) 10
UNVEILED [56] 5-7-12^{1} (7*) S Drowne (10) *prmnt, pushed alng hfwy, sn wknd*.......... (25 to 1 op 20 to 1) 11
101^{8} BUSTER [65] 5-8-13 G Bardwell (8) *beh, hrd rdn 4 fs out, no response*.......... (50 to 1 op 33 to 1) 12
Dist: ½l, sht-hd, 2½l, 2l, hd, nk, ½l, 1l, 3½l, 1½l. 1m 24.67s. a 1.27s (12 Ran).
SR: 41/26/16/33/11/17/9/24/24/ (R Kiernan), A Moore

198 Daily Star Challenge Handicap Qualifier CLASS F (0-70 4-y-o and up) £2,905 1¼m ....(3:50)

169^{7} CARLOWITZ (USA) [54] 5-8-5 (7*) B Russell (3) *sn pushed alng to track ldrs, led one furlong out, rdn out.* .... (13 to 2 op 7 to 1 tchd 8 to 1) 1
110^{4} BALLYRANTER [48] 4-8-4 Dale Gibson (4) *chsd ldrs, rdn alng and hdwy o'r 3 fs out, ran on wl und pres ins last, jst fld*.......... (9 to 1 op 7 to 1) 2
139* LOWAWATHA [58] 5-8-11 (5*) Stephen Davies (9) *dsptd ld, wnt on o'r 3 fs out, hdd one out, one pace.* .... (5 to 1 op 9 to 2 tchd 11 to 2) 3
157* PIGALLE WONDER [59] (bl) 5-9-3 D Biggs (5) *hld up, rdn o'r 3 fs out, hdwy over 2 out, sn one pace.* .... (4 to 1 fav tchd 9 to 2) 4
142^{4} AMENABLE [70] 8-10-0 J McLaughlin (10) *cl up till rdn and wknd aftr 3 fs out*.......... (9 to 1 op 7 to 1) 5
128^{4} NORDANSK [40] 4-7-10^{3} N Adams (1) *dsptd ld till hdd o'r 3 fs out, wknd over one out*......(16 to 1 tchd 20 to 1) 6
169^{2} KILLICK [55] 5-8-13 J Quinn (7) *cl up, pushed alng o'r 4 fs out, wknd 3 out*.......... (9 to 2 op 7 to 2) 7
114^{3} PREMIER DANCE [40] (v) 6-7-12 T Williams (8) *chsd ldrs, effrt 4 fs out, sn btn*.......... (7 to 1 tchd 8 to 1) 8
SHARQUIN [35] 6-7-7 G Bardwell (11) *missed break, sn reco'red, mid-div till wknd 3 fs out.* .... (33 to 1 op 25 to 1) 9
114^{4} SHARP THISTLE [35] (bl) 7-7-7 S Wood (6) *beh, cld hfwy, sn wknd*.......... (12 to 1 tchd 14 to 1) 10
128^{5} MERSEYSIDE MAN [51] (v) 7-8-4 (5*) K Rutter (2) *strted slwly, al beh, tld off*.. (10 to 1 op 6 to 1 tchd 11 to 1) 11
Dist: Sht-hd, 1½l, 10l, ¾l, 2½l, ½l, 1l, 12l, 4l, 12l. 2m 4.26s. a 1.06s (11 Ran).
SR: 42/33/42/23/32/-/11/-/-/ (K Higson), A Moore

199 Dorothy L. Sayers Handicap CLASS F (0-70 4-y-o and up) £2,733 1½m..... (4:20)

171* BREAKDANCER (Ire) [57] 4-9-5 W Ryan (10) *hld up, hdwy o'r 4 fs out, led appr 2 out, sn clr, ran on wl.* .... (3 to 1 op 2 to 1) 1
114 DEBACLE (USA) [62] 4-9-10 W Woods (11) *cl up, ev ch o'r 2 fs out, one pace frm over one out*... (8 to 1 op 12 to 1) 2
141* MODEST HOPE (USA) [63] 6-10-0 J McLaughlin (5) *wth ldr, led o'r 3 fs out till appr 2 out, one pace.* .... (9 to 4 fav tchd 5 to 2) 3
158^{4} INDIAN TERRITORY [39] (v) 4-8-1 T Williams (4) *trkd ldrs, pushed alng o'r 4 fs out, kpt on one pace.* .... (8 to 1 op 7 to 1) 4
114^{5} TAUNTING (Ire) [50] 5-9-1 J Williams (7) *pld hrd, hld up beh, hdwy frm o'r one furlong out, nvr nrr.* .... (8 to 1 op 7 to 1) 5
SINCLAIR LAD (Ire) [60] 5-9-4 (7*) S Drowne (2) *trkd ldrs till pushed alng and wknd 4 fs out*.. (12 to 1 tchd 14 to 1) 6
158^{3} TENAYESTELIGN [35] 5-8-0 S Dawson (1) *led till hdd o'r 3 fs out, wknd*.......... (13 to 2 op 7 to 1 tchd 6 to 1) 7
141^{7} COOL SOCIETY (USA) [53] 4-9-1 J Quinn (6) *nvr on terms wth ldrs*.......... (8 to 1 op 6 to 1) 8
4698a^{9} SPRING FORWARD [28] (v) 9-7-7 S Wood (3) *strted slwly, sn reco'red, in tch till wknd over 4 fs out, tld off.* .... (33 to 1) 9
Dist: 6l, 3l, 3l, 3½l, 7l, 5l, nk, 10l. 2m 31.42s. a 2.12s (9 Ran).
SR: 30/23/21/-/-/-/ (J Jannaway), W R Muir

200 Ladbroke All Weather Trophy Handicap Qualifier CLASS F (0-75 3-y-o and up) £2,950 1m.......................... (4:50)

155^{2} EASTLEIGH [63] 4-8-10 (7*) D Carson (5) *mid-div, hdwy and not much room 2 fs out, swtchd rght and ran on strly to ld cl hme*.......... (6 to 1 op 13 to 2) 1
142^{3} SCOTS LAW [52] (bl) 6-8-6 D Biggs (4) *led, clr appr fnl furlong, ct cl hme.* (11 to 2 co-fav op 5 to 1 tchd 6 to 1) 2
157^{3} APOLLO RED [49] 4-8-3 A McGlone (10) *trkd ldrs, ev ch o'r 2 fs out, sn hrd rdn and one pace.* (11 to 2 co-fav op 5 to 1 tchd 6 to 1) 3
77^{5} AMETHYSTINE (USA) [56] 7-8-3 (7*) S Drowne (3) *trkd ldrs, kpt on one pace fnl 2 fs*.......... (10 to 1 op 8 to 1) 4
184^{5} MADAGANS GREY [65] (bl) 5-9-5 W Ryan (9) *strted slwly, hdwy o'r 2 fs out, one pace frm over one out.* .... (11 to 2 co-fav op 5 to 1 tchd 6 to 1) 5
169^{6} LOOKINGFORARAINBOW (Ire) [72] 5-9-12 N Day (6) *cl up till rdn and wknd o'r one furlong out.* .... (13 to 2 op 6 to 1 tchd 7 to 1) 6
177^{6} WELLSY LAD (USA) [54] 6-8-8 S Wood (12) *took keen hold, prmnt till wknd o'r 2 fs out*..... (12 to 1 tchd 14 to 1) 7
CHEVEUX MITCHELL [74] (v) 6-10-0 Lorna Vincent (2) *nvr on terms*.......... (20 to 1 op 16 to 1) 8
144^{7} NORTH ESK (USA) [68] 4-9-8 M Tebbutt (7) *mid-div till wknd o'r 2 fs out*....... (7 to 1 op 5 to 1 tchd 8 to 1) 9
157^{4} DAM CERTAIN (Ire) [56] 4-8-10 J Quinn (8) *beh, rdn alng o'r 4 fs out, nvr on terms*... (15 to 2 op 6 to 1 tchd 8 to 1) 10
TURTLE BEACH [66] 4-9-6 W Newnes (1) *trkd ldr till wknd quickly 3 fs out*.......... (20 to 1) 11
OUR EDDIE [58] 4-8-12 N Adams (11) *outpcd, tld off 4 fs out*.......... (33 to 1 tchd 40 to 1) 12
Dist: 1l, 3½l, 2½l, 1l, 6l, nk, 2l, ½l, 1l, 1½l. 1m 37.50s. a 1.30s (12 Ran).
SR: 30/16/2/1/7/-/ (J E Bigg), R Hollinshead

CAGNES-SUR-MER (FR) (good)
Sunday February 21st

201 Prix Policeman (3-y-o) £13,142 1¼m (2:50)

173^{2} PRINCE DIANON (Fr) 8-10 A Bredillet,.......... 1
132* FAY WRAY (Fr) 9-0 G Elorriaga-Santos,.......... 2
105* VILLAGE STORM (Fr) 9-0 O Peslier,.......... 3
173* SALBUS 8-10 J Reid,.......... 12

Dist: Hd, 1l, 1l, 3l, 2l. 2m 6.10s. (12 Ran).

SOUTHWELL (A.W) (std)
Monday February 22nd
Going Correction: PLUS 0.40 sec. per fur.

202 Edingley Claiming Stakes CLASS F (4-y-o and up) £2,322 1½m. . . . . (2:20)

94* TEMPERING 7-9-11 S Wood (1) *made all, quickened clr aftr 4 fs, styd on wl fnl 2....* (5 to 2 on tchd 9 to 4 on) 1
188² LOCK KEEPER (USA) 7-8-9 J Quinn (5) *mid-div, hdwy hfwy, chsd ldr 3 fs out, sn hrd drvn and one paced.* ....(8 to 1 op 6 to 1) 2
30² SWEET REVIVAL 5-8-0 Dale Gibson (2) *chsd ldrs, rdn o'r 4 fs out, sn btn.*..................(9 to 1 op 8 to 1) 3
128² MAJAL (Ire) 4-9-8 D Nicholls (8) *chsd ldrs, rdn o'r 4 fs out, sn btn.*..................(8 to 1 op 6 to 1) 4
BUCK COMTESS (USA) 4-8-6 (5*) B Doyle (6) *beh, some hdwy 3 fs out, one pace.* ....(15 to 2 op 6 to 1 tchd 8 to 1) 5
148 BATTUTA 4-8-1 Alex Greaves (4) *al beh, tld off fnl 3 fs.* ....(25 to 1 op 20 to 1) 6
164⁶ QUALITAIR IDOL 4-7-7 G Bardwell (3) *chsd ldrs, rdn hfwy, sn lost pl.*..................(16 to 1 op 14 to 1) 7
179⁶ RESISTING (USA) 5-8-8 (3*) S D Williams (7) *cl up 3 fs, sn rdn and wknd hfwy, tld off fnl three furlongs.* (33 to 1) 8

Dist: 6l, 7l, 1½l, 2½l, 30l, 3l, 6l. 2m 45.70s. a 11.80s (8 Ran).
SR: 41/13/-/9/-/ (David W Chapman), D W Chapman

203 Beckingham Handicap CLASS E (0-90 3-y-o) £3,143 1m. . . . . (2:50)

15* BRACKENTHWAITE [57] 7-7 J Fanning (3) *hld up in tch, rdn and hdwy o'r 2 fs out, styd on to ld wl ins fnl furlong*.................. (2 to 1 op 7 to 4 tchd 13 to 8) 1
178⁴ ROSE FLYER (Ire) [57] 7-7 S Wood (1) *led, quickened clr o'r 3 fs out, rdn over one out, hdd and no extr wl ins last.* ....(9 to 2 op 7 to 2 tchd 5 to 1) 2
4762a⁵ TANAGOME (USA) [70] 8-2¹ (5*) O Pears (5) *hld up in tch, rdn 3 fs out, kpt on one pace fnl 2.* ....(7 to 1 op 5 to 1 tchd 8 to 1) 3
109* GOLDEN KLAIR [85] 9-7 J Quinn (4) *hld up in tch, rdn alng and outpcd 3 fs out, styd on und pres appr fnl furlong.* .... (11 to 8 fav op Evens tchd 6 to 4) 4
4697a⁵ NANCY (Ire) [57] 7-4⁴ (7*) Claire Balding (2) *chsd ldr, rdn o'r 3 fs out, grad wknd.*. (16 to 1 op 10 to 1 tchd 20 to 1) 5

Dist: 1½l, 1½l, 2½l, ½l. 1m 47.50s. a 8.50s (5 Ran).
SR: -/-/3/10/-/ (Alex Gorrie), T D Barron

204 Fenton Maiden Stakes CLASS F (3-y-o) £2,070 1m. . . . . (3:20)

149⁴ KINGSTON BROWN (bl) 9-0 M Hills (1) *made all, quickened clr 2 and a half fs out, unchlgd.* (7 to 4 fav tchd 9 to 4) 1
PACIFIC SPIRIT 8-9 Dale Gibson (3) *outpcd and beh, rdn 3 fs out, styd on wl fnl 2.* ....(14 to 1 op 12 to 1 tchd 16 to 1) 2
93⁵ SCOFFERA 8-9 Kim Tinkler (9) *cl up, rdn 3 fs out, sn one pace*..................(14 to 1 op 10 to 1) 3
ICTERINA (USA) 8-4 (5*) Stephen Davies (8) *mid-div, effrt and hdwy hfwy, rdn 3 fs out, sn btn.* (13 to 1 op 7 to 4) 4
162² GLOWING PATH 9-0 J Quinn (4) *in tch, rdn 3 fs out, sn one paced*..................(6 to 1 op 5 to 1) 5
SAXON SHORE (USA) 8-9 Dean McKeown (5) *in tch, hdwy hfwy, effrt and rdn 3 fs out, wknd 2 out.* ....(15 to 8 op 7 to 4 tchd 2 to 1) 6
62 TEMPLE HILL 8-9 S Morris (2) *al outpcd and beh.* ....(50 to 1 op 33 to 1) 7
NOBLE MEASURE (Ire) (bl) 9-0 S Webster (7) *al outpcd and beh*..................(33 to 1 op 20 to 1) 8
151 THE CUT 8-9 L Charnock (6) *chsd ldrs 3 fs, sn lost pl and beh fnl three*..................(50 to 1 op 33 to 1) 9

Dist: 7l, hd, 2½l, 1½l, 1½l, 8l, 2½l. 1m 47.70s. a 8.70s (9 Ran).
SR: 18/-/-/-/-/ (H E Lhendup Dorji), D R Loder

205 Claypole Handicap CLASS F (0-70 4-y-o and up) £2,364 7f. . . . . (3:50)

163⁶ DREAM CARRIER (Ire) [65] 5-9-13 Alex Greaves (8) *beh, wide strt, gd hdwy 2 fs out, rdn and led o'r one out, cmftbly*..................(3 to 1 op 5 to 2 tchd 7 to 2) 1
163² DIAMOND INTHE DARK (USA) [54] (v) 5-9-2 L Charnock (4) *chsd ldrs, rdn 2 fs out, styd on appr fnl furlong, no ch wth wnr*..................(5 to 1 tchd 9 to 2 and 11 to 2) 2
177³ THE DREAM MAKER (Ire) [45] 4-8-0 (7*) M Humphries (3) *beh, hdwy 2 fs out, rdn and styd on fnl furlong.* ....(6 to 1 tchd 7 to 1) 3
161* THEMAAM [66] 4-10-0 Dean McKeown (9) *chsd ldrs, rdn o'r 2 fs out, kpt on one pace.* ....(5 to 2 fav op 2 to 1 tchd 11 to 4) 4
163⁸ COMISKEY PARK (Ire) [33] (bl) 4-7-9 S Wood (6) *cl up, effrt and ev ch 2 fs out, sn rdn and wknd o'r one out.* ....(12 to 1 tchd 14 to 1 and 16 to 1) 5
27⁴ SHANNON EXPRESS [47] (bl) 6-8-9 J Quinn (1) *cl up, led aftr 2 fs, rdn two out, hdd and wknd o'r one out.* ....(8 to 1 op 14 to 1) 6
163⁴ BAYIN (USA) [36] 4-7-12 N Adams (2) *mid-div, effrt and rdn 3 fs out, no hdwy*..................(8 to 1 op 7 to 1) 7
163⁹ MORPICK [47] (bl) 6-8-4 (5*) Stephen Davies (5) *sn led, hdd aftr 2 fs, rdn and wknd two and a half out.* ....(8 to 1 tchd 10 to 1) 8
161 CRIMSON CONSORT (Ire) [33] 4-7-5³ (7*) Claire Balding (7) *al rear*..................(25 to 1) 9

Dist: 3l, nk, 2l, 1½l, sht-hd, 4l, hd, 6l. 1m 32.70s. a 6.60s (9 Ran).
SR: 56/36/26/41/3/16/-/3/-/ (David Barron Racing Club), T D Barron

206 Clapwell Maiden Stakes CLASS F (3-y-o and up) £2,070 6f. . . . . (4:20)

151² HERSHEBAR (bl) 3-8-5 S Webster (3) *mid-div, hdwy o'r 2 fs out, rdn to ld over one out, kpt on.* ....(7 to 4 fav op 6 to 4 tchd 2 to 1) 1
151⁴ MUSICAL PHONE (bl) 3-8-5 Dean McKeown (4) *led, rdn 2 fs out, hdd and one pace appr fnl furlong.* ....(13 to 2 op 6 to 1 tchd 8 to 1) 2
LADY ROXANNE 4-8-9 (7*) D Salt (9) *in tch, hdwy 3 fs out, rdn and ev ch one and a half out, sn one paced.* ....(4 to 1 op 7 to 4) 3
188⁶ NEVENTER (Fr) 4-9-7 V Smith (6) *beh, hdwy 2 fs out, styd on und pres fnl furlong*..................(9 to 1 op 6 to 1) 4
176 THE TONDY (Ire) 5-9-7 D Nicholls (1) *mid-div, rdn and kpt on one pace fnl 2 fs, nvr dngrs*.....(33 to 1 op 20 to 1) 5
PRETTY CHIC 4-9-7 S Wood (5) *beh, wide strt, styd on fnl 2 fs, not rch ldrs.* ....(4 to 1 op 6 to 1 tchd 7 to 1 and 8 to 1) 6
NOT ALL BLISS 5-9-2 Alex Greaves (8) *beh, wide strt, rdn 2 fs out, nvr dngrs*..................(33 to 1 op 20 to 1) 7
131 LONELY LASS 7-9-2 J Quinn (2) *cl up till rdn and wknd 2 fs out*..................(8 to 1 op 6 to 1) 8
161 ANGEL'S WING 4-8-9 (7*) Marie Plowright (7) *nvr a factor.* ....(33 to 1 op 20 to 1) 9
LAST TYPHOON 3-7-12¹ (3*) F Norton (10) *chsd ldr till rdn and wknd 2 fs out*..................(20 to 1 tchd 33 to 1) 10

Dist: 1½l, 2l, 3½l, 3l, 1½l, 2l, 1½l, 5l, 2l. 1m 19.50s. a 6.10s (10 Ran).
SR: 17/11/14/5/-/-/ (Mrs P A Barratt), S R Bowring

207 Dunham-on-Trent Handicap CLASS F (0-70 4-y-o and up) £2,364 6f. . . . . . . (4:50)

194³ QUATRE FEMME [50] 6-9-4 G Bardwell (8) *chsd ldrs, hdwy 2 and a half fs out, sn rdn, led wl o'r one out, all out.* ....(6 to 1 op 9 to 2) 1
177² LORD NASKRA (USA) [56] 4-9-7 (3*) Emma O'Gorman (9) *beh, wide strt, gd hdwy 2 fs out, rdn and styd on fnl furlong*..................(13 to 2 op 7 to 1) 2
131⁴ VELOCE (Ire) [56] (bl) 5-9-10 A Mackay (1) *beh, hdwy 2 fs out, kpt on und pres fnl furlong*..................(10 to 1) 3
180² STRIP CARTOON (Ire) [44] (bl) 5-8-12 J Quinn (3) *cl up, effrt and ev ch 2 fs out, sn rdn, kpt on one pace appr fnl furlong*..................(11 to 4 fav op 2 to 1 tchd 3 to 1) 4
134⁸ KALAR [42] 4-8-10 S Wood (6) *cl up, effrt to chal 2 fs out, sn rdn and wknd fnl furlong*..................(12 to 1) 5
180⁶ DRUMMER'S DREAM (Ire) [42] (v) 5-8-10 Dale Gibson (7) *hdwy to chase ldrs 2 fs out, sn rdn and one pace.* ....(9 to 1 op 8 to 1) 6
180* LAST STRAW [44] 5-8-5 (7*,7ex) Claire Balding (5) *led, rdn and hdd wl o'r one furlong out, sn wknd.* ....(100 to 30 op 2 to 1 tchd 7 to 2) 7
166⁵ TOSHIBA COMET [46] (bl) 6-9-0 D Nicholls (2) *chsd ldrs for 3 fs, sn wknd*..................(5 to 1 tchd 11 to 2) 8
91 INNOCENT GEORGE [51] 4-9-5 L Charnock (4) *chsd ldrs to hfwy, sn wknd*..................(20 to 1) 9

Dist: ½l, 2½l, ½l, 1½l, 2½l, ¾l, 3l, 3½l. 1m 18.70s. a 5.30s (9 Ran).
SR: 46/50/40/26/18/8/7/-/-/ (C John Hill), C J Hill

LINGFIELD (A.W) (std)
Thursday February 25th
Going Correction: MINUS 0.30 sec. per fur.

208 Gironde Claiming Stakes CLASS F (3-y-o) £2,282 7f. . . . . (1:50)

160* STARDUST EXPRESS 8-7 Dean McKeown (1) *cl up, rdn to ld 3 fs out, rallied whn chlgd ins last, ran on wl.* ....(11 to 8 fav tchd 6 to 4 and 5 to 4) 1
143⁵ PERSIAN GUSHER (Ire) (e/s) 8-3 A McGlone (2) *hld up in cl tch gng wl, chsd wnr frm 2 fs out, sn ev ch, no extr close hme*..................(6 to 4 tchd 7 to 4) 2
191³ GREENWICH CHALENGE (v) 8-1 (7*) D McCabe (3) *led till hdd wl o'r 4 fs out, wknd over one out.* ....(4 to 1 op 9 to 4) 3
183² GENESIS FOUR (bl) 7-10 (5*) B Doyle (4) *took keen hold, wth ldr, led wl o'r 4 fs out till hdd 3 out, wknd.* ....(12 to 1 op 10 to 1 tchd 14 to 1) 4

Dist: ½l, 10l, 5l. 1m 25.89s. a 2.49s (4 Ran).
SR: 24/18/-/-/ (Mrs R A Johnson), M Johnston

209 Alpine Double Glazing Maiden Stakes CLASS F (3-y-o) £2,208 1¼m. . . . . (2:20)

185[5] NEDAARAH 8-9 W Newnes (8) *trkd ldrs, led 3 fs out, clr appr last, pushed out*...........(16 to 1 tchd 20 to 1) 1
57[2] SPANISH REFUGE 9-0 Dean McKeown (4) *beh, rdn alng 4 fs out, hdwy o'r one out, styd on.* ....(3 to 1 op 7 to 4 tchd 7 to 2) 2
185[3] HALHAM TARN (Ire) (e/s) 9-0 J Williams (1) *mid-div, cld o'r 2 fs out, one pace whn slightly hmpd ins last.* ....(13 to 2 op 8 to 1 tchd 10 to 1 and 6 to 1) 3
129[3] UMHAMBI 8-9 W Ryan (10) *cl up, led 5 fs out to 3 out, one pace*..........................(2 to 1 fav op 7 to 2) 4
83[3] WESTRAY (Fr) 9-0 J Quinn (9) *in tch, effrt o'r 2 fs out, btn whn slightly hmpd ins last.* ....(10 to 1 op 6 to 1 tchd 12 to 1) 5
160[2] ARAWA 8-9 M Hills (5) *nvr on terms.* ....(11 to 1 op 8 to 1 tchd 14 to 1) 6
MR GENEAOLOGY (USA) 8-11 (3*) A Tucker (3) *strted slwly, al beh*............................(8 to 1 tchd 7 to 1) 7
95[6] VADDALLIAN 9-0 G Carter (6) *led aftr 3 fs, hdd 5 out, wknd*............................(33 to 1 op 20 to 1) 8
APRIL IN KENTUCKY (USA) 8-2 (7*) G Milligan (7) *strted slwly, nvr gng pace*................(14 to 1 op 8 to 1) 9
RUSTY REEL 8-9 (5*) B Doyle (2) *led 3 fs, sn wknd.* ....(8 to 1 op 5 to 1) 10

Dist: 2½l, 2l, nk, 1½l, 6l, 15l, 4l, 1½l, ½l. 2m 8.31s. a 5.11s (10 Ran).
SR: 14/14/10/4/6/-/ (T C Marshall), C C Elsey

210 William Hill Amateur Riders' Handicap CLASS E (0-70 4-y-o and up) £3,054 1m 5f ....(2:50)

141[2] STRAT'S LEGACY [50] 6-10-11 (5*) Mrs D Arbuthnot (13) *chsd ldrs, led wl o'r one furlong out, ran on well.* ....(6 to 1 op 4 to 1) 1
199[2] DEBACLE (USA) [62] 4-11-11 Miss A Harwood (3) *cl up, led briefly blw 2 fs out, kpt on one pace*...........(10 to 1) 2
182* SERIOUS ACTION [38] 4-10-1 Miss E Bronson (2) *led til hdd blw 2 fs out, rdn and one pace.* (5 to 4 on op 11 to 10) 3
182[8] BEAM ME UP SCOTTY (Ire) [53] 4-11-2 Mr R Teal (1) *trkd ldrs, reminders 4 fs out, styd on one pace.* ....(14 to 1 op 10 to 1 tchd 16 to 1) 4
ELECTROJET [27] 5-9-7 Miss I Diana W Jones (9) *chsd ldrs, outpcd o'r 3 fs out, styd on ins last*...........(50 to 1) 5
199[7] TENAYESTELIGN [35] 5-10-1 Miss K Marks (14) *beh, hdwy to chase ldg grp aftr 5 fs, outpcd o'r 2 furlongs out.* ....(25 to 1 op 14 to 1) 6
85[6] BREEZED WELL [52] 7-10-13 (5*) Mrs H Noonan (12) *trkd ldrs, cld 4 fs out, sn outpcd*.......(16 to 1 op 14 to 1) 7
SOLID STEEL (Ire) [42] 5-10-3 (5*) Mr K Goble (8) *in tch, no hdwy frm 4 fs out*...............(25 to 1 op 16 to 1) 8
126[7] WRITTEN AGREEMENT [35] 5-9-10 (5*) Mrs C Peacock (11) *trkd ldrs to hfwy*............................(50 to 1) 9
MARIOLINO [32] 6-9-7 (5*) Miss J Southcombe (4) *nvr better than mid-div*........(20 to 1 op 16 to 1 tchd 25 to 1) 10
PHIL-BLAKE [36] 6-10-2 Mrs E Mellor (5) *wth ldr til wknd 3 fs out*.....................................(20 to 1) 11
25[4] MILLY BLACK (Ire) [38] 5-9-13 (5*) Mrs J Gault (10) *in tch, pushed alng hfwy, sn wknd*.......(14 to 1 op 10 to 1) 12
175[4] KOVALEVSKIA [37] 8-9-12 (5*) Miss L Hide (6) *nvr dngrs.* ....(10 to 1 op 6 to 1) 13
82[7] PARISIAN [35] 8-9-11[1] (5*) Miss A Purdy (7) *rcd wide, beh, hdwy aftr 4 fs, wknd o'r 5 furlongs out*.......(33 to 1) 14
ALBURY GREY [32] 6-9-7 (5*) Miss E Mills (15) *trkd ldrs for 4 fs, sn drpd out, tld off*..........................(50 to 1) 15
TYNRON DOON [65] 4-11-9 (5*) Miss S Broadley (16) *strted slwly, rdr lost irons, pld up aftr one furlong*...(20 to 1) pu

Dist: 2l, 3½l, 7l, 6l, 2l, sht-hd, 1l, hd, ¾l, sht-hd. 2m 49.10s. a 6.10s (16 Ran).
SR: 30/35/4/5/-/-/ (Jack Blumenow), D W P Arbuthnot

211 Daily Star Challenge Handicap Qualifier CLASS F (0-70 4-y-o and up) £2,905 1¼m ....(3:20)

169[5] COLTRANE [67] (v) 5-9-13 Dean McKeown (12) *led til hdd appr 3 fs out, rallied to ld ag'n approaching last, ran on und pres*....................(5 to 2 fav op 7 to 4) 1
12[6] TADORA (Ire) [51] 4-8-9 M Hills (4) *trkd ldrs, ev ch o'r one furlong out, ran on wl*............(12 to 1 op 8 to 1) 2
CAMDEN'S RANSOM (USA) [68] (e/s) 6-10-0 J Williams (8) *beh, gd hdwy o'r 4 fs out, ev ch one out, no extr.* ....(13 to 2 op 5 to 1 tchd 7 to 1) 3
84* SLIGHT RISK [63] (e/c) 4-9-7 G Bardwell (6) *trkd ldrs, led appr 3 fs out till hdd approaching last, one pace.* ....(9 to 2 op 3 to 1 tchd 5 to 1) 4
155[4] STORM FREE (USA) [49] 7-8-9 N Carlisle (11) *trkd ldr til o'r 3 fs out, wknd over 2 out.* ....(11 to 1 op 10 to 1 tchd 12 to 1) 5
182 SPRING TO THE TOP [45] 6-8-0[2] (7*) S Drowne (5) *sn pushed alng, chsd ldrs till wknd o'r 3 fs out.* ....(25 to 1 op 20 to 1) 6
GRAND HONDA (Ire) [47] 4-8-0 (5*) B Doyle (1) *nvr on terms.* ....(10 to 1 op 8 to 1) 7
4771a[6] PARKING BAY [61] (bl) 6-9-4 (3*) J Weaver (7) *beh, cld hfwy, wknd 3 fs out*..........(13 to 2 op 7 to 1 tchd 8 to 1) 8
DARK VISION [35] 4-7-0 (7*) D Wright (10) *al beh.* ....(66 to 1 op 33 to 1) 9
84[4] VA UTU [43] 5-8-3 G Carter (9) *beh, effrt 4 fs out, sn eased.* ....(5 to 1 tchd 6 to 1) 10
LAMASTRE [40] 4-7-12 N Adams (3) *outpcd, tld off.* ....(33 to 1 op 25 to 1) 11

Dist: ½l, 1l, 1½l, 7l, 7l, 2l, 3l, 2l, sht-hd, 30l. 2m 7.27s. a 4.07s (11 Ran).
SR: 42/23/40/30/4/-/ (M L Oberstein), Lord Huntingdon

212 Seine Handicap CLASS D (0-90 3-y-o and up) £3,806 5f......................(3:50)

195[3] CRECHE [86] (bl) 4-9-7 (7*) E Husband (8) *trkd ldr, hrd rdn o'r one furlong out, led ins last, all out.* ....(20 to 1 op 16 to 1 tchd 25 to 1) 1
187[3] EWALD (Ire) [57] 5-7-13 T Williams (3) *led til hdd ins fnl furlong, no extr und pres cl hme*.. (5 to 1 tchd 11 to 2) 2
191* LUCAYAN TREASURE [79] (v) 3-8-6 (7ex) M Hills (4) *chsd ldg pair, rapid hdwy ins fnl furlong, fnshd wl, jst fld.* ....(6 to 4 fav op 11 to 10 tchd 13 to 8) 3
187[2] LE CHIC [53] 7-7-9 S Wood (1) *chsd ldg pair, one pace appr fnl furlong*....................(7 to 2 op 9 to 2) 4
180 HINARI VIDEO [52] 8-7-8 J Fanning (5) *sn outpcd, hdwy ins fnl furlong, not rch ldrs.* ....(20 to 1 op 16 to 1 tchd 25 to 1) 5
99[4] RHYTHMIC DANCER [75] 5-9-3 Dean McKeown (2) *reared strt and lost many ls, not reco'r*.... (10 to 1 op 8 to 1) 6
MISDEMEANOURS GIRL (Ire) [59] 5-7-10 (5*) B Doyle (6) *sn outpcd*..................................(14 to 1) 7
196* DAANIERA (Ire) [82] (bl) 3-8-9 (7ex) J Quinn (7) *chsd ldg pair til wknd wl o'r one furlong out*..... (8 to 1 op 6 to 1) 8

Dist: Hd, nk, 5l, ½l, 2l, 4l, 1l. 59.20s. a 1.00s (8 Ran).
SR: 64/34/40/9/6/21/-/-/ (Brian Pollins), Mrs N Macauley

213 Rhone Handicap CLASS F (0-80 3-y-o) £2,820 1¼m...................... (4:20)

203* BRACKENTHWAITE [62] 8-6 (5ex) Alex Greaves (2) *hld up in cl tch, al gng wl, quickened to ld appr fnl furlong, sn clr, imprsv*........ (13 to 8 fav op 2 to 1 tchd 6 to 4) 1
129* ARCTIC GUEST (Ire) [51] 7-9 T Williams (6) *cl up, led 2 fs out to appr last, one pace*... (2 to 1 op 6 to 4 tchd 9 to 4) 2
143[3] KRYPTOS (USA) [65] 8-9 Dean McKeown (5) *trkd ldrs, pushed alng o'r 3 fs out, styd on one pace.* ....(7 to 2 op 3 to 1 tchd 4 to 1) 3
143[6] ABSOLUTELY FACT (USA) [77] 9-7 W Newnes (4) *hld up, took keen hold, cld o'r 4 fs out, ev ch appr last, wknd.* ....(7 to 1 tchd 10 to 1) 4
185[7] HUSH BABY (Ire) [55] 7-6 (7*) D Wright (1) *trkd ldr till rdn and wknd 3 fs out*....(33 to 1 op 16 to 1 tchd 50 to 1) 5
100[3] MEDLAND (Ire) [54] 7-12 J Quinn (3) *led till hdd 2 fs out, wknd*............................(10 to 1 op 7 to 1) 6

Dist: 3½l, 1½l, 1½l, 2l, sht-hd. 2m 10.15s. a 6.95s (6 Ran).
(Alex Gorrie), T D Barron

SOUTHWELL (A.W) (std)
Friday February 26th

Going Correction: MINUS 0.20 sec. per fur. (race 1), PLUS 0.35 (2,3,4,5,6)

214 Wellow Claiming Stakes CLASS F (3-y-o) £2,301 5f...................... (2:10)

206* HERSHEBAR (bl) 8-5 (5*) O Pears (5) *bumped strt, hdwy hfwy, led o'r one furlong out, ran on wl.* ....(5 to 4 fav tchd 11 to 10) 1
149[5] EXPRESS MARIECURIE (Ire) (bl) 8-6 Alex Greaves (6) *wth ldrs, ev ch 2 fs out, ran on one pace ins fnl furlong.* ....(9 to 2 op 3 to 1 tchd 5 to 1) 2
151[9] PALACEGATE GIRL 7-3 (7*) A Daly (1) *wth ldrs, ev ch 2 fs out, wknd one furlong out*....................(10 to 1) 3
151[8] CRACKER JACK (bl) 8-5 J Fanning (9) *slight ld o'r 3 fs, unbl to quicken fnl furlong*......(25 to 1 op 20 to 1) 4
151[5] APOLLO DE ORIENTE 8-0 (7*) G Parkin (3) *no ch fnl 2 fs.* ....(14 to 1 op 10 to 1) 5
178[6] BURBLE 7-12 S Wood (4) *bumped strt, hdwy hfwy, rdn 2 fs out, no headway*.... (5 to 1 op 9 to 2 tchd 11 to 2) 6
151[6] VILAMAR (Ire) 7-12 J Quinn (8) *speed 3 fs.* ....(5 to 1 op 7 to 1 tchd 8 to 1) 7
CELTIC CHERRY 7-7 (7*) Claire Balding (2) *speed o'r 3 fs, wknd quickly over one furlong out.* ....(25 to 1 op 20 to 1) 8
196[3] FOREST FLYER 8-0 G Bardwell (10) *wth ldrs 3 fs, sn lost pl.* ....(14 to 1 op 10 to 1) 9
OVER THE CLIFFS (Ire) 7-7 (7*) Kim McDonnell (7) *nvr trbld ldrs*..........................(25 to 1 op 20 to 1) 10

Dist: 6l, 2½l, sht-hd, 3 ¾l, nk, 4l, 2½l, 1l, 25l. 1m 0.20s. a 2.30s (10 Ran).
SR: 30/2/-/-/-/-/ (Mrs P A Barratt), S R Bowring

215 Claypole Maiden Stakes CLASS F (3-y-o and up) £2,070 1m..................(2:40)

193[2] GREEN'S FAIR (Ire) 3-8-5 M Hills (3) *made virtually all, clr wl o'r one furlong out, cmftbly.* ....(9 to 4 on op 11 to 8 on) 1
161[7] SUNKALA SHINE 5-9-10 L Charnock (5) *hdwy 3 fs out, ran on wl fnl furlong, no ch wth wnr*... (12 to 1 op 8 to 1) 2
206[4] NEVENTER (Fr) 4-9-10 V Smith (7) *chsd ldrs, second 2 fs out, wknd fnl furlong*............(10 to 1 op 6 to 1) 3

NIP 5-8-12 (7*) P McCabe (1) *styd on fnl 2 fs, nvr nr to chal*..................................(33 to 1) 4
HIGH CHAIR 3-8-0 Dale Gibson (8) *some hdwy fnl 2 fs, not trble ldrs*..........................(25 to 1 op 10 to 1) 5
SOMNIFERE (USA) 3-7-11² (5*) Stephen Davies (6) *chsd ldrs, btn 2 fs out*......................(7 to 2 op 6 to 4) 6
190⁴ GIRTON DEGREE 4-8-12 (7*) S Sanders (4) *wth wnr 2 fs, wknd quickly two furlongs out*..........(12 to 1) 7
179⁸ MOUNTAIN GLOW 6-9-5 (5*) K Rutter (9) *prmnt till wknd quickly 3 fs out*..........................(33 to 1) 8
ACIDOSIS 4-9-10 S Wood (2) *slow to strt, al rear div.* ....(33 to 1 op 16 to 1) 9
Dist: 7l, 3l, 4l, 12l, sht-hd, hd, 10l, 2l. 1m 46.70s. a 7.70s (9 Ran).
SR: 18/16/7/-/-/-/ (Richard Green (Fine Paintings)), M Bell

216 Thurgaton Handicap CLASS E (0-100 4-y-o and up) £3,067 1m..................(3:10)

169³ MENTALASANYTHIN [58] 4-8-0 A Mackay (5) *al cl up, led o'r 3 fs out, rdn and kpt on wl*......(2 to 1 op 7 to 4) 1
155* NO SUBMISSION (USA) [86] 7-10-0 S Wood (4) *al cl up, rdn fnl 2 fs, unbl to quicken ins final furlong.* ....(15 to 8 fav op 2 to 1 tchd 9 to 4) 2
MOSCOW DYNAMO [64] 6-8-3 (3*) F Norton (3) *tucked in beh, effrt o'r 3 fs out, ran on one pace fnl 2 furlongs.* ....(14 to 1 op 25 to 1) 3
4765a³ DEBSY DO (USA) [68] 4-8-5 (5*) O Pears (1) *wth ldr, ev ch o'r 3 fs out till wknd 2 furlongs out*.. (7 to 1 op 6 to 1) 4
130* KING PARROT (Ire) [57] 5-7-6 (7*) J Wilkinson (2) *led o'r 4 fs, wknd rpdly 2 furlongs out.* ....(9 to 4 op 6 to 4 tchd 5 to 2) 5
Dist: 4l, 4l, sht-hd, 20l. 1m 44.80s. a 5.80s (5 Ran).
SR: 41/57/23/26/-/ (Mrs M O'Donnell), A Bailey

217 Beesthorpe Maiden Stakes CLASS F (4-y-o and up) £2,070 7f................(3:40)

161² MAROWINS 4-9-0 J Quinn (6) *al prmnt, effrt o'r 2 fs out, led over one furlong out, rdn out*.... (9 to 2 op 5 to 2) 1
147⁹ BLACK BOY (Ire) 4-8-11 (3*) F Norton (4) *gd hdwy fnl 2 fs, ran on wl final furlong, nrst finish.* ....(7 to 1 op 5 to 1 tchd 8 to 1) 2
161⁴ SPEED OIL 4-8-8¹ (7*) H Bastiman (5) *gd hdwy wl o'r one furlong out, kpt on fnl furlong*..... (12 to 1 op 8 to 1) 3
48⁷ PRECIOUS CAROLINE (Ire) 5-8-9 W Woods (8) *al prmnt, ev ch 2 fs out, unbl to quicken fnl furlong.* ....(12 to 1 op 10 to 1) 4
206³ LADY ROXANNE 4-8-2 (7*) J Wilkinson (1) *hld up, ran on fnl 2 fs, nvr nr to chal.* ....(3 to 1 fav op 2 to 1 tchd 7 to 2) 5
FATHOM FIVE (Ire) 4-8-9 J Williams (9) *al abt middle div, one pace fnl 2 fs*..................(20 to 1 op 14 to 1) 6
ALNEZ (Ire) 5-9-0 R Price (3) *led aftr 2 fs, hdd o'r one furlong out, wknd quickly*........ (25 to 1 op 20 to 1) 7
163³ BLYTON STAR (Ire) 5-9-0 S Webster (11) *wth ldrs, ev ch 2 fs out, sn rdn and btn*.................(4 to 1 op 6 to 1) 8
206⁶ PRETTY CHIC 4-9-0 D Nicholls (10) *al rear div,* ....(5 to 1 tchd 11 to 2) 9
4731a⁵ BETTER STILL (Ire) 4-8-9 Dale Gibson (2) *beh fnl 2 fs.* ....(16 to 1 op 12 to 1) 10
108⁷ THE OLD MITRE 5-8-2 (7*) S Sanders (7) *led 2 fs, chsd ldrs till wknd o'r two furlongs out*..... (16 to 1 op 12 to 1) 11
Dist: Hd, 1½l, 1½l, 1½l, ¾l, 2½l, 4l, 8l, 5l, 5l. 1m 32.90s. a 6.80s (11 Ran).
SR: 35/34/29/19/14/12/9/-/-/ (Whitehills Racing Syndicate), E J Alston

218 Ravenshead Handicap CLASS E (0-90 3-y-o and up) £3,171 6f..................(4:10)

170⁵ PRIME MOVER [68] (v) 5-9-2 L Charnock (3) *chsd ldrs, led jst ins fnl furlong, rdn out*..............(5 to 2 op 2 to 1) 1
207² LORD NASKRA (USA) [56] 4-8-1 (3*) Emma O'Gorman (9) *rcd wide, ev ch 2 fs out, no extr ins fnl furlong.* ....(2 to 1 fav op 13 to 8) 2
147 BRISAS [46] (bl) 6-7-8 J Fanning (2) *led hfwy, hdd 2 fs out, led ag'n o'r one furlong out, headed jst ins fnl furlong, no extr*..................................(14 to 1 op 12 to 1) 3
194² CHOICE LOT [45] (v) 6-7-0 (7*) D Wright (7) *beh till hdwy frm hfwy, unbl to quicken fnl 2 fs.* (6 to 1 tchd 7 to 1) 4
166⁴ APPLEDORN [79] 6-9-6 (7*) S Sanders (6) *wth ldrs, slight ld 2 fs out, hdd o'r one furlong out, wknd quickly fnl furlong*................. (8 to 1 op 6 to 1 tchd 9 to 1) 5
CELESTIAL KEY (USA) [85] 3-8-12 (5*) O Pears (1) *kpt on fnl 2 fs, not trble ldrs*................ (16 to 1 op 12 to 1) 6
207⁵ KALAR [45] 4-7-7 S Wood (5) *nvr nr to chal.* ....(14 to 1 op 10 to 1) 7
166⁸ AFRICAN CHIMES [80] 6-9-11 (3*) S D Williams (8) *chsd ldrs till wknd quickly 2 fs out.* ....(17 to 2 op 14 to 1 tchd 16 to 1) 8
150³ THE CUCKOO'S NEST [50] 5-7-12 N Adams (4) *slight ld to hfwy, sn wknd 2 fs out*.......... (12 to 1 tchd 14 to 1) 9
Dist: Nk, ½l, 4l, sht-hd, 1l, 3½l, 2l, 20l. 1m 17.90s. a 4.50s (9 Ran).
SR: 54/41/29/12/45/31/-/20/-/ (Mrs M E Brooks), D Burchell

219 Skedby Handicap CLASS E (0-85 4-y-o and up) £3,054 1¾m....................(4:40)

165* HORIZON (Ire) [67] (bl) 5-9-7 D Biggs (7) *made all, styd on wl*..................(11 to 4 fav op 7 to 4 tchd 3 to 1) 1
175* COLERIDGE [76] (bl) 5-9-11 (5*,7ex) K Rutter (8) *al chasing ldrs, ev ch 2 fs out, unbl to quicken fnl furlong.* ....(7 to 2 op 5 to 2 tchd 4 to 1) 2
165² WELL AND TRULY [43] 6-7-11 J Quinn (3) *chsd ldrs, ev ch 2 fs out, ran on one pace*............. (5 to 1 op 4 to 1) 3
189* SUGEMAR [61] 7-8-12 (3*) S D Williams (5) *chsd ldrs, ev ch 2 fs out, wknd one furlong out.* .... (13 to 2 op 6 to 1 tchd 7 to 1) 4
125⁴ STEPPEY LANE [70] 8-9-10 Dean McKeown (4) *hld up, styd on fnl 3 fs, nvr dngrs*.... (7 to 2 op 9 to 2 tchd 5 to 1) 5
120⁷ SANDMOOR DENIM [55] 6-8-9 S Webster (1) *nvr better than mid-div*..................(33 to 1 op 20 to 1) 6
192⁴ WITCHES COVEN [54] 4-8-1 (3*) F Norton (9) *chsd ldrs till rdn and btn 5 fs out.* (25 to 1 op 20 to 1 tchd 33 to 1) 7
MOUNTAIN RETREAT [62] 7-9-2 J Williams (10) *al mid-div.* ....(50 to 1 op 33 to 1) 8
189³ EIRE LEATH-SCEAL [49] (v) 6-8-3 G Bardwell (2) *prmnt to hfwy, sn rdn and btn*............................(12 to 1) 9
111⁶ ROYAL VERSE (Fr) [41] 6-7-9² Dale Gibson (11) *beh most of way*........................... (40 to 1 op 33 to 1) 10
164² AMOUR ROYAL [59] 6-8-13 D Nicholls (6) *refused to race in 1st furlong*..................(20 to 1 op 16 to 1) pu
Dist: 8l, 1½l, 15l, 15l, 2l, 10l, 10l, 15l, 8l. 3m 11.70s. a 11.70s (11 Ran).
SR: 39/32/-/-/-/-/ (Mrs Solna Thomson Jones), T Thomson Jones

LINGFIELD (A.W) (std)
Saturday February 27th
Going Correction: MINUS 0.15 sec. per fur.

220 Racings Response To Bosnia Maiden Stakes CLASS F (3-y-o) £2,174 7f....(2:10)

196² PURBECK CENTENARY 9-0 Dean McKeown (7) *led aftr 2 and a half fs, made rst, ran on wl last.* ....(5 to 2 op 3 to 1 tchd 4 to 1) 1
SCORCHER (Ire) 8-9 (5*) B Doyle (1) *hit rail and lost tch aftr 2 fs, hdwy and ran on strly to go second ins last.* ....(20 to 1 op 12 to 1) 2
168⁴ GOOD IMAGE 9-0 D Nicholls (4) *led for 2 and a half fs, rdn wl o'r one out, one pace*..........(20 to 1 op 12 to 1) 3
168³ QUELQUE CHOSE 9-0 M Hills (5) *chsd ldrs, rdn and hdwy 3 fs out, one pace last*..............(5 to 4 fav op 6 to 4) 4
172² WATERLORD (Ire) (bl) 9-0 W Newnes (6) *in frnt rnk till wknd entering fnl furlong.* ....(9 to 4 op 6 to 4 tchd 5 to 2 and 11 to 4) 5
NO GAIN 8-2 (7*) Kim McDonnell (2) *al beh, lost tch hfwy.* ....(33 to 1 op 16 to 1) 6
62⁹ LOBELIA (Ire) 8-2 (7*) M Jermy (3) *slwly away, al beh.* ....(25 to 1 op 12 to 1) 7
Dist: 1½l, 2½l, 2l, 1l, 3l, 2l. 1m 28.79s. a 5.39s (7 Ran).
SR: 3/-/-/-/ (The Hammond Partnership), P Howling

221 Aid To Croatia Claiming Stakes CLASS F (4-y-o and up) £2,467 5f.............(2:40)

212* CRECHE (bl) 4-8-8 (7*) M Humphries (3) *led for one furlong, led ag'n 2 out, ran on gmely*..........(7 to 2 op 5 to 2) 1+
195* LITTLE SABOTEUR 4-8-4 W Ryan (2) *slwly into strd and outpcd early, hdwy o'r one furlong out, ran on wl ins.* ....(11 to 8 fav op 5 to 4 tchd 6 to 4) 1+
195² ANOTHER EPISODE (Ire) 4-9-7 J Carroll (4) *led aftr one furlong, hdd 2 out, rdn and wknd entering last.* ....(6 to 4 op 2 to 1 tchd 9 to 4) 3
HARRY'S COMING 9-7-12² (7*) S Drowne (1) *sn outpcd, al beh*..................... (8 to 1 op 5 to 1 tchd 10 to 1) 4
Dist: Dd-ht, 7l, 2½l. 59.94s. a 1.74s (4 Ran).
SR: 51/40/29/1/ (Brian Pollins & Mrs P J Makin), Mrs N Macauley & P J Makin

222 Medjugorje Appeal Fund Handicap CLASS D (0-100 4-y-o and up) £5,692 7f..... (3:10)

101* SPENCER'S REVENGE [81] 4-9-7 Dean McKeown (2) *al in tch on ins, squeezed through inside fnl furlong to ld cl hme*.................................... (2 to 1 fav) 1
200⁸ CHEVEUX MITCHELL [73] (v) 6-8-13 G Carter (5) *led very early, al prmnt, led appr fnl furlong, hrd rdn and hdd nr finish*.............(12 to 1 op 8 to 1 tchd 14 to 1) 2
197* INVOCATION [76] 6-9-2 N Adams (1) *slwly into strd, sn led, hdd appr fnl furlong, ran on.* ....(9 to 2 op 4 to 1 tchd 5 to 1) 3
142* ALLINSON'S MATE (Ire) [84] 5-9-10 Alex Greaves (6) *beh till hdwy o'r 2 fs out, ran on und pres ins last.* ....(5 to 2 tchd 11 to 4) 4
MERLINS WISH (USA) [80] 4-8-13 (7*) D Gibbs (7) *al prmnt, rdn and kpt on one pace fnl furlong.* ....(12 to 1 op 10 to 1) 5
197⁴ MAC'S FIGHTER [76] (bl) 8-8-9 (7*) B Russell (3) *beh whn pushed alng frm hfwy, hrd rdn 2 fs out, one pace.* ....(13 to 2 op 11 to 2) 6
155⁵ APPEALING TIMES (USA) [70] (bl) 4-8-7 (3*) Emma O'Gorman (4) *in tch whn rdn hfwy, sn beh, tld off.* ....(7 to 1 op 6 to 1 tchd 15 to 2) 7
Dist: Sht-hd, ¾l, nk, nk, 2½l, 10l. 1m 25.48s. a 2.08s (7 Ran).
SR: 60/51/52/59/54/42/6/ (Lord Crawshaw), Lord Huntingdon

223 Children Of The Balkans Handicap CLASS E (0-80 3-y-o and up) £3,289 6f...... (3:40)

4751a^{3} SPENDER [40] 4-7-9^{2} N Adams (8) *al in tch, wnt second wl o'r one furlong out, ran on und pres to ld well ins last.* ....(16 to 1) 1
180^{3} LOVE LEGEND [69] 8-9-10 J Williams (4) *beh till hdwy o'r 2 fs out, rdn ins last and ran on wl to line.* ....(7 to 2 fav tchd 4 to 1) 2
180^{5} SIR TASKER [62] 5-8-12 (5*) B Doyle (7) *led aftr one furlong, rdn and hdd wl ins last, kpt on*....(8 to 1) 3
170^{6} MISTER JOLSON [65] 4-8-13 (7*) S Drowne (2) *led 1st furlong, rdn o'r one out, one pace*..... (4 to 1 op 7 to 2) 4
197^{7} SAMSOLOM [60] 5-9-1 Dean McKeown (9) *chsd ldrs till wknd entering fnl furlong*........ (7 to 1 tchd 8 to 1) 5
207^{8} TOSHIBA COMET [47] (e/s) 6-8-2^{1} Alex Greaves (3) *al abt same pl, no hdwy ins fnl 2 fs*...... (12 to 1 op 10 to 1) 6
176^{4} SALLY'S SON [64] 7-9-2 (3*) Emma O'Gorman (6) *rcd wide, rdn and outpcd appr fnl furlong*.... (5 to 1 op 9 to 2) 7
SHARP GAZELLE [57] 3-7-3 (7*) Kim McDonnell (5) *prmnt till wknd o'r 3 fs out, tld off*....(16 to 1) 8
70^{5} SIRMOOR (Ire) [52] (v) 4-8-7 A McGlone (10) *al towards rear, tld off*.... (10 to 1 op 7 to 1) 9
195^{6} BLAZING SENSATION [49] 5-8-4 G Carter (1) *very slwly away, nvr got into race, tld off*.... (14 to 1 op 10 to 1) 10

Dist: ½l, nk, 4l, hd, 1l, 1l, 10l, 15l, 25l. 1m 13.02s. a 2.22s (10 Ran).
SR: 19/46/38/25/19/2/15/-/-/ (The Entrepreneurs), P W Harris

224 People Of Sarajevo Amateur Riders' Handicap CLASS E (0-70 4-y-o and up) £3,054 1¼m...................... (4:10)

8^{5} NATIVE CHIEFTAN [56] (e/s) 4-10-9 (5*) Mr T Cuff (6) *al prmnt in chasing grp, wnt second 3 fs out, rdn and styd on to ld nr finish*.... (16 to 1) 1
159* GOLD BLADE [60] 4-11-4 Mrs L Pearce (12) *hld up in rear, hdwy 3 fs out, rdn appr last, swtchd rght and ran on ins, jst fld*.... (4 to 1 jt-fav tchd 9 to 2) 2
198^{3} LOWAWATHA [59] 5-11-0 (5*) Mrs L Morris (3) *sn led, clr aftr 2 fs, wknd one furlong out, ct nr finish.* .... (13 to 2 op 9 to 2 tchd 7 to 1) 3
169 RIPSNORTER (Ire) [61] 4-11-0 (5*) Miss A Purdy (7) *mid-div, rdn 2 fs out, kpt on one pace.* .... (9 to 1 op 7 to 1 tchd 10 to 1) 4
198* CARLOWITZ (USA) [58] 5-10-13 (5*) Mr K Goble (9) *mid-div, rdn 3 fs out, one pace aftr*.... (6 to 1 op 4 to 1) 5
169^{8} MASTER HYDE (USA) [70] 4-12-0 Mr R Teal (4) *prmnt in chasing grp, wknd appr fnl furlong.* .... (11 to 2 op 9 to 2) 6
130^{5} NORTHERN CONQUEROR (Ire) [33] 5-9-2 (5*) Mrs J Naughton (2) *chsd ldr to 5 fs out, wknd wl o'r one furlong out.* .... (6 to 1 op 10 to 1) 7
SINGING DETECTIVE [33] 6-9-2 (5*) Miss Elaine Mills (8) *led early, ran wide 1st bend, sn beh, tld off*.... (33 to 1) 8
85 WAYWARD SON [35] 4-9-7^{5} (5*) Miss M Bridger (10) *al beh, tld off*.... (33 to 1) 9
158* ALBERT [51] 6-10-11 Miss E Bronson (1) *sn struggling in rear, tld off, fnshd lme*.... (4 to 1 jt-fav op 5 to 2) 10
131 INSWINGER [33] 7-9-2 (5*) Mr G Kille (11) *mid-div till wknd 5 fs out, sn tld off*.... (16 to 1 op 14 to 1) 11

Dist: Nk, sht-hd, 4l, nk, ½l, sht-hd, 15l, 3½l, 1½l, 25l. 2m 10.90s. a 7.70s (11 Ran).
SR: 36/39/39/31/29/38/2/-/-/ (Mrs S R Crowe), S Dow

225 Zagreb Medical Centre Handicap CLASS E (0-80 4-y-o and up) £3,498 1½m..... (4:40)

125^{3} SWORD MASTER [80] 4-10-0 N Day (6) *trkd ldr, led 4 fs out, styd on wl*.... (9 to 2 op 7 to 2 tchd 5 to 1) 1
171^{2} AWESOME POWER [74] 7-9-11 W Ryan (4) *al in tch, ev ch appr fnl furlong, rdn and no imprsn ins.* .... (15 to 8 fav op 9 to 4 tchd 7 to 4) 2
4782a^{6} BOOKCASE [72] (e/s) 6-9-9 J Williams (1) *in rear, styd on ins fnl 2 fs, nvr nr to chal*.... (10 to 1 tchd 12 to 1) 3
158^{2} SUPER LUNAR [60] 9-8-11 G Carter (5) *trkd ldrs, rdn o'r 2 fs out, sn btn*.... (5 to 1 tchd 6 to 1) 4
LORD BELMONTE (Ire) [48] 4-7-10^{3} N Adams (2) *led till hdd 4 fs out, wknd quickly.* .... (20 to 1 op 33 to 1 tchd 50 to 1 and 66 to 1) 5
BABY WIZZARD [45] 4-7-0 (7*) D Wright (3) *al beh.* .... (20 to 1 op 14 to 1 tchd 25 to 1) 6
199* BREAKDANCER (Ire) [66] 4-9-0 M Hills (7) *rcd in tch, rdn 3 fs out, sn btn*.... (2 to 1 op 6 to 4) 7

Dist: 2½l, 8l, 1½l, 5l, sht-hd, 7l. 2m 35.30s. a 6.00s (7 Ran).
SR: 36/28/10/-/ (Ian A Vogt), Bob Jones

SOUTHWELL (A.W) (std)
Monday March 1st

Going Correction: PLUS 0.45 sec. per fur. (races 1,2,3,4,5), PLUS 0.35 (6)

226 Pint And Cigar Apprentice Handicap Class E (0-70 4-y-o and up) £2,427 2m..... (2:10)

94^{6} MASTER FOODBROKER (Ire) [64] (bl) 5-9-11 (3*) D McCabe (9) *sluggish strt, improved to go hndy hfwy, led o'r one furlong out, ran on wl.* .... (25 to 1 op 14 to 1 tchd 33 to 1) 1
210 KOVALEVSKIA [37] 8-8-1 A Tucker (1) *nvr far away, effrt and drvn alng last 2 fs, styd on same pace.* .... (10 to 1 op 8 to 1) 2
175^{2} BEDOUIN PRINCE (USA) [50] (bl) 6-9-0 Stephen Davies (2) *patiently rdn, smooth hdwy to join issue entering strt, ridden and kpt on same pace last 2 fs.* .... (6 to 1 op 5 to 1 tchd 13 to 2) 3
179* MR POPPLETON [58] 4-9-3 J Weaver (8) *set steady pace, quickened up entering strt, hdd o'r one out, no extr.* .... (11 to 4 op 3 to 1 tchd 4 to 1) 4
165^{6} ELIZA WOODING [30] (v) 5-7-8 D Wright (7) *slow away, reco'red aftr 2 fs to track ldr, rdn alng two furlongs out, rallied*.... (10 to 1 op 6 to 1) 5
125^{2} QUALITAIR RHYTHM (Ire) [56] 5-9-3 (3*) G Mitchell (6) *trkd ldg trio, ev ch o'r 2 fs out, fdd.* .... (2 to 1 fav tchd 9 to 4 and 7 to 4) 6
175^{5} LAFKADIO [40] (bl) 6-8-4^{1} O Pears (4) *tucked away on ins, effrt and drvn alng hfwy, fdd appr strt.* .... (12 to 1 op 10 to 1 tchd 14 to 1) 7
192^{2} SOUL TRADER [45] 4-8-4 F Norton (3) *co'red up on ins, feeling pace and rdn entering strt, sn btn.* .... (16 to 1 op 8 to 1) 8
18^{3} DANCING DAYS [32] (bl) 7-7-10 M Humphries (5) *chsd ldrs, struggling and lost grnd hfwy, tld off.* .... (11 to 1 op 8 to 1 tchd 12 to 1) 9

Dist: 3½l, 2½l, 2l, ½l, 10l, 2½l, 5l, 5l. 3m 55.20s. a 28.70s (9 Ran).
(Broughton Thermal Insulation), W J Musson

227 Owners And Trainers Bar Claiming Stakes Class G (4-y-o and up) £2,574 7f.....(2:40)

54^{7} CLAUDIA MISS 6-8-4 Dean McKeown (16) *nvr far away, led o'r 2 fs out, hld on wl ins fnl furlong.* .... (6 to 1 tchd 7 to 1) 1
190* SILKY SIREN (bl) 4-8-4 J Quinn (11) *trkd ldg 5, drvn up to chal entering fnl furlong, jst hld.* .... (7 to 4 fav op 5 to 4 tchd 2 to 1) 2
MOST SURPRISING (Ire) 4-7-10 (7*) M Humphries (5) *patiently rdn, improved centre last 2 fs, ran on wl towards finish*.... (20 to 1 op 16 to 1) 3
205^{8} MORPICK (v) 6-8-2 (5*) Stephen Davies (1) *led aftr 2 fs, hdd o'r two furlongs out, rdn and one pace.* .... (25 to 1 op 20 to 1) 4
13^{8} LILY'S LOVER (USA) 7-8-5 L Charnock (9) *chsd ldg half dozen, came very wide last 2 fs, kpt on same pace.* .... (10 to 1 op 7 to 1) 5
135^{8} CAL'S BOY 4-8-9 R Lappin (10) *improved frm midfield to go hndy hfwy, drvn alng last 2 fs, one pace.* .... (33 to 1 op 25 to 1) 6
188^{3} FIABA 5-8-0^{3} (3*) F Norton (4) *swtchd ins to improve frm off the pace hfwy, styd on, nvr able to chal.* .... (7 to 1 tchd 8 to 1) 7
200 TURTLE BEACH (v) 4-8-12 W Newnes (15) *bustled alng in midfield, effrt o'r 2 fs out, not pace to chal.* .... (14 to 1 op 12 to 1) 8
188^{7} MAHZOOZ 4-8-7 J McLaughlin (14) *drvn alng to keep up, styd on last 2 fs, nvr nrr*.... (33 to 1 op 20 to 1) 9
190^{3} POP TO STANS (bl) 4-8-9 G Bardwell (12) *chsd alng to keep up, styd on last 2 fs, nvr nrr*.... (9 to 1 op 5 to 1) 10
176* FARM STREET 6-8-0 (7*) B Russell (3) *wth ldrs, drvn alng hfwy, fdd 2 fs out*.... (7 to 2 op 4 to 1 tchd 9 to 2) 11
WEEKEND GIRL 4-7-10 N Adams (2) *sluggish strt, nvr a factor*.... (33 to 1 op 20 to 1) 12
ROSE GEM (Ire) 4-8-4 Dale Gibson (7) *pressed ldrs for o'r 4 fs, fdd*.... (14 to 1 op 12 to 1) 13
206^{5} THE TONDY (Ire) 5-9-1 D Nicholls (13) *chases alng beh ldg bunch, some hdwy o'r 2 fs out, nvr dngrs.* .... (33 to 1 op 20 to 1) 14
188^{8} TIBBY HEAD (Ire) (bl) 5-8-5 G Carter (6) *broke fst to ld for 2 fs, fdd und pres o'r two furlongs out.* .... (33 to 1 op 25 to 1) 15
190^{8} KACHINA MAID 8-7-12 S Wood (8) *sluggish strt, nvr able to reco'r*.... (33 to 1 op 20 to 1) 16

Dist: ½l, 2l, 1l, ½l, 2l, hd, 4l, 2l, 2½l, 5l. 1m 32.80s. a 6.70s (16 Ran).
SR: 37/35/28/29/25/23/13/13/2/ (G Whorton), W W Haigh

228 Tatt's 2000 Bar Handicap Class E (0-70 3-y-o) £2,343 7f......................... (3:10)

203^{2} ROSE FLYER (Ire) [55] 8-9 (7*) D McCabe (2) *made all, quickened to go clr o'r 2 fs out, began to tire ins last, rdn out*.... (13 to 2 op 6 to 1) 1
149^{2} JORDYWRATH [57] 9-4 J McLaughlin (3) *took keen hold, rstrained till hdwy hfwy, effrt fnl furlong, ran on.* .... (9 to 2 op 6 to 1 tchd 13 to 2) 2
172* STEVIE'S WONDER (Ire) [52] 8-13 T Quinn (1) *last away, improved to join wnr aftr 2 fs, hrd rdn last two furlongs, one pace*.... (13 to 2 op 6 to 1) 3
193* DON'T BE SAKI (Ire) [58] 9-0 (5*) O Pears (6) *chsd alng to go pace hfwy, styd on last 2 fs, nrst finish.* .... (12 to 1 op 7 to 1) 4

178^{2} PYTCHLEY DAWN [50] 8-6 (5*) Stephen Davies (4) *chsd ldrs, swtchd centre and effrt 2 fs out, styd on same pace.* ....(3 to 1 jt-fav tchd 11 to 4) 5
FORMAESTRE (Ire) [58] 8-12 (7*) J Tate (7) *bustled alng to keep up hfwy, styd on last 2 fs, nvr nrr*........(25 to 1) 6
162* NIKKI NOO NOO [58] 9-5 J Quinn (5) *bustled alng to go pace, nvr able to trble ldrs.* (3 to 1 jt-fav op 5 to 2 tchd 100 to 30) 7
186^{4} DIAMOND LUCY [60] (bl) 9-4 (3*) Emma O'Gorman (8) *pressed ldg pair till fdd last 2 fs*......(9 to 1 op 7 to 1) 8
Dist: 1½l, 2l, 1½l, nk, 1½l, 10l, 2l. 1m 34.70s. a 8.60s (8 Ran).
SR: 20/17/6/7/-/1/-/-/ (A M Packaging Ltd), M C Chapman

229 Saddle Bar Claiming Stakes Class G (4-y-o and up) £2,448 1½m............ (3:40)

175^{3} ATLANTIC WAY 5-8-8 G Bardwell (9) *pushed alng to improve frm midfield hfwy, swtchd outsd to ld o'r one furlong out, styd on wl.* ....(11 to 2 op 5 to 1 tchd 8 to 1) 1
192* KARAMOJA 4-8-8 T Quinn (3) *chsd alng to improve frm off the pace hfwy, led o'r 2 fs out till over one out, not quicken*.............................(4 to 1 op 3 to 1) 2
148^{5} RED INDIAN 7-9-1 Dean McKeown (10) *settled gng wl, drw level 2 fs out, not quicken appr fnl furlong.* ....(12 to 1 op 10 to 1) 3
179^{5} MISS LAWN (Fr) 5-8-1 (5*) Stephen Davies (12) *pressed ldrs till lost grnd hfwy, styd on ag'n last 2 fs, nvr nrr.* ....(25 to 1 op 20 to 1) 4
164* SOL ROUGE (Ire) 4-7-9 (7*) Nicola Howarth (6) *set gd pace, hdd and drvn alng o'r 2 fs out, no extr.* ....(10 to 1 op 7 to 1) 5
189^{2} LA REINE ROUGE (Ire) 5-8-3 (3*) F Norton (8) *improved frm midfield to track ldr hfwy, fdd und pres 2 fs out.* ....(11 to 1 op 8 to 1) 6
$4671a^{9}$ I'M CURIOUS 4-7-13^{4} (7*) B Russell (1) *chsd ldrs, hrd at work hfwy, fdd appr strt*.........(50 to 1 op 33 to 1) 7
202^{2} LOCK KEEPER (USA) 7-9-1 J Quinn (5) *settled midfield, feeling pace hfwy, btn appr strt.* ....(5 to 1 op 4 to 1 tchd 6 to 1) 8
152 MAI PEN RAI 5-8-7 N Adams (7) *chsd alng to go pace hfwy, nvr a factor*... (25 to 1 op 20 to 1 tchd 33 to 1) 9
69^{4} MON PETITNAMOUR (Ire) 4-8-13 W Ryan (2) *steadied strt, hld up and al beh*.....(7 to 1 op 12 to 1 tchd 14 to 1) 10
92* ANNACURRAGH (Ire) 4-8-7 G Carter (11) *chsd ldg half dozen to hfwy, wknd quickly, tld off.* ....(5 to 2 fav op 6 to 4) 11
ACE REPORTER 4-7-13 L Charnock (4) *reared and lost grnd strt, reco'red aftr 2 fs, lost tch hfwy, tld off.* ....(20 to 1 op 16 to 1) 12
Dist: 3l, 8l, 5l, nk, 1½l, 10l, hd, sht-hd. 2m 46.90s. a 13.00s (12 Ran).
SR: 18/12/3/-/-/-/ (C John Hill), C J Hill

230 Members Bar Maiden Stakes Class D (3-y-o) £2,427 1½m.................. (4:10)

213^{5} HUSH BABY (Ire) 8-2 (7*) D Wright (8) *made most, hdd briefly o'r 2 fs out, hld on grimly ins fnl furlong.* ....(14 to 1 op 7 to 1 tchd 16 to 1) 1
162^{3} BARSAL (Ire) 9-0 Alex Greaves (9) *nvr far away, nosed ahead o'r 2 fs out, sn hdd, ev ch fnl furlong, jst hld.* ....(3 to 1 op 7 to 2 tchd 11 to 4 and 4 to 1) 2
SOLOMAN SPRINGS (USA) 8-9 (5*) O Pears (6) *rcd freely in frnt rnk, bustled alng whn pace quickened last 3 fs, styd on, better for race*....... (11 to 10 fav op 2 to 1) 3
CAROJANGO 9-0 M Hills (4) *chsd ldg 5, hrd at work aftr a m, styd on last 2 fs*................. (5 to 1 op 3 to 1) 4
TURFMANS VISION 9-0 W Ryan (7) *settled strt, improved into midfield hfwy, sn drvn alng, rallied last 2 fs.* ....(20 to 1 op 16 to 1) 5
132^{9} MOUNTAIN WILLOW (v) 8-9 Dean McKeown (2) *trkd ldg half dozen, hrd at work hfwy, styd on last 2 fs.* ....(11 to 2 op 9 to 4 tchd 6 to 1) 6
129^{7} FREE DANCER 8-9 N Adams (5) *chsd ldg quartet, lost grnd hfwy, rdn alng last 2 fs, one pace.* ....(33 to 1 op 20 to 1) 7
204^{8} NOBLE MEASURE (Ire) (bl) 9-0 S Webster (3) *pressed ldg pair for a m, sn struggling*.........(33 to 1 op 25 to 1) 8
72^{6} PERSIAN STAR (Fr) 8-9 T Quinn (1) *struggling to go pace hfwy, nvr a factor*................ (20 to 1 op 14 to 1) 9
Dist: Sht-hd, 1½l, 2½l, 2l, hd, ½l, 3l, 6l. 2m 52.30s. a 18.40s (9 Ran).
(John Peters), C N Allen

231 Paddock Bar Handicap Class E (0-70 3-y-o and up) £2,364 5f.................. (4:40)

207^{4} STRIP CARTOON (Ire) [48] (bl) 5-8-7 (7*) B Russell (9) *beh and bustled alng hfwy, rapid hdwy stand side to ld cl hme*..............................(11 to 2 op 9 to 2) 1
187^{4} COMET WHIRLPOOL (Ire) [57] (bl) 3-8-9 J Quinn (4) *al hndy, nosed ahead entering fnl furlong, hdd and not quicken cl hme*...............................(7 to 1 op 9 to 2) 2
194^{7} ARC LAMP [49] 7-8-12 (3*) S D Williams (3) *nvr far away, rdn to draw level ins fnl furlong, no extr cl hme.* ....(9 to 1 op 12 to 1) 3
212^{2} EWALD (Ire) [57] 5-9-9 Dean McKeown (1) *tried to make all, hdd and rdn entering fnl furlong, no extr.* ....(100 to 30 op 5 to 2 tchd 4 to 1) 4
188^{5} MARIETTE LARKIN [42] 4-8-8 J Fanning (10) *sluggish strt, beh till ran on wl appr fnl furlong, nrst finish.* ....(16 to 1 op 14 to 1) 5
205^{5} COMISKEY PARK (Ire) [33] (bl) 4-7-13 S Wood (2) *chsd alng far side, effrt hfwy, not quicken appr fnl furlong.* ....(16 to 1 op 14 to 1) 6
180^{4} LINCSTONE BOY (Ire) [58] (bl) 5-9-10 S Webster (8) *broke wl to show gd speed for o'r 3 fs*........ (10 to 1 op 7 to 1) 7
SLADES HILL [62] 6-10-0 Alex Greaves (7) *bustled alng to keep up, nvr able to trble ldrs.* ....(20 to 1 op 12 to 1 tchd 25 to 1) 8
207* QUATRE FEMME [57] 6-9-4 (5*,7ex) Stephen Davies (5) *dwlt, nvr able to reco'r.* ....(5 to 2 fav op 3 to 1 tchd 100 to 30) 9
147 MISS EL ARAB (Ire) [52] (v) 5-9-1 (3*) F Norton (6) *gd speed in frnt rnk 3 fs, fdd*.................(25 to 1 op 20 to 1) 10
180 LONG LAST [28] 4-7-8 G Bardwell (11) *gd speed stand side for o'r 3 fs, fdd*................................(33 to 1) 11
Dist: ½l, hd, ½l, 3l, 2l, nk, nk, 2l, ¾l, ½l. 1m 2.50s. a 4.60s (11 Ran).
SR: 43/36/41/47/20/3/27/30/17/ (Mrs Irene Pryce), S R Bowring

LINGFIELD (A.W) (std)
Thursday March 4th
Going Correction: MINUS 0.05 sec. per fur.

232 Marco Polo Apprentice Handicap Class E (0-80 4-y-o and up) £3,054 1m....... (2:10)

184* BELMOREDEAN [77] 8-10-0 F Norton (10) *al hndy, led o'r 2 fs out, clr fnl furlong, cmftbly*... (3 to 1 fav op 5 to 2) 1
184^{3} EXPRESS SERVICE [60] 4-8-11 Emma O'Gorman (5) *al prmnt, ev ch o'r 2 fs out, rdn and no extr fnl furlong.* ....(11 to 2 op 4 to 1) 2
SAAHI (USA) [76] 4-9-13 K Rutter (7) *beh till rdn and ran on strly fnl one and a half fs, fnshd wl.* ....(12 to 1 op 8 to 1 tchd 14 to 1) 3
KILLY [68] 4-9-5 J Weaver (6) *trkd ldrs, rdn and ev ch o'r one furlong out, sn btn*.............(8 to 1 op 6 to 1) 4
152 SAREEN EXPRESS (Ire) [43] 5-7-8 D Wright (1) *beh till styd on fnl 2 fs, nvr nrr*..............................(6 to 1) 5
205^{2} DIAMOND INTHE DARK (USA) [54] (v) 5-8-5 O Pears (8) *led 4 fs out till hdd o'r 2 out, wknd appr fnl furlong.* ....(11 to 2 op 5 to 1 tchd 13 to 2) 6
197 UNVEILED [56] 5-8-7 S Drowne (4) *nvr nr to chal.* ....(20 to 1 op 14 to 1 tchd 25 to 1) 7
200^{4} AMETHYSTINE (USA) [54] 7-8-5 Stephen Davies (9) *nvr a factor*.................(13 to 2 op 6 to 1 tchd 7 to 1) 8
157^{6} ALBERT THE BOLD [60] (v) 4-8-11 M Humphries (3) *chsd ldrs till no hdwy fnl 3 fs*..........(16 to 1 op 10 to 1) 9
CHINA SKY [42] 5-7-7^{7} (7*) A Whelan (2) *led till hdd 4 fs out, wknd quickly*................(33 to 1 op 20 to 1) 10
Dist: 2½l, sht-hd, nk, 2l, nk, 2l, 3½l, 12l, 8l. 1m 40.12s. a 3.92s (10 Ran).
SR: 49/24/39/30/-/9/5/-/-/ (Fred Honour), R J O'Sullivan

233 Rational Combi-Steamer Claiming Stakes Class G (3-y-o) £2,325 7f............(2:40)

183^{4} MISTER BLAKE (bl) 8-12 (3*) Emma O'Gorman (2) *sn chsd alng, hdwy o'r 3 fs out, chlgd appr fnl furlong, sstnd run to ld post*...................... (7 to 2 op 5 to 2) 1
208* STARDUST EXPRESS 9-1 Dean McKeown (3) *chsd ldrs, rdn to ld 2 fs out, ct post.* ....(13 to 8 on op 6 to 4 on tchd 11 to 8 on) 2
178^{3} PIRATES GOLD (Ire) 9-3 T Quinn (1) *wth ldr, led o'r 3 fs out till hdd over 2 out, sn wknd*........ (5 to 1 op 4 to 1) 3
THREEOFUS 8-4 (5*) Stephen Davies (4) *sn outpcd, some hdwy fnl furlong, no dngr.* ....(50 to 1 op 20 to 1 tchd 66 to 1) 4
GATE OF HEAVEN 7-12^{5} (3*) F Norton (5) *made most till hdd o'r 3 fs out, wknd*..... (14 to 1 op 7 to 1 tchd 16 to 1) 5
Dist: Hd, 12l, sht-hd, 2l. 1m 27.88s. a 4.48s (5 Ran).
SR: 29/28/ (Red Seven Stable), W A O'Gorman

234 Drake Handicap Class C (0-90 4-y-o and up) £3,984 1¼m.................... (3:10)

198^{4} PIGALLE WONDER [58] 5-8-9 D Biggs (7) *trkd ldr, led o'r 4 fs out, quickened 2 out, hrd rdn and hld on gmely ins last*..................................(6 to 1 op 9 to 2) 1
225^{2} AWESOME POWER [74] 7-9-11 W Ryan (2) *patiently rdn gng wl, pld out to chal appr fnl furlong, edgd rght and styd on one pace*.... (9 to 4 fav op 5 to 2 tchd 3 to 1) 2
202^{4} MAJAL (Ire) [62] 4-8-12 D Nicholls (1) *cl up, rdn and ev ch 2 fs out, not quicken*...... (3 to 1 op 5 to 2 tchd 4 to 1) 3
184^{2} APPLIANCEOFSCIENCE [46] 6-7-11 J Quinn (8) *chsd ldrs, rdn o'r 2 fs out, kpt on ins last.* ....(8 to 1 op 6 to 1 tchd 10 to 1) 4
4757a* SIR NORMAN HOLT (Ire) [58] 4-8-8 R Lappin (6) *took keen hold, in tch till outpcd 3 fs out, sn btn.* ....(10 to 1 op 6 to 1) 5
128^{9} MODESTO (USA) [42] (bl) 5-7-7 S Wood (5) *led till hdd o'r 4 fs out, sn lost pl*.....(16 to 1 op 14 to 1 tchd 20 to 1) 6

197^2 RURAL LAD [62] 4-8-9 (3*) D Harrison (4) *hld up in tch, took clr order 4 fs out, sn ev ch, rdn and btn o'r 2 out.* ....(6 to 1 op 9 to 2) 7
190^2 JUVENARA [52] 7-7-10 (7*) M Humphries (3) *beh till shrtlvd effrt 4 fs out, sn wknd.* ....(12 to 1 op 10 to 1 tchd 14 to 1) 8
Dist: Nk, 3l, ½l, 7l, ¾l, ½l, 4l. 2m 9.26s. a 6.06s (8 Ran).
SR: 29/44/25/9/6/-/7/-/ (Miss Nicola M Pfann), R J O'Sullivan

235 Daily Star Challenge Handicap Qualifier Class E (0-70 4-y-o and up) £2,782 1½m ....(3:40)

210^* STRAT'S LEGACY [55] 6-9-3 (3*,5ex) J Weaver (10) *patiently rdn, smooth hdwy frm 4 fs out to ld o'r 2 out, sn quickened clr, pushed out*...(9 to 4 fav tchd 5 to 2) 1
199^6 SINCLAIR LAD (Ire) [57] 5-9-8 W Ryan (4) *hld up and beh, hdwy 3 fs out, styd on appr fnl furlong, nvr nrr.* ....(10 to 1 op 8 to 1 tchd 12 to 1) 2
103^7 FLASH OF STRAW (Ire) [36] (bl) 4-7-12 T Williams (6) *handily plcd, effrt o'r 2 fs out, sn ev ch, rdn and one pace appr fnl furlong*..................(10 to 1 tchd 12 to 1) 3
229^6 LA REINE ROUGE (Ire) [37] 5-7-13 (3*) F Norton (9) *chsd ldrs, ev ch o'r 2 fs out, sn no extr*....... (16 to 1 op 14 to 1) 4
210^2 DEBACLE (USA) [64] (bl) 4-9-12 W Woods (2) *led till hdd o'r 2 fs out, wknd appr fnl furlong*......(4 to 1 op 7 to 2) 5
215^4 NIP [32] 5-7-11[2] D Biggs (11) *mid-field, effrt o'r 3 fs out, sn one pace*..........................(16 to 1 op 14 to 1) 6
182^3 EL DOMINIO [53] 5-9-4 T Quinn (14) *in tch, hmpd o'r 3 fs out, sn lost pl and eased*.............(4 to 1 op 7 to 2) 7
114^6 WESSEX MILORD [28] 8-7-4[4] (7*) Claire Balding (7) *beh til moderate hdwy fnl 2 fs, nvr a threat.* ....(20 to 1 op 25 to 1 tchd 33 to 1) 8
DOUBLE THE STAKES (USA) [40] 4-8-2 R Lappin (13) *wth ldr till rdn and lost pl o'r 3 fs out*.. (33 to 1 op 20 to 1) 9
211^7 GRAND HONDA (Ire) [47] 4-8-4 (5*) B Doyle (12) *prmnt, rdn o'r 4 fs out, sn wknd*.............. (16 to 1 op 14 to 1) 10
199^9 SPRING FORWARD [28] (v) 9-7-7 S Wood (8) *al beh.* ....(50 to 1) 11
152 COOL PARADE (USA) [47] 5-8-12 J Quinn (3) *chsd ldg grp till wknd o'r 4 fs out*............. (20 to 1 op 14 to 1) 12
SAFE ARRIVAL (USA) [54] 5-9-5 M Tebbutt (1) *prmnt for 3 fs, sn lost pl, wl beh frm 5 furlongs out*...........(25 to 1) 13
SAIF AL ADIL (Ire) [50] 4-8-7 (5*) Stephen Davies (5) *al beh.* ....(25 to 1) 14
Dist: 7l, 3½l, 3½l, 1½l, 6l, 2l, nk, 1½l, 4l, 3½l. 2m 35.23s. a 5.93s (14 Ran).
SR: 41/29/-/-/16/-/ (Jack Blumenow), D W P Arbuthnot

236 Nestle Handicap Class G (0-60 3-y-o and up) £2,807 5f.......................(4:10)

187^* SERIOUS HURRY [53] 5-9-10 T Quinn (8) *led o'r a furlong, rgned ld over 2 out, styd on wl fnl furlong.* ....(9 to 4 fav op 2 to 1 tchd 5 to 2) 1
231^2 COMET WHIRLPOOL (Ire) [57] (bl) 3-9-0 J Quinn (5) *chsd ldrs, ran on appr fnl furlong, one pace ins last.* (7 to 2) 2
207^7 LAST STRAW [45] 5-8-9 (7*) Claire Balding (3) *chsd ldrs on ins, effrt wl o'r one furlong out, kpt on.* ....(7 to 1 op 5 to 1) 3
187^5 PALACEGATE GOLD (Ire) [43] (bl) 4-8-7 (7*) S Drowne (6) *beh till styd on wl appr fnl furlong, nvr nrr.* .... (10 to 1 op 9 to 1) 4
218^7 KALAR [42] (bl) 4-8-13 S Wood (10) *prmnt on outsd, ev ch o'r 2 fs out, sn one paced.* ....(11 to 1 op 10 to 1 tchd 12 to 1) 5
212^5 HINARI VIDEO [52] 8-9-9 Dean McKeown (1) *chsd ldrs, rdn aftr 2 fs, no hdwy fnl two.* ....(13 to 2 op 6 to 1 tchd 7 to 1) 6
156^5 TEE-EMM [57] 3-8-7 (7*) L Carter (2) *led aftr one and a half fs till hdd o'r 2 out, sn wknd.* ....(13 to 2 op 7 to 1 tchd 6 to 1) 7
ALL THE GIRLS (Ire) [37] 4-8-8[2] J Williams (9) *slwly away, outpcd*.. (20 to 1) 8
195^5 GRAND TIME [50] 4-9-0 (7*) D Wright (4) *mid-field, hrd rdn o'r 3 fs out, sn btn*.................(10 to 1 op 9 to 1) 9
Dist: 1½l, ½l, ¾l, 1l, ½l, 4l, sht-hd, 1l. 1m 0.86s. a 2.66s (9 Ran).
SR: 52/36/36/31/26/34/9/2/11/ (Richard Berenson), C C Elsey

237 Alpine Double Glazing Maiden Stakes Class D (3-y-o) £2,208 1¼m.........(4:40)

185^2 DARING PAST 9-0 W Ryan (2) *al hndy, effrt o'r 2 fs out, came wide and styd on strly ins last to ld cl hme.* ....(11 to 4 op 2 to 1 tchd 3 to 1) 1
178^5 ASHOVER 9-0 Alex Greaves (5) *pld hrd, al prmnt, led wl o'r 2 fs out, hard rdn and ran on till hdd cl hme.* ....(11 to 4 op 7 to 2 tchd 5 to 1) 2
209^2 SPANISH REFUGE 9-0 Dean McKeown (1) *tucked away, short of room whn pace quickened o'r 2 fs out, rcvred to hold ev ch over one out, ran on.* ....(Evens fav op 11 to 10 on tchd 6 to 5) 3
193^3 PRINCE OF SOUL 9-0 J McLaughlin (7) *hld up in tch, effrt o'r 3 fs out, sn no imprsn.* ....(16 to 1 op 7 to 1 tchd 20 to 1) 4
$4755a^8$ DOOGAREY 9-0 C Avery (3) *prmnt till wknd 2 fs out.* .... (50 to 1 op 25 to 1) 5
83^9 UNIVERSAL (Fr) 8-9 D Biggs (4) *led till hdd wl o'r 2 fs out, wknd quickly, tld off*.............(50 to 1 op 20 to 1) 6
Dist: Hd, hd, 8l, 1½l, 15l. 2m 11.72s. a 8.52s (6 Ran).
SR: 10/9/8/ (Keith Sturgis), R Boss

SOUTHWELL (A.W) (std)
Friday March 5th
Going Correction: PLUS 0.40 sec. per fur.

238 Rufford Maiden Apprentice Stakes Class G (3-y-o and up) £2,070 1m......... (2:10)

$4669a^6$ CAPTAIN MARMALADE 4-9-10 K Rutter (4) *mid-div, hdwy and wide strt, led o'r one and a half fs out, sn clr.* .... (14 to 1 op 16 to 1) 1
ABSALOM'S PILLAR 3-8-6 O Pears (8) *outpcd and beh, hdwy 3 fs out, styd on wl fnl 2 furlongs.* .... (14 to 1 op 10 to 1) 2
148^7 BAHER (USA) 4-9-5 (5*) Carol Davison (6) *chsd ldrs, hdwy 3 fs out, ev ch 2 furlongs out, sn rdn and one pace appr fnl furlong*..........(7 to 2 op 4 to 1 tchd 3 to 1) 3
204^2 PACIFIC SPIRIT 3-8-1 F Norton (2) *chsd ldr, bustled alng hfwy, led 2 and a half fs out till hdd one and a half furlongs out, sn wknd.* ....(7 to 4 fav op 6 to 4 tchd 2 to 1) 4
217^2 BLACK BOY (Ire) 4-9-10 S D Williams (1) *dwlt, hdwy to chase ldrs hfwy, rdn and one pace o'r 2 fs out.* ....(5 to 2 op 9 to 4 tchd 3 to 1) 5
FIRST HOME 6-9-10 T G McLaughlin (9) *sn outpcd and beh*...(33 to 1) 6
215^9 ACIDOSIS 4-9-5 (5*) Carl Llewellyn (5) *cl up till rdn and wknd 3 fs out*.......................................(33 to 1) 7
206 LAST TYPHOON 3-8-1 N Kennedy (7) *prmnt to hfwy, sn wknd*... (33 to 1) 8
205^7 BAYIN (USA) (bl) 4-9-10 D Harrison (3) *led and sn clr, rdn and hdd 2 and a half fs out, wknd quickly.* ....(8 to 1 op 6 to 1 tchd 9 to 1) 9
Dist: 2l, 3l, 4l, 2½l, 8l, hd, 10l, 5l. 1m 47.90s. a 8.90s (9 Ran).
SR: 25/1/10/-/-/-/ (Mrs Carol Whitwood), D T Thom

239 Tuxford Handicap Class C (0-100 3-y-o and up) £3,275 1m.......................(2:40)

184^4 SIRTELIMAR (Ire) [65] 4-9-5 A Mackay (4) *made all, rdn 2 fs out, ran on wl.* ....(5 to 2 op 9 to 4 tchd 11 to 4 and 3 to 1) 1
203^4 GOLDEN KLAIR [85] 3-9-7 J Quinn (5) *in tch, effrt and hdwy 3 fs out, rdn o'r one furlong out, kpt on.* .... (5 to 1 op 4 to 1 tchd 11 to 2) 2
216^* MENTALASANYTHIN [63] 4-8-10 (7*,5ex) D Wright (2) *prmnt, effrt and ev ch 2 fs out, sn rdn and kpt on one pace.* ....(7 to 4 fav tchd 2 to 1) 3
$4724a^*$ ABERDEEN HEATHER [88] (e/s) 3-9-10 J Williams (1) *hld up in tch, hdwy o'r 2 fs out, styd on und pres fnl furlong.* .... (9 to 1 op 7 to 1 tchd 10 to 1) 4
203^3 TANAGOME (USA) [70] 3-8-1 (5*) O Pears (6) *in tch, hdwy to chase wnr 3 fs out, rdn 2 furlongs out, grad wknd.* .... (11 to 2 op 5 to 1 tchd 6 to 1) 5
SHIRLEY'S TRAIN (USA) [67] 4-9-4 (3*) D Harrison (3) *prmnt, rdn 3 fs out, sn wknd.* ....(11 to 1 op 10 to 1 tchd 12 to 1) 6
172^4 QUICK SILVER BOY [58] 3-7-8[1] N Adams (7) *chsd ldrs till wknd hfwy, sn wl beh*.............(25 to 1 op 20 to 1) 7
Dist: 2l, nk, 2½l, 1½l, 8l, 30l. 1m 45.90s. a 6.90s (7 Ran).
SR: 50/46/41/40/17/8/-/ (D W Price), R C Spicer

240 Skegby Claiming Stakes Class G (3-y-o) £2,280 1m....................... (3:10)

167^2 HOTSOCKS 8-4 (7*) Kim McDonnell (1) *hld up and beh, gd hdwy 3 fs out, led ins fnl furlong, styd on wl.* ....(4 to 1 op 3 to 1) 1
228^4 DON'T BE SAKI (Ire) 8-3 (5*) O Pears (3) *al prmnt, effrt 2 fs out, rdn to ld appr fnl furlong, hdd and no extr ins last.* ....(5 to 2 op 2 to 1) 2
214^7 VILAMAR (Ire) 7-1[1] (7*) D Wright (7) *led aftr one furlong, rdn 2 fs out, hdd and one pace appr fnl furlong.* ....(12 to 1 op 8 to 1) 3
228^7 NIKKI NOO NOO 8-10 J Quinn (6) *in tch, effrt and rdn 2 fs out, wknd appr fnl furlong*...... (2 to 1 fav op 6 to 4) 4
204^3 SCOFFERA 8-8 Kim Tinkler (2) *led one furlong, prmnt till rdn and wknd 3 fs out*...(7 to 1 op 5 to 1 tchd 8 to 1) 5
167^6 WEALTHYWOO 7-9 Dale Gibson (4) *in tch and sn pushed alng, rdn and wknd wl o'r 2 fs out.* ....(6 to 1 op 7 to 1 tchd 8 to 1 and 10 to 1) 6
168^5 GIRTON BELLE (bl) 7-8[1] N Adams (5) *prmnt till rdn and wknd 3 fs out*................. (25 to 1 op 20 to 1) 7
Dist: 2½l, 2½l, 2½l, 1l, 8l, 12l. 1m 49.80s. a 10.80s (7 Ran).
(The Marketing And Distribution Group), Pat Mitchell

241 Normanton Handicap Class D (0-80 4-y-o and up) £2,364 7f..................(3:40)

216^4 DEBSY DO (USA) [68] 4-9-0 (5*) O Pears (7) *al prmnt, hdwy to ld o'r 2 fs out, sn clr, rdn and hld on wl fnl furlong.* ....(3 to 1 op 5 to 2) 1

218² LORD NASKRA (USA) [58] 4-8-6 (3*) Emma O'Gorman (2) *chsd ldrs and scrubbed alng, wide strt, gd hdwy o'r one furlong out, styd on wl ins last.* ....(6 to 4 fav op 7 to 4 tchd 9 to 4 and 5 to 2) 2
216³ MOSCOW DYNAMO [64] 6-8-12 (3*) F Norton (8) *chsd ldrs, hdwy 2 and a half fs out, sn chasing wnr, rdn and kpt on one pace fnl furlong*..............(7 to 1 op 5 to 1) 3
SHUJAN (USA) [73] 4-9-10 R Price (9) *mid-div, hdwy 2 fs out, styd on fnl furlong, nrst finish.* ....(14 to 1 op 10 to 1 tchd 16 to 1) 4
QUESTION OF DEGREE [50] 7-8-1⁷ Kim Tinkler (10) *slwly into strd, hdwy o'r 2 fs out, kpt on fnl furlong, nrst finish*..............................(20 to 1 op 14 to 1) 5
134⁹ COMPANY CASH [50] (bl) 5-8-1 J Fanning (5) *sn led and clr, hdd o'r 2 fs out, soon wknd*.........(12 to 1 op 9 to 1) 6
48⁸ LOOTING (USA) [42] 7-7-0 (7*) Kim McDonnell (1) *cl up till rdn and wknd 2 fs out*............(25 to 1 op 20 to 1) 7
155³ NELLIE DEAN [48] 4-7-13 Dale Gibson (6) *prmnt, rdn 3 fs out, grad wknd*....... (13 to 2 op 5 to 1 tchd 7 to 1) 8
SLEEPLINE FANTASY [60] 8-8-11 J Quinn (3) *chsd ldrs, rdn 3 fs out, sn wknd*................. (10 to 1 tchd 8 to 1) 9
227 KACHINA MAID [42] 8-7-1¹ (7*) D Wright (4) *slwly into strd, al beh*..............................(50 to 1 op 33 to 1) 10
Dist: Hd, 1l, 3l, 1½l, 8l, hd, ¾l, 6l, 10l. 1m 32.50s. a 6.40s (10 Ran).
SR: 51/40/43/43/15/-/ (S G Norton), S G Norton

242 Retford Handicap Class C (0-100 4-y-o and up) £2,794 6f......................(4:10)

221* CRECHE [89] (bl) 4-9-8 (7*,7ex) E Husband (6) *made all, quickened clr o'r 2 fs out, rdn one furlong out, hld on wl*.................... (11 to 1 op 5 to 1 tchd 12 to 1) 1
222⁷ APPEALING TIMES (USA) [70] 4-8-7 (3*) Emma O'Gorman (5) *mid-div, hdwy o'r 2 fs out, styd on fnl furlong.* ....(25 to 1 op 16 to 1 tchd 33 to 1) 2
166* ROSEATE LODGE [88] 7-10-0 G Carter (1) *chsd ldrs till outpcd hfwy, gd hdwy 2 fs out, rdn and wknd entering fnl furlong*..................(5 to 4 fav op 11 to 10) 3
212⁷ MISDEMEANOURS GIRL (Ire) [59] 5-7-9¹ (5*) B Doyle (8) *hdwy o'r 2 fs out, styd on fnl furlong.* ....(11 to 1 op 8 to 1) 4
218⁴ CHOICE LOT [53] (v) 6-7-7 S Wood (2) *chsd ldrs, rdn o'r 2 fs out, no imprsn*..................(10 to 1 op 14 to 1) 5
223³ SIR TASKER [62] 5-7-13 (3*) F Norton (4) *cl up till rdn and wknd o'r 2 fs out*.....................(5 to 1 op 3 to 1) 6
231⁹ QUATRE FEMME [57] 6-7-11 (7ex) J Quinn (3) *cl up till rdn and wknd o'r 2 fs out.* ....(9 to 2 op 5 to 1 tchd 11 to 2 and 6 to 1) 7
Dist: 1l, 3l, 1½l, 4l, 2½l, 1½l. 1m 17.90s. a 4.50s (7 Ran).
SR: 73/50/56/21/ (Brian Pollins), Mrs N Macauley

243 Milton Handicap Class C (0-90 4-y-o and up) £2,301 1½m...................(4:40)

199³ MODEST HOPE (USA) [63] 6-8-10 J McLaughlin (1) *mid-div, effrt and hdwy to chase ldr 4 fs out, led o'r 2 furlongs out, drvn clr*.............................(4 to 1 tchd 9 to 2) 1
202* TEMPERING [85] 7-10-4 (5ex) S Wood (2) *led and sn clr, rdn 3 fs out, soon hdd, wknd fnl furlong.* ....(9 to 2 op 7 to 2) 2
4714a² FIVE TO SEVEN (USA) [84] 4-9-9 (5*) O Pears (4) *chsd ldr, rdn 4 fs out, kpt on one pace.* ....(13 to 2 op 7 to 1 tchd 6 to 1) 3
148⁹ WESTFIELD MOVES (Ire) [57] 5-8-4 J Quinn (5) *mid-div, effrt and rdn 4 fs out, kpt on one pace.* ....(8 to 1 tchd 10 to 1) 4
219* HORIZON (Ire) [72] (bl) 5-9-5 (5ex) D Biggs (6) *chsd ldr, scrubbed alng and feeling pace hfwy, rdn and wknd 4 fs out*..........(5 to 4 fav op 5 to 4 on tchd 11 to 8) 5
165 KRONPRINZ (Ire) [46] (bl) 5-7-11 (7*) Darren Moffatt (3) *in tch, rdn alng hfwy, beh fnl 4 fs*.......(33 to 1 op 25 to 1) 6
Dist: 7l, 2½l, 2l, 20l, 5l. 2m 44.50s. a 10.60s (6 Ran).
SR: 38/46/37/9/-/-/ (J McManamon), R C Spicer

LINGFIELD (A.W) (std)
Saturday March 6th
Going Correction: MINUS 0.15 sec. per fur.

244 Taurus Claiming Stakes Class G (4-y-o and up) £2,656 7f..................(2:05)

KNOCK TO ENTER (USA) 5-9-3 J Williams (3) *trkd ldrs, led appr fnl furlong, easily.* ....(12 to 1 op 10 to 1 tchd 14 to 1) 1
33⁴ ABSONAL 6-7-13 A McGlone (4) *midfield till gd hdwy o'r 3 fs out, kpt on und pres fnl furlong, no ch wth wnr.* ....(5 to 2 fav op 9 to 4 tchd 2 to 1) 2
197 RESPECTABLE JONES 7-8-11 W Ryan (7) *midfield till hdwy 3 fs out, styd on fnl furlong, nvr nrr.* .... (7 to 1 op 6 to 1 tchd 15 to 2) 3
187⁶ RUSHANES 6-7-12 (5*) B Doyle (5) *wth ldr, led jst o'r 2 fs out, hdd and no extr appr fnl furlong.* ....(14 to 1 op 10 to 1 tchd 16 to 1) 4
200³ APOLLO RED 4-8-1 N Adams (1) *led till hdd jst o'r 2 fs out, sn wknd*............(12 to 1 op 10 to 1 tchd 14 to 1) 5

222⁶ MAC'S FIGHTER (bl) 8-8-7 D Biggs (9) *midfield till ran on o'r 2 fs out, one pace appr fnl furlong.* ....(4 to 1 op 7 to 2 tchd 9 to 2) 6
4799a SUNSET STREET (Ire) (e/s) 5-7-13 J Quinn (13) *midfield, no hdwy fnl 2 fs*..........................(20 to 1 op 12 to 1) 7
221⁴ HARRY'S COMING 9-7-12² (7*) S Drowne (10) *midfield, rdn alng hfwy, nvr trbld ldrs*...........(10 to 1 op 7 to 1) 8
WESSEX WARRIOR (v) 7-7-13 T Williams (2) *sn scrubbed alng, nvr able to chal.* ....(25 to 1 op 20 to 1 tchd 33 to 1) 9
131 SUMMER EXPRESS (bl) 4-8-1 Dale Gibson (11) *in tch till rdn and wknd 2 fs out.* ....(14 to 1 op 10 to 1 tchd 16 to 1) 10
197³ COURTING NEWMARKET 5-8-0 (3*) F Norton (6) *trkd ldrs till wknd o'r 2 fs out*.. (12 to 1 op 8 to 1 tchd 14 to 1) 11
217⁷ ALNEZ (Ire) 5-8-11 R Price (8) *midfield early, beh fnl 3 fs.* ....(7 to 1 op 8 to 1) 12
SUPREME OPTIMIST (bl) 9-7-13 A Mackay (12) *al outpcd.* ....(40 to 1 op 33 to 1 tchd 50 to 1) 13
43 DAL MISS 6-7-8 S Wood (14) *chsd ldrs till lost pl frm hfwy*............... (40 to 1 op 33 to 1 tchd 50 to 1) 14
Dist: 3l, 2l, hd, 6l, 1½l, sht-hd, 6l, 2l, 1l, 6l. 1m 25.01s. a 1.61s (14 Ran).
SR: 63/36/42/33/13/14/5/-/-/ (R B Payne), M Williams

245 Ascom Tele-nova Handicap Class E (0-70 3-y-o) £2,978 1¼m................ (2:35)

237² ASHOVER [60] 9-0 Alex Greaves (7) *hld up, pushed alng 5 fs out, hdwy o'r 2 furlongs out, came wide hme turn, sstnd run to ld cl home*..............(5 to 1 op 9 to 2) 1
213² ARCTIC GUEST (Ire) [52] 8-6 Dean McKeown (6) *pushed alng to track ldr, chlgd frm 2 fs out, led 50 yards out till ct cl hme*..............(7 to 2 op 11 to 4 tchd 4 to 1) 2
209³ HALHAM TARN (Ire) [54] (e/s) 8-8 J Williams (1) *slwly into strd, beh till gd hdwy o'r 3 fs out, ev ch ins last, one pace*..........................(12 to 1 op 8 to 1) 3
4676a³ WITHOUT A FLAG (USA) [57] 8-4 (7*) Michael Hunt (10) *slwly away, rcd wide, hdwy 5 fs out, sn ev ch, rallied ins last.* ....(25 to 1 op 20 to 1) 4
204* KINGSTON BROWN [67] (bl) 9-7 T Quinn (8) *led aftr 2 fs till wknd fnl furlong and hdd last 50 yards.* ....(4 to 1 op 3 to 1 tchd 9 to 2) 5
185 ROSIE'S GOLD [50] 7-13 (5*) Stephen Davies (5) *chsd ldrs, rdn alng o'r 5 fs out, sn lost pl*.....(14 to 1 op 16 to 1) 6
209* NEDAARAH [53] 8-7 W Newnes (3) *prmnt 3 fs, sn niggled alng and struggling frm hfwy, eased whn btn.* ....(9 to 4 fav op 2 to 1) 7
4778a⁷ QUATTRO [46] (bl) 8-0¹ R Price (9) *sn rdn alng to go pace, in tch till wknd o'r 4 fs out.* ....(14 to 1 op 10 to 1 tchd 16 to 1) 8
100⁴ ASCOM PAGER TOO [49] 8-3 J Quinn (2) *al beh, tld off.* ....(25 to 1 op 20 to 1) 9
167⁷ BUCKSKI ECHO [43] 7-11³ S Dawson (4) *led 2 fs, wknd 5 furlongs out, tld off*...............(33 to 1 op 25 to 1) 10
Dist: Nk, 1½l, sht-hd, 2l, 10l, 6l, hd, 12l, 5l. 2m 9.22s. a 6.02s (10 Ran).
SR: 25/16/15/17/23/-/ (Timothy Cox), T D Barron

246 Rapporteur Stakes Class C (4-y-o and up) £5,484 1¼m...................... (3:05)

169⁹ RAPPORTEUR (USA) 7-9-5 W Newnes (1) *enterprisingly rdn, led aftr 3 fs, ridden three furlongs out, clr one out, hld on gmely*......................(11 to 4 op 5 to 2) 1
169* MULCIBER 5-9-5 M Hills (5) *hld up in tch, ev ch o'r 2 fs out, hng rght over one out, ran on wl und pres ins last.* ....(3 to 1 tchd 7 to 2) 2
DOUBLE FLUTTER 4-8-9 T Quinn (2) *tucked away, hdwy, 3 fs out, sn ev ch, rdn and wknd wl o'r one out.* ....(11 to 4 op 9 to 4) 3
216² NO SUBMISSION (USA) 7-9-5 S Wood (4) *prmnt till lost pl aftr 4 fs, sn wl beh, some hdwy fnl 2 furlongs.* ....(5 to 2 fav tchd 11 to 4) 4
NOORA'S ROSE (NZ) 4-8-6 J Penza (6) *took keen hold, led 3 fs, rdn alng o'r 4 furlongs out, wknd quickly, tld off.* ....(14 to 1 op 16 to 1) 5
229 MON PETITNAMOUR (Ire) 4-8-13 Dean McKeown (3) *wl beh fnl 5 fs, tld off*......................(50 to 1 op 33 to 1) 6
Dist: ½l, 10l, 1l, 30l, dist. 2m 7.99s. a 4.79s (6 Ran).
SR: 42/41/11/19/-/-/ (Richard Berenson), C C Elsey

247 Conquest Cup Handicap Class B (0-110 4-y-o and up) £7,440 1m........... (3:40)

CHATHAM ISLAND [64] 5-7-12 (5*) B Doyle (11) *wth ldr till wnt on o'r 3 fs out, clr fnl furlong, styd on strly.* ....(12 to 1 op 8 to 1 tchd 14 to 1) 1
198⁵ AMENABLE [67] 8-8-6 J McLaughlin (8) *hld up and beh, shaken up and plenty to do entering strt, ran on strly fnl furlong, nvr nrr*.. (12 to 1 op 10 to 1 tchd 14 to 1) 2
222⁵ MERLINS WISH (USA) [80] 4-9-5 T Quinn (5) *al prmnt, rdn 3 fs out, still ev ch wl o'r one furlong out, not quicken.* ....(5 to 1 jt-fav op 4 to 1 tchd 11 to 2) 3
PAY HOMAGE [89] 5-10-0 M Hills (1) *prmnt till rdn and lost pl o'r 4 fs out, styd on ag'n fnl furlong.* ....(10 to 1 op 8 to 1 tchd 12 to 1) 4

224[4] RIPSNORTER (Ire) [59] 4-7-12 N Carlisle (3) *hld up and beh, rdn and rapid hdwy frm wl o'r one furlong out, nvr nrr*..........(14 to 1 op 8 to 1) 5
222[4] ALLINSON'S MATE (Ire) [84] 5-9-9 Alex Greaves (6) *hld up, hdwy on outsd 3 fs out, came wide hme turn, ran on fnl furlong, nvr nrr*..........(5 to 1 jt-fav tchd 6 to 1) 6
197[9] MASNUN (USA) [80] 8-9-5 D Biggs (4) *sn chsd alng in midfield, no hdwy fnl 2 fs.* ....(6 to 1 op 4 to 1 tchd 15 to 2) 7
DANCE ON SIXPENCE [58] (v) 5-7-11 J Quinn (9) *chsd ldg grp, ev ch o'r 2 fs out, wknd wl over one out.* ....(33 to 1 op 16 to 1) 8
234[7] RURAL LAD [62] 4-7-12 (3*) D Harrison (12) *al prmnt, chsd wnr into strt, sn wknd.* ....(8 to 1 tchd 10 to 1 and 7 to 1) 9
4803a[4] DASWAKI (Can) [85] 5-9-10 B Rouse (10) *prmnt 3 fs, sn lost pl and no further imprsn*..........(10 to 1 op 6 to 1) 10
232[2] EXPRESS SERVICE [61] 4-8-0[4] (3*) Emma O'Gorman (7) *dwlt, beh till gd hdwy 4 fs out, sn chasing ldrs, wknd fnl 2 furlongs*..........(9 to 1 op 5 to 1) 11
222[2] CHEVEUX MITCHELL [75] (v) 6-9-0 G Carter (2) *led till hdd o'r 3 fs out, sn btn*......(6 to 1 op 9 to 2 tchd 7 to 1) 12
Dist: 3l, hd, sht-hd, ½l, hd, 2l, 1½l, hd, 3l, 2l. 1m 38.56s. a 2.36s (12 Ran).
SR: 36/30/42/50/18/42/32/5/8/ (B H Voak), C E Brittain

248 Alpine Double Glazing Maiden Stakes Class D (3-y-o) £2,208 1m..........(4:10)

62[6] HEART OF SPAIN 9-0 W Ryan (7) *al hndy, led wl o'r one furlong out, sn quickened clr.* ....(4 to 1 op 3 to 1 tchd 9 to 2) 1
220[3] GOOD IMAGE 9-0 D Nicholls (8) *led till hdd wl o'r one furlong out, not pace of wnr.* ....(13 to 2 op 10 to 1 tchd 11 to 1) 2
220[2] SCORCHER (Ire) 8-9 (5*) B Doyle (6) *ran in snatches, chsd ldrs till lost pl and drpd last wl o'r 2 fs out, ran on ag'n ins last*..........(7 to 4 fav op 6 to 4 tchd 2 to 1) 3
183[3] CHILTERN HUNDREDS (USA) 8-7 (7*) D McCabe (1) *beh till kpt on fnl 2 fs, nvr able to chal*...... (5 to 1 op 4 to 1) 4
213[6] MEDLAND (Ire) 9-0 J Quinn (4) *beh till hdwy 4 fs out, sn chasing ldrs, rdn and wknd wl o'r 2 out.* ....(10 to 1 op 8 to 1) 5
204[6] SAXON SHORE (USA) 8-9 Dean McKeown (2) *tracking ldrs whn snatched up aftr 3 fs, sn lost pl, no further imprsn.* ....(9 to 2 op 11 to 4) 6
220[6] NO GAIN 8-2 (7*) Kim McDonnell (5) *beh till short lived effrt 4 fs out, sn wknd*..........(33 to 1 op 20 to 1) 7
209[8] VADDALLIAN 9-0 G Carter (3) *al beh, tld off.* ....(33 to 1 op 20 to 1) 8
Dist: 8l, 5l, ¾l, 1½l, 1l, ½l, 12l. 1m 40.08s. a 3.88s (8 Ran).
SR: 24/-/-/-/-/ (J S Hobhouse), P J Makin

249 Ladbroke All Weather Trophy Handicap Final Class B (3-y-o and up) £7,310 7f (4:40)

144* HENIU (USA) [70] (v) 4-9-8 T Quinn (5) *led one furlong, trkd ldr, rgned advantage wl o'r one furlong out, rdn clr.* .....(11 to 4 fav op 3 to 1 tchd 100 to 30 and 5 to 2) 1
222[3] INVOCATION [76] 6-10-0 N Adams (4) *midfield till hdwy 3 fs out, kpt on fnl furlong, no ch wth wnr.* ....(9 to 1 op 8 to 1 tchd 11 to 1) 2
131* NOBBY BARNES [63] 4-9-1 J Williams (3) *beh till gd hdwy and crrd wide 2 fs out, ran on, nvr nrr.* ....(9 to 1 op 8 to 1 tchd 10 to 1) 3
200[2] SCOTS LAW [56] (bl) 6-8-8 D Biggs (12) *led aftr one furlong till hdd wl o'r a furlong out, wknd*..........(7 to 1) 4
200[9] NORTH ESK (USA) [66] 4-9-4 M Tebbutt (1) *chsd ldrs, rdn o'r 2 fs out, one pace*..........(25 to 1 op 20 to 1) 5
157[5] SARUM [56] 7-8-8 Dale Gibson (7) *beh, rdn alng and some hdwy frm 2 fs out, one pace fnl furlong.* ....(10 to 1 op 7 to 1 tchd 11 to 1) 6
87[6] MEESON TIMES [55] 5-8-7 M Hills (6) *beh till styd on frm o'r one furlong out, nvr trbld ldrs.* ....(12 to 1 tchd 14 to 1 and 10 to 1) 7
207[3] VELOCE (Ire) [55] (v) 5-8-7 A Mackay (9) *chsd ldrs, hrd rdn wl o'r 2 fs out, sn lost pl*..........(10 to 1 op 12 to 1) 8
197[6] KISSAVOS [67] (v) 7-9-5 W Newnes (10) *chsd ldrs till rdn and lost pl o'r 3 fs out*..........(10 to 1 tchd 11 to 1) 9
200[7] WELLSY LAD (USA) [52] 6-8-4 S Wood (2) *trkd ldrs till rdn and wknd 3 fs out*..........(14 to 1 op 25 to 1) 10
144[8] BANBURY FLYER [59] 5-8-6 (5*) A Garth (8) *midfield, rdn and no hdwy whn came wide wl o'r a furlong out, sn beh*..........(16 to 1 op 14 to 1 tchd 20 to 1) 11
223[7] SALLY'S SON [62] 7-8-11 (3*) Emma O'Gorman (13) *slwly away, sn reco'red to chase ldrs till rdn and wknd 3 fs out*..........(14 to 1 op 12 to 1) 12
144[5] AIN'TLIFELIKETHAT [50] (bl) 6-8-2 G Carter (11) *missed break, hdwy to midfield aftr 3 fs, came wide hme turn, sn wknd, eased whn btn*..........(6 to 1 op 5 to 1) 13
Dist: 4l, 1½l, ¾l, sht-hd, 3l, nk, 1½l, 5l, nk, ½l. 1m 25.47s. a 2.07s (13 Ran).
SR: 61/55/37/28/37/18/16/11/8/ (Henryk de Kwiatkowski), Lord Huntingdon

SOUTHWELL (A.W) (std)
Monday March 8th
Going Correction: PLUS 0.40 sec. per fur.

250 Odds Against Maiden Stakes Class D (3-y-o) £2,070 6f..........(2:30)

156[3] BELLE SOIREE 8-6 (3*) J Weaver (6) *chsd ldrs, led appr fnl quarter-m, drvn out.* (2 to 1 jt-fav op 7 to 2 tchd 4 to 1) 1
MISS WHITTINGHAM (Ire) 8-2 (7*) P Roberts (9) *led early, styd wth ldrs, no extr fnl 100 yards.* (12 to 1 op 8 to 1) 2
DUVEEN (Ire) 8-9 (5*) M Fenton (3) *reminders early, sn wl beh, hdwy und pres 2 fs out, styd on strly towards finish*..........(7 to 2 op 5 to 1 tchd 7 to 1) 3
4791a[6] MUDGEE 8-9 Alex Greaves (2) *chsd ldrs, outpcd 2 fs out, kpt on grimly towards finish*....... (7 to 1 op 5 to 1) 4
206[2] MUSICAL PHONE (bl) 9-0 Dean McKeown (4) *sn led, hdd o'r 2 fs out, rdn and one pace fnl furlong.* (2 to 1 jt-fav op 11 to 10) 5
HAWAYMYSON (Ire) 9-0 W Newnes (5) *nvr far away, kpt on same pace und pres fnl 2 fs*....... (8 to 1 op 4 to 1) 6
WHAT BLISS 8-2 (7*) Carl Llewellyn (8) *missed break, beh, ran wide entering strt, styd on towards finish.* ....(33 to 1 op 25 to 1) 7
136[6] BIG-W 8-9 (5*) O Pears (7) *prmnt to hfwy.* ....(33 to 1 op 20 to 1) 8
NIGHTMARE LADY 8-9 J McLaughlin (1) *missed break, al rear*..........(33 to 1 op 25 to 1) 9
Dist: ¾l, 1l, 1½l, hd, 2l, 5l, 3½l, ½l. 1m 20.90s. a 7.50s (9 Ran).
(Paul Gibbons), P M McEntee

251 Banker Claiming Stakes Class G (4-y-o and up) £2,280 1m..........(3:00)

246[4] NO SUBMISSION (USA) 7-9-0 S Wood (1) *made virtually all, quickened clr o'r 2 fs out, drvn out.* ....(11 to 8 on op 7 to 4 on tchd 5 to 4 on) 1
BESCABY BOY 7-8-11 J Williams (5) *wnt clr second o'r 2 fs out, kpt on, nvr able to chal*..........(14 to 1 op 8 to 1) 2
176[5] DIGGER DOYLE 4-8-1 (3*) F Norton (3) *chsd ldrs, sn drvn alng and outpcd, kpt on fnl 2 fs.* ....(10 to 1 op 8 to 1 tchd 12 to 1) 3
188* ROUND BY THE RIVER 4-8-4 Dean McKeown (7) *chsd ldrs, rdn and outpcd 2 fs out, no dngr aftr.* ....(7 to 4 op 2 to 1 tchd 9 to 4) 4
133[2] NORTH FLYER 4-8-2 L Charnock (6) *wth wnr to 3 fs out.* ....(20 to 1 op 14 to 1 tchd 25 to 1) 5
SIE AMATO (Ire) 4-8-7 D Biggs (2) *prmnt early, drvn alng and struggling hfwy*..........(16 to 1 op 12 to 1) 6
206[7] NOT ALL BLISS 5-8-1[4] Alex Greaves (4) *sn wl last.* ....(66 to 1 op 33 to 1) 7
Dist: 2l, 6l, 2l, 10l, 7l, 15l. 1m 44.90s. a 5.90s (7 Ran).
SR: 60/51/26/20/ (T S Redman), D W Chapman

252 Smokescreen Handicap Class C (0-100 3-y-o) £4,347 7f..........(3:30)

239[2] GOLDEN KLAIR [85] 9-4 (3*) J Weaver (7) *slwly away, beh till hdwy 2 fs out, styd on to ld nr finish.* ....(11 to 2 op 5 to 1) 1
215* GREEN'S FAIR (Ire) [71] 8-7 M Hills (6) *sn led, quickened clr 2 fs out, hdd and no extr cl hme*......(4 to 1 op 3 to 1) 2
213[4] ABSOLUTELY FACT (USA) [76] 8-12 W Newnes (8) *nvr far away, kpt on same pace fnl 2 fs*.....(10 to 1 op 7 to 1) 3
228[2] JORDYWRATH [59] 7-9[2] A Mackay (10) *chsd ldrs, rdn 2 fs out, one pace*..........(2 to 1 fav op 5 to 1) 4
233* MISTER BLAKE [74] (bl) 8-7 (3*,7ex) F Norton (2) *sn beh and pushed alng, styd on appr fnl furlong.* ....(8 to 1 op 7 to 1 tchd 12 to 1) 5
228* ROSE FLYER (Ire) [65] 7-8 (7*,7ex) D McCabe (1) *missed break, sn midfield, one pace frm hfwy.* ....(9 to 1 op 8 to 1) 6
ASTRAC TRIO (USA) [70] (bl) 8-3[2] (5*) O Pears (9) *sluggish strt, beh whn ran wide entering strt, nvr on terms.* ....(20 to 1) 7
233[2] STARDUST EXPRESS [71] 8-7 Dean McKeown (4) *chsd ldrs, struggling to keep up hfwy, no ch aftr.* ....(6 to 1 op 9 to 2) 8
4691a[6] NUTTY BROWN [60] 7-10 Dale Gibson (5) *chsd ldrs, drvn alng hfwy, sn lost pl*..........(14 to 1 tchd 16 to 1) 9
BIRCHWOOD SUN [78] 9-0 W Ryan (3) *missed break, al beh*..........(25 to 1 op 20 to 1) 10
Dist: 1½l, 7l, ¾l, 2½l, 1½l, 1½l, hd, 1½l, 2l. 1m 31.80s. a 5.70s (10 Ran).
SR: 64/45/29/10/17/3/3/3/-/ (C John Hill), C J Hill

253 In The Frame Claiming Stakes Class G (4-y-o and up) £2,385 7f..........(4:00)

249 SALLY'S SON 7-7-11[2] (3*) F Norton (13) *al hndy, led appr fnl quarter-m, drvn out, styd on strly.* ....(6 to 1 op 4 to 1) 1
197[5] ON Y VA (USA) 6-8-3 D Biggs (11) *al chasing ldrs, styd on fnl 2 fs*..........(4 to 1 op 3 to 1 tchd 5 to 1) 2
227* CLAUDIA MISS 6-8-4 Dean McKeown (7) *chsd ldrs till outpcd hfwy, kpt on fnl furlong*..... (6 to 1 op 4 to 1) 3
161[3] WEE SARAH 5-8-2 Alex Greaves (6) *sn wl beh, gd hdwy appr fnl furlong, fnshd strly*...... (25 to 1 op 14 to 1) 4
215[3] NEVENTER (Fr) 4-9-0 V Smith (4) *sluggish strt, beh till kpt on fnl 2 fs*..........(33 to 1 op 20 to 1) 5

227 ROSE GEM (Ire) 4-7-13 Dale Gibson (1) *led till o'r 2 fs out, sn wknd*.......................... (20 to 1 op 14 to 1) 6
195[4] SAVAHRA SOUND 8-9-8 D Nicholls (2) *trkd ldrs, effrt 2 fs out, sn rdn and wknd*... (7 to 2 op 5 to 1 tchd 6 to 1) 7
194[6] GRUBBY 4-7-8[4] (7*) M Humphries (10) *nvr better than mid-div*........................ (33 to 1 op 20 to 1) 8
227[7] FIABA 5-7-8 J Fanning (8) *nvr trble ldrs*. .... (14 to 1 op 10 to 1) 9
218* PRIME MOVER (v) 5-8-8 L Charnock (12) *sn chasing ldrs, effrt o'r 2 fs out, soon lost pl*. ....(11 to 4 fav op 5 to 2 tchd 9 to 4) 10
227[6] CAL'S BOY (bl) 4-8-4 R Lappin (5) *chsd ldrs till fdd 3 fs out*. .... (33 to 1 op 20 to 1) 11
217[9] PRETTY CHIC 4-8-5 (5*) O Pears (9) *al beh*. .... (33 to 1 op 20 to 1) 12
217[4] PRECIOUS CAROLINE (Ire) (bl) 5-7-11 S Wood (3) *missed break, al rear*.................. (20 to 1 op 16 to 1) 13

Dist: 3l, 2½l, hd, 4l, sht-hd, 2l, sht-hd, 1½l, 2l, 2l. 1m 32.50s. a 6.40s (13 Ran).
SR: 30/26/19/16/16/-/17/-/-/ (W A O'Gorman), W A O'Gorman

254 Dead Cert Handicap Class C (0-95 4-y-o and up) £3,143 1½m................(4:30)

243[2] TEMPERING [82] 7-10-0 S Wood (1) *set str pace, sn clr, styd on und pres fnl furlong, all out*. .... (2 to 1 fav tchd 6 to 4) 1
219[4] SUGEMAR [64] 7-8-3 (7*) D McCabe (7) *effrt to chase wnr 3 fs out, sn rdn, kpt on fnl furlong*.... (5 to 1 op 6 to 1) 2
226[3] BEDOUIN PRINCE (USA) [50] 6-7-10 N Adams (4) *sn beh and drvn alng, hdwy hfwy, styd on same pace fnl 3 fs*. .... (11 to 2 op 9 to 2 tchd 6 to 1) 3
243[3] FIVE TO SEVEN (USA) [84] 4-9-8 (5*) O Pears (6) *chsd wnr, drvn alng hfwy, fdd fnl half-m*. ....(4 to 1 op 7 to 2 tchd 9 to 2) 4
200[6] LOOKINGFORARAINBOW (Ire) [72] 5-9-4 N Day (3) *wtd wth, effrt 4 fs out, sn rdn and wknd*. .... (11 to 2 op 4 to 1 tchd 6 to 1) 5
4732a[3] FALCONS DAWN [52] 6-7-12 A Mackay (2) *chsd wnr till rdn and wknd 3 fs out*..........(12 to 1 tchd 14 to 1) 6
175[9] CASTLE SECRET [69] 7-9-1 L Charnock (5) *sn struggling and drvn alng, tld off hfwy*...... (50 to 1 op 25 to 1) 7

Dist: 1l, 3l, 10l, 15l, 5l, 15l. 2m 45.10s. a 11.20s (7 Ran).
SR: 50/30/10/21/ (David W Chapman), D W Chapman

255 Hot Money Handicap Class C (0-100 3-y-o and up) £3,492 5f...................(5:00)

223[2] LOVE LEGEND [70] (bl) 8-8-9 T Quinn (7) *chsd ldrs, rdn and outpcd hfwy, kpt on to ld fnl 100 yards*. ....(5 to 2 fav op 11 to 4 tchd 3 to 1) 1
231[4] EWALD (Ire) [59] 5-7-7 (5*) B Doyle (3) *made most, hdd and no extr ins fnl furlong*............ (4 to 1 tchd 9 to 2) 2
214* HERSHEBAR [68] (bl) 3-7-7 N Adams (5) *struggled to go pace, hdwy o'r one furlong out, ran on wl towards finish*...........................(5 to 1 op 5 to 2) 3
56[6] MAID WELCOME [64] (bl) 6-7-11[1] (7*) Madeleine Smith (6) *trkd ldrs, prog to dispute ld o'r one furlong out, kpt on same pace*.......................(16 to 1 op 12 to 1) 4
242* CRECHE [96] (bl) 4-10-0 (7*,7ex) E Husband (2) *pushed alng to keep up, styd on one pace fnl 2 fs*. ....(100 to 30 op 4 to 1 tchd 3 to 1) 5
231[8] SLADES HILL [62] 6-8-1 Alex Greaves (4) *trkd ldrs till grad wknd fnl 2 fs, better for race*. .... (14 to 1 op 8 to 1 tchd 16 to 1) 6
212[4] LE CHIC [55] 7-7-8 S Wood (1) *rcd upsides to hfwy, sn lost pl*............................(6 to 1 op 7 to 1) 7

Dist: 1½l, 1½l, 2l, ½l, 6l, 1½l. 1m 1.90s. a 4.00s (7 Ran).
SR: 55/38/27/29/59/1/-/ (George S Thompson), D W P Arbuthnot

NAAS (IRE) (good to yielding)
Saturday March 13th
Going Correction: PLUS 0.25 sec. per fur.

256 Fishery EBF (C & G) Maiden (3-y-o) £3,450 6f...............................(2:00)

READY (Ire) 9-0 W J Supple (13)..................(4 to 1) 1
TEAZEL BOY 9-0 P V Gilson (12)............. (7 to 4 fav) 2
KERB CRAWLER 9-0 S Craine (3)..................(10 to 1) 3
KHARASAR (Ire) 9-0 R Hughes (4)..................(9 to 2) 4
BRIGHT STORM (Ire) 9-0 C Roche (9)..................(5 to 1) 5
SOMERTON BOY (Ire) 8-10 (4*) W J Smith (8).....(33 to 1) 6
FRIAR STREET (Ire) 8-8 (6*) P Carberry (7).........(12 to 1) 7
LUCKY PRINCE (Ire) 9-0 P Shanahan (5)............(7 to 1) 8
BENE MERENTI (Ire) 9-0 N G McCullagh (1)....... (8 to 1) 9
CLANFLUTHER (Ire) 9-0 D V Smith (10)............ (33 to 1) 10
TEXAS FRIDAY (Ire) 8-12 (2*) R M Burke (11)......(20 to 1) 11
PHASE IN 9-0 D Manning (6)......................(33 to 1) 12
CHAMPAGNE NIGHT (Fr) 8-6 (8*) R V Skelly (2)... (20 to 1) 13

Dist: ¾l, 1l, nk, 3½l. 1m 16.80s. a 7.30s (13 Ran).
(Mrs Anne Coughlan), Kevin Prendergast

257 Tenderleen Horsefeed EBF Maiden (3-y-o) £4,140 1m.......................... (3:30)

FARMAAN (Ire) 9-0 J P Murtagh (15).......... (5 to 4 fav) 1
CARRICK PIKE (USA) 9-0 C Roche (22)........... (5 to 2) 2
SCHMEICHEL (Ire) 9-0 N Byrne (18)............. (16 to 1) 3
DIFFERENT TIMES (Ire) 9-0 S Craine (4)...........(7 to 1) 4
DAHLIA'S BEST (USA) 9-0 W J Supple (20)........(7 to 1) 5
MY TRELAWNY (Ire) 8-9 (2*) R M Burke (10).......(14 to 1) 6
ABSOLUTE JAMBOREE 8-6 (8*) J J Stack (1).....(25 to 1) 7
TOUCHING MOMENT (Ire) 9-0 P V Gilson (3).....(10 to 1) 8
NORDIC HALO (Ire) 8-3 (8*) T E Durcan (14).......(20 to 1) 9
WHITECRAITS (Ire) 8-11 R Hughes (12)..........(16 to 1) 10
QUIETEST (Ire) (bl) 8-11 Joanna Morgan (16)......(33 to 1) 11
ISLAND VISION (Ire) 8-8 (6*) B J Walsh,...........(33 to 1) 12
TANGO IN PARIS (Arg) 8-8 (6*) P Carberry (5).....(20 to 1) 13
POLITICAL DOMAIN (Ire) 9-0 P Shanahan (8).......(10 to 1) 14
THE SALTY FROG (Ire) 9-0 W J O'Connor (13).....(25 to 1) 15
MANGANS HILL (Ire) 8-11 N G McCullagh (6).....(40 to 1) 16
TREBLE BOB (Ire) 9-0 D V Smith (19)............(33 to 1) 17
ONODI (Ire) 8-3 (8*) M W Martin (11)..............(33 to 1) 18
DENZILLE LANE (Ire) 9-0 A J Nolan (2)............(25 to 1) 19
SALZAAD (Ire) 8-9 (2*) D G O'Shea (17)..........(16 to 1) 20
GIRARDELLI (Ire) 8-4 (10*) J Smullen (21).........(25 to 1) 21
SPORTSTYLE (Ire) 9-0 K J Manning (7)............(20 to 1) 22

Dist: 1l, nk, 4½l, ½l. 1m 44.90s. a 9.10s (22 Ran).
(H H Aga Khan), John M Oxx

258 Johnstown Fillies EBF Race (3-y-o) £3,450 7f...................................(4:30)

WEEKEND MADNESS (Ire) 8-7 W J O'Connor (15) (20 to 1) 1
ELEGANT BLOOM (Ire) 9-0 P Shanahan (4).... (5 to 4 fav) 2
TARTAN LADY (Ire) 9-0 S Craine (13).............(12 to 1) 3
SHAIKALA (Ire) 9-0 D Hogan (12)..................(5 to 1) 4
SLEET (Ire) 8-7 P V Gilson,........................(12 to 1) 5
PERNILLA (Ire) 9-0 C Roche (6)....................(9 to 4) 6
SOUNDPROOF (Ire) 9-0 K J Manning (16).........(12 to 1) 7
RETICENT BRIDE (Ire) 8-7 P Lowry (17)...........(25 to 1) 8
KENTUCKY BABY (Ire) 9-0 N Byrne (8).............(20 to 1) 9
TEGEMEZA (Ire) 8-5 (2*) R M Burke (1)...........(20 to 1) 10
COPSEWOOD (Ire) 7-13 (8*) J M Buckley (3).......(33 to 1) 11
TEBRE (USA) 8-7 W J Supple (5).................(10 to 1) 12
BOBADIL (Ire) 7-11 (10*) P J Smullen (11).........(33 to 1) 13
TRES JOUR (Ire) 8-7 D Manning (9)...............(20 to 1) 14
CORAL SOUND (Ire) 8-7 R Hughes (10)............(14 to 1) 15
BRASS BUTTON (Ire) 8-7 N G McCullagh (2)......(20 to 1) 16
NORDIC SUCCESS (Ire) 8-1 (6*) J A Heffernan (14) (16 to 1) 17

Dist: 1l, 1l, ¾l, 2½l. 1m 27.50s. a 4.90s (17 Ran).
SR: 46/50/47/45/30/-/ (Yoshiki Akazawa), P Aspell

LINGFIELD (A.W) (std)
Tuesday March 16th
Going Correction: MINUS 0.05 sec. per fur.

259 Tonbridge Claiming Stakes Class F (Div I) (3-y-o and up) £2,511 1m........... (1:25)

232[3] SAAHI (USA) 4-9-7 (5*) K Rutter (6) *sn pushed alng in rear, rapid hdwy o'r one furlong out, sstnd run to ld nr finish*...... (6 to 1 op 11 to 2 tchd 6 to 1 and 7 to 1) 1
237* DARING PAST 3-8-4 W Ryan (7) *cl up, led 4 fs out, battled on gmely whn chlgd fnl 2 furlongs, hdd close hme*. .... (13 to 2 op 5 to 1 tchd 7 to 1) 2
186[3] ERLKING (Ire) 3-8-4 A Munro (9) *trkd ldrs, rdn and ev ch ins fnl furlong, not quicken*. .... (3 to 1 op 11 to 4 tchd 7 to 2) 3
251* NO SUBMISSION (USA) 7-9-12 S Wood (5) *led till hdd 4 fs out, cl up, kpt on one pace frm o'r one out*. .... (11 to 10 fav op Evens tchd 6 to 5) 4
WILD AND LOOSE 5-9-7 T Quinn (8) *in tch, effrt o'r 3 fs out, sn one pace*. ....(15 to 2 op 7 to 1 tchd 8 to 1 and 10 to 1) 5
4802a UP THE PUNJAB 4-8-10 Candy Morris (4) *trkd ldrs till wknd 3 fs out*.......................... (33 to 1 op 20 to 1) 6
4677a[6] JULIASDARKINVADER 3-8-0 N Adams (1) *chsd ldrs, reminders appr hfwy, sn wknd*.... (33 to 1 op 25 to 1) 7
167[5] LITTLE KARLIE (Den) 3-7-4 (7*) D Wright (3) *chsd ldrs to hfwy*.............................. (33 to 1 op 20 to 1) 8
SYMMETRICAL 4-9-1 W Newnes (2) *cl up for o'r 3 fs, sn pushed alng and drpd out quickly, tld off*.....(33 to 1) 9

Dist: 1½l, sht-hd, 1½l, 4l, 15l, 3l, 1½l, 20l. 1m 39.98s. a 3.78s (9 Ran).
SR: 49/22/21/38/21/-/ (Martin N Peters), C Weedon

260 Tonbridge Claiming Stakes Class F (Div II) (3-y-o and up) £2,489 1m........... (1:55)

244[6] MAC'S FIGHTER (bl) 8-9-2 (3*) J Weaver (6) *presssed ldr, led 5 fs out, hdd o'r one out, rallied to ld ag'n ins last, ran-on*...................................... (5 to 2 op 2 to 1) 1
4799a[6] PRECIOUS AIR (Ire) 5-9-0 B Rouse (9) *ldg grp, rdn to gain slight advantage o'r one furlong out, hdd and one pace last 100 yards*........................ (12 to 1 op 10 to 1) 2
244[3] RESPECTABLE JONES 7-9-7 W Ryan (4) *hdwy 4 fs out, promissing run frm 2 out, no extr last 50 yards*. ....(6 to 5 fav op 5 to 4 on tchd 5 to 4) 3
TROPICAL JUNGLE (USA) 3-8-4 D Biggs (7) *slwly into strd, styd on frm rear appr last 2 fs, not trble ldrs*. .... (25 to 1 op 14 to 1) 4

244[7] SUNSET STREET (Ire) (e/s) 5-9-1 T Quinn (5) *ldg grp till rdn and wknd appr fnl furlong.* ....(6 to 1 op 5 to 1 tchd 7 to 1) 5
SOOTY TERN 6-9-5 N Adams (8) *led for 3 fs, wknd o'r 2 out*....(12 to 1 op 10 to 1 tchd 14 to 1) 6
SUNBEAM CHARLIE 3-8-0 Candy Morris (1) *settled in mid-div, rdn and outpcd frm hfwy*....(33 to 1) 7
LUCY BELLE (Ire) 4-8-7 (3*) D Harrison (2) *strted slwly, al outpcd*....(33 to 1 op 25 to 1) 8
214 OVER THE CLIFFS (Ire) 3-7-7 G Bardwell (3) *sn pushed alng towards rear, nvr on terms*....(50 to 1) 9
Dist: Nk, nk, 5l, 2½l, 8l, 3½l, 8l, 12l. 1m 40.78s. a 4.58s (9 Ran).
SR: 30/24/30/-/1/-/ (Christopher Lane), R J O'Sullivan

261 Alpine Double Glazing Apprentice Maiden Stakes Class D (4-y-o and up) £2,208 1¼m ....(2:25)

211[5] STORM FREE (USA) 7-9-1 J Weaver (1) *hld up beh, steady hdwy o'r 3 fs out, styd on to ld cl hme.* ....(6 to 1 op 5 to 1) 1
139[2] SET THE FASHION (v) 4-9-0 D Harrison (3) *led for 2 fs, led ag'n 5 out, clr o'r two out, ct cl hme.* ....(5 to 4 on op 6 to 4 on) 2
8[4] SIMON ELLIS (Ire) 4-9-0 A Tucker (8) *led aftr 2 fs till 5 out, hrd rdn 3 out, one pace*....(10 to 1 op 6 to 1) 3
82[2] DOC'S COAT 8-9-1 F Norton (4) *sn pushed alng to chase ldrs, outpcd frm o'r 4 fs out.* ....(9 to 4 op 5 to 2 tchd 11 to 4) 4
ROGERSON 5-9-1 B Russell (6) *strted slwly, nvr on terms.* ....(20 to 1) 5
171[6] PEACH BRANDY 4-8-9 S Drowne (2) *al beh.* ....(50 to 1 op 25 to 1) 6
210 PARISIAN 8-9-1 Claire Balding (5) *trkd ldrs to hfwy, tld off*....(50 to 1 op 25 to 1) 7
DIVINE GLORY 4-8-9 B Doyle (7) *trkd ldrs, rdn 5 fs out, wknd, tld off*....(50 to 1 op 25 to 1) 8
Dist: Hd, 12l, 4l, 5l, 7l, 20l, nk. 2m 10.23s. a 7.03s (8 Ran).
SR: 26/24/-/-/-/ (E J S Gadsden), L G Cottrell

262 Goodwins Handicap Class D (0-80 3-y-o) £3,143 7f....(2:55)

208[2] PERSIAN GUSHER (Ire) [66] (e/s) 9-0 T Quinn (4) *pressed ldrs, led wl o'r 2 fs out, pushed clr over one out, not extended*....(3 to 1 tchd 7 to 2) 1
183* MARK'S CLUB (Ire) [63] (bl) 8-11 D Biggs (2) *slwly into strd, pushed alng hfwy, ran on frm rear appr fnl furlong, took second pl nr finish*....(6 to 1 op 4 to 1) 2
252[2] GREEN'S FAIR (Ire) [71] 9-5 M Hills (1) *in tch, pushed alng frm hfwy, chsd wnr o'r one furlong out, no imprsn ins last*....(11 to 8 fav op 5 to 4 tchd 13 to 8) 3
191[2] PINE RIDGE LAD (Ire) [73] (bl) 9-7 Dean McKeown (5) *led till o'r 2 fs out, rdn and one pace appr last.* ....(5 to 1 op 9 to 2 tchd 6 to 1) 4
168* SQUIRE YORK [64] 8-12 W Newnes (3) *dwlt, sn cl up, pushed alng 3 fs out, wknd o'r one out.* ....(6 to 1 op 9 to 2) 5
Dist: 1l, 1½l, 2½l, 3l. 1m 27.72s. a 4.32s (5 Ran).
SR: 30/24/27/21/3/ (Gravy Boys Racing), S Dow

263 Spring Handicap Class E (0-70 3-y-o and up) £2,847 6f....(3:25)

223* SPENDER [43] 4-8-8 N Adams (1) *made all, rdn clr appr fnl furlong, drvn out*....(5 to 2 fav op 2 to 1) 1
236[8] HINARI VIDEO [50] 8-9-1 Dean McKeown (2) *trkd ldrs, hrd rdn o'r one furlong out, kpt on cl hme.* ....(7 to 1 op 6 to 1) 2
ZINBAQ [39] 7-8-4 T Williams (3) *pushed alng to chase ldrs, hrd rdn o'r one furlong out, ran on cl hme.* ....(16 to 1 op 14 to 1) 3
242[6] SIR TASKER [63] 5-9-9 (5*) B Doyle (5) *trkd wnr, rdn o'r one furlong out, one pace ins last*....(6 to 1 op 5 to 1) 4
156[4] THE INSTITUTE BOY [69] (bl) 3-9-6 S Webster (4) *took keen hold, trkd ldrs, rdn and one pace appr fnl furlong.* ....(7 to 1 op 6 to 1) 5
4789a[3] LITMORE DANCER [39] 5-7-11 (7*) Michael Bradley (9) *strted slwly, nvr on terms*....(20 to 1 op 14 to 1) 6
244[4] RUSHANES [60] 6-9-4 (7*) B Russell (8) *outpcd.* ....(8 to 1 tchd 9 to 1 and 10 to 1) 7
236[4] PALACEGATE GOLD (Ire) [43] (bl) 4-8-8 W Ryan (6) *chsd ldrs to hfwy*....(5 to 1 tchd 11 to 2) 8
CHESHIRE ANNIE (Ire) [55] 4-9-3 (3*) A Tucker (7) *sn pushed alng, beh frm hfwy*....(6 to 1 op 14 to 1 tchd 16 to 1) 9
Dist: 1½l, 1½l, nk, 1½l, ½l, 4l, 2½l, 1l. 1m 13.72s. a 2.92s (9 Ran).
SR: 30/31/14/37/23/5/10/-/-/ (The Entrepreneurs), P W Harris

264 Tunbridge Wells Handicap Class E (0-70 4-y-o and up) £2,856 1¼m....(3:55)

211[3] CAMDEN'S RANSOM (USA) [70] 6-9-9 (5*) B Doyle (10) *handily plcd aftr 4 fs, led wl o'r one out, shaken up to go clr clsg stages*....(7 to 2 op 5 to 1) 1
198[2] BALLYRANTER [52] 4-8-9 J Quinn (3) *ldg grp, led o'r 3 fs out, hdd wl over one out, ran same pace.* ....(3 to 1 fav op 5 to 2 tchd 7 to 2) 2
198[8] PREMIER DANCE [36] 6-7-8 G Bardwell (2) *beh till rdn and hdwy 2 fs out, styd on one pace appr last.* ....(14 to 1 op 8 to 1) 3
SALBYNG [60] 5-9-4 M Hills (7) *mid-div, hrd rdn and one pace ins last 2 fs*....(8 to 1 op 7 to 1) 4
8[9] ROCKY BAY [36] 4-7-0 (7*) D Wright (9) *improved frm rear 4 out, hrd rdn and no imprsn on ldrs from 2 fs out.* ....(33 to 1 op 25 to 1) 5
234[4] APPLIANCEOFSCIENCE [45] 6-7-10 (7*) P McCabe (8) *mid-div, rdn 4 fs out, no extr last 2 furlongs*....(14 to 1) 6
234* PIGALLE WONDER [60] (bl) 5-9-4 D Biggs (4) *ldg grp, led o'r 5 fs out till over 3 out, wknd over one out.* ....(5 to 1 op 9 to 2 tchd 11 to 2) 7
113[3] DANCING BOAT [36] 4-7-7 S Wood (12) *jnd ldrs aftr 4 fs, rdn and wknd o'r 3 out*....(14 to 1 op 10 to 1) 8
225[4] SUPER LUNAR [57] 9-9-1 G Carter (6) *al racing towards rear*....(10 to 1 op 8 to 1) 9
WINGED WHISPER (USA) [50] 4-8-4 (3*) D Harrison (5) *pld hrd early, nvr nr to chal*....(20 to 1) 10
SAYSANA [37] 6-7-9[9] (7*) B Russell (1) *chsd frnt rnk for 6 fs, sn wknd*....(50 to 1) 11
152[4] ROYAL ACCLAIM [37] (v) 8-7-9[2] N Adams (11) *effrt frm rear o'r 6 fs out, rdn and wknd 4 out*....(25 to 1 op 20 to 1) 12
211[2] TADORA (Ire) [54] 4-8-11 T Quinn (14) *led till hdd o'r 5 fs out, wknd appr last 2 furlongs, tld off.* ....(8 to 1 op 6 to 1 tchd 10 to 1) 13
241 KACHINA MAID [40] 8-7-12[8] (3*) F Norton (13) *ldg grp to hfwy, drpd rear fnl 4 fs, tld off*....(33 to 1) 14
Dist: 5l, nk, 4l, ¾l, 4l, 3l, ½l, 1l, 1½l, 4l, ¾l. 2m 7.81s. a 4.61s (14 Ran).
SR: 63/34/18/34/7/9/18/-/11/ (Bob Cullen), D R C Elsworth

265 Pantiles Handicap Class E (0-70 4-y-o and up) £2,611 1½m....(4:25)

235[4] LA REINE ROUGE (Ire) [34] 5-7-12[2] (3*) F Norton (8) *trkd ldrs, led o'r 4 fs out, clr 2 out, easily.* ....(12 to 1 tchd 14 to 1) 1
235* STRAT'S LEGACY [63] 6-10-0 T Quinn (2) *trkd ldrs, chsd wnr frm o'r 3 fs out, hrd rdn 2 out, eased whn no imprsn ins last*....(5 to 4 fav op Evens tchd 11 to 8) 2
235[2] SINCLAIR LAD (Ire) [57] 5-9-8 W Ryan (1) *wtd wth, pushed alng and effrt o'r 4 fs out, styd on.* ....(7 to 2 op 4 to 1 tchd 9 to 2) 3
200 OUR EDDIE [55] (v) 4-9-4 W Newnes (7) *cl up, led briefly o'r 4 fs out, one pace frm nxt*....(25 to 1 op 20 to 1) 4
182[4] DR ZEVA [38] 7-7-10 (7*) D Wright (3) *nvr nr to chal.* ....(13 to 2 op 6 to 1 tchd 7 to 1) 5
235[3] FLASH OF STRAW (Ire) [33] (bl) 4-7-10 T Williams (4) *mid-div, pushed alng hfwy, wknd*....(11 to 2 op 4 to 1) 6
210 PHIL-BLAKE [30] 6-7-9 N Adams (6) *led, took gd hold, hdd o'r 4 fs out, wknd*....(20 to 1 op 16 to 1 tchd 25 to 1) 7
171[4] IRON BARON (Ire) [48] 4-8-6 (5*) A Garth (5) *strted slwly, al beh*....(12 to 1 tchd 14 to 1) 8
Dist: 7l, 2l, 2½l, nk, 5l, 15l, ¾l. 2m 36.79s. a 7.49s (8 Ran).
SR: 4/19/9/-/-/ (L J Hawkings), Mrs A Knight

ST-CLOUD (FR) (good)
Tuesday March 16th
Going Correction: PLUS 0.35 sec. per fur.

266 Prix Maurice Caillault (Listed) (3-y-o) £14,337 1¼m 110yds....(3:20)

FANTASTIC DREAM (Ire) 8-11 D Boeuf, ... 1
4753a* SAWASDEE (Fr) 9-1 J Boisnard, ... 2
BRAZANY (USA) 8-11 C Asmussen, ... 3
TASHTIYANA (Ire) 8-8 W Mongil, ... 4
Dist: ½l, 1½l, 1½l, 3l. 2m 2.00s. a 9.50s (5 Ran).
SR: 39/42/35/29/ (Yazid Saud), E Lellouche

DOWN ROYAL (IRE) (good)
Wednesday March 17th

267 Calor Gas Maiden (3-y-o) £1,380 7f..(3:50)

MISS TWIN PEAKS (Ire) 8-11 W J O'Connor (3)....(3 to 1) 1
PENNINE MIST (Ire) 8-7 (4*) W J Smith (6)....(9 to 4 fav) 2
RUNNING GUEST (Ire) 8-11 N G McCullagh (2)....(8 to 1) 3
MARY'S CASE (Ire) 9-0 E A Leonard (8)....(7 to 1) 4+
WILDE (Ire) 9-0 G Curran (1)....(8 to 1) 4+
257 SPORTSTYLE (Ire) 9-0 N Byrne (9)....(14 to 1) 6
257 DENZILLE LANE (Ire) 9-0 A J Nolan (10)....(14 to 1) 7
WARREN STREET (Ire) 9-0 A Munro (5)....(3 to 1) 8
257 MANGANS HILL (Ire) 8-9 (2*) R M Burke (4)....(14 to 1) 9
TANDRAGEE STARLET (Ire) 8-11 Joanna Morgan (7) ....(20 to 1) 10
Dist: 2l, sht-hd, nk, dd-ht. (Time not taken) (10 Ran).
(Mrs H H Morriss), Michael Kauntze

268 Moira Handicap (0-75 3-y-o) £1,208 7f ....(4:20)

BOBROSS (Ire) [-] 8-5 (6*) J A Heffernan (6)....(14 to 1) 1
SLIGHTLY SCRUFFY (Ire) [-] 8-10 P Lowry (9)....(10 to 1) 2

ROOTSMAN (Ire) [-] 8-12 (8*) T J Daly (7) .... (8 to 1) 3
FASTAFLOW (Ire) [-] 8-8 (6*) B J Walsh (8) ...... (7 to 4 fav) 4
LOWLACK [-] 8-7 (4*) W J Smith (3) .... (7 to 1) 5
RATES RELIEF (Ire) [-] 9-3 W J O'Connor (4) .... (4 to 1) 6
KELLSBORO LASS (Ire) [-] 9-7 N G McCullagh (5) .. (7 to 2) 7
PHILIP PATRICK (Ire) [-] 8-13 A Munro (1) .... (7 to 1) 8
COMMANDER JOHN (Ire) [-] 8-6 (2*) R M Burke (2) (14 to 1) 9
BRIGENSER (Ire) [-] 8-8 (8*) R V Skelly (10) .... (4 to 1) 10

Dist: 3l, 2l, ¾l, 1l. (Time not taken) (10 Ran).
(Mrs P D McCreery), Peter McCreery

LEOPARDSTOWN (IRE) (yielding)
Wednesday March 17th

Going Correction: PLUS 0.25 sec. per fur. (races 1,2), PLUS 0.70 (3,4)

269 Castrol Formula RS EBF Maiden (2-y-o) £4,830 5f. .... (2:10)

CITY NIGHTS (Ire) 9-0 P Shanahan (4) .... (7 to 2) 1
CORINADO (Ire) 9-0 C Roche (3) .... (11 to 10 fav) 2
OLIVER MESSEL (Ire) 9-0 W J Supple (1) .... (5 to 1) 3
AVONDALE FOREST (Ire) 8-11 K J Manning (8) .... (6 to 1) 4
OVERALL MAJORITY (Ire) 8-9 (2*) D G O'Shea (9) .. (8 to 1) 5
BONNIE CRATHIE (Ire) 8-11 P V Gilson (6) .... (7 to 1) 6
TREJOLY PIGEONS (Ire) 9-0 J P Murtagh (5) .... (8 to 1) 7
MUSICAL BANKER 9-0 S Craine (2) .... (10 to 1) 8
TRIMBLEMILL (Ire) 9-0 B Coogan (7) .... (5 to 1) 9

Dist: Sht-hd, 1l, 3l, ¾l. 1m 3.30s. a 4.60s (9 Ran).
SR: 33/32/28/13/10/-/ (R E Sangster), D K Weld

270 Burmah Castrol EBF Delmaine Race (3-y-o and up) £5,520 5f. .... (2:40)

SUMY 3-9-1 J P Murtagh (1) .... (7 to 2) 1
DIAMONDS GALORE (Can) 8-10-7 P Shanahan (6) .... (7 to 4 fav) 2
LAVINIA FONTANA (Ire) 4-10-4 P V Gilson (3) ...... (7 to 2) 3
PERSIAN CREEK (Ire) 4-10-2 C Roche (7) .... (6 to 1) 4
4684a[6] CHEVIOT AMBLE (Ire) 5-10-1 J F Egan (4) .... (6 to 1) 5
CAURSELLE (Ire) 4-9-11 K J Manning (5) .... (7 to 1) 6
SOME FUN 6-9-8 S Craine (2) .... (20 to 1) 7

Dist: 1l, nk, 4l, 2½l. 1m 2.40s. a 3.70s (7 Ran).
SR: 52/68/64/46/35/-/-/ (Sheikh Mohammed), John M Oxx

271 Burmah Castrol 21st Anniversary Trophy Race (3-y-o) £4,830 7f. .... (3:20)

NORDIC FOX (Ire) 9-5 C Roche (4) .... (11 to 10 fav) 1
ARABIC TREASURE (USA) 9-0 P Shanahan (1) ...... (2 to 1) 2
TIRIZI (Ire) 9-0 R Hughes (3) .... (11 to 4) 3
SKIPO (USA) 8-9 D V Smith (5) .... (25 to 1) 4
RONDELLI (Ire) 9-0 K J Manning (2) .... (14 to 1) 5

Dist: 1l, 4l, 3½l, 7l. 1m 33.60s. a 8.20s (5 Ran).
SR: 56/48/36/20/4/ (Mrs Catherine Shubotham), J S Bolger

272 Burmah Castrol Lincolnshire Trial Handicap (0-105 4-y-o and up) £6,900 1m. (4:50)

4685a[2] TONY'S FEN [-] 4-8-5 W J Supple (7) .... (5 to 1) 1
4684a[8] NORDIC PAGEANT (Ire) [-] 4-9-11 C Roche (12) (7 to 4 fav) 2
4683a[2] NINJA DANCER (USA) [-] 4-9-10 P Shanahan (9) ... (7 to 1) 3
NORDIC DISPLAY (Ire) [-] 5-7-2 (8*) R T Fitzpatrick (11) .... (12 to 1) 4
WINNING HEART [-] (bl) 6-9-10 J P Murtagh (4) .... (7 to 1) 5
BARNAGEERA BOY (Ire) [-] 4-6-13 (8*) P P Murphy (2) .... (25 to 1) 6
SHIRWAN (Ire) [-] 4-8-2 (2*) D G O'Shea (6) .... (10 to 1) 7
LIFEWATCH VISION [-] 6-10-0 R Dolan (1) .... (10 to 1) 8
PURPLE EMPEROR (Fr) [-] 4-7-7[1] (10*) D W O'Sullivan (5) .... (7 to 1) 9
4686a OLD TALKA RIVER [-] 6-7-7[3] (8*) D J O'Donohoe (13) (6 to 1) 10
MONTEFIORE [-] 8-8-12 J F Egan (3) .... (10 to 1) 11
KAZKAR (Ire) [-] (bl) 5-8-13 P V Gilson (8) .... (12 to 1) 12
DRUMAALER [-] 5-6-13 (8*) L O'Shea (10) .... (12 to 1) 13

Dist: 1l, sht-hd, ¾l, 2l. 1m 46.20s. a 8.20s (13 Ran).
SR: 52/69/67/37/59/-/ (Mrs C Harrington), Kevin Prendergast

MAISONS-LAFFITTE (FR) (soft)
Thursday March 18th

Going Correction: PLUS 0.40 sec. per fur.

273 Prix Altipan (Listed) (4-y-o and up) £14,337 1m. .... (2:50)

BURDUR 5-8-11 C Le Scrill, ... 1
4726a[6] ARCHANGE (USA) 4-8-11 F Head, ... 2
KENBU (Fr) 4-8-12 C Asmussen, ... 3
COMPOTA (Fr) 4-8-8 D Boeuf, ... 4

Dist: ½l, hd, 1l, sht-hd, 1½l, 1l, ¾l. 1m 42.30s. a 6.80s (8 Ran).
SR: 43/41/41/34/ (M Kura), Y Porzier

SOUTHWELL (A.W) (std)
Thursday March 18th

Going Correction: PLUS 0.15 sec. per fur.

274 Badminton Handicap Class C (0-90 4-y-o and up) £3,289 1m. .... (2:10)

239[3] MENTALASANYTHIN [64] 4-8-9 A Mackay (9) *ldg grp, led o'r 2 out, rdn out.* .... (4 to 1 fav op 3 to 1) 1
247[5] RIPSNORTER (Ire) [59] 4-8-4 N Carlisle (1) *hld up beh, ran on frm 2 out, kpt on wl und pres nr finish.* .... (11 to 2 op 5 to 1 tchd 6 to 1) 2
177* QUINZII MARTIN [64] (v) 5-8-9 J Williams (2) *wl in tch, rdn and not quicken appr fnl furlong.* ... (6 to 1 op 9 to 2) 3
241[4] SHUJAN (USA) [71] 4-9-2 R Price (3) *chsd ldrs til lost pl 3 out, ran on ag'n ins fnl furlong.* ... (5 to 1 tchd 6 to 1) 4
189[4] KATY'S LAD [60] 6-7-12 (7*) J Bramhill (6) *pressed ldrs, rdn and not quicken o'r one out.* .... (16 to 1 op 8 to 1) 5
BATTLE COLOURS (Ire) [79] 4-9-10 G Duffield (4) *led til hdd o'r 2 out, no extr.* .... (8 to 1 op 7 to 1) 6
247 EXPRESS SERVICE [60] 4-8-3[1] (3*) Emma O'Gorman (7) *slwly into strd, hdwy hfwy, pushed alng and one pace appr fnl furlong.* .... (12 to 1 op 8 to 1) 7
205[4] THEMAAM [65] 4-8-10 Dean McKeown (11) *cl up til rdn and wknd o'r one out.* .... (11 to 2 op 9 to 2) 8
4663a[7] CEE-JAY-AY [60] 6-8-5 J Carroll (5) *slwly into strd, prog on ins o'r 2 out, one pace appr fnl furlong.* .... (14 to 1 op 12 to 1 tchd 16 to 1) 9
RED KITE [62] 4-8-2 (5*) M Fenton (8) *chsd ldrs to hfwy, sn rdn alng and lost pl.* .... (8 to 1 op 10 to 1) 10
234[8] JUVENARA [49] 7-7-8 G Bardwell (10) *drpd rear aftr 3 fs, tld off.* .... (20 to 1 op 16 to 1) 11

Dist: 1l, 2½l, 1l, nk, 1½l, ½l, ¾l, ½l, 8l, 30l. 1m 45.60s. a 6.60s (11 Ran).
SR: 14/6/3/7/-/9/ (Mrs M O'Donnell), A Bailey

275 Windsor Claiming Stakes Class G (3-y-o) £2,385 6f. .... (2:40)

106[4] LARN FORT 8-4 J Fanning (1) *made all, rdn out ins fnl furlong, kpt on wl.* .... (10 to 1 op 7 to 1) 1
239[5] TANAGOME (USA) (v) 8-13 (5*) O Pears (3) *dwlt, prog frm rear o'r 2 out, jnd ldrs and hng lft und pres ins fnl furlong, no extr on line.* (3 to 1 op 7 to 1 tchd 8 to 1) 2
252[8] STARDUST EXPRESS 8-12 Dean McKeown (8) *cl up, rdn alng and not quicken o'r one out, rallied last 100 yards.* .... (2 to 1 fav op 6 to 4 tchd 9 to 4) 3
240[2] DON'T BE SAKI (Ire) 7-13 J Quinn (2) *pressed ldrs, rdn and one pace frm 2 out.* .... (4 to 1 op 11 to 4) 4
4772a[6] IRISH ROOTS (Ire) (v) 7-13 (3*) F Norton (9) *ldg grp, rdn and btn appr fnl furlong.* .... (9 to 1 op 6 to 1) 5
250[2] MISS WHITTINGHAM (Ire) 8-5 J Carroll (6) *mid-div, pushed alng and no prog frm o'r 2 out.* ..... (6 to 1 op 7 to 2) 6
KENTUCKY DREAMS 8-10 A Mackay (4) *nvr on terms.* .... (12 to 1 op 10 to 1 tchd 14 to 1) 7
RUM TEMPEST 8-6 L Charnock (7) *outpcd, eased whn btn last 2 fs.* .... (16 to 1) 8
233[5] GATE OF HEAVEN 7-10 (5*) A Garth (5) *chsd ldrs for o'r 3 fs, sn wknd and eased..* (16 to 1 op 20 to 1 tchd 25 to 1) 9

Dist: Hd, 1l, 4l, sht-hd, 12l, ¾l, 3½l, 6l. 1m 18.20s. a 4.80s (9 Ran).
SR: 12/25/15/-/-/-/ (R T Cartwright), T Fairhurst

276 Chatsworth Handicap Class C (0-100 4-y-o and up) £4,347 7f. .... (3:10)

218[5] APPLEDORN [77] 6-9-10 T Quinn (7) *hdwy frm rear hfwy, str brst to ld entering fnl furlong, ran on.* .... (9 to 1 op 7 to 1) 1
247[9] RURAL LAD [61] 4-8-8 J McLaughlin (2) *led til hdd entering fnl furlong, kpt on und pres.* .... (7 to 1 op 6 to 1) 2
205* DREAM CARRIER (Ire) [72] 5-9-5 Alex Greaves (6) *cld on ldrs aftr 2 fs, disputing ld whn squeezed for room ins fnl furlong, no extr.* .... (7 to 4 fav tchd 2 to 1) 3
241* DEBSY DO (USA) [71] 4-8-13 (5*) O Pears (1) *chsd ldrs, rdn and one pace appr fnl furlong.* ...... (4 to 1 op 3 to 1) 4
242[2] APPEALING TIMES (USA) [72] 4-9-2 (3*) Emma O'Gorman (3) *wl in tch, rdn alng o'r 2 out, kpt on one pace.* .... (11 to 2 op 7 to 2) 5
232[9] ALBERT THE BOLD [58] 4-8-5 N Adams (8) *jnd ldrs aftr one furlong, rdn and wknd wl o'r one out.* .... (16 to 1 op 14 to 1 tchd 20 to 1) 6
218[8] AFRICAN CHIMES [75] (bl) 6-9-1 (7*) D McCabe (5) *pld hrd, prmnt till lost pl aftr 3 fs, rnwd effrt 2 out, no imprsn.* .... (8 to 1 op 6 to 1) 7
27[6] HAWAII STORM (Fr) [66] 5-8-13 Dale Gibson (4) *al outpcd.* .... (10 to 1 op 8 to 1 tchd 11 to 1) 8

Dist: 1½l, 1l, 1l, 3l, 2½l, 1l, ¾l. 1m 32.40s. a 6.30s (8 Ran).
SR: 31/10/18/14/6/ (Mrs B Facchino), B A McMahon

277 Bramham Handicap Class C (0-90 3-y-o) £3,201 6f. .... (3:45)

218[6] CELESTIAL KEY (USA) [85] 9-1 (5*) O Pears (2) *made virtually all, rdn and found extr ins fnl furlong, styd on gmely.* .... (8 to 1 op 6 to 1 tchd 9 to 1) 1
212[3] LUCAYAN TREASURE [86] (v) 9-7 L Dettori (7) *hld up wl in tch, dsptd ld on bridle appr fnl furlong, rdn and found no extr last 100 yards.* .... (5 to 4 on op 11 to 10 tchd 5 to 4) 2

WINTERING (Ire) [75] 8-10 G Duffield (5) *pushed alng and outpcd 1st 2 fs, rdn and effrt o'r two out, no imprsn on first two appr fnl furlong*..........(6 to 1 op 5 to 2) 3
COCKERHAM RANGER [64] 7-13 G Carter (3) *chsd ldrs, rdn and outpcd appr fnl furlong*.... (8 to 1 op 4 to 1) 4
252^{6} ROSE FLYER (Ire) [60] 7-2 (7*) Darren Moffatt (6) *pressed wnr til rdn and lost pl wl o'r one out.* ....(8 to 1 op 7 to 1 tchd 9 to 1) 5
37^{4} GIRL NEXT DOOR [58] 7-7 S Wood (1) *missed break, effrt hfwy, not quicken ins last 2 fs*..... (8 to 1 tchd 9 to 1) 6
214^{2} EXPRESS MARIECURIE (Ire) [58] (bl) 7-6^{6} (7*) Claire Balding (4) *broke wl, drpd rear aftr 2 fs.* ....(11 to 1 op 12 to 1 tchd 10 to 1) 7

Dist: ¾l, 10l, ½l, sht-hd, ¾l, 4l. 1m 16.90s. a 3.50s (7 Ran).
SR: 54/52/1/-/ (M J Brodrick), S G Norton

278 Osberton Claiming Stakes Class G (4-y-o and up) £2,364 1½m.................(4:15)

254* TEMPERING 7-9-7 S Wood (11) *made all, clr hfwy, shaken up 2 out, eased nr finish.* ....(5 to 2 on op 7 to 2 on tchd 9 to 4 on) 1
229^{3} RED INDIAN 7-8-11 Dean McKeown (2) *cld on wnr frm 5 out, rdn and not quicken 2 out, no imprsn fnl furlong.* ....(6 to 1 op 5 to 1) 2
226^{5} ELIZA WOODING (v) 5-7-10 G Bardwell (9) *al wl plcd, rdn and outpcd frm 5 out*.......... (12 to 1) 3
PIMS CLASSIC 5-8-11 L Dettori (7) *improved frm rear hfwy, sn rdn alng, no prog last 4 fs.* (10 to 1 op 8 to 1) 4
YANKEE FLYER 6-7-9 (7*) D Wright (3) *beh till some hdwy hfwy, no imprsn on ldrs last 4 furlong.* .... (25 to 1 op 20 to 1) 5
OSSIE 4-8-0 (5*) Stephen Davies (5) *chsd wnr til 5 out, sn wknd*.......... (33 to 1 op 25 to 1) 6
202^{8} RESISTING (USA) 5-7-9 (7*) D McCabe (8) *beh, lost tch aftr 3 fs*.......... (50 to 1 op 33 to 1) 7
ROCK THE BARNEY (Ire) 4-8-11 T Quinn (4) *al in rear.* .... (16 to 1 op 10 to 1) 8
211^{6} SPRING TO THE TOP 6-8-6^{1} W Newnes (6) *chsd ldrs for 7 fs, sn wknd*.......... (12 to 1 op 8 to 1) 9
TAMASHA 4-7-8 N Adams (10) *mid-div to hfwy, sn lost tch, tld off*.......... (16 to 1 op 12 to 1) 10
219 AMOUR ROYAL 6-9-1 L Charnock (1) *refused to race aftr leaving stalls*.......... (20 to 1 op 16 to 1) 11

Dist: 4l, 15l, 3l, 10l, nk, sht-hd, 10l, 2l, 20l. 2m 42.80s. a 8.90s (11 Ran).
SR: 36/18/-/-/-/-/ (David W Chapman), D W Chapman

279 Burghley Handicap Class E (0-70 4-y-o and up) £2,427 1¾m...................(4:45)

219^{5} STEPPEY LANE [66] 8-10-0 Dean McKeown (11) *hdwy frm rear 6 out, rdn to ld wl ins fnl furlong, edgd lft and kpt on*.......... (7 to 1 op 6 to 1 tchd 8 to 1) 1
254^{2} SUGEMAR [64] 7-9-5 (7*) D McCabe (2) *improved frm rear 5 out, led 2 out, hdd and not quicken wl ins fnl furlong.* .... (13 to 2 op 7 to 2) 2
219^{3} WELL AND TRULY [45] 6-8-7 T Quinn (1) *chsd ldr, led 5 out, hdd 2 out, ran on same pace*.......... (5 to 1 op 2 to 1) 3
INTRICACY [60] 5-9-5 (3*) F Norton (4) *beh til rdn and styd on wl last 2 fs, nrst at finish*.......(12 to 1 op 10 to 1) 4
202^{3} SWEET REVIVAL [37] 5-7-13 Dale Gibson (6) *al chasing frnt rnk, effrt o'r 3 out, no imprsn last 2 fs.* .... (12 to 1 op 10 to 1) 5
254^{3} BEDOUIN PRINCE (USA) [49] (bl) 6-8-6 (5*) Stephen Davies (9) *dwlt, rdn to improve hfwy, no extr appr last 2 fs.* ....(4 to 1 tchd 5 to 1) 6
224^{8} SINGING DETECTIVE [32] 6-7-8^{1} N Adams (12) *wl plcd til wknd o'r 3 out*.......... (33 to 1 op 25 to 1) 7
HILLZAH (USA) [66] 5-10-0 M Hills (8) *hndy pos, dsptd ld 5 out till wknd o'r 2 out*.......... (5 to 2 fav op 16 to 1) 8
217^{3} SPEED OIL [47] 4-8-6 J Fanning (7) *clr ldr til wknd and hdd 5 out, tld off*..........(11 to 1 op 7 to 1) 9
210^{5} ELECTROJET [31] 5-7-6^{6} (7*) Claire Balding (5) *sn beh, lost tch bef hfwy, tld off*..........(33 to 1 op 25 to 1) 10
235^{6} NIP [32] 5-7-8 S Wood (3) *chsd ldrs for 9 fs, tld off.* .... (33 to 1 op 20 to 1) 11
4721a^{3} NOTED STRAIN (Ire) [53] 5-9-1 L Dettori (10) *mid-div till rdn and wknd 6 out, tld off*..........(8 to 1 op 5 to 1) 12

Dist: 1l, 4l, 2l, 1l, 1½l, 8l, ¾l, dist, 12l, 1l. 3m 10.80s. a 10.80s (12 Ran).
SR: 27/23/-/7/-/-/ (Dr C I Emmerson), W W Haigh

NAVAN (IRE) (yielding)
Saturday March 20th

280 Wilkinstown EBF Maiden (3-y-o and up) £3,450 5f.......................... (1:30)

256^{3} KERB CRAWLER 3-8-12 S Craine (3)..........(2 to 1 fav) 1
MACGILLYCUDDY (Ire) (bl) 4-9-5 (6*) C Everard (12) (12 to 1) 2
SHOOT THE DEALER (Ire) 3-8-9 B Coogan (2)..... (8 to 1) 3
GOLD BRAISIM (Ire) 3-8-9 C Roche (18)..........(9 to 2) 4
256^{8} SOMERTON BOY (Ire) 3-8-12 P Shanahan (17).....(9 to 2) 5
256^{7} FRIAR STREET (Ire) 3-8-12 R Hughes (11)..........(9 to 1) 6
SANS CERIPH (Ire) 3-8-9 W J O'Connor (15).......(8 to 1) 7
256^{9} BENE MERENTI (Ire) 3-8-12 N G McCullagh (14)... (9 to 1) 8
PERSIAN RENDEZVOUS (Ire) 3-8-12 P V Gilson (4) (14 to 1) 9
KILTIMONY 3-8-7 (2*) R M Burke (16)..........(12 to 1) 10
SISTER CARMEL (Ire) 3-8-9 K J Manning (1)......(25 to 1) 11
LAUNCH INTO SONG (Ire) 3-8-4 (8*) J J Stack (8). (20 to 1) 12
258 BOBADIL (Ire) 3-7-13 (10*) P J Smullen (10).......(33 to 1) 13
CAMEY'S CHOICE (Ire) 3-8-9 N Byrne (13)....... (33 to 1) 14
SHESLOOKINATME (Ire) 4-9-3 (8*) R V Skelly (9).. (33 to 1) 15
SANDCHORUS (Ire) 3-8-12 A J Nolan (6).........(14 to 1) 16
DIGNIFIED (Ire) 3-8-5 (4*) W J Smith (19).......... (14 to 1) 17
LARGO KEY (Ire) 3-8-9 W J Supple (5).......... (10 to 1) 18
GOLDEN TARGET (USA) 3-8-9 G Curran (7)...... (12 to 1) 19

Dist: ½l, 2l, nk, hd. 1m 3.80s. (19 Ran).
(T Corden), T Stack

281 Derrinstown Apprentice Series Handicap (0-75 5-y-o and up) £3,795 1¼m..... (2:00)

FERRYCARRIG HOTEL (Ire) [-] 4-8-4 (4*) J A Heffernan (12) ....(8 to 1) 1
4686a ARLINGTON HEIGHTS (Ire) [-] 4-9-10 (4*) B J Walsh (6) ....(8 to 1) 2+
COOLRAIN LADY (Ire) [-] 3-7-13^{3} R M Burke,..... (12 to 1) 2+
WINTER DREAMS (Ire) [-] 4-8-6 (8*) T Hagger (23). (20 to 1) 4
SHANKORAK [-] 6-8-12^{1} (4*) P Carberry (4).......(12 to 1) 5
TWO MAGPIES [-] 6-6-13 (8*) G Mylan (9)........ (12 to 1) 6
DIAMOND CLUSTER [-] 3-7-1 (6*) R T Fitzpatrick (11) ....(16 to 1) 7
SIMPLY GRAND [-] 6-8-4 (8*) G Coogan (19)......(25 to 1) 8
RATTLE AND HUM [-] 6-9-3 (6*) T J Daly (17)....... (8 to 1) 9
POWER SOURCE (Ire) [-] 5-7-11 (8*) P J Smullen (21) ....(25 to 1) 10
BALLYSPARKLE (Ire) [-] 3-7-6^{1} (6*) B A Hunter (2)...(8 to 1) 11
ARDLEA HOUSE (Ire) [-] 4-6-13 (8*) D Quirke (13).......... 12
STEEL GEM (Ire) [-] 4-8-8 D G O'Shea (1).........(20 to 1) 13
DOBIE (USA) [-] 5-9-5 (8*) J J Byrne (18).......... (12 to 1) 14
RIENZI [-] 9-7-8 (8*) P M Donohue (5)............ (14 to 1) 15
272 OLD TALKA RIVER [-] 6-9-9 (4*) C Everard (22)..... (8 to 1) 16
258^{9} KENTUCKY BABY (Ire) [-] (bl) 3-8-0 (2*) W J Smith (10) .... (4 to 1 fav) 17
MUMMYS BEST [-] (bl) 7-8-7 (6*) R V Skelly (8)....(50 to 1) 18
THE BOWER (Ire) [-] 4-8-2 (6*) J J Mullins (3)......(12 to 1) 19
DARCARI ROSE (Ire) [-] 4-8-8 (6*) D J O'Donohue (14) ....(20 to 1) 20
COMMAND 'N CONTROL [-] 4-8-10 (8*) W M Lynch (16) ....(8 to 1) 21
DAHAR'S LOVE (USA) [-] 4-8-6 (8*) J Cornally (15) (16 to 1) 22
SOUTHERN RULE [-] (bl) 6-7-1 (6*) P P Murphy (7) (12 to 1) 23

Dist: 3l, dd-ht, 6l, 1l. 2m 15.40s. (23 Ran).
(J C Lacy), T F Lacy

282 Staffordstown Stud EBF Fillies Maiden (3-y-o) £4,140 1¼m................... (2:30)

SPECIAL PAGEANT (Ire) 9-0 C Roche (7).....(7 to 4 jt-fav) 1
LADIES GALLERY (Ire) 8-12 (2*) R M Burke (20)... (33 to 1) 2
ANDANTE (Ire) 9-0 W J O'Connor (12).......... (20 to 1) 3
MAYASTA (Ire) 9-0 K J Manning (11).......... (33 to 1) 4
UNCERTAIN AFFAIR (Ire) 9-0 P Shanahan (21)..... (7 to 1) 5
ARAN EXILE 9-0 R Hughes (10).......... (10 to 1) 6
WICKLOW WAY (Ire) 9-0 W J Supple (18)..........(8 to 1) 7
MANZALA (USA) 9-0 J P Murtagh (19).......(7 to 4 jt-fav) 8
LIMAHEIGHTS (Ire) 8-4 (10*) P J Smullen (4).......... 9
BERESFORD LADY (Ire) 9-0 P V Gilson (17).......(10 to 1) 10
SELUNE (Fr) 9-0 N G McCullagh (14).......... (10 to 1) 11
INISHMOT (Ire) 8-6 (8*) R F Skelly (16)..........(33 to 1) 12
DARK HYACINTH (Ire) 9-0 S Craine (5).......... (10 to 1) 13
GLAS AGUS OR (Ire) 8-8 (6*) J A Heffernan (3).... (14 to 1) 14
258 COPSEWOOD (Ire) 8-0^{1}4 P Carberry (6)..........(14 to 1) 15
TANHONEY (Ire) 9-0 G Curran (1)..........(20 to 1) 16
GOLDEN SPHINX (Ire) 9-2^{2} D P Fagan (8).......... (33 to 1) 17
257 ONODI (Ire) 8-6 (8*) M W Martin (13).......... (50 to 1) 18
ADJAIYBA (USA) 8-12 (2*) D G O'Shea (9)........ (20 to 1) 19
RAYJOHN GIRL (Ire) 8-4 (10*) G Coogan (2).......(33 to 1) 20
LEOS LITTLE BIT (Ire) 8-4 (10*) B Fenton (15)..... (33 to 1) 21

Dist: 3l, hd, 2½l, sht-hd, 3l. 2m 17.40s. (21 Ran).
(D H W Dobson), J S Bolger

ST-CLOUD (FR) (good)
Saturday March 20th
Going Correction: PLUS 0.25 sec. per fur.

283 Prix Exbury (Group 3) (4-y-o and up) £23,895 1¼m...................... (2:10)

URBAN SEA (USA) 4-8-8 M Boutin, *prmnt, second strt, rdn o'r one furlong out, quickened to ld ins fnl furlong, drvn out*..........(23 to 10 fav) 1
145^{3} MARILDO (Fr) 6-8-9 G Guignard, *led, quickened 2 fs out, hrd rdn and hdd ins last, ran on*..........(48 to 10) 2
FUNNY BABY (Fr) 5-9-2 A Badel, *7th strt, hdwy o'r one furlong out, ran on ins last*.......... (15 to 1) 3
PRINCE POLINO (USA) 4-8-11 F Head, *hld up, 5th strt, effrt 2 fs out, one pace fnl furlong*..........(14 to 1) 4
SHEIKH DANCER 6-8-11 C Asmussen, *mid-div, 4th strt, hdwy 2 fs out, btn appr fnl furlong*.......... (17 to 2) 5
DAMPIERRE (USA) 5-9-2 T Jarnet, *prmnt, 3rd strt, rdn wl o'r one furlong out, sn btn*..........(37 to 10) 6

4674a[2] MICHEL GEORGES 5-8-11 C Le Scrill, *last to strt, some hdwy 2 fs out, sn btn*..........(17 to 1) 7
SHEBA DANCER (Fr) 4-8-12 D Boeuf, *nvr dngrs*. (24 to 10) 8
Dist: 1l, 2l, 1l, hd, 1l, ½l, 3l. 2m 9.20s. a 5.20s (8 Ran).
SR: 67/66/69/62/61/64/58/53/ (D Tsui), J Lesbordes

SOUTHWELL (A.W) (std)
Wednesday March 24th
Going Correction: PLUS 0.25 sec. per fur. (races 1,2,3,4,5), MINUS 0.30 (6)

284 Blackbird Maiden Stakes Class D (3-y-o and up) £3,377 1m..................(2:10)

KEYWAY (USA) 3-8-4 G Duffield (4) *made most, hrd pressed o'r one furlong out, ran on strly und pres*. ....(6 to 1 op 9 to 2 tchd 7 to 1) 1
MOON STRIKE (Fr) 3-8-2[1] (3*) Emma O'Gorman (6) *nvr far away, quickened through on ins to chal o'r one furlong out, edgd lft, rdn and no extr*. ....(2 to 1 fav op 11 to 10) 2
220[4] QUELQUE CHOSE 3-8-4 D Holland (9) *patiently rdn, steady hdwy hfwy, came wide strt, styd on, nvr able to chal*..........(7 to 2 op 5 to 2) 3
TEJANO GOLD (USA) 3-8-4 T Quinn (7) *nvr far away, effrt and drvn alng o'r 2 fs out, ran green, one pace*. ....(6 to 1 op 5 to 1) 4
4791a[9] TELEPHONIC (USA) 3-8-4 C Nutter (8) *sluggish strt, bustled alng to improve entering strt, ran green o'r 2 fs out, no imprsn*..........(16 to 1 op 14 to 1) 5
230[8] NOBLE MEASURE (Ire) (bl) 3-8-1[4] (7*) G Strange (2) *pushed alng in midfield, effrt on ins hfwy, nvr able to rch ldrs*. ....(20 to 1 op 14 to 1) 6
FUTURE FAME (USA) 4-9-7 A Munro (5) *led early, styd hndy till fdd und pres 2 fs out*......(16 to 1 op 8 to 1) 7
159[4] PRINCESS DECHTRA (Ire) 4-9-2 W Ryan (11) *pressed ldg pair, rdn o'r 2 fs out, fdd*.......... (10 to 1) 8
SUMMERS DREAM 3-7-13 N Adams (3) *broke wl to show speed in frnt rnk for o'r 5 fs, fdd*...(25 to 1 op 20 to 1) 9
233[4] THREEOFUS 3-7-13 (5*) Stephen Davies (12) *struggling to hold pl hfwy, sn tld off*..........(12 to 1 op 16 to 1) 10
ALICANTE 6-9-4 (3*) S D Williams (10) *struggling to keep up hfwy, tld off*..........(25 to 1 op 20 to 1) 11
Dist: ¾l, 10l, nk, ½l, 1½l, 8l, 8l, 1½l, 8l, 10l. 1m 45.90s. a 6.90s (11 Ran).
SR: 17/15/-/-/-/-/ (B Haggas), Sir Mark Prescott

285 Robin Claiming Stakes Class G (4-y-o and up) £2,385 6f......................(2:40)

276* APPLEDORN 6-8-11 T Quinn (5) *al travelling wl, quickened through on ins to ld o'r one furlong out, readily*. .... (5 to 4 on tchd Evens) 1
255[5] CRECHE (bl) 4-9-3 (7*) D Carson (2) *sluggish strt, reco'red quickly to press ldg pair, led over 2 out till over one furlong out, no ch wth wnr*..........(3 to 1 op 7 to 4) 2
138 JOVIAL KATE (USA) 6-8-1 T Williams (4) *tried to make all, hdd o'r 2 fs out, rdn and not quicken*. ....(14 to 1 tchd 16 to 1) 3
276[5] APPEALING TIMES (USA) 4-8-7 (3*) Emma O'Gorman (6) *broke wl, outpcd and struggling hfwy, ran on well appr fnl furlong, nrst finish*....... (5 to 1 tchd 9 to 2) 4
41[6] PESIDANAMICH (Ire) (bl) 5-8-5 (5*) Stephen Davies (1) *drvn alng to chase ldg trio, hrd at work o'r 2 fs out, sn btn*. .... (12 to 1 op 10 to 1) 5
SALADAN KNIGHT 8-8-8 Alex Greaves (7) *broke wl to show gd speed in frnt rnk for o'r 3 fs, fdd*. .... (20 to 1 op 12 to 1) 6
IMPORTANT DECISION 4-8-5 S Wood (3) *sluggish strt, al wl outpcd*..........(33 to 1 op 20 to 1) 7
Dist: 6l, 2l, ¾l, 2l, 7l, 12l. 1m 16.90s. a 3.50s (7 Ran).
SR: 57/46/15/21/13/-/-/ (Mrs B Facchino), B A McMahon

286 Starling Handicap Class D (0-80 3-y-o) £3,114 1m.......................... (3:10)

124* DORAZINE [70] 9-3 J Quinn (2) *patiently rdn, bustled alng to improve last 2 fs, ran on to ld cl hme*. ....(11 to 4 fav op 6 to 4 tchd 3 to 1) 1
262[3] GREEN'S FAIR (Ire) [74] 9-7 T Quinn (6) *dictated pace aftr one furlong, quickened to go clr o'r 2 fs out, ran on jst ct*..........(4 to 1 tchd 5 to 1 and 7 to 2) 2
62* RECORD LOVER (Ire) [61] 8-8 A Munro (4) *nvr far away, hrd at work whn pace lifted o'r 2 fs out, rallied fnl furlong*.......... (4 to 1 op 7 to 2) 3
240* HOTSOCKS [56] 7-10 (7*) Kim McDonnell (1) *settled in last pl, effrt on ins o'r 2 fs out, kpt on, nvr able to chal*. .... (11 to 2 op 4 to 1 tchd 6 to 1) 4
252[7] ASTRAC TRIO (USA) [68] 9-1 K Darley (7) *pressed ldg pair, hrd at work o'r 2 fs out, sn outpcd*. ....(16 to 1 op 14 to 1 tchd 20 to 1) 5
172[3] TAKE YOUR PARTNER (Ire) [59] 8-6 Dean McKeown (5) *led for a furlong, styd hndy till hrd drvn o'r 2 fs out, fdd*. .... (13 to 2 op 11 to 2) 6
252[4] JORDYWRATH [58] 8-5 A Mackay (3) *trkd ldg trio, feeling pace and drvn alng o'r 2 fs out, sn btn*. ....(7 to 1 op 6 to 1) 7
Dist: 1l, 2l, 4l, 4l, ¾l, 1½l. 1m 46.10s. a 7.10s (7 Ran).
SR: 27/28/9/-/ (C John Hill), C J Hill

287 Thrush Handicap Class D (0-80 4-y-o and up) £3,201 1¾m..................(3:40)

243[5] HORIZON (Ire) [77] (bl) 5-10-0 D Biggs (1) *made all, steadied hfwy, quickened up ag'n o'r 2 fs out, kpt on strly*. ....(3 to 1 op 5 to 2) 1
229[2] KARAMOJA [53] 4-8-1 A Munro (7) *nvr far away, effrt and drvn alng last 2 fs, styd on, not rch wnr*. ....(7 to 2 op 3 to 1 tchd 4 to 1) 2
226[6] QUALITAIR RHYTHM (Ire) [56] (v) 5-8-0 (7*) G Mitchell (4) *al ldg 3, ev ch appr strt, styd on same pace last 2 fs*. .... (7 to 2 op 11 to 4) 3
4662a PONDERED BID [42] (bl) 9-7-0 (7*) Kim McDonnell (6) *last and pushed alng, outpcd and beh hfwy, some late hdwy, nvr dngrs*..........(33 to 1) 4
229* ATLANTIC WAY [54] 5-8-5 J Quinn (5) *settled gng wl, prmsg effrt aftr a m, rdn and btn entering strt*. ....(11 to 4 fav op 9 to 4 tchd 3 to 1) 5
254[7] CASTLE SECRET [61] 7-8-12 L Charnock (8) *trkd ldg quartet, hrd at work aftr a m, sn lost tch*. .... (12 to 1 op 20 to 1) 6
278[4] PIMS CLASSIC [46] 5-7-11 N Carlisle (2) *co'red up on ins, struggling to keep up hfwy, sn lost tch*........(12 to 1) 7
175[7] AS D'EBOLI (Fr) [55] (bl,e/s) 6-8-6 K Fallon (3) *wth ldrs to hfwy, sn tld off*.......... (25 to 1 op 16 to 1) 8
Dist: 3½l, 2½l, 15l, 2l, 2½l, 5l, 15l. 3m 9.30s. a 9.30s (8 Ran).
SR: 56/22/23/-/-/ (Mrs Solna Thomson Jones), T Thomson Jones

288 Woodpecker Maiden Stakes Class D (4-y-o and up) £3,377 1½m................(4:10)

118 HIERARCH (USA) 4-9-5 Dean McKeown (13) *al gng wl, led well o'r 4 fs out, quickened clr last 2 furlongs, ran on strly*.......... (7 to 2 op 7 to 2) 1
261[4] DOC'S COAT 8-9-7 T Quinn (3) *patiently rdn, improved into midfield hfwy, styd on wl last 2 fs, nrst finish*. .... (20 to 1 op 14 to 1) 2
DEDUCE 4-9-5 M Hills (8) *nvr far away, ev ch and drvn alng o'r 2 fs out, styd on same pace*. .... (13 to 8 fav op Evens tchd 7 to 4) 3
MRS JAWLEYFORD (USA) 5-9-2 J Carroll (6) *slwly into strd, given time to reco'r, improved over 2 fs out, ran on finish*..........(10 to 1 op 8 to 1) 4
BRANDON GROVE 5-9-2 Alex Greaves (1) *settled gng wl, prmsg effrt appr strt, kpt on same pace last 2 fs*. .... (10 to 1 op 14 to 1 tchd 16 to 1) 5
PONTYNYSWEN 5-9-2 (5*) Stephen Davies (10) *al chasing ldrs, feeling pace appr strt, styd on one pace*. .... (14 to 1 op 12 to 1) 6
MILIYEL 4-9-0 A Munro (12) *chsd ldg bunch, feeling pace appr strt, one pace last 2 fs*.......... (9 to 1 op 8 to 1) 7
225[5] LORD BELMONTE (Ire) 4-9-2 (3*) J Weaver (9) *wth ldrs, led o'r 5 fs out till over 4 furlongs out, btn entering strt*. ....(20 to 1) 8
LOCH GARANNE 5-9-2 N Connorton (5) *settled off the pace, a lot to do hfwy, styd on wl last 2 fs, nvr plcd to chal*.......... (10 to 1 op 8 to 1) 9
RESTLESS MINSTREL (USA) 4-9-0 (5*) L Newton (2) *dictated pace till hdd o'r 5 fs out, fdd entering strt*. ....(7 to 1 tchd 6 to 1) 10
179[2] MULAWIH (USA) 5-9-2 (5*) O Pears (11) *pressed ldrs, hrd at work and lost pl hfwy, tld off*. ....(10 to 1 tchd 12 to 1 and 14 to 1) 11
THE METROPOLE (Ire) 4-9-2 (3*) S D Williams (4) *wth ldrs to hfwy, tld off entering strt*..........(20 to 1) 12
BLUE POINT (Ire) 4-9-0 W Ryan (7) *sluggish strt, struggling hfwy, tld off*.......... (16 to 1 op 14 to 1) 13
Dist: 1½l, 2½l, 4l, ½l, 1½l, 3l, 4l, ½l, 15l, 4l. 2m 43.60s. a 9.70s (13 Ran).
SR: 38/37/30/19/18/20/7/4/-/ (The Queen), Lord Huntingdon

289 Blue Tit Handicap Class C (0-90 3-y-o and up) £4,878 5f.......................(4:40)

277* CELESTIAL KEY (USA) [92] 3-9-4 (5*,7ex) O Pears (1) *rcd alng far side, nvr far away, kpt on grimly to ld cl hme*. .... (7 to 1 op 11 to 2 tchd 8 to 1) 1
166[6] TINO TERE [69] 4-8-6 (7*) P Roberts (9) *tried to make all centre, kpt on und pres fnl furlong, jst ct*. ....(8 to 1 op 6 to 1) 2
277[3] WINTERING (Ire) [75] 3-8-6 G Duffield (5) *nvr far away, ev ch and drvn alng o'r one furlong out, kpt on und pres*. .... (9 to 1 op 7 to 1 tchd 10 to 1) 3
221* LITTLE SABOTEUR [75] 4-9-5 W Ryan (8) *trkd ldrs, effrt and drvn alng last 2 fs, kpt on same pace*. ....(7 to 2 fav op 5 to 1 tchd 3 to 1) 4
231* STRIP CARTOON (Ire) [51] (bl) 5-7-9 J Quinn (11) *wl plcd stands side, drvn alng last 2 fs, not quicken*. ....(9 to 2 op 5 to 1 tchd 6 to 1) 5
249[7] MEESON TIMES [53] 5-7-11 T Williams (10) *rcd midfield, outpcd and drvn alng hfwy, styd on wl fnl furlong*. .... (14 to 1 op 12 to 1) 6
231[3] ARC LAMP [50] 7-7-8 Dale Gibson (7) *chsd alng to keep up, nvr able to rch ldrs*.......... (5 to 1 tchd 9 to 2) 7

276^{7} AFRICAN CHIMES [75] (bl) 6-8-12 (7*) D McCabe (4) *early speed, hrd at work hfwy, sn btn*...(25 to 1 op 20 to 1) 8
253^{7} SAVAHRA SOUND [84] 8-10-0 D Nicholls (2) *chsd ldg bunch to hfwy, eased whn btn.* ....(20 to 1 op 16 to 1 tchd 25 to 1 and 33 to 1) 9
255^{4} MAID WELCOME [62] (bl) 6-7-13 (7*) J Marshall (12) *gd speed stands side for 3 fs, fdd.* (15 to 2 op 7 to 1 tchd 8 to 1) 10
DAYTONA BEACH (Ire) [74] 3-8-5 K Darley (3) *early speed, struggling hfwy, eased whn btn.* ....(12 to 1 op 10 to 1 tchd 14 to 1) 11
SO SUPERB [58] 4-8-2 J Lowe (6) *missed break, nvr able to reco'r*.................(20 to 1 op 14 to 1) 12
Dist: Hd, ½l, 1½l, 1½l, ¾l, 5l, sht-hd, ½l, 2l, ½l. 58.90s. a 1.00s (12 Ran).
SR: 59/48/39/46/16/15/-/16/23/ (M J Brodrick), S G Norton

DONCASTER (good to firm)
Thursday March 25th
Going Correction: MINUS 0.35 sec. per fur.

290 Raceform Apprentice Handicap Class E (0-80 4-y-o and up) £3,261 1½m..... (1:55)

NORTHERN GRADUATE (USA) [63] 4-8-13 S Maloney (11) *patiently rdn, steady hdwy on outsd o'r 3 fs out, drvn to ld appr fnl furlong, kpt on.* ....(10 to 1 op 8 to 1 tchd 12 to 1) 1
251^{2} BESCABY BOY [62] 7-9-0 S D Williams (14) *trkd ldg half-dozen, nosed ahead wl o'r one furlong out, hdd appr last, kpt on*....................(8 to 1 tchd 10 to 1) 2
279^{2} SUGEMAR [57] 7-8-4 (5*) D McCabe (3) *trkd ldg bunch, ev ch and edgd lft appr fnl furlong, kpt on und pres.* ....(9 to 1 op 8 to 1 tchd 10 to 1) 3
KALKO [58] 4-8-8 N Kennedy (10) *wtd wth, improved on outsd o'r 3 fs out, ev ch whn edgd lft and put head in air appr fnl furlong, no extr.* ....(9 to 1 op 8 to 1 tchd 7 to 1 and 10 to 1) 4
ROUSITTO [66] 5-8-13 (5*) J Dennis (1) *trkd ldg bunch, improved on ins o'r 2 fs out, staying on towards finish.* ....(14 to 1 op 12 to 1 tchd 16 to 1) 5
219^{9} EIRE LEATH-SCEAL [49] 6-7-10 (5*) J Marshall (7) *tried to make all, clr o'r 3 fs out, wknd and hdd wl over one furlong out*....................(20 to 1 op 16 to 1) 6
GREAT MAX (Ire) [68] (v) 4-9-1 (3*) K Rutter (12) *settled midfield, reminder appr strt, improved last 2 fs, styd on*..................(11 to 2 fav op 5 to 1 tchd 6 to 1) 7
265^{3} SINCLAIR LAD (Ire) [60] 5-8-7 (5*) S Drowne (2) *co'red up on ins, effrt and drvn alng over 2 fs out, kpt on same pace.* ....(16 to 1 tchd 20 to 1) 8
BROUGHTON'S TANGO (Ire) [51] 4-7-10 (5*) D Wright (16) *beh and drvn alng entering strt, styd on last 2 fs, nvr nrr*..................(10 to 1 op 7 to 1 tchd 11 to 1) 9
254^{4} FIVE TO SEVEN (USA) [72] 4-9-5 (3*) O Pears (8) *trkd ldr, hrd at work whn pace lifted o'r 3 fs out, fdd.* ....(12 to 1 tchd 14 to 1) 10
4788a DEMOKOS (Fr) [41] 8-7-2 (5*) Darren Moffatt (4) *settled in rear, improved last 3 fs, nrst finish.* ....(50 to 1 op 25 to 1) 11
279^{3} WELL AND TRULY [43] 6-7-6^{2} (5*) A Garth (13) *trkd ldg trio, ev ch and drvn alng o'r 3 fs out, fdd last 2 furlongs.* ....(14 to 1 op 16 to 1) 12
LABURNUM [76] 5-9-7 (7*) D Thomas (6) *patiently rdn, steady hdwy on outsd o'r 3 fs out, nvr nr to chal.* ....(10 to 1 op 7 to 1 tchd 12 to 1) 13
LEGION OF HONOUR [70] 5-9-8 J Weaver (5) *chsd ldg 5, hrd at work o'r 3 fs out, fdd*......(16 to 1 op 12 to 1) 14
4698a^{7} POST IMPRESSIONIST (Ire) [59] 4-8-9 F Norton (20) *co'red up on ins, effrt over 3 fs out, fdd last 2 furlongs.* ....(25 to 1 op 14 to 1) 15
RIMOUSKI [41] 5-7-6^{4} (5*) Claire Balding (17) *missed break, nvr able to reco'r*..................(12 to 1 op 14 to 1) 16
QUEENS TOUR [41] 8-7-7^{5} (5*) S McCarthy (15) *struggling to keep up hfwy, nvr a factor*..... (50 to 1 op 20 to 1) 17
ARRASTRA [49] 5-8-1 D Harrison (19) *trkd ldg quartet for o'r a m, wknd over 2 fs out.* ....(10 to 1 op 9 to 1 tchd 12 to 1) 18
PARADISE NAVY [78] 4-9-11 (3*) B Doyle (9) *pressed ldg pair till wknd quickly last 3 fs*.....(25 to 1 op 16 to 1) 19
227^{9} MAHZOOZ [54] 4-7-11 (7*) Elizabeth Turner (18) *al struggling in rear, nvr a factor*........ (50 to 1 op 25 to 1) 20
Dist: ½l, sht-hd, hd, 2½l, 1½l, nk, sht-hd, 3l, ½l, 2½l. 2m 32.06s. a 1.56s (20 Ran).
SR: 41/41/35/33/38/18/34/27/10/ (P D Savill), Mrs M Reveley

291 Philip Cornes Brocklesby Conditions Stakes Class D (2-y-o) £3,687 5f.....(2:30)

BANDON CASTLE (Ire) 8-8 (3*) D Harrison (6) *wth ldr, led aftr one furlong, sprinted clr ins fnl furlong, readily.* ....(10 to 1 tchd 8 to 1 and 12 to 1) 1
INDIAN DREAMER 8-11 M Hills (9) *nvr far away, effrt and bustled alng o'r one furlong out, kpt on, no ch wth wnr*..............................(7 to 2 op 7 to 4) 2
CULSYTH FLYER 8-11 W Ryan (1) *chsd ldrs on outsd, effrt and drvn alng o'r one furlong out, kpt on wl.* ....(8 to 1 op 7 to 1 tchd 10 to 1) 3
TOP SHOW (Ire) 8-11 A Munro (3) *missed break, improved into midfield hfwy, ran on wl fnl furlong, can improve.* ....(8 to 1 tchd 10 to 1) 4
VALIANT MAN 8-11 J Williams (12) *al chasing ldrs, feeling pace and bustled alng hfwy, nvr able to chal.* ....(12 to 1 op 10 to 1) 5
ME NEITHER 8-6 J Carroll (2) *ran green to hfwy, effrt and drvn alng 2 fs out, nvr able to chal.* ....(9 to 2 op 9 to 4 tchd 5 to 1) 6
MAKE THE BREAK 8-11 B Rouse (4) *broke fst, led a furlong, styd hndy till fdd o'r one furlong out.* ....(3 to 1 fav op 7 to 2 tchd 9 to 4) 7
CLOSE TO REALITY 8-11 K Fallon (8) *chsd alng to go pace to hfwy, steady hdwy o'r one furlong out, nvr able to chal*..................(8 to 1 op 7 to 1 tchd 12 to 1) 8
SALVOR (Ire) 8-11 J Fanning (11) *unruly in stalls, missed break, nvr able to reco'r*......... (20 to 1 tchd 25 to 1) 9
HILTONS TRAVEL (Ire) 8-6 (5*) Stephen Davies (10) *gd speed on ins, ran green and hng lft hfwy, wknd quickly.* ....(20 to 1 op 16 to 1) 10
CLANCY'S EXPRESS 8-11 J Comber (7) *sluggish strt, chsd alng to go pace, nvr a threat.* ....(20 to 1 tchd 25 to 1 and 16 to 1) 11
Dist: 3½l, 2½l, ½l, 5l, hd, 1½l, 1½l, 1l, nk, 20l. 1m 0.53s. a 1.73s (11 Ran).
SR: 27/13/3/1/-/-/ (The Riston Racing Partnership), B S Rothwell

292 Raceform Update Handicap Class D (0-85 3-y-o and up) £3,817 5f............. (3:05)

AMRON [76] 6-9-9 N Carlisle (5) *trkd ldg bunch, drvn through entering fnl furlong, kpt on to ld last 50 yards.* ....(8 to 1 op 7 to 1) 1
EAGER DEVA [81] 6-9-9 (5*) S Wynne (13) *nvr far away, improved to ld o'r one furlong out, rdn and ct last 50 yards*..... (9 to 1 op 10 to 1 tchd 12 to 1 and 8 to 1) 2
289^{7} ARC LAMP [58] 7-8-5 Dale Gibson (10) *chsd alng in midfield, gd hdwy appr fnl furlong, ran on wl.* ....(16 to 1 op 14 to 1) 3
223^{4} MISTER JOLSON [60] 4-8-7 W Carson (3) *bustled alng in midfield, improved o'r one furlong out, ran on finish.* ....(7 to 1 jt-fav op 6 to 1) 4
255^{6} SLADES HILL [60] 6-8-7 Alex Greaves (9) *nvr far away, effrt and drvn alng o'r one furlong out, ran on same pace*..............................(20 to 1 op 14 to 1) 5
255^{2} EWALD (Ire) [59] 5-8-1 (5*) B Doyle (1) *wth ldr, hrd at work whn pace quickened o'r one furlong out, no extr.* ....(7 to 1 jt-fav tchd 8 to 1) 6
MISS MOVIE WORLD [57] 4-8-4 A Munro (7) *trkd ldrs, hrd at work 2 fs, unbl to quicken*........ (8 to 1 op 7 to 1) 7
99^{7} MARTINA [64] 5-8-11 J Williams (14) *settled midfield, effrt and bustled alng hfwy, kpt on, nvr nrr.* ....(16 to 1 op 14 to 1) 8
140^{3} BOLD HABIT [80] 8-9-13 R Cochrane (12) *sluggish strt, steady hdwy 2 fs out, rng on whn not much room fnl furlong, nvr nrr*..................(10 to 1 tchd 12 to 1) 9
SIGAMA (USA) [78] 7-9-8 (3*) N Kennedy (6) *dictated pace for o'r 3 fs, no extr*..............(14 to 1 tchd 16 to 1) 10
DRUM SERGEANT [76] (bl) 6-9-9 Pat Eddery (4) *sluggish strt, drvn alng to go pace hfwy, staying on finish.* ....(15 to 2 op 8 to 1 tchd 7 to 1) 11
263^{4} SIR TASKER [63] 5-8-10 T Quinn (2) *sluggish strt, chsd alng on outsd hfwy, not pace to chal.* ....(9 to 1 op 8 to 1 tchd 10 to 1) 12
GANESHAYA [53] (bl) 4-8-0 J Lowe (8) *settled midfield, drvn alng hfwy, no imprsn*...... (16 to 1 tchd 20 to 1) 13
FIRST GOLD [67] 4-9-0 M Birch (11) *beh and pushed alng hfwy, nvr a threat*.................(20 to 1 op 16 to 1) 14
231 MISS EL ARAB (Ire) [52] 5-7-13 J Quinn (15) *patiently rdn, stumbled and hit rng rail o'r 2 fs out, eased whn no ch.* ....(66 to 1 op 50 to 1 tchd 100 to 1) 15
Dist: 1l, 1½l, hd, ½l, 1½l, ½l, hd, ¾l, ½l, ½l. 59.49s. a 0.69s (15 Ran).
SR: 60/61/32/33/31/24/20/26/39/ (Roy Peebles), J Berry

293 Doncaster 2000 Mile Class A (Listed Race) (3-y-o and up) £11,062 1m.......... (3:35)

MELLOTTIE 8-9-6 J Lowe (5) *last and hld up, niggled alng hfwy, weaved through to ld wl ins fnl furlong, ran on*......................(5 to 2 jt-fav tchd 3 to 1) 1
ALFLORA (Ire) 4-9-3 J Penza (7) *tried to make all, ran on und pres fnl furlong, ct towards finish.* (5 to 2 jt-fav op 2 to 1) 2
KARINGA BAY 6-9-8 B Rouse (8) *al hndy, ev ch and drvn alng last 2 fs, kpt on same pace*.....(7 to 1 op 11 to 2) 3+
244* KNOCK TO ENTER (USA) 5-9-3 J Williams (6) *patiently rdn, swtchd ins and shaken up o'r one furlong out, fnshd wl*.......................... (20 to 1 tchd 25 to 1) 3+
PEARL ANGEL 4-9-1 L Dettori (3) *trkd ldg quartet, effrt and drvn alng o'r one furlong out, not quicken.* ....(8 to 1 op 6 to 1) 5
NOMINATOR 3-8-3 W Ryan (1) *chsd ldrs, effrt and drvn alng o'r one furlong out, one pace.* ....(11 to 2 op 4 to 1 tchd 6 to 1) 6
246^{3} DOUBLE FLUTTER 4-8-12 W Newnes (4) *chsd ldg half-dozen, effrt and rdn wl o'r one furlong out, sn outpcd.* ....(25 to 1 op 20 to 1) 7

TOP REGISTER (USA) 4-9-3 A Munro (2) *al wl plcd, ev ch and drvn alng o'r one furlong out, fdd.* .... (10 to 1 op 12 to 1) 8
247² AMENABLE 8-9-3 W Woods (9) *co'red up beh ldrs, effrt hfwy, hrd at work over one furlong out, sn btn.* .... (25 to 1 op 33 to 1 tchd 50 to 1) 9
Dist: ½l, 1½l, dd-ht, 2½l, ½l, ¾l, 6l, 2l. 1m 37.18s. a 0.38s (9 Ran).
SR: 58/53/53/48/38/24/31/18/12/ (Mrs J G Fulton), Mrs M Reveley

294 Forte Ladies Only Handicap Class E (0-80 4-y-o and up) £3,494 1¼m 60yds.... (4:05)

224 ALBERT [44] 6-8-9 (5*) Mrs D Arbuthnot (7) *confidently rdn, improved on ins entering strt, quickened ahead o'r one out, easily*........................ (8 to 1 op 11 to 2) 1
4707a⁶ THE KARAOKE KING [50] (bl) 4-9-0 (5*) Mrs J Boggis (1) *nvr far away, nosed ahead briefly wl o'r one furlong out, kpt on, no ch wth wnr*...(7 to 1 op 6 to 1 tchd 8 to 1) 2
DAWN FLIGHT [66] 4-10-7 Mrs Maxine Cowdrey (15) *settled in rear, improved to take clr order 3 fs out, styd on appr fnl furlong*.................................. (14 to 1) 3
4662a³ BALZINO (USA) [55] 4-9-10 Mrs S Cumani (18) *settled off the pace, swtchd ins and rapid hdwy whn badly baulked o'r one furlong out, ran on, nvr nrr.* ....(7 to 1 op 8 to 1 tchd 9 to 1) 4
265⁴ OUR EDDIE [45] (v) 4-8-9 (5*) Mrs M Busby (5) *settled midfield, effrt on ins o'r 3 fs out, kpt on same pace.* (25 to 1) 5
9⁸ MAY SQUARE (Ire) [44] 5-8-11² (5*) Miss D Pomeroy (17) *dashed up frm off the pace to ld hfwy, hdd and rdn wl o'r one furlong out, sn btn*....... (20 to 1 op 16 to 1) 6
225* SWORD MASTER [73] 4-10-9 (5*) Miss Diana J Jones (16) *trkd ldg bunch, effrt and drvn alng o'r 3 fs out, kpt on, nvr able to chal*......(7 to 2 fav op 3 to 1 tchd 4 to 1) 7
274² RIPSNORTER (Ire) [61] 4-9-11 (5*) Miss A Purdy (4) *wth ldrs, hrd at work whn pace quickened o'r 3 fs out, no extr.* ....(10 to 1 tchd 11 to 1) 8
210⁷ BREEZED WELL [55] 7-9-11⁸ (5*) Mrs H Noonan (10) *chsd ldg bunch, feeling pace and drvn alng o'r 2 fs out, no imprsn*......................... (16 to 1 tchd 20 to 1) 9
199⁵ TAUNTING (Ire) [53] 5-9-9 Miss S A Billot (14) *pressed ldrs, drvn alng entering strt, fdd o'r 2 fs out*.......(16 to 1) 10
BRENDA HUNT (Ire) [45] 4-8-9 (5*) Mrs S Moore (9) *beh and drvn alng hfwy, nvr able to rch ldrs.* .... (100 to 1 op 50 to 1) 11
4710a REZA [48] 5-9-4⁹ (5*) Mrs C Hirst (2) *in tch till rdn alng entering strt, sn btn*.......................... (50 to 1) 12
CHEEKY POT [44] (bl) 5-8-9 (5*) Miss M Carson (6) *chsd alng beh ldg bunch, nvr trbld ldrs.* .... (14 to 1 op 12 to 1 tchd 16 to 1) 13
LOTS OF LUCK [64] 10-10-6 Mrs L Pearce (13) *settled to track ldg bunch, effrt entering strt, sn rdn and btn.* ....(5 to 1 op 7 to 2) 14
CHIEF OF STAFF [80] 4-11-2 (5*) Mrs C Wilkinson (11) *reluctant to race, lost many ls strt, nvr a factor.* .... (16 to 1 op 14 to 1) 15
SHAHNIZAM (USA) [48] 9-9-4¹ Miss P Robson (8) *trkd ldg quartet till fdg entering strt*...... (50 to 1 op 33 to 1) 16
67 KAYMONT [44] 5-8-9 (5*) Miss J Bond (12) *dictated pace to hfwy, wknd quickly entering strt.* .... (100 to 1 op 50 to 1) 17
MILLIE (USA) [44] 5-8-9 (5*) Miss S Judge (3) *wl plcd on ins, losing grnd whn clipped heels of rival and f appr strt.* ....(50 to 1) f
Dist: 3½l, ¾l, 3½l, 1½l, ½l, hd, 1l, hd, 5l, hd. 2m 12.21s. a 5.51s (18 Ran).
SR: 9/7/21/3/-/-/16/2/-/ (T S M S Riley-Smith), D A Wilson

295 'Back A Winner By Train' Handicap Class C (0-95 3-y-o) £5,005 1¼m 60yds.... (4:35)

DUTOSKY [73] 8-7 W Carson (3) *trkd ldg trio, drvn ahead o'r one furlong out, hld on grimly ins fnl furlong.* ....(10 to 1 tchd 11 to 1) 1
186* BROUGHTONS FORMULA [63] 7-11 J Quinn (2) *tucked away in midfield, baulked and snatched up o'r 2 fs out, rallied and bumped over one out, fnshd wl, unlucky.* ....(8 to 1 op 6 to 1) 2
DOC COTTRILL [72] 8-6 K Fallon (6) *co'red up on ins, improved but no room over one furlong out, swtchd sharply rght, ran on wl.* .... (11 to 2 op 6 to 1 tchd 7 to 1) 3
MONDRAGON [75] 8-9 R Cochrane (12) *patiently rdn, steady hdwy o'r 2 fs out, styd on finish.* ....(7 to 1 tchd 8 to 1) 4
186² DEE RAFT (USA) [80] 9-0 D Holland (9) *led aftr 3 fs till o'r one furlong out, rdn and no extr.* .... (11 to 2 op 5 to 1 tchd 6 to 1) 5
WAHEM (Ire) [75] 8-9 L Dettori (1) *led for 3 fs, hrd drvn o'r 2 furlongs out, fdd*........(7 to 1 op 8 to 1 tchd 9 to 1) 6
BRIGANTE DI CIELO [86] 9-6 B Raymond (13) *chsd ldg bunch, effrt on outsd 3 fs out, kpt on same pace.* ....(14 to 1 tchd 16 to 1) 7
ARGYLE CAVALIER (Ire) [70] 8-4 G Carter (5) *chsd ldrs till rdn and fdd o'r 2 fs out*............(12 to 1 op 14 to 1) 8
ARC BRIGHT (Ire) [68] 8-2 A Munro (4) *trkd ldg quartet till fdd und pres o'r 2 fs out.* .... (16 to 1 op 20 to 1 tchd 14 to 1) 9
MOON CARNIVAL [74] 8-8 J Reid (7) *in tch till wknd quickly o'r 2 fs out*.............(20 to 1 tchd 25 to 1) 10
PERSIAN REVIVAL (Fr) [87] 9-7 T Quinn (10) *trkd ldrs, badly hmpd and snatched up o'r one furlong out, not rcvr.* ....(12 to 1 tchd 14 to 1) 11
213* BRACKENTHWAITE [59] 7-7 J Fanning (11) *settled in last pl, feeling pace and hrd at work entering strt, nvr dngrs*....(3 to 1 fav op 5 to 2 tchd 2 to 1 and 7 to 2) 12
209⁷ MR GENEAOLOGY (USA) [76] (bl) 8-10 W Ryan (8) *struggling to keep up hfwy, tld off last 3 fs.* ....(33 to 1 op 25 to 1) 13
Dist: ¾l, hd, 3½l, hd, 1½l, 1½l, 1l, ¾l, 1½l, 1½l. 2m 9.01s. a 2.31s (13 Ran).
SR: 34/22/30/26/30/22/30/12/8/ (Lord Matthews), R J R Williams

ST-CLOUD (FR) (soft)
Thursday March 25th
Going Correction: PLUS 0.30 sec. per fur.

296 Prix Ronde de Nuit (Listed) (3-y-o) £14,337 1¼m 110yds......................(2:50)

4693a⁴ ACCOMMODATING (USA) 8-9 F Head,.................. 1
APPLIANCE 8-9 S Guillot,.............................. 2
AIR REVEUSE (Ire) 8-9 C Asmussen,.................. 3
MY FABULEUSE (Fr) 8-9 G Guignard,.................. 4
Dist: 3l, 2l, 2½l, ½l, 1l, 5l. 2m 18.00s. a 7.50s (7 Ran).
SR: 52/46/42/37/ (Mme F Boutin), F Boutin

THURLES (IRE) (yielding)
Thursday March 25th

297 Silvermines Maiden (3-y-o) £2,243 1½m 110yds............................(4:00)

MAN OF ARRAN (Ire) 8-12 (2*) R M Burke (13).... (14 to 1) 1
257⁷ ABSOLUTE JAMBOREE 9-0 S Craine (5)..........(7 to 1) 2
MAJESTIC JOHN (Ire) 8-12 (2*) D G O'Shea (1)....(14 to 1) 3
ANY MINUTE NOW (Ire) 9-0 J P Murtagh (16)..... (14 to 1) 4
282 GLAS AGUS OR (Ire) 8-5 (6*) J A Heffernan (14) (5 to 4 fav) 5
GIFT OF PEACE (Ire) 8-11 P V Gilson (3)...........(6 to 1) 6
257 TANGO IN PARIS (Arg) 8-8 (6*) P Carberry (12).... (12 to 1) 7
282 TANHONEY (Ire) 8-11 G Curran (8)...............(12 to 1) 8
257 ISLAND VISION (Ire) 9-0 W J Supple (7).......... (14 to 1) 9
BIZANA (Ire) 9-0 R Hughes (6)....................(8 to 1) 10
IRISH WEDDING (Ire) 8-11 W J O'Connor (2)......(10 to 1) 11
MILLMOUNT (Ire) 8-11 P Shanahan (17)...........(7 to 1) 12
257 TREBLE BOB (Ire) 8-10 (4*) W J Smith (11)....... (10 to 1) 13
RED ROOSTER (Ire) 8-6 (8*) J A Nagle (10)........ (20 to 1) 14
258 BRASS BUTTON (Ire) 8-11 N G McCullagh (9).... (12 to 1) 15
Dist: 1l, 4½l, ½l, sht-hd. 2m 54.90s. (15 Ran).
(Patrick O'Leary), Patrick O'Leary

298 Galtee Handicap (4-y-o and up) £2,243 2m ....(5:00)

SYLVIA FOX [-] 6-9-7 P Shanahan (13).........(7 to 4 fav) 1
SHARP INVITE [-] 6-8-1 W J Supple (10).......... (8 to 1) 2
CEDAR COURT (Ire) [-] (bl) 5-9-11 C F Swan (17)..(10 to 1) 3
FINAL FAVOUR (Ire) [-] 4-9-5 J P Murtagh (5)..... (12 to 1) 4
RANDOM PRINCE [-] 9-7-1 (8*) P P Murphy (15)....(8 to 1) 5
STYLE AND CLASS [-] 4-8-11 D Manning (9)......(14 to 1) 6
MARIAN YEAR [-] 7-7-11 (4*) W J Smith (18)...... (14 to 1) 7
KINVARA LADY (Ire) [-] 4-6-11 (10*) L O'Shea (7).. (50 to 1) 8
SIMPLY SWIFT [-] 6-9-7 S Craine (8)..............(9 to 2) 9
LYPHARD ABU (Ire) [-] 5-9-11 C Roche (6).........(8 to 1) 10
PRINCE YAZA [-] 6-9-11 W J O'Connor (1)....... (14 to 1) 11
WOODFIELD ROSE [-] 4-8-1 (10*) B Fenton (14)...(33 to 1) 12
AEGEAN FANFARE (Ire) [-] 4-9-12 R Hughes (12)..(12 to 1) 13
PRINCE PERICLES (Ire) [-] 4-9-1 (10*) J F Clarke (11) ....(20 to 1) 14
281 RIENZI [-] 9-8-10 P V Gilson (2)................. (14 to 1) 15
NISHA SOCIETY (Ire) [-] (bl) 4-9-2 N G McCullagh (3) ....(33 to 1) 16
STRAWBERRY DOLLAR [-] (bl) 8-8-10 (2*) D G O'Shea (16) ....(33 to 1) 17
FAMOUS DANCER [-] 5-8-1 (8*) B Bowens (4).... (14 to 1) 18
Dist: 1l, ¾l, 2l, ½l. 3m 47.00s. (18 Ran).
(Mrs C L Weld), D K Weld

DONCASTER (good to firm)
Friday March 26th
Going Correction: MINUS 0.30 sec. per fur.

299 South Yorkshire Maiden Selling Stakes Class F (2-y-o) £2,243 5f............(1:40)

BEST KEPT SECRET 9-0 J Carroll (7) *nvr far away, drvn alng hfwy, led o'r one furlong out, rdn clr.* ....(6 to 1 op 3 to 1) 1
RISKIE THINGS 8-9 B Rouse (12) *wth ldr, chsd alng o'r one furlong out, kpt on wl.* ....(7 to 1 op 10 to 1 tchd 6 to 1) 2

TURTLE ROCK 9-0 K Darley (11) *sluggish strt, ran green and a lot to do hfwy, rapid hdwy entering fnl furlong, fnshd wl.*.........(9 to 4 fav tchd 11 to 4 and 2 to 1) 3

SADDAM THE LOG 8-9 A Mackay (8) *made most for o'r 3 fs, fdd ins last.*..............(3 to 1 op 5 to 1 tchd 5 to 2) 4

ROCKABYE BAILEYS 8-9 Dean McKeown (9) *nvr far away, feeling pace and drvn alng 2 fs out, no extr.* ....(12 to 1 op 8 to 1 tchd 14 to 1) 5

LYING EYES 8-9 T Sprake (13) *chsd alng in midfield, styd on und pres appr fnl furlong, nrst finish.* ....(14 to 1 op 12 to 1 tchd 20 to 1) 6

RUSTUS 8-9 S Webster (6) *bustled alng in midfield hfwy, ran on wl ins fnl furlong, nvr nrr.* (25 to 1 op 20 to 1) 7

DUCHESS DAISY 8-9 Kim Tinkler (5) *missed break, bustled alng thrght, nvr dngrs.*...........(14 to 1 op 10 to 1) 8

YOUNG MEDIC 8-7 (7*) G Parkin (10) *missed break, nvr able to reco'r.*.....................(25 to 1 op 16 to 1) 9

GENERAL FAIRFAX (Ire) 9-0 T Quinn (3) *sn drvn alng to go pace, nvr a factor.*...(16 to 1 op 14 to 1 tchd 20 to 1) 10

DOUBLE-D (Ire) 8-4 (5*) M Fenton (1) *broke wl to show early pace, rdn alng hfwy, sn btn.* ....(9 to 1 op 6 to 1 tchd 12 to 1) 11

KALAKAFU 8-9 L Dettori (4) *chsd alng to keep up, nvr a threat.*...............(16 to 1 op 12 to 1 tchd 20 to 1) 12

LADY SWIFT 8-9 A Munro (2) *sluggish strt, drvn alng on outsd hfwy, sn btn.*..(16 to 1 op 12 to 1 tchd 20 to 1) 13

Dist: 2½l, 2½l, nk, 1½l, 1½l, 2½l, 7l, 2l, 2½l, hd. 1m 1.49s. a 2.69s (13 Ran).

SR: 16/1/-/-/-/-/ (Manny Bernstein (Racing) Ltd), J Berry

300 Doncaster Exhibition Centre Maiden Stakes Class D (3-y-o) £2,880 7f.....(2:10)

THUNDER RIVER (Ire) 9-0 T Quinn (7) *wth ldr, nosed ahead o'r one furlong out, shaken up fnl furlong, pushed out.* ....(10 to 1 op 12 to 1) 1

SECRET ALY (Can) 8-9 (5*) B Doyle (11) *tried to make all, hdd and drvn alng o'r one furlong out, rallied.* (8 to 1) 2

COMPLETE MADNESS 9-0 M Hills (5) *nvr far away, hrd at work whn pace lifted o'r 2 fs out, kpt on same pace.* ....(13 to 8 fav op 7 to 4 tchd 2 to 1) 3

HOSTILE WITNESS (Ire) 9-0 Pat Eddery (4) *sluggish strt, drvn into midfield hfwy, styd on und pres last 2 fs.* ....(9 to 1 op 8 to 1) 4

IMPERIAL TOKAY (USA) 9-0 D Holland (1) *very slwly away, improved on outsd hfwy, ran green, no imprsn.* ....(9 to 1 op 8 to 1 tchd 10 to 1) 5

SALVATORE GIULIANO 9-0 J Lowe (9) *ducked lft strt, improved into midfield hfwy, sn drvn alng and no imprsn.*..........................(25 to 1 op 20 to 1) 6

ROSIE O'REILLY (Ire) 8-9 K Fallon (8) *broke wl to show gd speed in frnt rnk for o'r 5 fs, fdd.*..(50 to 1 op 33 to 1) 7

RICH ASSET (Ire) 9-0 A Culhane (6) *missed break, nvr able to reco'r.*............(25 to 1 op 20 to 1 tchd 33 to 1) 8

4697a DICKINS 9-0 K Darley (3) *missed break, al struggling.* ....(25 to 1 op 20 to 1) 9

L'AIGLE D'OR (USA) 9-0 Paul Eddery (2) *sluggish strt, struggling thrght.*...................(3 to 1 op 2 to 1) 10

SMITH N'ALLAN 9-0 N Day (10) *trkd ldrs, hrd at work whn pace quickened o'r 2 fs out, sn btn.* ....(25 to 1 tchd 33 to 1) 11

Dist: Nk, 10l, 2½l, 2½l, 8l, 5l, 1½l, nk, 1l, 2½l. 1m 26.12s. a 2.72s (11 Ran).

SR: 28/27/-/-/-/-/ (Mrs Elaine Mitchell), M J Heaton-Ellis

301 Holroyd Construction Group Handicap Stakes Class C (0-95 3-y-o and up) £4,160 6f..................................(2:40)

GORINSKY (Ire) [67] 5-8-3 J Carroll (6) *made all, hrd pressed appr fnl furlong, kpt on strly.* (9 to 2 jt-fav tchd 11 to 2) 1

242[4] MISDEMEANOURS GIRL (Ire) [68] 5-7-13 (5*) B Doyle (7) *nvr far away, ev ch and drvn alng o'r one furlong out, kpt on.*..........................(14 to 1 tchd 12 to 1) 2

170[3] ASSIGNMENT [76] 7-8-12 R Cochrane (8) *al wl plcd, ev ch and drvn alng ins fnl furlong, ran on same pace.* ....(6 to 1 tchd 7 to 1) 3

ADWICK PARK [82] 5-9-4 M Hills (5) *drvn alng to show gd speed thrght, not quicken ins fnl furlong.* ....(5 to 1 op 9 to 2 tchd 11 to 2) 4

255* LOVE LEGEND [72] 8-8-8 T Quinn (9) *nvr far awy, ev ch and drvn alng 2 fs out, kpt on same pace.* (9 to 2 jt-fav op 7 to 2 tchd 5 to 1) 5

SEA DEVIL [79] 7-9-1 N Connorton (2) *patiently rdn, improved into midfield hfwy, staying on finish.* ....(12 to 1) 6

CASTLEREA LAD [73] 4-8-9 Pat Eddery (4) *patiently rdn, drvn to improve hfwy, prmsg effrt whn not clr run and snatched up ins fnl furlong.*........(8 to 1 op 10 to 1) 7

DENSBEN [84] 9-9-6 K Fallon (1) *steadied strt, improved frm hfwy, rng on finish.*...........(10 to 1 op 7 to 1) 8

SENSE OF PRIORITY [92] 4-10-0 K Darley (10) *sluggish strt, chsd alng and some hdwy whn hmpd and checked o'r 2 fs out, no imprsn.*..............(20 to 1 op 16 to 1) 9

HALBERT [78] 4-9-0 J Reid (11) *broke wl to show speed 4 fs, fdd.*..............(11 to 1 op 10 to 1 tchd 12 to 1) 10

252[9] NUTTY BROWN [74] 3-7-10 Dale Gibson (3) *drvn alng on outsd, feeling pace hfwy, sn btn.* (20 to 1 tchd 25 to 1) 11

Dist: 1l, 1½l, hd, nk, ¾l, nk, ¾l, 5l, 1½l, 1l. 1m 12.72s. a 1.32s (11 Ran).

SR: 27/24/26/31/20/24/17/25/13/ (William Robertson), J Berry

302 William Hill Spring Mile Handicap Class B (4-y-o and up) £18,910 1m.......... (3:10)

274[9] CEE-JAY-AY [55] 6-8-4 J Carroll (16) *sluggish strt, improved centre o'r 2 fs out, led appr fnl furlong, sprinted clr.*......................(25 to 1 op 20 to 1) 1

249* HENIU (USA) [64] (v) 4-8-13 (5ex) T Quinn (17) *wth ldrs stands side thrght, kpt on wl fnl furlong.* ....(6 to 1 fav op 9 to 2 tchd 13 to 2) 2

249[9] KISSAVOS [50] 7-7-10 (3*) F Norton (24) *chsd alng wth stands side bunch, styd on strly appr fnl furlong, fnshd wl.*.......................................(25 to 1) 3

INDIAN SLAVE (Ire) [67] 5-8-13 (3*) D Harrison (5) *chsd far side bunch, rdn to improve last 2 fs, ran on wl.* ....(14 to 1 tchd 16 to 1) 4

264[4] SALBYNG [60] 5-8-9 D Holland (18) *wth ldrs stands side, drvn alng o'r one furlong out, ran on same pace.* ....(16 to 1 tchd 18 to 1) 5

247[6] ALLINSON'S MATE (Ire) [72] 5-9-7 Alex Greaves (9) *trkd far side ldrs, improved o'r 2 fs out, rng on finish.* ....(10 to 1 op 12 to 1 tchd 14 to 1) 6

254[6] FALCONS DAWN [54] 6-8-0 (3*) A Tucker (19) *bustled alng to improve stands side o'r 2 fs out, ran on finish.* ....(25 to 1 op 33 to 1) 7

247* CHATHAM ISLAND [69] 5-8-13 (5*,5ex) B Doyle (4) *chsd ldg pair far side for o'r 5 fs, not quicken.* ....(10 to 1 tchd 14 to 1) 8

LEIF THE LUCKY (USA) [69] 4-9-4 N Connorton (8) *chsd far side bunch, improved o'r 2 fs out, styd on.*.... (33 to 1) 9

211* COLTRANE [62] (v) 5-8-11 A Munro (11) *wth ldrs stands side for o'r 5 fs, no extr.* ....(14 to 1 op 12 to 1 tchd 16 to 1) 10

DOMICKSKY [67] 5-9-2 Paul Eddery (22) *trkd ldrs stands side, led hfwy to appr fnl furlong, no extr.* ....(14 to 1 op 16 to 1) 11

TAHITIAN [67] 4-9-2 K Fallon (13) *wth ldrs stands side till fdd o'r one furlong out.* (9 to 1 op 8 to 1 tchd 10 to 1) 12

254[5] LOOKINGFORARAINBOW (Ire) [57] 5-8-6 N Day (14) *chsd stands side bunch, drvn alng o'r 2 fs out, no imprsn.* ....(25 to 1 op 33 to 1) 13

242[3] ROSEATE LODGE [70] 7-9-5 G Carter (12) *in tch, effrt and drvn alng o'r 2 fs out, no imprsn.* ....(11 to 1 op 10 to 1 tchd 12 to 1) 14

HABETA (USA) [59] 7-8-8 G Duffield (10) *chsd alng far side, nvr able to rch chalg pos.*....... (14 to 1 tchd 16 to 1) 15

GANT BLEU (Fr) [60] 6-8-9 A Culhane (6) *trkd far side bunch, led that grp o'r one furlong out, fdd.*..(33 to 1) 16

232[4] KILLY [68] 4-9-3 W Carson (2) *wth ldr far side for o'r 6 fs, fdd.*..(14 to 1) 17

SPANISH VERDICT [68] 6-8-10 (7*) C Teague (3) *led far side bunch till wknd and hdd o'r one furlong out.* (33 to 1) 18

274* MENTALASANYTHIN [68] 4-9-3 A Mackay (7) *chsd alng far side to keep up hfwy, nvr a threat.*........... (20 to 1) 19

AFFIDARE (Ire) [63] 4-8-12 J Lowe (23) *chsd alng wth stands side bunch, fdd o'r 2 fs out.*...........(50 to 1) 20

LEAP IN THE DARK (Ire) [62] 4-8-11 Pat Eddery (20) *slight ld stands side to hfwy, fdd 2 fs out.* ....(16 to 1 op 14 to 1 tchd 20 to 1) 21

274 RED KITE [62] (bl) 4-8-6 (5*) M Fenton (21) *wth ldrs stands side till wknd last 2 fs.*........................(20 to 1) 22

200[5] MADAGANS GREY [67] 5-9-2 R Cochrane (15) *gd speed stands side for o'r 5 fs, fdd.*..................(33 to 1) 23

Dist: 2½l, sht-hd, hd, nk, hd, nk, sht-hd, ¾l, ¾l, ½l. 1m 38.11s. a 1.31s (23 Ran).

SR: 34/35/20/36/28/39/20/34/32/ (Richard Jinks), J Berry

303 Cystic Fibrosis Research Cup Handicap Stakes Class C (0-90 4-y-o and up) £6,400 2 ¼m................................ (3:40)

SNOW BOARD [59] 4-7-9 W Carson (1) *tucked away gng wl, not much room entering strt, not clr run o'r 2 fs out and over one out, led ins last, ran on well.* ....(7 to 4 fav op 9 to 4) 1

TAROUDANT [60] 6-8-2 K Darley (8) *patiently rdn, improved frm midfield o'r 2 fs out, styd on und pres.* ....(12 to 1 op 10 to 1) 2

JACK BUTTON (Ire) [78] 4-9-0 N Day (5) *trkd ldr, led appr strt, rdn and hdd fnl furlong, one pace.* ....(8 to 1 op 10 to 1) 3

AVRO ANSON [58] 5-8-0[1] N Connorton (10) *settled midfield, not much room appr strt, effrt and edgd lft o'r 2 out, one pace.*...................(4 to 1 tchd 9 to 2) 4

164[8] ADMINISTER [52] (bl) 5-7-1 (7*) D Wright (3) *beh and a lot to do hfwy, rapid hdwy appr fnl furlong, fnshd wl.* ....(50 to 1 op 33 to 1) 5

SILLARS STALKER (Ire) [51] 5-7-7 J Lowe (14) *patiently rdn, improved frm off the pace o'r 2 fs out, styd on und pres, nvr nrr.*........................(5 to 1 tchd 9 to 2) 6

FARSI [86] 5-10-0 R Cochrane (16) *wtd wth, chsd alng to improve frm off the pace o'r 2 fs out, styd on, no imprsn.*.........................(12 to 1 tchd 14 to 1) 7

FRENCH IVY (USA) [83] 6-9-11 K Fallon (4) *chsd ldg bunch, effrt on ins o'r 2 fs out, nvr able to chal.* ....(50 to 1 op 33 to 1) 8
CREEAGER [66] 11-8-8 J Williams (12) *hld up and beh, drvn alng and hdwy o'r 2 fs out, not rch ldrs.* (20 to 1) 9
25⁶ POSTAGE STAMP [64] 6-8-6 T Quinn (15) *nvr far away, ev ch and rdn o'r 2 fs out, no extr*...(14 to 1 tchd 16 to 1) 10
182⁵ AUDE LA BELLE (Fr) [73] 5-8-12 (3*) F Norton (11) *patiently rdn, imprvg on ins whn badly baulked o'r 2 fs out, not rcvr*........(16 to 1 op 14 to 1) 11
279⁶ BEDOUIN PRINCE (USA) [51] (bl) 6-7-7 N Adams (13) *trkd ldrs, feeling pace and losing grnd whn hmpd o'r 2 fs out*........(33 to 1 op 25 to 1) 12
137⁷ GREEN LANE (USA) [71] 5-8-10 (3*) J Weaver (9) *settled to track ldg bunch, feeling pace entering strt, nvr dngrs.* ....(16 to 1 op 14 to 1) 13
226⁷ LAFKADIO [51] 6-7-0 (7*) Darren Moffatt (6) *trkd ldrs, ev ch entering strt, fdd o'r 2 fs out*.......(50 to 1 op 33 to 1) 14
CHARLIE DICKINS [51] 9-7-7 N Carlisle (7) *trkd ldg trio to strt, fdd*........(66 to 1 op 50 to 1) 15
165 CARDEA CASTLE (Ire) [51] 5-7-7 S Wood (2) *led till appr strt, wknd and lost tch o'r 3 fs out.* ....(100 to 1 op 50 to 1) 16
Dist: 1½l, hd, 1½l, hd, 1½l, 5l, ¾l, nk, hd, 1½l. 3m 56.00s. a 4.00s (16 Ran).
SR: -/-/3/-/-/-/7/2/-/ (J Hanson), B W Hills

304 Richards Cystic Fibrosis Maiden Stakes Class D (3-y-o) £2,880 1m..........(4:10)

MARASTANI (USA) 9-0 J Reid (7) *al hndy, drvn to nose ahead o'r 2 fs out, ran on gmely ins fnl furlong.* ....(5 to 2 fav tchd 11 to 4 and 2 to 1) 1
KINEMA RED (USA) 9-0 Pat Eddery (6) *co'red up in mid-field, swtchd outsd to draw level over 2 fs out, hrd rdn fnl furlong, jst hld*...... (9 to 2 op 3 to 1 tchd 5 to 1) 2
BITTER'S END (Ire) 9-0 W R Swinburn (12) *al tracking ldrs, feeling pace hfwy, ev ch o'r one out, hrd rdn and ran on towards finish*........ (10 to 1 tchd 12 to 1) 3
ERTLON 9-0 J Penza (5) *tried to make all, hdd and drvn alng o'r 2 fs out, wknd and edgd lft fnl furlong.* ....(11 to 2 op 4 to 1 tchd 6 to 1) 4
CIVIL LAW (Ire) 9-0 L Dettori (11) *nvr far away, feeling pace and drvn alng o'r 2 fs out, not quicken.* ....(11 to 1 op 10 to 1 tchd 12 to 1) 5
ABJAR 9-0 A Munro (13) *chsd alng in midfield hfwy, styd on last 2 fs, nrst finish.* ....(14 to 1 op 12 to 1 tchd 16 to 1) 6
STYLISH ROSE (Ire) 8-9 J Lowe (2) *broke wl to show gd speed in frnt rnk for o'r 5 fs, fdd*...(25 to 1 op 20 to 1) 7
PEACEFULL REPLY (USA) 9-0 R Lappin (14) *rcd very freely in midfield to hfwy, kpt on same pace last 2 fs.* (20 to 1) 8
HONEY GUIDE 9-0 W Woods (8) *sluggish strt, effrt and pushed alng hfwy, nvr able to chal*........ (33 to 1) 9
COLLIER BAY 9-0 R Cochrane (15) *last hfwy, nvr able to trble ldrs*........(16 to 1 op 20 to 1) 10
WHITE CREEK (Ire) 9-0 J Carroll (4) *broke wl to show speed for o'r 5 fs, fdd*........ (4 to 1 op 6 to 1 tchd 7 to 1) 11
GRENOBLE (Ire) 8-9 K Darley (3) *sluggish strt, effrt and chsd alng on outsd hfwy*........(33 to 1) 12
CHIEF'S SONG 9-0 D Holland (9) *sluggish strt, badly baulked and snatched up o'r 5 fs out, effrt hfwy, edgd lft, sn btn*........ (11 to 1 op 8 to 1 tchd 12 to 1) 13
MR LUCIANO (Ire) 9-0 P Smith (10) *chsd ldrs for o'r 5 fs, fdd*........(25 to 1) 14
BOLD LINE 8-9 Dale Gibson (1) *struggling to keep up hfwy, sn btn*........ (33 to 1 op 25 to 1) 15
Dist: Hd, nk, 3½l, 6l, 1½l, 3½l, ¾l, 1l, ½l, 1½l. 1m 37.92s. a 1.12s (15 Ran).
SR: 47/46/45/34/16/11/ (Cecil J Hedigan), G Harwood

CURRAGH (IRE) (soft)
Saturday March 27th
Going Correction: PLUS 1.00 sec. per fur. (races 1,5,6), PLUS 1.40 (2,3,4,7)

305 Irish Life Investment Managers (EBF) Maiden (2-y-o) £4,830 5f........... (2:00)

COIS NA TINE (Ire) 9-0 C Roche (7)........ (5 to 4 fav) 1
269⁹ TRIMBLEMILL (Ire) 9-0 B Coogan (6)........(8 to 1) 2
269⁴ AVONDALE FOREST (Ire) 8-11 S Craine (1)........(10 to 1) 3
GENUINE BID (Ire) 9-0 J P Murtagh (5)........(9 to 1) 4
269⁶ BONNIE CRATHIE (Ire) 8-11 P V Gilson (8)........(12 to 1) 5
269³ OLIVER MESSEL (Ire) 9-0 W J Supple (2)........(5 to 2) 6
SPRING FORCE (Ire) 9-0 W J O'Connor (4)........(10 to 1) 7
ASTRO REEF (Ire) 9-0 P Shanahan (3)........(14 to 1) 8
DEARMISTERSHATTER (Ire) 9-0 Joanna Morgan (9) ....(20 to 1) 9
BOY IN BLACK (Ire) 9-0 N G McCullagh (10)........(25 to 1) 10
Dist: ½l, sht-hd, ¾l, 2l. 1m 7.00s. a 8.70s (10 Ran).
SR: 26/24/20/20/9/-/ (Niall Quinn), J S Bolger

306 Irish Life Assurance EBF Race (3-y-o) £4,140 1m........................ (2:30)

SHAHZADI (Ire) 8-8 D Hogan (8)........(12 to 1) 1
257* FARMAAN (Ire) 8-12 R Hughes (1)........(3 to 1) 2
PERFECT IMPOSTER (Ire) 9-2 C Roche (2).. (11 to 10 fav) 3
GENERAL CHAOS (Ire) 8-8 P V Gilson (9)........ (14 to 1) 4
256* READY (Ire) 8-12 W J Supple (7)........(9 to 2) 5
SIR SLAVES 8-11 P Shanahan (3)........(12 to 1) 6
257³ SCHMEICHEL (Ire) 8-8 S Craine (5)........(8 to 1) 7
TAKE NO CHANCES (Ire) 8-11 W J O'Connor (6)... (8 to 1) 8
Dist: ½l, ¾l, 1l, ¾l. 1m 50.90s. a 14.30s (8 Ran).
SR: 47/49/51/40/42/ (H H Aga Khan), John M Oxx

307 Kilbelin Handicap (0-85) (0-85 3-y-o) £3,105 1m 1f............................(3:00)

TOPOGRAPHE (Fr) [-] 8-13 (8*) D J O'Donohoe (13) ....(4 to 1 fav) 1
281² COOLRAIN LADY (Ire) [-] 8-5¹ R Hughes (11)..... (13 to 2) 2
NEVER BACK DOWN (Ire) [-] 8-13 N G McCullagh (7) ....(13 to 2) 3
268* BOBROSS (Ire) [-] 8-4 (6*,5ex) J A Heffernan (8)... (10 to 1) 4
281 KENTUCKY BABY (Ire) [-] (bl) 8-10 S Craine (5)....(8 to 1) 5
268⁷ KELLSBORO LASS (Ire) [-] 9-1 J P Murtagh (6)....(14 to 1) 6
267⁸ WARREN STREET (Ire) [-] 8-8 D Hogan (10)........(14 to 1) 7
CARAVELLE LAD (Ire) [-] 8-8 P V Gilson (3)........ (8 to 1) 8
268³ ROOTSMAN (Ire) [-] 9-0 W J Supple (12)........ (14 to 1) 9
MOUNT OVAL (Ire) [-] 8-7 (2*) D G O'Shea (14).... (20 to 1) 10
268 BRIGENSER (Ire) [-] 8-10 K J Manning (15)........ (16 to 1) 11
268² SLIGHTLY SCRUFFY (Ire) [-] 8-4 P Lowry (9)........(14 to 1) 12
NORDIC UNION (Ire) [-] 8-11 C Roche (1)........(13 to 2) 13
IBDA [-] 8-9 (6*) B J Walsh (2)........ (6 to 1) 14
GLANCE CARD (Ire) [-] 8-7 B Coogan (4)........ (16 to 1) 15
Dist: Hd, 2½l, 1½l, 2l. 2m 7.40s. a 17.90s (15 Ran).
SR: 28/11/11/3/-/-/ (Mrs A J F O'Reilly), D K Weld

308 Irish Life Lincolnshire Handicap (0-110) (0-110 4-y-o and up) £9,750 1m..... (3:30)

272* TONY'S FEN [-] 4-8-2 (4ex) W J Supple (11)....(4 to 1 fav) 1
FAYDINI (Ire) [-] 4-8-2 N G McCullagh (10)........ (16 to 1) 2
SEDOV (USA) [-] 4-6-13 (8*) P P Murphy (21)........(12 to 1) 3
SALMON EILE (Ire) [-] 5-9-4 S Craine (12)........(8 to 1) 4
BALLYKETT PRINCE (Ire) [-] (bl) 5-9-7 K J Manning (18) ....(14 to 1) 5
DONNASOO (Ire) [-] 4-7-7 Joanna Morgan (6)........(20 to 1) 6
281² ARLINGTON HEIGHTS (Ire) [-] 4-7-1² (8*) R T Fitzpatrick (7) ....(16 to 1) 7
272³ NINJA DANCER (USA) [-] 4-8-9 (8*) D J O'Donohoe (8) ....(7 to 1) 8
MAGIC ARTS (Ire) [-] 5-7-5 (2*) D G O'Shea (14)... (33 to 1) 9
272⁵ WINNING HEART [-] (bl) 6-9-3 J P Murtagh (16)... (12 to 1) 10
4684a⁵ KAYFA (Ire) [-] 4-7-12 (6*) J A Heffernan (3)........ (12 to 1) 11
FOREST CONCERT (Ire) [-] 4-7-13 (2*) R M Burke (5) ....(14 to 1) 12
272⁷ SHIRWAN (Ire) [-] 4-7-7 (4*) W J Smith (19)........ (20 to 1) 13
ORMSBY (Ire) [-] 4-9-10 P Shanahan (9)........(14 to 1) 14
272 MONTEFIORE [-] 8-8-5 P V Gilson (4)........ (16 to 1) 15
272² NORDIC PAGEANT (Ire) [-] 4-9-4 C Roche (2)........ (6 to 1) 16
272 KAZKAR (Ire) [-] 5-8-6 R Hughes (13)........(16 to 1) 17
PENNINE PASS (Ire) [-] 4-7-8⁹ (8*) R V Skelly (17)..(16 to 1) 18
SIMPLY AMBER (Ire) [-] 5-7-7 A J Nolan (1)........ (33 to 1) 19
FOR REG (Ire) [-] 4-8-10 J D Eddery (15)........ (14 to 1) 20
Dist: Hd, ½l, 1½l, 1½l. 1m 50.80s. a 14.20s (20 Ran).
SR: 43/42/31/51/49/-/ (Mrs C Harrington), Kevin Prendergast

309 James & Karl Hannan (QR) Race (4-y-o and up) £4,155 2m................(4:00)

TIME FOR A RUN 6-11-3 Mr E Bolger (27)........(7 to 1) 1
RISZARD (USA) 4-11-3 Mr A P O'Brien (17)........(7 to 1) 2
FORCE SEVEN 6-10-9 (5*) Mrs S McCarthy (9)....(14 to 1) 3
I'VE TOPPED IT 8-11-3 Mr J A Flynn (7)........(10 to 1) 4
MRS DOESKIN (Ire) 5-11-5 Mr T Mullins (25)........(7 to 1) 5
4685a⁹ SANNDILA (Ire) 5-10-7 (7*) Mr E Norris (18).....(9 to 4 fav) 6
ARCTIC WEATHER (Ire) 4-10-12 (5*) Mr D Valentine (4) ....(12 to 1) 7
PAGET 6-10-10 (7*) Mr A K Wyse (3)........ (20 to 1) 8
BAYROUGE (Ire) 5-10-7 (7*) Mr R P Cody (26)......(6 to 1) 9
DUNFERNE CLASSIC (Ire) 4-11-3 Mr A J Martin (21) ....(16 to 1) 10
GALAVOTTI (Ire) 4-10-11¹ (7*) Mr J A Hayes (11).. (14 to 1) 11
CURRENCY BASKET (Ire) 4-11-3 (3*) Mr D Marnane (23) ....(5 to 1) 12
INDIANA GOLD (Ire) 5-10-7 (7*) Ms W Fox (10).... (20 to 1) 13
OPEN THE GATE 8-11-0 (3*) Mr S R Murphy (13).. (16 to 1) 14
LEGAL ADVISER 6-10-10 (7*) Mr E Kelly (28)......(12 to 1) 15
FRENCHMANS BUCK 8-10-10 (7*) Mr B Moran (15) ....(16 to 1) 16
MILTONFIELD 4-11-0 (3*) Miss C Hutchinson (24). (16 to 1) 17
LAY ONE ON YA (Ire) 5-10-10 (7*) Mr T N Cloke (1) (14 to 1) 18
NICKY'S RUN 6-10-12 (5*) Mr D P Murphy (8).....(16 to 1) 19
GILT DIMENSION 6-11-3 Mr W P Mullins (5)........ (12 to 1) 20
SYLVAN TEMPEST 7-10-10 (7*) Mr E Henley (16).. (20 to 1) 21
ALBERTS LADY (Ire) 4-10-7 (7*) Mr B Lennon (2).. (50 to 1) 22
COLLECTED (Ire) 4-10-7 (7*) Miss C Roger (12)... (33 to 1) 23
ALTEREZZA (USA) (bl) 6-10-10 (7*) Mr J A Nash (22) ....(10 to 1) 24
DAMODAR 4-10-10 (7*) Mr H F Cleary (14)........ (20 to 1) 25
SILVER GIPSEY 7-10-7 (7*) Mr K O'Sullivan (29)... (33 to 1) 26
CAHERASS KATE 8-10-10 (7*) Mr G Hogan (19)... (50 to 1) 27

PRECISE TIMING 5-10-10 (7*) Mr K Dempsey (6)..(12 to 1) 28
LA MAJA (Ire) 4-10-11 (3*) Miss M Olivefalk (20)...(25 to 1) 29
Dist: ½l, 4½l, 1½l, 6l. 3m 49.70s. a 28.20s (29 Ran).
SR: 9/8/-/1/-/-/ (John P McManus), E J O'Grady

310 Sunnyhill Handicap (0-90) (0-90 3-y-o and up) £3,105 6f......................(4:30)

CONS PRINCE (Ire) [-] 3-7-8 Joanna Morgan (9)....(7 to 1) 1
272⁶ BARNAGEERA BOY (Ire) [-] 4-6-13 (8*) B J Halligan (10) ....(10 to 1) 2
LORD GLENVARA (Ire) [-] 5-7-1 (8*) P P Murphy (11) ....(25 to 1) 3
FANTANTE (Ire) [-] 4-8-0 (2*) D G O'Shea (12).....(12 to 1) 4
LADY PRESIDENT (Ire) [-] 4-7-13 (2*) R M Burke (1) (11 to 2) 5
ISLAND HEATHER (Ire) [-] (bl) 5-9-1 K J Manning (15) ....(16 to 1) 6
WALLY WALLENSKY (Ire) [-] 3-8-6 R Hughes (3)....(7 to 1) 7
MAGIC DON (Ire) [-] 4-7-12 (8*) R T Fitzpatrick (14) (14 to 1) 8
HONORARY PRINCE (Ire) [-] 4-8-8 W J Supple (13) ....(4 to 1 fav) 9
ALBONA [-] (bl) 5-8-9 C Roche (2)...............(8 to 1) 10
SWEET NASHA (Ire) [-] 4-9-10 J P Murtagh (5)....(11 to 2) 11
MEMSAHB [-] 4-9-5 P Shanahan (7)...............(7 to 1) 12
270⁷ SOME FUN [-] 6-9-1 S Craine (4)...............(10 to 1) 13
THATCHING CRAFT (Ire) [-] 4-9-3 W J O'Connor (6) (12 to 1) 14
LUTE AND LYRE (Ire) [-] 4-9-8 (6*) C Everard (8)...(12 to 1) 15
Dist: 4½l, ¾l, 1½l, ½l. 1m 21.10s. a 10.60s (15 Ran).
(Vincent McFadden), D P Kelly

311 Black Ditch EBF Maiden (3-y-o) £3,450 7f ....(5:00)

KURDISTAN (Ire) 9-0 W J O'Connor (9)...........(10 to 1) 1
257⁴ DIFFERENT TIMES (Ire) 9-0 S Craine (24)..........(8 to 1) 2
256⁴ KHARASAR (Ire) 9-0 J P Murtagh (1)............(9 to 2) 3
L'EQUIPE (Ire) 8-6 (8*) M F Ryan (28)............(20 to 1) 4
SUAVE GROOM (Ire) 9-0 P Shanahan (3).......(7 to 4 fav) 5
BRITANNIA BAY (Ire) 9-0 P V Gilson (22)..........(11 to 2) 6
ROUNDWOOD ROSE (Ire) 8-11 W J Supple (17)..(14 to 1) 7
DRIFT APART (Ire) 8-11 G Curran (12)............(12 to 1) 8
280⁹ PERSIAN RENDEZVOUS (Ire) 9-0 E A Leonard (19) (25 to 1) 9
258⁵ SLEET (Ire) 8-3 (8*) J J Mullins (15)............(14 to 1) 10
STATION HOUSE (Ire) 9-0 N G McCullagh (10)....(14 to 1) 11
256 PHASE IN 8-6 (8*) J M Buckley (13)...............(33 to 1) 12
SARA MAURETTE (Ire) 8-11 N Byrne (20).........(25 to 1) 13
FAIRY BRIDE (Ire) 8-5 (6*) J A Heffernan (27).......(20 to 1) 14
BOB THE YANK (Ire) 8-12 (2*) R M Burke (25).....(20 to 1) 15
SHOWBOAT MELODY (Ire) 8-11 B Coogan (21)....(25 to 1) 16
REGAL PRETENDER (Ire) 9-0 R Hughes (4).......(33 to 1) 17
PENNY A DAY (Ire) 8-6 (8*) B A Hunter (11).......(20 to 1) 18
PLEASE WIDD (Ire) 8-11 K J Manning (18)........(12 to 1) 19
GREEN LIFE 8-11 C Roche (23)...............(12 to 1) 20
282 ADJAIYBA (USA) 8-5 (6*) B J Walsh (8)...........(50 to 1) 21
PERSIAN GEM (Ire) 8-11 J D Eddery (26).........(12 to 1) 22
SHY WIN (Ire) 8-3 (8*) P P Murphy (6)...........(50 to 1) 23
257 THE SALTY FROG (Ire) 8-4 (10*) T M Finn (16).....(50 to 1) 24
BIRTHPLACE (Ire) 8-12 (2*) D G O'Shea (5).......(14 to 1) 25
280 GOLDEN TARGET (USA) 8-11 E McCabe (2)......(20 to 1) 26
CALIANDAK (Ire) 9-0 D Hogan (14)...............(8 to 1) 27
Dist: ¾l, 1l, 2½l, sht-hd. 1m 37.40s. a 14.20s (27 Ran).
SR: 34/32/29/21/20/-/ (C S Gaisford-St Lawrence), Michael Kauntze

DONCASTER (good to firm) Saturday March 27th

Going Correction: MINUS 0.15 sec. per fur. (races 1,2,4,5,6), MINUS 0.40 (3,7)

312 EBF 'Superpower' Maiden Stakes Class D (2-y-o) £3,289 5f..................(2:00)

CAPE MERINO 8-9 M Birch (5) *made all, drw clr o'r one out, cmftbly*...............(33 to 1 op 25 to 1) 1
BOLD ARISTOCRAT (Ire) 9-0 S Perks (3) *wth ldr, rdn o'r one out, kpt on, no ch with wnr.* ....(8 to 1 op 10 to 1 tchd 7 to 1) 2
HILL FARM KATIE 8-9 L Dettori (2) *cl up, rdn 2 out, one paced*...............(10 to 1 op 16 to 1 tchd 8 to 1) 3
JASARI (Ire) 9-0 Pat Eddery (8) *beh till styd on fnl 2 fs, nrst finish*...............(5 to 1 tchd 6 to 1 and 9 to 2) 4
MONKEY MAGIC (Ire) 9-0 J Carroll (4) *trkd ldrs till hmpd and stumbled aftr one and a half fs, not reco'r.* ....(11 to 4 fav op 5 to 2 tchd 3 to 1) 5
SWEET WHISPER 8-9 K Darley (7) *wnt lft strt, beh, hdwy und pres hfwy, wknd o'r one out*....(5 to 1 op 3 to 1) 6
MAIDEN EFFORT 8-9 M Roberts (6) *chsd ldrs till wknd 2 out*...............(100 to 30 op 7 to 4) 7
MUCKROSS PARK 8-9 A Munro (1) *sn beh, tld off.* ....(12 to 1 tchd 14 to 1) 8
Dist: 4l, 1½l, nk, hd, ½l, 2½l, 12l. 1m 1.88s. a 3.08s (8 Ran).
SR: 18/7/-/-/-/ (Hugh Ellis), A Smith

313 'Raceform Horses In Training' Maiden Stakes Class D (3-y-o) £3,348 6f.....(2:30)

GARNOCK VALLEY 9-0 J Carroll (6) *made all, ran on wl.* ....(9 to 2 op 4 to 1) 1
GRAN SENORUM (USA) 9-0 A Munro (10) *slwly into strd, mid-div, pushed alng hfwy, styd on wl fnl 2 fs, not rch wnr*...............(7 to 2 jt-fav op 5 to 2) 2
FRIENDLY BRAVE (USA) 9-0 Pat Eddery (8) *prmnt, rdn o'r one out, kpt on same pace*......(7 to 2 jt-fav op 9 to 4) 3
ABLE CHOICE (Ire) 9-0 L Piggott (4) *beh till ran on wl fnl 2 fs, nrst finish*...............(5 to 1 tchd 6 to 1) 4
RED FAN (Ire) 9-0 N Connorton (3) *slwly into strd, beh till ran on wl fnl 2 fs, nrst finish*.... (16 to 1 tchd 20 to 1) 5
FOLLY VISION (Ire) 8-9 J Reid (9) *wth ldr till wknd o'r one out*............... (14 to 1 op 16 to 1) 6
FLASHMAN 9-0 M Roberts (7) *slwly into strd, sn chasing ldrs, swtchd and effrt hfwy, soon rdn and btn.* .... (9 to 1 op 12 to 1) 7
193⁵ MAGICATION 8-2 (7*) Claire Balding (2) *al beh*.... (33 to 1) 8
EXPORT MONDIAL 9-0 L Dettori (5) *prmnt till wknd 2 out.* ....(11 to 1 op 8 to 1 tchd 12 to 1) 9
SOLO CHARTER 9-0 P Robinson (1) *al beh*.......(25 to 1) 10
Dist: 1½l, 2½l, 2½l, 1l, hd, 6l, 1½l, 1l, 8l. 1m 13.64s. a 2.24s (10 Ran).
SR: 37/31/21/11/7/1/ (Robert Aird), J Berry

314 Hayselden Audi VW Doncaster Shield Class B Conditions Stakes (4-y-o and up) £7,002 1½m...................... (3:00)

SHAMBO 6-9-3 M Roberts (2) *trkd ldr, led 3 out, rdn and ran on wl*............(13 to 8 op 7 to 4 tchd 6 to 4) 1
YOUNG BUSTER (Ire) 5-9-2 W R Swinburn (3) *hld up gng wl, effrt o'r one out, sn rdn and no imprsn.* ....(13 to 8 on op 2 to 1 on tchd 6 to 4 on) 2
243* MODEST HOPE (USA) 6-9-0 A Mackay (1) *led till hdd 3 out, wknd o'r one out, eased whn btn fnl furlong.* ....(14 to 1 op 25 to 1 tchd 33 to 1) 3
Dist: ¾l, 12l. 2m 34.91s. a 4.41s (3 Ran).
SR: 11/8/-/ (Mrs C E Brittain), C E Brittain

315 William Hill Lincoln Handicap Class B (4-y-o and up) £48,412 1m.............(3:40)

HIGH PREMIUM [80] 5-8-8 K Fallon (5) *rcd far side, led aftr 3 fs, made rst, rdn o'r one out, styd on wl.* ....(16 to 1 tchd 20 to 1) 1
MIZAAYA [96] 4-9-10 W R Swinburn (6) *rcd far side, effrt 2 out, sn rdn and styd on wl*............... (12 to 1 op 10 to 1) 2
WILL OF STEEL [76] 4-7-13 (5*) B Doyle (9) *rcd far side, in tch, effrt 2 out, styd on wl und pres*..........(40 to 1) 3
4744a³ RINGLAND (USA) [79] 5-8-0 (7*) Darren Moffatt (4) *rcd far side, hld up, pushed alng o'r 3 out, styd on wl fnl furlong*...............(40 to 1) 4
LAUREL QUEEN (Ire) [74] 5-8-2² J Carroll (7) *rcd far side, in tch, kpt on wl fnl furlong*........(16 to 1 tchd 20 to 1) 5
BEWARE OF AGENTS [88] 4-9-2 Dean McKeown (2) *chsd ldrs far side, onepaced fnl 2 fs*.....(20 to 1 op 16 to 1) 6
BUZZARDS BELLBUOY [73] 4-8-1 J Quinn (18) *rcd stands side, hld up, effrt 3 out, not much room 2 out, styd on wl fnl furlong*.........(10 to 1 op 8 to 1 tchd 11 to 1) 7
ROYAL SEATON [85] 4-8-13 S Whitworth (23) *in tch stands side, swtchd and effrt 3 out, styd on wl frm 2 out.* ....(33 to 1) 8
222* SPENCER'S REVENGE [74] 4-7-13 (3*,5ex) D Harrison (1) *rcd far side, in tch till outpcd o'r 3 out, styd on fnl furlong*...............(12 to 1) 9
IMPERIAL BID (Fr) [73] 5-8-1 L Charnock (8) *prmnt far side till wknd 2 out*...............(50 to 1) 10
ASHDREN [75] 6-8-3 A Munro (19) *rcd stands side, in tch, kpt on fnl 2 fs, nvr dngrs.* ....(13 to 1 op 12 to 1 tchd 14 to 1) 11
WELL APPOINTED (Ire) [81] (bl) 4-8-9 D Holland (16) *rcd stands side, hld up, hdwy hfwy, wknd o'r one out.* ....(50 to 1) 12
EFHARISTO [89] 4-9-3 M Roberts (13) *prmnt till led stands side grp o'r 2 out, wknd entering fnl furlong.* ....(12 to 1 op 10 to 1) 13
AMAZING FEAT (Ire) [90] 4-9-4 K Darley (11) *rcd stands side, in tch, effrt o'r 2 out, no hdwy.* ....(10 to 1 op 7 to 1 tchd 11 to 1) 14
WALKING THE PLANK [73] 4-8-1 P Robinson (17) *rcd stands side, prmnt till wknd o'r 2 out*......... (66 to 1) 15
247³ MERLINS WISH (USA) [80] 4-8-8 B Rouse (10) *rcd stands side, in tch till wknd o'r 2 out*...............(33 to 1) 16
4782a AKKAZAO (Ire) [75] 5-7-12 (5*) N Gwilliams (12) *rcd stands side, prmnt till wknd o'r 2 out*............... (50 to 1) 17
GOLDEN CHIP (Ire) [75] 5-8-0 (3*) S Maloney (24) *led stands side grp till wknd o'r 2 out*...............(33 to 1) 18
274⁴ SHUJAN (USA) [73] 4-8-1 R Price (15) *rcd stands side, al beh*...............(16 to 1) 19
247 DASWAKI (Can) [77] 5-8-5² Pat Eddery (20) *rcd stands side, al beh*...............(7 to 1 fav op 10 to 1) 20
247⁷ MASNUN (USA) [80] 8-8-8 D Biggs (14) *rcd stands side, in tch till wknd o'r 2 out*...............(33 to 1) 21
MILLSOLIN (Ire) [76] 5-8-4 G Carter (22) *rcd stands side, in tch till wknd o'r 2 out*.........(10 to 1 tchd 12 to 1) 22
289⁸ AFRICAN CHIMES [77] (bl) 6-7-12 (7*) D McCabe (3) *led far side grp 3 fs, sn wknd and beh*...............(100 to 1) 23

PETITE-D-ARGENT [87] 4-9-1 L Piggott (21) *prmnt stands side till wknd quickly o'r 2 out, eased, tld off.* ....(13 to 1 op 12 to 1 tchd 11 to 1 and 14 to 1) 24
Dist: ½l, ¾l, 1½l, 3½l, hd, 1l, sht-hd, sht-hd, 2l, 1½l. 1m 37.90s. a 1.10s (24 Ran).
SR: 60/74/52/50/34/47/29/40/28/ (P A Leonard), Mrs J R Ramsden

316 Cammidge Trophy Class A (Listed Race) (3-y-o and up) £11,257 6f............(4:15)

REGAL CHIMES 4-9-2 A Munro (7) *made all, rdn o'r one out, hld on wl*..................(50 to 1 op 33 to 1) 1
SILCA-CISA 4-8-11 G Carter (11) *chsd ldrs, rdn 2 out, kpt on wl*...............(16 to 1 op 20 to 1 tchd 25 to 1) 2
285* APPLEDORN 6-8-11 L Dettori (4) *beh till styd on fnl 2 fs, nrst finish*..................(20 to 1 tchd 25 to 1) 3
MONTENDRE 6-9-7 J Reid (6) *in tch, kpt on same pace fnl 2 fs*..............................(6 to 1 op 4 to 1) 4
THOURIOS (v) 4-9-7 L Piggott (9) *chsd ldrs till wknd 2 out.* ....(5 to 4 fav op 6 to 4 tchd 6 to 5) 5
TAUFAN BLU (Ire) (bl) 4-8-11 Dean McKeown (8) *beh, sn pushed alng, some late hdwy, nvr dngrs.* .... (20 to 1 op 16 to 1) 6
NIGHT MELODY (Ire) 3-8-2 K Darley (5) *nvr nr to chal.* ....(16 to 1 op 14 to 1) 7
FYLDE FLYER 4-9-7 J Carroll (2) *chsd ldrs till wknd 2 out.* .... (5 to 1 op 4 to 1 tchd 11 to 2) 8
4702a* SWING LOW 4-9-9 Pat Eddery (3) *in tch, hdwy hfwy, wknd 2 out*..........................(7 to 1 op 6 to 1) 9
SPANISH STORM (Ire) 4-9-2 W Woods (10) *sn beh.* .... (25 to 1 op 20 to 1) 10
4666a^{6} BRANSTON ABBY (Ire) 4-8-11 M Roberts (1) *dwlt, in tch till wknd 2 out, eased whn btn.* .... (9 to 1 op 8 to 1 tchd 10 to 1) 11
Dist: ¾l, ½l, 2½l, 1½l, sht-hd, sht-hd, 1½l, 3l, 10l, hd. 1m 12.28s. a 0.88s (11 Ran).
SR: 66/58/56/56/50/39/29/42/32/ (Michael Sturgess), B A McMahon

317 Insurex Expo-Sure Group Handicap Class C (0-90 3-y-o) £4,751 7f............. (4:45)

MR BUTCH [68] 8-7 Pat Eddery (8) *hld up, smooth hdwy 3 out, led o'r one out, ran on wl.* (3 to 1 fav tchd 7 to 2) 1
WORDSMITH (Ire) [62] 8-1 P Robinson (5) *in tch, effrt 2 out, kpt on fnl furlong*.......(9 to 2 op 5 to 1 tchd 6 to 1) 2
MOVE SMARTLY (Ire) [63] 8-2 G Carter (4) *trkd ldrs, slight ld wl o'r one out, sn hdd, one pace.* (10 to 1 op 7 to 1) 3
UMBUBUZI (USA) [72] 8-11 R Lappin (2) *prmnt, ev ch o'r one out, kpt on same pace.* .... (14 to 1 op 10 to 1 tchd 16 to 1) 4
PRINCELY FAVOUR (Ire) [82] 9-7 B Rouse (9) *beh till styd on fnl 2 fs, nvr nrr*..........................(8 to 1 tchd 10 to 1) 5
277^{5} ROSE FLYER (Ire) [57] 7-10 S Wood (3) *slwly into strd, sn wth ldr, slight ld o'r 3 out till hdd wl over one out, soon wknd*..........................(12 to 1 op 10 to 1) 6
COSTA VERDE [80] 9-5 A Munro (6) *beh, effrt o'r 2 out, no hdwy*............................ (9 to 1 op 7 to 1 tchd 10 to 1) 7
SHADOW JURY [67] 8-6 K Darley (7) *in tch till lost pl hfwy, no dngr aftr*........... (9 to 1 op 8 to 1 tchd 10 to 1) 8
BEZIQUE (USA) [78] (bl) 9-3 M Roberts (1) *led till hdd o'r 3 out, sn wknd*..........................(7 to 2 op 9 to 4) 9
Dist: 1l, 4l, 5l, 1½l, 1½l, 1l, sht-hd, 1½l. 1m 26.31s. a 2.91s (9 Ran).
SR: 34/25/14/8/13/-/3/-/-/ (G Herridge), M R Channon

318 Mitsubishi Diamond Vision Maiden Stakes Class D (3-y-o) £3,494 1¼m 60yds...(5:15)

MAJORITY (Ire) 9-0 M Roberts (2) *trkd ldrs, led o'r one out, easily*..............(11 to 10 fav op 6 to 4 tchd Evens) 1
YAHMI (Ire) 9-0 M Hills (6) *chsd ldr, led o'r 2 out, hdd over one out, kpt on, no ch wth wnr.* .... (10 to 1 op 8 to 1 tchd 11 to 1) 2
RIVER NORTH (Ire) 9-0 K Darley (4) *beh, styd on wl fnl 3 fs, nrst finish*............................(16 to 1 op 14 to 1) 3
BROWN'S (Fr) 9-0 L Dettori (10) *led till hdd o'r 2 out, wknd over one out*...........................(3 to 1 op 4 to 1) 4
WINGS COVE 9-0 C Dwyer (1) *chsd ldrs till wknd o'r 2 out.* .... (25 to 1 op 20 to 1 tchd 33 to 1) 5
DEBOS 9-0 W R Swinburn (11) *in tch, effrt 4 out, no hdwy*...................................(7 to 1 op 5 to 1) 6
SIR EDWARD HENRY (Ire) 9-0 R Lappin (5) *al beh.* .... (33 to 1 op 20 to 1) 7
RANZEL 9-0 G Hind (3) *al beh*........ (12 to 1 op 8 to 1) 8
KEEP YOUR DISTANCE 8-7 (7*) Darren Moffatt (8) *sddl slpd, lost tch 4 out*.........................(20 to 1 op 25 to 1) 9
VICTORIAN FLOWER 8-4 (5*) B Doyle (9) *slwly into strd, al beh*...........................(20 to 1 tchd 25 to 1) 10
Dist: ¾l, 5l, 1½l, 10l, 6l, 12l, 2l, 8l, hd. 2m 7.50s. a 0.80s (10 Ran).
SR: 51/49/39/36/16/4/ (Sheikh Mohammed), B W Hills

LINGFIELD (A.W) (std)
Saturday March 27th
Going Correction: MINUS 0.25 sec. per fur.

319 Wellington Handicap Class E (0-70 4-y-o and up) £2,322 7f...................(2:20)

249^{4} SCOTS LAW [55] (bl) 6-9-2 (3*) J Weaver (8) *made all, hrd rdn o'r one furlong out, jst hld on.* (5 to 1 tchd 6 to 1) 1
249^{6} SARUM [54] 7-9-4 C Rutter (3) *chsd ldrs, rdn o'r 3 fs out, styd on wl ins last*..................(7 to 1 op 5 to 1) 2
217^{5} LADY ROXANNE [52] 4-9-2 W Newnes (9) *trkd ldr, rdn wl o'r one furlong out, kpt on.* .... (8 to 1 tchd 9 to 1 and 10 to 1) 3
260^{5} SUNSET STREET (Ire) [53] (e/s) 5-9-3 W Ryan (6) *midfield, rdn ove 2 fs out, kpt on fnl furlong, nrst finish.* .... (14 to 1 op 12 to 1) 4
263^{3} ZINBAQ [39] 7-8-3 S O'Gorman (4) *beh till styd on o'r one furlong out, nvr nrr*...................(7 to 1 op 5 to 1) 5
249^{3} NOBBY BARNES [63] 4-9-13 G Duffield (2) *sn pushed alng to chase ldr, rdn and wknd appr fnl furlong.* ....(7 to 2 fav op 9 to 2) 6
274^{3} QUINZII MARTIN [64] (v) 5-9-7 (7*) S McCarthy (5) *beh early, nvr able to chal*.................. (5 to 1 op 9 to 2) 7
247^{8} DANCE ON SIXPENCE [54] (v) 5-9-4 V Smith (7) *chsd ldrs, rdn 3 fs out, sn wknd*.............(8 to 1 tchd 10 to 1) 8
241^{7} LOOTING (USA) [36] 7-7-7 (7*) Kim McDonnell (10) *beh frm hfwy*..............................(20 to 1 tchd 33 to 1) 9+
263^{6} LITMORE DANCER [38] 5-7-13 (3*) F Norton (1) *beh and drpd out o'r 3 fs out, no hdwy*.....(20 to 1 op 14 to 1) 9+
Dist: Nk, hd, 2½l, hd, 2l, ¾l, 5l, 4l, dd-ht. 1m 25.84s. a 2.44s (10 Ran).
SR: 42/40/37/30/15/33/32/7/-/ (Mrs R J Doorgachurn), R J O'Sullivan

320 Adam 'Sweet Thing' Kean Claiming Stakes Class F (3-y-o and up) £1,882 6f ....(2:50)

170^{7} SOBA GUEST (Ire) 4-9-3 (3*) Emma O'Gorman (2) *trkd ldr gng wl, led o'r 2 fs out, pushed out, cmftbly.* ....(3 to 1 tchd 7 to 2) 1
260^{3} RESPECTABLE JONES 7-9-8 W Ryan (3) *hld up, hdwy o'r 2 fs out, styd on fnl furlong*........(3 to 1 tchd 7 to 2) 2
285^{2} CRECHE (bl) 4-9-3 (7*) E Husband (4) *led till hdd o'r 2 fs out, sn rdn and btn.* ....(6 to 4 on op 7 to 4 on tchd 11 to 8 on) 3
LOON 5-8-13 (3*) J Weaver (1) *sn rdn alng and struggling aftr 2 fs*..........................(33 to 1 op 20 to 1) 4
Dist: 2½l, 4l, 7l. 1m 13.12s. a 2.32s (4 Ran).
SR: 30/22/8/-/ (Richard Jinks), J Berry

321 Daily Star Challenge Handicap Qualifier Class E (0-70 4-y-o and up) £2,684 1¼m ....(3:25)

224^{2} GOLD BLADE [62] 4-9-8 W Ryan (7) *patiently rdn, smooth hdwy frm 4 fs out, shaken up to ld o'r one out, ran on.* ....(2 to 1 fav op 5 to 2 tchd 7 to 4) 1
224^{3} LOWAWATHA [62] 5-9-9 M Tebbutt (3) *chsd ldrs, hdwy to chal frm o'r 2 fs out, led briefly wl over one out, ran on und pres*..............(13 to 2 op 5 to 1 tchd 7 to 1) 2
261^{2} SET THE FASHION [50] (v) 4-8-10 G Duffield (6) *set gd pace till hdd wl o'r one furlong out, no extr.* ....(4 to 1 tchd 5 to 1) 3
264^{3} PREMIER DANCE [35] 6-7-7[4] (7*) S McCarthy (8) *chsd ldrs, ev ch o'r 2 fs out, kpt on same pace*.. (9 to 1 op 8 to 1) 4
234^{6} MODESTO (USA) [35] (bl) 5-7-7[2] (5*) A Garth (2) *dsptd ld 3 fs, sn rdn and lost pl, kpt on ag'n ins last.* ....(14 to 1 op 16 to 1 tchd 20 to 1) 5
249^{5} NORTH ESK (USA) [64] 4-9-10 W Newnes (9) *hld up till some hdwy 4 fs out, sn rdn and no imprsn*.....(10 to 1) 6
264^{7} PIGALLE WONDER [59] (bl) 5-9-3 (3*) J Weaver (5) *chsd ldrs till wknd 3 fs out*..................(8 to 1 tchd 9 to 1) 7
224* NATIVE CHIEFTAN [59] (e/s) 4-9-2 (3*) F Norton (1) *rdn alng aftr 4 fs, sn struggling*..............(6 to 1 op 9 to 2) 8
HIGHTOWN-PRINCESS (Ire) [35] (v) 5-7-3 (7*) Kim McDonnell (4) *slwly into strd, al beh.* ....(40 to 1 op 33 to 1 tchd 50 to 1) 9
Dist: 1½l, 5l, 2½l, 1½l, ¾l, 10l, 5l, 1½l. (Time not taken) (9 Ran).
(Paul G Jacobs), N A Graham

322 Halifax Handicap Class D (0-80 4-y-o and up) £3,055 1½m.....................(3:55)

265* LA REINE ROUGE (Ire) [46] 5-7-10[1] (3*) F Norton (4) *trkd ldrs, chlgd frm o'r 2 fs out, led over one out, hld on grimly*..........................(2 to 1 fav op 7 to 4) 1
MAJESTIC IMAGE [73] 7-9-4 (7*) J Wilkinson (2) *tucked in hndy, rdn and outpcd o'r 2 fs out till ran on strly over fnl furlong, gng on finish*............ (9 to 2 op 7 to 2) 2
DAY OF HISTORY (Ire) [44] 4-7-8[1] Dale Gibson (5) *took keen hold, wth ldr till wnt on and quickened pace o'r 3 fs out, hld over one out, rallied*........(8 to 1 op 5 to 1) 3
234^{2} AWESOME POWER [76] 7-10-0 W Ryan (6) *hld up, rdn o'r 2 fs out, kpt on ins last*..................(3 to 1 op 7 to 2) 4
58^{5} MR WISHING WELL [48] (e/s) 7-8-0 C Rutter (3) *hld up in tch, rdn o'r 2 fs out, ran on appr fnl furlong till no extr ins last*..........................(10 to 1 op 8 to 1) 5
210^{4} BEAM ME UP SCOTTY (Ire) [48] 4-7-12 S O'Gorman (1) *led till hdd o'r 3 fs out, wknd.* ....(9 to 2 op 5 to 1 tchd 6 to 1) 6
Dist: ¾l, sht-hd, sht-hd, sht-hd, 25l. 2m 36.05s. a 6.75s (6 Ran).
SR: -/12/-/13/-/-/ (L J Hawkings), Mrs A Knight

323 Alpine Double Glazing Maiden Stakes Class D (3-y-o) £2,880 6f............(4:25)

QUINSIGIMOND 8-9 G Duffield (6) *trkd ldr gng wl, led o'r 2 fs out, sn clr, eased fnl furlong.* ....(6 to 4 on op 5 to 4 on) 1
HALL BANK COTTAGE 8-9 R P Elliott (5) *chsd ldg pair, rdn o'r 2 fs out, came wide hme turn, kpt on ins last.* ....(7 to 2 op 3 to 1 tchd 4 to 1) 2
250[5] MUSICAL PHONE (bl) 9-0 D Nicholls (4) *broke wl, led till rdn and hdd o'r 2 fs out, sn outpcd..* (8 to 1 op 5 to 1) 3
SLEEPTITE (Fr) 9-0 W Newnes (1) *outpcd early, some hdwy hfwy, no imprsn fnl furlong..* .(7 to 1 op 3 to 1) 4
TOP GUNNER (Ire) 9-0 D Gibson (2) *al outpcd, tld off.* ....(11 to 2 op 3 to 1 tchd 6 to 1) 5

Dist: 4l, ¾l, 1½l, 30l. 1m 14.25s. a 3.45s (5 Ran).
(A E T Mines), Sir Mark Prescott

324 Stirling Handicap Class E (0-70 3-y-o) £2,154 5f.......................... (5:00)

PRESS THE BELL [55] 8-8 G Duffield (4) *broke wl and sn led, shaken up 2 fs out, ran on strly.* (9 to 4 jt-fav op 2 to 1) 1
263[5] THE INSTITUTE BOY [68] (bl) 9-7 S Webster (2) *pld hrd tracking ldr, rdn 2 fs out, kpt on same pace.* ....(7 to 2 op 3 to 1 tchd 11 to 4 and 4 to 1) 2
220* PURBECK CENTENARY [63] 9-2 W Newnes (1) *trkd ldrs, rdn 2 fs out, unbl to quicken*.......(5 to 2 tchd 3 to 1) 3
236[2] COMET WHIRLPOOL (Ire) [58] (bl) 8-11 S O'Gorman (3) *hld up in tch, effrt o'r one furlong out, no imprsn ins last.* ....(9 to 4 jt-fav op 2 to 1 tchd 5 to 2) 4

Dist: 2l, 1l, sht-hd. 1m 0.23s. a 2.03s (4 Ran).
SR: 28/33/24/18/ (Sydney Mason), J Berry

WARWICK (firm)
Saturday March 27th
Going Correction: MINUS 0.50 sec. per fur. (races 1,2), MINUS 0.20 (3,4,5,6,7)

325 Old Milverton Maiden Fillies Stakes Class D (2-y-o) £3,377 5f..................(2:15)

TUTU SIXTYSIX 8-11 R Cochrane (1) *trkd ldr, led 2 fs out, rdn out*................ (9 to 2 op 4 to 1 tchd 5 to 1) 1
BELLA PARKES 8-11 T Quinn (4) *led till hdd 2 fs out, ran green, kpt on ins last.* .... (11 to 10 on op 6 to 4 on tchd Evens) 2
PARADISE NEWS 8-11 N Day (7) *prmnt on outsd, came wide hfwy, ran on ins fnl furlong.* (25 to 1 op 12 to 1) 3
BEARALL (Ire) 8-11 R Perham (6) *sn pushed alng, ran on wl ins fnl 2 fs*..........(8 to 1 op 5 to 1 tchd 10 to 1) 4
FORMIDABLE LASS 8-11 N Carlisle (2) *speed for 3 fs.* .... (20 to 1 op 12 to 1) 5
ROSIE VALENTINE 8-6 (5*) O Pears (9) *speed till came wide into strt, no further hdwy.* ....(6 to 1 op 4 to 1 tchd 7 to 1) 6
CARLTON CROWN (USA) 8-11 J Lowe (10) *outpcd, nvr on terms*.......................... (33 to 1 op 20 to 1) 7
LEESON STREET LADY (Ire) 8-11 Paul Eddery (3) *slwly away, al beh*......................(33 to 1 op 16 to 1) 8
WILKS DREAM (Ire) 8-11 T Sprake (8) *al beh.* .... (14 to 1 op 8 to 1) 9
HI-RUBY 8-8 (3*) A Tucker (5) *slwly away, tld off frm hfwy*........................ (20 to 1 op 12 to 1) 10

Dist: ¾l, 1½l, 1l, 6l, ¾l, ¾l, nk, 2½l, 25l. 59.90s. a 1.70s (10 Ran).
SR: 13/10/4/-/-/-/ (Mrs Ann Gover), R Boss

326 Tote/Racing Post Ten To Follow Maiden Stakes Class D (3-y-o and up) £3,318 5f ....(2:45)

TRIOMING 7-9-7 N Adams (1) *made all, clr 2 fs out, kpt on*....................(20 to 1 op 14 to 1 tchd 25 to 1) 1
THE FED 3-8-8 A Culhane (8) *mid-div, rdn and hdwy o'r one furlong out, ran on wl*.......... (3 to 1 op 2 to 1) 2
217[8] BLYTON STAR (Ire) 5-9-7 S Webster (5) *slwly into strd, rdn and hdwy appr fnl furlong, kpt on.* ....(14 to 1 op 12 to 1 tchd 20 to 1) 3
214[4] CRACKER JACK (bl) 3-8-8 G Baxter (3) *al prmnt, chsd wnr 2 fs out till one pace ins last*.......(20 to 1 op 12 to 1) 4
YUNUS EMRE (Ire) 3-8-1 (7*) J O'Dwyer (2) *slwly away, in rear, some late hdwy*................(12 to 1 tchd 14 to 1) 5
BARASSIE 3-8-3 A Clark (4) *chsd wnr till wknd 2 fs out.* ....(10 to 1 op 20 to 1 tchd 25 to 1) 6
RICKY'S TORNADO (Ire) 4-9-7 J Williams (6) *speed to hfwy, sn btn*.............................(6 to 4 fav op Evens) 7
WILL'S LEGACY 3-8-8 Paul Eddery (7) *slwly away, al beh.* ....(15 to 2 op 6 to 1 tchd 8 to 1) 8
4668a[8] LAID BACK BEN 3-8-9[1] R Cochrane (9) *in tch till ran wide trng into strt, no ch aftr*........ (20 to 1 tchd 33 to 1) 9

Dist: 1½l, ½l, 2l, 2½l, 5l, 2½l, 2½l, 2l. 59.60s. a 1.40s (9 Ran).
SR: 29/10/21/-/-/-/ (A A King), A P Jones

327 Binton Claiming Stakes Class F (4-y-o and up) £2,243 1m......................(3:15)

227[2] SILKY SIREN (bl) 4-8-4 Paul Eddery (16) *trkd ldr till wnt on hfwy, clr 2 fs out, eased ins last.* ....(5 to 2 fav tchd 11 to 4) 1
SHALOU 4-8-2 (7*) T G McLaughlin (10) *rcd in tch, rdn and hdwy 3 fs out, kpt on, no ch wth wnr.* ....(25 to 1 op 20 to 1 tchd 33 to 1) 2
261* STORM FREE (USA) 7-8-9 N Carlisle (8) *nvr far away, hdwy 3 fs out, ran on ins last*..... (8 to 1 tchd 9 to 1) 3
200* EASTLEIGH 4-8-10 (7*) D Carson (5) *in rear till hdwy ins fnl 2 fs, nvr nrr*..................(6 to 1 op 5 to 1) 4
139[5] MARSH WARBLER 5-7-12 (7*) P McCabe (12) *al prmnt, chsd wnr into strt, outpcd and wknd ins last.* (50 to 1) 5
MADRAJ (Ire) 5-9-3 T Sprake (6) *mid-div, ran on ins fnl 2 fs, nvr nrr*.. (25 to 1 op 16 to 1) 6
MEXICAN DANCER 4-7-13[2] (7*) S Drowne (7) *mid-div, made some late hdwy*........................(12 to 1) 7
259[5] WILD AND LOOSE 5-8-13 J Williams (2) *slwly away, styd on fnl 2 fs, nvr nrr*.....(4 to 1 op 7 to 2 tchd 9 to 2) 8
ALLIMAC NOMIS 4-8-4 (7*) G Mitchell (9) *in rear till some late hdwy*.......................(33 to 1 op 20 to 1) 9
232[5] SAREEN EXPRESS (Ire) 5-8-7 G Bardwell (11) *al mid-div.* ....(25 to 1 op 20 to 1) 10
SUPER FLYER (Ire) 4-8-5 A McGlone (4) *chsd ldrs till wknd 2 fs out*............... (25 to 1 op 20 to 1) 11
253 PRECIOUS CAROLINE (Ire) 5-8-2 J Penza (13) *al towards rear*.............................(33 to 1 op 20 to 1) 12
227[3] MOST SURPRISING (Ire) (bl) 4-8-9 R Cochrane (14) *chsd ldrs till weakenen quickly 2 fs out.* (12 to 1 op 10 to 1) 13
COBBLERS HILL 4-8-3 T Lang (18) *al beh.* ....(16 to 1 tchd 14 to 1) 14
133[6] SEASIDE MINSTREL 5-8-5 J Lowe (1) *slwly away, al beh.* ....(16 to 1 tchd 20 to 1) 15
278[8] ROCK THE BARNEY (Ire) 4-8-13 T Quinn (3) *al beh.* .... (25 to 1 op 20 to 1) 16
217[6] FATHOM FIVE (Ire) 4-8-0 N Adams (15) *al beh.* ....(25 to 1 op 20 to 1) 17
SEEMENOMORE 4-8-8 R Perham (17) *prmnt till wknd quickly 3 fs out*..............................(50 to 1) 18
227 FARM STREET 6-7-12 (7*) B Russell (20) *led to hfwy, wknd rpdly 3 fs out*..............................(8 to 1 tchd 9 to 1) 19
YOUNG JAMES 5-8-4 (3*) A Tucker (19) *al beh, tld off fnl 3 fs*... (50 to 1) 20

Dist: 2l, hd, 1½l, sht-hd, hd, hd, 3l, 3½l, hd, hd. 1m 39.00s. a 2.20s (20 Ran).
SR: 33/32/31/34/21/32/19/19/6/ (S Nixon), M C Pipe

328 Rothmans Royals North South Challenge Series Handicap Class D (0-80 3-y-o) £3,655 1m........................ (3:45)

4730a* EASTERN MEMORIES (Ire) [76] 9-7 B Raymond (11) *al gng wl, wnt second 3 fs out, shaken up to ld ins last, very easily*...................(9 to 1 op 6 to 1 tchd 10 to 1) 1
4778a* STRICTLY PERSONAL (USA) [71] 9-2 R Cochrane (1) *slwly into strd, hld up in rear til 2 fs out, swtchd lft and ran on strly ins last*................(7 to 2 fav tchd 4 to 1) 2
CREDIT SQUEEZE [64] 8-6 (3*) A Tucker (3) *mid-div, hdwy o'r 2 fs out, ran on ins last*.......... (16 to 1 op 14 to 1) 3
220[5] WATERLORD (Ire) [67] 8-5 (7*) D Wright (9) *led till hdd ins fnl furlong, one pace*..............(20 to 1 op 14 to 1) 4
4794a[3] MAJOR TRIUMPH (Ire) [66] 8-11 N Day (2) *prmnt till one pace fnl 2 fs*...................(12 to 1 tchd 16 to 1) 5
RACING TELEGRAPH [72] 9-3 M Wigham (4) *pld hrd, prmnt till one pace fnl 3 fs*.........(14 to 1 op 10 to 1) 6
BAYDON BELLE (USA) [67] 8-12 J Lowe (6) *slwly away, hdwy hfwy, one pace fnl 2 fs*........(10 to 1 op 7 to 1) 7
248* HEART OF SPAIN [68] 8-13 T Quinn (5) *sn rdn alng, in frnt rnk till wknd quickly o'r one furlong out.* ....(5 to 1 op 4 to 1) 8
248[3] SCORCHER (Ire) [60] (bl) 8-5 J Penza (8) *sn beh.* .... (9 to 1 op 8 to 1 tchd 10 to 1) 9
OUR SHADEE (USA) [60] 8-5 G Bardwell (7) *prmnt till o'r halway*..........................(20 to 1 op 16 to 1) 10
144 ESTHAL (Ire) [73] 8-11 (7*) S Drowne (10) *in tch for 5 fs.* ....(12 to 1 op 20 to 1) 11
215[6] SOMNIFERE (USA) [66] 8-11 Paul Eddery (12) *trkd ldr till wknd quickly 3 fs out*............ (12 to 1 op 10 to 1) 12

Dist: 1½l, hd, 1l, 2½l, 3½l, sht-hd, nk, ¾l, ¾l, 2l. 1m 39.20s. a 2.40s (12 Ran).
SR: 47/37/29/29/20/15/9/9/-/ (Jim Horgan), R Hannon

329 Dunsmore Handicap Class C (0-90 4-y-o and up) £4,878 1¼m 169yds.........(4:20)

4807a[5] NIGHT CLUBBING (Ire) [75] 4-8-13 T Quinn (7) *al prmnt on outsd, led o'r one furlong out, stretched out wl ins.* ....(9 to 1 op 6 to 1 tchd 10 to 1) 1
MYFONTAINE [60] 6-7-13 G Bardwell (3) *hld up, hdwy on outsd o'r 2 fs out, ran on und pres ins last.* .... (11 to 2 op 6 to 1 tchd 13 to 2) 2
246[2] MULCIBER [70] 5-8-9 W Carson (9) *trkd ldr, ev till wknd entering fnl furlong.* (5 to 2 fav op 9 to 4 tchd 3 to 1) 3
KNOCK KNOCK [89] 8-10-0 R Cochrane (1) *hld up in rear, hdwy 2 fs out, one pace*..........................(3 to 1) 4

264* CAMDEN'S RANSOM (USA) [70] 6-8-9 J Williams (2) *pld hrd, effrt 3 fs out, one pace fnl 2*..... (3 to 1 op 7 to 2) 5
SMILING CHIEF (Ire) [59] 5-7-12^{1} T Sprake (6) *prmnt till wknd one furlong out*............ (14 to 1 op 16 to 1) 6
MR ZIEGFELD (USA) [56] (bl) 4-7-8^{1} N Adams (4) *led till hdd o'r one furlong out, wknd quickly*. (33 to 1 op 25 to 1) 7
RULLY [77] 4-9-1 J Penza (5) *pld hrd, prmnt till wknd wl o'r 2 fs out*...................... (25 to 1 op 20 to 1) 8
38 BASSIO (Bel) [62] 4-7-7 (7*) D Wright (8) *al towards rear, rdn 4 fs out, sn btn*................ (50 to 1 op 33 to 1) 9

Dist: ¾l, 4l, 2½l, 1½l, 2l, 4l, 10l, nk. 2m 18.90s. a 6.10s (9 Ran).
SR: 17/1/3/17/-/-/ (Sheikh Essa Bin Mubarak), R Akehurst

330 Wellesbourne Handicap Class E (0-70 3-y-o and up) £3,287 6f.................. (4:50)

MARTINOSKY [60] 7-9-9 N Day (8) *al prmnt, rdn 2 fs out, ran on strly to ld nr finish*........ (16 to 1 op 14 to 1) 1
138^{9} HITCHIN A RIDE [40] 6-8-3^{6} J Comber (3) *hld up in rear, gd hdwy to track wnr appr fnl furlong, ran on strly to go second nr finish*.................................. (25 to 1) 2
263* SPENDER [43] 4-8-6 N Adams (5) *chsd ldrs, led wl o'r one furlong out, clrly entering last, ct cl hme*. .... (7 to 2 fav tchd 4 to 1) 3
244^{8} HARRY'S COMING [63] 9-9-5 (7*) S Drowne (11) *slwly away, hdwy 2 fs out, ran on wl*....(16 to 1 op 14 to 1) 4
263^{7} RUSHANES [57] 6-9-6 T Quinn (2) *chsd ldrs, one pace appr fnl furlong*........................(12 to 1 tchd 10 to 1) 5
LEIGH CROFTER [58] (bl) 4-9-7 J Williams (7) *mid-div, ran on ins fnl 2 fs*.....................(16 to 1 tchd 20 to 1) 6
4716a^{6} JOHN O'DREAMS [43] 8-8-6 T Sprake (19) *chsd ldrs, rdn 2 fs out, one pace*.................. (25 to 1 op 16 to 1) 7
4787a^{8} RED SOMBRERO [50] 4-8-13 J Lowe (4) *al mid-div, one pace fnl 2 fs*..................(25 to 1 op 20 to 1) 8
218^{3} BRISAS [42] (bl) 6-8-5 G Baxter (9) *al mid-div*. .... (12 to 1 op 10 to 1) 9
SLIP-A-SNIP [54] 6-9-0 (3*) A Tucker (18) *chsd ldr, led briefly wl o'r one furlong out, sn wknd*. ....(14 to 1 op 25 to 1 tchd 33 to 1) 10
4681a* NOBLE POWER (Ire) [65] 4-10-0 R Cochrane (10) *sn rdn alng, al towards rear*............(12 to 1 tchd 16 to 1) 11
MURPHY'S HOPE (Ire) [66] 3-9-1 B Raymond (14) *nvr on terms*.............................(10 to 1 tchd 12 to 1) 12
242^{5} CHOICE LOT [44] (v) 6-8-4 (3*) N Kennedy (13) *outpace, al towards rear*...................(20 to 1 op 16 to 1) 13
SPECTACLE JIM [50] 4-8-13 G Bardwell (16) *al towards rear*.. (25 to 1) 14
TAKE IT IN CASH [48] 4-8-11 Paul Eddery (1) *chsd ldrs till rdn 2 fs out, sn btn*............. (10 to 1 tchd 12 to 1) 15
134 BEATLE SONG [62] 5-9-11 W Carson (6) *al beh*. ....(7 to 1 op 6 to 1) 16
231^{7} LINCSTONE BOY (Ire) [55] (bl) 5-9-4 M Wood (12) *led till hdd wl o'r one furlong out, wknd quickly*. .... (12 to 1 op 10 to 1) 17
CHEREN BOY [37] 4-7-7 (7*) D Wright (15) *al beh*. (66 to 1) 18
SUPER DEB [56] (bl) 6-9-0 (5*) L Newton (17) *speed till wknd rpdly wl o'r 2 fs out*.......... (33 to 1 op 20 to 1) 19

Dist: ½l, nk, 1½l, 1l, 1½l, nk, 1½l, 2½l, sht-hd, 1½l. 1m 14.10s. a 2.40s (19 Ran).
SR: 37/15/17/31/21/16/-/1/-/ (D B Clark), G C Bravery

331 Coventry Cup Handicap Class E (0-70 4-y-o and up) £3,416 1¾m 194yds....... (5:20)

PHAROAH'S GUEST [45] 6-8-7 W Carson (5) *al prmnt, pushed alng frm hfwy, led one furlong out, styd on wl*. ....(11 to 4 fav op 5 to 2 tchd 3 to 1) 1
RAGAMUFFIN ROMEO [65] 4-9-10 Paul Eddery (8) *hld up, rdn and hdwy 3 fs out, dsptd ldr appr fnl furlong, no extr ins*............................. (20 to 1 op 14 to 1) 2
ANGELICA PARK [38] 7-8-0 J Penza (7) *hld up in rear, gd hdwy 2 fs out, swtchd lft ins last, ran on strly*. .... (15 to 2 op 6 to 1) 3
JANISKI [47] (v) 10-8-2 (7*) D Wright (6) *hld up in rear, hdwy ins fnl 2 fs, nvr nrr*..........(10 to 1 op 8 to 1) 4
PINISI [33] 8-7-9^{2} N Carlisle (14) *al prmnt, led 4 fs out, rdn and hdd one out, wknd ins*........(33 to 1 op 20 to 1) 5
EURIDICE (Ire) [60] 4-9-5 T Sprake (12) *chsd ldrs, no hdwy fnl 2 fs*.................................. (5 to 1 op 8 to 1) 6
111^{8} ROMANIAN (Ire) [43] 5-8-5 T Quinn (4) *chsd ldr, led 6 fs out, hdd 4 out, wkng whn slightly hmpd ins last*. .... (11 to 2 op 9 to 2 tchd 6 to 1) 7
ELSA [40] 4-7-13 A McGlone (1) *in tch till wknd wl o'r one furlong out*...................... (16 to 1 op 14 to 1) 8
182^{6} LYPH (USA) [45] 7-8-4 (3*) A Tucker (10) *beh, rdn hfwy, nvr on terms*......................... (8 to 1 op 7 to 1) 9
PERFORATE [43] (bl) 4-8-2 S Dawson (15) *rcd in tch, no hdwy fnl 4 fs*....... (14 to 1 tchd 16 to 1 and 12 to 1) 10
ANAR (Ire) [45] 4-8-1 (3*) N Kennedy (13) *prmnt till o'r hfwy, rdn 6 fs out, wknd stdly*.....(10 to 1 op 8 to 1) 11
FERMAIN [46] 4-8-5 N Adams (3) *hld up in mid-div, wknd 3 fs out*............................ (33 to 1 op 25 to 1) 12
JUNE'S LEAR FAN (Can) [51] 4-8-10 G Bardwell (2) *led till hdd 6 fs out, wknd o'r 2 out*....... (20 to 1 op 14 to 1) 13
HYMN BOOK (Ire) [62] 4-9-7 J Lowe (11) *al beh*. ....(33 to 1 op 25 to 1) 14

Dist: 1½l, 1l, 2½l, sht-hd, nk, 3½l, 1½l, 1½l, hd, 5l. 3m 11.90s. a 3.60s (14 Ran).
SR: 27/42/17/23/8/31/13/5/11/ (E Reitel), N A Twiston-Davies

FOLKESTONE (good to firm)
Monday March 29th
Going Correction: PLUS 0.10 sec. per fur. (races 1,2,3,7), NIL (4,5,6)

332 Alkham Handicap Class E (0-70 4-y-o and up) £3,002 1m 1f 149yds........... (1:50)

HERE HE COMES [33] 7-7-10 J Quinn (14) *slwly into strd, beh till smooth hdwy frm 4 fs out, swtchd ins to chal o'r one out, rdn to ld inside last*. ....(9 to 4 fav op 6 to 4 tchd 5 to 2) 1
210^{6} TENAYESTELIGN [32] 5-7-9^{2} S Dawson (13) *nvr far away, led o'r one furlong out till hdd and unbl to quicken ins last*.............................(25 to 1 op 20 to 1) 2
4817a^{5} DANCING BEAU (Ire) [52] 4-9-0 M Roberts (7) *trkd ldr, led o'r 2 fs out till hdd over one out, no extr*. .... (10 to 1 op 8 to 1) 3
BUSMAN (Ire) [66] 4-10-0 T Quinn (8) *midfield till hdwy 4 fs out, sn chasing ldrs, rdn and one pace frm 2 out*. ....(10 to 1 tchd 11 to 1) 4
SKIMMER HAWK [40] 4-8-2 N Carlisle (5) *al hndy, ev ch wl o'r one furlong out, sn rdn and wknd*. .... (20 to 1 op 12 to 1) 5
ALMOST A PRINCESS [48] 5-8-11 R Cochrane (3) *beh till styd on fnl 2 fs, nvr trbld ldrs*. ....(8 to 1 op 10 to 1 tchd 11 to 1) 6
264^{6} APPLIANCEOFSCIENCE [41] 6-7-11 (7*) P McCabe (6) *midfield, rdn alng o'r 4 fs out, no real imprsn*. .... (14 to 1 op 12 to 1) 7
BRONZE RUNNER [30] (bl) 9-7-0 (7*) Antoinette Armes (12) *hld up and beh till hdwy on outsd o'r 3 fs out, nvr able to chal*...............................(20 to 1 op 12 to 1) 8
114^{8} PRINCE ROONEY (Ire) [54] 5-8-10 (7*) S Drowne (4) *hld up in midfield till lost pl frm o'r 3 fs out*. .... (20 to 1 op 12 to 1) 9
103^{9} UP ALL NIGHT [43] 4-8-5 G Bardwell (2) *sn rdn alng, al beh*..................................(25 to 1 op 20 to 1) 10
4696a RED INK [52] 4-9-0 Pat Eddery (9) *trkd ldrs till wknd wl o'r 3 fs out*............................ (16 to 1 op 12 to 1) 11
JARZON DANCER [30] 5-7-7 E Johnson (1) *al beh*. .... (20 to 1 op 10 to 1) 12
239* SIRTELIMAR (Ire) [59] 4-9-7 A Mackay (10) *led till hdd o'r 2 fs out, sn wknd*....... (5 to 1 op 7 to 2 tchd 11 to 2) 13
229^{5} SOL ROUGE (Ire) [37] 4-7-13^{1} G Carter (11) *prmnt 2 fs, sn lost pl and wl beh*.....(10 to 1 op 8 to 1 tchd 12 to 1) 14

Dist: 1l, 6l, sht-hd, 3l, nk, 1l, 1½l, 1l, 6l, nk. 2m 5.30s. a 7.70s (14 Ran).
SR: 15/12/19/32/-/-/ (E Harrington), R Akehurst

333 Levy Board Handicap Class E (0-70 3-y-o and up) £3,002 6f 189yds............(2:20)

MR NEVERMIND (Ire) [60] 3-8-4^{1} B Rouse (10) *trkd ldrs, led and veered sharply lft to stands rail wl o'r one furlong out, hld on cmftbly*..................(6 to 1 op 4 to 1) 1
ROYAL DARTMOUTH (USA) [49] 8-8-9 J Williams (4) *slwly into strd, reco'red to chase ldrs, chalg whn slightly impeded wl over one furlong out, kpt on*.. .... (11 to 2 op 7 to 2) 2
4803a^{8} PRECIOUS WONDER [64] 4-9-10 R Cochrane (8) *hmpd aftr 2 fs and sn wl beh, gd hdwy frm o'r one out, fnshd well*. ....(10 to 1 tchd 12 to 1) 3
BELLATRIX [44] 5-8-4^{2} M Roberts (2) *rdn to ld for 2 fs, styd hndy and ev ch wl o'r one out, unbl to quicken*. .... (8 to 1 op 12 to 1) 4
319^{6} NOBBY BARNES [58] 4-9-4 G Duffield (1) *chsd ldrs, rdn o'r 2 fs out, kpt on same pace appr last*. ....(4 to 1 fav op 5 to 1 tchd 11 to 2 and 7 to 2) 5
DUTY SERGEANT (Ire) [52] (bl) 4-8-12 A Munro (7) *beh, rdn o'r 2 fs out, styd on ins last, nvr nrr*. (6 to 1 op 9 to 2) 6
MISS PRECOCIOUS [35] 5-7-9^{2} J Quinn (5) *led aftr 2 fs, sn clr, hdd wl o'r one out, soon wknd*. (25 to 1 op 20 to 1) 7
200 DAM CERTAIN (Ire) [56] 4-8-13 (3*) D Harrison (3) *chsd ldrs, rdn and effrt wl o'r one furlong out, wknd ins last*. ....(7 to 1 op 8 to 1 tchd 9 to 1) 8
319^{4} SUNSET STREET (Ire) [57] 5-9-3 T Quinn (9) *al beh*. ....(7 to 1 op 6 to 1 tchd 8 to 1) 9
BARBEZIEUX [33] 6-7-0 (7*) Sharon Millard (6) *sn in rear, came wide hme turn, tld off*....... (33 to 1 op 20 to 1) 10

Dist: 1l, 1½l, sht-hd, hd, 1½l, ½l, 2l, 25l. 1m 25.90s. a 5.00s (10 Ran).
SR: 25/27/37/16/29/18/ (K Higson), G L Moore

334 Aldington Rating Related Maiden Stakes Class F (0-65 3-y-o) £2,243 6f 189yds (2:50)

SPRING SIXPENCE 8-9 G Duffield (9) *chsd ldr, chlgd frm 2 fs out, led jst ins last, drvn clr*. .... (11 to 2 op 5 to 1 tchd 6 to 1) 1
248^{2} GOOD IMAGE 9-0 Pat Eddery (3) *sn led, jnd frm 2 fs out, hdd and no extr jst ins last*.......... (5 to 1 op 9 to 2) 2
KOA 9-0 G Carter (6) *beh till ran on fnl furlong, nvr trbld ldrs*................ (4 to 1 fav op 3 to 1 tchd 9 to 2) 3

2485 MEDLAND (Ire) 8-11 (3*) D Harrison (11) *chsd ldrs till rdn and no hdwy frm 2 fs out*..........(33 to 1 op 20 to 1) 4
TEXAS COWGIRL (Ire) 8-9 W Hood (8) *trkd ldrs, ev ch 2 fs out, wknd o'r one out*..............(8 to 1 op 4 to 1) 5
EASTERN GLOW 8-9 W Woods (7) *slwly away and sn wl beh, hdwy o'r 3 fs out, kpt on ins last*. ....(16 to 1 op 10 to 1) 6
PURE MADNESS (USA) 9-0 J Quinn (2) *chsd ldrs till wknd frm 2 fs out*...................(12 to 1 tchd 14 to 1) 7
WHO'S THE BEST (Ire) 9-0 S Whitworth (12) *beh early, nvr able to chal*...................(10 to 1 tchd 11 to 1) 8
PETITE LOUIE 8-4 (5*) N Gwilliams (13) *midfield, rdn o'r 3 fs out, no imprsn*..................(33 to 1 op 20 to 1) 9
BEAT THE BAGMAN (Ire) 9-0 C Avery (5) *slwly away, nvr a dngr*..............................(33 to 1 op 20 to 1) 10
209 RUSTY REEL (bl) 9-0 M Roberts (10) *beh, rdn 3 fs out, no hdwy*...................(7 to 1 op 6 to 1 tchd 8 to 1) 11
2096 ARAWA 8-9 T Quinn (1) *trkd ldrs till rdn and wknd frm wl o'r 2 fs out*.................... (16 to 1 tchd 14 to 1) 12
CANADIAN EAGLE 8-2 (7*) B Russell (4) *slwly into strd, sn in rear*...............(10 to 1 op 8 to 1 tchd 12 to 1) 13
Dist: 3½l, 5l, ½l, nk, ½l, 2½l, 1½l, 1½l, 1½l, 1½l. 1m 25.60s. a 4.70s (13 Ran).
SR: 35/29/14/12/6/-/ (C I T Racing Ltd), J R Fanshawe

335 Shorncliffe Median Auction Maiden Stakes Class F (3-y-o) £2,243 6f............ (3:20)

MR VINCENT 8-11 (3*) D Harrison (4) *pld hrd and rstrained early, produced frm o'r one furlong out, ran on to ld last 50 yards, cleverly*. ....(15 to 8 fav op Evens tchd 9 to 4) 1
ROYAL INTERVAL 9-0 T Sprake (1) *led, quickened the pace 2 fs out, rdn and hdd last 50 yards*. ....(2 to 1 op 7 to 4 tchd 6 to 4) 2
SILVER GROOM (Ire) 9-0 S Whitworth (2) *trkd ldg pair, effrt wl o'r one furlong out, wknd ins last*. ....(5 to 1 tchd 8 to 1) 3
TRINITY HALL 8-9 R Hills (3) *wth ldr till wknd frm 2 fs out*. ....(9 to 4 op 3 to 1) 4
Dist: Nk, 4l, 12l. 1m 16.50s. a 5.50s (4 Ran).
(Mrs Shirley Robins), G Lewis

336 Rochester Conditions Stakes Class D (3-y-o) £3,807 5f...................... (3:50)

SABRE RATTLER 9-8 Pat Eddery (1) *made all, shaken up 2 fs out, ran on wl*........... (6 to 4 on tchd 5 to 4 on) 1
KAMAATERA (Ire) 8-10 W R Swinburn (2) *took keen hold, rdn to chal wl o'r one furlong out, sn btn*. ....(11 to 10 op Evens tchd 5 to 4) 2
Won by 2l. 1m 1.20s. a 2.60s (2 Ran).
SR: 56/36/ (H B Hughes), J Berry

337 Headcorn Maiden Fillies Auction Stakes Class E (2-y-o) £2,924 5f............ (4:20)

MADAME GREGOIRE 8-11 R Cochrane (7) *dsptd ld till o'r 2 fs out, sn rdn, ran on gmely to lead ins last*. ....(5 to 2 tchd 7 to 2) 1
ANTONIA'S FOLLY 8-11 Pat Eddery (6) *sn prmnt on outsd, led o'r 2 fs out till hdd ins last, edgd lft and kpt on*. .... (15 to 8 fav op 5 to 4 on tchd 2 to 1) 2
FLAIR LADY 8-11 T Sprake (9) *dwlt, reco'red to chase ldrs on outsd till outpcd 2 fs out, ran on ins last*. .... (10 to 1 op 7 to 1) 3
STARISK 8-11 R Hills (3) *dsptd ld till o'r 2 fs out, kpt on same pace fnl furlong*. ....(12 to 1 op 10 to 1 tchd 14 to 1) 4
EUROPHARM LASSIE 8-11 B Rouse (8) *al prmnt, rdn and ev ch one furlong out, no extr wl ins last*. ....(7 to 2 op 7 to 1 tchd 3 to 1) 5
FOREVER BLUSHING 8-4 (7*) S Drowne (5) *slwly away, outpcd*..............(33 to 1 op 20 to 1 tchd 40 to 1) 6
KISS NO TELL (Ire) 8-11 N Day (2) *chsd ldrs 2 fs, sn beh*. .... (12 to 1 op 8 to 1 tchd 14 to 1) 7
MACE EL REEM 8-11 M Roberts (4) *very slow away, some hdwy hfwy, ran green and wknd wl o'r one furlong out*.................(12 to 1 op 10 to 1 tchd 14 to 1) 8
Dist: 1l, 1l, ½l, hd, 6l, 4l, ¾l. 1m 2.80s. a 4.20s (8 Ran).
SR: 13/9/5/3/2/ (Mrs James Eustace), J M P Eustace

338 Kingsnorth Handicap Class E (0-70 3-y-o) £2,924 1½m...................... (4:50)

ONE VOICE (USA) [55] 9-5 G Duffield (7) *trkd ldr, kicked into ld o'r 4 fs out, pushed out, cmftbly*. ....(7 to 2 op 7 to 1 tchd 8 to 1) 1
PRESTON GUILD (Ire) [48] 8-12 R Cochrane (3) *took keen hold, al hndy, chsd wnr frm o'r 4 fs out, no imprsn fnl furlong*.........................(7 to 4 fav op 2 to 1) 2
EARLY TO RISE [55] 9-5 M Roberts (6) *beh, pushed alng frm hfwy, styd on fnl 2 fs, nvr a dngr*. ....(7 to 1 op 6 to 1 tchd 8 to 1) 3
2095 WESTRAY (Fr) [54] 9-4 J Quinn (1) *chsd ldrs, effrt o'r 3 fs out to chase ldg pair, sn wknd*. .... (5 to 1 op 7 to 2 tchd 11 to 2) 4

724 BADAWI (Fr) [57] 9-0 (7*) G Forster (5) *beh till effrt 7 fs out, rdn and wknd o'r 4 out*. .... (10 to 1 op 5 to 1 tchd 12 to 1) 5
DANGER BABY [50] (v) 9-0 N Day (2) *led till hdd o'r 4 fs out, sn rdn and wknd*.............(25 to 1 op 10 to 1) 6
835 HONORARY GUEST [50] 9-0 J Reid (4) *chsd ldrs, rdn o'r 3 fs out, 4th and wkng whn broke leg and f ins last, destroyed*.........................(5 to 1 op 7 to 2) f
Dist: 4l, 15l, 6l, 1½l, 7l. 2m 41.50s. a 11.00s (7 Ran).
SR: 7/-/-/-/ (Pinnacle Racing Stable), Sir Mark Prescott

HAMILTON (soft)
Monday March 29th

Going Correction: PLUS 0.65 sec. per fur. (races 1,2,6), PLUS 0.80 (3,4,5)

339 Chatelherault Claiming Stakes Class F (3-y-o) £2,243 1m 1f 36yds............. (2:10)

PALACEGATE SUNSET 8-13 J Carroll (6) *sluggish strt, drvn up to ld aftr 2 fs, hdd 4 furlongs out, rallied to lead wl ins fnl furlong, rdn out*. .... (13 to 8 fav op 7 to 4 tchd 2 to 1 and 6 to 4) 1
FRIENDLY KNIGHT 8-5 K Darley (1) *trkd ldg quartet, feeling pace and niggled alng hfwy, styd on grimly to chal wl ins fnl furlong, ran on*......... (33 to 1 op 20 to 1) 2
4717a6 GOODBYE MILLIE 8-21 (5*) O Pears (3) *nvr far away, brght wide strt, ch ins fnl furlong, one pace und pres*. ....(9 to 2 op 3 to 1 tchd 5 to 1) 3
1787 DESIRABLE MISS (bl) 7-101 (7*) J Marshall (5) *trkd ldg pair, ev ch hfwy, hrd drvn fnl furlong, one pace*. .... (33 to 1 op 20 to 1) 4
NICKNAME 8-13 K Fallon (2) *led for 2 fs, styd hndy till rgned ld 4 furlongs out, wknd and ct wl ins fnl furlong*. ....(5 to 1 op 3 to 1 tchd 8 to 1) 5
230* HUSH BABY (Ire) 7-9 (7*) D Wright (4) *last and hld up, rdn whn pace lifted hfwy, btn o'r 2 fs out*. ....(7 to 4 op 5 to 2) 6
Dist: Nk, 1½l, ½l, nk, 6l. 2m 6.90s. a 12.90s (6 Ran).
(Palacegate Corporation Ltd), J Berry

340 Strathclyde Park Apprentice Handicap Class E (0-80 3-y-o and up) £3,183 1m 65yds............................. (2:40)

2056 SHANNON EXPRESS [45] (v) 6-8-2 Claire Balding (12) *made all, clr hfwy, strd shortened fnl furlong, jst lasted*. ....(10 to 1) 1
SALDA [71] 4-9-11 (3*) G Parkin (6) *sluggish strt, chsd alng to take clr order hfwy, styd on und pres fnl furlong, jst hld*...............................(6 to 1 op 4 to 1) 2
CHANTRY BELLINI [42] 4-7-93 (7*) K Sked (11) *trkd ldg pair, rdn o'r 3 fs out, styd on grimly fnl furlong, nrst finish*..............................(20 to 1 op 16 to 1) 3
BRECKENBROUGH LAD [56] 6-8-13 J Tate (9) *trkd ldg bunch, outpcd and edgd rght o'r 3 fs out, styd on wl fnl furlong, nvr nrr*.....................(7 to 1 op 6 to 1) 4
THE DANDY DON (Ire) [50] 4-7-13 (8*) C Teague (10) *trkd ldg half dozen, effrt and chsd alng o'r 2 fs out, kpt on same pace*..(14 to 1) 5
DRUMDONNA (Ire) [67] 3-7-13 (8*) P Roberts (4) *sluggish strt, last hfwy, effrt on outsd o'r 3 fs out, nvr nrr*. ....(6 to 1 op 5 to 1) 6
302 MENTALASANYTHIN [68] 4-9-1 (10*) W Hollick (1) *trkd ldg 5, feeling pace and rdn hfwy, not pace to chal*. ....(11 to 4 fav op 5 to 2 tchd 3 to 1) 7
SELF EXPRESSION [68] 5-9-1 (10*) D Thomas (3) *in tch, effrt and drvn alng appr strt, nvr able to rch ldrs*. ....(7 to 1 op 4 to 1) 8
4705a GOLD SURPRISE (Ire) [50] 4-8-2 (5*) J Dennis (7) *settled midfield, drvn alng to go pace hfwy, nvr dngrs*. ....(8 to 1 op 7 to 1) 9
DIET [65] 7-9-5 (3*) R Havlin (2) *chsd ldrs to strt, fdd und pres last 3 fs*......... (14 to 1 op 12 to 1 tchd 16 to 1) 10
111 VANDA'S GIRL [36] 5-7-0 (7*) F Savage (8) *chsd ldr till fdd quickly 3 fs out, eased whn btn*.................. (50 to 1) 11
Dist: Nk, nk, sht-hd, 4l, 4l, 2½l, 1½l, 3l, 6l, 12l. 1m 54.00s. a 10.00s (11 Ran).
SR: 18/43/13/26/8/-/6/1/-/ (R Cottam), E J Alston

341 'Home In On Hamilton' Handicap Class D (0-80 3-y-o) £3,201 6f 5yds.......... (3:10)

2752 TANAGOME (USA) [70] (v) 8-8 (5*) O Pears (3) *nvr far away, nosed ahead o'r 2 fs out, hdd ins last, rallied to ld post*. ....(4 to 1 op 3 to 1 tchd 9 to 2) 1
PEEDIE PEAT [60] 8-3 K Darley (4) *steadied strt, improved to draw level o'r 2 fs out, nosed ahead ins fnl furlong, jst ct*..............................(6 to 1 op 4 to 1) 2
CARNBREA SNIP [78] 9-7 M Hills (1) *co'red up beh ldrs, effrt and bustled alng last 2 fs, not quicken*. ....(5 to 1 op 3 to 1) 3
HIGH ROMANCE [56] 7-6 (7*) Darren Moffatt (5) *wl plcd on outsd, dsptd ld hfwy, rdn and fdd o'r one furlong out*. .... (8 to 1 op 14 to 1 tchd 7 to 1) 4

4708a7 ANUSHA [66] 8-9 J Carroll (2) *led stands side till o'r 2 fs out, wknd quickly appr fnl furlong.* (3 to 1 jt-fav op 7 to 4) 5
EGG [69] (bl) 8-12 Alex Greaves (6) *wnt rght and lost grnd strt, effrt and drvn alng hfwy, outpcd last 2 fs.* ....(3 to 1 jt-fav op 4 to 1) 6
Dist: Sht-hd, 6l, 4l, 5l, 2½l. 1m 18.70s. a 8.00s (6 Ran).
SR: 35/24/18/ (S G Norton), S G Norton

342 Bothwell Road Claiming Stakes Class F (3-y-o) £2,243 5f 4yds................ (3:40)

CHARITY EXPRESS (Ire) 8-10 J Carroll (1) *sluggish strt, bustled alng to ld hfwy, styd on strly fnl furlong.* ....(9 to 4 on tchd 5 to 2 on and 2 to 1 on) 1
GO FLIGHTLINE (Ire) 8-13 M Hills (2) *broke wl to ld to hfwy, rdn o'r one furlong out, kpt on same pace.* ....(9 to 4 op 2 to 1) 2
SELVOLE 8-1 J Fanning (3) *sluggish strt, struggling to go pace hfwy, btn 2 fs out*..............(7 to 1 op 12 to 1) 3
Dist: 2l, 10l. 1m 5.40s. a 7.10s (3 Ran).
SR: 34/29/-/ (C G Davey), J Berry

343 Campsie Maiden Auction Stakes Class F (2-y-o) £2,243 5f 4yds.............. (4:10)

STEADFAST ELITE (Ire) 8-9 K Darley (2) *chsd ldr, hng badly lft 2 fs out, styd on grimly to ld wl ins fnl furlong.* ....(10 to 1 op 6 to 1) 1
2913 CULSYTH FLYER 8-7 (7*) M Humphries (6) *tried to make all, gng wl 2 fs out, wknd and hdd well ins fnl furlong.* ....(13 to 8 op Evens tchd 2 to 1) 2
MAD ABOUT MEN 8-9 J Carroll (4) *hmpd and crrd rght strt, badly outpcd till ran on wl ins fnl furlong.* ....(8 to 1 op 3 to 1) 3
JOYRIDER 9-0 M Hills (1) *pressed ldg pair, rdn whn slightly hmpd 2 fs out, btn o'r one furlong out.* ....(6 to 4 fav op 2 to 1) 4
GOOD SPIRITS 8-9 K Fallon (5) *hmpd and crrd rght strt, al struggling, tld off*.................. (12 to 1 op 8 to 1) 5
MARBLE 8-2 (7*) Darren Moffatt (3) *rstless in stalls, swrvd and uns rdr sn aftr strt.* ....(12 to 1 op 8 to 1 tchd 14 to 1 and 16 to 1) ur
Dist: 2l, 5l, 3½l, 15l. 1m 5.90s. a 7.60s (6 Ran).
SR: 23/20/-/ (Steadfast Engineering Company Ltd), J J O'Neill

344 Hamilton Enterprise Development Co. Median Auction Maiden Stakes Class E (3-y-o) £2,795 1½m 17yds............ (4:40)

MARROS MILL 8-9 M Hills (2) *nvr far away, drvn ahead o'r 2 fs out, jnd fnl furlong, kpt on wl.* ....(13 to 8 fav op 7 to 4 on tchd 7 to 4) 1
VAIGLY SUNTHYME 9-0 S Morris (4) *in tch, drvn alng to improve aftr a m, ev ch ins fnl furlong, edgd rght, no extr cl hme..*(7 to 1 op 6 to 1 tchd 5 to 1 and 8 to 1) 2
MOONLIGHT ECLIPSE 9-0 K Fallon (3) *chsd alng to go early pace, drvn along to improve o'r 2 fs out, styd on nvr dngrs..*.......................... (8 to 1 op 7 to 1) 3
2302 BARSAL (Ire) 9-0 Alex Greaves (6) *led aftr a furlong, quickened clr, steadied hfwy, hdd o'r 2 out, sn btn.* ....(4 to 1 op 3 to 1 tchd 9 to 2) 4
958 MEESON IMPOSSIBLE 9-0 K Darley (1) *led one furlong, styd hndy till fdd und pres 2 fs out.* ....(25 to 1 op 33 to 1 tchd 14 to 1) 5
INNOCENT ABROAD (Den) 8-9 A Culhane (5) *chsd ldg trio, rdn aftr a m, sn lost tch*........... (11 to 4 op 5 to 1) 6
Dist: 1½l, 12l, 5l, 8l, 4l. 2m 53.30s. a 20.30s (6 Ran).
(Alasdair Simpson), M Bell

MAISONS-LAFFITTE (FR) (good to soft) Monday March 29th

345 Prix Cor de Chasse (Listed) (3-y-o and up) £14,337 6f........................ (2:40)

CHARME SLAVE (Fr) 5-9-4 W Mongil,.................... 1
SILICON BAVARIA (Fr) 6-9-1 M Boutin,.................. 2
4702a6 CRACK REGIMENT (USA) 5-9-4 E Saint-Martin,........... 3
CARDOUN (Fr) 4-9-9 D Boeuf,............................ 4
MEDAILLE D'OR 5-9-9 G Guignard,...................... 6
Dist: Hd, sht-hd, sht-hd, 1½l, nk, 1l, 4l, sht-nk, ¾l. 1m 10.07s. a 0.57s (11 Ran).
SR: 63/59/61/65/-/ (J Nahoum), R Collett

LEICESTER (firm) Tuesday March 30th

Going Correction: MINUS 0.50 sec. per fur. (races 1,2,3,7), MINUS 0.35 (4,5,6)

346 Bescaby Maiden Stakes Class D (3-y-o) £3,494 1m 8yds.................... (2:00)

EMBANKMENT (Ire) 9-0 J Reid (1) *trkd ldrs gng wl, led well o'r one furlong out, sn clr, pushed out, cmftbly.* ....(5 to 2 fav op 4 to 1 tchd 9 to 4) 1
SUN OF SPRING 9-0 M Roberts (11) *wth ldr, led o'r 3 fs out till hdd wl over one out, not pace of wnr.* ....(4 to 1 op 3 to 1) 2
RUNAWAY PETE (USA) 9-0 T Quinn (9) *midfield till prmsg effrt o'r 3 fs out, kpt on fnl furlong.* (10 to 1 op 7 to 1) 3
ZAAHEYAH (USA) 8-9 W R Swinburn (5) *slwly away, hdwy 3 fs out, no imprsn o'r one out*...... (9 to 2 op 8 to 1) 4
SABEEL 8-9 A Munro (12) *chsd ldrs, rdn alng wl o'r 2 fs out, unbl to quicken*............. (20 to 1 op 16 to 1) 5
1246 MISS OFFIE 8-9 W Ryan (8) *trkd ldrs, rdn wl o'r 2 fs out, sn btn*......................... (40 to 1 op 50 to 1) 6
MASTER BEVELED 9-0 N Adams (10) *slwly into strd, nvr able to chal*...................................(50 to 1) 7
M'BEBE 9-0 D Holland (4) *hld up and beh, moderate hdwy fnl 2 fs, nvr plcd to chal.* ....(12 to 1 op 10 to 1 tchd 14 to 1) 8
FIELD OF STARS 9-0 R Cochrane (2) *pld hrd, led till hdd o'r 3 fs out, wknd quickly*.......... (9 to 2 op 5 to 4) 9
1934 HOOCHIECOOCHIE MAN (Ire) 9-0 R Price (7) *hld up, nvr trbld ldrs*.......................................(50 to 1) 10
WIRED FOR SOUND 9-0 Lorna Vincent (6) *in tch on outsd till lost pl fnl 2 and a half fs*.......(40 to 1 op 33 to 1) 11
2845 TELEPHONIC (USA) 9-0 C Nutter (3) *al beh.* ....(40 to 1 op 33 to 1) 12
Dist: 4l, ¾l, 8l, 2½l, 1l, 2l, hd, sht-hd, 1l, 2l. 1m 36.20s. a 1.10s (12 Ran).
SR: 24/12/10/-/-/-/ (Lady Tennant), R Hannon

347 Loddington Conditions Stakes Class D (3-y-o) £3,201 5f 218yds.............. (2:30)

LORD OLIVIER (Ire) 8-10 M Tebbutt (6) *tucked in hndy, led jst o'r one furlong out, rdn out.* .... (6 to 1 op 5 to 1 tchd 13 to 2) 1
ROGER THE BUTLER (Ire) 8-10 M Hills (2) *led till hdd jst o'r one furlong out, ran on wl.* ....(5 to 2 op 6 to 4 tchd 100 to 30 and 7 to 2) 2
BRIGG FAIR 9-0 J Reid (5) *hld up in tch, hdwy 2 fs out, kpt on ins last*..................(6 to 4 fav op 6 to 4) 3
ARADANZA 8-10 T Quinn (1) *al prmnt, rdn 2 fs out, wknd fnl furlong*..............(4 to 1 op 7 to 1 tchd 8 to 1) 4
SISON (Ire) 8-3 (7*) G Parkin (3) *hld up, rdn o'r 2 fs out, no real imprsn*.......................... (40 to 1 op 33 to 1) 5
PALACEGATE TOUCH 9-0 G Carter (7) *beh, rdn and shrt-lvd effrt o'r 2 fs out, sn btn*......... (10 to 1 op 7 to 1) 6
THE SHARP BIDDER (Ire) 8-10 W Ryan (4) *wth ldr till rdn and wknd fnl 2 fs, sn wl beh*.......(16 to 1 op 14 to 1) 7
Dist: 1½l, 2l, 2l, 2l, hd, 10l. 1m 9.90s. b 0.50s (7 Ran).
SR: 46/40/36/24/16/19/-/ (Miss V R Jarvis), W Jarvis

348 Billesdon Selling Stakes Class G (3-y-o and up) £2,070 5f 2yds.............. (3:00)

2774 COCKERHAM RANGER 3-8-13 G Carter (6) *chsd ldrs, rdn o'r 2 fs out, squeezed through to ld ins last, pushed clr.* ....(5 to 2 fav op 9 to 4 tchd 2 to 1) 1
THE RIGHT TIME (bl) 8-9-12 L Dettori (1) *made most till hdd ins fnl furlong, no extr.* ....(9 to 1 op 12 to 1 tchd 14 to 1) 2
865 TOMMY TEMPEST 4-9-7 T Quinn (7) *broke wl, al prmnt, ev ch jst o'r one furlong out, unbl to quicken.* ....(10 to 1 op 12 to 1 tchd 14 to 1) 3
GREAT HALL 4-9-12 J Williams (8) *chsd ldrs, rdn 2 fs out, ran on ins last*.................. (33 to 1 op 25 to 1) 4
2777 EXPRESS MARIECURIE (Ire) (bl) 3-8-8 A Munro (5) *gd speed to hfwy, sn rdn and lost pl.* ....(9 to 1 op 8 to 1 tchd 10 to 1) 5
PARFAIT AMOUR 4-9-7 W Carson (4) *wth ldrs to hfwy, sn rdn alng and wknd wl o'r one furlong out.* ....(100 to 30 op 7 to 4) 6
2632 HINARI VIDEO 8-9-12 M Roberts (2) *speed 2 fs, sn rdn alng and wknd*..............(3 to 1 op 4 to 1 tchd 9 to 2) 7
BOULABAS (Ire) 4-9-7 R Cochrane (3) *chsd ldrs, rdn hfwy, no imprsn*.......................................(25 to 1) 8
Dist: 2½l, hd, ¾l, 4l, ½l, 1½l, 1l. 59.50s. a 0.80s (8 Ran).
SR: 33/36/30/32/-/9/8/-/ (J Berry), J Berry

349 Kingfisher Handicap Class E (0-70 4-y-o and up) £3,209 1m 3f 183yds....... (3:30)

211 VA UTU [44] 5-8-2 C Rutter (8) *patiently rdn, pld wide and gd hdwy frm 4 fs out, led 2 out, jnd ins last, all out.* ....(9 to 1 op 12 to 1) 1
2905 ROUSITTO [66] 5-9-10 W Ryan (3) *hld up and beh, steady hdwy frm 3 fs out, chlgd ins last, jst fld.* ....(5 to 1 op 7 to 2) 2
2906 EIRE LEATH-SCEAL [49] 6-8-7 M Wigham (9) *hld up in midfield, gd hdwy 4 fs out and sn ev ch, no extr ins last.* ....(9 to 1 op 8 to 1) 3
WILKINS [68] 4-9-10 G Carter (16) *trkd ldr, led 5 fs out till hdd 2 out, unbl to quicken*........ (10 to 1 op 8 to 1) 4
MOON SPIN [64] 4-9-6 W Carson (5) *hld up in midfield, rdn 3 fs out, styd on appr fnl furlong.* ....(8 to 1 op 6 to 1) 5

SAINT CIEL (USA) [65] 5-9-9 W Newnes (15) *trkd ldrs, ev ch 3 fs out, wknd appr last*........(12 to 1 op 8 to 1) 6
ZEALOUS KITTEN (USA) [55] 5-8-8 (5*) B Doyle (6) *wl beh till styd on fnl 2 fs, nvr nrr*...........(12 to 1 op 10 to 1) 7
1896 BALAAT (USA) [41] 5-7-9³ (7*) D McCabe (4) *midfield, effrt o'r 4 fs out, nvr able to chal*.......(25 to 1 op 20 to 1) 8
2152 SUNKALA SHINE [61] 5-9-5 K Fallon (14) *chsd ldrs, niggled alng 5 fs out, stdly lost pl.* .... (3 to 1 fav op 5 to 2 tchd 4 to 1 and 9 to 2) 9
LLOYDS DREAM [38] 4-7-8¹ J Quinn (7) *al rear div.* ....(66 to 1 op 50 to 1) 10
ROCKY ROMANCE [43] 6-8-1⁸ A Munro (10) *trkd ldrs till wknd o'r 3 fs out*..................(50 to 1 op 33 to 1) 11
2795 SWEET REVIVAL [37] 5-7-9⁵ (3*) N Kennedy (2) *beh, shrtlvd effrt and wndrd o'r 4 fs out, no further imprsn.* ....(16 to 1 op 12 to 1) 12
1655 HEIR OF EXCITEMENT [39] 8-7-11⁷ (3*) F Norton (11) *beh, effrt o'r 3 fs out, sn btn*...........(33 to 1 op 16 to 1) 13
235 SAIF AL ADIL (Ire) [37] 4-7-7 G Bardwell (13) *rdn to ld early, hdd 5 fs out, sn wknd, tld off*......(33 to 1 op 20 to 1) 14
4662a TEN HIGH (Ire) [38] 4-7-8¹ N Adams (1) *prmnt till wknd 5 fs out, sn in rear, tld off*...........(100 to 1 op 50 to 1) 15

Dist: Sht-hd, 3l, hd, 5l, 3l, hd, 1½l, ½l, 2½l, 8l. 2m 31.20s. a 2.70s (15 Ran).
SR: 20/41/18/34/20/17/6/-/8/ (M Quinn), M R Channon

350 Greyhound Handicap Class D (0-80 4-y-o and up) £3,348 1m 1f 218yds........ (4:00)

2434 WESTFIELD MOVES (Ire) [55] 5-8-5 J Quinn (2) *chsd ldrs on ins, jnd issue frm 3 fs out, led inside last, all out.* ....(9 to 1 op 14 to 1) 1
LOBILIO (USA) [67] 4-9-2 M Roberts (11) *made virtually all till hdd ins fnl furlong, ran on gmely, jst fld.* .... (2 to 1 fav op 9 to 4 tchd 3 to 1 and 7 to 4) 2
2902 BESCABY BOY [62] 7-8-12 J Williams (6) *patiently rdn, pld wide and hdwy frm 3 fs out, kpt on one pace fnl furlong*............................(11 to 2 op 4 to 1) 3
3027 FALCONS DAWN [54] 6-8-4 G Baxter (7) *hld up in tch, gd hdwy o'r 3 fs out, ran on one pace appr last.* ....(10 to 1 op 7 to 1) 4
GLIDE PATH (USA) [77] 4-9-12 M Hills (3) *hld up, hdwy wl o'r 2 fs out, nvr able to chal*.........(11 to 2 op 5 to 1) 5
SWIFT SILVER [58] 6-8-8 J Reid (1) *rcd wide early, in tch till no hdwy fnl 3 fs*..............(14 to 1 op 12 to 1) 6
1034 VINTAGE [75] 8-9-11 W Carson (5) *hld up in midfield, rdn o'r 3 fs out, sn no imprsn*..........(16 to 1 op 14 to 1) 7
GRAND VITESSE (Ire) [79] 4-9-7 (7*) Mark Denaro (8) *wth ldr, ev ch and hng lft o'r 3 fs out, wknd wl over one out.* ....(14 to 1 op 10 to 1) 8
LONG FURLONG [50] 5-8-0 N Adams (10) *slwly into strd, pld hrd on ins, nvr rchd ldrs*...... (20 to 1 op 16 to 1) 9
HIT THE FAN [66] 4-9-1 Pat Eddery (4) *wth ldrs on outsd, rdn alng 5 fs out, wknd wl o'r 3 out.* (7 to 1 op 5 to 1) 10
1598 GONE BUST (Ire) [50] 4-7-10 (3*) A Tucker (9) *chsd ldrs till rdn and wknd o'r 3 fs out*....................(33 to 1) 11

Dist: Hd, 3l, 3½l, 5l, 4l, ½l, ½l, 10l, nk, ½l. 2m 5.10s. a 2.20s (11 Ran).
SR: 34/44/34/19/31/5/21/23/-/ (A G Wakley), H J Collingridge

351 Levy Board Claiming Stakes Class E (3-y-o) £2,489 1m 1f 218yds............(4:30)

GENERAL CHASE 8-5 J Williams (7) *al hndy, led on ins o'r 2 fs out, styd on wl*............. (5 to 2 fav op 6 to 4) 1
1296 ANN HILL (Ire) 8-1 (7*) M Humphries (4) *hld up and beh, came wide and hdwy frm 4 fs out, wndrd fnl 2 furlongs, kpt on wl ins last*.....................(6 to 1 op 5 to 1) 2
STAPLEFORD LASS 8-6 W Woods (5) *tucked away, hdwy o'r 3 fs out, hng lft wl over 2 out, drifted rght and kpt on one pace und pres fnl furlong.* ....(5 to 1 op 11 to 2 tchd 13 to 2 and 7 to 4) 3
2397 QUICK SILVER BOY 8-9 L Charnock (6) *pld hrd, led till hdd o'r 2 fs out, unbl to quicken*........ (9 to 2 op 4 to 1) 4
2304 CAROJANGO 9-0 (7*) J O'Dwyer (2) *hld up in tch, imprvg on outsd whn slightly hmpd wl o'r 2 fs out, one pace.* .... (5 to 1 op 11 to 4) 5
KESANTA 8-4 T Sprake (3) *wth ldr till wknd fnl 3 fs.* ....(25 to 1 op 16 to 1) 6
4801a9 BEYOND THE LIMIT 8-4 T Quinn (1) *trkd ldrs, ev ch 3 fs out, sn btn*..........(18 to 1 op 16 to 1 tchd 25 to 1) 7
1678 GENERAL LINK 8-9 W Carson (9) *trkd ldrs till lost pl o'r 4 fs out*............................(33 to 1 op 20 to 1) 8
284 THREEOFUS 8-9 G Bardwell (8) *hld up, rdn o'r 3 fs out, no hdwy*..(33 to 1) 9

Dist: 1½l, 2l, ¾l, 4l, 2½l, 1½l, 2½l, 1l. 2m 8.30s. a 5.40s (9 Ran).
SR: 2/2/-/-/1/-/ (John Astbury), P G Murphy

352 Keythorpe Maiden Fillies Stakes Class D (3-y-o) £3,289 7f 9yds...............(5:00)

SEHAILAH 8-11 L Piggott (2) *broke wl, made virtually all, rdn and ran on ins last.* ....(15 to 2 op 12 to 1 tchd 14 to 1) 1
HAZY KAY (Ire) 8-11 A Munro (4) *al prmnt in centre, ev ch o'r one furlong out, unbl to quicken ins last.* ....(85 to 40 fav op 7 to 4 tchd 9 to 4) 2
LAKE POOPO (Ire) 8-11 D Holland (8) *al prmnt, rdn o'r 2 fs out, kpt on ins last*...(20 to 1 op 16 to 1 tchd 33 to 1) 3
BINT AL BALAD (Ire) 8-11 G Carter (6) *al prmnt, ev ch o'r one furlong out, sn rdn and one pace.* ....(12 to 1 op 7 to 1) 4
EXHIBIT AIR (Ire) 8-11 J Reid (10) *al prmnt far rail, ev ch frm 2 fs out, no extr ins last*...... (20 to 1 op 12 to 1) 5
RANI (Ire) 8-11 M Roberts (5) *nvr far away, ev ch o'r one furlong out, sn btn*.....(5 to 2 op 2 to 1 tchd 11 to 4) 6
RISPOTO 8-11 C Nutter (9) *chsd ldrs, shaken up wl o'r 2 fs out, no hdwy*.................... (33 to 1 op 25 to 1) 7
SAKURA QUEEN (Ire) 8-11 W Woods (7) *in tch till rdn and wknd fnl 3 fs*........(16 to 1 op 33 to 1 tchd 50 to 1) 8
ASTERN (USA) 8-11 Pat Eddery (3) *slwly into strd, reco'red to chase ldr, effrt over 3 fs out, wknd.* .... (11 to 2 op 4 to 1) 9
CHAMPAGNE GRANDY 8-11 T Quinn (1) *veered lft strt, reco'red to chase ldrs till lost pl frm hfwy.* ....(33 to 1 op 20 to 1) 10

Dist: 2l, ½l, ½l, ½l, 4l, ½l, 7l, nk, 1½l. 1m 24.30s. a 2.40s (10 Ran).
SR: 9/3/1/-/-/-/ (Ali K Al Jafleh), Mrs L Piggott

NEWCASTLE (good)
Tuesday March 30th

Going Correction: PLUS 0.15 sec. per fur. (races 1,2,3), MINUS 0.10 (4,5,6)

353 'Monkey Business' Median Auction Maiden Fillies Stakes Class F (3-y-o) £2,355 6f.......................... (2:15)

CHILLY BREEZE 8-11 G Duffield (3) *hld up in tch, led 2 out, pushed out, cmftbly.* ....(9 to 4 on op 2 to 1 on tchd 7 to 4 on) 1
KILLY'S FILLY 8-11 J Carroll (2) *cl up, led hfwy, hdd 2 out, sn rdn and no imprsn*............. (11 to 4 op 5 to 2) 2
NITEOWLADY 8-11 K Darley (1) *led to hfwy, sn wknd and beh*................................ (7 to 1 op 6 to 1) 3

Dist: 2½l, 15l. 1m 17.13s. a 5.13s (3 Ran).
SR: 12/2/-/ (P G Goulandris), Sir Mark Prescott

354 'Horse Feathers' Maiden Stakes Class D (2-y-o) £3,172 5f...................(2:45)

2914 TOP SHOW (Ire) 9-0 K Darley (5) *trkd ldr, led o'r 2 out, ran on wl*............................ (7 to 2 op 7 to 4) 1
ARTA 9-0 A Culhane (4) *in tch, hdwy to chase wnr frm 2 out, kpt on, no imprsn*............ (13 to 2 op 4 to 1) 2
PRECISION EDGE (Ire) 8-10¹ D Nicholls (3) *prmnt till wknd 2 out*.................(14 to 1 op 12 to 1 tchd 16 to 1) 3
SALTPETRE (Ire) 8-7 (7*) J Marshall (6) *led till hdd o'r 2 out, sn wknd*.......................(14 to 1 op 12 to 1) 4
GRANDMAN (Ire) 9-0 R Hills (2) *prmnt till wknd 2 out.* ....(4 to 1 op 7 to 2 tchd 5 to 1) 5
SING SONG BLUES 9-0 J Carroll (1) *sn outpcd and beh.* ......(11 to 8 fav op 7 to 4 tchd 2 to 1 and 11 to 10) 6

Dist: 1½l, 7l, nk, 3l, 6l. 1m 3.09s. a 4.19s (6 Ran).
SR: 31/25/-/ (P J White), K W Hogg

355 'Go West' Sprint Handicap Class C (0-90 3-y-o and up) £4,498 5f............. (3:15)

PENNY HASSET [67] 5-9-0 T Lucas (5) *in tch, hdwy to ld ins fnl furlong, ran on wl*...........(8 to 1 op 6 to 1) 1
2922 EAGER DEVA [81] 6-9-9 (5*) S Wynne (2) *trkd ldrs, chlgd ins fnl furlong, no extr towards finish.* ....(11 to 4 op 9 to 4) 2
EVER SO LONELY [55] 4-7-9 (7*) D Wright (3) *led till hdd and no extr ins fnl furlong*.......... (14 to 1 op 12 to 1) 3
292* AMRON [83] 6-10-2 (7ex) N Carlisle (7) *chsd ldrs, ev ch entering fnl furlong, one paced.* ....(6 to 4 fav tchd 7 to 4) 4
2926 EWALD (Ire) [59] 5-8-6 Dean McKeown (1) *sn pushed alng and beh, some late hdwy, nvr dngrs.* (8 to 1 op 6 to 1) 5
2927 MISS MOVIE WORLD [57] 4-8-4 J Fanning (6) *chsd ldrs, ev ch o'r one out, wknd fnl furlong*....(11 to 2 op 9 to 2) 6
289 SO SUPERB [58] 4-8-5 J Lowe (4) *prmnt till wknd 2 out.* ....(25 to 1 op 16 to 1) 7

Dist: 1½l, ½l, ¾l, 2½l, hd, 1l. 1m 2.55s. a 3.65s (7 Ran).
SR: 42/50/22/47/13/10/7/ (Mrs Anne Henson), M W Easterby

356 'At The Circus' Handicap Class E (0-70 4-y-o and up) £2,976 2m 19yds..........(3:45)

GREY POWER [56] 6-9-3 K Darley (9) *hld up and beh, hdwy 5 out, styd on wl und pres fnl 2 fs to ld post.* ....(9 to 2 op 7 to 2) 1
CHANTRY BARTLE [35] 7-7-10 J Fanning (5) *trkd ldrs, led 3 fs out, rdn o'r one out, ct post.* (5 to 2 fav tchd 3 to 1) 2
DESERT MIST [47] (bl) 4-7-10 (7*) C Teague (8) *chsd ldrs, reminders hfwy, kpt on und pres fnl 3 fs*....... (5 to 1) 3
HOT STAR [52] 7-8-13 J Lowe (2) *hld up, hdwy 5 fs out, kpt on same pace frm 3 out*...... (10 to 1 tchd 11 to 1) 4
COST EFFECTIVE [35] 6-7-10³ A Mackay (10) *in tch, ev ch 3 fs out, kpt on same pace*..................... (16 to 1) 5
ONLY A ROSE [48] 4-8-4 N Connorton (7) *prmnt, ev ch 3 fs out, sn wknd*....... (11 to 1 op 10 to 1 tchd 12 to 1) 6

ONE FOR THE POT [63] 8-9-7 (3*) J Weaver (3) *hld up, effrt o'r 3 fs out, sn btn*..................(8 to 1 op 6 to 1) 7
BEST GUN [55] (bl) 4-8-11 J Carroll (6) *led till hdd 3 fs out, wknd quickly*..................(16 to 1 op 14 to 1) 8
4742a[9] BRIDGE PLAYER [40] 6-7-8 (7*) D Wright (11) *sn beh, lost tch 5 fs out*..................(16 to 1 op 12 to 1) 9
288[7] MILIYEL [45] (v) 4-8-1 N Carlisle (1) *prmnt till wknd quickly 4 fs out*..................(8 to 1 op 6 to 1) 10
Dist: Hd, 1½l, 2l, sht-hd, 15l, 8l, 12l, 5l, 2½l. 3m 35.71s. a 9.71s (10 Ran).
(J P S Racing), Mrs M Reveley

357 'Animal Crackers' Maiden Stakes Class D (3-y-o) £3,055 1¼m 32yds...........(4:15)

UM ALGOWAIN (USA) 9-0 Paul Eddery (2) *led early, sn tracking ldr, led 4 fs out, quickened o'r 2 out, pushed out*..................(13 to 8 op Evens tchd 7 to 4) 1
EATON ROW (USA) 9-0 S Whitworth (1) *trkd ldrs, effrt o'r 2 fs out, ev ch entering last, no extr und pres.* ....(4 to 1 op 5 to 2) 2
MOUNT FUJI 9-0 R Hills (5) *hld up, hdwy o'r 3 fs out, rdn wl over one out, sn outpcd*......(11 to 8 fav op 2 to 1) 3
KARIB 8-9 K Darley (4) *in tch till wknd o'r 2 fs out.* ....(20 to 1) 4
GROGFRYN 8-9 J Carroll (3) *in tch till wknd o'r 2 fs out.* ....(14 to 1 op 10 to 1 tchd 16 to 1) 5
51[8] BADENOCH BURNER 9-0 Kim Tinkler (6) *pld hrd early and sn led, hdd 4 fs out, wknd quickly 3 out, tld off.* ....(100 to 1 op 33 to 1) 6
Dist: ¾l, 15l, 4l, 6l, dist. 2m 13.63s. a 7.13s (6 Ran).
SR: 18/16/-/ (Sheikh Ahmed Al Maktoum), M R Stoute

358 'Duck Soup' Handicap Class D (0-80 3-y-o and up) £3,260 1¼m 32yds..........(4:45)

TANODA [42] 7-7-8[1] J Lowe (6) *made all, rdn o'r one furlong out, ran on wl*..................(6 to 1 op 5 to 1) 1
JAZILAH (Fr) [64] 5-9-2 K Darley (3) *trkd ldr, effrt 3 fs out, rdn 2 out, kpt on, no imprsn.* ....(11 to 8 fav op 5 to 4 tchd 6 to 4) 2
4735a[2] COMMON COUNCIL [72] 4-9-9 G Duffield (5) *hld up in tch, effrt 3 out, styd on fnl furlong*......(10 to 1 op 8 to 1) 3
LORD LAMBSON [42] 4-7-7 J Fanning (1) *chsd ldrs, ev ch 2 fs out, one paced*.....(14 to 1 op 12 to 1 tchd 16 to 1) 4
MAD MILITANT (Ire) [77] 4-9-9 (5*) S Wynne (4) *beh, hdwy 4 fs out, kpt on same pace frm 2 out*... (7 to 1 op 6 to 1) 5
GOLDEN TORQUE [67] 6-8-12 (7*) H Bastiman (7) *beh, effrt 3 fs out, no hdwy*..................(13 to 2 op 5 to 1) 6
PHILGUN [58] 4-8-6 (3*) S Maloney (2) *chsd ldrs till wknd o'r 2 fs out*..................(7 to 2 op 3 to 1) 7
KHALLOOF (Ire) [66] 4-9-3 D Nicholls (8) *al beh, lost tch 3 fs out*..................(33 to 1 op 25 to 1) 8
Dist: 2l, 1l, ¾l, ¾l, 1½l, 2l, 20l. 2m 10.83s. a 4.33s (8 Ran).
SR: 26/44/49/17/50/38/24/-/ (Mel Brittain), M Brittain

ST-CLOUD (FR) (good)
Tuesday March 30th

359 Prix la Camargo (Listed) (3-y-o) £14,337 1m..............................(2:10)

SHOWGUM (Fr) 9-2 A Junk,.......................... 1
LA GROUPIE (Fr) 9-2 O Doleuze,.......................... 2
KIRUNA (USA) 9-2 T Jarnet,.......................... 3
ARMEE DE L'AIR 9-2 E Saint-Martin,.......................... 4
Dist: Sht-hd, 1½l, nk, 1½l, 2l, 2l, 6l. 1m 44.50s. a 6.00s (8 Ran).
SR: 12/11/6/5/ (Mme C Miremad), G Milbank

360 Prix Omnium II (Listed) (3-y-o) £14,337 1m ....(2:40)

BIGSTONE (Ire) 9-2 D Boeuf,.......................... 1
LE BALAFRE (Fr) 9-2 O Peslier,.......................... 2
SEATON DELAVAL (USA) 9-2 T Jarnet,.......................... 3
SEMILLON 9-2 A Badel,.......................... 4
Dist: 2l, nk, 1½l, nk, hd, 5l, 1½l, hd, 5l. 1m 40.90s. a 2.40s (10 Ran).
SR: 66/60/59/54/ (D Wildenstein), E Lellouche

CATTERICK (good)
Wednesday March 31st
Going Correction: PLUS 0.10 sec. per fur. (races 1,4,7), MINUS 0.05 (2,3,5,6)

361 Springtime Limited Stakes Class F (0-60 3-y-o) £2,601 5f.................... (2:20)

324* PRESS THE BELL 8-11 J Carroll (6) *broke fst, made all, drw clr frm hfwy, eased*...... (2 to 1 fav op 11 to 10) 1
95[3] GUSSIE FINK-NOTTLE (Ire) 8-11 Alex Greaves (3) *chsd wnr most of way, kpt on, no imprsn fnl furlong.* ....(15 to 2 op 8 to 1 tchd 7 to 1) 2
MILBANK CHALLENGER 8-11 M Birch (4) *chsd ldg trio, hrd at work 2 fs out, kpt on same pace.* ....(9 to 1 op 8 to 1) 3
LUCKY MILL 8-3 (3*) N Kennedy (8) *sluggish strt, chsd alng to improve last 2 fs, ran on finish.* ....(10 to 1 op 6 to 1) 4
DEAD CALM 8-11 Dean McKeown (12) *rcd wide thrght, improved frm midfield 2 fs out, ran on wl finish.* ....(16 to 1 op 12 to 1) 5
324[4] COMET WHIRLPOOL (Ire) (bl) 8-11 J Quinn (9) *broke wl to show gd speed for o'r 2 fs, fdd*...... (7 to 1 op 10 to 1) 6
214[9] FOREST FLYER 7-13 (7*) J Marshall (5) *bustled alng to keep up, nvr able to trble ldrs*..................(20 to 1) 7
29[4] DON'T TELL JEAN 8-6 L Charnock (7) *drvn alng in midfield, nvr nr to chal*..........(100 to 1 op 50 to 1) 8
BRIGADORE GOLD 8-6 R Lappin (1) *sluggish strt, chsd alng thrght, nvr dngrs*.. (7 to 1 op 6 to 1 tchd 8 to 1) 9
29[5] BROADSTAIRS BEAUTY (Ire) 8-8 (3*) S D Williams (10) *chsd ldrs, hrd at work hfwy, sn btn, virtually pld up o'r one furlong out*..........(12 to 1 op 10 to 1) 10
PRESSURE OFF (bl) 8-8 (3*) J Weaver (11) *sn outpcd and drvn alng, nvr dngrs*............(100 to 1 op 50 to 1) 11
SIMPLY SUPERB 8-11 T Lucas (2) *slow to break, wl beh whn pld up lme a furlong out*..... (20 to 1 op 16 to 1) pu
Dist: 4l, 1½l, 2l, ¾l, 2½l, 3½l, 4l, ½l, 3½l, 2½l. 1m 0.90s. a 3.40s (12 Ran).
SR: 39/23/17/4/6/-/ (Sydney Mason), J Berry

362 Forcett Park Selling Stakes Class G (3-y-o and up) £2,364 7f..................(2:50)

ROYAL GIRL 6-9-6 N Connorton (2) *al hndy, drvn long 2 fs out, styd on grimly to ld wl ins fnl furlong.* ....(9 to 2 op 5 to 2 tchd 5 to 1) 1
CLEDESCHAMPS 4-9-2 S Morris (9) *dsptd ld, drvn alng last 2 fs, styd on same pace*..................(20 to 1) 2
UCKERBY MOOR (v) 4-9-2 (5*) O Pears (5) *sluggish strt, given time to reco'r, effrt and not much room fnl furlong, ran on*..................(100 to 1) 3
285[6] SALADAN KNIGHT 8-9-11 D Nicholls (1) *made most, quickened o'r 2 fs out, wknd and hdd wl ins fnl furlong.* ....(15 to 2 op 7 to 1 tchd 8 to 1) 4
72[7] ARAGON KING 3-8-5 K Fallon (3) *al chasing ldrs, feeling pace and drvn alng o'r 2 fs out, no imprsn.* ....(14 to 1 op 12 to 1) 5
AARDVARK (bl) 7-9-4 (7*) E Husband (6) *trkd ldg bunch, chsd alng whn pace quickened o'r 2 fs out, no extr.* ....(7 to 1 op 5 to 1) 6
275[7] KENTUCKY DREAMS 3-8-2 (3*) J Weaver (10) *chsd ldg trio for o'r 4 fs, fdd*.......... (7 to 1 op 5 to 1 tchd 8 to 1) 7
OUR MICA 3-8-5 J Carroll (12) *chsd ldg 5, feeling pace o'r 2 fs out, sn btn*..........(13 to 2 op 6 to 1 tchd 7 to 1) 8
228[6] FORMAESTRE (Ire) 3-7-11 (7*) J Tate (7) *chsd alng to keep up hfwy, came wide strt, no imprsn.* ....(7 to 2 fav op 3 to 1) 9
CHAMPENOISE 5-9-2 S Webster (13) *in tch, chsd alng to keep up hfwy, fdd entering strt*..................(16 to 1) 10
DOMDOM 3-8-5 Dean McKeown (11) *sluggish strt, reco'ring whn hmpd and snatched up appr hfwy, not rcvr*..................(50 to 1) 11
FREE STYLE 7-9-2 J Lowe (8) *chsd ldg bunch to hfwy, sn struggling*..................(50 to 1) 12
253[5] NEVENTER (Fr) 4-9-4 (3*) S D Williams (4) *bolted gng to post, missed break, al struggling*.. (12 to 1 op 10 to 1) 13
Dist: 2l, sht-hd, 1½l, 2l, 5l, 3½l, ¾l, 5l, 1½l, 1½l. 1m 27.80s. a 4.80s (13 Ran).
SR: 29/19/23/22/-/1/ (Miss S E Hall), Miss S E Hall

363 Gods Solution Handicap Class D (0-80 3-y-o and up) £3,406 7f................. (3:20)

24[5] TYRONE FLYER [48] 4-8-5 N Carlisle (7) *made all, drvn alng to quicken last 2 fs, hld on grimly fnl furlong.* ....(7 to 1 op 6 to 1) 1
MCA BELOW THE LINE [56] (v) 5-8-8 (5*) O Pears (12) *nvr far away, hrd drvn ins fnl furlong, ran on, edgd lft cl hme*..................(20 to 1 op 16 to 1) 2
232[6] DIAMOND INTHE DARK (USA) [53] (v) 5-8-10 T Lucas (6) *chsd alng in midfield, staying on fnl furlong whn not much room cl hme*..........(12 to 1 op 10 to 1) 3
LEAVE IT TO LIB [59] 6-8-9 (7*) J Tate (10) *trkd ldg quartet, effrt and drvn alng last 2 fs, styd on.* (8 to 1 op 7 to 1) 4
WILD PROSPECT [56] 5-8-13 M Birch (9) *trkd wnr, ev ch o'r one furlong out, kpt on same pace.* ....(10 to 1 op 8 to 1) 5
227 THE TONDY (Ire) [37] 5-7-8 J Fanning (8) *nvr far away, effrt and bustled alng last 2 fs, not quicken.* ....(100 to 1 op 50 to 1) 6
SECOND COLOURS (USA) [62] 3-8-3 K Darley (3) *hld up and beh, niggled alng to improve 2 fs out, eased whn btn fnl furlong*..................(4 to 1 op 3 to 1) 7
MARY MACBLAIN [41] 4-7-12 J Quinn (1) *chsd ldg bunch, hrd at work o'r 2 fs out, no imprsn*..........(14 to 1) 8
DOKKHA OYSTON (Ire) [71] 5-10-0 J Carroll (2) *sluggish strt, improved o'r 2 fs out, not rch ldrs.* ....(6 to 1 op 5 to 1 tchd 7 to 1) 9
276[3] DREAM CARRIER (Ire) [70] 5-9-13 Alex Greaves (4) *trkd ldg half dozen, chsd alng on ins o'r 2 fs out, no extr.* ....(100 to 30 fav op 7 to 2 tchd 4 to 1) 10
39[5] SCOTTISH PARK [63] 4-9-6 G Duffield (5) *sluggish strt, nvr able to reco'r*..................(10 to 1) 11

4764a^{8} CASHTAL DAZZLER [49] (bl) 6-8-6 L Charnock (11) *chsd ldg 5 till fdd last 2 fs*.................. (25 to 1 op 20 to 1) 12
Dist: ½l, ¾l, sht-hd, nk, 3l, nk, ¾l, 1l, 4l, nk. 1m 27.50s. a 4.50s (12 Ran).
SR: 18/24/19/24/20/-/-/-/20/ (J Naughton), Miss Gay Kelleway

364 Toytop Condition Stakes Class D (2-y-o) £3,231 5f.......................... (3:50)

291^{2} INDIAN DREAMER 8-10 M Hills (1) *made all, clr whn ran green and drifted rght o'r one furlong out, kpt on wl.* ....(11 to 10 on op 5 to 4 tchd 6 to 4) 1
312^{3} HILL FARM KATIE 8-6^{1} L Dettori (6) *chsd ldg pair, hrd at work hfwy, styd on fnl furlong, no imprsn.* .... (7 to 1 op 11 to 2 tchd 8 to 1) 2
UP THE MARINERS (Ire) 8-5 R P Elliott (3) *chsd ldg trio, effrt and ran green hfwy, styd on fnl furlong.* .... (33 to 1 op 25 to 1) 3
312^{8} MUCKROSS PARK 8-5 K Darley (4) *sluggish strt, chsd alng to keep up hfwy, kpt on, nvr nrr.* .... (50 to 1 op 33 to 1) 4
RICH HARMONY 8-10 W Newnes (2) *sluggish strt, chsd alng thrght, nvr dngrs..* (4 to 1 op 2 to 1 tchd 9 to 2) 5
TEETOTALLER (Ire) 8-10 J Carroll (7) *sluggish strt, wndrd aftr 2 fs, nvr a factor*.................. (5 to 1 op 3 to 1) 6
NORTHGATE RAVER 8-6^{1} M Wigham (5) *broke wl to chase wnr for 2 fs, wknd quickly two furlongs out.* .... (20 to 1 op 14 to 1) 7
Dist: 3½l, 2½l, 2½l, 2½l, hd, 6l. 1m 1.80s. a 4.30s (7 Ran).
SR: 20/2/-/-/ (R B Holt), M Bell

365 Yarm Handicap Class C (0-90 4-y-o and up) £4,624 1m 5f 175yds................ (4:20)

WHITE WILLOW [69] 4-8-9 K Darley (4) *made most, hrd drvn o'r 2 fs out, jnd ins fnl furlong, hld on wl.* ....(9 to 2 op 7 to 2) 1
STAR PLAYER [85] 7-9-11 (3*) J Weaver (1) *patiently rdn, improved on bit entering strt, drw level fnl furlong, edgd lft, not go past*..............(10 to 1 op 8 to 1) 2
PATROL [59] 4-7-13 N Carlisle (8) *chsd ldg trio, hrd at work whn pace quickened o'r 2 fs out, one pace.* .... (33 to 1 op 20 to 1) 3
TRUBEN (USA) [80] 4-9-6 L Dettori (6) *nvr far away, feeling pace and drvn alng o'r 2 fs out, not quicken.* ....(5 to 2 fav op 7 to 4) 4
290^{4} KALKO [58] 4-7-9 (3*) N Kennedy (7) *chsd ldg half dozen, hrd at work entering strt, sn outpcd.* ....(3 to 1 tchd 7 to 2 and 11 to 4) 5
CHIEF MINISTER (Ire) [82] 4-9-8 K Fallon (2) *scrubbed alng most of way, nvr rch ldrs.* ....(11 to 2 op 4 to 1 tchd 6 to 1) 6
TOUR LEADER (NZ) [62] 4-8-2 Alex Greaves (3) *dsptd ld to strt, fdd o'r 2 fs out*............ (20 to 1 op 16 to 1) 7
CO-CHIN (Ire) [66] 4-8-6 J Quinn (5) *chsd ldrs, struggling to hold pl hfwy, sn lost tch*.........(14 to 1 tchd 16 to 1) 8
Dist: Hd, 5l, ¾l, 4l, 1l, sht-hd, 15l. 3m 3.80s. a 8.30s (8 Ran).
SR: 5/23/-/3/-/ (Mrs H North), Mrs M Reveley

366 Whorlton Handicap Class E (0-70 3-y-o and up) £3,106 1½m 44yds.............. (4:50)

DEB'S BALL [54] 7-9-5 J Quinn (3) *wtd wth, hrd at work aftr a m, styd on wl to ld entering fnl furlong, drw clr.* .... (10 to 1 op 8 to 1) 1
198^{9} SHARQUIN [30] 6-7-9^{2} J Lowe (12) *settled midfield, improved to nose ahead o'r one furlong out, hdd entering last, one pace*................(14 to 1 tchd 16 to 1) 2
DUGGAN [45] 6-8-10 L Dettori (8) *chsd ldg quartet, effrt and drvn alng o'r 2 fs out, styd on same pace.* ....(9 to 1 op 8 to 1) 3
278* TEMPERING [45] 7-8-10 S Wood (4) *tried to make all, clr hfwy, wknd and hdd o'r one furlong out.* ....(9 to 4 fav op 6 to 4 tchd 5 to 2) 4
PRIDE OF PENDLE [47] 4-8-10 Paul Eddery (6) *nvr far away, hrd at work whn pace quickened entering strt, fdd*................................ (14 to 1 op 12 to 1) 5
FANATICAL (USA) [50] 7-8-12 (3*) J Weaver (1) *settled gng wl, effrt and drvn alng entering strt, no imprsn.* .... (10 to 1 op 8 to 1) 6
294 CHEEKY POT [33] (bl) 5-7-12 L Charnock (2) *chsd clr ldr, drvn alng o'r 2 fs out, fdd*........... (8 to 1 op 7 to 1) 7
OLLIVER DUCKETT [35] 4-7-12 Dale Gibson (10) *pld hrd, wth ldrs to strt, fdd*.............. (25 to 1 op 20 to 1) 8
165^{9} RUPPLES [28] 6-7-4^{4} (7*) Claire Balding (7) *in tch, chsd alng hfwy, btn entering strt*.......(50 to 1 op 33 to 1) 9
290 DEMOKOS (Fr) [28] 8-7-7 J Fanning (9) *trkd ldg 5 for a m, fdd entering strt*....... (8 to 1 op 12 to 1 tchd 7 to 1) 10
LADY DONOGHUE (USA) [49] 4-8-12 K Darley (11) *chsd ldrs, hrd at work entering strt, sn btn.* ....(12 to 1 op 10 to 1) 11
EXPLOSIVE SPEED (USA) [59] 5-9-10 Dean McKeown (5) *struggling to keep up hfwy, nvr a factor.* ....(7 to 1 op 6 to 1) 12
Dist: 4l, ½l, 2½l, 8l, 1½l, 2½l, ½l, ½l, 2l, sht-hd. 2m 40.80s. a 5.80s (12 Ran).
SR: 41/9/23/18/2/4/ (J Calvert), D Moffatt

367 Oran Maiden Stakes Class D (3-y-o) £3,172 5f................................. (5:20)

PRIMULA BAIRN 8-9 K Fallon (6) *patiently rdn, improved on outsd to ld entering last, ran on wl.* ....(4 to 1 op 5 to 1 tchd 7 to 2) 1
250^{6} HAWAYMYSON (Ire) 8-11 (3*) J Weaver (1) *chsd alng in midfield, improved to ld o'r one furlong out, hdd entering last, one pace*................ (16 to 1 op 14 to 1) 2
275^{6} MISS WHITTINGHAM (Ire) 8-9 J Carroll (4) *slight ld for o'r 3 fs, rdn and no extr*................ (20 to 1 op 14 to 1) 3
SABO THE HERO 9-0 G Duffield (3) *sluggish strt, chsd alng to pick up hfwy, ran on wl fnl furlong.* ....(5 to 1 op 4 to 1) 4
KIMMY'S PRINCESS 8-9 R Cochrane (2) *dsptd ld for o'r 3 fs, fdd*.................. (9 to 2 op 2 to 1 tchd 5 to 1) 5
INDIAN SECRET (Ire) 9-0 J Fortune (5) *sluggish strt, bustled alng thrght, nvr dngrs*........(25 to 1 op 20 to 1) 6
WINDRUSH BOY 9-0 J Reid (7) *wth ldg pair, hrd at work and edgd lft 2 fs out, eased whn btn.* ....(6 to 4 fav op 5 to 4) 7
Dist: 1½l, 3½l, hd, ¾l, 4l, 7l. 1m 1.70s. a 4.20s (7 Ran).
SR: 21/20/1/5/ (Kavli), Mrs J R Ramsden

BRIGHTON (good (races 1,2,3,4), good to soft (5,6))
Thursday April 1st
Going Correction: PLUS 0.05 sec. per fur.

368 Elm Grove Claiming Stakes Class F (4-y-o and up) £2,243 5f 213yds............ (2:15)

232^{7} UNVEILED 5-8-4 W Carson (4) *settled towards rear, pushed alng appr hfwy, rdn and ran on to ld entering fnl furlong, quickened clr*..... (Evens fav op 6 to 4 on) 1
223^{9} SIRMOOR (Ire) (v) 4-8-7 A McGlone (2) *made most of rng til hdd entering fnl furlong, sn outpcd.* (5 to 2 op 6 to 4) 2
ORATEL FLYER (v) 6-7-10 (7*) Nicola Howarth (3) *pressed ldr, ev ch 2 out, not quicken fnl furlong.* .... (33 to 1 op 8 to 1) 3
ALPHONSO 4-9-3 S Whitworth (1) *wl in tch, effrt und pres and hng rght 2 out, found no extr.* ....(3 to 1 op 6 to 1 tchd 7 to 1) 4
264 SAYSANA 6-8-2 Candy Morris (5) *in tch, rdn and one pace frm 2 out*........................(33 to 1 op 10 to 1) 5
Dist: 7l, ¾l, 2l, 1l. 1m 12.90s. a 4.50s (5 Ran).
SR: 6/-/ (Mrs K M Burge), R J Hodges

369 Roedean Handicap Class C (0-90 3-y-o and up) £4,371 5f 213yds................ (2:50)

223^{5} SAMSOLOM [58] 5-8-11 J Quinn (5) *trkd ldrs, rdn to ld and edgd lft o'r one out, drvn out*....(8 to 1 op 6 to 1) 1
SHIKARI'S SON [72] 6-9-11 T Quinn (2) *in tch, not clr run on ins 2 out, swtchd rght o'r one out, styd on nr finish.* ....(4 to 1 op 3 to 1 tchd 9 to 2) 2
232^{8} AMETHYSTINE (USA) [59] 7-8-12 W Carson (4) *led for one furlong, pressed ldr til squeezed for room o'r one out, not rcvr*................(4 to 1 op 3 to 1 tchd 9 to 2) 3
249^{2} INVOCATION [75] 6-10-0 N Adams (1) *slwly into strd, led aftr one furlong, hdd und pres o'r one out, kpt on same pace*.............................(11 to 2 op 5 to 1) 4
301^{2} MISDEMEANOURS GIRL (Ire) [68] 5-9-2 (5*) B Doyle (3) *al outpcd in rear*................ (5 to 4 fav tchd 13 to 8) 5
Dist: ¾l, 2l, ¾l, 8l. 1m 11.90s. a 3.50s (5 Ran).
SR: 33/44/23/36/-/ (The Hammond Partnership), P Howling

370 Hollingbury Conditions Stakes Class D (3-y-o) £3,026 6f 209yds.............. (3:25)

284* KEYWAY (USA) 8-12 G Duffield (4) *chsd ldr, led o'r 3 out, rdn clr one out, eased nr finish.* .... (9 to 1 op 5 to 1 tchd 10 to 1) 1
262* PERSIAN GUSHER (Ire) 8-12 M Roberts (1) *slwly into strd, jnd ldrs 3 out, ev ch 2 out, edgd lft and no extr appr fnl furlong*..............(14 to 1 op 6 to 1 tchd 16 to 1) 2
TYCHONIC 8-10 Pat Eddery (5) *handily plcd, pushed alng o'r 2 out, eased whn btn fnl furlong.* ....(7 to 4 on op Evens tchd 11 to 10) 3
WYNONA (Ire) 8-13 W R Swinburn (3) *chsd ldrs til 2 out, eased whn btn*........................ (7 to 2 op 7 to 4) 4
SOVIET EXPRESS 8-10 T Quinn (2) *led for o'r 3 fs, virtually pld up last 2 furlongs, tld off.* ....(20 to 1 op 10 to 1 tchd 25 to 1) 5
Dist: 7l, 3½l, ½l, 25l. 1m 27.30s. a 7.30s (5 Ran).
(B Haggas), Sir Mark Prescott

371 Falmer Rating Related Maiden Stakes Class E (0-70 3-y-o) £2,872 7f 214yds (4:00)

DANA SPRINGS (Ire) 8-9 J Comber (2) *hld up in tch, jnd ldr 2 out, led jst o'r one out, styd on cleverly.* .... (13 to 2 op 4 to 1) 1

SMARGINATO (Ire) 9-0 W Carson (1) *chsd ldr till led o'r 2 out, rdn and hdd jst over one out, no extr.* ....(11 to 10 on op 6 to 4 on tchd Evens) 2
HALF A DOZEN (USA) 8-9 W R Swinburn (3) *hld up in rear, effrt 3 out, sn rdn alng, lost tch o'r one out.* ....(5 to 1 op 6 to 1) 3
328[5] MAJOR TRIUMPH (Ire) (bl) 8-9 N Day (4) *led, clr hfwy, hdd o'r 2 out, sn wknd and lost tch.* ....(3 to 1 op 4 to 1 tchd 9 to 2) 4
Dist: 2½l, 20l, 25l. 1m 41.00s. a 8.60s (4 Ran).
(G Howard-Spink), R Hannon

372 Churchill Square Maiden Stakes Class D (3-y-o) £3,318 1m 1f 209yds......... (4:35)

ERICOLIN (Ire) 9-0 M Roberts (2) *ldg grp, led o'r 2 out, shaken up and styd on ins fnl furlong.* ....(11 to 10 fav op 11 to 10 on tchd 6 to 4) 1
ALYDUNCAN (USA) 9-0 T Quinn (9) *slwly into strd, hdwy to ld aftr 2 fs, hdd o'r two out, rdn and kpt on same pace*..................(7 to 4 op 2 to 1 tchd 13 to 8) 2
PHROSE 9-0 J Reid (1) *led for 2 fs, pressed ldrs, rdn alng o'r two out, ran on ins fnl furlong.* ....(6 to 1 op 7 to 2 tchd 8 to 1) 3
259[7] JULIASDARKINVADER 9-0 Candy Morris (8) *handily plcd til rdn and wknd frm 2 out*........(50 to 1 op 20 to 1) 4
HARLESTONE BROOK 9-0 W Carson (4) *styd on frm rear last 2 fs, nvr nrr*.....(16 to 1 op 10 to 1 tchd 20 to 1) 5
MY HARVINSKI 9-0 S Whitworth (5) *in tch til wknd o'r 2 out*.............................(14 to 1 op 6 to 1) 6
MRS NICE GUY 8-9 G Duffield (3) *steadied leaving stalls, al rear div*...........(16 to 1 op 8 to 1 tchd 20 to 1) 7
259[8] LITTLE KARLIE (Den) 8-2 (7*) D Wright (7) *mid-div til wknd o'r 3 out*.......................(50 to 1 op 20 to 1) 8
260[7] SUNBEAM CHARLIE 9-0 N Adams (6) *chsd ldrs to hfwy, drpd out quickly, tld off.* ....(33 to 1 op 20 to 1 tchd 50 to 1) 9
Dist: 1l, ¾l, 7l, 3½l, 4l, 12l, hd, 30l. 2m 14.50s. a 16.30s (9 Ran).
(Sheikh Marwan Al Maktoum), C E Brittain

373 Sheepcote Valley Handicap Class E (0-70 3-y-o and up) £2,976 1m 3f 196yds...(5:05)

287[5] ATLANTIC WAY [42] 5-8-2 J Quinn (8) *mid-div, ran on o'r 3 out, led over one out, styd on wl*....(11 to 2 op 7 to 2) 1
294[2] THE KARAOKE KING [50] (bl) 4-8-8 J Reid (2) *trkd ldrs, led o'r 2 out, hdd und pres and edgd rght over one out, one pace*.........................(9 to 4 fav op 5 to 4) 2
FLY FOR GOLD (Ire) [51] 4-8-9 T Quinn (12) *swtchd to stands side o'r 3 out, ran on and wndrd badly lft appr fnl furlong, no imprsn on wnr*..... (7 to 1 tchd 8 to 1) 3
4800a[7] BUGLET [58] 3-7-8[1] N Carlisle (11) *pressed ldrs, led o'r 4 out till over 2 out, no extr appr fnl furlong.* ....(16 to 1 op 10 to 1) 4
AL SHANY [50] 7-8-5 (5*) N Gwilliams (10) *effrt frm rear o'r 3 out, not trble ldrs last 2 fs*........(33 to 1 op 20 to 1) 5
182 CASTLE GALAH [35] (v) 6-7-9[6] (5*) B Doyle (5) *effrt o'r 3 out, wknd over 2 out*.......................(25 to 1 op 20 to 1) 6
4759a[8] JOLI'S GREAT [50] 5-8-10 D Biggs (7) *improved aftr hfwy, wknd o'r 3 out*...............(4 to 1 op 5 to 1 tchd 6 to 1) 7
265[5] DR ZEVA [33] 7-7-2[2] (7*) D Wright (4) *cl up, led 6 out till o'r 4 out, wknd frm 3 out*..............................(8 to 1) 8
78[8] THIN RED LINE [44] (v) 9-8-4 M Roberts (1) *in tch till wknd 4 out, eased whn btn*.............(16 to 1 op 10 to 1) 9
NORTHERN LION [36] 10-7-10[3] N Adams (13) *led for 6 fs, wknd quickly, tld off*.............(33 to 1 op 25 to 1) 10
Dist: 2½l, 5l, 2l, 2½l, 1l, 4l, 4l, 3l, dist. 2m 42.50s. a 15.00s (10 Ran).
(C John Hill), C J Hill

SOUTHWELL (A.W) (std)
Thursday April 1st
Going Correction: MINUS 0.25 sec. per fur. (races 1,6), PLUS 0.25 (2,3,4,5)

374 Narcissus Maiden Auction Stakes Class F (2-y-o) £2,444 5f....................(2:25)

312[2] BOLD ARISTOCRAT (Ire) 9-0 S Perks (5) *cl up, led 2 fs out, sn clr, very easily*..............(Evens fav tchd 5 to 4) 1
DUBALL REMY 8-9 S O'Gorman (4) *in tch, rdn alng hfwy, styd on fnl furlong*...............(20 to 1 op 10 to 1) 2
MR BLOBBY (Ire) 9-0 J Carroll (8) *led, rdn and hdd 2 fs out, wknd fnl furlong*.....................(7 to 1 op 5 to 2) 3
299[5] ROCKABYE BAILEYS 8-9 Dean McKeown (2) *pressed ldrs, rdn and wknd o'r 2 fs out.* ....(10 to 1 op 5 to 1 tchd 12 to 1) 4
CRUISING CHICK 8-4 (5*) O Pears (7) *chsd ldrs 2 fs, outpcd and beh hfwy, some hdwy fnl furlong.* ....(20 to 1 op 14 to 1) 5
MARCH OF TIME 9-0 Paul Eddery (6) *slwly away, sn outpcd and beh*.........................(7 to 2 op 5 to 1) 6
BURNTWOOD MELODY 9-0 A Munro (3) *slwly into strd, al outpcd and beh*........(13 to 2 op 4 to 1 tchd 7 to 1) 7
Dist: 10l, hd, 3½l, ½l, 1l, ½l. 1m 0.30s. a 2.40s (7 Ran).
SR: 27/-/-/-/ (Mrs J Hughes), R Hollinshead

375 Primrose Apprentice Stakes Handicap Class G (0-70 4-y-o and up) £2,070 1m ....(2:55)

264 ROYAL ACCLAIM [33] (v) 8-7-11[10] (7*) Michael Bradley (4) *in tch, outpcd and swtchd outsd 3 fs out, gd hdwy 2 out, styd on to ld wl ins last*......................(14 to 1) 1
238* CAPTAIN MARMALADE [56] 4-9-6 K Rutter (6) *hld up, hdwy 2 and a half fs out, rdn to ld ins fnl furlong, hdd and no extr wl inside last*....... (7 to 2 op 9 to 4 tchd 4 to 1) 2
217* MAROWINS [50] 4-9-0 F Norton (2) *slwly into strd and beh, gd hdwy 2 fs out, rdn to ld entering fnl furlong, sn hdd and no extr*.........(6 to 1 op 5 to 1 tchd 13 to 2) 3
216[5] KING PARROT (Ire) [57] 5-9-7 D Harrison (5) *led, rdn one and a half fs out, hdd and wknd entering fnl furlong.* ....(6 to 1 op 3 to 1) 4
241[2] LORD NASKRA (USA) [60] 4-9-10 Emma O'Gorman (10) *in tch, gd hdwy hfwy, wide strt, ev ch o'r one furlong out, sn rdn and wknd*............. (5 to 2 fav tchd 3 to 1) 5
HATAAL (Ire) [33] (v) 4-7-6 (5*) Claire Balding (3) *slwly into strd and beh, some hdwy fnl 2 fs*...(20 to 1 op 16 to 1) 6
264 WINGED WHISPER (USA) [47] 4-8-8 (3*) A Garth (8) *chsd ldrs, ev ch o'r 2 fs out, sn rdn and btn.* ....(25 to 1 op 33 to 1) 7
241[5] QUESTION OF DEGREE [43] 7-8-7 S Maloney (9) *chsd ldrs till rdn and wknd wl o'r 2 fs out*..... (5 to 1 op 6 to 1) 8
284 ALICANTE [36] 6-7-10[1] (5*) D McCabe (1) *chsd ldrs, rdn and wknd 3 fs out*.................................(33 to 1) 9
4710a VERRO (USA) [30] (bl) 6-7-8 N Kennedy (7) *cl up, wknd quickly o'r 3 fs out, tld off*..........(14 to 1 op 16 to 1) 10
Dist: ½l, 1l, 1½l, 1½l, 6l, 4l, nk, 5l, dist. 1m 45.60s. a 6.60s (10 Ran).
SR: 14/35/26/28/26/-/ (J M Bradley), J M Bradley

376 Cyclamen Claiming Stakes Class F (4-y-o and up) £2,243 7f..................(3:30)

STOPROVERITATE 4-9-2 N Connorton (2) *hld up, gd hdwy 2 and a half fs out, effrt to ld ins last, ran on.* ....(8 to 1 op 6 to 1) 1
GALLERY ARTIST (Ire) 5-8-5[3] (7*) S Eiffert (9) *chsd ldrs, hdwy to ld 2 and a half fs out, rdn and hdd ins last, no extr*....................(6 to 1 op 7 to 2 tchd 13 to 2) 2
319[9] LITMORE DANCER 5-7-11 (7*) Michael Bradley (8) *hld up and beh, wide strt, gd hdwy 2 fs out, rdn and styd on same pace fnl furlong*........... (16 to 1 tchd 25 to 1) 3
253[3] CLAUDIA MISS 6-9-2 Dean McKeown (6) *al prmnt, effrt 2 fs out, rdn and ev ch one out, not quicken ins last.* ....(7 to 2 op 3 to 1 tchd 4 to 1) 4
253* SALLY'S SON 7-8-8 (3*) Emma O'Gorman (7) *prmnt, effrt and ev ch 2 fs out, sn rdn and wknd appr last.* ....(6 to 4 fav tchd 13 to 8) 5
285[5] PESIDANAMICH (Ire) (bl) 5-8-6 (7*) S Mulvey (4) *led 3 fs, sn rdn, wknd 2 and a half out*.........(7 to 1 op 5 to 1) 6
327 MOST SURPRISING (Ire) (bl) 4-9-5 J O'Reilly (3) *cl up, led aftr 3 fs til 2 and a half out, sn btn.* ....(14 to 1 tchd 16 to 1) 7
285[7] IMPORTANT DECISION 4-8-13 D Nicholls (10) *slwly into strd and outpcd, al rear*....................... (33 to 1) 8
238[7] ACIDOSIS 4-8-7 J Fanning (5) *chsd ldrs to hfwy, sn wknd.* ....(33 to 1) 9
Dist: 2l, 1½l, hd, 1l, 3l, 12l, 2½l, sht-hd. 1m 32.50s. a 6.40s (9 Ran).
SR: 32/19/9/20/12/5/ (John D Clark), S G Norton

377 Tulip Maiden Stakes Class D (3-y-o) £3,084 1½m.............................(4:05)

ROVEREDO (USA) 9-0 L Dettori (3) *trkd ldrs, hdwy to join lder hfwy, led 2 and a half fs out, sn clr, eased fnl furlong*..........................(6 to 4 tchd 13 to 8) 1
BILJAN (USA) 9-0 A Munro (1) *led, rdn and hdd 2 and a half fs out, styd on one pace, no ch wth wnr.* ....(Evens fav op 2 to 1 on tchd 11 to 10) 2
PUGET DANCER (USA) 8-4 (5*) M Fenton (2) *in tch, rdn o'r 4 fs out, sn wknd*.....................(5 to 1 op 4 to 1) 3
230[7] FREE DANCER 8-9 J Lowe (5) *chsd ldr to hfwy, sn wknd and lost tch*.....................(25 to 1 op 20 to 1) 4
230[5] TURFMANS VISION 9-0 W Ryan (4) *hld up, effrt and some hdwy hfwy, sn rdn and wknd*..... (20 to 1 op 16 to 1) 5
Dist: 2½l, 5l, 15l, 12l. 2m 43.40s. a 9.50s (5 Ran).
SR: 35/30/15/-/-/ (Edward St George), D R Loder

378 Lilac Handicap Class E (0-70 3-y-o) £2,898 1m..................................(4:40)

4770a[5] CERTAIN WAY (Ire) [52] 8-4 M Birch (1) *cl up, led hfwy, rdn clr 2 fs out, styd on wl*...(6 to 1 op 5 to 1 tchd 7 to 2) 1
250[3] DUVEEN (Ire) [52] 7-13 (5*) M Fenton (8) *in tch, hdwy 3 fs out, not much room and swtchd 2 out, sn rdn, styd on one pace*............ (Evens fav op 5 to 4 tchd 6 to 4) 2
252[5] MISTER BLAKE [69] 9-4 (3*) Emma O'Gorman (9) *in tch, effrt and hdwy 2 and a half fs out, sn rdn and one pace*..........(11 to 2 op 3 to 1 tchd 13 to 2) 3
RAD [63] 9-1 W Woods (6) *hld up, hdwy 3 fs out, rdn and edgd lft 2 out, sn one pace.* ....(12 to 1 op 10 to 1 tchd 14 to 1) 4

240[5] SCOFFERA [44] 7-10 Kim Tinkler (2) *led to hfwy, cl up till rdn 2 fs out*.......... (14 to 1 op 8 to 1 tchd 16 to 1) 5
40[3] I'M A DREAMER (Ire) [66] 9-4 Dean McKeown (7) *chsd ldrs, rdn o'r 3 fs out, sn wknd*........... (7 to 1 op 5 to 1) 6
DOC SPOT [60] 8-12 G Carter (4) *hmpd strt, al rear*. .... (14 to 1 op 10 to 1 tchd 16 to 1) 7
162[5] BOULMERKA [43] (bl,e/s) 7-9[5] (3*) N Kennedy (3) *al rear*. .... (20 to 1 op 16 to 1) 8
284[6] NOBLE MEASURE (Ire) [45] (bl) 7-11 L Charnock (5) *chsd ldrs till rdn and wknd o'r 3 fs out*. (25 to 1 op 14 to 1) 9

Dist: 4l, 3l, ¾l, 5l, 2l, 1½l, 3l, 7l. 1m 45.70s. a 6.70s (9 Ran).
SR: 20/8/16/8/-/-/ (M J Rogers), C Tinkler

379 Forget-me-not Handicap Class E (0-70 3-y-o and up) £2,976 5f.................. (5:10)

292 SIR TASKER [63] (v) 5-9-12 L Dettori (1) *cl up, effrt to chal o'r one furlong out, rdn to ld ins last, ran on*. ....(6 to 1 op 4 to 1) 1
SUPERLATIVEMAXIMUS (Ire) [52] 5-9-1 D Holland (4) *al cl up, led one and a half fs out, sn rdn and hdd ins last, kpt on und pres*.................... (11 to 1 op 7 to 1) 2
289[5] STRIP CARTOON (Ire) [51] (bl) 5-8-7 (7*) G Strange (6) *chsd ldrs, effrt and hdwy appr fnl furlong, sn rdn, styd on ins last*................(4 to 1 op 7 to 1 tchd 8 to 1) 3
LANGTONIAN [55] (bl) 4-9-4 J Carroll (8) *al cl up, led hfwy till one and a half fs out, rdn and wknd entering fnl furlong*.......................... (5 to 1 op 2 to 1) 4
289 MAID WELCOME [62] (bl) 6-9-4 (7*) E Husband (7) *led to hfwy, sn rdn, one pace fnl 2 fs*. .... (11 to 1 op 8 to 1 tchd 12 to 1) 5
207[6] DRUMMER'S DREAM (Ire) [41] (v) 5-8-4 Dale Gibson (3) *badly outpcd and beh, drvn alng hfwy, styd on fnl furlong, nvr dngrs*................. (7 to 1 op 6 to 1) 6
253[8] GRUBBY [36] 4-7-8 (5*) A Garth (2) *outpcd and beh, rdn alng hfwy, styd on und pres fnl furlong, nvr dngrs*. .... (20 to 1 op 14 to 1) 7
250* BELLE SOIREE [50] 3-7-13[1] (3*) J Weaver (9) *outpcd and drvn alng aftr 2 fs, no hdwy*. ....(3 to 1 fav op 4 to 1 tchd 5 to 2) 8
250[7] WHAT BLISS [42] 3-7-7 J Fanning (5) *gd speed 2 fs, rdn alng hfwy, sn lost pl*.. (20 to 1 op 16 to 1) 9

Dist: Nk, nk, 2l, 3½l, 1½l, nk, ½l, 2½l. 59.90s. a 2.00s (9 Ran).
SR: 47/35/33/29/22/-/ (J F Coupland), J L Harris

BEVERLEY (good to firm)
Friday April 2nd
Going Correction: PLUS 0.25 sec. per fur.

380 Hutton Cranswick Maiden Stakes Class D (3-y-o and up) £3,348 5f.............(1:50)

284[2] MOON STRIKE (Fr) 3-8-12 D Nicholls (6) *in tch, effrt hfwy, styd on wl to ld ins fnl furlong*................(9 to 4) 1
4664a[9] MISS BRIGHTSIDE 5-9-5 S Webster (5) *broke wl, led till hdd ins fnl furlong, kpt on*.................. (33 to 1) 2
313[5] RED FAN (Ire) 3-8-12 N Connorton (1) *beh, hdwy 2 fs out, kpt on ins fnl furlong*.............. (6 to 1 op 5 to 1) 3
PRESS GALLERY 3-8-12 G Duffield (4) *slwly into strd, beh, hdwy hfwy, ev ch o'r one furlong out, not quicken ins last*.............. (15 to 8 fav op 6 to 4 tchd 2 to 1) 4
CHICAGO (Ire) 3-8-12 M Birch (2) *chsd ldrs till wknd and eased o'r 2 fs out*................. (20 to 1 op 16 to 1) 5
NEWBURY COAT 3-8-12 W Carson (3) *pressed ldr, rdn hfwy, wknd o'r one furlong out*..... (7 to 2 op 3 to 1) 6
OSCAR THE SECOND (Ire) 3-8-12 J Fanning (7) *in tch, drvn alng hfwy, grad wknd*.......................(20 to 1) 7

Dist: ½l, 1½l, nk, 8l, 2½l, 10l. 1m 6.60s. a 4.90s (7 Ran).
SR: 25/30/17/16/ (S Fustok), W A O'Gorman

381 Scarborough Claiming Stakes Class F (2-y-o) £2,243 5f...................... (2:20)

JIMMY THE SKUNK (Ire) 8-10 J Carroll (5) *hmpd strt, in tch, effrt and swtchd o'r one furlong out, quickened to ld ins last, rdn out*................ (6 to 4 fav op 7 to 4) 1
PORTITE SOPHIE 8-6 M Wigham (8) *led till hdd and no extr ins fnl furlong*..............(14 to 1 tchd 16 to 1) 2
XAMDIVAD (Ire) 8-2[1] M Wood (2) *chsd ldrs, rdn o'r 2 fs out, not quicken fnl furlong*.......... (12 to 1 op 10 to 1) 3
ASHEN 8-5 M Birch (9) *chsd ldrs, hmpd 3 fs out, sn drvn alng, one pace ins fnl*.............(3 to 1 tchd 4 to 1) 4
BATIEN'S RIVER 8-9 Dale Gibson (10) *beh, rdn hfwy, styd on fnl furlong, nvr dngrs*..........(8 to 1 op 10 to 1) 5
299[9] YOUNG MEDIC 8-2 J Fanning (6) *squeezed out strt, beh, rdn to improve o'r one furlong out, kpt on ins last*. ....(20 to 1) 6
PARKSIDE LADY 8-1 (3*) S Maloney (4) *took fierce hold, in tch, drvn alng aftr 2 fs, no imprsn*. .... (13 to 2 op 4 to 1 tchd 7 to 1) 7
CRY OF THE DOLPHIN 8-9 Dean McKeown (1) *in tch on outsd till rdn and wknd frm hfwy*. (16 to 1 op 12 to 1) 8
364[4] MUCKROSS PARK 8-4 (5*) A Garth (7) *in tch, sn pushed alng, wknd o'r 2 fs out*.........................(12 to 1) 9
RED GRIT (Ire) 8-5 J Lowe (3) *beh, rdn bef hfwy, sn btn*. .... (20 to 1 op 14 to 1) 10

Dist: 1½l, 1½l, 1½l, 1½l, 1l, ½l, 1½l, 3l, 8l. 1m 7.60s. a 5.90s (10 Ran).
SR: 3/-/-/-/-/-/ (J David Abell), J Berry

382 Bridlington Bay Handicap Class E (0-70 4-y-o and up) £2,976 2m 35yds...... (2:50)

303[2] TAROUDANT [60] 6-9-9 K Darley (8) *trkd ldr, improved to ld o'r 2 fs out, styd on strly fnl furlong*. ....(Evens fav op 11 to 10 tchd 5 to 4) 1
KING WILLIAM [34] 8-7-11 J Lowe (3) *hld up and beh, gd hdwy 4 fs out, ev ch o'r 2 out, wknd ins fnl furlong*. ....(10 to 1 tchd 8 to 1) 2
356[5] COST EFFECTIVE [30] 6-7-7 G Bardwell (7) *mid-div, effrt o'r 5 fs out, styd on ins fnl furlong, not pace to chal*. ....(13 to 2 op 6 to 1) 3
58[6] LUKS AKURA [39] (v) 5-7-9 (7*) M Baird (11) *led til hdd o'r 2 fs out, rdn and grad wknd*........ (20 to 1 op 14 to 1) 4
TROJAN LANCER [50] 7-8-13 G Duffield (5) *hld up and beh, effrt o'r 3 fs out, kpt on fnl furlong, nvr dngrs*. .... (11 to 1 op 10 to 1 tchd 12 to 1) 5
ENKINDLE [30] 6-7-2[2] (7*) Darren Moffatt (2) *chsd ldrs, drvn alng 4 fs out, not quicken*...................(33 to 1) 6
VASILIEV [65] (bl) 5-10-0 Dean McKeown (10) *hld up in rear, hdwy 6 fs out, no imprsn entering strt*. .... (12 to 1 op 14 to 1) 7
294[4] BALZINO (USA) [55] 4-9-0 K Fallon (6) *settled towards rear, rdn to improve 5 fs out, wknd o'r 2 out*. ....(4 to 1 op 7 to 2) 8
ICE MAGIC [50] 6-8-13 J Carroll (9) *chsd ldrs, effrt o'r 3 fs out, sn wknd, tld off*.........................(20 to 1) 9
ESCAPE TALK [30] 6-7-7 J Fanning (1) *hld up in tch, rdn o'r 4 fs out, sn wknd, tld off*..................(33 to 1) 10
SUM MEDE [46] (bl) 6-8-4 (5*) A Garth (4) *hld up in rear, drvn alng 6 fs out, sn lost tch, tld off*.........(20 to 1) 11

Dist: 3½l, 1½l, 2½l, 6l, ¾l, 5l, 5l, 5l, 12l, 3½l. 3m 43.70s. a 14.70s (11 Ran).
SR: 3/-/-/-/-/-/ (G A Farndon), Mrs M Reveley

383 Withernsea Handicap Class D (0-80 4-y-o and up) £3,289 7f 100yds............(3:20)

315 GOLDEN CHIP (Ire) [75] 5-10-0 K Darley (2) *chsd ldrs, rdn to ld o'r one furlong out, styd on gmely fnl furlong*. ....(3 to 1 fav op 5 to 2) 1
219[6] SANDMOOR DENIM [58] 6-8-11 S Webster (7) *in tch, short of room o'r 2 fs out, swtchd over one out, kpt on, no extr wl ins last*.............(11 to 2 op 5 to 1 tchd 6 to 1) 2
260[6] SOOTY TERN [50] 6-8-3 N Adams (8) *led til hdd o'r 3 fs out, rgned ld over 2 out, headed over one out, sn wknd*. .... (11 to 2 op 5 to 1) 3
253[4] WEE SARAH [59] 5-8-12 Alex Greaves (6) *hld up in rear, styd on fnl 2 fs, nvr dngrs*........... (6 to 1 op 9 to 2) 4
WHO'S TEF (Ire) [54] 5-8-4 (3*) S Maloney (3) *chsd ldg 3, effrt o'r three fs out, not quicken over one out*. ....(9 to 2 op 5 to 1) 5
177[7] MANULEADER [60] (bl) 4-8-13 D Nicholls (4) *in tch, rdn alng o'r 3 fs out, wknd over one out*..........(25 to 1) 6
BLUE GRIT [60] 7-8-13 J Lowe (5) *beh, rdn o'r 2 fs out, no imprsn*.......................... (6 to 1 op 5 to 1) 7
QUIET VICTORY [40] (bl) 6-7-7 J Fanning (1) *wth ldr, led o'r 3 fs out, hdd over 2 out, sn btn*......(8 to 1 op 12 to 1) 8

Dist: 1l, 7l, ¾l, 2l, 1l, 2½l, 3½l. 1m 36.40s. a 6.10s (8 Ran).
SR: 51/31/2/9/-/1/-/-/ (A H Jackson), A P Stringer

384 Hornsea Mere Handicap Class C (0-90 4-y-o and up) £4,371 1m 1f 207yds...... (3:50)

290* NORTHERN GRADUATE (USA) [63] 4-8-8 K Darley (2) *made all, hld on gmely whn hrd pressed fnl furlong*. .... (7 to 4 on op 2 to 1 on) 1
FIRST BID [58] 6-8-3 J Fanning (4) *nvr far away, improved on bit o'r 2 fs out, rdn to draw level ins fnl furlong, no extr towards finish*.....(5 to 1 op 9 to 2 tchd 11 to 2) 2
4749a[2] TALENTED TING (Ire) [70] 4-9-1 Dale Gibson (3) *hld up in last pl, lost tch 3 fs out*............ (11 to 2 op 5 to 1) 3
259[4] NO SUBMISSION (USA) [83] 7-10-0 D Nicholls (1) *chsd ldrs, lost grnd hfwy, wknd entering strt*.. (7 to 1 op 6 to 1) 4

Dist: Nk, 15l, nk. 2m 10.10s. a 8.70s (4 Ran).
SR: 32/26/8/20/ (P D Savill), Mrs M Reveley

385 Leconfield Maiden Fillies Stakes Class D (3-y-o) £3,114 1m 1f 207yds......... (4:25)

SEEK THE PEARL 8-11 G Duffield (5) *chsd ldrs, effrt o'r 2 fs out, led ins fnl furlong, styd on wl*. (12 to 1 op 10 to 1) 1
HOOSIE 8-11 M Birch (2) *wth ldr, led o'r one furlong out, hdd ins last, no extr*.................(4 to 1 op 3 to 1) 2
SUNRISE MORNING (USA) 8-11 W Carson (4) *led til hdd o'r one furlong out, rdn and not quicken*. .... (11 to 8 on op 11 to 10 on tchd 11 to 10) 3
OMIDJOY (Ire) 8-11 W Woods (1) *hld up in cl tch, hdwy appr strt, rdn and wknd 2 fs out*. ....(7 to 2 op 5 to 1 tchd 11 to 2 and 6 to 1) 4
SMOCKING 8-11 M Hills (3) *chsd ldrs til rdn and wknd o'r 2 fs out*............................(8 to 1 op 10 to 1) 5

Dist: 3½l, 5l, 7l, 15l. 2m 10.70s. a 9.30s (5 Ran).
SR: 29/22/12/-/-/ (Cheveley Park Stud), J R Fanshawe

KEMPTON (good to soft)
Friday April 2nd
Going Correction: PLUS 1.00 sec. per fur. (race 1), PLUS 0.45 (2,3,4,5,6)

386 Polyanthus Maiden Auction Stakes Class D (2-y-o) £3,377 5f. . . . . (2:15)

MILLION AT DAWN (Ire) 8-3 (3*) D Harrison (6) *slwly into strd, rdn to ld 2 fs out, pushed out ins last, cmftbly.* . . . . (11 to 2 op 4 to 1 tchd 6 to 1) 1
299² RISKIE THINGS 8-0 A McGlone (3) *al prmnt on outsd, kpt on one pace fnl furlong.* (7 to 1 op 6 to 1 tchd 8 to 1) 2
RISKY AFFAIR 8-7 Paul Eddery (8) *chsd ldrs, rdn hfwy, one pace fnl furlong.* . . . . (5 to 1 op 3 to 1) 3
THATCHERELLA 8-1¹ D Holland (1) *slwly away, gd hdwy 2 fs out, rdn and kpt on one pace fnl furlong.* . . . . (14 to 1 op 10 to 1 tchd 16 to 1) 4
SELHURST PARK LAD (Ire) 8-9 Pat Eddery (2) *pushed alng frm strt, wknd appr fnl furlong.* . . . . (11 to 2 op 5 to 2) 5
NO WHAT I MEAN (Ire) 8-0 J Quinn (4) *speed till wknd 2 fs out.* . . . . (10 to 1 op 20 to 1 tchd 8 to 1) 6
LORD SKY 8-9 T Quinn (7) *trkd ldr, led briefly o'r 2 fs out, sn wknd.* . . . . (9 to 4 fav op 5 to 2 tchd 3 to 1) 7
PHONE ME UP 8-11 B Raymond (9) *led till hdd o'r 2 fs out, drpd out quickly.* . . . . (8 to 1 op 5 to 1) 8
COLONEL SINCLAIR (Ire) 8-5 W Ryan (5) *outpcd frm strt, lost tch 2 fs out.* . . . . . . (10 to 1 op 6 to 1 tchd 12 to 1) 9
Dist: 3l, 1½l, sht-hd, 7l, 3½l, 2½l, 2½l, nk. 1m 6.44s. a 8.24s (9 Ran).
SR: 27/9/10/3/-/-/ (Million In Mind Partnership (2)), G A Pritchard-Gordon

387 Florence Nagle Girl Apprentices Handicap Class F (0-70 4-y-o and up) £2,534 1m 1f . . . . (2:45)

294* ALBERT [43] 6-7-10 (5*,5ex) Sharon Millard (4) *hld up in rear, steady hdwy o'r 2 fs out, str brst and squeezed through ins fnl furlong, ran on strongly.* . . . . (7 to 2 op 2 to 1 tchd 4 to 1) 1
329⁵ CAMDEN'S RANSOM (USA) [70] 6-10-0 Tracey Purseglove (10) *slwly away, settled in rear till hdwy 3 fs out, led entering last, sn hdd, ran on.* . . . . . . (10 to 1 op 7 to 1) 2
GEBLITZT [35] 9-7-3¹ (5*) Wendy Jones (11) *rdn to dispute ld aftr 2 fs, wnt on 3 furlongs out, hdd entering last, kpt on one pace.* . . . . (100 to 1 op 50 to 1) 3
85³ THUNDERING [35] 8-7-7 Claire Balding (6) *chsd ldrs, rdn appr fnl furlong, kpt on one pace.* (16 to 1 op 12 to 1) 4
290⁸ SINCLAIR LAD (Ire) [60] 5-9-4 Debbie Biggs (9) *wl in rear till hdwy appr fnl furlong, ran on, nvr nrr.* . . . . (16 to 1 op 14 to 1) 5
SHINING JEWEL [66] 6-9-10 Sally Radford-Howes (8) *mid-div, hdwy on ins 3 fs out, ev ch appr last, one pace.* . . . . (16 to 1 op 14 to 1) 6
294⁶ MAY SQUARE (Ire) [40] 5-7-12 Madeleine Smith (3) *led till hdd 3 fs out, wknd appr last.* . . . . . (16 to 1 op 14 to 1) 7
QUANTITY SURVEYOR [58] 4-9-2 Emma O'Gorman (2) *trkd ldrs till wknd 2 fs out.* . . . . (7 to 1 op 6 to 1) 8
332² TENAYESTELIGN [35] 5-7-7 Antoinette Armes (5) *in tch on outsd, no hdwy fnl 2 fs.* . (8 to 1 op 5 to 1 tchd 9 to 1) 9
LUCKY NOIRE [61] 5-9-5 Gaye Harwood (7) *slwly away, swtchd lft and effrt o'r 2 fs out, sn btn.* . . . . (9 to 1 op 8 to 1 tchd 10 to 1) 10
FRONT PAGE [40] 6-7-12 Kim McDonnell (1) *prmnt to hfwy, sn beh, tld off.* . . . . (5 to 2 fav op 4 to 1) 11
Dist: 1l, 2½l, ¾l, 1l, sht-hd, 3½l, 2½l, 2l, 2½l, 12l. 2m 1.14s. a 11.14s (11 Ran).
SR: -/6/-/-/-/-/ (T S M S Riley-Smith), D A Wilson

388 Laburnum Conditions Stakes Class C (3-y-o) £4,157 1m. (3:15)

EUROLINK THUNDER 8-12 Pat Eddery (4) *al prmnt, rdn to join ldr appr fnl furlong, nosed ahead wl ins final furlong, jst hld on.* . . . . . (5 to 1 op 6 to 1 tchd 13 to 2) 1
293⁶ NOMINATOR 9-4 W Ryan (2) *led till hdd wl ins fnl furlong, fought back gmely, jst fld.* . . . . (6 to 1 op 4 to 1 tchd 7 to 1) 2
PORT LUCAYA 8-10 L Dettori (6) *chsd ldrs, pushed alng frm hfwy, ran on und pres ins fnl furlong.* . . . . (5 to 1 op 4 to 1 tchd 11 to 2) 3
AZHAR 8-10 W R Swinburn (1) *in rear, hdwy o'r 2 fs out, outpcd appr last.* . . . . (25 to 1 op 12 to 1) 4
NEEDLE GUN (Ire) 8-10 M Roberts (3) *hld up, rdn o'r 2 fs out, no further hdwy.* . . . . (5 to 4 fav op Evens tchd 11 to 8) 5
PALACE PAGEANT (USA) 8-10 R Cochrane (5) *al beh, lost tch o'r 2 fs out.* . . . . (11 to 2 op 4 to 1) 6
DEVILRY 8-12 Paul Eddery (7) *trkd ldr to 3 fs out, rdn and sn btn.* . . . . (25 to 1 op 12 to 1) 7
Dist: Sht-hd, 1l, 6l, ¾l, 12l, 7l. 1m 43.51s. a 6.71s (7 Ran).
SR: 51/56/45/27/25/-/-/ (Eurolink Group Plc), J L Dunlop

389 Jonnie Mullings Memorial Handicap Class C (0-100 4-y-o and up) £4,624 1½m. . (3:45)

225³ BOOKCASE [72] 6-8-4 J Williams (4) *hld up in rear, hdwy o'r 3 fs out, str run ins last, led last strd.* . . . . (8 to 1 op 10 to 1 tchd 7 to 1) 1
BIGWHEEL BILL (Ire) [78] 4-8-8 Pat Eddery (1) *led 1st 2 fs, trkd ldr, led two out, rdn and ct last strd.* . . . . (4 to 1 op 7 to 2 tchd 9 to 2) 2
SECRET SOCIETY [80] 6-8-12 R Cochrane (5) *al prmnt in chasing grp, ev ch entering fnl furlong, ran on.* . . . . (5 to 1 op 7 to 2) 3
ABSENT RELATIVE [61] 5-7-7 J Quinn (2) *al in tch, ev ch 2 fs out, one pace fnl furlong.* . . . . (8 to 1 op 5 to 1) 4
POINCIANA [70] 4-8-0 A McGlone (6) *in chasing grp, rdn 3 fs out, outpcd appr last.* . . . . (12 to 1 op 10 to 1) 5
GREEK GOLD (Ire) [80] 4-8-10 W R Swinburn (8) *led aftr 2 fs, sn clr, hdd two furlongs out, wknd entering last.* . . . . (7 to 4 fav op 6 to 4 tchd 9 to 5) 6
SONG OF SIXPENCE (USA) [96] 9-10-0 J Reid (7) *al beh, rdn 3 fs out, no hdwy.* . . . . (12 to 1 op 10 to 1 tchd 14 to 1) 7
NEWTON POINT [71] 4-7-12 (3*) D Harrison (3) *in tch till drpd out 3 fs out, tld off.* . . . . (20 to 1 op 16 to 1) 8
Dist: Sht-hd, ½l, 1½l, ¾l, ¾l, 3½l, 20l. 2m 42.76s. a 11.76s (8 Ran).
SR: 26/29/32/10/15/23/34/-/ (Adept (80) Ltd), D R C Elsworth

390 Magnolia Stakes Class A (Listed Race) (4-y-o and up) £10,254 1¼m. . . . . (4:15)

CAPTAIN HORATIUS (Ire) 4-9-6 J Reid (6) *hld up towards rear, hdwy to ld 2 fs out, sn clr, easily.* . . . . (4 to 1 op 3 to 1) 1
HALF A TICK (USA) 5-9-6 T Quinn (4) *slwly away, rapid hdwy 5 fs out to press ldrs, ev ch 2 furlongs out, ran on one pace.* . . . . (7 to 2 op 3 to 1 tchd 9 to 2) 2
CASPIAN TERN (USA) 4-8-6 A Munro (3) *trkd ldrs, led briefly o'r 2 fs out, sn outpcd.* . . . . (4 to 1 op 5 to 1) 3
SOIREE (Ire) 4-8-6 D Holland (8) *hld up, styd on ins fnl 3 fs, nvr nr to chal.* . . . . (11 to 4 fav op 9 to 4 tchd 3 to 1) 4
BOLOARDO 4-8-11 M Roberts (2) *chsd ldr, led o'r 3 fs out, rdn and hdd over 2 out, sn btn, eased.* . . . . (9 to 1 op 6 to 1 tchd 10 to 1) 5
MASTER PLANNER 4-8-11 R Cochrane (5) *chsd ldrs till lost pl 4 fs out, eased whn btn.* . . . . (16 to 1 op 12 to 1) 6
DURSHAN (USA) 4-8-11 S Whitworth (1) *hld up, rdn o'r 3 fs out, sn btn, eased.* . . . (25 to 1 op 20 to 1 tchd 33 to 1) 7
BOBZAO (Ire) 4-9-6 Pat Eddery (7) *led till hdd o'r 3 fs out, eased whn btn.* . . . . (13 to 2 op 5 to 1 tchd 7 to 1) 8
Dist: 4l, 3l, 1½l, 15l, 1½l, 4l, 7l. 2m 12.31s. a 10.51s (8 Ran).
SR: 46/38/18/15/-/ (D R Hunnisett), J L Dunlop

391 Syringa Handicap Class C (0-90 3-y-o and up) £4,878 7f. . . . . (4:45)

LITTLE ROUSILLON [55] 5-7-7 J Penza (1) *al prmnt, rdn to ld o'r 2 fs out, ran on wl.* . . . . (7 to 1 op 6 to 1 tchd 11 to 2 and 8 to 1) 1
SAGEBRUSH ROLLER [73] 5-8-11 Pat Eddery (5) *wtd wth in mid-div, hdwy o'r 2 fs out, wnt second entering last, ran on, no imprsn.* . . . . (100 to 30 fav op 3 to 1 tchd 4 to 1) 2
253² ON Y VA (USA) [56] 6-7-8 J Quinn (4) *rcd in tch, ev ch 2 fs out, ran on one pace.* . . . . (4 to 1 tchd 11 to 2) 3
244² ABSONAL [67] 6-8-2 (3*) D Harrison (14) *hld up in tch, rdn and hdwy o'r 2 fs out, styd on ins last.* . . . . (10 to 1 tchd 12 to 1) 4
NEPTUNE'S PET [83] 5-9-7 J Reid (6) *hld up, ran on ins fnl 2 fs, not rch ldrs.* . . . . (12 to 1 op 10 to 1 tchd 14 to 1) 5
HOPEFUL BID (Ire) [68] 4-8-6 B Raymond (3) *al abt same pl, one pace ins fnl 2 fs.* . . . . (16 to 1 op 10 to 1) 6
MOUGINS (Ire) [90] 4-9-9 (5*) A Procter (8) *slwly away, some hdwy fnl 2 fs, nvr nr to chal.* (14 to 1 op 10 to 1) 7
FOOLISH TOUCH [58] 11-7-10 A Mackay (9) *al towards rear.* . . . . (16 to 1 op 12 to 1) 8
ELTON LEDGER (Ire) [66] 4-8-4¹ J Fortune (11) *chsd ldr for 3 fs, wknd o'r 2 out.* . . . . (33 to 1 op 25 to 1) 9
RISE UP SINGING [66] 5-7-11 (7*) D McCabe (7) *al in rear.* . . . . (16 to 1 op 14 to 1) 10
TALENT (USA) [83] (v) 5-9-7 A Munro (13) *chsd ldrs, rdn 3 fs out, wknd o'r one out.* . . . . (12 to 1 op 10 to 1 tchd 14 to 1) 11
247 CHEVEUX MITCHELL [74] (v) 6-8-12 T Quinn (12) *led till hdd o'r 2 fs out, sn btn, eased.* . . . . (10 to 1 op 6 to 1) 12
SAND TABLE [82] 4-9-6 M Roberts (2) *mid-div, beh fnl 3 fs.* . . . . (12 to 1 op 7 to 1) 13
SYLVAN SABRE (Ire) [66] 4-8-4 S O'Gorman (10) *mid-div till drpd out to rear hfwy, tld off.* . . . . (14 to 1 op 12 to 1 tchd 16 to 1) 14
Dist: 2l, 2½l, 1½l, 1½l, nk, 5l, 2l, nk, sht-hd, 1½l. 1m 30.01s. a 5.91s (14 Ran).
SR: 38/50/25/31/42/26/33/-/2/ (Fayzad Thoroughbred Limited), W R Muir

MAISONS-LAFFITTE (FR) (soft)
Friday April 2nd
Going Correction: PLUS 0.50 sec. per fur.

392 Prix Right Royal (Listed) (4-y-o and up) £14,337 1m 7f 110yds. . . . . (2:10)

CUTTING REEF (Ire) 4-8-8 A Badel, ... 1
GOLD SCRIPT (Fr) 4-8-11 M Boutin, ... 2
NORTHERN PARK (USA) 5-9-1 T Jarnet, ... 3
IN QUARTO 4-8-11 D Boeuf, ... 4
Dist: 1½l, 1l, 1½l, 1l, 6l. 3m 26.10s. a 13.10s (6 Ran).
SR: 41/42/45/39/ (Mme M Bollack-Badel), Mme M Bollack-Badel

BEVERLEY (good to firm)
Saturday April 3rd
Going Correction: PLUS 0.25 sec. per fur. (races 1,2,4,5,6), PLUS 0.05 (3)

393 Martin Plenderleith Conditions Stakes Class D (3-y-o) £3,357 1m 1f 207yds. (1:00)

NEWTON'S LAW (Ire) 8-10 Pat Eddery (3) *made all, quickened clr o'r 2 fs out, easily*.... (5 to 4 fav op 5 to 4 on) 1
ZIMZALABIM 8-12 W Carson (1) *chsd ldg pair, improved to chase wnr o'r 2 fs out, no imprsn.* (9 to 4 op 6 to 4) 2
NURYANDRA 8-5 P Robinson (2) *chsd ldr till wknd o'r 2 fs out, eased*........................... (9 to 4 op 4 to 1) 3
Dist: 8l, 15l. 2m 8.10s. a 6.70s (3 Ran).
SR: 54/40/3/ (R E Sangster), P W Chapple-Hyam

394 Steve Massam Selling Stakes Class G (3-y-o) £2,070 7f 100yds. .... (1:30)

HOT OFF THE PRESS 8-11 A Culhane (7) *in tch, effrt o'r 2 fs out, led one furlong out, hld on wl ins last.* .... (7 to 2 tchd 3 to 1 and 4 to 1) 1
339[4] DESIRABLE MISS (v) 8-6 M Wigham (4) *led til hdd one furlong out, rallied ins last*....... (5 to 1 tchd 11 to 2) 2
284[9] SUMMERS DREAM 8-6 K Fallon (6) *chsd ldr, rdn alng hfwy, no extr fnl furlong*..................... (12 to 1) 3
250[9] NIGHTMARE LADY 8-6 W Woods (1) *slwly into strd, beh, effrt and came wide strt, veered rght fnl furlong, no imprsn*.. (20 to 1) 4
PRINCE SONGLINE 8-11 W Carson (8) *chsd ldrs, effrt whn short of room 2 fs out, not quicken appr last.* .... (11 to 4 op 6 to 4) 5
KRAYYAN DAWN 8-11 S Dawson (2) *in tch, rdn 3 fs out, not quicken fnl 2 furlongs*...................... (25 to 1) 6
275[4] DON'T BE SAKI (Ire) 8-6 (5*) O Pears (5) *chsd ldrs, rdn o'r 3 fs out, wknd wl over one furlong out.* ....(6 to 4 fav op 9 to 4) 7
162[8] RED EDGE 8-6 E Johnson (3) *hld up, rdn alng appr strt, sn lost tch*........................ (20 to 1 op 16 to 1) 8
Dist: Hd, 2l, 1½l, 3l, 1½l, 8l, ½l. 1m 37.70s. a 7.40s (8 Ran).
SR: 14/8/2/-/-/ (R M Whitaker), R M Whitaker

395 Peter Adamson Maiden Auction Stakes Class F (2-y-o) £2,243 5f. .... (2:00)

OCHOS RIOS (Ire) 8-11 (3*) D Harrison (12) *sn outpcd and beh, swtchd outsd hfwy, rapid hdwy o'r one furlong out, led wl ins last*..........................(7 to 1 op 5 to 1) 1
GAELIC STAR (Ire) 9-0 R Cochrane (9) *nvr far away, led 2 fs out, sn rdn, hdd wl ins fnl furlong, no extr.* ....(6 to 1 op 8 to 1) 2
GALLIC GENT 9-0 W Carson (10) *chsd ldrs, chlgd o'r 2 fs out, ev ch ins last, not quicken towards finish.* (8 to 1) 3
KINGFISHER GREY 9-0 D Nicholls (13) *chsd ldrs, drvn alng hfwy, not quicken ins fnl furlong.* .... (20 to 1 op 14 to 1) 4
CARAPELLE 8-9 M Birch (4) *in tch, effrt and rdn 2 fs out, one pace fnl furlong*............ (16 to 1 op 14 to 1) 5
DON PEPE 9-0 K Fallon (6) *mid-div, rdn alng hfwy, one pace o'r one furlong out*............ (4 to 1 op 7 to 2) 6
MUZZ (Ire) 9-0 Dean McKeown (11) *made most till hdd 2 fs out, grad wknd*.....(11 to 4 fav op 5 to 2 tchd 3 to 1) 7
SHUTTLECOCK 9-0 Dale Gibson (1) *slwly into strd, beh and sn pushed alng, styd on appr fnl furlong, nvr dngrs*....................................(20 to 1 op 14 to 1) 8
299 LADY SWIFT 8-9 K Darley (2) *beh and sn rdn alng, nvr dngrs*.. (20 to 1) 9
291[6] ME NEITHER 8-9 G Carter (3) *in tch, effrt hfwy, grad wknd*................................ (4 to 1 op 7 to 2) 10
354[4] SALTPETRE (Ire) 9-0 M Wigham (14) *prmnt, drvn alng hfwy, wknd wl o'r one furlong out*...........(10 to 1) 11
EN-CEE-TEE 9-0 J Fanning (7) *in tch till rdn and wknd frm hfwy*........................ (20 to 1 op 16 to 1) 12
MIDNIGHT HUNTER 9-0 S Webster (8) *beh and sn pushed alng, nvr a factor*...............................(16 to 1) 13
SHARPISH WORDS 8-11 (3*) F Norton (5) *slwly into strd, al struggling in rear*.............................(20 to 1) 14
Dist: 1½l, ½l, 4l, nk, 1l, 2½l, 2l, 2l, ½l, 3½l. 1m 5.70s. a 4.00s (14 Ran).
SR: 25/19/17/1/-/-/ (Mrs H A Burn), B S Rothwell

396 Chris Langmore Handicap Class E (0-70 4-y-o and up) £2,950 1m 1f 207yds... (2:30)

278[2] RED INDIAN [35] 7-7-7 J Fanning (6) *hld up and beh, gd hdwy o'r 2 fs out, led over one furlong out, sn clr, ran on wl ins last*.................. (9 to 4 fav op 3 to 1) 1
366[2] SHARQUIN [35] 6-7-7 J Lowe (5) *hld up, effrt whn no room 2 fs out, styd on appr fnl furlong, not rch wnr.* ....(9 to 2 op 5 to 1) 2
290[3] SUGEMAR [61] 7-9-2 (3*) S D Williams (8) *hld up and beh, effrt o'r one furlong out, kpt on ins last, nvr nr to chal.* ....(9 to 2 op 7 to 2) 3
302 TAHITIAN [67] 4-9-11 K Fallon (3) *dwlt, sn reco'red to chase ldrs, effrt whn short of room over one furlong out, not quicken ins last*.................... (3 to 1 op 2 to 1) 4
VALATCH [43] 5-8-1[1] P Robinson (10) *led aftr one furlong til hdd o'r one furlong out, sn btn*.. (8 to 1 op 25 to 1) 5
235 COOL PARADE (USA) [47] 5-8-1[1] (5*) O Pears (4) *led a furlong, styd hndy, effrt 2 fs out, grad wknd.* (14 to 1) 6
217 BETTER STILL (Ire) [42] 4-7-7 (7*) C Adamson (9) *missed break, sn reco'red to chase ldr, drvn entering strt, wknd over one furlong out*....... (20 to 1 op 16 to 1) 7
MALINDI BAY [47] 5-8-5 E Johnson (7) *tucked away on ins, drvn alng o'r 2 fs out, fdd*........ (33 to 1 op 25 to 1) 8
13[9] CHARIOTEER [43] 4-8-1 Dale Gibson (1) *hld up, effrt 3 fs out, wkng whn hmpd o'r 2 furlongs out.* .... (10 to 1 op 8 to 1) 9
294 SHAHNIZAM (USA) [44] 9-8-2[3] K Darley (2) *in tch on outsd, lost pl 4 fs out, tld off fnl 2 furlongs*.......... (20 to 1) 10
Dist: 1½l, 4l, ¾l, ¾l, 1½l, 1½l, 2½l, 6l, dist. 2m 10.70s. a 9.30s (10 Ran).
SR: 11/8/26/30/4/5/ (Dave Marshall), W W Haigh

397 BBC Radio Humberside Handicap Class C (0-95 3-y-o) £5,190 1m 100yds. ..... (3:05)

RIBHI (USA) [78] 8-12 W Carson (4) *unruly stalls, hld up in tch, effrt and swtchd outsd wl o'r one furlong out, ran on to ld a furlong out, edgd rght, sn clr.* (3 to 1 jt-fav op 7 to 4) 1
HI NOD [70] 8-4 N Connorton (5) *chsd ldrs, effrt and rdn o'r 2 fs out, one pace ins fnl furlong.* (4 to 1 op 7 to 2) 2
LATIN LEADER [70] 8-4 P Robinson (2) *chsd ldr, led 2 fs out, hdd one furlong out, one pace.* (3 to 1 jt-fav op 4 to 1 tchd 11 to 4) 3
BRANDONHURST [87] 9-7 R Cochrane (6) *chsd ldrs, effrt and swtchd ins o'r one furlong out, not much room entering fnl furlong, one pace*...... (5 to 1 op 6 to 1) 4
286[2] GREEN'S FAIR (Ire) [74] 8-8 K Darley (3) *sn led, hdd 2 fs out, one pace whn hmpd o'r one furlong out.* ....(7 to 2 tchd 4 to 1) 5
LANCASTER PILOT [71] 8-5[1] A Culhane (1) *hld up in last pl, lost tch hfwy, tld off.* .... (12 to 1 op 14 to 1 tchd 10 to 1) 6
Dist: 5l, ½l, 1½l, 10l, 20l. 1m 48.40s. a 5.60s (6 Ran).
SR: 46/23/21/33/-/-/ (Hamdan Al-Maktoum), D Morley

398 Dave Taviner Handicap Class E (0-70 3-y-o) £3,131 7f 100yds. .... (3:35)

MY BEST VALENTINE [65] 9-4 (3*) F Norton (1) *in tch, improved o'r 2 fs out, led over one out, styd on wl ins last*.............................. (10 to 1 tchd 12 to 1) 1
SOOJAMA (Ire) [43] 7-13 S Dawson (4) *slwly into strd, beh till hdwy 2 fs out, kpt on ins last, not rch wnr.* .... (16 to 1 op 14 to 1) 2
317[6] ROSE FLYER (Ire) [52] 8-1 (7*) D McCabe (8) *led till hdd o'r one furlong out, not quicken ins last.* .... (12 to 1 op 9 to 1) 3
HEATHYARDS GEM [65] 9-7 R Cochrane (2) *slwly into strd, in rear till improved 2 fs out, styd on ins last, nvr dngrs.* ....(8 to 1 tchd 7 to 1) 4
RUBY COOPER [52] 8-8 W Carson (9) *chsd ldrs, drvn alng hfwy, one pace ins fnl furlong*.......(7 to 1 op 6 to 1) 5
259[2] DARING PAST [55] 8-11 Dean McKeown (6) *chsd ldrs, chlgd o'r 2 fs out, rdn and sn wknd.* ....(2 to 1 fav op 9 to 4 tchd 5 to 2) 6
PAAJIB (Ire) [57] 8-13 M Birch (7) *hld up, effrt entering strt, one pace appr fnl furlong*......... (14 to 1 op 10 to 1) 7
275* LARN FORT [54] 8-10 J Fanning (10) *pressed ldr, chlgd o'r 2 fs out, fdd over one furlong out*......(6 to 1 op 5 to 1) 8
CARDINAL DOGWOOD (USA) [60] 9-2 M Wigham (5) *in tch, drvn alng and lost pl hfwy, sn btn.* (16 to 1 op 12 to 1) 9
250[4] MUDGEE [50] 8-6 Alex Greaves (11) *chsd ldrs, drvn o'r 2 fs out, sn btn*........................ (6 to 1 op 5 to 1) 10
BODY LANGUAGE [56] 8-12 K Fallon (3) *hld up, improved on outsd hfwy, wknd o'r 2 fs out*... (8 to 1 op 11 to 2) 11
Dist: 3½l, hd, 1l, 1½l, ½l, nk, 1½l, hd, 1½l, 1½l. 1m 37.00s. a 6.70s (11 Ran).
SR: 35/2/10/20/2/3/4/-/1/ (The Valentines), P W Harris

LINGFIELD (good)
Saturday April 3rd
Going Correction: MINUS 0.15 sec. per fur.

399 EBF Tandridge Maiden Stakes Class D (2-y-o) £3,406 5f. .... (1:40)

MISS AMY LOU (Ire) 8-9 J Carroll (1) *made all, trkd o'r frm far side, clr whn hng lft ins last, ran on.* ....(5 to 1 op 4 to 1 tchd 6 to 1) 1
KERRIE-JO 8-9 J Williams (10) *al in tch, swtchd rght appr fnl furlong, ran on wl.* .... (10 to 1 op 16 to 1 tchd 20 to 1) 2

KENNET BOY 9-0 T Quinn (9) *slwly away, making hdwy whn hng rght o'r 2 fs out, wnt lft entering last, ran on.* ....(3 to 1 fav op 11 to 10 tchd 4 to 1) 3
312[4] JASARI (Ire) 9-0 M Roberts (2) *chsd ldrs stands side, short of room ins fnl furlong, ran on cl hme.* ....(5 to 1 op 9 to 4 tchd 11 to 2) 4
MARJORIE'S MEMORY (Ire) 8-9 W Ryan (3) *slwly into strd, al mid-div on outsd*........ (10 to 1 op 14 to 1) 5
ZUNO STAR (USA) 9-0 Paul Eddery (11) *in tch, no hdwy ins fnl 2 fs*........................(6 to 1 op 16 to 1) 6
SWEET CAROLINE 8-9 A Munro (8) *mid-div whn slightly hmpd 2 fs out, one pace aftr*.......(16 to 1 op 10 to 1) 7
WINDOW DISPLAY 9-0 C Rutter (12) *broke wl, chsd wnr till wknd appr fnl furlong*..........(6 to 1 op 16 to 1) 8
JUST GREENWICH 8-4 (5*) N Gwilliams (6) *mid-div whn slightly hmpd o'r 2 fs out, nvr dngrs aftr.* ....(20 to 1 op 12 to 1) 9
THE KAMIKAZE QUEEN 8-9 R Perham (4) *outpcd, al beh.* ....(20 to 1 op 12 to 1 tchd 25 to 1) 10
KOMPLICITY 9-0 N Day (7) *sn struggling in rear.* ....(10 to 1 op 7 to 1 tchd 11 to 1) 11
SON OF HADEER 9-0 G Duffield (5) *made hdwy aftr slow strt, wknd 2 fs out*...............(16 to 1 tchd 25 to 1) 12
Dist: 1½l, nk, sht-hd, 4l, nk, 3l, sht-hd, ½l, 3l, 4l. 1m 5.70s. a 8.80s (12 Ran).
(B R Allen), J Berry

400 Leisure Projects Rated Class B (0-100 3-y-o) £6,407 7f........................ (3:40)

IHTIRAZ [90] 8-13 R Hills (3) *trkd ldr, led wl o'r one furlong out, ran on well.* (12 to 1 op 8 to 1 tchd 14 to 1) 1
SHAMAM (USA) [84] 8-7 M Hills (6) *mid-div till hdwy appr fnl furlong, ran on*.............(12 to 1 tchd 14 to 1) 2
MR MARTINI (Ire) [96] 9-5 M Roberts (7) *led, pushed alng frm hfwy, hdd wl o'r one furlong out, one pace ins last.* ....(6 to 1 op 5 to 1 tchd 7 to 1) 3
CARELAMAN [98] 9-7 W Ryan (8) *hld up in mid-div, shaken up o'r one furlong out, ran on wl.* ....(25 to 1 op 14 to 1) 4
328* EASTERN MEMORIES (Ire) [84] 8-7 B Raymond (9) *hld up, short of room 2 fs out, shaken up appr fnl furlong, found little*........(5 to 4 fav op 7 to 4 tchd 11 to 10) 5
NEW CAPRICORN (USA) [96] 9-5 G Duffield (5) *prmnt till wknd appr fnl furlong.* (6 to 1 op 8 to 1 tchd 10 to 1) 6
EAST LIBERTY (USA) [94] 9-3 L Dettori (10) *prmnt till wknd quickly wl o'r one out*........ (12 to 1 tchd 14 to 1) 7
ANNIVERSAIRE [84] 8-7 N Day (11) *al beh.* ....(50 to 1 op 20 to 1) 8
MULLITOVER [85] 8-8 T Quinn (1) *stumbled on leaving stalls, sn in tch on far side, wknd o'r 2 fs out.* ....(6 to 1 op 5 to 1 tchd 7 to 1) 9
BOLD SEVEN (Ire) [84] 8-7 R Lappin (4) *in tch till wknd 2 fs out*........................(50 to 1 op 20 to 1) 10
Dist: 1½l, sht-hd, ¾l, ½l, 3l, 5l, 2½l, 8l, ¾l. 1m 24.94s. a 4.24s (10 Ran).
SR: 20/9/20/20/4/7/ (Hamdan Al-Maktoum), H Thomson Jones

401 Aintree Handicap Class D (0-80 4-y-o and up) £3,260 5f........................ (4:20)

THE NOBLE OAK (Ire) [55] 5-7-12 (7*) Gina Faulkner (8) *made all, ran on wl fnl furlong*...........(12 to 1 op 8 to 1) 1
MISS VAXETTE [73] 4-9-2 (7*) M Humphries (3) *hld up in rear, hdwy appr fnl furlong, ran on to go second nr finish*........................(10 to 1 op 6 to 1) 2
4804a[6] JOE SUGDEN [55] 9-8-5 W Newnes (2) *hld up, rdn and hdwy appr fnl furlong, ran on ins.* (12 to 1 op 7 to 1) 3
236* SERIOUS HURRY [56] 5-8-6 T Quinn (4) *trkd wnr, rdn appr fnl furlong, one pace cl hme.* ....(11 to 4 op 2 to 1 tchd 3 to 1) 4
320* SOBA GUEST (Ire) [73] 4-9-9 J Carroll (5) *chsd ldrs till wknd appr fnl furlong*..........(9 to 4 fav op 7 to 4) 5
223 BLAZING SENSATION [47] (bl) 5-7-11[2] D Biggs (7) *nvr on terms*........................(25 to 1 op 10 to 1) 6
292[9] BOLD HABIT [78] 8-10-0 L Dettori (1) *al beh.* ....(7 to 1 op 5 to 1) 7
301 HALBERT [75] 4-9-11 M Roberts (6) *prmnt till wknd wl o'r one furlong out*........ (9 to 2 op 7 to 1 tchd 8 to 1) 8
Dist: 1l, ½l, 1½l, 3l, 5l, 2½l, hd. 58.94s. a 2.04s (8 Ran).
SR: 35/49/29/24/29/-/4/-/ (M McCormack), M McCormack

LINGFIELD (A.W) (std)
Saturday April 3rd
Going Correction: MINUS 0.30 sec. per fur.

402 Daily Star Challenge Final Handicap Class B (4-y-o and up) £7,310 1¼m........ (2:10)

321[5] MODESTO (USA) [47] (v) 5-7-7 N Carlisle (3) *al prmnt, trkd ldr aftr 4 fs, hrd rdn and ran on to ld wl ins last.* ....(33 to 1) 1
321* GOLD BLADE [66] 4-8-12 T Quinn (11) *al prmnt, rdn o'r 2 fs out, ran on ins fnl furlong*.......(4 to 1 fav op 3 to 1) 2
302 COLTRANE [71] (v) 5-9-3 A Munro (4) *led till rdn and hdd wl ins fnl furlong*.................. (9 to 1 op 12 to 1) 3
115* EL VOLADOR [82] 6-9-7 (7*) B Russell (6) *sn pushed alng, rdn 4 fs out, ran on gmely ins last.* ....(5 to 1 tchd 11 to 2 and 9 to 2) 4
171[3] PRESENT TIMES [48] 7-7-8[1] N Adams (14) *al prmnt, rdn 3 fs out, wknd wl o'r one out*.................. (33 to 1) 5
302 LOOKINGFORARAINBOW (Ire) [70] (v) 5-9-2 N Day (9) *sn in mid-div, chsd ldrs frm hfwy, rdn and wknd appr fnl furlong*........................(14 to 1 op 12 to 1) 6
293[9] AMENABLE [69] 8-9-1 A Mackay (10) *beh till styd on fnl 2 fs, nvr nrr*............ (10 to 1 op 8 to 1 tchd 12 to 1) 7
264[2] BALLYRANTER [52] 4-7-12 J Quinn (7) *beh, styd on fnl 2 fs, nvr nrr*............. (12 to 1 op 10 to 1 tchd 14 to 1) 8
321[2] LOWAWATHA [64] 5-8-5 (5*) K Rutter (1) *trkd ldr 1st 4 fs, wknd 3 out*........................(6 to 1 op 7 to 1) 9
211[4] SLIGHT RISK [63] (e/c) 4-8-9 G Bardwell (12) *chsd ldrs, rdn 4 fs out, wknd o'r 2 out*.........(20 to 1 op 16 to 1) 10
114* FERDIA (Ire) [71] 4-9-3 W Ryan (8) *al in rear.* ....(14 to 1 op 10 to 1) 11
265[2] STRAT'S LEGACY [64] 6-8-7 (3*) J Weaver (5) *prmnt early, wknd hfwy*........................ (10 to 1 op 7 to 1) 12
321[6] NORTH ESK (USA) [63] 4-8-9 W Newnes (2) *mid-div, rdn o'r 3 fs out, sn btn*........................(25 to 1) 13
264 TADORA (Ire) [51] 4-7-11 D Biggs (13) *beh frm hfwy.* ....(20 to 1 op 14 to 1) 14
Dist: ½l, nk, nk, 6l, 2l, sht-hd, sht-hd, 5l, nk, ¾l. 2m 5.55s. a 2.35s (14 Ran).
SR: 26/44/48/58/12/30/28/10/12/ (D Bass), K O Cunningham-Brown

403 Rothmans Royals North South Challenge Series Handicap Class D (4-y-o and up) £5,208 1m........................ (2:40)

333[5] NOBBY BARNES [62] 4-8-12 J Williams (1) *hld up in rear, swtchd to outsd hfwy, smooth hdwy o'r 2 fs out, led wl ins last*........................(12 to 1 op 8 to 1) 1
198[7] KILLICK [54] 5-8-4 J Quinn (9) *trkd ldr, led o'r 3 fs out, rdn and hdd wl ins last*.............. (12 to 1 op 10 to 1) 2
302* CEE-JAY-AY [57] 6-8-7 J Carroll (12) *slwly away, rcd on outsd in rear, hdwy o'r 2 fs out, ran on, nvr nrr.* ....(7 to 2 fav op 2 to 1) 3
224[6] MASTER HYDE (USA) [68] 4-9-4 S O'Gorman (6) *hld up, hdwy o'r 2 fs out, hng lft ins last, no extr*..... (12 to 1) 4
274[6] BATTLE COLOURS (Ire) [77] 4-9-13 G Duffield (4) *al prmnt, rdn o'r 2 fs out, kpt on one pace, hmpd cl hme.* ....(9 to 2 op 5 to 1 tchd 11 to 2) 5
327[4] EASTLEIGH [71] 4-9-0 (7*) D Carson (5) *al mid-div, not quicken ins fnl 2 fs*..................(12 to 1 op 10 to 1) 6
315 MASNUN (USA) [78] 8-9-7 (7*) B Russell (3) *beh, hdwy o'r 2 fs out, rdn, nvr nrr*..............(12 to 1 tchd 14 to 1) 7
319[2] SARUM [54] 7-8-4 C Rutter (7) *mid-div, slightly hmpd wl o'r one furlong out, one pace aftr*....(7 to 1 op 9 to 1) 8
276[8] HAWAII STORM (Fr) [64] 5-9-0 N Adams (8) *al in rear.* ....(33 to 1 op 25 to 1) 9
319* SCOTS LAW [57] 6-8-7 D Biggs (2) *led till hdd o'r 3 fs out, wknd quickly appr last, eased*......(10 to 1 op 7 to 1) 10
241[9] SLEEPLINE FANTASY [57] 8-8-7 N Carlisle (10) *prmnt till wknd o'r 2 fs out*.....(12 to 1 op 20 to 1 tchd 25 to 1) 11
332 SIRTELIMAR (Ire) [73] 4-9-9 A Mackay (11) *prmnt till wknd quickly o'r 3 fs out, tld off*..........(12 to 1 op 8 to 1) 12
Dist: ½l, 1l, 1½l, 2½l, nk, sht-hd, hd, 12l, nk, 3l. 1m 38.43s. a 2.23s (12 Ran).
SR: 29/19/19/25/26/19/25/-/-/ (T S M S Riley-Smith), D A Wilson

404 Kentucky Derby Trial Conditions Stakes Class C (3-y-o) £5,060 1¼m.........(3:10)

239[4] ABERDEEN HEATHER 8-10 J Williams (2) *settled in rear, shaken up and hdwy 3 fs out, hng fire appr last, ran on strly ins to ld nr finish.* (11 to 4 op 7 to 2 tchd 5 to 2) 1
201 SALBUS 9-0 T Quinn (5) *rcd on outsd, hdwy to ld 2 fs out, rdn and ct nr finish.* (12 to 1 op 14 to 1 tchd 25 to 1) 2
NOYAN 9-2 M Hills (4) *led till hdd 2 fs out, rallied wl till wknd ins last*....................(2 to 1 fav op 6 to 4) 3
SUIVEZ 8-10 L Dettori (3) *trkd ldr, rdn 3 fs out, wknd wl o'r one out*.............(6 to 1 op 7 to 1 tchd 5 to 1) 4
ALDERNEY PRINCE (USA) 8-10 A Munro (1) *trkd ldrs, outpcd 2 fs out*.............. (5 to 2 op 2 to 1 tchd 3 to 1) 5
Dist: Nk, 4l, 8l, 3½l. 2m 7.11s. a 3.91s (5 Ran).
SR: 27/30/24/2/-/ (Major H S Cayzer), D R C Elsworth

405 Chair Limited Stakes Class F (3-y-o) £2,467 1m........................ (4:50)

JUST YOU DARE (Ire) 8-11 G Duffield (1) *pld hrd, al prmnt, rdn wl o'r one furlong out, ran on to ld well ins last.* ....(5 to 4 on op 6 to 4) 1
228[3] STEVIE'S WONDER (Ire) 8-6 (5*) N Gwilliams (4) *hld up, hdwy hfwy, led 2 fs out, rdn and hdd wl ins last.* ....(12 to 1 op 8 to 1 tchd 14 to 1) 2
304[8] PEACEFULL REPLY (USA) 8-11 R Lappin (2) *pld hrd, al prmnt, rdn and ev ch ins last, wknd cl hme.* ....(15 to 2 op 5 to 1 tchd 8 to 1) 3
284[4] TEJANO GOLD (USA) 8-11 T Quinn (7) *in rear, came wide into strt, rdn and ran on strly ins fnl furlong.* ....(11 to 1 op 10 to 1 tchd 14 to 1) 4
71[3] CONVOY (bl) 8-11 W Ryan (5) *al prmnt, led o'r 3 fs out, hdd 2 out, wknd appr last*......... (7 to 2 tchd 4 to 1) 5
286[4] HOTSOCKS 7-13 (7*) Kim McDonnell (8) *al in rear.* ....(7 to 1 tchd 10 to 1) 6

223[8] SHARP GAZELLE 8-6 W Newnes (6) *hld up in rear, nvr on terms*..........(20 to 1 op 14 to 1) 7
ADMIRED 8-6 N Carlisle (3) *set steady pace, hdd o'r 3 fs out, sn btn*..........(16 to 1 op 10 to 1 tchd 20 to 1) 8
Dist: ½l, 1½l, nk, 2½l, 3½l, 8l, 6l. 1m 41.12s. a 4.92s (8 Ran).
(Mrs David Thompson), Sir Mark Prescott

GELSENKIRCHEN (GER) (good to soft)
Sunday April 4th

406 Grosser Preis der Gelsenkirchener Wirtschaft (Group 2) (4-y-o and up) £24,490 1¼ m..........(4:15)

CARLTON (Ger) 4-9-2 P Schiergen, *led to 4 fs out, led one out, drvn out*.......... 1
SUGUNAS (Ger) 5-9-2 T Hellier, *trkd ldr, led 4 fs out to one out, fnshd wl*.......... 2
EMBARCADERO (Ger) 5-9-0 A Best, *rear till hdwy wl o'r one furlong out, fnshd well*.......... 3
LE JARDIN (Ger) 5-8-12 M Hofer, *hld up, hdwy wl o'r 2 fs out, ran on one pace fnl furlong*.......... 4
HELL DRIVER (Fr) 7-9-0 L Charnock, *nrst at finish*.......... 5
FRIEDLAND (USA) 5-9-0 J Reid, *3rd to strt, one pace fnl furlong*.......... 6
TWIST AND TURN 4-9-2 M Rimmer, *prmnt, 5th strt, one pace fnl 2 fs*.......... 7
FRISCOLINO (Ger) 5-9-0 L Mader, *nvr a factor*.......... 8
DAJRAAN (Ire) 4-9-4 S Guillot, *prmnt, 4th strt, wknd o'r 2 fs out*.......... 9
INHERITANCE (Ire) (bl) 5-9-2 Susanne Berneklint, *beh fnl 4 fs*.......... 0
HERO'S LIGHT (USA) 4-8-9 F Johansson, *beh fnl 4 fs*.......... 0
HONDO MONDO (Ire) (bl) 5-9-4 K Woodburn, *al beh*.......... 0
ZOHAR (Ger) 4-9-4 A Helfenbein, *in tch for o'r 6 fs*.......... 0
Dist: 1l, 1½l, nk, 2½l, 1½l, nk. 2m 8.30s. (13 Ran).

LONGCHAMP (FR) (soft)
Sunday April 4th
Going Correction: PLUS 0.30 sec. per fur.

407 Prix d'Harcourt (Group 2) (4-y-o and up) £35,842 1¼m..........(3:05)

283[2] MARILDO (Fr) (bl) 6-8-11 G Guignard (11) *made all, quickened 2 and a half fs out, ran on wl, jst hld on*. (92 to 10) 1
4728a[3] DEAR DOCTOR (Fr) 6-9-4 C Asmussen (10) *4th strt, effrt 2 fs out, quickened one out, ran on wl, jst fld*. (6 to 4 fav) 2
POLYTAIN (Fr) 4-9-4 W Mongil (1) *3rd strt, quickened 2 fs out, wknd cl hme*..........(15 to 1) 3
APPLE TREE (Fr) 4-9-4 T Jarnet (4) *5th strt, rdn 2 and a half fs out, no extr*..........(63 to 10) 4
4728a VERT AMANDE (Fr) 5-9-1 E Legrix (9) *6th strt, effrt 2 and a half fs out, one pace*..........(14 to 1) 5
DADARISSIME (Fr) 4-8-11 F Head (2) *nrst finish*.. (22 to 1) 6
MODHISH (Ire) 4-9-1 M Roberts (3) *mid-div whn hmpd aftr 5 fs, one paced after*..........(15 to 1) 7
PONDORO 4-8-11 D Boeuf (12) *al beh*..........(69 to 10) 8
PETIT LOUP (USA) 4-9-4 W Swinburn (5) *al rear*.. (18 to 1) 9
283[3] FUNNY BABY (Fr) 5-8-11 A Badel (8) *second strt, wknd quickly 2 and a half fs out*..........(68 to 10) 0
OUMNAZ (Fr) 4-8-11 N Jeanpierre (7) *al beh*..........(40 to 1) 0
ADIEU AU ROI (Ire) 4-9-1 M Boutin (6) *refused to race, lft and took no part*..........(14 to 1) I
Dist: Hd, nk, ¾l, 1½l, 1½l, ¾l, 1½l, 1½l, 1½l, ¾l. 2m 7.70s. a 5.60s (12 Ran).
SR: 71/77/76/74/68/61/63/56/60/ (D Smaga), D Smaga

408 Prix de Courcelles (Listed) (3-y-o) £14,337 1¼m 110yds..........(4:40)

TALLOIRES (USA) 8-11 M Roberts,.......... 1
REGENCY 8-11 W Swinburn,.......... 2
HUNTING HAWK (Ire) 8-11 T Jarnet,.......... 3
BADOLATO (USA) 8-11 W Mongil,.......... 4
Dist: ½l, ½l, 2l, ½l, 1½l, 4l, 1l, 6l. 2m 16.80s. a 7.80s (9 Ran).
SR: 51/50/49/45/ (P de Moussac), A Fabre

SOUTHWELL (A.W) (std)
Monday April 5th
Going Correction: PLUS 0.15 sec. per fur.

409 Daffodil Handicap Class E (0-70 3-y-o and up) £2,950 6f..........(2:15)

277[6] GIRL NEXT DOOR [54] 3-8-7 J O'Reilly (11) *al prmnt, wnt second 2 fs out, led ins last, pushed out*..........(12 to 1 op 8 to 1) 1
223[6] TOSHIBA COMET [43] (bl) 6-8-9 J Quinn (7) *towards rear till hdwy o'r 2 fs out, styd on gmely, not rch wnr*..........(9 to 1 op 8 to 1) 2
330[9] BRISAS [47] (bl) 6-8-13 J Fanning (3) *led aftr 2 fs, rdn and hdd ins last, one pace*..........(5 to 1 op 4 to 1) 3
376[5] SALLY'S SON [62] 7-9-11 (3*) Emma O'Gorman (10) *al in tch on outsd, kpt on one pace fnl 2 fs*..........(4 to 1 fav op 9 to 2 tchd 11 to 2) 4
PAR DE LUXE [31] 6-7-11 A Mackay (4) *towards rear on outsd, kpt on one pace fnl 2 fs*..........(33 to 1) 5
379[7] GRUBBY [36] 4-7-11 (5*) A Garth (1) *prmnt on ins, no hdwy fnl 2 fs*..........(12 to 1 op 14 to 1 tchd 16 to 1) 6
236[9] GRAND TIME [47] (v) 4-8-13 G Bardwell (5) *led 1st 2 fs, rdn hfwy, sn btn*..........(9 to 1 op 12 to 1) 7
327 COBBLERS HILL [52] 4-9-4 T Lang (2) *slwly away, al beh*..........(16 to 1 tchd 20 to 1) 8
249 WELLSY LAD (USA) [50] 6-9-2 D Nicholls (6) *in tch to hfwy*..........(6 to 1 op 9 to 2 tchd 13 to 2) 9
285[3] JOVIAL KATE (USA) [51] 6-9-3 J Lowe (9) *speed to hfwy*..........(5 to 1 op 4 to 1) 10
MALCESINE (Ire) [40] 4-8-6 G Carter (8) *al beh*.... (16 to 1) 11
Dist: ¾l, 2½l, 1½l, sht-hd, 1l, ½l, 1l, 1l, 5l, 3½l. 1m 19.30s. a 5.90s (11 Ran).
(M G Vines), A A Hambly

410 Trillium Claiming Stakes Class F (3-y-o) £2,243 7f..........(2:45)

362[9] FORMAESTRE (Ire) 8-3 (5*) O Pears (2) *wtd wth, cld on ldrs o'r 2 fs out, ran on strly to ld appr last, all out*..........(8 to 1 op 7 to 1 tchd 9 to 1) 1
378[3] MISTER BLAKE (bl) 9-0 (3*) Emma O'Gorman (5) *trkd ldr till passed by wnr appr fnl furlong, rallied ins last, jst fld*..........(Evens fav op 6 to 4 on) 2
275[5] IRISH ROOTS (Ire) (v) 8-9 M Birch (4) *led, rdn and hdd appr fnl furlong, one pace final 50 yards*..........(5 to 2 op 7 to 2 tchd 4 to 1) 3
334[6] EASTERN GLOW 8-6 W Woods (1) *al same pl, lost tch hfwy*..........(11 to 2 op 7 to 2 tchd 6 to 1) 4
ACHY BREAKY 8-9 J O'Reilly (3) *reared up leaving stalls, tld off frm hfwy*..........(11 to 1 op 6 to 1 tchd 12 to 1) 5
Dist: Hd, 1½l, 12l, 25l. 1m 33.70s. a 7.60s (5 Ran).
SR: -/4/ (S G Norton), S G Norton

411 Hyacinth Handicap Class D (0-80 3-y-o and up) £3,231 7f..........(3:15)

DUNE RIVER [68] 4-9-5 M Tebbutt (1) *led aftr 2 fs, hdd jst ins last, rallied to ld ag'n nr finish*..........(7 to 1 op 8 to 1 tchd 5 to 1) 1
276[4] DEBSY DO (USA) [70] 4-9-2 (5*) O Pears (6) *trkd ldrs, gd hdwy o'r 2 fs out, led jst ins fnl furlong, rdn and hdd nr finish*..........(8 to 1 op 6 to 1) 2
375[5] LORD NASKRA (USA) [60] 4-8-8 (3*) Emma O'Gorman (2) *towards rear on ins, kpt on inside fnl 2 fs, nvr nrr*..........(6 to 1 op 8 to 1 tchd 10 to 1) 3
315 ASHDREN [74] 6-9-11 A Munro (7) *al same pl, pushed alng o'r 2 fs out, one pace*... (4 to 1 tchd 7 to 2 and 9 to 2) 4
319[7] QUINZII MARTIN [62] (v) 5-8-13 J Williams (5) *in rear till effrt o'r 2 fs out, nvr nr to chal*..........(10 to 1) 5
AITCH N'BEE [76] 10-9-13 L Dettori (8) *nvr on terms*..........(4 to 1 op 5 to 1) 6
375[2] CAPTAIN MARMALADE [56] 4-8-2 (5*) K Rutter (3) *slwly away, effrt outsd o'r 2 fs out, nvr dngrs*..........(7 to 2 fav tchd 3 to 1 and 4 to 1) 7
276[2] RURAL LAD [62] 4-8-13 M Hills (4) *led 2 fs, rdn 3 out, sn btn*..........(8 to 1 op 7 to 1) 8
Dist: Hd, 5l, nk, 1½l, 3l, hd, 6l. 1m 30.90s. a 4.80s (8 Ran).
SR: 49/50/25/38/21/26/5/-/ (D R Loder), D R Loder

412 Crocus Maiden Stakes Class D (3-y-o) £3,276 1½m..........(3:45)

LORD NITROGEN (USA) 9-0 M Hills (2) *made all, pushed clr o'r 3 fs out, eased ins last, unchlgd*..........(2 to 1 on op 7 to 2 on tchd 7 to 4 on) 1
295[9] ARC BRIGHT (Ire) 9-0 W Ryan (1) *trkd wnr 1st 4 fs, wnt second ag'n four out, sn no ch wth winner*..........(2 to 1 op 11 to 4 tchd 7 to 2) 2
377[4] FREE DANCER 8-9 N Adams (3) *pld hrd, rdn to chase wnr aftr 4 fs, wknd four out*..........(10 to 1 op 8 to 1) 3
Dist: 15l, 12l. 2m 41.60s. a 7.70s (3 Ran).
SR: 41/11/-/ (John Purcell), M Bell

413 Bluebell Selling Stakes Class G (3-y-o) £2,070 1½m..........(4:15)

339[3] GOODBYE MILLIE 8-2 (5*) O Pears (3) *pld hrd early, al in tch, wnt second o'r 2 fs out, led appr last, edgd lft ins*..........(4 to 1 op 5 to 2) 1
351[3] STAPLEFORD LASS 8-7 W Woods (5) *hld up, hdwy hfwy, wnt second 4 fs out, led 3 out, hdd appr fnl furlong, held whn slightly short of room ins*. (2 to 1 jt-fav op 9 to 4 tchd 5 to 2) 2
245[6] ROSIE'S GOLD 8-2 (5*) Stephen Davies (2) *trkd ldr 1st 5 fs, rdn 3 furlongs out, kpt on one pace*. (7 to 1 op 5 to 1) 3
BAEZA (bl) 8-12 L Dettori (4) *led till hdd 3 fs out, sn hrd rdn, no response, eased, tld off*. (2 to 1 jt-fav op 5 to 2 tchd 3 to 1) 4
SOCIETY LOVER (USA) 8-7 M Hills (1) *al beh, lost tch hfwy, tld off*..........(6 to 1 op 3 to 1) 5
Dist: 1½l, 1½l, 30l, 5l. 2m 46.30s. a 12.40s (5 Ran).
(Lintscan Ltd (Corbett Bookmakers)), S G Norton

414 Rose Median Auction Maiden Stakes Class D (3-y-o) £3,114 7f............(4:45)

CYPRIAN DANCER (USA) 9-0 T Quinn (5) *led aftr one furlong, wnt clr o'r 2 out, ran green unchlgd.* ....(11 to 2 op 5 to 2) 1
SAXON MAGIC 8-9 J Quinn (2) *beh till hdwy o'r 2 fs out, rdn and styd on to go second ins last.* ....(7 to 1 op 8 to 1 tchd 9 to 1) 2
SYLVAN STARLIGHT 8-9 G Duffield (4) *sn trkd wnr, rdn 2 fs out, one pace fnl furlong*.........(5 to 2 tchd 11 to 4) 3
OCARA (USA) 8-9 L Dettori (3) *chsd ldrs, rdn 2 fs out, no hdwy*................(5 to 4 fav op Evens tchd 6 to 4) 4
ACCESS FESTIVALS 9-0 R Cochrane (1) *led 1st furlong, sn beh, nvr dngrs aftr*..................(8 to 1 op 12 to 1) 5
Dist: 4l, 1l, 2½l, 3½l. 1m 32.80s. a 6.70s (5 Ran).
SR: 15/-/ (C Shiacolas), P F I Cole

415 Wallflower Handicap Class E (0-70 3-y-o) £2,847 1m.......................... (5:15)

378* CERTAIN WAY (Ire) [57] 8-11 (5ex) M Birch (2) *outpcd early, rdn and hdwy 3 fs out, led wl o'r one out, ridden and styd on*............(13 to 8 fav op 5 to 4 tchd 7 to 4) 1
245^{5} KINGSTON BROWN [67] (bl) 9-7 L Dettori (5) *led aftr one furlong, hdd wl o'r one out, rdn and pressed wnr till no extr fnl stages*.......................(9 to 2 op 7 to 2) 2
124^{2} PERSONIMUS [39] 7-7 J Fanning (4) *sn trkd ldr, passed by wnr 2 fs out, rallied one out, kpt on one pace.* ....(9 to 1 op 6 to 1) 3
237^{3} SPANISH REFUGE [60] (v) 9-0 Dean McKeown (3) *slwly away, sn rdn alng, nvr on terms.* ....(7 to 4 op 9 to 4 tchd 3 to 1) 4
378^{5} SCOFFERA [44] (bl) 7-12 Kim Tinkler (1) *led 1st furlong, rdn hfwy, lost tch wl o'r 2 fs out, tld off.* (12 to 1 op 7 to 1) 5
Dist: 1½l, ½l, 6l, 20l. 1m 47.40s. a 8.40s (5 Ran).
(M J Rogers), C Tinkler

FOLKESTONE (soft)
Tuesday April 6th

Going Correction: PLUS 0.70 sec. per fur. (races 1,2,5,7), PLUS 0.15 (3,4,6)

416 Saltwood Handicap Class E (0-70 4-y-o and up) £3,365 1m 1f 149yds........ (1:45)

ALDERBROOK [69] 4-9-13 Paul Eddery (5) *hld up, al gng wl, hdwy 5 fs out, led on bit one out, very cheekily.* ....(5 to 1 op 3 to 1) 1
332* HERE HE COMES [40] 7-7-12 (7ex) J Quinn (7) *hld up, steady hdwy frm 5 fs out, rdn to ld o'r 2 out, hdd one out, kpt on und pres.* ....(Evens fav op 11 to 10 tchd 5 to 4) 2
189^{5} L'UOMO CLASSICS [64] 6-9-8 A Clark (6) *mid-div, sn pushed alng, effrt 3 fs out, styd on, not pace to chal.* ....(16 to 1 op 8 to 1) 3
349 LLOYDS DREAM [37] 4-7-9 N Carlisle (11) *beh, pushed alng and hdwy o'r 2 fs out, styd on, nvr nrr.* ....(40 to 1 op 25 to 1 tchd 50 to 1) 4
332^{6} ALMOST A PRINCESS [48] 5-8-6 T Quinn (14) *trkd ldr till rdn and wknd o'r 2 fs out*.......(12 to 1 tchd 16 to 1) 5
ANATROCCOLO [43] 6-8-1 C Rutter (2) *led til hdd o'r 2 fs out, wknd*........ (25 to 1 op 20 to 1 tchd 33 to 1) 6
402 NORTH ESK (USA) [67] 4-9-11 G Carter (12) *nvr on terms wth ldrs*..........................(33 to 1 op 16 to 1) 7
USAIDIT [69] 4-9-8 (5*) N Gwilliams (8) *al beh.* ....(20 to 1 op 10 to 1 tchd 25 to 1) 8
211^{8} PARKING BAY [61] 6-9-2 (3*) D Harrison (10) *nvr better than mid-div*..........................(14 to 1 op 10 to 1) 9
STRIKING IMAGE (Ire) [59] (v) 4-9-3 B Rouse (1) *nvr better than mid-div*........ (16 to 1 op 10 to 1 tchd 20 to 1) 10
DAZZLING FIRE (Ire) [58] 4-9-2 W Newnes (3) *trkd ldrs til rdn and wknd o'r 4 fs out*.......... (12 to 1 op 8 to 1) 11
MASTAMIST [38] (bl) 4-7-10 N Adams (9) *al beh.* ....(33 to 1 op 20 to 1) 12
332 SOL ROUGE (Ire) [36] 4-7-4^{3} (7*) Nicola Howarth (13) *trkd ldrs till rdn and lost pl quickly aftr 3 fs.* ....(40 to 1 op 25 to 1) 13
320^{4} LOON [53] 5-8-11 D Biggs (4) *missed break and lost many ls strt, al beh*.....................(33 to 1 op 20 to 1) 14
329^{7} MR ZIEGFELD (USA) [49] (bl) 4-8-7 A McGlone (15) *sn rdn alng, trkd ldrs till drpd out o'r 4 fs out.* ....(33 to 1 op 20 to 1) 15
Dist: Nk, 10l, 6l, 10l, 2½l, nk, 7l, 1l, 1½l, 5l. 2m 10.70s. a 13.10s (15 Ran).
SR: 50/20/24/-/-/-/ (E Pick), Mrs J Cecil

417 'Privy Councillor' Maiden Stakes Class D (3-y-o) £3,523 6f 189yds.............(2:15)

TABKIR (USA) 9-0 W Carson (3) *cl up, led aftr 2 fs till hdd ins last, shaken up and ran on ag'n to ld close hme.* ....(5 to 1 op 3 to 1) 1
NESSUN DORMA 8-11 (3*) F Norton (10) *trkd ldg trio, hdwy to chase wnr o'r one furlong out, led ins last till hdd cl hme*............(5 to 2 op 6 to 4 tchd 11 to 4) 2
JETBEEAH (Ire) 8-9 G Carter (11) *slwly into strd, sn in tch, hdwy 2 fs out, ran green and one pace ins last.* ....(6 to 1 op 5 to 1 tchd 7 to 1) 3
SYLVANIA (Ire) 9-0 B Rouse (9) *cl up, sn rdn alng, ev ch o'r 2 fs out, one pace*.... (2 to 1 fav op 7 to 4 tchd 9 to 4) 4
JUST JAMIE 9-0 Paul Eddery (4) *slwly into strd and beh, styd on frm o'r one furlong out, nrst finish.* ....(20 to 1 op 12 to 1 tchd 33 to 1) 5
AL MOULOUKI 9-0 R Cochrane (1) *beh, styd on frm o'r one furlong out, nvr nrr.* (33 to 1 op 20 to 1 tchd 50 to 1) 6
323^{4} SLEEPTITE (Fr) 9-0 W Newnes (2) *beh, effrt hfwy, not pace to chal*...............(25 to 1 op 20 to 1 tchd 33 to 1) 7
MARAT (USA) 9-0 T Quinn (7) *led 2 fs, cl up, ev ch o'r two furlongs out, wknd*............... (20 to 1 op 12 to 1) 8
TOCCATELLA 8-9 R Perham (5) *mid-div till wknd o'r 2 fs out*...............(25 to 1 op 16 to 1 tchd 33 to 1) 9
BAYFAN (Ire) 9-0 A McGlone (6) *nvr dngrs.* ....(33 to 1 op 20 to 1 tchd 50 to 1) 10
CAVALIER PRINCE (Ire) 9-0 S Whitworth (8) *trkd ldrs till rdn and wknd o'r 3 fs out, drpd out quickly, tld off.* ....(33 to 1 op 20 to 1) 11
Dist: Nk, 2½l, 6l, 4l, 2l, ¾l, sht-hd, ¾l, sht-hd, 25l. 1m 30.70s. a 9.80s (11 Ran).
SR: 26/25/12/-/-/-/ (Hamdan Al-Maktoum), J L Dunlop

418 Levy Board Apprentices' Handicap Class G (0-70 3-y-o) £2,427 6f............. (2:45)

245 BUCKSKI ECHO [38] 7-4^{2} (5*) D Toole (5) *al prmnt, led briefly o'r one and a half fs out, led ag'n ins last, shade cmftbly*..........................(33 to 1 op 20 to 1) 1
ANOTHER JADE [63] 9-1 (3*) L Newton (1) *trkd ldrs, led one and a half fs out till hdd and no extr und pres ins last.* ....(6 to 1 op 4 to 1 tchd 13 to 2) 2
SUPERENSIS [46] 7-12 (3*) Kim McDonnell (8) *broke wl, cl up till outpcd o'r one furlong out.* ....(10 to 1 op 8 to 1 tchd 12 to 1) 3
CLEAR LOOK [65] 9-3 (3*) T G McLaughlin (10) *trkd ldrs till outpcd fnl 2 fs*.....................(7 to 2 fav op 5 to 1) 4
326^{9} LAID BACK BEN [45] 8-0 Stephen Davies (2) *cl up, led o'r 2 fs out till hdd over one and a half out, wknd.* (20 to 1) 5
BURISHKI [52] 8-2 (5*) J O'Dwyer (4) *strted slwly, beh, styd on frm o'r one furlong out, unbl to chal.* ....(8 to 1 op 7 to 1) 6
334 ARAWA [48] 7-12 (5*) S McCarthy (11) *led till hdd o'r 2 fs out, wknd*........................ (12 to 1 op 8 to 1) 7
313^{6} FOLLY VISION (Ire) [64] 8-12 (7*) D O'Neill (7) *outpcd frm hfwy*..............................(6 to 1 op 7 to 2) 8
262^{2} MARK'S CLUB (Ire) [66] 9-4 (3*) A Procter (6) *outpcd.* ....(6 to 1 op 7 to 2) 9
DRAGONMIST (Ire) [48] 8-0 (3*) B Russell (9) *sn outpcd.* ....(12 to 1 op 10 to 1) 10
TOFF SUNDAE [52] 8-2 (5*) S Mulvey (3) *nvr on terms.* ....(9 to 1 op 6 to 1) 11
KENSWORTH LADY [54] 8-9 C Hodgson (12) *outpcd.* ....(7 to 1 tchd 8 to 1) 12
Dist: ½l, 10l, ¾l, 1l, 5l, ¾l, 2½l, 1½l, nk, 1½l. 1m 16.30s. a 5.30s (12 Ran).
SR: -/14/-/-/-/ (T M Jones), T M Jones

419 Chatham Claiming Stakes Class F (3-y-o and up) £2,243 5f..................(3:15)

330^{4} HARRY'S COMING 9-9-2 W Carson (5) *made all, shaken up and quickened o'r 2 fs out, cmftbly.* ....(2 to 1 tchd 5 to 2) 1
COPPERMILL LAD 10-8-12 A Munro (3) *cl up, hrd rdn o'r one furlong out, kpt on ins last*......(9 to 2 op 3 to 1) 2
AQUADO 4-9-10 W Newnes (8) *cl up, pushed alng o'r 2 fs out, outpcd appr last*.............(14 to 1 op 10 to 1) 3
288 BLUE POINT (Ire) 4-8-11 N Carlisle (7) *cl up, rdn 3 fs out, sn outpcd*..........................(33 to 1 op 16 to 1) 4
HEBER SPRING (Ire) 3-8-8 A McGlone (1) *lft at strt, took no part*.......... (11 to 10 fav op 5 to 4 on tchd 6 to 5) l
Dist: 1l, 10l, 2½l. 1m 4.20s. a 5.60s (5 Ran).
SR: 5/-/ (Mrs D A Wetherall), R J Hodges

420 Gravesend Handicap Class E (0-70 4-y-o and up) £3,209 1m 7f 92yds......... (3:45)

148^{3} ISLAND BLADE (Ire) [49] 4-8-4^{1} T Quinn (12) *hld up beh ldrs, cld o'r 6 fs out, led 2 out, sn clr, eased bef line.* ....(4 to 1 fav op 9 to 2 tchd 5 to 1) 1
261^{6} PEACH BRANDY [40] 4-7-9^{2} N Adams (13) *chsd ldrs, led 6 fs out till hdd 2 out, one pace*.....(50 to 1 op 33 to 1) 2
331 PERFORATE [43] 4-7-12 A McGlone (7) *sn pushed alng in rear, hrd rdn o'r 2 fs out, rapid hdwy ins last, fnshd wl.* ....(20 to 1 op 12 to 1) 3
THOR POWER (Ire) [40] 4-7-2 (7*) Kim McDonnell (6) *beh, hdwy o'r 6 fs out, one pace frm over 2 out.* ....(14 to 1 op 10 to 1) 4
34^{3} SCOTONI [48] 7-8-6 D Biggs (9) *trkd ldrs, hrd rdn o'r 2 fs out, sn wknd*..........................(6 to 1 op 4 to 1) 5
BOLD RESOLUTION (Ire) [70] 5-10-0 G Carter (2) *hld up beh ldg grp, hdwy 6 fs out, hrd rdn 3 out, sn btn, better for race*.................................(13 to 2 op 8 to 1) 6
ALICE'S MIRROR [45] 4-8-0 J Quinn (10) *trkd ldrs till wknd o'r 5 fs out*..........................(14 to 1 op 10 to 1) 7

287[2] KARAMOJA [60] 4-9-1 A Munro (14) *trkd ldr, rdn hfwy, outpcd frm o'r 3 fs out.* (13 to 2 op 5 to 1 tchd 7 to 1) 8
331[9] LYPH (USA) [42] (bl) 7-7-11 (3*) A Tucker (11) *chsd ldrs till wknd o'r 4 fs out.* (14 to 1 op 10 to 1) 9
DECIDING BID [36] 7-7-8[1] N Carlisle (5) *beh, hrd rdn and hdwy o'r 4 fs out, sn btn.* (100 to 1 op 33 to 1) 10
279[4] INTRICACY [56] 5-9-0 D Holland (15) *led till hdd 6 fs out, wknd und pres.* (6 to 1 op 9 to 2) 11
CORINTHIAN GOD (Ire) [40] 4-7-9 W Carson (8) *sn struggling in rear.* (7 to 1 op 5 to 1 tchd 8 to 1) 12
229[7] I'M CURIOUS [38] 4-7-4[4] (7*) Nicola Howarth (4) *sn pushed alng to go pace, al beh.* (50 to 1 op 20 to 1) 13
73[7] BURSANA [38] 7-7-10[8] (5*) A Garth (1) *chsd ldrs to hfwy.* (66 to 1 op 33 to 1) 14
235[7] EL DOMINIO [50] 5-8-8 G Bardwell (3) *al beh, tld off.* (10 to 1 op 6 to 1) 15
HAWKISH (USA) [54] 4-8-9 W Ryan (16) *al beh, tld off.* (16 to 1 op 10 to 1 tchd 20 to 1) 16

Dist: 5l, 1l, ¾l, 15l, ½l, 12l, 2l, 4l, 6l, 7l. 3m 38.80s. a 20.30s (16 Ran).
(The Lime Street Racing Syndicate), R Akehurst

421 Gillingham Limited Stakes Class E (4-y-o and up) £3,002 5f. (4:15)

292[4] MISTER JOLSON 4-8-11 W Carson (2) *cl up, led o'r 2 fs out, hrd rdn over one out, ran on wl.* (2 to 1 fav op 5 to 2 tchd 11 to 4) 1
330[5] RUSHANES 6-8-11 T Quinn (10) *wth ldr, ev ch 2 fs out, sn hrd rdn and one pace.* (6 to 1 op 5 to 1 tchd 8 to 1) 2
CALL TO THE BAR (Ire) 4-8-11 A Clark (9) *trkd ldrs, sn pushed alng, pld out o'r 2 fs out, one pace appr last.* (11 to 1 op 5 to 1 tchd 12 to 1) 3
4669a[4] LADY SABO 4-8-6 Paul Eddery (1) *missed break and beh, steady hdwy ins fnl furlong, nrst finish.* (13 to 2 op 4 to 1 tchd 7 to 1) 4
WE'RE ALL GAME 4-8-6 P Robinson (4) *led till wndrd hdd o'r 2 fs out, wknd appr last.* (9 to 1 op 7 to 1 tchd 10 to 1) 5
IRON KING 7-8-11 W Newnes (5) *missed break, nvr on terms.* (10 to 1 op 6 to 1 tchd 11 to 1) 6
NO QUARTER GIVEN 8-8-11 W Ryan (7) *outpcd.* (7 to 2 op 9 to 4) 7
326* TRIOMING 7-8-11 N Adams (6) *cl up till slightly hmpd o'r 2 fs out, sn btn.* (10 to 1 op 7 to 1) 8
BELTHORN 4-8-6 A Munro (3) *speed to hfwy.* (20 to 1 op 10 to 1) 9

Dist: 3½l, ½l, 2l, 1l, 1½l, 1l, 6l, 3½l. 1m 2.30s. a 3.70s (9 Ran).
SR: 38/24/22/9/5/4/ (J W Mursell), R J Hodges

422 Dartford Median Auction Maiden Stakes Class F (3-y-o) £2,243 1½m. (4:45)

FOREVER SHINEING 8-9 R Cochrane (2) *hld up beh ldrs, al gng smoothly, hrd rdn to ld appr fnl furlong, ran on wl.* (9 to 4 op 2 to 1 tchd 6 to 4) 1
372[3] PHROSE 9-0 W Carson (3) *pld hrd, trkd ldrs, led o'r 2 fs out, hdd and one pace und pres appr last.* (2 to 1 on op 6 to 4 on tchd Evens) 2
4717a PONDERING 9-0 T Quinn (5) *beh, hdwy o'r 3 fs out, styd on one pace.* (9 to 1 op 4 to 1 tchd 10 to 1) 3
STARLIGHT ROSE (Ire) 8-9 A McGlone (11) *chsd ldrs, pushed alng 3 fs out, one pace.* (33 to 1 op 20 to 1) 4
EVE'S TREASURE 8-9 G Bardwell (8) *pld hrd, trkd ldg pair, rdn o'r 3 fs out, sn btn.* (33 to 1 op 20 to 1) 5
CANDARELA 8-9 Paul Eddery (4) *trkd ldr, led briefly wl o'r 2 fs, sn btn.* (20 to 1 op 10 to 1) 6
304 MR LUCIANO (Ire) 9-0 Paul Smith (9) *nvr on terms.* (33 to 1 op 20 to 1 tchd 50 to 1) 7
ITS UNBELIEVABLE 9-0 R Price (6) *al beh.* (33 to 1 op 20 to 1 tchd 50 to 1) 8
DOTTY'S WALKER (Fr) 8-9 D Biggs (1) *al beh.* (33 to 1 op 20 to 1 tchd 50 to 1) 9
MY SISTER LUCY 8-9 S Whitworth (7) *set slow pace, hdd wl o'r 2 fs out, wknd quickly, tld off.* (33 to 1 op 20 to 1) 10
ROUSILLA 8-9 P Robinson (10) *al beh, tld off.* (33 to 1 op 20 to 1 tchd 50 to 1) 11

Dist: 2½l, 6l, ¾l, 2½l, 3½l, 3l, 4l, ¾l, 12l, 15l. 2m 53.70s. a 23.20s (11 Ran).
(Lord Matthews), R J R Williams

PONTEFRACT (good)
Tuesday April 6th
Going Correction: NIL (races 1,3,4,5), MINUS 0.15 (2,6,7)

423 Beast Fair Maiden Stakes Class D (3-y-o) £3,406 1¼m 6yds. (2:40)

WHITE MUZZLE 9-0 J Reid (1) *in tch, cld hfwy, led o'r one furlong out, sn clr, easily.* (11 to 8 on tchd Evens) 1
BLUE GROTTO (Ire) (v) 9-0 G Duffield (7) *chsd ldr, drvn alng 3 fs out, styd on ins last.* (11 to 2 op 8 to 1 tchd 9 to 1 and 5 to 1) 2
LIJAAM (Ire) 9-0 W R Swinburn (11) *in tch, improved hfwy, drvn o'r 2 fs out, kpt on ins last.* (9 to 1 op 7 to 1) 3
CHAMPAGNE 'N ROSES 8-9 L Dettori (8) *led till o'r one furlong out, sn btn.* (16 to 1 op 14 to 1) 4
RISING WOLF 9-0 R Hills (5) *mid-div, chsd alng o'r 3 fs out, not quicken entering strt.* (25 to 1 op 12 to 1) 5
TEACHER (Ire) 9-0 B Raymond (6) *slwly into strd, beh till hdwy fnl 2 fs, nvr nr to chal.* (12 to 1) 6
LEAGUE LEADER (Ire) 9-0 Dean McKeown (10) *hld up in tch, effrt and rdn o'r 3 fs out, no imprsn entering strt.* (12 to 1 op 8 to 1 tchd 14 to 1) 7
DUPLICATE 9-0 M Birch (2) *beh, chsd alng 4 fs out, nvr on terms.* (33 to 1 op 20 to 1) 8
JAVA QUEEN (USA) 8-9 M Hills (3) *mid-div, improved to track ldrs o'r 3 fs out, rdn and wknd entering strt.* (14 to 1 tchd 16 to 1) 9
FARANDOLE 9-0 M Roberts (4) *chsd ldrs, rdn alng o'r 3 fs out, wknd.* (8 to 1 op 9 to 2) 10
THE BRACKETEER 9-0 D Wilkinson (9) *al beh, lost tch fnl 3 fs, tld off.* (300 to 1 op 100 to 1) 11

Dist: 5l, hd, 6l, 3½l, hd, 1½l, 7l, 1½l, ¾l, 20l. 2m 17.10s. a 8.90s (11 Ran).
SR: 11/1/-/-/-/-/ (Luciano Gaucci), P W Chapple-Hyam

424 Bentley Memorial Selling Stakes Class G (3-y-o and up) £2,406 6f. (3:10)

MURRAY'S MAZDA (Ire) 4-9-12 J Carroll (1) *in tch, effrt entering strt, sstnd run to ld wl ins fnl furlong.* (8 to 1 op 7 to 1) 1
CLANROCK 3-8-8 A Culhane (4) *chsd ldrs, led wl o'r one furlong out, sn shaken up, hdd well ins last.* (3 to 1 fav tchd 7 to 2) 2
FLETCHER'S BOUNTY (Ire) 4-9-7 K Darley (2) *beh, drvn alng hfwy, hdwy o'r one furlong out, kpt on ins last.* (100 to 30 op 11 to 4 tchd 7 to 2) 3
348[8] BOULABAS (Ire) 4-9-7 M Wigham (5) *mid-div, pushed alng hfwy, one pace o'r one furlong out.* (33 to 1) 4
376[6] PESIDANAMICH (Ire) (bl) 5-9-12 M Roberts (10) *wth ldr, led o'r 2 fs out till wl over one out, sn btn.* (8 to 1 op 7 to 1) 5
289[6] MEESON TIMES 5-9-7 J Lowe (6) *beh, effrt o'r 2 fs out, kpt on fnl furlong, nvr dngrs.* (6 to 1 tchd 7 to 1) 6
253[9] FIABA 5-9-7 K Fallon (7) *chsd ldrs, drvn alng o'r 2 fs out, sn one pace.* (25 to 1 op 16 to 1) 7
362 NEVENTER (Fr) 4-9-7 V Smith (11) *rear, drvn alng o'r 2 fs out, no imprsn.* (20 to 1) 8
353[3] NITEOWLADY 3-7-10 (7*) C Teague (9) *chsd ldrs, rdn and wknd o'r 2 fs out.* (16 to 1) 9
LIBERTY GLEN 4-9-2 J Williams (8) *beh, rdn hfwy, nvr on terms.* (33 to 1) 10
323[3] MUSICAL PHONE (v) 3-8-8 Dean McKeown (3) *led till o'r 2 fs out, sn wknd.* (8 to 1) 11

Dist: ¾l, 6l, 4l, ½l, 1½l, sht-hd, 5l, hd, sht-hd, 7l. 1m 17.60s. a 2.90s (11 Ran).
SR: 36/15/4/-/-/-/ (Murray Grubb), J Berry

425 Landbridge Shipping Handicap Class C (0-90 3-y-o and up) £5,526 1m 4yds. (3:40)

302[9] LEIF THE LUCKY (USA) [69] 4-8-8 N Connorton (10) *in tch, improved to ld o'r one furlong out, drvn out ins last.* (11 to 2 jt-fav op 6 to 1) 1
COOL LUKE (Ire) [80] 4-9-5 J Fanning (9) *hld up, hdwy o'r 3 fs out, styd on strly ins last.* (11 to 1 op 10 to 1 tchd 12 to 1) 2
247[4] PAY HOMAGE [89] 5-10-0 M Hills (2) *hld up, hdwy o'r 2 fs out, kpt on same pace ins last.* (7 to 1 tchd 8 to 1) 3
315[4] RINGLAND (USA) [80] 5-8-12 (7*) Darren Moffatt (6) *chsd ldrs, drvn appr strt, one pace o'r one furlong out.* (7 to 1 op 6 to 1 tchd 8 to 1) 4
302 HABETA (USA) [58] 7-7-11 J Lowe (3) *beh, hdwy entering strt, styd on wl fnl furlong, nvr dngrs.* (6 to 1 op 5 to 1 tchd 13 to 2) 5
274[5] KATY'S LAD [63] 6-8-2 J Fortune (12) *led till o'r one furlong out, sn btn.* (8 to 1) 6
315 IMPERIAL BID (Fr) [72] 5-8-11 L Charnock (11) *chsd ldrs, ev ch 2 fs out, sn wknd.* (33 to 1 op 25 to 1) 7
AFFORDABLE [60] 5-7-13 Dale Gibson (1) *chsd ldrs, rdn and wknd o'r 2 fs out.* (25 to 1) 8
350[4] FALCONS DAWN [54] 6-7-0 (7*) D Wright (13) *mid-div, drvn alng o'r 2 fs out, sn one pace.* (9 to 1 op 8 to 1 tchd 10 to 1) 9
HOB GREEN [72] 4-8-11 K Fallon (4) *hld up in rear, effrt o'r 2 fs out, no imprsn.* (11 to 2 jt-fav op 5 to 1 tchd 6 to 1) 10
JALMUSIQUE [83] 7-9-8 M Birch (8) *trkd ldr, shaken up o'r 2 fs out, sn wknd.* (16 to 1 op 14 to 1) 11
294 CHIEF OF STAFF [75] 4-9-0 M Wigham (5) *slwly into strd, beh, struggling hfwy.* (25 to 1) 12
315[5] LAUREL QUEEN (Ire) [72] 5-8-11 J Carroll (7) *mid-div, improved o'r 3 fs out, sn rdn and wknd.* (7 to 1) 13

Dist: 1½l, 1½l, 2½l, 1l, 1½l, ½l, 2½l, 1l, 1l, 5l. 1m 46.40s. a 4.30s (13 Ran).
SR: 30/36/40/23/-/-/5/-/-/ (Miss Betty Duxbury), Miss S E Hall

426 Fryston Conditions Stakes Class C (4-y-o and up) £4,082 1¼m 6yds. (4:10)

314[2] YOUNG BUSTER (Ire) 5-9-7 M Hills (6) *made all, clr o'r 3 fs out, shaken up and styd on wl appr last.* (11 to 8 on op Evens) 1

BREAK BREAD (USA) 4-9-7 J Reid (3) *in tch, improved o'r 2 fs out, kpt on fnl furlong, no extr nr finish.* ....(9 to 2 op 7 to 2) 2
4711a³ LUPESCU 5-8-13 L Dettori (5) *chsd ldrs, effrt o'r 2 fs out, edgd lft and sn one pace*.....(5 to 2 tchd 9 to 4) 3
AJZEM (USA) 4-8-10 W R Swinburn (4) *chsd ldr, drvn alng 3 fs out, wknd entering strt*........(14 to 1 op 12 to 1) 4
PHARLY DANCER 4-8-10 Dean McKeown (1) *settled in last pl, rdn alng hfwy, sn lost tch, tld off.* ....(100 to 1 op 66 to 1) 5
Dist: 1½l, 12l, 7l, 10l. 2m 13.90s. a 5.70s (5 Ran).
SR: 50/47/15/-/-/ (Mollers Racing), G Wragg

427 Levy Board Handicap Class D (0-80 4-y-o and up) £3,435 2m 1f 22yds......... (4:40)

303⁴ AVRO ANSON [59] 5-9-5 N Connorton (3) *chsd ldr, rdn to ld o'r 2 fs out, styd on gmely ins last.* (7 to 2 jt-fav op 3 to 1 tchd 4 to 1) 1
356² CHANTRY BARTLE [35] 7-7-9 J Fanning (7) *chsd ldrs, rdn 4 fs out, ev ch o'r one out, not quicken ins last, lft second cl hme*..........(7 to 1 op 6 to 1) 2
288³ DEDUCE [71] 4-9-13 M Hills (5) *in tch, improved to chase ldrs o'r 2 fs out, not quicken ins last.* ....(7 to 1 op 6 to 1 tchd 8 to 1) 3
SHOOFE (USA) [64] 5-9-10 M Roberts (10) *chsd ldrs, rdn and weaakened o'r 2 fs out*..........(7 to 1 op 6 to 1) 4
303 LAFKADIO [35] 6-7-9 A Mackay (6) *hld up in rear, hdwy o'r 4 fs out, rdn and no extr entering strt.* ....(20 to 1 op 16 to 1) 5
MYSTIC MEMORY [64] 4-9-6 K Darley (2) *settled rear, improved hfwy, sn rdn, eased whn btn o'r one furlong out*..........(10 to 1 op 8 to 1) 6
TRICYCLE (Ire) [40] 4-7-10 J Lowe (4) *led till o'r 2 fs out, no extr*..........(25 to 1 op 20 to 1) 7
303⁹ CREEAGER [66] 11-9-12 J Williams (8) *hld up, improved into midfield hfwy, rdn and wknd o'r 2 fs out.* (20 to 1) 8
303⁵ ADMINISTER [53] (bl) 5-8-13 G Duffield (12) *mid-div, drvn alng 4 fs out, no imprsn*..........(7 to 1 tchd 8 to 1) 9
PATROCLUS [50] 8-8-10 S Dawson (1) *hld up and beh, rdn 5 fs out, nvr on terms*..........(12 to 1 op 20 to 1) 10
STAGE PLAYER [52] 7-8-12 L Dettori (9) *chsd ldrs, rdn and wknd o'r 4 fs out, tld off*..........(16 to 1 op 14 to 1) 11
303⁶ SILLARS STALKER (Ire) [51] 5-8-11 K Fallon (11) *hld up in rear, rdn o'r 4 fs out, hdwy over 2 out, ev ch whn rdr lost iron and uns cl hme.* (7 to 2 jt-fav op 3 to 1 tchd 4 to 1) ur
Dist: 2l, 2½l, 7l, ½l, ½l, 1½l, 6l, 2½l, 10l, 10l. 3m 56.20s. a 16.70s (12 Ran).
(B P Skirton), M J Camacho

428 Spring Three Year Old Maiden Fillies Stakes Class D £3,348 6f........... (5:10)

TAALIF 8-11 R Hills (8) *wth ldr, effrt 2 fs out, ran on to ld ins last, hld on gmely*..........(7 to 1 op 6 to 1) 1
VICTORIA HALL 8-11 G Duffield (5) *led till ins fnl furlong, no extr nr finish*..........(10 to 1 op 20 to 1) 2
CROIRE (Ire) 8-11 M Hills (7) *in tch, outpcd hfwy, hdwy 2 fs out, kpt on wl fnl furlong*........(12 to 1 op 8 to 1) 3
PUTOUT 8-11 L Dettori (3) *chsd ldrs gng wl, effrt entering strt, no extr fnl furlong.* (5 to 2 jt-fav op 3 to 1 tchd 7 to 2) 4
LAMSONETTI 8-4 (7*) G Parkin (1) *slwly into strd, beh, hdwy to chase ldrs hfwy, rdn and one pace fnl furlong.* ....(33 to 1) 5
LIKE THE SUN (USA) 8-11 W R Swinburn (4) *in tch, effrt o'r 2 fs out, not quicken over one out.* (5 to 2 jt-fav op 7 to 4 tchd 13 to 8) 6
BALIANA 8-11 A Culhane (6) *sn chsd alng beh ldrs, no imprsn entering strt*..........(7 to 1 op 5 to 1) 7
ALBEIT 8-11 N Connorton (10) *beh, sn pushed alng, nvr dngrs*..........(25 to 1 op 20 to 1) 8
323² HALL BANK COTTAGE 8-11 Dean McKeown (11) *in tch to hfwy*..........(14 to 1 op 12 to 1) 9
FINAL OAK 8-11 J Fortune (12) *in tch on outsd, effrt hfwy, wknd entering strt*..........(20 to 1 op 16 to 1) 10
121⁵ WELL TRIED (Ire) 8-11 K Darley (2) *sn outpcd*.....(33 to 1) 11
367⁵ KIMMY'S PRINCESS 8-11 M Roberts (9) *chsd ldrs, wkng whn hmpd entering strt, eased*...(12 to 1 tchd 10 to 1) 12
Dist: Nk, 2½l, nk, 3l, 5l, 4l, nk, nk, 1½l, 10l. 1m 18.20s. a 3.50s (12 Ran).
SR: 9/8/-/-/-/-/ (Hamdan Al-Maktoum), H Thomson Jones

429 Barbican Limited Stakes Class E (3-y-o and up) £2,794 5f..................(5:40)

355* PENNY HASSET 5-9-5 T Lucas (3) *in tch, effrt o'r 2 fs out, ran on to ld ins last, kpt on*.. (6 to 4 on op 11 to 8 on) 1
323* QUINSIGIMOND 3-8-7 G Duffield (5) *chsd ldrs, effrt entering strt, ev ch ins fnl furlong, not quicken nr finish.* ....(11 to 4 op 5 to 2) 2
SUPER ROCKY 4-9-3 (7*) H Bastiman (2) *chsd ldr, led aftr one furlong, clr entering strt, hdd ins last, no extr.* ....(14 to 1 op 12 to 1) 3
379⁴ LANGTONIAN 4-9-7 (3*) Emma O'Gorman (4) *missed break, cld hfwy, wide strt, rdn and veered lft o'r one furlong out, no imprsn*.......... (10 to 1 tchd 12 to 1) 4
262⁴ PINE RIDGE LAD (Ire) (bl) 3-8-12 Dean McKeown (1) *led one furlong, styd hndy, drvn hfwy, wknd entering strt.* ....(8 to 1 op 7 to 1) 5
Dist: 1l, 2l, 3½l, 3½l. 1m 4.50s. a 3.30s (5 Ran).
SR: 24/8/17/3/-/ (Mrs Anne Henson), M W Easterby

ST-CLOUD (FR) (soft)
Tuesday April 6th
Going Correction: PLUS 0.75 sec. per fur.

430 Prix Edmond Blanc (Group 3) (4-y-o and up) £23,895 1m....................(2:25)

TAKE RISKS (Fr) 4-9-2 M Boutin (6) *hld up, last strt, hdwy on outsd to ld one furlong out, sn clr, imprsv.* ....(121 to 10) 1
SHANGHAI (USA) 4-9-6 C Asmussen (3) *mid-div, 4th strt, lost pl 2 fs out, ran on ag'n fnl furlong*.........(5 to 2) 2
KITWOOD (USA) 4-9-6 T Jarnet (7) *mid-div, 5th strt, effrt 2 fs out, kpt on*..........(18 to 10 fav) 3
ACTEUR FRANCAIS (USA) 5-9-2 S Guillot (5) *mid-div, 3rd strt, ev ch and unbl to quicken o'r one furlong out.* ....(32 to 10) 4
ROBIN DES PINS (USA) 5-9-2 E Saint-Martin (2) *prmnt, second strt, led o'r one furlong out till one out, wknd.* ....(5 to 2) 5
273⁴ COMPOTA (Fr) 4-8-8 D Boeuf (1) *nvr plcd to chal.* ....(92 to 10) 6
4711a⁵ IRISH SOURCE 4-8-8 O Peslier (4) *nvr dngrs*..... (22 to 1) 7
273* BURDUR 5-8-11 C Le Scrill (8) *led till wknd sn aftr entering strt*..........(44 to 10) 8
Dist: 3l, 2l, ½l, 1½l, 3l, ½l, 10l. 1m 46.30s. a 7.80s (8 Ran).
SR: 75/70/64/58/53/36/34/7/ (D Tsui), J Lesbordes

MAISONS-LAFFITTE (FR) (soft)
Wednesday April 7th
Going Correction: PLUS 0.55 sec. per fur.

431 Prix Djebel (Listed) (3-y-o) £14,337 7f (2:25)

KINGMAMBO (USA) 9-2 C Asmussen, *rcd in second till ld ins fnl furlong, rdn out, jst hld on*.......... (42 to 10) 1
ZAFONIC (USA) 9-2 Pat Eddery, *pld hrd in 3rd, rdn and ev ch one furlong out, kpt on*..........(10 to 1 on) 2
KASHANI (USA) 9-2 T Jarnet, *led till ins fnl furlong, ran on on und pres*..........(10 to 1 on) 3
ASTAIR (Fr) 9-2 W Mongil, ... 4
Dist: Sht-hd, sht-hd, 8l. 1m 28.70s. a 6.10s (4 Ran).
SR: 68/67/66/42/ (S S Niarchos), F Boutin

432 Prix Imprudence (Listed) (3-y-o) £14,337 7f ....(2:55)

WIXON (Fr) 9-2 C Asmussen, ... 1
ELIZABETH BAY (USA) 9-2 T Jarnet, ... 2
MISS ELODIE (Fr) 9-2 T Gillet, ... 3
LENCLOITRE (Fr) 9-2 M Boutin, ... 4
Dist: 2l, 1l, ¾l, 4l. 1m 31.90s. a 9.30s (5 Ran).
SR: 20/14/11/9/ (Allen E Paulson), F Boutin

RIPON (good)
Wednesday April 7th
Going Correction: PLUS 0.45 sec. per fur.

433 EBF Spa Welter Maiden Stakes Class D (2-y-o) £3,172 5f...................... (2:25)

KIERCHEM (Ire) 9-0 D Nicholls (2) *trkd ldr, led o'r 2 out, pushed clr fnl furlong.* ....(16 to 1 op 20 to 1 tchd 14 to 1) 1
RAPIER POINT (Ire) 9-0 Dale Gibson (1) *led till hdd o'r 2 out, kpt on, no ch wth wnr*.........(11 to 2 op 5 to 1) 2
312⁵ MONKEY MAGIC (Ire) 9-0 G Carter (7) *chsd ldrs, drvn alng hfwy, kpt on same pace.* ....(11 to 8 fav op 6 to 4 tchd 11 to 10) 3
SWEETINGS PISCES 9-0 M Birch (8) *sn pushed alng, some hdwy fnl furlong, nvr dngrs*.......(14 to 1 op 12 to 1) 4
354² ARTA 9-0 A Culhane (6) *wth ldr, ev ch 2 out, wknd appr fnl furlong*............(7 to 2 tchd 3 to 1 and 4 to 1) 5
INDIAN CRYSTAL 8-9 Dean McKeown (5) *al chasing ldrs, no hdwy fnl 2 fs*..........(10 to 1 op 8 to 1) 6
354⁵ GRANDMAN (Ire) 8-7 (7*) Darren Moffatt (9) *sn beh.* ....(10 to 1 op 8 to 1 tchd 12 to 1) 7
RAVEN'S RETURN (Ire) 9-0 W Ryan (3) *slwly into strd, al beh*..........(12 to 1 op 8 to 1) 8
STEANARD BOY 9-0 J Fanning (4) *sn beh, lost tch hfwy.* ....(16 to 1 op 14 to 1) 9
Dist: 3l, 1l, ¾l, 2l, 1l, hd, 8l, 12l. 1m 3.70s. a 5.70s (9 Ran).
SR: 31/19/15/12/4/-/ (Mrs D Miller), R F Fisher

434 Studley Royal Handicap Class E (0-70 3-y-o) £3,132 1½m 60yds.............. (3:00)

338[2] PRESTON GUILD (Ire) [48] 8-4 W Carson (11) *made virtually all, styd on gmely fnl furlong.* ....(4 to 1 tchd 9 to 2) 1
295[2] BROUGHTONS FORMULA [65] (bl) 9-7 R Cochrane (9) *mid-div, effrt 2 out, drw level ins fnl furlong, no extr cl hme.* ....(7 to 2 fav tchd 4 to 1) 2
203[5] NANCY (Ire) [49] 8-5 K Darley (8) *trkd ldrs, rdn 3 out, not much room 2 out, styd on wl towards finish...* (14 to 1) 3
MERRY MERMAID [48] 8-4 L Charnock (4) *trkd ldrs, effrt 3 out, ev ch 2 out, no extr*....(12 to 1) 4
CHALLENGER ROW (Ire) [48] 8-4 N Connorton (1) *in tch, hdwy 4 out, kpt on same pace fnl 2 fs*.... (14 to 1) 5
THE WHERE WITHAL [52] 8-8 G Duffield (14) *mid-div, effrt 3 out, kpt on same pace*....(9 to 2 tchd 5 to 1) 6
MASTER FIDDLER [60] 9-2 J Fanning (6) *pld hrd, trkd ldr till wknd o'r one out*.... (33 to 1 op 20 to 1) 7
SAFETY IN NUMBERS [50] 8-6 Dean McKeown (15) *nvr nr to chal*....(12 to 1 tchd 14 to 1) 8
344[4] BARSAL (Ire) [60] 9-2 M Roberts (13) *pld hrd, mid-div, effrt o'r 2 out, no hdwy*....(14 to 1) 9
300[9] DICKINS [50] 8-6 W Ryan (12) *nvr dngrs.* .... (33 to 1 op 20 to 1) 10
GREYSTYLE [45] 8-1 J Lowe (3) *beh, some hdwy o'r 3 out, sn btn*....(33 to 1) 11
WONDERFUL YEARS (USA) [50] 8-6 K Fallon (2) *nvr dngrs.* ....(8 to 1 op 10 to 1 tchd 12 to 1 and 7 to 1) 12
SURE RIGHT (Ire) [61] 9-3 M Hills (5) *al beh*....(14 to 1) 13
SAVINGS BANK [60] 9-2 Alex Greaves (10) *prmnt till wknd 2 out*....(16 to 1 op 14 to 1) 14
HASTA LA VISTA [43] 7-13[7] (7*) C Munday (7) *in tch till wknd quickly o'r 2 out, tld off*.... (14 to 1) 15

Dist: Nk, 3½l, hd, hd, 2l, ¾l, sht-hd, 1½l, 1½l, 5l. 2m 52.40s. a 17.40s (15 Ran).

(Lady Matthews), R J R Williams

435 Galphay Conditions Stakes Class D (3-y-o) £3,318 1m 1f....(3:30)

BENEFICIAL 8-12 M Hills (6) *trkd ldrs, pushed alng o'r 2 out, styd on wl to ld ins fnl furlong, all out.* ....(11 to 2 op 5 to 1 tchd 6 to 1) 1
TRUE HERO (USA) 8-12 M Roberts (1) *wnt lft strt, hld up, hdwy to ld 2 out, hdd ins fnl furlong, kpt on...* (4 to 1) 2
VISTO SI STAMPI (Ire) 8-12 W Carson (4) *led, rdn 3 out, hdd 2 out, one pace*....(2 to 1 op 9 to 4 tchd 5 to 2) 3
295 PERSIAN REVIVAL (Fr) 8-10 T Quinn (3) *wth ldr till wknd 2 out*.... (10 to 1 op 12 to 1) 4
COSMIC STAR 8-7 W Woods (5) *in tch till wknd 3 out.* .... (33 to 1 op 25 to 1) 5
DECLASSIFIED (USA) 8-10 R Cochrane (2) *trkd ldrs, chlgd 3 out, sn rdn and wknd.* ....(6 to 4 fav op 5 to 4 tchd 13 to 8) 6

Dist: Hd, 7l, 6l, 3l, ½l. 1m 57.70s. a 6.70s (6 Ran).
SR: 59/58/37/17/5/6/ (Exors Of The Late Sir Robin McAlpine), G Wragg

436 Fountains Handicap Class C (0-90 3-y-o and up) £5,526 6f....(4:00)

301* GORINSKY (Ire) [73] 5-8-12 G Carter (2) *made all, ran on wl*.... (13 to 2 op 5 to 1) 1
SARTIGILA [59] 4-7-12 J Quinn (6) *in tch, not much room 2 out, swtchd and ran on wl nr finish*.... (16 to 1) 2
BEAU VENTURE (USA) [89] 5-9-11 (3*) N Kennedy (11) *trkd ldrs, kpt on wl fnl furlong*.... (25 to 1) 3
FACE THE FUTURE [57] 4-7-10 N Adams (18) *sn chasing ldrs, kpt on wl fnl furlong*.... (14 to 1) 4
292 DRUM SERGEANT [76] (bl) 6-9-1 M Roberts (3) *mid-div, hdwy to chase wnr 2 out, no extr towards finish.* ....(7 to 1 tchd 8 to 1) 5
OUR RITA [77] 4-9-2 R Cochrane (9) *in tch, styd on wl fnl 2 fs, not rch ldrs*....(14 to 1) 6
CUMBRIAN WALTZER [88] 8-9-13 M Birch (8) *mid-div, no hdwy fnl 2 fs*....(10 to 1 op 7 to 1) 7
301[7] CASTLEREA LAD [73] 4-8-12 W Ryan (4) *mid-div, effrt o'r 2 out, one pace*....(7 to 1 op 6 to 1) 8
340 DIET [65] (v) 7-8-1 (3*) F Norton (7) *wth ldr, rdn o'r 2 out, fdd*....(14 to 1) 9
301[6] SEA DEVIL [79] 7-9-4 N Connorton (12) *mid-div, effrt 2 out, one pace*.... (9 to 2 fav op 5 to 1) 10
BERNSTEIN BETTE [71] 7-8-10 T Quinn (1) *nvr dngrs.*, ... (9 to 1 op 12 to 1) 11
CALEMAN [79] 4-9-4 J Reid (14) *nvr dngrs*....(12 to 1) 12
PAGEBOY [73] 4-8-12 Dale Gibson (5) *sn beh.* ....(16 to 1 tchd 14 to 1) 13
LUCEDEO [75] 9-9-0 Dean McKeown (10) *nvr dngrs.* ....(33 to 1) 14
348[6] PARFAIT AMOUR [62] 4-8-1 W Carson (19) *rcd alone centre, beh frm hfwy*.... (20 to 1 op 16 to 1) 15
301[9] SENSE OF PRIORITY [89] 4-10-0 K Darley (17) *sn beh.* ....(20 to 1) 16
CATHERINES WELL [75] 10-9-0 T Lucas (16) *sn beh.* ....(16 to 1 op 12 to 1) 17
355[7] SO SUPERB [56] 4-7-9 J Lowe (13) *sn beh*....(33 to 1) 18
MACS MAHARANEE [65] 6-8-4 J Fanning (15) *sn beh.* ....(33 to 1) 19

Dist: 1½l, nk, sht-hd, nk, sht-hd, 2½l, ¾l, 3l, 1½l, 5l. 1m 15.80s. a 5.20s (19 Ran).
SR: 48/28/57/24/42/42/43/25/5/ (William Robertson), J Berry

437 Sawley Handicap Class E (0-70 3-y-o) £3,288 1¼m....(4:30)

378[2] DUVEEN (Ire) [52] 7-12 (5*) M Fenton (17) *in tch, hdwy to ld wl o'r one out, ran on well*....(8 to 1 op 7 to 1) 1
SOLARTICA (USA) [66] 9-3 G Carter (11) *beh, steady hdwy hfwy, ran on strly fnl furlong, not rch wnr.* ....(11 to 2 fav op 6 to 1 tchd 7 to 1) 2
MOUSSAHIM (USA) [66] 9-3 W R Swinburn (2) *beh, hdwy o'r 3 out, kpt on same pace frm 2 out.* (6 to 1 op 9 to 2) 3
GOLD DESIRE [45] 7-10 J Lowe (14) *led till hdd wl o'r one out, one pace*....(33 to 1) 4
MAD MYTTON [55] 8-6 A Mackay (18) *prmnt, ev ch o'r 2 out, one pace*.... (20 to 1 op 16 to 1 tchd 25 to 1) 5
351[2] ANN HILL (Ire) [56] 8-0 (7*) M Humphries (7) *beh, hdwy 4 out, kpt on same pace frm 2 out*....(10 to 1 op 8 to 1) 6
KISS IN THE DARK [60] 8-11 K Darley (15) *nvr dngrs.* ....(14 to 1 op 10 to 1) 7
317[3] MOVE SMARTLY (Ire) [63] 9-0 R Cochrane (8) *in tch, effrt o'r 2 out, no hdwy*....(6 to 1 op 5 to 1) 8
HAZARD A GUESS (Ire) [58] 8-9 K Fallon (6) *sn beh, nvr dngrs*....(12 to 1 op 7 to 1 tchd 14 to 1) 9
SON OF SHARP SHOT (Ire) [70] 9-7 W Carson (9) *nvr plcd to chal*.... (10 to 1 op 6 to 1) 10
STAR MINSTREL (Ire) [68] 9-5 J Reid (12) *sn beh, hmpd aftr 3 fs*.... (20 to 1 op 14 to 1) 11
BLAKES BEAU [65] 9-2 M Birch (3) *in tch, no hdwy fnl 3 fs.* .... (12 to 1 op 16 to 1) 12
MILNGAVIE (Ire) [49] 8-0 J Fanning (4) *in tch till wknd 3 out*.... (12 to 1 op 14 to 1) 13
PRIME PAINTER [61] 8-12[1] D Nicholls (1) *prmnt till wknd o'r 3 out*.... (25 to 1 op 20 to 1) 14
344[6] INNOCENT ABROAD (Den) [53] 8-4 A Culhane (13) *wth ldr, ev ch 3 out, sn wknd*....(20 to 1) 15
237[4] PRINCE OF SOUL [47] 7-12 J Quinn (16) *slwly into strd, sn tracking ldrs, wknd o'r 3 out*.... (16 to 1 op 14 to 1) 16
RUBIDIAN [50] 8-1[2] G Duffield (5) *beh most of way.* .... (16 to 1 op 14 to 1) 17
NEVER IN TOUCH [43] 7-8[1] G Bardwell (10) *slwly into strd, al beh*....(33 to 1 op 50 to 1) 18

Dist: 1l, 2½l, ¾l, 4l, nk, 5l, 1½l, nk, ¾l, 6l. 2m 14.40s. a 10.40s (18 Ran).
SR: 30/42/37/14/16/16/10/10/4/ (Mrs D Weatherby), M Bell

438 Markington Conditions Stakes Class D (4-y-o and up) £3,172 1½m 60yds....(5:00)

DARU (USA) (v) 4-9-11 M Roberts (1) *hld up in tch, shaken up to ld jst ins fnl furlong, easily.* ....(14 to 1 on op 10 to 1 on) 1
MURPHYS WAY 4-8-2[1] (5*) O Pears (2) *cl up, rdn alng 3 out, led 2 out, hdd jst ins fnl furlong, kpt on, no ch wth wnr*....(33 to 1 tchd 50 to 1) 2
TAWAFIJ (USA) 4-8-11 K Darley (5) *hld up, effrt 2 out, kpt on same pace*.... (20 to 1 op 16 to 1) 3
303 GREEN LANE (USA) 5-9-1 J Reid (3) *led till hdd 4 out, wknd 3 out*.... (14 to 1 op 12 to 1) 4
288 MULAWIH (USA) 5-8-13 M Birch (4) *trkd ldrs, led 4 out, hdd and wknd 2 out*....(50 to 1 op 33 to 1) 5

Dist: 2l, 5l, ½l, 2l. 2m 48.10s. a 13.10s (5 Ran).
SR: 35/12/7/10/4/ (Sheikh Mohammed), J H M Gosden

439 Grantley Median Auction Maiden Stakes Class F (3-y-o) £2,511 1m....(5:30)

JALCANTO 9-0 K Darley (7) *pld hrd early, hld up, effrt and swtchd wl o'r 2 out, styd on well und pres to ld post*....(3 to 1 op 4 to 1 tchd 9 to 2) 1
HE'S A KING (USA) 9-0 W Carson (6) *made most, rdn o'r 3 out, kpt on wl, ct post.* ....(13 to 8 fav op 5 to 4 tchd 15 to 8 and 2 to 1) 2
FEATHER FACE 9-0 J Reid (3) *in tch, steady hdwy to dispute ld o'r one out, no extr towards finish.* .... (10 to 1 op 8 to 1) 3
238[2] ABSALOM'S PILLAR 9-0 W Newnes (4) *beh, hdwy 2 out, kpt on fnl furlong*....(10 to 1 op 8 to 1) 4
4755a[5] COVEN MOON 8-9 J Quinn (5) *in tch till wknd o'r 2 out.* .... (16 to 1 op 14 to 1) 5
VOLUNTEER POINT (Ire) 9-0 J Fortune (1) *dsptd ld till wknd 3 out*....(33 to 1) 6
CHIPPENDALE LADD (Can) 8-9 (5*) Stephen Davies (8) *trkd ldrs till wknd o'r 2 out.* (5 to 2 op 9 to 4 tchd 11 to 4) 7
CICERONE 9-0 G Hind (2) *pld hrd early, trkd ldrs, ev ch 2 out, sn rdn and wknd quickly*....(16 to 1 op 14 to 1) 8

Dist: Sht-hd, ¾l, 4l, 3l, 1l, 1½l, 6l. 1m 47.00s. a 8.70s (8 Ran).
SR: 24/23/21/9/-/ (William A Davies), Mrs M Reveley

BRIGHTON (good)
Thursday April 8th
Going Correction: MINUS 0.20 sec. per fur.

440 Levy Board Apprentice Handicap Class E (0-80 3-y-o and up) £2,924 7f 214yds. (2:00)

MOLLY SPLASH [49] 6-7-8³ (7*) S James (10) *hld up, hdwy o'r one furlong out, str run to ld ins last.* .... (10 to 1 op 8 to 1) 1
294 TAUNTING (Ire) [50] 5-7-8 (5*) S McCarthy (9) *prmnt, hdwy and ran on ins fnl furlong, jst fld.* (16 to 1 op 12 to 1) 2
333³ PRECIOUS WONDER [64] 4-8-13 A Procter (6) *trkd ldrs, led o'r 2 fs out till over one out, one pace.* ....(5 to 2 fav op 9 to 4 tchd 11 to 4) 3
MARZOCCO [49] 5-7-12 L Newton (5) *mid-div, hdwy o'r 2 fs out, ev ch over one out, one pace.* .... (5 to 1 op 3 to 1 tchd 11 to 2) 4
327² SHALOU [49] 4-7-12 T G McLaughlin (2) *cl up, led 2 and a half fs out till appr two out, led o'r one out till hdd and wknd ins last*.......... (9 to 2 op 7 to 2 tchd 5 to 1) 5
261³ SIMON ELLIS (Ire) [44] (bl) 4-7-7 D Wright (8) *led to 2 and a half fs out*............ (14 to 1 op 10 to 1 tchd 16 to 1) 6
329⁹ BASSIO (Bel) [52] 4-8-1 G Forster (3) *hld up in mid-div, effrt and hdwy o'r one furlong out, sn btn.* ....(20 to 1 op 16 to 1 tchd 25 to 1) 7
321⁸ NATIVE CHIEFTAN [79] 4-9-9 (5*) A Martinez (1) *prmnt till wknd wl o'r 2 fs out*... (14 to 1 op 8 to 1 tchd 16 to 1) 8
QUICK STEEL [51] 5-7-11 (3*) S Mulvey (7) *dwlt, nvr on terms*........................ (10 to 1 op 6 to 1) 9
248⁴ CHILTERN HUNDREDS (USA) [65] 3-7-9 (3*) D McCabe (4) *al beh.*..(10 to 1) 10

Dist: Hd, 3½l, nk, 1l, hd, hd, 4l, 2l, 2½l. 1m 35.80s. a 3.40s (10 Ran).
SR: 9/9/12/-/-/-/-/9/-/ (R M Cyzer), C A Cyzer

441 Pyecombe Maiden Stakes Class D (3-y-o) £3,465 1m 1f 209yds................. (2:30)

318³ RIVER NORTH (Ire) 9-0 K Darley (9) *hld up beh, hdwy wl o'r 2 fs out, squeezed through to ld ins last, cleverly.* ....(9 to 4 op 7 to 2) 1D
CONSPICUOUS (Ire) 9-0 T Quinn (3) *cl up, led aftr 2 fs out, hdd and no extr und pres ins last.* .... (9 to 1 op 8 to 1 tchd 16 to 1) 1
304² KINEMA RED (USA) 9-0 Paul Eddery (6) *co'red up beh ldg trio, rdn to chal 2 fs out, ev ch over one out, one pace.* .... (11 to 10 on op 2 to 1 on tchd Evens) 2
SAFIR (USA) 9-0 R Hills (5) *led till aftr 2 fs out, one pace* ....(8 to 1 op 5 to 1) 3
260⁴ TROPICAL JUNGLE (USA) 9-0 D Biggs (1) *chsd ldrs till outpcd fnl 2 fs*.................... (50 to 1 op 20 to 1) 4
DESERT CHALLENGER (Ire) 9-0 J Reid (7) *chsd ldrs, outpcd frm wl o'r 2 fs out.* .... (16 to 1 op 10 to 1 tchd 20 to 1) 5
334⁹ PETITE LOUIE 8-4 (5*) N Gwilliams (8) *cl up, pushed alng 4 fs out, sn wknd*................... (50 to 1 op 20 to 1) 6
IKHTIRAA (USA) 9-0 R Price (2) *keen hold, al beh.* .... (50 to 1 op 20 to 1) 7
323⁵ TOP GUNNER (Ire) 9-0 R Cochrane (10) *beh, reminders hfwy, no response*.. (66 to 1 op 33 to 1 tchd 100 to 1) 8
372⁹ SUNBEAM CHARLIE 8-7 (7*) B Russell (11) *rcd alone on outsd, cocked jaw and collided wth rls aftr 2 fs, sn tld off, pld up*.......... (66 to 1 op 33 to 1 tchd 100 to 1) pu

Dist: ½l, nk, 2½l, 3½l, 3l, 3½l, 5l, 2½l. 2m 3.20s. a 5.00s (10 Ran).
SR: 30/29/28/23/16/10/ (Fahd Salman), P F I Cole

442 Ovingdean Handicap Class D (0-80 4-y-o and up) £3,318 1m 3f 196yds........ (3:00)

322³ DAY OF HISTORY (Ire) [47] 4-8-1 D Biggs (8) *wtd wth in mid-div, cld o'r 4 fs out, hrd rdn one out, ran on gmely to ld ins last*.......... (11 to 2 op 4 to 1 tchd 6 to 1) 1
STATE OF AFFAIRS [40] 6-7-10 S Dawson (7) *slwly into strd, beh, hdwy frm 5 fs out, ev ch ins last, ran on.* .... (13 to 2 tchd 7 to 1 and 5 to 1) 2
PRINCE HANNIBAL [72] 6-10-0 J Reid (4) *hld up in mid-div, hdwy on bit o'r 3 fs out, ev ch appr last, rdn and no extr*......................................(12 to 1 op 10 to 1) 3
373* ATLANTIC WAY [46] 5-8-2 (4ex) J Quinn (5) *cl up, pushed alng 3 fs out, ev ch one out, not quicken.* ....(7 to 2 fav op 9 to 4) 4
332⁴ BUSMAN (Ire) [66] 4-9-6 T Quinn (1) *sn led, clr aftr 3 fs, rallied und pres whn chlgd 2 out, hdd ins last, no extr.* ....(8 to 1 tchd 9 to 1) 5
349* VA UTU [48] 5-8-4 (4ex) C Rutter (2) *chsd ldrs, rdn 3 fs out, outpcd appr 2 out, styd on*.............(7 to 1 op 6 to 1) 6
332 UP ALL NIGHT [43] 4-7-4 (7*) D Wright (3) *trkd ldrs to hfwy.* .... (50 to 1 op 33 to 1) 7
373⁵ AL SHANY [50] 7-8-1 (5*) N Gwilliams (11) *trkd ldrs, sn pushed alng, btn o'r 4 fs out*..... (20 to 1 tchd 25 to 1) 8
322⁵ MR WISHING WELL [41] 7-7-11³ S O'Gorman (6) *al beh.* .... (11 to 2 op 6 to 1 tchd 7 to 1) 9
SARAZAR (USA) [61] 4-8-8 (7*) L Carter (10) *al beh.* ....(8 to 1 op 6 to 1) 10
DON'T GIVE UP [57] 5-8-13 Paul Eddery (9) *trkd ldrs till wknd hfwy*..(33 to 1) 11

Dist: Hd, 2l, ½l, ¾l, 2l, 8l, ½l, 2½l, 6l, 1½l. 2m 32.20s. a 4.70s (11 Ran).
SR: 16/10/38/11/27/7/ (R M Cyzer), C A Cyzer

443 Woodingdean Maiden Fillies Stakes Class D (3-y-o) £3,377 7f 214yds...........(3:30)

ALYAKKH (Ire) 8-11 R Hills (7) *wth ldr, rdn to ld appr 2 fs out, hng lft o'r one out, ran on.* (5 to 4 on tchd Evens) 1
4794a² PATSY GRIMES 8-11 K Darley (3) *led till appr 2 fs out, kpt on und pres*..........(16 to 1 op 12 to 1 tchd 20 to 1) 2
SWIFT SPRING (Fr) 8-11 T Quinn (6) *trkd ldrs, ev ch appr fnl furlong, not quicken*..............(5 to 1 op 7 to 2) 3
CASHELL 8-11 R Cochrane (2) *trkd ldrs, rdn o'r 3 fs out, one pace*.........................(3 to 1 op 5 to 2) 4
RAFIF (USA) 8-11 J Reid (5) *hld up beh ldrs, effrt o'r 2 fs out, hng lft over one out, better for race.* ....(10 to 1 op 5 to 1) 5
KEEP SAFE 8-11 D Biggs (1) *ran green, sn pushed alng in rear, outpcd hfwy*... (25 to 1 op 10 to 1 tchd 33 to 1) 6
334 CANADIAN EAGLE 8-11 Paul Eddery (4) *slwly into strd, al beh, tld off*..........(50 to 1 op 20 to 1 tchd 66 to 1) 7

Dist: ¾l, sht-hd, 1l, 2l, 15l, 12l. 1m 36.50s. a 4.10s (7 Ran).
SR: 12/10/9/6/ (Hamdan Al-Maktoum), H Thomson Jones

444 Brighton Festival Handicap Class C (0-95 3-y-o) £4,624 6f 209yds............. (4:00)

ABBEY'S GAL [82] 9-7 R Cochrane (4) *hld up beh, cld 3 fs out, ran on to ld ins last, readily.* .... (100 to 30 op 9 to 4 tchd 7 to 2) 1
FINAL FRONTIER (Ire) [64] 8-3 J Quinn (3) *led till ins fnl furlong, no extr*.... (15 to 8 fav op 2 to 1 tchd 7 to 4) 2
LAKAB (USA) [74] 8-13 R Hills (1) *cl up, ev ch o'r one furlong out, sn one pace.* ....(6 to 1 op 4 to 1 tchd 7 to 1) 3
GLEN MILLER [66] 8-5 T Quinn (2) *cl up, effrt and not much room wl o'r one furlong out, sn btn.* ....(4 to 1 op 7 to 2 tchd 9 to 2) 4
RAGING THUNDER [66] 8-5 K Darley (5) *in tch, sn pushed alng, hrd rdn o'r 2 fs out, wknd.* .... (11 to 2 op 4 to 1 tchd 6 to 1) 5

Dist: 2l, 3½l, ½l, 5l. 1m 21.80s. a 1.80s (5 Ran).
SR: 59/35/34/24/9/ (Jerrard Williamson), I A Balding

445 Southwick Median Auction Maiden Stakes Class F (2-y-o) £2,243 5f 59yds...... (4:30)

312⁶ SWEET WHISPER 8-9 K Darley (4) *cl up, hrd rdn o'r one furlong out, ran on to ld wl ins last, all out.* ....(4 to 1 tchd 5 to 1) 1
PETRATHENE 8-9 S Whitworth (1) *sn pushed alng to go pace, rdn and hdwy appr fnl furlong, ran on wl.* .... (20 to 1 op 6 to 1) 2
SOUTHDOWN GIRL 8-9 R Cochrane (2) *outpcd and plenty to do hfwy, rapid prog ins fnl furlong, fnshd fst.* .... (20 to 1 op 10 to 1 tchd 33 to 1) 3
386³ RISKY AFFAIR 9-0 Paul Eddery (5) *cl up, led 2 and a half fs out till wl ins last, no extr*......(6 to 4 fav tchd 9 to 4) 4
337⁴ STARISK 8-9 R Hills (6) *trkd ldrs, hrd rdn and ev ch 2 fs out, outpcd appr last, eased.* ....(9 to 2 op 5 to 2 tchd 5 to 1) 5
386² RISKIE THINGS (v) 8-9 B Rouse (3) *led to 2 and a half fs out, wknd quickly*...................(7 to 2 op 9 to 4) 6
WOOLY BULLY 8-2 (7*) D Toole (7) *slwly into strd, outpcd.* ....(25 to 1 op 12 to 1) 7

Dist: Nk, nk, sht-hd, 8l, 12l, 3l. 1m 4.60s. a 4.50s (7 Ran).
(P D Savill), R Hannon

446 Seven Dials Conditions Stakes Class D (2-y-o) £3,388 5f 59yds................ (5:00)

325* TUTU SIXTYSIX 8-10 T Quinn (2) *rcd in 3rd, pld out o'r one furlong out, ran on to ld ins last, readily.* ....(7 to 2 op 2 to 1) 1
337* MADAME GREGOIRE 8-8 R Cochrane (3) *trkd ldr, hrd rdn o'r one furlong out, level briefly ins last, one pace.* ....(5 to 4 fav op 6 to 4 tchd 7 to 4) 2
364* INDIAN DREAMER 8-10 (5*) M Fenton (1) *led till ins fnl furlong, one pace*........(6 to 4 op 5 to 4 tchd Evens) 3

Dist: 2½l, 2½l. 1m 3.60s. a 3.50s (3 Ran).
SR: 5/-/-/ (Mrs Ann Gover), R Boss

HAMILTON (heavy)
Thursday April 8th

Going Correction: PLUS 1.10 sec. per fur. (races 1,2,6,7), PLUS 1.20 (3,4,5)

447 Springfield Rating Related Maiden Stakes Class F (3-y-o) £2,243 1m 65yds..... (2:10)

THE PREMIER EXPRES 9-0 G Duffield (6) *trkd ldr, led 2 fs out, clr one out, styd on wl*... (3 to 1 jt-fav tchd 4 to 1) 1
398⁹ CARDINAL DOGWOOD (USA) (bl) 9-0 M Wigham (1) *chsd ldrs, sn pushed alng, rdn 3 fs out, styd on wl fnl furlong*.............(3 to 1 jt-fav tchd 11 to 4 and 7 to 2) 2
240³ VILAMAR (Ire) 8-9 K Fallon (5) *led till hdd 2 fs out, sn btn.* ....(7 to 1 op 6 to 1 tchd 8 to 1) 3
SUDDEN SPIN 9-0 G Carter (2) *in tch till wknd 3 fs out.* ....(4 to 1) 4
4724a⁹ FESTIN 9-0 Dale Gibson (4) *in tch, rdn o'r 3 fs out, sn wknd*................(100 to 30 op 7 to 4 tchd 7 to 2) 5
SAINTED SUE 8-9 L Charnock (3) *al beh.* .... (33 to 1 op 20 to 1) 6

Dist: 3½l, 6l, 5l, 4l, ½l. 1m 57.80s. a 13.80s (Flag start) (6 Ran).

SR: 29/18/-/ (Ron Davison), W Bentley

448 Calder Handicap Class E (0-70 4-y-o and up) £3,028 1m 65yds................(2:40)

376* STOPROVERITATE [57] 4-9-6 (5ex) N Connorton (5) *mid-div, hdwy to ld o'r one furlong out, styd on wl und pres.* ....(3 to 1 fav op 7 to 2 tchd 5 to 2) 1
110⁶ BOROCAY [38] 5-8-1 L Charnock (8) *beh, styd on und pres fnl 3 fs, not rch wnr.* (14 to 1 op 10 to 1 tchd 16 to 1) 2
358* TANODA [46] 7-8-9 (5ex) M Wigham (1) *sn ld, hdd 4 fs out, led ag'n 2 out, soon headed and no extr.* ....(5 to 1 op 11 to 2 tchd 6 to 1) 3
302 RED KITE [58] 4-9-7 M Hills (9) *prmnt, dsptd ld 4 fs out till wknd 2 out*.............(8 to 1 op 7 to 1 tchd 9 to 1) 4
235⁹ DOUBLE THE STAKES (USA) [40] 4-8-3 G Carter (10) *cl up, slight ld 4 fs out, hdd 2 out, one paced.* ....(33 to 1 op 25 to 1) 5
387⁸ QUANTITY SURVEYOR [58] 4-9-7 G Duffield (6) *in tch till wknd 3 fs out*......... (11 to 2 op 6 to 1 tchd 5 to 1) 6
396⁷ BETTER STILL (Ire) [42] 4-8-5 Dale Gibson (12) *sn beh, nvr dngrs*............(33 to 1 op 25 to 1) 7
AEGAEN LADY [50] 4-8-10 (3*) J Weaver (7) *al beh.* .... (11 to 2 op 5 to 1 tchd 7 to 1) 8
STRAW THATCH [65] 4-10-0 S Webster (3) *sn wl beh.* ....(33 to 1 op 25 to 1) 9
DEPUTY TIM [46] 10-8-9 Dean McKeown (2) *in tch till wknd 3 fs out*............ (10 to 1 op 8 to 1) 10
340³ CHANTRY BELLINI [42] 4-8-5 J Fanning (4) *in tch till wknd 3 fs out*............(6 to 1 op 5 to 1 tchd 7 to 1) 11
Dist: 2½l, 3l, 4l, 5l, 1½l, 1½l, 2l, hd, 1½l, 6l. 1m 59.10s. a 15.10s (Flag start) (11 Ran).
SR: 16/-/-/-/-/ (John D Clark), S G Norton

449 Earn Selling Stakes Class G (2-y-o) £2,070 5f 4yds............................(3:10)

DUNDEELIN 8-6 J Lowe (1) *slwly into strd, hng rght thrght, beh till hdwy fnl furlong, kpt on wl to ld post.* ....(15 to 2 op 5 to 1 tchd 8 to 1) 1
299⁶ LYING EYES 7-13 (7*) P McCabe (5) *cl up, rdn o'r one furlong out, kpt on to ld wl ins last, ct post.* ....(3 to 1 tchd 4 to 1) 2
381⁵ BATIEN'S RIVER 8-6 Dale Gibson (2) *slight ld till hdd one furlong out, kpt on, hng lft towards finish.* ....(5 to 2 op 7 to 2 tchd 4 to 1) 3
343³ MAD ABOUT MEN 8-6 G Carter (3) *trkd ldrs, led one furlong out, hdd wl ins last, btn whn slightly hmpd cl hme*............(5 to 4 fav op 5 to 4 on tchd 11 to 8) 4
FREE TYSON 8-11 L Charnock (4) *cl up till wknd o'r one furlong out*............ (16 to 1 op 7 to 1) 5
Dist: Sht-hd, ¾l, 3½l, 4l. 1m 10.10s. a 11.80s (5 Ran).
(Charles Castle), B Ellison

450 Avon Handicap Class D (0-80 3-y-o) £3,114 5f 4yds............................(3:40)

TWO MOVES IN FRONT (Ire) [68] 8-13 G Carter (6) *made all, clr o'r one furlong out, rdn and ran on wl.* ....(9 to 2 op 4 to 1 tchd 5 to 1) 1
289³ WINTERING (Ire) [76] 9-7 G Duffield (4) *trkd ldr, rdn o'r one furlong out, kpt on, no imprsn.* (6 to 4 fav tchd 2 to 1) 2
ASHGORE [68] 8-13 Dean McKeown (1) *in tch, pushed alng hfwy, one pace*............(9 to 2 op 3 to 1) 3
342² GO FLIGHTLINE (Ire) [69] 9-0 M Hills (5) *cl up till wknd 2 fs out*............(3 to 1 tchd 7 to 2) 4
317⁸ SHADOW JURY [63] 8-8 S Wood (3) *trkd ldrs till grad lost pl frm 2 fs out*............(16 to 1 op 14 to 1) 5
342³ SELVOLE [50] 7-9² J Lowe (2) *chsd ldrs till wknd quickly 2 fs out*............(33 to 1 op 20 to 1) 6
Dist: 7l, 7l, nk, ½l, 8l. 1m 7.10s. a 8.80s (6 Ran).
SR: 43/23/-/ (Robert Aird), J Berry

451 Glen Rating Related Maiden Stakes Class F (3-y-o) £2,243 5f 4yds.............(4:10)

341⁴ HIGH ROMANCE 8-2 (7*) Darren Moffatt (4) *chsd ldrs, rdn to ld ins fnl furlong, hng lft towards finish.* ....(3 to 1 tchd 7 to 2) 1
353² KILLY'S FILLY 8-9 G Carter (1) *led early, cl up, ev ch ins fnl furlong, no extr towards finish*.... (3 to 1 tchd 4 to 1) 2
DAYJUZ (Ire) 9-0 Dean McKeown (5) *sn ld, hdd and no extr ins fnl furlong*............(7 to 4 fav op 5 to 4) 3
326⁴ CRACKER JACK (bl) 9-0 J Fanning (3) *in tch, effrt and ev ch o'r one furlong out, sn rdn and wknd.* ....(9 to 1 op 10 to 1 tchd 8 to 1) 4
214⁵ APOLLO DE ORIENTE 9-0 D Nicholls (2) *chsd ldrs till wknd quickly 2 fs out*............ (14 to 1 op 12 to 1) 5
Dist: 1l, 1½l, 8l, 10l. 1m 9.20s. a 10.90s (5 Ran).
(W K Curran), D Moffatt

452 Dunwan Median Auction Maiden Fillies Stakes Class E (3-y-o) £2,717 1m 3f 16yds ....(4:40)

BAY QUEEN 8-11 M Hills (5) *trkd ldrs, led 2 fs out, pushed clr, cmftbly*......... (5 to 4 fav op Evens tchd 11 to 8) 1
DANCES WITH GOLD 8-11 Dean McKeown (2) *led till hdd 2 fs out, no extr*............(6 to 1 op 7 to 2) 2
A BADGE TOO FAR (Ire) 8-11 J Fanning (1) *hld up, effrt o'r 2 fs out, sn rdn and one pace*........(7 to 2 tchd 3 to 1) 3
GOLDMIRE 8-11 D Nicholls (3) *in tch till wknd 3 fs out.* ....(5 to 1 op 4 to 1) 4
304 GRENOBLE (Ire) 8-11 G Duffield (4) *chsd ldr, pushed alng 4 fs out, wknd 3 out*.......(7 to 1 op 6 to 1 tchd 8 to 1) 5
Dist: 2½l, 8l, 6l, 4l. 2m 51.10s. a 31.10s (5 Ran).
(B J Warren), M Bell

453 Levy Board Handicap Class E (0-70 3-y-o and up) £3,209 1m 5f 9yds.......... (5:10)

358⁷ PHILGUN [58] 4-9-0 (3*) S Maloney (3) *mid-div, hdwy to ld 2 fs out, styd on wl und pres*.........(9 to 1 op 6 to 1) 1
356⁴ HOT STAR [52] 7-8-13 J Lowe (9) *ran in snatches, mid-div, pushed alng hfwy, hdwy 4 fs out, outpcd 3 out, styd on wl appr last, not rch wnr.* ....(5 to 1 op 4 to 1 tchd 6 to 1) 2
PERSUASIVE [58] 6-9-5 Dale Gibson (2) *hld up and beh, hdwy o'r 3 fs out, chlgd over one out, wknd fnl furlong.* ....(12 to 1 op 8 to 1) 3
331⁶ EURIDICE (Ire) [60] 4-9-2 (3*) J Weaver (7) *beh, hdwy to track ldrs hfwy, ev ch 3 fs out, kpt on same pl.* .... (5 to 1 op 9 to 2 tchd 11 to 2) 4
GREY COMMANDER [34] 5-7-9 J Fanning (6) *mid-div, effrt o'r 3 fs out, kpt on same pace*......(12 to 1 op 10 to 1) 5
288⁹ LOCH GARANNE [42] 5-8-3 N Connorton (5) *trkd ldrs, ev ch o'r 2 fs out, sn rdn and btn.* ....(2 to 1 fav op 6 to 4 tchd 9 to 4) 6
137⁶ MINGUS (USA) [51] 6-8-12 D Nicholls (10) *hld up, effrt 3 fs out, no real hdwy*....(12 to 1 op 10 to 1 tchd 14 to 1) 7
356⁹ BRIDGE PLAYER [40] (bl) 6-7-8 (7*) Darren Moffatt (8) *chsd ldr, led hfwy, hdd and wknd 2 fs out.* ....(16 to 1 op 10 to 1 tchd 20 to 1) 8
DOUBLE SHERRY [43] 4-8-2 G Carter (4) *prmnt till wknd o'r 2 fs out*............(33 to 1 op 20 to 1) 9
78 LATOUR [48] 5-8-9 L Charnock (11) *led to hfwy, sn wknd.* ....(12 to 1) 10
BEAU QUEST [65] (bl) 6-9-12 M Hills (1) *al beh.* ....(16 to 1 op 14 to 1) 11
Dist: 1l, 2½l, 3½l, 1½l, 4l, 3½l, 10l, 10l, 15l, 8l. 3m 16.60s. a 30.60s (Flag start) (11 Ran).
(C D Barber-Lomax), C W C Elsey

LEICESTER (good)
Thursday April 8th
Going Correction: PLUS 0.25 sec. per fur.

454 Knighton Maiden Auction Stakes Class F (2-y-o) £2,691 5f 2yds..............(2:20)

386⁴ THATCHERELLA 8-9 D Holland (2) *al prmnt, led appr fnl furlong, ran on wl*............(6 to 1 op 9 to 2) 1
MR ROUGH 9-0 M Tebbutt (12) *al prmnt, dsptd ld 2 fs out, kpt on one pace ins.* ....(10 to 1 op 14 to 1 tchd 16 to 1 and 25 to 1) 2
GIGUE 8-9 J Williams (7) *hld up, rdn and hdwy appr fnl furlong, fnshd wl*............ (25 to 1 op 16 to 1) 3
395² GAELIC STAR (Ire) 9-0 W Ryan (13) *al frnt rnk, ev ch entering fnl furlong, kpt on one pace.* .... (7 to 2 fav op 3 to 1 tchd 9 to 2 and 5 to 1) 4
325³ PARADISE NEWS 8-9 N Day (8) *al prmnt, led 2 fs out, hdd appr last, kpt on one pace*..........(4 to 1 op 5 to 1) 5
CYARNA QUINN (Ire) 8-9 W Newnes (3) *chsd ldrs, one pace ins fnl 2 fs*............(16 to 1) 6
PRIVATE FIXTURE (Ire) 9-0 W Carson (9) *slwly away, nvr on terms*............ (11 to 1 op 6 to 1 tchd 12 to 1) 7
CAPITAL LADY (Ire) 8-6 (3*) D Harrison (11) *chsd ldrs, no hdwy fnl 2 fs*.........(13 to 2 op 5 to 1 tchd 10 to 1) 8
PETITE BIJOU 8-9 W Woods (10) *al beh.* .... (33 to 1 op 20 to 1) 9
BLURRED IMAGE (Ire) 9-0 B Raymond (5) *in tch to hfwy, sn drpd out*............ (9 to 1 op 5 to 1) 10
SPORTING HEIR (Ire) 9-0 N Adams (6) *slwly away, al beh.* .... (25 to 1 op 20 to 1) 11
THE FERNHILL FLYER (Ire) 8-9 Pat Eddery (4) *led till hdd 2 fs out, drpd out quickly*............ (5 to 1 op 9 to 4) 12
GRANDEE 9-0 A Munro (1) *very slwly away, al beh.* .... (16 to 1 op 14 to 1) 13
Dist: ¾l, ½l, ¾l, nk, 2½l, nk, sht-hd, 1l, 5l, 2½l. 1m 3.60s. a 4.90s (13 Ran).
SR: 22/24/17/19/13/3/7/1/-/ (George Mortimer), J Akehurst

455 Burton Overy Selling Stakes Class G (3-y-o) £2,070 5f 218yds.............. (2:50)

352 CHAMPAGNE GRANDY 8-9 J Williams (9) *nvr far away, rdn to ld wl o'r one furlong out, sn clr, easily.* .... (15 to 2 op 12 to 1 tchd 7 to 1) 1
KILDEE LAD 9-0 N Adams (3) *led till hdd wl o'r one furlong out, kpt on one pace*............(10 to 1) 2
313⁸ MAGICATION 8-2 (7*) Claire Balding (8) *outpcd, rdn and ran on ins last 2 fs, nvr nrr.* .... (9 to 1 op 7 to 1 tchd 10 to 1) 3

MIDLIN 8-9 L Dettori (2) *slwly away, hdwy 2 fs out, hng rght appr last, one pace*............(13 to 2 op 7 to 2) 4

362[8] OUR MICA 9-5 Pat Eddery (7) *in frnt rnk, rdn 2 fs out, sn outpcd*..............................(6 to 1 op 4 to 1) 5

240[6] WEALTHYWOO (bl) 8-7 (7*) C Hawksley (10) *slwly into strd, hdwy hfwy, rdn and wknd appr fnl furlong*.. (16 to 1) 6

286[7] JORDYWRATH (v) 9-5 W Newnes (4) *chsd ldrs, wkng whn hmpd o'r one furlong out*............(8 to 1 op 5 to 1) 7

240[7] GIRTON BELLE 8-6 (3*) D Harrison (6) *speed till wknd 2 fs out*..(33 to 1) 8

328 ESTHAL (Ire) 8-12 (7*) S Drowne (11) *speed to o'r hfwy*. ....(4 to 1 op 7 to 2) 9

CALISAR 9-5 L Piggott (5) *broke wl, prmnt till wknd 2 fs out*..............(7 to 2 fav tchd 4 to 1 and 9 to 2) 10

BOLD TREASURE (Ire) 8-6 (3*) S D Williams (1) *in tch to hfwy, sn beh*........................(50 to 1 op 33 to 1) 11

Dist: 8l, 2½l, 1½l, 3½l, hd, 2l, 1l, sht-hd, ½l, 5l. 1m 15.00s. a 4.60s (11 Ran).

SR: 33/6/-/-/-/-/ (Grandy Girls), M R Channon

456 Kibworth Handicap Class E (0-70 3-y-o and up) £3,468 1m 1f 218yds............ (3:20)

SUPERTOP [53] 5-9-0 W R Swinburn (8) *nvr far away, rdn to ld appr fnl furlong, ran on wl*.. (12 to 1 op 10 to 1) 1

ALTERMEERA [50] 5-8-11 G Bardwell (14) *al prmnt, hrd rdn and ev ch o'r one furlong out, kpt on one pace*. ....(16 to 1) 2

349[6] SAINT CIEL (USA) [65] 5-9-12 W Newnes (9) *led till hdd appr fnl furlong, kpt on one pace*............(16 to 1) 3

IN THE MONEY (Ire) [63] 4-9-10 W Ryan (15) *hld up, hdwy 3 fs out, styd on, nvr nrr*........................ (20 to 1) 4

4757a[4] JOLTO [47] 4-8-8 L Dettori (5) *hld up, hdwy ins fnl 3 fs, nvr dngrs*..........................(20 to 1 op 16 to 1) 5

387* ALBERT [51] 6-8-12 J Williams (11) *hld up in mid-div, some hdwy fnl 2 fs, nvr dngrs*. ....(7 to 2 fav op 4 to 1 tchd 9 to 2) 6

BLACKPATCH HILL [57] 4-9-4 W Carson (10) *trkd ldrs, no hdwy fnl 3 fs*......................(14 to 1 op 10 to 1) 7

350[9] LONG FURLONG [50] 5-8-11 N Adams (3) *towards rear, styd on fnl 2 fs, nvr nrr*......................(20 to 1) 8

FERN HEIGHTS [51] 6-8-9 (3*) A Tucker (1) *slwly away, some late hdwy, nvr dngrs*..................(25 to 1) 9

NEARCTIC BAY (USA) [43] 7-8-4 N Carlisle (18) *al mid-div*. ....(20 to 1 op 16 to 1) 10

327[6] MADRAJ (Ire) [56] 5-9-3 Pat Eddery (6) *hld up, nvr nr to chal*..............................(9 to 1 op 5 to 1) 11

4780a* DISPUTED CALL (USA) [66] 4-9-13 D Holland (7) *chsd ldrs, rdn 3 fs out, wknd quickly*. ....(17 to 2 op 5 to 1 tchd 9 to 1) 12

314[3] MODEST HOPE (USA) [60] 6-9-7 M Roberts (4) *chsd ldr, rdn o'r 3 fs out, sn wknd*..................(8 to 1 op 7 to 1) 13

315 SHUJAN (USA) [67] 4-10-0 L Piggott (17) *chsd ldrs, wknd 3 fs out, eased whn btn*.. (9 to 1 op 8 to 1 tchd 12 to 1) 14

290 POST IMPRESSIONIST (Ire) [59] 4-9-3 (3*) F Norton (16) *al beh*.............................(20 to 1 op 16 to 1) 15

DODGY DANCER [60] (bl) 3-8-2 A Munro (13) *al beh*. ....(9 to 1 op 20 to 1) 16

238[5] BLACK BOY (Ire) [50] 4-8-6 (5*) O Pears (12) *in tch till wknd o'r 3 fs out*........................(25 to 1 op 20 to 1) 17

FAIRY WISHER (Ire) [50] 4-8-8 (3*) D Harrison (19) *al beh*. ....(25 to 1) 18

GUEST PLAYER [45] (bl) 6-7-13 (7*) M Jermy (2) *al beh*. ....(50 to 1) 19

Dist: 3½l, nk, 4l, hd, 3l, 6l, 5l, sht-hd, 1½l, ½l. 2m 11.30s. a 8.40s (19 Ran).

SR: 41/31/45/35/18/16/10/-/-/ (Mrs G A Godfrey), P W Harris

457 Langham Maiden Stakes Class D (3-y-o) £3,289 1m 3f 183yds................(3:50)

ACANTHUS (Ire) 9-0 B Raymond (7) *trkd ldrs, led wl o'r one furlong out, ran on well*. ....(16 to 1 op 10 to 1 tchd 20 to 1) 1

KASSAB 9-0 W Carson (4) *hld up, hdwy 5 fs out, led briefly 2 out, rdn and ev ch till no extr and eased cl hme*..............(9 to 4 jt-fav op 5 to 4 tchd 5 to 2) 2

300[4] HOSTILE WITNESS (Ire) 9-0 M Roberts (1) *hld up in rear, hdwy o'r 3 fs out, rdn and one pace appr last*. ....(4 to 1 op 9 to 2) 3

377[2] BILJAN (USA) 9-0 A Munro (3) *trkd ldr, led 4 fs out, hdd 2 out, rdn and one pace*...(5 to 1 op 4 to 1 tchd 6 to 1) 4

ROMALITO 9-0 D Holland (6) *al in rear, rdn 2 fs out, kpt on one pace*......................(25 to 1 op 16 to 1) 5

351[8] GENERAL LINK 9-0 W Newnes (5) *led till hdd 4 fs out, wknd o'r 2 out, eased, tld off*......(66 to 1 op 20 to 1) 6

OCTOBER BREW (USA) 9-0 Pat Eddery (2) *al beh, lost tch 3 fs out, tld off*..............(9 to 4 jt-fav op 7 to 2) 7

Dist: 1½l, 2½l, 1½l, 1½l, 20l, 8l. 2m 40.60s. a 12.10s (7 Ran).

SR: 8/5/-/-/ (Cuadra Africa), J L Dunlop

458 Harborough Fillies Handicap Class D (0-80 4-y-o and up) £3,435 1m 8yds....... (4:20)

SWEET MIGNONETTE [57] 5-8-4 (3*) F Norton (6) *hld up, rdn and hdwy 2 fs out, ran on strly to ld wl ins last*. ....(9 to 2 op 4 to 1 tchd 5 to 1) 1

MUMMYS ROCKET [45] 4-7-9 A Mackay (8) *hld up, hdwy o'r 2 fs out, rdn and ev ch ins last, outpcd cl hme*. ....(14 to 1 op 16 to 1 tchd 20 to 1) 2

327* SILKY SIREN [61] (bl) 4-8-11 M Roberts (1) *rcd keenly, led, came o'r to stands rail, clr 2 fs out, hdd wl ins last*. ....(2 to 1 fav op 9 to 4 tchd 7 to 4 and 5 to 2) 3

293[7] DOUBLE FLUTTER [78] 4-10-0 Pat Eddery (10) *trkd ldr, rdn 2 fs out, sn btn and eased*. ....(11 to 4 op 5 to 2 tchd 3 to 1 and 100 to 30) 4

MISSY-S (Ire) [43] 4-7-7 N Carlisle (9) *hld up, hdwy o'r 2 fs out, not pace to chal*..............(12 to 1 op 8 to 1) 5

MA BELLA LUNA [73] 4-9-9 W Carson (5) *hld up, outpcd 2 fs out, nvr dngrs*....................(7 to 1 op 5 to 1) 6

246[6] MON PETITNAMOUR (Ire) [43] 4-7-7 G Bardwell (11) *prmnt far side, rdn frm hfwy, lost tch fnl 2 fs*. ....(20 to 1 op 16 to 1) 7

330 BEATLE SONG [60] 5-8-3 (7*) S Drowne (2) *chsd ldrs, wknd o'r 2 fs out*......................(16 to 1 tchd 20 to 1) 8

ABSOLUTLEY FOXED [54] 4-8-4 A Munro (7) *in tch, wkng whn hmpd 2 fs out*..................................(33 to 1) 9

190[5] MERRYHILL MADAM [58] 4-8-8 L Dettori (3) *prmnt to hfwy, sn beh*...........................(20 to 1 op 16 to 1) 10

4756a[2] CHANCE REPORT [43] 5-7-7[3] (3*) N Kennedy (12) *speed to hfwy*.............................(20 to 1 op 16 to 1) 11

114 ITHKURNI (USA) [50] 4-8-0 N Adams (4) *al beh*.... (33 to 1) 12

Dist: 2l, sht-hd, 12l, 4l, ¾l, 4l, 5l, 5l, 3½l, nk. 1m 41.50s. a 6.40s (12 Ran).

SR: 27/9/24/5/-/-/ (Ron Whitehead), Mrs M Reveley

459 Simon De Montfort Maiden Stakes Class D (3-y-o) £3,903 1m 8yds.............(4:50)

SOVIET LINE (Ire) 9-0 P D'Arcy (12) *in tch till lost pl hfwy, 5th entering fnl furlong, hrd rdn and str brst to ld nr finish*..........................(25 to 1 op 14 to 1) 1

EL GAHAR 9-0 W Ryan (16) *hld up, hdwy 3 fs out, led appr fnl furlong, ran on, ct cl hme*. ....(4 to 1 op 5 to 1 tchd 6 to 1) 2

QAMOOS (Ire) 9-0 N Carlisle (18) *al prmnt, rdn and ran on ins fnl furlong*..................(25 to 1 op 14 to 1) 3

WESTERN CAPE (USA) 9-0 Pat Eddery (8) *al frnt rnk, ev ch entering fnl furlong, ran on one pace*. ....(4 to 1 op 7 to 2 tchd 9 to 2) 4

KASSBAAN (USA) 9-0 W R Swinburn (9) *led, hng badly rght and hdd appr fnl furlong, sn btn*. ....(5 to 1 op 7 to 2) 5

KHISAL (Can) 9-0 D Holland (10) *prmnt till outpcd ins fnl 2 fs*..................................(25 to 1 op 20 to 1) 6

DIVINE BOY 9-0 P Robinson (17) *prmnt till wknd wl o'r one furlong out*.......................................(50 to 1) 7

LT WELSH (USA) 9-0 L Dettori (14) *mid-div, rdn o'r 2 fs out, eased ins last*...................(12 to 1 op 16 to 1) 8

MAJOR YAASI (USA) 9-0 B Raymond (7) *mid-div, nvr nr to chal*..............................(12 to 1 tchd 16 to 1) 9

TOP CEES 9-0 N Adams (6) *slwly away, nvr on terms*. ....(20 to 1 op 50 to 1) 10

MAP OF STARS (USA) 9-0 M Roberts (13) *chsd ldrs, rdn o'r 3 fs out, wknd 2 out*.. (2 to 1 fav op Evens tchd 9 to 4) 11

SPECIAL DAWN (Ire) 9-0 W Newnes (11) *al mid-div*. ....(25 to 1 op 16 to 1) 12

TOP RANK 9-0 J Williams (1) *al beh*.. (16 to 1 op 10 to 1) 13

NOMADIC FIRE 9-0 M Tebbutt (4) *prmnt for 5 fs*. ....(50 to 1 op 33 to 1) 14

MONSIEUR DUPONT (Ire) 9-0 A Munro (2) *al beh*. ....(25 to 1 op 14 to 1) 15

MUHTASHIM (Ire) 9-0 W Carson (15) *in tch for 5 fs*. ....(12 to 1 op 8 to 1 tchd 14 to 1) 16

STOCKFORCE 9-0 R Perham (5) *rdn alng frm hfwy, al towards rear*...(50 to 1) 17

HARD EIGHT 9-0 A McGlone (3) *al beh*. ....(25 to 1 op 14 to 1) 18

Dist: ½l, 1l, ½l, 3½l, 3l, 1½l, 2l, sht-hd, hd, nk. 1m 43.90s. a 8.80s (18 Ran).

(Maktoum Al Maktoum), M R Stoute

460 Butler Handicap Class C (0-95 3-y-o) £4,878 5f 2yds.................... (5:20)

MAGIC ORB [63] 7-10 A Mackay (8) *mid-div, hdwy 2 fs out, hrd rdn and ran on to ld wl ins last*. ....(11 to 1 op 10 to 1 tchd 12 to 1) 1

LAUREL DELIGHT [80] 8-13 Pat Eddery (5) *broke wl, led, rdn one furlong out, hdd well ins*. .... (100 to 30 fav op 3 to 1 tchd 4 to 1) 2

HOTARIA [66] 7-13 N Carlisle (2) *al prmnt, rdn and ev ch entering fnl furlong, kpt on one pace*. ....(10 to 1 op 12 to 1) 3

4668a* ARAGROVE [67] 8-0[2] A Munro (4) *al frnt rnk, hrd rdn and ev ch one furlong out, kpt on one pace*. ....(8 to 1 op 5 to 1) 4

MY BONUS [81] 8-11 (3*) D Harrison (3) *mid-div, ran on fnl furlong, nvr dngrs*................ (10 to 1 op 6 to 1) 5

289 DAYTONA BEACH (Ire) [71] 8-4 W Ryan (1) *outpcd, made some late hdwy*..................(10 to 1 tchd 12 to 1) 6

TROON [88] 9-7 L Piggott (9) *outpcd, nvr on terms*. ....(13 to 2 op 10 to 1 tchd 12 to 1) 7

RAIN SPLASH [80] 8-6 (7*) Claire Balding (7) *al beh*. ....(25 to 1 op 20 to 1) 8

341[3] CARNBREA SNIP [78] 8-11 L Dettori (11) *prmnt far side, hrd rdn 2 fs out, wknd appr last*.....(9 to 2 op 3 to 1) 9
324[2] THE INSTITUTE BOY [65] (bl) 7-12 N Adams (6) *chsd ldrs till rdn and wknd appr fnl furlong*. (12 to 1 tchd 14 to 1) 10
MEADMORE MAGIC [74] 8-4 (3*) F Norton (10) *prmnt till rdn and wknd wl o'r one furlong out*. ....(11 to 1 op 8 to 1 tchd 12 to 1) 11
Dist: 1½l, 1½l, sht-hd, 3½l, hd, 4l, 2½l, 2½l, hd, nk. 1m 2.30s. a 3.60s (11 Ran).
SR: 35/46/26/26/26/15/16/-/-/ (M Olden), J L Spearing

LONGCHAMP (FR) (soft)
Thursday April 8th
Going Correction: PLUS 0.60 sec. per fur.

461 Prix Lord Seymour (Listed) (4-y-o and up) £14,337 1½m..................... (2:50)

SHARP COUNSEL (Fr) 4-9-2 D Boeuf, ... 1
KARMISYK (Fr) 4-8-11 C Asmussen, ... 2
283[4] PRINCE POLINO (USA) 4-8-11 F Head, ... 3
4754a[4] GLORIA MUNDI (Fr) 6-8-13 W Mongil, ... 4
Dist: ¾l, 1½l, ¾l, 1½l, 1½l, 1½l, 4l. 2m 40.80s. a 11.50s (8 Ran).
SR: 59/52/49/49/ (Mme J Sabban), E Lellouche

HAYDOCK (soft)
Saturday April 10th
Going Correction: PLUS 0.55 sec. per fur. (races 1,2,6,7), PLUS 0.10 (3,4,5)

462 Cheadle Hulme Conditions Stakes Class B (4-y-o and up) £6,385 2m 45yds..... (1:10)

303[3] JACK BUTTON (Ire) 4-8-10 N Day (5) *trkd ldrs, pushed alng 5 fs out, hdwy to ld 2 out, sn clr, ran on strly*. ....(11 to 10 on op Evens) 1
CRYSTAL SPIRIT 6-9-0 M Hills (2) *led, wide strt to stands rls, quickened 4 fs out, rdn and hdd 2 out, kpt on*. ....(3 to 1 tchd 7 to 2) 2
303[7] FARSI 5-9-0 W Ryan (1) *hld up in tch, hdwy 4 fs out, effrt 3 out, sn rdn and one pace*. ....(4 to 1 op 3 to 1 tchd 9 to 2) 3
NORTHERN RARITY (USA) 4-8-11[1] D Nicholls (3) *trkd ldr, hdwy to chal o'r 3 fs out, sn rdn and ev ch, wknd 2 out*. ....(14 to 1 op 20 to 1) 4
303[8] FRENCH IVY (USA) 6-9-0 K Fallon (4) *hld up in tch, hdwy 4 fs out, sn rdn and wknd*........(14 to 1 op 10 to 1) 5
Dist: 4l, 3½l, nk, 12l. 3m 43.10s. a 17.10s (5 Ran).
SR: 14/14/10/6/-/ (A And B Racing), Bob Jones

463 Matthew Peacock Maiden Stakes Class D (3-y-o) £3,720 7f 30yds.............. (1:40)

RIVER LIFE 9-0 C Rutter (5) *in tch, hdwy o'r 3 fs out, chlgd 2 out, sn rdn, ran on to ld wl ins last*. (4 to 1 op 7 to 2) 1
WALI (USA) 9-0 M Hills (4) *cl up, led hfwy, rdn 2 fs out, hdd and no extr wl ins last*.......... (6 to 1 op 5 to 1) 2
KASSERHOM (USA) 9-0 G Hind (3) *slwly into strd, hld up, hdwy on outsd 3 fs out, rdn and ev ch entering fnl furlong, sn no extr*.................... (5 to 1 op 7 to 2) 3
352[4] BINT AL BALAD (Ire) 8-9 W R Swinburn (1) *trkd ldrs, effrt 3 fs out, sn ev ch, rdn 2 out, soon wknd*. ....(9 to 4 fav op 5 to 2 tchd 11 to 4) 4
SHAMGAAN (USA) 9-0 B Raymond (2) *led to hfwy, sn rdn, wknd 2 fs out*...................... (5 to 1 op 7 to 2) 5
SOLOMON'S DANCER (USA) 9-0 Dean McKeown (7) *in tch, rdn o'r 3 fs out, sn btn*..............(7 to 1 op 6 to 1) 6
NORTHGATE FIREMAN 9-0 M Wigham (6) *chsd ldrs, rdn and wknd 3 fs out, sn beh*..........................(33 to 1) 7
Dist: Hd, 1l, 4l, 1½l, 2½l, 20l. 1m 34.90s. a 7.70s (7 Ran).
SR: 44/43/40/23/23/15/-/ (Fahd Salman), P F I Cole

464 Field Marshal Stakes Class A (Listed) (3-y-o) £10,575 5f..................... (2:10)

SEA GAZER (Ire) 8-11 K Darley (4) *led, rdn one and a half fs out, hdd one out, rallied und pres to ld wl ins last*. .... (13 to 2 op 7 to 1 tchd 8 to 1) 1
UP AND AT 'EM 9-4 B J Coogan (2) *chsd ldrs, smooth hdwy to chal 2 furlong out, led one out, rdn, edgd rght, hdd wl ins last*..... (7 to 4 fav op 9 to 4 tchd 5 to 2) 2
LUCKY PARKES 8-6 G Duffield (7) *cl up, rdn o'r 2 fs out, grad wknd*..(8 to 1) 3
347* LORD OLIVIER (Ire) 8-11 M Tebbutt (8) *hdwy hfwy, rdn 2 fs out, sn one pace*....................(7 to 1 op 6 to 1) 4
347[2] ROGER THE BUTLER (Ire) 8-11 M Hills (6) *hmpd strt, hdwy o'r 2 fs out, sn rdn and one pace*.....(9 to 2 op 7 to 2) 5
336* SABRE RATTLER 9-1 G Carter (3) *chsd ldrs 3 fs, sn btn*. ....(5 to 1 tchd 6 to 1) 6
ANSELLMAN 9-1 B Raymond (5) *al rear*.........(12 to 1) 7
336[2] KAMAATERA (Ire) 8-11 W R Swinburn (1) *chsd ldrs till rdn and wknd haflway, sn beh*.... (20 to 1 tchd 25 to 1) 8
Dist: Nk, 3½l, 2l, 2½l, 3l, 2l, 3l. 1m 0.90s. a 2.10s (8 Ran).
SR: 65/71/45/42/32/24/16/-/ (P D Savill), T D Barron

465 Beamish Stout Rated Class B (0-100 4-y-o and up) £6,291 6f.................. (2:40)

SIR HARRY HARDMAN [86] 5-8-10 B Raymond (1) *made all, quickened one and a half fs out, kpt on wl fnl furlong*. ....(4 to 1 op 3 to 1) 1
DOMINUET [83] 8-8-7 J Lowe (2) *hld up, gd hdwy o'r 2 fs out, rdn and chsd wnr appr last, kpt on*. ....(15 to 2 op 7 to 1 tchd 8 to 1) 2
301[8] DENSBEN [84] 9-8-8 K Fallon (6) *chsd ldrs, rdn wl o'r one furlong out, kpt on*.................(7 to 2 tchd 4 to 1) 3
HARD TO FIGURE [97] 7-9-0 (7*) S Drowne (7) *hld up in tch, effrt 2 fs out and not much room, sn rdn and kpt on one pace fnl furlong*........(13 to 2 op 7 to 1 tchd 6 to 1) 4
301[4] ADWICK PARK [83] 5-8-7 M Hills (4) *chsd wnr, rdn 2 fs out, sn wknd*.................................(6 to 1 op 5 to 1) 5
ECHO-LOGICAL [88] 4-8-12 K Darley (5) *chsd ldrs, effrt and rdn 2 fs out, kpt on one pace*. ....(11 to 4 fav op 5 to 2 tchd 3 to 1) 6
THE AUCTION BIDDER [83] 6-8-7 W Ryan (3) *chsd ldrs, rdn 2 fs out, wknd appr last*......... (20 to 1 tchd 25 to 1) 7
Dist: 1l, 1½l, ½l, ½l, ½l, 2½l. 1m 15.40s. a 3.80s (7 Ran).
SR: 32/25/20/31/15/18/3/ (P D Hobbs), F H Lee

466 J & K Palmer Maiden Auction Stakes Class E (2-y-o) £2,924 5f.................. (3:10)

MOSCOW ROAD 9-0 A McGlone (1) *wnt lft strt, sn cl up, led 2 fs out, rdn and hng left appr last, jst hld on*. ....(6 to 1 op 5 to 1) 1
381[2] PORTITE SOPHIE 8-9 M Wigham (4) *chsd ldrs, effrt and hdwy 2 fs out, rdn and styd on wl ins last, jst fld*. ....(10 to 1 op 8 to 1) 2
291[8] CLOSE TO REALITY 9-0 K Fallon (2) *outpcd and swrvd lft hfwy, sn rdn and styd on wl fnl furlong*. ....(7 to 1 tchd 10 to 1) 3
ROCKY TWO 9-0 A Mackay (6) *mid-div, effrt 2 fs out, styd on last, nrst finish*............. (14 to 1 tchd 16 to 1) 4
HEATHYARDS CRUSADE (Ire) 9-0 W Ryan (5) *outpcd till styd on fnl 2 fs, nrst finish*......... (14 to 1 op 8 to 1) 5
SONNETEER 9-0 M Birch (3) *outpcd till styd on wl fnl 2 fs, nrst finish*..........(7 to 2 fav op 5 to 2 tchd 4 to 1) 6
364[2] HILL FARM KATIE 8-9 M Hills (8) *led till hdd and wknd 2 fs out*...(6 to 1) 7
291 HILTONS TRAVEL (Ire) 9-0 S Webster (7) *cl up, rdn o'r 2 fs out and sn wknd*....................(14 to 1 op 20 to 1) 8
MONKEY MUSIC 9-0 G Carter (10) *slwly away, ran green, al outpcd and beh*......(4 to 1 op 7 to 2 tchd 9 to 2) 9
CHINESE TREASURE (Ire) 9-0 N Day (9) *chsd ldrs, rdn 2 fs out, sn wknd*..........(13 to 2 op 5 to 1 tchd 7 to 1) 10
Dist: Sht-hd, 2l, 1½l, sht-hd, hd, 1½l, sht-hd, ½l, 3½l. 1m 4.10s. a 5.30s (10 Ran).
SR: 4/-/-/-/-/-/ (G C Sampson), R Hannon

467 Levy Board Apprentices Handicap Class E (0-80 3-y-o) £2,795 7f 30yds......... (3:40)

DAILY SPORT DON [62] 8-10 (3*) D Gibbs (3) *chsd ldr, wndrd badly 3 fs out, led 2 out, kpt on fnl furlong*. ....(3 to 1 op 5 to 2) 1
PANTHER (Ire) [66] 9-3 P Johnson (1) *beh, wide strt to stands' rls, hdwy and ev ch 2 fs out, sn rdn, kpt on same pace*...............(4 to 1 op 7 to 2 tchd 9 to 2) 2
RED LEADER (Ire) [70] 9-2 (5*) L Aspell (2) *led and sn clr, rcd alone centre fnl 4 fs, hdd and wknd quickly 2 out*. ....(11 to 10 on op 5 to 4 on) 3
TTYFRAN [64] 9-1 J Dennis (4) *chsd ldrs till rdn and wknd 3 fs out*................(6 to 1 tchd 5 to 1 and 7 to 1) 4
Dist: 2l, 20l, 4l. 1m 37.20s. a 10.00s (4 Ran).
SR: 9/7/-/-/ (Roldvale Limited), R Hannon

468 Holiday Club Pontins Handicap Class C (0-95 3-y-o) £4,836 1¼m 120yds..... (4:10)

PERSIAN BRAVE (Ire) [93] 9-5 M Hills (9) *led, wide to stands rls strt, quickened o'r 2 fs out, hdd entering last, rallied to ld last 100 yards*............. (10 to 1 tchd 12 to 1) 1
KEY TO MY HEART (Ire) [82] 8-8 Dean McKeown (5) *hld up, gd hdwy 2 and a half fs out, effrt and rdn to ld entering last, hdd and no extr last 100 yards*. .... (20 to 1 op 16 to 1) 2
MOORISH [82] 8-8 B Raymond (8) *in tch, hdwy o'r 2 fs out, rdn and styd on appr last*. .... (7 to 1 tchd 8 to 1 and 6 to 1) 3
295[8] ARGYLE CAVALIER (Ire) [67] 7-7[3] (3*) N Kennedy (7) *hld up and beh, hdwy 3 fs out, rdn 2 out, kpt on one pace*. ....(16 to 1 op 14 to 1) 4
328[2] STRICTLY PERSONAL (USA) [74] 8-0 G Hind (3) *slwly away, hdwy 4 fs out, sn pushed alng, styd on fnl 2 furlongs, nvr dngrs*................(7 to 2 tchd 4 to 1) 5
295[3] DOC COTTRILL [73] 7-8 (5*) B Doyle (4) *mid-div, effrt and hdwy 3 fs out, rdn and one pace 2 out*. ....(85 to 40 fav op 3 to 1) 6
295[4] MONDRAGON [74] 7-7 (7*) Darren Moffatt (1) *cl up till rdn and wknd o'r 3 fs out*...............(6 to 1 op 5 to 1) 7
NEMEA (USA) [80] 8-6 G Carter (10) *chsd ldrs, rdn 3 fs out, sn wknd*..................... (6 to 1 op 4 to 1) 8

HEATHYARDS BOY [95] 9-7 W Ryan (6) *rdn 3 fs out, sn wknd*.. (16 to 1) 9
HARPOON LOUIE (USA) [82] 8-8 K Darley (2) *cl up till rdn and wknd o'r 3 fs out.* (10 to 1 op 8 to 1 tchd 12 to 1) 10
Dist: 1l, 2l, 1½l, 2l, nk, 3l, 3l, 6l, 4l. 2m 21.90s. a 10.90s (10 Ran).
SR: 54/41/37/19/22/20/15/15/18/ (Persian Partnership), M Bell

KEMPTON (soft)
Saturday April 10th
Going Correction: PLUS 1.00 sec. per fur. (races 1,3), PLUS 0.70 (2,4,5,6,7,8)

469 EBF Redfern Maiden Stakes Class D (2-y-o) £3,289 5f...................... (2:15)

291^{5} VALIANT MAN 9-0 J Williams (8) *chsd ldrs, hdwy 2 fs out, led wl ins last, ran on well*........ (20 to 1 op 14 to 1) 1
291^{7} MAKE THE BREAK 9-0 B Rouse (9) *led, clr appr fnl furlong, tired and hdd wl ins last, no extr.* .... (11 to 2 op 4 to 1 tchd 6 to 1) 2
GENERAL SHIRLEY (Ire) 9-0 T Quinn (6) *pushed alng thrght, cl up, ev ch 2 fs out, ran on close hme, improve.* ....(9 to 2 op 4 to 1 tchd 5 to 1) 3
BOLD CYRANO (Ire) 8-9 (5*) Stephen Davies (2) *cl up till pushed alng and one pace appr fnl furlong.* ....(33 to 1 tchd 40 to 1) 4
NORTHERN CELADON (Ire) 9-0 P Robinson (4) *sn pushed alng in rear, some hdwy ins fnl furlong.* ....(9 to 1 op 8 to 1 tchd 6 to 1 and 10 to 1) 5
SILVER WEDGE (USA) 9-0 Pat Eddery (5) *nvr gng pace.* .... (6 to 1 op 9 to 2 tchd 13 to 2) 6
LIVELY STREAM 9-0 R Cochrane (10) *missed break, slwly into strd, nvr on terms*..........(4 to 1 fav op 5 to 2) 7
PERSIAN HERITAGE 9-0 A Munro (1) *strted slwly, al beh.* ....(16 to 1 op 12 to 1 tchd 20 to 1) 8
IVA'S FLYER (Ire) 8-9 W Carson (7) *slwly into strd, rdn and cld hfwy, eased whn btn wl o'r one furlong out.* ....(6 to 1 op 4 to 1 tchd 7 to 1) 9
STORM 9-0 N Carlisle (11) *sn outpcd, tld off.* .... (20 to 1 op 14 to 1) 10
Dist: 1½l, sht-hd, 2½l, ½l, sht-hd, 3l, nk, 2l, 5l. 1m 6.53s. a 8.33s (10 Ran).
SR: 33/27/26/16/14/13/1/-/-/ (J Rose), J Wharton

470 Stark Maiden Stakes Class D (Div I) (3-y-o and up) £3,377 7f...................(2:45)

HILARY GERRARD (USA) 3-8-9 P Robinson (7) *hld up in tch, hdwy on outsd wl o'r one furlong out, led fnl 50 yards. ran on strly*................(14 to 1 op 12 to 1) 1
FLASHFEET 3-8-9 L Dettori (9) *cl up, stumbled hfwy, ev ch appr 2 fs out, rdn and ran on ins last.* .... (5 to 2 op 6 to 4 tchd 11 to 4) 2
SO INTREPID (Ire) 3-8-9 Paul Eddery (6) *keen hold early, trkd ldrs, led one and a half fs out till hdd and no extr fnl 50 yards*......................(10 to 1 op 12 to 1) 3
WAINWRIGHT (USA) 4-9-10 M Roberts (3) *led to one and a half fs out, one pace*... (11 to 2 op 5 to 1 tchd 6 to 1) 4
NEGD (USA) 3-8-9 P D'Arcy (1) *missed break, beh, rdn and hdwy o'r 2 fs out, ran on ins last.* ....(7 to 1 op 5 to 1 tchd 8 to 1) 5
KHATTAT (USA) 3-8-9 W Carson (8) *hld up, hdwy and ev ch 2 fs out, sn rdn and btn.* ....(2 to 1 fav op 7 to 4 tchd 6 to 4) 6
419^{3} AQUADO 4-9-10 N Carlisle (5) *cl up till wknd o'r 3 fs out.* .... (33 to 1 op 25 to 1) 7
ICE STRIKE (USA) 4-9-10 J Williams (4) *pld hrd, al beh.* .... (33 to 1 op 20 to 1) 8
$4664a^{7}$ KINNEGAD KID 4-9-5 R P Elliott (2) *keen hold, rcd wide, in tch to hfwy*....................................(50 to 1) 9
Dist: 1½l, 1l, 1l, ¾l, 12l, 1l, 1½l, nk. 1m 34.59s. a 10.49s (9 Ran).
SR: 11/6/3/15/-/-/ (Martin Myers), Mrs J Cecil

471 Queen Elizabeth Handicap Class C (0-90 3-y-o) £4,667 6f..................... (3:15)

313^{*} GARNOCK VALLEY [81] 9-3 Pat Eddery (9) *al gng wl, made all, clr o'r one furlong out, ran on well.* ....(4 to 1 op 3 to 1 tchd 9 to 2) 1
SECOND CHANCE (Ire) [74] 8-10 M Roberts (3) *pushed alng to chase ldrs, kpt on one pace fnl 2 fs. 1* ....(6 to 1 tchd 7 to 1) 2
335^{4} TRINITY HALL [61] 7-11 S Dawson (5) *mid-div, hdwy o'r one furlong out, ran on*.......... (16 to 1 op 14 to 1) 3
317^{5} PRINCELY FAVOUR (Ire) [80] 9-2 B Rouse (7) *sn pushed alng, chsd ldrs, one pace fnl 2 fs.* ....(7 to 2 fav tchd 4 to 1) 4
330 MURPHY'S HOPE (Ire) [65] 8-1[1] D Holland (8) *trkd ldrs till wknd appr 2 fs out*..... (9 to 1 op 7 to 1 tchd 10 to 1) 5
NABJELSEDR [85] 9-7 W Carson (6) *outpcd, effrt o'r one furlong out, ran on ins last, nrst finish.* .... (6 to 1 op 5 to 1 tchd 13 to 2) 6
313^{3} FRIENDLY BRAVE (USA) [77] 8-8 (5*) N Gwilliams (4) *nvr on terms*....................................(7 to 1 tchd 8 to 1) 7
212^{8} DAANIERA (Ire) [75] (bl) 8-11 J Quinn (2) *wth wnr till wknd o'r 2 fs out*..................... (16 to 1 op 10 to 1) 8
WALNUT BURL (Ire) [60] 7-10 C Avery (1) *outpcd, al beh, tld off*....................(12 to 1 op 10 to 1 tchd 14 to 1) 9
Dist: 5l, ½l, ¾l, ¾l, sht-hd, 1l, 15l, 2½l. 1m 18.93s. a 8.13s (9 Ran).
SR: 60/33/18/34/16/35/23/-/-/ (Robert Aird), J Berry

472 BonusPrint Masaka Conditions Stakes Class B (3-y-o) £9,662 1m..........(3:45)

NICER (Ire) 8-11 D Holland (10) *strted slwly, hld up beh, hdwy 4 fs out, tacked to stands rail strt, led 2 out, sn clr*..................(14 to 1 op 12 to 1 tchd 16 to 1) 1
AJFAN (USA) 8-9 R Hills (12) *trkd ldrs, led briefly o'r 2 fs out, ran on wl.* (3 to 1 jt-fav op 2 to 1 tchd 100 to 30) 2
BRIGHT GENERATION (Ire) 8-11 A Munro (2) *trkd ldrs, ev ch appr 2 fs out, one pace.* (5 to 1 op 9 to 2 tchd 11 to 2) 3
ZENITH 8-9 L Dettori (9) *hld up beh, hdwy 3 fs out, one pace 2 out*......................(16 to 1 tchd 20 to 1) 4
HOLLY GOLIGHTLY 8-11 J Reid (7) *pld hrd, chsd ldrs, no hdwy frm o'r 2 fs out*..............(20 to 1 op 16 to 1) 5
FABRIANA 8-9 T Quinn (8) *beh, hdwy o'r one furlong out, nrst finish*....................................(33 to 1) 6
RAPID REPEAT (Ire) 8-9 Paul Eddery (1) *cl up till lost pl o'r 3 fs out, styd on one pace ins last.* .... (12 to 1 op 20 to 1 tchd 25 to 1) 7
HELVELLYN (USA) 8-9 M Roberts (11) *led till o'r 2 fs out, wknd and eased.* (3 to 1 jt-fav tchd 11 to 4 and 100 to 30) 8
KATIBA (USA) 8-11 W Carson (6) *hld up beh, shrtlvd effrt wl o'r 2 fs out, sn btn*....(7 to 1 op 6 to 1 tchd 8 to 1) 9
WHITE SHADOW (Ire) 9-1 Pat Eddery (3) *trkd ldrs till wknd o'r 2 fs out, eased*........(8 to 1 op 7 to 1 tchd 9 to 1) 10
348^{5} EXPRESS MARIECURIE (Ire) 8-9 T Sprake (5) *wth ldr till wknd 3 fs out*....................................(100 to 1) 11
252^{*} GOLDEN KLAIR 8-11 R Cochrane (4) *al beh.* .... (12 to 1 op 20 to 1) 12
Dist: 3½l, 3l, 3l, ¾l, 5l, ½l, 8l, ¾l, 1½l, hd. 1m 46.10s. a 9.30s (12 Ran).
SR: 41/28/21/10/10/-/ (Mrs J M Corbett), B W Hills

473 Chatsworth Rated Class B (0-100 4-y-o and up) £6,256 1½m.................... (4:15)

329^{*} NIGHT CLUBBING (Ire) [80] 4-8-9 T Quinn (8) *trkd ldrs, led o'r 2 fs out till ins last, rallied to ld cl hme.* ....(5 to 1 op 7 to 2 tchd 11 to 2) 1
UNFORGIVING MINUTE [86] 4-9-1 Paul Eddery (7) *trkd ldrs, rdn to ld ins fnl furlong, hdd cl hme.* ....(5 to 1 tchd 11 to 2) 2
389^{7} SONG OF SIXPENCE (USA) [90] 9-9-7 J Reid (4) *hld up, hdwy and ev ch o'r 2 fs out, no extr ins last*... (20 to 1) 3
CRYSTAL CROSS (USA) [78] 4-8-7 L Dettori (2) *trkd ldrs, drvn alng o'r 3 fs out, one pace*... (5 to 1 tchd 11 to 2) 4
389^{3} SECRET SOCIETY [80] 6-8-11 R Cochrane (5) *hld up, effrt and cld o'r 2 fs out, sn one pace.* .... (7 to 2 fav tchd 4 to 1) 5
389^{*} BOOKCASE [76] 6-8-7 J Williams (3) *hld up beh, effrt o'r 2 fs out, sn btn*..........(6 to 1 op 5 to 1 tchd 13 to 2) 6
FLIGHT LIEUTENANT (USA) [82] 4-8-11 W Newnes (9) *trkd ldr till rdn and wknd o'r 2 fs out*..............(10 to 1) 7
169 MOONLIGHT QUEST [80] 5-8-11 Pat Eddery (6) *led till o'r 2 fs out, wknd*.......................... (10 to 1 op 8 to 1) 8
Dist: Hd, 2l, 2½l, 2½l, 3l, 2l, hd. 2m 47.16s. a 16.16s (8 Ran).
SR: 17/22/24/5/4/ (Sheikh Essa Bin Mubarak), R Akehurst

474 BonusPrint Easter Stakes Class A (Listed Race) (3-y-o) £14,312 1m........... (4:45)

RIGHT WIN (Ire) 8-10 J Reid (7) *keen hold, cl up, led 3 fs out, quickened clr o'r one out.* .... (Evens fav tchd 11 to 10 on) 1
ARMAN'S SAX (Ire) 9-0 L Dettori (2) *keen hold, hld up, cld and ev ch 2 fs out, one pace und pres.* ....(11 to 2 op 4 to 1) 2
STAR MANAGER (USA) 8-10 T Quinn (3) *cl up, rdn and ev ch 2 fs out, one pace*....(9 to 1 op 8 to 1 tchd 10 to 1) 3
370^{*} KEYWAY (USA) 8-10 G Duffield (1) *led, rdn o'r 4 fs out, hdd 3 out, wknd*...........(11 to 2 op 5 to 1 tchd 6 to 1) 4
LAW COMMISSION 8-10 J Williams (4) *pld hrd, in cl tch, effrt o'r 2 fs out, sn outpcd*.......... (5 to 1 op 4 to 1) 5
Dist: 6l, nk, 10l, 8l. 1m 47.38s. a 10.58s (5 Ran).
SR: 21/7/2/-/-/ (Conal Kavanagh), R Hannon

475 Durante Handicap Class D (0-80 3-y-o and up) £3,728 7f........................ (5:15)

$4757a$ TENDER MOMENT (Ire) [64] 5-8-12 A Munro (5) *chsd ldrs, hdwy to ld appr fnl furlong, ran on wl*........(10 to 1) 1
440^{3} PRECIOUS WONDER [65] 4-8-13 Pat Eddery (8) *mid-div, hdwy o'r 2 fs out, ran on wl und pres ins last.* ....(7 to 1 op 6 to 1) 2
369^{4} INVOCATION [73] 6-9-7 N Adams (13) *led till appr fnl furlong, no extr*..................(12 to 1 tchd 14 to 1) 3
391^{6} HOPEFUL BID (Ire) [67] 4-9-1 J Reid (2) *mid-div, effrt o'r 2 fs out, styd on one pace*......... (12 to 1 tchd 14 to 1) 4
PHARAOH'S DANCER [72] 6-9-6 M Roberts (10) *keen hold, trkd ldrs, not much room 2 fs out, ran on.* ....(7 to 1 op 5 to 1) 5

302 DOMICKSKY [67] 5-9-1 Paul Eddery (15) *trkd ldrs, ev ch wl o'r one furlong out, rdn and one pace.* ....(13 to 2 fav op 7 to 1) 6
SUPEROO [74] 7-9-8 W Newnes (11) *beh, hdwy o'r one furlong out, nrst finish*..........(20 to 1 op 16 to 1) 7
401[7] BOLD HABIT [75] 8-9-9 R Cochrane (14) *beh, styd on fnl 2 fs, nvr nrr*....................(16 to 1 op 14 to 1) 8
391 SYLVAN SABRE (Ire) [64] (v) 4-8-12 G Duffield (12) *pld hrd, hld up beh, effrt o'r 2 fs out, no imprsn*........(25 to 1) 9
411[8] RURAL LAD [61] 4-8-4 (5*) A Garth (7) *snatched up strt, mid-div, effrt and not much room o'r 2 fs out, no imprsn*..................(9 to 1 op 8 to 1 tchd 10 to 1) 10
LAHOOB (USA) [69] 4-9-3 L Dettori (16) *hld up, hdwy to hold ev ch o'r 2 fs out, sn btn and eased.* ....(8 to 1 op 7 to 1) 11
315 DASWAKI (Can) [73] 5-9-7 B Rouse (17) *trkd ldrs till wknd quickly appr 2 fs out*..............(8 to 1 tchd 10 to 1) 12
327[8] WILD AND LOOSE [70] 5-9-4 J Williams (6) *nvr dngrs.* ....(12 to 1) 13
TROOPING (Ire) [78] 4-9-12 W Carson (9) *hld up beh, shrt-lvd effrt whn not much room o'r one furlong out.* ....(16 to 1 op 14 to 1) 14
QUEEN OF SHANNON (Ire) [72] 5-9-6 M Tebbutt (4) *nvr better than mid-div*..........(14 to 1 op 12 to 1) 15
GLADEER (Ire) [60] 4-8-3 (5*) N Gwilliams (3) *trkd ldrs till wknd quickly 3 fs out, fnshd 16th, disqualified.* ....(66 to 1 op 50 to 1) 16D
391 RISE UP SINGING [63] 5-8-11 J Quinn (1) *al beh, tld off.* ....(20 to 1 op 16 to 1) 17

Dist: ½l, 2l, 2½l, 1½l, ¾l, ¾l, hd, 1l, ¾l, ½l. 1m 32.65s. a 8.35s (17 Ran).
SR: 46/45/47/33/33/26/31/31/17/ (Ray Richards), C E Brittain

476 Stark Maiden Stakes Class D (Div II) (3-y-o and up) £3,348 7f....................(5:45)

YAQTHAN (Ire) 3-8-9 R Hills (7) *wth ldr, led o'r 2 fs out, rdn and hld on wl*......(15 to 8 fav op 5 to 4 tchd 2 to 1) 1
BOLD THATCHER 3-8-9 Paul Eddery (6) *pld hrd, trkd ldrs, str chal und pres ins last, ran on wl.* (5 to 1 op 7 to 1) 2
RITTO 3-8-9 M Roberts (3) *trkd ldrs, pushed alng o'r 3 fs out, sn one pace*..................(5 to 1 tchd 13 to 2) 3
EXCLUSION 4-9-10 W Newnes (5) *pld hrd, chsd ldrs, outpcd 3 fs out*..........................(6 to 1 op 9 to 2) 4
TWICE THE GROOM (Ire) 3-8-9 Pat Eddery (8) *led till o'r 2 fs out, eased whn btn ins last.* ....(4 to 1 op 7 to 2 tchd 3 to 1) 5
PRIVATE JET (Ire) 4-9-10 T Quinn (1) *wnt lft strt, trkd ldrs till wknd hfwy*......(20 to 1 op 12 to 1 tchd 25 to 1) 6
CONCINNITY (USA) 4-9-10 J Reid (4) *al beh.* ....(25 to 1 op 20 to 1) 7
327 ROCK THE BARNEY (Ire) 4-9-10 B Rouse (2) *al beh.* ....(50 to 1) 8

Dist: Nk, 3l, 12l, nk, 5l, hd, 1½l. 1m 32.69s. a 8.59s (8 Ran).
SR: 40/39/30/9/-/ (Hamdan Al-Maktoum), H Thomson Jones

KEMPTON (soft)
Monday April 12th

Going Correction: PLUS 1.00 sec. per fur. (races 1,3,4,5,6), PLUS 0.95 (2,7)

477 Redshank Maiden Fillies Stakes Class D (2-y-o) £3,289 5f....................(2:00)

RISKY 8-11 B Raymond (4) *frnt rnk, led appr 2 fs out, drvn out fnl furlong, styd on wl.* ....(100 to 30 fav op 6 to 4 tchd 7 to 2) 1
337[2] ANTONIA'S FOLLY 8-11 G Carter (7) *made most till appr 2 fs out, one pace ins last.* ....(9 to 2 op 4 to 1 tchd 11 to 2) 2
399[2] KERRIE-JO 8-11 R Cochrane (6) *sn rdn alng to chase ldrs, ev ch and hng rght entering fnl 2 fs, one pace final furlong*................(7 to 2 op 4 to 1 tchd 5 to 1) 3
ALZIANAH 8-8 (3*) D Harrison (5) *handily plcd till rdn and outpcd appr 2 fs out, kpt on one pace frm one out.* ....(4 to 1 tchd 7 to 2) 4
LIGHTNING BELLE 8-11 J Reid (2) *slwly away, reco'red to track ldrs, fdd entering fnl 2 fs.* ....(8 to 1 op 10 to 1 tchd 14 to 1) 5
PIP'S DREAM 8-11 D Biggs (1) *outpcd.* ....(20 to 1 op 16 to 1 tchd 25 to 1) 6
337[5] EUROPHARM LASSIE 8-11 B Rouse (3) *sn drvn alng to chase ldrs till wknd entering fnl 2 fs.* ....(8 to 1 tchd 10 to 1) 7

Dist: 2l, sht-hd, ¾l, 5l, 8l, 1½l. 1m 6.54s. a 8.34s (7 Ran).
SR: 30/22/21/18/ (Roldvale Limited), R Hannon

478 Harcros Queen's Prize Handicap Class C Qualifier for the Harcros Timber and Building Supplies Ltd Stakes(0-90 4-y-o and up) £8,025 2m....................(2:35)

RODEO STAR (USA) [51] 7-7-8[4] (5*) B Doyle (9) *made all, drvn alng appr fnl furlong, styd on gmely ins last.* ....(12 to 1 op 10 to 1) 1
ROBINGO (Ire) [81] (bl) 4-9-7 A Munro (7) *hld up, improved 4 fs out, str brst ins last, not rch wnr.* ....(13 to 2 op 5 to 1 tchd 7 to 1) 2
TOP SPIN [83] 4-9-9 S Whitworth (8) *hld up in rear, drvn alng 5 fs out, hdwy and brght stands side 3 out, effrt 2 out, one pace*.........(10 to 1 op 8 to 1 tchd 12 to 1) 3
365* WHITE WILLOW [75] 4-9-1 B Raymond (2) *nvr far away, pressed wnr o'r 4 fs out, effrt and wknd over 2 out.* ....(15 to 2 op 6 to 1 tchd 8 to 1) 4
BRANDON PRINCE (Ire) [80] (bl) 5-9-10 R Cochrane (4) *hld up, hdwy 6 fs out, effrt appr 3 out, sn btn.* ....(9 to 1 op 8 to 1 tchd 10 to 1) 5
382* TAROUDANT [66] 6-8-10 L Piggott (5) *trkd ldrs, brght stands side and wknd o'r 3 fs out.* (4 to 1 jt-fav op 9 to 2 tchd 5 to 1) 6
SPECTACULAR DAWN [78] 4-9-4 J Reid (6) *nvr on terms.* ....(16 to 1 tchd 20 to 1) 7
IOTA [73] 4-8-13 M Roberts (10) *mid-div, rdn alng o'r 4 fs out, wknd appr 3 out.* (4 to 1 jt-fav op 7 to 2 tchd 9 to 2) 8
BROOM ISLE [60] 5-7-12[1] (7*) S Mulvey (3) *in tch, wknd 4 fs out*..........................(33 to 1 op 25 to 1) 9
BARDOLPH (USA) [79] 6-9-2 (7*) T G McLaughlin (1) *hld up in tch, rdn and wknd 6 fs out*........(9 to 1 op 8 to 1) 10
REQUESTED [73] 6-9-3 G Carter (11) *rear, improved hfwy, rdn and wknd 3 fs out, tld off*..... (14 to 1 op 12 to 1) 11

Dist: ½l, 10l, 15l, 3½l, 15l, 2½l, ½l, ¾l, 10l, 30l. 3m 44.64s. a 20.14s (11 Ran).
SR: 32/57/49/26/31/2/7/1/-/ (J C Bradbury), N Tinkler

479 Crinkley Bottom Handicap Class C (0-90 4-y-o and up) £5,005 6f.............(3:05)

EFRA [62] 4-8-5 S Raymont (8) *hld up in rear, improved entering fnl 2 fs, led ins last, ran on wl.* ....(16 to 1 op 14 to 1 tchd 20 to 1) 1
SO RHYTHMICAL [79] 9-9-8 A Munro (4) *mid-div, hdwy ins fnl 2 fs, led briefly entering last, ran on one pace.* ....(6 to 1 op 5 to 1) 2
301[3] ASSIGNMENT [76] 7-9-5 R Cochrane (1) *trkd ldrs, led o'r 3 fs out, hdd and no extr entering last.* ....(9 to 2 fav op 4 to 1) 3
BODARI [78] 4-9-4 (3*) D Harrison (7) *led for o'r 2 fs, in tch, ev ch two out, sn one pace.* ....(9 to 1 op 8 to 1 tchd 10 to 1) 4
SURREY RACING [73] 5-9-2 B Rouse (3) *trkd ldrs, styd on one pace ins last*.....(12 to 1 op 14 to 1 tchd 16 to 1) 5
4796a[5] TRUTHFUL IMAGE [70] 4-8-13 D Biggs (5) *beh, styd on one pace appr fnl furlong, nvr nrr.* ....(11 to 1 op 10 to 1 tchd 12 to 1) 6
BAYSHAM (USA) [75] 7-9-4 M Roberts (2) *prmnt, ev ch appr 2 fs out, wknd wl o'r one out.* ....(11 to 2 op 5 to 1 tchd 6 to 1) 7
HOW'S YER FATHER [81] 7-9-10 L Piggott (10) *speed for o'r 3 fs*....................(15 to 2 op 8 to 1 tchd 9 to 1) 8
326[7] RICKY'S TORNADO (Ire) [72] 4-8-10 (5*) B Doyle (6) *speed for o'r 3 fs*......................(16 to 1 tchd 20 to 1) 9
4681a[2] FACE NORTH (Ire) [55] 5-7-12 G Carter (9) *speed 4 fs.* ....(5 to 1 op 7 to 2) 10

Dist: ½l, 2½l, ½l, 2½l, ½l, sht-hd, 12l, 2l, 10l. 1m 20.90s. a 10.10s (10 Ran).
SR: 9/24/11/11/-/-/ (Mrs P Jubert), R Hannon

480 Westminster-Motor Taxi Insurance Rosebery Rated Class B (0-105 4-y-o and up) £12,792 1¼m.................... (3:40)

LUCKY GUEST [89] 6-9-4 L Piggott (3) *hld up in tch, hdwy 3 fs out, led appr last, shaken up, ran on wl.* ....(7 to 1 op 6 to 1 tchd 15 to 2) 1
HOST (Ire) [86] 4-9-1 M Roberts (7) *in tch, led aftr 4 fs till o'r one out, one pace*.........(5 to 2 fav tchd 11 to 4) 2
329[4] KNOCK KNOCK [88] 8-9-3 R Cochrane (2) *hld up, kpt on fnl 2 fs, nvr nrr*....................(8 to 1 op 6 to 1) 3
YILDIZ [80] 4-8-9 R Hills (4) *chsd ldrs, effrt o'r 2 fs out, sn btn*...................(4 to 1 op 3 to 1 tchd 9 to 2) 4
315 WELL APPOINTED (Ire) [80] 4-8-9 J O'Reilly (1) *beh, kpt on one pace ins fnl 2 fs, nvr nrr*..... (16 to 1 tchd 20 to 1) 5
THE POWER OF ONE [78] 4-8-7 W Ryan (6) *keen hold, beh, styd on fnl 2 fs, nvr nrr.* ....(33 to 1 op 25 to 1 tchd 40 to 1) 6
PELORUS [79] 8-8-5 (3*) D Harrison (8) *slwly away, nvr on terms*....................(7 to 1 op 6 to 1 tchd 15 to 2) 7
259* SAAHI (USA) [78] 4-8-7 J Reid (5) *pressed ldrs, effrt 3 fs out, sn btn*....................(8 to 1 tchd 9 to 1) 8
YOUNG FREEMAN (USA) [92] 4-9-7 B Raymond (9) *led 4 fs, in tch till wknd four out.* ....(9 to 1 op 8 to 1 tchd 10 to 1) 9

Dist: 3½l, 2l, 6l, ½l, ¾l, 2½l, 30l, 20l. 2m 16.68s. a 14.88s (9 Ran).
SR: 55/45/43/23/22/18/14/-/-/ (Windflower Overseas Holdings Inc), J L Dunlop

481 Quail Conditions Stakes Class C (3-y-o and up) £4,517 6f....................(4:10)

BOLD LEZ 6-9-3 R Cochrane (5) *wtd wth, improved 3 fs out, led appr last, drvn out, kpt on wl.* ....(9 to 2 op 4 to 1 tchd 5 to 1) 1

A PRAYER FOR WINGS 9-9-2 A Munro (7) *hld up, rdn and styd on frm o'r 2 fs out, ran on ins last, no ch wth wnr.* .... (13 to 2 op 5 to 1 tchd 7 to 1) 2
4712a* NIGHT JAR 6-9-1 (3*) D Harrison (6) *in tch, led appr 2 fs out, hdd and one pace approaching last.* .... (9 to 4 fav tchd 7 to 4) 3
DUPLICITY (Ire) 5-9-0 J Reid (2) *in tch, drvn alng appr 2 fs out, one pace o'r one out.* .... (5 to 1 op 7 to 2) 4
181^{6} I'LLEAVEITOYOU (Ire) 3-8-1 G Carter (1) *trkd ldrs, rdn and lost pl appr 2 fs out.* .... (25 to 1 tchd 33 to 1) 5
ROCKY WATERS (USA) 4-9-4 B Rouse (4) *led till appr 2 fs out, sn btn.* .... (10 to 1 op 12 to 1) 6
VENTURE CAPITALIST (bl) 4-9-2 L Piggott (3) *chsd ldrs 4 fs.* .... (9 to 2 op 4 to 1) 7

Dist: 3l, 1½l, 1l, 10l, 2l, 3½l. 1m 19.12s. a 8.32s (7 Ran).
SR: 57/44/40/32/ (Ansells Of Watford), M J Haynes

482 Fifield Maiden Stakes Class D (3-y-o) £3,816 1¼m. .... (4:40)

MAGICAL RETREAT (USA) 8-9 D Biggs (8) *hld up in mid-div, improved 4 fs out, led entering last, all out.* .... (16 to 1 op 12 to 1 tchd 20 to 1) 1
SEREN QUEST 8-6 (3*) D Harrison (14) *wtd wth, hdwy 3 fs out, led briefly appr last, ran on cl hme.* .... (66 to 1 op 33 to 1 tchd 100 to 1) 2
MASHAIR (USA) 8-9 R Hills (4) *chsd ldrs, led o'r 2 fs out till over one out, one pace ins last.* .... (8 to 1 op 7 to 1 tchd 12 to 1) 3
LICORNE 8-9 W Ryan (10) *nvr far away, led o'r 3 fs out till over 2 out, wknd appr last.* .... (9 to 4 fav op 5 to 2 tchd 2 to 1) 4
PERO 9-0 M Roberts (9) *beh till styd on one pace ins last 2 fs.* .... (7 to 1 op 5 to 1 tchd 8 to 1) 5
HATTA RIVER (USA) 9-0 A Munro (16) *pressed ldrs, drvn alng o'r 2 fs out, sn btn.* .... (8 to 1 tchd 10 to 1) 6
ISLE OF PEARLS (USA) 9-0 P D'Arcy (3) *slwly away, moderate hdwy fnl 2 fs, nvr nrr.* .... (20 to 1 op 10 to 1) 7
PURPLE SPLASH 9-0 B Raymond (11) *dwlt, beh till styd on one pace ins fnl 2 fs.* .... (66 to 1 op 20 to 1) 8
BALLON 8-9 J Penza (13) *cl up, led briefly 4 fs out, sn wknd.* .... (16 to 1 op 12 to 1 tchd 20 to 1) 9
4708a^{8} CASHABLE 9-0 S O'Gorman (15) *nvr on terms.* .... (66 to 1 op 33 to 1) 10
CIRCUS COLOURS 9-0 B Rouse (6) *in tch to hfwy.* .... (20 to 1 op 12 to 1 tchd 25 to 1) 11
YELLOW RATTLE 8-9 B Procter (12) *chsd ldrs till rdn and wknd o'r 4 fs out.* .... (33 to 1 op 20 to 1 tchd 50 to 1) 12
ESERIE DE CORES (USA) 8-9 (5*) C Hodgson (2) *rear, improved hfwy, fdd 3 fs out.* .... (66 to 1 op 33 to 1 tchd 100 to 1) 13
SMUGGLER'S POINT (USA) 9-0 J Reid (5) *dwlt, al rear.* .... (10 to 1 op 9 to 2) 14
385^{5} SMOCKING 8-9 R Cochrane (17) *nvr on terms.* .... (20 to 1 op 12 to 1) 15
REMEMBER THE NIGHT 9-0 G Carter (7) *in tch 5 fs.* .... (66 to 1 op 33 to 1 tchd 100 to 1) 16
DANNY BOY 9-0 L Piggott (1) *led to 4 fs out, sn rdn and wknd.* .... (4 to 1 tchd 5 to 1) 17

Dist: Hd, 3½l, 12l, 4l, ½l, sht-hd, 6l, 6l, 6l, ¾l. 2m 17.21s. a 15.41s (17 Ran).
SR: 41/40/33/9/6/5/4/-/-/ (R M Cyzer), C A Cyzer

483 CPM Field Marketing Handicap Class D (0-80 3-y-o) £3,611 1m. .... (5:10)

335* MR VINCENT [74] 9-2 (3*) D Harrison (1) *towards rear, improved o'r 2 fs out, str run ins last to ld last strds.* .... (11 to 2 op 5 to 1 tchd 6 to 1) 1
245^{4} WITHOUT A FLAG (USA) [57] 8-2 D Biggs (5) *in tch, jnd ldr 2 fs out, hrd rdn and ev ch ins last, styd on.* .... (8 to 1 tchd 7 to 1) 2
317^{9} BEZIQUE (USA) [72] (bl) 9-3 M Roberts (11) *led, jnd 2 fs out, hdd and no extr cl hme.* (9 to 2 jt-fav op 5 to 1 tchd 6 to 1) 3
SEA BARON [68] 8-13 G Carter (10) *dwlt, beh till hdwy 3 fs out, styd on ins last.* ... (7 to 1 op 8 to 1 tchd 10 to 1) 4
LUNAR RISK [54] 7-13^{2} A Munro (13) *hld up beh, styd on one pace o'r 2 fs out.* .... (25 to 1) 5
328^{9} SCORCHER (Ire) [56] 8-1 J Penza (3) *mid-div, improved hfwy, drvn alng o'r 2 fs out, sn btn.* .... (14 to 1) 6
BOBBYSOXER [76] 9-7 J Reid (6) *nvr better than mid-div.* .... (14 to 1) 7
SUPREME MASTER [70] 9-1 B Raymond (2) *nvr trble ldrs.* .... (14 to 1 op 12 to 1) 8
333* MR NEVERMIND (Ire) [67] 8-12 B Rouse (12) *in tch, rdn o'r 2 fs out, sn wknd.* .... (6 to 1 op 5 to 1 tchd 13 to 2) 9
MISTY SILKS [70] 8-8 (7*) P McCabe (9) *al rear*... (25 to 1) 10
BAULKING TOWERS [48] 7-5^{5} (7*) Gina Faulkner (4) *chsd ldrs till wknd 4 fs out.* .... (50 to 1) 11
MANON LESCAUT [57] 7-11 (5*) L Newton (14) *pressed ldrs, drvn alng o'r 2 fs out, sn wknd.* .... (10 to 1) 12
AMERICAN SWINGER (USA) [63] 8-8 R Cochrane (8) *nvr trble ldrs.* .... (9 to 2 jt-fav op 3 to 1 tchd 5 to 1) 13

Dist: 1l, nk, ¾l, 5l, 1½l, 5l, 10l, ¾l, 2l, 1½l. 1m 49.33s. a 12.33s (13 Ran).
SR: 34/14/28/22/-/-/ (Mrs Shirley Robins), G Lewis

LONGCHAMP (FR) (soft)
Monday April 12th
Going Correction: PLUS 0.70 sec. per fur.

484 Prix Finlande (Listed) (3-y-o) £14,337 1m 1f .... (2:15)

INTREPIDITY 8-9 T Jarnet, ... 1
ALICE SPRINGS (USA) 8-9 G Guignard, ... 2
4738a* MADELEINE'S DREAM (USA) 8-13 C Asmussen, ... 3
INSIJAAM (USA) 8-9 W R Swinburn, ... 4

Dist: ½l, sht-hd, hd, 2l, ¾l, 1½l, 2½l, ½l, 1½l. 2m 0.80s. a 11.80s (11 Ran).
SR: 12/11/14/9/ (Sheikh Mohammed), A Fabre

485 Prix Noailles (Group 2) (3-y-o) £34,839 1m 3f. .... (3:20)

FORT WOOD (USA) 9-2 W R Swinburn (2) *rcd in second, led aftr one furlong, rdn and effrt 2 fs out, ran on wl, comfortable.* .... (31 to 10) 1
MARCHAND DE SABLE (USA) 9-2 D Boeuf (4) *led for one furlong, second and effrt 2 fs out, unbl to trble wnr.* .... (Evens fav) 2
266^{2} SAWASDEE (Fr) 9-2 J Boisnard (5) *4th strt, prog into 3rd o'r one furlong out, not rch ldrs.* .... (7 to 1) 3
ARINTHOD (Fr) 9-2 F Head (1) *rcd in 5th, hrd rdn 2 fs out, ran on one pace.* .... (78 to 10) 4
SISMART (Fr) 9-2 T Jarnet (3) *3rd strt, wknd 2 fs out.* .... (22 to 10) 5

Dist: ½l, 1½l, ½l, 1½l. 2m 31.50s. a 16.30s (5 Ran).
SR: 16/15/12/11/8/ (Sheikh Mohammed), A Fabre

MALLOW (IRE) (heavy)
Monday April 12th

486 Holiday Maiden (3-y-o and up) £2,243 5f .... (2:40)

280^{2} MACGILLYCUDDY (Ire) (bl) 4-9-0 (8*) R V Skelly (5) .... (5 to 2 fav) 1
CARRIG STAR (Ire) 4-9-0 (8*) J J Stack (3) .... (10 to 1) 2
TOUGH AS TEAK (Ire) 3-8-8 (2*) R M Burke (1) .... (10 to 1) 3
280^{4} GOLD BRAISIM (Ire) 3-8-7 C Roche (12) .... (4 to 1) 4
257 GIRARDELLI (Ire) 3-8-0 (10*) P J Smullen (2) ...... (20 to 1) 5
280 KILTIMONY 3-8-7 P V Gilson (7) .... (7 to 1) 6
SHESOMETHINGELSE (Ire) 3-7-11 (10*) D W O'Sullivan (10) .... (20 to 1) 7
280^{5} SOMERTON BOY (Ire) 3-8-10 P Shanahan (8) ...... (5 to 1) 8
280^{8} BENE MERENTI (Ire) (bl) 3-8-10 N G McCullagh (11) (9 to 1) 9
FOREST 3-8-10 S Craine (6) .... (9 to 1) 10
YELLOW PRINCESS (Ire) 3-8-7 D Manning (9) .... (10 to 1) 11
RICH LIFE (Ire) 3-8-10 D V Smith (14) .... (20 to 1) 12
280 LARGO KEY (Ire) 3-8-7 W J Supple (13) .... (12 to 1) 13
MRS SCHILLACI (Ire) 4-9-5 N Byrne (4) .... (20 to 1) 14

Dist: 2½l, hd, 1½l, 2½l. 1m 4.30s. (14 Ran).
(Mrs Rita Hale), Patrick Prendergast

487 Buttevant Apprentice Handicap (3-y-o and up) £2,243 1m 1f. .... (3:40)

4686a^{3} FONTANAYS (Ire) [-] 5-8-11 P P Murphy (4) .... (7 to 1) 1
THE BERUKI (Ire) [-] 3-7-12 D J O'Donohoe (9) .. (12 to 1) 2
307^{2} COOLRAIN LADY (Ire) [-] 3-9-0^{3} T P Treacy (1) .. (2 to 1 fav) 3
ONOMATOPOEIA (Ire) [-] 3-8-7 (2*) W J Walsh (5) .. (10 to 1) 4
HAWAIAN TASCA (Ire) [-] 4-8-5 (2*) B Carson (2) .... (8 to 1) 5+
257 QUIETEST (Ire) [-] (bl) 3-7-10 (2*) D O'Callaghan (14) .... (12 to 1) 5+
281^{6} TWO MAGPIES [-] 6-8-3 T J Daly (3) .... (8 to 1) 7
MAZELLA (Ire) [-] 4-8-12 (2*) S P Cooke (6) .... (12 to 1) 8
281 POWER SOURCE (Ire) [-] 5-8-13 (2*) P J Smullen (7) (10 to 1) 9
4686a MAY WE DANCE (Ire) [-] 4-9-9 R V Skelly (8) .... (8 to 1) 10
281^{7} DIAMOND CLUSTER [-] 3-7-8 R T Fitzpatrick (13) . (10 to 1) 11
4686a^{4} NORDIC SIGN (Ire) [-] 4-9-9 M W Martin (10) .... (7 to 1) 12
ASTRA (Ire) [-] 4-9-10 M F Ryan (16) .... (8 to 1) 13
298 WOODFIELD ROSE [-] 4-8-11 (2*) B Fenton (17) ... (12 to 1) 14
281 THE BOWER (Ire) [-] 4-9-2 (2*) P M Donohue (12) .. (10 to 1) 15
MOLDAVIA [-] 7-9-13 J J Stack (15) .... (6 to 1) 16
281 DAHAR'S LOVE (USA) [-] 4-9-8 (2*) J Cornally (18) (10 to 1) 17
DONMIR LOVEBIRD (Ire) [-] 3-8-8 A J Beale (11) .. (14 to 1) 18

Dist: ½l, 1½l, 2½l, dd-ht. 2m 14.40s. (18 Ran).
(E A MacRedmond), B V Kelly

488 City Fillies Maiden (3-y-o) £2,243 1m 1f .... (4:20)

TARAKANA (USA) 9-0 R Hughes (9) .... (6 to 4 on) 1
282^{4} MAYASTA (Ire) 9-0 P V Gilson (4) .... (7 to 1) 2
257^{6} MY TRELAWNY (Ire) 8-12 (2*) R M Burke (7) ...... (10 to 1) 3
267^{2} PENNINE MIST (Ire) 9-0 P Shanahan (6) .... (13 to 2) 4
SOLAS ABU (Ire) 9-0 C Roche (16) .... (7 to 1) 5
282 INISHMOT (Ire) 8-6 (8*) R V Skelly (1) .... (14 to 1) 6
311^{8} DRIFT APART (Ire) 9-0 G Curran (11) .... (10 to 1) 7
LADY GLOW (Ire) 9-0 D Hogan (13) .... (16 to 1) 8
311 SHOWBOAT MELODY (Ire) 9-0 B Coogan (3) ..... (16 to 1) 9

297[8] TANHONEY (Ire) 8-6 (8*) D M McCullagh (14)......(16 to 1) 10
STEADY DEAR (Ire) 9-0 N G McCullagh (5).......(16 to 1) 11
SUNBED SUE (Ire) 8-6 (8*) R T Fitzpatrick (2).....(16 to 1) 12
DUCHESS AFFAIR (Ire) (bl) 9-0 Joanna Morgan (12) (20 to 1) 13
GIG TIME (Ire) 8-4 (10*) B Fenton (18)............(20 to 1) 14
282 LEOS LITTLE BIT (Ire) 9-0 W J O'Connor (10).....(16 to 1) 15
282 RAYJOHN GIRL (Ire) 8-4 (10*) G Coogan (8)........(16 to 1) 16
257 SALZAAD (Ire) 8-12 (2*) D G O'Shea (15).........(16 to 1) 17
282[6] ARAN EXILE 9-0 S Craine (17)..................(10 to 1) 18
Dist: 3½l, 10l, 4l, hd. 2m 12.90s. (18 Ran).
(H H Aga Khan), John M Oxx

489 Easter (C & G) Maiden (3-y-o) £2,243 1m 1f ....(4:50)

257[8] TOUCHING MOMENT (Ire) 9-0 P V Gilson (1).....(14 to 1) 1
306[7] SCHMEICHEL (Ire) 9-0 N Byrne (2)................(8 to 1) 2
297[2] ABSOLUTE JAMBOREE 9-0 S Craine (8)...........(8 to 1) 3
311[5] SUAVE GROOM (Ire) (bl) 9-0 P Shanahan (4)... (6 to 4 fav) 4
TORC MOUNTAIN (Ire) 9-0 W J Supple (10).......(14 to 1) 5
267[7] DENZILLE LANE (Ire) (bl) 9-0 A J Nolan (3)........(20 to 1) 6
311 THE SALTY FROG (Ire) 9-0 G Curran (12).........(25 to 1) 7
BOLD NOT BEAT (Ire) 8-12 (2*) R M Burke (9).....(20 to 1) 8
PALACE PARADE (USA) 9-0 W J O'Connor (6)....(12 to 1) 9
297 TREBLE BOB (Ire) 8-10 (4*) W J Smith (7).........(20 to 1) 10
ERBIL (Ire) 9-0 D Hogan (5)......................(5 to 2) 11
SPRING MARATHON (USA) 8-6 (8*) R V Skelly (13) (14 to 1) 12
NORDIC HABITAT (Ire) 9-0 C Roche (14)...........(8 to 1) 13
Dist: ½l, nk, 3l, 7l. 2m 14.00s. (13 Ran).
(Mrs H D McCalmont), C Collins

NOTTINGHAM (good)
Monday April 12th

Going Correction: PLUS 0.30 sec. per fur. (races 1,2,3), PLUS 0.35 (4,5,6)

490 'Easter Egg' Selling Stakes Class G (2-y-o) £2,070 5f 13yds.................... (2:10)

BEV'S FOLLY 8-6 W Carson (1) *swrvd lft strt, made virtually all, hld on.* ....(9 to 4 fav op 5 to 2 tchd 11 to 4 and 2 to 1) 1
ROSE OF GLENN 8-6 J Quinn (7) *slwly into strd, outpcd till hdwy o'r one furlong out, ran on wl towards finish.* ....(14 to 1) 2
MISS RISKY 8-7[1] L Dettori (3) *al cl up, rdn o'r a furlong out, one pace*........ (100 to 30 op 5 to 2 tchd 7 to 2) 3
ENTENTE CORDIALE (Ire) 8-4 (7*) Kim McDonnell (2) *al prominnent, ran on one pace appr fnl furlong.* ....(6 to 1 op 5 to 1 tchd 7 to 1) 4
381[3] XAMDIVAD (Ire) 8-6 M Wood (8) *sn pushed alng, some hdwy appr fnl furlong, nvr able to chal.* ....(3 to 1 op 5 to 2 tchd 7 to 2) 5
374[4] ROCKABYE BAILEYS 8-6 Dean McKeown (4) *chsd ldrs, rdn hfwy, no imprsn*.................. (12 to 1 op 10 to 1) 6
399 THE KAMIKAZE QUEEN 8-6 R Perham (5) *wth ldrs stands side o'r 3 fs*................(20 to 1 op 16 to 1) 7
BESSIE'S WILL 8-6 Dale Gibson (6) *strted slwly, al beh and outpcd, tld off*................(20 to 1 op 12 to 1) 8
Dist: Nk, 2½l, 1l, 1l, nk, nk, 15l. 1m 4.10s. a 5.90s (8 Ran).
SR: 4/3/-/-/-/ (Mrs Beverley Thompson), J Berry

491 Robin Hood Median Auction Maiden Stakes Class E (3-y-o) £2,872 5f 13yds ....(2:40)

CRIME OFTHECENTURY 8-9 T Quinn (2) *hld up gng wl, led on bit appr fnl furlong, easily.* ....(13 to 8 fav op 9 to 4 tchd 6 to 4) 1
BELLSABANGING 9-0 J Quinn (6) *led aftr 2 fs till appr fnl furlong, no ch wth wnr.* .... (11 to 2 op 5 to 1 tchd 6 to 1) 2
428[9] HALL BANK COTTAGE 8-9 Dean McKeown (1) *chsd alng thrght, kpt on appr fnl furlong, not pace to chal.* ....(12 to 1 op 8 to 1) 3
4741a MUSICAL TIMES 8-6 (3*) F Norton (7) *lost pl aftr 2 fs, sn drvn alng, kpt on appr fnl furlong.* ....(14 to 1 op 12 to 1) 4
KELLY MAC 9-0 W Carson (4) *wth ldrs, rdn 2 fs out, sn btn*..........................(15 to 8 op Evens tchd 2 to 1) 5
4687a[9] MY FOXY LADY 8-9 L Dettori (3) *strted slwly, al beh.* ....(20 to 1) 6
380[5] CHICAGO (Ire) 9-0 G Duffield (5) *led 2 fs, hrd rdn and wknd wl o'r a furlong out*...... (12 to 1 tchd 14 to 1) 7
Dist: 1½l, 5l, 1½l, 1l, hd, 2½l. 1m 2.40s. a 4.20s (7 Ran).
SR: 41/40/15/9/10/4/-/ (Christopher Wright), P F I Cole

492 'Family Day Out' Handicap Class E (0-70 3-y-o and up) £3,339 6f 15yds....... (3:10)

HONEY SEEKER [58] 4-9-2 K Darley (5) *hld up, swtchd rght hfwy, shaken up to ld a furlong out, sn clr.* ....(11 to 1 op 12 to 1) 1
379[3] STRIP CARTOON (Ire) [50] (bl) 5-8-1 (7*) G Strange (18) *led till hdd a furlong out, sn outpcd.* ....(5 to 1 fav tchd 11 to 2) 2
348[4] GREAT HALL [43] 4-8-1 A Mackay (9) *rdn alng hfwy, hdwy blw dist, ran on wl fnl furlong*.... (14 to 1 op 12 to 1) 3
HIGHBORN (Ire) [47] 4-8-5[2] Dean McKeown (6) *slwly into strd, hdwy o'r 2 fs out, kpt on und pres fnl furlong.* ....(25 to 1 op 20 to 1) 4
127[2] WELL BOUGHT (Ire) [39] 4-7-11[3] (3*) F Norton (4) *rcd alone centre, hdwy 2 fs out, ran on*................ (14 to 1) 5
391[9] ELTON LEDGER (Ire) [62] 4-8-13 (7*) J Tate (7) *hld up, effrt o'r 2 fs out, not rch ldrs*........... (20 to 1 op 16 to 1) 6
GREY CHARMER (Ire) [53] 4-8-11 Dale Gibson (8) *nvr nr to chal*.................................. (20 to 1 op 16 to 1) 7
LORD HIGH ADMIRAL (Can) [67] 5-9-11 R Perham (16) *chsd ldr stands side 4 fs, sn wknd*........(9 to 1 op 10 to 1) 8
ABIGAILS BOY (Hol) [56] 4-9-0 G Hind (17) *in tch, rdn blw dist, not pace to chal*............. (12 to 1 tchd 14 to 1) 9
368* UNVEILED [58] 5-9-2 W Carson (14) *nvr nr ldrs.* .... (13 to 2 op 5 to 1) 10
330 NOBLE POWER (Ire) [65] 4-9-9 L Dettori (19) *nvr a factor.* ....(8 to 1 op 10 to 1 tchd 12 to 1) 11
330 TAKE IT IN CASH [46] 4-8-4 T Quinn (2) *rcd far side, speed to hfwy*... (14 to 1) 12
TWILIGHT FALLS [46] 8-8-4 L Charnock (10) *trkd ldrs 4 fs, sn wknd*.........................(16 to 1 op 12 to 1) 13
429[3] SUPER ROCKY [65] 4-9-2 (7*) H Bastiman (12) *speed o'r 4 fs*...(14 to 1 op 8 to 1) 14
421[7] NO QUARTER GIVEN [70] 8-10-0 G Duffield (1) *rcd far side, prmnt to hfwy*................................(14 to 1) 15
326[3] BLYTON STAR (Ire) [48] 5-8-6[2] S Webster (11) *outpcd.* ....(14 to 1) 16
409[2] TOSHIBA COMET [50] (bl) 6-8-8 J Quinn (15) *outpcd.* .... (11 to 1 op 12 to 1) 17
HARRY'S GEM (Ire) [39] 5-7-4 (7*) Darren Moffatt (3) *al beh.* .... (25 to 1 op 33 to 1) 18
333 BARBEZIEUX [35] 6-7-0 (7*) Sharon Millard (13) *beh frm hfwy*................... (33 to 1 op 20 to 1) 19
Dist: 4l, nk, sht-hd, 2l, 1½l, 4l, 2l, sht-hd, 1½l, nk. 1m 16.60s. a 5.10s (19 Ran).
SR: 36/12/4/7/-/8/ (P D Savill), T Thomson Jones

493 Rothmans Royals North South Challenge Series Handicap Class D (0-80 3-y-o) £4,045 1m 54yds................... (3:45)

BARIK (Ire) [78] 9-7 W Carson (7) *wtd wth in rear, steady hdwy to nose ahead one furlong out, cheekily.* ....(11 to 8 on op 11 to 10) 1
317[4] UMBUBUZI (USA) [70] 8-13 S Perks (5) *al wl-plcd, led o'r 2 fs out to one furlong out, kpt on, no ch wth wnr.* ....(12 to 1) 2
334[3] KOA [65] 8-8 T Quinn (3) *al prmnt, led 4 fs out till o'r 2 out, styd on same pace*...............(7 to 1 op 5 to 1) 3
334* SPRING SIXPENCE [63] 8-6 G Duffield (9) *trkd ldrs, shaken up 2 fs out, swtchd rght appr last, unbl to quicken.* ....(9 to 2 op 3 to 1) 4
LEGAL ARTIST (Ire) [54] 7-11 Dale Gibson (6) *hld up, effrt und pres 2 fs out, nvr able to chal*............(20 to 1) 5
WOLF POWER (Ire) [62] 8-5 K Darley (8) *hdwy o'r 2 fs out, nvr nrr*............................(7 to 1 op 12 to 1) 6
BOISTEROUS [50] 7-0 (7*) Kim McDonnell (2) *led aftr a furlong to 4 out, rdn and wknd blw dist*........(33 to 1) 7
SILKY HEIGHTS (Ire) [60] 8-3 L Charnock (1) *led a furlong, cl up till wknd 2 fs out*........... (14 to 1 op 12 to 1) 8
DIVINE RAIN [60] 8-3 J Quinn (10) *al in rear.* .... (16 to 1 op 10 to 1) 9
286[5] ASTRAC TRIO (USA) [68] 8-8 (3*) F Norton (4) *al beh.* .... (20 to 1 op 16 to 1) 10
Dist: ½l, 2l, 2l, ½l, hd, 2l, 2½l, 2½l, ¾l. 1m 50.40s. a 10.40s (10 Ran).
(Hamdan Al-Maktoum), A C Stewart

494 Easter Bonnet Conditions Stakes Class D (3-y-o) £3,318 1m 1f 213yds......... (4:15)

AZZILFI 8-10 L Dettori (5) *patiently rdn, smooth hdwy to ld o'r 2 fs out, very easily.* ....(9 to 4 fav op 7 to 2 tchd 2 to 1) 1
BUROOJ 8-10 Dean McKeown (3) *hld up and beh, gd hdwy o'r 2 fs out, chsd wnr appr fnl furlong, kpt on.* ....(6 to 1 op 9 to 2) 2
4703a[9] FRESCADE (USA) 8-10 T Quinn (6) *ran in snatches, hdwy und pres o'r 3 fs out, wknd blw dist.* (10 to 1 op 8 to 1) 3
SHARJAH (USA) 9-0 G Duffield (2) *chsd ldrs, ev ch till wknd wl o'r a furlong out.* ....(7 to 2 op 3 to 1 tchd 4 to 1) 4
ALMAMZAR (USA) 8-10 K Darley (1) *led aftr 2 fs till hdd and wknd o'r two furlongs out*..... (11 to 1 op 8 to 1) 5
DYAB (USA) 8-12 W Carson (7) *hld up and beh, drvn alng hfwy, effrt o'r 2 fs out, no imprsn*....(9 to 2 op 7 to 2) 6
393[3] NURYANDRA 8-2 (3*) F Norton (4) *led 2 fs, prmnt till wknd two furlongs out*...... (6 to 1 op 5 to 1 tchd 13 to 2) 7
Dist: 2l, 7l, 1½l, 2½l, sht-hd, 6l. 2m 10.60s. a 7.60s (7 Ran).
SR: 55/51/37/38/29/30/11/ (Prince A A Faisal), J L Dunlop

495 'Easter Bunny' Handicap Class E (0-70 4-y-o and up) £3,339 1¾m 15yds........ (4:45)

ENFANT DU PARADIS (Ire) [35] 5-7-13 W Carson (18) *settled mid-div, hdwy 3 fs out, led wl ins last, hld on grimly.* ....(10 to 1 op 8 to 1 tchd 12 to 1) 1

61[2] MIZYAN (Ire) [58] 5-9-5 (3*) F Norton (10) *in rear, rdn alng hfwy, styd on fnl 2 fs, fnshd wl.*. (5 to 2 fav op 3 to 1) 2

WHITE RIVER [36] 7-8-0 A Mackay (5) *al wl plcd, led o'r 2 fs out till hdd and no extr well ins fnl furlong*... (14 to 1) 3

331[4] JANISKI [47] (v) 10-8-11 S Webster (6) *patiently rdn, hdwy 3 fs out, styd on ins fnl furlong*....(11 to 1 op 10 to 1) 4

NOTABLE EXCEPTION [51] 4-8-12 K Darley (16) *hld up and beh, steady prog o'r 2 fs out, nrst at finish.* ....(8 to 1 op 7 to 1) 5

FULL QUIVER [46] (v) 8-8-10 G Duffield (12) *wtd wth, prog to join ldr blw dist, rdn and wknd appr fnl furlong.* ....(18 to 1 op 14 to 1 tchd 20 to 1) 6

350 HIT THE FAN [63] 4-9-10 L Dettori (4) *ran on fnl 2 fs, nvr nrr*....(9 to 1 op 7 to 1) 7

349[3] EIRE LEATH-SCEAL [49] 6-8-13 S Perks (13) *prmnt till rdn and wknd o'r 2 fs out.* ....(11 to 1 op 10 to 1 tchd 12 to 1) 8

287[4] PONDERED BID [33] (bl) 9-7-4 (7*) Kim McDonnell (8) *led till hdd and wknd o'r 2 fs out*.... (20 to 1) 9

126[4] FIRST FLING (Ire) [52] 4-8-13 G Hind (2) *pressed ldrs till rdn and wknd o'r 2 fs out.* ....(18 to 1 op 14 to 1 tchd 20 to 1) 10

HYDEONIUS [33] 8-7-11 L Charnock (1) *nvr a factor.* ....(25 to 1) 11

25[8] HONEY DANCER [56] 9-9-6 R Perham (7) *cl up to hfwy, grad lost tch*.... (16 to 1 tchd 14 to 1) 12

382[9] ICE MAGIC [46] 6-8-10 Dean McKeown (15) *beh, effrt entering strt, wknd o'r 3 fs out*.... (25 to 1 op 16 to 1) 13

182[2] HUNTING GROUND [51] 5-9-1 J Quinn (11) *chsd ldrs o'r 2 fs, sn lost tch*....(10 to 1 tchd 12 to 1) 14

349 ROCKY ROMANCE [30] 6-7-8[6] (5*) N Gwilliams (14) *wth ldr ten fs, sn lost tch, tld off*.... (16 to 1 op 25 to 1) 15

135[3] GEE DOUBLE YOU [41] 7-8-5 Dale Gibson (17) *cl up o'r 8 fs, sn wknd, tld off*....(14 to 1 tchd 20 to 1) 16

373[2] THE KARAOKE KING [52] (bl) 4-8-13 T Quinn (9) *prmnt o'r 8 fs, sn wknd, tld off*....(4 to 1 op 6 to 1 tchd 7 to 2) 17

Dist: 1l, ½l, 2l, 3l, 6l, 1½l, 5l, 1l, sht-hd, 6l. 3m 11.90s. a 14.00s (17 Ran).
SR: -/15/-/-/-/- (P A Taylor), P D Evans

WARWICK (soft)
Monday April 12th

Going Correction: PLUS 0.35 sec. per fur. (races 1,6), PLUS 0.50 (2,3,4,5,7)

496 Lions Club International Median Auction Maiden Fillies' Stakes Class E (2-y-o) £3,054 5f.... (1:45)

CARRIE KOOL 8-11 W Woods (3) *cl up, led one and a half furlong out, edgd lft, rdn out*....(12 to 1 tchd 16 to 1) 1

325[4] BEARALL (Ire) 8-11 A McGlone (1) *cl up, led o'r 2 fs out till one and a half out, kpt on wl.* ....(6 to 4 fav op 7 to 4 tchd 2 to 1) 2

COLNE VALLEY 8-8 (3*) A Tucker (2) *cl up, ev ch 2 fs out, kpt on one pace*....(14 to 1 op 10 to 1) 3

312[7] MAIDEN EFFORT 8-11 Paul Eddery (8) *chsd ldrs, one pace fnl 2 fs*....(13 to 2 op 9 to 2) 4

HOLLINGTON SONG 8-11 W Newnes (5) *sn chsd alng, styd on frm o'r one furlong out*....(25 to 1 op 16 to 1) 5

MONKEY MONEY (Ire) 8-11 M Hills (9) *broke wl, sn outpcd.* ....(7 to 2 op 5 to 2) 6

337[3] FLAIR LADY 8-11 T Sprake (6) *cl up, led till ran wide wide o'r 2 fs, wknd*.... (7 to 2 op 11 to 4 tchd 4 to 1) 7

GRANMAS DELIGHT 8-11 G Bardwell (4) *sn pushed alng, nvr on terms*....(14 to 1 op 10 to 1) 8

Dist: 1l, 5l, 2l, 2l, ¾l, ¾l, 2l. 1m 4.00s. a 5.80s (8 Ran).
SR: 16/12/-/-/-/- (Miss T Williams), A Hide

497 West Midlands Conditions Stakes Class D (4-y-o and up) £3,143 7f.... (2:15)

THOUSLA ROCK (Ire) 4-8-11 Paul Eddery (4) *trkd ldrs, led one furlong out, rdn and ran on gmely.* ....(13 to 2 op 7 to 1 tchd 6 to 1) 1

POWERFUL EDGE 4-8-10 M Hills (6) *trkd ldrs, rdn alng o'r 2 fs out, ev ch ins last, kpt on und pres.* ....(7 to 4 op 5 to 4 tchd 15 to 8) 2

BRIGADE 4-8-11 M Tebbutt (3) *trkd ldr, led 2 and a half fs out till one out, swshd tail and one pace und pres.* ....(16 to 1 op 10 to 1) 3

LORD CHICKNEY (USA) 4-9-4 D Holland (2) *slwly into strd, hld up, effrt on ins 2 fs out, sn no imprsn and eased.* ....(6 to 4 fav op 5 to 4) 4

363* TYRONE FLYER 4-9-0 N Carlisle (1) *led, sn clr, hdd and wknd 2 and a half fs out.* ....(8 to 1 op 16 to 1 tchd 20 to 1) 5

LOUISVILLE BELLE (Ire) 4-8-11 N Adams (5) *al beh.* ....(33 to 1 op 20 to 1) 6

Dist: Nk, 2l, 12l, 3l, 6l. 1m 30.00s. a 6.20s (6 Ran).
SR: 57/55/50/21/8/- (R E Sangster), P W Chapple-Hyam

498 BBC CWR Handicap Class E (0-70 3-y-o and up) £3,416 1¼m 169yds.... (2:45)

387[9] TENAYESTELIGN [34] 5-7-13 S Dawson (8) *hld up in mid-div, hdwy o'r 3 fs out, led appr last, edgd lft, ran on.* ....(14 to 1 op 12 to 1) 1

LEGUARD EXPRESS (Ire) [32] (bl) 5-7-4 (7*) D Wright (12) *led till appr fnl furlong, rallied*....(33 to 1) 2

HIGHLY SECURE [50] 6-9-1 Paul Eddery (17) *hld up gng wl in mid-div, rdn alng and hdwy 3 fs out, hrd ridden and ev ch o'r one out, one pace*.... (7 to 1 op 4 to 1) 3

387[5] SINCLAIR LAD (Ire) [59] 5-9-3 (7*) S Drowne (15) *strted slwly, beh, swtchd rght and hdwy 2 fs out, styd on wl, nrst finish*....(14 to 1 op 12 to 1) 4

332[5] SKIMMER HAWK [39] 4-8-3 N Carlisle (1) *trkd ldrs, outpcd fnl 2 fs*.... (20 to 1) 5

IRISH GROOM [40] (bl) 6-8-0 (5*) A Garth (16) *mid-div, hdwy 4 fs out, wknd o'r 2 out*....(12 to 1 op 10 to 1) 6

GILBERT'S GIRL [35] 6-7-11 (3*) N Kennedy (5) *beh, hdwy wl o'r 3 fs out, styd on, nvr nrr*.... (14 to 1 op 12 to 1) 7

RAGTIME SONG [40] 4-8-4 A McGlone (3) *trkd ldrs, wknd wl o'r 2 fs out*....(16 to 1 op 14 to 1) 8

CRYSTAL STONE [60] 3-8-1 (3*) A Tucker (11) *mid-div, sn rdn alng, nvr rch chalg pos*.... (16 to 1 op 14 to 1) 9

251[6] SIE AMATO (Ire) [47] 4-8-11 J Fortune (19) *trkd ldrs, rdn and wknd o'r 2 fs out*....(7 to 1 op 6 to 1) 10

DRINKS PARTY (Ire) [36] 5-8-1 J Lowe (2) *al beh.* ....(5 to 1 fav op 7 to 1) 11

387[3] GEBLITZT [30] 9-7-2 (7*) Wendy Jones (6) *nvr dngrs.* ....(16 to 1 op 14 to 1) 12

349 SAIF AL ADIL (Ire) [30] 4-7-8 G Bardwell (13) *chsd ldrs, sn pushed alng, wknd 5 fs out*....(50 to 1) 13

CONSTRUCTIVIST (Ire) [59] (bl) 4-9-2 (7*) C Hawksley (9) *trkd ldrs, pushed alng o'r 3 fs out, wknd quickly.* ....(14 to 1 op 33 to 1) 14

VANUATU (Ire) [48] 4-8-12 N Adams (4) *chsd ldrs till wknd o'r 4 fs out*....(14 to 1 op 12 to 1) 15

DYD [51] 5-9-2 W Newnes (10) *al beh.* (25 to 1 op 20 to 1) 16

FIRST HEIRESS (Ire) [49] 4-8-13 A Clark (14) *chsd ldrs, hrd rdn and wknd hfwy*....(9 to 1 op 7 to 1 tchd 10 to 1) 17

RED JACK (Ire) [45] 4-8-9 D Holland (18) *mid-div, hrd rdn and wknd 5 fs out, tld off*....(16 to 1) 18

Dist: Nk, 4l, 12l, 3l, 1l, sht-hd, 1l, nk, 3½l, hd. 2m 26.60s. a 13.80s (18 Ran).
SR: 1/-/8/-/-/-/ (G J King), D Marks

499 Easter Claiming Stakes Class F (3-y-o) £2,243 1½m 115yds.... (3:15)

98[5] MRS SNUGGS (Ire) 8-6 W Woods (1) *chsd ldrs, pushed alng and lost pl o'r 5 fs out, hdwy over one out, styd on to ld ins last*.... (12 to 1 op 14 to 1) 1

230[6] MOUNTAIN WILLOW (v) 8-8 W Newnes (5) *trkd ldrs, led o'r 2 fs out, hrd rdn and hdd ins last, one pace.* ....(9 to 2 op 4 to 1 tchd 5 to 1) 2

295 MR GENEAOLOGY (USA) (h,bl) 8-11 (3*) A Tucker (10) *strted slwly and sn reminders, hdwy o'r 5 fs out, ev ch ins last, no extr*.... (14 to 1) 3

437[6] ANN HILL (Ire) 8-1 (7*) M Humphries (7) *hld up beh, hdwy o'r 3 fs out, sn one pace*....(6 to 1 op 5 to 1) 4

351[7] BEYOND THE LIMIT 8-4 S Dawson (8) *trkd ldrs, pushed alng o'r 4 fs out, sn wknd*....(33 to 1) 5

422[3] PONDERING 8-11 Paul Eddery (4) *nvr gng wl, hrd rdn hfwy, no response*....(3 to 1 fav op 6 to 1) 6

4675a[6] HOBEY CAT 8-5 M Hills (3) *led till o'r 2 fs out, wknd quickly*.... (7 to 1 op 6 to 1) 7

351[6] KESANTA 7-9 (7*) S Lanigan (2) *keen hold, trkd ldr till wknd quickly o'r 4 fs out, sddl slpd*.... (33 to 1) 8

KIAWAH 8-6 G Bardwell (11) *al beh, tld off fnl 2 fs.* ....(11 to 2 op 5 to 1) 9

MERITRE (Ire) 8-2 N Adams (9) *in tch till wknd o'r 4 fs out, tld off*....(20 to 1) 10

OLIVIA VAL 8-5 (3*) N Kennedy (6) *strted slwly, sn tld off, pld up ins fnl furlong*....(16 to 1) pu

Dist: 1l, sht-hd, 10l, 5l, 3l, 3½l, 15l, 8l, 15l. 2m 54.30s. a 16.40s (11 Ran).
(Shane T Ryan), M H Tompkins

500 High Tensile Bolts Handicap Class D (0-80 4-y-o and up) £3,348 1¼m 169yds... (3:45)

416* ALDERBROOK [74] 4-9-8 (5ex) Paul Eddery (7) *hld up, cld 4 fs out, not much room 2 furlongs out, sn swtchd rght, shaken up to ld close hme*.... (11 to 8 fav op 11 to 10) 1

4689a ACHELOUS [53] (v) 6-8-2[1] D Holland (9) *led, rallied whn chlgd ins fnl furlong, hdd and no extr cl hme.* ....(33 to 1 op 20 to 1) 2

425[6] KATY'S LAD [63] 6-8-12 J Fortune (3) *trkd ldrs, rdn and one pace fnl 2 fs*....(11 to 2 op 5 to 1) 3

329[2] MYFONTAINE [64] 6-8-13 G Bardwell (5) *trkd ldrs, cld o'r 3 fs out, hrd rdn and ev ch 2 out, wknd appr last.* ....(3 to 1 op 5 to 2 tchd 7 to 2) 4

358[5] MAD MILITANT (Ire) [76] 4-9-5 (5*) S Wynne (6) *dwlt, sn in tch, effrt and no hdwy fnl 3 fs*....(10 to 1 op 16 to 1) 5

SCENIC DANCER [53] 5-8-2[2] W Woods (8) *al beh.* ....(20 to 1 op 14 to 1) 6

402* MODESTO (USA) [51] (v) 5-8-0 N Carlisle (1) *trkd ldr till rdn and wknd o'r 4 fs out*....(8 to 1 op 7 to 1) 7

4767a^{3} MAPLE BAY (Ire) [64] 4-8-12 M Hills (2) *trkd ldrs till rdn and wknd 4 fs out, tld off*........ (16 to 1 op 14 to 1) 8
L'ACQUESIANA [44] (bl) 5-7-2^{2} (7*) D Wright (4) *al beh, tld off*..............................(100 to 1 op 66 to 1) 9
Dist: 1½l, 8l, 1½l, 6l, 15l, 2½l, 20l, sht-hd. 2m 26.00s. a 13.20s (9 Ran).
SR: 30/7/1/-/-/-/ (E Pick), Mrs J Cecil

501 P. J. Rowan Handicap Class E (0-70 3-y-o and up) £3,235 5f...................(4:15)

GOODY FOUR SHOES [46] 5-8-6 G Bardwell (11) *chsd ldrs, led ins fnl furlong, ran on wl*.....(16 to 1 op 12 to 1) 1
330^{2} HITCHIN A RIDE [43] 6-8-3 J Comber (14) *beh, hdwy ins fnl furlong, fnshd wl*.................. (10 to 1 op 5 to 1) 2
263^{8} PALACEGATE GOLD (Ire) [45] 4-8-0^{2} (7*) S Drowne (7) *beh, hdwy o'r one furlong out, kpt on.* (16 to 1 op 14 to 1) 3
330^{7} JOHN O'DREAMS [43] 8-8-3 T Sprake (18) *chsd ldrs, rdn and kpt on one pace ins last, fnshd lme.* .... (12 to 1 op 9 to 1) 4
333^{7} MISS PRECOCIOUS [33] 5-7-2^{2} (7*) D Wright (19) *beh, hrd rdn o'r one furlong out, styd on*..............(33 to 1) 5
117^{7} BRIGHT PARAGON (Ire) [46] 4-7-13 (7*) C Hawksley (20) *wnt rght strt, beh, plenty to do strt, hdwy o'r one furlong out, nrst finish*..........................(20 to 1 op 14 to 1) 6
LET'S GO LOCHY [45] 7-8-5^{2} M Hills (13) *cl up, ev ch whn jinked rght and hit rail o'r one furlong out, not rcvr.* .... (8 to 1 op 25 to 1 tchd 7 to 1) 7
319^{9} LOOTING (USA) [39] 7-7-13^{3} R Price (1) *beh, styd on ins fnl furlong, nrst finish*..................................(33 to 1) 8
330 LINCSTONE BOY (Ire) [53] (bl) 5-8-13 M Wood (3) *wth ldr, led o'r 2 fs out till hdd and one pace ins last.* .... (16 to 1 op 14 to 1) 9
CLEAN GATE [33] (bl) 4-7-7 E Johnson (4) *nvr rch ldrs.* ....(33 to 1) 10
MACFARLANE [68] 5-10-0 D Holland (9) *prmnt, hrd rdn and ev ch wl o'r one furlong out, eased whn btn.* .... (12 to 1 op 8 to 1) 11
421^{2} RUSHANES [55] 6-9-1 Paul Eddery (6) *rdn alng to chase ldrs, no hdwy fnl 2 fs*........... (5 to 1 fav op 8 to 1) 12
CONVENIENT MOMENT [64] 3-8-9 (3*) Emma O'Gorman (15) *nvr dngrs*.......................... (8 to 1 op 7 to 1) 13
292 GANESHAYA [51] (bl) 4-8-11 N Carlisle (12) *chsd ldrs till wknd wl o'r one furlong out*......(16 to 1 op 14 to 1) 14
419^{2} COPPERMILL LAD [47] 10-8-7 C Avery (10) *outpcd.* .... (10 to 1 op 8 to 1 tchd 11 to 1) 15
401^{3} JOE SUGDEN [55] 9-9-1 W Newnes (16) *outpcd.* .... (12 to 1 op 10 to 1) 16
330 SLIP-A-SNIP [54] 6-8-11 (3*) A Tucker (2) *cl up, ev ch o'r one furlong out, sn wknd and eased*...(12 to 1 op 20 to 1) 17
421^{8} TRIOMING [52] (bl) 7-8-12 A Clark (8) *led til hdd o'r 2 fs out, wknd quickly*.............................(20 to 1) 18
368^{2} SIRMOOR (Ire) [47] (v) 4-8-7 A McGlone (17) *outpcd, tld off.* .... (14 to 1 op 10 to 1) 19
Dist: 3l, hd, ¾l, nk, sht-hd, ½l, 1½l, sht-hd, sht-hd, ¾l. 1m 2.80s. a 4.60s (19 Ran).
SR: 35/20/21/16/5/17/14/2/15/ (A G Newcombe), C J Hill

502 Pearl Run Limited Stakes Class E (3-y-o) £3,028 1½m 115yds................. (4:45)

295 MOON CARNIVAL 8-6 A Clark (1) *al gng wl, hld up beh ldrs, hdwy to ld one furlong out, rdn out.* ....(7 to 4 fav op 6 to 4) 1
SHYNON 8-11 M Tebbutt (4) *led till one furlong out, no extr*................................(9 to 2 op 7 to 2) 2
412^{2} ARC BRIGHT (Ire) 8-11 Paul Eddery (8) *trkd ldrs, rdn 4 fs out, ev ch 2 out, one pace*........................ (7 to 2) 3
378^{7} DOC SPOT 8-11 J Fortune (7) *wtd wth, effrt o'r 4 fs out, sn one pace*.......................... (8 to 1 op 7 to 1) 4
230^{9} PERSIAN STAR (Fr) 8-6 N Carlisle (2) *trkd ldrs, pushed alng o'r 5 fs out, wknd over 2 furlongs out.* .... (50 to 1 op 20 to 1) 5
PAPER DAYS 8-11 A Dicks (6) *hld up beh, shrtlvd effrt o'r 4 fs out*......................... (20 to 1 op 16 to 1) 6
422^{4} STARLIGHT ROSE (Ire) 8-6 A McGlone (9) *pld hrd, trkd ldrs till wknd quickly o'r 2 fs out*........(8 to 1 op 7 to 1) 7
351^{9} THREEOFUS 8-11 G Bardwell (5) *al beh.* .... (33 to 1 op 20 to 1) 8
Dist: 2½l, 5l, 7l, 2l, 4l, 8l, 4l. 2m 54.00s. a 16.10s (8 Ran).
(Lavinia Duchess Of Norfolk), Lady Herries

NEWCASTLE (heavy)
Tuesday April 13th

Going Correction: PLUS 0.85 sec. per fur. (races 1,5,6), PLUS 0.60 (2,3,4)

503 Balaclava Army Benevolent Fund Handicap Stakes Class E (0-70 3-y-o) £2,560 7f ....(2:30)

394^{2} DESIRABLE MISS [42] (v) 8-4 J Lowe (5) *made all, clr 2 fs out, rdn and ran on wl fnl furlong*...(5 to 1 op 4 to 1) 1
394* HOT OFF THE PRESS [48] 8-10 A Culhane (3) *chsd ldrs, rdn and hdwy 2 fs out, styd on fnl furlong, not rch wnr.* ....(5 to 1 op 4 to 1) 2
PUBLIC WAY (Ire) [56] 9-4 S Webster (2) *prmnt till lost pl and beh hfwy, swtchd and gd hdwy 2 fs out, rdn and one pace fnl furlong.* (14 to 1 op 12 to 1 tchd 16 to 1) 3
CONTRACT ELITE (Ire) [58] 9-6 N Connorton (6) *chsd wnr, effrt o'r 2 fs out, sn rdn and wknd appr fnl furlong.* ....(4 to 1 jt-fav op 4 to 1 tchd 5 to 1) 4
346 TELEPHONIC (USA) [47] 8-9 G Duffield (7) *chsd wnr, rdn o'r 2 fs out, wknd wl over one furlong out.* ....(6 to 1 op 7 to 1) 5
NELLIE'S GAMBLE [52] 9-0 K Darley (1) *hld up, effrt and pushed alng 3 fs out, sn btn.* (4 to 1 jt-fav op 4 to 1 tchd 9 to 2) 6
93^{4} ROBIX (Ire) [55] 9-3 W Newnes (4) *al rear.* .... (14 to 1 op 12 to 1 tchd 16 to 1) 7
335^{3} SILVER GROOM (Ire) [59] 9-7 D Nicholls (8) *in tch, rdn 3 fs out, sn wknd and beh*... (7 to 1 op 7 to 1 tchd 8 to 1) 8
Dist: 1½l, 1½l, 6l, 2l, 5l, 7l, 10l. 1m 34.23s. a 10.23s (8 Ran).
SR: 26/27/30/14/-/ (Mel Brittain), M Brittain

504 Crimea Army Benevolent Fund Rating Related Maiden Stakes Class F (3-y-o) £2,243 6f........................... (3:00)

QUEEN OF THE QUORN 8-9 W Newnes (3) *made all, rdn 2 fs out, styd on wl*.................(10 to 1 op 8 to 1) 1
361^{3} MILBANK CHALLENGER 9-0 M Birch (4) *chsd wnr, rdn 2 fs out, kpt on und pres*............. (11 to 1 op 10 to 1) 2
341^{2} PEEDIE PEAT (bl) 9-0 K Darley (2) *in tch, outpcd and rdn 2 fs out, styd on fnl furlong.* .... (7 to 4 fav op 7 to 4 tchd 2 to 1 and 6 to 4) 3
424^{2} CLANROCK 9-0 A Culhane (1) *in tch, effrt and hdwy 2 fs out, sn rdn and one pace*........... (9 to 2 op 4 to 1) 4
367^{4} SABO THE HERO 9-0 G Duffield (6) *unruly stalls, chsd ldrs, effrt and rdn o'r 2 fs out, sn btn.* .... (7 to 2 op 11 to 4) 5
FLY TO THE END (USA) (bl) 9-0 J Fortune (5) *unruly stalls, slwly away and pushed alng, hrd rdn hfwy, beh and eased fnl 2 fs*......................(6 to 1 op 4 to 1) 6
Dist: 1½l, hd, 3l, 3l, 15l. 1m 19.78s. a 7.78s (6 Ran).
SR: 11/10/9/ (Lord Crawshaw), G M Moore

505 Light Brigade Army Benevolent Fund Handicap Stakes Class D (0-80 4-y-o and up) £3,200 6f...................... (3:30)

391^{2} SAGEBRUSH ROLLER [75] 5-9-10 M Birch (6) *trkd ldrs gng wl, hdwy on bit 2 fs out, shaken up to ld ins fnl furlong, quickened clr*......(6 to 4 fav op 5 to 4 tchd 13 to 8) 1
70* PRETONIC [67] 5-9-2 J Lowe (4) *chsd ldr, led one and a half fs out, rdn and hdd ins last*.... (4 to 1 op 5 to 2) 2
4692a^{9} SONDERISE [64] 4-8-13 W Newnes (1) *chsd ldrs, rdn 2 fs out, styd on fnl furlong.* (5 to 1 op 6 to 1 tchd 7 to 1) 3
436^{9} DIET [62] (v) 7-8-8 (3*) F Norton (2) *led, rdn 2 fs out, sn hdd and wknd fnl furlong*.............. (4 to 1 op 7 to 2) 4
383^{7} BLUE GRIT [59] 7-8-8 S Webster (5) *slwly away, al rear.* .... (11 to 1 op 8 to 1) 5+
358^{8} KHALLOOF (Ire) [52] (bl) 4-7-8 (7*) C Teague (3) *prmnt till rdn and wknd 2 fs out*...........(33 to 1 op 25 to 1) 5+
Dist: 3½l, 1½l, 1l, ½l, dd-ht. 1m 19.47s. a 7.47s (6 Ran).
SR: 33/11/2/ (A K Collins), J W Watts

506 Cavalry Army Benevolent Fund Median Auction Maiden Stakes Class D (2-y-o) £2,880 5f......................... (4:00)

299^{4} SADDAM THE LOG 8-9 A Mackay (4) *made all, rdn o'r one furlong out, edgd rght ins last, styd on.* ....(7 to 4 fav op 6 to 4 tchd 2 to 1) 1
DISTINCTIVE AIR 9-0 W Newnes (5) *cl up, hdwy to chal 2 fs out, rdn and ev ch appr fnl furlong, not quicken.* .... (8 to 1 op 6 to 1 tchd 10 to 1) 2
JUST BILL 9-0 T Lucas (6) *dwlt, sn cl up, effrt to chal 2 fs out, soon rdn, ran green and wknd appr fnl furlong.* ....(7 to 2 op 9 to 4) 3
MINNESOTA VIKING 9-0 K Darley (3) *sn outpcd, rdn and styd on fnl 2 fs*..................... (6 to 1 op 3 to 1) 4
LAUREL ROMEO (Ire) 9-0 J Carroll (2) *dwlt, sn cl up, rdn and outpcd hfwy*.... (3 to 1 op 9 to 4 tchd 100 to 30) 5
Dist: 1½l, 4l, 3½l, sht-hd. 1m 5.29s. a 6.39s (5 Ran).
SR: 27/26/10/-/-/ (Mrs M O'Donnell), A Bailey

507 Infantry Army Benevolent Fund Rating Related Maiden Stakes Class E (0-70 3-y-o) £2,560 1¼m 32yds............... (4:30)

EFIZIA 8-9 J Lowe (2) *chsd ldrs, hdwy o'r 3 fs out, sn rdn, led 2 out, ran on*................ (6 to 4 fav op Evens) 1
434^{9} BARSAL (Ire) 9-0 D Nicholls (1) *trkd ldr, hdwy 4 fs out, led 2 and a half out, sn rdn and hdd, kpt on one pace.* .... (7 to 1 op 8 to 1 tchd 10 to 1) 2
CAMEO KIRBY (Fr) 9-0 J Fortune (4) *slwly away, sn in tch, hdwy on outer 3 fs out, rdn 2 out, one pace.* ....(9 to 4 op 7 to 4 tchd 5 to 2) 3
304 WHITE CREEK (Ire) 9-0 J Carroll (3) *led, hdd and wknd 2 and a half fs out*....... (4 to 1 op 3 to 1 tchd 9 to 2) 4
Dist: 1½l, 2l, 12l. 2m 27.10s. a 20.60s (4 Ran).
(Mrs H I S Calzini), Mrs M Reveley

508 Inkerman Army Benevolent Fund Handicap Stakes Class D (0-80 3-y-o and up) £2,880 1¼m 32yds.................. (5:00)

3586 GOLDEN TORQUE [66] 6-8-13 (7*) H Bastiman (5) *dwlt, hld up in tch, gd hdwy on outer o'r 2 fs out, rdn to chal ins last, edgd lft, styd on to ld line.* (4 to 1 jt-fav op 3 to 1) 1
PERSONAL HAZARD [66] (v) 4-9-6 M Birch (6) *trkd ldr, effrt to ld 2 fs out, sn rdn, ct on line......* (5 to 1 op 7 to 2) 2
4483 TANODA [47] 7-8-1 J Lowe (2) *led, rdn and hdd 2 fs out, sn one paced......................* (4 to 1 jt-fav op 3 to 1) 3
3409 GOLD SURPRISE (Ire) [49] 4-8-3¹ J Fortune (7) *chsd ldrs, lost pl 4 fs out, rdn and styd on fnl 2 furlongs.* (12 to 1) 4
SALU [58] (bl) 4-8-9 (3*) F Norton (4) *trkd ldr, effrt and hdwy 4 fs out, rdn 3 out, sn wknd.* ....(9 to 2 op 5 to 1 tchd 4 to 1) 5
TAKE BY STORM (Ire) [70] 4-9-10 W Newnes (1) *trkd ldrs, rdn 3 fs out, sn wknd.................* (6 to 1 op 5 to 1) 6
SHADANZA (Ire) [48] 4-7-13 (3*) S Maloney (3) *prmnt, hdwy 4 fs out, rdn 3 out, sn wknd.* .... (10 to 1 op 8 to 1 tchd 12 to 1) 7
Dist: Sht-hd, 6l, 1½l, 4l, 4l, 4l. 2m 23.87s. a 17.37s (7 Ran).
SR: 19/18/-/-/ (Trevor J Smith), R Bastiman

NEWMARKET (good)
Tuesday April 13th
Going Correction: PLUS 0.10 sec. per fur.

509 Constant Security Maiden Stakes Class D (3-y-o) £3,622 1½m.................. (2:00)

OAKMEAD (Ire) 8-9 J Reid (5) *patiently rdn, improved hfwy, ran green and shaken up o'r 2 fs out, styd on strly to ld ins last...................* (8 to 1 op 10 to 1) 1
2453 HALHAM TARN (Ire) 9-0 W Carson (4) *trkd ldg 5, drvn to ld o'r 2 fs out, hrd driven and hdd ins last, one pace.* .... (33 to 1 op 16 to 1) 2
ALINOVA (USA) 8-9 M Roberts (10) *nvr far away, rdn to draw level o'r 2 fs out, kpt on same pace ins last.* ....(9 to 4 fav op 6 to 4 tchd 5 to 2) 3
ERCKULE 8-9 (5*) B Doyle (2) *co'red up on ins, effrt hfwy, rdn and swtchd over 2 fs out, fnshd wl.* .... (12 to 1 op 8 to 1 tchd 14 to 1) 4
3045 CIVIL LAW (Ire) 9-0 L Dettori (6) *steadied strt, improved into midfield hfwy, rdn and styd on same pace last 2 fs.* .... (8 to 1 op 7 to 1 tchd 10 to 1) 5
3722 ALYDUNCAN (USA) 9-0 T Quinn (11) *wth ldr, led aftr 2 and a half fs till o'r two out, fdd.........* (4 to 1 op 5 to 1) 6
COMMANCHE CREEK 9-0 R Cochrane (3) *drpd out strt, effrt and bustled alng hfwy, no imprsn last 3 fs.* ....(8 to 1 op 6 to 1) 7
OLD RED (Ire) 9-0 Pat Eddery (7) *trkd ldg quartet, drvn alng whn pace quickened o'r 2 fs out, fdd.* ....(6 to 1 op 5 to 1) 8
4225 EVE'S TREASURE 8-9 G Bardwell (8) *led 2 and a half fs, hndy till wknd rpdly o'r two out, tld off.* .... (50 to 1 op 33 to 1) 9
3727 MRS NICE GUY 8-9 D Biggs (9) *trkd ldg trio, losing grnd whn hmpd 4 fs out, tld off..........*(50 to 1 op 25 to 1) 10
Dist: 2½l, ½l, 1½l, 3½l, 7l, hd, 6l, 30l, 20l. 2m 36.92s. a 7.32s (10 Ran).
SR: 34/34/28/30/23/9/8/-/-/ (R E Sangster), P W Chapple-Hyam

510 Stetchworth Maiden Stakes Class D (3-y-o) £3,655 6f............................ (2:35)

MATILA (Ire) 8-9 R Hills (6) *nvr far away, narrow ld frm o'r 2 fs out till quickened clr fnl furlong, pushed out.* .... (10 to 1 op 5 to 1 tchd 12 to 1) 1
AGHAR (Ire) 9-0 M Roberts (1) *al wl plcd, ev ch and bustled alng o'r 2 fs out, rallied fnl furlong, no chance wth wnr...........................* (7 to 1 op 4 to 1) 2
NAFUTH (USA) 9-0 W Carson (4) *made most till o'r 2 fs out, rdn and one pace ins last.* ....(9 to 4 fav op 7 to 4 tchd 5 to 2) 3
RESIST THE FORCE (USA) 9-0 D Biggs (2) *patiently rdn, smooth hdwy on bit to draw level o'r 2 fs out, wknd last 50 yards...............*(5 to 2 tchd 3 to 1 and 9 to 4) 4
LORD BOTHWELL (USA) 9-0 J Reid (7) *struggling to go pace hfwy, nvr a threat.* .... (11 to 2 op 4 to 1 tchd 7 to 1) 5
TARTIB (Ire) 9-0 T Quinn (5) *dsptd ld to hfwy, eased whn btn appr fnl furlong............*(20 to 1 tchd 25 to 1) 6
SCENT OF POWER 9-0 Pat Eddery (3) *chsd alng to go pace hfwy, nvr a factor...................* (10 to 1 op 5 to 1) 7
Dist: 6l, ¾l, 1l, ½l, 2l, 2½l. 1m 14.11s. a 2.71s (7 Ran).
SR: 53/34/31/27/25/17/7/ (Hamdan Al-Maktoum), R W Armstrong

511 Abernant Stakes Class A (Listed) (3-y-o and up) £9,768 6f.................... (3:05)

SPLICE 4-8-11 W R Swinburn (2) *patiently rdn, shaken up to improve on outsd o'r one furlong out, kpt on strly to ld last 50 yards........*(6 to 1 op 10 to 1 tchd 12 to 1) 1
3164 MONTENDRE 6-9-8 J Reid (3) *nvr far away, drvn through on ins to chal fnl furlong, kpt on wl.* (4 to 1 jt-fav op 3 to 1 tchd 9 to 2) 2
ARTISTIC REEF 4-9-2 Pat Eddery (1) *nvr far away, drvn to ld ins fnl furlong, hdd and one pace last 50 yards.* ....(6 to 1 op 9 to 2) 3
SURPRISE OFFER (bl) 3-8-3 M Roberts (4) *keen hold, led aftr 2 and a half fs till ins last, rdn and no extr.* .... (13 to 2 op 5 to 1 tchd 7 to 1) 4
3168 FYLDE FLYER (v) 4-9-8 L Piggott (6) *led 2 and a half fs, rallied and ev ch o'r one out, not quicken nr finish.* ....(6 to 1 tchd 13 to 2) 5
HAMAS (Ire) 4-9-8 W Carson (5) *sluggish strt, bustled alng to improve hfwy, effrt o'r one furlong out, no extr.* ....(4 to 1 jt-fav tchd 5 to 1) 6
3162 SILCA-CISA 4-8-11 T Quinn (8) *pressed ldg pair till wknd appr fnl furlong, eased...............*(6 to 1 op 9 to 2) 7
Dist: ½l, ½l, 1½l, 1½l, 2½l, 10l. 1m 13.39s. a 1.99s (7 Ran).
SR: 69/78/70/51/64/54/3/ (Cheveley Park Stud), J R Fanshawe

512 Shadwell Stud Nell Gwyn Stakes Class A (Group 3) (3-y-o) £21,961 7f......... (3:40)

NICHE 9-0 L Piggott (2) *set modest pace, quickened appr fnl furlong, drvn out.* ....(11 to 1 op 14 to 1 tchd 10 to 1) 1
ZARANI SIDI ANNA (USA) 8-9 B Raymond (7) *trkd ldg 5, bustled alng to improve last 2 fs, ran on nr finish.* ....(11 to 2 op 4 to 1) 2
SAYYEDATI 9-0 W R Swinburn (6) *stumbled strt, improved on outsd gng wl hfwy, ev ch entering fnl furlong, not quicken cl hme.....* (11 to 8 fav op 5 to 4 tchd 7 to 4) 3
TOOCANDO (Ire) 8-9 R Cochrane (4) *sluggish strt, drvn into midfield hfwy, styd on und pres fnl furlong, nvr nrr...............................*(16 to 1 tchd 20 to 1) 4
MARINA PARK 8-12 Dean McKeown (3) *rcd freely in frnt rnk for o'r 5 fs, eased whn btn...* (10 to 1 tchd 12 to 1) 5
MAGIQUE ROND POINT (USA) 8-9 W Ryan (5) *pressed ldg trio 5 fs, wknd ins last..........*(14 to 1 tchd 16 to 1) 6
BASHAYER (USA) 8-9 W Carson (8) *trkd ldrs, hrd drvn o'r 2 fs out, sn btn........* (4 to 1 op 5 to 2 tchd 9 to 2) 7
EXCLUSIVELY YOURS 8-9 L Dettori (1) *rcd freely in frnt rnk for o'r 4 fs, wknd quickly......*(50 to 1 op 33 to 1) 8
Dist: 1½l, sht-hd, 2l, nk, 4l, sht-hd, 25l. 1m 27.07s. a 3.57s (8 Ran).
SR: 57/47/51/40/42/27/26/-/ (Lord Carnarvon), R Hannon

513 Ladbroke Handicap Class C (0-95 4-y-o and up) £7,310 1¼m................. (4:10)

LOKI (Ire) [81] 5-9-0 (3*) D Harrison (4) *patiently rdn, last hfwy, improved o'r 2 fs out, led ins last, drvn out.* .... (5 to 1 op 9 to 2 tchd 11 to 2) 1
3506 SWIFT SILVER [57] 6-7-7 J Quinn (3) *nvr far away, led o'r one furlong out till ins last, edgd lft and rght, no extr cl hme.................* (7 to 1 op 10 to 1 tchd 12 to 1) 2
3502 LOBILIO (USA) [71] 4-8-7 L Dettori (7) *settled midfield, feeling pace and lost grnd 4 fs out, rallied appr last, styd on...............* (5 to 1 op 4 to 1 tchd 11 to 2) 3
RUTLAND WATER (USA) [67] 6-8-3² T Quinn (6) *trkd ldrs, improved to chal o'r 2 fs out, one pace whn hmpd and snatched up ins last.* ....(9 to 2 fav op 4 to 1 tchd 11 to 2) 4
SURREY DANCER [74] 5-8-10 B Raymond (8) *co'red up on ins, effrt and drvn alng last 2 fs, edgd lft appr last, styd on same pace nr finish.* .... (12 to 1 op 10 to 1 tchd 14 to 1) 5
BOLD STROKE [89] 4-9-11 W Carson (2) *nvr far away, effrt and drvn alng o'r 2 fs out, not quicken ins last.* .... (10 to 1 op 8 to 1 tchd 12 to 1) 6
MAHOOL (USA) [80] 4-9-2 W R Swinburn (10) *led till o'r one furlong out, fdd und pres.........* (20 to 1 op 16 to 1) 7
402 SLIGHT RISK [60] (e/c) 4-7-10 G Bardwell (5) *wth ldrs, feeling pace and drvn alng 2 fs out, fdd.......* (33 to 1) 8
315* HIGH PREMIUM [87] 5-9-9 K Fallon (9) *tucked away on ins, effrt hfwy, losing grnd whn squeezed out appr fnl furlong, eased..........................*(6 to 1 op 4 to 1) 9
CONISTON WATER (USA) [83] 4-9-5 M Roberts (1) *patiently rdn, improved on outsd hfwy, ridden and btn 2 fs out.* ....(8 to 1 op 7 to 1 tchd 9 to 1) 10
Dist: 1½l, 1l, 1½l, nk, 3l, 6l, ¾l, 2l, ¾l. 2m 8.58s. a 5.88s (10 Ran).
SR: 54/27/39/32/38/47/26/4/27/ (Michael H Watt), G Lewis

514 Chris Blackwell Memorial Handicap Class C (0-95 3-y-o) £5,481 7f............. (4:40)

3703 TYCHONIC [69] 8-1 D Holland (9) *co'red up in midfield, drvn through appr fnl furlong, styd on wl to ld on line.* ....(11 to 4 fav op 5 to 2 tchd 3 to 1) 1
4009 MULLITOVER [83] 9-1 W Ryan (8) *sluggish strt, improved into midfield hfwy, led o'r one furlong out, ran on, jst ct.......................................* (10 to 1 tchd 12 to 1) 2
JERVIA [86] 9-4 M Roberts (12) *nvr far away, ev ch and drvn alng o'r one furlong out, kpt on same pace.* .... (11 to 1 op 8 to 1 tchd 12 to 1) 3
3975 GREEN'S FAIR (Ire) [69] 7-12² (5*) M Fenton (7) *sluggish strt, drvn alng to keep up hfwy, styd on wl fnl furlong, nvr nrr...............................*(14 to 1 tchd 16 to 1) 4

GROVE DAFFODIL (Ire) [74] 8-6 P Robinson (13) *wth ldr, ev ch and drvn alng appr fnl furlong, kpt on same pace.* .... (9 to 1 op 8 to 1 tchd 10 to 1) 5
346* EMBANKMENT (Ire) [89] 9-7 J Reid (2) *chsd ldrs, effrt und pres last 2 fs, kpt on one pace......* (7 to 1 tchd 6 to 1) 6
MY PATRIARCH [83] 9-1 T Quinn (6) *sluggish strt, improved into midfield hfwy, styd on fnl furlong, nrst finish.............................*(12 to 1 op 10 to 1) 7
DALALAH [77] 8-9 R Hills (5) *chsd ldrs for o'r 5 fs.* .... (12 to 1 op 10 to 1 tchd 14 to 1) 8
FORMAL AFFAIR [80] 8-12 D Biggs (4) *frnt rnk 5 fs.* .... (16 to 1 op 10 to 1 tchd 20 to 1) 9
334 RUSTY REEL [62] 7-8 J Penza (10) *wth ldrs 5 fs, wknd quickly...*(33 to 1) 10
352* SEHAILAH [85] 9-3 L Piggott (11) *led till hdd and wknd o'r one furlong out........* (15 to 2 op 7 to 1 tchd 8 to 1) 11
TAJDIF (USA) [82] 9-0 W Carson (3) *speed 5 fs, eased whn btn....................* (15 to 2 op 6 to 1 tchd 8 to 1) 12
IRISH DOMINION [80] 8-12 Pat Eddery (1) *rcd wide, chsd ldrs 5 fs...............*(11 to 1 op 8 to 1 tchd 12 to 1) 13
Dist: Sht-hd, 2l, 1½l, sht-hd, ½l, 5l, ¾l, 2½l, 2½l, ½l. 1m 27.21s. a 3.71s (13 Ran).
SR: 42/55/52/30/34/47/26/18/13/ (K Abdulla), B W Hills

515 Museum Maiden Stakes Class D (3-y-o) £3,752 1¼m...................... (5:10)

COMMANDER IN CHIEF 9-0 Pat Eddery (7) *wth ldr, led o'r 3 fs out, quickened clr fnl furlong, imprsv.* ....(Evens fav op 5 to 4 tchd 11 to 10 on) 1
SILVERDALE (USA) 9-0 M Roberts (3) *settled midfield, improved to chase wnr last 2 fs, ran on, prmsg.* .... (5 to 1 op 5 to 2 tchd 11 to 2) 2
SPIN DOCTOR (Ire) 9-0 R Cochrane (1) *steadied strt, improved into midfield hfwy, steady hdwy fnl furlong, improve...............*(9 to 1 op 6 to 1 tchd 10 to 1) 3
ARKAAN (USA) 9-0 W R Swinburn (6) *trkd ldg quartet, effrt and shaken up last 2 fs, styd on same pace.* ....(7 to 1 op 5 to 1 tchd 8 to 1) 4
WARSPITE 9-0 P Robinson (8) *wth ldrs, chsd alng appr fnl furlong, one pace.* .... (33 to 1 op 20 to 1 tchd 50 to 1) 5
FIRM BUT FAIR 8-11 (3*) J Weaver (9) *settled off the pace, hdwy last 2 fs, ran on, prmsg.* .... (33 to 1 op 20 to 1 tchd 50 to 1) 6
LEAR KING (USA) 9-0 T Quinn (10) *co'red up on ins, shaken up over 2 fs out, nvr plcd to chal.* .... (14 to 1 op 10 to 1 tchd 16 to 1) 7
LATHERON (Ire) 9-0 R Hills (4) *trkd ldg 5, chsd alng last 2 fs, no imprsn......*(10 to 1 op 8 to 1 tchd 14 to 1) 8
PALACE OF GOLD 9-0 D Biggs (12) *sluggish strt, bustled alng hfwy, nvr able to chal........*(33 to 1 op 20 to 1) 9
RIBBOLD 9-0 L Dettori (13) *led till o'r 3 fs out, fdd appr last.................*(16 to 1 op 12 to 1 tchd 20 to 1) 10
304⁹ HONEY GUIDE 9-0 W Woods (5) *chsd ldrs, wknd last 2 fs.* ....(33 to 1 op 20 to 1 tchd 50 to 1) 11
LIVONIAN 9-0 W Carson (2) *pressed ldg pair till fdd last 2 fs...* (12 to 1 tchd 14 to 1) 12
RAVENSPUR (Ire) 9-0 W Ryan (11) *swshd tail and drvn alng aftr 2 fs, nvr a threat.........*(33 to 1 op 20 to 1) 13
Dist: 6l, ½l, 1½l, ½l, ½l, 6l, 2l, 3½l, 15l, 7l. 2m 7.65s. a 4.95s (13 Ran).
SR: 61/49/48/45/44/43/31/27/20/ (K Abdulla), H R A Cecil

WARWICK (soft)
Tuesday April 13th
Going Correction: PLUS 0.70 sec. per fur. (races 1,3,4,5,6,7), PLUS 0.60 (2)

516 Warwick Castle Maiden Fillies Stakes Class D (Div I) (3-y-o and up) £3,435 1m ....(1:50)

MIDNIGHT HEIGHTS 3-8-8 A McGlone (6) *al in tch, led 2 fs out, drvn out..........* (13 to 2 op 5 to 1 tchd 7 to 1) 1
RED COTTON 3-8-8 Paul Eddery (11) *led 1st 2 fs, settled in beh ldrs, chlgd and ev ch ins fnl two furlongs, no extr nr finish...............................* (4 to 1 op 2 to 1) 2
ON GOLDEN POND (Ire) 3-8-8 A Munro (13) *mid-div, styd on fnl 2 fs, nvr nrr.....* (11 to 2 op 8 to 1 tchd 5 to 1) 3
LOVE IN THE MIST (USA) 3-8-8 M Hills (8) *chsd ldrs, one pace fnl 2 fs.* .... (9 to 4 fav op 6 to 4 tchd 5 to 2 and 11 to 4) 4
CHERHILL (Ire) 3-8-3 (5*) Stephen Davies (4) *al prmnt, led briefly o'r 2 fs out, wknd appr last...* (8 to 1 op 6 to 1) 5
CHOUETTE 3-8-1 (7*) D McCabe (5) *drpd out in rear, made some late hdwy.....................* (25 to 1 op 14 to 1) 6
KATIE EILEEN (USA) 3-8-8 A Clark (7) *wl beind till some late prog............*(18 to 1 op 20 to 1 tchd 33 to 1) 7
TINA'S ANGEL 6-9-10 J Comber (9) *al towards rear, nvr on terms........................* (100 to 1 op 33 to 1) 8
4740a⁸ WHYALLA RAIN 3-8-1 (7*) J Dennis (12) *mid-div, wknd 2 fs out...............................* (66 to 1 op 33 to 1) 9
352⁹ ASTERN (USA) 3-8-8 G Hind (10) *broke wl, led aftr 2 fs, hdd o'r two out, wknd quickly....* (14 to 1 op 10 to 1) 10
161 RUBY VISION (Ire) 4-9-10 N Adams (2) *dsptd ld to hfwy, sn beh...............................*(100 to 1 op 33 to 1) 11
GAMEFULL GOLD 4-9-5 (5*) D Meredith (3) *mid-div, outpcd frm hfwy.........................* (50 to 1 op 25 to 1) 12
Dist: 2l, 4l, 1½l, ¾l, 1½l, 2l, 2l, 10l, 4l, 1½l. 1m 46.60s. a 9.80s (12 Ran).
SR: 31/25/13/8/6/1/-/5/-/ (Ettore Landi), J L Dunlop

517 Hatton Country World Maiden Auction Stakes Class F (2-y-o) £2,070 5f..... (2:20)

343² CULSYTH FLYER 9-0 M Hills (10) *al prmnt on outsd, led jst ins fnl furlong, ran on wl........*(9 to 4 fav op 7 to 4) 1
CHICKAWICKA (Ire) 9-0 S Whitworth (5) *al prmnt, ev ch entering fnl furlong, ran on.* ....(10 to 1 op 14 to 1 tchd 16 to 1) 2
374³ MR BLOBBY (Ire) 9-0 G Carter (4) *mid-div, ran on wl ins fnl 2 fs, nvr nrr.......................*(6 to 1 op 5 to 1) 3
OBVIOUS RISK 9-0 Paul Eddery (6) *mid-div, rdn and ran on strly ins fnl furlong.* (5 to 2 op 2 to 1 tchd 11 to 4) 4
SWEET DECISION (Ire) 8-9 N Adams (2) *slwly away, led aftr one furlong, hdd jst ins last, kpt on one pace.* ....(33 to 1 op 20 to 1) 5
CRAFTY CRICKETER 9-0 S Dawson (1) *led 1st furlong, rdn o'r one out, one pace..............*(33 to 1 op 20 to 1) 6
SHEILOBLIGE 8-9 B Rouse (3) *mid-div, nvr got into race.* .... (10 to 1 op 8 to 1) 7
PRIMOST 9-0 A McGlone (9) *outpcd thrght.* .... (25 to 1 op 20 to 1) 8
MALLAM WATERS (Ire) 8-9 A Munro (11) *speed to hfwy.* .... (6 to 1 op 4 to 1 tchd 13 to 2) 9
CLUBS ARE TRUMPS (Ire) 9-0 C Rutter (7) *slwly away, al beh...............................*(33 to 1 op 20 to 1) 10
COURT SERENADE 8-9 J Comber (8) *in tch early, beh frm hfwy...............................* (33 to 1 op 20 to 1) 11
Dist: ¾l, nk, ¾l, sht-hd, 4l, ½l, 1l, ½l, 1l, 5l. 1m 5.20s. a 7.00s (11 Ran).
SR: 20/17/16/13/7/-/ (W Cully), R Hollinshead

518 Motor Heritage Trust Claiming Stakes Class G (3-y-o) £2,070 6f............(2:50)

TRENTESIMO (Ire) 9-3 G Carter (5) *made all, drw clr appr fnl furlong, unchlgd..........*(6 to 4 fav tchd 13 to 8) 1
DOCTOR-J (Ire) 8-6 (7*) D Wright (6) *outpcd and sn drvn alng, hdwy on outsd o'r 2 fs out, ran on to go second ins last...*(4 to 1) 2
151* ALWAYS BAILEYS 8-8 R P Elliott (3) *chsd wnr till wknd fnl furlong...............................*(7 to 4 tchd 2 to 1) 3
BECKY BOO 8-0² R Price (7) *al outpcd.........* (33 to 1) 4
SHARP IMP 8-10 B Rouse (8) *sn rdn, wnt 3rd hfwy, wknd wl o'r one furlong out.........................* (12 to 1) 5
Dist: 3l, 3l, 4l, 3½l. 1m 19.70s. a 8.00s (5 Ran).
SR: 27/11/ (B R Allen), J Berry

519 Coventry Citizen Rating Related Maiden Stakes Class E (0-70 3-y-o) £3,076 7f (3:20)

KNYAZ 9-0 N Carlisle (6) *al prmnt, rdn and ran on wl to ld well ins fnl furlong...............*(33 to 1 op 25 to 1) 1
328⁴ WATERLORD (Ire) 8-7 (7*) D Wright (2) *led, rdn entering fnl furlong, hdd wl ins.....*(4 to 1 tchd 9 to 2 and 7 to 2) 2
357⁵ GROGFRYN 8-9 G Carter (7) *chsd ldr till one pace ins fnl furlong...................................*(7 to 1 tchd 8 to 1) 3
FITZROY LAD 9-0 C Rutter (1) *al prmnt, one pace appr fnl furlong...*(20 to 1) 4
AGENDA ONE 8-9 Dale Gibson (5) *mid-div, kpt on one pace fnl 2 fs........................*(20 to 1 op 16 to 1) 5
334 BEAT THE BAGMAN (Ire) 9-0 C Avery (4) *mid-div, nvr nr to chal..........* (16 to 1 op 20 to 1 tchd 25 to 1) 6
417⁶ AL MOULOUKI 9-0 W Hood (10) *in rear, styd on ins fnl 2 fs...................................*(14 to 1 op 6 to 1) 7
INFANTRY GLEN 9-0 N Adams (11) *chsd ldrs till wknd o'r 2 fs out......................* (33 to 1 op 25 to 1) 8
248⁸ VADDALLIAN 9-0 Paul Eddery (9) *mid-div, no hdwy fnl 2 fs...* (33 to 1) 9
LADY RELKO 8-9 S Dawson (13) *mid-div till wknd o'r 2 fs out.................* (10 to 1 op 8 to 1 tchd 11 to 1) 10
SOPHISTICATED AIR 8-9 M Hills (3) *very slwly away, nvr got into race.......* (13 to 8 fav op 5 to 4 tchd 7 to 4) 11
INONDER 8-9 B Rouse (12) *al beh...............*(33 to 1) 12
237⁶ UNIVERSAL (Fr) 8-9 N Day (8) *in tch to hfwy.* .... (50 to 1 op 33 to 1) 13
Dist: 1½l, 2l, 6l, nk, hd, sht-hd, 3½l, 5l, nk, 3½l. 1m 33.50s. a 9.70s (13 Ran).
SR: 28/23/12/-/-/-/ (Terence M Molossi), L G Cottrell

520 Philip Gomm Final Fling England's Historic Heartland Handicap Class D (0-80 4-y-o and up) £3,494 1½m 115yds... (3:50)

290⁹ BROUGHTON'S TANGO (Ire) [51] 4-7-7 (7*) D McCabe (8) *hld up in mid-div, hdwy 3 fs out, led one and a half out, quickened clr.......................* (12 to 1 op 8 to 1) 1
ROSGILL [66] 7-8-10 (7*) S Mulvey (1) *hld up, hdwy 5 fs out, rdn o'r 2 out, styd on to go second ins last.* ....(6 to 1 op 4 to 1) 2
287³ QUALITAIR RHYTHM (Ire) [60] (v) 5-8-11 Dale Gibson (6) *al in tch, rdn 2 fs out, kpt on one pace....* (6 to 1 op 8 to 1) 3

MONARDA [66] 6-9-3 A Munro (2) *al prmnt, wnt second o'r 2 fs out, outpcd appr fnl furlong*.....(8 to 1 op 4 to 1) 4
STORM DUST [65] 4-9-0 G Carter (9) *chsd ldrs, hdwy to hold ev ch 2 fs out, kpt on one pace*..(5 to 1 op 4 to 1) 5
JIMLIL [77] 5-9-9 (5*) Stephen Davies (7) *al mid-div, styd on one pace fnl 2 fs*.....................(16 to 1 op 14 to 1) 6
416 STRIKING IMAGE (Ire) [59] 4-8-8 B Rouse (10) *led till hdd one and a half fs out, sn btn*...... (20 to 1 op 16 to 1) 7
MAHRAJAN [56] 9-8-7 M Hills (13) *wtd wth, effrt on outsd o'r 2 fs out, nvr dngrs*. ....(14 to 1 op 12 to 1 tchd 16 to 1) 8
MAJOR BUGLER (Ire) [75] 4-9-10 C Rutter (3) *hld up, rdn 2 fs out, nvr dngrs*...........................(9 to 2 fav op 4 to 1) 9
EASTERN MAGIC [51] 5-8-2[1] Paul Eddery (12) *chsd ldrs till wknd o'r 2 fs out*................................... (14 to 1) 10
331 HYMN BOOK (Ire) [58] (bl) 4-8-2 (5*) C Hodgson (11) *chsd ldr till wknd quickly o'r 2 fs out*...... (50 to 1 op 33 to 1) 11
EIGHTANDAHALF (Ire) [70] 4-9-5 A Clark (4) *al struggling in rear*..................................(25 to 1 op 16 to 1) 12
ALQAIRAWAAN [70] 4-9-5 A McGlone (5) *al beh*. .... (14 to 1 op 8 to 1) 13

Dist: 5l, 1½l, 2l, nk, 4l, 1½l, hd, hd, ½l, 10l. 2m 52.30s. a 14.40s (13 Ran).
SR: 30/37/28/30/26/32/9/7/23/ (S P Lansdown), M J Heaton-Ellis

521 N.A.C. Events And Exhibitions Handicap Class E (0-70 3-y-o and up) £3,675 7f (4:20)

HOMEMAKER [56] 3-8-0 C Rutter (5) *chsd ldrs, rdn to ld jst ins fnl furlong, drvn out*. ....(14 to 1 op 10 to 1 tchd 16 to 1) 1
MAINLY ME [56] 4-9-1 M Tebbutt (19) *hld up in mid-div, str brst ins fnl furlong, jst fld*.........(33 to 1 op 14 to 1) 2
391[3] ON Y VA (USA) [56] 6-9-1 M Hills (6) *nvr far away, chlgd and ev ch entering fnl furlong, one pace ins*. ....(9 to 2 fav op 5 to 1 tchd 7 to 1) 3
OLD COMRADES [55] 6-9-0 A Munro (7) *al prmnt, led 3 fs out, rdn and hdd jst ins last, kpt on gmely*. ....(8 to 1 op 6 to 1) 4
332[9] PRINCE ROONEY (Ire) [50] 5-8-2 (7*) S Drowne (17) *alway prmnt, one pace appr fnl furlong*. ....(12 to 1 tchd 20 to 1) 5
CHANDIGARH [53] 5-8-12 Dale Gibson (9) *nvr far away, ev ch 2 fs out, one pace ins last*.......(33 to 1 op 14 to 1) 6
328[6] RACING TELEGRAPH [70] 3-9-0 M Wigham (10) *mid-div, ran on one pace ins fnl 2 fs*.........(12 to 1 op 8 to 1) 7
JUST A STEP [65] 7-9-3 (7*) Gina Faulkner (18) *al abt same pl*..(20 to 1 op 10 to 1) 8
330 SPECTACLE JIM [48] 4-8-7 N Day (3) *chsd ldrs till outpcd ins fnl 2 fs*......................(33 to 1 tchd 50 to 1) 9
330[8] RED SOMBRERO [48] 4-8-7 A Clark (16) *nvr on terms*. ....(20 to 1 tchd 25 to 1) 10
4760a[3] LADY LACEY [49] 6-8-8 R Price (14) *in rear, nvr nr to chal*. ....(20 to 1 op 16 to 1 tchd 25 to 1) 11
375[7] WINGED WHISPER (USA) [47] (bl) 4-8-1 (5*) A Garth (2) *slwly away, sn in tch, wknd o'r 2 fs out*. ....(33 to 1 tchd 40 to 1) 12
319[5] ZINBAQ [39] 7-7-12 A McGlone (12) *mid-div, no hdwy fnl 3 fs*..........................(8 to 1 op 6 to 1 tchd 9 to 1) 13
350 GONE BUST (Ire) [40] 4-7-10 (3*) A Tucker (13) *nvr on terms*. ....(25 to 1) 14
COURT MINSTREL [59] 4-9-4 C Avery (1) *slwly away, nvr got into race*.......................(33 to 1 op 14 to 1) 15
KISMETIM [60] 3-8-4 R Perham (15) *al beh*. ....(25 to 1 op 16 to 1) 16
FLYING WIND [49] 4-8-8 B Rouse (11) *al beh*. ....(33 to 1 op 20 to 1) 17
403[9] HAWAII STORM (Fr) [51] 5-8-10 N Adams (4) *made most till hdd 3 fs out, wknd rpdly*. ....(20 to 1 op 14 to 1 tchd 25 to 1) 18
320[2] RESPECTABLE JONES [68] 7-9-8 (5*) S Wynne (20) *speed on outsd to hfwy, sn beh*.............(14 to 1 op 10 to 1) 19
MERLS PEARL [38] 4-7-11 S Dawson (8) *al beh*. ....(25 to 1 op 20 to 1) 20

Dist: ½l, 1½l, sht-hd, 1½l, ½l, ¾l, ¾l, 2l, 2½l, ½l. 1m 33.00s. a 9.20s (20 Ran).
SR: 22/35/30/28/18/19/19/27/4/ (Racecourse Farm Racing), P G Murphy

522 Warwick Castle Maiden Fillies Stakes Class D (Div II) (3-y-o and up) £3,406 1m ....(4:50)

ANDROMAQUE (USA) 3-8-8 T Sprake (2) *trkd ldr, led hfwy, quickened clr wl o'r one out, eased ins*. ....(2 to 1 fav op 5 to 4 tchd 9 to 4) 1
SHOPTILLYOUDROP 3-8-8 B Rouse (3) *al prmnt, rdn o'r 2 fs out, styd on to go second fnl furlong*. ....(33 to 1 op 20 to 1) 2
MISS KINABALU 3-8-8 M Hills (6) *led to hfwy, outpcd fnl 2 fs*..........................(5 to 1 op 8 to 1 tchd 9 to 2) 3
WILLOW RIVER (Can) 3-8-8 G Hind (8) *beh till hdwy 3 fs out, not pace to chal*...............(12 to 1 op 5 to 1) 4
NATCHEZ TRACE 4-9-10 S O'Gorman (11) *beh till gd hdwy o'r 3 fs out, one pace fnl 2*.......(25 to 1 op 14 to 1) 5
FAIRFIELDS CONE 10-9-3 (7*) Michelle Thomas (1) *in rear till hdwy 3 fs out, styd on one pace*. ....(50 to 1 op 33 to 1) 6
WHAT LOLA WANTS (Ire) 3-8-8 A Dicks (12) *al towards rear*...............................(20 to 1 tchd 25 to 1) 7
385[3] SUNRISE MORNING (USA) 3-8-3 (5*) Stephen Davies (10) *chsd ldrs, rdn o'r 2 fs out, wknd over one out*. ....(4 to 1 op 3 to 1 tchd 9 to 2) 8
LAURA 4-9-10 N Carlisle (7) *slwly away, sn prmnt, rdn and wknd 3 fs out*.......(5 to 1 op 6 to 1 tchd 7 to 1) 9
LADY GAIL 3-8-8 C Rutter (9) *in tch to hfwy, tld off*. ....(14 to 1 tchd 16 to 1) 10
NATIVE NOBLE 3-8-8 G Carter (5) *nvr on terms, tld off*. ....(33 to 1 op 20 to 1) 11
LEGAL RISK 3-8-8 Dale Gibson (13) *prmnt to hfwy, tld off*. ....(33 to 1 op 20 to 1) 12

Dist: 7l, ½l, 1½l, 2l, 1l, ½l, 4l, sht-hd, 25l, 6l. 1m 47.40s. a 10.60s (12 Ran).
SR: 19/-/-/-/1/-/ (Dr Carlos E Stelling), R Charlton

NEWMARKET (good)
Wednesday April 14th
Going Correction: NIL

523 Geoffrey Barling Maiden Fillies Stakes Class D (3-y-o) £3,752 7f...........(2:00)

STELLA MYSTIKA (USA) 8-11 M Roberts (1) *patiently rdn, not clr run o'r 2 fs out, quickened to ld appr last, ran on wl*.........................(6 to 4 on op 6 to 4 on) 1
SEASONAL SPLENDOUR (Ire) 8-11 D Biggs (10) *wtd wth, improved on outsd hfwy, lost action and wnt lft 2 fs out, rallied, not quicken last 50 yards*. ....(16 to 1 op 10 to 1 tchd 20 to 1) 2
ANEESATI 8-11 W R Swinburn (9) *patiently rdn, swtchd rght to improve o'r 2 fs out, hmpd over one out, ev ch entering last, kpt on same pace*......(7 to 1 op 3 to 1) 3
DANCING SPIRIT (Ire) 8-11 J Reid (6) *nvr far away, ev ch and drvn alng last 2 fs, kpt on same pace*. ....(25 to 1 op 10 to 1 tchd 33 to 1) 4
DITTISHAM (USA) 8-11 T Quinn (3) *led, hrd drvn o'r 2 fs out, hdd appr last, sn btn*......... (25 to 1 op 12 to 1) 5
ALLIGRAM (USA) 8-11 Pat Eddery (7) *wth ldr, feeling pace and drvn alng o'r 2 fs out, fdd*. ....(10 to 1 op 5 to 1 tchd 11 to 1) 6
352[8] SAKURA QUEEN (Ire) 8-11 W Woods (5) *chsd ldrs, drvn alng whn hmpd 2 fs out, no imprsn*. ....(66 to 1 op 33 to 1) 7
SUMMER FLOWER 8-11 M Hills (4) *sluggish strt, chsd alng and no imprsn whn hmpd 2 fs out*. ....(16 to 1 op 10 to 1 tchd 20 to 1) 8
CORAL GEM 8-11 R Hills (2) *unruly strt, slwly away, no imprsn whn hmpd 2 fs out*........(33 to 1 op 14 to 1) 9
SWORD SAIL 8-11 L Piggott (8) *rcd wide, chasing ldrs whn hmpd 2 fs out, eased when btn*. ....(10 to 1 op 7 to 1 tchd 12 to 1) 10

Dist: 2½l, 1l, 2½l, sht-hd, 2½l, 4l, 3½l, ½l, hd. 1m 27.14s. a 3.64s (10 Ran).
SR: 42/34/31/23/22/14/2/-/-/ (Sheikh Mohammed), L M Cumani

524 Swaffham Rated Class B (0-105 4-y-o and up) £7,438 7f.......................(2:35)

315[3] WILL OF STEEL [85] 4-8-7 K Fallon (3) *tucked away on ins, drvn through fnl furlong, ran on wl to ld last 50 yards*. ....(13 to 2 op 9 to 2 tchd 7 to 1) 1
LITTLE BEAN [96] 4-9-4 M Hills (6) *trkd ldg trio, led appr fnl furlong, hdd and not quicken last 50 yards*. ....(11 to 10 fav op 11 to 8) 2
HERORA (Ire) [87] 4-8-9 W Carson (1) *nvr far away, drw level appr fnl furlong, rdn and not quicken nr finish*. ....(15 to 2 op 6 to 1 tchd 8 to 1) 3
EURO FESTIVAL [93] 4-9-1 Pat Eddery (7) *last and hld up, swtchd outsd and effrt last 2 fs, styd on*. ....(11 to 2 op 7 to 1 tchd 5 to 1) 4
315[6] BEWARE OF AGENTS [88] 4-8-10 Dean McKeown (5) *dsptd ld, led hfwy till appr fnl furlong, one pace*. ....(11 to 2 op 4 to 1 tchd 6 to 1) 5
GILT THRONE [99] 6-9-7 P Robinson (4) *narrow ld to hfwy, fdd und pres last 2 fs*. (16 to 1 op 12 to 1 tchd 20 to 1) 6

Dist: 2l, ½l, 1½l, ½l, 15l. 1m 26.05s. a 2.55s (6 Ran).
SR: 55/60/49/50/43/9/ (K E Wheldon), Mrs J R Ramsden

525 Earl Of Sefton EBF Stakes Class A (Group 3) (4-y-o and up) £21,804 1m 1f......(3:05)

EZZOUD (Ire) (v) 4-8-10 W R Swinburn (9) *settled gng wl, led 2 fs out, crrd head high fnl furlong, pushed out*. ....(5 to 1 op 3 to 1 tchd 11 to 2) 1
CLOUD OF DUST 4-8-10 T Quinn (13) *trkd ldrs, drvn to chal entering fnl furlong, ran on one pace ins last*. ....(11 to 1 op 8 to 1 tchd 12 to 1) 2
LORD OF THE FIELD 6-8-13 G Duffield (12) *patiently rdn, drvn to improve on outsd fnl 2 fs, ran on wl*... (33 to 1) 3
LUCKY LINDY (Ire) (bl) 4-9-1 Pat Eddery (3) *nvr far away, ev ch and drvn alng appr fnl furlong, styd on same pace*.......(6 to 1 op 5 to 1 tchd 7 to 1) 4
TIK FA (USA) (v) 4-8-10 B Raymond (11) *tucked away in midfield, effrt and bustled alng o'r 2 fs out, styd on same pace*.......... (20 to 1 op 14 to 1 tchd 25 to 1) 5
IRISH MEMORY 4-8-13 C Roche (8) *jinked lft strt, reco'red to chase ldrs, not quicken last 2 fs*.. (9 to 1 op 12 to 1) 6

ARMARAMA 4-8-12 A Munro (7) *co'red up in midfield, effrt and drvn alng over 2 fs out, no imprsn.* ....(16 to 1 op 12 to 1 tchd 20 to 1) 7
SHUAILAAN (USA) 4-8-10 M Roberts (1) *al hndy, led o'r 3 fs out to 2 out, fdd.* (11 to 4 fav op 3 to 1 tchd 5 to 2) 8
426² BREAK BREAD (USA) 4-8-13 J Reid (2) *in tch, chsd alng stands side hfwy, no imprsn last 2 fs.* ....(8 to 1 op 7 to 1 tchd 10 to 1) 9
390⁴ SOIREE (Ire) 4-8-7 W Carson (6) *settled midfield, hrd drvn o'r 3 fs out, eased whn btn 2 out...* (14 to 1 op 12 to 1) 10
YOUNG SENOR (USA) 4-8-10 M Hills (4) *reluctant to enter stalls, in tch, effrt and chsd alng hfwy, nvr nr to chal.* ....(7 to 1 op 5 to 1 tchd 8 to 1) 11
KRISTIANSTAD 4-8-10 L Dettori (5) *settled off the pace, effrt hfwy, lost tch last 2 fs.....* (20 to 1 tchd 25 to 1) 12
PERFAY (USA) 5-8-10 R Hills (10) *led till o'r 3 fs out, fdd und pres over 2 out.............* (50 to 1 tchd 66 to 1) 13
Dist: 1½l, nk, ¾l, 3l, nk, hd, hd, 5l, 1½l, 7l. 1m 51.42s. a 1.72s (13 Ran).
SR: 71/66/68/68/54/56/54/51/39/ (Maktoum Al Maktoum), M R Stoute

526 European Free Handicap Class A (Listed Race) (3-y-o) £18,034 7f. ....(3:40)

SO FACTUAL (USA) [112] 9-6 Pat Eddery (7) *nvr far away, led wl o'r one furlong out, quickened ins last, ran on strly.*..........................(8 to 1 tchd 10 to 1) 1
REVELATION (Ire) [106] 9-0 J Reid (2) *al frnt rnk, led briefly hfwy, veered rght o'r one furlong out, ran on strly nr finish.*..............................(3 to 1 jt-fav op 11 to 4 tchd 100 to 30) 2
SALATIN (USA) [108] 9-2 W Carson (6) *led, hdd briefly hfwy, bustled alng and headed wl o'r one furlong out, kpt on same pace.* ....(15 to 2 op 8 to 1 tchd 9 to 1 and 7 to 1) 3
SILVER WIZARD (USA) [112] 9-6 L Piggott (3) *settled beh ldrs, effrt and pushed alng hfwy, rdn and no imprsn appr fnl furlong......* (7 to 2 op 11 to 4 tchd 4 to 1) 4
DARBONNE (USA) [109] 9-3 T Quinn (5) *patiently rdn, shaken up to chal whn squeezed and snatched up o'r one furlong out, swtchd rght, styd on.* ....(20 to 1 op 16 to 1) 5
LOST SOLDIER (USA) [106] 9-0 M Roberts (1) *chsd ldrs, feeling pace and drvn alng o'r 2 fs out, nvr able to chal.* ....(12 to 1 op 8 to 1 tchd 14 to 1) 6
PETARDIA [113] 9-7 W R Swinburn (4) *al last, niggled alng to keep up hfwy, nvr a threat.* ....(3 to 1 jt-fav op 11 to 4 tchd 100 to 30) 7
Dist: ½l, 1½l, 1½l, nk, 5l, 1l. 1m 26.23s. a 2.73s (7 Ran).
SR: 65/57/54/53/49/31/35/ (K Abdulla), G Harwood

527 Ladbroke Racing Handicap Class C (0-90 4-y-o and up) £5,299 1½m.......... (4:10)

THINKING TWICE (USA) [62] 4-8-5 W Carson (11) *pld hrd, trkd ldg quartet, drvn to ld ins fnl furlong, kpt on wl.* ....(8 to 1 op 6 to 1) 1
384* NORTHERN GRADUATE (USA) [68] 4-8-11 K Darley (5) *patiently rdn, chsd alng to improve o'r 2 fs out, styd on und pres ins last.* (5 to 1 fav tchd 11 to 2 and 9 to 2) 2
MISS PIN UP [66] 4-8-9 D Biggs (12) *tucked away on ins, swtchd lft to improve o'r one furlong out, kpt on wl last 50 yards.*........................(16 to 1 tchd 100 to 1) 3
AMBIGUOUSLY REGAL (USA) [75] 4-9-4 G Duffield (1) *nvr far away, led wl o'r 3 fs out till ins last, rdn and no extr*.................(12 to 1 op 10 to 1 tchd 14 to 1) 4
290 LABURNUM [76] 5-9-4 (3*) J Weaver (7) *co'red up, swtchd ins to improve over 3 fs out, edgd lft and rght, nvr plcd to chal*...............................(8 to 1 op 7 to 1) 5
HELLO MY DARLING (Ire) [60] 5-8-5 T Quinn (13) *trkd ldg trio, bustled alng whn pace quickened last 2 fs, no extr.* ....(16 to 1 op 14 to 1 tchd 20 to 1) 6
DOM WAC [70] 5-9-1 M Hills (2) *wtd wth, improved into midfield o'r 3 fs out, rdn and no imprsn fnl furlong.* .... (8 to 1 tchd 7 to 1 and 9 to 1) 7
LYPHANTASTIC (USA) [85] 4-10-0 W R Swinburn (8) *patiently rdn, shaken up and undrd o'r 3 fs out, nvr rch ldrs..* (8 to 1 op 7 to 1 tchd 9 to 1) 8
365⁶ CHIEF MINISTER (Ire) [82] 4-9-11 K Fallon (4) *sluggish strt, beh till improved und pres o'r 2 fs out, nvr nrr.* ....(10 to 1 op 8 to 1) 9
349² ROUSITTO [71] 5-9-2 R Cochrane (3) *sluggish strt, chsd alng and in tch hfwy, no imprsn last 3 fs.* ....(8 to 1 op 6 to 1 tchd 10 to 1) 10
SOVEREIGN PAGE (USA) [69] 4-8-12 B Raymond (6) *trkd ldg 5, lost grnd o'r 2 fs out, sn btn.* ....(16 to 1 tchd 20 to 1) 11
FARMER'S PET [78] 4-9-7 L Dettori (10) *led till wl o'r 3 fs out, wknd quickly 2 out*..........(20 to 1 op 14 to 1) 12
ALCOY (Ire) [50] 4-7-7 J Quinn (9) *trkd ldr, bustled alng whn pace lifted o'r 2 fs out, sn btn.* (14 to 1 op 12 to 1) 13
Dist: ¾l, ¾l, 1½l, hd, 5l, hd, nk, 1½l, 1l, 12l. 2m 35.75s. a 6.15s (13 Ran).
SR: 30/34/30/36/38/12/21/33/27/ (Million In Mind Partnership (2)), N J Henderson

528 Bartlow Maiden Auction Fillies Stakes Class D (2-y-o) £3,622 5f............(4:45)

POMMES FRITES (Ire) 8-11 L Piggott (8) *made all, shaken up to quicken appr fnl furlong, ran on strly.* ....(5 to 4 fav op 6 to 4) 1
INDIAHRA 8-11 K Darley (5) *chsd ldg trio, kpt on strly ins fnl furlong, not rch wnr*...........(20 to 1 op 16 to 1) 2
NAKITA 8-4 (7*) G Forster (3) *sluggish strt, chsd alng to improve last 2 fs, styd on finish.* ....(11 to 2 op 6 to 1 tchd 5 to 1) 3
ACCESS ADVANTAGE 8-11 R Cochrane (9) *chsd ldg pair, drvn alng whn pace quickened o'r one furlong out, no extr*..............................(20 to 1 op 12 to 1) 4
CAPPUCHINO (Ire) 8-11 A Munro (4) *trkd ldg quartet, feeling pace and drvn alng last 2 fs, no imprsn.* ....(8 to 1 op 6 to 1 tchd 10 to 1) 5
HIPS'N HAWS (Ire) 8-11 M Hills (2) *chsd wnr for o'r 3 fs, rdn and no extr*........ (13 to 2 op 5 to 1 tchd 7 to 1) 6
399⁷ SWEET CAROLINE 8-11 J Reid (1) *pushed alng in midfield, nvr trble ldrs*..............(33 to 1 op 20 to 1) 7
QUEENS STROLLER (Ire) 8-11 W Carson (6) *sluggish strt, not reco'r*............(10 to 1 op 6 to 1 tchd 12 to 1) 8
MISS PARAMOUNT 8-11 M Roberts (11) *sluggish strt, chsd alng, nvr wnt pace....*(10 to 1 op 7 to 1 tchd 12 to 1) 9
SALT STONE (Ire) 8-11 P Robinson (7) *chsd alng in midfield hfwy, sn btn*................(33 to 1 op 20 to 1) 10
374² DUBALL REMY 8-11 Pat Eddery (10) *struggling aftr 2 fs, nvr dngrs*..........................(14 to 1 op 10 to 1) 11
Dist: 1½l, 5l, nk, 1½l, nk, nk, 1½l, 2½l, ¾l, 6l. 1m 1.09s. a 2.49s (11 Ran).
SR: 47/41/21/20/14/13/12/6/-/ (Lord Carnarvon), R Hannon

529 Wood Ditton Stakes Class D (3-y-o) £6,316 1m................................(5:15)

FLUVIAL (Ire) 9-0 Pat Eddery (8) *made most till ins fnl furlong, rallied gmely to ld on line*............(6 to 1) 1
MT TEMPLEMAN (USA) 9-0 L Dettori (3) *beh and chsd alng hfwy, gd hdwy o'r 2 fs out, led ins fnl furlong, jst ct.* ....(10 to 1) 2
KARSHI 9-0 G Duffield (9) *patiently rdn, steady hdwy last 2 fs, ran on, prmsg*...............................(16 to 1) 3
MECKLENBURG (Ire) 9-0 M Roberts (6) *tucked away in midfield, effrt and drvn alng o'r 2 fs out, rallied, eased whn btn last 50 yards*......................(5 to 2 fav) 4
SHARAAR (USA) 9-0 N Day (18) *nvr far away, ev ch entering fnl furlong, kpt on, improve*..............(20 to 1) 5
BARRATRY 9-0 A McGlone (14) *speed in frnt rnk till rdn and no extr fnl furlong*........................(7 to 1) 6
TEJ SINGH (USA) 9-0 R Cochrane (16) *nvr far away, effrt and drvn alng last 2 fs, kpt on same pace nr finish.* ....(8 to 1) 7
MUTAMANNI 9-0 W Carson (19) *chsd ldrs, effrt and drvn alng hfwy, styd on, nvr able to chal*...........(8 to 1) 8
FABULOUS MTOTO 9-0 T Quinn (13) *chsd ldrs, feeling pace and drvn alng hfwy, no imprsn last 2 fs*...(8 to 1) 9
HADDAAJ (Ire) 9-0 B Raymond (5) *speed for o'r 4 fs, fdd 2 out*..(20 to 1) 10
MAASHAI LAWM (Ire) 9-0 P Robinson (15) *chsd alng in midfield hfwy, not pace to chal*..............(20 to 1) 11
PREMIATA (Ire) 8-9 J Lowe (10) *sluggish strt, improved into midfield hfwy, nvr plcd to chal*...........(5 to 1) 12
CURTELACE 9-0 J Reid (4) *trkd ldrs, drw level o'r 3 fs out, fdd appr last*...................................(12 to 1) 13
TILTY (USA) 9-0 R Perham (11) *sluggish strt, nvr able to reco'r*.......................................(20 to 1) 14
ELEGANT HUSSAR 9-0 J Penza (12) *struggling to go pace hfwy, nvr a factor*..............................(20 to 1) 15
AJDAYT (USA) 9-0 L Piggott (17) *chsd ldrs 5 fs, eased whn btn*...(14 to 1) 16
LIWAN (USA) 9-0 R Hills (2) *tracking ldr whn broke leg and pld up o'r 2 fs out, destroyed*.............(6 to 1) pu
Dist: Sht-hd, 3l, sht-hd, hd, 1½l, sht-hd, 1l, ½l, 2l, nk. 1m 41.04s. a 3.84s (17 Ran).
SR: 42/41/32/31/30/25/24/21/19/ (K Abdulla), J H M Gosden

PONTEFRACT (soft)
Wednesday April 14th
Going Correction: PLUS 0.40 sec. per fur.

530 Strawberry Hill Handicap Class E (0-70 3-y-o and up) £3,262 1¼m 6yds..... (2:45)

349 SWEET REVIVAL [35] 5-8-3 J Fortune (2) *in tch, effrt 3 out, chlgd o'r one out, kpt on und pres to ld ins fnl furlong.* ....(16 to 1 op 14 to 1) 1
331 ANAR (Ire) [45] 4-8-8 (5*) O Pears (1) *led till hdd ins fnl furlong, kpt on*..............................(14 to 1) 2
456* SUPERTOP [58] 5-9-12 (5ex) Paul Eddery (5) *in tch, styd on und pres fnl 2 fs*...............(7 to 1 op 6 to 1) 3
425⁹ FALCONS DAWN [54] (bl) 6-9-5 (3*) A Tucker (6) *pld hrd early, prmnt, ev ch 2 out, one pace.* ....(9 to 1 op 8 to 1 tchd 10 to 1) 4
EVERSO IRISH [43] 4-8-11 D Holland (4) *chsd ldrs, kpt on same pace fnl 3 fs*................ (14 to 1 op 12 to 1) 5
TIGER SHOOT [48] 6-9-2 A Shoults (11) *in tch, styd on fnl 2 fs, nvr dngrs*........(11 to 1 op 10 to 1 tchd 12 to 1) 6
366⁵ PRIDE OF PENDLE [43] 4-8-11 W Newnes (3) *prmnt till wknd 2 out*....................... (20 to 1 op 16 to 1) 7

437* DUVEEN (Ire) [57] 3-8-1 (5*,5ex) M Fenton (10) *prmnt till wknd o'r 2 fs out*... (5 to 2 fav op 9 to 4 tchd 11 to 4) 8
327⁹ ALLIMAC NOMIS [39] 4-8-0 (7*) G Mitchell (7) *nvr nr to chal*...(20 to 1) 9
396* RED INDIAN [42] 7-8-10 J Fanning (15) *hld up, effrt 3 out, sn btn*...(13 to 2 op 6 to 1) 10
ESSAYEFFSEE [49] 4-8-10 (7*) Darren Moffatt (18) *prmnt till wknd 3 fs out*... (13 to 2 op 8 to 1) 11
BEAUMOOD [39] 7-8-2 (5*) Stephen Davies (16) *sn chasing ldrs, wknd o'r 2 fs out*... (33 to 1) 12
302 LEAP IN THE DARK (Ire) [59] 4-9-13 W Ryan (8) *chsd ldrs till wknd o'r 2 fs out*...(33 to 1 op 25 to 1) 13
SPRAY OF ORCHIDS [51] 4-9-5 T Lucas (12) *sn beh*. ...(16 to 1 tchd 20 to 1) 14
375⁹ ALICANTE [35] 6-7-10 (7*) D McCabe (9) *sn beh*... (33 to 1) 15
294 REZA [33] 5-7-12 (3*) F Norton (14) *sn beh*... (33 to 1) 16
NEGATORY (USA) [51] 6-9-5 V Smith (13) *dwlt, al beh, tld off*... (33 to 1) 17

Dist: ¾l, 5l, 1½l, 1½l, hd, 1½l, 3½l, 4l, 3l, 6l. 2m 18.70s. a 10.50s (17 Ran).
SR: 24/32/35/28/14/18/10/-/-/ (C S Tateson), J A Glover

531 Ossett Selling Stakes Class G (3-y-o and up) £2,721 1m 4yds...(3:15)

ROMOLA NIJINSKY 5-8-11 D Holland (13) *cl up, led wl o'r 2 out, clr over one out, easily*... (16 to 1 op 14 to 1) 1
284⁷ FUTURE FAME (USA) 4-8-13 (3*) D Harrison (14) *in tch, effrt 3 out, chsd wnr frm o'r one out, kpt on, no imprsn*. ...(14 to 1) 2
78⁷ HOT PUNCH 4-9-2 W Newnes (15) *mid-div, pushed alng hfwy, styd on wl frm 2 out*...(20 to 1) 3
376⁴ CLAUDIA MISS 6-9-2 Dale Gibson (19) *in tch, effrt 3 out, kpt on fnl 2 fs*...(9 to 2 jt-fav op 4 to 1 tchd 5 to 1) 4
66⁵ BARLEY CAKE 3-7-9 J Fanning (16) *hld up, hdwy 3 out, staying on whn hmpd one out, nrst finish*. ...(20 to 1 op 14 to 1) 5
375* ROYAL ACCLAIM (v) 8-9-0 (7*) Michael Bradley (17) *in tch, hdwy o'r 2 out, edgd lft and wknd one out*. ...(16 to 1 op 14 to 1) 6
279⁹ SPEED OIL 4-8-10¹ (7*) H Bastiman (12) *chsd ldrs till wknd 2 out*...(11 to 1 op 12 to 1) 7
120⁹ FUTURES GIFT (Ire) (bl) 4-9-7 S Webster (21) *chsd ldrs till wknd o'r one out*... (25 to 1) 8
ANFIELD SALLY 7-9-2 Paul Eddery (8) *chsd ldrs till wknd 2 out*... (25 to 1 op 33 to 1) 9
424³ FLETCHER'S BOUNTY (Ire) 4-8-9 (7*) Darren Moffatt (10) *mid-div, pushed alng hfwy, no hdwy*...(9 to 2 jt-fav op 4 to 1 tchd 5 to 1) 10
IBSEN 5-9-2 W Ryan (4) *nvr nr to chal*. ...(11 to 2 op 5 to 1 tchd 6 to 1) 11
253 CAL'S BOY 4-9-2 S Perks (6) *cl up till wknd 2 out*. ...(50 to 1) 12
376⁸ IMPORTANT DECISION 4-9-2 S Wood (7) *nvr dngrs*. ...(100 to 1) 13
362⁶ AARDVARK (bl) 7-9-0 (7*) E Husband (3) *led till hdd wl o'r 2 out, sn wknd*... (16 to 1) 14
STRANGERSINTHENITE (bl) 4-9-2 L Charnock (20) *mid-div, wknd o'r 2 out*...(50 to 1) 15
383⁶ MANULEADER (bl) 4-9-7 D Nicholls (5) *prmnt till wknd o'r 2 out*...(16 to 1 op 20 to 1) 16
334⁸ WHO'S THE BEST (Ire) 3-7-7 (7*) D Wright (18) *sn beh*. ... (13 to 2 op 5 to 1 tchd 7 to 1) 17
PALM LAGOON (Ire) 4-9-2 M Birch (11) *cl up till wknd 3 out*...(16 to 1) 18
WAXING LYRICAL 6-8-6 (5*) O Pears (2) *dwlt, al beh*. ... (33 to 1 op 50 to 1) 19
ANNA MANANA (bl) 4-9-2 J O'Reilly (9) *al beh*. ... (16 to 1 op 12 to 1) 20
50⁶ CYRILL HENRY (Ire) 4-9-2 N Connorton (1) *lost tch 3 out, tld off*...(33 to 1) 21

Dist: 6l, 1½l, ½l, 1l, 1½l, 1½l, 4l, 5l, 1½l, 3½l. 1m 49.90s. a 7.80s (21 Ran).
SR: 28/15/10/8/-/5/ (Mrs L A Windsor), P D Evans

532 St Giles Fillies Handicap Class D (0-80 3-y-o) £3,260 6f...(3:45)

418² ANOTHER JADE [63] 9-1 S Whitworth (9) *trkd ldrs, hmpd o'r one out, ran on wl to ld well ins fnl furlong*. ...(7 to 2 jt-fav op 4 to 1 tchd 9 to 2) 1
398³ ROSE FLYER (Ire) [53] 7-12 (7*) D McCabe (5) *led, clr o'r one out, hdd and no extr wl ins fnl furlong*. ...(7 to 1 tchd 8 to 1) 2
4773a⁴ BRIGHT GEM [54] 8-6 J Fanning (3) *cl up, rdn and ducked rght o'r one out, kpt on same pace*. (12 to 1 op 10 to 1) 3
398⁴ HEATHYARDS GEM [65] 9-3 W Ryan (2) *in tch, some hdwy fnl 2 fs, nvr dngrs*...(7 to 2 jt-fav op 3 to 1) 4
MARIBELLA [59] 8-8 (3*) F Norton (8) *chsd ldrs, one pace fnl 2 fs*... (9 to 1 op 8 to 1) 5
RUSSIA WITH LOVE [59] 8-11 Paul Eddery (7) *in tch, effrt whn hmpd o'r one out, not rcvr*...(8 to 1) 6
341⁵ ANUSHA [64] (bl) 9-2 J Carroll (4) *chsd ldrs, rdn whn hmpd o'r one out, sn btn*... (13 to 2 op 6 to 1 tchd 7 to 1) 7
361⁸ DON'T TELL JEAN [41] 7-7 S Wood (6) *cl up, pushed alng hfwy, hmpd o'r one out, sn btn*...(25 to 1 op 33 to 1) 8
IBTIKAR (USA) [69] 9-7 D Holland (1) *dwlt, beh whn badly hmpd o'r one furlong out*...(13 to 2 op 6 to 1) 9

Dist: 1½l, 1½l, 1l, nk, 3l, 1½l, 7l, 2l. 1m 22.30s. a 7.60s (9 Ran).
(Mrs Rita J Kaplan), A P Jarvis

533 Weft Gate Conditions Stakes Class C (4-y-o and up) £4,747 1m 4yds...(4:15)

390⁵ BOLOARDO 4-8-12 M Birch (3) *trkd ldr, effrt o'r one out, kpt on wl to ld ins fnl furlong*. ...(4 to 1 op 6 to 1 tchd 7 to 2) 1
PETO 4-8-12 W Ryan (4) *led, rdn one out, hdd ins fnl furlong, no extr*. ...(6 to 4 on op 5 to 4 on tchd 6 to 5 on) 2
RAMBO'S HALL 8-9-10 Dean McKeown (1) *steadied strt, hld up, pushed alng o'r 3 out, kpt on wl fnl furlong*. ...(4 to 1 op 5 to 2) 3
480⁵ WELL APPOINTED (Ire) 4-8-11 D Holland (2) *in tch till wknd 2 fs out, eased whn btn, tld off*. ... (9 to 1 op 20 to 1 tchd 8 to 1) 4

Dist: 2l, nk, 30l. 1m 49.90s. a 7.80s (4 Ran).
SR: 29/23/34/-/ (B H Voak), C E Brittain

534 Lady Balk Median Auction Maiden Stakes Class D (3-y-o) £3,260 1¼m 6yds...(4:50)

LAVENDER COTTAGE 8-6 (3*) F Norton (7) *dwlt, beh, hdwy 4 out, led one out, kpt on wl*. ...(14 to 1 op 10 to 1 tchd 16 to 1) 1
352³ LAKE POOPO (Ire) 8-9 D Holland (10) *hld up, hdwy 4 out, led entering fnl fs, sn hdd, kpt on*. ...(11 to 8 fav op 5 to 4 tchd 11 to 10 and 6 to 4) 2
439⁴ ABSALOM'S PILLAR 9-0 W Newnes (4) *trkd ldrs, effrt 2 out, ch o'r one out, kpt on same pace*. ... (12 to 1 op 10 to 1) 3
344³ MOONLIGHT ECLIPSE 8-9 (5*) Stephen Davies (9) *sn tracking ldrs, chlgd o'r one out, wknd ins fnl furlong*. ...(33 to 1 tchd 40 to 1) 4
4691a HALMANERROR 9-0 J Carroll (1) *led till hdd entering fnl furlong, sn btn*...(66 to 1 op 50 to 1) 5
MOIDART 8-9 Dean McKeown (6) *dwlt, beh, effrt 2 out, no real hdwy*...(16 to 1 op 14 to 1) 6
378⁹ NOBLE MEASURE (Ire) (bl) 8-7 (7*) G Strange (2) *wth ldr till wknd o'r one out*...(66 to 1 op 50 to 1) 7
357³ MOUNT FUJI 9-0 Paul Eddery (5) *in tch, effrt 2 out, sn btn*. ... (11 to 4 op 5 to 2 tchd 3 to 1) 8
GORDON'S BROTHER (Ire) 9-0 N Connorton (3) *prmnt early, lost tch frm 4 out, tld off*... (50 to 1 op 33 to 1) 9
346⁵ SABEEL 8-9 W Ryan (8) *in tch till wknd quickly 2 out, tld off*...(7 to 1 op 8 to 1) 10

Dist: Nk, 4l, 2½l, 2½l, 1l, sht-hd, 3½l. 2m 22.70s. a 14.50s (10 Ran).
(Sheikh Mohammed), G Wragg

535 Garforth Handicap Class E (0-70 3-y-o) £3,054 5f...(5:20)

MY GODSON [57] (bl) 8-4 (5*) O Pears (1) *beh, hdwy 2 out, led one out, sn clr*...(5 to 1) 1
255³ HERSHEBAR [66] (bl) 8-11 (7*) G Strange (8) *chsd ldrs, effrt 2 out, kpt on fnl furlong, no ch wth wnr*...(3 to 1 jt-fav op 4 to 1) 2
PLUM FIRST [67] 9-5 D Nicholls (7) *trkd ldr, led o'r 2 out, hdd one out, wknd ins fnl furlong*... (5 to 1) 3
COVENT GARDEN GIRL [57] 8-9 T Lucas (3) *beh, some late hdwy, nvr dngrs*...(5 to 1) 4
4668a⁹ BROOKLANDS EXPRESS [60] 8-12 D Wilkinson (4) *chsd ldrs till wknd o'r one out*... (14 to 1 op 10 to 1) 5
379⁹ WHAT BLISS [41] (bl) 7-7 S Wood (2) *chsd ldrs till wknd 2 out*... (20 to 1 op 16 to 1) 6
TOM PIPER [69] 9-7 J Carroll (5) *led till hdd o'r 2 out, wknd over one out*... (3 to 1 jt-fav tchd 7 to 2) 7

Dist: 3½l, 2½l, 6l, 1½l, 3l, 3½l. 1m 7.00s. a 5.80s (7 Ran).
SR: 19/14/5/-/ (P Hampshire), B Beasley

LONGCHAMP (FR) (heavy)
Thursday April 15th
Going Correction: PLUS 1.00 sec. per fur.

536 Prix de Guiche (Group 3) (3-y-o) £23,895 1m 1f 55yds...(2:50)

4693a³ RANGER (Fr) 9-2 W Mongil (9) *6th strt, hdwy 2 fs out, chlgd two furlongs out, led one and a half out, ran on wl*... (164 to 10) 1
HAWK SPELL (USA) 9-2 E Legrix (8) *4th strt, effrt 2 fs out, no extr*... (18 to 1) 2D
4713a* SIN KIANG (Fr) 9-2 T Jarnet (7) *trkd ldrs, 5th strt, hmpd 2 fs out, swtchd, ran on wl*... (37 to 10) 2
EXTRA POINT 9-2 C Asmussen (3) *second strt, effrt 2 fs out, styd on wl*...(58 to 10) 4
266* FANTASTIC DREAM (Ire) 9-2 D Boeuf (2) *led strt, rdn and wknd quickly o'r one and a half fs out*...(21 to 10) 5
KADOUNOR (Fr) 9-2 O Doleuze (4) *nvr dngrs*. ...(18 to 10 fav) 6
RAPHAELO (Fr) 9-2 O Peslier (6) *nvr dngrs*... (14 to 1) 7
SOLDIER COVE (USA) 9-2 E Saint-Martin (1) *3rd strt, wknd quickly 2 fs out*...(15 to 1) 8

Dist: 1½l, ½l, hd, nose, 1½l, 4l, 1l. 2m 5.70s. a 13.70s (9 Ran).
SR: 35/32/31/30/29/26/18/16/ (Mme P Demercastel), P Demercastel

NAD AL SHEBA (DUB) (good)
Thursday April 15th

537 **Conditions Race (3-y-o) £2,248 1m.......**

GHURRAH (Ire) 8-11 P Brette,........................... 1
DAYFLOWER (USA) 8-5 D Batteate,...................... 2
NAKUPITA (Ire) 8-5 P Woods,........................... 3
Dist: 3½l, 8l, 1 ¾l. 1m 40.57s. (8 Ran).
(K K Al Nabooda), P Rudkin

NEWMARKET (good)
Thursday April 15th
Going Correction: MINUS 0.15 sec. per fur.

538 **Granby Maiden Stakes Class D (3-y-o) £3,947 7f.......................... (2:00)**

LOWER EGYPT (USA) 9-0 M Roberts (9) *settled midfield, rdn hfwy, str run ins fnl furlong, led last strds.* ....(11 to 4 fav op 3 to 1) 1
AUTUMNIS (USA) 9-0 Pat Eddery (7) *patiently rdn, hdwy frm off the pace last 2 fs, led ins last, jst ct.* ....(10 to 1 op 7 to 1 tchd 11 to 1) 2
DRAMANICE (USA) 9-0 L Dettori (4) *nvr far away, nosed ahead centre o'r 2 fs out, hdd fnl furlong, ran on same pace*................................(5 to 1 op 3 to 1) 3
STONEY VALLEY 9-0 Paul Eddery (11) *al hndy, rdn and ev ch fnl furlong, ran on same pace.* ....(12 to 1 op 10 to 1 tchd 14 to 1) 4
ANORAK (USA) 9-0 R Cochrane (2) *settled off the pace, hdwy last 2 fs, ran on und pres, nvr nrr.* ....(14 to 1 op 16 to 1 tchd 25 to 1) 5
BIG SKY 9-0 W Ryan (6) *al hndy, led briefly wl o'r 2 fs out, rdn and no extr fnl furlong.* ....(11 to 2 op 5 to 2 tchd 6 to 1) 6
WISHAM (USA) 9-0 B Raymond (16) *tucked away on ins, swtchd centre o'r 2 fs out, rng on finish.* ....(14 to 1 op 8 to 1 tchd 16 to 1) 7
GLEN ECHO (Ire) 9-0 T Quinn (18) *trkd ldg bunch, improved on ins to flter o'r 2 fs out, not quicken fnl furlong*..............(14 to 1 op 10 to 1 tchd 16 to 1) 8
SCUSI 9-0 J Reid (1) *chsd alng to go early pace, improved centre o'r 2 fs out, ran on finish.* ....(14 to 1 op 8 to 1 tchd 16 to 1) 9
TIMOTHY CASEY 9-0 V Smith (15) *unruly at strt, broke wl to ld till hdd well o'r 2 fs out, fdd.* ....(20 to 1 op 16 to 1 tchd 25 to 1) 10
AROOM 9-0 W Carson (17) *wth ldrs, ev ch till wknd and eased o'r one furlong out.* ....(10 to 1 op 7 to 1 tchd 11 to 1) 11
FASHIONABLE DANCER 9-0 A Munro (5) *settled midfield, feeling pace o'r 2 fs out, grad wknd.* ....(33 to 1 op 25 to 1) 12
BURNT IMP (USA) 9-0 M Hills (8) *steadied strt, effrt and niggled alng hfwy, nvr dngrs.* ....(25 to 1 op 20 to 1 tchd 33 to 1) 13
MUJAWAB 9-0 R Hills (10) *wth ldrs till wknd o'r a furlong out*..............................(20 to 1 op 25 to 1) 14
RED WHIRLWIND 9-0 W R Swinburn (13) *bustled alng in midfield hfwy, nvr a threat.* ....(25 to 1 op 16 to 1 tchd 33 to 1) 15
422[7] MR LUCIANO (Ire) (v) 9-0 M Tebbutt (14) *chsd alng to go pace thrght, nvr a factor*.........(66 to 1 op 50 to 1) 16
FULL FEATHER (USA) 9-0 D Holland (12) *missed break, nvr able to reco'r*.....................(33 to 1 op 16 to 1) 17
DODDINGTON PLAYER (Ire) 9-0 A Culhane (3) *missed break, al last*...........................(50 to 1 op 33 to 1) 18
Dist: Hd, 1l, sht-hd, 3½l, hd, nk, ¾l, 1½l, 2l, 1½l. 1m 26.08s. a 2.58s (18 Ran).
SR: 46/45/42/41/30/29/28/26/21/ (Sheikh Mohammed), J H M Gosden

539 **Tote/Racing Post Ten To Follow Rated Class B (0-105 4-y-o and up) £7,327 1¾m ....(2:35)**

4671a* DIME BAG [79] 4-8-7 D Holland (2) *trkd ldg pair, led o'r 6 fs out, hrd pressed entering last, styd on gmely.* ....(3 to 1 fav op 2 to 1 tchd 100 to 30) 1
365[2] STAR PLAYER [90] 7-9-7 L Dettori (3) *patiently rdn, improved on bit to chal entering fnl furlong, put head in air, not go past*......(6 to 1 op 9 to 2 tchd 13 to 2) 2
NOT IN DOUBT (USA) [88] 4-9-2 C Rutter (7) *trkd ldg trio, rdn whn pace quickened o'r 3 fs out, styd on und pres last, nrst finish*.......................... (4 to 1 op 7 to 2) 3
145 FLY AWAY SOON (USA) [80] 5-8-8 (3*) D Harrison (4) *dictated pace till hdd o'r 6 fs out, remained hndy till rdn and no extr fnl furlong.* ....(9 to 1 op 6 to 1 tchd 10 to 1) 4
303 AUDE LA BELLE (Fr) [76] 5-8-4 (3*) F Norton (1) *trkd ldr, pld outsd and effrt o'r 3 fs out, rdn and no imprsn appr fnl furlong*.............................. (8 to 1 op 7 to 1) 5
MULL HOUSE [76] 6-8-7 W Carson (6) *trkd ldg quartet, rdn whn pace lifted o'r 3 fs out, sn outpcd.* ....(4 to 1 tchd 9 to 2) 6
115[6] LYN'S RETURN (Ire) [79] 4-8-4 (3*) A Tucker (5) *last and hld up, swtchd centre and effrt o'r 3 fs out, sn rdn and btn.* ....(33 to 1 op 25 to 1 tchd 40 to 1) 7
Dist: ¾l, 3½l, 1l, hd, 6l, 15l. 3m 3.75s. a 7.75s (7 Ran).
SR: -/7/-/-/ (R J McAlpine), B W Hills

540 **Feilden Stakes Class A (Listed Race) (3-y-o) £9,768 1m 1f...................(3:05)**

PLACERVILLE (USA) 8-11 Pat Eddery (6) *led early, styd hndy till led ag'n o'r 3 fs out, hdd appr last, rallied to ld ins last, kpt on gmely.* ....(11 to 8 on op 5 to 4 on tchd 11 to 10 on) 1
DESERT TEAM (USA) 8-11 C Roche (3) *trkd ldrs, nosed ahead o'r 4 fs out, hdd and lost grnd over 3 out, rallied und pres fnl furlong, fnshd wl*.... (12 to 1 op 10 to 1) 2
YELTSIN 8-11 W Ryan (5) *patiently rdn, hdwy frm off the pace o'r 3 fs out, ran on grimly fnl furlong, prmsg.* ....(10 to 1 tchd 12 to 1) 3
TIOMAN ISLAND 9-0 T Quinn (4) *tucked away in midfield, effrt hfwy, rdn o'r 3 fs out, staying on finish.* ....(16 to 1 op 14 to 1 tchd 20 to 1) 4
IOMMELLI (Ire) 8-11 L Dettori (9) *nvr far away, ev ch and drvn alng o'r 2 fs out, kpt on same pace.* ....(50 to 1 op 33 to 1) 5
PEMBROKE (USA) 9-0 M Roberts (2) *patiently rdn, improved to ld wl o'r one furlong out, hdd ins last, wknd and eased last 50 yards.* ....(6 to 1 op 7 to 2 tchd 13 to 2) 6
ALJAZZAF 8-11 W R Swinburn (8) *chsd ldg bunch, feeling pace and drvn alng o'r 3 fs out, styd on und pres, nvr nrr*.............................. (33 to 1 op 16 to 1) 7
304[3] BITTER'S END (Ire) 8-11 J Reid (7) *nvr far away, drw level o'r 3 fs out, rdn and no extr appr last.* ....(8 to 1 op 12 to 1) 8
TAAHHUB (Ire) 8-11 W Carson (1) *sn led, hdd o'r 4 fs out, rdn over 3 out, soon btn*..........(14 to 1 op 10 to 1) 9
Dist: ½l, ½l, 1½l, hd, 1½l, hd, ½l, 8l. 1m 51.11s. a 1.41s (9 Ran).
SR: 56/54/52/50/46/44/40/38/14/ (K Abdulla), H R A Cecil

541 **Craven Stakes Class A (Group 3) (3-y-o) £23,135 1m....................... (3:40)**

EMPEROR JONES (USA) 8-9 R Cochrane (1) *al hndy, drw level und pres entering fnl furlong, kpt on grimly to ld post*................. (14 to 1 op 10 to 1 tchd 16 to 1) 1
WHARF (USA) 8-12 Pat Eddery (9) *nvr far away, nosed ahead entering fnl furlong, ran on, jst ct.* ....(4 to 1 op 3 to 1 tchd 9 to 2) 2
VENTIQUATTROFOGLI (Ire) 8-9 W Carson (6) *patiently rdn, swtchd to race alone stands side entering fnl furlong, fnshd strly*..........(25 to 1 op 20 to 1 tchd 33 to 1) 3
BARATHEA (Ire) 8-9 M Roberts (5) *al hndy, rdn to draw level appr fnl furlong, no extr cl hme.* ....(11 to 10 on tchd Evens and 5 to 4 on) 4
IVORY FRONTIER (Ire) 8-12 C Roche (4) *trkd ldg quartet, rdn appr fnl furlong, rallied gmely.* ....(33 to 1 op 25 to 1 tchd 40 to 1) 5
CHADDLEWORTH (Ire) 8-9 J Reid (7) *patiently rdn, improved on outsd to nose ahead o'r one furlong out, hdd entering last, better for race*... (10 to 1 op 7 to 1) 6
388[2] NOMINATOR 8-9 W Ryan (2) *wth ldr, led briefly o'r 2 fs out, hrd drvn and not much room entering fnl furlong, no extr*............. (11 to 1 op 12 to 1 tchd 14 to 1) 7
REDENHAM (USA) 8-9 L Piggott (8) *dictated pace, quickened hfwy, hdd o'r one furlong out, rdn whn not much room entering last, eased when btn.* ....(16 to 1 op 14 to 1 tchd 20 to 1) 8
CANASKA STAR 8-9 L Dettori (3) *sluggish strt, chsd alng to keep up hfwy, not pace of ldrs.* (25 to 1 op 20 to 1) 9
Dist: Sht-hd, ½l, sht-hd, nk, 2l, ½l, 2l, 4l. 1m 37.80s. a 0.60s (9 Ran).
SR: 68/70/65/64/66/57/55/49/37/ (Sheikh Mohammed), J H M Gosden

542 **Ladbrokes Boldboy Sprint Handicap Class C (0-95 3-y-o) £7,180 6f............. (4:10)**

380* MOON STRIKE (Fr) [73] 7-13 A Munro (10) *tucked away on ins, drvn through to ld inside fnl furlong, idled, rdn out*..................................(5 to 1 op 9 to 2) 1
PRINCESS OBERON (Ire) [84] 8-10 M Hills (7) *tried to make all, hdd and drvn alng fnl furlong, rallied.* ....(25 to 1 op 20 to 1 tchd 33 to 1) 2
PAIR OF JACKS (Ire) [75] 8-1 W Woods (2) *wth ldr, rdn entering fnl furlong, styd on.* ....(14 to 1 op 12 to 1 tchd 16 to 1) 3
ABTAAL [90] 9-2 R Hills (6) *trkd ldrs, effrt and drvn alng o'r 2 fs out, unbl to quicken fnl furlong*......... (8 to 1) 4
NORTHERN BIRD [85] 8-11 D Holland (1) *nvr far away, rdn whn pace quickened last 2 fs, one pace.* ......(9 to 2 jt-fav op 4 to 1 tchd 7 to 2) 5
347[5] SISON (Ire) [80] 8-6 A Culhane (4) *settled midfield, effrt und pres o'r 2 fs out, kpt on, nvr able to chal.* ....(8 to 1 op 6 to 1 tchd 9 to 1) 6

347^{7} THE SHARP BIDDER (Ire) [80] 8-6 W Ryan (8) *chsd ldg quartet, rdn o'r 2 fs out, no extr*... (25 to 1 op 20 to 1) 7
SHEILA'S SECRET (Ire) [95] 9-7 J Reid (5) *in tch, chsd alng to go pace hfwy, nvr a threat.*
.... (8 to 1 op 10 to 1 tchd 12 to 1) 8
317* MR BUTCH [75] 8-1 W Carson (3) *chsd ldrs, rdn hfwy, sn btn*............................ (9 to 2 jt-fav op 5 to 1) 9
277^{2} LUCAYAN TREASURE [91] (v) 9-3 L Dettori (9) *chsd ldrs, feeling pace and reminders hfwy, eased whn btn 2 fs out*.................... (9 to 1 op 5 to 1 tchd 10 to 1) 10
Dist: ¾l, ½l, 1½l, nk, sht-hd, sht-hd, 5l, nk, 6l. 1m 13.27s. a 1.87s (10 Ran).
SR: 30/38/27/36/30/24/23/18/-/ (S Fustok), W A O'Gorman

543 EBF Stuntney Maiden Stakes Class D (2-y-o) £3,622 5f...................... (4:45)

WAJIBA RIVA (Ire) 9-0 Pat Eddery (1) *pressed ldr, quickened up to ld o'r one furlong out, ran on strly.*
.... (5 to 1 op 7 to 1) 1
MONTAYA 9-0 W R Swinburn (9) *chsd alng to improve far side hfwy, effrt ins fnl furlong, kpt on same pace.*
.... (7 to 2 jt-fav op 7 to 1 tchd 3 to 1) 2
GREATEST 9-0 R Price (7) *al hndy, rdn whn pace quickened o'r one furlong out, rallied.*
.... (13 to 2 op 5 to 1 tchd 7 to 1) 3
386^{7} LORD SKY 9-0 T Quinn (6) *tried to make all, hdd appr fnl furlong, rdn and no extr*....... (7 to 2 jt-fav op 5 to 2) 4
DOWN D ISLANDS 9-0 J Reid (8) *broke wl, ran green and lost pl hfwy, ran on ag'n fnl furlong, prmsg.*
.... (10 to 1 op 8 to 1 tchd 11 to 1) 5
FRANKLY MY DEAR 9-0 R Cochrane (3) *speed to chase ldrs for o'r 3 fs, no extr*... (12 to 1 op 10 to 1 tchd 14 to 1) 6
ERRIS BOY 9-0 A Clark (4) *sluggish strt, chsd alng to improve hfwy, fdd wl o'r one furlong out.*
.... (12 to 1 tchd 16 to 1) 7
374^{6} MARCH OF TIME 9-0 Paul Eddery (5) *chsd alng to go pace hfwy, nvr able to trble ldrs.*
.... (25 to 1 op 16 to 1 tchd 33 to 1) 8
BALI WARRIOR (Ire) 9-0 M Hills (2) *lost many ls strt, nvr able to reco'r*...................... (8 to 1 op 4 to 1) 9
Dist: 2l, 2½l, 1½l, ½l, 1½l, 3½l, 1½l, 7l. 1m 0.75s. a 2.15s (9 Ran).
SR: 42/34/24/18/16/10/ (The Winning Team), R Hannon

RIPON (soft)
Thursday April 15th

Going Correction: PLUS 0.35 sec. per fur. (races 1,2,5), PLUS 0.60 (3,4,6)

544 EBF Cocked Hat Supreme Maiden Stakes Class D (2-y-o) £3,260 5f............ (2:15)

LAMBENT 8-9 W Newnes (2) *in tch, pushed alng hfwy, ran on wl fnl furlong to ld post*.... (20 to 1 op 14 to 1) 1
STIMULANT 8-9 G Duffield (6) *chsd ldrs, sn pushed alng, led jst ins fnl furlong, ct post.*
.... (13 to 8 fav op 11 to 10 tchd 7 to 4) 2
433^{2} RAPIER POINT (Ire) 9-0 Dean McKeown (7) *cl up, led hfwy, hdd jst ins fnl furlong, kpt on wl.*
.... (9 to 4 op 2 to 1 tchd 5 to 2) 3
BOLLIN MARY 8-9 M Birch (5) *led to hfwy, cl up till wknd o'r one out*............................ (10 to 1 op 8 to 1) 4
364^{3} UP THE MARINERS (Ire) 8-9 R P Elliott (1) *hng rght, chsd ldrs till wknd o'r one out.*
.... (12 to 1 op 10 to 1 tchd 14 to 1) 5
ARKINDALE SPIRIT (Ire) 9-0 T Lucas (9) *nvr dngrs.*
.... (25 to 1 op 12 to 1) 6
PRINCE SKYBURD 9-0 L Charnock (3) *dwlt, al beh.*
.... (25 to 1 op 20 to 1) 7
NOSMO KING (Ire) 9-0 J Carroll (8) *sn beh.*
.... (6 to 1 op 7 to 1) 8
FLYING VISION (Ire) 8-9 S Morris (4) *sn beh.*
.... (33 to 1 op 25 to 1) 9
Dist: Sht-hd, nk, 7l, nk, 6l, ½l, sht-hd, 1l. 1m 3.60s. a 5.60s (9 Ran).
SR: 18/17/21/-/-/-/ (R L Heaton), E Weymes

545 Cocked Hat Quality Claiming Stakes Class F (3-y-o and up) £2,831 5f.......... (2:45)

292^{8} MARTINA 5-8-7 J Williams (3) *in tch, hdwy 2 out, ran on wl to ld ins fnl furlong, sn clr*................. (4 to 1) 1
221^{3} ANOTHER EPISODE (Ire) 4-9-7 J Carroll (5) *cl up, led hfwy, hdd ins fnl furlong, no extr*...... (7 to 4 fav op 2 to 1) 2
355^{3} EVER SO LONELY (bl) 4-8-0 (7*) D Wright (1) *led to hfwy, wknd entering fnl furlong*.......... (2 to 1 op 7 to 4) 3
289^{9} SAVAHRA SOUND 8-9-6 D Nicholls (7) *sn pushed alng and beh, some late hdwy, nvr dngrs.*
.... (12 to 1 op 10 to 1 tchd 14 to 1) 4
DARDANELLE 3-7-0 (7*) Darren Moffatt (8) *chsd ldrs, no hdwy fnl 2 fs*.................................. (66 to 1) 5
CORONA GOLD 3-8-3^{1} K Fallon (9) *dwlt, sn wl beh, nvr dngrs*............................ (12 to 1 op 10 to 1) 6
BALLAD DANCER 8-8-12 G Duffield (2) *dwlt, al beh.*
.... (10 to 1 op 8 to 1) 7
Dist: 4l, 2½l, hd, ¾l, 7l, 1l. 1m 2.10s. a 4.10s (7 Ran).
SR: 46/44/20/32/2/-/-/ (M J Yarrow), J Wharton

546 Cocked Hat 'Cock O'the North' Handicap Class C (0-90 3-y-o) £5,385 1m...... (3:15)

405* JUST YOU DARE (Ire) [65] 8-1 G Duffield (4) *pld hrd early, in tch, effrt 3 out, led one out, drvn out*..... (15 to 8 jt-fav op 7 to 4 tchd 2 to 1) 1
447* THE PREMIER EXPRES [65] 8-1^{1} (6ex) K Darley (1) *cl up, jnd ldr 5 out, slight ld 2 out, hdd one out, kpt on wl.*
.... (11 to 2 tchd 6 to 1) 2
317^{2} WORDSMITH (Ire) [66] 8-2 K Fallon (5) *hld up in tch, effrt o'r 2 out, kpt on same pace*............... (15 to 8 jt-fav op 7 to 4 tchd 2 to 1) 3
378^{6} I'M A DREAMER (Ire) [62] 7-12 Dale Gibson (2) *chsd ldrs, pushed alng 4 out, no hdwy*....... (14 to 1 op 12 to 1) 4
MHEMEANLES [85] 9-4 (3*) S Maloney (3) *led, hdd 2 out, wknd one out, eased whn btn*....... (5 to 1 op 4 to 1) 5
Dist: 1½l, 1½l, 3l, 7l. 1m 46.50s. a 8.20s (5 Ran).
SR: 36/31/27/14/16/ (Mrs David Thompson), Sir Mark Prescott

547 Cocked Hat 21st Birthday Handicap Class D (0-80 3-y-o) £3,622 1½m 60yds.... (3:45)

372^{5} HARLESTONE BROOK [56] 8-2 G Carter (1) *sn cl up, quickened to ld o'r 2 out, styd on wl.*
.... (4 to 1 op 7 to 2 tchd 9 to 2) 1
434^{8} SAFETY IN NUMBERS [50] 7-10 J Quinn (2) *trkd ldrs, effrt o'r 2 out, ev ch one out, no extr towards finish.*
.... (7 to 2 op 4 to 1 tchd 9 to 2) 2
MANILA BAY (USA) [75] 9-2 (5*) M Fenton (4) *hld up, hdwy 3 out, sn ev ch, wknd entering fnl furlong.*
.... (4 to 1 op 7 to 2) 3
434^{2} BROUGHTONS FORMULA [65] (bl) 8-4 (7*) D McCabe (3) *trkd ldrs, effrt o'r 2 out, sn btn.*
.... (7 to 4 fav op 6 to 4 tchd 15 to 8) 4
434^{7} MASTER FIDDLER [60] 8-6 J Fanning (5) *led, hdd and wkng whn f o'r 2 out*........................ (10 to 1) f
Dist: 1l, 3½l, hd. 2m 51.70s. a 16.70s (5 Ran).
SR: -/-/5/-/-/ (J L Dunlop), J L Dunlop

548 Cocked Hat Paris Apprentice Handicap Class E (0-70 4-y-o and up) £2,924 5f (4:15)

348^{3} TOMMY TEMPEST [40] 4-7-12 P McCabe (5) *made all, clr one out, hld on wl*................. (11 to 2 op 9 to 2) 1
363^{9} DOKKHA OYSTON (Ire) [70] 5-9-6 (8*) P Roberts (2) *beh, outpcd and behind till ran on strly fnl 2 fs, not rch wnr.*
.... (7 to 1 op 6 to 1) 2
GONDO [70] 6-9-4 (10*) S Knott (1) *beh, hdwy hfwy, kpt on wl fnl furlong*.................... (9 to 1 op 8 to 1) 3
348^{7} HINARI VIDEO [44] 8-7-8 (8*) M Baird (4) *in tch, pushed alng hfwy, styd on wl fnl furlong, nrst finish.*
.... (8 to 1 op 7 to 1 tchd 9 to 1) 4
236^{3} LAST STRAW [41] 5-7-13 Claire Balding (7) *prmnt till wknd 2 out*............................ (6 to 1 op 5 to 1) 5
348^{2} THE RIGHT TIME [45] (bl) 8-8-3 G Parkin (10) *al chasing ldrs, no hdwy fnl 2 fs*............ (6 to 1 op 9 to 2) 6
4744a GENERAL JOHN (Ire) [70] 4-9-4 (10*) C Adamson (8) *slwly into strd, beh till some late hdwy, nvr dngrs.*
.... (25 to 1 op 16 to 1) 7
4744a BEST EFFORT [61] 7-9-5 V Halliday (3) *beh frm hfwy.*
.... (14 to 1 op 10 to 1) 8
236^{5} KALAR [47] (bl) 4-8-5 D McCabe (9) *prmnt till wknd o'r one out*.................. (10 to 1 op 8 to 1 tchd 11 to 1) 9
421^{5} WE'RE ALL GAME [60] 4-9-4 S Mulvey (6) *prmnt till wknd 2 out*........................ (5 to 1 fav op 7 to 1) 10
Dist: 1l, ¾l, hd, 2½l, 1l, ¾l, 1½l, sht-hd, 3l. 1m 2.80s. a 4.80s (10 Ran).
SR: 23/49/46/19/6/6/28/13/-/ (Mrs Elaine M Burke), K R Burke

549 Cocked Hat Service Stakes Rating Related Maiden Class E (0-70 3-y-o) £3,080 1m .... (4:50)

371^{2} SMARGINATO (Ire) 9-0 G Carter (3) *trkd ldr frm 5 out, rdn to ld o'r one out, ran on wl*..... (11 to 8 fav op 7 to 4) 1
MISSA BREVIS (USA) 8-9 G Duffield (6) *hld up in tch, effrt o'r 2 out, sn rdn, styd on fnl furlong.*
.... (100 to 30 op 2 to 1 tchd 7 to 2) 2
467^{2} PANTHER (Ire) 9-0 K Darley (1) *prmnt, lft in led 5 out, hdd o'r one out, one paced*........................ (6 to 1) 3
YOUNG TESS 8-9 S Webster (2) *beh, kpt on fnl 2 fs, not trble ldrs*........................... (8 to 1 op 7 to 1) 4
301 NUTTY BROWN 8-9 (5*) O Pears (4) *trkd ldr till crrd wide bend 5 out, no dngr aftr*....... (10 to 1 tchd 12 to 1) 5
SKY WISH 9-0 M Birch (5) *led till hng badly lft and ran wide bend 5 out, some hdwy till lost pl o'r 2 out, eased fnl furlong, bit slpd*..... (7 to 1 op 8 to 1 tchd 9 to 1) 6
Dist: 3l, sht-hd, 4l, 12l, 20l. 1m 47.80s. a 9.50s (6 Ran).
SR: 30/16/20/3/-/-/ (Gerecon Italia), J L Dunlop

TIPPERARY (IRE) (heavy)
Thursday April 15th

550 Bruff Maiden (3-y-o) £2,760 1m 1f... (2:30)

MISS MISTLETOES (Ire) 8-11 S Craine (4) .... (8 to 1) 1
RAJAURA (Ire) 8-11 R Hughes (11) ....(2 to 1) 2
311 STATION HOUSE (Ire) 9-0 P V Gilson (9) ....(8 to 1) 3
311² DIFFERENT TIMES (Ire) 9-0 W J O'Connor (7) (15 to 8 fav) 4
297⁶ GIFT OF PEACE (Ire) 8-5 (6*) J A Heffernan (12).... (7 to 1) 5
PERFECT POET (Ire) 8-6 (8*) J J Stack (2) .... (25 to 1) 6
258 TEBRE (USA) 8-11 W J Supple (1) ....(12 to 1) 7
KATIES VISION (Ire) 8-11 N G McCullagh (5) .... (25 to 1) 8
BLAZING SPECTACLE (Ire) 9-0 P Shanahan (8) .... (8 to 1) 9
SIMPLE DANCER (Ire) 8-6 (8*) P P Murphy (10) ....(25 to 1) 10
MUSWELL BROOK (Ire) 9-0 K J Manning (6) ....(7 to 1) 11
311 SHY WIN (Ire) 8-3 (8*) R V Skelly (13) ....(25 to 1) 12
EILEENS HOPE (Ire) 8-11 J F Egan (3) ....(10 to 1) 13

Dist: 1l, 1l, hd, 9l. 2m 6.80s. (13 Ran).

(R E Sangster), T Stack

551 Kilfrush Race (3-y-o and up) £2,760 7f ....(3:00)

311³ KHARASAR (Ire) 3-8-9 D Hogan (3) .... (5 to 2) 1
RELENTLESS BOY (Ire) 3-9-2 S Craine (1) .... (8 to 1) 2
MOUMAYAZ (USA) 3-9-2 K J Manning (5)......... (Evens fav) 3
311⁹ PERSIAN RENDEZVOUS (Ire) 3-8-9 P V Gilson (2) (12 to 1) 4
306⁶ SIR SLAVES 3-9-2 P Shanahan (4) ....(9 to 2) 5
CARHUE STAR (Ire) 3-8-4 (2*) R M Burke (7)...... (25 to 1) 6
SORRECA (Ire) 4-8-11 (10*) P J Smullen (6) ....(50 to 1) 7

Dist: 1½l, hd, 2½l, nk. 1m 46.50s. (7 Ran).

(H H Aga Khan), John M Oxx

552 Aherlow Race (3-y-o) £2,760 1½m...(3:30)

IMAD (USA) 9-0 W J Supple (5) .... (12 to 1) 1
257² CARRICK PIKE (USA) (bl) 9-0 K J Manning (16) (Evens fav) 2
282 SELUNE (Fr) 8-11 N G McCullagh (1) .... (10 to 1) 3
282⁵ UNCERTAIN AFFAIR (Ire) 8-11 P Shanahan (13).... (7 to 2) 4
311 BIRTHPLACE (Ire) 9-0 R Hughes (10) ....(8 to 1) 5
297⁴ ANY MINUTE NOW (Ire) 8-12 (2*) R M Burke (14)..(10 to 1) 6
KIDAMIYA (Ire) 8-5 (6*) J A Heffernan (7) ....(12 to 1) 7
MONTEJUSTICE (Ire) 8-11 N Byrne (8) ....(20 to 1) 8
SKERRIES BELL 8-11 P V Gilson (9) ....(8 to 1) 9
CHRISTY MOORE (Ire) (bl) 9-0 R Dolan (2) ....(16 to 1) 10
POSITIVE VIEW (Ire) 9-0 W J O'Connor (3) ....(16 to 1) 11
258 CORAL SOUND (Ire) 8-11 S Craine (11) .... (10 to 1) 12
297 RED ROOSTER (Ire) 9-0 B Coogan (12) .... (20 to 1) 13
EFFICIENT FUNDING (Ire) 8-11 J F Egan (6) ...... (20 to 1) 14
488 STEADY DEAR (Ire) 8-3 (8*) R T Fitzpatrick (15)....(12 to 1) 15
CREHELP EXPRESS (Ire) 8-3 (8*) B Bowens (4) ... (20 to 1) pu

Dist: ½l, ½l, 2½l, 1l. 2m 59.00s. (16 Ran).

(Hamdan Al-Maktoum), Kevin Prendergast

553 Junction Race (4-y-o and up) £3,450 1½m ....(4:00)

309² RISZARD (USA) 4-9-0 K J Manning (3) .... (4 to 1) 1
DOWLAND (USA) 5-9-4 W J O'Connor (5) .... (9 to 2) 2
YUKON GOLD (Ire) (bl) 4-9-9 P V Gilson (4) .... (2 to 1 fav) 3
4727a⁵ ONESIXNINE (Ire) 5-9-3 P Shanahan (7) ....(10 to 3) 4
SHUIL AR AGHAIDH 7-8-6 W J Supple (6) ....(12 to 1) 5
LACKEL (Ger) 5-8-8 (6*) J A Heffernan (8)........ (20 to 1) 6
TAGANINI (Ire) 5-9-0 S Craine (9)................ (33 to 1) 7
THE RIDGE BOREEN 9-8-9 N Byrne (2) .... (50 to 1) 8

Dist: 5l, 2½l, 4l, 1l. 2m 57.90s. (8 Ran).

(Henryk de Kwiatkowski), J S Bolger

NEWBURY (good)
Friday April 16th
Going Correction: PLUS 0.75 sec. per fur. (races 1,2,5), PLUS 0.60 (3,4,6)

554 EBF Beckhampton Maiden Stakes Class D (2-y-o) £3,557 5f 34yds..............(2:10)

TURTLE ISLAND (Ire) 9-0 J Reid (6) *trkd ldrs, led appr fnl furlong, sn quickened clr.*
....................(13 to 8 fav op 5 to 4 tchd 7 to 4) 1
PASSING PLAYER (USA) 9-0 M Hills (7) *missed break, shaken up 2 fs out, hdwy o'r one out, ran on ins last.*
.... (20 to 1 op 8 to 1 tchd 33 to 1) 2
BASKERVILLE 9-0 A Munro (5) *cl up, led briefly o'r one furlong out, one pace.*
.....................(14 to 1 op 10 to 1 tchd 20 to 1) 3
399⁶ ZUNO STAR (USA) 9-0 Pat Eddery (8) *cl up, lost pl hfwy, sn rdn, kpt on ins fnl furlong.*
.........................(6 to 1 op 7 to 2 tchd 7 to 1) 4
399³ KENNET BOY 9-0 T Quinn (3) *cl up, led hfwy till o'r one furlong out, wknd ins last.*
.........................(7 to 2 op 2 to 1 tchd 9 to 2) 5
LEGAL CONQUEST 8-9 W Newnes (4) *sn pushed alng, nvr on terms*......................... (33 to 1 op 12 to 1) 6
PETER ROWLEY 9-0 W Carson (2) *wth ldr, led briefly aftr 2 fs, wknd two out*...... (9 to 2 op 5 to 1 tchd 4 to 1) 7
BID FOR BLUE 9-0 M Roberts (1) *slwly into strd, sn led, hdd hfwy, wknd*..................... (7 to 1 op 3 to 1) 8

Dist: 5l, 2l, ¾l, 1½l, 2l, 3l, 5l. 1m 7.68s. a 7.38s (8 Ran).

SR: 31/11/3/-/-/ (R E Sangster), P W Chapple-Hyam

555 Newbury Racecourse Shopping Arcade Rated Class B (0-105 4-y-o and up) £6,164 5f 34yds...........................(2:40)

OLIFANTSFONTEIN [86] (bl) 5-8-7 G Carter (6) *cl up, led one furlong out, rdn and ran on wl.*
.... (16 to 1 op 20 to 1 tchd 10 to 1) 1
INHERENT MAGIC (Ire) [86] 4-8-7 W Carson (5) *wth ldr, ev ch one furlong out, ran on.*
.... (11 to 2 op 6 to 1 tchd 13 to 2) 2
316* REGAL CHIMES [100] 4-9-7 A Munro (2) *led, rdn and hdd one furlong out, one pace.*
.... (100 to 30 op 2 to 1 tchd 7 to 2) 3
PLAIN FACT [86] 8-8-7 M Hills (3) *in tch, pushed alng 2 fs out, outpcd o'r one out, styd on ins last.*
...........................(4 to 1 tchd 9 to 2) 4
ALLTHRUTHENIGHT (Ire) [86] 4-8-7 J Reid (4) *trkd ldrs till wknd wl o'r one furlong out.*
.... (8 to 1 op 7 to 1 tchd 10 to 1) 5
TERRHARS (Ire) [92] 5-8-13 T Quinn (1) *trkd ldrs till wknd appr fnl furlong*....(5 to 2 fav op 2 to 1 tchd 11 to 4) 6

Dist: 2l, nk, 5l, 1½l, 1½l. 1m 5.68s. a 5.38s (6 Ran).

SR: 64/56/69/35/29/29/ (Trevor Painting), R Simpson

556 Gainsborough Stud Fred Darling Stakes Class A (Group 3) (3-y-o) £23,463 7f 64yds ....(3:10)

SUEBOOG (Ire) 9-0 W R Swinburn (6) *trkd ldrs, led appr fnl furlong, shaken up, ran on wl*......(5 to 2 op 7 to 4) 1
RIBBONWOOD (USA) 9-0 M Roberts (2) *beh, pld out o'r 2 fs out, rdn and hdwy over one out, styd on ins last.*
.... (10 to 1 op 7 to 1) 2
SECRAGE (USA) 9-0 D Holland (1) *cl up, led o'r 3 fs out till appr last, one pace*............(2 to 1 fav tchd 5 to 2) 3
THAWAKIB (Ire) 9-0 W Carson (4) *sn led, hdd o'r 3 fs out, wknd over one out.*
..................(3 to 1 tchd 11 to 4 and 100 to 30) 4
SHAMISEN 9-0 L Dettori (3) *cl up, pushed alng o'r 3 fs out, hrd rdn 2 out, wknd.* (25 to 1 op 14 to 1 tchd 33 to 1) 5
GUV'S JOY (Ire) 9-0 Pat Eddery (5) *beh but in tch, effrt o'r 3 fs out, sn outpcd*... (25 to 1 op 20 to 1 tchd 33 to 1) 6
472⁵ HOLLY GOLIGHTLY 9-0 J Reid (7) *trkd ldrs, wide into strt, wknd appr 3 fs out, tld off*........(14 to 1 op 20 to 1) 7

Dist: 3½l, nk, 4l, 8l, 1½l, 15l. 1m 35.22s. a 7.92s (7 Ran).

SR: 46/35/34/22/ (Mohamed Obaida), C E Brittain

557 Peter Smith Memorial Maiden Stakes Class D (3-y-o) £3,752 1m 3f 5yds... (3:40)

CAIRO PRINCE (Ire) 9-0 J Reid (9) *chsd ldrs, led one and a half fs out, ran on strly, imprsv.*
.... (10 to 1 op 6 to 1 tchd 12 to 1) 1
MASTER CHARLIE 9-0 M Hills (5) *hld up in mid-div, cld o'r 4 fs out, sn not much room, kpt on wl frm over one out.*
.... (50 to 1 op 25 to 1 tchd 66 to 1) 2
SAINT KEYNE 9-0 A McGlone (2) *chsd ldrs, not much room o'r 3 fs out, swtchd rght over 2 out, hng lft frm over one out, ran on*.......... (12 to 1 op 8 to 1 tchd 14 to 1) 3
SCOTSMAN (Ire) 9-0 M Roberts (6) *led to one and a half fs out, one pace*...................(7 to 2 op 3 to 1) 4
SPRING TO ACTION 9-0 L Dettori (1) *trkd ldrs, ev ch 2 fs out, sn rdn and one pace.*
.........................(4 to 1 op 7 to 2 tchd 6 to 1) 5
RAINBOW LAKE 8-9 Pat Eddery (8) *trkd ldrs, ev ch 2 fs out, wknd one out*.............. (5 to 4 fav op 5 to 4 on) 6
HILL OF DREAMS 9-0 R Cochrane (10) *slwly into strd, beh, hdwy 4 fs out, sn outpcd, eased 2 out.*
.... (16 to 1 op 12 to 1 tchd 20 to 1) 7
PRIDWELL 9-0 S Raymont (4) *strted slwly, hdwy 3 fs out, wknd 2 out, eased*.................(33 to 1 op 25 to 1) 8
4801a ONE MORE POUND 9-0 R Perham (11) *cl up, rdn alng 5 fs out, wknd 3 out*.................(50 to 1 op 33 to 1) 9
RITZY 8-9 W Newnes (3) *al beh*......(50 to 1 op 33 to 1) 10
BARRAAK 9-0 W Carson (7) *al beh.*
.....................(25 to 1 op 16 to 1 tchd 33 to 1) 11
318⁸ RANZEL 9-0 G Hind (12) *trkd ldrs, wknd o'r 3 fs out, tld off*..................................(50 to 1 op 25 to 1) 12

Dist: 7l, ½l, 2½l, hd, 5l, 4l, 3l, 2l, 2l, nk. 2m 27.94s. a 11.74s (12 Ran).

SR: 49/35/34/29/28/13/10/-/-/ (R E Sangster), P W Chapple-Hyam

558 Stroud Green Handicap Class C (0-100 3-y-o) £4,836 1m......................(4:10)

400⁵ EASTERN MEMORIES (Ire) [82] 8-6 Pat Eddery (4) *made all, clr appr fnl furlong, shaken up, ran on wl.*
............(13 to 2 op 7 to 1 tchd 8 to 1 and 6 to 1) 1
LYFORD CAY (Ire) [89] 8-13 M Hills (11) *hld up in tch gng wl, effrt 2 fs out, ran on ins last.*
.........................(6 to 1 op 3 to 1 tchd 7 to 1) 2
400³ MR MARTINI (Ire) [97] 9-7 M Roberts (9) *hld up beh, hdwy 2 fs out, kpt on*.................(10 to 1 tchd 12 to 1) 3
AFTER THE LAST [86] 8-10 J Reid (6) *hld up gng wl, cld 2 fs out, ran on ins last, better for race.* (8 to 1 tchd 9 to 1) 4

ECU DE FRANCE (Ire) [85] 8-9 W Carson (5) *trkd ldrs, shaken up 2 fs out, kpt on, better for race.* ....(12 to 1 op 10 to 1) 5
YOUNG ERN [93] 9-3 T Quinn (3) *cl up, rdn 2 fs out, wknd ins last, better for race*............(7 to 1 tchd 8 to 1) 6
CATHERINEOFARAGON [85] 8-9 J Williams (1) *keen hold, trkd ldrs, effrt 2 fs out, sn btn*..... (16 to 1 op 14 to 1) 7
286* DORAZINE [71] 7-9 J Quinn (8) *hld up beh, shrtlvd effrt 2 fs out*.................(13 to 2 op 5 to 1 tchd 7 to 1) 8
GROUND NUT (Ire) [76] 8-0 C Rutter (2) *cl up, rdn 2 fs out, wknd quickly*..............................(33 to 1) 9
EMPIRE POOL [90] 9-0 W R Swinburn (10) *trkd ldrs till wknd o'r 2 fs out*..................(14 to 1 op 12 to 1) 10
SECRET ASSIGNMENT (USA) [72] 7-10³ D Biggs (7) *trkd ldrs, pushed alng o'r 2 fs out, sn not much room and btn*..............................(12 to 1 tchd 10 to 1) 11
MARIUS (Ire) [79] 8-3 D Holland (12) *hld up, pushed alng o'r 3 fs out, sn btn.* (11 to 2 fav op 9 to 2 tchd 6 to 1) 12
Dist: 2l, ¾l, 1l, ¾l, nk, 2½l, 12l, 1½l, 3l, ½l. 1m 47.30s. a 10.20s (12 Ran).
SR: 29/30/36/22/19/26/10/-/-/ (Jim Horgan), R Hannon

559 Thatcham Handicap Class C (0-95 4-y-o and up) £4,878 2m..................(4:40)

226* MASTER FOODBROKER (Ire) [70] 5-9-2 (7*) D McCabe (8) *hld up beh, hdwy 4 fs out, shaken up to ld wl ins last, ran on well*..........................(10 to 1 tchd 12 to 1) 1
94³ CITY LINE [47] 4-7-10⁹ (3*) A Tucker (3) *chsd ldrs, led o'r 3 fs out till wl ins last, no extr.* ....(11 to 1 op 10 to 1 tchd 12 to 1) 2
288* HIERARCH (USA) [74] 4-9-9 A Munro (10) *trkd ldrs, rdn and ev ch appr fnl furlong, no extr.* ....(5 to 1 op 4 to 1 tchd 11 to 2) 3
VADO VIA [47] 5-8-0 G Carter (4) *hld up, rdn and hdwy 3 fs out, btn o'r 2 out, styd on same pace.* ....(5 to 1 op 4 to 1 tchd 11 to 2) 4
MANZOOR SAYADAN (USA) [67] 5-9-6 S Whitworth (9) *hld up, rdn and hdwy o'r 3 fs out, hrd ridden and ch over 2 out, btn over one out.* ....(14 to 1 op 12 to 1 tchd 16 to 1) 5
420 INTRICACY [56] 5-8-6 (3*) F Norton (6) *mid-div, pushed alng 6 fs out, no imprsn strt*....... (20 to 1 op 14 to 1) 6
389⁵ POINCIANA [69] 4-9-4 M Roberts (7) *hld up, hdwy 4 fs out, sn btn*..............(9 to 2 fav op 4 to 1 tchd 5 to 1) 7
420⁴ THOR POWER (Ire) [44] 4-7-0 (7*) Kim McDonnell (1) *trkd ldrs, rdn and wknd o'r 3 fs out*.... (20 to 1 op 16 to 1) 8
420³ PERFORATE [44] (bl) 4-7-7 N Adams (2) *trkd ldr, led hfwy till o'r 4 fs out, wknd*...(9 to 1 op 8 to 1 tchd 10 to 1) 9
ULURU (Ire) [75] 5-9-9 (5*) S Wynne (11) *led to hfwy, led o'r 4 fs out till over 3 out, wknd.* ....(16 to 1 op 12 to 1 tchd 20 to 1) 10
4813a⁹ GO SOUTH [60] (bl) 9-8-13 Pat Eddery (5) *hld up beh, drpd out o'r 4 fs out, tld off.* ....(6 to 1 tchd 13 to 2 and 11 to 2) 11
Dist: ½l, 1½l, 10l, 10l, 2½l, 2l, hd, 1½l, 5l, dist. 3m 48.09s. a 22.09s (11 Ran).
(Broughton Thermal Insulation), W J Musson

OAKLAWN PARK (USA) (firm)
Friday April 16th

560 Apple Blossom Handicap (Grade 1) (4-y-o and up) £198,675 1m 110yds.............

PASEANA (Arg) 6-8-12 C McCarron,...........(5 to 2 on) 1
LOOIE CAPOTE (USA) 4-8-3 K Desormeaux,..... (11 to 1) 2
LUV ME LUV ME NOT (USA) 4-8-2 W Martinez,... (35 to 1) 3
QUEEN OF TRIUMPH (USA) 4-8-0 F Arguello Jr,.. (15 to 1) 4
ERICA'S DREAM (USA) 5-8-1² L Snyder,......... (36 to 1) 5
LOW TOLERANCE (USA) 4-8-4 M Smith,........(69 to 10) 6
SOUTHERN TRUCE (USA) 5-8-5 C Nakatani,.... (38 to 10) 7
SIDE OUT FRONT (USA) 5-8-1⁴ S Romero,....... (36 to 1) 8
RICHARD'S LASS (USA) 5-8-0 J Chavez,....... (15 to 1) 9
Dist: 3½l, 4½l, nk, hd, ½l, ½l, ½l, 4l. 1m 41.80s. (9 Ran).
(S H Craig), R McAnally

ST-CLOUD (FR) (heavy)
Friday April 16th
Going Correction: PLUS 0.70 sec. per fur.

561 Prix Penelope (Group 3) (3-y-o) £23,895 1¼m 110yds.......................(2:25)

WEMYSS BIGHT 8-11 T Jarnet (3) *second strt, chlgd 2 fs out, led one and a half out, ran on wl*.......(24 to 10) 1
4693a* DANCIENNE (Fr) 8-11 D Boeuf (7) *3rd strt, hdwy 2 and a half fs out, led two out till one and a half out, eased whn btn*.......................(17 to 10 fav) 2
4753a³ MISS KADROU (Fr) 8-11 W Mongil (1) *last strt, hdwy o'r 2 fs out, not rch ldrs*......................(25 to 1) 3
FINIR EN BEAUTE (Fr) 8-11 S Guillot (6) *6th strt, effrt 2 fs out, kpt on fnl furlong*................... (87 to 10) 4
296* ACCOMMODATING (USA) 8-11 F Head (2) *led strt till 2 fs out, rdn and wknd one and a half furlongs out.* ....(22 to 10) 5
MOLESNES (USA) 8-11 O Peslier (4) *4th strt, nvr dngrs.* ....(19 to 1) 6
GIFT OF THE NIGHT (USA) 8-11 E Legrix (5) *nvr dngrs.* ....(10 to 1) 7
Dist: 4l, 6l, 1l, 5l, 4l, 4l. 2m 20.50s. a 10.00s (7 Ran).
SR: 71/63/51/49/39/31/23/ (K Abdulla), A Fabre

562 Prix Charles et Henry Rouher (Listed) (4-y-o and up) £14,337 1¼m.......... (3:25)

SERRANT (USA) 5-9-2 T Jarnet,........................ 1
SEBA LA ROUGE (Fr) 6-8-12 W Mongil,................. 2
4737a³ SAKURA BERING (USA) 4-8-12 O Doleuze,............... 3
4737a² MATARUN (Ire) 5-8-12 N Jeanpierre,..................... 4
Dist: 1l, 1½l, sht-hd, 1½l, 3l, 1½l, nose. 2m 16.70s. a 12.70s (8 Ran).
SR: 45/39/36/35/ (D Wildenstein), A Fabre

THIRSK (good)
Friday April 16th
Going Correction: PLUS 0.15 sec. per fur. (races 1,2,4,6), PLUS 0.30 (3,5)

563 Briton Rating Related Maiden Stakes Class D (3-y-o) £3,084 6f............(2:15)

450³ ASHGORE 9-0 Dean McKeown (4) *dsptd ld till led o'r 3 fs out, rdn appr fnl furlong, edgd lft and ran on wl ins last*..............(4 to 1 op 5 to 1 tchd 6 to 1) 1
418⁸ FOLLY VISION (Ire) 8-9 K Darley (6) *trkd ldrs, swtchd to chal appr fnl furlong, sn rdn and kpt on wl.* ....(9 to 2 op 4 to 1) 2
SARANGANI BAY (USA) 9-0 Paul Eddery (5) *dsptd ld o'r 2 fs, cl up, ev ch appr fnl furlong, sn rdn, wknd ins last.* ....(Evens fav op 6 to 4 on tchd 11 to 10) 3
300 SMITH N'ALLAN 9-0 N Day (2) *chsd ldrs till rdn and wknd 2 fs out*......................(25 to 1 op 20 to 1) 4
SCORED AGAIN 9-0 A Culhane (3) *in tch, effrt 2 fs out, sn rdn and wknd appr last*............(7 to 1 op 5 to 1) 5
ANDRULA MOU 8-9 T Lucas (1) *al rear.* ....(16 to 1 op 12 to 1) 6
Dist: ½l, 3½l, 4l, 1½l, 10l. 1m 15.20s. a 5.20s (6 Ran).
SR: 14/7/-/ (Harvey Ashworth), M Johnston

564 Knayton Claiming Stakes Class F (2-y-o) £2,601 5f......................... (2:50)

381⁷ PARKSIDE LADY 7-12² (3*) S Maloney (6) *made all, rdn o'r one furlong out, jst hld on*..........(9 to 1 op 6 to 1) 1
PALACEGATE JO (Ire) 8-3 J Carroll (4) *outpcd and beh, drvn alng and edgd lft hfwy, styd on strly entering fnl furlong, wnt left and jst fld*......(2 to 1 fav op 9 to 4) 2
449³ BATIEN'S RIVER 7-11¹ (3*) D Harrison (2) *al cl up, rdn and ev ch ins fnl furlong, no extr nr finish.* ....(3 to 1 op 9 to 4) 3
WINGS AHEAD 8-2 K Darley (1) *chsd ldrs, hng rght 2 fs out, sn wknd*...........................(11 to 2 op 5 to 1) 4
TILQUHILLIE ROSE 8-6¹ T Lucas (5) *slwly away, al rear.* ....(12 to 1 op 10 to 1) 5
381 RED GRIT (Ire) 8-1 L Charnock (3) *cl up, ev ch 2 fs out, sn rdn, hng rght and wknd o'r one out.* ....(16 to 1 op 20 to 1 tchd 33 to 1) 6
LASTOTHEBRADFIELDS 8-3⁴ R P Elliott (7) *al beh.* ....(13 to 2 op 6 to 1) 7
Dist: Sht-hd, nk, 6l, 8l, sht-hd, 15l. 1m 1.90s. a 4.70s (7 Ran).
SR: 6/9/4/-/ (Mrs Margaret Liles), M H Easterby

565 Birdforth Handicap Class E (0-70 4-y-o and up) £3,209 7f.......................(3:20)

302 GANT BLEU (Fr) [59] 6-9-3 A Culhane (1) *trkd ldrs gng wl, effrt to ld entering fnl furlong, ran on.* ....(8 to 1 op 7 to 1) 1
363⁵ WILD PROSPECT [56] 5-8-11 (3*) S Maloney (4) *led to 3 fs out, cl up, rdn and ev ch entering last, kpt on.* ....(7 to 1 co-fav op 6 to 1) 2
409⁹ WELLSY LAD (USA) [52] (bl) 6-8-10 S Wood (5) *cl up, led 3 fs out till rdn and hdd entering last, kpt on.* ....(20 to 1 op 16 to 1) 3
340⁵ THE DANDY DON (Ire) [49] 4-8-7 K Fallon (15) *mid-div, hdwy 3 fs out, rdn and styd on last 2 furlongs.* ....(9 to 1 op 5 to 1 tchd 10 to 1) 4
362² CLEDESCHAMPS [48] 4-8-6 S Morris (10) *cl up, effrt to chal o'r 2 fs out, rdn over one out, wknd entering last.* ....(17 to 2 op 7 to 1 tchd 9 to 1) 5
403⁴ MASTER HYDE (USA) [63] 4-9-7 Paul Eddery (6) *chsd ldrs, effrt and rdn 2 fs out, one pace appr last.* ....(16 to 1 op 12 to 1) 6
LOMBARD SHIPS [48] 6-8-6 A Mackay (7) *chsd ldrs, rdn 2 fs out, wknd ins last*.............(14 to 1 op 12 to 1) 7
JOKIST [54] 10-8-12 N Day (11) *mid-div, effrt and hdwy 2 fs out, sn rdn and kpt on one pace.* (14 to 1 op 12 to 1) 8
383² SANDMOOR DENIM [58] 6-9-2 S Webster (8) *beh, hdwy 3 fs out, sn rdn, not rch ldrs*..... (7 to 1 co-fav op 5 to 1) 9
363 SCOTTISH PARK [60] 4-9-4 G Duffield (2) *mid-div till hmpd and lost pl hfwy, some hdwy fnl 2 fs*........ (20 to 1) 10

362* ROYAL GIRL [60] 6-9-1 (3*) D Harrison (14) *chsd ldrs, rdn 2 fs out, sn btn*............... (7 to 1 co-fav tchd 8 to 1) 11
492 TWILIGHT FALLS [46] 8-8-4 N Connorton (3) *al mid-div.* .... (14 to 1 op 12 to 1) 12
363 DREAM CARRIER (Ire) [67] 5-9-11 Alex Greaves (9) *al rear.* .... (12 to 1 op 10 to 1) 13
391[8] FOOLISH TOUCH [56] 11-9-0 Dale Gibson (12) *slwly into strd, al beh*.................................(10 to 1) 14
PATIENCE PLEASE [58] 4-9-2 M Birch (16) *chsd ldrs, rdn and wknd o'r 2 fs out*............ (12 to 1 op 14 to 1) 15
LAWNSWOOD JUNIOR [61] 6-9-5 K Darley (13) *al rear.* .... (14 to 1 op 12 to 1) 16

Dist: ½l, nk, ½l, 1½l, hd, 1l, hd, ½l, 2½l, 2½l. 1m 28.90s. a 6.10s (16 Ran).
SR: 43/38/33/28/22/36/18/23/25/ (E C Alton), R M Whitaker

566 Hambleton Conditions Stakes Class C (3-y-o) £4,119 5f...................... (3:50)

316[7] NIGHT MELODY (Ire) 8-10 K Darley (6) *chsd ldrs, effrt and hdwy appr fnl furlong, rdn ins last to ld nr line.* ....(11 to 4 jt-fav op 5 to 2) 1
PALACEGATE EPISODE (Ire) 9-1 J Carroll (2) *cl up, led aftr one furlong, rdn appr last, hdd and no extr nr finish.* ....(11 to 4 jt-fav op 5 to 2 tchd 3 to 1) 2
RISTON LADY (Ire) 8-6 (3*) D Harrison (1) *cl up, effrt to chal entering fnl furlong, sn rdn and edgd rght, no extr nr finish*...............(12 to 1 op 20 to 1 tchd 25 to 1) 3
SAINT EXPRESS 8-12 A Culhane (3) *chsd ldrs, outpcd hfwy, kpt on fnl 2 fs, nvr dngrs*......(4 to 1 op 3 to 1) 4
SATANK (USA) 9-2 G Duffield (5) *led one furlong, cl up till rdn and wknd 2 fs out*...(7 to 2 op 3 to 1 tchd 4 to 1) 5
JOBIE 8-10 N Day (4) *outpcd and beh frm hfwy*. (10 to 1) 6

Dist: Hd, ½l, 6l, 2½l, 10l. 59.80s. a 2.60s (6 Ran).
SR: 59/63/55/34/28/-/ (P D Savill), R Hannon

567 Sowerby Maiden Stakes Class D (3-y-o) £3,201 1½m...................... (4:20)

457[2] KASSAB 9-0 R Hills (2) *made all, rdn 2 fs out, styd on strly ins last*.........................(6 to 4 fav op 5 to 4) 1
ANCHOR STONE 9-0 W Ryan (3) *trkd ldr, took clr order 4 fs out, effrt to chal 2 and a half out, sn rdn, one pace appr last*...............(9 to 4 op 5 to 2 tchd 2 to 1) 2
459[6] KHISAL (Can) 9-0 G Duffield (6) *hdwy to chase ldrs hfwy, effrt 4 fs out, sn rdn and wknd 2 out.* ....(4 to 1 tchd 5 to 1) 3
HATITH (Ire) 9-0 Paul Eddery (7) *chsd ldrs, rdn 5 fs out, sn one pace*........................... (6 to 1 op 4 to 1) 4
CARA'S PRIDE 8-9 Dale Gibson (4) *beh and green, sn pushed alng, styd on fnl 3 fs*...... (25 to 1 op 16 to 1) 5
HYDE'S HAPPY HOUR 9-0 Kim Tinkler (5) *al rear, tld off fnl 4 fs*...........................(33 to 1 op 20 to 1) 6
344[5] MEESON IMPOSSIBLE (bl) 9-0 J Fortune (1) *chsd ldrs to hfwy, sn lost pl and tld off fnl 4 fs.* (33 to 1 op 25 to 1) 7

Dist: 3½l, 8l, 5l, hd, 12l, 30l. 2m 40.50s. a 10.30s (7 Ran).
SR: 33/26/10/-/ (Hamdan Al-Maktoum), J L Dunlop

568 Oakstripe Claiming Handicap Class F (0-70 3-y-o and up) £2,959 6f........ (4:50)

177[8] JUST BOB [58] 4-9-8 J Fortune (16) *dwlt, hdwy hfwy, led one and a half fs out, hrd rdn ins last and jst hld on.* .... (20 to 1 op 16 to 1) 1
492[2] STRIP CARTOON (Ire) [50] (bl) 5-8-7 (7*) G Strange (17) *led, hdd one and a half fs out, rdn and rallied ins last.* .... (11 to 2 op 5 to 1 tchd 6 to 1) 2
362[4] SALADAN KNIGHT [54] 8-9-4 D Nicholls (12) *mid-div, hdwy o'r 2 fs out, sn rdn, edgd lft and one pace appr last.* ....(8 to 1 tchd 10 to 1) 3
176[7] SULLY'S CHOICE (USA) [47] (bl) 12-8-11 S Wood (13) *cl up, ev ch 2 fs out, sn rdn and one pace*. (14 to 1 op 10 to 1) 4
424[6] MEESON TIMES [47] 5-8-11 K Darley (14) *hdwy hfwy, rdn and kpt on fnl 2 fs*........................ (16 to 1 op 14 to 1) 5
380[2] MISS BRIGHTSIDE [40] 5-8-4 S Webster (15) *chsd ldrs, rdn 2 fs out, sn one pace*....(6 to 1 op 5 to 1 tchd 13 to 2) 6
398[8] LARN FORT [52] 3-8-4 R Hills (18) *beh, hdwy 2 fs out, sn one pace*...............(15 to 2 op 7 to 1 tchd 9 to 1) 7
CRAIL HARBOUR [36] (v) 7-8-0 Dale Gibson (2) *mid-div, effrt and some hdwy 2 fs out, not rch ldrs*..... (20 to 1) 8
424* MURRAY'S MAZDA (Ire) [58] 4-9-8 (5ex) J Carroll (9) *mid-div, effrt hfwy, sn rdn and btn.* ....(9 to 2 fav op 5 to 1 tchd 4 to 1) 9
421[4] LADY SABO [64] 4-10-0 Paul Eddery (3) *chsd ldrs to hfwy, sn btn*..............................(9 to 1 op 7 to 1) 10
194[4] HANSOM LAD [39] 10-8-3 Dean McKeown (11) *nvr dngrs.* .... (16 to 1 op 14 to 1) 11
ARABAT [59] (v) 6-9-9 Jaki Houston (7) *nvr rch ldrs.* .... (20 to 1 op 16 to 1) 12
DARK AND STORMY [48] 3-8-0 A Mackay (1) *al beh.* .... (50 to 1 op 33 to 1) 13
253[6] ROSE GEM (Ire) [57] 4-9-7 K Fallon (6) *cl up till rdn and wknd o'r 2 fs out*..................(20 to 1 op 16 to 1) 14
BREEZE AWAY [60] 4-9-3 (7*) G Parkin (5) *in tch to hfwy, sn beh*..................................(16 to 1 op 14 to 1) 15
275[9] GATE OF HEAVEN [41] 3-7-7 E Johnson (10) *al rear.* .... (50 to 1 op 20 to 1) 16
424 LIBERTY GLEN [40] 4-8-4 G Bardwell (8) *al beh.* .... (33 to 1 op 20 to 1) 17

Dist: Hd, 6l, 2l, sht-hd, 2½l, 1½l, 1½l, ½l, 3l, ½l. 1m 15.40s. a 5.40s (17 Ran).
SR: 18/9/-/-/-/-/ (J Fotherby), S E Kettlewell

AQUEDUCT (USA) (firm)
Saturday April 17th

569 Wood Memorial Invitational (Grade 1) (3-y-o) £198,675 1m 1f.....................

STORM TOWER (USA) 9-0 R Wilson,............(26 to 10) 1
TOSSOFTHECOIN (USA) 9-0 R Romero,..........(16 to 1) 2
MARKED TREE (USA) 9-0 P Day,..........(16 to 10 jt-fav) 3
DUC D'SLIGOVIL (USA) 9-0 Julie Krone,..........(16 to 1) 4
MARCO BAY (USA) 9-0 A Madrid,................(11 to 1) 5
OZAN (USA) 9-0 E Maple,................(16 to 10 jt-fav) 6
AS INDICATED (USA) 9-0 C Bisono,.............(56 to 10) 7
TAKIN' NAMES (USA) 9-0 R Migliore,.............(55 to 1) 8
CLASSI ENVOY (USA) 9-0 R Davis,...............(80 to 1) 9
COUNTRY STORE (USA) 9-0 C Perret,.................... 0
ROHWER (USA) 9-0 J Chavez,..................(59 to 1) 0
TRI FOR THE GOLD (USA) 9-0 M Vigliotti,........(41 to 1) 0

Dist: 2l, ¾l, ½l, 1l, ¾l, 3½l, 2 ¼l, 2l, nk, 4½l. 1m 48.50s. (12 Ran).
(Summa Stable), B Perkins Jr

KEENELAND (USA) (firm)
Saturday April 17th

570 Ashland Stakes (Grade 1) (3-y-o) £113,889 1m 110yds...............................

LUNAR SPOOK (USA) 8-9 S Sellers,............(26 to 10) 1
AVIE'S SHADOW (USA) 8-3 G Gomez,............(12 to 1) 2
ROAMIN RACHEL (USA) 8-3 C Antley,..........(5 to 4 on) 3
FUTURE PRETENSE (USA) 8-0 J Bravo,.......... (17 to 1) 4
SHE'S A LITTLE SHY (USA) 8-3 K Bourque,....... (19 to 1) 5
HEY HAZEL (Can) 8-9 D Seymour,...............(13 to 1) 6
SENTIMENTALDIAMOND (USA) 8-6 M Johnston, (74 to 10) 7

Dist: 2½l, ½l, nk, 1 ¾l, 4l, 5l. 1m 43.40s. (7 Ran).
(Omoyglare Stud Farm),

LEOPARDSTOWN (IRE) (yielding to soft)
Saturday April 17th
Going Correction: PLUS 0.25 sec. per fur. (races 1,2), PLUS 0.40 (3,4,5,6,7)

571 Corrig EBF Maiden (2-y-o) £4,830 5f (2:00)

KLY GREEN 9-0 K J Manning (3).................. (3 to 1) 1
CATCH A DREAM (Ire) 8-9 (2*) R M Burke (13).....(16 to 1) 2
BARTOK (Ire) 9-0 P V Gilson (7)..................(10 to 1) 3
269[8] MUSICAL BANKER 8-6 (8*) J J Stack (2)..........(20 to 1) 4
COMMON RUMPUS (Ire) 9-0[3] J P Murtagh (4).... (20 to 1) 5
LA BERTA (Ire) 8-11 W J O'Connor (10)........... (14 to 1) 6
SHARP PHASE (Ire) 9-0 S Craine (12)..............(7 to 1) 7
PAUGIM (Ire) 9-0 P Shanahan (1)..................(7 to 1) 8
YAHTHAB (Ire) 9-0 W J Supple (9)...............(6 to 4 fav) 9
MON PANACHE (Ire) 8-11 R Hughes (8)........... (14 to 1) 10
PETER'S POWER (Ire) 9-0 L Piggott (5)...........(10 to 1) 11
WHEREWILITALL END (Ire) 9-0 J F Egan (11)..... (10 to 1) 12

Dist: Hd, ¾l, 1l, 1½l. 1m 3.40s. a 4.70s (12 Ran).
SR: 31/27/27/23/17/-/ (Maktoum Al Maktoum), J S Bolger

572 Eden Handicap (0-100 3-y-o and up) £3,450 5f................................. (2:30)

310[8] MAGIC DON (Ire) [-] 4-7-6 (8*) R T Fitzpatrick (13) (25 to 1) 1
308[6] DONNASOO (Ire) [-] 4-8-10 Joanna Morgan (5)....(12 to 1) 2
DESERT THUNDER (Ire) [-] (bl) 4-10-0 P Shanahan (3) ....(10 to 1) 3
486[9] BENE MERENTI (Ire) [-] 3-7-10[4] (8*) R V Skelly (2) (33 to 1) 4
280[3] SHOOT THE DEALER (Ire) [-] 3-7-9 (2*) D G O'Shea (9) ....(8 to 1) 5
280* KERB CRAWLER [-] (bl) 3-7-6 (8*) P P Murphy (14) (13 to 2) 6
FAIRYDEL (Ire) [-] 3-6-11 (10*) L O'Shea (8)....... (14 to 1) 7
RECOLLECTION (Ire) [-] 4-7-9 (8*) B J Halligan (4) (33 to 1) 8
310 MEMSAHB [-] 4-8-11 B Coogan (10).............(20 to 1) 9
UKUD (USA) [-] 3-8-6 W J Supple (6)..............(6 to 1) 10
270* SUMY [-] 3-9-6 J P Murtagh (11)..............(2 to 1 fav) 11
310 LUTE AND LYRE (Ire) [-] 4-9-8 L Piggott (1)...... (12 to 1) 12
NORDIC OAK (Ire) [-] 5-9-1 (6*) J A Heffernan (15).. (6 to 1) 13
KO SAMAT [-] 8-7-10 (2*) R M Burke (12).........(33 to 1) 14
SALLUSTAR [-] 8-7-13 (4*) W J Smith (16).........(12 to 1) 15
CLANDOLLY (Ire) [-] 5-8-11 D V Smith (7).........(16 to 1) 16

Dist: Nk, 1½l, nk, nk. 1m 2.10s. a 3.40s (16 Ran).
SR: 43/52/64/35/31/-/ (Mrs Anne Coughlan), J T Gorman

573 Leopardstown 1,000 Guineas Trial (Listed Race) (3-y-o) £8,625 7f..............(3:00)

MIAMI SANDS (Ire) 8-10 R Hughes (4) *trkd ldr, prog to ld 3 fs out, sn rdn, kpt on wl*....................(5 to 2 fav) 1
258* WEEKEND MADNESS (Ire) 8-10 W J O'Connor (1) *strted slwly, sn wl plcd, prog to chal 2 fs out, no extr ins last.* ....(7 to 1) 2
306^{8} TAKE NO CHANCES (Ire) 8-10 P V Gilson (8) *hld up, rdn and prog o'r 2 fs out, ran on strly fnl furlong.* (20 to 1) 3
258^{2} ELEGANT BLOOM (Ire) 8-10 P Shanahan (6) *wl plcd, rdn 3 fs out, wknd one out*....................(4 to 1) 4
SABAYA (USA) 8-10 W J Supple (2) *mid-div, rdn o'r 2 fs out, swtchd rght, prog ins last*....................(11 to 2) 5
I HAVE TO SAY (Ire) 8-10 G Curran (9) *led to 3 fs out, sn rdn, wknd o'r one out*....................(33 to 1) 6
258^{3} TARTAN LADY (Ire) 8-10 S Craine (7) *al rear*....................(9 to 1) 7
PREPONDERANCE (Ire) 8-10 L Piggott (5) *wl plcd till rdn and wknd o'r 2 fs out, eased fnl furlong*....................(9 to 1) 8
258^{6} PERNILLA (Ire) 8-10 K J Manning (3) *strted slwly, prog 3 fs out till swrvd lft through rls 125 yards out*..... (8 to 1) ro

Dist: 1l, sht-hd, 3l, hd. 1m 34.10s. a 8.70s (9 Ran).
SR: 8/5/4/-/-/-/ (Dieter H Hofemeier), John M Oxx

574 Leopardstown 2,000 Guineas Trial (Listed Race) (3-y-o) £8,625 7f..............(3:30)

MASSYAR (Ire) 8-10 R Hughes (3) *wl plcd, prog to chal o'r one furlong out, ran on strly to ld ins last half-furlong.* ....(6 to 1) 1
FATHERLAND (Ire) 9-3 L Piggott (2) *led, rdn o'r one furlong out, hdd ins last half-furlong, eased cl hme.* ....(13 to 8 on) 2
271* NORDIC FOX (Ire) 8-10 K J Manning (6) *trkd ldrs, rdn and prog 3 fs out, no extr strt*....................(4 to 1) 3
KHORAZ (USA) 8-10 Jacqueline Freda (1) *trkd ldr, rdn 3 fs out, wknd ins last*....................(8 to 1) 4
271^{5} RONDELLI (Ire) 8-10 J A Heffernan (4) *strted slwly, al rear, rdn 3 fs out, not quicken*....................(25 to 1) 5
UPWARD SURGE (Ire) 8-10 P Shanahan (5) *al rear, rdn 3 fs out, not quicken*....................(14 to 1) 6

Dist: 2l, 3½l, ½l, 6l. 1m 31.40s. a 6.00s (6 Ran).
SR: 48/49/31/29/11/-/ (H H Aga Khan), John M Oxx

575 Connell Handicap (0-85 4-y-o and up) £3,450 1½m...................... (4:00)

298 LYPHARD ABU (Ire) [-] 5-8-0[1] (6*) J A Heffernan (14) (14 to 1) 1
MASAI WARRIOR [-] 6-9-3 (2*) R M Burke (12) .... (16 to 1) 2
NAIYSARI (Ire) [-] 5-9-4 J P Murtagh (11).......... (10 to 1) 3
ASSURING (Ire) [-] 5-9-2 K J Manning (22).......... (7 to 1) 4
$4685a^{3}$ BITOFABANTER [-] 6-9-3 N Byrne (19)........(6 to 1 jt-fav) 5
309 ALTEREZZA (USA) [-] (bl) 6-8-13 P Shanahan (20) (12 to 1) 6
MARILYN (Ire) [-] 4-8-12 J F Egan (6).............. (12 to 1) 7
309 LEGAL ADVISER [-] 6-9-5 D Manning (5).......... (16 to 1) 8
NATURAL ABILITY [-] 8-8-12 (6*) P Carberry (13).. (10 to 1) 9
HIDDEN LIGHT (Ire) [-] 4-9-4 P V Gilson (3)........ (10 to 1) 10
281^{9} RATTLE AND HUM [-] 6-8-13 R Hughes (1)........ (12 to 1) 11
SAKANDA (Ire) [-] 4-8-13 (8*) T P Treacy (17)...... (10 to 1) 12
MARIYDA (Ire) [-] 4-9-6 (8*) M F Ryan (8).......... (20 to 1) 13
OFTEN AHEAD (Ire) [-] 5-9-7 N G McCullagh (9)... (14 to 1) 14
281 STEEL GEM (Ire) [-] 4-7-12 Joanna Morgan (4).... (14 to 1) 15
$4685a^{6}$ GREEN GLEN (USA) [-] 4-9-0 L Piggott (2).... (6 to 1 jt-fav) 16
TIME IT RIGHT (Ire) [-] 4-9-6 J Ely (7)..............(14 to 1) 17
298 PRINCE PERICLES (Ire) [-] 4-8-5 W J Supple (15) (20 to 1) 18
281 OLD TALKA RIVER [-] (bl) 6-8-9 (8*) D J O'Donohoe (21) ....(20 to 1) 19
LET IT RIDE (Ire) [-] 4-7-13 (4*) W J Smith (16)..... (14 to 1) 20
DOMINO'S RING (Ire) [-] 4-10-0 W J O'Connor (18) (20 to 1) 21
272^{9} PURPLE EMPEROR (Fr) [-] 4-9-7 S Craine (10).... (12 to 1) 22

Dist: 1½l, 1l, ½l, 2l. 2m 41.80s. a 10.80s (22 Ran).
SR: 31/42/39/36/33/-/ (D Bernie), J S Bolger

576 Ballysax Race (Listed Race) (3-y-o) £8,625 1¼m........................... (4:30)

SHANDON LAKE (Ire) 8-11 K J Manning (6) *made all, rdn o'r 3 fs out, styd on wl*....................(4 to 1) 1
DANSE ROYALE (Ire) 8-9[1] L Piggott (2) *trkd ldrs, chlgd 2 fs out, no extr cl hme, swshd tail und pres*........(7 to 1) 2
SINISSIPI (USA) 9-0 J P Murtagh (8) *mid-div, prog strt to chal fnl furlong, kpt on*....................(9 to 2) 3
282* SPECIAL PAGEANT (Ire) 8-8 J A Heffernan (4) *trkd ldr, rdn o'r 3 fs out, wknd over one out*....................(14 to 1) 4
257^{5} DAHLIA'S BEST (USA) 8-11 W J Supple (3) *hld up, prog 5 fs out, no extr strt*....................(25 to 1) 5
306^{2} FARMAAN (Ire) 8-11 R Hughes (7) *hld up till some prog 2 fs out*....................(8 to 1) 6
BABUSHKA (Ire) 8-8 S Craine (1) *al rear*..........(25 to 1) 7
ROYAL BALLERINA (Ire) 8-8 W J O'Connor (5) *strted slwly, sn wl plcd, rdn and wknd 3 fs out*..........(9 to 4 fav) 8
307* TOPOGRAPHE (Fr) 8-11 P Shanahan (9) *trkd ldrs till rdn and wknd 4 fs out*....................(15 to 2) 9

Dist: ½l, hd, 3½l, 3l. 2m 12.20s. a 7.50s (9 Ran).
SR: 62/59/63/50/47/-/ (J P Hill), J S Bolger

577 Arkendale EBF Maiden (3-y-o) £3,450 1m ....(5:00)

MANDE MERCHANT (Ire) 8-11[3] (6*) C Everard (5)..(10 to 1) 1
DAFTARI (Ire) 9-0 D Hogan (4)................. (9 to 4 fav) 2
ABEL TASMAN (USA) 9-0 P V Gilson (15).......... (5 to 1) 3
TRILLICK (Ire) 8-5 (6*) J A Heffernan (1).......... (10 to 1) 4
VALUEWISE (Ire) 8-13[2] J P Murtagh (2)............(16 to 1) 5
CLEAR ABILITY (Ire) 8-11 P Shanahan (3)......... (3 to 1) 6
ROLANDS GIRL (Ire) 8-3 (8*) M W Martin (9)...... (50 to 1) 7
267^{3} RUNNING GUEST (Ire) 8-11 N G McCullagh (6)... (14 to 1) 8
PLUM LICK (Ire) 8-4[1] (8*) T E Durcan (13).......... (9 to 1) 9
SUEKAR (Ire) 8-9 (2*) D G O'Shea (7)..............(8 to 1) 10
BOTHSIDESNOW (Ire) 9-0 R Hughes (16)..........(14 to 1) 11
ARZAAQ (USA) 9-0 W J Supple (8)............... (10 to 1) 12
ANOTHER FIDDLE (Ire) 9-0 S Craine (11).......... (12 to 1) 13
256 CLANFLUTHER (Ire) 9-0 D V Smith (12).......... (33 to 1) 14
STATE PRINCESS (Ire) 8-3 (8*) P P Murphy (14)... (14 to 1) 15
KERMIS (Fr) 9-0 J F Egan (10)....................(33 to 1) 16

Dist: Hd, ½l, 1l, nk. 1m 46.20s. a 8.20s (16 Ran).
SR: 25/24/22/16/17/-/ (Miss E Oxx), John M Oxx

NEWBURY (good)
Saturday April 17th
Going Correction: PLUS 0.60 sec. per fur.

578 P. C. L. Burghclere Conditions Stakes Class B (3-y-o) £6,280 1m 3f 5yds... (2:00)

393* NEWTON'S LAW (Ire) 8-12 Pat Eddery (4) *sn led, shaken up one furlong out, hrd rdn ins last, jst hld on.* .... (11 to 10 on tchd 5 to 4 on and Evens) 1
BLUE JUDGE (Ire) 8-12 C Roche (2) *trkd ldr, pushed alng 5 fs out, hrd rdn 2 out, rallied ins last, jst fld.* ....(4 to 1 op 5 to 1) 2
372* ERICOLIN (Ire) 8-12 M Roberts (6) *hld up beh, hdwy o'r 2 fs out, sn ev ch, once pace appr last.* (12 to 1 op 10 to 1) 3
185* MARCO MAGNIFICO (USA) 8-10 W Carson (1) *trkd ldrs, shaken up 3 fs out, wknd o'r one out.* (8 to 1 op 6 to 1) 4
JACKPOT STAR 8-12 J Reid (5) *hld up beh, effrt o'r 2 fs out, sn wknd*..........(13 to 2 op 6 to 1 tchd 7 to 1) 5
404^{5} ALDERNEY PRINCE (USA) 8-10 A Munro (3) *trkd ldg trio, hdwy 3 fs out, btn 2 out*........... (25 to 1 op 12 to 1) 6

Dist: Sht-hd, 10l, 4l, 3l, 8l. 2m 27.02s. a 10.82s (6 Ran).
SR: 56/55/35/25/21/3/ (R E Sangster), P W Chapple-Hyam

579 Lanes End John Porter EBF Stakes Class A (Group 3) (4-y-o and up) £20,439 1½m 5yds.............................. (2:30)

LINPAC WEST 7-8-12 L Dettori (3) *hld up, swtchd rght o'r 2 fs out, led one and a half out, ran on wl.* .... (25 to 1 op 20 to 1 tchd 33 to 1) 1
4727a* SPRING 4-8-7 W Carson (4) *hld up in tch, pushed alng and cld o'r 2 fs out, chsd wnr appr last, no extr.* ....(100 to 30 op 11 to 4 tchd 7 to 2) 2
ALWAYS FRIENDLY 5-8-9 A Munro (1) *strted slwly, hld up, rdn and hdwy to hold ev ch 2 fs out, styd on ins last.* .... (15 to 2 op 7 to 1 tchd 8 to 1) 3
ASSESSOR (Ire) 4-9-2 J Reid (7) *in cl tch, ev ch o'r 2 fs out, styd on*.............. (11 to 2 op 4 to 1 tchd 6 to 1) 4
MASHAALLAH (USA) 5-9-4 M Roberts (6) *led, rdn alng o'r 3 fs out, hdd one and a half out, wknd.* ....(7 to 4 fav op 6 to 4 tchd 15 to 8) 5
314* SHAMBO 6-9-1 Pat Eddery (5) *trkd ldr, ev ch 2 fs out, btn o'r one out*.............(15 to 2 op 8 to 1 tchd 7 to 1) 6
JAPE (USA) 4-8-10 R Cochrane (2) *trkd ldrs, ev ch 2 fs out, rdn and btn quickly.* (16 to 1 op 14 to 1 tchd 20 to 1) 7

Dist: 2l, 1l, 2½l, nk, 4l, 3½l. 2m 41.92s. a 12.32s (7 Ran).
SR: 47/38/38/40/41/30/18/ (Linpac Group Limited), C W C Elsey

580 Singer & Friedlander Greenham Stakes Class A (Group 3) (3-y-o) £22,383 7f (3:00)

INCHINOR 9-0 L Dettori (8) *hld up gng wl, shaken up and quickened to ld one furlong out, ran on well und pres.* ....(7 to 2 op 5 to 2 tchd 4 to 1) 1
SHARP PROD (USA) 9-0 B Raymond (3) *led to one furlong out, rallied und pres, kpt on wl*....(14 to 1 op 12 to 1) 2
TINNERS WAY (USA) 9-0 Pat Eddery (5) *hld up, swtchd rght and cld o'r one furlong out, sn ev ch, hrd rdn and one pace ins last*.................... (6 to 1 op 9 to 2) 3
RUSTIC CRAFT (Ire) 9-0 J Williams (7) *hld up beh, pushed alng hfwy, outpcd o'r 2 fs out, styd on ins last.* ....(20 to 1 tchd 25 to 1) 4
BASIM (USA) 9-0 C Roche (2) *cl up, pushed alng hfwy, hrd rdn and ev ch 2 fs out, wknd o'r one out.* ....(9 to 4 fav op 2 to 1 tchd 5 to 2) 5
FIRM PLEDGE (USA) 9-0 A Munro (1) *trkd ldrs, ev ch 2 fs out, wknd quickly o'r one out, better for race.* .... (11 to 2 op 4 to 1) 6
SON PARDO 9-0 J Reid (4) *cl up, pushed alng 3 fs out, btn appr 2 out*............ (13 to 2 op 10 to 1 tchd 6 to 1) 7

Dist: Nk, ¾l, 10l, 2l, 2½l, 4l. 1m 30.38s. a 6.28s (7 Ran).
SR: 69/68/66/36/30/22/10/ (Sir Philip Oppenheimer), R Charlton

581 Ladbrokes Spring Handicap Class B (0-105 4-y-o and up) £17,993 1m 7yds (3:30)

TISSISAT (USA) [83] 4-9-1 L Dettori (20) *beh, hdwy 2 fs out, led appr last, ran on wl*.........(20 to 1 tchd 25 to 1) 1

RISK MASTER [82] 4-9-0 R Hills (2) *beh, hdwy and not much room 2 fs out, swtchd rght o'r one out, ran on wl.* ....(20 to 1 op 14 to 1) 2
315[8] ROYAL SEATON [85] 4-9-3 S Whitworth (8) *beh, hdwy 3 fs out, rdn appr last, kpt on wl.*....(12 to 1 tchd 14 to 1) 3
391[5] NEPTUNE'S PET [83] 5-9-1 J Reid (12) *mid-div, hdwy o'r 2 fs out, kpt on.*..........(14 to 1) 4
524* WILL OF STEEL [87] 4-9-5 (7ex) K Fallon (11) *hld up in mid-div, hdwy o'r one furlong out, sn one pace*...(6 to 1 jt-fav tchd 7 to 1) 5
KING ATHELSTAN (USA) [96] 5-10-0 B Raymond (15) *keen hold, trkd ldrs, led briefly o'r one furlong out, one pace, better for race*..........(33 to 1) 6
293[3] KNOCK TO ENTER (USA) [90] 5-9-8 J Williams (9) *beh, hdwy o'r one furlong out, styd on, nrst finish.* ....(9 to 1 op 8 to 1 tchd 10 to 1) 7
PORT SUNLIGHT (Ire) [80] 5-8-12 A McGlone (3) *chsd ldrs, hrd rdn one furlong out, sn no extr.* ....(14 to 1 tchd 16 to 1) 8
315 EFHARISTO [89] 4-9-7 M Roberts (7) *chsd ldrs, not much room o'r 2 fs out, sn rdn and btn.*..........(6 to 1 jt-fav op 11 to 2 tchd 7 to 1) 9
DAWNING STREET (Ire) [90] 5-9-8 W Carson (16) *chsd ldrs, rdn o'r 2 fs out, btn over one out.* ....(9 to 1 op 7 to 1 tchd 10 to 1) 10
391 TALENT (USA) [81] (v) 5-8-13 A Munro (18) *trkd ldrs till wknd wl o'r one furlong out, eased.* ....(16 to 1 tchd 20 to 1) 11
425[3] PAY HOMAGE [89] 5-9-7 S O'Gorman (10) *trkd ldrs, rdn 2 fs out, wknd o'r one out*..........(16 to 1 tchd 20 to 1) 12
391 SAND TABLE [80] 4-8-12 B Rouse (17) *al beh.* ....(25 to 1 op 20 to 1 tchd 33 to 1) 13
HIGHLAND MAGIC (Ire) [76] 5-8-8 C Rutter (4) *al beh.* ....(20 to 1) 14
475[3] INVOCATION [73] 6-8-5 N Adams (5) *trkd ldrs, led 3 fs out till hdd and wknd o'r one out*.....(25 to 1 op 20 to 1) 15
GOOGLY [73] 4-8-5 G Bardwell (19) *hld up beh, effrt 4 fs out, sn btn*..........(20 to 1) 16
SUNDAY'S HILL [93] 4-9-11 R Cochrane (6) *al beh.* ....(25 to 1 op 20 to 1 tchd 33 to 1) 17
AMAZE [90] (bl) 4-9-8 Paul Eddery (14) *al beh.* ....(14 to 1 tchd 16 to 1) 18
CONFRONTER [78] 4-8-10 G Carter (1) *led to 3 fs out, wknd quickly*.......(20 to 1 op 16 to 1 tchd 25 to 1) 19
480[8] SAAHI (USA) [76] 4-8-3 (5*) K Rutter (13) *al beh, wide into strt, tld off*..........(33 to 1) 20

Dist: 1½l, ½l, 2½l, nk, sht-hd, nk, 2l, nk, ¾l, ¾l. 1m 43.29s. a 7.49s (20 Ran).

SR: 61/55/56/46/49/57/50/34/42/ (The Queen), I A Balding

582 Ben Michaelson 80th Birthday Maiden Stakes Class D (3-y-o) £4,175 1m....(4:00)

PLANETARY ASPECT (USA) 9-0 J Reid (6) *al gng wl, trkd ldrs, led ins fnl furlong, ran on well.* ....(6 to 4 fav op Evens tchd 2 to 1) 1
CLOUDED ELEGANCE 9-0 L Dettori (22) *chsd ldrs, hdwy and ev ch one furlong out, ran on wl.* ....(6 to 1 op 14 to 1) 2
GONE FOR A BURTON (Ire) 9-0 T Sprake (13) *trkd ldrs, led one and a half fs out till ins last, no extr*.....(66 to 1) 3
PREROGATIVE 9-0 R Cochrane (9) *mid-div, hdwy 3 fs out, styd on frm o'r one out.* ....(20 to 1 op 14 to 1 tchd 25 to 1) 4
ARID 9-0 M Roberts (10) *keen hold, chsd ldrs, shaken up and kpt on frm o'r one furlong out, improve.* ....(8 to 1 op 5 to 1 tchd 9 to 1) 5
GREEN CHILI 8-9 R Hills (18) *chsd ldrs gng wl, kpt on one pace fnl 2 fs, prmsg*..........(33 to 1) 6
SCARLET TUNIC (USA) 9-0 B Raymond (1) *mid-div, styd on fnl 2 fs, nrst finish*....(14 to 1 op 8 to 1 tchd 16 to 1) 7
ALLESCA 8-9 R Price (2) *cl up till rdn and wknd wl o'r one furlong out*..........(66 to 1) 8
BEVERLY KNIGHT 9-0 C Rutter (20) *cl up, led 2 fs out to one and a half out, wknd*........(50 to 1 op 66 to 1) 9
300[5] IMPERIAL TOKAY (USA) 9-0 J Williams (5) *hld up beh, swtchd lft and effrt 2 fs out, sn btn.* ....(25 to 1 op 20 to 1) 10
FOX SPARROW 9-0 S Raymont (21) *hld up beh, nvr rchd chalg pos*..........(25 to 1 op 33 to 1) 11
346[7] MASTER BEVELED 9-0 N Adams (7) *chsd ldrs till wknd appr 3 fs out*..........(66 to 1) 12
WINNING APPEAL (Fr) 8-9 Pat Eddery (19) *led to 2 fs out, wknd*..........(14 to 1 op 10 to 1 tchd 16 to 1) 13
BELFRY GREEN (Ire) 9-0 A Clark (11) *beh, effrt 3 fs out, sn btn*..........(66 to 1) 14
417 BAYFAN (Ire) 9-0 B Rouse (3) *beh, effrt and not much room 4 fs out, sn btn*..........(66 to 1) 15
313[2] GRAN SENORUM (USA) 9-0 A Munro (8) *trkd ldrs till wknd 3 fs out*..........(6 to 1 op 4 to 1) 16
MOST EQUAL 9-0 G Carter (12) *nvr dngrs*.......(66 to 1) 17
346[8] M'BEBE 9-0 R Street (14) *al beh*..........(66 to 1) 18
417[5] JUST JAMIE 9-0 Paul Eddery (16) *al beh.* ....(25 to 1 op 20 to 1 tchd 33 to 1) 19
TRIPPIANO 9-0 A McGlone (4) *cl up, rdn alng 3 fs out, wknd*..........(10 to 1 tchd 14 to 1) 20
SULA MOON 8-9 K Fallon (17) *nvr dngrs*........(66 to 1) 21
300[6] SALVATORE GIULIANO 9-0 W Carson (15) *trkd ldrs 3 fs, sn beh*..........(25 to 1 op 20 to 1 tchd 33 to 1) 22

Dist: 2l, ¾l, 2½l, 4l, ½l, 2½l, hd, 2l, ¾l, ½l. 1m 48.17s. a 11.07s (22 Ran).

SR: 6/-/-/-/-/-/ (R E Sangster), P W Chapple-Hyam

583 Bridget Maiden Fillies Stakes Class D (3-y-o) £3,817 7f..........(4:30)

WINGED VICTORY (Ire) 8-11 L Dettori (5) *trkd ldrs, led o'r one furlong out, quickened clr, imprsv.* ....(11 to 2 op 4 to 1 tchd 6 to 1) 1
NUMBER ONE SPOT 8-11 Pat Eddery (7) *led till o'r one furlong out, one pace.* ....(100 to 30 fav op 2 to 1 tchd 7 to 2) 2
ABBRAAK (USA) 8-11 B Raymond (8) *cl up, ev ch 2 fs out, one pace appr last*..........(8 to 1 op 5 to 1) 3
SWEET THATCH (Ire) 8-6 (5*) Stephen Davies (14) *beh, hdwy 2 fs out, styd on*..........(8 to 1 tchd 12 to 1) 4
CORN CIRCLE (Ire) 8-11 J Reid (13) *hld up, hdwy o'r 2 fs out, sn ev ch, one pace appr last.* ....(8 to 1 op 10 to 1 tchd 14 to 1) 5
MIGAVON 8-11 R Cochrane (12) *chsd ldrs, cld hfwy, ev ch o'r 2 fs out, wknd*..........(50 to 1 tchd 66 to 1) 6
ARRASAS LADY 8-11 N Adams (6) *mid-div, rdn alng hfwy, outpcd frm o'r 2 fs out*.....(100 to 1 op 66 to 1) 7
SUMMER WIND (Ire) 8-11 J Williams (11) *al beh.* ....(14 to 1 op 10 to 1 tchd 16 to 1) 8
SHEFFORD 8-11 B Rouse (10) *al beh*..........(33 to 1) 9
SURFINA 8-11 M Roberts (9) *chsd ldrs, pushed alng hfwy, wknd quickly appr 2 fs out.* ....(10 to 1 op 8 to 1 tchd 12 to 1) 10
TRIPLE SALKO (Ire) 8-11 C Rutter (1) *cl up till wknd o'r 2 fs out*..........(33 to 1 op 20 to 1) 11
AKHLAK (Ire) 8-11 W Carson (4) *cl up till wknd quickly 2 fs out*..........(11 to 2 op 9 to 2 tchd 6 to 1) 12
CLANDESTINE AFFAIR (Ire) 8-11 R Hills (2) *chsd ldrs till wknd wl o'r 2 fs out*..........(20 to 1 op 16 to 1) 13
MISS MICHELLE 8-11 S Whitworth (3) *strted slwly, sn tld off*..........(50 to 1 op 33 to 1) 14

Dist: 6l, 1½l, nk, nk, 3l, 4l, hd, 5l, 1½l, ½l. 1m 34.02s. a 9.92s (14 Ran).

SR: 11/-/-/-/-/-/ (Paul Mellon), I A Balding

584 Levy Board Seventh Handicap Class C (0-90 3-y-o) £4,920 1½m 5yds.......(5:00)

344* MARROS MILL [79] 9-0 Pat Eddery (7) *trkd ldr, led briefly 4 fs out, bumped 2 out, led appr last, ran on wl.* ....(9 to 2 op 5 to 1 tchd 4 to 1) 1
72* HIGH SUMMER [62] 7-11 N Adams (2) *al hndy, led o'r 3 fs out, edgd lft 2 out, hdd appr last, kpt on one pace.* ....(4 to 1 op 11 to 4) 2
457[3] HOSTILE WITNESS (Ire) [73] 8-8 M Roberts (6) *in tch, effrt o'r one out, ran on ins last*.........(4 to 1 tchd 5 to 1) 3
388[7] DEVILRY [86] 9-7 Paul Eddery (5) *in tch, effrt o'r one furlong out, one pace*..........(10 to 1) 4
457[5] ROMALITO [68] 8-3 G Carter (1) *in tch, rdn o'r 2 fs out, nvr dngrs*..........(10 to 1 op 8 to 1 tchd 12 to 1) 5
422* FOREVER SHINEING [75] 8-10 R Cochrane (8) *in tch, rdn o'r 2 fs out, wknd ins last.* ....(7 to 2 fav op 2 to 1 tchd 4 to 1) 6
441[4] SAFIR (USA) [78] 8-13 W Carson (3) *led to 4 fs out, sn rdn and btn*..........(5 to 1 tchd 6 to 1) 7

Dist: 2l, ¾l, 2l, ½l, 4l, 6l. 2m 48.16s. a 18.56s (7 Ran).

(Alasdair Simpson), M Bell

OAKLAWN PARK (USA) (firm)
Saturday April 17th

585 Arkansas Derby (Grade 1) (dirt) (3-y-o) £198,675 1m 1f..........

ROCKAMUNDO (USA) 8-6 C Borel,..........(108 to 1) 1
KISSIN KRIS (USA) 8-10 J Santos,..........(16 to 1) 2
FOXTRAIL (USA) 8-10 C McCarron,..........(63 to 10) 3
MI CIELO (USA) 8-6 A Gryder,..........(93 to 10) 4
DIAZO (USA) 8-6 K Desormeaux,..........(47 to 10) 5
RAGTIME REBEL (USA) 8-10 L Quinonez,........(74 to 1) 6
OVER JACK MOUNTAIN (USA) 8-6 W Martinez, (10 to 7 on) 7
PROUDEST ROMEO (USA) 8-6 F Arguello Jr,....(91 to 10) 8
DALHART (USA) 8-10 M Smith,..........(10 to 7 on) 9
AGGRESSIVE CHIEF (USA) 8-6 J Bailey,..........(30 to 1) 10

Dist: 1½l, nose, hd, hd, 1l, hd, nk, 6l, 5l. 1m 48.00s. (10 Ran).

(G & Mary West), O Glass Jr

THIRSK (good)
Saturday April 17th

Going Correction: PLUS 0.30 sec. per fur. (races 1,2,6), PLUS 0.40 (3,4,5,7)

586 Clifton Conditions Stakes Class D (2-y-o) £3,318 5f..........(2:15)

299* BEST KEPT SECRET 8-10 J Carroll (5) *slwly away and hng lft, sn pushed alng, hdwy hfwy, led o'r one and a half fs out, rdn out*..................(2 to 1 fav op 3 to 1) 1
395* OCHOS RIOS (Ire) 8-7 (3*) D Harrison (6) *chsd ldrs, effrt 2 fs out, ev ch entering fnl furlong, sn rdn, edgd lft and not quicken*................(5 to 2 op 5 to 2 tchd 3 to 1) 2
LEPINE (Ire) 8-10 G Duffield (3) *outpcd and beh, gd hdwy hfwy, rdn and ch appr fnl furlong, kpt on.* ....(5 to 1 op 7 to 2) 3
343* STEADFAST ELITE (Ire) 8-5 K Darley (1) *cl up, effrt and led briefly 2 fs out, sn hdd and btn*......(9 to 2 op 3 to 1) 4
399 KOMPLICITY 8-10 N Day (4) *led till rdn and hdd 2 fs out, sn wknd*............(25 to 1 op 20 to 1 tchd 33 to 1) 5
BLASTER BATES (USA) 8-11[1] D Nicholls (2) *slwly into strd, outpcd and rear till styd on fnl furlong.* .... (16 to 1 op 12 to 1) 6
FIRE MUSIC 8-10 L Charnock (7) *al outpcd in rear.* .... (33 to 1 op 20 to 1) 7
Dist: 1½l, 1½l, 5l, 2½l, 2l, 10l. 1m 1.90s. a 4.70s (7 Ran).
SR: 32/26/20/-/ (Manny Bernstein (Racing) Ltd), J Berry

587 Michael Foster Memorial Conditions Stakes Class B (3-y-o and up) £4,931 6f ....(2:50)

511[5] FYLDE FLYER (v) 4-9-7 J Carroll (1) *cl up, effrt to ld and wnt rght one and a half fs out, sn rdn and ran on.* .... (11 to 4 op 6 to 4) 1
DOUBLE BLUE 4-9-0 Dean McKeown (6) *led, pushed alng hfwy, hdd and swtchd o'r one and a half fs out, rdn to chal entering last, hng lft, kpt on*............(5 to 2 jt-fav op 7 to 2 tchd 9 to 4) 2
HOPE HALL (Ire) 5-9-0 A Culhane (3) *chsd ldrs, effrt and swtchd 2 fs out, sn rdn, kpt on one pace.* .... (66 to 1 op 33 to 1) 3
481[2] A PRAYER FOR WINGS 9-9-2 W Ryan (2) *outpcd till styd on fnl 2 fs*..........(7 to 2 op 4 to 1 tchd 9 to 2) 4
345[6] MEDAILLE D'OR (v) 5-9-8 G Duffield (5) *chsd ldrs, rdn o'r 2 fs out, sn btn*..... (5 to 2 jt-fav op 5 to 2 tchd 3 to 1) 5
Dist: 1l, 4l, 1½l, 3l. 1m 15.40s. a 5.40s (5 Ran).
SR: 35/24/8/4/-/ (Blackpool Gazette & Herald Ltd), J Berry

588 Thirsk Classic Trial Conditions Stakes Class B (3-y-o) £9,594 1m..........(3:20)

COLWAY ROCK (USA) 8-10 G Duffield (2) *squeezed strt and outpcd, hdwy 4 fs out, effrt 2 furlongs out, rdn to ld ins fnl furlong, ran on wl*.................. (16 to 1) 1
435* BENEFICIAL 8-12 M Hills (5) *trkd ldrs, gd hdwy o'r 2 fs out, led over one furlong out, rdn and hdd ins last, kpt on*.............................. (3 to 1 op 9 to 2) 2
388* EUROLINK THUNDER 9-0 K Darley (3) *cl up, ev ch 2 fs out, sn rdn, one pace entering fnl furlong*........(9 to 4 jt-fav op 3 to 1) 3
BLUES TRAVELLER (Ire) 8-12 D Holland (4) *cl up, effrt to ld 2 fs out, sn rdn, hdd o'r one furlong out and soon one pace*.............. (9 to 2 op 4 to 1 tchd 5 to 1) 4
304[4] ERTLON 8-10 M Birch (1) *led till hdd 2 fs out, sn wknd and eased*........................(25 to 1 op 20 to 1) 5
ARDKINGLASS 9-4 W Ryan (6) *cl up, effrt and ev ch o'r 2 fs out, sn rdn, wknd over one and a half furlongs out, eased whn btn*.................(9 to 4 jt-fav op 6 to 4) 6
Dist: Nk, 2½l, 1l, 12l, 20l. 1m 42.90s. a 7.00s (6 Ran).
SR: 39/40/34/29/-/-/ (R Coleman), J W Watts

589 Straightlace Limited Stakes Class E (3-y-o and up) £3,002 1½m...............(3:50)

456[4] IN THE MONEY (Ire) 4-9-12 W Ryan (3) *mid-div, gd hdwy 4 fs out, effrt to ld o'r 2 out, hdd briefly appr last, rdn and quickened clr in last*........... (7 to 1 op 8 to 1) 1
508* GOLDEN TORQUE 6-9-5 (7*) H Bastiman (6) *hld up and beh, gd hdwy o'r 3 fs out, rdn to ld briefly appr fnl furlong, sn hdd and not quicken*... (3 to 1 op 11 to 4) 2
294[7] SWORD MASTER 4-9-12 N Day (2) *led, rdn and hdd o'r 2 fs out, kpt on one pace.* ....(9 to 4 fav op 5 to 2 tchd 11 to 4) 3
BELLTON 5-9-12 T Lucas (7) *cl up, effrt and ev ch 2 and a half fs out, rdn and wknd o'r one furlong out.* ....(100 to 30 op 3 to 1 tchd 7 to 2) 4
4689a[9] JAMES IS SPECIAL (Ire) 5-9-12 J Quinn (4) *chsd ldrs, rdn and wknd o'r 2 fs out*.......................(14 to 1) 5
366 EXPLOSIVE SPEED (USA) 5-9-12 G Duffield (9) *hld up and beh, pushed alng hfwy, nvr a factor*............(10 to 1) 6
MEDIA STAR 8-9-7 D Nicholls (1) *chsd ldrs, rdn and wknd 3 fs out*....................................(50 to 1) 7
366[8] OLLIVER DUCKETT 4-9-12 Dale Gibson (8) *chsd ldrs till wknd 5 fs out, sn beh*..............(50 to 1 op 33 to 1) 8
Dist: 3l, 4l, 3l, 3½l, 6l, 15l, 15l. 2m 41.60s. a 11.40s (8 Ran).
SR: 46/40/32/26/19/7/-/-/ (J E Bigg), R Hollinshead

590 Byland Rating Related Maiden Stakes Class F (3-y-o) £2,579 7f............ (4:20)

447[5] FESTIN (bl) 9-0 Dale Gibson (2) *cl up, hdwy to ld one and a half fs out, edgd rght, rdn and edged lft entering last, jst hld on, fnshd 1st, plcd second*... (10 to 1 op 8 to 1) 1D
439[8] CICERONE 9-0 G Hind (7) *chsd ldrs, hdwy 3 out, effrt 2 out, not clr run and swtchd entering last, fnshd wl, finished second, plcd 1st*......... (20 to 1 op 16 to 1) 1
NORTHERN BLUFF (v) 9-0 G Duffield (6) *led, rdn and hdd 2 fs out, kpt on und pres*............ (6 to 1 op 5 to 1) 3
PYRRHIC DANCE 9-0 M Hills (1) *mid-div, effrt and pushed alng o'r 2 fs out, styd on fnl furlong.* ....(4 to 1 op 5 to 2 tchd 9 to 2) 4
418[4] CLEAR LOOK 8-2 (7*) T G McLaughlin (3) *chsd ldrs, effrt to ld 2 fs out, sn rdn, hdd and wknd appr fnl furlong.* ....(11 to 4 fav op 5 to 2) 5
BREAKING HEARTS (Ire) 8-9 K Darley (5) *hld up, hdwy 3 fs out, rdn and kpt on one pace fnl 2 furlongs.* ....(20 to 1 op 16 to 1 tchd 25 to 1) 6
313[7] FLASHMAN 9-0 S Perks (10) *chsd ldrs, hdwy on outer and ev ch 2 fs out, rdn and wknd appr fnl furlong.* ....(4 to 1 op 6 to 1) 7
CONTRAC COUNTESS (Ire) (bl) 8-6 (3*) D Harrison (9) *cl up till rdn and wknd o'r 2 fs out.* ....(8 to 1 op 10 to 1 tchd 7 to 1) 8
275[8] RUM TEMPEST 9-0 M Birch (8) *al rear*..........(33 to 1) 9
367[6] INDIAN SECRET (Ire) 9-0 J Fortune (4) *al rear.* ....(16 to 1 op 14 to 1) 10
Dist: Sht-hd, ¾l, 1½l, ½l, 5l, 2½l, 1½l, 2l, hd. 1m 31.60s. a 8.80s (10 Ran).
SR: 10/9/7/2/-/-/ (Miss S Moore), P Calver

591 Thomas Lord Handicap Class C (0-90 3-y-o and up) £5,089 5f..................(4:50)

355[5] EWALD (Ire) [57] 5-8-0 (5*) B Doyle (12) *chsd ldr, rdn appr fnl furlong, styd on to ld ins last.* (11 to 1 op 10 to 1) 1
292[5] SLADES HILL [59] 6-8-7 Alex Greaves (8) *chsd ldrs, effrt 2 fs out, rdn and edgd rght entering fnl furlong, ran on.* .... (13 to 2 op 6 to 1 tchd 7 to 1) 2
MISTERTOPOGIGO (Ire) [85] 3-9-8 D Nicholls (10) *led, rdn and hdd ins last, no extr.* .... (5 to 1 fav op 5 to 1 tchd 11 to 2 and 9 to 2) 3
STORITHS (Ire) [87] 3-9-10 M Birch (15) *dwlt and beh, gd hdwy 2 fs out, effrt whn hmpd entering fnl furlong, not reco'r*.............................(9 to 1 op 8 to 1) 4
450[5] SHADOW JURY [64] 3-8-1[1] K Darley (5) *in tch, effrt 2 fs out, rdn and one pace entering fnl furlong.* ....(16 to 1 op 14 to 1) 5
355[6] MISS MOVIE WORLD [55] 4-8-3 L Charnock (14) *chsd ldrs, rdn o'r 2 fs out, sn one pace.* ....(7 to 1 op 6 to 1 tchd 8 to 1) 6
379* SIR TASKER [61] (v) 5-8-9 D Holland (13) *chsd ldrs, effrt and rdn one and a half fs out, wknd ins last.* .... (11 to 2 op 5 to 1 tchd 6 to 1) 7
NED'S BONANZA [67] 4-9-1 S Webster (7) *in tch, effrt and some hdwy 2 fs out, nvr dngrs*................(25 to 1) 8
436 LUCEDEO [75] 9-9-9 Dean McKeown (6) *nvr rchd ldrs.* ....(14 to 1 op 14 to 1 tchd 16 to 1) 9
436 CATHERINES WELL [74] 10-9-8 T Lucas (3) *nvr rchd ldrs.* ....(16 to 1 op 14 to 1) 10
436 MACS MAHARANEE [61] 6-8-9 W Ryan (4) *al rear.* .... (50 to 1 op 25 to 1) 11
436 PAGEBOY [70] 4-9-4 Dale Gibson (9) *dwlt, al beh.* (12 to 1) 12
SINGING STAR [76] 7-9-3 (7*) Claire Balding (2) *slwly away, al beh*..................................(20 to 1) 13
436[2] SARTIGILA [61] 4-8-9 G Duffield (1) *al beh.* ....(6 to 1 op 5 to 1) 14
Dist: 2l, sht-hd, 1½l, nk, 1l, ½l, 1½l, ¾l, 1½l, 1½l. 1m 1.40s. a 4.20s (14 Ran).
SR: 37/31/45/41/17/15/19/19/24/ (Mark Johnston Racing Ltd), M Johnston

592 Levy Board Handicap Class D (0-80 3-y-o and up) £3,757 1m..................(5:20)

384[4] NO SUBMISSION (USA) [79] 7-9-13 S Wood (9) *chsd ldrs, hdwy to chal 2 fs out, rdn to ld entering fnl furlong, ran on*.............................(20 to 1 op 16 to 1) 1
383* GOLDEN CHIP (Ire) [77] 5-9-11 K Darley (13) *chsd ldrs, led o'r 3 fs out, rdn 2 furlongs out, hdd entering fnl furlong, no extr nr finish.* (9 to 1 op 8 to 1 tchd 10 to 1) 2
383[4] WEE SARAH [56] 5-8-4 Alex Greaves (8) *in tch, hmpd 5 fs out, hdwy 3 furlongs out, ev ch appr fnl furlong, sn rdn and not quicken*................ (20 to 1 op 14 to 1) 3
FOREVER DIAMONDS [74] 6-9-8 M Birch (2) *chsd ldrs, ev ch 2 fs out, sn rdn, kpt on same pace.* .... (12 to 1 op 10 to 1 tchd 14 to 1) 4
402[7] AMENABLE [80] 8-9-9 (5*) A Garth (7) *dwlt, hdwy hfwy, rdn and styd on wl fnl 2 fs, nrst finish*........ (20 to 1) 5
425 HOB GREEN [71] 4-9-2 (3*) D Harrison (6) *mid-div, hdwy on inner 3 fs out, rdn and one pace wl o'r one furlong out.* ....(4 to 1 op 5 to 1 tchd 7 to 1) 6
340* SHANNON EXPRESS [47] (v) 6-7-4[2] (7*) Claire Balding (17) *mid-div, hdwy o'r 2 fs out, kpt on*..............(14 to 1) 7
400[8] ANNIVERSAIRE [77] 3-8-10 N Day (5) *in tch, rdn o'r 2 fs out, sn wknd*.................................... (25 to 1) 8
SUPREME BOY [60] 4-8-8 F Norton (16) *mid-div, effrt and hdwy o'r 2 fs out, one pace*........(20 to 1 op 16 to 1) 9
403[3] CEE-JAY-AY [62] 6-8-10 J Carroll (18) *slwly away, al rear.* .... (7 to 1 op 6 to 1 tchd 15 to 2) 10
BOURSIN (Ire) [74] 4-9-8 W Newnes (10) *in tch whn hmpd 5 fs out, sn lost pl*..................(12 to 1 op 20 to 1) 11

LEGEND DULAC (Ire) [52] 4-8-0 P Robinson (11) *cl up, effrt to chal o'r 3 fs out, sn rdn and wknd.* ....(25 to 1 op 20 to 1) 12
MAJOR MOUSE [73] 5-9-7 Dean McKeown (14) *dwlt, al rear*....(16 to 1 op 14 to 1) 13
3157 BUZZARDS BELLBUOY [73] 4-9-7 J Quinn (3) *al beh.* ....(7 to 2 fav op 7 to 2 tchd 9 to 2) 14
3583 COMMON COUNCIL [72] 4-9-6 G Duffield (15) *al beh.* ....(12 to 1 op 10 to 1 tchd 14 to 1) 15
3843 TALENTED TING (Ire) [69] 4-9-3 Dale Gibson (12) *al beh.* ....(12 to 1 op 10 to 1) 16
THORNTON GATE [70] (bl) 4-8-13 (5*) O Pears (1) *led till hdd o'r 3 fs out, wknd quickly and eased.* ....(16 to 1 op 16 to 1 tchd 20 to 1) 17
Dist: 1l, ½l, 1½l, nk, 2½l, nk, 5l, hd, 1l, 5l. 1m 43.90s. a 8.00s (17 Ran).
SR: 41/36/13/26/31/14/ (T S Redman), D W Chapman

CAPANNELLE (ITY) (good)
Sunday April 18th

593 Premio Natale di Roma (Group 3) (4-y-o and up) £28,793 1m.... (3:30)

PROSPECTIVE RULER (USA) 5-8-9 D Holland, ... 1
EL DINERO (Ire) 5-8-9 S Soto, ... 2
ANOTHER BOB (USA) 5-8-9 Jacqueline Freda, ... 3
NIGHT MANOEUVRES 4-8-9 S Landi, ... 4
MINSTREL'S AGE (USA) 4-8-9 M Vargui, ... 5
AMANDHLA (Ire) 5-8-9 B Jovine, ... 6
KAA (Ire) 5-8-9 S Morales, ... 7
SULDA 5-8-9 L Sorrentino, ... 8
JUNK BOND 5-8-9 L Ficuciello, ... 9
TITI STATILIO (Ire) 4-8-9 O Fancera, ... 10
Dist: Nk, 1½l, ½l, 1 ¼l, sht-hd, 2l, ¾l, 1½l, 15l. 1m 39.20s. (10 Ran).
(R C Thompson), G Pucciatti

FRANKFURT (GER) (good)
Sunday April 18th

594 Grosser Preis der Steigenberger Hotels (Group 3) (3-y-o) £28,571 1¼m.... (3:10)

MONSUN (Ger) 8-9 P Schiergen, *rcd in 4th, hdwy to track ldr 2 fs out, led ins last, jst hld on*.... 1
KOMTUR (USA) 8-11 K Woodburn, *led till ins fnl furlong, rallied gmely, jst fld*.... 2
LASKO (Ger) 8-9 A Starke, *mid-div, 4th strt, kpt on, nvr dngrs*.... 3
TROPICAL KING (Ger) 9-2 M Rimmer, *3rd strt, unbl to quicken*.... 4
DUKE OF FUN (Fr) 8-9 G Schick, *trkd ldr till wknd 4 fs out.* 5
TI ZINO (Fr) 8-9 M Hofer, *al beh*.... 6
DAMP (USA) 8-9 T Hellier, *al rear, tld off*.... 7
Dist: Nose, 2l, 3½l, ¾l, 8l, dist. 2m 6.44s. (7 Ran).
(Baron G Von Ullmann), H Jentzsch

SHA TIN (HK) (yielding)
Sunday April 18th

595 Hong Kong International Bowl (Listed) (3-y-o and up) £173,060 7f.... (7:40)

GLEN KATE 6-8-11 C Black (1)....(24 to 1) 1
HELENE STAR (NZ) 4-9-0 G Mosse (9).... (17 to 10 fav) 2
QUICKEN AWAY 7-9-0 B Marcus (8)....(83 to 10) 3
CARDMANIA (USA) 7-9-0 A Cruz (10)....(86 to 10) 4
KADBRIDGE (NZ) (v) 5-9-0 D Gauci (7)....(13 to 1) 5
THE KINGFIGHTER (Aus) 5-9-0 G Eades (3).... (14 to 1) 6
ZAPARRI (Aus) 6-9-0 S Marshall (5)....(13 to 1) 7
3165 THOURIOS 4-9-0 T Quinn (14)....(14 to 1) 8
CARRY ON WINNING 6-9-0 F Coetzee (11)....(64 to 1) 9
3452 SILICON BAVARIA (Fr) 6-8-11 M Boutin (6).... (10 to 1) 0
2702 DIAMONDS GALORE (Can) 8-9-0 M Kinane (12) (67 to 10) 0
STORAIA (Aus) (v) 5-9-0 D Oliver (4).... (25 to 1) 0
LORD TRIDAN (NZ) 5-9-0 G Grylis (13).... (23 to 1) 0
HOKUSEI CIBOULETTE (Jpn) 5-9-0 N Sugai (2)... (19 to 1) 0
Dist: Sht-hd, 1½l, 4l, ¾l, 1l, sht-hd, 2 ¼l, sht-hd, 1 ¾l, sht-hd. 1m 22.20s. (14 Ran).
(Lord Matthews), H R A Cecil

596 Hong Kong International Cup (Group 3) (3-y-o and up) £222,506 1m 1f.... (8:55)

ROMANEE CONTI (NZ) 4-8-11 G Childs (9).... (23 to 1) 1
FRAAR (USA) 5-9-0 M Clarke (8).... (10 to 1) 2
CHARMONNIER (USA) 5-9-0 C Black (1).... (11 to 1) 3
MOTIVATION (Arg) 5-9-0 D Beadman (2).... (30 to 1) 4
RIVER VERDON 6-9-0 B Marcus (5).... (10 to 6 on) 5
283* URBAN SEA (USA) 4-8-11 W R Swinburn (13)... (86 to 10) 6
293* MELLOTTIE 8-9-0 J Lowe (3).... (29 to 1) 7
COZZENE'S PRINCE (Can) 6-9-0 D Penna (10)... (25 to 1) 8
SOUND PRINT (Ire) 5-9-0 F Coetzee (14).... (35 to 1) 9
3902 HALF A TICK (USA) 5-9-0 T Quinn (6).... (37 to 1) 0
WONDERFUL WORLD 6-9-0 A Cruz (12).... (13 to 1) 0
ON THE BEACH (NZ) 5-8-11 P Johnson (11).... (38 to 1) 0
RASPUTIN'S REVENGE (NZ) 5-9-0 A Matthews (4) (27 to 1) 0
HARD ROCK (Aus) 6-9-0 M Sng (7).... (71 to 1) 0
Dist: 1l, 1l, ¾l, nk, 1 ¾l, 1½l, 4l, 4l, 1 ¼l, sht-hd. 1m 22.20s. (14 Ran).

SANTA ANITA (USA) (firm)
Sunday April 18th

597 San Juan Capistrano Invitational Handicap (Grade I) (4-y-o and up) £145,695 1¾m ....

KOTASHAAN (Fr) 5-8-9 K Desormeaux, ...(10 to 9 on) 1
4769a* BIEN BIEN (USA) 4-8-7 C McCarron, ...(3 to 1) 2
4769a FRAISE (USA) 5-8-11 P Valenzuela, ...(18 to 10) 3
CARNIVAL BABY (USA) 5-8-1 D Flores, ... (14 to 1) 4
4769a5 CAMPAGNARDE (Arg) 6-8-0 J Garcia, ... (18 to 10) 5
Dist: Nose, 1 ¼l, 10l, 3½l. 2m 45.00s. (5 Ran).
(J Wertheimer), Mrs C Head

BALLINROBE (IRE) (soft)
Monday April 19th

598 Inishmaine Handicap (0-65 3-y-o and up) £2,243 1¼m.... (4:00)

487* FONTANAYS (Ire) [-] 5-9-0 (3ex) S Craine (8)....(4 to 1 fav) 1
2983 CEDAR COURT (Ire) [-] (bl) 5-9-13 C F Swan (10)... (9 to 2) 2
4875 HAWAIAN TASCA (Ire) [-] 4-7-11 (10*) B Carson (11) (10 to 1) 3
TINCO PALENO [-] 9-9-3 (2*) R M Burke (13).... (10 to 1) 4
280 SISTER CARMEL (Ire) [-] 3-8-10 K J Manning (5).. (16 to 1) 5
TANAMANDA (Ire) [-] 4-8-13 (3ex) G Curran (12)... (20 to 1) 6
MR GERAN (Ire) [-] 4-8-10 (8*) R V Skelly (2).... (20 to 1) 7
4686a8 THE MAN FROM COOKS (Ire) [-] 4-9-10 R Hughes (9) ....(8 to 1) 8
MRS BARTON (Ire) [-] 5-9-5 (6*) J R Barry (6)....(12 to 1) 9
DIPIE (Ire) [-] 5-8-10 (8*) D J O'Donohoe (7).... (9 to 1) 10
SOLAR FLASH (Ire) [-] 4-8-3 (6*) B Bowens (1).... (8 to 1) 11
487 THE BOWER (Ire) [-] 4-9-4 P V Gilson (14).... (10 to 1) 12
HARARE SUN (Ire) [-] 4-8-5 (8*) R T Fitzpatrick (3) (20 to 1) 13
4878 MAZELLA (Ire) [-] 4-9-0 J F Egan (16).... (5 to 1) 14
SIGHTSEER (Ire) [-] 4-8-13 (6*) C Everard (17)....(12 to 1) 15
2988 KINVARA LADY (Ire) [-] 4-6-13 (8*) P P Murphy (4) (20 to 1) 16
DANCE THIS TUNE (USA) [-] 4-8-10 N G McCullagh (15) ....(9 to 1) 17
ZIO MARIANO (Ire) [-] 3-7-11 (2*) D G O'Shea (18) (25 to 1) 18
Dist: 2l, 15l, 2l, 3½l. 2m 43.10s. (18 Ran).
(E A MacRedmond), B V Kelly

599 Claremorris Handicap (0-65 3-y-o and up) £2,243 6f.... (5:00)

4686a THE MAIN CHOICE (Ire) [-] (bl) 4-8-12 (6*) P Carberry (4) ....(25 to 1) 1
BOLD MOLLY (Ire) [-] 4-8-3 (2*) R M Burke (2)....(12 to 1) 2
TAUTEN (Ire) [-] 3-9-2 S Craine (10)....(10 to 1) 3
4686a MUGNANO [-] 7-9-4 (8*) D J O'Donohoe (9)....(14 to 1) 4
281 SOUTHERN RULE [-] 6-7-4 (8*) P P Murphy (1)....(9 to 1) 5
3105 LADY PRESIDENT (Ire) [-] 4-9-2 (8*) R V Skelly (13) ....(7 to 4 fav) 6
SWEET REALM [-] 4-8-0 (4*) W J Smith (8).... (14 to 1) 7
RUSTIC-ORT (Ire) [-] (bl) 5-8-11 N Byrne (7)....(10 to 1) 8
4863 TOUGH AS TEAK (Ire) [-] (bl) 3-8-12 R Hughes (12) (6 to 1) 9
VOUVRAY (Ire) [-] 3-9-1 Joanna Morgan (11).... (8 to 1) 10
3104 FANTANTE (Ire) [-] 4-9-11 P V Gilson (5).... (5 to 1) 11
487 DAHAR'S LOVE (USA) [-] 4-9-10 W J Supple (6)...(10 to 1) 12
487 DONMIR LOVEBIRD (Ire) [-] (bl) 3-9-0 D V Smith (3) (16 to 1) 13
Dist: ½l, 3l, nk, sht-hd. 1m 30.70s. (13 Ran).
(Mrs C Roper), B V Kelly

BRIGHTON (good)
Monday April 19th

Going Correction: MINUS 0.10 sec. per fur.

600 Levy Board Handicap Class E (0-70 3-y-o and up) £3,002 5f 59yds.... (2:00)

5013 PALACEGATE GOLD (Ire) [45] 4-8-6 W Carson (2) *hld up in midfield, swtchd rght and hdwy 2 fs out, led wl ins last, ran on*....(5 to 1 jt-fav op 4 to 1) 1
348* COCKERHAM RANGER [64] 3-9-0 L Piggott (4) *trkd ldrs, not clr run o'r one furlong out, swtchd lft and kpt on und pres ins last*.... (6 to 1 op 5 to 1) 2
3243 PURBECK CENTENARY [54] 3-8-4 M Roberts (12) *made most till wl ins fnl furlong, no extr*...(7 to 1 op 5 to 1) 3
5017 LET'S GO LOCHY [43] 7-8-4 D Holland (6) *chsd ldrs, rdn and hdwy 2 fs out, sn ev ch, no extr fnl furlong.* ....(11 to 2 op 5 to 2 tchd 6 to 1) 4
416 LOON [51] (bl) 5-8-9 (3*) J Weaver (5) *slwly away, swtchd wide and hdwy o'r 2 fs out, kpt on, nvr nrr*... (33 to 1) 5

501[9] LINCSTONE BOY (Ire) [53] 5-9-0 S Webster (1) *prmnt on ins, rdn and no hdwy fnl 2 fs.* ....(9 to 1 op 12 to 1 tchd 14 to 1) 6
AGIL'S PET [55] 3-8-5 B Rouse (3) *slwly into strd, wl beh till styd on fnl 2 fs, nvr nr to chal.* (14 to 1 op 12 to 1) 7
401[4] SERIOUS HURRY [54] 5-9-1 T Quinn (8) *rdn to chase ldr, ev ch o'r one furlong out, wknd ins last.* ....(5 to 1 jt-fav op 4 to 1) 8
421[6] IRON KING [67] 7-10-0 W Newnes (9) *slwly away and sn beh, moderate hdwy fnl 2 fs, no dngr.* ....(12 to 1 op 8 to 1 tchd 14 to 1) 9
4708a LADY OF SHADOWS [49] 3-7-13 C Rutter (7) *al rear.* ....(20 to 1) 10
501[5] MISS PRECOCIOUS [32] 5-7-0 (7*) D Wright (11) *sn rdn alng on outsd, beh hfwy.* (12 to 1 op 10 to 1 tchd 14 to 1) 11
263[9] CHESHIRE ANNIE (Ire) [55] 4-8-13 (3*) A Tucker (10) *al beh.* ....(8 to 1 op 10 to 1) 12
455[2] KILDEE LAD [56] 3-8-6 N Adams (13) *slwly into strd, sn chsd alng on outsd, eased whn btn appr last.* ....(14 to 1 op 12 to 1) 13

Dist: 1l, sht-hd, 1½l, 1½l, nk, 1l, sht-hd, 1½l, 2½l, sht-hd. 1m 3.60s. a 3.50s (13 Ran).
SR: 12/16/5/-/1/2/-/-/5/ (R J Hodges), R J Hodges

601 Prince Of Wales Conditions Stakes Class C (4-y-o and up) £4,464 1m 3f 196yds (2:30)

SPINNING 6-9-10 R Cochrane (1) *pld hrd, made all, shaken up o'r one furlong out, sn clr, easily.* (11 to 1 on op 10 to 1 on tchd 8 to 1 on and 14 to 1 on) 1
390[7] DURSHAN (USA) 4-8-9 S Whitworth (2) *settled last, niggled alng o'r 4 fs out, ran on to chase wnr over 2 out, no imprsn.* ....(12 to 1 op 6 to 1) 2
322* LA REINE ROUGE (Ire) 5-8-7 F Norton (3) *trkd ldr, ev ch 3 fs out, sn rdn and wknd, eased whn btn.* ....(25 to 1 op 10 to 1) 3

Dist: 6l, 25l. 2m 33.40s. a 5.90s (3 Ran).
SR: 39/12/-/ (Paul Mellon), I A Balding

602 Conflans Maiden Stakes Class D (3-y-o) £3,552 7f 214yds.................. (3:00)

WOODWARDIA (USA) 8-9 D Holland (5) *slwly away and beh, hdwy hfwy, ev ch 2 fs out, sstnd run to ld cl hme, gmely.*..........(5 to 4 fav tchd 11 to 8 and 11 to 10) 1
GREEN KILT 9-0 A Munro (13) *al hndy, rdn to ld o'r one furlong out, hdd cl hme.* ....(11 to 2 op 5 to 1 tchd 9 to 2 and 6 to 1) 2
SCORCHED AIR 8-9 J Williams (3) *hld up in midfield, hdwy o'r 2 fs out, kpt on, not rch ldrs.* ....(12 to 1 op 10 to 1 tchd 14 to 1) 3
BOHEMIAN CROWN (USA) 9-0 M Roberts (16) *prmnt, led 2 fs out till o'r one out, no extr.* ....(11 to 2 op 4 to 1 tchd 6 to 1) 4
457[7] OCTOBER BREW (USA) 8-11 (3*) D Harrison (2) *in tch, ev ch o'r 2 fs out, sn rdn, kpt on same pace.* ....(10 to 1 op 7 to 1 tchd 12 to 1) 5
TASSET (Can) 9-0 T Quinn (17) *beh, rdn alng hfwy, kpt on fnl 2 fs, not pace to chal.* ....(14 to 1 op 8 to 1 tchd 20 to 1) 6
IJAB (Can) 9-0 W Carson (14) *made most to 2 fs out, sn lost pl, eased whn btn.*..........(33 to 1 op 16 to 1) 7
459 SPECIAL DAWN (Ire) 9-0 W Newnes (12) *beh till styd on fnl 2 fs, nvr nrr.*..........(20 to 1 op 12 to 1) 8
372[4] JULIASDARKINVADER 9-0 Candy Morris (1) *chsd ldrs, rdn and ev ch o'r 3 fs out, sn btn.*..........(33 to 1) 9
WOODMANS STAR 8-9 (5*) K Rutter (6) *nvr better than mid-div.*..........(33 to 1 op 20 to 1) 10
394[5] PRINCE SONGLINE 9-0 R Cochrane (9) *al rear.* ....(33 to 1 op 20 to 1) 11
459[7] DIVINE BOY 9-0 L Piggott (8) *slwly away, reco'red to midfield hfwy, eased whn btn fnl furlong.* ....(7 to 1 op 10 to 1) 12
BARSLEY 8-9 (5*) B Doyle (11) *al beh.* (50 to 1 op 33 to 1) 13
414[5] ACCESS FESTIVALS 9-0 M Tebbutt (15) *al beh.* ....(50 to 1 op 33 to 1) 14
ARRAS ROYALE (v) 9-0 N Adams (7) *chsd ldrs to hfwy, sn wknd.*..........(50 to 1) 15
PETITE JESS 8-9 F Norton (4) *slwly into strd, sn rdn alng, al struggling.*..........(33 to 1 op 20 to 1) 16
129[8] AIR COMMAND (Bar) 9-0 G Bardwell (10) *prmnt, rdn and ev ch o'r 3 fs out, wknd quickly.*..........(50 to 1) 17

Dist: Nk, 5l, ¾l, 2l, sht-hd, nk, 1½l, 4l, 2½l, 2½l. 1m 36.10s. a 3.70s (17 Ran).
SR: 28/32/12/15/9/8/7/2/-/ (K Abdulla), B W Hills

603 Town Purse Handicap Class E (0-70 4-y-o and up) £3,235 7f 214yds............(3:30)

232* BELMOREDEAN [60] 8-9-5 (3*) J Weaver (10) *beh early, hdwy 3 fs out, pld wide wl o'r one out, sstnd run to ld cl hme.*..........(7 to 1 op 5 to 1) 1
157[2] BUDDY'S FRIEND (Ire) [57] 5-9-5 R Cochrane (5) *hld up and beh, gd hdwy frm o'r 2 fs out, squeezed through to chal one out, kpt on.*..........(8 to 1 op 7 to 1 tchd 9 to 1) 2
302[5] SALBYNG [60] 5-9-8 D Holland (17) *al prmnt, led wl o'r 2 fs out till hdd cl hme.*.....(15 to 2 op 7 to 1 tchd 8 to 1) 3
260[2] PRECIOUS AIR (Ire) [52] 5-9-0 B Rouse (6) *handily plcd, ev ch o'r 2 fs out, kpt on one pace und pres.* ....(15 to 2 op 6 to 1 tchd 8 to 1) 4
440[2] TAUNTING (Ire) [53] 5-9-1 T Quinn (2) *trkd ldrs, rdn 3 fs out, ran on o'r one out till no extr ins last.* ....(10 to 1 tchd 12 to 1) 5
456[5] JOLTO [47] 4-8-9 W Newnes (8) *al prmnt, ev ch 2 fs out, no extr appr last.*..........(10 to 1 op 7 to 1) 6
440[9] QUICK STEEL [50] 5-8-5 (7*) S Mulvey (16) *beh till styd on fnl one and a half fs, nvr nr to chal.* ....(20 to 1 op 16 to 1 tchd 25 to 1) 7
383[3] SOOTY TERN [47] 6-8-9 N Adams (3) *chsd ldrs, rdn and ev ch 3 fs out, wknd wl o'r one out.*... (10 to 1 op 8 to 1) 8
THAMES GLOW [62] 4-9-10 J Williams (7) *beh till moderate hdwy fnl 2 fs, no dngr.*..........(14 to 1 tchd 20 to 1) 9
403 SLEEPLINE FANTASY [59] 8-9-7 W Carson (12) *midfield, rdn and hdwy to chase ldrs o'r 2 fs out, wknd appr last.* ....(14 to 1 op 12 to 1) 10
332 RED INK [48] 4-8-5 (5*) B Doyle (11) *beh early, nvr a dngr.* ....(20 to 1 op 14 to 1) 11
332[3] DANCING BEAU (Ire) [52] 4-9-0 M Roberts (9) *chsd ldrs, rdn and ev ch on outsd o'r 3 fs out, sn btn.* ....(13 to 2 fav op 7 to 1 tchd 6 to 1) 12
387 LUCKY NOIRE [60] 5-9-1 (7*) P Houghton (14) *beh, rdn and came wide o'r 3 fs out, no real imprsn.* ....(9 to 1 op 8 to 1 tchd 10 to 1) 13
333[6] DUTY SERGEANT (Ire) [50] (bl) 4-8-12 A Munro (15) *wth ldrs, ev ch o'r 3 fs out, wknd.* ....(10 to 1 op 8 to 1 tchd 11 to 1) 14
OYSTON'S LIFE [46] 4-8-8 C Rutter (13) *led till wl o'r 2 fs out, sn wknd.*..........(33 to 1 op 25 to 1) 15
403 SCOTS LAW [51] 6-8-13 A Clark (4) *speed 2 fs, struggling hfwy.*.......... (20 to 1 op 14 to 1) 16
STORM RISK [51] 4-8-13 F Norton (1) *wth ldrs till rdn and lost pl hfwy.*..........(33 to 1) 17

Dist: ½l, 1l, 3½l, 2l, 1½l, ¾l, ¾l, ½l, nk, ¾l. 1m 35.90s. a 3.50s (17 Ran).
SR: 44/39/39/20/15/4/5/-/13/ (Fred Honour), R J O'Sullivan

604 Sidney Thompson Memorial Conditions Stakes Class C (4-y-o and up) £3,995 6f 209yds............................ (4:00)

369[2] SHIKARI'S SON 6-8-12 T Quinn (1) *patiently rdn, hdwy and not much room o'r one furlong out, ridden to ld ins last, sn clr.*.......... (7 to 2 tchd 3 to 1 and 4 to 1) 1
465[4] HARD TO FIGURE 7-8-13 L Piggott (3) *al prmnt, led wl o'r one furlong out, hrd rdn and hdd ins last, no extr.* ....(Evens fav op 2 to 1 on tchd 11 to 10) 2
497[3] BRIGADE 4-8-10 M Tebbutt (4) *led till wl o'r one furlong out, edgd lft and not quicken.* ....(7 to 2 op 4 to 1 tchd 5 to 1) 3
475[2] PRECIOUS WONDER 4-8-10 T Williams (5) *chsd ldrs, rdn hfwy, sn no imprsn.* (25 to 1 op 16 to 1 tchd 33 to 1) 4
AMADEUS AES (v) 4-8-10 R Cochrane (2) *prmnt, rdn hfwy, wknd fnl 2 fs.*..........(10 to 1 op 7 to 1) 5

Dist: 4l, 5l, 2l, 2½l. 1m 23.70s. a 3.70s (5 Ran).
SR: 32/21/3/-/-/ (Alan Spargo), J White

605 Petworth Handicap Class C (0-90 4-y-o and up) £4,709 6f 209yds................(4:30)

315 MILLSOLIN (Ire) [75] 5-9-4 T Quinn (11) *nvr far away, rdn to chal one furlong out, ran on to ld last strds.* ....(11 to 2 op 3 to 1 tchd 6 to 1) 1
157[7] TYRIAN PURPLE (Ire) [62] 5-8-5 D Holland (10) *led, hrd rdn frm wl o'r one furlong out, ran on gmely till ct last strds.*..........(14 to 1 op 12 to 1) 2
436 CALEMAN [79] 4-9-8 R Cochrane (4) *chsd ldrs, swtchd lft and rdn to chal o'r one furlong out, not quicken ins last.*..........(7 to 1 op 5 to 1 tchd 8 to 1) 3
369[3] AMETHYSTINE (USA) [59] 7-8-2 W Carson (3) *al hndy, rdn to chal o'r one furlong out, no extr wl ins last.* ....(4 to 1 op 5 to 1 tchd 6 to 1) 4
EN ATTENDANT (Fr) [85] 5-10-0 B Raymond (9) *al hndy on outsd, rdn and hng rght wl o'r one furlong out, kpt on ins last.*..........(8 to 1 op 7 to 1 tchd 10 to 1) 5
475[6] DOMICKSKY [65] 5-8-8 M Roberts (8) *chsd ldrs, rdn and not clr run o'r one furlong out, sn one pace.* ....(7 to 2 fav op 4 to 1 tchd 9 to 2) 6
403[7] MASNUN (USA) [75] 8-9-1 (3*) J Weaver (7) *beh, hdwy 2 fs out, wknd appr last.*.....(8 to 1 op 5 to 1 tchd 9 to 1) 7
BIG BLUE [81] 4-9-5 (5*) B Doyle (5) *outpcd and wl beh early, some hdwy fnl 2 fs, nvr able to chal.* ....(12 to 1 op 7 to 1) 8
244 COURTING NEWMARKET [50] 5-7-0 (7*) D Wright (1) *trkd ldrs, rdn and wknd wl o'r 2 fs out.* ....(25 to 1 op 16 to 1 tchd 33 to 1) 9
HELIOS [78] 5-9-7 L Piggott (2) *wth ldr, shaken up and lost pl o'r 2 fs out, eased whn btn.* ....(8 to 1 op 7 to 1 tchd 9 to 1) 10
WILD POPPY [50] (v) 4-7-7 G Bardwell (6) *rdn alng aftr 2 fs, sn struggling.*..... (100 to 1 op 50 to 1 tchd 150 to 1) 11

Dist: Hd, 1l, 1l, ½l, sht-hd, 1l, 3l, nk, 3l, 6l. 1m 22.90s. a 2.90s (11 Ran).
SR: 50/36/50/27/51/30/37/34/2/ (Normandy Developments (London)), R Akehurst

606 Orleans Limited Stakes Class D (0-75 3-y-o) £3,611 5f 213yds.................(5:00)

532* ANOTHER JADE 8-6 S Whitworth (3) *al hndy gng wl, led o'r one furlong out, pushed clr ins last, readily.* ....(3 to 1 tchd 100 to 30) 1
471² SECOND CHANCE (Ire) 8-11 M Roberts (12) *sn rdn alng, hdwy o'r 2 fs out, ev ch over one out, not quicken ins last, no chance wth wnr.* ....(9 to 4 fav op 3 to 1 tchd 7 to 2) 2
NO EXTRAS (Ire) 8-11 B Rouse (8) *rear early, hdwy whn not clr run o'r 2 fs out, edgd rght over one out, ran on.* ....(8 to 1 op 7 to 1 tchd 9 to 1) 3
418⁹ MARK'S CLUB (Ire) 8-11 A Clark (9) *beh and outpcd till ran on fnl 2 fs, nvr nrr.*.................... (20 to 1 op 14 to 1) 4
STORMY HEIGHTS 8-6 A Munro (10) *chsd ldrs on outsd, rdn o'r 2 fs out, not quicken appr last.* ....(10 to 1 op 12 to 1) 5
370² PERSIAN GUSHER (Ire) 8-11 T Quinn (7) *chsd ldrs, rdn and wkng whn hmpd o'r one furlong out, no extr.* ....(5 to 1 op 7 to 2) 6
236⁷ TEE-EMM 8-11 C Rutter (11) *led till o'r one furlong out, sn wknd.*.............................(33 to 1 op 25 to 1) 7
262⁵ SQUIRE YORK (bl) 8-11 J Williams (5) *missed break, wl beh till some hdwy fnl one and a half fs, no dngr.* ....(16 to 1 op 12 to 1) 8
519⁷ AL MOULOUKI 8-11 R Cochrane (4) *slwly away, al beh.* ....(33 to 1 op 20 to 1) 9
MELODYS DAUGHTER 8-3 (3*) A Tucker (2) *wth ldrs, ev ch 3 fs out, not much room, sn wknd.* .... (9 to 1 op 6 to 1 tchd 10 to 1) 10
BONITA BEE 8-6 N Adams (6) *slwly away, al beh.* ....(25 to 1 op 12 to 1) 11
460 THE INSTITUTE BOY 8-11 S Webster (1) *hng lft thrght, al prmnt, wkng whn hmpd o'r 2 fs out, not rcvr.* ....(16 to 1 op 10 to 1) 12

Dist: 2l, 3½l, 5l, 1½l, hd, hd, 2½l, 1½l, ¾l, 1l. 1m 10.70s. a 2.30s (12 Ran).
SR: 34/31/17/-/-/-/ (Mrs Rita J Kaplan), A P Jarvis

EDINBURGH (soft)
Monday April 19th

Going Correction: PLUS 0.15 sec. per fur. (race 1), PLUS 0.25 (2,3,4,5,6)

607 Carberry Maiden Auction Stakes Class F (2-y-o) £1,630 5f....................(2:10)

454⁶ CYARNA QUINN (Ire) 8-9 G Duffield (1) *made all, drvn alng to quicken o'r one furlong out, ran on strly.* ....(11 to 8 fav op 5 to 4 tchd 7 to 4) 1
454 THE FERNHILL FLYER (Ire) 8-9 G Carter (4) *chsd alng and ran green most of way, kpt on ins fnl furlong, fnshd wl.* ....(3 to 1 op 11 to 4) 2
395 EN-CEE-TEE 9-0 K Darley (7) *pressed ldg pair, jnd wnr 2 fs out, no extr fnl furlong.* ....(16 to 1 op 20 to 1 tchd 14 to 1) 3
TENDER NORTH 8-9 Dale Gibson (3) *drvn alng to go pace, improved last 2 fs, nvr able to chal.* (14 to 1 op 8 to 1) 4
NORBECK (Ire) 9-0 S Morris (6) *sluggish strt, chsd alng to cl hfwy, not pace to chal.* ....(6 to 1 op 5 to 1 tchd 7 to 1) 5
354³ PRECISION EDGE (Ire) 8-10¹ D Nicholls (2) *unruly, sweating, broke wl to dispute ld to hfwy, wknd quickly and eased o'r one furlong out.* .... (13 to 2 op 5 to 1 tchd 7 to 1) 6
449⁵ FREE TYSON 9-0 L Charnock (5) *sluggish strt, chsd alng thrght, nvr wnt pace.*..............(25 to 1 op 20 to 1) 7

Dist: 2½l, 1½l, 2½l, 2l, 5l, 2½l. 1m 2.20s. a 4.40s (7 Ran).
SR: 22/12/11/-/ (M Quinn), M R Channon

608 Tennents Spring Handicap Class E (0-70 3-y-o) £1,945 1m 3f 32yds...........(2:40)

434⁶ THE WHERE WITHAL [50] 9-2 G Duffield (6) *trkd ldr, drvn ahead wl o'r 2 fs out, styd on grimly fnl furlong.* .... (11 to 10 fav op 6 to 4 tchd 13 to 8) 1
129⁹ BUZZ-B-BABE [47] 8-13 K Darley (5) *patiently rdn, improved frm off the pace hfwy, ev ch and ridden fnl furlong, ran on same pace.*........(33 to 1 op 20 to 1) 2
339* PALACEGATE SUNSET [52] 9-4 G Carter (1) *sluggish strt, rdn alng in last pl, styd on und pres last 2 fs, nvr nrr.* ....(5 to 2 op 9 to 4) 3
WEAVER GEORGE (Ire) [45] (bl) 8-11 Dale Gibson (4) *took keen hold, trkd ldg trio, hrd drvn and not quicken appr fnl furlong*..........................(33 to 1 op 20 to 1) 4
413* GOODBYE MILLIE [51] 8-12 (5*) O Pears (2) *chsd ldg 5, hrd at work o'r 2 fs out, not pace to chal.* (6 to 1 op 5 to 1) 5
437⁴ GOLD DESIRE [44] 8-10 M Wigham (8) *dictated pace, quickened hfwy, hdd wl o'r 2 fs out, fdd.* ....(6 to 1 op 5 to 1) 6
318⁷ SIR EDWARD HENRY (Ire) [55] 9-7 S Perks (7) *trkd ldg quartet, rdn and not handle bend into strt, btn 2 fs out.* .... (16 to 1 op 14 to 1 tchd 20 to 1) 7
LUCKY OWL [46] 8-5 (7*) R Havlin (3) *steadied strt, niggled alng to keep up hfwy, outpcd last 3 fs.* ....(25 to 1 op 20 to 1) 8

Dist: 1½l, 2½l, nk, 4l, 1½l, 4l, 5l. 2m 32.20s. a 12.70s (8 Ran).
SR: 3/-/-/-/-/ (W E Sturt), Sir Mark Prescott

609 Inveresk Rating Related Maiden Stakes Class F (0-60 3-y-o) £1,693 1m 16yds (3:10)

RAGGERTY (Ire) 9-0 G Carter (8) *sluggish strt, improved to chase ldg quartet entering strt, ran on und pres to ld last 50 yards*.........(14 to 1 op 6 to 1 tchd 16 to 1) 1
4697a⁷ MAASTRICHT 9-0 G Duffield (6) *led early, settled till led ag'n entering strt, hrd drvn fnl furlong, ct last 50 yards*............ (5 to 2 jt-fav op 6 to 4 tchd 11 to 4) 2
4695a⁴ NORTH ARDAR 9-0 R P Elliott (2) *nvr far away, ev ch and drvn alng entering strt, styd on same pace last 2 fs.* ....(7 to 2 op 9 to 2 tchd 5 to 1) 3
437 INNOCENT ABROAD (Den) 8-9 A Culhane (5) *patiently rdn, improved to fitter o'r 2 fs out, ridden and one pace.* ....(10 to 1 op 12 to 1 tchd 14 to 1) 4
437 PRIME PAINTER 9-0 D Nicholls (1) *sn led, hdd and drvn alng entering strt, no extr last 2 fs*... (6 to 1 op 5 to 1) 5
4761a⁶ FREDDIE JACK 9-0 S Perks (7) *slow away, reco'red aftr 2 fs, hrd at work whn pace quickened entering strt, no imprsn*.............................(20 to 1 op 14 to 1) 6
4695a⁹ SUPREME SOVIET 9-0 K Darley (4) *chsd alng in rear, nvr able to trble ldrs*.................. (50 to 1 op 33 to 1) 7
437⁵ MAD MYTTON 9-0 A Mackay (3) *chsd ldg trio, hrd at work and lost grnd 3 fs out, tld off*...............(5 to 2 jt-fav op 11 to 4 tchd 3 to 1) 8

Dist: 1l, 2l, 2½l, 3l, 1½l, 1l, dist. 1m 48.50s. a 10.00s (8 Ran).
(Norman Jackson), J Berry

610 Aberlady Selling Handicap Class G (0-60 3-y-o and up) £1,679 7f 15yds....... (3:40)

376² GALLERY ARTIST (Ire) [49] 5-9-1 (7*) S Eiffert (11) *patiently rdn, bustled alng to improve o'r 2 fs out, ran on grimly to ld post*.............................(4 to 1 op 5 to 2) 1
448 CHANTRY BELLINI [41] (bl) 4-9-0 K Darley (9) *nvr far away, led o'r 2 fs out, ran on und pres, ct post.* ....(9 to 1 op 7 to 1) 2
548⁴ HINARI VIDEO [44] 8-9-3 R P Elliott (5) *al hndy, led briefly o'r 2 fs out, rdn and outpcd appr fnl furlong.* ....(6 to 1 tchd 8 to 1) 3
4688a J'ARRIVE [43] 4-8-11 (5*) C Hodgson (7) *trkd ldrs, hrd at work whn pace quickened last 2 fs, one pace.* ....(12 to 1 op 10 to 1) 4
COOL ENOUGH [36] 12-8-9 K Fallon (10) *patiently rdn, bustled alng to improve on ins o'r 2 fs out, not pace to chal*................(7 to 2 fav op 3 to 1 tchd 4 to 1) 5
127³ MU-ARRIK [48] (bl) 5-9-7 G Duffield (4) *chsd ldg bunch, hrd at work hfwy, kpt on, nvr nrr.* .... (6 to 1 tchd 5 to 1 and 13 to 2) 6
MISS MAGENTA (Ire) [33] 5-8-6² A Culhane (8) *last and chsd alng hfwy, styd on late, nvr dngrs.* (14 to 1 op 10 to 1) 7
448⁷ BETTER STILL (Ire) [38] (v) 4-8-11 Dale Gibson (3) *in tch, came wide and rdn strt, nvr able to chal.* ....(14 to 1 op 10 to 1) 8
RAVECINO [38] 4-8-11 L Charnock (12) *dictated pace till hdd and fdd o'r 2 fs out*......................(50 to 1) 9
MISS HOSTESS [20] (bl) 6-7-7 S Wood (6) *chsd ldg bunch to strt, sn rdn and btn.* ....(14 to 1 op 25 to 1 tchd 33 to 1) 10
448⁵ DOUBLE THE STAKES (USA) [36] 4-8-9 G Carter (2) *settled midfield, feeling pace and rdn entering strt, sn btn.* ....(8 to 1 op 6 to 1) 11
505⁵ KHALLOOF (Ire) [52] (bl) 4-9-11 D Nicholls (1) *wth ldrs to strt, wknd quickly o'r 2 fs out*..... (14 to 1 op 12 to 1) 12

Dist: Sht-hd, 8l, ½l, 1½l, nk, ¾l, 4l, sht-hd, 5l, sht-hd. 1m 32.20s. a 7.00s (12 Ran).
SR: 29/20/-/-/-/-/ (Rae Guest), R Guest

611 North Berwick Median Auction Maiden Stakes Class E (3-y-o) £1,630 7f 15yds ....(4:10)

459³ QAMOOS (Ire) 9-0 R Hills (3) *trkd ldr, hrd drvn to nose ahead 2 fs out, styd on wl to go clr fnl furlong, eased.* ....(6 to 1 on op 8 to 1 on) 1
451² KILLY'S FILLY 8-9 G Carter (4) *tried to make all, hdd and rdn 2 fs out, kpt on same pace*...... (8 to 1 op 7 to 1) 2
RUNRIG (Ire) 8-2 (7*) R Havlin (1) *wtd wth, came wide strt, effrt and chsd alng o'r 2 fs out, styd on one pace.* .... (9 to 1 op 7 to 1 tchd 10 to 1) 3
SEVERE STORM 9-0 K Darley (5) *trkd ldg pair, effrt and drvn alng o'r 2 fs out, outpcd fnl furlong*......(66 to 1) 4
SENSABO 8-4 (5*) O Pears (2) *chsd ldg trio till wknd und pres last 2 fs*...................(50 to 1 tchd 66 to 1) 5

Dist: 2½l, 3l, 5l, 6l. 1m 34.50s. a 9.30s (5 Ran).
(Hamdan Al-Maktoum), H Thomson Jones

612 Dalmeny Handicap Class E (0-70 3-y-o) £1,826 7f 15yds.................... (4:40)

SILVER STANDARD [50] 8-7 G Duffield (3) *made all, hrd pressed o'r 2 fs out, styd on wl to go clr ag'n ins fnl furlong*............(100 to 30 op 5 to 2 tchd 7 to 2) 1

504^3 PEEDIE PEAT [64] 9-7 K Darley (1) *patiently rdn, drvn alng to improve on ins last 2 fs, ran on, nrst finish.* ....(6 to 4 fav op 2 to 1) 2

503^3 PUBLIC WAY (Ire) [56] 8-13 Dale Gibson (4) *al hndy, ev ch and drvn alng o'r 2 fs out, not quicken fnl furlong.* ....(3 to 1 op 5 to 2 tchd 7 to 2) 3

410* FORMAESTRE (Ire) [53] 8-5 (5*) O Pears (2) *nvr far away, effrt on outsd o'r 2 fs out, one pace fnl furlong.* ....(3 to 1 op 2 to 1) 4

Dist: 2½l, ½l, 3½l. 1m 34.70s. a 9.50s (4 Ran).

(Lord Swaythling), J W Watts

LONGCHAMP (FR) (soft)
Monday April 19th
Going Correction: PLUS 0.40 sec. per fur.

613 Prix de Fontainebleau (Group 3) (3-y-o) £23,895 1m........................ (2:55)

ZIETEN (USA) 9-2 T Jarnet (1) *rcd in second, effrt o'r 2 and a half fs out, led two and a half furlongs out, ran on wl*..................................(10 to 1 on) 1

360^4 SEMILLON 9-2 A Badel (2) *3rd strt, effrt o'r 2 fs out, ran on, not rch wnr*..............................(72 to 10) 2

DANAKAL (USA) 9-2 W Mongil (6) *4th strt, effrt and hrd rdn o'r 2 fs out, one pace clsg stages*.......... (57 to 10) 3

GLORIEUX DANCER (Fr) 9-2 G Guignard (3) *5th strt, some late hdwy*.....................................(76 to 10) 4

FRASER RIVER (USA) 9-2 S Guillot (4) *led, rdn o'r 2 and a half fs out, wknd strt*......................(10 to 1 on) 5

LASTING GRACE (Ire) (bl) 9-2 M Boutin (5) *3rd strt, wknd quickly*...(26 to 1) 6

Dist: 1½l, 1½l, 1½l, 1½l, 6l. 1m 44.20s. a 6.70s (6 Ran).

SR: 50/45/40/35/30/12/ (Sheikh Mohammed), A Fabre

NOTTINGHAM (good)
Monday April 19th
Going Correction: PLUS 0.15 sec. per fur. (races 1,2), MINUS 0.20 (3,4,5,6,7)

614 Aboyeur Selling Stakes Class G (3-y-o) £2,070 6f 15yds.................... (2:20)

DAILYSPORTDUTCH 8-6 N Carlisle (7) *cl up, led hfwy, rdn and ran on fnl furlong.* (7 to 1 op 4 to 1 tchd 8 to 1) 1

HY WILMA 7-13 (7*) S Drowne (12) *chsd ldrs, effrt and hdwy 2 fs out, rdn and ev ch ins last, kpt on.* ....(12 to 1 op 10 to 1 tchd 16 to 1) 2

342* CHARITY EXPRESS (Ire) 8-6 J Carroll (8) *dwlt, sn chasing ldrs, rdn and ev ch appr fnl furlong, one pace ins last.* ....(11 to 10 on op Evens tchd 5 to 4 on) 3

JAKE THE PAKE (Ire) 8-11 A Shoults (10) *beh till styd on fnl 2 fs, nrst finish*.....................(25 to 1 op 16 to 1) 4

455^4 MIDLIN 8-7^1 L Dettori (13) *chsd ldrs, rdn and one pace fnl 2 fs*.....................................(8 to 1 op 6 to 1) 5

428 FINAL OAK 8-6 J Fortune (5) *cl up, rdn 2 fs out, wknd entering fnl furlong*...............(25 to 1 op 12 to 1) 6

455^3 MAGICATION 7-13 (7*) Claire Balding (2) *in tch, rdn and one pace fnl 2 fs*...................(14 to 1 op 10 to 1) 7

518^3 ALWAYS BAILEYS 8-6 Dean McKeown (9) *chsd ldrs, rdn hfwy, sn wknd*.........(13 to 2 op 4 to 1 tchd 7 to 1) 8

455^6 WEALTHYWOO 7-13 (7*) C Hawksley (4) *al rear.* ....(33 to 1 op 25 to 1) 9

4805a MOVING IMAGE (Ire) 8-9^3 C Dwyer (6) *led to hfwy, grad wknd*...............................(14 to 1 op 8 to 1) 10

518^4 BECKY BOO 8-6 R Price (11) *al rear.* (25 to 1 op 14 to 1) 11

GLEAM OF GOLD 8-6 S Dawson (1) *slwly away, al beh.* ....(33 to 1 op 14 to 1) 12

417^9 TOCCATELLA 8-6 R Perham (3) *lost pl and beh frm hfwy.* ....(10 to 1 op 20 to 1 tchd 33 to 1) 13

Dist: 1l, 1l, 1½l, 1l, 2l, 1½l, 3l, 1½l, nk, 3½l. 1m 15.90s. a 4.40s (13 Ran).

SR: 22/18/14/13/5/-/ (Brian T Eastick), Miss Gay Kelleway

615 Felstead Claiming Stakes Class F (3-y-o and up) £2,668 5f 13yds.............(2:50)

FOLLOWMEGIRLS 4-8-7 (5*) A Garth (12) *mid-div, rdn and hdwy 2 fs out, styd on to ld wl ins fnl furlong.* ....(25 to 1 op 20 to 1 tchd 33 to 1) 1

292^3 ARC LAMP 7-9-1 J Fortune (13) *chsd ldrs, swtchd and effrt to chal appr fnl furlong, rdn and ev ch ins last, edgd lft and no extr*... (6 to 1 tchd 13 to 2 and 7 to 1) 2

METAL BOYS 6-9-2 (5*) S Wynne (3) *al prmnt, effrt 2 fs out and ev ch ins last, edgd rght and no extr.* ....(5 to 1 op 4 to 1 tchd 11 to 2 and 6 to 1) 3

289^2 TINO TERE 4-9-9 J Carroll (1) *cl up, led 2 fs out, rdn, hdd and wknd ins fnl furlong.* ....(13 to 2 op 7 to 2 tchd 7 to 1) 4

401* THE NOBLE OAK (Ire) (bl) 5-8-13 (7*) Gina Faulkner (5) *cl up, ev ch entering fnl furlong, sn rdn and wknd.* ....(14 to 1 op 12 to 1) 5

289^4 LITTLE SABOTEUR 4-9-2 W Ryan (9) *chsd ldrs, hdwy 2 fs out, rdn and ev ch appr fnl furlong, wkng whn hmpd ins last*..........(11 to 4 fav op 9 to 4 tchd 3 to 1) 6

379^2 SUPERLATIVEMAXIMUS (Ire) 5-8-12 (7*) Claire Balding (6) *cl up, led aftr 2 fs to two furlongs out, grad wknd.* ....(20 to 1 op 16 to 1) 7

545* MARTINA 5-9-0 J Quinn (4) *in tch, rdn 2 fs out, sn btn.* ....(9 to 2 op 7 to 2 tchd 5 to 1) 8

419* HARRY'S COMING 9-8-11 (7*) S Drowne (2) *nvr rch ldrs.* .... (9 to 1 op 12 to 1) 9

28^9 CUMBRIAN CAVALIER 4-8-12 R Lappin (7) *al rear.* (50 to 1) 10

4719a NORDOORA (Ire) 4-8-7 L Dettori (10) *slwly into strd, al rear*..(33 to 1) 11

RISKMEMAY 4-8-9 J O'Reilly (8) *wnt rght strt, al rear.* ....(50 to 1) 12

501 SLIP-A-SNIP (bl) 6-8-10 (3*) S D Williams (11) *led 2 fs, prmnt till rdn and wknd two furlongs out*...........(14 to 1) 13

Dist: 1l, ½l, ¾l, 2l, 2½l, 1l, hd, ½l, 1½l, 2l. 1m 2.10s. a 3.90s (13 Ran).

SR: 35/34/38/37/26/12/11/5/7/ (Exors Of The Late Mr J Martin), Mrs A L M King

616 Oh So Sharp Fillies Conditions Stakes Class C (4-y-o and up) £4,073 1m 1f 213yds ....(3:20)

DELVE (Ire) 4-8-12 Pat Eddery (2) *made all, clr 4 fs out, pushed alng and quickened 2 furlongs out, styd on wl ins last*.... (13 to 8 on op 5 to 4 on tchd 11 to 10 on) 1

293^5 PEARL ANGEL 4-9-0 L Dettori (1) *trkd ldrs, hdwy o'r 3 fs out, rdn to chal one and a half furlongs out, kpt on one pace*.............(3 to 1 op 9 to 4 tchd 100 to 30) 2

ROCKAWHILE (Ire) 4-8-12 W Ryan (3) *hld up, hdwy o'r 3 fs out, effrt and rdn to chal appr fnl furlong, one pace ins last*......................................(4 to 1 op 7 to 4) 3

522^6 FAIRFIELDS CONE 10-8-3 (7*) Michelle Thomas (4) *chsd wnr till wknd o'r 3 fs out, sn beh*..............(33 to 1) 4

Dist: 3l, nk, 20l. 2m 6.60s. a 3.60s (4 Ran).

SR: 42/38/35/-/ (Exors Of The Late Sir Robin McAlpine), J L Dunlop

617 Michelozzo Conditions Stakes Class C (4-y-o and up) £4,073 1¾m 15yds...... (3:50)

ALLEGAN (USA) 4-8-12 Pat Eddery (1) *set gd pace, quickened wl o'r one furlong out, styd on strly.* ....(7 to 2 on op 3 to 1 on) 1

CASTLE COURAGEOUS 6-8-13 J Reid (4) *hld up in tch, hdwy 4 fs out, pushed alng to take clr order 2 furlongs out, sn rdn and one pace appr fnl furlong.* ....(9 to 1 op 6 to 1 tchd 10 to 1) 2

LONG SILENCE (USA) 4-8-3 P Robinson (5) *chsd ldr, pushed alng 4 fs out, rdn to chal 2 furlongs out, sn one pace*..................................(7 to 1 op 9 to 2) 3

FLAKEY DOVE 7-8-5 W Ryan (2) *al rear.* ....(14 to 1 op 16 to 1 tchd 20 to 1) 4

462^4 NORTHERN RARITY (USA) 4-8-8 J Quinn (3) *chsd ldr to 6 fs out, sn rdn and wknd 3 furlongs out.* ....(33 to 1 op 20 to 1) 5

Dist: 3½l, 1l, 3l, ¾l. 3m 4.20s. a 6.30s (5 Ran).

SR: 7/1/ (K Abdulla), H R A Cecil

618 Call Boy Handicap Class D (0-80 4-y-o and up) £3,640 1¾m 15yds..............(4:20)

ASIAN PUNTER (Ire) [66] 4-8-8 (7*) N Varley (9) *beh, hdwy and pushed alng 3 fs out, styd on appr fnl furlong to ld on line*.............................(16 to 1 op 12 to 1) 1

349^9 SUNKALA SHINE [55] 5-8-6 Dean McKeown (13) *chsd ldr, led o'r 3 fs out and sn clr, rdn appr fnl furlong, ct on line*................................(10 to 1 op 8 to 1) 2

TEXAN TYCOON [71] 5-9-8 L Dettori (14) *hld up and beh, hdwy 3 fs out, effrt 2 furlongs out and sn rdn, styd on.* ....(5 to 1 op 7 to 2 tchd 11 to 2) 3

365^7 TOUR LEADER (NZ) [58] 4-8-7 Alex Greaves (5) *in tch, effrt and hdwy 2 fs out, sn rdn and kpt on*......... (20 to 1) 4

PROVENCE [70] 6-9-7 G Hind (7) *beh till styd on fnl 2 fs, nrst finish*........................ (25 to 1 op 20 to 1) 5

4813a PEAK DISTRICT [45] 7-7-10 J Quinn (12) *mid-div, gd hdwy 7 fs out, rdn 3 furlongs out, kpt on one pace*...(25 to 1) 6

456 SHUJAN (USA) [64] 4-8-13 M Hills (3) *prmnt till rdn and one pace fnl 3 fs*..................(14 to 1 op 20 to 1) 7

294^3 DAWN FLIGHT [67] 4-9-2 W Ryan (4) *chsd ldrs, rdn 2 fs out, wknd appr fnl furlong*.............(9 to 1 op 10 to 1) 8

HIGH GRADE [47] 5-7-8^3 (7*) C Hawksley (6) *nvr rch ldrs.* ....(20 to 1 op 16 to 1) 9

FAMOUS BEAUTY [49] 6-7-11^4 (7*) L Aspell (10) *slwly away, nvr a factor*...............(16 to 1 op 14 to 1) 10

442^3 PRINCE HANNIBAL [75] 6-9-12 J Reid (15) *hld up and beh, gd hdwy 6 fs out, effrt and ch 2 furlongs out, sn rdn, edgd rght and wknd*... (6 to 1 op 8 to 1 tchd 10 to 1) 11

382^5 TROJAN LANCER [47] 7-7-12 J Lowe (16) *hld up and beh, gd hdwy 6 fs out, rdn and wknd 2 furlongs out.* ....(9 to 2 fav op 5 to 2) 12

456 NEARCTIC BAY (USA) [42] 7-7-7 N Carlisle (1) *chsd ldrs, rdn 4 fs out, wknd 3 furlongs out*.... (33 to 1 tchd 50 to 1) 13

287* HORIZON (Ire) [66] (bl) 5-9-3 D Biggs (8) *led, hdd o'r 3 fs out, wknd 2 furlongs out.* ....(6 to 1 op 5 to 1 tchd 7 to 1) 14

CHUCKLESTONE [69] 10-9-6 Pat Eddery (11) *chsd ldrs, rdn alng 6 fs out, sn wknd*............(16 to 1 op 12 to 1) 15
NOBLE SOCIETY [49] 5-8-0² R Price (2) *prmnt till wknd o'r 4 fs out*..................................(50 to 1) 16
Dist: Sht-hd, 2½l, nk, 2l, 1½l, nk, 1l, 1l, ½l, 1½l. 3m 3.90s. a 6.00s (16 Ran).
SR: 13/3/14/-/8/-/ (Rory C Leader), A Hide

619 Slip Anchor Conditions Stakes Class D (4-y-o and up) £3,084 1m 54yds........(4:50)

IMPERIAL BALLET (Ire) 4-8-10 Pat Eddery (5) *trkd ldrs gng wl, quickened to ld one and a half fs out and sn clr.* ....(7 to 4 on op 6 to 4 on) 1
PATER NOSTER (USA) 4-9-0 L Dettori (4) *hld up in tch, hdwy 3 fs out, effrt and rdn 2 furlongs out, kpt on.* ....(5 to 2 op 6 to 4 tchd 11 to 4) 2
524⁵ BEWARE OF AGENTS 4-8-13 Dean McKeown (1) *cl up, led aftr 2 fs out, rdn two furlongs out, sn hdd and not quicken*...........................(7 to 1 op 10 to 1) 3
VANBOROUGH LAD 4-8-10 D Biggs (3) *led 2 fs, cl up till rdn and wknd two furlongs out*... (50 to 1 op 33 to 1) 4
533⁴ WELL APPOINTED (Ire) 4-8-12 J O'Reilly (2) *in tch, effrt and hdwy 3 fs out, sn rdn and btn.* (33 to 1 op 20 to 1) 5
Dist: 2½l, ¾l, 3l, ½l. 1m 44.40s. a 4.40s (5 Ran).
SR: 5/1/ (R E Sangster), H R A Cecil

620 Coronach Handicap Class D (0-80 3-y-o and up) £3,465 1m 1f 213yds........ (5:20)

358² JAZILAH (Fr) [66] 5-9-0 W Ryan (12) *cl up, hdwy to ld 3 fs out, hdd entering fnl furlong, rdn to lead wl ins last, ran on strly*.................... (7 to 2 fav op 5 to 1) 1
513² SWIFT SILVER [59] 6-8-7² J Reid (10) *mid-div, hdwy 4 fs out, effrt 2 furlongs out, rdn to chal entering fnl furlong, no extr nr finish*........... (6 to 1 tchd 7 to 1) 2
MARCHMAN [58] 8-8-6¹ Pat Eddery (5) *trkd ldrs, gd hdwy o'r 2 fs out, rdn to ld briefly entering fnl furlong, no extr nr finish*.....................(12 to 1 op 8 to 1) 3
416² HERE HE COMES [47] 7-7-9² S Dawson (3) *hld up and beh, hdwy o'r 2 fs out, sn rdn and kpt on.* (5 to 1 op 3 to 1) 4
350* WESTFIELD MOVES (Ire) [60] 5-8-8 J Quinn (11) *chsd ldrs, hdwy o'r 3 fs out, chlgd 2 furlongs out, sn rdn and wknd*.................(7 to 1 op 6 to 1 tchd 8 to 1) 5
350⁵ GLIDE PATH (USA) [74] 4-9-8 M Hills (7) *mid-div, effrt and hdwy 4 fs out, rdn and wknd o'r 2 furlongs out.* .... (13 to 2 op 5 to 1 tchd 7 to 1) 6
456³ SAINT CIEL (USA) [65] 5-8-13 R Perham (2) *cl up, rdn and ev ch 3 fs out, grad wknd fnl 2 furlongs.* ....(14 to 1 tchd 16 to 1) 7
YOUNG GEORGE [45] 6-7-7 J Lowe (14) *dwlt, nvr rch ldrs.* .... (14 to 1 op 12 to 1) 8
500⁸ MAPLE BAY (Ire) [64] 4-8-12 N Carlisle (8) *cl up till rdn and wknd o'r 3 fs out*........................... (25 to 1) 9
500² ACHELOUS [52] (v) 6-8-0 P Robinson (1) *led, hdd and wknd 3 fs out*...................... (8 to 1 op 6 to 1) 10
279⁸ HILLZAH (USA) [66] 5-9-0 Dean McKeown (4) *dwlt, al rear.* .... (16 to 1 op 14 to 1) 11
WRETS [80] 4-9-7 (7*) C Hawksley (9) *al beh.* .... (33 to 1 op 25 to 1) 12
327 SEEMENOMORE [45] 4-7-0 (7*) F Savage (13) *beh frm hfwy*..(50 to 1) 13
521 MERLS PEARL [45] 4-7-2² (7*) Darren Moffatt (6) *chsd ldrs 6 fs, sn wknd*...................... (33 to 1 op 25 to 1) 14
Dist: 2l, 1l, ¾l, 2½l, 3l, 1l, hd, 2½l, 3l, ½l. 2m 6.10s. a 3.10s (14 Ran).
SR: 49/38/35/22/30/38/27/6/20/ (S Aitken), Mrs M Reveley

FOLKESTONE (good (races 1,2,3,6,8), good to soft (4,5,7)) Tuesday April 20th

Going Correction: PLUS 0.10 sec. per fur. (races 1,2,3,6,8), MINUS 0.15 (4,5,7)

621 Tim Freeman Claiming Stakes Class G (Div I) (4-y-o and up) £2,070 1m 1f 149yds ....(1:50)

224⁷ NORTHERN CONQUEROR (Ire) 5-8-7 D Holland (4) *hld up, hdwy o'r 2 fs out, led wl ins last, readily.* .... (13 to 2 op 7 to 2) 1
327³ STORM FREE (USA) 7-8-13 N Carlisle (1) *hld up beh ldg grp, led appr 2 fs out till hdd and no extr wl ins last.* ....(11 to 10 on op 11 to 10 tchd 5 to 4 on) 2
373⁹ THIN RED LINE (v) 9-8-7 S Whitworth (3) *hld up beh, hdwy 2 fs out, sn one pace*.................(8 to 1 op 5 to 1) 3
498⁸ RAGTIME SONG 4-8-5 T Quinn (2) *chsd ldrs, rdn o'r 2 fs out, wknd*......................... (12 to 1 op 8 to 1) 4
138⁷ EMERALD EARS 4-7-13² (3*) J Weaver (8) *hld up in rear, effrt o'r one furlong out, not pace to chal.* ....(16 to 1 op 10 to 1 tchd 25 to 1) 5
DEVONIAN (USA) 4-8-9 R Cochrane (9) *took keen hold, led til hdd appr 2 fs out, wknd*........ (12 to 1 op 8 to 1) 6
YAAFOOR (USA) (v) 4-8-2 (3*) A Tucker (7) *trkd ldr till rdn and wknd appr 2 fs out.* .... (16 to 1 op 10 to 1 tchd 20 to 1) 7

416 MASTAMIST (bl) 4-8-3 N Adams (5) *trkd ldrs, rdn alng 5 fs out, sn lost pl*..................... (25 to 1 op 14 to 1) 8
190⁶ WOOD KAY (Ire) 4-8-4² W Ryan (6) *trkd ldrs till wknd quickly 2 fs out*...... (14 to 1 op 16 to 1 tchd 33 to 1) 9
Dist: 1l, 7l, 4l, sht-hd, 3½l, 2l, 6l, 5l. 2m 5.30s. a 7.70s (9 Ran).
SR: 26/30/10/-/-/-/ (Mrs J T Naughton), T J Naughton

622 Tim Freeman Claiming Stakes Class G (Div II) (4-y-o and up) £2,070 1m 1f 149yds ....(2:20)

NATURAL LAD (bl) 8-8-9 G Duffield (2) *trkd ldr, led o'r 5 fs out, hrd rdn 2 out, all out*.......(5 to 2 fav op 5 to 1) 1
AMLAK (USA) 4-8-11 J Quinn (8) *trkd ldrs, chsd wnr fnl 2 fs, hrd rdn o'r one out, kpt on wl*.... (6 to 1 op 6 to 1) 2
PRINCESS EVITA (Fr) 4-7-12¹ (3*) D Harrison (5) *in tch, cld 4 fs out, one pace frm 2 out.* .... (10 to 1 tchd 8 to 1 and 12 to 1) 3
333⁹ SUNSET STREET (Ire) 5-8-3 C Rutter (4) *pld hrd, hld up beh, cld o'r 2 fs out, outpcd over one out, styd on one pace*................................ (3 to 1 op 6 to 4) 4
458⁷ MON PETITNAMOUR (Ire) (bl) 4-8-7 (5*) B Doyle (6) *missed break, in tch, rdn 3 fs out, nvr on terms.* .... (8 to 1 op 4 to 1 tchd 10 to 1) 5
261⁵ ROGERSON 5-8-7 Candy Morris (9) *missed break, in tch till outpcd frm o'r 3 fs out.* ....(25 to 1 op 20 to 1 tchd 33 to 1) 6
COLONEL FAIRFAX 5-8-1 G Carter (7) *trkd ldrs till rdn and wknd 2 fs out, eased*................(8 to 1 op 4 to 1) 7
331 JUNE'S LEAR FAN (Can) 4-8-13 M Roberts (3) *led til hdd o'r 5 fs out, wknd quickly*............ (6 to 1 tchd 7 to 1) 8
500⁹ L'ACQUESIANA (v) 5-8-0 D Biggs (1) *al beh, tld off.* .... (20 to 1 op 12 to 1) 9
Dist: ½l, 3l, 3½l, sht-hd, 15l, 1½l, 1l, 15l. 2m 5.10s. a 7.50s (9 Ran).
SR: 30/31/15/10/18/-/ (Thomas Dyer), C Weedon

623 Walmer Apprentice Maiden Stakes Class G (3-y-o and up) £2,070 6f 189yds... (2:50)

PRAIRIE GROVE 3-8-2 (8*) Mark Denaro (3) *hdwy 3 fs out, ran on strly to ld ins last, sn clr.* ....(5 to 2 op 3 to 1 tchd 7 to 2) 1
BREAKFAST BOOGIE 3-8-2 (3*) N Varley (8) *led aftr one furlong, clr 3 fs out, hdd and no extr ins last.* .... (11 to 2 op 5 to 1 tchd 6 to 1) 2
335² ROYAL INTERVAL 3-8-2 (8*) S Lanigan (9) *chsd clr ldr aftr one furlong, kpt on one pace frm o'r one furlong out.* .... (15 to 8 fav op Evens tchd 2 to 1) 3
417⁸ MARAT (USA) 3-8-10 D McCabe (7) *trkd ldrs, lost pl hfwy, effrt and styd on frm o'r one furlong out.* .... (14 to 1 op 12 to 1) 4
TAKE THE MICK 3-8-5 (5*) J Wilkinson (5) *chsd ldrs, effrt and one pace fnl 2 fs*.............. (33 to 1 op 20 to 1) 5
394⁶ KRAYYAN DAWN 3-8-10 S Mulvey (2) *sn outpcd, nvr on terms*............................. (33 to 1 op 20 to 1) 6
458² MUMMYS ROCKET 4-8-9 (10*) W Hollick (4) *outpcd.* ....(4 to 1 op 2 to 1 tchd 9 to 2) 7
TRESARIA (Ire) 3-7-11 (8*) D Toole (1) *speed 2 fs, sn beh.* .... (33 to 1 op 20 to 1) 8
346 WIRED FOR SOUND 3-8-5³ (8*) R Painter (6) *led one furlong, cl up till wknd quickly o'r 2 fs out.* .... (16 to 1 op 14 to 1 tchd 20 to 1) 9
Dist: 2l, nk, 3l, nk, 8l, hd, 3l, 1½l. 1m 25.70s. a 4.80s (9 Ran).
SR: 34/23/27/18/17/-/ (Giles Gleadell), R Hannon

624 Barham Median Auction Maiden Stakes Class E (3-y-o) £3,080 6f............(3:20)

380⁴ PRESS GALLERY 9-0 G Duffield (9) *cl up, led hfwy, ran on wl*......................... (7 to 2 op 4 to 1 tchd 5 to 1) 1
THE LITTLE FERRET 9-0 B Rouse (4) *led til hdd hfwy, one pace frm o'r one furlong out.* ....(5 to 4 fav op 6 to 4 on tchd 6 to 4) 2
471⁹ WALNUT BURL (Ire) 9-0 J Reid (6) *trkd ldrs, one pace fnl 2 fs*.................................(33 to 1 op 12 to 1) 3
DEVIOUS DANCER 9-0 T Sprake (8) *trkd ldrs, rdn 2 fs out, one pace*.............(14 to 1 op 20 to 1 tchd 25 to 1) 4
TIP ME UP 8-9 M Roberts (11) *outpcd, rdn and hdwy appr fnl furlong, styd on, nrst finish.* ....(6 to 1 op 5 to 1 tchd 8 to 1) 5
GALLOP TO GLORY 9-0 T Quinn (12) *wth ldrs till wknd quickly 2 fs out*.................. (50 to 1 op 25 to 1) 6
JULY BRIDE 8-9 Candy Morris (10) *nvr plcd to chal.* .... (50 to 1 op 25 to 1) 7
LANZAMAR 8-9 C Rutter (3) *outpcd.* (50 to 1 op 25 to 1) 8
476⁵ TWICE THE GROOM (Ire) 9-0 W Newnes (1) *outpcd.* .... (11 to 2 op 5 to 1 tchd 6 to 1) 9
4747a⁸ WESTERN VALLEY 8-9 G Bardwell (5) *sn pushed alng, beh frm hfwy*......................... (50 to 1 op 20 to 1) 10
SHARP PROSPECT 9-0 Paul Eddery (13) *beh frm hfwy,* .... (16 to 1 op 10 to 1) 11
459 STOCKFORCE 9-0 R Perham (2) *al beh.* .... (33 to 1 op 20 to 1 tchd 50 to 1) 12
SENCINI 8-9 D Holland (7) *outpcd, tld off.* .... (25 to 1 op 12 to 1) 13
Dist: 2l, 6l, 2l, hd, 1½l, sht-hd, 2l, hd, hd, nk. 1m 13.10s. a 2.10s (13 Ran).
SR: 40/32/8/-/-/-/ (Lord Howard de Walden), Mrs J Cecil

625 Margate Claiming Stakes Class G (2-y-o) £2,070 5f. . . . . (3:50)

399[8] WINDOW DISPLAY 8-6 M Roberts (11) *trkd ldrs, rdn o'r one furlong out, ran on to ld wl ins last.* . . . . (15 to 2 op 6 to 1 tchd 8 to 1) 1
LITTLE EMMELINE 7-9 N Carlisle (8) *fst away, led til hdd wl ins fnl furlong, no extr*. . . . . . (33 to 1 op 12 to 1) 2
446[2] MADAME GREGOIRE 8-9 R Cochrane (9) *tacked across to stands side wth ldr, hrd rdn wl o'r one furlong out, one pace*. . . . . (6 to 4 fav op 7 to 4 tchd 2 to 1) 3
445[4] RISKY AFFAIR 8-5 (3*) D Harrison (3) *chsd ldrs, sn rdn alng, kpt on one pace frm o'r one furlong out.* . . . . (9 to 4 tchd 5 to 2 and 2 to 1) 4
IMPERIAL BAILIWICK (Ire) 8-7 N Adams (1) *chsd ldrs, sn pushed alng, one pace fnl 2 fs*. . . . . . (16 to 1 op 8 to 1) 5
337[6] FOREVER BLUSHING 7-9[2] J Quinn (2) *nvr on terms wth ldrs*. . . . . (25 to 1 op 12 to 1 tchd 33 to 1) 6
299 DOUBLE-D (Ire) 7-12 (7*) J O'Dwyer (6) *sn beh.* . . . . (16 to 1 op 8 to 1 tchd 20 to 1) 7
490[3] MISS RISKY 8-1 A McGlone (4) *outpcd*. (4 to 1 op 5 to 2) 8
517[6] CRAFTY CRICKETER 8-4 S Dawson (10) *sn outpcd.* . . . . (25 to 1 op 20 to 1) 9
445[7] WOOLY BULLY 7-7 G Bardwell (5) *outpcd, tld off.* . . . . (33 to 1 op 20 to 1) 10

Dist: Nk, 2l, 1l, nk, 5l, ½l, 2l, 8l, 4l. 1m 1.20s. a 2.60s (10 Ran).
SR: 25/13/19/14/12/-/ (Sheet & Roll Convertors Ltd), M R Channon

626 Levy Board Handicap Class E (0-70 4-y-o and up) £3,365 1m 7f 92yds. . . . . (4:20)

427[4] SHOOFE (USA) [64] 5-9-11 M Roberts (5) *took keen hold early, trkd ldrs, rdn alng 3 fs out, styd on wl to ld ins fnl furlong*. . . . . (9 to 2 op 5 to 1 tchd 6 to 1) 1
420* ISLAND BLADE (Ire) [54] 4-8-13 T Quinn (13) *hld up, cld o'r 4 fs out, rdn to ld over one out till hdd and no extr ins last*. . . . . (15 to 8 fav op 7 to 4 tchd 2 to 1) 2
PRIDE OF BRITAIN (Can) [49] 4-8-8 N Carlisle (6) *cl up, led ten fs out, hdd one out, one pace.* . . . . (8 to 1 op 7 to 1 tchd 10 to 1) 3
495 HUNTING GROUND [51] 5-8-12 J Quinn (2) *beh, hdwy on ins o'r one furlong out, styd on, nrst finish.* . . . . (16 to 1 op 14 to 1 tchd 20 to 1) 4
FORGE [40] 5-7-10 (5*) B Doyle (16) *trkd ldrs, outpcd o'r 5 fs out, styd on one pace frm over 2 out.* . . . . (16 to 1 op 14 to 1 tchd 20 to 1) 5
SMILINGATSTRANGERS [52] (v) 5-8-13 G Bardwell (7) *hld up in mid-div, effrt o'r 2 fs out, one pace.* . . . . (10 to 1 op 7 to 1) 6
442[7] UP ALL NIGHT [35] 4-7-1 (7*) D Wright (8) *beh, hdwy o'r one furlong out, nvr nrr.* (16 to 1 op 14 to 1 tchd 20 to 1) 7
420[2] PEACH BRANDY [38] 4-7-11 N Adams (15) *chsd ldrs, no hdwy fnl 3 fs*. . . . . (10 to 1 op 7 to 1) 8
CHAKALAK [60] 5-9-7 G Carter (17) *nvr nr to chal.* . . . . (25 to 1) 9
AEDEAN [51] 4-8-10 A McGlone (10) *hld up in mid-div, hdwy wl o'r 2 fs out, btn over one out.* . . . . (12 to 1 op 10 to 1 tchd 14 to 1) 10
520[7] STRIKING IMAGE (Ire) [58] 4-9-3 B Rouse (11) *led til heded ten fs out, wknd o'r 2 furlongs out*. (25 to 1 op 20 to 1) 11
CANADIAN BOY (Ire) [37] 4-7-10[3] D Biggs (9) *sn beh.* . . . . (66 to 1 op 50 to 1 tchd 100 to 1) 12
CHASMARELLA [38] 8-7-13[3] Candy Morris (4) *trkd ldrs, beh fnl 3 fs*. . . . . (33 to 1) 13
SUREN [60] (bl) 7-9-7 A Clark (14) *chsd ldrs, hmpd and lost pl o'r 6 fs out*. . . . . (33 to 1) 14
498 DRINKS PARTY (Ire) [36] 5-7-9[5] (7*) C Hawksley (3) *al beh.* . . . . (14 to 1 op 12 to 1) 15
416[4] LLOYDS DREAM [35] 4-7-8[1] Dale Gibson (12) *al beh, tld off*. . . . . (33 to 1) 16

Dist: 1l, hd, 3½l, ½l, 1l, ¾l, 2l, ½l, 3½l, ¾l. 3m 28.40s. a 9.90s (16 Ran).
SR: 28/15/9/9/-/8/-/-/11/ (Ali K Al Jafleh), D Morley

627 Folkestone Fillies Conditions Stakes Class D (3-y-o and up) £3,084 5f. . . . . (4:50)

491* CRIME OFTHECENTURY 3-8-2 T Quinn (3) *cl up, slight advantage 2 fs out, ran on wl.* . . . . (5 to 4 on op Evens tchd 11 to 10) 1
YAKIN (USA) 3-8-0 R Hills (4) *cl up, ev ch appr fnl furlong, one pace*. . . . . (11 to 8 op 5 to 4 on tchd 6 to 4) 2
BELLS OF LONGWICK 4-8-13 T Williams (2) *in tch, led hfwy till hdd 2 fs out, ev ch one out, one pace.* . . . . (9 to 1 op 4 to 1 tchd 10 to 1) 3
545[3] EVER SO LONELY 4-8-6 (7*) D Wright (1) *led til hdd hfwy, wknd o'r one furlong out.* . . . . (33 to 1 op 14 to 1 tchd 40 to 1) 4

Dist: 3l, 1½l, 3l. 59.90s. a 1.30s (4 Ran).
SR: 47/33/40/28/ (Christopher Wright), P F I Cole

628 Dover Handicap Class E (0-70 3-y-o and up) £3,287 1½m. (5:20)

456[7] BLACKPATCH HILL [54] 4-9-0 W Carson (3) *trkd ldrs, led wl o'r one furlong out, pushed out.* . . . . (4 to 1 op 3 to 1 tchd 9 to 2) 1
520* BROUGHTON'S TANGO (Ire) [55] 4-8-8 (7*,4ex) D McCabe (4) *beh, hdwy o'r 3 fs out, hrd rdn over one out, ran on.* . . . . (5 to 2 fav op 3 to 1 tchd 4 to 1) 2
498* TENAYESTELIGN [38] 5-7-13 (4ex) S Dawson (17) *hld up in mid-div, headway 3 fs out, styd on one pace.* . . . . (12 to 1 op 8 to 1 tchd 14 to 1) 3
152[5] ADMIRALS SECRET (USA) [64] 4-9-10 R Cochrane (8) *mid-div, hdwy 3 fs out, not much room on ins wl o'r one out, one pace*. (14 to 1 op 10 to 1) 4
434* PRESTON GUILD (Ire) [54] 3-7-8 N Adams (6) *al hndy, led briefly aftr one furlong, led ag'n 3 fs out till hdd wl o'r one out, wknd*. (5 to 1 tchd 6 to 1) 5
338[3] EARLY TO RISE [56] 3-7-10[2] D Biggs (14) *trkd ldrs till wknd wl o'r one furlong out*. . . . . . . (14 to 1 op 10 to 1) 6
403[2] KILLICK [40] 5-8-1 J Quinn (18) *led one furlong, trkd ldrs till wknd 2 fs out*. . . . . (8 to 1 op 10 to 1 tchd 12 to 1) 7
34[7] ILDERTON ROAD [40] 6-7-8 (7*) D Wright (11) *mid-div, staying on whn hmpd o'r 2 fs out, sn btn.* . . . . (33 to 1 op 20 to 1) 8
420 EL DOMINIO [47] 5-8-8 J Reid (13) *beh, hdwy o'r 4 fs out, sn btn*. (20 to 1 op 12 to 1) 9
476[8] ROCK THE BARNEY (Ire) [49] 4-8-9 B Rouse (15) *nvr better than mid-div*. . . . . (33 to 1 op 20 to 1) 10
416[3] L'UOMO CLASSICS [63] 6-9-10 A Clark (7) *cl up, led o'r 8 fs out till hdd and wknd 3 out*. . . . . . . (14 to 1 op 10 to 1) 11
PRINCESS ERMYN [55] 4-9-1 Dale Gibson (12) *al beh.* . . . . (25 to 1 op 14 to 1) 12
JULFAAR (USA) [56] 6-9-3 G Bardwell (2) *beh, cld 6 fs out, rdn 4 out, sn wknd*. . . . . (33 to 1 op 20 to 1) 13
456 POST IMPRESSIONIST (Ire) [55] 4-9-1 F Norton (10) *al beh.* . . . . (33 to 1 op 20 to 1) 14
QUALITAIR MEMORY (Ire) [34] 4-7-8[1] J Penza (16) *chsd alng beh ldg grp, behind frm hfwy.* . . . . (14 to 1 op 12 to 1 tchd 16 to 1) 15
SIMPLY (Ire) [64] 4-9-3 (7*) T G McLaughlin (9) *al beh.* . . . . (20 to 1 op 12 to 1 tchd 25 to 1) 16
TEMPELHOF (Ire) [59] 4-9-2 (3*) D Harrison (1) *led aftr 2 fs, hdd 8 furlongs out, wknd 6 out*. . . . (16 to 1 op 10 to 1) 17

Dist: 2l, 3l, sht-hd, 7l, sht-hd, ¾l, 1½l, 3l, sht-hd, ¾l. 2m 38.30s. a 7.80s (17 Ran).
SR: 34/31/9/33/-/-/ (J L Dunlop), J L Dunlop

MAISONS LAFFITTE (FR) (soft)
Tuesday April 20th

629 Prix Sir Gallahad (Listed) (4-y-o and up) £14,337 1m. . . . . (2:55)

NORTHERN CRYSTAL 5-9-6 S Guillot, ... 1
BALLINAMALLARD (USA) 4-8-8 O Peslier, ... 2
BOUT EN BOUT (Fr) 4-8-11 B Marchand, ... 3
PORTICO (USA) 4-9-2 F Head, ... 4

Dist: Nk, 2l, hd, 2½l, ½l, 5l, 10l. 1m 36.50s. a 1.80s (8 Ran).
SR: 73/60/57/61/ (Sheikh Mohammed), A Fabre

CATTERICK (good to soft)
Wednesday April 21st

Going Correction: PLUS 0.40 sec. per fur. (races 1,2,3,4,6,7), PLUS 0.50 (5)

630 Aspiring Jockeys Apprentice Maiden Stakes Class F (3-y-o) £2,579 7f. . . . . (2:10)

417[2] NESSUN DORMA 9-0 F Norton (8) *trkd ldrs, smooth hdwy on inner 3 fs out, rdn to ld entering last, cmftbly.* . . . . (11 to 10 on op 5 to 4 on tchd Evens) 1
549[3] PANTHER (Ire) 9-0 N Kennedy (6) *cl up, ev ch 2 fs out, sn rdn and outpcd, styd on ins last*. . . (10 to 1 op 8 to 1) 2
CHICKCHARNIE 9-0 O Pears (3) *led, rdn 2 fs out, hdd entering last, no extr*. . . . . (16 to 1 tchd 20 to 1) 3
463[5] SHAMGAAN (USA) 8-9 (5*) K Pattinson (9) *outpcd and beh till styd on fnl 2 fs, nrst finish*. . . . (7 to 2 tchd 4 to 1) 4
BROOMHOUSE LADY 8-4 (5*) M Baird (10) *cl up till rdn and wknd 3 fs out*. . . . . (66 to 1 op 50 to 1) 5
423[8] DUPLICATE 9-0 S Maloney (2) *nvr rchd ldrs.* . . . . (10 to 1 op 8 to 1) 6
MUNNASIB (Fr) 8-9 (5*) J Tate (1) *cl up till rdn and wknd 2 and a half fs out*. (6 to 1 op 7 to 2) 7
CARLTON EXPRESS (Ire) 8-9 (5*) C Teague (4) *al outpcd and beh*. . . . . (40 to 1 op 25 to 1) 8
534[9] GORDON'S BROTHER (Ire) 9-0 A Tucker (5) *dwlt, outpcd and beh*. . . . . (50 to 1) 9

Dist: 1l, ½l, 3l, 2l, 3l, 5l, ½l, 1½l. 1m 30.50s. a 7.50s (9 Ran).
SR: 30/27/25/16/5/1/ (H H Morriss), G Wragg

631 Jockey Cap Maiden Stakes Class D (3-y-o) £3,735 5f 212yds. . . . . (2:45)

367[3] MISS WHITTINGHAM (Ire) 8-9 J Carroll (1) *trkd ldr, effrt and quickened to ld entering fnl furlong, sn clr.* . . . . (7 to 1 tchd 6 to 1) 1
JIZYAH 8-9 R Hills (2) *led, shaken up and hdd entering fnl furlong, sn btn*. . . . . (10 to 1 on tchd 9 to 1 on) 2

Won by 5l. 1m 18.10s. a 7.10s (2 Ran).

SR: 1/-/ (J W Barrett), J Berry

632 'Win With The Tote' Handicap Class D (0-85 4-y-o and up) £3,377 1½m 44yds ....(3:20)

MERRY NUTKIN [67] 7-9-0 K Darley (7) *hld up, gd hdwy 4 fs out, effrt 2 out and sn led, rdn and ran on wl ins last.* ....(12 to 1 op 7 to 1) 1
FAIR FLYER (Ire) [57] 4-8-3 R P Elliott (6) *al prmnt, effrt and not clr run 2 fs out, swtchd wide and styd on strly ins last, jst fld*..............(8 to 1 op 10 to 1 tchd 12 to 1) 2
366* DEB'S BALL [60] 7-8-7 J Quinn (2) *in tch, hdwy o'r 3 fs out, effrt to chal one and a half out and sn ev ch, rdn and one pace ins last*.................... (9 to 2 op 4 to 1) 3
25^{5} CONTINUITY [53] 4-7-6 (7*) D Wright (5) *hld up and beh, hdwy o'r 2 fs out, styd on ins last, hng lft nr finish.* ....(14 to 1 op 12 to 1) 4
CANNY CHRONICLE [81] 5-10-0 P Robinson (4) *hld up, effrt and some hdwy 2 fs out, nvr rchd ldrs*.....(5 to 1) 5
290 LEGION OF HONOUR [70] 5-9-3 A Munro (8) *dsptd ld to hfwy, cl up till wknd wl o'r 2 fs out*..........(12 to 1) 6
508^{2} PERSONAL HAZARD [66] (v) 4-8-12 M Birch (3) *dsptd ld till led hfwy, rdn o'r 2 fs out and sn hdd, wknd.* .... (100 to 30 fav op 11 to 4 tchd 7 to 2) 7
DRUMMER HICKS [80] 4-9-12 Dean McKeown (1) *in tch, effrt and hdwy 3 fs out, sn rdn and btn, eased appr last*..................(4 to 1 tchd 7 to 2 and 9 to 2) 8

Dist: Hd, 2l, ¾l, 10l, 2l, 1½l, 8l. 2m 46.30s. a 11.30s (8 Ran).
SR: 36/24/24/14/23/8/-/-/ (Robert F S Newall), Mrs M Reveley

633 Hurgill Lodge Conditions Stakes Class D (3-y-o) £3,420 7f....................(3:50)

WILLSHE GAN 8-5 K Fallon (2) *trkd ldr, quickened o'r 2 fs out, rdn to chal over one out, styd on to ld entering last, ran on*.......................(10 to 1 op 8 to 1) 1
SPICE AND SUGAR 8-5 A Munro (3) *set steady pace, quickened o'r 2 fs out, rdn over one out, hdd entering last, no extr*.......................(10 to 1 op 6 to 1) 2
CARBON STEEL (Ire) 8-12 D Holland (1) *hld up, rdn and not quicken o'r 2 fs out, styd on und pres entering last, no extr nr finish.* ....(17 to 2 on op 6 to 1 on tchd 9 to 1 on) 3

Dist: ¾l, 2l. 1m 32.70s. a 9.70s (3 Ran).
(H Hewitson), Denys Smith

634 Sedbury Handicap Class D (0-80 3-y-o) £3,348 5f......................... (4:20)

367* PRIMULA BAIRN [63] 8-8 K Fallon (4) *chsd ldrs, rdn wl o'r one furlong out, styd on to ld ins last.* ....(4 to 1 op 3 to 1) 1
361* PRESS THE BELL [70] 9-1 J Carroll (6) *led, rdn o'r one furlong out, hdd and no extr ins last.* ....(5 to 4 fav op 6 to 4) 2
450^{2} WINTERING (Ire) [76] 9-7 G Duffield (8) *chsd ldrs, rdn and hdwy 2 fs out, sn one pace*.........(11 to 2 op 4 to 1) 3
$4687a^{5}$ JOTRA [51] 7-10 N Carlisle (7) *beh till styd on wl appr fnl furlong, nrst finish*.............. (25 to 1 op 16 to 1) 4
451^{4} CRACKER JACK [48] (bl) 7-7 S Wood (9) *in tch, effrt and hdwy 2 fs out, sn rdn and one pace.* .... (25 to 1 op 16 to 1) 5
BOLD COUNTY [72] 9-3 Dean McKeown (1) *chsd ldrs till rdn 2 fs out, sn wknd*...............(9 to 1 op 6 to 1) 6
398 MUDGEE [48] 7-0 (7*) D Wright (3) *chsd ldrs 3 fs, sn wknd.* .... (20 to 1 op 16 to 1) 7
361^{4} LUCKY MILL [53] 7-9 (3*) N Kennedy (10) *cl up, rdn 2 fs out, sn wknd*.......................... (8 to 1 op 5 to 1) 8
106^{7} MATTHEW DAVID [48] (bl) 7-7 J Lowe (5) *al rear.* .... (16 to 1 op 14 to 1) 9
361^{7} FOREST FLYER [48] 7-7 G Bardwell (2) *al outpcd and beh.* ....(33 to 1 op 25 to 1) 10

Dist: 1½l, 6l, 1½l, nk, nk, 1½l, 3l, 3l, 12l. 1m 2.60s. a 5.10s (10 Ran).
SR: 42/43/25/-/-/13/ (Kavli), Mrs J R Ramsden

635 Richmond Conditions Stakes Class D (3-y-o) £3,084 1½m 44yds............. (4:50)

423* WHITE MUZZLE 8-12 J Reid (3) *hld up, hdwy on bit 2 fs out, led one and a half out, sn clr, unchlgd.* ....(13 to 8 on op 2 to 1 on) 1
SOUL EMPEROR 8-10 A Munro (4) *cl up, led 2 and a half fs out, rdn and hdd one and a half out, one pace.* .... (14 to 1 op 10 to 1) 2
SCULLER (USA) 8-10 W Ryan (2) *led, pushed alng o'r 4 fs out, hdd 2 and a half out and sn one pace.* ....(7 to 2 op 3 to 1 tchd 4 to 1) 3
377* ROVEREDO (USA) 8-12 L Dettori (1) *trkd ldrs till broke leg and pld up o'r 3 fs out, dead*........(5 to 1 op 3 to 1) pu

Dist: 6l, ½l. 2m 44.00s. a 9.00s (4 Ran).
SR: 57/43/42/-/ (Luciano Gaucci), P W Chapple-Hyam

636 Spring Handicap Class E (0-70 3-y-o and up) £3,235 7f....................... (5:20)

QUINTA ROYALE [53] 6-8-12 G Duffield (12) *beh and wide strt, gd hdwy 2 fs out, led one out and ran on wl.* ....(10 to 1 op 8 to 1) 1
358^{4} LORD LAMBSON [41] 4-8-0 A Munro (4) *in tch, effrt and hdwy 2 fs out, sn rdn, styd on ins last.* ....(10 to 1 op 8 to 1) 2
375^{3} MAROWINS [43] 4-8-2 J Quinn (2) *hld up, hdwy 3 fs out, effrt and ch appr last, sn rdn and kpt on one pace.* ....(7 to 1 op 6 to 1) 3
302 ROSEATE LODGE [69] 7-9-11 (3*) J Weaver (11) *in tch, hdwy to ld o'r one and a half fs out, sn rdn, hdd one out and one pace*.............. (5 to 1 fav tchd 11 to 2) 4
610^{5} COOL ENOUGH [36] 12-7-9 N Carlisle (13) *hld up and beh, hdwy 3 fs out, rdn and kpt on one pace fnl 2 furlongs.* ....(8 to 1 op 6 to 1) 5
241^{6} COMPANY CASH [46] (bl) 5-8-5 Dean McKeown (9) *cl up, effrt to ld o'r 2 fs out, hdd and wknd one and a half out*........................(11 to 1 op 10 to 1) 6
521^{9} SPECTACLE JIM [48] 4-8-7 N Day (3) *chsd ldrs, rdn 2 fs out, sn btn*....................(33 to 1 op 20 to 1) 7
497^{5} TYRONE FLYER [51] 4-8-5 (5*) Stephen Davies (6) *led, rdn and hdd o'r 2 fs out, sn wknd*........(6 to 1 op 5 to 1) 8
458 CHANCE REPORT [37] 5-7-9^{2} (3*) N Kennedy (7) *al rear.* ....(16 to 1 op 14 to 1) 9
545^{7} BALLAD DANCER [53] 8-8-12 K Darley (5) *al rear.* ....(14 to 1 tchd 16 to 1) 10
THROW AWAY LINE [46] 4-8-5^{1} S Webster (8) *cl up till rdn and wknd wl o'r 2 fs out*.......... (50 to 1 op 33 to 1) 11
GLENFIELD GRETA [58] 5-9-3 W Ryan (10) *beh frm hfwy.* ....(16 to 1) 12
425^{8} AFFORDABLE [59] 5-8-13 (5*) O Pears (1) *prmnt till rdn and wknd wl o'r 2 fs out.* ....(13 to 2 op 8 to 1 tchd 6 to 1) 13

Dist: 1½l, hd, ½l, 2½l, 6l, 1½l, 1l, 1l, hd, ½l. 1m 30.50s. a 7.50s (13 Ran).
SR: 28/11/12/36/-/-/ (Laurie Snook), W G M Turner

EVRY (FR) (good) Wednesday April 21st

637 Prix Servanne (Listed) £14,337 6f....(2:55)

DAUBERVAL (USA) 4-9-4 T Jarnet,...................... 1
BERINSFIELD 3-8-7 S Guillot,........................ 2
345* CHARME SLAVE (Fr) 5-9-7 W Mongil,.................... 3
TOP SALSE (Fr) 3-8-7 C Asmussen,..................... 4

Dist: 2½l, nk, nk, 2l, 1½l, 3l, 2l. 1m 10.84s. a 0.54s (9 Ran).
SR: 63/42/55/40/ (Sheikh Mohammed), A Fabre

638 Prix d'Angerville (Listed) (3-y-o) £14,337 1m...............................(3:55)

SKI PARADISE (USA) 9-2 T Jarnet,...................... 1
SHIR DAR (Fr) 9-2 O Peslier,............................ 2
BORODISLEW (USA) 9-2 F Head,......................... 3
BINT LARIAAF (USA) 9-2 O Doleuze,..................... 4

Dist: 1l, 1½l, 2l, 5l. 1m 39.36s. a 1.96s (5 Ran).
SR: 43/40/35/29/ (Zenya Yoshida), A Fabre

GOWRAN PARK (IRE) (heavy) Wednesday April 21st

639 Gowran Maiden (3-y-o) £2,760 1m...(2:30)

ADVOCAT (Ger) 9-0 M J Kinane (13).............. (6 to 4) 1
PENNINE'S DAUGHTER 8-11 B Coogan (7)...... (12 to 1) 2
311^{4} L'EQUIPE (Ire) 9-0 R Hughes (16)............ (11 to 8 fav) 3
MAGIC ROYALE (Ire) 8-11 R Dolan (8)............(33 to 1) 4
550^{5} GIFT OF PEACE (Ire) (bl) 8-11 C Roche (1)........(12 to 1) 5
552^{9} SKERRIES BELL 8-11 P V Gilson (12)............(14 to 1) 6
486^{6} KILTIMONY 8-3 (8*) J J Mullins (9)................(16 to 1) 7
BLUE DIANA (Ire) 8-11 J F Egan (15)..............(12 to 1) 8
PRINTOUT (Ire) 8-13^{2} J P Murtagh (11).............(12 to 1) 9
488^{9} SHOWBOAT MELODY (Ire) 8-1 (10*) G Coogan (5) (14 to 1) 10
311 REGAL PRETENDER (Ire) 9-0 N Byrne (3)........ (14 to 1) 11
NEWYORK CONNECTION (Ire) 8-1 (10*) D Cullen Jnr (14) ....(50 to 1) 12
267^{4} MARY'S CASE (Ire) 9-0 E A Leonard (4)........... (16 to 1) 13
552 STEADY DEAR (Ire) 8-3 (8*) R T Fitzpatrick,.......(25 to 1) 14
HIGHLAND ARK (Ire) 9-0 G Curran (2)............(14 to 1) 15

Dist: 3l, 2l, 4l, ½l. 1m 51.70s. (15 Ran).
(Sheikh Mohammed), John M Oxx

640 Bennettsbridge Handicap (0-80 3-y-o and up) £2,760 7f......................(3:00)

WHEATSHEAF LADY (Ire) [-] 3-8-13^{1} J P Murtagh (11) ....(16 to 1) 1
AULD STOCK (Ire) [-] 3-8-6 J D Eddery (5).........(8 to 1) 2
281 DOBIE (USA) [-] (bl) 5-9-8 M J Kinane (8).......(5 to 2 fav) 3
BELMARTIN [-] 7-9-6 (8*) J J Mullins (3)............ (8 to 1) 4
310 THATCHING CRAFT (Ire) [-] 4-9-5 (6*) J A Heffernan (1) ....(14 to 1) 5
ARDGILLIAN (Ire) [-] 3-8-7 N G McCullagh (12)....(16 to 1) 6

599⁷ SWEET REALM [-] 4-6-13 (8*) P P Murphy (4)..... (16 to 1) 7
SAMOT (Ire) [-] 3-8-6 J F Egan..................(10 to 1) 8
310⁶ ISLAND HEATHER (Ire) [-] (bl) 5-9-3 (6*) P Carberry (6) ....(10 to 1) 9
NORDIC SAINT (Ire) [-] 4-8-11 C Roche (9).........(7 to 1) 10
EVERY ONE KNOWS (USA) [-] 4-9-3 (8*) M F Ryan (13) ....(12 to 1) 11
ALSHOU (Ire) [-] 4-8-12 B Coogan (2)............(10 to 1) 12
310 ALBONA [-] 5-9-3 S Craine (14)..................(10 to 1) 13
FLORAL STREET [-] 4-9-3 (6*) C Everard (15).......(7 to 1) 14
GRAND PRINCESS (Ire) [-] 5-9-3 K J Manning (10) (14 to 1) 15
Dist: Sht-hd, 2l, 1½l, 3½l. 1m 38.40s. (15 Ran).
(Thomas Mullins), P Mullins

BEVERLEY (good to soft)
Thursday April 22nd
Going Correction: PLUS 0.25 sec. per fur.

641 Captain Storie Maiden Stakes Class D (3-y-o and up) £3,143 5f............... (2:10)

CYNIC 3-8-8 G Duffield (1) *cl up, led aftr one furlong, shaken up o'r one out, kpt on gmely ins last.* .... (5 to 4 fav op 11 to 10 tchd 11 to 8) 1
587³ HOPE HALL (Ire) 5-9-10 A Culhane (4) *pressed wnr, ev ch fnl furlong, no extr nr finish*..................(7 to 4) 2
313⁹ EXPORT MONDIAL 3-8-13 M Tebbutt (5) *led one furlong, styd hndy, chsd alng hfwy, not quicken appr last.* ....(8 to 1 tchd 10 to 1) 3
LIDA'S DELIGHT (Ire) 3-8-13 T Lucas (3) *unruly strt, slwly into strd, beh, ran green, sn pushed alng, hdwy o'r one furlong out, kpt on ins last*........(20 to 1 op 16 to 1) 4
CLOUDY REEF 3-8-8 W Ryan (2) *chsd ldrs, rdn o'r 2 fs out, wknd appr last*..................(9 to 1 op 8 to 1) 5
Dist: 1½l, 2½l, 2½l, ½l. 1m 7.90s. a 6.20s (5 Ran).
SR: -/5/ (Lord Derby), J W Watts

642 Brian Boyes Claiming Stakes Class F (3-y-o) £2,243 1m 1f 207yds............(2:45)

LOCK TIGHT (USA) 9-1 A Culhane (16) *hld up, hdwy o'r 2 fs out, led ins last, ran on wl*...... (14 to 1 op 12 to 1) 1
459 NOMADIC FIRE 8-13 W Ryan (14) *hld up in rear, improved entering strt, swtchd outsd one furlong out, kpt on nr finish*..............................(7 to 1 op 4 to 1) 2
608³ PALACEGATE SUNSET (v) 8-12 J Carroll (4) *nvr far away, chlgd entering strt, led one furlong out, edgd lft, hdd ins last, no extr*....(5 to 1 jt-fav op 6 to 1 tchd 9 to 2) 3
531⁵ BARLEY CAKE 7-10 J Fanning (12) *beh, hdwy 2 fs out, hng lft fnl furlong, no extr*..........................(20 to 1) 4
452² DANCES WITH GOLD 8-6 Dean McKeown (15) *led to one furlong out, not quicken*..........(13 to 2 op 6 to 1) 5
413² STAPLEFORD LASS 8-1 W Woods (3) *chsd ldrs, drvn alng 2 fs out, one pace*..................(6 to 1 op 7 to 1) 6
493⁹ DIVINE RAIN 8-11 R Cochrane (17) *chsd ldrs, ev ch o'r one furlong out, sn btn*................(12 to 1 op 7 to 1) 7
424 MUSICAL PHONE 8-3 K Fallon (11) *in tch, effrt o'r 2 fs out, kpt on same pace over one out*..................(20 to 1) 8
WORKINGFORPEANUTS (Ire) 8-8⁴ M Wigham (8) *beh, hdwy o'r one furlong out, styd on wl fnl furlong.* ....(14 to 1 op 12 to 1) 9
4717a BONNY PRINCESS 7-5 (7*) K Sked (1) *chsd ldrs, rdn and wknd wl o'r one furlong out*......(14 to 1 op 25 to 1) 10
CLAIRIFICATION (Ire) 8-7 W Newnes (13) *slwly into strd, beh, effrt entering strt, kpt on fnl furlong, nvr dngrs.* ....(14 to 1 op 10 to 1) 11
434 HASTA LA VISTA 8-11 T Lucas (2) *mid-divisin, rdn o'r 2 fs out, wknd*.......... (25 to 1 op 20 to 1 tchd 33 to 1) 12
PRINCE PALACIO 8-9 N Connorton (9) *sn beh, rdn 4 fs out, no imprsn entering strt*..........................(12 to 1) 13
SOCIAL VISION (Ire) 8-11 M Birch (7) *beh, rdn alng 3 fs out, nvr on terms*.................(25 to 1 op 20 to 1) 14
MANX MONARCH 8-1³ K Darley (5) *chsd ldrs, drvn o'r 2 fs out, sn wknd*......................(15 to 2 op 6 to 1) 15
493 ASTRAC TRIO (USA) 8-11 F Norton (6) *mid-div, rdn alng 3 fs out, wknd*..........................(20 to 1) 16
BACKSTABBER 8-11 J Quinn (10) *settled midfield, rdn alng o'r 2 fs out, sn btn*........ (5 to 1 jt-fav op 6 to 1) 17
Dist: ½l, 1½l, 3l, 1½l, 1½l, nk, sht-hd, sht-hd, 1½l, nk. 2m 12.00s. a 10.60s (17 Ran).
SR: 20/17/13/-/-/-/ (E R Thomas), R M Whitaker

643 Charles Greig Rated Class B (0-95 3-y-o) £6,326 7f 100yds.................... (3:15)

444* ABBEY'S GAL [89] 9-1 L Dettori (7) *chsd ldrs, led o'r one furlong out, swshd tail and jmpd path ins last, ran on.* ....(9 to 2 op 5 to 1) 1
SHINTILLO (Ire) [84] 8-10 R Cochrane (4) *hld up in last pl, rdn 2 fs out, kpt on fnl furlong*. (3 to 1 jt-fav op 5 to 2) 2
CHEVROTAIN [88] (v) 9-0 M Roberts (6) *keen hold, wth ldr, led o'r 2 fs out till over one out, no extr.* ....(11 to 2 op 5 to 1) 3
514² MULLITOVER [83] 8-9 W Ryan (2) *hld up in tch, effrt 2 fs out, one pace fnl furlong*.......(3 to 1 jt-fav op 5 to 2) 4
435⁴ PERSIAN REVIVAL (Fr) [84] 8-10 T Quinn (3) *narrow ld till o'r 2 fs out, wknd*..............(11 to 1 op 14 to 1) 5
SILVERLOCKS [88] 9-0 N Connorton (1) *in tch, pushed alng hfwy, wknd fnl 2 fs*........(14 to 1 tchd 16 to 1) 6
400* IHTIRAZ [95] 9-7 R Hills (5) *chsd ldrs, rdn 3 fs out, wknd 2 out*..........................(11 to 2 op 5 to 1) 7
Dist: 1l, 3½l, 2l, ¾l, nk, 5l. 1m 35.70s. a 5.40s (7 Ran).
SR: 48/40/33/22/21/24/16/ (Jerrard Williamson), I A Balding

644 Brian Oughtred Handicap Class D (0-85 3-y-o) £3,752 1m 1f 207yds..........(3:45)

452* BAY QUEEN [66] 7-12¹ (5*) M Fenton (10) *chsd ldrs, led o'r one furlong out, kpt on wl fnl furlong.* ....(7 to 1 op 5 to 1) 1
439² HE'S A KING (USA) [77] 8-13 T Quinn (5) *hld up, improved on outsd hfwy, ev ch o'r one furlong out, kpt on nr finish*..............................(5 to 1 op 6 to 1) 2
304 COLLIER BAY [66] 8-2 J Carroll (9) *hld up, rdn o'r 2 fs out, styd on wl fnl furlong.* ....(2 to 1 fav tchd 5 to 2 and 7 to 4) 3
437³ MOUSSAHIM (USA) [66] 8-2 Paul Eddery (1) *hld up, chsd ldr aftr 4 fs, led o'r 3 out till over one out, edgd lft and not quicken fnl furlong*..............(9 to 2 op 7 to 2) 4
FORT VALLY [68] 8-4 J Fortune (7) *keen hold, hld up, rdn 3 fs out, one pace whn baulked o'r one out.* ....(25 to 1 op 20 to 1) 5
397³ LATIN LEADER [70] 8-6 P Robinson (8) *hld up, effrt 3 fs out, wndrd o'r one out, sn btn*..... (6 to 1 tchd 7 to 1) 6
532⁴ HEATHYARDS GEM [65] 8-1 A Munro (2) *nvr far away, ev ch o'r 2 fs out, wknd over one out.* (12 to 1 op 10 to 1) 7
MATARIS [73] 8-9 W Carson (6) *sn led, hdd o'r 3 fs out, rdn and wknd 2 out, eased*.............. (9 to 1 op 7 to 1) 8
398⁷ PAAJIB (Ire) [57] 7-7 J Lowe (4) *led early, chsd ldrs till lost pl hfwy*.............................. (25 to 1) 9
QAFFAL (USA) [85] 9-7 R Hills (3) *hld up in rear, shaken up entering strt, sn lost tch*........(14 to 1 op 12 to 1) 10
Dist: 1½l, sht-hd, 2l, 6l, 3½l, 3l, 3l, 5l, 7l. 2m 10.20s. a 8.80s (10 Ran).
SR: 25/33/21/17/7/2/ (B J Warren), M Bell

645 George Cullington Handicap Class E (0-70 4-y-o and up) £3,390 1m 1f 207yds...(4:15)

531* ROMOLA NIJINSKY [51] 5-8-13 (7ex) D Holland (14) *dsptd ld, led o'r 2 fs out, drvn out fnl furlong.* ....(13 to 2 fav op 6 to 1 tchd 7 to 1) 1
384² FIRST BID [60] 6-9-8 J Fanning (7) *in tch, hdwy 2 fs out, rdn and not quicken ins last*........(7 to 1 op 5 to 1) 2
4788a⁴ KINOKO [52] 5-9-0 K Darley (6) *settled rear, hdwy o'r 2 fs out, ev ch entering last, no extr.* ....(9 to 1 op 8 to 1 tchd 10 to 1) 3
448⁸ AEGAEN LADY [49] 4-8-8 (3*) J Weaver (10) *hld up, improved on ins 3 fs out, hmpd 2 out, one pace one out.* ....(12 to 1 op 14 to 1) 4
REMANY [63] 4-9-11 R Hills (15) *mid-div, rdn o'r 2 fs out, one pace one out*..............(12 to 1 op 10 to 1) 5
382⁷ VASILIEV [62] (bl) 5-9-10 R Cochrane (12) *missed break, beh till styd on strly fnl 2 fs*..........................(20 to 1) 6
530² ANAR (Ire) [45] 4-8-2 (5*) O Pears (9) *chsd ldrs, pushed alng o'r 3 fs out, one pace 2 out*..........................(7 to 1) 7
530⁷ PRIDE OF PENDLE [43] 4-8-5 W Newnes (3) *in tch, rdn o'r 3 fs out, wknd 2 out*..............(20 to 1 op 16 to 1) 8
396³ SUGEMAR [60] 7-9-8 L Dettori (13) *chsd ldrs, rdn and wknd fnl 2 fs*..........................(14 to 1) 9
508⁷ SHADANZA (Ire) [48] 4-8-7 (3*) S Maloney (5) *slwly into strd, beh, rdn o'r 3 fs out, kpt on fnl furlong, no imprsn.* ....(33 to 1) 10
498 SIE AMATO (Ire) [47] 4-8-9 J Fortune (4) *chsd ldrs, rdn and wknd o'r 2 fs out*..........................(20 to 1) 11
DORADUS [50] 5-8-12 K Fallon (19) *mid-div, drvn o'r 3 fs out, sn btn*............(9 to 1 op 8 to 1 tchd 10 to 1) 12
500³ KATY'S LAD [61] 6-9-9 T Quinn (17) *made most till hdd and wknd o'r 2 fs out*..............(10 to 1 op 7 to 1) 13
373⁷ JOLI'S GREAT [46] 5-8-8 D Biggs (16) *mid-div, rdn o'r 4 fs out, no imprsn*..............(14 to 1 op 12 to 1) 14
340⁴ BRECKENBROUGH LAD [57] 6-9-5 J Lowe (2) *al rear.* ....(14 to 1 op 12 to 1) 15
ROYAL COMEDIAN [52] 4-9-0 J Quinn (18) *hld up in rear, effrt 3 fs out, no imprsn*....................(33 to 1) 16
438⁵ MULAWIH (USA) [57] 5-9-5 M Birch (11) *in tch, hmpd 2 fs out, sn wknd*..........................(33 to 1) 17
BLYOSTKA (USA) [40] 4-8-2 G Duffield (1) *al rear, tld off.* ....(33 to 1) 18
366⁴ TEMPERING [41] 7-8-3 S Wood (8) *al struggling, tld off.* ....(14 to 1 tchd 16 to 1) 19
Dist: 1½l, nk, 3l, hd, ½l, 6l, 1½l, 1½l, hd, sht-hd. 2m 9.80s. a 8.40s (19 Ran).
SR: 40/46/37/28/41/39/10/5/19/ (Mrs L A Windsor), P D Evans

646 ALD William Hodgson Maiden Stakes Class D (3-y-o and up) £3,640 1m 100yds ....(4:45)

CHATOYANT 3-8-11 G Duffield (14) *dwlt, sn reco'red to track ldrs, led ins fnl furlong, kpt on wl.* ....(12 to 1 op 10 to 1) 1
318⁴ BROWN'S (Fr) 3-8-11 D Holland (15) *led till ins fnl furlong, rallied*.................. (9 to 2 op 7 to 1 tchd 8 to 1) 2

AL SENAFI (Ire) 3-8-11 R Cochrane (6) *in tch, effrt 2 fs out, ran on ins last*......... (9 to 2 op 4 to 1 tchd 11 to 2) 3
459[2] EL GAHAR 3-8-11 W Ryan (2) *hld up, effrt o'r 2 fs out, edgd rght and not quicken fnl furlong.* ....(6 to 4 fav op 11 to 10) 4
APACHE SQUAW 3-8-6 N Connorton (4) *hld up, styd on fnl 2 fs, nvr plcd to chal*.............. (50 to 1 op 25 to 1) 5
346[4] ZAAHEYAH (USA) 3-8-6 B Raymond (5) *mid-div, pushed alng o'r 2 fs out, sn wknd*......... (14 to 1 op 12 to 1) 6
BRESIL (USA) 4-9-12 S Whitworth (10) *chsd ldrs, rdn and wknd 2 fs out*..................... (50 to 1 op 25 to 1) 7
288[5] BRANDON GROVE 5-9-7 Alex Greaves (1) *beh, rdn o'r 2 fs out, not pace to chal*.................. (50 to 1 op 25 to 1) 8
529 HADDAAJ (Ire) 3-8-11 M Roberts (9) *mid-div, rdn alng hfwy, no imprsn*.................... (14 to 1 op 8 to 1) 9
MOST SIOUXTABLE 3-8-6 J Fanning (11) *slwly into strd, beh, rdn o'r 3 fs out, no imprsn*.... (33 to 1 op 25 to 1) 10
459[8] LT WELSH (USA) 3-8-11 L Dettori (16) *hld up in tch, effrt o'r 2 fs out, sn btn*.................(12 to 1 op 8 to 1) 11
ISLAND KNIGHT (Ire) 4-9-12 D Biggs (8) *trkd le ader, rdn and wknd 2 fs out*................(33 to 1 op 16 to 1) 12
459 MUHTASHIM (Ire) 3-8-11 W Carson (12) *mid-div, lost pl entering strt*.................... (14 to 1 op 10 to 1) 13
522[9] LAURA 4-9-7 R Hills (13) *beh, rdn o'r 2 fs out, tld off.* .... (25 to 1 op 20 to 1) 14
CALYMAR 7-9-7 (5*) O Pears (7) *in tch, rdn o'r 3 fs out, sn wknd, tld off*.................. (100 to 1 op 25 to 1) 15
CROMER'S EXPRESS (v) 4-9-12 J Lowe (3) *al rear, tld off.* ....(150 to 1 op 50 to 1 tchd 200 to 1) 16

Dist: ½l, nk, 4l, 10l, ½l, ½l, 2l, ¾l, ¾l, nk. 1m 50.10s. a 7.30s (16 Ran).
SR: 19/17/16/4/-/-/ (Lord Derby), J W Watts

MALLOW (IRE) (soft)
Thursday April 22nd

647 Mallow Handicap (0-75 3-y-o) £2,243 1½m ....(4:00)

487[2] THE BERUKI (Ire) [-] 7-8[3] (8*) D J O'Donohoe (9) (9 to 4 jt-fav) 1
SCANNO'S CHOICE (Ire) [-] 8-0 W J Supple (3) ... (12 to 1) 2
281 BALLYSPARKLE (Ire) [-] (bl) 8-10 C Roche (4) ...... (8 to 1) 3
487 DIAMOND CLUSTER [-] 7-1 (8*) R T Fitzpatrick (8) (12 to 1) 4
307[6] KELLSBORO LASS (Ire) [-] 9-4 P Shanahan (6) ..... (7 to 1) 5
307[7] WARREN STREET (Ire) [-] 8-11 M J Kinane (2) ......(6 to 1) 6
489[3] ABSOLUTE JAMBOREE [-] 9-7 S Craine (1) .. (9 to 4 jt-fav) 7
HOMERS FOLLY (Ire) [-] 6-13 (8*) P P Murphy (5) .. (20 to 1) 8
IRISH MISTRESS (Ire) [-] 7-8 (2*) D G O'Shea (7) ...(12 to 1) 9

Dist: 4l, ½l, 3½l, 11l. 3m 0.60s. (9 Ran).
(Mrs Geraldine Treacy), S J Treacy

648 Kinsale (Fillies) Race (3-y-o and up) £2,243 1m 1f..............................(4:30)

573[7] TARTAN LADY (Ire) 3-8-10 S Craine (3) .... (5 to 2) 1
488[7] DRIFT APART (Ire) 3-8-3 W J Supple (1) .... (10 to 1) 2
KIROV PREMIERE 3-8-8 C Roche (9) ....(5 to 4 fav) 3
RAIN RITE (Ire) 4-9-1 (10*) B Fenton (2) ....(6 to 1) 4
PHARELLA 5-9-9 (6*) C Everard (10) .... (12 to 1) 5
TRIBAL MEMORIES (Ire) 3-7-11 (6*) J J Behan (6) .. (8 to 1) 6
NORDICOLINI (Ire) 3-7-13 (4*) W J Smith (4) .... (7 to 1) 7
311 FAIRY BRIDE (Ire) 3-7-13[2] (6*) J A Heffernan (7) ... (10 to 1) 8

Dist: 1l, 2½l, 1l, 9l. 2m 4.10s. (8 Ran).
(John Thompson), T Stack

649 Cork (C & G) Maiden (3-y-o) £2,243 1m 1f ....(5:00)

550[4] DIFFERENT TIMES (Ire) 9-0 C Roche (3) ....(5 to 4 on) 1
489[2] SCHMEICHEL (Ire) 9-0 N Byrne (5) ....(5 to 2) 2
256[8] LUCKY PRINCE (Ire) (bl) 9-0 M J Kinane (1) ....(7 to 1) 3
VLADIVOSTOK 8-6 (8*) R V Skelly (7) .... (10 to 1) 4
550[6] PERFECT POET (Ire) 9-0 S Craine (4) .... (8 to 1) 5
489 TREBLE BOB (Ire) 8-10 (4*) W J Smith (6) ....(25 to 1) 6
268[9] COMMANDER JOHN (Ire) 8-6 (8*) P P Murphy (8) (16 to 1) 7
552 RED ROOSTER (Ire) 9-0 B Coogan (2) ....(16 to 1) 8

Dist: 3½l, 4½l, 2½l, sht-hd. 2m 7.40s. (8 Ran).
(Park Beech Racing Syndicate), Liam Browne

CARLISLE (heavy)
Friday April 23rd

Going Correction: PLUS 0.70 sec. per fur. (races 1,2,3,4), PLUS 0.90 (5,6)

650 Kestrel Claiming Stakes Class F (4-y-o and up) £2,243 6f 206yds............(2:15)

531[4] CLAUDIA MISS 6-8-11 Dean McKeown (3) *chsd ldrs, rdn 2 fs out, styd on to ld ins last*.........(8 to 1 op 5 to 1) 1
565[7] LOMBARD SHIPS 6-8-7 A Mackay (8) *cl up, led 2 and a half fs out, rdn and hdd ins fnl furlong, kpt on.* ....(6 to 1 op 5 to 1) 2
448* STOPROVERITATE 4-9-1 N Connorton (11) *mid-div, hdwy on inner 2 fs out, sn rdn and styd on one pace.* ....(15 to 8 fav op 5 to 2) 3
521 RESPECTABLE JONES 7-9-2 S Perks (7) *beh, hdwy o'r 2 fs out, kpt on, nvr dngrs*............... (8 to 1 op 6 to 1) 4
565 DREAM CARRIER (Ire) 5-9-3 Alex Greaves (4) *hld up, hdwy 3 fs out, sn rdn and no imprsn*....... (8 to 1 op 5 to 1) 5
SHALABIA 4-8-4 J Carroll (9) *prmnt, ev ch o'r 2 fs out, sn rdn and wknd*..............(5 to 1 op 3 to 1) 6
362[3] UCKERBY MOOR (v) 4-8-10 (5*) O Pears (12) *chsd ldrs, rdn o'r 2 fs out, sn btn*.......................... (12 to 1) 7
424[7] FIABA (bl) 5-7-8 (7*) Darren Moffatt (1) *cl up till rdn and wknd 2 fs out*..............................(12 to 1) 8
MR SNAIL 5-9-3 G Duffield (10) *led till hdd and wknd 2 and a half fs out*................ (8 to 1 tchd 12 to 1) 9
EDDIE WALSHE 8-8-5 K Fallon (6) *dwlt, al rear*.. (33 to 1) 10
205[9] CRIMSON CONSORT (Ire) (v) 4-8-5 Kim Tinkler (5) *al rear.* ....(50 to 1) 11

Dist: Nk, 4l, 6l, 3½l, 1l, nk, 4l, 3l, 12l, nk. 1m 34.50s. a 9.10s (11 Ran).
SR: 34/29/25/8/-/-/ (G Whorton), W W Haigh

651 Golden Eagle Handicap Class C (0-90 3-y-o and up) £5,216 7f 214yds..........(2:45)

425* LEIF THE LUCKY (USA) [74] 4-9-2 N Connorton (8) *in tch, hdwy 3 fs out, led on bit 2 furlongs out and sn clr.* ....(3 to 1 fav op 5 to 2) 1
JUNGLE KNIFE [70] 7-8-5 (7*) S Mulvey (7) *hld up and beh, hdwy 3 fs out, rdn 2 furlongs out, kpt on, no ch wth wnr*.. (5 to 1) 2
475 LAHOOB (USA) [69] 4-8-11 B Raymond (5) *prmnt, hdwy and hmpd o'r 2 fs out, swtchd ins and effrt appr fnl furlong, sn rdn and not much room, one pace.* ....(7 to 2 op 9 to 2) 3
HAMADRYAD (Ire) [82] 5-9-5 (5*) O Pears (6) *hld up and beh till styd on fnl 2 fs, nrst finish*..... (14 to 1 op 12 to 1) 4
WILSONIC [78] 4-9-6 Dean McKeown (9) *cl up, effrt and rdn to ld briefly 2 and a half fs out, sn hdd, edgd rght and wknd entering fnl furlong.* .... (15 to 2 op 6 to 1 tchd 10 to 1) 5
340[2] SALDA [72] 4-9-0 A Culhane (4) *led till rdn and hdd 2 and a half fs out, sn wknd*.............(5 to 1 op 4 to 1) 6
448[9] STRAW THATCH [63] (bl) 4-8-5 J Lowe (2) *al rear.* .... (20 to 1 op 16 to 1) 7
340[8] SELF EXPRESSION [66] 5-8-8 K Fallon (3) *al beh.* ....(14 to 1 op 10 to 1) 8
302 SPANISH VERDICT [67] 6-8-9 G Duffield (1) *prmnt till wknd o'r 3 fs out*......................... (10 to 1 op 8 to 1) 9

Dist: 4l, 2½l, 1½l, 1½l, 5l, 2l, 1½l, hd. 1m 47.50s. a 9.60s (9 Ran).
SR: 42/26/17/25/16/-/ (Miss Betty Duxbury), Miss S E Hall

652 Harcros Timber & Building Supplies Stayers Championship Series Handicap Qualifier Class D (0-75 3-y-o) £3,882 1½m ....(3:15)

502[2] SHYNON [53] 8-0 (7*) S Mulvey (3) *made all, rdn 2 fs out, styd on wl*.........(13 to 8 fav op 11 to 8 tchd 7 to 4) 1
502[4] DOC SPOT [59] 8-13 J Fortune (5) *hld up, gd hdwy on inner 2 and a half fs out, chlgd and ev ch one and a half furlongs out, sn rdn and one pace.* .... (16 to 1 op 14 to 1) 2
434[5] CHALLENGER ROW (Ire) [48] 8-2 N Connorton (8) *chsd ldrs, effrt and rdn 2 and a half fs out, plugged on one pace.* ....(4 to 1 tchd 9 to 2) 3
344[2] VAIGLY SUNTHYME [67] 9-7 S Morris (4) *chsd ldrs, hdwy 3 fs out, sn rdn and wknd 2 furlongs out*.........(5 to 1) 4
434[3] NANCY (Ire) [49] 8-3 Dale Gibson (6) *hld up, hdwy 4 fs out, effrt and rdn o'r 2 furlongs out, sn wknd.* ....(5 to 1 tchd 11 to 2) 5
434 SAVINGS BANK [58] 8-12 Alex Greaves (7) *al rear.* ....(14 to 1 op 8 to 1) 6
162[4] MRS DAWSON [50] (v) 8-4 G Hind (1) *pld hrd, chsd wnr till wknd o'r 3 fs out*............. (12 to 1 tchd 10 to 1) 7

Dist: 10l, 5l, 15l, 1l, 20l, 20l. 2m 45.90s. a 15.90s (7 Ran).
SR: 18/4/-/-/ (M P Bowring), M H Tompkins

653 Sparrow Hawk Maiden Stakes Class D (3-y-o) £3,406 1½m................... (3:45)

423[3] LIJAAM (Ire) 9-0 B Raymond (5) *made all, clr 3 fs out, unchlgd.* (7 to 4 on op 2 to 1 on tchd 13 to 8 on and 6 to 4 on) 1
357[4] KARIB 8-9 J Carroll (3) *in tch, effrt 3 fs out, sn rdn and no imprsn*............................(12 to 1 op 8 to 1) 2
502[3] ARC BRIGHT (Ire) 9-0 S Perks (4) *chsd wnr, rdn o'r 3 fs out and sn one pace*.........(5 to 1 op 9 to 2 tchd 6 to 1) 3
452[4] GOLDMIRE 8-9 K Fallon (6) *mid-div, effrt o'r 4 fs out, sn rdn and one pace*..............................(16 to 1) 4
439[6] VOLUNTEER POINT (Ire) 9-0 J Fortune (8) *prmnt till wknd o'r 4 fs out*......................... (20 to 1 op 16 to 1) 5
339[5] NICKNAME 9-0 Raymond Berry (7) *hld up and beh, nvr a factor*.. (8 to 1) 6
RAQS ASSAYF 9-0 A Culhane (2) *al rear.* .... (20 to 1 op 16 to 1) 7

EVERGREEN TANGO 9-0 Dean McKeown (1) *hld up, effrt and some hdwy 4 fs out, sn rdn and lost pl.* .... (12 to 1 op 6 to 1) 8
Dist: 25l, 2l, 1½l, 8l, 5l, 12l, 15l. 2m 46.90s. a 16.90s (8 Ran).
SR: 15/-/-/-/-/ (Maktoum Al Maktoum), A A Scott

654 Buzzard Fillies Conditions Stakes Class D (4-y-o and up) £3,055 5f 207yds......(4:15)

316 BRANSTON ABBY (Ire) 4-9-10 G Duffield (1) *trkd ldrs, hdwy on bit to chal 2 fs out, shaken up to ld fnl furlong, pushed clr*........(5 to 2 op 9 to 4 tchd 11 to 4) 1
436[6] OUR RITA 4-8-10 G Hind (2) *hld up, hdwy o'r 2 fs out, sn rdn, styd on one pace fnl furlong.* ....(7 to 4 fav op 15 to 8) 2
STACK ROCK 6-9-5 K Fallon (3) *cl up, led hfwy, rdn and hdd appr fnl furlong, one pace*...... (5 to 2 op 7 to 4) 3
NIFTY FIFTY (Ire) 4-8-11 J Carroll (4) *led till hdd and wknd quickly hfwy, eased*.................................. (5 to 1) 4
Dist: 5l, 1l, dist. 1m 20.30s. a 7.30s (4 Ran).
SR: 72/38/43/-/ (J David Abell), M Johnston

655 Peregrine Falcon Handicap Class E (0-70 3-y-o and up) £3,287 5f 207yds...... (4:50)

568[2] STRIP CARTOON (Ire) [50] (bl) 5-8-7 (7*) G Strange (8) *made all, rdn 2 fs out, styd on gmely fnl furlong.* ....(3 to 1 op 6 to 4) 1
565 TWILIGHT FALLS [46] 8-8-10 N Connorton (6) *in tch, hdwy 2 fs out, sn rdn, styd on wl fnl furlong.* ....(7 to 4 fav op 7 to 2) 2
568[8] CRAIL HARBOUR [36] (v) 7-8-0 Dale Gibson (9) *chsd wnr, rdn wl o'r one furlong out, wknd ins last.* .... (13 to 2 op 5 to 1 tchd 7 to 1) 3
438[3] TAWAFIJ (USA) [60] 4-9-10 S Webster (2) *hld up, hdwy o'r 2 fs out, sn rdn and kpt on one pace.* .... (9 to 1 op 7 to 1 tchd 10 to 1) 4
568 BREEZE AWAY [60] 4-9-10 A Culhane (7) *chsd ldrs, rdn 2 fs out, sn btn*..........................(10 to 1 op 8 to 1) 5
KATIE-A (Ire) [51] 4-9-1 J Lowe (5) *chsd ldrs, rdn o'r 2 fs out, sn btn*...........................(16 to 1 op 10 to 1) 6
ROUTING [55] 5-9-5 G Duffield (4) *slwly away, effrt and some hdwy hfwy, sn wknd*...... (12 to 1 tchd 10 to 1) 7
BOLD PHILIP [52] 3-8-4 L Charnock (3) *al rear.* ....(25 to 1 op 12 to 1) 8
565 ROYAL GIRL [60] 6-9-10 Dean McKeown (1) *pushed alng hfwy and some hdwy, wknd wl o'r one furlong out, eased*................. (17 to 2 op 7 to 1 tchd 9 to 1) 9
Dist: ½l, 3l, 2½l, 2l, nk, 1l, 1l, 1½l. 1m 22.30s. a 9.30s (9 Ran).
SR: 22/16/-/8/-/-/ (Mrs Irene Pryce), S R Bowring

MAISONS LAFFITTE (FR) (good)
Friday April 23rd

656 Prix Montenica (Listed) (3-y-o) £14,337 1m ....(3:00)

CAESOUR (USA) 9-2 C Asmussen,....................... 1
SHARMAN (USA) 9-2 T Jarnet,........................... 2
NEW CYBERIAN (USA) 9-2 S Guillot,..................... 3
GUEST OF HONOR (Fr) 9-2 W Mongil,..................... 4
Dist: 1½l, ½l, sht-hd, ½l. 1m 37.80s. a 3.10s (5 Ran).
SR: 56/51/49/48/ (S Niarchos), F Boutin

SANDOWN (good)
Friday April 23rd
Going Correction: NIL (races 1,3), PLUS 0.10 (2,4,5,6,7)

657 Kelvin International Services Median Auction Maiden Fillies Stakes Class D (2-y-o) £3,532 5f 6yds..................... (2:00)

ROHITA (Ire) 8-11 Pat Eddery (3) *cl up, led 2 fs out, drvn out*.................(2 to 1 fav tchd 7 to 4 and 9 to 4) 1
JADE PET 8-11 J Reid (1) *trkd ldrs, ev ch ins fnl furlong, swshd tail und pres, kpt on*........(10 to 1 op 6 to 1) 2
CIRCLE OF FRIENDS (Ire) 8-11 T Quinn (10) *trkd ldrs, ev ch 2 fs out, one pace appr last, better for race.* .... (12 to 1 op 8 to 1) 3
625[5] IMPERIAL BAILIWICK (Ire) 8-11 N Adams (6) *chsd ldrs, rdn 2 fs out, kpt on wl frm one out.* .... (25 to 1 op 33 to 1 tchd 50 to 1) 4
477[3] KERRIE-JO 8-11 J Williams (11) *chsd ldrs, outpcd 2 fs out, styd on*.................................... (5 to 1 op 7 to 2) 5
528[3] NAKITA 8-11 M Roberts (7) *strted slwly, sn rdn alng to chase ldrs, btn 2 fs out*....................(6 to 1 op 7 to 2) 6
496[5] HOLLINGTON SONG 8-11 W Newnes (8) *led to 2 fs out, wknd o'r one out*.... (50 to 1 op 33 to 1 tchd 66 to 1) 7
FOOTSTEPS (Ire) 8-11 A Munro (2) *trkd ldrs, rdn and wknd hfwy*............ (9 to 1 op 8 to 1 tchd 12 to 1) 8
ABBOTS DAUGHTER 8-11 D Holland (5) *dwlt, nvr on terms*.............................. (12 to 1 op 6 to 1) 9
445[2] PETRATHENE 8-11 S Whitworth (12) *broke wl, trkd ldrs till wknd 2 fs out*........ (10 to 1 op 8 to 1 tchd 12 to 1) 10
PETITE POET 8-11 W Woods (9) *slwly into strd, sn pushed alng, hmpd aftr 2 fs, nvr a factor.* ....(33 to 1 tchd 50 to 1) 11
MRS JOGGLEBURY 8-8 (3*) S D Williams (4) *strted slwly, al beh*.........................(50 to 1 op 33 to 1 tchd 66 to 1) 12
Dist: Nk, 3½l, ¾l, 1l, ¾l, 1l, 2l, 1½l, hd, nk. 1m 2.32s. a 2.82s (12 Ran).
SR: 40/39/25/22/18/15/11/3/-/ (B J Taylor), M R Channon

658 Forte Conditions Stakes Class C (3-y-o) £4,658 1m 14yds.................. (2:35)

388[3] PORT LUCAYA (bl) 8-10 L Dettori (7) *trkd ldrs, led 2 fs out, ran on wl fnl furlong.* (11 to 2 op 6 to 1 tchd 13 to 2) 1
FRET (USA) 8-10 A Munro (3) *trkd ldrs, ev ch 2 fs out, ran on one pace*...................(10 to 1 tchd 11 to 1) 2
BIN AJWAAD (Ire) 8-12 M Roberts (9) *hld up, not much room 3 fs out and o'r 2 out, rdn and hdwy over one out, one pace ins last*.....(9 to 4 fav op 7 to 4 tchd 5 to 2) 3
FITZCARRALDO (USA) 8-10 R Cochrane (6) *keen hold, trkd ldrs, one pace fnl 2 fs*...(11 to 2 op 5 to 1 tchd 6 to 1) 4
TYKEYVOR (Ire) 8-12 P Robinson (2) *wtd wth beh, drpd out 4 fs out, hdwy on ins 2 out, rdn and btn one out.* ....(14 to 1 op 20 to 1 tchd 25 to 1 and 12 to 1) 5
SERIOUS 8-12 W R Swinburn (8) *hld up, hrd rdn o'r 2 fs out, no imprsn*........ (5 to 1 op 4 to 1 tchd 11 to 2) 6
510[4] RESIST THE FORCE (USA) 8-10 D Biggs (1) *slwly into strd, sn trkd ldrs, rdn and wknd appr fnl furlong.* ....(25 to 1 op 20 to 1) 7
414* CYPRIAN DANCER (USA) 8-12 T Quinn (4) *led to 2 fs out, wknd*... (20 to 1 op 25 to 1 tchd 33 to 1 and 16 to 1) 8
470* HILARY GERRARD (USA) 8-12 W Ryan (5) *hld up, rdn alng o'r 2 fs out, no response, tld off*.....(10 to 1 op 8 to 1) 9
Dist: 1l, nk, 6l, 2½l, nk, 2½l, 1l, 12l. 1m 44.87s. a 5.77s (9 Ran).
SR: 21/18/19/-/-/-/ (Edward St George), R Hannon

659 Ring & Brymer Handicap Class C (0-90 3-y-o and up) £5,186 5f 6yds............ (3:05)

492[8] LORD HIGH ADMIRAL (Can) [67] 5-8-8 M Roberts (10) *keen hold, led aftr one furlong, drvn out.* ....(10 to 1 op 8 to 1 tchd 12 to 1) 1
479[4] BODARI [78] 4-9-2 (3*) D Harrison (7) *trkd ldrs, ev ch ins fnl furlong, ran on*...................(12 to 1 op 14 to 1) 2
PADDY CHALK [82] 7-9-9 J Reid (9) *mid-div, rdn and hdwy o'r one furlong out, ran on.* .... (25 to 1 op 20 to 1 tchd 33 to 1) 3
492* HONEY SEEKER [64] 4-8-5 (6ex) K Darley (3) *sn pushed alng in mid-div, hdwy 2 fs out, kpt on.* .... (13 to 2 op 5 to 1 tchd 7 to 1) 4
421* MISTER JOLSON [64] 4-8-5 W Carson (1) *prmnt stands side, edgd rght one furlong out, sn hrd rdn, not quicken*.........................(16 to 1 op 12 to 1) 5
301[5] LOVE LEGEND [71] (v) 8-8-12 T Quinn (8) *trkd ldrs, pushed alng hfwy, hrd rdn o'r one furlong out, one pace.* ....(12 to 1 tchd 14 to 1) 6
479[2] SO RHYTHMICAL [79] 9-9-6 A Munro (5) *chsd ldrs, rdn and one pace o'r one furlong out.* .... (10 to 1 op 8 to 1 tchd 12 to 1) 7
FASCINATION WALTZ [73] 6-8-11 (3*) S D Williams (16) *hld up gng wl, steady hdwy ins fnl furlong, nrst finish.* .... (12 to 1 op 14 to 1 tchd 16 to 1) 8
401[8] HALBERT [71] (bl) 4-8-12 Pat Eddery (14) *trkd ldrs, hrd rdn o'r one furlong out, eased whn btn ins last.* .... (10 to 1 op 8 to 1) 9
555* OLIFANTSFONTEIN [80] (bl) 5-9-7 (6ex) G Carter (12) *chsd ldrs, pushed alng hfwy, sn btn*...(9 to 2 fav op 4 to 1) 10
369[5] MISDEMEANOURS GIRL (Ire) [70] 5-8-6 (5*) B Doyle (17) *trkd ldrs, effrt o'r one furlong out, not much room and eased ins last*.......... (9 to 1 op 8 to 1 tchd 10 to 1) 11
AUGHFAD [87] 7-10-0 W Newnes (6) *al beh*.........(33 to 1) 12
401[2] MISS VAXETTE [74] 4-9-1 L Dettori (4) *sn pushed alng in rear, hrd rdn 2 furlong out, no response.* ....(16 to 1 op 12 to 1) 13
4752a[3] PALEY PRINCE (USA) [76] 7-9-3 W R Swinburn (13) *chsd ldrs, effrt 2 fs out, eased whn btn ins last.* ....(20 to 1 op 16 to 1) 14
PETRACO (Ire) [75] 5-9-2 W Ryan (2) *prmnt stands side till wknd o'r one furlong out*..........(33 to 1 op 25 to 1) 15
LETSBEONESTABOUTIT [76] 7-9-3 Paul Eddery (11) *led one furlong, chsd ldrs, wknd 2 fs out.* (20 to 1 op 16 to 1) 16
479[9] RICKY'S TORNADO (Ire) [72] 4-8-13 J Williams (15) *outpcd, tld off*...........................(33 to 1 op 25 to 1) 17
Dist: Nk, hd, nk, ½l, ½l, 1½l, ¾l, 1l, hd, 2½l. 1m 2.02s. a 2.52s (17 Ran).
SR: 44/54/57/38/36/41/43/34/28/ (E J G Young), M J Heaton-Ellis

660 Gardner Merchant Mile Class A (Group 2) (4-y-o and up) £35,325 1m 14yds.... (3:40)

4682a[2] ALHIJAZ 4-9-6 W Carson (3) *trkd ldr, led one and a half fs out, drvn out*............(6 to 1 op 5 to 1 tchd 7 to 1) 1
HAZAAM (USA) 4-9-0 M Roberts (5) *hld up, keen hold, rdn o'r 2 fs out, sn not much room, ran on wl fnl furlong.* ....(6 to 1 op 9 to 2) 2
ZAAHI (USA) 4-9-0 R Hills (6) *led to one and a half fs out, one pace*.......... (7 to 4 fav op 6 to 4 tchd 15 to 8) 3

STUBASS (Ire) 4-9-4 R Cochrane (2) *trkd ldrs, effrt and cld 2 fs out, ev ch o'r one out, one pace.* ......(20 to 1 op 14 to 1) 4
ENHARMONIC (USA) 6-9-0 L Dettori (4) *hld up, effrt o'r 2 fs out, not pace to chal*......(33 to 1 op 25 to 1) 5
525^4 LUCKY LINDY (Ire) (bl) 4-9-4 Pat Eddery (7) *trkd ldrs, pushed alng 3 fs out, wknd o'r one out.* ......(11 to 4 tchd 3 to 1) 6
MOJAVE 4-9-0 W R Swinburn (1) *hld up, pld hrd, effrt o'r 2 fs out, sn btn*......(14 to 1 op 10 to 1 tchd 16 to 1) 7
Dist: Nk, 2l, hd, 1½l, 1l, 6l. 1m 43.08s. a 3.98s (7 Ran).
SR: 58/51/45/48/39/40/18/ (Prince A A Faisal), J L Dunlop

661 Autobar Group Rated Class B (0-100 4-y-o and up) £6,040 2m 78yds............ (4:10)

478^2 ROBINGO (Ire) [87] (bl) 4-9-0 A Munro (4) *hld up, pushed alng hfwy, hdwy 5 fs out, led o'r 2 out, clr ins last.* ......(2 to 1 fav op 6 to 4) 1
539^6 MULL HOUSE [76] 6-8-7 W Carson (6) *chsd ldrs, pushed alng o'r 2 fs out, styd on wl frm over one out, eased whn hld ins last*...... (10 to 1 op 8 to 1 tchd 11 to 1) 2
478 BARDOLPH (USA) [79] 6-8-10 T Quinn (8) *cl up, led briefly wl o'r 2 fs out, one pace.* ......(9 to 1 op 6 to 1 tchd 10 to 1) 3
478 REQUESTED [76] 6-8-7 J Reid (5) *led 2 fs, trkd ldrs, rdn 3 out, styd on frm two out, no extr ins last.* ......(33 to 1 op 16 to 1) 4
539^2 STAR PLAYER [90] (bl) 7-9-4 (3*) J Weaver (1) *hld up beh, styd on ins last, nvr dngrs.* ......(4 to 1 op 5 to 1 tchd 11 to 2) 5
478^5 BRANDON PRINCE (Ire) [80] (bl) 5-8-11 R Cochrane (7) *hld up beh, effrt 2 fs out, not pace to chal, sn eased.* ......(10 to 1 op 8 to 1) 6
STAR QUEST [76] 6-8-7 Pat Eddery (2) *cl up, led briefly aftr 2 fs, effrt o'r 3 out, btn two out.* ......(9 to 1 op 8 to 1 tchd 10 to 1) 7
365^4 TRUBEN (USA) [80] 4-8-7 L Dettori (3) *cl up, led aftr 3 fs till wl o'r 2 out, wknd*......(7 to 1 op 5 to 1 tchd 8 to 1) 8
Dist: 4l, ½l, 3l, 5l, 2½l, 10l, 10l. 3m 38.79s. a 9.79s (8 Ran).
SR: 18/7/9/3/12/ (M & N Plant Ltd), M C Pipe

662 Lockhart Catering Equipment Maiden Fillies' Stakes Class D (3-y-o) £3,688 1¼m 7yds................................ (4:45)

TALENTED 8-11 W Carson (3) *trkd ldrs, lost pl and pushed alng 4 fs out, led 2 out, ran on gmely ins last.* ......(15 to 8 fav op 5 to 2 tchd 11 to 4) 1
DANCING PRIZE (Ire) 8-11 Paul Eddery (15) *hld up in mid-div, cld 2 fs out, ran on wl fnl furlong.* ......(25 to 1 op 12 to 1) 2
REINE DE NEIGE 8-11 W R Swinburn (13) *hld up in mid-div gng wl, hdwy 2 fs out, sn not much room, rdn and one pace ins last*...... (10 to 1 op 5 to 1 tchd 11 to 1) 3
BELLA BALLERINA 8-11 Pat Eddery (8) *trkd ldrs, ev ch o'r one furlong out, one pace and eased whn hld ins last.* ......(7 to 1 op 5 to 1) 4
385^2 HOOSIE 8-11 L Dettori (12) *chsd ldrs, cld and ev ch 2 fs out, one pace o'r one out*...... (14 to 1 tchd 16 to 1) 5
SING A RAINBOW (Ire) 8-7 J Williams (6) *beh, hdwy o'r one furlong out, styd on, nvr nrr*...... (50 to 1 op 20 to 1) 6
SEA SIREN 8-11 W Newnes (2) *trkd ldrs, rdn and no hdwy fnl 2 fs*......(14 to 1 tchd 16 to 1) 7
USK THE WAY 8-7 W Ryan (7) *sn pushed alng in rear, nvr on terms*...... (6 to 1 op 3 to 1 tchd 13 to 2) 8
HAUNTED WOOD (USA) 8-11 M Roberts (14) *pld hrd, cl up, led briefly o'r 2 fs out, wkng whn not much room ins last*......(11 to 2 op 5 to 1 tchd 6 to 1) 9
DUTCH DEBUTANTE 8-11 G Carter (1) *al beh.* ......(50 to 1 op 33 to 1) 10
MISS SHAGRA (USA) 8-7 K Darley (5) *led till o'r 2 fs out, btn whn hmpd over one out*...... (33 to 1 op 16 to 1) 11
EYE WITNESS (Ire) 8-7 A Munro (11) *trkd ldrs, ev ch o'r 2 fs out, btn whn hmpd over one out.* ......(16 to 1 op 10 to 1 tchd 20 to 1) 12
DREAM BABY 8-7 M Hills (4) *beh, shrtlvd effrt o'r 2 fs out.* ......(50 to 1 op 20 to 1) 13
RANEEN ALWATAR 8-11 R Cochrane (9) *beh, hdwy 2 fs out, sn btn and eased.* ......(25 to 1 op 16 to 1 tchd 33 to 1) 14
IMPECCABLE TASTE 8-7 D Biggs (10) *sn beh.* ......(33 to 1 op 20 to 1) 15
Dist: Nk, 1l, 3l, 2l, ½l, ¾l, hd, nk, 5l, 1l. 2m 11.12s. a 7.22s (15 Ran).
SR: 35/34/32/26/22/17/19/14/17/ (P G Goulandris), J L Dunlop

663 Town & County Catering Handicap Class C (0-95 3-y-o and up) £5,186 1¼m 7yds (5:20)

387^2 CAMDEN'S RANSOM (USA) [70] 6-8-4 (5*) B Doyle (2) *hld up, plenty to do strt, hdwy wl o'r one furlong out, str run to ld cl hme*...... (10 to 1 tchd 9 to 1) 1
513^4 RUTLAND WATER (USA) [65] 6-8-4 T Quinn (16) *hld up in tch, led o'r 2 fs out, sn hrd rdn, hdd cl hme.* ......(4 to 1 tchd 9 to 2) 2
513* LOKI (Ire) [86] 5-9-8 (3*,5ex) D Harrison (11) *strted slwly, plenty to do strt, hdwy 2 fs out, ran on wl fnl furlong.* ......(7 to 2 fav op 4 to 1 tchd 3 to 1) 3
473^6 BOOKCASE [73] 6-8-12 J Williams (6) *hld up in mid-div, hdwy o'r 2 fs out, crrd head awkwardly and one pace frm over one out*...... (16 to 1 op 14 to 1 tchd 20 to 1) 4
304* MARASTANI (USA) [88] 3-8-9 J Reid (10) *mid-div, hdwy and ev ch 2 fs out, sn one pace.* ......(5 to 1 op 7 to 1 tchd 8 to 1) 5
ROSE ALTO [85] 5-9-10 W R Swinburn (5) *mid-div, hdwy on ins 2 fs out, one pace inside last.* ......(12 to 1 tchd 14 to 1) 6
513^5 SURREY DANCER [74] 5-8-13 W Ryan (7) *mid-div, drvn alng 2 fs out, styd on*...(9 to 1 op 8 to 1 tchd 10 to 1) 7
KNOWTH (Ire) [69] 4-8-8 R Perham (9) *chsd ldrs, lost pl and hmpd appr 2 fs out, kpt on ins last.* (33 to 1 op 25 to 1) 8
BLUE FLAG (USA) [74] 4-8-13 L Dettori (15) *trkd ldrs till wknd 2 fs out*...... (33 to 1 op 16 to 1) 9
WAVE HILL [79] 4-9-4 K Darley (3) *beh, shrtlvd effrt and not much room o'r 2 fs out.* ......(33 to 1 op 20 to 1 tchd 40 to 1) 10
480^2 HOST (Ire) [86] 4-9-11 M Roberts (4) *trkd ldrs, rdn alng 4 fs out, btn o'r 2 out*...... (7 to 1 op 6 to 1 tchd 8 to 1) 11
440^8 NATIVE CHIEFTAN [75] 4-9-0 A Munro (13) *trkd ldr, wknd o'r 2 fs out*...... (33 to 1 op 25 to 1) 12
FIELDRIDGE [86] 4-9-11 M Hills (14) *led till o'r 2 fs out, wknd*......(33 to 1 op 25 to 1 tchd 40 to 1) 13
329^3 MULCIBER [70] 5-8-9 W Carson (12) *chsd ldrs, wknd wl o'r 2 fs out*...... (12 to 1 op 10 to 1 tchd 14 to 1) 14
391^7 MOUGINS (Ire) [89] 4-9-9 (5*) A Procter (1) *reluctant to race, lost many ls strt, al beh.* ......(33 to 1 op 20 to 1 tchd 40 to 1) 15
LEGAL EMBRACE (Can) [70] 4-8-9 G Carter (8) *trkd ldrs till wknd o'r 2 fs out*......(33 to 1 op 20 to 1 tchd 40 to 1) 16
Dist: Hd, ¾l, 2½l, sht-hd, 2½l, nk, 1½l, 1½l, 3½l, 1½l. 2m 9.54s. a 5.64s (16 Ran).
SR: 49/43/62/44/40/50/38/30/32/ (Bob Cullen), D R C Elsworth

CURRAGH (IRE) (heavy)
Saturday April 24th
Going Correction: PLUS 1.25 sec. per fur. (races 1,2,3,4,6), PLUS 1.10 (5,7)

664 Loughbrown (E.B.F.) Race (2-y-o) £5,865 5f ....(2:00)

IL CARAVAGGIO (Ire) 8-10 M J Kinane (5)......(6 to 4 fav) 1
GIULIO ROMANO (Ire) 8-3^1 (8*) T E Durcan (4)...... (5 to 1) 2
CORLEONIE (Ire) 8-10 W J Supple (2)......(4 to 1) 3
JOMACOON (Ire) 7-13 (8*) B A Hunter (3)......(9 to 4) 4
MUSICAL SUNSET (Ire) 8-10 P V Gilson (1)...... (5 to 1) 5
Dist: 3½l, hd, 2½l, 7l. 1m 7.30s. a 9.00s (5 Ran).
SR: 41/27/26/13/-/ (Andrea Schiavi), D K Weld

665 Athasi Stakes (Listed) (3 & 4-y-o) £8,625 7f ....(2:30)

ASEMA (USA) 3-8-11 M J Kinane (10) *trkd ldrs, smooth prog to chal o'r a furlong out, sn rdn, led ins last, styd on wl*......(9 to 4 fav) 1
270^3 LAVINIA FONTANA (Ire) 4-9-7 P V Gilson (9) *dsptd ld till wnt on o'r 3 fs out, hdd ins last, no extr*...... (13 to 2) 2
488* TARAKANA (USA) 3-8-6 R Hughes (8) *hld up, gd prog whn rdn one and a half fs out, kpt on ins last*...... (5 to 2) 3
573 PERNILLA (Ire) 3-8-6 J A Heffernan (6) *hld up till gd prog to chal und 2 fs out, kpt on*......(12 to 1) 4
LADAKIYA (USA) 3-8-6 D Hogan (7) *dsptd ld till hdd o'r 3 fs out, rdn 2 out, wknd ins last*......(10 to 1) 5
MILLIE'S CHOICE (Ire) 4-9-7 W J Supple (4) *trkd ldrs, prog whn rdn one and a half fs out, wknd ins last.* (20 to 1) 6
573^2 WEEKEND MADNESS (Ire) 3-8-6 W J O'Connor (1) *mid-div, rdn 2 fs out, not quicken*......(13 to 2) 7
NAIVITY (Ire) 4-9-7 J Ely (2) *al rear*......(50 to 1) 8
573^3 TAKE NO CHANCES (Ire) 3-8-6 P Shanahan (3) *mid-div, rdn 2 fs out, sn wknd*......(10 to 1) 9
270^6 CAURSELLE (Ire) 4-9-7 J P Murtagh (5) *wl plcd, chlgd 2 fs out, sn wknd, eased ins last*...... (20 to 1) 10
Dist: 1l, ½l, ¾l, 1½l. 1m 36.80s. a 13.60s (10 Ran).
SR: 24/31/14/12/7/-/ (Allen E Paulson), D K Weld

666 Somfy International Handicap (0-90 3-y-o and up) £3,795 1m..................(3:00)

PRIVATE GUY (Ire) [-] (bl) 4-9-9 M J Kinane (3)...... (6 to 1) 1
311* KURDISTAN (Ire) [-] 3-8-10 W J O'Connor (6)......(5 to 1) 2
310* CONS PRINCE (Ire) [-] 3-8-2 Joanna Morgan (7)......(7 to 1) 3
ACCELL (Ire) [-] 4-7-13 (2*) W J Supple (1)......(20 to 1) 4
ELIZABETH'S PET (Ire) [-] 3-8-5 R Hughes (13)......(10 to 1) 5
306^4 GENERAL CHAOS (Ire) [-] 3-8-5 P V Gilson (8)..(5 to 2 fav) 6
272 DRUMAALER [-] 5-8-6 (2*) R M Burke (2)......(20 to 1) 7
DESERT CALM (Ire) [-] 4-9-0 (6*) B J Walsh (12)... (10 to 1) 8
310 SWEET NASHA (Ire) [-] 4-9-11 N G McCullagh (10) (16 to 1) 9
GLOWING VALUE (Ire) [-] 3-9-2 J P Murtagh (4)... (16 to 1) 10
272^4 NORDIC DISPLAY (Ire) [-] 5-8-7^2 (8*) M W Martin (5) (7 to 1) 11
4686a CISEAUX (USA) [-] 4-9-7 P Shanahan (11)...... (20 to 1) 12
BASIE NOBLE [-] (bl) 4-8-11 (6*) J J Behan (9).... (10 to 1) 13

Dist: ¾l, 3l, 1½l, 5½l. 1m 52.40s. a 15.80s (13 Ran).
SR: 22/7/-/-/-/-/ (Michael W J Smurfit), D K Weld

667 Victor McCalmont Tetrarch Stakes (Group 3) (3-y-o) £14,375 7f................ (3:30)

COLLEGE CHAPEL 8-9 W J Supple (1) *hld up till prog 2 fs out to ld o'r 100 yards out, cmftbly*............(12 to 1) 1
MASTER TRIBE (Ire) 8-9 P V Gilson (3) *trkd ldr till led o'r 4 fs out, rdn 2 out, hdd over 100 yards out, kpt on.* ....(9 to 4 fav) 2
574[3] NORDIC FOX (Ire) 8-9 W J O'Connor (5) *wl plcd, rdn o'r 2 fs out, no extr fnl furlong*................(5 to 1) 3
MYSTERIOUS WAYS (Ire) 8-9 P Shanahan (2) *hld up, little room till rdn and swtchd rght one furlong out, ran on.* ....(4 to 1) 4
UNUSUAL HEAT (USA) 8-9 M J Kinane (4) *wl plcd, rdn 2 fs out, not quicken, wknd fnl furlong*.........(100 to 30) 5
TIMOURID (USA) 8-9 R Hughes (6) *led till hdd o'r 4 fs out, rdn 2 out, wknd one out*......................(9 to 2) 6
Dist: 3l, hd, 1l, 6l. 1m 36.10s. a 12.90s (6 Ran).
SR: 33/24/23/20/2/-/ (Mrs M V O'Brien), M V O'Brien

668 Corrib Handicap (0-95 3-y-o) £6,900 1¼m ....(4:00)

307[3] NEVER BACK DOWN (Ire) [-] 8-0[1] W J Supple (4) ...(5 to 1) 1
576[4] SPECIAL PAGEANT (Ire) [-] 8-11 (6*) J A Heffernan (5) ....(5 to 1) 2
SHREWD IDEA [-] 9-6 W J O'Connor (1)..........(13 to 2) 3
TIGHT FIST (Ire) [-] 7-10 (6*) J J Behan (8)........(20 to 1) 4
DOYROY (Ire) [-] 8-0 J D Eddery (2)..............(12 to 1) 5
CALL MY GUEST (Ire) [-] 7-2[2] (8*) R T Fitzpatrick (9) (20 to 1) 6
282 BERESFORD LADY (Ire) [-] 7-8 (2*) D G O'Shea (7)..(6 to 1) 7
VINEY (USA) [-] (bl) 8-6 M J Kinane (6)...........(15 to 2) 8
306* SHAHZADI (Ire) [-] 8-13 D Hogan (3)............(5 to 2 fav) 9
Dist: 3l, ½l, 2½l, hd. 2m 19.70s. a 16.90s (9 Ran).
SR: 27/38/40/17/14/-/ (Mount Juliet), W P Mullins

669 Warren (E.B.F.) Maiden (3-y-o) £3,440 1m ....(4:30)

HUSHANG (Ire) 9-0 J P Murtagh (15).........(10 to 9 on) 1
GOODNIGHT KISS 8-11 M J Kinane (2)..............(3 to 1) 2
FLORA WOOD (Ire) 8-5 (6*) B J Walsh (17)........(20 to 1) 3
SAFFRON CROCUS 8-9 (2*) D G O'Shea (7)......(10 to 1) 4
MONOPOLY MONEY (Ire) 9-0 P V Gilson (5)......(10 to 1) 5
489[9] PALACE PARADE (USA) 9-0 W J O'Connor (10)....(14 to 1) 6
INDIGENT (Ire) 8-5 (6*) W J Supple (11)..............(9 to 1) 7
RASSETTE (Ire) 8-5 (6*) J A Heffernan (1)..........(14 to 1) 8
HELLO EXCUSE ME (USA) 9-0 G Curran (6)........(20 to 1) 9
311 PENNY A DAY (Ire) 8-6 (8*) B A Hunter (14)........(20 to 1) 10
ARROGANT LADY 8-3 (8*) J J Mullins (9)..........(33 to 1) 11
VERITABLE GALLERY (Ire) 9-0 N G McCullagh (3) (12 to 1) 12
LORD CHIEF (Ire) 9-0 N Byrne (12)...............(14 to 1) 13
ANOTHER FLYER (Ire) 8-12 (2*) R M Burke (8).....(33 to 1) 14
CAROLINA RUA (USA) 8-11 B Coogan (16)..........(12 to 1) 15
577[7] ROLANDS GIRL (Ire) 8-7[4] (8*) M W Martin (13).....(25 to 1) 16
Dist: 3½l, ¾l, 5l, 1l. 1m 52.80s. a 16.20s (16 Ran).
SR: 7/-/-/-/-/-/ (H H Aga Khan), John M Oxx

670 Mooresbridge Stakes (Listed) (4-y-o and up) £8,625 1¼m..................... (5:00)

308[4] SALMON EILE (Ire) 5-8-12 J P Murtagh (6) *hld up, prog 2 fs out to ld one out, styd on*....................(11 to 2) 1
525[6] IRISH MEMORY 4-9-10 W J O'Connor (1) *led 1st 2 fs, then trkd ldr till prog to dispute ld two out, hdd one out, kpt on*...(2 to 1 fav) 2
553[3] YUKON GOLD (Ire) (bl) 4-8-12 P V Gilson (4) *trkd ldr till led aftr 2 fs, jnd two out, hdd one out, no extr*..... (9 to 2) 3
APPROACH THE BENCH (Ire) 5-9-7 W J Supple (5) *strted slwly, rear till gd prog 2 out, wknd ins last*.....(4 to 1) 4
GAELIC MYTH (USA) 6-8-12 S Craine (2) *mid-div, rdn 3 fs out, wknd one out*..............................(11 to 2) 5
308 ORMSBY (Ire) 4-9-7 M J Kinane (3) *mid-div, prog 2 fs out, wknd one out*.................................(11 to 2) 6
Dist: 1l, ½l, 5½l, 1½l. 2m 18.00s. a 15.20s (6 Ran).
SR: 56/66/53/51/39/-/ (Mrs M C O'Connor), Patrick Joseph Flynn

HOLLYWOOD (USA) (firm)
Saturday April 24th

671 The Californian (Grade 1) (3-y-o and up) £145,695 1m 1f..........................

LATIN AMERICAN (USA) 5-8-4 G Stevens,..... (179 to 10) 1
MISSIONARY RIDGE 6-8-4 K Desormeaux,..... (33 to 10) 2
MEMO (Chi) 6-8-6 P Atkinson,..................(71 to 10) 3
SIR BEAUFORT (USA) 6-8-8 P Valenzuela,.....(6 to 5 fav) 4
REIGN ROAD (USA) 5-8-4 E Delahoussaye,..... (48 to 10) 5
PORTOFERRAIO (Arg) 5-8-4 A Solis,............ (45 to 1) 6
HAVE FUN (USA) 4-8-4 C Nakatani,............ (67 to 10) 7
Dist: 5l, 3l, hd, 5l, 7l, 1½l. 1m 46.92s. (7 Ran).
(Sheikh Mohammed), A Fabre

LEICESTER (good)
Saturday April 24th

Going Correction: PLUS 0.20 sec. per fur. (races 1,3,7,8), PLUS 0.05 (2,4,5,6)

672 Redmile Maiden Stakes Class D (Div I) (3-y-o and up) £4,077 1m 1f 218yds.....(2:20)

PREMIER LEAGUE (Ire) 3-8-6 J Quinn (5) *made all, quickened clr wl o'r one furlong out, styd on*......(4 to 1 jt-fav op 7 to 1) 1
441[2] CONSPICUOUS (Ire) 3-7-13 (7*) T G McLaughlin (7) *ran on 3 fs out, rdn and edgd rght ins last, kpt on*....(4 to 1 jt-fav op 7 to 1 tchd 10 to 1) 2
PRINCESS KRIS 3-8-1 P Robinson (9) *hdwy o'r 3 fs out, rdn and one pace ins last 2*........(12 to 1 op 6 to 1) 3
DREAMS ARE FREE (Ire) 3-8-1 W Ryan (18) *ldg grp, rdn alng and not quicken 2 fs out, styd on ins last.* ....(7 to 1 op 3 to 1) 4
DANSEUSE FRANCAISE (Ire) 3-8-2[1] M Hills (3) *mid-div, effrt o'r 3 fs out, wknd 2 out*.......(20 to 1 op 12 to 1) 5
MOSHAAJIR (USA) 3-8-7[1] W R Swinburn (13) *slwly into strd, improved hfwy, effrt o'r 3 fs out, no extr 2 out.* ....(9 to 1 op 5 to 1 tchd 10 to 1) 6
GENERAL MOUKTAR 3-8-6 W Woods (10) *chsd ldrs, rdn and wknd 2 fs out*...................(33 to 1 op 16 to 1) 7
SUMMER PAGEANT 3-8-4[3] N Day (12) *wl plcd, rdn and lost pos appr last 2 fs*..............(16 to 1 op 8 to 1) 8
BITTER ALOE 4-9-10 L Dettori (19) *effrt frm rear o'r 3 fs out, not trble frnt rnk*............(16 to 1 op 10 to 1) 9
557 RITZY 3-8-1 J Lowe (4) *cl up till wknd 3 fs out.* ....(33 to 1 op 20 to 1) 10
MASTER REACH 4-9-10 R Perham (14) *al beh.* ....(33 to 1 op 25 to 1) 11
529[8] MUTAMANNI 3-8-6 B Rouse (1) *chsd ldrs, wknd o'r 3 fs out*................................(5 to 1 op 5 to 2) 12
CHAPEL OF BARRAS (Ire) 4-9-10 J Williams (15) *slwly into strd, al rear*..................(33 to 1 op 16 to 1) 13
522[2] SHOPTILLYOUDROP 3-7-12 (3*) D Harrison (8) *hndy 6 fs, sn btn*..................(12 to 1 op 8 to 1 tchd 14 to 1) 14
INDIAN FLASH (Ire) 3-8-1 G Bardwell (6) *beh aftr 4 fs.* ....(33 to 1 op 16 to 1) 15
MR WOODCOCK 8-9-10 F Norton (2) *slwly into strd, sn in tch, wknd 3 fs out*.................(20 to 1 op 14 to 1) 16
FISIO SANDS 4-9-5 D Nicholls (17) *al rear, tld off.* ....(33 to 1 op 25 to 1) 17
RONEO (USA) 5-9-3 (7*) S Curran (16) *al beh, tld off.* ....(33 to 1 op 20 to 1) 18
D SEVEN 3-8-8[2] M Tebbutt (11) *al rear, tld off.* ....(33 to 1 op 25 to 1) 19
Dist: 3l, 1½l, 2l, 12l, hd, 2½l, 1½l, 5l, sht-hd, ¾l. 2m 9.10s. a 6.20s (19 Ran).
SR: 50/44/36/32/9/13/7/2/12/ (Miss P Rovera), J E Banks

673 Gadsby Median Auction Maiden Stakes Class F (2-y-o) £3,161 5f 2yds....... (2:50)

NERA 8-9 L Dettori (6) *made virtually all stands side, quickened clr fnl furlong, imprsv.* ....(6 to 4 fav tchd 7 to 4) 1
LADY HIGHFIELD 8-9 A Clark (14) *ran on frm 2 fs out, fnshd wl*..........................(33 to 1 op 20 to 1) 2
HALI (Ire) 9-0 F Norton (4) *dwlt, hdwy 2 fs out, styd on ins last*...(33 to 1) 3
454[2] MR ROUGH 9-0 M Tebbutt (10) *wl plcd, hng rght and one pace appr fnl furlong*... (6 to 1 op 7 to 2 tchd 7 to 1) 4
433[4] SWEETINGS PISCES 8-11 (3*) S Maloney (1) *pressed wnr, rdn and not quicken 2 fs out, kpt on ins last.* ....(16 to 1 op 8 to 1) 5
528[5] CAPPUCHINO (Ire) 8-6 (3*) Emma O'Gorman (9) *chsd ldrs, rdn alng 2 fs out, no imprsn fnl furlong.* ....(10 to 1 op 6 to 1) 6
517[4] OBVIOUS RISK 9-0 R Perham (16) *cl up, ev ch 2 fs out, outpcd fnl furlong*...... (5 to 1 op 4 to 1 tchd 7 to 1) 7
ABLEST SON 9-0 M Hills (8) *slwly into strd, trkd ldrs aftr one furlong, not quicken 2 out*......(14 to 1 op 7 to 1) 8
JUST HARRY 9-0 G Bardwell (11) *nvr nrr.* ....(25 to 1 op 20 to 1) 9
NORTHERN STARLIGHT 9-0 N Adams (13) *ldg grp 3 fs.* ....(33 to 1 op 20 to 1) 10
BELLROI (Ire) 9-0 P Robinson (2) *slwly into strd, nvr nr to chal*..........................(20 to 1 op 10 to 1) 11
517[9] MALLAM WATERS (Ire) 8-6 (3*) D Harrison (17) *nvr better than mid-div*..................(33 to 1 op 14 to 1) 12
MARINER BOY (Ire) 8-7 (7*) S Sanders (3) *nvr on terms.* ....(33 to 1 op 25 to 1) 13
NORTHERN STORM (Ire) 9-0 W Woods (19) *led far side grp 3 fs, wknd*.................. (33 to 1 op 20 to 1) 14
SUN CHIEF (Ire) 9-0 R Street (21) *strted slwly, al beh.* ....(16 to 1 op 8 to 1) 15
TIMBER BROKER 9-0 J Williams (5) *slwly away, al rear.* ....(33 to 1 op 20 to 1) 16
517[7] SHEILOBLIGE 8-9 B Rouse (20) *outpcd.* ....(20 to 1 op 10 to 1) 17

PARISH WALK (Ire) 8-9 (5*) A Garth (15) *outpcd.* (33 to 1 op 20 to 1) 18
CARELESS LADY 8-9 J Quinn (7) *slwly into strd, al rear.* (33 to 1 op 25 to 1) 19
544^{9} FLYING VISION (Ire) 8-9 S Morris (12) *outpcd hfwy.* (33 to 1) 20
454 GRANDEE 9-0 J Lowe (18) *pressed far side ldr 3 fs, wknd quickly, tld off* (33 to 1 op 25 to 1) 21
Dist: 3½l, 1l, 1½l, nk, 2½l, hd, 1½l, 2l, ¾l, 2½l. 1m 1.70s. a 3.00s (21 Ran).
SR: 40/26/27/21/20/5/9/3/-/ (Lady Portman), Mrs J Cecil

674 Madagans Handicap Class D (0-80 3-y-o and up) £4,110 1m 3f 183yds........ (3:20)

KAISER WILHELM [77] 4-10-0 W Ryan (21) *mid-div, hdwy o'r 2 fs out, led appr last, easily* (9 to 1 op 7 to 1) 1
530^{6} TIGER SHOOT [48] 6-8-0 G Bardwell (14) *led till appr fnl furlong, kpt on same pace* (8 to 1 op 7 to 1) 2
FREE MOVER (Ire) [77] 4-10-0 L Dettori (11) *wl plcd, not quicken 2 fs out, styd on fnl furlong.* (9 to 1 op 20 to 1) 3
MUCH SOUGHT AFTER [75] 4-9-12 M Tebbutt (8) *in tch, effrt 3 fs out, one pace ins last 2* (25 to 1 op 14 to 1) 4
508^{3} TANODA [47] 7-7-13 J Lowe (16) *pressed ldrs, no extr und pres 2 fs out* (12 to 1 op 10 to 1) 5
645^{3} KINOKO [52] 5-7-13 (5*) A Garth (12) *hld up, ran on appr last 2 fs, nrst finish* (5 to 1 fav op 6 to 1) 6
INCOLA [57] 7-8-2 (7*) Antoinette Armes (20) *handily plcd, rdn and ev ch o'r 2 fs out, btn one out.* (12 to 1 op 10 to 1) 7
520^{8} MAHRAJAN [52] 9-8-4 P Robinson (3) *late hdwy, nvr nrr.* (20 to 1 op 14 to 1) 8
442^{5} BUSMAN (Ire) [66] (bl) 4-9-3 W Woods (7) *hld up, prog 5 fs out, wknd 2 out* (20 to 1 op 14 to 1) 9
WASSL THIS THEN (Ire) [71] 4-9-8 R Price (9) *nvr nr to chal.* (20 to 1 op 12 to 1) 10
473^{8} MOONLIGHT QUEST [75] 5-9-13 M Hills (13) *trkd frnt rnk till lost pl o'r 2 fs out* (25 to 1 op 14 to 1) 11
527 ROUSITTO [68] 5-9-6 W R Swinburn (15) *mid-div, improved 3 fs out, wknd and eased o'r one out.* (10 to 1 op 8 to 1 tchd 12 to 1) 12
520 ALQAIRAWAAN [67] 4-9-4 B Rouse (19) *wl plcd 9 fs.* (12 to 1 op 7 to 1) 13
350^{3} BESCABY BOY [65] 7-9-3 J Williams (1) *al rear.* (9 to 1 op 8 to 1 tchd 10 to 1) 14
530^{5} EVERSO IRISH [43] 4-7-8 Dale Gibson (17) *hld up, brief effrt 4 fs out, wknd 3 out* (33 to 1 op 16 to 1) 15
520 EIGHTANDAHALF (Ire) [60] 4-8-11 A Clark (2) *rear most of way* (33 to 1 op 25 to 1) 16
382^{8} BALZINO (USA) [53] 4-7-13 (5*) Stephen Davies (10) *al beh.* (10 to 1 op 5 to 1) 17
182^{7} MALENOIR (USA) [51] 5-8-0 (3*) D Harrison (6) *nvr on terms.* (33 to 1 op 25 to 1) 18
559^{5} MANZOOR SAYADAN (USA) [60] 5-8-12 S Whitworth (18) *wl plcd till rdn and wknd 3 fs out* (14 to 1 op 12 to 1) 19
199^{8} COOL SOCIETY (USA) [58] 4-8-9 N Day (5) *beh hfwy.* (33 to 1 op 25 to 1) 20
Dist: 2l, 1½l, 2½l, ¾l, ½l, 1½l, 7l, ½l, ½l, ¾l. 2m 38.00s. a 9.50s (20 Ran).
SR: 43/11/36/29/-/4/6/-/-/ (Charles H Wacker III), H R A Cecil

675 Madagans Leicestershire Stakes Class A (Listed Race) (4-y-o and up) £9,768 7f 9yds .... (3:50)

316^{9} SWING LOW 4-9-4 B Rouse (2) *hld up, sstnd run to ld o'r one furlong out, rdn out* (10 to 1 op 9 to 1) 1
497^{2} POWERFUL EDGE 4-8-12 L Dettori (6) *hld up, hdwy and not clr run 2 fs out, wndrd o'r one out, ran on und pres nr finish, fnshd second, plcd 3rd.* (10 to 1 op 12 to 1) 2D
315^{2} MIZAAYA 4-8-12 W R Swinburn (1) *wth ldrs, rdn alng o'r 2 fs out, hmpd and lost pl over one out, rallied ins last, fnshd 3rd, plcd second* (11 to 4 fav op 7 to 2) 2
581 SUNDAY'S HILL 4-8-12 J Quinn (7) *pressed ldr, led 2 fs out till o'r one out, ran on same pace.* (33 to 1 op 20 to 1) 4
533^{3} RAMBO'S HALL 8-8-12 D Nicholls (3) *hld up rear, rdn o'r 2 fs out, styd on ins last* (9 to 2 op 5 to 1 tchd 4 to 1) 5
CASTEDDU 4-9-4 W Ryan (5) *hld up rear, rcd alone far side frm hfwy, kpt on fnl furlong.* (16 to 1 op 10 to 1) 6
481* BOLD LEZ 6-8-12 J Williams (11) *led to 2 fs out, wknd o'r one out* (10 to 1 op 8 to 1 tchd 11 to 1) 7
A-TO-Z (Ire) 4-8-13 M Hills (10) *in tch gng wl till rdn and btn appr fnl furlong* (7 to 2 op 3 to 1 tchd 4 to 1) 8
481^{3} NIGHT JAR 6-8-10 D Harrison (8) *in tch 5 fs.* (9 to 1 op 7 to 1 tchd 10 to 1) 9
316^{8} TAUFAN BLU (Ire) (v) 4-8-7 J Lowe (4) *outpcd most of way.* (33 to 1 op 20 to 1) 10
316^{3} APPLEDORN 6-8-7 P Robinson (9) *dwlt, nvr nr to chal.* (25 to 1 op 20 to 1) 11
Dist: ½l, hd, 2l, 1½l, ½l, ¾l, 2½l, 3½l, ½l, ½l. 1m 26.10s. a 4.20s (11 Ran).
SR: 46/38/37/31/26/30/22/15/1/ (Roldvale Limited), R Hannon

676 Rothmans Royals North South Challenge Series Handicap Class D (0-80 4-y-o and up) £3,915 1m 8yds................ (4:20)

315 WALKING THE PLANK [70] 4-9-5 P Robinson (1) *handily plcd, quickened to ld ins fnl furlong, ran on.* (25 to 1 op 20 to 1) 1
JADE VALE [69] 4-9-4 M Hills (6) *in tch, jnd ldrs o'r 2 fs out, ev ch fnl furlong, jst fld* (9 to 1 op 12 to 1) 2
$4749a^{5}$ PENNY DROPS [67] 4-8-13 (3*) D Harrison (2) *ran on wl 2 fs out, styd on nr line* (10 to 1 op 8 to 1) 3
592^{4} FOREVER DIAMONDS [74] 6-9-6 (3*) S Maloney (15) *wth ldrs, led 3 fs out till ins last, no extr.* (8 to 1 op 9 to 2) 4
458* SWEET MIGNONETTE [63] 5-8-12 F Norton (7) *hld up, hdwy o'r 2 fs out, rdn and one pace fnl furlong.* (7 to 2 fav tchd 9 to 2) 5
479^{5} SURREY RACING [73] 5-9-8 B Rouse (8) *styd on wl frm rear last 2 fs, nrst finish.* (10 to 1 op 7 to 1 tchd 11 to 1) 6
402^{8} BALLYRANTER [48] 4-7-11 J Quinn (17) *ldg grp, rdn and no hdwy 2 fs out* (20 to 1 op 14 to 1) 7
COURAGEOUS KNIGHT [72] 4-9-7 R Perham (12) *nvr nrr.* (25 to 1 op 14 to 1) 8
458^{6} MA BELLA LUNA [73] 4-9-8 W R Swinburn (13) *nvr better than mid-div* (14 to 1 op 8 to 1) 9
448^{4} RED KITE [57] 4-7-13 (7*) J O'Dwyer (3) *wl plcd for o'r 5 fs, wknd* (20 to 1 op 12 to 1) 10
565 FOOLISH TOUCH [54] 11-8-3 N Day (9) *jnd ldrs 3 fs out, sn ev ch, wknd wl o'r one out* (25 to 1 op 16 to 1) 11
568^{5} MEESON TIMES [45] 5-7-8[1] J Lowe (16) *prmnt for o'r 4 fs.* (25 to 1 op 20 to 1) 12
ANNABELLE ROYALE [66] 7-9-1 L Dettori (4) *led 5 fs, sn wknd* (20 to 1 tchd 16 to 1) 13
JAHANGIR (Ire) [75] 4-9-10 M Tebbutt (5) *effrt o'r 3 fs out, eased whn btn ins last 2* (14 to 1 op 16 to 1) 14
391^{4} ABSONAL [65] 6-9-0 J Williams (11) *nvr trble ldrs.* (20 to 1 op 12 to 1) 15
$4758a^{3}$ KINGCHIP BOY [55] 4-8-4 G Bardwell (10) *rear most of way* (25 to 1 op 16 to 1) 16
NILE DELTA (Ire) [72] 4-9-7 W Ryan (14) *pressed ldrs till drpd out quickly 2 fs out, tld off* (7 to 1 op 4 to 1) 17
Dist: Nk, 2l, nk, 3l, ¾l, 2l, ½l, 1½l, 3½l, 6l. 1m 39.50s. a 4.40s (17 Ran).
SR: 45/43/35/41/21/29/-/20/16/ (Michael White), P T Walwyn

677 Woolsthorpe Handicap Class C (0-90 3-y-o and up) £5,427 5f 218yds............ (4:50)

LANGUEDOC [58] 6-7-11 L Charnock (10) *pressed ldr, rdn to ld ins fnl furlong, hld on* (33 to 1 op 20 to 1) 1
MASSIBA (Ire) [85] 4-9-7 (3*) D Harrison (12) *led till ins fnl furlong, rallied cl hme* (20 to 1 op 14 to 1) 2
436^{7} CUMBRIAN WALTZER [88] 8-9-10 (3*) S Maloney (21) *chsd ldrs, rdn and effrt 3 fs out, outpcd 2 out.* (11 to 1 op 7 to 1 tchd 12 to 1) 3
479* EFRA [67] 4-8-6 S Raymont (17) *mid-div, hrd rdn and styd on frm 2 fs out, not rch wnr* (8 to 1 co-fav op 7 to 1 tchd 9 to 1) 4
JIGSAW BOY [77] 4-9-2 J Williams (11) *styd on last 2 fs, nrst finish* (8 to 1 co-fav op 12 to 1) 5
252 BIRCHWOOD SUN [76] 3-8-3 W Ryan (2) *outpcd till ran on strly ins fnl 2 fs* (33 to 1) 6
COOLABA PRINCE (Ire) [67] 4-8-3 (3*) N Kennedy (5) *chsd stands side ldrs till outpcd o'r 2 fs out.* (20 to 1 op 12 to 1) 7
521^{2} MAINLY ME [60] 4-7-13 G Bardwell (16) *nvr able to chal.* (10 to 1 op 8 to 1) 8
369* SAMSOLOM [63] 5-8-2 J Quinn (19) *nvr rch frnt rnk.* (16 to 1 op 12 to 1) 9
330* MARTINOSKY [64] 7-8-3 N Day (1) *speed stands side to hfwy* (9 to 1 op 10 to 1 tchd 8 to 1) 10
ROCA MURADA (Ire) [61] 4-8-0[3] P Robinson (4) *outpcd hfwy* (12 to 1 op 14 to 1 tchd 16 to 1) 11
STAR GODDESS (USA) [74] 4-8-13 B Rouse (14) *ldg grp till wknd o'r 2 fs out* (9 to 1 op 20 to 1) 12
292 FIRST GOLD [65] 4-8-4 A Clark (18) *outpcd.* (33 to 1 op 20 to 1) 13
436 BERNSTEIN BETTE [71] 7-8-10 M Hills (22) *slwly into strd, not reco'r* (12 to 1 op 14 to 1) 14
479^{6} TRUTHFUL IMAGE [70] 4-8-9 D Biggs (20) *mid-div, hrd rdn hfwy, no prog* (16 to 1 op 12 to 1) 15
475^{8} BOLD HABIT [74] 8-8-13 D Nicholls (8) *nvr rch ldrs.* (20 to 1 op 14 to 1) 16
87 HARDLINER [70] 4-8-9 W Woods (7) *prmnt stands side, wknd hfwy* (33 to 1) 17
505^{2} PRETONIC [67] 5-8-6 T Williams (3) *speed to hfwy.* (10 to 1 op 8 to 1) 18
RED ROSEIN [89] 7-10-0 L Dettori (15) *chsd ldrs far side for o'r 3 fs* (25 to 1 op 16 to 1) 19
465^{2} DOMINUET [84] 8-9-9 J Lowe (9) *outpcd* (8 to 1 co-fav op 7 to 1 tchd 9 to 1) 20
208^{3} GREENWICH CHALENGE [76] 3-8-3 Dale Gibson (6) *led stands side grp to hfwy* (25 to 1 op 20 to 1) 21
320^{3} CRECHE [62] (bl) 4-8-1 F Norton (13) *pressed ldrs 3 fs, wknd quickly* (16 to 1 op 12 to 1) 22
Dist: Hd, 2½l, 2l, ½l, ½l, 1½l, hd, sht-hd, 2l, ¾l. 1m 13.10s. a 2.70s (22 Ran).
SR: 35/61/54/25/33/18/15/7/9/ (Mrs H H Wane), Martyn Wane

678 Spring Handicap Class E (0-70 3-y-o and up) £3,522 1m 1f 218yds............ (5:20)

351* GENERAL CHASE [62] 3-7-11 (5*) Stephen Davies (3) *ran on 4 fs out, rdn alng 2 out, led und pres ins last.* ....(8 to 1 op 7 to 1 tchd 9 to 1) 1
EDGE OF DARKNESS [55] 4-8-10 (3*) D Harrison (5) *in tch, effrt and swtchd rght 2 fs out, ev ch one out, not quicken last 50 yards*........(12 to 1 op 10 to 1) 2
373³ FLY FOR GOLD (Ire) [51] 4-8-9 R Price (9) *sn wth ldrs, kpt on one pace fnl furlong*........(8 to 1 op 10 to 1) 3
456² ALTERMEERA [50] 5-8-8 G Bardwell (1) *ldg grp, led 3 fs out till hdd and no extr ins last.* ....(6 to 1 fav op 5 to 1 tchd 7 to 1) 4
FOX CHAPEL [63] 6-9-4 (3*) S Maloney (16) *improved on outsd 4 fs out, edgd lft and not quicken 2 out.* ....(20 to 1 op 16 to 1) 5
4759a⁶ SARAH-CLARE [51] 5-8-9 R Perham (15) *wl plcd, ev ch 2 fs out, btn one out*........(7 to 1 op 6 to 1 tchd 8 to 1) 6
LIGHT-HEARTED LADY [56] 5-9-0 J Williams (6) *hdwy on outsd 4 fs out, no extr und pres 2 out.* ....(16 to 1 tchd 20 to 1) 7
141 CAL NORMA'S LADY (Ire) [53] 5-8-11 W Woods (8) *led to 3 fs out, eased whn btn o'r one out*........(25 to 1 op 14 to 1) 8
521 WINGED WHISPER (USA) [44] (bl) 4-7-11 (5*) A Garth (17) *slwly into strd, effrt frm rear o'r 2 fs out, not trble ldrs.* ....(33 to 1 op 25 to 1) 9
DON'T FORGET MARIE (Ire) [64] 3-8-4 S Raymont (10) *moderate prog frm rear o'r 3 fs out, nrst finish.* ....(20 to 1 op 16 to 1) 10
BIT ON THE SIDE (Ire) [58] 4-9-2 J Quinn (12) *beh till effrt and swtchd rght o'r 2 fs out, not rch ldrs*........(14 to 1) 11
396⁴ TAHITIAN [66] 4-9-10 P Robinson (11) *trkd ldrs 7 fs, sn wknd*........(8 to 1 op 6 to 1) 12
FATHER HAYES (USA) [64] 5-9-8 N Day (19) *mid-div, wknd 4 fs out*........(16 to 1 op 14 to 1) 13
GEORGE ROPER [66] 3-8-6 B Rouse (7) *settled mid-div, no prog frm hfwy*........(20 to 1 op 16 to 1) 14
470⁸ ICE STRIKE (USA) [51] 4-8-9 S Whitworth (13) *in tch 6 fs.* ....(33 to 1 op 25 to 1) 15
YAAKUM [53] 4-8-6 (5*) L Newton (4) *beh fnl 4 fs.* ....(20 to 1 op 14 to 1) 16
SOLID (Ire) [47] 5-8-5 D Biggs (14) *in tch 6 fs.* ....(12 to 1 op 33 to 1) 17
470⁷ AQUADO [51] 4-8-9 J Lowe (18) *strted slwly, al beh.* ....(16 to 1 op 12 to 1) 18

Dist: 2½l, nk, hd, 6l, hd, ¾l, 2½l, sht-hd, 1½l, 1½l. 2m 10.90s. a 8.00s (18 Ran).
SR: 28/34/29/27/28/15/18/10/-/ (T R Pearson), D Burchell

679 Redmile Maiden Stakes Class D (Div II) (3-y-o and up) £4,077 1m 1f 218yds.....(5:50)

SHAREEK (USA) 3-8-7¹ W R Swinburn (8) *wl plcd, shaken up to ld o'r one furlong out, rdn out.* ....(6 to 4 on tchd Evens) 1
RAFTERS 4-9-10 N Day (10) *pressed ldrs, ev ch ins fnl furlong, not quicken nr line*........(33 to 1 op 16 to 1) 2
FORMATO UNI (Ire) 3-8-6 A Clark (16) *in tch, not much room and swtchd lft o'r 2 fs out, styd on ins last.* ....(12 to 1 op 7 to 1) 3
COLORFUL AMBITION 3-8-6 P D'Arcy (6) *made most till o'r 2 fs out, wknd fnl furlong*........(16 to 1 op 8 to 1) 4
CROMARTY 3-8-1 J Lowe (5) *ldg grp, led o'r 2 fs out, hdd and wknd over one out*........(16 to 1 op 8 to 1) 5
CALL THE GUV'NOR 4-9-10 W Ryan (9) *slwly into strd, beh till ran on appr last 2 fs, no imprsn on ldrs.* ....(10 to 1 op 6 to 1 tchd 12 to 1) 6
GUESTWICK 3-8-6 M Hills (1) *chsd frnt rnk till outpcd o'r 3 fs out*........(16 to 1 op 12 to 1 tchd 20 to 1) 7
ELA BILLANTE 3-8-1 P Robinson (14) *nvr trble ldrs.* ....(33 to 1 op 16 to 1) 8
BAYRAK (USA) 3-8-6 S Whitworth (18) *hld up beh, rdn and effrt o'r 3 fs out, no imprsn*........(33 to 1 op 16 to 1) 9
423⁶ TEACHER (Ire) 3-7-13 (7*) J Tate (7) *slwly into strd, al rear.* ....(25 to 1 op 12 to 1) 10
MOVE A MINUTE (USA) 4-9-10 J Williams (17) *nvr on terms.* ....(11 to 1 op 8 to 1 tchd 9 to 2 and 12 to 1) 11
FLAMING MIRACLE (Ire) 3-7-13 (7*) T G McLaughlin (15) *al beh*........(33 to 1 op 16 to 1) 12
582 MOST EQUAL 3-8-6 N Adams (19) *in tch till rdn and lost pl o'r 3 fs out*........(33 to 1 op 20 to 1) 13
SHARE A MOMENT (Can) 3-7-13 (7*) M Humphries (2) *lost pl hfwy*........(20 to 1 op 10 to 1) 14
MISTRESS BEE (USA) 4-9-5 F Norton (12) *jnd ldrs o'r 5 fs out, wknd quickly 3 out*........(33 to 1 op 16 to 1) 15
522⁵ NATCHEZ TRACE 4-9-5 L Dettori (11) *nvr on terms.* ....(10 to 1 op 25 to 1 tchd 33 to 1) 16
516 GAMEFULL GOLD 4-9-5 S Dawson (13) *beh hfwy*. (33 to 1) 17
534 SABEEL 3-8-1 J Quinn (3) *chsd ldrs 6 fs, drpd out quickly.* ....(33 to 1 op 20 to 1) 18

Dist: ½l, 4l, hd, ¾l, 12l, nk, nk, nk, hd, ½l. 2m 10.40s. a 7.50s (18 Ran).
SR: 38/54/28/27/20/19/ (Maktoum Al Maktoum), M R Stoute

RIPON (good)
Saturday April 24th

Going Correction: PLUS 0.05 sec. per fur. (races 1,2), PLUS 0.20 (3,4,5,6,7)

680 Topcliffe Maiden Auction Fillies' Stakes Class D (2-y-o) £3,348 5f...........(2:10)

DANCE OF THE SWANS (Ire) 8-11 Dean McKeown (4) *beh, hdwy 2 fs out, chlgd ins fnl furlong, sn led, styd on wl towards finish*........(16 to 1 op 14 to 1) 1
SINNERS REPRIEVE 8-11 K Darley (1) *dwlt, beh, gd hdwy hfwy, ran on to ld briefly ins fnl furlong, rallied towards finish*........(7 to 2 fav op 9 to 2) 2
MY LIFETIME LADY (Ire) 8-11 S Perks (3) *led or dsptd ld til hdd ins fnl furlong, no extr*........(5 to 1 tchd 6 to 1) 3
DESIRE'S DREAM 8-11 M Wigham (10) *led or dsptd ld, rdn alng o'r one furlong out, not quicken ins last.* ....(14 to 1 tchd 12 to 1) 4
BUSTLE'EM (Ire) 8-11 G Duffield (11) *chsd ldrs on outsd, effrt and rdn 2 fs out, one pace fnl furlong.* ....(20 to 1 op 14 to 1) 5
TENPIN PROPHET (Ire) 8-11 D Holland (2) *chsd ldrs, rdn hfwy, improved wl o'r one furlong out, wknd ins last.* ....(6 to 1 op 9 to 2) 6
ORIENTAL AIR (Ire) 8-11 W Newnes (7) *chsd ldrs, effrt and rdn o'r 2 fs out, wknd over one furlong out.* ....(7 to 1 op 6 to 1) 7
HOTCROFT 8-11 A Culhane (5) *beh and sn pushed alng, nvr able to chal*........(14 to 1 op 12 to 1) 8
RANDONNEUR (Ire) 8-11 J Carroll (9) *dwlt, sn chasing ldrs, rdn hfwy, grad wknd*........(5 to 1 op 9 to 2) 9
TITANIA'S DANCE (Ire) 8-11 R Hills (6) *beh and sn pushed alng, nvr on terms*........(9 to 2 tchd 4 to 1 and 5 to 1) 10
SOTTISES (Ire) 8-11 J Fortune (8) *slwly into strd, al in rear*........(16 to 1 op 12 to 1) 11

Dist: Sht-hd, 2½l, ¾l, 3½l, ½l, ¾l, ¾l, 2l, nk, 10l. 1m 2.50s. a 4.50s (11 Ran).
SR: 12/11/1/-/-/-/ (S A B Dinsmore), P C Haslam

681 Aldborough Selling Stakes Class G (3-y-o and up) £2,637 1¼m................(2:40)

VELVET HEART (Ire) 3-8-1 E Johnson (16) *sn beh, gd hdwy o'r 2 fs out, str run fnl furlong to ld towards finish.* ....(20 to 1 op 14 to 1) 1
CUMBRIAN RHAPSODY 3-8-1 K Darley (11) *mid-div, effrt and swtchd ins 3 fs out, ran on to ld inside fnl furlong, hdd towards finish.* (12 to 1 op 14 to 1 tchd 10 to 1) 2
508⁴ GOLD SURPRISE (Ire) 4-9-10 J Fortune (21) *chsd ldrs, improved o'r 3 fs out, led 2 out, hdd ins last, no extr.* ....(10 to 1 op 7 to 1) 3
DELPIOMBO 7-9-10 K Fallon (18) *hld up, improved wl o'r 2 fs out, chlgd entering fnl furlong, not quicken.* ....(9 to 1 op 10 to 1) 4
PRINCESS OF ORANGE 4-9-5 S Webster (7) *hld up and beh, improved 3 fs out, not quicken appr fnl furlong.* ....(33 to 1) 5
GAY MING 4-9-2 (7*) J Dennis (20) *slwly into strd, beh, effrt and hdwy 4 fs out, kpt on ins fnl furlong.* ....(16 to 1 op 20 to 1 tchd 14 to 1) 6
452³ A BADGE TOO FAR (Ire) 3-8-1 G Hind (23) *in tch, effrt and rdn 3 fs out, no extr o'r one furlong out.* ....(9 to 1 op 8 to 1 tchd 10 to 1) 7
507⁴ WHITE CREEK (Ire) (v) 3-8-6 J Carroll (17) *led, clr entering strt, hdd 2 fs out, sn wknd*........(10 to 1 op 7 to 1) 8
531³ HOT PUNCH 4-9-10 W Newnes (19) *trkd ldrs, rdn hfwy, wknd 3 fs out*........(10 to 1 op 8 to 1) 9
531⁹ ANFIELD SALLY 7-9-9 Paul Eddery (22) *chsd ldrs, rdn 3 fs out, grad wknd*........(20 to 1 tchd 25 to 1) 10
LODESTAR (Ire) 5-10-0 Kim Tinkler (6) *beh til styd on fnl 2 fs, nvr dngrs*........(12 to 1 op 8 to 1) 11
MASTER OF THE ROCK (bl) 4-9-10 B Raymond (24) *settled mid-div, drvn alng o'r 3 fs out, sn one pace.* ....(10 to 1 op 8 to 1) 12
448 DEPUTY TIM 10-9-7 (7*) H Bastiman (14) *in tch, pushed alng hfwy, wknd o'r 2 fs out*........(20 to 1 op 16 to 1) 13
453⁹ DOUBLE SHERRY 4-9-5 A Culhane (1) *in tch, rdn alng 4 fs out, grad wknd*........(25 to 1) 14
NOT YET 9-9-9 (5*) S Wynne (4) *slwly into strd, beh till kpt on fnl 2 fs, nvr dngrs*........(20 to 1 op 25 to 1) 15
602 PETITE JESS 3-8-1 N Carlisle (12) *chsd ldrs til rdn and wknd 3 fs out*........(25 to 1 op 20 to 1) 16
RUN MILADY 5-9-5 D Wilkinson (9) *slwly into strd, sn beh and detached, some hdwy o'r one furlong out, nvr nrr.* ....(33 to 1) 17
458⁹ ABSOLUTLEY FOXED 4-9-5 R Hills (3) *in tch til rdn and wknd fnl 3 fs*........(20 to 1) 18
398 BODY LANGUAGE 3-8-1 G Carter (2) *mid-div, rdn entering strt, wknd o'r 3 fs out*........(10 to 1 tchd 8 to 1) 19
620 HILLZAH (USA) 5-10-0 Dean McKeown (10) *hld up, came wide strt, rdn and no imprsn fnl 3 fs.* ....(11 to 2 fav op 5 to 1 tchd 6 to 1) 20
375⁶ HATAAL (Ire) (v) 4-8-12 (7*) Claire Balding (5) *al struggling in rear*........(25 to 1 op 33 to 1) 21
STRATHELLA 6-9-0 (5*) O Pears (15) *beh, rdn entering strt, sn wknd*........(33 to 1) 22
HENBURY HALL (Ire) 5-10-0 D Holland (13) *in tch, effrt 3 fs out, wknd quickly*........(16 to 1) 23
4670a AFFIRMED'S DESTINY (USA) (bl) 4-9-10 S Perks (8) *mid-div, lost pl hfwy, tld off*........(33 to 1) 24

Dist: Nk, 1½l, 2l, 3½l, ½l, 1½l, 12l, 1l, ½l, 2½l. 2m 12.10s. a 8.10s (24 Ran).

SR: 11/10/30/26/14/17/ (Gordon Milne), P C Haslam

682 C. B. Hutchinson Memorial Challenge Cup Handicap Stakes Class C (0-90 4-y-o and up) £7,765 2m......................(3:10)

GOOD HAND (USA) [80] 7-9-13 N Connorton (3) *settled mid-div, rdn o'r 3 fs out, styd on wl to ld ins fnl furlong.* ....(14 to 1 tchd 16 to 1) 1

303* SNOW BOARD [68] 4-8-11 D Holland (2) *in tch, niggled alng frm hfwy, improved 4 fs out, led o'r one furlong out, hng rght, hdd ins last, no extr.* ....(6 to 4 fav op 2 to 1) 2

462* JACK BUTTON (Ire) [83] 4-9-12 G Duffield (14) *in tch, pushed alng 6 fs out, improved o'r 2 furlongs out, edgd rght, ev ch over one out, no extr ins last*........(8 to 1) 3

DOMINANT SERENADE [50] 4-7-7 S Wood (4) *chsd ldrs, hdwy o'r 3 fs out, ev ch whn crrd rght over one furlong out and ins fnl furlong, not quicken.* ....(12 to 1 op 10 to 1 tchd 14 to 1) 4

453^{2} HOT STAR [53] 7-8-0 J Fanning (12) *settled mid-div, rdn to improve o'r 2 fs out, one pace ins fnl furlong.* (20 to 1) 5

427^{2} CHANTRY BARTLE [46] 7-7-0 (7*) D Wright (10) *chsd ldrs, rdn alng 3 fs out, wknd o'r one out.* ....(25 to 1 op 20 to 1) 6

NIJMEGEN [68] 5-9-1 B Raymond (7) *nvr far away, rdn 4 fs out, led o'r 2 furlongs out, hdd over one out, sn btn.* ....(12 to 1) 7

SARAWAT [81] 5-10-0 W Newnes (9) *chsd ldrs, led aftr 5 fs, hdd 4 furlongs out, sn btn and eased.* ....(16 to 1 op 14 to 1) 8

356* GREY POWER [62] 6-8-9 K Darley (13) *hld up in rear, effrt o'r 3 fs out, sn no imprsn*..........(14 to 1 op 12 to 1) 9

420^{6} BOLD RESOLUTION (Ire) [67] 5-9-0 G Carter (5) *settled midfield, drvn alng o'r 3 fs out, wknd 2 out.* ....(7 to 1 op 6 to 1) 10

427^{3} DEDUCE [73] 4-9-2 Paul Eddery (8) *led 5 fs, styd hndy, rgned ld 4 furlongs out, hdd o'r 2 furlongs out, sn btn.* ....(12 to 1 tchd 14 to 1) 11

559* MASTER FOODBROKER (Ire) [73] (bl) 5-8-13 (7*) D McCabe (1) *hld up in rear, rdn alng 4 fs out, no imprsn.* (10 to 1) 12

OUR AISLING [75] 5-9-3 (5*) O Pears (11) *beh, effrt o'r 3 fs out, sn wknd*......................(16 to 1 op 14 to 1) 13

527^{5} LABURNUM [75] 5-9-8 K Fallon (6) *hld up and wl beh, rdn to improve o'r 3 fs out, sn lost tch*...(10 to 1 op 8 to 1) 14

Dist: 1½l, 1l, hd, 1½l, 2½l, 5l, ¾l, nk, 2½l, 2l. 3m 38.10s. a 13.10s (14 Ran).

SR: 14/-/10/-/-/-/ (Mrs M M Haggas), J W Watts

683 Yorkshire Television Handicap Class D (0-80 3-y-o) £3,980 6f..............(3:45)

MARGARET'S GIFT [74] 9-3 J Carroll (1) *in tch, outpcd and drvn alng o'r 2 fs out, hdwy over one out, str run to ld wl ins last*.........................(10 to 1 op 8 to 1) 1

471^{7} FRIENDLY BRAVE (USA) [75] (bl) 9-4 W Newnes (8) *prmnt, led aftr a furlong, shaken up o'r one furlong out, hdd wl ins last*.......................(16 to 1 op 14 to 1) 2

460^{3} HOTARIA [65] 8-8 A Culhane (14) *chsd ldrs, drvn 2 fs out, not quicken fnl furlong*........... (14 to 1 op 12 to 1) 3

504^{2} MILBANK CHALLENGER [60] (v) 8-3 K Darley (3) *led a furlong, chsd ldrs, drvn alng hfwy, kpt on same pace ins fnl furlong*..................................(10 to 1) 4

FOR THE PRESENT [70] 8-13 Alex Greaves (9) *chsd ldrs, pushed alng hfwy, not quicken fnl furlong.* ....(14 to 1 tchd 16 to 1) 5

535^{2} HERSHEBAR [66] (bl) 8-2 (7*) G Strange (13) *rcd on wide outsd, effrt o'r 2 fs out, not quicken fnl furlong.* ....(12 to 1) 6

535* MY GODSON [66] (bl) 8-4 (5*) O Pears (10) *beh til styd on o'r one furlong out, nvr nr to chal*............(16 to 1) 7

SPECIAL ONE [73] 9-2 R Hills (7) *cl up til rdn and wknd o'r one furlong out*..................... (9 to 1 op 7 to 1) 8

334^{5} TEXAS COWGIRL (Ire) [57] 7-7 (7*) D Wright (12) *mid-div, effrt and rdn o'r 2 fs out, wknd appr fnl furlong.* ....(16 to 1 op 14 to 1) 9

444^{4} GLEN MILLER [64] (bl) 8-7 G Duffield (18) *sn pushed alng on outsd, wknd o'r one furlong out.* (9 to 1 op 8 to 1) 10

563* ASHGORE [68] 8-11 Dean McKeown (17) *in tch on outsd, rdn hfwy, wknd fnl 2 fs.* ....(9 to 2 fav op 6 to 1 tchd 7 to 1 and 4 to 1) 11

KENNEDYS PRIMA [71] 9-0 B Raymond (11) *sn beh, no dngr frm hfwy*...................(16 to 1 op 14 to 1) 12

451^{3} DAYJUZ (Ire) [59] 8-2 G Carter (4) *in tch, rdn alng hfwy, grad wknd*....................(14 to 1 tchd 16 to 1) 13

460^{8} RAIN SPLASH [78] 9-0 (7*) Claire Balding (2) *beh and sn pushed alng, nvr on terms*...................(25 to 1) 14

CALL ME I'M BLUE (Ire) [66] 8-9 N Carlisle (16) *in tch to hfwy, sn outpcd and beh*..........(12 to 1 op 10 to 1) 15

467^{4} TTYFRAN [62] 8-5 R Lappin (5) *al struggling in rear.* ....(20 to 1) 16

535^{4} COVENT GARDEN GIRL [54] 7-11 S Wood (6) *hmpd strt, al in rear*..............................(16 to 1 op 14 to 1) 17

MAKE MINE A DOUBLE [56] 7-13 A McGlone (15) *mid-div til wknd frm hfwy*................(20 to 1 op 16 to 1) 18

Dist: ½l, 3½l, ½l, 1l, ½l, 1½l, 1l, 1½l, ½l, ½l. 1m 14.90s. a 4.30s (18 Ran).

SR: 41/40/16/9/15/9/3/6/-/ (Mrs T G Holdcroft), J Berry

684 Langthorpe Rated Class B (0-95 3-y-o) £6,616 1¼m......................(4:15)

441* RIVER NORTH (Ire) [84] 8-13 K Darley (2) *settled mid-div, effrt o'r 3 fs out, improved to ld over one furlong out, sprinted clr ins last*............(11 to 4 fav op 4 to 1) 1

472^{7} RAPID REPEAT (Ire) [89] 9-4 Paul Eddery (13) *in tch, rdn 3 fs out, kpt on ins fnl furlong, no ch wth wnr.* ....(10 to 1 op 12 to 1) 2

295* DUTOSKY [78] 8-7 N Connorton (10) *chsd ldrs, led o'r 2 fs out, hdd over one out, kpt on same pace ins last.* ....(8 to 1 op 7 to 1) 3

397* RIBHI (USA) [86] 9-1 R Hills (11) *hld up, imprvg whn short of room o'r 2 fs out, sn swtchd, one pace appr fnl furlong*..................................(6 to 1) 4

THE SEER [84] 8-13 D Holland (5) *hld up and beh, improved 3 fs out, nvr plcd to chal*...(9 to 1 op 8 to 1) 5

482* MAGICAL RETREAT (USA) [78] 8-7 G Carter (6) *hld up, rdn to improve o'r 3 fs out, wknd and eased over one furlong out*..................................(10 to 1) 6

NICO MIKE [83] 8-12 W Newnes (12) *settled midfield, no room 4 fs out, swtchd and no imprsn fnl 2 furlongs.* ....(14 to 1) 7

468^{9} HEATHYARDS BOY [92] 9-7 S Perks (9) *keen hold, hld up, drvn alng 4 fs out, wknd wl o'r 2 furlongs out.* (20 to 1) 8

385* SEEK THE PEARL [84] 8-13 G Duffield (7) *chsd ldrs, hmpd 4 fs out and o'r 2 out, grad lost pl*... (11 to 1 op 10 to 1) 9

546^{5} MHEMEANLES [82] 8-11 K Fallon (8) *mid-div, drvn alng 3 fs out, sn btn*......................(9 to 1 op 7 to 1) 10

TOTALLY UNIQUE (USA) [80] (v) 8-9 J Carroll (3) *led a furlong and a half, styd hndy, rgned ld o'r 3 fs out till over 2 out, fdd*..................................(16 to 1) 11

FORTENSKY (USA) [91] 9-3 (3*) J Weaver (4) *hld up, rdn o'r 3 fs out, no imprsn*..................... (9 to 1 op 8 to 1) 12

ANAXAGORAS [81] 8-10 B Raymond (1) *chsd ldrs, led aftr a furlong and a half, hdd o'r 3 out, sn btn*.... (12 to 1) 13

Dist: 3½l, 1½l, 3½l, 10l, 2½l, 3½l, ¾l, 2½l, 3l, 8l. 2m 10.30s. a 6.30s (13 Ran).

SR: 56/54/40/41/19/8/6/13/-/ (P D Savill), Lady Herries

685 Roecliffe Handicap Class D (0-80 3-y-o) £3,882 1m.........................(4:45)

549* SMARGINATO (Ire) [73] 9-4 G Carter (4) *in tch, improved to ld wl o'r 2 fs out, clr over one out, edgd rght and styd on well*..........................(7 to 4 fav op 11 to 4) 1

328^{3} CREDIT SQUEEZE [64] 8-6 (3*) A Tucker (12) *keen hold early, hld up, hdwy 3 fs out, kpt on fnl furlong, no ch wth wnr*............(11 to 1 op 10 to 1 tchd 12 to 1) 2

503^{2} HOT OFF THE PRESS [51] 7-10^{1} J Penza (11) *in tch, imprvg whn hng lft 2 fs out, not quicken ins last.* ....(10 to 1 op 8 to 1) 3

630^{2} PANTHER (Ire) [66] 8-11 W Newnes (3) *chsd ldrs, drvn alng o'r 2 fs out, kpt on same pace over one out.* ....(12 to 1 tchd 10 to 1) 4

437^{9} HAZARD A GUESS (Ire) [57] 8-2 K Fallon (8) *beh, came wide strt, hdwy 2 fs out, styd on ins last, nvr dngrs.* ....(11 to 1 op 7 to 1 tchd 12 to 1) 5

493^{2} UMBUBUZI (USA) [73] 9-4 S Perks (10) *led a furlong and a half, styd hndy, rgned ld o'r 3 fs out, hdd wl over 2 out, sn btn*.................. (9 to 1 op 6 to 1 tchd 10 to 1) 6

4766a* DANCE TO ORDER (Ire) [76] 9-7 G Duffield (14) *cl up, led aftr a furlong and a half, hdd o'r 3 out, grad wknd.* ....(10 to 1 op 8 to 1) 7

CUBIST (Ire) [73] 9-4 Paul Eddery (6) *chsd ldrs on ins, drvn alng 3 fs out, grad wknd*.........(10 to 1 tchd 11 to 1) 8

NORTHERN CHIEF [58] 8-3 K Darley (2) *chsd ldrs, ev ch o'r 2 fs out, sn wknd*..........................(10 to 1 op 8 to 1) 9

516^{6} CHOUETTE [59] 7-11 (7*) D McCabe (9) *al in rear.* ....(20 to 1 op 16 to 1) 10

BARDIA [48] 7-5^{5} (7*) Claire Balding (7) *mid-div til wknd wl o'r 2 fs out*..........................(50 to 1 op 33 to 1) 11

NORLING (Ire) [62] 8-7 Kim Tinkler (1) *al beh, lost tch 3 fs out, tld off*.................................... (20 to 1) 12

Dist: 4l, 1½l, 3½l, ½l, 1½l, ½l, ¾l, 3½l, 5l, 7l. 1m 43.70s. a 5.40s (12 Ran).

SR: 47/26/8/12/1/12/13/8/-/ (Gerecon Italia), J L Dunlop

686 Levy Board Maiden Stakes Class D (3-y-o) £3,669 1¼m.......................(5:20)

482 CIRCUS COLOURS 9-0 W Newnes (4) *trkd ldr, led o'r 2 fs out, pushed clr fnl furlong*........(14 to 1 op 12 to 1) 1

SHIRLEY ROSE 8-9 Dean McKeown (10) *chsd ldrs, drvn alng o'r 3 fs out, kpt on same pace ins last.* ....(14 to 1 op 10 to 1) 2

SAVOY TRUFFLE (Fr) 8-9 A McGlone (9) *in tch, rdn to improve o'r 3 fs out, one pace over one furlong out.* ....(5 to 1 op 7 to 2) 3

MOUNT ROSE 8-11 (3*) J Weaver (8) *chsd ldrs, rdn alng entering strt, kpt on same pace fnl 2 fs.* ....(8 to 1 op 7 to 1) 4

BLUSHING BARADA (USA) 8-9 J Fortune (3) *chsd ldrs til rdn and wknd o'r 2 fs out*........ (14 to 1 op 12 to 1) 5

534^{5} HALMANERROR 9-0 J Carroll (5) *hld up, improved hfwy, not quicken o'r 2 fs out*.......................... (25 to 1) 6

423^{5} RISING WOLF 9-0 K Fallon (6) *in tch, drvn alng entering strt, wknd o'r 2 fs out*.............. (6 to 1 op 7 to 1) 7

AMIARGE 9-0 M Wigham (1) *hld up, rdn 4 fs out, no imprsn*..........(16 to 1 op 33 to 1 tchd 14 to 1) 8
423 FARANDOLE 9-0 G Duffield (7) *beh and early reminders, effrt entering strt, sn btn*........ (12 to 1 tchd 14 to 1) 9
459[5] KASSBAAN (USA) 9-0 B Raymond (11) *sn led and clr, hdd o'r 2 fs out, wknd quickly*.......(13 to 8 fav op 6 to 4) 10
TUSCANIA 8-9 Kim Tinkler (2) *missed break, beh, took clr order hfwy, fdd o'r 3 fs out, tld off*...........(33 to 1) 11
Dist: 4l, 1½l, 10l, 2l, 1½l, ¾l, 2½l, 4l, nk, 15l. 2m 12.10s. a 8.10s (11 Ran).
SR: 39/26/23/8/-/1/ (Exors Of The Late Sir Robin McAlpine), J L Dunlop

SANDOWN (good to soft)
Saturday April 24th
Going Correction: PLUS 0.35 sec. per fur. (races 1,5), PLUS 0.65 (2,3,4)

687 Pizza Hut Maiden Stakes Class D (2-y-o) £3,629 5f 6yds.................... (2:20)

543[2] MONTAYA 9-0 A Geran (7) *cl up, led hfwy, rdn out.* .... (5 to 1 tchd 4 to 1 and 11 to 2) 1
469[6] SILVER WEDGE (USA) 9-0 Pat Eddery (14) *led to hfwy, hrd rdn o'r one furlong out, ev ch ins last, no extr.* ....(4 to 1 fav op 3 to 1 tchd 9 to 2) 2
469[7] LIVELY STREAM 9-0 R Cochrane (8) *chsd ldrs, cld und pres and ev ch one furlong out, one pace.* .... (10 to 1 op 6 to 1 tchd 11 to 1) 3
SMART FAMILY (USA) 9-0 T Quinn (9) *chsd ldrs and sn pushed alng, rdn 2 fs out, kpt on.* ....(8 to 1 op 5 to 1 tchd 9 to 1) 4
ALCOVE 9-0 L Piggott (4) *sn outpcd, hdwy o'r one furlong out, styd on, nrst finish.* .... (5 to 1 tchd 7 to 1 and 9 to 2) 5
PERSIAN AFFAIR (Ire) 8-9 (5*) M Fenton (12) *al prmnt, rdn alng and one pace fnl 2 fs.* .... (16 to 1 op 10 to 1 tchd 20 to 1) 6
WICKLOW BOY (Ire) 9-0 J Comber (10) *sn beh, styd on wl fnl furlong, better for race*........ (25 to 1 op 14 to 1) 7
MISTER BLOY 9-0 W Carson (2) *cl up, pushed alng and ev ch o'r one furlong out, wknd, better for race.* ....(8 to 1 tchd 10 to 1) 8
NONIOS (Ire) 9-0 T Sprake (6) *cl up til rdn and wknd one furlong out, improve.* .... (20 to 1 op 33 to 1 tchd 50 to 1) 9
PRINCE BABAR 9-0 W Hood (13) *jinked sn aftr strt and almost uns rdr, nvr on terms.* .... (33 to 1 op 20 to 1 tchd 50 to 1) 10
CALLING (USA) 9-0 A Munro (5) *al beh.* .... (33 to 1 op 20 to 1 tchd 50 to 1) 11
ROYAL CAPE 9-0 M Roberts (3) *slwly away, sn in tch til wknd hfwy*.......... (12 to 1 op 6 to 1 tchd 14 to 1) 12
RICHARD'S ERROR 8-7 (7*) C Hawksley (11) *sn outpcd.* .... (33 to 1 op 25 to 1 tchd 40 to 1) 13
THE SPIVE 9-0 A Mackay (15) *strted slwly, sn tld off.* ....(33 to 1 tchd 50 to 1) 14
Dist: Hd, 1½l, 2½l, ¾l, hd, 1l, 2l, 2½l, nk, 1½l. 1m 4.19s. a 4.69s (14 Ran).
SR: 41/40/34/24/21/20/16/8/-/ (Malcolm Parrish), J M Troy

688 Thresher Classic Trial Class A (Group 3) (3-y-o) £29,376 1¼m 7yds...........(2:55)

435[2] TRUE HERO (USA) 8-11 R Cochrane (5) *cl up, took keen hold, pushed alng 2 fs out, ran on wl to ld ins last, readily*.............................(7 to 1 op 5 to 1) 1
540* PLACERVILLE (USA) 8-11 Pat Eddery (1) *led til hdd ins fnl furlong, hrd rdn, kpt on.* ....(7 to 4 fav op 11 to 8 tchd 2 to 1) 2
318* MAJORITY (Ire) 8-11 M Roberts (4) *cl up, took keen hold, ev ch 2 fs out, sn rdn and one pace.* .... (11 to 4 op 5 to 2 tchd 3 to 1) 3
541[8] REDENHAM (USA) 8-11 L Piggott (2) *trkd ldrs, brght wide strt, ev ch appr 2 fs out, one pace und pres.* ....(9 to 2 op 3 to 1 tchd 5 to 1) 4
540[5] IOMMELLI (Ire) 8-11 D Biggs (6) *pld hrd in tch, outpcd 3 fs out, kpt on wl frm o'r one out*....(20 to 1 tchd 33 to 1) 5
435[3] VISTO SI STAMPI (Ire) 8-11 W Carson (7) *al beh, tld off fnl 4 fs*................................. (7 to 1 op 6 to 1) 6
Dist: ½l, 3l, nk, ½l, 8l. 2m 16.54s. a 12.64s (6 Ran).
SR: 36/35/29/28/27/11/ (Sheikh Mohammed), J H M Gosden

689 T.G.I. Friday's Gordon Richards EBF Stakes Class A (Group 3) (4-y-o and up) £21,519 1¼m 7yds................. (3:30)

RUBY TIGER 6-8-12 T Quinn (1) *trkd ldrs, pushed alng 2 fs out, led o'r one out, shaken up cl hme.* ....(9 to 2 op 4 to 1 tchd 5 to 1) 1
GREAT PALM (USA) 4-9-1 A Munro (2) *cl up, led 2 fs out till hdd o'r one out, ev ch ins last, no extr und pres close hme*.....................(11 to 2 op 5 to 1 tchd 6 to 1) 2
533* BOLOARDO 4-8-10 W Carson (3) *cl up, lost pl 5 fs out, drpd rear 2 furlongs out, hdwy ins last, styd on wl.* ....(16 to 1 tchd 20 to 1) 3
SILVER WISP (USA) 4-8-10 Pat Eddery (4) *hld up beh, pushed alng o'r 4 fs out, hrd rdn over 2 out, no imprsn til cld ins last, lost 3rd close hme.* ....(5 to 2 fav op 13 to 8) 4
426* YOUNG BUSTER (Ire) 5-8-10 L Piggott (5) *sn clr ld, hdd 2 fs out, wknd ins last*.......(7 to 2 op 3 to 1 tchd 4 to 1) 5
MASAD (Ire) 4-9-3 R Cochrane (6) *hld up beh, effrt o'r 3 fs out, no imprsn*........ (5 to 1 op 9 to 2 tchd 11 to 2) 6
Dist: ½l, 2½l, hd, 1½l, 1l. 2m 12.60s. a 8.70s (6 Ran).
SR: 76/78/68/67/64/69/ (Mrs Philip Blacker), P F I Cole

690 Country Club Hotels Rated Class B (0-100 3-y-o) £12,776 1m 14yds............ (4:40)

558* EASTERN MEMORIES (Ire) [90] 8-8 (7*) D Gibbs (13) *made all, clr 4 fs out, ran on wl whn pressed ins fnl furlong.* ....(8 to 1 tchd 9 to 1) 1
400[6] NEW CAPRICORN (USA) [95] 9-6 Pat Eddery (2) *al prmnt, hrd rdn o'r one furlong out, ev ch ins last, one pace cl hme*.............................(14 to 1 op 12 to 1) 2
514[6] EMBANKMENT (Ire) [87] 8-5 (7*) Mark Denaro (5) *trkd ldrs, rdn o'r 2 fs out, ev ch ins last, one pace.* .... (20 to 1 op 16 to 1 tchd 25 to 1) 3
404* ABERDEEN HEATHER [84] 8-4 (5*) B Doyle (10) *beh, hdwy wl o'r one furlong out, kpt on, nvr nrr.* .... (12 to 1 op 10 to 1) 4
388[4] AZHAR [90] 9-1 M Roberts (4) *wtd wth beh, effrt wl o'r 2 fs out, styd on, nrst finish.* ....(9 to 1 op 8 to 1 tchd 7 to 1 and 10 to 1) 5
REGAL AURA (Ire) [85] 8-10 A Munro (6) *trkd ldrs till and wknd 2 fs out*................... (14 to 1 op 12 to 1) 6
493* BARIK (Ire) [90] 9-1 W Carson (1) *trkd ldrs, smooth hdwy to hold ev ch 3 fs out, rdn o'r 2 out, wknd quickly over one out*........ (6 to 5 on op 5 to 4 on tchd 11 to 10 on) 7
397[4] BRANDONHURST [85] 8-10 S O'Gorman (9) *hld up, effrt o'r 2 fs out, no imprsn.* .... (14 to 1 op 12 to 1 tchd 16 to 1) 8
CONEYBURY (Ire) [96] 9-7 R Cochrane (12) *hld up, effrt 3 fs out, nvr on terms*...............(10 to 1 tchd 12 to 1) 9
TOP PET (Ire) [88] 8-13 T Quinn (11) *led chasing grp til wknd o'r 2 fs out*.....(20 to 1 op 16 to 1 tchd 25 to 1) 10
404[2] SALBUS [92] (v) 9-3 C Rutter (7) *chsd ldrs til wknd o'r 2 fs out*............................ (25 to 1 op 20 to 1) 11
443[2] PATSY GRIMES [82] 8-7 A Mackay (3) *mid-div til wknd 3 fs out*...(100 to 1) 12
Dist: 3l, nk, 6l, ¾l, 3½l, 2l, ½l, hd, nk, 8l. 1m 46.66s. a 7.56s (12 Ran).
SR: 65/61/52/31/35/19/18/11/21/ (Jim Horgan), R Hannon

691 Lansbury Hotels Handicap Class C (0-100 3-y-o) £4,508 5f 6yds.............. (5:15)

460* MAGIC ORB [69] 7-8 A Mackay (5) *hld up in tch gng wl, rdn to ld ins fnl furlong, ran on well.* .... (5 to 1 op 3 to 1 tchd 11 to 2) 1
SOBER LAD (Ire) [75] 8-0 W Carson (2) *cl up, led o'r 3 fs out till hdd over one out, rallied und pres ins last.* .... (6 to 1 op 5 to 1 tchd 13 to 2) 2
SIMPLY SOOTY [80] 8-0 (5*) B Doyle (4) *cl up, outpcd hfwy, styd on wl ins fnl furlong*.....(7 to 2 jt-fav op 5 to 1) 3
347[4] ARADANZA [96] 9-7 Pat Eddery (1) *trkd ldrs, rdn to ld o'r one furlong out, hdd and one pace ins last.* .... (6 to 1 op 9 to 2 tchd 13 to 2) 4
566[6] JOBIE [75] 8-0 A Munro (6) *in tch, hmpd and drpd rear 3 fs out, not reco'r*.................... (10 to 1 op 14 to 1) 5
510[2] AGHAR (Ire) [82] 8-7 M Roberts (3) *cl up, ev ch 2 fs out, one pace appr last, eased*............ (5 to 1 tchd 11 to 2) 6
542[2] PRINCESS OBERON (Ire) [86] 8-6 (5*) M Fenton (7) *led til hdd o'r 3 fs out, wknd 2 out, eased*..........(7 to 2 jt-fav op 5 to 2 tchd 4 to 1) 7
Dist: 1½l, ½l, nk, 3l, 2l, 1½l. 1m 3.34s. a 3.84s (7 Ran).
SR: 38/38/41/56/23/22/20/ (M Olden), J L Spearing

SAN SIRO (ITY) (firm)
Saturday April 24th

692 Premio Ambrosiano (Group 3) (4-y-o and up) £29,022 1¼m................... (4:00)

406[2] SUGUNAS (Ger) 5-8-11 A Boschert, *rcd in 4th, 3rd strt, led wl o'r one furlong out, ran on well*..........(14 to 10) 1
407 FUNNY BABY (Fr) 5-8-9 A Badel, *al cl up, wnt second 5 fs out, jnd ldr o'r 3 out, one pace*.......... (11 to 10 fav) 2
TAFF'S ACRE (Ire) 4-8-11 O Fancera, *trkd ldr till led 5 fs out, hdd wl o'r one out, one pace*........... (43 to 10) 3
GOLDEN MINTAGE (USA) 5-8-9 A Parravani, *5th strt, styd on fnl 2 fs, nvr plcd to chal*.................. (16 to 1) 4
REDIPUGLIA (Ire) 4-8-9 B Jovine, *led for 5 fs, sn wknd.* ....(14 to 1) 5
4682a[9] ASTRO DI LUCE (USA) 4-8-9 J Heloury, *al rear.* (71 to 10) 6
Dist: 3l, hd, 1 ¼l, hd, 14l. 2m 2.60s. (6 Ran).
(Gestut Fahrhof), A Wohler

ST-CLOUD (FR) (good to soft)
Saturday April 24th

Going Correction: PLUS 0.35 sec. per fur.

693 Prix Corrida (Group 3) (4-y-o and up) £23,895 1¼m 110yds.............. (2:30)

DIESE (USA) 4-8-11 T Jarnet, *led, quickened o'r 2 fs out, ran on wl*..............(6 to 5 fav) 1
4306 COMPOTA (Fr) 4-8-11 C Asmussen, *hld up in rear, 6th strt, quickened one and a half fs out, ran on wl.* ....(10 to 1) 2
PAIX BLANCHE (Fr) 4-8-11 D Boeuf, *trkd ldrs, 4th strt, prog to go second 2 fs out, rdn and one pace one and a half out*..............(27 to 10) 3
4711a8 RIVER NYMPH (USA) 4-9-2 F Head, *mid-div, 5th strt, effrt 2 fs out, wknd one and a half out*..............(11 to 1) 4
4307 IRISH SOURCE 4-8-11 O Peslier, *trkd ldr, second strt, rdn and unbl to quicken one and a half fs out*.....(24 to 1) 5
2838 SHEBA DANCER (Fr) 4-9-2 E Legrix, *3rd strt, rdn and wknd sn aftr entering straight*..............(28 to 10) 6
4754a* LADY OF PERSIA (USA) 6-8-11 G Guignard, *al rear.* ....(14 to 1) 7

Dist: 1½l, nk, 2½l, 1l, nose, 2l. 2m 17.40s. a 6.90s (7 Ran).
SR: 65/62/61/61/54/58/49/ (K Abdulla), A Fabre

CAPANNELLE (ITY) (good)
Sunday April 25th

694 Premio Regina Elena (Group 2) (3-y-o) £51,416 1m.......................(3:40)

ANCESTRAL DANCER 8-11 M Hills, *hld up, 5th strt, hdwy to ld 2 fs out, rdn out*.............. 1
FIRM FRIEND (Ire) 8-11 Jacqueline Freda, *hld up, 7th strt, hdwy on rls fnl 2 fs, nrst finish*.............. 2
SEEING (USA) 8-11 F Jovine, *4th strt, hdwy fnl 2 fs, nrst finish*.............. 3
LOVE OF SILVER (USA) 8-11 M Roberts, *3rd strt, jnd ldrs o'r 3 fs out, ev ch over one out, no extr ins last*.............. 4
AISLA (USA) 8-11 V Mezzatesta, *hld up, last strt, ran on fnl 2 fs, nrst finish*.............. 5
JEU DE CARTES (USA) 8-11 M Pasquale, *nvr able to chal.* 6
SHIVANI 8-11 A Luongo, *nvr nrr*.............. 7
LIFTING (Ire) 8-11 H McMahon, *nvr dngrs*.............. 8
ZAIRA DA CESENA (USA) 8-11 S Soto, *led for 6 fs*.............. 9
FOOLISH HEART (Ire) 8-11 L Sorrentino, *6th strt, wknd o'r 2 fs out*.............. 0
SHE'S ANNA 8-11 L Ficuciello, *pressed ldr till wknd quickly aftr strt*.............. 0

Dist: ½l, ½l, ¾l, sht-nk, 2l, hd, 1 ¼l, nose, 3½l, 3l. 1m 39.90s. (11 Ran).
(Innlaw Racing), M Bell

COLOGNE (GER) (good)
Sunday April 25th

695 Gerling Preis (Group 2) (4-y-o and up) £29,592 1½m.................... (3:40)

PROTEKTOR (Ger) 4-9-0 T Hellier, *rcd in 3rd, led and drifted rght one and a half fs out, ran on wl*.............. 1
4067 TWIST AND TURN 4-9-2 B Raymond, *trkd ldr till led 3 fs out, hdd one and a half furlongs out, kpt on*.............. 2
4077 MODHISH (Ire) 4-9-4 S Guillot, *hld up, hmpd whn chalg one and a half fs out, swtchd to outsd, fnshd fst*.............. 3
4063 EMBARCADERO (Ger) 5-9-0 A Best, *6th strt, ran on fnl 2 fs*.............. 4
APIS (Ger) 4-9-0 O Schick, *cl 4th strt, no extr fnl 2 fs*.............. 5
CHESA PLANA 4-8-9 M Rimmer, *al rear*.............. 6
406 ZOHAR (Ger) 4-9-4 A Helfenbein, *led till 3 fs out, sn wknd.* 7

Dist: ½l, ½l, 3½l, 2l, 5l, 8l. 2m 31.45s. (7 Ran).
(D Joswich), A Lowe

LONGCHAMP (FR) (soft)
Sunday April 25th

Going Correction: PLUS 0.55 sec. per fur.

696 Prix Greffulhe (Group 2) (3-y-o) £37,091 1 ¼m 110yds.......................(2:40)

4083 HUNTING HAWK (Ire) 9-2 T Jarnet (1) *trkd ldr till led 2 fs out, ran on wl*..............(6 to 5 fav) 1
360* BIGSTONE (Ire) 9-2 D Boeuf (2) *3rd strt, quickened o'r 2 fs out, hrd rdn fnl furlong, not rch wnr*..............(7 to 2) 2
408* TALLOIRES (USA) 9-2 G Guignard (5) *led till 2 fs out, sn rdn and one pace*..............(28 to 10) 3
5366 KADOUNOR (Fr) 9-2 O Doleuze (3) *4th strt, hrd rdn 2 fs out, nvr able to chal*..............(51 to 10) 4
2663 BRAZANY (USA) 9-2 C Asmussen (6) *nvr dngrs.* (69 to 10) 5
FASTNESS (Ire) 9-2 F Head (4) *al last*..............(14 to 1) 6

Dist: 1½l, 1½l, ¾l, 4l, ¾l. 2m 18.40s. a 9.40s (6 Ran).
SR: 66/63/60/58/50/48/ (Sheikh Mohammed), A Fabre

697 Prix de la Grotte (Group 3) (3-y-o) £23,895 1m..............................(3:40)

BAYA (USA) 9-2 T Jarnet (1) *4th strt, swtchd o'r 2 fs out, chlgd one and a half out, led one out, ran on wl.* ....(6 to 5 jt-fav) 1
GOLD SPLASH (USA) 9-2 O Doleuze (2) *second strt, led 2 fs out to one out, kpt on one pace*..............(13 to 10) 2
HAWK BEAUTY (USA) 9-2 E Legrix (6) *3rd and hrd rdn strt, styd on fnl furlong*..............(10 to 1) 3
3593 KIRUNA (USA) 9-2 P Bodin (4) *led to 2 fs out, sn rdn and wknd*..............(6 to 5 jt-fav) 4
GRANSE OAKS (USA) 9-2 C Asmussen (3) *5th strt, no hdwy fnl 2 fs*..............(42 to 10) 5
359* SHOWGUM (Fr) 9-2 A Junk (7) *nvr dngrs*..............(78 to 10) 6

Dist: 2l, nk, ¾l, 2l, 4l. 1m 45.10s. a 6.60s (6 Ran).
SR: 69/63/62/60/54/42/ (Sheikh Mohammed), A Fabre

PONTEFRACT (soft)
Monday April 26th

Going Correction: PLUS 0.30 sec. per fur.

698 EBF Tote Maiden Stakes Class D (2-y-o) £3,435 5f........................ (2:45)

4338 RAVEN'S RETURN (Ire) 9-0 S Perks (9) *made all, shaken up o'r one furlong out, hld on gmely ins last*..... (16 to 1) 1
4698 PERSIAN HERITAGE 9-0 R Cochrane (8) *in tch, effrt and rdn alng o'r 2 fs out, kpt on wl fnl furlong, jst hld.* ....(13 to 2 op 5 to 1) 2
3256 ROSIE VALENTINE 8-9 M Roberts (13) *wth ldr, ev ch o'r one furlong out, not quicken ins last.* ....(10 to 1 op 7 to 1) 3
5062 DISTINCTIVE AIR 9-0 W Newnes (4) *chsd ldrs on ins, ev ch o'r one furlong out, no extr inside last.* ....(7 to 2 op 4 to 1 tchd 9 to 2) 4
4663 CLOSE TO REALITY 9-0 K Fallon (7) *chsd ldrs, ev ch o'r one furlong out, wknd ins last.* ....(7 to 2 op 4 to 1 tchd 5 to 1 and 3 to 1) 5
5542 PASSING PLAYER (USA) 9-0 M Hills (6) *in tch, shaken up entering strt, no imprsn.* ....(9 to 4 fav op 7 to 4 tchd 13 to 8) 6
5866 BLASTER BATES (USA) 9-0 D Nicholls (2) *hld up, drvn alng hfwy, not pace to chal*..............(33 to 1) 7
THREEPENNY-BRIDGE 9-0 T Sprake (12) *chsd ldrs on outsd, wknd entering strt*.............. (16 to 1 op 14 to 1) 8
4337 GRANDMAN (Ire) 8-7 (7*) Darren Moffatt (10) *beh, sn pushed alng, nvr on terms*..............(25 to 1) 9
DIAMOND FRONTIER (Ire) 9-0 G Duffield (5) *chsd ldrs, drvn aftr 2 fs, grad lost pl*..............(12 to 1) 10+
TIMES ZANDO 8-9 J Fortune (3) *slwly into strd, al beh.* ....(40 to 1 op 33 to 1) 10+
673 FLYING VISION (Ire) 8-9 G Bardwell (1) *sn pushed alng in rear, lost tch hfwy*..............(100 to 1) 12
HARPO'S SPECIAL 9-0 Raymond Berry (11) *dwlt, nvr a factor*..............(33 to 1 op 25 to 1) 13

Dist: Sht-hd, 1l, 1½l, 1½l, 1½l, 2l, 2½l, nk, 2½l, dd-ht. 1m 6.10s. a 4.90s (13 Ran).
SR: 32/31/22/21/15/9/1/-/-/ (A S Hill), R Hollinshead

699 Tote Credit Selling Stakes Class G (3-y-o) £2,448 1½m 8yds................. (3:15)

4996 PONDERING (v) 8-12 M Roberts (5) *patiently rdn, hdwy to ld o'r 3 fs out, ridden entering strt, ran on wl fnl furlong*..............(5 to 1 op 6 to 1 tchd 13 to 2) 1
4992 MOUNTAIN WILLOW (v) 8-7 L Dettori (9) *chsd ldrs, outpcd and drvn alng o'r 2 fs out, kpt on fnl furlong, took second on line*......(15 to 8 fav op 7 to 4 tchd 2 to 1) 2
4993 MR GENEAOLOGY (USA) (h,bl) 8-12 R Price (4) *slwly into strd, sn reco'red to midfield, rdn and ev ch over 2 fs out, edgd lft over one out, no extr.* ....(9 to 2 op 7 to 2 tchd 5 to 1) 3
6085 GOODBYE MILLIE 8-9 (5*) O Pears (3) *settled mid-div, improved on ins o'r 3 fs out, not quicken entering strt.* ....(8 to 1 tchd 9 to 1) 4
5025 PERSIAN STAR (Fr) 8-7 W Newnes (12) *hld up, effrt 5 fs out, not pace to chal*..............(33 to 1) 5
423 THE BRACKETEER 8-12 D Wilkinson (11) *hld up, rdn 5 fs out, no imprsn frm 3 out*..............(50 to 1) 6
437 STAR MINSTREL (Ire) (bl) 8-12 J Reid (13) *cl up, led aftr 2 fs till o'r 3 out, wknd over two out, tld off.* ....(5 to 1 op 4 to 1) 7
5099 EVE'S TREASURE 8-7 G Bardwell (6) *chsd ldrs, rdn alng o'r 4 fs out, wknd over 3 out, tld off.* ....(16 to 1 op 14 to 1) 8
531 WHO'S THE BEST (Ire) 8-12 J Lowe (7) *led 2 fs, chsd ldrs, wknd o'r 3 out, tld off*..............(12 to 1) 9
5035 TELEPHONIC (USA) 8-12 G Duffield (2) *hld up in rear, effrt 5 fs out, wknd 3 out, tld off.* ....(20 to 1 op 25 to 1 tchd 33 to 1) 10
3396 HUSH BABY (Ire) 8-7 (7*) G Forster (8) *chsd ldrs, rdn and wknd o'r 3 fs out*..............(20 to 1) 11
5028 THREEOFUS 8-12 R Cochrane (1) *hld up, drvn 5 fs out, wknd, tld off*..............(50 to 1) 12
WILD EXPRESSION 8-12 M Wood (10) *settled rear, drvn 4 fs out, sn btn, tld off*..............(33 to 1) 13

Dist: 1½l, sht-hd, 8l, 25l, 6l, ½l, 12l, hd, 1l, 1½l. 2m 45.80s. a 10.80s (13 Ran).
SR: 26/18/22/8/-/-/ (Paul Deakin), S Dow

700 Tote Dual Forecast Handicap Class D (0-80 3-y-o and up) £3,980 6f............. (3:45)

505⁵ BLUE GRIT [59] 7-8-7 J Lowe (10) *beh, sn pushed alng, hdwy and squeezed through on ins o'r one furlong out, led inside last, styd on wl*........ (25 to 1 op 16 to 1) 1
505* SAGEBRUSH ROLLER [82] 5-10-2 G Duffield (15) *beh, hdwy entering strt, edgd lft and ran on strly fnl furlong*............................(6 to 1 tchd 11 to 2) 2
636 BALLAD DANCER [53] 8-7-8 (7*) Darren Moffatt (9) *beh, styd on wl frm o'r one furlong out, nvr nrr.* .... (33 to 1 op 25 to 1) 3
505³ SONDERISE [62] 4-8-10 W Newnes (11) *mid-div, rdn and hdwy o'r one furlong out, no extr ins last.* ....(14 to 1 tchd 16 to 1) 4
501⁶ BRIGHT PARAGON (Ire) [46] 4-7-6⁵ (7*) C Hawksley (8) *led 2 fs, chsd ldrs, drvn alng o'r two out, no extr fnl furlong.* ....(14 to 1) 5
565³ WELLSY LAD (USA) [53] (bl) 6-8-1 W Carson (1) *chsd ldrs, led aftr 2 fs, shaken up entering strt, hdd ins last, sn btn*.................. (9 to 1 op 10 to 1) 6
4690a⁸ AYR RAIDER [61] 6-8-2 (7*) R Havlin (2) *slwly into strd, beh and sn rdn, hdwy on outsd entering strt, kpt on ins last, nrst finish*..................(20 to 1 tchd 25 to 1) 7
591 PAGEBOY [66] (bl) 4-9-0 Dale Gibson (5) *in tch, rdn hfwy, one pace o'r one furlong out*.................(10 to 1) 8
429* PENNY HASSET [73] 5-9-7 T Lucas (4) *chsd ldrs, drvn alng hfwy, wknd appr fnl furlong*.......(13 to 2 op 6 to 1) 9
475⁵ PHARAOH'S DANCER [72] 6-9-6 M Roberts (7) *nvr far away, effrt and rdn o'r 2 fs out, wknd appr last.* ....(3 to 1 fav tchd 7 to 2) 10
591⁶ MISS MOVIE WORLD [54] 4-8-2 P Robinson (6) *in tch, pushed alng appr strt, wknd o'r one furlong out.* .... (14 to 1 op 12 to 1) 11
655² TWILIGHT FALLS [45] 8-7-7³ (3*) N Kennedy (12) *in tch, rdn alng hfwy, wknd*.......(6 to 1 tchd 9 to 2 and 7 to 1) 12
440⁷ BASSIO (Bel) [50] 4-7-12 N Carlisle (13) *slwly into strd, al beh*............................(16 to 1) 13
615² ARC LAMP [58] 7-8-6 J Fortune (14) *chsd ldrs, drvn alng o'r 2 fs out, wknd entering strt*.... (20 to 1 op 14 to 1) 14
107⁵ HONEY VISION [45] (bl) 4-7-7 G Bardwell (16) *beh, sn pushed alng, nvr on terms*.........(20 to 1 op 14 to 1) 15
CRAIGIE BOY [72] 3-8-3 (5*) O Pears (3) *slwly into strd, al struggling*.................. (40 to 1 op 33 to 1) 16

Dist: Nk, 1½l, 1½l, 1½l, hd, ½l, 2l, 2l, 1l, ½l. 1m 19.50s. a 4.80s (16 Ran).
SR: 33/55/20/23/1/7/13/10/9/ (C Michael Wilson), M Dods

701 Tote Bookmakers Conditions Stakes Class C (4-y-o and up) £5,826 1m 4yds.... (4:15)

525⁵ TIK FA (USA) (v) 4-9-1 B Raymond (1) *trkd ldr, rdn alng entering strt, ran on to ld ins fnl furlong, kpt on wl.* ....(9 to 4 on op 5 to 2 on tchd 2 to 1 on) 1
ARANY 6-8-12 P Robinson (2) *led, shaken up 2 fs out, hdd ins last, not quicken*.....(7 to 4 op 6 to 4 tchd 2 to 1) 2

Won by 3½l. 1m 48.10s. a 6.00s (2 Ran).
SR: 47/33/ (Abdullah Ali), B Hanbury

702 Tote Marathon Handicap Class E (0-70 4-y-o and up) £3,106 2m 5f 122yds...... (4:45)

GRACE CARD [42] 7-8-6 R Cochrane (5) *chsd ldg pair, led o'r 4 fs out, clr appr strt, easily.* .... (11 to 10 fav op Evens tchd 5 to 4) 1
427⁸ CREEAGER [56] 11-9-3 (3*) S D Williams (7) *hld up rear, improved o'r 2 fs out, rdn and no extr fnl furlong.* .... (10 to 1 op 8 to 1 tchd 12 to 1) 2
382⁶ ENKINDLE [29] 6-7-0 (7*) Darren Moffatt (4) *mid-div, lost pl one m out, drvn alng 4 fs out, styd on wl frm 2 out, nvr dngrs*.......................... (50 to 1 tchd 66 to 1) 3
427⁵ LAFKADIO [32] 6-7-10 J Lowe (1) *beh, improved one m out, rdn alng o'r 4 fs out, wknd appr strt.* ....(14 to 1 tchd 16 to 1 and 12 to 1) 4
427 SILLARS STALKER (Ire) [57] 5-9-2 (5*) O Pears (10) *in tch, rdn alng o'r 3 fs out, wknd entering strt.* ....(3 to 1 tchd 100 to 30) 5
626⁴ HUNTING GROUND [48] 5-8-12 W Newnes (11) *hld up beh, rdn to improve 6 fs out, wknd wl o'r 3 out, tld off.* ....(8 to 1 tchd 9 to 1) 6
438⁴ GREEN LANE (USA) [63] 5-9-13 J Reid (8) *in tch, cld hfwy, drvn alng 4 fs out, wknd, tld off*.... (10 to 1 op 8 to 1) 7
MY SWAN SONG [31] 8-7-8⁴ (5*) A Garth (2) *dwlt, hld up rear, rdn o'r 4 fs out, sn btn, eased 2 out, tld off.* .... (25 to 1 op 20 to 1) 8
PRECIOUS MEMORIES [30] 8-7-8¹ N Carlisle (9) *led till o'r 4 fs out, sn wknd, tld off*........ (100 to 1 tchd 200 to 1) 9
BE MY HABITAT [42] 4-8-0 W Carson (12) *chsd ldr, rdn one m out, wknd o'r 4 fs out, tld off*....(16 to 1 op 14 to 1) 10

Dist: 7l, ½l, 2½l, 6l, 10l, 7l, ¾l, 20l, 3l. 5m 11.20s. a 31.20s (10 Ran).
(G A Farndon), Mrs M Reveley

703 Tote Placepot Conditions Stakes Class D (4-y-o and up) £3,201 1¼m 6yds..... (5:15)

BADIE (USA) 4-8-11 W Carson (3) *chsd ldrs, outpcd and rdn entering strt, str run and edgd lft ins fnl furlong, sn led, kpt on wl*.................. (7 to 4 op 13 to 8) 1
525 SOIREE (Ire) 4-8-10 J Reid (4) *hld up last, hdwy o'r 2 fs out, ev ch ins last, no extr.* ....(11 to 8 fav tchd 6 to 4 and 5 to 4) 2
79² MARTINI EXECUTIVE (bl) 5-8-10 K Fallon (2) *led, clr aftr one furlong, shaken up o'r 2 out, hdd ins last, one pace*..(50 to 1) 3
DESERT ZONE (USA) 4-8-10 L Dettori (1) *chsd ldr, effrt o'r 2 fs out, chlgd over one out, ev ch whn bumped ins last, sn one pace*.......................(14 to 1 op 25 to 1) 4
FAWZ (Ire) 4-8-5 R Price (5) *keen hold, hld up, rdn 3 fs out, wknd o'r one out*.......(4 to 1 tchd 9 to 2 and 7 to 2) 5

Dist: ¾l, 2l, ½l, 12l. 2m 19.30s. a 11.10s (5 Ran).
SR: 16/13/9/8/-/ (Hamdan Al-Maktoum), J L Dunlop

SLIGO (IRE) (heavy) Monday April 26th

704 Strandhill (C & G) Maiden (3-y-o) £2,243 6f 110yds............................ (3:00)

489⁴ SUAVE GROOM (Ire) (bl) 9-0 M J Kinane (4).... (11 to 8 on) 1
BOCANDE (Ire) 9-0 S Craine (5)......................... (7 to 1) 2
551⁴ PERSIAN RENDEZVOUS (Ire) 9-0 P V Gilson (2).... (2 to 1) 3
GOODIES TWO STEP (Ire) 8-12 (2*) R M Burke (3) (12 to 1) 4
489⁶ DENZILLE LANE (Ire) (bl) 9-0 A J Nolan (1)........(16 to 1) 5

Dist: ¾l, 7l, 1½l, 8l. 1m 36.90s. (5 Ran).
(Dr Anne J F Gillespie), D K Weld

705 Ballymote Fillies Maiden (3-y-o) £2,243 6f 110yds............................ (3:30)

488⁴ PENNINE MIST (Ire) 9-0 M J Kinane (8)............(6 to 1) 1
ELLE A TED (Ire) 9-0 W J Supple (3)...................(12 to 1) 2
BUSINESS CENTRE (Ire) 8-8 (6*) J J Behan (10)...(20 to 1) 3
JU JU'S GIRL (Ire) 9-0 K J Manning (5)........(10 to 9 on) 4
280 DIGNIFIED (Ire) 9-0 P Shanahan (4)..............(16 to 1) 5
311 SLEET (Ire) 9-0 P V Gilson (7)..........................(7 to 1) 6
PERSIAN LIGHT (Ire) 8-4 (10*) A J Dempsey (1)... (20 to 1) 7
599³ TAUTEN (Ire) 9-0 S Craine (6)........................(7 to 2) 8
SMOULDERING (Ire) 9-0 W J O'Connor (9)....... (10 to 1) 9
488 RAYJOHN GIRL (Ire) 9-0 A J Nolan (2)............(50 to 1) 10

Dist: 4l, 2l, 2l, 11l. 1m 37.70s. (10 Ran).
(Mrs Sean M Collins), D K Weld

706 Four Lanterns Handicap (0-70 4-y-o and up) £2,760 1½m.................... (5:00)

575⁶ ALTEREZZA (USA) [-] (bl) 6-10-0 M J Kinane (11)... (3 to 1) 1
575 STEEL GEM (Ire) [-] (bl) 4-8-13 W J O'Connor (4).. (10 to 1) 2
JESSIE'S BOY (Ire) [-] 4-7-5 (2*) D G O'Shea (9)... (33 to 1) 3
575* LYPHARD ABU (Ire) [-] 5-9-4 (6*,4ex) J A Heffernan (2) .... (7 to 4 fav) 4
BANKONIT (Ire) [-] 5-8-11 W J Supple (1).........(12 to 1) 5
281 MUMMYS BEST [-] 7-8-10 (8*) R V Skelly (6)......(20 to 1) 6
281⁴ WINTER DREAMS (Ire) [-] 4-8-9 (10*) T Hagger (7).. (4 to 1) 7
487 ASTRA (Ire) [-] (bl) 4-8-13 (6*) J R Barry (10)........(8 to 1) 8
598⁶ TANAMANDA (Ire) [-] 4-8-2 (6*) J J Behan (8).......(7 to 1) 9
TIME IS UP (Ire) [-] 4-9-0 (4*) W J Smith (5).........(7 to 1) 10
SENSITIVE KING (Ire) [-] 5-7-12 (2*) R M Burke (3).. (9 to 1) 11

Dist: ½l, 2l, 5l, 7l. 3m 23.10s. (11 Ran).
(M G Hynes), D K Weld

SOUTHWELL (A.W) (std) Monday April 26th

Going Correction: PLUS 0.05 sec. per fur.

707 Wensleydale Rating Related Maiden Stakes Class E (3-y-o) £2,743 7f..... (2:30)

609³ NORTH ARDAR 9-0 Dean McKeown (4) *trkd ldr on outsd, led o'r 2 fs out, pushed out.* .... (5 to 2 op 9 to 4 tchd 11 to 4) 1
362⁵ ARAGON KING 8-11 (3*) J Weaver (2) *led till hdd o'r 2 fs out, one pace aftr*...................... (7 to 1 op 5 to 1) 2
414² SAXON MAGIC 8-9 J Quinn (3) *chsd ldrs, rdn 3 fs out, some hdwy 2 out, one pace aftr*....... (5 to 4 fav op Evens) 3
NEWINSKY 8-9 (5*) Stephen Davies (1) *al same pl, lost tch wl o'r 2 fs out*....................... (14 to 1 op 8 to 1) 4
GALEJADE 8-9 A Mackay (5) *jinked rght leaving stalls, al struggling in rear*....... (4 to 1 op 3 to 1 tchd 9 to 2) 5

Dist: 5l, 2l, 15l, 15l. 1m 32.30s. a 6.20s (5 Ran).
SR: 12/-/ (L Webster), M Johnston

708 Gloucester Selling Stakes Class G (2-y-o) £2,070 5f.......................... (3:00)

607³ EN-CEE-TEE 8-11 J Fanning (12) *nvr far away, hdwy o'r 2 fs out, led over one out, edgd rght, cmftbly.* .... (7 to 2 op 4 to 1 tchd 9 to 2 and 5 to 1) 1
KANGRA VALLEY 8-6 Dean McKeown (9) *led till hdd o'r one furlong out, ran on one pace*... (12 to 1 op 8 to 1) 2
490⁷ THE KAMIKAZE QUEEN 8-6 R Perham (7) *al prmnt, outpcd appr fnl furlong*................. (33 to 1 op 20 to 1) 3

325⁹ WILKS DREAM (Ire) 7-13 (7*) P McCabe (5) *mid-div, rdn and styd on appr fnl furlong, nvr nrr.* ....(25 to 1 op 12 to 1) 4
VIVS FUTURE (Ire) 8-6 N Day (8) *hld up, hdwy ins fnl 2 fs, nvr nrr*................ (17 to 2 op 3 to 1 tchd 9 to 1) 5
490² ROSE OF GLENN 8-6 J Quinn (11) *broke wl, sn rdn and lost pl hfwy, styd on ag'n ins fnl furlong.* ....(4 to 1 op 5 to 2 tchd 9 to 2) 6
490⁸ BESSIE'S WILL 8-6 A Mackay (2) *chsd ldr till wknd wl o'r one furlong out*.................. (33 to 1 op 25 to 1) 7
374⁵ CRUISING CHICK 8-6 F Norton (10) *al outpcd.* ....(20 to 1 op 16 to 1) 8
ALICE OF LOXLEY 8-6 N Connorton (13) *slwly away, al beh*................................(33 to 1 op 25 to 1) 9
SE VENDE (Ire) 8-11 J Carroll (14) *speed for 3 fs.* ....(3 to 1 fav tchd 7 to 2 and 11 to 4) 10
299⁸ DUCHESS DAISY (bl) 8-6 Kim Tinkler (6) *al beh.* ....(20 to 1 op 8 to 1) 11
395 SALTPETRE (Ire) (bl) 8-11 M Wigham (1) *rcd alone far side, in tch till wknd 2 fs out*.......... (20 to 1 op 10 to 1) 12
CHEEKY CHAPPY 8-11 S Wood (4) *slwly away, al beh.* ....(20 to 1 op 12 to 1) 13
337⁸ MACE EL REEM 8-6 D Biggs (3) *in tch early, outpcd frm hfwy*......................................(14 to 1) 14

Dist: 3½l, 4l, 1½l, hd, 1l, 1½l, 3l, 1½l, nk, 3½l. 1m 2.10s. a 4.20s (14 Ran).
SR: 18/-/-/-/-/-/ (North Cheshire Trading & Storage Ltd), T Fairhurst

709 Leicester Claiming Stakes Class F (4-y-o and up) £2,691 1½m................(3:30)

645 TEMPERING 7-9-7 S Wood (2) *made all, clr aftr 4 fs, eased ins last, unchlgd.* ....(7 to 4 fav op 11 to 10 on tchd 2 to 1) 1
MUST BE MAGICAL (USA) 5-8-9 G Hind (6) *hld up, hdwy 4 fs out, styd on to go second cl hme*........... (10 to 1) 2
520³ QUALITAIR RHYTHM (Ire) (v) 5-8-9 D Biggs (11) *hld up, hdwy 7 fs out, chsd wnr furlongs out till no extr nr finish*.......................... (4 to 1 op 2 to 1) 3
332⁷ APPLIANCEOFSCIENCE 6-8-2 (7*) P McCabe (5) *beh, styd on fnl 3 fs, nvr dngrs*.......................... (20 to 1) 4
227 POP TO STANS 4-9-0 M Wigham (7) *in rear, effrt 4 fs out, nvr nr to chal*.............................. (10 to 1) 5
442⁹ MR WISHING WELL (e/s) 7-8-7 C Rutter (13) *beh till hdwy o'r 3 fs out, nvr nr to chal*.......... (7 to 1 op 6 to 1) 6
BOOGIE BOPPER (Ire) (v) 4-8-13 J Quinn (10) *chsd ldrs till lost tch hfwy*..........(6 to 1 op 5 to 1 tchd 13 to 2) 7
DASHING FELLOW (Ire) 5-8-8 S Whitworth (1) *chsd ldrs to hfwy, sn beh*................................ (25 to 1) 8
396⁵ VALATCH 5-8-13 J Carroll (4) *al beh.* (12 to 1 op 25 to 1) 9
495⁹ PONDERED BID (bl) 9-7-13 (7*) Kim McDonnell (8) *al beh.* ....(33 to 1) 10
416 DAZZLING FIRE (Ire) 4-8-10 Dean McKeown (3) *chsd wnr till wknd quickly 4 fs out*.........(10 to 1 op 14 to 1) 11
SWYNFORD FLYER 4-8-6 L Charnock (9) *in tch to hfwy, sn beh, tld off*.................................. (33 to 1) 12

Dist: 10l, nk, 8l, 1l, 1½l, 8l, 5l, nk, nk, 10l. 2m 42.20s. a 8.30s (12 Ran).
SR: 30/-/-/-/-/-/ (David W Chapman), D W Chapman

710 Edam Handicap Class E (0-70 3-y-o and up) £3,106 1m......................(4:00)

295 BRACKENTHWAITE [68] 3-8-7 (7*) V Halliday (9) *wl in rear till gd hdwy 2 fs out, led jst ins last, all out.* ....(6 to 1 op 7 to 2) 1
415* CERTAIN WAY (Ire) [60] 3-8-3 (3*) S Maloney (4) *al prmnt, led 3 fs out, hdd jst ins last, rallied gmely und pres, just fld*.................................(9 to 1 op 8 to 1) 2
592⁵ AMENABLE [67] 8-10-0 W Woods (6) *beh till hdwy on outsd o'r 3 fs out, ev ch 2 out, one pace.* .... (7 to 2 fav op 5 to 1 tchd 11 to 2 and 3 to 1) 3
363³ DIAMOND INTHE DARK (USA) [54] (v) 5-9-1 Dean McKeown (1) *al prmnt, one pace fnl 2 fs*...... (12 to 1 op 10 to 1) 4
4680a⁸ HARCLIFF [58] 4-9-0 (5*) K Rutter (12) *towards rear till styd on towards fnl 2 fs, nvr dngrs.* (16 to 1 op 25 to 1) 5
274⁷ EXPRESS SERVICE [59] 4-9-3 (3*) Emma O'Gorman (5) *in tch till outpcd fnl 2 fs*............... (16 to 1 op 14 to 1) 6
565⁵ CLEDESCHAMPS [46] 4-8-7 S Morris (15) *slwly away, sn in tch, wknd o'r 2 fs out*..................... (14 to 1) 7
650³ STOPROVERITATE [61] 4-9-8 N Connorton (13) *al beh.* ....(8 to 1 op 5 to 1) 8
622⁴ SUNSET STREET (Ire) [51] 5-8-12 C Rutter (10) *al towards rear*..(14 to 1) 9
409 JOVIAL KATE (USA) [51] 6-8-12 J Carroll (8) *led till hdd 3 fs out, rdn and wknd wl o'r one out*............ (20 to 1) 10
OBSIDIAN GREY [60] 6-9-0 (7*) S Sanders (14) *nvr on terms.* .... (20 to 1 op 16 to 1) 11
4764a GREEN'S SEAGO (USA) [54] 5-9-1 J Quinn (7) *in tch till wknd o'r 2 fs out*............ (33 to 1 op 20 to 1) 12
4669a³ KING'S GUEST (Ire) [64] 4-9-11 W Ryan (11) *al beh.* .... (12 to 1 op 7 to 1) 13
ROCK SONG (Ire) [52] 4-8-13 G Hind (16) *mid-div till wknd o'r 2 fs out*........................ (20 to 1 op 16 to 1) 14
492⁴ HIGHBORN (Ire) [48] 4-8-9 J Fanning (2) *prmnt to o'r hfwy, wkng whn clipped heels of another horse, uns rdr over 2 fs out*............. (10 to 1 op 12 to 1 tchd 9 to 1) ur

Dist: Hd, 8l, 2½l, 1l, 5l, 2l, 2l, 1l, 1l, 3l. 1m 43.10s. a 4.10s (15 Ran).
SR: 45/36/34/13/14/-/ (Alex Gorrie), T D Barron

711 Gouda Fillies Handicap Class E (0-70 3-y-o) £2,976 7f.......................(4:30)

503⁶ NELLIE'S GAMBLE [50] 8-1 (3*) S Maloney (11) *wtd wth, hdwy to go second 2 fs out, led o'r one out, sn clr.* ....(10 to 1 op 8 to 1) 1
PENNY BANGER (Ire) [50] 8-4 Dean McKeown (8) *outpcd, hdwy 2 fs out, styd on to go second ins last.* ....(10 to 1 op 7 to 1) 2
447³ VILAMAR (Ire) [41] 7-9¹ J Quinn (4) *led till hdd o'r one furlong out, one pace*......................(14 to 1) 3
532² ROSE FLYER (Ire) [58] 8-5 (7*) D McCabe (13) *slwly away, in rear till hdwy o'r 2 fs out, nvr nrr.* (5 to 1 op 4 to 1) 4
LOWRIANNA (Ire) [48] 8-2 A Mackay (6) *slwly away, sn chsd ldrs, one pace fnl 2 fs*...................(16 to 1) 5
532⁵ MARIBELLA [59] 8-13 F Norton (10) *mid-div, effrt o'r 2 fs out, nvr nr to chal*..........................(12 to 1) 6
606⁵ STORMY HEIGHTS [64] 9-4 S Whitworth (1) *in frnt rnk till wknd 2 fs out*................. (10 to 1 op 12 to 1) 7
MALZETA (Ire) [45] 7-13 E Johnson (9) *nvr on terms.* ....(12 to 1) 8
519³ GROGFRYN [59] 8-13 J Carroll (3) *al beh, lost tch 3 fs out.* ....(8 to 1) 9
394⁷ DON'T BE SAKI (Ire) [54] 8-8 N Connorton (7) *al beh.* ....(12 to 1) 10
4762a⁶ JOELLISE [43] 7-4 (7*) Claire Balding (5) *rdn hfwy, al beh.* ....(33 to 1) 11
455* CHAMPAGNE GRANDY [67] 9-7 Lorna Vincent (2) *in frnt rnk till wknd o'r 2 fs out.* ....(9 to 2 fav op 4 to 1 tchd 5 to 1) 12
CHUMMY'S FRIEND (Ire) [47] 7-8 (7*) S McCarthy (12) *beh frm hfwy*.............................(10 to 1 op 4 to 1) 13

Dist: 10l, 2½l, 2l, 2½l, hd, 5l, 1½l, 2l, 1½l, nk. 1m 30.80s. a 4.70s (13 Ran).
SR: 25/-/-/-/-/-/ (C R Galloway), A P Stringer

712 Cheddar Median Auction Maiden Stakes Class F (3-y-o) £2,243 1m..........(5:00)

TRIANGLEPOINT (Ire) 8-9 W Hood (4) *trkd ldr, led o'r 2 fs out, sn hdd, ran on to ld ag'n jst ins last, pushed out.* ....(15 to 2 op 5 to 1 tchd 8 to 1 and 10 to 1) 1
CASTEL ROSSELO 9-0 F Norton (7) *sn pushed alng, cruised into ld 2 fs out, put ears back and hng rght jst ins last, not run on.* ....(5 to 2 on op 4 to 1 on tchd 9 to 4 on) 2
MARATHIA 8-9 W Woods (6) *chsd ldrs, outpcd o'r 2 fs out, styd on ag'n ins last*............. (25 to 1 op 33 to 1) 3
422⁶ CANDARELA 8-9 N Day (2) *led till hdd o'r 2 fs out, sn btn.* .... (14 to 1 op 10 to 1) 4
GRANDERISE (Ire) 9-0 L Charnock (1) *al beh, no ch fnl 3 fs.* ....(33 to 1) 5
583 TRIPLE SALKO (Ire) 8-9 C Rutter (3) *sn rdn alng, al beh, tld off*...................(7 to 1 op 5 to 1) 6
KERRIA 8-9 Alex Greaves (5) *slwly away, al beh, tld off.* ....(20 to 1 tchd 25 to 1) 7

Dist: 1½l, ¾l, 12l, 4l, 15l, hd. 1m 46.30s. a 7.30s (7 Ran).
(S A Meacock), G A Pritchard-Gordon

713 Cheshire Maiden Stakes Class D (3-y-o) £3,289 5f.......................... (5:30)

504⁵ SABO THE HERO (v) 9-0 G Duffield (3) *made all, edgd rght and drvn out fnl furlong*..... (2 to 1 jt-fav tchd 9 to 4) 1
641⁵ CLOUDY REEF 8-9 W Ryan (4) *chsd wnr, ev ch appr fnl furlong, no imprsn ins last*....(2 to 1 jt-fav op 11 to 8) 2
418⁵ LAID BACK BEN 8-9 (5*) Stephen Davies (6) *al same pl, sn rdn alng, no hdwy fnl furlong.* .... (9 to 1 op 7 to 1 tchd 10 to 1) 3
ADAMPARIS 8-9 N Day (2) *in tch to hfwy.* .... (11 to 4 op 9 to 4) 4
455 BOLD TREASURE (Ire) (v) 8-9 Dean McKeown (5) *al outpcd.* ....(33 to 1) 5
ASCOM PAGER (Ire) 8-9 F Norton (1) *al struggling in rear.* .... (33 to 1 op 20 to 1) 6

Dist: 1½l, 2l, 4l, ½l, 10l. 1m 1.40s. a 3.50s (6 Ran).
SR: 35/24/21/ (Mrs David Thompson), Sir Mark Prescott

WINDSOR (good to soft)
Monday April 26th

Going Correction: PLUS 0.40 sec. per fur. (races 1,4,6), PLUS 0.05 (2,3,5)

714 Torrish Claiming Stakes Class F (3-y-o and up) £1,912 1m 67yds...............(5:50)

327⁷ MEXICAN DANCER 4-8-4 (7*) S Drowne (10) *hdwy 4 fs out, styd on frm o'r one out to ld cl hme.* ....(10 to 1 op 7 to 1 tchd 11 to 1) 1
CAPE PIGEON (USA) 8-9-5 A Munro (11) *sn prmnt, led gng wl 3 fs out, shaken up fnl furlong, ct cl hme.* (5 to 1 jt-fav op 3 to 1 tchd 6 to 1) 2
622* NATURAL LAD (bl) 8-9-4 A Clark (16) *al pressing ldrs, ev ch 2 fs out, one pace fnl furlong.* .... (9 to 1 op 6 to 1 tchd 10 to 1) 3

198[6] NORDANSK 4-9-2 C Avery (20) *hdwy 4 fs out, styd on frm 2 out*... (14 to 1 op 10 to 1) 4
418 TOFF SUNDAE 3-8-0[1] (3*) J Weaver (17) *mid-div, styd on same pace frm o'r 2 fs out*... (20 to 1 tchd 25 to 1) 5
523[8] SUMMER FLOWER 3-7-10 D Biggs (19) *nvr rch ldrs.* ... (9 to 1 op 5 to 1 tchd 10 to 1) 6
436 SENSE OF PRIORITY 4-9-12 K Darley (21) *led to 3 fs out, wknd o'r 2 out*... (9 to 1 op 4 to 1 tchd 10 to 1) 7
498 CONSTRUCTIVIST (Ire) 4-9-0 (3*) D Harrison (18) *nvr better than mid-div*... (20 to 1) 8
622[9] L'ACQUESIANA (v) 5-8-2 (7*) T G McLaughlin (2) *nvr dngrs.* ... (33 to 1 op 20 to 1) 9
521[5] PRINCE ROONEY (Ire) 5-9-2 T Williams (13) *prmnt, ev ch 3 fs out, sn wknd*... (14 to 1 op 10 to 1 tchd 20 to 1) 10
161[6] SURE SHOT NORMAN 4-9-2 J Williams (5) *nvr rch ldrs.* ... (25 to 1 op 20 to 1) 11
FAILAND 6-8-10 N Adams (15) *chsd ldrs till wknd o'r 3 fs out*... (33 to 1 op 20 to 1) 12
351[5] CAROJANGO 3-8-6 M Hills (12) *beh hfwy.* ... (12 to 1 op 10 to 1 tchd 14 to 1) 13
416[6] ANATROCCOLO 6-9-4 L Piggott (6) *prmnt till wknd o'r 3 fs out*... (16 to 1) 14
531[2] FUTURE FAME (USA) 4-9-3 R Hills (7) *nvr better than mid-div*... (14 to 1 op 10 to 1) 15
518[2] DOCTOR-J (Ire) 3-8-4 T Quinn (3) *nvr rch ldrs.* ... (13 to 2 op 6 to 1 tchd 8 to 1) 16
417[4] SYLVANIA (Ire) 3-8-8 B Rouse (8) *beh hfwy*... (5 to 1 jt-fav tchd 9 to 2) 17
NORDIC FLASH 6-9-2 G Carter (4) *beh most of way.* ... (33 to 1 op 20 to 1) 18
615 CUMBRIAN CAVALIER 4-9-0 R Lappin (9) *unruly stalls, sn beh*... (33 to 1 op 20 to 1) 19
CALCUTTA QUEEN (bl) 4-8-6 (3*) A Tucker (14) *prmnt early, sn beh*... (14 to 1 op 10 to 1 tchd 16 to 1) 20

Dist: ¾l, 2l, 2½l, 3½l, 1l, ¾l, ½l, ¾l, ½l, 1½l. 1m 48.30s. a 7.30s (20 Ran).
SR: 37/43/36/26/1/-/20/9/-/ (Mrs Y Moffatt), P G Murphy

715 EBF Blue Charm Maiden Fillies Stakes Class D (2-y-o) £3,915 5f 10yds......(6:15)

477[2] ANTONIA'S FOLLY 8-11 G Carter (9) *sn in tch, led 3 fs out, edgd lft, ran on fnl furlong.* ... (9 to 2 op 7 to 2 tchd 5 to 1) 1
SINGULAR SENSATION 8-11 D Holland (3) *hdwy 3 fs out, chlgd one and a half out, not quicken fnl furlong.* ... (12 to 1 op 7 to 1) 2
HIGHLY FASHIONABLE (Ire) 8-11 T Quinn (5) *trkd ldrs, rdn 2 fs out, styd on same pace ins last.* ... (7 to 1 op 3 to 1 tchd 10 to 1) 3
454[3] GIGUE 8-11 J Williams (7) *hdwy hfwy, swtchd rght 2 fs out, one pace frm o'r one out.* ... (5 to 1 op 4 to 1 tchd 6 to 1) 4
496[3] COLNE VALLEY 8-8 (3*) A Tucker (8) *chsd ldrs, no imprsn frm o'r one furlong out*... (20 to 1 op 12 to 1) 5
528[6] HIPS'N HAWS (Ire) 8-11 M Hills (6) *pressed ldrs, ev ch o'r 2 fs out, sn wknd.* ... (4 to 1 fav op 7 to 2 tchd 9 to 2 and 3 to 1) 6
FORGOTTEN LADY (Ire) 8-4 (7*) T G McLaughlin (11) *pressed ldrs to hfwy*... (20 to 1 op 16 to 1 tchd 25 to 1) 7
454[8] CAPITAL LADY (Ire) 8-8 (3*) D Harrison (12) *led aftr one furlong to 3 out, sn wknd.* ... (20 to 1 op 10 to 1 tchd 25 to 1) 8
GRECIAN GARDEN 8-11 Pat Eddery (1) *early speed.* ... (5 to 1 op 9 to 4 tchd 11 to 2) 9
445[6] RISKIE THINGS 8-11 B Rouse (13) *speed to hfwy.* ... (14 to 1 op 10 to 1 tchd 16 to 1) 10
FOREMMA 8-11 Paul Eddery (4) *outpcd.* ... (20 to 1 op 8 to 1) 11
TERMITE 8-11 N Adams (2) *led one furlong, sn beh.* ... (33 to 1 op 25 to 1) 12
FAST BEAT 8-11 R Perham (10) *dwlt, outpcd.* ... (33 to 1 op 25 to 1) 13

Dist: 2½l, nk, nk, 4l, 1l, nk, sht-hd, 2l, 1½l, 3½l. 1m 3.10s. a 4.10s (13 Ran).
SR: 20/10/9/8/-/-/ (Chris Deuters), J Berry

716 Elite Handicap Class C (0-95 3-y-o) £5,089 5f 10yds............................(6:40)

TRUE PRECISION [66] 8-4 A Munro (14) *trkd ldrs, led one and a half fs out, rdn out*... (10 to 1 op 7 to 1) 1
FLORAC (Ire) [55] 7-1[1] (7*) D Wright (11) *hdwy o'r 2 fs out, swtchd lft one and a half out, ran on, not pace of wnr.* ... (20 to 1 op 16 to 1 tchd 25 to 1) 2
460[5] MY BONUS [79] 9-0 (3*) D Harrison (13) *prmnt, led 2 fs out to one and a half out, styd on one pace.* ... (10 to 1 op 6 to 1) 3
371[4] MAJOR TRIUMPH (Ire) [62] (bl) 8-0 D Biggs (7) *beh, hdwy one and a half fs out, ran on*... (20 to 1 op 16 to 1) 4
558[7] CATHERINEOFARAGON [83] 9-7 J Williams (6) *effrt hfwy, no imprsn frm o'r one furlong out.* ... (9 to 1 op 14 to 1 tchd 8 to 1) 5
606[2] SECOND CHANCE (Ire) [76] 9-0 M Roberts (12) *chsd ldrs, no prog fnl 2 fs*... (13 to 2 op 5 to 1 tchd 7 to 1) 6
634[2] PRESS THE BELL [70] 8-8 Pat Eddery (15) *made most to 2 fs out, sn wknd*... (15 to 8 fav op 5 to 2 tchd 11 to 4) 7
MINSHAAR [70] 8-8 Paul Eddery (8) *prmnt till wknd 2 fs out*... (16 to 1 op 14 to 1) 8
460[9] CARNBREA SNIP [75] 8-13 M Hills (10) *pressed ldrs, ev ch o'r 2 fs out, sn wknd*... (12 to 1 op 8 to 1) 9
FIRST OPTION [73] 8-11 K Darley (5) *chsd ldrs to hfwy.* ... (10 to 1 op 6 to 1) 10
FIVE ISLANDS [71] 8-9 T Quinn (9) *in tch, sn drvn alng, wknd 2 fs out*... (16 to 1 op 14 to 1 tchd 20 to 1) 11
AVRIL ETOILE [62] 8-0 C Avery (4) *outpcd.* ... (25 to 1 op 14 to 1) 12
514 IRISH DOMINION [77] 9-1 R Hills (3) *outpcd.* ... (20 to 1 op 16 to 1 tchd 25 to 1) 13
SKULLCAP [62] 8-0[2] G Carter (1) *sn outpcd.* ... (20 to 1 op 14 to 1) 14

Dist: ¾l, 2½l, 1l, ½l, nk, 3l, nk, nk, ½l, 1l. 1m 1.50s. a 2.50s (14 Ran).
SR: 45/31/45/24/43/35/17/16/20/ (T R Lock), J D Bethell

717 Dusty Miller Handicap Class D (0-80 3-y-o) £3,687 1m 3f 135yds................(7:10)

371* DANA SPRINGS (Ire) [72] 9-4 Pat Eddery (10) *hld up, hdwy 3 fs out, hrd drvn fnl furlong to ld last strds.* ... (5 to 1 op 9 to 2 tchd 6 to 1) 1
373[4] BUGLET [55] 7-8 (7*) D McCabe (8) *hdwy 3 fs out, led one out, sn drvn, ct last strds.* ... (14 to 1 op 12 to 1 tchd 16 to 1) 2
502* MOON CARNIVAL [70] 9-2 A Clark (7) *hdwy to track ldrs o'r 4 fs out, led 2 out, hdd one out, styd on same pace.* ... (5 to 2 fav op 2 to 1) 3
509[2] HALHAM TARN (Ire) [75] 9-2 (5*) A Procter (14) *trkd ldrs, ev ch 2 fs out, outpcd*... (11 to 1 op 10 to 1 tchd 12 to 1) 4
502[6] PAPER DAYS [48] 7-8[1] N Adams (11) *pressed ldrs, chlgd frm 3 fs out till wknd 2 out*... (10 to 1 tchd 12 to 1) 5
457[4] BILJAN (USA) [70] 9-2 A Munro (2) *in tch till fdd o'r 2 fs out*... (10 to 1 tchd 14 to 1) 6
441[8] IKHTIRAA (USA) [56] 8-2 R Hills (5) *led till hdd and wknd 2 fs out*... (20 to 1 op 16 to 1 tchd 25 to 1) 7
602[5] OCTOBER BREW (USA) [70] 8-13 (3*) D Harrison (3) *hdwy 5 fs out, no prog frm 3 out.* (7 to 1 op 6 to 1 tchd 8 to 1) 8
482 CASHABLE [60] 8-6[1] J Williams (4) *sn beh*... (33 to 1) 9
245[2] ARCTIC GUEST (Ire) [49] 7-9[1] T Williams (9) *prmnt one m.* ... (5 to 1 op 9 to 2 tchd 11 to 2) 10
PISTOLS AT DAWN (USA) [64] 8-10 K Darley (13) *chsd ldrs till wknd ins fnl 3 fs.* (16 to 1 op 12 to 1 tchd 20 to 1) 11
434 SURE RIGHT (Ire) [59] 8-0 (5*) M Fenton (12) *chsd ldrs till rdn 4 fs out, sn btn*...(20 to 1 op 16 to 1 tchd 25 to 1) 12
MR COPYFORCE [54] 8-0 A McGlone (6) *prmnt early, sddl slpd, tld off*... (20 to 1 op 14 to 1 tchd 25 to 1) 13

Dist: Hd, 1l, 3½l, 2½l, 1l, 3l, 3½l, ¾l, hd, 2½l. 2m 33.70s. a 10.70s (13 Ran).
SR: 43/25/38/36/4/24/4/11/-/ (G Howard-Spink), R Hannon

718 Lady Caroline Fillies Conditions Stakes Class D (2-y-o) £3,435 5f 10yds......(7:40)

LEMON SOUFFLE 8-8 L Piggott (1) *trkd ldrs, led one and a half fs out, quickened clr ins last,* ... (3 to 1 op 2 to 1 tchd 7 to 2) 1
607* CYARNA QUINN (Ire) 8-8 Pat Eddery (9) *sn led, pushed alng hfwy, hdd one and a half fs out, kpt on, not pace of wnr*... (100 to 30 op 5 to 1 tchd 11 to 4) 2
445* SWEET WHISPER 8-8 K Darley (10) *broke wl, outpcd, styd on frm o'r one furlong out.* ... (10 to 1 op 6 to 1 tchd 11 to 1) 3
ISABELLA SHARP 8-8 M Hills (7) *al chasing ldrs. one pace fnl 2 fs*... (12 to 1 op 10 to 1 tchd 16 to 1) 4
386* MILLION AT DAWN (Ire) 8-9 (3*) D Harrison (5) *prmnt till wknd ins fnl 2 fs.* (5 to 2 fav op 2 to 1 tchd 100 to 30) 5
386[6] NO WHAT I MEAN (Ire) 8-8 B Rouse (8) *nvr gng pace of ldrs.* ... (25 to 1 op 16 to 1 tchd 33 to 1) 6
496* CARRIE KOOL 8-10 W Woods (4) *prmnt, ev ch 2 fs out, sn wknd*... (14 to 1 op 10 to 1 tchd 16 to 1) 7
446* TUTU SIXTYSIX 8-11 (5*) M Fenton (6) *pressed ldrs to hfwy.* ... (5 to 1 op 3 to 1 tchd 11 to 2) 8
490* BEV'S FOLLY 8-1 (7*) D McCabe (2) *early speed.* ... (25 to 1 op 14 to 1) 9

Dist: 2½l, 2½l, nk, 1l, 1½l, ¾l, 1½l, 10l. 1m 2.50s. a 3.50s (9 Ran).
SR: 29/19/9/8/8/-/ (Lord Carnarvon), R Hannon

719 Mar Lodge Rating Related Maiden Stakes Class E (3-y-o and up) £2,355 1m 67yds ....(8:10)

COMANCHE COMPANION 3-8-4 A Munro (10) *in tch, led ins fnl 2 fs, ran on wl*... (4 to 1 fav op 6 to 1) 1
MISBELIEF 3-8-4 G Carter (3) *hdwy o'r 3 fs out, ev ch over one out, not quicken*... (8 to 1 op 6 to 1 tchd 9 to 1) 2
444[5] RAGING THUNDER 3-8-9 K Darley (11) *mid-div, hdwy 4 fs out, styd on fnl furlong*... (16 to 1 op 8 to 1) 3
521[6] CHANDIGARH 5-9-10 J Williams (15) *gd hdwy o'r 2 fs out, fnshd wl*... (20 to 1 tchd 16 to 1 and 25 to 1) 4
304 CHIEF'S SONG 3-8-9 D Holland (2) *prmnt, ev ch o'r 2 fs out, one pace*... (10 to 1 op 6 to 1) 5
STORM VENTURE (Ire) 3-8-9 R Cochrane (14) *prmnt, led 3 fs out till hdd and wknd ins fnl 2 furlongs.* ... (7 to 1 op 10 to 1) 6
KEEP ME IN MIND (Ire) 4-9-10 T Sprake (1) *prmnt till wknd ins fnl 3 fs*... (33 to 1 op 25 to 1) 7
507[3] CAMEO KIRBY (Fr) 3-8-9 B Raymond (16) *nvr rch ldrs.* ... (10 to 1 tchd 12 to 1 and 9 to 1) 8

456 FAIRY WISHER (Ire) 4-9-2 (3*) D Harrison (4) *prmnt, led 5 fs out to 4 out, sn wknd*..............(33 to 1 op 25 to 1) 9
QUEEN WARRIOR 4-9-5 Pat Eddery (5) *prmnt for o'r 5 fs.* ....(9 to 1 op 8 to 1 tchd 7 to 1 and 10 to 1) 10
498 RED JACK (Ire) 4-9-10 S Whitworth (9) *nvr dngrs.* ....(33 to 1 op 20 to 1) 11
439[5] COVEN MOON 3-8-4 J Quinn (8) *prmnt, wth ldrs 4 fs out, sn wknd*..........................(25 to 1 op 16 to 1) 12
APACHE MYTH 3-8-4 T Quinn (12) *led to 5 fs out, led 4 out to 3 out, wknd quickly.* ....(12 to 1 op 6 to 1 tchd 14 to 1) 13
PERDITION (Ire) 3-8-4 M Hills (6) *nvr dngrs.* ....(14 to 1 op 8 to 1 tchd 16 to 1) 14
BALLET 3-8-4 M Roberts (20) *in tch to hfwy.* ....(7 to 1 op 6 to 1 tchd 8 to 1) 15
519[8] INFANTRY GLEN 3-8-9 N Adams (13) *beh hfwy.* ....(33 to 1 op 25 to 1) 16
476[7] CONCINNITY (USA) 4-9-10 A McGlone (7) *al beh.* ....(33 to 1 op 25 to 1) 17
522 LADY GAIL 3-8-4 A Mackay (18) *chsd ldrs 5 fs.* ....(25 to 1 op 14 to 1 tchd 33 to 1) 18
519[4] FITZROY LAD 3-8-4 (5*) B Doyle (21) *sn beh.* ....(33 to 1 op 20 to 1) 19
32[9] GREY WATCH (bl) 3-8-4 D Biggs (19) *al beh.* ....(33 to 1 op 20 to 1) 20
Dist: 2l, 3l, 2l, hd, ½l, nk, 1l, 2½l, 2l, sht-hd. 1m 48.70s. a 7.70s (20 Ran).
SR: 24/18/14/23/7/5/19/1/3/ (Drofmor Racing), T J Naughton

BATH (good)
Tuesday April 27th

Going Correction: PLUS 0.45 sec. per fur. (races 1,2,3), PLUS 0.70 (4,5,6)

720 Spa Selling Stakes Class G (3-y-o) £2,406 5f 11yds..........................(2:30)

602 AIR COMMAND (Bar) 8-7 G Bardwell (4) *drvn alng to chase ldrs, led one furlong out, all out*...(33 to 1 op 20 to 1) 1
614[2] HY WILMA 8-0 (7*) S Drowne (10) *rdn and hdwy frm 2 fs out, ran on ins last, not quite get up.* (6 to 1 op 4 to 1) 2
606[7] TEE-EMM 8-12 W Newnes (8) *led till hdd one furlong out, kpt on same pace, dead-heated for 3rd pl.* ....(8 to 1 op 12 to 1 tchd 14 to 1) 3+
SPENMAX (Ire) 8-7 T Sprake (7) *hdwy 2 fs out, rdn and kpt on same pace ins last, dead-heated for 3rd pl.* ....(14 to 1 op 20 to 1 tchd 33 to 1) 3+
467[3] RED LEADER (Ire) 8-12 T Quinn (6) *drvn and hdwy to chase ldrs 3 fs out, wknd o'r one furlong out.* ....(6 to 4 fav op 6 to 4 tchd 5 to 4 and 7 to 4) 5
GAYNOR GOODMAN (Ire) 8-2 G Hind (5) *slwly into strd, al beh*..................................(33 to 1 op 20 to 1) 6
CREAGMHOR 8-7 J Williams (3) *al outpcd.* ....(13 to 2 op 12 to 1 tchd 6 to 1) 7
TOUCH SILVER 8-12 D Holland (1) *chasing ldrs whn faltered and lost pos aftr one and a half fs.* ....(6 to 1 op 9 to 2) 8
326[6] BARASSIE (bl) 8-4[2] A Clark (9) *dwlt, al outpcd.* ....(12 to 1 op 6 to 1 tchd 14 to 1) 9
600 LADY OF SHADOWS (v) 8-2 D Biggs (11) *sn outpcd.* ....(20 to 1 op 14 to 1 tchd 25 to 1) 10
CLARE'S BOY 8-7 N Adams (2) *prmnt till wknd ins fnl 2 fs*..................................(33 to 1 op 20 to 1) 11
Dist: ¾l, nk, dd-ht, 3l, 2½l, 1l, 8l, 1½l, 8l, ½l. 1m 6.20s. a 5.70s (11 Ran).
SR: 24/21/25/20/13/-/ (J J Bridger), J J Bridger

721 Tripleprint Handicap Class E (0-70 3-y-o and up) £3,210 5f 11yds.............(3:00)

421[3] CALL TO THE BAR (Ire) [53] 4-8-11 A Clark (6) *chsd ldrs, rdn and edgd lft o'r one furlong out, led ins last, all out, fnshd 1st, disqualified*...............(6 to 1 op 4 to 1) 1D
409[8] COBBLERS HILL [52] 4-8-10 T Lang (11) *hdwy frm 2 fs out, chlgd and ev ch wl ins last, jst fld, fnshd second, plcd 1st*..................................(33 to 1 op 20 to 1) 1
659[5] MISTER JOLSON [64] 4-9-1 (7*) S Drowne (3) *chsd ldrs till led ins fnl 2 fs, hdd and not quicken inside last, fnshd 3rd, plcd second*.....(4 to 1 fav op 3 to 1 tchd 9 to 2) 2
SIR JOEY (USA) [63] 4-9-7 J Williams (5) *dwlt, hdwy on outsd o'r one furlong out, fnshd wl, finished 4th, plcd 3rd*..................................(5 to 1 op 6 to 1) 3
491[2] BELLSABANGING [61] 3-8-8 T Williams (2) *pressed ldrs, wkng whn hmpd and snatched up o'r one furlong out, fnshd 5th, plcd 4th*.....(13 to 2 op 6 to 1 tchd 7 to 1) 4
CASTLE MAID [35] 6-7-7 N Carlisle (4) *mid-div, hdwy 2 fs out, one pace fnl furlong, fnshd 6th, plcd 5th.* ....(25 to 1 op 20 to 1) 5
CEE-EN-CEE [66] (v) 9-9-10 T Quinn (1) *mid-div, nvr gng pace of ldrs*..........................(8 to 1 tchd 12 to 1) 7
492 BARBEZIEUX [39] 6-7-11[4] F Norton (7) *some prog frm o'r one furlong out*..........................(50 to 1 op 20 to 1) 8
600[9] IRON KING [67] 7-9-11 W Newnes (10) *outpcd.* ....(16 to 1 op 10 to 1) 9
600[3] PURBECK CENTENARY [54] 3-8-1 D Biggs (9) *led till hdd and wknd ins fnl 2 fs.* ....(12 to 1 op 10 to 1 tchd 14 to 1) 10

548* TOMMY TEMPEST [50] 4-8-8 S Whitworth (13) *chsd ldrs o'r 3 fs*..................................(12 to 1 op 8 to 1) 11
421[9] BELTHORN [50] 4-8-8 G Bardwell (12) *speed 3 fs.* ....(25 to 1 op 16 to 1) 12
418* BUCKSKI ECHO [47] 3-7-3[2] (7*) D Toole (14) *al outpcd.* ....(11 to 1 op 8 to 1 tchd 12 to 1) 13
518[5] SHARP IMP [48] 3-7-9 N Adams (8) *outpcd.* ....(20 to 1 op 14 to 1) 14
KARUKERA [55] 3-8-2 D Holland (15) *mid-div till wknd 2 fs out*..................................(20 to 1 op 14 to 1) 15
Dist: Sht-hd, 1l, 1l, sht-hd, sht-hd, 2½l, ¾l, ¾l, 8l, 3l. 1m 5.60s. a 5.10s (15 Ran).
SR: 40/38/46/41/27/11/32/2/27/ (Miss S Steel), C R Barwell

722 Corston Conditions Stakes Class D (4-y-o and up) £3,145 5f 11yds.............(3:30)

CASE LAW 6-9-0 G Duffield (1) *led till hdd ins fnl 2 fs, rallied to ld ag'n inside last, jst hld on.* ....(Evens fav tchd 5 to 4) 1
CRADLE DAYS 4-9-2 D Holland (8) *hdwy on outsd 2 fs out, str run fnl furlong, jst fld.* ....(5 to 1 op 3 to 1 tchd 11 to 2) 2
555[5] ALLTHRUTHENIGHT (Ire) 4-9-0 R Cochrane (5) *dwlt, outpcd, hdwy appr fnl furlong, ran on wl.* ....(11 to 1 op 8 to 1 tchd 12 to 1) 3
627[3] BELLS OF LONGWICK 4-8-7 T Williams (4) *chsd ldrs, led ins fnl 2 fs, hdd and outpcd inside last.* ....(10 to 1 op 8 to 1) 4
FARFELU 6-9-2 T Quinn (2) *prmnt, not rdn o'r one furlong out, not much room fnl furlong, not rcvr.* ....(15 to 2 op 5 to 1 tchd 8 to 1) 5
4692a[8] LOVE RETURNED 6-8-5 R Hills (3) *pld hrd, outpcd frm hfwy*..................(7 to 1 op 5 to 1 tchd 8 to 1) 6
479[8] HOW'S YER FATHER 7-9-0 (7*) S Drowne (6) *sn outpcd.* ....(14 to 1 op 10 to 1 tchd 16 to 1) 7
659 OLIFANTSFONTEIN (bl) 5-9-6 G Carter (7) *outpcd frm hfwy, eased whn btn fnl furlong.* ....(8 to 1 op 7 to 1 tchd 9 to 1) 8
Dist: Sht-hd, ¾l, nk, ½l, 3½l, ¾l, 2l. 1m 5.10s. a 4.60s (8 Ran).
SR: 53/54/49/41/48/23/36/27/ (Mrs David Thompson), Sir Mark Prescott

723 Empire Handicap Class D (0-80 4-y-o and up) £3,535 1m 3f 144yds........... (4:00)

589[3] SWORD MASTER [68] 4-9-5 N Day (5) *pushed alng to stay in tch hfwy, hdwy 4 fs out, led 2 and a half furlongs out, sn clr, hld on wl*... (5 to 1 op 4 to 1 tchd 11 to 2) 1
442[2] STATE OF AFFAIRS [44] 6-7-10 S Dawson (9) *hld up and beh, steady hdwy ins fnl 2 fs, not rch wnr.* ....(5 to 1 op 4 to 1 tchd 11 to 2) 2
159[2] LEXUS (Ire) [42] 5-7-8 N Adams (8) *beh till hdwy 3 fs out, kpt on same pace ins fnl 2 furlongs.* ....(12 to 1 op 10 to 1 tchd 14 to 1) 3
442* DAY OF HISTORY (Ire) [53] 4-8-4 D Biggs (6) *prmnt whn badly hmpd 4 fs out, ran on ag'n fnl 2 furlongs.* ....(6 to 1 op 5 to 1 tchd 13 to 2) 4
601[3] LA REINE ROUGE (Ire) [47] 5-7-13 F Norton (7) *in tch, hdwy to chase ldrs 3 fs out, wknd frm 2 furlongs out.* ....(14 to 1 op 10 to 1) 5
366[6] FANATICAL (USA) [46] 7-7-12 T Williams (12) *chsd ldrs, led 4 fs out till hdd 2 and a half furlongs out, sn wknd.* ....(14 to 1 tchd 16 to 1) 6
BLAZON OF TROY [63] 4-9-0 S Whitworth (1) *prmnt for a m.* ....(16 to 1 op 12 to 1 tchd 20 to 1) 7
416[7] NORTH ESK (USA) [61] 4-8-12 G Carter (10) *nvr rchd ldrs.* ....(20 to 1 op 14 to 1 tchd 25 to 1) 8
605 WILD POPPY [42] (v) 4-7-7 G Bardwell (14) *beh frm hfwy.* ....(50 to 1 op 25 to 1) 9
520[4] MONARDA [65] 6-9-3 T Quinn (3) *prmnt, led 6 fs out, hdd 4 furlongs out, wknd quickly 3 furlongs out.* ....(5 to 2 fav tchd 3 to 1 and 2 to 1) 10
626 STRIKING IMAGE (Ire) [52] 4-8-3 D Holland (11) *led one furlong, styd frnt rnk till wknd o'r 3 fs out.* ....(25 to 1 op 20 to 1) 11
327 SEASIDE MINSTREL [53] 5-8-2[2] (5*) C Hodgson (4) *in tch 7 fs*..................................(33 to 1 op 20 to 1) 12
LITERARY CRITIC (Ire) [53] 4-8-1 (3*) A Tucker (2) *led aftr one furlong till hdd 6 fs out, wknd quickly*....(50 to 1) 13
Dist: 2½l, 3l, 7l, sht-hd, 8l, 1½l, 10l, ¾l, nk, 1l. 2m 40.30s. a 13.30s (13 Ran).
SR: 52/24/16/12/6/-/2/-/-/ (Ian A Vogt), Bob Jones

724 Blathwayt Rating Related Maiden Stakes Class F (3-y-o) £2,770 1¼m 46yds... (4:30)

346 HOOCHIECOOCHIE MAN (Ire) 9-0 R Price (11) *rdn alng 4 fs out, hdwy to ld 2 and a half furlongs out, ridden out.* ....(16 to 1 op 12 to 1 tchd 20 to 1) 1
185[8] BOXBOY 9-0 S Whitworth (7) *hdwy frm 3 fs out, ran on fnl furlong, no imprsn on wnr*....... (66 to 1 op 33 to 1) 2
SKY BURST 8-9 N Carlisle (9) *in tch, hdwy 4 fs out, chlgd 3 furlongs out, one pace fnl 2 furlongs.* ....(25 to 1 op 16 to 1) 3
405[4] TEJANO GOLD (USA) 9-0 T Quinn (8) *prmnt, dsptd ld 4 fs out, one pace frm o'r 2 furlongs out.* ....(6 to 1 op 4 to 1 tchd 7 to 1) 4

BURNING COST 8-9 N Day (6) *chsd ldrs till led 4 fs out, hdd and btn 2 and a half furlongs out.* ....(12 to 1 op 10 to 1 tchd 14 to 1) 5
521 KISMETIM 9-0 W Newnes (14) *beh till styd on frm o'r 2 fs out*..........(33 to 1 op 20 to 1) 6
483[2] WITHOUT A FLAG (USA) 9-0 D Biggs (2) *prmnt, rdn 3 fs out, sn wknd*.......(11 to 4 fav op 9 to 4 tchd 3 to 1) 7
519 UNIVERSAL (Fr) 8-4 (5*) B Doyle (12) *slwly into strd, nvr rchd ldrs*..........(50 to 1 op 25 to 1) 8
377[3] PUGET DANCER (USA) 8-9 R Cochrane (13) *nvr dngrs.* ....(5 to 1 op 4 to 1) 9
516[7] KATIE EILEEN (USA) 8-9 A Clark (16) *mid-div, effrt 4 fs out, sn wknd*..........(16 to 1 op 12 to 1 tchd 20 to 1) 10
SPARKY'S SONG 8-9 J Williams (1) *nvr better than mid-div*..........(12 to 1 op 10 to 1 tchd 14 to 1) 11
602[9] JULIASDARKINVADER 9-0 Candy Morris (5) *beh most of way*..........(33 to 1 op 20 to 1) 12
JIHAAD (USA) 9-0 R Hills (3) *in tch, chsd ldrs 5 fs out, wknd rpdly*..........(6 to 1 op 4 to 1 tchd 7 to 1) 13
447[2] CARDINAL DOGWOOD (USA) (bl) 9-0 M Wigham (4) *sn led, hdd and wknd quickly 4 fs out.* ....(15 to 2 op 6 to 1 tchd 8 to 1) 14
SHEER ECSTASY 8-11 (3*) J Weaver (17) *al beh.* ....(50 to 1 op 20 to 1) 15
4677a AMBIVALENTATTITUDE 9-0 G Carter (15) *chsd ldrs 6 fs.* ....(66 to 1 op 33 to 1) 16

Dist: 1½l, 2½l, 2½l, 2½l, 2l, 2l, 1½l, 1½l, ¾l, 1½l. 2m 21.70s. a 15.30s (16 Ran).
SR: 19/16/6/6/-/-/ (Christopher Wright), D W P Arbuthnot

725 Hawkesbury Handicap Class D (0-80 3-y-o) £3,379 1¼m 46yds.................. (5:00)

437 SON OF SHARP SHOT (Ire) [69] 9-1 R Cochrane (4) *hld up, hdwy to ld 2 and a half fs out, clr o'r one furlong out, readily*..........(9 to 4 fav op 2 to 1 tchd 5 to 2) 1
GRAND APPLAUSE (Ire) [70] 9-2 S Whitworth (11) *beh, steady hdwy frm 3 fs out, ran on fnl furlong, not rch wnr*..........(14 to 1 op 8 to 1 tchd 16 to 1) 2
372[6] MY HARVINSKI [67] 8-13 D Holland (12) *hld up, hdwy 3 fs out, hrd drvn to chase wnr o'r one furlong out, one pace*.......(13 to 2 op 6 to 1 tchd 7 to 1 and 11 to 2) 3
286[3] RECORD LOVER (Ire) [55] 7-12 (3*) D Harrison (10) *hdwy 5 fs out, stumbled 4 furlongs out, some prog frm o'r one furlong out*..........(5 to 1 op 4 to 1 tchd 11 to 2) 4
LA DELITZIA (USA) [65] 8-11 T Quinn (9) *prmnt, led o'r 3 fs out, hdd 2 and a half furlongs out, sn btn.* ....(10 to 1 op 7 to 1) 5
502[7] STARLIGHT ROSE (Ire) [50] 7-10 S Dawson (1) *chsd ldrs 7 fs.* ....(16 to 1 op 12 to 1) 6
23[2] BICHETTE [65] 8-11 B Rouse (7) *prmnt for 7 fs.* ....(6 to 1 tchd 8 to 1) 7
204[5] GLOWING PATH [49] 7-9 J Quinn (5) *al beh.* ....(10 to 1 tchd 12 to 1) 8
472 EXPRESS MARIECURIE (Ire) [63] 8-9 R Price (8) *pressed ldrs 6 fs*..........(25 to 1 op 20 to 1) 9
444[3] LAKAB (USA) [72] 9-4 R Hills (2) *sn led, hdd o'r 3 fs out, wknd rpdly*..........(13 to 2 op 6 to 1 tchd 8 to 1) 10
GOLD TASSEL [75] 9-7 J Comber (6) *slwly away, rapid hdwy 5 fs out, sn wknd, tld off*.....(14 to 1 op 8 to 1) 11

Dist: 1½l, nk, 8l, ¾l, 5l, 6l, 3½l, 10l, nk, dist. 2m 21.40s. a 15.00s (11 Ran).
SR: 23/21/17/-/-/-/ (Windflower Overseas Holdings Inc), J L Dunlop

LONGCHAMP (FR) (soft)
Tuesday April 27th
Going Correction: PLUS 0.75 sec. per fur.

726 Prix d'Hedouville (Group 3) (4-y-o and up) £23,895 1½m...................... (2:25)

461* SHARP COUNSEL (Fr) 4-8-11 D Boeuf (5) *al cl up, 4th strt, hdwy 2 fs out, led o'r one out, ran on wl*.....(5 to 4 on) 1
DARIYOUN (USA) 5-9-6 F Head (6) *led early, trkd ldr, chlgd 2 fs out, ev ch ins last, ran on wl*..........(7 to 1) 2
NON PARTISAN (USA) 4-9-4 T Jarnet (4) *rcd in 3rd to strt, hdwy 2 fs out, hrd rdn one out, kpt on same pace.* ....(24 to 10) 3
407 OUMNAZ (Fr) 4-9-2 N Jeanpierre (3) *last to strt, some prog o'r 2 fs out, hrd rdn and one pace frm over one out.* ....(14 to 1) 4
DOWN THE FLAG (USA) (bl) 6-8-9 C Le Scrill (2) *sn led, hdd o'r one out out, one pace*..........(37 to 1) 5
461[3] PRINCE POLINO (USA) 4-8-11 C Asmussen (1) *nvr able to chal*..........(7 to 2) 6

Dist: Nk, 2½l, 1l, hd, ½l. 2m 41.60s. a 12.50s (6 Ran).
SR: 62/70/63/59/51/52/ (F Guidotti), E Lellouche

NOTTINGHAM (good to soft)
Tuesday April 27th
Going Correction: PLUS 0.25 sec. per fur. (races 1,5,6,7), PLUS 0.40 (2,3,4)

727 Trent Bridge Handicap Class E (0-70 4-y-o and up) £3,494 1¾m 15yds..........(2:15)

674[6] KINOKO [52] 5-8-13 K Darley (7) *mid-div, hdwy 4 fs out, str run to ld ins last, styd on wl.* (10 to 1 tchd 12 to 1) 1
402[6] LOOKINGFORARAINBOW (Ire) [55] 5-9-2 N Connorton (4) *hld up, hdwy o'r 2 fs out, effrt and edgd lft appr last, ran on*..........(12 to 1 op 10 to 1) 2
618[6] PEAK DISTRICT [45] 7-8-6 Pat Eddery (13) *led, rdn 2 fs out, hdd wl ins last, no extr.* ....(11 to 1 op 10 to 1 tchd 12 to 1) 3
349[7] ZEALOUS KITTEN (USA) [55] 5-8-11 (5*) Stephen Davies (1) *hld up, hdwy 3 fs out, rdn and kpt on appr last.* ....(9 to 1 op 10 to 1 tchd 11 to 1) 4
OUR SLIMBRIDGE [38] 5-7-13 J Quinn (15) *hld up, hdwy 3 fs out, rdn and one pace appr last*... (8 to 1 op 4 to 1) 5
527[3] MISS PIN UP [67] 4-9-12 J Reid (2) *hld up, hdwy 3 fs out, rdn and ch 2 out, sn one pace.* (7 to 1 jt-fav op 6 to 1) 6
495[8] EIRE LEATH-SCEAL [44] 6-8-5 A Munro (17) *chsd ldr, rdn 2 fs out, wknd appr last*..........(14 to 1 op 10 to 1) 7
495* ENFANT DU PARADIS (Ire) [41] 5-8-2 W Carson (18) *chsd ldrs, effrt and ch o'r 2 fs out, sn rdn and wknd.* ....(7 to 1 jt-fav op 6 to 1) 8
SELDOM IN [33] 7-7-1 (7*) Darren Moffatt (9) *chsd ldrs, rdn 3 fs out, wknd*..........(16 to 1 op 12 to 1) 9
INTREPID LASS [39] 6-7-7 (7*) Antoinette Armes (3) *chsd ldrs, rdn 3 fs out, wknd wl o'r one out*..........(20 to 1) 10
453[5] GREY COMMANDER [32] 5-7-0 (7*) D Wright (6) *in tch till lost pl aftr 3 fs, hdwy three out, rdn 2 out, sn one pace.* ....(20 to 1) 11
495[3] WHITE RIVER [39] 7-8-0 A Mackay (20) *chsd ldrs, effrt and ev ch o'r 2 fs out, sn rdn, wknd appr last.* ....(10 to 1 tchd 12 to 1) 12
UNDERWYCHWOOD (Ire) [45] 5-8-6 R Perham (10) *chsd ldrs, rdn o'r 4 fs out, sn wknd*..........(33 to 1) 13
331[2] RAGAMUFFIN ROMEO [69] 4-10-0 Paul Eddery (8) *al rear.* ....(12 to 1) 14
618 FAMOUS BEAUTY [49] 6-8-3 (7*) L Aspell (11) *dwlt, hdwy hfwy, effrt and ch 2 fs out, sn rdn and wknd.* ....(20 to 1 op 16 to 1) 15
442[8] AL SHANY [43] 7-7-13 (5*) N Gwilliams (12) *nvr rch ldrs.* ....(33 to 1 op 25 to 1) 16
559[6] INTRICACY [50] (v) 5-8-11 L Dettori (14) *chsd ldrs to hfwy, sn lost pl*..........(20 to 1) 17
626* SHOOFE (USA) [69] 5-10-2 (5ex) M Roberts (19) *hdwy to chase ldrs 6 fs out, rdn and wknd 3 out.* ....(8 to 1 op 6 to 1) 18
DOMAIN [55] (bl) 5-9-2 J Lowe (16) *mid-div, hdwy 6 fs out, rdn 3 out, sn wknd*..........(33 to 1) 19
BARTON PRIDE (Ire) [44] 4-8-3 J Carroll (5) *al rear.* ....(33 to 1 op 20 to 1) 20

Dist: 1l, ¾l, 1l, 2l, ¾l, hd, ½l, sht-hd, 2l, sht-hd. 3m 12.60s. a 14.70s (20 Ran).
(Anthony White), K W Hogg

728 Tavern Claiming Stakes Class F (3-y-o) £2,243 6f 15yds...................... (2:45)

361[5] DEAD CALM (v) 8-11 L Dettori (10) *trkd ldrs, hdwy 2 fs out, led appr last, sn clr*..........(100 to 30 fav op 3 to 1) 1
549[5] NUTTY BROWN (bl) 8-12 (5*) O Pears (5) *led, rdn 2 fs out, hdd appr last, one pace*..........(7 to 2 op 3 to 1) 2
410[3] IRISH ROOTS (Ire) (v) 8-11 M Birch (7) *cl up, rdn 2 fs out, sn one pace*..........(4 to 1 op 7 to 2) 3
MELODIC DRIVE 9-7 W Ryan (3) *chsd ldrs, rdn 2 fs out, kpt on one pace*..........(25 to 1) 4
545[5] DARDANELLE 7-11 (5*) A Garth (4) *cl up, effrt 2 fs out, rdn and ev ch whn hng lft appr last, sn wknd.* ....(11 to 1 op 10 to 1) 5
545[6] CORONA GOLD 8-13 K Fallon (8) *chsd ldrs, rdn and outpcd 2 fs out, styd on ins last*..........(6 to 1 op 5 to 1) 6
428[8] ALBEIT 8-6 N Connorton (12) *nvr rch ldrs*..........(8 to 1) 7
614 GLEAM OF GOLD 8-6 C Rutter (2) *chsd ldrs, rdn hfwy, sn wknd*..........(16 to 1) 8
357[6] BADENOCH BURNER 8-7 Kim Tinkler (11) *prmnt, rdn 2 fs out, sn wknd*..........(16 to 1) 9
394[8] RED EDGE 8-0 E Johnson (9) *beh hfwy.* ....(33 to 1 op 25 to 1) 10
DIAMONDS 'N PEARLS 8-13 M Tebbutt (6) *slwly away, wnt rght, al outpcd, tld off fnl 2 fs.* (16 to 1 op 12 to 1) 11

Dist: 3l, 1½l, 1½l, 1½l, ½l, 4l, 7l, 1l, 10l, 12l. 1m 16.80s. a 5.30s (11 Ran).
SR: 39/33/21/25/-/9/ (Mrs S R Brook), C Tinkler

729 Headingley Conditions Stakes Class C (3-y-o) £4,232 6f 15yds................ (3:15)

SPECIFIED (USA) 8-11 Pat Eddery (7) *trkd ldrs, swtchd and hdwy to ld entering fnl furlong, sn rdn, edgd rght, ran on*..........(7 to 4 fav op 5 to 4) 1
ROCK SYMPHONY 9-1 B Raymond (3) *cl up, rdn to ld appr fnl furlong, hdd entering last, kpt on wl und pres.* ....(10 to 1 op 6 to 1) 2
CARRANITA (Ire) 8-1 (5*) Stephen Davies (2) *chsd ldrs, rdn 2 fs out, ev ch till wknd ins last*...... (7 to 1 op 12 to 1) 3
542[8] SHEILA'S SECRET (Ire) 8-10 K Darley (6) *led, rdn 2 fs out, hdd and wknd o'r one out*..........(8 to 1 op 6 to 1) 4
526[6] LOST SOLDIER (USA) 8-13 M Roberts (1) *cl up, ev ch 2 fs out, sn rdn and wknd*..........(9 to 4 op 7 to 4) 5
481[5] I'LLEAVEITOYOU (Ire) 8-11 W Ryan (4) *chsd ldrs, rdn 2 fs out, sn wknd*..........(20 to 1 op 16 to 1) 6

464^{7} ANSELLMAN 9-5 L Dettori (5) *chsd ldrs, rdn and wknd 2 fs out*................................(6 to 1 tchd 5 to 1) 7
Dist: Hd, 1½l, 2l, 2l, 2l, 6l. 1m 16.40s. a 4.90s (7 Ran).
SR: 47/50/35/31/26/16/-/ (K Abdulla), J H M Gosden

730 Old Trafford Median Auction Maiden Stakes Class E (2-y-o) £3,339 5f 13yds ....(3:45)

SNIPE HALL 8-9 P Robinson (6) *chsd ldrs far side, hdwy 2 fs out, led one out, sn clr.* ....(12 to 1 op 10 to 1 tchd 14 to 1) 1
PALACEGATE JACK (Ire) 9-0 J Carroll (14) *led stands side, rdn and hng lft one and a half fs out, hdd one out, wknd ins last*....................(5 to 2 fav op 2 to 1) 2
ROYAL INSIGNIA 9-0 A Munro (19) *chsd ldrs stands side, rdn 2 fs out, kpt on wl fnl furlong*... (4 to 1 op 3 to 1) 3
JOHNNIE THE JOKER 9-0 Dean McKeown (8) *mid-div, styd on wl fnl furlong*..............................(20 to 1) 4
673 PARISH WALK (Ire) 9-0 J Lowe (17) *mid-div, hdwy fnl 2 fs.* ....(50 to 1) 5
ABSOLUTELY FAYRE 9-0 M Roberts (10) *mid-div, styd on fnl 2 fs*..................................(10 to 1 op 20 to 1) 6
466^{7} HILL FARM KATIE 8-9 Paul Eddery (4) *cl up far side, rdn 2 fs out, sn wknd*..................(25 to 1 tchd 33 to 1) 7
399^{9} JUST GREENWICH 8-9 J Reid (11) *prmnt stands side, rdn and wknd 2 fs out*..............................(33 to 1) 8
466^{4} ROCKY TWO 9-0 A Mackay (18) *nvr rch ldrs.* ....(14 to 1 op 12 to 1) 9
554^{6} LEGAL CONQUEST 8-9 L Dettori (15) *nvr dngrs.* ....(16 to 1 op 14 to 1) 10+
STORM REGENT 9-0 W Woods (1) *nvr rch ldrs*...(33 to 1) 10+
LUNAR MISSION (Ire) 9-0 K Darley (13) *dwlt, rear till some late hdwy*..............................(14 to 1 op 8 to 1) 12
586^{5} KOMPLICITY 9-0 N Connorton (2) *speed far side 3 fs.* ....(33 to 1) 13
IMPOSING GROOM (Ire) 9-0 W Carson (3) *nvr rch ldrs.* ....(12 to 1 op 7 to 1) 14
543^{5} DOWN D ISLANDS 9-0 Pat Eddery (5) *prmnt far side, rdn hfwy, sn wknd*..........(3 to 1 op 5 to 2 tchd 4 to 1) 15
BOLDANDPRETTY 8-9 K Fallon (16) *al rear.* ....(20 to 1 op 14 to 1) 16
466^{5} HEATHYARDS CRUSADE (Ire) 9-0 W Ryan (12) *prmnt stands side, rdn and wknd 2 fs out.* ....(14 to 1 op 10 to 1) 17
386^{8} PHONE ME UP 9-0 B Raymond (7) *al rear.* ....(16 to 1 op 14 to 1) 18
INDIAN CASTLE (Ire) 9-0 R Perham (9) *beh hfwy.* (50 to 1) 19
Dist: 3l, hd, 4l, 1l, ½l, nk, 1l, sht-hd, 1l, dd-ht. 1m 3.30s. a 5.10s (19 Ran).
SR: 33/26/25/9/5/3/ (Mrs R T Watson), J Wharton

731 Edgbaston Handicap Class D (0-80 4-y-o and up) £3,757 1m 1f 213yds........(4:15)

500* ALDERBROOK [77] 4-9-13 Paul Eddery (16) *in tch, cld 4 fs out, hdwy 2 out, sn led, ran on wl fnl furlong.* ....(7 to 4 fav tchd 2 to 1) 1
663^{7} SURREY DANCER [73] 5-9-9 W Ryan (5) *in tch, hdwy 4 fs out, chsd wnr one and a half out, rdn, edgd lft, kpt on fnl furlong*..........................(7 to 1 op 8 to 1) 2
520^{6} JIMLIL [74] 5-9-5 (5*) Stephen Davies (1) *chsd ldrs, ev ch 2 fs out, sn rdn, one pace*......................(14 to 1) 3
498^{4} SINCLAIR LAD (Ire) [58] 5-8-8 W Carson (13) *hld up beh, hdwy 3 fs out, rdn and kpt on one pace frm 2 out.* ....(8 to 1 op 6 to 1) 4
37 TOUCH ABOVE [51] 7-8-1 Alex Greaves (3) *in tch, rdn alng 3 fs out, styd on appr last*.........................(20 to 1) 5
239^{6} SHIRLEY'S TRAIN (USA) [56] 4-8-6 M Roberts (4) *chsd ldr, led 2 and a half fs out, rdn and hdd o'r one and a half out, wknd*..........................(10 to 1 op 7 to 1) 6
396^{8} MALINDI BAY [43] 5-7-7 E Johnson (10) *beh, styd on fnl 3 fs, nvr dngrs*..........................(50 to 1 op 33 to 1) 7
4701a ALDINGTON PEACH [46] 4-7-10² A Mackay (12) *sn led, rdn 3 fs out, hdd 2 and a half out, wknd.* ....(33 to 1 op 25 to 1) 8
589^{6} EXPLOSIVE SPEED (USA) [53] 5-8-3³ J Carroll (6) *nvr rch ldrs*..............................(20 to 1 op 14 to 1) 9
363^{8} MARY MACBLAIN [43] 4-7-0 (7*) Darren Moffatt (2) *al mid-div*..............................(25 to 1 op 50 to 1) 10
VALLANCE [78] 5-10-0 Pat Eddery (7) *chsd ldrs, rdn and wknd o'r 2 fs out*..................(10 to 1 op 7 to 1) 11
456^{6} ALBERT [49] 6-7-13 A McGlone (9) *nvr rch ldrs.* ....(10 to 1 op 7 to 1) 12
BENTICO [60] 4-8-5 (5*) K Rutter (14) *al rear.* ....(14 to 1 op 12 to 1) 13
SIBERIAN BREEZE [44] (v) 5-7-8¹ J Lowe (17) *al rear.* ....(50 to 1) 14
HIGHLAND FLAME [43] 4-7-0 (7*) D Wright (15) *chsd ldrs, rdn 3 fs out, sn wknd*..............................(33 to 1) 15
513^{7} MAHOOL (USA) [76] 4-9-12 B Raymond (11) *chsd ldrs, rdn and wknd o'r 2 fs out*..............(12 to 1 op 7 to 1) 16
Dist: 1½l, 2l, 3½l, 1½l, 1½l, 4l, sht-hd, 1l, nk, 2½l. 2m 11.00s. a 8.00s (16 Ran).
SR: 58/51/48/25/15/17/-/-/3/ (E Pick), Mrs J Cecil

732 Oval Maiden Fillies Stakes Class D (3-y-o) £3,816 1m 54yds....................(4:45)

ZAJIRA (Ire) 8-11 W Carson (2) *hld up, hdwy o'r 3 fs out, swtchd outsd over one out, str run to ld wl ins last.* ....(10 to 1 tchd 12 to 1) 1
SEROTINA (Ire) 8-11 M Tebbutt (6) *dwlt, hdwy on ins o'r 3 fs out, not clr run 2 out, rdn appr last, kpt on.* (16 to 1) 2
BALNAHA 8-11 M Hills (14) *hld up, hdwy o'r 3 fs out, led wl over one and a half out, sn rdn, hdd and no extr well ins last*..........(9 to 2 op 4 to 1 tchd 5 to 1) 3
583^{6} MIGAVON 8-11 Paul Eddery (11) *chsd ldr, effrt and ev ch 2 fs out, sn rdn, kpt on one pace*... (25 to 1 op 33 to 1) 4
MYSILV 8-11 P Robinson (5) *led, rdn and hdd o'r 2 fs out, kpt on one pace*..................(33 to 1 op 25 to 1) 5
583^{3} ABBRAAK (USA) 8-11 B Raymond (12) *chsd ldrs, hdwy to ld briefly o'r 2 fs out, rdn and wknd wl over one out.* ....(7 to 2 fav op 6 to 4 tchd 4 to 1) 6
BY QUEEN (Ire) 8-11 J Lowe (3) *beh, styd on fnl 2 fs.* ....(50 to 1) 7
443^{3} SWIFT SPRING (Fr) 8-4 (7*) J D Smith (10) *hld up, some hdwy 3 fs out, not rch ldrs*..........(14 to 1 op 7 to 1) 8
523^{6} ALLIGRAM (USA) 8-11 Pat Eddery (7) *chsd ldrs, rdn o'r 2 fs out, sn btn*..........................(9 to 2 op 3 to 1) 9
PURE MISK 8-11 W Ryan (9) *al rear*...(12 to 1 op 8 to 1) 10
MULLED ALE (Ire) 8-11 W Woods (4) *nvr a factor.* (33 to 1) 11
516^{3} ON GOLDEN POND (Ire) 8-11 A Munro (15) *in tch, rdn and wknd o'r 3 fs out*..........................(7 to 1 op 4 to 1) 12
IMAGERY 8-11 L Dettori (1) *nvr a factor*........ (20 to 1) 13
DESERT GIRL 8-11 K Darley (8) *slwly away, al rear.* ....(12 to 1 op 10 to 1) 14
SHARP SILK 8-11 C Rutter (13) *prmnt, rdn and wknd o'r 3 fs out*......................................(20 to 1) 15
Dist: 2½l, 2l, 2l, 3l, nk, ¾l, 2½l, ¾l, 6l, sht-hd. 1m 48.10s. a 8.10s (15 Ran).
SR: 6/-/-/-/-/-/ (Hamdan Al-Maktoum), R W Armstrong

733 Lords Handicap Class E (0-70 3-y-o) £3,753 1m 54yds..........................(5:15)

516* MIDNIGHT HEIGHTS [70] 9-7 A McGlone (7) *chsd ldrs, hdwy on ins to ld 2 fs out, sn clr, rdn and ran on fnl furlong*..............(5 to 2 fav op 7 to 2 tchd 4 to 1) 1
398^{6} DARING PAST [53] 8-4 W Ryan (11) *mid-div, hdwy 4 fs out, not clr run 3 out, sn rdn, styd on wl appr last.* ....(14 to 1 op 10 to 1) 2
GENSERIC (Fr) [70] 9-7 W Carson (6) *in tch, hdwy o'r 2 fs out, sn rdn, styd on same pace*.... (16 to 1 op 14 to 1) 3
503* DESIRABLE MISS [47] (v) 7-11² (3*) S Maloney (13) *chsd ldrs, hdwy 3 fs out, rdn and one pace 2 out.* ....(14 to 1 tchd 16 to 1) 4
326^{5} YUNUS EMRE (Ire) [52] 8-3 M Roberts (8) *beh, styd on wl fnl 2 fs, nrst finish*.................(12 to 1 op 10 to 1) 5
546^{3} WORDSMITH (Ire) [64] 9-1 K Fallon (1) *slwly into strd, some hdwy fnl 2 fs, nvr dngrs*............(10 to 1 op 7 to 1) 6
437 NEVER IN TOUCH [42] (bl) 7-0 (7*) D Wright (9) *slwly into strd, styd on wl fnl 2 fs*.............................(33 to 1) 7
467* DAILY SPORT DON [65] 9-2 Pat Eddery (12) *in tch, hdwy 4 fs out, sn rdn, wknd 3 out*.............(8 to 1 op 6 to 1) 8
493^{6} WOLF POWER (Ire) [62] 8-13 K Darley (4) *hld up in tch, hdwy to ld briefly o'r 2 fs out, sn rdn, wknd wl over one out*.........(11 to 2 op 7 to 1 tchd 8 to 1 and 5 to 1) 9
346^{6} MISS OFFIE [49] 8-0 A Munro (10) *nvr rch ldrs*....(25 to 1) 10
QUEENS CONTRACTOR [65] 9-2 J Reid (15) *wth ldr, effrt and ev ch 2 fs out, sn rdn and wknd.* ....(11 to 1 op 10 to 1 tchd 12 to 1) 11
405^{2} STEVIE'S WONDER (Ire) [54] 8-0 (5*) N Gwilliams (5) *nvr rch ldrs*................(12 to 1 op 10 to 1 tchd 14 to 1) 12
313 SOLO CHARTER [55] 8-6 P Robinson (3) *nvr a factor.* ....(14 to 1 op 12 to 1) 13
519^{6} BEAT THE BAGMAN (Ire) [50] 8-1 Dale Gibson (14) *nvr a factor*..............................(20 to 1 op 16 to 1) 14
493^{5} LEGAL ARTIST (Ire) [54] 8-5 B Raymond (16) *cl up, effrt and ev ch 2 fs out, sn rdn, wknd quickly.* ....(16 to 1 op 14 to 1) 15
4709a7 WORKING TITLE (Ire) [65] 9-2 M Hills (17) *al rear.* (16 to 1) 16
642 MANX MONARCH [58] 8-9 J Lowe (2) *led till hdd and wknd quickly o'r 2 fs out*.........(33 to 1 op 25 to 1) 17
Dist: 1l, 5l, sht-hd, 2½l, ½l, 2½l, ¾l, nk, 1½l, hd. 1m 49.30s. a 9.30s (17 Ran).
(Ettore Landi), J L Dunlop

ASCOT (good)
Wednesday April 28th
Going Correction: NIL (races 1,2,3,4,6), MINUS 0.25 (5)

734 Insulpak Conditions Stakes Class B (3-y-o) £8,616 1m............................... (2:00)

POLKA DANCER 8-11 W R Swinburn (5) *trkd ldr aftr 3 fs, led o'r 2 out, ran on wl*.......(4 to 1 co-fav op 3 to 1) 1
472^{4} ZENITH 8-11 L Dettori (3) *wtd wth, hdwy wl o'r 2 fs out, rdn to go second appr last, kpt on.* ....(4 to 1 co-fav op 3 to 1) 2
BRIGHT SPELLS 8-11 J Williams (1) *hld up, hdwy o'r 2 fs out, kpt on one pace last.* ....(4 to 1 co-fav op 5 to 2 tchd 9 to 2) 3
LACERTA (Ire) 8-11 J Reid (6) *hld up, hdwy 2 fs out, styd on, nvr nrr*..........................(8 to 1 op 6 to 1) 4

472[9] KATIBA (USA) (bl) 8-13 W Carson (4) *led till hdd o'r 2 fs out, sn btn*..........(6 to 1 op 5 to 1 tchd 7 to 1) 5
472[6] FABRIANA 8-11 D Holland (2) *prmnt till wknd appr fnl furlong*..............(20 to 1 op 16 to 1 tchd 25 to 1) 6
NA-AYIM (Ire) 8-11 R Hills (7) *hld up in rear, lost tch o'r 2 fs out*..................(11 to 2 op 6 to 1 tchd 7 to 1) 7
482[9] BALLON 8-11 M Roberts (9) *trkd ldr for 3 fs, rdn o'r 2 out, stdly wknd*..........................(33 to 1 op 16 to 1) 8
514 SEHAILAH 8-13 L Piggott (8) *hld up in tch, wknd o'r 2 fs out, eased*..........(20 to 1 op 14 to 1 tchd 25 to 1) 9
Dist: 1½l, 1½l, sht-hd, 3l, nk, 1½l, 3l, 2½l. 1m 43.95s. a 4.45s (9 Ran).
SR: 30/25/20/19/12/9/4/-/-/ (S J Richmond-Watson), J R Fanshawe

735 Insulpak Sagaro EBF Stakes Class A (Group 3) (4-y-o and up) £26,892 2m 45yds ....(2:30)

ROLL A DOLLAR 7-8-12 B Rouse (1) *trkd ldr, led 3 fs out, rdn and styd on gmely fnl furlong*.
..................................(12 to 1 tchd 14 to 1) 1
579[4] ASSESSOR (Ire) 4-9-0 T Quinn (5) *hld up, hdwy hfwy, rdn 2 fs out, no imprsn cl hme*..................(15 to 8 jt-fav op 6 to 4 tchd 2 to 1) 2
601* SPINNING 6-8-12 R Cochrane (6) *pld hrd, hld up in rear, hdwy o'r 3 fs out, rdn and no imprsn ins last*.
..........................(7 to 2 op 4 to 1 tchd 9 to 2) 3
539[3] NOT IN DOUBT (USA) 4-8-8 W Newnes (3) *set steady pace, quickened aftr 4 fs, hdd 3 out, rallied wl fnl furlong*.
..........................(16 to 1 op 14 to 1 tchd 20 to 1) 4
438* DARU (USA) (v) 4-8-8 M Roberts (2) *hld up, hdwy o'r 2 fs out, kpt on one pace fnl furlong*............(15 to 8 jt-fav op 6 to 4) 5
JUSTICE (Fr) 5-9-4 L Dettori (4) *trkd ldrs till wknd 5 fs out, virtually pld up appr last, tld off*.
......................(33 to 1 op 25 to 1 tchd 40 to 1) 6
Dist: Nk, hd, ¾l, 1l, 25l. 3m 42.36s. a 17.36s (6 Ran).
(K Higson), D R C Elsworth

736 White Rose Conditions Stakes Class B (3-y-o) £9,399 1¼m.................... (3:05)

540[4] TIOMAN ISLAND 8-12 T Quinn (2) *trkd ldr, rdn to ld o'r one furlong out, drvn out*.
........................(7 to 4 fav op 2 to 1 tchd 5 to 2) 1
ZIND (Ire) 8-10 J Reid (1) *hld up in tch, chlgd and ev ch one and a half fs out, one pace ins*.
..............................(2 to 1 op 11 to 10 on) 2
TOMOS 8-10 M Roberts (3) *led, rdn and hdd o'r one furlong out, one pace aftr*.
........................(10 to 1 op 14 to 1 tchd 16 to 1) 3
KING PARIS (Ire) 9-0 M Hills (4) *hld up, stumbled on path and lost pl o'r 4 fs out, hdwy 2 out, not pace to chal*.
..........................(4 to 1 op 9 to 2 tchd 5 to 1) 4
388[6] PALACE PAGEANT (USA) 8-10 R Cochrane (5) *hld up, rdn and hdwy o'r 2 fs out, sn outpcd*..............(10 to 1) 5
Dist: 1½l, ¾l, 2½l, 2l. 2m 12.44s. a 8.74s (5 Ran).
SR: 11/6/4/3/-/ (H R H Sultan Ahmad Shah), P F I Cole

737 Insulpak Victoria Cup Handicap Class B (0-110 4-y-o and up) £20,387 7f...... (3:40)

475* TENDER MOMENT (Ire) [69] 5-7-7[3] (5*) B Doyle (18) *chsd ldrs far side, hdwy o'r one furlong out, str run to ld nr finish*..........................(16 to 1 tchd 20 to 1) 1
KAYVEE [92] 4-9-4 W R Swinburn (21) *trkd ldrs far side, led appr fnl furlong, ran on, hdd nr finish*.
.................................(25 to 1 tchd 33 to 1) 2
302[4] INDIAN SLAVE (Ire) [67] 5-7-7 J Quinn (16) *al prmnt far side grp, dsptd ld entering fnl furlong, ran on wl ins*.
.................................(14 to 1 tchd 16 to 1) 3
391* LITTLE ROUSILLON [67] 5-7-7 J Penza (6) *nvr far away, ev ch entering fnl furlong, ran on one pace*.
........................(25 to 1 op 20 to 1 tchd 33 to 1) 4
581[9] EFHARISTO [88] (bl) 4-9-0 M Roberts (5) *chsd ldrs, ev ch appr fnl furlong, kpt on one pace*. ....(11 to 1 co-fav op 10 to 1) 5
605* MILLSOLIN (Ire) [81] 5-8-7 (6ex) T Quinn (13) *nvr far away, ev ch one furlong out, one pace*. ....(11 to 1 co-fav op 12 to 1 tchd 10 to 1) 6
592[6] HOB GREEN [69] 4-7-9 J Lowe (1) *hld up on stands side, hdwy appr fnl furlong, not rch ldrs*. ......(11 to 1 co-fav op 8 to 1 tchd 12 to 1) 7
581 CONFRONTER [77] 4-8-3 C Rutter (22) *led far side grp, trkd o'r towards stands hfwy, dsptd ld entering fnl furlong, one pace*..............(25 to 1 tchd 33 to 1) 8
581 HIGHLAND MAGIC (Ire) [75] 5-8-1 D Holland (11) *towards rear, styd on appr fnl furlong, nvr nrr*.
..................................(12 to 1 op 14 to 1) 9
425 LAUREL QUEEN (Ire) [69] 5-7-9 L Charnock (4) *led till hdd o'r one furlong out, sn wknd*....(25 to 1 tchd 33 to 1) 10
475 TROOPING (Ire) [76] 4-8-2 W Carson (12) *outpcd, nvr rchd ldrs*..................................(12 to 1 op 10 to 1) 11
524[4] EURO FESTIVAL [92] 4-9-4 Pat Eddery (17) *nvr on terms*.
.............(11 to 1 co-fav op 10 to 1 tchd 12 to 1) 12
581[5] WILL OF STEEL [90] 4-9-2 K Fallon (9) *al beh*.
......................(12 to 1 op 10 to 1 tchd 14 to 1) 13
475[7] SUPEROO [74] 7-7-11 (3*) D Harrison (8) *mid-div, nvr on terms*...........................(14 to 1 tchd 20 to 1) 14
581[7] KNOCK TO ENTER (USA) [90] 5-9-2 J Williams (14) *al beh*.
....................................(14 to 1 op 12 to 1) 15
465[6] ECHO-LOGICAL [88] 4-9-0 K Darley (10) *al towards rear*.
....................................(12 to 1 op 10 to 1) 16
NOBLE PET [91] 4-9-3 B Raymond (3) *al beh*.
....................................(33 to 1 op 25 to 1) 17
390[6] MASTER PLANNER [98] 4-9-10 D Biggs (2) *trkd ldr till wknd quickly 2 fs out*.............(33 to 1 op 25 to 1) 18
479[3] ASSIGNMENT [76] 7-8-2 T Williams (20) *al towards rear*.
....................................(25 to 1 op 20 to 1) 19
604[4] PRECIOUS WONDER [69] 4-7-9 N Adams (7) *outpcd thrght*...........................(33 to 1 op 25 to 1) 20
604* SHIKARI'S SON [81] 6-8-7 (6ex) R Cochrane (15) *al beh*.
..............................(16 to 1 tchd 20 to 1) 21
581[2] RISK MASTER [86] 4-8-12 R Hills (19) *speed far side to hfwy*..........(11 to 1 co-fav op 10 to 1 tchd 12 to 1) 22
Dist: Nk, nk, 1½l, sht-hd, ¾l, nk, nk, nk, nk, 1½l. 1m 28.21s. a 1.91s (22 Ran).
SR: 51/73/47/42/62/53/40/47/44/ (Ray Richards), C E Brittain

738 Garter Conditions Stakes Class B (2-y-o) £6,396 5f......................... (4:10)

543* WAJIBA RIVA (Ire) 9-1 Pat Eddery (4) *nvr far away and al gng wl, led well o'r one furlong out, edgd lft, pushed out, cmftbly*.
......(11 to 8 fav op 5 to 4 tchd 11 to 10 and 6 to 4) 1
RIVER DEEP (USA) 8-12 A Munro (9) *outpcd, gd hdwy appr fnl furlong, ran on wl*. (13 to 2 op 4 to 1 tchd 7 to 1) 2
454* THATCHERELLA 8-7 D Holland (5) *al prmnt, ev ch 2 fs out, rdn and kpt on one pace ins last*.
.....................(16 to 1 op 10 to 1 tchd 20 to 1) 3
399* MISS AMY LOU (Ire) 8-10 J Carroll (3) *led till hdd wl o'r one furlong out, edgd rght and one pace ins last*.
......................(7 to 1 op 8 to 1 tchd 10 to 1) 4
586[2] OCHOS RIOS (Ire) 8-12 D Harrison (10) *outpcd, ran on fnl furlong*..............(20 to 1 op 25 to 1 tchd 33 to 1) 5
469* VALIANT MAN 9-1 J Reid (6) *speed to hfwy*.
..............................(16 to 1 tchd 25 to 1) 6
FRENCH GIFT 8-7 J Williams (1) *al outpcd*.
......................(11 to 2 op 5 to 1 tchd 7 to 1) 7
625* WINDOW DISPLAY 8-12 G Carter (7) *speed till wknd o'r one furlong out*......(20 to 1 op 16 to 1 tchd 25 to 1) 8
325[7] CARLTON CROWN (USA) 8-7 T Quinn (8) *al beh*.
.................................(50 to 1 op 66 to 1) 9
STOMPIN 8-12 M Roberts (11) *swrvd rght strt, al beh*.
......................(14 to 1 op 12 to 1 tchd 16 to 1) 10
Dist: 3½l, ¾l, ½l, 1½l, 2l, ¾l, 5l, 2l, sht-hd. 1m 1.61s. a 1.31s (10 Ran).
SR: 50/33/25/26/22/17/6/-/-/ (The Winning Team), R Hannon

739 Chobham Apprentice Handicap Class E (0-90 4-y-o and up) £4,464 1½m..... (4:40)

628[2] BROUGHTON'S TANGO (Ire) [57] 4-8-7 (3*) D McCabe (9) *hld up, steady hdwy 3 fs out, ran on strly to ld 50 yards out*.................................(9 to 2 op 5 to 1) 1
527[7] DOM WAC [66] 5-9-6 M Fenton (12) *hld up, gd hdwy on ins 3 fs out, led one out, hdd 50 yards out*.
......................................(7 to 1 tchd 8 to 1) 2
674[9] BUSMAN (Ire) [66] 4-9-2 (3*) Kim McDonnell (6) *hld up, hdwy o'r 2 fs out, ran on, not rch 1st two*.
..............................(20 to 1 op 16 to 1) 3
226[2] KOVALEVSKIA [39] 8-7-2 (5*) Sharon Millard (8) *wtd wth, hdwy o'r 2 fs out, kpt on one pace ins last*.....(33 to 1) 4
ALLMOSA [48] 4-7-10 (5*) D Gibbs (4) *hdwy on outsd o'r 4 fs out, ran wide into strt, styd on ins last*.
..................(25 to 1 op 20 to 1 tchd 33 to 1) 5
WESTERN DYNASTY [65] 7-9-0 (5*) P McCabe (13) *led aftr 2 fs, rdn and hdd one furlong out, no extr*.
..............................(16 to 1 tchd 20 to 1) 6
PROSEQUENDO (USA) [65] 6-9-5 N Gwilliams (11) *hld up, hdwy 5 fs out, ev ch 2 furlongs out, sn btn*.
...................(20 to 1 op 16 to 1 tchd 25 to 1) 7
628* BLACKPATCH HILL [58] 4-8-11 (4ex) Stephen Davies (2) *hld up in tch, rdn 2 fs out, one pace*.
.....................(2 to 1 fav op 7 to 4 tchd 9 to 4) 8
622[5] MON PETITNAMOUR (Ire) [40] 4-7-4 (3*) Darren Moffatt (3) *slwly away, nvr on terms*..........(25 to 1 op 33 to 1) 9
495 ROCKY ROMANCE [39] 6-7-6[2] (3*) C Hawksley (1) *al beh*.
....(100 to 1) 10
513[3] LOBILIO (USA) [71] (bl) 4-9-10 B Doyle (7) *led 1st 2 fs, rdn 4 out, sn wknd*.........................(11 to 2 op 5 to 1) 11
ACROBATE (USA) [70] 4-9-6 (3*) A Procter (5) *al beh*.
.......................(25 to 1 op 20 to 1 tchd 33 to 1) 12
632[2] FAIR FLYER (Ire) [57] 4-8-10 O Pears (14) *dsptd ld, wkng whn hit rail o'r 2 fs out, sn beh*.....(9 to 2 op 5 to 1) 13
626[7] UP ALL NIGHT [40] 4-7-4 (3*) D Wright (10) *prmnt till lost tch 4 fs out*...............(33 to 1 tchd 40 to 1) 14
Dist: ½l, 1½l, 1½l, hd, ¾l, nk, ¾l, 1½l, 12l, 2½l. 2m 36.00s. a 7.80s (14 Ran).
SR: 18/27/23/-/1/17/16/6/-/ (S P Lansdown), M J Heaton-Ellis

HAMILTON (soft)
Thursday April 29th

Going Correction: PLUS 0.60 sec. per fur. (races

1,2,5,6), PLUS 0.45 (3,4)

740 Eaglesham Limited Stakes Class F (4-y-o and up) £2,534 1m 1f 36yds......... (2:05)

645* ROMOLA NIJINSKY 5-8-6 K Darley (7) *trkd ldg pair, led 2 fs out, pushed clr, cmftbly*........(5 to 4 on op 11 to 10) 1
645⁴ AEGAEN LADY 4-8-6 J Carroll (6) *chsd ldrs, hdwy o'r 2 fs out, rdn appr last, kpt on same pace, no ch wth wnr.* .... (5 to 1 tchd 6 to 1 and 7 to 1) 2
620 ACHELOUS (v) 6-8-8 (3*) S D Williams (4) *made most till hdd 2 fs out, sn rdn and one pace*...(11 to 2 op 4 to 1) 3
SRIVIJAYA 6-8-4 (7*) Darren Moffatt (1) *patiently rdn, hdwy o'r 4 fs out, sn ridden and no extr.* ....(8 to 1 op 5 to 1) 4
645 BRECKENBROUGH LAD 6-8-4 (7*) V Halliday (2) *tucked away on ins, shrtlvd effrt 4 fs out, sn btn.* .... (11 to 1 op 7 to 1 tchd 12 to 1) 5
TINA MEENA LISA 4-8-6 J Lowe (5) *chsd ldrs till wknd 4 fs out*................................ (66 to 1 op 33 to 1) 6
531 STRANGERSINTHENITE (bl) 4-8-11 L Charnock (8) *dsptd ld till wknd quickly frm 4 fs out, sn wl beh*......(100 to 1) 7
ARAGON AYR 5-8-11 N Connorton (3) *hld up, rdn alng 4 fs out, sn wl beh*.....................(25 to 1 op 14 to 1) 8

Dist: 3l, 3l, 7l, 1½l, 8l, 15l, 15l. 2m 3.50s. a 9.50s (8 Ran).
SR: 33/24/20/-/-/ (Mrs L A Windsor), P D Evans

741 Bellshill Claiming Stakes Class F (3-y-o) £2,422 1m 65yds.................. (2:35)

532⁷ ANUSHA 8-2 J Carroll (6) *rstrained early, rdn and outpcd 4 fs out, styd on ag'n frm o'r 2 out to ld appr last, sn clr, cmftbly*.............................(4 to 1 op 3 to 1) 1
339² FRIENDLY KNIGHT 8-5 K Darley (3) *trkd ldrs, led o'r 3 fs out, hdd over one out, unbl to quicken.* ....(5 to 1 op 4 to 1) 2
455 CALISAR 8-7 T Sprake (2) *wtd wth till effrt 4 fs out, rdn and ev ch o'r 2 out, wknd appr last.* (8 to 1 op 5 to 1) 3
ALWAYS RISKY 8-1 (7*) R Havlin (1) *rstrained early, effrt 4 fs out, ev ch o'r 2 out, sn rdn and btn.* ....(7 to 2 op 4 to 1 tchd 9 to 2) 4
733⁴ DESIRABLE MISS (v) 8-4 J Lowe (5) *led till hdd o'r 3 fs out, sn rdn alng, wknd wl over one out*...(4 to 1 op 7 to 2) 5
549⁶ SKY WISH 8-9 N Connorton (4) *hng lft thrght, trkd ldr, rdn wl o'r 3 fs out, wknd.* .... (3 to 1 fav op 5 to 2 tchd 4 to 1 and 5 to 1) 6

Dist: 3½l, 8l, 5l, ¾l, 2½l. 1m 52.80s. a 8.80s (6 Ran).
SR: 30/22/-/ (Yahya Nasib), J Berry

742 Glengoyne Single Highland Malt Scotch Whisky Handicap Class E (0-70 3-y-o) £2,768 6f 5yds.................... (3:05)

418⁶ BURISHKI [50] 8-0 (7*) D Wright (4) *trkd ldrs, led hfwy, pld clr fnl furlong*..........................(7 to 1 op 6 to 1) 1
428⁵ LAMSONETTI [56] 8-13 A Culhane (3) *beh till rdn and effrt on ins o'r 2 fs out, kpt on inside last.* (9 to 2 op 7 to 2) 2
451* HIGH ROMANCE [54] 8-4 (7*) Darren Moffatt (7) *chsd ldrs, effrt 2 fs out, ran on one pace*........(7 to 2 op 5 to 2) 3
591⁵ SHADOW JURY [63] 9-6 K Darley (1) *chsd ldrs, rdn and ev ch 2 fs out, wknd ins last.* .... (9 to 4 fav op 3 to 1 tchd 4 to 1) 4
631* MISS WHITTINGHAM (Ire) [61] 9-4 (7ex) J Carroll (2) *hld up in tch on outsd, effrt 2 fs out, wknd appr last.* ....(9 to 2 op 7 to 2 tchd 5 to 1) 5
4717a MY BALLYBOY [64] (bl) 9-7 A Mackay (5) *beh and outpcd till moderate hdwy fnl one and a half fs, nvr able to chal*.............................. (16 to 1 op 7 to 1) 6
634⁹ MATTHEW DAVID [48] (bl) 8-5 J Lowe (6) *broke wl, led to hfwy, sn wknd*....................(33 to 1 op 16 to 1) 7

Dist: 3l, sht-hd, ½l, 6l, 1½l, 3l. 1m 16.60s. a 5.90s (7 Ran).
SR: 29/23/20/27/1/-/-/ (Giles W Pritchard-Gordon), G A Pritchard-Gordon

743 Coatbridge Maiden Auction Stakes Class F (2-y-o) £2,444 5f 4yds............. (3:35)

466⁸ HILTONS TRAVEL (Ire) (v) 9-0 S Webster (5) *made all far side, sn clr, unchlgd.* (10 to 1 op 7 to 1 tchd 12 to 1) 1
MONKEY'S WEDDING 9-0 J Carroll (3) *made most stands side, rdn o'r one furlong out, ran on same pace ins last, no ch wth wnr*.....................(3 to 1 tchd 2 to 1) 2
TRENDY DANCER (Ire) 8-9 (5*) O Pears (4) *prmnt stands side, effrt wl o'r one furlong out, not quicken ins last.* .... (20 to 1 op 8 to 1) 3
BACCANALIA (Ire) 9-0 D Nicholls (6) *prmnt stands side till wknd fnl furlong*..... (13 to 2 op 6 to 1 tchd 12 to 1) 4
343 MARBLE 8-9 N Connorton (7) *hng rght leaving stalls and slwly away, some hdwy 2 fs out, wknd o'r one out.* .... (20 to 1 op 10 to 1) 5
607⁴ TENDER NORTH 8-9 K Darley (1) *outpcd stands side, rdn hfwy, no imprsn*................ (3 to 1 op 6 to 4) 6
466² PORTITE SOPHIE 8-9 M Wigham (2) *prmnt 2 fs stands side, sn rdn alng and lost pl quickly.* (2 to 1 fav tchd 3 to 1) 7

Dist: 4l, nk, 2½l, 4l, 8l, ½l. 1m 5.80s. a 7.50s (7 Ran).
(Mrs Dot Jones), E J Alston

744 Drumloch Rating Related Maiden Stakes Class E (3-y-o and up) £2,691 1½m 17yds ....(4:05)

CHIAPPUCCI (Ire) (v) 3-8-5 J Carroll (2) *hld up gng wl, smooth hdwy to ld o'r 2 fs out, sn clr, easily.* ....(6 to 4 op 7 to 4 tchd 5 to 4) 1
642⁵ DANCES WITH GOLD 3-8-0 J Lowe (3) *led till hdd o'r 2 fs out, not pace of wnr*.......... (Evens fav op 5 to 4 on) 2
559⁸ THOR POWER (Ire) 4-9-12 K Darley (1) *trkd ldr, rdn and ev ch 3 fs out, one pace*....(13 to 2 op 4 to 1 tchd 7 to 1) 3
ACQUISITION (bl) 6-9-12 S Webster (4) *sn last, lost tch fnl 5 fs*......(20 to 1 op 12 to 1 tchd 33 to 1 and 50 to 1) 4

Dist: 5l, 1½l, 10l. 2m 49.10s. a 16.10s (4 Ran).
SR: 2/-/10/-/ (M A Jarvis), M A Jarvis

745 East Kilbride Handicap Class E (0-70 3-y-o and up) £2,950 1½m 17yds..........(4:35)

SHAMSHOM AL ARAB (Ire) [34] 5-7-6 (7*) Darren Moffatt (5) *took keen hold, al hndy, led wl o'r 3 fs out, clr frm 2 out, styd on strly.* ....(9 to 1 op 10 to 1 tchd 8 to 1 and 14 to 1) 1
453³ PERSUASIVE [57] 6-9-8 Dale Gibson (4) *wtd wth, gd hdwy wl o'r 2 fs out, sn chasing wnr, no imprsn fnl furlong.* ....(6 to 4 fav op 5 to 4 tchd 7 to 4) 2
453* PHILGUN [60] 4-9-7 (3*) S Maloney (1) *al tracking ldrs, rdn and effrt o'r 2 fs out, kpt on same pace.* ....(2 to 1 op 5 to 2 tchd 7 to 4) 3
530 BEAUMOOD [34] 7-7-6 (7*) D Wright (8) *trkd ldrs till rdn and one pace frm o'r 2 fs out*...... (33 to 1 op 16 to 1) 4
WEST WITH THE WIND [48] 6-8-13 J Lowe (7) *wtd wth, effrt o'r 3 fs out, sn btn.* .... (10 to 1 op 7 to 1 tchd 12 to 1) 5
453⁷ MINGUS (USA) [47] 6-8-12 D Nicholls (6) *hld up and beh, rdn wl o'r 2 fs out, nvr able to chal.* .... (14 to 1 op 10 to 1 tchd 16 to 1) 6
18⁸ INVISIBLE ARMOUR [42] 4-7-13 (7*) C Adamson (3) *trkd ldr till ran wide bend o'r 5 fs out, sn lost pl.* .... (20 to 1 op 14 to 1) 7
LOCAL DEALER [33] 5-7-12 L Charnock (2) *led till hdd wl o'r 3 fs out, sn wknd*... (9 to 1 op 8 to 1 tchd 10 to 1) 8

Dist: 3½l, 5l, 4l, 3½l, 2½l, 4l, ½l. 2m 46.60s. a 13.60s (8 Ran).
SR: 21/37/29/-/3/ (Miss Maha Kalaji), S G Norton

NEWMARKET (good)
Thursday April 29th
Going Correction: MINUS 0.15 sec. per fur.

746 Timanfaya Conditions Stakes Class C (3-y-o) £5,070 7f..................... (2:00)

580⁶ FIRM PLEDGE (USA) 9-0 A Munro (6) *confidently rdn, drw level 2 fs out, led appr fnl furlong, lnd wl.* ....(11 to 8 fav op 6 to 4) 1
510* MATILA (Ire) 8-9 W Carson (1) *nvr far away, bustled alng whn pace lifted o'r one furlong out, kpt on wl towards finish*..............................(4 to 1 op 6 to 1) 2
300* THUNDER RIVER (Ire) 9-0 M J Kinane (3) *dictated pace for o'r 5 fs, rallied ins last, kpt on.* .... (25 to 1 op 14 to 1 tchd 33 to 1) 3
583* WINGED VICTORY (Ire) 8-9 L Dettori (5) *al hndy, nosed ahead 2 fs out, hdd appr last, fdd towards finish.* .... (5 to 1 op 9 to 2 tchd 11 to 2) 4
MYSTIC GODDESS (USA) 9-1 W R Swinburn (2) *last and hld up, effrt o'r 2 fs out, rdn and outpcd entering fnl furlong*...............(10 to 1 op 8 to 1 tchd 12 to 1) 5
FACTUAL (USA) 9-0 Pat Eddery (4) *settled to track ldr, hrd rdn and bustled alng o'r one furlong out, sn btn.* .... (9 to 2 op 7 to 4 tchd 11 to 2) 6

Dist: 1½l, ¾l, 1½l, 3l, 2½l. 1m 26.02s. a 2.52s (6 Ran).
SR: 46/36/39/29/26/17/ (Fahd Salman), P F I Cole

747 P.R.S. Professional Revenue Services Handicap Class C (0-95 3-y-o) £5,692 7f ....(2:30)

EASY ACCESS (Ire) [86] 9-7 M J Kinane (3) *patiently rdn, improved 2 fs out, drvn through to ld appr last, faltered ins last, hld on wl*..................(10 to 1 op 7 to 1) 1
313⁴ ABLE CHOICE (Ire) [75] 8-10 L Piggott (1) *trkd ldr centre, drvn up to draw level ins fnl furlong, ran on, jst hld.* ....(9 to 2 op 4 to 1) 2
538 TIMOTHY CASEY [75] 8-10 Pat Eddery (7) *fractious at strt, wtd wth, improved frm off the pace 2 fs out, ev ch ins last, kpt on same pace.* (13 to 2 op 5 to 1 tchd 7 to 1) 3
380³ RED FAN (Ire) [69] 8-4 G Duffield (8) *chsd far side ldr, ev ch und pres appr fnl furlong, no extr.* ....(11 to 4 fav op 9 to 4 tchd 3 to 1) 4
71² MISS GORGEOUS (Ire) [77] 8-9 (3*) Emma O'Gorman (6) *clr ldr centre, led briefly 2 fs out, fdd ins last.* ....(12 to 1 op 8 to 1 tchd 14 to 1) 5
483³ BEZIQUE (USA) [72] (bl) 8-7 M Roberts (9) *set fst pace far side, hdd and rdn 2 fs out, fdd.* ....(7 to 2 op 4 to 1 tchd 5 to 1) 6

471[6] NABJELSEDR [85] 9-6 W Carson (2) *last and drvn alng most of way, nvr a threat*.......... (13 to 2 op 5 to 1) 7
Dist: Nk, 1½l, 1½l, 2½l, 4l, sht-hd. 1m 26.39s. a 2.89s (7 Ran).
SR: 48/36/31/20/20/3/15/ (N Ahamad), R Hannon

748 Madagans Pretty Polly Stakes Class A (Listed Race) (3-y-o) £12,652 1¼m...(3:00)

684[6] MAGICAL RETREAT (USA) 8-10 D Biggs (1) *enterprisingly rdn, set steady pace till quickened o'r 3 out, kpt on strly fnl furlong*..... (20 to 1 op 33 to 1 tchd 16 to 1) 1
472[3] BRIGHT GENERATION (Ire) 9-1 A Munro (3) *patiently rdn, pld out to improve o'r 2 fs out, dngrs fnl furlong, no extr cl hme.* ....(5 to 2 op 6 to 4 tchd 11 to 4 and 11 to 4) 2
PAMZIG (USA) 8-10 D Holland (4) *trkd ldg trio, rdn whn pace lifted o'r 2 fs out, kpt on same pace.* .... (100 to 30 op 5 to 2 tchd 7 to 2) 3
FAYFA (Ire) 8-13 Pat Eddery (2) *settled gng wl, prmsg effrt 3 fs out, sn rdn, no imprsn fnl furlong.* ....(11 to 8 fav op 6 to 4 tchd 13 to 8) 4
443* ALYAKKH (Ire) 8-10 R Hills (5) *trkd wnr, feeling pace and lost grnd o'r 2 fs out, sn struggling.* (8 to 1 tchd 9 to 1) 5
Dist: ¾l, 2l, ¾l, 10l. 2m 8.64s. a 5.94s (5 Ran).
SR: 22/25/16/17/-/ (R M Cyzer), C A Cyzer

749 Madagans 1000 Guineas Stakes Class A (Group 1) (3-y-o) £107,063 1m.......(3:40)

512[3] SAYYEDATI 9-0 W R Swinburn (4) *steadied strt, improved into midfield and swtchd outsd hfwy, led wl o'r one out, ran on strly ins last*.............(4 to 1 op 5 to 2) 1
512* NICHE 9-0 L Piggott (8) *tried to make all, hdd and drvn alng wl o'r one furlong out, rallied gmely, kpt on.* .... (6 to 1 op 7 to 1 tchd 15 to 2) 2
472[2] AJFAN (USA) 9-0 R Hills (11) *trkd ldrs, feeling pace and drvn alng o'r 2 fs out, rallied ins last, fnshd wl.* ....(33 to 1 tchd 40 to 1) 3
FELAWNAH (USA) 9-0 W Carson (9) *settled midfield, improved entering last 2 fs, rng on wl finish.* ....(33 to 1 tchd 50 to 1) 4
537[2] DAYFLOWER (USA) 9-0 L Dettori (7) *trkd ldrs, improved frm midfield appr fnl furlong, ran on strly finish.* ....(33 to 1 tchd 40 to 1) 5
LYRIC FANTASY (Ire) 9-0 M J Kinane (12) *trkd ldr, ev ch and bustled alng o'r one furlong out, not quicken last 100 yards*.............................. (14 to 1 tchd 16 to 1) 6
512[2] ZARANI SIDI ANNA (USA) 9-0 B Raymond (10) *tucked away beh ldrs, effrt and bustled alng 2 fs out, styd on ins last, nvr nrr*............................(5 to 1 tchd 11 to 2) 7
432[2] ELIZABETH BAY (USA) 9-0 M Roberts (2) *edgy bef race, rdn to go pace hfwy, styd on, nvr able to trble ldrs.* ....(9 to 4 fav op 2 to 1 tchd 5 to 2) 8
556[3] SECRAGE (USA) 9-0 Pat Eddery (5) *nvr far away, ev ch and drvn alng o'r one furlong out, no extr ins last.* ....(16 to 1 tchd 20 to 1) 9
STAR FAMILY FRIEND (Ire) 9-0 P Robinson (1) *chsd ldg bunch, rdn hfwy, not pace to chal*..........(100 to 1) 10
432* WIXON (Fr) 9-0 C Asmussen (6) *settled midfield, effrt hfwy, struggling 2 fs out, fdd*.... (14 to 1 tchd 16 to 1) 11
523* STELLA MYSTIKA (USA) 9-0 R Cochrane (3) *moved poorly to post, sluggish strt, nvr a factor.* ....(16 to 1 tchd 20 to 1) 12
Dist: ½l, hd, 1½l, ½l, hd, nk, 1l, 1l, 7l, 1l. 1m 37.34s. a 0.14s (12 Ran).
SR: 80/78/77/72/70/69/68/65/62/ (Mohamed Obaida), C E Brittain

750 Fairfax House Rated Stakes Handicap Class B (0-105 4-y-o and up) £9,611 6f ....(4:15)

511* SPLICE [102] 4-9-5 W R Swinburn (6) *patiently rdn, improved to show ahead o'r one furlong out, ran on strly last 50 yards*.............(4 to 1 jt-fav op 4 to 1) 1
587[2] DOUBLE BLUE [94] 4-8-11 Dean McKeown (3) *al hndy, rdn o'r one furlong out, rallied gmely towards finish.* ....(4 to 1 jt-fav op 3 to 1 tchd 9 to 2) 2
604[2] HARD TO FIGURE [97] 7-9-0 W Carson (8) *chsd ldrs, rdn hfwy, swtchd ins to improve o'r one out, fnshd fst.* ....(8 to 1 tchd 9 to 1) 3
GARAH [104] 4-9-7 Pat Eddery (10) *led, rcd alone far side, rdn and hdd o'r one furlong out, kpt on same pace.* .... (7 to 1 op 6 to 1 tchd 15 to 2) 4
481[7] VENTURE CAPITALIST [93] (bl) 4-8-10 M J Kinane (1) *jinked lft leaving stalls, improved into midfield hfwy, shaken up and ran on wl fnl furlong.* .... (7 to 1 op 6 to 1 tchd 15 to 2) 5
481[4] DUPLICITY (Ire) [96] 5-8-13 M Roberts (5) *settled to track ldg bunch, pushed alng to improve o'r 2 fs out, ran on.* .... (13 to 2 op 5 to 1) 6
GREEN DOLLAR [90] 10-8-7 M Tebbutt (9) *pushed up frm midfield to join issue hfwy, rdn o'r one furlong out, fdd*.................(16 to 1 op 20 to 1 tchd 25 to 1) 7
FINJAN [90] 6-8-7 A Munro (2) *trkd ldg quartet, rdn o'r one furlong out, no extr.* .... (25 to 1 op 20 to 1 tchd 33 to 1) 8
436[3] BEAU VENTURE (USA) [90] 5-8-7 B Raymond (4) *trkd ldg trio, ev ch o'r 2 fs out, rdn and no extr.* .... (15 to 2 op 6 to 1 tchd 8 to 1) 9
524[6] GILT THRONE [95] 6-8-12 P Robinson (7) *broke wl to show gd speed in frnt rnk 4 fs, fdd.* .... (25 to 1 op 20 to 1 tchd 33 to 1) 10
Dist: 1l, nk, hd, sht-hd, 1½l, ¾l, hd, 2½l, 3l. 1m 12.08s. a 0.68s (10 Ran).
SR: 73/61/63/69/57/54/45/44/34/ (Cheveley Park Stud), J R Fanshawe

751 Rex Cohen Memorial Maiden Stakes Class D (3-y-o) £4,971 1m...........(4:45)

WAGON MASTER (Fr) 9-0 R Hills (18) *tucked away in midfield, bustled through to ld ins fnl furlong, ran on wl*..............................(25 to 1 tchd 33 to 1) 1
MISTLE CAT (USA) 9-0 W Woods (15) *wth ldr, led o'r 2 fs out, till ins fnl furlong, kpt on wl*............. (33 to 1) 2
540[8] BITTER'S END (Ire) 9-0 M J Kinane (6) *al hndy, ev ch and drvn alng 2 fs out, kpt on same pace.* ....(7 to 2 fav op 3 to 1 tchd 4 to 1) 3
529[4] MECKLENBURG (Ire) 9-0 M Roberts (9) *wth ldrs, hng rght und pres o'r one furlong out, no extr.* ....(6 to 1 op 5 to 1 tchd 7 to 1) 4
529[2] MT TEMPLEMAN (USA) 9-0 L Dettori (11) *nvr far away, ev ch and not much room o'r one furlong out, unbl to quicken*.................(9 to 2 op 4 to 1 tchd 5 to 1) 5
WINGED VICTORY (USA) 9-0 R Cochrane (21) *lost many ls strt, given time to reco'r, ran on wl last 2 fs, prmsg.* .... (9 to 1 op 7 to 1 tchd 10 to 1) 6
THALEROS 9-0 L Piggott (17) *broke wl to show gd speed in frnt rnk for 6 fs, fdd*..................(7 to 1 op 6 to 1) 7
529[6] BARRATRY 9-0 A McGlone (8) *settled midfield, feeling pace and bustled alng o'r 2 fs out, staying on finish.* ....(12 to 1 tchd 14 to 1) 8
529[3] KARSHI 9-0 G Duffield (4) *beh and chsd alng hfwy, styd on frm off the pace last 2 fs, nvr nrr.* ....(8 to 1 tchd 9 to 1) 9
BALE BREAKER (USA) 9-0 N Day (14) *beh and chsd alng hfwy, styd on last 2 fs, nrst finish.* (33 to 1 op 25 to 1) 10
DAWALIB (USA) 9-0 W Carson (16) *made most till hdd o'r 2 fs out, fdd entering fnl furlong*.....(6 to 1 tchd 7 to 1) 11
582[5] ARID 9-0 Pat Eddery (19) *trkd ldg bunch, effrt o'r 3 fs out, outpcd last 2 furlongs*............ (7 to 1 tchd 8 to 1) 12
DARMSTADT (USA) 9-0 G Hind (7) *settled off the pace, steady hdwy o'r 2 fs out, nvr plcd to chal*..... (33 to 1) 13
529 AJDAYT (USA) 9-0 B Raymond (13) *sluggish strt, nvr able to reco'r*.........................(33 to 1 op 20 to 1) 14
TINSASHE (Ire) 8-9 M Tebbutt (12) *settled midfield, effrt hfwy, wknd and eased last 2 fs*.............. (33 to 1) 15
529 MAASHAI LAWM (Ire) 9-0 P Robinson (5) *pushed alng in midfield hfwy, no imprsn*........(33 to 1 tchd 50 to 1) 16
DON TOCINO 9-0 A Munro (1) *trkd ldrs, effrt hfwy, grad wknd*.............................(33 to 1 op 25 to 1) 17
MOULTAZIM (USA) 9-0 W R Swinburn (2) *chsd alng in midfield hfwy, fdd*.... (11 to 2 op 5 to 1 tchd 6 to 1) 18
HOPEFUL PROSPECT 8-9 G Carter (20) *drvn alng in midfield hfwy, sn lost tch*.......................... (33 to 1) 19
CAST THE LINE 9-0 Dean McKeown (3) *struggling to go pace hfwy, nvr a factor*.......... (25 to 1 op 20 to 1) 20
Dist: 1½l, 1½l, ½l, 3½l, 1½l, 1½l, sht-hd, ½l, 2½l, ½l. 1m 39.06s. a 1.86s (20 Ran).
SR: 54/49/44/42/31/26/21/20/18/ (Hamdan Al-Maktoum), A C Stewart

752 Coombe House Maiden Stakes Class D (3-y-o) £4,581 7f.....................(5:15)

KHUBZA 8-11 A McGlone (4) *made all, hrd pressed o'r one furlong out, kpt on strly.* .... (16 to 1 op 8 to 1 tchd 20 to 1) 1
GHOST TREE (Ire) 8-11 M Roberts (9) *trkd ldg 5, drvn up to chal o'r one furlong out, kpt on same pace fnl furlong.* ....(5 to 4 fav op 6 to 4) 2
523[9] CORAL GEM 8-11 R Hills (6) *trkd ldg half dozen, improved 2 fs out, styd on one pace fnl furlong.* .... (33 to 1 op 20 to 1) 3
523[4] DANCING SPIRIT (Ire) 8-11 M J Kinane (8) *broke wl to show gd speed in frnt rnk for o'r 5 fs, no extr.* .... (6 to 1 op 4 to 1 tchd 13 to 2) 4
PRINCESS HAYLEY 8-11 Pat Eddery (11) *chsd alng to go pace, styd on last 2 fs, nvr nrr*..... (6 to 1 tchd 7 to 1) 5
CRYSTAL REAY 8-11 R Cochrane (3) *beh and ran green hfwy, steady hdwy o'r one furlong out, nrst finish.* ....(8 to 1 op 4 to 1 tchd 9 to 1) 6
ROCK THE BOAT 8-11 L Dettori (5) *sluggish strt, swtchd rght to improve hfwy, kpt on, nvr able to chal.* ....(12 to 1 op 8 to 1 tchd 16 to 1) 7
FADAKI HAWAKI (USA) 8-11 W R Swinburn (1) *al hndy, rdn 2 fs out, fdd fnl furlong.* .... (9 to 1 op 7 to 1 tchd 10 to 1) 8
624[5] TIP ME UP 8-11 D Biggs (10) *broke wl to show gd speed for o'r 5 fs, no extr*.................(12 to 1 op 12 to 1) 9
FRANCIA 8-11 W Woods (2) *chsd alng to keep up hfwy, nvr dngrs*.............................(50 to 1 op 33 to 1) 10
583[9] SHEFFORD 8-11 R Price (7) *wth ldrs, feeling pace and drvn alng 2 fs out, fdd*.............. (50 to 1 op 33 to 1) 11
Dist: 2l, 1½l, 2l, 1½l, 3l, 1½l, 1½l, 1½l, 4l, hd. 1m 25.56s. a 2.06s (11 Ran).
SR: 50/44/39/33/28/19/14/9/4/ (Sheikh Mohammed), H R A Cecil

PUNCHESTOWN (IRE) (good to yielding)
Thursday April 29th

753 Irish Kidney Association Private Sweepstakes (4-y-o and up) £0 1m 5f. . . . . (5:45)

BRAVEFOOT 5-12-2 O Byrne (24) . . . . (6 to 1) 1
BLUEJACKET (Ire) 5-11-10 Susan Shortt (9) . . . . . . (10 to 1) 2
575 TIME IT RIGHT (Ire) 4-11-13 James Nolan (19) . . (5 to 2 fav) 3
PERSIAN HAZE (Ire) 4-11-13 Jane Martin (11) . . . . . . (6 to 1) 4
BLENHEIM PALACE (USA) 6-11-13 Richard Ranaghan (7) . . . . (10 to 1) 5
SOOTH 6-11-10 Dan McSorley (8) . . . . (25 to 1) 6
PIER THIRTY NINE 7-11-13 D O'Brien (6) . . . . (10 to 1) 7
BRAVE STAR 7-11-10 Audrey Powell (13) . . . . (20 to 1) 8
SLANEY ENCORE (Ire) 5-11-10 T Carberry (26) . . . . (7 to 2) 9
TERINGETTE (Hun) 5-12-5 Charles O'Reilly (12) . . . (25 to 1) 10
DEEP IN GREEK 7-11-10 Liam O'Flynn (4) . . . . (16 to 1) 11
AT YOUR SERVICE (Ire) 4-11-10 J Byrne (2) . . . . (10 to 1) 12
MIDNIGHT COURT (USA) 10-12-11 Claire Cremin (16) . . . . (10 to 1) 13
TESALIA (Spa) 4-11-13 Capt David C Foster (15) . . (10 to 1) 14
WHO'S FOOLING WHO 7-11-13 Frank Ward (3) . . (12 to 1) 15
LANTERN LUCK (Ire) 5-11-10 Michael Duke (5) . . . (14 to 1) 16
ONE FOR LUCK (Ire) 5-11-13 David Moloney (18) (10 to 1) 17
LISMEEN JOY 6-11-10 Jane Bradbury (25) . . . . (25 to 1) 18
DEEPRUNONTHEPOUND (Ire) 5-11-10 Robin McMullen (23) . . . . (20 to 1) 19
LE BRAVE 7-11-10 David Cox (22) . . . . (20 to 1) 20
CAPDOO LADY (Ire) 5-11-10 Paul Boland (27) . . . . (20 to 1) 21
GRANVILLE GRILL 8-12-2 F Berry (10) . . . . (8 to 1) 22
VISIONARY (Ire) 5-11-10 D Bennett (17) . . . . (14 to 1) 23
572 KO SAMAT 8-11-13 Linda Young (1) . . . . (14 to 1) 24
SKATE (Ire) 5-11-10 Alice Reeves-Smyth (20) . . . . . (25 to 1) su

Dist: ¾l, hd, 15l. 3m 18.70s. (25 Ran).

(S Macklin), J H Scott

SALISBURY (good)
Thursday April 29th
Going Correction: PLUS 0.05 sec. per fur.

754 Almond Apprentice Handicap Class G (0-70 3-y-o and up) £2,700 6f 212yds (2:20)

327 SAREEN EXPRESS (Ire) [42] 5-7-10 (5*) S McCarthy (8) *mid-div till hdwy 2 fs out, hrd rdn and ran on strly to get up on line*. . . . . (33 to 1 op 20 to 1) 1
603⁷ QUICK STEEL [50] (bl) 5-8-9 S Mulvey (20) *al prmnt, led 2 fs out, sn clr, wknd ins last, ct on line*. . . . . (5 to 1 fav op 10 to 1) 2
521⁴ OLD COMRADES [55] 6-8-9 (5*) Mark Denaro (15) *al prmnt, outpcd 2 fs out, ran on ins last*. . . . . . (8 to 1 op 6 to 1) 3
PROUD BRIGADIER (Ire) [51] 5-8-5 (5*) R Painter (6) *mid-div till styd on ins fnl 2 fs*. . . . . (14 to 1 op 10 to 1) 4
521* HOMEMAKER [60] 3-8-0 (5*) R Waterfield (19) *mid-div, styd on fnl 2 fs*. . . . . (6 to 1 op 5 to 1) 5
531⁶ ROYAL ACCLAIM [47] (v) 8-8-1 (5*) Michael Bradley (16) *in tch till one pace fnl 2 fs*. . . . . (25 to 1 op 14 to 1) 6
ANDY JACK [51] 4-8-7 (3*) J O'Dwyer (18) *led till hdd 2 fs out, one pace aftr*. . . . . (50 to 1 op 33 to 1) 7
521³ ON Y VA (USA) [56] 6-8-8 (7*) Sarah Thompson (11) *prmnt till outpcd fnl 2 fs*. . . . . (10 to 1 op 7 to 1) 8
333² ROYAL DARTMOUTH (USA) [51] 8-8-10 D Gibbs (12) *slwly away, hdwy 2 fs out, nvr dngrs*. . . . . . (9 to 1 op 6 to 1) 9
SINGERS IMAGE [59] (v) 4-9-1 (3*) Tracey Purseglove (2) *slwly away, nvr rch ldrs*. . . . . (16 to 1 op 10 to 1) 10
714 PRINCE ROONEY (Ire) [48] 5-8-2 (5*) G Strange (17) *chsd ldrs far side, lost tch o'r 2 fs out*. . . (16 to 1 op 14 to 1) 11
521⁸ JUST A STEP [63] 7-9-3 (5*) Gina Faulkner (3) *al beh*. . . . . (14 to 1 op 12 to 1 tchd 16 to 1 and 20 to 1) 12
PRINCE RODNEY [69] 4-9-7 (7*) A Whelan (1) *prmnt stands side till o'r hfwy*. . . . . (14 to 1) 13
DAVROB [59] 3-7-11 (7*) Wendy Jones (13) *chsd ldrs till wknd o'r 2 fs out*. . . . . (33 to 1 op 20 to 1) 14
440⁵ SHALOU [47] 4-8-6 P McCabe (14) *prmnt till wknd o'r 2 fs out*. . . . . (16 to 1 op 14 to 1) 15
403⁸ SARUM [47] 7-8-1 (5*) J Wilkinson (10) *chsd ldrs to hfwy, sn beh*. . . . . (20 to 1 op 14 to 1) 16
SEA PRODIGY [51] 4-8-10 D McCabe (5) *in tch stands side to hfwy*. . . . . (33 to 1 op 20 to 1) 17
531 IBSEN [49] 5-8-8 G Mitchell (9) *al beh*. (25 to 1 op 14 to 1) 18
4675a RISK PROOF [57] 3-7-9 (7*) D O'Neill (7) *in tch stands side for 4 fs*. . . . . (25 to 1 op 16 to 1) 19
SUDANOR (Ire) [43] 4-8-2 J Tate (4) *al beh*. . . . . (16 to 1 op 12 to 1) 20

Dist: Sht-hd, ¾l, 3l, 1½l, hd, 2l, ¾l, nk, 2l, sht-hd. 1m 29.81s. a 4.21s (20 Ran).

SR: 29/36/39/26/16/16/14/17/11/ (Don Hazzard), Mrs J C Dawe

755 Pentland Conditions Stakes Class D (3-y-o) £3,348 1m 1f 209yds. . . . . (2:50)

459* SOVIET LINE (Ire) 9-0 P D'Arcy (6) *hld up in tch, al gng wl, squeezed through to ld o'r 2 fs out, stretched clr, very easily*. . . . . (9 to 4 co-fav op 6 to 5) 1
4703a BOBBIE DEE 7-13 (3*) D Harrison (4) *hld up in tch, hdwy to go second 3 fs out, ev ch 2 out, rdn and one pace*. . . . . (9 to 4 co-fav op 2 to 1 tchd 5 to 2) 2
DOUBLE BASS (USA) 8-10 W Ryan (5) *nvr far away, rdn whn bumped 3 fs out, sn outpcd*. . . . . (9 to 4 co-fav op 5 to 2 tchd 3 to 1) 3
BONAR BRIDGE (USA) 8-7 J Reid (2) *led till hdd o'r 2 fs out, sn btn, eased*. . . . . (16 to 1 op 12 to 1) 4
ZILFI (USA) 8-10 T Quinn (1) *al beh, ran wide on bend bef hfwy, nvr a factor*. . . . . (8 to 1 op 6 to 1 tchd 10 to 1) 5
ELECTROLYTE 8-2 (5*) Stephen Davies (3) *pld hrd, trkd ldr till wknd 3 fs out*. . . . . (40 to 1 op 20 to 1) 6

Dist: 5l, 7l, ¾l, 12l, 2½l. 2m 9.92s. a 5.92s (6 Ran).

SR: 46/24/18/13/-/-/ (Maktoum Al Maktoum), M R Stoute

756 Lauderdale Handicap Class D (0-80 4-y-o and up) £4,207 1m. . . . . (3:20)

WAKIL (Ire) [55] 4-8-3 N Carlisle (6) *trkd ldrs, led 2 fs out, drvn out, jst hld on*. . . . (9 to 1 op 8 to 1 tchd 10 to 1) 1
WAKI GOLD (USA) [66] 6-9-0 Lorna Vincent (13) *trkd ldrs, rdn 2 fs out, ran on wl ins last, jst fld*. . . . . (33 to 1 op 20 to 1) 2
581 SAND TABLE [79] 4-9-13 W Ryan (10) *hld up in rear, swtchd lft and hdwy 2 fs out, ran on wl ins last, nvr nrr*. . . . . (14 to 1 op 12 to 1 tchd 16 to 1) 3
479⁷ BAYSHAM (USA) [75] 7-9-9 S Whitworth (3) *chsd ldrs, ev ch 2 fs out, kpt on one pace*. . . . . (14 to 1 tchd 16 to 1) 4
619⁴ VANBOROUGH LAD [64] 4-8-12 M Hills (1) *in tch nr side, rdn o'r one furlong out, one pace*. (14 to 1 op 10 to 1) 5
350⁸ GRAND VITESSE (Ire) [75] 4-9-9 J Reid (15) *led till hdd 2 fs out, one pace aftr*. . . . . (5 to 1 fav op 6 to 1) 6
581 GOOGLY [72] 4-9-6 G Bardwell (17) *mid-div, ran on ins fnl 2 fs, nvr nrr*. (10 to 1 op 7 to 1) 7
475 DASWAKI (Can) [71] 5-9-5 B Rouse (12) *chsd ldrs till wknd wl o'r one furlong out*. . . . . (14 to 1 op 10 to 1) 8
581 SAAHI (USA) [70] (bl) 4-8-13 (5*) K Rutter (16) *nvr on terms*. . . . . (20 to 1 op 16 to 1) 9
603⁹ THAMES GLOW [62] 4-8-10 J Williams (11) *chsd ldrs till wknd wl o'r one furlong out*. . . . . (15 to 2 op 6 to 1 tchd 9 to 1) 10
391 CHEVEUX MITCHELL [72] 6-9-6 C Rutter (2) *hld up, rdn and hdwy o'r 2 fs out, wknd appr last*. . . . . (14 to 1 op 10 to 1) 11
476⁴ EXCLUSION [75] 4-9-9 W Newnes (4) *al towards rear*. . . . . (6 to 1 op 10 to 1) 12
DUCKEY FUZZ [57] 5-8-5 Paul Eddery (5) *al beh*. . . . . (25 to 1 op 16 to 1) 13
315 AKKAZAO (Ire) [73] 5-9-2 (5*) N Gwilliams (7) *al beh*. . . . . (16 to 1 op 12 to 1) 14
521 COURT MINSTREL [57] 4-8-5 C Avery (8) *al beh*. . . . . (20 to 1 op 16 to 1) 15
HEAVYWEIGHT (Ire) [55] 4-8-0 (3*) A Tucker (9) *slwly away, al beh*. . . . . (50 to 1 op 33 to 1) 16
BROADWAY RUCKUS (Can) [56] 4-8-4 S O'Gorman (14) *in tch to hfwy, sn beh, tld off*. . . . . (33 to 1 op 25 to 1) 17
YOUNG MAX [67] 4-9-1 T Quinn (18) *speed to hfwy, tld off*. . . . . (16 to 1 tchd 20 to 1) 18

Dist: Hd, ¾l, 3l, ½l, 1½l, 3l, 1½l, nk, ¾l, 2l. 1m 44.28s. a 4.78s (18 Ran).

SR: 23/33/44/31/18/24/12/6/4/ (E J S Gadsden), L G Cottrell

757 Douglas Rated Class B (0-95 4-y-o and up) £7,556 1¾m. . . . . (3:50)

473⁴ CRYSTAL CROSS (USA) [76] 4-8-8 M Hills (2) *trkd ldr, led 3 fs out, styd on wl*. (9 to 4 op 7 to 4) 1
617² CASTLE COURAGEOUS [87] 6-9-7 J Reid (3) *hld up, rdn 4 fs out, hdwy to chase wnr fnl furlong*. . . . . (7 to 4 fav op 6 to 4 tchd 2 to 1) 2
473⁵ SECRET SOCIETY [78] 6-8-12 J Williams (7) *hld up in rear, gd hdwy o'r 2 fs out, styd on ins last*. . . . . (7 to 2 op 11 to 4) 3
601² DURSHAN (USA) [81] 4-8-13 S Whitworth (6) *hld up, hdwy o'r 4 fs out, ev ch 3 out till wknd entering last*. . . . . (7 to 1 op 5 to 1 tchd 8 to 1) 4
628⁹ EL DOMINIO [73] 5-8-7 J Quinn (5) *al in rear*. . . . . (33 to 1) 5
559 ULURU (Ire) [73] 5-8-7 T Williams (4) *led till hdd 3 fs out, wknd wl o'r one out*. . . . . (14 to 1 op 12 to 1) 6
RICH PICKINGS [75] 4-8-7 G Bardwell (1) *pld hrd, trkd ldrs till wknd wl o'r 4 fs out*. . . . . (66 to 1 op 50 to 1) 7

Dist: 2l, 1½l, 3l, 7l, 10l, 5l. 3m 9.87s. a 12.17s (7 Ran).

(Urs E Schwarzenbach), I A Balding

758 Levy Board Limited Stakes Class F (3-y-o and up) £3,004 6f. . . . . (4:20)

BLUE TOPAZE 5-9-5 J Williams (5) *mid-div, hdwy frm hfwy, led one furlong out, rdn out*. . . (7 to 1 op 8 to 1) 1
PETONELLAJILL 3-8-0 (7*) Mark Denaro (2) *in rear till gd hdwy appr fnl furlong, fnshd strly*. . . . . (14 to 1 op 12 to 1 tchd 16 to 1) 2
POLAR STORM (Ire) 3-8-7 J Reid (8) *mid-div, hdwy 2 fs out, ran on ins last*. . . . (15 to 2 op 8 to 1 tchd 10 to 1) 3

428² VICTORIA HALL 3-8-7 N Carlisle (4) *trkd ldrs, led 2 fs out, hdd one out, wknd cl hme.* ....(7 to 1 op 6 to 1 tchd 8 to 1) 4
FAY'S SONG (Ire) 5-9-5 T Quinn (7) *chsd ldrs, one pace entering fnl furlong.* ....(9 to 2 op 5 to 1 tchd 6 to 1 and 4 to 1) 5
501 RUSHANES 6-9-10 W Newnes (15) *led till hdd 2 fs out, no extr ins last*......................(20 to 1 op 14 to 1) 6
475⁹ SYLVAN SABRE (Ire) (v) 4-9-10 S Whitworth (13) *beh till hdwy 2 fs out, wknd ins last*.......(16 to 1 op 10 to 1) 7
471⁵ MURPHY'S HOPE (Ire) 3-8-12 W Ryan (6) *chsd ldrs till wknd 2 fs out, eased*.............(14 to 1 op 10 to 1) 8
JEREMIAHS BOY 3-8-12 Paul Eddery (10) *slwly away, effrt hfwy, nvr dngrs.* ....(9 to 4 fav op 2 to 1 tchd 3 to 1 and 7 to 2) 9
615* FOLLOWMEGIRLS 4-9-0 (5*) A Garth (14) *beh, rdn hfwy, no hdwy 2 fs out, eased*............(12 to 1 op 7 to 1) 10
602 ARRAS ROYALE 3-8-12 N Adams (1) *speed on nrside to hfwy*............................(50 to 1 op 25 to 1) 11
NIGEL'S LUCKY GIRL 5-9-5 C Dwyer (9) *in rear whn hmpd sn aftr hfwy, nvr on terms*...(33 to 1 op 25 to 1) 12
519 LADY RELKO 3-8-7 S Dawson (12) *trkd ldrs till wknd quickly 2 fs out*....................(33 to 1 op 25 to 1) 13
327 STALLED (Ire) 3-8-12 T Rogers (11) *al towards rear.* ....(20 to 1 op 10 to 1) 14

Dist: 2l, nk, 1l, 1½l, 3½l, 3l, hd, 1½l, 1½l, 1l. 1m 16.14s. a 3.64s (14 Ran).
SR: 38/18/17/13/19/10/ (M S Saunders), P G Murphy

759 Morriston Maiden Stakes Class D (Div I) (3-y-o) £3,552 1m....................(4:50)

582² CLOUDED ELEGANCE 9-0 M Hills (10) *al frnt rnk, jnd ldr o'r 2 fs out, led jst ins last, ran on wl.* ....(9 to 4 op 7 to 4 tchd 3 to 1) 1
SIMPLY FINESSE 9-0 T Quinn (5) *al prmnt, led o'r 2 fs out, hdd jst ins last, no extr.* ....(12 to 1 op 8 to 1 tchd 14 to 1) 2
582⁹ BEVERLY KNIGHT 9-0 C Rutter (6) *pld hrd, rstrained in rear, hdwy 2 fs out, styd on, nvr nrr.* ....(33 to 1 op 20 to 1) 3
538⁵ ANORAK (USA) 8-11 (3*) J Weaver (2) *wtd wth in tch, hdwy 2 fs out, hng lft appr last, one pace.* ....(5 to 4 fav op 7 to 4 tchd 2 to 1) 4
582 FOX SPARROW 9-0 S Raymont (11) *hld up, ran on ins fnl 2 fs, nvr nrr*......................(16 to 1 op 10 to 1) 5
SLIVOVITZ 9-0 W Ryan (16) *chsd ldrs till outpcd appr fnl furlong*..........................(16 to 1 op 8 to 1) 6
RUE REMBRANDT (USA) 9-0 Paul Eddery (14) *led for 2 fs, prmnt till wknd wl o'r one furlong out, eased.* ....(16 to 1 op 8 to 1) 7
439⁷ CHIPPENDALE LADD (Can) 8-9 (5*) Stephen Davies (15) *hld up, hdwy on ins sn aftr hfwy, one pace fnl 2 fs.* ....(14 to 1 op 10 to 1) 8
SIMPLY A HERO (Ire) 9-0 J Williams (8) *slwly away, al beh.* ....(14 to 1 op 8 to 1) 9
MAGIC FAN (Ire) 9-0 N Adams (13) *prmnt till wknd o'r 2 fs out*............................(50 to 1 op 20 to 1) 10
TURTLE POWER 9-0 S Whitworth (1) *al beh.* ....(25 to 1 op 12 to 1) 11
582 BAYFAN (Ire) 9-0 B Rouse (4) *al beh.* (66 to 1 op 33 to 1) 12
HARD ROCK MINER 8-11 (3*) A Tucker (7) *al beh.* ....(66 to 1 op 20 to 1) 13
MUMAYYAZ (Ire) 9-0 N Carlisle (3) *in tch to hfwy, sn beh.* ....(12 to 1 op 6 to 1) 14
DONTDRESSFORDINNER 9-0 G Bardwell (9) *led aftr 2 fs, hdd o'r two out, wknd quickly, tld off.* ....(100 to 1 op 33 to 1) 15

Dist: 3l, 1l, ½l, 2½l, ¾l, ½l, 1½l, 6l, 8l, ½l. 1m 44.81s. a 5.31s (15 Ran).
SR: 26/17/14/12/4/2/ (Mrs Michael Wates), I A Balding

760 Sutherland Handicap Class E (0-70 4-y-o and up) £3,236 6f....................(5:20)

492⁷ GREY CHARMER (Ire) [51] 4-8-13 W Newnes (2) *hld up in rear, hdwy on outsd o'r one furlong out, fnshd strly to ld nr finish*......................(16 to 1 op 14 to 1) 1
479 FACE NORTH (Ire) [55] 5-9-3 T Quinn (5) *hld up, rdn and hdwy 2 fs out, led wl ins last, tchd off cl hme.* ....(7 to 1 op 8 to 1 tchd 10 to 1) 2
436⁴ FACE THE FUTURE [57] 4-9-5 N Adams (1) *al prmnt, led briefly ins fnl furlong, no extr nr finish.* ....(5 to 1 fav op 8 to 1) 3
521 ZINBAQ [36] 7-7-12 T Williams (10) *hld up, hdwy o'r one furlong out, ran on wl, nvr nrr*..............(12 to 1) 4
492³ GREAT HALL [44] (bl) 4-8-1 (5*) Stephen Davies (15) *led till hdd ins fnl furlong, no extr*......(14 to 1 op 10 to 1) 5
600* PALACEGATE GOLD (Ire) [53] 4-8-8 (7*,6ex) S Drowne (4) *hld up, hdwy on outsd 2 fs out, ran on, nvr nrr.* ....(9 to 1 op 7 to 1 tchd 10 to 1) 6
302 AFFIDARE (Ire) [60] 4-9-8 W Ryan (16) *trkd ldrs, ev ch entering fnl furlong, one pace*.....(20 to 1 op 10 to 1) 7
330⁶ LEIGH CROFTER [58] (v) 4-9-6 J Williams (11) *hld up, ran on fnl furlong, nvr nrr.* ....(9 to 1 op 10 to 1 tchd 12 to 1) 8
MY RUBY RING [55] 6-9-0 (3*) D Harrison (17) *hld up, nvr nr to chal*.........................(16 to 1 op 12 to 1) 9
501 COPPERMILL LAD [48] 10-8-10 J Reid (3) *in rear, hdwy fnl 2 fs, nvr nrr*..........(14 to 1 op 10 to 1 tchd 16 to 1) 10
501 MACFARLANE [66] 5-9-11 (3*) J Weaver (19) *prmnt far side till wknd appr fnl furlong*........(12 to 1 op 10 to 1) 11
501⁸ LOOTING (USA) [34] 7-7-10 J Quinn (8) *chsd ldrs till wknd wl o'r one furlong out*..........(16 to 1 op 12 to 1) 12
PRINCESS JESSICA [35] 6-7-7³ (7*) D McCabe (12) *speed to hfwy*......................................(20 to 1) 13
ORCHARD BAY [34] 4-7-9² (3*) A Tucker (18) *al beh.* ....(50 to 1 op 33 to 1) 14
501² HITCHIN A RIDE [45] 6-8-7 J Comber (20) *al beh.* ....(7 to 1 tchd 6 to 1 and 8 to 1) 15
4725a CONISTON LAKE (Ire) [64] 4-9-12 B Rouse (13) *speed to hfwy*......................................(20 to 1) 16
605⁹ COURTING NEWMARKET [44] 5-8-6² S Whitworth (14) *al beh*...........................(20 to 1 op 14 to 1) 17
411³ LORD NASKRA (USA) [58] 4-9-3 (3*) Emma O'Gorman (9) *al beh*..................(12 to 1 op 10 to 1 tchd 14 to 1) 18
603 OYSTON'S LIFE [46] 4-8-8 C Rutter (7) *al towards rear.* ....(33 to 1 op 20 to 1) 19
492 UNVEILED [58] 5-9-6 M Hills (6) *speed till wknd wl o'r one furlong out*......................(14 to 1 op 10 to 1) 20

Dist: ¾l, nk, hd, nk, 1½l, hd, hd, nk, 1l, ½l. 1m 16.26s. a 3.76s (20 Ran).
SR: 30/31/32/10/17/20/26/23/19/ (Miss S Previte), C James

761 Morriston Maiden Stakes Class D (Div II) (3-y-o) £3,523 1m....................(5:50)

459 TOP CEES 9-0 N Adams (2) *hld up, hdwy on outsd o'r 2 fs out, sn rdn, styd on to ld nr finish*...........(33 to 1) 1
529⁹ FABULOUS MTOTO 9-0 J Williams (14) *trkd ldr, led ins fnl furlong, hdd cl hme*.................(3 to 1 op 7 to 4) 2
470² FLASHFEET 9-0 M Hills (9) *led till rdn and hdd ins fnl furlong, no extr*..................(6 to 4 on op 5 to 4) 3
510⁵ LORD BOTHWELL (USA) 8-9 (5*) Stephen Davies (6) *beh, rdn and hdwy 3 fs out, kpt on one pace ins fnl 2.* ....(14 to 1 op 7 to 1) 4
PLAY WITH ME (Ire) 8-9 W Ryan (16) *nvr far away, ran on one pace ins fnl 2 fs*...............(12 to 1 op 10 to 1) 5
MIDYAN BLUE (Ire) 9-0 B Rouse (10) *prmnt till rdn and wknd fnl furlong*..................(20 to 1 op 10 to 1) 6
SEASON'S STAR 8-9 S Dawson (11) *nvr on terms.* (33 to 1) 7
482 ESERIE DE CORES (USA) 8-9 (5*) C Hodgson (15) *mid-div, hrd rdn o'r 3 fs out, sn btn*............(66 to 1 op 33 to 1) 8
AZRAG (Ire) 9-0 S Whitworth (3) *beh, rdn and effrt o'r 2 fs out, sn btn*.......................(33 to 1 op 20 to 1) 9
624⁸ LANZAMAR 8-9 C Rutter (8) *chsd ldrs till wknd 2 fs out.* ....(66 to 1 op 33 to 1) 10
602⁶ TASSET (Can) 9-0 T Quinn (5) *nvr gng wl in rear, rdn hfwy, sn btn*........(11 to 1 op 5 to 1 tchd 12 to 1) 11
BANG ON TIME 9-0 J Quinn (4) *al beh.* ....(66 to 1 op 33 to 1) 12
CRIMINAL RECORD (USA) 8-11 (3*) D Harrison (12) *al beh.* ....(20 to 1 op 8 to 1) 13
582 JUST JAMIE 9-0 Paul Eddery (7) *al beh.* ....(33 to 1 op 16 to 1) 14

Dist: Nk, 1½l, sht-hd, 2½l, 1½l, 10l, ½l, sht-hd, ¾l, ¾l. 1m 46.08s. a 6.58s (14 Ran).
SR: 7/6/1/-/-/-/ (Mrs P W Harris), P W Harris

CHURCHILL DOWNS (USA) (firm)
Friday April 30th

762 Kentucky Oaks (Grade 1) (3-y-o) £126,642 1m 1f....................................

DISPUTE (USA) 8-9 J D Bailey,..................(51 to 10) 1
ELIZA (USA) 8-9 P Valenzuela,..................(5 to 3 on) 2
QUINPOOL (USA) 8-9 Julie Krone,..................(34 to 1) 3
570² AVIE'S SHADOW (USA) 8-9 G Stevens,..........(60 to 1) 4
BOOTS 'N JACKIE (USA) 8-9 F Arguello, Jr,......(17 to 1) 5
DREAM MARY (USA) 8-9 R Romero,..............(95 to 10) 6
AZTEC HILL (USA) 8-9 M Smith,..................(63 to 10) 7
SUM RUNNER (USA) 8-9 P Day,..................(14 to 1) 8
570* LUNAR SPOOK (USA) 8-9 S Sellers,.............(95 to 10) 9
570⁵ SHE'S A LITTLE SHY (USA) 8-9 K Desormeaux,...(62 to 1) 0
CORMORANT'S FLIGHT (USA) 8-9 M Luzzi,......(47 to 1) 0

Dist: 1 ¼l, nk, nk, 3½l, ½l, 1 ¾l, hd, 6l, 4l, 7l. 1m 52.40s. (11 Ran).
(O M Phipps), C R McGaughey

HAMILTON (soft)
Friday April 30th

Going Correction: PLUS 0.40 sec. per fur. (races 1,2,7), PLUS 0.30 (3,4,5,6)

763 Holy Loch Rating Related Maiden Stakes Class F (3-y-o) £2,511 1m 65yds.....(2:15)

681⁸ WHITE CREEK (Ire) (v) 9-0 J Carroll (2) *al hndy, effrt 4 fs out, led o'r 2 out, styd on wl.* ....(16 to 1 op 12 to 1 tchd 20 to 1) 1
284³ QUELQUE CHOSE 9-0 K Darley (6) *tucked in hndy, rdn and effrt o'r 2 fs out, kpt on ins last.* (9 to 2 op 4 to 1) 2

609² MAASTRICHT 9-0 G Duffield (1) *took keen hold, trkd ldr, led o'r 4 fs out till hdd over 2 out, kpt on same pace.* .... (5 to 2 tchd 9 to 4 and 11 to 4) 3
549⁴ YOUNG TESS 8-9 S Webster (5) *hld up in tch, rdn and outpcd o'r 3 fs out, kpt on ins last, nvr nrr.* .... (6 to 5 on op 5 to 4 tchd 5 to 4 on) 4
ROSMARINO 9-0 N Connorton (4) *hld up, rdn o'r 3 fs out, no imprsn*........................ (25 to 1 op 12 to 1) 5
609⁵ PRIME PAINTER 9-0 D Nicholls (3) *led till hdd o'r 4 fs out, sn rdn, wknd appr last*.......... (33 to 1 op 14 to 1) 6
Dist: 1½l, sht-hd, hd, 2l, nk. 1m 54.60s. a 10.60s (6 Ran).
(J K Brown), J Berry

764 Plumb Center Handicap Class D (0-80 3-y-o) £3,655 1m 65yds.................(2:45)

437 MILNGAVIE (Ire) [45] 7-7 J Fanning (5) *al hndy, rdn 2 fs out, ran on strly to ld cl hme.* .... (7 to 1 op 8 to 1 tchd 10 to 1) 1
AWESTRUCK [73] 9-7 G Duffield (3) *chsd ldr, led 3 fs out, jnd ins last and ct cl hme.* .... (15 to 2 op 5 to 1 tchd 8 to 1) 2
608⁶ GOLD DESIRE [46] 7-8¹ J Lowe (7) *led till hdd 3 fs out, sn rdn and kpt on wl*.............. (12 to 1 tchd 16 to 1) 3
503⁴ CONTRACT ELITE (Ire) [56] 8-4 N Connorton (1) *chsd ldrs, ev ch frm 3 fs out, no extr ins last.* .... (4 to 1 op 7 to 2 tchd 9 to 2) 4
546² THE PREMIER EXPRES [65] 8-13 K Darley (2) *in tch, effrt 4 fs out, sn rdn and one pace.* .... (2 to 1 fav op 5 to 2 tchd 3 to 1) 5
609* RAGGERTY (Ire) [58] 8-6 (5ex) J Carroll (6) *hld up, short lived effrt o'r 4 fs out, sn rdn and no extr.* .... (7 to 2 op 2 to 1 tchd 4 to 1) 6
286⁶ TAKE YOUR PARTNER (Ire) [57] 8-5 T Williams (4) *sn rdn alng, outpcd till hdwy 2 fs out, soon wknd.* .... (16 to 1 op 8 to 1) 7
Dist: Nk, 2l, 1½l, 2½l, 1½l, 7l. 1m 52.30s. a 8.30s (7 Ran).
SR: 4/31/-/-/4/-/-/ (A S Robertson), M Johnston

765 Levy Board Claiming Stakes Class F (3-y-o and up) £2,601 6f 5yds..............(3:15)

548² DOKKHA OYSTON (Ire) 5-9-6 J Carroll (2) *slwly into strd, reco'red to ld aftr a furlong and a half, clr 2 out, easily.* .... (9 to 4 on tchd 2 to 1 on) 1
728² NUTTY BROWN (v) 3-8-5 (5*) O Pears (4) *led one and a half fs, sn outpcd, kpt on und pres clsg stages, no ch wth wnr*................................(4 to 1 op 7 to 2) 2
FRANCIS ANN 5-8-0 (7*) R Havlin (3) *pld hrd, wth ldrs on outsd, rdn o'r 2 fs out, wknd appr last.* ....(9 to 2 op 7 to 2 tchd 5 to 1) 3
BAFFIE 4-9-7 N Connorton (1) *lost tch frm hfwy.* .... (100 to 1 op 20 to 1) 4
Dist: 2½l, 6l, 1½l. 1m 16.10s. a 5.40s (4 Ran).
SR: 34/14/-/-/ (Murray Grubb), J Berry

766 Firth Of Clyde Handicap Class E (0-70 3-y-o) £2,795 5f 4yds................... (3:50)

742⁴ SHADOW JURY [63] 9-6 K Darley (1) *broke wl, made all, pushed clr fnl 2 fs, easily*........... (9 to 4 op 5 to 2) 1
504⁴ CLANROCK [56] 8-13 A Culhane (2) *chsd ldr, rdn o'r 2 fs out, styd on same pace*............ (3 to 1 op 5 to 2) 2
742³ HIGH ROMANCE [54] 8-4 (7*) Darren Moffatt (3) *chsd ldg pair, rdn and rdr drpd whip o'r 2 fs out, sn no imprsn.* ....(2 to 1 fav op 5 to 2) 3
501 CONVENIENT MOMENT [64] 9-7 J Carroll (4) *dwlt, rdn hfwy, sn lost tch*.................. (5 to 1 op 3 to 1) 4
Dist: 3l, 2½l, 7l. 1m 3.10s. a 4.80s (4 Ran).
SR: 40/21/9/-/ (P D Savill), D W Chapman

767 Loch Goil Claiming Stakes Class F (2-y-o) £2,511 5f 4yds.................... (4:20)

381* JIMMY THE SKUNK (Ire) 8-8 J Carroll (1) *made all, shaken up and edgd lft appr fnl furlong, ran on wl.* .... (11 to 10 on op 6 to 5 tchd 5 to 4) 1
PASSION SUNDAY 8-8 K Darley (4) *slwly into strd, sn reco'red to chase ldr, rdn 2 fs out, kpt on wl.* ....(9 to 4 op 7 to 4 tchd 5 to 2) 2
564³ BATIEN'S RIVER 7-9 Dale Gibson (3) *prmnt on outsd till rdn o'r 2 fs out, btn appr last*....... (5 to 1 op 4 to 1) 3
KING ACRYLIC (Ire) 8-0 J Lowe (2) *sn drvn alng, no imprsn frm hfwy*........................ (7 to 1 tchd 8 to 1) 4
Dist: 1½l, 3½l, 2½l. 1m 3.20s. a 4.90s (4 Ran).
SR: 26/20/-/-/ (J David Abell), J Berry

768 EBF Loch Striven Median Auction Maiden Fillies Stakes Class E (2-y-o) £2,691 5f 4yds.................................. (4:50)

449² LYING EYES 8-4 (7*) P McCabe (3) *sn rdn and outpcd till styd on frm o'r one furlong out, led nr finish, gmely.* ....(7 to 1 op 5 to 1) 1
698³ ROSIE VALENTINE 8-6 (5*) O Pears (2) *led, clr o'r one furlong out, wknd and hdd nr finish.* .... (11 to 8 op 6 to 4) 2
607² THE FERNHILL FLYER (Ire) 8-11 J Carroll (1) *wth ldr, rdn frm 2 fs out, ran green and wknd appr last.* .... (Evens fav tchd 11 to 10 and 5 to 4) 3
Dist: ½l, 7l. 1m 4.00s. a 5.70s (3 Ran).
SR: 13/11/-/ (A K Holbrook), W G M Turner

769 Loch Long Limited Stakes Class D (3-y-o and up) £3,590 1m 3f 16yds......... (5:20)

478⁴ WHITE WILLOW 4-9-12 K Darley (5) *in tch, hdwy to ld wl o'r one furlong out, pushed clr ins last, cmftbly.* ....(11 to 8 fav op 5 to 4 tchd 6 to 4) 1
290⁷ GREAT MAX (Ire) (v) 4-9-12 G Duffield (2) *al hndy, chlgd frm wl o'r one furlong out, no extr ins last.* .... (7 to 2 tchd 4 to 1 and 3 to 1) 2
589² GOLDEN TORQUE 6-9-5 (7*) H Bastiman (3) *patiently rdn, gd hdwy on outsd o'r 3 fs out, wknd fnl furlong.* .... (3 to 1 op 11 to 4 tchd 4 to 1) 3
508⁶ TAKE BY STORM (Ire) 4-9-12 J Carroll (4) *hld up in tch, effrt o'r 3 fs out, rdn and one pace fnl 2.* ....(7 to 1 op 5 to 1) 4
INVERTIEL 9-9-12 N Connorton (6) *trkd ldr, led o'r 3 fs out till hdd wl over one out, sn wknd.* (100 to 1 op 66 to 1) 5
GHYLLDALE 5-9-7 A Culhane (1) *led till hdd o'r 3 fs out, wknd quickly*................(100 to 1 op 50 to 1) 6
Dist: 2½l, 2½l, 2l, 10l, 5l. 2m 30.00s. a 10.00s (6 Ran).
SR: 56/51/46/42/22/7/ (Mrs H North), Mrs M Reveley

MAISONS LAFFITTE (FR) (soft)
Friday April 30th
Going Correction: PLUS 0.25 sec. per fur.

770 Prix Rose de Mai (Listed) (3-y-o) £14,337 1¼m 110yds....................... (2:25)

ROYALE CHANTOU (Fr) 9-2 C Le Scrill,.................. 1
484⁴ INSIJAAM (USA) 9-2 O Doleuze,......................... 2
ENCOREMOI (USA) 9-2 F Head,......................... 3
FRESHER 9-2 O Benoist,............................... 4
Dist: Nk, 1½l, ½l, hd, ½l, ½l, 1l, 3l, 2l. 2m 14.60s. a 6.90s (10 Ran).
SR: 59/58/55/54/ (G Gallot), Y Porzier

NEWMARKET (good)
Friday April 30th
Going Correction: MINUS 0.35 sec. per fur. (race 1), MINUS 0.10 (2,3,4,5,6,7)

771 Lucinda Stopford-Sackville Ladies Handicap Class E (0-80 3-y-o and up) £5,127 7f ....(2:00)

475 RISE UP SINGING [59] (bl) 5-9-10 (5*) Mrs J Musson (27) *made all far side, clr last 2 fs, readily.* .... (10 to 1 op 12 to 1 tchd 16 to 1) 1
302³ KISSAVOS [51] 7-9-2 (5*) Miss A Elsey (21) *chsd ldrs centre, styd on ins fnl furlong, not rch wnr.* .... (12 to 1 op 10 to 1) 2
411⁶ AITCH N'BEE [76] 10-11-4 Mrs Maxine Cowdrey (7) *rcd centre, improved frm midfield o'r 2 fs out, fnshd wl.* .... (14 to 1 op 12 to 1 tchd 16 to 1) 3
411⁷ CAPTAIN MARMALADE [53] 4-9-9 Miss I Diana W Jones (3) *settled midfield, hdwy centre last 2 fs, ran on strly.* .... (25 to 1 op 20 to 1) 4
475 RURAL LAD [60] 4-9-11 (5*) Mrs L Lawson (5) *chsd ldrs stands side, drvn alng last 2 fs, styd on.* .... (25 to 1 op 20 to 1) 5
WELLINGTON ROCK (USA) [76] 4-11-4 Mrs S Cumani (28) *wth wnr far side, chsd alng last 2 fs, one pace.* .... (14 to 1 op 12 to 1) 6
470⁴ WAINWRIGHT (USA) [79] 4-11-7 Mrs L Pearce (24) *rcd far side, pressed ldg pair, drvn alng o'r one furlong out, no extr*.............(3 to 1 fav op 2 to 1 tchd 100 to 30) 7
RELENTLESS PURSUIT (Ire) [70] 5-10-7 (5*) Mrs J Chapple-Hyam (18) *patiently rdn, hdwy last 2 fs, fnshd wl.* .... (25 to 1 op 20 to 1 tchd 33 to 1) 8
387⁶ SHINING JEWEL [65] 6-10-2 (5*) Mrs M Haggas (26) *chsd ldrs far side, styd on wl last 2 fs, nvr nrr.* .... (14 to 1 op 12 to 1) 9
67⁵ DON'T DROP BOMBS (USA) [44] 4-9-0 Miss J Feilden (17) *improved frm midfield last 2 fs, styd on, nvr nrr.* .... (14 to 1 tchd 20 to 1 and 12 to 1) 10
492⁶ ELTON LEDGER (Ire) [59] 4-9-10 (5*) Miss T Bracegirdle (1) *led stands side grp till fdd last 2 fs.* .... (14 to 1 op 12 to 1 tchd 16 to 1) 11
HIGHEST PRAISE (USA) [58] 10-9-9 (5*) Miss S Francome (6) *chsd ldrs stands side for o'r 5 fs, no extr*....... (33 to 1) 12+
294⁸ RIPSNORTER (Ire) [58] 4-9-9 (5*) Miss A Purdy (23) *chsd alng far side, not pace to trble ldrs.* .... (20 to 1 op 16 to 1 tchd 25 to 1) 12+
4708a³ HERETICAL MISS [62] (bl) 3-8-13 (5*) Mrs J Boggis (13) *rcd freely centre, speed 5 fs, fdd*....... (25 to 1 op 20 to 1) 14
ACROSS THE BAY [70] (v) 6-10-12 Miss J Winter (11) *wth ldrs stands side for o'r 5 fs, no extr.* (25 to 1 op 20 to 1) 15

403* NOBBY BARNES [58] 4-9-9 (5*) Miss J Sandford-Johnson (16) *bustled alng hfwy, no imprsn last 2 fs.* ......(10 to 1 op 8 to 1) 16
714^{5} TOFF SUNDAE [58] 3-9-0^{5} (5*) Miss Elaine Mills (15) *drvn alng in midfield hfwy, nvr dngrs.* (33 to 1 op 20 to 1) 17
TRUNDLEY WOOD [71] 3-9-8 (5*) Miss L Hide (25) *chsd alng hfwy, nvr rch ldrs...* (25 to 1 op 20 to 1 tchd 33 to 1) 18
BLOCKADE (USA) [79] 4-11-2 (5*) Mrs G Bell (22) *bustled alng far side hfwy, nvr a threat...* (14 to 1 op 10 to 1) 19+
274^{8} THEMAAM [61] 4-10-3 Miss A Harwood (12) *chsd alng in midfield, not pace to trble ldrs.....*(25 to 1 op 16 to 1) 19+
411* DUNE RIVER [72] 4-11-0 Miss J Allison (4) *speed stands side 5 fs, fdd.............*(12 to 1 op 10 to 1 tchd 14 to 1) 21
700 BASSIO (Bel) [50] 4-9-3^{2} (5*) Miss R Lowes (10) *chsd alng hfwy, sn btn......* (50 to 1 tchd 66 to 1) 22
492 TAKE IT IN CASH [46] 4-8-11 (5*) Miss S Duckett (9) *chsd ldrs stands side, hrd drvn o'r 2 fs out, sn btn.* ......(33 to 1 tchd 50 to 1) 23
SAIFAN [57] 4-9-9^{1} (5*) Mrs L Morris (19) *struggling hfwy, sn btn......*(25 to 1 tchd 33 to 1) 24
ALNASRIC PETE (USA) [52] 7-9-8 Mrs D Arbuthnot (8) *struggling hfwy..........*(16 to 1 tchd 20 to 1 and 14 to 1) 25
LOOSE ZEUS (USA) [56] 4-9-7 (5*) Mrs C Wall (20) *feeling pace hfwy, sn lost tch......* (25 to 1 tchd 33 to 1) 26
224^{9} WAYWARD SON [49] 4-9-5^{10} (5*) Miss M Bridger (14) *missed break, drvn alng and some hdwy aftr 2 fs, sn lost tch.* ......(100 to 1) 27
Dist: 3l, 2l, hd, hd, sht-hd, 1l, nk, 1l, nk, ¾l. 1m 25.86s. a 2.36s (27 Ran).
SR: 43/26/45/21/27/42/42/32/24/ (Mrs Rita Brown), W J Musson

772 Eastern Electricity Handicap Class C (0-100 3-y-o) £6,160 1m.............(2:35)

400^{2} SHAMAM (USA) [85] 8-10 W Carson (1) *al frnt rnk, quickened to ld o'r one furlong out, ran on gmely.* ......(7 to 1 op 6 to 1 tchd 15 to 2) 1
295^{6} WAHEM (Ire) [73] 7-7 (5*) B Doyle (10) *set steady pace, quickened 3 fs out, hdd o'r one out, rallied.* ......(7 to 1 op 6 to 1 tchd 9 to 1) 2
SATIN DANCER [81] 8-6 M Roberts (11) *nvr far away, drvn up on outsd to chal entering fnl furlong, ran on.* ......(9 to 1 op 7 to 1 tchd 10 to 1) 3
514^{4} GREEN'S FAIR (Ire) [69] 7-8 J Quinn (5) *trkd ldg bunch, bustled alng whn pace quickened 3 fs out, styd on, not pace to chal...........*(9 to 1 op 8 to 1 tchd 11 to 1) 4
514^{7} MY PATRIARCH [81] 8-6 T Quinn (4) *tucked away in midfield, swtchd ins to improve o'r 2 fs out, not quicken fnl furlong................* (7 to 1 op 5 to 1 tchd 15 to 2) 5
514^{5} GROVE DAFFODIL (Ire) [74] 7-13^{2} P Robinson (7) *trkd ldrs, ev ch 2 fs out, sn rdn and not quicken.* ......(9 to 2 fav op 3 to 1) 6
370^{4} WYNONA (Ire) [96] 9-7 W R Swinburn (9) *settled midfield, effrt and drvn alng o'r 2 fs out, one pace.* ......(25 to 1 op 16 to 1 tchd 33 to 1) 7
523^{2} SEASONAL SPLENDOUR (Ire) [82] 8-7 D Biggs (6) *co'red up beh ldrs, effrt and rdn 2 fs out, sn btn.* ......(9 to 1 op 7 to 1) 8
471^{4} PRINCELY FAVOUR (Ire) [80] 8-5 M J Kinane (3) *chsd ldrs, feeling pace 3 fs out, sn btn.* ......(10 to 1 tchd 9 to 1 and 12 to 1) 9
DON'T JUMP (Ire) [77] 7-11^{2} (7*) S Mulvey (8) *reared strt, reco'red to join ldr aftr 2 fs, fdd over one out.* ......(33 to 1 tchd 40 to 1) 10
45^{2} EXCESS BAGGAGE (Ire) [71] 7-10 N Carlisle (2) *in tch, struggling whn pace quickened 3 fs out, sn btn.* ......(12 to 1) 11
Dist: Nk, nk, 2½l, 1½l, 1½l, 4l, ¾l, 2l, 1½l, 2l. 1m 39.21s. a 2.01s (11 Ran).
SR: 54/41/48/28/35/23/33/17/9/ (Hamdan Al-Maktoum), P T Walwyn

773 Harcros Timber & Building Supplies Stayers Championship Series Rated Qualifier Class B (0-105 4-y-o and up) £7,438 1½m.............................(3:05)

BRIER CREEK (USA) [101] 4-9-7 M Roberts (2) *trkd ldg trio, swtchd outsd to ld briefly o'r one furlong out, ran on wl to lead well ins last...*(5 to 1 op 4 to 1 tchd 6 to 1) 1
DUKE OF EUROLINK [99] 4-9-5 R Cochrane (1) *tucked away beh ldg 4, led o'r one furlong out, rdn and hdd wl ins last..................*(4 to 1 op 3 to 1 tchd 9 to 2) 2
CASTLE CAVALIER [90] 5-8-11 C Dwyer (4) *wth ldr, led briefly wl o'r one furlong out, styd on same pace last 100 yards.............* (7 to 1 op 12 to 1 tchd 14 to 1) 3
QUICK RANSOM [87] 5-8-8 Dean McKeown (5) *set slow pace, quickened o'r 6 fs out, hdd and wknd wl over one out.........................*(11 to 4 fav op 9 to 4) 4
473^{3} SONG OF SIXPENCE (USA) [90] 9-8-11 J Reid (6) *trkd ldg pair, drvn alng and not much room o'r one furlong out, sn outpcd..........................*(7 to 2 op 5 to 2) 5
MUHARIB (USA) [97] 4-9-3 W Carson (7) *pld hrd to hfwy, sn lost tch......................*(14 to 1 tchd 16 to 1) 6
Dist: Hd, 2½l, 5l, 2½l, 25l. 2m 36.25s. a 6.65s (6 Ran).
SR: 29/26/13/ (Sheikh Mohammed), J H M Gosden

774 Jockey Club Stakes Class A (Group 2) (4-y-o and up) £33,794 1½m..........(3:40)

ZINAAD 4-8-9 W R Swinburn (3) *patiently rdn, bustled alng whn pace lifted 2 fs out, styd on strly to ld cl hme.* ......(3 to 1 fav op 7 to 2 tchd 9 to 2) 1
407^{4} APPLE TREE (Fr) (bl) 4-9-0 T Jarnet (6) *nvr far away, quickened to ld o'r 3 fs out, clr appr last, wknd and hdd cl hme...............*(13 to 2 op 5 to 1 tchd 8 to 1) 2
JEUNE 4-8-9 R Cochrane (7) *missed break, improved aftr one m, effrt entering fnl furlong, styd on same pace.* ......(4 to 1 op 7 to 2) 3
525^{8} SHUAILAAN (USA) 4-8-9 M Roberts (1) *trkd ldg 4, effrt und pres last 2 fs, kpt on one pace.* ......(11 to 2 op 7 to 2 tchd 6 to 1) 4
579^{5} MASHAALLAH (USA) 5-9-0 J Reid (2) *wth ldr, led o'r 5 fs out till over 3 out, no extr ins last.* ......(7 to 1 op 6 to 1 tchd 8 to 1) 5
ANNE BONNY 4-8-6 T Quinn (4) *trkd ldrs, bustled alng to improve o'r 2 fs out, no imprsn....* (12 to 1 op 16 to 1) 6
GARDEN OF HEAVEN (USA) 4-8-12 W Carson (8) *trkd ldg pair, feeling pace and lost grnd o'r 2 fs out, sn btn.* ......(13 to 2 op 6 to 1 tchd 7 to 1) 7
SILVERNESIAN (USA) 4-9-0 L Piggott (5) *narrow ld till o'r 5 fs out, tld off appr last......* (12 to 1 tchd 14 to 1) 8
Dist: Nk, 2l, ¾l, 4l, 2½l, 1l, 25l. 2m 31.40s. a 1.80s (8 Ran).
SR: 65/69/60/58/55/42/46/-/ (Maktoum Al Maktoum), M R Stoute

775 Newmarket Stakes Class A (Listed Race) (3-y-o) £12,771 1¼m................(4:10)

TENBY 9-4 Pat Eddery (3) *trkd ldr, drvn to ld o'r 2 fs out, hrd pressed fnl furlong, ran on gmely.* ......(6 to 5 fav op Evens tchd 5 to 4) 1
582* PLANETARY ASPECT (USA) 8-10 J Reid (4) *nvr far away, drw level ins fnl furlong, ran on, jst hld.* ......(9 to 2 op 11 to 4) 2
540^{2} DESERT TEAM (USA) 8-10 C Roche (5) *led till o'r 2 fs out, hrd rdn appr last, no extr..........* (7 to 2 op 9 to 2) 3
SHAIBA (USA) 8-10 M Roberts (2) *al hndy, hrd drvn whn pace quickened o'r 2 fs out, one pace.* ......(9 to 2 tchd 5 to 1 and 4 to 1) 4
474^{3} STAR MANAGER (USA) 8-10 T Quinn (1) *patiently rdn, swtchd outsd to chal hfwy, ridden and outpcd last 2 fs.* ......(25 to 1 tchd 33 to 1) 5
Dist: ½l, 3½l, 1½l, 3l. 2m 5.15s. a 2.45s (5 Ran).
SR: 70/61/54/51/45/ (K Abdulla), H R A Cecil

776 Arlington Maiden Auction Stakes Class E (2-y-o) £4,337 5f..................(4:40)

MILD REBUKE 8-2 M Hills (20) *dsptd ld far side, led wl o'r one furlong out, ran on strly.* ......(5 to 1 fav op 4 to 1 tchd 3 to 1 and 11 to 2) 1
543^{8} MARCH OF TIME (bl) 8-7 R Cochrane (6) *led stands side grp, drvn alng fnl furlong, kpt on............*(33 to 1) 2
ANZIO (Ire) 8-7 L Dettori (2) *wth ldr stands side, drvn alng o'r one furlong out, kpt on same pace.* ......(9 to 1 op 7 to 1 tchd 10 to 1) 3
MAZEEKA (Ire) 8-2 A Munro (11) *nvr far away, improved o'r one furlong out, ran on wl......*(16 to 1 op 8 to 1) 4
KINGSWELL PRINCE (Ire) 8-11 T Quinn (7) *trkd ldrs far side, ev ch hfwy, not quicken ins fnl furlong.* ......(10 to 1 op 8 to 1) 5
CRYSTAL MAGIC 8-2 A McGlone (21) *narrow ld far side grp for o'r 3 fs, no extr.* (11 to 2 op 7 to 2 tchd 6 to 1) 6
454^{7} PRIVATE FIXTURE (Ire) 8-7 J Reid (9) *settled midfield, chsd alng to improve o'r one furlong out, prmsg.* ......(25 to 1 op 20 to 1 tchd 33 to 1) 7
454^{4} GAELIC STAR (Ire) 8-11 W Ryan (3) *chsd ldg pair stands side for o'r 3 fs, no extr.* ......(11 to 1 op 8 to 1 tchd 12 to 1) 8
543^{4} LORD SKY 8-8 (7*) T G McLaughlin (17) *speed far side for o'r 3 fs, fdd.............*(7 to 1 op 5 to 1 tchd 8 to 1) 9
528^{8} QUEENS STROLLER (Ire) 8-6 D Holland (23) *chsd far side grp for o'r 3 fs, wknd..........* (14 to 1 tchd 16 to 1) 10
625^{4} RISKY AFFAIR 8-8 (3*) D Harrison (19) *chsd alng in midfield, styd on last 2 fs, nvr nrr.....* (20 to 1 op 12 to 1) 11
LUCY'S GOLD 8-2 D Biggs (10) *missed break, styd on last 2 fs, nrst finish.....................*(33 to 1) 12
543^{7} ERRIS BOY 9-1 A Clark (22) *speed to chase far side grp 3 fs, wknd.......................* (20 to 1) 13
QUEEN'S TRUST 8-2 W Carson (8) *drvn alng hfwy, no imprsn..............*(14 to 1 op 12 to 1 tchd 16 to 1) 14
TWIN CREEKS 8-7 Paul Eddery (18) *bustled alng hfwy, nvr a threat...............*(25 to 1 op 20 to 1) 15
SHERIFF 9-1 R Hills (4) *drvn alng, nvr able to rch ldrs.* ......(33 to 1 op 20 to 1) 16
528^{4} ACCESS ADVANTAGE 8-2 M Roberts (1) *chsd ldg trio stands side 3 fs.........*(7 to 1 op 6 to 1 tchd 10 to 1) 17
HE SHALL REIGN 8-7 W Newnes (12) *chsd alng in midfield, nvr a threat.................*(20 to 1 op 16 to 1) 18
BURES (Ire) 8-7 P Robinson (5) *slwly away, not reco'r.* ......(20 to 1 op 16 to 1) 19
CONNECT (Ire) 9-5 B Rouse (15) *struggling hfwy, nvr dngrs............................*(25 to 1 op 20 to 1) 20
PRIMA SILK 8-2 G Bardwell (14) *al struggling.* ......(33 to 1 op 20 to 1 tchd 40 to 1) 21
SPORTING START 9-1 N Adams (13) *unruly strt, al beh.* ......(33 to 1) 22

VICEROY RULER 9-5 S Whitworth (16) *struggling hfwy, sn lost tch*.......................................(33 to 1) 23
Dist: 2½l, nk, nk, ¾l, 2l, sht-hd, nk, ¾l, sht-hd, ½l. 1m 0.57s. a 1.97s (23 Ran).
SR: 39/34/33/27/33/16/20/23/24/ (P D Player), D R Loder

777 Newmarket Challenge Whip Class G (3-y-o) £0 1m..........................(5:10)

WINTER FOREST (USA) 9-0 M Roberts (1)................ 1
Walked over. (Time not taken) (1 Ran).
SR: -/ (Sheikh Mohammed), H R A Cecil

CAPANNELLE (ITY) (good to soft) Saturday May 1st

778 Premio Niccolo Dell'Arca (3-y-o) £11,207 1¼m 110yds..........................(3:30)

DI CIACOMO 8-7 F Jovine,.............................. 1
ROSTOCK (Ity), *dead-heated for 2nd, btn 1 1/4l, disqualified for hampering sddlback and plcd last*........... 2D
MARAAN (Ity) 8-9 B Jovine, *dead-heated wth Rostock for 2nd pl but plcd second outrght following disqualificaton of Rostock*.................................. 2
PASCOLI (Ity) 8-7 O Fancera, *fnshd 4th, plcd 3rd*......... 3
Dist: 1 ¼l, dd-ht, 1 ¼l, sht-hd. 2m 17.10s. (6 Ran).
(Scuderia Erasec), J L Dunlop

CHURCHILL DOWNS (USA) (firm) Saturday May 1st

779 Kentucky Derby (Grade 1) (3-y-o) £487,351 1¼m....................................

SEA HERO (USA) 9-0 J Bailey (6)................(13 to 1) 1
PRAIRIE BAYOU (USA) 9-0 M Smith (5)......(44 to 10 fav) 2
WILD GALE (USA) 9-0 S Sellers (13)............(85 to 10) 3
PERSONAL HOPE (USA) 9-0 G Stevens (7)......(82 to 10) 4
585^{5} DIAZO (USA) 9-0 K Desormeaux (18)............(17 to 1) 5
CORBY (USA) 9-0 C McCarron (17)..............(17 to 1) 6
585^{2} KISSIN KRIS (USA) 9-0 J Santos (2).............(16 to 1) 7
SILVER OF SILVER (USA) 9-0 J Vasquez (9)......(85 to 10) 8
585^{6} RAGTIME REBEL (USA) 9-0 R Lester (14).......(85 to 10) 9
585* ROCKAMUNDO (USA) 9-0 C Borel (8)............(10 to 1) 0
569* STORM TOWER (USA) 9-0 R Wilson (1)...........(9 to 1) 0
569^{2} TOSSOFTHECOIN (USA) 9-0 L Pincay, Jr (11)... (85 to 10) 0
UNION CITY (USA) 9-0 P Valenzuela (4).........(59 to 10) 0
BULL INTHE HEATHER (USA) 9-0 W Ramos (10) (52 to 10) 0
DIXIELAND HEAT (USA) 9-0 R Romero (15).......(21 to 1) 0
WALLENDA (USA) 9-0 P Day (16)................(12 to 1) 0
TRUTH OF IT ALL (USA) 9-0 J Valasquez (3).....(85 to 10) 0
585^{4} MI CIELO (USA) 9-0 A Gryder (12)..............(85 to 10) 0
EL BAKAN (USA) 9-0 C Perret (19)..............(85 to 10) 0
Dist: 2½l, hd, nk, 3l, hd, ¾l, 2l, nose, 2l, 4l. 2m 2.40s. (19 Ran).
(Rokeby Stables), M Miller

HAYDOCK (good) Saturday May 1st

Going Correction: MINUS 0.20 sec. per fur. (races 1,3,4,5,6), PLUS 0.10 (2)

780 Henry Cooke Lumsden Maiden Fillies Stakes Class D (3-y-o) £3,525 1¼m 120yds ....(1:00)

GISARNE (USA) 8-11 W Newnes (6) *wtd wth, smooth hdwy 4 fs out, led one out, shaken up and ran on wl, readily*.............(7 to 4 fav op 2 to 1 tchd 6 to 4) 1
482^{4} LICORNE 8-11 W Ryan (3) *hld up, rdn and hdwy o'r 2 out, styd on wl ins last, nrst finish*..... (5 to 2 tchd 3 to 1) 2
TAHDID 8-11 R Hills (5) *trkd ldr, led o'r 3 fs out, hdd one out, kpt on*..........................(7 to 1 op 5 to 1) 3
FAIR TO THE WIND (USA) 8-11 B Raymond (1) *trkd ldg pair till rdn o'r 3 fs out, sn one pace*...... (9 to 2 op 3 to 1) 4
BRONZE MAQUETTE (Ire) 8-11 C Rutter (4) *chsd ldrs, niggled alng 4 fs out, kpt on same pace fnl 2*.
.... (14 to 1 op 10 to 1) 5
ROSE NOBLE (USA) 8-11 J Carroll (2) *took keen hold and rstrained early, rdn 3 fs out, ran green and wknd*.
.... (14 to 1 op 10 to 1) 6
PRINCESS TATEUM (Ire) 8-11 Dean McKeown (7) *led till hdd o'r 3 fs out, sn rdn and lost pl*. (10 to 1 tchd 8 to 1) 7
Dist: 1½l, hd, 4l, 1l, 1½l, ¾l. 2m 19.55s. a 8.55s (7 Ran).
(Racing Welfare), J L Dunlop

781 Arthur Andersen Conditions Stakes Class B (3-y-o) £8,090 5f..................(1:30)

566^{2} PALACEGATE EPISODE (Ire) 9-3 J Carroll (1) *broke fst, made all, rdn out fnl furlong*.
.... (6 to 5 on tchd 11 to 10 on and 5 to 4 on) 1
566* NIGHT MELODY (Ire) 9-2 K Darley (2) *slwly into strd, al chasing rival in vain, rdn o'r 2 fs out, no imprsn*.
..................................(Evens op 11 to 10 on) 2
Won by 3½l. 1m 1.18s. a 2.38s (2 Ran).
SR: 65/50/ (Palacegate Corporation Ltd), J Berry

782 Halliwell Landau Spring Trophy Rated Class A (Listed Race) (0-105 3-y-o and up) £9,228 7f 30yds.................... (2:00)

524^{2} LITTLE BEAN [97] 4-9-3 Paul Eddery (7) *al hndy, led o'r one furlong out, ran on gmely*.
...................(9 to 4 fav op 2 to 1 tchd 11 to 4) 1
619^{3} BEWARE OF AGENTS [91] 4-8-11 Dean McKeown (2) *hld up, pld wide and hdwy frm 2 fs out, ran on ins last, fnshd wl*........................ (12 to 1 tchd 14 to 1) 2
619^{2} PATER NOSTER (USA) [98] 4-9-4 P Robinson (3) *tucked in hndy, rdn o'r 2 fs out, kpt on wl ins last*.
..................(7 to 2 tchd 4 to 1 and 100 to 30) 3
675^{4} SUNDAY'S HILL [96] 4-9-2 J Quinn (5) *rcd keenly, led till hdd o'r one furlong out, hrd rdn and battled on wl*.
.... (10 to 1 op 8 to 1) 4
BAND ON THE RUN [97] 6-9-3 R Hills (1) *trkd ldr, not much room frm o'r 2 fs out till no extr wl ins last*.
.................................(6 to 1 tchd 13 to 2) 5
315 AMAZING FEAT (Ire) [91] 4-8-11 K Darley (6) *pld hrd and rstrained early, effrt o'r 3 fs out, sn hard rdn and wknd appr last*...........................(9 to 2 op 3 to 1) 6
4726a^{2} TWO LEFT FEET [101] 6-9-2 (5*) K Rutter (4) *hld up in tch, pld wide and rdn 3 fs out, sn btn*.....(8 to 1 op 6 to 1) 7
Dist: ½l, sht-hd, sht-hd, 1½l, 3l, 10l. 1m 31.88s. a 4.68s (7 Ran).
SR: 11/3/9/6/2/-/-/ (Sir Philip Oppenheimer), G Wragg

783 Bacon And Woodrow Conditions Stakes Class C (4-y-o and up) £4,303 2m 45yds ....(2:35)

682^{3} JACK BUTTON (Ire) 4-9-5 N Day (5) *hld up in tch, niggled alng frm hfwy, led o'r 3 fs out, drw clr appr last, easily*.
...............................(13 to 8 on op 5 to 4 on) 1
BOKARO (Fr) 7-9-0 W Newnes (1) *al hndy, ev ch frm 3 fs out, rdn and not pace of wnr appr last*.
.........................(4 to 1 op 7 to 2 tchd 5 to 1) 2
539^{5} AUDE LA BELLE (Fr) 5-8-6 (7*) D Wright (4) *wtd wth, hdwy o'r 4 fs out, sn rdn and kpt on one pace*.
....(5 to 1 op 3 to 1) 3
559^{9} PERFORATE (bl) 4-8-11 J Quinn (2) *led for 5 fs, sn lost pl*.
....................................(20 to 1 op 12 to 1) 4
617^{5} NORTHERN RARITY (USA) 4-8-11 P Robinson (3) *trkd ldr, led aftr 5 fs till hdd o'r 3 out, wknd*. (5 to 1 op 7 to 2) 5
Dist: 6l, 6l, 3½l, nk. 3m 36.30s. a 10.30s (5 Ran).
(A And B Racing), Bob Jones

784 Royal Scottish Assurance Maiden Stakes Class D (3-y-o) £3,590 7f 30yds......(3:05)

439^{3} FEATHER FACE 9-0 W Newnes (2) *trkd ldr, led o'r 3 fs out, hrd rdn and hld on wl ins last*..... (3 to 1 tchd 7 to 2) 1
582 GRAN SENORUM (USA) 9-0 C Rutter (6) *wtd wth, hdwy 3 fs out, sn rdn alng, styd on wl ins last*.
....(5 to 1 op 3 to 1) 2
529^{7} TEJ SINGH (USA) 8-11 (3*) J Weaver (4) *al hndy, shaken up and hng rght frm wl o'r 2 fs out, kpt on ins last*.
...................(6 to 5 on op 5 to 4 on tchd Evens) 3
MOON FLASK (Ire) 9-0 T Sprake (1) *tucked away, rdn and effrt o'r 2 fs out, not much room appr fnl furlong, one pace*.............................. (5 to 1 op 4 to 1) 4
INOVAR 9-0 K Fallon (5) *sn last and rcd wide, moderate hdwy fnl 2 fs, no dngr*.
.....................(25 to 1 op 20 to 1 tchd 33 to 1) 5
RARE OCCURANCE 9-0 J Quinn (3) *led till hdd o'r 3 fs out, sn wknd*......................... (33 to 1 op 25 to 1) 6
Dist: ½l, sht-hd, 2½l, 8l, 1½l. 1m 33.13s. a 5.93s (6 Ran).
(J A Mountain), M McCormack

785 Lambert Smith Hampton Handicap Class C (0-90 3-y-o and up) £4,844 1m 3f 200yds ....(3:35)

632^{6} LEGION OF HONOUR [65] 5-8-7 (7*) V Halliday (2) *made all, hrd rdn frm o'r 2 fs out, jst hld on*... (9 to 1 op 5 to 1) 1
527^{4} AMBIGUOUSLY REGAL (USA) [74] 4-9-9 P Robinson (6) *took keen hold, al tracking ldr, chlgd frm o'r 2 fs out, ran on wl nr finish*...................(2 to 1 fav tchd 7 to 4) 2
589^{5} JAMES IS SPECIAL (Ire) [49] 5-7-12 J Quinn (4) *in tch, niggled alng and outpcd o'r 5 fs out, styd on fnl 2 furlongs, ran on nr finish*.
...............................(15 to 2 op 10 to 1 tchd 12 to 1) 3
527^{9} CHIEF MINISTER (Ire) [78] 4-9-13 K Fallon (3) *slwly into strd, niggled alng frm o'r 5 fs out, some late hdwy, nvr able to chal*........................ (4 to 1 op 5 to 2) 4
389^{2} BIGWHEEL BILL (Ire) [79] 4-9-9 (5*) Stephen Davies (5) *al hndy, niggled alng frm hfwy, wknd wl o'r 2 fs out*.
...................................(9 to 4 tchd 5 to 2) 5
TIME FOR A FLUTTER [74] 4-9-9 W Newnes (1) *hld up in tch till wknd frm 3 fs out, tld off*....(10 to 1 op 7 to 1) 6
Dist: Hd, nk, 6l, 15l, 10l. 2m 33.72s. a 3.92s (6 Ran).

SR: 37/45/19/36/7/-/ (Robson/Pattinson Partnership), M P Naughton

NAAS (IRE) (good)
Saturday May 1st
Going Correction: NIL (race 1), PLUS 0.10 (2,3,4,5)

786 Grange Con E.B.F. Maiden (2-y-o) £3,795 5f.................................(2:00)

5717 SHARP PHASE (Ire) 8-8 (6*) J J Behan (15)....... (16 to 1) 1
5715 COMMON RUMPUS (Ire) 8-11 J P Murtagh (3)....... (5 to 1) 2
THE PUZZLER (Ire) 9-0 P V Gilson (10)........ (3 to 1 fav) 3
SOMETHING SUPER 9-0 W J Supple (9).......... (8 to 1) 4
3057 SPRING FORCE (Ire) 9-0 J F Egan (16)........... (10 to 1) 5
GALLIC VICTORY (Ire) 9-0 P Shanahan (12)......... (7 to 1) 6
5714 MUSICAL BANKER 9-0 S Craine (14)............... (7 to 1) 7
SHIOWEN (Ire) 9-0 M J Kinane (2)............... (5 to 1) 8
ROYAL THIMBLE (Ire) 8-11 A J Nolan (11)......... (20 to 1) 9
JOIN FORCES (Ire) 9-0 R Hughes (13)............ (10 to 1) 10
ALKILIM (Ire) 8-9 (2*) D G O'Shea (7)............ (14 to 1) 11
CLANCY NOSSEL (Ire) 8-8 (6*) B J Walsh (4)...... (16 to 1) 12
EASTROP DANCER (Ire) 8-6 (8*) R V Skelly (8)..... (16 to 1) 13
LUDDEN LADY (Ire) 8-11 E A Leonard (6).......... (20 to 1) 14
TREASURE RING (Ire) 8-11 K J Manning (5)...... (11 to 2) 15
305 BOY IN BLACK (Ire) 9-0 N G McCullagh (1)....... (33 to 1) 16

Dist: 1l, 1l, 1½l, sht-hd. 1m 1.10s. a 3.10s (16 Ran).
SR: 38/31/30/24/23/-/ (Marvin Malmuth), Liam Browne

787 Woodlands Handicap (0-100 3-y-o and up) £6,900 7f......................... (3:00)

2705 CHEVIOT AMBLE (Ire) [-] 5-9-8 (6*) J R Barry (15).. (10 to 1) 1
6656 MILLIE'S CHOICE (Ire) [-] 4-9-11 W J Supple (9)... (10 to 1) 2
308 KAYFA (Ire) [-] 4-8-11 (6*) P Carberry (3)......... (10 to 1) 3
308 FOREST CONCERT (Ire) [-] 4-8-8 (6*) J J Behan (16) (7 to 1) 4
5512 RELENTLESS BOY (Ire) [-] 3-8-2 (4*) W J Smith (12) (10 to 1) 5
666 BASIE NOBLE [-] (bl) 4-8-6 N G McCullagh (13)... (16 to 1) 6
2584 SHAIKALA (Ire) [-] 3-8-4 (2*) D G O'Shea (6)... (10 to 3 fav) 7
5722 DONNASOO (Ire) [-] 4-8-6 Joanna Morgan (8)...... (8 to 1) 8
ALALJA (Ire) [-] 3-8-13 J F Egan (1).............. (8 to 1) 9
5723 DESERT THUNDER (Ire) [-] (bl) 4-9-10 M J Kinane (5) (5 to 1) 10
6405 THATCHING CRAFT (Ire) [-] 4-8-7 S Craine (11)... (14 to 1) 11
JUST FOUR (Ire) [-] 4-7-34 (8*) R T Fitzpatrick (2).. (33 to 1) 12
DIXIE FAVOR (USA) [-] 4-8-9 Ann O'Rourke (17)... (14 to 1) 13
6404 BELMARTIN [-] 7-8-10 P V Gilson (18)........... (10 to 1) 14
GALLARDINI (Ire) [-] 4-9-8 K J Manning (10)...... (10 to 1) 15
640 EVERY ONE KNOWS (USA) [-] 4-8-7 R Hughes (14) (16 to 1) 16
308 SIMPLY AMBER (Ire) [-] 5-7-101 (8*) R V Skelly (7) (20 to 1) pu

Dist: Sht-hd, nk, 1½l, 1l. 1m 27.00s. a 4.40s (17 Ran).
SR: 59/55/46/38/27/-/ (Michael W J Smurfit), Patrick Joseph Flynn

788 Broadfield EBF Race (3-y-o) £3,450 1m ....(3:30)

COLOUR PARTY (USA) 8-10 (6*) P Carberry (7)..... (7 to 1) 1
IDRIS (Ire) 9-2 M J Kinane (1).................. (3 to 1 on) 2
VIA PARIGI (Ire) 9-0 K J Manning (6)............ (5 to 1) 3
SEMPLE STADIUM (Ire) 8-9 P V Gilson (3)........ (10 to 1) 4
ATLANTIC ADIOS (Ire) 9-0 P Shanahan (2)......... (8 to 1) 5
639 MARY'S CASE (Ire) 8-9 J F Egan (4)............ (100 to 1) 6
577 KERMIS (Fr) 8-9 E A Leonard (5)............... (100 to 1) 7

Dist: Nk, 3l, ½l, 14l. 1m 41.20s. a 5.40s (7 Ran).
SR: 33/32/21/14/ (C S Gaisford-St Lawrence), Michael Kauntze

789 Saggart Handicap (0-80 3-y-o) £4,140 1m 3f ....(4:00)

668* NEVER BACK DOWN (Ire) [-] 9-1 (6*,7ex) P Carberry (11) .... (2 to 1 fav) 1
LADY TYONE (Ire) [-] 9-3 J P Murtagh (14)........ (6 to 1) 2
307 BRIGENSER (Ire) [-] 8-7 P Shanahan (13).......... (16 to 1) 3
6402 AULD STOCK (Ire) [-] 9-0 J F Egan (12)........... (5 to 1) 4
307 SLIGHTLY SCRUFFY (Ire) [-] 7-11 (8*) R T Fitzpatrick (5) .... (12 to 1) 5
SIENNA SOUND (Ire) [-] 8-12 (6*) J J Behan (3).... (10 to 1) 6
PULMICORT [-] 8-7 R Hughes (4)................ (16 to 1) 7
6688 VINEY (USA) [-] (bl) 9-7 M J Kinane (6).......... (8 to 1) 8
MICKS DELIGHT (Ire) [-] 8-11 S Craine (10)....... (12 to 1) 9
3078 CARAVELLE LAD (Ire) [-] 8-9 P V Gilson (9)....... (12 to 1) 10
LAKE OF LOUGHREA (Ire) [-] 8-7 W J Supple (15) (16 to 1) 11
GLENBRACK [-] 8-13 J D Eddery (7)............ (14 to 1) 12
6473 BALLYSPARKLE (Ire) [-] (bl) 8-82 K J Manning (2).. (10 to 1) 13
3074 BOBROSS (Ire) [-] 8-5 (6*) J A Heffernan (1)........ (9 to 1) 14
550 SHY WIN (Ire) [-] 8-0 N G McCullagh (8)........... (33 to 1) pu

Dist: 1l, ¾l, hd, 2½l. 2m 27.60s. a 11.10s (15 Ran).
SR: 7/1/-/-/-/-/ (Mount Juliet), W P Mullins

790 Tipper Fillies E.B.F. Maiden (3-y-o and up) £3,450 1¼m.......................... (4:30)

5502 RAJAURA (Ire) 3-8-9 R Hughes (18)............ (7 to 4 fav) 1
5776 CLEAR ABILITY (Ire) (bl) 3-8-9 M J Kinane (16)...... (4 to 1) 2
2823 ANDANTE (Ire) 3-8-7 (2*) R M Burke (15).......... (8 to 1) 3
VALONA (Ire) 3-8-9 K J Manning (12).............. (8 to 1) 4
KILTIMAGH (Ire) 3-8-9 N Byrne (6)............... (14 to 1) 5
HAANEM 3-8-9 W J Supple (10).................. (10 to 1) 6
2822 LADIES GALLERY (Ire) 3-8-9 P V Gilson (17)....... (7 to 1) 7
HOPESVILLE (Ire) 3-8-3 (6*) J A Heffernan (5)...... (14 to 1) 8
552 EFFICIENT FUNDING (Ire) 3-8-9 J F Egan (7)...... (25 to 1) 9
2679 MANGANS HILL (Ire) 3-8-9 N G McCullagh (3).... (33 to 1) 10
552 CORAL SOUND (Ire) (bl) 3-8-9 S Craine (9)....... (12 to 1) 11
SPECIAL OFFER (Ire) 3-8-112 J P Murtagh (8)..... (14 to 1) 12
OVERCAST (Ire) 3-8-9 G Curran (14)............ (10 to 1) 13
282 ONODI (Ire) 3-8-3 (6*) J J Behan (13)............. (66 to 1) 14
MOONLIGHT PARTNER (Ire) 3-8-9 D Manning (11) (14 to 1) 15
WHY ME LINDA (Ire) 4-9-3 (8*) R V Skelly (2)...... (20 to 1) 16
VROOM VROOM (Ire) 3-8-9 P Shanahan (4)....... (66 to 1) 17

Dist: Sht-hd, sht-hd, 4½l, 5l. 2m 15.10s. a 11.10s (17 Ran).
(H H Aga Khan), John M Oxx

NEWMARKET (good)
Saturday May 1st
Going Correction: MINUS 0.30 sec. per fur.

791 Culford Conditions Stakes Class C (3-y-o) £4,436 1½m...................... (2:00)

515* COMMANDER IN CHIEF 8-13 Pat Eddery (4) *trkd ldr, pushed alng 5 furlong out, led 3 out, quickened clr fnl furlong, easily.* ....(5 to 2 on op 3 to 1 on tchd 9 to 4 on) 1
509* OAKMEAD (Ire) 8-8 J Reid (6) *chsd 1st 2, not quicken o'r 3 fs out, rdn and styd on ins last, no imprsn on wnr.* ....(10 to 1 op 6 to 1 tchd 11 to 1) 2
5782 BLUE JUDGE (Ire) 8-13 C Roche (1) *led to 3 fs out, wknd out of second pl ins last*.............(9 to 2 tchd 5 to 1) 3
5156 FIRM BUT FAIR 8-11 R Cochrane (5) *al 4th, rdn and outpcd o'r four fs out, kpt on frm 2 out.* ....(20 to 1 op 14 to 1 tchd 25 to 1) 4
6847 NICO MIKE 8-11 L Dettori (2) *al beh, rdn and lost tch frm 4 fs out, tld off*...(50 to 1 op 20 to 1 tchd 66 to 1) 5

Dist: 3½l, 1½l, 10l, dist. 2m 32.05s. a 2.45s (5 Ran).
SR: 39/27/29/7/-/ (K Abdulla), H R A Cecil

792 Mayer Parry Rated Class B (0-100 4-y-o and up) £9,976 1¼m................(2:30)

MUHAYAA (USA) [90] 4-8-13 W R Swinburn (11) *pressed ldrs, led o'r one furlong out, rdn out.* ....(16 to 1 op 14 to 1 tchd 20 to 1) 1
4732 UNFORGIVING MINUTE [88] 4-8-11 Pat Eddery (9) *wl plcd, quickened to ld o'r 2 fs out, hdd over one out, rallied last strds*..............(11 to 2 op 5 to 1 tchd 6 to 1) 2
525 KRISTIANSTAD [93] 4-9-2 M Roberts (10) *al handily plcd, ev ch entering fnl furlong, not quicken last 50 yards.* ....(12 to 1 op 10 to 1 tchd 14 to 1) 3
4807 PELORUS [84] 8-8-4 (3*) D Harrison (1) *strted slwly, ran on frm rear last 2 fs, nrst finish*.......(16 to 1 op 20 to 1) 4
4803 KNOCK KNOCK [88] 8-8-11 R Cochrane (3) *steadied strt, hld up, hdwy 3 fs out, not rch wnr appr last.* ....(5 to 1 tchd 6 to 1) 5
CRYSTADO (Fr) [98] 4-9-7 J Williams (12) *mid-div, kpt on one pace last 2 fs*....(25 to 1 op 20 to 1 tchd 33 to 1) 6
4809 YOUNG FREEMAN (USA) [85] (bl) 4-8-8 M Hills (2) *hld up rear, improved 3 fs out, not trble frnt rnk frm 2 out..* ....(16 to 1 op 14 to 1) 7
BARFORD LAD [84] 6-8-7 L Dettori (4) *trkd ldrs, rdn and no extr o'r one furlong out*........ (16 to 1 op 14 to 1) 8
5136 BOLD STROKE [87] 4-8-10 W Carson (6) *led one furlong, ldg grp, rdn and wknd 2 out.* ....(9 to 4 fav op 2 to 1 tchd 5 to 2) 9
GYMCRAK PREMIERE [98] (bl) 5-9-7 G Duffield (5) *pld hrd in mid-div, drpd rear o'r 2 fs out.* ....(12 to 1 op 10 to 1 tchd 14 to 1) 10
WELSH MILL (Ire) [87] 4-8-10 A Munro (8) *led aftr one furlong till o'r 2 out, sn btn*....... (12 to 1 op 10 to 1) 11
TALOS (Ire) [84] 5-8-7 D Holland (7) *al beh, tld off last 4 fs.* ....(25 to 1 op 20 to 1 tchd 16 to 1) 12

Dist: Hd, 1½l, 2l, sht-hd, 3½l, ¾l, nk, 1½l, 6½l, ¾l. 2m 3.60s. a 0.90s (12 Ran).
SR: 60/57/59/46/49/52/37/35/35/ (Maktoum Al Maktoum), A A Scott

793 Philip Cornes Nickel Alloys Maiden Stakes Class D (2-y-o) £4,542 5f............(3:00)

GOLD LAND (USA) 9-0 A Munro (3) *trkd ldrs, shaken up to ld o'r one furlong out, quickened clr, easily.* ....(2 to 1 fav op 6 to 4 tchd 9 to 4) 1
GROTTO POOL (USA) 9-0 G Duffield (6) *led till appr fnl furlong, kpt on same pace.* .... (9 to 2 op 5 to 1 tchd 11 to 2) 2
6879 NONIOS (Ire) 9-0 W Ryan (11) *mid-div, effrt o'r one furlong out, styd on ins last*....... (20 to 1 tchd 16 to 1) 3
687 ROYAL CAPE 9-0 D Holland (4) *cl up, ev ch till rdn and outpcd ins fnl furlong*............(20 to 1 op 12 to 1) 4
BLUE BOMBER 9-0 W R Swinburn (9) *pressed ldrs, wknd one furlong out, eased whn btn.* ....(9 to 2 op 7 to 2 tchd 5 to 1) 5
BALLAH SHACK (USA) 8-11 (3*) D Harrison (10) *outpcd till some late prog*...... (20 to 1 op 12 to 1 tchd 25 to 1) 6
STRADISHALL 9-0 L Dettori (1) *ldg grp till wknd wl o'r one furlong out*......... (25 to 1 op 20 to 1 tchd 33 to 1) 7

KELLYSI 9-0 T Quinn (7) *handily plcd for 3 fs, no extr.*
....................(14 to 1 op 12 to 1 tchd 16 to 1) 8
MEMORABLE 8-7 (7*) S Mulvey (8) *slwly into strd, al outpcd*..............(20 to 1 op 12 to 1 tchd 25 to 1) 9
EXTRA BONUS 9-0 R Cochrane (2) *strted slwly, effrt frm rear hfwy, nvr dngrs*...........(16 to 1 tchd 20 to 1) 10
TONDRES (USA) 9-0 M Roberts (5) *strted slwly, sn mid-div, no prog frm 2 fs out.*
....................(7 to 1 op 4 to 1 tchd 15 to 2) 11
Dist: 4l, ¾l, sht-hd, 2½l, 3l, ½l, 1l, 3½l, 1l, hd. 1m 0.52s. a 1.92s (11 Ran).
SR: 32/16/13/12/2/-/ (Fahd Salman), P F I Cole

794 2000 Guineas Stakes Class A (Group 1) (3-y-o) £110,871 1m..................(3:40)

431[2] ZAFONIC (USA) 9-0 Pat Eddery (10) *hld up towards rear, hdwy on outsd 3 fs out, quickened to ld wl ins last 2, sn clr, imprsv*....... (6 to 5 on op Evens tchd 5 to 4 on) 1
541[4] BARATHEA (Ire) 9-0 M Roberts (6) *towards rear, prog frm hfwy, led briefly 2 out, sn hdd and outpcd, kpt on gmely ins fnl*.........(10 to 1 op 8 to 1 tchd 11 to 1) 2
658[3] BIN AJWAAD (Ire) 9-0 B Raymond (4) *beh, made up considerable grnd last 2 fs, nrst finish.*
....................(66 to 1 op 50 to 1 tchd 100 to 1) 3
526[7] PETARDIA (bl) 9-0 M Hills (5) *hdwy frm rear 3 fs out, wnt 3rd one out, not quicken*....................(66 to 1) 4
526[4] SILVER WIZARD (USA) 9-0 L Piggott (9) *led for o'r 4 fs, rdn and kpt on 2 out, btn appr last.* (25 to 1 tchd 33 to 1) 5
580* INCHINOR 9-0 L Dettori (11) *pushed alng o'r 3 fs out, styd on one pace frm 2 out.*
....................(11 to 1 op 14 to 1 tchd 10 to 1) 6
541[2] WHARF (USA) 9-0 W R Swinburn (12) *handily plcd till rdn and outpcd o'r one furlong out*.... (7 to 1 tchd 8 to 1) 7
541* EMPEROR JONES (USA) 9-0 R Cochrane (8) *hld up in mid-div, effrt o'r 2 fs out, sn rdn and btn*.........(20 to 1) 8
541[7] NOMINATOR 9-0 W Ryan (15) *pressed ldr, led o'r 3 fs out to 2 out, sn outpcd*....................(100 to 1) 9
541[6] CHADDLEWORTH (Ire) 9-0 J Reid (7) *hld up towards rear, effrt o'r 2 fs out, nvr dngrs.*
....................(9 to 1 op 7 to 1 tchd 10 to 1) 10
541[5] IVORY FRONTIER (Ire) 9-0 C Roche (2) *mid-div, rdn alng hfwy, nvr on terms*....................(33 to 1) 11
526[2] REVELATION (Ire) 9-0 W J O'Connor (14) *pressed ldrs till lost pl o'r 2 fs out*............... (33 to 1 op 25 to 1) 12
474* RIGHT WIN (Ire) 9-0 T Quinn (1) *cl up 5 fs, wknd quickly.*
....................(20 to 1 tchd 25 to 1) 13
540[6] PEMBROKE (USA) 9-0 W Carson (13) *in tch till rdn and wknd o'r 2 fs out*....................(20 to 1) 14
Dist: 3½l, 3l, 1½l, nk, nk, 3½l, 2l, hd, ¾l, ½l. 1m 35.32s. b 1.88s (14 Ran).
SR: 92/81/72/67/66/65/54/48/47/ (K Abdulla), A Fabre

795 Palace House Stakes Class A (Group 3) (3-y-o and up) £20,232 5f..............(4:15)

PARIS HOUSE 4-8-10 J Carroll (15) *pressed ldrs, rdn to ld o'r one furlong out, ridden out, hld on cl hme.*
....................(9 to 1 op 10 to 1 tchd 11 to 1) 1
637* DAUBERVAL (USA) 4-8-10 M Roberts (5) *hdwy o'r one furlong out, fnshd strly, jst fld*...............(10 to 1) 2
LOCHSONG 5-8-7 W Carson (16) *led aftr 2 fs till o'r one out, kpt on gmely und pres nr finish.*
....................(11 to 2 op 9 to 2 tchd 6 to 1) 3
511[3] ARTISTIC REEF 4-8-10 L Dettori (14) *ldg grp, not quicken 2 fs out, styd on wl fnl 100 yards*...............(16 to 1) 4
464[2] UP AND AT 'EM 3-8-0 Paul Eddery (4) *settled rear, styd on und pres appr fnl furlong, nrst finish.*
....................(5 to 2 fav op 2 to 1 tchd 11 to 4) 5
BUNTY BOO 4-8-7 T Quinn (1) *chsd ldrs, ran on one pace ins fnl furlong*................. (50 to 1 tchd 66 to 1) 6
555[3] REGAL CHIMES 4-8-10 A Munro (17) *in tch, no extr appr fnl furlong*....................(33 to 1 op 25 to 1) 7
464* SEA GAZER (Ire) 3-8-0 K Darley (10) *led 2 fs, wl plcd till wknd o'r one out*......(10 to 1 op 7 to 1 tchd 12 to 1) 8
SPANIARDS CLOSE 5-8-10 W R Swinburn (12) *slwly into strd, nvr better than mid-div.*
....................(10 to 1 op 16 to 1 tchd 20 to 1) 9
MILLYANT 3-7-11 D Harrison (9) *rdn alng o'r 2 fs out, nvr trble ldrs*....................(14 to 1 op 10 to 1) 10
722* CASE LAW 6-8-10 G Duffield (13) *broke wl, pushed alng and outpcd hfwy*...............(12 to 1 tchd 14 to 1) 11
FREDDIE LLOYD (USA) 4-8-10 Pat Eddery (7) *speed to hfwy, sn btn*...........(8 to 1 op 6 to 1 tchd 9 to 1) 12
BIT OF A LARK 5-8-10 R Cochrane (6) *outpcd.*
....................(50 to 1 op 33 to 1) 13
566[4] SAINT EXPRESS 3-8-0 J Penza (3) *nvr able to chal.*
....................(33 to 1 tchd 40 to 1) 14
566[5] SATANK (USA) 3-8-1[1] R Hills (11) *early pace, no prog frm hfwy*....................(33 to 1) 15
ANONYMOUS 3-7-11 G Bardwell (8) *slwly into strd, al outpcd*....................(50 to 1 tchd 66 to 1) 16
Dist: Nk, nk, 1½l, ¾l, ¾l, hd, ½l, 2½l, 1½l, hd. 58.75s. a 0.15s (16 Ran).
SR: 63/62/58/55/42/46/48/36/36/ (P E T Chandler), J Berry

796 Ladbrokes Handicap Class C (0-90 3-y-o and up) £11,647 6f..................(4:45)

436[8] CASTLEREA LAD [71] 4-8-10 W Ryan (15) *in tch, led entering fnl furlong, rdn out*.........(10 to 1 tchd 12 to 1) 1
677 MARTINOSKY [64] 7-8-3 M Hills (12) *hld up, swtchd lft o'r one furlong out, kpt on und pres nr finish.*
....................(14 to 1 op 16 to 1 tchd 20 to 1) 2
460[7] TROON [88] 3-9-2 L Piggott (17) *on heels of ldrs, ev ch appr fnl furlong, rdn and edgd lft, styd on cl hme.*
....................(14 to 1 tchd 12 to 1 and 16 to 1) 3
YES [54] 5-7-0 (7*) Kim McDonnell (13) *cl up, led o'r 2 fs out till entering last, ran on same pace.*
....................(40 to 1 op 33 to 1 tchd 50 to 1) 4
4768a FIGHTER SQUADRON [61] (bl) 4-8-0 G Duffield (8) *hld up, hdwy and hmpd o'r one furlong out, kpt on nr finish.*
....................(25 to 1 op 20 to 1 tchd 33 to 1) 5
654[2] OUR RITA [77] 4-9-2 R Cochrane (14) *hld up, cld on ldrs and not clr run appr fnl furlong, eased whn btn final 100 yards*............ (11 to 1 op 8 to 1 tchd 12 to 1) 6
700 MISS MOVIE WORLD [54] (bl) 4-7-7 J Fanning (10) *cl up, ev ch o'r 2 fs out till over one out, no extr und pres.*
....................(25 to 1) 7
542* MOON STRIKE (Fr) [78] 3-8-6 A Munro (16) *mid-div, effrt 2 fs out, styd on one pace ins last.*
....................(11 to 4 fav op 4 to 1 tchd 5 to 2) 8
NAGIDA [80] 4-9-5 Pat Eddery (1) *nvr nr to chal.*
....................(14 to 1 op 16 to 1 tchd 12 to 1) 9
501* GOODY FOUR SHOES [54] 5-7-7 G Bardwell (18) *rear, rdn alng appr last 2 fs, nvr dngrs.*
....................(15 to 2 op 7 to 1 tchd 8 to 1) 10
659[8] FASCINATION WALTZ [73] 6-8-12 B Raymond (4) *hld up, effrt o'r 2 fs out, hmpd and snatched up appr last, sn btn*.................... (8 to 1 op 6 to 1 tchd 9 to 1) 11
659 AUGHFAD [85] 7-9-10 J Reid (2) *wth ldrs for o'r 4 fs.*
....................(33 to 1 op 25 to 1) 12
677* LANGUEDOC [64] 6-8-0 (3*) D Harrison (11) *led for o'r 3 fs, wknd over one out*... (12 to 1 op 10 to 1 tchd 14 to 1) 13
4752a[7] TAUBER [63] 9-8-2 S O'Gorman (6) *speed to hfwy.*
....................(40 to 1 op 33 to 1 tchd 50 to 1) 14
465[3] DENSBEN [83] 9-9-8 M Roberts (9) *in tch 3 fs, wknd quickly*..............(10 to 1 op 8 to 1 tchd 11 to 1) 15
TEMPLE FORTUNE (USA) [72] 4-8-11 W Carson (3) *outpcd.*
....................(14 to 1 tchd 16 to 1) 16
SURE LORD (Ire) [69] 4-8-8 T Quinn (5) *al beh.*
....................(40 to 1 op 33 to 1 tchd 50 to 1) 17
Dist: ¾l, 1l, 1l, hd, 1l, nk, hd, 1l, hd, ½l. 1m 12.41s. a 1.01s (17 Ran).
SR: 40/30/39/12/18/30/6/18/27/ (Mrs Tess Graham), R Hollinshead

797 Chippenham Park Maiden Stakes Class D (3-y-o) £4,347 6f....................(5:15)

538[6] BIG SKY 9-0 W Ryan (6) *pressed ldr, rdn to ld o'r one furlong out, hng lft ins last, kpt on.* (5 to 2 op 6 to 4) 1
428[4] PUTOUT 8-9 L Dettori (2) *ldg grp, ev ch o'r one furlong out, crrd lft ins last, not quicken und pres.*
....................(5 to 1 op 4 to 1) 2
ROBLEU 8-7 (7*) Gaye Harwood (3) *led till o'r one furlong out, kpt on same pace*.............(50 to 1 op 20 to 1) 3
MITHI AL GAMAR (USA) 8-9 W R Swinburn (5) *mid-div, outpcd o'r 2 fs out, styd on ins last.* (7 to 1 op 8 to 1) 4
INDERAPUTERI 8-9 T Quinn (7) *trkd ldrs, rdn and one pace 2 fs out*........ (20 to 1 op 14 to 1 tchd 25 to 1) 5
541[9] CANASKA STAR 9-0 Pat Eddery (4) *slwly into strd, sn hndy, ev ch o'r one furlong out, not much room and swtchd rght ins last, not rcvr.*
....................(7 to 4 fav op 6 to 4 tchd 9 to 4) 6
PERSIAN CHIMES (Ire) 9-0 G Duffield (9) *mid-div, outpcd appr last 2 fs*.................... (33 to 1) 7
510[6] TARTIB (Ire) 9-0 W Carson (1) *slwly into strd, al beh, lost tch o'r 2 fs out*.................. (10 to 1 op 20 to 1) 8
519 INONDER 8-9 J Williams (8) *al beh, lost tch appr last 2 fs.*
....................(50 to 1 tchd 66 to 1) 9
Dist: 1½l, 1½l, sht-hd, sht-hd, ¾l, 6l, 6l, 5l. 1m 12.91s. a 1.51s (9 Ran).
SR: 34/23/22/16/15/17/ (L Marinopoulos), H R A Cecil

ST-CLOUD (FR) (heavy)
Saturday May 1st
Going Correction: PLUS 1.05 sec. per fur.

798 Prix de Barbeville (Group 3) (4-y-o and up) £23,895 1¾m 110yds............... (3:25)

407[6] DADARISSIME (Fr) 4-9-0 F Head, *last strt, effrt 2 and a half fs out, rdn one and a half out, quickened to ld cl hme*....................(31 to 10) 1
SOUGHT OUT (Ire) 5-9-1 C Asmussen, *led strt, jnd o'r 2 fs out, quickened clr over one and a half furlongs out, ct cl hme*....................(11 to 10 fav) 2
TURGEON (USA) 7-8-12 G Guignard, *4th strt, effrt o'r 2 fs out, jnd ldrs over one and a half furlong out, one pace.*
....................(42 to 10) 3
4674a[4] GRAND FLOTILLA (USA) 6-8-9 D Boeuf, *8th strt, effrt o'r 2 fs out, jnd ldrs over one and a half out, one pace.*
....................(77 to 10) 4
461[4] GLORIA MUNDI (Fr) 6-8-8 W Mongil, *7th strt, effrt o'r 2 fs out, one pace*....................(22 to 1) 5
406[9] DAJRAAN (Ire) 4-9-2 T Jarnet, *al mid-div*...... (42 to 10) 6

COMMENDABLE (Ire) 5-9-2 Joel Boisnard, *3rd strt, chlgd o'r 2 and a half fs out, sn wknd*..............(98 to 10) 7
CIUDADELLA (Fr) 4-8-8 C Le Scrill, *al rear*........(46 to 1) 8
392* CUTTING REEF (Ire) 4-8-6 A Badel, *second strt, rdn and wknd quickly*................................(12 to 1) 9
392³ NORTHERN PARK (USA) 5-8-11 O Poirier, *5th strt, sn wknd*...(33 to 1) 10
Dist: ¾l, ½l, 2½l, ¾l, ½l, 8l, 3l, 3l, 5l. 3m 19.10s. a 17.60s (10 Ran).
SR: 76/75/71/63/60/67/51/37/29/ (Sir J Goldsmith), G Bridgland

THIRSK (good)
Saturday May 1st

Going Correction: PLUS 0.10 sec. per fur. (races 1,3,4,5), PLUS 0.15 (2,6)

799 May Maiden Stakes Class D (3-y-o and up) £3,699 1½m...................... (2:15)

681² CUMBRIAN RHAPSODY 3-7-11 (3*) S Maloney (1) *patiently rdn, dashed up to join issue entering strt, led appr fnl furlong, ran on wl*..............(14 to 1 tchd 16 to 1) 1
POINT THE WAY (Ire) 3-8-0 G Carter (10) *nvr far away, led o'r 2 fs out till appr last, ran on same pace*. ....(7 to 4 fav tchd 2 to 1 and 13 to 8) 2
567³ KHISAL (Can) 3-8-6¹ M Wigham (5) *settled midfield, improved entering strt, styd on, not pace to chal*. ....(8 to 1 op 6 to 1) 3
679⁶ CALL THE GUV'NOR 4-9-10 A McGlone (3) *tucked away on ins, effrt and bustled alng entering strt, one pace last 2 fs*..................(4 to 1 tchd 9 to 2 and 7 to 2) 4
COMBELLINO 3-8-5 N Adams (4) *led 4 fs, styd hndy till fdd wl o'r one out, better for race*. (10 to 1 tchd 9 to 1) 5
482⁷ ISLE OF PEARLS (USA) 3-8-5 P D'Arcy (13) *chsd ldg bunch, effrt and drvn alng aftr a m, no imprsn*. ....(11 to 1 op 8 to 1 tchd 12 to 1) 6
646⁷ BRESIL (USA) 4-9-10 S Whitworth (2) *patiently rdn, hdwy into midfield o'r 2 fs out, nvr plcd to chal*. ....(50 to 1 op 33 to 1) 7
ABALENE 4-9-10 G Hind (6) *in tch, chsd alng to keep up hfwy, nvr a threat*..............(66 to 1 op 50 to 1) 8
FAIRWAYS ON TARGET 7-9-10 J Lowe (9) *hld up, al beh*. ....(16 to 1 op 14 to 1) 9
438² MURPHYS WAY 4-9-0 (5*) O Pears (14) *wth ldrs, feeling pace and rdn entering strt, fdd*......(7 to 1 op 6 to 1) 10
679 MISTRESS BEE (USA) 4-9-5 M Tebbutt (8) *sluggish strt, nvr able to reco'r*......................(33 to 1 op 25 to 1) 11
CHAJOTHELYTBRIGADE (Ire) 3-7-7 (7*) Darren Moffatt (7) *unruly at strt, led aftr 4 fs till after 2 out, sn btn*. ....(66 to 1 op 50 to 1) 12
646⁸ BRANDON GROVE 5-9-5 Alex Greaves (11) *wth ldrs till fdd entering strt*..................................(33 to 1) 13
VIENNA WOODS 6-9-10 T Lucas (12) *trkd ldg half dozen, drvn alng aftr a m, tld off last 2 fs*. (20 to 1 op 16 to 1) 14
Dist: 1½l, 7l, 3½l, nk, 1½l, ½l, 2½l, 8l, 1½l, 2l. 2m 36.10s. a 5.90s (14 Ran).
SR: 39/36/28/39/19/16/34/29/13/ (Cumbrian Industrials Ltd), M H Easterby

800 Business Furniture Centre Handicap Class D (0-80 3-y-o and up) £3,816 5f (2:45)

700⁴ SONDERISE [62] 4-8-11 N Carlisle (22) *trkd ldrs, effrt and not clr run o'r one furlong out, quickened through to ld ins last, ran on*.........(15 to 2 op 7 to 1 tchd 8 to 1) 1
591⁸ NED'S BONANZA [65] 4-9-0 J Lowe (16) *tucked away gng wl, improved to chal appr fnl furlong, kpt on*. ....(14 to 1 op 16 to 1 tchd 12 to 1) 2
700³ BALLAD DANCER [49] 8-7-5 (7*) Darren Moffatt (21) *settled midfield, str run entering fnl furlong, fnshd fst*. ....(15 to 2 op 7 to 1 tchd 8 to 1) 3
591² SLADES HILL [60] 6-8-9 Alex Greaves (17) *nvr far away, led wl o'r one furlong out till hdd and not quicken ins last*................(11 to 2 fav op 6 to 1 tchd 5 to 1) 4
SOBERING THOUGHTS [45] 7-7-8⁸ (7*) M Humphries (13) *shaped wl, in frnt rnk thrght, prmsg*. ....(33 to 1 op 25 to 1) 5
591* EWALD (Ire) [64] 5-8-8 (5*) B Doyle (9) *broke wl to show speed centre, tacked o'r to stands' side grp hfwy, kpt on same pace*.............................(9 to 1 op 8 to 1) 6
MISS ARAGON [47] 5-7-10 F Norton (5) *chsd alng to improve frm midfield hfwy, styd on ins fnl furlong*. ....(25 to 1) 7
600⁶ LINCSTONE BOY (Ire) [53] (bl) 5-8-2³ M Wood (19) *broke fst to ld stands' side 3 fs, no extr ins last*. ....(16 to 1 op 14 to 1) 8
591 MACS MAHARANEE [58] 6-8-7 G Hind (6) *settled midfield, drvn alng to improve o'r one furlong out, not pace to chal*..................................(33 to 1 op 25 to 1) 9
PRINCE BELFORT [60] 5-8-5¹ (5*) O Pears (14) *wth ldrs, ev ch till fdd appr fnl furlong*....................(20 to 1) 10
591 CATHERINES WELL [71] 10-9-6 T Lucas (23) *co'red up on ins, swtchd centre over one furlong out, kpt on stdly finish*..............................(10 to 1 op 8 to 1) 11
HERE COMES A STAR [67] 5-9-2 S Morris (3) *chsd ldg bunch, hrd at work 2 fs out, no imprsn*........(25 to 1) 12
PRECENTOR [59] (bl) 7-8-1 (7*) K Sked (20) *co'red up wth stands' side bunch, effrt and not much room over one furlong out, eased whn btn*........(14 to 1 op 12 to 1) 13
YOURS OR MINE (Ire) [49] 5-7-12 S Wood (11) *gd speed in frnt rnk for o'r 3 fs, fdd*.......................(20 to 1) 14
591 SINGING STAR [76] 7-9-4 (7*) Claire Balding (1) *sluggish strt, nvr a factor*..............(25 to 1 op 20 to 1) 15
MASTER POKEY [61] 9-8-7⁴ (7*) P Johnson (12) *sluggish strt, rcd centre, nvr plcd to chal*...............(33 to 1) 16
401⁵ SOBA GUEST (Ire) [70] 4-9-5 G Carter (4) *rcd alone far side, gd speed 3 fs, wknd*.............(10 to 1 tchd 11 to 1) 17
492 SUPER ROCKY [67] 4-8-9 (7*) H Bastiman (18) *chsd ldrs for 3 fs, fdd*...................................(12 to 1) 18
677 GREENWICH CHALENGE [71] 3-8-10 M Wigham (8) *chsd alng to go pace hfwy, nvr dngrs*.............(25 to 1) 19
DAILY SPORT AUGUST [45] 4-7-8⁸ (7*) D McCabe (10) *bustled alng to keep up hfwy, nvr dngrs*..........(66 to 1) 20
615 RISKMEMAY [44] 4-7-7 J O'Reilly (7) *chsd ldrs, struggling hfwy, sn btn*.................................(66 to 1) 21
FILICAIA [58] 7-8-7 Kim Tinkler (15) *sluggish strt, al wl beh*. ....(25 to 1 op 20 to 1) 22
Dist: ¾l, 1½l, ½l, nk, nk, 1½l, nk, nk, 1½l, hd. 1m 0.50s. a 3.30s (22 Ran).
SR: 46/46/24/33/17/35/12/17/21/ (Mrs D Wright), N Tinkler

801 Thirsk Hunt Cup Handicap Class C (0-90 3-y-o and up) £12,330 1m........... (3:20)

676⁴ FOREVER DIAMONDS [74] 6-9-0 M Birch (4) *sluggish strt, imprvg whn trapped on rls and plenty to do o'r one furlong out, weaved through to ld ins last, ran on*. ....(8 to 1 tchd 9 to 1) 1
592 CEE-JAY-AY [60] 6-8-0 G Carter (2) *sluggish strt, improved and not much room last 2 fs, squeezed through fnl furlong, ran on wl*...................................(14 to 1) 2
651⁹ SPANISH VERDICT [65] 6-7-12 (7*) C Teague (1) *tried to make all, rdn last 2 fs, hdd and no extr ins last*. ....(25 to 1 op 20 to 1) 3
651⁴ HAMADRYAD (Ire) [82] 5-9-3 (5*) O Pears (6) *sluggish strt, beh and a lot to do entering strt, gd hdwy on outsd o'r one furlong out, fnshd wl*.........................(14 to 1) 4
302⁶ ALLINSON'S MATE (Ire) [72] 5-8-12 Alex Greaves (10) *settled midfield, swtchd outsd to improve o'r one furlong out, kpt on same pace*...................(14 to 1 op 12 to 1) 5
530⁴ FALCONS DAWN [55] (bl) 6-7-9² A Mackay (3) *trkd ldr, hrd at work last 2 fs, no extr ins last*...(20 to 1 op 16 to 1) 6
592* NO SUBMISSION (USA) [84] 7-9-10 S Wood (16) *patiently rdn, brght wide to improve last 2 fs, kpt on, not pace to chal*............................(14 to 1 op 10 to 1) 7
302² HENIU (USA) [65] (v) 4-8-5 Dean McKeown (9) *nvr far away, hrd at work whn pace quickened 2 fs out, fdd*. ....(4 to 1 jt-fav op 5 to 1) 8
603³ SALBYNG [61] 5-8-1 N Carlisle (7) *chsd ldg bunch, drvn alng o'r one furlong out, no imprsn*. ....(14 to 1 op 12 to 1) 9
651⁸ SELF EXPRESSION [64] 5-8-4 J Lowe (13) *settled in rear, improved entering strt, not rch ldrs*. ....(16 to 1 op 12 to 1) 10
651* LEIF THE LUCKY (USA) [82] 4-9-8 N Connorton (5) *bustled alng in midfield hfwy, nvr a threat*.........(4 to 1 jt-fav op 7 to 2 tchd 9 to 2) 11
592² GOLDEN CHIP (Ire) [79] 5-9-2 (3*) S Maloney (12) *co'red up on ins, hrd at work over 2 fs out, no imprsn*. ....(12 to 1 op 10 to 1) 12
ATHERTON GREEN (Ire) [66] 3-7-7³ (3*) N Kennedy (11) *chsd alng in midfield hfwy, nvr dngrs*...............(33 to 1) 13
398* MY BEST VALENTINE [74] 3-8-1 F Norton (14) *chsd ldg bunch for o'r 6 fs, fdd*...........(12 to 1 op 10 to 1) 14
605⁶ DOMICKSKY [63] 5-7-12 (5*) B Doyle (15) *shwd up in frnt rnk for o'r 5 fs, fdd*...(12 to 1 op 14 to 1 tchd 10 to 1) 15
565* GANT BLEU (Fr) [63] 6-8-3 A Culhane (8) *wth ldrs, feeling pace 2 fs out, wknd and eased appr fnl furlong*. ....(12 to 1 op 10 to 1) 16
Dist: 1½l, 1½l, ¾l, ½l, hd, 1½l, 3l, 1½l, 1½l, 1l. 1m 40.10s. a 4.20s (16 Ran).
SR: 49/30/30/45/33/15/39/11/2/ (Mrs J B Russell), M H Easterby

802 Rothmans Royals North South Challenge Series Handicap Class C (0-90 3-y-o) £5,208 7f.......................... (3:50)

397² HI NOD [67] 8-2 N Connorton (12) *nvr far away, drvn ahead entering last 2 fs, sn hdd, rgned ld appr fnl furlong, ran on wl*.............(5 to 2 fav tchd 9 to 4) 1
TARNSIDE ROSAL [70] 8-5 M Birch (10) *patiently rdn, improved on outsd to ld briefly o'r one furlong out, nudged lft and no extr ins last*.... (14 to 1 op 12 to 1) 2
683* MARGARET'S GIFT [81] 9-2 G Carter (11) *al tracking ldrs, improved last 2 fs, styd on finish*.....(5 to 1 op 9 to 2) 3
NITOUCHE [70] 8-5 W Woods (3) *pressed ldg pair, led o'r 2 fs out till wl over one out, sn btn*..............(16 to 1) 4
405³ PEACEFULL REPLY (USA) [64] 7-13 N Carlisle (9) *al pressing ldrs, hrd at work o'r one furlong out, no extr*. ....(12 to 1 tchd 14 to 1) 5
677⁶ BIRCHWOOD SUN [74] 8-9 S Perks (8) *last and bustled alng hfwy, styd on, nvr nrr*..............(10 to 1) 6
SPRING SUNRISE [67] 8-2 F Norton (7) *chsd alng in midfield hfwy, outpcd last 2 fs*.................(12 to 1) 7

SO SO [83] 9-4 Alex Greaves (5) *chsd ldg bunch till wknd last 2 fs*......................................(8 to 1) 8
685^{7} DANCE TO ORDER (Ire) [71] 8-6 C Nutter (1) *sluggish strt, nvr a factor*.........................(7 to 1 op 6 to 1) 9
711^{4} ROSE FLYER (Ire) [58] 7-7 S Wood (6) *wth ldr, crrd wide bend hfwy, sn led, hdd o'r 2 fs out, fdd.* ....(16 to 1 op 20 to 1) 10
BENZOE (Ire) [86] 9-7 T Lucas (4) *led, not handle bend and ran wide hfwy, sn hdd, squeezed out entering strt, soon btn*..........................(11 to 1 op 8 to 1) 11
Dist: 2l, 2l, 6l, 1½l, 2l, ½l, hd, sht-hd, 5l, 5l. 1m 27.00s. a 4.20s (11 Ran).
SR: 36/33/38/9/-/2/-/8/-/ (Brian Nordan), M J Camacho

803 Millgate Maiden Stakes Class D (3-y-o) £3,406 7f.......................... (4:25)

630^{3} CHICKCHARNIE 8-9 (5*) O Pears (3) *led o'r 2 fs out, kpt on wl ins last*..........(8 to 1 op 5 to 1) 1
476^{2} BOLD THATCHER 9-0 N Adams (6) *chsd ldg 5, drvn alng to improve o'r one furlong out, styd on wl.* ....(6 to 4 on op 11 to 10 tchd 6 to 5) 2
CELESTIAL CHOIR 8-9 Dale Gibson (1) *sluggish strt, given time to reco'r, effrt over one furlong out, kpt on wl.* ....(33 to 1 op 20 to 1) 3
BEAUMONT (Ire) 9-0 M Wigham (7) *chsd ldg half dozen, rdn 2 fs out, ran on finish.* ....(8 to 1 op 10 to 1 tchd 7 to 1) 4
BROUGHTON'S PORT 8-7 (7*) D McCabe (2) *patiently rdn, shaken up to improve o'r one furlong out, prmsg.* ....(20 to 1 op 14 to 1) 5
ROYAL MUSIC 9-0 G Carter (8) *led, hdd and drvn alng o'r 2 fs out, sn btn*....................(8 to 1 op 6 to 1) 6
VIKING WATERS 8-9 J Fortune (5) *sluggish strt, took clr order hfwy, fdd o'r one furlong out.* ....(12 to 1 op 10 to 1 tchd 14 to 1) 7
641^{4} LIDA'S DELIGHT (Ire) 9-0 T Lucas (4) *chsd ldg pair, hng badly rght und pres last 2 fs, sn lost tch.* ....(12 to 1 op 10 to 1) 8
PRIMITIVE GIFT 8-9 J Lowe (9) *dug toes in leaving stalls, refused to race, took no part*......(16 to 1 op 12 to 1) I
Dist: ½l, 1l, 1½l, 1½l, 3½l, 12l, nk. 1m 27.90s. a 5.10s (9 Ran).
SR: 34/32/24/24/19/8/ (Mrs P A Barratt), B Beasley

804 Market Place Median Auction Maiden Stakes Class F (2-y-o) £2,780 5f..... (4:55)

SPORTING WARRIOR (Ire) 9-0 S Morris (6) *nvr far away, edgd lft o'r one furlong out, kpt on grimly to ld last 100 yards*..........................(12 to 1 op 33 to 1) 1
CERTIFICATE-X 8-9 Dean McKeown (12) *al hndy, hrd at work o'r one furlong out, kpt on wl.* ....(7 to 2 fav op 5 to 1) 2
ALLWIGHT THEN (Ire) 9-0 S Perks (13) *tried to make all, hdd and drvn alng fnl furlong, no extr.* ....(4 to 1 op 7 to 2) 3
WHARFEDALE MUSIC 8-9 A Culhane (16) *unruly in stalls, missed break, steady hdwy on ins last 2 fs, prmsg.* ....(9 to 1 op 10 to 1) 4
517^{3} MR BLOBBY (Ire) 9-0 G Carter (3) *wth ldg trio, edgd rght und pres o'r one furlong out, no extr.* ....(11 to 2 op 5 to 1) 5
708 CHEEKY CHAPPY 9-0 D Nicholls (1) *al chasing ldrs, feeling pace hfwy, kpt on ins fnl furlong*......... (33 to 1) 6
TRYSAIL 8-6 (3*) S D Williams (11) *chsd ldg quartet, bustled alng hfwy, kpt on, nvr able to chal.* ....(8 to 1 op 7 to 1) 7
DEMI-PLIE 9-0 F Norton (10) *sluggish strt, styd on last 2 fs, nvr nrr*..........................(8 to 1 op 7 to 1) 8
SPRING STAR 8-9 N Connorton (7) *bustled alng to go pace, styd on, nvr dngrs*..........................(20 to 1) 9
544^{7} PRINCE SKYBURD 9-0 M Birch (8) *chsd alng to keep up, nvr nr to chal*.................................. (33 to 1) 10
CHILIOLA 8-6 (3*) S Maloney (9) *sluggish strt, beh till ran on last 2 fs, nvr nrr*..................(9 to 1 op 8 to 1) 11
544^{6} ARKINDALE SPIRIT (Ire) 9-0 T Lucas (14) *drvn alng to keep up, nvr a factor*........................... (20 to 1) 12
RIVA'S BOOK (USA) 9-0 D Wilkinson (5) *drvn alng thrght, nvr dngrs*..................(14 to 1 tchd 16 to 1) 13
EXPRESS LINE 8-9 S Whitworth (4) *bustled alng thrght, nvr dngrs*........................(16 to 1 op 14 to 1) 14
UNKNOWN STAR 9-0 J O'Reilly (2) *unruly in stalls, nvr a factor*...................................... (33 to 1) 15
Dist: 1½l, 1l, 1½l, ¾l, 1½l, ¾l, ½l, 1l, ½l, hd. 1m 2.00s. a 4.80s (15 Ran).
SR: 19/8/9/-/-/-/ (Mrs Margaret Clarke), J M Carr

DUSSELDORF (GER) (good) Sunday May 2nd

805 Arag-Preis (Group 2) 3yo Fillies £48,980 1m................................(4:05)

QUEBRADA (Ire) 8-11 A Tylicki, *broke wl, trkd ldr, led 2 fs out, sn clr, imprsv*.................................. 1
SECONDIA 8-11 A Boschert, *4th strt, ran on fnl 2 fs, no ch wth wnr*... 2
AMBRA (Fr) 8-11 L Mader, *3rd strt, kpt on one pace fnl 2 fs*.. 3
RHODE ISLAND (Ger) 8-11 S Eccles, *led o'r 6 fs, one pace.* 4
SOOTY SWIFT (Ire) 8-11 M Hills, *mid-div, 7th strt on ins, kpt on one pace fnl furlong*.............................. 5
VAL D'ISERE (Ger) 8-11 A Starke, *hdwy 2 out, no extr fnl furlong*.. 6
DSHAMILJA (Ger) 8-11 A Helfenbein,.................... 7
NOUVELLE REINE (Ger) 8-11 G Bocskai,................... 8
MEDDICINA 8-11 A Best,................................. 9
ELACATA (Ger) 8-11 M Rimmer,........................... 10
FLAMBOYANT (Ger) 8-11 11
352^{2} HAZY KAY (Ire) 8-11 W Newnes,........................ 12
Dist: 5l, 2½l, nk, ½l, 1 ¾l, 4½l, 5l. 1m 39.77s. (12 Ran).
(Gestut Fahrhof), H Jentzsch

GOWRAN PARK (IRE) (good to yielding) Sunday May 2nd

806 Copper Beech Maiden (3-y-o and up) £2,760 6f......................... (2:30)

486^{4} GOLD BRAISIM (Ire) 3-8-6 C Roche (3)...........(10 to 1) 1
KINDNESS ITSELF (Ire) 3-8-6 M J Kinane (11).. (7 to 4 on) 2
572^{4} BENE MERENTI (Ire) 3-8-9 N G McCullagh (9).... (12 to 1) 3
YONOKA (Fr) 4-8-12 (8*) R V Skelly (13).......... (40 to 1) 4
WHAT MAGIC (Ire) 3-8-2 (4*) W J Smith (1)....... (12 to 1) 5
MATTABOY TWO (Ire) 4-9-0 (6*) J R Barry (12)... (100 to 1) 6
BARRY'S PRINCESS (Ire) 4-9-3 W J O'Connor (6) (25 to 1) 7
669^{3} FLORA WOOD (Ire) 3-8-6 W J Supple (14)........(10 to 3) 8
486 RICH LIFE (Ire) 3-8-9 P Shanahan (4).............(20 to 1) 9
GEALLAINNBAN (Ire) 3-8-9 E A Leonard (5).......(25 to 1) 10
550 EILEENS HOPE (Ire) 3-8-6 P V Gilson (7).......... (16 to 1) 11
LADY ASHLING (Ire) 5-8-12^{1} (6*) P Carberry (10) (100 to 1) 12
551^{7} SORRECA (Ire) 4-8-7 (10*) P J Smullen (8).......(100 to 1) 13
486 YELLOW PRINCESS (Ire) 3-8-6 D Manning (2).... (33 to 1) 14
Dist: Nk, 1½l, 3l, 1½l. 1m 13.70s. (14 Ran).
(Saeed Suhail), J S Bolger

807 Mountain Ash Handicap (0-90 4-y-o and up) £2,760 1¾m.................... (3:00)

4685a* PHARFETCHED [-] 4-9-0 J P Murtagh (11).........(7 to 2) 1
575^{2} MASAI WARRIOR [-] 6-9-0 (2*) R M Burke (12)..... (6 to 1) 2
4685a^{4} SHANTALLA BAY [-] 6-8-3 N G McCullagh (9)......(10 to 1) 3
4685a MAYFIELD PRINCE (Ire) [-] 4-8-8 (6*) B Bowens (16) (10 to 1) 4
AIYBAK (Ire) [-] 5-9-13 M J Kinane (2)........ (15 to 8 fav) 5
BEAUMONT HOUSE (Ire) [-] 4-8-10 W J Supple (8) (12 to 1) 6
AQUINAS [-] 7-6-13 (8*) P P Murphy (4)........... (25 to 1) 7
575 OFTEN AHEAD (Ire) [-] 5-9-4 R Hughes (14)........(8 to 1) 8
553^{6} LACKEL (Ger) [-] 5-9-4 (10*) C McCormack (1).... (20 to 1) 9
MUNSIF (Fr) [-] 6-7-10^{1} (8*) R V Skelly (13).........(25 to 1) 10
706^{3} JESSIE'S BOY (Ire) [-] 4-7-8^{1} A J Nolan (6)........(25 to 1) 11
4685a DIRECT LADY (Ire) [-] 4-9-8 C Roche (7)...........(8 to 1) 12
TRANQUIL BEAUTY (Ire) [-] 4-8-0 (2*) D G O'Shea (5) ....(16 to 1) 13
OPEN MARKET (USA) [-] 4-9-5 P Shanahan (15).. (20 to 1) 14
575 HIDDEN LIGHT (Ire) [-] 4-9-1 P V Gilson (3)....... (12 to 1) 15
Dist: 2l, 3l, 6l, hd. 3m 11.20s. (15 Ran).
(James Shanahan), Mrs A M O'Brien

808 Avonmore Classic Trial Race (3-y-o and up) £5,520 1m 1f 130yds............ (3:30)

271^{4} SKIPO (USA) 3-8-7 M J Kinane (5)...............(11 to 1) 1
ALOUETTE 3-8-9 C Roche (1).............. (6 to 4 jt-fav) 2
668^{9} SHAHZADI (Ire) 3-8-10 D Hogan (4)................(7 to 1) 3
PORTRAIT GALLERY (Ire) 3-8-12 P V Gilson (3) ..(6 to 4 jt-fav) 4
FLAME OF PERSIA (Ire) 3-8-7 W J O'Connor (2)....(9 to 2) 5
Dist: Sht-hd, 2½l, 1l, 20l. 2m 6.70s. (5 Ran).
(Allen E Paulson), D K Weld

LONGCHAMP (FR) (heavy) Sunday May 2nd

Going Correction: PLUS 1.00 sec. per fur.

809 Prix Vanteaux (Group 3) 3yo Fillies £23,895 1m 1f 55yds.........................(1:15)

CORRAZONA (USA) 9-2 O Doleuze, *led, quickened 2 fs out, ran on wl, drw clr*............................... 1
561^{5} ACCOMMODATING (USA) 9-2 F Head, *hld up, effrt o'r one furlong out, one pace*.............................. 2
BROKEN PEACE (USA) 9-2 T Jarnet, *second strt, effrt o'r 2 fs out, wknd over one out*............................ 3
Dist: 8l, 4l. 2m 5.80s. a 13.50s (3 Ran).
SR: 34/10/-/ (J Wertheimer), Mme C Head

810 Prix Ganay (Group 1) Colts & Fillies (4-y-o and up) £59,537 1¼m 110yds........(2:50)

407^{5} VERT AMANDE (Fr) 5-9-2 D Boeuf, *3rd strt, hdwy 2 out, chlgd appr fnl furlong, ran on wl to ld 60 yards out*... . 1

OPERA HOUSE 5-9-2 M Roberts, *led wl o'r 2 fs out, rdn two out, ct 60 yards out, ran on* 2
MISIL (USA) 5-9-2 L Dettori, *last strt, sn rdn, hdwy fnl 2 fs, kpt on* 3
4072 DEAR DOCTOR (Fr) 6-9-2 C Asmussen, *second strt, rdn 2 fs out, btn one and a half out, kpt on one pace* 4
407* MARILDO (Fr) 6-9-2 G Guignard, *4th strt, effrt 2 out, no extr fnl furlong* 5
4073 POLYTAIN (Fr) 4-9-2 W Mongil, *7th strt, sn rdn and outpcd, ran on ins fnl furlong* 6
ARCANGUES (USA) 5-9-2 T Jarnet, *5th strt, rdn and btn 2 fs out* 7
BOSTON TWO STEP (USA) 6-9-2 W R Swinburn, *led till wl o'r 2 out, wknd quickly* 8

Dist: Sht-nk, 3l, nk, sht-nk, sht-hd, 10l, 20l. 2m 21.10s. a 12.10s (8 Ran).
SR: 86/85/79/78/77/76/56/16/ (E Sarasola), E Lellouche

811 Prix de Suresnes (Listed) 3yo Colts & Geldings £14,337 1¼m 110yds...... (4:25)

HERNANDO (Fr) 9-2 C Asmussen, 1
OKEEDOKEE (Fr) 9-2 O Doleuze, 2
IRISH PROSPECTOR (Fr) 9-2 G Guignard, 3
EPAPHOS (Ger) 9-0 (2*) E Legrix, 4
4693a2 DERNIER EMPEREUR (USA) 9-2, 5

Dist: ½l, 2½l, 4l, 4l. 2m 25.60s. a 16.80s (5 Ran).
SR: 39/38/33/25/17/ (S S Niarchos), F Boutin

DONCASTER (good)
Monday May 3rd

Going Correction: MINUS 0.25 sec. per fur. (races 1,3,4), MINUS 0.10 (2,5,6,7)

812 Wiseton Maiden Auction Stakes Class D (2-y-o) £3,435 5f.................... (2:20)

6802 SINNERS REPRIEVE 8-9 M Birch (2) *cl up, quickened to ld 2 fs out, kpt on nr finish.* (5 to 4 fav op 11 to 8 tchd 6 to 4) 1
4695 NORTHERN CELADON (Ire) 9-0 P Robinson (8) *chsd ldrs, rdn 2 fs out, styd on wl ins last*..... (7 to 2 op 3 to 1) 2
4336 INDIAN CRYSTAL 8-9 Dean McKeown (9) *led, hdd 2 fs out, sn rdn, one pace appr last*.......... (8 to 1 op 6 to 1) 3
698 HARPO'S SPECIAL 9-0 K Fallon (10) *chsd ldrs, rdn 2 fs out, kpt on same pace*................(25 to 1 op 20 to 1) 4
KARSEAM (Ire) 9-0 N Connorton (6) *dwlt, in rear till styd on wl appr fnl furlong*........... (25 to 1 op 20 to 1) 5
FUSSY SIOUX 8-9 L Charnock (11) *chsd ldrs, rdn o'r 2 fs out, sn one paced*............... (25 to 1 op 16 to 1) 6
DRAGON MAN 9-0 Dale Gibson (7) *chsd ldrs 3 fs.* (16 to 1 op 14 to 1) 7
STUDFORD GIRL 8-9 T Lucas (1) *slwly away, effrt and gd hdwy hfwy, sn rdn and wknd wl o'r one furlong out.* (25 to 1 op 20 to 1) 8
YO (Ire) 8-9 B Raymond (3) *in tch till rdn hfwy, sn wknd.* (14 to 1 op 10 to 1) 9
6806 TENPIN PROPHET (Ire) 8-9 J Fanning (4) *chsd ldrs, rdn alng hfwy, sn wknd*............(25 to 1 op 20 to 1) 10
OLYMPIC BID 8-9 J Carroll (5) *al outpcd and beh.* (5 to 1 op 7 to 2) 11

Dist: Nk, 2l, 1½l, sht-hd, 1½l, 4l, ½l, 1½l, ½l, 2½l. 1m 1.57s. a 2.77s (11 Ran).
SR: 15/19/6/5/4/-/ (Mrs J B Mountifield), M H Easterby

813 May Day Holiday Limited Stakes Class F (0-65 3-y-o) £3,199 1¼m 60yds...... (2:50)

724* HOOCHIECOOCHIE MAN (Ire) 8-11 R Price (13) *mid-div, gd hdwy 3 fs out, effrt 2 out, rdn to ld appr last, edgd lft and styd on*.................... (4 to 1 fav op 9 to 4) 1
5464 I'M A DREAMER (Ire) 8-11 Dean McKeown (12) *mid-div, steady hdwy 3 fs out, rdn appr last, styd on wl.* (12 to 1) 2
6868 AMIARGE 8-11 M Wigham (4) *mid-div, hdwy and not clr run 2 and a half fs out, swtchd rght and sn rdn, styd on wl fnl furlong*.............................. (20 to 1) 3
5828 ALLESCA 8-6 R Street (10) *beh, hdwy o'r 3 fs out, swtchd ins, hmpd 2 out, switched wide, rdn and ran on strly fnl furlong*..........................(8 to 1 op 6 to 1) 4
KAWASIR (Can) 8-11 N Carlisle (5) *chsd ldrs, effrt to ld o'r 2 fs out, rdn and hdd appr last, btn whn wkng and hmpd ins last*........................... (16 to 1 op 14 to 1) 5
6424 BARLEY CAKE 8-6 J Fanning (1) *mid-div, gd hdwy on inner 3 fs out, ev ch 2 out, sn rdn and wknd entering last*...................................(20 to 1 op 14 to 1) 6
GYPSY CRYSTAL (USA) 8-6 A Culhane (8) *beh, styd on fnl 2 fs, nrst finish*......................... (25 to 1 op 20 to 1) 7
4344 MERRY MERMAID 8-6 L Charnock (3) *al chasing ldrs, rdn and one pace o'r 2 fs out*.......... (14 to 1 op 12 to 1) 8
4933 KOA 8-11 P Robinson (14) *chsd ldr, rdn 3 fs out, grad wknd*.................(5 to 1 op 4 to 1 tchd 11 to 2) 9
6306 DUPLICATE 8-11 M Birch (9) *hld up and beh, effrt and some hdwy 2 fs out, nvr dngrs*.......(10 to 1 op 6 to 1) 10
4770a8 LOCHORE 8-11 A McGlone (16) *nvr rch ldrs.* (12 to 1 op 14 to 1 tchd 16 to 1) 11
4104 EASTERN GLOW 8-6 W Woods (7) *slwly into strd, al rear.* (20 to 1) 12
B B GLEN 8-71 M Tebbutt (18) *mid-div, effrt and some hdwy o'r 3 fs out, sn btn*...........(12 to 1 op 7 to 1) 13
434 DICKINS 8-11 B Raymond (11) *chsd ldrs, rdn and wknd 3 fs out*........................(25 to 1 op 20 to 1) 14
4134 BAEZA 8-11 F Norton (2) *led, rdn 3 fs out, sn hdd and wknd*.............................(12 to 1 op 10 to 1) 15
6427 DIVINE RAIN 8-11 W Hood (20) *cl up, rdn and wknd wl o'r 2 fs out*......................... (25 to 1 op 20 to 1) 16
6428 MUSICAL PHONE 8-11 K Fallon (19) *chsd ldrs, wknd 3 fs out*.............................. (33 to 1 op 20 to 1) 17
7177 IKHTIRAA (USA) (bl) 8-11 W Carson (17) *mid-div, rdn 4 fs out, sn lost pl*...................... (7 to 1 op 8 to 1) 18
6082 BUZZ-B-BABE 8-11 J Carroll (6) *al beh.* (20 to 1 op 16 to 1 tchd 25 to 1) 19

Dist: ½l, 1½l, sht-hd, sht-hd, 2l, 1l, 3½l, ½l, nk, 2l. 2m 12.12s. a 5.42s (19 Ran).
SR: 33/32/29/23/27/18/16/9/13/ (Christopher Wright), D W P Arbuthnot

814 Coal Miner Handicap Class C (0-100 4-y-o and up) £5,071 6f.................... (3:20)

3554 AMRON [82] 6-9-2 N Carlisle (6) *steadied strt, hdwy o'r 2 fs out, effrt and rdn to ld ins last, ran on.* (11 to 2 op 5 to 1) 1
676 NILE DELTA (Ire) [66] 4-8-0 A McGlone (11) *trkd ldr, hdwy to ld o'r 2 fs out, rdn, hdd and not quicken ins last.* (5 to 1 op 4 to 1) 2
677 PRETONIC [65] 5-7-13 J Lowe (9) *al prmnt, ev ch 2 fs out, sn rdn and kpt on one pace*........ (8 to 1 tchd 9 to 1) 3
677 FIRST GOLD [65] 4-7-131 P Robinson (4) *cl up on outer till hmpd and lost pl aftr 2 fs, swtchd ins and gd hdwy two out, rdn, styd on fnl furlong*.....(10 to 1 tchd 11 to 1) 4
677 RED ROSEIN [89] 7-9-9 J Carroll (3) *steadied strt and hld up, hdwy 2 fs out, kpt on wl fnl furlong, nrst finish.* (8 to 1 op 10 to 1) 5
436 SEA DEVIL [79] 7-8-13 N Connorton (2) *prmnt on outer, hng rght thrght, rdn and one pace fnl 2 fs.* (7 to 1 op 6 to 1) 6
5487 GENERAL JOHN (Ire) [67] 4-8-1 Dale Gibson (10) *led, rdn and hdd o'r 2 fs out, sn wknd*.......(12 to 1 op 8 to 1) 7
7002 SAGEBRUSH ROLLER [82] 5-9-2 B Raymond (8) *chsd ldrs, effrt and rdn o'r 2 fs out, edgd lft and sn btn.* (9 to 2 jt-fav op 7 to 2) 8
6777 COOLABA PRINCE (Ire) [66] 4-8-0 W Carson (5) *cl up on outer, hamperd and lost pl 2 fs out, not reco'r.* (9 to 2 jt-fav op 4 to 1 tchd 5 to 1) 9

Dist: ¾l, 2½l, sht-hd, 1½l, ¾l, hd, ¾l, ¾l. 1m 12.66s. a 1.26s (9 Ran).
SR: 47/28/17/16/34/21/8/20/1/ (Roy Peebles), J Berry

815 Bawtry Claiming Stakes Class F (4-y-o and up) £2,758 5f...................... (3:55)

6158 MARTINA 5-8-1 J Fanning (8) *trkd ldrs, swtchd and effrt to chal appr fnl furlong, quickened to ld ins last, ran on*................................. (7 to 1 op 6 to 1) 1
5917 SIR TASKER 5-9-0 P Robinson (7) *cl up, rdn to chal and ev ch entering fnl furlong, no extr*....(14 to 1 op 12 to 1) 2
5452 ANOTHER EPISODE (Ire) 4-9-0 J Carroll (2) *led, rdn 2 fs out, hdd and no extr ins last*............(11 to 4 op 5 to 2) 3
6153 METAL BOYS 6-8-8 B Raymond (6) *in tch, effrt and hdwy 2 fs out, sn rdn, styd on ins last*........... (9 to 4 fav) 4
7226 LOVE RETURNED 6-9-5 M Tebbutt (5) *in tch, smooth hdwy o'r 2 fs out, ev ch appr last, sn rdn and wknd.* (11 to 2 op 9 to 2 tchd 6 to 1) 5
5683 SALADAN KNIGHT (v) 8-8-2 F Norton (1) *chsd ldrs, rdn o'r 2 fs out, sn wknd*.................(14 to 1 tchd 16 to 1) 6
4796a7 BELATED 4-9-0 Dale Gibson (3) *al rear.* (6 to 1 op 5 to 1) 7
DANDY DESIRE 4-8-4 Dean McKeown (4) *al rear.* (33 to 1 op 25 to 1) 8

Dist: 1½l, nk, 1½l, sht-hd, 3l, ¾l, 2½l. 59.72s. a 0.92s (8 Ran).
SR: 44/51/50/38/48/19/28/8/ (M J Yarrow), J Wharton

816 Intake Handicap Class D (0-80 3-y-o) £3,687 1¾m 132yds............... (4:25)

457* ACANTHUS (Ire) [80] 9-7 W Carson (1) *prmnt, rdn alng hfwy, sn outpcd, hrd ridden o'r 3 fs out, styd on to ld appr last, ran on wl*....(5 to 2 op 7 to 4 tchd 11 to 4) 1
5472 SAFETY IN NUMBERS [53] 7-8 J Lowe (2) *hld up, gd hdwy o'r 3 fs out, effrt and ev ch appr last, sn rdn and styd on*.................................. (6 to 1 op 7 to 1) 2
3854 OMIDJOY (Ire) [70] 8-11 W Woods (4) *chsd ldrs, effrt and hdwy to chal 2 fs out, sn rdn and ev ch till wknd entering fnl furlong*.............(20 to 1 op 16 to 1) 3
653* LIJAAM (Ire) [80] 9-7 B Raymond (5) *pld hrd, led, rdn 3 fs out, drifted rght 2 furlongs out, hdd and wknd appr last*............... (13 to 8 fav op 6 to 4 tchd 7 to 4) 4
5845 ROMALITO [64] 8-5 N Carlisle (6) *prmnt, chsd ldr frm hfwy, rdn and wknd o'r one furlong out.* (14 to 1 tchd 16 to 1) 5
4684 ARGYLE CAVALIER (Ire) [66] 8-7 A Culhane (3) *hld up, took clr order 4 fs out, sn rdn alng, hng rght and beh fnl 2 furlongs*...............................(9 to 2 tchd 5 to 1) 6

Dist: 1½l, 3l, nk, ¾l, 3½l. 3m 9.33s. a 4.83s (6 Ran).
SR: 44/14/25/34/16/11/ (Cuadra Africa), J L Dunlop

817 Carr Hill Conditions Stakes Class D (3-y-o) £3,348 1m. .... (4:55)

538* LOWER EGYPT (USA) 9-0 J Carroll (4) *trkd ldrs, hdwy to chal 2 fs out, sn led, rdn and ran on wl fnl furlong.* ....(6 to 5 jt-fav op 6 to 4 tchd 13 to 8) 1
526³ SALATIN (USA) 9-4 W Carson (3) *set gd pace, quickened 3 fs out, rdn 2 out, sn hdd, rallied und pres entering fnl furlong, no extr nr finish*..................(6 to 5 jt-fav op 11 to 10 on tchd 5 to 4 on) 2
463⁶ SOLOMON'S DANCER (USA) 8-10 Dean McKeown (5) *chsd ldrs, rdn 3 fs out, sn one paced*.... (50 to 1 op 33 to 1) 3
611* QAMOOS (Ire) 8-12 N Carlisle (2) *chsd ldr, rdn o'r 3 fs out, sn wknd*.......................(11 to 1 op 7 to 1) 4
642* LOCK TIGHT (USA) 8-10 A Culhane (6) *hld up, effrt and rdn 2 and a half fs out, no hdwy*. (20 to 1 op 14 to 1) 5
Dist: 1l, 10l, 3l, 3l. 1m 40.09s. a 3.39s (5 Ran).
SR: 37/38/ (Sheikh Mohammed), J H M Gosden

818 Sandall Beat Handicap Class C (0-90 3-y-o and up) £4,793 1m..................(5:25)

592 BUZZARDS BELLBUOY [70] 4-9-1 Dale Gibson (1) *chsd ldrs, rdn alng 3 fs out, styd on und pres to ld wl ins last, hld on gmely*......................(11 to 2 op 9 to 2) 1
565⁶ MASTER HYDE (USA) [61] 4-8-6 P Robinson (4) *hld up, effrt and hng lft 2 fs out, sn rdn, styd on to chal wl ins last, kpt on*............................(8 to 1 tchd 9 to 1) 2
605⁵ EN ATTENDANT (Fr) [83] 5-10-0 B Raymond (2) *trkd ldrs gng wl, hdwy on bit to ld 2 and a half fs out, rdn and hdd well ins last, not run on*.....(3 to 1 fav op 4 to 1) 3
592⁹ SUPREME BOY [58] 4-8-3 F Norton (8) *al prmnt, effrt 2 fs out, rdn to chal entering fnl furlong, sn btn.* ....(8 to 1 op 7 to 1) 4
BLOW DRY (Ire) [84] 3-9-2 A Culhane (5) *in tch, effrt 2 fs out, rdn and wknd appr fnl furlong*. (8 to 1 op 7 to 1) 5
592 LEGEND DULAC (Ire) [50] 4-7-9 J Lowe (7) *led, hdd 2 and a half fs out, sn wknd*..............(14 to 1 op 12 to 1) 6
592³ WEE SARAH [58] 5-8-3 W Carson (6) *hld up and beh, effrt and hdwy 3 fs out, sn rdn and btn*. (5 to 1 tchd 9 to 2) 7
CAUSLEY [76] 8-9-0 (7*) S Sanders (9) *cl up, rdn 3 fs out, sn wknd*.............(10 to 1 op 8 to 1 tchd 12 to 1) 8
737 LAUREL QUEEN (Ire) [69] 5-9-0 J Carroll (3) *hld up and beh, effrt and rdn 3 fs out, no hdwy*... (7 to 1 tchd 13 to 2) 9
Dist: Sht-hd, 3l, 2½l, 7l, 3l, 1½l, 3l, 8l. 1m 39.11s. a 2.41s (9 Ran).
SR: 53/43/56/23/15/-/ (N H Gardner), H J Collingridge

DOWN ROYAL (IRE) (good to firm) Monday May 3rd

819 British Midland Diamond Maiden (3-y-o and up) £1,380 1½m................(3:30)

267⁶ SPORTSTYLE (Ire) 3-8-7 N G McCullagh (4)...... (10 to 1) 1
282 DARK HYACINTH (Ire) 3-8-4 W J Supple (2)........(7 to 1) 2
669 LORD CHIEF (Ire) 3-8-12⁵ J P Murtagh (5)........(10 to 1) 3
552⁶ ANY MINUTE NOW (Ire) 3-8-5 (2*) R M Burke (11).. (5 to 1) 4
INNOCENT MAN (Ire) 3-8-1 (6*) J J Behan (7).....(12 to 1) 5
553⁸ THE RIDGE BOREEN 9-9-12 N Byrne (6).........(25 to 1) 6
649⁴ VLADIVOSTOK 3-8-7 S Craine (3)................(7 to 2) 7
WINE BROKER 8-9-12 R Hughes (10)............(50 to 1) 8
SOLSTRAND (Ire) 3-7-10² (10*) D Cullen Jnr (8)....(33 to 1) 9
DALKEY ISLAND (Ire) 3-8-7 D Hogan (9).....(11 to 10 fav) ur
Dist: Sht-hd, nk, sht-hd, 20l. (Time not taken) (10 Ran).
(F Dunne), F Dunne

820 Antrim E.B.F. Maiden (2-y-o) £2,070 5f ....(4:00)

LONG GALLERY (Ire) 9-0 W J Supple (4).......... (5 to 2) 1
PEACE TOKEN (Ire) 8-11 B Coogan (6)............(9 to 2) 2
571 PETER'S POWER (Ire) 9-0 S Craine (2)...........(7 to 1) 3
FIONN DE COOL (Ire) 9-0 C Roche (7)......... (Evens fav) 4
ABSOLUTE RULER (Ire) (bl) 9-0 J P Murtagh (5)...(20 to 1) 5
BAKER HILL (Ire) 9-0 N G McCullagh (3)..........(25 to 1) 6
ONTHEOTHEREND (Ire) 9-0 N Byrne (1)..........(14 to 1) 7
Dist: 3l, hd, 3½l, 1l. (Time not taken) (7 Ran).
(Mrs M J Grassick), M J Grassick

KEMPTON (good (races 1,3,4,5), good to firm (2,6,7)) Monday May 3rd

Going Correction: MINUS 0.05 sec. per fur. (races 1,3,4,5), MINUS 0.10 (2,6,7)

821 Sporting Bears Maiden Fillies Stakes Class D (3-y-o) £3,728 1m...........(2:10)

523³ ANEESATI 8-6 (5*) B Doyle (9) *ldg grp, shaken up to ld ins fnl furlong, pushed out, jst hjeld on.* .... (100 to 30 fav op 3 to 1 tchd 7 to 2) 1
TOCHAR BAN (USA) 8-11 J Williams (12) *str run frm reear o'r one fs out, fnshd fst*............(11 to 2 op 4 to 1) 2
ALASKAN PRINCESS (Ire) 8-11 T Quinn (6) *wth ldrs, led o'r 3 fs out till ins last, ran on*........ (12 to 1 op 7 to 1) 3
DUKRAME 8-11 W Newnes (14) *hdwy frm rear hfwy, kpt on wl last 2 fs.* ....(9 to 1 op 10 to 1 tchd 12 to 1 and 8 to 1) 4
KENESHA (Ire) 8-11 C Rutter (10) *mid-div, riden and styd on one pace last 2 fs*...............(50 to 1 op 33 to 1) 5
ALTA VICTORIA (Ire) 8-11 S Raymont (4) *steadied strt, rear till ran on fnl 2 fs*.... (12 to 1 op 20 to 1 tchd 33 to 1) 6
TAP ON AIR 8-11 M Roberts (8) *wl plcd, rdn and not quicken appr last 2 fs.* (5 to 1 op 4 to 1 tchd 11 to 2) 7
ARAADH (USA) 8-11 R Hills (11) *mid-div, cld on ldrs o'r 3 fs out, no hdwy ins last 2*.............. (7 to 1 op 9 to 2) 8
ZANZE (USA) 8-11 R Cochrane (13) *beh, effrt 3 fs out, no imprsn on ldrs appr last.* ....(12 to 1 op 10 to 1 tchd 14 to 1) 9
HAVEN OF LOVE (Ire) 8-4 (7*) Michael Hunt (5) *led till ran wide and hdd on bend o'r 3 fs out, sn wknd.* ....(50 to 1 op 33 to 1) 10
GLINT OF AYR 8-11 A Clark (3) *in tch, effrt o'r 3 fs out, btn over 2 out*..................................(33 to 1) 11
522³ MISS KINABALU 8-11 Paul Eddery (1) *pressed ldrs till lost pl ins fnl 2 fs*.....................(14 to 1 op 12 to 1) 12
GABHADERA 8-11 S Whitworth (2) *mid-div to hfwy.* ....(50 to 1) 13
SWISS MOUNTAIN 8-11 S O'Gorman (7) *nvr dngrs.* ....(50 to 1 op 25 to 1) 14
443⁶ KEEP SAFE 8-11 D Biggs (16) *pushed alng in mid-div till drpd rear hfwy*................ (50 to 1 op 25 to 1) 15
SUPPER WITH SUSIE 8-4 (7*) Sharon Millard (15) *outpcd, tld off*.......................................(50 to 1) 16
Dist: Nk, ¾l, 1½l, 2½l, ½l, hd, ½l, 2½l, 1½l, ½l. 1m 40.09s. a 3.29s (16 Ran).
SR: 42/41/39/34/26/24/23/21/13/ (Mohamed Obaida), C E Brittain

822 'Helping Children Through Sport' Conditions Stakes Class D (4-y-o and up) £3,143 1¾m. .... (2:40)

617³ LONG SILENCE (USA) 4-8-5 Paul Eddery (7) *led 2 fs, chsd ldr, led o'r two out, rdn out wl ins last.* .... (5 to 4 on op 6 to 4 on tchd 11 to 10 on) 1
757⁴ DURSHAN (USA) 4-8-10 Pat Eddery (2) *wl plcd, cld on wnr o'r 2 fs out, rdn and not quicken over one out, rallied ins last, not quicken nr finish.* ....(11 to 4 op 5 to 2 tchd 9 to 4 and 3 to 1) 2
BALADIYA 6-8-0 (5*) Stephen Davies (4) *led aftr 2 fs, clr appr hfwy, hdd o'r two out, ran on same pace.* ....(25 to 1 op 33 to 1) 3
663 NATIVE CHIEFTAN (v) 4-8-13 M Roberts (3) *str hold, hld up in rear till effrt 3 fs out, no imprsn on ldrs ins last 2.* ....(12 to 1 tchd 16 to 1) 4
MATCHING GREEN 4-8-5 J Williams (5) *mid-div, effrt o'r 3 fs out, outpcd frm 2 out*..........(8 to 1 tchd 10 to 1) 5
626⁹ CHAKALAK 5-8-12 T Quinn (6) *dsptd 3rd pl 4 fs, lost place, hdwy 5 out, outpcd o'r 2 out*......(12 to 1 op 33 to 1) 6
727 INTRICACY 5-8-5 W Newnes (1) *settled rear, rdn alng o'r 3 fs out, not rch ldrs*............... (33 to 1 op 25 to 1) 7
Dist: ¾l, 2½l, 2l, 2½l, 1½l, 1½l. 3m 12.03s. a 14.03s (7 Ran).
(W S Farish III), Mrs J Cecil

823 Shield Club Fillies Conditions Stakes Class D (3-y-o) £3,231 6f............(3:10)

BROCKTON DANCER 8-8 L Piggott (2) *slwly into strd, hdwy o'r 2 fs out, led one out, rdn out.* ....(10 to 1 tchd 12 to 1) 1
512⁴ TOOCANDO (Ire) 8-10 R Cochrane (6) *trkd ldrs, rdn and not much room o'r one furlong out, swtchd lft, fnshd strly*................(11 to 8 fav op Evens tchd 6 to 4) 2
GOLDEN GUEST 8-8 Paul Eddery (4) *slwly into strd, improved o'r 2 fs out, ran on wl fnl furlong.* .... (9 to 1 op 14 to 1 tchd 16 to 1) 3
627² YAKIN (USA) 8-8 R Hills (8) *led 5 fs, no extr last 100 yards.* ....(6 to 1 op 7 to 1 tchd 8 to 1) 4
627* CRIME OFTHECENTURY 9-0 T Quinn (5) *trkd ldr till o'r one furlong out, wknd fnl 150 yards.* ....(4 to 1 op 5 to 2 tchd 9 to 2) 5
512⁶ MAGIQUE ROND POINT (USA) 9-0 W Ryan (3) *mid-div, no imprsn on ldrs frm 2 fs out.* .... (6 to 1 op 5 to 1 tchd 13 to 2) 6
DESERT NOMAD 8-8 C Rutter (7) *outpcd most of way.* ....(66 to 1 op 50 to 1) 7
AUNTIE GINGER 8-8 M Roberts (1) *speed to hfwy, sn wknd, tld off*..............(66 to 1 tchd 100 to 1) 8
Dist: ½l, nk, 1l, 2½l, 2½l, 7l, 15l. 1m 13.37s. a 2.57s (8 Ran).
SR: 37/37/34/30/26/16/-/-/ (Mrs D A La Trobe), R Hannon

824 'Sparks' Jubilee Handicap Class B (0-105 4-y-o and up) £17,757 1m........... (3:40)

581 PAY HOMAGE [88] 5-9-1 L Piggott (9) *hld up, hdwy frm 3 fs out, led ins last, ran on.* .... (12 to 1 op 14 to 1 tchd 16 to 1) 1
737⁹ HIGHLAND MAGIC (Ire) [75] 5-8-2 C Rutter (4) *sstnd run ins last 2 fs, fnshd strly und pres*.....(10 to 1 op 14 to 1) 2

581 DAWNING STREET (Ire) [90] 5-9-3 Pat Eddery (13) *pressed ldrs, ev ch entering fnl furlong, not quicken last 100 yards*..............(5 to 1 fav op 4 to 1 tchd 11 to 2) 3
TAPIS ROUGE (Ire) [100] 4-9-13 M Roberts (6) *chsd ldr, led 2 fs out, hdd and one pace ins last*. (12 to 1 tchd 16 to 1) 4
581⁴ NEPTUNE'S PET [83] 5-8-7 (3*) D Harrison (3) *beh till ran on fnl 2 fs, nrst finish*..................(6 to 1 tchd 7 to 1) 5
581³ ROYAL SEATON [88] 4-9-1 S Whitworth (8) *hld up, hdwy o'r 2 fs out, styd on ins last*. ....(12 to 1 op 10 to 1 tchd 16 to 1) 6
302⁸ CHATHAM ISLAND [69] 5-7-7² (5*) B Doyle (2) *trkd ldrs, chlgd 3 fs out, wknd wl o'r one out*. ....(14 to 1 tchd 16 to 1 and 12 to 1) 7
581⁸ PORT SUNLIGHT (Ire) [80] 5-8-7 R Cochrane (11) *hdwy frm rear o'r 2 fs out, no imprsn on ldrs appr last*. ....(9 to 1 op 8 to 1) 8
HIGH LOW (USA) [81] 5-8-8 J Quinn (1) *led 6 fs*. ....(6 to 1 op 5 to 1) 9
MISS HAGGIS [84] 4-8-11 W Ryan (12) *handily plcd, rdn and wknd wl o'r one furlong out*. ....(25 to 1 op 20 to 1 tchd 33 to 1) 10
651⁵ WILSONIC [78] 4-8-5 T Quinn (7) *mid-div, wknd last 3 fs*. ....(16 to 1 op 12 to 1) 11
425² COOL LUKE (Ire) [82] 4-8-9 W Newnes (5) *in tch for o'r 5 fs*. ....(8 to 1 op 7 to 1 tchd 9 to 1) 12
426⁴ AJZEM (USA) [88] 4-9-1 Paul Eddery (10) *wl plcd till wknd 3 fs out*............. (20 to 1 op 16 to 1 tchd 25 to 1) 13
Dist: ½l, 1½l, ½l, ½l, 1½l, 2l, 1l, nk, 1l, 2½l. 1m 38.42s. a 1.62s (13 Ran).
SR: 71/56/66/74/55/55/30/38/38/ (Miss A V Hill), I A Balding

825 Classic Cars Maiden Stakes Class D (3-y-o) £3,523 1m.....................(4:10)

538³ DRAMANICE (USA) 9-0 L Piggott (7) *handily plcd, quickened to ld o'r one furlong out, pushed clr*. ....(11 to 4 fav op 3 to 1 tchd 9 to 4) 1
GONE TROPPO 9-0 W Ryan (4) *strted slwly, beh till ran on o'r 3 fs out, styd on wl ins last, not rch wnr*. .... (8 to 1 op 6 to 1 tchd 10 to 1) 2
DARECLIFF (USA) 9-0 S Raymont (2) *pressed ldrs, rdn alng o'r 2 fs out, not quicken over one out, styd on same pace*..........(10 to 1 op 6 to 1 tchd 12 to 1) 3
538⁸ GLEN ECHO (Ire) 9-0 T Quinn (1) *ran on frm rear last 2 fs, nrst finish*............. (9 to 1 op 8 to 1 tchd 11 to 1) 4
529⁵ SHARAAR (USA) 9-0 N Day (10) *in tch, cld on ldrs o'r 3 fs out, chlgd 2 out, one pace fnl furlong*. ....(10 to 1 op 6 to 1 tchd 11 to 1) 5
300³ COMPLETE MADNESS 9-0 R Hills (3) *mid-div, cld on ldrs o'r 3 fs out, not clr run over 2 out, outpcd over one out*. ....(14 to 1 op 12 to 1 tchd 16 to 1) 6
AJMAAN (USA) 9-0 M Roberts (11) *led till o'r one furlong out, no extr*............ (6 to 1 op 4 to 1 tchd 7 to 1) 7
582⁴ PREROGATIVE 9-0 Pat Eddery (9) *pressed ldrs, ev ch 2 fs out, wknd fnl furlong*... (9 to 2 op 4 to 1 tchd 5 to 1) 8
NAIF (USA) 9-0 R Cochrane (18) *in tch in mid-div, rdn and ran on one pace last 2 fs*. .... (15 to 2 op 6 to 1 tchd 8 to 1) 9
515 LIVONIAN 9-0 J Williams (12) *prog frm rear last 2 fs, not trble ldrs*...........(25 to 1 op 16 to 1 tchd 33 to 1) 10
JURA FOREST 9-0 Paul Eddery (8) *mid-div most of way*. .... (25 to 1 op 20 to 1) 11
582 BELFRY GREEN (Ire) 9-0 A Clark (17) *ldg grp till wknd o'r 2 fs out*.. (50 to 1) 12
538 FASHIONABLE DANCER 8-9 (5*) B Doyle (5) *wl plcd till lost pos frm 3 fs out*.................(33 to 1 op 20 to 1) 13
582 IMPERIAL TOKAY (USA) 8-11 (3*) D Harrison (13) *nvr nr to chal*.................................(50 to 1 op 33 to 1) 14
CALIBRATE 9-0 W Newnes (15) *beh, effrt 3 fs out, not rch ldrs*...................................(50 to 1 op 33 to 1) 15
459 HARD EIGHT 9-0 S Whitworth (16) *al beh*. .... (50 to 1 op 33 to 1) 16
4709a⁵ HILLSDOWN BOY (Ire) (v) 9-0 C Rutter (6) *al rear*. .... (50 to 1 op 33 to 1) 17
BRAVE HERO (USA) 9-0 D Biggs (14) *al rear*. .... (50 to 1 op 33 to 1) 18
Dist: 2l, ½l, ½l, hd, 2½l, 1l, ¾l, 1l, nk, hd. 1m 40.34s. a 3.54s (18 Ran).
SR: 41/35/33/31/30/22/19/17/14/ (W S Farish III), Mrs J Cecil

826 'Support Sparks' Selling Stakes Class E (3-y-o and up) £3,442 1½m..........(4:40)

699³ MR GENEAOLOGY (USA) (h,bl) 3-8-5 W Newnes (9) *slwly into strd, hdwy on outsd o'r 3 fs out, styd on to ld ins last, drw clr nr finish*....(5 to 1 op 9 to 2 tchd 6 to 1) 1
527⁶ HELLO MY DARLING (Ire) 5-9-13 T Quinn (18) *wl plcd, led o'r 2 fs out, hdd and outpcd ins last*. ....(4 to 1 fav op 7 to 2 tchd 9 to 2) 2
PENNINE LAD (Ire) 3-8-5 J Comber (4) *led 2 fs, in tch, rallied two out, styd on fnl furlong*. .... (25 to 1 op 20 to 1) 3
699* PONDERING (v) 3-8-8 M Roberts (14) *ran on frm rear last 2 fs, fnshd strly*...........(9 to 2 op 5 to 2 tchd 5 to 1) 4
LOCH DUICH 7-9-13 R Cochrane (16) *wl plcd, ev ch 2 fs out till ins last, not quicken*. ....(12 to 1 op 10 to 1 tchd 14 to 1) 5
483⁸ SUPREME MASTER 3-8-5 S Raymont (20) *hmpd aftr 3 fs, ran on frm rear from three out, nrst finish*. ....(10 to 1 op 8 to 1) 6
628 PRINCESS ERMYN 4-9-5 A Clark (10) *steadied into mid-div aftr 2 fs, hdwy o'r two out, one pace fnl furlong*. ....(20 to 1) 7
318 VICTORIAN FLOWER 3-8-2² Paul Eddery (19) *beh till some late prog*.................................... (20 to 1) 8
179⁷ LAJADHAL (Fr) 4-9-10 J Williams (11) *moderate late prog, nvr nrr*.................................. (50 to 1 op 33 to 1) 9
244⁹ WESSEX WARRIOR (v) 7-9-10 S O'Gorman (1) *led aftr 2 fs till o'r two out, sn wknd*...........(25 to 1 op 16 to 1) 10
642 BACKSTABBER 3-8-5 J Quinn (12) *in tch till wknd 3 fs out*..................... (9 to 1 op 8 to 1 tchd 10 to 1) 11
672⁵ DANSEUSE FRANCAISE (Ire) 3-8-1¹ R Hills (8) *trkd ldr, rdn and wknd 2 fs out*..................(9 to 2 op 8 to 1) 12
709 PONDERED BID (bl) 9-9-13 S Whitworth (3) *ldg grp till lost pos o'r 2 fs out*..................(25 to 1 op 20 to 1) 13
495 ICE MAGIC 6-9-13 W Ryan (7) *mid-div, rdn and no prog frm o'r 3 fs out*..................(50 to 1 op 33 to 1) 14
724⁸ UNIVERSAL (Fr) 3-7-9 (5*) B Doyle (17) *outpcd*. ....(50 to 1 op 33 to 1) 15
183⁵ PREMIER BLUES (Fr) 3-8-0 D Biggs (2) *nvr rch ldrs*. ....(20 to 1 op 16 to 1) 16
HUNTED 6-9-10 C Rutter (13) *nvr better than mid-div, wknd 3 fs out*..................... (50 to 1 op 25 to 1) 17
THE GORROCK (bl) 4-9-7 (3*) D Harrison (15) *chsd ldrs for o'r 7 fs*..........................(50 to 1 op 33 to 1) 18
MALLYPHA (Fr) (bl) 9-9-13 N Day (5) *in tch 7 fs, tld off*. .... (25 to 1 op 16 to 1) 19
Dist: 3l, sht-hd, 2l, hd, 1l, 3l, 6l, ½l, 1½l, nk. 2m 36.64s. a 5.64s (19 Ran).
SR: 23/39/16/15/33/9/17/-/9/ (B Pooler), R F Johnson Houghton

827 Epsom Owners & Trainers Handicap Class D (0-80 3-y-o) £3,552 1m 1f....(5:10)

483 AMERICAN SWINGER (USA) [60] 8-5 Paul Eddery (9) *made virtually all, rdn o'r one furlong out, quickened clr last 100 yards*............ (10 to 1 op 8 to 1 tchd 12 to 1) 1
725² GRAND APPLAUSE (Ire) [70] 9-1 S Whitworth (11) *hdwy on outsd 4 fs out, rdn alng o'r 2 out, styd on wl nr finish*. ....(9 to 2 op 5 to 1 tchd 11 to 2 and 4 to 1) 2
602⁴ BOHEMIAN CROWN (USA) [76] 9-7 M Roberts (14) *ldg grp, rdn o'r 2 fs out, outpcd over one out, kpt on nr finish*. ....(13 to 2 op 6 to 1 tchd 8 to 1) 3
THE EXECUTOR [72] 9-3 T Quinn (2) *pressed wnr, ev ch 2 fs out, rdn and one pace ins last*..... (20 to 1 op 16 to 1) 4
328⁷ BAYDON BELLE (USA) [65] 8-7 (3*) D Harrison (6) *wl plcd, pushed alng o'r 3 fs out, no extr frm 2 out*. ....(7 to 1 op 5 to 1 tchd 8 to 1) 5
MR DINGLE [53] 7-12 J Quinn (12) *slwly into strd, rear till some hdwy last 2 fs*..............(10 to 1 tchd 12 to 1) 6
684 TOTALLY UNIQUE (USA) [75] 9-1 (5*) M Fenton (13) *settled mid-div, shaken up and no hdwy o'r 3 fs out*. ....(20 to 1 op 14 to 1) 7
PRIMO FIGLIO [76] 9-7 S Raymont (5) *nvr rch ldrs*. ....(14 to 1 tchd 20 to 1) 8
623* PRAIRIE GROVE [72] 9-3 L Piggott (1) *in tch in mid-div, rdn and no hdwy 3 fs out*. .....(100 to 30 fav op 3 to 1 tchd 11 to 4 and 7 to 2) 9
NIGHT EDITION [53] 7-12¹ C Rutter (8) *wl plcd till rdn and wknd o'r 2 fs out*..................(20 to 1 op 16 to 1) 10
483⁵ LUNAR RISK [52] 7-4 (7*) Kim McDonnell (10) *in tch for o'r 6 fs*..................(12 to 1 op 10 to 1 tchd 14 to 1) 11
483⁷ BOBBYSOXER [72] 9-3 Pat Eddery (4) *rear most of way*. ....(10 to 1 tchd 12 to 1) 12
MOON WATCH [60] 8-5 D Biggs (3) *al beh*. .... (10 to 1 op 7 to 1) 13
568 DARK AND STORMY [48] 7-6⁶ (7*) C Hawksley (7) *al rear*. .... (50 to 1 op 33 to 1) 14
Dist: 5l, sht-hd, nk, 5l, ¾l, 1l, 1½l, 3l, 2½l, sht-hd. 1m 52.75s. a 2.75s (14 Ran).
SR: 36/31/36/31/9/-/9/9/-/ (Triple (Crowners I), P W Harris

NEWCASTLE (good to soft) Monday May 3rd

Going Correction: PLUS 0.25 sec. per fur. (races 1,2,3), PLUS 0.40 (4,5,6)

828 Lucky Dip Claiming Stakes Class F (3-y-o and up) £1,646 7f.................(2:15)

763* WHITE CREEK (Ire) (v) 3-8-13 (3*,4ex) J Weaver (11) *hld up, gd hdwy to ld 3 out, ran on wl*....... (4 to 1 op 7 to 2) 1
531 FLETCHER'S BOUNTY (Ire) 4-9-4 K Darley (3) *hld up, rdn to chase wnr 2 out, styd on, no imprsn*..........(10 to 1) 2
800³ BALLAD DANCER 8-9-1 (5*) Darren Moffatt (5) *led till hdd 3 out, kpt on same pace*.........(7 to 2 jt-fav op 5 to 2) 3
MR ABBOT 3-8-9 (3*) S Maloney (6) *in tch, rdn 3 out, sn btn*..................... (20 to 1 op 16 to 1) 4
CAPTAIN BRAMSTAN (Ire) 5-8-7 (5*) O Pears (10) *dwlt, hld up, some hdwy hfwy, nvr dngrs*... (33 to 1 op 25 to 1) 5
650⁴ RESPECTABLE JONES 7-10-0 S Perks (4) *dwlt, hld up, effrt hfwy, no hdwy*................(6 to 1 op 5 to 1) 6

610* GALLERY ARTIST (Ire) 5-8-11 (7*) S Eiffert (8) *cl up till wknd 3 out*.........................(7 to 2 jt-fav tchd 3 to 1) 7
531 PALM LAGOON (Ire) (v) 4-9-4 G Duffield (9) *prmnt till wknd 3 out*..........................(10 to 1 tchd 12 to 1) 8
362 DOMDOM 3-8-6 S Wood (2) *chsd ldrs to hfwy, wknd quickly, tld off*...................(20 to 1 op 25 to 1) 9
BARGEE (USA) 4-9-10 R Lappin (7) *prmnt early, wknd quickly hfwy, tld off*..........................(33 to 1) 10
Dist: 2½l, 2½l, 10l, 5l, 2½l, 2l, 2l, 15l, 2½l. 1m 32.26s. a 8.26s (10 Ran).
SR: 4/-/-/-/-/ (J K Brown), J Berry

829 Helter Skelter Handicap Class E (0-70 3-y-o) £1,618 6f........................ (2:45)

614* DAILYSPORTDUTCH [66] 9-7 K Darley (9) *cl up, led hfwy, ran on wl*..........................(5 to 1 op 4 to 1) 1
535^{3} PLUM FIRST [66] 9-7 D Nicholls (7) *prmnt, chsd wnr frm hfwy, styd on, no imprsn*...........(5 to 1 op 9 to 2) 2
409* GIRL NEXT DOOR [49] 8-2^{3} (5*) O Pears (5) *trkd ldrs, swtchd o'r 2 out, rdn over one out, kpt on same pace*. ....(5 to 1 op 4 to 1) 3
590^{9} RUM TEMPEST [47] (bl) 8-2^{2} G Duffield (10) *in tch, effrt und pres o'r 2 out, kpt on same pace*. .... (20 to 1 op 16 to 1) 4
BECKYHANNAH [43] 7-12^{3} (3*) S Maloney (4) *wth ldrs till wknd o'r 2 out*...... (14 to 1 op 16 to 1 tchd 20 to 1) 5
742^{7} MATTHEW DAVID [43] (bl) 7-7 (5*) Darren Moffatt (6) *beh till some late hdwy, nvr dngrs*......(14 to 1 tchd 16 to 1) 6
532^{6} RUSSIA WITH LOVE [59] 9-0 S Perks (8) *in tch, rdn o'r 2 out, sn btn*..................................... (7 to 1) 7
634^{4} JOTRA [49] (v) 8-4 J Penza (2) *sn led, hdd hfwy, rdn and wknd*..........................(9 to 2 jt-fav op 5 to 1) 8
SPORTING SPIRIT [48] 8-3 S Wood (3) *al beh*. ....(14 to 1 tchd 16 to 1) 9
GLISSO (Ire) [55] 8-7 (3*) J Weaver (1) *al beh, tld off*. ....(9 to 2 jt-fav op 4 to 1) 10
Dist: 3½l, ½l, 1½l, 6l, 2l, 3l, 2½l, 5l, 12l. 1m 17.41s. a 5.41s (10 Ran).
SR: 29/15/-/-/-/-/ (Brian T Eastick), Miss Gay Kelleway

830 Big Dipper Maiden Auction Stakes Class F (2-y-o) £1,562 5f...................(3:15)

BROCTUNE GOLD 9-0 K Darley (3) *prmnt, chsd ldr 2 out, hrd rdn o'r one out, kpt on wl to ld cl hme*. ....(6 to 5 fav op 13 to 8 tchd 2 to 1) 1
ANTANANARIVO (Ire) 8-11 (3*) J Weaver (2) *led, clr 2 out, rdn and edgd lft ins fnl furlong, ct cl hme*. ....(9 to 2 op 4 to 1 tchd 5 to 1) 2
715^{8} CAPITAL LADY (Ire) 8-9 S Wood (6) *in tch, kpt on same pace fnl 2 fs*............(8 to 1 op 7 to 1 tchd 9 to 1) 3
MICHELLISA 8-6 (3*) S Maloney (4) *slwly into strd, beh till some late hdwy, nvr dngrs*........ (12 to 1 op 10 to 1) 4
386^{9} COLONEL SINCLAIR (Ire) 9-0 S Perks (5) *chsd ldr till wknd 2 out*..................................(9 to 1 op 8 to 1) 5
CAPTAIN KEYSTONE 9-0 D Nicholls (7) *sn beh*. ....(7 to 2 op 5 to 2) 6
ANOTHER GOVERNOR 9-0 G Duffield (1) *dwlt, in tch till wknd hfwy*............................ (5 to 1 op 7 to 2) 7
Dist: ¾l, 8l, 2½l, 5l, 4l, 3l. 1m 3.29s. a 4.39s (7 Ran).
SR: 37/34/-/-/ (D Playforth), Mrs M Reveley

831 Bank Holiday Handicap Class D (0-85 3-y-o and up) £3,557 1½m 93yds..........(3:50)

674^{4} MUCH SOUGHT AFTER [73] 4-9-7 G Duffield (3) *trkd ldrs, led o'r 2 out, styd on wl*...........(4 to 1 tchd 9 to 2) 1
661^{8} TRUBEN (USA) [74] 4-9-5 (3*) J Weaver (1) *hld up, effrt o'r 2 out, kpt on wl fnl furlong*. .... (13 to 2 op 6 to 1 tchd 7 to 1) 2
645^{2} FIRST BID [63] 6-8-11 J Penza (8) *dwlt, sn tracking ldr, chlgd o'r 2 out, ev ch till no extr fnl furlong*. ....(4 to 1 op 9 to 2 tchd 7 to 2) 3
SUNDERLAND ECHO [63] 4-8-11 K Darley (4) *led, hdd o'r 2 out, hng lft over one out, kpt on wl towards finish*. .... (9 to 4 fav tchd 5 to 2) 4
589^{4} BELLTON [65] 5-8-10 (3*) S Maloney (7) *in tch, hdwy hfwy, pushed alng o'r 3 out, kpt on fnl furlong*. ....(7 to 1 op 8 to 1) 5
769^{3} GOLDEN TORQUE [70] 6-8-11 (7*) H Bastiman (2) *hld up, effrt o'r 2 out, no hdwy*........... (6 to 1 tchd 7 to 1) 6
BATTLE STANDARD (Can) [75] 6-9-9 S Perks (6) *trkd ldrs, rdn 3 out, sn btn*................. (20 to 1 op 16 to 1) 7
GREAT HEIGHTS [80] (bl) 6-9-9 (5*) O Pears (5) *refused to race*.......................................(14 to 1) I
Dist: 1½l, nk, sht-hd, 1½l, ½l, 3l. 2m 49.61s. a 11.91s (8 Ran).
SR: 38/36/24/23/22/26/25/-/ (The Msa Partnership), D Morley

832 Caterpillar Maiden Stakes Class D (3-y-o and up) £3,435 1¼m 32yds..........(4:20)

515^{3} SPIN DOCTOR (Ire) 3-8-5 (3*) J Weaver (4) *chsd ldr, led o'r 2 out, sn clr, eased fnl furlong, very easily*. ....(9 to 1 on op 6 to 1 on tchd 10 to 1 on) 1
672 MR WOODCOCK 8-9-10 K Darley (3) *in tch, pushed alng 4 out, wnt second 2 out, kpt on, no ch wth wnr*. ....(7 to 1 op 6 to 1) 2
300^{8} RICH ASSET (Ire) 3-8-8 S Perks (1) *wl beh till styd on well fnl 2 fs, nrst finish*.................. (33 to 1 op 20 to 1) 3
653^{5} VOLUNTEER POINT (Ire) 3-8-5 (3*) S Maloney (2) *chsd ldrs till wknd 2 out*.................... (25 to 1 op 16 to 1) 4
547 MASTER FIDDLER 3-8-8 R Lappin (5) *led, clr hfwy, hdd o'r 2 out, wknd quickly*.................(11 to 1 op 10 to 1) 5
Dist: 6l, 3l, 10l, 6l. 2m 16.14s. a 9.64s (5 Ran).
SR: 39/43/21/1/-/ (Princess Nicholas Von Preussen), L M Cumani

833 Roundabout Handicap Class E (0-70 3-y-o) £1,660 1m........................ (4:50)

546* JUST YOU DARE (Ire) [68] 9-7 G Duffield (6) *in tch, rdn to ld entering fnl furlong, hld on wl*. .... (6 to 5 on op 5 to 2 tchd 3 to 1) 1
567^{6} HYDE'S HAPPY HOUR [48] 8-1 Kim Tinkler (7) *in tch, effrt o'r 2 out, styd on wl und pres fnl furlong*. ....(9 to 1 op 12 to 1 tchd 14 to 1) 2
764^{5} THE PREMIER EXPRES [65] 9-4 R Lappin (4) *wth ldr, led 3 out, hdd entering fnl furlong, one pace*. ....(7 to 1 op 5 to 1) 3
685^{3} HOT OFF THE PRESS [50] 8-3 J Penza (5) *chsd ldrs, ev ch o'r one out, wknd fnl furlong*. ....(13 to 2 op 5 to 1 tchd 7 to 1) 4
612^{3} PUBLIC WAY (Ire) [55] 8-8 S Wood (8) *reared up strt and started slwly, nvr trbld ldrs*........ (10 to 1 op 8 to 1) 5
711* NELLIE'S GAMBLE [55] 8-5 (3*,5ex) S Maloney (9) *nvr trbld ldrs*....................(4 to 1 op 3 to 1 tchd 9 to 2) 6
MOUNTAIN HIGH (Fr) [66] 9-5 K Darley (2) *in tch till wknd 3 out*..(10 to 1) 7
644^{9} PAAJIB (Ire) [52] 8-5 S Perks (3) *led till hdd 3 out, sn btn*. ....(20 to 1) 8
733^{7} NEVER IN TOUCH [40] (bl) 7-2 (5*) Darren Moffatt (1) *dwlt, tld off most of way*............... (50 to 1 op 33 to 1) 9
Dist: ¾l, 2l, 1½l, 8l, 3l, 8l, sht-hd, 1½l. 1m 46.43s. a 7.43s (9 Ran).
SR: 44/22/33/13/-/-/ (Mrs David Thompson), Sir Mark Prescott

WARWICK (good to firm)
Monday May 3rd
Going Correction: MINUS 0.15 sec. per fur.

834 Levy Board Apprentice Handicap Class G (0-70 3-y-o and up) £2,952 1m....... (1:45)

ROSIETOES (USA) [38] 5-7-11^{5} (5*) Mark Denaro (2) *trkd ldrs, led wl o'r one furlong out, ran on well*... (16 to 1) 1
521 LADY LACEY [47] (v) 6-7-13 (7*) D Griffiths (6) *beh, hdwy appr fnl furlong, fnshd wl*........ (12 to 1 op 10 to 1) 2
603^{2} BUDDY'S FRIEND (Ire) [60] 5-8-9 (10*) Sarah Thompson (3) *beh, hdwy 3 fs out, styd on frm o'r one out*. ....(7 to 1 op 6 to 1) 3
754^{4} PROUD BRIGADIER (Ire) [51] 5-8-2 (8*) R Painter (21) *mid-div, cld o'r 3 fs out, kpt on one pace ins last*. ....(8 to 1 op 6 to 1) 4
603^{8} SOOTY TERN [44] 6-7-9 (8*) Michael Bradley (15) *chsd ldrs, kpt on one pace fnl 2 furlong*....... (10 to 1 op 8 to 1) 5
ARAGONA [40] 4-7-13 D Gibbs (5) *beh, styd on fnl 2 fs, nrst finish*.......................... (25 to 1 op 20 to 1) 6
NAVARESQUE [40] 8-7-10 (3*) J O'Dwyer (18) *led aftr one furlong, hng rght and came wide into strt, hdd wl o'r one furlong out, wknd*...............................(20 to 1) 7
714* MEXICAN DANCER [55] 4-8-6 (8*,7ex) R Waterfield (20) *led one furlong, cl up till wknd ins fnl furlong*. ....(7 to 2 fav op 8 to 1) 8
636^{4} ROSEATE LODGE [69] 7-10-0 P McCabe (10) *beh, hdwy 2 fs out, nvr nrr*............................(7 to 1 op 10 to 1) 9
603^{5} TAUNTING (Ire) [50] 5-8-4 (5*) S McCarthy (17) *nvr better tha mid-div*...........(10 to 1 op 7 to 1 tchd 12 to 1) 10
714 SURE SHOT NORMAN [42] (v) 4-7-10 (5*) D Toole (8) *chsd ldrs till wknd o'r 3 fs out*........ (33 to 1 op 25 to 1) 11
264^{5} ROCKY BAY [34] 4-7-3^{1} (5*) M Baird (1) *strted slwly, nvr dngrs*............................... (25 to 1 op 20 to 1) 12
498^{6} IRISH GROOM [44] (bl) 6-8-3^{12} (7*) L Aspell (22) *prmnt till wknd 2 fs out*....................... (20 to 1 op 16 to 1) 13
623^{5} TAKE THE MICK [50] 3-7-5 (5*) J Wilkinson (11) *nvr dngrs*. .... (20 to 1 op 12 to 1) 14
678^{9} WINGED WHISPER (USA) [40] (bl) 4-7-6 (7*) F Savage (13) *strted slwly, al beh*..................(33 to 1 op 20 to 1) 15
636^{2} LORD LAMBSON [42] 4-8-0^{2} (3*) G Parkin (14) *nvr dngrs*. ....(11 to 1 op 10 to 1 tchd 12 to 1) 16
GIVE ME HOPE (Ire) [34] 5-7-5^{3} (5*) J Bramhill (7) *al beh*. ....(50 to 1 op 40 to 1 tchd 66 to 1) 17
FAIRFORD [50] 4-8-9 S Mulvey (16) *trkd ldrs till rdn and wknd o'r 2 fs out*..................(66 to 1 op 25 to 1) 18
492 HARRY'S GEM (Ire) [35] 5-7-7^{6} (7*) L Suthern (4) *al beh*. .... (66 to 1 op 33 to 1) 19
WALK THAT WALK [67] 4-9-7 (5*) K Pattinson (12) *al beh*. .... (50 to 1 op 33 to 1) 20
LOFTY DEED (USA) [59] 3-8-0 (5*) Sally Radford-Howes (19) *al beh*.................................(25 to 1 op 20 to 1) 21
Dist: 2½l, ½l, ¾l, ¾l, 3l, 1½l, sht-hd, ¾l, nk, ¾l. 1m 39.40s. a 2.60s (21 Ran).
SR: 26/27/38/27/18/5/-/14/26/ (Mrs Anne Yearley), L G Cottrell

835 Alveston Maiden Fillies' Stakes Class D (3-y-o) £3,552 1m..................(2:15)

PRINCESS HAIFA (USA) 8-11 W R Swinburn (1) *made all, hrd rdn o'r one furlong out, hld on wl.* ....(5 to 1 op 4 to 1 tchd 11 to 2) 1

732[3] BALNAHA 8-11 M Hills (9) *trkd ldrs, drw level o'r one furlong out, hrd rdn and not quicken.* ...... (11 to 10 on op 5 to 4 tchd 11 to 8 and 6 to 4) 2

HARD TASK 8-8 (3*) A Tucker (3) *cl up, effrt and one pace fnl 2 fs.*..........................(16 to 1 op 8 to 1) 3

522[7] WHAT LOLA WANTS (Ire) 8-11 A Dicks (5) *slwly into strd, sn in tch, kpt on one pace fnl 2 fs.* (33 to 1 op 16 to 1) 4

662 EYE WITNESS (Ire) 8-11 A Munro (7) *cl up, pushed alng o'r 2 fs out, sn wknd.*.....................(11 to 2 op 8 to 1) 5

UNNAB 8-11 G Carter (2) *strted slwly, in tch, shaken up 2 fs out, not pace to chal.*............(10 to 1 op 4 to 1) 6

582[6] GREEN CHILI 8-11 D Holland (10) *hdwy to track ldrs aftr 2 fs, pld out o'r two furlongs out, wknd appr last, eased.* ....(5 to 1 op 4 to 1) 7

728[8] GLEAM OF GOLD 8-11 S Dawson (8) *trkd ldrs till wknd o'r 3 fs out.*.......................... (50 to 1 op 20 to 1) 8

PHASE ONE (Ire) 8-11 N Adams (6) *missed break, al beh.* ....(33 to 1 op 16 to 1) 9

Dist: ¾l, 5l, 1½l, 3½l, 1½l, 2½l, 8l, 6l. 1m 40.30s. a 3.50s (9 Ran).
SR: 27/25/10/5/-/-/ (Sheikh Ahmed Al Maktoum), M R Stoute

836 Stoneleigh Park Polo Club Handicap Class D (0-80 3-y-o) £3,699 7f............. (2:45)

444[2] FINAL FRONTIER (Ire) [66] 8-7 A Munro (1) *trkd ldrs, led wl o'r one furlong out, drvn out.* ....(4 to 1 fav op 7 to 2 tchd 9 to 2) 1

685[2] CREDIT SQUEEZE [66] 8-4 (3*) A Tucker (3) *beh, hdwy o'r one furlong out, sn hrd rdn, hng lft and no extr cl hme.* .... (13 to 2 op 6 to 1 tchd 7 to 1) 2

606[3] NO EXTRAS (Ire) [69] 8-10 B Rouse (2) *strted slwly, sn reco'red, mid-div, cld 3 fs out, effrt over one furlong out, kpt on one pace.*...............(7 to 1 tchd 8 to 1) 3

519[2] WATERLORD (Ire) [66] 8-0 (7*) D Wright (5) *led til hdd wl o'r one furlong out, one pace.* ....(12 to 1 op 8 to 1 tchd 14 to 1) 4

370[5] SOVIET EXPRESS [68] 8-2 (7*) T G McLaughlin (6) *trkd ldrs, pushed alng 2 fs out, one pace*.....(20 to 1 op 14 to 1) 5

4761a* MR CUBE (Ire) [60] 7-10[2] (7*) J D Smith (9) *mid-div, no hdwy fnl 2 fs*...............................(20 to 1 op 14 to 1) 6

516[4] LOVE IN THE MIST (USA) [61] 8-2 M Hills (12) *chsd ldrs til wknd 2 fs out.*..........................(5 to 1 op 4 to 1) 7

JULIET BRAVO [63] 8-4 G Carter (14) *beh, effrt 3 fs out, no response*.............(12 to 1 op 6 to 1 tchd 20 to 1) 8

592[8] ANNIVERSAIRE [71] 8-12 R Perham (7) *nvr on terms.* ....(20 to 1 op 16 to 1) 9

719 FITZROY LAD [55] 7-10 N Adams (8) *nvr dngrs.* ....(33 to 1 op 20 to 1) 10

397[6] LANCASTER PILOT [64] 8-0[2] (7*) G Parkin (10) *trkd ldrs til wknd 2 fs out.*......................(25 to 1 op 20 to 1) 11

747[5] MISS GORGEOUS (Ire) [77] 9-1 (3*) Emma O'Gorman (4) *beh, effrt and came wide into strt, sn btn.* ....(9 to 1 op 12 to 1 tchd 14 to 1 and 8 to 1) 12

REGALSETT [80] 9-0 (7*) D Gibbs (11) *al beh.* ....(20 to 1 op 10 to 1) 13

602[7] IJAB (Can) [70] 8-11 J Fortune (13) *nvr gng wl, al beh, tld off 3 fs out.*..........................(12 to 1 op 7 to 1) 14

Dist: Nk, 1l, 4l, 2½l, ¾l, 5l, 2½l, 1½l, 2½l, 1l. 1m 26.50s. a 2.70s (14 Ran).
SR: 37/36/36/21/15/5/ (A D Spence), R Akehurst

837 Stonebridge Limited Stakes Class F (4-y-o and up) £2,243 6f...................(3:15)

163 TOP ONE 8-8-11 G Bardwell (1) *trkd ldrs, cld o'r one furlong out, swtchd rght ins last, ran on to ld close hme*...................................(12 to 1 op 8 to 1) 1

710 HIGHBORN (Ire) 4-8-11 G Hind (2) *led aftr one furlong, cl up, led ag'n ins last till hdd close hme.* ....(25 to 1 op 12 to 1) 2

409[4] SALLY'S SON 7-8-9[1] (3*) Emma O'Gorman (4) *trkd ldrs, ev ch und pres ins fnl furlong, no extr cl hme.* ....(8 to 1 op 8 to 1) 3

800[4] SLADES HILL 6-8-11 Alex Greaves (10) *cl up, led hfwy till hdd and one pace ins last*.....(9 to 2 co-fav op 5 to 2) 4

721[5] CASTLE MAID 6-8-6 A Dicks (7) *outpcd, hdwy appr fnl furlong, fnshd wl*................ (25 to 1 op 20 to 1) 5

719[9] FAIRY WISHER (Ire) 4-8-6 A Munro (6) *mid-div, hrd rdn o'r one furlong out, kpt on ins last.* (20 to 1 tchd 50 to 1) 6

442 DON'T GIVE UP (bl) 5-8-4 (7*) N Varley (3) *strted slwly, beh, hdwy o'r one furlong out, kpt on*............ (50 to 1) 7

760[8] LEIGH CROFTER (v) 4-8-4 (7*) S Drowne (18) *mid-div, no hdwy fnl 2 fs*..... (9 to 2 co-fav op 6 to 1 tchd 3 to 1) 8

760 HITCHIN A RIDE 6-8-11 B Rouse (13) *outpcd, styd on ins fnl furlong, nrst finish*...........(14 to 1 op 16 to 1) 9

SCARLET PRINCESS 5-8-6 T Sprake (8) *nvr dngrs.* ....(20 to 1) 10

BATCHWORTH BOUND 4-7-13 (7*) D Wright (15) *nvr on terms*.....................(20 to 1 op 10 to 1) 11

409[5] PAR DE LUXE 6-8-6 A Mackay (12) *nvr dngrs.* ....(50 to 1 op 20 to 1) 12

531 CAL'S BOY (bl) 4-8-8 (3*) A Tucker (17) *outpcd.* ....(50 to 1 op 20 to 1) 13

492 BLYTON STAR (Ire) (bl) 5-8-11 S Webster (9) *outpcd.* ....(12 to 1 op 16 to 1 tchd 25 to 1) 14

227 WEEKEND GIRL 4-8-1 (5*) A Garth (5) *strted slwly, al beh.* ....(50 to 1 op 33 to 1) 15

285[4] APPEALING TIMES (USA) 4-8-11 J Fortune (14) *al beh.* ....(14 to 1 op 10 to 1) 16

244 DAL MISS (bl) 6-8-6 N Adams (11) *trkd ldrs till wknd 2 fs out*...........................(50 to 1 op 20 to 1) 17

548 WE'RE ALL GAME 4-8-1 (5*) C Hodgson (16) *trkd ldrs till wknd quickly o'r 2 fs out*..........(12 to 1 op 10 to 1) 18

655[5] BREEZE AWAY 4-8-7[1] W R Swinburn (19) *led o'r one furlong, cl up til wknd 2 fs out*..................(9 to 2 co-fav op 5 to 1 tchd 6 to 1) 19

Dist: ½l, hd, 1l, 2l, hd, ¾l, hd, 2l, sht-hd, 4l. 1m 14.60s. a 2.90s (19 Ran).
SR: 21/19/18/14/1/-/2/1/-/ (C John Hill), C J Hill

838 C.I.U. Charity Handicap Class D (0-80 3-y-o) £3,201 1½m 115yds..............(3:45)

547* HARLESTONE BROOK [61] 9-2 G Carter (5) *trkd ldrs, led appr 2 fs out, clr o'r one out, cmftbly.* ....(7 to 4 jt-fav op 6 to 4 tchd 15 to 8 and 2 to 1) 1

WARM SPELL [66] 9-7 B Rouse (2) *hld up, hmpd 5 fs out, hdwy o'r one out, kpt on*..................(4 to 1 op 3 to 1) 2

717[5] PAPER DAYS [45] 8-0 N Adams (8) *sn led, hdd appr 2 fs out, one pace*.......... (8 to 1 tchd 9 to 1 and 7 to 1) 3

BRANSBY ROAD (Ire) [49] 8-4 A Munro (3) *chsd ldrs, effrt and hng lft o'r one furlong out, one pace.* ....(12 to 1 op 7 to 1 tchd 14 to 1) 4

644[4] MOUSSAHIM (USA) [66] 9-7 W R Swinburn (7) *hld up beh, effrt 3 fs out, no imprsn on ldrs*..............(7 to 4 jt-fav op 5 to 2 tchd 11 to 4) 5

338[6] DANGER BABY [44] 7-13 G Bardwell (1) *chsd ldrs, pushed alng o'r 6 fs out, wknd over 2 out.* (33 to 1 op 20 to 1) 6

498[9] CRYSTAL STONE [57] 8-9 (3*) A Tucker (6) *trkd ldr til wknd o'r 4 fs out*.......................(20 to 1 op 16 to 1) 7

443[7] CANADIAN EAGLE [44] 7-6 (7*) D Wright (4) *hld up, al beh, tld off*..............................(33 to 1 op 20 to 1) 8

Dist: 2l, ½l, 1½l, 5l, 3½l, 5l, 4l. 2m 44.50s. a 6.60s (8 Ran).
SR: 17/18/-/-/4/ (J L Dunlop), J L Dunlop

839 EBF Primrose Maiden Fillies' Stakes Class D (2-y-o) £3,552 5f............(4:15)

657[4] IMPERIAL BAILIWICK (Ire) 8-11 N Adams (10) *made virtually all, edgd lft ins fnl furlong, jst hld on.* ....(9 to 1 op 3 to 1) 1

718[4] ISABELLA SHARP 8-11 M Hills (2) *wth ldr, ev ch ins fnl furlong, ran on*...... (Evens fav op 2 to 1 tchd 9 to 4) 2

673[6] CAPPUCHINO (Ire) 8-8 (3*) Emma O'Gorman (8) *chasing grp, styd on one pace frm o'r one furlong out.* ....(16 to 1 op 14 to 1) 3

PRIMO STAMPARI 8-11 B Rouse (5) *chasing grp, styd on frm o'r one furlong out, better for race.* .... (8 to 1 op 5 to 1 tchd 10 to 1) 4

RAMBOLD 8-11 T Williams (1) *dwlt, beh, hdwy o'r one furlong out, nrst finish*............(33 to 1 op 20 to 1) 5

657[9] ABBOTS DAUGHTER 8-11 D Holland (9) *chsd ldg trio till wknd 2 fs out*......... (10 to 1 op 6 to 1 tchd 12 to 1) 6

469[9] IVA'S FLYER (Ire) 8-11 G Carter (7) *cl up til squeezed out wl o'r one furlong out, not rcvr.* ....(7 to 1 op 6 to 1 tchd 8 to 1) 7

HIGHLAND WARNING 8-11 W R Swinburn (3) *outpcd.* ....(7 to 1 op 5 to 1) 8

496[4] MAIDEN EFFORT (bl) 8-11 G Bardwell (11) *chasing grp, wknd 2 fs out*......................(33 to 1 op 16 to 1) 9

JANE HERRING 8-4 (7*) S Drowne (12) *strted slwly, outpcd*..............................(33 to 1 op 20 to 1) 10

REIGNING ROYAL 8-11 A Dicks (4) *outpcd, sn tld off.* ....(33 to 1 op 20 to 1) 11

Dist: Sht-hd, 5l, 1½l, 2½l, ¾l, 1½l, ½l, 3½l, 1½l. 1m 0.80s. a 2.60s (11 Ran).
SR: 30/29/9/3/-/-/ (Dr Ian R Shenkin), M D I Usher

840 Warwick Spring Handicap Class E (0-70 4-y-o and up) £3,416 1¼m 169yds... (4:45)

620[4] HERE HE COMES [45] 7-8-10 A Munro (3) *trkd ldrs, rdn to ld o'r 2 fs out, clr over one out, ran on wl*. ...(4 to 1 jt-fav op 3 to 1 tchd 9 to 2) 1

ATHAR (Ire) [60] 4-9-6 (5*) K Rutter (1) *strted slwly, beh, hdwy 2 fs out, hng lft ins last, one pace.* ....(20 to 1 op 8 to 1) 2

678[7] LIGHT-HEARTED LADY [54] 5-8-12 (7*) S Drowne (6) *hdwy to chase ldrs 4 fs out, drvn alng o'r one out, kpt on.* ....(10 to 1 op 20 to 1 tchd 8 to 1) 3

530* SWEET REVIVAL [41] 5-8-6 J Fortune (18) *trkd ldrs till lost pl hfwy, hdwy 2 fs out, one pace.* (10 to 1 tchd 12 to 1) 4

620[2] SWIFT SILVER [59] 6-9-3 (7*) D McCabe (15) *hld up and beh, hdwy o'r one furlong out, nvr nrr.* ....(5 to 1 op 3 to 1) 5

603 DANCING BEAU (Ire) [49] 4-9-0 G Carter (20) *hld up beh, hdwy 3 fs out, sn one pace*........ (14 to 1 op 10 to 1) 6

NORTHERN TRIAL (USA) [52] 5-9-3 T Williams (4) *hdwy to track ldrs hfwy, ch whn hmpd o'r 2 fs out, eased when btn over one out*.................. (33 to 1 op 20 to 1) 7

78 TENDRESSE (Ire) [43] 5-8-8 G Bardwell (9) *beh, hmpd o'r 4 fs out, hdwy over one out, nrst finish.* .... (12 to 1 op 10 to 1) 8

CRACKLING [53] 4-9-4 S Dawson (12) *nvr dngrs.*
.... (12 to 1 op 10 to 1 tchd 16 to 1) 9
456[9] FERN HEIGHTS [48] 6-8-13 C Avery (14) *al beh.*
.... (33 to 1 op 25 to 1) 10
620[7] SAINT CIEL (USA) [63] 5-9-7 (7*) D Wright (19) *beh, cld hfwy, wknd 3 out*................. (16 to 1 op 5 to 1) 11
REGGAE BEAT [50] 8-8-8 (7*) G Mitchell (2) *al beh.*
.... (20 to 1 op 16 to 1) 12
349[5] MOON SPIN [59] (bl) 4-9-10 M Hills (11) *led, sn clr, hdd o'r 2 fs out, wknd*...................... (7 to 1 op 3 to 1) 13
498[3] HIGHLY SECURE [50] 6-9-1 W R Swinburn (13) *trkd ldrs till wknd 3 fs out*........................... (4 to 1 jt-fav) 14
CHADWICK'S GINGER [42] 5-8-2 (5*) C Hodgson (16) *trkd ldrs till wknd quickly o'r 2 fs out.*
.... (16 to 1 op 25 to 1 tchd 12 to 1) 15
672 MASTER REACH [55] 4-9-6 R Perham (8) *cl up, hmpd aftr 2 fs, wknd quickly 3 furlongs out*....(33 to 1 op 20 to 1) 16
LORD OBERON (Ire) [56] 5-9-7 D Holland (5) *al beh, tld off.*
.... (12 to 1 op 8 to 1) 17

Dist: 2½l, 1½l, ¾l, 3½l, ¾l, 1l, nk, sht-hd, ½l, 1½l. 2m 18.50s. a 5.70s (17 Ran).
SR: 23/33/24/9/20/8/9/-/8/ (E Harrington), R Akehurst

CHESTER (good to firm)
Tuesday May 4th
Going Correction: MINUS 0.40 sec. per fur.

841 Lily Agnes Conditions Stakes Class C (2-y-o) £6,137 5f 16yds................ (2:10)

477* RISKY 8-8 Pat Eddery (1) *made virtually all, sprinted clr fnl furlong, eased.* (11 to 8 fav op 5 to 4 tchd 6 to 4) 1
586* BEST KEPT SECRET 8-13 J Carroll (4) *chsd ldg pair, effrt and drvn o'r one furlong out, not pace of wnr.*
.................................(4 to 1 op 3 to 1) 2
738[3] THATCHERELLA 8-5 D Holland (3) *chsd ldrs, drvn to improve o'r one furlong out, ran on, nvr nrr.*
.................................(4 to 1 op 5 to 2) 3
517* CULSYTH FLYER 8-10 W Ryan (6) *trkd ldg trio, feeling pace and edgd lft o'r one furlong out, rallied.*
.... (12 to 1 op 10 to 1) 4
506* SADDAM THE LOG 8-8 A Mackay (5) *dsptd ld, rdn o'r one furlong out, no extr.* (10 to 1 op 12 to 1 tchd 14 to 1) 5
544* LAMBENT 8-8 W Newnes (7) *broke wl, bustled alng hfwy, no imprsn appr fnl furlong*......... (10 to 1 op 8 to 1) 6
743[7] PORTITE SOPHIE 8-5 A Munro (2) *chsd ldrs, struggling hfwy, kpt on fnl furlong*......... (33 to 1 op 20 to 1) 7

Dist: 4l, ¾l, 1½l, 1l, sht-hd, nk. 1m 1.30s. a 1.00s (7 Ran).
SR: 34/23/12/11/5/4/-/ (Roldvale Limited), R Hannon

842 Crabwall Manor Hotel Maiden Stakes Class D (3-y-o) £7,408 1¼m 75yds...(2:40)

538[4] STONEY VALLEY 9-0 J Reid (8) *settled gng wl, drvn through to ld appr fnl furlong, pushed out.*
.....................(7 to 4 fav op 2 to 1 tchd 9 to 4) 1
BARON FERDINAND 9-0 R Cochrane (3) *patiently rdn, improved gng wl appr strt, not clr run and swtchd o'r one out, fnshd strly*.... (9 to 1 op 7 to 1 tchd 10 to 1) 2
515[2] SILVERDALE (USA) (v) 9-0 M Roberts (5) *trkd ldr, effrt and hrd drvn entering strt, found little.*
.........................(9 to 4 op 2 to 1 tchd 5 to 2) 3
BAWAETH (USA) 8-9 W Carson (9) *chsd ldg trio, drvn and not much room entering strt, eased whn btn fnl furlong*.................. (7 to 1 op 4 to 1 tchd 15 to 2) 4
672[2] CONSPICUOUS (Ire) 9-0 A Munro (1) *tried to make all, hdd and drvn appr fnl furlong, no extr.*
.... (12 to 1 op 10 to 1) 5
672 MUTAMANNI 9-0 R Hills (11) *settled midfield, effrt and bustled alng appr strt, no imprsn.*
.... (16 to 1 op 14 to 1 tchd 20 to 1) 6
515[5] WARSPITE 9-0 P Robinson (6) *trkd ldg pair, rdn o'r one furlong out, no extr*... (10 to 1 op 7 to 1 tchd 12 to 1) 7
509[5] CIVIL LAW (Ire) 9-0 S Perks (7) *squeezed out strt, reco'red to chase ldrs for over 5 fs, fdd*..... (16 to 1 op 12 to 1) 8
KEDGE 9-0 W R Swinburn (10) *trkd ldrs in 7th, rdn o'r 3 fs out, sn btn*.......... (25 to 1 op 20 to 1 tchd 33 to 1) 9
482[2] SEREN QUEST 8-9 D Harrison (4) *tucked away in midfield, feeling pace and lost grnd o'r 3 fs out, sn btn.*
.... (14 to 1 op 16 to 1 tchd 12 to 1) 10
712[5] GRANDERISE (Ire) 9-0 L Charnock (2) *pld hrd for 3 fs, sn tld off*................. (66 to 1 op 33 to 1 tchd 100 to 1) 11

Dist: Nk, 2½l, 1½l, 3l, 2½l, sht-hd, 6l, hd, 3½l, 30l. 2m 9.99s. a 0.89s (11 Ran).
SR: 50/49/44/36/35/30/29/17/16/ (R E Sangster), P W Chapple-Hyam

843 Dalham Chester Vase Class A (Group 3) (3-y-o) £33,526 1½m 66yds..........(3:10)

ARMIGER 8-11 Pat Eddery (2) *moved poorly to post, bustled alng to improve o'r 2 fs out, led ins fnl furlong, styd on wl*....... (6 to 4 on op 2 to 1 on tchd 11 to 8 on) 1
668[3] SHREWD IDEA 8-11 G Duffield (6) *led for one furlong, styd hndy till led wl o'r one out, hdd ins last, kpt on.*
.... (25 to 1) 2
468* PERSIAN BRAVE (Ire) 8-11 M Hills (1) *led aftr one furlong till wl o'r one out, rdn and styd on same pace.*
.... (8 to 1 op 14 to 1) 3
557* CAIRO PRINCE (Ire) 8-11 J Reid (5) *unsuited to course, last and struggling till ran on wl und pres fnl furlong, nrst finish*.................(9 to 2 op 4 to 1 tchd 5 to 1) 4
688[3] MAJORITY (Ire) 8-11 M Roberts (4) *chsd ldg trio, rdn 2 fs out, not quicken*...... (6 to 1 op 5 to 1 tchd 13 to 2) 5
494[3] FRESCADE (USA) 8-11 A Munro (3) *trkd ldg quartet, feeling pace and drvn alng appr strt, no extr.*
.... (33 to 1 op 25 to 1) 6

Dist: 2½l, 1½l, hd, 3½l, sht-hd. 2m 35.32s. b 1.48s (6 Ran).
SR: 63/58/55/54/47/46/ (K Abdulla), H R A Cecil

844 Tote Credit Rated Class B (0-105 3-y-o) £12,351 7f 122yds.................. (3:40)

643* ABBEY'S GAL [95] 8-12 R Cochrane (1) *last and hld up, effrt and not clr run entering strt, swtchd ins to ld fnl furlong, ran on wl*.................(7 to 2 op 3 to 1) 1
558[4] AFTER THE LAST [90] 8-7 J Reid (2) *tucked away on ins, not clr run entering strt, swtchd to brst through fnl furlong, ran on*....... (3 to 1 tchd 7 to 2 and 11 to 4) 2
643[3] CHEVROTAIN [90] (v) 8-7 M Roberts (6) *trkd ldr, nosed ahead o'r one furlong out, hdd ins last, kpt on.*
.................................(7 to 1 op 5 to 1) 3
558[2] LYFORD CAY (Ire) [92] 8-9 Pat Eddery (7) *nvr far away, swtchd outsd and ev ch o'r one furlong out, ran on.*
..................(11 to 4 fav op 5 to 2 tchd 3 to 1) 4
AMAAM AMAAM [90] 8-7 G Duffield (5) *made most for o'r 5 fs, kpt on same pace fnl furlong*.... (10 to 1 op 8 to 1) 5
NO RESERVATIONS (Ire) [93] 8-7 (3*) D Harrison (3) *trkd ldg quartet, rdn 2 fs out, fdd*.......... (11 to 1 op 10 to 1) 6
633[3] CARBON STEEL (Ire) [104] 9-7 D Holland (4) *fly-jmpd leaving stalls, chsd ldrs in last pl for 5 fs, sn btn*...(10 to 1) 7

Dist: ¾l, 1l, ¾l, sht-hd, 7l, 5l. 1m 33.00s. a 1.00s (7 Ran).
SR: 38/31/28/28/25/7/3/ (Jerrard Williamson), I A Balding

845 Great Cheshire Handicap Class C (0-90 4-y-o and up) £8,708 1¼m 75yds.... (4:10)

663[6] ROSE ALTO [84] 5-9-11 G Duffield (1) *nvr far away, quickened ahead o'r one furlong out, drvn out.*
.................................(7 to 1 op 5 to 1) 1
628[7] KILLICK [52] 5-7-0 (7*) D Wright (2) *tucked away in midfield, drvn to improve 2 fs out, ran on wl und pres fnl furlong*..(33 to 1) 2
527 SOVEREIGN PAGE (USA) [64] 4-8-5 M Roberts (9) *patiently rdn, swtchd rght to improve appr fnl furlong, ran on one pace*............... (7 to 1 op 6 to 1 tchd 8 to 1) 3
PICKLES [53] 5-7-8[1] Dale Gibson (7) *settled gng wl, improved entering strt, styd on ins fnl furlong.*
.... (25 to 1 op 33 to 1 tchd 20 to 1) 4
801[6] FALCONS DAWN [52] 6-7-7 J Quinn (4) *chsd ldg grp, effrt und pres fnl 2 fs, kpt on one pace.* (16 to 1 op 14 to 1) 5
480[4] YILDIZ [77] 4-9-4 D Holland (12) *trkd ldg pair, rdn o'r one furlong out, not quicken.*
.........................(7 to 1 op 6 to 1 tchd 8 to 1) 6
703[4] DESERT ZONE (USA) [87] 4-10-0 R Cochrane (14) *co'red up on ins, hdwy appr strt, not quicken last 2 fs.*
.... (33 to 1 op 25 to 1) 7
GILDERDALE [80] 11-9-7 M Hills (6) *co'red up in midfield, effrt and drvn over 2 fs out, one pace.*
...............................(14 to 1 tchd 12 to 1) 8
340[7] MENTALASANYTHIN [64] 4-8-5 A Mackay (10) *chsd ldrs in 7th, feeling pace appr strt, no imprsn.*
.... (16 to 1 op 14 to 1 tchd 20 to 1) 9
402[2] GOLD BLADE [57] 4-7-12 W Carson (5) *co'red up on ins, unbl to handle bend and checked aftr 3 fs, effrt over three out, sn btn*.....(9 to 2 fav op 7 to 2 tchd 5 to 1) 10
389[6] GREEK GOLD (Ire) [78] 4-9-5 W R Swinburn (11) *wth ldr, led o'r 6 fs out till wknd quickly over one out.*
.... (11 to 2 op 9 to 2 tchd 6 to 1) 11
674[5] TANODA [52] 7-7-7 J Lowe (13) *led till o'r 6 fs out, wknd quickly appr strt*.................(33 to 1 op 25 to 1) 12
678 TAHITIAN [63] 4-8-4 K Fallon (3) *last and hld up, effrt and niggled alng hfwy, not rch ldrs.*
.... (10 to 1 op 7 to 1 tchd 12 to 1) 13
589* IN THE MONEY (Ire) [73] 4-9-0 W Ryan (8) *in tch, feeling pace and lost grnd o'r 3 fs out, tld off.*
.... (10 to 1 op 12 to 1) 14

Dist: ½l, 1½l, 2½l, sht-hd, 1l, 1½l, sht-hd, hd, 1½l, nk. 2m 9.71s. a 0.61s (14 Ran).
SR: 64/31/40/24/22/45/52/44/27/ (T & J Vestey), J R Fanshawe

846 Prince Of Wales Handicap Class C (0-100 3-y-o) £7,252 6f 18yds............. (4:40)

191[4] PLAY HEVER GOLF [75] 8-3 D Holland (5) *made all, clr hfwy, ran on strly fnl furlong.*
.... (14 to 1 op 12 to 1 tchd 16 to 1) 1
606* ANOTHER JADE [73] 8-1 M Roberts (2) *chsd ldrs, improved frm off the pace appr fnl furlong, ran on finish.*
.................................(9 to 4 fav op 3 to 1) 2
450* TWO MOVES IN FRONT (Ire) [78] 8-6 J Carroll (6) *chsd ldg pair, effrt and drvn alng fnl 2 fs, styd on.*
.... (11 to 2 op 4 to 1 tchd 6 to 1) 3

591^4 STORITHS (Ire) [87] 9-1 W R Swinburn (8) *settled to track ldg grp, feeling pace hfwy, swtchd wide to improve fnl furlong, nvr nrr*........(5 to 1 op 3 to 1 tchd 11 to 2) 4
542^7 THE SHARP BIDDER (Ire) [79] 8-7 W Ryan (9) *chsd alng in midfield, styd on appr fnl furlong, nvr nrr*. .... (20 to 1 op 14 to 1) 5
400 BOLD SEVEN (Ire) [79] 8-4 (3*) N Kennedy (7) *sluggish strt, bustled alng to improve last 2 fs, nvr nrr*. ....(20 to 1 op 16 to 1) 6
SOUTHERN MEMORIES (Ire) [75] 8-3 W Carson (4) *chsd ldg grp, feeling pace hfwy, nvr able to chal*. ....(8 to 1 op 6 to 1) 7
289* CELESTIAL KEY (USA) [93] 9-2 (5*) O Pears (1) *settled gng wl, effrt and shaken up hfwy, outpcd last 2 fs*. ....(15 to 2 op 7 to 1 tchd 8 to 1) 8
606 MELODYS DAUGHTER [65] (bl) 7-7 J Lowe (3) *chsd wnr, rdn o'r 2 fs out, fdd*.................(14 to 1 op 12 to 1) 9
634* PRIMULA BAIRN [72] 8-0 A Munro (10) *trkd ldg trio, rdn 2 fs out, sn btn*...........(11 to 2 op 5 to 1 tchd 9 to 2) 10

Dist: 1½l, 2l, 5l, 1l, hd, 2½l, 4l, hd, nk. 1m 12.78s. b 0.72s (10 Ran).
SR: 53/45/42/31/19/18/4/6/-/ (R A Popely), T J Naughton

LIMERICK (IRE) (good to firm)
Tuesday May 4th

847 Adare Fillies Maiden (3-y-o) £2,245 7f ....(5:30)

488^3 MY TRELAWNY (Ire) 8-12 (2*) R M Burke (12) ..... (10 to 1) 1
SAFAYN (USA) 9-0 M J Kinane (17) .... (5 to 2) 2
639^2 PENNINE'S DAUGHTER 9-0 B Coogan (18) ....(7 to 4 fav) 3
ALASKAN GIRL (Ire) 9-0 D Manning (11) ....(20 to 1) 4
311 PERSIAN GEM (Ire) 9-0 J D Eddery (1) .... (12 to 1) 5
MISS MARESE (Ire) 9-0 K J Manning (15) ....(25 to 1) 6
705^7 PERSIAN LIGHT (Ire) 8-4 (10*) A J Dempsey (13) .. (20 to 1) 7
ICEFLOW (Fr) 9-0 P V Gilson (4) ....(7 to 1) 8
648^8 FAIRY BRIDE (Ire) 9-0 N G McCullagh (6) ....(20 to 1) 9
TROPICAL LAKE (Ire) 9-0 S Craine (14) ....(8 to 1) 10
MYRO BALANNE (Ire) 9-0 W J Supple (16) .... (50 to 1) 11
NURSES RUN (Ire) 8-8 (6*) J J Behan (7) .... (12 to 1) 12
639 STEADY DEAR (Ire) 9-0 G Curran (5) ....(33 to 1) 13
648^6 TRIBAL MEMORIES (Ire) 9-0 E McCabe (9) ....(14 to 1) 14
486^7 SHESOMETHINGELSE (Ire) 8-4 (10*) D W O'Sullivan (8) ....(20 to 1) 15
551^6 CARHUE STAR (Ire) 9-0 W J O'Connor (2) .... (14 to 1) 16
488 SUNBED SUE (Ire) 9-0 Joanna Morgan (10) ....(33 to 1) 17
488 SALZAAD (Ire) 8-12 (2*) D G O'Shea (3) .... (20 to 1) 18

Dist: Sht-hd, ¾l, 2l, sht-hd. 1m 27.90s. (18 Ran).
(J C Harley), J C Harley

848 Kilmallock (C & G) Maiden (3-y-o and up) £2,245 7f.......................... (6:00)

256^2 TEAZEL BOY 3-8-9 P V Gilson (7) .... (6 to 4 on) 1
489^5 TORC MOUNTAIN (Ire) 3-8-9 W J Supple (13) .....(10 to 1) 2
550 MUSWELL BROOK (Ire) 3-8-9 K J Manning (6) .....(7 to 1) 3
486^2 CARRIG STAR (Ire) 4-8-13 (8*) J J Stack (9) ....(12 to 1) 4
669 PENNY A DAY (Ire) 3-8-9 C Roche (2) ....(20 to 1) 5
649^3 LUCKY PRINCE (Ire) (bl) 3-8-9 M J Kinane (8) ......(5 to 1) 6
577 BOTHSIDESNOW (Ire) 3-8-9 R Hughes (4) ....(14 to 1) 7
489^8 BOLD NOT BEAT (Ire) 3-8-7 (2*) R M Burke (1) ..... (16 to 1) 8
CELESTIAL CROWN (Ire) 3-8-9 P Shanahan (10) ... (4 to 1) 9
MILLERS MILL (Ire) 3-8-9 S Craine (15) .... (14 to 1) 10
SPEED DEMON 3-8-1 (8*) R T Fitzpatrick (12) ....(25 to 1) 11
ROCKY (Ire) 3-8-5 (4*) W J Smith (14) ....(20 to 1) 12
550 SIMPLE DANCER (Ire) 3-8-1 (8*) P P Murphy (5) ....(16 to 1) 13
ASSERT STAR 3-8-3 (6*) J A Heffernan (11) ....(20 to 1) 14
THREE MUSKETEERS (Ire) 4-9-7 W J O'Connor (3) (25 to 1) 15

Dist: 2l, 1½l, ¾l, 2l. 1m 27.10s. (15 Ran).
(James McNeil), C Collins

849 Rathkeale Apprentice Handicap (0-70 3-y-o and up) £2,245 1¼m.............. (6:30)

647* THE BERUKI (Ire) [-] 3-7-13 (4*,8ex) P P Murphy (16) (7 to 2) 1
575 RATTLE AND HUM [-] 6-9-7 (4*) T J Daly (10) ..... (14 to 1) 2
308^9 MAGIC ARTS (Ire) [-] 5-9-12 (2*) J R Barry (2) ..... (16 to 1) 3
VICOSA (Ire) [-] (bl) 4-7-9 W J Smith (12) .... (16 to 1) 4
598^8 THE MAN FROM COOKS (Ire) [-] 4-9-3 (2*) C Everard (13) ....(10 to 1) 5
STEEL CHIMES (Ire) [-] 4-9-0 (4*) D J O'Donohoe (15) ....(8 to 1) 6
666^4 ACCELL (Ire) [-] 4-9-2 (2*) P Carberry (17) .... (2 to 1 fav) 7
598 SOLAR FLASH (Ire) [-] 4-8-0 (4*) B Bowens (1) ..... (12 to 1) 8
550^8 KATIES VISION (Ire) [-] 3-7-12 (4*) R T Fitzpatrick (8) (20 to 1) 9
598 KINVARA LADY (Ire) [-] 4-7-3 (4*) B J Halligan (6) .. (25 to 1) 10
598 THE BOWER (Ire) [-] 4-8-6 (4*) J J Mullins (7) ......(33 to 1) 11
598 MAZELLA (Ire) [-] (bl) 4-8-3 (6*) S P Cooke (3) ..... (12 to 1) 12
487^7 TWO MAGPIES [-] 6-7-4 (6*) G M Moylan (5) ....(10 to 1) 13
INAUGURATION (Ire) [-] 4-9-3 (6*) J Wixted (18) ... (14 to 1) 14
640 ALSHOU (Ire) [-] 4-9-2 (6*) G Coogan (4) ....(14 to 1) 15
598^3 HAWAIAN TASCA (Ire) [-] 4-7-11^3 (6*) B Carson (11) (8 to 1) 16
RIYADH DANCER (Ire) [-] 3-7-13 (2*) J J Behan (14) (20 to 1) 17
647^8 HOMERS FOLLY (Ire) [-] (bl) 3-7-9^8 (6*) B Fenton, ..(33 to 1) 18

Dist: 1½l, 1½l, ¾l, sht-hd. 2m 6.70s. (18 Ran).
(Mrs Geraldine Treacy), S J Treacy

850 Shannon Race (3-y-o) £2,245 1½m.. (7:00)

SIRSAN (Ire) 9-0 R Hughes (5) ....(20 to 1) 1
649* DIFFERENT TIMES (Ire) 9-7 S Craine (7) .... (6 to 4 fav) 2
LUSTRINO (USA) 9-0 M J Kinane (11) ....(7 to 2) 3
639^8 BLUE DIANA (Ire) 8-11 J F Egan (6) ....(8 to 1) 4
489* TOUCHING MOMENT (Ire) 9-7 P V Gilson (10) ..... (6 to 1) 5
297* MAN OF ARRAN (Ire) 9-5 (2*) R M Burke (4) ....(6 to 1) 6
790^9 EFFICIENT FUNDING (Ire) 8-11 W J O'Connor (2) (20 to 1) 7
297^3 MAJESTIC JOHN (Ire) 9-0 J P Murtagh (1) ....(10 to 1) 8
257^9 NORDIC HALO (Ire) 8-11 C Roche (3) .... (6 to 1) 9
639 HIGHLAND ARK (Ire) 8-6 (8*) R V Skelly (12) ...... (40 to 1) 10
WESTERN FRONTIER (Ire) 8-6 (8*) J M Buckley (8) (50 to 1) 11
RYE HILL QUEEN (Ire) 8-11 D Manning (9) ....(25 to 1) 12

Dist: Nk, sht-hd, 1½l, 1l. 2m 33.20s. (12 Ran).
(J M Vander-Poel), M J Grassick

851 Foynes Maiden (4-y-o and up) £2,245 1½m ....(7:30)

CORONADO (Ire) 5-10-0 W J Supple (14) ...... (5 to 4 fav) 1
309 GALAVOTTI (Ire) 4-10-0 C Roche (7) ....(7 to 1) 2
SHAREEF ALLIANCE (Ire) 4-10-0 K F O'Brien (17) (10 to 1) 3
487 MAY WE DANCE (Ire) 4-9-5 (6*) C Everard (1) ..... (14 to 1) 4
RIENROE (Ire) 4-9-11 M J Kinane (11) ....(6 to 1) 5
THIS IS MY LIFE (Ire) 4-10-0 G Curran (15) .... (25 to 1) 6
787 JUST FOUR (Ire) 4-9-3 (8*) R T Fitzpatrick (18) .... (50 to 1) 7
PRINCE TAUFAN (Ire) 4-9-8 (6*) P Carberry (12) ... (14 to 1) 8
JUPITER JIMMY 4-10-0 J Magee (13) ....(12 to 1) 9
KESS (Ire) 4-9-3 (8*) B Bowens (4) ....(66 to 1) 10
STEEL MIRROR 4-10-0 P V Gilson (2) ....(12 to 1) 11
GLAD'S NIGHT (Ire) 4-9-11 M Kelly (16) ....(20 to 1) 12
CLEEVAUN (Ire) 5-10-0 K J Manning (6) ....(20 to 1) 13
VON CARTY (Ire) 4-9-11 N Byrne (3) ....(33 to 1) 14
SIR HENRY KNYVET (Ire) 4-10-0 R Hughes (8) .... (20 to 1) 15
RIYASHA (Ire) 5-9-11 C F Swan (10) .... (50 to 1) 16
INCREDIBLE JOHN (Ire) (bl) 4-10-0 J P Murtagh (5) (66 to 1) 17
NATIVE CHAMPION (Ire) 4-10-0 T J Ryan (9) ......(66 to 1) 18

Dist: 3l, 3l, 1½l, 2l. 2m 28.60s. (18 Ran).
(Lord White Of Hull), M J Grassick

852 Garryowen Handicap (0-65 4-y-o and up) £2,245 2m.......................... (8:00)

598^9 MRS BARTON (Ire) [-] 5-9-5 (6*) J R Barry (12) ..(7 to 4 fav) 1
298* SYLVIA FOX [-] 6-9-12 M J Kinane (2) ....(100 to 30) 2
SERJITAK [-] 6-8-5 (8*) P P Murphy (11) .... (12 to 1) 3
ZUHAL [-] 5-9-0 (8*) J J Behan (6) .... (25 to 1) 4
598^2 CEDAR COURT (Ire) [-] 5-9-13 C F Swan (14) ...... (7 to 1) 5
298 AEGEAN FANFARE (Ire) [-] 4-9-12 R Hughes (15) .. (16 to 1) 6
309 INDIANA GOLD (Ire) [-] 5-8-0 Joanna Morgan (9) .. (25 to 1) 7
RACK RATE (Ire) [-] 5-10-0 W J O'Connor (7) ......(33 to 1) 8
298 PRINCE YAZA [-] 6-9-5 (6*) C Everard (16) ....(10 to 1) 9
706^5 BANKONIT (Ire) [-] 5-9-2 P Shanahan (4) .... (25 to 1) 10
MOTILITY [-] 6-9-5 (6*) P Carberry (18) ....(12 to 1) 11
HAWKFIELD (Ire) [-] 4-9-8 J P Murtagh (10) ....(16 to 1) 12
298^4 FINAL FAVOUR (Ire) [-] 4-9-7 S Craine (5) ....(9 to 2) 13
PLUMBOB (Ire) [-] (bl) 4-8-5 N G McCullagh (13) .. (16 to 1) 14
VIVERE (Ire) [-] 4-9-1 P V Gilson (1) ....(20 to 1) 15
487 WOODFIELD ROSE [-] 4-7-9 (10*) B Fenton (8) ....(33 to 1) 16
FROMTHEGETGO (Ire) [-] 4-9-6 W J Supple (3) ... (20 to 1) 17
706^8 ASTRA (Ire) [-] (bl) 4-9-10 J F Egan (17) ....(25 to 1) 18

Dist: ¾l, hd, hd, ½l. 3m 26.80s. (18 Ran).
(Mrs Patrick Flynn), Patrick Joseph Flynn

LONGCHAMP (FR) (soft)
Tuesday May 4th
Going Correction: PLUS 0.75 sec. per fur.

853 Prix du Pont-Neuf (Listed) (3-y-o) £14,337 7f................................(3:25)

MATELOT (USA) 8-12 T Jarnet, ... 1
638^3 BORODISLEW (USA) 8-8 F Head, ... 2
ASTUDILLO (Ire) 9-2 P Julien, ... 3
4753a^2 EMBROS (USA) 8-11 E Saint-Martin, ... 4

Dist: 1l, 2l, ½l, 1l, 6l, 1½l. 1m 26.70s. a 7.20s (7 Ran).
SR: 69/62/64/57/ (Sheikh Mohammed), A Fabre

CHESTER (good to firm)
Wednesday May 5th
Going Correction: MINUS 0.40 sec. per fur.

854 Sefton Maiden Fillies' Stakes Class D (3-y-o) £6,940 7f 2yds................. (2:10)

ARJUZAH (Ire) 8-11 W Carson (1) *tucked away, not clr run and swtchd appr fnl furlong, brst through to ld last 75 yards*.........................(5 to 4 fav op 7 to 4) 1
428^3 CROIRE (Ire) 8-11 M Hills (5) *trkd ldg quartet, swtchd outsd to ld entering fnl furlong, edgd lft and sn hdd, kpt on one pace*...................(10 to 1 op 8 to 1) 2

523^{5} DITTISHAM (USA) 8-11 Pat Eddery (3) *tried to make all, rdn and hdd entering fnl furlong, no extr.* ....(4 to 1 op 3 to 1 tchd 9 to 2) 3
516^{5} CHERHILL (Ire) 8-11 J Reid (4) *trkd ldr, hrd at work whn pace lifted o'r one furlong out, one pace.* ....(14 to 1 op 10 to 1) 4
LANDRAIL (USA) 8-11 M Roberts (2) *sluggish strt, bustled alng to keep up hfwy, nvr nr to chal.* ....(13 to 2 op 5 to 1 tchd 7 to 1) 5
516^{2} RED COTTON 8-11 W R Swinburn (6) *chsd ldg pair, feeling pace o'r 2 fs out, sn btn.* (11 to 2 op 3 to 1 tchd 6 to 1) 6
Dist: ½l, 3l, 1½l, ¾l, 7l. 1m 25.62s. a 0.22s (6 Ran).
SR: 52/50/41/36/34/13/ (Hamdan Al-Maktoum), J H M Gosden

855 Cheshire Regiment Handicap Class C (0-95 3-y-o) £8,552 1½m 66yds...... (2:40)

423^{7} LEAGUE LEADER (Ire) [75] 8-12 W R Swinburn (7) *trkd ldr aftr 2 fs, quickened und pres to nose ahead ins fnl furlong, drvn out*.... (11 to 2 op 4 to 1) 1
468^{2} KEY TO MY HEART (Ire) [84] 9-7 Dean McKeown (6) *settled gng wl, improved frm midfield to draw level entering fnl furlong, ran on, jst hld.* ....(17 to 2 op 10 to 1 tchd 7 to 1) 2
644^{3} COLLIER BAY [69] 8-6 W Carson (4) *made most, quickened und pres o'r 3 fs out, hdd ins fnl furlong, one pace.* ....(2 to 1 fav op 5 to 2) 3
468^{3} MOORISH [82] 9-5 A Munro (8) *pld hrd, trkd ldg trio, effrt and bustled alng o'r 3 fs out, one pace.* ....(6 to 1 op 5 to 1) 4
$4790a^{3}$ SPRING FLYER (Ire) [61] 7-12 A Mackay (5) *chsd ldg bunch, effrt und pres o'r 3 fs out, not quicken.* ....(20 to 1 tchd 16 to 1) 5
LAMU LADY (Ire) [80] 9-3 J Reid (1) *trkd ldg 5, rdn o'r 3 fs out, outpcd last 2 furlongs*.... (11 to 1 op 10 to 1) 6
423^{2} BLUE GROTTO (Ire) [80] (v) 9-3 Pat Eddery (2) *pld hrd, dsptd ld till settled aftr 2 fs, fdd und pres two furlongs out*....(5 to 1 tchd 9 to 2) 7
295^{5} DEE RAFT (USA) [79] 9-2 D Holland (3) *trkd ldg bunch, effrt and scrubbed alng o'r 3 fs out, sn lost tch.* ....(17 to 2 op 8 to 1 tchd 9 to 1) 8
Dist: Nk, 1l, 3l, 2l, 6l, ¾l, 15l. 2m 38.41s. a 1.61s (8 Ran).
SR: 33/41/24/31/6/13/11/-/ (Lord Weinstock), M R Stoute

856 Shadwell Stud Cheshire Oaks Class A (Listed Race) (3-y-o) £23,815 1m 3f 79yds ....(3:10)

ABURY (Ire) 8-11 J Reid (3) *trkd ldg quartet, hrd at work hfwy, styd on grimly fnl furlong to ld last strds.* ....(9 to 2 op 3 to 1 tchd 5 to 1) 1
512^{7} BASHAYER (USA) 8-11 W Carson (1) *trkd ldr, led o'r 5 fs out, 3 ls clr ins last, eased and idled, ct post.* ....(2 to 1 fav op 9 to 4 tchd 5 to 2) 2
748* MAGICAL RETREAT (USA) 8-11 D Biggs (5) *nvr far away, ev ch whn rdr drpd whip entering strt, kpt on same pace*.... (5 to 1 op 4 to 1) 3
602* WOODWARDIA (USA) 8-11 Pat Eddery (6) *settled in last pl, effrt and bustled alng last 3 fs, kpt on same pace.* ....(11 to 2 op 9 to 2 tchd 6 to 1) 4
662^{3} REINE DE NEIGE 8-11 W R Swinburn (2) *trkd ldg trio, drvn alng and ch 2 fs out, not quicken*.... (7 to 1 op 6 to 1) 5
556^{5} SHAMISEN 8-11 M Roberts (4) *dictated pace, hdd and drvn alng hfwy, wknd quickly appr strt.* ....(13 to 2 op 6 to 1 tchd 7 to 1) 6
Dist: Hd, 3½l, 2l, sht-hd, 12l. 2m 25.21s. a 1.91s (6 Ran).
SR: 33/32/25/21/20/-/ (R E Sangster), P W Chapple-Hyam

857 Ladbroke Chester Cup Handicap Class B (4-y-o and up) £27,050 2¼m 117yds (3:40)

478* RODEO STAR (USA) [65] 7-7-13 N Carlisle (16) *confidently rdn, al hndy, quickened through to ld o'r one furlong out, readily*.... (9 to 1 op 10 to 1) 1
783* JACK BUTTON (Ire) [87] 4-9-3 (3ex) N Day (1) *trkd ldg half dozen, swtchd outsd to improve o'r one furlong out, fnshd wl*.... (12 to 1) 2
WELSHMAN [62] 7-7-10 J Quinn (7) *trkd ldr, led aftr 4 and a half fs till o'r one out, kpt on same pace.* ....(10 to 1 op 12 to 1) 3
BALASANI (Fr) [65] 7-7-13 W Carson (14) *co'red up on ins, drvn to improve appr strt, styd on und pres.* ....(9 to 1 op 8 to 1 tchd 10 to 1) 4
661* ROBINGO (Ire) [90] (bl) 4-9-6 A Munro (17) *trkd ldg quartet, drw level und pres o'r 3 fs out, one pace last.* ....(15 to 2 op 7 to 1 tchd 8 to 1) 5
661^{3} BARDOLPH (USA) [76] 6-8-10 T Quinn (11) *led for o'r 4 fs, styd hndy and rallied appr strt, no extr fnl furlong.* ....(7 to 1 jt-fav op 8 to 1) 6
702^{6} HUNTING GROUND [59] (bl) 5-7-7 A Mackay (9) *patiently rdn, took clr order fnl circuit, styd on one pace last 2 fs.* ....(200 to 1) 7
NATIVE MISSION [70] 6-8-4 L Charnock (3) *nvr far away, hrd at work o'r 3 fs out, one pace*... (9 to 1 op 10 to 1) 8
783^{3} AUDE LA BELLE (Fr) [70] 5-8-4 F Norton (10) *settled midfield, scrubbed alng aftr one circuit, rallied, fdd entering strt*.... (33 to 1 op 25 to 1) 9
495^{2} MIZYAN (Ire) [62] (bl) 5-7-10 Dale Gibson (12) *rcd freely in frnt rnk, ev ch and drvn alng appr strt, fdd.* ....(14 to 1 op 16 to 1 tchd 20 to 1) 10
462^{5} FRENCH IVY (USA) [78] 6-8-12 W R Swinburn (2) *settled off the pace, drvn alng to improve fnl circuit, btn 3 fs out.* ....(25 to 1) 11
661^{5} STAR PLAYER [90] 7-9-10 L Piggott (19) *in tch on outsd, effrt fnl circuit, rdn appr strt, no response.* ....(14 to 1 op 16 to 1) 12
539* DIME BAG [80] 4-8-10 D Holland (15) *ran in snatches, drvn alng fnl circuit, no imprsn*.... (7 to 1 jt-fav op 11 to 2) 13
478^{3} TOP SPIN [83] 4-8-13 S Whitworth (6) *trkd ldg bunch, struggling to keep up appr strt, sn btn.* ....(20 to 1 tchd 16 to 1) 14
682 OUR AISLING [73] 5-8-7^{6} (5*) O Pears (4) *settled off the pace, improved on outsd o'r 6 fs out, fdd appr strt.* ....(12 to 1 op 14 to 1) 15
682* GOOD HAND (USA) [84] 7-9-4 N Connorton (8) *trkd ldg bunch for o'r a circuit, struggling hfwy, sn btn.* ....(16 to 1 tchd 14 to 1) 16
682 BOLD RESOLUTION (Ire) [64] 5-7-12 D Biggs (13) *re-plated bef race, chsd ldg bunch till wknd quickly o'r 4 fs out.* ....(16 to 1 op 20 to 1) 17
427^{9} ADMINISTER [62] 5-7-10^{6} (3*) N Kennedy (5) *chsd alng to keep in tch aftr one circuit, nvr a factor, uns rdr after line*.... (100 to 1) 18
Dist: 2l, 2l, 1½l, sht-hd, 3l, nk, 1l, hd, ¾l, 2½l. 4m 2.51s. a 3.01s (Flag start) (18 Ran).
(J C Bradbury), N Tinkler

858 Boodle & Dunthorne Diamond Rated Class B (0-105 3-y-o) £7,492 5f 16yds...... (4:10)

ELLE SHAPED (Ire) [90] 8-9 M Roberts (5) *trkd ldg pair, drvn ahead appr fnl furlong, sprinted clr.* ....(6 to 1 tchd 13 to 2) 1
464^{3} LUCKY PARKES [102] 9-7 J Carroll (2) *wth ldr, led briefly o'r one furlong out, sn rdn and outpcd.* ....(5 to 2 op 2 to 1 tchd 11 to 4) 2
691^{4} ARADANZA [96] 9-1 Pat Eddery (3) *chsd ldg trio, hrd at work o'r one furlong out, no extr*.... (5 to 1 op 4 to 1) 3
591^{3} MISTERTOPOGIGO (Ire) [88] 8-7 J Reid (1) *dictated pace for o'r 3 fs, sn rdn and btn*.... (2 to 1 fav op 6 to 4) 4
566^{3} RISTON LADY (Ire) [97] 8-13 (3*) D Harrison (4) *chsd ldg quartet till fdd und pres o'r one furlong out.* ....(5 to 1 tchd 9 to 2) 5
Dist: 3½l, 4l, 2½l, sht-hd. 59.94s. b 0.36s (5 Ran).
SR: 62/60/38/20/28/ (J E Marsden), S G Norton

859 Red Dragon Maiden Stakes Class D (2-y-o) £4,825 5f 16yds.................... (4:40)

REDOUBTABLE (USA) 9-0 Pat Eddery (1) *settled aftr fst break, quickened through on ins to ld o'r one furlong out, sn clr.* ...(11 to 10 on op Evens tchd 5 to 4 on and 11 to 10) 1
730^{2} PALACEGATE JACK (Ire) 9-0 J Carroll (2) *tried to make all, hdd o'r one furlong out, no ch wth wnr.* ....(9 to 4 op 7 to 4) 2
554^{3} BASKERVILLE 9-0 A Munro (4) *wth ldr, hrd at work o'r one furlong out, sn outpcd.* ....(13 to 2 op 5 to 1 tchd 7 to 1) 3
DINOT (Ire) 9-0 S Perks (5) *pressed ldg pair for o'r 3 fs, sn btn*.... (13 to 2 op 7 to 1 tchd 8 to 1 and 6 to 1) 4
Dist: 5l, 3l, 8l. 1m 1.22s. a 0.92s (4 Ran).
SR: 42/22/10/-/ (B E Nielsen), R Hannon

EDINBURGH (good)
Wednesday May 5th

Going Correction: MINUS 0.20 sec. per fur. (races 1,2,3,4,5), MINUS 0.40 (6,7)

860 Edinburgh Castle Median Auction Maiden Stakes Class E (3-y-o) £2,752 1m 16yds ....(2:20)

646^{2} BROWN'S (Fr) 8-9 (5*) Stephen Davies (5) *made all, rdn o'r 2 fs out, clr appr fnl furlong.* ....(6 to 1 on op 8 to 1 on tchd 5 to 1 on) 1
611^{3} RUNRIG (Ire) 8-9 G Duffield (6) *chsd ldrs, effrt and hdwy to chal o'r 2 fs out, sn rdn and one pace.* ....(7 to 1 op 6 to 1) 2
447^{4} SUDDEN SPIN 9-0 G Carter (4) *cl up, ev ch 2 and a half fs out, sn rdn and one pace*.... (10 to 1 op 8 to 1) 3
630^{8} CARLTON EXPRESS (Ire) 9-0 K Fallon (1) *outpcd and beh hfwy, some hdwy fnl 2 fs, nvr a factor*.... (33 to 1) 4
611^{4} SEVERE STORM 9-0 D Nicholls (2) *chsd ldrs, rdn o'r 3 fs out and sn wknd*.... (33 to 1) 5
MAJOR JACK 9-0 J Fanning (3) *dwlt, al rear.* ....(20 to 1 op 25 to 1) 6
Dist: 10l, ¾l, 12l, 8l, 3½l. 1m 41.60s. a 3.10s (6 Ran).
SR: 30/-/-/ (F M Kalla), P W Chapple-Hyam

861 Dalkeith Selling Handicap Class G (0-60 3-y-o and up) £2,473 1m 16yds...... (2:50)

409 MALCESINE (Ire) [40] 4-8-11 J Fortune (15) *al cl up, led 2 and a half fs out, sn hdd, rdn and styd on to ld wl ins last*......(20 to 1 tchd 25 to 1) 1
769^5 INVERTIEL [55] 9-9-12 J Fanning (14) *trkd ldrs, hdwy 4 fs out, led 2 out, sn rdn, hdd and no extr wl ins last.*......(10 to 1) 2
710^4 DIAMOND INTHE DARK (USA) [53] (v) 5-9-10 T Lucas (13) *trkd ldrs till lost pl hfwy, rdn 2 fs out, styd on ins last.*......(8 to 1 op 7 to 1) 3
610^2 CHANTRY BELLINI [44] (bl) 4-9-1 K Darley (11) *mid-div, hdwy 3 fs out, rdn and one pace appr fnl furlong.*......(3 to 1 fav tchd 7 to 2) 4
610^4 J'ARRIVE [41] 4-8-7 (5*) C Hodgson (8) *chsd ldrs, rdn and ch o'r 2 fs out, sn one pace*......(12 to 1 op 10 to 1) 5
681 DEPUTY TIM [42] 10-8-10^4 (7*) H Bastiman (4) *mid-div, hdwy 3 fs out, rdn and hng lft 2 out, sn one pace.*......(16 to 1 op 14 to 1) 6
754^6 ROYAL ACCLAIM [47] (v) 8-8-11 (7*) Michael Bradley (2) *beh till styd on fnl 2 fs, nvr dngrs*......(10 to 1 op 8 to 1) 7
376^3 LITMORE DANCER [41] 5-8-12 R Cochrane (10) *al mid-div.*......(8 to 1 op 7 to 1) 8
610^7 MISS MAGENTA (Ire) [30] 5-8-1 J Lowe (3) *nvr rch ldrs.*......(14 to 1 op 8 to 1) 9
396^6 COOL PARADE (USA) [45] 5-9-2 G Carter (7) *nvr a factor.*......(12 to 1 op 8 to 1) 10
VERDANT BOY [48] 10-9-5 K Fallon (5) *al rear*......(12 to 1) 11
771 BASSIO (Bel) [50] (bl) 4-9-0 (7*) Mick Denaro (12) *nvr a factor*......(12 to 1 op 10 to 1) 12
710 JOVIAL KATE (USA) [41] 6-8-12 G Duffield (6) *chsd ldrs, rdn 3 fs out, sn wknd*......(20 to 1) 13
681 ANFIELD SALLY [35] 7-8-1 (5*) Darren Moffatt (9) *in tch till rdn and wknd 3 fs out.*......(25 to 1 op 33 to 1 tchd 20 to 1) 14
447^6 SAINTED SUE [40] 3-7-12^3 (3*) S Maloney (16) *led, hdd and wknd quickly 2 and a half fs out*......(100 to 1) 15
531^8 FUTURES GIFT (Ire) [37] (bl) 4-8-8 S Webster (1) *rear till broke leg and pld up aftr 3 fs, destroyed*......(14 to 1) pu
Dist: ¾l, 3½l, 2½l, hd, 1½l, hd, 1l, ½l, ½l, nk. 1m 42.10s. a 3.60s (16 Ran).
SR: 19/32/19/2/-/-/ (F Cunliffe), Capt J Wilson

862 Arthurs Seat Maiden Handicap Class E (0-70 3-y-o and up) £2,951 7f 15yds.. (3:20)

606^9 AL MOULOUKI [51] 3-8-7 R Cochrane (4) *mid-div, gd hdwy on inner 3 fs out, rdn to ld o'r one and a half furlongs out and sn clr, eased nr finish.*......(5 to 1 op 7 to 1 tchd 8 to 1) 1
655^4 TAWAFIJ (USA) [60] 4-10-0 K Darley (10) *chsd ldrs, effrt 3 fs out, led 2 furlongs out, sn hdd and rdn, kpt on one pace*......(7 to 1 op 6 to 1) 2
610 MISS HOSTESS [25] (bl) 6-7-2 (5*) Darren Moffatt (8) *beh, effrt and hdwy 2 fs out, rdn and styd on wl fnl furlong.*......(25 to 1 op 16 to 1) 3
590^3 NORTHERN BLUFF [63] (v) 3-9-5 G Duffield (9) *led, wide strt, rdn and hdd 2 fs out, kpt on same pace.*......(3 to 1 op 2 to 1) 4
655^8 BOLD PHILIP [48] (bl) 3-8-4 J Fortune (6) *chsd ldrs, rdn o'r 2 fs out, sn one pace*......(12 to 1 op 16 to 1) 5
565^4 THE DANDY DON (Ire) [50] 4-9-4 K Fallon (3) *hld up, effrt and hdwy 3 fs out, sn rdn and no imprsn.*......(5 to 2 fav op 2 to 1 tchd 3 to 1) 6
711^2 PENNY BANGER (Ire) [50] 3-8-6 J Lowe (5) *chsd ldrs till rdn and wknd wl o'r 2 fs out*......(7 to 1 op 5 to 1) 7
UMBRIA [42] 4-8-10 C Dwyer (2) *chsd ldrs, rdn 2 and a half fs out, no hdwy*......(14 to 1 op 6 to 1) 8
BRUSH WOLF (USA) [35] 4-8-3 G Carter (1) *al rear.*......(14 to 1 op 12 to 1) 9
503^7 ROBIX (Ire) [50] (bl) 3-8-3 (3*) S Maloney (7) *cl up, rdn wl o'r 2 fs out and sn wknd*......(16 to 1 op 12 to 1) 10
Dist: 3l, 1½l, 1½l, sht-hd, 5l, 2l, ½l, 3l, nk. 1m 28.60s. a 3.40s (10 Ran).
SR: 21/33/-/14/-/-/ (G Jabre), J W Payne

863 Levy Board Claiming Handicap Class G (4-y-o and up) £2,579 1½m 31yds...... (3:50)

622^3 PRINCESS EVITA (Fr) [30] 4-7-12 J Fanning (9) *al prmnt, hdwy 3 fs out, rdn to ld one and a half furlongs out and ran on wl*......(5 to 1 op 7 to 2) 1
628 POST IMPRESSIONIST (Ire) [51] 4-9-0 (5*) Stephen Davies (14) *led, hdd 5 fs out, cl up till led ag'n 2 and a half furlongs out, rdn and headed one and a half furlongs out, kpt on*......(17 to 2 op 5 to 1 tchd 9 to 1) 2
620^8 YOUNG GEORGE [40] 6-8-8 J Lowe (1) *hld up and beh, gd hdwy 3 fs out, rdn appr fnl furlong and styd on.*......(4 to 1 op 3 to 1) 3
681^3 GOLD SURPRISE (Ire) [48] 4-9-2 J Fortune (6) *al chasing ldrs, effrt 2 fs out, rdn and kpt on one pace ins fnl furlong*......(7 to 2 fav op 5 to 2 tchd 4 to 1) 4
681^9 HOT PUNCH [43] 4-8-11 R Cochrane (15) *in tch, effrt on inner and hdwy 3 fs out, rdn 2 furlongs out, one pace.*......(12 to 1 op 10 to 1) 5
RAPID MOVER [32] (bl) 6-8-0^5 G Carter (2) *cl up, ev ch o'r 2 fs out, sn rdn and wknd appr fnl furlong.*......(8 to 1 tchd 10 to 1) 6
681 MASTER OF THE ROCK [46] (bl) 4-9-0 D Nicholls (13) *beh, hdwy 3 fs out, sn rdn and plugged on same pace.*......(20 to 1 op 16 to 1) 7
DOTS DEE [27] 4-7-4 (5*) Darren Moffatt (12) *mid-div, effrt and hdwy o'r 3 fs out, sn rdn and wknd*......(33 to 1) 8
495 HYDEONIUS [28] 8-7-10 S Wood (5) *mid-div, hdwy on outer o'r 2 fs out, sn rdn and btn.* (16 to 1 op 12 to 1) 9
164^5 LORD ADVOCATE [40] (v) 5-8-8 K Fallon (4) *nvr a factor.*......(10 to 1 op 8 to 1) 10
MRS NORMAN [40] 4-8-8 S Webster (7) *al rear*... (50 to 1) 11
4715a^8 REACH FOR GLORY [47] 4-9-1 T Lucas (3) *chsd ldrs till wknd o'r 4 fs out*......(11 to 1 op 7 to 1 tchd 12 to 1) 12
JOSEPH'S WINE (Ire) [43] 4-8-11 M Tebbutt (8) *al rear.*......(16 to 1 op 10 to 1) 13
JOHN NAMAN (Ire) [57] 4-9-11 G Duffield (11) *prmnt, hdwy to ld 5 fs out, rdn and hdd 2 and a half furlongs out, sn wknd*......(10 to 1) 14
Dist: 2l, ¾l, 1l, ½l, 2l, ¾l, 3l, 1l, sht-hd, hd. 2m 40.40s. a 7.60s (14 Ran).
(S Lury), R Guest

864 Charlotte Square Median Auction Maiden Stakes Class F (3-y-o) £2,460 1½m 31yds ......(4:20)

413^3 ROSIE'S GOLD 8-9 M Tebbutt (4) *made all, rdn o'r 2 fs out, hrd drvn ins last and hld on wl*...(25 to 1 op 20 to 1) 1
725^3 MY HARVINSKI 8-9 (5*) Stephen Davies (7) *hld up, hdwy o'r 2 fs out, rdn to chal entering fnl furlong, kpt on wl.*......(15 to 8 op 6 to 4 tchd 11 to 8 and 2 to 1) 2
SANTA STELLAR 8-9 G Duffield (3) *chsd wnr, rdn and ev ch 2 fs out, wknd entering fnl furlong.*......(16 to 1 op 8 to 1) 3
509^7 COMMANCHE CREEK 9-0 R Cochrane (6) *trkd ldrs, stumbled bend aftr 2 fs, rdn alng o'r 4 furlongs out, swtchd and hrd drvn two furlongs out, sn one pace*......(6 to 4 on op 5 to 4 on tchd Evens) 4
611^5 SENSABO 8-9 K Fallon (5) *hld up, hdwy to chal 2 fs out, sn rdn and wknd appr fnl furlong.*......(66 to 1 op 100 to 1) 5
653^2 KARIB 8-9 K Darley (2) *hld up, rapid hdwy to chase wnr 5 fs out, rdn and ev ch o'r 2 furlongs out, wknd appr fnl furlong*......(10 to 1 op 7 to 1) 6
653^4 GOLDMIRE 8-9 J Lowe (1) *chsd ldrs, rdn o'r 3 fs out, wknd 2 furlongs out*......(14 to 1 op 12 to 1) 7
Dist: Sht-hd, 4l, 2l, 3½l, nk, 7l. 2m 41.20s. a 8.40s (7 Ran).
(Mrs Rosalie Hawes), D Morris

865 Princes Street Maiden Auction Stakes Class F (2-y-o) £2,448 5f............ (4:50)

DON'T BE KOI (Ire) 8-9 G Duffield (6) *chsd ldr, led hfwy, cmftbly*......(5 to 1 op 5 to 2) 1
395^6 DON PEPE 9-0 R Cochrane (5) *chsd ldrs, effrt o'r 2 fs out, sn rdn and not quicken ins last.*......(5 to 2 op 4 to 1 tchd 9 to 4) 2
673^4 MR ROUGH 9-0 M Tebbutt (1) *chsd ldrs, rdn 2 fs out, kpt on one pace*......(2 to 1 fav tchd 3 to 1) 3
FLOATING TRIAL 8-9 G Carter (2) *chsd ldrs, rdn 2 fs out, kpt on ins fnl furlong*......(8 to 1 op 4 to 1) 4
FORREST MASTER (Ire) 9-0 J Fanning (8) *dwlt, sn in tch, rdn and kpt on one pace appr fnl furlong.*......(20 to 1 op 12 to 1) 5
STARICA (Ire) 8-9 K Darley (4) *dwlt, sn pushed alng, styd on fnl 2 fs*......(25 to 1 op 16 to 1) 6
698 TIMES ZANDO 8-9 J Fortune (3) *slwly away and wnt lft strt, sn in tch, rdn hfwy, wknd wl o'r one furlong out.*......(25 to 1) 7
395^4 KINGFISHER GREY 9-0 D Nicholls (7) *led to hfwy, sn wknd*......(9 to 2 op 4 to 1 tchd 5 to 1) 8
Dist: 2l, 2½l, ¾l, 1l, ½l, 4l, 7l. 59.90s. a 2.10s (8 Ran).
SR: 13/10/-/-/-/ (The 2nd Kingsley House Partnership), M Johnston

866 Castle Handicap Class D (0-80 3-y-o and up) £3,143 5f......................(5:20)

568* JUST BOB [65] 4-10-0 J Fortune (1) *dwlt, hdwy hfwy, swtchd rght appr fnl furlong and rdn to ld nr finish.*......(5 to 1 op 4 to 1) 1
800^6 EWALD (Ire) [64] 5-9-13 R Cochrane (6) *cl up, ev ch whn crrd badly lft thrght fnl 2 fs, no extr nr finish, fnshd 3rd, plcd second.*......(9 to 4 fav op 11 to 4 tchd 3 to 1 and 2 to 1) 2
LOCAL HEROINE [71] 3-9-10 G Carter (7) *chsd ldrs, ev ch whn crrd badly lft ins fnl furlong, not quicken nr finish, fnshd 4th, plcd 3rd.*......(9 to 2 op 4 to 1 tchd 5 to 1) 3
429^4 LANGTONIAN [55] (bl) 4-9-1 (3*) Emma O'Gorman (9) *cl up, led hfwy and sn hng badly lft thrght fnl 2 fs, hdd nr line, fnshd second, plcd 4th.*......(5 to 1 op 4 to 1 tchd 6 to 1) 4
655^6 KATIE-A (Ire) [49] 4-8-12 K Darley (10) *slwly into strd, rdn hfwy, styd on fnl furlong, nvr dngrs.*......(12 to 1 op 7 to 1) 5
436 SO SUPERB [52] (e/c) 4-9-1 J Lowe (5) *cl up, rdn 2 fs out, sn wknd*......(7 to 1 tchd 10 to 1) 6
450^6 SELVOLE [47] 3-7-7 (7*) Claire Balding (3) *chsd ldrs o'r 3 fs.*......(14 to 1 op 16 to 1) 7
231 LONG LAST [30] 4-7-7 J Fanning (4) *led to hfwy, sn wknd.*......(25 to 1 op 20 to 1 tchd 33 to 1) 8

548[8] BEST EFFORT [60] 7-9-9 K Fallon (8) *slwly away, al outpcd*.................................(10 to 1 op 6 to 1) 9
MINSK [38] 7-8-1[8] G Duffield (2) *rdn and outpcd frm hfwy*.
.................................(50 to 1 op 33 to 1) 10
Dist: Sht-hd, sht-hd, 1l, 3l, sht-hd, 1½l, sht-hd, 1½l, 2l. 59.20s. a 1.40s (10 Ran).
SR: 46/43/36/35/11/13/-/-/9/ (J Fotherby), S E Kettlewell

EVRY (FR) (soft)
Wednesday May 5th

867 Prix Matchem (Listed) (3-y-o) £14,337 1m 1f.................................(2:50)

360[2] LE BALAFRE (Fr) 8-9 O Peslier,.................................. 1
MINYDOUN (Ire) 8-9 F Head,.................................. 2
536 HAWK SPELL (USA) 8-9 E Legrix,.................................. 3
360[3] SEATON DELAVAL (USA) 8-9 T Jarnet,.................................. 4
HURTEVENT (Fr) 8-9 D Boeuf,.................................. 7
Dist: 1l, ¾l, nk, ½l, 1½l, sht-hd, 4l, sht-nk. 1m 56.86s. (9 Ran).
(Comte J de Lastours), N Clement

NAVAN (IRE) (good to firm (race 1), good (2,3))
Wednesday May 5th

868 Dunsany Handicap (0-75 3-y-o and up) £2,762 6f.................................(5:30)

599[5] SOUTHERN RULE [-] (bl) 6-7-7 Joanna Morgan (4) (14 to 1) 1
486 FOREST [-] 3-9-1 S Craine (1).................................(7 to 1) 2
310[9] HONORARY PRINCE (Ire) [-] 4-9-12 R Hughes (23) (8 to 1) 3
AFTERGLOW (Ire) [-] 4-8-13 O O'Shea,.................................(16 to 1) 4
BELLE OF DREAMS (Ire) [-] (bl) 5-8-7 W J Supple (18)
.................................(25 to 1) 5
FILL MY GLASS [-] 9-7-11 A J Nolan (16)..........(25 to 1) 6
486* MACGILLYCUDDY (Ire) [-] (bl) 4-9-7 (6*) J J Behan (9)
.................................(4 to 1 fav) 7
ABEREDW (Ire) [-] 3-8-10 M J Kinane (14).........(8 to 1) 8
RETURN JOURNEY (Ire) [-] 4-9-6 (8*) R T Fitzpatrick (6)
.................................(14 to 1) 9
640[6] ARDGILLIAN (Ire) [-] 3-9-6 N G McCullagh (5).....(12 to 1) 10
310[2] BARNAGEERA BOY (Ire) [-] 4-8-13 N Byrne (21)....(6 to 1) 11
705[3] BUSINESS CENTRE (Ire) [-] 3-8-1 (8*) P P Murphy (7)
.................................(16 to 1) 12
PILGRIM BAY (Ire) [-] 3-8-13 D Manning (17)......(14 to 1) 13
599 FANTANTE (Ire) [-] 4-8-12 (8*) J J Mullins (22).....(12 to 1) 14
599[2] BOLD MOLLY (Ire) [-] 4-7-12 (2*) R M Burke (8).....(8 to 1) 15
256 CHAMPAGNE NIGHT (Fr) [-] 3-8-9 (8*) R V Skelly (20)
.................................(12 to 1) 16
JOHNS DANCER (Ire) [-] (bl) 4-7-10 (2*) D G O'Shea (19)
.................................(33 to 1) 17
4684a DSHAMILJA [-] 6-8-10 (8*) D McCullagh (2).......(16 to 1) 18
AVALONIA (Ire) [-] 3-8-4 J F Egan (13)..........(14 to 1) 19
RED VERONA [-] 4-7-8 (4*) W J Smith (12)........(20 to 1) 20
572 SALLUSTAR [-] 8-9-13 D V Smith (15)..........(12 to 1) 21
572[7] FAIRYDEL (Ire) [-] 3-9-1 K J Manning (10)..........(8 to 1) 22
577[4] TRILLICK (Ire) [-] 3-9-3 J P Murtagh (11)..........(5 to 1) 23
Dist: Hd, 1½l, sht-hd, ¾l. 1m 12.40s. (23 Ran).
(Malachy McKenna), Malachy McKenna

869 Airlie Stud EBF Maiden (2-y-o) £4,487 5f.................................(6:00)

305[4] GENUINE BID (Ire) 9-0 J P Murtagh (8)...........(7 to 2) 1
SEE YOU (Ire) 9-0 W J Supple (3)..................(8 to 1) 2
664[2] GIULIO ROMANO (Ire) 9-0 C Roche (2)...... (3 to 1 jt-fav) 3
305[2] TRIMBLEMILL (Ire) 9-0 B Coogan (9)..............(7 to 2) 4
SUMMERHILL SPECIAL (Ire) 8-11 Joanna Morgan (4)
.................................(25 to 1) 5
DON'T KNOW (Ire) 9-0 K J Manning (6).............(10 to 1) 6
571[8] PAUGIM (Ire) 9-0 M J Kinane (1)............ (3 to 1 jt-fav) 7
571[6] LA BERTA (Ire) 8-11 W J O'Connor (7).............(8 to 1) 8
Dist: 1l, nk, hd, 1½l. 1m 3.80s. (8 Ran).
(M A Ryan), Declan Gillespie

870 Old Rectory Fillies Maiden (3-y-o and up) £3,452 1¼m.................................(6:30)

MAMOURA (Ire) 3-8-10 R Hughes (13).........(9 to 4 fav) 1
CREATIVE CRAFT (USA) 3-8-10 M J Kinane (4).....(5 to 1) 2
282[7] WICKLOW WAY (Ire) 3-8-10 W J Supple (11).......(7 to 1) 3
790 SPECIAL OFFER (Ire) 3-8-10 J P Murtagh (19)..... (20 to 1) 4
VELMA (USA) 3-8-10 P Shanahan (2)..............(14 to 1) 5
311 GREEN LIFE 3-8-10 C Roche (5)..................(12 to 1) 6
CELESTIAL BLISS (USA) 3-8-10 W J O'Connor (7)..(5 to 1) 7
297[5] GLAS AGUS OR (Ire) 3-8-10 K J Manning (10)....(10 to 1) 8
ALIBAR'S PET (Ire) 3-8-4 (6*) J A Heffernan (14)....(10 to 1) 9
790 MOONLIGHT PARTNER (Ire) 3-8-10 N G McCullagh (9)
.................................(12 to 1) 10
ELA-MANA-SUE (Ire) 4-9-12 C F Swan (1)..........(50 to 1) 11
MY SPECIAL GUEST (Ire) 3-8-10 B Coogan (12)....(8 to 1) 12
552 CREHELP EXPRESS (Ire) 3-8-4 (6*) B Bowens (17) (20 to 1) 13
ALDENA (Ire) 3-8-10 D Manning (15).............(33 to 1) 14
806 SORRECA (Ire) 4-9-2 (10*) P J Smullen (16).......(50 to 1) 15
REALTHOGUE GIRL (Ire) 4-9-2 (10*) T Hagger (18) (50 to 1) 16
488 ARAN EXILE 3-8-10 S Craine (6)................(10 to 1) 17
Dist: 2½l, 5l, 2l, sht-hd. 2m 8.50s. (17 Ran).
(H H Aga Khan), John M Oxx

SALISBURY (firm)
Wednesday May 5th

Going Correction: MINUS 0.60 sec. per fur. (races 1,2,3), MINUS 0.35 (4,5,6)

871 Warminster Rating Related Maiden Stakes Class F (3-y-o and up) £2,856 5f.....(2:30)

721[4] BELLSABANGING 3-8-11 T Williams (2) *broke wl, al prmnt, rdn to ld ins fnl furlong*.
.................(9 to 4 fav op 5 to 2 tchd 11 to 4) 1
623[2] BREAKFAST BOOGIE 3-7-13 (7*) N Varley (11) *led, edgd lft wl o'r one furlong out, strted and hdd ins last*.
.................................(4 to 1 tchd 9 to 2) 2
615[7] SUPERLATIVEMAXIMUS (Ire) 5-9-7 W Newnes (10) *rcd keenly, trkd ldr till no hdwy ins fnl 2 fs*.
.....................(16 to 1 op 12 to 1 tchd 20 to 1) 3
716 AVRIL ETOILE 3-8-6 A McGlone (8) *chsd ldrs till wknd wl o'r one furlong out*..................(7 to 1 op 5 to 1) 4
563[2] FOLLY VISION (Ire) 3-8-6 R Hills (6) *beh, rdn and some hdwy o'r one furlong out, one pace*. (9 to 2 op 4 to 1) 5
582 SALVATORE GIULIANO 3-8-11 W Ryan (1) *rear till effrt 2 fs out, nvr nr to chal*..................(14 to 1 op 8 to 1) 6
PERFECT PASSION 3-8-6 G Bardwell (9) *mid-div, hrd rdn 2 fs out, sn btn*.....................(33 to 1 op 20 to 1) 7
4720a[5] THE ORDINARY GIRL (Ire) 3-8-6 N Adams (4) *chsd ldrs till wknd 2 fs out*.................(16 to 1 op 10 to 1) 8
713[3] LAID BACK BEN 3-8-11 Paul Eddery (7) *outpcd*.
.................................(33 to 1 op 25 to 1) 9
JEWEL THIEF 3-8-11 J Williams (3) *outpcd*.
.................................(16 to 1 op 12 to 1) 10
475 GLADEER (Ire) 4-8-11 (5*) N Gwilliams (5) *al struggling*.
.................................(33 to 1 op 20 to 1) 11
Dist: 2l, 7l, 1½l, 3l, ¾l, 1½l, 1l, ½l, ½l, 3l. 59.40s. b 0.40s (11 Ran).
SR: 45/32/19/-/-/-/ (Mrs Marion Wickham), D R Laing

872 John Smith's Maiden Stakes Class D (3-y-o) £4,240 6f.....................(3:00)

FOURFORFUN 8-7 (7*) A Whelan (1) *rcd on outsd, hdwy 2 fs out, ran on strly to ld wl ins last*. (33 to 1 op 20 to 1) 1
JAAZIM 9-0 A Clark (4) *mid-div, hdwy 2 fs out, fnshd wl*.
.....................(14 to 1 op 10 to 1 tchd 16 to 1) 2
538 AROOM 9-0 R Hills (12) *chsd ldr, ev ch ins fnl furlong, no extr cl hme*..............(5 to 1 op 7 to 2 tchd 6 to 1) 3
683[2] FRIENDLY BRAVE (USA) (bl) 9-0 W Newnes (19) *led till wl ins fnl furlong, kpt on*.
.................(8 to 1 tchd 10 to 1 and 12 to 1) 4
BALLET SHOES (Ire) 8-9 Paul Eddery (14) *prmnt, rdn o'r one furlong out, ran on wl ins last*...(6 to 1 op 4 to 1) 5
PETERSFORD GIRL (Ire) 8-9 R Perham (17) *chsd ldrs, one pace appr fnl furlong*.............. (7 to 1 op 8 to 1) 6
LOCH PATRICK 9-0 C Avery (15) *prmnt till rdn and wknd wl o'r one furlong out*............(50 to 1 op 33 to 1) 7
MARCHMAIN 9-0 R Street (10) *mid-div, ran on one pace fnl 2 fs*...........(16 to 1 op 10 to 1 tchd 20 to 1) 8
752[4] DANCING SPIRIT (Ire) 8-9 B Raymond (5) *al mid-div*.
.... (9 to 1 op 10 to 1 tchd 12 to 1) 9
OARE SPARROW 8-9 P Robinson (16) *rear till hdwy 2 fs out, one pace appr last*............(16 to 1 op 12 to 1) 10
BOLTROSE 8-9 (5*) A Garth (2) *outpcd*.
.................................(50 to 1 op 33 to 1) 11
691[6] AGHAR (Ire) 9-0 J Williams (11) *al mid-div*.
.................................(12 to 1 op 7 to 1) 12
583[5] CORN CIRCLE (Ire) 8-9 W Ryan (18) *slwly into strd, sn chasing ldrs, wknd wl o'r one furlong out*.
.................................(3 to 1 fav tchd 7 to 2) 13
BLOWING (USA) 9-0 M Perrett (13) *al beh*.
.................................(20 to 1 op 10 to 1) 14
582 MASTER BEVELED 9-0 N Adams (6) *al beh*.
.................................(50 to 1 op 33 to 1) 15
CHILI LADY 8-9 T Sprake (9) *nvr on terms*.
.................................(20 to 1 op 10 to 1) 16
606 BONITA BEE 8-9 A McGlone (7) *al beh*.
.................................(50 to 1 op 33 to 1) 17
624[6] GALLOP TO GLORY 8-11 (3*) J Weaver (3) *mid-div, lost tch hfwy*.............................. (50 to 1 op 33 to 1) 18
752[9] TIP ME UP 8-5[3] (7*) Michael Hunt (8) *al beh*.
.................................(20 to 1 op 14 to 1) 19
624 STOCKFORCE 9-0 B Rouse (20) *al beh*.
.................................(33 to 1 tchd 50 to 1) 20
Dist: ¾l, sht-hd, nk, sht-hd, 3l, 2l, 1½l, 1l, sht-hd, ½l. 1m 12.40s. b 0.10s (20 Ran).
SR: 30/27/26/25/19/7/4/-/-/ (Mrs R F Knipe), R Hannon

873 Druids Rating Related Maiden Stakes Class D (3-y-o) £3,172 1m..........(3:30)

582 TRIPPIANO 9-0 W Ryan (5) *trkd ldr, led o'r 2 fs out, hdd appr last, rallied and fought back to ld jst ins last.* ....(100 to 30 op 7 to 4 tchd 7 to 2) 1
BARBOUKH 8-9 J Williams (1) *settled rear, rapid hdwy 2 fs out to ld appr last, hdd jst ins last, one pace.* ....(11 to 10 on op 6 to 4) 2
538 BURNT IMP (USA) 9-0 B Raymond (7) *led till o'r 2 fs out, one pace aftr*..........(9 to 1 op 5 to 1 tchd 10 to 1) 3
SMART DAISY 8-9 Paul Eddery (3) *chsd ldrs till wknd 2 fs out*....................(11 to 2 op 5 to 1 tchd 6 to 1) 4
418 DRAGONMIST (Ire) 8-9 N Adams (2) *slwly away, al struggling*....................(33 to 1 op 14 to 1) 5
725 GOLD TASSEL 8-9 S Raymont (6) *al towards rear, lost tch 2 fs out*....................(12 to 1 op 6 to 1) 6
Dist: 1½l, 7l, 4l, 10l, 3l. 1m 41.00s. a 1.50s (6 Ran).
SR: 6/-/-/ (Mrs Mark Burrell), H R A Cecil

874 Courage Trophy Handicap Class C (0-95 4-y-o and up) £5,677 1¾m.......... (4:00)

661^{4} REQUESTED [70] 6-9-2 M Perrett (4) *trkd ldr, led o'r 2 fs out, sn clr, very easily*..........(5 to 1 tchd 6 to 1) 1
757^{3} SECRET SOCIETY [78] 6-9-10 Paul Eddery (2) *hld up, took clr order 6 fs out, rdn and styd on to take second close hme*....................(5 to 1 op 4 to 1) 2
618 HORIZON (Ire) [62] (bl) 5-8-8 R Hills (9) *led till o'r 2 fs out, one pace and lost second cl hme*...(16 to 1 op 14 to 1) 3
663^{4} BOOKCASE [72] 6-9-4 J Williams (3) *hld up, hdwy o'r 3 fs out, not rch ldrs*........(11 to 2 op 5 to 1 tchd 6 to 1) 4
661^{7} STAR QUEST [73] 6-9-5 W Ryan (5) *chsd ldrs till wknd o'r 2 fs out*..........(14 to 1 op 12 to 1) 5
739^{2} DOM WAC [66] 5-8-7 (5*) M Fenton (1) *hld up, hdwy 6 fs out, rdn 3 out, sn btn*..........(3 to 1 fav op 7 to 4) 6
559^{7} POINCIANA [66] 4-8-11 B Raymond (6) *beh, rdn 4 fs out, sn btn*..........(7 to 1 op 6 to 1 tchd 8 to 1) 7
TEMPLE KNIGHT [66] 4-8-11 W Newnes (7) *mid-div till wknd 3 fs out*..........(12 to 1 op 10 to 1) 8
495 HONEY DANCER [51] 9-7-10^{2} (3*) A Tucker (8) *al beh, lost tch hfwy, tld off*..........(33 to 1 tchd 50 to 1) 9
Dist: 8l, ½l, 2½l, 4l, 2½l, 3l, 3l, dist. 2m 58.39s. a 0.69s (9 Ran).
SR: 46/38/21/26/19/7/ (G S Beccle), R Akehurst

875 Fosters Handicap Class C (0-100 3-y-o) £4,836 1m 1f 209yds................(4:30)

459^{9} MAJOR YAASI (USA) [80] 8-7 B Raymond (14) *made all, rdn ins fnl furlong, hld on gmely*......(5 to 1 tchd 4 to 1) 1
644* BAY QUEEN [72] 7-12^{4} (5*) M Fenton (7) *nvr far away, rdn and hdwy to press wnr ins fnl furlong, no imprsn cl hme*....................(10 to 1 op 6 to 1) 2
PISTOL RIVER (Ire) [85] 8-12 A McGlone (13) *chsd ldrs, rdn appr fnl furlong, one pace.* ....(12 to 1 op 10 to 1 tchd 14 to 1) 3
295^{7} BRIGANTE DI CIELO [83] 8-10 S Raymont (5) *hld up, steady hdwy ins fnl 2 fs, nvr nrr.* ....(7 to 1 op 8 to 1 tchd 6 to 1) 4
494^{6} DYAB (USA) [84] 8-11 R Hills (8) *chsd wnr till wknd entering fnl furlong*..........(14 to 1 op 12 to 1) 5
684^{3} DUTOSKY [77] 8-4 N Adams (1) *hld up in tch, hdwy 3 fs out, one pace appr last.* (7 to 1 op 6 to 1 tchd 8 to 1) 6
558^{5} ECU DE FRANCE (Ire) [85] 8-12 W Ryan (10) *trkd ldrs till wknd wl o'r one furlong out.* ....(4 to 1 fav op 3 to 1 tchd 9 to 2) 7
LATEST FLAME (Ire) [79] 8-6 W Newnes (4) *hld up, effrt 2 fs out, wknd appr last*..........(25 to 1 op 20 to 1) 8
690^{4} ABERDEEN HEATHER [83] 8-10 J Williams (2) *hld up, some hdwy 3 fs out, wknd o'r one out.* (10 to 1 tchd 12 to 1) 9
584^{4} DEVILRY [83] 8-10 Paul Eddery (6) *al beh.* ....(12 to 1 tchd 14 to 1) 10
690^{6} REGAL AURA (Ire) [83] 8-10 A Clark (3) *al beh.* ....(14 to 1 op 10 to 1 tchd 16 to 1) 11
472 GOLDEN KLAIR [82] 8-6 (3*) J Weaver (9) *al beh.* ....(16 to 1 op 10 to 1 tchd 20 to 1) 12
459 TOP RANK [86] 8-13 B Rouse (11) *slwly away, al struggling*....................(20 to 1) 13
YAJEED (USA) [94] 9-0 (7*) J Tate (12) *hld up in tch, wknd 3 fs out*....................(25 to 1 op 16 to 1) 14
Dist: Hd, 2½l, ½l, hd, 2½l, 2½l, 2l, hd, 5l, 2½l. 2m 6.76s. a 2.76s (14 Ran).
SR: 30/21/29/26/26/14/17/7/10/ (Mohamed Suhail), J R Fanshawe

876 Wincanton Maiden Stakes Class D (3-y-o) £3,915 1½m...................... (5:00)

557^{2} MASTER CHARLIE 9-0 W Newnes (8) *al gng, hdwy 3 fs out, led o'r one out, pushed out.* ....(7 to 2 op 2 to 1 tchd 4 to 1 and 9 to 2) 1
318^{2} YAHMI (Ire) 9-0 R Hills (12) *trkd ldrs, led o'r 2 fs out, hdd over one out, one pace*........(5 to 2 fav tchd 7 to 2) 2
567^{2} ANCHOR STONE 9-0 W Ryan (9) *trkd ldr, dsptd ld 5 fs out to 3 out, rdn to keep 3rd fnl furlong.* ....(5 to 1 op 4 to 1 tchd 11 to 2) 3
755^{4} BONAR BRIDGE (USA) 9-0 S Raymont (13) *led till o'r 2 fs out, kpt on one pace*.............. (20 to 1 op 14 to 1) 4
679^{7} GUESTWICK 9-0 A McGlone (11) *hld up in rear, hdwy o'r 2 fs out, styd on, nvr nrr*.......... (25 to 1 op 20 to 1) 5
557^{7} HILL OF DREAMS 9-0 Paul Eddery (5) *rear till styd on fnl 3 fs, nvr nr to chal*..................(10 to 1 op 8 to 1) 6
441^{5} TROPICAL JUNGLE (USA) 9-0 P Robinson (2) *beh till hdwy 4 fs out, nvr nr to chal*........... (25 to 1 op 20 to 1) 7
672^{6} MOSHAAJIR (USA) 9-0 B Raymond (10) *al mid-div, no hdwy fnl 2 fs*..........(16 to 1 op 12 to 1 tchd 20 to 1) 8
515 RAVENSPUR (Ire) 9-0 W Woods (4) *rear till hdwy on outsd 4 fs out, rdn and edgd lft o'r 2 out, one pace.* ....(25 to 1 op 16 to 1 tchd 33 to 1) 9
679 MOST EQUAL 9-0 N Adams (7) *al beh, tld off fnl 2 fs.* ....(50 to 1 op 33 to 1) 10
672 RITZY 8-9 Dale Gibson (6) *al beh, tld off.* ....(50 to 1 op 33 to 1) 11
582^{7} SCARLET TUNIC (USA) 9-0 B Rouse (1) *beh, effrt on outsd hfwy, sn btn, tld off*..........(5 to 1 op 7 to 2) 12
662^{6} SING A RAINBOW (Ire) 8-9 J Williams (3) *al beh, tld off.* ....(8 to 1 op 4 to 1 tchd 10 to 1) 13
724^{2} BOXBOY 9-0 G Bardwell (14) *chsd ldrs early, tld off fnl 3 fs*....................(20 to 1 op 14 to 1) 14
Dist: 3l, 8l, nk, nk, nk, 1l, 2½l, 2l, 10l, 2l. 2m 32.35s. a 0.35s (14 Ran).
SR: 55/49/33/32/31/30/28/23/19/ (David R Watson), I A Balding

BRIGHTON (firm)
Thursday May 6th
Going Correction: MINUS 0.60 sec. per fur.

877 EBF St Ann's Wells Maiden Stakes Class D (2-y-o) £3,318 5f 59yds.............(2:00)

554^{8} BID FOR BLUE 9-0 L Piggott (3) *made all, stretched out wl fnl furlong.* ....(11 to 4 fav op 5 to 2 tchd 9 to 4 and 3 to 1) 1
730^{8} JUST GREENWICH 8-9 J Reid (8) *al second, drw clr wth wnr wl o'r one furlong out, rdn and no imprsn cl hme.* ....(33 to 1 op 20 to 1) 2
SUPER SYMPHONIC 9-0 P Robinson (9) *chsd ldrs, rdn hfwy, outpcd ins fnl 2 fs.* ....(14 to 1 op 5 to 1 tchd 16 to 1) 3
657^{7} HOLLINGTON SONG 8-9 W Newnes (2) *chsd ldrs, outpcd fnl 2 fs*....................(9 to 2 op 7 to 1) 4
399 SON OF HADEER 9-0 Paul Eddery (4) *slwly away, rdn to get in tch, nvr nr to chal*.......... (25 to 1 op 20 to 1) 5
673^{8} ABLEST SON 8-9 (5*) M Fenton (5) *slwly away, hdwy hfwy, nvr nr to chal*................(6 to 1 op 5 to 1) 6
554^{5} KENNET BOY 9-0 T Quinn (11) *slwly away, some hdwy 2 fs out, nvr on terms*.................(9 to 2 op 2 to 1) 7
HUMMINBIRDPRINCESS 8-9 N Adams (1) *slwly away, al beh*....................(25 to 1 op 12 to 1) 8
445^{3} SOUTHDOWN GIRL 8-9 R Cochrane (6) *speed to hfwy.* .... (9 to 2 tchd 5 to 1 and 4 to 1) 9
CLASSICAL DON (Ire) 9-0 S Whitworth (7) *al beh.* ....(12 to 1 op 10 to 1 tchd 14 to 1) 10
687 THE SPIVE 9-0 G Bardwell (10) *al beh, lost tch 2 fs out, tld off*.................... (33 to 1) 11
Dist: Nk, 8l, 1½l, ¾l, ¾l, 1½l, 4l, hd, 1½l, 8l. 1m 0.10s. (11 Ran).
SR: 37/31/4/-/-/-/ (David Thompson), R Hannon

878 Hollingbury Claiming Stakes Class F (3-y-o) £2,243 6f 209yds..............(2:30)

FANFOLD (Ire) 8-4 T Quinn (5) *hld up in tch, pld out wide 2 fs out, rdn and ran on wl to ld ins last.* ....(3 to 1 tchd 4 to 1) 1
4724a^{7} PATONG BEACH 8-4 R Hills (3) *nvr far away, wnt second 2 fs out, led appr last, rdn and hdd wl ins.* ....(10 to 1 op 6 to 1) 2
741^{3} CALISAR 8-7 T Sprake (7) *led, hdd appr fnl furlong, ran on one pace und pres*..............(10 to 1 op 6 to 1) 3
233^{3} PIRATES GOLD (Ire) 8-13 P Robinson (9) *mid-div, rdn and styd on wl ins fnl 2 fs, nvr nrr.* ....(7 to 2 op 3 to 1 tchd 5 to 1) 4
RACHELLY 8-4 R Perham (6) *towards rear, styd on one pace fnl 2 fs, nvr dngrs.* ....(20 to 1 op 12 to 1 tchd 25 to 1) 5
755^{5} ZILFI (USA) (bl) 9-7 C Rutter (8) *prmnt, wnt second hfwy, rdn and wknd 2 fs out*..............(7 to 1 op 4 to 1) 6
623^{6} KRAYYAN DAWN 8-3 S Dawson (13) *chsd ldr to hfwy, wknd o'r 2 fs out*..........(33 to 1 op 16 to 1) 7
MR JAZZ DANCER (Ire) 8-9 J Williams (1) *al beh.* ....(25 to 1 op 10 to 1 tchd 33 to 1) 8
KUTAN (Ire) 8-4 (3*) A Tucker (12) *slwly away, al beh.* ....(16 to 1 op 12 to 1) 9
724 AMBIVALENTATTITUDE 8-3 N Adams (4) *chsd ldrs till wknd o'r 2 fs out*..........(33 to 1 op 25 to 1) 10
720^{2} HY WILMA 8-4 W Carson (10) *nvr gng wl, al beh, eased, tld off*............(11 to 4 fav op 2 to 1 tchd 3 to 1) 11
INTERVIEW 8-2 T Williams (2) *al beh, tld off.* ....(33 to 1 op 10 to 1) 12
Dist: 1l, 2l, ½l, 7l, ¾l, 1½l, 1½l, nk, ¾l, 8l. 1m 20.40s. a 0.40s (12 Ran).
SR: 21/18/15/19/-/4/ (Miss Judy Smith), R Akehurst

879 Jim Taylor Memorial Handicap Class E (0-70 4-y-o and up) £3,054 1m 3f 196yds ....(3:00)

MUNDAY DEAN [53] (bl) 5-8-11 J Reid (2) *nvr far off pace, led o'r 2 fs out, rdn clr*...(8 to 1 op 6 to 1 tchd 9 to 1) 1

373[8] DR ZEVA [35] 7-7-0 (7*) Kim McDonnell (4) *hld up in rear, gd hdwy o'r 3 fs out, ran on to chase wnr ins fnl 2.*
.... (25 to 1 op 20 to 1) 2
ROCQUAINE BAY [40] 6-7-12 C Rutter (5) *in rear, rdn and hdwy 3 fs out, styd on, nvr nrr.*
.... (8 to 1 op 7 to 1 tchd 10 to 1) 3
495[6] FULL QUIVER [43] (v) 8-8-1 G Bardwell (6) *hld up, hdwy 3 fs out, sn rdn, kpt on one pace.*
.... (10 to 1 op 12 to 1 tchd 14 to 1) 4
500[6] SCENIC DANCER [49] (v) 5-8-7 W Woods (9) *in rear till hdwy 3 fs out, styd on ins fnl 2....* (10 to 1 op 12 to 1) 5
498[7] GILBERT'S GIRL [35] 6-7-7 E Johnson (3) *trkd ldrs, rdn o'r 2 fs out, one pace aftr.* (6 to 1 op 8 to 1 tchd 12 to 1) 6
628[4] ADMIRALS SECRET (USA) [65] 4-9-4 (5*) K Rutter (7) *hld up towards rear, rdn and hdwy o'r 2 fs out, nvr nr to chal.*
.... (7 to 2 fav tchd 3 to 1) 7
442[4] ATLANTIC WAY [48] 5-8-6 N Adams (8) *wtd wth, hdwy o'r 3 fs out, nvr rch ldrs.*.................. (13 to 2 op 7 to 2) 8
235[5] DEBACLE (USA) [70] 4-10-0 W Carson (1) *made most till hdd o'r 2 fs out, sn btn.* (11 to 2 op 5 to 1 tchd 7 to 1) 9
621[3] THIN RED LINE [38] (v) 9-7-8[3] (5*) B Doyle (12) *chsd ldrs till wknd o'r 2 fs out.*................ (14 to 1 op 10 to 1) 10
674 ALQAIRAWAAN [63] 4-9-7 B Rouse (11) *al beh.*
.... (8 to 1 op 5 to 1 tchd 9 to 1) 11
678 AQUADO [45] 4-8-3 N Carlisle (10) *dsptd ld till wknd wl o'r 2 fs out.*.............................. (20 to 1 op 14 to 1) 12
628 SIMPLY (Ire) [60] 4-8-11 (7*) T G McLaughlin (13) *in tch till wknd quickly o'r 3 fs out, tld off...*(33 to 1 op 25 to 1) 13
Dist: 2l, 5l, nk, hd, 1½l, ¾l, nk, 7l, 10l, 1l. 2m 29.40s. a 1.90s (13 Ran).
SR: 6/-/-/-/-/-/ (I Kerman), R J O'Sullivan

880 Vardean Maiden Stakes Class D (3-y-o) £3,552 1m 1f 209yds................. (3:30)

352[5] EXHIBIT AIR (Ire) 8-9 L Piggott (10) *trkd ldr, led o'r 2 fs out, ran on, cmftbly*......................... (9 to 2 tchd 5 to 1) 1
CAPTAIN'S GUEST (Ire) 9-0 R Hills (4) *rcd in tch, hdwy o'r 2 fs out, ran on to go second ins last.*
.... (13 to 2 op 6 to 1 tchd 7 to 1) 2
509[6] ALYDUNCAN (USA) 9-0 M Perrett (7) *al prmnt, wnt second o'r 2 fs out, wknd ins last.*..........(8 to 1 op 9 to 2) 3
761 TASSET (Can) 9-0 T Quinn (6) *beh and rdn alng, hdwy o'r 2 fs out, not rch ldrs*.................(16 to 1 op 7 to 1) 4
CANOPUS 9-0 J Reid (1) *chsd ldrs, rdn o'r 2 fs out, kpt on one pace.*................(7 to 2 op 2 to 1 tchd 4 to 1) 5
MONSIGNOR PAT (USA) 9-0 W Ryan (9) *chsd ldrs, one pace fnl 2 fs*.................(10 to 1 op 4 to 1 tchd 12 to 1) 6
443[4] CASHELL (v) 8-9 W Carson (2) *pld hrd, led till hdd o'r 2 fs out, sn btn.......* (100 to 30 fav op 7 to 2 tchd 5 to 1) 7
OLIVADI (Ire) 9-0 R Cochrane (13) *beh, some late hdwy, nvr dngrs.*...............(14 to 1 op 7 to 1 tchd 16 to 1) 8
4801a[2] ONE OFF THE RAIL (USA) 9-0 B Rouse (14) *mid-div, wknd o'r 2 fs out*............................ (20 to 1 op 14 to 1) 9
237[5] DOOGAREY 9-0 J Williams (3) *al beh.* (50 to 1 op 33 to 1) 10
JAFETICA 8-9 T Williams (5) *mid-div till wknd 3 fs out.*
.... (50 to 1 op 33 to 1) 11
PERSIANSKY (Ire) 9-0 N Carlisle (11) *al beh.*
.... (20 to 1 op 12 to 1) 12
SIDE BAR 9-0 P Robinson (8) *al beh.* (50 to 1 op 33 to 1) 13
RISKY ROSIE 8-9 S Dawson (12) *sn wl beh, tld off.*
.... (50 to 1 op 33 to 1) 14
Dist: 2½l, 2l, hd, 2l, nk, 2½l, 10l, 6l, 1½l, sht-hd. 1m 58.50s. a 0.30s (14 Ran).
SR: 32/32/28/27/23/22/12/-/-/ (Archie Hornall), R Hannon

881 Corn Exchange Handicap Class E (0-70 3-y-o and up) £3,080 6f 209yds...... (4:00)

91[5] DANCING SENSATION (USA) [34] 6-8-4[1] T Quinn (3) *al in tch, led 2 fs out, sn clr, eased nr finish.......*(9 to 2 jt-fav op 7 to 2 tchd 5 to 1) 1
636[8] TYRONE FLYER [49] 4-9-2 (3*) J Weaver (4) *led till hdd 2 fs out, one pace aftr.....* (12 to 1 op 7 to 1 tchd 14 to 1) 2
636* QUINTA ROYALE [57] 6-9-13 Paul Eddery (9) *trkd ldrs, rdn 2 fs out, ran on one pace.*
.... (11 to 2 op 4 to 1 tchd 6 to 1) 3
714 ANATROCCOLO [41] 6-8-11 J Reid (2) *chsd ldr till rdn o'r 2 fs out, one pace aftr.*..........(12 to 1 tchd 14 to 1) 4
605[4] AMETHYSTINE (USA) [58] 7-10-0 W Carson (5) *chsd ldrs, rdn 2 fs out, no hdwy.*.......................(9 to 2 jt-fav op 7 to 2 tchd 5 to 1) 5
FIVEOFIVE (Ire) [61] 3-9-5 W Newnes (11) *chsd ldrs, rdn and ev ch o'r 2 fs out, sn btn.*.....(12 to 1 op 10 to 1) 6
CHARMED KNAVE [53] 8-9-4 (5*) N Gwilliams (8) *hld up, short lived effrt o'r 2 fs out, nvr on terms.*
.... (7 to 1 op 14 to 1) 7
603 DUTY SERGEANT (Ire) [46] 4-9-2 J Williams (6) *nvr on terms.*............. (7 to 1 op 6 to 1 tchd 8 to 1) 8
4807a[8] OSGATHORPE [40] 6-8-10 N Adams (7) *al beh.*
.... (50 to 1 op 33 to 1) 9
677 ROCA MURADA (Ire) [58] 4-10-0 P Robinson (1) *nvr on terms.*...................... (14 to 1 op 6 to 1) 10
CHUMMY'S IDEA (Ire) [45] 3-8-3 R Hills (10) *al beh.*
.... (12 to 1 op 10 to 1) 11
HOLD FAST (Ire) [38] 5-8-8 T Williams (12) *al beh, tld off.*
..................................(33 to 1 tchd 50 to 1) 12
521 FLYING WIND [47] (bl) 4-9-3 B Rouse (13) *speed on outsd to hfwy, sn beh, tld off.*............(20 to 1 tchd 25 to 1) 13

Dist: 3l, nk, 3l, sht-hd, 2l, 1½l, 2l, ½l, 2l, 3l. 1m 19.60s. b 0.40s (13 Ran).
SR: 33/39/46/21/37/22/21/8/-/ (Chelgate Public Relations Ltd), R Akehurst

882 Coldean Maiden Handicap Class E (0-70 3-y-o and up) £3,183 5f 213yds...... (4:30)

4699a[4] SAKHAROV [41] 4-8-10 P Robinson (5) *hld up in tch, rdn 2 fs out, ran on strly ins last, led cl hme.*
.... (16 to 1 op 12 to 1 tchd 20 to 1) 1
501 CLEAN GATE [30] (bl) 4-7-13 E Johnson (3) *led, rdn entering fnl furlong, ct nr finish.*.......(16 to 1 op 10 to 1) 2
683[9] TEXAS COWGIRL (Ire) [54] 3-8-7 (5*) B Doyle (11) *al prmnt, ev ch 2 fs out, kpt on one pace.*
.... (9 to 1 op 8 to 1 tchd 12 to 1) 3
590[5] CLEAR LOOK [58] 3-9-2 T Quinn (7) *mid-div, rdn entering fnl furlong, ran on, nvr nrr.*
..........................(5 to 1 op 4 to 1 tchd 6 to 1) 4
1[5] KAFIOCA (Ire) [48] 3-8-6 A McGlone (2) *chsd ldr frm hfwy, rdn 2 fs out, wknd appr last.*
.... (16 to 1 op 12 to 1 tchd 20 to 1) 5
492[5] WELL BOUGHT (Ire) [39] 4-8-8 W Carson (8) *hld up in rear, swtchd rght and hdwy o'r 2 fs out, sn rdn and no imprsn, eased ins last.*
..........................(9 to 4 fav op 2 to 1 tchd 5 to 2) 6
330 CHEREN BOY [34] 4-8-3 N Adams (9) *towards rear, made some late hdwy*........................ (33 to 1 op 20 to 1) 7
4794a[4] MARWELL MITZI [49] 3-8-7 G Bardwell (1) *mid-div, no hdwy fnl 2 fs*..........................(16 to 1 op 14 to 1) 8
623[3] ROYAL INTERVAL [66] 3-9-10 T Sprake (6) *speed to hfwy.*
..................................(7 to 1 op 5 to 1) 9
837[5] CASTLE MAID [32] 6-8-1 N Carlisle (10) *al in rear.*
.... (4 to 1 op 9 to 2 tchd 11 to 2) 10
754[7] ANDY JACK [51] 4-9-6 W Newnes (12) *chsd ldr to hfwy, sn drpd out*......................... (25 to 1 op 20 to 1) 11
837 BLYTON STAR (Ire) [44] 5-8-13 T Williams (13) *chsd ldrs till wknd o'r 2 fs out*................(25 to 1 op 14 to 1) 12
600[5] LOON [49] (bl) 5-9-1 (3*) J Weaver (4) *slwly away, al beh.*
.... (12 to 1 op 7 to 1) 13
Dist: Nk, 2½l, sht-hd, 2l, ¾l, 2½l, nk, 1½l, 1½l, 5l. 1m 8.10s. b 0.30s (13 Ran).
SR: 30/18/21/24/6/5/-/-/4/ (J R Good), M A Jarvis

CARLISLE (good)
Thursday May 6th

Going Correction: MINUS 0.15 sec. per fur. (races 1,2,4,5), PLUS 0.10 (3,6)

883 Buttermere Claiming Stakes Class F (3-y-o and up) £2,758 5f 207yds............ (2:20)

710 OBSIDIAN GREY 6-8-3 (7*) S Sanders (7) *chsd ldrs, hdwy 2 fs out, rdn to ld appr fnl furlong, hld on gmely.*
.... (25 to 1 op 14 to 1) 1
GUV'NORS GIFT 3-7-11[2] (7*) S Mulvey (12) *mid-div, hdwy hfwy, rdn to chal entering fnl furlong, kpt on.*
..................................(9 to 1 op 5 to 1) 2
700[7] AYR RAIDER (v) 6-9-2 G Duffield (14) *chsd ldrs, effrt and hdwy 2 fs out, rdn to chal entering fnl furlong, no extr nr finish*.............. (9 to 1 op 8 to 1 tchd 10 to 1) 3
728* DEAD CALM (v) 3-8-5 M Birch (9) *beh, hdwy hfwy, effrt and not much room appr fnl furlong, kpt on one pace.*
.... (17 to 2 op 7 to 1 tchd 9 to 1) 4
728[6] CORONA GOLD 3-8-5 S Morris (3) *in tch, rdn and kpt on one pace fnl 2 fs*.....................(25 to 1 op 12 to 1) 5
765* DOKKHA OYSTON (Ire) 5-9-6 G Carter (11) *trkd ldrs, effrt 2 fs out, rdn and one pace appr fnl furlong.*
..................................(3 to 1 fav op 9 to 2) 6
716[4] MAJOR TRIUMPH (Ire) (bl) 3-8-8 N Day (15) *dwlt and beh, gd hdwy on inner hfwy, rdn wl o'r one furlong out and sn one pace*.......................................(10 to 1) 7
612[4] FORMAESTRE (Ire) 3-7-5 (7*) Claire Balding (17) *cl up, rdn o'r 2 fs out, grad wknd.*
.... (20 to 1 op 33 to 1 tchd 16 to 1) 8
532[3] BRIGHT GEM 3-7-12 J Fanning (1) *al mid-div.*
.... (16 to 1 op 14 to 1) 9
815[4] METAL BOYS 6-9-4 S Perks (10) *cl up, effrt and led briefly 2 fs out, sn hdd and wknd appr fnl furlong.*
..................................(8 to 1 op 6 to 1) 10
244 SUMMER EXPRESS 4-8-3 (7*) C Hawksley (16) *led, rdn and hdd 2 fs out, wkng and btn whn squeezed out appr fnl furlong*...................... (25 to 1 op 14 to 1) 11
610[9] RAVECINO 4-8-5 L Charnock (4) *chsd ldrs till rdn and wknd 2 fs out*........... (100 to 1 op 50 to 1) 12
815[7] BELATED 4-9-5 Dale Gibson (6) *al rear.*
.... (11 to 1 op 6 to 1) 13
728[7] ALBEIT 3-7-12 J Lowe (8) *sn outpcd and beh.*
.... (50 to 1 op 33 to 1) 14
720[3] SPENMAX (Ire) 3-7-7[1] (7*) P McCabe (5) *al rear, collapsed entering fnl furlong, dead.*
.... (14 to 1 op 10 to 1 tchd 16 to 1) f
275[3] STARDUST EXPRESS 3-8-9 Dean McKeown (13) *in tch till wknd 2 fs out, beh whn brougth dwn entering fnl furlong*......................... (14 to 1 op 10 to 1) bd
Dist: Sht-hd, ¾l, 2½l, 2l, ½l, hd, hd, 2l, nk, 1½l. 1m 15.80s. a 2.80s (16 Ran).
SR: 22/13/24/3/-/8/ (D J Allen), B A McMahon

884 Ennerdale Rating Related Maiden Stakes Class F (3-y-o) £2,623 5f 207yds..... (2:50)

611² KILLY'S FILLY 8-9 G Carter (7) *made all, rdn clr 2 fs out, jst hld on*.......... (3 to 1 op 9 to 2) 1
614⁷ MAGICATION 8-2 (7*) Claire Balding (5) *outpcd and beh, hdwy and rdn alng hfwy, styd on und pres ins fnl furlong*.......... (12 to 1 tchd 16 to 1) 2
534⁷ NOBLE MEASURE (Ire) (bl) 8-7 (7*) G Strange (2) *cl up, rdn alng hfwy, kpt on one pace fnl 2 fs*..........(33 to 1) 3
CANNY LAD 9-0 Dean McKeown (4) *chsd ldrs, rdn o'r 2 fs out, sn one pace*..... (3 to 1 op 2 to 1 tchd 100 to 30) 4
683⁴ MILBANK CHALLENGER (v) 9-0 M Birch (6) *cl up, rdn o'r 2 fs out, sn btn*.......... (11 to 8 fav op 5 to 4) 5
535⁵ BROOKLANDS EXPRESS 9-0 D Wilkinson (3) *chsd ldrs to hfwy, sn lost pl and beh*..........(16 to 1 op 10 to 1) 6
728⁹ BADENOCH BURNER 9-0 Kim Tinkler (1) *outpcd and beh frm hfwy*.......... (100 to 1 op 50 to 1) 7
Dist: Nk, 3½l, 5l, 6l, 3l, 6l. 1m 16.80s. a 3.80s (7 Ran).
SR: 1/-/-/-/ (Raymond Kilgour Holdings Ltd), J Berry

885 Bassenthwaite Handicap Class D (0-80 3-y-o and up) £3,915 7f 214yds...... (3:20)

4733a⁷ GOOD FOR THE ROSES [48] 7-8-4 G Carter (8) *chsd ldr, effrt 2 fs out, rdn to ld one furlong out, styd on wl*.......... (9 to 1 op 8 to 1 tchd 10 to 1) 1
425⁵ HABETA (USA) [58] 7-9-0 G Duffield (2) *mid-div, hdwy o'r 2 fs out, sn rdn, styd on ins last*.......... (100 to 30 fav op 3 to 1 tchd 7 to 2) 2
NEITHER NOR [63] 4-8-12 (7*) D McCabe (14) *hld up and beh, hdwy o'r 2 fs out, rdn and styd on wl fnl furlong*.......... (9 to 1 op 7 to 1 tchd 10 to 1) 3
AMERICAN HERO [65] 5-9-7 S Perks (4) *led, rdn 2 fs out, hdd one furlong out, wknd ins last*.......... (33 to 1 op 20 to 1) 4
VENTURE FOURTH [45] 4-8-1 J Fanning (9) *hld up and beh, steady hdwy fnl 2 fs, nrst finish*... (20 to 1 op 16 to 1) 5
703³ MARTINI EXECUTIVE [61] (bl) 5-9-0 (3*) S D Williams (6) *chsd ldrs, rdn o'r 2 fs out, sn one pace*.... (5 to 1 op 7 to 2) 6
632⁷ PERSONAL HAZARD [69] (v) 4-9-11 M Birch (7) *hld up and beh, hdwy fnl 2 fs, nvr dngrs*.......... (9 to 1 op 8 to 1 tchd 10 to 1) 7
710 KING'S GUEST (Ire) [64] 4-9-6 D Nicholls (3) *chsd ldrs, rdn 3 fs out, wknd wl o'r one furlong out*.......... (14 to 1 op 12 to 1) 8
651⁷ STRAW THATCH [58] 4-9-0 S Webster (1) *al rear*. (12 to 1) 9
BOLD MELODY [55] 4-8-11 Dale Gibson (10) *al rear*.......... (12 to 1 tchd 14 to 1) 10
SLY PROSPECT (USA) [47] 5-8-3 L Charnock (5) *in tch to hfwy, sn lost pl*.......... (33 to 1 op 16 to 1) 11
655⁷ ROUTING [55] 5-8-11 Dean McKeown (13) *slwly away, al beh*.......... (16 to 1 op 14 to 1) 12
710⁸ STOPROVERITATE [61] 4-9-3 N Connorton (12) *in tch, rdn 3 fs out and sn btn*...... (9 to 1 op 7 to 1 tchd 10 to 1) 13
HAND ON HEART (Ire) [61] 4-8-12 (5*) O Pears (11) *chsd ldrs till wknd quickly 3 fs out, sn beh*..........(20 to 1) 14
Dist: 2½l, nk, nk, 6l, ¾l, 2l, hd, sht-hd, nk, nk. 1m 42.40s. a 4.50s (14 Ran).
SR: 35/37/41/42/4/18/20/14/7/ (Trow Lane Farm), M McCormack

886 Wastwater Selling Stakes Class G (2-y-o) £2,448 5f.......... (3:50)

730⁷ HILL FARM KATIE 8-6 G Duffield (11) *al cl up, effrt 2 fs out, led one furlong out, ran on wl*.... (8 to 1 tchd 10 to 1) 1
564* PARKSIDE LADY (bl) 8-11 M Birch (8) *cl up, led hfwy, sn rdn, hdd and not quicken one furlong out*.......... (4 to 1 op 7 to 1) 2
730⁹ ROCKY TWO 8-4 (7*) S Sanders (3) *outpcd and beh till styd on wl fnl 2 fs, nrst finish*..... (12 to 1 op 10 to 1) 3
454⁵ PARADISE NEWS 8-6 N Day (10) *led to hfwy, cl up and ev ch appr fnl furlong, sn rdn and no extr ins last*.......... (9 to 4 fav op 6 to 4 tchd 5 to 2) 4
496⁶ MONKEY MONEY (Ire) 8-6 G Carter (9) *al chasing ldrs, rdn 2 fs out, kpt on one pace appr fnl furlong*.......... (10 to 1 op 8 to 1) 5
BROOKHEAD LADY 8-6 N Connorton (1) *chsd ldrs, hdwy on outer 2 fs out, sn rdn and one pace appr fnl furlong*.......... (25 to 1 op 20 to 1) 6
EASY FOR ME 8-11 J Fanning (5) *nvr rch ldrs*.......... (20 to 1 op 14 to 1) 7
804⁶ CHEEKY CHAPPY 8-11 D Nicholls (7) *pld hrd, trkd ldrs, effrt o'r one furlong out, sn rdn and wknd ins fnl furlong*.......... (10 to 1 op 8 to 1) 8
381⁸ CRY OF THE DOLPHIN 8-6 Dale Gibson (4) *cl up till rdn and wknd 2 fs out*..... (13 to 2 op 9 to 2 tchd 7 to 1) 9
490⁵ XAMDIVAD (Ire) 8-6 M Wood (12) *al rear*.......... (9 to 1 op 8 to 1) 10
708⁴ WILKS DREAM (Ire) 7-13 (7*) D McCabe (6) *chsd ldrs to hfwy, sn wknd*.......... (25 to 1 op 20 to 1) 11
Dist: 2½l, 2l, sht-hd, 1½l, 1½l, nk, ¾l, 1½l, 2½l, 3½l. 1m 4.10s. a 4.10s (11 Ran).
(Dennis Newton), P D Evans

887 Crummock Water Apprentice Handicap Class E (0-70 4-y-o and up) £3,080 5f (4:20)

800⁵ SOBERING THOUGHTS [36] 7-7-13 M Humphries (9) *cl up, effrt to ld one and a half fs out, kpt on*.......... (7 to 2 fav op 3 to 1) 1
655* STRIP CARTOON (Ire) [56] (bl) 5-9-0 (5*) G Strange (3) *cl up, effrt and ev ch entering fnl furlong, sn rdn and not quicken*.......... (6 to 1 op 5 to 1 tchd 13 to 2) 2
LOFT BOY [59] 10-9-1 (7*) K Sked (10) *mid-div, swtchd outsd and hdwy appr fnl furlong, sn rdn and styd on wl ins last*.......... (14 to 1 op 12 to 1) 3
568⁹ MURRAY'S MAZDA (Ire) [61] 4-9-10 S Giles (1) *chsd ldrs, effrt and hdwy appr fnl furlong, sn rdn and kpt on same pace*.......... (7 to 1 op 5 to 1) 4
610 KHALLOOF (Ire) [48] (bl) 4-8-6 (5*) C Teague (5) *beh till styd on wl appr fnl furlong, nrst finish*. (33 to 1 op 20 to 1) 5
700⁵ BRIGHT PARAGON (Ire) [46] 4-8-9 C Hawksley (11) *chsd ldrs, rdn appr fnl furlong, kpt on one pace*.......... (11 to 2 op 4 to 1) 6
721⁸ BARBEZIEUX [30] 6-7-7 D McCabe (2) *beh, hdwy 2 fs out, rdn and styd on fnl furlong*.......... (11 to 2 op 3 to 1) 7
655³ CRAIL HARBOUR [34] 7-7-11 G Forster (4) *al mid-div*.......... (6 to 1 tchd 7 to 1) 8
548⁹ KALAR [46] (bl) 4-8-6 (3*) Claire Balding (8) *cl up, led hfwy till hdd and wknd one and a half fs out*.......... (14 to 1 op 12 to 1) 9
MY ABBEY [62] 4-9-4 (7*) S Knott (6) *led to hfwy, sn lost pl and beh*.......... (14 to 1 op 12 to 1 tchd 16 to 1) 10
409⁶ GRUBBY [33] 4-7-10 A Garth (7) *al outpcd and beh*.......... (20 to 1 op 14 to 1) 11
Dist: 1½l, ½l, ½l, ½l, ¾l, hd, 2½l, 3l, 2l, 6l. 1m 2.40s. a 2.40s (11 Ran).
SR: 22/36/37/37/22/17/ (Mrs Lynn Campion), J L Eyre

888 Loweswater Handicap Class E (0-70 3-y-o) £3,002 1½m.......... (4:50)

608* THE WHERE WITHAL [54] 9-4 G Duffield (3) *chsd ldr, rdn o'r 2 fs out, hrd drvn and styd on to ld entering fnl furlong*......... (11 to 10 on op 5 to 4 on tchd Evens) 1
652³ CHALLENGER ROW (Ire) [43] 8-7 N Connorton (1) *led, rdn 2 fs out, faltered and hdd entering fnl furlong, kpt on*.......... (6 to 1 op 10 to 1) 2
717² BUGLET [55] 9-5 N Day (5) *trkd ldrs, effrt and rdn 3 fs out, sn one pace*.......... (11 to 4 op 2 to 1) 3
608⁴ WEAVER GEORGE (Ire) [43] 8-7 Dale Gibson (4) *prmnt, rdn o'r 3 fs out, sn one pace*.......... (16 to 1 op 14 to 1 tchd 20 to 1) 4
CARNEA [42] 8-6 L Charnock (7) *in tch, rdn o'r 3 fs out, sn wknd*.......... (16 to 1) 5
437⁷ KISS IN THE DARK [57] 9-7 Dean McKeown (2) *al rear*.......... (6 to 1 tchd 7 to 1) 6
72⁸ DORMSTON BOYO [35] 7-6 (7*) C Hawksley (6) *in tch, sddl slpd and wl beh fnl 4 fs*.......... (50 to 1 op 33 to 1) 7
Dist: 2l, 5l, 2½l, 8l, 3½l, 25l. 2m 38.30s. a 8.30s (7 Ran).
SR: 33/18/20/3/ (W E Sturt), Sir Mark Prescott

CHESTER (good to firm)
Thursday May 6th
Going Correction: MINUS 0.40 sec. per fur.

889 EBF Sceptre Maiden Fillies' Stakes Class D (2-y-o) £4,792 5f 16yds.......... (2:10)

544² STIMULANT 8-11 W R Swinburn (2) *made most, hdd briefly hfwy, quickened clr ins fnl furlong*.......... (8 to 1 op 5 to 1 tchd 9 to 1) 1
715² SINGULAR SENSATION 8-11 D Holland (5) *al hndy, drvn to draw level hfwy, kpt on same pace fnl furlong*.......... (6 to 1 op 5 to 1 tchd 13 to 2) 2
657² JADE PET 8-11 Pat Eddery (1) *wth ldr, led briefly hfwy, hrd drvn o'r one furlong out, sn outpcd*.......... (2 to 1 on tchd 15 to 8 on) 3
325² BELLA PARKES 8-11 J Carroll (3) *not act on course, chsd alng and outpcd till ran on fnl furlong, nrst finish*.......... (6 to 1 op 5 to 1 tchd 13 to 2) 4
Dist: 5l, ½l, 1½l. 1m 2.27s. a 1.97s (4 Ran).
SR: 18/ (Lord Derby), J W Watts

890 180th Year Of Dee Stakes Class A (Listed Race) (3-y-o) £24,790 1¼m 75yds....(2:40)

588² BENEFICIAL 8-10 M Hills (4) *settled gng wl, swtchd outsd to ld o'r one furlong out, easily*. (5 to 2 fav op 9 to 4) 1
588⁴ BLUES TRAVELLER (Ire) 8-13 D Holland (6) *trkd ldg pair, hrd drvn whn pace quickened o'r one furlong out, styd on*.......... (7 to 1 op 6 to 1) 2
578* NEWTON'S LAW (Ire) 9-1 Pat Eddery (1) *set str pace, steadied hfwy, hdd o'r one furlong out, no extr*.......... (7 to 2 op 3 to 1) 3
658² FRET (USA) 8-10 A Munro (3) *trkd ldg trio, feeling pace and rdn 2 fs out, not quicken*.......... (9 to 2 op 4 to 1 tchd 5 to 1) 4
672* PREMIER LEAGUE (Ire) 8-13 J Quinn (2) *wth ldr, hrd drvn appr strt, sn btn*..... (11 to 1 op 12 to 1 tchd 14 to 1) 5
DESERT SECRET (Ire) 9-3 W R Swinburn (5) *last and hld up, effrt hfwy, outpcd last 3 fs*...... (9 to 2 op 4 to 1) 6
Dist: 4l, hd, 1½l, 5l, 4l. 2m 7.98s. b 1.12s (6 Ran).
SR: 66/61/62/54/47/43/ (Exors Of The Late Sir Robin McAlpine), G Wragg

891 Grahams Machinery Sales Rated Class B (0-100 4-y-o and up) £7,508 5f 16yds (3:10)

654[3] STACK ROCK [92] 6-9-1 K Fallon (6) *trkd ldr, quickened to ld o'r one furlong out, kpt on wl.* ....(8 to 1 op 7 to 1 tchd 9 to 1) 1
555[4] PLAIN FACT [85] 8-8-8 D Holland (2) *trkd ldg 4, swtchd ins to chal entering fnl furlong, kpt on.* (8 to 1 op 6 to 1) 2
NEVER IN THE RED [84] (v) 5-8-7 J Carroll (4) *settled midfield, hrd drvn and swtchd outsd o'r one furlong out, fnshd wl.*..................(4 to 1 jt-fav tchd 9 to 2) 3
555[2] INHERENT MAGIC (Ire) [84] 4-8-7 M Roberts (3) *chsd ldg pair, effrt and hrd drvn o'r one furlong out, no extr.* ....(4 to 1 jt-fav tchd 7 to 2) 4
750[8] FINJAN [86] 6-8-9 A Munro (7) *chsd alng to improve frm off the pace last 2 fs, fnshd wl.*......(9 to 1 op 8 to 1) 5
627[4] EVER SO LONELY [84] 4-8-0 (7*) D Wright (1) *led for o'r 3 fs, fdd und pres ins last.* ....(20 to 1 tchd 25 to 1 and 16 to 1) 6
659 PETRACO (Ire) [84] 5-8-4 (3*) D Harrison (5) *nvr far away, hrd drvn 2 fs out, sn btn.*........................(14 to 1) 7
CRYSTAL JACK (Fr) [88] 5-8-11 B Raymond (8) *speed on outsd 3 fs.*..............................(5 to 1 op 7 to 1) 8
795 BIT OF A LARK [98] 5-9-7 Pat Eddery (9) *last and bustled alng hfwy, nvr able to chal.*.........(7 to 1 op 6 to 1) 9

Dist: ½l, 1½l, ½l, 3l, ¾l, 1½l, 3½l, 7l. 59.97s. b 0.33s (9 Ran).
SR: 68/59/52/50/40/35/29/19/1/ (Castle Racing), E J Alston

892 Ormonde EBF Stakes Class A (Group 3) (4-y-o and up) £30,981 1m 5f 89yds.....(3:40)

579[6] SHAMBO 6-9-2 M Roberts (2) *patiently rdn, improved appr strt, drifted lft o'r one furlong out, led ins last, ran on wl.*...................... (7 to 1 tchd 15 to 2) 1
617* ALLEGAN (USA) 4-8-11 Pat Eddery (4) *led, hdd and drvn alng ins fnl furlong, one pace.*.....(3 to 1 tchd 7 to 2) 2
774* ZINAAD 4-9-2 W R Swinburn (1) *trkd ldg pair, effrt and not much room entering strt, ev ch ins fnl furlong, one pace.*........ (6 to 5 on op 11 to 8 on tchd 6 to 4 on) 3
FURTHER FLIGHT 7-8-11 M Hills (3) *steadied strt, improved to chal appr strt, wkng whn hmpd o'r one furlong out, sn btn.*...............(11 to 2 op 6 to 1) 4
735[6] JUSTICE (Fr) 5-9-2 A Munro (5) *trkd ldr, struggling to hold pl aftr one m, btn 2 fs out.*......(33 to 1 tchd 50 to 1) 5

Dist: 1l, hd, 6l, 12l. 2m 50.45s. a 0.45s (5 Ran).
SR: 43/36/40/23/4/ (Mrs C E Brittain), C E Brittain

893 Wynn Handicap Class C (0-90 4-y-o and up) £7,356 7f 122yds................(4:10)

801[2] CEE-JAY-AY [60] 6-8-5 J Carroll (5) *missed break, weaved through appr fnl furlong, ran on wl to ld last strds.* ....(3 to 1 jt-fav op 9 to 2) 1
249[8] VELOCE (Ire) [55] 5-8-0 F Norton (3) *settled midfield, led ins fnl furlong, ct last strds.* ....(14 to 1 op 12 to 1 tchd 16 to 1) 2
458[3] SILKY SIREN [63] (bl) 4-8-8 Pat Eddery (1) *nvr far away, effrt on ins appr fnl furlong, kpt on.* ....(3 to 1 jt-fav op 5 to 2) 3
605[2] TYRIAN PURPLE (Ire) [64] 5-8-9 D Holland (6) *led till hdd and rdn ins fnl furlong, no extr.*.....(5 to 1 op 4 to 1) 4
592 BOURSIN (Ire) [72] 4-9-3 J Fortune (4) *trkd ldr, hrd drvn appr fnl furlong, no extr.* ....(11 to 1 op 10 to 1 tchd 12 to 1) 5
623[7] MUMMYS ROCKET [48] 4-7-0 (7*) D Wright (2) *struggling hfwy, styd on fnl furlong, nvr nrr.* (14 to 1 op 10 to 1) 6
333[8] DAM CERTAIN (Ire) [53] 4-7-9 (3*) D Harrison (7) *tucked away in midfield, ev ch and rdn 2 fs out, fdd.* ....(11 to 1 op 16 to 1) 7
605[8] BIG BLUE [79] 4-9-10 M Roberts (8) *missed break, hdwy hfwy, shaken up o'r one furlong out, nvr plcd to chal.* ....(9 to 1 op 8 to 1 tchd 10 to 1) 8
710 ROCK SONG (Ire) [52] 4-7-11 J Quinn (10) *chsd ldrs for o'r 5 fs.*...............................(33 to 1 op 25 to 1) 9
650[2] LOMBARD SHIPS [50] 6-7-9 A Mackay (9) *chsd ldg trio to hfwy, wknd quickly 2 fs out.*.......(8 to 1 op 10 to 1) 10

Dist: Hd, 1l, 1l, 2l, 2½l, 1½l, 1½l, 5l, 20l. 1m 32.00s. (10 Ran).
SR: 46/40/45/43/45/13/13/34/-/ (Richard Jinks), J Berry

894 Eaton Handicap Class D (0-80 3-y-o and up) £7,148 1½m 66yds..............(4:40)

845[2] KILLICK [41] 5-7-0 (7*) D Wright (1) *nvr far away, drvn alng to ld ins fnl furlong, kpt on wl.*..........(3 to 1 jt-fav op 5 to 2) 1
745[3] PHILGUN [60] 4-8-9 (3*) S Maloney (9) *al hndy, led o'r 3 fs out till ins last, one pace.*........... (9 to 1 op 8 to 1) 2
727[7] EIRE LEATH-SCEAL [44] 6-7-10 J Lowe (7) *led early, styd hndy, led o'r 4 fs out till over 3 out, kpt on same pace.* ....(7 to 1 op 8 to 1 tchd 9 to 1) 3
723[6] FANATICAL (USA) [46] 7-7-12 A Munro (2) *chsd ldg 4, drvn alng 2 fs out, sn outpcd.*........... (14 to 1 op 10 to 1) 4
727[8] ENFANT DU PARADIS (Ire) [41] 5-7-7 J Quinn (3) *made most till o'r 4 fs out, fdd entering strt.*... (10 to 1 op 8 to 1) 5
500[5] MAD MILITANT (Ire) [72] 4-9-10 W R Swinburn (4) *patiently rdn, drvn up to chal 2 fs out, no extr.*.........(3 to 1 jt-fav op 9 to 2) 6
678 DON'T FORGET MARIE (Ire) [62] 3-7-9[1] D Biggs (5) *chsd ldrs till wknd entering strt.* ....(10 to 1 op 8 to 1 tchd 11 to 1) 7
674 WASSL THIS THEN (Ire) [69] 4-9-7 R Price (6) *chsd ldrs, hrd drvn o'r 2 fs out, fdd...* (15 to 2 op 6 to 1 tchd 8 to 1) 8
ROSE GLEN [61] 7-8-13 A Mackay (8) *last and hld up, nvr trble ldrs.*.............................(8 to 1 op 7 to 1) 9

Dist: 2½l, 2l, 5l, ½l, 2½l, 2½l, 5l, ½l. 2m 36.44s. b 0.36s (9 Ran).
SR: 34/48/28/20/14/40/6/22/13/ (Esprit de Corps Racing), A Bailey

TIPPERARY (IRE) (good to firm) Thursday May 6th

895 Crescent Race (4-y-o and up) £2,762 1½m ....(5:30)

SLEET SKIER 6-9-10 M J Kinane (6)..............(7 to 2) 1
GARABAGH (Ire) 4-9-7 J P Murtagh (5)............(9 to 2) 2
553* RISZARD (USA) 4-9-5 C Roche (4)............ (5 to 2 fav) 3
GLYER (USA) 4-9-0 S Craine (9).................(12 to 1) 4
POLLYS GLOW (Ire) 4-8-10 (6*) J A Heffernan (11) (12 to 1) 5
308 WINNING HEART 6-8-11 R Hughes (7)...........(10 to 1) 6
EBONY AND IVORY (Ire) 4-9-7 W J Supple (10)... (12 to 1) 7
NEMURO (USA) 5-9-4 (6*) P Carberry (2).........(25 to 1) 8
MARCOVALDO (Ire) 4-8-9 P V Gilson (3).........(50 to 1) 9
272[8] LIFEWATCH VISION 6-9-7 P Shanahan (1)........(14 to 1) 10
553[2] DOWLAND (USA) 5-9-5 W J O'Connor (8).........(4 to 1) 11

Dist: 1l, 1l, 1l, 2½l. 2m 34.20s. (11 Ran).
(A J O'Reilly), D K Weld

896 Tipperary Auction Race (2-y-o) £2,762 5f ....(6:30)

FOLLOW THE BREEZE (Ire) 8-8 S Craine (8).......(7 to 1) 1
571[2] CATCH A DREAM (Ire) 8-0 (2*) R M Burke (4).......(5 to 2) 2
305[3] AVONDALE FOREST (Ire) 7-10 (6*) J J Behan (6) (7 to 4 fav) 3
786 EASTROP DANCER (Ire) 8-5 J F Egan (11)........(20 to 1) 4
ZOE BAIRD 8-0 (2*) D G O'Shea (2)...............(14 to 1) 5
305[5] BONNIE CRATHIE (Ire) 7-8 (8*) J J Mullins (9)...... (9 to 1) 6
ASTRADANE (Ire) 8-5 M J Kinane (1)..............(8 to 1) 7
571 MON PANACHE (Ire) 8-8 R Hughes (7)..............(14 to 1) 8
SHARE A DREAM (Ire) 8-2 D Manning (3).........(14 to 1) 9
I HAVE A DREAM (Ire) 8-8 G Curran (12)..........(12 to 1) 10
GAELIC HEATHER (Ire) 8-2 D V Smith (5).........(20 to 1) 11
FORTY QUID (Ire) 8-8 W J Supple (13).............(7 to 1) 12
820[7] ONTHEOTHEREND (Ire) 7-11 (8*) R T Fitzpatrick (10) ....(33 to 1) 13

Dist: Hd, 1l, 4l, sht-hd. 1m 0.00s. (13 Ran).
(T Harty), J H Johnson

897 Topaz Sprint Stakes (Listed Race) (3-y-o and up) £8,627 5f...................(7:00)

DAWNSIO (Ire) 3-8-7 R Hughes (4) *wl plcd, prog 2 fs out, quickened to ld well ins last.*.................. (10 to 1) 1
BRADAWN BREEVER (Ire) (bl) 4-9-6 W J Supple (3) *led till hdd and no extr wl ins fnl furlong.*.........(5 to 4 fav) 2
4684a* DASHING COLOURS (Ire) 4-9-8 J P Murtagh (5) *rear, styd on wl ins fnl furlong, not rch ldrs.*............(14 to 1) 3
572 SUMY (bl) 3-8-10 W J O'Connor (2) *wl plcd, rdn and no extr ins fnl furlong.*...............................(9 to 1) 4
551[3] MOUMAYAZ (USA) 3-8-10 C Roche (7) *rear, rdn and kpt on one pace fnl 2 fs.*..............................(9 to 1) 5
TROPICAL (bl) 3-9-0 M J Kinane (8) *wl plcd, rdn and wknd ins fnl furlong.*..................................(5 to 1) 6
EL ZORRO DORADO (Ire) 3-8-10 S Craine (1) *trkd ldr, rdn and lost pl one furlong out, wknd quickly.*......(4 to 1) 7
ORTHORHOMBUS 4-9-6 Joanna Morgan (6) *al rear.* ....(25 to 1) 8

Dist: 1l, ¾l, hd, hd. 57.60s. (8 Ran).
(Lady Clague), John M Oxx

898 Laburnum Handicap (0-90 3-y-o) £2,762 1m 1f.................................(7:30)

551[5] SIR SLAVES [-] (bl) 8-10 M J Kinane (6)............(6 to 1) 1
640* WHEATSHEAF LADY (Ire) [-] 8-13 (4ex) J P Murtagh (3) ....(7 to 1) 2
311 PHASE IN [-] 7-6 (2*) D G O'Shea (4)..............(5 to 1) 3
666[6] GENERAL CHAOS (Ire) [-] 8-10 P V Gilson (8)...... (6 to 1) 4
666[2] KURDISTAN (Ire) [-] 9-1 W J O'Connor (1)...... (5 to 4 fav) 5
LA CENERENTOLA (Ire) [-] 8-1 W J Supple (2).... (10 to 1) 6
668[4] TIGHT FIST (Ire) [-] 8-0 (6*) J J Behan (5)...........(8 to 1) 7

Dist: 2l, 1½l, hd, hd. 1m 52.50s. (7 Ran).
(Andrea Schiavi), D K Weld

BEVERLEY (good to firm) Friday May 7th

Going Correction: NIL

899 Houghton Maiden Stakes Class D (3-y-o) £3,720 5f......................... (2:20)

JADE CITY 9-0 K Fallon (10) *beh, gd hdwy 2 out, ran on wl to ld fnl furlong.*...................(20 to 1 op 16 to 1) 1

HUMBER'S SUPREME (Ire) (bl) 8-6 (3*) D Harrison (12) *made most till hdd and no extr ins fnl furlong.* .... (25 to 1 op 20 to 1 tchd 50 to 1) 2

803^{8} LIDA'S DELIGHT (Ire) 9-0 T Lucas (8) *cl up, kpt on fnl 2 fs.* .... (14 to 1) 3

57^{5} FRIENDLY SMILE 8-9 G Carter (9) *al chasing ldrs, no extr fnl 2 fs.* .... (16 to 1 op 12 to 1) 4

641^{3} EXPORT MONDIAL 9-0 M Tebbutt (15) *wth ldrs till grad wknd 2 out.* .... (9 to 2 op 5 to 1 tchd 4 to 1) 5

MOLLY BRAZEN 8-9 G Hind (13) *dwlt, some hdwy hfwy, not rch ldrs.* .... (12 to 1 op 8 to 1) 6

CUMBRIAN CALYPSO 8-11 (3*) S Maloney (11) *dwlt, beh till some late hdwy, nvr dngrs.* .. (14 to 1 tchd 12 to 1) 7

538^{9} SCUSI 9-0 W Ryan (4) *slightly hmpd strt, sn pushed alng, nvr dngrs.* .... (11 to 10 on op Evens tchd 6 to 5) 8

563^{5} SCORED AGAIN 9-0 A Culhane (2) *prmnt till wknd 2 out.* .... (10 to 1 op 8 to 1 tchd 12 to 1) 9

COLFAX CLASSIC 8-9 N Carlisle (7) *al beh.* .... (25 to 1 op 16 to 1) 10

563^{6} ANDRULA MOU 8-9 L Charnock (14) *in tch to hfwy.* .... (16 to 1 op 14 to 1) 11

491^{4} MUSICAL TIMES 8-9 F Norton (6) *sn beh.* .... (25 to 1 op 16 to 1) 12

614^{6} FINAL OAK 8-2 (7*) S Sanders (1) *in tch to hfwy.* (50 to 1) 13

JESSICA SUE 8-9 S Webster (5) *slightly hmpd strt, al beh.* .... (33 to 1 op 20 to 1) 14

Dist: 1l, 1½l, nk, 1½l, ½l, sht-hd, ¾l, ½l, 2l, ¾l. 1m 4.80s. a 3.10s (14 Ran).

SR: 38/29/28/22/21/14/18/15/13/ (Norman Jackson), J G FitzGerald

900 Lund Claiming Stakes Class F (2-y-o) £2,243 5f. .... (2:50)

SURPRISE BREEZE 7-13 N Carlisle (11) *prmnt, rdn to ld ins fnl furlong, ran on wl.* .... (10 to 1 tchd 8 to 1 and 7 to 1) 1

564^{2} PALACEGATE JO (Ire) 8-4 G Carter (10) *led till edgd lft and hdd ins fnl furlong, no extr.* .... (7 to 4 on op 6 to 4 on tchd 11 to 8 on) 2

BESCABY GIRL 8-3 K Fallon (13) *in tch, hdwy hfwy, chalg whn hmpd ins fnl furlong, not reco'r.* .... (8 to 1 tchd 9 to 1 and 10 to 1) 3

LUNAR RHAPSODY 8-0 L Charnock (7) *in tch, styd on und pres fnl 2 fs, nvr dngrs.* .... (16 to 1 op 12 to 1) 4

544^{8} NOSMO KING (Ire) 8-8 W Ryan (9) *cl up till grad wknd 2 out.* .... (14 to 1 op 10 to 1) 5

BUNNY RUN 8-1 (3*) S Maloney (8) *chsd ldrs till wknd 2 out.* .... (10 to 1 op 6 to 1) 6

804 UNKNOWN STAR 8-10 A Proud (3) *prmnt till wknd 2 out.* .... (33 to 1 op 20 to 1) 7

299^{7} RUSTUS 7-7^{1} (7*) C Hawksley (1) *chsd ldrs to hfwy.* .... (20 to 1 op 14 to 1) 8

CLASSIC MISS (Ire) 8-4 S Webster (5) *prmnt till wknd 2 out.* .... (50 to 1 op 25 to 1) 9

381^{6} YOUNG MEDIC (v) 8-5 F Norton (12) *al beh.* .... (14 to 1 op 16 to 1 tchd 25 to 1) 10

673 GRANDEE (bl) 7-12 (7*) S Sanders (6) *prmnt to hfwy.* .... (50 to 1 op 33 to 1) 11

564^{7} LASTOTHEBRADFIELDS 8-1^{7} (7*) C Munday (4) *al beh.* .... (25 to 1 op 20 to 1) 12

NINE PIPES (Ire) 8-7 B Raymond (2) *dwlt, al beh, tld off.* .... (33 to 1 op 20 to 1) 13

Dist: 2l, 1½l, 3½l, 3½l, 1½l, 5l, nk, 3½l, 2l, hd. 1m 4.80s. a 3.10s (13 Ran).

SR: 23/20/13/-/-/-/ (D R Brotherton), R M Whitaker

901 Harcros Timber & Building Supplies Stayers Championship Series Handicap Qualifier Class E (0-70 4-y-o and up) £3,340 2m 35yds. .... (3:20)

382^{2} KING WILLIAM [34] 8-8-3 Alex Greaves (3) *hld up, smooth hdwy 6 out, led o'r 2 out, styd on wl, easily.* .... (9 to 2 fav tchd 5 to 1) 1

682^{6} CHANTRY BARTLE [41] 7-8-10 S Webster (11) *al cl up, chlgd o'r 2 out, kpt on, no ch wth wnr.* .... (11 to 2 op 9 to 2) 2

702^{4} LAFKADIO [32] (bl) 6-8-1 G Carter (9) *in tch, hdwy 6 out, chlgd o'r 2 out, kpt on.* (9 to 1 op 8 to 1 tchd 11 to 1) 3

331^{5} PINISI [33] 8-8-2 N Carlisle (5) *hld up, hdwy hfwy, effrt 3 out, kpt on same pace.* .... (10 to 1 tchd 12 to 1) 4

702^{3} ENKINDLE [24] 6-7-2 (5*) Darren Moffatt (1) *in tch, styd on fnl 3 fs, not trble ldrs.* .... (9 to 1 op 6 to 1) 5

SAFARI PARK [31] 4-7-11^{3} (3*) D Harrison (6) *chsd ldrs, one pace frm 3 out.* .... (25 to 1) 6

REXY BOY [26] (v) 6-7-9^{1} L Charnock (13) *chsd ldrs till wknd 5 out.* .... (14 to 1) 7

18^{7} SIR PAGEANT [58] (bl) 4-9-7 (3*) S D Williams (2) *trkd ldrs, led 7 out, hdd o'r 2 out, wknd quickly.* .... (14 to 1 op 12 to 1) 8

KIRKMAN'S KAMP [36] (v) 8-8-5^{1} B Raymond (8) *led till hdd 7 out, sn wknd.* .... (14 to 1 op 10 to 1) 9

IZITALLWORTHIT [37] 4-8-3 G Hind (4) *mid-div, hdwy and ev ch 3 out, sn rdn and wknd quickly.* .... (20 to 1) 10

495^{5} NOTABLE EXCEPTION [51] 4-9-3 W Ryan (10) *beh most of way.* .... (5 to 1 op 4 to 1) 11

356^{3} DESERT MIST [50] (bl) 4-9-2 K Fallon (12) *al beh, tld off.* .... (6 to 1) 12

709^{9} VALATCH [41] 5-8-3 (7*) G Forster (7) *prmnt till wknd 5 out, tld off.* .... (16 to 1) 13

Dist: 5l, ½l, 4l, ½l, 5l, 20l, nk, 7l, 2½l, nk. 3m 37.30s. a 8.30s (13 Ran).

SR: 6/8/-/-/-/-/ (Group 1 Racing (1991) Ltd), J L Spearing

902 Humberside Apprentice Handicap Class F (0-70 4-y-o and up) £2,691 1m 100yds (3:50)

676^{5} SWEET MIGNONETTE [62] 5-9-11 F Norton (1) *in tch, hdwy 3 out, led jst ins fnl furlong, styd on wl.* .... (11 to 8 fav op 6 to 4 tchd 5 to 4) 1

681 DOUBLE SHERRY [35] 4-7-7 (5*) M Baird (8) *al chasing ldrs, kpt on wl ins fnl furlong.* .... (20 to 1) 2

676^{7} BALLYRANTER [46] 4-8-4 (5*) C Hawksley (4) *wth ldr, ev ch one out, no extr ins fnl furlong.* .... (5 to 1 op 4 to 1 tchd 11 to 2) 3

592^{7} SHANNON EXPRESS [47] (v) 6-8-5 (5*) Claire Balding (7) *made most till hdd and wknd jst ins fnl furlong.* .... (7 to 1 op 6 to 1 tchd 8 to 1) 4

565^{9} SANDMOOR DENIM [58] 6-9-2 (5*) G Strange (3) *hld up, hdwy 3 out, rdn o'r one out, no imprsn.* .... (9 to 2 tchd 5 to 1) 5

565^{8} JOKIST [52] 10-8-8 (7*) S Jones (6) *beh, effrt whn not clr run 2 out, one pace.* ..... (8 to 1 op 7 to 1 tchd 9 to 1) 6

565 PATIENCE PLEASE [56] 4-9-5 S Maloney (5) *prmnt till wknd 2 out.* .... (7 to 1 op 6 to 1) 7

396^{9} CHARIOTEER [40] 4-7-10 (7*) C Adamson (2) *tld off frm hfwy.* .... (20 to 1) 8

Dist: ½l, 1l, 3l, hd, 1½l, 3l, dist. 1m 48.90s. a 6.10s (8 Ran).

SR: 20/-/-/-/1/ (Ron Whitehead), Mrs M Reveley

903 Everingham Median Auction Maiden Stakes Class D (3-y-o) £3,947 1m 1f 207yds .... (4:20)

VISTEC EXPRESS (Ire) 9-0 W Ryan (6) *made all, styd on strly fnl 2 fs.* .... (4 to 1 op 3 to 1) 1

BEST APPEARANCE (Ire) 9-0 K Fallon (2) *in tch, hdwy 3 out, styd on wl fnl furlong.* .... (14 to 1 op 10 to 1) 2

679^{3} FORMATO UNI (Ire) 9-0 G Carter (3) *trkd ldr gng wl, effrt o'r 2 out, sn rdn and one pace.* .... (15 to 8 on op 6 to 4 on tchd 11 to 8 on) 3

642 SOCIAL VISION (Ire) 9-0 L Charnock (5) *chsd ldrs till outpcd 4 out.* .... (100 to 1 op 50 to 1) 4

642 CLAIRIFICATION (Ire) 8-9 N Carlisle (4) *in tch till lost pl 5 out.* .... (50 to 1 op 25 to 1) 5

MOW WAAL (USA) 8-9 B Raymond (1) *chsd ldrs till wknd o'r 2 out.* .... (6 to 1 op 7 to 2) 6

Dist: 5l, nk, 12l, nk, hd. 2m 7.50s. a 6.10s (6 Ran).

SR: 39/29/28/4/-/-/ (A L R Morton), H R A Cecil

904 Settrington Handicap Class E (0-70 3-y-o and up) £3,157 1m 3f 216yds. .... (4:50)

745* SHAMSHOM AL ARAB (Ire) [40] 5-7-12 (5*,6ex) Darren Moffatt (6) *chsd ldrs, led 3 out, rdn and styd on wl.* .... (9 to 4 fav op 7 to 4) 1

618 TROJAN LANCER [43] 7-8-6 W Ryan (3) *beh till styd on wl fnl 2 fs, nrst finish.* ..... (4 to 1 op 7 to 2 tchd 9 to 2) 2

745^{5} WEST WITH THE WIND [48] 6-8-11 S Webster (1) *beh, hdwy o'r 3 out, styd on fnl 2 fs.* .... (14 to 1 op 12 to 1) 3

645^{6} VASILIEV [62] (bl) 5-9-11 G Carter (2) *cl up, chlgd 3 out, kpt on same pace.* .... (10 to 1 tchd 12 to 1) 4

382^{4} LUKS AKURA [36] (v) 5-7-6 (7*) M Baird (10) *cl up, led aftr 4 fs till hdd 3 out, grad wknd.* .... (6 to 1 op 11 to 2) 5

ILLOGICAL [35] (v) 6-7-12 L Charnock (9) *beh, hdwy 4 out, wknd o'r 2 out.* .... (16 to 1 tchd 20 to 1) 6

STATIA (Ire) [33] 5-7-10^{3} Kim Tinkler (8) *prmnt early, in tch till wknd o'r 3 out.* .... (25 to 1) 7

530 ALICANTE [31] (bl) 6-7-8^{1} N Carlisle (7) *chsd ldrs till wknd o'r 3 out.* .... (33 to 1) 8

366^{3} DUGGAN [45] 6-8-8 B Raymond (5) *beh most of way, virtually pld up fnl furlong, tld off.* (5 to 2 op 7 to 2) 9

LINPAC EXPRESS [44] (v) 4-8-0 (7*) C Hawksley (4) *led 4 fs, cl up till wknd quickly o'r 3 out, tld off.* ..... (20 to 1) 10

Dist: 3l, nk, nk, 6l, 10l, 8l, 1½l, 25l, ¾l. 2m 37.20s. a 6.20s (10 Ran).

SR: 27/24/28/41/3/-/ (Miss Maha Kalaji), S G Norton

CARLISLE (good)
Friday May 7th

Going Correction: MINUS 0.10 sec. per fur. (races 1,2,3,6), MINUS 0.20 (4,5)

905 Irthing Rating Related Maiden Stakes Class F (3-y-o) £2,422 1½m. .... (2:40)

763^{6} PRIME PAINTER 9-0 D Nicholls (2) *made all, quickened 2 and a half fs out, rdn and ran on wl fnl furlong.* .... (7 to 2 op 9 to 2) 1

652^{2} DOC SPOT 9-0 J Fortune (3) *trkd ldrs, hdwy 4 fs out, chsd wnr 2 out, sn rdn and kpt on.* .... (2 to 1 fav op 5 to 2) 2

SASSAMOUSE 8-9 W Woods (5) *hld up, hdwy o'r 3 fs out, sn rdn and one pace.* .... (9 to 2 op 3 to 1) 3

653^{3} ARC BRIGHT (Ire) 9-0 K Darley (6) *trkd ldrs, effrt 3 fs out, rdn 2 out and sn wknd.* .... (5 to 2 op 2 to 1) 4

422 MY SISTER LUCY 8-9 S Whitworth (4) *hld up, effrt and rdn 4 fs out, sn wknd*..........(33 to 1) 5
LADY ADARE (Ire) 8-9 M Birch (1) *trkd ldr, rdn alng 4 fs out, sn lost pl*..........(25 to 1) 6
Dist: 3½l, 6l, 4l, 20l, 2½l. 2m 37.40s. a 7.40s (6 Ran).
SR: 14/7/-/ (Mrs Sue Fletcher), R F Fisher

906 Derwent Claiming Stakes Class F (3-y-o and up) £2,780 6f 206yds..........(3:10)

650* CLAUDIA MISS 6-8-13 Dean McKeown (1) *chsd ldrs, hdwy 2 fs out, rdn and styd on ins last to ld on line.*..........(9 to 2 op 5 to 1 tchd 6 to 1) 1
650[6] SHALABIA 4-8-6 (5*) O Pears (5) *chsd ldrs, hdwy 3 fs out, led appr last, sn rdn, ct on line*....(14 to 1 op 12 to 1) 2
545[4] SAVAHRA SOUND 8-9-10 D Nicholls (12) *chsd ldrs, hmpd 3 fs out, effrt and hdwy to chal appr fnl furlong, sn rdn and kpt on*..........(8 to 1 op 10 to 1) 3
HOMILE 5-8-10 M Birch (6) *mid-div, hdwy 3 fs out, styd on ins last*..........(12 to 1 op 10 to 1) 4
754 JUST A STEP 7-9-2 W Newnes (7) *chsd ldr, rdn 2 fs out, sn one pace*..........(3 to 1 fav op 7 to 4) 5
885 SLY PROSPECT (USA) 5-8-9 (5*) A Garth (14) *hld up, hdwy o'r 2 fs out, sn rdn, one pace*..........(33 to 1) 6
828[6] RESPECTABLE JONES 7-9-6 S Perks (10) *nvr rch ldrs.*..........(14 to 1 tchd 16 to 1) 7
429[5] PINE RIDGE LAD (Ire) (bl) 3-8-2 J Lowe (9) *led and sn clr, rdn 2 fs out, hdd and wknd appr last.*..........(6 to 1 op 4 to 1) 8
700 TWILIGHT FALLS 8-8-12 N Connorton (2) *al mid-div.*..........(12 to 1 tchd 14 to 1) 9
741[4] ALWAYS RISKY 3-8-2[1] G Duffield (8) *mid-div, hdwy outer 3 fs out, rdn and wknd 2 out*..........(7 to 1 tchd 8 to 1) 10
765[4] BAFFIE 4-9-5 J Fortune (15) *slwly into strd, al rear.*..........(33 to 1) 11
679 GAMEFULL GOLD 4-8-9 P Robinson (11) *nvr a factor.*..........(100 to 1) 12
646 MOST SIOUXTABLE 3-8-7 J Fanning (13) *nvr rchd ldrs.*..........(12 to 1) 13
KABELIA 5-8-7 J Carroll (4) *al rear*..........(100 to 1) 14
PERSIAN LION 4-9-0 K Darley (3) *al beh, tld off fnl 3 fs.*..........(100 to 1) 15
Dist: Hd, 1l, 2l, nk, 2l, 1½l, 1l, 2½l, 1½l, ½l. 1m 28.60s. a 3.20s (15 Ran).
SR: 40/37/47/27/32/24/25/4/6/ (G Whorton), W W Haigh

907 Eamont Handicap Class E (0-70 3-y-o) £3,209 6f 206yds..........(3:40)

828* WHITE CREEK (Ire) [50] (v) 8-5 (5ex) J Carroll (8) *chsd ldrs, rdn o'r 2 fs out, styd on to ld ins last.*..........(11 to 10 fav op 5 to 4 tchd 6 to 4) 1
685[4] PANTHER (Ire) [66] 9-7 K Darley (2) *cl up, hdwy to ld o'r 2 fs out, rdn appr fnl furlong, hdd and no extr ins last.*..........(12 to 1 op 10 to 1) 2
GWEEK (Ire) [53] 8-8 P Robinson (10) *al prmnt, effrt and ev ch appr fnl furlong, sn rdn and kpt on one pace.*..........(11 to 2 op 6 to 1 tchd 9 to 2) 3
568[7] LARN FORT [50] 8-5 J Fanning (3) *chsd ldr, effrt and ev ch 2 fs out, sn rdn and one pace appr last.*..........(14 to 1 op 12 to 1) 4
504* QUEEN OF THE QUORN [62] 9-3 W Newnes (1) *led, rdn and hdd o'r 2 fs out, grad wknd*..........(7 to 1 op 6 to 1) 5
304 BOLD LINE [50] 8-5 Dale Gibson (12) *nvr rchd ldrs.*..........(33 to 1 op 25 to 1) 6
ADMISSION (Ire) [50] 8-5 N Connorton (11) *mid-div, effrt and hdwy on inner 2 fs out, rdn and wknd appr last.*..........(33 to 1 op 25 to 1) 7
710[2] CERTAIN WAY (Ire) [60] 9-1 M Birch (6) *in tch, hdwy on outer 3 fs out, sn rdn and wknd 2 out.*..........(11 to 2 op 6 to 1 tchd 7 to 1) 8
609[6] FREDDIE JACK [52] 8-7 R Lappin (5) *slwly away, al rear.*..........(33 to 1 op 25 to 1) 9
ORIENTAL PRINCESS [50] 8-0 (5*) A Garth (4) *slwly into strd, al rear*..........(33 to 1 op 25 to 1) 10
FORMIDABLE LIZ [47] 8-2[1] G Duffield (9) *in tch to hfwy, sn lost pl*..........(14 to 1 op 12 to 1 tchd 20 to 1) 11
Dist: 1½l, ¾l, ½l, 5l, 1l, ¾l, 8l, 3½l, nk, sht-hd. 1m 29.70s. a 4.30s (11 Ran).
SR: 16/27/12/7/4/-/ (J K Brown), J Berry

908 Caldew Maiden Stakes Class D (2-y-o) £3,435 5f..........(4:10)

WIXI (Ire) 8-9 P Robinson (5) *hld up, hdwy 2 fs out, rdn and styd on wl ins last to ld nr finish.*..........(6 to 1 op 4 to 1) 1
698[2] PERSIAN HERITAGE 9-0 G Duffield (4) *hdwy 2 fs out, rdn appr fnl furlong, styd on to ld ins last, hdd and no extr nr finish*..........(9 to 4 fav op 7 to 4 tchd 5 to 2) 2
RAFFERTY'S RULES (Ire) 9-0 Raymond Berry (1) *cl up, hdwy to ld one and a half fs out, hdd and no extr ins fnl furlong*..........(8 to 1 op 7 to 1 tchd 10 to 1) 3
GOLDEN STAR (Ire) 9-0 J Fanning (6) *in tch, rdn alng o'r 2 fs out, kpt on ins last*..........(7 to 1 op 5 to 1) 4
CALL TO MIND (Ire) 9-0 M Birch (11) *slwly away, hdwy fnl 2 fs, nrst finish*..........(14 to 1 op 10 to 1) 5
698[7] BLASTER BATES (USA) 9-0 D Nicholls (8) *cl up, led hfwy till rdn and hdd one and a half fs out, sn wknd.*..........(7 to 1 op 10 to 1 tchd 12 to 1) 6
PETE AFRIQUE (Ire) 9-0 K Darley (9) *beh till some hdwy fnl furlong*..........(20 to 1 op 7 to 1) 7
WESTCOAST 9-0 Dean McKeown (10) *nvr rchd ldrs.*..........(25 to 1 op 20 to 1) 8
364[5] RICH HARMONY 9-0 W Newnes (3) *led to hfwy, sn wknd.*..........(8 to 1 op 7 to 1) 9
743[4] BACCANALIA (Ire) 9-0 J Lowe (7) *cl up to hfwy, sn lost pl.*..........(20 to 1 op 16 to 1) 10
433[3] MONKEY MAGIC (Ire) 9-0 J Carroll (12) *chsd ldrs, rdn 2 fs out, sn wknd*..........(7 to 2 op 11 to 4) 11
804 EXPRESS LINE 8-9 S Whitworth (2) *beh frm hfwy.*..........(25 to 1 op 20 to 1) 12
Dist: Hd, 3½l, ½l, 2½l, sht-hd, 4l, ¾l, 3l, 6l, 2½l. 1m 2.20s. a 2.20s (12 Ran).
SR: 31/35/21/19/9/8/ (Mrs K Dooley), M H Tompkins

909 Esk Handicap Class E (0-70 3-y-o and up) £3,261 5f 207yds..........(4:40)

800[7] MISS ARAGON [47] 5-8-6 P Robinson (8) *in tch, hdwy 2 fs out, led entering fnl furlong, sn clr.* (8 to 1 op 7 to 1) 1
700* BLUE GRIT [66] 7-9-11 (7ex) J Lowe (5) *beh, hdwy 2 fs out, rdn and styd on wl ins last*..........(5 to 1 jt-fav op 9 to 2 tchd 11 to 2) 2
591 SARTIGILA [61] 4-9-6 G Duffield (6) *mid-div, effrt and rdn appr fnl furlong, styd on wl ins last.*..........(5 to 1 jt-fav op 9 to 2) 3
887[7] BARBEZIEUX [34] 6-7-6[6] (7*) D McCabe (13) *in tch, hdwy 2 fs out, effrt and ev ch appr last, sn rdn and not quicken*..........(8 to 1 op 10 to 1) 4
800 MASTER POKEY [61] 9-8-13 (7*) P Johnson (3) *beh till styd on wl fnl furlong*..........(25 to 1 op 20 to 1) 5
636[5] COOL ENOUGH [34] 12-7-2[2] (7*) C Teague (2) *beh till styd on wl fnl furlong*..........(16 to 1 op 14 to 1) 6
610[6] MU-ARRIK [45] (bl) 5-8-4 W Newnes (1) *in tch, rdn and one pace fnl 2 fs*..........(33 to 1) 7
568 ARABAT [59] (v) 6-9-4 Jaki Houston (11) *nvr rch ldrs.*..........(8 to 1 op 12 to 1) 8
505[4] DIET [60] (v) 7-9-5 N Connorton (4) *led 2 fs, cl up till rdn and wknd o'r one out.*..........(11 to 1 op 12 to 1 tchd 10 to 1) 9
409[3] BRISAS [39] (bl) 6-7-12 J Fanning (10) *cl up, rdn and wknd appr fnl furlong*..........(9 to 1 op 8 to 1 tchd 10 to 1) 10
4687a[4] COLMAR [46] 3-7-8[1] Dale Gibson (9) *cl up, rdn o'r one furlong out, sn wknd*..........(25 to 1) 11
4660a[8] SUPER BENZ [69] 7-9-9 (5*) O Pears (16) *cl up, led aftr 2 fs till hdd and wknd quickly entering last.*..........(9 to 1 op 10 to 1 tchd 8 to 1) 12
610[3] HINARI VIDEO [43] 8-8-2 R P Elliott (12) *chsd ldrs 3 fs, sn wknd*..........(7 to 1 tchd 8 to 1) 13
330 CHOICE LOT [40] 6-7-13 A Mackay (14) *in tch till lost pl hfwy, sn beh*..........(25 to 1) 14
Dist: 3l, ½l, ½l, 1½l, hd, nk, sht-hd, 3l, 3l, ½l. 1m 14.90s. a 1.90s (14 Ran).
SR: 30/37/30/1/22/-/4/17/6/ (T Charlesworth), Miss L C Siddall

910 Eden Handicap Class E (0-70 3-y-o and up) £3,106 1¾m 32yds..........(5:10)

632[4] CONTINUITY [53] 4-9-0 (3*) J Weaver (12) *hld up and beh, hdwy 5 fs out, effrt and led o'r 2 out, ran on wl.*..........(7 to 1 op 8 to 1 tchd 6 to 1) 1
652* SHYNON [62] 3-8-6 P Robinson (4) *led, rdn and hdd o'r 2 fs out, kpt on*..........(2 to 1 tchd 9 to 4) 2
702* GRACE CARD [47] 7-8-12 (5ex) K Darley (3) *al chasing ldrs, effrt and hdwy 3 fs out, rdn 2 out, kpt on one pace.*..........(7 to 4 fav op 13 to 8 tchd 15 to 8) 3
CORNET [49] (v) 7-9-0 N Connorton (2) *chsd ldrs, effrt and ev ch 3 fs out, sn rdn and wknd fnl 2 furlongs.*..........(50 to 1 op 33 to 1) 4
681 HILLZAH (USA) [57] 5-9-1 (7*) H Bastiman (9) *hld up and beh, hdwy 5 fs out, rdn and styd on one pace fnl 2 furlongs*..........(20 to 1) 5
427[7] TRICYCLE (Ire) [37] 4-8-1 J Lowe (10) *chsd ldr, rdn 3 fs out, wknd 2 out*..........(7 to 1) 6
616[4] FAIRFIELDS CONE [55] 10-9-1 (5*) D Meredith (6) *mid-div, hdwy o'r 4 fs out, rdn 3 out, sn btn*..........(16 to 1) 7
MONTPELIER LAD [63] 6-10-0 D Nicholls (5) *al mid-div.*..........(20 to 1) 8
111[5] BLUE DISC [34] 8-7-8 (5*) A Garth (7) *chsd ldrs, rdn and wknd o'r 4 fs out*..........(20 to 1) 9
ALPHA HELIX [28] (v) 10-7-7 J Fanning (11) *al rear.*..........(50 to 1 op 33 to 1) 10
727 BARTON PRIDE (Ire) [44] 4-8-8 G Duffield (13) *chsd ldrs, rdn hfwy, sn lost pl*..........(50 to 1) 11
GREAT ORATION (Ire) [43] 4-8-7 R P Elliott (8) *al rear, tld off fnl 4 fs*..........(100 to 1) 12
Dist: 2l, hd, 8l, 1½l, 8l, 1½l, ½l, 6l, sht-hd, 2½l. 3m 7.30s. a 9.50s (12 Ran).
(Mrs Stella Barclay), E J Alston

DOWNPATRICK (IRE) (good to firm) Friday May 7th

911 Downpatrick Mares Maiden (4-y-o and up) £1,207 1m 5f..........(7:00)

PRETTY NICE (Ire) 5-10-0 R Hughes (3)........... (7 to 2) 1
CAMDEN BUZZ (Ire) 5-10-0 C F Swan (6)...... (2 to 1 on) 2
MOSARAT (Ire) 4-9-4 (10*) D Behan (8)........... (33 to 1) 3
706[7] WINTER DREAMS (Ire) 4-10-0 W J O'Connor (1)... (7 to 1) 4
SARAKAYA 8-10-0 W J Supple (7)............... (12 to 1) 5
598 SIGHTSEER (Ire) 4-10-0 H Rogers (2)............ (16 to 1) 6
BACK TO BLACK (Ire) 4-9-4 (10*) M G Cleary (9).. (33 to 1) 7
GRADH MO CROI (Ire) 5-9-8 (6*) B Bowens (4)..... (16 to 1) 8
SHY GAL (Ire) 5-10-0 P L Malone (10)............ (33 to 1) 9
AMME ENAEK (Ire) 4-9-8 (6*) P Carberry (5)....... (16 to 1) ur
Dist: ½l, 8l, ½l, nk. (Time not taken) (10 Ran).
(K M Campbell), M J Grassick

912 Caithness Handicap (0-60 3-y-o and up) £1,380 1m 3f 208yds................ (7:30)

SENSE OF VALUE [-] 4-9-6 J P Murtagh (11)....... (7 to 2) 1
647[4] DIAMOND CLUSTER [-] 3-7-3 (8*) R T Fitzpatrick (12) .... (10 to 1) 2
598* FONTANAYS (Ire) [-] 5-9-10 (5ex) S Craine (8)... (5 to 2 fav) 3
TOUCHDOWN [-] 6-9-4 R Hughes (2)............ (10 to 1) 4
281 ARDLEA HOUSE (Ire) [-] 4-7-9 (6*) J J Behan (9)... (10 to 1) 5
ALVATUR (Ire) [-] 4-8-8 N Byrne (6)............... (25 to 1) 6
GREEK CHIME (Ire) [-] 4-10-0 P McWilliams (15).. (12 to 1) 7
297[9] ISLAND VISION (Ire) [-] 3-8-0 (10*) I Browne (5).... (20 to 1) 8
PEPPERS PET (Ire) [-] 5-9-7 C F Swan (13)....... (16 to 1) 9
647[2] SCANNO'S CHOICE (Ire) [-] 3-8-4 W J Supple (7)... (5 to 1) 10
ST AIDAN (Ire) [-] 5-7-5 (2*) D G O'Shea (3)....... (12 to 1) 11
LOVE OF ERIN (Ire) [-] 4-7-9 Joanna Morgan,...... (16 to 1) 12
PERSIAN EMPRESS (Ire) [-] 4-8-4 (4*) W J Smith (10) .... (25 to 1) 13
NO SIR ROM [-] 7-9-5 (6*) J A Heffernan (1)....... (12 to 1) 14
552 CHRISTY MOORE (Ire) [-] 3-8-0 J F Egan (4)...... (20 to 1) 15
Dist: 3l, 2½l, 1l, sht-hd. (Time not taken) (15 Ran).
(F Dunne), F Dunne

LINGFIELD (good (races 1,2), good to firm (3,4,5))

Friday May 7th

Going Correction: MINUS 0.15 sec. per fur.

913 Hawthorn Maiden Stakes Class D (2-y-o) £3,611 5f.......................... (2:30)

HIGH DOMAIN (Ire) 9-0 J Reid (12) *led aftr 2 fs, wndrd lft o'r one out, rdn out*..... (9 to 2 op 7 to 1 tchd 8 to 1) 1
554[7] PETER ROWLEY 9-0 Pat Eddery (9) *pressed ldrs, rdn and styd on one pace ins fnl furlong*..... (7 to 1 op 7 to 2) 2
STRAIGHT ARROW 9-0 A Munro (8) *chsd frnt rnk, ran on o'r one furlong out, styd on ins last.* .... (14 to 1 op 7 to 1 tchd 16 to 1) 3
KNIGHTRIDER 9-0 J Quinn (6) *in tch, hdwy 2 fs out, not quicken o'r one out.* (20 to 1 op 33 to 1 tchd 50 to 1) 4
469[2] MAKE THE BREAK 9-0 B Rouse (11) *led 2 fs, no extr two out*.................................. (7 to 2 op 2 to 1) 5
JUST FLAMENCO 9-0 D Biggs (2) *improved 2 fs out, no imprsn on ldrs ins last*........... (20 to 1 tchd 33 to 1) 6
PRINCE DANZIG (Ire) 9-0 C Rutter (10) *outpcd most of way.* .... (33 to 1 op 16 to 1 tchd 50 to 1) 7
BENFLEET 9-0 R Hills (3) *nvr on terms.* .... (20 to 1 op 10 to 1) 8
AQUA VIVA (bl) 9-0 R Cochrane (7) *ldg grp for o'r 3 fs.* .... (6 to 4 fav op 2 to 1 tchd 9 to 4) 9
687 RICHARD'S ERROR 9-0 Paul Eddery (13) *outpcd.* .... (25 to 1 op 14 to 1 tchd 33 to 1) 10
291 CLANCY'S EXPRESS 9-0 M Hills (5) *speed on outsd to hfwy, sn lost pl*.................. (50 to 1 op 20 to 1) 11
DURANDETTE 8-9 G Bardwell (4) *strted slwly, al beh.* .... (50 to 1 op 33 to 1) 12
BITE THE BULLET 9-0 J Williams (1) *outpcd.* .... (33 to 1 op 20 to 1 tchd 50 to 1) 13
Dist: 1½l, ½l, 5l, nk, nk, 2l, 3½l, 2½l, ½l, ½l. 59.69s. a 2.79s (13 Ran).
SR: 29/23/21/1/-/-/ (Mrs S J Stovold), M McCormack

914 Sharron Murgatroyd Center Parcs Ladies Handicap Stakes Class F (0-70 4-y-o and up) £2,560 7f........................ (3:30)

834[7] NAVARESQUE [40] 8-9-10 Miss J Southcombe (10) *made virtually all, kpt on wl fnl furlong.* .... (25 to 1 tchd 16 to 1 and 33 to 1) 1
771[9] SHINING JEWEL [65] 6-11-7 Mrs J Crossley (5) *ran on frm 2 fs out, fnshd strly*..... (9 to 1 op 10 to 1 tchd 7 to 1) 2
771[4] CAPTAIN MARMALADE [53] 4-10-9 Miss I Diana W Jones (11) *settled rear, hdwy o'r one furlong out, fnshd wl.* .... (6 to 1 op 5 to 1 tchd 7 to 1) 3
760 COURTING NEWMARKET [42] 5-9-12 Miss S A Billot (12) *pressed ldrs, ev ch entering fnl furlong, not quicken.* .... (20 to 1 op 10 to 1) 4
771 ALNASRIC PETE (USA) [52] 7-10-8 Mrs E Mellor (15) *beh till styd on one pace wl o'r one furlong out.* .... (12 to 1 op 8 to 1 tchd 14 to 1) 5
131[6] BILL MOON [54] 7-10-10 Miss J Feilden (14) *ldg grp, ev ch 2 fs out, no extr ins last*.............. (7 to 1 op 5 to 1) 6
603 RED INK [42] 4-9-12 Miss T Bracegirdle (13) *nvr better than mid-div*......................... (20 to 1 op 10 to 1) 7
4780a[9] KALOKAGATHOS [35] 4-9-5 Miss L Eaton (16) *outpcd till ran on ins last 2 fs, nrst finish*.... (100 to 1 op 33 to 1) 8
771* RISE UP SINGING [64] (bl) 5-11-6 (5ex) Mrs J Musson (3) *hld up, hdwy o'r 2 fs out, one pace appr last.* .... (11 to 4 fav op 3 to 1 tchd 7 to 2 and 5 to 2) 9
676 ABSONAL [62] 6-11-4 Mrs L Pearce (9) *chsd ldrs 5 fs, fnshd lme, destroyed*......... (6 to 1 op 4 to 1 tchd 13 to 2) 10
RAG TIME BELLE [32] 7-9-2 Miss J Winter (7) *in tch, hrd rdn 3 fs out, wknd o'r one out.* .... (25 to 1 op 20 to 1 tchd 33 to 1) 11
621[8] MASTAMIST [31] (bl) 4-9-1 Mrs G Rees (8) *beh most of way.* .... (25 to 1 op 20 to 1) 12
700[6] WELLSY LAD (USA) [53] (bl) 6-10-9 Mrs Maxine Cowdrey (6) *wl plcd, effrt 3 fs out, shaken up and no hdwy 2 out, eased whn btn*..................... (12 to 1 op 8 to 1) 13
603 LUCKY NOIRE [58] 5-11-0 Miss A Harwood (1) *pressed ldrs for o'r 5 fs*......................... (12 to 1 op 7 to 1) 14
85 MARDIOR [30] (bl) 5-9-0 Miss L Hide (4) *mid-div till wknd o'r 2 fs out*........................ (33 to 1 op 20 to 1) 15
MAY HILLS LEGACY (Ire) [58] 4-11-0 Mrs D Arbuthnot (2) *cl up on outsd to hfwy, veered lft and lost pl o'r 2 fs out.* .... (16 to 1 op 14 to 1 tchd 20 to 1) 16
Dist: 1l, 1½l, ½l, sht-hd, 1½l, 1½l, ¾l, 1l, ½l, ¾l. 1m 25.37s. a 4.67s (16 Ran).
SR: 24/46/29/16/25/22/5/-/22/ (Mrs D Pickford), R J Hodges

915 McCall Group Conditions Stakes Class D (3-y-o) £3,318 7f.................. (4:00)

746[4] WINGED VICTORY (Ire) 8-9 R Cochrane (4) *hld up rear, hdwy o'r one furlong out, str brst to ld last 50 yards.* .... (4 to 1 op 7 to 2) 1
558[6] YOUNG ERN 8-10 L Piggott (7) *hld up in mid-div, not clr run wl o'r one furlong out, quickened to ld one out, hdd last 50 yards*........................ (3 to 1 op 7 to 2) 2
400[4] CARELAMAN 8-10 W Carson (3) *in tch, pushed alng hfwy, not quicken o'r one furlong out, ran on nr finish*................ (11 to 4 fav op 5 to 2 tchd 7 to 2) 3
476* YAQTHAN (Ire) 9-0 R Hills (2) *pressed ldr, ev ch one furlong out, ran on same pace*.. (8 to 1 op 5 to 1 tchd 9 to 1) 4
624* PRESS GALLERY 8-12 Paul Eddery (6) *led 6 fs, no extr.* .... (13 to 2 op 5 to 1 tchd 7 to 1) 5
FORTHWITH 8-7 M Hills (8) *outpcd in rear till styd on fnl furlong, not rch ldrs*............. (33 to 1 op 20 to 1) 6
472 WHITE SHADOW (Ire) 8-13 Pat Eddery (1) *strted slwly, pushed alng to cl aftr 3 fs, wknd and eased ins last 2.* .... (7 to 1 op 5 to 1) 7
658[8] CYPRIAN DANCER (USA) 9-0 T Quinn (5) *trkd frnt rnk, one pace appr fnl furlong*.......... (20 to 1 op 12 to 1) 8
Dist: 1l, 2½l, nk, ½l, nk, sht-hd, 1½l. 1m 23.28s. a 2.58s (8 Ran).
SR: 41/39/31/34/30/24/29/25/ (Paul Mellon), I A Balding

916 Victoria Trading Handicap Class E (0-70 3-y-o and up) £3,183 5f............. (4:30)

600[8] SERIOUS HURRY [53] 5-8-11 T Quinn (10) *pressed ldrs, led 2 fs out, rdn out*...................... (8 to 1 op 10 to 1) 1
716[2] FLORAC (Ire) [51] 3-7-6 (7*) D Wright (12) *ldg grp, lost pl hfwy, ran on o'r one furlong out, kpt on nr line.* .... (15 to 8 fav op 9 to 4 tchd 7 to 4) 2
721[2] MISTER JOLSON [64] 4-9-8 W Carson (3) *reminders aftr 2 fs, cld on ldrs two out, not quicken ins last.* .... (6 to 1 op 5 to 1 tchd 13 to 2) 3
492 NO QUARTER GIVEN [70] 8-10-0 R Cochrane (7) *hld up, ran on appr fnl furlong, nrst finish.* .... (16 to 1 op 12 to 1 tchd 20 to 1) 4
614 MOVING IMAGE (Ire) [61] 3-8-9 C Dwyer (5) *rear till ran on strly fnl furlong, fnshd wl*......... (33 to 1 op 20 to 1) 5
4719a* PEERAGE PRINCE [67] (bl) 4-9-11 A Munro (4) *in tch, styd on one pace frm 2 fs out.* .... (10 to 1 op 12 to 1 tchd 14 to 1) 6
721 BELTHORN [50] 4-8-8 G Bardwell (11) *ldg grp, hrd rdn o'r one furlong out, no extr.* .... (33 to 1 op 20 to 1 tchd 40 to 1) 7
600[2] COCKERHAM RANGER [65] 3-8-13 A Geran (6) *reared strt, sn in tch, hmpd o'r one furlong out, not rcvr.* .... (15 to 2 op 5 to 1 tchd 8 to 1) 8
615[5] THE NOBLE OAK (Ire) [60] 5-9-4 J Reid (2) *speed on outsd, not quicken appr fnl furlong*...... (10 to 1 op 6 to 1) 9
800[8] LINCSTONE BOY (Ire) [50] (bl) 5-8-8 J Williams (9) *led 3 fs.* .... (12 to 1 op 10 to 1) 10
6 CAMINO A RONDA [37] 4-7-2 (7*) Kim McDonnell (13) *early speed, outpcd hfwy*.............. (50 to 1 op 33 to 1) 11
501 JOE SUGDEN [55] 9-8-13 C Rutter (8) *pressed ldrs 3 fs.* .... (14 to 1 op 12 to 1) 12
SKI CAPTAIN [56] 9-9-0 Paul Eddery (1) *al rear.* .... (16 to 1 op 12 to 1) 13
Dist: 1l, 2l, hd, ½l, ½l, sht-hd, sht-hd, nk, 2½l, 1½l. 59.52s. a 2.62s (13 Ran).
SR: 30/14/29/34/13/27/9/13/17/ (Richard Berenson), C C Elsey

917 Marley Goldseal Plus Limited Stakes Class E (3-y-o and up) £3,131 7f 140yds .... (5:00)

SOAKING 3-8-11 B Rouse (8) *pressed ldr, led 2 fs out, jst hld on*.............. (14 to 1 op 10 to 1 tchd 16 to 1) 1

4754 HOPEFUL BID (Ire) 4-9-10 Pat Eddery (5) *hld up in mid-div, str brst fnl furlong, jst fld.* .... (6 to 1 op 5 to 1 tchd 13 to 2) 2
677 BERNSTEIN BETTE 7-9-5 R Cochrane (11) *hld up, str run ins fnl furlong, fnshd wl.* .... (6 to 1 op 5 to 1 tchd 13 to 2) 3
719* COMANCHE COMPANION 3-8-6 D Holland (12) *wl plcd, ev ch und pres fnl furlong, not quicken nr line.* .... (100 to 30 fav op 3 to 1 tchd 5 to 2) 4
8349 ROSEATE LODGE 7-9-10 T Quinn (7) *hdwy frm rear o'r 2 fs out, outpcd ins last.* .... (10 to 1 op 8 to 1) 5
4834 SEA BARON 3-8-11 J Williams (1) *improved frm rear 3 fs out, no extr appr last.* ....(10 to 1 tchd 12 to 1) 6
SANTANA LADY (Ire) 4-9-5 J Reid (6) *pressed ldrs till out-pcd o'r one furlong out.* (8 to 1 op 6 to 1 tchd 9 to 1) 7
663 MULCIBER 5-9-10 M Hills (10) *led for o'r 5 fs, sn btn.* ....(8 to 1 op 6 to 1 tchd 9 to 1) 8
4057 SHARP GAZELLE 3-8-3 (3*) A Tucker (9) *nvr better than mid-div.* ....(33 to 1 op 20 to 1) 9
519* KNYAZ 3-8-11 A Munro (4) *in tch in mid-div, effrt 3 fs out, wknd 2 out.* ....(12 to 1 op 7 to 1) 10
ACARA (Ire) 4-9-5 J Quinn (13) *chsd ldrs for o'r 4 fs.* .... (33 to 1 op 20 to 1) 11
756 DUCKEY FUZZ 5-9-10 Paul Eddery (2) *outpcd.* .... (33 to 1 op 20 to 1) 12
737 PRECIOUS WONDER 4-9-10 L Piggott (3) *al rear.* .... (10 to 1 op 12 to 1 tchd 14 to 1) 13
Dist: Nk, nk, ¾l, 5l, ½l, 3½l, sht-hd, 2l, 4l, 3½l. 1m 31.30s. a 3.00s (13 Ran).
SR: 35/47/41/26/29/14/11/15/-/ (K Higson), G L Moore

LINGFIELD (A.W) (std)
Friday May 7th
Going Correction: NIL

918 Courvoisier Claiming Stakes Class F (4-y-o and up) £2,556 1¼m. .... (3:00)

6212 STORM FREE (USA) 7-8-11 A Munro (8) *hld up gng wl, cld on ldrs 4 fs out, shaken up to ld one out, not extended.* .... (6 to 1 op 5 to 1 tchd 13 to 2) 1
8017 NO SUBMISSION (USA) 7-9-1 S Wood (1) *trkd ldr, pushed alng and outpcd o'r 3 fs out, lost pl, ran on strly ins last.* ....(3 to 1 op 2 to 1 tchd 100 to 30) 2
7106 EXPRESS SERVICE (bl) 4-8-3 (3*) Emma O'Gorman (3) *led till hdd und pres one furlong out, no extr.* .... (14 to 1 op 8 to 1) 3
7569 SAAHI (USA) 4-8-9 (5*) K Rutter (5) *hld up rear, hdwy o'r 2 fs out, not rch ldrs fnl furlong.* ....(7 to 2 op 9 to 2 tchd 5 to 1) 4
3224 AWESOME POWER 7-8-9 D Holland (4) *ldg grp, rdn alng 5 fs out, wknd o'r 2 out.* ....(15 to 8 fav op 2 to 1 tchd 5 to 2) 5
4795a4 KING OF NORMANDY (Ire) 4-8-5 T Williams (7) *beh aftr 3 fs.* .... (33 to 1 op 12 to 1) 6
BARUD (Ire) 5-8-5 N Adams (6) *strted slwly, al beh, tld off.* .... (100 to 1 op 25 to 1) 7
Dist: 1l, 1l, 3½l, 7l, 10l, 25l. 2m 7.42s. a 4.22s (7 Ran).
SR: 55/57/46/47/28/4/-/ (E J S Gadsden), L G Cottrell

919 May Handicap Class E (0-70 3-y-o and up) £2,924 1¼m. .... (5:30)

621* NORTHERN CONQUEROR (Ire) [32] 5-7-7⁵ (5*) B Doyle (5) *ran on frm rear appr hfwy, led o'r 3 fs out, pushed clr approaching last.* ..(9 to 4 fav op 5 to 2 tchd 11 to 4) 1
2945 OUR EDDIE [49] (v) 4-8-10 N Adams (9) *trkd ldrs, ev ch 3 fs out, one pace appr last.* .... (16 to 1 op 20 to 1 tchd 25 to 1) 2
4029 LOWAWATHA [62] 5-9-4 (5*) Stephen Davies (8) *beh till ran on o'r 3 fs out, styd on one pace fnl furlong.* ....(6 to 1 op 5 to 1) 3
3877 MAY SQUARE (Ire) [37] 5-7-12 T Sprake (10) *ldg grp, led o'r 4 fs out till over 3 out, cl 3rd whn hmpd on bend 2 out, sn btn.* .... (12 to 1 op 14 to 1 tchd 16 to 1) 4
456 DISPUTED CALL (USA) [66] 4-9-13 M Hills (7) *chsd ldrs till outpcd 3 fs out.* .... (4 to 1 tchd 5 to 1) 5
7257 BICHETTE [65] 3-8-10 B Rouse (11) *wl plcd till rdn and wknd o'r 3 fs out.* .... (8 to 1 op 5 to 1) 6
1586 WITH GUSTO [35] 6-7-10 D Biggs (6) *nvr nrr.* .... (16 to 1 op 14 to 1 tchd 20 to 1) 7
RIVAL BID (USA) [67] 5-10-0 N Day (12) *nvr trble frnt rnk.* .... (12 to 1 op 8 to 1 tchd 14 to 1) 8
840 HIGHLY SECURE [50] 6-8-11 Paul Eddery (4) *mid-div, rdn and drpd out last 3 fs.* (10 to 1 op 8 to 1 tchd 11 to 1) 9
2084 GENESIS FOUR [48] (bl) 3-7-7 E Johnson (2) *led to hfwy, sn wknd.* .... (20 to 1 op 10 to 1) 10
3728 LITTLE KARLIE (Den) [48] 3-7-0 (7*) D Wright (1) *outpcd.* .... (33 to 1 op 20 to 1) 11
731 HIGHLAND FLAME [43] (bl) 4-8-4 J Quinn (3) *pressed ldrs, led briefly 5 fs out, wknd o'r 3 out.* (25 to 1 op 20 to 1) 12
Dist: 4l, 2½l, 2l, 2½l, nk, 4l, 5l, 2l. 2m 9.50s. a 6.30s (12 Ran).
SR: 16/25/33/4/28/10/-/10/-/ (Mrs J T Naughton), T J Naughton

ST-CLOUD (FR) (good to soft)
Friday May 7th
Going Correction: PLUS 0.50 sec. per fur.

920 Prix du Muguet (Group 3) (4-y-o and up) £35,842 1m. .... (2:25)

HATOOF (USA) 4-9-1 W R Swinburn (3) *second strt, rdn and quickened 2 fs out, led jst o'r one out, ran on wl.* ....(3 to 1) 1
4302 SHANGHAI (USA) 4-9-1 C Asmussen (4) *3rd strt, rdn 2 fs out, wnt second one out, ran on gmely fnl furlong, not rch wnr.* ....(9 to 5 fav) 2
629* NORTHERN CRYSTAL 5-9-0 T Jarnet (1) *led till jst o'r one furlong out, kpt on one pace.* ....(28 to 10) 3
430* TAKE RISKS (Fr) 4-9-0 M Boutin (2) *4th strt, rdn 2 fs out, hrd ridden and one pace fnl furlong.* .... (23 to 10) 4
4304 ACTEUR FRANCAIS (USA) 5-9-0 D Boeuf (5) *al rear.* ....(93 to 10) 5
Dist: ¾l, 1½l, ½l, 2l. 1m 43.60s. a 5.10s (5 Ran).
SR: 85/83/77/75/69/ (Maktoum Al Maktoum), Mrs C Head

BATH (firm)
Saturday May 8th
Going Correction: MINUS 0.20 sec. per fur. (races 1,4,5,6), MINUS 0.35 (2,3,7)

921 Midford Maiden Fillies Stakes Class D (3-y-o) £3,582 1m 5yds. .... (1:40)

6723 PRINCESS KRIS 8-11 Pat Eddery (12) *in tch, improved to ld 2 fs out, sn clr, easily.* ....(Evens fav op 11 to 8 tchd 6 to 4) 1
4144 OCARA (USA) 8-11 M Tebbutt (10) *hdwy o'r 2 fs out, kpt on to go second ins last, no ch wth wnr.* .... (10 to 1 op 7 to 1) 2
522 LEGAL RISK (v) 8-11 S Whitworth (3) *cl up, led o'r 3 fs out, hdd 2 out, one pace.* (40 to 1 op 25 to 1 tchd 50 to 1) 3
SUSQUEHANNA DAYS (USA) 8-11 R Cochrane (9) *al chasing ldrs, no prog last 2 fs.* ....(7 to 2 op 5 to 2 tchd 4 to 1) 4
7805 BRONZE MAQUETTE (Ire) 8-4 (7*) T G McLaughlin (14) *cl up till wknd wl o'r one out.* .... (10 to 1 op 8 to 1 tchd 14 to 1) 5
5237 SAKURA QUEEN (Ire) 8-11 W Woods (7) *missed break, ran on last 2 fs, not rch ldrs.* .... (12 to 1 op 10 to 1 tchd 16 to 1) 6
583 CLANDESTINE AFFAIR (Ire) 8-11 S Dawson (13) *effrt on outsd o'r 3 fs out, wknd 2 out.* .... (25 to 1 op 16 to 1 tchd 33 to 1) 7
MY MINNIE 8-4 (7*) S Drowne (4) *missed break, late hdwy, nrst finish.* .... (50 to 1 op 25 to 1) 8
I'M YOURS 8-11 A McGlone (1) *led o'r 4 fs, lost pl over 2 out.* ....(7 to 1 op 4 to 1) 9
SHALHOLME 8-11 N Adams (8) *shrtlvd effrt 3 fs out.* .... (50 to 1 op 33 to 1) 10
IS SHE QUICK 8-11 R Perham (6) *struggling frm hfwy.* .... (50 to 1 op 25 to 1) 11
624 SENCINI 8-11 A Munro (2) *pressed ldrs till wknd ins last 3 fs.* ....(50 to 1 op 25 to 1) 12
821 SUPPER WITH SUSIE 8-11 M Wigham (5) *al trailing, tld off.* ....(50 to 1 op 33 to 1) 13
SUEENA 8-11 T Sprake (11) *al in rear, tld off.* .... (50 to 1 op 25 to 1) 14
Dist: 5l, 3l, 1½l, ½l, 1½l, 3l, 1½l, ¾l, 2l, 2½l. 1m 41.30s. a 2.30s (14 Ran).
SR: 39/24/15/10/8/3/ (Exors Of The Late Mrs V Hue-Williams), M R Stoute

922 Pulteney Maiden Auction Stakes Class F (2-y-o) £2,833 5f 11yds. ....(2:10)

ROBELLION 9-0 R Price (13) *broke wl, al frnt rnk, ran on und pres to ld last 50 yards.* ....(7 to 2 op 4 to 1 tchd 5 to 2) 1
5175 SWEET DECISION (Ire) 8-9 M Wigham (14) *led til hdd last 50 yards.* .... (16 to 1 op 12 to 1) 2
6737 OBVIOUS RISK 9-0 A McGlone (5) *al handily plcd, kpt on same pace last 2 fs.* ... (10 to 1 op 7 to 1 tchd 12 to 1) 3
5172 CHICKAWICKA (Ire) 9-0 S Whitworth (4) *chsd ldr, ev ch wl o'r one furlong out, wknd fnl furlong.* .... (13 to 2 op 5 to 1) 4
ARABOYBILL 9-0 R Perham (6) *nrst finish.* .... (50 to 1 op 25 to 1) 5
5436 FRANKLY MY DEAR 9-0 R Cochrane (10) *speed 3 fs.* .... (9 to 2 op 7 to 2 tchd 11 to 2) 6
7154 GIGUE 8-9 Pat Eddery (1) *speed to hfwy.* ....(7 to 4 fav op 5 to 2 tchd 11 to 4) 7
EMMA GRIMES (Ire) 8-9 A Munro (3) *chsd ldrs to hfwy.* .... (16 to 1 op 14 to 1 tchd 20 to 1) 8
RITA'S JOY 8-9 T Sprake (16) *nvr dngrs.* .... (25 to 1 op 16 to 1 tchd 33 to 1) 9
MR MYSTICAL (Ire) 9-0 B Rouse (2) *outpcd.* .... (33 to 1 op 20 to 1) 10
4549 PETITE BIJOU 8-9 W Woods (8) *outpcd.* .... (50 to 1 op 25 to 1) 11
STAR SPEEDER (Ire) 8-2 (7*) B Russell (9) *slwly away, al beh.* .... (20 to 1 op 12 to 1) 12

WHITCHURCH SILK (Ire) 8-9 M Tebbutt (7) *nvr gng pace.* .... (33 to 1 op 20 to 1) 13

MISS TRIANGLE 8-9 G Bardwell (11) *al struggling.* .... (20 to 1 op 12 to 1 tchd 33 to 1) 14

SUPPRESSION (bl) 8-9 N Adams (12) *strted slwly, tld off.* .... (50 to 1 op 25 to 1) 15

Dist: ½l, 3l, 3½l, 4l, nk, 3l, 1½l, sht-hd, ½l, 1½l. 1m 1.80s. a 1.30s (15 Ran).

SR: 39/32/25/11/-/-/ (George S Thompson), D W P Arbuthnot

923 James & Cowper Handicap Class C (0-90 3-y-o and up) £4,760 5f 11yds....... (2:40)

HEAVENLY RISK [80] 3-8-8 A McGlone (4) *al chasing frnt rnk, kpt on und pres to ld wl ins fnl furlong.* .... (16 to 1 op 12 to 1) 1

EL YASAF (Ire) [83] 5-9-7 B Rouse (14) *al cl up, led jst ins fnl furlong, hdd towards finish.* .... (16 to 1 op 20 to 1 tchd 25 to 1) 2

FIVESEVENFIVEO [71] 5-8-2 (7*) S Drowne (3) *wth ldrs, led 2 fs out till jst ins last, not quicken.* ....(11 to 2 jt-fav op 7 to 2) 3

659^{6} LOVE LEGEND [70] (v) 8-8-8 A Munro (9) *al chasing ldrs, styd on fnl furlong.*.................. (8 to 1 tchd 9 to 1) 4+

555^{6} TERRHARS (Ire) [90] 5-10-0 R Perham (1) *al hndy, kpt on wl ins fnl furlong.*.... (10 to 1 op 8 to 1 tchd 11 to 1) 4+

721^{3} SIR JOEY (USA) [63] 4-8-1 N Adams (2) *led 3 fs, no extr fnl furlong.*........................(11 to 2 jt-fav op 5 to 1) 6

659 PALEY PRINCE (USA) [76] 7-9-0 R Cochrane (12) *hdwy appr fnl furlong, nvr able to chal.*..............(14 to 1) 7

722^{4} BELLS OF LONGWICK [74] 4-8-12 T Williams (10) *chsd ldrs till wknd appr fnl furlong.*.......... (6 to 1 op 9 to 2) 8

722^{7} HOW'S YER FATHER [80] 7-9-4 T Sprake (11) *al in rear.* .... (16 to 1 op 12 to 1 tchd 20 to 1) 9

796^{8} MOON STRIKE (Fr) [78] 3-8-3 (3*) Emma O'Gorman (7) *missed break, nvr in the hunt.* ....(8 to 1 op 7 to 1 tchd 9 to 1) 10

GONE SAVAGE [90] 5-10-0 Pat Eddery (5) *wth ldrs till wknd quickly appr fnl furlong.* .... (8 to 1 tchd 7 to 1 and 9 to 1) 11

721^{7} CEE-EN-CEE [66] (v) 9-8-1 (3*) A Tucker (6) *missed break, al struggling.*.......................(7 to 1 tchd 8 to 1) 12

Dist: 1½l, hd, ½l, dd-ht, 2½l, sht-hd, 1l, ¾l, 2½l, 3l. 1m 1.20s. a 0.70s (12 Ran).

SR: 45/52/39/36/56/19/31/25/28/ (Roldvale Limited), R Hannon

924 Box Handicap Class E (0-70 4-y-o and up) £3,521 2m 1f 34yds.................. (3:10)

626^{6} SMILINGATSTRANGERS [52] (v) 5-9-0 G Bardwell (5) *gd prog 4 fs out, hrd drvn appr fnl furlong, led ins last, all out.*................... (11 to 1 op 10 to 1 tchd 12 to 1) 1

495^{4} JANISKI [47] (v) 10-8-2 (7*) D Wright (7) *steadied strt, gd hdwy 4 fs out, led 3 furlongs out, edgd rght o'r one out, hdd ins last, styd on.*............(10 to 1 tchd 11 to 1) 2

SURCOAT [51] 6-8-13 T Williams (3) *prog 6 fs out, rdn to chal 2 and a half furlongs out, kpt on same pace.* ....(8 to 1 op 6 to 1 tchd 9 to 1) 3

BRIGGSMAID [59] 5-9-7 M Tebbutt (10) *wtd wth, steady hdwy aftr 6 fs, no real prog last 3 furlongs.* .... (14 to 1 op 10 to 1 tchd 16 to 1) 4

427 PATROCLUS [50] 8-8-12 S Dawson (12) *in rear till styd on fnl 2 fs, not rch ldrs.*............. (16 to 1 op 10 to 1) 5

783^{4} PERFORATE [41] 4-8-0^{3} A Munro (9) *beh till styd on fnl 2 fs, nrst finish*....... (14 to 1 op 10 to 1 tchd 16 to 1) 6

331* PHAROAH'S GUEST [51] 6-8-13 M Wigham (11) *trkd ldrs till wknd o'r 2 fs out*.......... (6 to 1 jt-fav op 9 to 2) 7

618 CHUCKLESTONE [65] 10-9-13 Pat Eddery (6) *led 3 fs, sn pushed alng, lost pl o'r 4 furlongs out.* ....(7 to 1 op 5 to 1 tchd 8 to 1) 8

626^{5} FORGE [40] 5-8-2 J Comber (16) *pressed ldrs to hfwy.* .... (12 to 1 op 10 to 1 tchd 14 to 1) 9

TEL E THON [44] (bl) 6-8-6 T Sprake (17) *led aftr 3 fs till 7 out, wknd o'r 2 out.* (25 to 1 op 20 to 1 tchd 33 to 1) 10

FIGHT TO WIN (USA) [60] (v) 5-9-8 R Cochrane (13) *prmnt till wknd o'r 4 fs out*........................(6 to 1 jt-fav op 5 to 1 tchd 8 to 1) 11

559^{2} CITY LINE [50] 4-8-6 (3*) A Tucker (8) *rapid hdwy frm rear 7 fs out, wknd 4 furlongs out.* ....(8 to 1 op 6 to 1 tchd 9 to 1) 12

520 HYMN BOOK (Ire) [50] 4-8-2 (7*) S Drowne (2) *chsd ldrs till lost pl aftr 6 fs, rnwd effrt 8 furlongs out, wknd o'r 5 furlongs out.*....... (40 to 1 op 33 to 1 tchd 50 to 1) 13

727^{3} PEAK DISTRICT [49] 7-8-11 B Rouse (1) *cl up till lost pl quickly 3 fs out.*.................... (14 to 1 op 10 to 1) 14

OLD STEINE [57] 5-9-5 A McGlone (4) *cl up, led 7 fs out till 3 out, wknd quickly.* (16 to 1 op 14 to 1 tchd 20 to 1) 15

Dist: 1l, 4l, 1½l, 4l, ¾l, 1½l, 1l, 15l, 1l, sht-hd. 3m 47.30s. a 3.30s (15 Ran).

SR: 33/27/27/33/20/6/17/30/-/ (Middleton Scriven Investments Ltd), Mrs Barbara Waring

925 Somerset Conditions Stakes Class D (4-y-o and up) £3,348 1m 3f 144yds.....(3:40)

HIGHLAND DRESS 4-8-12 A Munro (2) *led aftr one furlong, quickened clr appr fnl furlong, imprsv.* ....(7 to 4 op 2 to 1 tchd 9 to 4) 1

SOURCE OF LIGHT 4-9-2 Pat Eddery (3) *hld up in last pl, smooth hdwy o'r 3 fs out, rdn over one out, kpt on, no ch wth wnr.*........(13 to 8 fav op 2 to 1 tchd 6 to 4) 2

703* BADIE (USA) 4-8-13 R Cochrane (6) *led one furlong, chsd wnr, stumbled 4 fs out, rdn alng and ev ch o'r 2 furlongs out, one pace.*................(9 to 4 op 6 to 4) 3

799^{7} BRESIL (USA) 4-8-10 S Whitworth (7) *hld up, no ch last 3 fs.*...... (16 to 1 op 33 to 1 tchd 50 to 1 and 14 to 1) 4

JADIDH 5-8-5 G Bardwell (4) *chsd ldrs, rdn 4 fs out, wknd 3 out.*...............(40 to 1 op 33 to 1 tchd 50 to 1) 5

672 CHAPEL OF BARRAS (Ire) 4-8-10 A McGlone (1) *al in rear.* .... (50 to 1 op 33 to 1 tchd 66 to 1) 6

Dist: 5l, ½l, 10l, 3l, 8l. 2m 32.00s. a 5.00s (6 Ran).

SR: 25/19/15/ (Sheikh Mohammed), M R Stoute

926 Radstock Rating Related Maiden Stakes Class D (0-75 3-y-o) £3,465 1¼m 46yds ....(4:10)

547^{3} MANILA BAY (USA) 9-0 A Munro (8) *took keen hold, hdwy 3 fs out, swtchd rght 2 out, led entering fnl furlong, readily*.............. (3 to 1 op 5 to 2 tchd 100 to 30) 1

717^{6} BILJAN (USA) 8-7 (7*) T G McLaughlin (9) *cl up, led 3 fs out till one out, kpt on.*............... (20 to 1 op 10 to 1) 2

EUPHONIC 9-0 R Cochrane (12) *wtd wth, prog 3 fs out, drvn alng o'r one out, styd on same pace.* ....(7 to 1 op 8 to 1 tchd 12 to 1) 3

761^{6} MIDYAN BLUE (Ire) 9-0 M Tebbutt (10) *chsd ldrs, no imprsn last 2 fs.*...........................(5 to 1 tchd 10 to 1) 4

717^{4} HALHAM TARN (Ire) 8-9 (5*) A Procter (4) *pressed ldrs till wknd 2 fs out.*..................... (5 to 1 op 5 to 2) 5

SO SAUCY 8-9 R Perham (5) *cl up till wknd 2 and a half fs out.*...................................... (66 to 1 op 25 to 1) 6

482^{6} HATTA RIVER (USA) 9-0 A McGlone (6) *no ch last 3 fs.* ....(8 to 1 op 5 to 1 tchd 9 to 1) 7

584^{3} HOSTILE WITNESS (Ire) 9-0 Pat Eddery (1) *led till hdd 3 fs out, sn lost pl*........(9 to 4 fav op 3 to 1 tchd 9 to 2) 8

733 WORKING TITLE (Ire) 9-0 B Rouse (7) *al trailing.* .... (66 to 1 op 25 to 1) 9

4805a^{9} WAR REQUIEM (Ire) 9-0 N Adams (3) *mid-div, struggling hfwy.*...................... (40 to 1 op 20 to 1 tchd 50 to 1) 10

BELL LAD (Ire) 9-0 M Wigham (11) *al in rear, tld off.* ....(66 to 1 op 25 to 1) 11

Dist: 1l, 2l, 5l, ½l, 2½l, ½l, 6l, 5l, sht-hd. 2m 10.20s. a 3.80s (11 Ran).

SR: 42/40/36/26/25/15/19/7/-/ (Fahd Salman), M Bell

927 Chapel Farm Handicap Class E (0-70 3-y-o) £3,202 5f 161yds.................(4:40)

HALLORINA [60] 9-2 G Bardwell (3) *al cl up, led jst ins fnl furlong, kpt on wl*.....(9 to 1 op 8 to 1 tchd 10 to 1) 1

602 PRINCE SONGLINE [50] 8-6^{1} R Cochrane (1) *slwly into strd, sn chasing ldrs, ev ch one furlong out, unbl to quicken.*.........................(12 to 1 tchd 16 to 1) 2

711 CHAMPAGNE GRANDY [65] 9-7 Pat Eddery (15) *al chasing ldrs, kpt on ins last.*.....(9 to 2 op 7 to 2 tchd 3 to 1) 3

4773a PAT POINDESTRES [49] 8-0 (5*) N Gwilliams (14) *led till hdd and no extr jst ins fnl furlong...* (20 to 1 tchd 33 to 1) 4

491^{6} MY FOXY LADY [48] 8-4 T Sprake (8) *styd on appr fnl furlong, nrst finish.* (14 to 1 op 33 to 1 tchd 40 to 1) 5

334^{2} GOOD IMAGE [59] 9-1 S Whitworth (9) *handily plcd, no imprsn last 2 fs.*........(9 to 1 op 5 to 1 tchd 10 to 1) 6

600^{7} AGIL'S PET [55] 8-11 B Rouse (5) *pressed ldrs till wknd o'r one furlong out.* ....(11 to 4 fav op 3 to 1 tchd 7 to 2 and 5 to 2) 7

797^{9} INONDER [40] 7-10 N Adams (11) *chsd frnt rnk, no prog last 2 fs.*............................(50 to 1 op 33 to 1) 8

882^{5} KAFIOCA (Ire) [48] (bl) 8-4 A McGlone (2) *al abt same pl.* ....(14 to 1 op 10 to 1 tchd 16 to 1) 9

418 KENSWORTH LADY [51] 8-4 (3*) A Tucker (16) *shrtlvd effrt hfwy.*................(11 to 1 op 10 to 1 tchd 20 to 1) 10

FIR COPSE [46] 8-2 A Munro (13) *outpcd.* ....(25 to 1 op 14 to 1) 11

720* AIR COMMAND (Bar) [56] 8-5 (7*) S Drowne (12) *speed to hfwy.*...... (17 to 2 op 8 to 1 tchd 7 to 1 and 9 to 1) 12

721 BUCKSKI ECHO [47] 8-3 S Dawson (4) *chsd ldrs 3 fs.* .... (14 to 1 op 8 to 1) 13

SUI GENERIS (Ire) [53] 8-9 R Perham (6) *outpcd.* ....(14 to 1 op 12 to 1 tchd 16 to 1) 14

742* BURISHKI [55] 8-4 (7*) D Wright (10) *al struggling.* ....(7 to 1 op 4 to 1) 15

DELAY NO MORE [50] 8-6 S O'Gorman (7) *slwly away, al trailing.*.......................(50 to 1 op 33 to 1) 16

Dist: 1½l, 2½l, nk, hd, 2l, nk, 2½l, 1l, sht-hd, 2l. 1m 10.80s. a 1.40s (16 Ran).

SR: 34/18/23/6/4/7/2/-/-/ (Mrs J A Thomson), W G R Wightman

BEVERLEY (good to firm (races 1,2,3,4,5,6), firm (7)) Saturday May 8th

Going Correction: MINUS 0.15 sec. per fur.

928 Kiplingcote Selling Stakes Class F (3-y-o) £2,646 1m 1f 207yds.............. (2:20)

813[6] BARLEY CAKE 8-9 J Fanning (4) *hld up beh, hdwy 3 fs out, effrt to ld ins last, ran on wl*.........(8 to 1 op 6 to 1) 1
HO-JOE (Ire) 9-0 K Fallon (12) *chsd ldrs, led o'r 2 out, sn rdn and hng rght, hdd and no extr entering fnl furlong*..............................(8 to 1 tchd 6 to 1) 2
761[8] ESERIE DE CORES (USA) 8-9 (5*) C Hodgson (8) *hld up and beh, hdwy on inner 2 fs out, not clr run and swtchd appr fnl furlong, styd on ins last.* (12 to 1 op 14 to 1) 3
744[2] DANCES WITH GOLD 8-9 J Lowe (1) *chsd ldrs, effrt and rdn o'r 2 fs out, kpt on one pace.* .... (8 to 1 op 5 to 1 tchd 10 to 1) 4
499[4] ANN HILL (Ire) 9-2 S Perks (3) *hld up, hdwy o'r 2 fs out, sn rdn and kpt on one pace.* .... (11 to 2 op 8 to 1 tchd 5 to 1) 5
394[3] SUMMERS DREAM 8-9 G Carter (13) *in tch, hdwy and ev ch 2 fs out, sn not much room, rdn and wknd appr fnl furlong*..............................(16 to 1 op 14 to 1) 6
653[8] EVERGREEN TANGO 9-0 Paul Eddery (11) *led 2 fs, cl up till rdn and wknd two furlongs out*... (25 to 1 op 14 to 1) 7
MARSHALL PINDARI 9-0 D Holland (10) *cl up, led aftr 2 fs till 4 out, rdn and wknd two out*.............. (33 to 1) 8
642[3] PALACEGATE SUNSET (v) 9-7 J Carroll (5) *hld up, hdwy 4 fs out, rdn and wknd wl o'r 2 out.* ....(6 to 1 op 9 to 2 tchd 7 to 1) 9
763[3] MAASTRICHT 9-0 G Duffield (14) *chsd ldrs, rdn alng 3 fs out, sn wknd*.......(11 to 4 fav op 2 to 1 tchd 7 to 2) 10
642 ASTRAC TRIO (USA) (v) 9-7 K Darley (6) *in tch till rdn and wknd o'r 3 fs out*............................. (25 to 1) 11
362[7] KENTUCKY DREAMS 8-9 (5*) O Pears (7) *cl up, led 4 fs out till hdd and hmpd o'r 2 furlongs out, sn wknd.* .... (20 to 1 op 16 to 1) 12
799 CHAJOTHELYTBRIGADE (Ire) 8-4 (5*) Stephen Davies (9) *cl up, ev ch o'r 2 fs out, sn rdn and wknd*........(33 to 1) 13
699 WILD EXPRESSION (v) 9-0 M Birch (2) *slwly into strd, middiv till lost pl and tld off fnl 3 fs*.............. (33 to 1) 14
Dist: 1½l, 2l, 2½l, 1½l, 12l, 1l, 12l, 2½l, 3½l, 2½l. 2m 7.30s. a 5.90s (14 Ran).
SR: 21/23/19/9/13/-/ (W J Dobson), T Fairhurst

929 Yorkshire Television Conditions Stakes Class D (3-y-o) £3,143 1m 3f 216yds (2:50)

635* WHITE MUZZLE 8-9 (5*) Stephen Davies (1) *hld up, hdwy and crrd wide 3 fs out, chsd ldr and rdn one and a half furlongs out, ran on to ld wl ins last.* .... (6 to 5 on op 11 to 10 on tchd Evens) 1
557[5] SPRING TO ACTION 8-7 G Carter (6) *led aftr 2 fs, clr 3 out, rdn appr fnl furlong, hdd and no extr wl ins last.* ....(7 to 1 op 6 to 1) 2
557[3] SAINT KEYNE 8-7 W Ryan (5) *hld up, effrt and hdwy 3 fs out, rdn and styd on appr fnl furlong.* .... (11 to 4 op 5 to 2 tchd 3 to 1) 3
534* LAVENDER COTTAGE 8-7 Paul Eddery (3) *cl up till rdn 3 fs out, sn wknd*........................(9 to 1 op 10 to 1) 4
578[4] MARCO MAGNIFICO (USA) 8-10 D Holland (4) *led 2 fs, chsd ldr till rdn and wknd o'r two furlongs out*.....(10 to 1) 5
799* CUMBRIAN RHAPSODY 8-7 M Birch (2) *al rear.* ....(16 to 1 tchd 20 to 1) 6
Dist: 1½l, 1½l, 10l, nk, 2½l. 2m 35.60s. a 4.60s (6 Ran).
SR: 36/26/23/3/5/-/ (Luciano Gaucci), P W Chapple-Hyam

930 Hypac Handicap Class C (0-90 3-y-o and up) £4,889 7f 100yds................(3:20)

771[5] RURAL LAD [60] 4-8-11 D Holland (7) *hld up gng wl, hdwy on ins 2 fs out, squeezed through and quickened to ld well inside last*.............................. (6 to 1) 1
565 SCOTTISH PARK [58] 4-8-9 G Duffield (8) *chsd ldrs, effrt 2 fs out amd sn rdn, styd on to ld entering fnl furlong, hdd and no extr wl ins last.* .... (9 to 1 op 8 to 1 tchd 10 to 1) 2
771 DUNE RIVER [70] 4-9-7 G Carter (1) *sn led, rdn 2 fs out, edgd lft and hdd entering fnl furlong, kpt on.* ....(11 to 2 op 5 to 1) 3
363[2] MCA BELOW THE LINE [58] (v) 5-8-4 (5*) O Pears (6) *trkd ldrs gng wl, not much room one and a half fs out, swtchd ins and hdwy till not clr run inside last, not reco'r*.............................. (9 to 2 op 4 to 1) 4
814[3] PRETONIC [65] 5-9-2 J Lowe (2) *chsd ldrs, pushed alng hfwy, rdn to chal and ev ch appr fnl furlong, sn one pace*............................(11 to 2 op 5 to 1) 5
251[4] ROUND BY THE RIVER [65] 4-9-2 Dale Gibson (5) *hld up, pushed alng and some hdwy hfwy, rdn wl o'r 2 fs out, no imprsn*.........................(8 to 1 op 7 to 1) 6
801 GOLDEN CHIP (Ire) [77] 5-10-0 K Darley (3) *cl up, effrt to chal 2 fs out, sn rdn and ev ch till wknd appr fnl furlong*...........................(4 to 1 fav op 7 to 2) 7+
676 JAHANGIR (Ire) [72] 4-9-9 B Raymond (4) *chsd ldrs, rdn o'r 2 fs out, wknd wl over one out.* ....(7 to 1 op 8 to 1 tchd 10 to 1) 7+
Dist: ½l, 1l, 2l, ½l, 2l, 1½l, dd-ht. 1m 33.00s. a 2.70s (8 Ran).
SR: 40/36/45/27/32/26/33/28/ (Vintage Racing), R C Spicer

931 Rapid Lad Handicap Class D (0-80 4-y-o and up) £4,737 1m 1f 207yds........ (3:50)

530[3] SUPERTOP [59] 5-8-8 Paul Eddery (11) *al prmnt, hdwy 2 fs out, rdn to ld entering fnl furlong, styd on wl.* .... (15 to 2 op 7 to 1 tchd 8 to 1) 1
740* ROMOLA NIJINSKY [60] 5-8-9 D Holland (10) *led 2 fs, cl up till led 4 out, rdn and hdd entering last, not quicken.* .... (6 to 1 op 11 to 2 tchd 13 to 2) 2
620[5] WESTFIELD MOVES (Ire) [58] 5-8-7 J Quinn (9) *chsd ldrs, effrt and bumped 2 fs out, sn rdn and styd on wl ins last*..................................(12 to 1 op 10 to 1) 3
620* JAZILAH (Fr) [69] 5-9-4 W Ryan (8) *al prmnt, effrt and hdwy to chal 2 fs out, ev ch till rdn and no extr entering fnl furlong*..........................(5 to 1 op 9 to 2) 4
739[8] BLACKPATCH HILL [62] 4-8-11 K Darley (13) *in tch, effrt and not much room 2 fs out, sn rdn, styd on one pace appr last*............................(13 to 2 op 11 to 2) 5
530 RED INDIAN [44] 7-7-7 J Fanning (15) *hld up and beh, hdwy o'r 2 fs out, rdn appr fnl furlong, kpt on.* (14 to 1) 6
396[2] SHARQUIN [44] 6-7-7 J Lowe (7) *hld up and beh, hdwy 3 fs out, rdn and kpt on fnl 2 furlongs.* .... (20 to 1 op 25 to 1) 7
645[9] SUGEMAR [56] 7-8-5 N Connorton (4) *chsd ldrs, rdn o'r 2 fs out, sn one pace*...............(16 to 1 tchd 20 to 1) 8
530 SPRAY OF ORCHIDS [48] 4-7-11 F Norton (14) *chsd ldrs till rdn and wknd 2 fs out*.............(25 to 1 op 20 to 1) 9
731[5] TOUCH ABOVE [48] 7-7-11 G Carter (2) *hld up, hdwy on outsd 2 out, sn rdn and wknd appr fnl furlong.* ....(7 to 2 fav tchd 4 to 1 and 3 to 1) 10
592 COMMON COUNCIL [70] 4-9-5 G Duffield (6) *in tch, rdn 2 fs out, wkng whn bumped one and a half furlongs out.* ....(16 to 1) 11
801 SELF EXPRESSION [60] 5-8-9 K Fallon (12) *nvr nr to chal.* ....(12 to 1 op 10 to 1 tchd 14 to 1) 12
ZEPPEKI (Ire) [60] 5-8-9 J Carroll (5) *nvr rch ldrs.* (33 to 1) 13
ZAMANAYN (Ire) [79] 5-10-0 M Birch (1) *cl up, led aftr 2 fs to 4 out, wknd, btn whn badly hmpd two out*.... (50 to 1) 14
645 ROYAL COMEDIAN [46] 4-7-9 Dale Gibson (3) *al rear, tld off fnl 3 fs*.................................... (25 to 1) 15
Dist: 1l, ½l, 1l, 1½l, 1½l, hd, hd, 1½l, 1l, 5l. 2m 5.90s. a 4.50s (15 Ran).
SR: 34/33/30/39/29/8/7/18/7/ (Mrs G A Godfrey), P W Harris

932 Crown Financial Management Challenge Trophy Handicap Class D (0-80 3-y-o) £3,720 1m 1f 207yds................(4:20)

685[5] HAZARD A GUESS (Ire) [54] 7-9 J Lowe (1) *hld up, hdwy on inner o'r 2 fs out, squeezed through appr fnl furlong, rdn to leaed ins last, kpt on*......... (6 to 1 op 5 to 1) 1
468[8] NEMEA (USA) [77] 9-4 G Carter (3) *slwly into strd, hld up, hdwy 3 fs out, swtchd one and a half out, rdn to chal ins last, no extr nr finish.* .... (11 to 2 op 5 to 1 tchd 6 to 1) 2
549[2] MISSA BREVIS (USA) [66] 8-7 G Duffield (6) *sn led, rdn 2 fs out, hdd and no extr ins last*......................(6 to 1) 3
642[2] NOMADIC FIRE [62] 8-3 Paul Eddery (7) *trkd ldrs, effrt and ev ch whn bumped 2 fs out, sn rdn and one pace appr last*...................................(11 to 2 op 5 to 1) 4
468[7] MONDRAGON [72] 8-13 K Darley (2) *hld up, hdwy 2 fs out, not clr run and swtchd appr fnl furlong, sn one pace.* ....(9 to 2 op 4 to 1) 5
644[2] HE'S A KING (USA) [80] 9-7 W Ryan (4) *pld hrd, chsd ldr, rdn o'r 2 fs out, sn wknd*.........(7 to 2 fav op 3 to 1) 6
558 MARIUS (Ire) [77] 9-4 D Holland (5) *chsd ldrs, pushed alng and hdwy 3 fs out, rdn to chal 2 out, wkng whn squeezed out appr last*...(7 to 1 op 6 to 1 tchd 8 to 1) 7
Dist: 1l, hd, 1½l, nk, 7l, 5l. 2m 8.00s. a 6.60s (7 Ran).
SR: -/21/9/2/11/5/-/ (Mrs D Ridley), Mrs J R Ramsden

933 Levy Board Median Auction Maiden Stakes Class E (2-y-o) £3,054 5f..... (4:50)

LEGATEE 8-9 K Darley (8) *chsd ldrs, hdwy 2 fs out, effrt and quickened to ld ins last, ran on.* (7 to 1 op 6 to 1) 1
673[5] SWEETINGS PISCES 9-0 M Birch (4) *led, rdn o'r one furlong out, hdd ins last, kpt on*........(4 to 1 op 5 to 1) 2
673[3] HALI (Ire) 9-0 F Norton (1) *cl up, rdn 2 fs out, ev ch appr fnl furlong, wknd ins last*..............(3 to 1 fav op 2 to 1) 3
564[5] TILQUHILLIE ROSE 8-9 T Lucas (7) *beh till styd on fnl 2 fs.* ....(16 to 1) 4
OVIDEO 8-9 G Duffield (2) *rdn and ev ch 2 fs out, wknd appr fnl furlong*.........................(4 to 1 op 7 to 2) 5
BROUGHTONS PARTNER 9-0 J Quinn (3) *chsd ldrs, rdn 2 fs out, wknd o'r one furlong out.* ....(10 to 1 op 7 to 1 tchd 12 to 1) 6
841[7] PORTITE SOPHIE 8-9 J Lowe (9) *cl up and sn pushed alng, wknd 2 fs out*..............(8 to 1 tchd 10 to 1) 7
NEZ CARRERA 9-0 A Culhane (6) *chsd ldrs and sn pushed alng, hdwy 2 fs out, rdn, edgd lft and wknd appr last.* ....(6 to 1 op 4 to 1) 8
BURRINGHAM BOY 8-9 (5*) O Pears (5) *slwly away and al outpcd, ran green, tld off*........ (14 to 1 op 10 to 1) 9
Dist: ¾l, 4l, ½l, 1l, 3l, 2½l, 4l. 1m 4.00s. a 2.30s (9 Ran).
SR: 34/36/20/13/9/2/ (Mrs J E Young), J Etherington

934 William Hill Handicap Class E (0-70 3-y-o) £3,261 7f 100yds................... (5:20)

685⁹ NORTHERN CHIEF [53] 8-8 J Carroll (8) *al chasing ldrs, hdwy 2 fs out, rdn to ld entering last, sn clr.* ....(9 to 1 op 8 to 1 tchd 10 to 1) 1
707* NORTH ARDAR [55] 8-10 G Duffield (7) *mid-div, hdwy 2 fs out, sn rdn and ev ch appr last, one pace.* ....(5 to 1 fav op 9 to 2) 2
612² PEEDIE PEAT [64] (bl) 9-5 K Darley (4) *sn led, rdn 2 fs out, hdd entering fnl furlong, no extr*... (10 to 1 op 8 to 1) 3
568 GATE OF HEAVEN [38] 7-2 (5*) Darren Moffatt (9) *chsd ldr, chlgd 2 fs out and ev ch till wknd entering last.* ....(33 to 1) 4
710* BRACKENTHWAITE [54] 8-2 (7*) V Halliday (2) *wl beh till styd on fnl 2 fs*........(11 to 2 op 4 to 1) 5
644⁷ HEATHYARDS GEM [62] 9-3 S Perks (5) *chsd ldrs, effrt and hdwy 2 fs out, rdn and ev ch appr fnl furlong, wkng whn hmpd entering last*........(8 to 1 op 7 to 1) 6
590 FESTIN [63] (bl) 9-4 Dale Gibson (12) *chsd ldrs, rdn o'r 2 fs out, wknd over one out*........(7 to 1) 7
683 TTYFRAN [58] 8-13 B Raymond (3) *nvr rch ldrs.* ....(14 to 1 op 12 to 1) 8
833⁹ NEVER IN TOUCH [38] 7-7 L Charnock (6) *al beh.* (33 to 1) 9
519 SOPHISTICATED AIR [66] 9-7 G Carter (11) *al rear.* ....(13 to 2 op 7 to 1 tchd 8 to 1) 10
WHO'S TOM (Ire) [50] 8-5 J Quinn (10) *pld hrd, beh hfwy.* ....(16 to 1 tchd 25 to 1) 11
646 MUHTASHIM (Ire) [60] 9-1 W Ryan (1) *al beh.* ....(15 to 2 op 6 to 1 tchd 8 to 1) 12

Dist: 3l, 1l, 3½l, 1½l, 1l, 2½l, ¾l, 1l, ½l, nk. 1m 34.20s. a 3.90s (12 Ran).
SR: 19/12/18/-/-/-/ (T C Chiang), M H Easterby

BELMONT PARK (USA) (firm) Saturday May 8th

935 Acorn Stakes (Grade 1) (3-y-o) £99,338 1m

SKY BEAUTY (USA) 8-9 M Smith,........(5 to 2 on) 1
EDUCATED RISK (USA) 8-9 J D Bailey,........(14 to 5) 2
IN HER GLORY (USA) 8-9 Julie Krone,........(73 to 10) 3
SILKY FEATHER (USA) 8-9 R Migliore,........(30 to 1) 4
STAR JOLIE (USA) 8-9 J Santos,........(18 to 1) 5
TUESDAY EDITION (USA) 8-9 R Davis,........(33 to 1) pu

Dist: 5l, 2½l, 5l, 1 ¾l. 1m 35.50s. (6 Ran).
(Georgia E Hofmann), H A Jerkens

DOWNPATRICK (IRE)Saturday May 8th

936 Jimmy Casement Bookmaker Fillies Maiden (3-y-o) £1,380 1m 3f 208yds (3:30)

790 MANGANS HILL (Ire) 8-6 (8*) P P Murphy (8)........(16 to 1) 1
SUNSET CAFE (Ire) 8-10 (4*) W J Smith (1)........(11 to 4) 2
639⁹ PRINTOUT (Ire) 8-12⁴ (6*) C Everard (4)........(11 to 4) 3
488⁶ INISHMOT (Ire) 8-8 (6*) J J Behan (6)........(13 to 2) 4
L-WAY FIRST (Ire) 9-0 N Byrne (2)........(5 to 1) 5
MULLAGHEA LASS (Ire) 8-6 (8*) T J Daly (3)........(14 to 1) 6
311 ADJAIYBA (USA) 8-6 (8*) J J Stack (5)........(5 to 2 fav) 7
STEPHENS GUEST (Ire) (bl) 9-0 J D Eddery (7)....(10 to 1) pu

Dist: 3l, 5l, 1½l, 1l. (Time not taken) (8 Ran).
(O Brady), Miss I T Oakes

937 Strangford Fuels Maiden (4-y-o and up) £1,380 1m 5f........(4:00)

HACKETTS CROSS (Ire) 5-9-8 (6*) C Everard (3) ....(11 to 10 fav) 1
PORT ERIN (USA) 4-9-3 (8*) J J Stack (1)........(5 to 4) 2
GONE LIKE THE WIND 6-10-0 N Byrne (5)........(20 to 1) 3
BOLD LILLIAN (Ire) 4-9-11 C F Swan (2)........(6 to 1) 4

Dist: 25l, hd, 1l. (Time not taken) (4 Ran).
(F Heffernan), Noel T Chance

LEOPARDSTOWN (IRE) (good) Saturday May 8th

938 Stepaside (EBF) Maiden (2-y-o) £4,830 6f ....(2:00)

571³ BARTOK (Ire) 9-0 P V Gilson (4)........(2 to 1) 1
CLIFDON FOG (Ire) 9-0 C Roche (1)........(10 to 9 on) 2
MARVIN'S FAITH (Ire) 9-0 S Craine (5)........(10 to 1) 3
786 LUDDEN LADY (Ire) 8-11 M J Kinane (3)........(25 to 1) 4
VENICE (Ire) 9-0 P Shanahan (8)........(10 to 1) 5
786 JOIN FORCES (Ire) 9-0 R Hughes (2)........(14 to 1) 6
YOUR VILLAGE (Ire) 8-11 K J Manning (6)........(12 to 1) 7
MONMOUTH PARK 8-12 (2*) R M Burke (9)........(16 to 1) 8
MAHASEAL (USA) 8-11 W J Supple (7)........(6 to 1) 9

Dist: 1l, 6l, 1½l, sht-hd. 1m 14.80s. a 3.30s (9 Ran).
SR: 22/18/-/-/-/-/ (Mrs G W Jennings), C Collins

939 Killiney Handicap (0-90 3-y-o and up) £3,105 6f........(2:30)

CLASSICAL AFFAIR (Ire) [-] 4-9-2 (8*) R V Skelly (5) (14 to 1) 1
806* GOLD BRAISIM (Ire) [-] 3-8-10 (5ex) C Roche (6)... (7 to 2) 2
306⁵ READY (Ire) [-] 3-9-6 W J Supple (9)........(5 to 2 fav) 3
572⁹ MEMSAHB [-] 4-9-6 M J Kinane (12)........(7 to 1) 4
MASTER WORK [-] (bl) 5-7-7 A J Nolan (2)........(33 to 1) 5
572* MAGIC DON (Ire) [-] 4-8-6 (8*) R T Fitzpatrick (4)....(7 to 1) 6
572⁸ RECOLLECTION (Ire) [-] 4-8-6 (8*) B J Halligan (8) (10 to 1) 7
787 EVERY ONE KNOWS (USA) [-] 4-9-0 (8*) M F Ryan (3) ....(12 to 1) 8
NEVER WRONG [-] 6-9-1 (8*) A J Beale (1)........(12 to 1) 9
GATE LODGE (Ire) [-] 3-9-6 W J O'Connor (11)........(6 to 1) 10
SMOKEY LAD [-] 9-9-7 (6*) J A Heffernan (10)........(14 to 1) 11

Dist: Sht-hd, ¾l, 1½l, 1l. 1m 13.30s. a 1.80s (11 Ran).
SR: 62/47/54/48/17/-/ (Paul Farrell), T M Walsh

940 Amethyst Stakes (Listed) (3-y-o and up) £8,625 1m........(3:00)

667⁵ UNUSUAL HEAT (USA) 3-8-11 M J Kinane (4) *led, jnd o'r 3 fs out till wnt clr 2 furlongs out, quickened wl, styd on strly*........(2 to 1) 1
MALVERNICO (Ire) 5-9-10 C Roche (2) *hld up till prog 2 fs out, kpt on und pres*........(9 to 2) 2
SHAHIK (USA) 3-8-11 W J Supple (1) *hld up, some prog 2 fs out, not quicken*........(3 to 1) 3
KARINIYD (Ire) 3-8-11 R Hughes (3) *trkd ldr till prog to dispute ld o'r 3 fs out, rdn and hdd 2 out, wknd bef last.* ....(7 to 4 fav) 4

Dist: 4l, 1½l, nk. 1m 44.60s. a 6.60s (4 Ran).
(Thomas T S Liang), D K Weld

941 Derrinstown Stud Derby Trial Stakes (Group 3) (3-y-o) £24,000 1¼m........(3:30)

306³ PERFECT IMPOSTER (Ire) 8-11 C Roche (2) *strted slwly, progess und pres o'r 3 fs out, led appr last, kpt on.* ....(4 to 1) 1
639* ADVOCAT (Ger) 8-11 J P Murtagh (1) *trkd ldrs, prog 2 fs out to dispute ld appr last, sn hdd and kpt on*....(4 to 1) 2
FORESEE 8-11 W J Supple (8) *hld up, rdn 4 fs out, prog strt, ran on strly fnl furlong*........(10 to 1) 3
669* HUSHANG (Ire) 8-11 M J Kinane (6) *mid-div, rdn 3 fs out, some prog strt, kpt on*........(5 to 2 fav) 4
576³ SINISSIPI (USA) 8-11 R Hughes (7) *dsptd ld till hdd aftr 4 fs, trkd ldr till chlgd and disputed lead und 2 furlongs, sn headed and wknd*........(4 to 1) 5
788* COLOUR PARTY (USA) 8-11 W J O'Connor (3) *dsptd ld, led aftr 4 fs till hdd bef one out, sn wknd*........(7 to 1) 6
BALLYKETT LADY (USA) 8-8 K J Manning (5) *mid-div, rdn 4 fs out, sn lost pl and wknd*........(14 to 1) 7
639³ L'EQUIPE (Ire) 8-11 J F Egan (4) *al rear, rdn and wknd bef 2 fs out, swshd tail und pres*........(12 to 1) 8

Dist: ½l, 1l, ¾l, 3l. 2m 7.90s. a 3.20s (8 Ran).
SR: 55/54/52/50/44/ (Michael W J Smurfit), J S Bolger

942 Phillipstown Handicap (0-95 4-y-o and up) £5,520 1m 1f........(4:00)

787³ KAYFA (Ire) [-] 4-9-2 (6*) P Carberry (7)........(3 to 1) 1
666 NORDIC DISPLAY (Ire) [-] 5-8-7 J A Heffernan (6)....(8 to 1) 2
4686a ROMAN FORUM (Ire) [-] (bl) 5-8-3 (2*) R M Burke (2) (12 to 1) 3
SHARASTAMINA (USA) [-] 4-8-5 N G McCullagh (4) (13 to 2) 4
666* PRIVATE GUY (Ire) [-] (bl) 4-9-0 (8*,5ex) D J O'Donohoe (8) ....(9 to 2) 5
308* TONY'S FEN [-] 4-9-3 (6*) B J Walsh (9)........(5 to 2 fav) 6
575 OLD TALKA RIVER [-] 6-8-6 R Hughes (1)........(16 to 1) 7
BOLD HABIBTI [-] 6-9-2 C Roche (5)........(9 to 1) 8

Dist: Hd, 2½l, 3l, sht-hd. 1m 56.20s. a 5.70s (8 Ran).
SR: 9/-/-/-/-/ (Vincent Loughnane), Noel Meade

943 Derrinstown Stud 1000 Guineas Trial Race (Listed) (3-y-o) £12,500 1m........(4:30)

576² DANSE ROYALE (Ire) 8-9 R Hughes (5) *led 1st half-furlong, trkd ldr till prog to ld bef 3 out, drifted rght fnl furlong, fnshd first, plcd second,reinstated*........(7 to 2) 1
EUROSTORM (USA) 8-9 P V Gilson (7) *mid-div till rdn and prog 2 fs out, kpt on wl fnl furlong, fnshd second,plcd 1st, Danse Royale reinstated, pld 2nd*........(3 to 1) 2
ADOLESCENCE (Ire) 8-9 P Shanahan (3) *hld up till prog 2 fs out, kpt on wl*........(16 to 1) 3
573⁵ SABAYA (USA) 8-9 W J Supple (6) *hld up, rdn 2 fs out, steady prog, kpt on*........(9 to 1) 4
TBAAREEH (USA) 8-9 C Roche (4) *rear, rdn 2 fs out, not quicken till some prog ins last*........(9 to 1) 5
CHANZI (USA) (bl) 8-12 M J Kinane (1) *trkd ldrs, rdn 2 fs out, wknd bef last*........(11 to 8 fav) 6
ATSUKO (Ire) 8-9 S Craine (2) *led aftr 1st half furlong, hdd bef 3 out, sn wknd, eased ins last*........(16 to 1) 7

Dist: Hd, 1½l, 1l, 6l. 1m 42.00s. a 4.00s (7 Ran).
SR: 22/23/17/14/ (Miss P F O'Kelly), M J Grassick

944 Kerrymount E.B.F. Maiden (3-y-o) £3,450 1 ½m........(5:00)

RAYSEKA (Ire) 8-11 R Hughes (9)........(9 to 4) 1
MOUSE BIRD (Ire) 9-0 J P Murtagh (3)........(10 to 1) 2
257 POLITICAL DOMAIN (Ire) 9-0 M J Kinane (8)........(10 to 1) 3
576⁵ DAHLIA'S BEST (USA) 9-0 W J Supple (4)........(5 to 1) 4
ALYREINA (USA) 8-11 C Roche (5)........(6 to 4 fav) 5

DANAMORE (Ire) 9-0 S Craine (6)..................(7 to 1) 6
850[8] MAJESTIC JOHN (Ire) 8-12 (2*) D G O'Shea (1)....(20 to 1) 7
489[7] THE SALTY FROG (Ire) 9-0 W J O'Connor (2)..... (33 to 1) 8
MISS PITTYPAT (Ire) 8-5 (6*) B Bowens (7)........(50 to 1) 9
Dist: 2½l, sht-hd, 8l, sht-hd. 2m 37.80s. a 6.80s (9 Ran).
SR: 17/15/14/-/-/-/ (H H Aga Khan), John M Oxx

LINGFIELD (good to firm)
Saturday May 8th
Going Correction: MINUS 0.20 sec. per fur.

945 William Hill May Rated Class B (0-95 3-y-o) £6,628 7f.......................... (1:45)

MOON OVER MIAMI [81] 8-12 J Reid (8) *trkd ldrs, led ins fnl furlong, edgd rght und pres, ran on wl.*
..................(20 to 1 op 16 to 1 tchd 25 to 1) 1
846[2] ANOTHER JADE [76] 8-2 (5*) B Doyle (13) *hld up, hdwy on ins o'r 2 fs out, led one out till hdd and no extr inside last*..................... (4 to 1 op 7 to 2 tchd 9 to 2) 2
729[6] I'LLEAVEITOYOU (Ire) [80] 8-11 C Rutter (6) *chsd ldrs, hmpd ins fnl furlong, kpt on wl und pres.*
..............................(20 to 1 tchd 25 to 1) 3
747[2] ABLE CHOICE (Ire) [78] 8-9 L Piggott (10) *cl up, led o'r 2 fs out till hdd one out, hmpd and one pace ins last.*
..................(7 to 2 fav tchd 3 to 1 and 4 to 1) 4
514[3] JERVIA [86] 9-3 M Roberts (7) *chsd ldrs, pushed alng 3 fs out, one pace*......... (5 to 1 tchd 9 to 2 and 11 to 2) 5
494[7] NURYANDRA [80] 8-11 M Hills (11) *wth ldr, hrd rdn o'r 2 fs out, wknd over one out.*
......................(12 to 1 op 16 to 1 tchd 20 to 1) 6
542[3] PAIR OF JACKS (Ire) [76] 8-7 P Robinson (4) *led til hdd o'r 2 fs out, wknd*............ (8 to 1 op 6 to 1 tchd 9 to 1) 7
716[6] SECOND CHANCE (Ire) [76] 8-7 W Newnes (12) *al beh.*
......................(14 to 1 op 12 to 1 tchd 16 to 1) 8
690 TOP PET (Ire) [85] 9-2 T Quinn (9) *al beh.*
.... (10 to 1 op 7 to 1) 9
643[4] MULLITOVER [86] 9-3 W R Swinburn (3) *chsd ldrs till wknd o'r 2 fs out*.............................. (12 to 1 op 7 to 1) 10
ROYAL DEED (USA) [76] 8-4 (3*) J Weaver (2) *hld up, swtchd lft and brief effrt o'r 2 fs out, sn btn.*
....(33 to 1 op 20 to 1) 11
RAKIS (Ire) [90] 9-7 W Carson (1) *rcd alone far side, in tch o'r 4 fs*..................................(20 to 1 op 12 to 1) 12
Dist: 1l, 2½l, sht-hd, 3l, hd, 5l, nk, 3l, ¾l, 7l. 1m 22.44s. a 1.74s (12 Ran).
SR: 51/43/39/36/35/28/9/8/8/ (Barry J Ross), C James

946 Champagne Ruinart Oaks Trial Stakes Class A (Listed Race) (3-y-o) £10,282 1m 3f 106yds.............................. (2:15)

791[2] OAKMEAD (Ire) 8-9 J Reid (5) *cl up, hrd rdn o'r 2 fs out, rallied to ld close hme*........ (2 to 1 jt-fav tchd 5 to 2) 1
662* TALENTED 8-9 W Carson (1) *trkd ldrs, lost pl o'r 4 fs out, rdn and hdwy over 2 out, hrd drvn to ld ins last, hdd cl hme*..................................(2 to 1 jt-fav op 7 to 4) 2
662[2] DANCING PRIZE (Ire) 8-9 W R Swinburn (3) *led aftr one furlong, rdn alng 3 fs out, hdd ins last, no extr.*
....(4 to 1 tchd 9 to 2) 3
BRIGHTSIDE (Ire) 8-9 T Quinn (4) *led one furlong, cl up, rdn 3 fs out, one pace frm 2 out.*
......................(12 to 1 op 8 to 1 tchd 14 to 1) 4
PRINCESS DAVID (USA) 8-9 M Roberts (6) *beh, styd on frm o'r one furlong out, nvr dngrs.*
......................(16 to 1 op 10 to 1 tchd 20 to 1) 5
755[2] BOBBIE DEE 8-9 J Williams (2) *in tch till wknd o'r 3 fs out, tld off*..................................(8 to 1 op 6 to 1) 6
Dist: Nk, 1½l, 2½l, 1½l, 10l. 2m 28.13s. a 3.93s (6 Ran).
SR: 33/32/29/24/21/1/ (R E Sangster), P W Chapple-Hyam

947 Alpine Double Glazing Derby Trial Stakes Class A (Group 3) (3-y-o) £33,836 1m 3f 106yds.............................. (2:45)

BOB'S RETURN (Ire) 9-0 P Robinson (9) *sn led, clr o'r 3 fs out, tired ins last, hrd rdn, all out.*
......................(14 to 1 op 12 to 1 tchd 16 to 1) 1
736* TIOMAN ISLAND 9-0 T Quinn (7) *cl up, chsd wnr fnl 3 fs, ran on ins last*.......... (5 to 1 op 9 to 2 tchd 6 to 1) 2
679* SHAREEK (USA) 9-0 W R Swinburn (5) *trkd ldrs, rdn alng 3 fs out, one pace*.............................(11 to 1 op 10 to 1) 3
494* AZZILFI 9-0 W Carson (2) *trkd ldrs, pushed alng o'r 5 fs out, hrd rdn over 2 out, kpt on.*
..................................(9 to 2 op 4 to 1 tchd 5 to 1) 4
540[3] YELTSIN 9-0 M Roberts (8) *wtd wth in rear, rdn alng o'r 4 fs out, not pace to chal.*
............................(5 to 4 fav op 6 to 4 tchd 7 to 4) 5
736[2] ZIND (Ire) 9-0 J Reid (4) *wtd wth in rear, rdn alng o'r 3 fs out, nvr on terms*.......(5 to 1 op 3 to 1 tchd 11 to 2) 6
761[2] FABULOUS MTOTO 9-0 J Williams (1) *slwly into strd, al beh, tld off*.....................(33 to 1 op 20 to 1) 7
BEAUMAN 9-0 M Hills (6) *trkd ldrs till wknd o'r 5 fs out, tld off*............. (66 to 1 op 50 to 1 tchd 100 to 1) 8
Dist: Nk, 2l, hd, 3l, sht-hd, 15l, 7l. 2m 25.34s. a 1.14s (8 Ran).
SR: 66/65/61/60/54/53/23/9/ (Mrs G A E Smith), M H Tompkins

948 Maxims Club Handicap Class D (0-80 3-y-o and up) £3,552 6f.................... (3:15)

760[2] FACE NORTH (Ire) [57] 5-8-10 T Quinn (5) *trkd ldrs, led ins fnl furlong, pushed out.*
..................(100 to 30 fav op 5 to 2 tchd 7 to 2) 1
4725a SYLVAN BREEZE [70] (v) 5-9-9 W Newnes (4) *cl up, led o'r 4 fs out till hdd and one pace ins last*.......... (33 to 1) 2
677 HARDLINER [65] 4-9-4 P Robinson (2) *in tch, shaken up o'r one furlong out, kpt on one pace*.......... (33 to 1) 3
568 LADY SABO [62] 4-8-12 (3*) D Harrison (8) *trkd ldrs, pushed alng hfwy, kpt on one pace*........ (6 to 1 tchd 7 to 1) 4
605[7] MASNUN (USA) [73] 8-9-9 (3*) J Weaver (6) *beh, hdwy o'r one furlong out, nrst finish.*
......................(10 to 1 op 8 to 1 tchd 12 to 1) 5
WHERE'S THE DANCE [69] 3-8-11 M Roberts (3) *trkd ldrs til wknd one furlong out, better for race.*
....(16 to 1 op 12 to 1) 6
677 TRUTHFUL IMAGE [67] (bl) 4-9-6 D Biggs (13) *hmpd strt, beh, hrd drvn o'r 2 fs out, nvr nrr.*
............................(11 to 2 op 9 to 2 tchd 6 to 1) 7
771 ACROSS THE BAY [69] (v) 6-9-8 W R Swinburn (9) *chsd ldrs, rdn alng o'r 2 fs out, sn btn*......(10 to 1 tchd 11 to 1) 8
760[5] GREAT HALL [44] (bl) 4-7-11 A Mackay (10) *led til hdd o'r 4 fs out, wknd 2 out*......(6 to 1 op 5 to 1 tchd 13 to 2) 9
615[9] HARRY'S COMING [61] 9-9-0 C Rutter (1) *cl up far side, rdn 2 fs out, sn btn*...(12 to 1 op 10 to 1 tchd 14 to 1) 10
GALLANT HOPE [51] 11-8-4 N Carlisle (12) *badly hmpd strt, al beh*..............................(12 to 1 op 16 to 1) 11
754[2] QUICK STEEL [53] 5-7-13 (7*) S Mulvey (11) *unruly stalls, almost uns rdr strt, rider lost irons, al tld off.*
....(6 to 1 op 4 to 1) 12
Dist: 1½l, 3l, ¾l, nk, ½l, 1½l, nk, 1l, 2½l, 1½l. 1m 10.68s. a 1.68s (12 Ran).
SR: 38/45/28/22/32/15/18/19/-/ (Normandy Developments (London)), R Akehurst

949 Overtons Restaurants Selling Stakes Class E (2-y-o) £3,640 5f............ (3:45)

715 RISKIE THINGS 7-13 (7*) Mark Denaro (11) *trkd ldrs, led one furlong out, ran on wl.*
......................(16 to 1 op 8 to 1 tchd 20 to 1) 1
496[8] GRANMAS DELIGHT 8-6 M Roberts (5) *trkd ldrs, shaken up o'r one furlong out, ran on wl.*
......................(12 to 1 op 8 to 1 tchd 14 to 1) 2
776 ERRIS BOY 8-11 M Hills (1) *al prmnt, ev ch one furlong out, one pace*............(4 to 1 op 3 to 1 tchd 5 to 1) 3
625[2] LITTLE EMMELINE 8-6 N Carlisle (9) *led til hdd one furlong out, one pace*..............(5 to 2 fav op 2 to 1) 4
625[6] FOREVER BLUSHING 7-13 (7*) D McCabe (4) *in tch, sn pushed alng, hdwy appr fnl furlong, styd on.*
....(33 to 1 op 20 to 1) 5
MISS IGLOO 8-6 W Newnes (14) *beh, styd on ins fnl furlong, nrst finish.* (16 to 1 op 10 to 1 tchd 20 to 1) 6
CHARISMA GIRL 8-6 T Quinn (2) *trkd ldrs, pld out and effrt o'r one furlong out, sn btn.*
......................(10 to 1 op 8 to 1 tchd 16 to 1) 7
MARTIAN FOREST 8-6 J Williams (3) *strted slwly, outpcd til styd on ins fnl furlong, nvr nrr.*
......................(16 to 1 op 10 to 1 tchd 20 to 1) 8
718[9] BEV'S FOLLY (bl) 8-3 (3*) J Weaver (10) *cl up til wknd wl o'r one furlong out*...... (10 to 1 op 7 to 1 tchd 12 to 1) 9
EL COHETE 8-6 (5*) B Doyle (15) *dwlt, al beh.*
......................(14 to 1 op 6 to 1 tchd 16 to 1) 10
337[7] KISS NO TELL (Ire) 8-3 (3*) D Harrison (6) *outpcd.*
......................(16 to 1 op 10 to 1 tchd 20 to 1) 11
490[4] ENTENTE CORDIALE (Ire) 8-11 W Carson (7) *cl up til wknd o'r one furlong out*.....(13 to 2 op 5 to 1 tchd 7 to 1) 12
730 INDIAN CASTLE (Ire) 8-11 J Reid (8) *dwlt, al beh.*
....(25 to 1 op 20 to 1) 13
SULLAMELL 8-11 C Rutter (13) *nvr gng pace, sn wl beh.*
......................(16 to 1 op 10 to 1 tchd 20 to 1) 14
BERKELEY HERO 8-11 P Robinson (12) *sn pld up, dismounted*............(25 to 1 op 20 to 1 tchd 33 to 1) pu
Dist: Nk, 1l, nk, 4l, nk, sht-hd, 2l, ½l, nk, nk. 1m 0.14s. a 3.24s (15 Ran).
SR: 7/6/7/1/-/-/ (Terry Pasquale), J S Moore

950 Europharm Group Maiden Stakes Class D (Div I) (3-y-o) £3,348 7f............. (4:15)

624[3] WALNUT BURL (Ire) 9-0 J Reid (11) *mid-div, hdwy 2 fs out, ev ch ins last, crrd lkeft cl hme, fnshd second, awarded race*..................(20 to 1 op 14 to 1 tchd 25 to 1) 1
784[2] GRAN SENORUM (USA) 9-0 T Quinn (8) *cl up, led o'r 3 fs out, shaken up one out, edgd lft, ran on, fnshd 1st, plcd second*......(7 to 2 co-fav op 3 to 1 tchd 4 to 1) 2
712[2] CASTEL ROSSELO 9-0 M Hills (9) *strted slwly, beh, hdwy wl o'r one furlong out, sn ev ch, one pace whn hmpd cl hme*..................(7 to 1 op 6 to 1 tchd 8 to 1) 3
THE LITTLE FERRET 9-0 S Raymont (4) *cl up, led 4 fs out till hdd o'r 3 out, one pace*..................(7 to 2 co-fav op 5 to 2 tchd 9 to 2) 4
470[3] SO INTREPID (Ire) 9-0 W R Swinburn (12) *led til hdd 4 fs out, cl up, ev ch one furlong out, wknd*....(7 to 2 co-fav op 3 to 1 tchd 4 to 1) 5

529 ELEGANT HUSSAR 8-9 (5*) B Doyle (5) *chsd ldrs, rdn and styd on one pace fnl 2 fs*..................... (20 to 1) 6
602 WOODMANS STAR 8-9 (5*) K Rutter (13) *chsd ldrs o'r 4 fs.* ....(50 to 1) 7
623[4] MARAT (USA) 9-0 W Newnes (6) *trkd ldrs til wknd wl o'r 2 fs out*............................(20 to 1 op 16 to 1) 8
TASSAGH BRIDGE (Ire) 8-4 (5*) M Fenton (14) *trkd ldrs till wknd 2 fs out*..(50 to 1) 9
519[9] VADDALLIAN 9-0 J Williams (3) *nvr dngrs*........(50 to 1) 10
751 DAWALIB (USA) 9-0 W Carson (1) *rcd alone far side, in tch till wknd 2 fs out*....................(6 to 1 op 7 to 2) 11
759 HARD ROCK MINER 8-7 (7*) S Mulvey (10) *sn outpcd.* ....(50 to 1) 12
CATEMPO (Ire) 9-0 C Rutter (2) *slwly into strd, in tch to hfwy, sn beh, tld off*..........................(50 to 1) 13

Dist: Hd, 1l, 4l, 2l, 1l, 4l, nk, 2½l, sht-hd, 1½l. 1m 24.23s. a 3.53s (13 Ran).
SR: 26/25/22/10/4/1/ (G Steinberg), L J Holt

951 Europharm Group Maiden Stakes Class D (Div II) (3-y-o) £3,348 7f.............(5:15)

538 FULL FEATHER (USA) 9-0 G Hind (4) *tacked across to stands rail, made virtually all, ran on wl.* ....(11 to 2 op 4 to 1 tchd 7 to 1) 1
510[3] NAFUTH (USA) 9-0 W Carson (11) *trkd ldrs, chsd wnr frm 2 fs out, sn hrd rdn, no response.* ....(6 to 5 fav op Evens tchd 5 to 4 on and 5 to 4) 2
WELL SUITED 9-0 J Reid (9) *chsd ldrs, one pace frm o'r 2 fs out*..............................(4 to 1 tchd 5 to 1) 3
417[7] SLEEPTITE (Fr) 9-0 D Biggs (2) *in tch, pushed alng hfwy, styd on ins last*......(14 to 1 op 12 to 1 tchd 16 to 1) 4
872 BLOWING (USA) 8-7 (7*) Gaye Harwood (8) *chsd ldrs til wknd o'r 2 fs out*.................(20 to 1 op 14 to 1) 5
FINDON ACADEMY (Ire) 9-0 Candy Morris (3) *cl up til wknd appr fnl 2 fs*.......................(50 to 1 op 20 to 1) 6
MISS COPYFORCE 8-9 W Newnes (6) *sn outpcd, hdwy o'r one furlong out, nrst finish*......(20 to 1 tchd 50 to 1) 7
583 MISS MICHELLE 8-6 (3*) D Harrison (7) *nvr on terms.* ....(50 to 1 op 20 to 1) 8
583[7] ARRASAS LADY 8-9 C Rutter (13) *outpcd, sn tld off, some late hdwy*..........................(50 to 1 op 33 to 1) 9
707[3] SAXON MAGIC 8-9 J Williams (12) *beh frm hfwy.* ....(10 to 1 op 12 to 1 tchd 16 to 1) 10
510[7] SCENT OF POWER 9-0 C Dwyer (1) *trkd ldrs to hfwy.* ....(16 to 1 op 12 to 1 tchd 20 to 1) 11
RUPERT'S REVENGE (Ire) 9-0 W Hood (5) *slwly into strd, al beh*..............................(50 to 1 op 20 to 1) 12

Dist: 1½l, 3½l, 7l, ½l, 1l, 5l, ½l, 3½l, 2½l, 2l. 1m 23.65s. a 2.95s (12 Ran).
SR: 35/30/19/-/-/-/ (Anthony Speelman), J H M Gosden

LINGFIELD (A.W) (std)
Saturday May 8th
Going Correction: PLUS 0.10 sec. per fur.

952 Teenoso Handicap Class D (0-80 4-y-o and up) £3,114 1m......................(4:45)

758[7] SYLVAN SABRE (Ire) [62] (v) 4-9-4 W Newnes (5) *cl up, led o'r 2 fs out, clr over one out, ran on wl.* ....(10 to 1 tchd 12 to 1) 1
754 SARUM [53] 7-8-9 C Rutter (4) *beh, hdwy o'r 4 fs out, hrd rdn over one out, not pace of wnr.* (7 to 2 tchd 4 to 1) 2
GRAND GUIGNOL [72] 5-10-0 M Hills (2) *led til hdd o'r 2 fs out, sn outpcd*.......(100 to 30 op 5 to 2 tchd 7 to 2) 3
458[5] MISSY-S (Ire) [48] 4-8-1 (3*) D Harrison (3) *in cl tch, rdn alng 3 fs out, wknd o'r one out*......(9 to 2 op 3 to 1) 4
834[3] BUDDY'S FRIEND (Ire) [53] 5-8-9 D Biggs (1) *trkd ldr till lost pl 5 fs out, rdn alng 3 out, wknd o'r one out.* ....(7 to 4 fav tchd 15 to 8) 5

Dist: 7l, 1l, ½l, 3½l. 1m 41.11s. a 4.91s (5 Ran).
SR: 42/12/28/2/-/ (Sir Wm Garthwaite), P Mitchell

COLOGNE (GER) (soft)
Sunday May 9th

953 Mehl Mulhens Rennen (Group 2) (3-y-o) £60,000 1m.............................(3:40)

KORNADO 9-2 A Best, *al prmnt, 3rd strt, led one and a half fs out, clr dist, ran on wl*........................ 1
NASR ALLAH (USA) 9-2 G Bocskai, *al prmnt, second strt, led 2 till hdd one and a half out, kpt on one pace*..... 2
IROKESE (Ger) 9-2 A Helfenbein, *6th strt, ran on one pace o'r one furlong out*................................ 3
526[5] DARBONNE (USA) 9-2 K Darley, *kpt on one pace fnl 2 fs, nvr dngrs*.. 4
613[4] GLORIEUX DANCER (Fr) 9-2 E Legrix, *4th strt, no hdwy fnl 2 fs*.. 5
LANDO (Ger) 9-2 A Tylicki, *trkd ldr till led aftr 2 fs till two out, one pace*.. 6
KOLN EXPRESS (USA) 9-2 W Ryan, *nvr nr to chal*........ 7
271[2] ARABIC TREASURE (USA) 9-2 M J Kinane, *al mid-div*..... 8
TINA'S KING (Ger) 9-2 A Boschert, *nvr a factor*.......... 9
588* COLWAY ROCK (USA) 9-2 G Duffield, *beh fnl 3 fs*......... 0
474[2] ARMAN'S SAX (Ire) 9-2 W Carson, *beh fnl 3 fs*........... 0
PHANTOMIC (USA) 9-2 H Horwart, *led for 2 fs, wknd rpdly strt*.. 0
PHARNAS 9-2 L Hammer-Hansen, *al rear*................ 0
FRANCESOLI (USA) 9-2 T Hellier, *beh fnl 2 fs*............ 0

Dist: 2½l, 1 ¾l, 1 ¼l, hd, hd, 1 ¾l, ¾l, ½l. 1m 36.39s. (14 Ran).
(Stall Granum), Bruno Schuetz

LONGCHAMP (FR) (good to soft)
Sunday May 9th

954 Dubai Poule d'Essai des Poulains (Group 1) (3-y-o) £119,474 1m..............(3:00)

431* KINGMAMBO (USA) 9-2 C Asmussen (5) *6th strt, rdn and hdwy 2 fs out, quickened to ld one and a half out, ran on wl*..(7 to 2) 1
794[3] BIN AJWAAD (Ire) 9-2 M Roberts (4) *8th strt, chlgd on outsd, rdn 2 fs out, ran on wl fnl furlong*... (102 to 10) 2
HUDO (USA) 9-2 E Saint-Martin (8) *3rd strt, ev ch 2 fs out, kpt on und pres*..........................(7 to 2) 3
613[2] SEMILLON 9-2 A Badel (7) *hld up and beh strt, ran on fnl furlong, nrst finish*..........................(13 to 1) 4
536[5] FANTASTIC DREAM (Ire) 9-2 D Boeuf (3) *nvr nrr*. (18 to 1) 5
637[2] BERINSFIELD 9-2 O Peslier (6) *chsd ldr, second strt, wknd o'r one furlong out*..........................(5 to 3 on) 6
BLUSH RAMBLER (USA) 9-2 W R Swinburn (2) *4th strt, rdn and no extr 2 fs out*..........................(54 to 10) 7
613* ZIETEN (USA) 9-2 T Jarnet (9) *7th strt, hdwy o'r 2 fs out, ev ch two out, wknd quickly*..........................(5 to 3 on) 8
580[3] TINNERS WAY (USA) 9-2 Pat Eddery (1) *led till one and a half fs out, wknd quickly*..........................(76 to 10) 9
746* FIRM PLEDGE (USA) 9-2 A Munro (10) *al rear, wl beh fnl 2 fs*..(26 to 1) 10

Dist: 1½l, 4l, ½l, sht-nk, nk, ½l, 5l, 2½l, 8l. 1m 39.10s. a 1.60s (10 Ran).
SR: 78/73/61/59/58/57/55/40/32/ (S S Niarchos), F Boutin

955 Prix Hocquart (Group 3) (3-y-o) £44,695 1 ½m..............................(3:35)

408[2] REGENCY 9-2 Pat Eddery (4) *trkd ldr, led o'r 3 fs out, ran on wl*..(2 to 1) 1
485[2] MARCHAND DE SABLE (USA) 9-2 D Bouef (3) *second 3 fs out, chlgd 2 out, no imprsn*..........................(27 to 10) 2
485[3] SAWASDEE (Fr) 9-2 J Boisnard (1) *3rd 3 fs out, kpt on one pace fnl quarter-m*..........................(15 to 1) 3
576* SHANDON LAKE (Ire) 9-2 C Roche (5) *5th strt, rdn o'r 2 fs out, kpt on one pace*..........................(17 to 1) 4
485[4] ARINTHOD (Fr) 9-2 F Head (8) *4th strt, no hdwy fnl 2 fs.* ....(98 to 10) 5
485* FORT WOOD (USA) 9-2 T Jarnet (7) *6th strt, rdn and btn 2 fs out*..........................(13 to 10 jt-fav) 6
ANGIO (USA) 9-2 M Boutin (9) *nvr dngrs*..........(39 to 1) 7
KNOWN LOVER (USA) 9-2 O Doleuze (6) *led till o'r 3 fs out, wknd*..(2 to 1) 8
CANADIAN SHIELD (Ire) 9-2 O Peslier (2) *3rd till wknd o'r 3 fs out*..........................(13 to 10 jt-fav) 9

Dist: 1½l, 6l, hd, 1½l, 2½l, 6l, dist, 4l. 2m 34.60s. a 5.50s (9 Ran).
SR: 47/44/32/31/28/23/11/-/-/ (K Abdulla), Mme C Head

956 Prix de Montretout (Listed) (4-y-o and up) £14,337 7f.........................(4:05)

GOTHLAND (Fr) 4-8-12 M Boutin,........................ 1
345[3] CRACK REGIMENT (USA) 5-8-12 E Saint-Martin,.......... 2
4712a[3] SHIVAREE (Fr) 4-8-12 W R Swinburn,.................... 3
VOLERIS (Fr) 4-9-2 C Asmussen,........................ 4

Dist: Nk, 1½l, sht-hd, 3l, ½l, ½l. 1m 22.40s. a 2.90s (7 Ran).
SR: 55/54/49/52/ (H Chalhoub), J Hammond

SAN SIRO (ITY) (heavy)
Sunday May 9th

957 Coppa d'Oro di Milano (Group 3) (4-y-o and up) £32,886 1m 7f.............(2:20)

DRUM TAPS (USA) 7-8-11 J Reid, *rcd in 3rd, swtchd outsd and prog to go second 4 fs out, led 2 and a half out, easily*.. 1
553[4] ONESIXNINE (Ire) 5-8-8 P Shanahan, *hld up, 4th strt, ran on fnl furlong*.. 2
JUNGLE DANCER (Ire) 5-8-11 D Holland, *led till 2 and a half fs out, one pace*.. 3
4727a[2] ALMANOR 4-8-11 B Jovine, *second strt, wknd fnl furlong*.. 4

Dist: 7l, 2l, ¾l. 3m 15.90s. (4 Ran).
(Yoshio Asakawa), Lord Huntingdon

958 Premio Emanuele Filiberto (Group 3) (3-y-o) £29,048 1¼m..................(3:40)

4704a* JOHNNY STECCHINO (USA) 9-2 J Reid, *rcd in 3rd to strt, hdwy 3 fs out, led 2 out, cmftbly*.......................... 1
4703a[6] CAMPALTO (Ire) 9-2 B Jovine, *6th strt, ran on fnl 2 fs, no imprsn*.. 2

688[5] IOMMELLI (Ire) 9-2 L Piggott, *hld up, 5th strt, styd on ins fnl furlong* 3
STEVE LUCKY (Ire) 9-2 G Forte, *nvr nrr* 4
4703a* WOOTTON RIVERS (USA) 9-2 D Holland, *second strt, wknd o'r 2 fs out* 5
BALBOA ROYAL (Ire) 9-2 G Bietolini, *led till wknd o'r 2 fs out* 6
COMMANCHE GOLD (Ire) 9-2 Jacqueline Freda, *strted slwly, al rear* 7
Dist: 1l, 3l, ¾l, sht-hd, nk, 2½l. 2m 6.50s. (7 Ran).
(Scuderia Lady M), L D'Auria

KILLARNEY (IRE) (good to firm)
Monday May 10th

959 Buckler Handicap (0-75 3-y-o and up) £3,452 1½m. .... (6:30)

DARK SWAN (Ire) [-] 3-7-7 (2*) D G O'Shea, ... (50 to 1) 1
789 GLENBRACK [-] 3-8-5 J F Egan (3) .... (8 to 1) 2
ANGAREB (Ire) [-] 4-8-11 P V Gilson (11) .... (6 to 1) 3
LAGRION (USA) [-] 4-9-4 N Byrne (2) .... (10 to 1) 4
936[4] INISHMOT (Ire) [-] 3-7-10 (6*) R V Skelly (6) .... (16 to 1) 5
280 BOBADIL (Ire) [-] 3-7-8 L O'Shea, ... (20 to 1) 6
LAKE HOTEL (Ire) [-] 4-9-3 M J Kinane (13) .... (12 to 1) 7
SOPHISM (USA) [-] 4-9-0 P Shanahan (7) .... (14 to 1) 8
CRAZY GAIL [-] 6-9-6 C F Swan (12) .... (6 to 1) 9
575 GREEN GLEN (USA) [-] 4-9-4 (6*) J J Behan (14) ... (5 to 1) 10
706[2] STEEL GEM (Ire) [-] (bl) 4-8-3 W J Supple (5) .. (10 to 3 fav) 11
ZVORNIK [-] 6-9-0 (6*) P Carberry (8) .... (10 to 1) 12
TENCA (Ire) [-] 3-7-13 A J Nolan (10) .... (12 to 1) 13
NORDIC SENSATION (Ire) [-] 4-9-0 K J Manning (4) (8 to 1) 14
575 PURPLE EMPEROR (Fr) [-] 4-10-0 S Craine (15) ... (12 to 1) 15
Dist: 1l, ¾l, hd, sht-hd. 2m 42.20s. (15 Ran).
(T J O'Mara), T J O'Mara

960 Three Lakes Hotel Maiden (3-y-o) £3,452 1m 100yds. .... (7:30)

TAWAR (Ire) 9-0 M J Kinane (6) .... (6 to 4 on) 1
806[8] FLORA WOOD (Ire) 8-11 W J Supple (5) .... (4 to 1) 2
806[5] WHAT MAGIC (Ire) 8-7 (4*) W J Smith (4) .... (10 to 1) 3
868 TRILLICK (Ire) 8-5 (6*) J A Heffernan (1) .... (10 to 1) 4
669[6] PALACE PARADE (USA) 9-0 J F Egan (2) .... (14 to 1) 5
704[2] BOCANDE (Ire) 9-0 S Craine (7) .... (4 to 1) 6
669[8] RASSETTE (Ire) 8-11 K J Manning (8) .... (12 to 1) 7
ARCH-T-GLEN (Ire) 8-6 (8*) D M McCullagh (9) .... (25 to 1) 8
847 SUNBED SUE (Ire) 8-11 Joanna Morgan (3) .... (50 to 1) 9
Dist: 1½l, 2l, 2½l, 7l. 1m 45.60s. (9 Ran).
(H H Aga Khan), John M Oxx

961 Quills Woolen Market Ladies Race (4-y-o and up) £3,625 1½m. .... (8:00)

309[3] FORCE SEVEN 6-10-2 Mrs S McCarthy (6) .... (2 to 1) 1
895[3] RISZARD (USA) 4-10-12 Miss C Hutchinson (3) (Evens fav) 2
309 CURRENCY BASKET (Ire) 4-10-12 Mrs M Mullins (2) (5 to 1) 3
ALL YOURS (Ire) 4-10-10 Miss J Lewis (7) .... (10 to 1) 4
UPPINGHAM 7-10-5 Miss C Bowden (5) .... (16 to 1) 5
851 VON CARTY (Ire) 4-10-2 Mrs F O'Sullivan (4) .... (33 to 1) 6
SUMMER FOX 6-10-5 Miss N Swan (9) .... (25 to 1) 7
CRAZY LADY 7-10-2 Mrs K Walsh (1) .... (33 to 1) 8
Dist: Hd, 1l, 7l, dist. 2m 42.20s. (8 Ran).
(Mrs C A Moore), P Mullins

REDCAR (good to firm (races 1,2), good (3,4,5,6,7))
Monday May 10th

Going Correction: MINUS 0.15 sec. per fur. (races 1,2), MINUS 0.05 (3,4,5,6,7)

962 Kilton Selling Stakes Class G (3-y-o and up) £2,070 7f. .... (2:15)

828[3] BALLAD DANCER 8-9-5 (5*) Darren Moffatt (15) *hld up, gd hdwy o'r 2 fs out, rdn to ld entering fnl furlong, ran on.* .... (13 to 2 op 6 to 1 tchd 7 to 1) 1
681[4] DELPIOMBO 7-9-7 K Fallon (1) *mid-div, hdwy 3 fs out, effrt and rdn 2 out, led briefly appr fnl furlong, sn hdd and one pace* .... (7 to 1 op 11 to 2) 2
828[2] FLETCHER'S BOUNTY (Ire) 4-9-7 K Darley (12) *sn beh, gd hdwy o'r 2 fs out, rdn and styd on entering fnl furlong.* .... (9 to 4 fav op 7 to 2 tchd 4 to 1) 3
813 EASTERN GLOW 3-8-4 W Woods (17) *slwly into strd, mid-div till hdwy o'r 2 fs out, rdn and kpt on one pace fnl furlong* .... (11 to 1 op 10 to 1 tchd 12 to 1) 4
548[6] THE RIGHT TIME (bl) 8-9-10 N Day (6) *cl up, led hfwy till o'r one furlong out, grad wknd* ..... (10 to 1 op 8 to 1) 5
590 INDIAN SECRET (Ire) 3-8-9 J Fortune (7) *cl up, effrt and ev ch 2 fs out, sn rdn and grad wknd.* .... (8 to 1 op 12 to 1 tchd 14 to 1) 6
650[9] MR SNAIL (bl) 5-9-10 M Roberts (16) *in tch, effrt and hdwy o'r 2 fs out, sn rdn and one pace.* .... (12 to 1 op 10 to 1 tchd 14 to 1) 7
650 CRIMSON CONSORT (Ire) (bl) 4-9-7 Kim Tinkler (4) *cl up, rdn o'r 3 fs out, sn wknd* .... (50 to 1) 8
BRAXTON BRAGG (Ire) 3-8-9 M Birch (5) *beh till some hdwy fnl 2 fs* .... (16 to 1 op 20 to 1) 9
SUPER CHARGE 4-9-4 (3*) S Maloney (14) *al mid-div.* .... (50 to 1) 10
YOUNG VALENTINE 4-9-10 A Culhane (2) *led to hfwy, sn rdn and wknd 2 fs out* .... (8 to 1 op 5 to 1) 11
PREMIER MAJOR (Ire) 4-9-7 Paul Eddery (11) *nvr rchd ldrs.* .... (25 to 1) 12
BLUE TRUMPET 3-8-9 Dale Gibson (9) *al rear.* .... (8 to 1 op 7 to 1) 13
636 THROW AWAY LINE 4-9-2 S Webster (13) *chsd ldrs to hfwy, sn lost pl* .... (33 to 1 op 20 to 1) 14
636[9] CHANCE REPORT 5-9-5 D Holland (10) *in tch to hfwy, sn beh* .... (20 to 1 op 16 to 1) 15
80 CIZARD (Ire) 3-8-4 N Connorton (8) *beh, hdwy o'r 2 fs out, sn rdn and wknd* .... (66 to 1) 16
133[7] CREPT OUT (Ire) 4-9-10 J Carroll (18) *al rear.* .... (16 to 1 op 14 to 1) 17
CREAM OF THE CROP (Ire) 5-9-4 (3*) S D Williams (3) *al beh.* .... (50 to 1 op 33 to 1) 18
Dist: 2½l, 1½l, ½l, 7l, 1½l, 1l, ¾l, hd, ½l, 4l. 1m 25.60s. a 3.80s (18 Ran).
SR: 37/26/21/2/1/-/ (W B Imison), Mrs P A Barker

963 Huntcliffe Fillies Handicap Class D (0-80 3-y-o) £3,465 7f. .... (2:45)

741* ANUSHA [60] 8-6 J Carroll (3) *in tch, hdwy 3 fs out, rdn wl o'r one out, styd on to ld ins last* .... (7 to 2 jt-fav op 5 to 2) 1
398[5] RUBY COOPER [52] 7-10[1] (3*) S Maloney (8) *led, rdn 2 fs out, hdd ins last, kpt on* .... (7 to 1 op 5 to 1) 2
SILENT EXPRESSION [70] 9-2 M Tebbutt (2) *stumbled strt and beh, hdwy hfwy, rdn and kpt on fnl 2 fs.* (7 to 2 jt-fav tchd 4 to 1) 3
742[2] LAMSONETTI [56] 8-2 Dale Gibson (4) *hld up, hdwy 3 fs out, sn rdn and one pace fnl 2 furlongs.* .... (9 to 2 op 7 to 2) 4
4687a[7] WALID'S PRINCESS (Ire) [55] 8-1 M Roberts (1) *cl up till rdn and wknd wl o'r 2 fs out* .... (6 to 1 op 4 to 1) 5
711[6] MARIBELLA [59] 8-5 F Norton (7) *chsd ldrs, rdn 3 fs out, sn wknd* .... (12 to 1 op 8 to 1) 6
683 RAIN SPLASH [75] 9-0 (7*) Claire Balding (6) *cl up to hfwy, sn wknd* .... (20 to 1 op 14 to 1 tchd 25 to 1) 7
644[5] FORT VALLY [64] 8-10 J Fortune (5) *chsd ldrs, rdn alng hfwy, wknd o'r 2 fs out* .... (8 to 1 op 7 to 1) 8
Dist: Nk, 3l, 1l, 5l, nk, 6l, 1½l. 1m 25.90s. a 4.10s (8 Ran).
SR: 15/6/15/-/-/ (Yahya Nasib), J Berry

964 'Worth Laying' Handicap Stakes Class E (0-70 4-y-o and up) £3,054 1m 1f. .... (3:15)

902* SWEET MIGNONETTE [62] 5-9-0 (7*) Gaye Harwood (11) *hld up and beh, hdwy on outer 3 fs out, rdn and styd on strly fnl furlong to ld nr line* ..... (9 to 4 fav op 7 to 2) 1
645[8] PRIDE OF PENDLE [37] 4-7-3 (7*) Kim McDonnell (7) *al prmnt, led 3 fs out, rdn entering last, hdd nr finish.* .... (13 to 2 op 6 to 1) 2
366 LADY DONOGHUE (USA) [45] 4-7-11 (7*) Wendy Jones (12) *chsd ldrs, effrt and ev ch whn sddld slpd 2 fs out, kpt on one pace* .... (25 to 1 op 33 to 1 tchd 20 to 1) 3
731 ALBERT [46] 6-7-12 (7*) Sharon Millard (1) *beh till hdwy 2 fs out, rdn and styd on wl last.* .... (11 to 2 op 9 to 2 tchd 6 to 1) 4
756[2] WAKI GOLD (USA) [69] 6-10-0 Lorna Vincent (10) *mid-div, hdwy 3 fs out, effrt and rdn 2 out, sn one pace.* .... (6 to 1 op 5 to 1 tchd 13 to 2) 5
498[5] SKIMMER HAWK [36] 4-7-2 (7*) Sally Radford-Howes (8) *chsd ldrs, rdn o'r 2 fs out, sn wknd.* .... (20 to 1 op 16 to 1) 6
714 FUTURE FAME (USA) [48] 4-8-7 Alex Greaves (4) *mid-div, effrt and hdwy 3 fs out, rdn 2 out, sn one pace.* (12 to 1) 7
727 DOMAIN [52] (bl) 5-8-4 (7*) Rebecca Bream (3) *nvr rchd ldrs* .... (50 to 1) 8
902[2] DOUBLE SHERRY [35] 4-7-4[3] (7*) Claire Balding (16) *beh till some hdwy fnl 2 fs, nvr dngrs* .... (7 to 1 op 6 to 1) 9
DOCTOR'S REMEDY [34] 7-7-4[4] (7*) Angela Gallimore (5) *prmnt, rdn 3 fs out, sn wknd* .... (33 to 1 tchd 25 to 1) 10
MURASIL (USA) [45] 4-8-4 Antoinette Armes (6) *led, hdd 3 fs out, sn wknd* .... (33 to 1 op 25 to 1) 11
731 MARY MACBLAIN [40] 4-7-13[10] (7*) Madeleine Smith (2) *chsd ldr, rdn o'r 3 fs out, sn wknd.* .... (16 to 1 op 14 to 1 tchd 20 to 1) 12
645 SIE AMATO (Ire) [41] 4-7-7 (7*) Adelle Gibbons (14) *prmnt to hfwy, sn lost pl* .... (14 to 1 tchd 16 to 1) 13
861 COOL PARADE (USA) [45] 5-7-11 (7*) Gina Faulkner (9) *al beh* .... (20 to 1 op 16 to 1) 14
49[6] MELTONBY [47] 4-8-6 Kim Tinkler (15) *al beh.* .... (33 to 1 op 25 to 1) 15
HIZEEM [35] 7-7-8[1] Jaki Houston (13) *al rear* .... (33 to 1) 16
Dist: Hd, 7l, 2½l, ¾l, 2l, 1l, 1½l, ½l, 1½l, sht-hd, 1l. 1m 53.30s. a 4.80s (16 Ran).
SR: 28/2/-/-/4/-/ (Ron Whitehead), Mrs M Reveley

965 Danby Maiden Stakes Class D (3-y-o) £3,552 1¼m. .... (3:45)

751[4] MECKLENBURG (Ire) 9-0 M Roberts (3) *hld up, hdwy 4 fs out, led o'r 2 out, hrd drvn fnl furlong, held on.* ....(2 to 1 on tchd 9 to 4 on and 7 to 4 on) 1
534[8] MOUNT FUJI 9-0 Paul Eddery (4) *trkd ldrs, hdwy o'r 2 fs out, rdn to chal appr last, kpt on wl.* ....(6 to 1 tchd 13 to 2) 2
DUNNELLON 8-9 N Connorton (2) *hld up, hdwy o'r 2 fs out, effrt on inner and ev ch ins last, not much room nr finish*..........................(8 to 1 op 7 to 1) 3
DEMURRER 9-0 K Fallon (5) *chsd ldrs, effrt to ld briefly 3 fs out, sn rdn and wknd wl o'r one furlong out.* ....(14 to 1 op 12 to 1) 4
SHADOWPLAY (Fr) 9-0 K Darley (6) *chsd ldrs, effrt and hdwy 4 fs out, sn rdn and wknd o'r 2 out.* ....(7 to 1 op 6 to 1) 5
630[7] MUNNASIB (Fr) 9-0 W R Swinburn (7) *led to 3 fs out, sn wknd*..........................(20 to 1 op 16 to 1) 6
Dist: Hd, 1l, 10l, 6l, 4l. 2m 10.30s. a 9.10s (6 Ran).
SR: 4/3/-/ (Sheikh Mohammed), H R A Cecil

966 Mackinlay Memorial Handicap Class E (0-70 3-y-o) £3,416 1¼m............ (4:15)

813[2] I'M A DREAMER (Ire) [58] 8-9 Dean McKeown (5) *mid-div, hdwy 3 fs out, led o'r 2 out, sn rdn, edgd lft and ran on gmely fnl furlong*..............................(8 to 1) 1
612* SILVER STANDARD [55] 8-6 M Roberts (10) *chsd ldrs on outer, outpcd o'r 2 fs out and sn rdn, ran on strly ins fnl furlong, nrst finish.* ....(9 to 2 fav op 5 to 1 tchd 11 to 2 and 4 to 1) 2
434 WONDERFUL YEARS (USA) [52] 8-3[2] K Fallon (2) *chsd ldrs, hdwy to chal 3 fs out, sn rdn and ev chgance till no extr wl ins last*........................ (16 to 1 op 10 to 1) 3
764[4] CONTRACT ELITE (Ire) [54] 8-5 N Connorton (12) *hld up and beh, gd hdwy on outer 3 fs out, effrt and ev ch o'r one out, sn rdn and kpt on ins last*.... (12 to 1 op 10 to 1) 4
672[8] SUMMER PAGEANT [67] 9-4 W R Swinburn (11) *hld up and beh, hdwy 2 fs out, effrt and rdn appr fnl furlong, styd on*.................................. (8 to 1 op 7 to 1) 5
608[7] SIR EDWARD HENRY (Ire) [51] 8-2[2] Paul Eddery (4) *chsd ldrs, hdwy to dispute ld o'r 3 fs out, rdn over 2 out, kpt on one pace*...................... (20 to 1 tchd 25 to 1) 6
733[5] YUNUS EMRE (Ire) [50] 7-8 (7*) J O'Dwyer (13) *beh, hdwy 3 fs out, rdn and squeezed through on inner entering fnl furlong, no extr ins last*.......................(10 to 1) 7
733[2] DARING PAST [57] 8-8 W Ryan (9) *hld up and beh, hdwy o'r 2 fs out, sn rdn and one pace appr fnl furlong.* ....(7 to 1 op 6 to 1 tchd 8 to 1) 8
764* MILNGAVIE (Ire) [47] 7-7 (5*) Darren Moffatt (7) *beh and pushed alng o'r 4 fs out, effrt 3 out and some hdwy, sn wknd*..................(13 to 2 op 5 to 1 tchd 7 to 1) 9
318[9] KEEP YOUR DISTANCE [55] 8-6 K Darley (14) *beh till styd on fnl 2 fs, nvr dngrs*..................(14 to 1 op 10 to 1) 10
435[5] COSMIC STAR [70] 9-7 W Woods (1) *cl up, led 4 fs out to 2 and a half out, sn wknd.* ....(15 to 2 op 12 to 1 tchd 14 to 1 and 7 to 1) 11
836 FITZROY LAD [54] 8-5 F Norton (15) *al beh*........ (33 to 1) 12
CLEAR HONEY (USA) [54] 8-5 D Holland (8) *led to 4 fs out, sn wknd*......................(12 to 1 op 10 to 1) 13
340[6] DRUMDONNA (Ire) [65] 9-2 J Carroll (6) *al rear.* ....(14 to 1 op 12 to 1) 14
764[3] GOLD DESIRE [45] (v) 7-10 Dale Gibson (3) *prmnt till rdn and wknd wl o'r 3 fs out*.......... (14 to 1 op 12 to 1) 15
Dist: ½l, sht-hd, nk, nk, 1½l, hd, 1½l, nk, hd, 2½l. 2m 8.60s. a 7.40s (15 Ran).
SR: 16/12/8/9/21/2/-/4/-/ (Dave Marshall), W W Haigh

967 Eston Handicap Class D (0-80 4-y-o and up) £3,494 2m 4yds.................(4:45)

MY DESIRE [67] 5-8-12 (5*) Darren Moffatt (10) *beh, hdwy on outer 4 fs out, rdn 2 out, edgd lft entering fnl furlong and styd on wl to ld nr finish.* .... (13 to 2 op 6 to 1 tchd 7 to 1) 1
799[4] CALL THE GUV'NOR [65] 4-8-12 W Ryan (5) *trkd ldrs, effrt to ld o'r 3 fs out, sn clr, rdn ins fnl furlong, ct nr finish.* ....(9 to 2 op 4 to 1 tchd 5 to 1) 2
618* ASIAN PUNTER (Ire) [72] 4-8-12 (7*) N Varley (2) *al chasing ldrs, effrt and rdn o'r 2 fs out, swtchd over one furlong out, kpt on ins last.* (4 to 1 fav op 9 to 2 tchd 5 to 1) 3
727[2] LOOKINGFORARAINBOW (Ire) [60] 5-8-10 N Day (11) *hld up and beh, gd hdwy on inner whn hmpd o'r 2 fs out, rdn and wknd entering fnl furlong*.................(6 to 1) 4
ARFEY (Ire) [61] 4-8-8 Dean McKeown (7) *track ldrs gng wl, effrt and hdwy 3 fs out, sn rdn and wknd o'r one furlong out*.........(16 to 1 tchd 20 to 1 and 14 to 1) 5
527 FARMER'S PET [75] 4-9-8 W R Swinburn (1) *led, rdn 4 fs out, sn hdd, edgd lft o'r 2 out, soon wknd.* ....(9 to 2 op 7 to 2) 6
674 MALENOIR (USA) [48] (v) 5-7-5 (7*) Claire Balding (6) *mid-div, effrt and some hdwy 4 fs out, sn rdn and wknd.* ....(33 to 1) 7
365[3] PATROL [59] 4-8-6 K Fallon (9) *hld up, hdwy 5 fs out, rdn and wknd wl o'r 2 out*..............(14 to 1 op 10 to 1) 8
BUSTINETTA [80] 4-9-13 K Darley (8) *hld up and beh, effrt and some hdwy 4 fs out, rdn and wknd 2 out.* .... (15 to 2 op 5 to 1 tchd 8 to 1) 9

471[4]a[7] HIGH FINANCE [43] 8-7-0 (7*) A Daly (3) *chsd ldrs to hfwy, sn lost pl and beh*.................(50 to 1 op 33 to 1) 10
TEDDY'S PLAY (USA) [78] 4-9-11 D Holland (4) *chsd ldr till rdn and wknd o'r 3 fs out*..........(7 to 1 op 5 to 1) 11
Dist: ½l, 2½l, 1l, 5l, 7l, 4l, 2½l, 3l, 3l, 8l. 3m 28.50s. a 5.50s (11 Ran).
SR: 40/34/38/28/21/28/-/5/23/ (Miss Jane Spensley), Mrs M Reveley

968 Ayton Median Auction Maiden Stakes Class F (2-y-o) £2,243 5f............ (5:15)

680[9] RANDONNEUR (Ire) 8-9 J Carroll (2) *made all, rdn and edgd rght fnl 2 fs, kpt on*.......... (6 to 1 op 11 to 2) 1
MOKAITE 8-9 K Darley (8) *chsd ldrs, rdn o'r one furlong out, styd on wl ins last*...................... (20 to 1) 2
812[5] KARSEAM (Ire) 9-0 M Tebbutt (9) *in tch, effrt and swtchd lft entering fnl furlong, rdn and ran on wl nr finish.* ....(4 to 1 tchd 7 to 2) 3
MISS MAH-JONG 8-9 Dean McKeown (6) *cl up, rdn and ev ch o'r one furlong out, wknd ins last.* ....(100 to 30 op 3 to 1 tchd 7 to 2) 4
673 NORTHERN STORM (Ire) 9-0 W Woods (7) *cl up, ev ch o'r one furlong out, rdn and hng lft entering fnl furlong, wknd*.. (10 to 1) 5
804[7] TRYSAIL 8-6 (3*) S D Williams (11) *cl up, rdn 2 fs out, wknd appr fnl furlong*................. (10 to 1 op 8 to 1) 6
IRISH PERFORMER 8-9 N Connorton (10) *beh till styd on fnl 2 fs*...........................(14 to 1 op 16 to 1) 7
GLENVALLY 8-9 J Fortune (3) *chsd ldrs to hfwy, sn wknd.* ....(20 to 1 op 16 to 1) 8
SHANNARA (Ire) 8-9 S Morris (12) *chsd ldrs, rdn 2 fs out, wknd appr fnl furlong*..............(20 to 1 op 33 to 1) 9
395[3] GALLIC GENT 9-0 M Birch (1) *speed to hfwy, sn lost pl.* .... (3 to 1 fav tchd 4 to 1) 10
JACKSON HOUSE 9-0 K Fallon (5) *al rear.* ....(10 to 1 op 8 to 1) 11
POT LEEK LADY 8-9 N Day (4) *al rear*.......... (12 to 1) 12
Dist: 1l, ½l, 1½l, 3l, ½l, ¾l, 1½l, 1½l, 3½l, ¾l. 1m 0.70s. a 4.00s (12 Ran).
SR: 10/6/9/-/-/-/ (J Nixon), J Berry

SOUTHWELL (A.W) (std)
Monday May 10th
Going Correction: NIL

969 Sweden Maiden Auction Stakes Class F (2-y-o) £2,243 5f....................(2:30)

776[4] MAZEEKA (Ire) 8-6 (3*) Emma O'Gorman (6) *made all, clr o'r one furlong out, kpt on ins fnl furlong.* ....(11 to 10 fav op 5 to 4 on tchd 13 to 8) 1
LEAP OF FAITH (Ire) 8-9 G Duffield (4) *sn outpcd and drvn alng, improved 2 fs out, kpt on ins fnl furlong, not rch wnr*..............................(5 to 2 op 6 to 4) 2
607[5] NORBECK (Ire) 9-0 S Morris (1) *chsd ldr, rdn hfwy, wknd o'r one furlong out*..................(7 to 1 op 8 to 1) 3
325[8] LEESON STREET LADY (Ire) 8-4 (5*) Stephen Davies (7) *chsd ldrs, sn pushed alng, wknd 2 fs out*.......... (33 to 1) 4
T O O MAMMA'S (Ire) 8-9 G Carter (3) *sn drvn alng in rear, not ch frm hfwy*...................(5 to 1 op 7 to 2) 5
830[5] COLONEL SINCLAIR (Ire) 9-0 S Perks (2) *sn drvn alng beh ldrs, fdd fnl 2 fs*..................(12 to 1 op 10 to 1) 6
708[9] ALICE OF LOXLEY 8-4 (5*) O Pears (5) *slwly into strd, al struggling in rear, tld off frm hfwy*.......... (50 to 1) 7
Dist: 1½l, 10l, 5l, 3l, nk, 7l. 1m 1.70s. a 3.80s (7 Ran).
SR: 19/13/-/-/ (S Fustok), W A O'Gorman

970 Spain Limited Stakes Class F (0-60 3-y-o and up) £2,243 7f..................(3:00)

754[8] ON Y VA (USA) 6-9-5 D Biggs (11) *chsd ldrs, improved to ld o'r one furlong out, sn clr, easily.* ....(2 to 1 fav op 3 to 1 tchd 4 to 1) 1
837[2] HIGHBORN (Ire) 4-9-10 G Hind (15) *in tch, effrt and rdn appr strt, not quicken ins fnl furlong*........ (10 to 1) 2
710[5] HARCLIFF 4-9-10 G Bardwell (6) *beh and sn rdn alng, improved entering strt, kpt on wl fnl furlong, nvr dngrs*..................................(8 to 1 op 3 to 1) 3
815[6] SALADAN KNIGHT (bl) 8-9-10 D Nicholls (4) *chsd ldrs, smooth hdwy to ld o'r 2 fs out, hdd over one furlong out, sn btn*..........................(9 to 1 op 6 to 1) 4
CATUNDRA (Ire) 5-8-12 (7*) Marie Plowright (5) *sn led, hdd o'r 2 fs out, kpt on same pace.* .... (20 to 1 op 14 to 1 tchd 25 to 1) 5
760 LORD NASKRA (USA) (bl) 4-9-7 (3*) Emma O'Gorman (2) *slwly away, beh, came wide strt, kpt on fnl 2 fs, nrst finish*..............................(6 to 1 op 4 to 1) 6
519[5] AGENDA ONE 3-8-4 (3*) A Tucker (3) *nvr far away, rdn alng 3 fs out, wknd o'r one furlong out.* ....(12 to 1 tchd 14 to 1) 7
728[3] IRISH ROOTS (Ire) (v) 3-8-12 G Duffield (1) *in tch, rdn hfwy, wknd fnl 2 fs*...............(6 to 1 op 5 to 1 tchd 13 to 2) 8
837 PAR DE LUXE 6-9-5 A Mackay (12) *mid-div, rdn alng hfwy, no imprsn*...................................(33 to 1) 9
754 DAVROB 3-8-12 G Carter (16) *mid-div, effrt and hdwy hfwy, wknd entering strt*..........(20 to 1 op 33 to 1) 10
GOTT'S DESIRE 7-9-10 N Adams (7) *mid-div, sn bustled alng, lost tch appr strt*...........(25 to 1 tchd 33 to 1) 11

424[4] BOULABAS (Ire) 4-9-5 M Wigham (9) *al beh, struggling frm hfwy*..........(20 to 1 op 12 to 1) 12
800 RISKMEMAY (bl) 4-9-5 A Proud (8) *beh and sn drvn alng, nvr a factor*..........(50 to 1) 13
636[6] COMPANY CASH (bl) 5-9-3 (7*) H Bastiman (10) *beh and sn rdn, nvr on terms*.... (16 to 1 op 12 to 1 tchd 20 to 1) 14
800 DAILY SPORT AUGUST 4-9-5 V Smith (13) *chsd ldrs till rdn and wknd quickly 2 fs out*........(20 to 1 op 33 to 1) 15
Dist: 2½l, 3l, 3½l, ¾l, ¾l, 1l, 2½l, 4l, hd, ½l. 1m 30.50s. a 4.40s (15 Ran).
SR: 39/36/27/16/9/12/ (Marriott Stables Limited), R J R Williams

971 France Handicap Class E (0-70 4-y-o and up) £3,131 1m......................(3:30)

771 THEMAAM [59] 4-9-8 D Biggs (13) *settled mid-div, improved entering strt, sstnd run to ld wl ins fnl furlong*..........(8 to 1 jt-fav tchd 10 to 1) 1
918[3] EXPRESS SERVICE [55] (bl) 4-9-1 (3*) Emma O'Gorman (15) *prmnt, led aftr 2 fs, clr o'r one furlongs out, hdd wl ins last*..........(17 to 2 op 6 to 1 tchd 9 to 1) 2
636[3] MAROWINS [50] 4-8-13 J Quinn (8) *hld up, improved 2 fs out, kpt on ins last, nrst finish*. ....(17 to 2 op 6 to 1 tchd 9 to 1) 3
610 DOUBLE THE STAKES (USA) [32] 4-7-9 G Bardwell (2) *in tch, drvn alng hfwy, ran on o'r one furlong out, no extr ins last*..........(20 to 1) 4
678[8] CAL NORMA'S LADY (Ire) [49] 5-8-9 (3*) D Harrison (1) *mid-div, effrt appr strt, kpt on same pace o'r one furlong out*..........(10 to 1 op 14 to 1 tchd 9 to 1) 5
645[7] ANAR (Ire) [45] 4-8-3 (5*) O Pears (16) *chsd ldrs till rdn and wknd wl o'r one furlong out*......(10 to 1 tchd 7 to 1) 6
771 RIPSNORTER (Ire) [60] 4-9-9 N Carlisle (3) *beh, effrt and rdn appr strt, kpt on ins fnl furlong*. ....(10 to 1 op 8 to 1) 7
498[2] LEGUARD EXPRESS (Ire) [36] (bl) 5-7-6 (7*) D Wright (7) *sn led, hdd aftr 2 fs, styd hndy, wknd two furlongs out*. ....(12 to 1) 8
861[3] DIAMOND INTHE DARK (USA) [52] (v) 5-9-1 T Lucas (4) *beh, drvn alng o'r 3 fs out, not pace to chal*. ....(10 to 1 op 8 to 1) 9
411[5] QUINZII MARTIN [61] 5-9-10 A Mackay (12) *hld up, nvr nr to chal*..........(9 to 1 op 6 to 1 tchd 10 to 1) 10
COLONNA (USA) [32] 7-7-9 J Lowe (11) *chsd ldrs til wknd and eased o'r 2 fs out*..........(50 to 1) 11
914[5] ALNASRIC PETE (USA) [55] 7-9-4 G Carter (6) *hld up, effrt 3 fs out, wknd and eased entering strt*. ....(9 to 1 op 6 to 1 tchd 10 to 1) 12
458 MERRYHILL MADAM [45] (v) 4-8-8 G Duffield (9) *beh, rdn alng hfwy, wknd 2 fs out*. ....(14 to 1 op 10 to 1 tchd 16 to 1) 13
DRY GIN [30] 10-7-7 E Johnson (10) *mid-div, sn lost pl, lost tch frm hfwy*..........(66 to 1 op 50 to 1) 14
771 NOBBY BARNES [65] 4-9-9 (5*) K Rutter (5) *dwlt, al beh*. ....(8 to 1 jt-fav op 5 to 1 tchd 10 to 1) 15
709 SWYNFORD FLYER [34] 4-7-11[4] L Charnock (14) *in tch, rdn alng 3 fs out, grad wknd*..........(50 to 1) 16
Dist: 1l, 1½l, 2½l, 1½l, hd, ½l, sht-hd, 1l, 12l, 2l. 1m 44.20s. a 5.20s (16 Ran).
SR: 30/23/13/-/-/-/7/-/-/ (Wetherby Racing Bureau Plc), T Thomson Jones

972 Germany Rating Related Maiden Fillies Stakes Class F (0-70 3-y-o) £2,243 7f (4:00)

862[7] PENNY BANGER (Ire) 8-11 T Williams (5) *made all, quickened clr o'r 2 fs out, styd on strly fnl furlong*. ....(5 to 2 fav op 2 to 1 tchd 11 to 4) 1
652[7] MRS DAWSON 8-11 G Hind (1) *hld up, effrt o'r 3 fs out, one pace fnl 2 furlongs, wnt second cl hme*. ....(100 to 30 op 5 to 2 tchd 7 to 2) 2
823[7] DESERT NOMAD 8-11 C Rutter (6) *trkd ldr, rdn whn rdr drpd whip wl o'r 3 fs out, one pace entering strt*. ....(3 to 1 op 5 to 2 tchd 100 to 30) 3
907 ORIENTAL PRINCESS 8-6 (5*) A Garth (4) *taken early to post, chsd ldg pair, effrt o'r 3 fs out, btn entering strt*. ....(16 to 1 op 10 to 1 tchd 20 to 1) 4
JENDORCET 8-11 J Fanning (3) *chsd ldrs, rdn 4 fs out, wknd o'r 2 furlongs out*..........(5 to 1 op 4 to 1) 5
GUANHUMARA 8-11 N Carlisle (2) *slwly into strd, beh, lost tch fnl 3 fs, tld off*...(7 to 1 op 6 to 1 tchd 8 to 1) 6
Dist: 8l, hd, 15l, ¾l, 3l. 1m 30.80s. a 4.70s (6 Ran).
SR: 27/3/2/ (R W Huggins), M Johnston

973 Italy Handicap Class E (0-70 3-y-o and up) £3,106 2m..........................(4:30)

739[4] KOVALEVSKIA [37] 8-8-11 G Bardwell (11) *beh and sn pushed alng, gd hdwy 6 fs out, sstnd run to ld o'r one furlong out, kpt on wl*.......(4 to 1 jt-fav tchd 5 to 1) 1
674[2] TIGER SHOOT [48] 6-9-8 J Lowe (8) *handily plcd, smooth hdwy to ld o'r 3 fs out, hdd over one furlong out, rdn and not quicken*..........(6 to 1 op 5 to 1) 2
626[3] PRIDE OF BRITAIN (Can) [55] 4-9-12 N Carlisle (9) *keen hold, chsd ldrs, led 6 fs out, hdd o'r 3 furlongs out, sn drvn, not quicken fnl 2 furlongs*..........(4 to 1 jt-fav op 5 to 1) 3
744[3] THOR POWER (Ire) [47] 4-9-4 G Duffield (12) *pressed ldg bunch, rdn o'r 3 fs out, not quicken entering strt*. ....(12 to 1 op 10 to 1) 4
4813a[8] SULUK (USA) [38] 8-8-5 (7*) M Humphries (15) *beh till styd on fnl 2 fs, nvr dngrs*....(6 to 1 op 4 to 1 tchd 7 to 1) 5
709[2] MUST BE MAGICAL (USA) [41] 5-9-1 G Hind (10) *hld up, effrt und pres hfwy, no imprsn entering strt*. ....(17 to 2 op 7 to 1 tchd 9 to 1) 6
303 BEDOUIN PRINCE (USA) [47] (bl) 6-9-2 (5*) C Hodgson (14) *chsd ldrs, led 7 fs out, hdd 6 furlongs out, wknd 4 furlongs out*........(11 to 1 op 10 to 1 tchd 12 to 1) 7
278[7] RESISTING (USA) [25] 5-7-13 E Johnson (3) *wl beh til some late hdwy, nvr dngrs*..........(50 to 1) 8
495 GEE DOUBLE YOU [40] 7-9-0 L Charnock (2) *slwly away, al in rear, tld off*.....(9 to 1 op 12 to 1 tchd 14 to 1) 9
709[8] DASHING FELLOW (Ire) [54] 5-9-9 (5*) O Pears (5) *in tch, rdn aftr 6 fs, lost touch frm hfwy, tld off*. ....(33 to 1 op 25 to 1) 10
699 HUSH BABY (Ire) [49] 3-7-13 G Carter (13) *led til hdd 7 fs out, sn drvn alng, wknd 4 furlongs out, tld off*. ....(12 to 1 op 8 to 1) 11
278[5] YANKEE FLYER [41] 6-9-1 A Mackay (4) *mid-div, rdn and lost tch hfwy, tld off*..........(25 to 1 op 20 to 1) 12
412[3] FREE DANCER [45] 3-7-9 J Fanning (7) *chsd ldrs, rdn aftr 7 fs, grad lost pl, tld off*..........(50 to 1) 13
4763a[5] BY FAR (USA) [29] 7-8-3 C Rutter (1) *very slwly away, al wl beh, tld off*..........(16 to 1 op 12 to 1) 14
530 NEGATORY (USA) [42] 6-9-2 V Smith (6) *in tch til lost pl aftr 6 fs, pld up lme hfwy*.......(33 to 1 tchd 50 to 1) pu
Dist: 2l, 6l, 2l, 12l, 2½l, 1½l, 12l, ½l, 3½l, 12l. 3m 45.00s. a 18.50s (15 Ran).
(D A Wilson), D A Wilson

974 Denmark Median Auction Maiden Stakes Class F (3-y-o) £2,243 5f............(5:00)

414[3] SYLVAN STARLIGHT (v) 8-9 G Duffield (2) *dwlt, early reminders, hdwy 2 fs out, ran on to ld entering fnl furlong, edgd lft and styd on wl*. ....(5 to 4 fav op 11 to 10 tchd 6 to 4) 1
491[7] CHICAGO (Ire) 9-0 T Lucas (3) *nvr far away, rdn hfwy, not quicken ins fnl furlong*......(10 to 1 tchd 12 to 1) 2
728[5] DARDANELLE 8-9 S Webster (5) *in tch, rdn hfwy, kpt on ins fnl furlong*..........(10 to 1 op 14 to 1) 3
MAGIC PEARL 8-9 N Carlisle (1) *chsd ldrs, improved to ld o'r one furlong out, hdd entering fnl furlong, sn btn*. ....(9 to 4 op 6 to 4) 4
538 DODDINGTON PLAYER (Ire) 9-0 S Perks (7) *dwlt, sn outpcd and beh, some late hdwy ins fnl furlong, nvr dngrs*. ....(10 to 1 op 20 to 1) 5
ARYAN VESPER 9-0 C Rutter (6) *chsd ldrs, chlgd hfwy, wknd one furlong out*. ....(11 to 1 op 10 to 1 tchd 12 to 1) 6
380[7] OSCAR THE SECOND (Ire) 9-0 J Fanning (4) *led til hdd o'r one furlong out, wknd quickly*.... (25 to 1 op 20 to 1) 7
Dist: 4l, 2½l, 1½l, 2½l, sht-hd, 2l. 1m 2.10s. a 4.20s (7 Ran).
SR: 11/-/-/-/ (Mrs R A Johnson), Sir Mark Prescott

WINDSOR (good to firm)
Monday May 10th
Going Correction: MINUS 0.20 sec. per fur.

975 Sloane Street Claiming Stakes Class F (3 & 4-y-o) £1,870 1m 67yds..........(6:15)

351[4] QUICK SILVER BOY 3-7-13 (5*) Stephen Davies (18) *made all, drvn and hld on wl fnl furlong*. ....(6 to 1 op 5 to 1 tchd 13 to 2) 1
834[8] MEXICAN DANCER 4-8-5 (7*) S Drowne (12) *al tracking ldrs, ev ch ins last, not quicken cl hme*. ....(7 to 1 op 16 to 1 tchd 33 to 1) 2
803[5] BROUGHTON'S PORT 3-8-1 (7*) D McCabe (8) *beh, gd hdwy on outsd frm 2 fs out, ran on*.......(100 to 30 jt-fav op 5 to 2 tchd 4 to 1) 3
754 PRINCE RODNEY 4-9-5 Pat Eddery (20) *hdwy and wnt sharply lft ins fnl 2 fs, ev ch inside last, fdd cl hme*. ....(100 to 30 jt-fav op 5 to 2 tchd 9 to 2) 4
FILOU FILANT (Fr) 3-7-12 (5*) B Doyle (9) *al chasing ldrs, styd on same pace fnl 2 fs*..........(20 to 1 op 8 to 1) 5
227[8] TURTLE BEACH 4-9-4 W Newnes (11) *pressed wnr till wknd o'r one furlong out*. ....(14 to 1 op 10 to 1 tchd 16 to 1) 6
834 ROCKY BAY 4-8-4 (7*) D Wright (5) *styd on fnl 2 fs, nrst finish*..........(33 to 1 op 25 to 1) 7
678 GEORGE ROPER 3-8-5 B Rouse (19) *chsd ldrs, rdn o'r 2 fs out, wknd ins fnl two furlongs*..... (16 to 1 op 8 to 1) 8
OPEN AGENDA (Ire) 4-9-4 R Wernham (6) *chsd ldrs till wknd o'r 2 fs out*..........(25 to 1 op 16 to 1) 9
621[5] EMERALD EARS 4-8-6 (3*) J Weaver (3) *prmnt, wkng whn hmpd one and a half fs out*.......(33 to 1 op 25 to 1) 10
SIMPLY GEORGE 4-9-0 A Munro (21) *dwlt, al beh*. ....(10 to 1 op 7 to 1) 11
521 GONE BUST (Ire) 4-9-0 L Piggott (17) *nvr rch ldrs*. ....(11 to 1 op 8 to 1 tchd 12 to 1) 12
245[9] ASCOM PAGER TOO 3-8-2 J Quinn (16) *mid-div whn hmpd ins fnl 2 fs, sn btn*..........(25 to 1 op 16 to 1) 13
699[7] STAR MINSTREL (Ire) (bl) 3-8-3 A Clark (7) *effrt hfwy, sn wknd*..........(8 to 1 op 6 to 1 tchd 10 to 1) 14
754 SUDANOR (Ire) (bl) 4-9-3 S Whitworth (4) *beh most of way*. ....(33 to 1 op 25 to 1) 15

419^4 BLUE POINT (Ire) 4-8-9 B Raymond (10) *in tch to hfwy.* .... (20 to 1 op 12 to 1) 16
FULL SIGHT (Ire) 4-8-10 (7*) G Mitchell (14) *dwlt, al beh.* .... (16 to 1 op 12 to 1) 17
GERRANS BAY (Ire) 4-9-5 J Williams (1) *beh most of way.* .... (33 to 1 op 20 to 1) 18
CHATWORTH GREY 3-8-1 N Adams (15) *al beh.* .... (33 to 1 op 20 to 1) 19
614 TOCCATELLA 3-7-12 A McGlone (2) *al beh.* .... (25 to 1 op 20 to 1) 20
NEEDWOOD NUGGET 3-8-3 P Robinson (13) *prmnt till wknd 3 fs out.*.......... (25 to 1 op 14 to 1) 21
Dist: ¾l, 1½l, nk, ¾l, 2½l, 3l, nk, 1½l, 1l, 2l. 1m 44.90s. a 3.90s (21 Ran).
SR: 7/13/4/14/-/3/ (T R Pearson), D Burchell

976 Mayfair Handicap Class E (0-70 3-y-o) £2,553 1m 3f 135yds................(6:40)

717^3 MOON CARNIVAL [70] 9-7 A Clark (8) *in tch, hdwy to ld ins fnl 2 fs, drvn out inside last.* .... (11 to 2 op 5 to 1 tchd 9 to 1) 1
530^8 DUVEEN (Ire) [57] 8-3 (5*) M Fenton (3) *al in tch, ev ch frm 2 fs out till outpcd ins last.*.......... (10 to 1 op 7 to 1) 2
725^4 RECORD LOVER (Ire) [55] 8-6 A Munro (4) *prmnt, pressed ldrs frm 2 fs out till one pace from o'r one furlong out.* ....(7 to 1 op 5 to 1 tchd 8 to 1) 3
838^2 WARM SPELL [66] 9-3 B Rouse (10) *in tch whn hmpd and lost pl 6 fs out, smooth hdwy to chal 4 furlongs out, ev ch o'r 2 furlongs out,one pace*... (4 to 1 fav op 6 to 1) 4
717 PISTOLS AT DAWN (USA) [61] 8-12 Pat Eddery (5) *al chasing ldrs, chlgd 4 fs out till outpcd fnl 2 furlongs.* ....(7 to 1 op 8 to 1 tchd 9 to 1) 5
628^5 PRESTON GUILD (Ire) [50] 8-1 W Carson (1) *made most till hdd and wknd ins fnl 2 fs*.......... (8 to 1 op 5 to 1) 6
483 MANON LESCAUT [54] 8-5 S Whitworth (11) *nvr rch ldrs.* .... (20 to 1 op 14 to 1 tchd 25 to 1) 7
724^6 KISMETIM [55] 8-6 W Newnes (6) *nvr better than mid-div.* .... (8 to 1 op 12 to 1 tchd 7 to 1) 8
628^6 EARLY TO RISE [50] 8-1 D Biggs (2) *prmnt till wknd 3 fs out.*.......... (20 to 1 op 16 to 1 tchd 25 to 1) 9
681 PETITE JESS [44] 7-9^2 J Quinn (15) *al beh.* .... (33 to 1 op 20 to 1) 10
SENSE OF HUMOUR [61] 8-12 M Hills (14) *chsd ldrs till wknd 3 fs out*.......... (25 to 1 op 20 to 1) 11
547^4 BROUGHTONS FORMULA [65] 8-9 (7*) D McCabe (7) *nvr rch ldrs*.......... (15 to 2 op 5 to 1 tchd 8 to 1) 12
557^9 ONE MORE POUND [52] 8-3^2 R Perham (9) *al beh.* .... (25 to 1 op 20 to 1) 13
761 BANG ON TIME [55] 8-6 J Williams (12) *wth ldr 6 fs out till wknd o'r 3 furlongs out*.......... (33 to 1 op 20 to 1) 14
642 BONNY PRINCESS [42] 7-6^6 (7*) K Sked (13) *al beh.* .... (33 to 1 op 20 to 1) 15
Dist: 2l, 3l, ½l, 2½l, sht-hd, nk, 1½l, 2l, sht-hd, 5l. 2m 29.80s. a 6.80s (15 Ran).
SR: 16/-/-/1/-/-/ (Lavinia Duchess Of Norfolk), Lady Herries

977 Piccadilly Handicap Class D (0-80 3-y-o) £4,110 5f 217yds................(7:05)

846^7 SOUTHERN MEMORIES (Ire) [75] 9-6 L Piggott (12) *al in tch, led one and a half fs out, readily.* (5 to 1 tchd 7 to 1) 1
683^8 SPECIAL ONE [73] 9-4 M Hills (3) *hdwy 2 fs out, ev ch one furlong out, one pace.* (15 to 2 op 5 to 1 tchd 8 to 1) 2
624^7 JULY BRIDE [53] 7-9 (3*) A Tucker (5) *beh, gd hdwy frm 2 fs out, styd on fnl furlong.* (8 to 1 op 6 to 1 tchd 9 to 1) 3
758^8 MURPHY'S HOPE (Ire) [62] 8-7 T Quinn (13) *led till hdd one and a half fs out, kpt on und pres, one pace.* .... (14 to 1 op 10 to 1 tchd 16 to 1) 4
872 GALLOP TO GLORY [58] 8-3 A Munro (11) *chsd ldrs till wknd appr fnl furlong.* .... (40 to 1 op 33 to 1 tchd 50 to 1) 5
471^8 DAANIERA (Ire) [72] 9-3 J Quinn (9) *dwlt, sn reco'red, wth ldrs but not much room 2 fs out, one pace.* .... (20 to 1 op 14 to 1) 6
758^3 POLAR STORM (Ire) [63] 8-8 J Williams (7) *hdwy hfwy, outpcd fnl 2 fs*................ (4 to 1 jt-fav op 4 to 1) 7
450^4 GO FLIGHTLINE (Ire) [67] 8-7 (5*) M Fenton (10) *speed o'r 3 fs*................ (12 to 1 op 7 to 1) 8
883^7 MAJOR TRIUMPH (Ire) [62] 8-7 B Raymond (8) *sn outpcd.* .... (14 to 1 op 10 to 1 tchd 16 to 1) 9
800 GREENWICH CHALENGE [68] 8-13 M Wigham (6) *outpcd.* .... (20 to 1 op 16 to 1 tchd 33 to 1) 10
532^9 IBTIKAR (USA) [67] 8-12 W Carson (1) *effrt hfwy, sn wknd.* .... (9 to 1 op 7 to 1 tchd 10 to 1) 11
691^2 SOBER LAD (Ire) [76] 9-7 Pat Eddery (2) *speed till fdd frm hfwy*................ (4 to 1 jt-fav op 5 to 1 tchd 11 to 2) 12
4773a* IOLITE [74] 9-0 (5*) K Rutter (14) *sn rdn, tld off fnl 2 fs.* .... (9 to 1 op 7 to 1 tchd 10 to 1) 13
Dist: 3l, nk, ½l, 2½l, sht-hd, 4l, 3l, 1l, ½l, ½l. 1m 11.80s. a 1.50s (13 Ran).
SR: 52/38/17/24/10/23/ (Jim Horgan), R Hannon

978 Serpentine Limited Stakes Class D (0-75 4-y-o and up) £4,045 1¼m 7yds..... (7:35)

756 AKKAZAO (Ire) 5-8-9 J Reid (11) *prmnt till lost pos 5 fs out, drvn and hdwy 4 furlongs out, hrd rdn fnl 2 furlongs till led cl hme*.......... (13 to 2 op 7 to 1 tchd 9 to 1) 1
663* CAMDEN'S RANSOM (USA) 6-8-9 (5*) B Doyle (12) *beh, gd hdwy frm 3 fs out, led appr fnl furlong, hdd and no extr cl hme*..........(11 to 10 fav op 5 to 4 tchd 6 to 4) 2D
628^8 ILDERTON ROAD 6-8-2 (7*) D Wright (13) *rdn and hdwy 3 fs out, styd on wl fnl furlong*...... (33 to 1 op 20 to 1) 2
663^9 BLUE FLAG (USA) 4-9-0 L Piggott (1) *made most till hdd o'r one furlong out, sn fdd.* .... (10 to 1 op 8 to 1 tchd 12 to 1) 3
SCOTTISH BAMBI 5-9-0 B Raymond (10) *prmnt till wknd ins fnl 2 fs*............ (5 to 1 op 7 to 2 tchd 11 to 2) 4
840 MASTER REACH 4-9-0 B Rouse (2) *some prog fnl 2 fs, not rch ldrs*.......... (33 to 1 tchd 40 to 1) 5
754 SINGERS IMAGE (v) 4-9-0 J Williams (3) *in tch, hdwy to chase ldrs 5 fs out, wknd o'r 2 furlongs out.* .... (16 to 1 op 14 to 1) 6
NORTH-WEST ONE (Ire) 5-9-0 V Smith (9) *rapid hdwy to chase ldrs 5 fs out, wknd o'r 2 furlongs out.* .... (50 to 1 op 33 to 1) 7
731 BENTICO 4-9-0 P Robinson (7) *dwlt, al beh.* .... (14 to 1 op 10 to 1 tchd 20 to 1) 8
756 YOUNG MAX 4-8-7 (7*) Tracey Purseglove (6) *prmnt, wth ldr 6 fs out, wknd quickly o'r 3 furlongs out.* .... (25 to 1 op 16 to 1 tchd 14 to 1) 9
FRUITFUL AFFAIR (Ire) 4-8-9 S Whitworth (4) *in tch till wknd hfwy*.......... (9 to 1 op 10 to 1 tchd 7 to 1) 10
ASSEMBLY DANCER 6-9-0 N Adams (8) *beh frm hfwy.* ....(33 to 1 tchd 40 to 1) 11
THEMEDA 4-8-2 (7*) B Russell (5) *beh most of way.* .... (16 to 1 op 10 to 1) 12
Dist: Hd, 1½l, 2½l, 2l, 7l, 5l, 3½l, ½l, ½l, 1½l. 2m 5.90s. a 3.40s (13 Ran).
SR: 41/45/37/37/33/19/9/2/1/ (T G Mills), T G Mills

979 Chelsea Conditions Stakes Class D (2-y-o) £3,655 5f 10yds.................... (8:05)

730* SNIPE HALL 8-8 P Robinson (1) *al prmnt, led jst ins last, drvn out*.......... (9 to 2 op 3 to 1 tchd 5 to 1) 1
528* POMMES FRITES (Ire) 8-10 L Piggott (3) *prmnt till led hfwy, hdd and not quicken ins last.* ....(9 to 4 on op 7 to 4 on tchd 6 to 4 on) 2
YA MALAK 8-11 R Cochrane (4) *chsd ldrs, effrt o'r one furlong out, styd on same pace ins last.* .... (15 to 2 op 4 to 1 tchd 9 to 1) 3
738^8 WINDOW DISPLAY 8-11 J Williams (5) *sn pushed alng to chase ldrs, styd on same pace fnl 2 fs.* .... (33 to 1 op 16 to 1 tchd 40 to 1) 4
776 VICEROY RULER 8-11 W Newnes (8) *sn drvn alng to stay in tch, styd on same pace frm o'r one furlong out.* .... (66 to 1 op 33 to 1 tchd 100 to 1) 5
STRAPPED 8-6 T Quinn (7) *outpcd*... (20 to 1 op 10 to 1) 6
466* MOSCOW ROAD 8-13 A McGlone (9) *led to hfwy, wkng whn faltered and hit rail one and a half fs out.* .... (14 to 1 op 8 to 1) 7
FOLLY FINNESSE 8-6 S Whitworth (6) *uns rdr stalls.* .... (50 to 1 op 25 to 1) ur
Dist: 1½l, 1½l, sht-hd, 2½l, 7l, 1l. 1m 1.50s. a 2.50s (8 Ran).
SR: 24/20/15/14/4/ (Mrs R T Watson), J Wharton

980 Green Park Median Auction Maiden Stakes Class F (3-y-o) £2,061 1¼m 7yds ....(8:35)

582^3 GONE FOR A BURTON (Ire) 9-0 Pat Eddery (11) *nvr far off the pace, hdwy 3 fs out, led 2 furlongs out, hrd drvn fnl furlong, hld on wl.* ....(11 to 10 on op 5 to 4 on tchd 6 to 4) 1
SHOW FAITH (Ire) 9-0 J Reid (15) *hld up in tch, str chal frm o'r one furlong out, not quicken cl hme.* .... (10 to 1 op 6 to 1 tchd 12 to 1) 2
813^4 ALLESCA 8-9 N Adams (14) *gd hdwy on rls 3 fs out, ev ch 2 furlongs out, eased whn hld fnl furlong.* .... (6 to 1 op 7 to 1 tchd 8 to 1 and 5 to 1) 3
MUTAWALI (Ire) 9-0 W Carson (21) *chsd ldrs, kpt on same pace fnl 2 fs*................(20 to 1 op 12 to 1) 4
724^5 BURNING COST 8-6 (3*) D Harrison (10) *led 6 fs out till hdd 2 furlongs out, sn btn*.......... (50 to 1 op 20 to 1) 5
759^6 SLIVOVITZ 9-0 P Robinson (7) *led 4 fs, styd prmnt, ev ch o'r 2 furlongs out, sn wknd*..........(25 to 1 op 16 to 1) 6
662 DUTCH DEBUTANTE 8-9 W Newnes (16) *beh till ran on frm o'r 2 fs out, nrst finish.* .... (20 to 1 tchd 16 to 1 and 25 to 1) 7
679 FLAMING MIRACLE (Ire) 9-0 T Quinn (13) *chsd ldrs till wknd 3 fs out*.......... (25 to 1 op 20 to 1 tchd 50 to 1) 8
534^6 MOIDART 8-9 S Whitworth (8) *effrt 5 fs out, wknd 3 furlongs out*.......... (25 to 1 op 12 to 1) 9
724 SPARKY'S SONG 8-9 M Hills (5) *nvr rchd ldrs.* .... (50 to 1 op 25 to 1) 10
751 TINSASHE (Ire) 8-9 B Rouse (3) *nvr better than mid-div.* .... (33 to 1 op 25 to 1 tchd 40 to 1) 11
751 CAST THE LINE 9-0 A McGlone (6) *beh most of way.* .... (50 to 1 op 20 to 1) 12
751 HOPEFUL PROSPECT 8-9 J Williams (20) *nvr dngrs.* .... (50 to 1 op 33 to 1) 13
422^8 ITS UNBELIEVABLE 8-7 (7*) T Fuggle (2) *effrt 6 fs out, sn wknd*................ (50 to 1) 14
755^6 ELECTROLYTE 8-9 (5*) Stephen Davies (1) *chsd ldrs till wknd 5 fs out*................ (50 to 1 op 33 to 1) 15

602 BARSLEY 8-9 (5*) B Doyle (19) *al beh.* (50 to 1 op 33 to 1) 16
POETIC FORM (Ire) 9-0 M Perrett (4) *al beh.* .... (50 to 1 op 33 to 1) 17
CHARLIE BIGTIME 9-0 B Raymond (12) *chsd ldrs till wknd o'r 3 fs out*............ (13 to 2 op 6 to 1 tchd 8 to 1) 18
761 CRIMINAL RECORD (USA) 9-0 A Munro (9) *mid-div till wknd 4 fs out*.................... (20 to 1 op 10 to 1) 19
732 IMAGERY 8-9 J Quinn (17) *sn beh*.... (50 to 1 op 33 to 1) 20
RUN TO AU BON (Ire) 9-0 R Cochrane (18) *al beh.* .... (16 to 1 op 8 to 1 tchd 20 to 1) 21
Dist: Nk, 10l, 1l, nk, 2l, 1½l, hd, hd, nk, nk. 2m 7.40s. a 4.90s (21 Ran).
SR: 31/30/5/8/2/3/ (H P Carrington), P J Makin

KILLARNEY (IRE) (firm)
Tuesday May 11th

981 Hotel Europe Handicap (0-70 3-y-o) £3,452 1m 100yds.........................(8:00)

TRYARRA (Ire) [-] 9-7 J P Murtagh (3)............ (4 to 1) 1
898[3] PHASE IN [-] 9-0 W J Supple (6).............. (7 to 4 fav) 2
639[5] GIFT OF PEACE (Ire) [-] 9-7 C Roche (9)........... (7 to 1) 3
868 CHAMPAGNE NIGHT (Fr) [-] 9-7 M J Kinane (2)... (12 to 1) 4
268[8] PHILIP PATRICK (Ire) [-] 8-12[1] (6*) P Carberry (7).. (14 to 1) 5
307 GLANCE CARD (Ire) [-] 9-3 B Coogan (5)......... (12 to 1) 6
257 WHITECRAITS (Ire) [-] 8-12 R Hughes (4).......... (7 to 2) 7
868 AVALONIA (Ire) [-] 8-8 J F Egan (12).............. (12 to 1) 8
MAZZARELLO (Ire) [-] 7-9 (4*) W J Smith (8)...... (25 to 1) 9
PHARUZAL [-] 9-3 S Craine (1)................... (7 to 1) 10
Dist: 2½l, 2l, 3l, ¾l. 1m 46.50s. (10 Ran).
(Mrs K Doyle), Mrs A M O'Brien

982 Castlerosse Hotel Fillies Maiden (3-y-o) £3,452 1m 3f.......................(8:30)

790[4] VALONA (Ire) 9-0 C Roche (5)...............(6 to 4 jt-fav) 1
669[4] SAFFRON CROCUS 9-0 M J Kinane (9)......(6 to 4 jt-fav) 2
870[9] ALIBAR'S PET (Ire) 9-0 J P Murtagh (8)...........(14 to 1) 3
847 TROPICAL LAKE (Ire) 9-0 S Craine (6)............(20 to 1) 4
648[2] DRIFT APART (Ire) 9-0 W J Supple (7)............(5 to 1) 5
DO-TELL-ME (Ire) 8-8 (6*) R V Skelly (10).........(33 to 1) 6
HAIL TO HOME (Ire) 9-0 R Hughes (2)............(33 to 1) 7
850 RYE HILL QUEEN (Ire) 9-0 D Manning (1).........(66 to 1) 8
CASTLETOWN (Ire) 9-0 P Shanahan (4).......... (14 to 1) 9
Dist: Nk, 14l, 7l, ¾l. 2m 28.80s. (9 Ran).
(William J Brennan), J S Bolger

MAISONS-LAFFITTE (FR) (heavy)
Tuesday May 11th
Going Correction: PLUS 0.30 sec. per fur.

983 Prix Petite Etoile (Listed) (3-y-o) £14,337 1m..................................(2:50)

BINT LARIAFF (USA) 9-2 F Head,........................ 1
359[2] LA GROUPIE (Fr) 9-2 O Doleuze,........................ 2
POLLY'S WIKA (USA) 9-2 C Asmussen,.................. 3
638[2] SHIR DAR (Fr) 9-2 K Desormeaux,...................... 4
Dist: Nk, ½l, 1l, ½l, ¾l, ¾l, 1½l, 5l, 3l. 1m 40.80s. a 5.30s (10 Ran).
SR: 59/58/56/53/ (Maktoum Al Maktoum), Mme C Head

YORK (good to soft)
Tuesday May 11th
Going Correction: PLUS 0.55 sec. per fur. (races 1,3), PLUS 0.20 (2,4,5,6)

984 EBF Zetland Maiden Fillies Stakes Class D (2-y-o) £5,117 5f....................(2:00)

QUEENBIRD 8-11 W Ryan (2) *trkd ldrs, hdwy 2 fs out, led o'r one out, rdn and ran on wl ins last.* .... (11 to 4 op 2 to 1 tchd 3 to 1) 1
738[7] FRENCH GIFT 8-11 J Williams (5) *chsd ldrs, hdwy 2 fs out, effrt and ev ch o'r one out, sn rdn, kpt on.* ....(9 to 4 fav op 2 to 1 tchd 5 to 2) 2
NIGHTITUDE 8-11 D Holland (3) *in tch, hdwy and ev ch o'r one furlong out, sn rdn, one pace ins last.* .... (15 to 2 op 7 to 1 tchd 8 to 1) 3
839[4] PRIMO STAMPARI 8-11 Pat Eddery (4) *wnt lft strt, sn led, rdn and hdd appr fnl furlong, soon btn.* ....(4 to 1 op 7 to 2) 4
NORDICO PRINCESS 8-11 S Perks (1) *cl up, rdn 2 fs out, wknd appr last*...... (16 to 1 op 14 to 1 tchd 20 to 1) 5
804[2] CERTIFICATE-X 8-11 Dean McKeown (6) *cl up till rdn and wknd 2 fs out*...................... (5 to 1 op 4 to 1) 6
Dist: 1½l, 2l, 1½l, 2½l, 2l. 1m 2.46s. a 5.16s (6 Ran).
SR: 49/43/35/29/19/11/ (A S Reid), H R A Cecil

985 Sotheby's Sledmere Conditions Stakes Class C (3-y-o) £4,274 1m 5f 194yds (2:30)

567* KASSAB 8-13 W Carson (4) *chsd ldr, rdn hfwy, chlgd 3 fs out, swtchd ins and hrd drvn appr one out, styd on to ld inside last*......................... (5 to 1 op 9 to 2) 1
509[3] ALINOVA (USA) 8-6 M Roberts (2) *led, rdn 2 and a half fs out, edgd rght o'r one out, hdd and no extr ins last.* .... (2 to 1 fav tchd 9 to 4) 2
843[6] FRESCADE (USA) 8-11 A Munro (1) *hld up, hdwy 5 fs out, ev ch 3 out, sn rdn and wknd*....... (9 to 2 op 7 to 2) 3
494[4] SHARJAH (USA) 8-13 Pat Eddery (6) *chsd ldrs, rdn o'r 4 fs out, sn wknd*....... (100 to 30 op 3 to 1 tchd 7 to 2) 4
679[4] COLORFUL AMBITION 8-11 W R Swinburn (5) *chsd ldrs, rdn o'r 5 fs out, sn beh*...............(5 to 1 op 9 to 2) 5
686[6] HALMANERROR 8-11 J Carroll (3) *beh hfwy, tld off fnl 5 fs*.................................(33 to 1 op 25 to 1) 6
Dist: 3l, 10l, 25l, 15l, dist. 3m 3.37s. a 8.37s (6 Ran).
SR: 43/30/15/ (Hamdan Al-Maktoum), J L Dunlop

986 Paul Caddick And MacGay Sprint Trophy Rated Class B Handicap (0-105 3-y-o and up) £10,237 6f.....................(3:00)

654* BRANSTON ABBY (Ire) [97] 4-8-13 M Roberts (14) *hld up, hdwy 2 fs out, rdn and quickened entering last to ld wl ins*............... (15 to 2 jt-fav op 8 to 1 tchd 7 to 1) 1
750[6] DUPLICITY (Ire) [95] 5-8-11 J Reid (11) *dwlt, beh till hdwy 2 fs out, rdn appr last, ran on wl ins.* .... (11 to 1 op 10 to 1 tchd 12 to 1) 2
891* STACK ROCK [95] 6-8-11 (3ex) K Fallon (13) *chsd ldrs, hdwy 2 fs out, rdn to ld entering last, hdd and no extr wl ins*..............................(11 to 1 op 8 to 1) 3
750[5] VENTURE CAPITALIST [93] (bl) 4-8-9 K Darley (4) *mid-div, hdwy o'r 2 fs out, ev ch entering last, no extr nr finish.* ....(10 to 1 tchd 11 to 1) 4
677[2] MASSIBA (Ire) [91] 4-8-7 B Raymond (7) *cl up centre, led aftr 2 fs, rdn wl o'r one out, hdd and wknd entering last*... (10 to 1) 5
677[3] CUMBRIAN WALTZER [91] 8-8-4 (3*) S Maloney (10) *chsd ldrs, rdn appr fnl furlong, edgd rght and one pace ins last*......................(17 to 2 op 8 to 1 tchd 9 to 1) 6
750 GILT THRONE [91] 6-8-7 P Robinson (12) *beh, styd on appr fnl furlong, nvr dngrs*.............(25 to 1 op 20 to 1) 7
737 MASTER PLANNER [94] 4-8-10 D Biggs (16) *beh, some hdwy fnl 2 fs, nvr dngrs*........................ (12 to 1) 8
465* SIR HARRY HARDMAN [91] 5-8-7 Pat Eddery (3) *cl up, ev ch 2 fs out, sn rdn, wknd appr last*......(8 to 1 op 6 to 1) 9
750[7] GREEN DOLLAR [91] 10-8-7 M Tebbutt (9) *al rear.* .... (16 to 1 op 14 to 1) 10
587* FYLDE FLYER [105] (v) 4-9-7 J Carroll (2) *o'rall ldr far side 2 fs, sn rdn, beh two out.* .... (11 to 1 op 10 to 1 tchd 12 to 1) 11
750[2] DOUBLE BLUE [94] 4-8-10 Dean McKeown (6) *chsd ldrs to hfwy, sn wknd*... (15 to 2 jt-fav op 7 to 1 tchd 8 to 1) 12
750[3] HARD TO FIGURE [95] 7-8-11 W Carson (15) *nvr a factor.* .... (9 to 1 op 8 to 1 tchd 10 to 1) 13
814[5] RED ROSEIN [91] 7-8-7 G Carter (1) *chsd ldr far side, effrt and rdn hfwy, sn btn and esaed*.............. (12 to 1) 14
Dist: Nk, ½l, hd, 3l, 1l, 1l, 1l, ½l, hd, 2½l. 1m 14.37s. a 4.37s (14 Ran).
SR: 78/75/73/70/56/52/48/47/42/ (J David Abell), M Johnston

987 Tattersalls Musidora Stakes Class A (Group 3) (3-y-o) £25,003 1¼m 85yds (3:35)

MARILLETTE (USA) 8-10 Pat Eddery (4) *hld up beh, hdwy 4 fs out, rdn to ld jst ins last, ran on.* .... (5 to 1 op 4 to 1 tchd 11 to 2) 1
IVIZA (Ire) 8-8 M Roberts (1) *hld up beh, hdwy 4 fs out, chlgd on outsd 2 out, sn rdn, ev ch entering last, kpt on*................................(11 to 2 op 4 to 1) 2
556* SUEBOOG (Ire) 8-12 W R Swinburn (3) *trkd ldrs, cld 3 fs out, led o'r 2 out, sn rdn, hdd ins last, wknd nr finish.* ....(2 to 1 on op 7 to 4 on tchd 13 to 8 on) 3
772[6] GROVE DAFFODIL (Ire) 8-8 P Robinson (2) *wnt clr, quickened 5 fs out, sn rdn, hdd o'r 2 out, soon wknd.* .... (66 to 1 op 33 to 1) 4
748[3] PAMZIG (USA) 8-8 D Holland (5) *chsd ldr, hdwy 4 fs out, rdn and ev ch o'r 2 out, sn wknd.* .... (10 to 1 op 8 to 1 tchd 11 to 1) 5
Dist: 1l, 1l, 6l, 3½l. 2m 15.69s. a 7.69s (5 Ran).
SR: 40/36/38/22/15/ (Sheikh Mohammed), J H M Gosden

988 Yorkshire Television Handicap Class C (0-90 4-y-o and up) £5,344 1m 3f 195yds ....(4:05)

785[2] AMBIGUOUSLY REGAL (USA) [75] 4-9-7 G Duffield (4) *chsd ldr, led o'r 3 fs out, rdn clr over 2 out, styd on wl und pres fnl furlong*......(4 to 1 fav op 5 to 1 tchd 7 to 2) 1
831[3] FIRST BID [63] 6-8-9 J Fanning (10) *al prmnt, chsd wnr 2 fs out, kpt on wl und pres fnl furlong.* (9 to 1 op 8 to 1) 2
769* WHITE WILLOW [75] 4-9-7 K Darley (9) *chsd ldrs, effrt and rdn 2 fs out, kpt on ins last*.........(7 to 1 op 5 to 1) 3
894[3] EIRE LEATH-SCEAL [47] 6-7-7 J Lowe (5) *led, rdn and hdd o'r 3 fs out, kpt on one pace*...............(20 to 1) 4
745[2] PERSUASIVE [57] 6-8-3 Dale Gibson (3) *hld up, hdwy 3 fs out, rdn 2 out, sn one pace.* .... (17 to 2 op 8 to 1 tchd 9 to 1) 5

723* SWORD MASTER [73] 4-9-5 N Day (1) *chsd ldrs, rdn 3 fs out, sn one pace*.........(9 to 1 op 7 to 1) 6
520[2] ROSGILL [67] 7-8-13 P Robinson (8) *al mid-div*. ....(9 to 1 op 7 to 1) 7
682 LABURNUM [72] 5-9-4 K Fallon (11) *hld up beh, hdwy fnl 2 fs, not rch ldrs*.......... (8 to 1 op 7 to 1 tchd 9 to 1) 8
HIGHFLYING [80] 7-9-12 W Newnes (14) *al rear*. ....(20 to 1 op 16 to 1 tchd 25 to 1) 9
739 FAIR FLYER (Ire) [60] 4-8-6 Dean McKeown (15) *mid-div, hdwy 4 fs out, sn rdn, wknd 3 out*. (10 to 1 op 12 to 1) 10
845 IN THE MONEY (Ire) [73] 4-9-5 W Ryan (12) *in tch, rdn and wknd 3 fs out*...................(20 to 1 tchd 16 to 1) 11
527[8] LYPHANTASTIC (USA) [82] 4-10-0 W R Swinburn (13) *wide to hfwy, prmnt till rdn and wknd 3 fs out*. ....(8 to 1 op 7 to 1) 12
PURITAN (Can) [73] 4-9-5 Kim Tinkler (16) *dwlt and bumped strt, al beh*.................................. (20 to 1) 13

Dist: ¾l, ½l, 1l, ¾l, nk, ¾l, ½l, 10l, 3l, hd. 2m 35.56s. a 7.56s (13 Ran).
SR: 55/41/52/22/30/45/37/41/29/ (George L Ohrstrom), Mrs J Cecil

989 Fitzwilliam Rated Class B Handicap (0-100 3-y-o) £6,674 1¼m 85yds........... (4:35)

843[3] PERSIAN BRAVE (Ire) [97] 9-7 M Hills (2) *made all, quickened clr 2 and a half fs out, unchlgd*. ....(7 to 2 fav op 3 to 1) 1
875[4] BRIGANTE DI CIELO [83] 8-7 B Raymond (11) *hld up, hdwy 3 fs out, rdn 2 out, kpt on, no ch wth wnr*. ....(5 to 1 op 9 to 2 tchd 11 to 2) 2
690[5] AZHAR [89] 8-13 M Roberts (3) *chsd ldrs, effrt 2 and a half fs out, sn rdn and one pace*. ....(9 to 1 op 8 to 1 tchd 10 to 1) 3
759* CLOUDED ELEGANCE [85] 8-9 Pat Eddery (5) *chsd ldrs, effrt 3 fs out, sn rdn and one pace*... (4 to 1 op 3 to 1) 4
684[5] THE SEER [83] 8-7 D Holland (1) *in tch, hdwy 3 fs out, rdn and one pace frm 2 out*. (9 to 1 op 8 to 1 tchd 10 to 1) 5
643[5] PERSIAN REVIVAL (Fr) [83] 8-7 A Munro (8) *beh, hdwy o'r 3 fs out, rdn 2 out, not rch ldrs*.... (16 to 1 tchd 20 to 1) 6
690[9] CONEYBURY (Ire) [92] 9-2 R Cochrane (4) *chsd ldrs, rdn and wknd 3 fs out*..............(10 to 1 tchd 11 to 1) 7
494[2] BUROOJ [88] 8-12 W Carson (9) *hld up beh, some hdwy 4 fs out, sn btn*......................(11 to 2 op 9 to 2) 8
BLUE BLAZER [87] 8-11 W Ryan (10) *mid-div, some hdwy 4 fs out, sn rdn and wknd*.............................. (16 to 1) 9
578[3] ERICOLIN (Ire) [88] 8-12 W R Swinburn (7) *chsd ldrs, effrt 4 fs out, sn rdn, wkng whn hmpd 3 out*. ....(12 to 1 op 10 to 1) 10
KADASTROF (Fr) [90] 9-0 T Quinn (6) *chsd wnr till rdn and wknd 3 fs out*...................(33 to 1 op 25 to 1) 11

Dist: 7l, ¾l, ½l, 2l, ¾l, 6l, 8l, 1l, hd, 7l. 2m 13.67s. a 5.67s (11 Ran).
SR: 71/43/47/42/36/34/31/11/8/ (Persian Partnership), M Bell

KEMPTON (good)
Wednesday May 12th
Going Correction: MINUS 0.05 sec. per fur. (races 1,4,6), MINUS 0.15 (2,3,5)

990 Ambition Apprentice Handicap Class E (0-80 3-y-o and up) £3,314 1m....... (6:05)

971 NOBBY BARNES [57] 4-8-2 (3*) T G McLaughlin (9) *hdwy o'r 2 fs out, rdn to ld entering last, styd on wl*. ....(14 to 1 op 10 to 1 tchd 20 to 1) 1
LANGTRY LADY [77] (v) 7-9-11 C Hodgson (3) *hdwy o'r 2 fs out, led briefly over one out, ran on same pace*. ....(12 to 1 op 8 to 1) 2
OVERPOWER [60] 9-8-3 (5*) S Mulvey (12) *ran on 2 fs out, effrt one out, one pace last 100 yards*. ....(12 to 1 op 8 to 1) 3
676 FOOLISH TOUCH [50] 11-7-9 (3*) D McCabe (8) *hld up in rear, str run o'r 2 fs out, kpt on ins last*. ....(14 to 1 op 12 to 1) 4
375[4] KING PARROT (Ire) [56] 5-7-13 (5*) J Wilkinson (14) *chsd ldrs, effrt 2 fs out, btn appr last*... (14 to 1 op 10 to 1) 5
709 DAZZLING FIRE (Ire) [54] 4-7-13 (3*) Kim McDonnell (16) *ran on frm 2 fs out, not rch ldrs*........(25 to 1 op 20 to 1) 6
756 CHEVEUX MITCHELL [70] (v) 6-8-13 (5*) Mark Denaro (6) *cl up, led o'r 2 fs out till over one out, sn wknd*. ....(16 to 1 op 12 to 1) 7
723 LITERARY CRITIC (Ire) [47] (bl) 4-7-9[7] (5*) G Milligan (18) *in tch, rdn and no prog o'r 2 fs out*... (50 to 1 op 33 to 1) 8
319[8] DANCE ON SIXPENCE [54] 5-7-13 (3*) C Hawksley (2) *trkd ldrs, hdwy o'r 3 fs out, ev ch 2 out, no extr appr last*. ....(16 to 1 op 10 to 1 tchd 20 to 1) 9
620 WRETS [75] 4-9-4 (5*) R Painter (4) *in tch, effrt o'r 2 fs out, no imprsn on ldrs appr last*..........(50 to 1 op 33 to 1) 10
827[8] PRIMO FIGLIO [76] 3-8-6 (5*) D Gibbs (10) *mid-div, lost pl o'r 3 fs out, kpt on one pace frm 2 out*. ....(14 to 1 op 10 to 1) 11
603[6] JOLTO [45] 4-7-4[2] (5*) D Toole (1) *led till o'r 2 fs out*. ....(20 to 1 op 16 to 1) 12
975[4] PRINCE RODNEY [67] 4-8-10 (5*) A Whelan (5) *ldg grp 6 fs*. ....(10 to 1 op 8 to 1 tchd 12 to 1) 13
440* MOLLY SPLASH [56] 6-7-13 (5*) S James (7) *nvr plcd to chal*.................. (9 to 1 op 7 to 1 tchd 12 to 1) 14
MR TATE (Ire) [58] 4-8-1 (5*) L Carter (15) *struggling hfwy*. ....(12 to 1 op 8 to 1) 15
931[2] ROMOLA NIJINSKY [60] 5-8-8 Stephen Davies (13) *in tch, rdn and no hdwy frm 3 fs out, eased whn btn*. ....(100 to 30 fav op 7 to 2 tchd 5 to 1) 16
600 CHESHIRE ANNIE (Ire) [53] 4-7-8 (7*) G Rothwell (11) *nvr on terms*............................ (50 to 1 op 25 to 1) 17
260* MAC'S FIGHTER [80] 8-9-11 (3*) B Russell (17) *al beh*. ....(16 to 1 op 10 to 1) 18
368[4] ALPHONSO [65] 4-8-13 B Doyle (20) *nvr rch ldrs*. ....(20 to 1 op 14 to 1) 19
KYRENIA GAME [67] 3-8-2 N Gwilliams (19) *outpcd most of way*........................... (16 to 1 op 12 to 1) 20

Dist: ½l, 2½l, 2l, 3l, 2l, ½l, ¾l, nk, 2l, 1l. 1m 40.31s. a 3.31s (20 Ran).
SR: 35/53/28/12/9/1/15/-/-/ (T S M S Riley-Smith), D A Wilson

991 Waterloo Maiden Stakes Class D (3-y-o) £3,406 7f.......................... (6:35)

797[3] ROBLEU 8-7 (7*) Gaye Harwood (8) *hld up towards rear, ran on o'r 2 fs out, led last 100 yards, styd on strly*. ....(14 to 1 op 8 to 1 tchd 16 to 1) 1
825[5] SHARAAR (USA) 9-0 M Roberts (2) *settled mid-div, ran on to ld 2 fs out, hdd und pres last 100 yards, no extr*. ....(10 to 1 op 8 to 1 tchd 12 to 1) 2
538[2] AUTUMNIS (USA) 9-0 Pat Eddery (5) *in 3rd pl till led o'r 3 fs out, hdd 2 out, eased whn btn ins last*. .... (11 to 8 op 6 to 4 tchd 7 to 4) 3
LINK RIVER (USA) 8-9 G Hind (3) *strted slwly, hdwy aftr 2 fs, rdn and wknd o'r one out*. ....(Evens fav tchd 11 to 10 on and 11 to 10) 4
719 APACHE MYTH 8-9 R Cochrane (4) *beh till styd on last 2 fs, not rch ldrs*.................. (20 to 1 tchd 33 to 1) 5
POCONO KNIGHT 9-0 C Avery (1) *outpcd in rear till ran on frm 2 fs out, nvr nrr*..........(100 to 1 op 50 to 1) 6
752 FRANCIA 8-9 W Woods (7) *wl plcd to hfwy, wkng whn hit rls o'r 2 fs out, not rcvr*...........(66 to 1 op 50 to 1) 7
871[7] PERFECT PASSION 8-9 G Bardwell (9) *led to hfwy, sn drpd out*.............................(100 to 1 op 50 to 1) 8
ST ALZINA (Ire) 9-0 A Munro (6) *chsd ldrs, ev ch o'r 3 fs out, sn wknd*......................... (66 to 1 op 50 to 1) 9

Dist: 3l, 3½l, 1½l, 2l, ¾l, 6l, 3l, 4l. 1m 27.56s. a 3.46s (9 Ran).
SR: 32/23/12/2/-/-/ (G Harwood), G Harwood

992 Kempton Business Centre Maiden Fillies Stakes Class D (3-y-o) £3,582 1m 1f (7:05)

662[4] BELLA BALLERINA 8-11 Pat Eddery (12) *hdwy o'r 3 fs out, led over one out, shaken up, cleverly*. ....(9 to 4 jt-fav op 2 to 1 tchd 7 to 4) 1
NASSMA (Ire) 8-11 G Carter (15) *slwly into strd, ran on 3 fs out, not quicken o'r one out, styd on*. ....(14 to 1 op 12 to 1) 2
821[2] TOCHAR BAN (USA) 8-11 J Williams (7) *slwly into strd, jnd ldrs aftr 3 fs, not quicken o'r 2 out, ran on ins last*. .... (9 to 4 jt-fav tchd 3 to 1) 3
752[3] CORAL GEM 8-11 M Roberts (8) *pld hrd, hdwy aftr 3 fs, one pace frm 2 out*......(6 to 1 op 5 to 1 tchd 15 to 2) 4
SINGER ON THE ROOF 8-11 M Hills (4) *ldg grp, ev ch 2 fs out, no extr fnl furlong*............(25 to 1 op 20 to 1) 5
662 RANEEN ALWATAR 8-11 R Cochrane (11) *hdwy 3 fs out, rdn and not much room 2 out, not rch ldrs fnl furlong*. ....(20 to 1 op 14 to 1 tchd 25 to 1) 6
821[5] KENESHA (Ire) 8-11 C Rutter (2) *led till o'r one furlong out, wknd*............................ (25 to 1 tchd 50 to 1) 7
CHASE THE STARS 8-11 W Newnes (14) *styd on last 2 fs, nvr nrr*..(33 to 1) 8
821 HAVEN OF LOVE (Ire) 8-11 D Biggs (1) *nvr rch frnt rnk*. ....(50 to 1) 9
TISZA 8-11 G Hind (16) *dwlt, beh till moderate late hdwy*. ....(14 to 1 op 12 to 1 tchd 16 to 1) 10
JOLIS ABSENT 8-11 M Tebbutt (3) *prmnt early, settled mid-div aftr 3 fs, nvr dngrs*.......................... (50 to 1) 11
583[8] SUMMER WIND (Ire) 8-8 (3*) D Harrison (9) *nvr better than mid-div*............................(33 to 1 op 25 to 1) 12
854[3] DITTISHAM (USA) 8-11 T Quinn (13) *pressed ldr, ev ch 3 fs out, wknd o'r one out*. (9 to 1 op 7 to 1 tchd 10 to 1) 13
ALYVAIR 8-11 A Clark (6) *nvr on terms*..............(33 to 1) 14
MISS PIMPERNEL 8-11 B Raymond (5) *outpcd*. ....(25 to 1 op 16 to 1 tchd 33 to 1) 15
DUSTY'S DARLING 8-11 P Robinson (17) *ldg grp till wknd o'r 2 fs out*........................(25 to 1 op 16 to 1) 16
672 SHOPTILLYOUDROP 8-11 B Rouse (10) *beh hfwy, tld off*. ....(33 to 1 op 25 to 1) 17

Dist: 1½l, 1½l, 4l, ½l, 2½l, ¾l, 2l, ¾l, 2½l, ½l. 1m 54.05s. a 4.05s (17 Ran).
SR: 16/11/6/-/-/-/ (Helena Springfield Ltd), M R Stoute

993 Ring & Brymer Conditions Stakes Class C (3-y-o and up) £4,195 5f............. (7:35)

675[7] BOLD LEZ 6-9-7 R Cochrane (3) *hld up rear, swtchd rght and ran on hfwy, led o'r one furlong out, pushed out*. ....(7 to 1 op 7 to 2 tchd 15 to 2) 1
464[6] SABRE RATTLER 3-9-3 Pat Eddery (2) *trkd ldrs, ev ch o'r one furlong out, not quicken last 100 yards*. ....(13 to 2 op 6 to 1 tchd 8 to 1) 2

871* BELLSABANGING 3-8-6 T Williams (4) *chsd ldrs till outpcd and rdn 2 fs out, ran on ins last.* ....(14 to 1 op 20 to 1 tchd 25 to 1) 3

795^{4} ARTISTIC REEF 4-9-2 W Carson (5) *made most for o'r 3 fs, kpt on same pace.* ....(Evens fav tchd 6 to 5 and 11 to 10 on) 4

POYLE GEORGE 8-9-2 J Williams (1) *beh, moderate effrt o'r one furlong out, no ch wth wnr.* ....(50 to 1 op 25 to 1) 5

587^{5} MEDAILLE D'OR (v) 5-9-12 A Munro (6) *pressed ldr till rdn and wknd quickly o'r one furlong out.* ....(10 to 1 op 6 to 1) 6

347^{3} BRIGG FAIR 3-8-10 J Reid (7) *slwly into strd, effrt hfwy, btn o'r one furlong out.* (6 to 1 op 5 to 1 tchd 13 to 2) 7

Dist: 2l, ¾l, ½l, 2l, 1l, sht-hd. 59.70s. a 1.50s (7 Ran).

SR: 72/60/46/54/46/52/35/ (Ansells Of Watford), M J Haynes

994 LBC Newstalk 97.3 FM Handicap Class E (0-70 3-y-o and up) £3,444 1½m..... (8:05)

727^{6} MISS PIN UP [67] 4-9-11 R Cochrane (4) *mid-div, ran on o'r 2 fs out, quickened to ld wl ins last.* ....(8 to 1 op 7 to 1 tchd 10 to 1) 1

714^{4} NORDANSK [44] 4-8-2 C Avery (14) *hld up, str run last 2 fs, fnshd wl*........(14 to 1 tchd 16 to 1 and 12 to 1) 2

TAYLORS PRINCE [54] (v) 6-8-12 J Quinn (3) *improved o'r 3 fs out, ran on to ld appr last, hdd and outpcd last 100 yards*...............(16 to 1 op 14 to 1 tchd 20 to 1) 3

879* MUNDAY DEAN [57] (bl) 5-9-1 (4ex) J Reid (10) *hdwy and not clr run o'r 2 fs out, hmpd and snatched up over one out, rallied last 100 yards*.... (6 to 1 jt-fav tchd 8 to 1) 4

FIERCE [57] (v) 5-9-1 A Munro (19) *hdwy on outsd 3 fs out, kpt on one pace fnl furlong*......(20 to 1 tchd 25 to 1) 5

739 ACROBATE (USA) [67] 4-9-11 J Williams (22) *ran on appr last 2 fs, nrst finish*.............. (33 to 1 op 25 to 1) 6

840^{9} CRACKLING [53] 4-8-11 S Dawson (16) *styd on appr last 2 fs, nrst finish*.................. (20 to 1 op 16 to 1) 7

520 EASTERN MAGIC [45] 5-8-3 G Carter (20) *pressed ldrs, ev ch o'r 2 fs out, styd on same pace.* (25 to 1 tchd 33 to 1) 8

620^{3} MARCHMAN [57] 8-9-1 Pat Eddery (1) *hdwy hfwy, led 2 fs out till appr last, no extr*. ....(6 to 1 jt-fav op 7 to 1 tchd 8 to 1) 9

389^{4} ABSENT RELATIVE [58] 5-9-2 M Roberts (12) *wl plcd, lost pos o'r 3 fs out, kpt on appr last.* ....(12 to 1 op 10 to 1 tchd 14 to 1) 10

678^{3} FLY FOR GOLD (Ire) [51] 4-8-9 T Quinn (15) *mid-div most of way*............................... (12 to 1 op 8 to 1) 11

756 HEAVYWEIGHT (Ire) [49] 4-8-4 (3*) A Tucker (7) *effrt frm rear o'r 5 fs out, no hdwy over 2 out*.............. (66 to 1) 12

678^{2} EDGE OF DARKNESS [56] 4-8-11 (3*) D Harrison (21) *improved into mid-div appr last 2 fs, no imprsn on frnt rnk*.................(12 to 1 op 10 to 1 tchd 14 to 1) 13

HYMNE D'AMOUR (USA) [50] 5-8-8 B Raymond (17) *led aftr 2 fs till hdd and wknd two out.* ....(11 to 1 op 8 to 1 tchd 12 to 1) 14

719^{7} KEEP ME IN MIND (Ire) [59] 4-9-3 T Sprake (11) *handily plcd till wknd and hmpd o'r 2 fs out.* ....(33 to 1 tchd 50 to 1) 15

618^{8} DAWN FLIGHT [67] 4-9-11 A Clark (2) *slwly into strd, sn rdn alng, effrt hfwy, wknd 3 fs out.* ....(20 to 1 op 16 to 1 tchd 25 to 1) 16

678 FATHER HAYES (USA) [62] 5-9-6 N Day (13) *nvr on terms.* ....(12 to 1 op 8 to 1) 17

MYSTERIOUS MAID (USA) [51] 6-8-9 M Wigham (5) *slwly into strd, al rear grp*.........................(20 to 1) 18

723^{7} BLAZON OF TROY [58] 4-9-2 S Whitworth (24) *wl plcd 9 fs.* ....(25 to 1 op 16 to 1) 19

879^{4} FULL QUIVER [43] (v) 8-7-8 (7*) D Wright (18) *led 2 fs, ev ch 3 out, wkng whn hmpd wl o'r one out.* ....(14 to 1 op 16 to 1 tchd 20 to 1) 20

739^{6} WESTERN DYNASTY [65] 7-9-9 D Biggs (6) *prmnt till lost pl quickly 3 fs out*............ (14 to 1 tchd 16 to 1) 21

628 JULFAAR (USA) [52] 6-8-10 G Bardwell (9) *ldg grp for o'r 9 fs, eased whn btn*..........................(33 to 1) 22

442 SARAZAR (USA) [54] 4-8-12 R Perham (23) *al beh.* ....(25 to 1 op 20 to 1) 23

Dist: 1l, ¾l, 2l, nk, sht-hd, hd, ¾l, hd, 1½l, 1½l. 2m 35.38s. a 4.38s (23 Ran).

SR: 49/24/32/31/30/39/24/14/25/ (E Baldwin), Pat Mitchell

995 Clubhouse Handicap Class C (0-90 3-y-o) £4,962 7f.......................... (8:35)

872* FOURFORFUN [70] 8-11 (5ex) B Raymond (5) *mid-div, ran on and edgd lft o'r one furlong out, rdn to ld nr line.* ....(9 to 4 fav op 6 to 4) 1

FAIRY STORY (Ire) [66] 8-7 T Quinn (3) *pressed ldr, ev ch ins fnl furlong, not quicken last strds.* ....(11 to 1 op 12 to 1 tchd 10 to 1) 2

624^{9} TWICE THE GROOM (Ire) [68] 8-9 W Newnes (9) *pld hrd, led aftr 2 fs till hdd nr finish.* ....(14 to 1 op 12 to 1 tchd 16 to 1) 3

OK BERTIE [78] 9-5 M Tebbutt (7) *hld up beh, ran on 2 fs out, styd on ins last.* (40 to 1 op 25 to 1 tchd 50 to 1) 4

252^{3} ABSOLUTELY FACT (USA) [62] 8-3 A Munro (1) *led 2 fs, rdn and crrd lft o'r one out, no extr.* ....(7 to 1 op 6 to 1 tchd 8 to 1) 5

761^{3} FLASHFEET [80] 9-7 M Hills (8) *in tch, rdn and one pace appr fnl furlong*.........(9 to 2 op 7 to 2 tchd 5 to 1) 6

483^{9} MR NEVERMIND (Ire) [67] 8-8 B Rouse (2) *mid-div, rdn alng o'r 2 fs out, crrd lft over one out, sn btn.* ....(11 to 2 op 8 to 1 tchd 5 to 1) 7

483 MISTY SILKS [65] 8-6 P Robinson (4) *outpcd.* ....(25 to 1 op 16 to 1) 8

471^{3} TRINITY HALL [62] 8-3 S Dawson (6) *in tch till rcd wide entering strt o'r 3 fs out, sn wknd*...(11 to 2 op 5 to 1) 9

Dist: ½l, sht-hd, 1l, 2½l, ½l, nk, 6l, nk. 1m 28.07s. a 3.77s (9 Ran).

SR: 35/29/30/37/13/29/15/-/-/ (Mrs R F Knipe), R Hannon

KILLARNEY (IRE) (firm)
Wednesday May 12th

996 RTE Eurovision Song Contest Handicap (0-75 4-y-o and up) £3,450 1m 100yds (4:00)

599^{8} RUSTIC-ORT (Ire) [-] (bl) 5-8-0 N G McCullagh (9) (16 to 1) 1

SEEK THE FAITH (USA) [-] (bl) 4-10-0 M J Kinane (6) ....(6 to 4 fav) 2

868^{3} HONORARY PRINCE (Ire) [-] 4-9-9 R Hughes (10).. (5 to 2) 3

640 FLORAL STREET [-] 4-9-7 (6*) C Everard (3)...... (10 to 1) 4

849^{3} MAGIC ARTS (Ire) [-] 5-9-5 (6*) J R Barry (4)........(7 to 1) 5

598^{4} TINCO PALENO [-] (bl) 9-8-9 (2*) R M Burke (1).....(8 to 1) 6

NORDIC RACE [-] 6-9-1 (6*) J A Heffernan (5).....(16 to 1) 7

849^{7} ACCELL (Ire) [-] 4-9-1 P Shanahan (7)............(11 to 2) 8

281 DARCARI ROSE (Ire) [-] 4-8-12 (4*) W J Smith (12) (16 to 1) 9

SIR ALWAH (Ire) [-] 4-8-10 W J O'Connor (8)......(16 to 1) 10

TUMBLE WOOD (Ire) [-] 5-7-1 (10*) M Maher (2)... (20 to 1) 11

Dist: 3l, nk, nk, 4l. 1m 44.10s. (11 Ran).

(J Kennedy), Edward Lynam

997 Baileys Irish Cream Race (3-y-o and up) £3,450 1m 3f........................ (4:30)

DESERT WISH 3-8-12 C Roche (4)............ (5 to 4 on) 1

944^{4} DAHLIA'S BEST (USA) 3-8-10 W J Supple (3)...... (2 to 1) 2

648^{4} RAIN RITE (Ire) 4-10-2 G M O'Neill (2).............(8 to 1) 3

850^{6} MAN OF ARRAN (Ire) 3-9-1 W J O'Connor (1)...... (7 to 1) 4

870 ELA-MANA-SUE (Ire) 4-9-11 C F Swan (5)........(20 to 1) 5

848 MILLERS MILL (Ire) 3-8-8 (2*) R M Burke (6)...... (16 to 1) f

Dist: 3l, 4l, 15l, 20l. 2m 28.50s. (6 Ran).

(Abdullah Ali), J S Bolger

YORK (good)
Wednesday May 12th

Going Correction: PLUS 0.45 sec. per fur. (races 1,3,6), PLUS 0.10 (2,4,5)

998 Dalton Conditions Stakes Class B (2-y-o) £6,017 6f............................ (2:00)

STONEHATCH (USA) 8-11 J Reid (3) *trkd ldrs, hdwy 2 fs out, quickened to ld appr last, edgd rght, sn clr, imprsv*............ (9 to 4 fav op 7 to 4 tchd 5 to 2) 1

812* SINNERS REPRIEVE 8-8 M Birch (8) *hld up, hdwy hfwy, effrt 2 fs out, sn ev ch, rdn and not quicken appr last.* ....(10 to 1 op 8 to 1) 2

830* BROCTUNE GOLD 8-11 K Darley (6) *hld up, hdwy hfwy, led o'r 2 fs out, sn rdn, hdd and one pace appr last.* ....(11 to 2 op 6 to 1 tchd 5 to 1) 3

687^{5} ALCOVE 8-11 L Piggott (4) *chsd ldrs, ev ch 2 fs out, sn rdn, wknd appr last*.......................(4 to 1 op 5 to 1) 4

395^{8} SHUTTLECOCK 8-11 Dale Gibson (9) *beh, styd on fnl 2 fs.* ....(33 to 1 op 25 to 1) 5

TIME STAR (USA) 8-11 A Munro (1) *chsd ldrs, rdn o'r 2 fs out, sn wknd*......................(11 to 2 op 4 to 1) 6

743* HILTONS TRAVEL (Ire) (v) 8-11 S Webster (2) *led till o'r 2 fs out, sn wknd and hng lft.* ....(20 to 1 op 16 to 1 tchd 25 to 1) 7

698* RAVEN'S RETURN (Ire) 8-13 S Perks (10) *nvr a factor.* ....(22 to 1 op 14 to 1 tchd 25 to 1) 8

543^{3} GREATEST 8-11 Pat Eddery (7) *chsd ldrs, wknd and bumped hfwy, sn beh.* (15 to 2 op 6 to 1 tchd 8 to 1) 9

718^{2} CYARNA QUINN (Ire) 8-6 G Duffield (5) *chsd ldrs, wknd o'r 2 fs out, beh whn hmpd over one out.* ....(10 to 1 tchd 12 to 1) 10

Dist: 6l, 3½l, 3½l, 3l, nk, 2l, 2½l, 1l, ½l. 1m 15.80s. a 5.80s (10 Ran).

SR: 35/8/-/-/-/-/ (R E Sangster), P W Chapple-Hyam

999 Middleton Fillies Conditions Stakes Class C (3-y-o) £5,024 1¼m 85yds........(2:30)

749^{5} DAYFLOWER (USA) 8-10 W R Swinburn (2) *trkd ldrs gng wl, hdwy on bit to ld 2 and a half fs out, sn clr, easily.* ....(Evens fav op 2 to 1 on tchd 11 to 10) 1

472^{8} HELVELLYN (USA) 8-8 M Roberts (1) *hld up, hdwy and pushed alng 4 fs out, chsd wnr frm 2 out, no impression*....................(3 to 1 op 7 to 2 tchd 4 to 1) 2

CHAIN DANCE 8-8 Pat Eddery (5) *slwly away, hdwy 4 fs out, effrt and rdn o'r 2 out, sn one pace.* ....(7 to 2 op 11 to 2) 3

SPARK (Ire) 8-8 K Darley (4) *prmnt, rdn 3 fs out, kpt on one pace*..........................(14 to 1 tchd 16 to 1) 4
FROSTY MORNING 8-8 W Carson (6) *led, rdn 3 fs out, sn hdd and wknd*.......(14 to 1 op 12 to 1 tchd 16 to 1) 5
681* VELVET HEART (Ire) 8-8 E Johnson (3) *hld up, hdwy hfwy, effrt o'r 3 fs out, sn rdn and wknd*. (33 to 1 op 25 to 1) 6
Dist: 5l, 1½l, ½l, 8l, ½l. 2m 14.10s. a 6.10s (6 Ran).
SR: 46/34/31/30/14/13/ (Maktoum Al Maktoum), S Seemar

1000 Homeowners Sprint Handicap Class B (0-105 3-y-o and up) £11,745 5f. . (3:00)

760 MACFARLANE [65] 5-7-10¹ F Norton (8) *chsd ldrs, hdwy 2 fs out, led o'r one out, ran on wl und pres*.....(16 to 1) 1
436⁵ DRUM SERGEANT [76] (bl) 6-8-7 T Quinn (2) *steadied strt, hdwy o'r 2 fs out, chlgd appr last, sn rdn, kpt on*. ....(14 to 1 op 12 to 1) 2
677 DOMINUET [84] 8-9-1 J Lowe (14) *mid-div, hdwy 2 fs out, sn rdn, styd on ins last*......................(16 to 1) 3
916³ MISTER JOLSON [65] 4-7-10 J Quinn (7) *beh, styd on fnl 2 fs, nrst finish*..................................(14 to 1) 4
436* GORINSKY (Ire) [81] 5-8-12 J Carroll (10) *led centre grp, o'rall ldr 2 fs out, sn rdn, hdd over one out, wknd*. ....(10 to 1) 5
795⁶ BUNTY BOO [97] 4-9-7 (7*) S Sanders (9) *dwlt, hdwy hfwy, effrt and ev ch one and a half fs out, sn rdn, wknd entering last*.....................(12 to 1 op 10 to 1) 6
700⁹ PENNY HASSET [73] 5-8-4 K Darley (4) *prmnt, outpcd hfwy, styd on appr fnl furlong*.... (14 to 1 op 12 to 1) 7
548³ GONDO [70] (v) 6-7-12 (3*) S Maloney (11) *beh, hdwy 2 fs out, sn rdn, kpt on*...(11 to 1 op 10 to 1 tchd 12 to 1) 8
659* LORD HIGH ADMIRAL (Can) [70] 5-8-1 M Roberts (13) *chsd ldrs, rdn 2 fs out, sn btn*. .... (15 to 2 op 7 to 1 tchd 8 to 1) 9
891⁷ PETRACO (Ire) [73] (bl) 5-7-11 (7*) D Wright (5) *prmnt, rdn and wknd o'r 2 fs out*...........(20 to 1 tchd 25 to 1) 10
355² EAGER DEVA [83] 6-9-0 L Piggott (6) *cl up, effrt 2 fs out, sn rdn, wknd o'r one out*.............(14 to 1 op 10 to 1) 11
750⁹ BEAU VENTURE (USA) [88] 5-9-2 (3*) N Kennedy (16) *al rear*..................................(11 to 1 op 12 to 1) 12
615⁴ TINO TERE [70] 4-7-8 (7*) Claire Balding (15) *led 3 fs on stands rls, wknd*................. (20 to 1 tchd 25 to 1) 13
700⁸ PAGEBOY [63] (bl) 4-7-8 Dale Gibson (3) *rcd far side, nvr a factor*..............................(25 to 1 op 20 to 1) 14
891² PLAIN FACT [85] 8-9-2 D Holland (12) *al rear*. .... (12 to 1 op 10 to 1) 15
722² CRADLE DAYS [93] 4-9-10 Pat Eddery (17) *chsd ldr stands rls, rdn o'r 2 fs out, sn btn*....... (6 to 1 fav op 7 to 1) 16
891⁴ INHERENT MAGIC (Ire) [80] 4-8-11 W Carson (1) *rcd far side, prmnt 4 fs, sn wknd*. ....(11 to 1 op 10 to 1 tchd 12 to 1) 17
Dist: 1l, 2l, 2½l, nk, 1l, nk, nk, nk, hd, sht-hd. 1m 1.19s. a 3.89s (17 Ran).
SR: 49/56/56/27/42/54/29/25/24/ (P Fetherston-Godley), M J Fetherston-Godley

1001 Tote Dante Stakes Class A (Group 2) (3-y-o) £60,156 1¼m 85yds......(3:35)

775* TENBY 9-0 Pat Eddery (1) *made all, quickened 3 fs out, pushed clr 2 out, easily*....... (3 to 1 on op 9 to 4 on) 1
775² PLANETARY ASPECT (USA) 9-0 J Reid (3) *trkd ldrs, hdwy 3 fs out, chsd wnr and rdn frm 2 out, no imprsn*. .... (15 to 2 op 5 to 1 tchd 8 to 1) 2
775⁴ SHAIBA (USA) 9-0 W R Swinburn (5) *chsd wnr, rdn 3 fs out, one pace 2 out*....... (14 to 1 op 12 to 1 tchd 16 to 1) 3
404³ NOYAN 9-0 M Hills (2) *chsd ldrs, rdn 3 fs out, sn btn*. .... (50 to 1 op 33 to 1 tchd 66 to 1) 4
TAOS (Ire) 9-0 M Roberts (4) *hld up beh, hdwy 4 fs out, rdn 3 out, sn btn*............ (11 to 2 op 7 to 2 tchd 6 to 1) 5
Dist: 3l, 1½l, 10l, 1l. 2m 12.36s. a 4.36s (5 Ran).
SR: 67/61/58/38/36/ (K Abdulla), H R A Cecil

1002 Hambleton Rated Class A Handicap (Listed Race) (0-110 4-y-o and up) £13,047 7f 202yds............... (4:05)

737 RISK MASTER [90] 4-8-9 R Hills (12) *hld up, hdwy 3 fs out, effrt appr one out, rdn to ld ins last, ran on gmely*. ....(16 to 1 op 20 to 1) 1
792 GYMCRAK PREMIERE [97] 5-9-2 K Darley (1) *hld up, hdwy 3 fs out, effrt appr fnl furlong, sn rdn, ev ch ins last till no extr cl hme*........(11 to 1 op 10 to 1 tchd 12 to 1) 2
737⁵ EFHARISTO [90] 4-8-9 M Roberts (4) *chsd ldrs, hdwy 2 fs out, squeezed through on ins to ld entering fnl furlong, sn rdn, hdd and no extr*..............(11 to 1 op 10 to 1) 3
581* TISSISAT (USA) [91] 4-8-10 J Reid (8) *chsd ldrs, effrt and swtchd outsd one and a half fs out, rdn and styd on wl ins last*.............................(13 to 2 op 7 to 1) 4
619* IMPERIAL BALLET (Ire) [99] 4-9-4 Pat Eddery (11) *trkd ldrs, hdwy 2 fs out, ev ch entering last, sn rdn and not quicken*..................... (3 to 1 fav tchd 11 to 4) 5
782⁵ BAND ON THE RUN [97] 6-9-2 T Quinn (2) *led, rdn 2 and a half fs out, hdd and wknd entering last*.........(7 to 1) 6
782³ PATER NOSTER (USA) [98] 4-9-3 L Piggott (5) *chsd ldr, effrt and ev ch 2 fs out, sn rdn and wknd*. ....(7 to 1 tchd 8 to 1) 7
675² MIZAAYA [102] 4-9-7 W R Swinburn (10) *prmnt, hdwy 2 fs out, sn ev ch, rdn and wknd entering last*. ....(6 to 1 op 13 to 2) 8
782² BEWARE OF AGENTS [91] 4-8-10 Dean McKeown (6) *al rear*..................................(10 to 1 op 12 to 1) 9
782* LITTLE BEAN [99] 4-9-4 Paul Eddery (9) *trkd ldrs, hdwy o'r 2 fs out, sn rdn, wknd one and a half out*. ....(9 to 2 op 5 to 1) 10
782⁷ TWO LEFT FEET [99] 6-9-4 G Duffield (7) *hld up, effrt and some hdwy 3 fs out, sn rdn and wknd*.........(16 to 1) 11
Dist: Nk, 2l, 1l, 1½l, 2½l, nk, sht-hd, 3l, hd, 2½l. 1m 39.09s. a 2.79s (11 Ran).
SR: 65/71/58/56/59/49/49/52/32/ (Mrs B Sumner), C A Horgan

1003 Wilkinson Memorial Conditions Stakes Class B (4-y-o and up) £6,504 6f 214yds........................ (4:35)

675⁶ CASTEDDU 4-9-4 W Carson (4) *trkd ldr, hdwy to ld 2 fs out, hrd drvn and ran on wl fnl furlong*. ....(Evens fav op 5 to 4 on tchd 11 to 10) 1
PETER DAVIES (USA) 5-8-12 W R Swinburn (3) *trkd ldrs, effrt 2 fs out, sn rdn, styd on wl und pres ins last*. ....(6 to 1 op 8 to 1) 2
737 EURO FESTIVAL 4-8-12 L Piggott (5) *hld up, hdwy 2 fs out, swtchd ins appr last, sn rdn, ran on wl nr finish*. ....(4 to 1 op 7 to 2) 3
986 HARD TO FIGURE 7-8-13 J Carroll (1) *trkd ldrs, hdwy 2 fs out, rdn and ev ch ins last, no extr nr finish*. ....(7 to 2 tchd 100 to 30) 4
604³ BRIGADE 4-8-12 M Tebbutt (2) *led to 2 fs out, sn wknd*. ....(16 to 1 op 14 to 1 tchd 20 to 1) 5
Dist: ¾l, hd, hd, 3½l. 1m 28.29s. a 6.59s (5 Ran).
SR: 52/44/43/43/31/ (Ettore Landi), J L Dunlop

BRIGHTON (firm)
Thursday May 13th
Going Correction: MINUS 0.40 sec. per fur.

1004 Henfield Maiden Stakes Class D (3-y-o and up) £3,318 1m 3f 196yds.... (1:55)

357² EATON ROW (USA) 3-8-7 Paul Eddery (6) *trkd ldrs, rdn o'r 2 out, led one furlong out, styd on wl*. .... (15 to 8 op 9 to 4 tchd 7 to 4) 1
679² RAFTERS 4-9-12 N Day (2) *led aftr 5 fs, gng wl 2 out, hdd entering last, rdn and not quicken*. .... (11 to 10 fav op 6 to 4 on tchd 5 to 4) 2
509⁸ OLD RED (Ire) 3-8-7 A Munro (1) *trkd ldrs, rdn o'r 4 out, styd on wl appr fnl furlong, nrst finish*. .... (9 to 1 op 7 to 1 tchd 10 to 1) 3
686⁴ MOUNT ROSE 3-8-4 (3*) J Weaver (7) *led for 5 fs, outpcd o'r 2 out, kpt on ag'n ins last*....... (10 to 1 op 7 to 1) 4
799⁶ ISLE OF PEARLS (USA) 3-8-7 R Hills (4) *settled rear, lost tch 4 fs out, sn beh*... (16 to 1 op 10 to 1 tchd 20 to 1) 5
799 MISTRESS BEE (USA) 4-9-7 M Tebbutt (3) *dwlt, hld up, lost action 4 fs out, virtually pld up ins last*. .... (66 to 1 op 33 to 1 tchd 100 to 1) 6
Dist: 1½l, hd, 1l, 10l, dist. 2m 28.60s. a 1.10s (6 Ran).
SR: 34/50/30/28/8/-/ (R E Sangster), P W Chapple-Hyam

1005 Goring Rating Related Maiden Stakes Class F (0-60 3-y-o and up) £2,243 1m 1f 209yds..................... (2:25)

NAHLATI (Ire) 3-7-10 (5*) B Doyle (9) *made all, rdn out ins fnl furlong*............(13 to 2 op 9 to 2 tchd 7 to 1) 1D
4778a³ MISS FASCINATION 3-8-1 G Duffield (6) *al prmnt, rdn o'r 2 fs out, ran on one pace ins last*...(4 to 1 fav op 3 to 1) 1
672 INDIAN FLASH (Ire) 3-8-1 G Bardwell (10) *al chasing wnr, hrd rdn 3 fs out, styd on, nvr able to chal*. ....(14 to 1 op 8 to 1) 2
557 BARRAAK 3-8-6 R Hills (4) *mid-div, rdn 3 fs out, styd on wl appr last, nrst finish*. (5 to 1 op 9 to 2 tchd 6 to 1) 3
719 CONCINNITY (USA) 4-9-8 A Munro (2) *rear till prog 3 out, styd on wl appr fnl furlong, nvr nrr*. ....(20 to 1 op 14 to 1) 4
COMEDY RIVER 6-9-1 (7*) J Tate (1) *strted slwly, beh, rdn and styd on fnl 2 fs, nvr dngrs*...(33 to 1 tchd 40 to 1) 5
724⁴ TEJANO GOLD (USA) 3-8-6 C Rutter (12) *prmnt till rdn and wknd wl o'r 2 fs out*. (8 to 1 op 6 to 1 tchd 9 to 1) 6
499⁹ KIAWAH 3-7-8 (7*) N Varley (16) *rear, brght wide and rdn entering strt, no prog fnl 2 fs*..... (14 to 1 op 12 to 1) 7
840⁷ NORTHERN TRIAL (USA) 5-9-8 T Williams (11) *nvr bey mid-div, no ch fnl 2 fs*.... (12 to 1 op 16 to 1 tchd 20 to 1) 8
724³ SKY BURST 3-8-1 N Carlisle (8) *trkd ldrs till rdn and wknd 3 fs out*............ (5 to 1 op 7 to 2 tchd 11 to 2) 9
754 SEA PRODIGY 4-9-8 W Newnes (5) *al rear, beh fnl 3 fs*. ....(25 to 1 op 20 to 1) 10
493⁷ BOISTEROUS (bl) 3-8-6 A Clark (7) *al rear, beh fnl 3 fs*. ....(33 to 1 op 20 to 1) 11
440⁶ SIMON ELLIS (Ire) 4-9-1 (7*) C Hawksley (13) *al rear, beh fnl 3 fs*.......................(25 to 1 op 14 to 1) 12
719 COVEN MOON (v) 3-8-1 J Quinn (14) *keen hold, trkd ldrs till wknd o'r 3 fs out*............. (14 to 1 op 10 to 1) 13

623[8] TRESARIA (Ire) 3-8-1 N Adams (3) *chsd ldrs, wnt prmnt hfwy, sn wknd and beh*.......... (50 to 1 op 33 to 1) 14
609[8] MAD MYTTON (v) 3-8-6 A Mackay (15) *prmnt 4 fs, wknd rpdly, tld off*..................... (14 to 1 op 10 to 1) 15
Dist: 1½l, sht-hd, ¾l, 1l, 3l, 1l, ½l, 4l, 2l, sht-hd. 2m 2.00s. a 3.80s (16 Ran).
SR: 9/6/5/8/22/16/-/-/5/ (N S Yong), M Jarvis

1006 Aldrington Conditions Stakes Class D (3-y-o) £3,026 1m 1f 209yds..... (2:55)

558 EMPIRE POOL 8-11 A Munro (4) *trkd ldr 6 fs out, led o'r 2 out, rdn appr last, ran on wl*..... (5 to 4 op 11 to 10) 1
KUSAMBA (USA) 9-1 Paul Eddery (1) *led one furlong, led ag'n 6 fs out till hdd o'r 2 out, rallied and ev ch ins last, ran on wl*.................. (6 to 4 on tchd 5 to 4 on) 2
973 HUSH BABY (Ire) 8-3 (7*) G Forster (2) *led aftr one furlong till 6 fs out, sn wknd and tld off*. .... (40 to 1 op 33 to 1 tchd 50 to 1) 3
Dist: Hd, dist. 2m 1.10s. a 2.90s (3 Ran).
SR: 28/31/-/ (The Queen), Lord Huntingdon

1007 Levy Board Maiden Handicap Class F (0-65 3-y-o and up) £2,915 7f 214yds ....(3:25)

DEEVEE [38] 4-8-1[1] G Duffield (2) *settled rear, prog hfwy, rdn 2 fs out, led wl ins last, ran on well*.....(5 to 1 co-fav op 4 to 1 tchd 11 to 2) 1
321[3] SET THE FASHION [48] (v) 4-8-11 J Carroll (9) *trkd ldrs, led o'r 2 fs out, rdn and hdd wl ins last, no extr*. (5 to 1 co-fav op 4 to 1) 2
590[4] PYRRHIC DANCE [58] 3-8-8 R Hills (3) *trkd ldrs, rdn and outpcd o'r 2 fs out, styd on ag'n ins last*....(5 to 1 co-fav op 4 to 1) 3
719[8] CAMEO KIRBY (Fr) [65] 3-8-8 (7*) J Tate (6) *prmnt, led briefly o'r 2 fs out, sn rdn and btn*. (7 to 1 tchd 8 to 1) 4
333[4] BELLATRIX [43] 5-8-1 (5*) B Doyle (7) *rear, rdn wl o'r 2 fs out, no imprsn on ldrs*........ (5 to 1 co-fav op 4 to 1) 5
725[5] LA DELITZIA (USA) [62] 3-8-5 (7*) T G McLaughlin (12) *mid-div, effrt 3 fs out, sn no prog*........ (7 to 1 op 6 to 1) 6
733 BEAT THE BAGMAN (Ire) [44] 3-7-8 Dale Gibson (11) *rear, nvr nrr*......................... (25 to 1 op 14 to 1) 7
759 MAGIC FAN (Ire) [54] 3-8-4 N Adams (4) *prmnt, rdn hfwy, sn btn*............... (11 to 1 op 7 to 1 tchd 12 to 1) 8
FULL SHILLING (USA) [65] (v) 4-10-0 T Williams (14) *dwlt, prog and cl up o'r 3 fs out, sn wknd, eased ins last*. ....(33 to 1) 9
ZHAAB [50] 3-8-0 C Avery (13) *al rear, no ch fnl 3 fs*. .... (33 to 1 op 20 to 1 tchd 40 to 1) 10
CHINAMAN [33] (bl) 4-7-10 G Bardwell (10) *strted very slwly, rdn alng and wl beh till kpt on fnl 2 fs*. .... (16 to 1 op 10 to 1 tchd 20 to 1) 11
238[9] BAYIN (USA) [43] 4-8-6[3] J Williams (1) *al rear, beh fnl 2 fs*. .... (33 to 1 op 20 to 1 tchd 40 to 1) 12
622[7] COLONEL FAIRFAX [34] (bl) 5-7-11[2] C Rutter (5) *led till o'r 2 fs out, wknd rpdly*............... (16 to 1 op 10 to 1) 13
Dist: 1½l, 5l, 3l, 1½l, ½l, 1½l, 1l, 1l, 3½l, hd. 1m 34.00s. a 1.60s (13 Ran).
SR: 15/20/2/-/-/-/ (D Turner), C J Benstead

1008 Madeira Handicap Class E (0-70 3-y-o) £3,131 7f 214yds............... (3:55)

JADIRAH (USA) [66] 9-5 R Hills (4) *rear, prog and hng lft 2 fs out, ran on ins last to ld fnl strd*. .... (5 to 1 op 7 to 2 tchd 11 to 2) 1
833* JUST YOU DARE (Ire) [74] 9-13 (6ex) G Duffield (6) *prmnt, rdn 2 fs out, led ins last, hdd fnl strd*. ....(5 to 4 fav op 5 to 4 on tchd 6 to 4) 2
418[3] SUPERENSIS [46] 7-6 (7*) Kim McDonnell (5) *led till ins fnl furlong, unbl to quicken*. ....(7 to 1 op 6 to 1 tchd 9 to 1) 3
836[6] MR CUBE (Ire) [60] 8-6 (7*) T G McLaughlin (7) *trkd ldrs, rdn and ev ch o'r 2 fs out, sn btn*. .... (6 to 1 op 7 to 1 tchd 11 to 2) 4
BILLYBACK [56] 8-2 (7*) T Beaver (10) *rear, rdn 3 fs out, kpt on, nvr dngrs*........ (20 to 1 op 12 to 1 tchd 33 to 1) 5
827 NIGHT EDITION [52] 8-5 C Rutter (1) *slwly into strd, last till ran on fnl 3 fs, nvr nrr*. .... (20 to 1 op 14 to 1 tchd 25 to 1) 6
679 SABEEL [60] 8-13 J Williams (8) *al rear, no imprsn on ldrs o'r 2 fs out*............................ (20 to 1 op 12 to 1) 7
882[8] MARWELL MITZI [49] 8-2 G Bardwell (9) *chsd ldrs, hrd rdn and wknd 2 fs out*.........................(25 to 1 op 14 to 1) 8
821 GABHADERA [45] (bl) 7-12 N Adams (3) *prmnt o'r 4 fs, wknd rpdly*.........(33 to 1 op 20 to 1 tchd 40 to 1) 9
714 DOCTOR-J (Ire) [58] 8-11 Paul Eddery (2) *wth ldr 3 fs, wknd rpdly*................. (15 to 2 op 6 to 1 tchd 8 to 1) 10
Dist: Sht-hd, 1l, 3½l, 2l, 2l, ¾l, 2l, 12l, 2l. 1m 35.30s. a 2.90s (10 Ran).
SR: 14/21/-/-/-/-/ (Hamdan Al-Maktoum), J L Dunlop

1009 Ditchling Fillies Conditions Stakes Class D (2-y-o) £3,201 5f 213yds (4:25)

496[2] BEARALL (Ire) 8-1 (7*) Mark Denaro (6) *pressed ldr till led o'r 2 fs out, rdn and ran on wl ins last*. ....(4 to 1 op 5 to 2 tchd 9 to 2) 1
657[8] FOOTSTEPS (Ire) 8-8 A Munro (1) *trkd ldg pair, rdn 2 fs out, styd on ins last, nvr able to chal*. .... (11 to 4 op 3 to 1 tchd 9 to 2) 2
657[5] KERRIE-JO 8-8 J Williams (4) *chsd ldrs, rdn o'r 2 fs out, hng rght appr last, kpt on*..................(9 to 4 jt-fav op 5 to 2 tchd 7 to 2) 3
839* IMPERIAL BAILIWICK (Ire) 8-12 N Adams (2) *led till rdn and hdd o'r 2 fs out, wknd ins last*. ....(9 to 4 jt-fav op 2 to 1 tchd 7 to 4 and 5 to 2) 4
657 PETRATHENE 8-5 (3*) B Doyle (5) *al last, ran wide entering strt, sn lost tch*................ (12 to 1 op 6 to 1) 5
Dist: 1½l, 2l, 2½l, 15l. 1m 10.00s. a 1.60s (5 Ran).
SR: 14/8/ (Mr And Mrs M Winterford), R Hannon

1010 Brighton Spring Handicap Class D (0-80 3-y-o) £3,143 5f 59yds..... (4:55)

460[4] ARAGROVE [65] 8-7 A Munro (5) *chsd ldg pair frm hfwy, hrd rdn 2 fs out, led wl ins last, ran on well*. (3 to 1 co-fav op 5 to 2 tchd 7 to 2) 1
829[3] GIRL NEXT DOOR [53] 7-9[2] A Proud (8) *mid-div, hrd rdn 2 fs out, ran on wl ins last, nrst finish*. .... (14 to 1 op 10 to 1) 2
716[7] PRESS THE BELL [73] 9-1 J Carroll (7) *pressed ldr till led 2 fs out, hdd wl ins last, no extr*.............(3 to 1 co-fav tchd 9 to 2) 3
716[3] MY BONUS [79] 9-0 (7*) D McCabe (2) *chsd ldrs, rdn 2 fs out, styd on wl ins last, nrst finish*.........(3 to 1 co-fav tchd 11 to 4 and 100 to 30) 4
720[3] TEE-EMM [57] 7-13 C Rutter (6) *led for 3 fs, rdn and wknd appr last*........... (12 to 1 op 10 to 1 tchd 16 to 1) 5
716[8] MINSHAAR [68] 8-10 Paul Eddery (3) *rdn o'r 2 fs out, al beh*................................ (6 to 1 op 10 to 1) 6
823[8] AUNTIE GINGER [52] 7-8[1] J Quinn (4) *keen hold, hld up in rear, no prog frm hfwy*........... (20 to 1 op 10 to 1) 7
716 FIVE ISLANDS [66] 8-1 (7*) T G McLaughlin (1) *chsd ldrs till wknd 2 fs out*..................... (20 to 1 op 10 to 1) 8
Dist: ¾l, nk, sht-hd, 2½l, 1l, ¾l, 2l. 1m 2.10s. a 2.00s (8 Ran).
SR: 11/-/15/20/-/ (K F Khan), L J Holt

LONGCHAMP (FR) (good to soft)
Thursday May 13th

Going Correction: PLUS 0.10 sec. per fur. (race 1), PLUS 0.30 (2)

1011 Prix de Saint-Georges (Group 3) (3-y-o and up) £23,895 5f.......... (2:55)

430[5] ROBIN DES PINS (USA) 5-9-2 C Asmussen (4) *hld up, rdn o'r one and a half fs out, led ins last, ran on wl*. ....(46 to 10) 1
MONDE BLEU 5-9-8 T Jarnet (2) *rear till rdn to chal one furlong out, took second cl hme*............(5 to 2 on) 2
345[4] CARDOUN (Fr) 4-9-2 D Boeuf (3) *rcd in 3rd, ev ch one furlong out, kpt on one pace*...............(5 to 2 on) 3
795[9] SPANIARDS CLOSE 5-9-0 B Raymond (6) *mid-div till rdn o'r 2 fs out, effrt over one out, one pace fnl furlong*. ....(14 to 1) 4
DREAM TALK 6-9-6 O Peslier (5) *led till hdd and wknd fnl furlong*................................ (28 to 10) 5
FIGHTING TEMERAIRE (Ire) 4-9-0 G Guignard (1) *trkd ldr, rdn and btn one and a half fs out*............(15 to 1) 6
Dist: Nk, ¾l, nk, 1l, 6l. 57.10s. a 1.60s (6 Ran).
SR: 80/85/76/73/75/45/ (S S Niarchos), F Boutin

1012 Prix de l'Avre (Listed) (3-y-o) £14,337 1 ½m.......................... (3:55)

FREEZING BIRD (USA) 9-2 O Doleuze, ... 1
INFRASONIC 9-2 T Jarnet, ... 2
KARAYOR (Fr) 9-2 G Dubroeucq, ... 3
DONDOOK (USA) 9-2 F Head, ... 4
Dist: 2½l, 1½l, 2l, nk, 1½l, sht-nk, 5l. 2m 41.70s. a 12.60s (8 Ran).
SR: 12/7/4/-/ (J Wertheimer), Mme C Head

TRAMORE (IRE) (good to firm)
Thursday May 13th

1013 Tramore Handicap (0-65 4-y-o and up) £2,245 1¾m.................. (7:30)

298[2] SHARP INVITE [-] 6-7-11 (6*) J J Behan (4).....(7 to 4 fav) 1
852[5] CEDAR COURT (Ire) [-] (bl) 5-10-0 C F Swan (6)...(13 to 2) 2
852* MRS BARTON (Ire) [-] 5-9-8 (6*,5ex) J R Barry (1)...(5 to 1) 3
575 LET IT RIDE (Ire) [-] 4-9-3 (6*) P Carberry (10)..... (20 to 1) 4
807[7] AQUINAS [-] 7-8-4 (6*) P P Murphy (14)........... (7 to 1) 5
PREMIER LEAP (Ire) [-] 4-8-8 (10*,5ex) B Fenton (11) (8 to 1) 6
852 MOTILITY [-] 6-9-5 (6*) C Everard (5)..............(16 to 1) 7
298 RIENZI [-] 9-7-11 (10*) P M Donohoe (7)..........(33 to 1) 8
912[9] PEPPERS PET (Ire) [-] (bl) 5-8-8 (8*) R T Fitzpatrick (8) ....(33 to 1) 9
706 SENSITIVE KING (Ire) [-] (bl) 5-8-3 (2*) R M Burke (9) (33 to 1) 10
SMOULDER (USA) [-] 5-9-7 R A Hennessy (13)....(25 to 1) 11

SOUND PERFORMANCE (Ire) [-] 4-9-8 (2*) D G O'Shea (12) ....(20 to 1) 12
912* SENSE OF VALUE [-] 4-9-8 (7ex) J P Murtagh (3) . . (11 to 2) 13
Dist: 4½l, 3½l, nk, 6l. 3m 2.00s. (13 Ran).
(Nicholas Quinlan), W P Mullins

1014 Suir Maiden (3-y-o) £2,245 1¾m (8:00)

819⁴ ANY MINUTE NOW (Ire) 9-0 R Hughes (4) .... (5 to 1) 1
552⁷ KIDAMIYA (Ire) 8-9 (2*) D G O'Shea (2) ....(7 to 4 fav) 2
936² SUNSET CAFE (Ire) (bl) 8-11 P V Gilson (1) ....(9 to 2) 3
819³ LORD CHIEF (Ire) 9-0 J P Murtagh (5) .... (9 to 4) 4
488 GIG TIME (Ire) 8-1 (10*) B Fenton (6) .... (33 to 1) 5
552⁸ MONTEJUSTICE (Ire) 8-11 N Byrne (3) .... (10 to 1) 6
850 HIGHLAND ARK (Ire) 8-8 (6*) R V Skelly (7) .... (20 to 1) 7
Dist: 6l, 2l, 7l, 11l. 3m 5.30s. (7 Ran).
(Mrs P W McGrath), Neil S McGrath

YORK (good) Thursday May 13th

Going Correction: PLUS 0.10 sec. per fur. (races 1,2,4,7), PLUS 0.15 (3,5,6)

1015 Glasgow Conditions Stakes Class C (3-y-o) £5,425 1¼m 85yds.......(2:00)

791* COMMANDER IN CHIEF 9-2 Pat Eddery (4) *led, quickened 4 fs out, pushed clr 2 and a half out, rdn o'r one out, hdd briefly ins last, styd on wl nr finish.* ....(9 to 2 on op 7 to 2 on tchd 10 to 3 on) 1
388⁵ NEEDLE GUN (Ire) 8-10 M Roberts (2) *trkd ldg pair, hdwy to chase wnr o'r 2 fs out, rdn to chal over one out, led briefly ins last, no extr.* (8 to 1 op 6 to 1 tchd 9 to 1) 2
NORFOLK HERO 8-12 T Quinn (1) *steadied strt, hld up, hdwy 4 fs out, sn rdn, one pace o'r 2 out.* .... (33 to 1 op 16 to 1) 3
842* STONEY VALLEY 8-12 J Reid (3) *trkd wnr, effrt 3 fs out, sn rdn, wknd o'r 2 out....* (13 to 2 op 4 to 1 tchd 7 to 1) 4
Dist: Nk, 7l, 4l. 2m 13.57s. a 5.57s (4 Ran).
SR: 57/50/38/30/ (K Abdulla), H R A Cecil

1016 Lambson Aviation Handicap Class C (0-95 3-y-o) £8,155 7f 202yds.... (2:30)

685* SMARGINATO (Ire) [84] 8-13 G Carter (2) *in tch, hdwy o'r 2 fs out, rdn over one out, styd on wl to ld ins last.* ....(10 to 1) 1
827* AMERICAN SWINGER (USA) [65] 7-8 (5ex) J Fanning (15) *sn led, set str pace, rdn clr 2 fs out, hdd and no extr ins last*..............................(17 to 2 op 10 to 1) 2
514* TYCHONIC [73] 8-2 D Holland (19) *chsd ldr, rdn o'r 2 fs out, kpt on*..........................(10 to 1 op 8 to 1) 3
690³ EMBANKMENT (Ire) [88] 9-3 Pat Eddery (1) *prmnt, rdn o'r 2 fs out, wknd appr last*.............................(14 to 1) 4
630* NESSUN DORMA [78] 8-7 F Norton (6) *chsd ldrs, rdn 3 fs out, one pace frm 2 out*...........(16 to 1 op 14 to 1) 5
643² SHINTILLO (Ire) [88] 9-3 R Cochrane (13) *hld up, hdwy on outsd 3 fs out, rdn and styd on 2 out, nrst finish.* ....(13 to 2 fav op 7 to 1 tchd 15 to 2) 6
SWEET ROMEO [80] 8-9 Dean McKeown (10) *mid-div, hdwy on outsd 3 fs out, sn rdn, no imprsn*.....(33 to 1) 7
643⁶ SILVERLOCKS [86] 9-1 N Connorton (3) *chsd ldrs, rdn 3 fs out, sn wknd*.......................(28 to 1 op 33 to 1) 8
400⁷ EAST LIBERTY (USA) [92] 9-7 M Hills (9) *hdwy and in tch hfwy, no prog fnl 2 fs*............ (33 to 1 op 25 to 1) 9
772⁷ WYNONA (Ire) [90] 9-5 W R Swinburn (18) *nvr rch ldrs.* ....(33 to 1) 10
439* JALCANTO [77] 8-6 K Darley (7) *steadied strt, mid-div hfwy, effrt o'r 2 fs out, no prog.* .... (9 to 1 op 8 to 1 tchd 10 to 1) 11
772* SHAMAM (USA) [88] 9-3 W Carson (4) *nvr rch ldrs.* ....(12 to 1 tchd 10 to 1) 12
483* MR VINCENT [78] 8-4 (3*) D Harrison (17) *mid-div, hdwy 4 fs out, sn rdn, wknd o'r 2 out*...................... (14 to 1) 13
GUSTAVIA (Ire) [85] 9-0 L Piggott (8) *al beh*....... (20 to 1) 14
GREAT STEPS [85] 9-0 G Hind (12) *mid-div, hdwy to join ldrs 4 fs out, sn rdn, wknd o'r 2 out*.................. (20 to 1) 15
346² SUN OF SPRING [79] 8-8 M Roberts (14) *al rear.* .... (10 to 1 op 8 to 1 tchd 11 to 1) 16
TOLEDO QUEEN (Ire) [78] 8-7 J Reid (16) *hmpd sn aftr strt, al beh*...................(9 to 1 op 8 to 1 tchd 10 to 1) 17
HEART BROKEN [77] 8-6 K Fallon (5) *al rear*......(33 to 1) 18
684 ANAXAGORAS [76] 8-5 J Fortune (11) *slwly into strd, mid-div hfwy, effrt and rdn 3 fs out, wknd quickly 2 out, eased*.............................(20 to 1 op 16 to 1) 19
Dist: 1l, 1½l, ¾l, 3½l, 3½l, ½l, nk, 1½l, 1½l, 1l, 1½l. 1m 39.14s. a 2.84s (19 Ran).
SR: 68/44/50/54/33/41/32/33/34/ (Gerecon Italia), J L Dunlop

1017 Bustardthorpe Handicap Class B (0-105 3-y-o) £14,490 6f 214yds. . (3:00)

802* HI NOD [74] 7-8 L Charnock (5) *chsd ldrs, hdwy 3 fs out, led appr last, styd on wl und pres*..........(5 to 1 jt-fav op 4 to 1 tchd 11 to 2) 1
641* CYNIC [82] 8-2 M Hills (4) *chsd ldrs, hdwy 2 fs out, rdn and ev ch ins last, kpt on.* ....(7 to 1 op 8 to 1 tchd 9 to 1) 2
588⁵ ERTLON [80] 8-0 M Roberts (7) *trkd ldrs gng wl, hdwy to ld o'r 2 fs out, rdn and hdd appr last, kpt on one pace.* .... (15 to 2 op 7 to 1 tchd 8 to 1) 3
802² TARNSIDE ROSAL [73] 7-7 J Lowe (3) *mid-div, hdwy 3 fs out, effrt 2 out, sn rdn, styd on ins last.* ....(8 to 1 op 7 to 1 tchd 9 to 1) 4
LOOK WHO'S HERE (Ire) [87] 8-7 T Quinn (2) *prmnt, effrt and ev ch o'r 2 fs out, sn hrd rdn, one pace appr last.* ....(12 to 1 tchd 14 to 1) 5
542⁵ NORTHERN BIRD [84] 8-4 D Holland (11) *hld up beh, hdwy on ins whn hmpd one and a half fs out, swtchd and styd on inside last*..................(8 to 1 op 7 to 1) 6
749 STAR FAMILY FRIEND (Ire) [101] 9-7 P Robinson (10) *nvr rch ldrs*......................... (14 to 1 tchd 16 to 1) 7
802⁶ BIRCHWOOD SUN [73] 7-7 J Fanning (9) *al rear.* .... (20 to 1 op 25 to 1) 8
747* EASY ACCESS (Ire) [90] 8-10 Pat Eddery (12) *al rear.* .... (5 to 1 jt-fav tchd 9 to 2) 9
846⁶ BOLD SEVEN (Ire) [79] 7-10 (3*) N Kennedy (1) *cl up, rdn and wknd 3 fs out*.............................. (25 to 1) 10
HAWAYAH (Ire) [75] 7-9 W Carson (6) *led, rdn and hdd o'r 2 fs out, sn wknd and hng lft*........(10 to 1 op 8 to 1) 11
633* WILLSHE GAN [86] 8-6 K Fallon (8) *chsd ldrs, rdn wl o'r 2 fs out, sn wknd*.....................(14 to 1 op 10 to 1) 12
Dist: 1½l, 1l, ¾l, nk, 2l, 5l, 2l, 1½l, ½l, 4l. 1m 25.57s. a 3.87s (12 Ran).
SR: 38/41/36/27/40/31/33/-/11/ (Brian Nordan), M J Camacho

1018 Polo Mints Yorkshire Cup Class A (Group 2) (4-y-o and up) £49,236 1m 5f 194yds....................... (3:35)

735² ASSESSOR (Ire) 4-9-0 T Quinn (5) *chsd ldrs, hdwy 3 fs out, led 2 out, sn rdn, edgd lft ins last, hld on wl.* .... (9 to 1 op 8 to 1 tchd 10 to 1) 1
892² ALLEGAN (USA) 4-8-9 Pat Eddery (4) *led, rdn and hdd 2 fs out, rallied and ev ch ins last, no extr nr finish.* .... (9 to 2 op 5 to 1 tchd 11 to 2) 2
735* ROLL A DOLLAR 7-8-10 B Rouse (6) *trkd ldrs, hdwy 3 fs out, effrt and ev ch 2 out, rdn and no extr ins last.* .... (12 to 1 op 10 to 1 tchd 14 to 1) 3
892* SHAMBO 6-8-13 W R Swinburn (8) *hld up, outpcd 3 fs out, sn rdn and hdwy 2 out, styd on wl und pres ins last.* .... (15 to 2 op 7 to 1) 4
579² SPRING 4-8-6 W Carson (3) *hld up, effrt and outpcd 3 fs out, sn rdn, styd on wl frm 2 out.* .... (9 to 4 fav op 5 to 2 tchd 3 to 1 and 2 to 1) 5
SAPIENCE 7-8-13 D Holland (2) *chsd ldrs, effrt and ev ch 3 fs out, sn rdn and wknd.* .... (7 to 1 op 5 to 1 tchd 15 to 2) 6
735⁵ DARU (USA) (v) 4-8-9 M Roberts (1) *trkd ldrs, hdwy 4 fs out, rdn 3 out, sn btn*...(13 to 2 op 5 to 1 tchd 7 to 1) 7
774⁵ MASHAALLAH (USA) 5-9-1 J Reid (7) *chsd ldr till rdn and wknd 3 fs out*.......... (15 to 2 op 6 to 1 tchd 8 to 1) 8
Dist: 1l, 1½l, hd, ½l, 7l, 1½l, 20l. 2m 59.23s. a 4.23s (8 Ran).
SR: 72/65/63/65/57/50/43/9/ (B E Nielsen), R Hannon

1019 Duke Of York Stakes Class A (Group 3) (3-y-o and up) £21,978 6f..... (4:05)

511⁶ HAMAS (Ire) 4-9-0 W Carson (5) *chsd ldrs, sn rdn alng, effrt appr fnl furlong, styd on to ld last 50 yards.* ....(14 to 1) 1
750⁴ GARAH 4-8-11 R Cochrane (1) *chsd ldrs, rdn and hdwy to ld entering fnl furlong, hdd and no extr last 50 yards.* ....(9 to 1 op 7 to 1) 2
511² MONTENDRE 6-9-0 J Reid (6) *beh, styd on wl appr fnl furlong*....................... (10 to 1 op 8 to 1) 3
795³ LOCHSONG 5-8-11 L Piggott (4) *led, sn clr, rdn o'r one furlong out, hdd and wknd entering last.* ....(11 to 4 op 5 to 2 tchd 9 to 4 and 3 to 1) 4
580⁷ SON PARDO 3-8-9 M Roberts (3) *chsd ldrs far side, rdn o'r 2 fs out, sn btn*.................. (20 to 1 op 16 to 1) 5
526* SO FACTUAL (USA) 3-8-4[1] Pat Eddery (9) *swtchd lft strt, hdwy o'r 2 fs out, sn rdn and no prog.* ....(7 to 4 fav op 2 to 1) 6
795 FREDDIE LLOYD (USA) 4-9-6 W R Swinburn (2) *chsd ldr 2 fs, sn rdn, beh frm two out*..........................(25 to 1) 7
729² ROCK SYMPHONY 3-8-3 J Fortune (7) *speed stands side to hfwy, sn rdn and beh*............. (33 to 1 op 25 to 1) 8
795⁷ REGAL CHIMES 4-9-0 T Quinn (10) *speed stands side to hfwy, sn rdn and beh*............. (33 to 1 op 25 to 1) 9
BLYTON LAD 7-9-0 S Webster (8) *speed stands side, rdn hfwy, pld up 2 and a half fs out, broke blood vessel.* .... (9 to 1 op 8 to 1 tchd 10 to 1) pu
Dist: ½l, 2l, 2l, 1l, 8l, ¾l, 12l, 2½l. 1m 12.22s. a 2.22s (10 Ran).
SR: 74/69/64/53/47/10/23/-/-/ (Hamdan Al-Maktoum), P T Walwyn

1020 EBF Yorkshire Maiden Stakes Class D (2-y-o) £5,952 6f.................(4:35)

STATE PERFORMER (USA) 9-0 J Reid (4) *dwlt, sn in tch, swtchd hfwy, quickened to ld o'r 2 fs out, soon clr.* .... (13 to 8 on op 5 to 4 on tchd 11 to 10 on) 1

STAR SELECTION 9-0 T Quinn (9) *al prmnt, effrt and ev ch 2 fs out, sn rdn, one pace appr last.* ....(8 to 1 op 5 to 1 tchd 9 to 1) 2
CLASSIC SKY (Ire) 9-0 W Ryan (3) *cl up, led briefly hfwy, sn rdn, one pace appr last.* ....(16 to 1 op 14 to 1 tchd 20 to 1) 3
PRINCE AZZAAN (Ire) 9-0 Pat Eddery (8) *slwly away and beh, styd on wl fnl 2 fs*..............(14 to 1 op 10 to 1) 4
CUT THE RED TAPE (Ire) 8-9 Dean McKeown (2) *chsd ldrs, rdn 2 fs out, one pace wl o'r one out.* ....(20 to 1 op 14 to 1) 5
908[4] GOLDEN STAR (Ire) 9-0 J Fanning (1) *chsd ldrs, rdn o'r 2 fs out, sn wknd*...................(20 to 1 op 14 to 1) 6
TABOOK (Ire) 9-0 W R Swinburn (6) *cl up, ev ch 2 fs out, sn rdn, wknd quickly*..... (6 to 1 op 4 to 1 tchd 13 to 2) 7
GREENFINCH (Can) 9-0 L Piggott (10) *slwly away, al rear.* ....(9 to 1 op 6 to 1) 8
291[9] SALVOR (Ire) 9-0 J Lowe (5) *led to hfwy, sn wknd.* ....(33 to 1 op 25 to 1) 9
DIVERTIMIENTO 9-0 K Fallon (7) *outpcd.* ....(33 to 1 op 16 to 1) 10
Dist: 2½l, ¾l, 4l, ¾l, 2l, 4l, ¾l, 3l, 6l. 1m 13.40s. a 3.40s (10 Ran).
SR: 50/40/37/21/13/10/ (R E Sangster), P W Chapple-Hyam

1021 Levy Board Seventh Race Rated Stakes (Handicap) Class B (0-105 4-y-o and up) £6,686 1¼m 85yds.... (5:05)

792* MUHAYAA (USA) [94] 4-8-10 W R Swinburn (2) *chsd ldr, led o'r 2 fs out, sn rdn, ran on wl fnl furlong.* ....(6 to 1 op 9 to 2) 1
480* LUCKY GUEST [96] 6-8-12 L Piggott (13) *hld up, hdwy 3 fs out, effrt and not clr run one and a half out, sn rdn, styd on ins last*..............(5 to 1 co-fav op 9 to 2) 2
MESLEH [100] 6-9-2 Pat Eddery (7) *hld up, hdwy 4 fs out, rdn and edgd lft one and a half out, styd on.* ....(5 to 1 co-fav op 7 to 2 tchd 11 to 2) 3
616[3] ROCKAWHILE (Ire) [93] 4-8-9 W Ryan (5) *in tch, hdwy 3 fs out, rdn to chal appr one out, ev ch till no extr wl ins last*...................(9 to 1 op 7 to 1 tchd 10 to 1) 4
663[3] LOKI (Ire) [91] 5-8-0 (7*) D Wright (12) *hld up beh, swtchd outsd o'r 2 fs out, styd on wl fnl furlong, not rch ldrs.* ....(5 to 1 co-fav tchd 9 to 2) 5
675[5] RAMBO'S HALL [105] 8-9-7 Dean McKeown (6) *hld up beh, styd on fnl 2 fs*..........(7 to 1 op 6 to 1 tchd 8 to 1) 6
PHILIDOR [91] 4-8-7 R Cochrane (4) *nvr rch ldrs.* ....(25 to 1 tchd 33 to 1) 7
632[8] DRUMMER HICKS [91] 4-8-2 (5*) C Hodgson (1) *chsd ldrs, rdn 4 fs out, sn wknd*.............................(33 to 1) 8
845[7] DESERT ZONE (USA) [91] 4-8-7 T Quinn (10) *chsd ldrs, rdn 3 fs out, wknd o'r 2 out*..........(33 to 1 tchd 50 to 1) 9
TURGENEV (Ire) [98] 4-9-0 M Roberts (3) *chsd ldrs till rdn and wknd 3 fs out*...............(8 to 1 tchd 10 to 1) 10
782[6] AMAZING FEAT (Ire) [91] 4-8-7 K Darley (9) *nvr rch ldrs.* ....(12 to 1 op 10 to 1 tchd 14 to 1) 11
525 PERFAY (USA) [91] 5-8-7 A McGlone (8) *al rear.* ....(33 to 1 op 25 to 1) 12
663 HOST (Ire) [91] 4-8-7 W Carson (11) *led, rdn 3 fs out, hdd o'r 2 out, sn wknd*...............(14 to 1 tchd 16 to 1) 13
Dist: ½l, 1½l, hd, 4l, 2½l, 1l, nk, 1½l, hd, 2l. 2m 12.72s. a 4.72s (13 Ran).
SR: 59/60/61/53/43/52/36/35/32/ (Maktoum Al Maktoum), A A Scott

LEOPARDSTOWN (IRE) (soft (race 1), good (2,3,4,5)) Friday May 14th

Going Correction: PLUS 0.80 sec. per fur. (races 1,2), PLUS 1.05 (3,4,5)

1022 Goodbody's Stockbrokers EBF Fillies Maiden (2-y-o) £5,444 6f........ (5:45)

DANISH (Ire) 8-10 W J O'Connor (10)............ (8 to 1) 1
BASSMAAT (USA) 8-10 C Roche (3)................. (9 to 4) 2
ASTRONAVE (Ire) 8-10 M J Kinane (9).............(6 to 1) 3
786[2] COMMON RUMPUS (Ire) 8-10 J P Murtagh (7)..... (5 to 1) 4
DANCING AT LUNASA (Ire) 8-10 P V Gilson (8)....(14 to 1) 5
664[4] JOMACOON (Ire) 8-10 K J Manning (2)...........(14 to 1) 6
EICHTERCUA (Ire) 8-10 J F Egan (4)..............(12 to 1) 7
RIDGE POOL (Ire) 8-10 R Hughes (5)..........(5 to 4 fav) 8
896 FORTY QUID (Ire) 8-10 W J Supple (6)............. (8 to 1) 9
786 ALKILIM (Ire) 8-4 (6*) J A Heffernan (1)........... (20 to 1) 10
Dist: ¾l, ¾l, hd, 8l. 1m 20.70s. a 9.20s (10 Ran).
SR: 8/5/2/1/-/-/ (Exors Of The Late Major Victor McCalmont), Michael Kauntze

1023 Evening Herald Handicap (0-80 3-y-o and up) £4,084 5f.............. (6:15)

572 CLANDOLLY (Ire) [-] 5-9-6 (6*) P Carberry (3)......(10 to 1) 1
939[6] MAGIC DON (Ire) [-] 4-8-10 (8*) R T Fitzpatrick (1).. (6 to 1) 2
939[4] MEMSAHB [-] (bl) 4-9-10 M J Kinane (2)..... (7 to 2 jt-fav) 3
868[4] AFTERGLOW (Ire) [-] 4-8-4 L O'Shea (11).........(14 to 1) 4
868 FAIRYDEL (Ire) [-] (bl) 3-7-11 (10*) P J Smullen (4)..(12 to 1) 5
939[2] GOLD BRAISIM (Ire) [-] 3-9-2 (6ex) C Roche (8) ..(7 to 2 jt-fav) 6
SOVEREIGN GRACE (Ire) [-] 4-10-0 P Shanahan (10) (7 to 1) 7
599[9] TOUGH AS TEAK (Ire) [-] (bl) 3-7-11 (2*) R M Burke (9) ....(10 to 1) 8
787[8] DONNASOO (Ire) [-] 4-9-12 R Hughes (6)..........(6 to 1) 9
939[7] RECOLLECTION (Ire) [-] 4-8-12 (6*) C Everard (7)..(14 to 1) 10
Dist: 3l, nk, 4l, ¾l. 1m 5.20s. a 6.50s (10 Ran).
SR: 62/42/47/11/11/-/ (Miss Gabrielle Byrne), Owen Weldon

1024 Andrex Savel Beg Stakes (Listed Race) (3-y-o and up) £8,479 1¾m (7:15)

895[2] GARABAGH (Ire) 4-9-7 J P Murtagh (6) *made all, quickened 5 ls clr 3 fs out, rdn appr last, hld on*.........(11 to 2) 1
EYELID 7-9-7 C F Swan (9) *hld up, prog 3 fs out, styd on strly ins last, jst fld*...........................(25 to 1) 2
VINTAGE CROP 6-9-7 M J Kinane (7) *hld up, prog 7 fs out, rdn 2 out, no extr ins last*..................(6 to 4 on) 3
MUIR STATION (USA) (bl) 5-9-7 K J Manning (4) *trkd ldr, rdn and lost pl 3 fs out, swtchd to chal on stands side one out, kpt on wl*...............................(8 to 1) 4
670[3] YUKON GOLD (Ire) (bl) 4-9-7 P V Gilson (5) *mid-div, rdn 2 fs out, no extr ins last*..............................(7 to 1) 5
668[2] SPECIAL PAGEANT (Ire) 3-7-11 J A Heffernan (2) *mid-div, prog 4 fs out, rdn 2 out, slightly hmpd one out, wknd.* ....(11 to 1) 6
895[4] GLYER (USA) 4-9-7 P Shanahan (10) *hld up, some prog 3 fs out, rdn and wknd 2 out*.........................(10 to 1) 7
944[7] MAJESTIC JOHN (Ire) 3-8-1[1] W J Supple (1) *mid-div, prog to track ldrs 7 fs out, rdn 4 out, sn wknd*...... (66 to 1) 8
LIGHTNING BUG 8-9-4 J F Egan (3) *al rear, rdn and wknd 4 fs out*..(50 to 1) 9
Dist: ½l, 1l, nk, ¾l. 3m 21.70s. a 25.70s (9 Ran).
(H H Aga Khan), John M Oxx

1025 Derrinstown Apprentice Series Handicap (0-80 3-y-o and up) £4,084 1¼m ....(7:45)

281* FERRYCARRIG HOTEL (Ire) [-] 4-8-4 (4*) J A Heffernan (15) ....(9 to 2) 1
NASSAU [-] 6-9-4 (8*) W J Walsh (14).............. (25 to 1) 2
942[2] NORDIC DISPLAY (Ire) [-] 5-9-0 (6*) M W Martin (11) (5 to 1) 3
807* PHARFETCHED [-] 4-9-8 (4*,4ex) P Carberry (7) (7 to 2 fav) 4
807[2] MASAI WARRIOR [-] 6-9-2 (8*) D J Finnegan (12)... (7 to 1) 5
849[2] RATTLE AND HUM [-] 6-8-9 (6*) T J Daly (1)........(7 to 1) 6
807 OPEN MARKET (USA) [-] 4-9-11 (2*) W J Smith (2) (14 to 1) 7
TOOLITTLE TOOLATE (Ire) [-] 4-8-11 R M Burke (5) (20 to 1) 8
898* SIR SLAVES [-] (bl) 3-8-10 (6*,5ex) D J O'Donohoe (4) ....(13 to 2) 9
789 LAKE OF LOUGHREA (Ire) [-] 3-7-3 (8*) J Cornally (13) ....(20 to 1) 10
THE BURSER [-] 7-9-0 (8*) W M Lynch (10)....... (10 to 1) 11
TALAYRA (Ire) [-] 3-8-9 D G O'Shea (8)............ (7 to 1) 12
Dist: Hd, 7l, ½l, 12l. 2m 21.20s. a 16.50s (12 Ran).
SR: 34/51/31/36/10/-/ (J C Lacy), T F Lacy

1026 A.C.C. Bank EBF (C&G) Maiden (3-y-o) £4,424 1¼m.............. (8:15)

788[4] SEMPLE STADIUM (Ire) 9-0 P V Gilson (1)......... (9 to 4) 1
848[7] BOTHSIDESNOW (Ire) 9-0 R Hughes (2)..........(33 to 1) 2
POLITICAL SURGE (USA) 9-0 M J Kinane (7)...(2 to 1 fav) 3
DEVIL'S HOLIDAY (USA) 9-0 W J O'Connor (3).....(7 to 1) 4
577 ARZAAQ (USA) 9-0 W J Supple (5).............. (20 to 1) 5
850 WESTERN FRONTIER (Ire) 9-0 D Manning (4).....(33 to 1) 6
Dist: ½l, 2l, 10l, 10l. 2m 23.10s. a 18.40s (6 Ran).
SR: 21/20/16/ (Mrs M V O'Brien), Charles O'Brien

NEWBURY (good) Friday May 14th

Going Correction: NIL

1027 Midgham Maiden Stakes Class D (3-y-o) £4,077 1m................ (2:05)

751[2] MISTLE CAT (USA) 9-0 W Woods (9) *made all, drvn and styd on wl fnl furlong.* (6 to 1 op 4 to 1 tchd 13 to 2) 1
RIVER BOARD 9-0 N Day (11) *hdwy frm 3 fs out, chsd wnr ins last, kpt on*......(25 to 1 op 20 to 1 tchd 33 to 1) 2
EL DUCO (USA) 9-0 Paul Eddery (1) *al tracking ldrs, drvn 2 fs out, one pace appr last*...... (4 to 1 jt-fav op 5 to 2) 3
GREENBANK (USA) 9-0 L Dettori (14) *hdwy o'r 2 fs out, kpt on fnl furlong*...................(20 to 1 op 14 to 1) 4
752[5] PRINCESS HAYLEY 8-9 W Carson (5) *chsd ldrs till wknd wl o'r one furlong out*........... (12 to 1 tchd 14 to 1) 5
YOUNG PETOSKI 9-0 A Munro (12) *prmnt till rdn and wknd ins fnl 2 fs*.................. (25 to 1 op 16 to 1) 6
TIME AGAIN 8-11 (3*) J Weaver (8) *beh till styd on fnl 2 fs.* ....(20 to 1 op 14 to 1) 7
LEARMONT (USA) 9-0 J Reid (2) *chsd ldrs till wknd o'r 2 fs out*.............................. (16 to 1 op 10 to 1) 8
TESHAMI (USA) 9-0 M Roberts (20) *effrt hfwy, sn wknd.* ....(4 to 1 jt-fav tchd 9 to 2 and 7 to 2) 9
515[7] LEAR KING (USA) 9-0 T Quinn (21) *beh, some prog fnl 2 fs.* ....(16 to 1 op 12 to 1 tchd 20 to 1) 10

759[3] BEVERLY KNIGHT 9-0 C Rutter (13) *prmnt till wknd o'r 2 fs out*..............................(14 to 1 op 20 to 1) 11
PROTON 9-0 W Newnes (7) *slwly into strd, nvr better than mid-div*..........(33 to 1 op 20 to 1) 12
CLIFTON GAME 9-0 J Williams (16) *al beh*.......(50 to 1) 13
MELLERIO 8-11 (3*) D Harrison (10) *beh most of way*. ....(50 to 1) 14
759[5] FOX SPARROW 9-0 S Raymont (15) *pld hrd, beh, nvr rch ldrs*.........................(20 to 1 tchd 25 to 1) 15
COLNBROOK (USA) 9-0 P D'Arcy (18) *speed for o'r 5 fs*. ....(9 to 2 op 7 to 2 tchd 5 to 1) 16
872 BONITA BEE 8-9 B Rouse (6) *nvr better than mid-div*. ....(50 to 1) 17
951[5] BLOWING (USA) 9-0 M Perrett (19) *al beh*.......(50 to 1) 18
951[3] WELL SUITED 9-0 L Piggott (4) *beh hfwy*. ....(14 to 1 op 10 to 1 tchd 16 to 1) 19
878[8] MR JAZZ DANCER (Ire) 9-0 N Adams (17) *sn beh*. (50 to 1) 20
Dist: ¾l, 3l, 2½l, 1l, 1½l, sht-hd, ½l, ½l, 1½l, sht-hd. 1m 39.68s. a 2.58s (20 Ran).
SR: 61/59/50/42/34/34/33/31/29/ (P K Chu), S P C Woods

1028 Harcros Stayers Championship Series Handicap Qualifier Class C (0-90 3-y-o and up) £6,004 1½m 5yds ....(2:40)

473* NIGHT CLUBBING (Ire) [84] 4-9-11 T Quinn (11) *trkd ldrs, pushed alng fnl 2 fs, styd on wl to ld cl hme*. ....(11 to 2 op 9 to 2 tchd 6 to 1) 1
816[4] LIJAAM (Ire) [80] 3-8-2 M Hills (8) *led aftr one furlong, clr 7 out, ran on wl whn chlgd frm 2 out, ct cl hme*. ....(8 to 1 tchd 10 to 1) 2
674[3] FREE MOVER (Ire) [77] 4-9-4 M Roberts (12) *mid-div, hdwy 4 fs out, drvn and styd on same pace 2 out*. ....(6 to 1 op 5 to 1) 3
DREAMS END [81] 5-9-8 R Cochrane (4) *beh, hdwy 3 fs out, not quicken 2 out*...................... (20 to 1) 4
MILLION IN MIND (Ire) [86] 4-9-13 W Newnes (2) *led one furlong, ev ch 3 fs out, one pace o'r 2 out*. ....(10 to 1 tchd 9 to 1) 5
MISS PLUM [80] 4-9-7 L Dettori (1) *chsd ldrs, wknd ins fnl 2 fs*.......................... (12 to 1 op 10 to 1) 6
731[3] JIMLIL [73] 5-9-0 W Ryan (3) *hdwy 3 fs out, no imprsn 2 out*................ (12 to 1 op 10 to 1 tchd 14 to 1) 7
422[2] PHROSE [77] 3-7-13 S Raymont (6) *al beh*. .... (16 to 1 op 20 to 1) 8
739[3] BUSMAN (Ire) [68] 4-8-2 (7*) Kim McDonnell (7) *al beh*. ....(16 to 1 op 12 to 1 tchd 20 to 1) 9
DISCORD [76] 7-9-0 (3*) D Harrison (9) *steadied strt, hdwy to chal 3 fs out, btn 2 out*.......... (10 to 1 op 7 to 1) 10
756[7] GOOGLY [69] 4-8-10 G Bardwell (10) *hdwy and rdn 4 fs out, btn o'r 2 out*..............(5 to 1 fav tchd 11 to 2) 11
672[9] BITTER ALOE [73] 4-9-0 W Carson (5) *str hold, in tch till wknd 3 fs out*.................... (7 to 1 op 12 to 1) 12
Dist: Nk, 2½l, 1½l, hd, 3l, nk, 1½l, 1½l, ¾l, ¾l. 2m 34.83s. a 5.23s (12 Ran).
SR: 59/35/46/47/51/39/31/13/20/ (Sheikh Essa Bin Mubarak), R Akehurst

1029 Juddmonte Lockinge Stakes Class A (Group 2) (3-y-o and up) £38,898 1m ....(3:10)

675* SWING LOW 4-9-0 L Piggott (6) *hld up in rear, hdwy 2 fs out, led ins last, ran on wl*........ (12 to 1 op 14 to 1) 1
794[7] WHARF (USA) 3-8-1 W Ryan (5) *prmnt, chlgd o'r one furlong out, rdn and styd on fnl furlong*. ....(4 to 1 op 5 to 2 tchd 9 to 2) 2
CULTURE VULTURE (USA) 4-9-2 T Quinn (4) *beh, not clr run frm 2 fs out, edgd lft jst ins last, fnshd wl*. ....(15 to 2 op 8 to 1 tchd 9 to 1 and 7 to 1) 3
293[2] ALFLORA (Ire) 4-9-0 W Carson (8) *led, quickened 3 fs out, rdn 2 out, hdd jst ins last, sn one pace*........ (20 to 1) 4
660[4] STUBASS (Ire) 4-9-3 R Cochrane (3) *mid-div, drvn and styd on same pace fnl 2 fs*. ....(15 to 2 op 5 to 1 tchd 8 to 1) 5
660[2] HAZAAM (USA) 4-9-0 M Roberts (2) *chsd ldrs till wknd ins fnl 2 fs*..........................(2 to 1 fav tchd 5 to 2) 6
FEMININE WILES (Ire) 4-8-11 J Reid (9) *chsd ldrs till rdn and wknd o'r 2 fs out*. (9 to 1 op 8 to 1 tchd 10 to 1) 7
675 POWERFUL EDGE 4-9-0 L Dettori (7) *in tch, rdn o'r 2 fs out, wkng whn bumped jst ins fnl furlong*. ....(20 to 1 tchd 25 to 1) 8
675[8] A-TO-Z (Ire) 4-8-11 M Hills (10) *nvr gng pace of ldrs*. ....(14 to 1 tchd 12 to 1) 9
660[6] LUCKY LINDY (Ire) (bl) 4-9-3 B Rouse (1) *pressed ldrs till wknd 2 and a half fs out*......... (14 to 1 op 12 to 1) 10
Dist: 1l, nk, ½l, 1l, 2½l, ¾l, 1½l, 6l, 5l. 1m 39.31s. a 2.21s (10 Ran).
SR: 67/51/65/61/61/50/45/43/22/ (Roldvale Limited), R Hannon

1030 Vodafone Group Fillies' Trial Stakes Class A (Listed Race) (3-y-o) £10,690 1¼m 6yds.......................... (3:40)

ATHENS BELLE (Ire) 8-9 W Carson (4) *str hold, in tch, rdn o'r 2 fs out, kpt on wl to ld last half-furlong*. ....(7 to 1 tchd 8 to 1) 1
748[4] FAYFA (Ire) 8-9 L Dettori (1) *sn led, drvn and styd on frm 2 fs out, hdd and not quicken last half-furlong*. ....(5 to 1 op 4 to 1 tchd 11 to 2) 2
556[2] RIBBONWOOD (USA) 8-9 M Roberts (2) *pld hrd, prmnt, ev ch frm 2 fs out till outpcd one out*. ....(2 to 1 fav op 7 to 4 tchd 9 to 4) 3
734[3] BRIGHT SPELLS 8-9 J Williams (7) *beh, shaken up 2 fs out, kpt on fnl furlong, not rch ldrs*................. (10 to 1) 4
734[4] LACERTA (Ire) 8-9 J Reid (5) *beh, rdn 3 fs out, sn btn*. ....(10 to 1 op 7 to 1) 5
694[4] LOVE OF SILVER (USA) 9-1 R Cochrane (6) *beh, effrt 4 fs out, btn o'r 2 out*.....(100 to 30 op 3 to 1 tchd 7 to 2) 6
856[3] MAGICAL RETREAT (USA) 8-12 D Biggs (3) *chsd ldrs, wknd ins fnl 3 fs*.............. (9 to 1 op 12 to 1 tchd 8 to 1) 7
Dist: ¾l, 3l, nk, 2l, 1½l, nk. 2m 7.90s. a 4.90s (7 Ran).
SR: 46/44/38/37/33/36/32/ (Lord Weinstock), R Charlton

1031 Lambourn Racing Welfare Conditions Stakes Class B (3-y-o) £8,208 6f 8yds ....(4:10)

729* SPECIFIED (USA) 8-13 W Carson (1) *led, lft clr and drvn out appr fnl furlong*. ....(3 to 1 tchd 5 to 2 and 100 to 30) 1
794 CHADDLEWORTH (Ire) 8-13 J Reid (3) *pressed ldr, ev ch 2 fs out, faltered and lost action o'r one out, eased, fnshd lme*............. (11 to 10 on op 6 to 4 on tchd Evens) 2
823* BROCKTON DANCER 8-8 L Piggott (2) *al 3rd, nvr gng pace of ldrs*..................................(3 to 1 op 2 to 1) 3
Dist: 7l, 5l. 1m 14.06s. a 2.36s (3 Ran).
SR: 52/24/-/ (K Abdulla), J H M Gosden

1032 Kingwood Stud Maiden Fillies Stakes Class D (2-y-o) £3,947 6f 8yds...(4:40)

VELVET MOON (Ire) 8-11 A Munro (11) *frnt rnk, led one and a half fs out, sn clr, ran green, easily*. ....(7 to 2 op 4 to 1) 1
MICHELLE HICKS 8-11 M Hills (3) *prmnt, shaken up o'r one furlong out, ran on, no ch wth wnr*. ....(9 to 1 op 10 to 1 tchd 12 to 1 and 8 to 1) 2
889[3] JADE PET 8-11 J Reid (10) *led to one and a half fs out, kpt on same pace*...........(7 to 1 op 6 to 1 tchd 10 to 1) 3
399[5] MARJORIE'S MEMORY (Ire) 8-11 W Ryan (7) *in tch, drvn and styd on frm o'r one furlong out*. ....(20 to 1 op 14 to 1 tchd 33 to 1) 4
GIFT BOX (Ire) 8-11 J Williams (6) *str hold, steadied, hdwy o'r one furlong out, kpt on*. ....(16 to 1 op 7 to 1 tchd 20 to 1) 5
MADURAI 8-11 T Quinn (5) *rcd keenly frnt rnk, wknd o'r one furlong out*......(14 to 1 op 10 to 1 tchd 16 to 1) 6
KISSING COUSIN (Ire) 8-11 M Roberts (4) *prmnt, shaken up 2 fs out, wknd o'r one out*. ....(5 to 4 fav op Evens tchd 11 to 8) 7
ROSE CIEL (Ire) 8-11 B Raymond (12) *drvn and effrt hfwy, sn wknd*............................(25 to 1 op 14 to 1) 8
ZORAHAYDA (Fr) 8-11 B Rouse (9) *outpcd*. ....(50 to 1 op 33 to 1) 9
LEGENDARY LADY 8-11 C Rutter (2) *chsd ldrs to hfwy*. ....(33 to 1 op 16 to 1) 10
MOCKINGBIRD 8-11 L Piggott (8) *dwlt, outpcd*. ....(7 to 1 tchd 10 to 1) 11
517 COURT SERENADE 8-11 W Newnes (13) *sn outpcd*. ....(50 to 1 op 33 to 1) 12
Dist: 5l, ½l, 2l, 5l, 4l, 1½l, 1½l, 2l, 1½l, 4l. 1m 14.07s. a 2.37s (12 Ran).
SR: 50/30/28/20/-/-/ (Fahd Salman), P F I Cole

ST-CLOUD (FR) (soft)
Friday May 14th
Going Correction: PLUS 0.30 sec. per fur.

1033 Prix Cleopatra (Group 3) (3-y-o) £23,895 1¼m 110yds.......... (2:25)

561* WEMYSS BIGHT 9-0 Pat Eddery (9) *led strt, rdn 2 and a half fs out, kpt on und pres fnl furlong*.... (10 to 7 on) 1
BRIGHT MOON (USA) (bl) 8-9 T Jarnet (6) *3rd strt, rdn 2 fs out, hmpd one and a half out, quickened one out, nrst finish*.. (9 to 2) 2
484[2] ALICE SPRINGS (USA) 8-9 G Guignard (7) *5th strt, rdn and quickened 2 fs out, chlgd one and a half out, kpt on last*.. (12 to 1) 3
770[2] INSIJAAM (USA) 8-9 W R Swinburn (4) *second strt, rdn 2 out, one pace fnl furlong*................. (88 to 10) 4
SHEMAKA (Ire) 9-0 W Mongil (5) *6th strt, rdn 2 fs out, no imprsn*.. (17 to 2) 5
ALLEGED SARON (USA) 8-9 C Asmussen (8) *nvr nrr*. ....(12 to 1) 6
770[4] FRESHER 8-9 O Benoist (2) *4th strt, rdn and wknd 2 fs out*..(13 to 1) 7
770[3] ENCOREMOI (USA) 8-9 F Head (1) *al rear*........(10 to 1) 8
561[3] MISS KADROU (Fr) 8-9 E Legrix (3) *al beh*........ (32 to 1) 9
Dist: Nose, sht-nk, 2½l, ¾l, ½l, 4l, 3l, 4l. 2m 16.80s. a 6.30s (9 Ran).
SR: 69/63/62/57/60/54/46/40/32/ (K Abdulla), A Fabre

THIRSK (soft)
Friday May 14th
Going Correction: PLUS 0.70 sec. per fur. (races 1,2,4,5,6,7,8), PLUS 0.55 (3)

1034 Station Road Claiming Stakes Class F (4-y-o and up) £3,027 1½m......(2:30)

416[5] ALMOST A PRINCESS 5-8-5 G Duffield (4) *al prmnt, hdwy to chase ldr 4 fs out, swtchd lft and rdn o'r one out, styd on to ld wl ins last.*.......... (14 to 1 op 12 to 1) 1
863[2] POST IMPRESSIONIST (Ire) 4-8-9 M Wigham (12) *cl up till rdn alng and outpcd hfwy, hdwy 3 fs out, styd on fnl 2 furlongs*.............................. (5 to 1 op 4 to 1) 2
148[8] LE TEMERAIRE 7-9-6 L Charnock (2) *led 3 fs, cl up till led 5 out, rdn and edgd rght o'r one out, hdd and no extr ins last*.............................. (20 to 1 op 16 to 1) 3
822[3] BALADIYA 6-8-10 (5*) Stephen Davies (8) *al prmnt, effrt and hdwy o'r 3 fs out, rdn and one pace 2 out.* .... (3 to 1 fav op 5 to 2 tchd 100 to 30) 4
678[5] FOX CHAPEL 6-8-9 (3*) S Maloney (18) *mid-div, hdwy 5 fs out, effrt and drvn alng 3 out, sn one pace.* ....(9 to 2 op 3 to 1 tchd 5 to 1) 5
RISING TEMPO (Ire) 5-8-13 (7*) D Wright (6) *beh till styd on fnl 2 fs*.. (33 to 1) 6
265[8] IRON BARON (Ire) 4-8-10 S Perks (13) *hld up, hdwy o'r 3 fs out, styd on fnl 2 furlongs, nvr dngrs.* .... (12 to 1 op 10 to 1) 7
740[6] TINA MEENA LISA 4-8-8[1] C Dwyer (10) *al mid-div.* .... (33 to 1 op 25 to 1) 8
834 WINGED WHISPER (USA) 4-8-3 (5*) A Garth (5) *in tch, hdwy hfwy, effrt and rdn o'r 3 fs out, sn wknd.* .... (50 to 1 op 33 to 1) 9
740[5] BRECKENBROUGH LAD 6-9-2 K Darley (19) *beh, effrt and some hdwy 4 fs out, nvr dngrs*..... (14 to 1 op 12 to 1) 10
CHECKPOINT CHARLIE 8-8-5 (7*) Antoinette Armes (16) *dwlt, rapid hdwy to ld aftr 3 fs, hdd 5 out and grad wknd*.............................. (8 to 1 op 6 to 1) 11
714[8] CONSTRUCTIVIST (Ire) 4-8-9 F Norton (11) *nvr a factor.* ....(20 to 1) 12
620[9] MAPLE BAY (Ire) 4-9-2 N Carlisle (14) *al rear.* .... (14 to 1 op 12 to 1) 13
GREY ANCONA (Ire) 4-9-2 M Birch (3) *al beh*......(50 to 1) 14
ALLEGRO CON BRIO 5-8-11 S Whitworth (9) *prmnt till rdn and wknd o'r 4 fs out, tld off*......(33 to 1 op 20 to 1) 15
SNEEK 5-8-7 (5*) O Pears (15) *chsd ldrs 7 fs, sn wknd, tld off*.. (50 to 1) 16
SKOLERN 9-9-0 J Fanning (7) *in tch to hfwy, sn lost pl, tld off*.. (33 to 1) 17

Dist: 1½l, 2l, 1½l, 1½l, 2l, ½l, 3l, 2l, 2l, 6l. 2m 45.80s. a 15.60s (17 Ran).
SR: 19/20/27/19/13/17/6/-/-/ (Laurie Snook), W G M Turner

1035 Mowbray Selling Stakes Class G (Div I) (3-y-o and up) £2,427 7f.......(3:00)

163 DESERT SPLENDOUR 5-9-12 J Lowe (5) *al prmnt, rdn and ev ch 2 fs out, styd on to ld wl ins last.* ....(5 to 1 op 3 to 1) 1
709[5] POP TO STANS 4-9-12 M Wigham (1) *hld up, gd hdwy on outer 2 and a half fs out, rdn to ld one and a half out, hdd and no extr wl ins last*......... (7 to 2 op 9 to 4) 2
531[7] SPEED OIL 4-9-0 (7*) H Bastiman (6) *dwlt, gd hdwy on outer 3 fs out, effrt to chal one and a half out, sn rdn and ev ch till no extr last.* ....(5 to 2 fav op 3 to 1 tchd 4 to 1) 3
834 FAIRFORD 4-9-7 F Norton (2) *cl up till lost pl hfwy, sn rdn and hdwy 2 fs out, one pace appr last*........(10 to 1) 4
4735a[7] CHAFF (v) 6-9-2 (5*) Stephen Davies (4) *chsd ldrs, rdn 3 fs out, sn wknd*.........................(12 to 1 tchd 14 to 1) 5
264[8] DANCING BOAT 4-9-7 J Quinn (10) *nvr dngrs.* ....(10 to 1 tchd 12 to 1) 6
887 GRUBBY 4-9-0 (7*) J Dennis (9) *sn led, wide strt, rdn o'r 2 fs out, hdd and wknd one and a half out.* ....(8 to 1 op 7 to 1) 7
PHILCO'S ANGEL 4-8-11 (5*) A Garth (8) *beh, gd hdwy on outer and wide strt, ev ch 3 fs out, sn rdn, hng badly lft and wknd 2 out*.................. (25 to 1 op 20 to 1) 8
828[5] CAPTAIN BRAMSTAN (Ire) 5-9-2 (5*) O Pears (7) *chsd ldrs, hdwy gng wl 4 fs out, rdn and wknd quickly 3 out, tld off*..............................(8 to 1 op 16 to 1) 9

Dist: 1l, nk, 3l, 6l, 2½l, 5l, 12l, 25l. 1m 32.70s. a 9.90s (9 Ran).
SR: 37/34/28/19/1/-/ (Cecil W Wardle), B R Cambidge

1036 Plasticisers 'Helta' Handicap Class D (0-80 3-y-o and up) £3,947 5f.... (3:30)

866[6] SO SUPERB [52] (bl) 4-8-1 J Lowe (20) *chsd ldrs stands side, effrt 2 fs out, rdn to ld ins last, ran on.* ....(14 to 1 tchd 12 to 1) 1
887[9] KALAR [46] (bl) 4-7-9 S Wood (16) *al cl up stands side, dsptd ld 2 fs out, rdn and no extr ins last.* .... (20 to 1 op 25 to 1) 2
800 PRINCE BELFORT [60] 5-8-4 (5*) O Pears (17) *al prmnt, effrt and ev ch o'r one furlong out, sn rdn and no extr ins last*............. (11 to 1 op 10 to 1 tchd 12 to 1) 3
891[6] EVER SO LONELY [56] 4-7-12 (7*) D Wright (22) *led stands side till dsptd ld 2 fs out, wknd ins last.* .... (6 to 1 op 11 to 2) 4
800* SONDERISE [69] 4-9-4 N Carlisle (18) *in tch stands side, effrt and hdwy 2 fs out, sn rdn, kpt on ins last.* ....(5 to 1 fav op 6 to 1 tchd 13 to 2) 5
INDIGO [79] 5-10-0 A Culhane (6) *clr ldr far side grp, ev ch whn hng rght appr fnl furlong, wknd ins last.* (33 to 1) 6
800[9] MACS MAHARANEE [57] 6-8-6 G Hind (8) *styd on fnl 2 fs, nrst finish*.................. (14 to 1 op 16 to 1) 7
659 MISS VAXETTE [73] 4-9-1 (7*) M Humphries (2) *rcd centre, beh till styd on fnl 2 fs*..........(14 to 1 tchd 12 to 1) 8
465[7] THE AUCTION BIDDER [77] 6-9-12 K Darley (11) *nvr rchd ldrs*.. (16 to 1) 9
BALLASECRET [78] 5-9-8 (5*) D Meredith (19) *cl up stands side till rdn and wknd one and a half fs out.* ....(14 to 1 op 12 to 1 tchd 16 to 1) 10
887[3] LOFT BOY [59] 10-8-1 (7*) K Sked (5) *rcd far side, beh frm hfwy*........................ (14 to 1 op 12 to 1) 11
677 BOLD HABIT [72] 8-9-7 M Wigham (9) *nvr rchd ldrs.* .... (20 to 1 op 16 to 1) 12
866[2] EWALD (Ire) [64] 5-8-13 Dean McKeown (10) *cl up stands side 3 fs, sn wknd*.................. (9 to 1 op 7 to 1) 13
4690a ADMIRALS REALM [62] 4-8-4 (7*) S Sanders (4) *rcd far side, beh frm hfwy*.................... (25 to 1 op 20 to 1) 14
796[7] MISS MOVIE WORLD [52] (bl) 4-8-1 L Charnock (12) *nvr a factor*..........................(14 to 1 op 12 to 1) 15
800 CATHERINES WELL [70] 10-9-5 T Lucas (3) *al rear.* ....(14 to 1 tchd 16 to 1) 16
4775a[5] ABSOLUTION [70] 9-9-5 N Connorton (21) *outpcd and beh frm hfwy*........................ (12 to 1 op 20 to 1) 17
800 SINGING STAR [73] 7-9-1 (7*) Claire Balding (7) *al rear.* .... (25 to 1 op 20 to 1) 18
758 FOLLOWMEGIRLS [59] 4-8-3 (5*) A Garth (1) *al beh.* .... (16 to 1 op 14 to 1) 19
138 SUPREME DESIRE [55] 5-8-4[4] S Webster (13) *al beh.* .... (25 to 1 op 20 to 1) 20

Dist: 1½l, ½l, 1l, nk, ½l, ¾l, 1l, 1½l, hd, 1½l. 1m 2.50s. a 5.30s (20 Ran).
SR: 36/24/36/28/40/48/23/35/33/ (N A Riddell), M Dods

1037 Rosedale Handicap Class D (0-80 3-y-o) £3,582 1m...................(4:00)

813 IKHTIRAA (USA) [51] 7-7 N Carlisle (3) *cl up, led aftr 2 fs, rdn two out, ran on wl*........... (16 to 1 op 20 to 1) 1
934* NORTHERN CHIEF [60] 8-2[2] (5ex) J Carroll (5) *chsd ldrs, hdwy 3 fs out, effrt 2 out and sn ev ch, rdn and no extr ins last*.............. (100 to 30 op 3 to 1 tchd 7 to 2) 2
733[9] WOLF POWER (Ire) [58] 8-0 K Darley (2) *chsd ldrs, hdwy on inner 3 fs out, ev ch 2 out, sn rdn and one pace appr last*............................... (10 to 1 op 8 to 1) 3
685[8] CUBIST (Ire) [68] 8-10 Dean McKeown (6) *led 2 fs, cl up, rdn two out, wknd appr last.* ....(11 to 1 op 10 to 1 tchd 12 to 1) 4
733* MIDNIGHT HEIGHTS [78] 9-6 A McGlone (9) *hld up in tch, hdwy 4 fs out, effrt on outer 2 out, sn rdn and wknd.* ....(2 to 1 fav op 6 to 4) 5
733[6] WORDSMITH (Ire) [62] 8-4 K Fallon (11) *slwly into strd, hdwy 4 fs out, rdn 2 out and sn wknd.* ....(5 to 1 op 4 to 1 tchd 6 to 1) 6
802[9] DANCE TO ORDER (Ire) [67] 8-9 G Duffield (8) *chsd ldrs, effrt 3 fs out, sn rdn and wknd o'r one and a half out.* .... (10 to 1 op 8 to 1) 7
521[7] RACING TELEGRAPH [68] 8-10 M Wigham (10) *al rear.* ....(9 to 1 op 7 to 1) 8

Dist: 2l, 2½l, 1½l, 5l, ½l, 4l, 1l. 1m 44.90s. a 9.00s (8 Ran).
SR: 28/31/21/26/21/3/-/-/ (Hamdan Al-Maktoum), R W Armstrong

1038 Mowbray Selling Stakes Class G (Div II) (3-y-o and up) £2,427 7f...... (4:30)

878[3] CALISAR 3-9-0 T Sprake (6) *chsd ldr, led 2 and a half fs out, sn rdn, hng lft one out, ran on und pres.* ....(5 to 1 tchd 9 to 2) 1
883* OBSIDIAN GREY 6-9-5 (7*) S Sanders (2) *chsd ldrs, effrt 2 fs out, rdn and swtchd rght o'r one out, ran on ins last.* ....(3 to 1 op 7 to 4) 2
532[8] DON'T TELL JEAN 3-8-4 L Charnock (5) *led, rdn and hdd 2 and a half fs out, rallied ins last.* ....(14 to 1 op 20 to 1 tchd 25 to 1) 3
883[6] DOKKHA OYSTON (Ire) 5-9-12 J Carroll (1) *chsd ldrs, hdwy 3 fs out, effrt 2 out, sn rdn and wknd entering fnl furlong*........................ (Evens fav op 6 to 4) 4
HERBRAND (Ire) 4-9-7 M Birch (7) *nvr rchd ldrs.* .... (8 to 1 op 7 to 1 tchd 10 to 1) 5
650[7] UCKERBY MOOR 4-9-7 S Webster (4) *beh frm hfwy.* ....(8 to 1 op 7 to 1) 6
837 WEEKEND GIRL 4-8-11 (5*) A Garth (8) *rdn hfwy, sn beh, tld off*...........................(33 to 1 op 20 to 1) 7
AUNTIE LORNA 4-9-2 G Duffield (9) *chsd ldrs, lost pl hfwy, sn tld off*........... (16 to 1 op 20 to 1 tchd 25 to 1) 8
NASHOON (Ire) 4-9-7 G Hind (10) *al beh, tld off fnl 3 fs.* .... (33 to 1 op 20 to 1) 9

Dist: ½l, 1½l, 3l, 6l, ½l, 15l, 2½l, 6l. 1m 33.40s. a 10.60s (9 Ran).
SR: 15/25/-/11/-/-/ (A Poole), W G M Turner

1039 Gordon Foster Maiden Stakes Class D (3-y-o and up) £3,816 1m....... (5:00)

REDSTELLA (USA) 4-9-10 A Culhane (3) al prmnt, led hfwy, rdn 2 fs out, ran on wl fnl furlong. .... (20 to 1 op 33 to 1) 1
844[5] AMAAM AMAAM 3-8-11 G Hind (5) led to hfwy, cl up, effrt to chal 2 fs out, sn hrd rdn, wknd ins last. .... (11 to 4 op 2 to 1 tchd 3 to 1) 2
842[5] CONSPICUOUS (Ire) 3-8-11 P Robinson (6) al prmnt, effrt 3 fs out, sn rdn and kpt on one pace... (9 to 2 op 5 to 1) 3
646[4] EL GAHAR 3-8-11 A McGlone (12) chsd ldrs, effrt and hdwy to chal o'r 2 fs, sn rdn and wknd appr last. .... (9 to 4 fav op 2 to 1 tchd 5 to 2) 4
803[3] CELESTIAL CHOIR 3-8-2[1] (5*) O Pears (10) hdwy hfwy, sn rdn and no imprsn................. (16 to 1 op 20 to 1) 5
803[4] BEAUMONT (Ire) 3-8-11 M Wigham (11) beh, hdwy 3 fs out, styd on fnl 2 furlongs, nvr dngrs............. (20 to 1) 6
ON BROADWAY 3-8-11 J Fortune (4) mid-div, some hdwy 3 fs out, sn rdn alng and no prog............... (50 to 1) 7
BALL GOWN 3-8-6 J Lowe (15) rcd wide and cl up till wknd 3 fs out................................ (50 to 1) 8
899[7] CUMBRIAN CALYPSO 3-8-8 (3*) S Maloney (7) nvr a factor. .... (16 to 1) 9
BROCTUNE BAY 4-9-10 K Darley (1) slwly into strd, al beh.. (12 to 1) 10
BILOELA 3-8-6 K Fallon (2) nvr rchd ldrs........ (33 to 1) 11
JUPITER STAR 4-9-10 C Dwyer (16) hld up, some hdwy 3 fs out, sn wknd.................................. (50 to 1) 12
EMERALD SANDS 3-8-6 J Carroll (13) beh frm hfwy. .... (20 to 1 op 50 to 1) 13
630[9] GORDON'S BROTHER (Ire) 3-8-11 N Connorton (9) al beh, tld off.. (50 to 1) 14
759 MUMAYYAZ (Ire) 3-8-11 R Hills (8) al beh, tld off. .... (11 to 1 op 10 to 1 tchd 12 to 1) 15

Dist: 4l, 1½l, 4l, 10l, ¾l, 1l, ½l, ½l, sht-hd, 1½l. 1m 47.60s. a 11.70s (15 Ran).
SR: 19/-/-/-/-/ (E R Thomas), R M Whitaker

1040 Dishforth Conditions Stakes Class D (3-y-o) £3,850 1m...............(5:30)

775[5] STAR MANAGER (USA) 8-10 S Perks (3) trkd ldrs, wide strt, smooth hdwy o'r 2 fs out, shaken up appr fnl furlong, led ins last, ran on...... (7 to 4 fav op Evens) 1
732* ZAJIRA (Ire) 8-9 R Hills (5) set steady pace, wide strt, quickened 3 fs out, rdn o'r one out, hdd and no extr ins last.................... (15 to 8 op 7 to 4 tchd 9 to 4) 2
633[2] SPICE AND SUGAR 8-5 Dean McKeown (1) in tch, styd far rail strt, sn rdn and no ch fnl 2 fs. ....(6 to 1 op 7 to 1 tchd 8 to 1) 3
BOLD AMUSEMENT 8-10 K Darley (2) dwlt, wide strt, rdn alng o'r 2 fs out and no hdwy...... (12 to 1 op 7 to 1) 4
784* FEATHER FACE 9-0 A Clark (7) chsd ldr, wide strt, effrt and ev ch 3 fs out, sn rdn and btn whn eased 2 out. .... (11 to 2 op 4 to 1) 5

Dist: 2l, 8l, 3l, 15l. 1m 49.60s. a 13.70s (5 Ran).
(M Arbib), P F I Cole

1041 Helmsley Handicap Class C (0-90 4-y-o and up) £4,836 2m............(6:00)

ENCORE UNE FOIS (Ire) [78] 4-9-8 Dean McKeown (4) al prmnt, rcd alone far rail strt, rdn 2 fs out, styd on to ld appr last, ran on.................. (12 to 1 op 8 to 1) 1
674* KAISER WILHELM [82] 4-9-12 A McGlone (8) led aftr 3 fs, wide strt, rdn and hdd appr last, kpt on. ....(3 to 1 fav op 11 to 4 tchd 7 to 2) 2
349[4] WILKINS [68] 4-8-12 G Carter (11) al prmnt, wide strt, effrt and ev ch 2 fs out, sn rdn and one pace. .... (100 to 30 op 3 to 1 tchd 7 to 2) 3
967[4] LOOKINGFORARAINBOW (Ire) [60] 5-8-7 N Connorton (3) hld up, gd hdwy 5 fs out, wide strt, effrt and ev ch o'r one out, sn rdn and wknd ins last. (12 to 1 op 8 to 1) 4
702[2] CREEAGER [56] 11-8-3 N Carlisle (2) in tch, effrt and rdn 4 fs out, wide strt, wknd 3 out. .... (8 to 1 op 10 to 1 tchd 12 to 1) 5
682[4] DOMINANT SERENADE [50] 4-7-8 S Wood (5) in tch, hdwy 4 fs out, rdn o'r 2 out and sn btn. ....(7 to 2 op 9 to 2 tchd 5 to 1) 6
CHAMPAGNE GOLD [63] 6-8-10 J Lowe (9) cl up, rcd wide, wknd 5 fs out, sn tld off......... (25 to 1 tchd 33 to 1) 7
KASHAN (Ire) [64] 5-8-11 J Carroll (10) hdwy aftr 6 fs and sn pushed alng, wknd 5 out and soon tld off. .... (33 to 1 op 20 to 1) 8
857[7] HUNTING GROUND [51] (bl) 5-7-12 J Quinn (1) al rear, tld off fnl 4 fs.......................(8 to 1 tchd 7 to 1) 9

Dist: 1l, 2½l, ½l, 3½l, 5l, dist, 6l, 2l. 3m 52.20s. a 28.20s (9 Ran).
(S & G Gutters), M Johnston

BADEN-BADEN (GER) (soft)
Saturday May 15th

1042 Oleander-Rennen (Group 3) (4-y-o and up) £30,612 2m............. (3:25)

695[4] EMBARCADERO (Ger) 5-8-9 M Rimmer, hld up, 6th 2 fs out, str run to ld last 50 yards............... (82 to 10) 1
798[3] TURGEON (USA) 7-8-9 C Asmussen, hld up, 5th strt, str run fnl 2 fs, jst fld.......................... (5 to 4 on) 2
DONGO (Pol) 6-8-9 A Boschert, led, quickened 5 fs out, clr 2 out, wknd and ct cl hme.................. (47 to 10) 3
GIRADON (Ire) 4-8-5 A Best, rcd in 4th, hmpd four fs out, ran on, not rch ldrs.......................... (129 to 10) 4
406* CARLTON (Ger) 4-8-11 P Schiergen, second and ev ch 2 fs out, wknd.......................................(4 to 1) 5
4694a[4] SAQUIACE (USA) 5-8-1[1] O Peslier, nvr plcd to chal. ....(25 to 1) 6
IBIANO (Ire) 4-8-5 K Woodburn, mid-div, ev ch 2 fs out, wknd.. (11 to 1) 7
HELENSVILLE (Ire) 5-8-2[2] M Santos, no show.... (24 to 1) 8

Dist: Sht-hd, hd, 3l, 2l, 3l, ¾l, 6l. 3m 32.57s. (8 Ran).
(Frau E Arras), B Schutz

1043 Scherping-Rennen (Listed) (3-y-o) £16,327 6f..................... (4:35)

NEW EUROPE 8-7 L Mader, mid-div, str run to ld fnl 100 yards... 1
DAILY SPORT'S GIFT 8-11 Meike Diedrichsen, hdwy to ld ins fnl furlong, sn hdd, kpt on............................. 2
781[2] NIGHT MELODY (Ire) 9-6 K Darley, mid-div, ran on fnl furlong, not rch ldrs.. 3
464[5] ROGER THE BUTLER (Ire) 9-2 M Rimmer, al prmnt, led hfwy, hdd and wknd ins fnl furlong.................. 4

Dist: 1l, 10l, ½l, nk, 3l, ½l. 1m 13.53s. (13 Ran).
(Stall Weissenhof), Frau E Mader

CURRAGH (IRE) (yielding)
Saturday May 15th
Going Correction: NIL (races 1,2,7), PLUS 0.55 (3,4,5,6)

1044 Milltown (EBF) Maiden (2-y-o) £5,250 6f.......................... (2:10)

938[3] MARVIN'S FAITH (Ire) 9-0 R Hughes (4).......... (11 to 2) 1
786[5] SPRING FORCE (Ire) 9-0 L Piggott (3)..............(8 to 1) 2
LITTLE MUSGRAVE (Ire) 9-0 M Roberts (2)....... (10 to 1) 3
786[4] SOMETHING SUPER 9-0 W J Supple (5).......... (7 to 1) 4
BIG STORY 8-11 C Roche (7).................. (5 to 4 fav) 5
820[6] BAKER HILL (Ire) 9-0 M Hills (1).................. (33 to 1) 6
ZIRAVELLO (Ire) 9-0 M J Kinane (8)................ (7 to 2) 7
571 WHEREWILITALL END (Ire) 9-0 J P Murtagh (6).... (10 to 1) 8

Dist: 1½l, 1l, 2l, 1l. 1m 15.60s. a 5.10s (8 Ran).
(Marvin Malmuth), Liam Browne

1045 Oral B. Marble Hill EBF Stakes (Listed Race) (2-y-o) £8,725 5f..........(2:40)

786[3] THE PUZZLER (Ire) 8-9 W J O'Connor (6) hld up, prog to ld jst und one furlong out, quickened wl..........(8 to 1) 1
269[2] CORINADO (Ire) 8-9 C Roche (3) wl plcd, rdn hfwy, lost pl o'r one furlong out, ran on strly last 100 yards. (3 to 1) 2
820* LONG GALLERY (Ire) 9-0 W J Supple (4) wl plcd, dsptd ld 2 fs out, led one out, sn hdd, no extr............ (8 to 1) 3
896[3] AVONDALE FOREST (Ire) 8-6 M Hills (5) rear, rdn 2 fs out, short of room, kpt on fnl furlong............(10 to 1) 4
664* IL CARAVAGGIO (Ire) 9-0 M J Kinane (1) led, rdn 2 fs out, hdd one out, sn wknd........................(11 to 10 fav) 5
869* GENUINE BID (Ire) 9-0 J P Murtagh (2) trkd ldr, rdn hfwy, not quicken...(8 to 1) 6
869[4] TRIMBLEMILL (Ire) 8-9 B Coogan (7) wl plcd, rdn 2 fs out, sn wknd..(14 to 1) 7

Dist: 3l, sht-hd, 1l, sht-hd. 1m 0.90s. a 2.60s (7 Ran).
SR: 43/31/35/23/30/-/-/ (Lady Richard Wellesley), Michael Kauntze

1046 Irish Equine Centre Handicap (0-90 3-y-o) £3,105 1m 3f............. (3:10)

789[9] MICKS DELIGHT (Ire) [-] 8-5 R Hughes (1).......... (6 to 1) 1
789[2] LADY TYONE (Ire) [-] 8-11 J P Murtagh (15)........ (5 to 1) 2
808[3] SHAHZADI (Ire) [-] 9-6 M J Kinane (11).............. (6 to 1) 3
668[6] CALL MY GUEST (Ire) [-] 8-3 W J Supple (8)...... (12 to 1) 4
789[5] SLIGHTLY SCRUFFY (Ire) [-] 7-5 (8*) R T Fitzpatrick (12) ....(14 to 1) 5
789* NEVER BACK DOWN (Ire) [-] 8-13 (6*,4ex) P Carberry (14) ....(5 to 1) 6
668[5] DOYROY (Ire) [-] (bl) 8-9 P Shanahan (10)..........(14 to 1) 7
789[8] VINEY (USA) [-] (bl) 8-7 (8*) D J O'Donohoe (13)... (14 to 1) 8
550* MISS MISTLETOES (Ire) [-] 9-1 L Piggott (7).... (9 to 2 fav) 9
640[8] SAMOT (Ire) [-] 8-2 (6*) P P Murphy (3)........... (10 to 1) 10
789[6] SIENNA SOUND (Ire) [-] 8-12 B Coogan (6)......... (10 to 1) 11
789[3] BRIGENSER (Ire) [-] 7-9 (6*) J J Behan (2).......... (13 to 2) 12
BENGALI (Ire) [-] 6-11 (10*) J P Cornally (9)....... (20 to 1) 13

Dist: Nk, 3½l, sht-hd, 1½l. 2m 30.20s. (13 Ran).
(M J McCarthy), Noel Meade

1047 Airlie/Coolmore Irish 2000 Guineas (Group 1) (3-y-o) £149,649 1m...(3:50)

794[2] BARATHEA (Ire) 9-0 M Roberts (1) *trkd ldr, rdn o'r 2 fs out to ld jst ins last, drifted lft, just hld on*......(7 to 4 on) 1
574[2] FATHERLAND (Ire) 9-0 L Piggott (9) *hld up, rdn o'r 2 fs out, str chal one out, drifted rght, jst fld*..........(11 to 2) 2
574* MASSYAR (Ire) 9-0 R Hughes (2) *mid-div, rdn 2 fs out, gd prog ins last, short of room clsg stages*........ (10 to 1) 3
658[4] FITZCARRALDO (USA) 9-0 W Swinburn (6) *led, rdn 3 fs out, hdd und 2 out, kpt on*........................ (40 to 1) 4
667[2] MASTER TRIBE (Ire) 9-0 P V Gilson (5) *trkd ldr till prog to chal 3 fs out, sn rdn, led und 2 out till hdd, wknd last 100 yards*..................................(20 to 1) 5
794 IVORY FRONTIER (Ire) 9-0 C Roche (3) *wl plcd, rdn 3 fs out, some prog one out, sn no extr*................. (20 to 1) 6
788[3] VIA PARIGI (Ire) 9-0 W J O'Connor (4) *hld up, rdn o'r 2 fs out, ran on wl fnl furlong*.................. (100 to 1) 7
667[3] NORDIC FOX (Ire) 9-0 K J Manning (11) *hld up, rdn o'r 2 fs out, some prog one out, sn wknd*.............(40 to 1) 8
667[4] MYSTERIOUS WAYS (Ire) 9-0 J P Murtagh (7) *wl plcd, rdn 3 fs out, sn wknd*..............................(20 to 1) 9
794[4] PETARDIA (bl) 9-0 M Hills (8) *wl plcd, rdn 3 fs out, wknd one and a half out*............................(9 to 1) 10
940* UNUSUAL HEAT (USA) 9-0 M J Kinane (10) *rear, rdn 2 fs out, not quicken, eased ins last*............... (16 to 1) 11

Dist: Hd, 1l, hd, ½l, ½l, hd, 4½l, 3½l, sht-hd, 5½l. 1m 43.00s. a 6.40s (11 Ran).

SR: 70/69/66/65/63/61/60/46/35/ (Sheikh Mohammed), L M Cumani

1048 Hotel Moyglare Manor Fillies EBF Maiden (3-y-o) £4,150 1¼m..... (4:30)

TAKAROUNA (USA) 8-12 J P Murtagh (7)...... (5 to 4 fav) 1
OENOTHERA (Ire) 8-12 L Piggott (4)............. (8 to 1) 2
488[5] SOLAS ABU (Ire) 8-12 C Roche (9).............. (10 to 1) 3
790[2] CLEAR ABILITY (Ire) (bl) 8-12 M J Kinane (8)....... (4 to 1) 4
KYRENIA 8-12 P Shanahan (13)................ (12 to 1) 5
NA-AMMAH (Ire) 8-12 W J Supple (5)........... (10 to 1) 6
790 OVERCAST (Ire) 8-12 E McCabe (14)............ (25 to 1) 7
639[6] SKERRIES BELL 8-12 P V Gilson (11)............ (14 to 1) 8
790[8] HOPESVILLE (Ire) 8-6 (6*) J A Heffernan (2)....... (16 to 1) 9
577 STATE PRINCESS (Ire) 8-12 R Hughes (1)........ (33 to 1) 10
552[3] SELUNE (Fr) 8-12 N G McCullagh (6)............ (11 to 1) 11
NEW LOVE (Ire) 8-8 (4*) W J Smith (3)............ (20 to 1) 12
870[7] CELESTIAL BLISS (USA) 8-12 W J O'Connor (12) (14 to 1) 13

Dist: 2l, 1l, ½l, 1l. 2m 14.70s. a 11.90s (13 Ran).

SR: 34/30/28/27/25/-/ (H H Aga Khan), John M Oxx

1049 Tattersalls Gold Cup (Group 2) (4-y-o and up) £28,750 1¼m...........(5:00)

GEORGE AUGUSTUS (USA) (bl) 5-9-1 M Roberts (5) *hld up, prog 2 fs out, short of room one out, quickened wl to ld cl hme*...................................(12 to 1) 1
525* EZZOUD (Ire) (bl) 4-8-12 W Swinburn (2) *mid-div, prog 2 fs out to ld one out, ct cl hme*.................(Evens fav) 2
670[4] APPROACH THE BENCH (Ire) 5-8-12 M J Kinane (1) *rear till prog 3 fs out, kpt on wl*.......................... (14 to 1) 3
774[7] GARDEN OF HEAVEN (USA) 4-9-1 W J O'Connor (6) *trkd ldr, led 4 fs out till one out, sn wknd*........... (7 to 1) 4
670[2] IRISH MEMORY 4-8-12 C Roche (4) *led till 4 fs out, sn rdn, wknd 2 out*...............................(10 to 1) 5
ENVIRONMENT FRIEND 5-8-12 G Duffield (3) *strted slwly, rear, stumbled 3 fs out, kpt on strt*............ (8 to 1) 6
689[4] SILVER WISP (USA) (bl) 4-8-12 L Piggott (7) *wl plcd, rdn 2 fs out, wknd one out*.............................(7 to 2) 7

Dist: Sht-hd, 3½l, 2l, sht-hd. 2m 11.50s. a 8.70s (7 Ran).

SR: 69/65/58/57/53/-/-/ (Sheikh Mohammed), John M Oxx

1050 Lumville Handicap (0-100 3-y-o and up) £6,900 6f..................(5:30)

939* CLASSICAL AFFAIR (Ire) [-] 4-8-4 (6*,3ex) R V Skelly (9) ....(10 to 1) 1
868[7] MACGILLYCUDDY (Ire) [-] (bl) 4-7-8[3] (6*) J J Behan (2) ....(10 to 1) 2
551* KHARASAR (Ire) [-] 3-7-9 (2*) D G O'Shea (4)... (7 to 2 fav) 3
640[9] ISLAND HEATHER (Ire) [-] (bl) 5-7-13[2] (4*) W J Smith (7) ....(20 to 1) 4
PETITE EPAULETTE [-] 3-8-1 N G McCullagh (3).. (33 to 1) 5
787* CHEVIOT AMBLE (Ire) [-] 5-9-9 (6*,3ex) J R Barry (15) ....(13 to 2) 6
666[3] CONS PRINCE (Ire) [-] (bl) 3-7-7 Joanna Morgan (14) (5 to 1) 7
787[2] MILLIE'S CHOICE (Ire) [-] 4-9-9 W J Supple (11).....(4 to 1) 8
COMMON BOND (Ire) [-] 3-7-10 (2*) R M Burke (12) (14 to 1) 9
HIGH TYCOON (Ire) [-] 3-8-11 M J Kinane (5)..... (11 to 2) 10
640 NORDIC SAINT (Ire) [-] 4-7-3[4] (8*) R T Fitzpatrick (6) (16 to 1) 11
960[3] WHAT MAGIC (Ire) [-] 3-7-1 (6*) P P Murphy (1)....(16 to 1) 12
939 SMOKEY LAD [-] 9-8-10 P V Gilson (8)........... (33 to 1) 13
939[9] NEVER WRONG [-] 6-7-12[2] (10*) G Coogan (10)...(20 to 1) 14

Dist: 3l, 6l, sht-hd, nk. 1m 14.00s. a 3.50s (14 Ran).

SR: 26/1/-/-/-/-/ (Paul Farrell), T M Walsh

HAMILTON (soft) Saturday May 15th

Going Correction: PLUS 0.50 sec. per fur.

1051 Horsell Anitec Claiming Stakes Class F (2-y-o) £1,847 6f 5yds......... (6:20)

767* JIMMY THE SKUNK (Ire) 9-0 J Carroll (3) *made all, shaken o'r over one out, sn clr, easily*. (7 to 4 on op 6 to 4 on) 1
998[5] SHUTTLECOCK 8-6 Dale Gibson (4) *in tch, sn pushed alng, styd on fnl 2 fs, no ch wth wnr*. (9 to 4 op 2 to 1) 2
865[5] FORREST MASTER (Ire) 8-6 J Fortune (1) *slwly into strd, sn chasing ldr, rdn hfwy, wknd 2 out*.. (8 to 1 op 5 to 1) 3
767[4] KING ACRYLIC (Ire) 8-2 C Avery (2) *sn beh*. .... (25 to 1 op 12 to 1) 4

Dist: 8l, 5l, 2½l. 1m 17.50s. a 6.80s (4 Ran).

SR: 24/ (J David Abell), J Berry

1052 Leggat Plant Amateur Riders' Handicap Class G (0-70 3-y-o and up) £1,730 5f 4yds....................... (6:50)

866* JUST BOB [65] 4-11-2 (5*) Mrs D Kettlewell (6) *cl up, led hfwy, hld on wl fnl furlong*. ....(11 to 4 fav op 2 to 1 tchd 3 to 1) 1
765[3] FRANCIS ANN [49] 5-10-5 Mr M Buckley (12) *in tch, hdwy hfwy, chlgd entering fnl furlong, kpt on und pres*. ....(9 to 2 op 4 to 1) 2
STATE FLYER [60] (v) 5-10-9 (7*) Mr S Walker (7) *slwly into strd, hdwy and ev ch 2 out, one pace*. .... (12 to 1 op 16 to 1) 3
909 CHOICE LOT [38] (bl) 6-9-8 Miss I Diana W Jones (9) *cl up, ev ch 2 out, one pace*..........................(33 to 1) 4
227[5] LILY'S LOVER (USA) [49] 7-10-0 (5*) Mr N Miles (1) *in tch, kpt on frm hfwy, not rch ldrs*......(10 to 1 op 14 to 1) 5
375 VERRO (USA) [40] (bl) 6-9-10[7] (5*) Miss A Purdy (10) *nvr dngrs*...................................... (8 to 1 op 9 to 1) 6
866 MINSK [45] 7-10-1[15] (7*) Miss F Barnes (8) *al beh*. .... (100 to 1 op 50 to 1) 7
837 WE'RE ALL GAME [56] 4-10-12 Miss S Baxter (3) *chsd ldrs to hfwy*........................(16 to 1 op 20 to 1) 8
721 TOMMY TEMPEST [50] 4-9-13 (7*) Miss Elaine Mills (4) *led to hfwy, sn wknd*...................(10 to 1 op 6 to 1) 9
887[5] KHALLOOF (Ire) [47] (bl) 4-9-10 (7*) Miss M Carson (2) *beh frm hfwy*....................... (12 to 1 op 14 to 1) 10
866[4] LANGTONIAN [55] 4-10-11 Mr D Parker (5) *beh frm hfwy*. ....(5 to 1 op 4 to 1) 11

Dist: Nk, 6l, ½l, 2½l, 2½l, 5l, 3½l, 1l, 2l, hd. 1m 5.80s. a 7.50s (11 Ran).

SR: 35/18/5/-/-/-/ (J Fotherby), S E Kettlewell

1053 Peter Yarwood Median Auction Maiden Stakes Class D (2-y-o) £3,172 5f 4yds........................ (7:20)

839[2] ISABELLA SHARP 8-9 J Fortune (2) *cl up, led 2 out, pushed out*.............(Evens fav tchd 5 to 4) 1
BRAILLE (Ire) 9-0 Dean McKeown (1) *chsd ldrs, kpt on wl fnl furlong*..........(10 to 1 op 12 to 1 tchd 14 to 1) 2
LUCIUS LOCKET (Ire) 9-0 J Carroll (6) *chsd ldrs, kpt on same pace fnl 2 fs*.................. (6 to 4 op 11 to 10) 3
KING RAT (Ire) 9-0 J Lowe (3) *slight ld till hdd 2 out, sn btn*.................. (33 to 1 op 20 to 1 tchd 50 to 1) 4
ALTOBY 9-0 S Webster (4) *dwlt, outpcd and wl beh till some late hdwy*.................(50 to 1 op 25 to 1) 5
TIME TO DANCE 8-6 (3*) J Weaver (5) *in tch to hfwy*. .... (12 to 1 op 8 to 1) 6

Dist: 1½l, 5l, 2l, 2½l, 8l. 1m 3.80s. a 5.50s (6 Ran).

SR: 35/34/14/6/-/-/ (Christopher Wright), M Bell

1054 Contractors Mechanical Plant Engineers Glasgow Branch Selling Handicap Class G (0-60 3-y-o and up) £1,702 1m 3f 16yds....................(7:50)

863[4] GOLD SURPRISE (Ire) [48] 4-9-10 J Fortune (7) *prmnt, led o'r 2 out, hld on wl und pres*. ....(9 to 2 op 3 to 1 tchd 5 to 1) 1
699[4] GOODBYE MILLIE [47] 3-8-0 (5*) Darren Moffatt (2) *in tch, pushed alng hfwy, rdn 4 out, hdwy 3 out, chlgd ins fnl furlong, no extr cl hme*. (4 to 1 op 7 to 2 tchd 9 to 2) 2
745[4] BEAUMOOD [31] (v) 7-8-4 (3*) J Weaver (3) *cl up, dsptd ld hfwy, led o'r 3 out, hdd over 2 out, rallied ins fnl furlong, no extr close hme*......... (6 to 1 tchd 7 to 1) 3
ABSOLUTELY RIGHT [45] 5-9-7 Dale Gibson (5) *hld up, hdwy hfwy, effrt o'r 3 out, kpt on same pace*. ....(3 to 1 fav op 5 to 1 tchd 6 to 1) 4
626 DRINKS PARTY (Ire) [30] (bl) 5-8-6 J Lowe (1) *in tch gng wl, rdn o'r 3 out, one pace*. (13 to 2 op 5 to 1 tchd 7 to 1) 5
928[7] EVERGREEN TANGO [50] 3-8-8 Dean McKeown (6) *led or dsptd ld till hdd o'r 3 out, sn wknd*. ....(20 to 1 op 16 to 1 tchd 25 to 1) 6
740[8] ARAGON AYR [26] 5-8-2[1] J Carroll (8) *nvr dngrs*. ....(5 to 1 op 8 to 1) 7
863 LORD ADVOCATE [37] (v) 5-8-13 K Fallon (9) *sn pushed alng, beh most of way*. ....(12 to 1 op 10 to 1 tchd 16 to 1) 8
BIJOU PRINCESS [20] 5-7-3 (7*) D Wright (4) *al beh*. ....(33 to 1) 9
880 DOOGAREY [45] 3-8-3 C Avery (10) *prmnt till wknd 5 out*. .... (20 to 1 op 16 to 1 tchd 25 to 1) 10

864[5] SENSABO [40] 3-7-12 J Fanning (11) *in tch till wknd o'r 4 out, tld off*...................... (25 to 1 tchd 33 to 1) 11
Dist: ½l, ½l, 3½l, 3½l, 10l, 1½l, 7l, 1l, hd. 2m 32.90s. a 12.90s (11 Ran).
SR: 36/16/17/24/2/-/ (J S Calvert), S E Kettlewell

1055 Lindsay Plant Rating Related Maiden Stakes Class E (3-y-o and up) £2,427 1½m 17yds..................... (8:20)

832[4] VOLUNTEER POINT (Ire) 3-8-5 J Fortune (5) *made all, styd on wl fnl 2 fs*........................(25 to 1 op 20 to 1) 1
679 SHARE A MOMENT (Can) 3-8-0 (5*) A Garth (3) *hld up, hdwy o'r 3 out, kpt on und pres fnl 2 fs, not rch wnr.* ....(10 to 1 op 6 to 1 tchd 12 to 1) 2
686[2] SHIRLEY ROSE 3-8-0 J Fanning (2) *hld up in tch, hdwy 4 out, rdn o'r 2 out, swshd tail, one pace.* ....(2 to 1 on op 5 to 2 on) 3
534[4] MOONLIGHT ECLIPSE 3-8-5 K Fallon (7) *in tch, outpcd 4 out, styd on und pres fnl 2 fs.* ....(11 to 2 op 4 to 1 tchd 6 to 1) 4
MATHAL (USA) 4-9-10 C Avery (6) *pld hrd early, trkd ldr till wknd 3 out*....................(33 to 1 op 25 to 1) 5
699[2] MOUNTAIN WILLOW (v) 3-8-0 J Lowe (1) *prmnt till wknd o'r 3 out*..........(4 to 1 op 6 to 1 tchd 7 to 1) 6
Dist: 2½l, 2½l, 2l, 5l, 2½l. 2m 48.30s. a 15.30s (6 Ran).
(Miss K S Bramall), Mrs S A Bramall

1056 Luddon Construction Handicap Class E (0-70 4-y-o and up) £2,616 1m 5f 9yds ....(8:50)

904* SHAMSHOM AL ARAB (Ire) [46] 5-8-5 (5*) Darren Moffatt (3) *trkd ldrs, led 2 out, styd on wl.* ....(11 to 8 fav op 6 to 4 tchd 2 to 1) 1
BEACHY HEAD [58] 5-9-8 J Carroll (1) *led till hdd 8 out, cl up, slight ld 3 out, headed 2 out, kpt on.* ....(4 to 1 op 5 to 2) 2
845[9] MENTALASANYTHIN [60] 4-9-10 A Mackay (2) *in tch, effrt 3 out, styd on wl fnl 2 fs.* ....(12 to 1 op 10 to 1 tchd 14 to 1) 3
682[5] HOT STAR [51] 7-9-1 J Fanning (6) *in tch, rdn o'r 3 out, kpt on same pace*..........(11 to 2 op 5 to 1 tchd 6 to 1) 4
863[6] RAPID MOVER [29] (bl) 6-7-0 (7*) D Wright (8) *wth ldr, led 8 out, hdd 3 out, fdd*........................(25 to 1 op 20 to 1) 5
910* CONTINUITY [59] 4-9-6 (3*) J Weaver (9) *hld up, effrt o'r 4 out, no real hdwy*.................. (5 to 1 tchd 6 to 1) 6
727 FAMOUS BEAUTY [46] 6-8-3 (7*) L Aspell (7) *dwlt, hld up, some hdwy 5 out, wknd o'r 3 out.* (16 to 1 op 14 to 1) 7
356[7] ONE FOR THE POT [58] 8-9-8 K Fallon (4) *hld up, effrt o'r 4 out, sn btn*........................(12 to 1 op 10 to 1) 8
Dist: 1½l, nk, 7l, 2½l, 7l, 3l, 3½l. 3m 4.00s. a 18.00s (8 Ran).
(Miss Maha Kalaji), S G Norton

LINGFIELD (good to firm)
Saturday May 15th
Going Correction: NIL

1057 Blue Max Maiden Stakes Class D (3-y-o) £3,669 6f................... (6:05)

872[7] LOCH PATRICK 9-0 A McGlone (10) *trkd ldr, led appr fnl furlong, rdn out*................ (14 to 1 op 10 to 1) 1
797[2] PUTOUT 8-9 L Dettori (4) *wtd wth, hdwy hfwy, ev ch entering fnl furlong, rdn and no extr cl hme.* .... (11 to 8 fav op 11 to 10 tchd 6 to 4) 2
872[4] FRIENDLY BRAVE (USA) (bl) 9-0 W Newnes (8) *led till hdd appr fnl furlong, ran on one pace.* ....(2 to 1 op 9 to 4 tchd 5 to 2 and 11 to 4) 3
797[8] TARTIB (Ire) 9-0 R Hills (6) *in rear, hdwy wl o'r one furlong out, nvr nr to chal*... (16 to 1 op 10 to 1 tchd 20 to 1) 4
797[5] INDERAPUTERI (bl) 8-9 A Munro (1) *prmnt early, lost pl hfwy, styd on fnl furlong, nvr dngrs.* ....(6 to 1 tchd 7 to 1) 5
882[9] ROYAL INTERVAL 9-0 T Sprake (5) *sn pushed alng, nvr nr to chal*...............(25 to 1 op 12 to 1 tchd 33 to 1) 6
CHEAT (USA) 9-0 N Day (11) *slwly into strd, sn in tch, rdn and wknd appr fnl furlong*........(14 to 1 op 4 to 1) 7
NANQUIDNO 8-9 G Bardwell (3) *al struggling in rear.* .... (50 to 1 op 33 to 1) 8
797[7] PERSIAN CHIMES (Ire) 9-0 W Hood (7) *speed to hfwy, sn beh*.................(25 to 1 op 16 to 1 tchd 33 to 1) 9
MAI-TU-TU 8-9 R Price (2) *very slwly away, al beh.* .... (50 to 1 op 20 to 1) 10
713[6] ASCOM PAGER (Ire) 8-9 C Rutter (9) *sn rdn, lost tch o'r 2 fs out*........................... (50 to 1 op 33 to 1) 11
Dist: 1l, ¾l, 3l, ½l, 2½l, 1½l, 10l, 8l, nk, ½l. 1m 12.60s. a 3.60s (11 Ran).
SR: 28/19/21/9/2/-/ (Miss E M L Coller), L J Holt

1058 Oastwell Wines Handicap Class E (0-80 3-y-o) £3,288 7f........... (7:05)

FIELD OF VISION (Ire) [56] 7-11 T Williams (14) *wtd wth on ins, rdn o'r 2 out, short of room appr last, squeezed through to ld inside fnl furlong*.... (10 to 1 op 8 to 1) 1
719 PERDITION (Ire) [62] 8-3 R Hills (12) *chsd ldrs, slightly bumped appr fnl furlong, ev ch ins last, ran on.* ....(25 to 1 op 20 to 1) 2
917* SOAKING [70] 8-11 B Rouse (13) *chsd ldr, led o'r 2 fs out, rdn and hdd ins last*.... (9 to 2 op 3 to 1 tchd 5 to 1) 3
836* FINAL FRONTIER (Ire) [70] 8-11 R Cochrane (7) *in tch, rdn and swtchd lft appr fnl furlong, ran on, no extr cl hme.* ....(7 to 2 fav op 5 to 1) 4
881[6] FIVEOFIVE (Ire) [59] 8-0 J Quinn (8) *hld up, styd on ins fnl 2 fs, nvr nrr*........... (12 to 1 op 14 to 1 tchd 20 to 1) 5
719[3] RAGING THUNDER [62] (bl) 8-0 (3*) D Harrison (11) *led till hdd o'r 2 fs out, one pace aftr.* ....(9 to 1 op 6 to 1 tchd 10 to 1) 6
950* WALNUT BURL (Ire) [77] 9-4 J Reid (3) *hld up, rdn and some hdwy 2 fs out, wknd ins last*... (8 to 1 op 7 to 1) 7
514[9] FORMAL AFFAIR [77] 9-4 D Biggs (4) *al mid-div, outpcd ins fnl 2 fs*............................(16 to 1 op 12 to 1) 8
801 MY BEST VALENTINE [73] 9-0 Paul Eddery (5) *mid-div, rdn 2 fs out, sn btn*..................... (8 to 1 op 14 to 1) 9
732 ON GOLDEN POND (Ire) [60] 8-1 A Munro (6) *al towards rear, rdn hfwy, wknd 2 fs out*..... (20 to 1 op 16 to 1) 10
ICE REBEL [52] 7-7 G Bardwell (9) *sn rdn in rear, nvr on terms*...(33 to 1) 11
945[3] I'LLEAVEITOYOU (Ire) [80] 9-7 T Quinn (10) *mid-div, rdn o'r 2 fs out, sn btn*......... (15 to 2 op 6 to 1 tchd 8 to 1) 12
733 QUEENS CONTRACTOR [61] 8-2 D Holland (1) *rcd alone far side, in tch till eased o'r one furlong out.* ....(25 to 1 op 20 to 1) 13
772 EXCESS BAGGAGE (Ire) [64] 8-5 B Raymond (2) *rcd wide early, trkd o'r to centre, beh frm hfwy, tld off.* ....(25 to 1 op 20 to 1) 14
Dist: ½l, ½l, ¾l, ¾l, 1l, 6l, ¾l, ½l, 1½l, sht-hd. 1m 24.38s. a 3.68s (14 Ran).
SR: 28/32/38/36/23/23/20/18/12/ (R W Huggins), M Johnston

1059 G. M. Benefit Consultants Handicap Class E (0-70 3-y-o and up) £3,150 6f ....(7:35)

MERRYHILL MAID (Ire) [60] 5-9-6 R Cochrane (13) *led aftr 2 and a half fs, rdn appr last, ran on wl.* ....(10 to 1 op 14 to 1 tchd 16 to 1) 1
836[8] JULIET BRAVO [60] 3-8-9 A Munro (2) *led far side aftr 2 fs, rdn and ran on ins fnl two*........ (14 to 1 op 10 to 1) 2
760[9] MY RUBY RING [54] 6-9-0 T Williams (16) *in tch stands side, short of room 2 fs out, swtchd lft, ran on ins last.* ....(13 to 2 op 5 to 1) 3
948 QUICK STEEL [53] 5-8-10 (3*) A Tucker (14) *hld up, rdn and hdwy 2 fs out, nvr nrr*........... (9 to 2 fav op 8 to 1) 4
760[3] FACE THE FUTURE [58] 4-9-4 Paul Eddery (9) *mid-div, hrd rdn o'r 2 fs out, kpt on one pace fnl furlong.* ....(15 to 2 op 5 to 1 tchd 8 to 1) 5
758[5] FAY'S SONG (Ire) [64] 5-9-10 T Quinn (4) *trkd o'r to stands side, pushed alng hfwy, styd on ins fnl 2 fs.* ....(6 to 1 op 5 to 1 tchd 7 to 1) 6
948 HARRY'S COMING [59] 9-9-5 T Sprake (11) *mid-div, rdn o'r 2 fs out, styd on one pace.* ....(10 to 1 op 8 to 1 tchd 12 to 1) 7
758 ARRAS ROYALE [45] 3-7-8 N Adams (15) *led for 2 and a half fs, rdn o'r two out, one pace.* (50 to 1 op 33 to 1) 8
WILD STRAWBERRY [50] 4-8-10 J Reid (8) *al mid-div, no hdwy fnl 2 fs*....................................... (20 to 1) 9
760 LOOTING (USA) [34] 7-7-8[1] J Quinn (6) *sn rdn, al outpcd.* ....(50 to 1 op 33 to 1) 10
4716a[8] FAIR ENCHANTRESS [46] 5-8-6 D Holland (3) *led far side 2 fs, wknd appr last, eased*..........(50 to 1 op 33 to 1) 11
948[3] HARDLINER [64] 4-9-10 W Woods (12) *al outpcd.* ....(8 to 1 op 6 to 1) 12
836[3] NO EXTRAS (Ire) [70] (v) 3-9-5 B Rouse (1) *speed on far side till wknd o'r one out.* (14 to 1 op 8 to 1 tchd 16 to 1) 13
760 OYSTON'S LIFE [40] 4-8-0 C Rutter (5) *sn outpcd, al beh.* ....(33 to 1) 14
SPRING HIGH [59] 6-9-5 G Bardwell (10) *al beh.* ....(14 to 1 tchd 16 to 1) 15
927[7] AGIL'S PET [53] (bl) 3-7-13 (3*) D Harrison (7) *speed till wknd 2 fs out*......... (12 to 1 op 8 to 1 tchd 14 to 1) 16
Dist: 2½l, hd, ¾l, 2l, ½l, 2l, ¾l, 1l, hd, 2l. 1m 11.87s. a 2.87s (16 Ran).
SR: 49/28/32/28/25/29/16/-/-/ (David Cahal), J L Harris

1060 Ashbourne Water Maiden Stakes Class D (3-y-o and up) £3,640 7f (8:05)

797[4] MITHI AL GAMAR (USA) 3-8-7 B Raymond (12) *trkd ldrs, led one furlong out, pushed out.* ....(2 to 1 fav op 11 to 4) 1
950[2] GRAN SENORUM (USA) 3-8-12 A Munro (14) *led for 2 fs, led ag'n o'r two out, hdd one out, no extr nr finish.* ....(3 to 1 op 9 to 4 tchd 100 to 30) 2
470[6] KHATTAT (USA) 3-8-12 R Hills (8) *pld hrd, hld up in tch, hdwy o'r one furlong out, edgd rght and one paced ins last*............(3 to 1 op 9 to 4 tchd 100 to 30) 3
646 ISLAND KNIGHT (Ire) 4-9-10 R Cochrane (7) *nvr far away, hdwy and ev ch o'r one furlong out, kpt on one pace.* ....(33 to 1 op 25 to 1) 4
248[7] NO GAIN 3-8-0 (7*) Kim McDonnell (11) *rcd keenly, led aftr 2 fs, hdd o'r two out, wknd appr last.* .... (50 to 1 op 33 to 1) 5

751 BALE BREAKER (USA) 3-8-12 N Day (1) *in tch in centre of course, rdn and wknd appr fnl furlong.* .... (12 to 1 op 7 to 1 tchd 14 to 1) 6
CLEVER MINSTREL (USA) 3-8-12 M Perrett (5) *mid-div, hdwy o'r 2 fs out, one pace aftr*.....(14 to 1 op 8 to 1) 7
WHATEVER'S RIGHT (Ire) 4-9-10 N Adams (13) *slwly away, nvr nr to chal*....................(33 to 1 op 20 to 1) 8
951[6] FINDON ACADEMY (Ire) 3-8-12 B Rouse (3) *al beh.* ....(33 to 1 op 20 to 1) 9
672 D SEVEN 3-8-5 (7*) C Hawksley (10) *in tch till outpcd o'r 2 fs out*.............................(50 to 1 op 33 to 1) 10
DYNAMIC GEORGE 3-8-12 W Newnes (9) *al beh.* ....(50 to 1 op 33 to 1) 11
LITTLE MISS RIBOT 3-8-7 J Reid (4) *sn outpcd, al beh.* ....(33 to 1 op 20 to 1) 12
825 BRAVE HERO (USA) 3-8-12 D Biggs (6) *chsd ldrs till wknd o'r 2 fs out*.......................(50 to 1 op 33 to 1) 13
950[9] TASSAGH BRIDGE (Ire) 3-8-7 J Quinn (2) *al beh.* ....(33 to 1 op 20 to 1) 14
Dist: ½l, 3½l, 2½l, 2l, ¾l, 2l, 2½l, hd, 5l, nk. 1m 24.20s. a 3.50s (14 Ran).
SR: 41/44/33/37/14/17/11/15/2/ (Maktoum Al Maktoum), M R Stoute

LINGFIELD (A.W) (std)
Saturday May 15th
Going Correction: NIL

1061 Cider Selling Stakes Class G (3-y-o) £2,454 1½m.................. (6:35)

717 ARCTIC GUEST (Ire) 9-0 T Williams (2) *wtd wth, steady hdwy to ld 4 fs out, sn clr, eased ins last.* ...(11 to 10 on op Evens tchd 11 to 10 and 5 to 4 on) 1
437 RUBIDIAN 9-0 T Quinn (3) *led till hdd 4 fs out, sn outpcd, hrd rdn to stay second fnl furlong*... (8 to 1 op 4 to 1) 2
699 THREEOFUS (bl) 9-0 R Cochrane (1) *al prmnt, rdn 4 fs out, pressed second to line.* ....(20 to 1 op 16 to 1 tchd 25 to 1) 3
905[3] SASSAMOUSE 8-9 W Woods (5) *in frnt rnk till rdn and wknd quickly 2 fs out*.............(7 to 2 tchd 4 to 1) 4
441[9] TOP GUNNER (Ire) 9-0 D Biggs (6) *slwly away, al wl beh.* ....(6 to 1 op 12 to 1 tchd 14 to 1) 5
826 DANSEUSE FRANCAISE (Ire) 8-2 (7*) R Adams (4) *al beh, lost tch hfwy, tld off*................ (8 to 1 op 6 to 1) 6
Dist: 10l, hd, 15l, 4l, 25l. 2m 38.53s. a 9.23s (6 Ran).
SR: 8/-/-/ (The Fairyhouse 1992 Partnership), M Johnston

1062 Gin & Tonic Handicap Class E (0-70 3-y-o) £2,831 1¼m............. (8:35)

880[9] ONE OFF THE RAIL (USA) [62] 9-6 B Rouse (6) *made all, quickened o'r 3 fs out, hld on wl ins last.* .... (5 to 1 op 4 to 1 tchd 11 to 2) 1
758 STALLED (Ire) [59] 9-3 R Cochrane (1) *hld up, outpcd o'r 3 fs out, hdwy wl over one out, ran on strly ins last.* ....(5 to 1 op 8 to 1) 2
724[7] WITHOUT A FLAG (USA) [58] 9-2 D Biggs (3) *chsd wnr till no extr ins fnl furlong.* .... (11 to 4 fav op 5 to 2 tchd 7 to 2 and 4 to 1) 3
733 LEGAL ARTIST (Ire) [48] 8-6 G Bardwell (5) *in tch, rdn o'r 3 fs out, kpt on one pace ins fnl 2.* .... (20 to 1 op 14 to 1 tchd 25 to 1) 4
764[7] TAKE YOUR PARTNER (Ire) [57] 9-1 T Williams (8) *hld up on outsd, hdwy o'r 3 fs out, ev ch 2 out, wknd appr last.* ....(5 to 1 op 5 to 2) 5
405[5] CONVOY [63] (bl) 9-7 T Quinn (7) *in tch till rdn 3 fs out, one pace aftr*...............................(6 to 1 op 5 to 1) 6
440 CHILTERN HUNDREDS (USA) [57] 8-8 (7*) D McCabe (4) *al beh, lost tch 4 fs out.* ....(6 to 1 op 8 to 1 tchd 9 to 1 and 5 to 1) 7
926[6] SO SAUCY [51] 8-9 R Hills (2) *in tch till wknd o'r 2 fs out.* ....(14 to 1 tchd 16 to 1) 8
Dist: ½l, 2l, ¾l, 1½l, 2l, 5l, 7l. 2m 9.85s. a 6.65s (8 Ran).
SR: 40/36/31/19/25/27/11/-/ (K Higson), A Moore

NEWBURY (good)
Saturday May 15th
Going Correction: MINUS 0.05 sec. per fur. (races 1,4), MINUS 0.15 (2,3,5,6,7)

1063 Crookham Median Auction Maiden Stakes Class D (2-y-o) £4,175 5f 34yds ....(2:00)

687 PRINCE BABAR 9-0 N Day (7) *in tch, drvn alng and ran green appr fnl furlong, styd on und pres to ld wl ins last*..................(20 to 1 op 16 to 1 tchd 25 to 1) 1
SERIOUS OPTION (Ire) 9-0 T Quinn (17) *hld up, prog hfwy, led briefly entering last, ran on same pace.* ....(8 to 1 op 5 to 1 tchd 9 to 1) 2
913[2] PETER ROWLEY 9-0 J Reid (10) *nvr far away, led o'r 3 fs out, hdd appr 2 out, led ag'n over one out, headed and one pace entering fnl furlong*...... (4 to 1 tchd 9 to 2) 3
DOLLAR GAMBLE (Ire) 9-0 B Raymond (1) *handily plcd, led o'r 2 fs out, hdd appr last, one pace*....... (20 to 1) 4
776 CONNECT (Ire) 9-0 W Newnes (2) *in tch, drvn alng and ev ch o'r one furlong out, sn one pace*............(33 to 1) 5
ELEVATOR SHAFT (Ire) 9-0 R Price (13) *trkd ldrs, drvn and one pace 2 fs out*..................(33 to 1 op 25 to 1) 6
PICCOLO 9-0 Pat Eddery (5) *strt slwly, reco'red to race in mid-div, rdn and effrt entering fnl 2 fs, sn one pace.* ....(3 to 1 fav tchd 4 to 1) 7
PARNASO (Ire) 9-0 A McGlone (6) *speed o'r 3 fs.* ....(33 to 1 op 20 to 1) 8
KILLING TIME 9-0 J Comber (16) *towards rear til styd on one pace entering fnl 2 fs, not trble ldrs.* ....(33 to 1 op 25 to 1) 9
RED VALERIAN 9-0 L Dettori (9) *hld up in mid-div, rdn and effrt hfwy, one pace*.......... (10 to 1 op 7 to 1) 10
MOUNT LEINSTER 9-0 J Williams (19) *nvr pace of ldrs.* ....(33 to 1 op 20 to 1) 11
BON TON 8-9 Paul Eddery (4) *nvr on terms.* ....(33 to 1 op 25 to 1) 12
SOLO TICKET 9-0 A Munro (12) *slwly into strd, nvr gng pace of ldrs*......... (20 to 1 op 12 to 1 tchd 25 to 1) 13
VERCINGETORIX (Ire) 8-11 (3*) D Harrison (8) *in tch to hfwy*............................(20 to 1 op 14 to 1) 14
RED NECK 8-9 (5*) Stephen Davies (15) *slwly away, nvr on terms*..(33 to 1) 15
839[8] HIGHLAND WARNING 8-6 (3*) J Weaver (14) *pressed ldrs o'r 2 fs*............................(33 to 1 op 16 to 1) 16
MR MORIARTY (Ire) 9-0 R Cochrane (18) *dwlt, nvr on terms*................(14 to 1 op 10 to 1 tchd 16 to 1) 17
EUROCHEM LAD (Ire) 9-0 B Rouse (3) *trkd ldrs, rdn alng hfwy, sn btn*.....................(16 to 1 tchd 33 to 1) 18
COMMENDATION DAY (Ire) 9-0 D Holland (11) *led o'r one furlong, remained in tch, fdd over one furlong out.* .... (12 to 1 op 7 to 1) 19
Dist: Hd, 3½l, 1½l, 1½l, hd, nk, hd, sht-hd, ¾l, nk. 1m 3.03s. a 2.73s (19 Ran).
SR: 40/39/25/19/13/12/11/10/9/ (Giles W Pritchard-Gordon), G A Pritchard-Gordon

1064 May Handicap Class C (0-90 3-y-o and up) £5,469 1¼m 6yds........... (2:30)

875 DEVILRY [80] 3-8-2 (3*) J Weaver (13) *hld up in midfield, gd prog entering fnl 2 fs, styd on wl ins last to ld cl hme.* .... (33 to 1 op 25 to 1) 1
LAST EMBRACE (Ire) [83] 4-9-7 (3*) D Harrison (18) *wtd wth, improved frm 2 fs out, ev ch wl ins last, kpt on.* ....(20 to 1 op 16 to 1) 2
792[8] BARFORD LAD [77] 6-9-4 A Munro (10) *hld up beh ldrs, improved 2 fs out, led appr fnl furlong, hdd and no extr cl hme*.............................(14 to 1 tchd 16 to 1) 3
771[7] WAINWRIGHT (USA) [78] 4-9-5 R Cochrane (21) *towards rear, hdwy entering fnl quarter m, effrt ins last, ran on*.................................. (14 to 1 op 10 to 1) 4
792[4] PELORUS [79] 8-9-6 J Williams (20) *slwly away, in rear til swtchd rght and hdwy 2 fs out, styd on strly ins last.* .... (12 to 1 op 10 to 1 tchd 14 to 1) 5
731 VALLANCE [75] 5-9-2 Paul Eddery (15) *wtd wth, hdwy 2 fs out, ev ch entering last, sn one pace.* ....(14 to 1 op 16 to 1 tchd 12 to 1) 6
663[2] RUTLAND WATER (USA) [68] 6-8-9 T Quinn (3) *pressed ldrs, drvn alng and ev ch entering fnl furlong, one pace ins last*................ (4 to 1 fav op 6 to 1 tchd 7 to 1) 7
792[7] YOUNG FREEMAN (USA) [80] (bl) 4-9-7 M Perrett (9) *pressed ldr, led o'r 3 fs out, hdd and one pace appr last.* ....(33 to 1 op 25 to 1) 8
CEZANNE [78] 4-9-5 Pat Eddery (14) *trkd ldrs, drvn alng 2 fs out, one pace*...................(14 to 1 op 10 to 1) 9
824[8] PORT SUNLIGHT (Ire) [77] 5-9-4 A McGlone (12) *patiently rdn, improved 2 fs out, not clr run and swtchd rght appr last, one pace*...(14 to 1 op 12 to 1 tchd 16 to 1) 10
CHAMBROS [61] 6-8-2 D Holland (1) *towards rear til improved o'r one furlong out, nvr plcd to chal.* ....(16 to 1 op 14 to 1) 11
731[2] SURREY DANCER [74] 5-9-1 B Raymond (4) *nvr far away, rdn alng 3 fs out, one pace entering fnl 2 furlongs.* ....(10 to 1 tchd 11 to 1) 12
739 LOBILIO (USA) [71] (bl) 4-8-9 (3*) B Doyle (17) *mid-div, effrt 3 fs out, sn btn*................. (16 to 1 tchd 20 to 1) 13
792[5] KNOCK KNOCK [87] 8-10-0 L Dettori (22) *wtd wth, improved o'r 2 fs out, sn not much room, one pace.* .... (16 to 1 op 20 to 1) 14
845[8] GILDERDALE [76] 11-9-3 R Hills (11) *hld up in mid-div, effrt and not much room 2 fs out, one pace.* ....(25 to 1 op 20 to 1) 15
840[5] SWIFT SILVER [59] 6-8-0 J Quinn (2) *trkd ldg grp, rdn and no hdwy 2 fs out*............... (14 to 1 tchd 16 to 1) 16
792[9] BOLD STROKE [84] 4-9-11 J Reid (19) *pressed ldrs, rdn o'r 2 fs out, sn btn*.................. (10 to 1 op 8 to 1) 17
785[6] TIME FOR A FLUTTER [70] 4-8-11 W Newnes (8) *nvr on terms*...........................(50 to 1 tchd 66 to 1) 18
731[4] SINCLAIR LAD (Ire) [54] 5-7-9 N Adams (7) *nvr trbld ldrs.* .... (16 to 1 op 12 to 1) 19
HAROLDON (Ire) [79] 4-9-1 (5*) Stephen Davies (16) *sn led, drvn alng and hdd appr 3 fs out, wknd entering fnl 2 furlongs*......................................(33 to 1) 20
679 MOVE A MINUTE (USA) [81] 4-9-8 B Rouse (5) *nvr on terms.* ....(33 to 1) 21
Dist: Sht-hd, hd, sht-hd, nk, 1l, 1½l, 1l, sht-hd, ¾l, nk. 2m 6.62s. a 3.62s (21

Ran).
SR: 40/58/51/51/51/45/35/45/42/ (Lady McIndoe), G Lewis

1065 Quantel Aston Park Stakes Class A (Listed Race) (4-y-o and up) £12,924 1m 5f 61yds....................(3:00)

773* BRIER CREEK (USA) 4-8-11 R Cochrane (4) *hld up towards rear, drvn alng and hdwy entering fnl 2 fs, styd on wl to ld ins last*.......... (11 to 4 op 5 to 2 tchd 3 to 1) 1
774^{4} SHUAILAAN (USA) 4-8-11 Pat Eddery (1) *led, rdn alng 2 fs out, hdd ins last, kpt on*.......... (9 to 4 fav op 6 to 4) 2
579* LINPAC WEST 7-9-3 B Raymond (2) *pressed ldr, drvn alng and ev ch appr fnl furlong, sn one pace.* ....(4 to 1 tchd 9 to 2) 3
UP ANCHOR (Ire) 4-8-12 A Munro (5) *trkd ldg pair, prog and ev ch appr 2 fs out, one pace approaching last.* ....(100 to 30 op 4 to 1 tchd 3 to 1) 4
MICHELOZZO (USA) 7-9-6 L Dettori (3) *wtd wth, drvn alng and outpcd frm 2 fs out*..........(14 to 1 tchd 16 to 1) 5
Dist: ½l, 3½l, 1½l, 30l. 2m 55.01s. a 8.81s (5 Ran).
(Sheikh Mohammed), J H M Gosden

1066 High Speed Production Handicap Class C (0-90 3-y-o and up) £5,754 6f 8yds......................... (3:30)

EVERGLADES (Ire) [81] 5-9-6 Paul Eddery (14) *hld up beh ldrs, drvn alng and improved frm o'r one furlong out, kpt on wl to ld cl hme*........................(20 to 1) 1
1000* MACFARLANE [71] 5-8-10 (7ex) D Holland (9) *pressed ldrs, drvn alng to ld one furlong out, hdd and not quicken cl hme*....... (9 to 1 op 10 to 1 tchd 12 to 1 and 8 to 1) 2
796^{9} NAGIDA [80] 4-9-2 (3*) J Weaver (15) *wtd wth, prog frm o'r one furlong out, styd on ins fnl furlong.* ....(12 to 1 tchd 14 to 1) 3
677^{5} JIGSAW BOY [75] 4-9-0 J Williams (22) *towards rear til styd on wl ins fnl furlong, nvr plcd to chal.* ....(7 to 1 fav tchd 8 to 1) 4
923^{9} HOW'S YER FATHER [79] 7-9-4 T Sprake (18) *wtd wth, prog 2 fs out, ran on one pace ins fnl furlong.* ....(25 to 1 op 20 to 1) 5
796^{6} OUR RITA [77] 4-9-2 R Cochrane (1) *hld up, kpt on frm o'r one furlong out, nvr nrr*.........(14 to 1 tchd 12 to 1) 6
CHILI HEIGHTS [83] 3-8-11 L Dettori (16) *rdn alng in mid-div, prog frm o'r one furlong out, styd on ins last.* ....(20 to 1) 7
923^{4} LOVE LEGEND [70] (v) 8-8-9 T Quinn (8) *trkd ldg grp, drvn alng hfwy, one pace appr 2 fs out.* ....(20 to 1 tchd 25 to 1) 8
659^{3} PADDY CHALK [83] 7-9-8 J Reid (17) *pressed ldrs, rdn and ev ch o'r one furlong out, sn one pace.* ....(8 to 1 op 10 to 1 tchd 12 to 1) 9
815* MARTINA [68] 5-8-4 (3*) D Harrison (7) *hld up beh ldrs, improved o'r 2 fs out, one pace appr last.* ....(20 to 1 op 16 to 1 tchd 25 to 1) 10
605^{3} CALEMAN [79] 4-9-4 Pat Eddery (13) *in tch, drvn alng to ld o'r one furlong out, sn hdd and btn.* ....(14 to 1 tchd 16 to 1) 11
796 FASCINATION WALTZ [72] 6-8-11 J Quinn (19) *nvr pace of ldrs*..................(12 to 1 op 10 to 1 tchd 14 to 1) 12
796^{4} YES [54] 5-7-0 (7*) Kim McDonnell (12) *pressed ldrs to hfwy*........................ (20 to 1 op 16 to 1) 13
737^{8} CONFRONTER [76] 4-9-1 A Munro (23) *nvr pace of ldrs.* ....(20 to 1 op 14 to 1) 14
659^{2} BODARI [80] 4-8-12 (7*) T G McLaughlin (2) *led o'r 4 fs, fdd.* ....(14 to 1 op 16 to 1) 15
691^{3} SIMPLY SOOTY [81] 3-8-6 (3*) B Doyle (11) *speed o'r 3 fs.* ....(12 to 1 op 14 to 1) 16
SEA-DEER [67] 4-8-6 N Adams (4) *al abt same pl*. (33 to 1) 17
986 GREEN DOLLAR [89] 10-9-9 (5*) Stephen Davies (3) *nvr on terms*.................(25 to 1 op 20 to 1 tchd 33 to 1) 18
700 PHARAOH'S DANCER [70] (bl) 6-8-9 W Newnes (10) *in tch, rdn o'r 2 fs out, btn whn hmpd wl over one furlong out.* .... (20 to 1 op 16 to 1) 19
986 RED ROSEIN [87] 7-9-7 (5*) K Rutter (6) *dwlt and lost many ls at strt, al beh*................ (33 to 1 op 25 to 1) 20
DARUSSALAM [72] 6-8-8 (3*) A Tucker (21) *nvr on terms.* .... (20 to 1 op 16 to 1) 21
Dist: Sht-hd, hd, 2l, hd, 1½l, hd, ¾l, ½l, ¾l, ½l. 1m 13.64s. a 1.94s (21 Ran).
SR: 61/50/58/45/48/40/34/29/40/ (Miss Sophie Oppenheimer), R Charlton

1067 London Gold Cup Rated Class B Handicap (0-100 3-y-o) £6,245 1½m 5yds......................... (4:00)

686* CIRCUS COLOURS [75] 8-11 Pat Eddery (8) *sn chasing ldr, led on bit 2 fs out, rdn out entering fnl furlong, eased cl hme*............... (2 to 1 fav op 6 to 4 tchd 9 to 4) 1
855* LEAGUE LEADER (Ire) [80] 9-2 Paul Eddery (2) *pressed ldrs, drvn alng 2 fs out, kpt on one pace ins last, no ch wth wnr*.............................(7 to 2 op 3 to 1) 2
584* MARROS MILL [83] 9-0 (5*) M Fenton (1) *led, drvn alng 3 fs out, hdd 2 out, sn one pace.* ....(6 to 1 op 5 to 1 tchd 13 to 2) 3
976^{4} WARM SPELL [71] 8-7 B Rouse (4) *wtd wth, improved o'r 2 fs out, btn appr last*................(10 to 1 op 8 to 1) 4
876^{4} BONAR BRIDGE (USA) [83] 9-5 J Reid (9) *patiently rdn, improved and effrt 2 fs out, one pace appr last.* ....(25 to 1 op 14 to 1 tchd 33 to 1) 5
842^{7} WARSPITE [78] 9-0 R Cochrane (6) *took keen hold in tch, effrt 2 fs out, sn btn.* (20 to 1 op 16 to 1 tchd 25 to 1) 6
826^{3} PENNINE LAD (Ire) [71] 8-4 (3*) D Harrison (7) *hld up in mid-div, rdn o'r 2 fs out, sn wknd*.... (25 to 1 tchd 33 to 1) 7
662^{5} HOOSIE [79] 9-1 L Dettori (5) *hld up, rdn o'r 2 fs out, brief effrt wl over one out, sn btn, eased ins last.* .... (9 to 1 op 8 to 1 tchd 10 to 1) 8
875* MAJOR YAASI (USA) [85] 9-7 B Raymond (3) *wtd wth, drvn alng 3 fs out, wknd 2 out*................ (6 to 1 op 5 to 1) 9
Dist: 1l, 1½l, hd, 2l, hd, 3½l, 1l, 5l. 2m 39.94s. a 10.34s (9 Ran).
(Exors Of The Late Sir Robin McAlpine), J L Dunlop

1068 Terry Driscoll Maiden Stakes Class D (3-y-o) £3,757 1¼m 6yds........(4:30)

825^{3} DARECLIFF (USA) 9-0 J Reid (20) *hld up beh ldrs, improved to ld entering fnl 2 fs, hdd entering final furlong, styd on ag'n to lead wl ins last.* ....(11 to 4 fav op 3 to 1 tchd 7 to 2) 1
GEORGE DILLINGHAM 9-0 N Adams (21) *wtd wth, prog frm 2 fs out, led entering fnl furlong, hdd wl ins last, not quicken*...........................(33 to 1 op 20 to 1) 2
CUTLASS (Ire) 8-9 B Procter (13) *pressed ldrs, led o'r 2 fs out, hdd entering fnl two furlongs, one pace.* ....(33 to 1 op 20 to 1) 3
BAMBURGH (USA) 9-0 B Raymond (11) *chsd ldrs, drvn alng and ev ch 2 fs out, sn btn.* ....(8 to 1 op 4 to 1 tchd 9 to 1) 4
827^{2} GRAND APPLAUSE (Ire) 9-0 S Whitworth (3) *hld up, rdn o'r 2 fs out, kpt on one pace ins last.* (8 to 1 tchd 10 to 1) 5
751 MOULTAZIM (USA) 9-0 A Munro (1) *trkd ldrs, drvn alng o'r 2 fs out, wknd appr last.* .... (10 to 1 op 7 to 1 tchd 12 to 1) 6
662^{7} SEA SIREN 8-9 W Newnes (4) *nvr far away, rdn appr 2 fs out, wknd approaching last*..... (8 to 1 tchd 10 to 1) 7
679 TEACHER (Ire) 8-7 (7*) J Tate (10) *hld up in mid-div, drvn and no prog frm 3 fs out*..........(33 to 1 op 20 to 1) 8
825 CALIBRATE 9-0 B Rouse (6) *pressed ldrs, rdn o'r 3 fs out, sn btn*..(33 to 1) 9
751 DARMSTADT (USA) 9-0 R Cochrane (8) *al abt same pl.* ....(14 to 1 tchd 16 to 1) 10
RIVIERE ACTOR (USA) 9-0 S Raymont (5) *nvr better than mid-div*............(20 to 1 op 10 to 1 tchd 25 to 1) 11
950^{6} ELEGANT HUSSAR 8-11 (3*) B Doyle (15) *nvr on terms.* ....(33 to 1 op 20 to 1) 12
BERING ISLAND (USA) 9-0 Pat Eddery (14) *nvr trbld ldrs.* .... (12 to 1 op 8 to 1 tchd 14 to 1) 13
759^{9} SIMPLY A HERO (Ire) 9-0 J Williams (17) *al beh*....(20 to 1) 14
880^{6} MONSIGNOR PAT (USA) 9-0 A McGlone (16) *hld up in tch, drvn alng 3 fs out, sn btn*.......(12 to 1 tchd 14 to 1) 15
SCORPIUS 9-0 Paul Eddery (2) *nvr trbld ldrs.* .... (20 to 1 op 14 to 1 tchd 25 to 1) 16
842^{9} KEDGE 9-0 M Perrett (12) *led, hdd appr 2 fs out, sn rdn and btn*...................................(33 to 1) 17
SPANISH SAHARA (Ire) 8-9 (5*) Stephen Davies (7) *nvr a threat*.......................... (20 to 1 op 14 to 1) 18
TARFSIDE (Ire) 9-0 L Dettori (18) *mid-div, effrt 4 fs out, sn eased, pld up appr 2 furlongs out, dismounted.* ....(16 to 1 op 20 to 1 tchd 14 to 1) pu
Dist: Nk, 5l, sht-hd, 1½l, 3½l, nk, 1l, sht-hd, ¾l, hd. 2m 8.04s. a 5.04s (19 Ran).
SR: 35/34/19/23/20/13/7/10/9/ (A D Latter), R Hannon

1069 Poulter 25th Anniversary Handicap Class C (0-90 3-y-o and up) £5,572 1m 7yds......................... (5:00)

676^{2} JADE VALE [73] 4-9-1 (3*) D Harrison (1) *handily plcd, drvn 2 fs out, styd on to ld ins last, kpt on wl.* ....(6 to 1 tchd 13 to 2) 1
PIQUANT [80] 6-9-11 B Raymond (10) *pressed ldrs, rdn appr 2 fs out, ev ch wl ins last, kpt on.* ....(16 to 1 op 12 to 1) 2
ALBEMINE (USA) [67] 4-8-12 Paul Eddery (3) *pressed ldr, led 2 fs out, hdd ins fnl furlong, ran on same pace.* ....(9 to 2 fav op 4 to 1 tchd 7 to 2) 3
676* WALKING THE PLANK [75] 4-9-6 R Cochrane (8) *hld up in mid-div, rdn alng o'r 2 fs out, improved over one furlong out, styd on*..................(7 to 1 op 10 to 1) 4
818* BUZZARDS BELLBUOY [75] 4-9-6 J Quinn (4) *nvr far away, rdn and ev ch 2 fs out, sn one pace.* .... (10 to 1 op 7 to 1) 5
719^{4} CHANDIGARH [53] 5-7-10^{1} (3*) A Tucker (11) *towards rear, drvn alng hfwy, styd on appr fnl furlong, nvr nrr.* ....(20 to 1 op 16 to 1) 6
737^{4} LITTLE ROUSILLON [67] 5-8-12 T Quinn (12) *led, hdd 2 fs out, wknd entering last.* .... (9 to 1 op 8 to 1 tchd 10 to 1) 7
663 WAVE HILL [72] 4-9-3 M Perrett (16) *nvr plcd to chal.* ....(12 to 1 tchd 14 to 1 and 16 to 1) 8
663 MOUGINS (Ire) [81] 4-9-12 J Williams (14) *dwlt, al beh.* ....(20 to 1 op 16 to 1) 9

756[5] VANBOROUGH LAD [63] 4-8-8 D Biggs (7) *wtd wth, some hdwy o'r one furlong out, sn btn.* ....(20 to 1 tchd 25 to 1) 10
690[8] BRANDONHURST [80] 3-8-7 (5*) Stephen Davies (13) *nvr on terms*....(12 to 1 op 10 to 1) 11
917[2] HOPEFUL BID (Ire) [69] 4-8-7 (7*) Mark Denaro (15) *pressed ldrs til wknd o'r 2 fs out.* ....(10 to 1 op 8 to 1 tchd 12 to 1) 12
CLAYBANK (USA) [83] 4-10-0 D Holland (9) *nvr a threat.* ....(25 to 1 op 16 to 1) 13
WILL SOON [66] 4-8-4 (7*) Antoinette Armes (6) *nvr dngrs.* ....(25 to 1 op 20 to 1) 14
497[6] LOUISVILLE BELLE (Ire) [66] 4-8-11 N Adams (17) *nvr dngrs*....(33 to 1 op 25 to 1) 15
824 MISS HAGGIS [81] 4-9-12 Pat Eddery (5) *nvr trbld ldrs.* ....(10 to 1 op 7 to 1 tchd 12 to 1) 16
Dist: Sht-hd, 1½l, 1½l, 2l, ¾l, sht-hd, nk, 2½l, nk, 3l. 1m 37.97s. a 2.17s (16 Ran).
SR: 53/59/41/44/38/14/27/31/32/ (Mrs S Bosher), J W Hills

PIMLICO (USA) (firm)
Saturday May 15th

1070 Preakness Stakes (Grade 1) (3-y-o) £266,887 1m 1f 110yds...............

779[2] PRAIRIE BAYOU (USA) 9-0 M Smith,........(22 to 10 fav) 1
CHEROKEE RUN (USA) 9-0 P Day,...........(94 to 10) 2
779 EL BAKAN (USA) 9-0 C Perret,.................(51 to 1) 3
779[4] PERSONAL HOPE (USA) 9-0 G Stevens,........(31 to 10) 4
779* SEA HERO (USA) 9-0 J D Bailey,...............(43 to 10) 5
WOODS OF WINDSOR (USA) 9-0 R Wilson,......(14 to 1) 6
779 ROCKAMUNDO (USA) 9-0 E Prado,............(97 to 10) 7
779[3] WILD GALE (USA) 9-0 S Sellers,...............(23 to 1) 8
HEGAR (USA) 9-0 J Ferrer,.......................(68 to 1) 9
KOLUCTOO JIMMY AL (USA) 9-0 C McCarron,...(18 to 1) 10
TOO WILD (USA) 9-0 H McCauley,..............(60 to 1) 0
779 UNION CITY (USA) 9-0 P Valenzuela,............(12 to 1) pu
Dist: ½l, 7l, nk, ¾l, 1 ¼l, 1l, ¾l, 1l, 6½l, 7½l. 1m 56.60s. (12 Ran).
(Loblolly Stable), T Bohannan

SOUTHWELL (A.W) (std)
Saturday May 15th

Going Correction: MINUS 0.10 sec. per fur. (races 1,6), PLUS 0.20 (2,3,4,5)

1071 Tulip Maiden Auction Stakes Class E (2-y-o) £2,976 5f...............(11:55)

768[3] THE FERNHILL FLYER (Ire) (v) 8-9 G Carter (3) *made all, rdn clr appr fnl furlong, ran on wl*......(5 to 1 op 3 to 1) 1
528 DUBALL REMY 8-9 S O'Gorman (1) *chsd ldg pair on outsd, rdn and swshd tail 2 fs out, kpt on ins last.* ....(12 to 1 op 6 to 1 tchd 14 to 1) 2
812[3] INDIAN CRYSTAL 8-9 Dean McKeown (2) *chsd ldr, rdn 2 fs out, unbl to quicken*..............(6 to 4 on op Evens) 3
KERAMIC 8-9 A Mackay (4) *missed break, wl beh till moderate late hdwy, nvr nrr*.......(20 to 1 op 8 to 1) 4
OVALWORLD 9-0 D Nicholls (5) *slwly away, outpcd.* ....(7 to 1 op 8 to 1 tchd 16 to 1) 5
MILLRIDGE (Ire) 8-9 W Woods (7) *chsd ldrs, sn rdn alng, wknd frm 2 out*...........(12 to 1 op 5 to 1) 6
MILLY'S PET 8-9 G Bardwell (6) *slwly away, al beh.* ....(16 to 1 op 10 to 1) 7
Dist: 3½l, 1½l, 5l, 1½l, 6l, 3l. 1m 0.90s. a 3.00s (7 Ran).
SR: 25/11/5/-/ (P J Evans), J Berry

1072 Begonia Selling Stakes Class G (3-y-o and up) £2,070 6f.............(12:25)

837 APPEALING TIMES (USA) 4-9-10 S Wood (2) *trkd ldr, led o'r 2 fs out, hdd briefly wl over one out, hld on gmely ins last*.............. (6 to 1 op 9 to 2 tchd 13 to 2) 1
887[4] MURRAY'S MAZDA (Ire) 4-9-10 G Carter (7) *midfield till gd hdwy frm o'r 2 fs out, chlgd fnl furlong, jst hld.* ....(5 to 2 op 2 to 1) 2
834 WALK THAT WALK 4-8-13[1] (7*) K Pattinson (5) *chsd ldrs, hdwy on ins wl o'r one furlong out, kpt on one pace.* ....(14 to 1 op 16 to 1 tchd 20 to 1) 3
SAMANTHAS JOY 3-7-11[1] (7*) S Sanders (10) *al prmnt, led briefly wl o'r one furlong out, sn hdd and btn.* ....(6 to 1 op 4 to 1) 4
837[3] SALLY'S SON 7-9-7 (3*) Emma O'Gorman (1) *led till hdd o'r 2 fs out, not much room and sn wknd.* ....(9 to 4 fav op 2 to 1 tchd 11 to 4) 5
424[8] NEVENTER (Fr) 4-9-5 V Smith (8) *slwly away, rdn alng to reco'r aftr 2 fs, no imprsn fnl two furlongs.* ....(14 to 1 op 12 to 1) 6
290 MAHZOOZ 4-9-5 M Wigham (6) *sn rdn alng, nvr able to chal*.............. (33 to 1 op 12 to 1) 7
970 RISKMEMAY (bl) 4-9-0 A Proud (4) *al towards rear.* ....(33 to 1 op 20 to 1) 8
615 NORDOORA (Ire) 4-9-0 F Norton (3) *wth ldrs till rdn, edgd lft and wknd o'r 2 fs out.* ....(20 to 1 op 16 to 1 tchd 25 to 1) 9
THRILL SEEKER (Ire) 4-8-7 (7*) S Mulvey (9) *slwly away, al beh*....(12 to 1 op 8 to 1) 10
Dist: Nk, 4l, 1l, sht-hd, nk, 6l, 1½l, 3l, ½l. 1m 18.90s. a 5.50s (10 Ran).
SR: 24/23/2/-/2/-/ (Miss N F Thesiger), D W Chapman

1073 Blackpool's Jonas Hotel And Mirabelle Communications Ltd Handicap Class E (0-70 3-y-o and up) £3,106 7f ....(12:55)

970[2] HIGHBORN (Ire) [52] 4-8-10 G Hind (9) *trkd ldr, led o'r 2 fs out, hld on grimly ins last.* ....(5 to 2 fav tchd 3 to 1 and 9 to 4) 1
902[5] SANDMOOR DENIM [54] 6-8-5 (7*) G Strange (5) *chsd ldrs, pushed up to chal frm o'r one furlong out, no extr cl hme*....(9 to 2 tchd 4 to 1) 2
970[6] LORD NASKRA (USA) [58] 4-8-13 (3*) Emma O'Gorman (6) *trkd ldrs, came wide to chal o'r 2 fs out, ran on one pace*....(12 to 1 op 8 to 1) 3
914 WELLSY LAD (USA) [48] (v) 6-8-6 S Wood (1) *led till hdd o'r 2 fs out, sn btn*....(14 to 1 op 10 to 1) 4
CHOIR PRACTICE [69] 6-9-13 C Rutter (7) *slwly into strd, beh till effrt o'r 2 fs out, sn one pace.* ....(8 to 1 tchd 12 to 1) 5
906[4] HOMILE [48] 5-7-13 (7*) S Sanders (4) *trkd ldg pair till wknd o'r 2 fs out*......(9 to 1 op 7 to 1 tchd 10 to 1) 6
893[9] ROCK SONG (Ire) [45] 4-8-3 F Norton (11) *beh early, hdwy 3 fs out, sn no further imprsn*......(25 to 1 op 16 to 1) 7
WALSHAM WITCH [60] 3-8-6 S Webster (3) *chsd ldrs till rdn and wknd frm wl o'r 2 fs out.* ....(20 to 1 op 14 to 1 tchd 25 to 1) 8
952* SYLVAN SABRE (Ire) [71] (v) 4-10-1 S Whitworth (10) *rcd wide in midfield, nvr able to chal.* ....(5 to 1 op 5 to 2 tchd 11 to 2) 9
971 QUINZII MARTIN [61] (v) 5-9-5 A Mackay (8) *tucked away, niggled alng o'r 3 fs out, sn wknd*...(12 to 1 op 8 to 1) 10
825 HILLSDOWN BOY (Ire) [56] (bl,e/s) 3-8-2 G Carter (2) *al beh.* ....(25 to 1 op 14 to 1) 11
Dist: Hd, 6l, ¾l, 1½l, 3l, 2l, 3l, sht-hd, 3l, sht-hd. 1m 30.90s. a 4.80s (11 Ran).
SR: 45/46/32/20/36/6/-/-/13/ (Yorkshire Racing Club Owners Group 1990), P S Felgate

1074 Camellia Claiming Stakes Class F (3-y-o) £2,243 1m................(1:25)

833[6] NELLIE'S GAMBLE 8-11 T Williams (10) *al hndy gng wl, led 2 fs out, clr fnl furlong, easily.* (15 to 8 fav op 5 to 2) 1
826 BACKSTABBER 8-7 G Hind (3) *led aftr 2 fs till hdd two furlongs out, not pace of wnr*.......(8 to 1 op 8 to 1) 2
MARCO CLAUDIO (Ire) 8-9 W Woods (5) *al prmnt, rdn alng wl o'r 2 fs out, sn one pace*........(33 to 1 op 10 to 1) 3
410[2] MISTER BLAKE (bl) 8-11 (3*) Emma O'Gorman (13) *chsd ldg bunch, rdn o'r 2 fs out, no imprsn*... (4 to 1 op 2 to 1) 4
725[8] GLOWING PATH (v) 8-7 S Whitworth (9) *hld up in midfield, rdn alng 3 fs, sn btn*...(11 to 2 tchd 7 to 1 and 9 to 2) 5
499 OLIVIA VAL 8-0 G Bardwell (2) *beh early, nvr nrr.* ....(33 to 1 op 16 to 1) 6
609[4] INNOCENT ABROAD (Den) 8-6[2] S Perks (4) *nvr able to chal*....(20 to 1 op 14 to 1) 7
764[6] RAGGERTY (Ire) (v) 8-10 G Carter (12) *midfield, shrtlvd effrt 3 fs out, sn btn*................(9 to 1 op 4 to 1) 8
970[8] IRISH ROOTS (Ire) (v) 8-8 F Norton (6) *led 2 fs, sn lost pl.* ....(12 to 1 op 8 to 1 tchd 14 to 1) 9
813 DIVINE RAIN 8-13 W Hood (11) *al towards rear.* ....(16 to 1 op 10 to 1 tchd 20 to 1) 10
903[5] CLAIRIFICATION (Ire) 8-13 (3*) S D Williams (1) *broke wl, sn lost pl and struggling*............(25 to 1 op 14 to 1) 11
928 KENTUCKY DREAMS 8-10 A Proud (7) *chsd ldrs to hfwy, sn rdn and wknd, tld off*.........(33 to 1 op 20 to 1) 12
394[4] NIGHTMARE LADY 7-12 D Biggs (8) *sn struggling, tld off.* ....(16 to 1 tchd 14 to 1) 13
Dist: 6l, 6l, nk, 6l, 10l, nk, 1½l, 1½l, ½l, ½l. 1m 45.60s. a 6.60s (13 Ran).
SR: 22/-/-/-/-/-/ (C R Galloway), A P Stringer

1075 Magnolia Handicap Class E (0-70 3-y-o and up) £3,054 1½m.......... (1:55)

618[7] SHUJAN (USA) [62] 4-10-0 G Carter (10) *made all, pld wl clr 3 fs out, unchlgd*........................(4 to 1 jt-fav op 5 to 1 tchd 7 to 1) 1
426[5] PHARLY DANCER [60] 4-9-12 S Webster (7) *midfield till gd hdwy o'r 3 fs out, wnt second over 2 out, no ch wth wnr*....(14 to 1 op 8 to 1) 2
448[2] BOROCAY [39] 5-8-5 E Johnson (11) *trkd ldr till rdn and unbl to quicken 3 fs out*............ (8 to 1 op 6 to 1) 3
931[8] SUGEMAR [60] 7-9-5 (7*) D McCabe (3) *trkd ldg pair, wkng whn hmpd 3 fs out, kpt on same pace.* (4 to 1 jt-fav tchd 9 to 2 and 7 to 1) 4
349 HEIR OF EXCITEMENT [32] 8-7-12 T Williams (8) *trkd ldr till no hdwy fnl 4 fs*....(7 to 1 op 4 to 1) 5
822[7] INTRICACY [56] 5-9-8 D Biggs (1) *outpcd and wl beh till some hdwy fnl 3 fs, not a dngr*......(10 to 1 op 7 to 1) 6
199[4] INDIAN TERRITORY [36] 4-7-9 (7*) C Hawksley (6) *midfield, rdn alng frm hfwy, sn no imprsn*... (12 to 1 op 8 to 1) 7

826[4] PONDERING [60] (e/s) 3-8-7 C Rutter (5) *slwly into strd, nvr nr to chal*..................... (11 to 2 op 3 to 1) 8
723[5] LA REINE ROUGE (Ire) [48] 5-9-0 F Norton (12) *trkd ldg bunch till rdn alng o'r 3 fs out, sn wknd.* ....(8 to 1 op 4 to 1) 9
975 FULL SIGHT (Ire) [50] 4-8-9 (7*) G Mitchell (2) *al rear div.* .... (14 to 1 op 10 to 1) 10
924 OLD STEINE [54] (bl) 5-9-6 D Nicholls (9) *handily plcd till wknd quickly frm o'r 3 fs out, tld off.* .... (12 to 1 op 8 to 1) 11
3 BUZZARDS CREST [27] 8-7-7 G Bardwell (4) *sn rdn alng in rear, tld off*..................................(20 to 1) 12
Dist: 8l, 6l, 8l, 4l, 2l, 3l, ½l, hd, 1½l, dist. 2m 42.00s. a 8.10s (12 Ran).
SR: 57/39/6/11/-/-/ (M J Polglase), R W Armstrong

1076 East Midland Electricity Handicap Class D (0-80 4-y-o and up) £3,260 5f ....(2:25)

916[6] PEERAGE PRINCE [69] (bl) 4-8-13 (7*) G Forster (2) *al prmnt, led jst ins fnl furlong, edgd lft and ran on.* ....(9 to 2 op 7 to 2 tchd 5 to 1) 1
379[5] MAID WELCOME [59] (bl) 6-8-3 (7*) Madeleine Smith (5) *led till hdd jst ins fnl furlong, kpt on.* ....(12 to 1 op 8 to 1 tchd 14 to 1) 2
800 SOBA GUEST (Ire) [77] 4-9-11 (3*) Emma O'Gorman (4) *al chasing ldrs, rdn o'r 2 fs out, kpt on, one pace.* ....(12 to 1 op 6 to 1 tchd 14 to 1) 3
NILU (Ire) [57] 5-8-1 (7*) S Sanders (1) *prmnt on outsd, rdn alng frm hfwy, not quicken appr fnl furlong.* .... (25 to 1 op 12 to 1) 4
815[2] SIR TASKER [65] (v) 5-9-2 F Norton (6) *slwly into strd, beh till hdwy 2 fs out, no extr fnl furlong.* ....(3 to 1 fav op 4 to 1 tchd 9 to 2) 5
887[2] STRIP CARTOON (Ire) [51] (bl) 5-8-0[5] (7*) G Strange (8) *prmnt till wknd o'r one furlong out.* (9 to 2 op 7 to 2) 6
948[2] SYLVAN BREEZE [60] (v) 5-8-11 S Whitworth (3) *sn rdn alng on outsd, beh fnl 2 and a half fs.* ....(9 to 2 op 7 to 2 tchd 11 to 2) 7
909 HINARI VIDEO [51] 8-8-2 T Williams (9) *speed to hfwy, sn btn*.................................. (10 to 1 op 6 to 1) 8
600[4] LET'S GO LOCHY [42] 7-7-7 G Bardwell (7) *struggling frm hfwy*.................................(10 to 1 op 4 to 1) 9
Dist: 1l, 2l, 1½l, nk, sht-hd, 1½l, ½l, 15l. 59.90s. a 2.00s (9 Ran).
SR: 56/42/52/26/33/18/21/10/-/ (David A Hobbs), Pat Mitchell

THIRSK (soft)
Saturday May 15th

Going Correction: PLUS 0.80 sec. per fur. (races 1,3,4), PLUS 0.15 (2,5,6,7)

1077 Elmire Maiden Fillies Stakes Class D (3-y-o) £3,435 1½m.............(2:15)

679[5] CROMARTY 8-11 W Ryan (8) *patiently rdn, improved to go hndy entering strt, led o'r 2 fs out, forged clr.* ....(9 to 4 jt-fav op 13 to 8) 1
MEANT TO BE 8-11 M Tebbutt (1) *trkd ldg trio, hrd at work last 2 fs, styd on same pace.* (12 to 1 op 25 to 1) 2
780[6] ROSE NOBLE (USA) 8-11 J Carroll (6) *dashed up to ld on outsd aftr 4 fs, hdd o'r 2 furlongs out, sn outpcd.* ....(8 to 1 tchd 7 to 1) 3
686[5] BLUSHING BARADA (USA) 8-11 J Fortune (7) *trkd ldg pair, struggling to hold pl whn ldrs quickened last 2 fs, fdd.* ....(12 to 1) 4
WAKT 8-11 W Carson (9) *struggling in midfield hfwy, nvr able to trble ldrs*.................. (8 to 1 tchd 7 to 1) 5
FOLLINGWORTH GIRL (Ire) 8-6 (5*) O Pears (10) *chsd alng to keep up hfwy, nvr a dngr*.......(50 to 1 op 25 to 1) 6
RESTRAINT 8-11 N Carlisle (2) *set modest pace 4 fs, struggling appr strt, sn lost tch*...... (20 to 1 tchd 25 to 1) 7
780[4] FAIR TO THE WIND (USA) 8-11 M Birch (4) *wth ldrs will wknd quickly entering strt, eased last 2 fs.* ..(9 to 4 jt-fav op 2 to 1 tchd 7 to 4) 8
HIGHLAND PRINCESS 8-11 L Charnock (3) *lost tch rpdly aftr 4 fs, virtually pld up in hme strt.* .... (33 to 1 op 20 to 1) 9
Dist: 15l, 5l, 2½l, 6l, 2l, 8l, 3l. 2m 45.60s. a 15.40s (9 Ran).
SR: 39/9/-/-/-/-/ (Sir David Wills), H R A Cecil

1078 Skipton Claiming Stakes Class F (2-y-o) £2,709 5f.................. (2:45)

680* DANCE OF THE SWANS (Ire) 8-6 Dean McKeown (5) *al gng best, shaken up to ld o'r one furlong out, readily.* ....(7 to 4 on op Evens) 1
395[5] CARAPELLE 7-11 (3*) S Maloney (2) *outpcd and drvn alng, improved frm off the pace appr fnl furlong, ran on wl.* .... (9 to 1 op 8 to 1 tchd 10 to 1) 2
812[8] STUDFORD GIRL 8-5 T Lucas (4) *led or dsptd ld, definite advantage hfwy, hdd o'r one out, kpt on same pace.* ....(16 to 1 op 12 to 1) 3
900[4] LUNAR RHAPSODY 8-2 L Charnock (1) *chsd alng to keep up, improved appr fnl furlong, nvr nrr.* .... (14 to 1 op 10 to 1) 4

708 SALTPETRE (Ire) 7-10 (7*) J Marshall (8) *led or dsptd ld to hfwy, veered badly lft o'r one furlong out, no extr.* ....(33 to 1) 5
949 KISS NO TELL (Ire) (bl) 7-3 (7*) D Wright (7) *broke smartly to show speed to hfwy, fdd appr fnl furlong.* .... (16 to 1 op 12 to 1) 6
900* SURPRISE BREEZE 8-4 A Culhane (3) *sn struggling to keep up, nvr a factor*................(4 to 1 op 5 to 2) 7
CONEY HILLS 8-2[3] (7*) G Parkin (6) *sn last and struggling, hng lft hfwy, nvr dngrs*........... (20 to 1 op 25 to 1) 8
Dist: 2½l, 1l, 1½l, 1l, ¾l, 3l, 1l. 1m 2.30s. a 5.10s (8 Ran).
SR: 5/-/-/-/-/ (S A B Dinsmore), P C Haslam

1079 Dibb Lupton Broomhead Cup Handicap Class C (0-95 3-y-o and up) £15,400 7f.................... (3:15)

675 TAUFAN BLU (Ire) [92] (bl) 4-9-9 (5*) O Pears (12) *trkd ldr, tacked o'r to ld stands side entering strt, drvn clr fnl furlong, eased*............... (14 to 1 op 12 to 1) 1
801* FOREVER DIAMONDS [81] 6-9-3 M Birch (6) *nvr far away, effrt and drvn alng o'r one furlong out, styd on not rch wnr*................. (7 to 4 fav op 5 to 2 tchd 3 to 1) 2
893* CEE-JAY-AY [66] 6-8-2[2] J Carroll (13) *steadied strt, improved to join issue 2 fs out, kpt on same pace fnl furlong*...........................(4 to 1 tchd 9 to 2) 3
1003[3] EURO FESTIVAL [90] 4-9-12 Dean McKeown (8) *settled to track ldrs, effrt and drvn alng 2 fs out, styd on same pace*.........(9 to 2 op 4 to 1 tchd 7 to 2 and 5 to 1) 4
801 GANT BLEU (Fr) [62] 6-7-12 Dale Gibson (15) *sluggish strt, improved to go hndy hfwy, rdn and not quicken appr fnl furlong*......................... (8 to 1 tchd 9 to 1) 5
796 DENSBEN [82] 9-9-4 K Fallon (2) *led early, styd hndy till wknd rpdly last 2 fs*................. (11 to 1 op 9 to 1) 6
962 YOUNG VALENTINE [57] 4-7-7 N Carlisle (11) *last and hld up, rcd alone far side in hme strt, nvr able to rch ldrs.* .... (33 to 1 op 25 to 1) 7
659[7] SO RHYTHMICAL [81] 9-8-12 (5*) Darren Moffatt (5) *sn led, set modest pace till hdd and pushed alng entering strt, fdd o'r one furlong out*...............(8 to 1 op 7 to 1) 8
POETS COVE [78] 5-9-0 A Clark (14) *trkd ldg bunch, struggling whn pace quickened o'r 2 fs out, nvr a threat.* ....(14 to 1) 9
Dist: 3½l, hd, ¾l, 4l, ½l, 3l, hd, 3½l. 1m 31.00s. a 8.20s (9 Ran).
SR: 75/53/37/59/19/37/3/26/12/ (Hambleton Lodge Equine Premix Ltd), B Beasley

1080 Easingwold Rating Related Maiden Stakes Class E (3-y-o) £3,106 1m (3:45)

602[8] SPECIAL DAWN (Ire) 9-0 W Ryan (10) *patiently rdn, improved frm off the pace 2 fs out, styd on grimly to ld nr finish*..............(3 to 1 tchd 5 to 2 and 7 to 2) 1
719[6] STORM VENTURE (Ire) 9-0 M Tebbutt (8) *al hndy, led and kicked for hme o'r 2 fs out, ct cl home.* ....(8 to 1 op 7 to 1) 2
MUTAKALLAM (USA) 9-0 N Carlisle (2) *wth ldr, came o'r to race stands side with one other entering strt, not quicken appr fnl furlong*..........(13 to 2 op 11 to 2) 3
752[7] ROCK THE BOAT 8-2 (7*) D Gibbs (6) *al hndy, swtchd to race stands side in hme strt, kpt on same pace appr fnl furlong*................................ (13 to 2 op 11 to 2) 4
907[2] PANTHER (Ire) 8-11 (3*) N Kennedy (3) *wth ldrs, hrd at work 2 fs out, fdd*.................. (6 to 1 op 9 to 2) 5
733[3] GENSERIC (Fr) 9-0 W Carson (1) *sn led, hdd o'r 2 fs out, wknd quickly*....... (5 to 2 fav op 3 to 1 tchd 7 to 2) 6
BOLLIN DUNCAN 9-0 M Birch (7) *led early, styd hndy till fdd und pres 2 fs out*............. (11 to 1 op 10 to 1) 7
304[7] STYLISH ROSE (Ire) 8-9 J Lowe (9) *sluggish strt, al trailing*..(20 to 1) 8
Dist: ¾l, 3l, 4l, 2½l, 1½l, 4l, 3½l. 1m 46.10s. a 10.20s (8 Ran).
SR: 43/41/32/15/12/7/-/-/ (Windflower Overseas Holdings Inc), J L Dunlop

1081 Dick Peacock Sprint Handicap Class D (0-75 3-y-o and up) £4,110 6f.... (4:15)

909[3] SARTIGILA [59] 4-9-3 Dean McKeown (7) *trkd ldg bunch, swtchd outsd to improve appr fnl furlong, kpt on to ld last fifty yards*.................. (8 to 1 tchd 10 to 1) 1
887* SOBERING THOUGHTS [45] 7-8-3 J Lowe (17) *tried to make all, hdd appr fnl furlong, rallied.* ....(4 to 1 tchd 9 to 2) 2
796 LANGUEDOC [64] 6-9-8 L Charnock (12) *al frnt rnk, nosed ahead appr fnl furlong, hdd and no extr last fifty yards*.................... (10 to 1 op 8 to 1) 3
814[4] FIRST GOLD [64] (bl) 4-9-8 M Birch (14) *al tracking ldrs, effrt and drvn alng o'r one furlong out, one pace.* ....(4 to 1 op 9 to 2 tchd 7 to 2 and 5 to 1) 4
962* BALLAD DANCER [59] 8-8-12 (5*,7ex) Darren Moffatt (16) *sluggish strt, steady hdwy frm off the pace last 2 fs, ran on*.........................(7 to 2 fav op 9 to 2 tchd 5 to 1) 5
700 CRAIGIE BOY [65] 3-8-12 Alex Greaves (13) *trkd ldg bunch, bustled alng o'r one furlong out, kpt on.* .... (25 to 1 op 20 to 1) 6
NORDAN RAIDER [62] 5-9-6 N Connorton (2) *took keen hold, improved into midfield hfwy, not rch ldrs.* ....(11 to 1 op 10 to 1 tchd 12 to 1) 7

796[5] FIGHTER SQUADRON [61] (bl) 4-9-2 (3*) S D Williams (4) *sn drvn alng to keep up, styd on fnl furlong, nvr nrr.* ....(14 to 1 op 12 to 1) 8
814[9] COOLABA PRINCE (Ire) [66] 4-9-10 W Carson (5) *settled off the pace, shaken up and steady hdwy 2 fs out, nvr plcd to chal*............(8 to 1 op 6 to 1) 9
460[6] DAYTONA BEACH (Ire) [68] 3-9-1 S Perks (3) *chsd alng to keep up, nvr a serious threat.* ....(16 to 1 op 14 to 1 tchd 20 to 1) 10
FLASHY'S SON [66] 5-9-10 M Tebbutt (8) *broke wl to show speed wth ldg quartet for o'r 3 fs, fdd.* ....(20 to 1 op 16 to 1) 11
866[9] BEST EFFORT [56] 7-9-0 K Fallon (6) *chsd alng in midfield, nvr trbld ldrs*............(20 to 1 op 16 to 1) 12
909[5] MASTER POKEY [59] 9-9-3 T Lucas (1) *sluggish strt, rcd wide, nvr dngrs*............(14 to 1 tchd 16 to 1) 13
Dist: ¾l, 1l, 2l, 2l, 2½l, ½l, 1l, 1½l, 5l, hd. 1m 13.80s. a 3.80s (13 Ran).
SR: 45/28/43/35/22/7/13/8/7/ (John Lishman), M D Hammond

1082 EBF Carlton Miniott Maiden Fillies Stakes Class D (2-y-o) £3,699 5f (4:45)

708[2] KANGRA VALLEY 8-11 Dean McKeown (15) *broke fst frm gd draw, made all, ran on wl fnl furlong.* ....(5 to 1 fav op 6 to 1 tchd 9 to 2) 1
900[3] BESCABY GIRL 8-11 L Charnock (11) *pressed wnr thrght, ev ch fnl furlong, one pace*............(6 to 1 op 9 to 2) 2
680[8] HOTCROFT 8-11 A Culhane (17) *al hndy, drvn alng o'r one furlong out, not quicken.* ....(13 to 2 op 10 to 1 tchd 6 to 1) 3
FAIR SWOP (Ire) 8-11 M Birch (10) *chsd ldg trio, effrt and drvn alng last 2 fs, one pace*............(10 to 1 op 6 to 1) 4
812[6] FUSSY SIOUX 8-11 T Lucas (13) *al tracking ldrs, swtchd outsd and effrt o'r one furlong out, not quicken.* ....(10 to 1 tchd 9 to 1 and 8 to 1) 5
KAYDARAJ 8-8 (3*) S Maloney (8) *chsd ldg bunch, flt out hfwy, no imprsn*............(14 to 1 op 12 to 1) 6
LUCKY LIZZY 8-11 M Wigham (6) *chsd ldrs, hrd at work hfwy, nvr dngrs*............(14 to 1 op 8 to 1) 7
LADY RISKY 8-4 (7*) D Gibbs (2) *sn outpcd and drvn alng, nvr a factor*............(7 to 1 op 6 to 1 tchd 5 to 1) 8
TREAD THE BOARDS 8-11 W Ryan (14) *al struggling to go pace, nvr dngrs*............(7 to 1 op 8 to 1) 9
GREY TOPPA 8-11 K Fallon (16) *slow to break, nvr a threat*............(10 to 1 op 14 to 1 tchd 9 to 1) 10
SHARP SUMMIT (Ire) 8-11 S Wood (5) *rcd wide, struggling thrght*............(14 to 1 op 12 to 1) 11
THREE OF HEARTS 8-4 (7*) M Humphries (3) *crrd rght strt, al struggling*............(25 to 1 op 20 to 1) 12
933[4] TILQUHILLIE ROSE 8-4 (7*) C Munday (1) *swrvd sharply rght leaving stalls, al beh*............(14 to 1) 13
Dist: 2l, 2l, nk, 4l, 2½l. 1m 2.50s. a 5.30s (13 Ran).
SR: 6/-/-/-/-/-/ (Mrs R T Watson), J Wharton

1083 'Bet With The Tote' Handicap Class C (0-95 3-y-o) £5,117 5f............(5:15)

829[2] PLUM FIRST [65] (bl) 7-11 (3*) S Maloney (1) *broke wl frm outsd draw to ld stands side, made all, edgd lft o'r one out, ran on*............(13 to 2 op 6 to 1 tchd 7 to 1) 1
716 FIRST OPTION [70] 8-5 M Birch (5) *settled to track ldrs, shaken up to improve o'r one furlong out, ran on* ....(9 to 2 op 4 to 1) 2
858[4] MISTERTOPOGIGO (Ire) [86] 9-2 (5*) O Pears (4) *patiently rdn, effrt and shaken up o'r one furlong out, ran on same pace*............(9 to 2 op 5 to 1 tchd 4 to 1) 3
802 BENZOE (Ire) [84] 9-5 T Lucas (7) *trkd ldg pair, effrt and drvn alng o'r one furlong out, not quicken.* ....(6 to 1 tchd 13 to 2) 4
829* DAILYSPORTDUTCH [74] 8-9 N Carlisle (3) *chsd wnr, hrd at work o'r one furlong out, fdd*............(3 to 1 jt-fav op 11 to 4) 5
691* MAGIC ORB [75] 8-10 A Mackay (6) *reluctant to enter stalls, sluggish strt, nvr a threat*............(3 to 1 jt-fav op 5 to 2) 6
Dist: 2½l, ¾l, 2½l, ¾l, 3½l. 1m 0.30s. a 3.10s (6 Ran).
SR: 39/34/47/35/22/9/ (Mrs Dyanne Benjamin), N Bycroft

BADEN-BADEN (GER) (soft)
Sunday May 16th

1084 Badener Meile (Group 3) (3-y-o and up) £30,612 1m............(3:25)

293[3] KARINGA BAY 6-9-7 B Rouse, *3rd strt, led 2 fs out, hng lft cl hme, cmftbly*............(69 to 10) 1
406[4] LE JARDIN (Ger) 5-9-1 M Rimmer, *mid-div, ran on fnl 2 fs, no imprsn on wnr*............(11 to 1) 2
660[5] ENHARMONIC (USA) 6-9-5 L Dettori, *6th strt, hdwy one and a half fs out, one pace ins last*............(7 to 2 fav) 3
AUTOCRACY (Ire) 4-9-1 K Woodburn, *hdwy fnl 2 fs, kpt on*............(30 to 1) 4
BANNIER (Ger) 6-9-5 D Wildman, *hld up in rear, hdwy fnl 2 fs, nrst finish*............(23 to 1) 5
MUTARJJAM (USA) 5-9-1 Meike Diedrichsen, *rear to strt, hdwy fnl 2 fs, nvr nrr*............(34 to 1) 6
RENOMEE (Ger) 5-9-1 G Bocskai, *nvr nr to chal.* (37 to 1) 7
THYER (USA) 4-9-1 A Boschert, *rcd in 4th to strt, ev ch 2 fs out, sn wknd*............(5 to 1) 8
NOTRE COPAIN (Ger) 6-9-1 A Best, *nvr nr to chal.* ....(16 to 1) 9
YOUNG MOON 7-9-7 J McLaughlin, *led for 2 fs, led 3 out till two out, sn wknd*............(20 to 1) 0
953[4] DARBONNE (USA) 3-8-1 K Darley, *6th strt, sn btn.* ....(42 to 10) 0
KONIGSLOWE 4-9-1 L Mader, *prmnt, 5th strt, wknd 2 fs out*............(11 to 1) 0
REZON (Su) 5-9-12 A Zakharov, *no show*............(28 to 1) 0
ALPHA FLASH (Ger) 5-9-1 A Helfenbein, *in tch 6 fs.* ....(83 to 10) 0
Dist: 2l, 3½l, ½l, nk, 1 ¼l, nk. 1m 38.30s. (14 Ran).
(K Higson), G L Moore

CAPANNELLE (ITY) (good to soft)
Sunday May 16th

1085 Premio Presidente della Repubblica (Group 1) (4-y-o and up) £57,151 1¼m............(3:30)

689[2] GREAT PALM (USA) 4-9-2 A Munro (8) *led aftr one furlong, quickened 2 out, unchlgd*............ 1
4682a[3] GUADO D'ANNIBALE (Ire) 4-9-2 F Jovine (2) *hdwy 5 fs out, 3rd strt, styd on fnl 2 furlongs, no imprsn*............ 2
689[6] MASAD (Ire) 4-9-2 R Cochrane (7) *trkd wnr till wknd fnl furlong*............ 3
4727a[3] BIG TOBIN (Ity) 4-9-2 O Fancera (5) *some prog fnl 2 fs, nvr able to chal*............ 4
689[3] BOLOARDO 4-9-2 W Carson (3) *5th strt, btn 2 fs out*..... 5
695[5] APIS (Ger) 4-9-2 O Schick (8) *al rear*............ 6
LABUAN CROOM (Ire) 4-9-2 A Luongo (6) *al rear*............ 7
4682a[5] GREEN SENOR (USA) 5-9-2 B Jovine (4) *led for one furlong, 4th strt, sn wknd*............ 8
Dist: 2l, 3½l, 3l, 2l, 7l, 2½l, 8l. 2m 2.40s. (8 Ran).
(Fahd Salman), P F I Cole

LONGCHAMP (FR) (good)
Sunday May 16th

1086 Dubai Poule d'Essai des Pouliches (Group 1) (3-y-o) £119,474 1m...(3:00)

484[3] MADELEINE'S DREAM (USA) 9-2 C Asmussen (5) *5th strt, rdn 2 fs out, quickened one out, led fnl strds.* (49 to 10) 1
638* SKI PARADISE (USA) 9-2 D Boeuf (4) *6th strt, rdn 2 fs out, led jst und one out, ct fnl strds*............(92 to 10) 2
697[2] GOLD SPLASH (USA) 9-2 O Doleuze (2) *3rd strt, led 2 fs out, hdd ins last, kpt on*............(37 to 10) 3
697* BAYA (USA) 9-2 T Jarnet (1) *slwly away, 4th strt, effrt 2 fs out, quickened one and a half out, kpt on.* (2 to 1 on) 4
NIDD (USA) 9-2 Pat Eddery (7) *last strt, some late prog, nvr nrr*............(15 to 2) 5
TENGA (USA) 9-2 E Saint-Martin (3) *led till wknd 2 fs out.* ....(49 to 10) 6
694[2] FIRM FRIEND (Ire) 9-2 Jacqueline Freda (6) *nvr nrr.* ....(27 to 1) 7
697[4] KIRUNA (USA) 9-2 O Peslier (8) *second strt, sn rdn and wknd*............(2 to 1 on) 8
Dist: Sht-hd, ¾l, sht-hd, 8l, 3l, sht-nk, 8l. 1m 36.40s. a 0.40s (8 Ran).
SR: 72/71/69/68/44/35/34/10/ (Allen E Paulson), F Boutin

1087 Prix Lupin (Group 1) (3-y-o) £59,205 1 ¼m 110yds............(3:35)

811* HERNANDO (Fr) 9-2 C Asmussen (3) *3rd strt, rdn into second 2 fs out, chlgd one and a half out, led ins last.* ....(32 to 10) 1
843* ARMIGER 9-2 Pat Eddery (1) *led till one and a half fs out, hrd rdn and no extr ins fnl furlong*............(2 to 1 on) 2
811[5] DERNIER EMPEREUR (USA) 9-2 T Jarnet (2) *second strt, rdn 2 fs out, one pace*............(9 to 2) 3
867[2] MINYDOUN (Ire) 9-2 F Head (5) *pld hrd, 4th strt, rdn 2 fs out, kpt on one pace*............(10 to 1) 4
536* RANGER (Fr) 9-2 G Guignard (4) *al last*............(15 to 2) 5
Dist: Nk, 2½l, nose, 2l. 2m 10.30s. a 1.50s (5 Ran).
SR: 66/65/60/59/55/ (S S Niarchos), F Boutin

1088 Prix de la Pepiniere (Listed) (4-y-o and up) £14,337 1¼m............(4:40)

693* DIESE (USA) 4-9-2 Pat Eddery,............ 1
4694a* EGYPTOWN (Fr) 4-9-2 O Doleuze,............ 2
629[2] BALLINAMALLARD (USA) 4-9-2 O Peslier,............ 3
4711a* HALESIA (USA) 4-9-2 F Head,............ 4
Dist: 2l, sht-nk, 3l, 1½l, ¾l. 2m 4.30s. a 2.20s (6 Ran).
SR: 60/56/55/49/ (K Abdulla), A Fabre

SAN SIRO (ITY) (good)
Sunday May 16th

1089 Premio Sirmione (Listed) (4-y-o and up) £20,173 1m................(3:30)

INNER CITY (Ire) 4-8-10 M Roberts, ... 1
692[4] GOLDEN MINTAGE (USA) 5-8-8 L Sorrentino, ... 2
593[4] NIGHT MANOEUVRES 4-8-8 S Landi, ... 3
DOMINATUS 7-8-8 M Esposito, ... 4
Dist: 2½l, 2l, 1½l, ¾l, 1l, 1½l. 1m 39.10s. (7 Ran).
(Sheikh Mohammed), L M Cumani

BATH (good)
Monday May 17th

Going Correction: MINUS 0.20 sec. per fur. (races 1,3,4,5,8), MINUS 0.50 (2,6,7)

1090 Timeform Day At Bath Median Auction Maiden Stakes Class F (3-y-o) £2,665 1m 5yds......................(2:15)

482 DANNY BOY 9-0 Pat Eddery (10) *nvr far away, hdwy hfwy, led one and a half fs out, drvn out*. ...(9 to 4 jt-fav tchd 5 to 2 and 2 to 1) 1
827[4] THE EXECUTOR 9-0 T Quinn (9) *made most till hdd one and a half fs out, kpt on one pace*. .... (9 to 2 tchd 5 to 1 and 4 to 1) 2
TWO LUMPS 9-0 R Cochrane (5) *mid-div, hdwy 3 fs out, one pace ins fnl 2*.................(12 to 1 op 8 to 1) 3
732[4] MIGAVON 8-9 Paul Eddery (3) *chsd ldrs, one pace fnl 2 fs*. ....(8 to 1 tchd 7 to 1) 4
872 MASTER BEVELED 9-0 N Adams (1) *slwly away, sn chsd ldrs, no hdwy fnl 2 fs*.............(50 to 1 op 20 to 1) 5
483 BAULKING TOWERS 9-0 M Perrett (2) *dsptd ld till rdn 3 fs out, sn btn*..................(50 to 1 op 33 to 1) 6
872 BOLTROSE 9-0 J Williams (4) *nvr rchd ldrs*. .... (33 to 1 op 12 to 1) 7
821[6] ALTA VICTORIA (Ire) 8-9 S Raymont (7) *settled in mid-div, nvr got into race*...(9 to 4 jt-fav op 5 to 2 tchd 2 to 1) 8
TREBLE LASS 8-9 A Munro (8) *in tch to hfwy*. .... (33 to 1 op 16 to 1) 9
MORAN BRIG 9-0 S O'Gorman (6) *al beh*. .... (14 to 1 op 6 to 1) 10
PRINCESS SHAWNEE 8-6 (3*) A Tucker (13) *al beh*. ....(33 to 1 op 20 to 1 tchd 66 to 1) 11
813 DICKINS 9-0 K Darley (12) *in tch to hfwy, beh aftr*. ....(25 to 1 op 12 to 1 tchd 33 to 1) 12
STRATTON FLYER 8-9 T Lang (11) *chsd ldrs till wknd quickly 3 fs out, tld off*..........(50 to 1 op 33 to 1) 13
Dist: 2½l, 5l, 2½l, 1l, 5l, hd, ¾l, ¾l, 5l, nk. 1m 40.90s. a 1.90s (13 Ran).
SR: 48/40/25/12/14/-/ (Ivan Twigden), R Hannon

1091 EBF Timeform Card Maiden Stakes Class D (2-y-o) £3,699 5f 11yds..(2:45)

DESERT LORE 9-0 L Piggott (13) *chsd ldrs, rdn to ld appr fnl furlong, all out*................ (3 to 1 tchd 4 to 1) 1
JACOB BOGDANI 9-0 T Quinn (2) *trkd ldr, led hfwy, hdd appr fnl furlong, rallied and ran on*. .... (10 to 1 op 7 to 1) 2
673 SUN CHIEF (Ire) 9-0 D Holland (17) *mid-div, hdwy 2 fs out, ran on wl fnl furlong*.............(14 to 1 op 10 to 1) 3
715[5] COLNE VALLEY 8-9 R Hills (12) *al prmnt, no extr ins fnl furlong*.........................(16 to 1 op 20 to 1) 4
ALPINE SKIER (Ire) 9-0 K Darley (11) *mid-div, styd on ins fnl 2 fs*..........................(16 to 1 op 7 to 1) 5
673 NORTHERN STARLIGHT 9-0 N Adams (7) *chsd ldrs, one pace appr fnl furlong*............ (25 to 1 op 14 to 1) 6
793[5] BLUE BOMBER 9-0 Pat Eddery (1) *led to hfwy, rdn and wknd wl o'r one furlong out*. ....(11 to 10 fav op 6 to 4 tchd Evens) 7
680 TITANIA'S DANCE (Ire) 8-9 M Hills (3) *wth ldrs, wkng whn not much room ins fnl furlong*......(14 to 1 op 7 to 1) 8
JULIA TONGA 8-9 J Williams (9) *nvr on terms*.... (33 to 1) 9
BANDAR PERAK 9-0 C Rutter (10) *slwly away, nvr on terms*...............(25 to 1 op 20 to 1 tchd 66 to 1) 10
ANOTHERONE TO NOTE 9-0 B Rouse (14) *slwly away, came o'r to race alone stands side, nvr dngrs*. .... (50 to 1 op 33 to 1) 11
MONSIEUR PETONG 9-0 Paul Eddery (5) *speed to hfwy*. .... (14 to 1 op 7 to 1) 12
913 BITE THE BULLET 9-0 J Quinn (6) *al beh*. .... (33 to 1 op 20 to 1) 13
839 REIGNING ROYAL 8-2 (7*) S Drowne (8) *slwly away, al beh*..(33 to 1) 14
SHE'S SWEET 8-9 W Newnes (16) *slwly away, al outpcd*. .... (50 to 1 op 33 to 1) 15
SILVER BRIEF 9-0 G Bardwell (15) *slwly away, al struggling in rear*...................(50 to 1 op 33 to 1) 16
Dist: Nk, 2½l, 1½l, 1½l, nk, 1½l, 2l, ½l, 2l, 2l. 1m 2.80s. a 2.30s (16 Ran).
SR: 4/3/-/-/-/-/ (The Queen), Lord Huntingdon

1092 Timeform Silver Tankard Maiden Stakes Class D (Div I) (3-y-o and up) £3,523 1¼m 46yds............ (3:15)

880[2] CAPTAIN'S GUEST (Ire) 3-8-11 R Hills (13) *mid-div, hdwy o'r 2 fs out, led jst ins last, ran on*. ....(100 to 30 jt-fav op 4 to 1 tchd 11 to 4) 1
BLACK DRAGON (Ire) 3-8-11 M Roberts (9) *mid-div, briefly lost pos on bend hfwy, rdn to ld 2 fs out, hdd jst ins last, btn whn eased cl hme*...............(9 to 2 op 2 to 1) 2
346[3] RUNAWAY PETE (USA) 3-8-11 T Quinn (8) *chsd ldrs, kpt on one pace fnl 2 fs*.......................(6 to 1 op 5 to 1) 3
825[8] PREROGATIVE 3-8-11 L Dettori (1) *trkd ldrs, ev ch 2 fs out, wknd appr last*. ....(100 to 30 jt-fav op 3 to 1 tchd 7 to 2) 4
BEAUCHAMP HERO 3-8-11 A McGlone (5) *sn chsd ldr, led o'r 3 fs out, hdd 2 out, soon btn*. ....(8 to 1 op 7 to 1 tchd 10 to 1) 5
COLWAY PRINCE (Ire) 5-9-12 R Cochrane (12) *al abt same pl, no hdwy fnl 2 fs*.............. (50 to 1 op 25 to 1) 6
925[6] CHAPEL OF BARRAS (Ire) 4-9-12 J Reid (3) *mid-div, no hdwy fnl 3 fs*..........................(33 to 1 op 14 to 1) 7
617[4] FLAKEY DOVE 7-9-7 J Williams (7) *hld up, hdwy hfwy, not pace to chal*......(10 to 1 op 7 to 1 tchd 12 to 1) 8
679[9] BAYRAK (USA) 3-8-11 W Carson (10) *nvr on terms*. ....(9 to 1 op 6 to 1 tchd 10 to 1) 9
951[8] MISS MICHELLE 3-8-3 (3*) D Harrison (11) *slwly away, nvr on terms*.........................(50 to 1 op 25 to 1) 10
BIJOU FIRE (NZ) 5-9-7 M Hills (15) *chsd ldrs till wknd o'r 3 fs out*......................(25 to 1 op 20 to 1 tchd 33 to 1) 11
826 THE GORROCK (bl) 4-9-12 M Perrett (14) *led till hdd o'r 3 fs out, wknd quickly*............... (100 to 1 op 20 to 1) 12
UNIFICATION (Ire) 4-9-7 R Perham (4) *al beh*. .... (50 to 1 op 20 to 1 tchd 66 to 1) 13
ARCTIC LINE 5-9-12 N Adams (2) *al beh, rdn o'r 3 fs out, sn tld off*.........................(50 to 1 op 25 to 1) 14
WHATONE BELL 3-8-11 B Rouse (6) *al beh, tld off*. .... (50 to 1 op 20 to 1) 15
Dist: 2½l, 3½l, nk, 3l, 10l, 1½l, 1l, hd, 1½l, 6l. 2m 9.90s. a 3.50s (15 Ran).
SR: 41/36/29/28/22/17/14/7/-/ (K J Buchanan), G Harwood

1093 Timeform Silver Tankard Maiden Stakes Class D (Div II) (3-y-o and up) £3,494 1¼m 46yds............ (3:45)

842[2] BARON FERDINAND 3-8-11 R Cochrane (1) *hld up, smooth hdwy o'r 3 fs out, led appr last, pushed out*. .... (5 to 2 on tchd 2 to 1 on) 1
663 FIELDRIDGE 4-9-12 J Reid (10) *led till hdd appr fnl furlong, kpt on wl*..... (10 to 1 op 14 to 1 tchd 20 to 1) 2
LEEWA (Ire) 3-8-11 M Roberts (9) *mid-div, hdwy 4 fs out, rdn o'r 2 out, kpt on one pace*..........(8 to 1 op 9 to 2) 3
538 RED WHIRLWIND 3-8-11 D Holland (6) *trkd ldrs, wnt second 4 fs out, ev ch till wknd entering fnl furlong*. ....(20 to 1 op 12 to 1) 4
SPICE BOX (USA) 3-8-11 L Dettori (4) *hld up, hdwy o'r 2 fs out, one pace ins last*...............(10 to 1 op 6 to 1) 5
CLASS ATTRACTION (USA) 4-9-7 M Perrett (8) *hld up in tch, rdn 2 fs out, no further hdwy*. (33 to 1 op 20 to 1) 6
876[8] MOSHAAJIR (USA) 3-8-11 B Raymond (14) *hld up, nvr nr to chal*...........................(33 to 1 op 14 to 1) 7
4763a[7] GESNERA 5-9-7 J Williams (15) *beh, some hdwy 4 fs out, nvr dngrs*..........................(66 to 1 op 33 to 1) 8
JONSALAN 3-8-11 W Newnes (5) *slwly away, nvr nr to chal*.................................. (25 to 1 op 14 to 1) 9
DIG IN THE RIBS (Ire) 3-8-11 K Darley (12) *al beh*. ....(33 to 1 op 14 to 1) 10
TAKE A FLYER (Ire) 3-8-4 (7*) S Drowne (13) *al beh*. ....(50 to 1 op 25 to 1) 11
ROLLING WATERS 3-8-11 E Johnson (7) *prmnt to hfwy, sn beh*..................................(50 to 1 op 33 to 1) 12
646[6] ZAAHEYAH (USA) 3-8-6 Paul Eddery (3) *al beh*. ....(16 to 1 op 14 to 1) 13
SANDRO (bl) 4-9-12 A Munro (11) *chsd ldrs till wknd o'r 3 fs out*.......................(25 to 1 op 10 to 1) 14
672 RONEO (USA) 5-9-12 R Perham (2) *chsd ldrs till wknd quickly o'r 3 fs out*............... (66 to 1 op 50 to 1) 15
Dist: 2l, 2½l, hd, sht-hd, 8l, 5l, 3l, ½l, 1l, nk. 2m 10.80s. a 4.40s (15 Ran).
SR: 32/43/23/22/21/15/ (Exors Of The Late Mrs J de Rothschild), R Charlton

1094 Timeform Perspective & Ratings Fillies Handicap Class D (0-80 3-y-o and up) £3,260 1m 5f 22yds......... (4:15)

ELAINE TULLY (Ire) [73] 5-9-7 J Reid (2) *led 1st furlong, trkd ldr, led wl o'r one furlong out, rdn out*. ....(11 to 2 op 5 to 1) 1
879[8] ATLANTIC WAY [48] 5-7-10 J Quinn (7) *hld up, rdn and gd hdwy o'r 2 fs out, ev ch entering last, ran on und pres*. ....(7 to 1 op 6 to 1 tchd 15 to 2) 2
840[2] ATHAR (Ire) [62] 4-8-10 A Munro (6) *hld up in mid-div, hdwy o'r 2 fs out, ev ch appr last, kpt on one pace*. .... (5 to 1 op 4 to 1 tchd 11 to 2) 3
831[2] TRUBEN (USA) [77] 4-9-11 L Dettori (8) *hld up, rdn o'r 2 fs out, outpcd appr last*...... (3 to 1 fav tchd 100 to 30) 4
478[7] SPECTACULAR DAWN [78] 4-9-12 W Carson (3) *led aftr one furlong, hdd wl o'r one out, wknd ins*. ....(7 to 2 tchd 4 to 1) 5
879[3] ROCQUAINE BAY [45] 6-7-7 N Adams (4) *al towards rear*. .... (13 to 2 op 5 to 1 tchd 7 to 1) 6

925[5] JADIDH [55] 5-8-3 G Bardwell (9) *prmnt, rdn o'r 3 fs out, sn btn*..................(20 to 1 op 16 to 1 tchd 25 to 1) 7
RUBY DAVIES [45] 7-7-7 N Carlisle (5) *prmnt till wknd o'r 3 fs out*..........................(66 to 1 op 50 to 1) 8
4671a[4] CHILD STAR (Fr) [53] 4-8-1 S Dawson (1) *al last, nvr got into race*..........................(14 to 1 op 12 to 1) 9
Dist: ½l, nk, 4l, nk, ¾l, 1½l, 8l, 6l. 2m 52.50s. a 4.20s (9 Ran).
SR: 39/13/26/33/33/-/5/-/-/ (F J Sainsbury), M J Heaton-Ellis

1095 Jock Johnstone Timeform Limited Stakes Class F (0-65 3-y-o) £2,581 5f 11yds........................(4:45)

927* HALLORINA 8-6 G Bardwell (6) *wl in rear till gd hdwy well o'r one furlong out, str run to ld well ins last.* ....(2 to 1 fav tchd 5 to 2) 1
927[3] CHAMPAGNE GRANDY 8-6 Pat Eddery (10) *mid-div till hdwy hfwy, rdn to ld o'r one furlong out, ct wl ins last.* ....(7 to 2 op 4 to 1 tchd 5 to 1) 2
871[8] THE ORDINARY GIRL (Ire) 8-6 N Adams (3) *prmnt, led hfwy, hdd appr fnl furlong, kpt on one pace.* ....(33 to 1 op 20 to 1) 3
713[2] CLOUDY REEF 8-6 K Darley (7) *chsd ldrs, ev ch appr fnl furlong, no extr ins*.... (9 to 1 op 8 to 1 tchd 10 to 1) 4
721 PURBECK CENTENARY 8-11 M Roberts (12) *chsd ldrs till wknd appr fnl furlong*............(20 to 1 op 12 to 1) 5
3677[7] WINDRUSH BOY 8-11 J Reid (1) *led to hfwy, rdn and wknd o'r one furlong out.* ....(6 to 1 op 5 to 1 tchd 13 to 2) 6
927 AIR COMMAND (Bar) 8-11 T Sprake (9) *outpcd, nvr on terms*..............................(33 to 1 op 25 to 1) 7
758[9] JEREMIAHS BOY 8-4 (7*) S Drowne (8) *outpcd frm hfwy.* ....(5 to 1 tchd 11 to 4) 8
720[7] CREAGMHOR 8-11 J Williams (2) *al beh.* ....(50 to 1 op 25 to 1) 9
846[9] MELODYS DAUGHTER 8-6 R Hills (11) *speed till wknd 2 fs out*...............................(12 to 1 tchd 14 to 1) 10
DISCO BOY 8-11 T Quinn (5) *speed to hfwy.* ....(33 to 1 op 20 to 1) 11
720 LADY OF SHADOWS (v) 8-6 C Rutter (4) *in tch early, beh frm hfwy*..............................(50 to 1 op 33 to 1) 12
Dist: 1½l, 2l, ¾l, 6l, nk, ½l, hd, 1½l, 1½l, ½l. 1m 1.50s. a 1.00s (12 Ran).
SR: 22/16/8/5/-/-/ (Mrs J A Thomson), W G R Wightman

1096 Timeform Raceview Handicap Class E (0-70 4-y-o and up) £2,976 5f 161yds ....(5:15)

948[7] TRUTHFUL IMAGE [67] (bl) 4-9-13 D Biggs (6) *trkd ldr, led 2 fs out, sn clr, eased nr finish*.......(5 to 1 tchd 4 to 1) 1
721 CALL TO THE BAR (Ire) [57] 4-9-3 A Clark (2) *al prmnt on ins, outpcd 2 fs out, rdn and ran on wl inside last.* ....(11 to 2 op 5 to 1 tchd 7 to 1) 2
758* BLUE TOPAZE [68] 5-10-0 J Williams (14) *mid-div, hdwy on outsd 2 fs out, ran on ins last, nvr nrr.* ....(9 to 2 fav op 7 to 2 tchd 11 to 2) 3
677[9] SAMSOLOM [63] 5-9-9 J Quinn (13) *hld up in tch, short of room wl o'r one furlong out, ran on ins last.* ....(20 to 1 op 12 to 1) 4
501 TRIOMING [50] 7-8-10 N Adams (5) *led till hdd 2 fs out, wknd entering last*..............(33 to 1 op 20 to 1) 5
837 SCARLET PRINCESS [42] 5-7-13[4] (7*) S Drowne (9) *chsd ldrs till wknd wl o'r one furlong out.* ....(16 to 1 op 14 to 1) 6
760 UNVEILED [56] 5-9-2 W Carson (8) *towards rear, some late hdwy, nvr nr to chal*..................(12 to 1 op 8 to 1) 7
721* COBBLERS HILL [56] 4-9-2 T Lang (1) *outpcd thrght.* ....(12 to 1 op 7 to 1) 8
771 ELTON LEDGER (Ire) [57] 4-9-3 B Raymond (11) *al towards rear*....................(6 to 1 op 7 to 1 tchd 8 to 1) 9
FARMER JOCK [51] 11-8-11 M Roberts (15) *rcd on ins in tch, wknd 2 fs out*................(16 to 1 op 10 to 1) 10
923 CEE-EN-CEE [64] (v) 9-9-10 T Quinn (7) *sn rdn, al beh.* ....(7 to 1 op 11 to 2 tchd 8 to 1) 11
409[7] GRAND TIME [42] 4-8-2 G Bardwell (10) *speed to hfwy.* ....(25 to 1 op 14 to 1) 12
948 GALLANT HOPE [51] 11-8-11 N Carlisle (3) *al beh.* ....(20 to 1 op 12 to 1) 13
758[6] RUSHANES [55] 6-9-1 J Reid (12) *prmnt till wknd hfwy.* ....(14 to 1 op 12 to 1 tchd 16 to 1) 14
DAWES OF NELSON [53] 8-8-13 W Newnes (4) *al in rear.* ....(20 to 1 op 16 to 1) 15
Dist: 2l, 2½l, hd, nk, 3l, 1½l, sht-hd, ¾l, 2l, 3½l. 1m 9.60s. a 0.20s (15 Ran).
SR: 52/34/35/29/15/-/3/2/-/ (P E Axon), M J Ryan

1097 Timeform Black Book & Ratings Handicap Class E (0-70 3-y-o and up) £2,875 1m 5yds......................(5:45)

834[4] PROUD BRIGADIER (Ire) [50] 5-8-10 T Quinn (11) *trkd ldrs, led o'r 2 fs out, sn clr, eased ins last.* (9 to 1 op 7 to 1) 1
836[2] CREDIT SQUEEZE [69] 3-9-3 R Hills (7) *hld up, hdwy 3 fs out, pld out and ran on ins fnl 2 furlongs.* ....(9 to 1 op 8 to 1) 2
754[5] HOMEMAKER [60] 3-8-8 J Williams (2) *hld up, hdwy 2 fs out, ran on, nvr nrr*...(10 to 1 op 8 to 1 tchd 11 to 1) 3
754* SAREEN EXPRESS (Ire) [45] 5-7-12 (7*) S McCarthy (6) *slwly away, in rear till hdwy ins fnl 2 fs, nvr nrr.* ....(20 to 1 op 12 to 1) 4
893[3] SILKY SIREN [63] (bl) 4-9-9 Pat Eddery (4) *led aftr one furlong, hdd o'r 2 out, one pace after.* ....(9 to 4 fav op 7 to 2 tchd 2 to 1) 5
834* ROSIETOES (USA) [49] 5-8-2 (7*) Mark Denaro (18) *trkd ldrs till wknd 2 fs out*......(12 to 1 op 6 to 1 tchd 14 to 1) 6
952[2] SARUM [44] 7-8-4 C Rutter (17) *towards rear, hdwy fnl 2 fs, nvr dngrs*.....................(20 to 1 op 14 to 1) 7
826[5] LOCH DUICH [61] 7-9-0 (7*) S Drowne (10) *chsd ldrs, no hdwy fnl 3 fs*..........................(33 to 1 op 20 to 1) 8
881[7] CHARMED KNAVE [51] 8-8-11 T Williams (8) *hld up, hdwy hfwy, wknd 2 fs out*...................(16 to 1 op 8 to 1) 9
ASTERIX [51] 5-8-11 W Newnes (9) *prmnt till wknd o'r 2 fs out*..(33 to 1) 10
978[5] SCOTTISH BAMBI [68] 5-9-7 (7*) D Gibbs (13) *chsd ldrs till wknd o'r 2 fs out*..............(12 to 1 tchd 14 to 1) 11
885* GOOD FOR THE ROSES [54] 7-9-0 J Reid (16) *nvr on terms.* ....(5 to 1 tchd 13 to 2) 12
328[8] HEART OF SPAIN [66] 3-9-0 B Raymond (15) *al towards rear*..................................(20 to 1 op 16 to 1) 13
521 RED SOMBRERO [45] 4-8-5 A Clark (3) *al beh*.... (33 to 1) 14
717[8] OCTOBER BREW (USA) [69] (bl) 3-9-0 (3*) D Harrison (12) *in tch to hfwy*.........(14 to 1 op 12 to 1 tchd 16 to 1) 15
837* TOP ONE [59] 8-9-2 (3*) J Weaver (1) *led 1st furlong, wknd hfwy*..............................(20 to 1 op 10 to 1) 16
458[8] BEATLE SONG [59] 5-9-5 G Bardwell (14) *al beh.* ....(20 to 1 op 14 to 1) 17
CHRISTIAN WARRIOR [52] 4-8-12 D Holland (5) *al beh, tld off*..................................(66 to 1 op 50 to 1) 18
Dist: 3l, 2l, 4l, 2l, 2½l, 3½l, nk, ¾l, 2l, hd. 1m 41.80s. a 2.80s (18 Ran).
SR: 30/28/13/-/10/-/ (M T Lawrance), M R Channon

EDINBURGH (soft)
Monday May 17th

Going Correction: PLUS 0.20 sec. per fur. (race 1), PLUS 0.35 (2,3,4,5,6)

1098 Child Friendly Maiden Auction Stakes Class E (2-y-o) £2,745 5f........(2:00)

968[4] MISS MAH-JONG 8-9 Dean McKeown (3) *led or dispute ld, ran green and hng rght wl o'r one furlong out, kpt on well towards finish.* ....(11 to 8 on op 7 to 4 on tchd 5 to 4 on) 1
466[9] MONKEY MUSIC 9-0 J Carroll (2) *sluggish strt, bustled alng to improve last 2 fs, fnshd wl*... (9 to 2 op 3 to 1) 2
730 STORM REGENT 9-0 W Woods (4) *led or dsptd ld, crowded wl o'r one furlong out, fdd towards finish.* ....(3 to 1 tchd 4 to 1) 3
IBERIAN MAGIC (Ire) 9-0 K Fallon (1) *sluggish strt, hrd at work to keep up hfwy, styd on late, nvr nrr.* ....(8 to 1 op 6 to 1 tchd 10 to 1) 4
Dist: 2l, 5l, ½l. 1m 2.40s. a 4.60s (4 Ran).
SR: 23/20/-/-/ (R Robinson (Wigan)), M Johnston

1099 Wimpey Homes Harlawhill Gardens Median Auction Maiden Stakes Class F (3-y-o) £2,451 1m 3f 32yds.... (2:30)

980[9] MOIDART 8-9 G Duffield (1) *al hndy, quickened ahead 6 fs out, rdn to go clr entering strt, unchlgd.* ....(5 to 2 fav op 3 to 1 tchd 100 to 30) 1
534[3] ABSALOM'S PILLAR 9-0 J Lowe (2) *trkd ldg bunch, pushed alng to improve entering strt, styd on, not rch wnr*..........................(4 to 1 op 5 to 2) 2
712[3] MARATHIA 8-9 W Woods (6) *trkd ldg quartet, shaken up to improve aftr a m, styd on fnl furlong.* ....(100 to 30 op 7 to 2 tchd 3 to 1) 3
864[3] SANTA STELLAR 8-9 Dean McKeown (8) *trkd ldr, not handle bend aftr 2 fs, rallied, one pace last two furlongs.* ....(9 to 2 op 4 to 1) 4
SWEETWATER MOON 8-9 J Fortune (4) *trkd ldg 5, effrt and came wide entering strt, ran green, btn 2 fs out.* ....(33 to 1) 5
860[5] SEVERE STORM 9-0 J Carroll (3) *dictated pace till hdd 6 fs out, fdd entering strt*.............(33 to 1 op 25 to 1) 6
TRI MY WAY (Ire) 8-9 J Fanning (5) *last and bustled alng most of way, tld off entering strt.* (66 to 1 op 33 to 1) 7
653[6] NICKNAME 9-0 Raymond Berry (7) *squeezed out strt, reco'red to settle on ins aftr 2 fs, lost tch entering strt, tld off*............... (14 to 1 op 6 to 1 tchd 16 to 1) 8
Dist: 6l, hd, ½l, 15l, 10l, 1½l, hd. 2m 30.60s. a 11.10s (8 Ran).
SR: 23/16/10/9/-/ (Sir David Wills), J R Fanshawe

1100 Edinburgh Gold Cup Handicap Class D (0-75 3-y-o) £3,825 1m 3f 32yds (3:00)

816[6] ARGYLE CAVALIER (Ire) [66] 9-4 J Carroll (3) *trkd ldg pair, drvn ahead appr fnl furlong, rdn out*........(6 to 4 jt-fav op 5 to 4 tchd 13 to 8) 1

903² BEST APPEARANCE (Ire) [69] 9-7 K Fallon (2) *made most, not handle paddock bend and hdd briefly aftr 3 fs, quickened o'r 2 furlongs out, headed appr last, one pace*..............(6 to 4 jt-fav op 11 to 8 tchd 7 to 4) 2
966⁹ MILNGAVIE (Ire) [47] 7-13 J Fanning (1) *dsptd ld, led briefly aftr 3 fs, hrd at work o'r 2 furlongs out, one pace.* ....(11 to 4 op 2 to 1) 3
Dist: 2l, 3½l. 2m 34.20s. a 14.70s (3 Ran).
(E H Jones (Paints) Ltd), F H Lee

1101 Wimpey Homes Gateside Selling Stakes Class G (3-y-o and up) £2,200 1m 16yds......................(3:30)

962² DELPIOMBO 7-9-7 K Fallon (6) *patiently rdn, squeezed through to ld o'r 2 fs out, gng clr whn edgd lft wl ins fnl furlong*.........................(5 to 4 fav tchd 6 to 4) 1
883⁸ FORMAESTRE (Ire) 3-8-3¹ (5*) O Pears (2) *co'red up, swtchd ins to improve over 2 fs out, styd on und pres towards finish*........ (11 to 2 op 4 to 1 tchd 6 to 1) 2
861⁴ CHANTRY BELLINI (bl) 4-9-2 N Connorton (1) *nvr far away, drw level and crowded o'r 2 fs out, rallied, not quicken towards finish*..........................(5 to 1 op 7 to 2) 3
861² INVERTIEL 9-9-10 J Fanning (7) *al wl plcd, led briefly and wndrd und pres o'r 2 fs out, outpcd ins last.* ....(5 to 1 op 7 to 2) 4
862⁵ BOLD PHILIP 3-8-9 J Lowe (3) *sluggish strt, dashed up to join issue aftr 2 fs, fdd und pres two furlongs out.* ....(12 to 1 op 10 to 1 tchd 14 to 1) 5
905⁶ LADY ADARE (Ire) (bl) 3-8-4 G Duffield (4) *trkd ldr, hrd at work o'r 2 fs out, fdd*...............(50 to 1 op 20 to 1) 6
LAUREL CONNECTION 4-9-7 J Carroll (5) *dictated pace, edgd away frm fence o'r 2 fs out, sn hdd and btn.* ....(25 to 1 op 16 to 1) 7
962⁷ MR SNAIL (bl) 5-9-10 J Fortune (8) *last thrght, lost tch entering strt*...........................(14 to 1 op 12 to 1) 8
Dist: 4l, ¾l, 3l, 7l, 10l, 3l, nk. 1m 46.30s. a 7.80s (8 Ran).
SR: 32/6/13/12/-/ (Paul Coulter), J G FitzGerald

1102 Wimpey Homes Farriers' Way Handicap Class E (0-70 3-y-o) £2,913 1m 16yds......................(4:00)

862* AL MOULOUKI [59] 9-6 W Hood (3) *sluggish strt, improved frm off the pace to ld o'r one furlong out, drvn clr.* ....(9 to 4 op 2 to 1 tchd 7 to 4 and 5 to 2) 1
KARINSKA [52] 8-13 G Duffield (4) *wth ldrs, drvn ahead o'r 2 fs out, hdd and veered rght fnl furlong, no extr.* ....(5 to 1 op 7 to 2) 2
963* ANUSHA [64] 9-4 (7*,4ex) P Roberts (5) *patiently rdn, improved on ins to flter o'r 2 fs out, no imprsn fnl furlong*...............(6 to 4 fav tchd 7 to 4 and 9 to 4) 3
741⁵ DESIRABLE MISS [47] (v) 8-8 J Lowe (1) *set str pace till checked and hdd appr strt, fdd 2 fs out.* ....(6 to 1 op 7 to 2) 4
QUESSONG [45] 8-6 R Lappin (2) *wth ldrs, led appr strt till o'r 2 fs out, sn btn*............. (16 to 1 op 14 to 1) 5
Dist: 3½l, 4l, 10l, 1½l. 1m 46.60s. a 8.10s (5 Ran).
SR: 27/9/9/-/-/ (G Jabre), J W Payne

1103 European Capital Handicap Class E (0-70 3-y-o and up) £2,788 7f 15yds ....(4:30)

SUSANNA'S SECRET [38] 6-7-12 (3*) S Maloney (6) *settled on ins, swtchd outsd and relentless prog last 2 fs, ran on grimly to ld cl hme*............... (7 to 1 op 4 to 1) 1
909² BLUE GRIT [65] 7-9-7 (7*) V Halliday (2) *nvr far away, led o'r 2 fs out, rdn and jst ct*........(2 to 1 fav op 7 to 4) 2
MASTER OFTHE HOUSE [44] 7-8-7 J Carroll (5) *trkd ldg bunch, feeling pace o'r 2 fs out, styd on, no imprsn.* .... (20 to 1 op 14 to 1) 3
909⁶ COOL ENOUGH [33] 12-7-10 J Lowe (1) *patiently rdn, bustled alng whn pace quickened o'r 2 fs out, not pace to chal*..................(9 to 2 op 4 to 1 tchd 5 to 1) 4
862³ MISS HOSTESS [30] 6-7-2 (5*) Darren Moffatt (3) *tongue tied, missed break, dashed up to ld aftr one furlong, hdd o'r 2 fs out, no extr.* ....(17 to 2 op 8 to 1 tchd 10 to 1) 5
934³ PEEDIE PEAT [64] 3-9-2 G Duffield (7) *trkd ldrs, hrd at work o'r 2 fs out, sn outpcd*..........(7 to 2 op 3 to 1) 6
PRINCIPAL PLAYER (USA) [59] 3-8-6 (5*) O Pears (4) *led early, styd hndy till fdd und pres o'r 2 fs out.* ....(33 to 1 op 14 to 1) 7
Dist: Nk, 7l, ½l, 1½l, 1½l, 6l. 1m 33.20s. a 8.00s (7 Ran).
SR: 4/30/-/-/ (Miss Maha Kalaji), S G Norton

MALLOW (IRE) (good)
Monday May 17th

1104 Kinsale Auction Race (2-y-o) £2,245 5f ....(6:00)

896⁶ BONNIE CRATHIE (Ire) 7-11 (2*) R M Burke (2)..... (6 to 1) 1
786⁹ ROYAL THIMBLE (Ire) 7-9 (4*) W J Smith (1)...... (12 to 1) 2
269⁵ OVERALL MAJORITY (Ire) 7-7 (6*) J J Behan (3)..(3 to 1 jt-fav) 3
DILIGENT DODGER (Ire) 8-8 W J Supple (8)........ (5 to 1) 4
896⁷ ASTRADANE (Ire) 7-10 (6*) P P Murphy (7)........(10 to 1) 5
896⁵ ZOE BAIRD 7-11 (2*) D G O'Shea (6)........ (3 to 1 jt-fav) 6
SOPHIE'S PET (Ire) 7-13 N G McCullagh (9)........(5 to 1) 7
786 BOY IN BLACK (Ire) 7-10 (6*) R V Skelly (5)....... (33 to 1) 8
896⁴ EASTROP DANCER (Ire) 8-2 J F Egan (4).........(11 to 2) 9
Dist: ¾l, hd, 1½l, ¾l. 1m 2.90s. (9 Ran).
(Mrs C Collins), C Collins

1105 Cobh Maiden (3-y-o and up) £2,245 5f ....(6:30)

MY-O-MY (Ire) 3-8-11 S Craine (6)........... (5 to 4 fav) 1
KILLEEN STAR (Ire) 3-9-0 W J Supple (15)........(10 to 1) 2
FIVE LITTLE GIRLS (Ire) 3-8-11 K J Manning (7)... (33 to 1) 3
848⁴ CARRIG STAR (Ire) 4-9-1 (8*) J J Stack (12).......(13 to 2) 4
572⁵ SHOOT THE DEALER (Ire) 3-8-11 B Coogan (16)..(11 to 2) 5
847⁷ PERSIAN LIGHT (Ire) 3-8-1 (10*) A J Dempsey (11) (20 to 1) 6
806⁷ BARRY'S PRINCESS (Ire) 4-8-10 (10*) T Hagger (9) (20 to 1) 7
806⁴ YONOKA (Fr) (bl) 4-9-3 (6*) R V Skelly (4)........... (7 to 1) 8
847⁹ FAIRY BRIDE (Ire) 3-8-11 W J O'Connor (8).......(16 to 1) 9
847 SHESOMETHINGELSE (Ire) 3-8-1 (10*) D W O'Sullivan (10) ....(25 to 1) 10
COTTAGE GUEST (Ire) 3-8-7 (4*) W J Smith (14)....(33 to 1) 11
MISS ANITA (Ire) 3-8-11 N G McCullagh (5).......(10 to 1) 12
806 EILEENS HOPE (Ire) 3-8-11 P V Gilson (13).......(14 to 1) 13
BRAZEN ANGEL (Ire) 3-8-11 J F Egan (2)..........(16 to 1) 14
806 YELLOW PRINCESS (Ire) 3-8-11 D Manning (1).. (330 to 1) 15
Dist: ½l, nk, ½l, sht-hd. 1m 2.10s. (15 Ran).
(R E Sangster), T Stack

1106 Fermoy Maiden (3-y-o and up) £2,245 1m 1f..........................(7:30)

TOPSEYS TIPPLE (Ire) 3-8-5 (6*) R V Skelly (2).... (14 to 1) 1
704⁴ GOODIES TWO STEP (Ire) 3-9-0 N G McCullagh (16) ....(50 to 1) 2
550³ STATION HOUSE (Ire) 3-9-0 P V Gilson (1).........(11 to 4) 3
489 ERBIL (Ire) 3-9-0 M J Kinane (8).................(11 to 2) 4
806³ BENE MERENTI (Ire) 3-9-0 J P Murtagh (9)....... (12 to 1) 5
847³ PENNINE'S DAUGHTER 3-8-11 B Coogan (6)......(6 to 1) 6
NO DUNCE (Ire) 3-8-5 (6*) J J Behan (4)...........(16 to 1) 7
256 TEXAS FRIDAY (Ire) 3-8-12 (2*) R M Burke (15).... (25 to 1) 8
HIND VISION (Ire) 3-8-11 J F Egan (3).............(33 to 1) 9
488² MAYASTA (Ire) 3-8-11 P Shanahan (11)......... (5 to 2 fav) 10
FAX ME NOW (Ire) 3-8-11 D Manning (7)........... (33 to 1) 11
DUNANY ROSE (Ire) 3-8-11 S Craine (5)...........(16 to 1) 12
DRESS DANCE (Ire) 3-9-0 W J O'Connor (12)......(16 to 1) 13
WHISKEY HALL (Ire) 4-9-8 (6*) P Carberry (14).... (50 to 1) 14
848 SPEED DEMON 3-8-6 (8*) R T Fitzpatrick (10).....(50 to 1) 15
SIMPLY PHRASED (Ire) 4-10-0 K J Manning (13).. (33 to 1) 16
Dist: ¾l, 3l, 2l, 1l. 1m 59.20s. (16 Ran).
(Duncan McGregor), Daniel J Murphy

1107 Lisgoold Claiming Race (3-y-o and up) £2,245 1m 1f...................(8:00)

912⁴ TOUCHDOWN 6-8-9 R Hughes (1)................(4 to 1) 1
297 MILLMOUNT (Ire) (bl) 3-7-9 (4*) W J Smith (12).... (12 to 1) 2
790⁵ KILTIMAGH (Ire) 3-7-13 N G McCullagh (3).....(3 to 1 fav) 3
649⁵ PERFECT POET (Ire) 3-7-6² (6*) J J Behan (2)...... (6 to 1) 4
HERMES GOLD (Ire) 3-6-11 (10*) J P Cornally (11) (10 to 1) 5
847 STEADY DEAR (Ire) 3-7-9 Joanna Morgan (9)...... (7 to 1) 6
BIT OF A THING (Ire) 3-7-4 (6*) P P Murphy (5).... (25 to 1) 7
848 THREE MUSKETEERS (Ire) (bl) 4-8-4 (6*) J A Heffernan (10) ....(33 to 1) 8
488 DUCHESS AFFAIR (Ire) 3-7-11 (2*) R M Burke (6)... (5 to 1) 9
DESTINATIONUNKNOWN (Ire) 4-9-2 M J Kinane (8) ....(14 to 1) 10
INNOCENT PARTY (Ire) 4-9-0 W J Supple (4)..... (10 to 1) 11
PENNINE PRINCE (Ire) (bl) 3-7-6⁴ (8*) R T Fitzpatrick (7) ....(12 to 1) 12
Dist: 1½l, 1l, 1½l, 1l. 1m 59.40s. (12 Ran).
(Mrs D T Hughes), D T Hughes

BEVERLEY (firm)
Tuesday May 18th

Going Correction: MINUS 0.40 sec. per fur. (races 1,6), MINUS 0.25 (2,3,4,5)

1108 Green Dragon Selling Stakes Class G (2-y-o) £2,070 5f..................(2:30)

886⁶ BROOKHEAD LADY 8-6 D Holland (5) *led aftr one furlong, pushed out fnl furlong, hld on wl.* ....(10 to 1 op 14 to 1 tchd 8 to 1) 1
900² PALACEGATE JO (Ire) 8-6 J Carroll (3) *in tch, effrt and wnt lft hfwy, ran on wl fnl furlong, no extr towards finish.* ....(5 to 1 op 3 to 1) 2
922⁹ RITA'S JOY 8-6 T Sprake (1) *led one furlong, cl up, one pace fnl furlong*.................(20 to 1 op 14 to 1) 3
767² PASSION SUNDAY 8-11 K Darley (8) *dwlt, sn pushed alng and beh, hdwy 2 fs out, wnt rght jst ins last, kpt on same pace*................. (9 to 4 on op 11 to 8 on) 4

949⁸ MARTIAN FOREST 8-6 J Williams (9) *prmnt till wknd entering fnl furlong*..............(14 to 1 op 12 to 1) 5
908⁸ WESTCOAST 8-11 J Fanning (6) *dwlt, sn prmnt, wkng whn slightly hmpd jst ins fnl furlong.*
..................................(33 to 1 op 20 to 1) 6
CARNEGIE BLUE 8-6 Paul Eddery (7) *wth ldrs till wknd o'r one furlong out*..........(16 to 1 op 10 to 1) 7
TEN TIMES TANGO 8-6 G Carter (2) *in tch till wknd 2 fs out*..............................(33 to 1 op 20 to 1) 8
Dist: Nk, 3½l, 1l, 1l, 4l, 2l, 1½l. 1m 5.20s. a 3.50s (8 Ran).
(J E Abbey), P D Evans

1109 Windmill Inn Maiden Stakes Class D (3-y-o) £3,201 7f 100yds.........(3:00)

CAVATINA 8-6 (3*) S D Williams (2) *trkd ldr, led 2 fs out, styd on wl*...................(14 to 1 op 12 to 1) 1
DIPLOMATIST 8-9 L Dettori (6) *cl up, chlgd 2 fs out, sn rdn and one pace*........................(3 to 1 op 2 to 1) 2
732⁵ MYSILV 8-9 P Robinson (1) *led till hdd 2 fs out, one pace.*
..................(13 to 8 fav op 6 to 4 tchd 11 to 8) 3
FLASHELLA (Ire) 8-9 J Lowe (3) *sn pushed alng and beh, styd on fnl 3 fs, nvr dngrs*.........(20 to 1 op 16 to 1) 4
1039⁵ CELESTIAL CHOIR 8-4 (5*) O Pears (7) *trkd ldrs, rdn o'r 2 fs out, sn wknd*........ (11 to 4 op 7 to 2 tchd 4 to 1) 5
JAMANE 9-0 G Carter (5) *dwlt, sn tld off.*
..................................(16 to 1 op 14 to 1) 6
KINTAVI 9-0 G Hind (4) *strted slwly, al tld off.*
..................................(16 to 1 op 14 to 1) 7
Dist: 3l, ½l, ¾l, 5l, 20l, 3l. 1m 32.30s. a 2.00s (7 Ran).
SR: 37/28/26/24/9/-/-/ (Hargate Stud And Racing Limited), T W Donnelly

1110 David Swannell Memorial Rated Class B Handicap (0-95 3-y-o and up) £6,396 1m 100yds..............(3:30)

824* PAY HOMAGE [93] 5-9-7 L Dettori (2) *hld up in tch, hdwy o'r 2 fs out, styd on wl to ld well ins last.*
..................................(2 to 1 fav op 11 to 4) 1
CUMBRIAN CHALLENGE (Ire) [92] 4-9-6 M Birch (4) *led till hdd and no extr wl ins fnl furlong.* (10 to 1 op 8 to 1) 2
458⁴ DOUBLE FLUTTER [79] 4-8-7 Paul Eddery (5) *prmnt, rdn o'r one furlong out, kpt on same pace.*
..................(6 to 1 op 11 to 2 tchd 13 to 2) 3
710³ AMENABLE [80] 8-8-8 Alex Greaves (7) *hld up, steady hdwy fnl 3 fs, nvr nr to chal*.......(16 to 1 op 12 to 1) 4
801 LEIF THE LUCKY (USA) [80] 4-8-8 N Connorton (1) *in tch, effrt o'r 2 fs out, one paced*.......... (9 to 2 op 7 to 2) 5
990² LANGTRY LADY [79] (v) 7-8-2 (5*) C Hodgson (8) *slwly into strd, hld up, effrt 2 fs out, sn btn*.... (9 to 2 op 7 to 2) 6
918² NO SUBMISSION (USA) [83] 7-8-11 S Wood (3) *prmnt till wknd 3 fs out*........ (6 to 1 op 11 to 2 tchd 13 to 2) 7
Dist: ¾l, 3l, hd, 1½l, 4l, 8l. 1m 44.80s. a 2.00s (7 Ran).
SR: 45/42/20/20/15/2/-/ (Miss A V Hill), I A Balding

1111 Angel Fillies Handicap Class D (0-80 3-y-o) £3,915 1m 1f 207yds......(4:00)

875² BAY QUEEN [80] 9-2 (5*) M Fenton (7) *trkd ldrs, led o'r one furlong out, ran on wl.* (11 to 2 op 9 to 2 tchd 6 to 1) 1
748⁵ ALYAKKH (Ire) [72] 8-13 N Carlisle (9) *led till hdd o'r one furlong out, kpt on same pace*....... (7 to 1 op 6 to 1) 2
437² SOLARTICA (USA) [70] 8-11 K Darley (2) *in tch, effrt 3 fs out, kpt on wl fnl furlong.*
.... (9 to 4 fav op 5 to 2 tchd 11 to 4 and 2 to 1) 3
813⁸ MERRY MERMAID [54] 7-9² L Charnock (1) *hld up, hdwy 3 fs out, styd on wl fnl furlong*......(33 to 1 op 25 to 1) 4
928* BARLEY CAKE [58] 7-13 J Fanning (10) *hld up, hdwy 3 fs out, not clr run o'r one out, kpt on same pace.* (12 to 1) 5
PERSIAN FOUNTAIN (Ire) [66] (v) 8-7 J Fortune (5) *cl up, rdn o'r 2 fs out, fdd*....................(16 to 1 op 14 to 1) 6
352⁷ RISPOTO [63] 8-4 G Duffield (3) *trkd ldrs till wknd 2 fs out.*
..................................(8 to 1 op 6 to 1) 7
875⁸ LATEST FLAME (Ire) [74] 9-1 Paul Eddery (4) *slwly into strd, hld up, effrt 3 fs out, not clr run 2 out, no ch aftr.*
..................................(10 to 1 op 8 to 1) 8
AMERIGUE [55] 7-10 J Lowe (6) *hld up, some hdwy 3 fs out, wknd 2 out*.......(17 to 2 op 12 to 1 tchd 8 to 1) 9
827 BOBBYSOXER [67] 8-8 G Carter (8) *in tch till wknd 2 fs out*.................. (5 to 1 tchd 9 to 2 and 11 to 2) 10
Dist: 1½l, hd, ½l, 2l, nk, 1½l, ¾l, hd, 1l. 2m 6.50s. a 5.10s (10 Ran).
SR: 31/20/17/-/-/7/1/10/-/ (B J Warren), M Bell

1112 Rose & Crown Handicap Class E (0-70 3-y-o and up) £3,235 1m 3f 216yds ....(4:30)

988⁴ EIRE LEATH-SCEAL [44] 6-8-4 J Lowe (13) *made virtually all, styd on wl fnl furlong.*
........................(5 to 1 op 6 to 1 tchd 13 to 2) 1
IN TRUTH [51] 5-8-11 L Dettori (2) *trkd ldrs, effrt o'r 2 fs out, ev ch one out, kpt on wl ins last.*
..................................(20 to 1 op 14 to 1) 2
508⁵ SALU [55] (bl) 4-9-1 G Duffield (10) *mid-div, steady hdwy 4 fs out, ev ch one out, kpt on wl*...... (8 to 1 op 7 to 1) 3

863⁷ MASTER OF THE ROCK [43] 4-8-3 N Connorton (11) *chsd ldrs, ev ch 2 fs out, kpt on same pace.*
..................................(16 to 1 tchd 20 to 1) 4
904⁵ LUKS AKURA [36] (v) 5-7-3 (7*) M Baird (1) *cl up, ev ch o'r one furlong out, one pace*....................(12 to 1) 5
LAMBSON [33] 6-7-7 N Carlisle (16) *trkd ldrs, kpt on same pace fnl 2 fs*...................................(33 to 1) 6
831⁶ GOLDEN TORQUE [67] 6-9-6 (7*) H Bastiman (6) *nvr nr to chal*....................................(8 to 1 op 7 to 1) 7
857⁸ NATIVE MISSION [68] 6-10-0 K Fallon (15) *mid-div, effrt o'r 2 fs out, no imprsn.*
.... (11 to 4 fav op 5 to 2 tchd 9 to 4 and 3 to 1) 8
681 NOT YET [35] 9-7-7³ (5*) A Garth (9) *nvr dngrs*....(16 to 1) 9
904³ WEST WITH THE WIND [48] 6-8-8 S Webster (4) *nvr dngrs.*
..................................(7 to 1 op 6 to 1) 10
382 ESCAPE TALK [33] 6-7-7 J Fanning (14) *mid-div till wknd o'r 2 fs out*...................................(33 to 1) 11
652⁵ NANCY (Ire) [51] 3-7-1¹ (7*) D Wright (3) *al beh*.... (20 to 1) 12
904⁷ STATIA (Ire) [35] 5-7-9² Kim Tinkler (7) *beh most of way.*
..................................(50 to 1) 13
863 JOSEPH'S WINE (Ire) [43] 4-8-3 Dean McKeown (8) *dwlt, al beh*..........(14 to 1 op 12 to 1 tchd 16 to 1) 14
ISOBAR [33] 7-7-7 S Wood (12) *wth wnr till wknd quickly o'r 4 fs out, tld off*..........................(50 to 1) 15
Dist: Nk, 1l, 1½l, 2l, ½l, 3½l, ½l, ¾l, ½l, 2l. 2m 35.50s. a 4.50s (15 Ran).
SR: 15/21/23/8/-/-/20/20/-/ (Mel Brittain), M Brittain

1113 Royal Standard Conditions Stakes Class D (3-y-o and up) £3,465 5f (5:00)

858² LUCKY PARKES 3-8-7 J Carroll (8) *made all, clr o'r one furlong out, very easily.*
....................(5 to 4 fav op 11 to 8 tchd 6 to 4) 1
986⁹ SIR HARRY HARDMAN 5-9-8 B Raymond (6) *chsd ldrs, styd on wl fnl furlong, no ch wth wnr.*
........................(15 to 2 op 6 to 1 tchd 8 to 1) 2
4666a⁷ SIZZLING SAGA (Ire) 5-9-6 (3*) S D Williams (11) *in tch, styd on fnl 2 fs*....................(14 to 1 tchd 16 to 1) 3
795 SAINT EXPRESS 3-8-9 A Culhane (7) *chsd ldr, one pace fnl 2 fs*......................... (11 to 2 op 5 to 1 tchd 6 to 1) 4
SABO SONG 3-8-0 Dale Gibson (10) *chsd ldrs till wknd o'r one furlong out*...............................(20 to 1) 5
846⁸ CELESTIAL KEY (USA) 3-8-12 (5*) O Pears (9) *in tch, no hdwy frm hfwy*.................. (16 to 1 op 14 to 1) 6
ABERGELE 3-8-11 K Fallon (3) *beh till styd on fnl 2 fs, nrst finish*...............................(16 to 1 op 14 to 1) 7
795 CASE LAW 6-9-8 G Duffield (2) *cl up, wkng whn slightly hmpd o'r one furlong out*...........(4 to 1 op 3 to 1) 8
ANOTHER LANE 6-8-9 J Williams (5) *in tch to hfwy.*
..................................(50 to 1 op 33 to 1) 9
PALLIUM (Ire) 5-9-4 N Connorton (4) *al beh*.......(33 to 1) 10
803* CHICKCHARNIE 3-8-9 L Charnock (1) *in tch to hfwy.*
..................................(25 to 1 op 16 to 1) 11
Dist: 6l, 1½l, ½l, 1½l, hd, 1½l, 1l, 1½l, 7l, nk. 1m 1.20s. b 0.50s (11 Ran).
SR: 63/54/49/33/18/34/22/29/10/ (Joseph Heler), J Berry

GOODWOOD (good to firm)
Tuesday May 18th
Going Correction: MINUS 0.20 sec. per fur. (races 1,2,3,5,7), NIL (4,6)

1114 Trehearne & Norman Maiden Stakes Class D (3-y-o) £3,557 7f........(2:10)

759² SIMPLY FINESSE 9-0 T Quinn (8) *cl up al gng wl, pld out well o'r one furlong out, led appr last, ran on well.*
........................(4 to 1 op 3 to 1 tchd 9 to 2) 1
825 BELFRY GREEN (Ire) 9-0 R Hills (5) *beh, hdwy 3 fs out, ran on wl fnl furlong*..................(66 to 1 op 33 to 1) 2
751 ARID 9-0 M Roberts (4) *cl up, pushed alng o'r 3 fs out, led briefly over one out, sn one pace*.............(5 to 2 jt-fav op 3 to 1 tchd 7 to 2) 3
872² JAAZIM 9-0 W Carson (7) *rcd freely, led til hdd o'r one furlong out, wknd ins last*..................(5 to 2 jt-fav op 6 to 4 tchd 3 to 1) 4
784⁴ MOON FLASK (Ire) 9-0 Pat Eddery (1) *trkd ldrs, rdn 3 fs out, btn wl o'r one out.* (11 to 4 op 5 to 2 tchd 3 to 1) 5
951⁴ SLEEPTITE (Fr) 9-0 D Biggs (2) *sn pushed alng in rear, nvr on terms*............(33 to 1 op 20 to 1 tchd 50 to 1) 6
950⁷ WOODMANS STAR 8-9 (5*) K Rutter (3) *al beh.*
..................................(50 to 1 op 25 to 1) 7
Dist: 2½l, hd, 5l, 6l, 2½l, 10l. 1m 26.85s. a 2.25s (7 Ran).
SR: 45/37/36/21/3/-/-/ (Food Brokers Ltd), R Akehurst

1115 Chichester Festival Theatre Handicap Class C (0-90 3-y-o) £4,751 1½m (2:40)

875³ PISTOL RIVER (Ire) [87] 9-7 J Reid (5) *trkd ldrs, lost pl 6 fs out, cld 3 out, led o'r one out, ran on wl.*
..................................(7 to 1 op 5 to 1) 1
827³ BOHEMIAN CROWN (USA) [76] 8-10 M Roberts (4) *trkd ldr, led 3 fs out till hdd o'r one out, kpt on.*
..................................(5 to 1 tchd 7 to 1) 2
780² LICORNE [78] 8-12 W Ryan (2) *in tch, pushed alng 5 fs out, ev ch 3 out, one pace o'r 2 out.*
.....................(100 to 30 op 9 to 2 tchd 3 to 1) 3

635[2] SOUL EMPEROR [84] 9-4 A Munro (7) *led til hdd 3 fs out, sn one pace*.............(10 to 1 tchd 12 to 1) 4
1068[5] GRAND APPLAUSE (Ire) [71] 8-5 S Whitworth (1) *hld up beh, cld and ev ch 3 fs out, wknd 2 out.* (8 to 1 tchd 9 to 1) 5
932[2] NEMEA (USA) [80] 9-0 Pat Eddery (6) *hld up in cl tch, hdwy o'r 4 fs out, wknd quickly 2 out, sn eased.*.....................................(7 to 1 op 5 to 1) 6
725* SON OF SHARP SHOT (Ire) [76] 8-10 W Carson (3) *ducked and uns rdr strt*...............(11 to 4 fav op 2 to 1) ur
Dist: 1l, 7l, ½l, 8l, 5l. 2m 40.80s. a 7.80s (7 Ran).
SR: 5/-/-/-/ (Paul Green), R Hannon

1116 A. R. Dennis Bookmakers Predominate Stakes Class A (Listed Race) (3-y-o) £21,540 1¼m.............. (3:10)

GEISWAY (Can) 8-12 L Piggott (3) *trkd ldrs, pld out and rapid hdwy und pres ins fnl furlong, led post.*......................(9 to 2 tchd 7 to 2 and 5 to 1) 1
890* BENEFICIAL 9-1 M Hills (6) *hld up gng wl, led one furlong out till ct post.*...........(6 to 4 on op 5 to 4 on tchd 11 to 10 on) 2
688[6] VISTO SI STAMPI (Ire) 8-12 Pat Eddery (1) *led til hdd one furlong out, kpt on one pace.*.....................(12 to 1 op 14 to 1 tchd 16 to 1) 3
817[2] SALATIN (USA) 8-12 W Carson (4) *hld up, hdwy 4 fs out, sn ev ch, rdn and one pace frm 2 out*....(4 to 1 op 3 to 1) 4
797[6] CANASKA STAR (bl) 8-12 T Quinn (2) *hld up beh, hdwy 2 fs out, one pace ins last*.........................(33 to 1) 5
MR MARTINI (Ire) (bl) 9-1 R Cochrane (5) *trkd ldr, rdn 2 fs out, one pace*..............(25 to 1 op 20 to 1) 6
Dist: Sht-hd, 2l, ¾l, sht-hd, nk. 2m 13.28s. a 7.78s (6 Ran).
SR: -/2/-/ (Paul Green), R Hannon

1117 Anne Frances Stevens Memorial Conditions Stakes Class D (3-y-o) £3,525 6f.............................. (3:40)

HALF TERM (USA) 8-10 M Roberts (2) *in tch, pushed alng hfwy, hdwy wl o'r one furlong out, led ins last, edgd lft, pushed out*.........(5 to 2 op 2 to 1 tchd 11 to 4) 1
464[4] LORD OLIVIER (Ire) 9-0 M Tebbutt (1) *cl up, ev ch ins fnl furlong, ran on*........(5 to 1 op 6 to 1 tchd 13 to 2) 2
511[4] SURPRISE OFFER (bl) 8-10 L Piggott (4) *led, sn clr, drifted rght blw 2 fs out, hdd ins last, one pace.*.................................(2 to 1 fav op 7 to 4) 3
746[6] FACTUAL (USA) 9-0 Pat Eddery (5) *slwly into strd, rdn alng thrght, in tch, effrt 2 fs out, short of room o'r one out, ran on*.............(4 to 1 op 3 to 1 tchd 9 to 2) 4
729[3] CARRANITA (Ire) 8-0 (5*) Stephen Davies (3) *in tch, outpcd and pushed alng hfwy, ran on und pres ins last.*.....................(12 to 1 op 14 to 1 tchd 10 to 1) 5
Dist: 2l, ½l, hd, 1l. 1m 12.03s. a 1.63s (5 Ran).
SR: 63/59/53/56/43/ (Sheikh Mohammed), J H M Gosden

1118 Festival Stakes Class A (formerly the Clive Graham Stakes) (Listed Race) (4-y-o and up) £10,575 1¼m.....(4:10)

4682a[7] RED BISHOP (USA) 5-9-1 M Roberts (2) *tacked ldrs, sn pushed alng whn pace quickened, pld out wl o'r one furlong out, sstnd run to ld appr last, eased cl hme.*.............(5 to 1 op 9 to 2 tchd 11 to 2) 1
390[8] BOBZAO (Ire) 4-9-1 J Reid (5) *hld up in tch, cld 2 fs out, not much room and swtchd lft one furlong out, ran on wl*...............(40 to 1 op 33 to 1 tchd 50 to 1) 2
774[3] JEUNE 4-9-4 R Cochrane (4) *reluctant ldr aftr one furlong, rcd freely, rdn alng o'r 2 fs out, hdd appr last, one pace*..............(5 to 4 fav op 11 to 8 tchd 7 to 4) 3
660[3] ZAAHI (USA) 4-9-4 R Hills (1) *hld up, cld o'r 4 fs out, ev ch 2 out, hmpd and squeezed out one furlong out.*.................................(7 to 2 op 5 to 2) 4
525[2] CLOUD OF DUST 4-8-13 T Quinn (3) *beh, pld hrd early, cld o'r 4 fs out, rdn and wknd 2 out*..... (7 to 2 op 2 to 1) 5
892[5] JUSTICE (Fr) 5-9-7 Pat Eddery (6) *led, set slow pace one furlong, cl up, stumbled 5 fs out, sn lost pl, tld off.*.........(40 to 1 op 33 to 1 tchd 50 to 1) 6
Dist: Nk, ¾l, 7l, 15l, 12l. 2m 11.33s. a 5.83s (6 Ran).
SR: 23/22/23/9/-/-/ (Ali Saeed), J H M Gosden

1119 Goodwood Aerodrome Claiming Stakes Class D (2-y-o) £3,687 6f (4:45)

969* MAZEEKA (Ire) 8-8 (3*) Emma O'Gorman (2) *cl up, led o'r 2 fs out, clr ins last, easily, fnshd lme.*.................................(7 to 2 tchd 11 to 4) 1
776 SHERIFF 8-9 R Hills (5) *in tch, rdn 2 fs out, ran on wl fnl furlong*..............(16 to 1 op 12 to 1 tchd 20 to 1) 2
708[6] ROSE OF GLENN 7-11[2] (5*) Stephen Davies (6) *led til hdd o'r 2 fs out, ran on one pace.*.....................(14 to 1 op 12 to 1 tchd 16 to 1) 3
718[3] SWEET WHISPER 8-8 Pat Eddery (10) *cl up, ev ch 2 fs out, one pace appr last.* (13 to 8 fav op 5 to 4 tchd 7 to 4) 4
949* RISKIE THINGS 7-12 (7*) Mark Denaro (8) *trkd ldrs, rdn o'r one furlong out, one pace*...... (10 to 1 tchd 12 to 1) 5
877[5] SON OF HADEER 8-11 J Quinn (9) *trkd ldrs till wknd appr fnl furlong*..........(20 to 1 op 14 to 1 tchd 25 to 1) 6
776 HE SHALL REIGN 8-13 W Carson (12) *in tch far side, swtchd rght o'r one furlong out, sn rdn and btn.*...................................(10 to 1 op 6 to 1) 7
776 RISKY AFFAIR 8-4 (3*) D Harrison (1) *chsd ldrs till wknd 2 fs out*...................(13 to 2 op 9 to 2 tchd 7 to 1) 8
469 STORM 8-5 W Newnes (11) *chsd ldrs far side, swtchd rght o'r 2 fs out, sn btn*....(20 to 1 op 16 to 1 tchd 25 to 1) 9
FIRST SHOT 8-11 W Ryan (3) *strted slwly, al beh.* (33 to 1) 10
THORNY BISHOP 8-13 G Bardwell (4) *pld hrd in rear grp, outpcd frm hfwy*...............(33 to 1 tchd 50 to 1) 11
657 PETITE POET 8-4 D Biggs (7) *sn outpcd.*..........(25 to 1 op 16 to 1 tchd 33 to 1) 12
Dist: 4l, ¾l, 2l, sht-hd, 1½l, hd, 2½l, sht-hd, sht-hd, 5l. 1m 14.03s. a 3.63s (12 Ran).
SR: 24/6/-/-/-/-/ (S Fustok), W A O'Gorman

1120 Cocked Hat Handicap Class E (0-70 4-y-o and up) £3,648 1m 1f...... (5:20)

169[4] REFLECTING (Ire) [66] 4-9-11 Pat Eddery (13) *hld up beh, rdn and hdwy 3 fs out, short of room one furlong out, quickened on bit to ld cl hme, cmftbly.*.....................(10 to 1 op 7 to 1 tchd 12 to 1) 1
756* WAKIL (Ire) [59] 4-9-4 A Munro (19) *trkd ldrs, led o'r one furlong out till hdd cl hme*........(8 to 1 tchd 10 to 1) 2
840 MOON SPIN [59] 4-9-4 W Carson (5) *trkd ldrs, led 3 fs out till hdd o'r one out, one pace.*...................(12 to 1 op 10 to 1 tchd 14 to 1) 3
881* DANCING SENSATION (USA) [44] 6-8-3[1] T Quinn (15) *trkd ldrs, rdn 2 fs out, one pace*..... (5 to 2 fav tchd 3 to 1) 4
840[6] DANCING BEAU (Ire) [47] 4-8-6 F Norton (16) *mid-div, hdwy o'r one furlong out, one pace ins last.*.................................(25 to 1 op 20 to 1) 5
402 TADORA (Ire) [48] 4-8-7 B Rouse (18) *mid-div, hdwy 3 fs out, one pace appr last*...........(33 to 1 op 20 to 1) 6
DOYCE [53] 4-8-12 R Cochrane (10) *beh, hrd rdn o'r one furlong out, nrst finish*...........(14 to 1 op 12 to 1) 7
NORMAN WARRIOR [44] 4-8-0 (3*) J Weaver (12) *beh, effrt o'r 2 fs out, nvr nrr*...............(25 to 1 op 20 to 1) 8
678[4] ALTERMEERA [50] 5-8-9 G Bardwell (14) *mid-div, hdwy 3 fs out, btn o'r one out*.......... (16 to 1 tchd 20 to 1) 9
914 LUCKY NOIRE [55] 5-8-9[2] (7*) P Houghton (3) *al beh.*...........................(25 to 1 op 20 to 1 tchd 14 to 1) 10
678 ICE STRIKE (USA) [46] (bl) 4-8-5 M Hills (2) *cl up, led aftr 2 fs till hdd 3 furlongs out, wknd*.... (33 to 1 tchd 50 to 1) 11
645[5] REMANY [63] 4-9-8 R Hills (20) *beh, hdwy o'r 2 fs out, sn btn*....................(10 to 1 op 7 to 1 tchd 11 to 1) 12
MISTY VIEW [65] 4-9-10 W Ryan (22) *al beh*..... (33 to 1) 13
ROLY WALLACE [55] 4-9-0 M Tebbutt (21) *al beh.* (33 to 1) 14
964[4] ALBERT [46] 6-8-5 J Quinn (1) *al beh.*......................(8 to 1 op 10 to 1 tchd 12 to 1) 15
CELIA BRADY [53] 5-8-12 W Newnes (17) *chsd ldrs, rdn and cld o'r 4 fs out, sn btn*.........(25 to 1 op 16 to 1) 16
834[2] LADY LACEY [48] (v) 6-8-7 R Price (7) *beh, hrd rdn and hdwy o'r 4 fs out, sn btn.*...........(12 to 1 op 10 to 1 tchd 14 to 1) 17
925[4] BRESIL (USA) [65] 4-9-10 S Whitworth (8) *al beh.*.................................(25 to 1 op 20 to 1) 18
990 JOLTO [45] 4-8-4 D Biggs (6) *chsd ldrs til wknd 4 fs out.*.................................(33 to 1 op 25 to 1) 19
978 YOUNG MAX [61] 4-8-13 (7*) Tracey Purseglove (9) *led 2 furlngs, trkd ldrs till wknd 4 fs out.*..............................(33 to 1 tchd 50 to 1) 20
Dist: ½l, 2½l, nk, ½l, 3l, hd, 1½l, nk, 1l, nk. 1m 56.04s. a 4.04s (20 Ran).
SR: 24/15/7/-/-/-/ (P A Leonard), J H M Gosden

MALLOW (IRE) (yielding) Tuesday May 18th

1121 Lee EBF Maiden (2-y-o) £3,064 5f ....(6:30)

820[2] PEACE TOKEN (Ire) 8-11 B Coogan (2)............(4 to 1) 1
JEDWA (Ire) 8-11 C Roche (4)...............(15 to 8 fav) 2
786[6] GALLIC VICTORY (Ire) 9-0 P Shanahan (5).........(7 to 2) 3
GREENCASTLE ROSE (Ire) 8-11 S Craine (6)..... (10 to 1) 4
CATWALKER (Ire) 9-0 M J Kinane (8)..............(7 to 1) 5
DASHING DANCER (Ire) 9-0 J D Eddery (1).......(14 to 1) 6
SALLY'S TRUST (Ire) 8-11 Joanna Morgan (3).....(20 to 1) 7
EASY STEP (Ire) (bl) 9-0 W J Supple (7)...........(8 to 1) 8
Dist: 2l, 2½l, 5½l, 1l. 1m 0.70s. (8 Ran).
(Mrs B Howard), J G Coogan

1122 Curraheen Maiden (3-y-o) £2,215 1m 5f.............................. (7:30)

PORTERSTOWN BOY (Ire) 9-0 M J Kinane (3)......(3 to 1) 1
TURNER PRIZE (Ire) 9-0 S Craine (10)..............(10 to 1) 2
870[3] WICKLOW WAY (Ire) 8-11 W J Supple (4)...........(6 to 1) 3
982[3] ALIBAR'S PET (Ire) 8-5 (6*) J A Heffernan (8).........(8 to 1) 4
552[2] CARRICK PIKE (USA) (bl) 9-0 C Roche (2)..... (2 to 1 fav) 5
936[5] L-WAY FIRST (Ire) 8-11 R Hughes (9)............(20 to 1) 6
848 ASSERT STAR 9-0 K J Manning (7)..................(25 to 1) 7
ABASIYA (USA) 8-11 J P Murtagh (6)...............(6 to 1) 8
DANCING VISION (Ire) 9-0 P V Gilson (1)..........(20 to 1) 9
1026[6] WESTERN FRONTIER (Ire) 9-0 P Shanahan (5)....(25 to 1) 10

Dist: Nk, 5l, sht-hd, 8l. 3m 8.50s. (10 Ran).
(Philip Monahan), D K Weld

1123 Duhallow Handicap (0-75 3-y-o) £2,215 1m 1f. . . . .(8:00)

1046^5 SLIGHTLY SCRUFFY (Ire) [-] 8-9 P Lowry (8) . . . . . . (10 to 1) 1
TINERANA (Ire) [-] 8-11 M J Kinane (2) . . . . (9 to 1) 2
981^* TRYARRA (Ire) [-] 9-7 (5ex) J P Murtagh (11) . . . .(7 to 2) 3
311 SARA MAURETTE (Ire) [-] 8-8^2 N Byrne (4) . . . .(6 to 1) 4
307^9 ROOTSMAN (Ire) [-] 9-2 W J Supple (3) . . . .(25 to 1) 5
789^4 AULD STOCK (Ire) [-] 9-1 (6*) J R Barry (5) . . . . . (5 to 4 fav) 6
868 BUSINESS CENTRE (Ire) [-] 8-2 (6*) J J Behan (10) (25 to 1) 7
280 LAUNCH INTO SONG (Ire) [-] 9-2 S Craine (9) . . . . .(25 to 1) 8
280^6 FRIAR STREET (Ire) [-] 8-12 (6*) P Carberry (1) . . . . . (8 to 1) 9
258 TRES JOUR (Ire) [-] 8-11 P Shanahan (6) . . . . (10 to 1) 10
Dist: Hd, 4½l, ¾l, 1l. 2m 0.20s. (10 Ran).
(Mrs S Andrews), J T Gorman

ST-CLOUD (FR) (good)
Tuesday May 18th
Going Correction: PLUS 0.25 sec. per fur.

1124 Prix Jean de Chaudenay (Group 2) (3-y-o and up) £35,842 1½m. . . . . . . (2:55)

695^3 MODHISH (Ire) 4-9-6 S Guillot (3) *mid-div, 5th strt, hdwy 2 fs out, str run fnl furlong, led last strds*. . . . . . (82 to 10) 1
774^2 APPLE TREE (Fr) (bl) 4-9-8 T Jarnet (1) *mid-div, 6th strt, effrt 2 fs out, ran on fnl furlong, jst fld*. . . . . (6 to 5 fav) 2+
LUAZUR (Fr) 4-9-2 C Asmussen (4) *led, rdn o'r one furlong out, ran on wl, hdd fnl strds*. . . . .(66 to 10) 2+
726^* SHARP COUNSEL (Fr) 4-9-2 D Boeuf (6) *rear, 7th strt, quickened 2 fs out, kpt on, not rch ldrs*. . . . . . .(46 to 10) 4
596^6 URBAN SEA (USA) 4-8-13 W R Swinburn (9) *trkd ldr, second strt, effrt 2 fs out, one pace fnl furlong*. (42 to 10) 5
726^4 OUMNAZ (Fr) 4-9-2 R Laplanche (5) *nvr rch ldrs*. (31 to 1) 6
693^2 COMPOTA (Fr) 4-8-13 O Peslier (7) *al rear*. . . . .(20 to 1) 7
695^* PROTEKTOR (Ger) 4-9-6 T Hellier (8) *trkd ldrs, 3rd strt, sn wknd*. . . . . (12 to 1) 8
DJAIS (Fr) 4-9-2 G Guignard (2) *rcd in 4th early, sn btn*. . . . .(14 to 1) 9
Dist: Sht-hd, dd-ht, 1½l, sht-nk, 2½l, nk, 3l, 6l. 2m 36.20s. a 6.20s (9 Ran).
SR: 74/75/69/66/62/60/56/57/41/ (Sheikh Mohammed), A Fabre

BADEN-BADEN (GER) (good)
Wednesday May 19th

1125 Preis der Hotellerie Baden-Baden (Listed) (3-y-o) £16,327 1m 1f. . . (2:10)

658^* PORT LUCAYA 8-9 L Dettori, *rcd in 3rd, quickened to ld 2 fs out, sn clr, easily*. 1
594^3 LASKO (Ger) 8-9 M Rimmer, *mid-div, hdwy 2 fs out, no ch wth wnr*. 2
AMARANT (Ger) 8-9 A Best, *mid-div till ran on wl clsg stages*. 3
ON YOUR MARK (Ger) 8-9 M Hills, *hld up, hdwy 2 fs out, nvr nrr*. 4
736^4 KING PARIS (Ire) 8-9 M Hills, ... 5
Dist: 2½l, 1 ¾l, 1½l, 1½l, 1 ¾l. 1m 50.64s. (10 Ran).
(Lucayan Stud), R Hannon

GOODWOOD (good to firm)
Wednesday May 19th
Going Correction: MINUS 0.15 sec. per fur.

1126 Finnboard Claiming Stakes Class D (3-y-o) £3,395 1½m. . . . .(2:10)

827 LUNAR RISK 8-6 W Ryan (4) *led till ins fnl 3 fs, sn drvn, led last strds, all out*. . . . .(7 to 4 tchd 11 to 10) 1
980 SPARKY'S SONG 8-2 R Hills (3) *trkd wnr, led ins fnl 3 fs, hng lft final quarter- m, hdd inside last, not quicken cl hme*. . . . .(11 to 8 on op 13 to 8 on tchd 5 to 4 on) 2
WILL HYDE 8-6 (5*) C Hodgson (2) *strted slwly, sn reco'red, 3rd till lost tch 3 fs out*. . . . . (7 to 1 op 4 to 1) 3
Dist: Nk, 20l. 2m 47.87s. a 14.87s (3 Ran).
(R Haim), W R Muir

1127 Citroen Xantia Sprint Handicap Class C (0-95 3-y-o and up) £4,962 6f. . (2:40)

796^* CASTLEREA LAD [77] 4-9-4 W Ryan (8) *hld up, hdwy o'r one furlong out, quickened to ld wl ins last*. . . . .(7 to 1 tchd 8 to 1) 1
948^5 MASNUN (USA) [71] 8-8-9 (3*) J Weaver (3) *hdwy 2 fs out, not much room and squeezed through ins last, ran on*. . . . .(9 to 2 fav op 6 to 1) 2
796 AUGHFAD [83] (v) 7-9-10 J Reid (9) *trkd ldrs, led o'r one furlong out, shaken up fnl furlong, ct cl hme*. . . . .(12 to 1 tchd 14 to 1) 3
VERDE ALITALIA (Ire) [77] 4-9-4 W Carson (5) *prmnt, ev ch 2 fs out till not quicken fnl furlong, better for race*. . . . . (12 to 1 op 10 to 1) 4
1000^5 GORINSKY (Ire) [81] 5-9-8 L Piggott (11) *led till o'r one furlong out, wknd ins last*. . . . . (15 to 2 op 6 to 1 tchd 8 to 1) 5
1036 BALLASECRET [78] 5-9-5 T Quinn (10) *pressed ldr, ev ch 2 fs out, wknd appr fnl furlong*. . . . . (20 to 1 op 16 to 1) 6
722^3 ALLTHRUTHENIGHT (Ire) [82] 4-9-9 Pat Eddery (13) *slwly into strd, hdwy hfwy, chsd ldrs 2 fs out, wknd o'r one out*. . . . . (13 to 2 op 6 to 1 tchd 7 to 1) 7
1066 BODARI [80] 4-9-4 (3*) D Harrison (2) *chsd ldrs 4 fs*. . . . . (11 to 1 op 8 to 1) 8
737 ASSIGNMENT [75] 7-9-2 T Williams (6) *sn rdn and outpcd*. . . . .(9 to 1 op 8 to 1) 9
659 LETSBEONESTABOUTIT [73] 7-8-7 (7*) B Russell (7) *sn outpcd*. . . . .(25 to 1) 10
923^8 BELLS OF LONGWICK [72] 4-8-13 W Newnes (1) *in tch, chsd ldrs o'r 2 fs out, sn wknd*. . . (14 to 1 tchd 16 to 1) 11
923^3 FIVESEVENFIVEO [72] 5-8-6 (7*) S Drowne (4) *outpcd*. . . . . (8 to 1 op 7 to 1 tchd 10 to 1) 12
796 TEMPLE FORTUNE (USA) [72] 4-8-13 A McGlone (12) *chsd ldrs till rdn and wknd o'r 2 fs out*. . . . . (14 to 1 op 12 to 1 tchd 16 to 1) 13
Dist: ½l, sht-hd, 3l, 1½l, ¾l, 2l, ½l, 1½l, nk, 1l. 1m 11.66s. a 1.26s (13 Ran).
SR: 61/53/64/46/44/38/34/30/19/ (Mrs Tess Graham), R Hollinshead

1128 Tripleprint Lupe Stakes Class A (Listed) (3-y-o) £14,230 1¼m. . . . . . . (3:10)

780^* GISARNE (USA) 8-11 W Carson (1) *chsd ldrs, pld out o'r 2 fs out, sn drvn, led appr fnl furlong, hld on wl*. . . . .(3 to 1 op 2 to 1 tchd 100 to 30) 1
YAWL 9-3 Pat Eddery (2) *led aftr half a furlong till appr fnl furlong, shaken up and no extr cl hme*. . . . .(9 to 4 fav op 7 to 4 tchd 3 to 1) 2
772^8 SEASONAL SPLENDOUR (Ire) 8-11 D Biggs (3) *beh, drvn o'r 2 fs out, styd on fnl furlong, not rch ldrs*. . . . .(20 to 1 op 16 to 1 tchd 25 to 1) 3
684^2 RAPID REPEAT (Ire) 8-11 Paul Eddery (7) *led for half a furlong, chsd ldr till 2 out, sn outpcd*. . . . . (9 to 2 tchd 4 to 1 and 5 to 1) 4
UPPER MOUNT CLAIR 8-11 T Quinn (5) *mid-div, rdn 3 fs out, one pace*. . . . . (9 to 1 op 8 to 1 tchd 10 to 1) 5
734^2 ZENITH 8-11 W Newnes (4) *slwly into strd, rdn 3 fs out, hng o'r 2 out, found nothing*. . . . . . . (7 to 2 op 4 to 1) 6
805 HAZY KAY (Ire) 8-11 W Ryan (6) *sn wl beh, tld off*. . . . .(33 to 1 tchd 40 to 1) 7
Dist: Hd, 3½l, hd, 4l, 3l, dist. 2m 10.15s. a 4.65s (7 Ran).
SR: 36/41/28/27/19/13/-/ (Racing Welfare), J L Dunlop

1129 Harcros Timber & Building Supplies Stayers Championship Series Rated Qualifier Class B Handicap (0-100 4-y-o and up) £6,117 1¾m. . . . . (3:40)

757^2 CASTLE COURAGEOUS [89] 6-9-7 J Reid (4) *chsd ldrs till lost pos and drvn frm 7 fs out, hdwy and edgd rght o'r 3 out, led 2 out, edged right, ran on*. . . . .(3 to 1 fav op 11 to 4) 1
822^2 DURSHAN (USA) [81] 4-8-13 Pat Eddery (6) *beh, rdn 3 fs out, styd on fnl 2 furlongs, no imprsn*. . . . . (11 to 2 op 5 to 1 tchd 6 to 1) 2
661^2 MULL HOUSE [75] 6-8-7 W Carson (7) *beh, rdn 4 fs out, ran on fnl 2 furlongs*. . . . . (4 to 1 op 7 to 2) 3
988 LYPHANTASTIC (USA) [82] 4-9-0 W Ryan (1) *sn chasing ldr, chlgd o'r 3 fs out, wknd frm 2 out*. (9 to 2 tchd 5 to 1) 4
INCHCAILLOCH (Ire) [78] 4-8-10 Paul Eddery (5) *led till 2 fs out, sn outpcd*. . . . .(16 to 1 tchd 20 to 1) 5
822^4 NATIVE CHIEFTAN [75] 4-8-7 A Munro (3) *beh, hdwy aftr 6 fs, chsd ldrs 5 furlongs out, wknd 2 and a half out*. . . . . (20 to 1 op 16 to 1 tchd 25 to 1) 6
857 DIME BAG [75] 4-8-7 T Quinn (2) *beh till hdwy aftr 6 fs, wkng whn slightly hmpd o'r 3 out*. . . . . (100 to 30 op 11 to 4 tchd 7 to 2) 7
Dist: 3l, 3l, 1½l, hd, ½l, 12l. 3m 4.17s. a 6.87s (7 Ran).
SR: 17/3/-/-/ (Lady Mary Mumford), Lady Herries

1130 Clive Graham Handicap Class D (0-80 3-y-o and up) £3,882 1m. . . . . . . (4:10)

676 KINGCHIP BOY [52] (v) 4-8-6 D Biggs (16) *str hold, chsd ldrs, strong chal fnl furlong, led last strds*. . . . .(14 to 1 tchd 16 to 1) 1
737 TROOPING (Ire) [73] 4-9-13 W Carson (9) *in tch, rdn frm 2 fs out, str chal fnl furlong, jst fld*. (6 to 1 jt-fav op 5 to 1) 2
756^8 DASWAKI (Can) [67] 5-9-7 B Rouse (3) *led for one furlong, led o'r 3 fs out, drvn frm over one out, hdd and no extr last strds*. . . . . (12 to 1 op 10 to 1 tchd 14 to 1) 3
756 COURT MINSTREL [54] 4-8-8 J Reid (14) *beh, plenty to do 2 fs out, pld out and hdwy o'r one out, fnshd wl*. . . . . (14 to 1 op 12 to 1) 4
990^* NOBBY BARNES [57] 4-8-4 (7*) T G McLaughlin (15) *beh, hdwy 3 fs out, not much room 2 out, ran on fnl furlong*. . . . . (6 to 1 jt-fav tchd 13 to 2) 5
801^9 SALBYNG [59] 5-8-13 Pat Eddery (13) *hdwy o'r 2 fs out, kpt on fnl furlong*. . . . . (7 to 1) 6

TIFFANY'S CASE (Ire) [60] 4-9-0 R Hills (17) *beh, some prog 2 fs out, one pace*.................(16 to 1 op 14 to 1) 7
771[2] KISSAVOS [53] 7-8-7 T Quinn (11) *chsd ldrs till wknd 2 fs out*........(9 to 1 op 10 to 1 tchd 11 to 1 and 8 to 1) 8
603 SLEEPLINE FANTASY [53] 8-8-7 N Carlisle (12) *chsd ldrs till wknd 2 fs out*..............................(16 to 1) 9
756[8] GRAND VITESSE (Ire) [74] 4-9-7 (7*) Mark Denaro (7) *in tch till wknd o'r 2 fs out*....(9 to 1 op 10 to 1 tchd 8 to 1) 10
1069 VANBOROUGH LAD [63] 4-9-3 L Piggott (4) *al beh*. ....(14 to 1 op 16 to 1) 11
818[8] CAUSLEY [73] 8-9-13 A Munro (8) *led aftr one furlong, hdd o'r 3 out, wknd quickly*.......(16 to 1 op 14 to 1) 12
530 LEAP IN THE DARK (Ire) [55] 4-8-9 W Ryan (6) *beh most of way*..(33 to 1) 13
LER CRU (Ire) [60] 4-9-0 T Williams (1) *al beh*. ....(33 to 1 op 20 to 1 tchd 50 to 1) 14
1062[7] CHILTERN HUNDREDS (USA) [60] 3-8-2 Paul Eddery (10) *nvr better than mid-div*..........(33 to 1 tchd 50 to 1) 15
ELEGANT TOUCH [68] 4-9-5 (3*) D Harrison (5) *al beh*. ....(14 to 1 op 12 to 1 tchd 16 to 1) 16
964[5] WAKI GOLD (USA) [69] 6-9-9 Lorna Vincent (2) *sn beh*. ....(16 to 1 op 12 to 1) 17
Dist: Sht-hd, nk, hd, 1½l, 3l, ½l, ½l, 2½l, 2l, 1½l. 1m 40.10s. a 2.90s (17 Ran).
SR: 31/51/44/30/28/21/20/11/3/ (Four Jays Racing Partnership), M J Ryan

1131 Goodwood House Maiden Stakes Class D (2-y-o) £3,915 6f........(4:45)

554[4] ZUNO STAR (USA) 9-0 Paul Eddery (3) *dsptd ld till led 2 fs out, drvn out fnl furlong*........ (20 to 1 tchd 33 to 1) 1
TIMELY EXAMPLE (USA) 9-0 T Quinn (10) *pushed alng frm hfwy, hdwy o'r one furlong out, fnshd wl*. ....(7 to 1 op 4 to 1 tchd 15 to 2) 2
SHEPHERD MARKET (Ire) 9-0 L Piggott (1) *str hold, dsptd ld, kpt on wl fnl furlong*........(10 to 1 tchd 12 to 1) 3
GREEN GOLIGHTLY (USA) 9-0 W Ryan (5) *hdwy 2 fs out, kpt on fnl furlong*............. (9 to 2 jt-fav op 5 to 1) 4
ROISIN CLOVER 8-9 A McGlone (13) *outpcd, rdn o'r 2 fs out, ran on fnl furlong*...........(33 to 1 op 20 to 1) 5
859[3] BASKERVILLE 9-0 A Munro (14) *made most till 2 fs out, fdd fnl furlong*.. (10 to 1) 6
913[7] PRINCE DANZIG (Ire) 9-0 C Rutter (9) *effrt frm 2 fs out, not pace of ldrs*.......................................(33 to 1) 7
UNBLEST 9-0 J Reid (2) *chsd ldrs till wknd fnl furlong*. ....(9 to 2 jt-fav op 4 to 1) 8
DUTY TIME 9-0 W Carson (4) *outpcd fnl 2 fs*. ....(8 to 1 op 6 to 1) 9
922[5] ARABOYBILL 8-9 (5*) Stephen Davies (12) *sn rdn, outpcd hfwy*.............................. (33 to 1 op 20 to 1) 10
CALYPSO MONARCH (Ire) 9-0 S Raymont (7) *hdwy 3 fs out, chlgd o'r 2 out, wknd over one out*. ....(11 to 2 op 5 to 1 tchd 6 to 1) 11
913 DURANDETTE 8-9 G Bardwell (11) *al rdn and outpcd*. ....(33 to 1) 12
MAJESTIC HEIGHTS (Ire) 9-0 Pat Eddery (8) *slwly into strd, al wl beh*..............(6 to 1 op 4 to 1 tchd 7 to 1) 13
CHIEF EXECUTIVE 9-0 J Williams (6) *slwly into strd, al beh*............................ (25 to 1 op 20 to 1) 14
Dist: ½l, ¾l, sht-hd, 2l, ¾l, sht-hd, nk, 2½l, ½l, 2l. 1m 13.45s. a 3.05s (14 Ran).
SR: 21/19/16/15/2/4/3/2/-/ (Vic Fatah), G Lewis

1132 Boxgrove Maiden Fillies' Stakes Class D (3-y-o) £3,980 7f........(5:20)

758[2] PETONELLAJILL 8-11 Pat Eddery (11) *in tch, drvn through on rls to ld wl ins last, gmely*. ....(4 to 1 tchd 5 to 1 and 7 to 2) 1
873[2] BARBOUKH 8-11 J Williams (4) *beh, hdwy o'r 2 fs out, ev ch ins last, not quicken*..............(4 to 1 op 3 to 1) 2
583 AKHLAK (Ire) 8-11 W Carson (6) *chsd ldrs till led o'r 3 fs out, hdd ins fnl 2 furlongs, rallied and ev ch inside last, one pace*............(16 to 1 op 12 to 1 tchd 20 to 1) 3
CHAPKA (Ire) 8-11 L Piggott (10) *trkd ldrs till led ins fnl 2 fs, hdd inside last, wknd cl hme*. ....(13 to 8 fav op 2 to 1 tchd 6 to 4) 4
995[9] TRINITY HALL 8-11 T Williams (1) *sn drpd rear and outpcd, drvn 2 fs out, styd on ins last*. ....(33 to 1 op 20 to 1 tchd 40 to 1) 5
THRIVING 8-11 J Reid (8) *slwly into strd, effrt and not much room ins fnl 3 fs, some prog final furlong*. ....(12 to 1 op 8 to 1) 6
CITY TIMES (Ire) 8-11 T Quinn (5) *mid-div, nvr rch ldrs*. ....(10 to 1 op 7 to 1) 7
872 CHILI LADY 8-11 T Sprake (9) *str hold, prmnt till wknd 2 fs out*..............(33 to 1 op 25 to 1 tchd 50 to 1) 8
4676a[6] VILLAVINA 8-11 C Rutter (3) *chsd ldrs, ev ch appr fnl 2 fs, wknd quickly*............................(50 to 1 op 25 to 1) 9
821 SWISS MOUNTAIN 8-11 W Newnes (2) *nvr rch ldrs*. ....(50 to 1 op 33 to 1) 10
EISHRELA 8-11 A Munro (7) *led till o'r 3 fs out, sn wknd*. ....(33 to 1 op 25 to 1 tchd 50 to 1) 11
Dist: 1l, sht-hd, 1l, 3l, ½l, 1½l, sht-hd, 3l, 5l, 1l. 1m 28.76s. a 4.16s (11 Ran).
SR: 19/16/15/12/3/1/ (Mrs J Cash), R Hannon

NOTTINGHAM (good to firm)

Wednesday May 19th

Going Correction: MINUS 0.30 sec. per fur. (races 1,2,6), PLUS 0.05 (3,4,5)

1133 Langwith Selling Handicap Class G (0-60 3-y-o) £2,763 1m 1f 213yds (2:20)

1005[8] KIAWAH [51] 8-6 (7*) N Varley (11) *co'red up beh ldrs, squeezed through to ld ins fnl furlong, drvn out*. ....(16 to 1 op 14 to 1) 1
888[3] BUGLET [56] 9-4 N Day (3) *settled midfield, not clr run 2 fs out, got through fnl furlong, ran on*. (8 to 1 op 6 to 1) 2
976[8] KISMETIM [55] 9-3 R Perham (4) *nvr far away, drvn through on ins to ld o'r one furlong out, hdd inside last, no extr*.....................(10 to 1 op 8 to 1) 3
699[9] WHO'S THE BEST (Ire) [45] 8-7 S Whitworth (19) *al hndy, drw level o'r 2 fs out, not quicken fnl furlong*. ....(5 to 1 op 8 to 1 tchd 12 to 1) 4
813[7] GYPSY CRYSTAL (USA) [41] 8-3 A Culhane (14) *patiently rdn, swtchd outsd to improve frm off the pace last 2 fs, ran on*............. (4 to 1 fav tchd 7 to 2 and 9 to 2) 5
415[5] SCOFFERA [49] 8-11 Kim Tinkler (17) *trkd ldr, nosed ahead o'r 2 fs out till over one out, edgd rght and wknd fnl furlong*......................(20 to 1 op 14 to 1) 6
894[7] DON'T FORGET MARIE (Ire) [55] 9-3 K Darley (6) *wth ldrs, hrd at work last 2 fs, no extr*.......(11 to 1 op 8 to 1) 7
934[8] TTYFRAN [54] 9-2 B Raymond (13) *patiently rdn, improved entering strt, no extr appr fnl furlong*. ....(14 to 1) 8
928[5] ANN HILL (Ire) [54] 9-2 S Perks (20) *sluggish strt, improved into midfield hfwy, not quicken last 2 fs*. ....(10 to 1 op 8 to 1) 9
963[6] MARIBELLA [59] 9-7 R Cochrane (8) *steadied strt, beh till some hdwy last 2 fs*...............(16 to 1 op 10 to 1) 10
1005 BOISTEROUS [45] (bl) 8-0 (7*) Kim McDonnell (12) *made most till hdd o'r 2 fs out, fdd appr fnl furlong*. ....(25 to 1 op 20 to 1) 11
826 UNIVERSAL (Fr) [40] 8-2 L Charnock (16) *improved frm midfield to take clr order entering strt, btn 2 fs out*. ....(25 to 1 op 20 to 1) 12
642[6] STAPLEFORD LASS [47] 8-9 W Woods (9) *sluggish strt, improved entering strt, nvr nr to chal*. ....(9 to 1 op 6 to 1 tchd 10 to 1) 13
976 PETITE JESS [40] 8-2 J Quinn (10) *chsd ldg half dozen till fdd o'r 2 fs out*.................... (25 to 1 op 14 to 1) 14
826 PREMIER BLUES (Fr) [44] 8-6 N Adams (2) *beh till styd on last 2 fs, nvr nrr*.................(20 to 1 op 14 to 1) 15
614 BECKY BOO [36] 7-12 J Lowe (5) *beh, some hdwy o'r 2 fs out, nvr dngrs*..................... (25 to 1 op 20 to 1) 16
928[4] DANCES WITH GOLD [50] 8-12 Dean McKeown (18) *pressed ldg pair, hrd at work o'r 2 fs out, fdd*.........(10 to 1) 17
499[7] HOBEY CAT [50] 8-12 G Duffield (7) *settled aftr fst break, feeling pace entering strt, sn btn*. (16 to 1 op 12 to 1) 18
928[6] SUMMERS DREAM [39] 8-1[1] G Carter (21) *patiently rdn, improved entering strt, fdd 2 fs out*. ....(16 to 1 op 14 to 1) 19
4800a[6] NIGELS PROSPECT [52] 9-0 A Mackay (1) *trkd ldg quartet to strt, fdd*.......................(25 to 1 op 14 to 1) 20
PRINCESS NEBIA [40] 8-2 E Johnson (15) *chsd ldg bunch to strt, sn btn*......................(25 to 1 op 20 to 1) 21
Dist: ½l, 2½l, 1l, ½l, 3l, 1l, 2½l, hd, hd, hd. 2m 7.40s. a 4.40s (21 Ran).
SR: 25/29/23/11/6/8/12/6/5/ (R S Field), J R Fanshawe

1134 Forest Handicap Class E (0-70 3-y-o) £3,261 1¾m 15yds............ (2:50)

838[3] PAPER DAYS [45] 7-10 N Adams (2) *trkd ldr, led appr strt till o'r one furlong out, rallied grimly to ld cl hme*. ....(10 to 1 op 5 to 1) 1
838* HARLESTONE BROOK [68] 9-5 G Carter (6) *settled midfield, hrd drvn to ld o'r one furlong out, ct cl hme*. ....(6 to 4 fav op 11 to 8 tchd 5 to 4) 2
816[5] ROMALITO [63] 9-0 R Cochrane (5) *trkd ldg half dozen, effrt und pres o'r 2 fs out, styd on same pace*. ....(12 to 1 op 10 to 1) 3
338* ONE VOICE (USA) [65] 9-2 G Duffield (11) *nvr far away, hrd at work entering strt, kpt on same pace last 2 fs*. ....(7 to 4 op 3 to 1) 4
724[9] PUGET DANCER (USA) [55] (v) 8-1 (5*) M Fenton (4) *wth ldrs, feeling pace and drvn alng o'r 2 fs out, no extr*. ....(12 to 1 op 7 to 1) 5
699[5] PERSIAN STAR (Fr) [42] 7-2 (5*) Darren Moffatt (9) *beh and chsd alng, improved frm off the pace last 2 fs, fnshd wl*. ....(20 to 1 op 16 to 1) 6
838[4] BRANSBY ROAD (Ire) [49] 8-0 J Quinn (8) *bustled alng to keep in tch aftr a m, not pace to chal*. (8 to 1 op 5 to 1) 7
SNUG SURPRISE [42] 7-7 J Fanning (7) *in tch, hrd at work aftr a m, sn btn*.......................... (50 to 1 op 33 to 1) 8
903[4] SOCIAL VISION (Ire) [50] 8-1 L Charnock (10) *sluggish strt, nvr able to trble ldrs*..................(50 to 1 op 33 to 1) 9
864* ROSIE'S GOLD [70] 9-7 M Tebbutt (1) *dictated pace till hdd appr strt, fdd 2 fs out*.........(14 to 1 op 10 to 1) 10
976 SENSE OF HUMOUR [61] 8-12 N Day (12) *sluggish strt, chsd alng to keep in tch aftr a m, sn btn*. ....(25 to 1 op 16 to 1) 11

MISS RIBBONS [52] 7-10 (7*) Kim McDonnell (3) *wl plcd on ins till wknd entering strt*..................(20 to 1) 12
Dist: Hd, 3½l, 4l, 1½l, 3½l, 12l, nk, 1½l, nk, 3l. 3m 3.30s. a 5.40s (12 Ran).
SR: -/8/-/-/-/-/ (M Dallimore), P G Murphy

1135 Cinderhill Maiden Stakes Class D (2-y-o) £3,874 5f 13yds............ (3:20)

793[2] GROTTO POOL (USA) 9-0 G Duffield (2) *made all, shaken up to quicken hfwy, ran on strly fnl furlong.* .... (9 to 4 on op 7 to 4 on tchd 6 to 4 on and 11 to 8 on) 1
730[4] JOHNNIE THE JOKER 9-0 Dean McKeown (1) *tucked away on ins, drvn through appr fnl furlong, ran on wl.* ....(10 to 1 op 7 to 2) 2
ELLARUTH (Ire) 8-9 P Robinson (11) *pushed alng to improve frm off the pace last 2 fs, fnshd wl.* .... (12 to 1 op 5 to 1) 3
877[2] JUST GREENWICH 8-9 K Darley (12) *pressed wnr, hrd at work appr fnl furlong, no extr*......(10 to 1 op 6 to 1) 4
GONE TO POT 9-0 J Lowe (6) *sn outpcd and bustled alng, swtchd ins hfwy, fnshd strly*....... (12 to 1 op 7 to 1) 5
BEDAZZLE 9-0 M Wigham (4) *sluggish strt, steady hdwy frm off the pace last 2 fs, ran on*... (50 to 1 op 20 to 1) 6
TARTAN GEM (Ire) 9-0 E Johnson (9) *sluggish strt, ran green and wndrd hfwy, nrst finish.* .... (50 to 1 op 33 to 1) 7
949 EL COHETE 9-0 S Whitworth (10) *co'red up in midfield, nvr plcd to chal*......................(50 to 1 op 33 to 1) 8
HELLABY 8-9 (5*) O Pears (7) *sluggish strt, pushed alng to improve hfwy, not rch ldrs*........ (33 to 1 op 16 to 1) 9
680 SOTTISES (Ire) 8-9 J Fortune (5) *broke wl to show gd speed 3 fs, fdd*..........................(25 to 1 op 16 to 1) 10
776 TWIN CREEKS 9-0 J Quinn (13) *steadied strt, improved hfwy, fdd o'r one furlong out*..... (33 to 1 op 16 to 1) 11
ZIGGYS BOY 9-0 N Adams (3) *sluggish strt, nvr able to reco'r*............................(50 to 1 op 33 to 1) 12
Dist: 3l, hd, 1½l, hd, nk, 3l, 1½l, 1l, ¾l, 1l. 1m 2.30s. a 4.10s (12 Ran).
SR: 23/11/5/-/3/2/ (Duke Of Devonshire), J A R Toller

1136 Flying Horse Maiden Fillies Stakes Class D (3-y-o) £3,289 5f 13yds..(3:50)

758[4] VICTORIA HALL 8-11 G Carter (7) *broke smartly, made all, quickened up fnl furlong, ran on, disqualified.* ....(5 to 2 op 3 to 1) 1D
872[5] BALLET SHOES (Ire) 8-11 R Cochrane (9) *wth wnr, hrd at work o'r one furlong out, unbl to quicken, fnshd second, awarded race*......... (5 to 4 fav op 11 to 10 on) 1
829[7] RUSSIA WITH LOVE 8-11 Dean McKeown (3) *nvr far away, effrt and drvn alng o'r one furlong out, styd on, fnshd 3rd, plcd second*...................(14 to 1 op 12 to 1) 2
NICHODOULA 8-11 G Duffield (2) *patiently rdn, not much room hfwy, swtchd ins and not clr run o'r one furlong out, ran on, better for race, fnshd 4th, plcd 3rd.* .... (14 to 1 op 12 to 1) 3
MANOR ADVENTURE 8-11 J Fortune (8) *sluggish strt, reco'red to show speed for over 3 fs, no extr, fnshd 5th, plcd 4th*.........................(8 to 1 tchd 10 to 1) 4
899[6] MOLLY BRAZEN 8-11 K Darley (6) *pressed ldrs, drifted lft und pres o'r one furlong out, no extr, fnshd 6th, plcd 5th*..............................(10 to 1 tchd 12 to 1) 5
SHE'S A BREEZE 8-11 M Birch (5) *chsd ldrs, effrt and bustled alng whn hmpd o'r one furlong out, eased when btn, fnshd 7th, plcd 6th*..... (33 to 1 op 25 to 1) 6
835[9] PHASE ONE (Ire) 8-11 N Adams (4) *outpcd and drvn alng, some hdwy o'r one furlong out, nvr nrr.* .... (33 to 1 op 25 to 1) 7
MIL BESOS 8-11 R Perham (1) *chsd ldrs, hrd at work hfwy, sn btn*...................(33 to 1 op 20 to 1) 8
963[4] LAMSONETTI (v) 8-11 A Culhane (10) *sluggish strt, reco'red to show speed on outsd till wknd over one furlong out*..........................(10 to 1 op 8 to 1) 9
Dist: 1½l, 1½l, ¾l, 2½l, 1l, 2l, nk, nk, 8l. 1m 1.40s. a 3.20s (10 Ran).
SR: 38/32/26/23/13/9/1/-/-/ (Lord Weinstock), R Charlton

1137 Bagthorpe Handicap Class D (0-80 3-y-o) £3,669 6f 15yds.......... (4:20)

683[3] HOTARIA [65] 8-12 A Culhane (7) *made all, quickened to go clr o'r one furlong out, ran on strly.* (11 to 2 op 3 to 1) 1
TUSCAN DAWN [71] 9-4 J Carroll (11) *nvr far away, hrd at work o'r one furlong out, kpt on same pace.* .... (6 to 1 op 11 to 2) 2
683 ASHGORE [66] 8-13 Dean McKeown (4) *al hndy, feeling pace and drvn alng 2 fs out, styd on.* ....(7 to 1 op 5 to 1 tchd 8 to 1) 3
683[6] HERSHEBAR [65] (bl) 8-5 (7*) G Strange (3) *beh and chsd alng hfwy, gd hdwy o'r one out, fnshd wl.* .... (8 to 1 op 10 to 1) 4
927 KENSWORTH LADY [48] 7-9 N Adams (9) *sluggish strt, reco'red to show gd speed thrght, one pace fnl furlong.* .... (14 to 1 op 20 to 1) 5
1010[6] MINSHAAR [68] 9-1 K Darley (6) *bustled alng wth chasing bunch, no imprsn appr fnl furlong.* .... (12 to 1 op 10 to 1 tchd 14 to 1) 6
747[4] RED FAN (Ire) [67] 9-0 N Connorton (10) *missed break, bustled alng to go pace, eased whn btn 2 fs out.* ....(3 to 1 fav op 11 to 4 tchd 7 to 2) 7
728[4] MELODIC DRIVE [58] 8-5 J Lowe (5) *took keen hold, not much room aftr 2 fs, nvr plcd to chal.* .... (10 to 1 op 6 to 1) 8
590[7] FLASHMAN [62] 8-9 G Carter (2) *drvn alng wth chasing bunch, eased whn btn last 2 fs*......(14 to 1 op 8 to 1) 9
945[7] PAIR OF JACKS (Ire) [74] 9-7 W Woods (8) *unruly in stalls, broke wl to show speed for o'r 3 fs, fdd.* .... (11 to 2 op 6 to 1 tchd 5 to 1) 10
Dist: 1½l, sht-hd, 1l, hd, 4l, 2½l, ½l, ½l, 12l. 1m 14.60s. a 3.10s (10 Ran).
SR: 42/42/36/31/13/17/6/-/-/ (Mrs Julia Richmond), R M Whitaker

1138 Langworth Apprentice Handicap Class G (0-70 3-y-o and up) £2,889 1m 54yds........................ (4:50)

964[3] LADY DONOGHUE (USA) [45] 4-7-12 (5*) Wendy Jones (7) *settled midfield, improved on ins to ld o'r one furlong out, readily*....... (5 to 1 fav tchd 11 to 2 and 6 to 1) 1
834[5] SOOTY TERN [42] 6-8-0 R Waterfield (16) *trkd ldg bunch, drvn alng to improve last 2 fs, no ch wth wnr*...(8 to 1) 2
931 SELF EXPRESSION [58] 5-8-8 (8*) D Thomas (1) *sluggish strt, improved frm off the pace last 2 fs, fnshd wl.* .... (12 to 1 op 7 to 1) 3
906[6] SLY PROSPECT (USA) [47] 5-8-0 (5*) C Webb (2) *swtchd ins to improve frm midfield last 2 fs, ran on.* .... (20 to 1 op 14 to 1 tchd 25 to 1) 4
845 TAHITIAN [58] 4-9-2 C Teague (5) *sluggish strt, beh till ran on wl last 2 fs, nrst finish*.......... (10 to 1 op 6 to 1) 5
930[3] DUNE RIVER [70] 4-9-6 (8*) I Hughes (18) *tried to make all, rdn and hdd o'r one furlong out, no extr.* .... (11 to 1 op 7 to 1) 6
861[7] ROYAL ACCLAIM [42] (v) 8-7-11 (3*) Michael Bradley (11) *beh till improved und pres last 2 fs, nvr nrr.* .... (14 to 1 op 10 to 1) 7
1073[2] SANDMOOR DENIM [56] 6-8-11 (3*) G Strange (17) *al chasing ldrs, came wide strt, kpt on, no imprsn.* ....(6 to 1 op 7 to 1) 8
GARTH [68] 5-9-4 (8*) L Aspell (12) *chsd ldg bunch, hrd at work 2 fs out, no imprsn*...........(33 to 1 op 20 to 1) 9
927[6] GOOD IMAGE [57] 3-7-12 (5*) D O'Neill (9) *nvr far away, hrd at work 2 fs out, sn btn*..........(12 to 1 op 8 to 1) 10
964[6] SKIMMER HAWK [36] (v) 4-7-8 Sally Radford-Howes (3) *chsd ldg bunch till wknd o'r 2 fs out*.... (16 to 1 op 12 to 1) 11
834 TAUNTING (Ire) [48] 5-8-6 S McCarthy (8) *struggling to go pace hfwy, nvr a threat*........... (14 to 1 op 10 to 1) 12
681 ABSOLUTLEY FOXED [35] 4-7-5[1] (3*) J Bramhill (14) *in tch to strt, sn btn*...................... (50 to 1 op 25 to 1) 13
962 CHANCE REPORT [35] 5-7-2 (5*) F Savage (10) *chsd ldg bunch to strt, sn btn*............. (25 to 1 op 20 to 1) 14
905[5] MY SISTER LUCY [47] 3-7-2 (5*) Martin Dwyer (6) *struggling to keep up hfwy, sn btn*........ (50 to 1 op 25 to 1) 15
990[5] KING PARROT (Ire) [56] 5-8-6 (8*) D Salt (15) *wth ldrs, hrd at work o'r 2 fs out, fdd.* .... (15 to 2 op 6 to 1 tchd 8 to 1) 16
990[8] LITERARY CRITIC (Ire) [43] (bl) 4-8-1 G Milligan (13) *chsd ldg quartet till fdd und pres o'r 2 fs out.* ....(14 to 1 tchd 16 to 1) 17
904 LINPAC EXPRESS [40] (bl) 4-7-12 A Whelan (4) *hrd at work on ins entering strt, tld off*........ (33 to 1 op 25 to 1) 18
Dist: 4l, 1½l, ½l, sht-hd, ½l, 1½l, sht-hd, 1½l, 1½l, ½l. 1m 43.40s. a 3.40s (18 Ran).
SR: 1/-/-/-/-/4/ (C C Buckley), Mrs M Reveley

CLONMEL (IRE) (good to firm) Thursday May 20th

1139 Cashel Handicap (0-75 3-y-o) £2,245 1 ½m.......................... (7:00)

912[8] ISLAND VISION (Ire) [-] 8-6 W J Supple (16)........(12 to 1) 1
912[2] DIAMOND CLUSTER [-] 7-12 (8*) R T Fitzpatrick (10) (7 to 1) 2
789[7] PULMICORT [-] 8-8 R Hughes (12)...............(11 to 2) 3
959 TENCA (Ire) [-] 8-13 J P Murtagh (13)............(12 to 1) 4
1046 BRIGENSER (Ire) [-] (bl) 8-13 P Shanahan (9).......(7 to 1) 5
1025 LAKE OF LOUGHREA (Ire) [-] 8-7 (6*) B J Walsh (8) (14 to 1) 6
912 SCANNO'S CHOICE (Ire) [-] 8-2 J F Egan (7)........(8 to 1) 7
639 REGAL PRETENDER (Ire) [-] 8-3 N G McCullagh (1) (14 to 1) 8
959* DARK SWAN (Ire) [-] 8-10 (2*,3ex) D G O'Shea (11) (3 to 1 fav) 9
959[5] INISHMOT (Ire) [-] 9-2 M J Kinane (17).............(5 to 1) 10
1014[6] MONTEJUSTICE (Ire) [-] 8-4 Joanna Morgan (2)... (14 to 1) 11
849[9] KATIES VISION (Ire) [-] 8-2 (6*) J J Behan (15)..... (12 to 1) 12
981[9] MAZZARELLO (Ire) [-] 7-4 (6*) P P Murphy (4)..... (10 to 1) 13
552 POSITIVE VIEW (Ire) [-] (bl) 7-11[1] (2*) R M Burke (14) (16 to 1) 14
489 NORDIC HABITAT (Ire) [-] 9-7 C Roche (3)......... (8 to 1) pu
Dist: ½l, 1l, ½l, 2l. 2m 44.30s. (15 Ran).
(Mrs M O'Connell), Kevin Prendergast

1140 Carrick (Fillies) Maiden (3-y-o and up) £2,245 1½m................... (7:30)

982[2] SAFFRON CROCUS 3-8-8 M J Kinane (3)...... (2 to 1 on) 1
911[2] CAMDEN BUZZ (Ire) 5-9-12 C F Swan (8)...........(4 to 1) 2

1106⁹ HIND VISION (Ire) 3-8-8 J F Egan (7) .... (20 to 1) 3
550⁷ TEBRE (USA) 3-8-8 W J Supple (9) .... (12 to 1) 4
936³ PRINTOUT (Ire) 3-8-2 (6*) J A Heffernan (2) .... (12 to 1) 5+
577⁹ PLUM LICK (Ire) 3-8-9¹ C Roche (1) .... (7 to 1) 5+
982⁴ TROPICAL LAKE (Ire) 3-8-8 S Craine (4) .... (16 to 1) 7
SAINT HILDA (Ire) 3-8-8 R Hughes (6) .... (12 to 1) 8
QUEENIES CHILD 6-9-12 W J O'Connor (5) ...... (25 to 1) 9
Dist: 1½l, 1l, 3l, nk, nk. 2m 42.60s. (9 Ran).
(Sheikh Mohammed), John M Oxx

1141 Roscrea Maiden (4-y-o and up) £2,245 2m. .... (8:00)

SOLBA (USA) 4-8-4 (10*) B Fenton (1) .... (9 to 1) 1
959⁹ CRAZY GAIL 6-8-11 J P Murtagh (9) .... (11 to 2) 2
852⁴ ZUHAL 5-8-5 (6*) J J Behan (10) .... (13 to 8 fav) 3
ROYAL OPTIMIST 9-8-2¹ (10*) A J Dempsey (2) ... (20 to 1) 4
1013² CEDAR COURT (Ire) (bl) 5-9-0 W J O'Connor (5) .... (7 to 4) 5
ALOHA (Ire) 4-8-11 M J Kinane (8) .... (12 to 1) 6
852 BANKONIT (Ire) (bl) 5-9-0 P Shanahan (12) .... (20 to 1) 7
REFINED HEIR 5-9-0 S Craine (11) .... (7 to 1) 8
BUZZ ALONG 7-8-7 (4*) W J Smith (3) .... (20 to 1) 9
852⁷ INDIANA GOLD (Ire) 5-8-11 Joanna Morgan (4) .... (16 to 1) 10
309 COLLECTED (Ire) 4-8-11 N Byrne (7) .... (20 to 1) 11
819⁶ THE RIDGE BOREEN 9-9-0 K J Manning (6) ...... (20 to 1) 12
Dist: 2½l, 1l, 8l, 1l. 3m 35.70s. (12 Ran).
(Three Counties Syndicate), Augustine Leahy

GOODWOOD (good to firm)
Thursday May 20th
Going Correction: PLUS 0.05 sec. per fur. (races 1,6,7), MINUS 0.15 (2,3,4,5)

1142 Payne And Gunter Fillies Conditions Stakes Class C (2-y-o) £4,232 6f (2:10)

657* ROHITA (Ire) 8-12 Pat Eddery (8) *hld up beh ldrs, led o'r one furlong out, quickened clr, cmftbly.*
.... (6 to 4 on op 5 to 4 on tchd Evens) 1
HADDIAH 8-10 J Reid (4) *sluggish strt, trkd ldrs, shaken up o'r one furlong out, ran on wl, prmsg.*
.... (12 to 1 op 5 to 1) 2
DIAMOND PARK (Ire) 8-10 B Raymond (6) *cl up, ev ch 2 fs out, kpt on one pace.* (16 to 1 op 6 to 1 tchd 20 to 1) 3
865* DON'T BE KOI (Ire) 8-10 T Quinn (1) *led til hdd 2 and a half fs out, rdn and one pace.*
.... (9 to 2 op 4 to 1 tchd 5 to 1) 4
715* ANTONIA'S FOLLY 8-12 G Carter (3) *cl up, led 2 and a half fs out till hdd o'r one out, wknd.*
.... (7 to 1 op 5 to 1 tchd 8 to 1) 5
SWAGGER LADY 8-10 M Hills (7) *strted slwly, sn reco'red, chsd ldrs till outpcd fnl 2 fs.*
.... (33 to 1 op 16 to 1 tchd 50 to 1) 6
922⁶ EMMA GRIMES (Ire) 8-3 (7*) Mark Denaro (5) *trkd ldrs till wknd o'r 2 fs out*..... (50 to 1 op 33 to 1 tchd 66 to 1) 7
URSULINE 8-10 L Piggott (2) *strted slwly, al outpcd.*
.... (12 to 1 op 5 to 1 tchd 14 to 1) 8
Dist: 3l, 2½l, 2l, 6l, ¾l, 5l, 2l. 1m 14.70s. a 4.30s (8 Ran).
SR: 18/4/-/-/-/ (B J Taylor), M R Channon

1143 Royal Sussex Regiment Handicap Class D (0-80 4-y-o and up) £3,552 1½m. .... (2:40)

620⁶ GLIDE PATH (USA) [70] 4-9-5 M Hills (11) *hld up in mid-div, hdwy to ld o'r 2 fs out, clr appr last, ran on wl.*
.... (8 to 1 tchd 10 to 1) 1
824⁷ CHATHAM ISLAND [67] 5-8-13 (3*) B Doyle (1) *mid-div, hdwy 3 fs out, chsd wnr frm o'r one out, ran on one pace*.. .... (14 to 1 tchd 16 to 1) 2
618 PRINCE HANNIBAL [75] 6-9-10 R Cochrane (9) *missed break, hld up beh, hdwy 2 fs out, styd on, nrst finish.*
.... (14 to 1 tchd 16 to 1) 3
674 MOONLIGHT QUEST [68] 5-9-3 L Dettori (15) *mid-div, rdn and hdwy 3 fs out, one pace und pres frm o'r one out.*
.... (16 to 1 op 14 to 1) 4
988⁶ SWORD MASTER [73] 4-9-8 N Day (12) *trkd ldrs, lost pl o'r 3 fs out, hrd rdn over one out, kpt on.*
.... (12 to 1 op 10 to 1) 5
785³ JAMES IS SPECIAL (Ire) [50] 5-7-13 J Quinn (8) *trkd ldrs, led 3 fs out till hdd o'r 2 out, wknd.*
.... (11 to 2 op 6 to 1 tchd 7 to 1) 6
618³ TEXAN TYCOON [74] 5-9-9 T Quinn (4) *chsd ldrs, drvn alng 3 fs out, btn o'r one out*............ (8 to 1 op 6 to 1) 7
874⁴ BOOKCASE [72] 6-9-7 J Williams (2) *beh, hrd rdn 4 fs out, hdwy o'r one out, nrst finish.*
.... (16 to 1 op 12 to 1 tchd 20 to 1) 8
994 KEEP ME IN MIND (Ire) [59] 4-8-8 T Sprake (7) *sn led til hdd o'r 4 fs out, wknd*.............................. (33 to 1) 9
988² FIRST BID [65] 6-9-0 L Piggott (5) *al beh.*
.... (8 to 1 tchd 9 to 1) 10
994⁴ MUNDAY DEAN [60] (bl) 5-8-9 J Reid (6) *trkd ldr, led o'r 4 fs out till hdd 3 out, wknd quickly.*
.... (100 to 30 fav op 3 to 1 tchd 7 to 2) 11
QUADRANT [73] 4-9-8 Candy Morris (13) *mid-div till wknd 3 fs out*.. (33 to 1) 12
879⁵ SCENIC DANCER [49] (v) 5-7-5 (7*) N Varley (3) *strted very slwly and lost many ls start, rapid hdwy to track ldrs hfwy, wknd o'r 3 fs out.*
.... (14 to 1 op 12 to 1 tchd 16 to 1) 13
440⁴ MARZOCCO [49] 5-7-12 T Williams (10) *al beh.*
.... (25 to 1 op 33 to 1) 14
EVERY ONE A GEM [50] 6-7-8 (5*) N Gwilliams (14) *al beh.*
.... (50 to 1) 15
Dist: 2l, ¾l, 1½l, ¾l, 2l, ¾l, hd, 7l, nk, 1l. 2m 40.87s. a 7.87s (15 Ran).
SR: 8/1/7/-/-/-/ (The Jampot Partnership), J W Hills

1144 Kidsons Impey Trophy Handicap Class C (0-90 3-y-o and up) £5,089 7f .... (3:10)

990⁷ CHEVEUX MITCHELL [70] (v) 6-8-11 Pat Eddery (1) *led til hdd 2 fs out, rallied und pres to ld ag'n cl hme.*
.... (10 to 1 op 7 to 1 tchd 12 to 1) 1
605 HELIOS [76] 5-9-3 J Reid (13) *cl up, led 2 fs out, rdn and hdd close hme*.................... (14 to 1 op 10 to 1) 2
818³ EN ATTENDANT (Fr) [83] 5-9-10 B Raymond (10) *hld up beh ldrs, cld 2 fs out, sn swtchd lft and one pace.* (5 to 1 co-fav tchd 11 to 2) 3
676 ANNABELLE ROYALE [65] 7-8-6 L Dettori (11) *pushed alng thrght, chsd ldrs, one pace frm o'r 2 fs out.*
.... (14 to 1 tchd 16 to 1) 4
893² VELOCE (Ire) [57] 5-7-12 F Norton (4) *trkd ldrs, drvn 3 out, one pace*.. .... (8 to 1 op 7 to 1) 5
DIGPAST (Ire) [85] 3-9-1 R Perham (8) *mid-div, pushed alng to cl 3 fs out, one pace frm 2 out.*
.... (20 to 1 op 14 to 1 tchd 25 to 1) 6
714² CAPE PIGEON (USA) [80] 8-9-4 (3*) J Weaver (7) *wtd wth in mid-div, effrt whn hmpd o'r one furlong out, kpt on.*
.... (5 to 1 co-fav tchd 11 to 2) 7
THE CAN CAN MAN [61] 6-8-2 R P Elliott (9) *trkd ldrs, drvn o'r 2 fs out, hng rght over one out.*
.... (14 to 1 op 12 to 1 tchd 16 to 1) 8
VAGANOVA (Ire) [76] 4-9-3 T Quinn (3) *rear, effrt and cld 3 fs out, sn btn*......... (12 to 1 op 8 to 1 tchd 14 to 1) 9
197 BUSTER [73] 5-9-0 G Bardwell (2) *sn rdn alng, al beh.*
.... (50 to 1) 10
948⁸ ACROSS THE BAY [67] (v) 6-8-8 M Hills (5) *cl up til wknd bef 2 fs out*..................... (14 to 1 tchd 16 to 1) 11
659⁹ HALBERT [68] 4-8-9 A McGlone (6) *mid-div, effrt whn not much room 2 fs out, sn rdn and no imprsn.*
.... (16 to 1 op 12 to 1 tchd 20 to 1) 12
676⁶ SURREY RACING [72] 5-8-13 B Rouse (14) *strted slwly, cld 3 fs out, sn btn.* (5 to 1 co-fav op 4 to 1 tchd 11 to 2) 13
771 HIGHEST PRAISE (USA) [56] 10-7-11 S O'Gorman (12) *al beh*.. .... (20 to 1) 14
Dist: Nk, 3l, ½l, ¾l, ¾l, ½l, 2l, 3l, nk, ½l. 1m 26.94s. a 2.34s (14 Ran).
SR: 46/51/49/29/19/34/38/13/19/ (Chitty Ltd), M R Channon

1145 Ivorbelle Maiden Stakes Class D (3-y-o) £3,465 1m 1f. .... (3:40)

AJALAN (Ire) 9-0 Pat Eddery (3) *hld up beh, hrd rdn 2 fs out, hdwy o'r one out, led ins last, ran on.*
.... (13 to 2 op 9 to 2 tchd 7 to 1) 1
751⁵ MT TEMPLEMAN (USA) 9-0 L Dettori (8) *trkd ldrs, not much room 2 fs out, squeezed through o'r one out, ran on*.. .... (5 to 2 jt-fav tchd 11 to 4) 2
751⁷ THALEROS 9-0 L Piggott (1) *trkd ldrs gng wl, led o'r one furlong out, hdd and one pace und pres ins last.*
.... (5 to 2 jt-fav tchd 9 to 4 and 11 to 4) 3
835³ HARD TASK 8-9 T Quinn (2) *cl up, led o'r 3 fs out till hdd over one out, ev ch entering last, one pace.*
.... (14 to 1 op 12 to 1 tchd 16 to 1) 4
803² BOLD THATCHER 9-0 Paul Eddery (6) *in tch, cld o'r 4 fs out, ev ch 2 out, one pace.*
.... (9 to 2 op 7 to 2 tchd 5 to 1) 5
TICKERTY'S GIFT 9-0 B Rouse (7) *al beh.*
.... (8 to 1 op 6 to 1) 6
980 POETIC FORM (Ire) 9-0 M Perrett (5) *al beh*....... (50 to 1) 7
759 TURTLE POWER 9-0 S Whitworth (4) *led til hdd o'r 3 fs out, wknd*.. (50 to 1) 8
Dist: 1l, 1½l, hd, 1l, 6l, 10l, 8l. 1m 57.40s. a 5.40s (8 Ran).
(Sultan Mohammed), M R Stoute

1146 SIS Live Action Claiming Stakes Class E (3-y-o and up) £3,903 1¼m. ... (4:10)

678⁶ SARAH-CLARE 5-8-10 T Quinn (10) *trkd ldrs, led o'r 2 fs out, rdn and ran on wl*........... (12 to 1 op 10 to 1) 1
918* STORM FREE (USA) 7-9-1 (3*) J Weaver (7) *trkd ldrs, ev ch 2 fs out, chsd wnr frm o'r one out, kpt on.*
.... (11 to 1 op 8 to 1 tchd 12 to 1) 2
PHARLY STORY 5-9-11 L Piggott (8) *hld up beh, hdwy o'r 2 fs out, sn not much room, ran on, too much to do.*
.... (6 to 4 fav tchd 15 to 8) 3
990³ OVERPOWER 9-9-0 P Robinson (15) *mid-div, hdwy o'r 2 fs out, kpt on und pres, nrst finish.*
.... (11 to 1 op 7 to 1 tchd 12 to 1) 4

714^{3} NATURAL LAD 8-9-3 A Clark (11) *chsd ldg grp, pushed alng and hdwy 4 fs out, one pace frm o'r 2 out.* ....(14 to 1 op 10 to 1) 5
918^{5} AWESOME POWER 7-8-12 (3*) D Harrison (17) *trkd ldrs, cld and ch 2 fs out, sn one pace und pres.* ....(16 to 1 op 12 to 1 tchd 20 to 1) 6
279 NOTED STRAIN (Ire) 5-9-0 Pat Eddery (1) *beh, hdwy o'r 3 fs out, nrst finish*..........(7 to 1 op 8 to 1 tchd 10 to 1) 7
926^{8} HOSTILE WITNESS (Ire) (bl) 3-8-4 A McGlone (19) *sn led, hdd o'r 3 fs out, wknd.* (8 to 1 op 7 to 1 tchd 10 to 1) 8
874^{8} TEMPLE KNIGHT 4-9-5 D Biggs (6) *nvr better than mid-div*..........(14 to 1 op 10 to 1) 9
WOLLBOLL 3-8-7 T Sprake (4) *nvr nrr.* ....(33 to 1 op 20 to 1) 10
879^{9} DEBACLE (USA) 4-9-3 M Perrett (14) *chsd ldrs till wknd o'r 2 fs out*..........(12 to 1 op 10 to 1 tchd 14 to 1) 11
731^{7} MALINDI BAY 5-9-0 E Johnson (16) *cl up, led o'r 3 fs out till over 2 out, wknd*..........(33 to 1 op 20 to 1) 12
CIRCUIT COURT (Ire) 5-9-8 S Whitworth (2) *al beh.* ....(20 to 1 op 14 to 1) 13
990^{6} DAZZLING FIRE (Ire) 4-8-9 W Newnes (20) *chsd ldrs 3 fs, sn beh*..........(20 to 1 op 16 to 1) 14
817^{5} LOCK TIGHT (USA) 3-8-10 A Culhane (5) *chsd ldrs, effrt wl o'r 2 fs out, sn wknd*..........(16 to 1 op 12 to 1) 15
CLEAR LIGHT 6-9-1 M Wigham (13) *al beh.* ....(33 to 1 op 25 to 1) 16
476^{6} PRIVATE JET (Ire) 4-8-13 T Williams (18) *al beh*....(33 to 1) 17
826 WESSEX WARRIOR (v) 7-9-1 G Bardwell (9) *chsd ldrs, effrt 4 fs out, sn wknd und pres*........ (33 to 1 op 25 to 1) 18
SHEER POWER (Ire) 4-9-1 J Reid (12) *al beh.* ....(25 to 1 tchd 33 to 1) 19
928^{3} ESERIE DE CORES (USA) 3-8-2 J Quinn (3) *cl up till wknd 3 fs out*..........(25 to 1 op 16 to 1 tchd 33 to 1) 20

Dist: ¾l, 4l, ¾l, hd, 2l, 8l, ¾l, 7l, hd, 1½l. 2m 10.92s. a 5.42s (20 Ran).
SR: 27/33/32/19/21/15/ (Miss Clare Coyne), R Akehurst

1147 Goodwood Park Hotel Golf And Country Club Claiming Stakes Class E (3-y-o) £3,080 6f.................. (4:45)

WALK THE BEAT 9-7 A Tucker (3) *in tch, hdwy to ld one furlong out, all out*.....(7 to 1 op 6 to 1 tchd 8 to 1) 1
878^{7} KRAYYAN DAWN 8-2 S Dawson (4) *in tch, outpcd and rdn o'r 2 fs out, rapid hdwy ins last, fnshd wl.* ....(50 to 1 op 33 to 1 tchd 66 to 1) 2
720^{5} RED LEADER (Ire) 8-0 (7*) T G McLaughlin (2) *fly-jmpd strt, beh, hdwy 2 fs out, sn ev ch, one pace und pres ins last.* ....(5 to 1 op 9 to 2 tchd 11 to 2) 3
733^{8} DAILY SPORT DON 7-13 (7*) D Gibbs (7) *trkd ldrs, ev ch 2 fs out, one pace*.......... (11 to 2 op 5 to 1 tchd 6 to 1) 4
771 TOFF SUNDAE 8-4 G Carter (8) *chsd ldrs, pushed alng hfwy, styd on und pres*..........(16 to 1 tchd 20 to 1) 5
977 SOBER LAD (Ire) 9-7 Pat Eddery (1) *hng rght thrght, led til hdd one furlong out, btn whn not much room cl hme.* ....(9 to 2 tchd 4 to 1) 6
927^{8} INONDER 7-11 N Adams (5) *cl up, rdn 2 fs out, ev ch o'r one out, eased whn hld ins last.* ....(50 to 1 op 33 to 1 tchd 66 to 1) 7
878^{2} PATONG BEACH 7-10^{2} (3*) D Harrison (10) *cl up, ev ch 2 fs out, sn rdn and btn*.......... (5 to 2 fav tchd 3 to 1) 8
950 HARD ROCK MINER 8-3 (7*) S Mulvey (6) *sn tld off, some modest late hdwy*....(50 to 1 op 33 to 1 tchd 66 to 1) 9
882^{3} TEXAS COWGIRL (Ire) (bl) 7-4 (7*) D Wright (9) *in tch, pushed alng hfwy, sn wknd und pres.* ....(11 to 2 op 9 to 2 tchd 6 to 1) 10

Dist: Hd, 1½l, 1l, nk, 1½l, 4l, 1½l, 1½l, 1l. 1m 13.97s. a 3.57s (10 Ran).
SR: 42/22/21/16/13/24/ (The Country Life Partnership), R Simpson

1148 Levin Down Apprentice Handicap Class F (0-70 3-y-o and up) £3,132 5f .... (5:20)

909^{4} BARBEZIEUX [36] 6-8-3 D McCabe (4) *outpcd, tld off hfwy, rapid hdwy ins fnl furlong, led final strds.* ....(8 to 1 op 7 to 1 tchd 9 to 1) 1
916^{9} THE NOBLE OAK (Ire) [59] 5-9-7 (5*) Gina Faulkner (2) *cl up, led wl ins fnl furlong till hdd close hme.* ....(10 to 1 op 7 to 1) 2
1036^{2} KALAR [42] (bl) 4-8-9 O Pears (12) *cl up, led o'r 2 fs out till hdd wl ins last*..... (4 to 1 fav op 7 to 2 tchd 9 to 2) 3
720^{6} GAYNOR GOODMAN (Ire) [44] 3-8-2 B Russell (13) *strted slwly, sn pushed alng to chase ldrs, hdwy und pres o'r one furlong out, ev ch ins last, no extr.* ....(25 to 1 op 20 to 1 tchd 33 to 1) 4
1010^{5} TEE-EMM [57] 3-8-10 (5*) L Carter (1) *cl up, rdn 2 fs out, one pace*..........(16 to 1 op 10 to 1 tchd 20 to 1) 5
916 JOE SUGDEN [53] 9-9-1 (5*) Debbie Biggs (7) *al prmnt, rdn o'r one furlong out, one pace*.....(14 to 1 op 10 to 1) 6
STOCKTINA [35] 6-7-13 (3*) D Gibbs (10) *chsd ldrs, kpt on und pres ins fnl furlong.* ....(20 to 1 op 16 to 1 tchd 25 to 1) 7
916* SERIOUS HURRY [61] 5-10-0 Stephen Davies (14) *al prmnt, ev ch one furlong out, wknd und pres ins last.* ....(7 to 1 op 5 to 1) 8
837 DAL MISS [37] (bl) 6-8-4^{14} (3*) Mark Denaro (11) *in tch, rdn o'r 2 fs out, one pace*..........(100 to 1 op 33 to 1) 9
326^{2} THE FED [62] 3-9-3 (3*) G Parkin (17) *chsd ldrs till wknd 2 fs out*..........(12 to 1 op 10 to 1 tchd 14 to 1) 10
1036^{4} EVER SO LONELY [56] 4-9-2 (7*) W Hollick (3) *chsd ldrs, rdn 2 fs out, wknd*..........(7 to 1 op 6 to 1) 11
760 COPPERMILL LAD [46] 10-8-6 (7*) Iona Wands (6) *outpcd.* ....(10 to 1 op 6 to 1) 12
916 SKI CAPTAIN [53] 9-9-6 D Wright (8) *chsd ldrs, in tch, rdn 2 fs out, nvr on terms*.......... (16 to 1 op 14 to 1) 13
927^{4} PAT POINDESTRES [47] 3-8-5 N Gwilliams (9) *led til hdd o'r 2 fs out, wknd*..........(7 to 1 op 8 to 1 tchd 10 to 1) 14
614^{9} WEALTHYWOO [41] (bl) 3-7-13 C Hawksley (16) *strted slwly, al beh*..........(50 to 1 op 25 to 1) 15
815^{8} DANDY DESIRE [42] 4-8-9 C Hodgson (15) *outpcd.* ....(25 to 1 op 20 to 1 tchd 33 to 1) 16

Dist: Nk, 2l, ½l, 1½l, 2l, ¾l, ½l, nk, 2½l, nk. 1m 0.20s. a 3.40s (16 Ran).
SR: 26/48/23/14/21/18/-/21/-/ (T S M S Riley-Smith), D A Wilson

LONGCHAMP (FR) (good to soft)
Thursday May 20th

Going Correction: PLUS 0.60 sec. per fur. (race 1), NIL (2)

1149 Prix La Force (Group 2) (3-y-o) £23,895 1¼m.......................... (3:00)

536^{2} SIN KIANG (Fr) 8-11 C Asmussen (5) *mid-div, second strt, led o'r 2 fs out, ran on wl, cmftbly*.......... (21 to 10) 1
811^{3} IRISH PROSPECTOR (Fr) 8-11 E Legrix (3) *rear early, 6th strt, hdwy 2 fs out, hrd rdn and ran on wl fnl furlong.* ....(17 to 1) 2
485^{5} SISMART (Fr) 8-11 T Jarnet (1) *mid-div, 7th strt, not clr run, nrst finish*..........(53 to 10) 3
ENJOY PLAN (USA) 8-11 F Head (4) *prmnt early, 3rd strt, one pace fnl one and a half fs*..........(9 to 1) 4
408^{4} BADOLATO (USA) 8-11 W Mongil (8) *4th strt, effrt 2 fs out, unbl to quicken*..........(27 to 1) 5
HUSBAND (USA) 8-11 M Boutin (2) *nvr dngrs*.... (20 to 1) 6
811^{2} OKEEDOKEE (Fr) 8-11 O Doleuze (9) *trkd ldr early, led strt, rdn and wknd 2 fs out*..........(13 to 10 fav) 7
NYEPI (Ire) 8-11 N Jeanpierre (6) *al rear*..........(36 to 1) 8
890^{4} FRET (USA) 8-11 A Munro (7) *broke wl, led briefly, 5th strt, sn wknd*.......... (86 to 10) 9

Dist: 1l, ½l, 1l, 1½l, 2½l, 2l, 5l, nose. 2m 12.90s. a 10.80s (9 Ran).
SR: 49/47/46/44/41/36/32/22/21/ (Mme Y Seydoux de Clausonne), A Fabre

NEWCASTLE (good to soft)
Thursday May 20th

Going Correction: PLUS 0.60 sec. per fur. (races 1,4,5,6), PLUS 0.35 (2,3)

1150 2d Tyrian Plum Claiming Stakes Class F (3-y-o) £2,579 7f.............. (2:30)

907^{5} QUEEN OF THE QUORN 8-2 J Fanning (4) *made all, clr 2 out, styd on wl*..........(5 to 1 op 4 to 1) 1
907^{7} ADMISSION (Ire) 8-3 N Connorton (2) *in tch, styd on und pres fnl 2 fs, no ch wth wnr*....... (33 to 1 op 20 to 1) 2
907* WHITE CREEK (Ire) (v) 8-9 J Carroll (1) *trkd ldrs, rdn o'r 2 out, sn btn*..........(11 to 4 op 9 to 4 tchd 3 to 1) 3
828^{4} MR ABBOT 7-12 (5*) Darren Moffatt (5) *wth ldr till wknd 3 out*..........(14 to 1 op 10 to 1 tchd 16 to 1) 4
LOGAN'S LUCK (USA) 9-5 K Darley (3) *hld up, rdn o'r 2 out, no imprsn, eased whn btn ins fnl furlong.* ....(6 to 4 on op 11 to 8 on) 5

Dist: 5l, 2½l, 8l, 3l. 1m 31.56s. a 7.56s (5 Ran).
SR: 38/24/22/-/-/ (Lord Crawshaw), G M Moore

1151 1856 British Guiana 1 Cent Three Year Old Handicap Class D (0-80) £3,427 5f .... (3:00)

683 COVENT GARDEN GIRL [50] 8-0 L Charnock (4) *trkd ldrs, led 2 out, ran on strly fnl furlong*....(7 to 2 op 4 to 1) 1
866^{3} LOCAL HEROINE [71] 9-7 J Carroll (3) *chsd ldrs, chlgd 2 out, kpt on same pace*..........(4 to 1 op 3 to 1) 2
766* SHADOW JURY [67] 9-3 K Darley (1) *cl up, led afer 2 fs till hdd two out, ev ch till wknd ins fnl furlong.* ....(15 to 8 fav op 6 to 4 tchd 2 to 1) 3
829^{8} JOTRA [49] (v) 7-13 W Carson (2) *beh till some late hdwy, nvr dngrs*..........(6 to 1 op 5 to 1) 4
884^{4} CANNY LAD [55] 8-5 K Fallon (5) *slight ld 2 fs, sn outpcd and beh*..........(8 to 1 op 5 to 1) 5

Dist: 5l, hd, 2½l, 6l. 1m 3.15s. a 4.25s (5 Ran).
SR: 36/37/32/4/-/ (New Covent Garden Flower Sales), M W Easterby

1152 Kleenex Club Stakes Class D Conditions Stakes For Two Yrs Old £3,765 5f .... (3:30)

841^{2} BEST KEPT SECRET 9-0 J Carroll (3) *chsd ldg pair, rdn to ld one out, kpt on wl*....... (7 to 4 on tchd 6 to 4 on) 1
998 CYARNA QUINN (Ire) 8-5 G Duffield (2) *slight ld till hdd o'r 2 out, ev ch til no extr ins fnl furlong.* ....(2 to 1 tchd 7 to 4) 2

SPRING LOADED 8-10 Dean McKeown (1) *cl up, quickened to ld o'r 2 out, hng lft, hdd one out, sn btn.* ....(8 to 1 op 4 to 1) 3
Dist: 1½l, 2½l. 1m 4.39s. a 5.49s (3 Ran).
SR: 25/10/5/ (Manny Bernstein (Racing) Ltd), J Berry

1153 3d 'New Carlisle' Envelope Handicap Class C (0-100 3-y-o) £7,050 1m (4:00)

1008² JUST YOU DARE (Ire) [73] 8-0 G Duffield (1) *trkd ldrs, led wl o'r one out, ran on well.* ....(5 to 2 fav op 2 to 1 tchd 11 to 4) 1
468⁶ DOC COTTRILL [71] 7-12 J Lowe (6) *hld up, hdwy o'r 2 out, chsd wnr fnl furlong, no imprsn.* ....(3 to 1 op 7 to 2 tchd 11 to 4) 2
844³ CHEVROTAIN [88] 9-1 M Birch (2) *in tch, drvn alng 2 out, kpt on same pace*....................(7 to 2 op 4 to 1) 3
643⁷ IHTIRAZ [94] 9-7 R Hills (4) *led till hdd wl o'r one out, sn wknd*....................(10 to 1) 4
1016 GREAT STEPS [85] 8-12 Dean McKeown (3) *trkd ldrs till wknd o'r 2 out*....................(7 to 1 op 6 to 1) 5
514 TAJDIF (USA) [80] 8-7 W Carson (5) *in tch till wknd o'r 2 out*....................(7 to 1 op 8 to 1) 6
Dist: 2½l, 3½l, 4l, 4l, 4l. 1m 47.13s. a 8.13s (6 Ran).
SR: 36/26/32/26/5/-/ (Mrs David Thompson), Sir Mark Prescott

1154 U.S.A. 'Boscawen' Paid 5 Cents Maiden Stakes Class D (3-y-o) £3,435 1¼m 32yds.................... (4:30)

476³ RITTO 9-0 G Duffield (3) *led till hdd o'r 4 out, remained cl up, led over one out, styd on wl*.....(3 to 1 op 5 to 2) 1
ROSSCOYNE 8-9 K Darley (5) *hld up, effrt 3 out, styd on wl fnl furlong, not rch wnr*....................(20 to 1) 2
980⁴ MUTAWALI (Ire) 9-0 W Carson (2) *cl up, slight ld o'r 4 out, hdd wl over one out, one paced*.... (4 to 1 tchd 9 to 2) 3
751⁸ BARRATRY 9-0 W Ryan (6) *in tch, effrt 3 out, styd on same pace*.................... (5 to 2 tchd 11 to 4) 4
RAHIL (Ire) 9-0 R Hills (4) *trkd ldrs, ch o'r one out, wknd fnl furlong*.......... (9 to 4 fav op 7 to 4 tchd 5 to 2) 5
NEVER SO BRAVE 9-0 N Connorton (1) *dwlt, hld up, effrt 4 out, wknd 3 out, tld off*........(20 to 1 op 16 to 1) 6
Dist: 2l, ¾l, 1l, 2l, 25l. 2m 21.19s. a 14.69s (6 Ran).
SR: 15/6/9/7/3/-/ (Sheikh Mohammed), B W Hills

1155 India 1/2 Anna Scarlet 'Scinde Dawk' Handicap Class D (0-80 3-y-o and up) £3,435 2m 19yds.............. (5:00)

661⁶ BRANDON PRINCE (Ire) [73] (bl) 5-9-9 W Ryan (2) *in tch gng wl, effrt o'r 2 out, styd on well und pres to ld towards finish*....................(3 to 1 op 7 to 2) 1
92⁵ VALSEUR (USA) [57] 4-8-5 J Fanning (5) *led, clr 3 out, rdn 2 out, hdd and no extr towards finish*. (6 to 1 op 5 to 1) 2
831* MUCH SOUGHT AFTER [78] 4-9-12 G Duffield (1) *trkd ldr, rdn o'r 2 out, wknd over one out*...(13 to 2 op 5 to 1) 3
967* MY DESIRE [70] 5-9-1 (5*,3ex) Darren Moffatt (6) *sn pushed alng and beh, some late hdwy und pres, nvr dngrs.* ....(15 to 8 fav op 7 to 4 tchd 2 to 1) 4
MY CHIARA [66] 7-9-2 N Connorton (4) *chsd ldrs till wknd 4 out*....................(10 to 1 tchd 12 to 1) 5
1056⁴ HOT STAR [51] 7-8-1 J Lowe (3) *al beh, tld off.* ....(7 to 1 op 8 to 1) 6
Dist: 2l, 6l, 10l, 2l, 15l. 3m 45.79s. a 19.79s (6 Ran).
SR: 7/-/2/ (R P B Michaelson), I A Balding

CATTERICK (soft)
Friday May 21st
Going Correction: PLUS 0.50 sec. per fur. (races 1,5,6,7), PLUS 0.35 (2,3,4)

1156 Croft Selling Stakes Class G (4-y-o and up) £2,448 1m 7f 177yds.... (2:20)

DECIDED (Can) 10-9-5 (5*) O Pears (11) *trkd ldrs, hdwy 4 fs out, led o'r one and a half out, sn clr, ran on.* ....(20 to 1 tchd 25 to 1) 1
1034² POST IMPRESSIONIST (Ire) 4-9-0 M Wigham (5) *in tch till rdn alng and lost pl 7 fs out, ridden and hdwy 3 out, kpt on und pres fnl 2 furlongs.* ....(9 to 4 fav tchd 5 to 2 and 2 to 1) 2
331³ ANGELICA PARK 7-9-5 M Birch (4) *trkd ldrs, hdwy to ld 5 fs out, rdn 2 out, sn hdd and one pace.* ....(11 to 2 op 5 to 1) 3
BARCHAM 6-9-7 (3*) D Harrison (9) *hld up, hdwy 4 fs out, rdn and one pace 2 out.* (15 to 2 op 6 to 1 tchd 8 to 1) 4
901⁵ ENKINDLE 6-9-2 J Fortune (10) *mid-div, rdn alng and outpcd 4 fs out, plugged on one pace und pres frm 2 out.* ....(14 to 1 op 12 to 1) 5
681 RUN MILADY 5-9-2 D Wilkinson (2) *hld up and beh, rdn alng and hdwy 5 fs out, one pace fnl 3 furlongs.* ....(33 to 1) 6
1034⁷ IRON BARON (Ire) 4-9-8 S Perks (1) *hld up and beh, hdwy o'r 4 fs out, sn rdn and no imprsn frm 2 out*....(6 to 1) 7
826 ICE MAGIC 6-9-10 A McGlone (3) *chsd ldrs, rdn 4 fs out, wknd o'r 2 out*.................... (33 to 1 op 25 to 1) 8
MISTIC GLEN (Ire) 4-8-7 (7*) V Halliday (6) *chsd ldrs till rdn and wknd 3 fs out*....................(10 to 1) 9
924⁷ PHAROAH'S GUEST 6-9-10 G Carter (8) *cl up, led 6 fs out to 5 out, sn rdn and wknd 3 out*......(9 to 2 op 3 to 1) 10
828 BARGEE (USA) 4-9-5 R Lappin (7) *sn led, hdd 6 fs out and soon lost pl, tld off frm 3 out*......(50 to 1 op 33 to 1) 11
Dist: 2l, sht-hd, 8l, 2l, 2l, 1½l, 1l, nk, 4l. 3m 46.30s. a 24.80s (11 Ran).
(Mrs C Lee), R Lee

1157 Doug Moscrop Sprint Handicap Class D (0-80 3-y-o) £3,348 5f......... (2:55)

COCONUT JOHNNY [53] 8-4 J Fanning (4) *al chasing ldr, rdn 2 fs out, styd on ins last to ld on line.* ....(14 to 1 op 10 to 1 tchd 16 to 1) 1
1151³ SHADOW JURY [67] 8-13 (5*) O Pears (3) *led, quickened clr 2 fs out, rdn fnl furlong, ct on line*... (5 to 1 op 7 to 2) 2
TREVORSNINEPOINTS [57] 8-3 (5*) Darren Moffatt (7) *al chasing ldrs, rdn 2 fs out, one pace appr last.* ....(7 to 2 tchd 3 to 1) 3
846 PRIMULA BAIRN [69] 9-6 M Birch (5) *chsd ldrs, effrt and rdn 2 fs out, sn one pace*......... (3 to 1 fav op 9 to 4) 4
899² HUMBER'S SUPREME (Ire) [57] (bl) 8-5 (3*) D Harrison (2) *effrt hfwy, sn rdn and nvr able to chal.* ....(9 to 2 op 4 to 1 tchd 5 to 1) 5
KIMBOLTON KORKER [65] 8-9 (7*) Claire Balding (6) *al rear.* .... (20 to 1 op 16 to 1) 6
614³ CHARITY EXPRESS (Ire) [70] 9-7 T Lucas (1) *very slwly away, al beh*....................(9 to 1 op 6 to 1) 7
535⁷ TOM PIPER [69] 9-6 G Carter (8) *chsd ldrs till rdn and wknd hfwy, sn beh*.................... (8 to 1) 8
Dist: Hd, 3½l, 2l, 1l, ¾l, 4l, nk. 1m 3.20s. a 5.70s (8 Ran).
SR: 11/24/-/4/-/ (Crestmart Ltd), G M Moore

1158 Stapleton Maiden Auction Fillies Stakes Class F (2-y-o) £2,713 5f (3:30)

680³ MY LIFETIME LADY (Ire) 8-11 S Perks (2) *made all, rdn and quickened clr fnl furlong.* ....(2 to 1 fav op 5 to 4 tchd 9 to 4) 1
865⁴ FLOATING TRIAL 8-11 G Carter (5) *cl up, effrt 2 fs out and ev ch till rdn and not quicken ins last.* ....(8 to 1 op 7 to 1) 2
DANGEROUS SHADOW 8-6 (5*) Darren Moffatt (10) *al prmnt, ev ch o'r one furlong out, sn rdn and one pace.* ....(5 to 1 op 4 to 1) 3
1078³ STUDFORD GIRL 8-11 T Lucas (3) *chsd ldrs, rdn o'r one furlong out and sn wknd.* ....(9 to 2 op 4 to 1 tchd 5 to 1) 4
812 TENPIN PROPHET (Ire) (bl) 8-8 (3*) D Harrison (11) *hdwy on outer o'r 2 fs out, sn rdn and kpt on one pace.* .... (12 to 1 op 10 to 1) 5
MACAROON LADY 8-11 Alex Greaves (4) *outpcd and beh till styd on fnl 2 fs*....................(25 to 1 op 20 to 1) 6
SILVER SLIPPER 8-11 A McGlone (7) *badly hmpd strt, effrt and some hdwy 2 fs out, sn rdn and no imprsn.* ....(5 to 1 op 3 to 1) 7
1082⁷ LUCKY LIZZY 8-11 M Wigham (1) *chsd ldrs 3 fs, sn rdn and wknd*...............(14 to 1 op 12 to 1 tchd 20 to 1) 8
CELTIC GOVERNESS 8-4 (7*) Claire Balding (8) *hmpd strt, al rear*....................(25 to 1 op 20 to 1) 9
968 POT LEEK LADY 8-11 J Fanning (9) *chsd ldrs till rdn and wknd 2 fs out*.................... (25 to 1 op 20 to 1) 10
743⁵ MARBLE 8-11 N Connorton (6) *swrvd badly rght strt, al beh*....................(25 to 1 op 20 to 1) 11
Dist: 2½l, 2l, 1l, 2l, 1½l, 1½l, 2l, ½l, 3l, nk. 1m 3.50s. a 6.00s (11 Ran).
SR: 12/2/-/-/-/-/ (Lifetime U K Ltd), R Hollinshead

1159 Pen Hill Claiming Stakes Class F (3-y-o and up) £2,646 5f........... (4:00)

962⁵ THE RIGHT TIME 8-8-9 (3*) D Harrison (5) *outpcd and beh, rdn 2 fs out, styd on wl ins last to ld on line*... (10 to 1) 1
815³ ANOTHER EPISODE (Ire) 4-9-3 (7*) P Roberts (2) *led, rdn appr fnl furlong, ct on line.* ....(11 to 8 fav op 6 to 4 tchd 5 to 4) 2
700 ARC LAMP 7-8-12 J Fortune (8) *al prmnt, rdn to chal ins fnl furlong, no extr nr finish*........ (9 to 2 op 7 to 2) 3
ANGELS ANSWER (Ire) 4-8-8 (5*) Darren Moffatt (6) *al prmnt, effrt and ev ch 2 fs out, sn rdn and wknd entering fnl furlong*.....(7 to 1 op 5 to 1 tchd 8 to 1) 4
974³ DARDANELLE (v) 3-7-8 S Wood (4) *chsd ldr 3 fs, sn rdn and wknd wl o'r one out*......... (16 to 1 op 12 to 1) 5
634⁵ CRACKER JACK (bl) 3-7-13 J Fanning (7) *in tch, rdn o'r 2 fs out and sn one pace*...............(16 to 1 op 12 to 1) 6
1038⁵ HERBRAND (Ire) 4-8-8 M Birch (3) *dwlt, al rear*...(12 to 1) 7
204⁹ THE CUT 3-7-10 A Mackay (1) *al outpcd and beh*. (50 to 1) 8
367² HAWAYMYSON (Ire) 3-8-7 G Carter (9) *outpcd and beh frm hfwy*....................(5 to 1 tchd 6 to 1) 9
Dist: Hd, hd, 2½l, 2l, 1l, 1½l, 3½l, 1l. 1m 2.30s. a 4.80s (9 Ran).
SR: 37/48/35/26/-/-/3/-/-/ (J H Myers), J Parkes

1160 Grinton Handicap Class E (0-70 3-y-o) £3,287 5f 212yds................ (4:30)

907^{4} LARN FORT [49] 8-3 J Fanning (7) *al prmnt, styd far side strt, rdn appr fnl furlong, led wl ins last.* .... (6 to 1 op 10 to 1) 1
871^{2} BREAKFAST BOOGIE [60] 8-7 (7*) N Varley (4) *sn led, sddl slpd and wide strt, rcd stands rls, rdn 2 fs out, hdd and no extr wl ins last.*........ (7 to 2 fav op 5 to 2) 2
934^{2} NORTH ARDAR [56] 8-10 R P Elliott (8) *al prmnt, wide strt, rdn and ev ch ins fnl furlong, not quicken nr finish.* .... (7 to 1 op 5 to 1) 3
907 FORMIDABLE LIZ [44] 7-11^{2} (3*) S Maloney (6) *al prmnt, styd far rls strt, rdn and ev ch o'r one furlong out, wknd ins last.*........ (25 to 1 op 20 to 1) 4
HELLO HOBSON'S (Ire) [67] 9-0 (7*) H Bastiman (2) *steadied strt and hld up, hdwy 2 fs out, styd on ins last.* .... (14 to 1 op 12 to 1) 5
1065^{5} MISSED THE BOAT (Ire) [57] 8-4 (7*) V Halliday (1) *al rear.* .... (16 to 1) 6
829^{4} RUM TEMPEST [44] (v) 7-12 N Carlisle (3) *al rear.* .... (10 to 1 op 8 to 1) 7
766^{3} HIGH ROMANCE [53] 8-2 (5*) Darren Moffatt (5) *nvr a factor*........ (10 to 1 op 8 to 1) 8
683^{7} MY GODSON [65] (bl) 9-0 (5*) O Pears (9) *cl up, wide strt, rdn and wknd 2 fs out*........ (6 to 1 tchd 11 to 2) 9
1010^{2} GIRL NEXT DOOR [50] 8-4 A Proud (10) *cl up, wide strt, rdn and wknd 2 fs out*........ (5 to 1 op 7 to 2) 10

Dist: Hd, ½l, 1½l, 3½l, 4l, ½l, 1½l, 2½l, 3l. 1m 17.20s. a 6.20s (10 Ran).

SR: 25/35/29/11/20/-/ (R T Cartwright), T Fairhurst

1161 Muker Rating Related Maiden Stakes Class F (0-60 3-y-o and up) £2,780 1 ½m 44yds........ (5:00)

763^{4} YOUNG TESS 3-8-1 N Connorton (12) *hld up, steady hdwy hfwy, led o'r 2 fs out, rdn fnl furlong, ran on.* .... (100 to 30 fav op 5 to 2 tchd 7 to 2) 1
905^{2} DOC SPOT 3-8-6 J Fortune (13) *in tch, lost pl hfwy, rdn alng and hdwy 3 fs out, effrt to chal one and a half out, ev ch, no extr nr finish.* (9 to 1 op 8 to 1 tchd 10 to 1) 2
813 DUPLICATE 3-8-6 M Birch (1) *mid-div, hdwy on inner hfwy, not clr run and swtchd o'r 2 fs out, ran on wl fnl furlong*........ (7 to 1 tchd 6 to 1) 3
921^{5} BRONZE MAQUETTE (Ire) 3-8-1 A McGlone (7) *in tch, hdwy 4 fs out and sn rdn alng, kpt on fnl 2 furlongs.* .... (11 to 2 op 4 to 1) 4
INTO THE FUTURE 6-9-7 (3*) S Maloney (4) *in tch, effrt 4 fs out, sn rdn, grad wknd fnl 2 furlongs*........ (50 to 1) 5
1005^{3} INDIAN FLASH (Ire) 3-7-12 (3*) D Harrison (8) *chsd ldrs, rdn o'r 3 fs out, grad wknd.* (11 to 2 op 4 to 1 tchd 6 to 1) 6
863 MRS NORMAN 4-9-5 S Webster (2) *nvr rchd ldrs.* (50 to 1) 7
507^{2} BARSAL (Ire) 3-8-6 N Carlisle (10) *cl up till rdn and wknd 3 fs out*........ (10 to 1 op 7 to 1) 8
1034^{8} TINA MEENA LISA 4-9-5 C Dwyer (17) *cl up, led o'r 4 fs out till hdd and wknd over 2 out*........ (33 to 1) 9
967^{8} PATROL 4-9-3 (7*) G Forster (6) *prmnt, rdn 4 fs out, wknd o'r 2 out*........ (12 to 1 op 10 to 1) 10
827 MOON WATCH 3-8-1 G Carter (15) *al rear, drvn alng hfwy*........ (6 to 1 op 8 to 1 tchd 5 to 1) 11
674 EIGHTANDAHALF (Ire) 4-9-3 (7*) G Parkin (14) *chsd ldrs, effrt and ch o'r 2 fs out, sn rdn and wknd.* .... (7 to 1 op 8 to 1 tchd 9 to 1) 12
DUKE OF DREAMS 3-8-1 (5*) Darren Moffatt (3) *al rear.* .... (8 to 1 op 10 to 1) 13
681 HATAAL (Ire) 4-8-12 (7*) Claire Balding (5) *nvr a factor.* .... (33 to 1) 14
901^{8} SIR PAGEANT (bl) 4-9-5 (5*) Stephen Davies (16) *sn led, hdd o'r 4 fs out and wknd quickly*....(20 to 1 tchd 16 to 1) 15

Dist: ½l, 2l, ¾l, 10l, 1½l, 3½l, 2l, 4l, ¾l, 1½l. 2m 49.40s. a 14.40s (15 Ran).

SR: 4/8/4/-/-/-/ (Miss Betty Duxbury), Miss S E Hall

1162 Wensley Maiden Stakes Class D (3-y-o) £3,201 5f 212yds........ (5:30)

624 SHARP PROSPECT 9-0 M Birch (2) *hld up, hdwy hfwy, effrt to chal o'r one furlong out, rdn to ld wl ins last, ran on*........ (12 to 1 op 10 to 1) 1
992 DITTISHAM (USA) 8-9 A McGlone (4) *led, wide strt, rdn o'r one furlong out, hng rght and hdd wl ins last, kpt on.* .... (7 to 4 on op 2 to 1 on) 2
803^{7} VIKING WATERS 8-9 J Fortune (3) *dwlt, sn cl up, rdn and outpcd hfwy, styd on und pres fnl 2 fs.* .... (10 to 1 op 12 to 1 tchd 14 to 1) 3
563^{4} SMITH N'ALLAN 9-0 N Carlisle (6) *chsd ldrs, rdn and wknd o'r 2 fs out*........ (10 to 1) 4
803^{6} ROYAL MUSIC 9-0 G Carter (1) *cl up till rdn and wknd o'r 2 fs out*........ (6 to 1 op 5 to 1) 5
CAUGHT REDHANDED (Ire) 8-6 (3*) D Harrison (5) *cl up, rdn hfwy, sn wknd*........ (17 to 2 op 8 to 1 tchd 9 to 1) 6
EVAHART 8-2 (7*) G Forster (7) *wl beh frm hfwy.* .... (20 to 1 op 14 to 1) 7

Dist: Sht-hd, 7l, 2½l, 4l, sht-hd, 15l. 1m 18.20s. a 7.20s (7 Ran).
SR: 16/10/-/-/ (The Pendley Associates), P W Harris

DUNDALK (IRE) (good)
Friday May 21st

1163 Carrolls Festival Handicap (0-70 3-y-o and up) £2,935 1m 1f........ (7:30)

SAIBOT (USA) [-] 4-10-0 M J Kinane (3)........ (9 to 4 fav) 1
912 ST AIDAN (Ire) [-] 5-7-3^{4} (8*) R T Fitzpatrick (2)........ (50 to 1) 2
849^{4} VICOSA (Ire) [-] (bl) 4-7-7 (2*) D G O'Shea (7)........ (6 to 1) 3
936* MANGANS HILL (Ire) [-] 3-8-5 (6*,5ex) P P Murphy (1) (7 to 1) 4
849 TWO MAGPIES [-] 6-7-2 (8*) L O'Shea (11)........ (10 to 1) 5
PICK'N HILL (Ire) [-] 5-7-1^{2} (8*) B J Halligan (10)... (50 to 1) 6
959^{7} LAKE HOTEL (Ire) [-] 4-9-2 (6*) C Everard (12)........ (10 to 1) 7
959^{8} SOPHISM (USA) [-] 4-9-5 P Shanahan (5)........ (6 to 1) 8
911^{6} SIGHTSEER (Ire) [-] 4-8-12 N Byrne (4)........ (16 to 1) 9
868 BARNAGEERA BOY (Ire) [-] 4-8-9 (4*) W J Smith (15) (7 to 1) 10
640^{7} SWEET REALM [-] 4-7-8^{1} (6*) J J Behan (6)........ (8 to 1) 11
981^{7} WHITECRAITS (Ire) [-] 3-8-5 S Craine (13)........ (7 to 1) 12
MAN OF STRAW [-] 7-7-12^{15} (10*) P J Smullen (9) (50 to 1) 13
599 VOUVRAY (Ire) [-] 3-8-8 Joanna Morgan (8)........ (16 to 1) 14
SPECIAL SECRET (Ire) [-] 5-8-0 J F Egan (16)........ (20 to 1) 15

Dist: 2l, ½l, nk, sht-hd. 2m 3.50s. (15 Ran).

(Michael W J Smurfit), D K Weld

1164 Dowdallshill Maiden (3-y-o) £2,245 7f 166yds........ (8:00)

960^{2} FLORA WOOD (Ire) 8-11 W J Supple (8)........ (9 to 2) 1
577^{2} DAFTARI (Ire) 9-0 M J Kinane (15)........ (5 to 2 on) 2
280^{7} SANS CERIPH (Ire) 8-11 W J O'Connor (12)........ (12 to 1) 3
BELLISSI (Ire) 8-1 (10*) P J Smullen (6)........ (33 to 1) 4
848^{3} MUSWELL BROOK (Ire) 9-0 K J Manning (7)........ (10 to 1) 5
639^{4} MAGIC ROYALE (Ire) 8-11 R Dolan (9)........ (16 to 1) 6
ROSE OF SUMMER (Ire) 8-11 P Shanahan (5)........ (12 to 1) 7
669 CAROLINA RUA (USA) 8-11 B Coogan (11)........ (33 to 1) 8
639 NEWYORK CONNECTION (Ire) 8-5 (6*) P P Murphy, ... (50 to 1) 9
DAIRINE'S DELIGHT (Ire) 8-11 J F Egan (10)........ (40 to 1) 10
SCALP (Ire) 9-0 N Byrne (2)........ (20 to 1) 11
I'M NO LADY (Ire) 8-5 (6*) J J Behan (1)........ (50 to 1) 12
847^{4} ALASKAN GIRL (Ire) 8-11 S Craine (3)........ (12 to 1) pu

Dist: ½l, nk, 1l, 6l. 1m 39.60s. (13 Ran).

(Steinbeck Syndicate), Kevin Prendergast

HAMILTON (soft)
Friday May 21st

Going Correction: PLUS 0.80 sec. per fur. (races 1,2,6), PLUS 0.40 (3,4,5)

1165 Linn Motor Group Handicap Class D (0-80 3-y-o) £3,687 1m 5f 9yds...(2:10)

888* THE WHERE WITHAL [60] 8-13 G Duffield (4) *al hndy, drw level o'r one furlong out, kpt on grimly to ld last 50 yards*........ (7 to 4 fav tchd 6 to 4 and 2 to 1) 1
816^{2} SAFETY IN NUMBERS [56] 8-9 K Fallon (3) *nvr far away, jnd ldr hfwy, led o'r 3 fs out, rdn fnl furlong, hdd last 50 yards*........ (9 to 4 op 5 to 2 tchd 2 to 1) 2
744* CHIAPPUCCI (Ire) [60] (v) 8-13 J Carroll (5) *tucked away on ins, effrt and bustled alng last 2 fs, styd on, not pace to chal*....... (3 to 1 op 5 to 2 tchd 7 to 2 and 11 to 4) 3
763^{5} ROSMARINO [52] 8-5 J Lowe (2) *patiently rdn, niggled alng whn pace lifted entering strt, not punished when btn fnl furlong*........ (16 to 1 op 6 to 1) 4
799^{3} KHISAL (Can) [68] 9-7 Dean McKeown (1) *set steady pace, quickened up entering strt, hdd o'r 3 out, wknd und pres appr fnl furlong.* (8 to 1 op 11 to 2 tchd 10 to 1) 5

Dist: ½l, 2l, 3l, 8l. 3m 7.30s. a 21.30s (5 Ran).

(W E Sturt), Sir Mark Prescott

1166 Blenheim Claiming Stakes Class F (4-y-o and up) £2,556 1m 1f 36yds..(2:40)

4663a MEDIA MESSENGER 4-8-12 K Fallon (1) *trkd ldr, led o'r 3 fs out till appr fnl furlong, rallied gmely to ld post.* .... (8 to 1 op 7 to 1 tchd 10 to 1) 1
740^{2} AEGAEN LADY 4-8-13 J Carroll (2) *patiently rdn, nosed ahead appr fnl furlong, edgd rght and idled, ct post.* .... (11 to 8 on op 11 to 10 on) 2
WAJEEB (USA) 4-9-6 G Duffield (4) *dictated pace till hdd o'r 3 fs out, wknd rpdly appr fnl furlong.* .... (11 to 8 op Evens tchd 6 to 4) 3
906 BAFFIE 4-8-11 Dean McKeown (3) *steadied strt, swtchd outsd and effrt o'r 3 fs out, sn rdn and btn.* .... (40 to 1 op 16 to 1 tchd 50 to 1) 4

Dist: Sht-hd, 12l, 10l. 2m 6.00s. a 12.00s (4 Ran).
SR: 29/29/12/-/ (Lord Lambton), Denys Smith

1167 Scottish Rifles Handicap Class E (0-70 3-y-o and up) £2,898 6f 5yds.... (3:10)

1052^{2} FRANCIS ANN [49] 5-8-10 (7*) R Havlin (6) *made most, shaken up to go clr entering fnl furlong, ran on strly.* .... (11 to 4 op 5 to 2 tchd 3 to 1) 1
884* KILLY'S FILLY [53] 3-8-11 J Carroll (3) *dsptd ld, hrd at work appr fnl furlong, not quicken*........ (6 to 1 op 3 to 1) 2

1052^{7} MINSK [32] 7-8-0^{7} T Sprake (5) *tucked away in midfield, effrt and not much room o'r one furlong out, styd on wl towards finish*.................. (66 to 1 op 33 to 1) 3
909^{8} ARABAT [56] (v) 6-9-10 K Fallon (4) *sluggish strt, chsd alng to go pace, ran on ins fnl furlong, nvr nrr*.
.... (5 to 1 tchd 6 to 1) 4
676 MEESON TIMES [42] 5-8-10 J Lowe (7) *bustled alng to match strds wth ldg pair, rdn and btn o'r one furlong out*.................... (14 to 1 op 12 to 1 tchd 16 to 1) 5
1076^{8} HINARI VIDEO [41] 8-8-9 Dean McKeown (2) *chsd ldg trio, hrd at work 2 fs out, sn outpcd*..... (10 to 1 op 8 to 1) 6
909* MISS ARAGON [54] 5-9-8 G Duffield (1) *chsd alng to keep up, effrt on outsd hfwy, nvr able to chal*.
.......................(9 to 4 fav op 5 to 2 tchd 2 to 1) 7
Dist: 2½l, sht-hd, 4l, 1l, 6l. 1m 16.60s. a 5.90s (7 Ran).
SR: 33/17/5/13/ (Miss L A Perratt), Miss L A Perratt

1168 Cameronians Conditions Stakes Class D (2-y-o) £3,622 6f 5yds...(3:40)

998^{3} BROCTUNE GOLD 8-10 G Duffield (3) *wth ldr, drvn ahead o'r one furlong out, kpt on strly*.... (11 to 4 op 5 to 2) 1
433* KIERCHEM (Ire) 9-0 D Nicholls (1) *trkd ldg trio till outpcd and wndrd 2 fs out, rallied ins last, ran on*.
.... (7 to 1 op 6 to 1 tchd 10 to 1) 2
1051* JIMMY THE SKUNK (Ire) 8-10 J Carroll (6) *broke smartly to ld for o'r 4 fs, rdn and no extr*.
.....................(6 to 4 fav op 7 to 4 tchd 11 to 8) 3
908* WIXI (Ire) 8-2 (7*) S Mulvey (4) *sluggish strt, reco'red to race in tch hfwy, not quicken last 2 fs*.
....................................(9 to 2 op 4 to 1) 4
979^{4} WINDOW DISPLAY 8-10 K Fallon (5) *chsd ldg pair, hrd at work hfwy, fdd*.................... (12 to 1 op 6 to 1) 5
449* DUNDEELIN 8-5 J Lowe (2) *sluggish strt, flt out last 2 fs*.
.... (16 to 1 op 12 to 1) 6
Dist: 3l, 1½l, 4l, 3l, 15l. 1m 16.30s. a 5.60s (6 Ran).
SR: 32/24/14/ (D Playforth), Mrs M Reveley

1169 Mandora Median Auction Maiden Stakes Class F (2-y-o) £2,511 5f 4yds ....(4:10)

SIGANCA 8-9 G Duffield (6) *nvr far away, drvn ahead ins fnl furlong, lnd wl*................... (3 to 1 op 2 to 1) 1
1053^{4} KING RAT (Ire) 9-0 Dean McKeown (2) *wth ldr, led aftr 2 fs, hrd rdn and hdd ins last, no extr*.
.... (11 to 2 op 6 to 1 tchd 5 to 1) 2
STARSPORT (Ire) 9-0 J Carroll (4) *sn outpcd and beh, improved last 2 fs, staying on finish*.
..........................(5 to 1 op 3 to 1 tchd 6 to 1) 3
698^{8} THREEPENNY-BRIDGE 9-0 T Sprake (5) *slight ld for 2 fs, hrd at work two furlongs out, sn btn*.
.... (8 to 1 op 6 to 1 tchd 10 to 1) 4
949^{3} ERRIS BOY 9-0 A Clark (3) *chsd alng to keep up, nvr able to trble ldrs*.................... (5 to 2 fav tchd 3 to 1) 5
PEASAN 8-7 (7*) S Mulvey (1) *unruly in stalls, missed break, nvr a factor*.............. (10 to 1 op 4 to 1) 6
Dist: 2l, 3l, 4l, 3½l, 2l. 1m 4.40s. a 6.10s (6 Ran).
SR: 13/10/-/ (Mrs B Long), M Bell

1170 Ramilles Rating Related Maiden Stakes Class F (3-y-o) £2,556 1m 3f 16yds.......................... (4:40)

DUSTY POINT (Ire) 9-0 Dean McKeown (1) *trkd ldg trio, drvn alng o'r 2 fs out, styd on grimly to ld last 50 yards*.
.... (10 to 1 op 5 to 1 tchd 12 to 1) 1
CORNFLAKE 8-9 K Fallon (6) *tried to make all, quickened clr o'r one furlong out, wknd and ct last 50 yards*.
....(33 to 1) 2
456 DODGY DANCER 9-0 Lorna Vincent (4) *chsd ldg quartet, effrt und pres 2 fs out, kpt on same pace*.
.... (14 to 1 op 8 to 1) 3
813 BUZZ-B-BABE 9-0 J Lowe (2) *last strt, und pres to improve fnl 2 fs, nvr nrr*.
.... (7 to 1 tchd 8 to 1 and 10 to 1) 4
932^{4} NOMADIC FIRE 9-0 G Duffield (3) *trkd ldr gng wl, effrt o'r 3 fs out, floundered, sn btn*..... (7 to 4 on op 5 to 4 on) 5
741^{2} FRIENDLY KNIGHT 9-0 J Carroll (5) *pressed ldg pair, struggling o'r 2 fs out, sn btn*............ (9 to 2 op 3 to 1) 6
Dist: 1l, 4l, 2l, 6l, 6l. 2m 35.50s. a 15.50s (6 Ran).
SR: 33/26/23/19/7/-/ (Abdullah Ali), B Hanbury

NEWMARKET (good)
Friday May 21st
Going Correction: MINUS 0.10 sec. per fur. (races 1,2,4,5,7), NIL (3,6)

1171 Ditch Maiden Fillies Stakes Class D (3-y-o and up) £3,492 6f.........(2:15)

WAFFLE ON 3-8-6 B Raymond (8) *dwlt, sn wth ldrs, ran on to ld ins fnl furlong, shaken up, cleverly*.
.... (12 to 1 op 10 to 1 tchd 14 to 1) 1
TRAPEZIUM 3-8-7^{1} R Cochrane (7) *led till rdn and hdd ins fnl furlong, no extr nr line*.
......(6 to 4 fav op 11 to 10 tchd 7 to 4 and 15 to 8) 2
823^{3} GOLDEN GUEST 3-8-6 Paul Eddery (4) *pressed ldr, rdn and not quicken o'r one out*........ (11 to 4 op 6 to 4) 3
854^{2} CROIRE (Ire) 3-8-6 M Hills (1) *effrt frm mid-div o'r 2 fs out, one pace appr last*.
.... (4 to 1 op 5 to 1 tchd 6 to 1 and 7 to 2) 4
AZOLA (Ire) 3-8-6 L Dettori (5) *in tch, pushed alng hfwy, outpcd last 2 fs*...... (16 to 1 op 10 to 1 tchd 20 to 1) 5
948^{6} WHERE'S THE DANCE 3-8-3 (3*) B Doyle (6) *ldg grp till wknd o'r 2 fs out*.......................(33 to 1 op 20 to 1) 6
WESTERING 3-8-6 P Robinson (2) *slwly into strd, al outpcd*..................................(33 to 1 op 20 to 1) 7
921^{9} I'M YOURS 3-8-6 J Reid (3) *al outpcd, lost tch appr last 2 fs*.......................................(33 to 1 op 16 to 1) 8
Dist: ¾l, 2l, 1½l, 1l, 3l, 2l, 8l. 1m 12.87s. a 1.47s (8 Ran).
SR: 51/49/40/34/30/18/10/-/ (T D Holland-Martin), J R Fanshawe

1172 Brandon Handicap Class C (0-100 4-y-o and up) £6,212 7f.............(2:45)

DRESS SENSE (Ire) [84] 4-9-2 R Cochrane (5) *towards rear, ran on 2 out, sstnd brst to ld last 25 yards*.
.... (10 to 1 op 8 to 1) 1
914^{9} RISE UP SINGING [64] (bl) 5-7-10 J Quinn (9) *led, clr 3 out, wknd and hdd last 25 yards*.
.......................(4 to 1 fav op 5 to 1 tchd 11 to 2) 2
524^{3} HERORA (Ire) [87] 4-9-5 W Carson (11) *chsd ldg grp, effrt 2 out, styd on one pace fnl furlong*.
.........................(15 to 2 op 6 to 1 tchd 8 to 1) 3
677 STAR GODDESS (USA) [74] 4-8-6 B Rouse (13) *rcd in 4th pl most of way, hrd rdn and one pace last 2 fs*.
..................................(14 to 1 tchd 16 to 1) 4
1066 GREEN DOLLAR [89] 10-9-7 M Tebbutt (2) *mid-div, effrt o'r 2 out, kpt on one pace fnl furlong*.
..................................(33 to 1 tchd 40 to 1) 5
737 SHIKARI'S SON [80] 6-8-12 T Quinn (4) *beh til effrt o'r 2 out, nvr nr to chal*.................................(20 to 1) 6
737 SUPEROO [71] 7-8-3 W Newnes (1) *hld up in rear, effrt o'r 2 out, eased whn btn appr fnl furlong*.
..................................(10 to 1 tchd 11 to 1) 7
792^{6} CRYSTADO (Fr) [95] 4-9-13 J Williams (8) *mid-div, rdn alng hfwy, no imprsn on ldrs last 2 fs*...(10 to 1 op 14 to 1) 8
604^{5} AMADEUS AES [78] (v) 4-8-5 (5*) C Hodgson (6) *pressed ldr til wknd o'r 2 out*.... (20 to 1 op 16 to 1 tchd 25 to 1) 9
737* TENDER MOMENT (Ire) [77] 5-8-6 (3*) B Doyle (12) *mid-div, rdn alng hfwy, nvr trbld frnt rnk*.
........................(7 to 1 op 6 to 1 tchd 8 to 1) 10
737^{2} KAYVEE [96] 4-10-0 W R Swinburn (3) *hld up in rear, improved 3 out, eased whn btn appr fnl furlong*.
.... (8 to 1 op 13 to 2) 11
MANGO MANILA [84] 8-9-2 Pat Eddery (7) *al in rear*.
..................................(6 to 1 op 5 to 1) 12
814^{7} GENERAL JOHN (Ire) [65] 4-7-11 Dale Gibson (10) *rcd in 3rd pl til wknd quickly o'r 2 out*....... (14 to 1 op 12 to 1) 13
Dist: ½l, 2l, 2l, nk, 3l, hd, 6l, 2½l, nk, 3l. 1m 25.91s. a 2.41s (13 Ran).
SR: 55/33/50/31/45/27/17/23/-/ (Sheikh Mohammed), L M Cumani

1173 Thurlow Handicap Class D (0-80 3-y-o and up) £4,971 1¾m............(3:20)

994* MISS PIN UP [71] 4-9-7 (4ex) D Biggs (9) *trkd ldrs, ran on 2 out, shaken up to ld ins fnl furlong, styd on*.
....(9 to 1 op 8 to 1) 1
682 DEDUCE [73] 4-9-9 M Hills (5) *ldg grp, led o'r 3 out till rdn and hdd ins fnl furlong, kpt on same pace*.
..................................(20 to 1 tchd 25 to 1) 2
723^{2} STATE OF AFFAIRS [47] 6-7-11 S Dawson (6) *hld up in rear, hdwy and not clr run o'r 3 out, ev ch over one out, not quicken*...............(14 to 1 op 8 to 1 tchd 16 to 1) 3
682 MASTER FOODBROKER (Ire) [73] (bl) 5-9-2 (7*) D McCabe (3) *hld up in rear, improved 4 out, no extr ins fnl furlong*.
..................................(20 to 1 tchd 25 to 1) 4
682^{2} SNOW BOARD [70] 4-9-6 W Carson (10) *al ldg grp, ev ch 2 out, sn btn*........ (11 to 2 fav op 7 to 2 tchd 6 to 1) 5
426 QUALITAIR SOUND (Ire) [43] 5-7-7 L Charnock (7) *improved 5 out, one pace last 2 fs*..........................(33 to 1) 6
857 MIZYAN (Ire) [59] (bl) 5-8-4 (5*) C Hodgson (13) *trkd ldrs, led 5 out till o'r 3 out, no hdwy last 2 fs*.
...........................(6 to 1 op 8 to 1 tchd 11 to 2) 7
988* AMBIGUOUSLY REGAL (USA) [79] 4-10-1 (4ex) T Kent (1) *improved frm rear hfwy, chlgd und pres o'r 2 out, no extr*..................(9 to 1 op 7 to 1 tchd 10 to 1) 8
727 RAGAMUFFIN ROMEO [69] 4-9-5 Paul Eddery (12) *nvr on terms*.............................(25 to 1 op 33 to 1) 9
994^{5} FIERCE [57] (v) 5-8-7 A Munro (16) *pressed ldrs, led 5 out, hdd and wknd o'r 3 out*.
.... (20 to 1 op 14 to 1 tchd 33 to 1) 10+
988^{8} LABURNUM [72] 5-9-5 (3*) J Weaver (11) *hdwy frm rear o'r 2 out, not rch frnt rnk*.......... (10 to 1 tchd 11 to 1) 10+
1041^{4} LOOKINGFORARAINBOW (Ire) [60] 5-8-10 N Day (15) *wl plcd for ten fs*.................. (12 to 1 tchd 14 to 1) 12
924^{2} JANISKI [51] (v) 10-8-1 G Bardwell (14) *trkd ldrs til wknd o'r 5 out*.......................(25 to 1 op 16 to 1) 13
924^{3} SURCOAT [51] 6-8-1 T Williams (2) *handily plcd, led hfwy till 5 out, grad lost pos*.......... (20 to 1 op 16 to 1) 14

785^{4} CHIEF MINISTER (Ire) [76] 4-9-12 J Reid (4) *al towards rear.* ....(8 to 1 op 7 to 1 tchd 9 to 1) 15
973 NEGATORY (USA) [43] 6-7-4^{4} (7*) C Hawksley (17) *slwly into strd, pld hrd, lost tch o'r 5 out, tld off.* ....(33 to 1 op 100 to 1) 16
826^{2} HELLO MY DARLING (Ire) [64] 5-9-0 T Quinn (8) *led to hfwy, tld off last 3 fs*....................(12 to 1 op 10 to 1) 17
Dist: ¾l, 2½l, 1½l, 1½l, 4l, 2½l, 3l, ½l, 5l, dd-ht. 3m 1.11s. a 5.11s (17 Ran).
SR: 56/56/25/48/42/7/18/32/21/ (E Baldwin), Pat Mitchell

1174 Thoroughbred Guild King Charles II Stakes Class A (Listed Race) (3-y-o) £9,768 7f..................... (3:50)

588^{3} EUROLINK THUNDER 8-12 R Cochrane (6) *trkd ldrs, reminders to ld o'r one out, rdn out*..........(3 to 1 jt-fav op 5 to 2 tchd 7 to 2) 1
844* ABBEY'S GAL 8-7 L Dettori (4) *hld up in rear, not clr run o'r 2 out, swtchd rght over one out, ran on strly.* ....(7 to 2 op 3 to 1 tchd 4 to 1) 2
HUMAM (Ire) 9-5 R Hills (2) *led til hdd o'r one out, styd on gmely ins fnl furlong*...............(12 to 1 op 8 to 1) 3
821* ANEESATI 8-7 W R Swinburn (8) *hld up in tch, prog hfwy, rdn and not quicken appr fnl furlong.* ....(16 to 1 op 12 to 1 tchd 20 to 1) 4
993^{7} BRIGG FAIR 8-12 J Reid (5) *slwly into strd, sn tracking ldrs, rdn alng 2 out, no imprsn appr fnl furlong.* ....(20 to 1 tchd 25 to 1) 5
854* ARJUZAH (Ire) 8-10 W Carson (7) *hld up in mid-div, effrt und pres 2 out, no hdwy fnl furlong*.........(3 to 1 jt-fav op 7 to 2 tchd 4 to 1) 6
746^{3} THUNDER RIVER (Ire) 8-12 T Quinn (3) *pressed ldr til wknd quickly o'r 2 out*.................. (12 to 1 op 8 to 1) 7
FELUCCA 8-7 Pat Eddery (1) *outpcd in rear til improved and swtchd rght hfwy, wknd o'r 2 out.* ....(6 to 1 op 5 to 1 tchd 13 to 2) 8
Dist: 1½l, ½l, 1½l, ½l, 2½l, 4l, 2l. 1m 25.60s. a 2.10s (8 Ran).
SR: 56/46/56/39/42/32/22/11/ (Eurolink Group Plc), J L Dunlop

1175 Cowlinge Claiming Stakes Class E (3-y-o) £3,236 1m................. (4:20)

883^{2} GUV'NORS GIFT 8-2 P Robinson (13) *in tch in mid-div, pushed alng o'r 2 out, styd on to ld ins fnl furlong, rdn clr*................................ (5 to 2 op 11 to 8) 1
963^{3} SILENT EXPRESSION 8-6 M Tebbutt (9) *trkd ldrs, rdn to ld 2 out, hdd and not quicken ins fnl furlong.* ....(9 to 4 fav op 3 to 1 tchd 4 to 1) 2
681^{7} A BADGE TOO FAR (Ire) 7-12 J Quinn (10) *rdn alng hfwy, improved 2 out, styd on one pace ins fnl furlong.* ....(20 to 1 tchd 25 to 1) 3
975^{5} FILOU FILANT (Fr) 8-4 (3*) B Doyle (7) *trkd ldg grp, rdn and one pace frm 2 out*.................(14 to 1 op 8 to 1) 4
THE SNOUT 7-9 (7*) D McCabe (8) *dwlt, hdwy frm rear o'r 2 out, nrst at finish.* (25 to 1 op 16 to 1 tchd 33 to 1) 5
761 JUST JAMIE 8-3 Paul Eddery (6) *pressed ldrs, led 3 out till 2 out, no extr ins fnl furlong.* ....(25 to 1 op 16 to 1 tchd 33 to 1) 6
PONTEVECCHIO MODA 8-10 Pat Eddery (3) *ldg grp, led hfwy til 3 out, btn o'r one out.* ....(6 to 1 op 5 to 1 tchd 13 to 2) 7
821 KEEP SAFE 7-12 D Biggs (1) *al beh, hrd rdn 3 out, no ch wth ldrs*......................... (20 to 1 op 16 to 1) 8
962 BLUE TRUMPET 7-12 (5*) M Fenton (12) *rcd in mid-div, outpcd appr last 2 fs*................ (20 to 1 op 12 to 1) 9
COUNTY GIRL (Ire) 8-6 W Ryan (2) *al in rear.* ....(20 to 1 op 12 to 1 tchd 25 to 1) 10
TEE GEE JAY 8-2 N Adams (5) *al beh.* ....(15 to 2 op 5 to 1 tchd 8 to 1) 11
975^{8} GEORGE ROPER (bl) 8-7 B Rouse (11) *led to hfwy, grad wknd*......................(14 to 1 op 12 to 1 tchd 16 to 1) 12
4805a^{5} RUANO 8-9 W Woods (4) *beh frm hfwy.* ....(16 to 1 op 14 to 1 tchd 20 to 1) 13
Dist: 2½l, nk, ½l, 1l, 1½l, 2l, 6l, 3l, 3½l, nk. 1m 40.43s. a 3.23s (13 Ran).
SR: 28/24/15/22/14/10/11/-/-/ (The Tompkins Team), M H Tompkins

1176 Ashley Maiden Stakes Class D (3-y-o) £3,947 1½m................... (4:55)

842^{3} SILVERDALE (USA) 9-0 W R Swinburn (4) *hld up, hdwy 4 out, cld on ldrs o'r 2 out, shaken up to ld ins fnl furlong*................ (9 to 2 op 6 to 1 tchd 7 to 1) 1
929^{3} SAINT KEYNE 9-0 Pat Eddery (9) *chsd ldr, led 5 out till rdn and hdd ins fnl furlong*.......... (Evens fav op 5 to 4) 2
ALASAD 9-0 R Hills (10) *ran on o'r 3 out, styd on one pace appr fnl furlong*....................... (33 to 1 op 20 to 1) 3
DARZEE 9-0 R Cochrane (13) *in tch, hrd rdn hfwy, lost pl o'r 3 out, styd on ag'n last 2 fs.* ....(20 to 1 op 12 to 1 tchd 25 to 1) 4
679^{8} ELA BILLANTE 8-9 P Robinson (8) *effrt o'r 3 out, no imprsn on ldrs last 2 fs*........... (33 to 1 op 20 to 1) 5
529 TILTY (USA) 9-0 T Quinn (6) *beh til effrt on outsd 4 out, not rch frnt rnk frm 2 out*............ (33 to 1 op 20 to 1) 6
KINGDOM OF SHADES (USA) 9-0 G Hind (11) *dwlt, beh till improved on outsd aftr 4 fs, no imprsn on ldrs last 3 furlongs*......................... (33 to 1 op 14 to 1) 7
KINCHENJUNGA 8-9 W Ryan (5) *slwly into strd, nvr on terms*................................(16 to 1 op 10 to 1) 8
842^{6} MUTAMANNI 9-0 W Carson (2) *chsd ldrs for 9 fs.* ....(20 to 1 op 10 to 1) 9+
946^{5} PRINCESS DAVID (USA) 8-9 Paul Eddery (16) *ldg grp to hfwy, grad lost pl*.................. (5 to 1 op 5 to 1) 9+
686^{7} RISING WOLF 9-0 M Hills (7) *hld up towards rear, nvr able to chal*.........(25 to 1 op 12 to 1 tchd 33 to 1) 11
ARMENIAN COFFEE (Ire) 9-0 B Rouse (14) *led for 7 fs, sn btn*................. (20 to 1 op 14 to 1 tchd 25 to 1) 12
799^{5} COMBELLINO 9-0 N Adams (3) *prmnt for 9 fs.* ....(33 to 1 op 20 to 1) 13
980 RUN TO AU BON (Ire) 8-11 (3*) J Weaver (15) *nvr better than mid-div, no hdwy last 3 fs*....(33 to 1 op 20 to 1) 14
BEDEVIL (USA) 9-0 L Dettori (1) *chsd ldrs, wnt second o'r 3 out, wknd over 2 out*.................. (16 to 1 op 10 to 1) 15
965^{5} SHADOWPLAY (Fr) 9-0 B Raymond (12) *wl plcd to hfwy, tld off last 3 fs*....... (25 to 1 op 16 to 1 tchd 33 to 1) 16
Dist: 1l, 3l, 2l, 6l, 3l, 3½l, 1½l, hd, dd-ht, ¾l. 2m 37.88s. a 8.28s (16 Ran).
SR: 17/15/9/5/-/-/ (Sheikh Mohammed), J H M Gosden

1177 Tuddenham Limited Stakes Class E (0-70 4-y-o and up) £4,110 7f.... (5:25)

737^{3} INDIAN SLAVE (Ire) 5-8-11 L Dettori (8) *settled in mid-div, rdn alng o'r 2 out, ran on to ld ins fnl furlong.* ......(100 to 30 fav op 9 to 2 tchd 5 to 1 and 3 to 1) 1
315 AFRICAN CHIMES 6-8-4 (7*) D McCabe (13) *pressed ldrs, ev ch appr fnl furlong, rallied und pres.* ....(25 to 1 op 20 to 1 tchd 33 to 1) 2
771 SAIFAN (bl) 4-8-6 (5*) C Hodgson (4) *wl plcd, ev ch 2 out, styd on und pres nr finish.* ....(20 to 1 op 14 to 1 tchd 25 to 1) 3
893^{5} BOURSIN (Ire) 4-8-11 W Newnes (14) *led till hdd and no extr ins fnl furlong*............... (8 to 1 tchd 7 to 1) 4
1073^{5} CHOIR PRACTICE 6-8-11 C Rutter (17) *pushed alng hfwy, styd on ins last 2 fs, not rch wnr.* ....(9 to 1 op 8 to 1 tchd 10 to 1) 5+
1081^{8} FIGHTER SQUADRON (bl) 4-8-8 (3*) S D Williams (2) *hld up, rdn alng and not much room ins last 2 fs, nrst at finish.* ....(20 to 1 op 14 to 1) 5+
917^{3} BERNSTEIN BETTE 7-8-6 W Ryan (5) *hld up in rear, swtchd rght and effrt 3 fs out, one pace appr fnl furlong*................... (7 to 1 op 5 to 1 tchd 8 to 1) 7
659^{4} HONEY SEEKER 4-8-11 Paul Eddery (1) *pushed alng and hdwy hfwy, not quicken ins last 2 fs.* (7 to 1 op 6 to 1) 8
LUCKNAM DREAMER 5-8-11 G Bardwell (16) *pressed ldr for 5 fs, wknd*.................... (33 to 1 op 20 to 1) 9
914^{2} SHINING JEWEL 6-8-4 (7*) G Milligan (9) *hld up, effrt o'r 2 out, no imprsn on ldrs fnl furlong.* (10 to 1 op 12 to 1) 10
758 NIGEL'S LUCKY GIRL 5-8-6 J Quinn (3) *nvr better than mid-div*........................... (33 to 1 op 20 to 1) 11
1059* MERRYHILL MAID (Ire) 5-8-7^{1} R Cochrane (7) *prmnt stands side for 5 fs*............(13 to 2 op 6 to 1 tchd 7 to 1) 12
760 CONISTON LAKE (Ire) 4-8-11 B Rouse (11) *dwlt, al outpcd.* ....(16 to 1 op 12 to 1 tchd 20 to 1) 13
329^{8} RULLY 4-8-8 (3*) B Doyle (6) *dwlt, al beh.* ....(33 to 1 op 20 to 1) 14
931 ZAMANAYN (Ire) 5-8-8 (3*) J Weaver (12) *in tch for o'r 4 fs.* ....(33 to 1 op 20 to 1) 15
TURRET GATES 4-8-11 Pat Eddery (15) *ldg grp to hfwy, sn drpd out*................ (10 to 1 tchd 12 to 1) 16
COURTENAY BEE 4-8-11 T Quinn (10) *chsd ldrs til wknd quickly hfwy*...................... (25 to 1 op 20 to 1) 17
Dist: 1½l, sht-hd, 3½l, ¾l, dd-ht, 1l, nk, 4l, 1½l, hd. 1m 26.31s. a 2.81s (17 Ran).
SR: 44/39/38/27/25/25/17/21/9/ (R Axford), R Guest

AYR (good to soft)
Saturday May 22nd

Going Correction: PLUS 0.40 sec. per fur. (races 1,2,3,4), PLUS 0.20 (5,6)

1178 Loganswell Maiden Stakes Class D (3-y-o and up) £3,291 1m.......... (2:20)

772 DON'T JUMP (Ire) 3-7-11 (7*) S Mulvey (2) *sluggish strt, dashed up on outsd to ld o'r 3 fs out, rdn out fnl furlong*................ (8 to 1 op 6 to 1 tchd 10 to 1) 1
662 MISS SHAGRA (USA) 3-8-4 P D'Arcy (8) *nvr far away, determined chal appr fnl furlong, kpt on same pace.* ....(4 to 1 tchd 5 to 1) 2
903^{3} FORMATO UNI (Ire) 3-8-9 G Carter (3) *patiently rdn, produced to chal o'r 2 fs out, ridden and not quicken fnl furlong*...................(9 to 4 fav tchd 3 to 1) 3
PERSIAN CHARMER (Ire) 3-8-9 J Fanning (9) *al hndy, led appr strt till o'r 3 fs out, one pace und pres.* ....(7 to 2 op 3 to 1 tchd 4 to 1) 4
860^{4} CARLTON EXPRESS (Ire) 3-8-9 J Fortune (5) *al hndy, rdn o'r 2 fs out, no extr*.......................(100 to 1) 5
I REMEMBER YOU (Ire) 3-8-9 S Perks (1) *led till hdd appr strt, fdd und pres last 3 fs.* ....(11 to 1 op 6 to 1 tchd 12 to 1) 6

824 WILSONIC 4-9-2 Dean McKeown (6) *trkd ldg bunch, not handle bend into strt, sn lost tch.* ....(7 to 2 op 3 to 1 tchd 4 to 1) 7
962⁹ BRAXTON BRAGG (Ire) 3-8-9 M Birch (7) *settled wth ldg bunch, rdn o'r 3 fs out, sn btn*............... (100 to 1) 8
860⁶ MAJOR JACK 3-8-9 K Darley (4) *struggling to hold pl hfwy, tld off in hme strt*..................... (200 to 1) 9
Dist: 2l, 3½l, 7l, 3½l, 1½l, 2l, 8l, dist. 1m 44.24s. a 6.54s (9 Ran).
SR: 40/34/28/7/-/-/ (Mark Tompkins Racing), M H Tompkins

1179 Kilbirnie Claiming Stakes Class E (3-y-o and up) £2,950 1¼m........ (2:50)

1074⁸ RAGGERTY (Ire) 3-8-3 G Carter (2) *sluggish strt, rapid hdwy on outsd to ld o'r 3 fs out, forged clr, won easing dwn*.................... (5 to 1 op 4 to 1 tchd 6 to 1) 1
999⁶ VELVET HEART (Ire) 3-8-8 E Johnson (4) *trkd ldg pair, rdn whn wnr quickened in strt, no imprsn.* ....(9 to 4 op 5 to 2) 2
642⁹ WORKINGFORPEANUTS (Ire) 3-7-6¹ (7*) D McCabe (8) *settled off the pace, imprvg whn not much room entering strt, styd on und pres, nrst finish*.... (5 to 1 op 6 to 1) 3
863³ YOUNG GEORGE 6-9-8 S Webster (1) *sluggish strt, improved frm off the pace last 3 fs, styd on fnl furlong.* ....(14 to 1 tchd 16 to 1) 4
470⁹ KINNEGAD KID 4-9-9 R P Elliott (3) *led early, styd hndy till fdd entering strt, tld off.* .... (12 to 1 op 10 to 1 tchd 16 to 1) 5
971⁴ DOUBLE THE STAKES (USA) (v) 4-9-4 S Perks (7) *sn led and clr, hdd entering strt, wknd rpdly, tld off.* .... (33 to 1 op 20 to 1) 6
1054* GOLD SURPRISE (Ire) 4-9-4 J Fortune (6) *pressed ldg trio, led briefly entering strt, eased and virtually pld up fnl furlong.* (7 to 4 fav op 6 to 4 tchd 2 to 1 and 9 to 4) 7
Dist: 4l, 1½l, sht-hd, 20l, 10l, dist. 2m 15.52s. a 10.52s (7 Ran).
SR: 24/21/8/31/ (Norman Jackson), J Berry

1180 Lochwinnoch Handicap Class D (0-85 3-y-o) £3,168 1m 5f 13yds....... (3:20)

910² SHYNON [65] 8-4 (7*) S Mulvey (1) *led early, styd hndy till led ag'n o'r 6 fs out, stayed on strly to go clr fnl furlong*.......................... (5 to 1 op 9 to 2) 1
905* PRIME PAINTER [64] 8-10 Gary Carter (3) *trkd ldg trio, improved und pres to press wnr o'r 2 fs out, one pace fnl furlong*............... (9 to 1 op 8 to 1 tchd 10 to 1) 2
929⁶ CUMBRIAN RHAPSODY [69] 9-1 M Birch (2) *settled midfield, drvn through to chase ldg pair last 2 fs, no imprsn.*................................(5 to 1 op 4 to 1) 3
966⁶ SIR EDWARD HENRY (Ire) [49] 7-9 J Fanning (7) *sluggish strt, bustled alng to improve on outsd entering strt, nvr able to chal*.......................(10 to 1 tchd 12 to 1) 4
932⁵ MONDRAGON [69] 9-1 K Darley (5) *chsd ldg bunch, rdn entering strt, nvr dngrs*......... (2 to 1 fav tchd 9 to 4) 5
976 BROUGHTONS FORMULA [63] (bl) 8-2 (7*) D McCabe (6) *settled midfield, rdn appr strt, sn struggling.* ....(8 to 1 op 5 to 1) 6
966 CLEAR HONEY (USA) [47] (bl) 7-7 E Johnson (8) *wth ldrs, rdn appr strt, sn lost tch*.......... (20 to 1 op 16 to 1) 7
1055* VOLUNTEER POINT (Ire) [65] 8-11 J Fortune (9) *edgy in stalls, sn led, hdd o'r 6 fs out, soon lost tch.* .... (11 to 1 op 10 to 1 tchd 12 to 1) 8
644 QAFFAL (USA) [75] 9-7 Dean McKeown (4) *trkd ldg quartet, rdn hfwy, sn tld off*............... (16 to 1 op 14 to 1) 9
Dist: 7l, 5l, 20l, 10l, 12l, 2½l, 25l, 1½l. 2m 57.65s. a 11.65s (9 Ran).
SR: 33/18/13/-/-/-/ (M P Bowring), M H Tompkins

1181 Irvine Handicap Class D (0-80 3-y-o) £3,187 7f...................... (3:50)

DANCING DOMINO [48] 8-0¹ K Darley (2) *led early, styd hndy till led ag'n o'r 2 fs out, kpt on strly.* ....(3 to 1 op 2 to 1) 1
1150³ WHITE CREEK (Ire) [65] (v) 9-3 G Carter (3) *nvr far away, not much room and swtchd outsd o'r 2 fs out, ran on und pres, not rch wnr.* ....(7 to 4 fav op 6 to 4 tchd 2 to 1) 2
966 GOLD DESIRE [41] 7-7 J Fanning (1) *sn led, hdd and drvn alng o'r 2 fs out, one pace*.......... (3 to 1 op 5 to 2) 3
725 LAKAB (USA) [69] (bl) 9-7 H Ballantine (4) *trkd ldrs, feeling pace and drvn alng hfwy, nvr able to chal.* ....(4 to 1 op 5 to 1 tchd 7 to 2) 4
Dist: 4l, 1l, 1½l. 1m 32.15s. a 8.15s (4 Ran).
SR: 6/11/-/7/ (P D Savill), M H Easterby

1182 Ochiltree Maiden Stakes Class D (2-y-o) £3,178 5f................. (4:20)

687⁸ MISTER BLOY 9-0 G Carter (4) *jinked rght strt, pressed ldg pair, swshd tail o'r one furlong out, kpt on to ld last 50 yards*......... (Evens fav tchd 5 to 4 on and 5 to 4) 1
WARTHILL WHISPERS 8-9 M Wigham (3) *broke fst to dispute ld, nosed ahead ins fnl furlong, hdd and no extr last 50 yards*.......................(20 to 1 op 33 to 1) 2
THE HAPPY LOON (Ire) 9-0 J Fortune (1) *drvn alng to ld, rdn and hdd ins fnl furlong, one pace.* .... (17 to 2 op 8 to 1) 3
968² MOKAITE 8-9 K Darley (5) *crrd rght strt, reco'red and swtchd lft hfwy, rdn and no extr over one furlong out.* ....(5 to 2 op 2 to 1) 4
WILLWIN 8-9 J Fanning (2) *sn struggling and outpcd, nvr nr to chal*.......................(10 to 1 op 14 to 1) 5
933⁶ BROUGHTONS PARTNER 8-7 (7*) D McCabe (7) *bumped strt, al wl outpcd*.....................(15 to 2 op 6 to 1) 6
Dist: 1½l, nk, 5l, 3½l, 5l. 1m 2.54s. a 4.44s (6 Ran).
SR: 31/20/24/ (H B Hughes), J Berry

1183 Kilwinning Handicap Class E (0-70 4-y-o and up) £2,740 5f......... (4:50)

1036* SO SUPERB [59] (bl) 4-9-3 S Webster (2) *pressed ldr, drvn alng o'r one furlong out, edgd rght und pres, kpt on wl.* ....(3 to 1 op 5 to 2) 1
1052* JUST BOB [68] 4-9-12 J Fortune (3) *drvn alng to go early pace, rallied to ld briefly wl o'r one furlong out, not quicken ins last.* (11 to 8 on op 5 to 4 on tchd 11 to 10 on and Evens) 2
1052 LANGTONIAN [55] (v) 4-8-13 G Carter (1) *broke fst to ld for o'r 3 fs, fdd*............ (11 to 4 op 5 to 2 tchd 3 to 1) 3
Dist: 3½l, 6l. 1m 1.98s. a 3.88s (3 Ran).
SR: 45/40/3/ (N A Riddell), M Dods

BELMONT PARK (USA) (firm)
Saturday May 22nd

1184 Shuvee Handicap (Grade 1) (3-y-o and up) £59,603 1m 110yds...............

TURNBACK THE ALARM (USA) 4-8-5 C Antley, ...(17 to 10 co-fav) 1
SHARED INTEREST (USA) 5-8-1 J D Bailey, ..(17 to 10 co-fav) 2
VIVANO (USA) 4-8-0 M Smith,.................. (76 to 10) 3
560⁴ QUEEN OF TRIUMPH (USA) 4-8-0 C Perret,..... (78 to 10) 4
S S SPARKLE (USA) 4-8-0 A Madrid,........... (96 to 10) 5
NANNERL (USA) 6-8-5 Julie Krone,.......(17 to 10 co-fav) 6
JEANO (USA) 5-8-1 R Davis,....................(84 to 10) 7
HAUNTING (USA) 5-8-2 J Santos,...............(19 to 1) 8
560⁹ RICHARD'S LASS (USA) 5-7-13 J Chavez,...... (78 to 10) 9
Dist: ¾l, 2l, nk, 1l, nose, hd, 2l, 22l. 1m 43.11s. (9 Ran).
(Moyglare Stud Farm), W Terrill

CARLISLE (good)
Saturday May 22nd

Going Correction: PLUS 0.25 sec. per fur. (races 1,2,6), PLUS 0.30 (3,4,5)

1185 Sands Centre Rating Related Maiden Stakes Class F (0-65 3-y-o) £2,075 7f 214yds........................ (6:10)

1007⁴ CAMEO KIRBY (Fr) 8-7 (7*) J Tate (1) *settled gng wl, improved to ld 2 fs out, shaken up and ran on well fnl furlong*....................... (3 to 1 jt-fav tchd 7 to 2) 1
1057⁶ ROYAL INTERVAL 9-0 T Sprake (6) *hld up in tch, rdn 4 fs out, hdwy on inner 2 out, kpt on ins last.* (3 to 1 jt-fav) 2
860³ SUDDEN SPIN (v) 8-7 (7*) P Roberts (2) *led till hdd 2 fs out, sn shaken up, not quicken fnl furlong.* ....(6 to 1 op 8 to 1) 3
880 PERSIANSKY (Ire) 9-0 Dean McKeown (7) *very unruly preliminaries, missed break, rcd keenly, took clr order hfwy, rdn and wknd o'r 2 fs out*... (5 to 1 tchd 9 to 2) 4
784⁵ INOVAR 8-11 (3*) S D Williams (4) *hld up, rdn 3 fs out, sn btn, tld off*.......................(20 to 1 op 16 to 1) 5
1103⁶ PEEDIE PEAT 9-0 M Birch (5) *chsd ldrs till rdn and wknd entering strt, tld off*.................. (7 to 2 op 3 to 1) 6
685 BARDIA 8-9 Kim Tinkler (3) *nvr far away, pushed alng entering strt, sn wknd, tld off*.... (50 to 1 op 33 to 1) 7
Dist: 1l, 1½l, 12l, 12l, 3½l, 1½l. 1m 45.10s. a 7.20s (7 Ran).
SR: 22/19/14/-/ (Maktoum Al Maktoum), A A Scott

1186 Lanes Claiming Stakes Class F (3-y-o and up) £2,302 6f 206yds........(6:40)

1038* CALISAR 3-8-9 T Sprake (5) *chsd ldrs, improved to ld wl o'r one furlong out, hld on gmely whn hrd pressed fnl furlong*...........................(3 to 1 fav op 11 to 4) 1
681⁵ PRINCESS OF ORANGE 4-8-12 (3*) S Maloney (9) *hld up, rdn to improve entering strt, ev ch and hng rght entering fnl furlong, kpt on*........... (12 to 1 tchd 16 to 1) 2
1052 KHALLOOF (Ire) (bl) 4-8-7 (7*) C Teague (13) *mid-div, effrt o'r 2 fs out, drifted lft over one out, ran on ins last.* .... (14 to 1 op 12 to 1) 3
893 LOMBARD SHIPS 6-8-7 A Mackay (14) *led aftr a furlong, hdd wl o'r one out, no extr*.......... (4 to 1 op 3 to 1) 4
884² MAGICATION 3-7-9 (7*) Claire Balding (2) *beh till styd on und pres fnl 2 fs, nrst finish*........ (6 to 1 op 7 to 1) 5
714⁷ SENSE OF PRIORITY 4-9-12 K Darley (11) *in tch, effrt and came wide strt, wknd o'r one furlong out.* .... (9 to 2 op 5 to 1 tchd 11 to 2) 6

883[9] BRIGHT GEM 3-7-12 J Fanning (7) *beh, effrt and rdn entering strt, no imprsn o'r one furlong out.* ....(7 to 1 tchd 8 to 1) 7
731[8] ALDINGTON PEACH 4-8-11 N Connorton (4) *led a furlong, styd hndy, rdn 3 fs out, grad wknd.* .... (10 to 1 op 12 to 1) 8
964 MELTONBY 4-8-9 Kim Tinkler (10) *al beh, nvr a factor.* .... (25 to 1 op 20 to 1) 9
1101[7] LAUREL CONNECTION 4-9-0 Dean McKeown (6) *chsd ldrs till rdn and wknd o'r 2 fs out, tld off*.........(20 to 1) 10
361 SIMPLY SUPERB 3-8-11 M Birch (1) *settled towards rear, rdn hfwy, grad lost tch, tld off.* ....(25 to 1 op 20 to 1 tchd 33 to 1) 11
WABWOM 4-8-11 (3*) S D Williams (8) *sn beh, sddl slpd and pld up aftr 3 fs*..........................(33 to 1) pu
Dist: Nk, ½l, 4l, 3½l, 3½l, sht-hd, 12l, nk, 8l, 6l. 1m 31.50s. a 6.10s (12 Ran).
SR: 30/35/32/13/-/10/ (A Poole), W G M Turner

1187 Carlisle Mitsubishi Handicap Class E (0-70 3-y-o) £2,490 5f........... (7:10)

1151* COVENT GARDEN GIRL [57] 8-8 (7ex) T Lucas (6) *dwlt, sn reco'red, led aftr a furlong, shaken up 2 fs out, hld on wl ins last*.........(13 to 8 fav op 11 to 8 tchd 7 to 4) 1
1083[2] FIRST OPTION [70] 9-7 K Darley (4) *dwlt, in tch, effrt and swtchd 2 fs out, styd on wl ins last.* ....(7 to 4 op 2 to 1 tchd 6 to 4) 2
883[4] DEAD CALM [61] (v) 8-12 Dean McKeown (1) *in tch on outer, effrt hfwy, not quicken ins fnl furlong.* ....(4 to 1 op 9 to 2) 3
909 COLMAR [43] 7-8[1] Dale Gibson (7) *led a furlong, remained prmnt, ev ch 2 fs out, wknd appr fnl furlong.* ....(9 to 1 op 8 to 1) 4
1151[4] JOTRA [49] 8-0 G Carter (3) *cl up, rdn hfwy, wknd wl o'r one furlong out*............ (10 to 1 op 8 to 1) 5
CANAZEI [44] (v) 7-9[2] Kim Tinkler (5) *beh and sn pushed alng, lost tch frm hfwy*...................... (33 to 1) 6
Dist: ½l, 4l, 1½l, 4l, 4l. 1m 4.50s. a 4.50s (6 Ran).
SR: 34/45/20/ (New Covent Garden Flower Sales), M W Easterby

1188 Evening News And Star Limited Stakes Class D (0-75 3-y-o and up) £3,546 5f 207yds............... (7:40)

411[2] DEBSY DO (USA) 4-8-11 (5*) O Pears (1) *led half a furlong, pressed ldr, shaken up o'r 2 fs out, rgned ld over one out, hld on wl ins last*.............(15 to 8 op 7 to 4) 1
1066[2] MACFARLANE 5-9-7 F Norton (2) *chsd ldg pair, effrt and swtchd o'r 2 fs out, sn rdn, kpt on ins last.* .... (6 to 5 on op 5 to 4 on tchd 11 to 10 on) 2
1038[4] DOKKHA OYSTON (Ire) 5-9-7 J Carroll (3) *stumbled leaving stalls, sn reco'red, led aftr half a furlong, rdn 2 fs out, hdd over one out, rallied, no extr wl ins last.* ....(4 to 1 tchd 9 to 2) 3
Dist: ½l, 1½l. 1m 17.50s. a 4.50s (3 Ran).
SR: 48/51/45/ (Lintscan Ltd (Corbett Bookmakers)), S G Norton

1189 Carlisle Castle Maiden Auction Stakes Class E (2-y-o) £2,803 5f 207yds......................... (8:10)

776[7] PRIVATE FIXTURE (Ire) 9-0 M Tebbutt (11) *dwlt, beh early, rdn to improve hfwy, effrt 2 fs out, sstnd run to ld wl ins last*....................... (2 to 1 fav tchd 5 to 2) 1
908[5] CALL TO MIND (Ire) 9-0 M Birch (4) *tried to make all, shaken up o'r 2 fs out, hdd wl ins last, kpt on.* ....(5 to 1 tchd 11 to 2) 2
299[3] TURTLE ROCK 9-0 K Darley (6) *chsd ldrs, bustled alng hfwy, kpt on same pace ins fnl furlong*.........(7 to 2) 3
812 OLYMPIC BID 8-9 J Carroll (1) *in tch on outer, effrt and rdn o'r 2 fs out, one pace ins last.* (14 to 1 op 12 to 1) 4
969[5] T O O MAMMA'S (Ire) 8-9 J Fortune (7) *chsd ldrs, rdn to chal o'r 2 fs out, slightly hmpd and veered rght over one out, no extr ins last*.....................(20 to 1) 5
730 IMPOSING GROOM (Ire) 9-0 G Carter (9) *in tch on ins, pushed alng o'r 2 fs out, one pace over one out.* .... (11 to 2 op 5 to 1) 6
564[4] WINGS AHEAD 9-0 J Fanning (2) *in tch on outer, effrt whn slightly hmpd o'r one furlong out, sn one pace.* ....(16 to 1 tchd 20 to 1) 7
812[7] DRAGON MAN 9-0 Dean McKeown (10) *beh, pushed alng hfwy, nvr dngrs*.............................(12 to 1) 8
SPORT RACING CLUB 8-4 (5*) Darren Moffatt (5) *sluggish strt, beh, detached and rdn hfwy, kpt on fnl furlong, no imprsn*..................(8 to 1 tchd 10 to 1) 9
SPRINGHEAD 8-9 F Norton (8) *in tch, rdn o'r 2 fs out, sn btn*................. (14 to 1 op 12 to 1 tchd 16 to 1) 10
1108[8] TEN TIMES TANGO 8-9 M Wigham (3) *wth ldr, drvn alng hfwy, wkng whn hmpd o'r one furlong out*....(33 to 1) 11
Dist: Hd, 3½l, hd, hd, 2l, 1½l, 2½l, 2½l, 2½l, 8l. 1m 18.60s. a 5.60s (11 Ran).
SR: 24/23/9/3/2/-/ (H J W Steckmest), W Jarvis

1190 Carlisle Cathedral Handicap Class E (0-70 4-y-o and up) £2,637 1½m (8:40)

931[5] BLACKPATCH HILL [61] 4-9-5 G Carter (16) *rcd freely, trkd ldr, led o'r 6 fs out, quickened clr over one out, eased ins last*...................... (5 to 2 fav tchd 3 to 1) 1
988[5] PERSUASIVE [57] 6-8-8 (7*) S Copp (12) *hld up and wl beh, gd hdwy and came wide strt, edgd rght ins fnl furlong, kpt on, not rch wnr*.................. (7 to 1 op 6 to 1) 2
910[5] HILLZAH (USA) [53] 5-8-8[4] (7*) H Bastiman (13) *slwly into strd, hmpd aftr a furlong, beh till hdwy entering strt, slightly hampered ins last, ran on.* (20 to 1 op 14 to 1) 3
1056* SHAMSHOM AL ARAB (Ire) [54] 5-8-7 (5*) Darren Moffatt (4) *hld up, took clr order aftr 4 fs, drvn alng entering strt, sn one pace*............ (9 to 2 op 7 to 2 tchd 5 to 1) 4
632[3] DEB'S BALL [60] 7-9-4 J Fanning (9) *hld up, improved to chase ldrs 3 fs out, rdn and kpt on same pace appr fnl furlong*...............................(8 to 1 tchd 10 to 1) 5
863[5] HOT PUNCH [43] 4-8-1 Dale Gibson (6) *in tch, drvn alng appr strt, not quicken*.......... (14 to 1 tchd 16 to 1) 6
527[2] NORTHERN GRADUATE (USA) [70] 4-10-0 K Darley (3) *chsd ldrs, effrt 4 fs out, rdn and no extr o'r 2 furlongs out.* ....(7 to 1 op 5 to 1) 7
SUNSET REINS FREE [37] (v) 8-7-9 F Norton (15) *chsd ldg pair, rdn o'r 4 fs out, sn btn*..................(20 to 1) 8
727 GREY COMMANDER [35] 5-7-7 A Mackay (11) *in tch till rdn and wknd o'r 3 fs out*......... (20 to 1 op 16 to 1) 9
745[6] MINGUS (USA) [44] 6-8-2 N Connorton (2) *hld up and beh, improved 2 fs out, nvr dngrs*.......(20 to 1 op 14 to 1) 10
845 TANODA [45] 7-7-10 (7*) J Marshall (5) *mid-div, effrt o'r 4 fs out, sn rdn, wknd entering strt*.............. (12 to 1) 11
1034* ALMOST A PRINCESS [51] 5-8-9 M Tebbutt (8) *mid-div, effrt and rdn o'r 5 fs out, wknd 3 furlongs out.* ....(10 to 1 tchd 12 to 1) 12
356[8] BEST GUN [50] (bl) 4-8-8 J Carroll (14) *sn led, hdd o'r 6 fs out, wknd over 3 furlongs out, eased over one out.* ....(20 to 1) 13
769[4] TAKE BY STORM (Ire) [64] 4-9-8 D Nicholls (1) *took keen hold, mid-divsion, took clr order aftr 4 fs, rdn and wknd four furlongs out*.........(12 to 1 tchd 14 to 1) 14
DON'T CRY [37] 5-7-9[2] Kim Tinkler (10) *beh, struggling fnl 4 fs, tld off*................... (66 to 1 tchd 100 to 1) 15
231[5] MARIETTE LARKIN [46] 4-8-4 Dean McKeown (7) *sn beh, lost tch o'r 4 fs out, tld off*...................... (33 to 1) 16
Dist: 2l, 1½l, 4l, 1½l, nk, ½l, 2½l, nk, hd, 2l. 2m 39.10s. a 9.10s (16 Ran).
SR: 44/36/29/22/25/7/33/-/-/ (J L Dunlop), J L Dunlop

CATTERICK (good to soft)
Saturday May 22nd
Going Correction: PLUS 0.45 sec. per fur.

1191 Swaledale Selling Handicap Class G (0-60 3-y-o) £2,322 1m 5f 175yds (2:15)

1054[2] GOODBYE MILLIE [50] 8-6 (5*) O Pears (4) *in tch, smooth hdwy 5 fs out, led wl o'r 2 furlongs out, clr appr fnl furlong*............................ (4 to 1 op 3 to 1) 1
1061[2] RUBIDIAN [42] 8-3 G Duffield (3) *led, quickened o'r 4 fs out, rdn and hdd wl over 2 furlongs out, kpt on one pace*............... (3 to 1 fav op 7 to 2 tchd 11 to 4) 2
928[9] PALACEGATE SUNSET [50] 8-11 Alex Greaves (9) *hld up and beh, headay 5 fs out and sn rdn alng, plugged on one pace und pres*...............................(4 to 1) 3
1055[6] MOUNTAIN WILLOW [55] (v) 9-2 A Clark (2) *mid-div, gd hdwy 5 fs out, effrt 3 furlongs out, sn rdn and wknd.* .... (6 to 1 op 7 to 1 tchd 11 to 2) 4
976 BONNY PRINCESS [40] 8-1 J Lowe (1) *chsd ldrs till lost pl 5 fs out, sn beh*...................(25 to 1 op 20 to 1) 5
888[5] CARNEA [40] 8-1 F Norton (10) *prmnt, chsd ldr aftr 5 fs till rdn and wknd 4 furlongs out*................ (12 to 1) 6
1073[8] WALSHAM WITCH [60] 9-4 (3*) S D Williams (5) *al rear.* .... (14 to 1 op 12 to 1) 7
864[7] GOLDMIRE [56] 9-3 N Connorton (8) *cl up, rdn 4 fs out and sn wknd*........................ (16 to 1 op 12 to 1) 8
NEWGATESKY [35] 7-5 (5*) Darren Moffatt (6) *in tch 4 fs, sn lost pl and beh frm hfwy*......... (50 to 1 op 33 to 1) 9
1038[3] DON'T TELL JEAN [40] 7-12 (3*) S Maloney (7) *chsd ldrs till wknd quickly o'r 5 fs out and sn tld off.* .... (9 to 1 op 8 to 1 tchd 10 to 1) 10
Dist: 3½l, sht-hd, 4l, 15l, ¾l, 6l, 7l, 12l, 8l. 3m 10.50s. a 15.00s (10 Ran).
SR: 9/-/1/-/-/-/ (Lintscan Ltd (Corbett Bookmakers)), S G Norton

1192 Gainford Median Auction Maiden Stakes Class D (3-y-o) £3,318 7f (2:45)

950[3] CASTEL ROSSELO 9-0 F Norton (9) *in tch, hdwy whn lft in ld 2 and a half fs out, badly hmpd two furlongs out, styd on to lead o'r one furlong out, ran on.* ....(9 to 2 op 4 to 1 tchd 5 to 1) 1
HATTON'S GEM 8-9 G Duffield (6) *slwly into strd, hdwy and wide strt whn hmpd 2 and a half fs out, sn rdn and styd on appr fnl furlong*.......... (4 to 1 tchd 9 to 2) 2
583[4] SWEET THATCH (Ire) 8-4 (5*) Stephen Davies (5) *in tch, wide strt, led briefly 2 fs out, sn rdn, hdd and one pace.* ....(15 to 8 fav op 6 to 4 tchd 2 to 1) 3
1016 HEART BROKEN 8-9 S Morris (4) *cl up, ev ch far rls whn badly hmpd 2 fs out, not reco'r*..... (9 to 1 op 10 to 1) 4

1039^{9} CUMBRIAN CALYPSO 8-11 (3*) S Maloney (3) *dwlt and beh, hmpd 2 and a half fs out, styd on fnl furlong, nvr a factor*.............. (14 to 1 op 12 to 1 tchd 16 to 1) 5
452^{5} GRENOBLE (Ire) 8-4 (5*) Darren Moffatt (8) *mid-div, rdn and beh frm hfwy*..................(33 to 1 op 20 to 1) 6
761 LANZAMAR 8-9 Dale Gibson (7) *led to hfwy, sn lost pl and beh*..(50 to 1) 7+
1136^{8} PHASE ONE (Ire) 8-9 J Lowe (2) *al rear, wl beh whn hmpd 2 and a half fs out*.................................(50 to 1) 7+
1027^{7} TIME AGAIN 8-11 (3*) J Weaver (1) *cl up, led hfwy till stumbled badly and uns rdr 2 and a half fs out*. ....(4 to 1 op 3 to 1) ur
Dist: 6l, 1½l, 4l, 8l, ½l, 2l, dd-ht. 1m 31.60s. a 8.60s (9 Ran).
SR: 18/-/-/-/-/-/ (Sir Philip Oppenheimer), G Wragg

1193 Rothmans Royals North South Challenge Series Handicap Class D (0-80 3-y-o and up) £3,622 7f......... (3:15)

862^{2} TAWAFIJ (USA) [61] 4-8-12 (5*) Stephen Davies (2) *chsd ldrs, effrt o'r 2 fs out, rdn to ld appr last, ran on strly*. ....(7 to 1 op 8 to 1) 1
818^{9} LAUREL QUEEN (Ire) [66] 5-9-8 Alex Greaves (6) *cl up, led hfwy, wide strt, rdn 2 fs out, hdd appr fnl furlong, one pace*..........................(8 to 1 op 10 to 1) 2
1081^{5} BALLAD DANCER [57] 8-8-8 (5*) Darren Moffatt (1) *hld up, effrt o'r 2 fs out, sn rdn and kpt on one pace*. ....(6 to 1 tchd 11 to 2) 3
1103^{2} BLUE GRIT [65] 7-9-7 J Lowe (5) *hld up, hdwy 2 fs out, sn rdn and one pace*..............(5 to 2 fav tchd 9 to 4) 4
1081* SARTIGILA [64] 4-9-3 (3*) S Maloney (7) *beh, effrt and pushed alng hfwy, no hdwy*..........(4 to 1 op 3 to 1) 5
909 SUPER BENZ [68] 7-9-7 (3*) S D Williams (3) *led to hfwy, cl up and wide strt, rdn o'r 2 fs out, grad wknd*. (10 to 1) 6
1081^{7} NORDAN RAIDER [62] 5-9-4 N Connorton (4) *chsd ldrs till wknd one and a half fs out, eased ins last*. ....(5 to 1 op 4 to 1) 7
Dist: 4l, 1½l, 2½l, 3l, 1l, 3½l. 1m 30.10s. a 7.10s (7 Ran).
SR: 44/37/23/23/13/14/-/ (Stephen Laidlaw), R Allan

1194 Yorkshire Television Limited Stakes Class F (0-60 3-y-o and up) £3,150 7f ....(3:45)

1102* AL MOULOUKI 3-8-13 W Hood (9) *hld up and beh, hdwy and wide strt, rdn 2 fs out, styd on to ld wl ins last*. ....(6 to 5 on op 6 to 4 tchd 5 to 4 on) 1
906* CLAUDIA MISS 6-9-5 Dale Gibson (11) *al prmnt, wide strt, effrt to chal 2 fs out, sn led, rdn and hdd wl ins last*. ....(13 to 2 op 4 to 1) 2
906^{5} JUST A STEP 7-9-10 A Clark (2) *sn led, wide strt, hdd o'r 2 fs out, soon rdn, kpt on fnl furlong*. (11 to 1 op 8 to 1) 3
636 GLENFIELD GRETA 5-9-5 F Norton (6) *mid-div, effrt and hdwy 2 fs out, sn rdn, kpt on one pace*. ....(16 to 1 op 12 to 1) 4
930^{2} SCOTTISH PARK 4-9-2 (3*) S Maloney (10) *chsd ldrs, wide strt, hdwy to ld 2 and a half fs out, sn rdn, hdd and wknd one and a half furlongs out*. (13 to 2 op 5 to 1) 5
833^{5} PUBLIC WAY (Ire) 3-8-13 J Lowe (4) *in tch, gd hdwy to chal 2 fs out, ev ch till rdn and wknd appr last*. ....(16 to 1 op 14 to 1) 6
931 ROYAL COMEDIAN 4-9-5 N Connorton (8) *chsd ldrs, effrt and ev ch 2 fs out, sn rdn and wknd*. ....(50 to 1 op 33 to 1) 7
710^{7} CLEDESCHAMPS 4-9-5 S Morris (7) *in tch, rdn 2 and a half fs out, sn btn*..............................(20 to 1) 8
1072* APPEALING TIMES (USA) 4-9-10 S Wood (3) *al rear*. ....(14 to 1 op 12 to 1) 9
565^{2} WILD PROSPECT 5-9-10 G Duffield (1) *cl up till rdn and wknd 3 fs out*..................(13 to 2 op 6 to 1) 10
Dist: 1½l, nk, 2l, 2l, 1½l, 3½l, sht-hd, 3l, 4l. 1m 31.40s. a 8.40s (10 Ran).
SR: 20/21/25/14/8/-/ (G Jabre), J W Payne

1195 William Edwin Neesham Memorial Handicap Class E (0-70 4-y-o and up) £3,080 1m 7f 177yds............(4:15)

MARDOOD [35] 8-7-7 S Wood (1) *hld up and beh, steady hdwy 6 fs out, led 3 out, hrd drvn and styd on gmely fnl furlong*...............(7 to 2 fav op 5 to 2 tchd 4 to 1) 1
KAYARTIS [39] 4-7-9 J Lowe (6) *mid-div, hdwy hfwy, effrt 3 fs out, chlgd 2 out, hrd drvn and ev ch, no extr nr line*. ....(9 to 2 op 4 to 1 tchd 7 to 2) 2
857 OUR AISLING [70] 5-9-9 (5*) O Pears (7) *trkd ldrs gng wl, hdwy 3 fs out, ev ch, rdn 2 out, sn one pace*. ....(5 to 1 tchd 11 to 2) 3
1056^{3} MENTALASANYTHIN [64] 4-9-6 A Mackay (3) *chsd ldrs, rdn 3 fs out, one pace fnl 2 furlongs*......(7 to 1 op 6 to 1) 4
645 DORADUS [45] 5-8-3 G Duffield (8) *chsd clr ldr till led 6 fs out, hdd 3 out, sn hrd rdn and wknd 2 out*. ....(11 to 2 op 8 to 1) 5
589^{7} MEDIA STAR [38] 8-7-10^{3} F Norton (4) *mid-div, hdwy o'r 4 fs out, rdn and one pace over 2 out*.............(33 to 1) 6
901^{7} REXY BOY [35] 6-7-6^{6} (7*) K Sked (10) *led and sn clr, hdd 6 fs out, cl up till wknd 3 out*........(25 to 1 op 20 to 1) 7
967^{7} MALENOIR (USA) [45] (v) 5-8-0 (3*) S Maloney (11) *chsd ldrs till rdn and wknd o'r 4 fs out*......(20 to 1 op 14 to 1) 8
901 NOTABLE EXCEPTION [48] 4-7-13 (5*) Darren Moffatt (5) *al rear, wl beh frm hfwy*. (8 to 1 tchd 7 to 1 and 9 to 1) 9
COLORADO INSIGHT [36] 5-7-8^{1} Dale Gibson (2) *in tch till lost pl and beh frm hfwy*..............................(33 to 1) 10
TOP WAVE [47] (bl) 5-8-5 N Connorton (9) *chsd ldrs till wknd 7 fs out, tld off fnl 3 furlongs*. (8 to 1 op 7 to 1) 11
Dist: Hd, 6l, 2l, 1½l, ½l, 10l, 5l, nk, 5l. 3m 38.60s. a 17.10s (11 Ran).
SR: -/-/7/-/-/-/ (J C Fretwell), P Leach

1196 Aldbrough Rating Related Maiden Stakes Class E (0-70 3-y-o and up) £2,717 5f 212yds.............. (4:45)

854^{4} CHERHILL (Ire) 3-8-1 (5*) Stephen Davies (2) *made all, rdn fnl 2 fs, styd on gmely ins last*. ....(11 to 10 fav op 5 to 4 on) 1
766^{2} CLANROCK 3-8-4 (7*) G Parkin (3) *cl up, rdn to dispute ld one and a half fs out, ev ch till no extr wl ins last*. ....(11 to 2 op 6 to 1) 2
HOY-LIEGH-RAG 3-8-11 G Duffield (1) *cl up, effrt and ev ch 2 fs out, sn rdn and wknd entering fnl furlong*. ....(3 to 1 op 7 to 2) 3
899^{3} LIDA'S DELIGHT (Ire) 3-8-11 T Lucas (4) *pld hrd, in tch, effrt 2 fs out, sn rdn and wknd appr fnl furlong*. ....(9 to 2 op 4 to 1) 4
Dist: ½l, 3½l, 1½l. 1m 17.90s. a 6.90s (4 Ran).
SR: 8/11/-/-/ (R E Sangster), P W Chapple-Hyam

CURRAGH (IRE) (yielding)
Saturday May 22nd

Going Correction: PLUS 0.70 sec. per fur. (races 1,3,4,5), PLUS 0.30 (2,6)

1197 Ballymany (E.B.F.) Maiden (2-y-o) £5,250 6f..................... (2:15)

1022^{4} COMMON RUMPUS (Ire) 8-11 J P Murtagh (1).....(8 to 1) 1
TANGO TRIO (Ire) 9-0 D V Smith (3)..............(20 to 1) 2
938^{2} CLIFDON FOG (Ire) 9-0 C Roche (11).......... (Evens fav) 3
MONTE MARIO (USA) 9-0 M J Kinane (6)..........(6 to 1) 4
OPULENT 9-0 P V Gilson (10)......................(10 to 3) 5
MOMENTS TO CARE (Ire) 8-11 N G McCullagh (7) (20 to 1) 6
GALLIC FLAIR (Ire) 9-0 J F Egan (9)..............(33 to 1) 7
938^{9} MAHASEAL (USA) 8-11 W J Supple (12)......... (20 to 1) 8
IMNOTAKROOK (Ire) 8-8 (6*) J A Heffernan (5).... (16 to 1) 9
ORANEDIN 9-0 P Shanahan (8).................. (20 to 1) 10
938^{6} JOIN FORCES (Ire) 9-0 R Hughes (4)..............(16 to 1) 11
THE MARDYKE (Ire) 9-0 W J O'Connor (13).......(20 to 1) 12
MONICA'S CHOICE (Ire) 9-0 K J Manning (2)..... (33 to 1) 13
Dist: 2½l, sht-hd, 2½l, ¾l. 1m 19.00s. a 8.50s (13 Ran).
SR: 11/4/3/-/-/-/ (Mrs Elizabeth Byrne), F Dunne

1198 Hotel Conrad Silver Race (Listed) (3-y-o) £8,625 1¼m............... (2:45)

941^{4} HUSHANG (Ire) 8-11 M J Kinane (3) *wl plcd, rdn 4 fs out, prog to chal 2 out, led o'r one out, kpt on*.......(7 to 2) 1
1047^{7} VIA PARIGI (Ire) 8-11 C Roche (5) *hld up, prog 2 fs out, styd on wl fnl furlong*..............................(13 to 2) 2
576^{8} ROYAL BALLERINA (Ire) 8-8 W J O'Connor (9) *wl plcd, rdn 2 fs out, kpt on well ins last*........................ (7 to 1) 3
941^{5} SINISSIPI (USA) 9-0 J P Murtagh (7) *led, rdn o'r 2 fs out, hdd over one out, sn wknd*.........................(10 to 1) 4
OISEAU DE FEU (USA) 8-8 R Hughes (2) *rear, prog o'r 2 fs out, rdn, kpt on fnl furlong*..........................(10 to 1) 5
1024^{6} SPECIAL PAGEANT (Ire) 8-8 K J Manning (6) *trkd ldr, rdn 3 fs out, little room 2 out, sn wknd*..................(16 to 1) 6
941^{2} ADVOCAT (Ger) 8-11 W R Swinburn (8) *wl plcd, trkd ldr o'r 2 fs out, little room, sn rdn, not quicken*... (13 to 8 fav) 7
808^{4} PORTRAIT GALLERY (Ire) 8-11 L Piggott (1) *rear, rdn o'r 2 fs out, not quicken*.................................(8 to 1) 8
808^{5} FLAME OF PERSIA (Ire) 8-8 W J Supple (4) *rear, rdn o'r 2 fs out, not quicken, eased ins last*................. (33 to 1) 9
Dist: 1½l, 2l, sht-hd, ½l. 2m 9.40s. a 6.60s (9 Ran).
SR: 61/58/51/56/49/-/ (H H Aga Khan), John M Oxx

1199 Maginn T.V. Handicap (0-100 3-y-o and up) £6,900 1m.................(3:15)

939^{3} READY (Ire) [-] 3-8-3 W J Supple (5)..................(8 to 1) 1
942* KAYFA (Ire) [-] 4-9-2 (6*,2ex) J A Heffernan (13).....(5 to 1) 2
SHARP REVIEW (Ire) [-] 5-9-10 M J Kinane (4).......(5 to 1) 3
898^{2} WHEATSHEAF LADY (Ire) [-] 3-8-1 D V Smith (10).. (9 to 1) 4
787^{6} BASIE NOBLE [-] (bl) 4-8-4 N G McCullagh (6)..... (9 to 1) 5
1106^{5} BENE MERENTI (Ire) [-] (bl) 3-7-2^{2} (8*) R T Fitzpatrick (7) ....(20 to 1) 6
939^{8} EVERY ONE KNOWS (USA) [-] 4-8-3 J F Egan (3)...(20 to 1) 7
787 GALLARDINI (Ire) [-] 4-9-9 C Roche (14)..........(14 to 1) 8
787 BELMARTIN [-] 7-7-13 (10*) P M Donohue (8).......(14 to 1) 9
898^{5} KURDISTAN (Ire) [-] 3-8-6 W J O'Connor (2)..........(10 to 1) 10
787^{7} SHAIKALA (Ire) [-] 3-8-1 (2*) D G O'Shea (11)..... (4 to 1 fav) 11
TINA'S CHARM (Ire) [-] 4-8-2 (2*) R M Burke (9)... (33 to 1) 12
CLASSIC MATCH (Ire) [-] 5-10-0 S Craine (12).....(33 to 1) 13
Dist: ½l, 3½l, hd, 2½l. 1m 44.80s. a 8.20s (13 Ran).
SR: 50/67/58/34/29/-/ (Mrs Anne Coughlan), Kevin Prendergast

1200 IAWS Irish 1,000 Guineas (Group 1) (3-y-o) £112,000 1m..............(3:50)

472* NICER (Ire) 9-0 M Hills (8) *hld up, little room o'r 2 fs out, sn gd prog to ld one and a half out, styd on strly.* (8 to 1) 1
669² GOODNIGHT KISS 9-0 P Shanahan (3) *rear, gd prog und 2 fs, sn rdn, no extr ins last*....................(25 to 1) 2
943* DANSE ROYALE (Ire) 9-0 L Piggott (6) *rear, rdn 2 fs out, gd prog fnl furlong*....................(16 to 1) 3
749⁴ FELAWNAH (USA) 9-0 W Carson (12) *trkd ldr till lost pos hfwy, sn rdn, prog to chal und 2 fs out, no extr fnl furlong*....................(13 to 2) 4
665³ TARAKANA (USA) 9-0 R Hughes (11) *wl plcd, smooth prog to track ldrs 2 fs out, sn rdn, not quicken*..... (25 to 1) 5
573* MIAMI SANDS (Ire) 9-0 J P Murtagh (4) *hld up, prog o'r 2 fs out, no extr fnl furlong*....................(20 to 1) 6
749⁷ ZARANI SIDI ANNA (USA) 9-0 W R Swinburn (13) *mid-div, rdn 3 fs out, some prog 2 out, wknd ins last.* (3 to 1 fav) 7
665* ASEMA (USA) 9-0 M J Kinane (14) *rear, some prog 3 fs out, rdn 2 out, not quicken*....................(6 to 1) 8
999* DAYFLOWER (USA) 9-0 L Dettori (7) *wl plcd, led o'r 4 fs out, rdn 2 out, sn hdd and wknd*...............(7 to 1) 9
943⁴ SABAYA (USA) 9-0 W J Supple (9) *wl plcd, trkd ldr hfwy, rdn 3 fs out, sn wknd*....................(66 to 1) 10
943³ ADOLESCENCE (Ire) 9-0 S Craine (1) *hld up till prog 3 fs out, sn wknd*....................(50 to 1) 11
749³ AJFAN (USA) 9-0 R Hills (2) *wl plcd, rdn bef hfwy, some prog 3 fs out, sn wknd*....................(6 to 1) 12
943² EUROSTORM (USA) 9-0 P V Gilson (5) *wl plcd till rdn and wknd o'r 3 and a half fs out, eased one and a half out.* ....(16 to 1) 13
943⁶ CHANZI (USA) 9-0 W J O'Connor (10) *led, rdn aftr 3 fs, sn hdd and wknd, eased three furlongs out, pld up ins last*....................(25 to 1) pu

Dist: 2l, sht-hd, 1½l, 2½l. 1m 44.20s. a 7.60s (14 Ran).
SR: 70/64/63/58/50/-/ (Mrs J M Corbett), B W Hills

1201 Greenlands Stakes (Group 3) (3-y-o and up) £11,500 6f..............(5:00)

667* COLLEGE CHAPEL 3-8-12 L Piggott (14) *hld up, prog o'r 2 fs out, sn led, kpt on wl*..............(11 to 10 fav) 1
665⁴ PERNILLA (Ire) 3-8-5 C Roche (8) *hld up, little room 2 fs out, prog o'r one out, quickened wl, kpt on*....(16 to 1) 2
4684a² STREET REBEL (Can) (bl) 5-9-8 S Craine (4) *rear, rdn 1st 3 fs, ridden ag'n o'r 2 out, ran on wl ins last*.... (12 to 1) 3
675⁹ NIGHT JAR 6-9-1 W R Swinburn (10) *wl plcd, rdn o'r 2 fs out, kpt on*....................(20 to 1) 4
1047⁸ NORDIC FOX (Ire) 3-8-8 K J Manning (6) *wl plcd, little room 2 fs out, hmpd one and a half out, kpt on*..... (20 to 1) 5
665² LAVINIA FONTANA (Ire) 4-9-1 P V Gilson (9) *wl plcd, chlgd 3 fs out, rdn 2 out, drifted lft and wknd*........(10 to 1) 6
595 DIAMONDS GALORE (Can) 8-9-4 M J Kinane (11) *wl plcd, chlgd 3 fs out, rdn one and a half out, sn wknd.* ....(10 to 1) 7
940³ SHAHIK (USA) 3-8-8 W J Supple (2) *wl plcd, little room 2 fs out, not quicken*....................(10 to 1) 8
787⁹ ALALJA (Ire) 3-8-5 J F Egan (12) *wl plcd till lost pos hfwy, sn rdn, wknd fnl furlong*.................... (20 to 1) 9
795⁵ UP AND AT 'EM 3-8-12 B Coogan (13) *wl plcd, prog to ld o'r 2 fs out, sn hdd, wknd ins last*............(11 to 2) 10
665 CAURSELLE (Ire) 4-9-1 R Hughes (1) *trkd ldr till rdn hfwy, wknd 2 out*....................(50 to 1) 11
897⁴ SUMY 3-8-8 W Carson (3) *trkd ldr till rdn 3 fs out, wknd 2 out*....................(12 to 1) 12
897³ DASHING COLOURS (Ire) 4-9-1 J P Murtagh (7) *rear, rdn and prog 2 fs out, wknd one out, eased*........(10 to 1) 13
897² BRADAWN BREEVER (Ire) (bl) 4-9-4 L Dettori (5) *led, rdn o'r 3 fs out, hdd 2 and a half out, sn wknd and eased.* ....(20 to 1) 14

Dist: 1l, 3l, sht-hd, nk. 1m 16.10s. a 5.60s (14 Ran).
SR: 70/59/64/56/48/-/ (Mrs M V O'Brien), M V O'Brien

1202 C.B.A. Handicap (0-100 3-y-o and up) £3,805 1¼m.................. (5:30)

942⁶ TONY'S FEN [-] 4-9-6 W J Supple (11)............ (7 to 1) 1
807⁴ MAYFIELD PRINCE (Ire) [-] 4-8-2² (6*) B Bowens (7) (10 to 1) 2
1025³ NORDIC DISPLAY (Ire) [-] 5-7-10 (8*) B A Hunter (1) (6 to 1) 3
648* TARTAN LADY (Ire) [-] 3-8-2 (2*) D G O'Shea (9).... (7 to 1) 4
807⁶ BEAUMONT HOUSE (Ire) [-] 4-8-2 J F Egan (10)...(12 to 1) 5
666⁹ SWEET NASHA (Ire) [-] 4-9-0 J P Murtagh (14).... (14 to 1) 6
850⁴ BLUE DIANA (Ire) [-] 3-7-7⁴ (6*) J J Behan (12).... (14 to 1) 7
942⁴ SHARASTAMINA (USA) [-] 4-8-2 N G McCullagh (4) ....(5 to 1 fav) 8
959⁴ LAGRION (USA) [-] 4-7-11² (2*) R M Burke (13)....(20 to 1) 9
895⁵ POLLYS GLOW (Ire) [-] 4-9-8 (6*) J A Heffernan (8)..(9 to 1) 10
648⁵ PHARELLA [-] 5-7-5 (6*) P P Murphy (5)............(9 to 1) 11
942⁵ PRIVATE GUY (Ire) [-] (bl) 4-9-5 M J Kinane (6)..... (6 to 1) 12
575 DOMINO'S RING (Ire) [-] (bl) 4-9-3 W J O'Connor (2) (20 to 1) 13
CINDYS BABY [-] 4-7-2³ (8*) R T Fitzpatrick (3)....(50 to 1) 14

Dist: Nk, hd, ½l, 1½l. 2m 11.20s. a 8.40s (14 Ran).
SR: 52/37/34/33/28/-/ (Mrs C Harrington), Kevin Prendergast

LINGFIELD (good to soft (races 1,3,5,6,7), good (2,4))
Saturday May 22nd

Going Correction: NIL (races 1,2,3,4,6,7), MINUS 0.15 (5)

1203 Daily Mail Racemail Maiden Auction Stakes Class D (2-y-o) £3,523 5f (2:00)

913³ STRAIGHT ARROW 9-0 A Munro (1) *broke wl, led aftr 2 fs, drw clr appr last, easily.* ....(11 to 8 fav op 6 to 4 tchd 7 to 4) 1
PERUSAL 9-0 J Reid (4) *slwly away, ran on wl fnl 2 fs, prmsg*..................(7 to 1 op 5 to 1 tchd 8 to 1) 2
979⁶ STRAPPED 8-6 (3*) B Doyle (7) *mid-div, rdn 2 fs out, kpt on one pace*..........(14 to 1 op 8 to 1 tchd 16 to 1) 3
REED MY LIPS (Ire) 9-0 Paul Eddery (8) *slwly away, styd on und pres ins fnl 2 fs.* (13 to 2 op 6 to 1 tchd 8 to 1) 4
793⁴ ROYAL CAPE 9-0 R Cochrane (3) *dsptd ld till outpcd fnl 2 fs*....................(4 to 1 op 9 to 4 tchd 9 to 2) 5
DEMON DANCER (Ire) 9-0 T Quinn (5) *speed till outpcd one and a half fs out*......(13 to 2 op 4 to 1 tchd 7 to 1) 6
MIGHTY KINGDOM (Ire) 8-9 W Newnes (6) *al beh.* .... (33 to 1 op 20 to 1) 7
708 MACE EL REEM 8-9 A Tucker (2) *led for 2 fs, outpcd and wknd quickly appr last*.......... (50 to 1 op 33 to 1) 8

Dist: 5l, 1l, 2½l, ½l, 1½l, 3l, 10l. 1m 0.16s. a 3.26s (8 Ran).
SR: 35/15/6/1/-/ (J R Bailey), Lord Huntingdon

1204 Daily Mail Handicap Class C (0-100 3-y-o) £7,570 1¼m............. (2:30)

989² BRIGANTE DI CIELO [86] 9-1 T Quinn (3) *hld up, hdwy 4 fs out, rdn 3 out, squeezed through to ld o'r one out, kpt on gmely*.................... (4 to 1 fav op 7 to 2) 1
761* TOP CEES [82] 8-11 N Adams (2) *hmpd early, in rear till gd hdwy on outsd 2 fs out, ran on strly ins last, nvr nrr.* ....(11 to 1 op 8 to 1 tchd 12 to 1) 2
635³ SCULLER (USA) [79] (bl) 8-8 W Newnes (12) *trkd ldrs, wnt second o'r 3 fs out, rdn and ev ch whn edgd lft over 2 furlongs out, rallied and kpt on.* ....(13 to 2 op 6 to 1 tchd 7 to 1) 3
926⁴ MIDYAN BLUE (Ire) [70] 7-10 (3*) N Kennedy (6) *pld hrd, in rear till gd hdwy o'r 2 fs out, styd on ins last.* ....(33 to 1 op 20 to 1) 4
772³ SATIN DANCER [83] (bl) 8-12 M Perrett (10) *slwly into strd, hdwy hfwy, rdn o'r 2 fs out, kpt on ins last.* ....(7 to 1 op 6 to 1 tchd 15 to 2) 5
875⁵ DYAB (USA) [84] 8-13 R Cochrane (7) *hld up in rear, hdwy o'r 2 fs out, ran on one pace.* ....(12 to 1 op 10 to 1 tchd 14 to 1) 6
985³ FRESCADE (USA) [87] 9-2 A Munro (1) *nvr far away, kpt on one pace fnl 2 fs*...............(12 to 1 op 10 to 1) 7
764² AWESTRUCK [72] 8-1 Paul Eddery (11) *led aftr one furlong, hdd o'r one out, sn wknd, eased nr finish.* ....(12 to 1 op 10 to 1) 8
772² WAHEM (Ire) [75] 8-1 (3*) B Doyle (4) *led for one furlong, styd in tch till rdn and wknd 2 out.* ....(8 to 1 op 7 to 1 tchd 9 to 1) 9
989 KADASTROF (Fr) [80] 8-9 B Rouse (13) *prmnt to hfwy, rdn and sn beh*...............(50 to 1 op 33 to 1) 10
630⁴ SHAMGAAN (USA) [66] 7-9¹ T Williams (5) *chsd ldrs, rdn o'r 3 fs out, wkng whn came wide into strt.* ....(6 to 1 op 5 to 1 tchd 7 to 1) 11
791⁵ NICO MIKE [75] 8-4 N Day (8) *al beh.* ....(20 to 1 tchd 25 to 1) 12
1015³ NORFOLK HERO [92] 9-7 J Reid (9) *in tch till wknd o'r 3 fs out, ran wide into strt, sn wl beh.* ....(15 to 2 op 10 to 1 tchd 7 to 1) 13

Dist: Hd, nk, nk, ¾l, ½l, 1½l, 2½l, 2½l, 10l, 7l. 2m 8.95s. a 3.95s (13 Ran).
SR: 62/57/53/43/54/54/54/34/32/ (P J Christey), R Hannon

1205 Daily Mail Leisure Stakes Class A (Listed Race) (3-y-o and up) £15,140 6f ....(3:00)

PIPS PRIDE 3-8-4 S Raymont (1) *made all, trkd o'r 2 stands side, clr two fs out, rdn ins last, jst hld on.* ....(6 to 1 op 4 to 1 tchd 13 to 2) 1
986* BRANSTON ABBY (Ire) 4-8-9 J Reid (8) *wtd wth, not much room o'r 2 fs out, ran on wl ins last, jst fld.* ....(9 to 4 fav op 5 to 2 tchd 11 to 4) 2
1019⁵ SON PARDO 3-8-4 T Quinn (7) *sn pushed alng to chase ldrs, no imprsn ins fnl 2 fs*......... (4 to 1 tchd 5 to 1) 3
986 FYLDE FLYER (v) 4-9-5 N Day (4) *chsd ldrs thrght, no imprsn ins fnl 2 fs*................(14 to 1 op 12 to 1) 4
MASTER OF PASSION 4-9-0 W Newnes (6) *al abt same pl, one pace ins fnl 2 fs*.............. (50 to 1 op 33 to 1) 5
993* BOLD LEZ 6-9-0 R Cochrane (10) *in rear, ran on fnl furlong, nvr nr to chal*.............. (9 to 2 op 4 to 1) 6
986² DUPLICITY (Ire) 5-9-0 Paul Eddery (5) *sn rdn, outpcd thrght*..............(11 to 1 op 10 to 1 tchd 12 to 1) 7
805⁵ SOOTY SWIFT (Ire) 3-7-13 B Doyle (3) *sn rdn, outpcd frm hfwy*............... (14 to 1 op 20 to 1 tchd 25 to 1) 8
MAGIC RING (Ire) 4-9-0 A Munro (2) *chsd wnr till wknd wl o'r one furlong out, better for race.* ....(8 to 1 op 7 to 1 tchd 9 to 1) 9

Dist: Hd, 2l, ¾l, 2l, hd, 1½l, 5l, hd. 1m 10.55s. a 1.55s (9 Ran).
SR: 59/63/50/62/49/48/42/7/21/ (Mrs V S Grant), R Hannon

1206 Daily Mail Dream Cottage Conditions Stakes Class C (4-y-o and up) £5,548 1m 3f 106yds.................. (3:30)

ANNA OF SAXONY 4-8-6[1] J Reid (3) *pld hrd, hld up in rear, hdwy to go second 2 fs out, led entering last, cmftbly*...... (15 to 8 on op 9 to 4 on tchd 7 to 4 on) 1
SHADOWS OF SILVER 5-8-5 A Munro (2) *led, styd on ins entering strt, hdd entering fnl furlong, kpt on one pace*..................(7 to 1 op 8 to 1 tchd 10 to 1) 2
925[3] BADIE (USA) 4-8-13 R Cochrane (1) *chsd ldr till hng rght 2 fs out, sn btn*..............(9 to 4 op 2 to 1 tchd 5 to 2) 3
Dist: 2½l, 6l. 2m 28.68s. a 4.48s (3 Ran).
SR: 47/41/37/ (Sheikh Mohammed), J H M Gosden

1207 OCS Sponsored Ladies Handicap Class E (0-80 3-y-o and up) £3,028 7f ....(4:00)

771[3] AITCH N'BEE [76] 10-11-5 M Cowdrey (6) *mid-div, hdwy 2 fs out, rdn and ran on to ld last strd*. .... (7 to 1 op 6 to 1 tchd 15 to 2) 1
914* NAVARESQUE [45] 8-9-2 Miss J Southcombe (14) *led, eased wl ins fnl furlong, shaken up, ct last strd*. .... (7 to 1 op 9 to 2 tchd 15 to 2) 2
914[3] CAPTAIN MARMALADE [53] 4-9-10 Miss I Diana W Jones (15) *in rear, hdwy and swtchd lft one and a half fs out, ran on wl, nvr nrr*...................(6 to 1 tchd 13 to 2) 3
754[3] OLD COMRADES [55] 6-9-9 (3*) Mrs L Lawson (7) *al prmnt, ev ch appr fnl furlong, ran on one pace*. .... (15 to 2 op 6 to 1 tchd 8 to 1) 4
771 HERETICAL MISS [60] 3-9-6 Mrs J Boggis (12) *al chasing ldrs, kpt on one pace fnl furlong*. (25 to 1 op 20 to 1) 5
1036 BOLD HABIT [69] 8-10-12 Mrs L Pearce (13) *hld up, hdwy o'r 2 fs out, one pace ins last*. ....(9 to 2 fav op 8 to 1 tchd 4 to 1) 6
1027 BLOWING (USA) [60] 3-9-6 Miss A Harwood (9) *prmnt, dsptd ld o'r one furlong out, wknd ins*. .... (10 to 1 op 12 to 1 tchd 16 to 1) 7
914[6] BILL MOON [53] 7-9-10 Miss J Feilden (2) *drawn low, sn came o'r to stand side, hdwy ins fnl 2 fs nvr nrr*. ....(12 to 1 tchd 14 to 1) 8
975[6] TURTLE BEACH [60] 4-10-0 (3*) Miss A Elsey (8) *chsd ldrs till wknd appr fnl furlong*.........(33 to 1 op 20 to 1) 9
971[7] RIPSNORTER (Ire) [56] 4-9-13 Miss A Purdy (10) *chsd ldrs till wknd wl o'r one furlong out*. .... (14 to 1 op 10 to 1 tchd 16 to 1) 10
YIMKIN BOOKRA [53] 5-9-7 (3*) Miss J Russell (11) *al towards rear*...........................(33 to 1 op 16 to 1) 11
971 ALNASRIC PETE (USA) [52] 7-9-9 Elain Mellor (16) *al beh*. ....(8 to 1 op 7 to 1 tchd 9 to 1) 12
978 ASSEMBLY DANCER [61] 6-10-1 (3*) Miss S Higgins (4) *strted on far side, sn came o'r to centre, nvr on terms*. .... (33 to 1 op 25 to 1 tchd 50 to 1) 13
581 INVOCATION [72] 6-10-12 (3*) Mrs J Moore (5) *rcd far side, no ch fnl 2 fs*..................(16 to 1 op 14 to 1) 14
EL CORTES (USA) [78] 4-11-7 Miss Y Haynes (1) *led far side, nvr on terms, fdd 2 fs out*.....(33 to 1 op 20 to 1) 15
771[8] RELENTLESS PURSUIT (Ire) [70] 5-10-10 (3*) Mrs J Chapple-Hyam (3) *rcd far side, tld off fnl 2 fs*. .... (16 to 1 op 14 to 1 tchd 20 to 1) 16
Dist: Sht-hd, ¾l, nk, 1l, 1l, 2l, 2½l, 1l, 1l, ½l. 1m 25.13s. a 4.43s (16 Ran).
SR: 51/19/25/26/17/34/8/4/8/ (Lady Herries), Lady Herries

1208 Daily Mail Classified Conditions Stakes Class D (4-y-o and up) £4,624 7f 140yds.......................... (4:30)

1029[4] ALFLORA (Ire) 4-8-10 R Cochrane (2) *hld up in tch, hdwy 3 fs out, sn wnt second, hrd rdn to ld wl ins last*. .... (11 to 10 fav op 5 to 4 on) 1
595[8] THOURIOS 4-9-4 J Reid (4) *led, rdn appr fnl furlong, hdd wl ins, no extr nr finish*. .... (11 to 4 op 5 to 2 tchd 3 to 1) 2
LEE ARTISTE 5-8-9 T Quinn (6) *hld up, hdwy 2 fs out, ev ch entering last, no imprsn ins*. .... (12 to 1 op 14 to 1 tchd 20 to 1) 3
1002[7] PATER NOSTER (USA) 4-9-0 Paul Eddery (1) *slwly away, rdn o'r 2 fs out, nvr nr to chal*. .... (13 to 2 op 9 to 2 tchd 7 to 1) 4
1002 TWO LEFT FEET 6-8-13 (5*) K Rutter (3) *hld up, rdn hfwy, lost tch 2 fs out*..................(10 to 1 tchd 12 to 1) 5
782[4] SUNDAY'S HILL 4-9-5 W Newnes (5) *chsd ldr till wknd o'r 2 fs out, sn btn*.......(14 to 1 op 10 to 1 tchd 16 to 1) 6
Dist: ½l, ¾l, 7l, 3l, 10l. 1m 30.42s. a 2.12s (6 Ran).
SR: 64/70/59/43/38/9/ (Circlechart Ltd), C E Brittain

1209 Daily Mail Circulation Handicap Class E (0-70 3-y-o and up) £3,158 6f.. (5:00)

923[6] SIR JOEY (USA) [63] 4-9-9 J Reid (10) *al prmnt, led one and a half fs out, pushed out*. ....(7 to 2 fav op 5 to 1 tchd 11 to 2) 1
760* GREY CHARMER (Ire) [56] 4-9-2 W Newnes (14) *hld up, hdwy 2 fs out, swtchd lft ins last, ran on strly*. ....(7 to 1 op 5 to 1) 2
760[6] PALACEGATE GOLD (Ire) [50] 4-8-10 A Munro (11) *hld up in tch, hdwy appr fnl furlong, ran on wl*. ....(8 to 1 op 6 to 1) 3
801 DOMICKSKY [61] 5-9-7 T Quinn (9) *hld up in tch, rdn 2 fs out, ran on ins last*.................(13 to 2 op 10 to 1) 4
1066 YES [51] 5-8-11 R Cochrane (6) *mid-div, ran on ins fnl furlong, nvr nrr*...................(12 to 1 op 10 to 1) 5
760[4] ZINBAQ [36] 7-7-10 T Williams (4) *rcd in mid-div, kpt on one pace ins fnl 2 fs*... (12 to 1 op 8 to 1 tchd 14 to 1) 6
677[4] EFRA [66] 4-9-12 S Raymont (3) *towards rear till hdwy appr fnl furlong, ran on, nvr nrr*. .... (10 to 1 tchd 12 to 1 and 9 to 1) 7
1059[3] MY RUBY RING [54] 6-8-7 (7*) Kim McDonnell (1) *chsd ldrs, led 2 fs out, sn hdd and wknd*. .... (10 to 1 op 8 to 1 tchd 11 to 1) 8
CAROMISH (USA) [53] 6-8-13 N Adams (8) *led for 2 fs, wknd wl o'r one out*. (14 to 1 op 12 to 1 tchd 16 to 1) 9
893[4] TYRIAN PURPLE (Ire) [63] 5-9-9 Paul Eddery (7) *in tch till wknd wl o'r one furlong out*.........(8 to 1 op 7 to 1) 10
1017 MOGWAI (Ire) [60] (bl) 4-9-6 A Tucker (15) *speed till wknd 2 fs out*...........................(14 to 1 tchd 20 to 1) 11
NAWWAR [51] 9-8-11 B Rouse (2) *slwly away, al beh*. .... (25 to 1 op 16 to 1 tchd 33 to 1) 12
KELLY'S KITE [36] 5-7-5[2] (7*) C Hawksley (16) *al in rear*. .... (20 to 1 op 14 to 1 tchd 25 to 1) 13
916[8] COCKERHAM RANGER [65] 3-9-1 A Geran (5) *led aftr 2 fs, rdn and hdd two out, sn btn, eased*. .... (14 to 1 op 10 to 1 tchd 16 to 1) 14
COURT PIANIST (Ire) [53] 3-8-3 R Perham (12) *slwly away, al beh, tld off*........(25 to 1 op 16 to 1 tchd 33 to 1) 15
Dist: 2l, hd, hd, hd, ½l, 2½l, 2l, ½l, 2l, 1½l. 1m 12.03s. a 3.03s (15 Ran).
SR: 48/33/26/36/25/8/28/8/5/ (Mrs A G Sims), P G Murphy

NEWMARKET (good)
Saturday May 22nd
Going Correction: PLUS 0.10 sec. per fur.

1210 Classic FM Celebrity Handicap Class G Celebrity Riders (0-60 4-y-o and up) £2,406 1m.................... (2:10)

723[3] LEXUS (Ire) [42] 5-10-10 Edward Hide (7) *hld up beh ldrs, hdwy to ld blw 2 fs out, pushed clr*. .... (7 to 1 op 10 to 1 tchd 12 to 1) 1
919* NORTHERN CONQUEROR (Ire) [48] 5-11-2 Walter Swinburn Snr (8) *mid-div, sn pushed alng, hdwy 2 fs out, styd on ins last*...........................(4 to 1 fav op 3 to 1) 2
818[6] LEGEND DULAC (Ire) [47] 4-11-1 Greville Starkey (9) *wth ldr, led 3 fs out, hdd blw 2 out, one pace*. ....(10 to 1 op 12 to 1) 3
837[7] DON'T GIVE UP [47] (bl) 5-11-1 Richard Linley (10) *chsd ldrs, kpt on one pace und pres fnl 2 fs*...............(20 to 1) 4
674 COOL SOCIETY (USA) [54] 4-11-8[2] John Francome (11) *rstrained strt, wtd wth beh, hdwy 2 fs out, styd on*. ....(25 to 1 op 33 to 1) 5
902[6] JOKIST [50] 10-11-4 Simon Sherwood (3) *wtd wth in tch, hdwy o'r 2 fs out, wknd ins last*. .... (14 to 1 op 12 to 1 tchd 16 to 1) 6
861* MALCESINE (Ire) [45] 4-10-13 Geoff Lewis (12) *led aftr 2 fs till hdd 3 out, wknd ins last*....... (14 to 1 op 10 to 1) 7
881[4] ANATROCCOLO [38] 6-10-6 Gianfranco Dettori (6) *led 2 fs, cl up, ev ch 3 out, sn wknd*........... (6 to 1 op 4 to 1) 8
676 RED KITE [53] 4-11-7 Peter Scudamore (5) *cl up, ev ch 3 fs out, wknd o'r 2 out*................(10 to 1 op 8 to 1) 9
952[4] MISSY-S (Ire) [43] 4-10-11 Paul Tulk (1) *cl up til wknd hfwy*. .... (14 to 1 op 8 to 1) 10
952[5] BUDDY'S FRIEND (Ire) [60] 5-12-0 Ron Barry (2) *in tch, hdwy to hold ev ch o'r 2 fs out, sn wknd*. ....(8 to 1 op 6 to 1 tchd 9 to 1) 11
771 DON'T DROP BOMBS (USA) [40] 4-10-8 Graham Thorner (4) *in tch to hfwy*..........(8 to 1 op 7 to 1 tchd 10 to 1) 12
Dist: 6l, 1l, sht-hd, 2l, 2½l, nk, ¾l, nk, ¾l, 3½l. 1m 44.06s. a 6.86s (12 Ran).
SR: 33/21/17/16/17/5/-/-/4/ (Marriott Stables Limited), R J R Williams

1211 Sunley Builds Maiden Auction Stakes Class D (2-y-o) £4,045 6f........(2:40)

THREATENING 8-0 G Bardwell (3) *pld hrd in rear, effrt whn hmpd 2 fs out, swtchd lft to chal when hng rght ins last, quickened to ld nr finish*. (33 to 1 op 20 to 1) 1
IRREPRESSIBLE (Ire) 8-11 Pat Eddery (13) *cl up, led o'r 3 fs till hdd close hme*....(5 to 2 fav op 2 to 1 tchd 3 to 1) 2
NICE WELCOME 8-2 W Woods (4) *chsd ldrs, chlgd 2 fs out, hng lft one out, one pace*.......(25 to 1 tchd 33 to 1) 3
INTERNATIONAL STAR (Ire) 8-5 (3*) Emma O'Gorman (12) *strted slwly, sn reco'red to track ldrs, ev ch 2 fs out, one pace*..................(33 to 1 op 20 to 1 tchd 50 to 1) 4
776[5] KINGSWELL PRINCE (Ire) 8-5 B Raymond (7) *trkd ldrs, rdn and edgd rght und pres 2 fs out, sn not clr run and one pace*..........................(5 to 1 op 3 to 1 tchd 11 to 2) 5
793[3] NONIOS (Ire) 8-5 W Ryan (2) *wtd wth, pld out to chal 3 fs out, sn hrd rdn and btn*. (3 to 1 op 5 to 2 tchd 7 to 2) 6

969[2] LEAP OF FAITH (Ire) 8-0 J Quinn (8) *chsd ldrs, rdn alng 3 fs out, wknd 2 out*........(15 to 2 op 5 to 1 tchd 8 to 1) 7
687[6] PERSIAN AFFAIR (Ire) 8-5 (5*) M Fenton (14) *wth ldrs till rdn and wknd 2 fs out.* (15 to 2 op 6 to 1 tchd 8 to 1) 8
793[9] MEMORABLE 8-8 P Robinson (10) *chsd ldrs, sn pushed alng, hrd rdn 3 out, wknd.* ....(25 to 1 op 16 to 1 tchd 33 to 1) 9
ORANGE PLACE (Ire) 8-5 J Carroll (5) *al beh.* ....(33 to 1 op 20 to 1 tchd 50 to 1) 10
ASKING FOR ACES 8-0 N Carlisle (6) *dwlt, al beh.* ....(33 to 1 op 20 to 1 tchd 50 to 1) 11
776 LUCY'S GOLD 8-0 D Biggs (9) *led til hdd o'r 3 fs, btn whn not much room 2 out.* (25 to 1 op 20 to 1 tchd 16 to 1) 12
MYSTERY MOON 8-0 A McGlone (1) *strted very slwly, al beh*...............................(14 to 1 op 33 to 1) 13
NOT THE NADGER 8-6 (3*) D Harrison (15) *cl up till wknd wl o'r 2 fs out*........(33 to 1 op 20 to 1 tchd 50 to 1) 14

Dist: ½l, 3½l, nk, 1l, sht-hd, 2½l, nk, sht-hd, nk, 3½l. 1m 15.12s. a 3.72s (14 Ran).
SR: 24/33/10/15/8/7/-/1/-/ (Lord Matthews), R J R Williams

1212 Bunty Scrope Maiden Stakes Class D (3-y-o) £3,947 1m...............(3:10)

980[2] SHOW FAITH (Ire) 9-0 Pat Eddery (10) *chsd ldrs, hdwy o'r 2 fs out, swtchd lft over one out, sn led, not extended.* ....(100 to 30 op 5 to 2 tchd 7 to 2) 1
LYPHARD'S DELTA (USA) 8-9 W Ryan (1) *trkd ldrs, led o'r 3 fs out till hdd over one out, kpt on.* ....(11 to 8 fav op 5 to 4 tchd 7 to 4) 2
825 JURA FOREST 9-0 P Robinson (8) *slwly into strd, beh, hdwy o'r 2 fs out, styd on.* ....(25 to 1 op 20 to 1 tchd 33 to 1) 3
686 KASSBAAN (USA) 9-0 B Raymond (6) *wtd wth, smooth hdwy 3 fs out, led briefly o'r one out, sn one pace.* ....(12 to 1 op 8 to 1 tchd 14 to 1) 4
825 LIVONIAN 9-0 J Williams (5) *beh, hdwy hfwy, styd on one pace fnl 2 fs*.........(20 to 1 op 16 to 1 tchd 25 to 1) 5
1027[8] LEARMONT (USA) 9-0 G Hind (13) *cl up, ev ch 3 fs out, wknd 2 out*..........(10 to 1 op 8 to 1 tchd 12 to 1) 6
1060 BRAVE HERO (USA) 9-0 D Biggs (9) *beh, hrd rdn 2 fs out, styd on, nrst finish*.............(33 to 1 tchd 50 to 1) 7
732 MULLED ALE (Ire) 8-9 W Woods (3) *trkd ldrs till wknd o'r 3 fs out*..........................(33 to 1 tchd 50 to 1) 8
MR BEAN 8-11 (3*) D Harrison (4) *al beh.* ....(33 to 1 tchd 50 to 1) 9
NAFIHA (USA) 8-9 R Price (7) *beh, sn reco'red to chase ldrs till wknd quickly over 2 fs out*... (33 to 1 tchd 50 to 1) 10
SHAHAADA (USA) 8-9 N Carlisle (11) *sn led, hdd o'r 3 fs out, soon rdn and wknd*..........(25 to 1 op 33 to 1) 11
991[6] POCONO KNIGHT 9-0 C Avery (12) *trkd ldrs till wknd o'r 3 fs out*..........................(33 to 1 tchd 25 to 1) 12
DESERT VENUS 8-9 J Quinn (2) *wth ldr, ev ch o'r 2 fs out, wknd quickly, eased ins last*.......(11 to 2 op 4 to 1) 13
MODAAYIN 9-0 K Fallon (14) *chsd ldrs till wknd quickly hfwy, tld off*....................(33 to 1 op 25 to 1) 14

Dist: 1½l, 2l, 2l, 1l, 5l, 1½l, 1l, nk, 4l, 1l. 1m 42.31s. a 5.11s (14 Ran).
SR: 35/25/24/18/15/-/ (I A N Wight), R Hannon

1213 Coral Handicap Class B (0-105 3-y-o) £22,905 6f.................... (3:40)

716* TRUE PRECISION [73] 7-10 L Charnock (3) *chsd ldrs, cld o'r 2 fs out, led one out, quickened clr*..........(7 to 1) 1
915[2] YOUNG ERN [94] 9-3 C Rutter (17) *trkd ldrs, led 2 fs out till hdd one out, no extr*..............................(7 to 1) 2
945[2] ANOTHER JADE [79] 8-2 S Whitworth (5) *trkd ldrs gng wl, ev ch o'r one furlong out, sn shaken up and one pace.* ....(8 to 1) 3
796[3] TROON [88] 8-11 J Williams (1) *towards rear, pushed alng and hdwy o'r one furlong out, styd on*.........(8 to 1) 4
977[2] SPECIAL ONE [74] 7-11 S Dawson (4) *outpcd, styd on ins fnl furlong, nrst finish*......................(14 to 1) 5
1083[5] DAILYSPORTDUTCH [74] (bl) 7-11 D Biggs (7) *led til hdd 2 fs out, wknd*..................................(20 to 1) 6
IN CASE (USA) [92] 9-1 Pat Eddery (10) *chsd ldrs, ev ch 2 fs out, sn wknd und pres*..........................(8 to 1) 7
844[7] CARBON STEEL (Ire) [98] 9-7 W Ryan (13) *dwlt, nvr on terms*..........................(25 to 1 tchd 33 to 1) 8
1010[4] MY BONUS [79] 7-13 (3*) D Harrison (9) *hld up, hdwy hfwy, not clr run frm o'r one furlong out.* ....(16 to 1 tchd 20 to 1) 9
858[3] ARADANZA [94] 9-3 P Robinson (8) *trkd ldrs, rdn 3 fs out, sn btn*..(20 to 1) 10
691[7] PRINCESS OBERON (Ire) [84] 8-2 (5*) M Fenton (12) *trkd ldrs to hfwy*..(12 to 1) 11
846[5] THE SHARP BIDDER (Ire) [77] 7-8[1] (7*) M Humphries (11) *slwly into strd, sn reco'red to track ldrs, wknd over 2 fs out*..(33 to 1) 12
915[5] PRESS GALLERY [88] 8-11 B Raymond (16) *cl up to hfwy.* ....(8 to 1 tchd 7 to 1) 13
823[4] YAKIN (USA) [86] 8-9 N Carlisle (14) *cl up to hfwy.* (12 to 1) 14
471* GARNOCK VALLEY [94] 9-3 J Carroll (15) *cl up til wknd quickly 2 fs out*..............(11 to 4 fav tchd 3 to 1) 15

Dist: 3l, ¾l, sht-hd, 4l, 5l, ¾l, 1l, nk, sht-hd, sht-hd. 1m 13.79s. a 2.39s (15 Ran).
SR: 46/55/37/45/15/-/10/12/-/ (T R Lock), J D Bethell

1214 Hambro Countrywide Charlotte Fillies Stakes Class A (Listed Race) (3-y-o) £10,029 6f.................... (4:10)

749[6] LYRIC FANTASY (Ire) 9-2 Pat Eddery (5) *broke fst, made all, eased cl hme.* (3 to 1 on op 11 to 4 on tchd 5 to 2 on) 1
MITHL AL HAWA 8-9 B Raymond (2) *hld up in tch, hdwy 2 fs out, kpt on und pres ins last, no ch wth wnr.* ....(13 to 2 op 9 to 2 tchd 7 to 1) 2
802[3] MARGARET'S GIFT 8-9 J Carroll (1) *cl up, pushed alng hfwy, one pace fnl 2 fs.* ....(20 to 1 op 25 to 1 tchd 33 to 1) 3
1017[7] STAR FAMILY FRIEND (Ire) (v) 9-2 P Robinson (6) *sn pushed alng to track ldrs, one pace fnl 2 fs.* ....(14 to 1 op 10 to 1 tchd 16 to 1) 4
729[4] SHEILA'S SECRET (Ire) 8-9 W Ryan (3) *nvr on terms.* ....(14 to 1 op 10 to 1) 5
1057[2] PUTOUT (bl) 8-9 D Biggs (4) *chsd wnr till wknd 2 fs out.* ....(16 to 1 op 20 to 1 tchd 25 to 1) 6

Dist: ¾l, 3l, 1½l, 2l, 4l. 1m 13.54s. a 2.14s (6 Ran).
SR: 71/61/49/50/35/19/ (Mrs John Magnier), R Hannon

1215 Harcros Racing Associates Handicap Class C (0-100 3-y-o and up) £5,435 5f ....(4:40)

883 METAL BOYS [74] 6-8-4 (3*) D Harrison (9) *in tch, hdwy und pres o'r one furlong out, ran on to ld cl hme.* ....(12 to 1 tchd 16 to 1) 1
1000 EAGER DEVA [82] 6-9-1 W Ryan (11) *cl up, led 2 fs out till ct close hme*...................(14 to 1 op 12 to 1) 2
993[5] POYLE GEORGE [90] 8-9-9 J Williams (14) *al prmnt, kpt on wl fnl furlong*.......(16 to 1 op 20 to 1 tchd 33 to 1) 3
986[8] MASTER PLANNER [92] 4-9-11 D Biggs (7) *sn pushed alng in mid-div, ran on wl und pres fnl furlong.* ....(10 to 1 op 8 to 1) 4
800[2] NED'S BONANZA [70] 4-8-3 A McGlone (8) *cl up, ev ch o'r one furlong out, ran on und pres.* (14 to 1 op 10 to 1) 5
986[3] STACK ROCK [95] 6-10-0 K Fallon (5) *cl up, ev ch appr fnl furlong, one pace.* .... (9 to 2 fav op 7 to 1 tchd 8 to 1 and 4 to 1) 6
814* AMRON [89] 6-9-8 N Carlisle (10) *beh, hdwy o'r one furlong out, ran on*................(10 to 1 tchd 12 to 1) 7
1000 BEAU VENTURE (USA) [87] 5-9-3 (3*) N Kennedy (13) *trkd ldrs, hrd rdn o'r one furlong out, one pace.* ....(14 to 1 op 10 to 1) 8
1036[6] INDIGO [79] 5-8-12 A Culhane (4) *chsd ldrs, btn o'r one furlong out*......................(14 to 1 op 10 to 1) 9
1000[2] DRUM SERGEANT [83] 6-9-2 B Raymond (6) *al beh.* ....(5 to 1 op 7 to 1 tchd 4 to 1) 10
977[6] DAANIERA (Ire) [70] 3-7-8 J Quinn (1) *missed break, outpcd.* ....(25 to 1 op 20 to 1 tchd 33 to 1) 11
1036[3] PRINCE BELFORT [62] 5-7-9 G Bardwell (3) *broke wl, sn outpcd*..............(12 to 1 op 10 to 1 tchd 14 to 1) 12
ASHTINA [91] 8-9-10 Pat Eddery (15) *led til hdd 2 fs out, wknd*................(14 to 1 op 10 to 1 tchd 16 to 1) 13
144 SADDLEHOME (USA) [70] 4-8-3 G Hind (12) *nvr on terms.* ....(20 to 1 op 33 to 1) 14
800 PRECENTOR [60] (bl) 7-7-7 L Charnock (2) *outpcd.* ....(16 to 1 op 14 to 1 tchd 20 to 1) 15

Dist: Sht-hd, 1l, hd, hd, hd, hd, 1l, 1l, nk, hd. 1m 1.23s. a 2.63s (15 Ran).
SR: 50/57/61/62/39/63/56/50/38/ (R J Wilkinson), Miss L C Siddall

1216 Subaru Maiden Stakes Class D (3-y-o) £3,655 1¾m.................. (5:15)

929[2] SPRING TO ACTION 9-0 Pat Eddery (7) *pld hrd, sn settled towards rear, cld 5 fs out, led on bit appr last, easily.* ....(11 to 8 fav op 5 to 4 tchd 13 to 8) 1
876[2] YAHMI (Ire) 9-0 W Ryan (1) *keen hold early, cl up, led 5 fs out till hdd appr last, one pace.* ....(5 to 2 op 7 to 4 tchd 11 to 4) 2
880[4] TASSET (Can) 9-0 C Rutter (6) *trkd ldrs, pushed alng o'r 3 fs out, sn one pace*... (14 to 1 op 10 to 1 tchd 20 to 1) 3
509[4] ERCKULE 8-11 (3*) B Doyle (2) *cl up, ev ch 3 fs out, sn hrd rdn and one pace*...... (9 to 2 op 6 to 1 tchd 4 to 1) 4
876[5] GUESTWICK 9-0 B Raymond (5) *in tch, pushed alng o'r 4 fs out, not pace to chal*............(10 to 1 op 7 to 1) 5
MARKETING MAN 9-0 J Quinn (4) *al beh, tld off.* ....(33 to 1 op 25 to 1 tchd 50 to 1) 6
980 CHARLIE BIGTIME 9-0 S O'Gorman (3) *set modest pace til hdd 5 fs out, drpd out quickly, tld off.* ....(14 to 1 op 12 to 1 tchd 20 to 1) 7

Dist: 3½l, 2l, sht-hd, 1l, dist, 12l. 3m 6.18s. a 10.18s (7 Ran).
SR: 12/5/1/-/ (The Queen), I A Balding

BADEN-BADEN (GER) (good)
Sunday May 23rd

1217 Grosser Preis der Wirtschaft (Group 2) (4-y-o and up) £65,306 1m 3f.. (3:25)

PLATINI (Ger) 4-9-7 M Rimmer, *rcd in 4th, swtchd outsd 2 fs out, led one and a half out, sn clr*.................. 1

406 HONDO MONDO (Ire) 5-9-4 A Best, *hld up, rear till 3 fs out, hdwy and ran on wl fnl furlong*.......... 2
1084* KARINGA BAY 6-9-2 B Rouse, *rcd in 5th, second one and a half fs out, lost second cl hme*.......... 3
SPORTIVO (USA) 4-9-0 P Schiergen, *mid-div, not much room 3 fs out, fnshd wl*.......... 4
689* RUBY TIGER 6-9-0 T Quinn, *trkd ldr, led 2 fs to one and a half out, unbl to quicken fnl furlong*.......... 5
695² TWIST AND TURN 4-9-2 W R Swinburn, *led till 2 fs out, kpt on one pace*.......... 6
692* SUGUNAS (Ger) 5-9-2 A Boschert, *cl up 2 fs out, wknd*... 7
SILVESTRO 8-9-2 T Jorgensen, *nvr nrr than mid-div*.... 8
810⁴ DEAR DOCTOR (Fr) 6-9-7 E Legrix,.......... 0
PEARL PANTHER 5-9-2 T Frick,.......... 0
TUSCAR ROCK (Fr) 4-9-0 S Guillemin,.......... 0
Dist: 4½l, nk, nk, ¾l, ½l, ¾l. 2m 15.36s. (11 Ran).
(Stall Steigenberger), B Schutz

LONGCHAMP (FR) (good to firm)
Sunday May 23rd

1218 Prix Saint-Alary (Group 1) (3-y-o) £61,302 1¼m.......... (2:55)

484* INTREPIDITY 9-2 T Jarnet (5) *4th strt, rdn 2 fs out, led one and a half out, ran on wl*..........(5 to 4 on) 1
561² DANCIENNE (Fr) 9-2 D Boeuf (4) *6th strt, rdn 2 fs out, hdwy one and a half out, chsd wnr ins last, no imprsn*. ....(58 to 10) 2
809² ACCOMMODATING (USA) 9-2 F Head (2) *last strt, rdn and hdwy 2 fs out, styd on one pace fnl furlong*... (15 to 1) 3
809* CORRAZONA (USA) 9-2 O Doleuze (3) *second strt, ev ch wl o'r one out, sn one pace*..........(6 to 4) 4
770* ROYALE CHANTOU (Fr) 9-2 C Le Scrill (1) *nvr rch ldrs*. ....(16 to 1) 5
697³ HAWK BEAUTY (USA) 9-2 C Asmussen (6) *3rd strt, rdn to ld 2 fs out, hdd one and a half out, wknd quickly*. ....(14 to 1) 6
MIXMATCH (Ire) 9-2 M de Smyler (7) *led till 2 fs out, sn wknd*..........(6 to 4) 7
Dist: 1l, 1½l, 1½l, sht-nk, 5l, 20l. 2m 4.80s. a 2.70s (7 Ran).
SR: 70/68/65/62/61/51/11/ (Sheikh Mohammed), A Fabre

1219 Prix Vicomtesse Vigier (Group 2) (4-y-o and up) £35,842 1m 7f 110yds (3:30)

798* DADARISSIME (Fr) 4-8-11 F Head (1) *hld up last, hdwy 3 fs out, 3rd strt, ran on to ld 100 yards out*...... (27 to 10) 1
798² SOUGHT OUT (Ire) 5-9-0 C Asmussen (4) *led, quickened o'r 2 fs out, rdn over one out, ct fnl 100 yards*. (10 to 7 on) 2
726³ NON PARTISAN (USA) 4-9-0 Pat Eddery (2) *rcd in 4th, effrt wl o'r one furlong out,, no extr appr fnl furlong*. ....(16 to 10) 3
798⁹ CUTTING REEF (Ire) 4-8-8 A Badel (3) *nvr dngrs*. (17 to 1) 4
726⁵ DOWN THE FLAG (USA) 6-8-11 C Le Scrill (5) *trkd ldr, second strt, ev ch 2 fs out, wknd appr fnl furlong*. ....(35 to 1) 5
LA POINTE 4-8-8 D Bonilla (6) *5th strt, sn rdn and wknd*. ....(12 to 1) 6
Dist: ¾l, 2l, 1½l, 1l, 15l. 3m 20.80s. a 4.30s (6 Ran).
SR: 46/47/45/37/39/21/ (Sir J Goldsmith), G Bridgland

1220 Prix de Pontarme (Listed) (3-y-o) £14,337 1m.......... (3:55)

GUIDE (Fr) 8-11 O Benoist,.......... 1
690² NEW CAPRICORN (USA) 8-11 Pat Eddery,.......... 2
SOMERSHAM (USA) 8-11 T Jarnet,.......... 3
613³ DANAKAL (USA) 8-11 W Mongil,.......... 4
Dist: Nk, 1l, sht-nk, sht-nk, ½l, 2l, sht-nk, 10l. 1m 38.40s. a 2.40s (9 Ran).
SR: 55/54/51/50/ (Exors of the late Sir Robin McAlpine), E Bartholomew

SAN SIRO (ITY) (good to firm)
Sunday May 23rd

1221 Premio Arcore (2-y-o) £11,207 5f (1:30)

ULTIMO IMPERATORE 8-7 W Carson,.......... 1
BLINDING SPEED 8-9 M Latorre,.......... 2
LONDON KID (Ire) 8-7 S Dettori,.......... 3
SPAGHETTI WESTERN (Ire) 8-7 A Munro,.......... 5
VEDO NUDO 8-7 M Hills,.......... 8
Dist: 3½l, nose, 2½l, ¾l, 2½l, ½l, 12l, 3l. 58.90s. (9 Ran).
(Gerecon Italia), J L Dunlop

1222 Oaks d'Italia (Group 1) (3-y-o) £103,764 1½m.......... (4:00)

748² BRIGHT GENERATION (Ire) 8-11 A Munro (1) *rcd in 5th, quickened on rls o'r one furlong out, led one out, ran on wl*..........(2 to 1) 1
ROSE VIOLET (USA) 8-11 F Jovine (8) *sn tracking ldrs, second strt, ev ch o'r one furlong out, one pace*. ....(24 to 1) 2
ZAFFERA (USA) 8-11 S Soto (2) *led till one furlong out, kpt on one pace*..........(53 to 10) 3
946² TALENTED 8-11 W Carson (11) *hld up, pld out 2 fs out, styd on ins last, not rch ldrs*.......... (17 to 10 fav) 4
694* ANCESTRAL DANCER 8-11 M Hills (4) *hld up, hdwy 3 fs out, one pace o'r one out*..........(62 to 10) 5
946⁴ BRIGHTSIDE (Ire) 8-11 G Duffield (6) *outpcd early, hdwy o'r 2 fs out, kpt on*..........(65 to 10) 6
PINTA (Ire) 8-11 Jacqueline Freda (3) *prmnt, 3rd strt, ev ch 2 fs out, sn wknd*..........(37 to 1) 7
PAESANELLA 8-11 E Botti (10) *4th strt, wknd o'r 3 fs out*. ....(21 to 1) 8
4713a² NICOTERA (Ire) 8-11 D Holland (9) *al rear*..........(12 to 1) 9
BIANCA VERGA (Ire) 8-11 M Tellini (5) *al beh*......(59 to 1) 10
Dist: 2½l, ¾l, sht-nk, 1l, nk, 2l, 5l, 2l, 2l. 2m 3.30s. (10 Ran).
(Fahd Salman), P F I Cole

AYR (good to soft)
Monday May 24th

Going Correction: PLUS 0.20 sec. per fur. (races 1,2,3), MINUS 0.15 (4,5,6)

1223 Crosshill Rating Related Maiden Fillies Stakes Class E (0-70 3-y-o) £2,792 1¼m.......... (2:30)

761⁵ PLAY WITH ME (Ire) 8-11 G Carter (2) *led 2 fs, remained prmnt, led two out, idled in frnt fnl furlong, eased cl hme*.......... (6 to 4 on op 5 to 4 on) 1
646⁵ APACHE SQUAW 8-11 N Connorton (3) *in tch, prog on outsd in strt to chal 2 fs out, ch one out, no imprsn ins last*.......... (6 to 1 op 4 to 1 tchd 7 to 1) 2
921⁶ SAKURA QUEEN (Ire) 8-11 W Woods (5) *led aftr 2 fs till hdd two out, kpt on one pace*........ (12 to 1 tchd 14 to 1) 3
522⁸ SUNRISE MORNING (USA) 8-11 D Holland (4) *in tch, effrt 2 fs out, sn rdn and no imprsn*...... (16 to 1 op 10 to 1) 4
932³ MISSA BREVIS (USA) 8-11 G Duffield (1) *trkd ldrs till wknd 2 fs out*..........(7 to 2 op 5 to 2) 5
Dist: 1½l, 1½l, 1½l, 1½l. 2m 22.31s. a 17.31s (5 Ran).
(Miss Katherine Gearon), J L Dunlop

1224 Cairnryan Maiden Stakes Class D (3-y-o and up) £3,265 1m 5f 13yds. .(3:00)

947⁶ ZIND (Ire) 3-8-5 D Holland (10) *in tch, 4th strt, rdn 2 fs out, styd on und pres to ld wl ins last, jst hld on*. ....(7 to 2 on op 3 to 1 on tchd 5 to 2 on) 1
THE LAUGHING LORD 7-9-10 M Birch (6) *trkd ldrs, second strt, effrt o'r one furlong out, styd on wl, jst fld*. .... (66 to 1 op 50 to 1) 2
783² BOKARO (Fr) 7-9-10 W Newnes (11) *prog to ld aftr 5 fs, clr 2 furlongs out, hdd and no extr fnl 100 yards*. .... (10 to 1 op 8 to 1) 3
832² MR WOODCOCK 8-9-10 K Darley (4) *trkd ldrs, 5th strt, kpt on one pace fnl 3 fs*..........(20 to 1 op 16 to 1) 4
799⁹ FAIRWAYS ON TARGET 7-9-10 Dean McKeown (1) *beh hfwy, styd on one pace in strt*..... (33 to 1 op 20 to 1) 5
BOOTIKIN 5-9-5 R Hills (8) *mid-div, no imprsn in strt*. ....(66 to 1) 6
876⁶ HILL OF DREAMS 3-8-5 G Carter (12) *beh to hfwy, prog to track ldrs into strt, wknd o'r 2 fs out*. (8 to 1 op 6 to 1) 7
RAGLAN LADY 6-8-12 (7*) Angela Gallimore (9) *al mid-div*. ....(66 to 1) 8
832³ RICH ASSET (Ire) 3-8-5 N Connorton (7) *trkd ldrs till lost pl and beh frm hfwy*..........(25 to 1 op 20 to 1) 9
799 MURPHYS WAY 4-9-5 G Duffield (2) *led 5 fs, fdd*. .... (25 to 1 op 20 to 1) 10
Dist: Sht-hd, 1½l, 8l, ½l, 1½l, nk, 4l, 25l, 4l. 2m 55.85s. a 9.85s (10 Ran).
SR: 19/37/34/18/17/9/ (F M Kalla), P W Chapple-Hyam

1225 Kilmacolm Handicap Class D (0-80 3-y-o) £3,707 1m.......... (3:30)

1016 TOLEDO QUEEN (Ire) [76] 9-3 D Holland (2) *rear, 6th strt, prog 2 fs out, chlgd ins last to ld cl hme* .... (7 to 2 tchd 3 to 1 and 4 to 1) 1
772⁴ GREEN'S FAIR (Ire) [68] 8-4 (5*) M Fenton (3) *mid-div, prog o'r 2 fs out, led over one out, hdd cl hme*. .... (11 to 2 op 7 to 2) 2
860² RUNRIG (Ire) [52] 7-7 J Fanning (7) *trkd ldrs, second strt, chlgd and ev ch one furlong out, no extr ins last*. .... (20 to 1 op 14 to 1) 3
802⁸ SO SO [80] 9-7 W Newnes (4) *rear till prog o'r 2 fs out, ran on wl ins last*.......... (12 to 1 op 10 to 1) 4
1102² KARINSKA [52] 7-7 N Carlisle (1) *trkd ldrs, effrt 2 fs out, no room and swtchd o'r one out, kpt on*. (6 to 1 op 7 to 1) 5
CUTTHROAT KID (Ire) [64] (bl) 8-5 K Darley (8) *trkd ldrs till wknd 2 fs out*......... (9 to 1 op 7 to 1 tchd 10 to 1) 6
966 DRUMDONNA (Ire) [58] (bl) 7-13¹ G Carter (6) *led, quickened up entering strt, hdd and wknd o'r one furlong out*.......... (16 to 1 op 12 to 1) 7
1008* JADIRAH (USA) [70] 8-11 R Hills (5) *al beh*. ....(9 to 4 fav tchd 2 to 1 and 5 to 2) 8
Dist: Nk, 2½l, ½l, nk, 5l, ½l, 12l. 1m 45.02s. a 7.32s (8 Ran).
SR: 17/8/-/10/-/ (R E Sangster), P W Chapple-Hyam

1226 Torranyard Limited Stakes Class E (0-70 3-y-o) £2,770 5f........... (4:00)

1157[2] SHADOW JURY 9-0 K Darley (3) *trkd ldr, shaken up to ld o'r one furlong out, pushed clr, easily.* .... (11 to 8 on op 13 to 8 on tchd 5 to 4 on) 1
977[8] GO FLIGHTLINE (Ire) (v) 8-4 (5*) M Fenton (1) *led till hdd o'r one furlong out, no extr*............(2 to 1 op 9 to 4) 2
866[7] SELVOLE 8-2 (7*) Claire Balding (2) *in tch, reminders and outpcd hfwy, no dngr aftr.* ....(33 to 1 op 25 to 1 tchd 40 to 1) 3
1157[8] TOM PIPER (bl) 9-0 G Carter (4) *chsd ldrs till wknd 2 fs out*..................................(5 to 1 op 4 to 1) 4

Dist: 2½l, 6l, 2½l. 1m 0.86s. a 2.76s (4 Ran).
SR: 30/15/-/-/ (P D Savill), D W Chapman

1227 Fenwick Median Auction Maiden Stakes Class E (2-y-o) £2,932 6f (4:30)

698[4] DISTINCTIVE AIR 9-0 W Newnes (10) *trkd ldrs, led wl o'r one furlong out, pushed out fnl furlong, hld on well.* ....(9 to 2 op 7 to 2) 1
933[5] OVIDEO 8-9 G Duffield (3) *chsd ldrs, styd on wl und pres to chal ins fnl furlong, no extr nr finish.* ....(10 to 1 tchd 11 to 1) 2
968[3] KARSEAM (Ire) 9-0 N Connorton (11) *chsd ldrs, rdn hfwy, kpt on wl fnl furlong*....(4 to 1 op 3 to 1 tchd 9 to 2) 3
865[6] STARICA (Ire) 8-9 Dale Gibson (2) *slwly into strd, beh, hdwy hfwy, kpt on same pace fnl furlong.* ....(20 to 1 op 14 to 1) 4
FEARLESS WONDER 9-0 M Birch (8) *beh till styd on fnl 2 fs, not rch ldrs*......................(8 to 1 op 5 to 1) 5
SNAKE PLISSKEN (Ire) 9-0 A Mackay (9) *slwly into strd, sn pushed alng, some hdwy o'r 2 fs out, wknd entering fnl furlong*.............(3 to 1 fav op 7 to 2 tchd 5 to 2) 6
MISTER PISTE (Ire) 9-0 J Fanning (6) *led till hdd wl o'r one out, fdd*..........................(33 to 1 op 20 to 1) 7
804 RIVA'S BOOK (USA) 9-0 R Hills (4) *prmnt to hfwy.* ....(14 to 1 op 10 to 1) 8
PARISIAN LOVER 9-0 K Darley (7) *chsd ldrs till wknd o'r 2 fs out*...................(4 to 1 op 3 to 1 tchd 9 to 2) 9
TYPOGRAPHER (Ire) 9-0 Dean McKeown (5) *slwly into strd, al beh*......................(20 to 1 op 10 to 1) 10
CURIE CRUSADER (Ire) 9-0 G Carter (1) *prmnt to hfwy.* ....(8 to 1 op 7 to 1 tchd 10 to 1) 11

Dist: Hd, 2½l, ¾l, 2l, 2l, 1½l, 4l, 3l, 5l, 4l. 1m 14.90s. a 4.00s (11 Ran).
SR: 2/-/-/-/-/-/ (T A Scothern), E Weymes

1228 Ballantrae Handicap Class E (0-70 3-y-o and up) £2,818 6f............. (5:00)

837[4] SLADES HILL [59] 6-9-9 K Darley (1) *in tch, steady hdwy o'r 2 fs out, led ins last, ran on wl*....(7 to 2 op 4 to 1) 1
1072[2] MURRAY'S MAZDA (Ire) [62] 4-9-5 (7*) P Roberts (6) *cl up, led o'r 2 fs out till hdd ins last, no extr.* ....(5 to 1 op 4 to 1) 2
1081[3] LANGUEDOC [64] 6-10-0 L Charnock (2) *trkd ldrs, drw level on bit entering fnl furlong, not much room, sn rdn and found nil*.....................(5 to 1 op 4 to 1) 3
883[3] AYR RAIDER [62] (v) 6-9-12 J Fanning (5) *beh, sn pushed alng, nvr dngrs*..................... (4 to 1 op 7 to 2) 4
1081[2] SOBERING THOUGHTS [47] 7-8-11 G Duffield (4) *chsd ldrs, rdn 2 out, no imprsn.* ....(11 to 4 fav op 5 to 2 tchd 3 to 1) 5
1103[7] PRINCIPAL PLAYER (USA) [59] 3-8-13 J Fortune (3) *led till hdd o'r 2 fs out, sn btn*........... (33 to 1 op 20 to 1) 6

Dist: 1l, ¾l, 2½l, nk, 4l. 1m 13.35s. a 2.45s (6 Ran).
SR: 42/41/40/28/12/-/ (James E Greaves), T D Barron

LEICESTER (good to firm) Monday May 24th

Going Correction: MINUS 0.30 sec. per fur.

1229 Wolvey Maiden Fillies Stakes Class D (Div I) (2-y-o) £3,260 5f 2yds.....(2:15)

ISHTIYAK 8-11 W Carson (1) *led aftr one furlong, quickened ins last, cmftbly*..............(9 to 4 op 5 to 4) 1
922[2] SWEET DECISION (Ire) 8-11 J Williams (3) *al in frnt rnk, rdn and ran on wl fnl furlong*......(10 to 1 op 7 to 2) 2
ELEUTHERA 8-11 L Dettori (10) *sn trkd ldrs, rdn and ev ch appr fnl furlong, one pace ins.* ....(13 to 8 fav op 2 to 1 tchd 5 to 2 and 6 to 4) 3
HEVER GOLF ROSE 8-11 Paul Eddery (4) *slwly away, hdwy frm hfwy, rdn appr fnl furlong, kpt on.* .... (66 to 1 op 20 to 1) 4
1091[4] COLNE VALLEY 8-11 T Quinn (8) *prmnt till rdn and wknd appr fnl furlong*................. (20 to 1 op 12 to 1) 5
CHINA ROBIN 8-11 R Cochrane (2) *al abt same pl, kpt on ins fnl furlong*.................... (33 to 1 op 14 to 1) 6
984[4] PRIMO STAMPARI 8-11 Pat Eddery (9) *led 1st furlong, wknd hfwy*.................. (7 to 2 op 2 to 1 tchd 5 to 1) 7
MATISSE 8-11 W R Swinburn (5) *slwly away, al struggling in rear*.............................(33 to 1 op 16 to 1) 8
CHARLIES DREAM (Ire) 8-11 S Whitworth (7) *chsd ldrs till drpd out hfwy*................... (50 to 1 op 25 to 1) 9
MAZZA 8-11 J Quinn (6) *slwly away, al beh.* .... (33 to 1 op 20 to 1) 10

Dist: 1½l, 2l, 3l, 2½l, 1l, 10l, 1½l, 1½l, 8l. 1m 0.60s. a 1.90s (10 Ran).
SR: 29/23/15/3/-/-/ (Hamdan Al-Maktoum), R W Armstrong

1230 Hickling Selling Handicap Class G (Div I) (0-60 3-y-o and up) £2,658 5f 218yds........................ (2:45)

327 FATHOM FIVE (Ire) [35] 4-8-5 J Williams (14) *hld up, gd hdwy appr fnl furlong, ran on strly to ld nr finish.* ....(33 to 1 op 20 to 1) 1
436 PARFAIT AMOUR [58] 4-10-0 A Culhane (12) *mid-div, hdwy 2 fs out, ran on wl ins last.* ....(20 to 1 op 14 to 1 tchd 25 to 1) 2
1097 ASTERIX [51] (v) 5-9-7 T Quinn (7) *al prmnt, led one and a half fs out, hrd rdn and hdd cl hme.* ....(9 to 1 op 12 to 1 tchd 16 to 1 and 8 to 1) 3
882[2] CLEAN GATE [34] (bl) 4-8-4 W Carson (2) *led stands side till hdd appr fnl furlong, drifted lft and no extr ins.* ....(5 to 1 jt-fav op 7 to 2) 4
882[7] CHEREN BOY [30] 4-8-0 N Adams (11) *nvr far away, ran on one pace ins fnl 2 fs*...........(14 to 1 op 12 to 1) 5
760 PRINCESS JESSICA [35] 6-7-12 (7*) D McCabe (16) *prmnt far side, rdn 2 fs out, kpt on one pace.* ....(14 to 1 op 33 to 1) 6
568[6] MISS BRIGHTSIDE [37] 5-8-7 S Webster (19) *led far side grp frm hfwy, wknd appr fnl furlong.* ....(6 to 1 op 4 to 1 tchd 13 to 2) 7
975 BLUE POINT (Ire) [30] 4-8-0 A Munro (8) *mid-div, kpt on one pace fnl 2 fs*......................(12 to 1 op 7 to 1) 8
975 EMERALD EARS [31] 4-8-1 G Bardwell (3) *pressed ldrs stands side, rdn o'r 2 fs out, sn wknd.* ....(14 to 1 op 12 to 1) 9
962[8] CRIMSON CONSORT (Ire) [33] (bl) 4-8-3 Kim Tinkler (18) *slwly away, nvr rch ldrs*......... (33 to 1 op 20 to 1) 10
1038[7] WEEKEND GIRL [23] 4-7-2 (5*) Darren Moffatt (9) *nvr nr to chal*..................................(33 to 1) 11
927 BURISHKI [55] (bl) 3-9-1 W R Swinburn (6) *beh till hdwy hfwy, ev ch till rdn and wknd appr fnl furlong.* ....(5 to 1 jt-fav op 4 to 1) 12
PRINCESS JESTINA (Ire) [32] 5-8-2 R Price (5) *speed on stands side to hfwy*.......................(33 to 1) 13
871 GLADEER (Ire) [52] 4-9-3 (5*) N Gwilliams (10) *al beh.* ....(33 to 1 op 20 to 1) 14
BLUEBELLA [39] 3-7-13 J Lowe (13) *al beh.* ....(16 to 1 op 10 to 1) 15
760 ORCHARD BAY [32] 4-8-2 A Tucker (1) *al beh.* ....(25 to 1 op 20 to 1) 16
970 DAVROB [56] 3-9-2 Paul Eddery (15) *al beh.* ....(16 to 1 op 12 to 1) 17
DICKENS LANE [51] 6-9-0 (7*) S Drowne (4) *slwly away, nvr got into race*...................... (8 to 1 op 6 to 1) 18
EVERSET (Fr) [53] 5-9-9 J Reid (20) *led far side to hfwy, sn btn, tld off*.......................(16 to 1 op 12 to 1) 19
970 DAILY SPORT AUGUST [30] 4-8-0 J Quinn (17) *al beh, tld off*..................................(20 to 1 op 14 to 1) 20

Dist: Hd, nk, 3l, ¾l, 3l, ½l, ½l, 1½l, 2l, 1½l. 1m 13.10s. a 2.70s (20 Ran).
SR: 1/23/15/-/-/-/ (Kevan R Kynaston), M Williams

1231 Silver Pheasant Fillies Conditions Stakes Class D (3-y-o) £3,465 7f 9yds ....(3:15)

556[7] HOLLY GOLIGHTLY 8-12 J Reid (3) *hld up in tch, hdwy hfwy, rdn wl o'r one furlong out, styd on to ld ins last.* ....(10 to 1 op 8 to 1) 1
752* KHUBZA 9-0 W Ryan (2) *trkd ldr, led o'r 2 fs out, hdd wl over one out, rallied and ran on ins last.* ....(2 to 1 fav op 5 to 2) 2
1016 GUSTAVIA (Ire) 8-12 L Dettori (10) *trkd ldrs, led wl o'r one furlong out, rdn and hdd ins last, kpt on.* ....(16 to 1 op 12 to 1) 3
SIWAAYIB 8-12 W R Swinburn (6) *hld up, hdwy hfwy, ev ch 2 fs out, outpcd appr last, eased.* ....(13 to 2 op 5 to 1 tchd 7 to 1) 4
VAYAVAIG 8-10 B Raymond (8) *hld up in tch, one pace fnl 2 fs*..................................(16 to 1 op 10 to 1) 5
823[5] CRIME OFTHECENTURY 9-2 T Quinn (4) *outpcd, nvr rch ldrs*..................................(12 to 1 op 10 to 1) 6
835* PRINCESS HAIFA (USA) 9-0 Paul Eddery (11) *trkd ldrs till rdn and wknd wl o'r one furlong out.* ....(9 to 1 op 7 to 1) 7
856[6] SHAMISEN 8-10 R Cochrane (12) *hld up, hdwy hfwy, wknd wl o'r one out.* ....(9 to 1 op 10 to 1 tchd 12 to 1 and 8 to 1) 8
1040[2] ZAJIRA (Ire) 9-0 W Carson (1) *al towards rear.* .... (7 to 1 op 6 to 1 tchd 15 to 2) 9
353* CHILLY BREEZE 8-5 (5*) K Rutter (5) *slwly away, al beh.* ....(25 to 1 op 16 to 1) 10
734[9] SEHAILAH 9-0 L Piggott (9) *led till hdd o'r 2 fs out, sn btn and eased, tld off*.................. (25 to 1 op 16 to 1) 11
556[6] GUV'S JOY (Ire) 9-0 Pat Eddery (7) *swrvd lft leaving stalls, al in rear, tld off*...................(16 to 1 op 10 to 1) 12

Dist: ½l, sht-hd, 5l, 2½l, 3l, 2½l, 2l, 2l, 1l, 12l. 1m 23.10s. a 1.20s (12 Ran).

SR: 49/49/46/31/21/18/8/-/-/ (Victor Behrens), R Hannon

1232 Hickling Selling Handicap Class G (Div II) (0-60 3-y-o and up) £2,637 5f 218yds........................ (3:45)

948[9] GREAT HALL [44] 4-9-1 J Williams (3) *hld up in rear, gd hdwy one and a half fs out, str brst to ld ins last, sn clr.* ....(8 to 1 tchd 10 to 1) 1
1159* THE RIGHT TIME [49] 8-9-3 (3*,5ex) D Harrison (5) *hld up, gd hdwy appr fnl furlong, ran on, nvr nrr.* ....(7 to 1 op 6 to 1 tchd 8 to 1) 2
837[8] LEIGH CROFTER [56] (v) 4-9-13 L Dettori (4) *hld up, gd hdwy to ld appr fnl furlong, hdd ins last, outpcd.* ....(7 to 1 op 4 to 1) 3
1148* BARBEZIEUX [36] 6-8-0 (7*) D McCabe (9) *slwly away, wl in rear till gd hdwy on stands side 2 fs out, one pace ins last*...(100 to 30 fav op 7 to 2 tchd 4 to 1 and 3 to 1) 4
909[7] MU-ARRIK [44] (bl) 5-8-8 (7*) G Parkin (1) *hld up, steady hdwy appr fnl furlong, ran on, nvr nrr.* ....(14 to 1 op 8 to 1) 5
600 KILDEE LAD [54] 3-9-1 Pat Eddery (10) *trkd ldrs, dsptd ld one and a half fs out, no extr ins last.* ....(14 to 1 op 12 to 1 tchd 16 to 1) 6
871[6] SALVATORE GIULIANO [50] (bl) 3-8-11 J Lowe (2) *mid-div, made some late hdwy, nvr dngrs.* ....(11 to 1 op 10 to 1 tchd 14 to 1) 7
1059[7] HARRY'S COMING [57] 9-10-0 W Carson (8) *trkd ldrs, till rdn and wknd appr fnl furlong*......(7 to 1 op 5 to 1) 8
934[4] GATE OF HEAVEN [35] 3-7-5 (5*) Darren Moffatt (6) *trkd ldr till wknd 2 fs out*..............................(33 to 1) 9
970 BOULABAS (Ire) [45] 4-9-2 M Wigham (14) *prmnt till wknd wl o'r one furlong out*.............(25 to 1 op 14 to 1) 10
861[8] LITMORE DANCER [37] (v) 5-8-8 R Cochrane (19) *slwly away, sn in tch, wknd 2 fs out*.....(20 to 1 op 16 to 1) 11
4756a[8] LIFE'S A BREEZE [43] 4-9-0 J Reid (18) *al towards rear.* ....(16 to 1 op 10 to 1) 12
1072[9] NORDOORA (Ire) [35] 4-8-6 J Carroll (7) *led till rdn and hdd appr fnl furlong, wknd quickly*..................(33 to 1) 13
1059[8] ARRAS ROYALE [42] 3-8-3 N Adams (15) *in tch to hfwy.* ....(20 to 1 op 33 to 1 tchd 50 to 1) 14
904[8] ALICANTE [28] (bl) 6-7-13 J Quinn (16) *al beh.* ....(50 to 1 op 33 to 1) 15
1035[7] GRUBBY [29] 4-7-9 (5*) A Garth (13) *gd speed till rdn 2 fs out, sn btn*.......................(25 to 1 op 14 to 1) 16
975 TOCCATELLA [37] (bl) 3-7-12[1] A McGlone (11) *al beh.* ....(33 to 1) 17

Dist: 2½l, ½l, 1l, ¾l, 2l, 1l, 1½l, 1½l, 2½l, 6l. 1m 12.20s. a 1.80s (17 Ran).
SR: 29/24/29/5/10/2/-/5/-/ (P D Cundell), P D Cundell

1233 Swannington Claiming Stakes Class F (3-y-o) £2,601 5f 2yds............(4:15)

518* TRENTESIMO (Ire) 9-7 J Carroll (7) *made all, lnd wl appr fnl furlong, cmftbly*...............(2 to 1 tchd 5 to 2) 1
1095[4] CLOUDY REEF 7-10 W Carson (3) *chsd wnr thrght, rdn o'r one furlong out, no imprsn.* ....(11 to 8 fav op 11 to 10 tchd 6 to 4) 2
1010[8] FIVE ISLANDS 8-3[1] T Quinn (2) *chsd ldrs, kpt on one pace fnl furlong*..........................(7 to 1 op 4 to 1) 3
926 BELL LAD (Ire) 8-7 M Wigham (1) *wtd wth, hdwy 2 fs out, nvr nr to chal*.................................(33 to 1) 4
1095[7] AIR COMMAND (Bar) 8-1 T Sprake (8) *trkd ldrs, rdn 2 fs out, wknd entering last*...........(12 to 1 op 10 to 1) 5
927 SUI GENERIS (Ire) 7-10 N Adams (5) *al in rear*....(25 to 1) 6
379[8] BELLE SOIREE (bl) 7-12 J Quinn (4) *outpcd early, rdn and some hdwy 2 fs out, sn btn.* ....(13 to 2 op 7 to 1 tchd 6 to 1) 7
974[6] ARYAN VESPER 8-1 C Rutter (6) *sn rdn, swshd tail and lost tch hfwy*...................(33 to 1 tchd 50 to 1) 8

Dist: 2½l, 2l, 3l, 2l, ½l, 4l, nk. 1m 0.90s. a 2.20s (8 Ran).
SR: 33/-/-/-/-/ (B R Allen), J Berry

1234 Wolvey Maiden Fillies Stakes Class D (Div II) (2-y-o) £3,231 5f 2yds.... (4:45)

NSX 8-11 T Quinn (1) *trkd ldrs, hrd rdn appr fnl furlong, ran on to ld cl hme*...(10 to 1 op 16 to 1 tchd 20 to 1) 1
657[3] CIRCLE OF FRIENDS (Ire) 8-11 Pat Eddery (3) *led, rdn appr fnl furlong, one pace and hdd cl hme.* ....(15 to 8 on op 7 to 4 on tchd 5 to 4 on) 2
889[4] BELLA PARKES 8-11 J Carroll (6) *chsd ldrs, rdn wl o'r one furlong out, one pace*...............(4 to 1 op 5 to 2) 3
BOLD GEM 8-11 B Raymond (5) *chsd ldr till wknd entering fnl furlong*........(11 to 1 op 16 to 1 tchd 8 to 1) 4
1063 BON TON 8-11 Paul Eddery (2) *lost tch for 3 fs.* ....(14 to 1 op 8 to 1) 5
ZANZARA (Ire) 8-11 J Lowe (4) *sn rdn, lost tch 2 fs out.* ....(66 to 1 op 33 to 1) 6

Dist: Nk, 3½l, ¾l, 6l, hd. 1m 0.70s. a 2.00s (6 Ran).
SR: 27/26/12/9/-/-/ (H R H Sultan Ahmad Shah), Miss Gay Kelleway

ROSCOMMON (IRE) (yielding)
Monday May 24th

1235 Hollywell Handicap (3-y-o and up) £2,245 1¼m.................. (7:30)

996[5] MAGIC ARTS (Ire) [-] 5-9-3 (6*) J A Heffernan (14)...(9 to 1) 1
851[5] RIENROE (Ire) [-] 4-9-1 M J Kinane (3)...............(5 to 2) 2
281[8] SIMPLY GRAND [-] 6-8-12 N Byrne (11)...........(16 to 1) 3
1046[4] CALL MY GUEST (Ire) [-] 3-8-5 W J Supple,.....(2 to 1 fav) 4
912[5] ARDLEA HOUSE (Ire) [-] 4-7-7[6] (6*) J J Behan (15) (14 to 1) 5
849 THE BOWER (Ire) [-] 4-7-11[9] (10*) P M Donohue (10) ....(20 to 1) 6
849[5] THE MAN FROM COOKS (Ire) [-] 4-8-11 C Roche (6) (7 to 1) 7
281 COMMAND 'N CONTROL [-] 4-9-4 J P Murtagh (1) (9 to 1) 8
868[9] RETURN JOURNEY (Ire) [-] 4-9-1 (6*) P Carberry (13) ....(12 to 1) 9
961[4] ALL YOURS (Ire) [-] 4-10-0 P Shanahan (8)........(16 to 1) 10
806[6] MATTABOY TWO (Ire) [-] 4-9-0 (6*) J R Barry (5)...(25 to 1) 11
959 PURPLE EMPEROR (Fr) [-] (bl) 4-10-0 S Craine (12) (20 to 1) 12
1107 DESTINATIONUNKNOWN (Ire) [-] 4-8-10 (4*) W J Smith (2) ....(50 to 1) 13
996[4] FLORAL STREET [-] 4-9-5 (6*) C Everard (7)........(8 to 1) 14
849 INAUGURATION (Ire) [-] 4-8-10 (8*) J Wixted (4)...(16 to 1) 15

Dist: 1½l, 1½l, ¾l, 6l. 2m 23.70s. (15 Ran).
(T J O'Mara), T J O'Mara

1236 Athleague Maiden (3-y-o) £2,245 1¼m ....(8:00)

1048[2] OENOTHERA (Ire) 8-11 S Craine (1)..........(11 to 8 fav) 1
1048[3] SOLAS ABU (Ire) 8-11 C Roche (10)..............(5 to 2) 2
GLAMOROUS BRIDE (Fr) 8-11 W J Supple (4)....(12 to 1) 3
1106[2] GOODIES TWO STEP (Ire) 9-0 N G McCullagh (5) (12 to 1) 4
819 DALKEY ISLAND (Ire) 9-0 R Hughes (8)...........(13 to 2) 5
SAFE CONDUCT (Ire) 9-0 J P Murtagh,...........(16 to 1) 6
FALCARRAGH (Ire) 9-0 J F Egan (3).............(20 to 1) 7
PARTICULAR (Ire) 8-10 (4*) W J Smith (6).........(16 to 1) 8
311 BOB THE YANK (Ire) 9-0 W J O'Connor (11)......(20 to 1) 9
982[8] RYE HILL QUEEN (Ire) 8-11 D Manning (7).........(50 to 1) 10
936[6] MULLAGHEA LASS (Ire) 8-11 N Byrne (14).......(50 to 1) 11
1048[8] SKERRIES BELL 8-3 (8*) J J Mullins (2)..........(14 to 1) 12
BLAKE'S FABLE (Ire) 8-11 P Shanahan (12).......(20 to 1) 13
GOLD AND BLUE (Ire) 8-11 M J Kinane (9).......(10 to 1) 14

Dist: 2l, 1l, 1½l, 4l. 2m 24.90s. (14 Ran).
(R E Sangster), T Stack

FOLKESTONE (firm (races 1,2,3,6), good to firm (4,5))
Tuesday May 25th

Going Correction: MINUS 0.15 sec. per fur. (races 1,2,3,6), MINUS 0.30 (4,5)

1237 Sellindge Claiming Stakes Class G (3-y-o and up) £2,469 1m 1f 149yds (1:45)

1130 WAKI GOLD (USA) 6-9-6 Pat Eddery (13) *made all, shaken up and styd on wl fnl furlong*...... (3 to 1 op 5 to 2) 1
1146[6] AWESOME POWER 7-9-12 D Holland (12) *ldg grp, chsd wnr appr fnl furlong, ran on clsg stages.* ....(6 to 1 op 5 to 1 tchd 7 to 1) 2
1146[4] OVERPOWER 9-9-8 P Robinson (9) *mid-div, ran on 3 out, not quicken ins last 2 fs.* ....(11 to 4 fav op 2 to 1 tchd 3 to 1) 3
1097[8] LOCH DUICH 7-9-6 W Carson (10) *pressed ldrs, hrd rdn and no extr appr fnl furlong.* ....(14 to 1 op 8 to 1 tchd 16 to 1) 4
754 RISK PROOF 3-8-7 S Whitworth (6) *improved frm hfwy, cld on ldrs 3 out, one pace appr fnl furlong.* ....(33 to 1 op 20 to 1 tchd 40 to 1) 5
861 BASSIO (Bel) 4-8-7 (7*) Michael Denaro (11) *hdwy o'r 3 fs out, rdn and not quicken wl over one out, wknd.* ....(33 to 1 op 20 to 1) 6
1090[5] MASTER BEVELED 3-8-5 J Williams (4) *hdwy 5 fs out, wknd o'r 2 out*........(8 to 1 op 12 to 1 tchd 16 to 1) 7
1130 ELEGANT TOUCH (v) 4-8-4 (7*) S Mulvey (2) *sn wl plcd, wknd last 2 fs*..............(7 to 1 op 5 to 1 tchd 8 to 1) 8
120[6] LORD NEPTUNE (v) 4-9-2 L Dettori (3) *chsd ldrs frm hfwy, wknd fnl 2 fs*.........(20 to 1 op 16 to 1 tchd 25 to 1) 9
NIPPER REED 3-8-11 A Tucker (5) *al rear.* ....(25 to 1 op 16 to 1 tchd 33 to 1) 10
838[8] CANADIAN EAGLE (bl) 3-7-8 N Adams (1) *slwly into strd, sn chasing ldrs, wknd 4 out.* ....(20 to 1 op 12 to 1 tchd 25 to 1) 11
975 CHATWORTH GREY 3-8-6 J Quinn (7) *settled in mid-div, beh fnl 3 fs, tld off*...............(25 to 1 op 20 to 1) 12
220[7] LOBELIA (Ire) 3-8-0 G Carter (8) *al in rear, tld off fnl 4 fs.* ....(33 to 1 op 16 to 1) 13

Dist: 1½l, 2l, 2l, ¾l, 2½l, 8l, 4l, 2½l, sht-hd, ¾l. 2m 3.90s. a 6.30s (13 Ran).
SR: 28/31/23/17/2/4/ (Mrs Susan Tate), M R Channon

1238 Glover Insurance Services Challenge Cup Handicap Class E (0-70 3-y-o and up) £3,416 1m 1f 149yds........ (2:15)

719[2] MISBELIEF [64] 3-9-8 G Carter (4) *hdwy o'r 3 out, led entering fnl furlong, eased nr finish*.........(4 to 1 jt-fav op 5 to 1 tchd 6 to 1) 1
840* HERE HE COMES [51] 7-9-10 A Munro (14) *settled in 4th pl, led o'r 2 out, hdd entering fnl furlong, kpt on same pace*..............(4 to 1 jt-fav op 3 to 1 tchd 9 to 2) 2
919[3] LOWAWATHA [40] 5-8-13 M Tebbutt (9) *ldg grp, ev ch frm o'r 2 out til one out, not quicken*. ....(11 to 2 op 6 to 1 tchd 7 to 1) 3
1062* ONE OFF THE RAIL (USA) [55] 3-8-6 (7*) B Russell (7) *str run 4 out, dsptd ld 3 out, no extr appr fnl furlong*. ....(8 to 1 op 6 to 1 tchd 10 to 1) 4
919[2] OUR EDDIE [42] (v) 4-9-1 J Quinn (2) *mid-div, effrt 3 out, rdn and btn o'r one out*. ....(14 to 1 op 12 to 1 tchd 16 to 1) 5
966[8] DARING PAST [54] (v) 3-8-12 G Duffield (11) *ran on frm rear last 2 fs, nvr nrr*...................(14 to 1 op 8 to 1) 6
1210[8] ANATROCCOLO [38] 6-8-11 L Dettori (1) *set str pace til hdd and wknd o'r 2 out*...(14 to 1 op 10 to 1 tchd 16 to 1) 7
456[8] LONG FURLONG [46] 5-9-5 N Adams (8) *outpcd*. ....(16 to 1 op 14 to 1) 8
1005 SEA PRODIGY [44] 4-9-3 R Cochrane (10) *beh most of way*. ....(33 to 1 op 20 to 1) 9
1120[6] TADORA (Ire) [48] 4-9-7 B Rouse (5) *al beh*. ....(16 to 1 op 12 to 1) 10
879 AQUADO [39] 4-8-12 Pat Eddery (3) *chsd ldrs to hfwy*. ....(14 to 1 op 10 to 1) 11
914 RAG TIME BELLE [30] 7-7-10 (7*) Wendy Jones (12) *wl plcd till wknd 4 out*.......(25 to 1 op 20 to 1 tchd 33 to 1) 12
813[5] KAWASIR (Can) [57] (v) 3-9-1 W Carson (13) *chsd ldr til lost pl o'r 3 out*..........................(6 to 1 op 9 to 2) 13
LAST APPEARANCE [42] 4-9-1 C Rutter (6) *mid-div til wknd frm hfwy*..........................(33 to 1 op 25 to 1) 14

Dist: 2l, nk, 3l, 2l, 3½l, 4l, 2½l, 6l, ¾l, nk. 2m 3.10s. a 5.50s (14 Ran).
SR: 38/36/24/18/16/6/ (T & J Vestey), J R Fanshawe

1239 Smeeth Median Auction Maiden Stakes Class F (3-y-o) £2,243 6f 189yds ....(2:45)

1057[5] INDERAPUTERI 8-9 A Munro (11) *wl in tch, hrd rdn o'r one out, ran on to ld nr line*............(6 to 1 op 8 to 1) 1
784[3] TEJ SINGH (USA) 9-0 R Cochrane (5) *chsd ldr, led und pres appr fnl furlong, hdd last strds*..............(9 to 4 jt-fav op 5 to 4) 2
COALISLAND 9-0 A McGlone (10) *led til appr fnl furlong, ran on one pace*..................(50 to 1 op 20 to 1) 3
921[3] LEGAL RISK (v) 8-9 S Whitworth (4) *trkd ldrs, ev ch o'r 2 fs out, no extr over one out*. ....(25 to 1 op 20 to 1 tchd 33 to 1) 4
1128[7] HAZY KAY (Ire) 8-9 W Carson (1) *ran on frm rear last 2 fs, nrst finish*.........................(7 to 1 op 5 to 1) 5
995[4] OK BERTIE 9-0 M Tebbutt (3) *hld up in tch, rdn and one pace frm 2 fs out*...(9 to 4 jt-fav op 5 to 2 tchd 3 to 1) 6
991[7] FRANCIA 8-9 L Dettori (7) *wl plcd, no extr ins last 2 fs*. ....(50 to 1 op 20 to 1) 7
950[4] THE LITTLE FERRET 9-0 B Rouse (6) *strted slwly, nvr on terms*..................... (9 to 2 op 7 to 2 tchd 5 to 1) 8
1060 DYNAMIC GEORGE 9-0 J Williams (2) *outpcd*. ....(50 to 1 op 20 to 1) 9
DISTANT DYNASTY 9-0 J Quinn (8) *chsd ldrs til wknd 3 fs out*...............................(50 to 1 op 20 to 1) 10

Dist: Sht-hd, 2l, 1½l, 2l, nk, ¾l, 3l, 10l, 5l. 1m 26.30s. a 5.40s (10 Ran).
(H R H Sultan Ahmad Shah), Miss Gay Kelleway

1240 Scottish Equitable Handicap Class E (0-70 3-y-o and up) £2,976 5f.... (3:15)

1232[4] BARBEZIEUX [38] 6-7-10[9] (7*) D McCabe (9) *slwly into strd, ran on frm rear o'r one furlong out, led nr line*. ....(9 to 2 op 3 to 1) 1
1096[5] TRIOMING [50] 7-8-8 N Adams (4) *led til hdd und pres nr line*..................(17 to 2 op 8 to 1 tchd 10 to 1) 2
927[2] PRINCE SONGLINE [53] 3-8-2 G Duffield (2) *outpcd til cld on ldrs 2 fs out, ev ch one out, rallied close hme*. ....(9 to 2 op 7 to 2) 3
1000[4] MISTER JOLSON [64] 4-9-8 W Carson (6) *pressed ldr, ev ch one furlong out, no extr nr finish*. ....(5 to 2 fav op 9 to 4 tchd 3 to 1) 4
721 SHARP IMP [45] (bl) 3-7-8 N Carlisle (10) *outpcd til styd on appr fnl furlong*...... (11 to 1 op 8 to 1 tchd 12 to 1) 5
ABSOLUTELY NUTS [70] 4-10-0 D Holland (3) *chsd frnt rnk, kpt on one pace frm o'r one furlong out*. ....(14 to 1 op 10 to 1 tchd 16 to 1) 6
1010[7] AUNTIE GINGER [48] 3-7-11 J Quinn (5) *pressed ldrs for 3 fs, fdd*...............................(14 to 1 tchd 16 to 1) 7
927[5] MY FOXY LADY [47] 3-7-10[1] F Norton (1) *outpcd most of way*..................(17 to 2 op 6 to 1 tchd 9 to 1) 8
1120 YOUNG MAX [56] (bl) 4-9-0 J Williams (7) *wl plcd to hfwy, sn btn*..........................(20 to 1 tchd 25 to 1) 9
1148[7] STOCKTINA [35] 6-7-7 G Bardwell (11) *cl up on outsd til wknd quickly o'r 2 fs out, tld off*...(14 to 1 op 12 to 1) 10

Dist: Nk, nk, 1l, 2½l, nk, 3½l, ½l, 5l, 15l. 59.90s. a 1.30s (10 Ran).
SR: 26/37/30/46/8/41/ (T S M S Riley-Smith), D A Wilson

1241 Westenhanger Median Auction Maiden Stakes Class E (2-y-o) £3,028 5f..............................(3:45)

1020[4] PRINCE AZZAAN (Ire) 9-0 W Carson (3) *made virtually all, kpt on strly ins fnl furlong*. .... (11 to 10 fav op Evens tchd 5 to 4 on and 5 to 4) 1
1071[4] KERAMIC 8-9 J Williams (4) *chsd ldrs, ran on o'r one furlong out, styd on nr finish*..... (50 to 1 op 20 to 1) 2
HELLO MISTER 9-0 D Holland (7) *veered rght leaving stalls, outpcd til styd on appr fnl furlong, not rch wnr nr finish*..........................(50 to 1 op 20 to 1) 3
687[7] WICKLOW BOY (Ire) 9-0 Pat Eddery (6) *cl up, ev ch 2 out, no extr ins fnl furlong*. (11 to 4 op 9 to 4 tchd 7 to 2) 4
1091 MONSIEUR PETONG 9-0 A Munro (1) *outpcd til moderate prog o'r one furlong out, no imprsn on ldrs*. ....(20 to 1 op 14 to 1 tchd 25 to 1) 5
THE MULTIYORKER (Ire) 8-9 P Robinson (5) *ldg grp til outpcd appr fnl furlong, eased whn btn*. ....(5 to 2 op 5 to 2) 6
949[7] CHARISMA GIRL 8-9 C Rutter (2) *outpcd aftr 2 fs*. ....(50 to 1 op 20 to 1) 7

Dist: 1l, 2½l, 2l, sht-hd, hd, 3½l. 1m 0.30s. a 1.70s (7 Ran).
SR: 36/27/22/14/13/7/-/ (K Al-Said), N A Callaghan

1242 Lympne Limited Stakes Class F (3-y-o and up) £2,243 1½m............(4:15)

1165* THE WHERE WITHAL 3-8-6 G Duffield (6) *chsd ldr, led briefly o'r 2 out, sn hdd, led wl ins fnl furlong, jst hld on*..................(2 to 1 fav op 9 to 4 tchd 7 to 2) 1
1120[7] DOYCE 4-9-5 R Cochrane (1) *mid-div, ran on o'r 3 out, led 2 out, hdd und pres wl ins fnl furlong, rallied and jst fld*...............................(10 to 1 op 5 to 1) 2
1005[4] BARRAAK 3-8-6 W Carson (11) *al racing in 3rd pl, outpcd o'r 2 out, styd on ag'n ins fnl furlong*. ....(9 to 2 op 5 to 2) 3
1005[5] CONCINNITY (USA) 4-9-10 A Munro (4) *hld up towards rear, ran on o'r 2 fs out, not rch ldrs*. ....(14 to 1 op 10 to 1) 4
1005[2] MISS FASCINATION 3-8-1 Paul Eddery (5) *settled in 4th pl, rdn o'r 2 out, wknd over one furlong out*. ....(7 to 2 op 5 to 2 tchd 5 to 1) 5
994[9] MARCHMAN 8-9-10 L Dettori (7) *mid-div, effrt 4 out, no hdwy appr last 2 fs*.................(13 to 2 op 8 to 1) 6
1034 CHECKPOINT CHARLIE 8-9-3 (7*) Antoinette Armes (2) *slwly into strd, nvr nr to chal*..... (16 to 1 op 10 to 1) 7
1415 NASEER (USA) 4-9-10 J Williams (10) *nvr on terms*. .... (14 to 1 op 8 to 1 tchd 16 to 1) 8
SURE PRIDE (USA) 5-9-10 Candy Morris (8) *chsd ldrs for 8 fs*..................(25 to 1 op 12 to 1 tchd 33 to 1) 9
712[4] CANDARELA 3-8-1 J Quinn (3) *hld up towards rear, lost tch fnl 4 fs*........................(33 to 1 op 20 to 1) 10
739[9] MON PETITNAMOUR (Ire) (bl) 4-9-5 S Whitworth (12) *led til o'r 2 fs out, wknd quickly*......... (33 to 1 op 20 to 1) 11
918[6] KING OF NORMANDY (Ire) 4-9-10 M Wigham (9) *al beh*. ....(33 to 1 op 20 to 1) 12

Dist: Sht-hd, 1½l, 7l, ¾l, 10l, ¾l, hd, 1l, 2l, 8l. 2m 38.50s. a 8.00s (12 Ran).
SR: -/6/-/-/-/-/ (W E Sturt), Sir Mark Prescott

MAISONS LAFFITTE (FR) (good) Tuesday May 25th

1243 Prix Lovelace (Listed) (4-y-o and up) £14,337 1m.................... (3:00)

430[8] BURDUR 5-9-2 C Le Scrill,...................................... 1
273[2] ARCHANGE (USA) 4-8-12 F Head,...................................... 2
WHAT KATY DID (USA) 4-8-8 T Jarnet,...................................... 3
THEATRICIAN (USA) 4-8-11 E Saint-Martin,...................................... 4

Dist: Nk, ¾l, ¾l, 1l, nk, 3l, 6l, 2½l. 1m 37.10s. a 2.40s (9 Ran).
SR: 60/55/49/50/ (M Kura), Y Porzier

SOUTHWELL (A.W) (std) Tuesday May 25th

Going Correction: PLUS 0.20 sec. per fur.

1244 Lynx Clubs Rating Related Maiden Stakes Class D (3-y-o) £2,997 1¾m ....(2:30)

980 ELECTROLYTE 9-0 W Ryan (2) *made all, rdn o'r 3 fs out, styd on wl fnl 2 furlongs*.......... (20 to 1 op 14 to 1) 1
816[3] OMIDJOY (Ire) 8-9 W Woods (4) *trkd ldrs, hdwy 4 fs out, effrt and rdn o'r 2 furlongs out, edgd lft and sn btn*. ....(5 to 1 on op 4 to 1 on) 2
1133 PREMIER BLUES (Fr) 8-9 D Biggs (3) *trkd ldrs, effrt o'r 3 fs out, sn rdn and wknd*............. (14 to 1 op 8 to 1) 3
980 ITS UNBELIEVABLE 9-0 Dale Gibson (1) *pld hrd, cl up, rdn alng o'r 5 fs out, wknd 4 furlongs out, sn lost tch*. ....(7 to 1 op 6 to 1 tchd 9 to 1) 4

Dist: 12l, 8l, 8l. 3m 13.30s. a 13.30s (4 Ran).
(Freemount Partnership), B Palling

1245 Puma Claiming Stakes Class F (2-y-o) £2,243 6f...................... (3:00)

1071* THE FERNHILL FLYER (Ire) (v) 8-9 J Carroll (9) *dwlt, sn in tch and led aftr one and a half fs, clr 3 furlongs out, rdn o'r one furlong out, jst hld on.* ....(11 to 8 on op 9 to 4 on tchd 5 to 4 on) 1
968 JACKSON HOUSE 9-0 K Fallon (1) *mid-div, effrt and hdwy 2 fs out, swtchd ins fnl furlong, ran on wl.* ....(12 to 1 op 6 to 1) 2
544⁵ UP THE MARINERS (Ire) 8-5 R P Elliott (5) *led o'r one furlong, prmnt and rdn hfwy, kpt on fnl 2 fs.* ....(12 to 1 op 10 to 1) 3
STORM HEIGHTS 8-1 K Darley (2) *beh till rdn and styd on fnl 2 fs, nrst finish*..............(12 to 1 op 7 to 1) 4
730 LEGAL CONQUEST 8-5 T Quinn (6) *wide strt, sn rdn and styd on wl fnl furlong.* (6 to 1 op 8 to 1 tchd 10 to 1) 5
1119⁹ STORM 7-7 (7*) D Wright (11) *rear till some hdwy fnl 2 fs.* ....(10 to 1 op 6 to 1) 6
657 MRS JOGGLEBURY 7-12 (7*) J Tate (12) *prmnt, hdwy to chase wnr hfwy, rdn and wknd wl o'r one furlong out.* ....(20 to 1 op 16 to 1) 7
804⁹ SPRING STAR 7-13 J Lowe (3) *chsd ldrs till wknd hfwy.* ....(12 to 1 op 10 to 1) 8
900 LASTOTHEBRADFIELDS 7-9 L Charnock (8) *al rear.* ....(33 to 1 op 25 to 1) 9
AGGIES DREAM 8-0 D Biggs (10) *al rear.* ....(14 to 1 op 7 to 1) 10
900⁷ UNKNOWN STAR (bl) 8-4 A Proud (7) *cl up, rdn hfwy, wknd 2 fs out*..............(25 to 1 op 20 to 1) 11
Dist: Hd, 2l, ¾l, hd, 1½l, 3½l, 6l, 2l, 1l, 2l. 1m 20.10s. a 6.70s (11 Ran).
(P J Evans), J Berry

1246 Subaru Impreza Handicap Class D (0-80 4-y-o and up) £3,289 7f.... (3:30)

1138⁸ SANDMOOR DENIM [58] 6-8-6 (7*) G Strange (3) *mid-div, gd hdwy 2 fs out, effrt to ld ins fnl furlong, cmftbly.* ....(6 to 1 op 7 to 1) 1
971² EXPRESS SERVICE [57] (bl) 4-8-9 (3*) Emma O'Gorman (9) *al prmnt, effrt and rdn 2 fs out, ev ch o'r one furlong out, kpt on ins last*..............(11 to 2 op 4 to 1) 2
650⁵ DREAM CARRIER (Ire) [71] 5-9-12 K Darley (6) *beh, hdwy 2 fs out, rdn and styd on strly ins last.* (7 to 1 op 8 to 1) 3
970³ HARCLIFF [54] (bl) 4-8-9 J Lowe (4) *led, hdd o'r 2 fs out, sn rdn and ev ch entering fnl furlong, no extr nr finish.* ....(6 to 1 op 4 to 1) 4
319³ LADY ROXANNE [52] (v) 4-8-4 (3*) D Harrison (5) *cl up, led o'r 2 fs out, rdn wl over one furlong out, headed and wknd ins last*.......... (11 to 2 op 5 to 1 tchd 6 to 1) 5
1073 QUINZII MARTIN [57] 5-8-12 A Mackay (1) *beh, hdwy fnl 2 fs, nrst finish*..............(12 to 1 tchd 14 to 1) 6
970* ON Y VA (USA) [60] 6-9-1 D Biggs (7) *chsd ldrs, rdn o'r 2 fs out, sn wknd*........(3 to 1 fav op 7 to 2 tchd 4 to 1) 7
1232 LITMORE DANCER [42] (v) 5-7-11 L Charnock (2) *slwly into strd, al rear*.............. (20 to 1) 8
916⁴ NO QUARTER GIVEN [69] 8-9-10 T Quinn (8) *cl up till rdn and wknd 3 fs out*..............(8 to 1 op 10 to 1) 9
Dist: 2½l, hd, sht-hd, 2l, hd, hd, 10l, 8l. 1m 31.10s. a 5.00s (9 Ran).
SR: 45/36/49/31/23/27/29/-/-/ (E H Lunness), S R Bowring

1247 Panther Handicap Class E (0-70 3-y-o) £3,054 1m.................... (4:00)

1074² BACKSTABBER [53] 8-7 G Hind (9) *al cl up, quickened to ld 2 fs out, sn clr, rdn out fnl furlong.* ....(13 to 2 op 7 to 1 tchd 6 to 1) 1
907⁸ CERTAIN WAY (Ire) [67] 9-7 M Birch (7) *beh, hdwy 3 fs out, rdn and styd on wl fnl furlong, not rch wnr.* ....(7 to 2 op 3 to 1 tchd 4 to 1) 2
MOHICAN BRAVE (Ire) [65] 9-5 K Fallon (10) *chsd ldrs, effrt 2 fs out, sn rdn and kpt on*.......... (12 to 1 op 10 to 1) 3
415² KINGSTON BROWN [67] 9-7 T Quinn (6) *chsd ldrs, effrt and rdn 2 fs out, wknd o'r one furlong out.* ....(11 to 2 op 4 to 1) 4
980 TINSASHE (Ire) [52] 8-6 J Carroll (1) *trkd ldrs, effrt on inner o'r 2 fs out, sn rdn and btn*.......... (8 to 1 op 6 to 1) 5
972* PENNY BANGER (Ire) [58] 8-12 Dean McKeown (5) *led, rdn and hdd 2 fs out, grad wknd.* ....(3 to 1 fav op 7 to 2 tchd 4 to 1) 6
713⁴ ADAMPARIS [60] 9-0 N Day (4) *prmnt, rdn 3 fs out, sn wknd*..............(8 to 1) 7
1102⁴ DESIRABLE MISS [42] (v) 7-10 L Charnock (3) *prmnt till rdn and wknd 3 fs out*..............(20 to 1) 8
1080⁵ PANTHER (Ire) [66] 9-6 K Darley (8) *hdwy hfwy, effrt and rdn o'r 2 fs out, sn wknd.* ....(8 to 1 op 7 to 1 tchd 9 to 1) 9
4695a⁸ DONTBETALKING (Ire) [51] 8-5 D Biggs (2) *chsd ldrs till hmpd and lost pl aftr 3 fs, sn beh*.............. (25 to 1) 10
Dist: 2l, ¾l, 4l, 6l, sht-hd, 10l, 5l, ¾l, 2l. 1m 45.20s. a 6.20s (10 Ran).
SR: 24/32/28/18/-/-/ (The Inn Crowd), Dr J D Scargill

1248 Tiger Limited Stakes Class F (3-y-o and up) £2,243 1½m........... (4:30)

973² TIGER SHOOT 6-9-12 J Lowe (5) *made all, rdn 2 fs out, ran on gmely fnl furlong*..........(7 to 2 tchd 4 to 1) 1
1075² PHARLY DANCER 4-9-12 Dean McKeown (8) *mid-div, hdwy 4 fs out, effrt and rdn to chal 2 furlongs out, ev ch till no extr ins last.* ....(100 to 30 op 11 to 4 tchd 7 to 2) 2
833⁷ MOUNTAIN HIGH (Fr) 3-8-8 K Fallon (4) *al prmnt, effrt and ev ch 3 fs out, sn rdn and one pace*...(9 to 2 op 4 to 1) 3
879⁷ ADMIRALS SECRET (USA) 4-9-7 (5*) K Rutter (1) *prmnt till lost pl and rdn alng hfwy, hdwy 3 fs out, styd on one pace und pres fnl 2 furlongs.* ....(9 to 4 fav op 5 to 4 tchd 11 to 4) 4
122 JALORE 4-9-12 W Ryan (3) *al outpcd and beh.* ....(40 to 1 op 33 to 1) 5
4813a² COSMIC DANCER (v) 6-9-12 W Woods (6) *nvr rchd ldrs.* ....(12 to 1 op 8 to 1) 6
ALILISA (USA) 5-9-7 N Day (7) *trkd ldrs, hdwy to chase wnr 5 fs out, rdn and wknd o'r 2 furlongs out.* .... (7 to 1 op 12 to 1) 7
971 COLONNA (USA) 7-9-5 (7*) Claire Balding (2) *prmnt till lost pl 5 fs out, sn beh and tld off fnl 3 furlongs.* ....(33 to 1 op 25 to 1) 8
Dist: 1l, 6l, 10l, 3l, ½l, 1½l, dist. 2m 42.90s. a 9.00s (8 Ran).
SR: 46/44/14/12/6/5/-/-/ (C V Lines), C V Lines

1249 Lion Handicap Class D (0-80 3-y-o and up) £3,348 5f.................. (5:00)

871³ SUPERLATIVEMAXIMUS (Ire) [53] 5-8-6 W Newnes (4) *chsd ldrs, hdwy 2 fs out, rdn to ld entering fnl furlong, ran on*.............. (8 to 1 op 7 to 1 tchd 9 to 1) 1
455⁵ OUR MICA [50] (bl) 3-7-8¹ L Charnock (6) *led, edgd lft 2 fs out, hdd entering fnl furlong, kpt on wl*.......(12 to 1) 2
548⁵ LAST STRAW [45] 5-7-5 (7*) Claire Balding (5) *chsd ldrs, effrt 2 fs out, rdn and ch ins last, kpt on*....... (8 to 1) 3
1036 EWALD (Ire) [59] 5-8-9 (3*) B Doyle (1) *chsd ldrs, rdn and swtchd o'r one furlong out, kpt on ins last.* (4 to 1 co-fav op 3 to 1) 4
1076* PEERAGE PRINCE [75] (bl) 4-9-7 (7*) G Forster (9) *prmnt stands rls, rdn 2 fs out, one pace appr last.* (4 to 1 co-fav op 7 to 2 tchd 9 to 2) 5
1076⁵ SIR TASKER [65] 5-9-4 T Quinn (3) *outpcd and beh, rdn and hdwy 2 fs out, nvr dngrs.* (4 to 1 co-fav op 5 to 1) 6
568⁴ SULLY'S CHOICE (USA) [47] 12-8-0 S Wood (8) *cl up stands side, rdn hfwy, sn wknd*.............. (20 to 1) 7
1076² MAID WELCOME [62] (bl) 6-8-8 (7*) Madeleine Smith (7) *cl up till rdn 2 fs out, sn wknd*........... (8 to 1 op 7 to 1) 8
887⁶ BRIGHT PARAGON (Ire) [41] 4-7-8¹ Dale Gibson (2) *slwly into strd, al outpcd and beh*.........(9 to 1 op 6 to 1) 9
Dist: ½l, ½l, 1l, 1½l, 1l, 2½l, 2l, 6l. 1m 1.40s. a 3.50s (9 Ran).
SR: 42/28/30/40/50/36/8/15/-/ (Ray Champion), J A Bennett

TRAMORE (IRE) (yielding) Tuesday May 25th

1250 Holiday Maiden (3-y-o and up) £2,245 1½m.......................... (7:00)

1202⁷ BLUE DIANA (Ire) 3-8-7 J F Egan (4).............. (5 to 2) 1
997² DAHLIA'S BEST (USA) (bl) 3-8-10 W J Supple (3) (5 to 4 fav) 2
1048⁹ HOPESVILLE (Ire) 3-8-5 (2*) D G O'Shea (2)........(7 to 1) 3
1122⁷ ASSERT STAR 3-8-10 N G McCullagh (6)........(16 to 1) 4
1107⁹ DUCHESS AFFAIR (Ire) 3-8-7 Joanna Morgan (9)..(20 to 1) 5
819² DARK HYACINTH (Ire) 3-8-7 R Hughes (1).........(5 to 1) 6
1024⁸ MAJESTIC JOHN (Ire) (bl) 3-8-8 (2*) R M Burke (7) (12 to 1) 7
TORCH SINGER 3-7-13 (8*) J J Mullins (5)........(10 to 1) 8
Dist: 1l, 2½l, 9l, 4½l. 2m 43.60s. (8 Ran).
(Mrs Anna Doyle), Patrick Joseph Flynn

1251 Waterford Crystal Handicap Trophy (0-60 3-y-o and up) £2,895 1m 1f (7:30)

1123⁴ SARA MAURETTE (Ire) [-] 3-9-0 N Byrne (13)........(7 to 1) 1
1107* TOUCHDOWN [-] 6-9-3 (6*,7ex) P P Murphy (12) (9 to 2 fav) 2
ANSEO (Ire) [-] 4-9-4 (6*) P Carberry (6)............(8 to 1) 3
TIGNES (Ire) [-] 5-9-0 (6*) C Everard (3)............(8 to 1) 4
I SAY AYE (Ire) [-] 4-9-10 (2*) R M Burke (14)...... (11 to 2) 5
868 FANTANTE (Ire) [-] 4-9-2 (10*) P Donohue (2)...... (10 to 1) 6
SHRAGRADDY LASS (Ire) [-] 3-8-10 N G McCullagh (7) ....(12 to 1) 7
849 RIYADH DANCER (Ire) [-] (bl) 3-8-13 J D Eddery (11) (10 to 1) 8
1013⁹ PEPPERS PET (Ire) [-] (bl) 5-8-12 (6*) R V Skelly (8) (10 to 1) 9
CASEY'S SHADOW (Ire) [-] 4-8-1 (8*) P O'Casey (15) ....(20 to 1) 10
CLANROSIE (Ire) [-] (bl) 4-9-0 (4*) W J Smith (10).. (16 to 1) 11
912 CHRISTY MOORE (Ire) [-] (bl) 3-8-0¹ W J Supple (1) (16 to 1) 12
1163² ST AIDAN (Ire) [-] 5-7-5 (2*) D G O'Shea (9)....... (11 to 2) 13
598⁷ MR GERAN (Ire) [-] 4-9-1 (6*) J J Behan (5)....... (14 to 1) 14
981⁸ AVALONIA (Ire) [-] 3-8-11 J F Egan (4)............(10 to 1) 15
Dist: Sht-hd, 3½l, ¾l, 2l. 2m 5.80s. (Flag start) (15 Ran).
(Michael John Wiley), Edward Lynam

1252 Dunmore East Maiden (3-y-o and up) £2,245 1m 1f.................. (8:00)

807 TRANQUIL BEAUTY (Ire) 4-9-5 (6*) C Everard (4)... (6 to 1) 1
647⁶ WARREN STREET (Ire) 3-8-8 (6*) J J Behan (8)....(10 to 1) 2
848² TORC MOUNTAIN (Ire) 3-9-0 R Hughes (6).....(5 to 2 fav) 3

705^{5} DIGNIFIED (Ire) 3-8-7 (4*) W J Smith (2)........... (8 to 1) 4
649^{8} RED ROOSTER (Ire) 3-9-0 N G McCullagh (7).....(33 to 1) 5
1046 SIENNA SOUND (Ire) 3-8-11 B Coogan (9)........(7 to 2) 6
NO DIPLOMACY (Ire) 4-9-11 C F Swan (10)........(14 to 1) 7
1026^{5} ARZAAQ (USA) (bl) 3-9-0 W J Supple (3).......... (8 to 1) 8
1123^{5} ROOTSMAN (Ire) 3-8-12 (2*) D G O'Shea (5)....... (6 to 1) 9
996^{7} NORDIC RACE 6-10-0 N Byrne (1).............. (12 to 1) 10
OUT OF STEP (Ire) 4-9-11 J F Egan (11)..........(20 to 1) 11
Dist: 1l, hd, 2½l, 2½l. 2m 8.00s. (11 Ran).
(Edward J Kearns), Edward J Kearns

BRIGHTON (firm)
Wednesday May 26th
Going Correction: MINUS 0.60 sec. per fur.

1253 Dome Claiming Stakes Class F (2-y-o) £2,243 5f 59yds................. (2:00)

1009^{4} IMPERIAL BAILIWICK (Ire) 8-9 N Adams (3) *trkd ldr, led 2 fs out till hdd one out, rallied und pres to ld ag'n nr finish*..... (15 to 8 op 7 to 4 tchd 2 to 1 and 13 to 8) 1
1119^{4} SWEET WHISPER (bl) 8-7 Pat Eddery (2) *led til hdd 2 fs out, rdn and led ag'n one out till headed cl hme.* ....(5 to 4 fav tchd 6 to 4) 2
804^{5} MR BLOBBY (Ire) 8-10 G Carter (4) *trkd ldg pair, hrd rdn wl o'r one furlong out, one pace*.... (13 to 2 op 9 to 2) 3
SEVEN UP CYD 8-4 C Rutter (5) *outpcd till ran on ins fnl furlong, better for race*........(33 to 1 op 12 to 1) 4
AERIAL VIEW 8-9 T Sprake (8) *nvr on terms.* .... (20 to 1 op 14 to 1) 5
FINISHING KIND 7-13 G Bardwell (6) *sn rdn alng, outpcd.* .... (33 to 1 op 16 to 1) 6
MY SONG OF SONGS 8-5 W Newnes (7) *sn outpcd.* .... (50 to 1 op 16 to 1) 7
1108^{5} MARTIAN FOREST 7-11 (3*) B Doyle (1) *missed break, ran wide into strt, al beh.* (20 to 1 op 8 to 1 tchd 25 to 1) 8
Dist: Nk, 1l, 6l, 1½l, 1½l, 2l, 2l. 1m 1.00s. a 0.90s (8 Ran).
SR: 14/11/10/-/-/ (Dr Ian R Shenkin), M D I Usher

1254 Victoria Gardens Selling Stakes Class G (2-y-o) £2,070 5f 213yds...... (2:30)

715^{9} GRECIAN GARDEN 8-6 Pat Eddery (9) *made all, shaken up 2 fs out, pushed out, cmftbly.* ....(7 to 4 fav op 5 to 4 tchd 15 to 8) 1
1108^{3} RITA'S JOY 8-6 T Sprake (6) *trkd ldrs, pushed alng and chsd wnr frm 2 fs out, ran on one pace.* .... (5 to 2 op 2 to 1 tchd 11 to 4) 2
BURMA STAR 8-6 R Cochrane (8) *hld up tracking ldrs, effrt wl o'r one furlong out, sn one paced.* ....(16 to 1 op 12 to 1 tchd 25 to 1) 3
949^{5} FOREVER BLUSHING 7-13 (7*) D McCabe (5) *outpcd, rdn 2 fs out, hng lft one out, ran on ins last.* .... (17 to 2 op 6 to 1 tchd 10 to 1) 4
949 ENTENTE CORDIALE (Ire) 8-4 (7*) Kim McDonnell (3) *chsd ldrs, no hdwy fnl 2 fs, fnshd lme, dead.* .... (12 to 1 op 7 to 1 tchd 14 to 1) 5
886^{5} MONKEY MONEY (Ire) 8-6 G Carter (1) *cl up till wknd ins fnl furlong*......................... (5 to 1 tchd 6 to 1) 6
1091 REIGNING ROYAL 8-6 J Quinn (7) *sn outpcd, tld off.* ....(20 to 1 op 12 to 1 tchd 25 to 1) 7
949 BERKELEY HERO 8-11 W Newnes (4) *sn pushed alng, tld off*..................................(50 to 1 op 33 to 1) 8
RISK A PICTURE 8-6 A Tucker (2) *missed break, al tld off.* .... (14 to 1 op 8 to 1) 9
Dist: 2½l, 1l, 2l, hd, ¾l, 15l, 8l, 20l. 1m 8.50s. a 0.10s (9 Ran).
SR: 18/8/4/-/-/-/ (Lord Carnarvon), R Hannon

1255 Grand Parade Rating Related Maiden Stakes Class E (0-70 3-y-o) £2,872 1m 3f 196yds...................... (3:00)

966^{5} SUMMER PAGEANT 8-9 W R Swinburn (5) *al hndy, led appr 2 fs out, sn clr, not extended.* ....(2 to 1 fav op 11 to 4 tchd 3 to 1) 1
926^{7} HATTA RIVER (USA) (bl) 9-0 W Carson (3) *rcd freely, led till hdd appr 2 fs out, ran on wl.* ....(20 to 1 op 10 to 1 tchd 25 to 1) 2
980^{7} DUTCH DEBUTANTE 8-9 W Newnes (6) *beh, styd on frm o'r one furlong out, nrst finish.* ....(16 to 1 op 14 to 1 tchd 20 to 1) 3
873^{3} BURNT IMP (USA) 9-0 T Quinn (1) *cl up, pushed alng 5 fs out, outpcd frm 3 out*....(7 to 1 op 9 to 2 tchd 8 to 1) 4
864^{4} COMMANCHE CREEK 9-0 R Cochrane (4) *in tch, hrd rdn 3 fs out, sn outpcd*....... (11 to 2 op 4 to 1 tchd 6 to 1) 5
827^{7} TOTALLY UNIQUE (USA) 9-0 M Hills (2) *al beh.* ....(5 to 1 op 5 to 1) 6
864^{2} MY HARVINSKI 9-0 J Reid (8) *hld up in cl tch, effrt 4 fs out, sn btn*............(3 to 1 op 5 to 2 tchd 7 to 2) 7
825 IMPERIAL TOKAY (USA) 9-0 D Holland (7) *al beh, tld off.* .... (8 to 1 op 7 to 1 tchd 12 to 1) 8
Dist: 3½l, 7l, 3l, 1l, 12l, 2l, 30l. 2m 26.80s. b 0.70s (8 Ran).
SR: 30/28/9/8/6/ (Cheveley Park Stud), J R Fanshawe

1256 Old Steine Rating Related Maiden Stakes Class D (0-80 3-y-o and up) £3,172 1m 1f 209yds............ (3:30)

1016 SUN OF SPRING 3-8-9 W R Swinburn (2) *trkd ldr, led appr 2 fs out, sn hrd rdn, ran on.* .... (11 to 4 op 2 to 1 tchd 3 to 1) 1
1058 ICE REBEL 3-8-9 W Newnes (1) *led, rdn o'r 3 fs out, hdd appr 2 out, rallied and ev ch ins last, one pace.* .... (66 to 1 op 33 to 1) 2
759^{4} ANORAK (USA) 3-8-9 R Cochrane (3) *trkd ldrs, ev ch appr 2 fs out, rdn and one pace approaching last.* .... (6 to 5 fav op 6 to 4 tchd Evens) 3
534^{2} LAKE POOPO (Ire) 3-8-4 D Holland (6) *hld up, cld o'r 3 fs out, slightly hmpd 2 out, ev ch und pres ins last, eased fnl strds*.......................(4 to 1 op 3 to 1 tchd 5 to 1) 4
480^{6} THE POWER OF ONE 4-9-10 J Reid (4) *hld up, took keen hold, drvn 2 fs out, not pace to chal.* (20 to 1 op 8 to 1) 5
AUSTRAL JANE 3-8-4 M Hills (5) *in cl tch till wknd 2 fs out*..................................(7 to 1 op 5 to 1) 6
Dist: 1l, sht-hd, sht-hd, 5l, 4l. 1m 59.70s. a 1.50s (6 Ran).
SR: 20/18/17/11/21/-/ (Sheikh Mohammed), M R Stoute

1257 Royal Pavilion Fillies Handicap Class E (0-70 3-y-o and up) £3,287 7f 214yds ....(4:00)

1058^{5} FIVEOFIVE (Ire) [58] 3-9-5 Pat Eddery (2) *wtd wth in cl tch, closed o'r 2 fs out, sn hrd rdn, led nr finish.* ....(2 to 1 op 5 to 2 tchd 11 to 4) 1
603^{4} PRECIOUS AIR (Ire) [51] 5-9-10 B Rouse (9) *cl up, ev ch ins fnl furlong, ran on*......(7 to 1 op 5 to 1 tchd 8 to 1) 2
1207^{2} NAVARESQUE [45] 8-9-4 T Quinn (8) *led, hrd rdn ins fnl furlong, ct cl hme*................(6 to 4 fav tchd 7 to 4) 3
873^{5} DRAGONMIST (Ire) [45] 3-7-13 (7*) D Wright (4) *in tch, ev ch o'r 2 fs out, sn one pace*..........(16 to 1 tchd 20 to 1) 4
991^{5} APACHE MYTH [62] 3-9-9 J Reid (3) *in cl tch till wknd quickly wl o'r 2 fs out.* (11 to 1 op 6 to 1 tchd 12 to 1) 5
964^{9} DOUBLE SHERRY [35] 4-8-8 G Bardwell (6) *took keen hold, in tch, rdn alng 4 fs out, sn btn*.....(16 to 1 op 8 to 1) 6
837 BATCHWORTH BOUND [50] 4-9-9 W Newnes (7) *cl up til wknd wl o'r 2 fs out.* (20 to 1 op 14 to 1 tchd 25 to 1) 7
977 IBTIKAR (USA) [60] 3-9-7 W Carson (1) *al beh.* .... (11 to 1 op 6 to 1 tchd 12 to 1) 8
834^{6} ARAGONA [38] 4-8-11 C Rutter (5) *al beh.* .... (11 to 1 op 6 to 1 tchd 12 to 1) 9
Dist: Nk, nk, 8l, 8l, 1l, 2l, sht-hd, 10l. 1m 32.20s. b 0.20s (9 Ran).
SR: 36/40/33/-/-/-/ (T A Foreman), N A Callaghan

1258 Brighton Centre Handicap Class C (0-100 3-y-o) £4,582 5f 59yds.... (4:30)

846* PLAY HEVER GOLF [83] 8-9 D Holland (1) *made all, rdn out*...............(9 to 4 jt-fav op 6 to 4 tchd 5 to 2) 1
1010* ARAGROVE [68] 7-8 C Avery (6) *outpcd, shaken up and hdwy 2 fs, styd on wl ins last.* .... (4 to 1 op 11 to 4 tchd 5 to 1) 2
1137^{2} TUSCAN DAWN [71] 7-11 W Carson (3) *chsd wnr, hrd rdn o'r one furlong out, one pace*................(9 to 4 jt-fav op 5 to 2 tchd 2 to 1) 3
858^{5} RISTON LADY (Ire) [92] 9-1 (3*) D Harrison (5) *trkd ldg pair, rdn o'r 2 fs out, wknd over one out.* ....(9 to 2 op 7 to 1 tchd 8 to 1) 4
1017 HAWAYAH (Ire) [73] 7-13 J Quinn (2) *in tch till outpcd o'r one furlong out*.................... (20 to 1 op 8 to 1) 5
795 ANONYMOUS [95] 9-4 (3*) B Doyle (4) *outpcd frm hfwy.* ....(10 to 1 tchd 14 to 1) 6
Dist: ½l, 3l, 7l, ½l, 3l. 59.30s. b 0.80s (6 Ran).
SR: 48/31/22/15/-/4/ (R A Popely), T J Naughton

HAMILTON (good to soft)
Wednesday May 26th
Going Correction: PLUS 0.10 sec. per fur. (races 1,2,3,4), MINUS 0.10 (5,6)

1259 Carfin Apprentice Handicap Class F (0-70 3-y-o) £2,422 1½m 17yds.. (2:20)

1180^{2} PRIME PAINTER [64] 9-2 (5*) L Aspell (3) *dictated pace, quickened hfwy, hrd pressed fnl furlong, kpt on wl.* .... (6 to 4 fav tchd 7 to 4) 1
966^{4} CONTRACT ELITE (Ire) [54] 8-3 (8*) G Mills (4) *patiently rdn shaken up to improve last 2 fs, not quicken last 50 yards*................ (2 to 1 op 7 to 4 tchd 9 to 4) 2
MOONSHINE DANCER [50] 8-1^{2} (8*) S Copp (2) *nvr far away, rdn last 2 furlong, sn outpcd.* (8 to 1 op 4 to 1) 3
1055^{2} SHARE A MOMENT (Can) [64] 9-4 (3*) J Dennis (1) *trkd wnr, feeling and drvn alng aftr a m, btn 2 fs out.* .... (100 to 30 op 5 to 2 tchd 7 to 2) 4
Dist: 1½l, 12l, 3½l. 2m 44.60s. a 11.60s (4 Ran).
SR: 3/ (Mrs Sue Fletcher), R F Fisher

1260 Courvoisier Cognac Classic Handicap Class D (0-80 3-y-o and up) £3,590 1m

3f 16yds. . . . . (2:50)

1190[2] PERSUASIVE [57] 6-9-3 Dale Gibson (5) *patiently rdn, quickened ahead o'r 2 fs out, idled in frnt, drvn out fnl furlong*. . . . . (9 to 4 fav op 2 to 1 tchd 5 to 2) 1

1075[3] BOROCAY [38] 5-7-12 L Charnock (3) *trkd ldg half dozen, improved o'r 2 fs out, swtchd ins fnl furlong, one pace*. . . . . (12 to 1 op 10 to 1) 2

988 FAIR FLYER (Ire) [57] 4-9-3 R P Elliott (9) *wtd wth, chsd alng to take clr order o'r 2 fs out, styd on finish*. . . . . (8 to 1 tchd 9 to 1 and 10 to 1) 3

1190 TANODA [45] 7-8-5 K Darley (1) *nvr far away, rdn 3 fs out, styd on one pace fnl 2 furlongs*. . . . (20 to 1 op 16 to 1) 4

894[2] PHILGUN [63] 4-9-6 (3*) S Maloney (2) *in tch, dashed up on outsd hfwy, rdn alng o'r 2 fs out, no extr*. . . . . (7 to 1 op 6 to 1) 5

845[3] SOVEREIGN PAGE (USA) [64] 4-9-10 B Raymond (8) *made most till hdd o'r 2 fs out, fdd und pres fnl furlong*. (5 to 2 op 9 to 4 tchd 11 to 4) 6

885[5] VENTURE FOURTH [42] 4-8-2 J Fanning (4) *nvr far away, rdn o'r 2 fs out, fdd*. . . . . (12 to 1 tchd 14 to 1) 7

885[7] PERSONAL HAZARD [64] (v) 4-9-10 M Birch (7) *tucked away on ins, feeling pace o'r 2 fs out, sn rdn and btn*. . . . . (14 to 1 op 10 to 1) 8

885[9] STRAW THATCH [54] 4-9-0 S Webster (6) *dsptd early ld, styd hndy till fdd und pres o'r 2 fs out*. . . . . (50 to 1 op 20 to 1) 9

Dist: 2l, 3½l, hd, 2l, 1l, 3½l, ¾l, 5l. 2m 27.30s. a 7.30s (9 Ran).
SR: 41/18/30/17/31/30/1/21/1/ (W G McHarg), Miss L A Perratt

1261 Auchingramot Claiming Stakes Class F (3-y-o and up) £2,399 1m 1f 36yds . . . . (3:20)

1166[2] AEGAEN LADY 4-9-1 J Carroll (4) *patiently rdn, shaken up to cruise ahead jst o'r one furlong out, quickened*. . . . . (3 to 1 tchd 7 to 2 and 4 to 1) 1

1110[7] NO SUBMISSION (USA) 7-9-10 S Wood (3) *set steady pace for 3 fs, styd hndy and pushed alng, rallied fnl furlong, kpt on*. . . . . (7 to 4 fav op 5 to 4) 2

1062[5] TAKE YOUR PARTNER (Ire) 3-7-11 J Fanning (1) *nvr far away, rdn o'r one furlong out, styd on towards finish*. . . . . (6 to 1 tchd 7 to 1) 3

MARIAN EVANS 6-8-9 A Mackay (2) *trkd ldrs, led and quickened pace aftr 3 fs, hdd appr fnl furlong, no extr*. . . . . (66 to 1 op 33 to 1) 4

38 BALLYMONEYBOY 4-9-2 P Robinson (5) *refused to come out of stalls, took no part*. . . . . (2 to 1 tchd 6 to 4 and 9 to 4) 5

Dist: 3l, 2½l, ½l. 2m 9.90s. a 15.90s (5 Ran).
(Ron Watkins), J Etherington

1262 Whirlies Selling Stakes Class G (3-y-o) £2,364 1m 65yds. . . . . (3:50)

1175* GUV'NORS GIFT 8-11 P Robinson (5) *settled gng wl, impeded and lost grnd o'r 2 out, sn plenty to do, ran on well to ld last 50 yards*. . . . . (8 to 1 on op 6 to 1 on tchd 9 to 2 on) 1

711[3] VILAMAR (Ire) 8-6 K Fallon (2) *trkd ldg trio, quickened ahead o'r 2 fs out, 3 ls clr ins last, ct last 50 yards*. . . . . (10 to 1 op 7 to 1) 2

1074 NIGHTMARE LADY 7-13 (7*) C Hawksley (1) *led early, styd upsides till led briefly o'r 2 fs out, sn rdn and one pace*. . . . . (25 to 1 op 16 to 1) 3

1090 DICKINS (bl) 8-11 K Darley (3) *sn led, hdd and hrd rdn o'r 2 fs out, wknd rpdly*. . . . . (12 to 1 op 10 to 1) 4

Dist: 1½l, 5l, 15l. 1m 51.50s. a 7.50s (4 Ran).
(The Tompkins Team), M H Tompkins

1263 Whitemoss Auction Maiden Stakes Class F (2-y-o) £2,623 6f 5yds. . . (4:20)

908[7] PETE AFRIQUE (Ire) 9-0 K Darley (4) *made all, quickened to go clr last 2 fs, not extended*. . . . . . . (7 to 2 op 9 to 4) 1

743[2] MONKEY'S WEDDING 9-0 J Carroll (6) *nvr far away, rdn 2 fs out, styd on grimly ins last, not rch wnr*. . . . . (10 to 1 op 7 to 1) 2

JOE JAGGER (Ire) 9-0 Dean McKeown (7) *broke wl, outpcd and hmpd hfwy, swtchd outsd last 2 fs, styd on well*. . . . . (10 to 1 op 7 to 1) 3

933[2] SWEETINGS PISCES 9-0 M Birch (9) *broke wl to show gd speed for o'r 4 fs, no extr*. . . . . (7 to 4 fav op 2 to 1 tchd 9 to 4) 4

776 BURES (Ire) 9-0 P Robinson (3) *rcd wide, effrt and drvn alng hfwy, outpcd last 2 fs*. . . . . (8 to 1 op 6 to 1) 5

933[7] PORTITE SOPHIE 8-9 M Wigham (8) *pressed ldrs, rdn o'r 2 fs out, fdd*. . . . . (25 to 1 op 12 to 1) 6

LADY-BO-K 8-9 N Day (2) *rcd wide, effrt hfwy, fdd und pres o'r one furlong out*. . . . . (7 to 2 op 7 to 4) 7

CHARLYMOON 8-2 (7*) C Hawksley (5) *missed break, nvr able to reco'r*. . . . . (25 to 1 op 16 to 1) 8

506[3] JUST BILL (bl) 9-0 K Fallon (1) *missed break, crossed o'r to join far side bunch aftr 2 fs, wknd quickly two furlongs out*. . . . . (10 to 1 op 8 to 1) 9

Dist: 6l, ½l, 2½l, 3l, 2½l, 4l, 3l, 2½l. 1m 13.40s. a 2.70s (9 Ran).
SR: 34/10/8/-/-/-/ (P D Savill), M W Easterby

1264 C.R.G.P. - Robertson Sprint Handicap Class E (0-70 3-y-o and up) £2,898 6f 5yds. . . . . (4:50)

1167[4] ARABAT [56] 6-9-4 K Fallon (2) *chsd alng to keep up, improved o'r one furlong out, kpt on wl to ld well ins last*. . . . . (5 to 1 op 7 to 2) 1

742[5] MISS WHITTINGHAM (Ire) [54] 3-8-6 J Carroll (5) *nvr far away, led 2 fs out till rdn and hdd wl ins fnl furlong*. . . . . (7 to 1 op 6 to 1) 2

1081 FLASHY'S SON [66] 5-9-7 (7*) C Adamson (3) *gd speed centre thrght, rdn and one pace ins fnl furlong*. . . . . (14 to 1 op 8 to 1) 3

1167* FRANCIS ANN [56] 5-8-11 (7*,5ex) R Havlin (4) *trkd ldg quartet, effrt and drvn alng last 2 fs, not pace to chal*. . . . . (9 to 4 fav op 2 to 1 tchd 5 to 2) 4

SILVER STONE BOY [32] 5-7-8 S Wood (8) *broke fst to ld for 4 fs, fdd und pres*. . . . . (8 to 1 tchd 10 to 1) 5

1103[5] MISS HOSTESS [34] (bl) 6-7-10[3] A Mackay (6) *sluggish strt, drvn alng to keep up, nvr a factor*. (14 to 1 op 12 to 1) 6

1095[9] CREAGMHOR [60] 3-8-12 R P Elliott (7) *chsd alng to show speed for o'r 3 fs, fdd*. . . . . (20 to 1 op 14 to 1) 7

1144[8] THE CAN CAN MAN [61] (bl) 6-9-9 Dean McKeown (1) *fst away, veered badly lft and lost pos hfwy, sn btn*. . . . . (3 to 1 tchd 7 to 2) 8

Dist: 2½l, 4l, 1l, ¾l, 5l, 2½l, 1½l. 1m 13.30s. a 2.60s (8 Ran).
SR: 40/18/24/10/-/ (Mrs H Wane), Martyn Wane

NEWBURY (good to soft)
Wednesday May 26th

Going Correction: PLUS 0.10 sec. per fur. (races 1,3), PLUS 0.50 (2,4,5,6)

1265 Boxford Maiden Stakes Class D (2-y-o) £3,699 5f 34yds. . . . . (6:20)

GOVERNOR GEORGE (USA) 9-0 L Piggott (14) *sn in tch, swtchd rght and hdwy o'r one furlong out, quickened smartly to ld wl ins last, easily*. . . . . (5 to 1 op 4 to 1 tchd 11 to 2) 1

CRAGGANMORE 9-0 M Hills (20) *chsd ldrs, led one and a half fs out, hdd wl ins last, kpt on*. (20 to 1 op 12 to 1) 2

1063[4] DOLLAR GAMBLE (Ire) 9-0 B Raymond (5) *pressed ldrs, ev ch frm 2 fs out till outpcd fnl furlong*. . . . . (11 to 2 op 3 to 1 tchd 6 to 1) 3

RAMANI (USA) 9-0 W R Swinburn (13) *trkd ldrs, led ins fnl 2 fs, sn hdd, one pace final furlong*. . . . . (11 to 1 op 8 to 1 tchd 12 to 1) 4

1032 MOCKINGBIRD 8-6 (3*) D Harrison (1) *chsd ldrs far side, styd on fnl furlong*. . . . . (9 to 1 op 12 to 1 tchd 8 to 1) 5

JEYPORE JO 9-0 J Reid (9) *mid-div, hdwy 2 fs out, kpt on fnl furlong*. . . . . (16 to 1 op 12 to 1) 6

ARKADY (Ire) 9-0 T Quinn (18) *chsd ldrs till wknd fnl furlong*. . . . . (20 to 1 op 10 to 1) 7

949[2] GRANMAS DELIGHT 8-9 G Duffield (8) *led till hdd ins fnl 2 fs, sn wknd*. . . . . (12 to 1 op 14 to 1 tchd 20 to 1) 8

HEATHCLIFF (Ire) 9-0 A Munro (15) *beh, pushed alng 2 fs out, ran on ins last*. . . . (11 to 1 op 6 to 1 tchd 12 to 1) 9

979 FOLLY FINNESSE 8-9 S Whitworth (12) *chsd ldrs 3 fs*. . . . . (33 to 1) 10

CHEF D'ETAT (USA) 9-0 D Holland (4) *chsd ldrs till wknd o'r one furlong out*. . . . . (9 to 2 fav op 4 to 1 tchd 5 to 1 and 7 to 2) 11

ROYALE FIGURINE (Ire) 8-9 N Adams (19) *dwlt, outpcd*. . . . . (33 to 1 op 20 to 1) 12

ROBERO 9-0 J Williams (10) *al outpcd*. . . . . (25 to 1 op 20 to 1 tchd 33 to 1) 13

1119 THORNY BISHOP 9-0 S Dawson (11) *outpcd*. . . . . (33 to 1 op 25 to 1) 14

738[9] CARLTON CROWN (USA) 8-9 D Biggs (2) *prmnt to hfwy*. . . . . (33 to 1) 15

QUEEN'S ADMIRAL 9-0 Pat Eddery (7) *outpcd*. . . . . (16 to 1 op 12 to 1 tchd 20 to 1) 16

AIR RAID (bl) 9-0 T Sprake (16) *al outpcd*. . . . . (33 to 1 op 25 to 1) 17

Dist: 1½l, 3½l, hd, 2½l, 1½l, nk, ½l, 1l, nk, ½l. 1m 3.72s. a 3.42s (17 Ran).

SR: 42/36/22/21/6/5/4/-/-/ (Lucayan Stud), R Hannon

1266 Basingstoke Claiming Stakes Class E (3-y-o) £2,976 1½m 5yds. . . . . . . (6:50)

826[6] SUPREME MASTER 8-12 Pat Eddery (5) *beh, drvn and hdwy frm 3 fs out, led one and a half furlongs out, ran on*. . . . . (4 to 1 jt-fav tchd 9 to 2 and 7 to 2) 1

826* MR GENEAOLOGY (USA) (h,bl) 8-11 W Newnes (6) *beh, hdwy o'r 2 fs out, crrd head high but ran on ins last, not rch wnr*. . . . . . . (4 to 1 jt-fav op 3 to 1 tchd 9 to 2) 2

980[8] FLAMING MIRACLE (Ire) (bl) 8-13 T Quinn (4) *beh till hdwy on rls 4 fs out, chlgd o'r 2 furlongs out, not quicken appr fnl furlong*. . . . . (12 to 1 op 10 to 1) 3

GALACTIC FURY 8-7[1] M Tebbutt (2) *in tch, rdn 3 fs out, styd on ag'n appr fnl furlong*. . . . (20 to 1 tchd 25 to 1) 4

1126* LUNAR RISK 8-7 A Munro (13) *chsd ldrs till led 3 and a half fs out, hdd one and a half furlongs out, sn wknd.* ....(9 to 1 op 8 to 1 tchd 10 to 1) 5
992 SUMMER WIND (Ire) 8-6 J Williams (14) *hdwy 4 fs out, wknd 2 furlongs out*...............(12 to 1 op 10 to 1) 6
1126[2] SPARKY'S SONG 8-2 R Hills (3) *in tch till wknd o'r 2 fs out*.....................(10 to 1 op 7 to 1 tchd 12 to 1) 7
976[9] EARLY TO RISE 9-2 D Biggs (1) *chsd ldrs, rdn 3 fs out, sn wknd*..............................(16 to 1 op 14 to 1) 8
976[7] MANON LESCAUT 7-11 (7*) D Wright (8) *mid-div, rdn 5 fs out, wknd 4 furlongs out.* ....(8 to 1 op 7 to 1 tchd 10 to 1) 9
KENNINGTON PROTON 8-1 A McGlone (12) *led till hdd 3 and a half fs out, sn btn*......................(33 to 1) 10
966 COSMIC STAR 8-11 W Woods (9) *chsd ldrs, rdn 3 fs out, sn wknd*..............................(7 to 1 op 3 to 1) 11
976 BANG ON TIME 8-5 N Adams (11) *chsd ldrs 9 fs.* ....(33 to 1 op 20 to 1) 12
STRAIGHT APPROACH (USA) 8-7 M Hills (10) *slwly into strd, al beh*......................(20 to 1 op 16 to 1) 13
1074[6] OLIVIA VAL 8-0 G Bardwell (7) *al beh.* (33 to 1 op 16 to 1) 14

Dist: 1l, 2l, 3½l, hd, 10l, ¾l, 1½l, 1l, 12l, 2½l. 2m 41.85s. a 12.25s (14 Ran).

SR: 36/33/31/18/17/-/-/1/-/ (Harry W Hopgood), R Hannon

1267 Castrol Handicap Class D (0-80 3-y-o and up) £4,659 6f 8yds..........(7:20)

1209[4] DOMICKSKY [61] 5-8-11 W Carson (6) *gd hdwy o'r 2 fs out, led one and a half furlongs out, rdn and styd on wl.* ....(10 to 1 tchd 12 to 1) 1
948* FACE NORTH (Ire) [64] 5-9-0 T Quinn (11) *in tch, rdn frm 2 fs out, ran on ins last.* ....(9 to 2 fav op 5 to 1 tchd 6 to 1) 2
1069 LOUISVILLE BELLE (Ire) [61] 4-8-8 (3*) D Harrison (8) *prmnt, ev ch appr fnl furlong, not quicken.* ....(25 to 1 tchd 33 to 1) 3
917 ACARA (Ire) [50] 4-8-0 J Quinn (12) *led till hdd one and a half fs out, still ev ch one furlong out, no extr.* ....(33 to 1 tchd 66 to 1) 4
1096[3] BLUE TOPAZE [68] 5-9-4 L Piggott (7) *hdwy ins fnl 2 fs, no imprsn final furlong*............(10 to 1 tchd 12 to 1) 5
1209[2] GREY CHARMER (Ire) [56] 4-8-6 W Newnes (2) *dwlt, hdwy ins fnl 2 fs, not quicken final furlong.* ....(9 to 1 op 8 to 1 tchd 10 to 1) 6
1059[4] QUICK STEEL [53] 5-8-3 Paul Eddery (13) *drvn alng in mid-div hfwy, not pace to chal*......(12 to 1 tchd 14 to 1) 7
1066[4] JIGSAW BOY [74] 4-9-10 J Williams (5) *beh, hdwy 3 fs out, one pace fnl 2 furlongs.* (11 to 2 op 5 to 1 tchd 6 to 1) 8
1096* TRUTHFUL IMAGE [73] (bl) 4-9-9 (6ex) D Biggs (4) *chsd ldrs, ev ch o'r one furlong out, sn wknd.* ....(9 to 1 op 5 to 1 tchd 10 to 1) 9
1066[8] LOVE LEGEND [70] (v) 8-9-6 A Munro (19) *chsd ldrs stands side 4 fs*.............(16 to 1 op 14 to 1 tchd 20 to 1) 10
1066[5] HOW'S YER FATHER [78] 7-10-0 M Hills (9) *beh, effrt o'r 2 fs out, sn wknd*.......................(14 to 1 op 10 to 1) 11
990 MAC'S FIGHTER [75] 8-9-4 (7*) B Russell (18) *al outpcd.* ....(33 to 1) 12
1059 SPRING HIGH [59] (bl) 6-8-9 G Bardwell (15) *pressed ldrs 4 fs*... (25 to 1) 13+
636[7] SPECTACLE JIM [44] 4-7-8 N Adams (3) *prmnt, ev ch o'r one furlong out, wknd quickly*............(100 to 1) 13+
796 GOODY FOUR SHOES [54] 5-8-4 G Duffield (17) *in tch to hfwy*............................ (14 to 1 op 12 to 1) 15
1066 DARUSSALAM [72] 6-9-8 Pat Eddery (10) *effrt hfwy, wknd 2 fs out*............................ (12 to 1 op 10 to 1) 16
1066 SEA-DEER [65] 4-9-1 J Reid (1) *beh whn hmpd 3 fs out, not reco'r*.. (33 to 1) 17
591[9] LUCEDEO [72] 9-9-8 W R Swinburn (16) *slwly into strd, al outpcd*...............(25 to 1 op 20 to 1 tchd 33 to 1) 18

Dist: 1l, nk, ½l, ½l, nk, ½l, ¾l, 1½l, 1l, ¾l. 1m 14.86s. a 3.16s (18 Ran).

SR: 46/45/41/28/44/31/26/44/37/ (M J Watson), M R Channon

1268 Kenneth Robertson Handicap Class D (0-80 3-y-o and up) £3,699 1m 5f 61yds ....(7:50)

994 WESTERN DYNASTY [61] 7-8-4 (7*) P McCabe (6) *chsd ldrs, led 4 fs out, came clr fnl 2 furlongs.* (20 to 1 op 14 to 1) 1
DARE TO DREAM (Ire) [61] 4-8-11 T Quinn (1) *sn tracking ldrs, chsd wnr fnl 2 fs, no imprsn*...........(11 to 2 jt-fav op 7 to 1 tchd 6 to 1) 2
739* BROUGHTON'S TANGO (Ire) [59] 4-8-2 (7*) D McCabe (19) *hdwy frm 4 fs out, styd on from o'r one furlong out.* ....(13 to 2 op 6 to 1 tchd 7 to 1) 3
739[7] PROSEQUENDO (USA) [65] 6-9-1 A Clark (2) *hdwy on rls 5 fs out, chlgd 4 furlongs out, one pace fnl 3 furlongs.* ....(20 to 1 tchd 25 to 1) 4
1064 CHAMBROS [57] 6-8-7 G Duffield (7) *chsd ldrs, rdn and one pace fnl 3 fs*.......(7 to 1 op 5 to 1 tchd 15 to 2) 5
1173[3] STATE OF AFFAIRS [47] 6-7-11 S Dawson (8) *pld hrd early, hdwy 3 fs out, one pace frm o'r 2 furlongs out.* ....(9 to 1 op 8 to 1 tchd 10 to 1) 6
822* LONG SILENCE (USA) [77] 4-9-13 Paul Eddery (16) *beh, hdwy o'r 3 fs out, wknd 2 furlongs out.* ....(7 to 1 op 6 to 1 tchd 8 to 1) 7
894[8] WASSL THIS THEN (Ire) [64] 4-9-0 R Price (9) *mid-div, rdn 3 fs out, wknd o'r 2 furlongs out.* ....(20 to 1 op 12 to 1 tchd 25 to 1) 8
822[5] MATCHING GREEN [63] 4-8-13 J Williams (5) *al beh.* .... (14 to 1 op 12 to 1) 9
994[6] ACROBATE (USA) [64] 4-9-0 W Carson (20) *nvr rch ldrs.* ....(11 to 2 jt-fav op 6 to 1 tchd 8 to 1) 10
1028[7] JIMLIL [71] 5-9-2 (5*) Stephen Davies (17) *chsd ldrs 9 fs.* ....(20 to 1) 11
994[8] EASTERN MAGIC [44] 5-7-8[1] J Quinn (15) *in tch 9 fs.* ....(20 to 1) 12
994 HEAVYWEIGHT (Ire) [46] 4-7-10[1] A Tucker (12) *led till hdd 4 fs out, wknd quickly*.........................(66 to 1) 13
1028 BITTER ALOE [66] 4-9-2 B Raymond (21) *al beh.* .... (20 to 1 op 16 to 1) 14
792 TALOS (Ire) [75] 5-9-11 D Holland (10) *slwly into strd, nvr better than mid-div*.............. (20 to 1 op 14 to 1) 15
1120 BRESIL (USA) [65] 4-9-1 S Whitworth (4) *al beh*... (33 to 1) 16
757[5] EL DOMINIO [43] 5-7-7 G Bardwell (14) *al beh*.... (33 to 1) 17
FATACK [60] 4-8-10 R Perham (13) *chsd ldrs 9 fs.* (66 to 1) 18
840[3] LIGHT-HEARTED LADY [54] 5-7-13[2] (7*) S Drowne (3) *al beh, wnt lme 2 fs out, pld up and dismounted.* ....(16 to 1 op 14 to 1 tchd 20 to 1) pu

Dist: 5l, ½l, nk, sht-hd, 2l, 6l, nk, 2l, 12l, 2½l. 2m 57.54s. a 11.34s (19 Ran).

SR: 49/39/36/41/32/18/36/22/17/ (M F Kentish), M J Ryan

1269 Hermitage Conditions Stakes Class C (4-y-o and up) £4,396 1¼m 6yds (8:20)

525 YOUNG SENOR (USA) 4-8-13 M Hills (6) *trkd ldr, led ins fnl 2 fs, quickened smartly, easily.* (10 to 1 op 8 to 1) 1
774[6] ANNE BONNY 4-8-8 W R Swinburn (9) *trkd ldrs, ev ch 2 fs out, rdn and kpt on fnl furlong, not pace of wnr.* ....(5 to 1 op 6 to 1) 2
1021[3] MESLEH 6-9-0 Pat Eddery (5) *hdwy 3 fs out, chsd ldrs 2 furlongs out, styd on one pace.* ....(9 to 4 fav tchd 2 to 1 and 5 to 2) 3
OH SO RISKY 6-8-10 J Williams (8) *beh, shaken up and hdwy frm 2 fs out, fnshd wl.* ....(14 to 1 op 16 to 1 tchd 20 to 1) 4
525[3] LORD OF THE FIELD 6-8-10 G Duffield (3) *beh, drvn alng o'r 3 fs out, no response*............ (7 to 2 op 9 to 4) 5
596 HALF A TICK (USA) 5-9-6 T Quinn (1) *beh, effrt o'r 3 fs out, wknd 2 furlongs out*....(7 to 1 op 6 to 1 tchd 15 to 2) 6
1177 TURRET GATES 4-8-10 J Quinn (4) *led till hdd and wknd ins fnl 2 fs*..................................(66 to 1) 7
1021 TURGENEV (Ire) 4-9-4 D Holland (2) *beh, hdwy o'r 3 fs out, wknd 2 and a half furlongs out.* ....(10 to 1 op 8 to 1 tchd 12 to 1) 8
BANDMASTER (USA) 4-8-10 B Raymond (7) *chsd ldrs till wknd frm 3 fs out*................. (33 to 1 op 25 to 1) 9

Dist: 2½l, 1l, hd, 2l, 8l, 3l, 4l, 8l. 2m 13.47s. a 10.47s (9 Ran).

SR: 44/34/38/33/29/23/7/7/-/ (Mollers Racing), G Wragg

1270 Burmah Handicap Class C (0-90 4-y-o and up) £6,056 7f 64yds.........(8:50)

MOROCCO (Ire) [74] 4-9-7 Paul Eddery (12) *hld up, hdwy 3 fs out, chlgd o'r one furlong out, led cl hme.* ....(12 to 1 op 10 to 1) 1
1144* CHEVEUX MITCHELL [72] (v) 6-9-5 (6ex) Pat Eddery (7) *led, rdn o'r one furlong out, ct cl hme*...........(5 to 1 jt-fav op 4 to 1 tchd 11 to 2) 2
LORD ALFIE [46] 4-7-7 J Quinn (13) *in tch, chlgd frm o'r one furlong out till no extr cl hme*....................(66 to 1) 3
475 QUEEN OF SHANNON (Ire) [70] 5-9-3 M Tebbutt (10) *hld up, hdwy o'r one furlong out, kpt on wl nr finish.* .... (25 to 1 op 20 to 1) 4
315 MERLINS WISH (USA) [76] 4-9-9 A McGlone (5) *hdwy o'r 2 fs out, styd on same pace fnl furlong.* ....(10 to 1 tchd 12 to 1) 5
TAKENHALL [66] 8-8-10 (3*) D Harrison (15) *chsd ldrs, rdn 3 fs out, not pace to chal*......... (10 to 1 tchd 12 to 1) 6
1066 PHARAOH'S DANCER [70] 6-9-3 W Newnes (9) *slwly into strd, nvr gng pace of ldrs*.........(16 to 1 op 20 to 1) 7
1069[7] LITTLE ROUSILLON [67] 5-9-0 A Munro (11) *sn chasing ldrs, rdn o'r 2 fs out, soon btn.* .... (6 to 1 op 9 to 2 tchd 13 to 2) 8
1069 CLAYBANK (USA) [81] 4-10-0 D Holland (1) *chsd ldrs, ev ch 2 fs out, sn btn*......(16 to 1 op 10 to 1 tchd 20 to 1) 9
885[3] NEITHER NOR [63] 4-8-10 G Duffield (4) *beh most of way.* .... (12 to 1 op 10 to 1) 10
737[6] MILLSOLIN (Ire) [80] 5-9-13 T Quinn (8) *chsd ldrs, wknd 2 fs out, eased whn btn fnl furlong.* (5 to 1 jt-fav op 4 to 1) 11
513 CONISTON WATER (USA) [80] 4-9-13 W Carson (6) *sn tracking ldrs, rdn and effrt 3 fs out, wknd o'r 2 furlongs out.* ....(8 to 1 tchd 12 to 1) 12
1069[9] MOUGINS (Ire) [78] 4-9-11 J Williams (3) *whipped round and uns rdr strt*..............(14 to 1 op 20 to 1) ur

Dist: Sht-hd, sht-hd, ½l, 4l, ¾l, ½l, nk, sht-hd, sht-hd, 1l. 1m 34.74s. a 7.44s (13 Ran).

SR: 50/47/20/42/36/24/26/22/35/ (Martin Myers), R Charlton

RIPON (good)
Wednesday May 26th

Going Correction: NIL (races 1,4,5,6), PLUS 0.10 (2,3)

1271 Ripon Cathedral Trust Appeal Claiming Stakes Class F (3-y-o) £2,905 1m .... (6:45)

1102[3] ANUSHA 8-6 J Fortune (1) *al prmnt, hdwy to ld 2 and a half fs out, sn quickened clr, eased nr finish.* .... (2 to 1 fav tchd 9 to 4) 1

1111[9] AMERIGUE 8-0 J Lowe (3) *hld up, hdwy 3 fs out, effrt to chase wnr one and a half out, sn rdn and one paced.* .... (7 to 2 tchd 4 to 1) 2

906 MOST SIOUXTABLE 8-6 J Fanning (6) *mid-div, hdwy 3 fs out, rdn and styd on appr last....* (20 to 1 op 16 to 1) 3

963[5] WALID'S PRINCESS (Ire) 7-13 (3*) S Maloney (7) *hld up and beh, hdwy 4 fs out, styd on fnl 2, not rch ldrs.* .... (11 to 1 op 10 to 1 tchd 12 to 1) 4

921[7] CLANDESTINE AFFAIR (Ire) 8-2 W Ryan (4) *hld up, effrt and hdwy on outer 3 fs out, rdn 2 out, one paced.* .... (17 to 2 op 6 to 1 tchd 9 to 1) 5

1178[8] BRAXTON BRAGG (Ire) 8-7 M Birch (8) *cl up, rdn 3 fs out, grad wknd....* .... (50 to 1) 6

1150[4] MR ABBOT 8-7 K Darley (12) *beh, styd on fnl 2 fs, nvr dngrs....* .... (12 to 1 tchd 14 to 1) 7

1109[6] JAMANE 9-7 G Hind (2) *sn outpcd and beh, styd on appr fnl furlong....* .... (50 to 1) 8

GLIMPSE OF HEAVEN 8-6 A Culhane (9) *cl up, led 4 fs out till 2 and a half out, sn wknd........* (9 to 1 op 8 to 1) 9

888[4] WEAVER GEORGE (Ire) (bl) 7-13 Dale Gibson (10) *led, hdd 4 fs out, grad wknd....* .... (16 to 1 op 12 to 1) 10

928 MAASTRICHT 7-12 (7*) G Milligan (5) *prmnt, ev ch 3 fs out, sn rdn and btn....* .... (7 to 1 op 6 to 1) 11

HARLOSH 8-0 (7*) V Halliday (11) *al rear.* .... (25 to 1 op 20 to 1) 12

Dist: 2½l, sht-hd, 5l, 2l, 1l, 5l, nk, 1l, ¾l, 3l. 1m 42.60s. a 4.30s (12 Ran).
SR: 28/14/19/-/-/-/ (Yahya Nasib), J Berry

1272 Lishman, Sidwell, Campbell And Price Maiden Stakes Class D (2-y-o) £3,205 5f............ (7:10)

979[3] YA MALAK 9-0 R Cochrane (9) *cl up, led on bit hfwy, sn clr, easily....* .... (11 to 8 on op Evens) 1

FAST EDDY 9-0 L Dettori (6) *al prmnt, chsd wnr fnl 2 fs, no impresison....* .... (3 to 1 op 7 to 4) 2

1082[6] KAYDARAJ 8-9 M Birch (11) *chsd ldrs, rdn 2 fs out, kpt on ins last....* .... (12 to 1 op 10 to 1) 3

MOSAIC GOLD 9-0 N Connorton (13) *beh, hdwy 2 fs out, styd on ins last....* .... (7 to 1) 4

DOCKYARD DORA 8-9 M Wigham (3) *chsd ldrs, rdn and one pace fnl 2 fs....* .... (33 to 1) 5

804 CHILIOLA 8-6 (3*) S Maloney (2) *hdwy hfwy, kpt on appr fnl furlong, improve....* .... (16 to 1 op 14 to 1) 6

506[4] MINNESOTA VIKING 9-0 K Darley (4) *outpcd till styd on fnl 2 fs....* .... (14 to 1 op 12 to 1) 7

HIGHFIELD LAD 9-0 J Fanning (8) *slwly into strd and beh, some late hdwy....* .... (25 to 1) 8

WOODTONG 9-0 S Webster (1) *outpcd and al beh.* .... (33 to 1) 9

DANTE'S RUBICON (Ire) 9-0 L Charnock (12) *chsd ldrs to hfwy, sn wknd....* .... (25 to 1 tchd 33 to 1) 10

804 ARKINDALE SPIRIT (Ire) 9-0 T Lucas (7) *sn outpcd, rdn alng hfwy, al beh....* .... (33 to 1) 11

DAUNTLESS FORT 8-9 J Fortune (5) *cl up 2 fs, sn rdn and wknd....* .... (33 to 1 op 25 to 1) 12

433[9] STEANARD BOY (bl) 9-0 D Nicholls (10) *led to hfwy, sn wknd....* .... (33 to 1) 13

Dist: 3½l, 2l, 1l, 2½l, 1½l, ½l, 2½l, 1l, 1½l, 1l. 1m 1.40s. a 3.40s (13 Ran).
SR: 42/28/15/16/1/-/ (G Jabre), J W Payne

1273 Touche Ross Handicap Stakes Class E (0-70 3-y-o) £2,565 6f......... (7:35)

683[5] FOR THE PRESENT [69] 9-7 K Darley (5) *cl up stands side, led hfwy, hrd rdn fnl furlong, hld on wl.* .... (10 to 1 tchd 11 to 1) 1

1160[4] FORMIDABLE LIZ [44] 7-10 J Lowe (3) *chsd ldrs, effrt and swtchd o'r one furlong out, rdn to dispute ld ins last, kpt on....* .... (12 to 1 op 10 to 1) 2

906[8] PINE RIDGE LAD (Ire) [61] 8-8 (5*) O Pears (8) *chsd ldrs, rdn and outpcd o'r 2 fs out, styd on wl ins last.* .... (14 to 1 tchd 16 to 1) 3

963[2] RUBY COOPER [56] 8-5 (3*) S Maloney (11) *al prmnt, effrt 2 fs out and sn rdn, ev ch entering fnl furlong, no extr nr finish....* .... (8 to 1 op 7 to 1) 4

1137[4] HERSHEBAR [65] (bl) 8-10 (7*) G Strange (10) *mid-div, hdwy and not clr run 2 fs out, swtchd and styd on ins last....* .... (12 to 1 op 10 to 1) 5

4791a[5] RED ADMIRAL [54] 8-6 R Cochrane (9) *chsd ldrs, rdn and one pace appr fnl furlong......* (20 to 1 tchd 16 to 1) 6

1187* COVENT GARDEN GIRL [55] 8-7 (5ex) T Lucas (4) *led to hfwy, cl up till rdn and wknd appr fnl furlong.* .... (2 to 1 fav op 5 to 2) 7

683 CALL ME I'M BLUE (Ire) [63] 9-1 D Nicholls (12) *nvr rch ldrs.* .... (9 to 1 op 8 to 1) 8

BLUE RADIANCE [66] 9-4 J Fanning (1) *chsd ldrs stands side o'r 3 fs....* .... (20 to 1 op 25 to 1) 9

MASTER PECKITT [44] 7-10 F Norton (2) *nvr a factor.* .... (50 to 1) 10

1160[3] NORTH ARDAR [56] 8-8 L Dettori (13) *in tch, effrt and rdn 2 fs out, sn btn....* .... (15 to 2 op 7 to 1) 11

829[5] BECKYHANNAH [42] 7-8[1] Dale Gibson (15) *prmnt to hfwy, sn wknd....* .... (20 to 1 tchd 25 to 1) 12

1081[6] CRAIGIE BOY [61] 8-13 Alex Greaves (6) *al rear...* (16 to 1) 13

829[6] MATTHEW DAVID [42] 7-8[1] L Charnock (7) *al rear.* (33 to 1) 14

974[2] CHICAGO (Ire) [53] 8-5[2] M Birch (14) *prmnt to hfwy, sn rdn and lost pl....* .... (12 to 1) 15

Dist: Hd, 1½l, nk, 1½l, ½l, sht-hd, sht-hd, 2l, sht-hd, 1½l. 1m 14.50s. a 3.90s (15 Ran).
SR: 41/15/26/20/23/10/10/17/12/ (Mrs J Hazell), T D Barron

1274 Amec Civil Engineering Handicap Stakes Class D (0-80 3-y-o and up) £3,850 1m............ (8:05)

885[2] HABETA (USA) [58] (bl) 7-8-6 J Lowe (14) *hld up, gd hdwy 2 fs out, effrt and not clr run o'r one out, swtchd and rdn to ld wl ins last, edgd rght, ran on...* (7 to 1 op 8 to 1) 1

930[7] JAHANGIR (Ire) [69] 4-9-3 W Ryan (3) *beh, gd hdwy 3 fs out, rdn and ev ch entering fnl furlong, no extr nr finish.* .... (12 to 1 tchd 14 to 1) 2

930[4] MCA BELOW THE LINE [58] (v) 5-8-6 S Webster (5) *hld up, gd hdwy o'r 2 fs out, effrt to dispute ld entering fnl furlong, rdn and no extr nr finish.* (11 to 1 op 10 to 1) 3

834 LORD LAMBSON [45] 4-7-7 J Fanning (13) *mid-div, hdwy and not clr run one and a half fs out, swtchd and styd on und pres ins last....* .... (25 to 1) 4

833[3] THE PREMIER EXPRES [65] 3-8-1 K Darley (8) *al prmnt, effrt and hdwy to ld 2 fs out, sn rdn, hdd and wknd entering fnl furlong....* .... (12 to 1 op 10 to 1) 5

1194[6] PUBLIC WAY (Ire) [57] 3-7-7 Dale Gibson (7) *beh, gd hdwy 2 fs out, sn rdn and ran on fnl furlong....* .... (33 to 1) 6

740[3] ACHELOUS [52] 6-7-11 (3*) S Maloney (6) *chsd ldrs, rdn 2 fs out, kpt on one pace.* (12 to 1 op 14 to 1 tchd 10 to 1) 7

1110[4] AMENABLE [80] 8-10-0 Alex Greaves (2) *hld up, steady hdwy 2 fs out, styd on ins last, nvr dngrs.* .... (25 to 1 op 20 to 1) 8

234[3] MAJAL (Ire) [70] 4-9-4 D Nicholls (10) *beh till styd on fnl 2 fs, nvr dngrs....* .... (25 to 1) 9

1138[6] DUNE RIVER [70] 4-9-4 L Dettori (12) *chsd ldrs, rdn o'r 2 fs out, sn wknd....* .... (14 to 1) 10

YFOOL [72] 3-8-8 P Robinson (16) *chsd ldrs till rdn and wknd o'r 2 fs out....* .... (16 to 1 op 12 to 1) 11

1138[3] SELF EXPRESSION [58] 5-8-6 K Fallon (4) *al rear.* .... (10 to 1 op 8 to 1) 12

1138* LADY DONOGHUE (USA) [45] 4-7-2 (5*) Darren Moffatt (1) *slwly into strd and beh, hdwy on outer 3 fs out, rdn 2 out and sn btn, eased fnl furlong.* .... (13 to 8 fav op 7 to 4 tchd 9 to 4) 13

885 ROUTING [55] 5-8-3[3] Dean McKeown (9) *pld hrd, chsd ldrs to ld 5 fs out, hdd and wknd 2 out.* (25 to 1 op 33 to 1) 14

1037* IKHTIRAA (USA) [58] 3-7-8[1] N Carlisle (11) *chsd ldr, rdn o'r 3 fs out, sn wknd....* .... (11 to 2 op 5 to 1) 15

ROYAL DIVA [74] 3-8-5 (5*) O Pears (15) *led, hdd 5 fs out, sn lost pl....* .... (20 to 1 op 16 to 1) 16

Dist: 1l, ½l, ¾l, 2½l, nk, nk, ¾l, ½l, 1l, 1l. 1m 41.50s. a 3.20s (16 Ran).
SR: 44/52/39/24/24/15/21/47/35/ (R D Bickenson), J W Watts

1275 Persimmon Homes Maiden Stakes Class D (3-y-o and up) £3,205 1¼m .... (8:35)

REFUGIO 3-8-9 W Ryan (14) *cl up, led 3 fs out, rdn appr last, ran on wl....* .... (7 to 2 op 3 to 1) 1

428[6] LIKE THE SUN (USA) 3-8-4 Dean McKeown (13) *hld up, gd hdwy o'r 2 fs out, effrt and rdn appr fnl furlong, styd on wl ins last....* .... (11 to 1 op 8 to 1) 2

842[8] CIVIL LAW (Ire) 3-8-9 L Dettori (6) *trkd ldrs, gd hdwy to chase wnr 2 fs out, sn rdn, kpt on one pace ins last.* .... (12 to 1 op 14 to 1) 3

1068 DARMSTADT (USA) 3-8-9 R Cochrane (16) *hld up, steady hdwy 2 fs out, rdn and ran on wl ins last.* .... (12 to 1 op 10 to 1 tchd 14 to 1) 4

965[2] MOUNT FUJI 3-8-9 F Norton (11) *prmnt, ev ch o'r 2 fs out, sn rdn and kpt on one pace.* .... (100 to 30 fav op 5 to 2 tchd 7 to 2) 5

SOUL DREAM (USA) 3-8-4 P Robinson (8) *chsd ldrs, rdn 2 fs out, wknd appr last....* .... (12 to 1) 6

1039 BROCTUNE BAY 4-9-10 K Darley (18) *hld up and beh till styd on fnl 2 fs....* .... (25 to 1) 7

HAYDON BRIDGE (Ire) 3-8-9 M Birch (12) *wl beh till styd on strly fnl 2 fs.........* (16 to 1 op 20 to 1 tchd 10 to 1) 8

ROYAL VACATION 4-9-10 J Fanning (5) *mid-div, hdwy on outer o'r 2 fs out, sn rdn and wknd wl over one out.* .... (33 to 1 op 25 to 1) 9

1004[2] RAFTERS 4-9-10 J Carroll (1) *mid-div, steady hdwy 3 fs out, effrt 2 out, sn rdn and wknd o'r one out.* .... (7 to 2 op 4 to 1) 10

1077[7] RESTRAINT 3-8-4 N Carlisle (17) *led, hdd 3 fs out, sn wknd....* .... (50 to 1 op 33 to 1) 11

FATAL SHOCK 3-8-4 J Lowe (10) *al rear.* .... (14 to 1 tchd 12 to 1) 12

1109[7] KINTAVI 3-8-9 G Hind (15) *beh, hdwy on outer 3 fs out, rdn and wknd wl o'r one out.....* (50 to 1 op 33 to 1) 13

836[9] ANNIVERSAIRE 3-8-9 N Day (2) *in tch, effrt 3 fs out, rdn and wknd wl o'r one out*..........(25 to 1) 14
215[5] HIGH CHAIR 3-8-4 Dale Gibson (7) *al rear*. ....(50 to 1 op 33 to 1) 15
1039[7] ON BROADWAY 3-8-9 J Fortune (9) *slwly into strd and beh, hdwy on outer 3 fs out, rdn and wknd o'r 2 out*. ....(33 to 1) 16
1034 GREY ANCONA (Ire) 4-9-10 M Wood (4) *chsd ldrs, rdn 4 fs out, sn wknd*..........(50 to 1 op 33 to 1) 17

Dist: 2l, nk, 1½l, 2l, 3½l, ¾l, 3l, 1l, ¾l, 2½l. 2m 8.80s. a 4.80s (17 Ran).
SR: 47/38/42/39/35/23/41/20/33/ (Sheikh Mohammed), H R A Cecil

1276 Glenfiddich Pure Malt Whisky Handicap Stakes Class E (0-70 4-y-o and up) £2,565 2m..........(9:05)

478[6] TAROUDANT [67] 6-10-0 K Darley (8) *trkd ldrs, hdwy 3 fs out, chlgd 2 out, sn rdn, put head in air, hrd drvn last, led last strd*..........(3 to 1 op 5 to 2) 1
1075* SHUJAN (USA) [62] 4-9-7 L Dettori (6) *led, rdn 2 fs out, ran on gmely, hdd last strd*. ....(5 to 2 fav op 5 to 2 tchd 3 to 1) 2
382[3] COST EFFECTIVE [33] 6-7-8[1] A Mackay (5) *hld up, hdwy o'r 3 fs out, rdn 2 out, styd on ins last*. ....(10 to 1 op 12 to 1) 3
290 RIMOUSKI [35] 5-7-10 J Lowe (11) *al prmnt, rdn 3 fs out, sn one pace*..........(16 to 1 op 20 to 1) 4
VAIN PRINCE [50] (bl) 6-8-11 L Charnock (4) *hdwy 6 fs out, rdn o'r 2 out, wknd appr last*..........(4 to 1 op 5 to 1) 5
727[9] SELDOM IN [33] 7-7-3 (5*) Darren Moffatt (10) *hld up, hdwy o'r 4 fs out, rdn and plugged on one pace fnl 2*. ....(13 to 2 op 6 to 1) 6
1195[7] REXY BOY [32] 6-7-7 S Wood (7) *prmnt till rdn o'r 4 fs out, sn wknd*..........(33 to 1) 7
1041[5] CREEAGER [56] 11-9-0 (3*) S D Williams (9) *hld up, hdwy 5 fs out, rdn and wknd o'r 2 out*..........(8 to 1 op 7 to 1) 8
910 BARTON PRIDE (Ire) [39] (bl) 4-7-12 J Fanning (3) *cl up till rdn and wknd o'r 3 fs out*..........(25 to 1 op 20 to 1) 9
ANOTHER EARL (USA) [33] 9-7-8[1] Dale Gibson (2) *al rear, tld off fnl 4 fs*..........(33 to 1) 10

Dist: Sht-hd, 2l, 4l, 1½l, nk, 8l, hd. 3m 31.50s. a 6.50s (10 Ran).
SR: 49/41/12/10/23/5/-/19/-/ (G A Farndon), Mrs M Reveley

BRIGHTON (firm)
Thursday May 27th
Going Correction: MINUS 0.45 sec. per fur.

1277 Freshfield Median Auction Maiden Stakes Class E (Div I) (2-y-o) £2,898 5f 213yds..........(2:00)

1020[3] CLASSIC SKY (Ire) 9-0 W R Swinburn (2) *tucked in hndy, hdwy to ld jst o'r one furlong out, drvn out to hold on*. ....(15 to 8 on op 11 to 10 on) 1
657[6] NAKITA 8-2 (7*) G Forster (5) *wth ldr, led o'r 2 fs out, hdd jst over one out, ran on wl*..........(14 to 1 op 6 to 1) 2
998[4] ALCOVE 9-0 L Piggott (3) *led till hdd o'r 2 fs out, still green and kpt on one pace*..........(9 to 4 op 5 to 4) 3
804[8] DEMI-PLIE 9-0 L Dettori (4) *chsd ldrs till rdn and no hdwy fnl 2 and a half fs*....(40 to 1 op 12 to 1 tchd 50 to 1) 4
TEXANNE (Bel) 8-9 I Ferguson (1) *missed break, last but in tch till rdn and no imprsn frm o'r 2 fs out*. ....(100 to 1 op 33 to 1) 5

Dist: Nk, 7l, 2l, 1l. 1m 10.40s. a 2.00s (5 Ran).
SR: 6/-/ (Saeed Suhail), B Hanbury

1278 Shoreham Maiden Stakes Class D (3-y-o) £3,435 6f 209yds..........(2:30)

SUNTARA (Ire) 8-9 M Roberts (3) *midfield, niggled alng hfwy, ran on to ld one furlong out, hld on wl*. ....(7 to 2 op 3 to 1 tchd 4 to 1) 1
1027[5] PRINCESS HAYLEY 8-9 W R Swinburn (8) *trkd ldrs, led o'r 2 fs out till hdd one out, battled on wl*. ....(3 to 1 op 7 to 2 tchd 9 to 2) 2
1171[3] GOLDEN GUEST 8-9 L Piggott (1) *al hndy, effrt and not much room o'r 2 fs out, ran on one pace und pres*. ....(11 to 8 fav op 5 to 4 on) 3
DOMULLA 9-0 T Quinn (4) *patiently rdn, hdwy o'r 2 fs out, kpt on*..........(10 to 1 op 5 to 1 tchd 12 to 1) 4
SENOR L'AMOUR 9-0 J Williams (5) *wl beh till ran on fnl one and a half fs, not rch ldrs*.....(50 to 1 op 33 to 1) 5
1060 LITTLE MISS RIBOT 8-9 L Dettori (7) *in tch on outsd, rdn hfwy, sn btn*..........(50 to 1 op 33 to 1) 6
992 DUSTY'S DARLING 8-9 P Robinson (9) *led till hdd o'r 2 fs out, wknd*..........(25 to 1 op 20 to 1 tchd 33 to 1) 7
1007[8] MAGIC FAN (Ire) (bl) 9-0 N Adams (6) *wth ldr, rdn and edgd lft o'r 2 fs out, sn wknd*..........(50 to 1 op 20 to 1) 8
921 SUEENA 8-2 (7*) S Drowne (2) *struggling frm hfwy*. ....(50 to 1 op 33 to 1) 9

Dist: Hd, 2l, 2l, 8l, ½l, 3l, ¾l, 2½l. 1m 22.00s. a 2.00s (9 Ran).
SR: 18/17/11/10/-/-/ (Sheikh Mohammed), B W Hills

1279 Freshfield Median Auction Maiden Stakes Class E (Div II) (2-y-o) £2,872 5f 213yds..........(3:00)

1063[5] CONNECT (Ire) 9-0 B Rouse (6) *made all, pushed clr o'r one furlong out, easily*. (5 to 2 op 9 to 4 tchd 3 to 1) 1
913[8] BENFLEET 9-0 R Hills (4) *wth ldr, rdn wl o'r one furlong out, not pace of wnr*..........(9 to 1 op 4 to 1) 2
1091[3] SUN CHIEF (Ire) 9-0 D Holland (1) *chsd ldrs, niggled alng wl o'r 2 fs out, sn one paced*. ....(5 to 4 fav op 5 to 4 on tchd 11 to 8) 3
913 RICHARD'S ERROR 9-0 Paul Eddery (2) *beh, some hdwy 2 fs out, unbl to chal*..........(33 to 1 op 10 to 1) 4
OLD HOOK (Ire) 9-0 Paul Smith (5) *chsd ldrs, rdn o'r 2 fs out, sn wknd*...... (66 to 1 op 33 to 1 tchd 100 to 1) 5
1009[3] KERRIE-JO (v) 8-9 J Williams (3) *prmnt on outsd, rdn o'r 2 fs out, wknd*........(100 to 30 op 3 to 1 tchd 4 to 1) 6

Dist: 5l, 3l, 3l, 1l, ¾l. 1m 10.50s. a 2.10s (6 Ran).
SR: 4/-/-/ (Mrs J A Hannon), B J Meehan

1280 Flanagan And Allen Handicap Class E (0-70 3-y-o and up) £3,054 7f 214yds..........(3:30)

1007* DEEVEE [45] 4-8-7 C Rutter (9) *trkd ldrs wide, hdwy o'r 2 fs out, led over one out, hrd rdn and jst hld on*. ....(9 to 2 tchd 4 to 1 and 5 to 1) 1
723[8] NORTH ESK (USA) [56] 4-9-4 M Wigham (3) *chsd ldrs, rdn and rapid hdwy o'r one furlong out, str run ins last, jst hld*..........(13 to 2 op 12 to 1 tchd 14 to 1) 2
1097* PROUD BRIGADIER (Ire) [57] 5-9-5 (7ex) Lorna Vincent (4) *slwly away and beh till smooth hdwy on ins 2 fs out, no extr fnl furlong*. (3 to 1 fav op 5 to 2 tchd 100 to 30) 3
978[6] MASTER REACH [50] (bl) 4-8-12 S Whitworth (6) *wth ldr, led hfwy till hdd o'r one furlong out, sn no extr*. ....(16 to 1 op 20 to 1 tchd 14 to 1) 4
1069 HOPEFUL BID (Ire) [66] 4-10-0 A McGlone (1) *wtd wth, rdn o'r 2 fs out, sn one pace*..........(5 to 1 op 4 to 1) 5
918[4] SAAHI (USA) [66] (bl) 4-10-0 Dale Gibson (2) *chsd ldrs till rdn and wknd 2 fs out*..........(16 to 1 op 14 to 1) 6
995[7] MR NEVERMIND (Ire) [64] (bl) 3-9-0 Candy Morris (7) *prmnt on outsd, effrt o'r 2 fs out, rdn and wknd wl over one out*..........(7 to 1 tchd 6 to 1) 7
837[9] HITCHIN A RIDE [44] 6-8-6 R Perham (5) *rdn and drpd last hfwy, sn no imprsn*. (16 to 1 op 14 to 1 tchd 20 to 1) 8
1257[3] NAVARESQUE [45] 8-8-7 T Sprake (8) *led to hfwy, sn rdn alng, wknd wl o'r one furlong out*. ....(4 to 1 op 3 to 1 tchd 9 to 2) 9

Dist: Sht-hd, 5l, ¾l, 2l, 2l, ½l, 2l, 7l. 1m 33.90s. a 1.50s (9 Ran).
SR: 17/27/13/4/14/8/ (D Turner), C J Benstead

1281 Seaford Selling Handicap Stakes Class G (0-60 3-y-o and up) £2,070 1m 3f 196yds..........(4:00)

621[4] RAGTIME SONG [34] 4-8-13 T Quinn (8) *al hndy, dashed into ld o'r 3 fs out, clr appr last, rdn out*. ....(11 to 1 op 8 to 1 tchd 12 to 1) 1
894[4] FANATICAL (USA) [40] 7-9-5 A Munro (7) *chsd ldrs, rdn on outsd frm o'r 2 fs out, kpt on ins last*. ....(5 to 1 tchd 11 to 2) 2
863* PRINCESS EVITA (Fr) [36] 4-8-12 (3*) D Harrison (11) *trkd ldrs, rdn o'r 3 fs out, kpt on one pace fnl 2*. ....(5 to 1 op 7 to 2 tchd 11 to 2) 3
1146[7] NOTED STRAIN (Ire) [49] 5-10-0 D Holland (2) *slwly away, wl beh early, hdwy 4 fs out, ran on appr last, nvr nrr*. ....(11 to 1 op 6 to 1 tchd 12 to 1) 4
332 JARZON DANCER [26] 5-8-5 W Newnes (6) *led till hdd o'r 3 fs out, sn one pace*..........(20 to 1 op 16 to 1) 5
863[8] DOTS DEE [24] 4-8-3 N Adams (9) *midfield, styd on same pace fnl 2 fs, nvr dngrs*..........(33 to 1 op 20 to 1) 6
1007 CHINAMAN [29] (bl) 4-8-8 J Williams (5) *wl beh till ran on fnl 2 fs, nvr nrr*..........(25 to 1 op 16 to 1) 7
719 RED JACK (Ire) [35] 4-9-0 S Whitworth (10) *midfield, rdn o'r 4 fs out, sn no hdwy*..........(20 to 1 op 16 to 1) 8
1064 SINCLAIR LAD (Ire) [49] 5-10-0 W Carson (1) *hld up, pushed alng and some hdwy 4 fs out, btn o'r 2 out*. ....(4 to 1 op 3 to 1 tchd 9 to 2) 9
1191[2] RUBIDIAN [42] 3-8-3 G Duffield (12) *wth ldr, niggled alng o'r 4 fs out, stdly lost pl*..........(11 to 4 fav op 5 to 1) 10
1175 GEORGE ROPER [57] 3-9-4 B Rouse (14) *rear div, some hdwy 2 fs out, nvr a threat*. ....(16 to 1 op 10 to 1 tchd 20 to 1) 11
863 REACH FOR GLORY [44] 4-9-9 Dale Gibson (4) *tucked away on ins, rdn and effrt 4 fs out, stdly wknd*. ....(14 to 1 op 10 to 1) 12
1054[9] BIJOU PRINCESS [16] (v) 5-7-9[1] A Tucker (13) *in tch till lost pl quickly o'r 5 fs out, sn in rear, tld off*. ....(33 to 1 tchd 40 to 1) 13
723 SEASIDE MINSTREL [47] 5-9-7 (5*) C Hodgson (3) *al beh, tld off*..........(25 to 1 op 20 to 1) 14

Dist: 3l, ¾l, ¾l, 7l, 2l, nk, 4l, 7l, sht-hd, 1½l. 2m 31.10s. a 3.60s (14 Ran).
SR: 9/9/3/14/-/-/ (William Alexander), R Akehurst

1282 Clayton Handicap Class E (0-70 3-y-o and up) £2,872 5f 213yds..........(4:30)

882* SAKHAROV [46] 4-8-6 P Robinson (5) *in tch, hdwy 2 fs out, led ins last, ran on strly.* ....(9 to 4 fav op 3 to 1 tchd 7 to 2) 1
1096 FARMER JOCK [51] 11-8-11 M Roberts (4) *beh till gd hdwy o'r 2 fs out, sstnd chal fnl furlong, jst hld.* ....(12 to 1 op 6 to 1 tchd 14 to 1) 2
796 SURE LORD (Ire) [68] 4-10-0 T Quinn (3) *led till hdd and wknd ins fnl furlong.* (12 to 1 op 8 to 1 tchd 14 to 1) 3
721⁹ IRON KING [64] (bl) 7-9-10 W Newnes (1) *slwly away, beh till ran on fnl 2 fs, nvr nrr.* .... (4 to 1 tchd 5 to 1) 4
LORINS GOLD [63] 3-8-13 A McGlone (2) *wth ldr, rdn o'r 2 fs out, sn unbl to quicken.* ....(14 to 1 op 10 to 1 tchd 16 to 1) 5
1209³ PALACEGATE GOLD (Ire) [50] 4-8-10 W Carson (7) *chsd ldrs, rdn alng wl o'r 2 fs out, sn btn.* ....(11 to 4 op 9 to 4 tchd 3 to 1) 6
483⁶ SCORCHER (Ire) [52] 3-7-13 (3*) B Doyle (6) *not look keen, sn rdn alng and al beh.*............(16 to 1 op 10 to 1) 7
1079⁷ YOUNG VALENTINE [53] 4-8-13 A Munro (8) *chsd ldrs on outsd till wknd wl o'r 2 fs out, sn in rear.* ....(14 to 1 op 10 to 1) 8
Dist: Nk, 4l, 1½l, ¾l, 5l, 1l, 2l. 1m 8.90s. a 0.50s (8 Ran).
SR: 28/32/33/23/9/ (J R Good), M A Jarvis

CARLISLE (good)
Thursday May 27th
Going Correction: MINUS 0.10 sec. per fur.

1283 Taunton Dry Blackthorn Claiming Stakes Class F (3-y-o) £2,467 1½m ....(2:20)

FUNNY CHOICE (Ire) 8-2 (5*) O Pears (2) *trkd ldr, pushed alng o'r 3 fs out, effrt and rdn to ld over one out, ran on und pres.*..............(6 to 1 op 5 to 1 tchd 13 to 2) 1
1191⁴ MOUNTAIN WILLOW (v) 8-5 K Darley (4) *led, rdn o'r 2 fs out, hdd over one out, kpt on und pres ins last.* ....(9 to 4 fav op 2 to 1) 2
1191³ PALACEGATE SUNSET (v) 9-3 J Carroll (1) *hld up, hdwy hfwy, effrt 3 fs out, sn hrd rdn and one pace.* ....(100 to 30 op 11 to 4 tchd 7 to 2) 3
1112 NANCY (Ire) 7-12² (3*) S Maloney (5) *hld up, hdwy hfwy, pushed alng 4 fs out, effrt and rdn 3 out, sn one pace.* ....(11 to 4 op 5 to 2) 4
972⁵ JENDORCET 8-1 J Fanning (6) *cl up, rdn 3 fs out, wknd wl o'r one out.*......................(9 to 1 op 6 to 1) 5
699⁶ THE BRACKETEER 8-8 K Fallon (3) *beh frm hfwy, tld off fnl 3 fs.*......................(33 to 1 tchd 50 to 1) 6
Dist: ½l, 2l, 3½l, hd, 25l. 2m 39.80s. a 9.80s (6 Ran).
(Lt-Col W L Monteith), P Monteith

1284 Heineken Export Handicap Class E (0-70 4-y-o and up) £3,287 7f 214yds ....(2:50)

1103⁴ COOL ENOUGH [33] 12-7-10 A Mackay (12) *hld up and beh, hdwy o'r 2 fs out, str run to ld entering fnl furlong, ran on.*..................... (12 to 1 op 10 to 1) 1
931 TOUCH ABOVE [46] 7-8-9 R Cochrane (8) *hld up and beh, hdwy o'r 2 fs out, rdn and ran on wl ins last.* ....(8 to 1 op 7 to 1) 2
EXPRESS GIFT [64] 4-9-8 (5*) Darren Moffatt (16) *hld up and beh, hdwy 2 fs out, ran on wl ins last.* ....(7 to 2 fav op 5 to 1 tchd 6 to 1) 3
565 LAWNSWOOD JUNIOR [59] 6-9-8 K Darley (7) *mid-div, hdwy 3 fs out, effrt and ev ch appr fnl furlong, sn rdn and one pace.*......................(8 to 1 op 7 to 1) 4
1210⁷ MALCESINE (Ire) [45] 4-8-8 J Fortune (19) *mid-div, effrt and hdwy whn not much room 2 fs out, swtchd and styd on wl ins last.*......................(14 to 1) 5
964² PRIDE OF PENDLE [43] 4-8-6 Dean McKeown (10) *chsd ldrs, rdn to ld o'r 2 fs out, hdd and wknd one out.* ....(8 to 1 op 5 to 1) 6
1034 SKOLERN [40] 9-8-3 J Fanning (17) *mid-div, effrt and hdwy 3 fs out, rdn 2 out and sn one pace.* ....(33 to 1 op 25 to 1) 7
975⁹ OPEN AGENDA (Ire) [57] 4-9-6 J Quinn (2) *chsd ldrs, hdwy 3 fs out, effrt and ev ch appr fnl furlong, sn rdn and wknd.*......................(20 to 1 op 12 to 1) 8
HYDROPIC [31] 6-7-8 S Wood (5) *hld up, hdwy on outer o'r 2 fs out, sn rdn and btn.*......(50 to 1 op 33 to 1) 9
964 MARY MACBLAIN [37] 4-7-12¹ (3*) S Maloney (6) *nvr rchd ldrs.*......................(20 to 1 op 14 to 1) 10
861 VERDANT BOY [46] 10-8-9 N Connorton (4) *al mid-div.* ....(20 to 1 op 14 to 1) 11
GOLDEN ANCONA [31] 10-7-8¹ L Charnock (13) *nvr a factor.*......................(50 to 1 op 33 to 1) 12
971⁶ ANAR (Ire) [45] 4-8-3 (5*) O Pears (18) *al rear.* ....(14 to 1 op 12 to 1) 13
902⁴ SHANNON EXPRESS [45] (v) 6-8-8 K Fallon (11) *cl up, led o'r 3 fs out till hdd and wknd over 2 out.* ....(10 to 1 op 8 to 1) 14
1138 ABSOLUTLEY FOXED [35] 4-7-12 J Lowe (14) *chsd ldrs to hfwy, sn wknd.*......................(33 to 1 op 25 to 1) 15
885⁴ AMERICAN HERO [65] 5-9-9 (5*) Stephen Davies (15) *led, hdd and rdn o'r 3 fs out, sn wknd...* (7 to 1 op 5 to 1) 16
931 ZEPPEKI (Ire) [54] 5-9-3 J Carroll (3) *al rear.*......(33 to 1) 17
1097 GOOD FOR THE ROSES [54] 7-9-3 A Clark (9) *prmnt to hfwy, sn lost pl.*..................... (9 to 1 op 10 to 1) 18
Dist: 1½l, 1½l, 1½l, hd, 1½l, 1l, ½l, 2l, 1½l, 2½l. 1m 42.30s. a 4.40s (18 Ran).
SR: 4/12/25/15/-/-/-/2/-/ (Mrs J R Ramsden), Mrs J R Ramsden

1285 Boddingtons Bitter Maiden Fillies Stakes Class D (3-y-o and up) £3,611 7f 214yds......................... (3:20)

835² BALNAHA 3-8-9 M Hills (6) *hld up and beh, hdwy 3 fs out, rdn to chal entering fnl furlong, edgd rght and styd on to ld nr finish.*......................(5 to 2 op 2 to 1) 1
AL SHAATI (Fr) 3-8-9 K Darley (8) *chsd ldrs, effrt 2 fs out, rdn to ld o'r one out, hdd and no extr nr finish.* ....(8 to 1 op 5 to 1 tchd 9 to 1) 2
752⁶ CRYSTAL REAY 3-8-9 R Cochrane (5) *hld up, hdwy 3 fs out, effrt 2 out and ev ch ins fnl furlong till no extr nr finish.*......................(85 to 40 fav op 2 to 1 tchd 9 to 4) 3
1039 BILOELA 3-8-9 K Fallon (10) *beh, gd hdwy o'r 2 fs out, staying on and ch ins fnl furlong whn not clr run, not rcvr.*......................(33 to 1 op 20 to 1) 4
732² SEROTINA (Ire) 3-8-9 M Tebbutt (1) *trkd ldrs gng wl, hdwy 3 fs out, led briefly entering fnl 2 furlongs, sn rdn and wknd.*...................... (5 to 2 op 2 to 1) 5
HUNTERS OF BRORA (Ire) 3-8-9 Dean McKeown (2) *slwly into strd, hdwy o'r 3 fs out, rdn and one pace fnl 2 furlongs.*......................(50 to 1 op 33 to 1) 6
SUSPECT 3-8-9 J Lowe (3) *chsd ldr, rdn 3 fs out, sn wknd.*...................... (100 to 1) 7
1132⁷ CITY TIMES (Ire) 3-8-9 M Birch (9) *chsd ldrs, rdn 3 fs out, wknd 2 out.*...................... (16 to 1 op 12 to 1) 8
906² SHALABIA 4-9-7 J Carroll (4) *led, rdn o'r 2 fs out, sn hdd and wknd.*.......... (20 to 1 op 16 to 1 tchd 25 to 1) 9
1099⁵ SWEETWATER MOON 3-8-9 J Fortune (7) *chsd ldrs to hfwy, sn lost pl and beh.*......................(100 to 1) 10
Dist: Hd, 1l, 1½l, 2½l, 5l, 3l, 4l, 1l, 10l. 1m 43.20s. a 5.30s (10 Ran).
SR: 4/3/-/-/-/-/ (Sir Philip Oppenheimer), G Wragg

1286 Heineken Lager Handicap Class E (0-70 3-y-o and up) £3,184 6f 206yds ....(3:50)

1101³ CHANTRY BELLINI [43] (bl) 4-8-5 N Carlisle (4) *chsd ldrs, hdwy 2 fs out, rdn to ld one out, sn clr.* ....(10 to 1 op 7 to 1) 1
KICK ON MAJESTIC (Ire) [33] 4-7-9 S Wood (11) *hdwy on inner 3 fs out, effrt and not clr appr fnl furlong, swtchd and ran on wl ins last.*......................(25 to 1 op 20 to 1) 2
CELESTINE [62] 4-9-10 J Fanning (1) *prmnt, chsd ldr hfwy, rdn and ev ch appr fnl furlong, not quicken ins last.*......................(20 to 1 op 16 to 1) 3
902³ BALLYRANTER [46] 4-8-8 J Quinn (14) *al chasing ldrs, rdn 2 fs out, kpt on one pace.*..............(8 to 1 op 7 to 1) 4
4710a KUMMEL KING [58] 5-9-6 K Fallon (8) *led, rdn 2 fs out, hdd and wknd appr fnl furlong.*.......(11 to 1 op 10 to 1) 5
1193³ BALLAD DANCER [57] 8-9-0 (5*) Darren Moffatt (10) *hld up and beh, hdwy 2 fs out, styd on und pres ins last.* ....(8 to 1 op 7 to 1 tchd 9 to 1) 6
962³ FLETCHER'S BOUNTY (Ire) [50] 4-8-12 M Birch (7) *hmpd strt and beh till styd on fnl 2 fs, nvr dngrs.* ....(9 to 1 op 7 to 1) 7
NORTHERN SPARK [52] 5-9-0 N Connorton (12) *nvr rchd ldrs.*......................(14 to 1 op 12 to 1) 8
1103* SUSANNA'S SECRET [44] 6-8-3 (3*,6ex) S Maloney (13) *prmnt, effrt 3 fs out, rdn to ld briefly one and a half out, sn hdd and wknd one out.* ....(7 to 2 fav op 3 to 1 tchd 4 to 1) 9
363⁷ SECOND COLOURS (USA) [61] 3-8-12 K Darley (2) *hld up, effrt o'r 2 fs out, no hdwy.* ....(6 to 1 op 4 to 1 tchd 13 to 2) 10
1035* DESERT SPLENDOUR [60] 5-9-8 J Lowe (5) *chsd ldrs, rdn 3 fs out, sn wknd.*...................... (10 to 1 op 7 to 1) 11
906⁹ TWILIGHT FALLS [49] 8-8-11 Dean McKeown (6) *stumbled strt, al rear.*........... (9 to 1 op 7 to 1 tchd 10 to 1) 12
885 HAND ON HEART (Ire) [58] 4-9-1 (5*) O Pears (9) *hld up, effrt and some hdwy on outer o'r 2 fs out, sn rdn and wknd.*......................(16 to 1 op 14 to 1) 13
Dist: 3l, 1l, nk, 1l, nk, ½l, 3½l, hd, 3½l, 2l. 1m 28.90s. a 3.50s (13 Ran).
SR: 28/9/35/18/27/25/16/7/-/ (Mrs J J Kirk Scott), C W Thornton

1287 Britvic Soft Drinks Limited Stakes Class F (3-y-o and up) £2,825 5f (4:20)

1228* SLADES HILL 6-9-7 R Cochrane (2) *trkd ldrs, hdwy 2 fs out, effrt to ld entering fnl furlong, ran on.* ....(9 to 2 op 7 to 2) 1
1157* COCONUT JOHNNY 3-8-12 J Fanning (4) *al prmnt, effrt and ev ch o'r one furlong out, sn rdn and kpt on.* ....(4 to 1 jt-fav tchd 9 to 2) 2
1157³ TREVORSNINEPOINTS 3-8-7 K Darley (13) *chsd ldrs, hdwy 2 fs out and dsptd ld one and a half out, sn rdn and edgd rght, no extr ins last.* ....(4 to 1 jt-fav tchd 7 to 2 and 9 to 2) 3

1081 MASTER POKEY 9-9-0 (7*) P Johnson (9) *in tch, hdwy and rdn o'r one furlong out, styd on ins last, nrst finish.* .... (20 to 1 op 14 to 1 tchd 25 to 1) 4
1052^{3} STATE FLYER 5-9-0 (7*) J Marshall (1) *in tch, effrt 2 fs out, sn rdn and kpt on ins last*....... (10 to 1 tchd 12 to 1) 5
1183* SO SUPERB (bl) 4-9-7 J Lowe (7) *cl up, effrt to dispute ld one and a half fs out, sn rdn, put head in air and wknd entering fnl furlong*.......................... (5 to 1) 6
1264^{7} CREAGMHOR 3-8-12 R P Elliott (11) *nvr a factor.* .... (50 to 1 op 33 to 1) 7
4716a^{3} ROCK OPERA (Ire) 5-9-0 (7*) V Halliday (6) *nvr rchd ldrs.* .... (25 to 1 op 20 to 1) 8
887 MY ABBEY 4-9-2 K Fallon (12) *led, rdn o'r 2 fs out, sn hdd and wknd*........................ (16 to 1 op 12 to 1) 9
1076^{4} NILU (Ire) 5-9-2 M Birch (10) *nvr rchd ldrs.* .... (14 to 1 op 12 to 1) 10
1036 LOFT BOY (bl) 10-9-7 Dean McKeown (8) *cl up, rdn o'r 2 fs out and sn wknd*................(9 to 1 op 7 to 1) 11
800 FILICAIA 7-9-2 Kim Tinkler (3) *very slwly away, al beh.* ....(20 to 1 tchd 15 to 1) 12
NORTH OF WATFORD 8-9-7 L Charnock (5) *beh frm hfwy.* ....(33 to 1) 13
Dist: 1l, ¾l, 1½l, sht-hd, 2½l, ¾l, ½l, 1l, 3l, 1l. 1m 2.60s. a 2.60s (13 Ran).
SR: 45/32/24/32/31/21/9/16/7/ (James E Greaves), T D Barron

1288 Bulmers Strongbow Handicap Class E (0-70 4-y-o and up) £3,080 1¾m 32yds ....(4:50)

682^{9} GREY POWER [62] 6-9-11 K Darley (4) *hld up, took clr order 4 fs out, hdwy 2 out, styd on to ld wl ins last.* ....(7 to 1 op 6 to 1) 1
1112 WEST WITH THE WIND [48] 6-8-11 J Lowe (2) *hld up in tch, hdwy 3 fs out, effrt to ld entering fnl furlong, sn rdn, hdd wl ins last*......... (9 to 1 op 8 to 1 tchd 10 to 1) 2
1056^{6} CONTINUITY [57] 4-9-6 K Fallon (7) *hld up, hdwy 3 fs out, effrt and not clr run appr fnl furlong, kpt on und pres ins last*............................. (4 to 1 tchd 9 to 2) 3
1190^{9} GREY COMMANDER [30] 5-7-7 A Mackay (5) *led, quickened 4 fs out and sn rdn, hdd 2 out, kpt on one pace.* .... (9 to 1 op 10 to 1 tchd 8 to 1) 4
924^{4} BRIGGSMAID [59] 5-9-8 M Tebbutt (6) *in tch, effrt and ev ch 2 fs out, sn rdn and btn*.......(2 to 1 fav op 5 to 2) 5
TRUMP [59] 4-9-8 J Carroll (1) *chsd ldr, hdwy to chal 3 fs out, rdn and slight ld 2 out, hdd and wknd one out.* ....(5 to 1 op 4 to 1) 6
DIZZY (USA) [65] 5-9-9 (5*) O Pears (8) *prmnt, effrt 3 fs out, rdn and ev ch 2 out, wknd appr last.* (6 to 1 op 5 to 1) 7
Dist: Nk, 1½l, nk, 4l, 3½l, 2l. 3m 19.10s. a 21.30s (7 Ran).
(J P S Racing), Mrs M Reveley

LONGCHAMP (FR) (good to firm)
Thursday May 27th

1289 Prix du Palais-Royal (Group 3) (3-y-o and up) £23,895 7f...............(2:55)

956^{4} VOLERIS (Fr) 4-9-4 C Asmussen (4) *3rd strt, rdn o'r one and a half fs out, chlgd over one out, led fnl 110 yards, ran on*.. (26 to 10) 1
920^{5} ACTEUR FRANCAIS (USA) 5-9-8 S Guillot (5) *second strt, effrt 2 fs out, led one and a half out, hdd last 110 yards, ran on*.................................... (54 to 10) 2
956^{2} CRACK REGIMENT (USA) 5-9-4 E Saint-Martin (6) *5th strt, effrt 2 fs out, chlgd one out, no extr fnl strds*... (6 to 1) 3
853* MATELOT (USA) 3-8-9 T Jarnet (2) *4th strt, effrt 2 fs out, chlgd fnl furlong, unbl to quicken cl hme*... (5 to 3 on) 4
637^{3} CHARME SLAVE (Fr) 5-9-4 W Mongil (3) *6th strt, rdn 2 fs out, one pace*.................................(14 to 1) 5
INFORMANT 3-8-9 F Head (1) *led till rdn and wknd quickly one and a half fs out*................ (16 to 1) 6
956^{3} SHIVAREE (Fr) 4-9-4 M Boutin (7) *al rear*............ (21 to 1) 7
Dist: Sht-hd, hd, sht-hd, 3l, sht-hd, 1½l. 1m 21.40s. a 1.90s (7 Ran).
SR: 65/68/63/53/53/43/47/ (J T L Jones), J E Hammond

1290 Prix de la Seine (Listed) (3-y-o) £14,337 1¼m.................. (3:55)

AUBE INDIENNE (Fr) 8-11 C Asmussen,................. 1
561^{4} FINIR EN BEAUTE (Fr) 8-11 S Guillot,.................. 2
ELITE GUEST (Ire) 8-11 N Jeanpierre,.................... 3
FORTROSE (USA) 8-11 F Head,......................... 4
Dist: ¾l, 3l, sht-nk, 2½l, sht-hd, 10l, 10l. 2m 7.10s. a 5.00s (8 Ran).
SR: 37/35/29/28/ (S Niarchos), Mme C Head

1291 Prix de la Porte de Madrid (Listed) (4-y-o and up) £14,337 1½m....... (4:25)

562* SERRANT (USA) 5-9-2 T Jarnet,.......................... 1
798^{4} GRAND FLOTILLA (USA) 6-8-12 D Boeuf,............... 2
726^{2} DARIYOUN (USA) 5-8-12 F Head,.......................... 3
LIYOUN (Ire) 5-8-12 W Mongil,.......................... 4
Dist: Nk, sht-hd, 2½l, 1½l. 2m 35.20s. a 6.10s (5 Ran).
SR: 29/24/23/18/ (D Wildenstein), A Fabre

DUNDALK (IRE) (yielding)
Friday May 28th

1292 Mountain Race (3-y-o) £2,245 1m 5f ....(6:00)

1122* PORTERSTOWN BOY (Ire) 9-5 M J Kinane (5).. (5 to 4 on) 1
944^{2} MOUSE BIRD (Ire) 8-12 J P Murtagh (1)........... (2 to 1) 2
552* IMAD (USA) 9-5 W J Supple (6)...................(8 to 1) 3
997^{4} MAN OF ARRAN (Ire) 9-5 C Roche (4).............(20 to 1) 4
850^{5} TOUCHING MOMENT (Ire) 9-5 P V Gilson (3)..... (12 to 1) 5
1163^{4} MANGANS HILL (Ire) 8-10 (6*) P P Murphy (2).....(25 to 1) 6
Dist: Hd, 1l, 7l, 1½l. 3m 3.60s. (6 Ran).
(Philip Monahan), D K Weld

1293 Newry Handicap (0-70 4-y-o and up) £2,245 7f 166yds............... (6:30)

1235^{5} ARDLEA HOUSE (Ire) [-] 4-7-7^{6} (6*) J J Behan (13)..(6 to 1) 1
ALBERTA ROSE (Ire) [-] 4-9-7 (6*) J R Barry (15) (7 to 2 fav) 2
1163 MAN OF STRAW [-] 7-7-1 (6*) P P Murphy (7)..... (33 to 1) 3
1050 NORDIC SAINT (Ire) [-] 4-9-4 (6*) J A Heffernan (10) (7 to 1) 4
IMPRIMATUR [-] 4-9-12 J F Egan (1)............(10 to 1) 5
MARTIN'S MARTINA (Ire) [-] 4-8-13 W J Supple (2) (25 to 1) 6
599^{4} MUGNANO [-] 7-9-4 (6*) P Carberry (6)............(4 to 1) 7
1235^{6} THE BOWER (Ire) [-] 4-7-10 (10*) P M Donohue (14) (12 to 1) 8
SUTTON CENTENARY (Ire) [-] (bl) 5-8-2 A J Nolan (12) ....(20 to 1) 9
868* SOUTHERN RULE [-] (bl) 6-8-0 Joanna Morgan (11) (4 to 1) 10
AUDACIOUS (Ire) [-] 4-8-6 D Manning (8).........(20 to 1) 11
868 SALLUSTAR [-] 8-10-0 J P Murtagh (5)...........(14 to 1) 12
TOP SLICE (Ire) [-] 5-9-12 W J O'Connor (3)....... (16 to 1) 13
REASON TO BELIEVE (Ire) [-] 4-9-2 N G McCullagh (9) ....(25 to 1) 14
ELLE VA BON [-] 11-7-8 (2*) D G O'Shea (4)...... (20 to 1) 15
Dist: 2l, 2l, sht-hd, hd. 1m 45.70s. (15 Ran).
(W Hennessy), Oliver Finnegan

1294 Centenary Handicap (0-70 3-y-o) £2,245 7f 166yds............... (7:00)

898^{6} LA CENERENTOLA (Ire) [-] 8-13 (6*) P Carberry (6) (10 to 1) 1
487^{3} COOLRAIN LADY (Ire) [-] 9-4 S Craine (4)...... (7 to 4 fav) 2
868^{8} ABEREDW (Ire) [-] 9-0 J P Murtagh (2)..............(5 to 1) 3
1123* SLIGHTLY SCRUFFY (Ire) [-] 9-5 (5ex) P Lowry (5).. (9 to 2) 4
268^{4} FASTAFLOW (Ire) [-] 9-4 W J Supple (7)............ (7 to 2) 5
RAFFERTY'S INNER (Ire) [-] 8-3 (8*) R T Fitzpatrick (1) ....(25 to 1) 6
COMMODITY MARKET (Ire) [-] 9-7 N G McCullagh (8) ....(10 to 1) 7
1163 VOUVRAY (Ire) [-] 9-1 Joanna Morgan (3).........(20 to 1) 8
SILVER SHARP (Ire) [-] 8-3 D Manning (10)........(20 to 1) 9
Dist: ½l, 4l, 2l, ¾l. 1m 48.10s. (9 Ran).
(Mrs Maureen Hunt), Noel Meade

1295 Seatown Maiden (4-y-o and up) £2,245 1m 1f.........................(8:00)

1235^{2} RIENROE (Ire) 4-8-11 M J Kinane (6)...........(Evens fav) 1
911^{4} WINTER DREAMS (Ire) 4-8-11 W J O'Connor (14).. (8 to 1) 2
598 DIPIE (Ire) 5-9-0 J P Murtagh (4).................(16 to 1) 3
HINTERLAND 6-9-0 S Craine (9).................. (13 to 2) 4
851 KESS (Ire) 4-8-5 (6*) B Bowens (10)...............(20 to 1) 5
575 PRINCE PERICLES (Ire) 4-9-0 W J Supple (7)..... (14 to 1) 6
COUNTESS PAHLEN (Ire) 4-8-11 Joanna Morgan (2) ....(66 to 1) 7
BELLE O' THE BAY (Ire) 4-8-5 (6*) J J Behan (1)... (50 to 1) 8
SALVATION 6-9-0 B Coogan (8)................... (14 to 1) 9
DYEGETME (Ire) 4-8-5 (6*) J A Heffernan (13)..... (25 to 1) 10
KARABAKH (Ire) 4-9-0 J F Egan (15)..............(25 to 1) 11
CHARIKAR (Ire) 4-9-0 P Shanahan (12)............(10 to 1) 12
851 RIYASHA (Ire) 5-8-11 G Curran (3)................(50 to 1) 13
DAMHSA (Den) 4-8-11 C Roche (5).................. (8 to 1) 14
Dist: 3l, 2½l, 2l, 1½l. 2m 11.90s. (14 Ran).
(Ovidstown Investments Ltd), D K Weld

HAYDOCK (soft)
Friday May 28th

Going Correction: PLUS 0.40 sec. per fur. (races 1,5,6), PLUS 0.55 (2,3,4,7)

1296 Bass Mild XXXX Maiden Auction Stakes Class D (2-y-o) £3,525 5f (2:00)

1063^{2} SERIOUS OPTION (Ire) 9-0 S Perks (5) *pushed alng to chase ldg trio, not clr run, swtchd twice o'r one furlong out, led ins last, eased*..... (11 to 10 on op 6 to 4 on) 1
528^{2} INDIAHRA 8-9 K Darley (3) *al hndy, drvn ahead o'r one furlong out, hdd ins last, ran on same pace.* .... (5 to 1 op 4 to 1 tchd 11 to 2) 2
ROOFTOP FLYER (Ire) 9-0 Pat Eddery (6) *broke wl to ld frm o'r 3 fs, eased whn btn, better for race.* .... (3 to 1 op 5 to 2 tchd 100 to 30) 3

LANCASHIRE LIFE (Ire) 9-0 K Fallon (4) *bustled alng to keep up, swtchd outsd hfwy, slightly hmpd o'r one out, no imprsn*............(25 to 1) 4

933^{8} NEZ CARRERA 9-0 A Culhane (2) *outpcd and drvn alng most of way, nvr a threat*..........(33 to 1 op 25 to 1) 5

PARIS SYMPHONY (Ire) 9-0 J Carroll (1) *broke fst to press ldg pair, hng lft und pres o'r one furlong out, sn btn.* ....(9 to 1 op 7 to 1) 6

Dist: ¾l, 4l, 6l, 4l, 2½l. 1m 3.60s. a 4.80s (6 Ran).
SR: 44/36/25/1/-/-/ (Lord Portman), P F I Cole

1297 Spinal Injuries Association Maiden Fillies Stakes Class D (3-y-o) £3,622 1m 3f 200yds.................. (2:30)

557^{6} RAINBOW LAKE 8-11 Pat Eddery (3) *led aftr 3 fs, quickened to go wl clr after a m, eased last 2 furlongs.* ....(11 to 8 fav op 11 to 10 tchd 6 to 4) 1

821^{8} ARAADH (USA) 8-11 R Hills (4) *trkd ldg trio, hrd at work to chase wnr last 2 fs, nvr dngrs*........(5 to 1 op 7 to 2) 2

965^{3} DUNNELLON 8-11 M Roberts (2) *chsd ldg quartet, bustled alng entering strt, one pace last 3 fs.* ....(5 to 2 op 9 to 4 tchd 11 to 4) 3

MAYDAY CALLING 8-6 (5*) M Fenton (1) *sluggish strt, reco'red to press ldg pair, struggling entering strt, sn btn*..............................(12 to 1 op 10 to 1) 4

1154^{2} ROSSCOYNE 8-11 K Darley (5) *set steady pace for 3 fs, styd hndy till fdd und pres entering strt.* ....(11 to 2 op 4 to 1) 5

Dist: 5l, 8l, 1l, 10l. 2m 41.59s. a 11.79s (5 Ran).
SR: 45/35/19/17/-/ (K Abdulla), H R A Cecil

1298 Elegant Resorts Handicap Class C (0-100 6-y-o and up) £4,962 1m 30yds ....(3:00)

581 AMAZE [88] 4-9-5 K Darley (3) *trkd ldg trio, drvn ahead wl o'r one furlong out, hrd pressed ins last, kpt on well.* ....(9 to 1 op 12 to 1) 1

1079^{3} CEE-JAY-AY [66] 6-7-11 L Charnock (4) *settled off the pace, prmsg effrt whn not clr run o'r one furlong out, swtchd lft, ran on*.........................(7 to 1 op 6 to 1) 2

701^{2} ARANY [81] 6-8-12 P Robinson (9) *nvr far away, hrd at work o'r one furlong out, rallied*...(8 to 1 tchd 7 to 1) 3

917^{5} ROSEATE LODGE [67] 7-7-12 J Quinn (2) *settled gng wl, cruised up on bit to draw level o'r one furlong out, rdn and found nothing*..........................(14 to 1) 4

1079^{2} FOREVER DIAMONDS [81] 6-8-12 M Birch (11) *co'red up beh ldrs, effrt and bustled alng last 2 fs, kpt on same pace*..............................(7 to 2 tchd 4 to 1) 5

676^{8} COURAGEOUS KNIGHT [71] 4-8-2 M Roberts (1) *led or dsptd ld, hrd at work o'r 2 fs out, no extr*......(10 to 1) 6

1069^{2} PIQUANT [83] 6-8-11 (3*) D Harrison (8) *led or dsptd ld, definite advantage o'r 2 fs out, hdd over one out, sn btn*............(100 to 30 fav op 5 to 2 tchd 7 to 2) 7

CORALS DREAM (Ire) [97] 4-10-0 W Woods (6) *chsd ldg 5, feeling pace and drvn alng o'r 2 fs out, no imprsn.* ....(25 to 1 op 20 to 1) 8

651^{6} SALDA [70] 4-8-1 G Duffield (10) *trkd ldg quartet, hrd at work o'r 2 fs out, no extr*..........(10 to 1 op 12 to 1) 9

737 WILL OF STEEL [89] 4-9-6 K Fallon (7) *missed break, chsd alng to keep up hfwy, nvr dngrs*.....(8 to 1 op 6 to 1) 10

Dist: 1l, 1½l, nk, 2l, 1½l, 3l, nk, 2½l, 2l. 1m 47.72s. a 7.12s (10 Ran).
SR: 66/41/51/36/44/29/32/45/10/ (Lady Katharine Phillips), Lady Herries

1299 Bass North West Rated Class B Handicap (0-95 3-y-o) £6,152 1¾m....(3:30)

816* ACANTHUS (Ire) [85] 9-7 Pat Eddery (5) *made most, und pres 3 fs out, styd on grimly to go wl clr ins fnl furlong.* ....(6 to 4 fav tchd 13 to 8) 1

1115^{2} BOHEMIAN CROWN (USA) [76] 8-12 M Roberts (6) *nvr far away, chsd wnr und pres last 2 fs, no imprsn.* ....(3 to 1 op 5 to 2) 2

1067^{3} MARROS MILL [83] 9-0 (5*) M Fenton (4) *al tracking ldrs, feeling pace and hrd drvn o'r 2 fs out, one pace.* ....(9 to 2 tchd 5 to 1) 3

1067^{5} BONAR BRIDGE (USA) [80] 9-2 W R Swinburn (3) *dsptd early ld, styd hndy till hrd drvn and not quicken last 2 fs*..(6 to 1) 4

855^{8} DEE RAFT (USA) [73] 8-9 D Holland (2) *in tch, effrt und pres entering strt, sn struggling*.....(8 to 1 op 7 to 1) 5

1100* ARGYLE CAVALIER (Ire) [71] 8-7 (3ex) J Carroll (1) *trkd ldg 5, hrd at work entering strt, sn btn*..............(8 to 1) 6

Dist: 10l, 1l, nk, 10l, 1½l. 3m 12.29s. a 14.79s (6 Ran).
SR: 36/7/12/8/-/-/ (Cuadra Africa), J L Dunlop

1300 Spinal Injuries Association Rating Related Maiden Stakes Class F (0-65 3-y-o) £2,684 6f................ (4:00)

1132^{5} TRINITY HALL 8-9 R Hills (1) *took keen hold, nvr far away, drvn through to nose ahead ins fnl furlong, kpt on*................ (13 to 8 fav op 6 to 4 tchd 7 to 4) 1

1196^{2} CLANROCK (v) 9-0 A Culhane (3) *tried to make all, hdd ins fnl furlong, rallied und pres.* ....(2 to 1 op 7 to 4 tchd 9 to 4) 2

1137^{9} FLASHMAN (bl) 9-0 S Perks (2) *wth ldr, hrd at work and ev ch appr fnl furlong, one pace*... (4 to 1 tchd 9 to 2) 3

SARAH HEIGHTS 8-6 (3*) D Harrison (4) *outpcd and struggling hfwy, nvr able to rch ldrs*....(11 to 2 op 5 to 1) 4

516^{9} WHYALLA RAIN 8-2 (7*) J Dennis (5) *chsd ldg pair, hrd at work o'r 2 fs out, sn btn*......... (14 to 1 tchd 16 to 1) 5

Dist: Nk, 1½l, 8l, ½l. 1m 19.72s. a 8.12s (5 Ran).
(S Starkey), C A Horgan

1301 Phurnacite Handicap Class C (0-90 3-y-o and up) £5,131 5f......... (4:30)

1000^{9} LORD HIGH ADMIRAL (Can) [70] 5-8-10 M Roberts (3) *made all, drvn alng to quicken clr o'r one furlong out, kpt on wl*.................................. (8 to 1 op 6 to 1) 1

1000^{3} DOMINUET [87] 8-9-13 J Lowe (10) *last and hld up, swtchd outsd to improve last 2 fs, ran on finish.* ....(6 to 1 op 11 to 2) 2

891^{3} NEVER IN THE RED [82] (v) 5-9-8 J Carroll (2) *trkd ldg quartet, effrt and drvn alng last 2 fs, not quicken.* ....(5 to 1 op 9 to 2) 3

1000^{8} GONDO [68] 6-8-8 K Fallon (8) *nvr far away, effrt und pres 2 fs out, one pace*.......... (4 to 1 fav op 7 to 2) 4

891^{8} CRYSTAL JACK (Fr) [88] 5-9-9 (5*) O Pears (7) *al hndy, hrd at work o'r one furlong out, no imprsn.* ....(8 to 1 tchd 9 to 1) 5

1215^{2} EAGER DEVA [82] 6-9-8 K Darley (1) *broke smartly to match strds wth ldr for o'r 2 fs, fdd.* ....(13 to 2 op 11 to 2 tchd 7 to 1) 6

1036^{5} SONDERISE [69] 4-8-9 N Carlisle (9) *pressed ldg trio, feeling pace and rdn 2 fs out, fdd*.....(6 to 1 tchd 13 to 2) 7

1127^{7} ALLTHRUTHENIGHT (Ire) [82] 4-9-8 Pat Eddery (4) *sluggish strt, chsd alng thrght, nvr dngrs*.....(5 to 1 op 4 to 1) 8

Dist: 1l, 5l, sht-hd, nk, nk, 1½l, 1½l. 1m 3.52s. a 4.72s (8 Ran).
SR: 42/55/30/15/34/27/8/15/ (E J G Young), M J Heaton-Ellis

1302 Knighton Group Conditions Stakes Class D (3-y-o) £3,552 1m 30yds (5:00)

890^{5} PREMIER LEAGUE (Ire) 9-0 J Quinn (6) *led till hdd o'r 3 fs out, rallied to ld ag'n over one out, ran on gmely.* ....(100 to 30 op 3 to 1 tchd 7 to 2) 1

646* CHATOYANT 9-0 G Duffield (1) *dashed up on ins aftr 2 fs, hrd at work to draw level o'r one out, kpt on wl.* ....(11 to 4 tchd 3 to 1) 2

1040* STAR MANAGER (USA) 9-0 S Perks (2) *patiently rdn, drvn up on outsd to chal o'r one furlong out, kpt on same pace*............................(5 to 2 fav op 9 to 4) 3

915^{4} YAQTHAN (Ire) 9-0 R Hills (5) *nvr far away, hrd at work to nose ahead briefly o'r one furlong out, no extr.* ....(4 to 1 op 7 to 2 tchd 9 to 2) 4

989^{6} PERSIAN REVIVAL (Fr) 8-10 M Birch (4) *wth wnr, led o'r 3 fs till over one out, no extr*............(10 to 1 op 8 to 1) 5

899* JADE CITY 9-0 K Fallon (3) *chsd alng to keep up hfwy, sn lost tch, tld off*..............(12 to 1 tchd 14 to 1) 6

Dist: ½l, 1½l, 1l, hd, 30l. 1m 50.54s. a 9.94s (6 Ran).
SR: 19/17/12/9/4/-/ (Miss P Rovera), J E Banks

PONTEFRACT (good)
Friday May 28th

Going Correction: MINUS 0.10 sec. per fur. (races 1,2,4,6), NIL (3,5)

1303 Friends of the Northern Racing School Fillies Conditions Stakes Class D (2-y-o) £3,231 6f.................. (6:45)

1211^{4} INTERNATIONAL STAR (Ire) 8-6 (3*) Emma O'Gorman (1) *slwly into strd, sn in tch, gd hdwy to ld jst ins fnl furlong, ran on wl*..................(5 to 2 op 2 to 1) 1

841^{6} LAMBENT 8-13 L Dettori (3) *trkd ldrs, rdn wl o'r one out, styd on fnl furlong*...................(7 to 1 op 5 to 1) 2

1078* DANCE OF THE SWANS (Ire) 8-13 K Darley (5) *trkd ldr, chlgd one out, sn rdn and btn.* ....(11 to 8 fav op 5 to 4 tchd 6 to 4) 3

1168^{4} WIXI (Ire) 8-13 P Robinson (6) *chsd ldr, kpt on fnl furlong.* ....(8 to 1 op 7 to 1) 4

1152^{2} CYARNA QUINN (Ire) 8-9 G Duffield (7) *led till hdd and wknd jst ins fnl furlong.* ....(6 to 1 op 7 to 1 tchd 8 to 1 and 9 to 1) 5

TAUFELIANE 8-9 Dean McKeown (2) *in tch, rdn hfwy, sn wknd*.. (50 to 1) 6

SPRING SENSATION 8-4 (5*) O Pears (4) *strted slwly, al beh, tld off*...................(100 to 1 op 50 to 1) 7

Dist: 2l, hd, ¾l, 1l, 8l, 30l. 1m 17.50s. a 2.80s (7 Ran).
SR: 27/23/22/19/11/-/-/ (N S Yong), W A O'Gorman

1304 Course Bookmakers Claiming Stakes Class F (4-y-o and up) £2,406 1m 4yds ....(7:10)

1101* DELPIOMBO 7-8-12 K Fallon (8) *in tch, gd hdwy 2 out, styd on to ld wl ins fnl furlong*...... (5 to 1 op 4 to 1) 1

1261² NO SUBMISSION (USA) 7-9-3 S Wood (9) *made most till hdd and no extr wl ins fnl furlong.* ....(9 to 2 op 3 to 1 tchd 5 to 1) 2
1130 CAUSLEY 8-8-13 L Dettori (10) *cl up, jnd ldr o'r 2 out, ev ch till no extr ins fnl furlong*.....(4 to 1 fav op 7 to 2) 3
1484 SILVER SAMURAI 4-8-4 (5*) O Pears (7) *chsd ldrs, effrt o'r 2 out, wknd over one out*....(14 to 1) 4
BROWNED OFF 4-8-7 M Roberts (13) *beh till styd on fnl 2 fs, nrst finish*.......(11 to 1 op 16 to 1 tchd 20 to 1) 5
893⁶ MUMMYS ROCKET 4-7-13² (5*) M Fenton (12) *nvr nrr.* ....(14 to 1) 6
931 COMMON COUNCIL (bl) 4-8-9 G Duffield (6) *chsd ldrs till wknd 2 out*....(10 to 1 op 12 to 1) 7
321⁴ PREMIER DANCE 6-8-7 A Mackay (3) *nvr dngrs.* (25 to 1) 8
NIMBLE DEER 4-8-6 Dean McKeown (4) *prmnt till wknd 2 out*....(6 to 1 op 5 to 1) 9
1159⁷ HERBRAND (Ire) 4-8-7 M Birch (2) *in tch till wknd 3 out.* ....(25 to 1 op 20 to 1) 10
914 MASTAMIST 4-8-7 P Robinson (1) *al beh.* ....(50 to 1 tchd 66 to 1) 11
681 AFFIRMED'S DESTINY (USA) 4-8-2 (5*) Darren Moffatt (11) *in tch till rdn and wknd hfwy, tld off*....(50 to 1) 12
622² AMLAK (USA) 4-8-11 J Quinn (5) *reared and uns rdr leaving stalls*.............(5 to 1 tchd 11 to 2 and 6 to 1) ur
Dist: 2l, hd, 6l, 3l, 1l, 1½l, 3l, 1½l, 3l, 12l. 1m 44.80s. a 2.70s (13 Ran).
SR: 46/45/40/18/7/-/1/-/-/ (Paul Coulter), J G FitzGerald

1305 William Hill Handicap Class E (0-70 3-y-o and up) £3,392 1½m 8yds (7:35)

1094² ATLANTIC WAY [48] 5-9-3 P Robinson (10) *hld up, smooth hdwy o'r 2 out, quickened to ld jst ins fnl furlong, sn clr, easily*....(8 to 1 op 6 to 1) 1
BOLD AMBITION [35] 6-8-1 (3*) S Maloney (11) *cl up, jnd ldr 3 out, slight ld o'r one out, sn hdd kpt on, no ch wth wnr*....(20 to 1 op 16 to 1) 2
1054³ BEAUMOOD [33] (v) 7-8-2 K Fallon (2) *prmnt, ev ch o'r one out, kpt on same pace*....(12 to 1) 3
1075⁸ PONDERING [62] (v) 3-8-13 M Roberts (15) *in tch, hdwy 4 out, ev ch o'r one out, one paced*... (8 to 1 op 10 to 1) 4
1112* EIRE LEATH-SEAL [53] 6-9-8 (5ex) M Wigham (3) *led till hdd o'r one out, wknd fnl furlong*....(12 to 1) 5
731⁹ EXPLOSIVE SPEED (USA) [47] 5-9-2 Dean McKeown (7) *in tch, kpt on same pace fnl 3 fs*.... (10 to 1 tchd 12 to 1) 6
1112⁴ MASTER OF THE ROCK [43] 4-8-12 N Connorton (16) *prmnt till wknd o'r one out*....(14 to 1 op 12 to 1) 7
1112² IN TRUTH [51] 5-9-6 L Dettori (14) *prmnt, effrt o'r 2 out, ev ch over one out, wknd fnl furlong*... (7 to 1 op 6 to 1) 8
349 TEN HIGH (Ire) [27] 4-7-10 L Charnock (13) *nvr nr ldrs.* ....(66 to 1 tchd 100 to 1) 9
1034 BRECKENBROUGH LAD [52] 6-9-7 K Darley (5) *hld up and beh, gd hdwy 4 out, ev ch 2 out, sn rdn and wknd.* ....(20 to 1 op 16 to 1) 10
1112³ SALU [55] (bl) 4-9-10 G Duffield (4) *hld up and beh, effrt 3 out, no real hdwy*....(6 to 1 co-fav tchd 13 to 2) 11
1075⁷ INDIAN TERRITORY [42] (v) 4-8-11 A Mackay (1) *mid-div, effrt 3 out, sn btn*....(20 to 1) 12
1143⁶ JAMES IS SPECIAL (Ire) [50] 5-9-5 J Quinn (12) *prmnt, ev ch 2 out, wknd quickly*....(6 to 1 co-fav tchd 7 to 1 and 15 to 2) 13
MOUJEEB (USA) [70] 3-9-7 W R Swinburn (8) *mid-div, effrt o'r 2 out, sn btn, eased fnl furlong*....(6 to 1 co-fav op 5 to 1) 14
TAURIAN PRINCESS [33] 4-7-11 (5*) Darren Moffatt (9) *in tch till wknd 4 out*....(25 to 1) 15
919 HIGHLAND FLAME [35] 4-8-4 Dale Gibson (6) *prmnt till wknd o'r 3 out*....(33 to 1) 16
Dist: 4l, ¾l, 1l, 1½l, 2l, 2l, hd, 2½l, 1½l, 2l. 2m 41.90s. a 6.90s (16 Ran).
SR: 34/13/9/18/24/14/6/13/-/ (C John Hill), C J Hill

1306 Tote Handicap Class D (0-80 3-y-o) £4,110 1m 4yds................ (8:05)

1037⁶ WORDSMITH (Ire) [58] 8-1 M Roberts (8) *hld up in tch, hdwy o'r 2 out, quickened to ld over one out, hng lft, sn clr, easily*....(6 to 1 tchd 13 to 2) 1
1153² DOC COTTRILL [71] 9-0 K Fallon (1) *in tch, effrt o'r 2 out, chlgd over one out, kpt on, no ch wth wnr.* ....(5 to 2 fav op 3 to 1 tchd 9 to 4) 2
780⁷ PRINCESS TATEUM (Ire) [70] 8-13 G Duffield (5) *trkd ldrs, slight ld wl o'r one out, sn hdd, kpt on same pace.* ....(10 to 1) 3
1037³ WOLF POWER (Ire) [58] 8-1 K Darley (7) *in tch, styd on fnl 2 fs, not trble ldrs*....(6 to 1 tchd 13 to 2) 4
1074⁴ MISTER BLAKE [60] (bl) 8-1¹ (3*) Emma O'Gorman (11) *cl up, slight ld 3 out, hdd wl o'r one out, wknd fnl furlong.* ....(14 to 1 op 12 to 1) 5
1039⁶ BEAUMONT (Ire) [68] 8-11 M Wigham (12) *beh, ran on wl fnl 2 fs, nrst finish*....(10 to 1 op 8 to 1) 6
437 BLAKES BEAU [62] 8-5 M Birch (13) *prmnt till wknd 2 out.* ....(20 to 1 tchd 25 to 1) 7
398² SOOJAMA (Ire) [52] 7-9⁵ (3*) B Doyle (10) *nvr dngrs.* ....(16 to 1 op 20 to 1) 8
907³ GWEEK (Ire) [56] 7-13³ P Robinson (6) *slight ld till hdd 3 out, wknd 2 out*....(9 to 2 tchd 4 to 1) 9
711⁵ LOWRIANNA (Ire) [50] 7-7 A Mackay (4) *in tch till wknd o'r 2 out*....(20 to 1) 10
685 NORLING (Ire) [52] 7-9 L Charnock (9) *sn beh.* ....(25 to 1 op 20 to 1) 11
1016⁷ SWEET ROMEO [78] 9-7 Dean McKeown (3) *wth ldr till wknd 3 out*....(9 to 1 op 8 to 1 tchd 10 to 1) 12
Dist: 5l, 1½l, 1½l, 3½l, 3½l, 3½l, ¾l, 2l, 7l, 2½l. 1m 45.50s. a 3.40s (12 Ran).
SR: 24/22/16/-/-/-/ (Sir Timothy Kitson), Mrs J R Ramsden

1307 Coral Handicap Class E (0-70 4-y-o and up) £3,366 1¼m 6yds....... (8:35)

840⁸ TENDRESSE (Ire) [43] 5-8-1 M Roberts (14) *hld up, steady hdwy 3 out, led ins fnl furlong, ran on wl.* ....(11 to 2 fav op 8 to 1) 1
TELEPHUS [46] 4-8-4 E Johnson (10) *in tch, steady hdwy to ld one out, hdd ins fnl furlong, kpt on wl.* ....(12 to 1 op 10 to 1 tchd 14 to 1) 2
674 BALZINO (USA) [50] 4-8-8 K Fallon (11) *beh, hdwy 3 out, wndrd und pres fnl furlong, nrst finish.* ....(16 to 1 op 14 to 1) 3
840⁴ SWEET REVIVAL [41] 5-7-13 J Fanning (2) *chsd ldrs, led o'r one out, sn hdd and wknd*.......(10 to 1 tchd 12 to 1) 4
978⁹ BENTICO [52] 4-8-10 P Robinson (1) *wth ldr, ev ch 2 out, one paced*....(14 to 1) 5
931³ WESTFIELD MOVES (Ire) [59] 5-9-3 J Quinn (16) *in tch, styd on fnl 2 fs, not touble ldrs*.......... (6 to 1 op 7 to 1) 6
645 KATY'S LAD [58] 6-9-2 J Fortune (13) *dwlt, in tch, effrt o'r 2 out, kpt on same pace, btn whn crrd rght ins fnl furlong*....(6 to 1 op 10 to 1) 7+
845⁵ FALCONS DAWN [51] 6-8-9 J Carroll (5) *made most till hdd o'r one out, btn whn hmpd ins fnl furlong.* ....(10 to 1 op 9 to 1) 7+
WESTHOLME (USA) [70] 5-9-11 (3*) S Maloney (18) *nvr dngrs*....(25 to 1 op 16 to 1) 9
931⁹ SPRAY OF ORCHIDS [43] 4-8-1 G Duffield (12) *nvr dngrs.* ....(14 to 1 op 12 to 1 tchd 10 to 1) 10
1112⁷ GOLDEN TORQUE [67] 6-9-4 (7*) H Bastiman (3) *in tch, no hdwy fnl 2 fs*....(16 to 1 op 14 to 1) 11
530 ESSAYEFFSEE [47] 4-8-5 K Darley (15) *in tch, effrt whn hmpd o'r 2 out, sn btn*.............(14 to 1 op 12 to 1) 12
1260⁷ VENTURE FOURTH [42] 4-8-0 S Wood (17) *in tch, hdwy hfwy, ev ch o'r 2 out, sn rdn and wknd quickly.* ....(25 to 1) 13
799 BRANDON GROVE [47] 5-8-5 Dean McKeown (9) *nvr dngrs.* ....(20 to 1) 14
904⁴ VASILIEV [62] (bl) 5-9-6 L Dettori (19) *nvr dngrs*... (12 to 1) 15
GALLANT JACK (Ire) [44] 4-8-2 A Mackay (4) *beh most of way*....(33 to 1 op 25 to 1) 16
971* THEMAAM [60] 4-9-4 D Biggs (6) *prmnt till wknd o'r 2 out.* ....(10 to 1 op 9 to 1) 17
78² EMPEROR ALEXANDER (Ire) [60] 5-9-1 (3*) S D Williams (8) *in tch till wknd o'r 2 out*....(20 to 1) 18
885⁶ MARTINI EXECUTIVE [58] (bl) 5-8-11 (5*) O Pears (7) *prmnt till wknd 3 out*....(20 to 1 op 16 to 1) 19
Dist: 1l, 4l, ½l, 2l, nk, nk, dd-ht, 1½l, 5l, 2½l. 2m 13.40s. a 5.20s (19 Ran).
SR: 35/36/32/22/29/35/33/26/42/ (C John Hill), C J Hill

1308 Brooke Group Maiden Stakes Class D (3-y-o) £3,348 6f................(9:05)

MIDHISH 9-0 W R Swinburn (5) *wth ldr, led o'r 2 out, quickened wl clr over one out, very easily.* ....(6 to 4 op Evens) 1
QUAVER (USA) 8-9 M Roberts (4) *in tch, effrt o'r 2 out, kpt on, no ch wth wnr*............(11 to 10 fav op 5 to 4) 2
899 COLFAX CLASSIC 8-9 J Fortune (1) *led till hdd o'r 2 out, sn btn*....(33 to 1 op 20 to 1) 3
SOBA UP 8-9 K Darley (3) *beh frm hfwy.* ....(9 to 1 op 8 to 1) 4
GRANVILLE CORNER 9-0 Dale Gibson (2) *sn beh, tld off.* ....(10 to 1 tchd 12 to 1) 5
Dist: 10l, 2½l, ½l, 15l. 1m 17.20s. a 2.50s (5 Ran).
SR: 38/-/ (Saeed Suhail), B Hanbury

SALISBURY (good to soft)
Friday May 28th

Going Correction: PLUS 0.10 sec. per fur. (races 1,3,4,5,6,7), NIL (2)

1309 Langford Apprentice Handicap Class G (0-70 3-y-o) £2,553 1m 1f 209yds ....(2:20)

976² DUVEEN (Ire) [61] 8-7 (6*) J O'Dwyer (13) *hdwy 6 fs out, chlgd frm 2 out, led one out, drvn out.* ....(6 to 1 op 9 to 2) 1
976⁶ PRESTON GUILD (Ire) [47] 7-13 N Varley (1) *led, clr 6 fs out, rdn frm 2 out, hdd one out, styd on.* ....(11 to 2 fav op 4 to 1 tchd 6 to 1) 2
976⁵ PISTOLS AT DAWN (USA) [58] 8-2 (8*) Wendy Jones (14) *mid-div, hdwy frm 2 fs out, no imprsn ins last.* ....(6 to 1 tchd 7 to 1) 3
1097³ HOMEMAKER [60] 8-4 (8*) R Waterfield (9) *mid-div, rdn 4 fs out, styd on appr fnl furlong.* ....(7 to 1 op 6 to 1 tchd 15 to 2) 4

1008[4] MR CUBE (Ire) [58] 8-0 (10*) A Daly (8) *hdwy 4 fs out, styd on same pace fnl 2 furlongs.* ....(9 to 1 op 10 to 1 tchd 12 to 1) 5
977[9] MAJOR TRIUMPH (Ire) [60] 8-12 S Mulvey (10) *hdwy 3 fs out, no imprsn fnl 2 furlongs.* ....(12 to 1 op 10 to 1 tchd 14 to 1) 6
1068[9] CALIBRATE [65] 9-3 D Gibbs (7) *beh, drvn alng o'r 4 fs out, nrst finish*..........(12 to 1 op 8 to 1 tchd 14 to 1) 7
1114[6] SLEEPTITE (Fr) [57] 7-13 (10*) T Thomas (12) *chsd ldrs till wknd o'r 2 fs out*.....(20 to 1 op 16 to 1 tchd 25 to 1) 8
827[6] MR DINGLE [51] 7-12 (5*) G Milligan (5) *chsd ldrs till wknd o'r 2 fs out*..........(12 to 1 op 10 to 1 tchd 14 to 1) 9
926 WAR REQUIEM (Ire) [54] 7-13 (7*) D Griffiths (3) *al beh.* ....(25 to 1 op 14 to 1) 10
1138 MY SISTER LUCY [45] 7-4 (7*) Martin Dwyer (11) *hdwy 5 fs out, wknd o'r 2 out*................(50 to 1 op 25 to 1) 11
1097 OCTOBER BREW (USA) [69] 8-11 (10*) M Payne (6) *chsd ldrs till wknd 3 fs out*..................(25 to 1 op 16 to 1) 12
1005 SKY BURST [61] 8-3 Mark Denaro (2) *beh most of way.* ....(6 to 1 op 9 to 2) 13
921 IS SHE QUICK [48] 7-9 (5*) S McCarthy (4) *beh, rdr lost irons 5 fs out, tld off.* (50 to 1 op 33 to 1 tchd 66 to 1) 14

Dist: ¾l, 6l, nk, nk, 1½l, nk, 3l, ½l, 2l, ¾l. 2m 11.18s. a 7.18s (14 Ran).
SR: 37/21/20/21/18/17/21/7/-/ (Mrs D Weatherby), M Bell

1310 Salisbury Conditions Stakes Class C (2-y-o) £4,910 5f................(2:50)

913* HIGH DOMAIN (Ire) 9-1 J Reid (4) *made virtually all, shaken up and kpt on wl fnl furlong.* ....(13 to 8 on op 6 to 4 on tchd 5 to 4 on) 1
877* BID FOR BLUE 9-1 L Piggott (2) *pressed wnr hfwy till rdn and not quicken ins last*.............(4 to 1 op 3 to 1) 2
1053* ISABELLA SHARP 8-10 M Hills (3) *chsd ldrs, drvn and styd on same pace appr fnl furlong.* ....(15 to 2 op 5 to 1 tchd 8 to 1) 3
776[3] ANZIO (Ire) 8-11 A Munro (1) *in tch, rdn and kpt on same pace fnl 2 fs.* ....(11 to 2 op 9 to 2 tchd 7 to 2 and 6 to 1) 4

Dist: Hd, 1½l, ¾l. 1m 2.55s. a 2.75s (4 Ran).
SR: 46/45/34/32/ (Mrs S J Stovold), M McCormack

1311 Netherhampton Maiden Fillies Stakes Class D (Div I) (3-y-o and up) £3,882 1m 1f 209yds.................. (3:20)

482[3] MASHAIR (USA) 3-8-6 W Carson (4) *hdwy 5 fs out, led o'r 2 out, quickened clr ins last.* ....(3 to 1 op 5 to 2 tchd 9 to 4) 1
946[3] DANCING PRIZE (Ire) 3-8-6 Paul Eddery (3) *al chasing ldrs, rdn alng frm 3 fs out, kpt on fnl furlong, not pace of wnr*...(11 to 10 on op 11 to 10 on tchd 6 to 5 and 5 to 4 on) 2
992[3] TOCHAR BAN (USA) 3-8-6 J Williams (2) *trkd ldrs 6 fs out, pushed alng and ran on frm o'r 2 furlongs out, one pace ins last*..........(4 to 1 op 5 to 1 tchd 13 to 2) 3
780[3] TAHDID 3-8-6 A Munro (5) *led 6 fs out, hdd o'r 2 out, sn outpcd*................(12 to 1 op 8 to 1 tchd 14 to 1) 4
KARDELLE 3-8-6 T Sprake (10) *beh, drvn and effrt o'r 3 fs out, wknd 2 furlongs out.* ....(33 to 1 op 20 to 1 tchd 40 to 1) 5
RASAYEL (USA) 3-8-6 B Raymond (1) *hld up in rear, styd on fnl 2 fs, not a dngr.* ....(20 to 1 op 10 to 1 tchd 25 to 1) 6
921[8] MY MINNIE 3-8-6 R Perham (9) *broke wl, sn beh, hdwy 6 fs out, wknd 3 out*.....(66 to 1 op 33 to 1 tchd 100 to 1) 7
ABET (USA) 3-8-6 J Reid (12) *chsd ldrs till wknd 3 fs out.* ....(20 to 1 op 12 to 1) 8
835[4] WHAT LOLA WANTS (Ire) 3-8-6 N Adams (7) *al beh.* ....(50 to 1 op 33 to 1 tchd 66 to 1) 9
AUNT ADA 4-9-7 M Perrett (6) *slwly into strd, al beh.* ....(66 to 1 op 33 to 1 tchd 100 to 1) 10
951[9] ARRASAS LADY 3-8-6 R Price (11) *sn beh.* ....(100 to 1 op 66 to 1) 11
1092 BIJOU FIRE (NZ) 5-9-7 M Hills (8) *led 4 fs, wknd four furlongs out*........(40 to 1 op 20 to 1 tchd 50 to 1) 12

Dist: 3½l, 1l, 1l, 2½l, nk, 3½l, 1l, 15l, 2½l, 1½l. 2m 10.15s. a 6.15s (12 Ran).
SR: 41/34/32/30/25/24/17/15/-/ (Hamdan Al-Maktoum), J L Dunlop

1312 Tryon Handicap Class D (0-80 3-y-o) £4,857 6f 212yds.............. (3:50)

977[7] POLAR STORM (Ire) [63] 8-8 J Reid (6) *came stands side prmnt, led 2 and a half fs out, drvn out.* ....(6 to 1 fav op 5 to 1 tchd 7 to 1) 1
772[9] PRINCELY FAVOUR (Ire) [76] 9-7 W Carson (14) *led aftr 2 fs far side, hdd two and a half furlongs out, styd on.* ....(13 to 2 op 5 to 1) 2
1147[4] DAILY SPORT DON [63] 8-8 Paul Eddery (1) *chsd ldrs stands side, kpt on same pace fnl 2 fs.* (9 to 1 op 6 to 1) 3
977[5] GALLOP TO GLORY [56] 8-1 C Rutter (5) *led 2 fs, styd prmnt stands side till outpcd fnl two furlongs.* ....(20 to 1 op 16 to 1 tchd 25 to 1) 4
503[8] SILVER GROOM (Ire) [55] 8-0 T Sprake (2) *chsd ldrs stands side till wknd o'r one furlong out.* (20 to 1 op 16 to 1) 5
751 DON TOCINO [69] 9-0 J Williams (4) *rcd stands side, outpcd fnl 2 fs*......................(16 to 1 op 12 to 1) 6
836[7] LOVE IN THE MIST (USA) [57] (bl) 8-2 S O'Gorman (3) *chsd ldrs stands side till wknd 2 fs out*............(12 to 1) 7
747[6] BEZIQUE (USA) [71] (bl) 9-2 R Cochrane (9) *pressed ldrs, came stands side and wknd frm 3 fs out.* ....(13 to 2 op 5 to 1 tchd 7 to 1) 8
802[7] SPRING SUNRISE [64] 8-9 F Norton (7) *some hdwy far side o'r 3 fs out, sn wknd*..............(12 to 1 op 10 to 1) 9
871[4] AVRIL ETOILE [56] 8-1 A McGlone (15) *chsd ldrs far side o'r 4 fs*..............................(12 to 1 op 14 to 1) 10
835[7] GREEN CHILI [64] 8-9 M Hills (13) *slwly into strd and wnt rght strt, sn chasing ldrs far side 4 fs.* (8 to 1 op 6 to 1) 11
813[9] KOA [62] 8-7 W Ryan (10) *chsd ldrs far side 4 fs.* ....(7 to 1 op 8 to 1 tchd 6 to 1) 12
690 PATSY GRIMES [67] 8-12 B Rouse (11) *speed to hfwy far side*..............................(20 to 1 op 16 to 1) 13
TIGERSPIKE (Ire) [52] 7-11 N Adams (8) *al beh stands side.* ....(20 to 1 op 16 to 1 tchd 25 to 1) 14
995[5] ABSOLUTELY FACT (USA) [59] 8-4 A Munro (12) *speed to hfwy far side*.................... (14 to 1 op 10 to 1) 15

Dist: 3½l, 2l, 1½l, ½l, ¾l, nk, 2½l, 2l, nk, 4l. 1m 30.55s. a 4.95s (15 Ran).
SR: 30/32/13/1/-/10/-/3/-/ (Dexam International Limited), Lady Herries

1313 Redenham Claiming Stakes Class G (3-y-o) £3,027 6f 212yds.........(4:20)

1175[6] JUST JAMIE 7-9[1] (7*) C Hawksley (4) *beh, gd hdwy frm 3 fs out, led o'r 2 out, hld on wl*.... (7 to 2 jt-fav op 4 to 1) 1
4675a[5] TONY'S MIST 8-11 J Reid (1) *prmnt, rcd alone stands side, str chal frm o'r 2 fs out, no extr cl hme.* ....(12 to 1 op 14 to 1) 2
752 SHEFFORD 8-6 R Cochrane (2) *beh, rdn 3 fs out, styd on wl fnl furlong*......................(20 to 1 op 16 to 1) 3
499[5] BEYOND THE LIMIT 8-1 W Carson (3) *sn in tch, rdn frm o'r 2 fs out, styd on same pace*.........(10 to 1 op 8 to 1) 4
1058[8] FORMAL AFFAIR 9-2 D Biggs (12) *chsd ldrs, no prog fnl 2 fs*.................(7 to 2 jt-fav op 5 to 2 tchd 4 to 1) 5
1059 NO EXTRAS (Ire) 9-2 B Rouse (9) *led aftr one furlong till hdd o'r 2 fs out, wknd over one furlong out.* ....(11 to 2 op 4 to 1) 6
917 KNYAZ 9-0 A Munro (11) *nvr gng pace of ldrs.* ....(6 to 1 op 4 to 1) 7
927 BUCKSKI ECHO 8-10 A Clark (8) *chsd ldrs till wknd frm 2 fs out*..........................(20 to 1 op 16 to 1) 8
624 WESTERN VALLEY 8-11 J Comber (5) *led one furlong, styd prmnt till wknd frm 3 fs out.* (20 to 1 tchd 33 to 1) 9
1007 ZHAAB 8-1 C Avery (7) *al beh*....................(33 to 1) 10
1147[5] TOFF SUNDAE 8-9 Paul Eddery (6) *beh frm hfwy.* ....(8 to 1 op 12 to 1) 11
758 LADY RELKO 8-1 S Dawson (10) *sn beh.* ....(25 to 1 op 20 to 1 tchd 33 to 1) 12

Dist: Nk, 1½l, 2l, nk, nk, 5l, 1½l, 3½l, 2½l, 1l. 1m 31.59s. a 5.99s (12 Ran).
SR: 8/17/7/-/10/9/ (A R Perry), G Lewis

1314 Durnford Conditions Stakes Class D (3-y-o) £3,687 1½m............(4:50)

947[2] TIOMAN ISLAND 9-4 T Quinn (2) *trkd ldr, led gng wl 3 fs out, shaken up o'r one furlong out, drvn out cl hme.* ....(7 to 4 fav tchd 9 to 4) 1
1092* CAPTAIN'S GUEST (Ire) 8-12 W Carson (5) *in tch, hdwy frm o'r 2 fs out, drvn and kpt on wl fnl furlong, not rch wnr*....................(13 to 2 op 8 to 1 tchd 6 to 1) 2
876* MASTER CHARLIE 8-12 M Hills (3) *chsd ldrs, ev ch 2 fs out, outpcd appr fnl furlong.* ....(100 to 30 op 9 to 2 tchd 5 to 1 and 3 to 1) 3
832* SPIN DOCTOR (Ire) 8-12 R Cochrane (6) *effrt o'r 3 fs out, no imprsn fnl 2 furlongs*..........(3 to 1 op 9 to 4) 4
EDBAYSAAN (Ire) 8-7 W Ryan (4) *beh, nvr rchd ldrs.* .... (8 to 1 op 7 to 1 tchd 12 to 1) 5
412* LORD NITROGEN (USA) 8-12 A Munro (1) *led till hdd 3 fs out, wknd o'r 2 furlongs out*.......(16 to 1 op 12 to 1) 6
929[4] LAVENDER COTTAGE 8-7 Paul Eddery (7) *nvr rchd ldrs.* ....(25 to 1 op 20 to 1) 7

Dist: ¾l, 2½l, 4l, 2½l, ½l, 7l. 2m 37.22s. a 5.22s (7 Ran).
SR: 64/56/51/43/33/37/18/ (H R H Sultan Ahmad Shah), P F I Cole

1315 Netherhampton Maiden Fillies Stakes Class D (Div II) (3-y-o and up) £3,882 1m 1f 209yds.................. (5:20)

672[4] DREAMS ARE FREE (Ire) 3-8-6 W Ryan (4) *led aftr one furling, drvn frm o'r 2 fs out, jst hld on.* .... (2 to 1 fav op 3 to 1 tchd 100 to 30) 1
1068[3] CUTLASS (Ire) 3-8-6 J Reid (3) *mid-div, hdwy 3 fs out, quickened to chal one furlong out, styd on, no extr cl hme*....... (5 to 2 op 9 to 4 tchd 2 to 1 and 11 to 4) 2
NAWAHIL 3-8-6 W Carson (9) *strted slwly, beh, gd hdwy frm 2 fs out, kpt on fnl furlong.* ....(6 to 1 op 7 to 2 tchd 13 to 2) 3
582 WINNING APPEAL (Fr) 3-8-6 S Raymont (1) *al chasing ldrs, one pace fnl 2 fs*..................(14 to 1 op 10 to 1) 4
821 GLINT OF AYR 3-7-13 (7*) Kim McDonnell (11) *chsd ldrs till wknd ins fnl 2 fs*.................. (50 to 1 op 33 to 1) 5
992[8] CHASE THE STARS 3-8-6 W Newnes (7) *mid-div, nvr rchd ldrs*..........(25 to 1 op 14 to 1 tchd 33 to 1) 6
RUFFLE 3-8-6 A Clark (2) *slwly into strd, sn in tch, effrt 4 fs out, wknd ins fnl 3 furlongs*...(12 to 1 tchd 14 to 1) 7

CHARLOTTE DUNDAS 3-8-6 R Cochrane (5) *slwly into strd, al in rear*......(5 to 1 op 5 to 2) 8

DASHING MARCH 4-9-7 R Price (6) *mid-div, drvn alng o'r 4 fs out, sn wknd*..................(100 to 1 op 50 to 1) 9

BELLEZZA 6-9-7 B Rouse (10) *led one furlong, wknd 3 fs out*..........(50 to 1 op 25 to 1 tchd 66 to 1) 10

880 JAFETICA 3-8-6 A Tucker (8) *rcd freely and beh, nvr dngrs*..................................(66 to 1 op 50 to 1) 11

Dist: Nk, 1l, 3l, nk, 4l, nk, 2l, 6l, 3½l, ½l. 2m 12.10s. a 8.10s (11 Ran).
SR: 21/20/18/12/11/3/2/-/1/ (R E Sangster), H R A Cecil

WARWICK (soft)
Friday May 28th

Going Correction: PLUS 0.30 sec. per fur. (races 1,3,4,5,6), PLUS 0.15 (2)

1316 Leam Handicap Stakes Amateur Riders Class F (0-70 3-y-o and up) £2,070 1m...................... (6:15)

4806a^{8} PUSEY STREET BOY [35] 6-8-10 (5*) Mrs S Bosley (7) *led for one furlong, trkd ldrs, led o'r one out, ran on wl.* ....(12 to 1 op 16 to 1) 1

970 GOTT'S DESIRE [37] (bl) 7-9-3^{5} (5*) Miss S Jakeway (9) *sstnd run frm 2 out, fnshd wl*..........(33 to 1 op 25 to 1) 2

GLENSCAR [41] 7-9-2 (5*) Miss T Spearing (16) *ran on 2 out, styd on ins fnl furlong*.......(33 to 1 op 16 to 1) 3

1172^{2} RISE UP SINGING [64] (bl) 5-10-11 (5*) Mrs J Musson (2) *led aftr one furlong, swtchd to stands side entering strt, hdd o'r one out, one pace*......(11 to 4 fav op 9 to 4) 4

1186^{4} LOMBARD SHIPS [45] (bl) 6-9-6 (5*) Miss D Pomeroy (1) *slwly into strd, sn chasing ldr, ev ch o'r one out, not quicken*..............(10 to 1 op 12 to 1 tchd 8 to 1) 5

1120 LADY LACEY [48] (v) 6-9-9 (5*) Miss K Greaney (8) *hdwy last 2 fs, rng on ins fnl furlong*.........(11 to 2 op 4 to 1) 6

914^{8} KALOKAGATHOS [35] 4-9-1 Miss L Eaton (22) *styd on one pace fnl 2 fs*..................................(20 to 1) 7

881^{9} OSGATHORPE [37] 6-8-12 (5*) Mrs A Usher (3) *wl plcd, wknd o'r one out*................(33 to 1 op 20 to 1) 8

STANE STREET (Ire) [47] 5-9-8 (5*) Mrs C Dunwoody (10) *towards rear hfwy, late prog*.....(40 to 1 op 25 to 1) 9

PINTAIL BAY [47] 7-9-12^{4} (5*) Miss A Owen (11) *nvr better than fnl placing*..............(20 to 1 op 16 to 1) 10

1207^{5} HERETICAL MISS [60] 3-9-9 (5*) Mrs J Boggis (4) *nvr nrr.* ....(8 to 1) 11

294^{9} BREEZED WELL [52] 7-9-13 (5*) Mrs H Noonan (25) *rcd in mid-div most of way*.............(33 to 1 op 16 to 1) 12

1090^{6} BAULKING TOWERS [46] 3-8-10^{1} (5*) Miss S Farrant (15) *chsd frnt rnk, no extr frm 2 out*....(50 to 1 op 25 to 1) 13

40 PETERED OUT [49] 3-9-3^{3} Miss P Robson (20) *nvr dngrs.* ....(50 to 1) 14

1186^{8} ALDINGTON PEACH [43] 4-9-9^{8} (5*) Mr W McLaughlin (14) *ldg grp for 6 fs, fdd*...............(33 to 1 op 20 to 1) 15

1073 HILLSDOWN BOY (Ire) [52] 3-9-1 (5*) Mr T Cuff (21) *nvr nr to chal*..(50 to 1) 16

64^{8} CELTIC BOB [47] 13-9-11^{3} (5*) Mr A Mitchell (13) *towards rear most of way*..............(50 to 1 op 33 to 1) 17

1238 RAG TIME BELLE [41] 7-9-7^{12} (5*) Miss J Russell (24) *speed to hfwy*....................(20 to 1 op 33 to 1) 18

1207 RIPSNORTER (Ire) [56] 4-10-3 (5*) Miss A Purdy (17) *nvr on terms*.......................(16 to 1 op 12 to 1) 19

883 SUMMER EXPRESS [55] 4-10-2 (5*) Miss C Spearing (5) *chsd ldrs for 6 fs*................(50 to 1 op 33 to 1) 20

1035^{4} FAIRFORD [47] 4-9-13 Miss I Diana W Jones (23) *wl plcd for o'r 4 fs*..............................(12 to 1 op 33 to 1) 21

244 SUPREME OPTIMIST [41] (bl) 9-9-7^{12} (5*) Mrs C Peacock (12) *al beh*..................................(50 to 1) 22

970^{7} AGENDA ONE [56] 3-9-10^{11} (5*) Mrs F Whitfield (19) *al towards rear*....................(50 to 1 op 25 to 1) 23

Dist: 1½l, ½l, ½l, 1½l, sht-hd, 1½l, 2½l, 1½l, 5l, sht-hd. 1m 44.30s. a 7.50s (23 Ran).
SR: 25/22/24/45/21/23/5/-/4/ (M A Wilkins), J R Bosley

1317 Packwood Median Auction Maiden Stakes Class E (2-y-o) £3,125 5f (6:50)

1063 MOUNT LEINSTER 9-0 N Adams (5) *made all, rdn clr o'r one out, styd on wl*.....(11 to 4 op 4 to 1 tchd 9 to 2) 1

886^{4} PARADISE NEWS 8-9 B Raymond (11) *ldg grp, und pres to chal 2 out, kpt on one pace ins fnl furlong*..... (8 to 1) 2

MAJOR SUCCESS (Ire) 9-0 D Holland (7) *chsd wnr, rdn and one pace appr fnl furlong*... (9 to 4 fav op 6 to 4) 3

877^{6} ABLEST SON 9-0 M Hills (8) *wl plcd, no extr o'r one furlong out*........... (13 to 2 op 7 to 1 tchd 8 to 1) 4

BELLAROY 8-4 (5*) Stephen Davies (10) *ran on appr fnl furlong, not rch wnr*. (20 to 1 op 14 to 1 tchd 25 to 1) 5

CA IRA (Ire) 8-9 J Williams (9) *in tch for o'r 3 fs.* ....(7 to 1 op 4 to 1) 6

528 SALT STONE (Ire) 8-2 (7*) S Mulvey (1) *nvr on terms.* .... (12 to 1 op 8 to 1) 7

922 WHITCHURCH SILK (Ire) 8-9 T Sprake (6) *pressed ldrs for 3 fs, grad wknd o'r one out*.......... (25 to 1 op 20 to 1) 8

SARASONIA 8-9 A McGlone (12) *outpcd*......... (33 to 1) 9

SILVERISTE (Ire) 9-0 G Bardwell (4) *slwly into strd, al outpcd*..............................(40 to 1 op 33 to 1) 10

Dist: 2½l, 2½l, ½l, 1½l, 1l, ½l, sht-hd, 1½l, 7l. 1m 2.40s. a 4.20s (10 Ran).
SR: 31/16/11/9/-/-/ (M & N Plant Ltd), P G Murphy

1318 Dudley Handicap Class D (0-80 4-y-o and up) £3,669 1¼m 169yds.....(7:20)

678 BIT ON THE SIDE (Ire) [58] 4-8-3 (7*) D McCabe (10) *hld up in last pl, ran on o'r 2 out, shaken up to ld ins fnl furlong, styd on*..............................(12 to 1) 1

663^{8} KNOWTH (Ire) [64] 4-9-2 T Quinn (4) *hld up towards rear, ran on 3 out, slight ld o'r one out, hng rght and hdd ins fnl furlong, no extr und pres*....(11 to 4 fav op 6 to 4) 2

1064 SURREY DANCER [72] (bl) 5-9-10 B Raymond (8) *hld up, prog 4 out, ev ch 2 out, outpcd appr fnl furlong.* ....(3 to 1 op 4 to 1) 3

840 SAINT CIEL (USA) [60] 5-8-5 (7*) D Wright (5) *pld hrd early stages, trkd ldr, led o'r 3 out, hdd and wknd over one out*.................................(8 to 1 op 6 to 1) 4

1069 WILL SOON [63] 4-9-1 C Rutter (9) *wl in tch, jnd ldrs o'r 3 out, btn over one furlong out*.......(7 to 1 op 10 to 1) 5

500^{4} MYFONTAINE [61] 6-8-13 G Bardwell (11) *ldg grp, ev ch o'r 2 fs out, sn rdn and lost pl*........ (4 to 1 tchd 7 to 2) 6

1094^{9} CHILD STAR (Fr) [53] 4-8-5 S Dawson (6) *led til hdd o'r 3 fs out, wknd quickly*................ (20 to 1 op 16 to 1) 7

1093 SANDRO [45] 4-7-11 N Adams (3) *al towards rear.* ....(25 to 1 op 20 to 1) 8

SHIRL [44] 4-7-10^{10} (7*) P McCabe (2) *pressed ldrs til wknd 4 fs out*......................................(33 to 1) 9

Dist: ½l, 5l, 2l, 5l, 6l, 1½l, 5l, nk. 2m 21.60s. a 8.80s (9 Ran).
SR: 39/44/42/26/19/5/ (Mike Hawkett), W J Musson

1319 Radway Stakes Claiming Class F (3-y-o) £2,070 1¼m 169yds........ (7:50)

ALLEGATION (bl) 8-9 A Munro (5) *chsd ldrs til checked and lost pl 4 furlong out, rdn and ran on 2 out, led one out, drw clr, easily.* (Evens fav op 5 to 4 on tchd 11 to 10) 1

1099^{2} ABSALOM'S PILLAR 8-3 J Lowe (6) *hld up in rear, rapid prog 4 fs out, led o'r one out, sn hdd and not quicken.* ....(15 to 8 op 7 to 4 tchd 2 to 1) 2

976 ONE MORE POUND 8-2^{2} R Perham (7) *wl in tch, led 5 out till o'r over five fs out, rdn and no extr.* ....(9 to 1 op 8 to 1) 3

1062^{8} SO SAUCY 7-10^{1} F Norton (1) *hld up, rdn alng and outpcd frm 2 fs out*............... (10 to 1 op 8 to 1) 4

FLYING AMY 7-10^{9} (7*) P McCabe (2) *wl plcd til rdn and outpcd fnl 2 fs*.................. (16 to 1 op 14 to 1) 5

1133 BECKY BOO 7-0 (7*) D Wright (4) *pld hrd, pressed ldr, led 6 fs out till 5 out, wknd 3 out*.....(50 to 1 op 33 to 1) 6

928^{8} MARSHALL PINDARI 8-0 T Sprake (3) *led til 6 fs out, lost pl 2 out, tld off*.................. (40 to 1 op 25 to 1) 7

Dist: 3l, ½l, 5l, 8l, 6l, 12l. 2m 24.20s. a 11.40s (7 Ran).
SR: 13/1/-/-/ (Fahd Salman), P F I Cole

1320 Coten End Maiden Stakes Class D (3-y-o and up) £3,640 7f........... (8:20)

ABSOLUTE MAGIC 3-8-13 M Hills (4) *handily plcd, rdn to ld o'r one furlong out, sn clr*.........(8 to 1 op 5 to 1) 1

1093^{6} CLASS ATTRACTION (USA) 4-9-5 M Perrett (2) *ldg grp, ev ch appr fnl furlong, not quicken.* (16 to 1 op 10 to 1) 2

854^{6} RED COTTON 3-8-8 Paul Eddery (1) *led til hdd o'r one furlong out, kpt on same pace*....... (3 to 1 op 7 to 4) 3

CATEQUIL (Can) 3-8-8 T Quinn (10) *hld up, cld on ldrs o'r 2 fs out, chlgd over one out, no extr clsg stages.* ....(5 to 2 fav op 9 to 4 tchd 2 to 1) 4

1175^{5} THE SNOUT 3-8-1 (7*) D McCabe (11) *ran on 3 fs out, rdn alng o'r one out, styd on ins fnl furlong.* ....(6 to 1 op 4 to 1) 5

837^{6} FAIRY WISHER (Ire) 4-9-5 A Munro (5) *settled in rear, no imprsn on ldrs last 2 fs*............ (12 to 1 op 33 to 1) 6

1069^{6} CHANDIGARH 5-9-10 J Williams (8) *wl plcd for 4 fs, fdd.* .... (12 to 1 op 10 to 1 tchd 16 to 1) 7

PHARLING 3-8-8 B Raymond (6) *towards rear most of way*............................. (20 to 1 op 12 to 1) 8

516 RUBY VISION (Ire) 4-9-5 N Adams (9) *pressed ldr til lost pl 2 fs out*.................................... (100 to 1) 9

FAMILY ROSE 4-9-3 (7*) S Mulvey (7) *dwlt, al beh.* (33 to 1) 10

872^{8} MARCHMAIN 3-8-13 J Lowe (12) *trkd ldrs for o'r 4 fs.* .... (12 to 1 op 7 to 1) 11

1034 ALLEGRO CON BRIO 5-9-10 S Whitworth (3) *hld up, sn pushed alng in rear, nvr on terms.* (50 to 1 op 20 to 1) 12

Dist: 2l, 1½l, hd, ½l, 8l, 2l, 1½l, 1½l, 10l, 2l. 1m 30.30s. a 6.50s (12 Ran).
SR: 33/33/17/16/14/1/ (Mrs Barbara Bassett), W J Haggas

1321 Banbury Handicap Class E (0-70 3-y-o and up) £3,297 1¾m 194yds.....(8:50)

857^{4} BALASANI (Fr) [65] 7-9-11 M Perrett (5) *hld up gng wl, improved frm hfwy, ran on 3 out, led ins fnl furlong, cleverly*........................(6 to 4 fav tchd 15 to 8) 1

727 INTREPID LASS [39] 6-7-6 (7*) Antoinette Armes (13) *led, sn clr, jnd 3 fs out, hdd and no extr ins fnl furlong.* ....(12 to 1 op 9 to 1 tchd 14 to 1) 2

1041^{7} CHAMPAGNE GOLD [55] 6-9-1 J Williams (8) *dwlt, cld on ldrs 5 fs out, ev ch 2 out, ran on one pace.* ....(33 to 1 tchd 40 to 1) 3

739⁵ ALLMOSA [48] 4-8-7 D Holland (12) *chsd ldg grp, rdn alng 2 fs out, not quicken*.....(5 to 1 op 8 to 1 tchd 9 to 1) 4
894⁵ ENFANT DU PARADIS (Ire) [40] 5-7-9 (5*) A Garth (7) *ran on fnl 2 fs, nvr nrr*.....................(9 to 1 op 6 to 1) 5
ROYAL PRINT (Ire) [42] 4-7-12 (3*) D Harrison (9) *styd on one pace frm 2 fs out, no ch wth wnr*...(20 to 1 op 16 to 1) 6
822⁶ CHAKALAK [60] 5-9-6 T Quinn (1) *wl in tch, rdn and no hdwy frm 2 fs out*..................(9 to 1 op 7 to 1) 7
727 WHITE RIVER [39] 7-7-13 A Tucker (6) *dwlt, beh most of way*..(14 to 1) 8
727 UNDERWYCHWOOD (Ire) [42] 5-8-2 G Bardwell (15) *wl plcd til hrd rdn and wknd 5 fs out*......(25 to 1 op 16 to 1) 9
901 IZITALLWORTHIT [34] 4-7-1¹ (7*) D Wright (14) *hld up in rear, nvr on terms*....(16 to 1 op 20 to 1 tchd 33 to 1) 10
826⁷ PRINCESS ERMYN [50] 4-8-9 A Clark (3) *chsd ldr, ev ch o'r 2 fs out, sn lost pl*..........(25 to 1 op 20 to 1) 11
1156⁸ ICE MAGIC [41] 6-8-1 A McGlone (4) *hdwy 6 fs out, chlgd and not quicken 2 out, wknd o'r one out.* ....(50 to 1 op 33 to 1) 12
453 BEAU QUEST [61] 6-9-7 J Lowe (10) *al beh.* ....(20 to 1 tchd 25 to 1) 13
924⁶ PERFORATE [42] 4-8-1⁷ A Munro (2) *rdn alng in rear hfwy, nvr dngrs*..............(8 to 1 op 7 to 1 tchd 9 to 1) 14
826⁹ LAJADHAL (Fr) [40] 4-7-13 T Sprake (11) *tld off*... (33 to 1) 15
Dist: 2l, 3l, 2½l, 1½l, 4l, nk, nk, sht-hd, hd, 2l. 3m 20.80s. a 12.50s (15 Ran).
SR: 31/3/16/5/-/-/11/-/-/ (M D Smith), M C Pipe

CAPANNELLE (ITY) (good)
Saturday May 29th

1322 Premio Lazio (Listed) (3-y-o) £20,173 1¼m..........................(3:00)

953 ARMAN'S SAX (Ire) 8-7 J Reid,.......................... 1
LISAMAUR (Ity) 8-7 S Soto,.......................... 2
4703a⁸ DARK STREET (Ire) 8-7 O Fancera,.......................... 3
CURE THE KING (Ire) 8-7 A Munro,.......................... 4
Dist: 1 ¼l, 2 ¾l, ¾l, 1l, 4½l, 3l. 2m 1.20s. (7 Ran).
(Gerecon Italia), J L Dunlop

1323 Premio Ellington (Group 2) (4-y-o and up) £47,428 1½m................(3:30)

1085⁴ BIG TOBIN (Ity) 4-8-9 O Fancera, *hld up, hdwy o'r 2 fs out, chsd ldr over one out, led fnl strds*.................. 1
390* CAPTAIN HORATIUS (Ire) 4-8-9 J Reid, *hld up, 3rd 3 fs out, led gng easily one and a half out, ct fnl strds*.......... 2
692⁵ REDIPUGLIA (Ire) 4-8-9 B Jovine, *rcd in 5th, kpt on ins fnl 2 fs, nvr nrr*.......................... 3
4682a⁶ ERDELISTAN (Fr) 6-8-9 M Tellini, *rcd in 4th, led 3 fs out till one and a half out, wknd cl hme*.......................... 4
JACK LANG 5-8-9 M Pasquale, *rcd in 3rd, effrt o'r 3 fs out, sn one pace*.......................... 5
FIRING LINE (Ire) 4-8-9 V Mezzatesta, *dsptd ld till led briefly o'r 3 fs out, wknd*.......................... 6
1065⁴ UP ANCHOR (Ire) 4-8-6 A Munro, *dsptd ld till wknd o'r 3 fs out*.......................... 7
KNOW THE WAY (Ity) 6-8-9 S Landi, *rcd in 6th till outpcd wl o'r 3 fs out, tld off*.......................... 8
Dist: Sht-hd, 2½l, ½l, 2½l, hd, 3½l, 12l. 2m 26.80s. (8 Ran).
(Lady Costanza Stable), L Camici

DONCASTER (good)
Saturday May 29th
Going Correction: NIL (races 1,3,4), MINUS 0.20 (2,5,6,7)

1324 EBF Zetland Maiden Stakes Class D (2-y-o) £3,640 6f................(2:20)

POLISH LAUGHTER (USA) 9-0 W R Swinburn (9) *co'red up in midfield, effrt 2 fs out, ran on wl to ld towards finish*..........................(10 to 1 op 6 to 1) 1
1053² BRAILLE (Ire) 9-0 Dean McKeown (8) *nvr far away, rdn to ld 2 fs out, hdd towards finish*..... (6 to 1 tchd 5 to 1) 2
730⁶ ABSOLUTELY FAYRE 9-0 J Fortune (11) *reared leaving stalls, mid-div, rdn 2 fs out, kpt on wl fnl furlong.* ....(16 to 1 op 12 to 1 tchd 20 to 1) 3+
JAZEEL (USA) 9-0 W Carson (16) *beh, imprvg whn no room appr 2 fs out, swtchd o'r one out, kpt on ins fnl furlong*..........................(11 to 8 fav op 6 to 4) 3+
1020⁶ GOLDEN STAR (Ire) 9-0 J Fanning (15) *led early, mid-div, sn rdn, improved 2 fs out, kpt on ins fnl furlong, nrst finish*..........................(25 to 1 op 12 to 1) 5
SCHNOZZLE (Ire) 8-11 (3*) D Harrison (6) *baulked leaving stalls, improved on outer o'r 2 fs out, sn rdn, no imprsn fnl furlong*..........................(33 to 1 op 25 to 1) 6
1020⁸ GREENFINCH (Can) 9-0 T Sprake (14) *beh and sn pushed alng, improved o'r 2 fs out, no imprsn fnl furlong.* ....(20 to 1 op 12 to 1) 7
1063⁷ PICCOLO 9-0 D Holland (7) *pressed ldg bunch, rdn 2 fs out, not quicken*..... (11 to 2 op 5 to 1 tchd 13 to 2) 8
1131 MAJESTIC HEIGHTS (Ire) 9-0 G Hind (13) *cl up, rdn hfwy, wknd o'r one furlong out*.........(20 to 1 op 14 to 1) 9
STORM LEADER 9-0 M Wigham (12) *beh, effrt and swtchd 2 fs out, not pace to chal*.......... (33 to 1 op 20 to 1) 10
STEPHENSONS ROCKET 9-0 G Carter (1) *slwly into strd, in tch, took clr order hfwy, rdn o'r 2 fs out, sn btn.* ....(20 to 1 op 12 to 1) 11
1135² JOHNNIE THE JOKER 9-0 D Nicholls (2) *nvr far away, drvn alng hfwy, wkng whn badly hmpd 2 fs out.* ....(11 to 1 op 8 to 1 tchd 12 to 1) 12
673 BELLROI (Ire) 8-7 (7*) S Mulvey (3) *in tch, rdn hfwy, wknd 2 fs out*..........................(25 to 1 op 20 to 1) 13
1082³ HOTCROFT 8-9 A Culhane (10) *sn led, hdd 2 fs out, soon wknd*..........................(16 to 1 op 10 to 1) 14
Dist: Sht-hd, 2l, dd-ht, 3l, 1l, 1½l, nk, 1½l, ¾l, 6l. 1m 14.84s. a 3.44s (14 Ran).
SR: 31/30/22/22/10/6/ (Juma Humaid), B Hanbury

1325 Northern Racing School Furniture Factors Ltd Apprentice Handicap Class E (0-80 4-y-o and up) £2,611 1m..........................(2:50)

964* SWEET MIGNONETTE [69] 5-9-1 (8*) S Copp (1) *hld up, effrt and swtchd o'r 3 fs out, hng rght 2 out, str run fnl furlong to ld last strd*..........(9 to 4 fav op 7 to 4) 1
1069⁴ WALKING THE PLANK [74] 4-10-0 D Harrison (4) *led til hdd o'r one furlong out, rallied to rgn ld ins fnl furlong, ct last strd*..............(5 to 2 op 9 to 4 tchd 11 to 4) 2
1193* TAWAFIJ (USA) [70] 4-9-10 Stephen Davies (6) *chsd ldrs, improved o'r 2 fs out, led over one out, hdd ins last, no extr*.......................... (3 to 1 tchd 7 to 2) 3
363⁴ LEAVE IT TO LIB [59] 6-8-13 J Tate (2) *trkd ldg pair, rdn 2 fs out, wknd appr fnl furlong*.......(7 to 1 tchd 15 to 2) 4
SIR ARTHUR HOBBS [56] 6-8-10 N Kennedy (5) *pressed ldr, rdn 3 fs out, wknd o'r one out*....... (9 to 1 op 8 to 1) 5
1186² PRINCESS OF ORANGE [50] 4-8-4 A Garth (3) *steadied strt, rstrained in rear, improved on outer hfwy, rdn, drifted rght and lost tch o'r 2 fs out*.......(12 to 1 op 10 to 1) 6
Dist: Sht-hd, 1l, 2½l, 8l, 12l. 1m 41.57s. a 4.87s (6 Ran).
SR: 12/16/9/ (Ron Whitehead), Mrs M Reveley

1326 Gazette & Herald Ryedale Handicap Stakes (Class C) (0-90 3-y-o) £5,089 6f..........................(3:20)

846⁴ STORITHS (Ire) [85] 9-7 W R Swinburn (5) *hld up, gd hdwy 2 fs out, swtchd outsd o'r one out, led one out, pushed out*..........................(5 to 2 fav op 4 to 1) 1
GREENLET (Ire) [80] 9-2 D Holland (9) *chsd ldrs gng wl, effrt appr fnl furlong, sn ev ch, not quicken towards finish*..........................(8 to 1 op 11 to 2) 2
ALASIB [75] 8-8 (3*) D Harrison (6) *chsd ldrs, ev ch o'r one furlong out, one pace ins last*........(8 to 1 op 7 to 1) 3
963⁷ RAIN SPLASH [70] 7-13 (7*) Claire Balding (3) *beh and sn rdn, improved 2 fs out, kpt on fnl furlong, no extr towards finish*.......................... (33 to 1 op 20 to 1) 4
347⁶ PALACEGATE TOUCH [84] 9-6 G Carter (8) *prmnt, led aftr a furlong, rdn 2 out, hdd one out, sn btn.* ....(6 to 1 op 9 to 2) 5
514⁸ DALALAH [75] 8-11 W Carson (1) *beh and sn pushed alng, effrt on outer hfwy, no imprsn o'r one furlong out.* ....(7 to 1 tchd 8 to 1) 6
977⁴ MURPHY'S HOPE (Ire) [62] 7-12 J Lowe (7) *led a furlong, styd upsides, ev ch wl o'r one out, sn btn.* ....(9 to 1 op 8 to 1 tchd 10 to 1) 7
542 LUCAYAN TREASURE [84] (v) 9-6 F Norton (4) *beh and sn pushed alng, lost tch o'r 2 fs out*....(15 to 2 op 5 to 1) 8
1137* HOTARIA [70] 8-6 A Culhane (2) *chsd ldrs, sn pushed alng, lost tch o'r 2 fs out, tld off*..........(9 to 2 op 3 to 1) 9
Dist: ¾l, 2½l, ½l, 2l, 1½l, 1½l, 15l, 8l. 1m 13.86s. a 2.46s (9 Ran).
SR: 58/50/35/28/34/19/ (Mrs M Irwin), J W Watts

1327 Gresley Median Auction Maiden Stakes Class E (3-y-o) £2,898 5f (3:50)

872³ AROOM 9-0 W Carson (7) *al frnt rnk, led hfwy, shaken up appr fnl furlong, kpt on ins last.* ....(2 to 1 on tchd 6 to 4 on) 1
VISIMOTION (USA) 9-0 W R Swinburn (3) *slight ld to hfwy, remained upsides, rdn and ev ch appr fnl furlong, no extr ins last*..........................(9 to 2 op 7 to 2) 2
1095 DISCO BOY 9-0 Dean McKeown (6) *chsd ldrs, effrt and not much room 2 fs out, kpt on ins last*.......(16 to 1) 3
1148 THE FED 9-0 A Culhane (1) *prmnt, rdn hfwy, not quicken appr fnl furlong*..........................(7 to 1 op 6 to 1) 4
974⁷ OSCAR THE SECOND (Ire) 9-0 J Fanning (5) *slwly into strd, beh, effrt and rdn 2 fs out, kpt on fnl furlong, no imprsn*..............(40 to 1 op 33 to 1 tchd 50 to 1) 5
683 DAYJUZ (Ire) 9-0 G Carter (2) *chsd ldrs, improved on outer hfwy, sn drvn alng, wknd appr fnl furlong*... (12 to 1) 6
SHALAKO 9-0 J Lowe (4) *dwlt, sn rdn in rear, wknd 2 fs out*..........................(33 to 1) 7
Dist: 1½l, 1½l, 2l, ¾l, sht-hd, 3l. 1m 1.59s. a 2.79s (7 Ran).
SR: 44/38/32/24/21/20/8/ (Hamdan Al-Maktoum), C J Benstead

1328 Hayselden Audi VW Handicap Class C (0-100 3-y-o and up) £4,836 1½m (4:20)

989[3] AZHAR [90] 3-8-8 W R Swinburn (1) *made all, rdn 3 fs out, hld on wl fnl quarter m*.........(9 to 2 fav op 7 to 2) 1
1028[4] DREAMS END [81] 5-9-3 R Cochrane (3) *settled midfield, imprvg whn no room o'r 2 fs out, squeezed through wl over one out, kpt on ins last, not rch wnr*. ....(6 to 1 tchd 13 to 2) 2
1173 LABURNUM [66] 5-8-2 D Holland (6) *steadied strt, hld up in rear, improved on inner 4 fs out, short of room 2 out, rdn and kpt on ins last*. (5 to 1 op 9 to 2 tchd 11 to 2) 3
894[6] MAD MILITANT (Ire) [69] 4-8-5 W Carson (5) *in tch, improved on outsd 3 fs out, rdn and not quicken appr fnl furlong*..................................(5 to 1) 4
1039* REDSTELLA (USA) [87] 4-9-9 A Culhane (2) *chsd ldrs, effrt and rdn 4 fs out, ev ch o'r 2 out, wkng whn hmpd appr fnl furlong*.....................(8 to 1 tchd 10 to 1) 5
AZUREUS (Ire) [72] 5-8-3 (5*) Darren Moffatt (4) *hld up, pushed alng to improve 5 fs out, no imprsn fnl quarter m*.....................(15 to 2 op 5 to 1 tchd 8 to 1) 6
785* LEGION OF HONOUR [68] 5-8-1 (3*) D Harrison (7) *wth ldr, rdn and ev ch 3 fs out, wknd 2 out*. (11 to 2 op 5 to 1) 7
KIVETON KABOOZ [88] 5-9-10 J Fortune (8) *chsd ldrs, effrt and rdn 3 fs out, wknd wl o'r one out*. ....(10 to 1 op 8 to 1 tchd 11 to 1) 8
Dist: 1l, nk, 3l, hd, 3l, 1½l, 2½l. 2m 32.26s. a 1.76s (8 Ran).
SR: 52/59/43/40/57/36/29/44/ (Sheikh Ahmed Al Maktoum), M R Stoute

1329 Jane McKerron's High Flier Romantic Novel Conditions Stakes Class D (3-y-o) £3,465 1¼m 60yds......... (4:50)

947[5] YELTSIN 8-11 R Cochrane (4) *trkd ldrs, improved to ld o'r 3 fs out, drvn out fnl furlong, eased cl hme*...(7 to 4 jt-fav op 6 to 4 tchd 2 to 1) 1
751* WAGON MASTER (Fr) 9-1 W Carson (6) *hld up in tch, smooth hdwy to chal o'r 2 fs out, shaken up over one out, edgd lft ins last, one pace*. (7 to 4 jt-fav op 5 to 2) 2
755* SOVIET LINE (Ire) 9-5 W R Swinburn (5) *hld up in tch, took clr order 3 fs out, rdn 2 out, eased whn btn ins fnl furlong*................(2 to 1 op 7 to 4 tchd 5 to 2) 3
947[8] BEAUMAN 8-11 Dean McKeown (3) *slight ld 2 fs, dsptd lead, rgned lead briefly o'r 3 out, sn drvn alng, wknd two out*...........(50 to 1 op 33 to 1 tchd 66 to 1) 4
658[9] HILARY GERRARD (USA) 9-1 M Birch (1) *pressed ldr 2 fs, made remainder til hdd o'r 3 out, sn lost tch*. .... (25 to 1 op 12 to 1) 5
Dist: 1l, 5l, 15l, 2l. 2m 9.45s. a 2.75s (5 Ran).
SR: 49/51/45/7/7/ (Sheikh Mohammed), H R A Cecil

1330 Frickley Maiden Stakes Class D (3-y-o) £3,611 1m................. (5:20)

825[9] NAIF (USA) 9-0 R Cochrane (8) *hld up in tch, improved to ld appr fnl quarter m, styd on gmely whn hrd pressed final furlong*.......(15 to 8 fav op 5 to 4 tchd 2 to 1) 1
751 AJDAYT (USA) 9-0 S Whitworth (6) *slwly into strd, beh, effrt and rdn 2 fs out, ran on to chal ins last, no extr nr finish*............................(12 to 1 op 10 to 1) 2
QUEENS CONSUL (Ire) 8-6 (3*) D Harrison (2) *chsd ldrs, effrt o'r 3 out fs, edgd rght over 2 out, ev ch over one out, not quicken wl ins last*..................(33 to 1) 3
1068 MONSIGNOR PAT (USA) 9-0 A McGlone (4) *trkd ldr, rdn appr strt, outpcd o'r 2 fs out, staying on finish*. .... (11 to 2 op 9 to 2) 4
MUSTAKIM (Ire) 9-0 W Carson (5) *chsd ldrs, rdn 3 fs out, hmpd o'r 2 out, sn btn*... (4 to 1 op 3 to 1 tchd 5 to 1) 5
1145[5] BOLD THATCHER (bl) 9-0 M Birch (3) *led till hdd appr fnl quarter m, grad wknd*...............(4 to 1 op 3 to 1) 6
437[8] MOVE SMARTLY (Ire) 9-0 R Lappin (1) *beh, effrt and rdn o'r 3 fs out, sn btn*................................(8 to 1) 7
1060 D SEVEN 8-7 (7*) C Hawksley (7) *beh and sn pushed alng, lost tch appr strt, tld off*......................(50 to 1) 8
Dist: Nk, ¾l, 6l, ½l, 2½l, 4l, dist. 1m 39.38s. a 2.68s (8 Ran).
SR: 36/35/28/15/13/5/-/-/ (Sultan Mohammed), L M Cumani

DOOMBEN (AUS) (heavy)
Saturday May 29th

1331 Doomben Cup (Group 1) (3-y-o and up) £88,636 1¼m 22yds............ (1:00)

ROUGH HABIT (NZ) 7-9-1 J Cassidy,..........(5 to 2 fav) 1
KIWI GOLFER 4-9-0 B Compton,................(10 to 1) 2
PALATE 3-8-6 L Dittman,.........................(14 to 1) 3
Dist: Nk, 1 ¼l. 2m 3.00s. (14 Ran).
(D Smith Et Al), J Wheeler

FAIRYHOUSE (IRE) (yielding to soft)
Saturday May 29th

1332 County Club (Dunshaughlin) E.B.F. Maiden (2-y-o) £4,140 6f........ (3:00)

1121[2] JEDWA (Ire) 8-11 C Roche (2)....................(6 to 1) 1
869[8] LA BERTA (Ire) 8-11 W J O'Connor (15).......... (14 to 1) 2
1104[4] DILIGENT DODGER (Ire) 9-0 W J Supple (5)....... (7 to 1) 3
STAGE LEFT EVEN (Ire) 9-0 S Craine (8)...........(3 to 1) 4
PEACE ROLE (USA) 9-0 M J Kinane (14).......(5 to 2 fav) 5
1044[2] SPRING FORCE (Ire) 9-0 K J Manning (11)....... (10 to 3) 6
VIVA VICTOR (Ire) 8-8 (6*) J J Behan (13).........(10 to 1) 7
BENAZIR LADY (Ire) 8-5 (6*) J A Heffernan (6).....(20 to 1) 8
DAYESS (USA) 9-0 P Shanahan (4).............(20 to 1) 9
1022[6] JOMACOON (Ire) 8-3 (8*) (3).....................(16 to 1) 10
869[5] SUMMERHILL SPECIAL (Ire) 8-11 Joanna Morgan (12) ....(16 to 1) 11
MONEYBROKER (Ire) 9-0 J P Murtagh (1)........(20 to 1) 12
PEARL OF ORIENT (Ire) 9-0 G Curran (10)..........(33 to 1) 13
BANK STATEMENT (Ire) 9-0 P V Gilson (9).........(8 to 1) 14
1044[6] BAKER HILL (Ire) 9-0 R Hughes (7)...............(20 to 1) 15
Dist: 3l, sht-hd, 2½l, 1½l. 1m 14.00s. (15 Ran).
(Hamad Ali), J S Bolger

1333 College Proteins E.B.F. Maiden (3-y-o and up) £4,140 7f...............(3:30)

806[2] KINDNESS ITSELF (Ire) 3-8-5 M J Kinane (18) (11 to 8 on) 1
1164[3] SANS CERIPH (Ire) 3-8-7[2] W J O'Connor (13)......(7 to 1) 2
847[5] PERSIAN GEM (Ire) 3-8-5 J D Eddery (15)........(20 to 1) 3
1050 WHAT MAGIC (Ire) 3-8-5 Joanna Morgan (7)......(14 to 1) 4
GLACIAL ARCTIC (USA) 3-8-8 P Shanahan (2).....(8 to 1) 5
LHOTSE (Ire) 3-8-6[1] S Craine (20)................(8 to 1) 6
ASTA MADERA (Ire) 3-8-5 J F Egan (1)..............(14 to 1) 7
669 ARROGANT LADY 3-8-5 P V Gilson (19).........(16 to 1) 8
847[6] MISS MARESE (Ire) 3-8-7[2] K J Manning (5).......(16 to 1) 9
MAJESTIC PADDY (Ire) 3-8-8 D V Smith (8).......(14 to 1) 10
DOREG (Ire) 3-8-8 R Hughes (17)...............(12 to 1) 11
TERESIAN GIRL (Ire) 3-8-5 D Manning (14).......(25 to 1) 12
PADDYS COCKTAIL (Ire) 3-8-5 W J Supple (12)... (14 to 1) 13
806 GEALLAINNBAN (Ire) 3-8-8 E A Leonard (16)..... (20 to 1) 14
BUTTERNUT (Ire) 3-8-2[7] (10*) A P Colgan (3)..... (25 to 1) 15
847 NURSES RUN (Ire) 3-7-9 (10*) B Carson (6)......(14 to 1) 16
KHASI HILLS (Ire) 3-8-3 (2*) D G O'Shea (9).......(20 to 1) 17
1164 DAIRINE'S DELIGHT (Ire) 3-7-13 (6*) P P Murphy (10) ....(25 to 1) 18
CAN'T RECALL (USA) 3-7-13 (6*) J J Behan (11).. (12 to 1) 19
1105[3] FIVE LITTLE GIRLS (Ire) 3-8-5 N G McCullagh (21) (14 to 1) 20
Dist: ½l, sht-hd, 2½l, 2½l. 1m 30.80s. (20 Ran).
(Lady Clague), John M Oxx

1334 Kepak Handicap (0-100 3-y-o) £8,280 1½m........................... (4:00)

941[7] BALLYKETT LADY (USA) [-] 8-10 C Roche (6)...... (7 to 2) 1
1046* MICKS DELIGHT (Ire) [-] 7-9 (6*,5ex) J J Behan (4) ....(6 to 4 fav) 2
1198[9] FLAME OF PERSIA (Ire) [-] 9-6 W J O'Connor (5)... (8 to 1) 3
1250* BLUE DIANA (Ire) [-] 8-8 (5ex) J F Egan (7).........(8 to 1) 4
1046[8] VINEY (USA) [-] (bl) 8-5[1] M J Kinane (2)...........(12 to 1) 5
849* THE BERUKI (Ire) [-] 7-1 (6*) P P Murphy (3)........(6 to 1) 6
1046[6] NEVER BACK DOWN (Ire) [-] 8-10 W J Supple (9) (13 to 2) 7
1202[4] TARTAN LADY (Ire) [-] 9-0 S Craine (1).............(6 to 1) 8
Dist: 1l, 6l, 1l, 3½l. 2m 46.20s. (8 Ran).
(Stephen Keating), J S Bolger

1335 Duggan Brothers E.B.F. Maiden (3-y-o) £4,140 1½m............... (4:30)

1048[4] CLEAR ABILITY (Ire) (bl) 8-11 M J Kinane (8).......(3 to 1) 1
1048[6] NA-AMMAH (Ire) 8-11 W J Supple (7).............(4 to 1) 2
1236[6] SAFE CONDUCT (Ire) 9-0 J P Murtagh (2)..........(8 to 1) 3
ERZADJAN (Ire) 9-0 D Hogan (3).....................(9 to 2) 4
1122[5] CARRICK PIKE (USA) (bl) 9-0 C Roche (9).........(7 to 1) 5
1122[2] TURNER PRIZE (Ire) 9-0 S Craine (6)........... (5 to 2 fav) 6
1140[3] HIND VISION (Ire) 8-11 J F Egan (4)..............(9 to 1) 7
MAXIXE (Ire) 9-0 P V Gilson (1)......................(7 to 1) 8
Dist: 2l, 1l, 1l, 13l. 2m 50.60s. (8 Ran).
(Moyglare Stud Farm), D K Weld

HAYDOCK (soft)
Saturday May 29th
Going Correction: PLUS 0.35 sec. per fur. (races 1,3,5,7), PLUS 0.15 (2,4,6)

1336 Harcros Timber & Building Supplies Stayers Championship Series Handicap Qualifier Class D (0-80 4-y-o and up) £6,524 1¾m................(2:00)

1260* PERSUASIVE [61] 6-8-11 (3ex) Dale Gibson (1) *patiently rdn, improved to ld appr fnl furlong, drvn out*. ....(4 to 1 op 11 to 4) 1
988[3] WHITE WILLOW [77] 4-9-13 M Hills (8) *tucked away in midfield, improved to ld 2 fs out, hdd and wndrd appr fnl furlong, one pace*..........(3 to 1 fav tchd 7 to 2) 2
967[9] BUSTINETTA [77] 4-9-13 P Robinson (5) *settled off the pace, drvn alng to improve last 2 fs, ran on und pres*. .... (14 to 1 op 10 to 1) 3
1173 CHIEF MINISTER (Ire) [71] 4-9-7 K Fallon (3) *sluggish strt, bustled alng to improve on outsd last 2 fs, nrst finish*. .... (15 to 2 op 6 to 1 tchd 8 to 1) 4

874[7] POINCIANA [63] (bl) 4-8-13 Pat Eddery (2) *settled gng wl, jnd ldr on bit o'r 2 fs out, rdn and no response.* .... (10 to 1 op 7 to 1) 5

988[9] HIGHFLYING [75] 7-9-11 J Carroll (7) *trkd ldg bunch, effrt and drvn alng entering strt, nvr able to chal.* .... (8 to 1 op 12 to 1) 6+

785[5] BIGWHEEL BILL (Ire) [75] 4-9-11 G Duffield (4) *settled aftr fst break, rnwd effrt und pres o'r 2 fs out, one pace.* .... (8 to 1 op 6 to 1) 6+

290 FIVE TO SEVEN (USA) [72] 4-9-3 (5*) O Pears (10) *chsd ldr, hrd at work o'r 2 fs out, sn btn*.... (20 to 1 op 14 to 1) 8

874[3] HORIZON (Ire) [62] (bl) 5-8-12 S Whitworth (9) *set gd pace, kicked for hme entering strt, hdd and wknd 2 fs out.* .... (11 to 1 op 10 to 1) 9

1028[6] MISS PLUM [78] 4-10-0 R Cochrane (6) *trkd ldg quartet, feeling pace entering strt, sn btn*... (11 to 1 op 8 to 1) 10

Dist: 1½l, hd, 2l, 2½l, 4l, dd-ht, 1½l, 7l, 1½l. 3m 8.15s. a 10.65s (10 Ran).

SR: 39/52/51/41/28/32/32/26/2/ (W G McHarg), Miss L A Perratt

1337 Sandy Lane Rated Stakes (Listed Race) (0-110 3-y-o) £9,681 6f.... (2:30)

1017[5] LOOK WHO'S HERE (Ire) [90] 8-7 G Duffield (5) *stumbled strt, improved on outsd hfwy, led o'r one furlong out, ran on wl*........ (4 to 1 op 7 to 2) 1

1113[6] CELESTIAL KEY (USA) [91] 8-8 K Fallon (1) *nvr far away, led briefly o'r one furlong out, rdn ins last, rallied.* .... (14 to 1 op 12 to 1) 2

977* SOUTHERN MEMORIES (Ire) [90] 8-7 L Piggott (6) *pressed ldg trio, hrd at work o'r one furlong out, kpt on same pace*........ (100 to 30 fav op 9 to 2 tchd 3 to 1) 3

1214[4] STAR FAMILY FRIEND (Ire) [96] (v) 8-13 P Robinson (2) *settled to track ldg quartet, effrt und pres o'r one furlong out, one pace*........ (6 to 1 op 9 to 2) 4

1117[2] LORD OLIVIER (Ire) [104] 9-7 M Tebbutt (7) *chsd ldr, hrd at work o'r one furlong out, no extr*.... (5 to 1 op 4 to 1) 5

1066 SIMPLY SOOTY [90] 8-7 S Whitworth (3) *broke wl to press ldg pair for o'r 4 fs, fdd*........ (16 to 1 op 20 to 1) 6

1043[4] ROGER THE BUTLER (Ire) [101] (bl) 9-4 M Hills (8) *broke fst frm gd draw, led and clr hfwy, wknd and hdd o'r one furlong out*........ (11 to 2 op 5 to 1) 7

858* ELLE SHAPED (Ire) [100] 9-3 R Cochrane (4) *drvn alng to keep up, nvr a factor*........ (11 to 2 op 5 to 1) 8

Dist: ½l, 3½l, ½l, 1l, ½l, 7l, 4l. 1m 14.74s. a 3.14s (8 Ran).

SR: 48/47/32/36/40/24/7/-/ (S L Edwards), B A McMahon

1338 Tote Credit Silver Bowl Handicap Class B (0-110 3-y-o) £20,387 1m 30yds........ (3:00)

855[4] MOORISH [80] 8-2 (7*) T G McLaughlin (8) *patiently rdn, shaken up to ld 2 fs out, sprinted clr.* .... (11 to 1 op 8 to 1) 1

989[7] CONEYBURY (Ire) [86] 9-1 R Cochrane (4) *steadied strt, improved frm off the pace o'r 2 fs out, styd on, no ch wth wnr*........ (16 to 1 op 14 to 1) 2

855[2] KEY TO MY HEART (Ire) [88] 9-3 K Fallon (5) *settled off the pace, weaved through fnl 2 fs, ran on, nrst finish.* .... (10 to 1) 3

1017[3] ERTLON [80] 8-9 M Hills (10) *hld up and beh, chsd alng to improve o'r 2 fs out, kpt on, nvr able to chal*... (14 to 1) 4

921* PRINCESS KRIS [79] 8-8 Pat Eddery (7) *dictated pace till hdd and wknd 2 fs out.* (5 to 1 op 4 to 1 tchd 11 to 2) 5

999[4] SPARK (Ire) [86] 8-12 (3*) S Maloney (2) *nvr far away, hrd at work 2 fs out, no extr*........ (20 to 1 op 16 to 1) 6

875[6] DUTOSKY [75] 7-11 (7*) N Varley (6) *trkd ldg quartet, und pres 2 fs out, fdd*....... (9 to 1 op 8 to 1 tchd 10 to 1) 7

1214[3] MARGARET'S GIFT [84] 8-13 J Carroll (9) *trkd ldr, feeling pace and rdn o'r 2 fs out, sn btn.* (12 to 1 tchd 14 to 1) 8

690[7] BARIK (Ire) [85] 9-0 R Hills (11) *coltish in paddock, improved to join wnr o'r one furlong out, put head on one side, found nothing*........ (4 to 1 jt-fav op 3 to 1 tchd 9 to 2) 9

844[2] AFTER THE LAST [89] 9-4 L Piggott (3) *rcd very freely, lost pl entering strt, sn btn*........ (4 to 1 jt-fav op 6 to 1) 10

EXPO MONDIAL (Ire) [92] 9-7 M Tebbutt (1) *drvn alng to go pace, al in rear*........ (40 to 1 op 33 to 1) 11

1080[2] STORM VENTURE (Ire) [69] 7-5 (7*) D Wright (12) *sweated badly, al wl beh*........ (14 to 1 tchd 16 to 1) 12

945[5] JERVIA [84] 8-13 G Duffield (13) *chsd ldg bunch til fdd und pres o'r 2 fs out*........ (16 to 1) 13

Dist: 6l, ¾l, 2l, 2½l, ½l, ¾l, ½l, nk, hd, 1l. 1m 46.76s. a 6.16s (13 Ran).

SR: 46/34/34/20/11/16/3/10/10/ (Fahd Salman), P F I Cole

1339 EBF St Helens Maiden Fillies Stakes Class D (2-y-o) £3,785 5f........ (3:30)

A SMOOTH ONE (Ire) 8-11 Pat Eddery (3) *sluggish strt, improved centre to ld o'r one furlong out, quickened away ins last*...... (5 to 4 fav op 11 to 10 tchd Evens) 1

1158[2] FLOATING TRIAL 8-11 J Carroll (1) *pressed ldr, led briefly 2 fs out, swshd tail und pres o'r one out, no extr.* .... (11 to 4 op 3 to 1 tchd 7 to 2) 2

544[4] BOLLIN MARY 8-8 (3*) S Maloney (2) *made most for o'r 3 fs, ran green, no extr fnl furlong*....... (5 to 1 op 3 to 1) 3

1203[3] STRAPPED 8-11 M Hills (4) *flt out the whole way, nvr a threat*........ (4 to 1 op 7 to 2) 4

Dist: 4l, 2½l, 1½l. 1m 2.69s. a 3.89s (4 Ran).

SR: 34/18/8/2/ (Bob Lalemant), R Hannon

1340 Eccles Maiden Stakes Class D (3-y-o) £3,915 1¼m 120yds........ (4:00)

PRINCESS BORGHESE (USA) 8-9 Pat Eddery (4) *made most, hrd pressed o'r 2 fs out, kpt on grimly ins last.* .... (9 to 4 op 7 to 4) 1

1068[2] GEORGE DILLINGHAM 9-0 G Duffield (5) *nvr far away, jnd wnr last 2 fs, rdn and not quicken nr finish.* .... (3 to 1 op 11 to 4) 2

751[3] BITTER'S END (Ire) (bl) 9-0 L Piggott (3) *al hndy, drw level o'r 2 fs out, not quicken und pres fnl furlong.* .... (13 to 8 fav op 2 to 1) 3

SASSIVER (USA) 9-0 S Perks (2) *lost many ls strt, drvn alng thrght, nvr nr to chal*........ (33 to 1 op 25 to 1) 4

926[2] BILJAN (USA) 8-7 (7*) T G McLaughlin (1) *trkd ldg pair, hrd at work o'r 2 fs out, sn struggling*.... (8 to 1 op 7 to 1) 5

1212 MODAAYIN 9-0 M Tebbutt (6) *chsd ldg quartet, lost grnd und pres o'r 2 fs out, tld off*....... (25 to 1 op 20 to 1) 6

Dist: 1l, 5l, 8l, 5l, 20l. 2m 20.21s. a 9.21s (6 Ran).

SR: 40/43/33/17/7/-/ (K Abdulla), H R A Cecil

1341 Orrell Apprentice Handicap Class E (0-80 3-y-o) £2,768 6f........ (4:30)

1213[3] ANOTHER JADE [79] 9-2 (5*) G McGrath (3) *sluggish strt, given time to reco'r, led entering fnl furlong, jst lasted.* .... (7 to 2 op 11 to 4) 1

1095[2] CHAMPAGNE GRANDY [63] 8-2 (3*) Mark Denaro (1) *chsd alng to improve frm off the pace last 2 fs, drw level ins last, faltered and jst hld*........ (4 to 1 tchd 7 to 2) 2

846[3] TWO MOVES IN FRONT (Ire) [77] 9-0 (5*) P Roberts (4) *tried to make all, hdd entering fnl furlong, rallied.* .... (5 to 2 fav tchd 3 to 1) 3

1083* PLUM FIRST [72] (bl) 9-0 V Halliday (2) *wth ldr, hrd at work o'r 2 fs out, btn appr fnl furlong*... (4 to 1 tchd 9 to 2) 4

934[6] HEATHYARDS GEM [60] 8-2 M Humphries (6) *unruly in stalls, chsd alng to show speed for o'r 4 fs, sn btn.* .... (10 to 1 tchd 9 to 1) 5

871[5] FOLLY VISION (Ire) [59] 7-12 (3*) D Gibbs (5) *broke wl to show speed to hfwy, wknd quickly o'r one furlong out.* .... (8 to 1 op 7 to 1) 6

Dist: Sht-hd, nk, 4l, 5l, 3½l. 1m 15.22s. a 3.62s (6 Ran).

SR: 53/36/49/28/-/-/ (Mrs Rita J Kaplan), A P Jarvis

1342 Shevington Rating Related Maiden Stakes Class D (3-y-o and up) £3,492 7f 30yds........ (5:00)

463[2] WALI (USA) 3-8-13 R Hills (2) *made all, shaken up to go clr o'r one furlong out, readily*..... (6 to 4 fav op 7 to 4) 1

872[9] DANCING SPIRIT (Ire) 3-8-8 L Piggott (4) *patiently rdn, effrt and shaken up o'r one furlong out, kpt on same pace*........ (9 to 2 op 4 to 1) 2

538[7] WISHAM (USA) 3-8-13 G Duffield (1) *steadied strt, effrt and bustled alng last 2 fs, not quicken.* .... (2 to 1 op 6 to 4 tchd 9 to 4) 3

995[6] FLASHFEET (bl) 3-8-13 M Hills (3) *nvr far away, hrd at work and drvn alng 2 fs out, one pace.* .... (7 to 2 op 3 to 1) 4

Dist: 3l, 2l, hd. 1m 36.93s. a 9.73s (4 Ran).

(Hamdan Al-Maktoum), P T Walwyn

KEMPTON (good)
Saturday May 29th
Going Correction: MINUS 0.15 sec. per fur.

1343 New England Conditions Stakes Class C (2-y-o) £4,327 6f........ (2:10)

793* GOLD LAND (USA) 8-13 T Quinn (2) *trkd ldr gng wl, led jst ins fnl 2 fs, clr one out, easily.* .... (4 to 1 on op 7 to 2 on tchd 5 to 1 on) 1

1131* ZUNO STAR (USA) 8-13 Paul Eddery (1) *led till hdd jst ins fnl 2 fs, kpt on but no ch wth wnr.* .... (15 to 2 op 5 to 1 tchd 8 to 1) 2

1168[5] WINDOW DISPLAY 8-11 J Williams (3) *al disputing 3rd, lost tch frm hfwy*.... (25 to 1 op 16 to 1 tchd 33 to 1) 3

MIDUSHI (USA) 8-6 K Darley (4) *dsptd 3rd till lost tch frm hfwy*........ (12 to 1 op 5 to 1) 4

Dist: 5l, 10l, 2½l. 1m 11.98s. a 1.18s (4 Ran).

SR: 57/37/-/-/ (Fahd Salman), P F I Cole

1344 Californian Maiden Stakes Class D (3-y-o) £4,272 1m........ (2:40)

417[3] JETBEEAH (Ire) 8-9 B Raymond (10) *beh, rapid hdwy on outsd frm 2 fs out, quickened smartly to ld wl ins last.* .... (11 to 2 op 9 to 2 tchd 6 to 1) 1

MUJAAZAFAH (USA) 9-0 M Roberts (4) *chsd ldrs, chlgd frm 2 fs out till led ins last, hdd and no quicken nr finish.* .... (3 to 1 fav op 9 to 4 tchd 7 to 2) 2

BLACK MISCHIEF 8-9 W Ryan (19) *pressed ldrs, str chal frm 2 fs out till outpcd ins last.* .... (11 to 2 op 3 to 1 tchd 6 to 1) 3

1212[6] LEARMONT (USA) 9-0 S Raymont (14) *chsd ldrs till led 4 fs out, hdd jst ins last, styd on.* .... (16 to 1 op 14 to 1 tchd 20 to 1) 4

PIXTON (Ire) 9-0 Paul Eddery (17) *beh, gd hdwy frm 2 fs out, fnshd wl*........ (16 to 1 op 14 to 1 tchd 20 to 1) 5

992[5] SINGER ON THE ROOF 8-9 L Dettori (3) *trkd ldrs on outsd, chlgd frm 2 fs out till wknd ins last.* .... (8 to 1 op 10 to 1 tchd 7 to 1) 6

PARANGO (USA) 9-0 T Quinn (18) *chsd ldrs, chlgd 3 fs out till wknd appr fnl furlong.* .... (8 to 1 op 6 to 1 tchd 10 to 1) 7

FUNNY HILARIOUS (USA) 8-9 D Biggs (7) *broke wl, steadied, hdwy o'r 2 fs out, no imprsn frm over one furlong out*.............................. (50 to 1 op 33 to 1) 8

MIND THE ROOF (Ire) 8-9 J Williams (15) *nvr rchd ldrs.* .... (14 to 1 op 10 to 1) 9

1027 PROTON 9-0 W Newnes (12) *mid-div, effrt 3 fs out, sn wknd*................ (16 to 1 op 14 to 1 tchd 20 to 1) 10

878[5] RACHELLY 8-9 R Perham (1) *mid-div most of way.* .... (50 to 1 op 25 to 1) 11

SEDGY'S SISTER 8-9 N Carlisle (2) *chsd ldrs till wknd o'r 2 fs out*........................ (50 to 1 op 33 to 1) 12

BORROWED AND BLUE 8-9 N Day (9) *slwly into strd, al beh*................................ (33 to 1 op 20 to 1) 13

NOBLE RISK 9-0 K Darley (5) *in tch early, sn beh.* .... (14 to 1 op 10 to 1) 14

JALIB (Ire) 9-0 B Rouse (6) *led 4 fs, sn wknd.* .... (16 to 1 op 12 to 1) 15

SIR KRISPIN 9-0 N Adams (13) *al beh.* .... (50 to 1 op 25 to 1) 16

1027 MELLERIO 9-0 W Woods (11) *al beh.* (50 to 1 op 33 to 1) 17

ROADRUNNER 9-0 G Bardwell (16) *al beh.* .... (50 to 1 op 33 to 1) 18

BEACON TOWERS 9-0 J Quinn (8) *prmnt to hfwy.* .... (50 to 1 op 25 to 1) 19

Dist: ¾l, 3l, sht-hd, 3l, 2l, ¾l, ½l, 1l, ¾l, 3½l. 1m 39.65s. a 2.85s (19 Ran).
SR: 34/37/23/27/18/7/10/3/-/ (Butti Mussabah), J R Fanshawe

1345 Crawley Warren Handicap Class C (0-95 4-y-o and up) £11,080 2m.. (3:10)

857[5] ROBINGO (Ire) [90] (bl) 4-10-0 M Roberts (5) *gd hdwy 5 fs out, drvn to ld one out, hld on wl.* .... (7 to 1 op 6 to 1 tchd 15 to 2) 1

DERAB (USA) [75] (bl) 7-9-1 J Williams (8) *chsd ldrs till led o'r 2 fs out, hdd one out, styd on same pace*... (33 to 1) 2

857* RODEO STAR (USA) [71] 7-8-11 N Carlisle (11) *chsd ldrs, chlgd one and a half fs out, not quicken.* .... (3 to 1 fav op 5 to 2 tchd 100 to 30) 3

618[5] PROVENCE [70] 6-8-10 Paul Eddery (4) *in tch, rdn alng hfwy and lost pl, drvn and styd on ag'n frm 3 fs out.* ....(8 to 1 op 7 to 1) 4

1094[7] JADIDH [53] 5-7-7 G Bardwell (10) *beh, rdn alng 5 fs out, styd on fnl 2 furlongs*..............................(100 to 1) 5

1173* MISS PIN UP [77] 4-9-1 D Biggs (9) *slwly into strd, some prog frm 3 fs out*...... (15 to 2 op 6 to 1 tchd 8 to 1) 6

857[6] BARDOLPH (USA) [75] 6-9-1 T Quinn (1) *chsd ldr, led 3 fs out, hdd o'r 2 out, sn wknd.* ....(7 to 1 op 6 to 1 tchd 8 to 1) 7

874[5] STAR QUEST [70] 6-8-10 L Dettori (2) *al beh.* ....(20 to 1 tchd 33 to 1) 8

967[2] CALL THE GUV'NOR [64] 4-8-2 W Ryan (12) *led till hdd 3 fs out, wknd quickly o'r 2 out.* .... (11 to 2 op 5 to 1 tchd 6 to 1) 9

1041[9] HUNTING GROUND [53] (bl) 5-7-7 A Mackay (6) *effrt 5 fs out, sn wknd*....................(25 to 1 tchd 33 to 1) 10

874[6] DOM WAC [67] 5-8-2 (5*) M Fenton (7) *al beh.* ....(16 to 1 op 14 to 1 tchd 20 to 1) 11

FAUGERON [82] 4-8-13 (7*) T Ashley (3) *slwly into strd, hdwy 9 fs out, wknd rpdly 6 out, tld off.* ....(16 to 1 tchd 14 to 1) 12

Dist: 3½l, 1½l, 3l, ½l, 6l, 8l, 5l, 2l, nk, 5l. 3m 27.41s. a 2.91s (12 Ran).
SR: 61/44/38/34/16/32/24/14/4/ (M & N Plant Ltd), M C Pipe

1346 Broking Handicap Class C (0-90 3-y-o and up) £5,216 1¼m............ (3:40)

731* ALDERBROOK [81] 4-9-8 Paul Eddery (6) *hdwy 5 fs out, led ins fnl 3 furlongs, ran on wl*....(3 to 1 fav tchd 7 to 2) 1

1028 GOOGLY [65] 4-8-6 G Bardwell (5) *beh, rapid hdwy o'r 2 fs out, str run fnl furlong, no imprsn cl hme.* ....(12 to 1 tchd 14 to 1) 2

1064[6] VALLANCE [75] 5-9-2 W Newnes (9) *mid-div, hdwy o'r 3 fs out, styd on ins fnl furlong.* .... (11 to 2 op 6 to 1 tchd 13 to 2) 3

1069[8] WAVE HILL [70] 4-8-11 K Darley (2) *gd hdwy 4 fs out, ev ch 2 furlongs out, sn outpcd*.............. (7 to 1 op 5 to 1) 4

1110[6] LANGTRY LADY [76] (v) 7-8-12 (5*) C Hodgson (10) *chsd ldrs till wknd frm 2 fs out*............ (12 to 1 tchd 14 to 1) 5

989[9] BLUE BLAZER [82] 3-8-8 B Raymond (13) *chsd ldrs, led o'r 3 fs out, sn hdd, wknd ins fnl 2 furlongs.* ....(12 to 1 tchd 14 to 1) 6

873* TRIPPIANO [83] 3-8-9 W Ryan (7) *beh, nvr rchd ldrs.* ....(7 to 1 op 6 to 1) 7

TOP SONG [63] 4-8-4 J Quinn (3) *chsd ldrs, led 4 fs out, hdd o'r 3 out, sn wknd*........... (14 to 1 op 12 to 1) 8

DEER HUNT [87] 4-10-0 T Quinn (12) *effrt 4 fs out, sn wknd*........................ (10 to 1 op 8 to 1) 9

875 REGAL AURA (Ire) [78] 3-8-4 M Roberts (4) *hdwy to chase ldrs 5 fs out, wknd o'r 3 out*....... (10 to 1 op 16 to 1) 10

592 TALENTED TING (Ire) [66] 4-8-7 W Woods (1) *nvr rchd ldrs.* ....(20 to 1) 11

978 THEMEDA [55] 4-7-10 N Carlisle (8) *al beh.* .... (33 to 1 op 25 to 1) 12

1207 ASSEMBLY DANCER [57] 6-7-12 N Adams (14) *led till hdd and wknd quickly 4 fs out*........(100 to 1 op 66 to 1) 13

1075[9] LA REINE ROUGE (Ire) [52] 5-7-7 A Mackay (11) *al beh.* .... (50 to 1 op 33 to 1 tchd 66 to 1) 14

Dist: ½l, 1½l, 2½l, ¾l, 1l, 15l, 2l, 5l, 3½l, 2½l. 2m 4.87s. a 3.07s (14 Ran).

SR: 62/45/52/42/46/35/6/-/11/ (E Pick), Mrs J Cecil

1347 Crawley Warren Heron Stakes Class A (Listed Race) (3-y-o) £14,312 1m ....(4:10)

1027* MISTLE CAT (USA) 8-12 W Woods (4) *made most till hdd ins fnl 2 fs, rallied to ld ag'n appr last, shaken up, jst hld on*................. (11 to 2 op 5 to 1 tchd 6 to 1) 1

1125* PORT LUCAYA (bl) 9-3 (5ex) L Dettori (5) *in tch, outpcd o'r 2 fs out, drvn and hdwy over one out, str chal ins last, jst fld*..................... (7 to 2 op 3 to 1 tchd 4 to 1) 2

588[6] ARDKINGLASS 9-3 W Ryan (1) *gd hdwy frm 4 fs out, led ins fnl 2 furlongs, hdd o'r one out, one pace.* ....(7 to 1 op 6 to 1 tchd 8 to 1) 3

1047[4] FITZCARRALDO (USA) 8-12 M Roberts (2) *prmnt, chlgd frm 6 fs out till outpcd from 3 out.* .... (5 to 1 op 9 to 4 tchd 11 to 2) 4

954 FIRM PLEDGE (USA) 8-12 T Quinn (3) *chsd ldrs, rdn o'r 2 fs out, sn btn*.......... (9 to 4 fav op 5 to 2 tchd 2 to 1) 5

RAPID SUCCESS (USA) 8-12 J Williams (8) *nvr gng pace of ldrs*..................(40 to 1 op 25 to 1 tchd 50 to 1) 6

URRY URRY URRY 8-7 D Biggs (7) *beh most of way.* .... (50 to 1 op 20 to 1) 7

300[2] SECRET ALY (Can) 8-12 B Raymond (6) *in tch whn hmpd o'r 4 fs out and drpd rear, nvr dngrs aftr.* .... (14 to 1 op 12 to 1) 8

Dist: Sht-hd, 1l, 4l, 1½l, 4l, 5l, 5l. 1m 38.30s. a 1.50s (8 Ran).

SR: 58/62/59/42/37/25/5/-/ (P K Chu), S P C Woods

1348 Underwriting Handicap Class C (0-95 3-y-o and up) £5,131 6f......... (4:40)

986[5] MASSIBA (Ire) [89] 4-9-1 (7*) D McCabe (6) *made virtually all, jst hld on*................................(12 to 1) 1

1066[9] PADDY CHALK [83] 7-9-2 Paul Eddery (13) *hld up, gd hdwy o'r one furlong out, str run fnl furlong, jst fld.* ....(8 to 1 tchd 9 to 1) 2

796[2] MARTINOSKY [67] 7-8-0 N Carlisle (15) *chsd ldrs, kpt on same pace ins last.* (11 to 2 fav op 7 to 1 tchd 5 to 1) 3

1079[8] SO RHYTHMICAL [81] 9-9-0 G Bardwell (12) *in tch, hdwy o'r one furlong out, kpt on fnl furlong.* .... (16 to 1 op 12 to 1) 4

986[4] VENTURE CAPITALIST [93] (bl) 4-9-12 B Raymond (9) *hdwy frm 2 fs out, styd on*.... (9 to 1 op 8 to 1 tchd 10 to 1) 5

ARABELLAJILL [90] 4-9-9 D Biggs (7) *pressed wnr till wknd o'r one furlong out*.................... (33 to 1) 6

891[5] FINJAN [86] 6-9-5 N Day (14) *pressed ldrs till wknd one furlong out*....................... (12 to 1 op 10 to 1) 7

716[5] CATHERINEOFARAGON [82] 3-8-5 J Williams (3) *chsd ldrs till wknd ins fnl 2 fs*............(16 to 1 tchd 20 to 1) 8

EASY LINE [85] 10-8-11 (7*) Michael Denaro (16) *nvr rchd ldrs*..............................(20 to 1 op 16 to 1) 9

BERTIE WOOSTER [85] 10-9-4 W Ryan (18) *nvr gng pace of ldrs*..................(20 to 1 op 16 to 1 tchd 25 to 1) 10

1066[7] CHILI HEIGHTS [82] 3-8-5 M Roberts (4) *outpcd.* .... (11 to 1 op 10 to 1) 11

923[4] TERRHARS (Ire) [90] 5-9-9 R Perham (10) *outpcd.* .... (16 to 1 op 14 to 1) 12

1127[3] AUGHFAD [87] (v) 7-9-6 W Newnes (8) *nvr gng pace of ldrs.* .... (9 to 1 op 8 to 1 tchd 10 to 1) 13

930[5] PRETONIC [64] 5-7-11 T Williams (11) *early speed.* .... (16 to 1 op 14 to 1) 14

BELFORT RULER [68] 6-8-1 N Adams (5) *outpcd.* (33 to 1) 15

1177[8] HONEY SEEKER [69] 4-8-2 K Darley (2) *outpcd.* ....(20 to 1 tchd 25 to 1) 16

1003[4] HARD TO FIGURE [95] 7-9-7 (7*) S Drowne (1) *outpcd.* ....(20 to 1 tchd 25 to 1) 17

1207 EL CORTES (USA) [75] 4-8-8 B Rouse (17) *outpcd.* .... (25 to 1 op 33 to 1) 18

Dist: Hd, 1½l, hd, ½l, 1½l, 1½l, ½l, ½l, ½l, ½l. 1m 12.09s. a 1.29s (18 Ran).
SR: 64/57/35/48/58/49/39/23/34/ (F J Sainsbury), M J Heaton-Ellis

LINGFIELD (good)
Saturday May 29th
Going Correction: PLUS 0.10 sec. per fur. (races 1,3), PLUS 0.05 (2,4)

1349 Hall Apprentice Maiden Stakes Class F (3-y-o) £2,448 1¼m. . . . . (6:15)

991^{2} SHARAAR (USA) 8-11 (3*) Sally Radford-Howes (3) *trkd ldr, led 6 fs out, pushed alng and ran on wl.* . . . .(3 to 1 op 2 to 1) 1
1028^{8} PHROSE 8-11 (3*) A Whelan (10) *cl up, effrt 2 fs out, one pace*. . . . . (9 to 2 op 5 to 1 tchd 11 to 2) 2
MORSTOCK 9-0 R Waterfield (9) *beh, hdwy o'r 6 fs out, cld on ldrs appr strt, one pace fnl 2 furlongs.* . . . . (20 to 1 op 12 to 1 tchd 25 to 1) 3
1092^{3} RUNAWAY PETE (USA) 9-0 J O'Dwyer (11) *beh till styd on frm o'r 2 fs out, nvr nrr.* . . . . (11 to 4 fav op 9 to 4 tchd 3 to 1 and 7 to 2) 4
1093^{4} RED WHIRLWIND 8-11 (3*) K Pattinson (7) *led til hdd 6 fs out, rdn 2 out, wknd appr last.* . . . . (3 to 1 op 9 to 4 tchd 100 to 30) 5
1007^{7} BEAT THE BAGMAN (Ire) 8-6 (8*) Iona Wands (5) *nvr better than mid-div*. . . . .(50 to 1 op 33 to 1) 6
1093 TAKE A FLYER (Ire) 9-0 G Milligan (4) *cl up till lost pl aftr 3 fs, no dngr after*. . . . .(33 to 1 tchd 50 to 1) 7
IMPERIAL FORTE 8-1 (8*) Sarah Thompson (8) *took keen hold, hld up, sn chsd ldrs till wknd wl o'r 2 fs out.* . . . . (20 to 1 op 16 to 1) 8
975 ASCOM PAGER TOO 8-9^{3} (3*) Debbie Biggs (6) *chsd ldrs, rdn alng o'r 3 fs out, btn over 2 out.* . . . . (33 to 1 op 20 to 1) 9
DO BE WARE 8-9 (5*) D O'Neill (2) *beh and sn pushed alng, reminder 3 fs out, no response*. . . . .(50 to 1 op 20 to 1) 10
1057 MAI-TU-TU 8-9 J Dennis (1) *rstrained strt, al beh, tld off.* . . . . (50 to 1 op 25 to 1) 11

Dist: 2l, 1½l, 6l, 2½l, 5l, 2l, 4l, 1½l, 6l, 12l. 2m 12.16s. a 7.16s (11 Ran).
SR: 38/34/31/19/14/4/ (Ali K Al Jafleh), W J Haggas

1350 EBF Lingfield Maiden Stakes Class D (2-y-o) £3,874 6f. . . . .(7:15)

TAMAR'S BRIGADE 8-9 A Clark (8) *in tch, cld o'r 2 fs out, led one out, drvn out, jst hld on*. . . . .(16 to 1) 1
MAKE A NOTE (USA) 9-0 K Darley (7) *dwlt, trkd ldrs, squeezed through on ins one furlong out, ev ch inside last, ran on wl, jst fld*. . . . . (8 to 1 op 10 to 1) 2
CABCHARGE PRINCESS (Ire) 8-9 P Robinson (1) *cl up, ev ch one furlong out, one pace ins last.* . . . . (9 to 1 op 12 to 1) 3
GLORIETTE 8-9 W Woods (11) *chsd ldrs, lost pl hfwy, rdn alng 2 fs out, kpt on wl fnl furlong.* . . . . (16 to 1 op 14 to 1 tchd 20 to 1) 4
877^{8} HUMMINBIRDPRINCESS 8-9 N Adams (15) *chsd ldrs, kpt on one pace ins fnl furlong*. . . . . (25 to 1) 5
MOMENT OF GLORY (Ire) 9-0 G Bardwell (14) *outpcd and beh, styd on ins fnl furlong, nrst finish.* . . . . (20 to 1 op 12 to 1) 6
1032^{9} ZORAHAYDA (Fr) 8-9 B Rouse (13) *led til hdd and hmpd one furlong out, wknd quickly*. . . . (14 to 1 op 12 to 1) 7
1091 BANDAR PERAK 9-0 C Rutter (9) *beh, effrt o'r 2 fs out, rdn out and styd on ins last*. . . . .(33 to 1) 8
913^{4} KNIGHTRIDER 9-0 W Newnes (12) *cl up, ev ch appr fnl furlong, eased whn hld ins last.* . . . .(7 to 2 fav op 3 to 1 tchd 4 to 1) 9
NO SPEECHES (Ire) 9-0 D Biggs (4) *outpcd, effrt o'r 2 fs out, nvr on terms*. . . . .(25 to 1 op 20 to 1) 10
SLASHER JACK (Ire) 9-0 R Perham (3) *outpcd.* . . . .(10 to 1 tchd 12 to 1) 11
SHFNAK (Ire) 9-0 M Roberts (5) *trkd ldrs, shaken up hfwy, wknd appr 2 fs out*. . . . . (10 to 1 op 7 to 1) 12
CHILIGRAY 9-0 B Raymond (16) *sn pushed alng in rear, nvr wnt pace*. . . . .(9 to 2 op 3 to 1 tchd 5 to 1) 13
TALYGARN 9-0 J Williams (2) *ran green, outpcd.* . . . . (25 to 1 op 16 to 1) 14
1063 MR MORIARTY (Ire) 9-0 N Day (6) *trkd ldrs till wknd quickly appr 2 fs out.* (14 to 1 op 12 to 1 tchd 16 to 1) 15
1203^{7} MIGHTY KINGDOM (Ire) 8-9 A Tucker (10) *outpcd.* (33 to 1) 16

Dist: Sht-hd, 4l, 2l, hd, ½l, nk, 1l, hd, 2½l, 2l. 1m 14.85s. a 5.85s (16 Ran).
(P R Cruden), M McCormack

1351 Corridor Handicap Class D (0-80 3-y-o) £3,669 1¼m. . . . . (8:15)

1133^{3} KISMETIM [53] 7-8 (3*) B Doyle (4) *trkd ldrs, led wl o'r 2 fs out, clr ins last, pushed out*. . . . . (7 to 2 op 5 to 1) 1
1037^{5} MIDNIGHT HEIGHTS [77] 9-7 B Raymond (7) *hld up, hdwy o'r 2 fs out, chsd wnr frm over one out, no extr.* . . . .(3 to 1 fav op 4 to 1 tchd 9 to 2) 2
880^{7} CASHELL [75] 9-5 M Roberts (3) *hld up in rear, pushed alng 3 fs out, pld out and hrd rdn o'r one out, styd on.* . . . .(11 to 2 tchd 13 to 2) 3
1062^{2} STALLED (Ire) [60] 8-4 D Biggs (10) *trkd ldrs, ev ch appr 2 fs out, sn one pace*. . . . . (7 to 1) 4
1058 QUEENS CONTRACTOR [58] 7-9 (7*) D McCabe (9) *led til hdd 7 fs out, cl up, ev ch o'r 2 out, one pace.* . . . . (20 to 1 op 16 to 1) 5
1111^{8} LATEST FLAME (Ire) [68] 8-12 W Newnes (2) *hld up, cld 5 fs out, rdn 3 out, sn btn.* (5 to 1 tchd 11 to 2 and 6 to 1) 6
873^{4} SMART DAISY [63] 8-7 S O'Gorman (6) *al beh.* . . . . (12 to 1 op 14 to 1) 7
1058 EXCESS BAGGAGE (Ire) [58] 8-2 N Carlisle (1) *cl up, led 7 fs out till hdd blw 3 out, wknd o'r 2 out.* . . . .(12 to 1 op 14 to 1 tchd 16 to 1) 8
558 SECRET ASSIGNMENT (USA) [67] 8-11 A Clark (8) *in tch, effrt o'r 3 fs out, wknd over 2 out.* . . . .(12 to 1 op 10 to 1 tchd 14 to 1) 9
972^{3} DESERT NOMAD [61] 8-5 C Rutter (5) *trkd ldr till wknd quickly o'r 6 fs out, pld up ins last, sddl slpd.* . . . . (25 to 1 op 14 to 1) pu

Dist: 2l, 5l, 2l, hd, 4l, ¾l, 6l, ½l. 2m 13.85s. a 8.85s (10 Ran).
SR: 5/25/13/-/-/-/ (The Kismetim Partnership), B J Meehan

1352 Bannister Handicap Class E (0-70 3-y-o and up) £3,122 5f. . . . . (8:45)

1095^{5} PURBECK CENTENARY [53] 3-8-6 K Darley (6) *made all, pushed out*. . . . . (12 to 1 op 14 to 1) 1
1240 STOCKTINA [33] 6-7-9 N Carlisle (9) *cl up, ev ch appr fnl furlong, one pace und pres*. . . . . . .(14 to 1 op 16 to 1) 2
1137^{5} KENSWORTH LADY [46] 3-7-13 N Adams (1) *mid-div, rdn o'r one furlong out, kpt on und pres ins last.* . . . . (11 to 1 op 14 to 1) 3
1267 SPRING HIGH [59] (bl) 6-9-0 (7*) C Scally (10) *cl up, pushed alng hfwy, kpt on one pace ins last*. . . . . (12 to 1) 4
1096^{2} CALL TO THE BAR (Ire) [60] 4-9-8 A Clark (13) *chsd ldrs, swtchd lft to chal 2 fs out, sn rdn and one pace.* . . . .(2 to 1 fav op 3 to 1 tchd 7 to 4) 5
916^{7} BELTHORN [47] 4-8-9 G Bardwell (12) *beh, swtchd lft 2 fs out, sn hrd rdn, styd on.* . . . .(11 to 1 op 10 to 1 tchd 12 to 1) 6
1059 HARDLINER [62] 4-9-10 W Woods (11) *chsd ldrs, rdn o'r one furlong out, wknd*. . . . . (11 to 1 op 8 to 1) 7
1230^{6} PRINCESS JESSICA [35] 6-7-4 (7*) D Wright (2) *nvr nrr.* . . . .(33 to 1) 8
1240* BARBEZIEUX [46] 6-8-1 (7*,4ex) D McCabe (3) *missed break and lost many ls strt, drvn alng o'r 2 fs out, too much to do*. . . . . (5 to 2 op 4 to 1 tchd 5 to 1) 9
1148^{8} SERIOUS HURRY [61] 5-9-9 W Newnes (14) *cl up til wknd blw 2 fs out*. . . . .(5 to 1 op 7 to 2) 10
4781a^{7} SHARPTINO [66] 4-9-7 (7*) B Russell (7) *outpcd.* . . . . (20 to 1 op 25 to 1) 11
1147^{9} HARD ROCK MINER [48] 3-7-12^{4} (7*) S Mulvey (8) *al beh.* . . . . (50 to 1 op 33 to 1) 12
SHADES OF JADE [52] 5-9-0 J Williams (5) *speed to hfwy.* . . . . (20 to 1 op 33 to 1) 13

Dist: 2½l, hd, 3l, ¾l, 1l, ½l, 3l, 1l, sht-hd, 1l. 1m 0.00s. a 3.10s (13 Ran).
SR: 35/14/17/27/25/8/21/-/-/ (The Hammond Partnership), P Howling

LINGFIELD (A.W) (std)
Saturday May 29th
Going Correction: PLUS 0.05 sec. per fur.

1353 Patio Selling Handicap Class G (0-60 3-y-o and up) £2,532 2m. . . . . . . (6:45)

879^{2} DR ZEVA [34] 7-8-6 (7*) D Wright (8) *hld up, steady hdwy frm 5 fs out, led one out, sn clr, cmftbly.* . . . . (4 to 1 tchd 9 to 2 and 7 to 2) 1
CARFAX [37] 8-9-2 W Newnes (7) *chsd ldrs, cld o'r 4 fs out, led briefly appr last, one pace.* . . . . (10 to 1 op 7 to 1 tchd 12 to 1) 2
1075^{6} INTRICACY [49] 5-10-0 M Roberts (2) *beh, pushed alng and hdwy hfwy, rdn along o'r 4 fs out, styd on frm over one out*. . . . .(7 to 2 fav op 5 to 1) 3
210^{9} WRITTEN AGREEMENT [29] 5-8-1 (7*) D McCabe (14) *trkd ldrs till lost pl appr 4 fs out, sn rdn alng, ran on ins last.* . . . . (33 to 1 op 25 to 1) 4
331^{7} ROMANIAN (Ire) [46] 5-9-11 M Perrett (3) *beh, effrt and hdwy o'r 4 fs out, ev ch 3 out, sn rdn and one pace.* . . . . (13 to 2 op 9 to 2) 5
1005 SIMON ELLIS (Ire) [40] 4-9-3 A Tucker (13) *trkd ldrs, effrt and one pace fnl 3 fs.* (25 to 1 op 14 to 1 tchd 33 to 1) 6
1156^{4} BARCHAM [40] 6-9-5 N Day (6) *cl up, led 4 fs out till hdd wl o'r 2 out, wknd*. . . . .(15 to 2 op 5 to 1 tchd 8 to 1) 7
402^{5} PRESENT TIMES [38] 7-9-3 N Adams (12) *chsd ldrs, cld up hfwy, led wl o'r 2 fs out, hdd appr last, wknd.* . . . . (10 to 1 op 7 to 1) 8
182^{9} CAROLES CLOWN [27] 7-7-13 (7*) D Toole (10) *al beh.* . . . . (14 to 1 op 16 to 1) 9
973^{9} GEE DOUBLE YOU [40] 7-9-5 J Williams (5) *led til hdd 7 fs out, wknd fnl 2 furlongs*. . . . . (25 to 1 op 16 to 1) 10
724 SHEER ECSTASY [42] 3-7-13 S Dawson (9) *al beh.* . . . . (20 to 1 op 16 to 1) 11
813 BAEZA [45] 3-8-2 K Darley (1) *beh, rdn alng o'r 7 fs out, no response*. . . . .(25 to 1 op 16 to 1 tchd 33 to 1) 12
332^{8} BRONZE RUNNER [25] (bl) 9-7-11 (7*) Antoinette Armes (11) *pld hrd, trkd ldrs aftr 6 fs, led 7 furlong out till hdd 4 out, wknd*. . . . . (14 to 1 op 12 to 1 tchd 16 to 1) 13

422[9] DOTTY'S WALKER (Fr) [45] 3-8-2 D Biggs (4) *sn beh, tld off.* .... (33 to 1 op 20 to 1) 14
Dist: 4l, 1½l, 1l, 2½l, 3l, ¾l, nk, 3l, 3l, 5l. 3m 30.48s. a 8.48s (14 Ran).
SR: 22/21/31/10/24/13/13/10/-/ (G R Butterfield), M Dixon

1354 King Post Maiden Handicap Class D (0-75 3-y-o and up) £3,231 7f.... (7:45)

1058[6] RAGING THUNDER [61] (bl) 3-9-8 K Darley (9) *trkd ldrs, led blw 2 fs out, rdn out.*................(6 to 1 op 9 to 2) 1
1062[3] WITHOUT A FLAG (USA) [59] 3-9-6 D Biggs (7) *beh, hdwy o'r 2 fs out, hrd rdn, no extr.*........(5 to 1 op 4 to 1) 2
1230[5] CHEREN BOY [30] 4-8-2 N Adams (10) *chsd ldrs, cld o'r 3 fs out, one pace appr last.* ....(16 to 1 op 12 to 1 tchd 20 to 1) 3
1076[7] SYLVAN BREEZE [56] (v) 5-10-0 W Newnes (1) *hld up beh, hdwy ins fnl furlong, ran on.* ....(8 to 1 op 7 to 1 tchd 9 to 1) 4
919 GENESIS FOUR [44] (bl) 3-8-2 (3*) B Doyle (5) *cl up, rdn 3 fs out, sn wknd.*....... (11 to 1 op 10 to 1 tchd 12 to 1) 5
977[3] JULY BRIDE [54] 3-9-1 B Rouse (8) *sn pushed alng, nvr gng pace.*.......... (5 to 2 fav op 3 to 1 tchd 7 to 2) 6
717[9] CASHABLE [53] (v) 3-9-0 J Williams (3) *led til hdd blw 2 fs out, wknd.*........................ (12 to 1 op 7 to 1) 7
882[6] WELL BOUGHT (Ire) [39] 4-8-11 B Raymond (2) *trkd ldr to hfwy, sn drpd out.*.....(6 to 1 op 9 to 2 tchd 13 to 2) 8
707[2] ARAGON KING [54] 3-8-8 (7*) D McCabe (4) *trkd ldrs to hfwy.*...............................(7 to 1 op 5 to 1) 9
JELLYROLL BLUES [29] 4-8-1 A Tucker (6) *outpcd frm hfwy.*............................... (50 to 1 op 25 to 1) 10
Dist: ¾l, 2½l, 2l, 3l, nk, ½l, 5l, 8l. 1m 28.24s. a 4.84s (10 Ran).
SR: 41/37/11/31/-/8/5/-/-/ (P D Savill), G Lewis

SOUTHWELL (A.W) (std)
Saturday May 29th
Going Correction: PLUS 0.10 sec. per fur.

1355 Randall Maiden Auction Stakes Class F (2-y-o) £1,380 5f.............. (6:30)

1211[7] LEAP OF FAITH (Ire) (bl) 8-9 L Dettori (6) *cl up, led hfwy, rdn clr appr fnl furlong, ran on.* .... (6 to 4 fav op 13 to 8 tchd 7 to 4 and 15 to 8) 1
GOLDEN GRAND 9-0 J Lowe (2) *chsd ldrs, effrt 2 fs out, styd on ins last.*.....................(5 to 1 op 4 to 1) 2
GREENSON (Ire) 9-0 T Quinn (3) *led, rdn and hdd hfwy, wknd wl o'r one furlong out.*...... (3 to 1 tchd 7 to 2) 3
NOORAN 9-0 J Carroll (4) *slwly away, outpcd and beh till styd on appr fnl furlong.*...........(11 to 2 op 9 to 2) 4
877 CLASSICAL DON (Ire) 9-0 G Hind (1) *chsd ldrs, rdn o'r 2 fs out, sn wknd.*....... (12 to 1 op 16 to 1 tchd 20 to 1) 5
1078[4] LUNAR RHAPSODY 8-9 T Lucas (7) *cl up 3 fs, sn rdn and wknd.*... (10 to 1) 6
MAZINA 8-9 A Culhane (5) *al outpcd and beh.* .... (12 to 1 op 11 to 1) 7
Dist: 2l, 5l, 4l, ½l, 1½l, 3l. 1m 2.20s. a 4.30s (7 Ran).
SR: 19/16/-/-/ (R M Stevenson), D R Loder

1356 Larwood Handicap Class E (0-70 3-y-o) £1,604 7f.................... (7:00)

836[5] SOVIET EXPRESS [65] (bl) 9-5 T Quinn (7) *made all, rdn 2 fs out, ran on wl ins last.*..............(6 to 1 op 9 to 2) 1
415[3] PERSONIMUS [41] 7-9[2] L Charnock (6) *chsd ldrs, hdwy o'r 2 fs out and sn disputing ld, rdn and ev ch till no extr nr finish.*.............................(6 to 1 op 5 to 1) 2
1247[4] KINGSTON BROWN [67] (bl) 9-7 L Dettori (3) *trkd ldrs, effrt and not much room 2 fs out, sn rdn, swtchd and ev ch till wknd ins last.*................... (9 to 4 fav op 2 to 1) 3
1137[8] MELODIC DRIVE [56] 8-10 J Lowe (4) *cl up, effrt and ev ch whn squeezed 2 fs out, sn hrd rdn and wknd.* ....(9 to 1 op 8 to 1) 4
1160* LARN FORT [55] 8-9 J Fanning (5) *outpcd and beh till styd on fnl 2 fs, nvr dngrs.* ....(5 to 2 op 11 to 4 tchd 3 to 1 and 9 to 4) 5
630[5] BROOMHOUSE LADY [53] 8-7 Dean McKeown (1) *cl up, rdn and not much room o'r 2 fs out, sn wknd.* ....(9 to 1 op 7 to 1) 6
713[5] BOLD TREASURE (Ire) [41] (v) 7-9[1] J Quinn (2) *sn outpcd and wl beh.*......................(20 to 1 op 14 to 1) 7
Dist: Hd, 2½l, 6l, 3l, 1l, 15l. 1m 31.00s. a 4.90s (7 Ran).
SR: 42/17/35/6/ (Brook Land), P F I Cole

1357 Vines Brothers Agricultural Contractors Limited Stakes Class D (3-y-o) £3,172 1m.................... (7:30)

1204[8] AWESTRUCK 8-11 G Duffield (1) *led, quickened o'r 2 fs out, rdn appr fnl furlong, ran on wl.* ....(100 to 30 op 3 to 1 tchd 7 to 2) 1
1247[2] CERTAIN WAY (Ire) 8-11 M Birch (2) *cl up, rdn 2 fs out, styd on ins last.*...........................(3 to 1 op 5 to 2) 2
1074* NELLIE'S GAMBLE 8-3 (3*) S Maloney (3) *cl up, effrt to chal 2 fs out, sn rdn and not quicken appr fnl furlong.* ....(13 to 8 fav op 2 to 1 tchd 9 to 4) 3
558[8] DORAZINE 8-6 J Quinn (5) *hld up in tch, hdwy o'r 2 fs out, effrt one and a half furlongs out, sn rdn and btn.* ....(3 to 1 op 5 to 2) 4
972[4] ORIENTAL PRINCESS 8-1 (5*) A Garth (4) *chsd ldrs, rdn hfwy, sn wknd, tld off fnl 2 fs.*.................(25 to 1) 5
Dist: 2l, 2l, 1½l, dist. 1m 44.10s. a 5.10s (5 Ran).
SR: 33/27/16/11/-/ (Mrs M M Haggas), W J Haggas

1358 Abacus Municipal Ltd. Claiming Stakes Class F (3-y-o and up) £1,380 7f ....(8:00)

614[4] JAKE THE PAKE (Ire) 3-8-3 D Holland (11) *slwly into strd, hdwy hfwy, effrt 2 ld one and a half fs out, pushed clr.* ....(6 to 1 op 5 to 1) 1
1194[9] APPEALING TIMES (USA) 4-8-12 S Wood (2) *chsd ldrs on inner till lost pl 3 fs out, sn rdn and styd on appr fnl furlong.*...................(9 to 4 fav op 5 to 2) 2
1101[2] FORMAESTRE (Ire) 3-7-7 (7*) Claire Balding (8) *al prmnt, effrt to chal 2 fs out and sn ev ch, rdn and one pace appr fnl furlong.*........(9 to 2 op 4 to 1 tchd 5 to 1) 3
1072[5] SALLY'S SON 7-8-7 (3*) Emma O'Gorman (7) *chsd ldrs, hdwy to ld o'r 2 fs out, sn rdn, hdd one and a half out, one pace.*........................... (4 to 1 op 7 to 2) 4
1038[6] UCKERBY MOOR 4-9-4 S Webster (1) *beh till styd on fnl 2 fs, nrst finish.*............ (14 to 1 op 12 to 1) 5
1072[3] WALK THAT WALK 4-8-4 (5*) O Pears (3) *chsd ldrs, rdn 3 fs out, sn btn.*.........................(7 to 1 op 5 to 1) 6
1074[9] IRISH ROOTS (Ire) (v) 3-7-13 F Norton (4) *al rear.* ....(14 to 1 op 10 to 1) 7
1160[7] RUM TEMPEST (v) 3-7-13 L Charnock (6) *al rear.* (33 to 1) 8
1237[9] LORD NEPTUNE 4-8-10 L Dettori (5) *cl up till rdn and wknd o'r 2 fs out.*........................... (14 to 1) 9
1186 WABWOM 4-8-9 (3*) S D Williams (10) *sn led, hdd and wknd o'r 2 fs out.*................................ (33 to 1) 10
Dist: 3l, nk, ½l, 3l, 6l, 3½l, 2l, 8l, 2l. 1m 31.10s. a 5.00s (10 Ran).
SR: 25/25/12/20/19/-/ (Buckland Thoroughbred), K R Burke

1359 Broad Median Auction Maiden Stakes Class F (3-y-o) £1,380 1½m..... (8:30)

980 CAST THE LINE 9-0 A McGlone (1) *beh and pushed alng till hdwy 5 fs out, rdn to ld one and a half out, styd on ins last.*.............................(6 to 1 op 4 to 1) 1
992 MISS PIMPERNEL 8-9 L Dettori (6) *chsd ldrs, rdn to ld briefly 2 fs out, swshd tail and hdd one and a half furlongs out, one pace.*..........(2 to 1 fav op 3 to 1) 2
1161[2] DOC SPOT 9-0 J Fortune (4) *chsd ldrs till rdn and outpcd o'r 5 fs out, styd on und pres fnl 2 furlongs, not pace to chal.*..................................(5 to 2 op 3 to 1) 3
980[5] BURNING COST 8-6 (3*) D Harrison (2) *cl up led aftr 2 fs, rdn 4 out, hdd two out, wknd appr last.* ....(4 to 1 op 3 to 1) 4
1077[6] FOLLINGWORTH GIRL (Ire) 8-4 (5*) O Pears (7) *chsd ldrs, rdn alng hfwy and sn lost pl, wl beh fnl 3 fs.* .... (9 to 1 op 16 to 1) 5
1099[4] SANTA STELLAR 8-9 Dean McKeown (3) *led 2 fs, cl up till rdn and wknd 4 furlongs out.*...... (13 to 2 op 5 to 1) 6
Dist: 1½l, sht-hd, 3½l, 10l, 25l. 2m 44.50s. a 10.60s (6 Ran).
SR: 6/-/2/ (D P Barrie), A C Stewart

1360 Gunn Handicap Class E (0-70 3-y-o) £1,520 5f..................... (9:00)

713* SABO THE HERO [57] (v) 9-2 G Duffield (1) *cl up, led 2 fs out, rdn appr last, ran on wl.* ....(5 to 4 fav op 11 to 8 tchd 6 to 4) 1
1249[2] OUR MICA [48] (v) 8-7 J Carroll (3) *led, rdn and hdd 2 fs out, kpt on und pres ins last.* .... (7 to 4 op 2 to 1 tchd 13 to 8) 2
1157[6] KIMBOLTON KORKER [62] 9-0 (7*) Claire Balding (5) *cl up till rdn and wknd o'r 2 fs out.*.....(20 to 1 op 14 to 1) 3
1159[5] DARDANELLE [39] 7-12 S Wood (2) *chsd ldrs, rdn hfwy, edgd lft and sn wknd.*...........................(10 to 1) 4
1072[4] SAMANTHAS JOY [49] 8-8 L Dettori (4) *cl up till rdn and wknd o'r 2 fs out.*......(7 to 2 op 4 to 1 tchd 3 to 1) 5
Dist: 1½l, 6l, ½l, 2½l. 1m 1.40s. a 3.50s (5 Ran).
SR: 42/27/17/-/-/ (Mrs David Thompson), Sir Mark Prescott

CAPANNELLE (ITY) (good to firm)
Sunday May 30th

1361 Premio Luigia Foggi (2-y-o) £13,448 5f ....(1:30)

MAASTRICHT (USA) 9-1 F Jovine,.............................. 1
SECRET NYMPH (USA) 8-12 V Mezzatesta,.............. 2
MOIANA (Ire) 8-12 M Pasquale,........................ 3
SUSPIRIA (Ire) 9-1 W Carson, *in tch till wknd appr fnl furlong.*.. 4
Dist: 2l, 5l, 2l, 1½l, nose, 2 ¼l, 1l. 59.50s. (8 Ran).
(Scuderia Cieffedi), L Brogi

1362 Premio W W F (Listed) (4-y-o and up) £20,173 7f.................... (2:05)

MOUNTAIN ASH 4-8-5 F Jovine, ... 1
1003* CASTEDDU 4-8-7 W Carson, ... 2
593* PROSPECTIVE RULER (USA) 5-9-0 A Munro, ... 3
593[9] JUNK BOND 5-8-7 Jacqueline Freda, ... 4
593[7] KAA (Ire) 5-8-7 A Corniani, ... 5
4702a VINTAGE ONLY 5-8-7 O Fancera, ... 6
VEIN OF GOLD (Ity) 4-8-7 V Mezzatesta, ... 7
DON ANTONIO (Ity) 4-8-7 A Arbau, ... 8
DOUBLOVA (Ire) 5-8-4 C Peraino, ... 9

Dist: Nk, 2½l, nose, 2l, ¾l, 1 ¼l, nk, 5l. 1m 23.50s. (9 Ran).
(Scuderia Azzurra), B Agriformi

1363 Premio Nearco (Listed) (4-y-o and up) £20,173 1m. .... (3:50)

GOLDEN BECHETT (Ire) 3-8-11 A Munro, ... 1
1016* SMARGINATO (Ire) 3-8-8 W Carson, ... 2
MAORI (Ity) 3-8-8 S Landi, ... 3
MISTER NAIF (USA) 3-8-8 F Jovine, ... 4
TONI BUIO (Ire) 3-8-8 A Parravani, ... 5
778[3] PASCOLI (Ity) 3-8-8 O Fancera, ... 6
BULLO (Ire) 3-8-8 M Pasquale, ... 7

Dist: 1l, 3l, ¾l, nk, nose, 2½l. 1m 38.30s. (7 Ran).
(Scuderia Golden Horse), G Fratini

1364 Derby Italiano (Group 1) (3-y-o) £264,377 1½m. .... (4:30)

929* WHITE MUZZLE 9-2 J Reid (3) *al prmnt, 4th strt, led 2 and a half furlong out, clr o'r one furlong out, ran on wl.* 1
1015[2] NEEDLE GUN (Ire) 9-2 M Roberts (14) *hdwy fnl 3 fs, second o'r one out, no imprsn.* 2
4703a[2] MR RICHARD (Ire) 9-2 V Mezzatesta (2) *cl up, hmpd 5 fs out, not clr run o'r 2 out, nrst finish.* 3
1012[2] INFRASONIC 9-2 Paul Eddery (8) *8th strt, hdwy 3 fs out, no extr appr fnl furlong.* 4
794 RIGHT WIN (Ire) 9-2 T Quinn (13) *hdwy fnl 2 fs, nrst finish.* 5
SCRIBANO 9-2 E Botti (7) *hdwy 4 fs out, pressed wnr o'r 2 out, no extr.* 6
4703a[3] MAD MARTIGAN 9-2 M Pasquale (1) *hdwy o'r 3 fs out, 4th one and a half furlongs out, no extr.* 7
958[2] CAMPALTO (Ire) 9-2 O Fancera (11) *prmnt for one m.* 8
989* PERSIAN BRAVE (Ire) 9-2 M Hills (15) *second strt, wknd 3 fs out.* 9
VAL SAUVAGE 9-2 E Saint-Martin (4) *nvr seen wth ch.* 0
1116[3] VISTO SI STAMPI (Ire) 9-2 W Carson (16) *led 5 fs out till o'r 3 out, wknd quickly.* 0
KHORAZ (USA) 9-2 Jacqueline Freda (9) *hdwy o'r 5 fs out, btn over 3 out.* 0
1047[5] MASTER TRIBE (Ire) 9-2 P V Gilson (6) *led o'r 3 fs out till over 2 out, sn wknd.* 0
958* JOHNNY STECCHINO (USA) 9-2 S Soto (12) *prmnt for one m.* 0
958[6] BALBOA ROYAL (Ire) 9-2 L Ficuciello (10) *nvr a factor.* 0
LIFE EXTENSION 9-2 G Bietolini (5) *led for 7 fs, sn wknd.* 0

Dist: 5l, hd, nk, 1l, 1l, 2½l, 2l, sht-nk, ¾l, 5l. 2m 24.50s. (16 Ran).
(Luciano Gaucci), P W Chapple-Hyam

1365 Premio Melton-Memorial Tudini (Group 2) (3-y-o and up) £48,011 6f .... (5:30)

4702a[7] SECRET THING (USA) 4-9-3 V Mezzatesta, ... 1
IMPREVEDIBILE (Ire) 3-8-8 A Parravani, ... 2
RAIN BROTHER (USA) 3-8-8 J Reid, ... 3
SPECIAL POWER (Ire) 6-9-3 S Soto, ... 4
4704a[6] VISCARDO (Ire) 3-8-8 E Botti, ... 5
4702a[4] HANTAYO YO (Ity) 7-9-3 A Luongo, ... 6
4702a[3] FLIGHT OF DESTINY 7-9-3 F Jovine, ... 7
ETEREA KING (Ire) 3-8-5 G Di Chio, ... 8
ARRANVANNA 5-9-0 Jacqueline Freda, ... 9
OSARIO 6-9-3 S Landi, ... 0
RIVER DEFENCES (USA) 4-9-3 A Munro, ... 0

Dist: Nk, ½l, ½l, 1l, ¾l, sht-hd, ½l, ½l, ¾l, 6l. 1m 9.60s. (11 Ran).
(Rita Incoronato), F Brogi

LONGCHAMP (FR) (firm)
Sunday May 30th

1366 Prix d'Ispahan (Group 1) (4-y-o and up) £59,737 1m 1f 55yds........ (2:55)

810[7] ARCANGUES (USA) 5-9-2 T Jarnet (7) *5th strt, effrt o'r 2 fs out, led one and a half out, ran on wl.* ....(66 to 10) 1
810[3] MISIL (USA) 5-9-2 L Dettori (8) *3rd strt, effrt o'r 2 fs out, ran on, no ch wth wnr.* ....(56 to 10) 2
920[2] SHANGHAI (USA) 4-9-2 C Asmussen (6) *4th strt, effrt and hmpd 2 fs out, swtchd one out, ran on.* .... (33 to 10) 3
920* HATOOF (USA) 4-8-13 W R Swinburn (3) *6th and came wide strt, effrt 2 fs out, sn no extr.* ....(11 to 10 jt-fav) 4
1088* DIESE (USA) 4-8-13 Pat Eddery (5) *second strt, chlgd 2 and a half fs out, sn wknd.* ....(38 to 10) 5
810[5] MARILDO (Fr) (bl) 6-9-2 G Guignard (2) *led till wknd quickly one and a half fs out.* .... (13 to 1) 6
MASSYOUNA (USA) (bl) 4-8-13 B Raymond (4) *trkd ldr, wknd quickly appr strt, tld off.* ....(11 to 10 jt-fav) 7

Dist: 1½l, ½l, 1½l, 6l, nk, 15l. 1m 50.70s. b 1.30s (7 Ran).
SR: 73/70/69/63/51/53/20/ (Daniel Wildenstein), A Fabre

1367 Prix Jean Prat (Group 1) (3-y-o) £59,737 1m 1f 55yds. .... (3:30)

867* LE BALAFRE (Fr) 9-2 O Peslier (4) *made most till o'r one furlong out, ran on to ld cl hme.* ....(57 to 10) 1
696[2] BIGSTONE (Ire) 9-2 D Boeuf (3) *3rd strt, led o'r one furlong out, ct cl hme.* .... (6 to 5 fav) 2
954[4] SEMILLON 9-2 A Badel (2) *last strt, hdwy on ins o'r 2 fs out, ran on.* ....(12 to 1) 3
794 REVELATION (Ire) 9-2 W R Swinburn (6) *4th strt, outpcd till styd on und pres fnl furlong, nrst finish.* ..... (26 to 1) 4
688[2] PLACERVILLE (USA) 9-2 Pat Eddery (7) *dsptd ld, second strt, ev ch o'r one furlong out, one pace.* .....(26 to 10) 5
696[4] KADOUNOR (Fr) 9-2 O Doleuze (9) *nvr able to chal.* ....(19 to 1) 6
650* CAESOUR (USA) 9-2 C Asmussen (8) *nvr able to chal.* ....(43 to 10) 7
1087[5] RANGER (Fr) 9-2 W Mongil (5) *al rear.* ....(19 to 1) 8

Dist: Nk, nk, sht-hd, ¾l, ½l, 2½l, ½l. 1m 53.10s. a 1.10s (8 Ran).
SR: 37/36/35/34/32/31/26/25/ (Comte J de Lastours), N Clement

1368 Prix de Bagatelle (Listed) (3-y-o) £14,337 1m. .... (4:00)

BROKEN PEACE (Fr) 9-2 T Jarnet, ... 1
853[2] BORODISLEW (USA) 9-2 F Head, ... 2
983[3] POLLY'S WIKA (USA) 9-2 C Asmussen, ... 3
MONDSEE 9-2 G Guignard, ... 4

Dist: 1½l, ¾l, 1½l, hd, 2l. 1m 39.70s. a 2.20s (6 Ran).
SR: 27/22/20/15/ (D Wildenstein), A Fabre

MUNICH (GER) (good)
Sunday May 30th

1369 Grosser Hertie Preis (Group 2) (3-y-o) £60,000 1m 3f. .... (3:10)

594* MONSUN (Ger) 9-2 P Schiergen, *al prmnt, 3rd strt, led and wnt clr o'r one furlong out, all out.* 1
594[2] KOMTUR (USA) 9-2 K Woodburn, *led till o'r one furlong out, rallied fnl furlong, fnshd wl.* 2
843[2] SHREWD IDEA 9-2 W J O'Connor, *trkd ldr, ev ch 2 fs out, one pace.* 3
947[4] AZZILFI 9-2 G Carter, *cld up 6 fs out, 4th strt, nvr able to chal.* 4
594[4] TROPICAL KING (Ger) 9-2 M Rimmer, *in tch, 5th strt, btn 2 fs out.* 5
WIRGILIAN (Ger) 9-2 N Grant, *nvr dngrs.* 6
HOBO (Ger) 9-2 R Hillis, *6th strt, sn btn.* 7
953[9] TINA'S KING (Ger) 9-2 A Boschert, *al beh.* 8
KASALTO (Ger) 9-2 H Ludewig, *al rear.* 9

Dist: Nk, 2½l, 1 ¼l, 5l, 1l, 7l, ¾l, 7l. 2m 17.35s. (9 Ran).
(Baron G Von Ullmann), H Jentzsch

HOLLYWOOD (USA) (firm)
Sunday May 30th

1370 Gamely Handicap (Grade 1) (3-y-o and up) £64,702 1m 1f. ....

TOUSSARD (USA) 4-8-4 K Desormeaux, ...(19 to 10) 1
GOLD FLEECE (USA) 5-8-2 C McCarron, ...(17 to 1) 2
BEL'S SCARLET (USA) 6-8-4 G Stevens, ...(55 to 10) 3
4769a[4] REVASSER (USA) 4-8-5 C Nakatani, ...(19 to 10) 4
WEDDING RING (Ire) 4-8-4 E Delahoussaye, ...(48 to 10) 5
MISS TURKANA (USA) 4-8-3 A Castanon, ...(29 to 1) 6
MIATUSCHKA (USA) 5-8-1 S Gonsalez Jr, ...(59 to 1) 7
MISTERIOSO 4-8-1 C Black, ...(17 to 1) 8
EXCHANGE (Can) 5-8-11 L Pincay Jr, ...(17 to 10 fav) 9

Dist: 1l, 1l, 2½l, ¾l, ½l, ½l, nk, nk. 1m 45.00s. (9 Ran).
(Juddmonte Farms), R Frankel

CHEPSTOW (soft)
Monday May 31st
Going Correction: PLUS 0.35 sec. per fur.

1371 St Arvans Median Auction Maiden Fillies Stakes Class F (3-y-o) £2,560 1½m 23yds. .... (2:00)

980[3] ALLESCA 8-11 N Adams (3) *trkd ldrs, pushed alng to go second o'r 3 fs out, led one out, rdn out.* ....(11 to 8 jt-fav op 11 to 10 tchd 6 to 4) 1
1077[2] MEANT TO BE 8-11 M Tebbutt (5) *trkd ldr, led 4 fs out, rdn and hdd one out, kpt on one pace.* ....(11 to 8 jt-fav op Evens tchd 6 to 4) 2
SCHOOLGIRL CRUSH 8-11 A Tucker (6) *slwly away, sn chasing ldrs, rdn hfwy and soon lost tch, styd on ag'n ins fnl 2 fs.* .... (50 to 1 op 20 to 1) 3

1242 CANDARELA 8-11 A Clark (4) *led till hdd 4 fs out, rdn and wknd wl o'r 2 out*.... (20 to 1 op 16 to 1 tchd 25 to 1) 4
NOEPROB (USA) 8-11 J Williams (2) *in rear till hdwy o'r 4 fs out, wknd wl over 2 out*. .... (11 to 2 op 5 to 1 tchd 6 to 1) 5
1090 STRATTON FLYER 8-11 T Lang (1) *al beh, lost tch 4 fs out*. .... (100 to 1 op 25 to 1) 6
Dist: 1½l, 10l, 7l, 3l, 15l. 2m 44.10s. a 12.60s (6 Ran).
SR: 13/10/-/ (Miss D G Kerr), I Usher 00

1372 Harcros Timber & Building Supplies Stayers Championship Series Handicap Qualifier Class D (0-80 3-y-o) £3,465 1½m 23yds............. (2:30)

1170* DUSTY POINT (Ire) [55] 7-11 (3*) D Harrison (5) *trkd ldrs, led 3 fs out, sn clr, easily*................(7 to 2 op 9 to 4) 1
1204 KADASTROF (Fr) [72] 9-3 S Dawson (1) *trkd ldr, led briefly o'r 3 fs out, kpt on one pace*...... (25 to 1 op 16 to 1) 2
1115 SON OF SHARP SHOT (Ire) [76] 9-7 G Duffield (3) *steadied strt, pld hrd, in rear till hdwy o'r 3 fs out, sn rdn, no imprsn*.....(5 to 4 on op 11 to 10 on tchd 11 to 8 on) 3
1067⁴ WARM SPELL [68] 8-13 B Rouse (4) *beh, effrt 4 fs out, nvr nr to chal*............. (3 to 1 op 7 to 2 tchd 4 to 1) 4
1266⁹ MANON LESCAUT [51] (bl) 7-10 N Adams (2) *led, sn clr, hdd o'r 3 fs out, soon rdn, drpd out quickly*. .... (33 to 1 op 10 to 1) 5
Dist: 8l, 2l, nk, 20l. 2m 41.40s. a 9.90s (5 Ran).
SR: 29/30/30/21/-/ (Abdullah Ali), B Hanbury

1373 Mercury Handicap Class D (0-80 4-y-o and up) £3,687 6f 16yds.........(3:00)

1209* SIR JOEY (USA) [69] 4-9-6 J Williams (7) *nvr far away, led o'r 2 fs out, drifted rght, rdn out*. ....(13 to 8 fav op 6 to 4) 1
1230³ ASTERIX [47] (v) 5-7-12 N Adams (2) *mid-div, hdwy on far side hfwy, ev ch entering fnl furlong, ran on wl*. ....(5 to 1 op 6 to 1 tchd 8 to 1) 2
1127⁶ BALLASECRET [77] 5-9-7 (7*) Michelle Thomas (5) *led till hdd o'r 2 fs out, kpt on one pace*...(20 to 1 op 10 to 1) 3
1096⁷ UNVEILED [54] 5-7-13¹ (7*) S Drowne (4) *outpcd early, ran on wl ins fnl 2 fs*.................. (16 to 1 op 8 to 1) 4
1096⁶ SCARLET PRINCESS [42] 5-7-7⁵ (5*) N Gwilliams (3) *chsd ldrs, kpt on one pace fnl 2 fs*........(10 to 1 op 5 to 1) 5
SWIFT ROMANCE (Ire) [53] 5-8-4 G Duffield (10) *broke wl, sn lost pl, hdwy 2 fs out, not rch ldrs*. ....(12 to 1 op 10 to 1 tchd 16 to 1) 6
756⁴ BAYSHAM (USA) [74] 7-9-11 S Whitworth (11) *in frnt on stands side, wknd entering fnl furlong*. ....(7 to 1 op 5 to 1) 7
1237⁸ ELEGANT TOUCH [65] (v) 4-9-2 M Perrett (9) *slwly away, wl in rear till styd on well ins fnl 2 fs, nvr nrr*. .... (20 to 1 op 12 to 1) 8
MUSTAHIL (Ire) [62] 4-8-13 R Perham (1) *chsd ldrs till outpcd appr fnl furlong, eased ins*. .... (40 to 1 op 16 to 1) 9
1096 RUSHANES [55] 6-8-6 A Clark (8) *chsd stands side ldr, wknd wl o'r one out*...............(16 to 1 op 10 to 1) 10
1177 CONISTON LAKE (Ire) [60] (v) 4-8-11 B Rouse (6) *prmnt till wknd rpdly wl o'r one out*.........(16 to 1 op 12 to 1) 11
Dist: ½l, 2l, hd, 1½l, 1l, nk, ½l, 1½l, ¾l, 5l. 1m 14.50s. a 5.00s (11 Ran).
SR: 48/24/46/22/4/11/31/20/11/ (Mrs A G Sims), P G Murphy

1374 St John Limited Stakes Class D (3-y-o and up) £3,289 1m 14yds....... (3:30)

1069* JADE VALE 4-9-2 (3*) D Harrison (2) *pld hrd, trkd ldr frm hfwy, rdn and led 2 fs out, pushed out*. ....(3 to 1 op 2 to 1) 1
1153* JUST YOU DARE (Ire) 3-8-12 G Duffield (1) *trkd ldr, led bef hfwy, hdd 2 fs out, rdn and kpt on one pace*. ....(11 to 10 fav op 6 to 4 tchd 7 to 4 and Evens) 2
MARINE DIVER 7-9-10 J Williams (3) *slwly away, settled in rear, ran on ins fnl 2 fs, nvr nrr*... (25 to 1 op 16 to 1) 3
1172⁴ STAR GODDESS (USA) 4-9-5 B Rouse (4) *hld up, hdwy 3 fs out, wknd appr last*...(11 to 2 op 6 to 1 tchd 13 to 2) 4
1064⁸ YOUNG FREEMAN (USA) (bl) 4-9-10 M Perrett (5) *in tch, rdn o'r 2 fs out, sn btn*..............(6 to 1 op 5 to 1) 5
1064 HAROLDON (Ire) 4-9-10 M Tebbutt (6) *led for 3 and a half fs, wknd 2 out*..................(25 to 1 op 14 to 1) 6
Dist: 2l, 1l, 4l, 2l, 8l. 1m 39.00s. a 6.60s (6 Ran).
SR: 48/35/44/27/26/2/ (Mrs S Bosher), J W Hills

1375 St Briavels Maiden Stakes Class D (3-y-o and up) £3,640 1m 14yds....(4:00)

825⁴ GLEN ECHO (Ire) 3-8-12 M Perrett (9) *al lying hndy, led 2 fs out, pushed out ins last, cmftbly*. ......(11 to 10 fav op 11 to 10 tchd 5 to 4 and Evens) 1
1092⁵ BEAUCHAMP HERO 3-8-12 J Williams (5) *hld up, hdwy o'r 2 fs out, ev ch entering last, ran on one pace*. ....(6 to 1 op 7 to 2) 2
HASTEN TO ADD (USA) 3-8-12 G Duffield (7) *prmnt till lost pl hfwy, kpt on ins fnl 2 fs*. .... (11 to 1 op 8 to 1 tchd 12 to 1) 3
1320² CLASS ATTRACTION (USA) 4-9-5 S Whitworth (3) *trkd ldr aftr 3 fs, led three out; hdd 2 out, one pace ins last*. ....(5 to 1 tchd 7 to 1) 4
558⁹ GROUND NUT (Ire) 3-8-12 S Dawson (10) *hld up in tch, ran on one pace fnl 2 fs*...............(16 to 1 op 8 to 1) 5
1114² BELFRY GREEN (Ire) 3-8-12 A Clark (11) *hld up, effrt o'r 2 fs out, edgd lft, wknd appr last*. ....(6 to 1 op 4 to 1 tchd 7 to 1) 6
813 MUSICAL PHONE 3-8-12 A Tucker (4) *led till hdd 3 fs out, sn btn*.......................... (50 to 1 op 20 to 1) 7
1007 BAYIN (USA) 4-9-10 B Rouse (1) *in tch far side till wknd o'r 2 fs out, eased*................ (40 to 1 op 20 to 1) 8
TOUT DE VAL 4-9-5 R Perham (2) *trkd ldr for 3 fs, wknd wl o'r 2 out*......................... (66 to 1 op 33 to 1) 9
1092 ARCTIC LINE (v) 5-9-10 N Adams (6) *al beh, lost tch o'r 2 fs out*............................ (50 to 1 op 25 to 1) 10
CHEEKY TUNE 4-9-10 B Procter (8) *speed to hfwy, sn beh, tld off*.............................(25 to 1 op 20 to 1) 11
Dist: 2l, 6l, 1l, 2l, 1½l, 12l, hd, 7l, 2l, 15l. 1m 39.30s. a 6.90s (11 Ran).
SR: 36/30/12/16/3/-/ (Seymour Cohn), G Harwood

1376 Badminton Rating Related Maiden Stakes Class E (0-70 3-y-o) £2,761 5f 16yds......................... (4:30)

721 KARUKERA 8-9 J Williams (5) *hld up, hdwy 2 fs out, swtchd rght appr last, hrd rdn to get up cl hme*. ....(6 to 1 op 5 to 1 tchd 13 to 2) 1
1233² CLOUDY REEF 8-9 G Duffield (1) *al in tch, led o'r 2 fs out, rdn and ran on, ct cl hme*........(6 to 4 fav op 7 to 4) 2
759 DONTDRESSFORDINNER 9-0 R Perham (3) *hld up in rear, gd hdwy o'r 2 fs out, ev ch entering last, one pace ins*. .... (28 to 1 op 12 to 1) 3
991⁸ PERFECT PASSION 8-9 S Whitworth (2) *led till hdd o'r 2 fs out, sn rdn, wknd appr last*....... (12 to 1 op 8 to 1) 4
1095³ THE ORDINARY GIRL (Ire) 8-9 N Adams (6) *speed till wknd wl o'r one furlong out*... (7 to 4 op 6 to 4 tchd 2 to 1) 5
1147⁷ INONDER (bl) 8-9 A Clark (4) *trkd ldrs till wknd 2 fs out*. .... (12 to 1 op 6 to 1 tchd 14 to 1) 6
871⁹ LAID BACK BEN 8-11 (3*) D Harrison (7) *speed to hfwy*. .... (12 to 1 op 8 to 1) 7
Dist: Nk, 3l, 3½l, 6l, 2½l, 2l. 1m 2.60s. a 5.60s (7 Ran).
SR: 18/17/10/-/ (Alex Smith), B R Millman

1377 Severn Handicap Class E (0-70 3-y-o) £3,178 7f 16yds................ (5:00)

1185* CAMEO KIRBY (Fr) [64] 8-12 (7*) J Tate (6) *slwly into strd, steady hdwy to ld hfwy, rdn appr fnl furlong, ran on wl*.................(15 to 8 fav op 2 to 1 tchd 5 to 2) 1
1138 GOOD IMAGE [54] 8-9 S Whitworth (3) *nvr far away, rdn to chase wnr 2 fs out, no extr ins last*. .... (6 to 1 op 5 to 1 tchd 13 to 2) 2
834 TAKE THE MICK [48] 8-3¹ R Perham (5) *hld up, gd hdwy o'r 2 fs out, outpcd appr last*. .... (10 to 1 op 20 to 1 tchd 33 to 1) 3
921 SHALHOLME [50] 8-5 N Adams (2) *in tch on far side, outpcd o'r 2 fs out, one pace aftr*. .... (20 to 1 op 10 to 1 tchd 25 to 1) 4
711 CHUMMY'S FRIEND (Ire) [47] 8-2 R Street (1) *led aftr one and a half fs, hdd hfwy, fdd ins fnl 2 furlongs*. .... (14 to 1 op 7 to 1) 5
761⁷ SEASON'S STAR [55] 8-10 S Dawson (8) *in tch till outpcd o'r 2 fs out, sn btn*......(7 to 1 op 5 to 1 tchd 8 to 1) 6
1095⁸ JEREMIAHS BOY [58] 8-6 (7*) S Drowne (7) *speed till o'r 2 fs out*.................. (7 to 1 op 5 to 1 tchd 8 to 1) 7
917⁹ SHARP GAZELLE [50] 8-5 A Tucker (9) *slwly away, al beh*. .... (20 to 1 op 12 to 1) 8
899⁵ EXPORT MONDIAL [66] 9-7 M Tebbutt (4) *led for one and a half fs, wknd wl o'r 2 furlongs out, eased, tld off*. .... (10 to 1 op 6 to 1 tchd 12 to 1) 9
Dist: 1½l, 4l, 4l, 3l, 8l, 1l, 1l, 10l. 1m 27.00s. a 7.00s (9 Ran).
SR: 37/22/4/-/-/-/ (Maktoum Al Maktoum), A A Scott

DONCASTER (good)
Monday May 31st

Going Correction: PLUS 0.30 sec. per fur. (races 1,2,4,5), PLUS 0.15 (3,6,7)

1378 EBF Vyner Maiden Stakes Class D (2-y-o) £3,201 5f.................. (2:20)

CLARINDA (Ire) 8-9 Paul Eddery (5) *led stands side, hdd o'r one furlong out, rallied gmely to ld nr finish*. ....(2 to 1 op 7 to 4 tchd 9 to 4) 1
ARZ (USA) 9-0 R Hills (4) *wtd wth, smooth hdwy 2 fs out, led appr fnl furlong, hdd and no extr nr finish*. .... (6 to 4 fav op 11 to 8 tchd 5 to 4 and 13 to 8) 2
WOODS VENTURE (Ire) 9-0 W Woods (3) *dsptd ld, shaken up blw dist, sn btn*..............(8 to 1 tchd 9 to 1) 3
913⁹ AQUA VIVA 9-0 A Geran (2) *slwly into strd, prog hfwy, ev ch 2 fs out, sn rdn and wknd*....... (4 to 1 op 7 to 2) 4
CASPIAN GOLD 9-0 Dean McKeown (1) *wth ldrs to hfwy, sn rdn, grad wknd*... (12 to 1 op 14 to 1 tchd 16 to 1) 5
Dist: Hd, 5l, 3l, 1½l. 1m 3.15s. a 4.35s (5 Ran).

SR: 38/42/22/10/4/ (Sheikh Mohammed), M R Stoute

1379 Shadwell Stud Apprentice Series Handicap Class F (0-80 3-y-o and up) £2,856 5f. .... (2:50)

1232[2] THE RIGHT TIME [47] 8-7-11 Darren Moffatt (8) *hld up, steady hdwy frm hfwy, quickened to ld ins fnl furlong, held on*......... (100 to 30 fav op 7 to 2 tchd 3 to 1) 1
737[7] HOB GREEN [69] 4-9-5 O Pears (7) *wth ldrs whn hmpd aftr one furlong, not much room 2 fs out, rapid hdwy appr fnl furlong, fnshd fst.* ....(7 to 2 op 4 to 1 tchd 9 to 2) 2
1036 CATHERINES WELL [70] 10-9-1 (5*) P Johnson (1) *slwly into strd, hdwy and swtchd rght aftr 2 fs, slight ld entering fnl furlong, sn hdd and no extr.* ....(9 to 2 op 5 to 1 tchd 6 to 1) 3
1249[3] LAST STRAW [43] 5-7-4 (3*) Claire Balding (3) *al cl up, rdn 2 fs out, ran on one pace*......... (5 to 1 op 6 to 1) 4
1036 FOLLOWMEGIRLS [59] 4-8-9 A Garth (5) *led a furlong, led 2 fs out till appr fnl furlong, one pace.* ....(9 to 1 op 8 to 1) 5
1081 BEST EFFORT [54] 7-8-4 V Halliday (4) *trkd ldrs, rdn alng hfwy, nvr nrr*........ (16 to 1 op 14 to 1) 6
1267 LUCEDEO [72] 9-9-8 M Humphries (6) *slwly into strd, al outpcd and beh*.................. (14 to 1 op 12 to 1) 7
1249[6] SIR TASKER [72] (v) 5-9-8 S D Williams (9) *rdn alng to ld aftr one furlong, hdd 2 fs out, sn lost tch, tld off.* ....(7 to 1 tchd 15 to 2) 8

Dist: ½l, hd, 2l, sht-hd, ½l, nk, 10l. 1m 2.73s. a 3.93s (8 Ran).
SR: 34/54/54/19/34/27/44/4/ (J H Myers), J Parkes

1380 Harewood Rated Class B Handicap (0-95 4-y-o and up) £6,430 2m 110yds ....(3:20)

857 GOOD HAND (USA) [84] 7-9-6 N Connorton (8) *hld up in rear, took clr order 3 fs out, led o'r one furlong out, hrd rdn, held on*........................(7 to 1 op 6 to 1) 1
1173[5] SNOW BOARD [73] (bl) 4-8-7 J Quinn (11) *chsd ldrs, 4th strt, led on bit 2 fs out, hdd appr fnl furlong, rallied und pres*........................(5 to 1 jt-fav op 9 to 2) 2
632* MERRY NUTKIN [73] 7-8-9 N Day (3) *al wl plcd, 5th strt, kpt on one pace fnl 2 fs*............(11 to 2 op 9 to 2) 3
857 FRENCH IVY (USA) [75] 6-8-11 K Fallon (4) *hld up in rear, hdwy o'r 2 fs out, nvr able to chal.* (16 to 1 op 20 to 1) 4
1041* ENCORE UNE FOIS (Ire) [84] 4-9-4 Dean McKeown (5) *al prmnt, second strt, slight ld o'r 2 fs out, sn hdd, hrd rdn and kpt on same pace*.. (7 to 1 op 7 to 1 tchd 6 to 1) 5
1155* BRANDON PRINCE (Ire) [80] (bl) 5-9-2 Paul Eddery (6) *wtd wth in rear, effrt and 6th strt, kpt on same pace fnl 2 fs.* .... (7 to 1 op 7 to 1 tchd 15 to 2) 6
1129[3] MULL HOUSE [72] 6-8-8 W Woods (10) *in rear, hdwy und pres 3 fs out, not rch ldrs*.......(5 to 1 jt-fav op 6 to 1) 7
857 STAR PLAYER [85] 7-9-2 (5*) O Pears (9) *hld up and beh, prog 4 fs out, rdn and hng lft 2 furlongs out, sn btn.* ....(14 to 1 op 16 to 1) 8
967[6] FARMER'S PET [73] 4-8-2 (5*) Darren Moffatt (7) *pressed ldrs till wknd 3 fs out*.............................. (12 to 1) 9
462[3] FARSI [82] (bl) 5-9-4 S Perks (2) *drpd rear aftr 4 fs, al beh.* ....(10 to 1) 10
1041[3] WILKINS [73] 4-8-7 G Carter (1) *led till hdd and wknd o'r 2 fs out*............(10 to 1 op 10 to 1 tchd 11 to 1) 11

Dist: Hd, 4l, 3l, nk, 1½l, 6l, 2l, 1½l, 4l, hd. 3m 42.11s. a 12.11s (11 Ran).
SR: 10/-/-/-/-/-/ (Mrs M M Haggas), J W Watts

1381 Toyota F. Cross & Sons Conditions Stakes Class D (2-y-o) £3,260 6f (3:50)

738[5] OCHOS RIOS (Ire) 8-11 J Quinn (5) *hld up, hdwy hfwy, led 2 fs out, pushed clr*...(10 to 1 op 10 to 1 tchd 12 to 1) 1
804* SPORTING WARRIOR (Ire) 8-11 S Morris (8) *trkd ldrs, effrt and ev ch 2 fs out, one pace*.................... (8 to 1) 2
1168* BROCTUNE GOLD 9-1 K Fallon (4) *al cl up, slight ld o'r 2 fs out, sn hdd, unbl to quicken*...(11 to 10 fav op 5 to 4) 3
687* MONTAYA 9-1 A Geran (2) *al wl plcd, hrd rdn 2 fs out, one pace*..............................(3 to 1 op 5 to 2) 4
841[4] CULSYTH FLYER 8-11 Paul Eddery (7) *sn rdn alng and outpcd, some hdwy appr fnl furlong, nvr nrr.* .... (12 to 1 op 12 to 1 tchd 14 to 1) 5
1098* MISS MAH-JONG 8-8 Dean McKeown (1) *rdn and lost pl hfwy, ran on ag'n ins fnl furlong.* (14 to 1 op 12 to 1) 6
1168[2] KIERCHEM (Ire) 9-1 D Nicholls (9) *led o'r 3 fs, rdn and wknd 2 furlongs out, tld off.* .... (11 to 2 op 6 to 1 tchd 7 to 1) 7
354* TOP SHOW (Ire) 9-1 G Carter (3) *outpcd, tld off.* .... (20 to 1 op 16 to 1) 8
HIT THE CANVAS (USA) 8-11 N Day (6) *strted slwly, swrvd lft and uns rdr sn aftr start*...... (25 to 1 op 20 to 1) ur

Dist: 3½l, 1l, 2l, 1l, ½l, 7l, 6l. 1m 17.13s. a 5.73s (9 Ran).
SR: 18/4/4/-/-/-/ (Mrs H A Burn), B S Rothwell

1382 St Leger Club Society Draw Handicap Class C (0-90 3-y-o and up) £4,793 7f ....(4:20)

1177[5] FIGHTER SQUADRON [60] (bl) 4-7-11 (5*) Darren Moffatt (11) *wtd wth, gd hdwy o'r one furlong out, quickened to ld ins fnl furlong, sn clr*........................(10 to 1) 1
1144[3] EN ATTENDANT (Fr) [81] 5-9-2 (7*) Antoinette Armes (8) *reared strt, hdwy hfwy, ev ch one furlong out, one pace*.......(9 to 2 op 5 to 1 tchd 11 to 2 and 6 to 1) 2
814[6] SEA DEVIL [77] 7-9-5 N Connorton (7) *hld up, gd hdwy 2 fs out, ran on one pace ins fnl furlong.* ....(12 to 1 op 9 to 1) 3
1137[3] ASHGORE [66] 3-7-11 J Quinn (9) *al wl plcd, ev ch a furlong out, unbl to quicken*...... (10 to 1 op 8 to 1) 4
814[8] SAGEBRUSH ROLLER [86] 5-10-0 K Fallon (10) *settled on heels of ldrs, quickened to ld o'r a furlong out, sn hdd and one pace*...................... (12 to 1 op 10 to 1) 5
1069 MISS HAGGIS [76] 4-9-4 G Carter (4) *wth ldrs, led o'r 2 fs out till appr fnl furlong, no extr*.. (16 to 1 op 25 to 1) 6
1270[2] CHEVEUX MITCHELL [73] (v) 6-9-1 N Day (6) *led till hdd o'r 2 fs out, sn rdn and btn.* .... (100 to 30 fav op 3 to 1 tchd 7 to 2) 7
991* ROBLEU [90] 3-9-0 (7*) Gaye Harwood (3) *gd speed on outsd o'r 5 fs*..........(11 to 2 op 5 to 1 tchd 6 to 1) 8
906[3] SAVAHRA SOUND [73] 8-8-10 (5*) O Pears (1) *pressed ldrs, ev ch 2 fs out, sn rdn and wknd*..............(10 to 1) 9
930[6] ROUND BY THE RIVER [62] 4-8-4 Dean McKeown (5) *in tch, rdn alng hfwy, sn btn.* ....(14 to 1 op 14 to 1 tchd 16 to 1) 10
818[2] MASTER HYDE (USA) [64] 4-8-6 Paul Eddery (2) *trkd ldrs, rdn alng o'r 2 fs out, sn lost tch*......(7 to 1 op 7 to 1) 11

Dist: 3l, ¾l, ½l, 1½l, 1½l, 1½l, ¾l, ¾l, 2½l, nk. 1m 28.93s. a 5.53s (11 Ran).
SR: 37/49/43/19/45/30/22/26/18/ (Claremont Management Services), J A Glover

1383 Yorkshire Stand Maiden Fillies Stakes Class D (3-y-o) £3,435 1¼m 60yds ....(4:50)

686[3] SAVOY TRUFFLE (Fr) 8-11 W Woods (5) *al cl up, 3rd strt, led o'r 2 fs out and ran on wl*....... (5 to 1 op 3 to 1) 1
992[2] NASSMA (Ire) 8-11 G Carter (7) *wtd wth, 4th strt, hdwy to chase wnr blw dist, no imprsn ins fnl furlong.* ....(5 to 4 on op Evens) 2
FOINERY 8-11 J Quinn (6) *strted slwly, sn reco'red, jnd ldr aftr 3 fs, second strt, ev ch 2 furlongs out, grad wknd*........................... (12 to 1 op 7 to 1) 3
992[4] CORAL GEM 8-11 Paul Eddery (4) *hld up in rear, 6th strt and gd hdwy to join ldrs 2 fs out, sn rdn and wknd.* .... (11 to 2 op 5 to 1 tchd 6 to 1) 4
1145[4] HARD TASK 8-11 Dean McKeown (3) *led till hdd o'r 2 fs out, sn wknd*......................(10 to 1 op 7 to 1) 5
992 TISZA 8-11 N Day (1) *al beh, 7th strt, tld off fnl 3 fs.* ....(10 to 1 op 10 to 1 tchd 12 to 1 and 8 to 1) 6
934 SOPHISTICATED AIR 8-11 N Connorton (8) *hld up, 5th strt, lost tch o'r 2 fs out, tld off*........(20 to 1 op 14 to 1) 7

Dist: 1½l, 8l, nk, sht-hd, 15l, hd. 2m 12.87s. a 6.17s (7 Ran).
SR: 51/48/32/31/30/-/ (L Marinopoulos), H R A Cecil

1384 Arksey Handicap Class D (0-80 3-y-o and up) £3,377 1½m............(5:20)

1190* BLACKPATCH HILL [67] 4-9-10 G Carter (4) *pressed ldr, second strt, led on bit 4 fs out, sn wl clr, eased towards finish*......................... (5 to 4 on op Evens) 1
994[3] TAYLORS PRINCE [54] (v) 6-8-11 J Quinn (7) *wtd wth in rear, 6th strt, hdwy to chase wnr o'r 2 fs out, no imprsn.* ....(4 to 1 op 4 to 1 tchd 9 to 2) 2
727* KINOKO [59] 5-9-2 Paul Eddery (1) *trkd ldrs, 3rd strt, rdn and outpcd 3 fs out*.................(8 to 1 op 7 to 1) 3
1138[5] TAHITIAN [57] 4-9-0 K Fallon (5) *slwly into strd, in rear, 7th strt, styd on fnl 2 fs, nvr nrr*..... (9 to 1 op 7 to 1) 4
978 FRUITFUL AFFAIR (Ire) [57] (bl) 4-9-0 N Day (2) *patiently rdn, 5th strt, shaken up o'r 3 fs out, no imprsn.* .... (25 to 1 op 16 to 1) 5
1100[2] BEST APPEARANCE (Ire) [69] 3-8-8 Dean McKeown (6) *mid-div, effrt and rdn 3 fs out, sn outpcd.* .... (10 to 1 op 7 to 1) 6
PERSIAN SOLDIER [53] 6-8-10 N Connorton (3) *led till hdd 4 fs out, sn outpcd, tld off*..........(11 to 1 op 8 to 1) 7

Dist: 2l, 7l, 3l, 2l, 6l, 6l. 2m 37.98s. a 7.48s (7 Ran).
SR: 53/36/27/19/15/-/-/ (J L Dunlop), J L Dunlop

DOWN ROYAL (IRE) (good to yielding) Monday May 31st

1385 Ballygowan Handicap (0-65 3-y-o and up) £1,207 7f.................(4:00)

1123[2] TINERANA (Ire) [-] 3-9-5 M J Kinane (12)....... (6 to 4 on) 1
1293[7] MUGNANO [-] 7-9-8 (6*) C Everard (8).............. (10 to 1) 2
868[6] FILL MY GLASS [-] 9-8-0 (4*) W J Smith (10)...... (12 to 1) 3
1123[7] BUSINESS CENTRE (Ire) [-] 3-8-8 (6*) J J Behan (5) (16 to 1) 4
BOLERO DANCER (Ire) [-] 5-8-13 N Byrne (13).... (20 to 1) 5
1023[4] AFTERGLOW (Ire) [-] 4-8-12 (8*) L O'Shea (6)...... (7 to 1) 6
1251[4] TIGNES (Ire) [-] 5-9-2 J F Egan (3).................. (6 to 1) 7
PERCY LANE (Ire) [-] 3-9-3 W J O'Connor (2)..... (12 to 1) 8
1293[3] MAN OF STRAW [-] 7-7-1 (6*) P P Murphy (1)..... (20 to 1) 9
868 BOLD MOLLY (Ire) [-] 4-8-6 (2*) R M Burke (9)..... (12 to 1) 10

1163[6] PICK'N HILL (Ire) [-] 5-7-7 Joanna Morgan (7)..... (14 to 1) 11
1163 SPECIAL SECRET (Ire) [-] 5-7-13 (8*) P O Casey (4) (33 to 1) 12
Dist: 3l, ½l, 1½l, 1l. (Time not taken) (12 Ran).
(Dr Paschal Carmody), E J O'Grady

1386 Lisnagarvey Maiden (3-y-o and up) £1,207 7f........................ (4:30)

486[8] SOMERTON BOY (Ire) 3-9-0 M J Kinane (3)........(3 to 1) 1
1105[2] KILLEEN STAR (Ire) 3-9-0 W J Supple (5).... (9 to 4 jt-fav) 2
847[8] ICEFLOW (Fr) 3-8-11 R Hughes (2)..........(9 to 4 jt-fav) 3
CLIFF EDGE (USA) 3-8-11 W J O'Connor (6).......(6 to 1) 4
790 WHY ME LINDA (Ire) 4-9-2 (6*) C Everard (7)......(20 to 1) 5
1333 MAJESTIC PADDY (Ire) 3-9-0 D V Smith (4)........(6 to 1) 6
Dist: 1½l, 1½l, 1½l, sht-hd. (Time not taken) (6 Ran).
(Philip Monahan), D K Weld

1387 Lisburn Claiming Race (2-y-o) £1,207 6f.............................. (5:00)

786[8] SHIOWEN (Ire) 8-11 M J Kinane (2)............(4 to 1 on) 1
1121[7] SALLY'S TRUST (Ire) 8-0 Joanna Morgan (3)......(10 to 1) 2
CAN BUT DREAM (Ire) 8-4 (2*) R M Burke (4)...... (5 to 1) 3
Dist: 2l, ½l. (Time not taken) (3 Ran).
(Miss K McGann), D K Weld

LEICESTER (good)
Monday May 31st
Going Correction: NIL

1388 Market Bosworth Median Auction Maiden Stakes Class F (3-y-o) £2,534 1m 8yds...................... (2:25)

1090[2] THE EXECUTOR 9-0 T Sprake (7) *hld up, not clr run and swtchd rght o'r 2 out, led wl over one out, sn clear, eased nr finish*.................(2 to 1 fav tchd 5 to 2) 1
PRETTY BABY 8-9 J Fanning (2) *ran on 3 out, outpcd o'r one out, no imprsn on wnr ins fnl furlong.*
.... (16 to 1 op 12 to 1) 2
1090[3] TWO LUMPS 9-0 S O'Gorman (6) *trkd ldrs, rdn and edgd rght 2 out, styd on one pace ins fnl furlong.*
....................................(5 to 1 op 3 to 1) 3
1058[2] PERDITION (Ire) 8-9 D Holland (4) *made most til hdd wl o'r one out, sn btn*.....................(5 to 2 op 9 to 4) 4
725[6] STARLIGHT ROSE (Ire) 8-9 E Johnson (1) *slwly into strd, beh til styd on last 2 fs, no ch wth ldrs.*
.... (20 to 1 op 12 to 1) 5
PREMIER STAR 8-9 (5*) M Fenton (10) *speed to hfwy.*
.... (14 to 1 op 8 to 1) 6
1008[7] SABEEL 8-9 A McGlone (8) *ldg grp for 6 fs, wknd.*
.... (20 to 1 op 14 to 1) 7
1133 NIGELS PROSPECT 9-0 A Mackay (9) *handily plcd, rdn and no hdwy entering last 2 fs*.... (50 to 1 op 25 to 1) 8
WARM TOES 8-9 P Robinson (3) *nvr able to chal.*
.... (25 to 1 op 16 to 1) 9
TRIBAT 8-2 (7*) J Marshall (5) *in tch til wknd o'r 2 out.*
.... (10 to 1 op 7 to 1) 10
Dist: 6l, 1½l, 3½l, 2½l, 8l, ¾l, nk, 2l, 10l. 1m 39.70s. a 4.60s (10 Ran).
SR: 31/8/8/-/-/-/ (Exors Of The Late Mrs J de Rothschild), R F Johnson Houghton

1389 Anstey Selling Handicap Class G (0-60 3-y-o and up) £3,036 1m 1f 218yds ....(2:55)

628 ROCK THE BARNEY (Ire) [45] 4-8-8 (5*) C Hodgson (7) *hld up, cld on ldrs frm 3 out, sstnd run to ld appr fnl furlong, ran on*...............(5 to 1 jt-fav op 33 to 1) 1
1133[7] DON'T FORGET MARIE (Ire) [50] 3-8-3 S Raymont (11) *chsd ldr, led o'r 3 out, hdd appr fnl furlong, styd on same pace*................................ (8 to 1 op 7 to 1) 2
1034[9] WINGED WHISPER (USA) [37] 4-7-12 (7*) D McCabe (5) *trkd ldrs, rdn and not quicken 2 out.*
.... (16 to 1 op 20 to 1 tchd 14 to 1) 3
1281[8] RED JACK (Ire) [35] 4-8-3 J Fanning (12) *wl plcd til lost pos hfwy, kpt on ag'n fnl 2 fs*....................(20 to 1) 4
1146 MALINDI BAY [36] 5-8-4 E Johnson (4) *mid-div, prmsg effrt o'r 3 out, outpcd appr fnl furlong.*
.... (10 to 1 op 14 to 1 tchd 9 to 1) 5
1120[8] NORMAN WARRIOR [42] 4-8-10 P Robinson (6) *beh til ran on o'r 2 out, nvr nrr*..................(7 to 1 op 6 to 1) 6
709[7] BOOGIE BOPPER (Ire) [53] (v) 4-9-2 (5*) Stephen Davies (14) *beh, rdn alng 4 out, some hdwy last 2 fs, not rch frnt rnk*.................................... (9 to 1 op 7 to 1) 7
1005[6] COMEDY RIVER [50] 6-9-4 Alex Greaves (19) *effrt frm rear o'r 3 out, wknd ins last 2 fs*........(12 to 1 op 10 to 1) 8
626 AEDEAN [48] 4-9-2 A Mackay (16) *wl in tch til lost pl o'r 2 out*................................(14 to 1 op 12 to 1) 9
1138[4] SLY PROSPECT (USA) [46] (v) 5-8-7 (7*) C Webb (1) *nvr on terms*.................................(14 to 1 op 12 to 1) 10
714[6] SUMMER FLOWER [55] 3-8-8 D Holland (9) *ldg grp til wknd o'r 2 out, eased whn btn*......(11 to 2 op 5 to 1) 11
964[8] DOMAIN [48] (bl) 5-8-9 (7*) A Daly (10) *pressed ldrs til lost pl o'r 3 out*..(20 to 1) 12

1133* KIAWAH [55] 3-8-1 (7*) N Varley (2) *hld up, cld on ldrs hfwy, ev ch o'r 2 out, found no extr*..........(5 to 1 jt-fav op 7 to 2 tchd 11 to 2) 13
REEL OF TULLOCH (Ire) [47] 4-9-1 A McGlone (3) *beh most of way*.................................(14 to 1 op 12 to 1) 14
834 SURE SHOT NORMAN [39] (v) 4-8-7 S O'Gorman (13) *led till o'r 3 out, sn wknd, tld off*......... (16 to 1 op 14 to 1) 15
975 GONE BUST (Ire) [36] (bl) 4-8-4 T Sprake (17) *rear grp most of way, tld off*.......................................(25 to 1) 16
Dist: ½l, 4l, 1½l, sht-hd, 2l, nk, 2l, 3l, 2l, nk. 2m 10.70s. a 7.80s (16 Ran).
SR: 21/10/4/-/-/1/11/4/-/ (Mrs Satu Marks), P Burgoyne

1390 Foxton Handicap Class D (0-80 3-y-o) £3,882 1m 8yds................ (3:25)

995[8] MISTY SILKS [60] 8-1 P Robinson (6) *handily plcd, squeezed for room 2 fs out, swtchd rght, led o'r one out, sn clr, styd on*.........(6 to 1 op 20 to 1 tchd 5 to 1) 1
724 JIHAAD (USA) [57] 7-12 A McGlone (5) *hld up in rear, str brst fnl furlong, fnshd fst*........... (8 to 1 op 6 to 1) 2
HADEER'S DANCE [80] 9-7 R Price (3) *trkd ldrs, slight advantage 2 fs out, hdd o'r one out, ran on one pace.*
....(8 to 1 op 6 to 1) 3
1225[2] GREEN'S FAIR (Ire) [68] 8-4 (5*) M Fenton (4) *hld up in rear, cld on ldrs o'r 2 out, one pace fnl furlong.*
..................(15 to 8 fav op 7 to 4 tchd 2 to 1) 4
1153[6] TAJDIF (USA) [73] 9-0 D Holland (1) *improved hfwy, ev ch 2 fs out, not quicken o'r one out.*
..........................(9 to 2 op 4 to 1 tchd 5 to 1) 5
1040[3] SPICE AND SUGAR [77] 8-11 (7*) D McCabe (2) *led til 2 fs out, sn btn*..........................(5 to 1 op 7 to 2) 6
TODDEN [52] 7-7 J Fanning (7) *pressed ldr, ev ch 2 fs out, wknd quickly*......................(14 to 1 op 10 to 1) 7
Dist: 1½l, 2½l, ½l, 2l, 3l, 6l. 1m 40.30s. a 5.20s (7 Ran).
SR: 9/1/16/2/1/-/-/ (P E Axon), M J Ryan

1391 Everards Tiger Best Bitter Claiming Stakes Class F (2-y-o) £2,668 5f 218yds ....(3:55)

1091[8] TITANIA'S DANCE (Ire) 8-2 (5*) M Fenton (12) *made all, sn clr, rdn and styd on ins fnl furlong.*
.... (7 to 1 op 8 to 1 tchd 10 to 1) 1
1119[5] RISKIE THINGS 8-2 (7*) Mark Denaro (9) *ldg grp, rdn to chal entering fnl furlong, not quicken last 50 yards.*
.... (8 to 1 op 10 to 1) 2
865[7] TIMES ZANDO 7-11[1] (5*) Stephen Davies (5) *hld up, hdwy o'r 2 fs out, one pace appr fnl furlong.*
.... (20 to 1 op 14 to 1) 3
1091[6] NORTHERN STARLIGHT 8-8 P Robinson (2) *ran on ins last 2 fs, not rch wnr*............(4 to 1 fav op 8 to 1) 4
WADDLE (Ire) 8-9 (7*) S Mulvey (4) *dwlt, effrt o'r 2 fs out, no imprsn on ldrs fnl furlong*........(9 to 1 op 4 to 1) 5
1189[7] WINGS AHEAD 8-10 J Fanning (3) *outpcd til ran on last 2 fs*..............(25 to 1 op 10 to 1 tchd 33 to 1) 6
1189[5] T O O MAMMA'S (Ire) 8-7 D Holland (7) *speed for o'r 3 fs.*
....(8 to 1) 7
768* LYING EYES 7-12 (7*) P McCabe (6) *broke wl, settled in mid-div, no prog frm 2 out*..........(9 to 2 op 3 to 1) 8
1245[4] STORM HEIGHTS 7-10 (7*) J Marshall (11) *trkd ldrs for 4 fs, wknd*..............................(14 to 1 op 8 to 1) 9
1277[4] DEMI-PLIE 9-2 A McGlone (10) *outpcd and rdn alng hfwy, nvr on terms*................(14 to 1 op 8 to 1) 10
BRIGHT VENUS 8-3 R Price (1) *veered lft aftr leaving stalls, al beh*.......................(20 to 1 op 10 to 1) 11
MOSS HOUSE (Ire) 9-2 S Raymont (8) *beh frm hfwy.*
....(8 to 1 op 5 to 2) 12
Dist: 2l, 2l, 2½l, 1½l, 1l, 1½l, 1½l, 6l, 4l, ½l. 1m 14.10s. a 3.70s (12 Ran).
SR: 19/13/-/-/-/-/ (Miss Lucille Boden), M Bell

1392 Tigers Apprentices' Handicap Class F (0-85 4-y-o and up) £2,489 1m 3f 183yds...................... (4:25)

BIG PAT [50] 4-8-10 (7*) Elizabeth Turner (4) *steadied leaving stalls, jnd ldrs hfwy, led 4 out, kpt on wl ins fnl furlong*..(10 to 1) 1
1268* WESTERN DYNASTY [66] 7-10-2 (3*,5ex) P McCabe (3) *cl up, led aftr 3 fs til 4 out, rallied ins fnl furlong.*
...................(6 to 4 fav op 5 to 4 tchd 13 to 8) 2
1064 SWIFT SILVER [56] 6-9-9 D McCabe (5) *settled towards rear, ran on 4 out, one pace last 2 fs.* (4 to 1 op 7 to 2) 3
1190[3] HILLZAH (USA) [57] 5-9-10 H Bastiman (8) *hld up in rear, hrd rdn 3 out, no imprsn on ldrs last 2 fs.*
......................................(7 to 1 op 6 to 1) 4
994 EDGE OF DARKNESS [56] 4-9-6 (3*) D Gibbs (1) *chsd ldrs till rdn and wknd o'r 2 out.*
..........................(7 to 1 op 6 to 1 tchd 8 to 1) 5
420 CORINTHIAN GOD (Ire) [35] 4-7-11 (5*) Sharon Millard (6) *led for 3 fs, dsptd ld hfwy til 4 out, wknd o'r 2 out.*
.... (10 to 1 op 8 to 1) 6
924 PEAK DISTRICT [49] 7-9-2 A Procter (7) *handily plcd, rdn and lost pl appr last 2 fs*......................(16 to 1) 7
1041[8] KASHAN (Ire) [60] (v) 5-9-10 (3*) Mark Denaro (2) *beh most of way, lost tch 4 out*.................(33 to 1 op 25 to 1) 8
Dist: ½l, 2l, 2½l, 2½l, 6l, hd, 6l. 2m 38.40s. a 9.90s (8 Ran).
SR: 4/19/5/1/-/ (Burton Park Country Club), J Pearce

1393 Lioness Maiden Fillies' Stakes Class D (2-y-o) £3,582 5f 218yds.......(4:55)

ELRAFA AH (USA) 8-11 R Hills (8) *strted slwly, ran on o'r 2 fs out, led over one out, quickened clr, imprsv.* ....(Evens fav tchd 6 to 4) 1
MARAGON 8-4 (7*) N Varley (9) *slwly into strd, sn chasing ldrs, led o'r 2 out, hdd and outpcd appr fnl furlong.* .... (8 to 1 op 12 to 1 tchd 7 to 1) 2
OMNIA (USA) 8-11 A Munro (4) *beh til ran on fnl furlong, nrst at finish*..........(11 to 2 op 3 to 1) 3
1142[6] SWAGGER LADY 8-11 P Robinson (3) *pressed ldrs, rdn and outpcd ins last 2 fs*..............(8 to 1 op 5 to 1) 4
ALACRITY 8-6 (5*) Stephen Davies (2) *in tch, cld on ldrs frm hfwy, one pace appr fnl furlong.* ....(14 to 1 op 10 to 1) 5
1032[8] ROSE CIEL (Ire) 8-11 S Raymont (5) *ldg grp til rdn and wknd hfwy*...................... (14 to 1 op 10 to 1) 6
YO KIRI-B 8-11 T Lucas (7) *led for o'r 3 fs, wknd quickly.* ....(33 to 1) 7
DYNAMIS (Ire) 8-11 A McGlone (1) *al outpcd.* ....(4 to 1 op 4 to 1 tchd 5 to 1 and 7 to 2) 8
Dist: 3l, 3½l, 2½l, 2l, 2l, 1½l, ½l. 1m 13.60s. a 3.20s (8 Ran).
SR: 33/21/7/-/-/ (Hamdan Al-Maktoum), H Thomson Jones

1394 Groby Handicap Class D (0-85 3-y-o and up) £3,915 5f 218yds........(5:25)

1232* GREAT HALL [51] 4-7-8 (7ex) A Mackay (5) *hld up in rear, str brst o'r one out, led ins fnl furlong, ran on.* ....(9 to 1 op 10 to 1) 1
YOURS BY RIGHT [81] 3-8-7 (7*) D McCabe (8) *ldg grp till outpcd and lost pos o'r 2 out, str brst ins fnl furlong, fnshd wl*...................................(8 to 1) 2
1066 RED ROSEIN [85] 7-10-0 P Robinson (4) *steadied leaving stalls, cld on ldrs o'r 2 out, ev ch one out, no extr last 100 yards*............ (12 to 1 op 8 to 1 tchd 14 to 1) 3+
ZEBOIM [70] (bl) 7-8-6 (7*) Kim McDonnell (7) *trkd ldrs, ev ch appr fnl furlong, rdn and one pace last 100 yards.* ....(20 to 1 tchd 16 to 1) 3+
993[3] BELLSABANGING [71] 3-8-4 R Hills (1) *made most of rng til hdd ins fnl furlong*..........................(4 to 1 jt-fav op 7 to 2 tchd 5 to 1) 5
1232[3] LEIGH CROFTER [56] (v) 4-7-13 R Price (6) *settled in mid-div, kpt on one pace last 2 fs.* ....(12 to 1 op 10 to 1 tchd 14 to 1) 6
1066[6] OUR RITA [76] 4-9-5 A Munro (9) *ldg grp til rdn and wknd o'r one out*..........................(5 to 1 op 6 to 1) 7
1177[5] CHOIR PRACTICE [64] (bl) 6-8-7 D Holland (2) *slwly into strd and hld up, effrt and hng o'r 2 out, sn btn.* ....(8 to 1 op 7 to 1) 8
1267 DARUSSALAM [72] 6-8-10 (5*) A Procter (3) *improved hfwy, effrt 2 out, wknd wl o'r one out.* ....(16 to 1 op 14 to 1) 9
1246[9] NO QUARTER GIVEN [70] 8-8-13 J Fanning (10) *cl up til wknd quickly 2 out*.............. (12 to 1 op 10 to 1) 10
814[2] NILE DELTA (Ire) [70] 4-8-13 A McGlone (11) *pressed ldrs, rdn and wknd 2 out, eased whn btn.* ....(4 to 1 jt-fav op 7 to 2 tchd 3 to 1) 11
Dist: ¾l, 2l, dd-ht, nk, 1½l, 1l, 1l, 3½l, 4l, 10l. 1m 12.60s. a 2.20s (11 Ran).
SR: 36/53/59/44/34/23/39/23/17/ (P D Cundell), P D Cundell

MULHEIM (GER) (good)
Monday May 31st

1395 Preis de Diana (Group 2) (3-y-o) £93,878 1m 3f..................(3:45)

ARKONA (Ger) 8-11 O Schick,.......................... 1
805* QUEBRADA (Ire) 8-11 A Tylicki,.......................... 2
OSTWAHL (Ire) 8-11 A Bond,.......................... 3
805 ELACATA (Ger) 8-11 M Rimmer,.......................... 4
805[2] SECONDIA 8-11 A Boschert,.......................... 5
SHINE SHARE (Ire) 8-11 W Newnes,.......................... 6
805[6] VAL D'ISERE (Ger) 8-11 M Hofer,.......................... 7
805[8] NOUVELLE REINE (Ger) 8-11 G Bocskai,.......................... 8
805[3] AMBRA (Fr) 8-11 L Mader,.......................... 9
Dist: 3l, 1½l, nk, 2l, 2½l, 15l, 4l, dist. 2m 23.91s. (9 Ran).
(Gestut Ebbesloh), H Blume

REDCAR (good)
Monday May 31st

Going Correction: MINUS 0.25 sec. per fur. (races 1,2,6,7), NIL (3,4,5)

1396 Coatham Bowl Median Auction Maiden Stakes Class D (3-y-o) £3,172 6f.............................(2:05)

FIRST PLAY 8-9 J Fortune (7) *broke wl, made all, shaken up o'r one furlong out, styd on well ins last.* .... (10 to 1 op 6 to 1 tchd 11 to 1) 1
1192[4] HEART BROKEN 8-9 L Piggott (8) *pressed ldrs on ins, effrt 2 fs out, styd on inside last.* ....(9 to 4 op 5 to 2 tchd 2 to 1) 2
1136[5] MOLLY BRAZEN 8-9 K Darley (9) *hld up, effrt 2 fs out, kpt on same pace ins last*..................(12 to 1 op 7 to 1) 3
EL ARZ 9-0 W Hood (5) *slwly into strd, ran green thrght, effrt 2 fs out, not quicken ins last.* ....(13 to 8 fav op 6 to 4) 4
428[7] BALIANA 8-9 A Culhane (6) *pressed ldrs, effrt 2 fs out, not quicken*..........................(11 to 2 op 9 to 2) 5
FORTIS PAVIOR (Ire) 8-7 (7*) G Parkin (2) *in tch, sn prmnt, effrt hfwy, not quicken o'r one furlong out.* ....(25 to 1 op 12 to 1) 6
PRESS ONWARD 8-9 T Williams (3) *trkd ldr, rdn hfwy, fdd 2 fs out*..........................(10 to 1 op 7 to 1) 7
FORDALLIA 8-9 J Lowe (1) *in tch on outsd, pushed alng hfwy, sn wknd*..........................(33 to 1 op 12 to 1) 8
1187[6] CANAZEI (v) 8-9 Kim Tinkler (4) *chsd ldrs, sn rdn, lost tch frm hfwy*.......................(100 to 1 op 20 to 1) 9
Dist: 1½l, 1½l, sht-hd, ¾l, 2l, 8l, 6l, 3½l. 1m 12.60s. a 2.90s (9 Ran).
SR: 7/1/-/-/-/-/ (Keith H Ewbank), J Berry

1397 Sandhills Claiming Stakes Class F (3-y-o and up) £2,601 6f........... (2:30)

1017[8] BIRCHWOOD SUN (bl) 3-8-8 K Darley (11) *beh and sn pushed alng, improved o'r 2 fs out, ran on to ld wl ins fnl furlong*..........................(4 to 1 op 5 to 2) 1
1060[4] ISLAND KNIGHT (Ire) 4-9-10 L Piggott (6) *nvr far away, improved to ld o'r one fs out, hdd wl ins last.* ....(9 to 1 op 6 to 1) 2
1228[3] LANGUEDOC 6-9-10 L Charnock (12) *trkd ldrs, led o'r 2 fs out, hdd over one out, one pace*......(9 to 1 op 8 to 1) 3
1188[3] DOKKHA OYSTON (Ire) (bl) 5-9-6 J Fortune (9) *trkd ldrs, rdn and swtchd o'r one furlong out, no extr ins last.* .... (5 to 1 op 4 to 1 tchd 11 to 2) 4
1187[3] DEAD CALM (v) 3-8-8 B Raymond (10) *chsd ldrs, drvn alng o'r 2 fs out, one pace fnl furlong*.....(8 to 1 op 6 to 1) 5
837 BREEZE AWAY 4-9-0 A Culhane (3) *chsd ldrs, rdn o'r 2 fs out, one pace fnl furlong*..........(14 to 1 op 12 to 1) 6
568 ROSE GEM (Ire) 4-8-8 (3*) S Maloney (1) *pressed ldrs, led hfwy, hdd o'r 2 fs out, sn one pace.* (33 to 1 op 25 to 1) 7
683 MAKE MINE A DOUBLE 3-8-4 J Lowe (7) *mid-div, rdn o'r 2 fs out, wknd over one out*.......... (25 to 1 op 16 to 1) 8
1113[5] SABO SONG 3-8-9 Dale Gibson (8) *beh, rdn haflway, no imprsn o'r one furlong out*.......(7 to 2 fav op 3 to 1) 9
1159[4] ANGELS ANSWER (Ire) 4-8-11 M Birch (13) *led 2 fs stands rail, sn drvn alng, wknd o'r two furlongs out.* ....(8 to 1 op 6 to 1) 10
MISS SIHAM (Ire) 4-8-11 G Hind (5) *prmnt, led aftr 2 fs, hdd hfwy, sn rdn and wknd*..................(33 to 1) 11
866[5] KATIE-A (Ire) 4-8-13 T Williams (2) *slwly into strd, nvr able to reco'r*..........................(33 to 1) 12
1230 CRIMSON CONSORT (Ire) (bl) 4-8-8 Kim Tinkler (4) *unruly stalls, beh, lost tch frm hfwy*................(100 to 1) 13
Dist: ½l, 1l, 3½l, ¾l, 1l, 1½l, 3½l, 1l, 2½l, 1½l. 1m 11.40s. a 1.70s (13 Ran).
SR: 30/44/40/22/7/9/ (P D Savill), R Hollinshead

1398 Zetland Gold Cup Handicap Class B (0-110 3-y-o and up) £16,180 1¼m ....(3:00)

684* RIVER NORTH (Ire) [90] 3-8-1 K Darley (12) *settled mdifield, rdn to improve o'r 2 fs out, led a furlong out, kpt on wl.* ....(15 to 8 fav op 9 to 4 tchd 5 to 2) 1
1021[7] PHILIDOR [84] 4-8-7 (3*) N Kennedy (14) *hld up, effrt whn not clr run 3 fs out, sn swtchd, ran on wl ins last.* ....(14 to 1 tchd 16 to 1) 2
1110[2] CUMBRIAN CHALLENGE (Ire) [94] 4-9-6 M Birch (5) *pressed ldr, led o'r 3 fs out, hdd one out, sn one pace.* ....(8 to 1 op 7 to 1) 3
1021[2] LUCKY GUEST [100] 6-9-12 L Piggott (4) *tucked away on ins, improved entering strt, rdn and no extr fnl 2 fs.* ....(6 to 1 op 8 to 1) 4
824 COOL LUKE (Ire) [79] 4-8-5 A Culhane (2) *hld up towards rear, improved on inner 4 fs out, not quicken o'r one out*.......................... (33 to 1 op 25 to 1) 5
1110[5] LEIF THE LUCKY (USA) [78] 4-8-4 J Lowe (6) *hld up, not clr run o'r 2 fs out, ran on fnl two furlongs, nrst finish.* .... (10 to 1 op 8 to 1 tchd 11 to 1) 6
1021[6] RAMBO'S HALL [102] 8-10-0 J Fortune (13) *hld up and beh, improved o'r 2 fs out, nvr nr to chal.* ....(20 to 1 op 14 to 1) 7
1143* GLIDE PATH (USA) [76] 4-7-12[3] (7*) T G McLaughlin (8) *in tch, took clr order o'r 3 fs out, wknd wl over one out.* ....(8 to 1 op 7 to 1) 8
1021[8] DRUMMER HICKS [79] 4-8-5 Dale Gibson (7) *in tch, drvn alng o'r 3 fs out, grad wknd.* .... (11 to 1 op 10 to 1 tchd 12 to 1) 9
801[4] HAMADRYAD (Ire) [82] 5-8-5 (3*) S Maloney (11) *hld up, improved on outer appr strt, rdn and wknd o'r 2 fs out, eased*..........................(16 to 1) 10
894* KILLICK [67] 5-7-0 (7*) D Wright (10) *in tch on outer till wknd o'r 2 fs out*.......................... (50 to 1) 11
1021* MUHAYAA (USA) [100] 4-9-12 B Raymond (9) *pressed ldrs, rdn 5 fs out, wknd wl o'r 2 out*................ (10 to 1) 12

893[8] BIG BLUE [75] (bl) 4-7-12 (3*) B Doyle (1) *made most till hdd o'r 3 fs out, sn btn*..............(10 to 1 tchd 11 to 1) 13
1178[7] WILSONIC [71] 4-7-11[1] T Williams (3) *chsd ldrs till rdn and wknd o'r 2 fs out*..................(50 to 1 op 33 to 1) 14
Dist: 1l, 3l, 2½l, 1½l, ¾l, 2½l, 1½l, 1½l, 3l, ¾l. 2m 5.00s. a 3.80s (14 Ran).
SR: 49/56/60/61/37/34/53/24/24/ (P D Savill), Lady Herries

1399 Dundas Fillies Handicap Class E (0-70 3-y-o) £3,157 1¼m............. (3:30)

1180[3] CUMBRIAN RHAPSODY [64] 9-2 (3*) S Maloney (10) *hld up, rdn to improve 3 fs out, sstnd run fnl 2 furlongs to ld ins last, styd on wl*.....(11 to 4 fav op 3 to 1 tchd 5 to 2) 1
1111 BOBBYSOXER [62] 9-3 L Piggott (3) *trkd ldr, led 4 fs out, shaken up o'r one out, swshd tail and hdd ins last, no extr*..............................(7 to 1 op 8 to 1) 2
1055[3] SHIRLEY ROSE [60] 9-1 T Williams (2) *settled midfield, improved 4 fs out, rdn and swtchd ins o'r 2 furlongs out, kpt on same pace inside last*...(7 to 1 tchd 8 to 1) 3
882[4] CLEAR LOOK [57] 8-5 (7*) T G McLaughlin (4) *hld up in rear, effrt on ins 3 fs out, rdn and not quicken entering last*..(8 to 1) 4
1133[6] SCOFFERA [44] 7-13 Kim Tinkler (6) *nvr far away, ev ch and edgd rght o'r 2 fs out, wknd appr fnl furlong.* ....(14 to 1 op 10 to 1) 5
1175[3] A BADGE TOO FAR (Ire) [53] 8-8 G Hind (7) *hld up, pushed alng to improve entering strt, wknd o'r 2 fs out.* (7 to 1) 6
631[2] JIZYAH [66] 9-7 N Carlisle (1) *trkd ldrs on ins till wknd quickly o'r 2 fs out*..................(8 to 1 tchd 10 to 1) 7
1074[7] INNOCENT ABROAD (Den) [48] 8-3 A Culhane (5) *hld up, rdn entering strt, btn o'r 2 fs out*.............(33 to 1) 8
934[9] NEVER IN TOUCH [38] (bl) 7-0 (7*) D Wright (9) *slwly into strd, sn detached and rdn, no imprsn entering strt.* ....(33 to 1) 9
1037[4] CUBIST (Ire) [66] 9-7 K Darley (11) *in tch on outer, rdn to improve o'r 3 fs out, wknd over 2 furlongs out.* ....(9 to 2 op 4 to 1 tchd 5 to 1) 10
1162[7] EVAHART [38] 7-7 L Charnock (8) *made most till hdd 4 fs out, sn btn and eased*...........................(33 to 1) 11
Dist: 2l, ¾l, 3l, sht-hd, 10l, 6l, 1½l, hd, 3l, 10l. 2m 8.30s. a 7.10s (11 Ran).
SR: 34/28/24/15/1/-/ (Cumbrian Industrials Ltd), M H Easterby

1400 Glaisdale Handicap Class E (0-70 3-y-o and up) £3,235 1¾m 19yds.... (4:05)

BILBERRY [39] 4-7-12 T Williams (6) *patiently rdn, improved on bit entering strt, led o'r 2 fs out, edgd rght and sn shaken up, ridden out ins last.* ....(20 to 1 op 16 to 1 tchd 25 to 1) 1
1190[7] NORTHERN GRADUATE (USA) [69] 4-10-0 K Darley (10) *settled mid-div, improved appr strt, led o'r 3 fs out, hdd over 2 out, sn rdn, not quicken ins last.* ....(9 to 4 tchd 11 to 4) 2
1179[4] YOUNG GEORGE [41] 6-8-0 J Lowe (1) *hld up and beh, hdwy entering strt, drvn alng 2 fs out, not quicken ins last*..................................(7 to 1 op 8 to 1) 3
STINGRAY CITY (USA) [62] 4-9-7 G Hind (5) *trkd ldrs, rdn entering strt, no extr fnl 2 fs.* ....(20 to 1 op 14 to 1 tchd 25 to 1) 4
1134[2] HARLESTONE BROOK [72] 3-8-11 L Piggott (9) *pressed ldg grp, rdn o'r 2 fs out, sn no imprsn, eased over one out.* ....(7 to 4 fav op 5 to 4) 5
1190[6] HOT PUNCH [38] 4-7-11 Dale Gibson (4) *hld up, pushed alng 6 fs out, effrt on outer 4 out, not quicken fnl 2 furlongs*..............................(16 to 1 op 12 to 1) 6
618[4] TOUR LEADER (NZ) [60] 4-9-5 M Birch (2) *nvr far away, led 4 fs out, hdd o'r 3 out, sn rdn and grad wknd.* ....(9 to 1 op 8 to 1) 7
1195[6] MEDIA STAR [36] 8-7-9[5] (3*) N Kennedy (8) *sluggish strt, in rear, rdn entering strt, nvr on terms.* ....(33 to 1 tchd 40 to 1) 8
53[5] SIGNOR SASSIE (USA) [54] 5-8-13 Kim Tinkler (7) *cl up, improved to dispute ld hfwy, rdn o'r 4 fs out, sn btn, tld off*..............................(25 to 1 op 16 to 1) 9
910[6] TRICYCLE (Ire) [34] (bl) 4-7-7 L Charnock (3) *took keen hold, led, jnd hfwy, hdd 4 fs out, sn wknd, tld off.* ....(10 to 1 op 8 to 1) 10
Dist: 1½l, nk, 12l, 1½l, 4l, 8l, 3½l, 3l, hd. 3m 4.60s. a 8.10s (10 Ran).
SR: 3/30/1/-/-/-/ (N Hetherton), C W C Elsey

1401 Spring Bank Holiday Maiden Auction Stakes Class D (2-y-o) £3,231 5f (4:40)

MR M-E-N (Ire) 9-0 J Fortune (1) *dwlt, sn prmnt, led 2 fs out, clr a furlong out, drvn out ins last.* ....(7 to 1 tchd 11 to 2) 1
CELESTIAL RUMOUR (Ire) 9-0 G Hind (9) *slwly away, beh and sn detached, rapid hdwy o'r one furlong out, fnshd wl*..............................(25 to 1 op 12 to 1) 2
830[2] ANTANANARIVO (Ire) 9-0 K Darley (7) *made most till hdd 2 fs out, sn drvn alng, one pace ins last.* ....(6 to 4 on tchd 11 to 10 on and Evens) 3
1152[3] SPRING LOADED 9-0 T Williams (2) *prmnt, drvn alng hfwy, not quicken appr fnl furlong.* ....(17 to 2 op 5 to 1 tchd 9 to 1) 4
680[4] DESIRE'S DREAM 8-9 M Wigham (5) *unruly stalls, dsptd ld 3 fs, sn drvn alng, kpt on same pace ins last.* ....(10 to 1 op 8 to 1 tchd 11 to 1) 5
ASTRAC (Ire) 9-0 L Piggott (4) *pressed ldrs, drvn alng o'r 2 fs out, one pace ins last*......................(10 to 1) 6
ONCE MORE FOR LUCK (Ire) 9-0 M Birch (8) *slwly into strd, beh, sn pushed alng, hdwy o'r one furlong out, nvr dngrs*..........................(10 to 1 op 7 to 1) 7
1020[9] SALVOR (Ire) 9-0 J Lowe (3) *dwlt, beh, pushed alng aftr 2 fs, no imprsn o'r one out*.........(16 to 1 op 20 to 1) 8
CAPTAIN TAFFY 9-0 B Raymond (6) *beh and sn outpcd, no dngr frm hfwy*..........................(16 to 1 op 8 to 1) 9
Dist: 2½l, sht-hd, sht-hd, sht-hd, ½l, nk, 1l, 4l. 59.50s. a 2.80s (9 Ran).
SR: 19/9/8/7/1/4/3/-/-/ (Manchester Evening News Ltd), J Berry

1402 Billingham Conditions Stakes Class D (3-y-o and up) £3,401 7f.........(5:15)

1003[5] BRIGADE 4-9-4 B Raymond (4) *pressed ldr, led o'r one furlong out, pushed out ins last*..... (9 to 2 op 5 to 2) 1
1040[4] BOLD AMUSEMENT 3-8-9 K Darley (3) *dwlt, sn chasing ldrs on inner, effrt and shaken up o'r one furlong out, kpt on ins last*.....................(11 to 2 op 5 to 1) 2
915[3] CARELAMAN 3-8-9 L Piggott (2) *nvr far away, effrt appr fnl furlong, sn one pace.* (11 to 8 on tchd 11 to 10 on) 3
1150* QUEEN OF THE QUORN 3-8-8 N Carlisle (5) *led, rdn 3 fs out, hdd o'r one out, sn btn.* ....(11 to 1 op 10 to 1 tchd 12 to 1) 4
641[2] HOPE HALL (Ire) 5-9-2 A Culhane (1) *hld up in last pl, shaken up 2 fs out, sn btn*.......... (9 to 1 op 8 to 1) 5
Dist: 1½l, 1l, 3½l, 5l. 1m 25.10s. a 3.30s (5 Ran).
SR: 28/14/11/-/-/ (D R Loder), D R Loder

SANDOWN (good to firm)
Monday May 31st

Going Correction: PLUS 0.05 sec. per fur. (races 1,4), MINUS 0.20 (2,3,5,6,7)

1403 Collchimie Maiden Fillies' Stakes Class D (2-y-o) £3,746 5f 6yds...(2:00)

DOUBLE DOWN 8-11 L Dettori (12) *pressed ldrs, rdn one furlong out, led ins last, ran on wl.* (10 to 1 op 5 to 1) 1
FAYROOZ (USA) 8-11 A Munro (9) *in tch, drvn alng and ev ch o'r one furlong out, not quicken ins last.* ....(5 to 4 fav op 11 to 10 tchd 11 to 8) 2
BRAARI (USA) 8-11 W Carson (17) *slwly away, improved o'r 2 fs out, kpt on one pace ins last.* ....(8 to 1 op 5 to 1 tchd 10 to 1) 3
KISSININTHEBACKROW (USA) 8-11 M Hills (6) *hld up, drvn alng 2 fs out, styd on one pace fnl furlong.* ....(33 to 1 op 20 to 1) 4
984[3] NIGHTITUDE 8-11 Pat Eddery (11) *led till appr last, one pace*..................(7 to 1 op 5 to 1 tchd 8 to 1) 5
WINSOME WOOSTER 8-11 M Roberts (8) *trkd ldrs, drvn alng hfwy, styd on same pace.* ....(33 to 1 op 16 to 1 tchd 40 to 1) 6
SHALBOURNE (USA) 8-11 J Reid (16) *wth ldr, led appr one furlong out, hdd entering last, fdd.* ....(15 to 2 op 8 to 1 tchd 10 to 1) 7
ZOLICA 8-11 J Carroll (1) *slwly away, rear till styd on one pace ins fnl 2 fs, not rch ldrs*...............(33 to 1) 8
MONAASSABAAT (USA) 8-11 W R Swinburn (2) *dwlt, beh, moderate hdwy o'r 2 fs out, sn one pace.* ....(7 to 1 op 5 to 1) 9
HANKYPANKYMANKI 8-11 T Quinn (7) *speed 3 fs.* ....(25 to 1 op 14 to 1 tchd 33 to 1) 10
839[5] RAMBOLD 8-4 (7*) C Hawksley (19) *speed to hfwy.* ....(50 to 1) 11
ZALAMERA 8-11 C Avery (18) *al mid-div*........(33 to 1) 12
CARTE BLANCHE 8-11 D Biggs (15) *speed to hfwy.* ....(33 to 1 op 20 to 1) 13
ANSELLADY 8-11 R Cochrane (21) *hld up in tch, lost pl o'r 2 fs out*.............(33 to 1 op 25 to 1 tchd 40 to 1) 14
DISH OF THE DAY (Ire) 8-11 C Rutter (3) *chsd ldrs to hfwy.* ....(33 to 1) 15
FOREST LOCH 8-11 F Norton (20) *mid-div, wkng whn not much room o'r 2 fs out*........................(50 to 1) 16
RAISA POINT 8-11 J Murray (4) *dwlt, al beh.* ....(33 to 1 op 20 to 1) 17
TINKER OSMASTON 8-11 J Curant (14) *dwlt, al beh.* ....(25 to 1 op 14 to 1) 18
1131 DURANDETTE 8-11 G Bardwell (13) *nvr dngrs*....(50 to 1) 19
Dist: 2l, 1½l, ½l, sht-hd, ¾l, nk, ½l, hd, ½l, 3½l. 1m 3.20s. a 3.70s (19 Ran).
SR: 28/20/14/12/11/8/7/5/4/ (J C Smith), I A Balding

1404 United Breweries Fillies Stakes Class A (Listed) (3-y-o and up) £11,860 1m 14yds......................... (2:35)

734* POLKA DANCER 3-8-8 W R Swinburn (5) *pressed ldr, led o'r 2 fs out, drvn out, ran on wl ins last.* ....(11 to 10 fav op Evens tchd 11 to 10 on) 1

823[6] MAGIQUE ROND POINT (USA) 3-8-9[1] J Reid (2) *chsd ldrs, ev ch whn edgd rght o'r one furlong out, no extr wl ins last*............(13 to 2 op 5 to 1 tchd 7 to 1) 2
INSTANT AFFAIR (USA) 3-8-8 T Quinn (3) *wtd wth, progess frm 2 fs out, swtchd outsd entering last, ran on.* ....(20 to 1 op 14 to 1) 3
844[6] NO RESERVATIONS (Ire) 3-8-8 R Cochrane (1) *wtd wth, drvn alng 3 fs out, styd on one pace ins last.* ....(33 to 1 op 20 to 1) 4
746[5] MYSTIC GODDESS (USA) 3-8-11 W Carson (6) *trkd ldrs, rdn 2 fs out, hmpd o'r one out, not rcvr.* ....(8 to 1 op 6 to 1) 5
992* BELLA BALLERINA 3-8-8 Pat Eddery (4) *led till appr 2 fs out, wkng whn short of room approaching last.* ....(3 to 1 op 5 to 2 tchd 7 to 2) 6
Dist: Nk, sht-hd, 2½l, 1l, 1½l. 1m 43.48s. a 4.38s (6 Ran).
SR: 4/4/2/ (S J Richmond-Watson), J R Fanshawe

1405 Cementone Beaver Henry II EBF Stakes Class A (Group 3) (4-y-o and up) £26,264 2m 78yds.......... (3:05)

1065* BRIER CREEK (USA) 4-8-10 M Roberts (7) *trkd ldrs, short of room o'r one furlong out, ran on strly ins last to ld last strds*............(7 to 2 op 3 to 1 tchd 4 to 1) 1
735[4] NOT IN DOUBT (USA) 4-8-10 L Dettori (5) *led one furlong, styd cl up, drvn alng appr 2 fs out, led entering last, hdd and no extr last strds.* ....(25 to 1 op 20 to 1 tchd 33 to 1) 2
1018* ASSESSOR (Ire) 4-9-2 T Quinn (1) *trkd ldrs, rdn 2 fs out, styd on ins last*............(5 to 1 op 7 to 2) 3
1018[7] DARU (USA) (v) 4-8-10 R Cochrane (4) *wtd wth, improved frm 2 fs out, kpt on ins last.* ....(16 to 1 op 14 to 1 tchd 12 to 1) 4
ARCADIAN HEIGHTS 5-8-12 W R Swinburn (8) *wtd wth, shaken up and styd on frm o'r one furlong out, nvr nr to chal*............(10 to 1 tchd 12 to 1) 5
1018[2] ALLEGAN (USA) 4-8-10 Pat Eddery (6) *cl up, rdn and effrt frm 2 fs out, one pace entering last, eased.* ....(4 to 1 op 7 to 2 tchd 9 to 2) 6
892[4] FURTHER FLIGHT 7-9-1 M Hills (2) *hld up, effrt appr 2 fs out, sn one pace.* (5 to 2 fav op 3 to 1 tchd 100 to 30) 7
774[8] SILVERNESIAN (USA) 4-9-2 W Carson (3) *led aftr one furlong, hdd and wknd entering last, eased.* ....(25 to 1 op 16 to 1 tchd 33 to 1) 8
Dist: Nk, ½l, hd, 1½l, nk, 3l, nk. 3m 39.64s. a 10.64s (8 Ran).
(Sheikh Mohammed), J H M Gosden

1406 UB Group Temple Stakes Class A (Group 2) (3-y-o and up) £35,325 5f 6yds.......................... (3:40)

795* PARIS HOUSE 4-9-7 J Carroll (7) *wth ldr, led 2 fs out, hrd rdn ins last, jst hld on.* (9 to 2 op 5 to 2 tchd 11 to 2) 1
WOLFHOUND (USA) 4-9-10 M Roberts (5) *nvr far away, drvn alng o'r one furlong out, ev ch ins last, ran on.* ....(5 to 1 op 11 to 2 tchd 6 to 1) 2
1019[2] GARAH 4-9-0 R Cochrane (3) *trkd ldrs, effrt ins fnl furlong, hld whn short of room cl hme.* ....(9 to 2 op 7 to 2 tchd 5 to 1) 3
1019[4] LOCHSONG 5-9-0 L Dettori (6) *led 3 fs, rdn and one pace o'r one out*............(4 to 1 fav op 3 to 1) 4
993[6] MEDAILLE D'OR (v) 5-9-3 J Reid (1) *towards rear, styd on appr fnl furlong, nvr nrr.* ....(33 to 1 op 25 to 1 tchd 40 to 1) 5
993[4] ARTISTIC REEF 4-9-3 T Quinn (10) *al abt same pl.* ....(25 to 1 op 20 to 1) 6
1011[4] SPANIARDS CLOSE 5-9-3 W R Swinburn (2) *chsd ldrs, rdn 2 fs out, sn outpcd*............(10 to 1 op 8 to 1) 7
1019* HAMAS (Ire) 4-9-3 W Carson (8) *in tch to hfwy.* ....(9 to 2 tchd 5 to 1) 8
923 GONE SAVAGE 5-9-3 Pat Eddery (4) *nvr on terms.* ....(33 to 1 tchd 40 to 1) 9
795 MILLYANT 3-8-5 M Hills (9) *chsd ldrs for o'r 2 fs.* ....(33 to 1 op 25 to 1) 10
Dist: Hd, ¾l, 2l, 1½l, 2l, 3l, 2½l, ½l, ¾l. 1m 0.99s. a 1.49s (10 Ran).
SR: 82/84/71/63/60/52/40/30/28/ (P E T Chandler), J Berry

1407 Kingfisher Lager Whitsun Cup Rated Class B Handicap (0-105 3-y-o and up) £15,636 1m 14yds.............. (4:10)

1110* PAY HOMAGE [98] 5-9-5 M Hills (7) *hld up, improved appr 2 fs out, led entering last, ran on strly.* ....(8 to 1 tchd 9 to 1) 1
663[5] MARASTANI (USA) [88] 3-7-11 C Rutter (5) *pressed ldrs, led appr fnl furlong, hdd entering last, kpt on same pace.* ....(10 to 1 tchd 12 to 1) 2
824[4] TAPIS ROUGE (Ire) [100] 4-9-7 M Roberts (3) *chsd ldrs, drvn alng 2 fs out, ev ch appr one out, one pace*...(7 to 2 jt-fav op 3 to 1 tchd 4 to 1) 3
1172* DRESS SENSE (Ire) [89] 4-8-10 R Cochrane (8) *wtd wth, prog entering fnl 2 fs, kpt on ins last*........(7 to 2 jt-fav op 3 to 1 tchd 4 to 1) 4
1002[4] TISSISAT (USA) [91] 4-8-12 L Dettori (4) *wtd wth, drvn alng o'r 2 fs out, sn no hdwy*............(5 to 1 op 6 to 1) 5
1002[3] EFHARISTO [90] 4-8-11 J Reid (9) *led 2 fs, chsd ldrs aftr, drvn alng and not clr run o'r one out, swtchd outsd, one pace*............(10 to 1) 6
1079[4] EURO FESTIVAL [92] 4-8-13 Pat Eddery (1) *patiently rdn, prog appr 2 fs out, wkng whn short of room approaching last*............(7 to 1 op 6 to 1 tchd 8 to 1) 7
792[3] KRISTIANSTAD [93] 4-9-0 W R Swinburn (6) *led aftr 2 fs, hdd appr last, fdd*............(7 to 1 tchd 8 to 1) 8
1172[8] CRYSTADO (Fr) [92] 4-8-13 T Quinn (2) *trkd ldrs, drvn alng and ev ch wl o'r 2 fs out, sn btn*...(20 to 1 op 16 to 1) 9
Dist: 2l, nk, sht-hd, 2l, nk, 2½l, nk, 5l. 1m 41.42s. a 2.32s (9 Ran).
SR: 46/18/41/29/25/23/17/17/1/ (Miss A V Hill), I A Balding

1408 UB International Handicap Class D (0-80 3-y-o) £4,318 7f 16yds..... (4:45)

1212[4] KASSBAAN (USA) [70] 8-12 W R Swinburn (10) *wtd wth, hdwy o'r one furlong out, str run ins last to ld last strds*............(4 to 1 jt-fav op 9 to 2 tchd 6 to 1) 1
1137 PAIR OF JACKS (Ire) [72] 9-0 J Carroll (2) *sn led, drvn alng o'r one furlong out, hdd and no extr last strds.* ....(25 to 1 op 16 to 1) 2
1058[4] FINAL FRONTIER (Ire) [70] 8-12 T Quinn (4) *in tch, rdn 2 fs out, ev ch ins last, kpt on*............(9 to 2 op 3 to 1) 3
1058* FIELD OF VISION (Ire) [60] 8-2 M Hills (5) *hld up in mid-div, prog 2 fs out, one pace one out*............(4 to 1 jt-fav op 7 to 2 tchd 9 to 2) 4
995[3] TWICE THE GROOM (Ire) [70] 8-12 M Roberts (8) *hld up, hdwy 2 fs out, styd on one pace ins last.* ....(9 to 1 op 7 to 1) 5
1097[2] CREDIT SQUEEZE [71] 8-13 R Cochrane (11) *hld up, prog frm o'r 2 fs out, rdn and one pace entering last.* ....(8 to 1 op 6 to 1) 6
1058[7] WALNUT BURL (Ire) [74] 9-2 C Avery (9) *nvr trble ldrs.* ....(16 to 1 op 10 to 1) 7
1057[3] FRIENDLY BRAVE (USA) [79] 9-7 J Reid (6) *hld up, rdn and not much room o'r one furlong out, not rcvr.* ....(12 to 1 op 10 to 1 tchd 14 to 1) 8
714 SYLVANIA (Ire) [69] 8-11 L Dettori (1) *pressed ldr, drvn alng 2 fs out, wknd appr last*............(14 to 1 tchd 16 to 1) 9
1037[8] RACING TELEGRAPH [62] 8-4 G Bardwell (7) *keen hold, mid-div, rdn alng o'r 2 fs out, fdd.* ....(8 to 1 op 7 to 1 tchd 9 to 1) 10
DANCING DIAMOND (Ire) [54] 7-10[1] F Norton (3) *chsd ldrs, rdn o'r 2 fs out, wknd appr last*...(33 to 1 op 25 to 1) 11
Dist: Sht-hd, hd, 1½l, ½l, sht-hd, 2½l, 2l, sht-hd, 4l, ¾l. 1m 30.43s. a 3.93s (11 Ran).
SR: 18/19/16/1/9/9/4/3/-/ (Maktoum Al Maktoum), A A Scott

1409 UB Coating Handicap Class D (0-80 4-y-o and up) £4,318 1¼m 7yds (5:20)

990 MR TATE (Ire) [56] 4-8-4 T Quinn (12) *pressed ldr, brght centre strt, led o'r 2 fs out, rdn appr last, styd on wl.* ....(12 to 1 op 10 to 1 tchd 14 to 1) 1
416[8] USAIDIT [67] 4-9-1 J Reid (7) *hld up, drvn alng 3 fs out, rapid hdwy to go second ins last.* (16 to 1 tchd 20 to 1) 2
1064 GILDERDALE [74] 11-9-8 M Hills (1) *pressed ldrs, led far side grp o'r 2 fs out, ev ch one out, one pace.* ....(7 to 1 tchd 8 to 1) 3
1130[2] TROOPING (Ire) [75] 4-9-9 W Carson (2) *trkd ldrs, rdn 2 fs out, ev ch appr last, one pace.* ....(7 to 2 fav op 3 to 1 tchd 4 to 1) 4
1064 PORT SUNLIGHT (Ire) [75] 5-9-9 R Cochrane (8) *hld up in mid-div, hmpd o'r 2 fs out, hdwy appr last, sn one pace.* ....(11 to 2 op 5 to 1 tchd 6 to 1) 5
1143[8] BOOKCASE [69] 6-9-3 Pat Eddery (10) *hld up, hdwy o'r 2 fs out, rdn and ev ch appr last, sn btn.* ....(11 to 2 op 5 to 1 tchd 6 to 1) 6
VIAGGIO [45] 5-7-7 G Bardwell (6) *nvr nr to chal.* (33 to 1) 7
1094[3] ATHAR (Ire) [64] 4-8-12 M Roberts (5) *hld up, rdn o'r 2 fs out, no hdwy*............(8 to 1 op 10 to 1) 8
1307[6] WESTFIELD MOVES (Ire) [59] 5-8-0 (7*) C Hawksley (11) *al abt same pl*............(10 to 1 op 8 to 1 tchd 7 to 1) 9
1028[3] FREE MOVER (Ire) [78] 4-9-12 L Dettori (9) *in tch, rdn and wknd o'r 2 fs out*............(9 to 1 op 7 to 1) 10
SLICK CHERRY [48] 6-7-10[2] F Norton (4) *nvr on terms.* ....(50 to 1 tchd 33 to 1) 11
845[6] YILDIZ [73] 4-9-7 W R Swinburn (13) *nvr dngrs.* ....(13 to 2 op 6 to 1 tchd 7 to 1) 12
1007[9] FULL SHILLING (USA) [61] (bl) 4-8-9 J Carroll (14) *led till hdd and wknd appr 2 fs out*.....(50 to 1 tchd 66 to 1) 13
Dist: 1½l, 2l, 1½l, 1½l, 1½l, 3l, 3l, ½l, 12l, sht-hd. 2m 6.87s. a 2.97s (13 Ran).
SR: 40/48/51/49/46/37/7/20/14/ (John Falvey), R Akehurst

ST-CLOUD (FR) (good)
Monday May 31st

1410 Prix du Lys (Group 3) (3-y-o) £23,895 1 ¾m........................ (1:55)

811[4] EPAPHOS (Ger) 8-11 E Legrix (6) *3rd strt, quickened 2 and a half fs out, led two out, sn clr, easily*......(78 to 10) 1
1012[3] KARAYOR (Fr) (bl) 8-11 G Dubroeucq (5) *second strt, chlgd 2 and a half fs out, styd on, no ch wth wnr.* ....(19 to 10 fav) 2

IS ME (Can) 8-11 T Jarnet (4) *4th strt, rdn 2 fs out, one pace*.....(26 to 10) 3
LUCIO (Ire) (bl) 8-11 F Head (2) *6th strt, nvr plcd to chal.*.....(15 to 1) 4
PAST DAYS (Fr) 8-11 M de Smyter (3) *nvr nrr*......(7 to 1) 5
KHRAUSS (Fr) 8-11 C Asmussen (1) *pld hrd early, led strt, hdd 2 fs out, wknd quickly*.....(3 to 1) 6
PALAIROS (Fr) 8-11 G Guignard (7) *5th strt, rdn and wknd 2 fs out*.....(9 to 1) 7
Dist: 5l, 2l, 4l, 2l, 1½l, 1l. 2m 59.30s. a 3.30s (7 Ran).
SR: 64/54/50/42/38/35/33/ (E Wanke), P Bary

1411 Prix de la Ville de Garches (Listed) (4-y-o and up) £14,337 1¼m....... (3:05)

692² FUNNY BABY (Fr) 5-9-2 A Badel,..... 1
1124⁷ COMPOTA (Fr) 4-8-8 D Boeuf,..... 2
D'ARROS (Ire) 4-9-2 C Asmussen,..... 3
DICK TRACY (Fr) 4-8-12 J Boisnard,..... 4
Dist: 1l, nk, hd, hd, 2l, 1½l, sht-nk, 1l. 2m 11.20s. a 7.20s (9 Ran).
SR: 30/20/27/22/ (Comtesse de Kerouara), Mme M Bollack-Badel

LEICESTER (good)
Tuesday June 1st
Going Correction: MINUS 0.05 sec. per fur.

1412 Tote Placepot Conditions Stakes Class C (3-y-o and up) £4,119 7f 9yds.....(2:30)

CATRAIL (USA) 3-8-6 M Roberts (1) *hld up, hdwy 3 fs out, led one and a half out, shaken up, cmftbly.*.....(11 to 10 fav op Evens tchd 6 to 4) 1
1208³ LEE ARTISTE 5-8-9 T Quinn (7) *tracking ldrs whn checked o'r 2 fs out, hdwy and edgd rght over one out, kpt on, not pace of wnr*........(11 to 2 op 2 to 1 tchd 6 to 1) 2
SHIRO 3-8-6 R Cochrane (4) *chsd ldrs, led o'r 2 fs out to one and a half out, kpt on one pace.*.....(6 to 1 op 7 to 1 tchd 9 to 1) 3
316 SPANISH STORM (Ire) 4-9-1 W Woods (5) *led till o'r 2 fs out, edgd lft, btn whn hmpd over one out.*.....(40 to 1 op 20 to 1) 4
915⁸ CYPRIAN DANCER (USA) 3-8-6 C Rutter (2) *str hold, chsd ldrs till wknd o'r one furlong out.* (40 to 1 op 20 to 1) 5
951* FULL FEATHER (USA) 3-8-6 L Dettori (6) *chsd ldr till wknd 2 fs out*.....(14 to 1 op 7 to 1) 6
Dist: 2½l, 4l, 3½l, 1½l, 12l. 1m 25.40s. a 3.50s (6 Ran).
SR: 34/29/14/12/-/-/ (Sheikh Mohammed), J H M Gosden

1413 Tote Each Way Selling Stakes Class G (2-y-o) £2,553 5f 218yds........(3:00)

LEFT STRANDED 8-11 W Woods (12) *trkd ldrs, rdn and edgd lft one furlong out, styd on to ld nr finish.*.....(11 to 4 op 6 to 1) 1
1254* GRECIAN GARDEN 8-11 Pat Eddery (8) *led, rdn o'r one furlong out, ct nr finish.*.....(7 to 4 fav op 5 to 4 tchd 2 to 1) 2
1253³ MR BLOBBY (Ire) 8-11 J Carroll (10) *pressed ldrs, ev ch 2 fs out till bumped and one pace one out.*.....(6 to 1 op 7 to 2) 3
886³ ROCKY TWO 8-11 T Quinn (2) *prmnt, one pace whn bumped one furlong out.*.....(7 to 1 op 6 to 1 tchd 8 to 1) 4
886⁷ EASY FOR ME 8-11 N Carlisle (1) *sn pushed alng, kpt on frm o'r one furlong out*.........(12 to 1 tchd 14 to 1) 5
1245³ UP THE MARINERS (Ire) 8-6 R P Elliott (3) *pressed ldrs, ev ch 2 fs out, sn outpcd.*.....(12 to 1 op 10 to 1 tchd 14 to 1) 6
900⁸ RUSTUS 8-6 N Adams (6) *beh, not pace to chal.*.....(33 to 1 op 16 to 1) 7
1091 BITE THE BULLET 8-11 J Quinn (7) *nvr gng pace of ldrs.*.........(14 to 1 op 16 to 1 tchd 25 to 1 and 10 to 1) 8
LITTLE HOOLIGAN 8-11 L Dettori (4) *dwlt, al outpcd.*.....(16 to 1 op 8 to 1) 9
JARZELA 7-13 (7*) J Marshall (5) *speed to hfwy.*.....(25 to 1 op 10 to 1) 10
JACQUI'S STAR (Ire) 8-11 D Holland (11) *outpcd.*.....(12 to 1 op 8 to 1) 11
922 MISS TRIANGLE 8-6 C Rutter (9) *sn outpcd.*.....(12 to 1 op 10 to 1) 12
Dist: 1l, 2½l, 2l, hd, 3l, 6l, nk, 1½l, 4l, 5l. 1m 14.30s. a 3.90s (12 Ran).
SR: 13/9/-/-/-/-/ (Brian Gubby Ltd), B Gubby

1414 Tote Credit Handicap Class E (0-70 3-y-o and up) £3,366 1m 1f 218yds.....(3:30)

931⁷ SHARQUIN [37] 6-7-9 A Mackay (13) *beh, drvn and hdwy frm 3 fs out, led ins last, driven out.*.....(12 to 1 tchd 16 to 1) 1
1238³ LOWAWATHA [40] 5-7-12 J Quinn (15) *chsd ldrs, led one and a half fs out till jst ins last, kpt on one pace.*.....(11 to 2 fav op 6 to 1 tchd 7 to 1) 2
1097 SCOTTISH BAMBI [65] 5-9-9 R Perham (11) *rdn 5 fs out, hdwy 3 out, led 2 out to one and a half out, one pace fnl furlong*.....(7 to 1 op 4 to 1 tchd 8 to 1) 3
1238⁵ OUR EDDIE [42] 4-7-7 (7*) C Hawksley (4) *al in tch, rdn and kpt on same pace fnl 2 fs*.....(20 to 1) 4
674 ROUSITTO [65] 5-9-9 W Ryan (19) *mid-div, hdwy 3 fs out, no imprsn frm 2 out*.....(16 to 1 op 14 to 1) 5
919⁸ RIVAL BID (USA) [67] 5-9-11 N Day (12) *beh, hdwy o'r 3 fs out, one pace frm 2 out.* (9 to 1 op 10 to 1 tchd 8 to 1) 6
994 FULL QUIVER [40] (v) 8-7-5 (7*) D Wright (16) *beh till some prog fnl 2 fs*.....(8 to 1 op 20 to 1) 7
ADDICTED TO LOVE [64] (bl) 4-9-8 T Sprake (3) *chsd ldrs, led 4 fs out to 2 out, sn btn*.....(12 to 1) 8
978* AKKAZAO (Ire) [70] 5-9-9 (5*) N Gwilliams (18) *pressed ldrs till wknd 3 fs out*.....(8 to 1 op 6 to 1) 9
845 GOLD BLADE [54] 4-8-12 T Quinn (9) *hdwy 5 fs out, chsd ldrs 3 out, sn wknd*.....(6 to 1 op 4 to 1) 10
1094⁸ RUBY DAVIES [37] 7-7-9² N Adams (17) *nvr rch ldrs.*.....(50 to 1) 11
994 MYSTERIOUS MAID (USA) [48] 6-8-6 G Bardwell (1) *nvr rch ldrs*.....(12 to 1 op 10 to 1) 12
1257⁹ ARAGONA [39] 4-7-11¹ C Rutter (2) *nvr dngrs*....(33 to 1) 13
784⁶ RARE OCCURANCE [48] 3-7-7 E Johnson (7) *made most to 4 fs out, wknd quickly*.....(50 to 1) 14
917⁷ SANTANA LADY (Ire) [66] 4-9-10 J Reid (8) *chsd ldrs, rdn and wknd 3 fs out*.....(6 to 1 op 4 to 1 tchd 13 to 2) 15
JUNCTION TWENTYTWO [50] 3-7-8⁶ (7*) B Russell (6) *pressed ldrs till wknd 3 fs out*.....(33 to 1) 16
1034 MAPLE BAY (Ire) [52] 4-8-10 N Carlisle (14) *beh most of way.*.....(33 to 1) 17
1161 MOON WATCH [50] (v) 3-7-4² (7*) N Varley (10) *nvr dngrs.*.....(14 to 1) 18
RADIO CAROLINE [40] 5-7-12⁹ (7*) S Mulvey (5) *chsd ldrs 5 fs*.....(33 to 1) 19
Dist: 1l, 3l, 2l, sht-hd, ¾l, nk, 1½l, 4l, 6l, 1½l. 2m 8.00s. a 5.10s (19 Ran).
SR: 25/26/45/18/40/40/12/33/31/ (M A Murphy), M Brittain

1415 Tote Fillies Conditions Stakes Class D (3-y-o) £3,525 5f 218yds.........(4:00)

1117⁵ CARRANITA (Ire) 8-8 M Roberts (3) *made all, drvn and wnt clr frm o'r one furlong out*..........(5 to 2 op 6 to 4) 1
1214⁵ SHEILA'S SECRET (Ire) 8-11 (5*) N Gwilliams (2) *chsd wnr thrght, no imprsn fnl furlong.*.....(6 to 1 op 5 to 1 tchd 8 to 1) 2
734⁵ KATIBA (USA) 8-12 W Carson (4) *rdn alng hfwy, styd on frm o'r one furlong out, kpt on cl hme.*.....(9 to 4 fav op 5 to 2 tchd 3 to 1) 3
1031³ BROCKTON DANCER (bl) 8-12 Pat Eddery (5) *in tch till outpcd fnl 2 fs*.....(7 to 2 op 3 to 1) 4
1231⁶ CRIME OFTHECENTURY 9-0 T Quinn (1) *str hold, steadied in rear, rdn o'r 2 fs out, no response.*.....(9 to 2 op 5 to 1 tchd 4 to 1) 5
Dist: 2½l, nk, 3l, 1l. 1m 13.20s. a 2.80s (5 Ran).
SR: 32/30/25/13/11/ (Lamb Lane Associates), B Palling

1416 Woodhouse Eaves Claiming Stakes Class F (3-y-o) £2,803 1m 8yds..(4:30)

972² MRS DAWSON 7-11 G Bardwell (3) *chsd ldrs on outsd, drvn and styd on wl fnl furlong to ld last strds.*.....(12 to 1 tchd 14 to 1) 1
1175² SILENT EXPRESSION 8-11 M Tebbutt (12) *in tch, led 2 and a half fs out, rdn fnl furlong, ct last strds.*.....(2 to 1 fav tchd 3 to 1) 2
733 MANX MONARCH 7-9¹ (5*) A Garth (1) *in tch, drvn and styd on same pace frm o'r one furlong out.*.....(11 to 1 op 33 to 1 tchd 10 to 1) 3
1257⁵ APACHE MYTH 8-7² J Reid (15) *al chasing ldrs, one pace fnl 2 fs*.....(4 to 1 op 3 to 1 tchd 5 to 1) 4
965⁶ MUNNASIB (Fr) (bl) 8-6 B Raymond (8) *hdwy o'r 2 fs out, sn wknd*.....(8 to 1 op 5 to 1) 5
1175 TEE GEE JAY (bl) 8-5 J Quinn (4) *some prog 3 fs out, no imprsn 2 out*.....(7 to 1 op 9 to 2) 6
1074 DIVINE RAIN (bl) 8-8 R Cochrane (5) *nvr rch ldrs.*.....(20 to 1 op 16 to 1) 7
1275 KINTAVI 9-0 A McGlone (14) *beh, some prog fnl 2 fs.*.....(20 to 1) 8
1062⁶ CONVOY (bl) 8-10 W Ryan (13) *nvr rch ldrs.*.....(12 to 1 op 8 to 1) 9
1074³ MARCO CLAUDIO (Ire) 8-12 L Dettori (16) *chsd ldrs till wknd o'r 2 fs out*.....(10 to 1 op 6 to 1) 10
1327⁷ SHALAKO 8-4¹ (7*) L Aspell (2) *al beh.* (33 to 1 op 25 to 1) 11
1027 MR JAZZ DANCER (Ire) 8-10 N Adams (7) *prmnt 4 fs.*.....(25 to 1 op 20 to 1) 12
1175 COUNTY GIRL (Ire) 8-1 P Robinson (17) *sn beh*....(20 to 1) 13
FRANKIE GOODMAN (Ire) 8-6 T Quinn (10) *al beh.*.....(16 to 1 op 7 to 1 tchd 20 to 1) 14
1271⁸ JAMANE 8-11 (3*) S D Williams (11) *al beh*........(20 to 1) 15
1175 RUANO (bl) 8-10 W Woods (9) *led till hdd and wknd quickly 2 and a half fs out*.....(25 to 1) 16
Dist: Nk, 4l, 2½l, 6l, 3l, nk, 1½l, 2l, 1½l, 2½l. 1m 38.50s. a 3.40s (16 Ran).
SR: 26/39/15/15/-/-/ (Mrs Susan Scargill), Dr J D Scargill

1417 Tote Dual Forecast Handicap Class E (0-70 3-y-o) £3,236 1m 3f 183yds (5:00)

1134[5] PUGET DANCER (USA) [51] (v) 8-1 (5*) M Fenton (3) *in tch early, rear and rdn 6 fs out, str run frm o'r 2 out, led appr last, drvn out.*..........(14 to 1 op 8 to 1) 1
1165[3] CHIAPPUCCI (Ire) [60] (v) 8-10 (5*) K Rutter (1) *hld up in rear, hdwy frm 3 fs out, ev ch ins last, one pace.* ....(8 to 1 op 6 to 1) 2
976[3] RECORD LOVER (Ire) [55] 8-10 B Raymond (2) *in tch, hdwy 5 fs out, led 4 out to 3 out, sn outpcd.* (6 to 1 op 5 to 1) 3
377[5] TURFMANS VISION [60] 9-1 W Ryan (9) *slwly into strd, hld up in rear, hdwy o'r 2 fs out, kpt on same pace fnl furlong.*..........(25 to 1 op 14 to 1) 4
1062[4] LEGAL ARTIST (Ire) [48] 8-3 A McGlone (7) *in tch, rdn 3 fs out, wknd 2 out.*..........(14 to 1 op 12 to 1) 5
1067[7] PENNINE LAD (Ire) [61] 8-9 (7*) D Wright (6) *led aftr 3 fs to 4 out, sn wknd.*..........(14 to 1 op 12 to 1) 6
1161[4] BRONZE MAQUETTE (Ire) [57] 8-12 T Quinn (12) *chsd ldrs, led 3 fs out till o'r one out, wknd rpdly.* ....(5 to 1 op 4 to 1 tchd 11 to 2) 7
733 STEVIE'S WONDER (Ire) [49] 7-13 (5*) N Gwilliams (4) *chsd ldrs till wknd o'r 2 fs out.*..........(7 to 2 fav op 8 to 1) 8
966[3] WONDERFUL YEARS (USA) [53] 8-8 R Cochrane (10) *beh, effrt o'r 3 fs out, sn wknd.*..........(5 to 1 op 3 to 1) 9
980[6] SLIVOVITZ [62] 9-3 P Robinson (11) *led 3 fs, wknd 4 out.* ....(10 to 1 op 6 to 1) 10
434 GREYSTYLE [40] 7-9 G Bardwell (5) *chsd ldrs 6 fs.* ....(25 to 1 op 20 to 1) 11
1068[8] TEACHER (Ire) [66] 9-7 W R Swinburn (8) *chsd ldrs 6 fs.* ....(8 to 1 op 5 to 1) 12
Dist: 2l, 6l, ¾l, sht-hd, 1l, nk, 7l, nk, 10l, 10l. 2m 36.10s. a 7.60s (12 Ran).
SR: 10/15/-/1/-/-/ (W J P Jackson), M Bell

REDCAR (good to firm)
Tuesday June 1st
Going Correction: MINUS 0.25 sec. per fur. (races 1,2,3,7), NIL (4,5,6)

1418 EBF Fillies Median Auction Maiden Stakes Class D (2-y-o) £3,465 6f (2:15)

ELECTION SPECIAL 8-11 M Tebbutt (10) *in tch, gd hdwy 2 fs out, led o'r one furlong out, sn clr.* ....(7 to 1 tchd 8 to 1 and 9 to 1) 1
830[4] MICHELLISA 8-11 Dean McKeown (4) *in tch, effrt and hdwy o'r one furlong out, sn rdn and ran on.* ....(25 to 1 op 16 to 1) 2
1009[2] FOOTSTEPS (Ire) 8-11 A Munro (5) *al cl up, ev ch o'r one furlong out, sn one pace.*..........(3 to 1 fav tchd 4 to 1) 3
680[7] ORIENTAL AIR (Ire) 8-11 W Newnes (13) *led, rdn and hdd o'r one furlong out, wknd ins last.* (14 to 1 op 12 to 1) 4
1135[3] ELLARUTH (Ire) 8-11 P Robinson (15) *cl up till rdn and wknd o'r one furlong out.*..........(4 to 1 op 7 to 2) 5
1272[5] DOCKYARD DORA 8-11 M Wigham (6) *chsd ldrs, rdn 2 fs out, kpt on one pace.*..........(50 to 1 op 25 to 1) 6
LEVEL EDGE 8-11 J Fortune (16) *slwly into strd and beh, hdwy fnl 2 fs, nrst finish.*..........(50 to 1 op 33 to 1) 7
DURHAM DRAPES 8-11 M Birch (11) *mid-div till styd on fnl 2 fs.*..........(14 to 1 tchd 12 to 1) 8
1158[3] DANGEROUS SHADOW 8-11 K Darley (8) *chsd ldrs, rdn 2 fs out, sn wknd.*..........(7 to 1 tchd 8 to 1) 9
968[7] IRISH PERFORMER 8-11 N Connorton (1) *chsd ldrs till rdn and wknd 2 fs out.*..........(25 to 1 op 14 to 1) 10
MISS MILLIPEDE 8-11 G Duffield (14) *nvr rchd ldrs.* ....(25 to 1) 11
900[6] BUNNY RUN 8-8 (3*) S Maloney (12) *nvr better than mid-div.*..........(33 to 1 op 20 to 1) 12
1234[6] ZANZARA (Ire) 8-11 J Lowe (9) *nvr a factor.* ....(33 to 1 op 25 to 1) 13
AJNAS (Ire) 8-11 R Hills (2) *cl up, ev ch one and a half fs out, sn rdn and wknd quickly appr last.* ....(7 to 2 op 2 to 1) 14
FADE AWAY (Ire) 8-11 K Fallon (3) *al rear.*..........(50 to 1) 15
Dist: 2½l, 2l, hd, ½l, hd, ½l, 1½l, ½l, ½l, hd. 1m 12.10s. a 2.40s (15 Ran).
SR: 19/9/1/-/-/-/ (J C Smith), J M P Eustace

1419 Redcar Amateur Riders' Maiden Handicap Class G (0-60 3-y-o and up) £2,532 6f.......... (2:45)

1232[5] MU-ARRIK [44] (bl) 5-10-5 (7*) Miss A Deniel (8) *cl up, led wl o'r one furlong out, ran on.* ....(9 to 1 op 8 to 1 tchd 10 to 1) 1
1264[5] SILVER STONE BOY [32] 5-10-0 Miss I Diana W Jones (10) *al chasing ldrs, effrt 2 fs out, sn rdn and wndrd, styd on ins last.*..........(10 to 1 op 5 to 1) 2
CASHMIRIANA (Ire) [53] 4-11-2 (5*) Mrs S Bosley (3) *chsd ldrs, swtchd rght wl o'r one furlong out, sn rdn and styd on ins last.*..........(14 to 1 op 12 to 1) 3
1273[2] FORMIDABLE LIZ [44] (bl) 3-10-3 Mrs L Pearce (14) *chsd ldrs, effrt and ev ch o'r one furlong out, sn rdn, edgd lft and wknd.*..........(7 to 4 fav op 2 to 1 tchd 9 to 4) 4
LETTERMORE [35] 3-9-8 Mr M Buckley (2) *mid-div, effrt 2 fs out, sn rdn and styd on ins last, nrst finish.* ....(12 to 1 op 8 to 1) 5
883[5] CORONA GOLD [50] (bl) 3-10-9 Mr R Hale (6) *mid-div, effrt and hdwy 2 fs out, kpt on ins last.* ....(15 to 2 op 8 to 1 tchd 7 to 1) 6
1148[9] DAL MISS [23] (bl) 6-9-5[10] (7*) Mrs C Peacock (11) *led, hng badly lft 2 fs out, sn hdd and wknd.* ....(20 to 1 op 14 to 1) 7
1187[4] COLMAR [39] 3-9-12 Miss L Eaton (7) *al mid-div.* ....(10 to 1 op 8 to 1) 8
646 CROMER'S EXPRESS [37] 4-9-12 (7*) Mrs D Wilkinson (15) *slwly into strd, pushed alng and hdwy hfwy, kpt on fnl 2 fs.*..........(33 to 1) 9
964 MURASIL (USA) [40] 4-10-8 Miss P Robson (4) *nvr a factor.* ....(14 to 1 op 12 to 1) 10
JUST-GO-AGAIN [49] 4-10-12 (5*) Mrs S Easterby (13) *al rear.*..........(33 to 1) 11
1230 BLUEBELLA [39] 3-9-7 (5*) Miss Diana J Jones (1) *prmnt o'r 3 fs, sn wknd.*..........(33 to 1) 12
1300[5] WHYALLA RAIN [40] 3-9-13 Miss L Perratt (5) *mid-div, rdn hfwy, sn wknd.*..........(20 to 1) 13
1233[4] BELL LAD (Ire) [40] 3-9-6 (7*) Miss H Callow (9) *chsd ldrs till sddl slpd badly hfwy, sn beh.*..........(12 to 1 op 8 to 1) 14
396 SHAHNIZAM (USA) [34] 9-10-2 Mr J Cambidge (12) *chsd ldrs till hmpd aftr one and a half fs, sn lost pl and beh, virtually pld up fnl furlong.*..........(33 to 1 op 25 to 1) 15
Dist: 1½l, ¾l, sht-hd, 1½l, ¾l, nk, ¾l, ¾l, ½l, ¾l. 1m 13.30s. a 3.60s (15 Ran).
SR: 24/6/24/5/-/2/ (Mick Burrowes), J S Wainwright

1420 Jamesons Irish Whiskey Sprint Handicap Class C (0-90 3-y-o and up) £4,920 5f.......... (3:15)

1301[6] EAGER DEVA [85] 6-9-12 K Darley (7) *cl up, led aftr one and a half fs, rdn appr last, ran on wl.* ....(11 to 2 op 5 to 1) 1
1215[5] NED'S BONANZA [69] 4-8-10 J Lowe (8) *chsd ldrs, hdwy 2 fs out, effrt to chal and ev ch ins last, sn rdn and no extr nr finish.*..........(4 to 1 fav tchd 9 to 2) 2
986[6] CUMBRIAN WALTZER [87] 8-10-0 M Birch (11) *beh, hdwy o'r one furlong out, ran on strly ins last.* ....(5 to 1 op 4 to 1) 3
1215 PRINCE BELFORT [61] 5-8-2 A Munro (9) *led one and a half fs, cl up, rdn and ev ch appr last till no extr nr finish.* ....(9 to 1 op 8 to 1) 4
1183[2] JUST BOB [68] 4-8-9 J Fortune (10) *chsd ldrs, effrt and rdn entering fnl furlong, ev ch till no extr nr finish.* ....(8 to 1) 5
1036 SINGING STAR [69] 7-8-3 (7*) Claire Balding (12) *badly hmpd aftr one furlong and drpd rear, hdwy 2 out, sn rdn and kpt on one pace.*..........(12 to 1 tchd 14 to 1) 6
1215* METAL BOYS [78] 6-9-2 (3*) D Harrison (2) *in tch on outer, rdn 2 fs out and sn one pace.*..........(11 to 2 op 5 to 1) 7
1286[6] BALLAD DANCER [56] 8-7-6 (5*) Darren Moffatt (5) *beh till styd on fnl 2 fs, nvr dngrs.*..........(12 to 1 tchd 14 to 1) 8
800 HERE COMES A STAR [67] 5-8-8 S Morris (4) *in tch, rdn 2 fs out, grad wknd.*..........(14 to 1 tchd 16 to 1) 9
1113[9] ANOTHER LANE [76] 6-9-3 W Newnes (1) *prmnt on outer, rdn hfwy and sn wknd.*..........(16 to 1 op 33 to 1) 10
GEMINI FIRE [68] 9-8-9 N Connorton (3) *al beh.*..........(33 to 1) 11
Dist: Nk, hd, nk, ½l, 2½l, 1½l, ½l, 1½l, 7l, 3½l. 57.90s. a 1.20s (11 Ran).
SR: 63/46/63/36/41/32/35/11/16/ (Mrs E G Faulkner), R Hollinshead

1421 Dormanstown Handicap Class E (0-70 3-y-o and up) £3,442 1m 1f.......... (3:45)

1120[3] MOON SPIN [59] 4-9-10 R Hills (16) *in tch, hdwy 3 fs out, led one and a half out, sn rdn and ran on wl ins last.* ....(11 to 4 fav op 3 to 1 tchd 7 to 2 and 5 to 2) 1
1103[3] MASTER OFTHE HOUSE [43] 7-8-8 Dean McKeown (9) *mid-div, hdwy 4 fs out, effrt 2 out and rdn to chal entering last, kpt on wl und pres.*..........(12 to 1) 2
971[5] CAL NORMA'S LADY (Ire) [47] 5-8-5 (7*) J Tate (8) *chsd ldrs, hdwy 3 fs out, effrt and rdn o'r one out, kpt on.* ....(12 to 1 tchd 10 to 1) 3
4744a[9] NO COMEBACKS [54] 5-9-5 K Fallon (11) *slwly away and beh, hdwy o'r 2 fs out, sn rdn and styd on ins last, nrst finish.*..........(16 to 1 op 20 to 1) 4
964[7] FUTURE FAME (USA) [44] 4-8-9 A Munro (13) *mid-div, hdwy 3 fs out, rdn and styd on frm 2 out, not rch ldrs.* ....(12 to 1 op 10 to 1 tchd 14 to 1) 5
1161[8] BARSAL (Ire) [51] 3-8-4 W Newnes (4) *chsd ldr, led 3 fs out, rdn 2 out, sn hdd and grad wknd.*..........(12 to 1) 6
JOMOVE [34] 4-7-13 K Darley (15) *mid-div, hdwy 4 fs out, effrt and rdn 2 out, sn wknd.*..........(5 to 1 op 4 to 1) 7
1274[5] THE PREMIER EXPRES [65] 3-9-4 G Duffield (6) *mid-div, effrt o'r 2 fs out, sn rdn and not rch ldrs.* ....(11 to 2 op 7 to 1) 8
1130 LEAP IN THE DARK (Ire) [50] (bl) 4-8-12 (3*) D Harrison (10) *in tch, rdn o'r 3 fs out, sn btn.*..........(12 to 1 op 10 to 1) 9
962 PREMIER MAJOR (Ire) [37] 4-8-2 L Charnock (2) *slwly away, al rear.*..........(20 to 1 op 16 to 1) 10
964 HIZEEM [28] (v) 7-7-7 J Fanning (7) *prmnt till rdn and wknd 3 fs out.*..........(33 to 1) 11
964 DOCTOR'S REMEDY [33] 7-7-5 (7*) Kim McDonnell (5) *al rear.*..........(16 to 1 op 12 to 1) 12+
RAHIF [58] (v) 5-9-9 S Webster (3) *led, hdd 3 fs out and sn wknd.*..........(33 to 1 op 25 to 1) 12+

AL-TORFANAN [40] 9-8-5 J Lowe (1) *chsd ldrs to hfwy, sn lost pl*..(66 to 1) 14
1150² ADMISSION (Ire) [51] 3-8-4 N Connorton (12) *al rear.* ....(12 to 1 op 10 to 1) 15
531 IMPORTANT DECISION [40] 4-8-5 S Wood (14) *al rear.* ....(50 to 1) 16
Dist: Hd, 1l, 2½l, 4l, 2l, 4l, 1l, 2½l, 2l, hd. 1m 54.10s. a 5.60s (16 Ran).
SR: 26/9/10/9/-/-/ (Mrs W R Hern), Major W R Hern

1422 Wilton Claiming Stakes Class F (3-y-o) £2,243 1¼m..................(4:15)

966* I'M A DREAMER (Ire) 9-4 Dean McKeown (5) *chsd ldrs, hdwy to ld 2 and a half fs out, sn clr, easily.* ....(3 to 1 fav tchd 7 to 2) 1
1179* RAGGERTY (Ire) 9-5 K Darley (6) *hld up and beh, hdwy 3 fs out, not clr run and swtchd 2 out, styd on fnl furlong.* ....(5 to 1 op 9 to 2) 2
1111⁵ BARLEY CAKE 8-4 J Fanning (7) *hld up and beh, hdwy o'r 3 fs out, rdn 2 out, kpt on one pace.* ....(7 to 2 op 4 to 1 tchd 9 to 2) 3
1319² ABSALOM'S PILLAR 8-13 J Lowe (2) *hld up, hdwy 3 fs out, sn rdn and one pace.* ....(5 to 1 op 9 to 2 tchd 11 to 2) 4
1261³ TAKE YOUR PARTNER (Ire) 8-2 T Williams (4) *nvr rch ldrs.* ....(10 to 1) 5
1262* GUV'NORS GIFT 8-7 G Duffield (3) *chsd ldrs, effrt and rdn 3 fs out, wknd o'r 2 out*..............(7 to 2 op 3 to 1) 6
1285 SWEETWATER MOON 8-4 J Fortune (1) *led, rdn and hdd 2 and a half fs out, sn wknd*...................(33 to 1) 7
Dist: 5l, 1l, 1½l, nk, 4l, 5l. 2m 10.20s. a 9.00s (7 Ran).
SR: 14/5/-/-/ (Dave Marshall), W W Haigh

1423 Skelton Rating Related Maiden Stakes Class F (3-y-o) £2,243 1¾m 19yds ....(4:45)

1242³ BARRAAK 9-0 R Hills (1) *trkd ldrs gng wl, hdwy 4 fs out, led 3 out, clr 2 out, easily.* ....(13 to 8 fav op 7 to 4 tchd 2 to 1) 1
1180⁵ MONDRAGON 9-0 J Lowe (6) *beh, hdwy and rdn 3 fs out, styd on frm 2 out, no ch wth wnr.* ....(9 to 2 op 7 to 2 tchd 5 to 1) 2
652⁴ VAIGLY SUNTHYME 9-0 S Morris (8) *hld up and beh, hdwy 4 fs out, rdn o'r 2 out, kpt on one pace.* ....(14 to 1 op 12 to 1) 3
1134³ ROMALITO 9-0 Dean McKeown (2) *trkd ldrs, hdwy to chase ldr hfwy, rdn 3 fs out and sn one pace.* ....(9 to 2 tchd 5 to 1) 4
1004⁵ ISLE OF PEARLS (USA) (v) 9-0 M Birch (3) *led, rdn and hdd 3 fs out, grad wknd*...............(8 to 1 tchd 9 to 1) 5
813³ AMIARGE 9-0 M Wigham (9) *chsd ldrs till wknd 5 fs out, sn beh*............................(6 to 1 tchd 7 to 1) 6
1055⁴ MOONLIGHT ECLIPSE 9-0 J Fortune (4) *prmnt till rdn and wknd o'r 3 fs out*..................................(16 to 1) 7
1248³ MOUNTAIN HIGH (Fr) 9-0 K Fallon (5) *hld up, hdwy hfwy, rdn and wknd o'r 3 fs out*......... (14 to 1 op 10 to 1) 8
711 JOELLISE 8-2 (7*) Claire Balding (7) *in tch, hdwy to join ldrs hfwy, wknd 5 fs out and tld off fnl 3 furlongs.* ....(100 to 1) 9
Dist: 7l, 2l, sht-hd, 2l, 15l, 2l, 12l, dist. 3m 7.30s. a 10.80s (9 Ran).
(Hamdan Al-Maktoum), Major W R Hern

1424 Kirkleatham Maiden Stakes Class D (3-y-o) £3,289 7f................(5:15)

1114³ ARID 9-0 G Hind (2) *made all, rdn one and a half fs out, edgd lft and ran on wl*.................. (7 to 4 jt-fav) 1
1060² GRAN SENORUM (USA) 9-0 A Munro (4) *al prmnt, effrt and ev ch whn bumped o'r one furlong out, hrd rdn, kpt on*............(7 to 4 jt-fav op 5 to 4 tchd 2 to 1) 2
1114⁴ JAAZIM 9-0 R Hills (7) *trkd ldrs, effrt and hng lft one and a half fs out, not clr run o'r one out, wknd ins last.* ....(11 to 4 op 3 to 1 tchd 100 to 30) 3
1162³ VIKING WATERS 8-4 (5*) O Pears (3) *beh till styd on fnl 2 fs*...................(16 to 1 op 20 to 1 tchd 25 to 1) 4
MUSTN'T GRUMBLE (Ire) 9-0 Kim Tinkler (5) *outpcd and beh till styd on fnl 2 fs*...................................(50 to 1) 5
974⁵ DODDINGTON PLAYER (Ire) 9-0 S Perks (6) *prmnt to hfwy, sn wknd*..(20 to 1) 6
STATE TACOMA 8-9 M Wigham (8) *al rear*........(50 to 1) 7
686 TUSCANIA 8-2 (7*) Claire Balding (1) *prmnt 3 fs, sn lost pl and beh*..(100 to 1) 8
Dist: ¾l, 1l, 12l, nk, 2½l, ½l, 3l. 1m 25.70s. a 3.90s (8 Ran).
SR: 15/13/10/-/-/ (Sheikh Mohammed), J H M Gosden

SANDOWN (firm)
Tuesday June 1st
Going Correction: MINUS 0.10 sec. per fur. (races 1,2,3,5,6), MINUS 0.25 (4)

1425 Douglas Cameron Claiming Stakes Class E (3-y-o and up) £3,363 1m 14yds.......................... (6:25)

1270 MOUGINS (Ire) (bl) 4-8-9 (5*) A Procter (7) *reluctant to strt, beh, hdwy on ins frm o'r 2 fs out, led inside last, pushed out*.................................(8 to 1 tchd 9 to 1) 1
836 REGALSETT 3-8-9 W Carson (3) *rcd freely, wth clr ldr, led o'r 4 fs out till hdd and no extr ins last.* ....(5 to 1 op 3 to 1) 2
650⁸ FIABA 5-8-4 J Quinn (8) *mid-div, swtchd rght and hdwy o'r one furlong out, styd on wl*.... (33 to 1 op 16 to 1) 3
975² MEXICAN DANCER 4-7-13¹ (7*) S Drowne (5) *chsd ldrs, drvn 2 fs out, kpt on*... (11 to 2 op 9 to 2 tchd 6 to 1) 4
VANROY 9-9-5 S Whitworth (1) *beh, effrt and not much room o'r 2 fs out, styd on, nrst finish.* ....(14 to 1 op 10 to 1) 5
328 OUR SHADEE (USA) 3-8-3 M Roberts (11) *trkd ldrs, pushed alng strt, hrd rdn 2 fs out, sn btn.* ....(12 to 1 op 10 to 1) 6
TAMBORITO (Ire) 4-8-12 D Holland (6) *strted slwly, beh, hrd drvn 3 fs out, nrst finish*..... (33 to 1 op 16 to 1) 7
1271* ANUSHA 3-8-6 J Carroll (12) *rcd freely, led aftr one furlong till o'r 4 out, wknd appr 2 out.* .... (100 to 30 fav op 3 to 1 tchd 7 to 2) 8
1304² NO SUBMISSION (USA) 7-9-3 J Williams (4) *prmnt in chasing grp till wknd o'r 2 fs out.* ....(7 to 2 op 4 to 1 tchd 9 to 2) 9
LADY BUNTING 6-8-4 S Dawson (10) *led one furlong, chsd clr ldrs till wknd o'r 2 out, tld off.* (50 to 1 op 33 to 1) 10
723⁹ WILD POPPY (v) 4-8-4 F Norton (2) *al beh, tld off.* ....(33 to 1 tchd 40 to 1) 11
Dist: 2l, nk, ¾l, 3l, 1½l, 3½l, 1½l, nk, 20l, 1½l. 1m 42.09s. a 2.99s (11 Ran).
SR: 43/32/26/25/30/9/7/-/6/ (Raymond Tooth), D R C Elsworth

1426 London Talkback Radio 1152AM Handicap Class D (0-80 3-y-o) £4,338 1m 3f 91yds....................(6:55)

717 MR COPYFORCE [50] 7-0 (7*) Antoinette Armes (15) *made all, ran on strly*........................(50 to 1 op 33 to 1) 1
1111³ SOLARTICA (USA) [70] 8-13 W R Swinburn (3) *chsd ldrs, rdn 2 fs out, kpt on ins last.* .... (13 to 2 op 6 to 1 tchd 8 to 1) 2
976* MOON CARNIVAL [77] 9-6 A Clark (4) *mid-div, swtchd rght o'r 2 fs out, kpt on und pres.* ....(11 to 2 fav op 5 to 1 tchd 6 to 1) 3
855³ COLLIER BAY [71] 9-0 W Carson (6) *hld up beh, rdn and hdwy 3 fs out, styd on*...............(7 to 1 op 5 to 1) 4
1266* SUPREME MASTER [64] 8-0 (7*,6ex) Mark Denaro (2) *trkd ldrs, kpt on one pace fnl 2 fs*.......(10 to 1 op 7 to 1) 5
772⁵ MY PATRIARCH [78] 9-7 Pat Eddery (7) *hld up beh, hrd rdn 2 fs out, kpt on, nvr nrr.* (8 to 1 op 6 to 1 tchd 9 to 1) 6
1180⁶ BROUGHTONS FORMULA [60] (bl) 7-10 (7*) D McCabe (5) *beh, hdwy 2 fs out, styd on*..... (16 to 1 tchd 20 to 1) 7
584² HIGH SUMMER [63] 8-3 (3*) D Harrison (1) *mid-div, drvn o'r 2 fs out, no imprsn*................(8 to 1 tchd 7 to 1) 8
1067⁸ HOOSIE [72] 9-1 M Roberts (8) *trkd ldrs till wknd o'r 2 fs out*.................................. (14 to 1 op 12 to 1) 9
813* HOOCHIECOOCHIE MAN (Ire) [62] 8-5 R Price (11) *mid-div, hrd rdn 2 fs out, sn btn*.............(8 to 1 op 7 to 1) 10
1027 LEAR KING (USA) [76] 9-5 T Quinn (13) *trkd ldrs till wknd o'r one furlong out*.................(12 to 1 tchd 14 to 1) 11
1212⁷ BRAVE HERO (USA) [63] 8-6 D Biggs (14) *keen hold, trkd ldr, wkng whn hmpd and lost pl o'r one furlong out.* ....(33 to 1) 12
966 KEEP YOUR DISTANCE [56] 7-13² K Darley (10) *beh, rdn and hdwy on ins o'r 3 fs out, hmpd and snatched up over 2 out*........................... (8 to 1 op 5 to 1) 13
1146 ESERIE DE CORES (USA) [51] 7-8¹ J Quinn (12) *al beh.* ....(33 to 1 op 25 to 1) 14
714 CAROJANGO [56] 7-13 F Norton (9) *mid-div, wknd fnl 3 fs.* ....(25 to 1 op 16 to 1) 15
Dist: 3½l, sht-hd, 1l, sht-hd, 2l, hd, 3l, ½l, 2½l, 1½l. 2m 23.79s. a 3.79s (15 Ran).
SR: 30/43/49/41/33/43/24/21/29/ (Copyforce Ltd), Miss B Sanders

1427 Brigadier Gerard Stakes Class A (Group 3) (4-y-o and up) £19,482 1¼m 7yds.......................... (7:25)

1118* RED BISHOP (USA) 5-8-10 M Roberts (2) *trkd ldg trio, cld 2 fs out, shaken up to ld ins last, cleverly.* ....(5 to 4 fav tchd 11 to 8) 1
925* HIGHLAND DRESS 4-8-10 W R Swinburn (1) *trkd ldr, led o'r 3 fs out to one out, one pace.* ....(7 to 2 op 11 to 4 tchd 4 to 1) 2
1269⁶ HALF A TICK (USA) 5-8-13 T Quinn (3) *hld up in last pl, effrt and not much room fnl 2 fs, ran on one pace.* .... (16 to 1 op 10 to 1) 3
1018⁶ SAPIENCE 7-9-1 Pat Eddery (4) *set modest pace, hdd 3 fs out, hrd rdn and rallied ins last.* ....(5 to 1 op 4 to 1 tchd 11 to 2) 4
689⁵ YOUNG BUSTER (Ire) 5-8-13 M Hills (6) *trkd ldg pair, cld 3 fs out, led briefly one out, wknd.* ....(9 to 2 op 4 to 1 tchd 5 to 1) 5
Dist: ¾l, ½l, hd, 2½l. 2m 8.83s. a 4.93s (5 Ran).
SR: 37/35/37/38/31/ (Ali Saeed), J H M Gosden

1428 Winalot National Stakes Class A (Listed Race) (2-y-o) £8,419 5f 6yds. (7:55)

859* REDOUBTABLE (USA) 9-1 T Quinn (5) *hld up in cl tch, led on bit 2 fs out, pushed out*.......(5 to 4 on tchd Evens) 1
841* RISKY 9-0 Pat Eddery (4) *led to 2 fs out, rallied gmely und pres*..............(2 to 1 op 7 to 4 tchd 9 to 4) 2
1272[2] FAST EDDY 8-12 L Dettori (2) *trkd ldrs, rdn appr 2 fs out, one pace*.............(12 to 1 op 10 to 1 tchd 14 to 1) 3
1032[2] MICHELLE HICKS 8-7 M Hills (1) *missed break, hld up in tch, rdn 2 fs out, no imprsn*.........(8 to 1 op 7 to 1) 4
1241[3] HELLO MISTER 8-12 D Holland (3) *cl up till wknd quickly ins fnl 2 fs, tld off*...............(66 to 1 op 33 to 1) 5
Dist: Hd, 2½l, ½l, 25l. 1m 0.95s. a 1.45s (5 Ran).
SR: 47/45/33/26/-/ (B E Nielsen), R Hannon

1429 LBC Newstalk 97.3 FM Mike Dickin Maiden Stakes Class D (3-y-o) £3,746 1¼m 7yds..................... (8:25)

1092[2] BLACK DRAGON (Ire) 9-0 M Roberts (9) *made all, pushed alng o'r 2 fs out, ran on strly*.......(13 to 2 op 9 to 2) 1
751[6] WINGED VICTORY (USA) 9-0 R Cochrane (13) *trkd ldrs, rdn alng o'r 2 fs out, pld out and ran on und pres ins last*. ....(11 to 8 on op 11 to 10) 2
515[4] ARKAAN (USA) 9-0 W R Swinburn (6) *trkd ldrs, ev ch 2 fs out, rdn and one pace appr last*. ....(6 to 1 op 9 to 2 tchd 13 to 2) 3
FROGMARCH (USA) 9-0 W Carson (10) *trkd wnr, ev ch 2 fs out, one pace appr last*. ....(33 to 1 op 16 to 1 tchd 40 to 1) 4
MOONSHINE LAKE 8-9 A McGlone (2) *mid-div, cld hfwy, hdwy o'r one furlong out, styd on*. (25 to 1 op 16 to 1) 5
1176 BEDEVIL (USA) 9-0 L Dettori (1) *beh, cld 3 fs out, drvn o'r 2 out, styd on*......... (12 to 1 op 16 to 1 tchd 20 to 1) 6
MIROSWAKI (USA) 9-0 D Holland (5) *beh, rdn alng o'r 2 fs out, nvr nrr*.........(50 to 1 op 33 to 1 tchd 100 to 1) 7
INTENTION (USA) 9-0 Paul Eddery (8) *beh, rdn 2 fs out, hdwy o'r one out, nrst finish*. ....(33 to 1 op 20 to 1 tchd 40 to 1) 8
1068 RIVIERE ACTOR (USA) 9-0 J Reid (4) *chsd ldrs till wknd o'r 2 fs out*............................ (33 to 1 op 16 to 1) 9
482 SMUGGLER'S POINT (USA) 9-0 J Carroll (12) *mid-div, snatched up whn short of room o'r 3 fs out, wknd over 2 out*.................(50 to 1 op 20 to 1 tchd 66 to 1) 10
THEME (Ire) 8-9 Pat Eddery (11) *missed break, al beh*. ....(9 to 1 op 6 to 1 tchd 10 to 1) 11
ONLY A MIRAGE 9-0 T Quinn (7) *al beh*. ....(50 to 1 op 33 to 1 tchd 66 to 1) 12
Dist: Nk, 1½l, sht-hd, 2½l, 1½l, 3l, 1½l, sht-hd, 1½l, 1½l. 2m 9.38s. a 5.48s (12 Ran).
SR: 35/34/31/30/20/22/16/13/12/ (Sheikh Mohammed), B W Hills

1430 London Racing Club Handicap Class D (0-80 3-y-o and up) £4,455 1¾m ....(8:55)

PHARAMINEUX [77] 7-9-12 T Quinn (2) *hld up in mid-div, hdwy on ins whn stumbled appr 2 fs out, sn reco'red, led approaching last, pushed out*. ....(4 to 1 fav tchd 5 to 1) 1
MUSE [71] 6-9-3 (3*) B Doyle (10) *chsd ldrs, cld aftr 6 fs, drvn 3 out, styd on wl*............. (8 to 1 op 7 to 2) 2
879 ALQAIRAWAAN [57] 4-8-6 B Rouse (3) *trkd ldrs, rdn o'r 2 fs out, styd on*.......................(12 to 1 op 8 to 1) 3
1321[3] CHAMPAGNE GOLD [55] 6-8-4 J Williams (13) *beh, pushed alng 4 fs out, styd on wl fnl furlong*. .... (10 to 1 op 8 to 1 tchd 12 to 1) 4
994 SARAZAR (USA) [50] 4-7-13 J Quinn (11) *trkd ldrs, rdn and one pace frm o'r 2 fs out*. ....(14 to 1 op 10 to 1 tchd 16 to 1) 5
880[3] ALYDUNCAN (USA) [78] 3-8-9 W Carson (9) *sn led, pushed alng 3 fs out, hdd appr last, one pace*. ....(8 to 1 tchd 7 to 1) 6
1129[5] INCHCAILLOCH (Ire) [75] 4-9-10 Paul Eddery (12) *cl up, rdn and ev ch 2 fs out, wknd ins last*. (12 to 1 tchd 14 to 1) 7
HEAVENLY WATERS [60] 4-8-9 J Reid (17) *beh, cld o'r 4 fs out, sn rdn and btn*.. (12 to 1 op 10 to 1 tchd 14 to 1) 8
287[6] CASTLE SECRET [72] 7-9-2 (5*) Stephen Davies (15) *nvr nrr*.................................(10 to 1 op 8 to 1) 9
BELAFONTE [55] 6-8-4 A Tucker (14) *trkd ldrs, rdn and wknd 3 fs out*......................... (10 to 1 op 8 to 1) 10
BALLY KNIGHT [55] 7-8-2[3] (5*) C Hodgson (7) *strted slwly, beh, hdwy o'r 2 fs out, btn over one out*....... (33 to 1) 11
1242[9] SURE PRIDE (USA) [51] 5-8-0[2] Candy Morris (5) *al beh*. .... (66 to 1 op 33 to 1) 12
WHERE ARE WE [45] 7-7-8[1] N Adams (8) *nvr better than mid-div*.. (66 to 1) 13
857 TOP SPIN [79] 4-10-0 S Whitworth (1) *al beh*. ....(9 to 1 op 8 to 1 tchd 10 to 1) 14
25[7] CATHOS (Fr) [49] 8-7-12 C Rutter (6) *al beh*. .... (20 to 1 op 14 to 1 tchd 25 to 1) 15
Dist: Hd, 1½l, sht-hd, ½l, 1l, 2½l, 1½l, 2½l, sht-hd, ¾l. 3m 3.28s. a 8.98s (15 Ran).
SR: 8/1/-/-/-/-/ (Nicholas Roteman), R Akehurst

SLIGO (IRE) (soft)
Tuesday June 1st

1431 N.C.F. Sligo Dairies Maiden (3-y-o and up) £2,962 1¾m................(7:00)

1107[2] MILLMOUNT (Ire) (bl) 3-8-3 (4*) W J Smith (3)...... (2 to 1) 1
1122[3] WICKLOW WAY (Ire) 3-8-7 W J Supple (4)......(3 to 1 on) 2
1122[6] L-WAY FIRST (Ire) 3-8-7 R Hughes (2)............(8 to 1) 3
Dist: Sht-hd, dist. 3m 28.70s. (3 Ran).
(T F Gammell), D K Weld

1432 Tattersalls Auction Race (2-y-o) £2,935 6f 110yds............... (7:30)

896[9] SHARE A DREAM (Ire) 8-0 (2*) R M Burke (7)......(12 to 1) 1
ALSTOMERIA 8-8 N G McCullagh (6)............ (12 to 1) 2
664[3] CORLEONIE (Ire) 9-0 W J Supple (3)...........(5 to 4 on) 3
1104[7] SOPHIE'S PET (Ire) 8-2 J F Egan (4).............. (7 to 1) 4
SLICK DEALER (Ire) 8-8 P Shanahan (5)............ (4 to 1) 5
269[7] TREJOLY PIGEONS (Ire) 8-8 (6*) J J Behan (1)..... (5 to 1) 6
Dist: 2l, 2l, 1l, ½l. 1m 32.50s. (6 Ran).
(Shared Dream Syndicate), J C Harley

1433 Collooney Apprentice Handicap (0-60 3-y-o and up) £2,245 6f 110yds.. (8:00)

1294[6] RAFFERTY'S INNER (Ire) [-] 3-9-5 R T Fitzpatrick (6) ....(14 to 1) 1
TAJANAMA (Ire) [-] 5-9-1 T P Treacy (2)..............(7 to 2) 2
1251* SARA MAURETTE (Ire) [-] 3-9-6 (2*,3ex) D A O'Sullivan (1) ....(5 to 2 fav) 3
1105[6] PERSIAN LIGHT (Ire) [-] 3-9-3 (2*) A J Dempsey (5). (5 to 1) 4
868[5] BELLE OF DREAMS (Ire) [-] (bl) 5-8-13 (2*) A J Beale (4) ....(6 to 1) 5
486[5] GIRARDELLI (Ire) [-] 3-8-13 (2*) P J Smullen (9).....(7 to 1) 6
870 SORRECA (Ire) [-] 4-9-5 (2*) T M Finn (3)..........(25 to 1) 7
868 DSHAMILJA [-] 6-10-0 D M McCullagh (8)........(10 to 1) ref
Dist: 1½l, sht-hd, 4½l, 2l. 1m 32.10s. (8 Ran).
(Ballykisteen Stud Ltd), J T Gorman

BEVERLEY (good to firm)
Wednesday June 2nd

Going Correction: MINUS 0.15 sec. per fur. (races 1,2,3,5,6), MINUS 0.05 (4)

1434 Scarborough Handicap Class D (0-80 4-y-o and up) £3,114 1m 100yds. (6:45)

1325* SWEET MIGNONETTE [69] 5-10-0 K Darley (6) *trkd ldrs, hdwy 3 fs out, rdn o'r one out, styd on to ld ins last*. ....(7 to 4 fav op 2 to 1 tchd 9 to 4) 1
1274[2] JAHANGIR (Ire) [69] 4-10-0 M Birch (4) *chsd ldr, hdwy to chal 2 fs out, sn rdn and ev ch till no extr ins last*. ....(7 to 2 op 3 to 1 tchd 4 to 1) 2
801[3] SPANISH VERDICT [65] 6-9-3 (7*) C Teague (1) *led, rdn 2 fs out, hdd entering fnl furlong, one pace*. ....(4 to 1 op 7 to 2) 3
1007[2] SET THE FASHION [52] (v) 4-8-11 Dean McKeown (3) *hld up in tch, hdwy 2 fs out, sn rdn and effrt appr fnl furlong, kpt on one pace*.....................(5 to 1 op 4 to 1) 4
1274[4] LORD LAMBSON [42] 4-8-1 J Fanning (5) *hld up in tch, hdwy 2 fs out, rdn and one pace entering fnl furlong*. ....(6 to 1 op 11 to 2 tchd 13 to 2) 5
1284 ZEPPEKI (Ire) [54] 5-8-13 S Wood (2) *trkd ldrs, effrt and hdwy 3 fs out, sn rdn and wknd 2 out*. .... (33 to 1 op 20 to 1) 6
Dist: 1l, ½l, ¾l, sht-hd, 10l. 1m 49.40s. a 6.60s (6 Ran).
(Ron Whitehead), Mrs M Reveley

1435 Welton Maiden Stakes Class D (3-y-o and up) £3,362 7f 100yds........(7:10)

UNDERWATER (USA) 4-9-7 S Raymont (1) *hld up, hdwy 3 fs out, led on bit entering fnl furlong, easily*. ....(5 to 4 on op 6 to 4 on) 1
1109[2] DIPLOMATIST 3-8-6 P Robinson (2) *cl up, effrt to ld 2 and a half fs out, sn rdn, hdd entering fnl furlong, no ch wth wnr*.............................(9 to 4 tchd 5 to 2) 2
1271 HARLOSH 3-8-11 K Darley (3) *led, rdn 3 fs out, sn hdd and wknd*......................... (25 to 1 tchd 33 to 1) 3
YOSHAARIK (Ire) 3-8-11 M Birch (4) *hld up in tch, effrt 3 fs out, sn rdn and btn*...............(4 to 1 tchd 9 to 2) 4
Dist: 1½l, 7l, 6l. 1m 35.00s. a 4.70s (4 Ran).
SR: 20/ (K Abdulla), R Charlton

1436 Habbershaws Bookmakers Handicap Class E (0-70 3-y-o and up) £4,562 7f 100yds........................ (7:35)

1058[9] MY BEST VALENTINE [70] 3-9-5 F Norton (18) *chsd ldrs, gd hdwy 3 fs out, effrt to ld entering fnl furlong, kpt on und pres*................................ (12 to 1) 1

1177[7] BERNSTEIN BETTE [60] 7-9-5 J Fanning (15) *prmnt, effrt and swtchd to chal fnl furlong, sn rdn and ev ch till no extr nr finish*......(11 to 2 fav op 9 to 2 tchd 6 to 1) 2
1284[5] MALCESINE (Ire) [45] 4-8-4 J Fortune (14) *chsd ldrs, hdwy to chal 2 fs out, sn rdn and ev ch till one pace ins last.* ....(16 to 1) 3
592 THORNTON GATE [68] 4-9-10 (3*) S Maloney (4) *steadied strt and beh, hdwy o'r 2 fs out, styd on wl ins last, nrst finish*..(20 to 1) 4
990[9] DANCE ON SIXPENCE [50] 5-8-9 J Quinn (16) *led 2 fs, cl up till led two out, sn rdn, hdd and wknd appr fnl furlong.* ....(20 to 1 op 16 to 1) 5
1038[2] OBSIDIAN GREY [60] 6-8-12 (7*) S Sanders (19) *cl up, led aftr 2 fs till rdn and hdd o'r two furlongs out, wknd.* ....(11 to 1 op 8 to 1) 6
MATTS BOY [49] 5-8-8 N Connorton (3) *hdwy 2 fs, kpt on ins last*..........................(12 to 1 op 20 to 1) 7
1287[5] STATE FLYER [60] (v) 5-8-12 (7*) J Marshall (7) *dwlt and beh, hdwy 2 fs out, styd on ins last, not rch ldrs.* ....(12 to 1 op 16 to 1) 8
1264* ARABAT [60] 6-9-5 (6ex) L Charnock (11) *al mid-div.* ....(11 to 1 op 8 to 1) 9
977 GREENWICH CHALENGE [63] 3-8-12 M Wigham (9) *nvr rch ldrs*..(33 to 1) 10
1194[2] CLAUDIA MISS [60] 6-9-5 Dean McKeown (12) *prmnt, rdn 3 fs out, sn wknd*....................(8 to 1 op 10 to 1) 11
BRAMBLES WAY [45] 4-8-4 S Webster (10) *in tch, effrt 3 fs out, sn rdn and wknd*..........................(25 to 1) 12
1079[5] GANT BLEU (Fr) [61] 6-9-6 A Culhane (17) *chsd ldrs, rdn o'r 2 fs out, sn btn*..............................(10 to 1) 13
1274 ROUTING [52] 5-8-11 S Perks (2) *al rear, wide strt and sn beh*..(25 to 1) 14
1186[3] KHALLOOF (Ire) [48] (bl) 4-8-0 (7*) C Teague (1) *hld up, hdwy on outer 3 fs out, sn rdn and btn.* ....(20 to 1 op 16 to 1) 15
1194 WILD PROSPECT [58] 5-9-3 M Birch (5) *chsd ldrs till rdn and wknd 3 fs out*..............(14 to 1 tchd 16 to 1) 16
1246[3] DREAM CARRIER (Ire) [60] 5-9-5 K Darley (6) *al rear.* ....(12 to 1 op 8 to 1) 17
1286* CHANTRY BELLINI [49] (bl) 4-8-8 (6ex) N Carlisle (8) *nvr a factor*..........................(10 to 1 op 8 to 1) 18

Dist: ¾l, 2l, ½l, ¾l, 2l, nk, hd, 6l, nk, ¾l. 1m 33.20s. a 2.90s (18 Ran).
SR: 44/42/21/42/22/26/14/24/6/ (The Valentines), P W Harris

1437 Hilary Needler Trophy Conditions Stakes Class C (2-y-o) £7,030 5f (8:05)

979* SNIPE HALL 8-10 P Robinson (3) *trkd ldrs, hdwy 2 fs out, quickened to ld ins last, sn rdn and ran on.* ....(11 to 8 fav op 5 to 4 tchd 11 to 10) 1
998[2] SINNERS REPRIEVE 8-10 M Birch (4) *cl up, led 2 fs out, rdn and hdd ins last, kpt on*........(3 to 1 op 5 to 2) 2
889* STIMULANT 8-10 N Connorton (2) *led, rdn and hdd 2 fs out, one pace appr last*..............(5 to 2 op 9 to 4) 3
933* LEGATEE 8-8 K Darley (1) *wnt lft strt, sn cl up and ev ch till wknd one and a half fs out*..... (8 to 1 op 12 to 1) 4

Dist: 1l, 3½l, 10l. 1m 4.00s. a 2.30s (4 Ran).
SR: 45/41/27/-/ (Mrs R T Watson), J Wharton

1438 Hurn Claiming Stakes Class F (4-y-o and up) £1,725 1m 3f 216yds.... (8:35)

1034[6] RISING TEMPO (Ire) 5-8-7 (7*) D Wright (4) *chsd ldg pair, hdwy o'r 3 fs out, rdn 2 out, styd on to ld wl ins last.* ....(8 to 1 op 7 to 1 tchd 9 to 1) 1
1034[3] LE TEMERAIRE 7-8-13 Kim Tinkler (1) *led and set str pace, clr o'r 2 fs out, sn rdn, hdd and no extr wl ins last.* ....(11 to 2 op 9 to 2 tchd 6 to 1) 2
1166[3] WAJEEB (USA) 4-8-7[1] M Birch (5) *in tch, rdn and lost pl 3 fs out, styd on und pres ins last, nvr dngrs.* ....(13 to 2 op 6 to 1 tchd 7 to 1) 3
1305 SALU (bl) 4-8-13 G Duffield (2) *chsd ldg pair, effrt and hdwy 3 fs out, sn rdn and one pace fnl 2 furlongs.* ....(3 to 1 fav op 7 to 2 tchd 4 to 1) 4
1281 REACH FOR GLORY (bl) 4-8-0 J Fanning (7) *cl up till rdn 3 fs out, wknd*....................(12 to 1 op 16 to 1) 5
DANZA HEIGHTS 7-8-10 K Darley (3) *mid-div, hdwy 4 fs out, rdn 2 and a half out, sn wknd.* (11 to 2 op 7 to 1) 6
1156[7] IRON BARON (Ire) 4-8-6[2] S Perks (8) *hld up, hdwy 4 fs out, rdn 2 and a half out, no imprsn*......(9 to 1 op 7 to 1) 7
4688a[8] SEA PADDY 5-8-9[2] (7*) H Bastiman (6) *al rear.* ....(12 to 1 op 8 to 1) 8
REAPERS REWARD 5-7-8 (5*) A Garth (10) *dwlt, al beh.* ....(33 to 1) 9
229 ANNACURRAGH (Ire) 4-8-7 M Wigham (9) *hld up, hdwy hfwy, rdn and wknd o'r 4 fs out, tld off.* ....(11 to 1 op 8 to 1) 10

Dist: ¾l, 5l, 1l, 2½l, 5l, 6l, ½l, 8l, 5l. 2m 38.40s. a 7.40s (10 Ran).
SR: 8/5/-/-/-/-/ (Mrs Diane Baugh), W Clay

1439 Derby Night Handicap Class E (0-70 3-y-o and up) £2,490 1m 3f 216yds ....(9:05)

1305[5] EIRE LEATH-SCEAL [49] 6-8-9 M Wigham (6) *made all, rdn 2 fs out, hrd drvn and ran on gmely ins last.* ....(7 to 1 op 6 to 1) 1
4812a SINGING REPLY (USA) [33] 5-7-7 N Carlisle (4) *al prmnt, effrt to chal 2 fs out, sn rdn and ev ch till no extr nr finish*...(25 to 1) 2
1143 FIRST BID [64] 6-9-10 J Fanning (8) *trkd ldrs gng wl, hdwy 2 fs out, effrt and ev ch whn not much room and not quicken ins last*.................. (9 to 2 tchd 5 to 1) 3
SAN PIER NICETO [45] 6-8-5 G Duffield (10) *prmnt, effrt 3 fs out, rdn 2 out, one pace appr last.* ....(14 to 1 op 12 to 1) 4
904[2] TROJAN LANCER [43] 7-8-3 K Darley (9) *hld up, hdwy 4 fs out, sn rdn and one pace appr last.* ....(7 to 4 fav tchd 2 to 1) 5
1111[4] MERRY MERMAID [49] 3-7-7 L Charnock (1) *hld up and beh, gd hdwy on inner 2 fs out, rdn and one pace appr fnl furlong*............(13 to 2 op 5 to 1 tchd 7 to 1) 6
1120[9] ALTERMEERA [49] 5-8-9 G Bardwell (7) *chsd ldrs, effrt and rdn 3 fs out, wndrd and wknd 2 out.* (9 to 1 op 10 to 1) 7
1384[3] KINOKO [59] 5-8-12 (7*) L Aspell (3) *mid-div, hdwy 4 fs, effrt and rdn o'r 2 furlongs out, sn one paced.* ....(7 to 1 tchd 15 to 2) 8
1190 DON'T CRY [37] 5-7-11[4] Kim Tinkler (5) *al rear*....(50 to 1) 9
681[6] GAY MING [44] 4-7-13 (5*) A Garth (2) *in tch till rdn and wknd 4 fs out*..(10 to 1) 10

Dist: Nk, 1l, ½l, 2l, 1l, 1½l, 4l, ½l, 4l. 2m 40.90s. a 9.90s (10 Ran).
(Mel Brittain), M Brittain

CURRAGH (IRE) (yielding to soft)
Wednesday June 2nd
Going Correction: PLUS 0.95 sec. per fur.

1440 Railway Bank Apprentice Handicap (0-75 3-y-o and up) £2,417 1m... (5:30)

1251[2] TOUCHDOWN [-] 6-8-8 (4*,9ex) G M Moylan (13)...(8 to 1) 1
WANDERING THOUGHTS (Ire) [-] 4-8-6 B Bowens (6) ....(14 to 1) 2
1294[2] COOLRAIN LADY (Ire) [-] 3-8-9 (2*) R T Fitzpatrick (2) (4 to 1) 3
1235[9] RETURN JOURNEY (Ire) [-] 4-9-5 (4*) J F Clarke (10) ....(12 to 1) 4
310[3] LORD GLENVARA (Ire) [-] 5-8-10 R V Skelly (7)....(10 to 1) 5
NUNIVAK (USA) [-] 5-9-6 B J Walsh (17)..........(10 to 1) 6
NORDIC MINE (Ire) [-] 3-7-12 (4*) D Casey (12)....(10 to 1) 7
1293[6] MARTIN'S MARTINA (Ire) [-] 4-8-3 (4*) B Fenton (9) (14 to 1) 8
1235* MAGIC ARTS (Ire) [-] 5-9-11 (4*,5ex) D W O'Sullivan (11) ....(7 to 1) 9
1046 BENGALI (Ire) [-] 3-7-12[1] (4*) I Browne (16)....... (20 to 1) 10
1293[2] ALBERTA ROSE (Ire) [-] 4-9-7 J R Barry (14)....(2 to 1 fav) 11
647[9] IRISH MISTRESS (Ire) [-] 3-7-3 (4*) J P Cornally (15) (20 to 1) 12
1199 TINA'S CHARM (Ire) [-] 4-9-10 (4*) D Callaghan (8) (14 to 1) 13
640[3] DOBIE (USA) [-] 5-9-12 (2*) D J O'Donohoe (4)..... (5 to 1) 14
YOUR UNCLE STANLEY (Ire) [-] 4-9-4 P P Murphy (5) ....(10 to 1) 15
MAGNUM STAR (Ire) [-] 4-9-2 (4*) W M Lynch (1).. (12 to 1) 16

Dist: Nk, ¾l, 2l, ½l. 1m 48.30s. a 11.70s (16 Ran).
SR: 37/30/33/39/24/-/ (Mrs D T Hughes), D T Hughes

1441 Curragh Bloodstock Trial E.B.F. Maiden (3-y-o) £2,417 1¼m..... (6:00)

1236[2] SOLAS ABU (Ire) 8-11 K J Manning (7)........ (7 to 4 fav) 1
SHIRLEY'S DELIGHT (Ire) 8-11 S Craine (4)........(8 to 1) 2
870[4] SPECIAL OFFER (Ire) 8-11 N G McCullagh (5).....(10 to 1) 3
SHEER OPULANCE (Ire) 9-0 P Shanahan (6).......(9 to 2) 4
UP SHE FLEW (USA) 8-11 W J O'Connor (10)......(14 to 1) 5
PALAIYTA (Ire) 8-11 D Hogan (1).............. (100 to 30) 6
552[5] BIRTHPLACE (Ire) 9-0 R Hughes (8)..................(8 to 1) 7
1106 DRESS DANCE (Ire) 9-0 D V Smith (9).............(14 to 1) 8
1236[5] DALKEY ISLAND (Ire) 8-12 (2*) D G O'Shea (11)... (10 to 1) 9
1105 BRAZEN ANGEL (Ire) 8-11 J F Egan (3).......... (16 to 1) 10
669[7] INDIGENT (Ire) 8-11 W J Supple (2)............... (9 to 1) 11

Dist: 8l, ¾l, nk, nk. 2m 19.90s. a 17.10s (11 Ran).
SR: 21/5/3/5/1/-/ (E R Madden), J S Bolger

1442 Hotel Keadeen E.B.F. Maiden (2-y-o) £3,452 6f..................... (6:30)

1332[3] DILIGENT DODGER (Ire) 9-0 W J Supple (13)...(3 to 1 fav) 1
1022[7] EICHTERCUA (Ire) 8-11 J F Egan (11)............(14 to 1) 2
938[4] LUDDEN LADY (Ire) 8-5 (6*) J J Behan (5)..........(8 to 1) 3
869[3] GIULIO ROMANO (Ire) 9-0 K J Manning (3)........ (9 to 2) 4
POSTPONE (Ire) 8-3 (8*) T E Durcan (4)............(8 to 1) 5
1197 MONICA'S CHOICE (Ire) 9-0 G Curran (10)....... (20 to 1) 6
MY RAGAMUFFIN (Ire) 8-11 N G McCullagh (7)... (20 to 1) 7
CAPATINA (Ire) 8-11 B Coogan (8)................. (4 to 1) 8
PARCACURRY PETE (Ire) 9-0 R Hughes (1)........(7 to 1) 9
BOLD EMIR 9-0 S Craine (6)........................(7 to 1) 10
OVER THE MAIGUE (Ire) 8-9 (2*) R M Burke (2)....(20 to 1) 11
896 GAELIC HEATHER (Ire) 8-11 W J O'Connor (9).... (14 to 1) 12

Dist: Sht-hd, ½l, 4l, ¾l. 1m 19.20s. a 8.70s (12 Ran).
SR: 40/36/34/21/15/-/ (Mrs D M Donohoe), Kevin Prendergast

1443 Michael Murphy Carpets E.B.F. Maiden (3-y-o and up) £2,417 1m (7:00)

1048[7] OVERCAST (Ire) 3-8-7 W J O'Connor (10)......... (7 to 1) 1
1164[2] DAFTARI (Ire) (bl) 3-8-10 D Hogan (7).........(11 to 8 fav) 2

577 SUEKAR (Ire) 3-8-7 R Hughes (11) .... (7 to 1) 3
MISS CARMELLA (Ire) 3-8-7 W J Supple (14) ...... (6 to 1) 4
1333^{7} ASTA MADERA (Ire) 3-8-7 J F Egan (9) .... (5 to 1) 5
NATIONAL FLAG (Fr) 3-8-8 (2*) D G O'Shea (1) .... (8 to 1) 6
1107^{8} THREE MUSKETEERS (Ire) 4-9-1 (6*) C Everard (3) (12 to 1) 7
WHAT A PLEASURE (Ire) 3-8-10 E A Leonard (5) ... (8 to 1) 8
JUST ONE CANALETTO 5-8-11 (10*) B Carson (4) (20 to 1) 9
DONTKISSTHEJOCKEY (Ire) 3-8-7 Joanna Morgan (2) .... (16 to 1) 10
1107 INNOCENT PARTY (Ire) 4-9-7 L O'Shea (13) ...... (20 to 1) 11
1295^{8} BELLE O' THE BAY (Ire) 4-8-12 (6*) J J Behan (6) .. (20 to 1) 12
Dist: Sht-hd, 2½l, 2l, 2½l. 1m 47.70s. a 11.10s (12 Ran).
SR: 41/43/32/26/18/-/ (Yoshiki Akazawa), P Aspell

1444 MC Loughlin Handicap (0-75 3-y-o and up) £2,417 6f. .... (7:30)

MACQUARIE RIDGE (USA) [-] 5-7-13^{1} W J Supple (7) .... (7 to 2 jt-fav) 1
1293^{5} IMPRIMATUR [-] 4-8-12 (6*) J J Behan (8) .... (8 to 1) 2
1050^{4} ISLAND HEATHER (Ire) [-] (bl) 5-9-6 (6*) C Everard (2) (5 to 1) 3
1251^{7} SHRAGRADDY LASS (Ire) [-] 3-8-0 N G McCullagh (1) .... (10 to 1) 4
1294^{5} FASTAFLOW (Ire) [-] 3-8-5 (6*) B J Walsh (10) .... (9 to 1) 5
1386* SOMERTON BOY (Ire) [-] 3-9-5 (5ex) P Shanahan (11) .... (7 to 2 jt-fav) 6
1294^{7} COMMODITY MARKET (Ire) [-] (bl) 3-9-0 N Byrne (4) .... (12 to 1) 7
1023^{2} MAGIC DON (Ire) [-] 4-9-0 (8*) R T Fitzpatrick (9) .... (9 to 2) 8
981 PHARUZAL [-] 3-8-9 S Craine (6) .... (10 to 1) 9
280 SHESLOOKINATME (Ire) [-] 4-7-10^{3} (10*) B Fenton (3) .... (25 to 1) 10
669^{9} HELLO EXCUSE ME (USA) [-] 3-8-9 J F Egan (5) .. (12 to 1) 11
Dist: Hd, hd, ½l, 4½l. 1m 18.60s. a 8.10s (11 Ran).
SR: 37/55/62/34/27/-/ (F B McEntee), D P Kelly

1445 Curragh Tintawn E.B.F. Maiden (3-y-o and up) £2,417 6f. .... (8:00)

LOCK'S HEATH (Can) 3-8-9 R Hughes (4) .... (5 to 1) 1
1200^{2} GOODNIGHT KISS 3-8-9 M J Kinane (1) .... (4 to 1 on) 2
JUNORIUS (Ire) 4-9-7 S Craine (3) .... (33 to 1) 3
1164 SCALP (Ire) 3-8-12 N Byrne (6) .... (20 to 1) 4
1252^{3} TORC MOUNTAIN (Ire) 3-8-12 W J Supple (8) ..... (10 to 1) 5
OICHE MHAITH 3-8-9 D Manning (2) .... (20 to 1) 6
1105^{8} YONOKA (Fr) 4-9-1 (6*) R V Skelly (7) .... (20 to 1) 7
PEARL DAWN (Ire) 3-8-1 (8*) R T Fitzpatrick (5) .. (33 to 1) 8
COULD BE LUCKY (Ire) 5-8-12 (6*) C Everard (9) .. (33 to 1) 9
Dist: 2½l, 6l, 1l, sht-hd. 1m 19.70s. a 9.20s (9 Ran).
SR: 25/15/3/-/-/-/ (Sheikh Mohammed), John M Oxx

EPSOM (good)
Wednesday June 2nd
Going Correction: MINUS 0.20 sec. per fur. (races 1,2,3,5,6), MINUS 0.10 (4)

1446 Energizer Woodcote Stakes Class A (Listed) (2-y-o) £10,430 6f. ...... (2:15)

MOCCASIN RUN (USA) 8-11 L Dettori (6) *sn trkd ldg pair, led 2 and a half fs out, pushed out, cmftbly.* ....(4 to 1 op 3 to 1 tchd 11 to 4 and 9 to 2) 1
984* QUEENBIRD 8-9 M J Kinane (8) *beh, swtchd rght wl o'r 2 fs out, hrd rdn and hdwy over one out, ran on.* ....(9 to 4 fav op 7 to 4) 2
922^{4} CHICKAWICKA (Ire) 8-11 S Whitworth (4) *cl up, ev ch o'r 2 fs out, rdn and kpt on wl.*.............(50 to 1 op 33 to 1) 3
687^{2} SILVER WEDGE (USA) 8-11 R Cochrane (7) *trkd ldrs, sn pushed alng, hrd rdn 3 fs out, one pace.* ....(4 to 1 op 7 to 2 tchd 9 to 2) 4
1063^{3} PETER ROWLEY 8-11 C Asmussen (1) *broke wl, chsd ldrs, rdn o'r 2 fs out, sn btn.*..........(10 to 1 tchd 12 to 1) 5
1279* CONNECT (Ire) 8-11 B Rouse (2) *sn led, hdd 2 and a half fs out, wknd.*........... (11 to 1 op 8 to 1 tchd 12 to 1) 6
1091^{5} ALPINE SKIER (Ire) 8-11 K Darley (3) *sn outpcd.* .... (20 to 1 op 16 to 1) 7
1241* PRINCE AZZAAN (Ire) 8-11 Pat Eddery (5) *beh, effrt o'r 2 fs out, sn btn and eased..* (5 to 1 op 4 to 1 tchd 11 to 2) 8
Dist: 1½l, 2l, 2½l, 3l, 3½l, 5l, 6l. 1m 9.92s. a 2.02s (8 Ran).
SR: 33/25/19/9/-/ (George Strawbridge), I A Balding

1447 Diomed Stakes Class A (Group 3) (3-y-o and up) £21,843 1m 114yds. .(2:45)

1084^{3} ENHARMONIC (USA) 6-9-7 L Dettori (2) *trkd ldrs gng wl, rdn to ld one furlong out, ran on well und pres.* ....(12 to 1 tchd 14 to 1) 1
1208^{2} THOURIOS 4-9-4 T Quinn (4) *led, rdn and quickened appr 2 fs out, hdd one out, rallied und pres, ran on wl.* .... (11 to 2 op 5 to 1 tchd 6 to 1) 2
1118^{4} ZAAHI (USA) 4-9-7 W Carson (1) *trkd ldrs, hrd rdn o'r one furlong out, kpt on one pace.* ....(4 to 1 op 7 to 2 tchd 9 to 2) 3
1174^{3} HUMAM (Ire) 3-8-6 R Hills (5) *trkd ldr, chlgd and ev ch 3 fs out, one pace appr 2 out.* (4 to 1 op 5 to 2 tchd 9 to 2) 4
1029^{5} STUBASS (Ire) 4-9-9 R Cochrane (3) *in tch, hrd drvn o'r 2 fs out, no imprsn.*.......(15 to 2 op 6 to 1 tchd 8 to 1) 5
1029* SWING LOW 4-9-9 L Piggott (8) *strted slwly, hld up beh, effrt o'r 2 fs out, no imprsn.*...(11 to 4 fav tchd 7 to 2) 6
701* TIK FA (USA) (v) 4-9-4 W R Swinburn (6) *hld up in tch, pushed alng o'r 3 fs out, btn over 2 out.* .... (12 to 1 op 14 to 1) 7
ROCALITY 4-8-13 M Roberts (7) *al beh.* .... (40 to 1 op 50 to 1 tchd 33 to 1) 8
Dist: Hd, 3l, 2l, ¾l, 3½l, 2½l, 3l. 1m 44.04s. a 2.04s (8 Ran).
SR: 52/48/42/21/36/25/12/-/ (The Queen), Lord Huntingdon

1448 Ever Ready Derby Class A (Group 1) (3-y-o) £447,580 1½m 10yds. ....(3:45)

1015* COMMANDER IN CHIEF 9-0 M J Kinane (6) *mid-div, hdwy o'r 4 fs out, led 2 and a half out, rdn clr.* .... (15 to 2 op 7 to 1 tchd 8 to 1) 1
791^{3} BLUE JUDGE (Ire) 9-0 B Raymond (3) *trkd ldrs, pushed alng o'r 3 fs out, styd on wl und pres frm over one out.* ....(150 to 1 op 100 to 1 tchd 200 to 1) 2
890^{2} BLUES TRAVELLER (Ire) 9-0 D Holland (13) *al prmnt, led 3 fs out, edgd lft und pres and hdd 2 and a half out, kpt on one pace.*....................(150 to 1 tchd 200 to 1) 3
843^{4} CAIRO PRINCE (Ire) 9-0 W Carson (9) *sn pushed alng in rear, hdwy und pres o'r 2 fs out, rapid headway ins last, fnshd wl.*.................. (50 to 1 tchd 40 to 1) 4
1047* BARATHEA (Ire) 9-0 M Roberts (1) *hld up in mid-div, cld 3 fs out gng wl, sn rdn, wknd appr last.* .... (11 to 1 op 10 to 1 tchd 12 to 1) 5
947* BOB'S RETURN (Ire) 9-0 P Robinson (2) *sn led, hdd 3 fs out, wknd 2 out.* ....(15 to 1 op 16 to 1 tchd 20 to 1 and 14 to 1) 6
688^{4} REDENHAM (USA) 9-0 T Quinn (15) *wtd wth beh, rdn alng o'r 3 fs out, styd on, not pace to chal.* ....(150 to 1 op 100 to 1 tchd 200 to 1) 7
WOLF PRINCE (USA) 9-0 L Dettori (8) *hld up towards rear, rdn o'r 5 fs out, nvr dngrs..*........ (40 to 1 op 50 to 1) 8
1047^{2} FATHERLAND (Ire) 9-0 L Piggott (5) *hld up in mid-div, effrt on ins o'r 3 fs out, sn rdn and btn.* ....(8 to 1 op 7 to 1 tchd 9 to 1) 9
1001* TENBY 9-0 Pat Eddery (10) *cl up, rdn and ev ch 3 fs out, btn whn squeezed out 2 and a half out, eased.* .... (5 to 4 on op 11 to 8 on tchd Evens) 10
775^{3} DESERT TEAM (USA) 9-0 C Roche (12) *trkd ldrs, pushed alng 7 fs out, wknd o'r 3 out.*.... (25 to 1 tchd 33 to 1) 11
1001^{2} PLANETARY ASPECT (USA) 9-0 J Reid (4) *trkd ldrs, effrt 4 fs out, wknd appr 3 out.* ....(16 to 1 op 14 to 1 tchd 20 to 1) 12
1116* GEISWAY (Can) 9-0 C Asmussen (16) *hld up, al beh.* .... (25 to 1 op 20 to 1 tchd 33 to 1) 13
1116^{5} CANASKA STAR 9-0 A Munro (7) *beh hfwy.* .... (200 to 1 tchd 300 to 1) 14
947^{3} SHAREEK (USA) 9-0 W R Swinburn (11) *mid-div, effrt 3 fs out, sn wknd.*..........(40 to 1 op 50 to 1) 15
1224* ZIND (Ire) (v) 9-0 R Cochrane (14) *chsd ldrs, reminders 5 fs out, wknd 4 out, tld off.* ....(150 to 1 op 100 to 1 tchd 200 to 1) 16
Dist: 3½l, 2½l, 3l, sht-hd, 5l, nk, 7l, nk, 1l, nk. 2m 34.51s. b 0.99s (16 Ran).
SR: 86/79/74/68/67/57/56/42/41/ (K Abdulla), H R A Cecil

1449 Night Rider Rated Class A Handicap (Listed Race) (0-105 3-y-o and up) £12,277 5f. .... (4:35)

923^{2} EL YASAF (Ire) [90] 5-9-1 D Holland (10) *al gng wl, trkd ldrs, not much room appr fnl furlong, quickened to ld ins last, easily.*..................(12 to 1 op 10 to 1) 1
1348 TERRHARS (Ire) [90] 5-9-1 R Perham (3) *al prmnt, led briefly one furlong out, ran on..* (12 to 1 tchd 14 to 1) 2
1000 CRADLE DAYS [91] 4-9-2 M Roberts (1) *outpcd, hrd rdn 2 fs out, hdwy o'r one out, styd on.* ....(9 to 1 op 8 to 1 tchd 10 to 1) 3
292 SIGAMA (USA) [90] 7-9-1 N Kennedy (6) *led to one furlong out, no extr.*.........(25 to 1 op 20 to 1 tchd 33 to 1) 4
1215^{3} POYLE GEORGE [90] 8-9-1 J Williams (8) *trkd ldrs, one pace frm o'r one furlong out.*........(7 to 1 op 6 to 1) 5
460^{2} LAUREL DELIGHT [90] 3-8-7 J Carroll (5) *chsd ldrs, rdn alng 2 fs out, one pace entering last.* .... (9 to 1 op 8 to 1 tchd 10 to 1) 6
1000^{6} BUNTY BOO [96] 4-9-7 T Quinn (4) *cl up till wknd entering fnl furlong.*..........(9 to 1 op 8 to 1 tchd 10 to 1) 7
722^{5} FARFELU [95] (bl) 6-9-6 W Carson (13) *sn pushed alng, nvr gng pace of ldrs.*.... (7 to 2 fav op 5 to 2 tchd 4 to 1) 8
1127^{8} BODARI [90] 4-9-1 A Munro (12) *chsd ldrs for o'r 3 fs.* .... (20 to 1 op 16 to 1) 9
729^{7} ANSELLMAN [98] (bl) 3-9-1 R Cochrane (9) *sn pushed alng, outpcd.*..................(16 to 1 op 14 to 1) 10
1215 ASHTINA [90] 8-9-1 Pat Eddery (7) *cl up, rdn o'r one furlong out, sn not much room, wknd ins last.* ....(7 to 1 op 6 to 1 tchd 8 to 1) 11
722^{8} OLIFANTSFONTEIN [90] (bl) 5-9-1 J Reid (11) *outpcd.* .... (14 to 1 op 12 to 1) 12
1258^{4} RISTON LADY (Ire) [92] (v) 3-8-9 D Harrison (2) *in tch to hfwy.*..........(25 to 1 op 20 to 1 tchd 33 to 1) 13
Dist: 1½l, 2l, nk, sht-hd, sht-hd, nk, ¾l, ¾l, 1½l, hd. 56.00s. a 1.30s (13 Ran).
SR: 65/59/52/50/49/40/53/49/41/ (J Naughton), T J Naughton

1450 Silver Seal Rated Class B Handicap (0-95 4-y-o and up) £12,230 1¼m 18yds ....(5:10)

1093^{2} FIELDRIDGE [80] 4-8-7 Pat Eddery (12) *trkd ldr, hrd rdn 2 fs out, led appr last, all out*......(10 to 1 tchd 11 to 1) 1

845* ROSE ALTO [87] 5-9-0 W R Swinburn (2) *trkd ldg pair, swtchd rght one and a half fs out, kpt on wl und pres fnl furlong*..........(11 to 2 fav op 5 to 1 tchd 6 to 1) 2

581 TALENT (USA) [80] (v) 5-8-7 A Munro (1) *led till appr fnl furlong, rallied und pres*........ (12 to 1 tchd 14 to 1) 3

824^{6} ROYAL SEATON [85] 4-8-12 J Williams (4) *hld up in cl tch, rdn alng 2 fs out, not much room one out, ran on one pace*.................... (6 to 1 op 5 to 1 tchd 7 to 1) 4

1146^{3} PHARLY STORY [90] 5-9-3 M Roberts (5) *hld up, rdn and cld o'r 2 fs out, one pace ins last*... (7 to 1 tchd 8 to 1) 5

824^{5} NEPTUNE'S PET [82] 5-8-9 J Reid (3) *mid-div, niggled alng 3 fs out, styd on*....(8 to 1 op 7 to 1 tchd 9 to 1) 6

1110^{3} DOUBLE FLUTTER [80] 4-8-7 Paul Eddery (10) *trkd ldrs, rdn 3 fs out, sn one pace*. ....(12 to 1 op 10 to 1 tchd 14 to 1) 7

1064 KNOCK KNOCK [85] 8-8-12 L Dettori (6) *hld up beh, effrt 2 fs out, no imprsn*........(8 to 1 op 7 to 1 tchd 9 to 1) 8

1064^{3} BARFORD LAD [80] 6-8-7 R Cochrane (7) *chsd ldrs, hrd rdn o'r 2 fs out, wknd*.............(10 to 1 op 7 to 1) 9

1002* RISK MASTER [94] 4-9-7 R Hills (11) *strted slwly, nvr on terms*................. (10 to 1 op 7 to 1 tchd 12 to 1) 10

978^{2} CAMDEN'S RANSOM (USA) [80] 6-8-4 (3*) B Doyle (8) *hld up, al beh*.........................(12 to 1 op 14 to 1) 11

1256^{5} THE POWER OF ONE [80] 4-8-7 B Raymond (9) *strted slwly, cld hfwy, sn wknd*......(50 to 1 tchd 66 to 1) 12

Dist: Sht-hd, hd, 1½l, hd, 2½l, nk, 4l, 1½l, sht-hd, 1l. 2m 7.18s. a 2.88s (12 Ran).

SR: 44/50/42/44/48/35/32/29/21/ (Mrs W Tulloch), C P E Brooks

1451 Craven Handicap Class C (0-100 3-y-o) £7,245 7f.....................(5:45)

1017^{6} NORTHERN BIRD [83] 8-12 D Holland (8) *hld up beh, cld o'r one furlong out, squeezed through to ld ins last, drvn out*.................... (5 to 1 op 4 to 1 tchd 11 to 2) 1

1016^{4} EMBANKMENT (Ire) [87] 9-2 W R Swinburn (1) *hld up, squeezed through appr fnl furlong, ran on und pres*. ....(8 to 1 op 6 to 1 tchd 9 to 1) 2

1016 MR VINCENT [76] 8-2 (3*) D Harrison (6) *trkd ldr, rdn o'r 2 fs out, ev ch ins last, one pace*. ....(12 to 1 op 10 to 1 tchd 14 to 1) 3

995* FOURFORFUN [80] 8-9 B Raymond (9) *in tch, pushed alng o'r 3 fs out, kpt on und pres ins last*. ....(8 to 1 op 6 to 1 tchd 9 to 1) 4

860* BROWN'S (Fr) [85] 9-0 M Roberts (7) *trkd ldrs, rdn alng o'r 3 fs out, hrd drvn 2 out, one pace*.... (8 to 1 op 7 to 1) 5

1213 ARADANZA [92] 9-7 Pat Eddery (5) *led till ins fnl furlong, no extr*.............. (14 to 1 op 12 to 1 tchd 16 to 1) 6

1114* SIMPLY FINESSE [78] 8-7 T Quinn (3) *beh, cld 3 fs out, sn rdn and one pace*....(2 to 1 fav op 9 to 4 tchd 5 to 2) 7

945* MOON OVER MIAMI [86] 9-1 J Reid (4) *trkd ldrs, rdn and one pace fnl 2 fs*........(15 to 2 op 7 to 1 tchd 8 to 1) 8

685^{6} UMBUBUZI (USA) [70] 7-13 W Carson (2) *prmnt, hrd rdn o'r 2 fs out, rallying whn hmpd and snatched up appr last*...............................(12 to 1 op 10 to 1) 9

Dist: Nk, hd, hd, ¾l, ½l, nk, ¾l, 12l. 1m 23.12s. a 2.72s (9 Ran).

SR: 36/39/27/30/33/38/23/29/-/ (John E Bradley), B W Hills

YARMOUTH (good) Wednesday June 2nd

Going Correction: NIL (races 1,2,3,4,5), MINUS 0.25 (6,7)

1452 Suffolk Maiden Stakes Class D (3-y-o) £4,127 1m 3yds................ (2:30)

991^{4} LINK RIVER (USA) 8-9 G Hind (5) *wth ldr till led o'r 3 fs out, ran on wl fnl furlong*.............(5 to 2 tchd 9 to 4) 1

825^{2} GONE TROPPO 9-0 W Ryan (3) *chsd ldrs, rdn 2 out, unbl to quicken one out*. ....(9 to 4 on op 5 to 2 on tchd 2 to 1 on) 2

1212 SHAHAADA (USA) 8-9 R Price (4) *al prmnt, in tch 2 fs out, ran on one pace fnl furlong*....... (25 to 1 op 14 to 1) 3

KEYLOCK (USA) 8-9 M Tebbutt (2) *led o'r 4 fs, rdn over 2 furlongs out, wknd wl over one furlong out*. ....(25 to 1 op 12 to 1) 4

1039 MUMAYYAZ (Ire) (bl) 9-0 N Carlisle (1) *prmnt to hfwy, sn wknd*............................(50 to 1 op 33 to 1) 5

Dist: 3½l, 7l, 4l, 10l. 1m 38.90s. a 3.10s (5 Ran).

SR: 49/43/17/5/-/ (Sheikh Mohammed), J H M Gosden

1453 Fleggs Selling Handicap Class G (0-60 3-y-o and up) £2,658 1m 3yds... (3:00)

1225^{5} KARINSKA [53] 3-8-10 G Duffield (9) *chsd ldrs far side, led o'r 2 fs out and rdn out*.............(6 to 1 op 4 to 1) 1

1138^{2} SOOTY TERN [43] 6-8-11 N Adams (17) *led stands side, rdn fnl furlong, no extr cl hme*. ....(6 to 1 op 5 to 1 tchd 7 to 1) 2

SHORT ENCOUNTER [40] 6-8-8 S Webster (20) *hdwy fnl 2 fs, not rch ldrs*................... (50 to 1 op 25 to 1) 3

STRIKE-A-POSE [57] 3-8-9 (5*) Stephen Davies (5) *hdwy fnl 2 fs, unbl to quicken final furlong*. ....(9 to 2 op 8 to 1 tchd 10 to 1 and 11 to 1) 4

1120 ROLY WALLACE [53] (bl) 4-9-7 M Wigham (2) *hdwy frm 2 fs out, kpt on fnl furlong*............. (12 to 1 op 8 to 1) 5

1138 SKIMMER HAWK [33] 4-8-1 N Carlisle (11) *kpt on fnl 2 fs, not trble ldrs*.....................(25 to 1 op 16 to 1) 6

861^{5} J'ARRIVE [39] 4-8-2 (5*) C Hodgson (7) *prmnt 5 fs*. ....(16 to 1 op 14 to 1) 7

LITTLE PARK [47] 4-9-1 V Smith (6) *no ch fnl 3 fs*. (33 to 1) 8

990^{4} FOOLISH TOUCH [47] 11-8-8 (7*) D McCabe (12) *slwly away, nvr trble ldrs*............ (4 to 1 fav op 5 to 1) 9

861^{9} MISS MAGENTA (Ire) [26] 5-7-8 J Lowe (18) *prmnt o'r 5 fs, sn wknd*.........................(20 to 1 op 12 to 1) 10

1144 HIGHEST PRAISE (USA) [52] 10-9-6 G Carter (8) *chsd ldrs 6 fs far side, sn wknd*..................(14 to 1 op 10 to 1) 11

1209 KELLY'S KITE [35] 5-7-10 (7*) C Hawksley (3) *nvr dngrs*. ....(14 to 1 op 10 to 1 tchd 16 to 1) 12

1237^{6} BASSIO (Bel) [46] 4-9-0 W Hood (19) *chsd ldrs stands side, no extr fnl 2 fs*........................(20 to 1 op 14 to 1) 13

1232 BOULABAS (Ire) [45] 4-8-13 Elizabeth Turner (1) *prmnt for 6 fs, sn lost pl*..........................(33 to 1 op 20 to 1) 14

1210^{9} RED KITE [53] (v) 4-9-7 M Hills (16) *prmnt 5 fs*. ....(14 to 1 op 12 to 1) 15

862^{9} BRUSH WOLF (USA) [32] 4-8-0 J Quinn (4) *led far side o'r 5 fs, wknd quickly*..................(25 to 1 op 16 to 1) 16

962^{4} EASTERN GLOW [44] 3-8-1 W Woods (13) *beh most of way, tld off*............... (12 to 1 op 10 to 1 tchd 14 to 1) 17

973^{8} RESISTING (USA) [29] (bl) 5-7-5¹ (7*) D Wright (10) *prmnt to hfwy, sn rdn and btn, tld off*...... (50 to 1 op 33 to 1) 18

1035^{2} POP TO STANS [60] 4-10-0 G Bardwell (15) *outpcd, tld off*. ....(20 to 1 op 14 to 1) 19

Dist: ¾l, 1l, 3l, ½l, 2½l, 2l, sht-hd, sht-hd, ¾l, 2l. 1m 40.50s. a 4.70s (19 Ran).

SR: 26/25/19/16/21/-/ (Saeed Manana), Sir Mark Prescott

1454 River Yare Median Auction Maiden Stakes Class E (3-y-o) £3,201 7f 3yds ....(3:30)

PONDICHERRY (USA) 8-11 W Woods (1) *hld up, hdwy 3 fs out, led one out and ran on wl*. ....(9 to 1 op 7 to 1 tchd 10 to 1) 1

583 SURFINA 8-11 W Newnes (4) *hld up, ran on fnl 2 fs, not trble wnr*...............(7 to 1 op 6 to 1 tchd 8 to 1) 2

1039^{8} BALL GOWN 8-11 J Lowe (7) *led till hdd one furlong out, unbl to quicken*.......... (8 to 1 op 6 to 1 tchd 9 to 1) 3

TREAD CAREFULLY 8-11 G Carter (6) *al prmnt, rdn 2 fs out, ran on one pace*........... (6 to 4 fav tchd 7 to 4) 4

1171^{7} WESTERING 8-11 M Tebbutt (2) *dwlt, sn prmnt, no hdwy fnl 2 fs*...................(100 to 30 op 4 to 1) 5

SING AS WE GO 8-11 N Day (3) *hld up, rdn and no hdwy fnl 2 fs*...............(20 to 1 op 25 to 1 tchd 16 to 1) 6

RISK THE WITCH 8-11 G Duffield (5) *prmnt till wknd o'r 2 fs out*................(12 to 1 op 10 to 1 tchd 14 to 1) 7

Dist: 3½l, 1½l, 5l, 2l, 3l, 10l. 1m 27.00s. a 3.80s (7 Ran).

SR: 40/29/24/9/3/-/-/ (High Point Bloodstock Ltd), S P C Woods

1455 Heydon Hall Handicap Class D (0-80 3-y-o) £3,557 6f 3yds........... (4:05)

1240^{3} PRINCE SONGLINE [53] 8-0 W Woods (2) *hld up, came through to ld o'r one furlong out and ran on wl*. ....(9 to 2 op 7 to 1 tchd 5 to 1) 1

836 MISS GORGEOUS (Ire) [73] 9-3 (3*) Emma O'Gorman (1) *wth ldr till led 3 fs out, hdd o'r one furlong out, no extr ins fnl furlong*......................(14 to 1 tchd 16 to 1) 2

1059^{2} JULIET BRAVO [63] 8-10 G Duffield (3) *chsd ldrs, ev ch 2 fs out, unbl to quicken fnl furlong*. (5 to 2 fav op 7 to 2) 3

945^{8} SECOND CHANCE (Ire) [74] 9-7 W Newnes (4) *hdwy fnl 2 fs, kpt on final furlong*.................(8 to 1 op 6 to 1) 4

TAJDID (Ire) [56] 8-3 N Carlisle (7) *wth ldrs, rdn 2 fs out, no hdwy fnl furlong*........(8 to 1 op 7 to 1 tchd 9 to 1) 5

1352* PURBECK CENTENARY [59] 8-6 (6ex) J Quinn (8) *al prmnt, ran on one pace fnl 2 fs*. (7 to 2 op 3 to 1 tchd 4 to 1) 6

977 IOLITE [68] 9-1 M Hills (5) *hdwy o'r 2 fs out, one pace fnl furlong*.......................... (9 to 1 op 12 to 1) 7

DUKE OF BUDWORTH [58] 7-12 (7*) S Mulvey (6) *hdwy o'r 2 fs out, sn wknd*.................. (12 to 1 op 10 to 1) 8

802 ROSE FLYER (Ire) [55] 8-2 G Bardwell (10) *led 3 fs, wknd quickly o'r 2 furlongs out*........ (16 to 1 op 14 to 1) 9

Dist: 1½l, ½l, 1l, nk, 2l, hd, 2½l, 2l. 1m 14.30s. a 3.30s (9 Ran).

SR: 20/34/22/29/10/5/13/-/-/ (Keith Sturgis), R Boss

1456 EBF Breckland Maiden Stakes Class D (2-y-o) £4,127 6f 3yds........(4:40)

FIRST TRUMP 9-0 M Hills (1) *trkd ldrs, led jst o'r one furlong out and pushed out*. ....(5 to 4 fav tchd 7 to 4 and 2 to 1) 1

THE FLYING PHANTOM 8-7 (7*) S Mulvey (6) *wth ldrs, ev ch o'r one furlong out, unbl to quicken fnl furlong*. ....(20 to 1 op 14 to 1 tchd 25 to 1) 2

ICY HOT (Ire) 9-0 W Ryan (2) *wth ldrs, ev ch o'r one furlong out, no extr ins fnl furlong*.. (7 to 2 op 2 to 1) 3

YAWARA 8-9 W Newnes (5) *made most till hdd jst o'r one furlong out, no extr*.................(7 to 1 op 5 to 1) 4
BERNIE'S SISTER (Ire) 8-9 W Hood (4) *kpt on one pace fnl 2 fs*.................(16 to 1 op 14 to 1) 5
MIAMI HURRICANE (Ire) 9-0 M Tebbutt (7) *nvr trble ldrs*.................(14 to 1) 6
CAZANOVE'S PET 8-9 N Day (8) *no ch fnl 2 fs*.................(25 to 1 op 20 to 1) 7
1098³ STORM REGENT 9-0 W Woods (9) *effrt hfwy, sn btn*.................(20 to 1 tchd 25 to 1) 8
BSHEER (USA) 9-0 G Duffield (3) *wth ldrs, ev ch wl o'r one furlong out, wknd quickly*.................(7 to 2 op 7 to 4) 9

Dist: 1l, sht-hd, 1½l, 3l, 1½l, sht-hd, ¾l, ½l. 1m 14.80s. a 3.80s (9 Ran).
SR: 24/20/19/8/-/-/ (Mollers Racing), G Wragg

1457 Royal Anglian Regiment Limited Stakes Class F (0-60 4-y-o and up) £2,601 1¾m 17yds............. (5:15)

1173⁷ MIZYAN (Ire) 5-8-11 J Quinn (9) *hld up, hdwy 2 fs out, ran on strly to ld last strd*.................(5 to 1 op 4 to 1) 1
994 JULFAAR (USA) 6-8-11 G Bardwell (10) *hld up, hdwy 3 fs out, ran on wl to ld ins fnl furlong, jst ct*.................(16 to 1 op 8 to 1) 2
1242² DOYCE 4-8-6 M Hills (6) *hld up, hdwy 3 fs out, led o'r one furlong out, no extr nr finish*.................(9 to 2 op 3 to 1) 3
994 FATHER HAYES (USA) 5-8-11 N Day (3) *chsd ldr, slight ld o'r 4 fs out, hdd and wknd over one furlong out*.................(2 to 1 fav op 4 to 1 tchd 7 to 1) 4
1288⁵ BRIGGSMAID 5-8-6 M Tebbutt (7) *hld up, hdwy and ev ch 3 fs out, wknd 2 furlongs out*.................(5 to 1 op 3 to 1) 5
1248⁶ COSMIC DANCER 6-8-11 W Woods (4) *5th strt, nvr nr to chal*.................(20 to 1 op 12 to 1) 6
1146 DEBACLE (USA) 4-8-11 M Perrett (1) *chsd ldrs, 4th strt, wknd 3 fs out*.................(14 to 1 op 8 to 1) 7
967⁵ ARFEY (Ire) 4-8-11 G Duffield (8) *led and sn wnt clr, wknd o'r 5 fs out, hdd over 4 furlongs out, soon btn*.................(11 to 1 op 8 to 1) 8
857 BOLD RESOLUTION (Ire) 5-8-11 G Carter (5) *rcd mid-div, effrt 3 fs out, wknd 2 furlongs out*... (6 to 1 op 4 to 1) 9
1242⁴ CONCINNITY (USA) 4-8-11 A McGlone (2) *chsd ldrs, ran on one pace fnl 2 fs, wknd quickly*.................(9 to 1 op 12 to 1 tchd 7 to 1) 10

Dist: Sht-hd, hd, 5l, 5l, 2½l, 5l, ½l, 5l, 3l. 3m 4.40s. a 7.40s (10 Ran).
(E Carter), J E Banks

1458 Radio Norfolk Apprentice Handicap Class G (0-70 3-y-o and up) £2,343 1¼m 21yds........................ (5:50)

1210* LEXUS (Ire) [47] 5-7-12 (10*) Sarah Thompson (7) *rcd mid-div, gd hdwy 2 fs out, led ins fnl furlong and styd on wl*.................(3 to 1 op 5 to 2) 1
1281⁶ DOTS DEE [32] 4-7-3¹ (5*) A Whelan (1) *chsd ldrs, led 2 fs out, hdd and unbl to quicken wl ins fnl furlong*.................(50 to 1 op 33 to 1) 2
1392² WESTERN DYNASTY [66] 7-9-3 (10*,5ex) T Beaver (5) *led entering strt, hdd 2 fs out, kpt on fnl furlong*.................(11 to 4 fav op 9 to 4 tchd 3 to 1) 3
709³ QUALITAIR RHYTHM (Ire) [60] 5-9-4 (3*) G Mitchell (6) *hld up, ran on fnl 2 fs, not rch ldrs*.................(6 to 1 op 8 to 1 tchd 9 to 1) 4
4771a BALLERINA BAY [67] (v) 5-9-11 (3*) S Eiffert (4) *hld up, hdwy o'r 3 fs out, ev ch 2 furlongs out, ran on one pace*.................(12 to 1 op 8 to 1 tchd 14 to 1) 5
1237³ OVERPOWER [58] 9-8-9 (10*) S Allen (10) *hdwy 4 fs out, ev ch 2 furlongs out, sn rdn and btn*.... (4 to 1 op 9 to 2) 6
1269⁷ TURRET GATES [63] 4-9-0 (10*) P Devlin (9) *led one furlong, chsd ldr till wknd o'r 2 fs out*.......(14 to 1 op 6 to 1) 7
1232 ALICANTE [32] (bl) 6-7-2 (5*) M Baird (3) *al rear div*.................(50 to 1 op 33 to 1) 8
LE COUTEAU [65] (bl) 3-8-7 (6*) Sally Radford-Howes (8) *led aftr one furlong, hdd entering strt (5 fs out), wknd 3 furlongs out and sn beh*.................(12 to 1 op 7 to 1) 9
BARBARY REEF (Ire) [39] 5-8-0 D Gibbs (2) *prmnt till wknd 3 fs out, sn no ch*.......(8 to 1 op 10 to 1 tchd 7 to 1) 10

Dist: ½l, 2½l, 1l, 1½l, hd, 6l, 2½l, 1½l, 10l. 2m 8.20s. a 4.20s (10 Ran).
SR: 27/11/40/32/36/26/19/-/-/ (Marriott Stables Limited), R J R Williams

BEVERLEY (good to firm)
Thursday June 3rd

Going Correction: PLUS 0.10 sec. per fur. (races 1,2,4,6), MINUS 0.20 (3,5)

1459 Brantingham Rating Related Maiden Stakes Class E (3-y-o) £2,950 1m 100yds........................ (2:20)

1080³ MUTAKALLAM (USA) 9-0 R Hills (3) *made all, rdn 2 fs out, ran on wl und pres ins last*.................(13 to 8 fav op 7 to 4 tchd 6 to 4) 1
1090⁸ ALTA VICTORIA (Ire) 8-9 R Cochrane (6) *prmnt, hdwy to chal 2 out, sn rdn and wndrd, ev ch whn rdr drpd reins appr fnl furlong, no extr*............ (5 to 2 op 7 to 4) 2
441⁶ DESERT CHALLENGER (Ire) 9-0 A McGlone (2) *in tch, pushed alng and some hdwy 3 fs out, hrd drvn and no imprsn fnl 2 furlongs*.................(6 to 1 op 9 to 2) 3
MENA 8-9 G Carter (5) *hld up and beh, hdwy o'r 3 fs out, sn rdn and one pace fnl 2 furlongs*...(6 to 1 op 5 to 1) 4
1421⁶ BARSAL (Ire) 9-0 Dean McKeown (1) *in tch, rdn 3 fs out, sn wknd*.................(14 to 1 op 10 to 1) 5
1080⁸ STYLISH ROSE (Ire) 8-9 J Lowe (4) *chsd ldr, rdn o'r 3 fs out and sn wknd*.................(25 to 1 op 33 to 1) 6

Dist: 2l, 7l, 1½l, 5l, ¾l. 1m 48.10s. a 5.30s (6 Ran).
SR: 33/22/6/ (Hamdan Al-Maktoum), H Thomson Jones

1460 Touch Above Handicap Class E (0-70 3-y-o and up) £3,028 1m 1f 207yds ....(2:55)

1238* MISBELIEF [69] 3-9-0 (5ex) G Carter (7) *trkd ldrs, hdwy o'r 3 fs out, effrt to chal 2 furlongs out, sn led, rdn and ran on wl fnl furlong*... (6 to 4 fav op 7 to 4 tchd 15 to 8) 1
931* SUPERTOP [63] 5-9-7 Paul Eddery (4) *in tch, hdwy on inner o'r 2 fs out, rdn and styd on ins last*.................(6 to 1 tchd 7 to 1) 2
1284² TOUCH ABOVE [47] 7-8-5¹ R Cochrane (9) *led, rdn 2 fs out, sn hdd and kpt on one pace*.................(9 to 2 op 7 to 2 tchd 5 to 1) 3
931⁶ RED INDIAN [40] 7-7-12 Dale Gibson (5) *hld up, gd hdwy o'r 2 fs out, effrt and rdn appr fnl furlong, kpt on one pace*.................(16 to 1 op 14 to 1) 4
1304* DELPIOMBO [62] 7-9-6 (5ex) K Fallon (10) *trkd ldrs till lost pl o'r 4 fs out, effrt and swtchd one and a half furlongs out, sn rdn and styd on ins last*.................(5 to 1 op 9 to 2 tchd 6 to 1) 5
1414* SHARQUIN [42] 6-8-0 (5ex) K Darley (6) *chsd ldrs, hdwy o'r 3 fs out, rdn 2 furlongs out and sn wknd*.................(9 to 1 op 7 to 1 tchd 10 to 1) 6
INFERRING [45] 5-8-3 L Charnock (1) *hld up, hdwy on outer 3 fs out, sn rdn and btn 2 furlongs out*.................(40 to 1 op 33 to 1) 7
1307 EMPEROR ALEXANDER (Ire) [60] 5-9-1 (3*) S D Williams (2) *al rear*.................(33 to 1 op 25 to 1) 8
1284* COOL ENOUGH [36] 12-7-8 (5ex) A Mackay (3) *al rear*.................(14 to 1 op 10 to 1 tchd 16 to 1) 9
SUNTAN (Fr) [70] 4-10-0 M Birch (8) *cl up, rdn o'r 4 fs out and sn lost pl*.................(33 to 1 op 25 to 1) 10

Dist: 2l, nk, nk, sht-hd, 3½l, 3l, 3l, 10l, 15l. 2m 8.00s. a 6.60s (10 Ran).
SR: 44/47/30/22/43/16/13/22/-/ (T & J Vestey), J R Fanshawe

1461 GRP Massey Two Year Old Trophy Conditions Stakes Class C (2-y-o) £6,512 5f.................... (3:25)

1263* PETE AFRIQUE (Ire) 8-10 K Darley (7) *chsd ldrs, hdwy to ld 2 fs out, rdn clr appr fnl furlong, ran on*.................(9 to 2 tchd 5 to 1) 1
1381* OCHOS RIOS (Ire) 8-12 (2ex) J Fortune (3) *hmpd strt and beh, hdwy and not clr run o'r 2 fs out, swtchd and ran on strly ins last*.................(7 to 2 co-fav) 2
1310* HIGH DOMAIN (Ire) 9-2 J Reid (1) *in tch, effrt and hdwy to chase wnr one and a half fs out, sn rdn, edgd rght and one pace entering fnl furlong*. (7 to 2 co-fav op 3 to 1) 3
1182* MISTER BLOY 8-12 J Carroll (9) *cl up, ev ch 2 fs out, sn rdn and wknd*.................(9 to 1 op 8 to 1 tchd 10 to 1) 4
374* BOLD ARISTOCRAT (Ire) 8-10 S Perks (5) *slwly into strd, sn chasing ldrs on outer, rdn 2 fs out and one pace*.................(9 to 1 op 7 to 1) 5
1381⁸ TOP SHOW (Ire) 8-12 J Lowe (2) *chsd ldrs, rdn o'r 2 fs out and sn btn*.................(33 to 1 op 25 to 1) 6
998⁷ HILTONS TRAVEL (Ire) (v) 8-10 S Webster (4) *al rear*.................(25 to 1 op 20 to 1 tchd 33 to 1) 7
1135* GROTTO POOL (USA) 8-12 P Robinson (6) *prmnt till rdn and wknd 2 fs out*.................(7 to 2 co-fav op 3 to 1) 8
1182² WARTHILL WHISPERS 8-5 G Carter (8) *led, hdd and wknd 2 fs out*.................(20 to 1 op 16 to 1) 9

Dist: 2l, 1½l, 3l, 1½l, nk, ¾l, 1l, 7l. 1m 4.00s. a 2.30s (9 Ran).
SR: 30/24/22/6/-/-/ (P D Savill), M W Easterby

1462 108th Year of the Watt Memorial Conditions Stakes Class D (4-y-o and up) £3,625 1m 3f 216yds........... (4:00)

1206* ANNA OF SAXONY 4-8-9 J Reid (2) *made virtually all, easily*........(15 to 2 on op 9 to 1 on tchd 7 to 1 on) 1
BOLD PURSUIT (Ire) 4-8-11 K Fallon (3) *trkd wnr, pushed alng to take clr order 3 fs out, rdn 2 furlongs out, sn one pace and no ch wth winner*.........(7 to 1 op 6 to 1) 2

Won by 3½l. 2m 44.80s. a 13.80s (2 Ran).
SR: -/-/ (Sheikh Mohammed), J H M Gosden

1463 Figham Apprentice Maiden Handicap Stakes Class E (0-75 3-y-o and up) £1,725 5f...................... (4:35)

1232 NORDOORA (Ire) [35] 4-8-7 (5*) G Strange (9) *made all, rdn appr fnl furlong, ran on wl*.................(16 to 1 op 12 to 1 tchd 20 to 1) 1

1230[7] MISS BRIGHTSIDE [37] 5-9-0 G Forster (5) *cl up, rdn and ev ch ins fnl furlong, not quicken nr finish.* ....(9 to 2 op 11 to 2 tchd 6 to 1) 2
1196[4] LIDA'S DELIGHT (Ire) [57] 3-9-7 (5*) P Johnson (1) *chsd ldrs, rdn 2 fs out, kpt on one pace*........(6 to 1 op 5 to 1) 3
1300[2] CLANROCK [59] (v) 3-9-11 (3*) G Parkin (8) *chsd ldrs, rdn 2 fs out, wknd appr last*........(5 to 2 fav tchd 11 to 4) 4
361[2] GUSSIE FINK-NOTTLE (Ire) [59] 3-10-0 V Halliday (3) *cl up, rdn o'r 2 fs out, sn btn*..............(13 to 2 op 5 to 1) 5
634[8] LUCKY MILL [50] 3-9-5 D Wright (4) *al rear.* ....(8 to 1 op 7 to 1) 6
1157[5] HUMBER'S SUPREME (Ire) [55] (bl) 3-9-5 (5*) L Aspell (6) *dwlt, hdwy hfwy, sn rdn, nvr dngrs.* (9 to 2 op 4 to 1) 7
711[9] GROGFRYN [59] 3-9-9 (5*) Ruth Coulter (7) *in tch, sn rdn and beh frm hfwy*.................................(12 to 1) 8
1273 BECKYHANNAH [40] 3-8-9 H Bastiman (2) *al rear.* (20 to 1) 9
Dist: Hd, 3½l, 2½l, hd, 2½l, sht-hd, 2½l, dd-ht. 1m 4.10s. a 2.40s (9 Ran).
SR: 30/31/29/21/20/1/5/-/-/ (David C Young), J L Harris

1464 Etton Maiden Stakes Class D (3-y-o and up) £3,435 1m 100yds...... (5:10)

817[3] SOLOMON'S DANCER (USA) 3-8-10 Dean McKeown (9) *trkd ldrs, pushed alng 2 fs out, rdn and styd on to ld wl ins last, ran on well.* ....(13 to 2 op 7 to 1 tchd 8 to 1 and 6 to 1) 1
854[5] LANDRAIL (USA) 3-8-5 D Holland (4) *trkd ldr, rdn 2 fs out and sn led, hdd and one pace wl ins last.* ....(7 to 2 op 5 to 2) 2
1275[3] CIVIL LAW (Ire) 3-8-10 W Ryan (3) *chsd ldrs, effrt 2 fs out, sn rdn and kpt on one pace.* ....(11 to 2 op 9 to 2 tchd 13 to 2) 3
MUFID (USA) 4-9-7 K Darley (8) *beh, steady hdwy o'r 2 fs out, sn rdn, styd on ins last, nrst finish.* ....(50 to 1 op 16 to 1) 4
1109[4] FLASHELLA (Ire) 3-8-5 J Lowe (6) *led, rdn 3 fs out, hdd entering fnl 2 furlongs, sn wknd*...(20 to 1 op 12 to 1) 5
1212[3] JURA FOREST 3-8-10 P Robinson (1) *dwlt, sn wth ldrs, rdn 3 fs out, wknd 2 out.* ....(6 to 5 fav op 11 to 10 on tchd 5 to 4) 6
1275 GREY ANCONA (Ire) 4-9-7 M Wood (2) *in tch, rdn 3 fs out, sn wknd*.........................(100 to 1 op 50 to 1) 7
4718a[3] JAMAICA BRIDGE 3-8-10 K Fallon (7) *al rear.* ....(20 to 1 op 16 to 1) 8
1416 SHALAKO 3-8-4[1] (7*) L Aspell (5) *prmnt to hfwy, sn rdn alng and lost pl*..................(50 to 1 op 33 to 1) 9
Dist: 2l, 1½l, 3½l, 3l, ½l, 6l, ¾l, 5l. 1m 48.40s. a 5.60s (9 Ran).
SR: 25/14/14/14/-/-/ (D D Hart), W W Haigh

CHANTILLY (FR) (soft)
Thursday June 3rd

1465 Prix du Gros-Chene (Group 2) (3-y-o and up) £35,842 5f..............(2:50)

1117[3] SURPRISE OFFER (bl) 3-8-9 B Raymond (2) *rcd in second, led one out till ins fnl furlong, rallied to ld on line.* ....(29 to 1) 1
1011[2] MONDE BLEU 5-9-2 S Guillot (6) *slwly away, plenty to do 3 fs out, str run to ld ins fnl furlong, hdd on line.* ....(10 to 7 on) 2
1406[4] LOCHSONG 5-8-13 F Head (1) *led till one furlong out, no extr*..(32 to 10) 3
1011* ROBIN DES PINS (USA) 5-9-2 C Asmussen (3) *slwly away, wl beh 3 fs out, ran on fnl 2, nvr nrr*........ (22 to 10) 4
ANOTHER CHARGER (Ire) (bl) 4-8-13 M Boutin (4) *mid-div till outpcd 2 fs out*.............................(18 to 1) 5
MAMMA'S TOO 4-8-9 M Hofer (7) *slwly away, al beh.* ....(19 to 1) 6
Dist: Sht-hd, 1½l, 1½l, 6l, sht-nk. 58.60s. a 1.10s (6 Ran).
SR: 68/74/65/62/35/30/ (Lord Carnarvon), R Hannon

CLONMEL (IRE) (good)
Thursday June 3rd

1466 Comeragh (Fillies) Maiden (3-y-o) £2,245 1½m................... (7:00)

982[5] DRIFT APART (Ire) 9-0 W J O'Connor (2)...........(5 to 1) 1
1250[3] HOPESVILLE (Ire) 9-0 M J Kinane (3)..........(2 to 1 fav) 2
1140[4] TEBRE (USA) (bl) 9-0 W J Supple (6)...............(3 to 1) 3
1250[6] DARK HYACINTH (Ire) 9-0 R Hughes (4).............(14 to 1) 4
870[6] GREEN LIFE 9-0 C Roche (7).........................(7 to 2) 5
EGALITE (Ire) 8-12 (2*) D G O'Shea (1)............ (20 to 1) 6
1236 RYE HILL QUEEN (Ire) 9-0 D Manning (5).......... (50 to 1) 7
Dist: 2l, 1½l, hd, 1l. 2m 50.90s. (7 Ran).
(Yoshiki Akazawa), P Aspell

1467 Ballymacarbry Maiden (4-y-o and up) £2,245 2m..................... (7:30)

PADASHPAN (USA) 4-8-8 (6*) J J Behan (4).........(7 to 2) 1
LAST GOODBYE 7-8-8 (6*) P P Murphy (14)...... (20 to 1) 2
1141[2] CRAZY GAIL 6-8-5 (6*) J A Heffernan (1).......... (6 to 1) 3
851[3] SHAREEF ALLIANCE (Ire) 4-9-0 W J Supple (5).... (8 to 1) 4
CARES OF TOMORROW 6-9-0 C Roche (7)...... (10 to 1) 5
1141[5] CEDAR COURT (Ire) (bl) 5-9-0 N Byrne (8).........(8 to 1) 6
1140[2] CAMDEN BUZZ (Ire) 5-8-11 S Craine (6).......(5 to 4 fav) 7
SHAYISTA 8-8-3 (8*) R T Fitzpatrick (13)..........(20 to 1) 8
961[5] UPPINGHAM 7-9-0 K J Manning (11)............ (33 to 1) 9
1295 KARABAKH (Ire) 4-9-0 J F Egan (10).............(50 to 1) 10
FARMER'S CROSS 9-9-0 P Shanahan (15)....... (25 to 1) 11
BROWN TOP 6-8-6 (8*) B Fenton (12)............(50 to 1) 12
FESTIVAL DREAMS 8-9-0 W J O'Connor (3)...... (14 to 1) 13
PHARACH (Ire) 4-9-0 N G McCullagh (2)......... (20 to 1) 14
Dist: 3l, 2½l, 1½l, 1½l. 3m 51.90s. (14 Ran).
(William Brennan), W P Mullins

1468 Clonmel Chemicals Tipperary Cup Handicap (0-90 4-y-o and up) £3,625 2m..........................(8:00)

281[5] SHANKORAK [-] 6-8-2 W J Supple (8).........(3 to 1 fav) 1
1013[3] MRS BARTON (Ire) [-] 5-8-3 J F Egan (5).......... (6 to 1) 2
CLIVEDEN GAIL (Ire) [-] 4-9-3 M J Kinane (12)......(7 to 1) 3
BANAIYKA (Ire) [-] 4-9-1 S Craine (4).............(10 to 1) 4
1025[5] MASAI WARRIOR [-] 6-8-12 (2*) R M Burke (6)..... (5 to 1) 5
4685a NANARCH (USA) [-] 9-7-11 (8*) R T Fitzpatrick (2).. (20 to 1) 6
807[9] LACKEL (Ger) [-] 5-9-10 C Roche (7)...............(12 to 1) 7
4685a DESERT SQUAW [-] 6-8-12 (2*) D G O'Shea (14).. (10 to 1) 8
4686a[2] THATCH AND GOLD (Ire) [-] 5-8-11 (6*) J R Barry (9) (10 to 1) 9
1235 ALL YOURS (Ire) [-] (bl) 4-8-11 P Shanahan (11)... (33 to 1) 10
WESBEST (Ire) [-] 4-8-4 N G McCullagh (13)...... (12 to 1) 11
961[3] CURRENCY BASKET (Ire) [-] 4-9-10 C F Swan (10) (12 to 1) 12
706 TIME IS UP (Ire) [-] 4-7-8 (4*) W J Smith (3)....... (12 to 1) 13
Dist: 3½l, 1l, nk, sht-hd. 3m 47.90s. (13 Ran).
(E J O'Mahony), Francis Berry

EPSOM (good)
Thursday June 3rd

Going Correction: MINUS 0.15 sec. per fur. (races 1,2,3,4,6), MINUS 0.40 (5)

1469 Nightingall Maiden Stakes Class D (3-y-o) £3,590 1¼m 18yds......... (2:00)

947[7] FABULOUS MTOTO 9-0 M Roberts (8) *took str hold in rear, pld wide and hdwy frm 2 fs out, styd on wl to ld cl hme*...................(4 to 1 op 7 to 2 tchd 9 to 2) 1
876 SING A RAINBOW (Ire) 8-9 A Munro (2) *gd hdwy on rls frm 3 fs out, led o'r 2 furlongs out, rdn fnl furlong, ct wl ins last*................(14 to 1 op 16 to 1 tchd 12 to 1) 2
1027[4] GREENBANK (USA) 9-0 L Dettori (9) *hld up, drvn and hdwy ins fnl 2 fs, one pace inside last.* ....(9 to 4 fav op 2 to 1 tchd 7 to 4) 3
1256[2] ICE REBEL 9-0 W Newnes (1) *led till hdd o'r 2 fs out, sn one pace*..............(9 to 1 op 8 to 1 tchd 12 to 1) 4
1060[7] CLEVER MINSTREL (USA) 9-0 M Perrett (7) *sn chasing ldrs, rdn 2 fs out, no imprsn.* ....(16 to 1 op 12 to 1 tchd 20 to 1) 5
1344 MELLERIO 8-11 (3*) D Harrison (3) *beh till hdwy 3 fs out, one pace fnl 2 furlongs*...........(33 to 1 op 25 to 1) 6
FOOLS ERRAND (Ire) 9-0 T Quinn (5) *beh, effrt 3 fs out, fdd 2 furlongs out*.........(13 to 2 op 9 to 2 tchd 7 to 1) 7
1067[6] WARSPITE 9-0 Pat Eddery (4) *chsd ldrs till wknd 2 fs out.* .... (11 to 2 op 5 to 1 tchd 6 to 1) 8
1315[4] WINNING APPEAL (Fr) 8-9 W R Swinburn (6) *chsd ldr till rdn and wknd ins fnl 2 fs*.........(16 to 1 op 12 to 1) 9
Dist: 1½l, 5l, 3½l, 1½l, hd, 1½l, 2½l, 2l. 2m 9.21s. a 4.91s (9 Ran).
SR: 36/28/23/16/13/12/9/4/-/ (Sheikh Ahmed Al Maktoum), D R C Elsworth

1470 Energizer Battery Maiden Stakes Class D (3-y-o) £3,622 6f........(2:30)

1278[4] DOMULLA 9-0 T Quinn (6) *chsd ldr 3 fs out, led one and a half furlongs out, drvn and kpt on wl.* ....(5 to 2 fav op 2 to 1 tchd 11 to 4) 1
1132[9] VILLAVINA 8-9 M Roberts (4) *in tch, rdn o'r 2 fs out, styd on wl fnl furlong, no extr cl hme.* (14 to 1 tchd 16 to 1) 2
1313[2] TONY'S MIST 9-0 Pat Eddery (3) *beh till styd on o'r 2 fs out, kpt on fnl furlong*.. (7 to 2 op 3 to 1 tchd 4 to 1) 3
THE BETHANIAN 9-0 A Munro (8) *led 4 fs out, rdn o'r 2 furlongs out, hdd one and a half furlongs out, sn outpcd*..........................(10 to 1 tchd 14 to 1) 4
1132[8] CHILI LADY 8-9 W R Swinburn (7) *nvr gng pace of ldrs.* .... (13 to 2 op 6 to 1 tchd 9 to 1) 5
1132 EISHRELA 8-9 J Williams (5) *al outpcd.* ....(33 to 1 tchd 50 to 1) 6
1057[4] TARTIB (Ire) 9-0 W Carson (9) *al beh and outpcd.* ....(9 to 2 op 3 to 1) 7
326[8] WILL'S LEGACY 8-11 (3*) D Harrison (2) *sn outpcd.* ....(16 to 1 op 14 to 1 tchd 25 to 1) 8
1136[9] MIL BESOS 8-9 G Duffield (1) *sn drvn into ld, hdd 4 fs out, wknd frm 3 furlongs out*.........(33 to 1 tchd 50 to 1) 9
Dist: ½l, 5l, hd, 5l, ¾l, 7l, 1½l, nk. 1m 10.50s. a 2.60s (9 Ran).
SR: 30/23/8/7/-/-/ (A W Boon), R Akehurst

1471 Energizer Conditions Stakes Class D (3-y-o and up) £4,558 1m 114yds (3:00)

1003[2] PETER DAVIES (USA) 5-9-2 L Dettori (7) *smooth hdwy frm o'r 2 fs out, quickened wl to ld last strds.* ....(3 to 1 op 2 to 1 tchd 7 to 2) 1
1029[8] POWERFUL EDGE 4-9-4 T Quinn (2) *in tch, chsd ldrs 3 fs out, led appr fnl furlong, sn drvn, ct last strds.* ....(5 to 2 fav op 6 to 4) 2
393[2] ZIMZALABIM 3-8-7 W Carson (6) *chsd ldr 6 fs out till led 2 and a half furlongs out, hdd appr fnl furlong, sn outpcd.*..........(11 to 4 op 3 to 1 tchd 5 to 2) 3
NASHVILLE BLUES (Ire) 4-9-3 M Hills (1) *beh, hdwy o'r 2 fs out, rdn over one furlong out, fdd ins last.* ....(9 to 1 op 8 to 1 tchd 10 to 1) 4
1090* DANNY BOY 3-8-9 Pat Eddery (3) *chsd ldr o'r 2 fs, wknd over two furlongs out..* (5 to 1 op 8 to 1 tchd 10 to 1) 5
1210[4] DON'T GIVE UP (bl) 5-8-9 (7*) N Varley (5) *al beh.* ....(100 to 1 tchd 200 to 1) 6
1238[7] ANATROCCOLO 6-9-1 W Newnes (4) *led till hdd 2 and a half fs out, wknd quickly*..... (100 to 1 tchd 200 to 1) 7
Dist: Hd, 4l, nk, 4l, 3l, 4l. 1m 43.73s. a 1.73s (7 Ran).
SR: 57/58/35/44/24/22/9/ (Lucayan Stud), D R Loder

1472 Ever Ready Coronation Cup Class A (Group 1) (4-y-o and up) £84,078 1½m 10yds.......................... (3:40)

810[2] OPERA HOUSE 5-9-0 M Roberts (7) *beh, hdwy o'r 2 fs out, hrd drvn fnl furlong and ran on wl to ld last strds.* ....(9 to 4 jt-fav op 6 to 4) 1
1049[6] ENVIRONMENT FRIEND 5-9-0 M Hills (3) *hdwy 3 fs out, led one and a half furlongs out, kpt on wl und pres till ct last strds, fnshd 3rd, plcd second.* ....(16 to 1 op 20 to 1 tchd 14 to 1) 2
1124[2] APPLE TREE (Fr) (bl) 4-9-0 T Jarnet (5) *trkd ldrs, led 2 and a half fs out, hdd one and a half out str chal, edgd lft, ct last strd, fnshd 2nd, plcd 3rd.* ....(11 to 2 op 5 to 1 tchd 7 to 1) 3
4728a[6] USER FRIENDLY 4-8-11 G Duffield (8) *pld hrd early, hdwy 3 fs out, rdn and hng badly lft ins fnl 2 furlongs, not reco'r.*.......... (9 to 4 jt-fav op 11 to 4 tchd 7 to 2) 4
1018[5] SPRING 4-8-11 W Carson (6) *prmnt till outpcd frm o'r 2 fs out.*..........(14 to 1 tchd 16 to 1) 5
892[3] ZINAAD 4-9-0 W R Swinburn (4) *chsd ldr till chlgd frm 5 fs out till wknd o'r 2 furlongs out.* ....(8 to 1 op 7 to 1 tchd 9 to 1) 6
1049[7] SILVER WISP (USA) 4-9-0 Pat Eddery (1) *led till hdd 2 and a half fs out, sn wknd.*..........(14 to 1 tchd 16 to 1) 7
1049[4] GARDEN OF HEAVEN (USA) 4-9-0 T Quinn (2) *prmnt, styd far side, wknd 3 fs out.*..........(20 to 1 tchd 25 to 1) 8
Dist: Hd, sht-hd, 5l, 6l, nk, 10l, 25l. 2m 35.13s. b 0.37s (8 Ran).
SR: 86/84/85/71/59/61/41/-/ (Sheikh Mohammed), M R Stoute

1473 Stanley Wootton Handicap Class D (0-80 3-y-o and up) £5,435 5f.... (4:10)

BORN TO BE [71] 4-9-7 M Roberts (7) *prmnt, led 2 fs out, hrd drvn and hld on wl fnl furlong.* ....(20 to 1 op 16 to 1 tchd 25 to 1) 1
1036[8] MISS VAXETTE [73] 4-9-2 (7*) M Humphries (3) *dwlt, hdwy 2 fs out, str chal fnl furlong, jst fld*...(10 to 1 op 8 to 1) 2
1352[2] STOCKTINA [43] 6-7-7 J Quinn (11) *hdwy 2 fs out, ev ch ins last, one pace*..........(14 to 1 op 12 to 1) 3
4796a[6] VERY DICEY [73] 5-9-9 W Woods (5) *trkd ldrs, chlgd 2 fs out till one pace fnl furlong*....... (16 to 1 op 14 to 1) 4
1096 GALLANT HOPE [49] (bl) 11-7-8[2] (7*) D McCabe (9) *beh and outpcd till ran on frm o'r one furlong out.* ....(8 to 1 op 10 to 1) 5
1066 MARTINA [68] 5-9-1 (3*) D Harrison (6) *hdwy ins fnl 2 fs, ran on*..........(5 to 1 fav op 6 to 1) 6
1249[5] PEERAGE PRINCE [67] (bl) 4-9-3 A Munro (1) *chsd ldrs till no imprsn fnl 2 fs.*.... (13 to 2 op 6 to 1 tchd 7 to 1) 7
MIAMI BANKER [49] (bl) 7-7-13 N Carlisle (12) *pressed ldrs 3 fs*..........(14 to 1 op 20 to 1) 8
1147[6] SOBER LAD (Ire) [73] (bl) 3-9-1 T Quinn (8) *led one furlong, styd prmnt till wknd 2 fs out.* ....(11 to 2 op 5 to 1 tchd 6 to 1) 9
815[5] LOVE RETURNED [76] 6-9-12 M Tebbutt (2) *speed o'r 3 fs.* ....(8 to 1) 10
1148[5] TEE-EMM [55] 3-7-11 C Rutter (4) *led aftr one furlong till hdd and wknd 2 fs out*.......... (12 to 1 op 10 to 1) 11
1127 LETSBEONESTABOUTIT [70] 7-8-13 (7*) B Russell (10) *al outpcd.*..........(16 to 1 op 14 to 1 tchd 20 to 1) 12
Dist: Sht-hd, 1l, 1½l, 1l, sht-hd, ¾l, nk, ¾l, hd, 2½l. 55.47s. a 0.77s (12 Ran).
SR: 52/53/19/43/15/33/29/10/23/ (J A Redmond), S Dow

1474 Staff Ingham Handicap Class D (0-80 3-y-o and up) £3,915 1m 114yds. (4:45)

1280* DEEVEE [51] 4-8-1[2] (4ex) G Duffield (2) *beh, plenty to do 2 fs out, drvn and rapid hdwy appr fnl furlong, led last strds*..........(8 to 1 op 7 to 1) 1
1120[4] DANCING SENSATION (USA) [43] 6-7-7 J Quinn (1) *trkd ldrs till led o'r 2 fs out, rdn fnl furlong, ct last strds.* ....(6 to 1 fav op 5 to 1 tchd 13 to 2) 2
1280[3] PROUD BRIGADIER (Ire) [58] 5-8-8 T Quinn (6) *al chasing ldrs, ev ch one furlong out, kpt on*... (7 to 1 op 6 to 1) 3
1120[5] DANCING BEAU (Ire) [47] 4-7-11 F Norton (8) *hdwy 3 fs out, rdn and kpt on frm o'r one furlong out.* ....(16 to 1 op 14 to 1 tchd 20 to 1) 4
754[9] ROYAL DARTMOUTH (USA) [50] 8-7-11 (3*) D Harrison (4) *beh till hdwy o'r 2 fs out, kpt on fnl furlong.* ....(10 to 1 tchd 11 to 1) 5
1130[5] NOBBY BARNES [59] 4-8-9 L Piggott (12) *sn in tch, shaken up and lost touch o'r 2 fs out.* ....(13 to 2 op 5 to 1 tchd 7 to 1) 6
1270[5] MERLINS WISH (USA) [76] (v) 4-9-12 Pat Eddery (9) *nvr rchd ldrs*..........(10 to 1 tchd 11 to 1) 7
1130[3] DASWAKI (Can) [68] 5-9-4 B Rouse (7) *chsd ldrs till wknd o'r 2 fs out*.......... (8 to 1 op 7 to 1 tchd 9 to 1) 8
1130* KINGCHIP BOY [55] (v) 4-8-5 D Biggs (5) *rcd alone far side, effrt o'r 2 fs out, sn wknd.* ....(8 to 1 op 7 to 1 tchd 9 to 1) 9
1130[6] SALBYNG [57] 5-8-7 L Dettori (3) *beh, effrt o'r 2 fs out, sn wknd*..........(9 to 1 op 8 to 1 tchd 10 to 1) 10
771 BLOCKADE (USA) [78] 4-10-0 M Hills (11) *led till hdd and wknd o'r 2 fs out*..........(20 to 1) 11
1204[9] WAHEM (Ire) [75] 3-8-13 M Roberts (10) *effrt 5 fs out, sn wknd*.......... (10 to 1 tchd 11 to 1) 12
Dist: Hd, ½l, ½l, ¾l, 8l, 1l, 1½l, ¾l, 1½l, ¾l. 1m 44.55s. a 2.55s (12 Ran).
SR: 30/21/34/21/22/7/21/8/-/ (D Turner), C J Benstead

CATTERICK (good)
Friday June 4th
Going Correction: MINUS 0.20 sec. per fur.

1475 'Cliffe' Maiden Fillies Stakes Class D (2-y-o) £3,231 5f................(2:20)

EVENING FALLS 8-11 K Darley (2) *broke wl, made all, clr o'r one furlong out, shaken up and styd on strly.* ....(16 to 1 op 12 to 1 tchd 20 to 1) 1
984[6] CERTIFICATE-X 8-11 Dean McKeown (1) *dwlt, sn rdn alng and in tch, effrt 2 fs out, kpt on ins last, no ch wth wnr.* ....(6 to 4 op 6 to 5) 2
1272[3] KAYDARAJ 8-11 M Birch (4) *chsd ldrs, drvn alng o'r 2 fs out, not quicken over one out.* ....(5 to 4 fav op 6 to 4 tchd 6 to 5) 3
BOLD TIME MONKEY 8-11 J Carroll (3) *in tch, sn pushed alng, effrt hfwy, no imprsn.* ....(15 to 2 op 5 to 1 tchd 8 to 1) 4
BALLARD RING (Ire) 8-11 L Charnock (6) *slwly into strd, beh and sn pushed alng, took clr order aftr 2 fs, hng lft and soon btn*..........(25 to 1 op 16 to 1) 5
1078[8] CONEY HILLS 8-11 A Culhane (5) *in tch, pushed alng, wknd quickly frm hfwy*.......... (16 to 1 op 10 to 1) 6
Dist: 2l, 3½l, 2l, 5l, 10l. 1m 0.60s. a 3.10s (6 Ran).
SR: 15/7/-/ (Mrs Carol J Welch), J L Spearing

1476 'Lambert Trot' Handicap Class D (0-80 3-y-o and up) £3,172 1½m 44yds (2:50)

1439[8] KINOKO [59] 5-8-12 K Darley (1) *steadied strt, patiently rdn, prog entering strt, ran on to ld appr fnl furlong, pushed out ins last*.....(15 to 8 op 6 to 4 tchd 2 to 1) 1
1305[2] BOLD AMBITION [40] 6-7-7 J Lowe (4) *led, rdn alng o'r 3 fs out, hdd appr last, one pace*....... (9 to 4 tchd 5 to 2) 2
1336[6] BIGWHEEL BILL (Ire) [75] 4-10-0 M Birch (2) *trkd ldr, pushed alng 4 fs out, came wide strt, not quicken fnl 2 furlongs*..........(7 to 4 fav) 3
SUPER BLUES [47] 6-8-0 J Fanning (3) *in tch, effrt and rdn o'r 3 fs out, wknd over one out*.... (16 to 1 op 10 to 1) 4
Dist: 2l, 2l, 1½l. 2m 40.10s. a 5.10s (4 Ran).
SR: 23/-/31/-/ (Anthony White), K W Hogg

1477 'Rapier' Claiming Stakes Class F (3-y-o) £2,444 1m 5f 175yds........(3:20)

1191* GOODBYE MILLIE 8-3 (5*) O Pears (4) *chsd ldrs on outsd, took clr order 4 fs out, rdn entering strt, led o'r one out, kpt on wl*..........(11 to 8 fav op 6 to 4 tchd 7 to 4) 1
1283[2] MOUNTAIN WILLOW 8-3 J Fortune (7) *led til hdd o'r one furlong out, not quicken ins last*.....(9 to 2 op 4 to 1) 2
499* MRS SNUGGS (Ire) 8-1 (7*) S Mulvey (5) *hld up in tch, drvn alng 5 fs out, improved o'r one out, edgd lft and kpt on ins last*..........(7 to 2 op 5 to 2) 3
1275 ON BROADWAY 8-10 J Fanning (1) *hld up in tch, shaken up o'r one furlong out, nvr plcd to chal.* ....(25 to 1 op 20 to 1) 4
1283[4] NANCY (Ire) 7-11 L Charnock (3) *trkd ldrs on ins, drvn alng 4 fs out, wknd o'r 2 out.* ....(12 to 1 op 14 to 1 tchd 16 to 1) 5
1093 DIG IN THE RIBS (Ire) 8-10 K Darley (6) *trkd ldrs, pushed alng hfwy, lost pl appr strt, sn btn*...(5 to 1 op 7 to 2) 6
928 ASTRAC TRIO (USA) 8-11 J Carroll (2) *hld up in last pl, rdn alng o'r 5 fs out, sn lost tch*........(50 to 1 op 33 to 1) 7
Dist: Nk, 1½l, 1l, 3l, 6l, ½l. 3m 0.70s. a 5.20s (7 Ran).
SR: 15/9/11/11/ (Lintscan Ltd (Corbett Bookmakers)), S G Norton

1478 Ronald Freeman Jewellers & Breitling Handicap Class D (0-80 3-y-o) £3,348 5f.............................. (3:50)

1273[8] CALL ME I'M BLUE (Ire) [63] 8-10 M Birch (1) *made all, clr o'r one furlong out, styd on strly*.... (5 to 1 op 9 to 2) 1
1187[2] FIRST OPTION [71] 9-4 K Darley (4) *chsd ldrs, effrt 2 fs out, not quicken ins last*. ....(3 to 1 tchd 100 to 30 and 11 to 4) 2
1083[6] MAGIC ORB [74] 9-7 Dean McKeown (6) *swrvd leaving stalls, in tch, pushed alng hfwy, edgd lft fnl furlong, not quicken*..............(7 to 1 tchd 8 to 1) 3
1287[2] COCONUT JOHNNY [56] (bl) 8-3 J Fanning (3) *nvr far away, effrt and rdn hfwy, sn btn*. ....(7 to 4 fav op 6 to 4 tchd 15 to 8) 4
1157[7] CHARITY EXPRESS (Ire) [66] 8-13 T Lucas (2) *slwly into strd, wl beh til styd on o'r one furlong out, nrrst finish*. .... (20 to 1 op 14 to 1) 5
1151[2] LOCAL HEROINE [71] 9-4 J Carroll (5) *in tch, drvn alng o'r 2 fs out, sn btn*....................(11 to 2 op 5 to 1) 6
Dist: 4l, 2½l, 2l, 1½l, 1½l. 59.00s. a 1.50s (6 Ran).
SR: 46/38/31/5/9/8/ (Harsh (Tipping Gears)), N Tinkler

1479 '25th Silver Streak' Rating Related Maiden Stakes Class F (0-60 3-y-o and up) £2,534 1½m 44yds.........(4:20)

1161[3] DUPLICATE 3-8-6 M Birch (2) *chsd ldrs, improved to ld o'r 2 fs out, drvn out ins last*......(5 to 4 fav tchd 11 to 8) 1
1266[3] FLAMING MIRACLE (Ire) (bl) 3-8-6 C Rutter (3) *in tch, effrt entering strt, sn ev ch, edgd lft fnl furlong, kpt on same pace*............................ (7 to 4 op 6 to 4) 2
1133[8] TTYFRAN 3-8-6 S Perks (4) *slwly into strd, rstrained in rear, improved o'r 3 fs out, no room frm over one out, kpt on ins last*.................. (16 to 1 op 14 to 1) 3
733 SOLO CHARTER 3-7-13 (7*) S Mulvey (5) *missed break, sn jnd pack, improved frm rear 4 fs out, rdn and hng lft o'r one out, no extr*..................... (7 to 1 op 5 to 1) 4
1259[4] SHARE A MOMENT (Can) 3-8-6 K Darley (6) *nvr far away, led 4 fs out, hdd o'r 2 out, wknd one out*. ....(8 to 1 op 6 to 1) 5
1156 BARGEE (USA) 4-9-8 R Lappin (1) *led till hdd 4 fs out, sn rdn alng, lost tch entering strt, tld off*. .... (66 to 1 op 33 to 1) 6
1038[9] NASHOON (Ire) 4-9-5 (3*) S Maloney (7) *hld up in tch, drvn alng hfwy, sn btn, tld off*........ (100 to 1 op 50 to 1) 7
Dist: 2l, 1½l, ½l, 1½l, dist, hd. 2m 43.30s. a 8.30s (7 Ran).
(G H Leatham), M H Easterby

1480 Leslie Petch Handicap Class E (0-70 3-y-o and up) £3,054 5f 212yds.. (4:50)

1167[2] KILLY'S FILLY [52] 3-8-12 J Carroll (12) *nvr far away, rdn to ld o'r one furlong out, ran on gmely whn hrd pressed wl ins last*..........................(7 to 1 op 6 to 1) 1
1059[5] FACE THE FUTURE [57] 4-9-12 M Birch (8) *mid-div, effrt 2 fs out, edgd lft appr fnl furlong, chlgd wl ins last, jst fld*.................. (9 to 2 fav op 4 to 1 tchd 5 to 1) 2
1228[5] SOBERING THOUGHTS [47] 7-8-11 (5*) O Pears (4) *reared leaving stalls, improved into midfield hfwy, drvn alng 2 fs out, kpt on same pace ins last*............. (6 to 1) 3
1416[3] MANX MONARCH [46] 3-8-1 (5*) A Garth (6) *mid-div, came wide strt, sn rdn, kpt on ins last*..... (8 to 1 op 7 to 1) 4
1230[2] PARFAIT AMOUR [58] 4-9-13 A Culhane (3) *mid-div, effrt and rdn appr strt, kpt on same pace ins fnl furlong*. .... (11 to 2 op 9 to 2) 5
1419* MU-ARRIK [48] (bl) 5-8-10 (7*,4ex) G Parkin (5) *chsd ldrs, rdn 2 fs out, one pace fnl furlong*. .... (11 to 2 op 9 to 2 tchd 6 to 1) 6
1287[4] MASTER POKEY [57] 9-9-5 (7*) P Johnson (2) *in tch, rdn alng 2 fs out, swtchd entering fnl furlong, not quicken*. ....(7 to 1 op 6 to 1) 7
ZINGER [28] 5-7-11 J Fanning (1) *al prmnt, ev ch o'r one furlong out, sn btn*..................(50 to 1 op 33 to 1) 8
1167[5] MEESON TIMES [50] (v) 5-9-5 K Darley (9) *sn led, came wide strt, hdd o'r one furlong out, soon btn*. .... (33 to 1 op 20 to 1) 9
970 COMPANY CASH [43] 5-8-12 Dean McKeown (7) *beh, drvn alng appr strt, no imprsn*..........(25 to 1 op 16 to 1) 10
1191 DON'T TELL JEAN [40] 3-8-0 L Charnock (11) *beh, pushed alng hfwy, nvr on terms*..........(25 to 1 op 20 to 1) 11
1419 BELL LAD (Ire) [40] 3-8-0 J Lowe (10) *dwlt, beh, rdn hfwy, sn wknd*......................................(14 to 1) 12
Dist: Sht-hd, 1½l, 1½l, sht-hd, hd, 1½l, sht-hd, 2l, 5l, 6l. 1m 13.10s. a 2.10s (12 Ran).
SR: 32/45/29/13/33/22/25/-/9/ (Raymond Kilgour Holdings Ltd), J Berry

EPSOM (good)
Friday June 4th
Going Correction: MINUS 0.20 sec. per fur.

1481 Flemington Maiden Auction Stakes Class E (2-y-o) £3,590 6f........ (2:00)

1203[2] PERUSAL 9-0 J Reid (8) *slwly into strd, plenty to do o'r 2 fs out, str run frm one and a half out to ld cl hme*. ....(5 to 2 op 3 to 1 tchd 2 to 1) 1
1131[3] SHEPHERD MARKET (Ire) 9-0 L Piggott (5) *led, edgd lft ins fnl 2 fs, rdn final furlong, ct cl hme*. ....(6 to 4 fav op 5 to 4 tchd 15 to 8) 2
812[2] NORTHERN CELADON (Ire) 9-0 P Robinson (3) *al chasing ldrs, kpt on same pace appr fnl furlong*. .... (11 to 2 op 4 to 1) 3
1063[8] PARNASO (Ire) 9-0 L Dettori (4) *al chasing ldrs, drvn and one pace ins fnl 2 fs*............... (33 to 1 op 16 to 1) 4
776[2] MARCH OF TIME (bl) 9-0 R Cochrane (7) *rdn and effrt o'r 2 fs out, wknd one and a half out*. ....(12 to 1 op 10 to 1 tchd 14 to 1) 5
1211 ASKING FOR ACES 8-9 T Quinn (2) *in tch whn hmpd ins fnl 2 fs, sn btn*.................... (33 to 1 op 25 to 1) 6
922 STAR SPEEDER (Ire) 8-2 (7*) B Russell (6) *outpcd*. .... (50 to 1 op 33 to 1) 7
NORISKI'MARINGER 9-0 Paul Eddery (1) *dwlt, outpcd*. ....(16 to 1 op 10 to 1 tchd 20 to 1) 8
SELHURSTPARK FLYER (Ire) 9-0 Pat Eddery (9) *chsd ldrs to hfwy*...................(8 to 1 op 5 to 1 tchd 9 to 1) 9
Dist: 1l, 1l, hd, 6l, 3½l, 1½l, sht-hd, 5l. 1m 10.75s. a 2.85s (9 Ran).
SR: 19/15/11/10/-/-/ (The Winning Team), R Hannon

1482 Alberta Rose Maiden Fillies Stakes Class D (3-y-o) £3,687 1m 114yds ....(2:30)

1132[2] BARBOUKH 8-11 Pat Eddery (3) *hld up, hdwy on bit to ld one and a half fs out, shaken up fnl furlong, cmftbly*. .... (9 to 4 fav op 5 to 2 tchd 2 to 1 and 11 to 4) 1
835[5] EYE WITNESS (Ire) 8-11 A Munro (5) *al chasing ldrs, rdn and kpt on fnl furlong, not pace of wnr*. ....(16 to 1 op 12 to 1 tchd 20 to 1) 2
1285[5] SEROTINA (Ire) 8-11 L Dettori (2) *chsd ldrs, styd far side, ev ch 2 fs out till outpcd ins last*. ....(7 to 1 op 6 to 1 tchd 8 to 1) 3
732[6] ABBRAAK (USA) 8-11 W R Swinburn (4) *led to one and a half fs out, sn outpcd*.. (9 to 1 op 8 to 1 tchd 10 to 1) 4
1132[3] AKHLAK (Ire) 8-11 W Carson (7) *chsd ldrs, rdn 2 fs out, swshd tail and wknd wl o'r one out*. (7 to 2 op 5 to 2) 5
KAPUCHKA (Ire) 8-11 J Reid (6) *slwly away, al outpcd*. ....(3 to 1 op 9 to 4 tchd 7 to 2) 6
1239[5] HAZY KAY (Ire) 8-11 M Roberts (1) *outpcd most of way*. .... (10 to 1 op 8 to 1) 7
Dist: Nk, 2½l, sht-hd, 3l, 4l, 5l. 1m 45.12s. a 3.12s (7 Ran).
SR: 25/24/16/15/6/-/-/ (R J McCreery), D R C Elsworth

1483 Kenilworth Handicap Class C (0-95 3-y-o) £7,205 1¼m 18yds....... (3:05)

1204[3] SCULLER (USA) [80] 9-3 Pat Eddery (3) *chsd ldrs, drvn alng 3 fs out, led appr 2 out, rdn out fnl furlong*. ....(100 to 30 fav op 3 to 1 tchd 4 to 1) 1
875[7] ECU DE FRANCE (Ire) [83] 9-6 W Ryan (5) *beh, pushed alng 3 fs out, hdwy to chal fnl furlong, outpcd cl hme*. ....(8 to 1 op 6 to 1) 2
1178* DON'T JUMP (Ire) [75] 8-12 P Robinson (1) *in tch till lost pos 6 fs out, ran on frm o'r 2 out, not rch ldrs*. ....(8 to 1 op 7 to 1 tchd 9 to 1) 3
880* EXHIBIT AIR (Ire) [80] 9-3 L Piggott (6) *chsd ldrs till lost pos o'r 4 fs out, rallied and ev ch 2 out, sn wknd*. ....(9 to 2 op 4 to 1 tchd 5 to 1) 4
1204[6] DYAB (USA) [83] (v) 9-6 W Carson (8) *slwly into strd, rapid hdwy 5 fs out, chlgd 4 out till wknd aftr 3 out*. ....(8 to 1 op 6 to 1) 5
1111* BAY QUEEN [84] 9-2 (5*) M Fenton (2) *effrt o'r 3 fs out, sn btn*.................... (9 to 2 op 7 to 2 tchd 5 to 1) 6
945[9] TOP PET (Ire) [82] 9-5 T Quinn (4) *led till o'r 2 fs out, wknd quickly*....................(8 to 1 tchd 10 to 1) 7
825 FASHIONABLE DANCER [70] 8-7 M Roberts (7) *al beh*. .... (16 to 1 op 12 to 1) 8
Dist: ¾l, 3½l, 3½l, 1½l, 5l, hd, 12l. 2m 7.05s. a 2.75s (8 Ran).
SR: 55/56/41/39/39/30/27/-/ (K Abdulla), H R A Cecil

1484 Sun Life Of Canada Northern Dancer Rated Class B Handicap (0-105 4-y-o and up) £11,998 1½m 10yds.....(3:40)

792 WELSH MILL (Ire) [90] 4-8-7 A Munro (2) *made all, sn clr, quickened 2 fs out, unchlgd*....... (10 to 1 op 12 to 1) 1
773[2] DUKE OF EUROLINK [100] 4-9-3 R Cochrane (5) *hld up, hdwy o'r 2 fs out, styd on to chase wnr ins last, no imprsn*........... (15 to 8 fav op 13 to 8 tchd 2 to 1) 2
1028* NIGHT CLUBBING (Ire) [90] 4-8-7 T Quinn (1) *chsd ldrs, trkd wnr o'r 3 fs out, rdn 2 out, one pace*. ....(4 to 1 op 9 to 2 tchd 7 to 2) 3
1018[3] ROLL A DOLLAR [104] 7-9-7 B Rouse (6) *beh, rdn 4 fs out, one pace*..............(11 to 2 op 9 to 2 tchd 6 to 1) 4
1269[8] TURGENEV (Ire) [96] 4-8-13 M Roberts (4) *improved hfwy, rdn and no imprsn frm 3 fs out*. ....(4 to 1 op 3 to 1 tchd 9 to 2) 5
773[5] SONG OF SIXPENCE (USA) [90] 9-8-7 J Reid (3) *chsd wnr for o'r one m, sn wknd*. ....(12 to 1 op 10 to 1 tchd 14 to 1) 6
Dist: 2½l, 2l, 3½l, 2½l, 3½l. 2m 37.18s. a 1.68s (6 Ran).
SR: 52/57/43/50/37/24/ (Lord Weinstock), Lord Huntingdon

1485 Tokyo Trophy Handicap Class C (0-100 3-y-o and up) £5,803 6f... (4:10)

197[8] RUNNING GLIMPSE (Ire) [75] 5-8-6 M Roberts (4) *trkd ldrs gng wl, led o'r one furlong out, cmftbly.* (5 to 1 jt-fav op 8 to 1) 1

1096[4] SAMSOLOM [62] 5-7-7 J Quinn (8) *al pressing ldrs, ev ch 2 fs out till outpcd ins last.* ...(10 to 1 op 14 to 1 tchd 16 to 1) 2

1373[3] BALLASECRET [77] 5-8-8 T Quinn (6) *chsd ldr, rdn ins fnl 2 fs, rallied inside last, kpt on*.........(8 to 1 op 7 to 1) 3

1127[5] GORINSKY (Ire) [80] 5-8-11 L Piggott (3) *led till o'r one furlong out, sn outpcd.* (15 to 2 op 7 to 1 tchd 8 to 1) 4

1205[7] DUPLICITY (Ire) [97] 5-10-0 J Reid (2) *beh, outpcd, drvn and kpt on frm o'r one furlong out, nrst finish.* ...(6 to 1 op 5 to 1 tchd 9 to 2) 5

1348 AUGHFAD [87] (v) 7-9-4 J Williams (5) *beh, shaken up and styd on frm o'r one furlong out.* ...(9 to 1 op 7 to 1 tchd 10 to 1) 6

1449[9] BODARI [78] 4-8-2 (7*) D McCabe (9) *chsd ldrs for o'r 3 fs.* ...(12 to 1 op 10 to 1) 7

1127[9] ASSIGNMENT [74] 7-8-5 R Cochrane (1) *chsd ldrs, rdn and wknd o'r 2 fs out*.....(11 to 1 op 10 to 1 tchd 12 to 1) 8

ROYAL ROLLER (Ire) [81] 3-8-3 G Bardwell (7) *slwly into strd, al beh*...(33 to 1) 9

1059[6] FAY'S SONG (Ire) [62] 5-7-0 (7*) D Wright (10) *outpcd.* ...(5 to 1 jt-fav op 4 to 1 tchd 11 to 2) 10

1172[5] GREEN DOLLAR [87] 10-9-4 M Tebbutt (11) *sn outpcd.* ...(8 to 1 op 7 to 1) 11

Dist: 1½l, ¾l, 1½l, 1l, nk, 2l, nk, nk, sht-hd, 1l. 1m 8.43s. a 0.53s (11 Ran).

SR: 57/38/50/47/60/49/32/27/24/ (Copyforce Ltd), Miss B Sanders

1486 Kentucky Claiming Stakes Class E (3-y-o) £3,905 1m 114yds..........(4:45)

975* QUICK SILVER BOY 8-8 J Reid (2) *made all, rdn and styd on wl frm 2 fs out.* ...(5 to 4 on op 6 to 4 on tchd 6 to 5 on) 1

878[4] PIRATES GOLD (Ire) 8-11 Dale Gibson (3) *chsd wnr, chlgd frm 2 fs out till outpcd ins last*....(11 to 10 tchd Evens) 2

Won by 4l. 1m 46.68s. a 4.68s (2 Ran).

SR: -/-/ (T R Pearson), D Burchell

GOODWOOD (good)
Friday June 4th

Going Correction: MINUS 0.25 sec. per fur. (races 1,2,4,5), MINUS 0.20 (3,6)

1487 Celer Et Audax Selling Stakes Class F (3-y-o and up) £3,027 7f.........(6:30)

754 PRINCE ROONEY (Ire) 5-9-2 (7*) S Drowne (12) *mid-div, hdwy o'r 2 fs out, sn ev ch, led jst ins last, rdn clr.* ...(20 to 1 op 16 to 1) 1

1312[5] SILVER GROOM (Ire) 3-8-1 (7*) D Wright (18) *beh, hdwy fnl 2 fs, ran on ins last, fnshd wl.* ...(11 to 1 op 10 to 1 tchd 12 to 1) 2

990 PRINCE RODNEY 4-9-9 W Carson (10) *beh, hdwy on ins o'r 2 fs out, edgd lft and kpt on inside last.* ...(6 to 1 op 5 to 1 tchd 13 to 2) 3

1194[3] JUST A STEP 7-9-9 J Reid (16) *trkd ldr, led 2 fs out, hdd and no extr jst ins last*...............(9 to 2 op 7 to 2) 4

1059 FAIR ENCHANTRESS (bl) 5-9-4 J Quinn (13) *led to 2 fs out, not quicken*...(33 to 1 op 20 to 1) 5

1027 BONITA BEE (bl) 3-8-3 A McGlone (14) *slwly away, reco'red to mid-div, not clr run over one furlong out, hng lft and kpt on ins last.* ...(16 to 1 op 14 to 1 tchd 20 to 1) 6

754 SHALOU 4-9-9 M Roberts (6) *al hndy, effrt on outsd o'r 2 fs out, sn ev ch, wknd appr last*... (20 to 1 op 16 to 1) 7

1313* JUST JAMIE 3-8-6 (7*) B Russell (15) *slwly into strd, reco'red to chase ldg grp, wknd fnl 2 fs.* ...(6 to 1 op 9 to 2) 8

1239 DISTANT DYNASTY 3-8-8 L Dettori (17) *chsd ldrs, wknd wl o'r one furlong out*... (33 to 1) 9

1316[8] OSGATHORPE 6-9-9 R Perham (3) *mid-div, rdn o'r 3 fs out, sn btn*... (33 to 1) 10

927 FIR COPSE 3-8-3 G Bardwell (1) *al rear.* ... (33 to 1 op 25 to 1) 11

1313 ZHAAB (bl) 3-8-3 C Avery (4) *al beh*...(33 to 1) 12

1207[9] TURTLE BEACH 4-9-9 W Newnes (2) *prmnt, rdn o'r 2 fs out, wknd over one out*...(33 to 1 op 20 to 1) 13

1147 TEXAS COWGIRL (Ire) 3-8-0 (3*) D Harrison (7) *al beh.* ... (12 to 1 op 10 to 1) 14

1147[2] KRAYYAN DAWN 3-8-8 S Dawson (8) *wl beh hfwy.* ... (10 to 1 op 7 to 1) 15

CALL THE BUREAU 4-9-9 W R Swinburn (11) *mid-div, rdn 3 fs out, sn wknd*....(4 to 1 fav op 10 to 1 tchd 11 to 1) 16

BOLD SETKO (Ire) 4-9-4 J Williams (9) *al beh.* ... (33 to 1 op 25 to 1) 17

Dist: 2½l, nk, sht-hd, 2l, 1½l, 3l, 1½l, ¾l, 5l, ½l. 1m 28.07s. a 3.47s (17 Ran).

SR: 31/8/22/21/10/-/1/-/-/ (D J Butler), P Butler

1488 Air Containers Golden Jubilee Handicap Class D (0-80 3-y-o) £3,640 1¼m ...(7:00)

1309* DUVEEN (Ire) [61] 7-13 (5*) M Fenton (7) *al hndy, led wl o'r one furlong out, styd on strly.* ...(3 to 1 op 11 to 4 tchd 7 to 2) 1

1111[2] ALYAKKH (Ire) [73] 9-2 R Hills (9) *set slow pace, hdd wl o'r one furlong out, sn hrd rdn, not quicken ins last.* ...(7 to 1 op 6 to 1 tchd 8 to 1) 2

1080* SPECIAL DAWN (Ire) [71] 9-0 W Carson (2) *handily plcd, rdn and outpcd o'r 3 fs out, kpt on ins last.* ...(13 to 8 fav op 7 to 4) 3

926[3] EUPHONIC [66] 8-9 L Dettori (6) *trkd ldrs, ev ch o'r 2 fs out, kpt on same pace und pres*.... (4 to 1 tchd 9 to 2) 4

1093[9] JONSALAN [66] 8-9 W Newnes (1) *trkd ldr, ev ch 2 fs out, sn rdn, not quicken fnl furlong.* ... (10 to 1 op 8 to 1 tchd 11 to 1) 5

875[9] ABERDEEN HEATHER [78] 9-7 J Williams (3) *in tch, effrt o'r 3 fs out, styd on same pace appr last.* ...(12 to 1 tchd 14 to 1) 6

1351[9] SECRET ASSIGNMENT (USA) [67] 8-10 A Clark (10) *hld up, outpcd o'r 4 fs out, kpt on und pres frm one and a half out, no dngr*...(33 to 1 op 25 to 1) 7

1130 CHILTERN HUNDREDS (USA) [52] 7-9 J Quinn (4) *hld up, rdn o'r 4 fs out, no imprsn*.........(50 to 1 op 20 to 1) 8

1313 LADY RELKO [54] (bl) 7-10[2] (3*) D Harrison (8) *hld up, rdn wl o'r 3 fs out, sn btn*...(50 to 1 tchd 66 to 1) 9

Dist: 1l, ½l, sht-hd, nk, 2½l, 4l, 2l, 5l. 2m 17.17s. a 11.67s (9 Ran).

(Mrs D Weatherby), M Bell

1489 Dinah Sheridan Maiden Stakes Class D (2-y-o) £5,385 6f..............(7:25)

CRAZY PAVING (Ire) 9-0 M Roberts (2) *beh, hdwy frm hfwy, not clr run 2 fs out, swtchd lft and led on bit jst o'r one out, ran green, sn clear, readily.* ...(11 to 1 op 8 to 1 tchd 12 to 1) 1

DANGER POINT 9-0 A Munro (3) *led aftr 2 fs, rdn two out, hdd jst o'r one out, not pace of wnr.* ... (12 to 1 op 8 to 1 tchd 14 to 1) 2

1131[2] TIMELY EXAMPLE (USA) 9-0 T Quinn (9) *sn pushed alng, prmnt till ran on same pace fnl one and a half fs.* ...(3 to 1 op 4 to 1) 3

RORY CREEK (USA) 9-0 L Dettori (10) *wtd wth, pushed alng and hdwy hfwy, sn ev ch, one pace fnl furlong.* ...(7 to 4 fav op 6 to 4 tchd 2 to 1) 4

1203[4] REED MY LIPS (Ire) 9-0 Paul Eddery (4) *wth ldrs, rdn o'r 2 fs out, sn btn*....... (10 to 1 op 12 to 1 tchd 14 to 1) 5

ROMAN REEL (USA) 9-0 B Rouse (5) *led 2 fs, styd hndy till wknd wl o'r one out.* (25 to 1 op 16 to 1 tchd 33 to 1) 6

BRAVE EDGE 9-0 J Reid (1) *slwly away, hdwy whn not clr run wl o'r one furlong out, sn wknd.* ... (10 to 1 op 12 to 1 tchd 14 to 1) 7

1131[9] DUTY TIME 9-0 W Carson (8) *prmnt till wknd o'r 2 fs out.* ...(9 to 1 op 10 to 1) 8

L'ETAT C'EST MOI (USA) 8-6 (3*) D Harrison (6) *prmnt, rdn o'r 2 fs out, wknd*... (12 to 1 tchd 14 to 1 and 10 to 1) 9

GRANBY BELL 9-0 J Williams (7) *slwly away, al beh.* ...(50 to 1 op 20 to 1 tchd 66 to 1) 10

Dist: 2½l, 2l, hd, 5l, 1l, ¾l, 1l, ½l, 12l. 1m 12.33s. a 1.93s (10 Ran).

SR: 37/27/19/18/-/-/ (R M Cyzer), C A Cyzer

1490 Wiley Handicap Class E (0-70 3-y-o and up) £3,465 1m..............(7:55)

1280[2] NORTH ESK (USA) [56] 4-9-0 M Wigham (4) *patiently rdn, hdwy 3 fs out, led o'r one out, ridden clr.* (7 to 2 jt-fav op 3 to 1 tchd 4 to 1) 1

1207[3] CAPTAIN MARMALADE [53] 4-8-11 M Roberts (5) *hld up beh, rdn and hdwy on outsd 2 fs out, kpt on ins last, nvr nrr*...(4 to 1 op 5 to 1 tchd 7 to 2) 2

1073[9] SYLVAN SABRE (Ire) [62] (v) 4-9-6 W Newnes (8) *led 2 fs, styd hndy, led o'r two out till over one out, wknd ins last*...(16 to 1 op 12 to 1 tchd 20 to 1) 3

1130[7] TIFFANY'S CASE (Ire) [59] 4-9-3 R Hills (7) *hld up in tch, hdwy 3 fs out, not much room 2 out, ran on one pace.* ...(5 to 1 tchd 7 to 1) 4

1270[3] LORD ALFIE [42] 4-8-0 J Quinn (10) *in tch, ev ch whn hmpd o'r 2 fs out, ran on in snatches.* (7 to 2 jt-fav op 5 to 2 tchd 4 to 1) 5

712* TRIANGLEPOINT (Ire) [65] 3-8-9 (3*) D Harrison (2) *handily plcd, ev ch whn edgd rght o'r 2 fs out, sn rdn and not quicken*...(14 to 1 op 8 to 1) 6

881[8] DUTY SERGEANT (Ire) [43] (bl) 4-8-1 A Munro (3) *led aftr 2 fs till o'r two out, wknd appr last, eased whn btn.* ...(20 to 1 tchd 33 to 1) 7

676[9] MA BELLA LUNA [70] 4-10-0 W Carson (6) *prmnt early, lost pl hfwy, sn no dngr.* (16 to 1 op 12 to 1 tchd 20 to 1) 8

840 LORD OBERON (Ire) [50] 5-8-8 T Quinn (9) *trkd ldrs, rdn and ev ch whn squeezed o'r 2 fs out, not rcvr, eased when btn*...(15 to 2 op 10 to 1 tchd 12 to 1) 9

Dist: 2½l, ¾l, nk, 2½l, 2l, 2½l, 3½l, 8l. 1m 40.21s. a 3.01s (9 Ran).

SR: 25/14/21/17/-/-/ (Alan J Speyer), D A Wilson

1491 Edmund Pocknell Memorial Claiming Stakes Class F (3-y-o) £2,872 1¾m ...(8:25)

1305[4] PONDERING (v) 8-2 A Munro (10) *al hndy, led 3 fs out, ran on strly fnl furlong*...(7 to 2 op 5 to 2) 1

1146[8] HOSTILE WITNESS (Ire) 8-8 J Reid (9) *hld up, effrt 3 fs out, styd on wl ins last, nvr nrr.* ....(9 to 2 op 3 to 1 tchd 5 to 1) 2
876[9] RAVENSPUR (Ire) 8-11 M Roberts (5) *trkd ldrs, ev ch o'r 2 fs out, swshd tail and ran on same pace und pres.* ....(6 to 1 tchd 7 to 1) 3
1372[5] MANON LESCAUT 7-2 (7*) D Wright (7) *hld up, hdwy on outsd o'r 3 fs out, sn rdn alng, flashed tail and one pace*.................(20 to 1 op 16 to 1 tchd 25 to 1) 4
1266[4] GALACTIC FURY 8-6 J Williams (1) *hld up in mid-div, lost pl o'r 3 fs out, styd on ins last*....(10 to 1 tchd 12 to 1) 5
1417[6] PENNINE LAD (Ire) 8-2 (3*) D Harrison (2) *handily plcd, rdn o'r 3 fs out, sn not quicken*...................(12 to 1) 6
926[9] WORKING TITLE (Ire) 8-4 R Hills (6) *led to 3 fs out, sn btn.* ....(20 to 1 op 14 to 1 tchd 25 to 1) 7
1266[2] MR GENEAOLOGY (USA) (h,bl) 8-6 W Newnes (8) *hld up, hdwy on outsd o'r 3 fs out, wndrd over one out, sn rdn, found little*..........(9 to 4 fav op 5 to 2 tchd 3 to 1) 8
1237 CHATWORTH GREY 7-10 J Quinn (4) *hld up beh, shrtlvd effrt o'r 4 fs out, tld off*...........(50 to 1 op 33 to 1) 9
1349 DO BE WARE 7-12 (7*) D McCabe (3) *wth ldr, wknd quickly hfwy, tld off*.............(50 to 1 op 33 to 1) 10

Dist: 2½l, 1l, 2½l, ¾l, 2½l, ½l, 2l, 30l, 3l. 3m 12.36s. a 15.06s (10 Ran).

(Paul Deakin), S Dow

1492 Cucumber Handicap Class E (0-70 3-y-o and up) £2,880 5f............. (8:55)

615[6] LITTLE SABOTEUR [64] 4-9-8 A Munro (12) *chsd ldg grp, swtchd rght and hdwy wl o'r one furlong out, led ins last, drvn out*................... (12 to 1 tchd 16 to 1) 1
1240[4] MISTER JOLSON [64] 4-9-8 W Carson (15) *beh, hdwy o'r one furlong out, ran on strly ins last, nrst finish.* ....(13 to 2 op 6 to 1 tchd 7 to 1) 2
1240[2] TRIOMING [49] 7-8-7 M Roberts (6) *in tch, led 2 fs out till ins last, no extr*....... (5 to 1 op 9 to 2 tchd 11 to 2) 3
1148[6] JOE SUGDEN [50] 9-8-8 L Dettori (9) *beh, hdwy wl o'r one furlong out, kpt on ins last*...... (16 to 1 tchd 20 to 1) 4
255[7] LE CHIC [48] 7-8-6 J Williams (11) *al prmnt, led aftr 2 fs to two out, ran on same pace ins last.* (16 to 1 op 12 to 1) 5
1249[9] BRIGHT PARAGON (Ire) [46] 4-8-4 J Quinn (8) *slwly away, beh till hdwy fnl one and a half fs, fnshd wl, nvr nrr.* ....(16 to 1 op 12 to 1 tchd 20 to 1) 6
1352[9] BARBEZIEUX [49] 6-8-0 (7*,7ex) D McCabe (5) *slwly away, beh till ran on fnl one and a half fs, not rch ldrs.* ....(8 to 1 op 10 to 1) 7
1148[4] GAYNOR GOODMAN (Ire) [44] 3-7-8 C Avery (3) *unruly strt, chsd ldrs stands side, not much room o'r one furlong out, kpt on ins last*...(14 to 1 op 10 to 1 tchd 16 to 1) 8
1148 COPPERMILL LAD [44] 10-7-9 (7*) Iona Wands (16) *slwly away, beh till kpt on fnl furlong, no dngr.* ....(33 to 1 op 25 to 1) 9
47 TREASURE TIME (Ire) [64] 4-9-8 Dale Gibson (4) *prmnt stands side till rdn and wknd o'r one furlong out.* ....(33 to 1 op 25 to 1) 10
1352 SERIOUS HURRY [61] 5-9-5 T Quinn (7) *prmnt in centre, rdn o'r one furlong out, wknd ins last*....... (12 to 1) 11
1148[2] THE NOBLE OAK (Ire) [61] 5-9-5 J Reid (2) *led 2 fs, stdly lost pl*.............................(7 to 2 fav op 9 to 2) 12
1148 SKI CAPTAIN [50] 9-8-8 Paul Eddery (14) *sn pushed alng far side, beh fnl 2 fs*..................(33 to 1 op 25 to 1) 13
1352 SHADES OF JADE [52] 5-8-10 S Whitworth (1) *speed stands side to hfwy, sn wknd*...........(33 to 1 op 25 to 1) 14
1127 TEMPLE FORTUNE (USA) [68] (bl) 4-9-12 R Hills (13) *prmnt far side, wknd quickly o'r one furlong out, eased whn btn*............................ (25 to 1 op 16 to 1) 15

Dist: ¾l, sht-hd, 1½l, nk, sht-hd, sht-hd, sht-hd, 3l, hd, hd. 58.98s. a 2.18s (15 Ran).

SR: 44/41/25/20/17/14/16/2/-/ (Mrs P J Makin), P J Makin

HAYDOCK (good to soft)
Friday June 4th
Going Correction: PLUS 0.25 sec. per fur. (races 1,2,3,4,5), NIL (6)

1493 Halsall Claiming Stakes Class F (3-y-o) £2,534 1¼m 120yds........ (6:45)

1133 STAPLEFORD LASS 8-1 W Woods (1) *trkd ldg trio, rdn and hng lft o'r 2 fs out, str brst to ld cl hme.* ....(6 to 1 op 4 to 1) 1
1309[3] PISTOLS AT DAWN (USA) 9-0 K Darley (2) *steadied aftr ldg early, hrd at work to nose ahead o'r one furlong out, ct cl hme.* ....(11 to 10 fav op 6 to 4 tchd 13 to 8 and Evens) 2
1133[9] ANN HILL (Ire) 8-1 N Carlisle (3) *nvr far away, drw level und pres o'r one furlong out, not go past last 50 yards.* ....(6 to 1 op 4 to 1) 3
1283[3] PALACEGATE SUNSET (bl) 8-10 J Fortune (6) *sluggish strt, sn reco'red and led, hdd wl over one furlong out, no extr*....................(11 to 4 op 2 to 1 tchd 3 to 1) 4
TRANQUIL LADY (Ire) 8-7[5] (7*) S Knott (5) *last and hld up, took clr order hfwy, rdn and btn o'r 2 fs out.* ....(16 to 1 op 12 to 1) 5

Dist: ¾l, hd, 2½l, 2½l. 2m 21.98s. a 10.98s (5 Ran).

SR: 3/14/-/4/-/ (S P C Woods), S P C Woods

1494 Burtonwood Brewery Handicap Class D (0-80 3-y-o and up) £3,611 6f.. (7:15)

1036[9] THE AUCTION BIDDER [74] 6-9-8 K Darley (7) *co'red up in midfield, drvn through to ld ins fnl furlong, hld on wl.* ....(20 to 1 op 16 to 1) 1
1144[5] VELOCE (Ire) [56] 5-8-4 F Norton (13) *tucked away in midfield, not clr run and swtchd outsd to improve o'r one furlong out, fnshd wl*.......... (9 to 1 op 10 to 1) 2
1177[4] BOURSIN (Ire) [65] 4-8-13 J Fortune (1) *nvr far away, tacked o'r to ld stands side over 2 fs out, hdd ins last, no extr*.................(13 to 2 op 6 to 1 tchd 7 to 1) 3
1397[3] LANGUEDOC [64] 6-8-12 L Charnock (4) *al hndy, ev ch and hrd at work appr fnl furlong, one pace.* .... (10 to 1 op 8 to 1) 4
1394[9] DARUSSALAM [72] 6-9-1 (5*) A Procter (3) *in tch, dashed up on outsd to fltter o'r one furlong out, not quicken.* ....(16 to 1 op 14 to 1) 5
1000[7] PENNY HASSET [72] 5-9-6 T Lucas (9) *al tracking ldrs, effrt hfwy, hrd at work o'r one furlong out, fdd.* ....(7 to 1) 6
1301[4] GONDO [68] (v) 6-9-2 K Fallon (14) *chsd alng on ins, swtchd outsd to improve hfwy, no imprsn fnl furlong.* ....(5 to 1 fav op 9 to 2) 7
1052[4] CHOICE LOT [45] (bl) 6-7-3[3] (7*) Claire Balding (10) *reared leaving stalls, improved frm off the pace hfwy, kpt on, nvr nrr*............(40 to 1 op 33 to 1 tchd 50 to 1) 8
1249[7] SULLY'S CHOICE (USA) [47] (bl) 12-7-9 S Wood (5) *broke smartly to dispute ld for o'r 3 fs, fdd.* ....(20 to 1 op 16 to 1) 9
1036 ADMIRALS REALM [60] 4-8-8 A Mackay (12) *chsd alng to go pace, nvr able to rch ldrs*.......(16 to 1 op 14 to 1) 10
1301[7] SONDERISE [69] 4-9-3 N Carlisle (8) *pushed alng in midfield, effrt hfwy, fdd o'r one furlong out.* ....(10 to 1 op 8 to 1) 11
1264[3] FLASHY'S SON [66] 5-9-0 G Duffield (6) *dictated pace for o'r 3 fs, fdd und pres*... (11 to 2 op 5 to 1 tchd 6 to 1) 12
1264[4] FRANCIS ANN [53] 5-7-12[4] (7*) R Havlin (2) *broke wl to show early speed, hrd drvn hfwy, sn btn.* ....(10 to 1 op 8 to 1) 13
ALMOST BLUE [80] 7-10-0 M Perrett (11) *al struggling to keep up, tld off appr fnl furlong*...(50 to 1 op 33 to 1) 14

Dist: Nk, 3½l, 1½l, 3l, 4l, hd, 2l, hd, 1½l, sht-hd. 1m 15.83s. a 4.23s (14 Ran).

SR: 53/34/29/22/18/2/ (Heathavon Stables Limited), R Hollinshead

1495 Famous Grouse Handicap Class D (0-80 3-y-o) £3,590 1¾m........ (7:45)

1180* SHYNON [72] 9-0 P Robinson (7) *trkd ldr, led and quickened o'r 3 fs out, styd on strly to remain clr fnl furlong.* ....(7 to 4 fav op 6 to 4) 1
1165[2] SAFETY IN NUMBERS [58] 8-0 K Darley (5) *patiently rdn, effrt entering strt, hrd at work o'r 2 fs out, rallied, not rch wnr*..............................(3 to 1 op 7 to 2) 2
1165[4] ROSMARINO [51] 7-7 J Fanning (4) *trkd ldg trio, ev ch whn edgd lft o'r one furlong out, styd on same pace.* ....(14 to 1 op 12 to 1) 3
1359[3] DOC SPOT [60] 8-2 J Fortune (2) *al hndy, effrt and bustled alng last 2 fs, kpt on one pace.* (13 to 2 op 6 to 1) 4
1216[5] GUESTWICK [79] 9-7 G Duffield (6) *niggled alng in last pl, no imprsn last 3 fs*..................(7 to 1 op 5 to 1) 5
DESERT LAUGHTER (Ire) [55] 7-11 N Carlisle (3) *trkd ldg bunch, hrd at work o'r 3 fs out, no imprsn*.... (33 to 1) 6
1134* PAPER DAYS [51] 7-7 N Adams (1) *dictated pace till hdd o'r 3 fs out, fdd und pres.* ....(11 to 2 op 5 to 1 tchd 6 to 1) 7

Dist: 3l, ½l, sht-hd, 6l, 6l, 1½l. 3m 7.61s. a 10.11s (7 Ran).

SR: 34/14/6/14/21/-/-/ (M P Bowring), M H Tompkins

1496 Mayfield Garage Handicap Class E (0-70 3-y-o) £3,366 1m 30yds.... (8:15)

VELASCO (Ire) [58] 9-1 G Duffield (3) *nvr far away, hrd at work 2 fs out, ran on grimly to ld last 50 yards.* ....(3 to 1 op 10 to 1 tchd 12 to 1) 1
1181* DANCING DOMINO [54] 8-11 K Darley (5) *tried to make all, quickened entering strt, wknd and worn dwn last 50 yards*........... (11 to 4 fav op 2 to 1 tchd 3 to 1) 2
1356[2] PERSONIMUS [38] 7-9 L Charnock (1) *trkd ldg 5, feeling pace o'r 2 fs out, styd on, no imprsn.* (10 to 1 op 8 to 1) 3
1262[2] VILAMAR (Ire) [50] 8-7 K Fallon (2) *trkd ldg bunch, hrd at work to improve o'r 2 fs out, not pace to chal.* ....(14 to 1 op 12 to 1) 4
1274[6] PUBLIC WAY (Ire) [55] 8-12 S Webster (8) *in tch, feeling pace and drvn alng entering strt, styd on, nvr able to chal*...(10 to 1) 5
1377* CAMEO KIRBY (Fr) [70] 9-6 (7*,6ex) J Tate (4) *trkd ldg quartet, effrt on outsd o'r 2 fs out, sn rdn and btn.* ....(4 to 1 op 5 to 2) 6
1037[2] NORTHERN CHIEF [62] 9-5 J Carroll (7) *trkd ldr, hrd rdn 3 fs out, btn o'r one out*.............. (6 to 1 op 9 to 2) 7
934 WHO'S TOM (Ire) [46] 8-3 A Mackay (9) *trkd ldg half dozen, fdd und pres o'r 3 fs out.* .... (10 to 1 op 8 to 1 tchd 12 to 1) 8

1192[7] LANZAMAR [47] 8-4 C Rutter (6) *pressed ldrs, struggling to hold pl o'r 3 fs out, sn lost tch*................(50 to 1) 9
Dist: 1½l, 8l, hd, 1½l, 10l, 1½l, 1½l, 2l. 1m 46.42s. a 5.82s (9 Ran).
SR: 44/35/-/6/6/-/ (G E Shouler), Sir Mark Prescott

1497 EBF Lancashire Life Maiden Stakes Class D (2-y-o) £3,523 6f........(8:45)

1272[4] MOSAIC GOLD 9-0 N Connorton (11) *made most, hrd pressed o'r one furlong out, kpt on strly.* ....(4 to 1 op 5 to 2) 1
ALPINE JOHNNY 9-0 S Perks (8) *al hndy, ev ch and drvn alng o'r one furlong out, better for race.* ....(16 to 1 op 14 to 1) 2
TO CROWN IT ALL (USA) 9-0 K Fallon (1) *nvr far away, effrt and drvn alng o'r one furlong out, kpt on same pace*................(12 to 1 op 7 to 1) 3
SECRET SERENADE 9-0 Dean McKeown (13) *settled midfield, imprvg whn hng lft o'r one furlong out, styd on.* ....(12 to 1 op 20 to 1 tchd 10 to 1) 4
877[3] SUPER SYMPHONIC 9-0 P Robinson (10) *dsptd ld for o'r 4 fs, rdn and no extr*................(14 to 1 op 10 to 1) 5
793 EXTRA BONUS 9-0 W Woods (4) *reared and lost many ls strt, improved on outsd last 2 fs, nvr nrr.* ....(20 to 1 tchd 25 to 1) 6
1063[9] KILLING TIME 9-0 B Raymond (6) *scrubbed alng in midfield, styd on last 2 fs, nvr nrr.* ....(11 to 4 fav op 5 to 2 tchd 7 to 2) 7
1169[3] STARSPORT (Ire) 9-0 J Carroll (5) *al chasing ldrs, hrd at work 2 fs out, no imprsn*................(5 to 1 op 4 to 1) 8
1227[5] FEARLESS WONDER 9-0 K Darley (3) *chsd alng to go pace, nvr rchd chalg pos*................(7 to 1 op 5 to 1) 9
SANDMOOR CHAMBRAY 9-0 M Birch (12) *sluggish strt, nvr able to trble ldrs*................(12 to 1 op 9 to 1) 10
1053[5] ALTOBY 9-0 S Webster (2) *chsd ldrs, hng badly lft hfwy, sn btn*................(25 to 1 op 20 to 1) 11
673 MARINER BOY (Ire) 9-0 J Fortune (7) *drvn alng to keep up aftr 2 fs, sn btn*................(50 to 1 op 20 to 1) 12
1221[8] VEDO NUDO 9-0 G Duffield (9) *broke wl to show speed for o'r 4 fs, wknd quickly*................(10 to 1 op 8 to 1) 13
Dist: 1½l, 1½l, nk, 1l, 1½l, nk, 3l, 2½l, hd, ¾l. 1m 16.83s. a 5.23s (13 Ran).
SR: 25/19/13/12/8/2/1/-/-/ (Miss Betty Duxbury), Miss S E Hall

1498 Red Rose Handicap Class G for Lady and Gentleman Amateur Riders (0-70 3-y-o and up) £2,679 1¼m 120yds ....(9:15)

1318[4] SAINT CIEL (USA) [60] 5-11-11 Mr M Buckley (15) *confidently rdn, wl-timed run frm off the pace to ld fnl furlong, readily*................(8 to 1 op 7 to 1) 1
387[4] THUNDERING [28] 8-9-7 Miss I Diana W Jones (10) *steadied aftr fst break, improved to ld after 2 fs out, hdd and one pace ins last*................(10 to 1) 2
994 DAWN FLIGHT [63] 4-12-0 Mrs M Cowdrey (17) *trkd ldg bunch, improved on outsd last 2 fs, not pace to chal.* ....(7 to 1 op 5 to 1) 3
1179[7] GOLD SURPRISE (Ire) [52] 4-11-0 (3*) Mrs D Kettlewell (8) *wtd wth, took clr order entering strt, eased whn btn ins fnl furlong*................(11 to 1 op 10 to 1 tchd 12 to 1) 4
COXANN [28] (bl) 7-9-4 (3*) Mr E Tolhurst (7) *nvr far away, hrd at work o'r 2 fs out, no extr*................(33 to 1) 5
1304[6] MUMMYS ROCKET [45] 4-10-7 (3*) Miss D Pomeroy (2) *ran in snatches, improved und pres o'r 2 fs out, one pace.* ....(14 to 1 op 12 to 1) 6
1284 VERDANT BOY [46] 10-10-8 (3*) Mr R D Green (13) *sluggish strt, improved into midfield entering strt, no imprsn last 2 fs*................(20 to 1) 7
1284[9] HYDROPIC [31] 6-9-7 (3*) Miss R Clark (9) *nvr far away, feeling pace and drvn alng aftr 2 fs out, not quicken.* ....(25 to 1) 8
1274[7] ACHELOUS [52] (bl) 6-11-3 Mr A Thornton (4) *wth ldrs, led appr strt till o'r 2 fs out, fdd.* (6 to 1 jt-fav op 5 to 1 tchd 13 to 2) 9
495 THE KARAOKE KING [52] (bl) 4-11-0 (3*) Mrs J Boggis (11) *pressed ldrs, hrd at work o'r 2 fs out, fdd.* (6 to 1 jt-fav op 5 to 1) 10
1120 LUCKY NOIRE [54] 5-11-5 Miss A Harwood (3) *sluggish strt, nvr able to reco'r*................(8 to 1 op 10 to 1) 11
1316[9] STANE STREET (Ire) [47] 5-10-9 (3*) Mrs C Dunwoody (1) *chsd ldrs till wknd 3 fs out*................(20 to 1) 12
1307[7] FALCONS DAWN [51] 6-11-2 Miss L Eaton (14) *trkd ldg bunch to strt, fdd*................(9 to 1 op 8 to 1) 13
1207 YIMKIN BOOKRA [51] 5-10-13 (3*) Miss J Russell (12) *chsd ldrs to strt, sn rdn and btn*................(20 to 1 op 16 to 1) 14
531 MANULEADER [52] (bl) 4-11-0 (3*) Mr G Evans (6) *sluggish strt, drvn into midfield hfwy, wknd entering strt.* ....(20 to 1) 15
1389 GONE BUST (Ire) [36] 4-10-1 Miss E Johnson Houghton (5) *led till hdd appr strt, fdd*................(20 to 1) 16
235 SAFE ARRIVAL (USA) [54] 5-11-2 (3*) Mrs L Morris (16) *pressed ldrs to strt, sn lost tch*................(25 to 1 op 20 to 1) 17
Dist: 3l, 10l, hd, 1½l, 2½l, sht-hd, 1½l, 1½l, 3½l, ¾l. 2m 20.75s. a 9.75s (17 Ran).
SR: 42/4/19/7/-/-/ (Tam Racing), F Jordan

SOUTHWELL (A.W) (std)
Friday June 4th
Going Correction: PLUS 0.20 sec. per fur. (races 1,7), NIL (2,3,4,5,6)

1499 Dorchester Maiden Auction Stakes Class F (2-y-o) £2,243 5f........(2:25)

1355[2] GOLDEN GRAND 9-0 D Biggs (6) *chsd ldrs, hdwy to ld o'r 2 fs out, sn rdn, edgd lft ins last, ran on.* ....(Evens fav op 5 to 4 tchd 6 to 4) 1
776 ACCESS ADVANTAGE 8-9 W Woods (3) *chsd ldrs, hdwy and ev ch 2 fs out, sn rdn, kpt on wl ins last.* ....(6 to 1 op 5 to 1 tchd 7 to 1) 2
743[3] TRENDY DANCER (Ire) 9-0 G Duffield (1) *cl up, rdn and ev ch o'r one furlong out, kpt on one pace ins last.* ....(15 to 2 op 5 to 1 tchd 8 to 1) 3
MISTER BEAT 9-0 K Fallon (2) *al prmnt, rdn and ev ch o'r one furlong out, kpt on one pace ins last.* ....(16 to 1 op 14 to 1 tchd 20 to 1) 4
LOVESCAPE 8-9 A Clark (8) *cl up, ev ch o'r one and a half fs out, sn rdn and wknd*................(8 to 1 op 3 to 1) 5
1082 SHARP SUMMIT (Ire) 8-9 S Wood (10) *led to hfwy, sn rdn and wknd wl o'r one furlong out*.. (16 to 1 op 14 to 1) 6
1189 TEN TIMES TANGO 8-9 M Wigham (4) *outpcd and beh till some late hdwy*................(33 to 1 op 20 to 1) 7
RENNYHOLME 9-0 S Morris (7) *cl up, rdn hfwy, wknd wl o'r one furlong out*...(12 to 1 op 25 to 1 tchd 33 to 1) 8
708[7] BESSIE'S WILL 8-9 A Mackay (5) *prmnt, rdn 2 fs out, sn wknd*................(25 to 1 op 20 to 1) 9
BILLPOSTER (Ire) 8-9 G Carter (11) *sn outpcd and beh frm hfwy*................(8 to 1 op 5 to 1) 10
CHIEF PRINTER 8-7 (7*) C Hawksley (9) *slwly away, al outpcd and beh*................(25 to 1 op 16 to 1) 11
Dist: ¾l, ½l, ½l, 3½l, 2½l, nk, hd, 3l, 8l, 8l. 1m 2.30s. a 4.40s (11 Ran).
SR: 32/24/27/25/6/-/ (D A Johnson), R J R Williams

1500 Savoy Rating Related Maiden Stakes Class F (3-y-o) £2,243 1m.......(3:00)

4718a[2] LAND O'LAKES (Ire) 9-0 G Duffield (2) *made all, rdn 2 fs out, ran on wl ins last*........(6 to 4 fav op 7 to 4 on) 1
1239[4] LEGAL RISK (v) 8-9 A Mackay (5) *cl up, effrt to chal 2 fs out and sn ev ch, kpt on one pace und pres.* ....(11 to 4 op 3 to 1) 2
1216[7] CHARLIE BIGTIME 9-0 Gay Kelleway (6) *steadied strt, gd hdwy o'r 3 fs out, rdn 2 out, sn one pace.* ....(4 to 1 tchd 6 to 1) 3
1175[9] BLUE TRUMPET 9-0 W Woods (3) *cl up, rdn o'r 2 fs out, grad wknd*................(10 to 1 tchd 14 to 1) 4
1134 MISS RIBBONS 8-9 N Adams (4) *chsd ldrs, rdn aftr 3 fs and sn lost pl, tld off fnl three furlongs.* ....(10 to 1 op 8 to 1) 5
SALT N VINEGAR (Ire) 9-0 R P Elliott (1) *dwlt, al rear, tld off fnl 3 fs*................(20 to 1 op 16 to 1) 6
Dist: 1½l, 2l, 4l, 25l, 6l. 1m 45.40s. a 6.40s (6 Ran).
SR: 4/-/-/ (G D Waters), Sir Mark Prescott

1501 Shoosmith & Harrison Handicap Class E (0-70 3-y-o) £3,002 1m........ (3:30)

1247[3] MOHICAN BRAVE (Ire) [65] 9-2 K Fallon (7) *in tch, hdwy on outer 3 fs out, effrt to chal 2 out, rdn to ld appr last, ran on*................(9 to 4 op 7 to 2) 1
1247* BACKSTABBER [58] 8-9 (5ex) G Hind (5) *cl up, led 2 fs out, sn rdn, hdd o'r one out, kpt on.* ....(2 to 1 fav op 6 to 4 tchd 9 to 4) 2
1357[3] NELLIE'S GAMBLE [70] 9-7 T Williams (1) *cl up, led hfwy, rdn and hdd 2 fs out, sn wknd.* ....(7 to 2 op 3 to 1 tchd 4 to 1) 3
4709a* PRECUSSION [67] 9-4 R Price (2) *outpcd and beh, some hdwy fnl 2 fs, nvr dngrs*................(8 to 1 op 5 to 1) 4
1306 LOWRIANNA (Ire) [44] 7-9 A Mackay (6) *hdwy on outer hfwy, rdn 3 fs out, sn btn.* ....(9 to 1 op 10 to 1 tchd 14 to 1) 5
MONET MONET MONET [47] 7-12 N Carlisle (4) *in tch, effrt and some hdwy hfwy, rdn 3 fs out and sn wknd.* ....(25 to 1 op 14 to 1) 6
1316 AGENDA ONE [46] 7-11 N Adams (3) *led to hfwy, sn rdn and wknd 3 fs out*................(16 to 1 op 14 to 1) 7
Dist: 1l, 10l, 6l, 4l, 2l, 2½l. 1m 44.10s. a 5.10s (7 Ran).
SR: 26/16/-/-/ (J Dick), J G FitzGerald

1502 East Midlands Electricity Handicap Class E (0-70 3-y-o and up) £2,872 7f ....(4:00)

1073* HIGHBORN (Ire) [57] 4-9-11 G Hind (3) *made all, quickened clr 3 fs out, eased nr finish.* ....(6 to 5 fav op 11 to 10 tchd 11 to 8) 1
1246* SANDMOOR DENIM [63] 6-9-10 (7*,5ex) G Strange (4) *hld up in tch, hdwy 3 fs out, chsd wnr fnl 2 furlongs, no imprsn*................(3 to 1 op 5 to 2 tchd 7 to 2) 2

1073[3] LORD NASKRA (USA) [54] (bl) 4-9-5 (3*) Emma O'Gorman (6) *cl up, effrt to chase wnr 3 fs out, sn rdn and wknd 2 out*..........(7 to 2 op 9 to 2) 3
VICTOR ROMEO [35] 4-7-12 (5*) Darren Moffatt (1) *chsd ldrs, rdn alng hfwy, sn wknd*..........(25 to 1 op 20 to 1 tchd 33 to 1) 4
1246[6] QUINZII MARTIN [57] (v) 5-9-11 A Mackay (2) *in tch, rdn alng hfwy, sn lost pl and beh*..........(7 to 1 op 6 to 1 tchd 8 to 1) 5
1313 TOFF SUNDAE [50] 3-8-8 G Carter (5) *cl up, rdn 3 fs out, sn wknd*..........(14 to 1 op 10 to 1) 6
Dist: 5l, 10l, ¾l, 7l, 20l. 1m 29.80s. a 3.70s (6 Ran).
SR: 56/47/8/ (Yorkshire Racing Club Owners Group 1990), P S Felgate

1503 Belgrave Handicap Class E (0-70 3-y-o) £3,002 6f.......... (4:30)

1264[2] MISS WHITTINGHAM (Ire) [48] 8-3 G Carter (7) *chsd ldrs, hdwy hfwy, led o'r 2 fs out, readily*..........(100 to 30 op 5 to 2 tchd 7 to 2) 1
1455* PRINCE SONGLINE [60] 9-1 (7ex) W Woods (6) *cl up, effrt and ev ch 2 fs out, sn rdn and one pace*..........(11 to 4 fav op 5 to 2) 2
883 STARDUST EXPRESS [66] 9-7 T Williams (2) *led, rdn and hdd o'r 2 fs out, one pace*..........(11 to 2 op 5 to 1 tchd 6 to 1) 3
1232[9] GATE OF HEAVEN [38] 7-2 (5*) Darren Moffatt (1) *chsd ldrs, rdn 3 fs out, sn wknd*..........(20 to 1) 4
1147[3] RED LEADER (Ire) [63] 8-11 (7*) T G McLaughlin (5) *chsd ldrs, rdn 3 fs out, sn wknd*..........(5 to 1 tchd 11 to 2) 5
711 DON'T BE SAKI (Ire) [51] 8-6 R P Elliott (4) *dwlt, al outpcd*..........(9 to 1 op 7 to 1) 6
1273 CHICAGO (Ire) [51] 8-6 G Duffield (9) *in tch till rdn and wknd hfwy*..........(10 to 1 tchd 12 to 1) 7
1192[7] PHASE ONE (Ire) [47] 8-2 N Adams (8) *al rear*.....(25 to 1) 8
WHISPERDALES [65] 9-6 S Morris (3) *beh, effrt and hdwy 3 fs out, sn rdn and wknd 2 out*....(25 to 1 op 20 to 1) 9
Dist: 2½l, sht-hd, 10l, ½l, 2½l, 2l, 1½l, 5l. 1m 17.10s. a 3.70s (9 Ran).
SR: 15/17/22/-/-/-/ (J W Barrett), J Berry

1504 Bloomsbury Maiden Stakes Class D (3-y-o) £3,084 1½m.......... (5:00)

1375[3] HASTEN TO ADD (USA) 9-0 G Duffield (4) *chsd ldrs and sn drvn alng, hdwy 5 fs out, led o'r 3 out, soon clr, easily*..........(11 to 8 on op 5 to 4 tchd 6 to 4 on) 1
1255[7] MY HARVINSKI 8-9 (5*) Stephen Davies (1) *led, rdn 4 fs out, hdd o'r 3 out, sn wknd*.. (7 to 2 op 7 to 4 tchd 4 to 1) 2
1099[3] MARATHIA 8-9 W Woods (3) *chsd ldr, rdn 5 fs out, wknd o'r 3 out*.......(100 to 30 op 5 to 2 tchd 7 to 2) 3
1146 WOLLBOLL 9-0 T Sprake (2) *chsd ldrs, rdn 5 fs out, sn btn*..........(12 to 1 op 10 to 1 tchd 14 to 1) 4
Dist: 8l, 6l, 2½l. 2m 41.40s. a 7.50s (4 Ran).
SR: 25/9/-/-/ (Pin Oak Stable), Sir Mark Prescott

1505 Eaton Handicap Class E (0-70 3-y-o) £2,950 5f.......... (5:30)

916[5] MOVING IMAGE (Ire) [49] 8-7 C Dwyer (2) *cl up, effrt 2 fs out and sn led, rdn and ran on ins last*.. (2 to 1 op 7 to 2) 1
1232[6] KILDEE LAD [54] 8-7 (5*) Stephen Davies (7) *chsd ldrs, rdn and ev ch o'r one furlong out, kpt on ins last*..........(9 to 1 op 8 to 1 tchd 10 to 1) 2
361[6] COMET WHIRLPOOL (Ire) [56] (bl) 8-7 (7*) G Forster (1) *cl up, ev ch one furlong out, sn rdn and no extr whn ins last*..........(7 to 1 op 6 to 1 tchd 8 to 1) 3
1226[2] GO FLIGHTLINE (Ire) [63] (v) 9-7 M Hills (5) *hmpd strt, chsd ldrs, rdn 2 fs out and kpt on one pace*..........(8 to 1 op 6 to 1) 4
1360[2] OUR MICA [48] (bl) 8-6 G Carter (3) *wnt rght strt, led, rdn 2 fs out, sn hdd, edgd lft and wknd*....(6 to 1 op 7 to 2) 5
1360* SABO THE HERO [62] (v) 9-6 (5ex) G Duffield (6) *hmpd strt, rdn to chase ldrs hfwy, sn btn*.. (6 to 4 fav op 11 to 8) 6
4741a MANADEL [39] (bl) 7-6 (5*) Darren Moffatt (4) *hmpd strt, sn outpcd and beh frm hfwy*..........(16 to 1 op 25 to 1 tchd 33 to 1) 7
Dist: 1l, ½l, nk, 3l, 5l, 1l. 1m 3.00s. a 5.10s (7 Ran).
SR: 11/12/12/18/ (Mrs Christine Rawson), H J Collingridge

ST-CLOUD (FR) (good)
Friday June 4th

1506 Prix de Royaumont (Group 3) (3-y-o) £23,895 1½m.......... (2:25)

APOGEE 9-2 T Jarnet (2) *3rd strt, led jst und 2 fs out, sn clr, imprsv*..........(5 to 2 on) 1
DIAMONAKA (Fr) 9-2 C Asmussen (4) *5th strt, rdn 2 fs out, chsd wnr one out, no extr*..........(48 to 10) 2
1290[3] ELITE GUEST (Ire) 9-2 D Boeuf (1) *last strt, rdn 2 fs out, kpt on*..........(97 to 10) 3
1128[4] RAPID REPEAT (Ire) 9-2 S Guillot (3) *second strt, chlgd 2 and a half fs out, kpt on one pace*..........(86 to 10) 4
OUBAVA (Fr) 9-2 E Saint-Martin (5) *4th strt, sn btn*..........(72 to 10) 5
1033[9] MISS KADROU (Fr) 9-2 E Legrix (6) *led till hdd and wknd und 2 fs out*..........(14 to 1) 6
Dist: 2l, 4l, nk, 1½l, 3l. 2m 33.50s. a 3.50s (6 Ran).
SR: 67/63/55/54/51/45/ (K Abdulla), A Fabre

WEXFORD (IRE) (good)
Friday June 4th

1507 Gowla Breeders (Fillies) Maiden (3-y-o and up) £2,762 1½m 170yds. (7:00)

SHAIYBARA (Ire) 3-8-7 M J Kinane (5)..........(6 to 4 fav) 1
1140[5] PLUM LICK (Ire) 3-8-7 K J Manning (3)..........(10 to 1) 2
1107[3] KILTIMAGH (Ire) 3-8-7 N G McCullagh (11)..........(8 to 1) 3
960[4] TRILLICK (Ire) 3-8-7 R Hughes (13)..........(8 to 1) 4
MYSTICAL CITY (Ire) 3-8-7 J Ely (6)..........(20 to 1) 5
648[7] NORDICOLINI (Ire) 3-8-7 P Shanahan (9)..........(20 to 1) 6
1140[8] SAINT HILDA (Ire) 3-8-1 (6*) J A Heffernan (7)..........(33 to 1) 7
QUIVAL (USA) 8-7 J F Egan (4)..........(16 to 1) 8
669 ROLANDS GIRL (Ire) 3-8-8[9] (8*) M W Martin (10)..(33 to 1) 9
943[7] ATSUKO (Ire) 3-8-7 S Craine (8)..........(3 to 1) 10
1295[5] KESS (Ire) 4-9-3 (6*) B Bowens (1)..........(33 to 1) 11
1048 NEW LOVE (Ire) 3-8-3 (4*) W J Smith (12)..........(20 to 1) 12
Dist: 4l, 7l, 1½l. 2m 41.00s. (12 Ran).
(H H Aga Khan), John M Oxx

1508 Katie Pats Bar And Restaurant Handicap (0-60 4-y-o and up) £2,762 2m.......... (8:00)

1013[4] LET IT RIDE (Ire) [-] 4-9-6 (6*) P Carberry (9)..........(10 to 1) 1
1141[3] ZUHAL [-] 5-9-7 (6*) C Everard (6)..........(7 to 1) 2
1013* SHARP INVITE [-] 6-8-9 (6*) J J Behan (14).....(5 to 4 fav) 3
753[2] BLUEJACKET (Ire) [-] 5-8-13 J F Egan (11)..........(20 to 1) 4
852[3] SERJITAK [-] 6-9-5 S Craine (3)..........(5 to 1) 5
1141[9] BUZZ ALONG [-] 7-9-1 (4*) W J Smith (1)..........(50 to 1) 6
852 VIVERE (Ire) [-] 4-9-1 P V Gilson (2)..........(33 to 1) 7
GO DEAS [-] 6-8-7 (6*) J Heffernan (10)..........(10 to 1) 8
PALACE GEM [-] 6-8-13 (8*) P O Casey (8)..........(10 to 1) 9
706[9] TANAMANDA (Ire) [-] 4-8-13 N G McCullagh (7)...(25 to 1) 10
1013[8] RIENZI [-] 9-8-0 (10*) P M Donohoe (5)..........(33 to 1) 11
996 TUMBLE WOOD (Ire) [-] 5-8-2 (8*) R T Fitzpatrick (13)..........(50 to 1) 12
852 HAWKFIELD (Ire) [-] (bl) 4-9-13 J P Murtagh (15)....(7 to 1) 13
SINGHANA (Ire) [-] 5-9-8 G Curran (4)..........(16 to 1) 14
937[3] GONE LIKE THE WIND [-] 6-7-9 Joanna Morgan (12)..........(50 to 1) 15
Dist: 2l, 1l, 6l, ¾l. 3m 42.30s. (15 Ran).
(J S Gutkin), E J O'Grady

CURRAGH (IRE) (yielding (races 1,5,7), good to yielding (2,3,4,6))
Saturday June 5th
Going Correction: PLUS 0.40 sec. per fur.

1509 Jockey Hall (E.B.F.) Maiden (2-y-o) £5,244 6f.......... (2:00)

LAKE COUNTRY (Ire) 8-11 J P Murtagh (6)..... (Evens fav) 1
869[6] DON'T KNOW (Ire) 9-0 K J Manning (1)..........(10 to 1) 2
1022[5] DANCING AT LUNASA (Ire) 8-11 P V Gilson (3).....(7 to 1) 3
GO MILLIE (Ire) 8-11 W J Supple (7)..........(6 to 1) 4
ALZUMA (Ire) 9-0 J F Egan (4)..........(3 to 1) 5
FABRIANO (USA) 9-0 D Hogan (2)..........(6 to 1) 6
1332 PEARL OF ORIENT (Ire) 9-0 G Curran (5)..........(33 to 1) 7
Dist: Nk, hd, hd, hd. 1m 18.00s. a 7.50s (7 Ran).
(Mrs M V O'Brien), M V O'Brien

1510 Blackmiller Hill E.B.F. Maiden (3-y-o) £3,450 1m 1f.......... (2:30)

FAMILY FORTUNE (Ire) 9-0 P V Gilson (8)..........(6 to 1) 1
KUDDAM (Ire) 8-11 M J Kinane (7)..........(100 to 30) 2
1026[2] BOTHSIDESNOW (Ire) 9-0 R Hughes (5)....... (5 to 2 fav) 3
SHEREGORI (Ire) 9-0 J P Murtagh (4)..........(5 to 1) 4
669[5] MONOPOLY MONEY (Ire) 9-0 P Shanahan (1)......(3 to 1) 5
CRISSY (Ire) 8-1 (10*) A P Colgan (2)..........(16 to 1) 6
Dist: 2½l, ½l, hd, 3l. 2m 4.60s. a 15.10s (6 Ran).
(Mrs M V O'Brien), Charles O'Brien

1511 Oaks Trial (Listed Race) (3-y-o and up) £8,625 1m 3f.......... (3:00)

944* RAYSEKA (Ire) 3-8-7 R Hughes (10) *made all, wl clr aftr 2 fs, rdn out fnl furlong*..........(7 to 2 fav) 1
1025[4] PHARFETCHED 4-9-8 J P Murtagh (5) *mid-div, rdn 4 fs out, styd on wl*..........(20 to 1) 2
1335* CLEAR ABILITY (Ire) (bl) 3-8-7 M J Kinane (2) *wl plcd, rdn 2 fs out, kpt on*..........(10 to 1) 3
RIYOOM (USA) 3-8-7 K J Manning (4) *wl plcd, gd prog 3 fs out, rdn and drifted lft o'r one out, wknd*..... (4 to 1) 4
790* RAJAURA (Ire) 3-8-7 D Hogan (8) *rear, rdn 3 fs out, steady prog frm 2 out*..........(10 to 1) 5

1198⁵ OISEAU DE FEU (USA) 3-8-7 P V Gilson (6) *trkd ldr, rdn 3 fs out, wknd o'r one out*..........................(5 to 1) 6
895⁷ EBONY AND IVORY (Ire) 4-9-8 W J Supple (3) *rear till some prog fnl 2 fs*..............................(10 to 1) 7
576⁷ BABUSHKA (Ire) 3-8-7 J D Eddery (7) *trkd ldr 2 fs, mid-div, rdn 3 furlongs out, sn wknd*..................(20 to 1) 8
1106* TOPSEYS TIPPLE (Ire) 3-8-7 P Shanahan (1) *al rear, rdn 3 fs out, not quicken*..............................(20 to 1) 9
1236* OENOTHERA (Ire) 3-8-7 S Craine (9) *mid-div, rdn and wknd 3 fs out, eased o'r one out*................(5 to 1) 10
Dist: 2½l, 4l, 3l, 1l. 2m 26.80s. (10 Ran).
(H H Aga Khan), John M Oxx

1512 Gallinule Stakes (Group 2) (3-y-o and up) £23,000 1¼m...............(3:30)

1047³ MASSYAR (Ire) 3-8-8 M J Kinane (3) *wl plcd, rdn to chal one and a half fs out, sn led, kpt on und pres.* ....(Evens fav) 1
1198* HUSHANG (Ire) 3-8-8 J P Murtagh (1) *dsptd ld 1st furlong, trkd ldr till prog to dispute lead one out, sn hdd, no extr*..(3 to 1) 2
1198⁴ SINISSIPI (USA) 3-8-8 R Hughes (6) *hld up till prog 3 fs out, kpt on wl fnl furlong*..........................(12 to 1) 3
843⁵ MAJORITY (Ire) 3-8-8 W J Supple (4) *dsptd ld 1st furlong, led, rdn 2 fs out, hdd and wknd one out*........(6 to 1) 4
953⁸ ARABIC TREASURE (USA) 3-8-8 P Shanahan (5) *al rear, rdn 3 fs out, not quicken*............................(12 to 1) 5
1198² VIA PARIGI (Ire) 3-8-8 K J Manning (2) *wl plcd, prog 5 fs out, rdn 3 out, sn wknd*...............................(6 to 1) 6
Dist: 1l, 2l, 1l, ½l. 2m 11.10s. a 8.30s (6 Ran).
SR: 51/49/45/43/42/-/ (H H Aga Khan), John M Oxx

1513 Horse France Fillies Handicap (0-90 3-y-o and up) £3,795 7f......... (4:00)

1440⁶ NUNIVAK (USA) [-] 5-8-3 (6*) R V Skelly (5).......(14 to 1) 1
787 DIXIE FAVOR (USA) [-] 4-9-3 (6*) J J Behan (7)....(14 to 1) 2
573⁴ ELEGANT BLOOM (Ire) [-] (bl) 3-9-5 M J Kinane (3) ....(5 to 2 fav) 3
1123⁶ AULD STOCK (Ire) [-] (bl) 3-8-9 J F Egan (10).......(8 to 1) 4
1444³ ISLAND HEATHER (Ire) [-] (bl) 5-9-3 R Hughes (12)..(6 to 1) 5
981³ GIFT OF PEACE (Ire) [-] 3-7-10 (6*) J A Heffernan (8) (12 to 1) 6
1050⁹ COMMON BOND (Ire) [-] 3-8-7 (8*) B Fenton (11)..(12 to 1) 7
1107⁵ HERMES GOLD (Ire) [-] 3-8-0 W J Supple (1)......(10 to 1) 8
1023⁶ GOLD BRAISIM (Ire) [-] 3-8-11 K J Manning (13)....(6 to 1) 9
668⁷ BERESFORD LADY (Ire) [-] 3-8-0 Joanna Morgan (4) ....(14 to 1) 10
JARGONEL (Ire) [-] 3-7-12¹ (2*) R M Burke (9).....(20 to 1) 11
996⁸ ACCELL (Ire) [-] 4-8-0 (2*) D G O'Shea (2).........(10 to 1) 12
WASSL'S NANNY (Ire) [-] 4-8-13 N G McCullagh (6) (16 to 1) 13
Dist: 1½l, sht-hd, 1l, nk. 1m 30.00s. a 6.80s (13 Ran).
SR: 35/44/39/26/33/-/ (Ratoath Hockey Club), T M Walsh

1514 Melitta Handicap (0-95 3-y-o and up) £6,900 1¼m.................. (4:30)

648³ KIROV PREMIERE [-] 3-7-10 (6*) J A Heffernan (10) (10 to 1) 1
308² FAYDINI (Ire) [-] 4-9-2 (4*) P Carberry (12)..........(8 to 1) 2
576⁶ FARMAAN (Ire) [-] 3-8-6 D Hogan (8)..................(5 to 1) 3
1202⁸ SHARASTAMINA (USA) [-] 4-8-4 N G McCullagh (1) (10 to 1) 4
1199⁴ WHEATSHEAF LADY (Ire) [-] 3-7-12 (6*) J J Behan (9) ....(10 to 1) 5+
1202⁵ BEAUMONT HOUSE (Ire) [-] 4-8-4 W J Supple (5).. (9 to 1) 5+
959² GLENBRACK [-] 3-7-1 (6*) P P Murphy (4)..........(9 to 1) 7
1164* FLORA WOOD (Ire) [-] 3-7-8 (2*) D G O'Shea (3)....(13 to 2) 8
808* SKIPO (USA) [-] 3-8-7 M J Kinane (7)..........(5 to 2 fav) 9
1202 DOMINO'S RING (Ire) [-] (bl) 4-9-5 R Hughes (13)..(33 to 1) 10
997 MILLERS MILL (Ire) [-] 3-7-7 A J Nolan (6)........(50 to 1) 11
753* BRAVEFOOT [-] 5-9-5 P V Gilson (2)...............(25 to 1) 12
MAXWELTON BRAES (Ire) [-] (bl) 4-8-4 J F Egan (11) ....(20 to 1) 13
Dist: 2l, ¾l, sht-hd, hd, dd-ht. 2m 11.30s. a 8.50s (13 Ran).
SR: 43/57/41/38/37/37/ (John L Wood), J S Bolger

1515 Curragh Camp Handicap (0-85 3-y-o and up) £3,105 5f...............(5:00)

1105⁵ SHOOT THE DEALER (Ire) [-] 3-7-11 (10*) G Coogan (6) ....(8 to 1) 1
1023³ MEMSAHB [-] (bl) 4-9-4 M J Kinane (4)........(4 to 1 fav) 2
599⁶ LADY PRESIDENT (Ire) [-] 4-7-10 (6*) J J Behan (5). (6 to 1) 3
1444⁸ MAGIC DON (Ire) [-] (bl) 4-8-4 (8*) R T Fitzpatrick (2) (7 to 1) 4
1386² KILLEEN STAR (Ire) [-] 3-8-8 W J Supple (9).........(8 to 1) 5
1023⁹ DONNASOO (Ire) [-] 4-9-2 (4*) W J Smith (10).....(14 to 1) 6
1023⁸ TOUGH AS TEAK (Ire) [-] (bl) 3-7-9 Joanna Morgan (11) ....(16 to 1) 7
1023* CLANDOLLY (Ire) [-] 5-9-8 (4*) P Carberry (3).......(5 to 1) 8
1050⁵ PETITE EPAULETTE [-] 3-8-13 (6*) R V Skelly (7)...(10 to 1) 9
572 LUTE AND LYRE (Ire) [-] 4-9-8 (6*) C Everard (12)..(10 to 1) 10
1250⁸ TORCH SINGER [-] 3-7-7³ (8*) J J Mullins (8).....(16 to 1) 11
1050 NEVER WRONG [-] 6-9-4 B Coogan (1)...........(12 to 1) 12
Dist: Sht-hd, ½l, 1l, 2l. 1m 2.50s. a 4.20s (12 Ran).
SR: 49/59/41/47/35/-/ (Samuel Murphy), J G Coogan

EDINBURGH (good)

Saturday June 5th

Going Correction: MINUS 0.05 sec. per fur.

1516 Gullane Rating Related Maiden Fillies Stakes Class E (0-70 3-y-o and up) £2,725 5f...................... (2:25)

1360³ KIMBOLTON KORKER 3-8-8 S Whitworth (3) *al prmnt, led o'r one out, pushed out*.........(2 to 1 tchd 5 to 2) 1
1054 SENSABO 3-8-1 (7*) R Havlin (6) *dwlt, rear, swtchd lft 2 fs out, effrt entering fnl furlong, kpt on.* ....(33 to 1 tchd 50 to 1) 2
1167³ MINSK 7-9-2 G Duffield (4) *cl up till lost pl hfwy, ran on ins last*..........................(8 to 1 op 7 to 1) 3
1136² RUSSIA WITH LOVE (bl) 3-8-8 K Darley (5) *led till hdd and wknd o'r one furlong out*..... (Evens fav op 5 to 4 on) 4
1360⁴ DARDANELLE 3-8-8 S Webster (1) *cl up 3 fs, kpt on one pace*..............................(20 to 1 op 16 to 1) 5
UPPANCE (bl) 5-9-2 J Fanning (2) *speed to hfwy, wknd 2 fs out*...............................(16 to 1 tchd 20 to 1) 6
Dist: 1½l, ¾l, 1½l, nk, 7l. 1m 1.60s. a 3.80s (6 Ran).
SR: 13/7/12/ (Classic Racing), J Balding

1517 Ochil Hills Claiming Stakes Class F (4-y-o and up) £2,377 1m 7f 16yds..(2:55)

1054⁸ LORD ADVOCATE (v) 5-7-12 (7*) V Halliday (3) *pressed ldr, led entering strt, hdd wl o'r one out, kpt on to ld ag'n ins last, all out*...... (14 to 1 op 10 to 1 tchd 16 to 1) 1
1400⁴ STINGRAY CITY (USA) 4-9-7 K Darley (6) *trkd ldrs, swtchd 2 out, chlgd one out, ev ch ins last, styd on.* ....(11 to 8 on op 11 to 10 on) 2
1156² POST IMPRESSIONIST (Ire) 4-8-10 G Duffield (5) *led till entering strt, rallied to rgn slight advantage wl o'r one furlong out, hdd and no extr ins last.* ....(7 to 4 op 2 to 1 tchd 9 to 4) 3
863 JOHN NAMAN (Ire) 4-8-2 (5*) O Pears (4) *rear, prog entering strt, effrt 2 fs out, not quicken ins last.* ....(11 to 1 op 7 to 1 tchd 12 to 1) 4
CARDENDEN (Ire) 5-8-9 J Lowe (1) *trkd ldrs till wknd entering strt*....................(66 to 1 op 50 to 1) 5
KINCARDINE BRIDGE (USA) 4-9-7 D Wilkinson (2) *beh, prog aftr 5 fs to track ldrs, wknd entering strt.* ....(66 to 1 op 50 to 1) 6
Dist: ½l, sht-hd, 1l, 20l, 8l. 3m 25.30s. a 13.30s (6 Ran).
(Mandarin Racing), M P Naughton

1518 Sheraton Grand Cup Handicap Stakes Class D (0-75 3-y-o) £3,551 5f... (3:25)

1226* SHADOW JURY [71] 9-7 K Darley (5) *led aftr a furlong, rdn ins last, kpt on wl*... (5 to 4 fav op 6 to 4 tchd 7 to 4) 1
1273⁷ COVENT GARDEN GIRL [61] 8-11 T Lucas (3) *cl up, rdn 2 fs out, kpt on ins last*..................(5 to 2 op 2 to 1) 2
1341⁴ PLUM FIRST [71] (bl) 9-7 S Whitworth (2) *chsd ldrs, rdn hfwy, no imprsn fnl 2 fs*.................(5 to 2 op 3 to 1) 3
1226³ SELVOLE [43] (bl) 7-7 J Fanning (1) *led one furlong, drifted lft and wknd hfwy, eased whn no ch.* ....(8 to 1 op 6 to 1) 4
Dist: ½l, 1½l, 20l. 1m 0.70s. a 2.90s (4 Ran).
SR: 44/32/36/-/ (P D Savill), D W Chapman

1519 Don't Blink Selling Stakes Class G (2-y-o) £2,274 5f.................. (3:55)

1108² PALACEGATE JO (Ire) (v) 8-6 J Carroll (1) *swrvd lft strt, chsd ldrs, quickened to ld one furlong out, rdn clr.* ....(5 to 4 on tchd 11 to 10 on) 1
1158⁶ MACAROON LADY 8-6 S Whitworth (4) *trkd ldr, led o'r one furlong out, sn hdd and no extr.* ....(3 to 1 tchd 7 to 2 and 4 to 1) 2
1108⁶ WESTCOAST (bl) 8-11 J Fanning (3) *led till hdd and wknd wl o'r one furlong out.* (8 to 1 op 6 to 1 tchd 10 to 1) 3
1169⁶ PEASAN 8-11 K Darley (6) *chsd ldrs, effrt o'r one out, wknd ins last*..................(25 to 1 op 14 to 1) 4
1078⁵ SALTPETRE (Ire) 8-11 M Wigham (7) *uns rdr leaving paddock and completed 2 circuits riderless, outpcd aftr one furlong, styd on ins last.* ....(12 to 1 op 10 to 1 tchd 14 to 1) 5
564⁶ RED GRIT (Ire) 8-6 J Lowe (2) *trkd ldrs, effrt whn wndrd and stumbled o'r one furlong out, sn btn.* ....(25 to 1 op 16 to 1) 6
886 XAMDIVAD (Ire) 8-2¹ (5*) O Pears (5) *al beh.* ....(10 to 1 op 7 to 1) 7
Dist: 3l, 8l, 1l, ¾l, 1l, 2l. 1m 1.70s. a 3.90s (7 Ran).
SR: 9/-/-/-/ (Palacegate Corporation Ltd), J Berry

1520 Rothmans Royals North South Challenge Series Handicap Class D (0-80 3-y-o and up) £3,707 1m 16yds.. (4:25)

1284⁴ LAWNSWOOD JUNIOR [58] 6-8-10 K Darley (3) *settled rear, prog o'r 2 fs out, swtchd and quickened wl to ld ins last, sn clr*.............. (7 to 2 tchd 4 to 1 and 9 to 2) 1
JUBRAN (USA) [67] 7-9-5 J Carroll (9) *al prmnt, chlgd and ev ch one furlong out, not quicken.* (13 to 2 op 6 to 1) 2

1274^3 MCA BELOW THE LINE [58] (v) 5-8-10 S Webster (6) in tch, prog 2 fs out, effrt o'r one out, kpt on one pace. ....(8 to 1 op 7 to 1 tchd 9 to 1) 3
1101^4 INVERTIEL [58] 9-8-7 (3*) S D Williams (10) trkd ldrs, prog to dispute ld o'r one furlong out, not quicken. ....(14 to 1 op 10 to 1) 4
1274* HABETA (USA) [62] (bl) 7-9-0 G Duffield (7) prmnt, effrt 2 fs out, sn rdn and not quicken. ....(6 to 4 fav op 5 to 2 tchd 11 to 4) 5
930^7 GOLDEN CHIP (Ire) [76] 5-10-0 F Norton (2) chsd ldrs, led 2 fs out till hdd and wknd ins last....(14 to 1 op 8 to 1) 6
862^6 THE DANDY DON (Ire) [49] 4-8-1 J Lowe (1) prmnt, effrt 2 fs out, sn rdn and btn...............(12 to 1 op 10 to 1) 7
1284^7 SKOLERN [41] 9-7-7 J Fanning (12) rear, some prog 3 fs out, not get on terms.............(25 to 1 op 20 to 1) 8
1284 AMERICAN HERO [61] 5-8-13 M Wigham (11) led one furlong, chsd ldr aftr till wknd o'r 2 out. ....(9 to 1 op 7 to 1 tchd 10 to 1) 9
1264^6 MISS HOSTESS [41] (bl) 6-7-7 E Johnson (4) in tch till wknd o'r 2 fs out..................(40 to 1 op 33 to 1) 10
1382^9 SAVAHRA SOUND [73] 8-9-6 (5*) O Pears (8) chsd alng to ld aftr one furlong, hdd and wknd 2 out. ....(20 to 1 op 16 to 1 tchd 25 to 1) 11
VALLEY OF TIME (Fr) [46] 5-7-12^{1}2 (7*) R Havlin (5) dwlt, al rear...........................(33 to 1 op 20 to 1) 12

Dist: 2l, 1l, ¾l, ½l, ½l, 3l, 1½l, 3½l, 5l, 1l. 1m 41.60s. a 3.10s (12 Ran).
SR: 44/47/35/33/35/47/11/-/7/ (Graham Treglown), J L Spearing

1521 Fisherrow Handicap Class E (0-70 4-y-o and up) £2,765 1m 3f 32yds... (4:55)

1260^4 TANODA [42] 7-8-1 G Duffield (1) trkd ldrs, chlgd one furlong out, kpt on und pres to ld last strd.....(7 to 1) 1
1190^4 SHAMSHOM AL ARAB (Ire) [51] 5-8-5 (5*) O Pears (2) prmnt, prog hme turn to ld 3 fs out, clr 2 out, rdn ins last, ct last strd...............(11 to 4 op 5 to 2 tchd 3 to 1) 2
931^4 JAZILAH (Fr) [69] 5-10-0 F Norton (3) rear, prog 3 fs out, kpt on one pace fnl 2 furlongs...... (5 to 2 fav op 11 to 4) 3
1307^2 TELEPHUS [51] 4-8-10 E Johnson (8) in tch in rear, prog entering strt, kpt on one pace fnl 2 fs. .... (3 to 1 op 11 to 4) 4
1112^9 NOT YET [34] (v) 9-7-7 J Fanning (5) rear, prog o'r 2 fs out, kpt on one pace.......(10 to 1 op 8 to 1 tchd 12 to 1) 5
1166* MEDIA MESSENGER [56] 4-9-1 J Carroll (6) prmnt, effrt 3 fs out, sn rdn and no imprsn..........(10 to 1 op 8 to 1) 6
1190 TAKE BY STORM (Ire) [61] 4-9-6 K Darley (7) in tch, effrt 3 fs out, sn rdn and btn................ (14 to 1 op 12 to 1) 7
1056^5 RAPID MOVER [38] (bl) 6-7-11^{1}1 (7*) R Havlin (9) led till 3 fs out, wknd 2 out...................(50 to 1 op 33 to 1) 8
ASTURIAS [38] 10-7-11 J Lowe (4) dsptd ld till wknd entering strt...................... (50 to 1 op 33 to 1) 9

Dist: Hd, 1½l, 2l, 1½l, ¾l, 1½l, 3l, ½l. 2m 25.40s. a 5.90s (9 Ran).
SR: 22/30/45/23/3/23/25/-/-/ (Mel Brittain), M Brittain

EPSOM (good to firm)
Saturday June 5th
Going Correction: MINUS 0.35 sec. per fur.

1522 Ever Ready Maiden Stakes Class D (3-y-o) £4,230 7f.................. (2:15)

1340^3 BITTER'S END (Ire) 9-0 Pat Eddery (1) pushed alng to ld, made all, shaken up and quickened clr appr last, easily........................... (6 to 4 fav op 11 to 10) 1
KNIGHT OF SHALOT (Ire) 9-0 J Reid (4) trkd ldrs, chsd wnr frm 3 fs out, no imprsn. ....(15 to 8 op 2 to 1 tchd 6 to 4 and 9 to 4) 2
872 OARE SPARROW 8-9 M Hills (6) trkd ldg pair, pushed alng 3 fs out, swshd tail and one pace und pres. .... (14 to 1 op 7 to 1) 3
1239^3 COALISLAND 9-0 A McGlone (5) trkd wnr, hrd rdn 3 fs out, outpcd............(9 to 1 op 6 to 1 tchd 10 to 1) 4
HOME SAFE 9-0 T Quinn (3) al beh. (20 to 1 tchd 25 to 1) 5
951^7 MISS COPYFORCE 8-9 W Newnes (2) al beh. ....(14 to 1 op 20 to 1 tchd 12 to 1) 6

Dist: 4l, 2½l, 5l, 3½l, 1½l. 1m 21.15s. a 0.75s (6 Ran).
SR: 52/40/27/17/6/-/ (Bob Lalemant), R Hannon

1523 Energizer Maiden Stakes Class D (2-y-o) £4,386 5f.................. (2:45)

ROXANIAN (Ire) 8-11 D Holland (10) trkd ldrs, led appr fnl furlong, ran on wl, jst hld on. ....(6 to 1 op 5 to 1 tchd 7 to 1) 1
CANASKA DANCER (Ire) 8-11 A Munro (7) outpcd, hdwy ins fnl furlong, fnshd fst, jst fld..... (6 to 1 op 4 to 1) 2
DANCES WITH RISK 8-6 M Hills (6) chsd ldrs, ran on wl ins fnl furlong..........(25 to 1 op 16 to 1 tchd 33 to 1) 3
1135^4 JUST GREENWICH (bl) 8-9 L Dettori (9) rcd freely, led till appr fnl furlong, no extr. ....(5 to 1 op 6 to 1 tchd 7 to 1) 4
KOONOONA LADY 7-13 (7*) D Wright (11) outpcd, hdwy ins fnl furlong, ran on, nrst finish. (33 to 1 op 20 to 1) 5
1265^8 GRANMAS DELIGHT 8-9 M Roberts (3) chsd ldrs, rdn 2 fs out, no imprsn..................... (10 to 1 op 8 to 1) 6
1350^7 ZORAHAYDA (Fr) 8-9 B Rouse (5) cl up till wknd o'r one furlong out.........(20 to 1 op 14 to 1 tchd 25 to 1) 7
1265^6 JEYPORE JO 9-0 J Reid (8) trkd ldrs, pushed alng hfwy, wknd.............. (4 to 1 fav op 3 to 1 tchd 9 to 2) 8
REGAL RAMBLER (Can) 8-8 (3*) D Harrison (2) outpcd. ....(8 to 1 op 6 to 1) 9
913^5 MAKE THE BREAK 9-0 Pat Eddery (1) trkd ldrs till wknd 2 fs out............................. (5 to 1 op 7 to 2) 10

Dist: Sht-hd, 1½l, 3l, 1l, nk, 4l, sht-hd, 2l, hd. 56.04s. a 1.34s (10 Ran).
SR: 35/34/23/14/7/9/ (Mrs Elaine Mitchell), M J Heaton-Ellis

1524 Energizer Handicap Class C (0-90 3-y-o) £10,885 1m 114yds...........(3:15)

684^4 RIBHI (USA) [83] 9-0 W Carson (1) chsd ldrs, cld o'r 3 fs out, led over one out, pushed out..... (3 to 1 fav op 4 to 1) 1
915^6 FORTHWITH [81] 8-12 M Hills (10) hld up, gd hdwy o'r 3 fs out, ev ch over one out, not quicken. ....(11 to 1 op 8 to 1 tchd 12 to 1) 2
1016 SHAMAM (USA) [88] 9-5 W R Swinburn (4) trkd ldrs, rdn alng o'r 2 fs out, kpt on ins last......(10 to 1 op 8 to 1) 3
1306^3 PRINCESS TATEUM (Ire) [70] 8-1 P Robinson (7) beh, hdwy o'r 2 fs out, one pace over one out.. (10 to 1 op 8 to 1) 4
578^5 JACKPOT STAR [86] 9-3 Pat Eddery (6) wtd wth in tch, effrt o'r 2 fs out, one pace. ....(7 to 1 op 6 to 1 tchd 8 to 1) 5
1144^6 DIGPAST (Ire) [83] 9-0 T Quinn (2) cl up, led o'r 2 fs out till over one out, wknd..............(5 to 1 tchd 11 to 2) 6
578^6 ALDERNEY PRINCE (USA) [82] 8-13 A Munro (5) trkd ldrs, rdn alng 3 fs out, sn btn...........(14 to 1 op 12 to 1) 7
1231^3 GUSTAVIA (Ire) [94] 9-11 L Dettori (8) hld up beh, effrt 3 fs out, no imprsn.......(12 to 1 op 10 to 1 tchd 14 to 1) 8
813 LOCHORE [62] 7-7 N Adams (3) led, came wide into strt, hdd o'r 2 fs out, wknd. ....(25 to 1 op 20 to 1 tchd 33 to 1) 9
1257* FIVEOFIVE (Ire) [62] 7-7 N Carlisle (9) hld up, cld hfwy, sn wknd.........(5 to 1 op 9 to 2 tchd 11 to 2) 10

Dist: 2½l, 2l, 1½l, 1½l, 1½l, 2l, 4l, ¾l, 12l. 1m 41.61s. b 0.39s (10 Ran).
SR: 61/51/52/29/40/32/25/25/-/ (Hamdan Al-Maktoum), D Morley

1525 Energizer Oaks Class A (Group 1) (3-y-o) £147,500 1½m 10yds....... (4:05)

1218* INTREPIDITY 9-0 M Roberts (9) stumbled aftr one furlong, pushed alng in rear, hdwy on outsd o'r 3 fs out, sstnd run to ld wl ins last, readily. ....(5 to 1 tchd 9 to 2 and 11 to 2) 1
1198^3 ROYAL BALLERINA (Ire) 9-0 W J O'Connor (14) trkd ldrs, pushed alng o'r 3 fs out, ev ch ins last, no extr cl hme. ....(33 to 1 tchd 50 to 1) 2
946* OAKMEAD (Ire) 9-0 L Dettori (1) trkd ldr, led wl o'r 2 fs out till hdd and no extr well ins last. ....(11 to 1 op 12 to 1 tchd 14 to 1) 3
987^3 SUEBOOG (Ire) 9-0 W R Swinburn (4) wtd wth in mid-div, hdwy to hold ev ch 2 fs out, hrd rdn o'r one out, wknd ins last.................(7 to 1 op 8 to 1 tchd 9 to 1) 4
1033* WEMYSS BIGHT 9-0 Pat Eddery (5) trkd ldrs, rdn o'r 2 fs out, wknd ins last......(11 to 2 op 5 to 1 tchd 6 to 1) 5
987^2 IVIZA (Ire) 9-0 R Cochrane (12) mid-div, rdn and cld o'r 3 fs out, sn no imprsn.................................(20 to 1) 6
856* ABURY (Ire) 9-0 J Reid (3) mid-div, reminder o'r 3 fs out, sn hrd rdn and btn...(25 to 1 op 20 to 1 tchd 28 to 1) 7
987* MARILLETTE (USA) 9-0 L Piggott (13) hld up towards rear, hdwy on ins o'r 3 fs out, wknd over one out. .... (9 to 1 op 8 to 1 tchd 10 to 1) 8
1128* GISARNE (USA) 9-0 C Asmussen (6) hld up, effrt and cld 3 fs out, hrd rdn and btn 2 out..... (20 to 1 op 16 to 1) 9
856^2 BASHAYER (USA) 9-0 W Carson (11) rstrained to track ldrs, rdn alng o'r 5 fs out, btn 3 out. ....(10 to 1 tchd 11 to 1) 10
987^4 GROVE DAFFODIL (Ire) (v) 9-0 P Robinson (7) slwly into strd, al beh.................................(200 to 1) 11
1128^2 YAWL 9-0 D Holland (8) sn led, hdd wl o'r 2 fs out, wknd quickly.........................(4 to 1 fav op 7 to 2) 12
808^2 ALOUETTE 9-0 C Roche (2) cl up, pushed alng 7 fs out, sn wknd...............(25 to 1 op 20 to 1 tchd 33 to 1) 13
946^6 BOBBIE DEE 9-0 J Williams (10) beh, cld to track ldrs hfwy, wknd 4 fs out.........(150 to 1 tchd 200 to 1) 14

Dist: ¾l, hd, 5l, hd, 2½l, sht-hd, hd, ¾l, 3l, 1½l. 2m 34.19s. b 1.31s (14 Ran).
SR: 71/69/68/58/57/52/51/50/48/ (Sheikh Mohammed), A Fabre

1526 Energizer Rated Class B Handicap (0-95 3-y-o) £6,016 1½m 10yds.. (4:40)

1256* SUN OF SPRING [80] 8-11 M Roberts (3) in tch, cld 4 fs out, led 2 out, rdn out.......(6 to 1 op 4 to 1 tchd 13 to 2) 1
1006* EMPIRE POOL [90] 9-7 A Munro (6) hld up, cld 3 fs out, ev ch ins last, no extr close hme......(8 to 1 tchd 10 to 1) 2
1028^2 LIJAAM (Ire) [84] 9-1 W R Swinburn (2) led, sn clr, hdd 2 fs out, rallied und pres. (3 to 1 op 5 to 2 tchd 100 to 30) 3
1067* CIRCUS COLOURS [80] 8-11 Pat Eddery (4) chsd clr ldr, cld 4 fs out, sn pushed alng, not much room 2 out, hrd rdn and no response. .... (11 to 10 on op 11 to 8 on tchd 11 to 10) 4
875 TOP RANK [79] 8-10 L Dettori (1) strted slwly, cld 4 fs out, rdn 2 out, wknd ins last........ (20 to 1 tchd 14 to 1) 5

Dist: 1½l, 1½l, 1½l, 4l. 2m 37.33s. a 1.83s (5 Ran).

SR: 37/44/35/28/19/ (Sheikh Mohammed), M R Stoute

1527 Abbots Hill Handicap Class C (0-90 4-y-o and up) £5,617 7f......... (5:10)

1097[5] SILKY SIREN [62] 4-8-0 (3*) D Harrison (14) *beh, rdn and hdwy 2 fs out, edgd lft and led one out, ran on wl.* ....(12 to 1 tchd 14 to 1) 1
1348[4] SO RHYTHMICAL [81] 9-9-8 Pat Eddery (5) *wth ldr, ev ch one furlong out, ran on*.......... (12 to 1 op 10 to 1) 2
1144[7] CAPE PIGEON (USA) [78] 8-9-5 A Munro (12) *beh, hdwy appr fnl furlong, styd on, nvr nrr.* .... (15 to 2 op 7 to 1 tchd 8 to 1) 3
1172[3] HERORA (Ire) [87] 4-10-0 M Roberts (15) *trkd ldrs, rng on whn squeezed for room one furlong out, not reco'r.* .... (9 to 1 op 10 to 1 tchd 12 to 1) 4
1207 INVOCATION [70] 6-8-11 N Adams (4) *trkd ldrs, led wl o'r 2 fs out to one out, one pace*.................. (25 to 1) 5
1172[6] SHIKARI'S SON [78] 6-9-5 P Robinson (16) *chsd ldrs gng wl, rdn alng and one pace frm o'r one furlong out.* .... (16 to 1 op 14 to 1) 6
1144[2] HELIOS [78] 5-9-5 J Reid (9) *trkd ldrs, rdn and one pace frm o'r one furlong out.* (11 to 2 jt-fav op 5 to 1 tchd 6 to 1) 7
1348 BELFORT RULER [68] 6-8-9 W Newnes (6) *chsd ldrs, hrd rdn o'r 2 fs out, sn btn*..............(20 to 1 op 16 to 1) 8
1267* DOMICKSKY [67] 5-8-8 W Carson (2) *nvr a factor.* ....(11 to 2 jt-fav op 5 to 1 tchd 6 to 1) 9
930* RURAL LAD [63] 4-8-4 D Holland (13) *al beh.* ....(11 to 1 op 10 to 1 tchd 12 to 1) 10
1144 ACROSS THE BAY [65] 6-8-6 L Dettori (7) *chsd ldrs, effrt 2 fs out, eased whn btn appr last*....(20 to 1 op 16 to 1) 11
1054[4] ABSOLUTELY RIGHT [52] 5-7-0 (7*) D Wright (8) *strted slwly, al beh*................................(33 to 1) 12
1130[9] SLEEPLINE FANTASY [52] 8-7-7 N Carlisle (11) *mid-div, beh fnl 2 fs*...................................... (20 to 1) 13
1209 TYRIAN PURPLE (Ire) [63] 5-8-1 (3*) B Doyle (3) *led till wl o'r 2 fs out, wknd*.....................(8 to 1 op 10 to 1) 14
1270 MILLSOLIN (Ire) [78] 5-9-5 T Quinn (1) *chsd ldrs, pushed alng hfwy, hrd rdn 2 fs out, wknd one out.* .... (9 to 1 op 7 to 1 tchd 10 to 1) 15
1352 SHARPTINO [64] 4-7-12 (7*) B Russell (10) *in tch to hfwy.* ....(33 to 1) 16

Dist: 1½l, hd, nk, 1½l, hd, ¾l, 2½l, hd, hd, hd. 1m 21.40s. a 1.00s (16 Ran).
SR: 37/51/47/55/33/40/38/20/18/ (S Nixon), M C Pipe

1528 Ebbisham Handicap Class D (0-80 3-y-o) £7,546 7f................... (5:40)

995[2] FAIRY STORY (Ire) [68] 9-3 D Holland (2) *made all, hrd rdn one furlong out, ran on gmely.* .... (13 to 2 op 6 to 1 tchd 7 to 1) 1
1132* PETONELLAJILL [72] 9-7 Pat Eddery (1) *trkd ldrs, rdn alng hfwy, ev ch ins fnl furlong, no extr und pres.* ....(11 to 4 fav op 3 to 1 tchd 7 to 2) 2
802[4] NITOUCHE [67] 9-2 W R Swinburn (11) *trkd ldrs, rdn 2 fs out, one pace*.................... (14 to 1 op 10 to 1) 3
1351 DESERT NOMAD [51] 8-0 C Rutter (3) *wth ldr, ev ch 2 fs out, one pace*.................. (33 to 1 op 25 to 1) 4
1341[2] CHAMPAGNE GRANDY [65] 9-0 P Robinson (4) *hld up beh, hdwy 2 fs out, one pace appr last.* .... (15 to 2 op 5 to 1 tchd 8 to 1) 5
916[2] FLORAC (Ire) [57] 8-6 M Roberts (10) *trkd ldrs, ev ch 3 fs out, wknd*............ (11 to 2 op 9 to 2 tchd 6 to 1) 6
1225[3] RUNRIG (Ire) [52] 8-1 A McGlone (6) *hld up beh, effrt o'r 2 fs out, no imprsn*.....(15 to 2 op 10 to 1 tchd 7 to 1) 7
878* FANFOLD (Ire) [63] 8-12 T Quinn (7) *trkd ldrs till wknd 2 fs out*..............................(5 to 1 op 3 to 1) 8
1175[7] PONTEVECCHIO MODA [67] 9-2 J Reid (9) *in tch till lost pl and ran wide appr strt.* .... (12 to 1 op 8 to 1 tchd 14 to 1) 9
711[7] STORMY HEIGHTS [60] 8-9 L Dettori (5) *beh hfwy.* .... (25 to 1 op 20 to 1 tchd 33 to 1) 10

Dist: 1l, 2l, 2½l, ½l, 3l, ¾l, 5l, ¾l, 2l. 1m 22.20s. a 1.80s (10 Ran).
SR: 39/40/29/5/17/-/ (The Fairy Story Partnership), J W Hills

HAYDOCK (good)
Saturday June 5th
Going Correction: MINUS 0.05 sec. per fur.

1529 Ribble Maiden Stakes Class D (2-y-o) £3,377 5f...................... (2:00)

804[3] ALLWIGHT THEN (Ire) 9-0 S Perks (4) *broke fst, made all, kpt on strly ins fnl furlong*.......... (4 to 1 op 7 to 2) 1
1135[5] GONE TO POT 9-0 W Ryan (5) *struggling to go early pace, improved last 2 fs, fnshd wl*.... (7 to 2 fav tchd 4 to 1) 2
NO MEAN CITY (Ire) 9-0 A Mackay (8) *missed break, last hfwy, steady hdwy appr fnl furlong, prmsg.* .... (14 to 1 op 10 to 1) 3
1401[6] ASTRAC (Ire) 9-0 N Connorton (1) *nvr far away, ran green hfwy, rallied fnl furlong, can improve.* ....(6 to 1 op 5 to 1) 4
1082 THREE OF HEARTS 8-2 (7*) M Humphries (7) *sluggish strt, chsd alng to pick up hfwy, kpt on wl fnl furlong.* .... (33 to 1 op 20 to 1) 5
CAPTAIN CARAT 9-0 K Fallon (6) *tucked away in midfield, shaken up last 2 fs, nvr plcd to chal.* ....(5 to 1 op 9 to 2 tchd 6 to 1) 6
698 DIAMOND FRONTIER (Ire) 9-0 G Carter (9) *chsd alng to keep up, styd on, nvr nrr*.........(12 to 1 op 10 to 1) 7
PETITE MAXINE 8-9 Paul Eddery (2) *speed to press ldg trio for 3 fs, no extr*..... (12 to 1 op 10 to 1 tchd 14 to 1) 8
1169[2] KING RAT (Ire) 9-0 Dean McKeown (3) *broke wl to show speed to hfwy, fdd o'r one furlong out.* ....(9 to 2 op 7 to 2) 9
1158[9] CELTIC GOVERNESS 8-2 (7*) Claire Balding (10) *sluggish strt, bustled alng stands side, no imprsn last 2 fs.* ....(25 to 1) 10

Dist: 1½l, nk, 1½l, hd, 2½l, hd, sht-hd, 1l, 4l. 1m 3.60s. a 4.80s (10 Ran).
(P J Cosgrove), F H Lee

1530 Weaver Handicap Class C (0-90 3-y-o and up) £4,920 1m 30yds...... (2:30)

1494[2] VELOCE (Ire) [56] 5-7-8 A Mackay (7) *patiently rdn, improved o'r 2 fs out, str run to ld ins last, edgd lft, drvn out*..........................(10 to 1 op 8 to 1) 1
1298[5] FOREVER DIAMONDS [80] 6-9-4 M Birch (6) *settled gng wl, improved to ld o'r one furlong out, hdd ins last, kpt on.* ....(6 to 1 tchd 7 to 1) 2
1298[2] CEE-JAY-AY [68] 6-8-6 G Carter (8) *sluggish strt, given time to reco'r, ran on fnl furlong, fnshd wl.* .... (11 to 2 op 6 to 1 tchd 5 to 1) 3
1346[5] LANGTRY LADY [74] (v) 7-8-12 D Biggs (10) *sluggish strt, drvn into midfield hfwy, effrt last 2 fs, ran on one pace.* .... (10 to 1 op 7 to 1) 4
1338* MOORISH [90] 3-8-10 (7*) T G McLaughlin (4) *took keen hold, wth ldr till hrd drvn o'r 2 fs out, sn outpcd.* ....(2 to 1 fav op 7 to 4 tchd 9 to 4) 5
1298[3] ARANY [81] 6-8-12 (7*) S Mulvey (5) *dictated pace till hdd wl o'r one furlong out, no extr*.....(10 to 1 op 7 to 1) 6
1274[8] AMENABLE [78] 8-9-2 Alex Greaves (1) *chsd ldg bunch, feeling pace and drvn alng o'r 2 fs out, no imprsn.* .... (12 to 1 op 10 to 1) 7
1284[3] EXPRESS GIFT [64] 4-7-11 (5*) Darren Moffatt (9) *pressed ldg trio till fdd und pres last 2 fs*..... (5 to 1 op 7 to 2) 8
1298 WILL OF STEEL [87] 4-9-11 K Fallon (2) *last and niggled alng, imprvg on ins whn hmpd and checked o'r one furlong out, not rcvr*............. (14 to 1 op 10 to 1) 9
GRANITTON BAY [72] 6-8-10 A Culhane (3) *wth ldrs, ev ch o'r 2 fs out, fdd*.....................................(50 to 1) 10

Dist: Nk, ¾l, ¾l, 4l, nk, ½l, 1l, 3½l, 4l. 1m 44.51s. a 3.91s (10 Ran).
SR: 15/38/24/28/21/22/17/-/12/ (Maximo Gonzalez), A Bailey

1531 Mersey Handicap Class C (0-90 4-y-o and up) £4,878 1¾m............ (3:00)

1305 JAMES IS SPECIAL (Ire) [45] 5-7-13 J Quinn (6) *patiently rdn, improved frm off the pace to ld o'r one furlong out, styd on wl*.......................(5 to 1 op 9 to 2) 1
1260[5] PHILGUN [60] 4-8-11 (3*) S Maloney (8) *nvr far away, drw level last 2 fs, led briefly o'r one out, kpt on same pace.* ....(6 to 1 op 5 to 1) 2
ROSINA MAE [70] 4-9-10 Dean McKeown (5) *al hndy, nosed ahead briefly wl o'r one furlong out, rdn and one pace ins last*.................... (8 to 1 op 6 to 1) 3
1195[4] MENTALASANYTHIN [60] 4-9-0 A Mackay (7) *set modest pace, made most till wl o'r one furlong out, rallied, not quicken towards finish.* .... (9 to 1 op 8 to 1 tchd 10 to 1) 4
1248[2] PHARLY DANCER [60] 4-9-0 D Biggs (4) *trkd ldr gng wl, rdn to draw level o'r one furlong out, eased whn btn last 50 yards*........... (7 to 1 op 6 to 1 tchd 8 to 1) 5
1156* DECIDED (Can) [50] 10-7-13 (5*) Darren Moffatt (3) *in tch, rdn whn pace lifted o'r 2 fs out, nvr able to chal.* ....(9 to 1 tchd 10 to 1) 6
988 PURITAN (Can) [67] 4-9-7 Kim Tinkler (1) *last strt, rdn o'r 2 fs out, no imprsn*....................(11 to 1 op 10 to 1) 7
1336* PERSUASIVE [64] 6-9-4 Dale Gibson (2) *hld up, struggling whn pace lifted o'r 2 fs out, sn btn.* .... (7 to 4 fav tchd 2 to 1) 8

Dist: 1l, 2½l, 1½l, 2l, 2½l, 2l, 8l. 3m 6.29s. a 8.79s (8 Ran).
SR: -/3/8/-/-/ (J A Thomas), H J Collingridge

1532 John Of Gaunt Stakes Class A (Listed Race) (3-y-o and up) £10,380 7f 30yds .... (3:30)

1337[2] CELESTIAL KEY (USA) 3-8-2 G Carter (1) *al hndy, drvn ahead one furlong out, kpt on grimly.* .... (11 to 4 op 4 to 1 tchd 5 to 2) 1
1002[6] BAND ON THE RUN 6-8-12 J Fortune (2) *tried to make all, hdd and rdn one furlong out, rallied.* ....(7 to 4 fav tchd 15 to 8) 2
660[7] MOJAVE (v) 4-9-8 Paul Eddery (4) *rcd freely, improved to fltter briefly o'r one furlong out, rdn and not run on.* ....(2 to 1 op 6 to 4) 3
1407[7] EURO FESTIVAL 4-8-12 Dean McKeown (3) *wth ldr, ev ch 2 fs out, sn fdd*........................(6 to 1 op 5 to 1) 4

Dist: ½l, 2l, 12l. 1m 31.96s. a 4.76s (4 Ran).
SR: 11/19/23/-/ (M J Brodrick), S G Norton

1533 Douglas Maiden Stakes Class D (3-y-o and up) £3,752 1¾m............(4:00)

1176[2] SAINT KEYNE 3-8-8 W Ryan (9) *al gng wl, led 4 fs out, clr last 2, easily*...(2 to 1 on op 9 to 4 on tchd 7 to 4 on) 1
1224[3] BOKARO (Fr) 7-9-12 G Carter (3) *patiently rdn, gd hdwy to fltter o'r 3 fs out, styd on same pace.* ....(11 to 1 op 8 to 1 tchd 12 to 1) 2
799[2] POINT THE WAY (Ire) 3-8-3 Paul Eddery (6) *trkd ldrs, improved entering strt, styd on last 2 fs.* ....(5 to 1 op 4 to 1) 3
1154[5] RAHIL (Ire) 3-8-8 R Hills (11) *nvr far away, jnd wnr o'r 3 fs out, wknd appr fnl furlong*.........(7 to 1 op 6 to 1) 4
1224[5] FAIRWAYS ON TARGET 7-9-12 Dean McKeown (2) *wtd wth, improved into midfield entering strt, nvr able to chal.* ....(20 to 1 op 16 to 1) 5
WORLD WITHOUT END (USA) 4-9-5 (7*) H Bastiman (7) *wth ldrs, ev ch appr strt, fdd 2 fs out*...(33 to 1 op 25 to 1) 6
1224[8] RAGLAN LADY 6-9-0 (7*) W Hawksley (4) *settled wth ldg bunch, feeling pace o'r 3 fs out, sn btn.* ....(66 to 1 op 50 to 1) 7
MAD CASANOVA (bl) 8-9-12 M Perrett (10) *chsd ldg bunch to strt, btn 3 fs out*............(50 to 1 op 33 to 1) 8
1349[7] TAKE A FLYER (Ire) 3-8-1 (7*) S Drowne (1) *sluggish strt, nvr able to reco'r*............(66 to 1 op 50 to 1) 9
1224[6] BOOTIKIN 5-9-7 K Fallon (5) *niggled alng to keep up aftr a m, nvr a factor*............(66 to 1 op 50 to 1) 10
BOLD REINE (Fr) 4-9-7 D Biggs (13) *chsd ldg bunch to strt, sn btn*............(66 to 1 op 50 to 1) 11
1093 RONEO (USA) (bl) 5-9-12 R Perham (8) *wth ldrs for o'r a m, sn tld off*............(100 to 1) 12

Dist: 5l, sht-hd, 4l, 12l, ½l, ½l, 1½l, 1l, 10l, ¾l. 3m 4.27s. a 6.77s (12 Ran).

SR: 19/27/3/-/-/-/ (Lord Howard de Walden), H R A Cecil

1534 Dee Handicap Class E (0-70 3-y-o) £3,470 1¼m 120yds............(4:30)

672[7] GENERAL MOUKTAR [60] 9-7 M Perrett (6) *wtd wth, improved gng wl to ld o'r one furlong out, drvn out.* ....(13 to 2 op 4 to 1) 1
932* HAZARD A GUESS (Ire) [56] 9-3 K Fallon (1) *last hfwy, dashed up on ins last 2 fs, ran on wl und pres.* ....(3 to 1 fav op 2 to 1 tchd 7 to 2) 2
1259[2] CONTRACT ELITE (Ire) [55] 9-2 A Mackay (7) *trkd ldr, drvn ahead o'r 3 fs out, hdd over one out, one pace.* ....(9 to 2 tchd 5 to 1) 3
1090[7] BOLTROSE [60] 9-7 J Quinn (3) *trkd ldg bunch, feeling pace o'r 2 fs out, sn struggling.* ....(25 to 1 op 20 to 1 tchd 33 to 1) 4
1212[8] MULLED ALE (Ire) [57] 9-4 W Woods (9) *trkd ldrs, rdn 3 fs out, fdd*............(16 to 1 op 12 to 1) 5
642 HASTA LA VISTA [43] 8-4 L Charnock (4) *rcd freely in frnt rnk till wknd quickly o'r 2 fs out*... (11 to 2 op 7 to 1) 6
905[4] ARC BRIGHT (Ire) [56] 9-3 W Ryan (5) *dictated pace till hdd o'r 3 fs out, sn btn*......(6 to 1 op 8 to 1 tchd 9 to 1) 7
833[4] HOT OFF THE PRESS [49] 8-10 A Culhane (2) *trkd ldg bunch, struggling to hold pl o'r 3 fs out, sn btn.* ....(5 to 1 op 9 to 2) 8
1306[7] BLAKES BEAU [55] 9-2 M Birch (8) *settled midfield, effrt entering strt, lost tch quickly o'r 2 fs out.* ....(10 to 1 op 8 to 1 tchd 12 to 1) 9
907[9] FREDDIE JACK [48] 8-9 R Lappin (10) *chsd ldrs to strt, sn tld off*............(20 to 1 op 14 to 1) 10

Dist: ½l, 6l, 2l, 4l, 2l, 1l, 1½l, 12l, 12l. 2m 16.97s. a 5.97s (10 Ran).

SR: 42/37/24/25/14/-/7/-/-/ (A S Helaissi), M C Pipe

LEICESTER (good to firm)
Saturday June 5th
Going Correction: MINUS 0.15 sec. per fur.

1535 Tipsters Table Median Auction Maiden Stakes Class F (2-y-o) £2,595 5f 2yds............(6:45)

1229[2] SWEET DECISION (Ire) 8-9 J Williams (1) *broke very fst, made all, eased ins fnl furlong.* ....(5 to 2 on op 9 to 4 on tchd 2 to 1 on) 1
1182[6] BROUGHTONS PARTNER 9-0 J Quinn (5) *slwly into strd, dsptd 3rd pl, styd on o'r one furlong out, not rch wnr.* ....(11 to 1 op 8 to 1 tchd 12 to 1) 2
GINGERILLO 9-0 Dean McKeown (3) *slwly into strd, ran on appr fnl furlong, not rch wnr.* ....(7 to 1 op 6 to 1 tchd 15 to 2) 3
CLARET BUMBLE 8-9 T Sprake (4) *dsptd 3rd pl, rdn and one pace last 2 fs*......(11 to 1 op 8 to 1 tchd 12 to 1) 4
UN PARFUM DE FEMME (Ire) 9-0 G Bardwell (2) *slwly into strd, al outpcd*......(14 to 1 op 12 to 1 tchd 16 to 1) 5
454 SPORTING HEIR (Ire) 9-0 R Price (6) *chsd wnr, rdn alng 2 out, wknd fnl furlong*............(33 to 1 op 20 to 1) 6

Dist: 8l, sht-hd, sht-hd, 1l, 2½l. 1m 1.10s. a 2.40s (6 Ran).

SR: 32/5/4/ (Mrs Diana Callard), M Williams

1536 Tele-ads Maiden Auction Fillies Stakes Class D (2-y-o) £3,231 5f 218yds............(7:15)

WANDERING ANGEL 8-11 L Dettori (4) *trkd ldrs, led o'r 2 fs out, pushed out*.... (13 to 8 fav op 7 to 4 tchd 2 to 1) 1
ENCORE M'LADY (Ire) 8-11 S Perks (6) *slwly into strd, improved hfwy, swtchd lft 2 out, styd on strly ins fnl furlong*............(12 to 1 op 8 to 1 tchd 14 to 1) 2
776 QUEEN'S TRUST 8-11 B Raymond (5) *chsd ldr, ev ch o'r 2 out, not quicken appr fnl furlong.* ....(3 to 1 tchd 5 to 2 and 100 to 30) 3
1317[7] SALT STONE (Ire) 8-4 (7*) S Mulvey (3) *sn rdn alng, kpt on frm 2 fs out, not trble ldrs.* ....(12 to 1 op 8 to 1 tchd 14 to 1) 4
1032 LEGENDARY LADY 8-11 J Williams (1) *hld up in rear, nvr pace to chal frm hfwy*... (7 to 1 op 6 to 1 tchd 8 to 1) 5
1211 LUCY'S GOLD 8-11 D Biggs (2) *outpcd til some prog und pres hfwy, wknd ins last 2 fs.* ....(5 to 1 op 4 to 1 tchd 11 to 2 and 6 to 1) 6
1135 SOTTISES (Ire) (bl) 8-11 A Munro (7) *led for o'r 3 fs, wknd quickly*............(20 to 1 tchd 25 to 1 and 33 to 1) 7

Dist: ½l, 2½l, 4l, 2½l, 2l, ½l. 1m 13.70s. a 3.30s (7 Ran).

SR: 13/1/1/1/-/ (Mrs P T Fenwick), D R Loder

1537 Mercury Night Fillies Handicap Class E (0-70 3-y-o and up) £2,553 5f 218yds............(7:45)

1267[5] BLUE TOPAZE [67] 5-9-13 J Williams (8) *slwly into strd, rdn alng and ran on o'r 2 out, str brst fnl furlong, led last strides*............(13 to 2 op 6 to 1 tchd 7 to 1) 1
1036[7] MACS MAHARANEE [56] 6-9-2 G Hind (7) *cld on ldrs hfwy, led ins fnl furlong, hdd last strds.* .... (4 to 1 fav op 9 to 2 tchd 5 to 1 and 7 to 2) 2
JOIN THE CLAN [44] 4-8-4 Dean McKeown (15) *pressed ldr, led o'r 2 out till ins fnl furlong, rallied gmely.* ....(33 to 1 op 20 to 1) 3
1209[8] MY RUBY RING [54] 6-9-0 T Williams (3) *ldg grp, rdn alng 2 out, one pace appr fnl furlong.* ....(9 to 1 op 10 to 1 tchd 11 to 1) 4
1267[3] LOUISVILLE BELLE (Ire) [62] 4-9-5 (3*) D Harrison (12) *ldg grp, lost pl entering last 2 fs, no extr.* ....(7 to 1 op 5 to 1 tchd 8 to 1) 5
882 CASTLE MAID [36] 6-7-10[2] D Biggs (14) *led til hdd o'r 2 out, wknd over one furlong out*... (14 to 1 op 12 to 1) 6
948[4] LADY SABO [60] 4-9-6 Paul Eddery (1) *slwly away, effrt o'r 2 fs out, not rch frnt rnk*............(6 to 1 op 7 to 1) 7
1136[4] MANOR ADVENTURE [64] 3-9-1 A Munro (9) *handily plcd til wknd 2 fs out*............(14 to 1) 8
971 MERRYHILL MADAM [48] 4-8-8 R Cochrane (11) *sn outpcd.* ....(25 to 1 op 20 to 1) 9
1373[4] UNVEILED [54] 5-9-0 M Roberts (4) *effrt frm rear hfwy, no imprsn on ldrs last 2 fs*............(8 to 1 op 9 to 1) 10
1230* FATHOM FIVE (Ire) [40] 4-8-0 J Quinn (6) *mid-div til drpd rear last 2 fs*.........(7 to 1 op 8 to 1 tchd 9 to 1) 11
1287 FILICAIA [54] 7-9-0 Kim Tinkler (10) *outpcd.* ....(20 to 1 op 16 to 1 tchd 25 to 1) 12
1230 WEEKEND GIRL [35] 4-7-9[5] (3*) N Kennedy (5) *mid-div, hng rght appr hfwy, sn btn*............(50 to 1) 13
1320[6] FAIRY WISHER (Ire) [44] 4-8-4 N Carlisle (2) *wl plcd for o'r 3 fs*............(20 to 1 tchd 25 to 1) 14
1137[6] MINSHAAR [64] 3-9-1 B Raymond (13) *ldg grp til wknd 2 fs out, tld off*............(16 to 1 op 14 to 1 tchd 20 to 1) 15

Dist: Nk, 1½l, 1½l, 2l, 1½l, 1½l, nk, sht-hd, 1l, sht-hd. 1m 12.40s. a 2.00s (15 Ran).

SR: 55/43/25/29/29/-/15/9/1/ (M S Saunders), M S Saunders

1538 Leicester Mercury Stakes Class A (Listed Race) (4-y-o and up) £9,594 1m 3f 183yds............(8:15)

SONUS (Ire) 4-9-0 W R Swinburn (5) *hld up in tch, cld on ldrs 4 out, rdn alng 2 out, led wl ins fnl furlong, jst held on*............(5 to 2 op 6 to 4 tchd 3 to 1) 1
ONLY ROYALE (Ire) 4-9-0 R Cochrane (2) *steadied leaving stalls and hld up, ran on frm rear 2 out, str brst fnl furlong, jst fld*............(100 to 30 op 9 to 2) 2
1065[2] SHUAILAAN (USA) (bl) 4-9-5 M Roberts (6) *handily plcd, led o'r 2 fs out till over one out, ev ch last 100 yards, not quicken nr line.* ......(11 to 8 fav op 6 to 4 tchd 7 to 4 and 2 to 1) 3
1085[5] BOLOARDO 4-9-0 W Carson (1) *trkd ldr, led o'r 4 out till over 2 out, led ag'n over one out till wl ins fnl furlong, no extr cl hme.* ....(9 to 1 op 10 to 1 tchd 11 to 1 and 12 to 1) 4
1206[2] SHADOWS OF SILVER 5-8-9 A Munro (3) *led til o'r 4 fs out, wknd 3 out, sn lost tch*............(20 to 1 op 16 to 1) 5
616[2] PEARL ANGEL 4-8-9 L Dettori (4) *settled in rear, rdn 4 out, lost tch o'r 2 fs out*....(16 to 1 op 8 to 1 tchd 14 to 1) 6

Dist: Sht-hd, nk, ¾l, 10l, 10l. 2m 29.40s. a 0.90s (6 Ran).

SR: 73/72/76/69/44/24/ (Sheikh Mohammed), J H M Gosden

1539 Sports Mercury Conditions Stakes Class D (3-y-o) £3,325 1m 3f 183yds............(8:45)

OLD PROVENCE 8-10 R Cochrane (1) *dwlt, sn tracking ldr, led aftr 3 fs, made rst, styd on wl frm 2 out.* ....(11 to 2 op 3 to 1 tchd 6 to 1 and 13 to 2) 1
1176* SILVERDALE (USA) 8-12 M Roberts (2) *slwly into strd, hld up beh, effrt 3 out, outpcd 2 out, styd on ag'n ins fnl furlong*....................(5 to 4 on op 11 to 10 on) 2
1116⁴ SALATIN (USA) 9-2 W Carson (3) *pld hrd, led for 3 fs, ev ch frm 2 out til not quicken one out.* ....(7 to 4 op 5 to 4 tchd 2 to 1) 3
Dist: 1½l, ½l. 2m 37.50s. a 9.00s (3 Ran).
(Sheikh Mohammed), L M Cumani

1540 Sporting Green Handicap Class D (0-80 3-y-o) £3,523 7f 9yds...... (9:15)

1194* AL MOULOUKI [69] 9-3 R Cochrane (1) *strted slwly, hdwy o'r 2 out, led one furlong out, drw clr, easily.* ....(11 to 8 fav tchd 6 to 4 and 13 to 8) 1
1388⁵ STARLIGHT ROSE (Ire) [48] 7-10³ T Williams (4) *rdn alng in rear 3 out, ran on 2 out, kpt on one pace fnl furlong.* ....(14 to 1 op 10 to 1) 2
1178⁴ PERSIAN CHARMER (Ire) [73] 9-7 W R Swinburn (5) *settled in 3rd pl, rdn alng o'r 2 out, ev ch over one furlong out, no extr clsg stages.* ....(7 to 2 op 4 to 1 tchd 9 to 2 and 5 to 1) 3
1382⁴ ASHGORE [66] 9-0 Dean McKeown (6) *trkd ldr, led 3 fs out, hdd one out, one pace*...(6 to 1 op 9 to 2 tchd 7 to 1) 4
1008³ SUPERENSIS [47] 7-2 (7*) Kim McDonnell (2) *mid-div, rdn alng and outpcd o'r 2 fs out*.........(6 to 1 op 4 to 1) 5
802⁵ PEACEFULL REPLY (USA) [61] 8-9 S Perks (7) *led for 4 fs, ev ch o'r one out, sn wknd.* ....(14 to 1 op 10 to 1 tchd 16 to 1) 6
129 SPECIAL RISK (Ire) [55] 7-12 (5*) M Fenton (3) *sn rdn alng and outpcd*..........(13 to 2 op 6 to 1 tchd 12 to 1) 7
Dist: 2½l, 1l, sht-hd, 5l, 8l, 4l. 1m 25.70s. a 3.80s (7 Ran).
SR: 30/1/23/15/ (G Jabre), J W Payne

BELMONT PARK (USA) (firm)
Saturday June 5th

1541 Nassau County Handicap (Grade 1) (3-y-o and up) £158,940 1m 1f..........

WEST BY WEST (USA) 4-8-2 J-L Samyn,....... (42 to 10) 1
VALLEY CROSSING (USA) 5-8-0 Julie Krone,.....(12 to 1) 2
STRIKE THE GOLD (USA) 5-8-5 C Perret,.......... (4 to 1) 3
DEVIL HIS DUE (USA) 4-8-11 H McCauley,.. (19 to 10 fav) 4
671² MISSIONARY RIDGE 6-8-5 K Desormeaux,...... (29 to 10) 5
OFFBEAT (USA) 4-8-0 J D Bailey,............... (15 to 1) 6
HONEST ENSIGN (USA) 5-8-2² J Santos,......... (31 to 1) 7
SAND LIZARD (USA) 4-8-0³ M Smith,.............(18 to 1) 8
Dist: ¾l, 1l, 3½l, ½l, 3l, 1 ¾l, nk. 1m 47.58s. (8 Ran).
(John Peace), George Arnold

1542 Belmont Stakes (Grade 1) (3-y-o) £294,397 1½m.......................

COLONIAL AFFAIR (USA) 9-0 Julie Krone (4) ... (139 to 10) 1
779⁷ KISSIN KRIS (USA) 9-0 J Santos (3)............ (13 to 1) 2
1070⁸ WILD GALE (USA) 9-0 S Sellers (14)............ (51 to 1) 3
779⁸ SILVER OF SILVER (USA) 9-0 J Vasquez (12)......(33 to 1) 4
VIRGINIA RAPIDS (USA) 9-0 E Maple (2)........ (49 to 10) 5
1070² CHEROKEE RUN (USA) 9-0 C Antley (1)......... (42 to 10) 6
1070⁵ SEA HERO (USA) 9-0 J D Bailey (11)............(32 to 10) 7
779 BULL INTHE HEATHER (USA) 9-0 J Chavez (6)....(20 to 1) 8
ANTRIM RD (USA) 9-0 R Migliore (13)............(63 to 1) 9
955⁵ ARINTHOD (Fr) 9-0 K Desormeaux (9)............(14 to 1) 0
RAGLAN ROAD (USA) 9-0 L Pincay Jr (7)...........(53 to 1) 0
ONLY ALPHA (USA) 9-0 R Davis (10)..............(88 to 1) 0
1070* PRAIRIE BAYOU (USA) 9-0 M Smith (5)......(27 to 10 fav) pu
Dist: 2 ¼l, ¾l, 2l, 1l, 7l, 2l, 3½l, 3l, ¾l, 7½l. 2m 29.97s. (13 Ran).
(Centennial Farms), F Schulhofer

SAN SIRO (ITY) (firm)
Saturday June 5th

1543 Premio Brunate (2-y-o) £5,603 6f (2:30)

1221⁵ SPAGHETTI WESTERN (Ire) 8-11 A Parravani, *made all, unchlgd*.. 1
AL SPANISH (Ire) 8-11 S Dettori,.. 2
BEL LORE (Ity) 8-11 A Marcialis,.. 3
Dist: 4l, 1l, 3l, ¾l, hd, nk, 3l, 2l, 2l, 1½l. 1m 13.60s. (11 Ran).
(Gerecon Italia), J L Dunlop

CHANTILLY (FR) (good to firm)
Sunday June 6th

1544 Prix du Jockey-Club Lancia (Grade 1) (3-y-o) £298,686 1½m...........(2:50)

1087* HERNANDO (Fr) 9-2 C Asmussen (1) *al in tch, 5th strt, rdn 2 fs out, quickened to ld one and a half out, ran on wl.* ....(2 to 1 fav) 1
1087³ DERNIER EMPEREUR (USA) 9-2 S Guillot (6) *hld up and tenth strt, hdwy o'r 2 fs out, took second one out, no imprsn*.......................................(25 to 1) 2
696* HUNTING HAWK (Ire) 9-2 T Jarnet (9) *7th strt, hdwy and not clr run o'r 2 fs out, styd on over one out.* (23 to 10) 3
890³ NEWTON'S LAW (Ire) 9-2 J Reid (8) *al prmnt, 3rd strt, rdn 2 fs out, kpt on one pace*.......................(21 to 1) 4
955* REGENCY 9-2 Pat Eddery (7) *trkd ldr, rdn to ld o'r 2 fs out, hdd and wknd over one and a half out.* (22 to 10) 5
1149⁵ BADOLATO (USA) 9-2 L Dettori (4) *6th strt, sn rdn and one pace*..(38 to 1) 6
1012* FREEZING BIRD (USA) 9-2 F Head (5) *nvr nrr*......(7 to 1) 7
1149* SIN KIANG (Fr) 9-2 E Legrix (10) *nvr rch ldrs*..... (11 to 1) 8
955⁴ SHANDON LAKE (Ire) 9-2 C Roche (11) *prmnt, 4th strt, rdn and wknd 2 fs out*.............................(41 to 1) 9
955⁶ FORT WOOD (USA) 9-2 W R Swinburn (3) *al beh.* (23 to 10) 0
955⁸ KNOWN LOVER (USA) 9-2 M de Smyter (2) *led till o'r 2 fs out*...(22 to 10) 0
Dist: 2½l, ¾l, ½l, 1½l, 1l, 2½l, 1l, 1½l, 2½l, 8l. 2m 27.20s. a 0.20s (11 Ran).
SR: 82/77/75/74/71/69/64/62/59/ (S S Niarchos), F Boutin

1545 Prix de Sandringham (Group 3) (3-y-o) £23,895 1m.................... (3:30)

1086² SKI PARADISE (USA) 8-11 T Jarnet, *hld up, 6th strt, led one and a half furlong out, eased cl hme*....(5 to 2 on) 1
ROUQUETTE 8-11 A Badel, *last strt, hdwy 2 fs out, ran on to take second on line*.................... (6 to 1) 2
697⁶ SHOWGUM (Fr) 8-11 A Junk, *3rd strt, second and hrd rdn one furlong out, no extr cl hme*............. (12 to 1) 3
983* BINT LARIAFF (USA) 8-11 W R Swinburn, *led till one and a half fs out, kpt on one pace*.................(76 to 10) 4
983² LA GROUPIE (Fr) 8-11 F Head, *4th strt, chlgd 2 fs out, wknd one out*...................................(52 to 10) 5
697⁵ GRANSE OAKS (USA) 8-11 C Asmussen, *5th strt, effrt 2 fs out, sn rdn and btn*...............................(68 to 10) 6
GAIRSIC (Fr) 8-11 G Benoit, *dwlt, reco'red to dispute, second strt, wknd quickly over 2 fs out*........ (6 to 1) 7
Dist: 3l, nose, nk, nk, 20l. 1m 36.90s. a 2.20s (7 Ran).
SR: 46/37/36/35/34/33/-/ (Zenya Yoshida), A Fabre

1546 Prix de la Jonchere (Group 3) (3-y-o) £23,895 1m.................... (5:00)

656² SHARMAN (USA) 8-11 T Jarnet, *6th strt, effrt 2 fs out, hrd rdn to ld fnl strds*.................................(36 to 10) 1
TRESOR DU MESNIL (Fr) 8-11 J Reid, *4th strt, hrd rdn one furlong out, hard ridden to take second cl hme.* ....(21 to 1) 2
1220* GUIDE (Fr) 8-11 O Benoist, *led till fnl strds*.... (57 to 10) 3
1367⁶ KADOUNOR (Fr) 9-3 O Peslier, *last strt, rdn 2 fs out, some late hdwy*..(49 to 10) 4
867³ HAWK SPELL (USA) 8-11 Pat Eddery, *3rd strt, chlgd one out, no extr ins fnl furlong*.................. (53 to 10) 5
954⁵ FANTASTIC DREAM (Ire) 8-11 F Head, *second strt, chlgd 2 out, one pace fnl furlong*................... (73 to 10) 6
954³ HUDO (USA) 8-11 C Asmussen, *5th strt, rdn and btn 2 fs out*.......................................(14 to 10 fav) 7
Dist: Sht-nk, nose, 1l, nose, nk, 6l. 1m 43.20s. a 8.50s (7 Ran).
(Sheikh Mohammed), A Fabre

SAN SIRO (ITY) (good to firm)
Sunday June 6th

1547 Premio Naviglio (3-y-o) £11,207 1½m ....(2:35)

DI GIACOMO 8-12 W Carson, *trkd ldr, rdn to ld one furlong out, ran on wl*.. 1
VEDAMIS 8-9 O Fancera,.. 2
SATELLITE GLINT 8-9 A Carboni,.................................. 3
Dist: 3l, 1l, ¾l, 2l, ½l. 2m 31.00s. (6 Ran).
(G Mazza), J L Dunlop

1548 Premio Emilio Turati (Group 2) (3-y-o and up) £43,331 1m........... (4:00)

1029³ CULTURE VULTURE (USA) 4-9-0 T Quinn, *rear early, 3rd strt, not clr run o'r 2 fs out, rdn to ld ins fnl furlong*... 1
1362³ PROSPECTIVE RULER (USA) 5-9-3 D Holland, *led, quickened wl o'r 3 fs out, ct ins fnl furlong*............... 2
VENTIQUATTROFOGLI (Ire) 3-8-7 W Carson, *pld hrd early, second strt, outpcd 2 fs out, rallied fnl furlong*....... 3
696⁵ BRAZANY (USA) 3-8-7 E Saint-Martin, *5th strt, kpt on one pace*.. 4
1089³ NIGHT MANOEUVRES 4-9-3 S Landi, *6th strt, ev ch o'r one furlong out, one pace*....................................... 5
1089² GOLDEN MINTAGE (USA) 5-9-3 L Sorrentino, *mid-div, one pace fnl 2 fs*.. 6
CAPOLAGO (Ire) 6-9-3 S Soto, *nvr able to chal*........... 7
1363* GOLDEN BECHETT (Ire) 3-8-7 A Munro, *in tch 5 fs*........ 8
593² EL DINERO (Ire) 5-9-3 O Fancera, *trkd ldr 3 fs, 4th strt, btn o'r 2 out*... 9

Dist: Nk, 1l, 2½l, ½l, ½l, hd, nose, 4l. 1m 39.20s. (9 Ran).
(Christopher Wright), P F I Cole

LEOPARDSTOWN (IRE) (good)
Monday June 7th

Going Correction: MINUS 0.10 sec. per fur. (races 1,4,5,6), NIL (2,3)

1549 Ascom Timeplex Handicap (75-95 3-y-o) £5,620 7f.................... (2:30)

LEGAL FLAIR (Ire) [-] 9-4 R Hughes (7)............ (3 to 1) 1
704* SUAVE GROOM (Ire) [-] (bl) 8-12 M J Kinane (4).... (5 to 1) 2
666 GLOWING VALUE (Ire) [-] (bl) 9-7 J P Murtagh (5)..(20 to 1) 3
1046⁹ MISS MISTLETOES (Ire) [-] 8-8 S Craine (6)........ (6 to 1) 4
1199* READY (Ire) [-] 9-7 W J Supple (3)............(13 to 8 fav) 5
1199⁶ BENE MERENTI (Ire) [-] 8-6 J F Egan (2)..........(16 to 1) 6
939 GATE LODGE (Ire) [-] 9-6 W J O'Connor (1)....... (10 to 1) 7
Dist: ½l, nk, ¾l, 1½l. 1m 28.00s. a 2.60s (7 Ran).
SR: 54/46/54/39/47/-/-/ (Miss P F O'Kelly), M J Grassick

1550 Acer E.B.F. Maiden (2-y-o) £5,344 6f ....(3:00)

1197⁴ MONTE MARIO (USA) 9-0 M J Kinane (8).........(11 to 4) 1
UNDER SIEGE (Ire) 9-0 J P Murtagh (2)........(2 to 1 fav) 2
1045² CORINADO (Ire) 9-0 C Roche (3)................ (9 to 4) 3
1332⁶ SPRING FORCE (Ire) (bl) 9-0 W J O'Connor (5)....(10 to 1) 4
QUASIMODO (Ire) 9-0 W J Supple (7).............. (9 to 1) 5
1044³ LITTLE MUSGRAVE (Ire) 9-0 J Carroll (6).......... (10 to 1) 6
NURMI (Ire) 9-0 J F Egan (4)....................... (12 to 1) 7
DANCING BRIEF (Ire) 8-12 (2*) D G O'Shea (1).... (20 to 1) 8
FANCY BOOTS (Ire) 8-9 (2*) R M Burke (9)........(20 to 1) 9
Dist: 2l, 1½l, 1l, 1l. 1m 16.00s. a 4.50s (9 Ran).
SR: 10/2/-/-/-/-/ (Saleh Y Al-Homaisi), D K Weld

1551 The Cara Ballyogan Stakes (Group 3) (3-y-o and up) £14,625 5f........(3:30)

795⁸ SEA GAZER (Ire) 3-8-8 K Darley (8) *dsptd ld, advantage 2 fs out, quickened 3 ls clr appr last, kpt on wl*..... (7 to 1) 1
1201 BRADAWN BREEVER (Ire) (bl) 4-9-2 W J Supple (7) *trkd ldrs, rdn 2 fs out, styd on strly und pres ins last.* ....(10 to 1) 2
781* PALACEGATE EPISODE (Ire) 3-8-5 J Carroll (1) *dsptd ld, hdd 2 fs out, sn rdn, kpt on one pace*........(100 to 30) 3
1201 DASHING COLOURS (Ire) 4-8-13 J F Egan (9) *trkd ldrs, rdn 2 fs out, kpt on*............................... (12 to 1) 4
1406⁷ SPANIARDS CLOSE 5-9-2 T Sprake (2) *mid-div, gd prog 2 fs out, rdn and no extr ins last*................(12 to 1) 5
897* DAWNSIO (Ire) 3-8-5 R Hughes (5) *hld up, prog 2 fs out, no extr ins last*..................................(3 to 1 fav) 6
1201⁷ DIAMONDS GALORE (Can) 8-9-2 M J Kinane (3) *al rear, rdn and wknd appr last*..............................(5 to 1) 7
1385⁶ AFTERGLOW (Ire) (bl) 4-8-13 L O'Shea (6) *al rear, rdn and wknd 2 fs out*..................................(100 to 1) 8
LEADING TIME (Fr) 4-9-2 C Roche (4) *mid-div, rdn and wknd 2 fs out*.....................................(11 to 1) 9
Dist: 1l, ¾l, ¾l, ½l. 1m 0.00s. a 1.30s (9 Ran).
SR: 68/72/58/63/64/-/ (P D Savill), T D Barron

1552 Compaq Glencairn Stakes (Listed) (4-y-o and up) £8,725 1m 1f........(4:00)

940² MALVERNICO (Ire) 5-8-9 C Roche (8) *wl-plcd, prog 2 fs out, quickened to ld ins last, kpt on*.............. (11 to 2) 1
1049³ APPROACH THE BENCH (Ire) 5-9-0 M J Kinane (1) *hld up, prog 2 fs out, kpt on strly ins last*..........(7 to 4 fav) 2
670* SALMON EILE (Ire) 5-9-0 J P Murtagh (11) *wl-plcd, prog to ld 2 fs out, hdd and no extr ins last*............(7 to 1) 3
308⁵ BALLYKETT PRINCE (Ire) (bl) 5-8-7 (2*) R M Burke (10) *mid-div, some prog 2 fs out, styd on strly ins last*...(10 to 1) 4
1024⁷ GLYER (USA) 4-8-9 S Craine (5) *led, hdd 2 fs out, rdn, eased whn btn cl hme*........................(20 to 1) 5
1201³ STREET REBEL (Can) (bl) 5-9-2 W J Supple (12) *mid-div, rdn 3 fs out, kpt on one pace*....................(7 to 1) 6
1199 CLASSIC MATCH (Ire) 5-8-9 Joanna Morgan (7) *mid-div, styd on one pace*.............................. (40 to 1) 7
PRE-EMINENT 6-9-0 W J Smith (3) *hld up, styd on fnl 2 fs.* ....(20 to 1) 8
895⁶ WINNING HEART 6-8-6 K Darley (2) *rear, kpt on strt without threatening ldrs*..................... (20 to 1) 9
BE MY HOPE (Ire) 4-8-6 R Hughes (13) *mid-div, rdn and wknd 2 fs out*...................................(14 to 1) 10
308⁸ NINJA DANCER (USA) 4-8-9 D V Smith (9) *al rear*. (20 to 1) 11
1050⁶ CHEVIOT AMBLE (Ire) 5-8-6 J F Egan (6) *mid-div, badly hmpd and lost pl 3 fs out, wknd*.............(12 to 1) 12
ESPRIT D'ETOILE (USA) (bl) 8-8-9 W J O'Connor (4) *trkd ldr, wknd quickly 3 fs out*..........................(20 to 1) 13
Dist: ½l, nk, 1l, 2l. 1m 52.80s. a 2.30s (13 Ran).
SR: 47/50/49/41/35/-/ (Mrs D Mahony), J S Bolger

1553 Mannesmann Tally Handicap (0-90 3-y-o) £4,240 1¼m............. (4:30)

1123³ TRYARRA (Ire) [-] 8-10 K Darley (7)................(8 to 1) 1
1046³ SHAHZADI (Ire) [-] 9-5 J P Murtagh (5)............ (9 to 2) 2
982* VALONA (Ire) [-] 9-1 C Roche (6)...................(5 to 1) 3
1334² MICKS DELIGHT (Ire) [-] 8-9 S Craine (4).......(2 to 1 fav) 4
1235⁴ CALL MY GUEST (Ire) [-] 8-2 W J Supple (3)....... (7 to 1) 5
1025⁹ SIR SLAVES [-] (bl) 9-5 M J Kinane (8)..............(9 to 1) 6
1139³ PULMICORT [-] 7-8 Joanna Morgan (1).......... (12 to 1) 7
RUPERT THE GREAT (Ire) [-] 8-5 J F Egan (9)..... (33 to 1) 8
959⁶ BOBADIL (Ire) [-] 7-5 (2*) D G O'Shea (11)........ (14 to 1) 9
1511⁹ TOPSEYS TIPPLE (Ire) [-] 9-1 R Hughes (10)...... (12 to 1) 10
1441⁸ DRESS DANCE (Ire) [-] (bl) 8-8 D V Smith (2)...... (33 to 1) 11
Dist: 1l, nk, nk. 2m 9.50s. a 4.80s (11 Ran).
SR: 38/45/40/33/-/-/ (Mrs K Doyle), Mrs A M O'Brien

1554 Racal Datacomm E.B.F. Race (3-y-o and up) £4,240 1¾m............(5:00)

1024³ VINTAGE CROP 6-10-9 M J Kinane (5).........(2 to 1 on) 1
1334* BALLYKETT LADY (USA) 3-9-2 C Roche (1)........(3 to 1) 2
1292³ IMAD (USA) 3-8-12 W J Supple (2).................(8 to 1) 3
EUROPE (USA) 3-8-6 (8*) T E Durcan (6)...........(8 to 1) 4
1014* ANY MINUTE NOW (Ire) 3-8-12 R Hughes (3)..... (33 to 1) 5
Dist: 2½l, 12l, 3l, 13l. 3m 2.20s. a 6.20s (5 Ran).
SR: 47/21/ (Michael W J Smurfit), D K Weld

NOTTINGHAM (good to firm)
Monday June 7th

Going Correction: MINUS 0.15 sec. per fur. (races 1,2,6), PLUS 0.10 (3,4,5)

1555 Radcliffe Selling Stakes Class G (2-y-o) £2,721 5f 13yds............ (2:30)

1403 TINKER OSMASTON 8-6 J Curant (10) *in tch, smooth hdwy to ld appr fnl furlong, pushed clr ins last.* ....(5 to 2 fav op 6 to 1) 1
1082⁸ LADY RISKY 8-6 Pat Eddery (3) *chsd ldrs, rdn and ev ch o'r one furlong out, edgd rght and not quicken ins last.* ....(5 to 1 op 2 to 1 tchd 6 to 1) 2
1418 BUNNY RUN 8-3 (3*) S Maloney (14) *hld up, effrt whn not clr run frm 2 fs out, ran on ins last*..(6 to 1 op 5 to 1) 3
1245⁷ MRS JOGGLEBURY 7-13 (7*) J Tate (9) *nvr far away, drvn alng 2 fs out, hng rght o'r one out, no extr.* ....(14 to 1 op 6 to 1) 4
1272 ARKINDALE SPIRIT (Ire) (bl) 8-11 T Lucas (7) *wth ldrs, ev ch o'r one furlong out, sn btn.* ....(7 to 1 op 8 to 1 tchd 14 to 1 and 9 to 2) 5
LADY WESTBURY (Ire) 8-6 S Whitworth (13) *al prmnt, led briefly o'r one furlong out, kpt on same pace ins last.* ....(6 to 1 op 7 to 1 tchd 12 to 1) 6
TITCH ON TIME 7-13 (7*) S Mulvey (1) *slwly into strd, beh and sn outpcd, improved 2 fs out, kpt on ins last.* ....(8 to 1 op 6 to 1) 7
949 SULLAMELL 8-4 (7*) S Drowne (4) *dwlt, in tch on outer, effrt 2 fs out, one pace whn baulked ins last.* ....(20 to 1 op 12 to 1) 8
1254⁶ MONKEY MONEY (Ire) 8-6 G Carter (2) *led til hdd o'r one furlong out, drvn alng and sn wknd.* ....(12 to 1 op 4 to 1) 9
ASTROLOGY 8-6 Kim Tinkler (12) *beh and sn pushed alng, rdn whn hmpd o'r one furlong out, not rcvr.* ....(20 to 1 op 12 to 1) 10
1413⁹ LITTLE HOOLIGAN 8-11 C Rutter (6) *slwly into strd, sn outpcd and drvn alng, nvr on terms.* ....(14 to 1 op 10 to 1) 11
1317 SILVERISTE (Ire) 8-11 W Newnes (5) *pushed alng beh ldg grp, fdd 2 fs out*..................(33 to 1 op 20 to 1) 12
969⁷ ALICE OF LOXLEY 8-6 R P Elliott (11) *beh and sn rdn alng, struggling frm hfwy*..............(33 to 1 op 20 to 1) 13
DOG AND GUN 8-11 B Raymond (8) *missed break, struggling thrght, tld off*.............. (33 to 1 op 12 to 1) 14
Dist: 3l, hd, 1½l, 1½l, hd, 1l, 1½l, sht-hd, ½l, 1l. 1m 2.70s. a 4.50s (14 Ran).
(Mrs S Foster), C N Williams

1556 EBF Plumtree Maiden Stakes Class D (2-y-o) £3,318 5f 13yds..........(3:00)

TORCH ROUGE 9-0 D Holland (1) *missed break, given time to reco'r, hdwy and switch ins over 2 fs out, led over one out, sn clr, easily*...............(3 to 1 op 6 to 4) 1
1265³ DOLLAR GAMBLE (Ire) 9-0 B Raymond (2) *pressed ldrs, ev ch whn baulked o'r one furlong out, not quicken ins last*...............................(4 to 1 op 3 to 1) 2
ASHKERNAZY (Ire) 8-9 W Carson (7) *led til hdd o'r 2 fs out, sn rdn alng, not quicken over one out.* ....(12 to 1 op 10 to 1) 3
IN MY LEAGUE (Ire) 9-0 M Hills (6) *in tch, drvn alng hfwy, wknd o'r one furlong out*..........(10 to 1 op 6 to 1) 4
1135⁹ HELLABY 9-0 Pat Eddery (3) *dwlt, sn in tch, rdn to have ev ch wl o'r one furlong out, wknd ins last.* ....(20 to 1 op 10 to 1) 5
859² PALACEGATE JACK (Ire) 9-0 G Carter (4) *nvr far away, led o'r 2 fs out, hdd over one out, edgd lft and sn btn.* ...(5 to 4 on op 11 to 10 on tchd 11 to 8 and 6 to 4) 6
1303⁶ TAUFELIANE 8-9 L Dettori (5) *chsd ldrs, drvn alng hfwy, sn lost tch*...............................(33 to 1) 7
Dist: 5l, 1½l, 1½l, 2½l, sht-hd, 6l. 1m 1.80s. a 3.60s (7 Ran).

SR: 13/-/-/-/ (J Hanson), B W Hills

1557 Bilborough Apprentice Rating Related Maiden Stakes Class F (3-y-o) £2,444 1 ¾m 15yds.................... (3:30)

1170[3] DODGY DANCER 8-9 (5*) R Painter (5) *nvr far away, effrt o'r 2 fs out, sstnd run to ld ins last, kpt on wl.* ....(13 to 8 fav op 6 to 4) 1
1534[7] ARC BRIGHT (Ire) 8-9 (5*) J Dennis (6) *set sedate pace, quickened clr entering strt, rdn 2 fs out, hdd ins last, no extr*............................(3 to 1 op 5 to 2) 2
928[2] HO-JOE (Ire) 9-0 S Maloney (4) *patiently rdn, improved 4 fs out, drvn o'r 2 out, not quicken entering last.* ....(9 to 4 op 7 to 4 tchd 5 to 2) 3
1133 PETITE JESS 8-6 (3*) N Gwilliams (3) *hld up in tch, improved o'r 3 fs out, pushed alng over 2 out, wknd appr last*........................(20 to 1 op 12 to 1) 4
1244[3] PREMIER BLUES (Fr) (bl) 8-4 (5*) Sarah Thompson (2) *cl up, pushed alng o'r 3 fs out, sn btn*....(20 to 1 op 10 to 1) 5
MERCH FACH (Ire) 8-4 (5*) S Drowne (1) *chsd ldrs, drpd rear 6 fs out, rdn 3 out, sn btn*......(10 to 1 op 7 to 1) 6

Dist: ¾l, 2½l, 5l, 6l, 10l. 3m 14.40s. a 16.50s (6 Ran).
(T W Langley), M R Channon

1558 Lowdham Conditions Stakes Class D (3-y-o) £3,318 1m 54yds........ (4:00)

736[5] PALACE PAGEANT (USA) 8-10 L Dettori (3) *nvr far away, improved on bit to ld o'r 3 fs out, rdn and ran on wl ins last*..............................(8 to 1 op 6 to 1) 1
825* DRAMANICE (USA) 9-0 L Piggott (5) *hld up in tch, improved on bit o'r 2 fs out, shaken up and ran on ins last, not rch wnr*.... (5 to 4 fav op 7 to 4 tchd 2 to 1) 2
529* FLUVIAL (Ire) 9-0 Pat Eddery (4) *pressed ldr, chlgd o'r 3 fs out, ev ch over one out, not quicken ins last.* ....(3 to 1 op 7 to 4) 3
540[9] TAAHHUB (Ire) 8-10 W Carson (2) *hld up in last pl, rdn alng o'r 2 fs out, nvr able to chal*.... (8 to 1 op 6 to 1) 4
1145* AJALAN (Ire) 9-0 W R Swinburn (1) *led til hdd o'r 3 fs out, sn btn, eased fnl furlong*.......... (5 to 1 op 11 to 4) 5

Dist: 2l, 2½l, 3l, 1½l. 1m 46.60s. a 6.60s (5 Ran).
SR: 9/7/ (Paul Mellon), I A Balding

1559 River Trent Conditions Stakes Class D (4-y-o and up) £3,172 1m 1f 213yds ....(4:30)

ST NINIAN 7-8-11 (3*) S Maloney (5) *bit slpd leaving stalls, hld up, not handle bend entering strt, improved to ld o'r 2 fs out, hng rght, styd on wl.* ....(3 to 1 op 5 to 2 tchd 100 to 30) 1
533[2] PETO 4-9-2 M Roberts (4) *prmnt in chasing grp, effrt and rdn o'r 2 fs out, not quicken ins last.* .... (Evens fav op 6 to 4 on) 2
1407[6] KRISTIANSTAD 4-9-2 Paul Eddery (2) *patiently rdn, effrt 2 fs out, kpt on ins fnl furlong.* ....(2 to 1 op 5 to 2 tchd 11 to 4) 3
990 WRETS 4-8-4[1] (7*) R Painter (1) *chsd clr ldr, pushed alng 3 fs out, wknd fnl furlong*......... (100 to 1 op 50 to 1) 4
ALMOSTAUTOMATIC (Ire) 4-8-10 W Newnes (3) *led and sn clr, hdd o'r 2 fs out, soon wknd*..(100 to 1 op 50 to 1) 5

Dist: 1½l, ½l, 4l, 15l. 2m 7.80s. a 4.80s (5 Ran).
SR: 62/61/60/46/16/ (M H Easterby), M H Easterby

1560 Sandiacre Handicap Class D (0-80 3-y-o and up) £3,435 5f 13yds.......(5:00)

1249[4] EWALD (Ire) [64] 5-9-5 L Dettori (11) *made all, hld on gmely whn hrd pressed ins fnl furlong*..... (8 to 1 op 4 to 1) 1
1379[3] CATHERINES WELL [70] 10-9-11 T Lucas (5) *beh, weaved through 2 fs out, chlgd ins last, hld cl hme.* ....(6 to 1 op 4 to 1 tchd 13 to 2) 2
1473[2] MISS VAXETTE [73] 4-9-7 (7*) M Humphries (9) *nvr far away, rdn to chal entering fnl furlong, no extr towards finish*............(7 to 2 fav op 5 to 2 tchd 4 to 1) 3
1473[7] PEERAGE PRINCE [67] (bl) 4-9-1 (7*) G Forster (13) *pressed ldrs, drvn 2 fs out, one pace ins last.* ....(8 to 1 tchd 10 to 1) 4
923[7] PALEY PRINCE (USA) [73] 7-10-0 W R Swinburn (10) *mid-div, rdn to improve 2 fs out, kpt on ins last.* ....(15 to 2 op 7 to 1 tchd 9 to 1) 5
1282[2] FARMER JOCK [54] 11-8-9 M Roberts (4) *beh, pushed alng to improve o'r 2 fs out, not quicken ins last.* ....(13 to 2 op 7 to 1 tchd 9 to 1) 6
1327[4] THE FED [54] 3-8-1 W Carson (12) *chsd ldrs, drvn alng 2 fs out, wknd appr last*............ (12 to 1 tchd 10 to 1) 7
1379[5] FOLLOWMEGIRLS [59] 4-8-9 (5*) A Garth (1) *swtchd rght strt, beh, rdn alng hfwy, no imprsn.* ....(16 to 1 op 10 to 1) 8
1287[6] SO SUPERB [62] (bl) 4-9-3 S Webster (7) *in tch, drvn hfwy, wknd o'r one furlong out.* ....(8 to 1 op 6 to 1 tchd 9 to 1) 9
1240[6] ABSOLUTELY NUTS [68] 4-9-9 D Holland (14) *taken early to post, speed stands side for o'r 3 fs, fdd.* ....(7 to 1 tchd 8 to 1) 10
1352[7] HARDLINER [60] 4-9-1 W Woods (8) *in tch, rdn alng hfwy, wknd o'r one furlong out*........(16 to 1 tchd 14 to 1) 11
1073[7] ROCK SONG (Ire) [46] 4-8-1[1] G Hind (6) *reared leaving stalls and lost many ls, nvr able to reco'r.* ....(33 to 1 op 25 to 1) 12
501 GANESHAYA [49] (bl) 4-8-4 N Carlisle (3) *slwly into strd, beh and sn outpcd, nvr a factor.* ....(16 to 1 tchd 20 to 1 and 14 to 1) 13
677 CRECHE [60] (bl) 4-8-8 (7*) Madeleine Smith (2) *rcd alone centre, speed 3 fs, fdd*.........................(20 to 1) 14

Dist: Sht-hd, nk, 1½l, 2l, 1½l, 1½l, ½l, 1½l, 1½l, ½l. 1m 0.30s. a 2.10s (14 Ran).
SR: 48/53/55/43/41/16/2/13/10/ (Mark Johnston Racing Ltd), M Johnston

PONTEFRACT (firm) Monday June 7th

Going Correction: MINUS 0.35 sec. per fur. (races 1,3,5), MINUS 0.50 (2,4,6)

1561 June Maiden Auction Stakes Class F (2-y-o) £3,027 5f...............(2:45)

1071[3] INDIAN CRYSTAL 8-9 Dean McKeown (12) *quickly away, made all, clr 2 fs out, rdn and ran on fnl furlong.* ....(8 to 1 op 6 to 1) 1
FORT ERIE 9-0 L Charnock (5) *al prmnt, effrt to chase wnr 2 fs out, sn rdn and one pace ins last.* ....(9 to 2 fav op 8 to 1) 2
776[8] GAELIC STAR (Ire) 9-0 R Cochrane (4) *in tch, effrt and hdwy 2 fs out, sn rdn and one pace fnl furlong.* ....(5 to 1 op 7 to 2) 3
BENEFICIARY 8-9 M Birch (1) *beh, gd hdwy on inner 2 fs out, styd on ins last, nrst finish*.... (10 to 1 op 8 to 1) 4
1263[2] MONKEY'S WEDDING 9-0 J Fortune (3) *chsd ldrs, rdn o'r 2 fs out, kpt on one pace.* (5 to 1 op 11 to 2 tchd 9 to 2) 5
1158[4] STUDFORD GIRL (v) 8-9 T Quinn (2) *cl up, rdn o'r 2 fs out, grad wknd*......................(14 to 1 tchd 16 to 1) 6
LEGAL TRAIN 9-0 G Duffield (9) *hdwy hfwy, styd on wl fnl 2 fs, better for race*................ (20 to 1 op 7 to 1) 7
FUN'N'FORTUNE 8-9 M Wigham (7) *nvr rch ldrs.* .... (33 to 1 op 25 to 1) 8
NON VINTAGE (Ire) 9-0 J Quinn (13) *slwly into strd and rear till some hdwy fnl 2 fs*....... (20 to 1 op 12 to 1) 9
1158[5] TENPIN PROPHET (Ire) (bl) 8-6 (3*) D Harrison (11) *al mid-div*..............................(20 to 1 op 14 to 1) 10
968 GALLIC GENT 9-0 P Robinson (10) *chsd ldrs, rdn 2 fs out, sn wknd*.................. (14 to 1 op 10 to 1) 11
1355[7] MAZINA 8-2 (7*) G Parkin (6) *nvr a factor.* .... (66 to 1 op 20 to 1) 12
793[7] STRADISHALL 9-0 N Day (8) *sn outpcd, beh frm hfwy.* ....(6 to 1 op 7 to 2) 13

Dist: 2½l, 2l, 2½l, sht-hd, 1l, sht-hd, ½l, sht-hd, 1½l, ¾l. 1m 3.20s. a 2.00s (13 Ran).
SR: 20/15/7/-/-/-/ (Mrs B A Matthews), M Johnston

1562 Dewsbury Selling Stakes Class G (3-y-o and up) £2,658 1¼m 6yds... (3:15)

1304[4] SILVER SAMURAI 4-9-11 J Lowe (7) *mid-div, gd hdwy on inner 2 and a half fs out, effrt to chal appr fnl furlong, led ins last, ran on*.. (7 to 2 fav op 9 to 2 tchd 3 to 1) 1
1319[4] SO SAUCY 3-7-11 (3*) B Doyle (15) *led, quickened 3 fs out, rdn o'r one out, hdd and no extr ins last.* ....(11 to 2 op 7 to 1) 2
1286[7] FLETCHER'S BOUNTY (Ire) 4-9-4 M Birch (13) *mid-div, steady hdwy 4 fs out, effrt to chase ldr 2 out, sn rdn and one pace*..........................(5 to 1 op 4 to 1) 3
1179[3] WORKINGFORPEANUTS (Ire) 3-7-11 (3*) D Harrison (5) *stumbled strt, sn in tch, rdn 3 fs out, edgd lft and kpt on one pace*.................... (9 to 2 tchd 5 to 1) 4
1358[3] FORMAESTRE (Ire) 3-8-2 (5*) O Pears (1) *al chasing ldrs, rdn and not clr run 2 and a half fs out, sn one pace.* ....(6 to 1 op 7 to 1) 5
1389[3] WINGED WHISPER (USA) 4-9-4 (7*) D McCabe (8) *al prmnt, rdn 3 fs out, wknd 2 out*................... (20 to 1) 6
1389[5] MALINDI BAY 5-9-4 E Johnson (6) *beh, hdwy and pushed alng 4 fs out, styd on fnl 2 furlongs, nvr dngrs.* (20 to 1) 7
1284 ABSOLUTLEY FOXED (bl) 4-8-13 A Mackay (14) *chsd ldrs, rdn 3 fs out and sn wknd*....(33 to 1 op 25 to 1) 8
METTERNICH 8-9-11 P Robinson (10) *al beh.* ....(9 to 1 op 7 to 1) 9
LADY RANDOLPH 4-8-13 M Wood (12) *in tch till wknd 4 fs out*..(50 to 1) 10
STORM VIXEN 4-8-13 G Duffield (11) *al rear.* .... (14 to 1 op 7 to 1) 11
BAJAN AFFAIR 3-8-0 Dale Gibson (3) *nvr rch ldrs.* (25 to 1) 12
962 SUPER CHARGE 4-9-4 S Morris (9) *al rear.* .... (50 to 1 op 33 to 1) 13
1191[9] NEWGATESKY 3-8-0 L Charnock (16) *cl up till rdn 4 fs out and sn wknd*..........................(50 to 1 op 33 to 1) 14
1161 HATAAL (Ire) 4-8-13 G Hind (2) *al beh.* (50 to 1 op 33 to 1) 15
MYLIEGE 9-9-11 S Wood (4) *al beh, tld off fnl 3 fs.* .... (50 to 1 op 25 to 1) 16

Dist: 1½l, 7l, 2½l, 2l, ¾l, 3½l, nk, 3l, 1½l, 1½l. 2m 11.50s. a 3.30s (16 Ran).
SR: 28/-/4/-/-/-/ (J D Cable), Mrs V A Aconley

1563 Hey Group Handicap Class D (0-80 3-y-o and up) £4,620 6f......... (3:45)

1480³ SOBERING THOUGHTS [47] 7-8-1 N Adams (9) *cl up, led 2 fs out, sn quickened clr, easily*..... (8 to 1 tchd 9 to 1) 1
1193⁴ BLUE GRIT [67] 7-9-7 J Lowe (4) *beh, hdwy 2 fs out, sn rdn, styd on ins last*.................(7 to 1 op 6 to 1) 2
1188* DEBSY DO (USA) [72] 4-9-7 (5*) O Pears (11) *cl up, effrt 2 fs out and sn ev ch, rdn and not quicken appr fnl furlong.* .... (10 to 1 op 8 to 1) 3
1273³ PINE RIDGE LAD (Ire) [62] 3-8-4 (3*) S D Williams (1) *led, hdd 2 fs out, grad wknd*.. (11 to 1 op 10 to 1 tchd 12 to 1) 4
1348 PRETONIC [63] 5-9-3 Dean McKeown (7) *in tch till lost pl hfwy, styd on und pres ins last.* .... (10 to 1 op 8 to 1 tchd 12 to 1) 5
1081⁴ FIRST GOLD [63] (bl) 4-9-3 M Birch (2) *chsd ldrs, effrt and rdn 2 fs out, sn one pace.* (9 to 2 co-fav op 5 to 1 tchd 11 to 2) 6
1287* SLADES HILL [63] 6-9-3 R Cochrane (10) *chsd ldrs, rdn 2 fs out, sn wknd*............... (9 to 2 co-fav tchd 5 to 1) 7
1167⁷ MISS ARAGON [54] 5-8-8 P Robinson (5) *chsd ldrs, effrt 2 fs out, sn rdn and wknd appr fnl furlong.* ....(8 to 1 op 7 to 1) 8
887⁸ CRAIL HARBOUR [41] (v) 7-7-9² Dale Gibson (6) *chsd ldrs till rdn and wknd 2 fs out*......... (33 to 1 op 25 to 1) 9
1348³ MARTINOSKY [67] 7-9-7 N Day (8) *al rear.* (9 to 2 co-fav tchd 5 to 1) 10

Dist: 5l, hd, 1½l, 5l, ¾l, 2l, sht-hd, 3½l, ½l. 1m 14.80s. a 0.10s (10 Ran).
SR: 43/43/47/22/12/9/1/-/-/ (W E Solomon), J L Eyre

1564 Pontefract Cup Handicap Class E (0-70 4-y-o and up) £2,976 2m 1f 216yds ....(4:15)

1195* MARDOOD [41] 8-8-4 S Wood (6) *hld up, hdwy 6 fs out, led 3 out, rdn appr fnl furlong, ran on wl.* ....(9 to 2 fav tchd 5 to 1) 1
1156³ ANGELICA PARK [41] 7-8-4 J Quinn (3) *hld up, hdwy 5 fs out, effrt to chase wnr 2 furlongs out, sn rdn and kpt on*................................(11 to 1 op 10 to 1) 2
1321⁶ ROYAL PRINT (Ire) [37] 4-7-11² (3*) D Harrison (8) *chsd ldrs, effrt 3 fs out, sn rdn and ev ch till no extr ins fnl furlong*.......................... (12 to 1 op 10 to 1) 3
1307³ BALZINO (USA) [50] 4-8-11 K Fallon (5) *hld up and beh, hdwy 3 fs out, styd on fnl furlong, not rch ldrs.* .... (16 to 1 op 12 to 1) 4
1276³ COST EFFECTIVE [34] 6-7-11 A Mackay (2) *mid-div, hdwy 4 fs out, rdn and one pace o'r 2 furlongs out.* ....(8 to 1 tchd 10 to 1) 5
1112⁵ LUKS AKURA [34] 5-7-11 J Lowe (4) *led 3 fs, cl up, rdn and one pace fnl three furlongs*...... (16 to 1 tchd 20 to 1) 6
973* KOVALEVSKIA [39] 8-8-2 G Bardwell (1) *beh, effrt and hdwy 3 fs out, sn rdn and one pace*.. (9 to 1 op 8 to 1) 7
924⁵ PATROCLUS [47] 8-8-10 S Dawson (12) *hld up, hdwy 4 fs out, sn rdn, nvr a factor*.............. (5 to 1 tchd 11 to 2) 8
1321⁹ UNDERWYCHWOOD (Ire) [38] 5-8-1¹ G Duffield (14) *in tch, rdn o'r 4 fs out, sn wknd.* .... (20 to 1 tchd 25 to 1 and 16 to 1) 9
1276⁸ CREEAGER [50] 11-8-10 (3*) S D Williams (9) *hld up and beh, effrt and some hdwy 3 fs out, sn wknd.* .... (9 to 1 op 10 to 1 tchd 8 to 1) 10
1155² VALSEUR (USA) [61] 4-9-8 J Fanning (10) *cl up, led 4 fs out to 3 out, sn wknd*................(10 to 1 tchd 11 to 1) 11
1276⁹ BARTON PRIDE (Ire) [34] (bl) 4-7-9² Dale Gibson (7) *prmnt till rdn and wknd o'r 3 fs out*.................. (33 to 1) 12
901³ LAFKADIO [31] 6-7-8 L Charnock (11) *al rear.* ....(14 to 1 tchd 16 to 1) 13
924⁸ CHUCKLESTONE [65] 10-10-0 T Quinn (13) *led aftr 3 fs till hdd and wknd 4 furlongs out.* ....(11 to 1 op 10 to 1 tchd 12 to 1) 14

Dist: ½l, ¾l, 5l, nk, sht-hd, hd, 10l, 5l, 2½l, sht-hd. 3m 57.40s. a 5.90s (14 Ran).
(J C Fretwell), P Leach

1565 Youngsters Conditions Stakes Class D (2-y-o) £3,114 6f.............. (4:45)

1296* SERIOUS OPTION (Ire) 9-0 T Quinn (1) *cl up, led 2 and a half fs out, rdn clr appr fnl furlong.* .... (Evens fav op 6 to 5 tchd 5 to 4) 1
1303* INTERNATIONAL STAR (Ire) 8-6 (3*) Emma O'Gorman (5) *cl up, effrt and ev ch 2 fs out, sn rdn, hng lft, one pace.* .... (13 to 8 op 11 to 8 tchd 7 to 4) 2
738⁶ VALIANT MAN 9-0 J Williams (2) *beh, swtchd wide strt and styd on und pres fnl furlong*...... (11 to 1 op 10 to 1) 3
1461⁵ BOLD ARISTOCRAT (Ire) 8-10 S Perks (4) *chsd ldrs, rdn 2 fs out, sn one pace*...... (10 to 1 op 8 to 1 tchd 11 to 1) 4
1461⁶ TOP SHOW (Ire) 9-0 J Lowe (3) *led, hdd 2 and a half fs out and sn wknd*............................(33 to 1 op 20 to 1) 5

Dist: 5l, ¾l, ½l, 3½l. 1m 17.80s. a 3.10s (5 Ran).
(Hon Piers Portman), P F I Cole

1566 Batley Handicap Class E (0-70 3-y-o and up) £3,080 1¼m 6yds.......(5:15)

1384⁴ TAHITIAN [57] 4-9-4 (7*) V Halliday (12) *hld up and beh, hdwy 3 fs out, effrt to ld and hng lft entering fnl furlong, ran on*...................(11 to 2 tchd 5 to 1) 1
1111⁶ PERSIAN FOUNTAIN (Ire) [63] 3-9-1 (3*) D Harrison (1) *mid-div, pushed alng 3 fs out, hdwy and not clr run one furlong out, styd on und pres ins last.* ....(12 to 1 tchd 10 to 1) 2
971³ MAROWINS [44] 4-8-12 K Fallon (4) *hld up and beh, hdwy 3 fs out, rdn o'r one out, styd on ins last*...... (12 to 1) 3
1307⁵ BENTICO [50] 4-9-4 P Robinson (10) *trkd ldrs, smooth hdwy to ld 2 fs out, rdn and hdd entering fnl furlong, sn btn*......................... (11 to 4 fav tchd 3 to 1) 4
1460⁶ SHARQUIN [43] 6-8-11 (6ex) M Wigham (11) *mid-div, hdwy on outer 3 fs out, rdn 2 out, one pace appr fnl furlong.* ....(10 to 1 tchd 12 to 1) 5
1133⁵ GYPSY CRYSTAL (USA) [39] (v) 3-7-8 J Lowe (3) *chsd ldrs, rdn 3 fs out, sn btn*............... (5 to 1 tchd 11 to 2) 6
1306⁵ MISTER BLAKE [57] (bl) 3-8-9 (3*) Emma O'Gorman (6) *chsd ldrs, rdn 3 fs out, wknd 2 out*......(16 to 1 op 14 to 1) 7
1307⁷ KATY'S LAD [57] 6-9-11 T Quinn (7) *chsd ldr till rdn and wknd o'r 3 fs out*...................(11 to 2 op 6 to 1) 8
1284 ANAR (Ire) [41] (v) 4-8-4 (5*) O Pears (5) *led, rdn 3 fs out, hdd and wknd 2 furlongs out*......(14 to 1 op 12 to 1) 9
1307⁴ SWEET REVIVAL [40] 5-8-8 J Fortune (8) *hld up, hdwy on outer 3 fs out, rdn and wknd 2 furlongs out.* .... (10 to 1 tchd 9 to 1 and 11 to 1) 10
842 GRANDERISE (Ire) [54] 3-8-9 L Charnock (9) *al beh.* .... (50 to 1 op 33 to 1) 11

Dist: 1l, hd, 5l, sht-hd, 10l, 5l, 1½l, 2l, nk, 2½l. 2m 10.40s. a 2.20s (11 Ran).
SR: 39/30/23/19/11/-/ (Exors Of The Late Mr K E Wheldon), Mrs J R Ramsden

TRALEE (IRE) (good) Monday June 7th

1567 Ardfert E.B.F. Maiden (2-y-o) £3,795 5f ....(2:00)

1442² EICHTERCUA (Ire) 8-11 P Shanahan (3)....... (2 to 1 fav) 1
1332⁷ VIVA VICTOR (Ire) 8-8 (6*) J J Behan (7)........... (3 to 1) 2
820⁴ FIONN DE COOL (Ire) 9-0 K J Manning (1)........(10 to 3) 3
SUSIE SUNSHINE (Ire) 8-5 (6*) J A Heffernan (2)....(7 to 1) 4
LAXEY LEAP (Ire) 8-11 N G McCullagh (4)......... (6 to 1) 5
EAS GEIPTINE 9-0 P V Gilson (6)................(20 to 1) 6

Dist: 1½l, hd, 3½l, 15l. 1m 5.00s. (6 Ran).
(Mrs P H O'Sullivan), K O'Sullivan

1568 Dennys Maiden (3-y-o and up) £3,450 1m...........................(2:30)

577³ ABEL TASMAN (USA) 3-8-9 P V Gilson (7)..... (5 to 4 fav) 1
BRAVE RAIDER (Ire) 3-8-9 P Shanahan (6).........(7 to 4) 2
1164⁴ BELLISSI (Ire) 3-8-6 N G McCullagh (4)............(6 to 1) 3
BLACK PIPER (Ire) 3-8-0 (6*) J J Behan (3)....... (20 to 1) 4
NORDIC GLARE (Ire) 3-8-9 K J Manning (2).......(11 to 2) 5
847 TRIBAL MEMORIES (Ire) 3-8-6 E McCabe (5)...... (20 to 1) 6
1333 GEALLAINNBAN (Ire) 3-8-9 E A Leonard (1).......(14 to 1) 7

Dist: 3l, ½l, nk, 2½l. 1m 48.60s. (7 Ran).
(David F Howard), C Collins

1569 Ballybeggan Racegoers Club Handicap (0-75 3-y-o and up) £3,450 7f (3:00)

1440² WANDERING THOUGHTS (Ire) [-] 4-8-5¹ P V Gilson (11) ....(5 to 2 fav) 1
787 THATCHING CRAFT (Ire) [-] 4-9-9 (4*) P Carberry (4) (8 to 1) 2
960⁷ RASSETTE (Ire) [-] 3-7-11² (6*) J A Heffernan (3)...(12 to 1) 3
996* RUSTIC-ORT (Ire) [-] (bl) 5-8-4 N G McCullagh (1).. (6 to 1) 4
1050² MACGILLYCUDDY (Ire) [-] 4-9-5 (6*) J J Behan (6).. (7 to 2) 5
789 BOBROSS (Ire) [-] 3-8-12 N Byrne (12)............. (12 to 1) 6
1105⁴ CARRIG STAR (Ire) [-] 4-9-4 K J Manning (7)...... (10 to 1) 7
849⁸ SOLAR FLASH (Ire) [-] 4-7-3 (6*) P P Murphy (10)... (8 to 1) 8
1023⁵ FAIRYDEL (Ire) [-] 3-7-13 (10*) P J Smullen (5)...... (8 to 1) 9
1163⁹ SIGHTSEER (Ire) [-] 4-8-3 A J Nolan (2)...........(14 to 1) 10
1235 INAUGURATION (Ire) [-] 4-9-4 E McCabe (9)....... (14 to 1) 11
705* PENNINE MIST (Ire) [-] 3-9-1 P Shanahan (8)......(13 to 2) 12

Dist: 1½l, nk, sht-hd, hd. 1m 31.60s. (12 Ran).
(W Mythen), Mrs A M O'Brien

LEOPARDSTOWN (IRE) (good) Tuesday June 8th

Going Correction: MINUS 0.10 sec. per fur. (races 1,2), MINUS 0.30 (3,4,5,6,7)

1570 Derrinstown Apprentice Handicap (0-80 3-y-o and up) £4,142 6f.... (6:00)

868 PILGRIM BAY (Ire) [-] 3-8-4 D G O'Shea (7)....... (10 to 1) 1
1513⁵ ISLAND HEATHER (Ire) [-] (bl) 5-9-2 (4*) C Everard (9) (4 to 1) 2+
1293⁴ NORDIC SAINT (Ire) [-] 4-8-7 (4*) J A Heffernan (8).. (8 to 1) 2+
939⁵ MASTER WORK [-] (bl) 5-7-4 (4*) P P Murphy (4)... (9 to 1) 4
996³ HONORARY PRINCE (Ire) [-] 4-8-10 (6*) T J Daly (10) ....(100 to 30 fav) 5
1386⁴ CLIFF EDGE (USA) [-] 3-8-7 (8*) T Hagger (11).... (10 to 1) 6

599 DAHAR'S LOVE (USA) [-] 4-7-10 (8*) J P Cornally (5) ....(20 to 1) 7
1106 SPEED DEMON [-] 3-7-3² (6*) R T Fitzpatrick (3)...(25 to 1) 8
868² FOREST [-] 3-8-4 (6*) J J Stack (2)....(9 to 2) 9
1444⁶ SOMERTON BOY (Ire) [-] (bl) 3-8-7 (6*,4ex) D J O'Donohoe (1) ....(8 to 1) 10
1050 SMOKEY LAD [-] 9-9-12 (2*) P Carberry (6)....(16 to 1) 11
Dist: Hd, dd-ht, 4l, 3l. 1m 14.60s. a 3.10s (11 Ran).
SR: 16/31/22/-/-/-/ (Frank A McNulty), E J O'Grady

1571 ACC Bank Silver Flash E.B.F. Stakes (Listed Race) (2-y-o) £8,627 6f...(6:30)

LAS MENINAS (Ire) 8-10 S Craine (6) *prog frm rear to track ldrs hfwy, str run to ld appr fnl furlong, kpt on wl.* ....(8 to 1) 1
1022* DANISH (Ire) 8-10 W J O'Connor (5) *dsptd ld to 2 fs out, kpt on und pres*....(5 to 2 fav) 2
1197* COMMON RUMPUS (Ire) 8-10 J P Murtagh (2) *rear, prog to track ldrs hfwy, not clr run 2 fs out, ran on fnl furlong.* ....(5 to 1) 3
ALJAWZA (USA) 8-10 M J Kinane (3) *wl plcd, rdn in 3rd o'r one furlong out, no extr fnl furlong*....(3 to 1) 4
1045⁴ AVONDALE FOREST (Ire) (bl) 8-10 C Roche (4) *wl plcd, led briefly o'r one furlong out, wknd*....(10 to 1) 5
VALID VICTRESS (Ire) 8-10 R Hughes (9) *wl plcd till rdn and wknd 2 fs out*....(8 to 1) 6
938⁷ YOUR VILLAGE (Ire) 8-10 K J Manning (7) *al rear.* (16 to 1) 7
1121⁴ GREENCASTLE ROSE (Ire) 8-10 W J Supple (1) *al rear.* ....(20 to 1) 8
1121* PEACE TOKEN (Ire) 8-10 B Coogan (8) *dsptd ld till rdn and hmpd 2 fs out, wknd quickly*....(5 to 1) 9
Dist: 1l, 1l, nk, 2l. 1m 13.50s. a 2.00s (9 Ran).
SR: 44/40/36/35/27/-/ (R E Sangster), T Stack

1572 Gandon Securities E.B.F. Race (3-y-o and up) £3,797 1½m....(7:00)

1198⁷ ADVOCAT (Ger) 3-9-3 M J Kinane (6)....(5 to 4 on) 1
1026* SEMPLE STADIUM (Ire) 3-9-5 P V Gilson (1)....(100 to 30) 2
LORD BENTLEY 3-9-3 C Roche (4)....(11 to 2) 3
1334³ FLAME OF PERSIA (Ire) 3-9-0 W J O'Connor (5)....(6 to 1) 4
850* SIRSAN (Ire) 3-9-3 R Hughes (2)....(12 to 1) 5
Dist: 1l, 1l, hd, 1l. 2m 34.70s. a 3.70s (5 Ran).
SR: 30/30/26/22/23/ (Sheikh Mohammed), John M Oxx

1573 Andrex E.B.F. Race (3-y-o and up) £3,452 1¼m....(7:30)

1026³ POLITICAL SURGE (USA) 3-8-13 M J Kinane (6) ....(13 to 8 on) 1
ROYAL VISION (Ire) 4-9-12 C Roche (4)....(10 to 1) 2
1250² DAHLIA'S BEST (USA) (bl) 3-8-13 W J Supple (5)..(10 to 1) 3
MADANIYYA (USA) 3-8-10 J P Murtagh (7)....(3 to 1) 4
1441² SHIRLEY'S DELIGHT (Ire) 3-8-10 R Hughes (8)....(8 to 1) 5
SEAWORTHY (Ire) 3-8-10 S Craine (3)....(10 to 1) 6
1467 KARABAKH (Ire) 4-9-12 J F Egan (2)....(50 to 1) 7
1333⁸ ARROGANT LADY 3-8-10 P V Gilson (1)....(20 to 1) 8
Dist: Hd, 4l, hd, 3½l. 2m 7.40s. a 2.70s (8 Ran).
SR: 42/54/33/29/22/ (Moyglare Stud Farms Ltd), D K Weld

1574 Goodbody Stockbrokers Handicap (0-75 3-y-o) £3,107 1m 1f....(8:00)

297 BIZANA (Ire) [-] 8-13 (4*) P Carberry (12)....(14 to 1) 1
1440³ COOLRAIN LADY (Ire) [-] 8-13 S Craine (6)....(9 to 2) 2
1433* RAFFERTY'S INNER (Ire) [-] 8-2 (8*,4ex) R T Fitzpatrick (2) ....(8 to 1) 3
1252² WARREN STREET (Ire) [-] 8-3 (6*) J J Behan (8)....(8 to 1) 4D
1139⁵ BRIGENSER (Ire) [-] (bl) 8-10 P Shanahan (7)....(13 to 2) 4
806⁹ RICH LIFE (Ire) [-] 8-11 M J Kinane (3)....(2 to 1 fav) 6
789 CARAVELLE LAD (Ire) [-] 8-11 P V Gilson (4)....(16 to 1) 7
307⁵ KENTUCKY BABY (Ire) [-] (bl) 8-13 N Byrne (11)....(10 to 1) 8
669 VERITABLE GALLERY (Ire) [-] 8-9 N G McCullagh (9) ....(14 to 1) 9
870 ALDENA (Ire) [-] 8-1 D Manning (1)....(50 to 1) 10
850⁷ EFFICIENT FUNDING (Ire) [-] 8-11 J F Egan (10)...(20 to 1) 11
267* MISS TWIN PEAKS (Ire) [-] 9-4 W J O'Connor (5)..(13 to 2) 12
Dist: ¾l, sht-hd, sht-hd, nk. 1m 54.60s. a 4.10s (12 Ran).
SR: 1/-/-/-/-/-/ (Breffni Syndicate), Noel Meade

1575 Cooney Carey Ferris E.B.F. Race (3-y-o and up) £3,797 7f....(8:30)

1050⁸ MILLIE'S CHOICE (Ire) 4-9-10 W J Supple (4)..(6 to 4 fav) 1
1333* KINDNESS ITSELF (Ire) 3-9-2 M J Kinane (1)....(7 to 2) 2
PRIVATE VIEWING (Ire) 3-9-3 P Shanahan (2)....(9 to 1) 3
1105* MY-O-MY (Ire) 3-9-0 S Craine (3)....(8 to 1) 4
ST MARTHA (Ire) 3-9-0 C Roche (5)....(5 to 2) 5
Dist: Hd, 2l, 1l, sht-hd. 1m 32.00s. a 6.60s (5 Ran).
(Colm McEvoy), Kevin Prendergast

1576 St. Vincents (Q.R) Flat Race (4-y-o and up) £3,107 1¾m....(9:00)

961² RISZARD (USA) 4-11-7 Mr A P O'Brien (4)....(11 to 8 fav) 1
4685a DUHARRA (Ire) (bl) 5-11-0 (7*) Mr J A Nash (1)....(7 to 2) 2
937* HACKETTS CROSS (Ire) 5-11-2 (3*) Mr A R Coonan (10) ....(8 to 1) 3
PERKNAPP 6-10-4 (7*) Mr G J Harford (8)....(16 to 1) 4
RISING WATERS (Ire) 5-11-0 (7*) Mrs D McDonagh (19) ....(25 to 1) 5
309 GILT DIMENSION 6-10-4 (7*) Mrs J M Mullins (13) (14 to 1) 6
753⁴ PERSIAN HAZE (Ire) 4-11-0 (7*) Mr P R Lenihan (3) (25 to 1) 7
MOUNTAIN BLOOM (Ire) 5-10-11 (5*) Mr D Valentine (5) ....(10 to 1) 8
308 KAZKAR (Ire) 5-10-12 (7*) Mr C M Healy (11)....(16 to 1) 9
309 LAY ONE ON YA (Ire) 5-10-4 (7*) Mr A K Wyse (15) (16 to 1) 10
1141⁶ ALOHA (Ire) 4-10-8 Mr J Queally (14)....(33 to 1) 11
TALINGANA (Ire) 4-10-3 (5*) Mr B R Hamilton (2).. (10 to 1) 12
1508 GONE LIKE THE WIND 6-10-4 (7*) Mr D McDonnell (18) ....(50 to 1) 13
MARTINS PARTY (bl) 8-10-1 (7*) Mr J P Brennan (9) ....(100 to 1) 14
COLLON BEAG 6-10-9 (7*) Mr M A Cahill (6)....(16 to 1) 15
AFAWI (Ire) 5-10-8 (3*) Mr R O'Neill (12)....(66 to 1) 16
RANDOM WALK 8-10-8 (3*) Mr D Marnane (7)....(66 to 1) 17
1141 THE RIDGE BOREEN 9-10-11 Mr M McNulty (16). (50 to 1) 18
Dist: 1½l, 3l, 1l, 3l. 3m 2.00s. a 6.00s (18 Ran).
SR: 33/30/22/12/16/-/ (Henryk de Kwiatkowski), J S Bolger

PONTEFRACT (firm)
Tuesday June 8th

Going Correction: MINUS 0.05 sec. per fur. (races 1,4), MINUS 0.30 (2,3,5,6)

1577 York & Westminster Apprentice Series Stakes Round One Class F Maiden (3-y-o) £2,684 6f....(2:45)

1186⁵ MAGICATION 8-6 Claire Balding (8) *chsd ldrs, hdwy to ld ins fnl furlong, pushed out.* (100 to 30 jt-fav op 3 to 1 tchd 4 to 1) 1
1396⁶ FORTIS PAVIOR (Ire) 8-11 G Parkin (1) *led till hdd ins fnl furlong, no extr*....(100 to 30 jt-fav op 5 to 2) 2
733 MISS OFFIE 8-1 (5*) J Dennis (3) *steadied strt, slwly into strd, beh till ran on fnl 2 fs, nrst finish.* ....(12 to 1 op 8 to 1) 3
1308³ COLFAX CLASSIC 8-6 J Tate (9) *prmnt, rdn wl o'r one out, one pace*....(4 to 1 op 9 to 2 tchd 5 to 1) 4
SELFISH LADY 7-13 (7*) F Savage (2) *chsd ldrs, hdwy and ran wide 2 out, wknd o'r one out*... (16 to 1 op 8 to 1) 5
1424⁷ STATE TACOMA 8-6 N Varley (4) *al beh.* ....(16 to 1 op 14 to 1) 6
1396⁸ FORDALLIA 8-5⁴ (5*) G Strange (6) *cl up till wknd o'r one out*....(16 to 1) 7
1162⁶ CAUGHT REDHANDED (Ire) 8-1 (5*) Sarah Thompson (7) *sn beh*....(6 to 1 op 4 to 1) 8
Dist: 2½l, 4l, 1½l, 1½l, 3l, 3l, 5l. 1m 17.40s. a 2.70s (8 Ran).
SR: 32/27/6/-/-/ (Mrs Stephen Allen), J Balding

1578 Grove Selling Handicap Class G (0-60 3-y-o and up) £2,763 1m 4yds...(3:15)

1284⁶ PRIDE OF PENDLE [40] 4-9-1 K Darley (3) *mid-div, hdwy 3 out, quickened to ld one out, ran on wl.* ....(4 to 1 fav op 5 to 1 tchd 11 to 2) 1
1453⁵ ROLY WALLACE [53] (bl) 4-10-0 M Wigham (7) *slwly into strd, beh, hdwy hfwy, ran on wl fnl furlong, not pace of wnr*....(10 to 1) 2
1436 KHALLOOF (Ire) [48] 4-9-2 (7*) C Teague (18) *mid-div, hdwy 3 out, chlgd one out, sn rdn and one pace.* ....(14 to 1 op 16 to 1) 3
1460⁹ COOL ENOUGH [39] 12-9-0 K Fallon (17) *beh till styd on fnl 2 fs, nrst finish*....(10 to 1 op 8 to 1) 4
1133 DANCES WITH GOLD [44] (bl) 3-8-8 Dean McKeown (5) *beh, hdwy hfwy, not clr run o'r one out, kpt on ins fnl furlong*....(8 to 1 tchd 9 to 1) 5
1284 MARY MACBLAIN [37] 4-8-12 P Robinson (6) *beh, styd on frm 3 out, not rch ldrs*....(12 to 1 tchd 14 to 1) 6
WAAZA (USA) [53] 4-9-9 (5*) O Pears (1) *prmnt, chlgd one out, sn rdn and wknd*....(25 to 1 op 20 to 1) 7
1073⁶ HOMILE [48] 5-9-2 (7*) S Sanders (8) *nvr trbld ldrs.* ....(14 to 1) 8
1358⁷ IRISH ROOTS (Ire) [53] (v) 3-9-3 M Birch (13) *cl up, led aftr 3 fs till hdd and wknd one out*....(33 to 1) 9
1480⁴ MANX MONARCH [46] 3-8-10 J Lowe (15) *mid-div, effrt 3 out, sn btn*....(6 to 1 op 5 to 1) 10
1421 PREMIER MAJOR (Ire) [37] 4-8-12 L Charnock (9) *in tch till wknd 3 out*.... (10 to 1 op 8 to 1 tchd 11 to 1) 11
1194⁸ CLEDESCHAMPS [45] 4-8-13 (7*) G Parkin (12) *cl up, dsptd ld 4 out to 3 out, wknd o'r one out.* (20 to 1 op 12 to 1) 12
861 ANFIELD SALLY [30] 7-8-5 N Connorton (2) *sn beh.* (50 to 1) 13
861⁶ DEPUTY TIM [42] 10-8-10 (7*) H Bastiman (10) *led 3 fs, prmnt till wknd wl o'r one out.* ....(10 to 1 op 8 to 1 tchd 12 to 1) 14
1419 JUST-GO-AGAIN [49] 4-9-10 J Fortune (11) *beh most of way*....(25 to 1 tchd 33 to 1) 15
1186⁹ MELTONBY [40] 4-9-1 Kim Tinkler (19) *chsd ldrs till wknd o'r 2 out*....(50 to 1 tchd 66 to 1) 16
1286² KICK ON MAJESTIC (Ire) [35] 4-8-10 S Wood (16) *beh most of way*....(7 to 1 tchd 6 to 1) 17

Dist: 2l, 2l, ¾l, 1½l, ½l, 1l, 1½l, ½l, 8l, 2½l. 1m 44.80s. a 2.70s (17 Ran).
SR: 25/32/21/10/-/1/14/4/-/ (W B Imison), P Calver

1579 St Johns Priory Handicap Class C (0-90 3-y-o) £5,299 1¼m 6yds... (3:45)

1016[5] NESSUN DORMA [76] 8-10 M Hills (5) *in tch, smooth hdwy to ld o'r one out, ran on wl*....... (5 to 1 tchd 11 to 2) 1
855[5] SPRING FLYER (Ire) [59] 7-7 A Mackay (4) *chsd ldrs, effrt o'r 2 out, kpt on wl fnl furlong.* ....(8 to 1 op 6 to 1 tchd 9 to 1) 2
1306* WORDSMITH (Ire) [68] 8-2 K Fallon (2) *hld up in tch, effrt 2 out, kpt on fnl furlong*.........(4 to 1 jt-fav op 5 to 2) 3
966[2] SILVER STANDARD [59] 7-7 J Lowe (1) *cl up, led wl o'r one out, sn hdd, wknd fnl furlong*...............(4 to 1 jt-fav tchd 9 to 2 and 7 to 2) 4
1016 JALCANTO [77] 8-11 K Darley (7) *beh till styd on fnl 2 fs, not trble ldrs*.................. (11 to 2 tchd 6 to 1) 5
684 MHEMEANLES [79] 8-13 M Birch (9) *chsd ldrs, effrt 2 out, sn btn*................. (7 to 1 op 8 to 1 tchd 13 to 2) 6
684[8] HEATHYARDS BOY [85] 9-5 W R Swinburn (6) *led till hdd and wknd wl o'r one out.* ....(11 to 1 op 10 to 1 tchd 12 to 1) 7
1225[6] CUTTHROAT KID (Ire) [61] 7-9 L Charnock (3) *al beh.* .... (16 to 1 op 10 to 1) 8
1338 EXPO MONDIAL (Ire) [87] 9-7 M Tebbutt (8) *cl up, rdn 3 out, wknd 2 out*.......................... (16 to 1 op 12 to 1) 9
Dist: 2l, 1l, 1l, 3l, 1l, 5l, 2½l, 2l. 2m 11.60s. a 3.40s (9 Ran).
SR: 32/11/18/7/19/19/15/-/8/ (H H Morriss), G Wragg

1580 EBF Thorne Maiden Fillies Stakes Class D (2-y-o) £3,318 6f........ (4:15)

1234[3] BELLA PARKES 8-9 J Carroll (3) *chsd ldrs, kpt on wl und pres to ld well ins fnl furlong*....... (11 to 2 op 5 to 1) 1
1020[5] CUT THE RED TAPE (Ire) 8-9 Dean McKeown (6) *slight ld till quickened o'r one out, hdd and no extr wl ins fnl furlong*..........(13 to 8 jt-fav op 7 to 4 tchd 6 to 4) 2
CELTIC CEILIDH 8-9 P Robinson (4) *dwlt, beh till styd on wl fnl 2 fs, nrst finish*............ (20 to 1 op 14 to 1) 3
PHYLIAN 8-9 W Woods (7) *in tch, kpt on same pace fnl 2 fs*..................(12 to 1 op 14 to 1 tchd 10 to 1) 4
889[2] SINGULAR SENSATION 8-9 D Holland (1) *cl up till wknd o'r one out*....... (13 to 8 jt-fav op 5 to 4 tchd 7 to 4) 5
1227[4] STARICA (Ire) 8-9 K Darley (5) *chsd ldrs till wknd o'r one out*.................................. (16 to 1 op 12 to 1) 6
Dist: 1l, 2½l, 1½l, 2½l, 2½l. 1m 17.70s. a 3.00s (6 Ran).
SR: 29/25/15/9/-/-/ (Joseph Heler), J Berry

1581 Ropergate Maiden Stakes Class D (3-y-o) £3,611 1¼m 6yds........... (4:45)

TREMOLANDO (USA) 9-0 Pat Eddery (6) *made all, quickened clr o'r one out, very easily.* ....(7 to 4 on op 11 to 8 on) 1
GRAEGOS (Ire) 9-0 A McGlone (2) *in tch, effrt o'r 2 out, styd on fnl furlong, no ch wth wnr.* (11 to 1 op 6 to 1) 2
1275[6] SOUL DREAM (USA) 8-9 P Robinson (1) *trkd ldr, one pace fnl 2 fs*.............................. (14 to 1 op 10 to 1) 3
646 LT WELSH (USA) 9-0 B Raymond (8) *cl up, rdn o'r 3 out, kpt on same pace*.......(9 to 1 op 8 to 1 tchd 10 to 1) 4
1154[3] MUTAWALI (Ire) 9-0 R Hills (5) *chsd ldrs, effrt 2 out, sn btn.* ....(8 to 1 op 6 to 1) 5
1275[8] HAYDON BRIDGE (Ire) 9-0 M Birch (7) *nvr nr to chal.* ....(12 to 1 tchd 10 to 1) 6
SCOTTISH WEDDING 8-4 (5*) O Pears (10) *nvr nr to chal.* .... (33 to 1 op 25 to 1) 7
62[2] DIWALI DANCER 9-0 A Mackay (9) *in tch till wknd 2 out.* .... (25 to 1 op 20 to 1) 8
Dist: 10l, ½l, nk, 1½l, 3l, 3½l, 6l. 2m 9.80s. a 1.60s (8 Ran).
SR: 54/34/28/32/29/23/11/4/ (K Abdulla), R Charlton

1582 Iron Bridge Handicap Class D (0-80 3-y-o) £3,318 1½m 8yds........ (5:15)

1372* DUSTY POINT (Ire) [61] 8-7[1] (5ex) W R Swinburn (7) *trkd ldrs gng wl, led o'r 2 out, drw clr, easily.* ....(13 to 8 fav op 5 to 4) 1
855[7] BLUE GROTTO (Ire) [75] 9-7 G Duffield (6) *led one furlong, cl up, slight ld o'r 2 out, sn hdd, kpt on same pace.* ....(5 to 1 op 7 to 1) 2
1399* CUMBRIAN RHAPSODY [69] 8-12 (3*,5ex) S Maloney (1) *prmnt, chlgd o'r 2 out, sn rdn and one pace.* ....(5 to 2 tchd 9 to 4) 3
1464[3] CIVIL LAW (Ire) [73] 9-5 K Darley (3) *led aftr one furlong till hdd and wknd o'r 2 out*........... (9 to 2 op 11 to 2) 4
1417 TEACHER (Ire) [66] (bl) 8-12 B Raymond (4) *al beh.* ....(16 to 1 op 14 to 1 tchd 20 to 1) 5
Dist: 6l, 1½l, 8l, 6l. 2m 40.40s. a 5.40s (5 Ran).
SR: 3/5/ (Abdullah Ali), B Hanbury

SALISBURY (good to firm) Tuesday June 8th

Going Correction: MINUS 0.10 sec. per fur. (races 1,2), MINUS 0.20 (3,4,5,6)

1583 Eddie Reavey Maiden Auction Fillies Stakes Class E (2-y-o) £3,183 6f (2:30)

GREAT DEEDS 8-11 T Quinn (9) *al in tch, led hfwy, clr entering fnl furlong, pushed out.* .... (100 to 30 fav op 5 to 2 tchd 7 to 2) 1
1403 HANKYPANKYMANKI 8-4 (7*) Mark Denaro (5) *hld up in tch, rdn 2 fs out, kpt on to go second wl ins last.* ....(4 to 1 op 5 to 2) 2
776 PRIMA SILK 8-11 D Biggs (1) *mid-div, hdwy and ev ch 2 fs out, hng lft, one pace ins last*.....(33 to 1 op 12 to 1) 3
477[7] EUROPHARM LASSIE 8-11 B Rouse (12) *rear till ran on ins fnl 2 fs, nvr nrr*................(14 to 1 op 10 to 1) 4
776 QUEENS STROLLER (Ire) 8-11 W Carson (2) *pushed alng in mid-div, styd on fnl 2 fs, nvr dngrs.* ....(6 to 1 op 4 to 1 tchd 7 to 1) 5
LIFE'S TOO SHORT (Ire) 8-8 (3*) D Harrison (16) *rear, kpt on fnl 2 fs, nvr dngrs*............. (10 to 1 tchd 12 to 1) 6
ADMIRALELLA 8-11 J Reid (8) *al mid-div, one pace ins fnl 2 fs*...................................... (16 to 1 op 8 to 1) 7
1241[2] KERAMIC 8-11 J Williams (15) *led to hfwy, rdn and wknd wl o'r one furlong out.* (11 to 2 op 4 to 1 tchd 6 to 1) 8
1350 MIGHTY KINGDOM (Ire) (bl) 8-11 Paul Eddery (14) *frnt rnk till wknd hfwy*.....................(33 to 1 op 20 to 1) 9
1317[6] CA IRA (Ire) 8-11 G Bardwell (4) *nvr on terms.* .... (10 to 1 op 6 to 1) 10
1317[8] WHITCHURCH SILK (Ire) 8-11 C Rutter (10) *speed to hfwy.* .... (33 to 1 op 20 to 1) 11
1245[5] LEGAL CONQUEST 8-11 W Newnes (11) *prmnt till wknd hfwy*................................ (20 to 1 op 14 to 1) 12
BIEN CUIT 8-11 N Carlisle (7) *slwly away, al struggling.* .... (33 to 1 op 20 to 1) 13
1032 COURT SERENADE (bl) 8-11 R Cochrane (3) *al beh.* ....(33 to 1) 14
1317[5] BELLAROY 8-6 (5*) Stephen Davies (13) *speed till rdn and wknd sn aftr hfwy*............(33 to 1 op 16 to 1) 15
Dist: 2l, 1l, 3l, hd, 4l, ¾l, 1l, 4l, 1½l, 2l. 1m 15.45s. a 2.95s (15 Ran).
SR: 26/18/14/2/1/-/ (Dubai Racing Syndicate), M R Channon

1584 Swanage Handicap Class C (0-90 3-y-o and up) £5,089 6f............. (3:00)

1282[3] SURE LORD (Ire) [66] 4-8-8 W Carson (10) *al prmnt, led hfwy, rdn and ran on ins fnl furlong.* .... (12 to 1 op 10 to 1) 1
1267[8] JIGSAW BOY [73] 4-9-1 J Williams (11) *drpd out and rear, short of room one and a half fs out, squeezed through and ran on wl fnl furlong.* ....(5 to 1 fav op 6 to 1 tchd 7 to 1) 2
1348 CHILI HEIGHTS [80] 3-8-13 L Dettori (1) *in tch, pushed alng hfwy, ran on ins furlong.* ....(16 to 1 op 12 to 1 tchd 20 to 1) 3
1213 PRESS GALLERY [87] 3-9-6 W Newnes (6) *al frnt rnk, rdn appr fnl furlong, one pace ins last.* (20 to 1 op 16 to 1) 4
1312[2] PRINCELY FAVOUR (Ire) [79] 3-8-12 T Quinn (3) *nvr far away, ev ch one and a half fs out, kpt on one pace.* ....(12 to 1 op 10 to 1 tchd 14 to 1) 5
1373[7] BAYSHAM (USA) [74] (bl) 7-9-2 R Price (12) *trkd ldrs, swtchd lft hfwy, sn rdn, kpt on one pace fnl furlong.* .... (7 to 1 op 6 to 1 tchd 15 to 2) 6
1348[2] PADDY CHALK [86] 7-10-0 J Reid (13) *hld up in tch, effrt appr fnl furlong, one pace ins last.* ....(15 to 2 op 6 to 1 tchd 8 to 1) 7
1267 HOW'S YER FATHER [77] 7-8-12 (7*) S Drowne (8) *hld up in rear, hdwy 2 fs out, nvr threaten ldrs.* ....(11 to 1 op 7 to 1 tchd 12 to 1) 8
1127[2] MASNUN (USA) [75] 8-9-0 (3*) J Weaver (9) *mid-div, rdn 2 fs out, one pace*............ (13 to 2 op 6 to 1 tchd 7 to 1) 9
1270* MOROCCO (Ire) [78] 4-9-6 Paul Eddery (7) *hld up, hdwy on outsd 2 fs out, wknd appr last*......(10 to 1 op 8 to 1) 10
1267[4] ACARA (Ire) [51] 4-7-7 J Quinn (2) *led to hfwy, wknd wl o'r one furlong out*..........(14 to 1 op 12 to 1) 11
1270 NEITHER NOR [61] 4-8-3 G Carter (4) *nvr got into race.* .... (20 to 1 op 16 to 1) 12
1348 BERTIE WOOSTER [83] 10-9-11 W Ryan (14) *hld up in rear, making hdwy whn no room wl o'r one furlong out, sn eased*...............................(16 to 1 op 14 to 1) 13
1267[9] TRUTHFUL IMAGE [76] (bl) 4-9-4 D Biggs (5) *al rear.* ....(10 to 1 op 7 to 1 tchd 12 to 1) 14
Dist: Nk, ½l, ¾l, ¾l, nk, sht-hd, hd, 1½l, nk, ¾l. 1m 14.44s. a 1.94s (14 Ran).
SR: 43/49/45/49/38/41/52/42/34/ (The Sussex Stud Limited), W R Muir

1585 Bishopstone Conditions Stakes Class D (3-y-o) £4,392 1¾m..........(3:30)

985* KASSAB 9-2 W Carson (3) *made all, pushed alng 4 fs out, ran on, cmftbly.* ....(11 to 8 on op 5 to 4 on tchd 6 to 4 on) 1
1077* CROMARTY 8-7 W Ryan (1) *rcd keenly, trkd wnr, rdn o'r 2 fs out, no imprsn ins last.* ....(11 to 8 op Evens tchd 6 to 4) 2
PAT OR ELSE 8-6[1] R Cochrane (2) *al last, effrt 2 fs out, kpt on one pace*.........(14 to 1 op 12 to 1 tchd 20 to 1) 3
Dist: 2½l, 1½l. 3m 7.92s. a 10.22s (Flag start) (3 Ran).
(Hamdan Al-Maktoum), J L Dunlop

1586 City Bowl Fillies Handicap Class D (0-80 3-y-o and up) £4,012 1½m (4:00)

992[6] RANEEN ALWATAR [75] 3-8-9 R Cochrane (5) *al prmnt, rdn 4 fs out, led jst ins last, styd on strly.* .... (9 to 1 op 8 to 1 tchd 10 to 1) 1
1094* ELAINE TULLY (Ire) [78] 5-10-0 J Reid (4) *made most till jst ins fnl furlong, kpt on one pace*..... (8 to 1 op 5 to 1) 2
1383[5] HARD TASK [73] 3-8-7 Paul Eddery (8) *trkd ldrs, dsptd ld 2 fs out, edgd lft, kpt on one pace fnl furlong.* .... (14 to 1 op 12 to 1) 3
973[3] PRIDE OF BRITAIN (Can) [52] 4-8-2 N Carlisle (3) *trkd ldr, ev ch one and a half fs out, outpcd*..... (9 to 1 op 6 to 1) 4
1305* ATLANTIC WAY [55] 5-8-5 L Dettori (10) *towards rear, styd on one pace ins fnl 3 fs.* (5 to 1 op 6 to 1 tchd 7 to 1) 5
914 MAY HILLS LEGACY (Ire) [54] 4-8-4 T Quinn (1) *hld up rear, hdwy on outsd 3 fs out, styd on one pace.* .... (16 to 1 tchd 20 to 1) 6
994[7] CRACKLING [50] 4-8-0 S Dawson (12) *rear, some hdwy ins fnl 3 fs, nvr dngrs*....... (7 to 1 op 5 to 1 tchd 8 to 1) 7
827[5] BAYDON BELLE (USA) [62] 3-7-3 (7*) D Wright (9) *hld up in tch, rdn 3 fs out, one pace aftr*..... (14 to 1 op 12 to 1) 8
1223* PLAY WITH ME (Ire) [70] 3-8-4 G Carter (6) *mid-div, no hdwy fnl 3 fs*.................. (7 to 2 fav tchd 3 to 1) 9
1268[9] MATCHING GREEN [60] 4-8-10 J Williams (7) *al beh.* .... (16 to 1 op 14 to 1 tchd 20 to 1) 10
1093[8] GESNERA [43] 5-7-7 J Quinn (13) *hld up rear, making hdwy whn hmpd o'r 2 fs out, not rcvr*......... (33 to 1) 11
1120 MISTY VIEW [63] 4-8-13 R Price (11) *rear, making hdwy whn hng rght o'r 2 fs out, sn btn.* (16 to 1 op 12 to 1) 12
644[8] MATARIS [70] 3-8-4 W Carson (2) *pld hrd in mid-div, drpd out fnl 3 fs*...................... (14 to 1 op 10 to 1) 13

Dist: 3l, sht-hd, 2l, 1½l, ½l, 1½l, 1½l, 1½l, nk, hd. 2m 35.13s. a 3.13s (13 Ran).
SR: 40/53/31/22/22/20/13/6/11/ (Sheikh Ahmed Al Maktoum), L M Cumani

1587 Laverstock Maiden Fillies Stakes Class D (3-y-o) £3,582 1m....... (4:30)

1212[2] LYPHARD'S DELTA (USA) 8-11 W Ryan (6) *chsd ldrs, pushed alng 2 fs out, styd on to ld cl hme.* ....(6 to 4 on op 11 to 8 on tchd 6 to 5 on) 1
1311[4] TAHDID 8-11 W Carson (9) *led, rdn o'r one furlong out, kpt on, ct cl hme*...... (11 to 2 op 7 to 2 tchd 6 to 1) 2
1320[4] CATEQUIL (Can) 8-11 T Quinn (14) *trkd ldrs, ev ch till wknd entering fnl furlong*........... (8 to 1 op 4 to 1) 3
COMMON LAW (Ire) 8-11 S Raymont (1) *prmnt, rdn o'r 2 fs out, one pace aftr.* ....(10 to 1 op 12 to 1 tchd 14 to 1 and 8 to 1) 4
1344[6] SINGER ON THE ROOF 8-11 L Dettori (11) *chsd ldrs, hrd rdn 2 fs out, sn btn*............... (10 to 1 op 8 to 1) 5
1342[2] DANCING SPIRIT (Ire) 8-11 J Reid (4) *in tch, rdn o'r 2 fs out, sn btn*.......................... (12 to 1 op 6 to 1) 6
NOMADIC QUEST (Ire) 8-11 Paul Eddery (7) *in tch to hfwy.* .... (12 to 1 op 7 to 1 tchd 14 to 1) 7
WADIA (USA) 8-11 B Rouse (10) *slwly away, al rear.* .... (33 to 1 op 20 to 1) 8
1278[6] LITTLE MISS RIBOT 8-11 A Clark (3) *speed till wknd o'r 2 fs out*.. (33 to 1) 9
MINTEEN 8-11 W Newnes (13) *al rear*.............. (33 to 1) 10
BELMONT PRINCESS (Ire) 8-11 N Adams (5) *slwly away, al beh*.. (33 to 1) 11
RIVERETTE 8-11 R Street (15) *al beh.* .... (25 to 1 op 20 to 1 tchd 33 to 1) 12
PADDINGTON GIRL (Ire) 8-11 G Carter (12) *al rear.* .... (20 to 1 op 12 to 1) 13
1311[7] MY MINNIE 8-4 (7*) S Drowne (8) *uns rdr aftr one furlong, clipped heels of another runner*.............. (33 to 1) ur

Dist: ½l, 7l, 2½l, ½l, 6l, 5l, 2l, 3½l, 5l, ¾l. 1m 41.32s. a 1.82s (14 Ran).
SR: 46/44/23/15/13/-/ (S Khaled), H R A Cecil

1588 Dorset Handicap Class E (0-70 3-y-o and up) £3,392 6f 212yds........ (5:00)

1097[9] CHARMED KNAVE [48] 8-8-11 T Williams (10) *al prmnt, led hfwy, drw clr appr fnl furlong, unnchlgd*...... (8 to 1) 1
1207[4] OLD COMRADES [55] 6-8-11 (7*) Mark Denaro (4) *chsd ldrs, hng lft o'r one furlong out, one pace.* ....(3 to 1 fav op 4 to 1) 2
229[9] MAI PEN RAI [37] 5-8-0 G Bardwell (1) *mid-div, rdn hfwy, ran on ins fnl 2 fs, nvr nrr*.................. (20 to 1) 3
1059[9] WILD STRAWBERRY [50] 4-8-13 B Rouse (6) *led to hfwy, kpt on one pace*.................... (20 to 1 op 16 to 1) 4
1096 CEE-EN-CEE [61] (bl) 9-9-10 T Quinn (13) *mid-div, some hdwy fnl 2 fs, nvr dngrs*........................ (10 to 1) 5
1209[6] ZINBAQ [36] 7-7-10 (3*) D Harrison (15) *chsd ldrs, one pace fnl 2 fs*............................ (5 to 1 op 9 to 2) 6
1284[8] OPEN AGENDA (Ire) [53] 4-9-2 R Wernham (9) *prmnt, pressed wnr 2 fs out, rdn and wknd appr last.* (10 to 1) 7
1373[2] ASTERIX [55] (v) 5-9-4 N Adams (2) *prmnt on outsd till wknd 2 fs out*..................................(7 to 1) 8
1207 ALNASRIC PETE (USA) [49] 7-8-12 W Newnes (8) *hld up, effrt o'r 2 fs out, nvr dngrs*.......... (14 to 1 op 12 to 1) 9
SIR OLIVER (Ire) [56] 4-8-12 (7*) S Drowne (7) *al rear.* .... (14 to 1) 10
1280[4] MASTER REACH [48] (bl) 4-8-11 S Whitworth (11) *frnt rnk till wknd o'r 2 fs out*............... (10 to 1 op 8 to 1) 11
SIR THOMAS BEECHAM [63] 3-9-2 C Rutter (5) *al rear.* .... (20 to 1) 12
1097 TOP ONE [57] 8-9-6 D Biggs (12) *speed to hfwy.* (10 to 1) 13
606[4] MARK'S CLUB (Ire) [64] 3-9-3 A Clark (3) *slwly away, al beh*................(12 to 1 op 10 to 1 tchd 14 to 1) 14
871 JEWEL THIEF [55] 3-8-8 J Williams (16) *al struggling, tld off fnl 2 fs*.............................. (20 to 1) 15

Dist: 6l, ¾l, sht-hd, ¾l, 1l, nk, 3l, 1l, 4l, hd. 1m 27.69s. a 2.09s (15 Ran).
SR: 44/33/13/25/34/6/22/15/6/ (Mrs M E Olsson), D R Laing

BEVERLEY (good to firm)
Wednesday June 9th
Going Correction: MINUS 0.30 sec. per fur. (races 1,2), MINUS 0.25 (3,4,5,6,7)

1589 'Quest For Knowledge' Sprint Handicap Class E (0-70 3-y-o and up) £3,106 5f............................. (2:00)

1463[3] LIDA'S DELIGHT (Ire) [57] 3-8-7 T Lucas (15) *pressed ldr, effrt 2 fs out, ran on gmely fnl furlong to ld last strds.* .... (12 to 1) 1
1463* NORDOORA (Ire) [35] 4-7-2 (5*) Darren Moffatt (11) *unruly at strt, tried to make all, rdn 2 fs out, ct last strds.* .... (10 to 1 op 8 to 1) 2
1563[8] MISS ARAGON [54] 5-8-9 (3*) S Maloney (16) *tucked away on ins, improved wl o'r one fs out, kpt on towards finish*.......................... (12 to 1 op 10 to 1) 3
1379* THE RIGHT TIME [49] 8-8-4 (3*) D Harrison (10) *settled midfield, rdn to improve 2 fs out, ran on wl ins fnl furlong*.............(9 to 2 fav op 5 to 1 tchd 4 to 1) 4
1160[9] MY GODSON [63] (bl) 3-8-8 (5*) O Pears (13) *mid-div, hdwy 2 fs out, ran on ins last*............ (16 to 1 op 14 to 1) 5
1420[9] HERE COMES A STAR [67] 5-9-11 S Morris (8) *beh, improved o'r one furlong out, ran on ins last, nvr nrr.* .... (14 to 1 op 12 to 1) 6
1148[3] KALAR [48] (bl) 4-8-6 S Wood (14) *in tch, drvn alng o'r 2 fs out, not quicken over one out*...... (8 to 1 tchd 9 to 1) 7
909 BRISAS [36] 6-7-8 J Fanning (2) *unruly strt, nvr far away, pushed alng aftr 2 fs, one pace wl o'r one out.* .... (25 to 1 op 20 to 1) 8
1420[8] BALLAD DANCER [56] 8-9-0 K Darley (7) *hld up, effrt on inner hfwy, no imprsn*.............................. (16 to 1) 9
1036 SUPREME DESIRE [51] 5-8-9 S Webster (9) *sn pushed alng in mid-div, one pace frm hfwy*..... (25 to 1 op 20 to 1) 10
1463[2] MISS BRIGHTSIDE [37] 5-7-9 J Lowe (12) *chsd ldrs, pushed alng 2 fs out, sn btn*........ (8 to 1 tchd 9 to 1) 11
1076[6] STRIP CARTOON (Ire) [57] (bl) 5-8-8 (7*) G Strange (6) *in tch, feeling pace o'r 2 fs out, sn btn*.... (14 to 1 op 12 to 1) 12
1420[4] PRINCE BELFORT [61] 5-9-5 D Holland (3) *towards rear on outer, sn rdn alng, not pace to chal.* .... (7 to 1 tchd 6 to 1) 13
1036 ABSOLUTION [69] 9-9-13 N Connorton (5) *beh, rdn alng hfwy, nvr a factor*.................................. (20 to 1) 14
1287[8] ROCK OPERA (Ire) [56] 5-8-7 (7*) V Halliday (1) *beh and sn pushed alng, struggling frm hfwy.* (20 to 1 op 16 to 1) 15
1215 PRECENTOR [55] 7-8-13 L Dettori (4) *beh, rdn alng hfwy, nvr on terms*......... (10 to 1 op 12 to 1 tchd 14 to 1) 16

Dist: Sht-hd, 1½l, ½l, 2½l, hd, nk, 2l, nk, 1l, sht-hd. 1m 2.80s. a 1.10s (16 Ran).
SR: 41/26/39/32/28/39/19/-/18/ (Patrington Haven Leisure Park), M W Easterby

1590 European Business And Management Claiming Stakes Class F (2-y-o) £2,243 5f............................ (2:30)

968* RANDONNEUR (Ire) 8-7 G Carter (5) *pressed ldr, led appr fnl furlong, pushed out ins last.* ....(9 to 4 fav op 5 to 2 tchd 3 to 1) 1
1108* BROOKHEAD LADY 8-2 D Holland (7) *chsd ldrs, rdn alng hfwy, styd on fnl furlong, wnt second cl hme.* ....(4 to 1 op 7 to 2) 2
1253* IMPERIAL BAILIWICK (Ire) 8-9 N Adams (8) *led, rdn 2 fs out, hdd appr fnl furlong, no extr ins last.* ....(5 to 1 op 4 to 1) 3
1108[4] PASSION SUNDAY 9-0 K Darley (9) *mid-div, shaken up o'r one furlong out, nvr nr to chal.* .... (11 to 2 op 5 to 1 tchd 9 to 2) 4
GENERAL GUBBINS 9-0 L Dettori (2) *slwly into strd, beh, improved o'r one furlong out, kpt on, nvr dngrs.* .... (14 to 1) 5
BRAMCOTE CENTURY 8-3 J Lowe (6) *missed break, sn pushed alng in rear, no imprsn frm hfwy.* .... (25 to 1 op 20 to 1) 6
1413[2] GRECIAN GARDEN 8-6 A Proud (4) *chsd ldrs on outer, sn rdn alng, wknd 2 fs out.* .... (11 to 2 op 5 to 1 tchd 6 to 1) 7
1053[6] TIME TO DANCE 7-13 J Fanning (1) *cl up on outer til rdn and wknd wl o'r one furlong out.* (20 to 1 tchd 8 to 1) 8
1245[8] SPRING STAR 7-9 A Mackay (3) *beh and sn pushed alng, struggling aftr 2 fs*.............................. (33 to 1) 9

1413 JACQUI'S STAR (Ire) 8-1 (3*) D Harrison (10) *beh and sn outpcd, lost tch frm hfwy*......... (25 to 1 op 20 to 1) 10
Dist: 1l, hd, 8l, 2l, 1l, 3½l, 1l, 2½l, 4l. 1m 3.20s. a 1.50s (10 Ran).
SR: 33/24/30/3/-/-/ (J Nixon), J Berry

1591 Eltherington Handicap Class E (0-70 3-y-o and up) £3,752 7f 100yds.. (3:00)

1304^{3} CAUSLEY [65] 8-9-11 B Raymond (8) *wth ldr, led 4 fs out, rdn 2 out, styd on wl ins last*........ (5 to 1 op 9 to 2) 1
1436^{2} BERNSTEIN BETTE [60] 7-9-6 J Fanning (11) *in tch on inner, improved to chase wnr 2 fs out, rdn and kpt on ins fnl furlong, no extr cl hme.* (7 to 2 fav tchd 3 to 1) 2
1316^{5} LOMBARD SHIPS [44] (bl) 6-8-4 A Mackay (13) *hld up towards rear, improved entering strt, kpt on fnl furlong, no extr towards finish*....... (14 to 1 op 12 to 1) 3
1434^{3} SPANISH VERDICT [65] 6-9-4 (7*) C Teague (2) *beh, rdn to improve entering strt, kpt on same pace ins last.* ....(7 to 1 tchd 13 to 2) 4
1165^{5} KHISAL (Can) [61] 3-8-11 M Birch (7) *hld up and beh, plenty to do whn not clr run o'r 2 fs out, kpt on wl fnl furlong, nvr nr to chal*........................(14 to 1) 5
818^{4} SUPREME BOY [55] 4-9-1 F Norton (3) *mid-div, effrt and rdn entering strt, sn one pace*...... (10 to 1 op 8 to 1) 6
1274 DUNE RIVER [68] 4-10-0 L Dettori (1) *trkd ldg bunch, effrt 3 fs out, wknd o'r one furlong out.* .... (11 to 1 op 10 to 1 tchd 12 to 1) 7
1286^{5} KUMMEL KING [58] 5-9-4 K Fallon (9) *in tch, rdn o'r 2 fs out, grad wknd*................ (12 to 1 tchd 11 to 1) 8
1436 CLAUDIA MISS [60] 6-9-6 Dean McKeown (5) *hld up, effrt entering strt, nvr able to chal*..... (14 to 1 op 16 to 1) 9
PIMSBOY [51] (bl) 6-8-8 (3*) D Harrison (6) *trkd ldrs til wknd o'r 2 fs out*.............................. (20 to 1) 10
1304 HERBRAND (Ire) [40] 4-7-12^{1} (3*) S Maloney (10) *beh, drvn alng appr strt, nvr on terms*....... (16 to 1 op 14 to 1) 11
899 ANDRULA MOU [52] 3-8-2 L Charnock (12) *led til hdd 4 fs out, sn drvn alng, wknd entering strt.* .... (25 to 1 op 20 to 1) 12
142^{5} GUESSTIMATION (USA) [49] 4-8-9 K Darley (4) *beh, drvn alng entering strt, sn btn*........ (14 to 1 tchd 16 to 1) 13
Dist: ¾l, nk, 3l, hd, nk, 2½l, 1½l, ½l, 3l, ½l. 1m 32.70s. a 2.40s (13 Ran).
SR: 47/40/23/35/20/23/28/13/13/ (Henry Pearce), B A McMahon

1592 University Of Humberside Handicap Class D (0-80 3-y-o and up) £3,655 1m 1f 207yds...................... (3:30)

1274 SELF EXPRESSION [56] 5-8-6 (7*) D Thomas (6) *made virtually all, quickened clr entering strt, styd on strly.* ....(8 to 1 op 7 to 1) 1
1460^{3} TOUCH ABOVE [49] 7-8-6 K Darley (1) *hld up, effrt and rdn 2 fs out, kpt on fnl furlong, not rch wnr.* ....(11 to 4 fav op 7 to 2 tchd 5 to 2) 2
1307^{9} WESTHOLME (USA) [69] 5-9-12 M Birch (10) *chsd ldrs on inner, rdn o'r 2 fs out, not quicken ins last.* ....(7 to 1 op 6 to 1) 3
1328^{6} AZUREUS (Ire) [70] 5-9-8 (5*) A Procter (3) *steadied strt, hld up, hdwy 2 fs out, baulked entering fnl furlong, styd on strly*............................. (7 to 1 op 6 to 1) 4
1421^{4} NO COMEBACKS [54] 5-8-11 K Fallon (9) *slwly into strd, hld up and beh, effrt and shaken up o'r one furlong out, kpt on ins last, nvr nrr*.............(6 to 1 op 5 to 1) 5
1318^{3} SURREY DANCER [71] 5-10-0 B Raymond (2) *in tch on outer, effrt and rdn entering strt, not quicken o'r one furlong out*........... (11 to 2 op 6 to 1 tchd 5 to 1) 6
1421^{9} LEAP IN THE DARK (Ire) [50] 4-8-7 L Dettori (4) *chsd ldrs, rdn entering strt, wknd o'r one furlong out.* .... (20 to 1 op 16 to 1) 7
1422^{3} BARLEY CAKE [55] 3-7-13 J Fanning (7) *tucked away on ins, effrt 2 fs out, sn one pace.* .... (10 to 1 op 8 to 1 tchd 11 to 1) 8
885^{8} KING'S GUEST (Ire) [61] 4-9-4 Dean McKeown (5) *wth ldr 4 fs, styd hndy till wknd quickly o'r 2 furlongs out.* ....(12 to 1) 9
1274^{9} MAJAL (Ire) [70] 4-9-13 D Nicholls (8) *dwlt, hld up, drvn alng entering strt, sn lost tch*......(16 to 1 op 12 to 1) 10
Dist: 2l, 1l, nk, ½l, 2½l, 2½l, sht-hd, 12l, 5l. 2m 5.50s. a 4.10s (10 Ran).
SR: 33/22/40/40/23/35/9/-/-/ (Jonathan Ramsden), Mrs J R Ramsden

1593 'Win With The Tote' Handicap Class D (0-80 3-y-o and up) £3,655 1m 3f 216yds....................... (4:00)

1345^{9} CALL THE GUV'NOR [62] 4-9-1 A McGlone (2) *pressed ldr, led o'r 6 fs out, crrd head high and hdd over 2 out, rallied to rgn ld ins fnl furlong, rdn out.* ....(7 to 2 fav op 4 to 1) 1
1260^{3} FAIR FLYER (Ire) [55] 4-8-8 R P Elliott (4) *chsd ldg pair, improved to ld o'r 2 fs out, hdd ins last, no extr.* ....(6 to 1 op 5 to 1) 2
1094^{4} TRUBEN (USA) [75] 4-10-0 L Dettori (1) *hld up in rear, effrt entering strt, ev ch one furlong out, sn one pace.* .... (11 to 2 op 5 to 1) 3
1438^{6} DANZA HEIGHTS [41] 7-7-8 J Fanning (6) *in tch, took clr order appr strt, rdn and one pace fnl 2 fs.* ....(7 to 1 op 5 to 1) 4

1398 KILLICK [54] 5-8-0 (7*) D Wright (5) *hld up in tch, effrt and rdn alng 2 fs out, not pace to chal*... (9 to 2 op 5 to 1) 5
1439* EIRE LEATH-SCEAL [54] 6-8-7 (5ex) M Wigham (7) *led til hdd o'r 6 fs out, styd hndy and sn rdn, wknd 2 furlongs out*...(6 to 1 op 5 to 1) 6
1288^{3} CONTINUITY [57] 4-8-10 K Fallon (3) *hld up and beh, pushed alng entering strt, no imprsn*...........(7 to 1) 7
Dist: 1½l, nk, 1½l, 1½l, ¾l, ¾l. 2m 35.70s. a 4.70s (7 Ran).
SR: 24/14/33/-/6/4/5/ (W H Ponsonby), H R A Cecil

1594 New University Maiden Stakes Class D (3-y-o and up) £3,465 1m 3f 216yds ....(4:30)

1216^{3} TASSET (Can) 3-8-8 T Quinn (2) *set sedate pace, pushed alng 4 fs out, hdd o'r one furlong out, rallied to rgn ld ins last, kpt on wl*................. (3 to 1 tchd 5 to 2) 1
MOSCOW SEA (USA) 3-8-8 A McGlone (1) *nvr far away, chlgd o'r 2 fs out, led over one furlong out, hdd ins last, no extr*.........(6 to 4 fav op 5 to 4 on tchd 13 to 8) 2
1311^{6} RASAYEL (USA) 3-8-3 D Holland (4) *hld up in tch, rdn to improve o'r 2 fs out, not quicken fnl furlong.* ....(9 to 4 op 3 to 1) 3
MISS RITA 4-9-5 M Wigham (5) *sluggish strt, hld up, shaken up entering strt, kpt on fnl furlong, nvr plcd to chal*............................ (25 to 1 op 33 to 1) 4
QUARTZ HILL (USA) 4-9-10 J Fanning (7) *chsd ldrs, rdn o'r 2 fs out, wknd over one furlong out*........... (33 to 1) 5
1077^{5} WAKT 3-8-3 Dean McKeown (3) *chsd ldrs on outer, rdn 3 fs out, sn ev ch, wknd 2 out*........ (20 to 1 op 14 to 1) 6
1533^{6} WORLD WITHOUT END (USA) 4-9-5 (5*) O Pears (6) *hld up in rear, lost tch entering strt*...... (33 to 1 op 25 to 1) 7
Dist: 1l, 1½l, 3½l, 2l, 3½l, 5l. 2m 40.90s. a 9.90s (7 Ran).
(Sheikh Mohammed), P F I Cole

1595 Polygon Quality Management Maiden Stakes Class D (3-y-o) £3,172 7f 100yds........................ (5:00)

951^{2} NAFUTH (USA) 9-0 D Holland (1) *in tch, imprvg whn not clr run o'r one furlong out, ran on to ld wl ins last.* ....(7 to 2 op 3 to 1) 1
1330^{3} QUEENS CONSUL (Ire) 8-9 Dean McKeown (2) *trkd ldr, improved to ld o'r one furlong out, hdd wl ins last, one pace*...............................(4 to 1 tchd 9 to 2) 2
1285^{2} AL SHAATI (Fr) 8-9 K Darley (5) *led, rdn o'r 2 fs out, hdd over one furlong out, not quicken ins last.* ....(7 to 4 fav op 2 to 1) 3
1171^{5} AZOLA (Ire) 8-9 B Raymond (3) *trkd ldrs on inner, not much room 2 fs out, rdn and sn btn.* (3 to 1 op 2 to 1) 4
KEEP BATTLING 9-0 J Fanning (4) *uns rdr gng to post, hld up in last pl, effrt on outer entering strt, ev ch wl o'r one furlong out, sn btn*....................... (33 to 1) 5
Dist: Nk, 5l, 1½l, 3l. 1m 32.70s. a 2.40s (5 Ran).
SR: 36/30/15/10/6/ (Hamdan Al-Maktoum), P T Walwyn

HAMILTON (good (races 1,2), good to soft (3,4,5,6)) Wednesday June 9th

Going Correction: MINUS 0.10 sec. per fur. (races 1,2,3), PLUS 0.15 (4,5,6)

1596 Sporting Club Of Mexico Selling Stakes Class G (3-y-o) £1,548 1m 65yds......................... (7:00)

1225^{7} DRUMDONNA (Ire) 8-11 J Fortune (2) *trkd ldr, led o'r 2 out, pushed out fnl furlong*........(7 to 4 on op 9 to 4 on) 1
4661a BOLD FLASH 8-11 Dale Gibson (3) *trkd ldrs, effrt 2 out, sn rdn and one pace*..................(5 to 2 tchd 3 to 1) 2
1185^{7} BARDIA 8-6 Kim Tinkler (1) *hld up, effrt 2 out, kpt on same pace*................(25 to 1 op 33 to 1 tchd 50 to 1) 3
1419 BLUEBELLA 8-6 S Perks (4) *led till hdd o'r 2 out, wknd entering fnl furlong.* ....(10 to 1 op 8 to 1 tchd 12 to 1 and 14 to 1) 4
Dist: 1½l, nk, 5l. 1m 51.30s. a 7.30s (4 Ran).
(Mrs Norma Peebles), J Berry

1597 Scottish Taverners Rating Related Maiden Stakes Class D (3-y-o and up) £3,318 1m 65yds............... (7:25)

1330^{2} AJDAYT (USA) 3-8-11 S Whitworth (4) *beh, gd hdwy 3 out, led wl o'r one out, sn clr, eased towards finish.* .... (5 to 4 fav op 6 to 4 tchd 13 to 8 and 2 to 1) 1
1540^{3} PERSIAN CHARMER (Ire) (v) 3-8-11 J Fortune (6) *led till hdd o'r 2 out, kpt on wl fnl furlong*...... (7 to 1 op 6 to 1) 2
563^{3} SARANGANI BAY (USA) 3-8-6 (5*) Stephen Davies (5) *in tch, rdn o'r 2 out, kpt on fnl furlong*....(4 to 1 tchd 9 to 2) 3
899^{8} SCUSI 3-8-11 J Carroll (2) *chsd ldr, led o'r 2 out, hdd wl over one out, sn wknd*...(7 to 2 op 5 to 2 tchd 4 to 1) 4
1349^{5} RED WHIRLWIND 3-8-11 K Darley (7) *in tch, effrt o'r 3 out, rdn over 2 out, sn btn*.............. (11 to 2 op 9 to 2) 5

1516[3] MINSK 7-9-3 S Webster (3) *chsd ldrs till wknd 3 out.* ....(66 to 1 op 50 to 1 tchd 100 to 1) 6
1261[4] MARIAN EVANS 6-9-3 A Mackay (1) *sn wl beh*...(100 to 1) 7
Dist: ¾l, 6l, nk, 6l, 10l, 12l. 1m 47.00s. a 3.00s (7 Ran).
SR: 39/37/19/18/ (Sheikh Ahmed Al Maktoum), A C Stewart

1598 Carlsberg-Tetley Alloa Maiden Auction Stakes Class E (2-y-o) £2,322 6f 5yds.......................... (7:55)

1324[2] BRAILLE (Ire) 9-0 Dean McKeown (6) *made all, pushed clr fnl furlong.* .... (2 to 1 on op 2 to 1 on tchd 6 to 4 on and 7 to 4 on) 1
1189[3] TURTLE ROCK 9-0 K Darley (3) *chsd ldrs, rdn o'r 2 out, kpt on, no ch wth wnr*.............(6 to 1 op 10 to 1) 2
WOODLAND WHISPER 8-9 Dale Gibson (9) *trkd ldrs, rdn o'r 2 out, one paced*...............(20 to 1 op 16 to 1) 3
1182[5] WILLWIN 8-9 L Charnock (5) *stumbled strt, sn in tch, kpt on same pace fnl 2 fs*..............(25 to 1 op 20 to 1) 4
1051[3] FORREST MASTER (Ire) 9-0 J Fortune (7) *chsd ldr till wknd wl o'r one out*.....................(14 to 1 op 10 to 1) 5
1098[4] IBERIAN MAGIC (Ire) 9-0 S Perks (2) *in tch, edgd rght hfwy, no hdwy*.................. (14 to 1 op 10 to 1) 6
354[6] SING SONG BLUES 9-0 J Carroll (8) *in tch till wknd o'r 2 out*........................... (10 to 1 op 6 to 1) 7
MOLLINSBURN (Ire) 9-0 A Mackay (1) *strted slwly, tld off till some late hdwy*..............(66 to 1 op 25 to 1) 8
865[8] KINGFISHER GREY 9-0 J Lowe (4) *rcd stands side, early speed, beh frm 2 out, tld off*......(33 to 1 tchd 50 to 1) 9
Dist: 8l, 2l, 2½l, sht-hd, 3½l, ¾l, 2l, 15l. 1m 14.10s. a 3.40s (9 Ran).
SR: 20/-/-/-/-/-/ (Kingsley Partnership), M Johnston

1599 Langs Supreme Scotch Whisky Handicap Class E (0-70 3-y-o and up) £2,427 5f 4yds........................ (8:25)

909[9] DIET [58] (v) 7-8-11 (7*) R Havlin (8) *made virtually all, hld on wl*...................(9 to 1 op 8 to 1 tchd 10 to 1) 1
1228[2] MURRAY'S MAZDA (Ire) [63] 4-9-9 J Carroll (9) *trkd ldrs, effrt o'r one out, kpt on wl towards finish, jst fld.* ....(3 to 1 fav op 7 to 2) 2
1420[5] JUST BOB [68] 4-10-0 J Fortune (3) *in tch, hdwy o'r 2 out, chlgd over one out, no extr ins fnl furlong.* ....(4 to 1 op 7 to 2 tchd 9 to 2) 3
1560[9] SO SUPERB [62] (bl) 4-9-8 S Webster (7) *squeezed strt, beh, hdwy wl o'r one out, kpt on und pres fnl furlong.* ....(6 to 1 op 7 to 1 tchd 8 to 1) 4
1480[9] MEESON TIMES [50] 5-8-5 (5*) O Pears (4) *prmnt, rdn 2 out, one paced*...............................(20 to 1) 5
1287 NORTH OF WATFORD [49] 8-8-9 L Charnock (10) *chsd ldrs, no hdwy fnl 2 fs*.................(12 to 1 op 20 to 1) 6
1286 SECOND COLOURS (USA) [58] 3-8-10 K Darley (1) *beh frm hfwy,*...............................(4 to 1 op 3 to 1) 7
1287[7] CREAGMHOR [52] 3-8-4 J Lowe (5) *sn beh.* ....(14 to 1 op 10 to 1 tchd 16 to 1) 8
1420 GEMINI FIRE [68] 9-10-0 Dean McKeown (2) *sn beh.* ....(20 to 1 op 16 to 1 tchd 25 to 1) 9
1516[6] UPPANCE [33] (bl) 5-7-7 A Mackay (6) *prmnt till wknd quickly 2 out*.....................(50 to 1 op 33 to 1) 10
Dist: Sht-hd, 1l, 1½l, 3l, ½l, 3l, 2½l, 2l, 1l. 1m 2.50s. a 4.20s (10 Ran).
SR: 35/39/40/28/4/1/ (Mrs M S J Clydesdale), Miss L A Perratt

1600 Tennents Amateur Riders' Maiden Handicap Class G (0-60 3-y-o and up) £1,646 1m 3f 16yds............. (8:55)

1521[8] RAPID MOVER [25] (bl) 6-10-1 (5*) Miss L Eaton (1) *made all, reminders 6 out, rdn 3 out, styd on wl.* ....(9 to 1 op 8 to 1) 1
888[2] CHALLENGER ROW (Ire) [46] 3-10-12 Mr S Swiers (8) *prmnt, trkd wnr frm 6 out, chlgd 4 out, rdn 2 out, styd on fnl furlong*....... (5 to 4 fav op 6 to 4 tchd 7 to 4) 2
1498[5] COXANN [26] (bl) 7-10-2 (5*) Mr E Tolhurst (7) *prmnt, chsd ldg pair frm 5 out, kpt on, no imprsn.* .... (9 to 1 op 7 to 1 tchd 10 to 1) 3
1170[4] BUZZ-B-BABE [47] 3-10-13 Mrs A Farrell (3) *in tch, outpcd 5 out, no dngr aftr*...... (9 to 2 op 4 to 1 tchd 5 to 1) 4
GAILY DANCE [30] 5-10-11 Mr A Thornton (4) *chsd ldrs, one paced 4 out*.......... (33 to 1 op 20 to 1 tchd 50 to 1) 5
MEESON CODE [24] 6-10-0 (5*) Mr V Lukaniuk (9) *in tch, hdwy to go prmnt 7 out, rdn 4 out, one paced.* ....(100 to 1 op 50 to 1) 6
BE THE BEST [37] 5-10-13 (5*) Mr R D Green (11) *dwlt, nvr nr ldrs*........................... (8 to 1 tchd 10 to 1) 7
1528[7] RUNRIG (Ire) [52] 3-10-13 (5*) Miss L Perratt (6) *chsd ldrs till wknd 4 out*.........................(4 to 1 op 5 to 2) 8
PAULINUS [40] 5-11-2 (5*) Miss M Carson (5) *chsd ldrs till wknd 4 out*.......................... (66 to 1 op 33 to 1) 9
TREBONKERS [33] 9-11-0[11] (5*) Mr M Kershaw (10) *wl beh frm hfwy*........................... (100 to 1 op 33 to 1) 10
745[7] INVISIBLE ARMOUR [39] 4-11-6 Mrs J Crossley (2) *beh most of way*...........................(16 to 1 op 10 to 1) 11
Dist: ½l, 3½l, 3l, ½l, ½l, 6l, 7l, 1l. 2m 31.90s. a 11.90s (11 Ran).
SR: 17/22/10/10/7/-/1/-/-/ (M B Gielty), T Craig

1601 Hamilton Advertiser Handicap Class E (0-70 4-y-o and up) £2,427 1m 5f 9yds .... (9:25)

1336[8] FIVE TO SEVEN (USA) [65] 4-9-9 (5*) O Pears (4) *trkd ldr, led o'r 4 out, hdd over 3 out, sn rdn, rallied fnl furlong to ld cl hme*.................. (9 to 2 op 4 to 1 tchd 5 to 1) 1
1531[4] MENTALASANYTHIN [60] 4-9-9 A Mackay (9) *trkd ldrs, led o'r 3 out, rdn fnl furlong, hdd and no extr cl hme.* ....(9 to 4 fav op 3 to 1 tchd 2 to 1) 2
1190 MINGUS (USA) [40] 6-8-3[1] K Fallon (1) *hld up, hdwy 4 out, kpt on fnl furlong, not rch ldrs.* (10 to 1 tchd 14 to 1) 3
SHAFFIC (Fr) [55] 6-9-4 K Darley (8) *hld up, effrt 4 out, styd on fnl 2 fs*..............................(5 to 1 op 7 to 2) 4
1288[4] GREY COMMANDER [31] 5-7-8[1] L Charnock (7) *led till hdd o'r 4 out, grad wknd*... (9 to 1 op 7 to 1 tchd 10 to 1) 5
1439[9] DON'T CRY [32] 5-7-9[2] Kim Tinkler (2) *in tch, effrt 4 out, no hdwy*..............................(66 to 1 op 50 to 1) 6
1389 REEL OF TULLOCH (Ire) [47] 4-8-10 Dean McKeown (5) *mid-div, effrt 4 out, wknd 2 out*....... (25 to 1 op 14 to 1) 7
1288[2] WEST WITH THE WIND [48] 6-8-11 J Lowe (6) *trkd ldrs, effrt 4 out, wknd o'r 2 out*.........(3 to 1 tchd 9 to 2) 8
910 ALPHA HELIX [32] (v) 10-7-9[2] Dale Gibson (3) *al beh, lost tch frm 6 out, tld off*...............(66 to 1 op 50 to 1) 9
Dist: Nk, 2½l, 1½l, 1½l, 1l, 7l, ½l, dist. 3m 0.70s. a 14.70s (9 Ran).
(The Five To Seven Partnership), S G Norton

KEMPTON (good)
Wednesday June 9th
Going Correction: MINUS 0.10 sec. per fur.

1602 LBC Newstalk 97.3 FM Maiden Auction Stakes Class F (2-y-o) £3,626 6f ....(6:40)

1350 SLASHER JACK (Ire) 9-0 Pat Eddery (7) *mid-div stands side, rdn and hdwy 2 fs out, ran on wl to ld nr finish.* ....(8 to 1 op 5 to 1 tchd 10 to 1) 1
1063 SOLO TICKET 9-0 J Reid (1) *led stands side grp, o'rall ldr appr fnl furlong, hdd cl hme*.................(12 to 1) 2
1211[6] NONIOS (Ire) 9-0 W Carson (18) *al in tch far side, led that grp one furlong out, wknd nr finish.* .... (5 to 1 op 4 to 1 tchd 11 to 2) 3
922 MR MYSTICAL (Ire) 9-0 B Rouse (2) *chsd ldrs stands side, outpcd 2 out, kpt on wl ins last.* (20 to 1 tchd 25 to 1) 4
1350[6] MOMENT OF GLORY (Ire) 9-0 R Cochrane (11) *mid-div, hdwy 2 fs out, ran on wl ins last.* ....(7 to 1 op 5 to 1 tchd 8 to 1) 5
1227[3] KARSEAM (Ire) 9-0 W Newnes (14) *al prmnt far side, no extr ins fnl furlong*..................(8 to 1 op 6 to 1) 6
1229[9] CHARLIES DREAM (Ire) 8-9 T Sprake (23) *led far side till one furlong out, wknd*............ (50 to 1 op 33 to 1) 7
CANDI DAS (Ire) 8-6 (3*) D Harrison (5) *chsd stands side grp, one pace ins fnl 2 fs.* (14 to 1 op 20 to 1 tchd 12 to 1) 8
528[7] SWEET CAROLINE 8-9 G Duffield (6) *pressed stands ldr till wknd o'r one furlong out*.........(50 to 1 op 33 to 1) 9
HAM N'EGGS 9-0 S Raymont (8) *chsd stands side grp till one pace fnl 2 fs*...............(12 to 1 op 14 to 1) 10
ROYAL INTERPRETER 8-11 (3*) J Weaver (3) *in tch stands side for 4 fs*.....................................(33 to 1) 11
1063 RED VALERIAN 9-0 L Dettori (13) *speed far side, wknd wl o'r one furlong out.* (4 to 1 fav op 3 to 1 tchd 9 to 2) 12
1063[6] ELEVATOR SHAFT (Ire) 9-0 F Norton (12) *towards rear till hdwy o'r 2 fs out, wknd appr last.* ....(15 to 2 op 6 to 1 tchd 8 to 1) 13
445[5] STARISK 8-9 T Williams (22) *chsd ldrs far side, wknd wl o'r one furlong out*..............(16 to 1 op 14 to 1) 14
LITTLE LUKE (Ire) 8-7 (7*) S Drowne (17) *al beh.* ....(50 to 1 op 33 to 1) 15
1253[4] SEVEN UP CYD 8-9 C Rutter (10) *in tch till wknd 2 fs out.* ....(20 to 1 tchd 25 to 1) 16
625[9] CRAFTY CRICKETER 9-0 S Dawson (21) *chsd ldrs far side, wknd quickly appr fnl furlong*.... (50 to 1 op 33 to 1) 17
LORD WELLINGTON (Ire) 9-0 M Perrett (20) *speed far side to hfwy*.................................(50 to 1 op 25 to 1) 18
DAVID BLUE (Ire) 9-0 C Avery (16) *slwly away, al in rear.* ....(50 to 1 op 33 to 1) 19
CURBRIDGE (Ire) 9-0 J Quinn (9) *outpcd thrght.* ....(50 to 1 op 33 to 1) 20
968[5] NORTHERN STORM (Ire) 9-0 W Woods (4) *in tch stands side to hfwy*.....................(12 to 1 tchd 14 to 1) 21
MLOUKIAH (Fr) 8-9 A Clark (15) *outpcd thrght.* ....(50 to 1 op 33 to 1) 22
Dist: ½l, 1l, ½l, 1l, hd, ½l, hd, 3l, ¾l, 1½l. 1m 14.68s. a 3.88s (22 Ran).
SR: 10/8/4/2/-/-/ (The Winning Team), R Hannon

1603 Eros Maiden Stakes Class D (3-y-o) £3,552 1½m................... (7:10)

1314[5] EDBAYSAAN (Ire) 9-0 W Ryan (2) *nvr far away, led 2 fs out, ran on wl*................ (5 to 2 fav tchd 2 to 1) 1
1176[4] DARZEE 9-0 R Cochrane (12) *chsd ldrs, ev ch 2 fs out, ran on one pace*..............(7 to 2 op 5 to 1 tchd 4 to 1) 2
1093[3] LEEWA (Ire) 9-0 M Roberts (10) *in tch till lost pl 3 fs out, ran on wl appr fnl furlong.* ....(4 to 1 op 7 to 2 tchd 5 to 1) 3
ELBURG (Ire) 9-0 M Hills (11) *led till hdd 2 fs out, no extr ins last*.......... (25 to 1 op 20 to 1 tchd 33 to 1) 4

1176[8] TILTY (USA) 9-0 R Perham (9) *beh till hdwy o'r 2 fs out, nvr nr to chal*............(25 to 1 op 20 to 1 tchd 33 to 1) 5
1224[7] HILL OF DREAMS 9-0 L Dettori (6) *hld up, styd on one pace fnl 3 fs*......................(14 to 1 op 12 to 1) 6
CYRUS THE BOLD (Ire) 9-0 J Reid (8) *al in rear, no hdwy fnl 3 fs*...............(14 to 1 op 8 to 1 tchd 16 to 1) 7
1068 BERING ISLAND (USA) 9-0 Pat Eddery (1) *chsd ldr to 3 fs out, sn btn and eased.*
.....................(14 to 1 op 12 to 1 tchd 16 to 1) 8
SUN GREBE (Ire) 8-9 G Duffield (7) *pld hrd, hmpd aftr 3 fs, swtchd lft three out, sn rdn and btn.*
.....................(20 to 1 op 16 to 1 tchd 25 to 1) 9
1093[5] SPICE BOX (USA) 9-0 S O'Gorman (4) *al towards rear, lost tch o'r 2 fs out*..........(8 to 1 op 7 to 1 tchd 9 to 1) 10
1176[8] KINCHENJUNGA 8-9 W R Swinburn (3) *mid-div till wknd o'r 3 fs out*.....................(14 to 1 tchd 16 to 1) 11
Dist: 3l, 3l, ½l, 1½l, 2l, 1½l, 3l, 1l, hd, 8l. 2m 36.40s. a 5.40s (11 Ran).
SR: 34/28/22/21/18/14/11/5/-/ (Sheikh Essa Bin Mubarak), H R A Cecil

1604 West End Final Handicap Class D (0-80 3-y-o and up) £3,786 1m... (7:40)

676[3] PENNY DROPS [67] 4-8-12 (3*) D Harrison (4) *hld up, hdwy on outsd 2 fs out, str run to ld nr finish.*
.................................(5 to 1 tchd 11 to 2) 1
1316[4] RISE UP SINGING [68] (bl) 5-9-2 Pat Eddery (9) *trkd ldr, led o'r 3 fs out, clr appr last, rdn and one pace, hdd nr finish*..................(7 to 1 op 6 to 1 tchd 8 to 1) 2
1274 YFOOL [70] 3-8-7 W R Swinburn (7) *beh till rdn and hdwy o'r 2 fs out, kpt on ins last.*
.....................(16 to 1 op 12 to 1 tchd 20 to 1) 3
1318[5] WILL SOON [58] 4-8-6 C Rutter (2) *nvr far away, rdn to go second appr fnl furlong, hng lft, one pace.*
.................................(8 to 1 tchd 10 to 1) 4
1474[6] NOBBY BARNES [59] 4-8-0 (7*) T G McLaughlin (6) *al prmnt, outpcd ins fnl 2 fs*..........(8 to 1 op 10 to 1) 5
1490[4] TIFFANY'S CASE (Ire) [59] 4-8-7 M Hills (14) *in rear, gd hdwy 3 fs out, wknd ins last.*
.........................(8 to 1 op 7 to 1 tchd 9 to 1) 6
1312* POLAR STORM (Ire) [73] 3-8-10 J Reid (11) *chsd ldrs, rdn o'r 2 fs out, sn btn*... (9 to 2 fav op 5 to 1 tchd 6 to 1) 7
1374[6] HAROLDON (Ire) [74] (v) 4-9-8 M Roberts (5) *in tch till no hdwy ins fnl 3 fs*...... (12 to 1 op 8 to 1 tchd 14 to 1) 8
1474[8] DASWAKI (Can) [68] 5-9-2 B Rouse (13) *led till hdd o'r 3 fs out, wknd stdly*..................(12 to 1 op 7 to 1) 9
1144[9] VAGANOVA (Ire) [74] 4-9-8 T Quinn (12) *in rear, some hdwy 3 fs out, not pace to chal.*
.....................(12 to 1 op 8 to 1 tchd 14 to 1) 10
1280[6] SAAHI (USA) [62] (bl) 4-8-10 G Duffield (10) *chsd ldrs till wknd o'r 2 fs out*....(33 to 1 tchd 25 to 1 and 50 to 1) 11
BARAHIN (Ire) [80] 4-10-0 A Clark (8) *refused to settle in rear, nvr got into race.*
.....................(33 to 1 op 20 to 1 tchd 50 to 1) 12
4790a[5] CHRISTIAN SPIRIT [71] 3-8-8 R Perham (3) *in tch till wknd quickly o'r 3 fs out*.. (33 to 1 op 20 to 1 tchd 50 to 1) 13
Dist: ¾l, 1½l, 1l, 2½l, ½l, 3½l, 1l, 2l, 5l, sht-hd. 1m 39.79s. a 2.99s (13 Ran).
SR: 44/43/29/25/18/16/8/17/5/ (Stanley J Sharp), Lord Huntingdon

1605 Business Day Limited Stakes Class F (3-y-o and up) £3,262 1¾m 92yds (8:10)

1242* THE WHERE WITHAL 3-8-6 G Duffield (7) *mid-div, pushed alng frm hfwy, gd hdwy to led nrly 2 fs out, rdn ins last, ran on gmely*.......(4 to 1 op 5 to 2 tchd 9 to 2) 1
1423* BARRAAK 3-8-6 W Carson (4) *sn in tch, wnt second aftr hfwy, rdn to ld o'r 2 fs out, soon hdd, rallied und pres and ran on gmely ins last.*
.....................(5 to 4 fav op 6 to 4 tchd 11 to 10) 2
1321[7] CHAKALAK 5-9-10 M Roberts (5) *trkd ldr to hfwy, lost pl 4 fs out, rallied appr last, fnshd strly.*
.....................................(33 to 1 op 25 to 1) 3
626[8] PEACH BRANDY 4-9-5 N Adams (2) *led till hdd o'r 2 fs out, one pace aftr*...........................(50 to 1 op 33 to 1) 4
4750a* AMAZON EXPRESS 4-9-10 T Quinn (1) *trkd ldrs, rdn o'r 3 fs out, one pace ins fnl 2.* (7 to 2 op 5 to 2 tchd 4 to 1) 5
1255[3] DUTCH DEBUTANTE 3-8-3[2] W Newnes (6) *hld up in rear, rdn o'r 4 fs out, some hdwy 3 out, not pace to chal.*
.................................(10 to 1 tchd 12 to 1) 6
879 SIMPLY (Ire) 4-9-10 J Quinn (10) *in tch till wknd o'r 3 fs out*.................................(50 to 1 op 33 to 1) 7
1414[5] ROUSITTO 5-9-10 W Ryan (9) *hld up in rear, effrt o'r 3 fs out, rdn and sn btn.* (16 to 1 op 14 to 1 tchd 20 to 1) 8
1268 EL DOMINIO (v) 5-9-10 G Bardwell (8) *hld up, al in rear, lost tch o'r 3 fs out, tld off*.......................(66 to 1) 9
FACT OR FICTION 7-9-3 (7*) Antoinette Armes (3) *prmnt early, rcd wide and lost tch by hfwy, tld off.*
.................................(50 to 1 op 33 to 1) 10
Dist: 1l, 1l, 6l, 2l, 5l, 1½l, 1½l, 12l, 15l. 3m 14.88s. (10 Ran).
(W E Sturt), Sir Mark Prescott

1606 ES Magazine Fillies Handicap Class E (0-70 3-y-o and up) £3,288 7f.... (8:40)

1471[7] ANATROCCOLO [35] 6-8-3 M Roberts (9) *al prmnt, led 3 fs out, hdd one and a half furlongs out, rallied to ld ag'n wl ins last, all out*..................(7 to 1 op 6 to 1) 1
1397[6] BREEZE AWAY [56] 4-9-10 J Reid (10) *chsd ldrs, rdn appr fnl furlong, ran on strly ins*........(8 to 1 op 6 to 1) 2
PANCHELLITA (USA) [50] 4-9-4 B Rouse (5) *wtd wth, gd hdwy o'r 2 fs out, ev ch ins last, no extr cl hme.*
.................................(10 to 1 op 16 to 1) 3
1209[9] CAROMISH (USA) [52] 6-9-6 N Adams (1) *al prmnt on outsd, led one and a half fs out, rdn and hdd wl ins last, no extr fnl stages.*
.........................(7 to 1 op 11 to 2 tchd 15 to 2) 4
1425[3] FIABA [49] 5-9-3 J Quinn (2) *hld up, hdwy o'r 2 fs out, kpt on one pace ins last*.... (13 to 2 op 7 to 1 tchd 8 to 1) 5
1132 SWISS MOUNTAIN [51] (v) 3-8-9 W Newnes (7) *trkd ldrs, ev ch entering fnl furlong, btn whn not much room nr finish*..............(16 to 1 op 14 to 1 tchd 20 to 1) 6
972[6] GUANHUMARA [47] (v) 3-8-5 M Hills (4) *in rear till hdwy appr fnl furlong, ran on wl ins, nvr nrr.*
.................................(25 to 1 op 20 to 1) 7
1344 SEDGY'S SISTER [57] 3-9-1 N Carlisle (3) *chsd ldrs till wknd sn aftr hfwy*...(16 to 1 op 12 to 1 tchd 20 to 1) 8
1059 AGIL'S PET [53] 3-8-11 L Dettori (6) *al in rear.*
.....................(10 to 1 op 8 to 1 tchd 12 to 1) 9
MISTY JENNI (Ire) [65] 3-9-9 T Quinn (8) *al beh.*
.....................(13 to 2 op 5 to 1 tchd 7 to 1) 10
1280[9] NAVARESQUE [48] 8-9-2 W Carson (11) *led aftr one furlong, hdd 3 out, sn btn.*
.....................(9 to 2 fav op 4 to 1 tchd 11 to 2) 11
1528 STORMY HEIGHTS [60] 3-9-4 Pat Eddery (12) *led for one furlong, lost tch wl o'r 2 fs out.*
.....................(14 to 1 op 10 to 1 tchd 16 to 1) 12
Dist: Nk, 1l, hd, ½l, ¾l, nk, 6l, 7l, 3½l, 1l. 1m 28.22s. a 4.12s (12 Ran).
SR: 17/37/28/29/24/14/9/1/-/ (Miss Samantha Dare), R A Bennett

1607 Londoner's Diary Handicap Class E (0-70 3-y-o and up) £3,236 1½m (9:10)

1143[4] MOONLIGHT QUEST [68] 5-9-12 L Dettori (5) *trkd ldrs, sstnd run frm 2 fs out, led 50 yards out, jst hld on.*
.....................(9 to 1 op 7 to 1 tchd 10 to 1) 1
1248* TIGER SHOOT [52] 6-8-10 W Newnes (3) *led hfwy, hdd one and a half fs out, ralled wl ins last, jst fld.*
.....................(9 to 1 op 6 to 1 tchd 10 to 1) 2
994[2] NORDANSK [45] 4-8-3 W Carson (2) *al in tch, led one and a half fs out, hdd wl ins last, rallied und pres, ran on.*
.....................(5 to 1 op 6 to 1 tchd 13 to 2) 3
674[7] INCOLA [54] 7-8-5 (7*) Antoinette Armes (10) *in rear, styd on ins fnl 2 fs, not rch ldrs.*
.........................(8 to 1 op 7 to 1 tchd 9 to 1) 4
1439[2] SINGING REPLY (USA) [35] 5-7-7 N Carlisle (7) *towards rear, styd on ins fnl 2 fs, nvr nrr.*
.....................(14 to 1 op 12 to 1 tchd 16 to 1) 5
1255* SUMMER PAGEANT [69] 3-8-11 W R Swinburn (1) *trkd ldrs, rdn o'r 2 fs out, wknd entering last.*
.................................(7 to 4 fav tchd 9 to 4) 6
919[5] DISPUTED CALL (USA) [63] 4-9-7 M Hills (13) *towards rear, hdwy 4 fs out, one pace ins fnl 2*...(10 to 1 op 7 to 1) 7
HALLOW FAIR [38] 8-7-10[3] T Williams (8) *slwly away, nvr got into race*..................(33 to 1 tchd 50 to 1) 8
1268 ACROBATE (USA) [62] 4-9-1 (5*) A Procter (6) *in rear till effrt 3 fs out, rdn and wknd o'r one out.*
.................................(10 to 1 tchd 12 to 1) 9
1392[6] CORINTHIAN GOD (Ire) [35] 4-7-7 G Bardwell (11) *al beh.*
.....................(16 to 1 op 20 to 1 tchd 25 to 1) 10
1237[5] RISK PROOF [54] 3-7-10 F Norton (4) *al beh.*
.................................(20 to 1 tchd 25 to 1) 11
1268 BITTER ALOE [60] (bl) 4-9-4 Pat Eddery (12) *led to hfwy, beh fnl 4 fs*......................(14 to 1 op 10 to 1) 12
719 GREY WATCH [52] 3-7-8[1] J Quinn (9) *chsd ldrs till wknd rpdly o'r 3 fs out, tld off*......................(50 to 1) 13
Dist: Nk, hd, 3½l, nk, 3l, 3l, 2l, 2l, 1l, 8l. 2m 36.06s. a 5.06s (13 Ran).
SR: 49/32/24/26/6/18/22/-/13/ (Mrs John Lamb), B Hanbury

TIPPERARY (IRE) (good (races 1,2,3), yielding (4)) Wednesday June 9th

1608 Elm E.B.F. Maiden (2-y-o) £3,797 5f ....(5:30)

1121[5] CATWALKER (Ire) 9-0 M J Kinane (1)..............(6 to 1) 1
WAVE THE WAND (Ire) 9-0 W J O'Connor (3)... (5 to 4 on) 2
1121[3] GALLIC VICTORY (Ire) 9-0 P Shanahan (2)...........(5 to 2) 3
1104[9] EASTROP DANCER (Ire) 9-0 J F Egan (4)..........(16 to 1) 4
1121[6] DASHING DANCER (Ire) 9-0 B Coogan (7)........(10 to 1) 5
1104[6] ZOE BAIRD 8-3 (8*) B Fenton (5)................ (8 to 1) 6
1197 JOIN FORCES (Ire) 9-0 R Hughes (6)............(12 to 1) 7
Dist: 2l, 4½l, 2l, ¾l. 59.70s. (7 Ran).
(R Salter-Townshend), E J O'Grady

1609 Golden Race (3-y-o) £2,762 1m 1f ....(6:00)

960* TAWAR (Ire) 9-7 M J Kinane (6)................(5 to 4 on) 1
848* TEAZEL BOY 9-7 P V Gilson (4)...................(2 to 1) 2
SHAWGATNY (USA) 9-4 C Roche (3)..............(4 to 1) 3
1106 DUNANY ROSE (Ire) 8-11 N G McCullagh (5)..... (33 to 1) 4

788[5] ATLANTIC ADIOS (Ire) 9-7 P Shanahan (2)........(10 to 1) 5
960[8] ARCH-T-GLEN (Ire) 8-6 (8*) D M McCullagh (1)....(33 to 1) 6
Dist: ½l, 7l, 4l, 1½l. 1m 54.30s. (6 Ran).
(H H Aga Khan), John M Oxx

1610 Roscrea Maiden (3-y-o and up) £2,762 7f..........................(6:30)

847[2] SAFAYN (USA) 3-8-11 M J Kinane (12)........(6 to 4 fav) 1
311[6] BRITANNIA BAY (Ire) 3-9-0 P V Gilson (6)........(100 to 30) 2
1443[4] MISS CARMELLA (Ire) 3-8-11 W J Supple (1).....(11 to 2) 3
1441 BRAZEN ANGEL (Ire) 3-8-5 (6*) J J Behan (4).....(20 to 1) 4
1333[3] PERSIAN GEM (Ire) 3-8-11 J D Eddery (9).........(4 to 1) 5
LADY NOBLE (Ire) 3-8-11 J F Egan (11)..........(14 to 1) 6
1106 FAX ME NOW (Ire) 3-8-11 D Manning (10).........(12 to 1) 7
1443 DONTKISSTHEJOCKEY (Ire) 3-8-11 Joanna Morgan (3) ....(20 to 1) 8
847 MYRO BALANNE (Ire) 3-8-11 W J O'Connor (7)...(33 to 1) 9
DOZING WIZZ (Ire) 3-8-11 G Curran (5)..........(20 to 1) 10
297 BRASS BUTTON (Ire) 3-8-11 N G McCullagh (8)...(25 to 1) 11
Dist: 1l, 5½l, 1½l, 4½l. 1m 35.10s. (11 Ran).
(Hamdan Al Maktoum), D K Weld

1611 Tipperary Handicap (0-80 3-y-o and up) £2,762 7f...................(7:00)

996[2] SEEK THE FAITH (USA) [-] (bl) 4-9-7 M J Kinane (8) ....(2 to 1 fav) 1
1333[2] SANS CERIPH (Ire) [-] 3-9-0 W J O'Connor (5)......(5 to 1) 2
1444* MACQUARIE RIDGE (USA) [-] 5-7-13[2] (4ex) W J Supple (9) ....(4 to 1) 3
1046 SAMOT (Ire) [-] (bl) 3-8-9 J F Egan (1)..........(10 to 1) 4
SECOND REVOLUTION (Ire) [-] 4-9-2 (8*) T E Durcan (6) ....(8 to 1) 5
1444[2] IMPRIMATUR [-] 4-8-7 (6*) J J Behan (7)..........(6 to 1) 6
1163 BARNAGEERA BOY (Ire) [-] 4-8-3 N G McCullagh (10) ....(12 to 1) 7
310[7] WALLY WALLENSKY (Ire) [-] 3-8-13 (4*) P Carberry (11) ....(8 to 1) 8
849 HAWAIAN TASCA (Ire) [-] (bl) 4-7-4[5] (8*) R T Fitzpatrick (2) ....(20 to 1) 9
309 PRECISE TIMING [-] 5-10-0 P Shanahan (3).......(20 to 1) 10
EDENS LANDING (Ire) [-] 3-8-3 (6*) P P Murphy (4) (16 to 1) 11
Dist: 1l, ½l, hd, 1l. 1m 36.60s. (11 Ran).
(M G Hynes), D K Weld

YARMOUTH (firm)
Wednesday June 9th

Going Correction: MINUS 0.35 sec. per fur. (races 1,2), MINUS 0.45 (3,4,5,6,7)

1612 Potter Heigham Handicap Class E (0-70 4-y-o and up) £2,924 1¼m 21yds ....(2:15)

1260[6] SOVEREIGN PAGE (USA) [61] 4-10-0 W Ryan (5) *hld up, cld o'r 3 fs out, swtchd rght 2 out, sn led, clr ins last.* ....(5 to 1 op 7 to 2) 1
1453[3] SHORT ENCOUNTER [40] 6-8-7 L Piggott (1) *hld up beh, hdwy o'r one furlong out, ran on*...(10 to 1 op 7 to 1) 2
1346 TALENTED TING (Ire) [58] 4-9-11 N Carlisle (3) *trkd ldrs, ev ch 2 fs out, one pace*.................(8 to 1 op 7 to 1) 3
1421[3] CAL NORMA'S LADY (Ire) [47] 5-8-7 (7*) J Tate (2) *led one furlong, cl up, led ag'n o'r 3 fs out till over 2 out, one pace*..........................(12 to 1 op 7 to 1) 4
1414[2] LOWAWATHA [41] 5-8-8 M Tebbutt (6) *trkd ldrs, led briefly o'r 2 fs out, one pace*.... (7 to 1 op 4 to 1 tchd 8 to 1) 5
1304 AMLAK (USA) [50] 4-9-3 J Quinn (8) *hld up, effrt 3 fs out, one pace*..........................(12 to 1 op 8 to 1) 6
1458 BARBARY REEF (Ire) [39] 5-8-6 G Bardwell (7) *chsd ldrs, pushed alng hfwy, btn 2 fs out.* ....(16 to 1 op 20 to 1 tchd 25 to 1 and 14 to 1) 7
1458* LEXUS (Ire) [47] 5-9-0 R Cochrane (10) *hld up beh, hrd rdn 4 fs out, no response.* ....(5 to 2 fav tchd 11 to 4 and 9 to 4) 8
MISTY GODDESS (Ire) [55] 5-9-3 (5*) K Rutter (9) *hld up beh, cld on ins o'r 2 fs out, wknd one out.* (20 to 1 op 8 to 1) 9
1007[5] BELLATRIX [41] 5-8-8 M Roberts (4) *pushed alng to ld aftr one furlong, hdd o'r 3 out, wknd over one out.* ....(14 to 1 op 10 to 1) 10
Dist: 6l, 1½l, nk, hd, nk, 1l, 2½l, nk, 15l. 2m 6.60s. a 2.60s (10 Ran).
SR: 53/20/35/23/16/24/11/14/21/ (Mrs J M Beeby), B Hanbury

1613 Charter Handicap Class E (0-70 3-y-o) £2,924 1¾m 17yds.............(2:45)

1061* ARCTIC GUEST (Ire) [45] 7-11 T Williams (1) *in cl tch, led on bit o'r 2 fs out, shaken up over one out, rdn out.* ....(11 to 4 jt-fav tchd 3 to 1 and 5 to 2) 1
1099* MOIDART [69] 9-7 G Duffield (6) *cl up, led briefly 3 fs out, kpt on und pres*..............(11 to 4 jt-fav op 9 to 4) 2
1180[9] QAFFAL (USA) [64] 9-2 R Hills (5) *trkd ldrs, rdn and one pace frm o'r 2 fs out*..............(16 to 1 op 10 to 1) 3
514 RUSTY REEL [56] 8-8 M Roberts (4) *led till ran wide on turn and hdd aftr one furlong, trkd ldrs til wknd 2 fs out, one pace fnl two furlongs*.....(16 to 1 op 12 to 1) 4
1417* PUGET DANCER (USA) [56] (v) 8-3 (5*,5ex) M Fenton (7) *in tch, pushed alng 5 fs out, outpcd 3 out, styd on.* ....(4 to 1 op 10 to 3 tchd 9 to 2) 5
UME RIVER (Ire) [60] 8-12 P Robinson (3) *al beh.* ....(11 to 1 op 5 to 1 tchd 12 to 1) 6
1305 MOUJEEB (USA) [67] (v) 9-5 W R Swinburn (2) *led aftr one furlong, rdn and hdd 3 fs out, eased whn btn.* ....(6 to 1 tchd 13 to 2) 7
Dist: 2l, hd, 2½l, 2l, nk, 10l. 3m 5.90s. a 8.90s (7 Ran).
(The Fairyhouse 1992 Partnership), M Johnston

1614 Hopton Conditions Stakes Class D (3-y-o) £4,798 5f 43yds............(3:15)

1113* LUCKY PARKES 9-2 J Carroll (2) *made all, shaken up o'r 2 fs out, hrd rdn over one out, ran on gmely.* ....(11 to 8 on op 11 to 10 on tchd 6 to 4 on) 1
1308* MIDHISH 9-0 W R Swinburn (4) *cl up gng wl, ev ch ins fnl furlong, no extr close hme*..........(11 to 4 op 2 to 1) 2
STEPANOV (USA) 8-10 M Roberts (3) *hld up in last pl, cld o'r 2 fs out, sn pushed alng, one pace.* ....(7 to 2 tchd 4 to 1) 3
1162* SHARP PROSPECT 9-0 Paul Eddery (1) *cl up till wknd o'r 2 fs out*...............(20 to 1 op 14 to 1 tchd 25 to 1) 4
Dist: 1l, ½l, 7l. 1m 0.40s. b 0.30s (4 Ran).
SR: 61/55/49/25/ (Joseph Heler), J Berry

1615 Tolhouse Selling Stakes Class G (2-y-o) £2,196 6f 3yds.............(3:45)

SAWTID 8-6 M Tebbutt (2) *hld up in cl tch, pushed alng hfwy, led o'r one furlong out, ran green, sn pushed clr.* ....(Evens fav op 2 to 1) 1
BADGER'S BEND 8-6 P Robinson (1) *in tch, rdn and hdwy o'r one furlong out, ran on, no ch wth wnr.* ....(9 to 2 op 7 to 2) 2
1355[5] CLASSICAL DON (Ire) 8-11 N Day (4) *led 2 fs, cl up, ev ch two furlongs out, sn outpcd.* ....(16 to 1 op 10 to 1 tchd 20 to 1) 3
RED QUEEN (Ire) 8-6 J Carroll (5) *cl up, led aftr 2 fs till hdd o'r one out, wknd*...(3 to 1 op 5 to 4 tchd 100 to 30) 4
490[6] ROCKABYE BAILEYS 8-6 M Roberts (3) *cl up till wknd o'r one furlong out*........(9 to 2 op 3 to 1 tchd 5 to 1) 5
Dist: 5l, 2l, 1½l, 1l. 1m 14.20s. a 3.20s (5 Ran).
(J B R Leisure Ltd), D Morris

1616 John Holdrich Maiden Fillies Stakes Class D (3-y-o) £3,720 7f 3yds...(4:15)

ETOSHA 8-11 M Hills (10) *beh, hdwy 2 fs out, led o'r one out, ran on wl*..................(10 to 1 op 14 to 1) 1
1212 DESERT VENUS 8-11 W R Swinburn (4) *slwly into strd, hdwy 2 fs out, ran on.* (9 to 1 op 6 to 1 tchd 10 to 1) 2
1171[2] TRAPEZIUM 8-11 M Roberts (6) *cl up, drvn o'r 2 fs out, ev ch over one out, one pace.* ....(5 to 4 on op Evens tchd 6 to 4) 3
1132[4] CHAPKA (Ire) 8-11 L Piggott (2) *hld up beh ldrs, hrd rdn 2 fs out, one pace*..............(4 to 1 op 5 to 2) 4
SIMAAT (USA) 8-11 R Hills (5) *mid-div, pushed alng o'r 2 fs out, styd on ins last*..............(16 to 1 op 8 to 1) 5
FUCHU 8-8 (3*) B Doyle (9) *led till hdd 3 fs out, wknd 2 out*..........................(33 to 1 op 12 to 1) 6
1278[2] PRINCESS HAYLEY 8-11 G Duffield (8) *trkd ldr, led o'r 3 fs out till hdd over one out, wknd*.....(10 to 1 op 6 to 1) 7
WAMDHA (Ire) (bl) 8-11 N Day (7) *cl up, keen hold early, ev ch 2 fs out, wknd*..................(40 to 1 op 14 to 1) 8
SHERGRESS 8-11 P Robinson (3) *al beh.* ....(16 to 1 op 20 to 1 tchd 25 to 1) 9
482 SMOCKING 8-11 Paul Eddery (1) *in tch till wknd quickly wl o'r 2 fs out*..................(40 to 1 op 20 to 1) 10
Dist: 2½l, nk, ¾l, 2l, 1½l, nk, 1½l, 3l, 6l. 1m 25.60s. a 2.40s (10 Ran).
SR: 14/6/5/3/-/-/ (A E Oppenheimer), G Wragg

1617 Blackfriars Maiden Stakes Class D (3-y-o) £4,045 1m 3yds............(4:45)

BLUE LION 9-0 M Hills (9) *missed break, mid-div, smooth hdwy 2 fs out, led o'r one out, rdn and ran on wl.* ....(13 to 8 fav op 11 to 10 tchd 7 to 4) 1
MITRAAS (USA) 9-0 R Hills (14) *trkd ldrs, led o'r 2 fs till hdd over one out, ran on wl*......(16 to 1 op 12 to 1) 2
1039[4] EL GAHAR 9-0 W Ryan (8) *trkd ldrs, rdn and ev ch appr fnl furlong, one pace und pres.* ....(9 to 2 op 5 to 1 tchd 6 to 1) 3
459 MAP OF STARS (USA) 9-0 W R Swinburn (3) *chsd ldrs, not much room wl o'r one furlong out, shaken up and ran on ins last*..........................(7 to 1 op 10 to 1) 4
BALI HERO (Ire) 9-0 Paul Eddery (15) *mid-div, pushed alng and cld 3 fs out, ev ch o'r 2 out, one pace.* ....(33 to 1 op 20 to 1) 5
1039[2] AMAAM AMAAM 9-0 M Roberts (11) *led til hdd wl o'r 2 fs out, wknd*..............(4 to 1 op 5 to 1 tchd 6 to 1) 6
602 DIVINE BOY 9-0 D Biggs (7) *beh, cld 3 fs out, sn no room, swtchd rght and kpt on ins last*..............(33 to 1) 7
1330[5] MUSTAKIM (Ire) 9-0 R Price (10) *trkd ldrs till wknd o'r 2 fs out*..........................(20 to 1 op 14 to 1) 8
951 RUPERT'S REVENGE (Ire) 9-0 W Hood (12) *beh, effrt and squeezed for room 3 fs out, sn btn*............(50 to 1) 9

MOHAYA (USA) 9-0 N Day (4) *outpcd.* (25 to 1 op 16 to 1) 10
HATTA SUNSHINE (USA) 9-0 G Hind (1) *cl up, ev ch 2 fs out, sn wknd*.... (33 to 1 op 20 to 1) 11
BITRAN 9-0 G Duffield (5) *al beh*.... (25 to 1 op 14 to 1) 12
CUT FINE 8-9 P Robinson (2) *trkd ldrs till wknd o'r 2 fs out*.... (16 to 1 op 10 to 1) 13
1435[4] YOSHAARIK (Ire) 9-0 M Tebbutt (6) *outpcd*. .... (33 to 1 op 25 to 1) 14
CHEVALIER VERT 8-11 (3*) B Doyle (13) *wth ldr, ev ch 3 fs out, wknd quickly wl o'r one out.* (33 to 1 op 20 to 1) 15
Dist: Nk, 2½l, 3½l, 2½l, hd, 1½l, 1½l, 4l, 1l, ¾l. 1m 38.70s. a 2.90s (15 Ran).
SR: 3/2/-/-/-/-/ (Sheikh Ahmed Bin Saeed Al Maktoum), G Wragg

1618 Levy Board Apprentice Handicap Class G (0-70 3-y-o and up) £2,259 6f 3yds.... (5:15)

1209[5] YES [51] 5-9-5 S Eiffert (7) *beh, hdwy appr 2 fs out, led wl o'r one out, ran on*.... (3 to 1 op 11 to 4) 1
1358[6] WALK THAT WALK [58] 4-9-12 K Pattinson (6) *beh, pushed alng hfwy, kpt on wl und pres fnl furlong.* .... (11 to 1 op 8 to 1 tchd 12 to 1) 2
1352[4] SPRING HIGH [56] (bl) 6-9-7 (3*) C Scally (5) *trkd ldg pair, pushed alng hfwy, one pace.* .... (100 to 30 op 3 to 1 tchd 7 to 2) 3
1160[2] BREAKFAST BOOGIE [63] 3-9-5 (3*) A Cairns (1) *led til hdd wl o'r one furlong out, no extr.* .... (9 to 4 fav op 11 to 4 tchd 3 to 1) 4
1320 FAMILY ROSE [40] 4-8-8 G Milligan (3) *outpcd.* .... (33 to 1 op 20 to 1) 5
1480[6] MU-ARRIK [49] (bl) 5-9-3 (7ex) P Houghton (2) *wth ldr, ev ch 2 fs out, wknd quickly*.... (5 to 1 tchd 11 to 2) 6
1172 GENERAL JOHN (Ire) [60] 4-9-6 (8*) J Gracey (4) *chsd ldrs till wknd o'r one furlong out.* .... (11 to 1 op 8 to 1 tchd 12 to 1) 7
Dist: ¾l, 2l, 1l, 6l, ½l, nk. 1m 13.40s. a 2.40s (7 Ran).
SR: 3/7/-/-/ (W F Coleman), D T Thom

BALLINROBE (IRE) (heavy)
Thursday June 10th

1619 Mayo Maiden (3-y-o and up) £2,245 6f .... (6:00)

1570[9] FOREST 3-9-0 S Craine (5).... (3 to 1) 1
MARKIEVICZ (Ire) 3-8-11 J F Egan (2).... (5 to 2 fav) 2
1445[5] TORC MOUNTAIN (Ire) 3-9-0 R Hughes (1).... (3 to 1) 3
1164[9] NEWYORK CONNECTION (Ire) 3-8-5 (6*) P P Murphy (9) .... (33 to 1) 4
1515[7] TOUGH AS TEAK (Ire) 3-8-12 (2*) R M Burke (4).... (10 to 1) 5
1386[5] WHY ME LINDA (Ire) (bl) 4-9-0 (6*) C Everard (6).... (8 to 1) 6
1105[9] FAIRY BRIDE (Ire) (bl) 3-8-11 N G McCullagh (7).... (12 to 1) 7
1164[6] MAGIC ROYALE (Ire) (bl) 3-8-5 (6*) J J Behan (8).... (6 to 1) 8
Dist: 2½l, 2l, 4½l, 7l. 1m 24.50s. (8 Ran).
(T Corden), T Stack

1620 Ballinrobe Handicap (0-65 3-y-o and up) £2,245 6f.... (7:00)

1444[4] SHRAGRADDY LASS (Ire) [-] 3-8-12 N G McCullagh (12) .... (3 to 1) 1
1515[3] LADY PRESIDENT (Ire) [-] 4-9-3 (6*) J J Behan (10) .... (9 to 4 fav) 2
1385[2] MUGNANO [-] 7-9-8 (6*) C Everard (11).... (9 to 2) 3
1385[4] BUSINESS CENTRE (Ire) [-] 3-9-2 J F Egan (5).... (7 to 1) 4
280 CAMEY'S CHOICE (Ire) [-] 3-8-11 N Byrne (13).... (12 to 1) 5
1433[7] SORRECA (Ire) [-] 4-8-12 (6*) R V Skelly (4).... (16 to 1) 6
1433[4] PERSIAN LIGHT (Ire) [-] 3-8-6 (10*) A J Dempsey (6) (8 to 1) 7
1105 SHESOMETHINGELSE (Ire) [-] 3-8-9 K J Manning (3) .... (16 to 1) 8
DESIGNED STEP (Ire) [-] (bl) 4-10-0 S Craine (8).... (12 to 1) 9
1433[5] BELLE OF DREAMS (Ire) [-] (bl) 5-8-10 (2*) R M Burke (9) .... (10 to 1) 10
268[5] LOWLACK [-] 3-9-0 (6*) P P Murphy (7).... (10 to 1) 11
Dist: 3½l, 6l, 4l, ¾l. 1m 23.30s. (11 Ran).
(Mrs J M Mullins), W P Mullins

1621 Anglers Handicap (0-60 3-y-o and up) £2,245 1¼m.... (7:30)

1163[5] TWO MAGPIES [-] 6-8-4 J F Egan (7).... (5 to 1) 1
FURTHER NOTICE (Ire) [-] 4-8-1 (2*) R M Burke (2) (16 to 1) 2
1440* TOUCHDOWN [-] 6-9-8 (6*,5ex) P P Murphy (4) (5 to 4 fav) 3
1139[2] DIAMOND CLUSTER [-] 3-7-11 (6*) R V Skelly (6).... (9 to 2) 4
1251 MR GERAN (Ire) [-] 4-9-1 (6*) J J Behan (5).... (16 to 1) 5
1251[8] RIYADH DANCER (Ire) [-] (bl) 3-8-4 (10*) S P Cooke (8) .... (10 to 1) 6
1107[4] PERFECT POET (Ire) [-] 3-9-1 S Craine (1).... (5 to 1) 7
Dist: Nk, 1l, 4l, 3l. 2m 42.20s. (7 Ran).
(E O'Riordan), M J Grassick

1622 Mayfly Maiden (3-y-o and up) £2,245 1 ¼m.... (8:00)

1236[4] GOODIES TWO STEP (Ire) 3-9-0 N G McCullagh (8) (9 to 4) 1
649[2] SCHMEICHEL (Ire) 3-9-0 N Byrne (10).... (7 to 4 fav) 2
898[7] TIGHT FIST (Ire) 3-9-0 K J Manning (2).... (8 to 1) 3
705[8] TAUTEN (Ire) 3-8-11 S Craine (5).... (7 to 1) 4
1252 NORDIC RACE 6-9-7 (6*) C Everard (3).... (16 to 1) 5
1507[4] TRILLICK (Ire) 3-8-11 R Hughes (1).... (6 to 1) 6
1252 OUT OF STEP (Ire) 4-9-4 (6*) J J Behan (9).... (16 to 1) 7
1139 INISHMOT (Ire) 3-8-11 J F Egan (7).... (12 to 1) 8
790 VROOM VROOM (Ire) 3-8-5 (6*) P P Murphy (4).... (14 to 1) su
Dist: 1½l, 7l, 2l, 20l. 2m 37.90s. (9 Ran).
(T Lucas), John Daly

CHEPSTOW (good to firm)
Thursday June 10th

Going Correction: MINUS 0.25 sec. per fur. (race 1), PLUS 0.05 (2,3,4,5,6)

1623 Orsino Amateur Riders Handicap Class G (0-70 3-y-o and up) £2,847 7f 16yds.... (6:00)

1487* PRINCE ROONEY (Ire) [50] 5-10-11 (5ex) Mrs J Crossley (16) *nvr far away stands side, hdwy o'r 2 fs out, ran on to ld fnl 50 yards*.... (11 to 2 fav op 9 to 2) 1
1207[8] BILL MOON [50] 7-10-11 Miss J Feilden (3) *al prmnt on outsd, led o'r 2 fs out, ran on, hdd 50 yards out.* .... (7 to 1 op 6 to 1) 2
914[4] COURTING NEWMARKET [42] 5-10-3 Miss J Southcombe (13) *trkd ldr to hfwy, styd in tch, outpcd fnl furlong.* .... (10 to 1 op 7 to 1) 3
881[3] QUINTA ROYALE [57] 6-10-13 (5*) Mrs J Gault (8) *led till hdd o'r 2 fs out, kpt on one pace aftr.* .... (7 to 1 op 8 to 1 tchd 9 to 1) 4
TEANARCO (Ire) [62] 5-11-9 Mrs P Nash (10) *al prmnt, outpcd ins fnl 2 fs*.... (9 to 1 op 12 to 1 tchd 8 to 1) 5
1316[2] GOTT'S DESIRE [43] (bl) 7-9-13 (5*) Miss S Jakeway (12) *towards rear till styd on ins fnl 2 fs.* .... (8 to 1 tchd 10 to 1) 6
COOCHIE [32] (bl) 4-9-4 (3*) Miss S Farrant (11) *very slwly away, wl in rear till ran on past btn horses fnl 2 fs.* .... (50 to 1 op 33 to 1) 7
1419[3] CASHMIRIANA (Ire) [53] 4-10-11 (3*) Mrs S Bosley (7) *al mid-div*.... (12 to 1 op 10 to 1) 8
1487 OSGATHORPE [35] 6-9-7 (3*) Mrs A Usher (9) *al abt same pl.* .... (25 to 1 op 20 to 1) 9
1207[7] BLOWING (USA) [58] 3-10-9 Miss A Harwood (18) *prmnt till wknd wl o'r one furlong out*.... (8 to 1 op 6 to 1) 10
SPANISH LOVE [43] 7-9-13 (5*) Mrs S Williams (17) *nvr on terms*.... (20 to 1 op 14 to 1) 11
1207 RELENTLESS PURSUIT (Ire) [67] 5-11-9 (5*) Mrs J Chapple-Hyam (2) *in tch till wknd wl o'r one furlong out.* .... (20 to 1 op 14 to 1) 12
1060[5] NO GAIN [60] 3-10-6 (5*) Mrs C Guest (15) *speed on stands side to hfwy*.... (25 to 1 op 16 to 1) 13
327[5] MARSH WARBLER [38] 5-9-8 (5*) Mrs C Dunwoody (6) *al in rear*.... (16 to 1 op 12 to 1) 14
KINTWYN [53] 3-10-4 Miss J Winter (4) *speed to hfwy.* .... (33 to 1 op 25 to 1) 15
GREEN'S STUBBS [32] 6-9-7 Mrs S Hobbs (14) *speed to hfwy*.... (50 to 1 op 33 to 1) 16
1230 PRINCESS JESTINA (Ire) [32] 5-9-2 (5*) Miss A Yardley (1) *prmnt till wknd hfwy*.... (50 to 1 op 33 to 1) 17
1097 CHRISTIAN WARRIOR [44] 4-10-0 (5*) Mrs C Peacock (5) *speed to hfwy*.... (50 to 1 op 33 to 1) 18
Dist: 1½l, 4l, 1½l, 1½l, 1½l, 1½l, nk, ½l, 2l, 1l. 1m 24.10s. a 4.10s (18 Ran).
SR: 37/32/12/22/22/-/-/2/-/ (D J Butler), P Butler

1624 EBF Median Auction Maiden Stakes Class E (2-y-o) £3,325 6f 16yds.. (6:30)

SECOND SIGHT (Ire) 9-0 M Roberts (9) *slwly into strd, sn rdn alng in mid-div, making hdwy whn swtchd lft 2 fs out, led jst ins last, drvn out*.... (5 to 1 op 3 to 1) 1
1403 RAMBOLD 8-9 T Williams (2) *al frnt rnk, led briefly one furlong out, ran on und pres.* .... (25 to 1 op 14 to 1 tchd 33 to 1) 2
MILLICENT NORTH 8-9 J Williams (6) *towards rear till hdwy hfwy, swtchd rght appr fnl furlong, ran on wl ins*.... (12 to 1 op 8 to 1 tchd 14 to 1) 3
1241[4] WICKLOW BOY (Ire) 9-0 J Reid (4) *trkd ldr, led 2 fs out, hdd one out, kpt on one pace.* .... (7 to 1 op 6 to 1 tchd 8 to 1) 4
1265[5] MOCKINGBIRD 8-9 A Munro (5) *chsd ldrs till appr fnl furlong*.... (7 to 2 fav tchd 4 to 1) 5
FAIRFIELD CHOICE 8-9 D Holland (11) *slwly away, hdwy hfwy, nvr nr to chal*.... (25 to 1 op 20 to 1) 6
1254[4] FOREVER BLUSHING 8-2 (7*) S Drowne (13) *prmnt till outpcd fnl 2 fs*.... (33 to 1 op 20 to 1) 7
1119[2] SHERIFF 9-0 M Hills (12) *in tch till wknd 2 fs out.* .... (4 to 1 op 3 to 1) 8
MELODY DANCER 9-0 W Carson (10) *slwly away, nvr on terms*.... (16 to 1 op 14 to 1) 9
1063 RED NECK 9-0 Paul Eddery (14) *speed till wknd 2 fs out.* .... (12 to 1 op 14 to 1 tchd 10 to 1) 10
913 CLANCY'S EXPRESS 9-0 R Price (7) *led till hdd 2 fs out, wknd quickly*.... (33 to 1 op 25 to 1) 11

SPEEDY SNAPS IMAGE 9-0 M Perrett (1) *slwly away, al beh*......................................(33 to 1) 12
BLAZING HEART 9-0 L Dettori (3) *slwly away, al beh*. ....(5 to 1 op 3 to 1) 13
Dist: 1½l, ¾l, hd, 5l, 1l, sht-hd, 2½l, 1½l, 4l, sht-hd. 1m 12.90s. a 3.40s (13 Ran).
SR: 38/27/24/28/3/-/ (Neil Greig), Sir Mark Prescott

1625 Tarmac Construction Fillies Maiden Stakes Class D (3-y-o) £3,348 1½m 23yds........................ (7:00)

662[9] HAUNTED WOOD (USA) 8-11 M Roberts (6) *made all, rdn and quickened wl appr fnl furlong, pushed out*. ....(7 to 2 op 9 to 4) 1
1315[2] CUTLASS (Ire) 8-11 J Reid (10) *trkd ldrs, hdwy to go second o'r 2 fs out, sn chlgd wnr, outpcd appr last*. ....(4 to 1 op 3 to 1) 2
1315[3] NAWAHIL 8-11 W Carson (2) *hld up in tch, rdn and hdwy o'r 2 fs out, kpt on one pace*. .... (2 to 1 fav op 9 to 4 tchd 11 to 4 and 7 to 4) 3
THREEMILESTONE (USA) 8-8 (3*) J Weaver (8) *wl in rear, hdwy 3 fs out, ran green, kpt on ins last*. ....(14 to 1 op 8 to 1 tchd 16 to 1) 4
1383[3] FOINERY 8-11 J Quinn (4) *trkd wnr early, styd in tch, rdn o'r 4 fs out, plugged on one pace ins fnl 3 furlongs*. ....(7 to 1 op 12 to 1) 5
1176[5] ELA BILLANTE 8-11 P Robinson (7) *hld up in tch, no hdwy fnl 3 fs*..........................(25 to 1 op 16 to 1) 6
SHE KNEW THE RULES (Ire) 8-11 C Rutter (5) *al in rear*. ....(25 to 1 op 14 to 1) 7
1297[2] ARAADH (USA) 8-11 N Carlisle (3) *in tch till wknd o'r 2 fs out*..........................(11 to 1 op 8 to 1 tchd 12 to 1) 8
1077[8] FAIR TO THE WIND (USA) 8-11 Paul Eddery (9) *trkd wnr aftr 2 fs till wknd quickly 3 out*....(14 to 1 op 10 to 1) 9
MY SET PEACE 8-11 M Perrett (1) *slwly away, wl beh frm hfwy, tld off*......................(66 to 1 op 50 to 1) 10
Dist: 2l, nk, sht-hd, 2½l, 1½l, 10l, 2½l, 10l, 12l. 2m 38.10s. a 6.60s (10 Ran).
SR: 37/33/32/31/26/23/3/-/-/ (Sheikh Mohammed), H R A Cecil

1626 Worthington Best Bitter Handicap Class E (0-70 3-y-o and up) £3,349 1¼m 36yds.................... (7:30)

1307* TENDRESSE (Ire) [51] 5-8-10 M Roberts (14) *hld up, steady hdwy 3 fs out, rdn to ld nr finish*. ....(7 to 1 op 5 to 1 tchd 15 to 2) 1
1414[3] SCOTTISH BAMBI [65] 5-9-10 R Perham (9) *nvr far away, led o'r one furlong out, rdn and hdd nr finish*. ....(6 to 1 tchd 7 to 1) 2
1238[2] HERE HE COMES [53] 7-8-12 A Munro (12) *hld up in tch, dsptd ld o'r 2 fs out, no extr wl ins fnl furlong*. ....(11 to 4 fav op 4 to 1 tchd 5 to 2) 3
1309 WAR REQUIEM (Ire) [48] 3-7-8 N Adams (13) *hld up, hdwy 4 fs out, led o'r 2 out, hdd appr last, kpt on one pace*. ....(40 to 1 op 25 to 1) 4
1120 CELIA BRADY [50] 5-8-9 C Rutter (7) *hld up in rear, hdwy 4 fs out, ran on ins fnl 2 furlongs*. (14 to 1 op 12 to 1) 5
1281[9] SINCLAIR LAD (Ire) [45] 5-7-13[2] (7*) S Drowne (8) *hld up, gd hdwy 3 fs out, rdn and ev ch 2 out, one pace ins last*. ....(9 to 1 op 8 to 1 tchd 10 to 1) 6
1316[6] LADY LACEY [47] (v) 6-8-6 R Price (10) *hld up, hdwy o'r 3 fs out, styd on, nvr nrr*.............(10 to 1 op 8 to 1) 7
1130 LER CRU (Ire) [57] 4-9-2 T Williams (6) *hmpd sn aftr strt, nvr rch ldrs*..........................(40 to 1 op 20 to 1) 8
1309[4] HOMEMAKER [60] 3-8-6 J Williams (4) *mid-div, no hdwy fnl 3 fs*..........................(13 to 2 op 5 to 1) 9
1064 TIME FOR A FLUTTER [64] (bl) 4-9-9 W Newnes (2) *trkd ldr till wknd o'r 2 fs out*...........(25 to 1 op 20 to 1) 10
SMART TEACHER (USA) [48] 3-7-8[1] J Quinn (11) *pld hrd, led till hdd o'r 2 fs out, sn btn*..... (33 to 1 op 25 to 1) 11
1146 CLEAR LIGHT [48] 6-8-7 M Wigham (15) *al beh*. ....(50 to 1 op 33 to 1) 12
50[8] BEIJA FLOR [34] 6-7-0 (7*) D Wright (3) *chsd ldrs till wknd o'r 2 fs out*..........................(50 to 1 op 33 to 1) 13
1005[9] NORTHERN TRIAL (USA) [47] 5-8-6 D Holland (1) *beh till hdwy 4 fs out, wknd wl o'r one out, eased*. ....(12 to 1 op 8 to 1 tchd 14 to 1) 14
1307 GALLANT JACK (Ire) [40] 4-7-13 A Tucker (5) *chsd ldrs, rdn o'r 3 fs out, sn btn*....(14 to 1 op 20 to 1 tchd 25 to 1) 15
Dist: Hd, 1½l, 1l, nk, ½l, ½l, 5l, 1½l, nk, 4l. 2m 10.40s. a 6.80s (15 Ran).
SR: 33/46/31/11/25/19/20/20/7/ (C John Hill), C J Hill

1627 Evening Selling Handicap Class G (0-60 3-y-o) £2,679 1m 14yds.... (8:00)

1133[4] WHO'S THE BEST (Ire) [42] 8-10 S Whitworth (6) *al prmnt, led jst ins fnl furlong, stretched out wl*. ....(4 to 1 op 9 to 2 tchd 5 to 1) 1
1247[8] DESIRABLE MISS [43] (v) 8-11 M Wigham (1) *rcd alone far side, led till hdd jst ins last, one pace*. ....(10 to 1 tchd 12 to 1) 2
813 B B GLEN [47] 8-10 (5*) C Hodgson (9) *chsd ldrs, rdn and outpcd sn aftr hfwy, kpt on ag'n ins fnl furlong*. ....(9 to 1 op 6 to 1) 3
711[8] MALZETA (Ire) [45] 8-6 (7*) D Wright (12) *beh till hdwy o'r 2 fs out, hng lft one out, ran on cl hme*. ....(14 to 1 op 10 to 1) 4
1414 JUNCTION TWENTYTWO [50] 9-4 J Williams (10) *slwly into strd, hld up, ran on ins fnl 2 fs, nvr nrr*. ....(25 to 1 op 16 to 1) 5
1262[3] NIGHTMARE LADY [35] 7-10 (7*) C Hawksley (15) *mid-div till hdwy hfwy, rdn 2 fs out, kpt on one pace*. ....(20 to 1 op 16 to 1) 6
1266[8] EARLY TO RISE [47] 9-1 M Roberts (14) *chsd ldrs, rdn o'r 2 fs out, one pace aftr*. (7 to 2 fav op 7 to 1 tchd 8 to 1) 7
1319[5] FLYING AMY [40] 8-8 T Sprake (2) *in frnt rnk, rdn 2 fs out, no extr and wknd ins last*......... (16 to 1 op 14 to 1) 8
1306[8] SOOJAMA (Ire) [44] 8-12 S Dawson (7) *nvr on terms*. ....(9 to 1 op 5 to 1 tchd 10 to 1) 9
878 AMBIVALENTATTITUDE [32] 8-0 N Adams (8) *nvr on terms*. ....(50 to 1 op 33 to 1) 10
1233[5] AIR COMMAND (Bar) [53] 9-7 L Dettori (4) *rcd in mid-div, lost tch fnl 2 fs*.......(11 to 1 op 10 to 1 tchd 14 to 1) 11
1315 JAFETICA [50] 9-4 W Newnes (5) *chsd ldrs till wknd o'r 2 fs out*..........................(20 to 1 op 14 to 1) 12
1419 WHYALLA RAIN [40] 8-8 J Reid (13) *in tch to hfwy*. ....(20 to 1 tchd 16 to 1) 13
1266 OLIVIA VAL [40] 8-8 T Williams (3) *al beh*. ....(10 to 1 op 7 to 1) 14
ANNIE ROSE [40] 8-8 C Rutter (11) *al beh*. ....(40 to 1 op 33 to 1) 15
1313[4] BEYOND THE LIMIT [50] 9-4 W Carson (16) *speed to hfwy, sn in rear*..............(11 to 2 op 6 to 1 tchd 7 to 2) 16
Dist: 3l, ½l, sht-hd, 1½l, 1l, 1½l, 1½l, 3l, 4l, nk. 1m 37.20s. a 4.80s (16 Ran).
SR: 30/22/24/21/21/3/10/-/-/ (Mrs Ann Jarvis), A P Jarvis

1628 Good Night Claiming Stakes Class F (3-y-o) £2,728 7f 16yds..........(8:30)

1416[2] SILENT EXPRESSION 8-3 (5*) C Hodgson (6) *trkd ldrs, al gng wl, led 2 fs out, sn clr, very easily*. ....(21 to 20 fav op 6 to 4 tchd 7 to 4 and Evens) 1
1388[8] NIGELS PROSPECT 8-5 J Williams (8) *towards rear till hdwy 2 fs out, ran on to go second ins last*. ....(20 to 1 tchd 25 to 1) 2
1186* CALISAR 8-11 T Sprake (10) *trkd ldr, led briefly o'r 2 fs out, sn outpcd*.................... (5 to 1 op 4 to 1) 3
1312[7] LOVE IN THE MIST (USA) (bl) 8-12 L Dettori (7) *led till hdd o'r 2 fs out, one pace aftr*. ....(4 to 1 tchd 9 to 2 and 7 to 2) 4
1313[3] SHEFFORD 8-4 M Roberts (3) *slwly into strd, sn pushed alng, rdn and hdwy o'r 2 fs out, kpt on one pace*. ....(5 to 1 op 4 to 1) 5
MOUNTAIN REACH 8-7 C Avery (5) *al towards rear*. ....(33 to 1 op 25 to 1) 6
BOY SOLDIER 8-8 (5*) N Gwilliams (2) *slwly away, sn trkd ldrs, rdn o'r 2 fs out, soon btn*..... (40 to 1 op 25 to 1) 7
RISKY TUESDAY 8-4 R Price (1) *slwly away, lost tch hfwy, tld off*......................(50 to 1 op 33 to 1) 8
1092 WHATONE BELL (bl) 8-2 (7*) Mark Denaro (4) *beh frm strt, tld off*..........................(40 to 1 op 33 to 1) 9
1057[8] NANQUIDNO 8-0 J Quinn (9) *chsd ldrs till wknd sn aftr hfwy, tld off*......................(40 to 1 op 25 to 1) 10
Dist: 8l, nk, ¾l, nk, 4l, sht-hd, 15l, nk, 1½l. 1m 23.80s. a 3.80s (10 Ran).
SR: 42/15/20/19/10/1/6/-/-/ (Mrs Rosalie Hawes), D Morris

HAMILTON (soft)
Thursday June 10th
Going Correction: PLUS 0.15 sec. per fur. (races 1,2,6), NIL (3,4,5)

1629 High Park Median Auction Maiden Stakes Class E (3-y-o) £2,769 1m 3f 16yds........................ (2:15)

1349[4] RUNAWAY PETE (USA) 9-0 K Darley (3) *made all, styd on wl frm 2 out*.................... (5 to 4 fav op 6 to 4) 1
880[5] CANOPUS 9-0 M Tebbutt (5) *trkd ldrs, effrt whn sligjhtly hmpd 2 out, styd on fnl furlong*. ....(6 to 4 op 5 to 4 tchd 7 to 4) 2
759[8] CHIPPENDALE LADD (Can) 8-9 (5*) Stephen Davies (1) *in tch, rdn o'r 3 out, kpt on same pace*. (9 to 2 op 7 to 2) 3
QUARRELLING 9-0 S Perks (2) *cl up, jnd wnr gng wl 4 out, edgd rght2 out, sn wknd*. ....(16 to 1 op 12 to 1 tchd 20 to 1) 4
DUSKY DUCHESS (Ire) 8-9 G Duffield (4) *sn lost tch, wl tld off*..........................(66 to 1 op 33 to 1) 5
Dist: 3½l, 3½l, 2½l, dist. 2m 29.00s. a 9.00s (5 Ran).
SR: 27/20/13/8/-/ (Thomas T S Liang), P F I Cole

1630 Howlet Row Handicap Class E (0-70 3-y-o) £3,080 1m 3f 16yds....... (2:45)

1534[2] HAZARD A GUESS (Ire) [56] 8-10 K Fallon (4) *hld up, hdwy 4 out, styd on und pres to ld wl ins fnl furlong*. ....(7 to 4 fav op 5 to 4 tchd 15 to 8) 1
1534[3] CONTRACT ELITE (Ire) [55] 8-9 A Mackay (1) *mid-div, steady hdwy to ld o'r 2 out, hdd and no extr wl ins last*. ....(12 to 1 op 10 to 1) 2

1299[6] ARGYLE CAVALIER (Ire) [67] 9-7 J Carroll (9) *in tch, effrt 3 out, styd on fnl furlong*..........(14 to 1 op 12 to 1) 3

1600[2] CHALLENGER ROW (Ire) [46] 8-0 G Duffield (8) *led aftr one furlong till hdd 8 out, cl up, led o'r 3 out, headed over 2 out, one paced*..................(6 to 1 op 5 to 1) 4

1100[3] MILNGAVIE (Ire) [45] 7-13 J Fanning (5) *chsd ldrs, one paced frm 2 out*......(14 to 1 op 12 to 1 tchd 16 to 1) 5

1179[2] VELVET HEART (Ire) [54] 8-8 E Johnson (7) *led one furlong, prmnt till wknd o'r 2 out.* ....(12 to 1 op 8 to 1 tchd 14 to 1) 6

1099[6] SEVERE STORM [47] 8-1 K Darley (2) *beh most of way, tld off*..................(66 to 1 op 33 to 1 tchd 100 to 1) 7

1170[2] CORNFLAKE [48] 8-2 J Lowe (6) *cl up, led 8 out till hdd wl o'r 3 out, sn wknd, tld off.* ....(7 to 2 op 3 to 1 tchd 4 to 1) 8

1223[4] SUNRISE MORNING (USA) [61] 8-10 (5*) Stephen Davies (3) *al beh, tld off*.......(14 to 1 op 12 to 1 tchd 16 to 1) 9

Dist: 1½l, 1½l, 1½l, 2l, 8l, 15l, 2l, 2½l. 2m 27.50s. a 7.50s (9 Ran).
SR: 38/34/43/19/14/7/ (Mrs D Ridley), Mrs J R Ramsden

1631 Stonefield Selling Handicap Class G (0-60 3-y-o and up) £2,322 5f 4yds ....(3:15)

1397 MISS SIHAM (Ire) [37] 4-8-9 G Hind (1) *rcd alng stands side, nvr far away, led one out, sn clr, cmftbly.* ....(8 to 1 op 6 to 1) 1

1183[3] LANGTONIAN [53] (bl) 4-9-8 (3*) Emma O'Gorman (3) *beh, hdwy hfwy, ev ch entering fnl furlong, kpt on.* ....(9 to 2 fav tchd 5 to 1) 2

1494[8] CHOICE LOT [37] (bl) 6-8-9[1] S Webster (4) *beh, styd on fnl 2 fs, nrst finish*......................(5 to 1 op 9 to 2) 3

1563[9] CRAIL HARBOUR [33] (bl) 7-8-5 Dale Gibson (5) *led till hdd and wknd one out*.....(5 to 1 op 9 to 2 tchd 11 to 2) 4

1327[6] DAYJUZ (Ire) [54] 3-9-4 S Perks (7) *prmnt till wknd entering fnl furlong*.....................(5 to 1 op 9 to 2) 5

1187[5] JOTRA [46] 3-8-10 A Culhane (6) *chsd ldrs, rdn 2 out, no hdwy*......(5 to 1 op 9 to 2 tchd 4 to 1 and 11 to 2) 6

1397[7] ROSE GEM (Ire) [56] 4-10-0 K Fallon (8) *chsd ldr till wknd 2 out*............................(20 to 1 op 16 to 1) 7

1599[8] CREAGMHOR [52] 3-9-2 J Lowe (2) *chsd ldrs till wknd 2 out*.....................(5 to 1 op 4 to 1 tchd 11 to 2) 8

Dist: 2½l, hd, 1½l, 3l, ½l, hd, hd. 1m 2.00s. a 3.70s (8 Ran).
SR: 21/27/10/-/1/-/8/-/ (Ardsley Racing), J Balding

1632 EBF Almada Maiden Stakes Class D (2-y-o) £3,289 5f 4yds...........(3:45)

730[3] ROYAL INSIGNIA 9-0 G Duffield (7) *made all, rdn o'r one out, ran on wl*................(5 to 4 fav tchd 6 to 4) 1

364[6] TEETOTALLER (Ire) 9-0 J Carroll (6) *chsd ldrs, kpt on wl fnl furlong*..........................(33 to 1 op 14 to 1) 2

1082 GREY TOPPA 8-9 K Fallon (3) *in tch, styd on und pres fnl 2 fs*.................................(50 to 1 op 33 to 1) 3

1403[7] SHALBOURNE (USA) 8-4 (5*) Stephen Davies (2) *cl up, rdn o'r one out, wknd fnl furlong.* ....(15 to 8 op 5 to 4 tchd 2 to 1) 4

1529[3] NO MEAN CITY (Ire) 9-0 A Mackay (4) *chsd ldrs till rdn and wknd 2 out*.......................(5 to 2 tchd 3 to 1) 5

SATLEY LASS 8-9 Dale Gibson (1) *in tch till wknd quickly 2 out, tld off*...................(50 to 1 op 33 to 1) 6

Dist: 2½l, 1½l, ¾l, 2½l, 15l. 1m 2.30s. a 4.00s (6 Ran).
SR: 20/10/-/ (Fahd Salman), M Bell

1633 P & O Containers Scotland Handicap Class D (0-80 3-y-o) £3,752 6f 5yds ....(4:15)

1326[4] RAIN SPLASH [68] 8-4 (7*) Claire Balding (5) *slightly hmpd strt, beh, hdwy hfwy, swtchd ins 2 out, led one out, all out*..................(10 to 1 op 8 to 1 tchd 12 to 1) 1

1231 CHILLY BREEZE [65] 8-8 G Duffield (8) *slightly hmpd strt, trkd ldrs, chlgd entering fnl furlong, swshd tail, kpt on towards finish*.................(3 to 1 tchd 100 to 30) 2

1196* CHERHILL (Ire) [66] 8-4 (5*) Stephen Davies (10) *cl up, led 2 out, hdd one out, one paced.* ....(4 to 1 op 3 to 1 tchd 9 to 2) 3

1397* BIRCHWOOD SUN [74] (bl) 9-3 (4ex) J Lowe (6) *slightly hmpd strt, beh till styd on und pres fnl 2 fs, nrst finish.* ....(12 to 1 op 8 to 1) 4

1341[3] TWO MOVES IN FRONT (Ire) [78] 9-7 J Carroll (2) *slight ld till hdd 2 out, wknd entering fnl furlong.* ......(85 to 40 fav op 9 to 4 tchd 11 to 4 and 2 to 1) 5

1503[3] STARDUST EXPRESS [63] 8-6 Dean McKeown (3) *wnt rght strt, trkd ldrs till wknd 2 out.* ....(14 to 1 op 10 to 1 tchd 16 to 1) 6

1326[3] ALASIB [75] 9-4 M Tebbutt (1) *cl up till wknd quickly 2 out*......................(7 to 1 op 6 to 1 tchd 8 to 1) 7

Dist: Hd, 2l, 1l, hd, 8l, 10l. 1m 15.00s. a 4.30s (7 Ran).
SR: 11/7/-/4/7/-/-/ (M Hill), J Balding

1634 Clyde Handicap Class E (0-70 3-y-o and up) £3,261 1m 65yds....... (4:45)

1496* VELASCO (Ire) [63] 3-8-10 (5ex) G Duffield (6) *prmnt, effrt 3 out, led wl o'r one out, styd on well.* ....(7 to 4 on tchd 6 to 4 on) 1

1498[4] GOLD SURPRISE (Ire) [52] 4-8-10 J Fortune (11) *led till hdd wl o'r one out, kpt on und pres.* ....(8 to 1 op 5 to 1 tchd 10 to 1) 2

425[7] IMPERIAL BID (Fr) [69] 5-9-13 K Fallon (4) *beh, gd hdwy o'r one out, no extr ins fnl furlong*.....(12 to 1 op 8 to 1) 3

1261* AEGAEN LADY [59] 4-9-3 J Carroll (3) *in tch, effrt 3 out, kpt on same pace*.................(5 to 1 tchd 6 to 1) 4

1421[8] THE PREMIER EXPRES [63] 3-8-5 (5*) Darren Moffatt (2) *sn cl up, ev ch o'r 2 out, one paced*........(8 to 1 op 6 to 1) 5

885 BOLD MELODY [51] 4-8-9 Dean McKeown (5) *in tch till wknd o'r 2 out*......(16 to 1 op 14 to 1 tchd 20 to 1) 6

1460 SUNTAN (Fr) [70] 4-10-0 A Culhane (1) *al beh.* ....(66 to 1 op 50 to 1) 7

1286 HAND ON HEART (Ire) [54] 4-8-9 (3*) S D Williams (8) *trkd ldrs, effrt 3 out, wknd 2 out*......(25 to 1 op 20 to 1) 8

Dist: 2½l, ½l, 2½l, 1½l, 3l, 2½l, 3½l. 1m 55.10s. a 11.10s (8 Ran).
(G E Shouler), Sir Mark Prescott

NEWBURY (good to firm)
Thursday June 10th
Going Correction: MINUS 0.35 sec. per fur. (races 1,2,5,6,7), MINUS 0.20 (3,4)

1635 Cork Gully Apprentice Median Auction Maiden Stakes Class E (3-y-o) £3,172 7f..................... (2:00)

1192 TIME AGAIN 9-0 J Weaver (4) *cl up, led one and a half fs out, pushed out.* ....(Evens fav op 5 to 4 on tchd 11 to 10) 1

1388[4] PERDITION (Ire) 8-9 D Harrison (5) *chsd ldrs, cld 2 fs out, hrd rdn appr last, kpt on.* ....(11 to 2 op 4 to 1 tchd 6 to 1) 2

SWEET DISORDER (Ire) 8-9 B Doyle (2) *chsd ldrs, pushed alng 3 fs out, hrd rdn one out, one pace.* ....(16 to 1 op 12 to 1 tchd 20 to 1) 3

1344 NOBLE RISK 8-9 (5*) A Whelan (9) *wtd wth in rear, effrt o'r 2 fs out, kpt on wl fnl furlong.* ....(12 to 1 op 10 to 1 tchd 14 to 1) 4

1540[5] SUPERENSIS (bl) 8-9 (5*) Kim McDonnell (1) *led, sn clr, tired and hdd one and a half fs out, wknd quickly.* ....(40 to 1 op 25 to 1) 5

1192[2] HATTON'S GEM 8-4 (5*) N Varley (3) *trkd ldrs, pushed alng hfwy, ev ch 2 fs out, wknd quickly one out.* ....(100 to 30 op 5 to 2 tchd 7 to 2) 6

SALLY OF THE ALLEY 8-4 (5*) B Russell (7) *al beh.* ....(33 to 1 op 20 to 1) 7

SELECTABLE 8-4 (5*) D Wright (8) *cl up, drvn appr 2 fs out, wknd*...............(50 to 1 op 33 to 1 tchd 66 to 1) 8

NATASHA NORTH 8-9 F Norton (6) *stumbled sn aftr strt, al tld off*...................(33 to 1 op 25 to 1) 9

Dist: 1l, 1½l, nk, 5l, 2l, 2½l, 4l, dist. 1m 25.95s. a 1.85s (9 Ran).
SR: 36/28/23/27/12/1/ (R J Shannon), L M Cumani

1636 George Smith Memorial Rated Class B Handicap (0-100 3-y-o and up) £6,477 7f..................... (2:30)

CROFT VALLEY [90] 6-8-11 T Quinn (3) *made all, sn clr, pushed alng appr fnl furlong, unchlgd.* ....(7 to 2 fav op 3 to 1) 1

1402* BRIGADE [93] 4-9-0 (3ex) L Dettori (5) *chsd wnr, pushed alng 3 fs out, hrd rdn o'r one out, kpt on.* ....(9 to 1 op 7 to 1 tchd 10 to 1) 2

481[6] ROCKY WATERS (USA) [94] 4-9-1 B Rouse (11) *hld up beh, cld hfwy, kpt on ins fnl furlong, nrst finish.* ....(14 to 1 op 12 to 1 tchd 16 to 1) 3

1204 NORFOLK HERO [87] 3-7-12 C Rutter (2) *in tch, hdwy 2 fs out, hrd rdn o'r one out, styd on*....(8 to 1 tchd 9 to 1) 4

737 NOBLE PET [89] 4-8-10 A Munro (9) *beh, rdn and hdwy o'r one furlong out, styd on, nvr nrr*.... (8 to 1 op 7 to 1) 5

474[5] LAW COMMISSION [99] 3-8-10 J Williams (1) *prmnt in chasing grp, rdn and one pace appr last*............. 6

1079* TAUFAN BLU (Ire) [100] (bl) 4-9-2 (5*) O Pears (6) *prmnt in chasing grp, pushed alng o'r 2 fs out, wknd.* ....(8 to 1 op 7 to 1) 7

PRENONAMOSS [86] 5-8-7 W Carson (7) *al beh.* ....(12 to 1 op 14 to 1 tchd 16 to 1) 8

1002[9] BEWARE OF AGENTS [91] 4-8-12 M Roberts (10) *beh, sn pushed alng, nvr on terms*........(7 to 1 tchd 8 to 1) 9

1298* AMAZE [91] 4-8-12 Paul Eddery (12) *al beh.* ....(8 to 1 op 7 to 1 tchd 9 to 1) 10

Dist: 1l, nk, hd, 2l, 1l, 3½l, 5l, 3½l, hd. 1m 23.91s. b 0.19s (10 Ran).
SR: 63/63/63/45/51/48/48/19/13/ (Miss Vivian Pratt), R Akehurst

1637 Coopers & Lybrand Summer Handicap Class C (0-100 3-y-o) £7,050 1½m 5yds......................... (3:00)

1068* DARECLIFF (USA) [87] 9-7 J Reid (2) *hld up in tch, cld on bit 2 fs out, led one and half out, shaken up, ran on wl.* ....(11 to 4 fav op 5 to 2) 1

1115[4] SOUL EMPEROR [80] 9-0 A Munro (3) *led to one and a half fs out, rallied und pres*........... (7 to 1 tchd 15 to 2) 2

989[5] THE SEER [81] 9-1 D Holland (1) *trkd ldg pair, ev ch whn not clr run on ins o'r one furlong out, sn outpcd, eased.* ....(4 to 1 op 3 to 1) 3
1204[4] MIDYAN BLUE (Ire) [70] 8-1 (3*) N Kennedy (5) *cl tch, hrd rdn 4 fs out, sn btn*...... (7 to 2 op 9 to 2 tchd 5 to 1) 4
1315* DREAMS ARE FREE (Ire) [80] 9-0 Pat Eddery (4) *trkd ldr, pushed alng entering strt, hrd rdn and ev ch 2 fs out, sn btn*...................... (3 to 1 op 2 to 1 tchd 7 to 2) 5
Dist: 1½l, 8l, ¾l, 1l. 2m 32.11s. a 2.51s (5 Ran).
SR: 58/48/33/20/28/ (A D Latter), R Hannon

1638 Ballymacoll Stud Stakes Class A (Listed Race) (3-y-o) £11,160 1¼m 6yds ....(3:30)

1297* RAINBOW LAKE 8-9 Pat Eddery (1) *made all, hrd rdn appr fnl furlong, sn quickened, hld on wl.* ....(11 to 8 fav op 5 to 4 tchd 13 to 8) 1
1311* MASHAIR (USA) 8-9 W Carson (7) *cl up, trkd wnr into strt, ev ch appr fnl furlong, hrd rdn, not quicken.* ....(7 to 2 op 3 to 1 tchd 4 to 1) 2
717* DANA SPRINGS (Ire) 8-9 L Dettori (6) *trkd ldrs, pushed alng and ev ch 2 fs out, one pace.* ....(20 to 1 op 14 to 1 tchd 25 to 1) 3
1128[3] SEASONAL SPLENDOUR (Ire) 8-9 M Roberts (5) *beh, pld out o'r 3 fs out, styd on frm over one out.* ....(10 to 1 op 12 to 1 tchd 14 to 1) 4
1344* JETBEEAH (Ire) 8-9 W R Swinburn (9) *beh, pushed alng o'r 4 fs out, hdwy over one out, nrst finish.* ....(5 to 1 op 6 to 1 tchd 8 to 1) 5
1030[5] LACERTA (Ire) 8-9 J Reid (3) *cl up, rdn 3 fs out, btn 2 out.* ....(25 to 1 op 14 to 1 tchd 33 to 1) 6
1404[4] NO RESERVATIONS (Ire) 8-9 R Cochrane (2) *in tch, rdn o'r 2 fs out, wknd*......... (25 to 1 op 16 to 1 tchd 33 to 1) 7
ARUSHA (Ire) 8-9 J Williams (8) *al beh.* ....(20 to 1 op 14 to 1) 8
1030[4] BRIGHT SPELLS 8-9 T Quinn (4) *mid-div, cld and ev ch 3 fs out, wknd und pres 2 out.* ....(8 to 1 op 7 to 1 tchd 9 to 1) 9
Dist: 1l, 5l, 2l, sht-hd, 5l, 2l, 3½l, hd. 2m 4.94s. a 1.94s (9 Ran).
SR: 56/54/44/40/39/29/25/18/17/ (K Abdulla), H R A Cecil

1639 Sikkens Masterstroke Conditions Stakes Class C (2-y-o) £5,708 6f 8yds ....(4:00)

718* LEMON SOUFFLE 8-7 L Piggott (2) *cl up, squeezed through on ins to ld 2 and a half fs out, sn clr, easily.* .... (5 to 4 fav op 11 to 10 on) 1
1063* PRINCE BABAR 8-12 N Day (1) *cl tch, hrd rdn 2 fs out, one pace*..................(3 to 1 op 5 to 2 tchd 100 to 30) 2
922* ROBELLION 8-10 T Quinn (3) *hng lft thrght, led to 2 and a half fs out, wknd*..................(7 to 4 tchd 2 to 1) 3
Dist: 6l, 7l. 1m 12.28s. a 0.58s (3 Ran).
SR: 39/20/-/ (Lord Carnarvon), R Hannon

1640 EBF Kennett Maiden Stakes Class D (2-y-o) £4,077 6f 8yds...........(4:30)

REPREHEND 9-0 R Cochrane (12) *dwlt, beh, pushed alng o'r 2 fs out, sstnd run to ld wl ins last, ran on well.* ....(14 to 1 op 12 to 1 tchd 16 to 1) 1
BLUEGRASS PRINCE (Ire) 9-0 Pat Eddery (5) *cl up, led o'r one furlong out till wl ins last, ran on.* ....(6 to 1 op 4 to 1 tchd 13 to 2) 2
793[6] BALLAH SHACK (USA) 9-0 Paul Eddery (16) *trkd ldrs, ev ch o'r one furlong out, ran on.* ....(14 to 1 op 12 to 1 tchd 16 to 1) 3
EIGHTEEN TWELVE 9-0 J Reid (6) *trkd ldrs, cld and ev ch one furlong out, not quicken.* ....(11 to 2 op 6 to 1 tchd 7 to 1 and 9 to 2) 4
DUELLO 9-0 J Quinn (15) *strted slwly, beh, pushed alng 2 fs out, hdwy ins last, ran on, prmsg.* ....(33 to 1 op 20 to 1) 5
SOUTHERN RIDGE 9-0 J Williams (2) *strted slwly, beh, shaken up and hdwy o'r one furlong out, nrst finish, better for race*...... (14 to 1 op 12 to 1 tchd 16 to 1) 6
1265 CHEF D'ETAT (USA) 9-0 M Roberts (8) *keen hold, in tch, shaken up hfwy, sn one pace*...... (6 to 1 tchd 7 to 1) 7
1119 FIRST SHOT 9-0 M Perrett (10) *prmnt, ev ch o'r 2 fs out, wknd*...............(25 to 1 op 20 to 1 tchd 33 to 1) 8
BLAIR CASTLE (Ire) 9-0 L Dettori (7) *trkd ldrs, pushed alng 2 fs out, sn wknd.* (100 to 30 fav op 3 to 1 tchd 7 to 2) 9
WILDFIRE (Swi) 9-0 T Quinn (4) *cl up, reminders 2 fs out, wknd o'r one out*....... (6 to 1 op 5 to 1 tchd 7 to 1) 10
IMPERIAL TREATMENT 9-0 W Newnes (3) *led aftr one furlong till hdd and wknd o'r one out.* ....(20 to 1 op 14 to 1) 11
TANBIH 9-0 W Carson (11) *pushed alng to chase ldrs, beh hfwy*...................(12 to 1 tchd 14 to 1) 12
SHARP THRILL 9-0 A Tucker (13) *strted slwly, sn in tch, hrd rdn o'r 2 fs out, no imprsn*................. (33 to 1) 13
KINGSCOURT JOHN-A (Ire) 9-0 B Rouse (14) *led one furlong, cl up till wknd hfwy, tld off*............ (33 to 1) 14
Dist: 1l, nk, 1l, 1½l, ¾l, hd, 1½l, ¾l, 2l, ½l. 1m 14.40s. a 2.70s (14 Ran).
SR: 4/-/-/-/-/-/ (Mrs C J Powell), R Hannon

1641 Levy Board Handicap Class D (0-80 3-y-o and up) £3,640 1m........ (5:00)

1346[4] WAVE HILL [68] 4-9-7 M Perrett (1) *hld up in tch, cld on bit 2 fs out, shaken up to ld ins last, readily.* ....(9 to 4 fav op 7 to 4 tchd 5 to 2) 1
1177[3] SAIFAN [66] (bl) 4-9-0 (5*) C Hodgson (2) *hld up, hdwy 3 fs out, led o'r one out till ins last, kpt on.* ....(8 to 1 op 6 to 1) 2
1307 THEMAAM [53] 4-8-6 Pat Eddery (3) *trkd ldrs, led 2 fs out till o'r one out, one pace.* ....(13 to 2 op 12 to 1 tchd 6 to 1) 3
1177 SHINING JEWEL [67] 6-9-6 L Piggott (4) *hld up in tch, cld 2 fs out, hrd rdn and one pace appr last.* ....(12 to 1 op 8 to 1 tchd 14 to 1) 4
MASTER EUROLINK [72] 4-9-11 R Cochrane (7) *hld up beh, hdwy und pres o'r one furlong out, nrst finish.* ....(15 to 2 op 10 to 1 tchd 7 to 1) 5
1130[8] KISSAVOS [51] 7-8-4 W Newnes (6) *hld up beh, hdwy o'r one furlong out, nvr nrr.* ....(10 to 1 op 8 to 1 tchd 11 to 1) 6
1425[2] REGALSETT [77] 3-9-5 M Roberts (9) *trkd ldrs, rdn o'r 2 fs out, sn btn*............(6 to 1 op 4 to 1 tchd 13 to 2) 7
1193[6] SUPER BENZ [65] 7-8-13 (5*) O Pears (5) *keen hold, cl up, ev ch 2 fs out, wknd*............... (8 to 1 tchd 9 to 1) 8
1267 MAC'S FIGHTER [72] (bl) 8-9-4 (7*) B Russell (11) *led to 2 fs out, wknd*...................... (16 to 1 op 14 to 1) 9
1145[8] TURTLE POWER [54] 3-7-10 A Tucker (10) *cl up, rdn alng 3 fs out, sn wknd*..................(25 to 1 tchd 33 to 1) 10
Dist: 1l, ½l, 2l, ½l, 2l, hd, 2½l, 10l, 12l. 1m 39.50s. a 2.40s (10 Ran).
SR: 29/24/9/17/20/-/7/-/-/ (J J Whelan), P R Hedger

SOUTHWELL (soft)
Thursday June 10th
Going Correction: NIL

1642 Himley Median Auction Maiden Stakes Class F (3-y-o) £2,243 1¼m ....(6:45)

MADAM GYMCRAK 8-9 Julie Bowker (7) *slwly away and beh, hdwy 4 fs out, wide strt, effrt 2 out, rdn to ld appr last, ran on*........................(20 to 1 op 14 to 1) 1
1388[2] PRETTY BABY 8-9 R Cochrane (2) *hld up, hdwy 5 fs out, chlgd 2 out, sn rdn, ev ch till wknd entering last.* ....(3 to 1 op 2 to 1) 2
932[6] HE'S A KING (USA) 9-0 W Ryan (1) *led, rdn 2 fs out, hdd appr last, sn one pace.* .... (5 to 4 on op 6 to 4 on tchd 11 to 10 on) 3
1316 HILLSDOWN BOY (Ire) 9-0 F Norton (6) *chsd ldrs, rdn o'r 3 fs out, sn one pace*............ (25 to 1 op 14 to 1) 4
MISTROY 8-9 A McGlone (5) *hld up, hdwy hfwy, ch 3 fs out, sn rdn, wknd 2 out*............ (7 to 1 op 3 to 1) 5
1388[6] PREMIER STAR 8-9 (5*) M Fenton (3) *mid-div, pushed alng and hdwy 4 fs out, sn hrd rdn, wknd 3 out.* ....(11 to 1 op 10 to 1 tchd 12 to 1) 6
1500[5] MISS RIBBONS 8-2 (7*) Kim McDonnell (8) *cl up, rdn and wknd o'r 2 fs out*............................... (25 to 1) 7
728 DIAMONDS 'N PEARLS 9-0 G Bardwell (4) *cl up, rdn and wknd quickly hfwy, tld off fnl 4 fs*........... (33 to 1) 8
Dist: 2l, 1½l, 5l, 7l, 1½l, hd, dist. 2m 19.70s. (8 Ran).
(The Gymcrak Thoroughbred Racing Club), M H Easterby

TIPPERARY (IRE) (soft (races 1,3,4), good (2))
Thursday June 10th

1643 Templemore E.B.F.Maiden (2-y-o) £3,797 5f........................ (5:30)

1608[2] WAVE THE WAND (Ire) 9-0 W J O'Connor (5) ... (2 to 1 on) 1
1104[3] OVERALL MAJORITY (Ire) 8-11 P Shanahan (2).... (3 to 1) 2
BRUGATTI (Ire) 8-11 J P Murtagh (1)..............(6 to 1) 3
1442 OVER THE MAIGUE (Ire) 8-11 G Curran (4)......... (16 to 1) 4+
RUSTIC LEAGUE (Ire) 9-0 W J Supple (3)..........(12 to 1) 4+
Dist: 4l, 3l, 9l, dd-ht. 1m 3.90s. (5 Ran).
(Exors Of The Late Major Victor McCalmont), Michael Kauntze

1644 Glen Handicap (0-80 4-y-o and up) £2,762 1m 1f.................. (6:00)

1295* RIENROE (Ire) [-] 4-8-11 M J Kinane (7)........ (Evens fav) 1
666[8] DESERT CALM (Ire) [-] 4-9-8 (6*) B J Walsh (3)..... (6 to 1) 2
997[3] RAIN RITE (Ire) [-] 4-9-11 C F Swan (1)............(8 to 1) 3
1235 FLORAL STREET [-] 4-9-5 (2*) D G O'Shea (6)......(8 to 1) 4
1440 ALBERTA ROSE (Ire) [-] 4-9-1 C Roche (8)......(100 to 30) 5
1106 SIMPLY PHRASED (Ire) [-] 4-7-7[2] (8*) B A Hunter (2) (20 to 1) 6
Dist: ¾l, 3½l, 3½l, hd. 2m 12.90s. (6 Ran).
(Ovidstown Investments Ltd), D K Weld

1645 Tipperary Handicap (0-80 3-y-o and up) £2,762 7f.................. (6:30)

1611^{2} SANS CERIPH (Ire) [-] 3-8-13 W J O'Connor (9) (3 to 1 fav) 1
1513^{8} HERMES GOLD (Ire) [-] 3-7-9 (10*) J P Cornally (2) (12 to 1) 2
1440^{5} LORD GLENVARA (Ire) [-] 5-8-3 W J Supple (8) .....(6 to 1) 3
1199^{5} BASIE NOBLE [-] 4-9-0 (6*) J R Barry (1) .... (100 to 30) 4
1570^{2} NORDIC SAINT (Ire) [-] 4-8-6 (6*) J A Heffernan (4) .. (6 to 1) 5
1440 DOBIE (USA) [-] (bl) 5-9-8 M J Kinane (6) .... (5 to 1) 6
1199^{9} BELMARTIN [-] 7-9-12 P V Gilson (7) ....(10 to 1) 7
1513 JARGONEL (Ire) [-] 3-8-2 (2*) D G O'Shea (3) ......(16 to 1) 8
704^{5} DENZILLE LANE (Ire) [-] 3-8-2 D V Smith (5) ...... (20 to 1) 9
Dist: Sht-hd, 2½l, 2l, 2l. 1m 46.30s. (9 Ran).

(Lady Clague), Michael Kauntze

1646 Coolmore Stud Concorde Stakes (Group 3) (3-y-o and up) £11,500 7f ....(7:00)

1201^{2} PERNILLA (Ire) 3-8-6 C Roche (7) *hld up, prog 3 fs out, dsptd ld one out, led wl ins last, held on*....(2 to 1 fav) 1
1551^{4} DASHING COLOURS (Ire) 4-9-2 P Shanahan (8) *hld up, prog 2 fs out, str chal ins last, jst fld*............ (6 to 1) 2
1552^{6} STREET REBEL (Can) (bl) 5-9-9 C F Swan (2) *wl plcd, prog to dispute ld one furlong out, hdd and no extr cl hme.* ....(6 to 1) 3
1200 SABAYA (USA) 3-8-6 W J Supple (6) *hld up, rdn 2 fs out, kpt on*..(10 to 1) 4
1201^{4} NIGHT JAR 6-9-2 B Raymond (5) *trkd ldr, dsptd ld and ev ch one furlong out, rdn and wknd quickly ins last.* ....(5 to 2) 5
DARK REEF 3-8-9 M J Kinane (4) *led, hdd and wknd quickly one furlong out*......................(13 to 2) 6
1611^{9} HAWAIAN TASCA (Ire) (bl) 4-9-5 J D Eddery (3) *mid-div, rdn and lost pl 3 fs out, wknd 2 out*.............. (100 to 1) 7
Dist: Sht-hd, ½l, 3l, 6l. 1m 45.20s. (7 Ran).

(T F Brennan), J S Bolger

CAPANNELLE (ITY) (good)
Friday June 11th

1647 Criterium di Roma (Group 3) (2-y-o) £28,874 6f.................... (3:30)

FRED BONGUSTO (Ire) 8-11 B Jovine, *made all, ran on wl, easily*... 1
SHOOT IN THE DARK (USA) 8-11 V Mezzatesta, *hdwy 2 fs out, ev ch entering fnl furlong, no extr*.............. 2
CASTEL RUNDEGG (Ity) 8-11 A Sauli, *ev ch 2 fs out, one pace*.. 3
HARTMAN 8-11 D Zarroli, *outpcd*........................ 4
ANOTHER BOLD (Ity) 8-11 G Di Chio, *outpcd*............ 5
GOLDEN BENGAL (USA) 8-11 G Ligas, *outpcd*........... 6
Dist: ¾l, 2½l, 4l, 2l, 4½l. 1m 10.10s. (6 Ran).

(Scuderia Super King), R Brogi

CHANTILLY (FR) (soft)
Friday June 11th
Going Correction: PLUS 0.15 sec. per fur.

1648 Prix d'Avilly-Saint-Leonard (Listed) (3-y-o) £14,337 1¼m 110yds.....(2:50)

TURNERS HILL 8-11 T Jarnet,........................... 1
JACKDIDI (Fr) 8-11 D Boeuf,............................ 2
KARMOUSIL (USA) 8-11 C Asmussen,.................... 3
TENET (Fr) 8-11 O Benoist,............................. 4
Dist: Hd, hd, 1½l, 1½l, 1½l, 6l. 2m 13.10s. a 6.50s (7 Ran).
SR: 48/47/46/43/ (K Abdulla), A Fabre

DUNDALK (IRE) (soft)
Friday June 11th

1649 Blackrock Maiden (3-y-o and up) £2,245 7f 166yds............... (6:30)

282^{8} MANZALA (USA) 3-8-11 D Hogan (6) ....(8 to 1) 1
GREAT CABARET (Ire) 3-9-0 M J Kinane (5) .... (5 to 4 on) 2
1252^{8} ARZAAQ (USA) (bl) 3-9-0 W J Supple (4) .... (10 to 1) 3
1445^{4} SCALP (Ire) 3-9-0 N Byrne (9) ....(7 to 1) 4
1513 BERESFORD LADY (Ire) 3-8-11 P V Gilson (14) ... (12 to 1) 5
1507^{6} NORDICOLINI (Ire) 3-8-1 (10*) J J Byrne, ... (10 to 1) 6
1551^{8} AFTERGLOW (Ire) (bl) 4-9-7 L O'Shea (13) .... (10 to 1) 7
788^{6} MARY'S CASE (Ire) 3-9-0 E A Leonard (2) .... (20 to 1) 8
1333 FIVE LITTLE GIRLS (Ire) 3-8-11 K J Manning (3) ... (12 to 1) 9
1568^{5} NORDIC GLARE (Ire) 3-9-0 C Roche (15) .... (5 to 1) 10
848 SIMPLE DANCER (Ire) 3-9-0 R Hughes (12) ....(33 to 1) 11
1333 KHASI HILLS (Ire) 3-8-9 (2*) D G O'Shea (8) .... (50 to 1) 12
577 CLANFLUTHER (Ire) 3-8-10 (4*) W J Smith (10) ....(50 to 1) 13
1333 DAIRINE'S DELIGHT (Ire) 3-8-11 J F Egan (1) ...... (25 to 1) 14
WILLY THE WEAVER (Ire) 3-8-5 (6*) P P Murphy (11) ....(50 to 1) 15
488^{8} LADY GLOW (Ire) 3-8-11 J P Murtagh (16) ....(6 to 1) 16
Dist: Hd, 1½l, 1l, 2½l. 1m 45.80s. (16 Ran).

(Dundalk Racing Club), John M Oxx

1650 Omeath E.B.F.Maiden (2-y-o) £3,107 7f 166yds........................ (7:00)

1332^{2} LA BERTA (Ire) 8-11 W J O'Connor (4) .... (6 to 4 fav) 1
1432^{3} CORLEONIE (Ire) (bl) 9-0 W J Supple (6) ....(10 to 1) 2
METROELLA (Ire) 8-11 R Hughes (3) .... (8 to 1) 3
SWIFT RIPOSTE (Ire) 9-0 C Roche (5) .... (3 to 1) 4
COPPER MOUNTAIN (Ire) 9-0 M J Kinane (2) ....(3 to 1) 5
1442^{9} PARCACURRY PETE (Ire) 8-10 (4*) P Carberry (7) ..(10 to 1) 6
FINAL OPERA (Ire) 8-5 (6*) J J Behan (11) .... (33 to 1) 7
1442^{7} MY RAGAMUFFIN (Ire) 8-11 J P Murtagh (8) .... (6 to 1) 8
THE PLAYER NOBLE (Ire) 9-0 P Shanahan (9) ...... (8 to 1) 9
NOBLE CHOICE (Ire) 8-11 N G McCullagh (1) ..... (14 to 1) 10
1550^{9} FANCY BOOTS (Ire) 8-9 (2*) R M Burke (10) ....(20 to 1) 11
Dist: 2½l, ½l, 5l, 3l. 1m 46.80s. (11 Ran).

(Mrs M Cattaneo), Michael Kauntze

1651 Mountain Bay Apprentice Handicap (0-60 3-y-o and up) £2,245 1m 1f (7:30)

1163^{3} VICOSA (Ire) [-] 4-8-2 (2*) P J Smullen (10) .... (9 to 2) 1
1139* ISLAND VISION (Ire) [-] 3-9-1 (2*) J F Clarke (14) .... (5 to 1) 2
1293^{9} SUTTON CENTENARY (Ire) [-] 5-8-7 (2*) D O'Sullivan (1) ....(16 to 1) 3
TOP GENERATION [-] 4-8-11 G Coogan (2) .... (16 to 1) 4
1293* ARDLEA HOUSE (Ire) [-] 4-8-9 (10ex) T J Daly (15) .. (5 to 1) 5
1251 ST AIDAN (Ire) [-] 5-8-1 (2*) G M Moylan (4) .... (8 to 1) 6
1295^{2} WINTER DREAMS (Ire) [-] 4-9-5 (2*) T Hagger (6) (5 to 2 fav) 7
1293^{8} THE BOWER (Ire) [-] 4-8-11 (2*) P M Donohoe (11) (10 to 1) 8
1385 PICK'N HILL (Ire) [-] 5-7-7 B J Halligan (3) .... (25 to 1) 9
870 REALTHOGUE GIRL (Ire) [-] 4-8-8 (2*) B Carson (5) (33 to 1) 10
912 LOVE OF ERIN (Ire) [-] 4-7-9 B A Hunter (12) ...... (25 to 1) 11
Dist: 1½l, 2l, 1½l, 4½l. 2m 13.80s. (11 Ran).

(T F Lacy), T F Lacy

1652 Carlingford Race (3-y-o) £2,245 1m 1f ....(8:00)

1441* SOLAS ABU (Ire) 9-4 C Roche (2) ....(Evens fav) 1
1514^{8} FLORA WOOD (Ire) 9-4 W J Supple (3) .... (6 to 1) 2
1026^{4} DEVIL'S HOLIDAY (USA) 9-0 W J O'Connor (5) ..... (8 to 1) 3
1292^{5} TOUCHING MOMENT (Ire) 9-7 P V Gilson (1) ...... (7 to 1) 4
BAHNASA (Ire) 8-11 M J Kinane (6) .... (2 to 1) 5
SHARP AT SIX (Ire) 9-0 P Shanahan (4) ....(16 to 1) 6
Dist: 4½l, 7l, 3½l, hd. 2m 12.80s. (6 Ran).

(E R Madden), J S Bolger

DONCASTER (soft)
Friday June 11th
Going Correction: PLUS 0.15 sec. per fur. (races 1,3,6), PLUS 0.45 (2,4,5)

1653 Holmfirth Conditions Stakes Class D (2-y-o) £3,451 5f................(6:50)

979^{7} MOSCOW ROAD 8-12 K Darley (3) *made all, rdn and hng lft frm 2 fs out, jnd wl ins last, ran on.* .... (11 to 2 op 7 to 2 tchd 6 to 1) 1+
776* MILD REBUKE 8-7 M Hills (2) *steadied strt, trkd ldg pair, smooth hdwy hfwy, shaken up o'r one furlong out, drw level wl ins fnl furlong*... (9 to 4 on op 7 to 4 on) 1+
1303^{5} CYARNA QUINN (Ire) 8-5 G Duffield (1) *pressed ldr, pushed alng aftr 2 fs, fdd o'r one out.* ....(4 to 1 op 7 to 2 tchd 9 to 2) 3
Dist: Dd-ht, 5l. 1m 2.60s. a 3.80s (3 Ran).
SR: 37/32/10/ (G C Sampson & P D Player), R Hannon & D R Loder

1654 Westside Magazine Group Handicap Class E (0-70 4-y-o and up) £3,184 2m 110yds....................... (7:20)

1195^{2} KAYARTIS [43] 4-8-0 J Lowe (14) *mid-div, improved hfwy, swept into ld o'r 3 fs out, clr 2 out, styd on wl.* .... (11 to 4 op 3 to 1 tchd 4 to 1) 1
1173^{6} QUALITAIR SOUND (Ire) [39] 5-7-11 L Charnock (8) *hld up towards rear, gd hdwy entering strt, chsd wnr fnl 2 fs, one pace*.. (12 to 1) 2
1400* BILBERRY [43] 4-8-0 (4ex) T Williams (1) *settled mid-div, improved on bit 6 fs out, ev ch 3 out, sn rdn and one pace*..............................(6 to 1 tchd 8 to 1) 3
1400^{8} MEDIA STAR [35] 8-7-0 (7*) D Wright (6) *missed break, beh, gd hdwy to chase ldrs entering strt, rdn alng 3 fs out, not quicken*......................(50 to 1 op 33 to 1) 4
ELITE REG [38] (bl) 4-7-9 J Quinn (4) *led and sn clr, rdn o'r 6 fs out, hdd appr strt, wknd over 3 out.* ....(5 to 2 fav op 2 to 1) 5
1564^{5} COST EFFECTIVE [36] 6-7-8^{1} A Mackay (15) *chsd ldr, rdn alng 6 fs out, one pace fnl half m.* (14 to 1 op 12 to 1) 6
1457^{6} COSMIC DANCER [44] (bl) 6-8-2^{1} W Woods (9) *nvr far away, led appr strt, hdd 3 fs out, sn btn.* .... (14 to 1 op 10 to 1) 7
1328^{3} LABURNUM [68] 5-9-5 (7*) V Halliday (11) *hld up and beh, shrtlvd effrt entering strt, sn btn, tld off.* ....(8 to 1 op 6 to 1) 8

1112 STATIA (Ire) [36] 5-7-8[1] Kim Tinkler (12) *in tch, lost pl hfwy, btn entering strt, tld off*..........(50 to 1 op 33 to 1) 9
1195[8] MALENOIR (USA) [38] (v) 5-7-5 (5*) Darren Moffatt (7) *missed break, beh, rdn appr strt, sn lost tch, tld off*...(33 to 1) 10
GOLDEN ISLE [55] 9-8-13 R Cochrane (3) *chsd ldrs, rdn entering strt, wknd o'r 3 fs out, tld off*. ....(16 to 1 op 10 to 1) 11
1564[4] BALZINO (USA) [50] 4-8-7 K Fallon (13) *hld up and wl beh, pushed alng entering strt, sn btn, tld off*. ....(9 to 1 op 6 to 1 tchd 10 to 1) 12
165[7] EQUITY CARD (Ire) [58] (v) 5-9-2 S Perks (2) *hld up, drvn hfwy, lost tch fnl half m, tld off*... (50 to 1 op 25 to 1) 13
Dist: 3½l, 6l, nk, 8l, hd, 5l, 20l, 1½l, ¾l, ¾l. 3m 47.10s. a 17.10s (13 Ran).
(Mrs J M Allen), Mrs M Reveley

1655 St John Ambulance Maiden Stakes Class D (3-y-o) £3,231 5f........(7:45)

1214[6] PUTOUT (bl) 8-9 D Biggs (4) *nvr far away, shaken up to ld a furlong out, kpt on wl*........ (6 to 4 fav op 5 to 4) 1
1505[2] KILDEE LAD 9-0 N Adams (8) *led til hdd one furlong out, edgd lft, kpt on same pace*...... (12 to 1 tchd 14 to 1) 2
OLYMPIA 8-9 J Lowe (7) *missed break, beh, pushed alng hfwy, improved o'r one furlong out, nrst finish*. .... (8 to 1 op 14 to 1) 3
1463[7] HUMBER'S SUPREME (Ire) (bl) 8-9 J Quinn (6) *in tch, rdn alng hfwy, not quicken fnl 2 fs*.... (12 to 1 op 10 to 1) 4
899[4] FRIENDLY SMILE 8-9 G Duffield (1) *beh on outer, rdn aftr 2 fs, not pace to chal*..............(14 to 1 op 12 to 1) 5
1162[5] ROYAL MUSIC 9-0 J Carroll (3) *chsd ldrs, drvn hfwy, lost tch o'r one furlong out*...........(14 to 1 op 12 to 1) 6
1396[4] EL ARZ 9-0 R Cochrane (2) *dwlt, beh and sn pushed alng, nvr on terms*....................... (7 to 4 op 9 to 4) 7
Dist: ¾l, 2½l, sht-hd, 5l, 2½l, 3½l. 1m 2.64s. a 3.84s (7 Ran).
SR: 33/35/20/19/ (Lord Tavistock), Mrs J Cecil

1656 Yorkshire Television Fillies Handicap Class D (0-80 3-y-o) £3,552 1m.. (8:15)

1459[6] STYLISH ROSE (Ire) [58] 8-8 J Lowe (5) *rcd keenly, made all, rdn and swshd tail 2 fs out, kpt on gmely ins last*. ....(25 to 1) 1
1242[5] MISS FASCINATION [56] 8-6 Paul Eddery (1) *in tch, improved 2 fs out, ran on to chal ins last, hld cl hme*. .... (5 to 1 op 11 to 2 tchd 9 to 2) 2
1285* BALNAHA [71] 9-7 M Hills (9) *slwly into strd, beh, steady hdwy 3 fs out, shaken up o'r one out, not quicken*. .... (7 to 4 fav op 2 to 1 tchd 9 to 4 and 5 to 2) 3
LA MENORQUINA (USA) [68] 9-4 R Cochrane (6) *beh, feeling pace and drvn alng entering strt, gd hdwy appr fnl furlong, fnshd wl*..... (13 to 2 op 11 to 2 tchd 7 to 1) 4
1528[3] NITOUCHE [67] 9-3 W Woods (4) *hld up, rdn o'r 2 fs out, sn one pace*.......... (5 to 1 tchd 11 to 2 and 6 to 1) 5
1300[4] SARAH HEIGHTS [46] 7-10 N Carlisle (7) *wth ldr, rdn o'r 2 fs out, wknd over one out*...... (16 to 1 op 14 to 1) 6
1351[6] LATEST FLAME (Ire) [63] 8-13 G Duffield (3) *trkd ldg pair, pushed alng o'r 2 fs out, fdd over one out*. ....(7 to 1 op 6 to 1) 7
NORTHERN JUDY (Ire) [46] 7-3 (7*) F Savage (2) *slwly into strd, in rear, rdn appr strt, effrt on outer 4 fs out, wknd o'r 2 out*...(33 to 1) 8
1271[3] MOST SIOUXTABLE [57] 8-7 J Fanning (8) *in tch, drvn alng o'r 3 fs out, sn btn, tld off*...........(8 to 1 op 7 to 1) 9
Dist: Sht-hd, 8l, ½l, hd, 2½l, 2½l, nk, 12l. 1m 44.48s. a 7.78s (9 Ran).
SR: 31/28/19/14/12/-/ (T McDonagh), P Cheesbrough

1657 Whitby Claiming Stakes Class F (3-y-o and up) £2,758 1½m............(8:45)

1034[4] BALADIYA 6-8-9 (5*) C Hodgson (11) *nvr far away, led appr strt, clr o'r 2 fs out, styd on*. ....(7 to 2 op 4 to 1 tchd 5 to 1) 1
1438[2] LE TEMERAIRE 7-9-7 Kim Tinkler (2) *al hndy, shaken up o'r 2 fs out, kpt on ins last, no ch wth wnr*. .... (11 to 2 op 5 to 1 tchd 6 to 1) 2
1438[7] IRON BARON (Ire) 4-9-2 S Perks (6) *mid-div, took clr order appr strt, effrt and swtchd lft 2 fs out, sn no imprsn*. .... (14 to 1 op 12 to 1) 3
1592[4] AZUREUS (Ire) 5-9-12 Dale Gibson (3) *hld up, rdn to improve o'r 3 fs out, one pace fnl 2 furlongs*. ....(5 to 2 fav op 5 to 4) 4
1275[9] ROYAL VACATION 4-9-12 R Cochrane (8) *hld up, effrt and rdn 3 fs out, eased whn btn wl o'r one out*.....(14 to 1) 5
SCOTTISH BALL 4-8-12 G Duffield (7) *in tch, drvn alng entering strt, wknd o'r 2 fs out*......(5 to 1 op 7 to 1) 6
653[7] RAQS ASSAYF 3-8-3[1] A Culhane (10) *nvr far away, drvn alng 3 fs out, btn 2 out*..........(25 to 1 tchd 33 to 1) 7
1304[5] BROWNED OFF 4-9-6 K Fallon (4) *missed break, beh, lost tch o'r 3 fs out, tld off*.........................(8 to 1) 8
799[8] ABALENE 4-9-4 (3*) S D Williams (9) *slwly into strd, beh, rdn appr strt, sn btn, tld off*.................. (33 to 1) 9
1357[5] ORIENTAL PRINCESS 3-7-8[3] (5*) A Garth (1) *led, hdd appr strt, quickly lost pl, tld off*....... (50 to 1 op 33 to 1) 10
Dist: 4l, 7l, 1½l, 8l, 1½l, 2½l, 15l, 15l, nk. 2m 42.29s. a 11.79s (10 Ran).
SR: 36/35/16/23/7/-/ (Mrs Rosalie Hawes), D Morris

1658 Pennine Handicap Class D (0-80 3-y-o and up) £3,377 7f..............(9:15)

1210[3] LEGEND DULAC (Ire) [47] 4-8-3 P Robinson (1) *dsptd ld centre, wnt on one furlong out, hld on wl*..... (12 to 1) 1
1496[2] DANCING DOMINO [54] 3-8-0 K Darley (2) *dsptd ld stands side, hdd one furlong out, ran on wl*. ....(6 to 4 fav op 2 to 1 tchd 9 to 4) 2
1436[9] ARABAT [62] 6-9-4 K Fallon (8) *dwlt, beh, improved 3 fs out, sn rdn, not quicken appr last*. (14 to 1 op 12 to 1) 3
655[9] ROYAL GIRL [56] 6-8-12 N Connorton (9) *chsd ldrs, effrt and rdn o'r 2 fs out, no extr over one out*. ....(10 to 1 op 8 to 1) 4
1394* GREAT HALL [56] 4-8-12 (5ex) A Mackay (10) *beh, drvn alng hfwy, nvr dngrs*................(5 to 1 op 6 to 1) 5
1382* FIGHTER SQUADRON [65] (bl) 4-9-4 (3*,5ex) S D Williams (3) *hld up, rdn to improve 3 fs out, wknd o'r one out*. ....(5 to 1 op 4 to 1) 6
1270[4] QUEEN OF SHANNON (Ire) [72] 5-10-0 M Tebbutt (7) *missed break, sn in tch, rdn 3 fs out, btn 2 out*. ....(5 to 1 op 9 to 2) 7
383[8] QUIET VICTORY [37] 6-7-7 N Carlisle (6) *chsd ldrs, wknd 2 fs out*..........................(20 to 1 op 14 to 1) 8
1266 COSMIC STAR [62] 3-8-8 W Woods (4) *chsd ldrs, pushed alng o'r 3 fs out, lost tch wl over one out*. ....(10 to 1 op 14 to 1 tchd 16 to 1) 9
Dist: Hd, 5l, 1½l, 2l, nk, 3½l, 3½l, 8l. 1m 29.69s. a 6.29s (9 Ran).
SR: 10/6/9/-/-/-/ (T J Wells), J L Harris

GOODWOOD (good)
Friday June 11th

Going Correction: PLUS 0.25 sec. per fur. (race 1), PLUS 0.30 (2,6), PLUS 0.35 (3,4,5)

1659 BBC South Today Handicap Amateur Riders Class F (0-70 3-y-o and up) £3,076 1m 1f..................(6:40)

1120 ALBERT [44] 6-9-12 (5*) Mrs D Arbuthnot (9) *hld up, hdwy o'r 2 fs out, rdn and ran on to ld wl ins last*. ....(11 to 4 fav op 7 to 2 tchd 4 to 1) 1
1474[4] DANCING BEAU (Ire) [47] 4-10-1 (5*) Mr T Cuff (16) *mid-div, rdn 2 fs out, ran on to go second cl hme*. ....(9 to 2 op 4 to 1 tchd 5 to 1) 2
1490[3] SYLVAN SABRE (Ire) [62] (v) 4-11-7 Mr R Teal (11) *prmnt, led 2 fs out, rdn and hdd wl ins last*.... (8 to 1 op 10 to 1) 3
1389[9] AEDEAN [48] 4-10-2 (5*) Mr M Ayres (5) *prmnt, led briefly 5 fs out, ev ch till wknd entering fnl furlong*. ....(33 to 1 tchd 50 to 1) 4
BROWN CARPET [29] (bl) 6-8-13[2] (5*) Miss D Pomeroy (2) *prmnt, led wl o'r 4 fs out to last, wknd appr last*. .... (14 to 1 op 16 to 1 tchd 25 to 1) 5
1316* PUSEY STREET BOY [39] 6-9-7 (5*) Mrs S Bosley (3) *nvr far away, rdn and wknd wl o'r one furlong out*. ....(9 to 2 op 4 to 1 tchd 5 to 1) 6
1498 LUCKY NOIRE [54] (bl) 5-10-13 Miss A Harwood (7) *hld up in rear, hdwy 3 fs out, rdn 2 out, not rch ldrs*. ....(7 to 1 op 8 to 1 tchd 9 to 1) 7
THRESHFIELD (USA) [58] 7-10-12 (5*) Mr C Curley (4) *rear, some late hdwy, nvr dngrs*. .... (9 to 1 op 6 to 1 tchd 10 to 1) 8
1498 YIMKIN BOOKRA [51] (v) 5-10-5 (5*) Miss J Russell (13) *al rear*..............................(50 to 1 op 25 to 1) 9
1371[4] CANDARELA [46] 3-9-2 (5*) Miss H Stubbings (10) *dsptd ld to hfwy, wknd o'r 2 fs out*...... (50 to 1 op 20 to 1) 10
PERMANENTLY PINK [27] 7-8-9 (5*) Mrs C Dunwoody (14) *prmnt early, sn mid-div, lost tch fnl 3 fs*. .... (50 to 1 op 25 to 1) 11
JONBEL [39] 5-9-7 (5*) Mr V Lukaniuk (12) *nvr on terms*. .... (50 to 1 op 33 to 1) 12
1281 GEORGE ROPER [56] 3-10-3[11] (5*) Mr J Keller (6) *slwly away, sn mid-div, rdn 4 fs out, wknd wl o'r 2 out*. .... (50 to 1 op 25 to 1) 13
1316 SUPREME OPTIMIST [29] (bl) 9-9-1[4] (5*) Mrs C Peacock (1) *led to 5 fs out, wknd*............ (50 to 1 op 25 to 1) 14
Dist: 2l, nk, 2l, 5l, ¾l, nk, ½l, 4l, ¾l, 1l. 2m 0.55s. a 8.55s (14 Ran).
SR: 22/19/33/13/-/-/ (T S M S Riley-Smith), D A Wilson

1660 EBF BBC Radio Berkshire Maiden Fillies Stakes Class D (2-y-o) £3,435 6f ....(7:05)

PALANA (USA) 8-9 L Dettori (2) *slwly into strd, hdwy hfwy, led 2 fs out, rdn ins last, jst hld on*. ....(3 to 1 fav op 7 to 4) 1
NORFOLK LAVENDER (Can) 8-9 A Munro (6) *led to 2 fs out, rallied wl ins last, jst fld*...........(8 to 1 op 10 to 1) 2
DOUCE MAISON (Ire) 8-6 (3*) B Doyle (3) *rear, hdwy 2 fs out, rdn and ran on ins last*.......(33 to 1 op 25 to 1) 3
1032[5] GIFT BOX (Ire) 8-9 J Williams (1) *reared strt, hld up, swtchd rght o'r 2 fs out, styd on ins last*. ....(9 to 2 op 5 to 1 tchd 6 to 1) 4
1403 FOREST LOCH 8-6 (3*) D Harrison (5) *rear, styd on ins fnl 2 fs, nvr nrr*......................... (33 to 1 op 25 to 1) 5

1032[4] MARJORIE'S MEMORY (Ire) 8-9 M Roberts (8) *chsd ldrs, rdn and ev ch appr fnl furlong, wknd ins.* ....(7 to 2 op 5 to 1 tchd 6 to 1 and 3 to 1) 6
1393[6] ROSE CIEL (Ire) 8-9 A McGlone (7) *chsd ldr to hfwy, in tch till wknd ins fnl furlong*..........(33 to 1 op 25 to 1) 7
BIRD OF TIME (Ire) 8-9 T Quinn (4) *speed till wknd 2 fs out.* ....(8 to 1 op 6 to 1 tchd 9 to 1) 8
RAJMAPATA 8-9 Pat Eddery (10) *prmnt on outsd, rdn hfwy, wknd wl o'r one furlong out.* ....(11 to 2 op 4 to 1 tchd 6 to 1) 9
673 SHEILOBLIGE 8-9 B Rouse (9) *beh, swtchd rght and hdwy hfwy, wknd quickly wl o'r one furlong out, tld off*..............................(33 to 1 op 25 to 1) 10
Dist: Sht-hd, 2l, 1½l, hd, sht-hd, 1½l, 4l, 3½l, 12l. 1m 15.33s. a 4.93s (10 Ran).
SR: 32/31/23/17/16/15/9/-/-/ (George Strawbridge), I A Balding

1661 BBC Radio Solent Handicap Class D (0-80 3-y-o) £3,523 1¼m........ (7:35)

CONTRACT COURT (USA) [72] 9-3 M Roberts (4) *trkd ldr, al gng wl, led 2 fs out, pushed clr ins last.* ....(14 to 1 tchd 12 to 1) 1
1488[5] JONSALAN [66] 8-11 Pat Eddery (5) *led, rdn o'r 2 fs out, sn hdd, ev ch till no extr ins last.* ....(11 to 4 op 7 to 2 tchd 4 to 1 and 5 to 2) 2
1460* MISBELIEF [75] 9-6 (4ex) G Carter (3) *chsd ldrs, rdn o'r 2 fs out, no imprsn.* (5 to 4 fav op 5 to 4 on tchd 11 to 8) 3
1487[2] SILVER GROOM (Ire) [53] 7-9 (3*) B Doyle (1) *al same pl, effrt o'r 3 fs out, kpt on one pace ins last.* ....(9 to 2 op 7 to 1) 4
1469[7] FOOLS ERRAND (Ire) [76] 9-7 T Quinn (6) *al last, lost tch o'r 2 fs out*...................................(7 to 1 op 11 to 2) 5
Dist: 3l, 2l, ½l, 8l. 2m 15.39s. a 9.89s (5 Ran).
SR: 39/27/32/9/16/ (R M Cyzer), C A Cyzer

1662 Three Keys Stakes Class D Claiming (3-y-o) £3,622 1½m............. (8:05)

1266[5] LUNAR RISK 8-11 A Munro (2) *hld up, hrd rdn to ld wl o'r one furlong out, drvn out.* ....(9 to 1 op 10 to 1 tchd 12 to 1 and 8 to 1) 1
876[7] TROPICAL JUNGLE (USA) 8-11 T Quinn (6) *chsd ldrs, rdn to ld 2 fs out, sn hdd, kpt on one pace.* ....(7 to 2 op 4 to 1) 2
1491[2] HOSTILE WITNESS (Ire) 8-8 Pat Eddery (3) *rear, hdwy 3 fs out, kpt on one pace*.......... (2 to 1 fav tchd 9 to 4) 3
1297[4] MAYDAY CALLING 7-12 (5*) M Fenton (1) *pld hrd, trkd ldrs, dsptd second hfwy, rdn o'r 3 fs out, sn lost pl, no dngr aftr*............................... (5 to 1 tchd 6 to 1) 4
1491[3] RAVENSPUR (Ire) (bl) 8-8 M Roberts (7) *led till o'r 3 fs out, not run on, sn btn*.......(7 to 2 op 9 to 4 tchd 4 to 1) 5
1417 SLIVOVITZ 8-11 D Holland (9) *chsd ldr, led o'r 3 fs out, hrd rdn and hdd 2 out, wknd quickly.* ....(12 to 1 tchd 14 to 1) 6
1126[3] WILL HYDE 8-3 S Dawson (5) *al beh, tld off.* ....(66 to 1 op 25 to 1 tchd 100 to 1) 7
1491[9] CHATWORTH GREY 7-8[1] (3*) B Doyle (8) *slwly away, al beh, tld off*....... (66 to 1 op 50 to 1 tchd 100 to 1) 8
Dist: 2l, 3½l, 12l, 2l, 2l, 8l, 8l. 2m 43.30s. a 10.30s (8 Ran).
SR: 36/32/22/-/-/ (R Haim), W R Muir

1663 BBC Radio Sussex And BBC Radio Surrey Claiming Stakes Class F (4-y-o and up) £2,880 1¼m............ (8:35)

1398[7] RAMBO'S HALL 8-9-7 Dean McKeown (3) *al in tch, led o'r 2 fs out, pushed clr, easily.* .... (2 to 1 on op 13 to 8 on tchd 6 to 4 on and 5 to 2 on) 1
1146* SARAH-CLARE 5-8-8 T Quinn (7) *mid-div, hdwy to go second o'r 2 fs out, kpt on und pres ins last, no ch wth wnr*...................(11 to 2 op 6 to 1 tchd 7 to 1) 2
1146[5] NATURAL LAD 8-8-5 (5*) Stephen Davies (5) *prmnt, kpt on to dispute second pl ins fnl furlong.* .... (33 to 1 op 16 to 1) 3
1298[6] COURAGEOUS KNIGHT 4-8-11 M Roberts (6) *beh, hdwy 3 fs out, kpt on, nvr nrr.* (10 to 1 op 8 to 1 tchd 12 to 1) 4
1130 VANBOROUGH LAD 4-8-9 A Munro (1) *rear but in tch, one pace ins fnl 3 fs*...... (25 to 1 op 14 to 1 tchd 33 to 1) 5
1237* WAKI GOLD (USA) 6-8-13 Pat Eddery (8) *led till o'r 2 fs out, rdn and wknd ins last*........... (11 to 2 tchd 6 to 1) 6
IMA RED NECK (USA) 4-8-13 A McGlone (2) *al rear.* .... (66 to 1 op 50 to 1 tchd 100 to 1) 7
COMMANCHERO 6-8-2 (7*) S Drowne (9) *slwly away, al rear*................................(33 to 1 op 20 to 1) 8
NOVA SPIRIT 5-9-5 M Wigham (4) *trkd ldr, wknd 3 fs out.* .... (66 to 1 op 50 to 1 tchd 100 to 1) 9
Dist: 3l, hd, 1l, ½l, 2½l, 4l, ½l, 2½l. 2m 13.85s. a 8.35s (9 Ran).
SR: 59/40/41/40/37/36/28/23/28/ (B Dixon), J A Glover

1664 University Of Sussex Handicap Class E (0-70 3-y-o and up) £2,831 6f.. (9:05)

1282[6] PALACEGATE GOLD (Ire) [50] 4-8-10 A Munro (2) *trkd ldrs, led one furlong out, drvn out*.......(11 to 2 op 7 to 2) 1
1492[9] COPPERMILL LAD [44] 10-7-11 (7*) Iona Wands (4) *beh, hdwy on outsd 2 fs out, ran on ins last.* ....(5 to 1 op 7 to 1 tchd 8 to 1) 2
1270[7] PHARAOH'S DANCER [68] 6-10-0 W Newnes (1) *slwly away, hdwy 2 fs out, ran on wl ins last.* ....(9 to 2 tchd 6 to 1) 3
1209 MOGWAI (Ire) [56] (v) 4-9-2 D Holland (8) *prmnt, rdn and ev ch one furlong out, no extr ins.* ....(9 to 1 op 10 to 1 tchd 12 to 1 and 8 to 1) 4
1280[7] MR NEVERMIND (Ire) [61] (bl) 3-8-12 B Rouse (6) *trkd ldr, led hfwy, rdn and hdd one furlong out, no extr.* ....(11 to 2 op 6 to 1 tchd 13 to 2 and 5 to 1) 5
1312[4] GALLOP TO GLORY [54] 3-8-5 M Roberts (5) *led to hfwy, rdn and wknd appr fnl furlong.* ....(4 to 1 fav op 3 to 1 tchd 9 to 2) 6
1267 SEA-DEER [61] 4-9-7 M Perrett (7) *outpcd, nvr got into race*..................... (9 to 1 op 8 to 1 tchd 10 to 1) 7
1487 KRAYYAN DAWN [58] 3-8-9 S Dawson (3) *outpcd.* .... (12 to 1 op 8 to 1 tchd 14 to 1) 8
Dist: ¾l, 1l, sht-hd, ½l, 4l, nk, 2l. 1m 15.09s. a 4.69s (8 Ran).
SR: 38/29/49/36/30/7/22/2/ (R J Hodges), R J Hodges

SANDOWN (good)
Friday June 11th

Going Correction: PLUS 0.20 sec. per fur. (races 1,4), PLUS 0.40 (2,3,5,6,7)

1665 Rosemary Maiden Auction Stakes Class D (2-y-o) £3,395 5f 6yds... (2:15)

BALANDRA BAY (Ire) 9-0 Pat Eddery (1) *chsd ldr, led hfwy, quickened clr o'r one out, styd on, easily.* ....(7 to 4 fav op 11 to 10 tchd 2 to 1) 1
GO WITH BO (Ire) 9-0 B Rouse (4) *trkd ldrs, chsd wnr entering last 2 fs, no imprsn fnl 100 yards.* .... (8 to 1 op 12 to 1 tchd 16 to 1) 2
1265 THORNY BISHOP 9-0 G Bardwell (5) *slwly into strd, beh till ran on o'r 2 out, one pace appr fnl furlong.* ....(33 to 1 tchd 50 to 1) 3
1339[4] STRAPPED (v) 8-9 T Quinn (2) *led to hfwy, sn rdn and btn.* .... (2 to 1 op 13 to 8) 4
1279[2] BENFLEET 9-0 L Dettori (3) *outpcd and reminders aftr 2 fs, lost tch frm hfwy*.....(3 to 1 op 5 to 2 tchd 7 to 2) 5
Dist: 3l, 5l, 1½l, 12l. 1m 3.88s. a 4.38s (5 Ran).
SR: 32/20/ (J A Lazzari), R Hannon

1666 Orleans Maiden Stakes Class D (2-y-o) £3,746 7f 16yds............ (2:50)

VENTA DE POSSA (USA) 9-0 L Dettori (4) *led aftr 2 fs, made rst, shaken up and styd on ins last, cleverly.* .... (16 to 1 op 12 to 1 tchd 20 to 1) 1
POTENTATE (USA) 9-0 A Munro (3) *ldg grp, ev ch frm one furlong out, not quicken last 100 yards.* ....(11 to 4 tchd 100 to 30) 2
SHARP TYCOON (Ire) 9-0 B Rouse (6) *towards rer till ran on last 2 fs, not rch wnr*.......... (33 to 1 op 16 to 1) 3
ALJAWAB (USA) 9-0 B Raymond (10) *handily plcd, rdn and not quicken 2 fs out, wknd fnl furlong.* .... (8 to 1 op 6 to 1 tchd 10 to 1) 4
MAKE A STAND 9-0 W Newnes (8) *in tch in mid-div, effrt on outsd o'r 2 out, pushed alng and no imprsn appr fnl furlong*............. (20 to 1 op 12 to 1 tchd 25 to 1) 5
1211[2] IRREPRESSIBLE (Ire) 9-0 Pat Eddery (7) *in tch, rdn to chal o'r 2 out, btn appr fnl furlong.* .. (11 to 10 fav op Evens tchd 11 to 10 on and 6 to 5) 6
1265[9] HEATHCLIFF (Ire) 9-0 D Holland (1) *led for 2 fs, pressed wnr till wknd two out*...................(10 to 1 op 6 to 1) 7
LUGANO 9-0 W R Swinburn (9) *strted slwly, al beh.* .... (25 to 1 op 14 to 1) 8
DEBLYN 9-0 G Bardwell (5) *beh frm hfwy.* .... (33 to 1 op 25 to 1 tchd 50 to 1) 9
FIGHTING SPIRIT 9-0 S Whitworth (2) *lost grnd leaving stalls, al rear grp*.... (50 to 1 op 25 to 1 tchd 66 to 1) 10
Dist: ¾l, 3½l, 1½l, 2l, 1½l, 3l, 2½l, 10l, ¾l. 1m 34.82s. a 8.32s (10 Ran).
SR: 17/15/4/-/-/-/ (Roldvale Limited), P A Kelleway

1667 Kidsons Impey Trophy (Handicap) Class C (0-90 3-y-o and up) £4,978 7f 16yds........................ (3:20)

703[5] FAWZ (Ire) [74] 4-9-5 Pat Eddery (9) *chsd ldr, led o'r 2 fs out, rdn out*.............(8 to 1 op 7 to 1 tchd 9 to 1) 1
1374[3] MARINE DIVER [73] 7-9-4 J Williams (5) *strted slwly, hdwy o'r 3 out, rdn and not quicken one furlong out, rallied nr line*........................... (7 to 1 op 5 to 1) 2
SYLVAN (Ire) [79] 4-9-10 B Raymond (11) *settled in mid-div, prog o'r 3 out, one pace ins fnl furlong*....... (20 to 1) 3
1060[8] WHATEVER'S RIGHT (Ire) [57] 4-8-2 R Perham (8) *improved on outsd frm 2 fs out, styd on, nrst at line.* ....(25 to 1 tchd 33 to 1) 4
1231[5] VAYAVAIG [83] 3-9-4 W R Swinburn (3) *hld up in mid-div, pushed alng o'r 2 out, ran on ins fnl furlong.* ....(7 to 1 tchd 8 to 1) 5

1394[2] YOURS BY RIGHT [81] 3-8-9 (7*) P McCabe (1) *rcd in 3rd pl till rdn and one pace 2 fs out*... (9 to 4 fav tchd 5 to 2) 6
1348[8] CATHERINEOFARAGON [80] 3-9-1 G Bardwell (4) *steadied leaving stalls, al towards rear*....... (9 to 1 op 7 to 1) 7
1270[6] TAKENHALL [64] 8-8-6 (3*) D Harrison (6) *rcd in 4th pl till rdn and lost pos o'r 2 fs out.* .... (15 to 2 op 7 to 1 tchd 8 to 1) 8
1412[5] CYPRIAN DANCER (USA) [84] 3-9-5 T Quinn (7) *al beh.* ....(10 to 1) 9
1382[7] CHEVEUX MITCHELL [75] (v) 6-9-6 C Rutter (10) *led till o'r 2 out, sn wknd, eased over one furlong out.* ....(8 to 1 op 5 to 1 tchd 9 to 1) 10

Dist: ½l, 2l, hd, sht-hd, 1½l, ¾l, 10l, 1l, 4l. 1m 33.16s. a 6.66s (10 Ran).

SR: 47/44/44/21/36/29/26/-/-/ (Jeremy Gompertz), R W Armstrong

1668 More Lane Claiming Stakes Class E (3-y-o and up) £2,843 5f 6yds....(3:50)

1406[9] GONE SAVAGE 5-9-5 Pat Eddery (1) *chsd ldr, led entering last 2 fs, pushed clr, cmftbly.* .... (11 to 10 fav tchd Evens and 6 to 5) 1
1420[7] METAL BOYS 6-9-2 (3*) D Harrison (5) *chsd ldrs till rdn and outpcd 2 fs out, styd on ag'n ins last, not rch wnr.* .... (6 to 1 op 5 to 1 tchd 13 to 2) 2
1560[5] PALEY PRINCE (USA) 7-9-6 W R Swinburn (6) *wl in tch, wnt second appr fnl furlong, wknd last 100 yards.* .... (8 to 1 op 10 to 1 tchd 11 to 1) 3
1095 MELODYS DAUGHTER (bl) 3-7-8 J Quinn (2) *led till hdd entering last 2 fs, one pace*........ (25 to 1 op 20 to 1) 4
1000 PLAIN FACT 8-9-5 D Holland (4) *in tch till rdn and outpcd 2 fs out*.............(2 to 1 op 6 to 4 tchd 9 to 4) 5
PRAIRIE DAWN 4-8-9 J Williams (3) *strted slwly, al wl beh.* .... (50 to 1 op 33 to 1 tchd 66 to 1) 6

Dist: 2½l, 1½l, ¾l, 2l, 5l. 1m 2.42s. a 2.92s (6 Ran).

SR: 66/56/51/22/39/9/ (Rex L Mead), G B Balding

1669 Allied Dunbar Handicap Class D (3-y-o and up) £4,221 1¾m............(4:25)

1380[7] MULL HOUSE [72] 6-9-6 W R Swinburn (11) *rcd in 4th pl, led wl o'r one furlong out, rdn out.* .... (9 to 1 op 8 to 1 tchd 10 to 1) 1
1430[4] CHAMPAGNE GOLD [58] 6-8-6 J Williams (10) *hdwy 6 out, ev ch frm o'r one furlong out, not quicken nr line.* ....(10 to 1 tchd 12 to 1) 2
1268[4] PROSEQUENDO (USA) [65] 6-8-13 A Clark (9) *mid-div, ran on 6 fs out, sstnd chal frm 2 out, kpt on same pace.* ....(8 to 1 op 7 to 1 tchd 9 to 1) 3
322[2] MAJESTIC IMAGE [73] 7-9-4 (3*) D Harrison (7) *ran on frm rear 3 fs out, rdn and swtchd lft o'r one out, styd on cl hme*..........(11 to 4 fav op 5 to 2 tchd 3 to 1) 4
1430[3] ALQAIRAWAAN [57] 4-8-5 B Rouse (4) *led for 2 fs, chsd ldr, led o'r two out, hdd over one out, ran on same pace.* .... (11 to 2 op 5 to 1 tchd 6 to 1) 5
988[7] ROSGILL [66] 7-9-0 P Robinson (1) *hld up, improved frm rear o'r 3 fs out, rdn and effrt over one out, no imprsn.* .... (9 to 1 op 6 to 1 tchd 10 to 1) 6
1457[9] BOLD RESOLUTION (Ire) [60] 5-8-8 M Roberts (5) *hld up in rear, effrt 3 fs out, no extr appr last.* (8 to 1 op 10 to 1) 7
ELEGANT KING (Ire) [65] 4-8-13 S Whitworth (12) *rcd in 3rd pl till wknd o'r 2 fs out.* .... (20 to 1 op 14 to 1 tchd 25 to 1) 8
1353[3] INTRICACY [47] 5-7-9 G Bardwell (8) *mid-div, rdn and effrt 3 fs out, wknd 2 out*.......... (14 to 1 op 12 to 1) 9
1430[5] SARAZAR (USA) [50] 4-7-12 J Quinn (2) *led aftr 2 fs, hdd o'r two out, lost tch over one out*.......(13 to 2 op 9 to 2) 10
APACHE PRINCE [60] 6-8-8 L Dettori (3) *rcd towards rear, lost tch 3 out, tld off*.....................................(50 to 1) 11
VITAL CLUE (USA) [80] 6-10-0 M Perrett (6) *al beh, lost tch 5 out, tld off*..................................(33 to 1 op 25 to 1) 12

Dist: ½l, 1½l, nk, sht-hd, 2½l, 6l, 2l, 1l, 4l, dist. 3m 7.54s. a 13.24s (12 Ran).

SR: 30/15/19/26/9/13/ (M Lowry), F J O'Mahony

1670 DTZ Debenham Thorpe Property Handicap Class C (0-100 3-y-o) £5,550 1m 1f..........................(5:00)

1069 BRANDONHURST [77] 8-11 L Dettori (8) *mid-div, ran on 3 fs out, swtchd lft 2 out, sstnd run to ld last strd.* ....(10 to 1 tchd 12 to 1) 1
1346[6] BLUE BLAZER [78] 8-12 B Raymond (2) *mid-div, cld on ldrs 3 fs out, led and edgd rght o'r one out, hdd on line.* ....(7 to 2 jt-fav op 5 to 2 tchd 4 to 1) 2
1483[3] DON'T JUMP (Ire) [75] 8-9 P Robinson (7) *sn led, clr appr hfwy, hdd o'r one furlong out, soon outpcd.* ....(7 to 1 op 5 to 1 tchd 8 to 1) 3
1388* THE EXECUTOR [79] 8-13 (5ex) T Sprake (1) *hld up in rear, hdwy o'r 2 fs out, one pace ins last.* ....(6 to 1 tchd 13 to 2) 4
1451[3] MR VINCENT [76] 8-7 (3*) D Harrison (6) *ldg grp, ev ch 2 fs out, not much room o'r one out, sn btn*.......(7 to 2 jt-fav op 4 to 1 tchd 5 to 1) 5
1346[7] TRIPPIANO [76] 8-10 Pat Eddery (4) *trkd ldrs, rdn and not quicken 2 fs out, not much room o'r one out, eased whn btn*.................. (6 to 1 tchd 5 to 1 and 13 to 2) 6

1016 WYNONA (Ire) [87] 9-7 W R Swinburn (5) *hld up in rear, moderate effrt o'r 3 fs out, not trble ldrs.* ....(10 to 1 tchd 14 to 1) 7
1471[5] DANNY BOY [85] 9-5 M Roberts (3) *prmnt till drpd rear 5 fs out*...................................(7 to 1 op 6 to 1) 8

Dist: Sht-hd, 6l, 1½l, sht-hd, 3l, 3½l, nk. 1m 57.82s. a 6.62s (8 Ran).

SR: 52/52/31/30/26/17/17/14/ (R P B Michaelson), I A Balding

1671 June Maiden Stakes Class D (3-y-o) £3,707 1¼m 7yds.............. (5:30)

1344[4] LEARMONT (USA) 9-0 M Roberts (8) *made all, pushed out fnl furlong, kpt on wl*.......... (13 to 8 fav op 2 to 1) 1
GRADIENT 9-0 W Newnes (5) *hdwy frm rear o'r 5 fs out, chsd wnr appr fnl furlong, styd on cl hme.* .... (10 to 1 op 7 to 1 tchd 12 to 1) 2
LAILATI (USA) 8-9 W R Swinburn (6) *trkd ldr, ev ch 2 fs out, shaken up and not quicken appr fnl furlong.* .... (15 to 2 op 5 to 1 tchd 8 to 1) 3
PISH KESH 8-9 A Clark (7) *chsd frnt rnk, rdn and one pace frm 2 fs out*.................. (33 to 1 op 16 to 1) 4
EL JUBAIL (Ire) 9-0 Pat Eddery (2) *strted slwly, effrt o'r 3 out, no imprsn last 2 fs.* (2 to 1 op 6 to 4 tchd 9 to 4) 5
MENHAAD (Ire) 8-9 S Whitworth (1) *slwly into strd, al rear grp*.................. (9 to 1 op 5 to 1 tchd 10 to 1) 6
VISHNU (USA) 9-0 A McGlone (4) *dwlt, nvr nr to chal.* .... (20 to 1 op 10 to 1 tchd 25 to 1) 7
MONAZITE 9-0 B Raymond (3) *in tch in mid-div till lost pl o'r 2 fs out*.................. (14 to 1 tchd 20 to 1) 8

Dist: ½l, 2½l, 3½l, 2½l, 1l, 2l, 2½l. 2m 15.94s. a 12.04s (8 Ran).

SR: 20/19/9/2/2/ (Sheikh Mohammed), J H M Gosden

SOUTHWELL (A.W) (std)

Friday June 11th

Going Correction: MINUS 0.25 sec. per fur.

1672 Spinal Injuries Association Maiden Auction Stakes Class F (2-y-o) £2,399 5f..............................(2:30)

933[3] HALI (Ire) 9-0 G Duffield (1) *sn outpcd and rdn alng, gd hdwy o'r 2 fs out, ridden to ld ins last, ran on.* ....(7 to 4 op Evens) 1
1339[2] FLOATING TRIAL 8-9 J Carroll (3) *led, rdn 2 fs out, hdd and no extr ins last*..... (6 to 4 fav tchd 7 to 4 and 2 to 1) 2
FUSSY HEN 8-9 L Charnock (4) *dwlt and beh, styd on fnl 2 fs*.. (5 to 1 op 3 to 1) 3
1499[6] SHARP SUMMIT (Ire) 8-9 S Wood (2) *cl up, rdn hfwy, sn wknd and edgd lft*..................(8 to 1 op 6 to 1) 4
1229 MAZZA 8-9 G Hind (5) *cl up, rdn and wknd 2 fs out.* ....(20 to 1 op 16 to 1) 5

Dist: ¾l, 4l, 1l, 2l. 1m 1.20s. a 3.30s (5 Ran).

SR: 9/1/ (Donald Cooper), Mrs N Macauley

1673 Supertherm Median Auction Maiden Stakes Class D (3-y-o) £3,084 1m (3:00)

1500[3] CHARLIE BIGTIME 8-11 (3*) J Weaver (2) *trkd ldrs, smooth hdwy to ld o'r one furlong out, sn clr.* ....(5 to 4 on op 6 to 4) 1
1005[7] TEJANO GOLD (USA) (bl) 8-7 (7*) T G McLaughlin (4) *led, rdn o'r 2 fs out, hdd and one pace over one out.* .... (9 to 4 op 11 to 10) 2
SURAGON 9-0 N Adams (3) *pld hrd, cl up, effrt to chal 2 fs out, sn rdn and wknd appr fnl furlong.* .... (6 to 1 op 8 to 1 tchd 10 to 1) 3
ZASTOI 9-0 R Price (1) *slwly away, al outpcd and wl beh.* ....(6 to 1 op 4 to 1) 4

Dist: 5l, 12l, 20l. 1m 42.10s. a 3.10s (4 Ran).

SR: 24/9/-/-/ (Ron Dawson), Miss Gay Kelleway

1674 Gala Clubs Selling Handicap Class G (0-60 3-y-o and up) £2,679 1m... (3:30)

975[7] ROCKY BAY [32] 4-8-0 A Mackay (12) *mid-div, hdwy 3 fs out, led 2 out, sn rdn and ran on gmely ins last.* .... (14 to 1 op 10 to 1) 1
1419[6] CORONA GOLD [50] (bl,e/s) 3-8-7 K Fallon (15) *al cl up, effrt to chal 2 fs out, sn rdn and ev ch till no extr nr finish*..............................(16 to 1 op 10 to 1) 2
1578[9] IRISH ROOTS (Ire) [46] (v) 3-8-3[3] (3*) J Weaver (5) *chsd ldrs, hdwy 3 fs out, rdn 2 out, kpt on one pace.* .... (12 to 1 op 7 to 1) 3
1232 LIFE'S A BREEZE [39] 4-8-0 (7*) D McCabe (10) *hld up and beh, gd hdwy o'r 2 fs out, rdn and ran on wl ins last, nrst finish*.................. (25 to 1 op 20 to 1) 4
1501[2] BACKSTABBER [58] 3-9-1 G Hind (9) *chsd ldrs, effrt 3 fs out, sn rdn, wknd appr last.* ....(11 to 8 fav tchd 5 to 4 and 6 to 4) 5
1422[5] TAKE YOUR PARTNER (Ire) [56] 3-8-13 T Williams (2) *chsd ldrs, rdn 2 fs, kpt on one pace*..... (12 to 1 op 6 to 1) 6
1191[7] WALSHAM WITCH [57] (bl) 3-8-9 (5*) C Hodgson (11) *mid-div, hdwy and wide strt, rdn 2 fs out, sn btn.* ....(12 to 1 tchd 14 to 1) 7
1453[6] SKIMMER HAWK [33] 4-8-1 G Duffield (13) *al mid-div.* .... (8 to 1 op 10 to 1) 8

906 PERSIAN LION [34] 4-8-2[4] R Price (3) *nvr rch ldrs.* (33 to 1) 9
531 CYRILL HENRY (Ire) [39] (v) 4-8-7 S Webster (1) *al rear.* ....(20 to 1 tchd 25 to 1) 10
1423[9] JOELLISE [39] (bl) 3-7-10 L Charnock (16) *cl up, led o'r 3 fs out, rdn and hdd 2 out, sn wknd*..............(50 to 1) 11
1358[4] SALLY'S SON [58] 7-9-12 S Wood (6) *al rear.* .... (16 to 1 op 6 to 1) 12
1035[3] SPEED OIL [41] (bl) 4-8-9 N Connorton (4) *nvr a factor.* ....(6 to 1 op 5 to 1 tchd 7 to 1 and 8 to 1) 13
1072[6] NEVENTER (Fr) [56] 4-9-10 D Nicholls (14) *slwly into strd, al rear*..............................(20 to 1 op 12 to 1) 14
620 MERLS PEARL [34] (bl) 4-8-2 N Adams (7) *led, hdd and wknd o'r 3 fs out*.....................(11 to 1 op 33 to 1) 15
742[6] MY BALLYBOY [50] (bl) 3-8-7 J Carroll (8) *al rear.* ....(14 to 1 op 12 to 1) 16

Dist: ½l, 1½l, sht-hd, 2½l, 2l, 2l, 2l, 2½l, 1½l, ½l. 1m 42.80s. a 3.80s (16 Ran).
SR: -/4/-/-/-/-/ (Miss Karen Harris), D Haydn Jones

1675 British Coal Nottinghamshire Group Handicap Class E (0-70 3-y-o) £3,080 7f ....(4:00)

966[7] YUNUS EMRE (Ire) [48] 8-3 K Fallon (9) *hld up, gd hdwy on outer o'r 2 fs out, rdn to ld over one out, ran on.* ....(14 to 1 op 10 to 1) 1
1496[3] PERSONIMUS [43] 7-12 L Charnock (7) *chsd ldrs, hdwy 3 fs out, effrt to ld briefly wl o'r one and a half out, sn hdd and kpt on one pace.* ....(6 to 1 op 7 to 1 tchd 8 to 1) 2
1137[7] RED FAN (Ire) [66] (bl) 9-7 N Connorton (2) *led, hdd 2 and a half fs out, sn hrd rdn and cl up till no extr entering fnl furlong*.............................. (8 to 1 op 6 to 1) 3
1634* VELASCO (Ire) [64] 9-5 (6ex) G Duffield (3) *beh and sn pushed alng, hdwy o'r 2 fs out, styd on und pres ins last.* (5 to 4 on op 5 to 4 on tchd Evens and 11 to 10) 4
1273 NORTH ARDAR [62] 9-3 T Williams (6) *chsd ldrs, effrt and hdwy to chal 2 fs out, sn rdn and wknd o'r one out.* ....(9 to 1 op 5 to 1) 5
1247 DONTBETALKING (Ire) [45] 8-0 N Adams (5) *chsd ldrs to hfwy, sn wknd*....................(25 to 1 op 20 to 1) 6
1397[5] DEAD CALM [60] (v) 8-12 (3*) J Weaver (1) *chsd ldrs, hdwy hfwy, rdn o'r 2 fs out, sn wknd.* ....(12 to 1 op 10 to 1 tchd 14 to 1) 7
1455[9] ROSE FLYER (Ire) [58] 8-6 (7*) D McCabe (4) *cl up, led 2 and a half fs out to one and a half out, grad wknd.* .... (10 to 1 op 8 to 1) 8
EASY TOUCH [47] 8-2 A Mackay (8) *slwly away, al beh.* .... (40 to 1 op 33 to 1) 9

Dist: 2½l, hd, hd, 1½l, 5l, ¾l, nk, nk. 1m 29.70s. a 3.60s (9 Ran).
SR: 9/-/18/15/8/-/ (Yucel Birol), M Bell

1676 Pretty Polly Limited Stakes Class E (0-70 4-y-o and up) £2,769 1½m (4:30)

1531[5] PHARLY DANCER 4-9-0 S Webster (1) *chsd ldrs, rdn o'r 2 fs out, styd on to ld entering last, ran on.* ....(6 to 1 op 5 to 1 tchd 7 to 1) 1
1276[2] SHUJAN (USA) 4-9-0 G Carter (2) *made most, quickened 3 fs out, rdn 2 out, hdd entering last, kpt on.* ....(5 to 2 on op 15 to 8 on tchd 7 to 4 on) 2
1075[4] SUGEMAR 7-8-7 (7*) D McCabe (6) *hld up, hdwy 4 fs out, effrt and rdn to chal one out, no extr wl ins last.* .... (8 to 1 op 11 to 2) 3
SMILES AHEAD 5-9-0 J Carroll (3) *cl up, rdn o'r 3 fs out, sn wknd*.. (12 to 1 op 8 to 1) 4
1566[9] ANAR (Ire) 4-8-9 (5*) O Pears (4) *in tch, rdn alng 5 fs out, effrt and wide strt, sn wknd*.......(12 to 1 op 10 to 1) 5
910 GREAT ORATION (Ire) 4-9-0 L Charnock (7) *in tch, effrt and some hdwy 5 fs out, sn wknd*...... (50 to 1 op 25 to 1) 6
1075[5] HEIR OF EXCITEMENT 8-9-0 T Williams (5) *chsd ldrs, rdn hfwy, wknd o'r 4 fs out, sn wl beh.* ....(20 to 1 op 14 to 1 tchd 25 to 1) 7

Dist: 1½l, hd, 20l, 8l, 1½l, 20l. 2m 36.20s. a 2.30s (7 Ran).
SR: 47/44/43/3/ (A Marucci), W W Haigh

1677 Bass Leisure/Spinal Injuries Association Handicap Class E (0-70 3-y-o and up) £2,976 5f..................(5:00)

1249* SUPERLATIVEMAXIMUS (Ire) [56] 5-9-2 (3*) J Weaver (7) *chsd ldrs, pushed alng hfwy, hdwy 2 fs out, rdn to chal, edgd lft appr fnl furlong, led ins last, ran on.* ....(11 to 4 fav op 2 to 1 tchd 3 to 1) 1
1492[3] TRIOMING [51] 7-9-0 N Adams (4) *chsd ldrs, hdwy and ev ch whn hmpd and swtchd entering fnl furlong, ran on.* ....(6 to 1 op 4 to 1 tchd 7 to 1) 2
1503* MISS WHITTINGHAM (Ire) [55] 3-8-10 (7ex) J Carroll (6) *outpcd and beh, styd on fnl 2 fs, nvr dngrs.* ....(3 to 1 op 11 to 4 tchd 100 to 30) 3
1492[5] LE CHIC [53] 7-9-2 S Wood (2) *led, clr o'r 2 fs out, rdn one and a half out, hdd and wknd entering last.* .... (5 to 1 op 4 to 1 tchd 11 to 2) 4
1394 NO QUARTER GIVEN [65] 8-10-0 G Duffield (3) *chsd ldrs, rdn and wknd 2 fs out.* (5 to 1 op 8 to 1 tchd 12 to 1) 5
1249[8] MAID WELCOME [60] (bl) 6-9-2 (7*) Madeleine Smith (1) *chsd ldrs, rdn and wknd o'r 2 fs out*..... (12 to 1 op 7 to 1) 6

1148 EVER SO LONELY [56] 4-8-12 (7*) W Hawksley (5) *chsd ldr, rdn 2 fs out, sn wknd*...............(11 to 1 op 7 to 1) 7

Dist: 1½l, 1l, sht-hd, 6l, 3l, ½l. 59.60s. a 1.70s (7 Ran).
SR: 46/35/27/32/20/3/-/ (Ray Champion), J A Bennett

YORK (good to soft)
Friday June 11th
Going Correction: PLUS 0.30 sec. per fur. (races 1,4,5,7), PLUS 0.45 (2,3,6)

1678 Merchant Adventurers Maiden Stakes Class D (3-y-o) £4,518 1m 5f 194yds ....(2:10)

985[2] ALINOVA (USA) 8-9 M Roberts (2) *made all, pushed clr o'r one out, easily*............(3 to 1 on tchd 11 to 4 on) 1
1426[4] COLLIER BAY 9-0 W Carson (3) *trkd wnr, effrt 3 out, no imprsn*.................(11 to 4 op 5 to 2 tchd 3 to 1) 2
567[5] CARA'S PRIDE 8-9 Dale Gibson (1) *in tch, pushed alng 4 out, btn 3 out*..................... (20 to 1 op 16 to 1) 3

Dist: 3l, 1l. 3m 7.11s. a 12.11s (3 Ran).
SR: 16/15/8/ (Sheikh Mohammed), H R A Cecil

1679 Stones Best Bitter Handicap Class C (0-100 3-y-o and up) £6,316 5f... (2:40)

1560[2] CATHERINES WELL [71] 10-7-13[1] K Darley (5) *in tch, hdwy and swtchd o'r one furlong out, ran on wl to ld well ins last*.....................(15 to 2 op 7 to 1 tchd 8 to 1) 1
1301[3] NEVER IN THE RED [81] (bl) 5-8-9 J Fortune (11) *cl up, led 2 fs out till hdd and no extr wl ins last*..........(8 to 1) 2
1188[2] MACFARLANE [75] 5-8-3 F Norton (3) *beh, styd on wl fnl 2 fs, nrst finish*..................... (8 to 1 op 10 to 1) 3
4672a[7] HEAVEN-LIEGH-GREY [68] 5-7-10 N Carlisle (7) *dwlt, beh, hdwy hfwy, styd on wl fnl furlong, nrst finish.* ....(16 to 1 tchd 20 to 1) 4
1494[7] GONDO [67] (bl) 6-7-2 (7*) D Wright (10) *prmnt, ev ch 2 fs out, one pace*..(12 to 1) 5
1406[5] MEDAILLE D'OR [100] (v) 5-10-0 R Cochrane (1) *mid-div, kpt on same pace fnl 2 fs*............................(12 to 1) 6
1215 DRUM SERGEANT [83] (bl) 6-8-11 L Piggott (2) *hld up, effrt o'r 2 fs out, no hdwy*............................(10 to 1) 7
1215[8] BEAU VENTURE (USA) [86] 5-8-11 (3*) N Kennedy (4) *mid-div, no hdwy fnl 2 fs*............................(12 to 1) 8
1113 PALLIUM (Ire) [72] 5-8-0 D Biggs (12) *in tch, no hdwy fnl 2 fs*.. (20 to 1) 9
1127[4] VERDE ALITALIA (Ire) [77] 4-8-5 W Carson (13) *prmnt till wknd 2 fs out*.......(7 to 2 fav op 5 to 2 tchd 4 to 1) 10
1420[2] NED'S BONANZA [69] 4-7-11 J Lowe (14) *chsd ldrs till wknd 2 fs out*..(8 to 1) 11
1083[4] BENZOE (Ire) [83] 3-8-3 Paul Eddery (9) *nvr nr ldrs.* .... (14 to 1 op 12 to 1) 12
1449[4] SIGAMA (USA) [78] 7-8-6 R Lappin (6) *led to 2 fs out, wknd quickly*...............(11 to 1 op 8 to 1 tchd 12 to 1) 13

Dist: 1½l, 1½l, ¾l, ¾l, ½l, ¾l, ½l, nk, 1½l, ¾l. 1m 0.59s. a 3.29s (13 Ran).
SR: 64/68/56/46/42/73/54/39/ (K Hodgson), M W Easterby

1680 Innovative Marketing Sprint Rated Class B Handicap (0-100 3-y-o and up) £14,114 6f..................... (3:10)

1301[2] DOMINUET [89] 8-8-10 J Lowe (4) *in tch gng wl, headay to ld ins fnl furlong, ran on well*.............(13 to 2 co-fav op 6 to 1) 1
1113[2] SIR HARRY HARDMAN [94] 5-9-1 R Cochrane (2) *mid-div, hdwy to ld wl o'r one furlong out, hdd and no extr ins last*.............................. (7 to 1 tchd 8 to 1) 2
1348[5] VENTURE CAPITALIST [93] (bl) 4-9-0 W Carson (1) *beh, hdwy o'r one furlong out, fnshd wl*........(13 to 2 co-fav op 6 to 1) 3
1394[3] RED ROSEIN [86] 7-8-7 G Carter (3) *dwlt, beh, hdwy 2 fs out, kpt on fnl furlong*.............. (7 to 1 op 6 to 1) 4
1205[6] BOLD LEZ [100] 6-9-7 J Reid (12) *beh, hdwy, hng lft and ev ch o'r one furlong out, wknd fnl furlong.* ....(7 to 1 op 6 to 1) 5
RESOLUTE BAY [86] 7-8-7 A Culhane (10) *in tch, outpcd o'r one furlong out, kpt on wl fnl furlong.* .... (50 to 1 op 33 to 1) 6
1113[3] SIZZLING SAGA (Ire) [100] 5-9-7 K Darley (7) *cl up, led o'r 2 fs out till wl over one out, sn wknd*...........(16 to 1) 7
986 DOUBLE BLUE [94] 4-9-1 Dean McKeown (11) *led till o'r 2 fs out, fdd*.......(13 to 2 co-fav op 6 to 1 tchd 7 to 1) 8
1205[5] MASTER OF PASSION [93] 4-9-0 L Piggott (9) *dwlt, sn in tch, one pace fnl 2 fs*... (15 to 2 op 8 to 1 tchd 7 to 1) 9
1348[7] FINJAN [86] 6-8-7 M Hills (13) *chsd ldrs, wkng whn hmpd o'r one furlong out*................(16 to 1 op 14 to 1) 10
1301[5] CRYSTAL JACK (Fr) [86] 5-8-7 Paul Eddery (6) *prmnt till wknd 2 fs out*..(14 to 1) 11
MACROBIAN [94] 9-9-1 M Birch (5) *prmnt to hfwy, wknd quickly, tld off*...................(16 to 1 op 12 to 1) 12

Dist: 1½l, 1½l, sht-hd, 2l, 2½l, hd, ½l, sht-hd, ½l, 5l. 1m 14.06s. a 4.06s (12 Ran).
SR: 69/68/61/53/59/35/48/40/38/ (Mrs Robert Heathcote), J L Spearing

1681 Shepherd Construction Apprentice Handicap Class E (0-90 4-y-o and up) £5,208 1m 3f 195yds............(3:40)

1336[6] HIGHFLYING [70] 7-8-13 J Tate (6) *trkd ldrs, hdwy to ld 2 fs out, styd on wl*......................(11 to 2 op 9 to 2) 1
1531[2] PHILGUN [60] 4-8-3 M Humphries (3) *trkd ldrs, effrt 3 fs out, styd on wl fnl furlong*.......(3 to 1 fav op 4 to 1) 2
1392* BIG PAT [57] 4-7-9 (5*,7ex) Elizabeth Turner (7) *sn cl up, led o'r 3 fs out to 2 out, kpt on same pace*. (5 to 1 op 4 to 1) 3
MELLABY (USA) [83] 5-9-7 (5*) K Pattinson (2) *in tch, outpcd 4 fs out, kpt on frm 2 out*.......... (5 to 1 op 7 to 2) 4
1328[7] LEGION OF HONOUR [65] 5-8-8 V Halliday (1) *led till o'r 3 fs out, fdd*............................ (8 to 1 tchd 9 to 1) 5
1328[5] REDSTELLA (USA) [85] 4-9-11 (3*) G Parkin (5) *prmnt, rdn 5 fs out, ev ch o'r 3 out, sn wknd*.
.... (9 to 1 op 8 to 1 tchd 10 to 1) 6
1307 GOLDEN TORQUE [66] 6-8-9 H Bastiman (9) *al beh*.
.....................................(10 to 1 tchd 11 to 1) 7
1593[5] KILLICK [54] 5-7-11 D Wright (8) *in tch, rdn o'r 3 fs out, sn btn*....................................(8 to 1 tchd 9 to 1) 8
1375[8] BAYIN (USA) [50] 4-7-7 C Hawksley (4) *al beh*.
.... (50 to 1 op 33 to 1) 9

Dist: ¾l, 2½l, 5l, 6l, 2½l, 3½l, ½l, ½l. 2m 35.97s. a 7.97s (9 Ran).
SR: 55/43/35/51/21/36/10/-/-/ (B Batey), G M Moore

1682 Harcros Timber And Building Supplies Ltd Stayers Championship Series Rated Qualifier Class B Handica (0-95 4-y-o and up) £6,396 1m 5f 194yds........................ (4:10)

773[4] QUICK RANSOM [85] 5-8-12 Dean McKeown (5) *trkd ldrs, not much room o'r 3 fs out, swtchd over 2 out, led over one out, styd on wl*. (7 to 2 fav op 3 to 1 tchd 4 to 1) 1
1328[2] DREAMS END [83] 5-8-10 R Cochrane (2) *hld up, hdwy o'r 2 fs out, ev ch entering last, kpt on, no imprsn*.
....(8 to 1 op 7 to 1) 2
1041[2] KAISER WILHELM [86] 4-8-13 W Ryan (7) *trkd ldrs, led o'r 2 fs out till over one out, one pace*.
.... (11 to 2 op 5 to 1 tchd 6 to 1) 3
682[8] SARAWAT [80] 5-8-7 F Norton (1) *prmnt, kpt on same pace frm 3 fs out*........................(7 to 1 tchd 8 to 1) 4
1129* CASTLE COURAGEOUS [94] 6-9-7 J Reid (4) *led till o'r 2 fs out, fdd*............................ (8 to 1 tchd 9 to 1) 5
757* CRYSTAL CROSS (USA) [82] 4-8-9 M Hills (6) *cl up, ev ch 3 fs out, wknd 2 out*......(13 to 2 op 6 to 1 tchd 7 to 1) 6
SATIN LOVER [87] 5-9-0 L Piggott (8) *al beh*.
.... (11 to 1 op 8 to 1) 7
1430* PHARAMINEUX [80] 7-8-7 (3ex) W Carson (3) *hld up, effrt 3 fs out, btn 2 out, eased fnl furlong*... (4 to 1 op 3 to 1) 8

Dist: 2½l, 3½l, hd, 7l, 1½l, 2½l, 7l. 3m 4.33s. a 9.33s (8 Ran).
SR: 47/40/36/29/29/14/14/-/ (J S Morrison), M Johnston

1683 University Of York Turf Club Conditions Stakes Class C (2-y-o) £4,553 6f ....(4:40)

1446[2] QUEENBIRD 8-13 W Ryan (4) *set steady pace, quickened hfwy, ran on strly fnl furlong*...(5 to 4 on tchd Evens) 1
1437[2] SINNERS REPRIEVE 8-13 M Birch (1) *trkd ldrs gng wl, effrt and chsd wnr o'r one furlong out, no imprsn*.
....(5 to 2 tchd 9 to 4) 2
1350* TAMAR'S BRIGADE 8-13 J Reid (3) *trkd ldrs, effrt o'r 2 fs out, kpt on wl fnl furlong*.......... (10 to 1 op 8 to 1) 3
1418* ELECTION SPECIAL 8-13 M Tebbutt (2) *wth ldr, rdn o'r 2 fs out, sn wknd*......................(9 to 2 op 7 to 2) 4
1229[8] MATISSE 8-11 Dean McKeown (5) *in tch till wknd 2 fs out*.
....(33 to 1) 5

Dist: 4l, 1½l, 4l, 2½l. 1m 17.02s. a 7.02s (5 Ran).
SR: 13/-/ (A S Reid), H R A Cecil

1684 Levy Board Rating Related Maiden Stakes Class D (0-80 3-y-o) £3,590 1¼m 85yds..................... (5:10)

1115[3] LICORNE 8-9 W Ryan (3) *trkd ldrs, led wl o'r one furlong out, pushed clr*.... (6 to 5 fav op 5 to 4 tchd 11 to 10) 1
1256[3] ANORAK (USA) 9-0 R Cochrane (2) *cl up, led o'r 4 fs out till wl over one out, kpt on, no ch wth wnr*.
.... (13 to 8 op 11 to 8) 2
1176 ARMENIAN COFFEE (Ire) 9-0 J Reid (4) *led till ran wide and hdd o'r 4 fs out, rdn over 3 out, wknd*.
.... (11 to 2 op 5 to 1) 3
1223[3] SAKURA QUEEN (Ire) 8-9 W Woods (1) *in tch till wknd o'r 2 fs out*.............................. (10 to 1 op 8 to 1) 4

Dist: 8l, 3½l, 3l. 2m 16.89s. a 8.89s (4 Ran).
SR: 38/27/20/9/ (Lord Howard de Walden), H R A Cecil

BATH (good (races 1,2,3), good to soft (4,5,6))

Saturday June 12th

Going Correction: PLUS 0.15 sec. per fur. (races 1,2), PLUS 0.25 (3,4), PLUS 0.30 (5,6)

1685 June Selling Stakes Class G (3-y-o and up) £2,658 1¼m 46yds......(2:00)

1626[6] SINCLAIR LAD (Ire) (bl) 5-9-3 (7*) S Drowne (3) *slwly into strd sn reco'red to track ldrs, hrd rdn 2 fs out, ran on fnl furlong, led last strides*...................(10 to 1) 1
1458[6] OVERPOWER 9-9-10 B Rouse (16) *hdwy 5 fs out, led on bit one and a half furlongs out, rdn ins last, ct last strds*.. (15 to 2) 2
AMBASSADOR ROYALE (Ire) (bl) 5-9-10 J Williams (14) *beh till hdwy frm 3 fs out, styd on same pace appr fnl furlong*...(5 to 1) 3
1146 DAZZLING FIRE (Ire) 4-8-12 (7*) Kim McDonnell (11) *hdwy 3 fs out, outpcd appr fnl furlong*............... (14 to 1) 4
1425[5] VANROY (v) 9-9-10 S Whitworth (2) *in tch, hdwy 3 fs out, rdn and hng rght 2 furlongs out, sn btn*.......(3 to 1) 5
1349[6] BEAT THE BAGMAN (Ire) 3-8-6 C Avery (5) *effrt 3 fs out, sn one pace*.. (50 to 1) 6
1375[9] TOUT DE VAL 4-9-0 R Perham (9) *nvr rch ldrs*....(50 to 1) 7
1471[6] DON'T GIVE UP (bl) 5-9-5 (5*) D Meredith (17) *chsd ldrs till led o'r 3 fs out, hdd and wknd one and a half furlongs out*..(14 to 1) 8
327 PRECIOUS CAROLINE (Ire) 5-9-0 J Lowe (6) *al beh*.
....(33 to 1) 9
327 YOUNG JAMES 5-9-5 A Tucker (18) *prmnt till ran wide and wknd 5 fs out*..................................... (50 to 1) 10
1353[6] SIMON ELLIS (Ire) 4-9-5 T Williams (10) *chsd ldrs till wknd 3 fs out*...(33 to 1) 11
763[2] QUELQUE CHOSE 3-8-6 D Holland (7) *chsd ldrs till wknd 4 fs out*...(5 to 2 fav) 12
1266 KENNINGTON PROTON 3-8-1 N Adams (4) *led till hdd and wknd o'r 2 fs out*.................................. (50 to 1) 13
1416 FRANKIE GOODMAN (Ire) 3-8-6 J Comber (8) *al beh*.
....(50 to 1) 14
1059 OYSTON'S LIFE 4-9-3 (7*) Antoinette Armes (13) *al beh*.
....(50 to 1) 15
ZINJAAL (Ire) 3-8-1 (5*) Stephen Davies (15) *pressed ldr till wknd 4 fs out*...(50 to 1) 16

Dist: Sht-hd, 3½l, 1½l, 1l, 5l, 2l, 1½l, 1l, 4l, 4l. 2m 16.30s. a 9.90s (16 Ran).
SR: 26/25/18/10/13/-/ (Miss R Dobson), R J Hodges

1686 Rothmans Royals North South Challenge Series Handicap Class D (0-80 3-y-o and up) £3,622 1m 5yds... (2:30)

BOLD ACRE [62] 3-8-10 (5*) Stephen Davies (9) *outpcd aftr 2 fs, hdwy on outsd after two furlongs out, styd on to ld last strds*............................(20 to 1 op 8 to 1) 1
1373[9] MUSTAHIL (Ire) [60] 4-9-10 R Perham (2) *broke wl, rdn to stay in tch aftr 2 fs, hdwy on rls to chal o'r one furlong out, led ins last, ct last strds*........(12 to 1 op 8 to 1) 2
1453[2] SOOTY TERN [45] 6-8-9 N Adams (8) *chsd ldrs till led 3 fs out, hdd ins last, no extr cl hme*.
...........................(6 to 1 op 4 to 1 tchd 13 to 2) 3
1097[4] SAREEN EXPRESS (Ire) [45] 5-8-9 J Lowe (1) *hld up, hdwy 3 fs out, ev ch one furlong out, styd on*.
....(6 to 1 op 4 to 1) 4
1474[3] PROUD BRIGADIER (Ire) [58] 5-9-8 P Robinson (3) *chsd ldrs, ev ch 2 fs out, wknd one furlong out*.
........................(9 to 4 fav tchd 5 to 2 and 2 to 1) 5
1120 ICE STRIKE (USA) [41] (bl) 4-8-5 D Holland (4) *led aftr one furlong, hdd 3 fs out, wknd 2 furlongs out*.
.... (6 to 1 op 14 to 1) 6
1257[2] PRECIOUS AIR (Ire) [54] 5-9-4 B Rouse (6) *effrt 3 fs out, not pace to chal*..........................(9 to 2 op 3 to 1) 7
1356* SOVIET EXPRESS [66] 3-8-12 (7*) D Goggin (5) *led one furlong, styd prmnt till ran wide 5 fs out, not reco'r*.
....(7 to 1 op 5 to 1) 8

Dist: Hd, ¾l, hd, 3½l, 5l, ¾l, 10l. 1m 45.80s. a 6.80s (8 Ran).
SR: 17/25/8/7/9/ (Mrs Marion C Morgan), D Burchell

1687 Electric Handicap Class D (0-80 3-y-o and up) £4,207 5f 161yds........(3:00)

1492[2] MISTER JOLSON [66] 4-9-0 J Williams (7) *hld up, hdwy 2 fs out, led o'r one out, drvn out, jst held on*.
........................(11 to 4 fav op 9 to 4 tchd 3 to 1) 1
1127 FIVESEVENFIVEO [71] 5-8-12 (7*) S Drowne (3) *in tch, hdwy o'r one furlong out, chlgd wl ins last, no extr cl hme*..................(13 to 2 op 9 to 2 tchd 7 to 1) 2
1485[3] BALLASECRET [77] 5-9-6 (5*) D Meredith (5) *led till o'r one furlong out, one pace, fnshd 3rd, disqualified*.
.........................(3 to 1 op 5 to 2 tchd 100 to 30) 3D
1473 LETSBEONESTABOUTIT [70] (v) 7-8-11 (7*) B Russell (4) *sn chasing ldrs, outpcd frm o'r one furlong out, fnshd 4th, plcd 3rd*..................(6 to 1 op 5 to 1 tchd 7 to 1) 3
1394[5] BELLSABANGING [71] 3-8-10 T Williams (2) *hmpd aftr one furlong, chsd ldrs till wknd ins last 2, fnshd 5th, plcd 4th*..(3 to 1 op 11 to 4) 4
COSSACK NOIR [47] 5-7-9[2] J Lowe (6) *slwly into strd, al beh, fnshd 6th, plcd 5th*.
...........................(14 to 1 op 33 to 1 tchd 40 to 1) 5

Dist: Nk, 2l, 2½l, 3l, 12l. 1m 13.30s. a 3.90s (6 Ran).
SR: 51/55/53/36/16/-/ (J W Mursell), R J Hodges

1688 BonusPrint Handicap Class D (0-80 4-y-o and up) £3,687 2m 1f 34yds (3:30)

7027 GREEN LANE (USA) [60] 5-8-10 R Perham (4) *trkd ldrs, drvn to ld 2 fs out, styd on wl.* (7 to 4 fav tchd 9 to 4) 1
10945 SPECTACULAR DAWN [75] 4-9-10 W Ryan (7) *led 4 fs, led ag'n 9 furlongs out, hdd 2 furlongs out, one pace.* ....(9 to 2 op 7 to 2) 2
13455 JADIDH [47] 5-7-11 J Lowe (5) *beh till hdwy 5 fs out, no imprsn fnl 3 furlongs....* (4 to 1 op 7 to 2 tchd 9 to 2) 3
13539 CAROLES CLOWN [44] 7-7-8[1] N Adams (6) *chsd ldrs till outpcd 5 fs out, styd on ag'n frm 3 furlongs out.* ....(25 to 1 op 16 to 1) 4
1430 TOP SPIN [75] (bl) 4-9-10 S Whitworth (1) *hdwy frm 6 fs out, wknd from 3 furlongs out.* ....(5 to 1 op 4 to 1 tchd 11 to 4) 5
15643 ROYAL PRINT (Ire) [44] 4-7-0 (7*) Kim McDonnell (8) *led aftr 4 fs, hdd 9 furlongs out, pressed ldr till wknd ins fnl 3 furlongs*.... (8 to 1 op 6 to 1) 6
1321 PERFORATE [47] (bl) 4-7-10[3] D Biggs (2) *al beh.* ....(25 to 1 op 16 to 1) 7
4788a CHARMED LIFE [51] 4-8-0 A Tucker (3) *sn beh, hdwy 7 fs out, wknd 4 furlongs out*...... (20 to 1 tchd 16 to 1) 8
Dist: 2l, 10l, hd, 1l, 3l, 5l, ½l. 3m 58.70s. a 14.70s (8 Ran).
SR: -/4/-/-/-/ (R N C Lynch), R Akehurst

1689 Charlcombe Maiden Auction Stakes Class E (2-y-o) £2,859 5f 11yds..(4:00)

13503 CABCHARGE PRINCESS (Ire) 8-9 P Robinson (4) *trkd ldrs, swtchd rght and chlgd one furlong out, sn led, ran on wl*.... (5 to 4 fav tchd 6 to 4 and Evens) 1
12657 ARKADY (Ire) 9-0 W Ryan (8) *chsd ldrs till led o'r 2 fs out, hdd ins last, one pace.* (5 to 1 op 3 to 1 tchd 11 to 2) 2
5178 PRIMOST 9-0 J Williams (6) *outpcd and beh till hdwy o'r one furlong out, kpt on ins.* ....(20 to 1 op 16 to 1 tchd 25 to 1) 3
14186 DOCKYARD DORA 8-9 M Wigham (1) *hdwy and rdn o'r one furlong out, styd on.* ....(7 to 1 op 6 to 1 tchd 8 to 1) 4
13173 MAJOR SUCCESS (Ire) 9-0 D Holland (5) *led till hdd o'r 2 fs out, wknd ins*.... (7 to 2 op 5 to 2 tchd 4 to 1) 5
15356 SPORTING HEIR (Ire) 9-0 N Adams (2) *outpcd frm hfwy.* ....(33 to 1 op 20 to 1) 6
RED SLANEY (Ire) 9-0 R Perham (7) *outpcd frm hfwy.* ....(10 to 1 op 7 to 1 tchd 11 to 1) 7
Dist: 1l, 2l, hd, 1l, 7l, ½l. 1m 5.30s. a 4.80s (7 Ran).
SR: 29/30/22/16/17/-/-/ (Computer Cab Racing Club), M H Tompkins

1690 Bedminster Limited Stakes Class F (0-60 3-y-o) £2,665 1m 3f 144yds (4:35)

1371* ALLESCA 8-6 N Adams (9) *hdwy 5 fs out, led 2 and a half furlongs out, sn clr, eased considerably ins last.* ....(11 to 4 tchd 3 to 1) 1
11332 BUGLET 8-6 J Williams (11) *chsd ldrs till led 4 fs out, hdd 2 and a half furlongs out, sn one pace.* ....(2 to 1 fav op 7 to 4 tchd 11 to 8) 2
1068 KEDGE 8-11 P Robinson (4) *chsd ldrs till outpcd 4 fs out, drvn and ran on ag'n frm 2 furlongs out.* ....(25 to 1 op 14 to 1) 3
13517 SMART DAISY 8-6 S O'Gorman (8) *chsd ldrs till rdn and one pace fnl 3 fs*..... (10 to 1 op 12 to 1 tchd 14 to 1) 4
7075 GALEJADE 8-6 A Tucker (3) *prmnt early, lost pl 6 fs out, styd on ag'n frm 3 furlongs out.* ....(33 to 1 op 16 to 1 tchd 40 to 1) 5
1557* DODGY DANCER 8-11 S Whitworth (2) *rapid hdwy 4 fs out, wknd ins fnl 3 furlongs.* ....(13 to 2 op 5 to 1 tchd 7 to 1) 6
1351* KISMETIM 8-11 R Perham (1) *drpd rear hfwy, nvr dngrs aftr*.... (8 to 1 op 6 to 1 tchd 9 to 1) 7
1309 IS SHE QUICK 8-6 R Price (6) *sn beh.* (50 to 1 op 25 to 1) 8
582 M'BEBE 8-11 D Biggs (10) *in tch till wknd 5 fs out.* ....(7 to 1 op 10 to 1) 9
13515 QUEENS CONTRACTOR (bl) 8-11 D Holland (5) *led till hdd and wknd 4 fs out*.... (16 to 1 op 12 to 1) 10
Dist: 1l, 1l, 3½l, 2½l, 10l, 3½l, 10l, 12l, 10l. 2m 38.90s. a 11.90s (10 Ran).
SR: 8/6/9/-/-/-/ (Miss D G Kerr), I Usher 00

BELMONT PARK (USA) (firm)
Saturday June 12th

1691 Hempstead Handicap (Grade 1) (3-y-o and up) £59,603 1m 1f..............

1184* TURNBACK THE ALARM (USA) 4-8-7 C Antley, ...(14 to 10 fav) 1
DEPUTATION (USA) 4-8-5 Julie Krone,.... (16 to 10) 2
YOU'D BE SURPRISED (USA) 4-8-0 J D Bailey,.. (43 to 10) 3
5606 LOW TOLERANCE (USA) 4-8-2 H McCauley,.... (99 to 10) 4
11844 QUEEN OF TRIUMPH (USA) 4-7-13 J Pezua,.... (29 to 1) 5
11843 VIVANO (USA) 4-7-13 M Smith,.... (88 to 10) 6
Dist: 1½l, nose, 14l, 1l, 1 ¾l. 1m 48.14s. (6 Ran).
(Moyglare Stud Farm), W Terrill

EVRY (FR) (soft)
Saturday June 12th
Going Correction: NIL (race 1), PLUS 0.15 (2,3)

1692 Prix La Fleche (2-y-o) £14,337 5f 110yds.......................(2:55)

FOXHOUND (USA) 9-2 T Jarnet,.... 1
ZINDARI (USA) 9-2 C Asmussen,.... 2
MELODIE ROYALE (Fr) 8-12 J-M Breux,.... 3
PETARD EXPRESS (Ire) 8-12 E Saint-Martin,.... 4
Dist: 1½l, 6l, 2½l. 1m 7.41s. a 2.41s (4 Ran).
SR: 54/48/20/10/ (Sheikh Mohammed), A Fabre

1693 Prix Melisande (Listed) (3-y-o) £13,337 1¼m.........................(3:30)

VIVIANA (USA) 9-2 T Jarnet,.... 1
TRICKY PRINCESS (Fr) 9-2 F Head,.... 2
VALLEY QUEST 9-2 E Saint-Martin,.... 3
10336 ALLEGED SARON (USA) 9-2 C Asmussen,.... 4
Dist: Nk, 1l, 1½l, 2l, 1½l, 4l. 2m 12.53s. a 8.53s (7 Ran).
SR: 32/31/29/26/ (K Abdulla), A Fabre

1694 Grand Prix d'Evry (Group 2) (4-y-o and up) £41,816 1½m...............(3:55)

1291* SERRANT (USA) 5-8-9 T Jarnet (5) *4th strt, led one and a half fs out, clr one out, hrd rdn, jst hld on...* (17 to 10) 1
1124* MODHISH (Ire) 4-8-13 S Guillot (1) *second strt, led 2 fs out, hdd one and a half out, rallied und pres fnl furlong, jst fld*.... (42 to 10) 2
810* VERT AMANDE (Fr) 5-9-2 D Boeuf (2) *rcd in 3rd, effrt and ev ch 2 fs out, one pace*.... (16 to 10 fav) 3
8106 POLYTAIN (Fr) 4-8-9 L Dettori (4) *led till 2 fs out, one pace.* ....(38 to 10) 4
GRAND PLAISIR (Ire) 4-8-9 F Head (3) *al rear*..... (10 to 1) 5
Dist: Nose, 3l, ½l, 6l. 2m 37.63s. a 6.83s (5 Ran).
SR: 45/48/45/37/25/ (D Wildenstein), A Fabre

HOLLYWOOD (USA) (firm)
Saturday June 12th

1695 Milady Handicap (Grade 1) (3-y-o and up) £62,583 1m 110yds..............

560* PASEANA (Arg) 6-8-13 C McCarron,.... (5 to 2 on) 1
BOLD WINDY (USA) 4-8-1 K Desormeaux,.... (83 to 10) 2
4729a7 RE TOSS (Arg) 6-8-1 E Delahoussaye,.... (88 to 10) 3
GUIZA (USA) 6-8-2 A Solis,.... (12 to 1) 4
SHES A SURE BET (USA) 4-8-1 J Garcia,.... (14 to 1) 5
STEFF GRAF (Brz) 5-8-2 D Flores,.... (44 to 1) 6
LA SPIA (USA) 4-8-2 C Black,.... (92 to 10) 7
Dist: Hd, 3l, 1l, ½l, 3½l, 4l. 1m 41.30s. (7 Ran).
(S H Craig), R McAnally

LINGFIELD (good)
Saturday June 12th
Going Correction: PLUS 0.35 sec. per fur.

1696 GSP Selling Handicap Class G (0-60 3-y-o and up) £2,805 7f........ (7:00)

12476 PENNY BANGER (Ire) [47] 3-8-9 T Williams (4) *cl up far side, o'rall ldr over 2 fs out, ran on wl.* ....(6 to 1 op 9 to 2 tchd 13 to 2) 1
1238 AQUADO [33] 4-8-5 G Carter (1) *cl up far side, ev ch o'r one furlong out, one pace*.... (20 to 1 op 12 to 1) 2
12464 HARCLIFF [54] (v) 4-9-12 J Lowe (13) *chsd ldrs stands side, hdwy to hold ev ch appr 2 fs out, one pace.* ....(8 to 1 op 7 to 1) 3
14875 FAIR ENCHANTRESS [46] (bl) 5-9-4 T Sprake (10) *wth ldr stands side, led briefly 3 fs out, ev ch appr 2 out, one pace*.... (12 to 1 op 10 to 1) 4
13738 ELEGANT TOUCH [54] (v) 4-9-12 M Perrett (14) *beh, styd on und pres o'r one furlong out, nvr dngrs*.... (6 to 1) 5
15376 CASTLE MAID [33] 6-8-5 D Biggs (11) *chsd ldrs stands side, no hdwy frm o'r 2 fs out.* ....(8 to 1 op 7 to 1 tchd 9 to 1) 6
1146 WESSEX WARRIOR [40] (v) 7-8-5 (7*) T G McLaughlin (7) *strted slwly, outpcd, styd on fnl furlong, nrst finish.* ....(25 to 1 op 16 to 1) 7
1389 SLY PROSPECT (USA) [44] 5-9-2 R Wernham (15) *cl up stands side till wknd 3 fs out*.... (7 to 1 op 12 to 1) 8
14877 SHALOU [44] 4-8-9 (7*) S Drowne (5) *in tch far side to hfwy*.... (14 to 1 op 12 to 1 tchd 16 to 1) 9
1453 HIGHEST PRAISE (USA) [49] 10-9-7 D Holland (3) *led far side grp till hdd 3 fs out, wknd.* ....(20 to 1 op 16 to 1 tchd 25 to 1) 10
14537 J'ARRIVE [36] 4-8-3 (5*) C Hodgson (8) *beh frm hfwy.* ....(14 to 1 op 10 to 1) 11

1233^6 SUI GENERIS (Ire) [47] 3-8-9 A Clark (9) *nvr on terms.* .... (25 to 1 op 16 to 1) 12
1346^8 TOP SONG [56] 4-10-0 T Quinn (6) *in tch far side, beh hfwy*.......................... (5 to 1 fav op 7 to 2) 13
1453 BOULABAS (Ire) [41] (bl) 4-8-13 G Bardwell (16) *cl up stands side to hfwy*........................ (25 to 1 op 20 to 1) 14
APACHEE FLOWER [51] 3-8-13 W Newnes (12) *al beh.* .... (25 to 1 op 20 to 1 tchd 25 to 1) 15
Dist: 2½l, 1½l, hd, 1½l, 5l, 2l, 1½l, 4l, 2l, ½l. 1m 27.65s. a 6.95s (15 Ran).
SR: 28/16/32/23/26/-/ (R W Huggins), M Johnston

1697 Pointer Handicap Class D (0-80 3-y-o) £4,012 7f........................ (8:00)

1390^5 TAJDIF (USA) [68] 8-9 D Holland (6) *hld up, cld and short of room 2 fs out, swtchd lft appr fnl furlong, led ins last, cleverly*.............................. (12 to 1 tchd 14 to 1) 1
1408^4 FIELD OF VISION (Ire) [60] 8-1 T Williams (12) *trkd ldrs, led appr fnl furlong till hdd and no extr ins last.* ....(5 to 1 op 4 to 1 tchd 6 to 1) 2
827^9 PRAIRIE GROVE [70] 8-11 A McGlone (11) *trkd ldrs, led 2 fs out till hdd appr last, one pace*..... (12 to 1 op 7 to 1) 3
1390^3 HADEER'S DANCE [80] 9-7 R Price (10) *mid-div, pushed alng o'r 4 fs out, styd on one pace frm 2 out.* .... (9 to 1 op 6 to 1 tchd 10 to 1) 4
1058^3 SOAKING [71] 8-12 B Rouse (8) *trkd ldrs, hrd rdn o'r 2 fs out, sn btn and eased.* ....(9 to 2 op 4 to 1 tchd 5 to 1 and 11 to 2) 5
1239* INDERAPUTERI [72] 8-13 K Darley (2) *in tch, rdn o'r 3 fs out, sn no imprsn*.............................. (5 to 1 op 7 to 1) 6
334^4 MEDLAND (Ire) [52] 7-0 (7*) Sharon Millard (9) *cl up, led 3 fs out till hdd 2 out, wknd*........... (16 to 1 op 14 to 1) 7
1060* MITHI AL GAMAR (USA) [73] 9-0 W R Swinburn (3) *hld up, rdn alng hfwy, hrd drvn o'r 2 fs out, sn btn.* .... (11 to 4 fav op 3 to 1 tchd 100 to 30) 8
683 GLEN MILLER [62] 8-3 G Carter (5) *hld up, hrd rdn o'r 2 fs out, no imprsn*...................... (20 to 1 op 16 to 1) 9
950^8 MARAT (USA) [53] 7-8 J Lowe (1) *beh, pushed alng 4 fs out, nvr on terms*....................... (14 to 1 op 12 to 1) 10
1436 GREENWICH CHALENGE [59] 8-0 E Johnson (7) *led til hdd 3 fs out, wknd appr 2 out*.............................. (33 to 1) 11+
NEWINGTON BUTTS (Ire) [63] 8-4^1 T Quinn (4) *chsd ldrs till wknd o'r 2 fs out*.....(16 to 1 op 14 to 1 tchd 20 to 1) 11+
Dist: 1½l, 2l, 3½l, 7l, ½l, 6l, 1½l, 1½l, ½l, ¾l. 1m 27.70s. a 7.00s (12 Ran).
SR: 27/14/18/17/-/-/ (Hamdan Al-Maktoum), D Morley

1698 Lurcher Maiden Stakes Class D (3-y-o and up) £3,699 6f................ (8:30)

872^6 PETERSFORD GIRL (Ire) 3-8-7 J Reid (14) *trkd ldr al gng wl, led on bit appr fnl furlong, rdn clr.* ....(3 to 1 fav op 11 to 4) 1
1354^4 SYLVAN BREEZE (v) 5-9-7 W Newnes (11) *led til hdd appr fnl furlong, one pace*.............. (6 to 1 tchd 7 to 1) 2
1397^2 ISLAND KNIGHT (Ire) 4-9-7 D Biggs (12) *trkd ldrs, hrd rdn o'r one furlong out, one pace*...... (7 to 1 tchd 4 to 1) 3
1424^3 JAAZIM 3-8-12 A Clark (6) *sn pushed alng to chase ldrs, outpcd frm 2 fs out*... (100 to 30 op 9 to 4 tchd 7 to 2) 4
1092 UNIFICATION (Ire) 4-8-9 (7*) T Ashley (3) *in tch til outpcd o'r 2 fs out*..(20 to 1) 5
GARRY'S CHOICE 4-9-7 Dale Gibson (1) *trkd ldrs til pushed alng hfwy, sn wknd*.......(14 to 1 op 14 to 1) 6
1344 JALIB (Ire) 3-8-12 B Rouse (10) *cl up till wknd quickly appr o'r fs out*............. (8 to 1 op 10 to 1 tchd 14 to 1) 7
1320^8 PHARLING 3-8-7 G Carter (2) *nvr on terms.* .... (25 to 1 op 14 to 1) 8
1396^7 PRESS ONWARD 3-8-7 T Williams (5) *cl up till rdn alng and outpcd frm hfwy.* .... (14 to 1 tchd 12 to 1 and 25 to 1) 9
UTRILLO (USA) 4-9-7 M Perrett (9) *outpcd.* .... (20 to 1 op 14 to 1) 10
732 DESERT GIRL 3-8-1^1 (7*) A Cairns (13) *beh frm hfwy.* ....(14 to 1 tchd 16 to 1) 11
JEAN BRODIE 3-8-7 T Lang (4) *strted slwly, sn reco'red to chase ldrs, outpcd frm hfwy, tld off*...........(50 to 1) 12
Dist: 6l, ¾l, 2½l, 10l, 2l, 1l, nk, ¾l, nk, nk. 1m 14.60s. a 5.60s (12 Ran).
SR: 23/13/10/-/-/-/ (T C Peters), Miss Jacqueline S Doyle

LINGFIELD (A.W) (std)
Saturday June 12th

Going Correction: MINUS 0.25 sec. per fur.

1699 Springer Handicap Class E (0-70 3-y-o and up) £2,660 1¼m............ (6:30)

1238^4 ONE OFF THE RAIL (USA) [66] 3-9-5 B Rouse (6) *trkd ldr, led o'r 4 fs out, rdn clr over one out, ran on wl.* ....(7 to 1 op 5 to 1) 1
723^4 DAY OF HISTORY (Ire) [44] 4-8-10 W Newnes (2) *in tch, hdwy 4 fs out, rdn o'r 2 out, one pace.* .... (3 to 1 op 11 to 4 tchd 100 to 30) 2
1146^2 STORM FREE (USA) [62] 7-10-0 J Reid (3) *trkd ldg pair, ev ch 3 fs out, sn one pace*.............. (4 to 1 op 3 to 1) 3
MY SPARKLING RING [28] 7-7-8^1 J Lowe (7) *trkd ldrs 4 fs, sn drpd rear, styd on ins last*...... (50 to 1 op 25 to 1) 4+
1210^2 NORTHERN CONQUEROR (Ire) [43] 5-8-9 G Carter (4) *beh, sn niggled alng, rdn to cl 3 fs out, soon btn.* ....(9 to 4 fav op 9 to 4) 4+
1210 DON'T DROP BOMBS (USA) [41] (v) 4-8-0 (7*) J Tate (1) *al beh*.................. (20 to 1 op 16 to 1 tchd 25 to 1) 6
500^7 MODESTO (USA) [49] (v) 5-9-1 T Quinn (5) *led til hdd o'r 4 fs out, wknd quickly*.......(7 to 1 op 6 to 1 tchd 8 to 1) 7
Dist: 3l, 1½l, 10l, dd-ht, 1½l, 2l. 2m 6.13s. a 2.93s (7 Ran).
SR: 51/36/51/-/12/7/11/ (K Higson), A Moore

1700 Mott MacDonald Rating Related Maiden Stakes Class E (0-70 3-y-o and up) £2,611 2m.................. (7:30)

NORSTOCK 6-9-5 R Price (2) *trkd ldr, led 5 fs out, drw clr o'r 2 out, easily*.................. (10 to 1 tchd 14 to 1) 1
1353^2 CARFAX 8-9-10 W Newnes (1) *beh, hdwy 4 fs out, styd on, no ch wth wnr*.......... (7 to 2 op 3 to 1 tchd 4 to 1) 2
288^2 DOC'S COAT 8-9-10 C Rutter (3) *beh, rdn alng hfwy, styd on und pres ins last, nrst finish*..............(2 to 1 jt-fav op 3 to 1) 3
202^7 QUALITAIR IDOL 4-8-12 (7*) Marie Plowright (5) *hld up towards rear, effrt o'r 4 fs out, nvr on terms.* .... (33 to 1 op 25 to 1) 4
1255^4 BURNT IMP (USA) 3-8-4 T Quinn (6) *led til hdd 5 fs out, sn wknd*........ (2 to 1 jt-fav op 11 to 10 tchd 9 to 4) 5
1061^3 THREEOFUS (bl) 3-8-4 G Bardwell (7) *prmnt, pushed alng hfwy, sn lost pl*..... (10 to 1 op 20 to 1 tchd 25 to 1) 6
1389 DOMAIN (bl) 5-9-10 J Lowe (8) *took keen hold early, cl up til wknd o'r 5 fs out*.................. (20 to 1 op 16 to 1) 7
TAPESTRY DANCER 5-9-10 M Perrett (4) *hld up in rear, lost tch o'r 5 fs out, tld off*......... (33 to 1 op 20 to 1) 8
Dist: 12l, 5l, nk, ½l, 15l, 4l, dist. 3m 28.65s. a 6.65s (8 Ran).
(Nick Quesnel), J White

1701 Retriever Limited Stakes Class F (0-65 3-y-o and up) £2,588 1m........ (9:00)

1354* RAGING THUNDER (bl) 3-8-13 K Darley (3) *hld up in rear, pushed alng 3 fs out, hdwy 2 out, led ins last, drvn out.* .... (11 to 4 op 9 to 4) 1
919^6 BICHETTE 3-8-8 B Rouse (2) *led one furlong, cl up, led ag'n appr 2 fs out till hdd and no extr ins last.* ....(7 to 1 tchd 8 to 1) 2
1246^7 ON Y VA (USA) 6-9-5 D Biggs (4) *wtd wth in mid-div, lost pl 3 fs out, sn not clr run, hdwy o'r one furlong out, ran on*..................... (8 to 1 op 6 to 1 tchd 9 to 1) 3
1097^7 SARUM 7-9-10 C Rutter (1) *chsd ldrs, pushed alng o'r 3 fs out, effrt on ins over one out, one pace inside last.* .... (12 to 1 op 10 to 1) 4
1453 BASSIO (Bel) (h) 4-9-10 W Hood (7) *trkd ldrs, cl 4 fs out, ev ch 2 out, wknd ins last*........... (50 to 1 op 33 to 1) 5
1426 BRAVE HERO (USA) 3-8-13 W Newnes (8) *trkd ldrs till wknd 3 fs out*....... (20 to 1 tchd 25 to 1 and 33 to 1) 6
1356^3 KINGSTON BROWN (bl) 3-8-13 T Quinn (9) *rdn thrght, led aftr one furlong till hdd appr 2 fs out, wknd.* ....(4 to 1 op 7 to 2 tchd 9 to 2 and 5 to 1) 7
235^8 WESSEX MILORD 8-9-3 (7*) Kim McDonnell (5) *al beh.* .... (50 to 1 op 33 to 1) 8
1500* LAND O'LAKES (Ire) 3-8-13 G Carter (6) *trkd ldrs till lost pl quickly aftr 2 fs*................ (9 to 4 fav op 2 to 1) 9
Dist: ¾l, sht-hd, 2½l, 1½l, 7l, 2½l, 3½l, ½l. 1m 39.20s. a 3.00s (9 Ran).
SR: 24/17/27/24/19/-/ (P D Savill), G Lewis

NOTTINGHAM (soft)
Saturday June 12th

Going Correction: PLUS 0.85 sec. per fur. (races 1,2,3,4,6), PLUS 0.70 (5)

1702 International Spinal Research Trust Selling Handicap Class G (0-60 3-y-o and up) £2,110 1¾m 15yds...... (6:15)

1248^5 JALORE [38] 4-8-12^3 M Tebbutt (7) *hld up, hdwy 6 fs out, jnd ldrs 4 out, led and edgd lft o'r one out, rdn out.* ....(8 to 1 tchd 10 to 1) 1
628 QUALITAIR MEMORY (Ire) [30] 4-8-1 (3*) S Maloney (5) *al prmnt, rdn and hdwy to ld 3 fs out, hdd and one pace o'r one out*.............................. (8 to 1 op 6 to 1) 2
1321^5 ENFANT DU PARADIS (Ire) [36] 5-8-10 W Carson (10) *led, rdn and hdd o'r 3 fs out, kpt on one pace.* ....(2 to 1 fav op 9 to 4 tchd 5 to 2) 3
1557^5 PREMIER BLUES (Fr) [38] (bl) 3-7-8^3 (3*) N Kennedy (4) *chsd ldrs, hdwy 4 fs out, ev ch 2 out, sn rdn and one paced.* ....(14 to 1 tchd 16 to 1) 4
973^6 MUST BE MAGICAL (USA) [23] 5-7-4 (7*) D Wright (9) *in tch, hdwy 5 fs out, rdn o'r 3 out, sn btn.* (8 to 1 op 6 to 1) 5
1191^5 BONNY PRINCESS [37] (bl) 3-7-7 N Carlisle (6) *in tch, hdwy 6 fs out, rdn and wknd o'r 3 out*... (14 to 1 op 33 to 1) 6
287^7 PIMS CLASSIC [42] 5-9-2 G Duffield (2) *prmnt, rdn and wknd o'r 4 fs out*..... (12 to 1 op 10 to 1 tchd 14 to 1) 7
1281^2 FANATICAL (USA) [42] 7-9-2 L Piggott (3) *chsd ldrs, rdn 5 fs out, sn wknd and beh*............ (5 to 1 op 7 to 2) 8
MOST INTERESTING [25] 8-7-13 S Dawson (1) *al rear, tld off fnl 4 fs*............................(9 to 1 op 8 to 1) 9

279 ELECTROJET [24] 5-7-7 (5*) Darren Moffatt (12) *chsd ldr, rdn and wknd 5 fs out, sn wl beh*.............. (33 to 1) 10
ALIZARI (USA) [50] 4-9-10 R P Elliott (8) *sn beh, tld off aftr 6 fs*.................................(20 to 1 op 16 to 1) 11
Dist: 4l, 1½l, 2l, 7l, 2l, 20l, 1½l, 1½l, 1½l, 30l. 3m 16.90s. a 19.00s (11 Ran).
SR: 27/11/14/-/-/-/ (R Hollinshead), R Hollinshead

1703 Nottingham Evening Post Handicap Class D (0-80 3-y-o) £3,465 1m 54yds ....(6:40)

1330[4] MONSIGNOR PAT (USA) [67] 8-11 L Piggott (5) *made all, quickened 4 fs out, rdn o'r 2 out, hrd drvn and styd on gmely ins last*...................... (7 to 2 op 3 to 1) 1
1037[7] DANCE TO ORDER (Ire) [62] 8-6 G Duffield (6) *chsd wnr, effrt 3 fs out, rdn to chal and ev ch 2 out, no extr wl ins last*..................(13 to 2 op 7 to 1 tchd 8 to 1) 2
1390[2] JIHAAD (USA) [61] 8-5 W Carson (1) *chsd ldrs, effrt and swtchd 2 fs out, rdn to chal entering last, sn no extr*. ....(2 to 1 fav op 3 to 1) 3
1238 KAWASIR (Can) [50] (v) 7-8 N Carlisle (3) *chsd ldrs, rdn 3 fs out, sn one paced*...... (13 to 2 op 5 to 1 tchd 7 to 1) 4
1540* AL MOULOUKI [77] 9-7 R Cochrane (2) *in tch, hdwy 3 fs out, rdn 2 out, sn btn*. (85 to 40 op 2 to 1 tchd 5 to 2) 5
1306 NORLING (Ire) [50] 7-8[1] J Quinn (7) *al rear*. ....(20 to 1 op 25 to 1) 6
Dist: 1l, 1½l, 8l, 7l, sht-hd. 1m 51.50s. a 11.50s (6 Ran).
SR: 30/22/16/ (Michael Poland), H R A Cecil

1704 Youngers Rating Related Maiden Stakes Class F (0-65 3-y-o) £2,162 1m 1f 213yds......................(7:10)

1306[6] BEAUMONT (Ire) 9-0 M Wigham (4) *hld up, hdwy 4 fs out, effrt 2 out, rdn to ld entering last, edgd lft and ran on*. ....(9 to 4 op 7 to 2 tchd 2 to 1) 1
921[4] SUSQUEHANNA DAYS (USA) 8-9 R Cochrane (1) *led, rdn 3 fs out, hdd and no extr entering last*. ....(100 to 30 op 9 to 4 tchd 7 to 2) 2
1223[2] APACHE SQUAW 8-9 W Carson (5) *chsd ldr, effrt 3 fs out, rdn 2 out, sn btn*.....(2 to 1 fav op 7 to 4 tchd 9 to 4) 3
1309[7] CALIBRATE 9-0 W Ryan (3) *in tch, effrt and hdwy 3 fs out, sn rdn and btn*..................... (6 to 1 op 5 to 1) 4
1178[5] CARLTON EXPRESS (Ire) (v) 9-0 L Piggott (7) *chsd ldrs, rdn and wknd 4 fs out*....(11 to 1 op 10 to 1 tchd 12 to 1) 5
Dist: 2½l, 20l, 15l, 25l. 2m 17.80s. a 14.80s (5 Ran).
SR: 37/27/ (Garth Thoroughbreds Ltd), J Pearce

1705 BBC Radio Nottingham Claiming Stakes Class F (3-y-o) £2,351 1m 54yds.......................... (7:40)

1109[3] MYSILV 8-6 P Robinson (2) *made all, rdn 3 fs out, clr appr last, easily*. .... (15 to 8 fav op 9 to 4 tchd 3 to 1 and 7 to 4) 1
1416* MRS DAWSON 8-10 A Proud (3) *al chasing wnr, effrt to chal 2 and a half fs out, sn rdn and one paced wl o'r one out*.............................. (4 to 1 op 5 to 1) 2
SHAMROCK DANCER (Ire) 7-13 (3*) S Maloney (6) *slwly into strd and beh, hdwy o'r 2 fs out, styd on wl ins last, nvr dngrs*..............................(16 to 1 op 33 to 1) 3
716 IRISH DOMINION 8-9 R Cochrane (5) *in tch, hdwy 4 fs out, rdn o'r 2 out, hrd drvn and one paced ins last*. ....(3 to 1 tchd 5 to 2) 4
1399[6] A BADGE TOO FAR (Ire) (v) 8-6 G Hind (10) *chsd ldrs, effrt and hdwy o'r 3 fs out, chlgd 2 out, sn rdn and wknd*. ....(5 to 1 tchd 6 to 1) 5
RIVER FIRE (Ire) 8-8 J Quinn (4) *chsd ldrs, rdn 3 fs out, sn wknd*.. (20 to 1) 6
BILLESCLOWN 8-11 M Wigham (8) *slwly into strd, al outpcd and beh*.................. (16 to 1 op 14 to 1) 7
HONEYMOON DAWN 8-1 (7*) D Wright (9) *nvr rch ldrs*. ....(33 to 1 op 25 to 1) 8
BLAKENEY'S DOUBLE (Ire) 8-8 (3*) S D Williams (1) *chsd ldrs, rdn and wknd quickly o'r 3 fs out*. ....(33 to 1 op 25 to 1) 9
Dist: 3½l, 3½l, nk, 1½l, 7l, 1½l, 10l, 20l. 1m 52.30s. a 12.30s (9 Ran).
SR: 13/6/-/-/-/-/ (Mrs C A Wall), C F Wall

1706 'Local Press For News' Maiden Stakes Class D (2-y-o) £3,757 6f 15yds ....(8:10)

1131[4] GREEN GOLIGHTLY (USA) 9-0 P Robinson (12) *al cl up, ev ch whn bumped one and a half fs out, sn rdn, styd on to ld nr finish*.......... (5 to 2 op 3 to 1 tchd 9 to 4) 1
1182[3] THE HAPPY LOON (Ire) 9-0 K Fallon (6) *wnt lft strt, chsd ldrs, hdwy hfwy, led o'r one furlong out, hng badly left, hdd nr finish*................(14 to 1 op 10 to 1) 2
1343[4] MIDUSHI (USA) 8-9 G Hind (8) *mid-div, rdn and styd on fnl 2 fs, nrst finish*............... (25 to 1 op 20 to 1) 3
673[9] JUST HARRY 9-0 M Tebbutt (10) *chsd ldrs, rdn and styd on fnl 2 fs*.............................(12 to 1 op 20 to 1) 4
1032[7] KISSING COUSIN (Ire) 8-9 M Roberts (7) *cl up, led 2 and a half fs out, rdn and edgd lft one and a half out, sn hdd and wknd ins last*..................(4 to 1 op 3 to 1) 5
1350 SHFNAK (Ire) 9-0 N Day (2) *beh, rdn alng hfwy, styd on fnl 2 fs*..................................(25 to 1 op 20 to 1) 6
FORGOTTEN DANCER (Ire) 9-0 B Raymond (5) *wl beh till styd on fnl 2 fs*....................(12 to 1 op 10 to 1) 7
LAUNE (Aus) 8-9 L Piggott (13) *led to 2 and a half fs out, sn wknd*............... (9 to 4 fav op 5 to 2 tchd 7 to 2) 8
ALLLEGSNOBRAIN 9-0 Paul Eddery (14) *nvr rch ldrs*. ....(25 to 1 op 20 to 1) 9
TAKHRIJ (USA) 9-0 W Carson (3) *beh frm hfwy*. ....(8 to 1 op 6 to 1) 10
WIZARD KING 9-0 G Duffield (4) *chsd ldrs to hfwy, sn wknd*...............(15 to 2 op 8 to 1 tchd 6 to 1) 11
ZOES PET 8-9 R Cochrane (9) *slwly away, al outpcd*. ....(25 to 1 op 20 to 1) 12
CRETAN GIFT 9-0 M Hills (11) *slwly away, al beh*. ....(12 to 1 op 10 to 1) 13
OUT OF FAVOUR (Ire) 9-0 C Dwyer (1) *al outpcd and wl beh*................................(25 to 1 op 16 to 1) 14
Dist: Nk, 2½l, nk, nk, 2l, 1½l, 6l, hd, 2l, ½l. 1m 19.20s. a 7.70s (14 Ran).
SR: 30/29/14/18/12/9/3/-/-/ (Raymond Anderson Green), M A Jarvis

1707 'Family Night Out' Handicap Class E (0-70 4-y-o and up) £2,870 1m 54yds ....(8:40)

1325[6] PRINCESS OF ORANGE [40] 4-7-13 (3*) S Maloney (12) *hld up, steady hdwy 4 fs out, led 2 furlongs out, sn rdn, ran on wl ins last*..................... (9 to 1 op 10 to 1) 1
1659[2] DANCING BEAU (Ire) [46] 4-8-8 M Roberts (11) *mid-div, hdwy on inner o'r 3 fs out, effrt to chal 2 out, sn rdn and ev ch till no extr nr line*..... (5 to 2 fav op 3 to 1) 2
448[6] QUANTITY SURVEYOR [54] 4-9-2 G Duffield (5) *chsd ldrs, effrt 4 fs out, sn rdn, ev ch o'r 2 out, soon one pace*. ....(9 to 2 op 6 to 1) 3
1490[9] LORD OBERON (Ire) [50] 5-8-12 Dean McKeown (13) *hld up, hdwy on outer o'r 4 fs out, rdn and one pace 2 out*. ....(8 to 1 op 7 to 1 tchd 9 to 1) 4
1490[5] LORD ALFIE [47] 4-8-9 S Whitworth (2) *chsd ldrs, hdwy to ld 3 fs out, hdd 2 out, sn wknd*.......(9 to 2 op 3 to 1) 5
1502[4] VICTOR ROMEO [35] (v) 4-7-6 (5*) Darren Moffatt (15) *sn rdn alng in mid-div, nvr rch ldrs*...... (20 to 1 op 14 to 1) 6
1286[4] BALLYRANTER [46] (v) 4-8-8 J Quinn (14) *in tch, effrt and hdwy 4 fs out, sn rdn and wknd 3 out*. ....(8 to 1 op 7 to 1) 7
1177 NIGEL'S LUCKY GIRL [55] 5-9-3 C Dwyer (6) *led, rdn and hdd 3 fs out, wknd quickly*........ (25 to 1 op 20 to 1) 8
1537[9] MERRYHILL MADAM [45] 4-8-7[2] R Cochrane (9) *dwlt, al rear*.................. (14 to 1 op 12 to 1 tchd 16 to 1) 9
1210 BUDDY'S FRIEND (Ire) [60] 5-9-1 (7*) Sarah Thompson (4) *chsd ldrs till rdn and wknd o'r 3 fs out*. ....(12 to 1 op 10 to 1) 10
BLAKE'S TREASURE [35] (bl) 6-7-11 N Carlisle (1) *cl up till wknd quickly o'r 4 fs out, sn tld off*. ....(25 to 1 op 16 to 1) 11
Dist: Hd, 10l, 1½l, ½l, 1l, 10l, hd, sht-hd, 1l. 1m 50.80s. a 10.80s (11 Ran).
SR: 31/36/14/5/-/-/ (David McDuffie), W M Brisbourne

SANDOWN (good to soft)
Saturday June 12th

Going Correction: PLUS 0.15 sec. per fur. (races 1,7), PLUS 0.50 (2,3,4,5,6)

1708 EBF Portman Square Maiden Fillies Stakes Class D (2-y-o) £3,454 5f 6yds ....(2:20)

1403[6] WINSOME WOOSTER 8-11 Pat Eddery (3) *al prmnt, led 2 fs out, drvn out fnl furlong, hld on gmely*. ....(6 to 5 fav op 5 to 4 tchd 11 to 8) 1
ROBIN LAKE (Ire) 8-11 A Munro (1) *slwly into strd, hdwy to chal one furlong out, rdn and pressed wnr to line*. ....(9 to 4 op 2 to 1 tchd 5 to 2) 2
1142[8] URSULINE 8-11 W R Swinburn (4) *led one furlong, ev ch till outpcd fnl furlong*.............. (14 to 1 tchd 20 to 1) 3
SISTER SUSAN 8-11 T Quinn (6) *speed till wknd one furlong out*............... (5 to 1 op 7 to 2 tchd 11 to 2) 4
BET A PLAN (Ire) 8-8 (3*) D Harrison (5) *led aftr one furlong to 2 out, wknd entering last*. ....(20 to 1 op 14 to 1 tchd 25 to 1) 5
DANCING ROSINA (Ire) 8-11 W Newnes (2) *slwly away, al rear, outpcd hfwy*................(50 to 1 op 25 to 1) 6
Dist: Sht-hd, 2½l, 1½l, hd, 3½l. 1m 4.39s. a 4.89s (6 Ran).
SR: 14/13/3/ (Miss Amanda J Rawding), P G Murphy

1709 Berkeley Square Claiming Stakes Class E (3-y-o) £2,835 1¼m 7yds (2:50)

1097 HEART OF SPAIN 8-5 W Newnes (8) *hld up, hdwy wl o'r 2 fs out, hrd rdn to ld well ins last*. .... (16 to 1 op 10 to 1 tchd 20 to 1) 1
1426[5] SUPREME MASTER 8-13 Pat Eddery (5) *trkd ldrs, quickened to ld 3 fs out, rdn and hdd wl ins last*. ....(3 to 1 fav op 4 to 1 tchd 11 to 4) 2
1306 SWEET ROMEO 8-7 Dean McKeown (2) *led to 3 fs out, rdn and edgd rght, outpcd appr last*..... (6 to 1 op 4 to 1) 3

1319[3] ONE MORE POUND 8-3 G Bardwell (4) *al mid-div, no hdwy ins fnl 3 fs*.................. (12 to 1 op 8 to 1) 4
1524[7] ALDERNEY PRINCE (USA) (bl) 8-12 A Munro (9) *prmnt, short of room and hmpd wl o'r 2 fs out, sn btn*. ....(7 to 2 op 5 to 2 tchd 4 to 1) 5
1371[5] NOEPROB (USA) 8-2 A McGlone (6) *al rear. wl beh hfwy*. .... (33 to 1 op 16 to 1) 6
1359[4] BURNING COST 7-10 (3*) D Harrison (3) *pld hrd, trkd ldr till wknd quickly 3 fs out*. .... (10 to 1 op 8 to 1 tchd 12 to 1) 7
1320[5] THE SNOUT 8-7 J Reid (7) *pld hrd, al rear, tld off*. .... (4 to 1 tchd 7 to 2 and 5 to 1) 8

Dist: 1l, 5l, 7l, ¾l, 5l, 4l, 20l. 2m 16.60s. a 12.70s (8 Ran).
SR: 14/20/4/-/-/ (Avon Industries Ltd), P J Makin

1710 Sloane Square Conditions Stakes Class C (3-y-o and up) £5,360 1m 14yds........................ (3:25)

1220[2] NEW CAPRICORN (USA) 3-8-5 Pat Eddery (1) *made all, shaken up appr fnl furlong, cmftbly*. ....(5 to 4 on op 11 to 8 on tchd 6 to 4 on) 1
1412[2] LEE ARTISTE 5-8-9 T Quinn (2) *trkd wnr, hrd rdn appr fnl furlong, no imprsn ins*. .... (2 to 1 op 11 to 10 tchd 9 to 4) 2
HEATHFIELD (USA) 3-8-3 A Munro (3) *pld hrd early, settled rear, effrt o'r 2 fs out, no imprsn, eased ins last*. .... (5 to 1 op 7 to 1 tchd 10 to 1) 3

Dist: 2½l, 10l. 1m 49.70s. a 10.60s (3 Ran).
(Kamal Bhatia), M A Jarvis

1711 Silver Gavel Handicap Class C (0-100 3-y-o and up) £7,002 1¼m 7yds (3:55)

1409[2] USAIDIT [68] 4-8-10 J Reid (7) *hld up, hdwy on ins o'r 2 fs out, led appr last, rdn clr*. ....(5 to 1 op 9 to 2 tchd 6 to 1) 1
1346[2] GOOGLY [68] 4-8-10 G Bardwell (2) *wtd wth, hdwy on outsd to ld 2 fs out, rdn and hdd appr last, kpt on one pace*. .....(100 to 30 fav op 3 to 1 tchd 11 to 4 and 7 to 2) 2
1566[4] BENTICO [51] 4-7-7 J Quinn (3) *pld hrd early, settled in mid-div, hdwy o'r 2 fs out, short of room appr last, ran on ins*.............. (12 to 1 op 14 to 1 tchd 16 to 1) 3
OPERA GHOST [82] 7-9-10 W R Swinburn (10) *al in tch, ev ch 2 fs out, wknd ins last, better for race*. .... (20 to 1 op 14 to 1) 4
1450[9] BARFORD LAD [77] 6-9-5 A Munro (8) *trkd ldrs, ev ch 2 fs out, rdn and sn btn*..... (8 to 1 op 7 to 1 tchd 9 to 1) 5
494[5] ALMAMZAR (USA) [89] 3-9-4 Pat Eddery (5) *led aftr 2 fs to 3 out, wknd wl o'r one out*. ....(9 to 1 op 8 to 1 tchd 10 to 1) 6
1450 CAMDEN'S RANSOM (USA) [74] 6-8-13 (3*) B Doyle (6) *in tch, led 3 fs out to 2 out, wknd*. ....(6 to 1 op 5 to 1 tchd 7 to 1) 7
1450[8] KNOCK KNOCK [82] 8-9-7 (3*) D Harrison (1) *al beh*. .... (16 to 1 op 14 to 1 tchd 20 to 1) 8
246* RAPPORTEUR (USA) [68] 7-8-10 W Newnes (9) *led 2 fs, rdn o'r two out, sn wknd, eased*. .... (25 to 1 op 14 to 1 tchd 33 to 1) 9
1064[7] RUTLAND WATER (USA) [67] 6-8-9 T Quinn (4) *al beh*. .... (13 to 2 op 9 to 2 tchd 7 to 1) 10

Dist: 3l, sht-hd, 2½l, 1l, 1½l, 2½l, 2½l, ½l, 3l. 2m 13.33s. a 9.43s (10 Ran).
SR: 52/46/28/54/47/43/36/39/24/ (Mrs Pauline Merrick), T G Mills

1712 Nicholas Attenborough Handicap Class E (0-70 4-y-o and up) £3,265 1m 3f 91yds...................... (4:30)

1120 REMANY [60] 4-9-9 W R Swinburn (10) *sn trkd ldr, hrd rdn to ld jst ins fnl furlong, just hld on*. ....(4 to 1 jt-fav tchd 9 to 2) 1
1392[3] SWIFT SILVER [57] 6-9-6 J Reid (2) *mid-div, hdwy 2 fs out, ran on ins last, edgd rght cl hme, jst fld*......(4 to 1 jt-fav op 7 to 2 tchd 9 to 2) 2
1414[7] FULL QUIVER [37] (v) 8-8-0 G Bardwell (8) *slwly away, settled rear, rdn and hdwy o'r 2 fs out, kpt on wl und pres ins last*.....................(10 to 1 op 8 to 1) 3
55[6] JADE GREEN [61] 4-9-10 T Quinn (1) *settled mid-div, rdn to ld o'r 2 fs out, hdd jst ins last, short of room and lost 3rd pl cl hme*.........(14 to 1 op 10 to 1 tchd 16 to 1) 4
1281* RAGTIME SONG [42] 4-8-5[1] W Newnes (4) *led till o'r 2 fs out, wknd appr last*...(10 to 1 op 8 to 1 tchd 11 to 1) 5
1414 GOLD BLADE [51] 4-9-0 A McGlone (6) *rear, effrt 3 fs out, nvr on terms*........... (7 to 1 op 8 to 1 tchd 10 to 1) 6
1389[4] RED JACK (Ire) [32] 4-7-9[2] Dale Gibson (7) *in tch till rdn and wknd 2 fs out*................(12 to 1 tchd 14 to 1) 7
1384[2] TAYLORS PRINCE [57] (v) 6-9-6 J Quinn (9) *al rear*. ....(9 to 2 op 3 to 1 tchd 5 to 1) 8
APRIL CITY [45] 4-8-8 G Carter (5) *trkd ldr early, in tch till wknd 2 fs out, eased*. (12 to 1 op 10 to 1 tchd 14 to 1) 9

Dist: Hd, nk, nk, 5l, 1½l, 2l, 6l, 5l. 2m 35.24s. a 15.24s (9 Ran).
SR: 14/10/-/12/-/-/ (A C Hall), J R Fanshawe

1713 Grosvenor Square Maiden Stakes Class D (3-y-o) £3,493 7f 16yds..(5:05)

1308[2] QUAVER (USA) 8-9 G Hind (8) *rcd keenly, led aftr 2 fs, shaken up jst ins last, cleverly*. ....(100 to 30 fav op 5 to 2 tchd 7 to 2) 1
PRIME OF LIFE (Ire) 9-0 S Raymont (1) *slwly away, rdn in mid-div o'r 2 fs out, ran on ins last, nvr nrr*. .... (11 to 2 op 16 to 1) 2
1342[3] WISHAM (USA) 9-0 W Newnes (7) *trkd ldrs, pressed wnr 2 fs out, kpt on one pace*. (11 to 2 op 4 to 1 tchd 6 to 1) 3
WINDRUSH LADY 8-9 Pat Eddery (6) *hld up rear, hdwy 2 fs out, eased whn btn ins last*..... (8 to 1 tchd 10 to 1) 4
1469[5] CLEVER MINSTREL (USA) 9-0 M Perrett (9) *led 2 fs, rdn two out, one pace*...................... (25 to 1 op 12 to 1) 5
1132[6] THRIVING 8-9 J Reid (5) *chsd ldrs, no hdwy fnl 2 fs*. .... (6 to 1 op 9 to 2 tchd 13 to 2) 6
DESERT TIME 9-0 W R Swinburn (4) *prmnt on outsd, ev ch o'r 2 fs out, wknd appr last*. .... (5 to 1 op 9 to 2 tchd 11 to 2) 7
1027 WELL SUITED 9-0 T Quinn (2) *al rear. rdn o'r 2 fs out, one pace*..................... (8 to 1 op 6 to 1 tchd 9 to 1) 8
LA POSADA 8-9 A McGlone (3) *in tch till rdn and wknd o'r 2 fs out*...................... (25 to 1 op 14 to 1) 9

Dist: Nk, 1½l, 3l, ½l, hd, nk, 1½l, 2l. 1m 33.77s. a 7.27s (9 Ran).
SR: 38/42/37/23/26/20/24/19/8/ (Sheikh Mohammed), J H M Gosden

1714 Leicester Square Apprentice Handicap Class F (0-70 3-y-o) £2,786 5f 6yds ....(5:35)

1528[5] CHAMPAGNE GRANDY [65] 8-8 (8*) R Painter (4) *outpcd early, str brst to go second one furlong out, ran on wl to ld 75 yards out*..........(11 to 2 op 9 to 2 tchd 6 to 1) 1
1455[6] PURBECK CENTENARY [60] 8-6 (5*) L Carter (8) *led, clr 2 fs out, hdd 75 yards out, no extr*. .... (15 to 2 op 10 to 1 tchd 7 to 1) 2
1505[4] GO FLIGHTLINE (Ire) [60] (v) 8-5 (6*) J O'Dwyer (9) *chsd ldrs, ran on ins fnl furlong*............ (5 to 1 tchd 11 to 2) 3
1516* KIMBOLTON KORKER [56] 8-4 (3*) Claire Balding (11) *chsd ldrs, kpt on one pace ins fnl furlong*. .... (5 to 1 op 3 to 1 tchd 11 to 2) 4
1258[3] TUSCAN DAWN [70] 8-13 (8*) P Roberts (6) *chsd ldr to one furlong out, one pace*. .... (7 to 2 fav op 5 to 1 tchd 11 to 2 and 3 to 1) 5
AHJAY [60] 8-3 (8*) Sharon Millard (2) *outpcd*. .... (10 to 1 op 14 to 1 tchd 16 to 1) 6
1313[8] BUCKSKI ECHO [45] 7-5 (5*) D Toole (5) *speed to hfwy*. .... (25 to 1 op 14 to 1 tchd 33 to 1) 7
1376[4] PERFECT PASSION [48] 7-8 (5*) Gina Faulkner (1) *outpcd*. .... (33 to 1 op 20 to 1) 8
1376[6] INONDER [42] 7-2 (5*) M Baird (7) *in tch to hfwy, outpcd*. .... (25 to 1 op 16 to 1 tchd 33 to 1) 9
1478[5] CHARITY EXPRESS (Ire) [62] 8-13 P McCabe (3) *strted slwly, nvr on terms*.....(13 to 2 op 5 to 1 tchd 7 to 1) 10
1233[7] BELLE SOIREE [47] 7-6[1] (7*) W Hawksley (12) *slwly away, outpcd*.........................(20 to 1 op 14 to 1) 11

Dist: 1l, nk, 2l, 1l, 3½l, ¾l, ½l, 1½l, 3l, sht-hd. 1m 3.30s. a 3.80s (11 Ran).
SR: 41/32/31/19/29/5/ (Grandy Girls), M R Channon

YORK (good to soft)
Saturday June 12th

Going Correction: PLUS 0.60 sec. per fur. (races 1,4,7), PLUS 0.15 (2,3,5,6)

1715 EBF Gwen Murless Stakes Class D (2-y-o) £4,308 6f.................. (2:15)

CARMOT 9-0 M Roberts (2) *led, rdn one furlong out, hdd and ran green ins last, kpt on und pres to ld cl hme*. ....(6 to 1 op 4 to 1) 1
1324[3] JAZEEL (USA) 9-0 W Carson (4) *wth ldr, rdn one furlong out, slight ld ins last, hdd and no extr cl hme*. .... (Evens fav op 6 to 4) 2
SAIHAT (Ire) 9-0 G Duffield (9) *in tch, hdwy o'r 2 fs out, one pace appr last*.........(13 to 2 op 7 to 2 tchd 7 to 1) 3
1350[2] MAKE A NOTE (USA) 9-0 K Darley (1) *wth ldrs, ev ch 2 fs out, wknd*............. (5 to 1 op 4 to 1 tchd 11 to 2) 4
908[6] BLASTER BATES (USA) 9-0 D Nicholls (7) *beh, styd on fnl 2 fs, not rch ldrs*.............. (33 to 1 op 20 to 1) 5
1497[2] ALPINE JOHNNY 9-0 S Perks (5) *prmnt till wknd o'r 2 fs out*.......................... (10 to 1 op 7 to 1) 6
1324[3] ABSOLUTELY FAYRE 9-0 Paul Eddery (8) *chsd ldrs, wknd o'r 2 fs out*......................... (10 to 1 op 6 to 1) 7
1135[6] BEDAZZLE 9-0 M Birch (6) *al beh*.... (33 to 1 op 20 to 1) 8
DOUBLE DANCER 9-0 L Charnock (3) *al beh*. .... (25 to 1 op 20 to 1) 9

Dist: Nk, 3½l, 1½l, 4l, 1½l, ½l, 3½l, 2½l. 1m 16.90s. a 6.90s (9 Ran).
SR: 34/33/19/13/-/-/ (Sheikh Mohammed), P F I Cole

1716 Cadogan Maiden Stakes Class D (3-y-o) £5,380 7f 202yds........... (2:45)

1429[4] FROGMARCH (USA) 9-0 W Carson (1) *led aftr one furlong, drw clr o'r one out, easily*............. (7 to 2 op 3 to 1) 1
LACOTTE (Ire) 9-0 M Roberts (3) *hld up, effrt o'r 2 fs out, rdn over one out, kpt on, no ch wth wnr*. .... (11 to 10 on op 11 to 8 on tchd Evens) 2

557⁴ SCOTSMAN (Ire) 9-0 C Rutter (4) *led one furlong, trkd wnr, effrt o'r 2 out, rdn over one out, one pace.* ....(4 to 1 op 6 to 1) 3
1595² QUEENS CONSUL (Ire) 8-2 (7*) J Tate (2) *trkd ldrs, rdn 2 fs out, sn btn*........(6 to 1 op 5 to 1) 4
Dist: 4l, ¾l, 1½l. 1m 42.85s. a 6.55s (4 Ran).
SR: 20/8/6/-/ (Lord Chelsea), Major W R Hern

1717 Queen Mother's Cup Lady Amateur Riders Conditions Class C (3-y-o and up) £10,113 1m 3f 195yds....... (3:15)

1328* AZHAR 3-9-12 Mrs M Cowdrey (6) *led aftr one furlong, clr 4 out, hld on wl fnl furlong.* ....(13 to 8 fav op Evens tchd 7 to 4) 1
1504* HASTEN TO ADD (USA) 3-9-8 Miss I Diana W Jones (2) *hld up, hdwy 5 fs out, chsd wnr 4 out, kpt on fnl furlong.* ....(7 to 1 op 4 to 1 tchd 8 to 1) 2
1021⁵ LOKI (Ire) 5-11-0 Miss A Dare (5) *in tch, hdwy to chase wnr 5 fs out, one pace 4 out*........(3 to 1 op 5 to 1) 3
1143⁵ SWORD MASTER 4-11-0 Miss Diana J Jones (1) *led one furlong, chsd ldrs, kpt on same pace und str pres fnl 4 fs*........(14 to 1 op 10 to 1) 4
59⁷ AREMEF (USA) 4-10-10 Mrs J Crossley (7) *beh, lost tch 5 fs out*........(14 to 1 op 8 to 1) 5
1450⁵ PHARLY STORY 5-11-0 Mrs L Pearce (4) *chsd wnr till wknd o'r 4 fs out, tld off.* ....(100 to 30 op 5 to 2 tchd 7 to 2) 6
1173 NEGATORY (USA) 6-10-10 Miss P Robson (3) *lost tch hfwy, tld off*........(100 to 1 op 50 to 1) 7
Dist: 1½l, 8l, nk, 8l, 20l, 4l. 2m 36.04s. a 8.04s (7 Ran).
SR: 50/43/47/46/26/-/-/ (Sheikh Ahmed Al Maktoum), M R Stoute

1718 William Hill Trophy Handicap Class B (0-105 3-y-o) £28,542 6f......... (3:45)

1451⁶ ARADANZA [94] 9-2 Paul Eddery (6) *prmnt, led 2 fs out, hld on wl fnl furlong*........(25 to 1 op 16 to 1) 1
1213⁴ TROON [88] 8-10 L Piggott (10) *hld up, not much room o'r 2 fs out, wnt lft wl over one out, ran on und str pres fnl furlong, jst fld*........(7 to 1 op 10 to 1) 2
1113⁷ ABERGELE [86] 8-8 K Fallon (12) *hld up, hdwy to chal entering fnl furlong, no extr nr finish.* ....(10 to 1 op 7 to 1) 3
1337* LOOK WHO'S HERE (Ire) [93] 9-1 (7ex) B Raymond (8) *trkd ldrs, effrt and hng lft 2 fs out, not much room fnl furlong, kpt on*........(6 to 1 op 5 to 1) 4
1213² YOUNG ERN [94] 9-2 C Rutter (7) *chsd ldrs, kpt on same pace fnl furlong*........(7 to 1) 5
923* HEAVENLY RISK [88] 8-3 (7*) Mark Denaro (2) *in tch, kpt on same pace fnl 2 fs*........(10 to 1 op 8 to 1) 6
1273* FOR THE PRESENT [78] 8-0² (7ex) K Darley (1) *led to 2 fs out, sn btn*........(14 to 1) 7
1337³ SOUTHERN MEMORIES (Ire) [87] 8-9 W Carson (9) *nvr dngrs*........(8 to 1 op 7 to 1) 8
1017² CYNIC [84] 8-6 G Duffield (5) *cl up, effrt whn squeezed and hmpd o'r one furlong out, sn no ch.* ....(6 to 1 tchd 11 to 2 and 13 to 2) 9
1341* ANOTHER JADE [79] 7-8 (7*) D Wright (11) *in tch, rdn 2 fs out, sn wknd*........(5 to 1 fav op 7 to 1 tchd 8 to 1) 10
1326² GREENLET (Ire) [80] 8-2 M Roberts (13) *in tch, rdn 2 fs out, sn wknd*........(7 to 1 tchd 6 to 1 and 8 to 1) 11
1213⁵ SPECIAL ONE [74] 7-10 S Dawson (4) *chsd ldrs till wknd 2 fs out*........(25 to 1 op 20 to 1) 12
1337⁸ ELLE SHAPED (Ire) [99] 9-2 (5*) O Pears (3) *cl up, rdn o'r 2 fs out, sn wknd*........(33 to 1 op 25 to 1) 13
Dist: Hd, ½l, 2l, 5l, 3l, 2½l, ¾l, 1½l, 3½l, ¾l. 1m 15.83s. a 5.83s (13 Ran).
SR: 57/50/46/45/26/8/ (Mrs P Lewis), M R Channon

1719 Daniel Prenn Royal Yorkshire Rated Class A Handicap (Listed Race) (0-105 3-y-o) £9,541 1¼m 85yds....... (4:15)

1398* RIVER NORTH (Ire) [99] 9-7 K Darley (2) *hld up, hdwy 6 fs out, led o'r one out, ran on wl.* ....(11 to 10 fav op Evens tchd 11 to 8) 1
1524⁵ JACKPOT STAR [90] 8-12 W Carson (3) *in tch, effrt 3 fs out, rdn o'r one out, kpt on wl fnl furlong.* ....(9 to 1 op 10 to 1 tchd 12 to 1) 2
1338³ KEY TO MY HEART (Ire) [90] 8-12 K Fallon (5) *prmnt, led 3 fs out till o'r one out, kpt on same pace.* (6 to 1 op 4 to 1) 3
1302⁵ PERSIAN REVIVAL (Fr) [90] (bl) 8-12 J Fortune (6) *led to 3 fs out, sn wknd*........(20 to 1 op 14 to 1) 4
1412³ SHIRO [91] 8-13 M Roberts (7) *slwly into strd, al beh.* ....(9 to 2 op 7 to 2) 5
1001⁴ NOYAN [97] (bl) 9-5 M Fenton (4) *prmnt till wknd 4 fs out.* ....(12 to 1 op 8 to 1 tchd 14 to 1) 6
999³ CHAIN DANCE [93] 9-1 Paul Eddery (1) *refused to race sn aftr strt*........(15 to 2 op 7 to 1 tchd 8 to 1) I
Dist: 2l, ¾l, 15l, 3½l, 6l. 2m 12.89s. a 4.89s (7 Ran).
SR: 74/61/59/29/23/17/-/ (P D Savill), Lady Herries

1720 Crawley Warren Handicap Class C (0-100 3-y-o and up) £10,672 1m 205yds........................ (4:45)

4782a⁹ DOUBLE ECHO (Ire) [67] 5-7-10 W Carson (2) *cl up, led wl o'r 2 fs out, rdn and ran on well fnl furlong.* ....(8 to 1 op 10 to 1 tchd 12 to 1) 1
TOP SHIEL [77] 5-8-6 R Cochrane (9) *in tch, effrt o'r 2 fs out, sn rdn, styd on fnl furlong*........(8 to 1 op 7 to 1) 2
1398⁵ COOL LUKE (Ire) [79] 4-8-8 J Fanning (4) *in tch, ev ch o'r 2 fs out, kpt on same pace*........(4 to 1 op 3 to 1) 3
1398³ CUMBRIAN CHALLENGE (Ire) [96] 4-9-11 M Birch (5) *trkd ldrs, ev ch o'r 2 fs out, one pace*........(4 to 1) 4
1434* SWEET MIGNONETTE [73] 5-8-2 K Darley (3) *hld up in tch, effrt o'r 2 fs out, no real hdwy*... (3 to 1 fav op 9 to 4) 5
ROYAL CITIZEN (Ire) [74] 4-8-3 L Charnock (6) *led to 3 fs out, sn wknd*........(20 to 1 op 16 to 1) 6
1125⁵ KING PARIS (Ire) [100] 3-9-3 M Hills (7) *cl up, rdn o'r 2 fs out, sn wknd*........(7 to 1 op 6 to 1) 7
845 GREEK GOLD (Ire) [74] 4-8-3 M Roberts (8) *al beh.* ....(7 to 1 op 6 to 1 tchd 8 to 1) 8
OPERATION WOLF [81] 7-8-10 Kim Tinkler (1) *beh, lost tch 4 fs out, tld off*........(16 to 1 op 12 to 1) 9
Dist: 3½l, 2½l, 2l, ½l, 6l, hd, nk, dist. 1m 57.12s. a 7.92s (9 Ran).
(Mrs John Lee), J D Bethell

1721 Michael Sobell Handicap Class C (0-90 3-y-o and up) £6,264 6f 214yds ....(5:15)

824² HIGHLAND MAGIC (Ire) [78] 5-9-7 M Roberts (9) *hld up, not much room 3 fs out, swtchd and hdwy o'r one out, ran on wl to ld ins last.* (2 to 1 fav tchd 5 to 2 and 7 to 4) 1
1436* MY BEST VALENTINE [76] 3-8-9 F Norton (6) *prmnt, led entering fnl furlong, sn hdd, no extr.* (6 to 1 op 5 to 1) 2
1530* VELOCE (Ire) [61] 5-8-4 A Mackay (2) *hld up in tch, hdwy 2 fs out, one pace fnl furlong*........(5 to 1 op 9 to 2) 3
818⁵ BLOW DRY (Ire) [80] 3-8-13 A Culhane (10) *hld up beh, ran on wl fnl 2 fs, nrst finish*........(7 to 1) 4
425 JALMUSIQUE [81] 7-9-10 M Birch (3) *led till entering fnl furlong, one pace*........(14 to 1 op 16 to 1) 5
1563³ DEBSY DO (USA) [72] 4-8-10 (5*) O Pears (1) *prmnt, rdn o'r 2 fs out, sn btn*........(15 to 2 op 7 to 1 tchd 8 to 1) 6
1177² AFRICAN CHIMES [67] 6-8-3 (7*) D McCabe (7) *pld hrd, in tch till wknd 3 fs out*........(8 to 1 tchd 7 to 1) 7
1527 RURAL LAD [61] 4-8-4 L Charnock (4) *mid-div, effrt 3 fs out, sn btn*........(10 to 1 tchd 12 to 1) 8
1530 GRANITTON BAY [69] 6-8-5 (7*) G Parkin (5) *mid-div, effrt 3 fs out, sn btn*........(25 to 1) 9
1494* THE AUCTION BIDDER [80] 6-9-9 K Darley (8) *trkd ldrs, effrt o'r 2 fs out, wknd quickly*..... (8 to 1 op 7 to 1) 10
Dist: ¾l, 2l, hd, 1½l, 3½l, hd, 2½l, 2½l, 10l. 1m 28.82s. a 7.12s (10 Ran).
SR: 63/49/38/46/52/32/26/12/12/ (Miss N Carroll), M J Fetherston-Godley

CHANTILLY (FR) (soft)
Sunday June 13th
Going Correction: PLUS 0.60 sec. per fur.

1722 Prix de Diane Hermes (Group 1) (3-y-o) £167,264 1¼m 110yds...... (2:40)

1033⁵ SHEMAKA (Ire) 9-2 G Mosse (1) *al prmnt, led appr strt, quickened 2 fs out, hrd rdn and ran on wl ins last.* ....(66 to 10) 1
1086⁴ BAYA (USA) 9-2 T Jarnet (4) *tenth strt, hdwy and not clr run 2 fs out, chlgd one and a half out, ran on wl.* ....(44 to 10) 2
1218² DANCIENNE (Fr) 9-2 F Head (12) *wl in rear till hdwy 2 fs out, fnshd well*........(5 to 2) 3
1218⁴ CORRAZONA (USA) 9-2 G Guignard (11) *hld up, hdwy 2 fs out, kpt on wl, not rch ldrs*........(83 to 10) 4
1033² BRIGHT MOON (USA) (bl) 9-2 D Boeuf (13) *prmnt, second strt, wknd fnl furlong*........(7 to 2) 5
1218⁵ ROYALE CHANTOU (Fr) 9-2 C Le Scrill (5) *8th strt, effrt 2 fs out, one pace*........(30 to 1) 6
1545² ROUQUETTE 9-2 A Badel (8) *9th strt, rdn 2 fs out, one pace*........(13 to 1) 7
1033³ ALICE SPRINGS (USA) 9-2 L Dettori (6) *4th strt, sn rdn and wknd*........(15 to 1) 8
1290* AUBE INDIENNE (Fr) 9-2 C Asmussen (9) *5th strt, sn rdn and btn*........(10 to 1) 9
1200⁹ DAYFLOWER (USA) 9-2 W R Swinburn (7) *7th strt, sn btn.* ....(36 to 1) 0
809³ BROKEN PEACE (USA) 9-2 S Guillot (14) *al beh*.... (7 to 2) 0
1218³ ACCOMMODATING (USA) 9-2 E Saint-Martin (3) *trkd ldrs, 3rd strt, wknd quickly 2 fs out*........(24 to 1) 0
1033⁷ FRESHER 9-2 O Benoist (2) *6th strt, wknd*........(44 to 1) 0
1545⁷ GAIRSIC (Fr) 9-2 G Benoit (10) *prmnt till wknd quickly appr strt, tld off*........(13 to 10 fav) 0
Dist: Nk, 1½l, 1½l, nose, 1½l, nk, 5l, ½l, ½l, ½l. 2m 16.00s. a 9.40s (14 Ran).
SR: 71/70/67/64/63/60/59/49/48/ (H H Aga Khan), A de Royer-Dupre

1723 Prix du Chemin de Fer du Nord (Group 3) (4-y-o and up) £23,895 1m.... (2:55)

AFRICANUS (Fr) 4-8-12 D Boeuf (4) *led strt, effrt 2 fs out, ran on wl*........(87 to 10) 1
1366³ SHANGHAI (USA) 4-8-12 C Asmussen (3) *3rd strt, effrt 2 fs out, some hdwy last, nvr able to chal*.....(11 to 10 fav) 2

956* GOTHLAND (Fr) 4-8-12 G Mosse (5) *second strt, effrt 2 fs out, one pace fnl furlong*.................... (10 to 1) 3
920³ NORTHERN CRYSTAL 5-9-1 T Jarnet (2) *4th strt, rdn o'r 2 fs out, nvr able to chal*.......................(4 to 1) 4
1243* BURDUR 5-8-12 C Le Scrill (1) *al last*...........(15 to 1) 5
Dist: ¾l, hd, ¾l, 4l. 1m 49.00s. a 14.30s (5 Ran).
E Lellouche

COLOGNE (GER) (good)
Sunday June 13th

1724 Zanders-Union-Rennen (Group 2) (3-y-o) £48,980 1m 3f..............(3:45)

953* KORNADO 9-2 A Best, *hld up, 6th strt, led one and a half fs out, rdn out*.. 1
STERNKONIG (Ire) 9-2 M Hofer, *hld up, hdwy and not clr run 2 fs out, fnshd wl*.. 2
ALTER ADEL 9-2 M J Kinane, *in rear till hdwy 4 fs out, 5th strt, not clr run one and a half out, ran on fnl furlong.* 3
1314* TIOMAN ISLAND 9-2 B Raymond, *led till one and a half fs out, kpt on wl*.. 4
CONCEPCION (Ger) 9-2 A Boschert, *hld up, 7th strt, chlgd o'r 2 fs out, ev ch one out, sn wknd*.................. 5
TACOMA PARK (Ger) 9-2 A Bond, *some hdwy fnl 2 fs, nvr nrr*.. 6
953⁶ LANDO (Ger) 9-2 A Tylicki, *trkd ldr, second strt, wknd o'r one furlong out*.. 7
953³ IROKESE (Ger) 9-2 A Helfenbein, *4th strt, sn btn*.......... 8
1369⁵ TROPICAL KING (Ger) 9-2 M Rimmer, *3rd strt, wknd quickly, tld off*.. 9
Dist: ½l, 1½l, nk, 1½l, 5l, 1l, hd, dist. 2m 13.09s. (9 Ran).
(Stall Granum), Bruno Schuetz

SAN SIRO (ITY) (good)
Sunday June 13th

1725 Premio Chiari (2-y-o) £11,207 7f 110yds........................(2:30)

TORRISMONDO (USA) 8-11 T Quinn, *made all, ran on wl.* 1
EL TEL (Fr) 8-11 A Munro, *rcd in 3rd, hdwy o'r one furlong out, no imprsn*.. 2
SORT CODE (USA) 8-11 S Soto,.. 3
Dist: 1½l, 1½l, 2½l, nk, 3½l, nk, 5l, 1l, 8l, 7l. 1m 36.50s. (13 Ran).
(Lord Portman), P F I Cole

1726 Premio Dyreen (2-y-o) £11,207 7f 110yds........................(4:00)

WHATCOMBE (USA) 8-8 A Munro, *rcd in 3rd, led 3 fs out, sn clr*.. 1
ALPRIDE (Ire) 8-8 L Sorrentino,.......................... 2
STREISAND 8-8 E Botti,.. 3
MICROLITE (USA) 8-8 T Quinn, *nvr able to chal*.......... 5
Dist: 2½l, 2l, 1½l, 1½l, 5½l, hd, ½l, nk, 13l. 1m 36.40s. (10 Ran).
(Fahd Salman), P F I Cole

1727 Premio Legnano-Memorial Mario Incisa della Rochetta (Group 3) (3-y-o and up) £29,586 1¼m..........(4:30)

1217⁵ RUBY TIGER 6-9-1 T Quinn, *rcd in rear, 6th strt, improved on outsd 4 fs out, led 2 and a half out, sn clr*.......... 1
4727a⁷ DAMA GRANDE 4-9-1 M Pasquale, *rcd in second, led strt, chlgd 2 and a half fs out, ran on wl*.................. 2
L'EREDITIERA (Ire) 4-9-1 O Fancera, *in rear, effrt 2 fs out, rdn fnl furlong, no extr*.................................. 3
OLLI STAR (Ire) 3-8-3 A Munro, *5th strt, styd on one pace fnl 3 fs*.. 4
TODESCHINA 3-8-3 B Jovine, *3rd strt, rdn 3 fs out, one pace*.. 5
ABLE LASSIE 5-9-1 J Tandari, *led till strt, rdn and wknd 2 fs out*.. 6
DARUBENA (Ity) 3-8-3 A Di Nardo, *4th strt, rdn 3 fs out, sn wknd*.. 7
LADY CARLOTTA (Ire) 4-9-1 A Marcialis, *nvr able to chal.* 8
VILNICA (Fr) 3-8-3 M Esposito, *al tld off*.................. 9
Dist: 1 ¾l, 3½l, nose, 2l, 3l, 7l, 12l, 3l. 2m 5.10s. (9 Ran).
(Mrs Philip Blacker), P F I Cole

BRIGHTON (good)
Monday June 14th
Going Correction: PLUS 0.10 sec. per fur.

1728 Bush At Kemp Town Handicap Class D (0-80 3-y-o and up) £3,172 5f 59yds..............................(2:00)

1352³ KENSWORTH LADY [47] 3-8-1 N Adams (1) *strted slwly, hld up beh ldrs, led ins fnl furlong, drvn out.* (3 to 1 jt-fav op 5 to 2) 1
1560⁶ FARMER JOCK [54] 11-9-2 M Roberts (3) *hld up, effrt o'r one furlong out, kpt on und pres ins last.* ....(7 to 2 tchd 4 to 1 and 100 to 30) 2
1492 SERIOUS HURRY [59] 5-9-7 T Quinn (5) *wth ldr, led o'r one furlong out, hdd and no extr ins last.* ....(14 to 1 op 6 to 1) 3
1492 TREASURE TIME (Ire) [62] 4-9-3 (7*) D Wright (6) *sn led, hdd o'r one furlong out, one pace*........(6 to 1 op 5 to 1) 4
1473 TEE-EMM [54] 3-8-8 L Dettori (4) *trkd ldg pair, drvn 2 fs out, sn btn*........................(10 to 1 op 6 to 1) 5
1473³ STOCKTINA [43] 6-8-5 J Quinn (2) *in tch, rdn and btn o'r 2 fs out, tld off*............(3 to 1 jt-fav tchd 100 to 30) 6
Dist: 1½l, 1½l, ½l, 2l, 15l. 1m 4.00s. a 3.90s (6 Ran).
SR: 20/29/28/29/5/-/ (P A Matthews), M Blanshard

1729 Bevendean Maiden Stakes Class D (3-y-o and up) £3,114 6f 209yds.... (2:30)

1424² GRAN SENORUM (USA) 3-8-11 A Munro (5) *cl up, led and hng lft und pres wl o'r one furlong out, rdn out.* ....(5 to 1 on op 4 to 1 on tchd 7 to 2 on) 1
1144 HALBERT (bl) 4-9-7 J Reid (3) *cl up, led 2 and a half fs out till wl o'r one out, hrd rdn, one pace.* ....(13 to 2 op 3 to 1 tchd 7 to 1) 2
1559⁵ ALMOSTAUTOMATIC (Ire) 4-9-7 L Dettori (1) *led to 2 and a half fs out, wknd*..... (12 to 1 op 8 to 1 tchd 14 to 1) 3
GATHERING 4-9-7 N Adams (4) *strted slwly, nvr on terms.* ....(33 to 1 op 20 to 1) 4
1349 MAI-TU-TU 3-8-6 A Tucker (2) *sn outpcd, tld off.* ....(100 to 1 op 25 to 1) 5
Dist: 3l, 5l, 6l, 20l. 1m 26.70s. a 6.70s (5 Ran).
SR: 7/8/ (Fahd Salman), P F I Cole

1730 Brighton Mile Challenge Trophy Handicap Class C (0-90 4-y-o and up) £4,582 7f 214yds............... (3:00)

1434⁴ SET THE FASHION [51] (v) 4-7-10 (3*) D Harrison (7) *trkd ldrs, swtchd lft 2 fs out, led o'r one out, drifted left, ran on strly*........................ (7 to 2 fav op 9 to 2) 1
1490* NORTH ESK (USA) [63] 4-8-11 M Wigham (3) *hld up rear, rdn and crrd lft o'r 2 fs out, kpt on wl fnl furlong.* ....(4 to 1 op 3 to 1) 2
1527⁶ SHIKARI'S SON [77] 6-9-11 T Quinn (6) *keen hold, trkd ldrs gng wl, ev ch o'r one furlong out, sn one pace.* ....(6 to 1 tchd 7 to 1) 3
1527⁷ HELIOS [77] 5-9-11 J Reid (5) *made most till o'r one furlong out, one pace*..................(12 to 1 op 7 to 1) 4
1530⁴ LANGTRY LADY [74] (v) 7-9-1 (7*) P McCabe (8) *hld up, effrt whn hmpd wl o'r 2 fs out, sn no imprsn.* ....(9 to 2 tchd 5 to 1) 5
1527³ CAPE PIGEON (USA) [80] 8-10-0 A Munro (1) *cl up, styd far side and led briefly entering strt, wknd o'r one furlong out*................................(8 to 1 op 5 to 1) 6
1447⁸ ROCALITY [73] 4-9-7 M Roberts (2) *hld up in tch, styd far side entering strt, outpcd o'r one furlong out, eased.* ....(6 to 1 tchd 13 to 2) 7
679 NATCHEZ TRACE [63] 4-8-11 L Dettori (4) *cl up, rdn and wknd wl o'r 2 fs out*..................(33 to 1 op 16 to 1) 8
Dist: 4l, hd, ¾l, 3l, 2½l, 6l, 3l. 1m 36.50s. a 4.10s (8 Ran).
SR: 36/36/49/47/35/33/8/-/ (The Queen), Lord Huntingdon

1731 Levy Board Handicap Class E (0-70 3-y-o and up) £2,821 1m 3f 196yds ....(3:30)

1607 CORINTHIAN GOD (Ire) [33] 4-8-0 M Roberts (3) *made most, hrd rdn 3 fs out, kpt on gmely*......(9 to 2 tchd 5 to 1) 1
1281³ PRINCESS EVITA (Fr) [37] 4-8-1 (3*) D Harrison (1) *wtd wth, cld o'r 3 fs out, rdn and ev ch entering last, no extr.* ....(9 to 2 tchd 5 to 1) 2
1242⁸ NASEER (USA) [49] 4-9-2 T Quinn (7) *hld up in cl tch, closed 5 fs out, ev ch und pres one out, not quicken.* ....(14 to 1 op 7 to 1 tchd 16 to 1) 3
723 MONARDA [61] (bl) 6-10-0 A Munro (2) *trkd ldrs, rdn 3 fs out, sn outpcd*........................ (5 to 1 op 5 to 2) 4
1094⁶ ROCQUAINE BAY [40] 6-8-7 C Rutter (4) *hld up, cld o'r 4 fs out, ev ch 3 out, wknd 2 out*....(7 to 2 jt-fav op 5 to 1) 5
1318⁹ SHIRL [35] 4-7-9 (7*) P McCabe (5) *cl up, wknd 4 fs out.* ....(12 to 1 op 8 to 1 tchd 14 to 1) 6
PIE HATCH (Ire) [42] 4-8-9 G Duffield (6) *wth ldr, wknd o'r 3 fs out, tld off*...... (7 to 2 jt-fav op 9 to 2 tchd 5 to 1) 7
Dist: 1l, sht-hd, 7l, hd, nk, 15l. 2m 36.30s. a 8.80s (7 Ran).
SR: 10/12/23/21/ (T S M S Riley-Smith), D A Wilson

1732 Royal Promenade Hotel Brighton Rating Related Maiden Fillies Stakes Class E (0-70 3-y-o) £2,847 1m 3f 196yds....................... (4:00)

1161⁶ INDIAN FLASH (Ire) 8-11 L Dettori (2) *made all, shaken up o'r one furlong out, not extended.* ....(15 to 2 op 6 to 1 tchd 8 to 1) 1
992⁹ HAVEN OF LOVE (Ire) 8-11 D Biggs (3) *hld up, hdwy to chase wnr frm wl o'r 2 fs out, hrd rdn over one out, no imprsn*........................ (8 to 1 tchd 9 to 1) 2

732[8] SWIFT SPRING (Fr) 8-11 T Quinn (6) *hld up, cld 4 fs out, outpcd o'r 2 out*........(11 to 4 op 5 to 2 tchd 3 to 1) 3
1315[5] GLINT OF AYR 8-11 W Carson (5) *trkd wnr, pushed alng 3 fs out, sn outpcd.* (85 to 40 fav op 2 to 1 tchd 9 to 4) 4
1359[2] MISS PIMPERNEL 8-11 B Raymond (1) *trkd ldrs, hrd rdn o'r 4 fs out, sn outpcd.* (11 to 4 op 5 to 2 tchd 3 to 1) 5
1501[7] AGENDA ONE 8-11 N Adams (4) *al beh, rdn alng o'r 5 fs out, sn lost tch, tld off.*
..............................(40 to 1 op 33 to 1 tchd 50 to 1) 6
Dist: 3l, 7l, hd, ½l, dist. (Time not taken) (6 Ran).
(Vijay Mallya), R Guest

1733 Moulsecoomb Rating Related Maiden Stakes Class E (0-70 3-y-o) £2,872 7f 214yds........................ (4:30)

1185[2] ROYAL INTERVAL 9-0 T Sprake (3) *in cl tch, not much room 3 fs out, squeezed through to ld wl o'r one out, sn clr, cmftbly*............ (5 to 1 op 4 to 1 tchd 13 to 2) 1
1524[4] PRINCESS TATEUM (Ire) 8-9 P Robinson (2) *beh, pushed alng appr strt, hrd rdn o'r 2 fs out, swtchd rght approaching last, kpt on one pace.*
..................................(11 to 8 on op Evens) 2
1092[9] BAYRAK (USA) 9-0 W Carson (5) *wth ldr, ev ch appr 2 fs out, rdn and no extr*.....(9 to 2 op 9 to 4 tchd 5 to 1) 3
4717a SHARRO 9-0 A Munro (1) *in cl tch, rdn o'r 3 fs out, sn btn.*
..................................(25 to 1 op 14 to 1) 4
1316 HERETICAL MISS 8-9 J Reid (4) *led till wl o'r one furlong out, wknd*............. (13 to 2 op 9 to 2 tchd 7 to 1) 5
Dist: 6l, 1½l, ¾l, 5l. 1m 37.10s. a 4.70s (5 Ran).
SR: 41/18/18/16/-/ (G L Barker), W G M Turner

1734 Peacehaven Apprentice Handicap Class F (0-70 3-y-o and up) £2,377 6f 209yds........................ (5:00)

1527* SILKY SIREN [68] 4-9-9 (5*) R Painter (5) *tld off appr strt, remained alone far side, rapid hdwy 2 fs out, led one out, pushed out.*
...........(7 to 2 op 3 to 1 tchd 11 to 4 and 4 to 1) 1
1487[3] PRINCE RODNEY [60] 4-9-3 (3*) Mark Denaro (4) *chsd ldg pair, cld 2 fs out, ev ch whn edgd lft und pres ins last, not quicken*...........(13 to 2 op 5 to 1 tchd 7 to 1) 2
1474[2] DANCING SENSATION (USA) [44] 6-7-10 (8*) T Ashley (1) *wth ldr, led 2 fs out to one out, one pace.*
......................(6 to 4 fav op 7 to 4 tchd 9 to 4) 3
1588* CHARMED KNAVE [54] 8-8-11 (3*,6ex) S Eiffert (2) *led to 2 fs out, wknd*............(9 to 2 op 2 to 1 tchd 5 to 1) 4
1267[7] QUICK STEEL [52] (v) 5-8-12 S Mulvey (3) *chsd ldg pair, rdn alng o'r 2 fs out, sn btn.*
........................(9 to 2 op 5 to 1 tchd 6 to 1) 5
Dist: Nk, 3l, 2l, 2l. (Time not taken) (5 Ran).
(S Nixon), M C Pipe

EDINBURGH (good)
Monday June 14th
Going Correction: PLUS 0.10 sec. per fur. (races 1,2,3,4), MINUS 0.25 (5,6)

1735 Cockenzie Rating Related Maiden Stakes Class E (0-70 3-y-o) £2,739 7f 15yds........................ (2:15)

1239[7] FRANCIA 8-2 (7*) J Tate (1) *trkd ldr, led wl o'r 2 out, drw clr, easily*........... (6 to 4 fav op 7 to 4 tchd 2 to 1) 1
1160[6] MISSED THE BOAT (Ire) 9-0 K Darley (5) *in tch, effrt 3 out, sn rdn, kpt on fnl 2 fs, no ch wth wnr.*
........................(13 to 8 op 5 to 4 tchd 7 to 4) 2
590[8] CONTRAC COUNTESS (Ire) (v) 8-9 S Wood (4) *chsd ldrs, effrt 3 out, sn rdn, styd on same pace.*
....(8 to 1 op 6 to 1) 3
991[9] ST ALZINA (Ire) 9-0 C Dwyer (3) *led till hdd wl o'r 2 out, sn wknd*..................(7 to 1 op 8 to 1 tchd 10 to 1) 4
884[6] BROOKLANDS EXPRESS (bl) 9-0 L Charnock (2) *al beh.*
....(12 to 1 op 8 to 1) 5
Dist: 4l, 5l, 6l, 3½l. 1m 30.60s. a 5.40s (5 Ran).
SR: 25/18/ (A B Atkins), A Hide

1736 Leith Claiming Stakes Class F (3-y-o and up) £2,460 7f 15yds.........(2:45)

1193[2] LAUREL QUEEN (Ire) 5-9-3 J Carroll (2) *cl up, led hfwy, shaken up and ran on wl fnl 2 fs.*
.......(21 to 20 fav op 5 to 4 tchd Evens and 11 to 8) 1
1436[6] OBSIDIAN GREY 6-8-8 Dean McKeown (9) *nvr far away, swtchd o'r one out, ran on wl fnl furlong, not rch wnr.*
....(7 to 2 op 5 to 2) 2
765[2] NUTTY BROWN (bl) 3-8-3 (5*) O Pears (4) *prmnt, ev ch 2 out, kpt on same pace*.............(20 to 1 op 14 to 1) 3
1285[9] SHALABIA 4-8-11 N Connorton (6) *dwlt, sn in tch, effrt o'r 2 out, one paced*...... (11 to 1 op 7 to 1 tchd 12 to 1) 4
1578 CLEDESCHAMPS 4-8-7 S Morris (3) *in tch, effrt 3 out, no hdwy*...............................(33 to 1 op 20 to 1) 5

1186[6] SENSE OF PRIORITY 4-9-8 K Darley (5) *hld up, hdwy hfwy, ev ch o'r 2 out, sn rdn and one paced.*
......................(10 to 1 op 5 to 1 tchd 12 to 1) 6
1578[3] KHALLOOF (Ire) 4-8-5 (7*) C Teague (8) *sn beh.*
......................(16 to 1 op 14 to 1 tchd 20 to 1) 7
1599* DIET (v) 7-8-7 (7*) R Havlin (7) *made most to hfwy, grad wknd*.................................(7 to 1 op 5 to 1) 8
1517[6] KINCARDINE BRIDGE (USA) 4-9-8 D Wilkinson (10) *al beh.*
......................................(300 to 1 op 200 to 1) 9
Dist: 2½l, ½l, 1½l, ½l, 2½l, 1l, 7l, 5l. 1m 29.50s. a 4.30s (9 Ran).
SR: 49/32/30/28/22/29/16/-/-/ (Laurel (Leisure) Limited), J Berry

1737 Levy Board Handicap Class E (0-70 3-y-o and up) £2,872 1m 16yds.. (3:15)

1520* LAWNSWOOD JUNIOR [63] 6-9-8 K Darley (6) *hld up in tch, steady hdwy to ld one out, ran on wl.*
....(7 to 2 fav op 3 to 1) 1
1436 ROUTING [47] 5-8-6 Dean McKeown (13) *slwly into strd, beh, hmpd o'r 4 out, hdwy 3 out, ran on wl fnl furlong, not rch wnr*.......................(10 to 1 op 7 to 1) 2
1436[4] THORNTON GATE [67] 4-9-9 (3*) S Maloney (8) *trkd ldrs, led wl o'r 2 out, hdd one out, one paced.*
....(9 to 2 op 3 to 1) 3
1274 LADY DONOGHUE (USA) [54] 4-8-13 J Carroll (11) *hld up, badly hmpd and crrd wide hfwy, styd on wl fnl 3 fs, nvr dngrs*..................(7 to 1 op 6 to 1 tchd 8 to 1) 4
1634[5] THE PREMIER EXPRES [62] (bl) 3-8-10 R Lappin (5) *nvr far away, kpt on same pace fnl 3 fs.* (12 to 1 tchd 14 to 1) 5
MONASTIC FLIGHT (Ire) [50] 3-7-12 S Wood (9) *in tch till badly hmpd and crrd wide hfwy, no dngr aftr.*
......................(11 to 2 op 5 to 1 tchd 10 to 1) 6
1534 FREDDIE JACK [45] 3-7-2 (5*) Darren Moffatt (1) *prmnt till badly hmpd and crrd wide hfwy, no dngr aftr.*
....(100 to 1) 7
1436[3] MALCESINE (Ire) [45] 4-8-4 J Lowe (2) *led aftr one furlong till hdd wl o'r 2 out, fdd.* (8 to 1 op 7 to 1 tchd 9 to 1) 8
1436 GANT BLEU (Fr) [59] 6-9-4 A Culhane (10) *hld up, badly hmpd aftr 4 out, nvr dngrs*........ (14 to 1 op 12 to 1) 9
TUMBLING (USA) [41] 5-8-0 L Charnock (3) *in tch till wknd 3 out*..........................(12 to 1 tchd 14 to 1) 10
1578[7] WAAZA (USA) [53] 4-8-7 (5*) O Pears (7) *beh, badly hmpd and crrd wide hfwy, no ch aftr*.................(14 to 1) 11
HILLTOWN BLUES [50] 4-8-9 M Birch (14) *in tch till wknd 3 out*..............................(25 to 1 op 20 to 1) 12
1629[5] DUSKY DUCHESS (Ire) [45] (v) 3-7-2[2] (7*) Claire Balding (12) *led one furlong, cl up till stumbled and uns rdr hfwy.*
......................................(300 to 1 op 200 to 1) ur
Dist: 1½l, hd, 5l, sht-hd, 2½l, 1l, 1½l, 3½l, 4l, 4l. 1m 43.80s. a 5.30s (13 Ran).
SR: 41/20/39/11/7/-/ (Graham Treglown), J L Spearing

1738 Millerhill Handicap Class E (0-70 4-y-o and up) £2,778 1m 7f 16yds..... (3:45)

1195[3] OUR AISLING [68] 5-9-7 (5*) O Pears (4) *trkd ldrs gng wl, led well o'r one out, rdn clr, easily.*
....(5 to 4 on op Evens) 1
1601[9] ALPHA HELIX [35] (v) 10-7-7 J Fanning (5) *cl up, slight ld o'r 3 out, hdd wl over one out, kpt on, no ch wth wnr.*
....(100 to 1 op 66 to 1) 2
1601[5] GREY COMMANDER [35] 5-7-7 L Charnock (6) *led till hdd o'r 3 out, ev ch 2 out, one paced.*
......................(11 to 1 op 7 to 1 tchd 12 to 1) 3
BLACKDOWN [56] 6-9-0 M Birch (1) *hld up, hdwy 3 out, one paced fnl 2 fs*.................. (16 to 1 op 10 to 1) 4
1400[3] YOUNG GEORGE [42] 6-8-0 J Lowe (3) *hld up, effrt o'r 3 out, no hdwy*........... (11 to 4 op 5 to 2 tchd 3 to 1) 5
1517[4] JOHN NAMAN (Ire) [43] 4-8-1 K Darley (2) *in tch, effrt 4 out, rdn 3 out, sn btn*..................... (7 to 1 op 5 to 1) 6
1421 DOCTOR'S REMEDY [35] 7-7-2[2] (7*) C Teague (7) *in tch till wknd o'r 4 out*............................(50 to 1 op 33 to 1) 7
Dist: 6l, 3½l, 2½l, 2½l, 7l, 4l. 3m 24.40s. a 12.40s (7 Ran).
SR: 3/-/-/-/ (A K Smeaton), S G Norton

1739 EBF Fillies Median Auction Maiden Stakes Class F (2-y-o) £2,540 5f (4:15)

PLAINSONG 8-11 N Connorton (5) *cl up, led aftr 2 fs, ran on wl fnl furlong*........(7 to 1 op 6 to 1 tchd 8 to 1) 1
1556[3] ASHKERNAZY (Ire) 8-11 K Darley (1) *slight ld 2 fs, sn pushed alng, kpt on wl fnl furlong.*
.... (5 to 4 on op 6 to 4 on tchd 11 to 10 on) 2
768[2] ROSIE VALENTINE 8-6 (5*) O Pears (6) *prmnt, ev ch 2 out, one paced*........... (100 to 30 op 5 to 2 tchd 7 to 2) 3
FORBIDDEN MONKEY 8-11 L Charnock (4) *chsd ldrs, kpt on same pace fnl 2 fs*.................. (25 to 1 op 16 to 1) 4
1189 SPRINGHEAD 8-11 Dean McKeown (7) *slwly into strd, beh till some late hdwy, nvr dngrs*..... (33 to 1 op 16 to 1) 5
395 ME NEITHER 8-11 J Carroll (3) *in tch till wknd 2 out.*
....(14 to 1 op 5 to 1) 6
1339[3] BOLLIN MARY 8-11 M Birch (2) *chsd ldrs till wknd 2 out.*
......................(13 to 2 op 5 to 1 tchd 7 to 1) 7
1418 FADE AWAY (Ire) 8-4 (7*) V Halliday (8) *beh frm hfwy.*
....(25 to 1 op 12 to 1) 8
Dist: 1½l, 3l, 1½l, 1l, 1½l, 8l, ½l. 1m 0.80s. a 3.00s (8 Ran).
SR: 12/6/-/-/-/ (Peter Innes), Denys Smith

1740 Tranent Handicap Class E (0-70 3-y-o) £2,845 5f...................... (4:45)

1478* CALL ME I'M BLUE (Ire) [72] 9-4 (5*) O Pears (9) *cl up, led hfwy, ran on wl fnl furlong.* ....(11 to 10 fav op 6 to 4 tchd 7 to 4) 1

1287[3] TREVORSNINEPOINTS [54] 8-5 K Darley (10) *slight ld to hfwy, chsd wnr aftr, kpt on, no imprsn.* ....(100 to 30 op 5 to 2 tchd 4 to 1) 2

1560[7] THE FED [54] 8-5 A Culhane (5) *wth ldrs, ev ch 2 out, kpt on same pace*......................(12 to 1 op 8 to 1) 3

1228[6] PRINCIPAL PLAYER (USA) [54] (bl) 8-2 (3*) S Maloney (6) *prmnt, kpt on same pace fnl 2 fs*... (20 to 1 op 14 to 1) 4

899 FINAL OAK [47] 7-12 J Fanning (1) *chsd ldrs, no hdwy fnl 2 fs*..................(25 to 1 op 14 to 1 tchd 33 to 1) 5

1463[6] LUCKY MILL [48] 7-13 R Lappin (7) *nvr dngrs.* ....(20 to 1 op 14 to 1) 6

1505[3] COMET WHIRLPOOL (Ire) [55] (bl) 7-13 (7*) G Forster (3) *nvr dngrs*.................. (8 to 1 op 6 to 1 tchd 9 to 1) 7

1516[2] SENSABO [42] 7-3[1] (5*) Darren Moffatt (2) *al beh.* ....(14 to 1 op 12 to 1) 8

1226[4] TOM PIPER [59] 8-10 J Carroll (4) *beh frm hfwy.* ....(16 to 1 op 12 to 1) 9

1503[9] WHISPERDALES [61] 8-12 S Morris (8) *beh frm hfwy.* ....(50 to 1 op 33 to 1) 10

Dist: 3½l, 1½l, ¾l, ½l, 1½l, nk, 1½l, hd, 7l. 59.40s. a 1.60s (10 Ran).
SR: 52/20/14/11/2/-/3/-/-/ (Harsh (Tipping Gears)), N Tinkler

WINDSOR (good to soft)
Monday June 14th

Going Correction: PLUS 0.15 sec. per fur. (races 1,2,4), PLUS 0.40 (3,5,6)

1741 Panmure Gordon Selling Stakes Class G (2-y-o) £2,514 5f 217yds (6:35)

1481[7] STAR SPEEDER (Ire) 7-13 (7*) B Russell (19) *wth ldr, led 2 fs out, rdn and edgd lft one out, pushed clr.* ....(3 to 1 fav op 6 to 1 tchd 9 to 1) 1

949[4] LITTLE EMMELINE 8-6 N Carlisle (9) *made most till hng lft and hdd 2 fs out, veered rght one out, ran on same pace*..............................(12 to 1 op 10 to 1) 2

1343[3] WINDOW DISPLAY 9-2 Paul Eddery (13) *sn chasing ldrs, one pace fnl 2 fs*....................(5 to 1 op 4 to 1) 3

REAL POPCORN (Ire) 8-6 G Carter (4) *ran on 2 fs out, no imprsn on wnr fnl furlong.* ....(12 to 1 op 8 to 1 tchd 14 to 1) 4

1253[5] AERIAL VIEW 8-11 T Sprake (10) *in tch, no prog frm 2 fs out*.............................. (33 to 1 op 20 to 1) 5

1555[8] SULLAMELL 8-11 L Dettori (17) *wl plcd, rdn alng and no extr frm 2 fs out*.....(12 to 1 tchd 20 to 1 and 8 to 1) 6

1555[2] LADY RISKY 8-6 Pat Eddery (11) *chsd ldrs, rdn and btn ins last 2 fs*..............................(4 to 1 op 3 to 1) 7

1602 LITTLE LUKE (Ire) 8-4 (7*) S Drowne (7) *nvr better plcd.* ....(33 to 1 op 25 to 1) 8

1583 CA IRA (Ire) (bl) 8-6 J Williams (16) *hndy for o'r 3 fs.* ....(25 to 1 op 12 to 1) 9

1555 LITTLE HOOLIGAN 8-11 C Rutter (14) *sn rdn alng, nvr trble frnt rnk*........(16 to 1 op 14 to 1 tchd 20 to 1) 10

877 THE SPIVE (bl) 8-11 G Bardwell (2) *mid-div most of way.* ....(33 to 1 op 25 to 1) 11

1265 AIR RAID 8-11 S Whitworth (12) *outpcd.* ....(33 to 1 op 25 to 1) 12

1391[5] WADDLE (Ire) 8-11 P Robinson (5) *in tch 4 fs.* .... (5 to 1 op 7 to 2 tchd 11 to 2) 13

MAN OF KASHMIR (Ire) 8-11 R Price (3) *nvr on terms.* ....(33 to 1) 14

1391 BRIGHT VENUS 8-6 N Adams (6) *early pace, btn hfwy.* ....(33 to 1 op 25 to 1) 15

1583 BIEN CUIT 8-3 (3*) D Harrison (8) *al beh.* ....(33 to 1 op 25 to 1) 16

1615[3] CLASSICAL DON (Ire) 8-11 N Day (15) *nvr dngrs.* ....(25 to 1 op 16 to 1) 17

MR GORDON BENNETT 8-11 J Quinn (1) *slwly into strd, outpcd*......................................(33 to 1) 18

SHAMINA 8-6 W Newnes (18) *outpcd, tld off.* ....(16 to 1 op 10 to 1 tchd 20 to 1) 19

Dist: 3l, 3½l, 2½l, 3l, ¾l, sht-hd, 1½l, ½l, nk, ½l. 1m 15.40s. a 5.10s (19 Ran).
SR: 8/-/-/-/-/-/ (Giles W Pritchard-Gordon), G Lewis

1742 Time Magazine Fillies Conditions Stakes Class D (2-y-o) £4,308 5f 10yds ....(7:05)

1310[3] ISABELLA SHARP 8-7 (5*) M Fenton (6) *made all, pushed clr appr fnl furlong.* (5 to 4 fav op 6 to 4 tchd 2 to 1) 1

1142[5] ANTONIA'S FOLLY 8-12 G Carter (7) *al chasing wnr, rdn alng 2 fs out, outpcd appr last.* ....(9 to 2 op 7 to 2 tchd 5 to 1) 2

1265 FOLLY FINNESSE 8-8 S Whitworth (5) *hld up in mid-div, styd on one pace frm 2 fs out*..... (50 to 1 op 33 to 1) 3

1234[2] CIRCLE OF FRIENDS (Ire) 8-8 Pat Eddery (3) *settled in 3rd pl, not quicken und pres 2 fs out.* ....(6 to 4 op Evens tchd 13 to 8) 4

625[3] MADAME GREGOIRE 8-10 R Cochrane (2) *rear, rdn and no hdwy last 2 fs*.....(16 to 1 op 8 to 1 tchd 20 to 1) 5

RANDOM 8-8 J Quinn (8) *sn outpcd, effrt on outsd 2 fs out, wknd appr last*..................(50 to 1 op 33 to 1) 6

Dist: 3½l, ¾l, ¾l, 1½l, 1½l. 1m 3.70s. a 4.70s (6 Ran).
SR: 19/5/-/ (Christopher Wright), M Bell

1743 Champagne Handicap Class E (0-70 3-y-o and up) £2,460 1m 67yds.. (7:35)

719 QUEEN WARRIOR [51] 4-8-12 Pat Eddery (15) *ldg grp, led 2 fs out, shaken up to go clr fnl furlong.* ....(13 to 2 op 8 to 1 tchd 6 to 1) 1

1474* DEEVEE [54] 4-9-1 G Duffield (18) *hld up, cld on ldrs 3 fs out, rdn and one pace fnl furlong.* (11 to 2 op 3 to 1) 2

1685[5] VANROY [63] (v) 9-9-10 L Dettori (11) *in tch, effrt 3 fs out, not quicken o'r one out.* ....(10 to 1 op 12 to 1 tchd 16 to 1) 3

1487 CALL THE BUREAU [62] 4-9-9 D Holland (14) *hdwy 3 fs out, not much room and swtchd lft o'r one out, styd on same pace*..............................(16 to 1 op 14 to 1) 4

1474[5] ROYAL DARTMOUTH (USA) [49] 8-8-10 S Whitworth (20) *led aftr one furlong to 2 out, no extr.* ....(7 to 1 op 6 to 1 tchd 8 to 1) 5

1453[9] FOOLISH TOUCH [44] 11-7-12 (7*) D McCabe (2) *hld up, hdwy clsg stages, nvr nrr.* ....(10 to 1 op 14 to 1 tchd 16 to 1) 6

1312[3] DAILY SPORT DON [63] 3-8-13 Paul Eddery (12) *in tch, rdn and btn 2 fs out*..........................(8 to 1 tchd 6 to 1) 7

1425[4] MEXICAN DANCER [55] 4-8-9 (7*) S Drowne (1) *mid-div, effrt 3 fs out, one pace 2 out.* ....(12 to 1 op 10 to 1 tchd 14 to 1) 8

1097[6] ROSIETOES (USA) [48] 5-8-2 (7*) Mark Denaro (4) *trkd ldrs till wknd 2 fs out*.....(16 to 1 op 12 to 1 tchd 20 to 1) 9

1490[7] DUTY SERGEANT (Ire) [39] 4-8-0[1] A Munro (10) *mid-div most of way*.......................(16 to 1 tchd 20 to 1) 10

1257[4] DRAGONMIST (Ire) [43] 3-7-1[1] (7*) D Wright (8) *nvr nr to chal*...............(16 to 1 op 20 to 1 tchd 14 to 1) 11

1311[9] WHAT LOLA WANTS (Ire) [58] 3-8-8 N Adams (17) *nvr rch frnt rnk*............ (20 to 1 op 16 to 1 tchd 25 to 1) 12

1409 FULL SHILLING (USA) [51] (v) 4-8-12 A Clark (16) *nvr better than mid-div*....................(33 to 1 tchd 50 to 1) 13

1344[9] MIND THE ROOF (Ire) [70] 3-9-6 J Williams (19) *outpcd most of way*..............(14 to 1 op 12 to 1 tchd 16 to 1) 14

1316[3] GLENSCAR [41] 7-8-2 M Roberts (6) *improved hfwy, wknd o'r 2 fs out*.........(5 to 1 fav op 4 to 1 tchd 11 to 2) 15

COOL COQUELIN (Ire) [40] 5-7-12 (3*) B Doyle (13) *nvr on terms*......................................(50 to 1) 16

1537 FAIRY WISHER (Ire) [42] 4-8-0 (3*) D Harrison (9) *outpcd.* ....(33 to 1 tchd 50 to 1) 17

1312 TIGERSPIKE (Ire) [49] 3-7-13 G Bardwell (5) *ldg grp till wknd last 2 fs*..............................(33 to 1) 18

1352[8] PRINCESS JESSICA [33] 6-7-8[1] J Quinn (21) *led one furlong, prmnt till wknd 3 out*.................. (33 to 1) 19

1304 MASTAMIST [35] (bl) 4-7-10[3] S Dawson (3) *strted slwly, al beh, tld off*.............................. (66 to 1) 20

Dist: 3½l, hd, 2l, ½l, 1l, ½l, nk, 2½l, nk, 1½l. 1m 48.40s. a 7.40s (20 Ran).
SR: 37/29/37/30/15/7/13/15/-/ (Christopher Spence), P T Walwyn

1744 Tilda Rice Handicap Class D (0-80 3-y-o and up) £4,932 5f 217yds..... (8:05)

1267[6] GREY CHARMER (Ire) [57] 4-8-8 W Newnes (5) *trkd far side ldrs, led entering fnl furlong, rdn out.* ....(7 to 1 tchd 5 to 1) 1

1177 MERRYHILL MAID (Ire) [67] 5-9-4 R Cochrane (3) *made most far side till entering fnl furlong, kpt on wl.* .... (16 to 1 op 14 to 1 tchd 20 to 1) 2

1095* HALLORINA [67] 3-8-9 G Bardwell (1) *ldg grp far side, kpt on one pace ins fnl furlong*.......... (8 to 1 op 6 to 1) 3

1527[8] BELFORT RULER [66] 6-9-3 Pat Eddery (2) *chsd far side grp, one pace appr fnl furlong.* ....(14 to 1 op 10 to 1 tchd 16 to 1) 4

1664[3] PHARAOH'S DANCER [68] 6-9-5 J Reid (17) *rcd stands side, hdwy o'r 2 out, kpt on one pace fnl furlong.* .... (13 to 2 op 8 to 1 tchd 10 to 1) 5

1527[5] INVOCATION [69] 6-9-6 N Adams (15) *ldg grp stands side, no extr appr fnl furlong*..........(14 to 1 op 12 to 1) 6

1436[5] DANCE ON SIXPENCE [48] 5-7-13 J Quinn (9) *chsd stands side grp, rdn and no extr o'r one furlong out.* ....(14 to 1 op 16 to 1 tchd 20 to 1 and 12 to 1) 7

1373* SIR JOEY (USA) [77] 4-10-0 J Williams (11) *rcd stands side, no imprsn fnl furlong.* ....(12 to 1 op 10 to 1 tchd 14 to 1) 8

1373[6] SWIFT ROMANCE (Ire) [53] 5-7-11 (7*) D McCabe (6) *rcd alng centre of course, outpcd frm hfwy.* ....(10 to 1 tchd 12 to 1) 9

1079[9] POETS COVE [76] 5-9-13 A Clark (14) *wl plcd stands side for 4 fs*..............................(33 to 1 op 25 to 1) 10

1537[4] MY RUBY RING [53] 6-8-4 T Williams (16) *cl up stands side, wknd o'r one furlong out*..........(8 to 1 op 14 to 1) 11

1527[9] DOMICKSKY [67] 5-9-4 C Rutter (12) *speed on stands side for 4 fs*................ (9 to 1 op 8 to 1 tchd 10 to 1) 12

1267[2] FACE NORTH (Ire) [66] 5-9-3 L Dettori (8) *nvr able to chal.* ....(11 to 2 fav op 7 to 2 tchd 6 to 1) 13

1327* AROOM [79] 3-9-7 W Carson (13) *no dngr frm 2 fs out.* ....(9 to 1 op 10 to 1 tchd 12 to 1 and 8 to 1) 14

1327[2] VISIMOTION (USA) [70] 3-8-12 D Holland (7) *prmnt stands side for o'r 3 fs.*......(11 to 1 op 10 to 1 tchd 12 to 1) 15
1282[4] IRON KING [62] 7-8-13 M Roberts (10) *rcd stands side, beh frm hfwy*....................................(12 to 1) 16
Dist: 1½l, 3½l, 1½l, 1l, nk, nk, sht-hd, 4l, 1½l, nk. 1m 13.70s. a 3.40s (16 Ran).
SR: 44/48/25/27/25/25/3/31/-/ (Miss S Previte), C James

1745 Dalham Hall Stud Handicap Class D (0-80 3-y-o) £3,552 1¼m 7yds... (8:35)

1372[4] WARM SPELL [66] 8-9 B Rouse (4) *chsd ldr, sstnd effrt frm 2 fs out, led wl ins last, ran on.*
..........................(7 to 2 op 5 to 2 tchd 4 to 1) 1
1426 HOOCHIECOOCHIE MAN (Ire) [57] 8-0 R Price (3) *hld up, cld on ldrs 4 fs out, led o'r 2 out, hdd und pres wl ins last*.................(9 to 4 fav op 2 to 1 tchd 5 to 2) 2
1306[4] WOLF POWER (Ire) [57] 8-0 J Quinn (2) *hld up rear, hdwy 4 fs out, rdn and outpcd 2 out*....... (7 to 2 tchd 3 to 1) 3
1314[7] LAVENDER COTTAGE [78] (bl) 9-7 M Roberts (5) *prog into 3rd hfwy, rdn and btn 2 fs out*..... (4 to 1 tchd 5 to 1) 4
1377[4] SHALHOLME [51] 7-8[1] N Adams (7) *in tch, rdn to ld o'r 3 fs out, hdd and wknd over 2 out*..... (25 to 1 op 12 to 1) 5
1312 ABSOLUTELY FACT (USA) [57] 8-0[1] G Duffield (6) *led till o'r 3 fs out, wknd und pres.*
.............................(10 to 1 op 8 to 1 tchd 12 to 1) 6
Dist: 1l, 8l, 5l, ¾l, 1½l. 2m 13.60s. a 11.10s (6 Ran).
SR: 24/13/-/8/-/-/ (K Higson), R Simpson

1746 Pavilion Median Auction Maiden Stakes Class F (3-y-o) £1,953 1¼m 7yds.......................... (9:05)

TEEN JAY 9-0 A Munro (5) *hld up, pushed alng 4 out, cld on ldrs frm 3 out, str brst und pres to ld nr finish.*
..........................(8 to 1 op 6 to 1 tchd 9 to 1) 1
LAMBAST 8-9 J Williams (8) *in tch, ran on o'r 3 fs out, led appr fnl furlong, hdd nr line.*
..............................(9 to 1 op 7 to 1 tchd 10 to 1) 2
EURYTHMIC 8-9 A McGlone (16) *ldg grp, led and hng lft o'r 2 fs out, hdd over one out, rallied nr finish.*
.....................(20 to 1 op 12 to 1 tchd 25 to 1) 3
1244[4] ITS UNBELIEVABLE 8-7 (7*) D Wright (18) *made most of rng till o'r 2 out, ran on one pace.*
.....................(33 to 1 op 50 to 1 tchd 66 to 1) 4
825[7] AJMAAN (USA) 9-0 M Roberts (12) *chsd ldg grp, rdn 3 fs out, ev ch 2 out, no extr fnl furlong.*
...................(6 to 5 on op 7 to 4 on tchd Evens) 5
1027 CLIFTON GAME 9-0 N Adams (11) *mid-div, rdn alng o'r 3 fs out, no imprsn on ldrs last 2 furlongs.*
.....................(20 to 1 op 12 to 1 tchd 25 to 1) 6
759[7] RUE REMBRANDT (USA) 9-0 Paul Eddery (2) *wl in tch, no hdwy frm 2 out*...... (10 to 1 op 5 to 1 tchd 11 to 1) 7
1371[3] SCHOOLGIRL CRUSH 8-9 A Tucker (17) *nvr nrr.*
..........(9 to 1 op 20 to 1 tchd 25 to 1 and 8 to 1) 8
1429 ONLY A MIRAGE 9-0 R Cochrane (3) *nvr able to chal.*
....(33 to 1 op 20 to 1) 9
ROSE OF MEDINA 8-9 W Newnes (6) *chsd ldrs till wknd 2 fs out*................(50 to 1 op 33 to 1 tchd 66 to 1) 10
1090[9] TREBLE LASS 8-9 D Holland (15) *ldg grp, rdn and wknd o'r 2 fs out*...........................(33 to 1 op 20 to 1) 11
1344 BORROWED AND BLUE 8-9 N Day (10) *wl in tch for o'r 7 fs*..(33 to 1 op 20 to 1) 12
1145[7] POETIC FORM (Ire) 9-0 A Clark (4) *nvr rch ldrs.*
....(50 to 1 tchd 66 to 1) 13
1092 MISS MICHELLE 8-9 C Rutter (13) *uns rdr and bolted bef strt, outpcd most of way*............ (50 to 1 op 33 to 1) 14
1090 MORAN BRIG 9-0 L Dettori (9) *nvr on terms.*
.....................(20 to 1 op 14 to 1 tchd 25 to 1) 15
FORGE GOLD 8-7 (7*) C Hawksley (1) *al beh.*
....(50 to 1 op 33 to 1) 16
1344 ROADRUNNER 9-0 G Bardwell (7) *towards rear most of way*.............................(50 to 1 tchd 66 to 1) 17
HEDGEHOG 8-9 J Quinn (14) *al beh, tld off*......(50 to 1) 18
Dist: Nk, ¾l, 3½l, 2l, 4l, 2½l, 1l, hd, ½l, nk. 2m 13.20s. a 10.70s (18 Ran).
SR: 33/27/25/23/19/11/6/-/3/ (Sheikh Mohammed), G Wragg

ASCOT (good to soft)
Tuesday June 15th
Going Correction: PLUS 0.30 sec. per fur.

1747 Queen Anne Stakes Class A (Group 2) (3-y-o and up) £53,194 1m...... (2:30)

1208* ALFLORA (Ire) 4-9-2 M J Kinane (6) *led till hdd one furlong out, rallied gmely und pres to get up ag'n cl hme.*
....(20 to 1) 1
1089* INNER CITY (Ire) 4-9-2 M Roberts (2) *settled in rear, hdwy 3 fs out, led one out, crrd head high, hdd cl hme.*
.... (6 to 4 fav tchd 7 to 4) 2
1029[6] HAZAAM (USA) 4-9-2 W R Swinburn (10) *nvr far away, swtchd rght o'r 2 fs out, hrd rdn appr last, one pace ins.*
......................(11 to 1 op 10 to 1 tchd 12 to 1) 3
1447[6] SWING LOW 4-9-5 T Quinn (9) *hld up in rear, hdwy 2 fs out, hrd rdn and ran on, nvr nrr.*
.....................(11 to 1 op 10 to 1 tchd 12 to 1) 4
1412* CATRAIL (USA) 3-8-5 R Cochrane (5) *pld hrd, in frnt rnk, rdn wl o'r one furlong out, wknd ins.*
.........................(5 to 1 op 7 to 2 tchd 11 to 2) 5
660* ALHIJAZ 4-9-8 W Carson (8) *trkd wnr till wknd 2 fs out.*
....(5 to 1 op 4 to 1) 6
1029[7] FEMININE WILES (Ire) 4-8-13 J Reid (4) *hld up, effrt 2 fs out, nvr on terms*.... (20 to 1 op 16 to 1 tchd 33 to 1) 7
CALLING COLLECT (USA) 4-9-2 C Asmussen (7) *prmnt on far side, rdn and wknd appr fnl furlong.*
.....................(16 to 1 op 20 to 1 tchd 25 to 1) 8
1471[2] POWERFUL EDGE 4-9-2 L Dettori (1) *mid-div til rdn and wknd o'r 2 fs out*....(40 to 1 op 33 to 1 tchd 50 to 1) 9
Dist: Nk, 1½l, ½l, 3½l, ¾l, 2l, 4l, 2l. 1m 43.16s. a 4.16s (9 Ran).
SR: 76/75/70/71/46/61/46/37/31/ (Circlechart Ltd), C E Brittain

1748 Prince Of Wales's Stakes Class A (Group 2) (3-y-o and up) £57,379 1¼m ....(3:05)

1367[5] PLACERVILLE (USA) 3-8-4 Pat Eddery (1) *took hold early, trkd ldr, hrd rdn 2 fs out, led ins last, drvn out.*
.........................(11 to 2 op 5 to 1 tchd 6 to 1) 1
1124[5] URBAN SEA (USA) 4-9-0 C Asmussen (12) *trkd ldrs, not much room 2 fs out, swtchd lft one out, ran on und pres*....................(8 to 1 op 7 to 1 tchd 9 to 1) 2
794[8] EMPEROR JONES (USA) 3-8-4 R Cochrane (2) *trkd ldrs, not much room o'r one furlong out, sn swtchd rght, hrd rdn and kpt on ins last*.......... (10 to 1 tchd 12 to 1) 3
1049* GEORGE AUGUSTUS (USA) (bl) 5-9-5 M Roberts (7) *hld up beh, hdwy o'r 2 fs out, one pace und pres ins last.*
..............................(5 to 1 jt-fav op 4 to 1) 4
1447* ENHARMONIC (USA) 6-9-3 L Dettori (10) *hld up in mid-div, rdn and hdwy 2 fs out, not much room and one pace appr last*..............(9 to 1 op 8 to 1 tchd 11 to 1) 5
1427[5] YOUNG BUSTER (Ire) 5-9-3 Paul Eddery (3) *led til hdd ins fnl furlong, kpt on one pace*.................. (20 to 1) 6
1512[6] VIA PARIGI (Ire) 3-8-4 W Carson (6) *hld up beh, hdwy on ins o'r 2 fs out, hrd rdn appr last, ran on.*
....(33 to 1 op 25 to 1) 7
1049[2] EZZOUD (Ire) (v) 4-9-3 W R Swinburn (5) *hld up beh, drvn 3 fs out, ran on ins last, nvr nr to chal*........(5 to 1 jt-fav op 4 to 1) 8
SPARTAN SHAREEF (Ire) 4-9-3 J Reid (4) *hdwy to track ldrs aftr 4 fs, rdn and wknd 2 out.*
.....................(33 to 1 op 25 to 1 tchd 50 to 1) 9
1029 LUCKY LINDY (Ire) 4-9-5 M J Kinane (8) *mid-div, rdn and btn quickly 2 fs out*..............(14 to 1 tchd 16 to 1) 10
1269* YOUNG SENOR (USA) 4-9-3 M Hills (11) *wtd wth in mid-div, pld out o'r 2 fs out, sn btn.*
.... (11 to 2 op 5 to 1 tchd 6 to 1) 11
Dist: Nk, ¾l, nk, 2l, sht-hd, hd, ½l, 4l, 1½l, 2½l. 2m 8.65s. a 4.95s (11 Ran).
SR: 71/80/68/82/76/75/61/73/65/ (K Abdulla), H R A Cecil

1749 St James's Palace Stakes Class A (Group 1) (3-y-o) £116,334 1m... (3:45)

954* KINGMAMBO (USA) 9-0 C Asmussen (4) *hld up on ins beh ldr, short of room 2 fs out, swtchd lft entering last, quickened and led wl inside.*
...............(5 to 2 on op 3 to 1 on tchd 2 to 1 on) 1
1364[2] NEEDLE GUN (Ire) 9-0 M Roberts (1) *styd on ins, led, rdn 2 fs out, hdd wl inside last, kpt on.*
............(13 to 2 op 7 to 1 tchd 8 to 1 and 6 to 1) 2
1548[3] VENTIQUATTROFOGLI (Ire) 9-0 W Carson (3) *tacked o'r to far side, trkd to ins 3 fs out, ev ch entering fnl furlong, ran on one pace*.... (16 to 1 tchd 14 to 1 and 20 to 1) 3
1029[2] WHARF (USA) 9-0 Pat Eddery (2) *trkd ldr far side, came o'r to ins 3 fs out, ev ch 2 out, faltered wl over one out, sn outpcd*...............................(5 to 1 op 7 to 2) 4
Dist: 1½l, ¾l, 3l. 1m 44.05s. a 4.55s (4 Ran).
SR: 68/63/61/52/ (S S Niarchos), F Boutin

1750 Coventry Stakes Class A (Group 3) (2-y-o) £26,766 6f................. (4:20)

998* STONEHATCH (USA) 8-13 J Reid (5) *hld up tracking ldrs, led appr fnl furlong, pushed out.*
.................(Evens fav op 7 to 4 on tchd 11 to 10) 1
1324* POLISH LAUGHTER (USA) 8-13 W R Swinburn (6) *led aftr one furlong, shaken up 2 fs out, hdd appr last, rallied wl*..................................(16 to 1 tchd 20 to 1) 2
738* WAJIBA RIVA (Ire) 8-13 Pat Eddery (4) *hld up, cld 2 fs out, not much room o'r one out, rdn and one pace ins last.*
..........................(5 to 2 op 3 to 1 tchd 7 to 2) 3
786* SHARP PHASE (Ire) 8-13 J J Behan (3) *led one furlong, cl up, ev ch 2 fs out, one pace appr last.*
.....................(25 to 1 op 20 to 1 tchd 33 to 1) 4
1489* CRAZY PAVING (Ire) 8-13 M Roberts (2) *wtd wth in tch, effrt 2 fs out, hrd rdn appr last, wknd.*
..........................(6 to 1 op 7 to 1 tchd 5 to 1) 5
1523[2] CANASKA DANCER (Ire) 8-13 A Munro (1) *trkd ldrs till rdn and wknd 2 fs out*................(16 to 1 op 25 to 1) 6
Dist: 1½l, ¾l, nk, 4l, 6l. 1m 18.15s. a 4.75s (6 Ran).
SR: 40/34/31/30/14/-/ (R E Sangster), P W Chapple-Hyam

1751 King Edward Vii Stakes Class A (Group 2) (3-y-o) £58,433 1½m. . (4:55)

1116[2] BENEFICIAL 8-8 M Hills (5) *hld up, hdwy o'r 3 fs out, sstnd run to ld wl ins last, rdn out.* ....(11 to 4 fav op 5 to 2 tchd 3 to 1) 1
1429[2] WINGED VICTORY (USA) 8-8 R Cochrane (3) *trkd ldrs, led 2 fs out, kpt on und pres, hdd wl ins last.* ....(12 to 1 op 16 to 1 tchd 20 to 1 and 10 to 1) 2
1369[4] AZZILFI 8-8 W Carson (1) *trkd ldr, led o'r 2 fs out, sn hdd, rallied wl ins last und pres.*..... (12 to 1 tchd 14 to 1) 3
941[3] FORESEE 8-8 M Roberts (7) *hld up, rdn sn aftr hfwy, short of room on ins 2 fs out, styd on wl inside last.* .... (11 to 2 op 5 to 1 tchd 13 to 2) 4
LINDON LIME (USA) 8-8 A Munro (8) *trkd ldrs, rdn and lost pl 3 fs out, kpt on one pace ins fnl 2.* .... (16 to 1 op 14 to 1 tchd 20 to 1) 5
1329* YELTSIN 8-8 Pat Eddery (6) *hld up in rear, effrt o'r 3 fs out, hrd rdn, one pace ins fnl 2*.... (5 to 1 tchd 6 to 1) 6
1448[4] CAIRO PRINCE (Ire) 8-8 J Reid (4) *in tch, cld on ldrs hfwy, outpcd 2 fs out, sn btn*...(4 to 1 op 5 to 2 tchd 9 to 2) 7
1001[3] SHAIBA (USA) 8-8 W R Swinburn (2) *led till hdd o'r 2 fs out, drpd out quickly, eased.* (8 to 1 op 7 to 1 tchd 9 to 1) 8

Dist: Nk, nk, nk, ½l, 1½l, 4l, 12l. 2m 33.88s. a 5.68s (8 Ran).
SR: 73/72/71/70/69/66/58/34/ (Exors Of The Late Sir Robin McAlpine), G Wragg

1752 Ascot Handicap Class C (0-90 4-y-o and up) £20,550 2½m. . . . . (5:30)

1321* BALASANI (Fr) [75] 7-9-1 M Perrett (14) *hld up towards rear, al gng wl, pld out and hdwy o'r 2 fs out, ran on to ld ins last, sn clr*..... (8 to 1 op 10 to 1 tchd 11 to 1) 1
1457[3] DOYCE [58] 4-7-9 G Bardwell (16) *mid-div, hdwy 6 fs out, rdn and ev ch 2 out, styd on wl fnl furlong.* ....(33 to 1 tchd 50 to 1) 2
857[2] JACK BUTTON (Ire) [90] 4-9-13 N Day (7) *beh, hdwy o'r 2 fs out, styd on wl und pres ins last.* (12 to 1 tchd 14 to 1) 3
1380[8] STAR PLAYER [81] 7-9-7 L Dettori (5) *hld up in mid-div, hdwy 5 fs out, not clr run o'r 2 out, sn led, hdd and one pace und pres ins last*.......... (25 to 1 tchd 33 to 1) 4
1380[2] SNOW BOARD [75] (bl) 4-8-12 W Carson (8) *chsd ldrs, cld 4 fs out, hrd rdn whn bumped 2 furlongs out and o'r one out, one pace*.......(7 to 1 fav op 8 to 1 tchd 9 to 1) 5
1468[2] MRS BARTON (Ire) [65] 5-8-5 M J Kinane (19) *chsd ldrs, rdn alng o'r 3 fs out, styd on*........(16 to 1 tchd 20 to 1) 6
1564* MARDOOD [53] 8-7-7 (3ex) S Wood (2) *hld up beh, hdwy wl o'r one furlong out, styd on well ins last, nvr nrr.* ....(12 to 1 tchd 14 to 1) 7
1605[3] CHAKALAK [55] 5-7-9 C Rutter (21) *beh, rdn and hdwy o'r 2 fs out, not clr run appr last, kpt on one pace.* .... (20 to 1 op 25 to 1) 8
1345[7] BARDOLPH (USA) [73] (bl) 6-8-13 T Quinn (15) *trkd ldrs, led 2 fs out to one and a half out, wknd.* ....(14 to 1 tchd 16 to 1) 9
1531[3] ROSINA MAE [71] 4-8-8 Dean McKeown (17) *chsd ldrs, ev ch 3 fs out, wknd wl o'r one out*.. (12 to 1 op 14 to 1) 10
1336[3] BUSTINETTA [77] 4-9-0 K Darley (3) *beh, hdwy o'r 2 fs out, wknd over one out*...(12 to 1 op 10 to 1 tchd 14 to 1) 11
1380* GOOD HAND (USA) [88] 7-10-0 J Reid (11) *al beh.* ....(16 to 1 tchd 20 to 1) 12
1533[2] BOKARO (Fr) [80] 7-9-6 Pat Eddery (22) *hld up in rear, al beh*..................(14 to 1 op 12 to 1 tchd 16 to 1) 13
1380[4] FRENCH IVY (USA) [73] 6-8-13 W R Swinburn (20) *mid-div till wknd fnl 3 fs*..........................(33 to 1 tchd 50 to 1) 14
1564[8] PATROCLUS [55] 8-7-9[2] S Dawson (12) *hld up, al beh.* ....(66 to 1) 15+
1276* TAROUDANT [71] 6-8-11 M Roberts (10) *mid-div till wknd wl o'r 2 fs out*..................... (12 to 1 op 10 to 1) 15+
1345[2] DERAB (USA) [79] (v) 7-9-5 J Williams (23) *beh, hdwy o'r 4 fs out, wknd over 2 out*........................ (20 to 1) 17
874* REQUESTED [80] 6-9-6 A Munro (13) *chsd ldrs, led 5 fs out to 2 furlongs out, wknd quickly.* (12 to 1 tchd 14 to 1) 18
1430[2] MUSE [77] 6-8-12 (5*) A Procter (6) *led aftr 2 fs till hdd 5 furlongs out, wknd.* (11 to 1 op 10 to 1 tchd 12 to 1) 19+
1268[2] DARE TO DREAM (Ire) [63] 4-8-0 A McGlone (9) *trkd ldrs till wknd o'r 4 fs out*..................(14 to 1 op 12 to 1) 19+
1173[4] MASTER FOODBROKER (Ire) [73] (bl) 5-8-6 (7*) D McCabe (1) *al beh*.....................(16 to 1 op 20 to 1) 21
1118[6] JUSTICE (Fr) [86] 5-9-12 C Asmussen (4) *al beh*... (33 to 1) 22
857[3] WELSHMAN [65] 7-8-5[2] R Cochrane (18) *led 2 fs, cl up til wknd o'r 3 furlongs out.* ....(14 to 1 op 12 to 1 tchd 16 to 1) 23

Dist: 3l, 1l, sht-hd, 1l, hd, ¾l, 3½l, hd, 2l, 2½l. 4m 31.81s. a 15.31s (23 Ran).
SR: 8/-/16/9/-/-/ (M D Smith), M C Pipe

CHANTILLY (FR) (soft)
Tuesday June 15th
Going Correction: PLUS 0.50 sec. per fur.

1753 Prix des Lilas (Listed) (3-y-o) £14,337 1m. . . . . (2:50)

1218[6] HAWK BEAUTY (USA) 8-9 D Boeuf, ... 1
1290[4] FORTROSE (USA) 8-9 E Saint-Martin, ... 2
694[5] AISLA (USA) 8-9 F Head, ... 3
TYSTHEA (Fr) 8-9 W Mongil, ... 4

Dist: Nk, 1l, 20l. 1m 44.50s. a 9.80s (4 Ran).
SR: 8/7/4/-/ (Ecurie I M Fares), P Bary

1754 Prix la Moskowa (Listed) (4-y-o and up) £14,337 1m 7f. . . . . (3:50)

1088[2] EGYPTOWN (Fr) 4-8-8 F Head, ... 1
1124[9] DJAIS (Fr) 4-8-12 G Guignard, ... 2
CORROUGE (USA) 4-8-12 T Jarnet, ... 3
1291[4] LIYOUN (Ire) 5-8-12 W Mongil, ... 4

Dist: 5l, ½l, 3l, 20l. 3m 19.10s. a 11.10s (5 Ran).
SR: 58/57/56/53/ (J Wertheimer), Mme C Head

CLONMEL (IRE) (yielding to soft (races 1,2), soft (3))
Tuesday June 15th

1755 Killenaule Claiming Race (3-y-o) £2,245 1½m. . . . . (6:30)

1507[7] SAINT HILDA (Ire) 7-8 (6*) R V Skelly (2).......... (14 to 1) 1
1514 MILLERS MILL (Ire) 8-7 W J O'Connor (12)....... (12 to 1) 2
1250[4] ASSERT STAR 7-11 (6*) J A Heffernan (13).........(8 to 1) 3
1507[3] KILTIMAGH (Ire) 8-0 N G McCullagh (9).......... (10 to 3) 4
GARDENVALE VIC (Ire) 8-1 J F Egan (5)..........(10 to 1) 5
1252[4] DIGNIFIED (Ire) 7-12 (4*) W J Smith (4).......... (6 to 1) 6
1140[7] TROPICAL LAKE (Ire) 8-6 S Craine (7)..............(8 to 1) 7
1431[2] WICKLOW WAY (Ire) 8-10 W J Supple (1)....... (2 to 1 fav) 8
1609[4] DUNANY ROSE (Ire) 7-12 (8*) B Fenton (11)...... (10 to 1) 9
ANIMATE (Ire) 8-0 (2*) D G O'Shea (8)............ (14 to 1) 10
1251 CHRISTY MOORE (Ire) (bl) 7-13[2] (2*) R M Burke (3) (20 to 1) 11
1252[5] RED ROOSTER (Ire) 8-9 N Byrne (14)........... (12 to 1) 12

Dist: 4l, hd, 4l, 1l. 2m 52.80s. (12 Ran).
(Liam O'Maobhuidhe), A P O'Brien

1756 Templemore Maiden (4-y-o and up) £2,245 1½m. . . . . (7:30)

1467[3] CRAZY GAIL 6-8-11 J P Murtagh (5)...........(Evens fav) 1
SIR SOOJE (Ire) 4-8-6 (8*) B Fenton (1)............(6 to 1) 2
1467[8] SHAYISTA 8-8-11 S Craine (2)......................(9 to 1) 3
LACKOTWINE (Ire) 4-8-11 W J Supple (8)........ (14 to 1) 4
1443[9] JUST ONE CANALETTO (bl) 5-9-0 W J O'Connor (3) (8 to 1) 5
1576 RANDOM WALK 8-9-0 K J Manning (4).......... (33 to 1) 6
1467[2] LAST GOODBYE 7-8-8 (6*) P P Murphy (7)........ (7 to 2) 7

Dist: 1l, 4l, 1l, 5l. 2m 57.80s. (7 Ran).
(S Bolger), A P O'Brien

1757 June Handicap (0-75 3-y-o and up) £2,245 1½m. . . . . (8:00)

1553[5] CALL MY GUEST (Ire) [-] 3-8-3 W J Supple (13) (4 to 1 fav) 1
706[4] LYPHARD ABU (Ire) [-] 5-9-5 K J Manning (9)...... (5 to 1) 2
1334[6] THE BERUKI (Ire) [-] 3-7-11 (6*) P P Murphy (1)....(11 to 2) 3
1431* MILLMOUNT (Ire) [-] (bl) 3-8-4 (4*,6ex) W J Smith (4) ....(10 to 1) 4
1235[3] SIMPLY GRAND [-] 6-8-11 N Byrne (2)........... (10 to 1) 5
1139[4] TENCA (Ire) [-] (bl) 3-7-12 (2*) D G O'Shea (11)..... (7 to 1) 6
297[7] TANGO IN PARIS (Arg) [-] 3-8-0 N G McCullagh (3) (16 to 1) 7
MISS DARCY (Ire) [-] 5-8-13 P Shanahan (6)...... (12 to 1) 8
1554[5] ANY MINUTE NOW (Ire) [-] 3-8-8[1] S Craine (10)... (10 to 1) 9
1508[8] GO DEAS [-] 6-7-12 Joanna Morgan (7)........... (6 to 1) 10
1508[4] BLUEJACKET (Ire) [-] 5-7-12 J F Egan (5).........(10 to 1) 11
POUNDWORLD (Ire) [-] 3-7-13 (2*) R M Burke (12) (16 to 1) 12

Dist: Sht-hd, 2½l, 6l, 1½l. 2m 54.50s. (12 Ran).
(Bezwell Fixings Ltd), Kevin Prendergast

THIRSK (good to firm)
Tuesday June 15th
Going Correction: MINUS 0.20 sec. per fur. (races 1,4,5,6,7), MINUS 0.10 (2,3)

1758 Bramcote School Scarborough Centenary Median Auction Maiden Stakes Class F (Div I) (2-y-o) £2,807 7f. . (2:15)

1227[2] OVIDEO 8-9 J Lowe (4) *al prmnt, effrt 2 fs out, led one out, ran on wl*... (11 to 10 on op 11 to 10 tchd 5 to 4) 1
968[8] GLENVALLY 8-9 D Holland (10) *chsd ldrs, effrt 2 out, ran on wl fnl furlong*.......................................(25 to 1) 2
730 KOMPLICITY 9-0 B Raymond (5) *cl up, led wl o'r 2 fs out, hdd one out, no extr*............(12 to 1 tchd 14 to 1) 3
1227[9] PARISIAN LOVER 9-0 K Darley (3) *hld up and beh, ran on wl fnl 2 fs, nrst finish*.............. (10 to 1 op 7 to 1) 4
730 HEATHYARDS CRUSADE (Ire) 9-0 S Perks (11) *in tch, kpt on same pace fnl 3 fs*............ (14 to 1 op 10 to 1) 5
1529[5] THREE OF HEARTS 8-2 (7*) M Humphries (6) *prmnt till wknd o'r one furlong out.* .... (15 to 2 op 5 to 1 tchd 8 to 1) 6
466[6] SONNETEER 8-11 (3*) S Maloney (7) *nvr dngrs.* ....(6 to 1 op 5 to 1) 7

1324 STORM LEADER 9-0 M Wigham (2) *led till hdd wl o'r 2 fs out, fdd*.........................(12 to 1 op 10 to 1) 8
1401⁹ CAPTAIN TAFFY 9-0 K Fallon (8) *beh frm hfwy*. ....(12 to 1 op 14 to 1 tchd 16 to 1) 9
PHIL THE TILL 9-0 Dale Gibson (12) *al beh*. ....(20 to 1 op 16 to 1) 10
KNAYTON LAD (Ire) 9-0 T Lucas (9) *dwlt, al beh*. ....(16 to 1 op 12 to 1 tchd 20 to 1) 11
Dist: ½l, 3½l, 2½l, ½l, 2l, 6l, ¾l, 5l, ½l, 6l. 1m 26.90s. a 4.10s (11 Ran).
SR: 13/11/5/-/-/-/ (Mrs S Cunliffe-Lister), J W Watts

1759 No. 6 Group Security Systems Selling Stakes Class G (2-y-o) £2,448 6f (2:45)

TWO D'S 8-6 M Birch (7) *hld up, effrt 2 out, ran on to ld ins fnl furlong*...................(10 to 1 op 7 to 1) 1
LUCKY FOURTEEN 8-8 (3*) S D Williams (13) *led till hdd and no extr ins fnl furlong*........(8 to 1 op 10 to 1) 2
1561 TENPIN PROPHET (Ire) (bl) 8-6 J Quinn (1) *beh till styd on fnl 2 fs, nrst finish*...............(10 to 1 op 7 to 1) 3
1272⁷ MINNESOTA VIKING 8-11 K Darley (4) *in tch, rdn o'r 2 fs out, styd on same pace*.........(6 to 4 fav tchd 7 to 4) 4
1590⁶ BRAMCOTE CENTURY 8-6 J Lowe (14) *prmnt, rdn hfwy, wknd o'r one furlong out*.........(12 to 1 op 10 to 1) 5
1227 TYPOGRAPHER (Ire) 8-11 T Williams (5) *beh till styd on fnl 2 fs, nrst finish*..................(20 to 1 op 16 to 1) 6
395 SHARPISH WORDS (bl) 8-11 S Webster (9) *chsd ldrs till outpcd hfwy, no dngr aftr*..................(20 to 1) 7
1555⁵ ARKINDALE SPIRIT (Ire) 8-11 T Lucas (6) *chsd ldrs till wknd 2 fs out*..................................(10 to 1) 8
886⁹ CRY OF THE DOLPHIN 8-6 Dale Gibson (2) *in tch, effrt o'r 2 fs out, sn btn*......................(10 to 1 op 8 to 1) 9
1391⁶ WINGS AHEAD (bl) 8-11 J Fanning (11) *cl up till wknd quickly 2 fs out*..........................(8 to 1 tchd 10 to 1) 10
900⁵ NOSMO KING (Ire) 8-11 J Carroll (12) *prmnt till wknd o'r 2 fs out*...............................(8 to 1 op 5 to 1) 11
1158⁸ LUCKY LIZZY 8-7¹ M Wigham (8) *chsd ldrs till wknd hfwy*..(12 to 1) 12
TOOGOODFORYOU 8-11 L Charnock (3) *al beh, tld off fnl furlong*..(20 to 1) 13
Dist: 1l, 3l, ½l, 4l, hd, nk, ½l, 1½l, 2l, nk. 1m 13.00s. a 3.00s (13 Ran).
SR: 20/21/4/7/-/-/ (M H Easterby), M H Easterby

1760 BBC Radio York Sport Handicap Class E (0-70 3-y-o) £3,262 6f......... (3:15)

1419⁴ FORMIDABLE LIZ [47] 7-12 J Lowe (16) *cl up, led o'r 2 out, wnt lft and drw clr entering fnl furlong*. ....(5 to 1 fav op 6 to 1 tchd 13 to 2) 1
1518³ PLUM FIRST [70] (bl) 9-7 S Whitworth (14) *led till hdd o'r 2 fs out, kpt on*....................(12 to 1 tchd 10 to 1) 2
1463⁵ GUSSIE FINK-NOTTLE (Ire) [59] 8-10 B Raymond (18) *wth ldrs, ev ch o'r one out, no extr fnl furlong*. .... (8 to 1 op 10 to 1 tchd 11 to 1) 3
1589⁵ MY GODSON [63] (bl) 8-9 (5*) O Pears (17) *in tch, kpt on same pace fnl 2 fs*............................(10 to 1) 4
491³ HALL BANK COTTAGE [49] 8-0 T Williams (13) *chsd ldrs, rdn o'r 2 fs out, one pace*..........(14 to 1 op 10 to 1) 5
1397⁸ MAKE MINE A DOUBLE [46] 7-11 J Quinn (3) *in tch, hrd rdn 2 fs out, no real hdwy*............(20 to 1 op 16 to 1) 6+
1577² FORTIS PAVIOR (Ire) [54] 8-5 A Culhane (11) *wth ldrs till wknd o'r one furlong out*...........(10 to 1 op 8 to 1) 6+
DUNNINGTON [43] 7-8 L Charnock (15) *nvr dngrs*. ....(25 to 1 op 16 to 1) 8
1480* KILLY'S FILLY [56] 8-7 J Carroll (6) *nvr dngrs*. .... (13 to 2 op 5 to 1 tchd 7 to 1) 9
1273⁹ BLUE RADIANCE [64] 9-1 J Fanning (7) *chsd ldrs till wknd 2 fs out*..................................(20 to 1) 10
1160⁵ HELLO HOBSON'S (Ire) [67] 8-11 (7*) H Bastiman (12) *dwlt, nvr dngrs*..........................(12 to 1 op 10 to 1) 11
1591 ANDRULA MOU [52] 8-3 K Fallon (19) *reared strt and lost grnd, nvr dngrs*..................(20 to 1 op 16 to 1) 12
884⁵ MILBANK CHALLENGER [59] (bl) 8-10 M Birch (4) *prmnt till wknd 2 fs out*...................(16 to 1 op 12 to 1) 13
1192⁵ CUMBRIAN CALYPSO [52] 8-0 (3*) S Maloney (5) *sn beh*. ....(16 to 1 op 14 to 1) 14
1136⁶ SHE'S A BREEZE [51] 8-2 N Adams (9) *sn beh*.... (33 to 1) 15
1503⁴ GATE OF HEAVEN [42] 7-2 (5*) Darren Moffatt (2) *chsd ldrs till wknd hfwy*...................(33 to 1 op 20 to 1) 16
1424⁶ DODDINGTON PLAYER (Ire) [52] 7-12 (5*) A Garth (8) *sn beh*. ....(25 to 1 op 20 to 1) 17
614⁸ ALWAYS BAILEYS [50] 8-1 R P Elliott (1) *in tch till wknd hfwy, fnshd lme*.................. (20 to 1 op 16 to 1) 18
Dist: 3½l, 1½l, sht-hd, 3l, sht-hd, dd-ht, 2½l, hd, 1½l, sht-hd. 1m 12.00s. a 2.00s (18 Ran).
SR: 32/41/24/27/1/-/5/-/-/ (J Johnson), M D Hammond

1761 BBC Radio York Fillies Handicap Class D (0-80 3-y-o and up) £3,752 1m ....(3:50)

1325⁴ LEAVE IT TO LIB [57] 6-8-5 (7*) J Tate (1) *made all, clr 3 fs out, rdn o'r one out, hld on wl*.......(7 to 2 op 3 to 1) 1
1225* TOLEDO QUEEN (Ire) [80] 3-9-10 D Holland (2) *in tch, effrt o'r 2 out, kpt on fnl furlong, not rch wnr*. ....(11 to 10 on op 11 to 10) 2
1390⁶ SPICE AND SUGAR [70] 3-9-0 B Raymond (4) *chsd wnr, effrt o'r 2 fs out, kpt on same pace*. ....(10 to 1 tchd 12 to 1) 3
1136 LAMSONETTI [54] 3-7-12 Dale Gibson (5) *beh, styd on fnl 2 fs, not rch ldrs*...................(14 to 1 op 16 to 1) 4
1326⁶ DALALAH [70] 3-9-0 R Hills (3) *chsd ldrs, effrt o'r 2 fs out, sn btn*..........................(7 to 1 tchd 8 to 1) 5
4696a⁹ BIDWEAYA (USA) [39] 6-7-8¹ N Adams (7) *al beh*. ....(12 to 1 op 10 to 1) 6
TRACHELIUM [70] 3-9-0 A Culhane (6) *al beh*. ....(20 to 1 op 16 to 1) 7
Dist: 1l, 3l, 1½l, nk, 4l, 10l. 1m 38.90s. a 3.00s (7 Ran).
SR: 29/38/19/-/13/-/-/ (Mrs C Calver), P Calver

1762 BBC Radio York News And Information Maiden Stakes Class D (3-y-o) £3,201 7f...................... (4:25)

1522² KNIGHT OF SHALOT (Ire) 9-0 D Holland (5) *made all, drw clr entering fnl furlong, easily*. ....(7 to 4 on op 6 to 4 on) 1
DAGNY JUEL (USA) 8-9 G Carter (3) *prmnt, ev ch 2 fs out, kpt on, no chance wth wnr*..........(4 to 1 op 5 to 2) 2
PHILNIC 9-0 J Carroll (7) *trkd ldrs, pushed alng and outpcd 3 fs out, no dngr aftr*..................(20 to 1) 3
1577⁵ SELFISH LADY 8-9 M Birch (6) *chsd wnr, ev ch o'r 2 fs out, sn rdn and wknd*...............(20 to 1 tchd 25 to 1) 4
642 PRINCE PALACIO 9-0 N Connorton (8) *chsd ldrs till wknd 3 fs out*..(25 to 1) 5
1424⁸ TUSCANIA 8-9 Kim Tinkler (4) *al beh*...............(50 to 1) 6
1577⁷ FORDALLIA 8-9 J Lowe (9) *al beh*.... (33 to 1 op 25 to 1) 7
Dist: 3½l, 8l, 1½l, 4l, 6l, 1l. 1m 26.30s. a 3.50s (7 Ran).
SR: 27/11/-/-/ (R E Sangster), P W Chapple-Hyam

1763 Bramcote School Scarborough Centenary Median Auction Maiden Stakes Class F (Div II) (2-y-o) £2,782 7f (5:00)

1189⁶ IMPOSING GROOM (Ire) 9-0 B Raymond (9) *trkd ldrs, led o'r one furlong out, ran on wl*..... (16 to 1 op 8 to 1) 1
1561⁹ NON VINTAGE (Ire) 9-0 M Birch (8) *in tch, rdn and hdwy 2 out, styd on wl fnl furlong*..........(8 to 1 tchd 10 to 1) 2
SWORDSMANSHIP 9-0 G Duffield (7) *prmnt, ev ch o'r one furlong out, one pace*...........(9 to 4 fav op 5 to 2) 3
506⁵ LAUREL ROMEO (Ire) 9-0 J Carroll (6) *led till hdd o'r one furlong out, fdd*........................(14 to 1 op 8 to 1) 4
1324 JOHNNIE THE JOKER 9-1¹ D Nicholls (10) *in tch, effrt and ch 2 fs out, rdn and one pace*....... (8 to 1 op 5 to 1) 5
1418⁷ LEVEL EDGE 8-9 K Fallon (4) *mid-div, effrt o'r 2 fs out, slightly hmpd over one out, sn btn*. ....(6 to 1 op 5 to 1 tchd 7 to 1) 6
1350⁴ GLORIETTE 8-9 W Woods (1) *beh, effrt 3 furlong out, no hdwy*..................................(7 to 2 op 9 to 4) 7
395 MIDNIGHT HUNTER 9-0 S Webster (5) *al beh*. ....(25 to 1 op 20 to 1) 8
1272⁹ WOODTONG (bl) 9-0 J Fanning (2) *pld hrd, trkd ldrs till wknd o'r 2 fs out*...................(20 to 1 op 16 to 1) 9
1082² BESCABY GIRL 8-9 L Charnock (3) *prmnt till wknd 2 fs out*..................................(8 to 1 op 6 to 1) 10
SONIC (Ire) 9-0 T Lucas (11) *slwly into strd, al beh*. ....(20 to 1 op 14 to 1) 11
Dist: 1½l, 2l, 1½l, 1l, 2l, 1l, 3½l, ¾l, ½l, 2½l. 1m 28.10s. a 5.30s (11 Ran).
(Ian Cameron), J L Dunlop

1764 Ernest Norris Memorial Handicap Class D (0-80 4-y-o and up) £3,525 1 ½m.......................... (5:35)

1143³ PRINCE HANNIBAL [75] 6-9-11 G Carter (1) *prmnt, led wl o'r 2 fs out, styd on und pres*. ....(9 to 2 op 7 to 2 tchd 5 to 1) 1
1593² FAIR FLYER (Ire) [55] 4-8-5 R P Elliott (3) *chsd ldrs, effrt o'r 2 fs out, rdn over one out, kpt on*.....(11 to 2 op 4 to 1) 2
1173⁸ AMBIGUOUSLY REGAL (USA) [78] 4-10-0 B Raymond (5) *cl up, led 7 fs out, hdd wl o'r 2 out, kpt on und pres fnl furlong*.............(7 to 2 fav op 5 to 2 tchd 4 to 1) 3
1457* MIZYAN (Ire) [65] 5-9-1 J Quinn (7) *in tch, effrt 3 fs out, kpt on fnl furlong*..........................(6 to 1 op 5 to 1) 4
1384⁷ PERSIAN SOLDIER [47] 6-7-6 (5*) Darren Moffatt (2) *led, hdd 7 fs out, chsd ldrs, one pace fnl 2 furlongs*. ....(14 to 1 op 12 to 1) 5
1305⁶ EXPLOSIVE SPEED (USA) [43] 5-7-7 J Lowe (8) *sn beh*. ....(4 to 1 op 9 to 2 tchd 5 to 1) 6
1400⁷ TOUR LEADER (NZ) [56] 4-8-6 M Birch (4) *al beh*. ....(8 to 1 op 12 to 1) 7
988 IN THE MONEY (Ire) [70] 4-9-6 S Perks (6) *al beh*. ....(14 to 1 op 12 to 1) 8
Dist: 1½l, sht-hd, sht-hd, 2½l, 4l, 1½l, 3½l. 2m 33.10s. a 2.90s (8 Ran).
SR: 58/35/57/43/20/8/18/25/ (D R Hunnisett), J L Dunlop

ASCOT (soft)
Wednesday June 16th
Going Correction: PLUS 0.90 sec. per fur. (races 1,4), PLUS 0.60 (2), PLUS 0.70 (3,5,6)

1765 Jersey Stakes Class A (Group 3) (3-y-o) £40,432 7f. . . . . (2:30)

1347^{3} ARDKINGLASS 9-1 W Ryan (13) *wl plcd centre, led o'r 2 fs out, rdn out*. . . . . (10 to 1 op 8 to 1 tchd 11 to 1) 1

1289^{4} MATELOT (USA) 9-1 T Jarnet (12) *hld up in centre, cld on ldr 2 fs out, ev ch wl ins last, no extr close hme*. . . . .(7 to 1 op 8 to 1 tchd 9 to 1) 2

1174^{2} ABBEY'S GAL 8-7 L Dettori (14) *rcd centre, in tch, ran on 2 fs out, ev ch und pres appr last, not quicken*. . . . . (9 to 1 op 8 to 1 tchd 10 to 1) 3

1174* EUROLINK THUNDER 9-1 R Cochrane (7) *in tch stands side, ev ch 2 fs out, edgd rght o'r one out, kpt on nr finish*. . . . .(12 to 1 op 10 to 1 tchd 14 to 1) 4

1367^{4} REVELATION (Ire) 8-10 T Quinn (6) *chsd stands side ldrs, rdn o'r 2 fs out, no imprsn fnl furlong*. . . . . (9 to 2 fav tchd 5 to 1) 5

1214^{2} MITHL AL HAWA 8-7 W R Swinburn (3) *wl plcd stands side, rdn alng hfwy, kpt on one pace last 2 fs*. . . . . (12 to 1 op 10 to 1) 6

1231* HOLLY GOLIGHTLY 8-7 J Reid (2) *slwly into strd, sn reco'red, trkd stands side ldrs, one pace last 2 fs*. . . . . (20 to 1 op 33 to 1 tchd 40 to 1) 7

1447^{4} HUMAM (Ire) 9-1 R Hills (5) *stands side, led aftr 2 fs, hdd and wknd o'r two out*. . . . . (20 to 1 op 14 to 1) 8

1337^{7} ROGER THE BUTLER (Ire) 8-10 M Hills (11) *rcd centre, hld up rear, effrt 3 fs out, no imprsn 2 out*. . . . . (50 to 1 op 33 to 1) 9

794 PEMBROKE (USA) 8-10 M Roberts (10) *pushed alng to chase ldrs in centre, wknd o'r 2 fs out*. . . . . (10 to 1 op 8 to 1 tchd 11 to 1) 10

1445^{2} GOODNIGHT KISS 8-7 M J Kinane (8) *speed centre to hfwy*. . . . .(6 to 1 op 9 to 2 tchd 13 to 2) 11

580^{4} RUSTIC CRAFT (Ire) 8-10 C Asmussen (1) *stands side, al beh*. . . . . (20 to 1 tchd 25 to 1) 12

1408^{8} FRIENDLY BRAVE (USA) 8-10 K Darley (9) *led centre grp till o'r 2 fs out, wknd quickly*. . . . .(100 to 1) 13

1347^{5} FIRM PLEDGE (USA) (bl) 8-10 A Munro (4) *led 2 fs stands side, wknd quickly 3 out*. . . . . (14 to 1 op 12 to 1 tchd 16 to 1) 14

941^{6} COLOUR PARTY (USA) 8-10 W J O'Connor (15) *cl up centre to hfwy, lost pl quickly, eased*. . . . . (40 to 1 op 33 to 1 tchd 50 to 1) 15

Dist: Nk, 2l, 1½l, 2½l, hd, 1½l, 1½l, ½l, 2½l, 8l. 1m 35.68s. a 9.38s (15 Ran).

SR: 55/54/40/43/30/26/21/24/17/ (Sir David Wills), H R A Cecil

1766 Queen Mary Stakes Class A (Group 3) (2-y-o) £28,152 5f. . . . .(3:05)

1428^{2} RISKY 8-8 W R Swinburn (6) *made virtually all, drw clr o'r one furlong out, easily*. . . . . (11 to 2 op 4 to 1 tchd 6 to 1) 1

1437* SNIPE HALL 8-8 P Robinson (2) *trkd ldrs, outpcd and rdn wl o'r one furlong out, kpt on well und pres fnl furlong*. . . . . (10 to 1 op 8 to 1 tchd 11 to 1) 2

1393* ELRAFA AH (USA) 8-8 R Hills (4) *trkd ldrs gng wl, rdn o'r one furlong out, styd on ins last*. . . . . (14 to 1 op 16 to 1 tchd 20 to 1) 3

1032* VELVET MOON (Ire) 8-8 A Munro (5) *wth wnr, ev ch one and a half fs out, sn outpcd*. . . . .(3 to 1 fav op 5 to 2 tchd 7 to 2) 4

1683* QUEENBIRD 8-8 W Ryan (9) *beh, rdn and hdwy o'r one furlong out, kpt on und pres*. . . . . (13 to 2 op 11 to 2 tchd 7 to 1) 5

1211* THREATENING 8-8 R Cochrane (10) *slwly into strd, cld on ldrs hfwy, outpcd o'r one furlong out*. . . . .(33 to 1 tchd 40 to 1) 6

1403* DOUBLE DOWN 8-8 L Dettori (1) *strted slwly, nvr gng wl, al beh*. . . . .(8 to 1 op 6 to 1 tchd 9 to 1) 7

1142* ROHITA (Ire) 8-8 Pat Eddery (7) *in tch, rdn o'r 2 fs out, btn over one out*. . . . .(9 to 2 op 4 to 1 tchd 5 to 1) 8

673* NERA 8-8 B Raymond (8) *cl up, pushed alng hfwy, wknd quickly*. . . . .(25 to 1 op 20 to 1 tchd 33 to 1) 9

1403^{5} NIGHTITUDE 8-8 M J Kinane (11) *speed to hfwy, sn wknd*. . . . .(33 to 1 tchd 50 to 1) 10

979^{2} POMMES FRITES (Ire) 8-8 L Piggott (3) *hld up beh, nvr on terms*. . . . . (14 to 1 op 20 to 1) 11

Dist: 5l, 2½l, sht-hd, 2l, ¾l, 10l, ½l, 2l, 1l, 1½l. 1m 4.75s. a 4.45s (11 Ran).

SR: 65/45/35/34/26/23/ (Roldvale Limited), R Hannon

1767 Coronation Stakes Class A (Group 1) (3-y-o) £109,537 1m. . . . . (3:45)

1086^{3} GOLD SPLASH (USA) 9-0 G Mosse (2) *trkd ldr, rdn to ld ins fnl furlong, styd on nr line*. . . . . (100 to 30 op 5 to 2 tchd 4 to 1) 1

749^{8} ELIZABETH BAY (USA) 9-0 T Jarnet (1) *hld up, hdwy and pld out o'r one furlong out, ran on ins last, styd on cl hme*. . . . .(7 to 2 op 3 to 1 tchd 4 to 1) 2

1200^{7} ZARANI SIDI ANNA (USA) (v) 9-0 W R Swinburn (5) *led, shaken up to go clr o'r 2 fs out, hdd ins last, kpt on same pace*. . . . .(10 to 1 op 8 to 1 tchd 12 to 1) 3

1200* NICER (Ire) 9-0 M Hills (4) *strted slwly, rdn alng in rear o'r 3 fs out, not rch ldrs und pres frm 2 out*. . . . .(7 to 4 fav op 5 to 4) 4

SUMOTO 9-0 Pat Eddery (3) *3rd pl till wknd rpdly o'r 2 fs out, sn tld off*. . . . . (13 to 2 op 8 to 1 tchd 6 to 1) 5

Dist: Nk, ¾l, 4l, 30l. 1m 47.68s. a 8.18s (5 Ran).

SR: 61/60/58/46/-/ (J Wertheimer), Mrs C Head

1768 Royal Hunt Cup Handicap Class B (3-y-o and up) £42,955 1m. . . . .(4:20)

1002^{5} IMPERIAL BALLET (Ire) [98] 4-8-12 Pat Eddery (19) *hld up, hdwy o'r 2 fs out, led one out, sn clr, easily*. . . . . (20 to 1 op 16 to 1) 1

1450^{4} ROYAL SEATON [85] 4-7-13 A Mackay (13) *mid-div, hdwy to ld o'r 2 fs out, hdd one out, one pace*. . . . .(12 to 1 tchd 14 to 1) 2

1398^{2} PHILIDOR [84] 4-7-9 (3*) N Kennedy (31) *in tch far side, hdwy to hold ev ch 2 fs out, outpcd appr last*. . . . .(14 to 1 tchd 16 to 1) 3

1450^{7} DOUBLE FLUTTER [79] 4-7-0 (7*) Antoinette Armes (27) *in tch far side, rdn o'r 2 fs out, styd on ins last*. . .(33 to 1) 4

1325^{2} WALKING THE PLANK [79] (v) 4-7-0 (7*) D Wright (7) *trkd ldrs, one pace fnl 2 fs*. . . . .(33 to 1) 5

1172 TENDER MOMENT (Ire) [79] 5-7-7^{3} (3*) B Doyle (16) *chsd ldrs, rdn alng o'r 2 fs out, one pace*. . . . . (20 to 1) 6

1374* JADE VALE [82] 4-7-10^{3} (3*,5ex) D Harrison (6) *chsd ldrs, led 4 fs out till o'r 3 out, one pace*. . . .(16 to 1 tchd 20 to 1) 7

1530^{2} FOREVER DIAMONDS [81] 6-7-9 F Norton (11) *chsd ldrs, rdn and no hdwy fnl 2 fs*. . . . . (14 to 1 tchd 16 to 1) 8

1663^{4} COURAGEOUS KNIGHT [79] 4-7-7 N Adams (23) *beh, hdwy und pres o'r one furlong out, nrst finish*. . . . .(50 to 1 tchd 66 to 1) 9

1450^{6} NEPTUNE'S PET [82] 5-7-10 J Lowe (32) *rcd alone far side to hfwy, ev ch 2 fs out, sn wknd*. . . . .(33 to 1) 10

1270^{8} LITTLE ROUSILLON [79] 5-7-0 (7*) Kim McDonnell (26) *nvr rch ldrs*. . . . . (33 to 1) 11

1552^{2} APPROACH THE BENCH (Ire) [110] 5-9-10 C Swan (10) *mid-div, no hdwy fnl 3 fs*. . . . .(33 to 1) 12

1069^{5} BUZZARDS BELLBUOY [79] 4-7-7 J Quinn (12) *chsd ldrs, shaken up o'r 2 fs out, sn btn*. . . . . .(50 to 1 op 33 to 1) 13

1552^{3} SALMON EILE (Ire) [103] 5-9-3 J Murtagh (25) *nvr dngrs*. . . . . (14 to 1 op 25 to 1) 14

1407^{6} EFHARISTO [90] 4-8-4 W Carson (4) *beh, hrd rdn and hdwy o'r 2 fs out, nvr nr to chal*. (14 to 1 tchd 16 to 1) 15

1130 GRAND VITESSE (Ire) [82] 4-7-10^{3} D Biggs (8) *led to 4 fs out, wknd*. . . . .(33 to 1 op 25 to 1) 16

1002^{2} GYMCRAK PREMIERE [100] 5-9-0 K Darley (30) *prmnt far side till wknd 3 fs out*. . . . .(10 to 1 tchd 12 to 1) 17

1471^{4} NASHVILLE BLUES (Ire) [89] 4-8-3 M Hills (2) *chsd ldrs stands side to hfwy*. . . . . (14 to 1 op 12 to 1) 18

1407^{3} TAPIS ROUGE (Ire) [100] 4-9-0 M Roberts (18) *chsd ldrs far side, rdn alng o'r 3 fs out, sn btn*. . . . .(15 to 2 fav op 8 to 1 tchd 10 to 1) 19

581^{6} KING ATHELSTAN (USA) [96] 5-8-10 B Raymond (29) *nvr rch ldrs*. . . . .(16 to 1 op 14 to 1 tchd 20 to 1) 20

1532^{2} BAND ON THE RUN [96] 6-8-10 T Quinn (3) *al beh*. . . . .(16 to 1 tchd 20 to 1) 21

513^{9} HIGH PREMIUM [87] 5-8-1 K Fallon (5) *trkd ldrs, led o'r 3 fs out till over 2 out, wknd*. . . . . (20 to 1 op 12 to 1 tchd 25 to 1) 22+

1409^{4} TROOPING (Ire) [79] 4-7-7 E Johnson (1) *al beh*. . . . .(20 to 1 tchd 25 to 1) 22+

1412^{4} SPANISH STORM (Ire) [97] 4-8-11 W Woods (15) *chsd ldrs to hfwy*. . . . .(50 to 1) 24

1527 MILLSOLIN (Ire) [81] 5-7-9^{1} S Dawson (21) *nvr dngrs*. . . . .(33 to 1) 25

1177* INDIAN SLAVE (Ire) [79] 5-7-7 (5ex) J Fanning (14) *chsd ldrs, pushed alng hfwy, sn wknd*. . . . . (33 to 1) 26

1720* DOUBLE ECHO (Ire) [79] 5-7-7 (7ex) L Charnock (28) *beh hfwy, eased whn btn ins last*. . . . . (25 to 1) 27

1298^{7} PIQUANT [84] 6-7-12^{1} A Munro (22) *prmnt far side, wknd hfwy, eased whn btn*. . . . . (25 to 1) 28

1270^{9} CLAYBANK (USA) [81] 4-7-9 Dale Gibson (17) *al beh*. . . . . (50 to 1 op 33 to 1) 29

1172 MANGO MANILA [86] 8-8-0^{2} R Hills (20) *al beh*. . . . .(20 to 1 tchd 25 to 1) 30

Dist: 1½l, 5l, 2l, nk, 1½l, 2½l, sht-hd, 2½l, 1l, 1l. 1m 47.40s. a 8.40s (30 Ran).

SR: 80/62/46/35/34/29/24/22/12/ (R E Sangster), H R A Cecil

1769 Queen's Vase Class A (Group 3) (3-y-o) £34,639 2m 45yds. . . . .(4:55)

1364^{4} INFRASONIC 8-11 Pat Eddery (4) *hld up, hdwy frm rear 6 fs out, shaken up to ld o'r one out, kpt on, cleverly*. . . . .(3 to 1 fav op 5 to 2 tchd 7 to 2) 1

1539^{2} SILVERDALE (USA) 8-11 M Roberts (3) *hld up in mid-div, ran on o'r 2 fs out, styd on one pace ins last*. . . . .(7 to 1 tchd 8 to 1) 2

1585* KASSAB 8-11 W Carson (7) *led till o'r 2 fs out, led wl over one out, sn hdd, ran on same pace*. . . . . (11 to 2 op 4 to 1 tchd 6 to 1) 3

1533* SAINT KEYNE 8-11 M J Kinane (5) *ldg grp, chsd ldr hfwy, led o'r 2 fs out till wl over one out, sn btn*. . . . .(5 to 1 op 9 to 2) 4

1216* SPRING TO ACTION 8-11 L Dettori (8) *in tch in mid-div, hdwy 4 fs out, wknd ins last 2*. . . . . (5 to 1 op 9 to 2 tchd 11 to 2) 5

1299* ACANTHUS (Ire) 8-11 B Raymond (2) *chsd ldr to hfwy, rdn alng o'r 5 fs out, wknd over 2 out*. (4 to 1 tchd 9 to 2) 6

1299[4] BONAR BRIDGE (USA) 8-11 T Quinn (6) *al beh.* ....(66 to 1 op 50 to 1 tchd 100 to 1) 7
1582[2] BLUE GROTTO (Ire) 8-11 W Ryan (1) *wl plcd till drpd rear quickly 7 fs out, tld off.* ....(40 to 1 op 50 to 1 tchd 100 to 1) 8
Dist: ¾l, 3½l, 2½l, 12l, ¾l, 4l, dist. 3m 46.47s. a 21.47s (8 Ran).
(K Abdulla), A Fabre

1770 Bessborough Handicap Class B (0-105 3-y-o and up) £19,737 1½m ....(5:30)

925[2] SOURCE OF LIGHT [94] 4-9-3 Pat Eddery (4) *steadied strt, hdwy to track ldr hfwy, led appr 2 fs out, hdd one out, led ins last, all out*...(11 to 1 op 10 to 1 tchd 12 to 1) 1
1484[5] TURGENEV (Ire) [93] 4-9-2 M Roberts (12) *sn pushed alng in mid-div, hdwy o'r 3 fs out, styd on und str pres ins last*..................(9 to 1 op 10 to 1 tchd 11 to 1) 2
1384* BLACKPATCH HILL [81] 4-8-4 W Carson (15) *trkd ldrs, led o'r 6 fs out till appr 2 out, led one out till ins last, no extr und pres*.......(4 to 1 fav op 7 to 2 tchd 9 to 2) 3
1064[2] LAST EMBRACE (Ire) [85] 4-8-5 (3*) D Harrison (10) *mid-div, hrd rdn and hdwy 4 fs out, styd on und pres.* ....(10 to 1 tchd 11 to 1 and 9 to 1) 4
1129[2] DURSHAN (USA) [82] 4-8-5 L Dettori (7) *prmnt, one pace o'r 2 fs out*....................(25 to 1 op 20 to 1) 5
ARBUSHA (USA) [102] 4-9-11 C Roche (6) *beh, hdwy 3 fs out, styd on und pres, nrst finish.* (50 to 1 op 33 to 1) 6
1511[2] PHARFETCHED [83] 4-8-6 W R Swinburn (14) *hld up beh, hdwy fnl 2 fs, nvr nrr.* (7 to 1 op 10 to 1 tchd 6 to 1) 7
1717[4] SWORD MASTER [72] 4-7-9 J Quinn (2) *chsd ldrs, lost pl hfwy, effrt o'r 3 fs out, sn outpcd.* ....(25 to 1 tchd 33 to 1) 8
1409[5] PORT SUNLIGHT (Ire) [70] 5-7-7 N Adams (18) *in tch, hdwy 4 fs out, btn o'r 2 out.* (11 to 1 op 10 to 1 tchd 12 to 1) 9
1269[4] OH SO RISKY [98] 6-9-2 (5*) A Procter (20) *nvr rch ldrs.* ....(12 to 1 tchd 14 to 1) 10
1398[8] GLIDE PATH (USA) [78] 4-8-1[3] M Hills (13) *al beh.* ....(20 to 1 op 16 to 1) 11
1129[4] LYPHANTASTIC (USA) [77] 4-8-0 K Darley (3) *trkd ldr, led briefly 7 fs out, wknd 4 out*.......(25 to 1 op 20 to 1) 12
1155[3] MUCH SOUGHT AFTER [77] 4-8-0[1] R Hills (9) *chsd ldrs, cld o'r 3 fs out, hrd rdn and wknd quickly over 2 out.* ....(25 to 1 op 20 to 1) 13
WHITECHAPEL (USA) [79] 5-8-2 A Munro (17) *in tch till drpd rear hfwy, tld off.* (9 to 1 op 6 to 1 tchd 10 to 1) 14
1607* MOONLIGHT QUEST [70] 5-7-7 (4ex) N Carlisle (16) *sn beh, tld off*....................(16 to 1 tchd 20 to 1) 15
1538[5] SHADOWS OF SILVER [81] 5-8-4 T Quinn (19) *led, sn clr, hdd 7 fs out, soon wknd, tld off*...(25 to 1 op 20 to 1) 16
Dist: ½l, nk, 7l, sht-hd, ¾l, nk, ¾l, 3l, 10l, nk. 2m 39.62s. a 11.42s (16 Ran).
SR: 73/71/58/48/44/62/42/29/21/ (K Abdulla), R Charlton

NOTTINGHAM (good to soft) Wednesday June 16th

Going Correction: PLUS 0.60 sec. per fur. (races 1,2,5,6,7), PLUS 0.55 (3,4)

1771 'Cover Drive' Apprentice Claiming Stakes Class G (3-y-o) £2,406 1m 1f 213yds....................(2:10)

1389[2] DON'T FORGET MARIE (Ire) 7-9 (5*) A Whelan (7) *prmnt, hdwy 3 fs out, effrt to ld 2 out, rdn appr last and ran on wl*....................(5 to 4 fav tchd 6 to 4) 1
1389 KIAWAH 8-0 (5*) N Varley (8) *hld up in tch, hdwy 3 fs out, not much room 2 out, squeezed through appr last, ran on und pres*....................(7 to 1 op 9 to 2) 2
1313[5] FORMAL AFFAIR 8-10 (5*) J D Smith (5) *led one furlong, prmnt till effrt and ev ch 2 out, sn rdn and kpt on one pace*....................(9 to 2 op 3 to 1) 3
1642[6] PREMIER STAR 8-10 (3*) M Fenton (4) *al prmnt, hdwy o'r 3 fs out, ev ch 2 out, sn rdn and wknd appr last.* ....(14 to 1 op 7 to 1) 4
1674[7] WALSHAM WITCH (bl) 8-4 (3*) C Hodgson (3) *pld hrd, led aftr one furlong, rdn and hdd 2 out, sn wknd.* ....(14 to 1 op 10 to 1) 5
1416[7] DIVINE RAIN 8-2 (5*) Michael Denaro (2) *cl up till rdn and wknd 3 fs out*....................(33 to 1 op 20 to 1) 6
1133 SUMMERS DREAM 7-9 (3*) A Garth (6) *trkd ldrs, effrt and ev ch 2 fs out, sn rdn and wknd*... (25 to 1 op 20 to 1) 7
1628[5] SHEFFORD 7-11 (5*) C Hawksley (1) *al rear, wl beh frm hfwy*....................(5 to 1 op 3 to 1) 8
Dist: 2l, 2l, 4l, 2l, 3l, 6l, 3½l. 2m 16.20s. a 13.20s (8 Ran).
SR: 14/15/21/11/1/ (Norman Harper), R Hannon

1772 'Yorker' Rating Related Maiden Stakes Class E (0-70 3-y-o and up) £2,847 1¾m 15yds.............(2:40)

1426[9] HOOSIE 3-8-1[2] (3*) J Weaver (7) *led 2 fs, chsd ldrs till led o'r 4 out, rdn over two out, styd on wl ins last.* ....(2 to 1 tchd 9 to 4) 1
1371[2] MEANT TO BE 3-8-2 G Duffield (8) *hld up, hdwy 5 fs out, effrt to chal 3 out, sn rdn and ev ch till no extr nr finish.* ....(15 to 8 fav op 6 to 4) 2
356 MILIYEL 4-8-12 (7*) D McCabe (6) *hld up and beh, hdwy 3 fs out, styd on ins last, nvr dngrs.* (16 to 1 op 14 to 1) 3
NAAWY 3-8-7 P D'Arcy (5) *chsd ldrs till rdn and outpcd o'r 3 fs out, plugged on one pace appr last.* ....(5 to 1 op 7 to 2) 4
1557[2] ARC BRIGHT (Ire) 3-8-0 (7*) J Dennis (1) *cl up, led aftr 2 fs till hdd o'r 4 out, sn wknd*..........(8 to 1 op 7 to 1) 5
1533[5] FAIRWAYS ON TARGET 7-9-10 W Newnes (2) *in tch, effrt and some hdwy 4 fs out, sn rdn and wknd wl o'r 2 out.* ....(11 to 2 tchd 7 to 1) 6
1700[7] DOMAIN (bl) 5-9-3 (7*) Rebecca Bream (4) *in tch, rapid hdwy aftr 3 fs to chase ldr, wknd quickly 5 out, sn beh.* ....(50 to 1 op 25 to 1) 7
Dist: ¾l, 8l, 1½l, 10l, 1½l, 12l. 3m 15.20s. a 17.30s (7 Ran).
(Sheikh Mohammed), C E Brittain

1773 EBF Maiden Stakes Class D (2-y-o) £3,435 5f 13yds................ (3:10)

1523[3] DANCES WITH RISK 8-9 G Hind (2) *cl up, led one and a half fs out and sn rdn, hdd ins last, rallied to ld nr finish*....................(7 to 4 fav op 5 to 4 on) 1
RESONANT 9-0 G Duffield (5) *cl up, effrt 2 fs out, rdn to ld ins last, hdd nr line*..... (9 to 2 op 5 to 1 tchd 6 to 1) 2
STELLOSO 9-0 M Tebbutt (6) *cl up, led hfwy, rdn and hdd one and a half fs out, wknd ins last.* ....(3 to 1 tchd 4 to 1) 3
1350[9] KNIGHTRIDER 9-0 J Williams (3) *chsd ldrs, rdn 2 fs out, kpt on ins last*....................(7 to 1 op 5 to 1) 4
BANDITA 8-9 R Perham (8) *chsd ldrs, hdwy 2 fs out, sn rdn, wknd appr fnl furlong*...... (50 to 1 op 25 to 1) 5
TANFIRION CHIEF 9-0 R P Elliott (7) *slwly into strd and beh till styd on fnl 2 fs, nrst finish.* (25 to 1 op 20 to 1) 6
ARAFARAZ 9-0 M Perrett (1) *slwly into strd, al beh.* ....(20 to 1) 7
TOTON LAD 9-0 W Newnes (4) *slwly away and hng lft thrght, rdn and chsd ldrs hfwy, sn wknd.* ....(12 to 1 op 20 to 1 tchd 10 to 1) 8
DEAR MADAM 8-9 G Carter (9) *led, rdn and hdd hfwy, sn wknd*.................. (6 to 1 op 5 to 1 tchd 7 to 1) 9
Dist: Sht-hd, 1½l, nk, 3l, 3½l, 10l, 3l, nk. 1m 4.10s. a 5.90s (9 Ran).
SR: 32/36/30/29/12/3/ (Roldvale Limited), G Lewis

1774 'Off Spinner' Claiming Stakes Class F (2-y-o) £2,623 6f 15yds..........(3:40)

1590[2] BROOKHEAD LADY 8-9 J Williams (10) *trkd ldrs, effrt and hdwy 2 fs out, rdn to ld ins last, ran on.* ....(3 to 1 fav tchd 4 to 1) 1
1535[4] CLARET BUMBLE 8-3 T Sprake (9) *cl up, led 2 and a half fs out, rdn and hdd ins last, no extr.* ....(6 to 1 tchd 5 to 1) 2
1254[2] RITA'S JOY 7-13 T Williams (6) *cl up, led briefly hfwy, sn rdn and hdd 2 and a half fs out, wknd appr last.* ....(6 to 1 op 5 to 1) 3
1418 IRISH PERFORMER 8-5 N Connorton (1) *cl up, ev ch o'r 2 fs out, sn rdn and wknd over one out.* (7 to 1 op 5 to 1) 4
1253[6] FINISHING KIND 8-0[1] G Duffield (7) *led to hfwy, sn rdn and one pace*.................... (14 to 1 op 12 to 1) 5
WHO'S CRYING NOW 7-6 (7*) P McCabe (2) *in tch on outer, rdn o'r 2 fs out and one pace*.......... (25 to 1) 6
CURTIS THE FIRST 8-10 W Newnes (3) *in tch on outer, rdn hfwy and one pace*................(16 to 1 op 14 to 1) 7
1403 DISH OF THE DAY (Ire) 8-13 C Rutter (8) *in tch to hfwy, sn lost pl*....................(10 to 1 op 8 to 1) 8
KOHIMA BOY 8-10 G Carter (11) *al rear.* .... (10 to 1 op 7 to 1) 9
1536[7] SOTTISES (Ire) 7-12[10] (7*) S Sanders (4) *dwlt, al beh.* ....(33 to 1) 10
1253[2] SWEET WHISPER (bl) 8-13 G Hind (5) *cl up 2 fs, sn lost pl and beh*....................(4 to 1 op 2 to 1) 11
Dist: 1½l, 4l, 1½l, 3½l, ¾l, nk, 3l, 3½l, 1½l, 7l. 1m 18.00s. a 6.50s (11 Ran).
SR: 31/19/-/-/-/-/ (J E Abbey), P D Evans

1775 'Cover Point' Handicap Class D (0-80 4-y-o and up) £3,483 2m 9yds... (4:10)

1601* FIVE TO SEVEN (USA) [70] 4-9-10 (5*,5ex) O Pears (2) *made all, clr hfwy, rdn 4 fs out, styd on wl fnl 2 furlongs.* .... (11 to 8 fav op Evens) 1
1586 MATCHING GREEN [60] 4-9-5 J Williams (3) *sn pushed alng, hdwy o'r 5 fs out, rdn and ev ch 3 out till one pace appr last*..........(7 to 4 op 2 to 1 tchd 6 to 4) 2
1564[7] KOVALEVSKIA [39] 8-7-12 T Williams (1) *chsd wnr, pushed alng to take clr order 5 fs out, sn rdn and ev ch till edgd rght and wknd wl o'r 2 out*........(11 to 4 op 5 to 2) 3
Dist: 3l, 20l. 3m 43.80s. a 19.60s (3 Ran).
SR: 15/2/-/ (The Five To Seven Partnership), S G Norton

1776 Test Cricket Fillies Handicap Class E (0-70 3-y-o) £3,183 1m 1f 213yds (4:40)

1562[2] SO SAUCY [44] 7-11 A Tucker (4) *sn led, rdn o'r 2 fs out, styd on strly ins last*................(7 to 2 op 4 to 1) 1

1074 CLAIRIFICATION (Ire) [47] 8-0 R Price (9) *hld up, gd hdwy 4 fs out, effrt to chal and ev ch 2 out, sn rdn, hng lft o'r one out and one pace*..............................(14 to 1) 2
1482[2] EYE WITNESS (Ire) [68] 9-7 C Rutter (10) *in tch, hdwy o'r 3 fs out, rdn and ev ch 2 out, sn edgd lft and one pace*. ....(5 to 2 fav op 2 to 1) 3
685 CHOUETTE [54] 8-7 W Newnes (6) *chsd ldrs, effrt and ev ch o'r 2 fs out, sn rdn and kpt on one pace*..... (9 to 1) 4
1257[8] IBTIKAR (USA) [54] 8-7 G Carter (7) *beh, hdwy o'r 4 fs out, sn rdn and not pace to rch ldrs*............... (10 to 1) 5
1627[2] DESIRABLE MISS [47] (v) 8-0[4] G Duffield (5) *chsd wnr, rdn 3 fs out and sn wknd*................................(8 to 1) 6
1501[3] NELLIE'S GAMBLE [50] 8-3 T Williams (8) *chsd ldrs, rdn 3 fs out and sn wknd*.. ....(4 to 1 op 9 to 2) 7
1080[4] ROCK THE BOAT [62] 9-1 S Raymont (1) *prmnt, rdn o'r 4 fs out and sn lost pl*.................. (11 to 2 op 9 to 2) 8
835[8] GLEAM OF GOLD [40] 7-0 (7*) F Savage (2) *al rear*. (33 to 1) 9
Dist: 5l, 1l, 2l, 6l, 2½l, 8l, nk, 5l. 2m 14.10s. a 11.10s (9 Ran).
SR: 32/25/44/26/14/2/ (L H J Ward), B J Meehan

1777 County Cricket Handicap Class D (0-80 3-y-o and up) £3,640 1m 54yds ....(5:10)

1707[3] QUANTITY SURVEYOR [54] 4-8-7 G Duffield (10) *hld up, hdwy 3 fs out, effrt and rdn 2 out, led ins last, ran on*. ....(7 to 1 op 6 to 1) 1
1530[7] AMENABLE [75] 8-10-0 Alex Greaves (6) *hld up, hdwy 3 fs out, ev ch whn not much room one and a half out, swtchd, rdn and every chance ins last, kpt on*. ....(8 to 1 op 6 to 1) 2
1626 NORTHERN TRIAL (USA) [47] (v) 5-7-7 (7*) P McCabe (8) *hld up, gd hdwy 3 fs out, rdn to ld appr last and edgd rght, hdd and not quicken ins last*...... (33 to 1 op 25 to 1) 3
1591* CAUSLEY [71] 8-9-3 (7*,6ex) S Sanders (9) *chsd ldr till led o'r 4 fs out, rdn 2 out, hdd and hmpd appr last, swtchd and kpt on one pace*... (11 to 2 op 4 to 1 tchd 6 to 1) 4
1298[9] SALDA [68] 4-9-0 (7*) G Parkin (1) *in tch, effrt and hdwy o'r 2 fs out, sn rdn, one pace*........(10 to 1 op 7 to 1) 5
1434[2] JAHANGIR (Ire) [70] 4-9-4 (5*) M Fenton (5) *chsd ldrs, hdwy 4 fs out, effrt to chal 3 out, sn rdn and ev ch till wknd entering last*.................(7 to 2 fav tchd 3 to 1) 6
1520[6] GOLDEN CHIP (Ire) [75] 5-9-7 (7*) V Halliday (11) *chsd ldrs, hdwy on outer 3 fs out, rdn 2 out and ev ch till wknd o'r one out*.............................. (8 to 1 op 6 to 1) 7
1591[7] DUNE RIVER [68] 4-9-7 M Tebbutt (3) *cl up till rdn and wknd 3 fs out*.................... (11 to 1 op 7 to 1) 8
1408[9] SYLVANIA (Ire) [64] (bl) 3-8-7 R Perham (7) *led, hdd o'r 4 fs out, sn wknd*.....................(9 to 2 op 10 to 1) 9
1438 ANNACURRAGH (Ire) [48] 4-8-1 G Carter (4) *sn outpcd and tld off fnl 5 fs*........................ (25 to 1 op 20 to 1) 10
Dist: 1½l, 1½l, 2½l, 1½l, nk, 5l, 3l, 8l. 1m 50.10s. a 10.10s (10 Ran).
SR: 16/32/-/15/7/8/ (Lady Fairhaven), Sir Mark Prescott

RIPON (good)
Wednesday June 16th
Going Correction: NIL (races 1,5), MINUS 0.10 (2,3,4,6,7)

1778 Richmond Conditions Stakes Class D (2-y-o) £3,114 6f.................(2:15)

1343[2] ZUNO STAR (USA) 9-1 Paul Eddery (6) *prmnt, effrt 2 out, led one out, ran on wl*. ....(11 to 8 on tchd 5 to 4 on and 6 to 5 on) 1
1152* BEST KEPT SECRET 9-5 J Carroll (1) *trkd ldrs, not much room frm hfwy till swtchd entering fnl furlong, ran on wl*.....................(100 to 30 op 7 to 2 tchd 3 to 1) 2
SKY DIVER 8-11 M Birch (5) *in tch, kpt on fnl furlong, nvr dngrs*..................................(20 to 1 op 14 to 1) 3
998[8] RAVEN'S RETURN (Ire) 9-1 S Perks (3) *prmnt till wknd o'r one out*..............................(20 to 1 op 12 to 1) 4
1497[3] TO CROWN IT ALL (USA) 8-11 Dean McKeown (7) *prmnt, pushed alng hfwy, wknd o'r one out*. (8 to 1 op 6 to 1) 5
446[3] INDIAN DREAMER 8-8 (7*) J O'Dwyer (2) *led till hdd and wknd one out*............................(12 to 1 op 8 to 1) 6
SPENVALLEY-KING 8-11 R Lappin (4) *al beh*. ....(50 to 1 op 33 to 1) 7
Dist: 1l, 7l, hd, ½l, 1l, ½l. 1m 13.90s. a 3.30s (7 Ran).
SR: 35/35/-/2/ (Vic Fatah), G Lewis

1779 Levy Board Handicap Class D (0-80 3-y-o and up) £3,406 1½m 60yds (2:50)

1681* HIGHFLYING [70] 7-9-3 (7*) J Tate (3) *trkd ldr frm 8 out, led 3 out, pushed clr from 2 out, cmftbly*. ....(7 to 4 on op 6 to 4 on tchd 11 to 8 on) 1
1224[4] MR WOODCOCK [51] 8-8-5 Dean McKeown (1) *led till hdd 3 out, kpt on, no ch wth wnr*........ (4 to 1 op 3 to 1) 2
1438[4] SALU [54] (bl) 4-8-8 M Birch (2) *hld up, some hdwy 4 out, no imprsn on 1st 2*.........................(9 to 1 op 7 to 1) 3
BOLD ELECT [68] 5-9-8 M Wigham (5) *trkd ldr 4 fs, in tch till wknd four out*..................(20 to 1 op 14 to 1) 4
1457[2] JULFAAR (USA) [64] 6-9-4 G Bardwell (4) *al beh*. ....(8 to 1 op 6 to 1) 5
Dist: 5l, 10l, 3½l, 5l. 2m 41.80s. a 6.80s (5 Ran).
SR: 30/1/ (B Batey), G M Moore

1780 City Of Ripon Handicap Class C (0-95 3-y-o) £7,700 1m................ (3:25)

1451[5] BROWN'S (Fr) [85] 9-2 (5*) Stephen Davies (2) *led aftr one furlong, made rst, rdn 2 out, styd on wl*. ....(9 to 2 tchd 5 to 1) 1
1357* AWESTRUCK [72] 8-8 N Day (9) *chsd ldrs, pushed alng 5 out, hdwy und pres o'r one out, kpt on ins fnl furlong*. .... (11 to 2 op 5 to 1) 2
1016[8] SILVERLOCKS [84] 9-6 Paul Eddery (1) *hld up, gd hdwy 4 out, ev ch 2 out, one pace*. ....(13 to 2 op 10 to 1 tchd 6 to 1) 3
1451[9] UMBUBUZI (USA) [69] 8-5 S Perks (7) *led one furlong, cl up till wknd o'r one out*. ....(11 to 1 op 10 to 1 tchd 12 to 1) 4
1017 WILLSHE GAN [82] 9-4 D Holland (4) *trkd ldrs, effrt o'r 3 out, kpt on same pace*........... (14 to 1 tchd 16 to 1) 5
474[4] KEYWAY (USA) [82] 9-4 C Nutter (5) *prmnt, pushed alng 4 out, wknd 2 out*..................(11 to 2 op 9 to 2) 6
CLIBURNEL NEWS (Ire) [75] 8-4 (7*) S Mulvey (6) *hld up, hdwy 3 out, wknd o'r one out, eased whn btn*. .... (14 to 1 op 12 to 1) 7
1338[6] SPARK (Ire) [84] 9-6 J Carroll (3) *in tch till wknd o'r 3 out*. .... (14 to 1 op 12 to 1) 8
Dist: ½l, 3½l, 6l, 2l, nk, 2½l, 4l. 1m 41.10s. a 2.80s (8 Ran).
SR: 53/38/39/6/13/12/-/-/ (F M Kalla), P W Chapple-Hyam

1781 Beaumonts Insurance Ladies' Derby Handicap Ladies Class F (0-70 3-y-o and up) £3,236 1½m 60yds......(4:00)

1143 SCENIC DANCER [43] 5-9-9 Miss L Hide (10) *hld up, gd hdwy 3 out, swtchd ins o'r 2 out, switched outsd over one out, quickened to ld inside fnl furlong, very easily*. .... (9 to 1 op 8 to 1 tchd 10 to 1) 1
1414 MYSTERIOUS MAID (USA) [43] 6-9-9 Mrs L Pearce (3) *trkd ldrs, led o'r 2 out, hdd over one out, kpt on, no ch wth wnr*.....................(11 to 2 op 8 to 1 tchd 5 to 1) 2
1259* PRIME PAINTER [68] 3-10-2 (3*) Miss A Yardley (8) *chsd ldr 9 out, led o'r 2 out, hdd over one out, one pace*. ....(6 to 1 tchd 7 to 1) 3
1498* SAINT CIEL (USA) [67] 5-11-5 Miss I Diana W Jones (2) *hld up, steady hdwy hfwy, ch 2 out, kpt on same pace*. ....(7 to 1 op 6 to 1) 4
1521[2] SHAMSHOM AL ARAB (Ire) [53] 5-10-5 Mrs J Crossley (1) *mid-div, hdwy hfwy, kpt on same pace frm 3 out*. ....(5 to 1 jt-fav op 4 to 1 tchd 11 to 2) 5
1430 CATHOS (Fr) [45] 8-9-11 Mrs D Arbuthnot (13) *beh till styd on fnl 3 fs, nrst finish*..............(8 to 1 tchd 10 to 1) 6
840 CHADWICK'S GINGER [40] 5-9-6 Miss S Baxter (9) *mid-div, effrt 4 out, kpt on same pace*.................(33 to 1) 7
1498[3] DAWN FLIGHT [63] (v) 4-11-1 Mrs M Cowdrey (5) *slwly into strd, led 9 out, hdd o'r 2 out, sn wknd*.........(7 to 1) 8
1460[7] INFERRING [42] 5-9-8 Miss A Deniel (12) *nvr dngrs*. .... (25 to 1 op 20 to 1) 9
1592[3] WESTHOLME (USA) [69] 5-11-7 Mrs S Easterby (14) *hld up, hdwy hfwy, wknd 3 out*......................(5 to 1 jt-fav op 4 to 1 tchd 11 to 2) 10
1600[3] COXANN [34] 7-8-11 (3*) Miss V Marshall (7) *prmnt early, beh frm hfwy*..................... (20 to 1 op 16 to 1) 11
1316 BREEZED WELL [49] 7-10-1 Mrs H Noonan (6) *prmnt till wknd o'r 2 out*..................... (33 to 1 op 20 to 1) 12
1439 GAY MING [39] 4-9-5 Mrs G Rees (15) *al beh*...... (20 to 1) 13
1305 BRECKENBROUGH LAD [45] 6-9-11 Miss P Robson (11) *beh frm hfwy*........................ (14 to 1 op 12 to 1) 14
1112[6] LAMBSON [34] 6-9-0 Mrs A Farrell (16) *prmnt to hfwy, sn wknd, tld off*..................(25 to 1 op 20 to 1) 15
1230 EVERSET (Fr) [50] 5-10-2 Mrs J Musson (4) *led till hdd 9 out, sn wknd, wl tld off*.......................(33 to 1) 16
Dist: 5l, 2l, ½l, 3½l, ½l, hd, 1½l, ¾l, 1½l, 2½l. 2m 41.80s. a 6.80s (16 Ran).
SR: 29/19/25/38/17/8/2/22/-/ (Anthony Hide), A Hide

1782 ACC Handicap Class D (0-80 3-y-o and up) £3,494 5f...................(4:35)

1589[9] BALLAD DANCER [55] 8-8-8 M Birch (5) *beh till ran on wl fnl 2 fs, led cl hme*....(11 to 1 op 10 to 1 tchd 12 to 1) 1
1175[5] SIMMIE'S SPECIAL [57] 5-8-10 S Perks (1) *cl up, led o'r one out, hdd close hme*................(12 to 1 op 10 to 1) 2
1599[3] JUST BOB [68] 4-9-0 (7*) J Tate (7) *slwly into strd, beh till gd hdwy 2 out, ev ch ins fnl furlong, no extr cl hme*. ....(9 to 2) 3
1473[4] VERY DICEY [71] 5-9-10 J Carroll (3) *slight ld till hdd o'r one out, kpt on wl*... (3 to 1 fav op 7 to 2 tchd 4 to 1) 4
1589 ROCK OPERA (Ire) [56] 5-8-9 Paul Eddery (4) *beh till ran on wl fnl furlong, nrst finish*..................(14 to 1) 5
1480[7] MASTER POKEY [55] 9-8-8 T Lucas (11) *chsd ldrs, no hdwy fnl 2 fs*......................(10 to 1 op 8 to 1) 6
1589 PRINCE BELFORT [62] 5-9-1 A McGlone (12) *chsd ldrs, no hdwy fnl 2 fs*.......................(8 to 1 op 6 to 1) 7
916 LINCSTONE BOY (Ire) [52] (bl) 5-8-5[3] S Webster (9) *chsd ldrs, no hdwy fnl 2 fs*. ....(11 to 1 op 16 to 1 tchd 10 to 1) 8

1599^{5} MEESON TIMES [41] (v) 5-7-8 G Bardwell (8) *chsd ldrs till wknd 2 out*.......................................(14 to 1) 9
1379^{8} SIR TASKER [66] 5-9-5 D Holland (2) *wth ldrs till wknd 2 out*...(10 to 1) 10
1677^{4} LE CHIC [47] (v) 7-7-9 (5*) Darren Moffatt (10) *swtchd far rail and gd early speed, wnt lft and wknd 2 out.* ....(7 to 1 op 6 to 1) 11
1494 ALMOST BLUE [75] 7-10-0 Dean McKeown (6) *sn beh.* ....(33 to 1) 12

Dist: ½l, sht-hd, sht-hd, 2½l, ½l, nk, sht-hd, 1½l, 2½l, 2½l. 1m 0.70s. a 2.70s (12 Ran).

SR: 40/40/50/52/27/24/30/19/2/ (W B Imison), P Calver

1783 Bedale Limited Stakes Class F (4-y-o and up) £3,002 1¼m............(5:05)

1612* SOVEREIGN PAGE (USA) 4-8-7 (7*) J Tate (7) *trkd ldrs gng wl, led o'r 4 out, clr one out, eased towards finish, cmftbly*..... (6 to 4 on op 11 to 8 on tchd 5 to 4 on) 1
1530^{8} EXPRESS GIFT 4-8-9 (5*) Darren Moffatt (2) *hld up, effrt 4 out, rdn 3 out, styd on, no ch wth wnr.* ....(11 to 2 op 7 to 2 tchd 6 to 1) 2
1460^{5} DELPIOMBO 7-8-11 (3*) S Maloney (3) *trkd ldrs, chsd wnr 4 out, rdn 3 out, kpt on same pace.* ....(4 to 1 op 7 to 2 tchd 9 to 2) 3
1634^{4} AEGAEN LADY 4-8-9 J Carroll (5) *hld up, effrt 3 out, rdn 2 out, sn btn*............(9 to 1 op 7 to 1 tchd 10 to 1) 4
1592^{9} KING'S GUEST (Ire) 4-9-0 Dean McKeown (6) *led till hdd o'r 4 out, fdd*......................(20 to 1 op 16 to 1) 5
1657^{2} LE TEMERAIRE 7-9-0 Kim Tinkler (4) *cl up till wknd 4 out.* ....(20 to 1 op 14 to 1) 6

Dist: 1½l, 2½l, 3½l, nk, 4l. 2m 8.50s. a 4.50s (6 Ran).

SR: 45/42/37/25/29/21/ (Mrs J M Beeby), B Hanbury

1784 Masham Maiden Stakes Class D (3-y-o) £3,640 1¼m...............(5:35)

1340^{2} GEORGE DILLINGHAM 9-0 Paul Eddery (13) *al prmnt, led wl o'r one out, all out.* ....(5 to 2 op 9 to 4 tchd 11 to 4 and 3 to 1) 1
1452^{2} GONE TROPPO 9-0 A McGlone (4) *prmnt, slight ld o'r 2 out, sn hdd, rallied fnl furlong, jst fld.* ....(6 to 4 fav tchd 7 to 4) 2
761^{4} LORD BOTHWELL (USA) 8-9 (5*) Stephen Davies (7) *in tch, hdwy 3 out, styd on fnl furlong*.....(8 to 1 op 6 to 1) 3
TRIPLE 9-0 D Holland (10) *mid-div, sn pushed alng, hdwy o'r 3 out, kpt on fnl furlong.* .... (7 to 1 op 9 to 1 tchd 10 to 1) 4
1068^{4} BAMBURGH (USA) 9-0 M Birch (12) *chsd ldr, chlgd o'r 2 out, wknd entering fnl furlong.* ....(8 to 1 op 7 to 1 tchd 9 to 1) 5
1429 SMUGGLER'S POINT (USA) 9-0 J Carroll (6) *in tch, effrt o'r 3 out, one pace*....................(16 to 1 op 14 to 1) 6
CIVIL ACTION (Ire) 9-0 A Culhane (5) *led till hdd o'r 2 out, sn wknd*...(33 to 1) 7
1275 FATAL SHOCK 8-9 G Bardwell (9) *in tch till wknd o'r 3 out.* ....(25 to 1 op 20 to 1) 8
LOWLANDS SCRIBE 8-9 S Webster (8) *nvr nr to chal.* ....(50 to 1) 9
185^{4} THATCHED (Ire) 9-0 N Day (2) *trkd ldrs till wknd 3 out.* ....(33 to 1) 10
GOLDEN SAVANNAH 9-0 T Lucas (1) *dwlt, al beh.* ....(50 to 1 op 33 to 1) 11
KAHLO 8-9 Dean McKeown (3) *dwlt, beh most of way.* ....(40 to 1 op 33 to 1) 12
1192^{6} GRENOBLE (Ire) 8-6 (3*) S Maloney (11) *al beh*.... (50 to 1) 13

Dist: Hd, 3½l, 1l, 1l, 3½l, 7l, ¾l, ½l, ½l, 2l. 2m 8.60s. a 4.60s (13 Ran).
SR: 44/43/36/34/32/25/11/4/3/ (Mrs P W Harris), P W Harris

ASCOT (soft)
Thursday June 17th
Going Correction: PLUS 0.55 sec. per fur. (races 1,3,5), PLUS 0.80 (2,4,6)

1785 King George V Handicap Class B (0-105 3-y-o) £19,412 1½m..... (2:30)

1671* LEARMONT (USA) [81] 8-8 (4ex) J Carroll (2) *in tch, cld on ldrs o'r 3 out, led and hng lft over 2 out, styd on wl fnl furlong*............(14 to 1 op 10 to 1 tchd 16 to 1) 1
1115* PISTOL RIVER (Ire) [92] 9-5 J Reid (12) *hld up in rear, prog o'r 3 out, chsd wnr appr fnl furlong, not quicken.* ....(7 to 1 jt-fav op 6 to 1 tchd 15 to 2) 2
1314^{3} MASTER CHARLIE [94] 9-7 L Dettori (8) *hld up, prog frm rear 4 out, ev ch o'r 2 out, ran on same pace*...(16 to 1) 3
1690* ALLESCA [75] 8-2 (4ex) N Adams (3) *hdwy o'r 4 fs out, led over 3 three till over 2 out, sn btn.* ....(10 to 1 op 8 to 1 tchd 11 to 1) 4
1299^{3} MARROS MILL [83] (v) 8-10 M Hills (10) *chases ldg grp, ch 3 fs out, outpcd appr last 2 furlongs.* ....(16 to 1 op 12 to 1 tchd 20 to 1) 5
844^{4} LYFORD CAY (Ire) [91] 9-4 D Holland (7) *hld up in rear, rdn alng o'r 2 fs out, kpt on ins fnl furlong, nrst at finish.* ....(16 to 1 op 12 to 1 tchd 20 to 1) 6
1429* BLACK DRAGON (Ire) [85] 8-12 M Roberts (16) *ldg grp, ev ch wl o'r 2 out, sn rdn and no extr*...........(7 to 1 jt-fav op 6 to 1 tchd 15 to 2) 7
1216^{2} YAHMI (Ire) [91] 9-4 R Hills (15) *pressed ldrs til lost pos o'r 2 fs out*...........................(25 to 1 op 20 to 1) 8
1526^{2} EMPIRE POOL [92] (v) 9-5 A Munro (13) *mid-div most of way*.............................(25 to 1 op 20 to 1) 9
540^{7} ALJAZZAF [94] 9-7 C Asmussen (18) *nvr better than mid-div*..(20 to 1) 10
1329^{4} BEAUMAN [81] 8-8 P Robinson (1) *wl plcd, led 7 out till o'r 3 fs out, sn wknd*.....(33 to 1 op 20 to 1 tchd 50 to 1) 11
1526^{4} CIRCUS COLOURS [80] 8-7 Pat Eddery (20) *trkd ldrs, rdn alng 5 fs out, wknd wl o'r 2 out*.....(8 to 1 op 6 to 1) 12
1375* GLEN ECHO (Ire) [83] 8-10 T Quinn (6) *handily plcd til weaked o'r 3 out, tld off*..........(14 to 1 op 10 to 1) 13
1064* DEVILRY [84] 8-8 (3*) J Weaver (11) *al beh, tld off.* ....(20 to 1 op 14 to 1 tchd 25 to 1) 14
1526^{3} LIJAAM (Ire) [84] 8-11 W R Swinburn (4) *led aftr one furlong, hdd 7 fs out, wknd und pres o'r 4 out, tld off.* ....(8 to 1 op 10 to 1) 15
1661* CONTRACT COURT (USA) [-] 8-3 Dean McKeown, *led one furlong, wknd 5 out, tld off*......................(20 to 1) 16

Dist: 2½l, 2½l, 8l, 4l, 2½l, 1½l, 1½l, 1½l, ¾l, 1½l. 2m 37.90s. a 9.70s (16 Ran).
SR: 63/69/66/31/31/34/25/28/26/ (Sheikh Mohammed), J H M Gosden

1786 Cork And Orrery Stakes Class A (Group 3) (3-y-o and up) £40,645 6f ....(3:05)

1201* COLLEGE CHAPEL 3-8-10 L Piggott (3) *trkd ldrs, smooth hdwy 2 fs out, shaken up to ld ins fnl furlong, rdn and ran on wl*......... (7 to 2 fav tchd 5 to 1 and 3 to 1) 1
KEEN HUNTER (USA) 6-9-7 M Roberts (6) *chsd ldrs, hdwy to ld o'r one one furlong out, edgd lft and hdd ins last, no extr*............. (12 to 1 op 10 to 1 tchd 14 to 1) 2
DOLPHIN STREET (Fr) 3-8-2 K Darley (11) *mid-div, hdwy whn short of room 2 fs out, not clr run briefly o'r one out, ran on ins last.* (6 to 1 tchd 13 to 2 and 11 to 2) 3
1019^{3} MONTENDRE 6-8-10 J Reid (13) *chsd ldrs, hdwy to hold ev ch o'r one furlong out, one pace und pres.* ....(14 to 1 op 12 to 1) 4
1406^{3} GARAH 4-8-7 Pat Eddery (8) *wth ldr, led o'r 2 fs out till hdd over one furlong out, wknd.* ....(10 to 1 op 8 to 1 tchd 11 to 1) 5
794^{5} SILVER WIZARD (USA) 3-8-2 A Munro (2) *chsd ldrs, pushed alng and lost pl hfwy, styd on wl fnl furlong.* ....(12 to 1 op 10 to 1) 6
1646^{3} STREET REBEL (Can) (bl) 5-9-0 S Craine (17) *outpcd til styd on ins fnl furlong, nrst finish*.... (50 to 1 op 33 to 1) 7
1406^{8} HAMAS (Ire) 4-9-0 W Carson (4) *led til hdd o'r 2 fs out, rdn and sn wknd*.....................(20 to 1 op 16 to 1) 8
1205^{4} FYLDE FLYER 4-8-10 J Carroll (19) *outpcd and sn rdn alng, hrd ridden 2 fs out, nvr on terms.* ....(25 to 1 tchd 33 to 1) 9
1201^{5} NORDIC FOX (Ire) 3-8-2 J A Heffernan (16) *sn reminders to go pace, beh, cld hfwy, outpcd frm 2 fs out.* ....(66 to 1 op 50 to 1) 10
1465^{2} MONDE BLEU 5-9-4 T Jarnet (9) *mid-div, effrt o'r 2 fs out, no imprsn*.....................(14 to 1 tchd 16 to 1) 11
1449^{3} CRADLE DAYS 4-8-10 M J Kinane (7) *chsd laders till wknd appr 2 fs out*..................(66 to 1 op 100 to 1) 12
1047 PETARDIA 3-8-10 M Hills (15) *chsd ldrs, pld and out and effrt 2 fs out, btn o'r one out*..... (25 to 1 tchd 33 to 1) 13
1365^{3} RAIN BROTHER (USA) 3-8-2 D Holland (1) *trkd ldrs stands side to hfwy*.....................(33 to 1 op 25 to 1) 14
1215^{6} STACK ROCK 6-8-7 K Fallon (5) *wth ldrs to hfwy, hrd rdn 2 fs out, wknd quickly*........... (50 to 1 op 33 to 1) 15
1447^{2} THOURIOS 4-8-10 T Quinn (10) *nvr on terms wth ldrs.* ....(12 to 1 op 8 to 1 tchd 14 to 1) 16
1205* PIPS PRIDE 3-8-13 L Dettori (14) *wth ldrs, ev ch 2 fs out, wknd und pres, eased whn btn.* ....(10 to 1 op 8 to 1 tchd 11 to 1) 17
1174^{5} BRIGG FAIR 3-8-2 R Hills (20) *speed to hfwy.* ....(100 to 1 op 66 to 1) 18
1031* SPECIFIED (USA) 3-8-2 Paul Eddery (12) *beh frm hfwy.* ....(14 to 1 op 12 to 1) 19

Dist: 1l, 1l, 3l, 2½l, 2½l, nk, hd, ½l, 1½l, ¾l. 1m 19.15s. a 5.75s (19 Ran).
SR: 77/84/61/57/44/29/40/39/33/ (Mrs M V O'Brien), M V O'Brien

1787 Gold Cup Class A (Group 1) (4-y-o and up) £107,464 2½m.............(3:45)

957* DRUM TAPS (USA) 7-9-2 L Dettori (6) *hld up, hdwy to ld o'r 4 fs out, hdd over 2 out, rdn to lead ag'n over one out, pushed clr*.........(13 to 2 op 9 to 2 tchd 7 to 1) 1
1405^{3} ASSESSOR (Ire) 4-9-0 T Quinn (4) *cld on ldrs 8 fs out, pushed alng o'r 4 out, led over 2 out, hdd and hng lft over one out, no extr.* (100 to 30 op 5 to 2 tchd 4 to 1) 2
1042^{2} TURGEON (USA) 7-9-2 M Roberts (10) *trkd ldrs, rdn alng o'r 3 out, one pace last 2 fs.* ....(20 to 1 op 16 to 1 tchd 25 to 1) 3
1219^{2} SOUGHT OUT (Ire) 5-8-13 C Asmussen (2) *pressed ldr til led 8 fs out, hdd o'r 4 out, wknd over 2 out.* .... (15 to 8 fav op 9 to 4 tchd 5 to 2 and 7 to 4) 4
1405^{5} ARCADIAN HEIGHTS 5-9-2 W R Swinburn (5) *hld up in rear, rdn and effrt o'r 3 out, no imprsn on ldrs appr last 2 fs*........................ (20 to 1 op 16 to 1 tchd 25 to 1) 5

1554* VINTAGE CROP 6-9-2 M J Kinane (8) *hld up towards rear, rdn alng 4 fs out, no hdwy appr last 2 furlongs.* .... (9 to 1 op 6 to 1 tchd 10 to 1) 6
1405[4] DARU (USA) (v) 4-9-0 R Cochrane (1) *settled in rear, cld on ldrs 4 fs out, rdn and wknd o'r 2 out.* .... (25 to 1 op 20 to 1) 7
1405[7] FURTHER FLIGHT 7-9-2 M Hills (7) *hld up in rear, pushed alng 4 fs out, sn btn, tld off.* .... (14 to 1 op 12 to 1 tchd 16 to 1) 8
1405[8] SILVERNESIAN (USA) 4-9-0 W Carson (3) *handily plcd, rdn and wknd o'r 4 fs out, eased over 2 out, tld off.* .... (33 to 1 op 25 to 1) 9
1405[6] ALLEGAN (USA) 4-9-0 Pat Eddery (9) *led for 12 fs, drpd rear quickly o'r 3 furlongs out, eased and tld off.* .... (12 to 1 tchd 10 to 1 and 14 to 1) 10
Dist: 3l, 6l, 7l, 3½l, sht-hd, 4l, 12l, 15l, 2½l. 4m 32.57s. a 16.07s (10 Ran).
SR: 51/46/42/32/31/30/24/14/-/ (Yoshio Asakawa), Lord Huntingdon

1788 Norfolk Stakes Class A (Group 3) (2-y-o) £24,249 5f. .... (4:20)

554* TURTLE ISLAND (Ire) 8-13 J Reid (1) *hld up, cld hfwy, led and drifted rght o'r one furlong out, sn clr.* .... (3 to 1 op 2 to 1 tchd 100 to 30) 1
1343* GOLD LAND (USA) 8-13 A Munro (3) *hld up tracking ldrs, hdwy and not clr run o'r one furlong out, bumped ins last, ran on wl nr finish.* (4 to 1 op 7 to 2 tchd 9 to 2) 2
1428* REDOUBTABLE (USA) 8-13 T Quinn (5) *cl up, led hfwy, hdd and crrd rght o'r one furlong out, swtchd lft ins last, no extr nr finish.* ....(15 to 8 fav op 7 to 4 tchd 9 to 4) 3
1045[3] LONG GALLERY (Ire) 8-13 M J Kinane (8) *hdwy to track ldrs hfwy, ev ch 2 fs out, sn hrd rdn and one pace.* .... (33 to 1 op 20 to 1) 4
1272* YA MALAK 8-13 R Cochrane (7) *slwly into strd, hld up in tch, rdn alng whn not much room o'r one furlong out, sn outpcd.* ....(13 to 2 op 8 to 1) 5
1461[3] HIGH DOMAIN (Ire) 8-13 L Dettori (2) *led to hfwy, wkng whn squeezed for room o'r one furlong out.* ....(20 to 1 tchd 25 to 1) 6
1556[2] DOLLAR GAMBLE (Ire) 8-13 Pat Eddery (4) *cl up till wknd o'r 2 fs out.* ....(14 to 1 op 33 to 1 tchd 50 to 1 and 10 to 1) 7
1265[2] CRAGGANMORE 8-13 M Hills (6) *cl up til wknd o'r 2 fs out.*.............................. (25 to 1 op 16 to 1) 8
Dist: 3½l, sht-hd, 4l, 1½l, 12l, nk, 4l. 1m 5.95s. a 5.65s (8 Ran).
SR: 66/52/51/35/29/ (R E Sangster), P W Chapple-Hyam

1789 Ribblesdale Stakes Class A (Group 2) (3-y-o) £59,407 1½m. .... (4:55)

556[4] THAWAKIB (Ire) 8-8 W Carson (4) *rcd keenly, made all, drw clr frm 3 out, pushed out, easily.* .... (5 to 2 fav tchd 3 to 1) 1
1525[6] IVIZA (Ire) (v) 8-8 M Roberts (7) *hld up in rear, rdn alng o'r 3 out, styd on last 2 fs, not quicken wl ins last.* ....(9 to 2 op 3 to 1) 2
1222[4] TALENTED 8-8 Pat Eddery (5) *trkd wnr most of way, rdn alng 5 fs out, hrd drvn and one pace frm 2 out.* ....(9 to 2 op 4 to 1 tchd 5 to 1) 3
1222* BRIGHT GENERATION (Ire) 9-0 A Munro (3) *ldg grp, rdn alng o'r 3 fs out, one pace last 2.* .... (11 to 2 op 5 to 1 tchd 6 to 1) 4
1525[7] ABURY (Ire) 8-8 J Reid (1) *slwly into strd, hld up in rear, rdn o'r 3 fs out, no imprsn on ldrs frm 2 out.* ....(9 to 2 op 3 to 1 tchd 5 to 1) 5
1030[7] MAGICAL RETREAT (USA) 8-8 T Quinn (8) *improved into mid-div appr hfwy, rdn alng o'r 4 fs out, one pace over 2 out.*..............................(20 to 1 tchd 25 to 1) 6
856[5] REINE DE NEIGE 8-8 W R Swinburn (2) *wl plcd till hrd rdn and wknd well o'r 2 fs out, tld off.* .... (33 to 1 op 25 to 1 tchd 50 to 1) 7
734[7] NA-AYIM (Ire) 8-8 R Hills (6) *in tch, rdn alng o'r 5 fs out, wknd 3 out, tld off.*................ (33 to 1 tchd 50 to 1) 8
Dist: 1½l, 4l, ½l, 2½l, nk, 20l, 3½l. 2m 38.53s. a 10.33s (8 Ran).
SR: 57/54/46/51/40/39/-/-/ (Hamdan Al-Maktoum), J L Dunlop

1790 Chesham Stakes Class A (Listed Race) (2-y-o) £19,912 6f. ....(5:30)

1020* STATE PERFORMER (USA) 9-0 J Reid (6) *hld up beh ldrs, smooth hdwy to ld o'r one furlong out, pushed clr, imprsv.*..........(13 to 8 on op 11 to 8 on tchd Evens) 1
998[6] TIME STAR (USA) 8-12 A Munro (7) *veered rght leaving stalls, sn led til hdd 2 fs out, styd on wl fnl furlong.* .... (10 to 1 op 6 to 1) 2
1265* GOVERNOR GEORGE (USA) 9-0 L Dettori (1) *hld up gng wl, smooth hdwy to ld 2 fs out, hdd o'r one out, wknd ins last.*.................................. (3 to 1 tchd 5 to 2) 3
IZZA 8-7 M J Kinane (3) *in tch, pushed alng and outpcd hfwy, shaken up o'r 2 fs out, styd on.* ....(25 to 1 tchd 33 to 1) 4
1489[9] L'ETAT C'EST MOI (USA) 8-7 Pat Eddery (4) *pld hrd, in cl tch till wknd o'r 2 fs out, tld off.* .... (16 to 1 op 20 to 1 tchd 25 to 1) 5
ALJATHAAB (USA) 8-12 M Roberts (5) *wth ldr till rdn and wknd 2 fs out, tld off.* (20 to 1 op 16 to 1 tchd 25 to 1) 6

1446[3] CHICKAWICKA (Ire) 8-12 S Whitworth (2) *wth ldr till wknd 2 fs out, tld off.*......(11 to 1 op 14 to 1 tchd 10 to 1) 7
Dist: 3½l, 2½l, 3½l, 20l, 1l, 2l. 1m 20.34s. a 6.94s (7 Ran).
SR: 57/41/33/12/ (R E Sangster), P W Chapple-Hyam

EVRY (FR) (good to soft)
Thursday June 17th
Going Correction: MINUS 0.10 sec. per fur. (race 1), NIL (2)

1791 Prix Hampton (Listed) (3-y-o and up) £14,337 6f. .... (3:00)

THREE FOR FANTASY (Ire) 3-8-6 N Jeanpierre, ... 1
1220[3] SOMERSHAM (USA) 3-8-9 S Guillot, ... 2
954[6] BERINSFIELD 3-8-9 D Boeuf, ... 3
1289[5] CHARME SLAVE (Fr) 5-9-5 W Mongil, ... 4
Dist: 2l, ½l, nk, nk, nk, 1l, ½l, 2l, 4l, 8l. 1m 11.54s. a 1.24s (10 Ran).
SR: 55/50/48/57/ (Anne de Contades), N Clement

NAAS (IRE) (soft)
Thursday June 17th
Going Correction: PLUS 0.70 sec. per fur. (races 1,4), PLUS 0.95 (2,3,5,6)

1792 Basin Street EBF Maiden (2-y-o) £3,797 6f. .... (5:45)

1650[8] MY RAGAMUFFIN (Ire) 8-11 J P Murtagh (1) ...... (25 to 1) 1
1509[2] DON'T KNOW (Ire) 9-0 K J Manning (10) ......(13 to 8 fav) 2
1550[7] NURMI (Ire) 9-0 J F Egan (5) .... (6 to 1) 3
1608[5] DASHING DANCER (Ire) 9-0 B Coogan (4) .... (7 to 1) 4
1550[4] SPRING FORCE (Ire) 9-0 P Shanahan (9) .... (3 to 1) 5
1650 NOBLE CHOICE (Ire) 8-11 N G McCullagh (7) ..... (16 to 1) 6
MAJESTIC MAN (Ire) 8-8 (6*) J J Behan (8) .... (12 to 1) 7
GREENRIDGE COURT (Ire) 8-3 (8*) B A Hunter (2) (25 to 1) 8
COUNTESS OUNAVARRA (Ire) 8-11 J D Eddery (6) (5 to 1) 9
Dist: ½l, 1½l, 3l, ¾l. 1m 18.00s. a 8.50s (9 Ran).
SR: 11/12/6/-/-/-/ (F Dunne), F Dunne

1793 Derrinstown Apprentice Series (3-y-o and up) £3,797 7f. ....(6:10)

1569[9] FAIRYDEL (Ire) 3-8-1 (6*) P J Smullen (5) ....(8 to 1) 1
258[8] RETICENT BRIDE (Ire) 3-8-2 (2*) W J Smith (1) . . (6 to 4 on) 2
1619[3] TORC MOUNTAIN (Ire) (bl) 3-8-3 (4*) R V Skelly (7) . .(9 to 2) 3
1649[3] ARZAAQ (USA) (bl) 3-8-3 (4*) B J Walsh (4) .... (9 to 2) 4
1333 BUTTERNUT (Ire) 3-8-0 (4*) J J Behan (3) ....(7 to 1) 5
BAYYINAT (USA) 3-7-13 (8*) D O'Callaghan (6) .... (12 to 1) 6
669 ANOTHER FLYER (Ire) 3-8-7 R M Burke (2) .... (33 to 1) 7
Dist: Nk, nk, 6l, ½l. 1m 32.70s. a 10.10s (7 Ran).
SR: 41/37/39/21/16/-/-/ (T F Lacy), T F Lacy

1794 Harristown Handicap (0-80 3-y-o and up) £2,762 1¼m. .... (7:05)

1553[9] BOBADIL (Ire) [-] 3-7-6 (2*) D G O'Shea (3) ....(12 to 1) 1
1202[2] MAYFIELD PRINCE (Ire) [-] 4-9-6 (6*) B Bowens (10) .... (5 to 2 fav) 2
BLASKET SUPREME (Ire) [-] 5-8-9 W J Supple (11) (12 to 1) 3
BRACKLOON BOY (Ire) [-] 4-8-13 P V Gilson (6) . . .(16 to 1) 4
1644[3] RAIN RITE (Ire) [-] 4-9-2 (8*) B Fenton (8) .... (8 to 1) 5
1514[4] SHARASTAMINA (USA) [-] 4-9-2 N G McCullagh (7) (7 to 2) 6
1644[4] FLORAL STREET [-] (bl) 4-9-0 (6*) C Everard (5) .... (9 to 1) 7
1025[7] OPEN MARKET (USA) [-] 4-9-11 P Shanahan (9) . . (12 to 1) 8
1574 WARREN STREET (Ire) [-] 3-7-13 J F Egan (4) ...... (7 to 1) 9
1440 BENGALI (Ire) [-] 3-7-0[3] (10*) J P Cornally (1) ......(20 to 1) 10
1440[9] MAGIC ARTS (Ire) [-] 5-9-2 (6*) J R Barry (12) ...... (8 to 1) 11
Dist: 1½l, 1½l, 1l, sht-hd. 2m 20.60s. a 16.60s (11 Ran).
SR: 9/38/18/20/30/-/ (T F Lacy), T F Lacy

1795 Athy Handicap (0-75 3-y-o and up) £2,762 5f. .... (7:30)

1515[4] MAGIC DON (Ire) [-] (bl) 4-9-0 (8*) R T Fitzpatrick (9) (8 to 1) 1
1620[3] MUGNANO [-] 7-8-8 (6*) B J Walsh (12) .... (7 to 1) 2
1620[2] LADY PRESIDENT (Ire) [-] 4-8-5 (6*) J J Behan (10) (5 to 1) 3
1620* SHRAGRADDY LASS (Ire) [-] 3-8-8 (6ex) N G McCullagh (5) .... (11 to 4 fav) 4
1649[7] AFTERGLOW (Ire) [-] (bl) 4-8-8 L O'Shea (4) ....(10 to 1) 5
1570[4] MASTER WORK [-] (bl) 5-7-13 A J Nolan (8) ...... (12 to 1) 6
868 RED VERONA [-] 4-7-7[4] (4*) W J Smith (3) .... (25 to 1) 7
1444[5] FASTAFLOW (Ire) [-] 3-8-9 W J Supple (7) ....(8 to 1) 8
1569[7] CARRIG STAR (Ire) [-] 4-9-0 (4*) P Carberry (2) ..... (8 to 1) 9
1515 TORCH SINGER [-] 3-8-6 P V Gilson (6) ....(33 to 1) 10
1649[9] FIVE LITTLE GIRLS (Ire) [-] 3-8-9 K J Manning (11) (12 to 1) 11
1515[2] MEMSAHB [-] (bl) 4-9-4 (10*) W J Walsh (1) .... (7 to 2) 12
Dist: Hd, ¾l, ¾l, ¾l. 1m 4.40s. a 6.40s (12 Ran).
SR: 50/41/35/29/26/-/ (Mrs Anne Coughlan), J T Gorman

1796 Kilcullen EBF Maiden (3-y-o) £3,452 1m. ....(8:00)

FAIRY LORE (Ire) 8-11 P V Gilson (5) ....(11 to 2) 1

1568^{3} BELLISSI (Ire) 8-11 K J Manning (7)...............(5 to 1) 2
1568^{2} BRAVE RAIDER (Ire) (bl) 9-0 P Shanahan (4).......(5 to 1) 3
1443^{3} SUEKAR (Ire) 8-11 R Hughes (1).............(11 to 8 fav) 4
1510^{6} CRISSY (Ire) 8-11 W J Supple (6)................(20 to 1) 5
705^{4} JU JU'S GIRL (Ire) 8-11 C Roche (3)..............(5 to 1) 6
1610^{6} LADY NOBLE (Ire) 8-11 J F Egan (2)..............(10 to 1) 7
FESTIVAL GIRL (Ire) 8-11 N G McCullagh (8)......(20 to 1) 8
Dist: ¾l, nk, 1½l, 1l. 1m 46.80s. a 11.00s (8 Ran).
SR: 46/44/46/38/35/ (M V O'Brien), Charles O'Brien

1797 W McDermott Kare Charity Private Stakes (4-y-o and up) £240 1m 3f (8:45)

1573^{7} KARABAKH (Ire) 4-11-7 John O'Connor (3)........(7 to 1) 1
575^{8} LEGAL ADVISER 6-11-13 Enda M Kelly (6).....(6 to 4 on) 2
WHOS FOOLING WHO 7-11-10 P O'Brien (11).....(8 to 1) 3
911^{9} SHY GAL (Ire) 5-11-12^{5} Padraig O'Cathan (8).....(20 to 1) 4
MISSED OPPORTUNITY (Ire) 5-11-10 James O'Haire (10) ....(12 to 1) 5
753^{8} BRAVE STAR 7-11-7 David Moloney (9)..........(12 to 1) 6
SAINTFIELD 10-11-10 M Burns Jnr (5)............(7 to 1) 7
ADAPT 9-12-8 John Tarrant (4)...................(5 to 1) 8
I SUPPOSE (bl) 8-12-7^{1}4 Sean Higgins (2)..........(20 to 1) 9
PARSONS EYRE (Ire) 5-11-7 Richard Ranaghan (1) (14 to 1) 10
KOI CORP 9-11-7 B Bjorner (7)..................(8 to 1) 11
Dist: 4l, 3½l, 11l. (Time not taken) (11 Ran).
(J P M O'Connor), W P Mullins

RIPON (good)
Thursday June 17th

Going Correction: MINUS 0.25 sec. per fur. (races 1,4), MINUS 0.30 (2,3,5,6)

1798 Leyburn Median Auction Maiden Stakes Class E (2-y-o) £3,236 5f (2:15)

1227^{7} MISTER PISTE (Ire) 9-0 J Fanning (2) *made all, styd on wl fnl furlong*.............(6 to 1 op 7 to 1 tchd 8 to 1) 1
698^{5} CLOSE TO REALITY 8-7 (7*) D Thomas (7) *al prmnt, effrt appr fnl furlong, ran on ins last.* ....(7 to 2 fav op 9 to 2 tchd 5 to 1) 2
1590^{5} GENERAL GUBBINS 9-0 B Raymond (9) *chsd ldrs, effrt entering fnl furlong, styd on wl*...(14 to 1 op 12 to 1) 3
1378^{5} CASPIAN GOLD 9-0 T Williams (8) *cl up, no extr fnl furlong*..............................(10 to 1 op 8 to 1) 4
ELUNED MAY 8-9 A Culhane (3) *al prmnt, no extr fnl furlong*...............(9 to 1 op 7 to 1 tchd 10 to 1) 5
1556^{5} HELLABY 9-0 W Ryan (10) *prmnt, styd on ins last.* ....(8 to 1 op 7 to 1) 6
MITSIS 9-0 A Mackay (14) *in tch, effrt o'r one furlong out, no imprsn ins last*..................(14 to 1 op 10 to 1) 7
DURANO 9-0 M Birch (13) *nvr on terms.* (8 to 1 op 6 to 1) 8
CELESTIAL DANCE 8-9 G Carter (15) *al rear.* ....(13 to 2 op 9 to 2 tchd 7 to 1) 9
FAIREY FIREFLY 8-9 N Connorton (4) *dwlt, al rear.* ....(16 to 1 op 12 to 1) 10
1561 GALLIC GENT 9-0 G Duffield (12) *chsd ldrs till wknd o'r one furlong out*......(11 to 1 op 10 to 1 tchd 12 to 1) 11
1158 POT LEEK LADY 8-9 R Lappin (6) *cl up till wknd o'r one furlong out*......................(33 to 1 op 25 to 1) 12
CREEK VALLEY 9-0 Raymond Berry (11) *al rear.* ....(16 to 1 op 12 to 1) 13
1499^{8} RENNYHOLME 9-0 S Morris (1) *nvr on terms.* ....(25 to 1 op 16 to 1) 14
LINSTONE LADY 8-9 J Fortune (5) *dwlt, al rear.* ....(10 to 1 op 8 to 1) 15
Dist: 2½l, hd, ½l, ½l, 2½l, 1½l, 1l, ½l, sht-hd, 1½l. 1m 0.00s. a 2.00s (15 Ran).
SR: 35/25/24/22/15/10/4/-/-/ (Major I C Straker), Miss L A Perratt

1799 Northallerton Apprentice Claiming Handicap Class F (0-70 3-y-o and up) £3,600 1m.................... (2:50)

1686^{3} SOOTY TERN [45] 6-8-1 (3*) Mark Denaro (15) *made virtually all, kpt on wl und pres fnl furlong.* ....(6 to 1 op 5 to 1) 1
1578* PRIDE OF PENDLE [44] 4-8-3 (4ex) J Tate (10) *al prmnt, chlgd 2 fs out, ev ch ins last, no extr cl hme.* ....(7 to 2 fav op 3 to 1 tchd 4 to 1) 2
1436 DREAM CARRIER (Ire) [56] 5-9-1 V Halliday (17) *al prmnt, effrt 2 fs out, kpt on one pace*....(14 to 1 tchd 16 to 1) 3
1496^{5} PUBLIC WAY (Ire) [55] 3-7-13 (5*) C Teague (9) *chsd ldrs, prog to chal 2 fs out, no extr ins last.* ....(20 to 1 op 12 to 1) 4
1562^{3} FLETCHER'S BOUNTY (Ire) [48] 4-8-2 (5*) S Copp (18) *in tch, prog to chal o'r one furlong out, wknd ins last.* ....(11 to 1 op 10 to 1) 5
1498^{7} VERDANT BOY [43] 10-8-2^{6} (5*) D Thomas (16) *al prmnt, effrt 2 fs out, no imprsn ins last*....(33 to 1 op 25 to 1) 6
906 ALWAYS RISKY [54] 3-8-1^{1} (3*) R Havlin (14) *cl up, ev ch 2 fs out, wknd o'r one out*..........................(25 to 1) 7
1436 CHANTRY BELLINI [48] 4-8-0 (7*) G Mills (3) *rear div, some prog 3 fs out, sn rdn and no imprsn.* (12 to 1 op 8 to 1) 8
1606^{2} BREEZE AWAY [53] 4-8-9 (3*) G Parkin (12) *prmnt till rdn and wknd 2 fs out*.................(11 to 2 op 9 to 2) 9
1527 ABSOLUTELY RIGHT [45] 5-8-4 D Wright (11) *slwly away, nvr nrr*..............(6 to 1 op 20 to 1 tchd 25 to 1) 10
1304^{9} NIMBLE DEER [65] 4-9-3 (7*) Sarah Senior (5) *pressed ldr, dsptd ld into strt till wknd 2 fs out.* ....(20 to 1 op 16 to 1 tchd 25 to 1) 11
1458^{2} DOTS DEE [34] 4-7-3^{1} (5*) A Whelan (2) *nvr on terms.* ....(14 to 1) 12
1148 DANDY DESIRE [40] 4-7-13 S Sanders (8) *prmnt till wknd 2 fs out*..(25 to 1) 13
1498 MANULEADER [47] (bl) 4-8-3 (3*) Claire Balding (13) *nvr on terms*..(25 to 1) 14
1151^{5} CANNY LAD [51] 3-7-7 (7*) F Savage (1) *nvr plcd to chal.* ....(12 to 1 op 10 to 1) 15
1578 DEPUTY TIM [47] 10-8-6^{1}2 (7*) John Alan Williams (4) *chsd ldrs till wknd o'r 3 fs out*.......... (25 to 1 op 20 to 1) 16
Dist: ½l, 4l, sht-hd, 2l, 1½l, 3l, 1½l, hd, 7l, ½l. 1m 40.30s. a 2.00s (16 Ran).
SR: 24/21/21/9/6/-/ (J M Bradley), J M Bradley

1800 Price Waterhouse Handicap Class D (0-80 3-y-o and up) £3,752 1¼m (3:25)

1783* SOVEREIGN PAGE (USA) [67] 4-8-12 (7*,6ex) J Tate (5) *rear, prog entering strt, led o'r 2 fs out, kpt on und pres fnl furlong.* (6 to 4 on op 11 to 8 on tchd 5 to 4 on and 6 to 5 on) 1
1414^{9} AKKAZAO (Ire) [69] 5-9-7 J Fortune (4) *pressed ldr, led o'r 3 fs out, hdd over 2 out, styd on wl ins last.* ....(14 to 1 op 12 to 1 tchd 16 to 1) 2
1592^{2} TOUCH ABOVE [47] 7-7-13 G Carter (9) *beh till prog entering strt, effrt 2 fs out, kpt on one pace ins last.* ....(9 to 1 op 8 to 1) 3
383^{5} WHO'S TEF (Ire) [51] 5-8-0 (3*) S Maloney (6) *in tch, prog to chal 2 fs out, ev ch o'r one out, no extr ins last.* ....(12 to 1 op 10 to 1) 4
1460^{2} SUPERTOP [64] 5-9-2 M Birch (1) *chsd ldrs, effrt 2 fs out, kpt on one pace fnl furlong*.........(11 to 2 op 5 to 1) 5
1194^{5} SCOTTISH PARK [59] 4-8-11 G Duffield (10) *rear, prog to track ldrs into strt, effrt 3 fs out, wknd o'r one out.* ....(16 to 1 op 14 to 1) 6
1398^{6} LEIF THE LUCKY (USA) [76] 4-10-0 N Connorton (3) *prog to press ldr entering strt, ev ch 3 fs out, wknd 2 out.* ....(7 to 1 op 8 to 1 tchd 9 to 1) 7
411^{4} ASHDREN [74] 6-9-12 W Ryan (8) *trkd ldrs, rdn 3 fs out, wknd 2 out*.......... (14 to 1 op 12 to 1 tchd 16 to 1) 8
1634^{7} SUNTAN (Fr) [65] 4-9-3 A Culhane (2) *led till o'r 3 fs out, wknd 2 out*...................... (33 to 1 op 20 to 1) 9
1177 RULLY [60] 4-8-12 W Newnes (7) *al beh.* ....(20 to 1 op 14 to 1) 10
Dist: Nk, 1½l, nk, 2l, ¾l, 8l, 8l, ¾l, 8l. 2m 6.70s. a 2.70s (10 Ran).
SR: 48/49/24/27/36/29/30/12/1/ (Mrs J M Beeby), B Hanbury

1801 Norman Wells Memorial Challenge Trophy Handicap Class C (0-90 3-y-o) £6,056 6f.................... (4:00)

1718^{7} FOR THE PRESENT [74] 8-12 B Raymond (3) *chsd ldrs, effrt 2 fs out, rdn to ld o'r one out, kpt on wl.* ....(5 to 1 op 4 to 1) 1
1213 THE SHARP BIDDER (Ire) [74] 8-12 W Ryan (2) *chsd ldrs, effrt whn hmpd o'r one out, swtchd and rnwd effort ins last, no extr cl hme*...............(12 to 1 op 10 to 1) 2
734^{8} BALLON [73] 8-11 W Newnes (7) *rdn hfwy, styd on ins last, nrst finish*..................(16 to 1 op 12 to 1) 3
1478^{2} FIRST OPTION [71] 8-9 M Birch (9) *trkd ldrs, effrt o'r one furlong out, sn rdn and wknd.* (11 to 4 fav op 9 to 2) 4
1633* RAIN SPLASH [75] 8-6 (7*,7ex) Claire Balding (8) *outpcd to hfwy, styd on fnl 2 fs*................(9 to 1 op 7 to 1) 5
1396* FIRST PLAY [69] 8-7 J Fortune (11) *cl up, slight ld hfwy, edgd lft o'r one furlong out, sn hdd and wknd.* ....(7 to 1 op 6 to 1) 6
1338^{9} BARIK (Ire) [83] 9-7 A McGlone (4) *pushed alng hfwy, effrt 2 fs out, not get on terms*........... (5 to 1 op 9 to 2) 7
1397^{9} SABO SONG [71] 8-9 Dale Gibson (6) *chsd ldrs, effrt 2 fs out, sn rdn and btn*............................(16 to 1) 8
1274 ROYAL DIVA [69] 8-7 N Connorton (10) *chsd ldrs for 4 fs, sn btn*........................... (20 to 1 op 16 to 1) 9
341^{6} EGG [67] 7-12 (7*) V Halliday (5) *al beh.* ....(20 to 1 op 16 to 1) 10
1326^{5} PALACEGATE TOUCH [82] (bl) 9-6 G Carter (1) *slight ld to hfwy, ev ch whn badly hmpd and snatched up one and a half fs out*..................................(8 to 1) 11
Dist: ½l, 6l, hd, 1l, 1½l, 1½l, hd, 1½l, 2½l, 15l. 1m 12.00s. a 1.40s (11 Ran).
SR: 40/38/13/10/10/-/6/-/-/ (Mrs J Hazell), T D Barron

1802 Hob Green Maiden Stakes Class D (3-y-o and up) £3,523 1½m 60yds.. (4:35)

1429^{5} MOONSHINE LAKE 3-7-13 A McGlone (5) *trkd ldr, quickened to ld hfwy, shaken up 2 fs out, pushed out ins last*...........(11 to 10 fav op 6 to 5 on tchd 5 to 4) 1
TREE OF LIFE 3-7-13 G Carter (8) *settled rear, prog entering strt, trkd ldrs 3 fs out, rdn 2 out, not quicken ins last*.........(6 to 1 op 7 to 1 tchd 8 to 1 and 5 to 1) 2
1297^{3} DUNNELLON 3-7-13 G Duffield (1) *pld hrd, not settled early, prog entering strt, trkd ldrs 3 fs out, no imprsn frm o'r one out*.......(10 to 1 op 6 to 1 tchd 11 to 1) 3

1429[3] ARKAAN (USA) 3-8-4 B Raymond (9) *al prmnt, trkd ldr into strt, rdn o'r 2 fs out, kpt on one pace.* ....(2 to 1 op 7 to 4 tchd 6 to 4) 4
646[9] HADDAAJ (Ire) 3-7-11 (7*) J Tate (10) *in tch, styd on one pace fnl 2 fs*..........(33 to 1 op 20 to 1) 5
BLUE LAWS (Ire) 3-8-4 L Charnock (2) *al prmnt, effrt 3 fs out, sn rdn and one paced*..........(33 to 1) 6
482[5] PERO 3-8-4 G Hind (4) *in tch, rdn 4 fs out, wknd 3 out.* ....(14 to 1 op 8 to 1) 7
EDITHMEAD (Ire) 3-7-13 F Norton (11) *rear, pushed alng entering strt, sn btn*..........(33 to 1 op 20 to 1) 8
1587 MINTEEN 3-7-6 (7*) D Wright (6) *led to hfwy, wknd entering strt*..........(33 to 1 op 25 to 1) 9
1275 HIGH CHAIR 3-7-13 Dale Gibson (3) *al rear*..... (50 to 1) 10
1617 MOHAYA (USA) 3-8-4 W Ryan (7) *al rear.* ....(33 to 1 op 25 to 1) 11
Dist: 1½l, 2½l, ½l, 1½l, 1½l, 8l, 2½l, nk, 7l, 10l. 2m 41.90s. a 6.90s (11 Ran).
(Sheikh Mohammed), H R A Cecil

1803 Middleham Maiden Stakes Class D (3-y-o) £3,523 1m..........(5:10)

516 ASTERN (USA) 8-9 G Hind (5) *wth ldr, slight ld 3 out, rdn 2 out, kpt on und pres ins last*..........(7 to 2 op 3 to 1) 1
443[5] RAFIF (USA) 8-9 A McGlone (4) *slight ld till hdd 3 out, rdn 2 out, styd on ins last.* ....(5 to 4 on op Evens tchd 11 to 8 on) 2
SHILKA 8-9 G Duffield (6) *trkd ldrs, cld up 3 out, sn rdn and one paced*..........(100 to 30 op 6 to 4 tchd 7 to 2) 3
4778a ALMONTY (Ire) 9-0 G Carter (1) *trkd ldrs, cld up 3 out, sn rdn and one paced*..........(33 to 1 op 25 to 1) 4
CHARLOTTES BILLO 9-0 M Birch (2) *dwlt, beh till cld up and ev ch 3 out, wknd o'r 2 out*..........(33 to 1 op 16 to 1) 5
Dist: ½l, 6l, 2l, 20l. 1m 41.30s. a 3.00s (5 Ran).
SR: 14/12/ (Sheikh Mohammed), J H M Gosden

ASCOT (soft)
Friday June 18th
Going Correction: PLUS 0.35 sec. per fur. (races 1,4), PLUS 0.55 (2,3,5,6)

1804 Windsor Castle Stakes Conditions Class B (2-y-o) £18,745 5f..........(2:30)

1583* GREAT DEEDS 8-6 T Quinn (2) *trkd ldrs, shaken up to ld 2 fs out, pushed out, cmftbly*..........(10 to 1 op 7 to 1) 1
1310[2] BID FOR BLUE 8-13 L Piggott (4) *handily plcd, rdn alng 2 fs out, styd on one pace ins last.* (12 to 1 tchd 16 to 1) 2
1590[3] IMPERIAL BAILIWICK (Ire) 8-8 N Adams (8) *slwly into strd, ran on frm rear ins last 2 fs, not rch wnr.* ....(50 to 1 op 33 to 1 tchd 66 to 1) 3
1381[4] MONTAYA 8-13 W R Swinburn (10) *led o'r 3 fs out to 2 out, sn rdn and one pace.* (20 to 1 op 12 to 1 tchd 25 to 1) 4
1632* ROYAL INSIGNIA 8-13 A Munro (5) *chsd ldrs, no extr appr fnl furlong*..........(10 to 1 op 8 to 1 tchd 11 to 1) 5
291* BANDON CASTLE (Ire) 8-13 D Harrison (6) *in tch, outpcd 2 fs out, eased whn btn ins last.* ....(16 to 1 op 12 to 1 tchd 20 to 1) 6
1475* EVENING FALLS 8-8 K Darley (9) *led for o'r one furlong, wknd quickly over one out*..........(33 to 1 op 20 to 1) 7
1032[3] JADE PET 8-6 J Reid (7) *in tch, rdn alng 2 fs out, no hdwy fnl furlong*..........(12 to 1 op 10 to 1) 8
1378[2] ARZ (USA) 8-11 R Hills (11) *speed 3 fs.* ....(8 to 1 op 7 to 1 tchd 10 to 1) 9
1523* ROXANIAN (Ire) 8-13 M J Kinane (1) *trkd ldrs, wknd hfwy.* ....(10 to 1 op 8 to 1) 10
1481[2] SHEPHERD MARKET (Ire) 8-11 M Hills (12) *in tch to hfwy, sn drpd out*..........(25 to 1 op 20 to 1 tchd 33 to 1) 11
PAPAGAYOS (Ire) 8-11 W Carson (3) *outpcd.* ....(20 to 1 tchd 16 to 1) 12
1045* THE PUZZLER (Ire) 9-3 W J O'Connor (13) *hld up, jnd ldrs hfwy, hng lft and ev ch 2 fs out, eased whn btn fnl furlong, fnshd lme.* ....(13 to 8 fav op 7 to 4 tchd 11 to 8) 13
Dist: 3l, hd, 3l, 3l, 3½l, ¾l, 4l, 1½l, ½l, 2l. 1m 4.18s. a 3.88s (13 Ran).
SR: 49/44/38/31/19/5/ (Dubai Racing Syndicate), M R Channon

1805 Hardwicke Stakes Class A (Group 2) (4-y-o and up) £56,700 1½m..........(3:05)

1118[3] JEUNE 4-8-9 R Cochrane (4) *pld hrd, rstrained in rear, hdwy o'r 2 fs out, led one and a half out, rdn out.* ....(7 to 2 tchd 9 to 2) 1
1427* RED BISHOP (USA) 5-8-9 M Roberts (1) *hld up, rdn and hdwy o'r 2 fs out, not quicken over one out, styd on wl cl hme*..........(11 to 4 fav op 7 to 4) 2
1427[2] HIGHLAND DRESS 4-8-9 C Asmussen (5) *trkd ldrs, wnt second 4 fs out, led o'r 2 out to one and a half out, rallied ins last*..........(7 to 2 tchd 100 to 30 and 4 to 1) 3
1427[4] SAPIENCE 7-8-12 Pat Eddery (2) *led till o'r 2 fs out, wknd wl over one out*..........(7 to 2 tchd 4 to 1) 4
1472[8] GARDEN OF HEAVEN (USA) 4-8-12 W Carson (3) *pld hrd, chsd ldr one m, wknd o'r 2 fs out, sn btn.* ....(7 to 1 op 8 to 1 tchd 10 to 1) 5
Dist: Nk, hd, 8l, 10l. 2m 39.43s. a 11.23s (5 Ran).
SR: 49/48/47/34/14/ (Exors Of The Late Sir Robin McAlpine), G Wragg

1806 Wokingham Handicap Class B (0-110 3-y-o and up) £39,640 6f..........(3:45)

1066[3] NAGIDA [84] 4-8-7 (3*) J Weaver (4) *in tch, ran on to ld wl o'r one furlong out, kpt on nr line.* ....(11 to 1 op 14 to 1 tchd 10 to 1) 1
1420[3] CUMBRIAN WALTZER [87] 8-8-13 M Birch (12) *chsd stands side grp, sstnd run frm o'r one furlong out, jst fld.* ....(13 to 1 op 14 to 1 tchd 12 to 1) 2
1348[6] ARABELLAJILL [90] 4-9-2 L Dettori (18) *trkd ldrs stands side, kpt on gmely und pres ins fnl furlong.* ....(20 to 1 tchd 25 to 1) 3
1485[4] GORINSKY (Ire) [80] 5-8-6 J Carroll (14) *made most stands side, hdd o'r one furlong out, rallied ins last.* ....(33 to 1 tchd 50 to 1) 4
1680[2] SIR HARRY HARDMAN [90] 5-9-2 B Raymond (6) *mid-div, hdwy and not much room 2 fs out, ran on ins last.* ....(11 to 1 op 12 to 1 tchd 14 to 1) 5
1348 HARD TO FIGURE [95] 7-9-7 W Carson (29) *rcd far side, rear till ran on o'r one furlong out, fnshd wl.* ....(25 to 1 op 20 to 1 tchd 33 to 1) 6
737 ECHO-LOGICAL [86] (bl) 4-8-12 K Darley (2) *cl up stands side, ev ch o'r one furlong out, ran on one pace.* ....(14 to 1 op 12 to 1) 7
1205[2] BRANSTON ABBY (Ire) [100] 4-9-12 M Roberts (30) *led far side grp 2 fs out, hdd and one pace ins last.* ....(9 to 1 op 8 to 1 tchd 10 to 1) 8
1079[6] DENSBEN [80] 9-8-6 K Fallon (19) *styd on last 2 fs, not rch ldrs*..........(40 to 1 op 33 to 1 tchd 50 to 1) 9
1215[7] AMRON [89] 6-9-1 N Carlisle (7) *chsd stands side grp, no extr appr fnl furlong*..........(20 to 1 op 16 to 1) 10+
1636[9] BEWARE OF AGENTS [91] 4-9-3 Dean McKeown (24) *mid-div, kpt on one pace fnl 2 fs.* ....(40 to 1 op 33 to 1 tchd 50 to 1) 10+
1382[5] SAGEBRUSH ROLLER [86] 5-8-12 G Duffield (26) *rcd far side, hrd rdn o'r one furlong out, one pace ins last.* ....(25 to 1 op 20 to 1 tchd 33 to 1) 12
1348* MASSIBA (Ire) [96] 4-9-1 (7*,7ex) D McCabe (20) *trkd frnt rnk, rdn and btn o'r one furlong out.* ....(25 to 1 op 20 to 1) 13
1584[3] CHILI HEIGHTS [82] 3-8-0 D Biggs (10) *outpcd most of way*..........(16 to 1 tchd 20 to 1) 14
CANTORIS [87] 7-8-13 R Cochrane (28) *rcd far side, nvr nr to chal*..........(25 to 1 tchd 33 to 1) 15
1584 MOROCCO (Ire) [84] 4-8-5 (5*,10ex) Stephen Davies (21) *in tch stands side, no hdwy 2 fs out.* (33 to 1 op 20 to 1) 16
1584 BERTIE WOOSTER [85] 10-8-11 L Piggott (13) *nvr nr to chal*..........(33 to 1 tchd 50 to 1) 17
1679[3] MACFARLANE [75] 5-8-1 F Norton (8) *handily plcd stands side, wknd last 2 fs*..........(25 to 1 op 20 to 1) 18
1537* BLUE TOPAZE [77] 5-8-3[2] (7ex) J Williams (22) *strted slwly, beh most of way*..........(25 to 1) 19
1680[7] SIZZLING SAGA (Ire) [100] 5-9-12 C Asmussen (15) *nvr on terms*..........(40 to 1 op 33 to 1 tchd 50 to 1) 20
1301[8] ALLTHRUTHENIGHT (Ire) [82] 4-8-8 W Newnes (17) *outpcd most of way*..........(40 to 1 op 33 to 1 tchd 50 to 1) 21
1449[2] TERRHARS (Ire) [90] 5-9-2 R Perham (3) *hld up in tch stands side, effrt and not much room 2 fs out, sn btn.* ....(33 to 1 op 25 to 1 tchd 50 to 1) 22
1668* GONE SAVAGE [97] 5-9-9 (7ex) W R Swinburn (27) *led far side grp 4 fs, sn wknd.* ....(40 to 1 op 25 to 1 tchd 50 to 1) 23
1215[4] MASTER PLANNER [92] 4-9-4 T Quinn (5) *wl plcd stands side for o'r 4 fs*..........(25 to 1 op 20 to 1) 24
1301* LORD HIGH ADMIRAL (Can) [77] 5-8-3 (7ex) Paul Eddery (11) *cl up stands side, wknd appr fnl furlong.* ....(16 to 1 op 14 to 1 tchd 20 to 1) 25
WATHIK (USA) [104] 3-9-8 R Hills (16) *nvr dngrs.* ....(40 to 1 op 33 to 1) 26
1668[5] PLAIN FACT [85] 8-8-11 M Hills (23) *outpcd.* ....(40 to 1 op 33 to 1 tchd 50 to 1) 27
1066* EVERGLADES (Ire) [86] 5-8-12 Pat Eddery (25) *rcd far side, in tch till no prog 2 fs out, eased whn btn.* ....(8 to 1 fav op 12 to 1 tchd 14 to 1) 28
1449 ASHTINA [91] 8-9-3 A Munro (9) *dsptd ld stands side 4 fs.* ....(33 to 1 op 25 to 1) 29
1485[6] AUGHFAD [83] (v) 7-8-9 J Reid (1) *early pace stands side, wknd hfwy*..........(25 to 1 tchd 28 to 1) 30
Dist: Nk, ¾l, sht-hd, 1½l, ½l, ½l, ½l, sht-hd, nk, dd-ht. 1m 18.11s. a 4.71s (30 Ran).
SR: 68/70/70/59/63/66/55/67/46/ (Miss U D Toller), J A R Toller

1807 King's Stand Stakes Class A (Group 2) (3-y-o and up) £60,361 5f..........(4:20)

ELBIO (v) 6-9-3 W R Swinburn (1) *slwly into strd, hrd rdn and hdwy to ld jst ins fnl furlong, pushed out.* ....(12 to 1 tchd 14 to 1) 1
1406[2] WOLFHOUND (USA) 4-9-3 M Roberts (3) *hld up in tch, swtchd rght appr fnl furlong, ran on und pres.* ....(11 to 10 on op 5 to 4) 2
1406* PARIS HOUSE 4-9-3 J Carroll (5) *prmnt, led wl o'r one furlong out till jst ins last, ran on one pace.* ....(4 to 1 op 3 to 1 tchd 9 to 2) 3

1019[7] FREDDIE LLOYD (USA) 4-9-3 J Reid (2) *led till o'r 2 fs out, outpcd, kpt on ins last.* ....(50 to 1 op 33 to 1 tchd 66 to 1) 4

1449* EL YASAF (Ire) 5-9-3 C Asmussen (6) *outpcd, effrt 2 fs out, rdn and one pace appr last*.................. (25 to 1) 5

1449[7] BUNTY BOO 4-9-0 T Quinn (8) *outpcd early, hdwy on outsd to ld o'r 2 fs out, hdd one and a half out, sn btn.* ....(66 to 1 op 100 to 1) 6

1214* LYRIC FANTASY (Ire) 3-8-7 Pat Eddery (4) *trkd ldr, ev ch 2 fs out, sn wknd, eased*..... (7 to 2 op 3 to 1 tchd 4 to 1) 7

1465* SURPRISE OFFER (bl) 3-8-10 B Raymond (7) *chsd ldrs to hfwy*............... (16 to 1 op 14 to 1 tchd 20 to 1) 8

Dist: 2l, sht-hd, 3½l, nk, 1½l, 6l, 2l. 1m 3.08s. a 2.78s (8 Ran).

SR: 82/74/73/59/58/49/18/13/ (Brian Brackpool), P J Makin

1808 Britannia Handicap Class B (0-105 3-y-o) £22,337 1m.............. (4:55)

1212* SHOW FAITH (Ire) [84] 8-5[3] Pat Eddery (20) *hld up in rear, quickened and ran on o'r 2 fs out, led wl ins last, rdn out*................(6 to 1 fav op 8 to 1 tchd 9 to 1) 1

1374[2] JUST YOU DARE (Ire) [80] 8-1 G Duffield (3) *handily plcd, rdn to ld o'r 2 fs out, hdd und pres ins last, kpt on.* ....(12 to 1 op 16 to 1 tchd 20 to 1) 2

1204* BRIGANTE DI CIELO [89] 8-10 T Quinn (19) *in tch, ev ch o'r 2 fs out, not quicken wl ins last.* ....(20 to 1 op 16 to 1 tchd 25 to 1) 3

1344[2] MUJAAZAFAH (USA) [83] 8-4 M Roberts (12) *improved hfwy, rdn and one pace appr fnl furlong.* ....(7 to 1 tchd 9 to 1) 4

1375[2] BEAUCHAMP HERO [78] 7-13 N Carlisle (22) *beh till cld on ldrs hfwy, ev ch o'r 2 fs out, no extr entering last.* ....(25 to 1 op 20 to 1) 5

1524* RIBHI (USA) [90] 8-11 W Carson (9) *hld up in rear, ran on o'r 2 fs out, styd on one pace appr last.* ....(10 to 1 tchd 11 to 1) 6

1342* WALI (USA) [85] 8-6 M Hills (16) *trkd ldrs, rdn and no extr 2 fs out*............................(16 to 1 op 12 to 1) 7

1530[5] MOORISH [89] 8-3 (7*) T G McLaughlin (24) *in tch, ev ch 2 fs out, wknd fnl furlong.* ....(11 to 1 op 12 to 1 tchd 10 to 1) 8

1524[6] DIGPAST (Ire) [79] 7-11 (3*) D Harrison (13) *moderate effrt on outsd 3 fs out, not rch frnt rnk.* (20 to 1 op 16 to 1) 9

1338[2] CONEYBURY (Ire) [89] 8-10 R Cochrane (4) *mid-div most of way, rdn alng o'r 3 fs out, no imprsn on ldrs.* ....(14 to 1 op 12 to 1 tchd 16 to 1) 10

1636[4] NORFOLK HERO [87] 8-8 C Rutter (8) *mid-div, no prog o'r 2 fs out*........................(14 to 1 op 20 to 1) 11

965* MECKLENBURG (Ire) [86] 8-7 W Ryan (6) *rear most of way.* ....(14 to 1 tchd 16 to 1) 12

WOODHAUNTER (USA) [84] 8-5 J Carroll (17) *trkd ldrs for o'r 5 fs*..........................(25 to 1 op 20 to 1) 13

1382[8] ROBLEU [88] 8-2 (7*) Gaye Harwood (2) *in tch till rdn and no prog 3 fs out*.................(50 to 1 tchd 66 to 1) 14

1408* KASSBAAN (USA) [74] 7-9 J Quinn (5) *trkd frnt rnk 5 fs.* ....(20 to 1 op 16 to 1 tchd 25 to 1) 15

1451[2] EMBANKMENT (Ire) [88] 8-9 W R Swinburn (10) *mid-div, und pres o'r 3 fs out, no further prog.* ....(25 to 1 op 20 to 1) 16

GYMCRAK TIGER (Ire) [88] 8-9 K Darley (15) *beh till improved hfwy, btn und pres o'r 2 fs out.* ....(20 to 1 op 14 to 1) 17

1338[4] ERTLON [80] 7-12 (3*) B Doyle (14) *effrt frm rear o'r 2 fs out, wknd wl over one out*.........(25 to 1 op 20 to 1) 18

1697[4] HADEER'S DANCE [80] 8-1 R Price (18) *in tch for o'r 4 fs.* ....(33 to 1 op 25 to 1) 19

1488[6] ABERDEEN HEATHER [74] 7-2 (7*) D Wright (11) *led aftr one furlong till o'r 2 out, wknd*...... (33 to 1 tchd 40 to 1) 20

1017[9] EASY ACCESS (Ire) [90] 8-11 L Dettori (23) *nvr able to chal.* ....(25 to 1 op 20 to 1 tchd 33 to 1) 21

1349* SHARAAR (USA) [82] 8-3 Paul Eddery (1) *in tch to hfwy.* ....(33 to 1 tchd 40 to 1) 22

602[2] GREEN KILT [83] 8-4 A Munro (25) *chsd ldrs 5 fs, sn btn.* ....(20 to 1 tchd 25 to 1 and 16 to 1) 23

1302[4] YAQTHAN (Ire) [89] 8-10 R Hills (7) *led one furlong, wknd hfwy*............................(25 to 1 op 20 to 1) 24

1765 COLOUR PARTY (USA) [100] (bl) 9-7 W J O'Connor (21) *slwly into strd, beh most of way*............. (50 to 1) 25

Dist: 1l, ½l, 1½l, nk, 3½l, sht-hd, 1½l, sht-hd, hd, 2½l. 1m 46.05s. a 7.05s (25 Ran).

SR: 51/44/51/40/34/35/29/28/17/ (I A N Wight), R Hannon

1809 Queen Alexandra Stakes Conditions Class B (4-y-o and up) £16,570 2¾m 34yds......................... (5:30)

1576* RISZARD (USA) 4-8-12 C Roche (6) *hld up, pushed alng one m out, ran on und pres fnl 2 fs to ld cl hme.* ....(9 to 2 op 3 to 1 tchd 5 to 1) 1

1752[3] JACK BUTTON (Ire) 4-9-2 N Day (12) *nvr far away, led o'r 3 fs out, hdd briefly appr last, rallied gmely und pres, ct cl hme*..........................(5 to 2 fav op 2 to 1) 2

1336 MISS PLUM 4-8-7 L Dettori (3) *hld up, hdwy 6 fs out, sn rdn, ran on strly ins fnl 2 furlongs.* (20 to 1 op 16 to 1) 3

1468 CURRENCY BASKET (Ire) 4-8-12 M J Kinane (13) *al frnt rnk, rdn to ld briefly o'r one furlong out, one pace ins last*........................... (12 to 1 tchd 14 to 1) 4

1752 BOKARO (Fr) 7-9-0 J Reid (8) *hld up rear, hdwy 4 fs out, short of room o'r 2 out, kpt on one pace.* ....(16 to 1 tchd 20 to 1) 5

1752[4] STAR PLAYER 7-9-0 Pat Eddery (14) *hld up in tch, lost pl 4 fs out, effrt o'r 2 out, one pace*..... (7 to 1 tchd 8 to 1) 6

1345[8] STAR QUEST 6-9-0 K Darley (10) *trkd ldrs, rdn 3 fs out, wknd appr 2 out*................ (66 to 1 op 50 to 1) 7

1752 GOOD HAND (USA) 7-9-4 M Birch (5) *trkd ldr to hfwy, sn rdn, no hdwy fnl 3 fs.* ....(16 to 1 op 14 to 1 tchd 20 to 1) 8

SWEET GLOW (Fr) 6-9-0 M Perrett (9) *hld up, rdn 6 fs out, lost tch 4 out*.......... (7 to 2 op 4 to 1 tchd 9 to 2) 9

ACROW LINE 8-9-0 Stephen Davies (11) *led, styd alone on ins hfwy, hdd o'r 3 fs out, sn rdn and wknd.* ....(33 to 1 op 20 to 1) 10

1752 REQUESTED 6-9-3 T Quinn (4) *hld up, effrt o'r 4 fs out, wknd wl over 2 out*............. (20 to 1 tchd 25 to 1) 11

1669[9] INTRICACY 5-8-9 M Roberts (1) *chsd ldrs, wnt second briefly one m out, wknd 5 fs out*... (25 to 1 op 50 to 1) 12

Dist: Sht-hd, ½l, 1½l, 1½l, 6l, 1½l, nk, sht-hd, 7l, nk. 5m 18.57s. a 31.57s (12 Ran).

(Henryk de Kwiatkowski), J S Bolger

AYR (good to soft)
Friday June 18th

Going Correction: PLUS 0.45 sec. per fur.

1810 Cunning Park Maiden Stakes Class D (2-y-o) £3,285 7f..................(2:15)

KEZIO RUFO (Ire) 9-0 M Wigham (4) *prmnt, pushed alng hfwy, outpcd 2 out, rallied und pres fnl furlong, hng lft towards finish*.................. (10 to 1 tchd 14 to 1) 1

1529[7] DIAMOND FRONTIER (Ire) 8-11 (3*) Emma O'Gorman (1) *prmnt, not much room frm 2 out, ran on wl fnl furlong, jst fld*.............................(50 to 1 op 16 to 1) 2

1391[3] TIMES ZANDO 8-9 J Fortune (3) *led, hrd pressed frm 3 out, hdd and no extr towards finish*....(40 to 1 op 20 to 1) 3

1715[5] BLASTER BATES (USA) 9-0 D Nicholls (6) *hld up in tch, smooth hdwy 3 out, chlgd 2 out, sn rdn, no extr fnl furlong*......................... (7 to 1 op 5 to 1) 4

1324[5] GOLDEN STAR (Ire) 9-0 J Fanning (7) *trkd ldrs, hdwy to chal o'r one furlong out, sn rdn, one pace.* ....(4 to 1 op 3 to 1) 5

865[2] DON PEPE 9-0 M Tebbutt (5) *hld up in tch, hdwy o'r 2 out, ev ch over one out, wknd fnl furlong.* (7 to 1 op 9 to 2) 6

GLIDINGONBY (Ire) 8-9 D Holland (2) *hld up in tch, effrt o'r 2 fs out, no hdwy.* ...(11 to 10 on op 5 to 4 on tchd Evens and 11 to 10) 7

Dist: Hd, sht-hd, 1l, ¾l, 3½l, nk. 1m 35.94s. a 11.94s (7 Ran).

(G Mazza), P A Kelleway

1811 Dalmilling Claiming Stakes Class F (3-y-o and up) £2,601 1m.......... (2:50)

1591[3] LOMBARD SHIPS (bl) 6-8-9 A Mackay (6) *hld up in tch, steady hdwy to ld o'r one furlong out, rdn and quickened clr fnl furlong*.................(4 to 1 op 7 to 2) 1

1592[8] BARLEY CAKE 3-7-11 J Fanning (4) *hld up in tch, effrt o'r 2 fs out, kpt on fnl furlong, no ch wth wnr.* ....(3 to 1 op 5 to 2) 2

1634[3] IMPERIAL BID (Fr) 5-9-6 D Holland (3) *cl up, led wl o'r 2 fs out, hdd over one out, one pace.* ....(5 to 4 fav op 11 to 10) 3

SAOIRSE (Ire) 5-9-0 (5*) Darren Moffatt (7) *beh, pushed alng hfwy, some late hdwy, nvr dngrs.* ....(25 to 1 op 20 to 1 tchd 33 to 1) 4

1634[2] GOLD SURPRISE (Ire) 4-9-4 J Fortune (2) *led till hdd wl o'r 2 out, fdd*.............. (9 to 2 op 4 to 1 tchd 5 to 1) 5

1634[8] HAND ON HEART (Ire) 4-8-12 (3*) S D Williams (1) *trkd ldrs, effrt o'r 2 fs out, sn rdn and btn.* ....(16 to 1 op 33 to 1 tchd 50 to 1) 6

Dist: 6l, nk, 1½l, 3l, sht-hd. 1m 46.78s. a 9.08s (6 Ran).

SR: 13/-/5/ (Mrs D M Mitchell), A Bailey

1812 Ben Handicap Class E (0-70 3-y-o) £2,736 1¼m.................. (3:25)

833[2] HYDE'S HAPPY HOUR [51] 9-0 J Fortune (4) *trkd ldrs gng wl, led 3 out, rdn o'r one furlong out, hld on well und pres*..............................(3 to 1 op 4 to 1) 1

1238[6] DARING PAST [51] (v) 9-0 M Tebbutt (5) *hld up, gd hdwy 3 fs out, rdn 2 out, ev ch fnl furlong, no extr.* ....(8 to 1 op 6 to 1) 2

1417 GREYSTYLE [35] 7-12 J Fanning (6) *in tch, effrt 3 out, ev ch till wknd 2 out*................. (16 to 1 op 12 to 1) 3

1630[2] CONTRACT ELITE (Ire) [54] 9-3 A Mackay (1) *hld up, hdwy to chal 3 out, sn rdn, wknd 2 out.* .... (5 to 2 fav tchd 3 to 1) 4

1579[4] SILVER STANDARD [58] 9-7 S Perks (2) *led till hdd 3 out, sn wknd, tld off*.................(3 to 1 op 9 to 4) 5

1357[2] CERTAIN WAY (Ire) [56] 9-5 L Charnock (3) *cl up till wknd quickly 3 out, wl tld off*..............(6 to 1 op 4 to 1) 6

Dist: 1½l, 6l, 3½l, 25l, 20l. 2m 15.48s. a 10.48s (6 Ran).

SR: 40/37/9/21/-/-/ (Travellers T Time Club), N Tinkler

1813 Muckhart Inn Median Auction Maiden Stakes Class E (3-y-o) £2,717 1m 5f 13yds. . . . . (4:00)

1256^{4} LAKE POOPO (Ire) 8-9 D Holland (4) *led aftr one furlong, drw wl clr frm o'r 3 fs out, very easily.* . . . .(7 to 2 on tchd 3 to 1 on and 4 to 1 on) 1
CAROUSEL MAGIC 9-0 S Perks (3) *slwly into strd, sn in tch, outpcd 5 fs out, kpt on frm 3 out, no ch wth wnr.* . . . . (15 to 2 op 7 to 1 tchd 8 to 1) 2
1359^{6} SANTA STELLAR 8-9 J Fanning (1) *led one furlong, chsd wnr till wknd o'r 3 out.* (4 to 1 op 7 to 2 tchd 9 to 2) 3
1416 MARCO CLAUDIO (Ire) 9-0 M Wigham (2) *in tch, sn pushed alng, outpcd 5 fs out, wl tld off.* . . . . . (8 to 1 op 7 to 1) 4
Dist: 30l, 20l, dist. 3m 6.00s. a 20.00s (4 Ran).
(R E Sangster), B W Hills

1814 Seafield Maiden Auction Stakes Class F (2-y-o) £2,399 5f. . . . . (4:35)

1561^{2} FORT ERIE 9-0 L Charnock (1) *made most, ran on wl fnl furlong.* . . . . (3 to 1 jt-fav tchd 7 to 2) 1
1475^{2} CERTIFICATE-X 8-9 J Fanning (7) *chsd ldrs, rdn o'r one furlong out, kpt on towards finish.* . .(4 to 1 op 3 to 1) 2
804^{4} WHARFEDALE MUSIC 8-9 A Mackay (2) *chsd ldrs, rdn hfwy, styd on fnl furlong.* . . . . (6 to 1 tchd 7 to 1 and 8 to 1) 3
LEADING PRINCESS (Ire) 8-9 D Holland (6) *slwly into strd, beh, hdwy hfwy, kpt on same pace fnl furlong.* . . . .(33 to 1 tchd 50 to 1) 4
WELSH MIST 8-9 M Tebbutt (3) *chsd ldrs, outpcd hfwy, no dngr aftr.* . . . .(3 to 1 jt-fav tchd 7 to 2) 5
NORTHGATE SYMPHONY 9-0 M Wigham (4) *sn beh.* . . . . (33 to 1 op 25 to 1 tchd 50 to 1) 6
1296^{6} PARIS SYMPHONY (Ire) 9-0 J Fortune (5) *dsptd ld till wknd o'r one furlong out.* . . . . . (9 to 2 op 3 to 1 tchd 5 to 1) 7
Dist: 4l, sht-hd, nk, ¾l, ¾l, 1l. 1m 3.69s. a 5.59s (7 Ran).
SR: 33/12/11/10/7/9/5/ (Richard Dawson), J F Bottomley

1815 Rozelle Handicap Class E (0-70 4-y-o and up) £2,745 5f. . . . . (5:05)

1782^{3} JUST BOB [68] 4-9-7 (7*) J Tate (9) *slwly into strd, sn in tch, led o'r one furlong out, ran on wl.* . . . .(7 to 2 jt-fav op 5 to 2 tchd 4 to 1) 1
1631^{2} LANGTONIAN [53] (bl) 4-8-10 (3*) Emma O'Gorman (2) *slwly into strd, hld up, steady hdwy hfwy, ev ch one furlong out, no extr fnl furlong.* . . . .(5 to 1 op 7 to 2 tchd 11 to 2) 2
1287 LOFT BOY [57] 10-8-10 (7*) K Sked (6) *in tch, effrt 2 fs out, ran on wl fnl furlong.* . . . .(12 to 1 tchd 14 to 1) 3
1379^{6} BEST EFFORT [53] 7-8-6 (7*) V Halliday (1) *sn beh and pushed alng, styd on fnl furlong, nvr dngrs.* . . . . (15 to 2 op 6 to 1 tchd 8 to 1) 4
BRAVE MELODY [34] 7-7-8 J Fanning (8) *cl up, led aftr 2 fs till hdd o'r one out, fdd.* . . . . (16 to 1 op 14 to 1 tchd 20 to 1) 5
1736^{8} DIET [65] (v) 7-9-4 (7*,7ex) R Havlin (4) *in tch, rdn 2 fs out, no hdwy.* . . . .(6 to 1 op 7 to 1 tchd 8 to 1) 6
1599^{4} SO SUPERB [62] (bl) 4-9-8 S Webster (7) *wth ldrs till wknd o'r one furlong out.* . . . . (11 to 2 op 5 to 1 tchd 6 to 1) 7
1599^{9} GEMINI FIRE [65] 9-9-11 J Fortune (5) *led 2 fs, wknd two out.* . . . . (16 to 1 op 12 to 1) 8
1492^{7} BARBEZIEUX [47] 6-8-7 M Wigham (3) *chsd ldrs till wknd 2 fs out.* . . . .(7 to 2 jt-fav tchd 4 to 1) 9
Dist: 1½l, ¾l, 2½l, 1½l, ½l, hd, 3l, 1l. 1m 3.40s. a 5.30s (9 Ran).
SR: 53/32/33/19/-/23/19/10/-/ (J Fotherby), S E Kettlewell

GOODWOOD (good)
Friday June 18th
Going Correction: PLUS 0.50 sec. per fur. (races 1,2,3,4,5), PLUS 0.30 (6)

1816 Ocean F.M. Maiden Stakes Class D (3-y-o and up) £3,523 1¼m. . . . . . . (6:35)

1178^{2} MISS SHAGRA (USA) 3-8-7 B Rouse (5) *pressed ldr, led o'r 4 fs out, rdn 2 out, styd on wl.* . . . . (100 to 30 op 7 to 4 tchd 7 to 2) 1
1349^{3} MORSTOCK 3-8-12 J Williams (1) *trkd ldrs, shaken up and prog 4 fs out, ev ch 2 out, one pace.* . . . .(4 to 1 op 9 to 2 tchd 5 to 1 and 7 to 2) 2
1533^{8} MAD CASANOVA (bl) 8-9-3 (7*) D McCabe (2) *rear, lost tch o'r 3 fs out, styd on 2 out, nvr able to chal.* . . . .(33 to 1) 3
POPSI'S LEGACY 6-9-5 N Adams (10) *beh, kpt on fnl 2 fs, nvr dngrs.* . . . .(50 to 1 op 33 to 1) 4
1285^{3} CRYSTAL REAY 3-8-7 R Cochrane (3) *trkd ldrs gng wl, swtchd to centre in strt, ev ch o'r 2 fs out, wknd rpdly.* . . . .(11 to 10 fav op 5 to 4 tchd 6 to 4) 5
1315^{6} CHASE THE STARS 3-8-7 K Fallon (4) *sn pushed alng in rear, nvr on terms.* . . . . .(9 to 1 op 5 to 1 tchd 10 to 1) 6
FOREST STAR (USA) 4-9-7 (3*) J Weaver (6) *led till o'r 4 fs out, wknd.* . . . . (14 to 1 op 10 to 1) 7
VILLAGE KID 4-9-10 C Avery (8) *mid-div, rdn o'r 4 fs out, sn wknd.* . . . .(50 to 1 op 20 to 1) 8
1311 AUNT ADA 4-9-5 W Newnes (7) *al beh.* . . . . (50 to 1) 9
1533 BOLD REINE (Fr) 4-8-12 (7*) S Drowne (9) *keen hold, prmnt till wknd hfwy, sn beh.* . . . .(50 to 1) 10
Dist: 3½l, 6l, 8l, 3½l, 1l, 1l, 1l, 6l, nk. 2m 17.06s. a 11.56s (10 Ran).
SR: 27/25/25/4/-/-/ (Maktoum Al Maktoum), M R Stoute

1817 Festival Of Speed Claiming Stakes Class E (3-y-o) £2,856 7f. . . . . (7:05)

1185^{4} PERSIANSKY (Ire) 8-5^{1} B Raymond (1) *al prmnt, rdn to chal 2 fs out, styd on strly to ld wl ins last.* . . . . (13 to 2 op 4 to 1 tchd 7 to 1) 1
1313^{6} NO EXTRAS (Ire) 8-6 B Rouse (7) *led o'r 5 fs out, rdn 2 out, hdd and no extr wl ins last.* . . . .(2 to 1 fav op 5 to 2 tchd 11 to 4) 2
1005 COVEN MOON (v) 7-13 J Quinn (5) *chsd ldrs, rdn 3 fs out, styd on one pace.* . . . .(16 to 1 op 12 to 1 tchd 20 to 1) 3
975^{3} BROUGHTON'S PORT 8-4 (7*) D McCabe (6) *hld up and wl beh, ran on fnl 2 fs, too much to do.* . . . .(11 to 4 op 7 to 2 tchd 4 to 1 and 9 to 2) 4
1487^{6} BONITA BEE (bl) 7-11 N Adams (10) *dwlt, chsd ldrs, rdn o'r 2 fs out, no prog.* . . . .(9 to 1 op 6 to 1 tchd 10 to 1) 5
1212 POCONO KNIGHT 8-4 C Avery (11) *sn rdn alng, nvr dngrs.* . . . .(7 to 1 tchd 8 to 1) 6
1458^{9} LE COUTEAU (bl) 8-3^{1} K Fallon (9) *rdn alng in rear, effrt hfwy, sn btn.* . . . .(14 to 1 op 7 to 1 tchd 16 to 1) 7
DOUBLE BOUNCE 8-8 W Newnes (4) *prmnt 2 fs, sn struggling.* . . . . (16 to 1 op 12 to 1 tchd 20 to 1) 8
878^{9} KUTAN (Ire) 8-2 G Bardwell (2) *mid-div, no ch fnl 3 fs.* . . . .(20 to 1 op 14 to 1 tchd 25 to 1) 9
878 INTERVIEW 8-5^{8} R Perham (8) *led for o'r one furlong, wknd rpdly bef hfwy.* . . . .(50 to 1 op 33 to 1) 10
DOUBLE DEALING (Ire) 7-10^{1} (7*) G Rothwell (3) *sn wl beh.* . . . . (25 to 1 op 20 to 1 tchd 33 to 1) 11
Dist: 2l, 1½l, nk, 6l, 3l, nk, 4l, 6l, 7l, 5l. 1m 31.44s. a 6.84s (11 Ran).
SR: 41/36/24/35/3/1/ (Mrs J M Beeby), B Hanbury

1818 Sky Sports Handicap Class D (0-80 3-y-o) £3,494 1m. . . . . (7:35)

1524^{9} LOCHORE [57] 7-13 A Tucker (4) *hld up beh, effrt 3 fs out, not clr run appr last, ran on ins last, jnd ldr last strd.* . . . . (20 to 1 op 12 to 1) 1+
1670^{2} BLUE BLAZER [78] 9-6 B Raymond (2) *set modest pace, quickened hfwy, rdn 2 fs out, ran on, jnd last strd.* . . . .(6 to 4 on op 6 to 5 on) 1+
1540^{2} STARLIGHT ROSE (Ire) [54] (v) 7-10^{3} T Williams (6) *keen hold, trcked ldrs, rdn to chal 2 furlong o sut, no extr ins last.* . . . .(11 to 2 op 9 to 2 tchd 6 to 1) 3
1584^{5} PRINCELY FAVOUR (Ire) [79] 9-7 B Rouse (5) *pld hrd, trkd ldr, rdn 3 fs out, wknd appr last.* . . . . (11 to 2 op 5 to 1 tchd 6 to 1) 4
1256^{6} AUSTRAL JANE [70] 8-12 J Reid (3) *trkd ldrs till wknd wl o'r 2 fs out.* . . . .(5 to 1 tchd 11 to 2) 5
Dist: Dd-ht, 2½l, 3l, 10l. 1m 47.03s. a 9.83s (5 Ran).
SR: -/19/-/3/-/ (Luke Devine & McHalapar Syndicate), R Ingram & B Hanbury

1819 Kincsem Claiming Stakes Class F (3-y-o) £2,611 1½m. . . . . (8:05)

1266^{6} SUMMER WIND (Ire) 7-11 (3*) B Doyle (3) *made virtually all, rdn 3 fs out, ran on wl fnl furlong.* . . . .(4 to 1 op 9 to 2) 1
1491^{5} GALACTIC FURY 8-7 J Williams (2) *prmnt, jnd wnr 4 fs out, wknd ins last.* . . . .(5 to 1 op 3 to 1) 2
1662^{2} TROPICAL JUNGLE (USA) 9-0 K Fallon (4) *trkd ldrs, rdn 2 fs out, nvr able to chal.* . . . . (11 to 10 on op 5 to 4 on tchd Evens) 3
1625^{7} SHE KNEW THE RULES (Ire) 8-0 C Rutter (5) *al beh, no ch fnl 4 fs.* . . . .(7 to 2 op 7 to 1 tchd 8 to 1) 4
1266 STRAIGHT APPROACH (USA) 8-5 R Perham (1) *rdn hfwy, sn wl beh.* . . . . (20 to 1 op 10 to 1) 5
Dist: 5l, 2l, 20l, 15l. 2m 47.30s. a 14.30s (5 Ran).
SR: 3/-/3/-/-/ (Ray Richards), D R C Elsworth

1820 Keren Harris Handicap Class D (0-80 4-y-o and up) £3,552 1¼m. . . . . (8:35)

1409^{6} BOOKCASE [68] 6-9-3 J Williams (8) *9th and pushed alng hfwy, prog to ld ins fnl furlong, drvn out.* . . . .(8 to 1 op 6 to 1 tchd 9 to 1) 1
1711^{2} GOOGLY [68] 4-9-3 G Bardwell (1) *8th hfwy, prog to ld briefly one furlong out, no extr nr finish.* . . . .(11 to 4 jt-fav tchd 3 to 1) 2
1318^{2} KNOWTH (Ire) [68] 4-9-3 J Reid (5) *6th hfwy, sn prmnt, ev ch one furlong out, unbl to quicken.* . . . .(11 to 4 jt-fav op 3 to 1 tchd 7 to 2) 3
1663^{3} NATURAL LAD [60] 8-8-4 (5*) Stephen Davies (2) *5th hfwy, ev ch one furlong out, one pace.* (10 to 1 tchd 12 to 1) 4
1607^{3} NORDANSK [45] 4-7-8 C Avery (3) *clr ldr hfwy, hdd and wknd one furlong out.* . . . (6 to 1 op 7 to 1 tchd 8 to 1) 5
1659* ALBERT [50] 6-7-8^{2} (7*,6ex) D McCabe (4) *last hfwy, ran on strly ins fnl furlong, nvr nrr.* . . . . (6 to 1 op 5 to 1 tchd 13 to 2) 6

1064 MOVE A MINUTE (USA) [75] 4-9-5 (5*) A Procter (6) *3rd hfwy, no ch appr fnl furlong.* .... (33 to 1 op 20 to 1 tchd 50 to 1) 7
1626² SCOTTISH BAMBI [65] 5-9-0 R Perham (9) *4th hfwy, no ch appr fnl furlong......* (9 to 1 op 5 to 1 tchd 10 to 1) 8
1414 SANTANA LADY (Ire) [63] 4-8-12 W Newnes (10) *second hfwy, sn wknd...................*(20 to 1 op 12 to 1) 9
990 MOLLY SPLASH [53] 6-8-2¹ K Fallon (7) *7th and rdn hfwy, sn beh..............*(16 to 1 op 14 to 1 tchd 20 to 1) 10
Dist: Hd, 1½l, hd, 1l, nk, 6l, 1l, 10l, 3½l. 2m 16.16s. a 10.66s (10 Ran).
SR: 46/45/42/33/16/20/33/21/-/ (Adept (80) Ltd), D R C Elsworth

1821 Priory Park Handicap Class E (0-70 3-y-o and up) £2,929 6f......... (9:05)

1606⁴ CAROMISH (USA) [52] 6-9-3 N Adams (4) *made all, clr one furlong out, cmftbly....*(4 to 1 op 5 to 1 tchd 11 to 2) 1
1588⁶ ZINBAQ [36] 7-8-1 T Williams (8) *rear to hfwy, ran on wl fnl furlong, nrst finish............*(6 to 1 tchd 7 to 1) 2
1485 FAY'S SONG (Ire) [59] 5-9-3 (7*) L Carter (2) *trkd ldrs, ran on one pace fnl furlong.* .... (11 to 2 op 5 to 1 tchd 7 to 1) 3
1664⁵ MR NEVERMIND (Ire) [61] (bl) 3-9-4 B Rouse (1) *chsd ldrs, styd on same pace fnl furlong.....*(7 to 1 tchd 9 to 1) 4
1232⁸ HARRY'S COMING [55] 9-9-6 J Williams (9) *wth wnr to hfwy, wknd appr fnl furlong.* .... (14 to 1 op 10 to 1 tchd 16 to 1) 5
1537 UNVEILED [54] 5-8-12 (7*) S Drowne (3) *al rear.* .... (14 to 1 op 10 to 1) 6
1664² COPPERMILL LAD [44] 10-8-9 J Reid (5) *beh hfwy, nvr nr to chal............* (2 to 1 fav op 9 to 4 tchd 15 to 8) 7
1485² SAMSOLOM [63] 5-10-0 J Quinn (6) *chsd ldrs to hfwy, no ch appr fnl furlong.....*(15 to 2 op 5 to 1 tchd 8 to 1) 8
1487 ZHAAB [39] (bl) 3-7-10 C Avery (7) *sn rdn alng, al beh.* .... (33 to 1 op 25 to 1 tchd 50 to 1) 9
Dist: 2½l, 1½l, 2l, nk, ½l, hd, 2l, 4l. 1m 15.26s. a 4.86s (9 Ran).
SR: 42/16/33/19/20/17/6/17/-/ (M D I Usher), M D I Usher

GOWRAN PARK (IRE) (yielding to soft)
Friday June 18th

1822 Dunnes Stores Ladies Fashion Series (3-y-o and up) £3,452 1m 1f 130yds .... (6:30)

1573⁴ MADANIYYA (USA) 3-8-11 Miss L Robinson (11)... (4 to 1) 1
1441⁵ UP SHE FLEW (USA) 3-8-11 Mrs C Doyle (6)......(14 to 1) 2
1252* TRANQUIL BEAUTY (Ire) 4-9-12 (2*) Miss M Butler (3) ....(12 to 1) 3
1652* SOLAS ABU (Ire) 3-9-9 (3ex) Miss I Leahy (12).. (5 to 4 on) 4
1610⁹ MYRO BALANNE (Ire) 3-8-9 (2*) Miss M Quigley (9) (33 to 1) 5
1620⁷ PERSIAN LIGHT (Ire) 3-8-11 (8ex) Miss M Olivefalk (1) ....(20 to 1) 6
1106⁷ NO DUNCE (Ire) 3-8-11 (8ex) Mrs S McCarthy (8)..(10 to 1) 7
1507 KESS (Ire) 4-9-6 (3ex) Miss C Rogers (4)..........(25 to 1) 8
849⁶ STEEL CHIMES (Ire) 4-10-1 (2*) Miss J McDowell (10) ....(16 to 1) 9
1441³ SPECIAL OFFER (Ire) (bl) 3-8-11 (3ex) Miss A H Marshall (5) ....(8 to 1) 10
1576⁶ GILT DIMENSION 6-9-12 (8ex) Mrs J M Mullins (7) (12 to 1) 11
267⁴ WILDE (Ire) 3-9-0 Miss A Gilsenan (2)............(14 to 1) 12
Dist: 3l, ¾l, ¾l, 5l. 2m 17.10s. (12 Ran).
(H H Aga Khan), John M Oxx

1823 Norelands Stud Fillies Trial Race (3-y-o and up) £4,982 1m 1f 130yds (7:00)

1201⁹ ALALJA (Ire) 3-8-12 (6*) J R Barry (5)..............(9 to 2) 1
1514* KIROV PREMIERE 3-9-1 K J Manning (2)..........(6 to 1) 2
1646⁴ SABAYA (USA) 3-8-13 W J Supple (9).............(4 to 1) 3
1552 CHEVIOT AMBLE (Ire) 5-10-2 J F Egan (8).........(6 to 1) 4
870* MAMOURA (Ire) 3-8-11 J P Murtagh (3)........(3 to 1 fav) 5
1511³ CLEAR ABILITY (Ire) (bl) 3-8-11 P Shanahan (7).... (6 to 1) 6
1514⁵ WHEATSHEAF LADY (Ire) 3-8-9 (6*) J J Behan (1)...(8 to 1) 7
1511⁸ BABUSHKA (Ire) 3-8-11 J D Eddery (4)...........(20 to 1) 8
Dist: Hd, 2l, 1l, 2½l. 2m 17.40s. (8 Ran).
(John Bernard O'Connor), Patrick Joseph Flynn

1824 Ormonde (E.B.F.) (C&G) Maiden (2-y-o) £3,797 6f................. (7:30)

1509⁵ ALZUMA (Ire) 9-0 J F Egan (4)............... (2 to 1 on) 1
305⁶ OLIVER MESSEL (Ire) 9-0 W J Supple (6).........(11 to 1) 2
BEAUCHAMP IMPERIAL 9-0 P Shanahan (7)..... (11 to 1) 3
1567² VIVA VICTOR (Ire) 9-0 R Hughes (8)...............(6 to 1) 4
1550⁸ DANCING BRIEF (Ire) 8-12 (2*) D G O'Shea (1).... (20 to 1) 5
1650⁶ PARCACURRY PETE (Ire) 9-0 N G McCullagh (5).. (20 to 1) 6
ZURYAF STAR (Ire) 9-0 S Craine (3)...............(14 to 1) 7
1567³ FIONN DE COOL (Ire) 9-0 K J Manning (2)........(10 to 1) 8
Dist: 2l, 1l, 5l, 6l. 1m 16.90s. (8 Ran).
(E Hannan), Patrick Joseph Flynn

1825 Rhone-Poulenc Seed Protection Handicap (0-80 3-y-o) £3,452 6f..(8:00)

1619* FOREST [-] 8-12 S Craine (1)......................(9 to 2) 1
1570* PILGRIM BAY (Ire) [-] 8-8 (2*,4ex) D G O'Shea (2)... (4 to 1) 2
1795⁴ SHRAGRADDY LASS (Ire) [-] 8-3 (6ex) N G McCullagh (8) ....(5 to 2 fav) 3
1549⁶ BENE MERENTI (Ire) [-] (bl) 8-10 (6*) R V Skelly (6) (10 to 1) 4
1433⁶ GIRARDELLI (Ire) [-] 7-7 (4*) W J Smith (9)........(10 to 1) 5
1513⁹ GOLD BRAISIM (Ire) [-] 9-4 K J Manning (3)........(6 to 1) 6
307 IBDA [-] 9-1 W J Supple (7).......................(6 to 1) 7
Dist: Nk, 1½l, 4½l, 6l. 1m 16.00s. (7 Ran).
(T Corden), T Stack

NEWMARKET (JULY) (good)
Friday June 18th
Going Correction: NIL (races 1,3,4,5), MINUS 0.10 (2,6)

1826 Histon Apprentice Handicap Class E (0-80 3-y-o) £3,655 5f........... (6:45)

1213⁹ MY BONUS [78] 9-4 (3*) L Newton (1) *led aftr one and a half fs, hrd rdn fnl furlong, hld on gmely.* ....(7 to 2 op 4 to 1) 1
1714³ GO FLIGHTLINE (Ire) [60] (v) 7-12 (5*) J O'Dwyer (3) *wtd wth, niggled alng and effrt 2 fs out, edgd lft and ran on wl ins last..............................*(9 to 4 op 2 to 1) 2
1455³ JULIET BRAVO [63] 8-1 (5*) N Varley (2) *al hndy, rdn o'r one furlong out, kpt on.* ....(2 to 1 fav op 2 to 1 tchd 7 to 4) 3
380⁶ NEWBURY COAT [70] 8-13 C Hodgson (5) *tucked away, rdn o'r 2 fs out, sn unbl to quicken.* .... (9 to 1 op 8 to 1 tchd 12 to 1) 4
1376⁵ THE ORDINARY GIRL (Ire) [54] 7-8 (3*) D Wright (4) *led one and a half fs, sn rdn and lost pl.* .... (13 to 2 op 6 to 1 tchd 7 to 1) 5
Dist: Nk, nk, 3½l, 7l. 1m 1.38s. a 2.68s (5 Ran).
SR: 53/34/36/29/-/ (Crazy Horse Bloodstock), D J S Cosgrove

1827 Antec International Handicap Class C (0-90 3-y-o and up) £5,481 1½m (7:15)

1681³ BIG PAT [56] 4-8-7 L Dettori (14) *trkd ldrs gng wl, led o'r one furlong out, rdn out.* .... (9 to 1 op 8 to 1 tchd 10 to 1) 1
1204⁵ SATIN DANCER [82] 3-9-4 K Darley (8) *patiently rdn, hdwy and not clr run wl o'r one furlong out, ran on ins last.* ....(14 to 1 op 10 to 1) 2
1426⁶ MY PATRIARCH [77] 3-8-13 W Carson (7) *midfield, rdn and outpcd 4 fs out, rallied o'r one out, kpt on.* ....(6 to 1 op 7 to 1) 3
1345⁶ MISS PIN UP [75] 4-9-12 D Biggs (9) *hld up and beh, hdwy o'r 2 fs out, rdn and ran on wl ins last, nvr nrr.* ....(9 to 1 op 8 to 1) 4
1028 DISCORD [73] 7-9-7 (3*) D Harrison (2) *hld up, effrt o'r 2 fs out, sn ev ch till wknd ins last...............* (10 to 1) 5
1669⁶ ROSGILL [66] 7-9-3 P Robinson (4) *took keen hold, prmnt, niggled alng 4 fs out, sn lost pl....* (16 to 1 op 14 to 1) 6
1637² SOUL EMPEROR [80] 3-9-2 A Munro (13) *led till hdd o'r one furlong out, sn btn.....................* (8 to 1) 7
1458³ WESTERN DYNASTY [70] 7-9-0 (7*) P McCabe (6) *in tch, ev ch 3 fs out, sn wknd..............*(14 to 1 op 10 to 1) 8
1173² DEDUCE [76] 4-9-13 Paul Eddery (12) *trkd ldrs till outpcd o'r 3 fs out, no further imprsn......* (12 to 1 op 8 to 1) 9
684⁹ SEEK THE PEARL [74] 3-8-10 G Duffield (10) *pld hrd, prmnt, ev ch 3 fs out, wknd.........*(14 to 1 op 12 to 1) 10
1417² CHIAPPUCCI (Ire) [63] (v) 3-7-13 G Carter (3) *rear till some hdwy 6 fs out, btn 3 out..........* (16 to 1 op 10 to 1) 11
1318* BIT ON THE SIDE (Ire) [64] 4-9-1 Pat Eddery (1) *steadied strt, hld up, hdwy 5 fs out, rdn and wknd o'r 2 out.* .... (11 to 2 op 8 to 1 tchd 10 to 1) 12
1064 LOBILIO (USA) [68] 4-9-5 M Roberts (11) *midfield till rdn 7 fs out, sn wknd.................*(5 to 1 fav op 8 to 1) 13
1345 FAUGERON [77] 4-10-0 T Quinn (5) *hld up, niggled alng o'r 6 fs out, sn wknd, tld off.......* (33 to 1 op 25 to 1) 14
Dist: 1½l, nk, sht-hd, ¾l, 5l, nk, 1½l, sht-hd, 8l, ½l. 2m 32.91s. a 4.11s (14 Ran).
SR: 40/48/42/54/50/33/31/33/38/ (Burton Park Country Club), J Pearce

1828 Videofax Maiden Stakes Class D (2-y-o) £3,915 6f.................. (7:45)

1428³ FAST EDDY 9-0 L Dettori (11) *trkd ldrs gng wl, led o'r one furlong out, sn pushed clr.* ....(6 to 4 fav op 7 to 4 tchd 11 to 8) 1
1310⁴ ANZIO (Ire) 9-0 W Carson (9) *led aftr one furlong, hdd o'r one furlong out, rdn and not pace of wnr.* ....(8 to 1 op 10 to 1) 2
1241⁶ THE MULTIYORKER (Ire) 8-9 P Robinson (2) *hld up, hdwy o'r 2 fs out, sn rdn and flashed tail over one out, no extr..................................*(25 to 1 op 20 to 1) 3
1131 CHIEF EXECUTIVE 9-0 M Roberts (3) *patiently rdn, ran green frm hfwy, some hdwy fnl one and a half fs, nvr nrr...............................* (25 to 1 op 20 to 1) 4
SANS ECOCIDE 9-0 G Duffield (1) *beh and outpcd till ran on fnl furlong, nvr nrr............* (33 to 1 op 16 to 1) 5
ALANEES 9-0 W R Swinburn (4) *prmnt on outsd, ev ch wl o'r one furlong out, sn wknd...........................*(6 to 1) 6

1489[2] DANGER POINT 9-0 A Munro (7) *prmnt till rdn and wknd wl o'r one furlong out..* (5 to 2 op 9 to 4 tchd 3 to 1) 7
1378[3] WOODS VENTURE (Ire) 9-0 W Woods (10) *prmnt till rdn 2 fs out, wknd.*..........(25 to 1) 8
1481[5] MARCH OF TIME 9-0 D Biggs (6) *led one furlong, rdn frm hfwy, sn wknd*..........(33 to 1 op 25 to 1) 9
PERHAPS 9-0 Paul Eddery (5) *sn rdn alng and outpcd.*..........(25 to 1 op 20 to 1) 10
LONE RISK 9-0 W Hood (8) *slwly away, al beh.*..........(16 to 1 op 12 to 1) 11
Dist: 4l, 2½l, 4l, 2½l, 1l, 2l, 2l, 3½l, 5l, 2½l. 1m 14.81s. a 3.11s (11 Ran).
SR: 38/22/7/-/-/-/ (Mrs Jenny Harris), D R Loder

1829 Chevington Claiming Stakes Class E (3-y-o) £3,262 1m..........(8:15)

1628* SILENT EXPRESSION 8-1[1] (5*) C Hodgson (10) *wth ldr, led gng wl o'r one furlong out, jst hld on.*..........(5 to 2 op 2 to 1) 1
1453[4] STRIKE-A-POSE 7-12 (3*) D Harrison (1) *hld up and beh, pld wide and gd hdwy o'r 2 fs out, sstnd chal ins last, jst fld*..........(9 to 1 op 8 to 1 tchd 12 to 1) 2
1273[4] RUBY COOPER 8-5 K Darley (12) *hld up in midfield, effrt o'r 2 fs out, styd on ins last.*..........(5 to 1 op 10 to 1 tchd 12 to 1) 3
1604[3] YFOOL 8-9 W R Swinburn (5) *prmnt, led aftr 2 fs till hdd o'r one furlong out, no extr*..........(9 to 4 fav op 2 to 1) 4
1453 EASTERN GLOW 8-2[1] W Woods (7) *prmnt on outsd, ev ch o'r one furlong out, wknd ins last.* (33 to 1 op 20 to 1) 5
1635[7] SALLY OF THE ALLEY 7-12 (7*) B Russell (9) *trkd ldg bunch, rdn 2 fs out, lost pl*..........(20 to 1) 6
1425[6] OUR SHADEE (USA) (bl) 8-12 M Wigham (11) *chsd ldg bunch, no hdwy fnl 2 fs*..........(20 to 1) 7
SABO'S EXPRESS 8-10 R Cochrane (4) *wl beh till some hdwy fnl one and a half fs, nvr nr to chal*..........(16 to 1) 8
1474 WAHEM (Ire) 9-4 M Roberts (3) *chsd ldrs, niggled alng hfwy, btn 2 out*..........(7 to 1 op 6 to 1) 9
1349[9] ASCOM PAGER TOO 8-5 Paul Eddery (14) *led 2 fs, stdly lost pl*..........(33 to 1) 10
O SO NEET 9-0 P Robinson (2) *slwly away, al beh.*..........(16 to 1 op 12 to 1) 11
1247[7] ADAMPARIS 8-5 W Carson (13) *trkd ldg bunch, niggled alng hfwy, sn wknd*..........(20 to 1 op 14 to 1) 12
1349[8] IMPERIAL FORTE 7-12[2] (7*) Sarah Thompson (6) *took keen hold, rstrained and beh, no imprsn frm hfwy.* (33 to 1) 13
1577[8] CAUGHT REDHANDED (Ire) 7-13 D Biggs (8) *midfield till rdn wl o'r 2 fs out, sn in rear*..........(33 to 1) 14
Dist: Sht-hd, 5l, nk, 2½l, 1½l, 1l, nk, 1½l, 2½l, 5l. 1m 42.66s. a 4.76s (14 Ran).
SR: 20/15/4/7/-/-/ (Mrs Rosalie Hawes), D Morris

1830 Kidsons Impey Trophy Handicap Class C (0-90 3-y-o and up) £5,754 7f..........(8:45)

1382[2] EN ATTENDANT (Fr) [82] 5-9-6 L Piggott (16) *wl plcd gng well, str run to ld ins fnl furlong, readily.*..........(7 to 1 op 8 to 1) 1
1280[5] HOPEFUL BID (Ire) [64] (bl) 4-8-2 K Darley (15) *al prmnt, led o'r 2 fs out, hdd over one out, kpt on.*..........(14 to 1 op 10 to 1) 2
1604[2] RISE UP SINGING [68] (bl) 5-8-6 W Carson (1) *wth ldr, led o'r one furlong out till hdd and no extr ins last.*..........(4 to 1 fav op 6 to 1) 3
1458[5] BALLERINA BAY [65] (v) 5-8-3 G Duffield (2) *trkd ldrs, ev ch o'r one furlong out, kpt on same pace*..........(20 to 1) 4
1721* HIGHLAND MAGIC (Ire) [83] 5-9-4 (3*,5ex) D Harrison (5) *wl beh till ran on fnl furlong, fnshd well, nvr nrr.*..........(13 to 2 op 6 to 1 tchd 7 to 1) 5
1667[3] SYLVAN (Ire) [79] 4-9-3 W R Swinburn (8) *beh, effrt on outsd o'r 2 fs out, wknd ins last*..........(12 to 1 op 10 to 1) 6
1382[6] MISS HAGGIS [74] 4-8-12 Pat Eddery (6) *took keen hold, trkd ldrs gng wl, not much room o'r one furlong out, eased whn btn*..........(7 to 1) 7
BRAVURA [79] 4-9-3 N Day (17) *prmnt till wknd wl o'r one furlong out*..........(33 to 1 op 25 to 1) 8
1066 CONFRONTER [76] 4-9-0 T Quinn (3) *trkd ldrs till wknd o'r 2 fs out*..........(16 to 1 op 14 to 1) 9
SET TABLE (USA) [72] 4-8-10 M Roberts (4) *led till hdd o'r 2 fs out, wknd*..........(9 to 1 op 8 to 1) 10
1527[4] HERORA (Ire) [88] 4-9-12 A McGlone (12) *nvr better than mid-div*..........(16 to 1 op 12 to 1) 11
1721[8] RURAL LAD [61] 4-7-6 (7*) D Wright (10) *midfield, rdn wl o'r 2 fs out, sn wknd*..........(25 to 1 op 20 to 1) 12
1144[4] ANNABELLE ROYALE [63] 7-8-1 A Munro (11) *midfield till wknd frm 3 fs out*..........(10 to 1 op 14 to 1) 13
1532[4] EURO FESTIVAL [90] 4-10-0 P Robinson (7) *beh, swtchd wide and effrt o'r 2 fs out, sn no extr.*..........(20 to 1 op 14 to 1) 14
1172[7] SUPEROO [69] 7-8-7 L Dettori (13) *midfield, shaken up o'r 2 fs out, no imprsn*..... (8 to 1 op 7 to 1 tchd 17 to 2) 15
1172[9] AMADEUS AES [74] (v) 4-8-7 (5*) C Hodgson (9) *pld hrd, midfield to hfwy, sn in rear*..........(33 to 1) 16
SATRAP (Ire) [87] 5-9-11 R Cochrane (14) *slwly into strd, al wl beh*..........(33 to 1 op 25 to 1) 17
Dist: 1½l, 1l, ½l, nk, 1½l, sht-hd, 1l, nk, nk, ¾l. 1m 27.45s. a 3.25s (17 Ran).
SR: 57/34/35/30/47/38/32/34/30/ (Mrs B Newton), B Hanbury

1831 Gazeley Maiden Stakes Class D (3-y-o) £4,012 1¼m..........(9:15)

IMAGINARY (Ire) 8-9 Pat Eddery (6) *took keen hold, al hndy, led wl o'r 2 fs out, sn clr, drvn out ins last.*..........(11 to 8 on op Evens tchd 11 to 10) 1
KITHANGA (Ire) 8-4 (5*) C Hodgson (14) *beh early, steady hdwy frm hfwy, rdn and styd on wl fnl furlong, prmsg.*..........(33 to 1) 2
MIDNIGHT POSTCARD (Fr) 8-9 W Ryan (4) *slwly into strd, hdwy o'r 3 fs out, ev ch over 2 out, kpt on fnl furlong.*..........(20 to 1 tchd 25 to 1) 3
MAMARA REEF 8-9 R Cochrane (5) *reluctant to enter stalls, in tch, ev ch o'r 2 fs out, not quicken ins last.*..........(10 to 1 tchd 12 to 1) 4
PEACHES POLLY 8-9 G Duffield (7) *pld hrd, trkd ldg grp on outsd, shaken up 3 fs out, one pace.*..........(7 to 1 op 10 to 1) 5
1429[6] BEDEVIL (USA) 9-0 L Dettori (16) *trkd ldrs, ev ch o'r 2 fs out, wknd over one out.* (7 to 2 op 7 to 2 tchd 4 to 1) 6
RUSSIAN EMPIRE 9-0 P D'Arcy (9) *in tch, rdn alng and ran green o'r 2 fs out, no imprsn*...(33 to 1 op 20 to 1) 7
MUTHAHB (Ire) 9-0 R Hills (13) *midfield, shaken up and ran green o'r 2 fs out, nvr nr to chal.*..........(20 to 1 op 16 to 1) 8
SHIP'S TWINE (Ire) 8-9 Paul Eddery (8) *midfield, rdn o'r 3 fs out, wknd over 2 out*..........(33 to 1 op 20 to 1) 9
980 HOPEFUL PROSPECT 8-9 K Darley (15) *led till hdd o'r 2 fs out, sn wknd*..........(33 to 1) 10
ROYAL BALLET (Ire) 8-9 A McGlone (10) *slwly into strd, al towards rear*..........(33 to 1) 11
1212[9] MR BEAN 8-11 (3*) D Harrison (12) *nvr able to chal.*..........(25 to 1 op 20 to 1) 12
COMFORTABLE 9-0 P Robinson (17) *missed break, al rear div*..........(33 to 1 op 25 to 1) 13
WANNABE 8-2 (7*) Jo Hunnam (11) *al towards rear and struggling*..........(33 to 1 op 20 to 1) 14
1176 RUN TO AU BON (Ire) 8-7 (7*) Michael Denaro (3) *rear div, rdn o'r 4 fs out, wknd*..........(33 to 1) 15
1216[6] MARKETING MAN 8-7 (7*) G Forster (2) *trkd ldr, reminder 6 fs out, wknd o'r 3 out, tld off*..........(33 to 1) 16
Dist: ½l, nk, 1½l, 5l, ¾l, nk, 2½l, nk, 3l, 3l. 2m 10.19s. a 7.99s (16 Ran).
SR: 5/4/3/-/-/-/ (K Abdulla), H R A Cecil

REDCAR (good to firm)
Friday June 18th

Going Correction: MINUS 0.20 sec. per fur. (races 1,3,5,7), MINUS 0.40 (2,4,6)

1832 Newton Claiming Stakes Class F (3-y-o and up) £2,243 1¼m..........(2:10)

1304[7] COMMON COUNCIL 4-8-11 (7*) J Marshall (5) *made most, quickened clr 3 fs out, ran on wl appr fnl furlong.*..........(8 to 1 op 11 to 2) 1
1392[5] EDGE OF DARKNESS 4-8-12 (3*) M Fenton (2) *hld up, hdwy 3 fs out, rdn 2 furlongs out, kpt on ins last.*..........(9 to 4 fav op 7 to 2 tchd 4 to 1) 2
KAGRAM QUEEN 5-9-5 G Carter (3) *al prmnt, effrt 2 fs out, sn rdn and kpt on one pace*..... (4 to 1 op 7 to 2) 3
1657[7] RAQS ASSAYF 3-8-4 A Culhane (4) *al prmnt, rdn 3 fs out, kpt on one pace fnl 2 furlongs*..........(20 to 1) 4
1271 WEAVER GEORGE (Ire) 3-7-13 (3*) S Maloney (10) *beh till styd on fnl 2 fs, nvr dngrs*..........(20 to 1) 5
1720[9] OPERATION WOLF 7-9-10 N Connorton (11) *in tch, hdwy 3 fs out, sn rdn and no imprsn*..........(8 to 1) 6
1438[8] SEA PADDY 5-8-13 (7*) H Bastiman (9) *slwly into strd and beh, hdwy o'r 2 fs out, not rch ldrs.* (16 to 1 op 12 to 1) 7
1464[7] GREY ANCONA (Ire) (v) 4-8-10 M Wood (1) *in tch, rdn 3 fs out and sn btn*..........(20 to 1 tchd 25 to 1) 8
1534[6] HASTA LA VISTA 3-8-8 T Lucas (6) *nvr rchd ldrs.*..........(16 to 1 tchd 20 to 1) 9
1676[6] GREAT ORATION (Ire) 4-9-2 A Clark (14) *slwly away, al beh*..........(25 to 1) 10
894[9] ROSE GLEN 7-8-11 A Tucker (7) *chsd ldrs, rdn 3 fs out, sn btn*..........(7 to 2 op 5 to 2) 11
1674 CYRILL HENRY (Ire) (v) 4-8-10 J Lowe (12) *in tch to hfwy, grad wknd*..........(33 to 1 op 25 to 1) 12
1161[5] INTO THE FUTURE 6-8-12 T Williams (13) *prmnt, rdn 4 fs out and sn wknd*..........(20 to 1) 13
1657[8] BROWNED OFF 4-9-6 P Robinson (8) *al beh, tld off fnl 3 fs.*..........(14 to 1 op 12 to 1) 14
Dist: 2l, ½l, 2½l, 3l, 1½l, 2l, 1½l, ¾l, 4l, ½l. 2m 5.50s. a 4.30s (14 Ran).
SR: 41/34/37/17/9/28/20/7/3/ (Mrs E E Newbould), M D Hammond

1833 NRS Handicap Class D (0-80 3-y-o) £3,494 7f..........(2:40)

1697[2] FIELD OF VISION (Ire) [60] 8-6 T Williams (5) *hld up in tch, gd hdwy o'r 2 fs out, led appr fnl furlong and sn clr.*..........(3 to 1 op 5 to 2) 1

1697* TAJDIF (USA) [73] 9-5 (5ex) S Whitworth (7) *trkd ldrs gng wl, effrt and not clr run one and a half fs out, squeezed through ins last and ran on, not rch wnr.* ....(2 to 1 fav op 9 to 4 tchd 5 to 2) 2
1330[6] BOLD THATCHER [70] 9-2 G Hind (9) *cl up, ev ch to fs out, sn rdn and not quicken appr fnl furlong.* ....(13 to 2 op 11 to 2) 3
1396[2] HEART BROKEN [67] 8-13 P Robinson (4) *trkd ldrs, effrt and ev ch 2 fs out, sn rdn and one pace appr fnl furlong*..........................(13 to 2 op 11 to 2) 4
1113 CHICKCHARNIE [75] 9-4 (3*) M Fenton (1) *led, rdn o'r 2 fs out, hdd and wknd over one furlong out.* ....(12 to 1 op 10 to 1) 5
MONTONE (Ire) [64] 8-10 A Culhane (3) *trkd ldrs, effrt o'r 2 fs out, sn rdn and wknd appr fnl furlong.* ....(11 to 1 op 8 to 1 tchd 12 to 1) 6
1633[4] BIRCHWOOD SUN [70] (bl) 9-2 J Lowe (2) *in tch, effrt and some hdwy 3 fs out, sn rdn and btn 2 furlongs out.* ....(13 to 2 op 11 to 2) 7
1760 MILBANK CHALLENGER [59] 8-2 (3*) S Maloney (8) *cl up till rdn and wknd o'r 2 fs out*..................(10 to 1) 8
1273 MASTER PECKITT [47] 7-7 S Wood (6) *al rear*.... (33 to 1) 9
Dist: 2½l, 1½l, 1½l, 2l, 2½l, hd, nk, 2l. 1m 23.40s. a 1.60s (9 Ran).
SR: 26/31/23/15/17/-/3/-/-/ (R W Huggins), M Johnston

1834 Brotton Seafoods Claiming Stakes Class E (4-y-o and up) £2,898 1¾m 19yds........................ (3:10)

1458[4] QUALITAIR RHYTHM (Ire) (v) 5-8-6 Dale Gibson (4) *trkd ldr, led 4 fs out, rdn o'r to furlongs out, ran on wl.* ....(Evens fav op 6 to 5 tchd 6 to 4) 1
1517[2] STINGRAY CITY (USA) (bl) 4-9-3 G Hind (2) *hld up, hdwy o'r 4 fs out, chsd wnr 3 furlongs out, sn rdn and one pace*..............................(9 to 4 op 7 to 4) 2
1438[3] WAJEEB (USA) 4-8-13 P Robinson (3) *led, rdn and hdd 4 fs out, sn wknd*.....................(11 to 4 op 5 to 2) 3
COSMIC RAY 8-9-7 J Lowe (1) *in tch till wknd quickly o'r 4 fs out, sn tld off*................ (20 to 1 op 16 to 1) 4
Dist: 1½l, 15l, 25l. 3m 6.50s. a 10.00s (4 Ran).
(R A Newson), I Campbell

1835 Suter Handicap Class C (0-90 3-y-o and up) £5,174 6f.............. (3:40)

1537[2] MACS MAHARANEE [60] 6-8-1 G Hind (7) *dwlt, swtchd to stands rls, gd hdwy hfwy, led one and a half fs out, rdn and ran on wl ins last.* ....(11 to 2 op 5 to 1 tchd 6 to 1 and 13 to 2) 1
1382[3] SEA DEVIL [77] 7-9-4 N Connorton (3) *beh, gd hdwy 2 fs out, rdn and styd on wl ins last*..............(12 to 1) 2
1436[8] STATE FLYER [58] (v) 5-7-6 (7*) G Forster (14) *outpcd and beh hfwy, rdn and styd on wl fnl 2 fs.* ....(16 to 1 tchd 20 to 1) 3
1584[4] PRESS GALLERY [87] 3-9-6 A Clark (4) *in tch, effrt and hdwy 2 fs out, sn ev ch till rdn and wknd entering last.* ....(6 to 1 op 4 to 1) 4
315 PETITE-D-ARGENT [87] 4-10-0 P Robinson (8) *trkd ldrs, effrt and hdwy 2 fs out, sn ev ch, rdn and wknd o'r one furlong out*.........(16 to 1 op 14 to 1 tchd 20 to 1) 5
1679[4] HEAVEN-LIEGH-GREY [68] 5-8-9 G Carter (5) *cl up on outer, ev ch 2 fs out, sn rdn and wknd appr fnl furlong.* ....(7 to 2 fav tchd 4 to 1) 6
FOOD OF LOVE [75] 5-9-2 S Whitworth (13) *led, rdn 2 fs out, sn hdd and wknd*.............................(20 to 1) 7+
EDUCATED PET [71] 4-8-12 T Williams (9) *cl up, rdn and ev ch o'r 2 fs out, sn btn*.............(20 to 1 op 16 to 1) 7+
1680 FINJAN [84] 6-9-8 (3*) S Maloney (11) *nvr rchd ldrs.* ....(14 to 1 tchd 12 to 1) 9
1589 ABSOLUTION [69] 9-8-10 J Lowe (1) *cl up on outer, rdn hfwy, sn wknd*....................(33 to 1 op 20 to 1) 10
1494[6] PENNY HASSET [70] 5-8-11 T Lucas (2) *prmnt to hfwy, sn wknd*..(10 to 1) 11
1668[2] METAL BOYS [78] 6-9-2 (3*) M Fenton (10) *in tch, effrt and hdwy o'r 2 fs out, sn rdn and btn*.... (7 to 1 op 6 to 1) 12
1494 FLASHY'S SON [63] 5-7-11 (7*) J Marshall (6) *cl up, rdn o'r 2 fs out and sn wknd*............... (14 to 1 op 16 to 1) 13
1494[3] BOURSIN (Ire) [63] 4-8-4 Dale Gibson (12) *chsd ldrs, effrt and rdn o'r 2 fs out, wknd quickly one and a half furlongs out*.......... (9 to 2 op 11 to 2 tchd 6 to 1) 14
Dist: ¾l, 3l, sht-hd, 2l, 1l, 1½l, dd-ht, ¾l, hd. ¾l. 1m 9.60s. b 0.10s (14 Ran).
SR: 41/55/24/44/44/21/22/18/28/ (John S Martin), P S Felgate

1836 Levy Board Handicap Class E (0-70 3-y-o) £3,106 1m 3f............. (4:10)

493[8] SILKY HEIGHTS (Ire) [56] 8-9 N Connorton (6) *in tch, hdwy 3 fs out, rdn and edgd lft appr fnl furlong, styd on to ld nr finish*..................(16 to 1 op 14 to 1) 1
1479* DUPLICATE [60] 8-10 (3*) S Maloney (5) *chsd ldrs, hdwy 3 fs out, led 2 furlongs out and sn rdn, hdd and no extr nr line*............................. (6 to 4 fav op 7 to 4) 2
WANZA [63] 9-2 E Johnson (4) *led and sn clr, rdn 3 fs out, hdd 2 furlongs out, wknd appr fnl furlong*.... (20 to 1) 3
1439[6] MERRY MERMAID [47] 8-0 Dale Gibson (2) *chsd ldrs, hdwy o'r 3 fs out and sn rdn, kpt on one pace*....... (10 to 1) 4

1161* YOUNG TESS [58] 8-8 (3*) M Fenton (8) *chsd ldrs, rdn 3 fs out, sn one pace*..... (100 to 30 op 7 to 2 tchd 3 to 1) 5
1223[5] MISSA BREVIS (USA) [61] 9-0 P Robinson (11) *hld up and beh, steady hdwy 3 fs out, rdn 2 furlongs out, not rch ldrs*............................ (8 to 1 tchd 10 to 1) 6
1170[5] NOMADIC FIRE [57] 8-10 S Whitworth (1) *in tch, effrt and some hdwy 4 fs out, sn rdn and wknd 3 furlongs out.* ....(8 to 1 op 7 to 1) 7
1161 DUKE OF DREAMS [55] 8-8 G Carter (10) *nvr rchd ldrs.* .... (12 to 1 op 10 to 1 tchd 14 to 1) 8
1422[2] RAGGERTY (Ire) [68] 9-0 (7*) G Parkin (9) *al rear.* ....(10 to 1 op 8 to 1) 9
1224[9] RICH ASSET (Ire) [47] (bl) 8-0 T Williams (3) *mid-div, hdwy to chase ldr hfwy, rdn and wknd 4 fs out.* ....(14 to 1 op 16 to 1 tchd 12 to 1) 10
1134[9] SOCIAL VISION (Ire) [43] (v) 7-10 J Lowe (7) *chsd ldr 4 fs, sn lost pl and behnd fnl four furlongs*...........(25 to 1) 11
Dist: Nk, 5l, hd, 2l, 2½l, 6l, 1l, 1l, 15l, hd. 2m 19.70s. a 4.30s (11 Ran).
SR: 30/33/26/9/16/14/-/-/5/ (Bernard Bloom), M J Camacho

1837 Ings Maiden Stakes Class D (2-y-o) £3,318 5f..................... (4:40)

TAKADOU (Ire) 9-0 P Robinson (7) *trkd ldrs, hdwy 2 fs out, quickened to ld ins fnl furlong and sn clr*..... (10 to 1) 1
1053[3] LUCIUS LOCKET (Ire) 9-0 G Carter (3) *cl up, led hfwy and sn rdn, edgd rght and hdd ins fnl furlong, not quicken.* ....(7 to 4 fav op 5 to 4) 2
1272[6] CHILIOLA 8-6 (3*) S Maloney (5) *hld up, hdwy hfwy, styd on fnl 2 fs, nrst finish*............ (6 to 1 op 4 to 1) 3
1523[4] JUST GREENWICH 8-4 (5*) N Gwilliams (1) *cl up, ev ch o'r 2 fs out, sn rdn and wknd appr fnl furlong.* ....(4 to 1 op 7 to 2) 4
LADY SHERIFF 8-9 T Lucas (8) *outpcd and beh till styd on fnl 2 fs*....................(14 to 1 op 10 to 1) 5
OAKLEY MANOR 8-9 T Williams (6) *chsd ldrs to hfwy, sn wknd*...........................(14 to 1 op 12 to 1) 6
DOCTOR JAMES (Ire) 9-0 J Lowe (4) *led to hfwy, sn rdn and wknd, eased fnl furlong.* ....(9 to 4 op 5 to 2 tchd 3 to 1 and 2 to 1) 7
1324 HOTCROFT 8-9 A Culhane (2) *cl up, rdn hfwy and sn wknd*..(8 to 1) 8
Dist: 3l, 1½l, ¾l, 1½l, ½l, 1l, 8l. 58.60s. a 1.90s (8 Ran).
SR: 22/10/-/-/-/ (F Tyldesley), Miss L C Siddall

1838 Grindale Rating Related Maiden Stakes Class E (3-y-o) £2,924 1m 3f ....(5:10)

1275[4] DARMSTADT (USA) 9-0 G Hind (4) *hld up, smooth hdwy 3 fs out, led on bit o'r one furlong out and sn clr, very easily.* (11 to 8 on op 6 to 4 on tchd 11 to 10 on and 6 to 5 on) 1
1255[2] HATTA RIVER (USA) (bl) 9-0 A Clark (1) *led, clr hfwy, rdn 3 fs out, hdd o'r one furlong out and no ch wth wnr.* ....(4 to 1 op 3 to 1) 2
1388[3] TWO LUMPS 9-0 S O'Gorman (3) *chsd ldr, rdn o'r 3 fs out and sn wknd*....................(9 to 2 op 7 to 2) 3
1384[6] BEST APPEARANCE (Ire) 8-11 (3*) S Maloney (5) *prmnt, rdn o'r 4 fs out and sn wknd.* ....(17 to 2 op 7 to 1 tchd 9 to 1) 4
1176 RISING WOLF (bl) 8-11 (3*) M Fenton (2) *chsd ldrs, rdn alng hfwy, wknd 4 fs out and sn beh*.... (10 to 1 op 8 to 1) 5
Dist: 6l, 12l, 4l, ½l. 2m 20.10s. a 4.70s (5 Ran).
SR: 31/19/ (Sheikh Mohammed), J H M Gosden

ASCOT (soft)
Saturday June 19th
Going Correction: PLUS 0.45 sec. per fur. (races 1,3,6), PLUS 0.35 (2,4,5,7)

1839 Ritz Club Fern Hill Rated Class A Handicap (Listed Race) (0-105 3-y-o) £12,467 1m................... (2:00)

1482* BARBOUKH [90] 8-13 Pat Eddery (5) *hld up in rear, hdwy on bit o'r one furlong out, led ins last, easily.* ....(8 to 1 op 10 to 1 tchd 7 to 1) 1
1524[2] FORTHWITH [90] 8-13 R Hills (1) *hdwy frm 2 fs out, ran on ins last, no ch wth wnr.* (7 to 2 op 4 to 1 tchd 3 to 1) 2
734[6] FABRIANA [90] 8-13 D Holland (4) *led aftr one furlong, hrd rdn frm 2 fs out, hdd jst last, not quicken.* ....(14 to 1 op 10 to 1) 3
1174[4] ANEESATI [94] 9-3 W R Swinburn (6) *al in tch, str chal frm o'r one furlong out till outpcd ins last.* .... (100 to 30 fav op 9 to 4 tchd 7 to 2) 4
1525 BOBBIE DEE [90] 8-13 J Williams (7) *sn prmnt, outpcd fnl 2 fs*...............(6 to 1 op 5 to 1 tchd 13 to 2) 5
1231[9] ZAJIRA (Ire) [90] 8-13 W Carson (3) *led one furlong, styd prmnt till wknd ins fnl 2 fs.* ....(9 to 1 op 8 to 1 tchd 10 to 1) 6
1128[6] ZENITH [98] 9-7 L Dettori (2) *chsd ldrs, rdn o'r 2 fs out, sn btn*..................(9 to 2 op 4 to 1 tchd 5 to 1) 7
Dist: 1½l, hd, ¾l, 1½l, 8l, 2l. 1m 47.50s. a 8.50s (7 Ran).
SR: 26/21/20/22/13/-/-/ (R J McCreery), D R C Elsworth

1840 Haagen Dazs Handicap Class D (0-80 3-y-o and up) £11,963 2m 45yds (2:30)

1586[4] PRIDE OF BRITAIN (Can) [53] 4-8-3 D Holland (1) *chsd ldrs, led 2 fs out, ran on wl.* ....(16 to 1 op 14 to 1 tchd 20 to 1) 1
1380[6] BRANDON PRINCE (Ire) [78] (bl) 5-10-0 L Dettori (7) *hdwy 4 fs out, styd on frm 2 furlongs out, no extr ins last.* ....(7 to 1 op 8 to 1 tchd 10 to 1 and 6 to 1) 2
1669[2] CHAMPAGNE GOLD [58] 6-8-8 J Williams (4) *beh till hdwy o'r 2 fs out, kpt on fnl furlong.* ....(9 to 1 op 8 to 1 tchd 10 to 1) 3
1676[2] SHUJAN (USA) [65] 4-9-1 R Hills (17) *led aftr one m, hdd 2 fs out, one pace*.................(14 to 1 tchd 16 to 1) 4
1688* GREEN LANE (USA) [66] 5-9-2 T Quinn (14) *mid-div, hdwy 5 fs out, no imprsn frm o'r 2 out.* ....(4 to 1 fav op 3 to 1 tchd 9 to 2) 5
559[3] HIERARCH (USA) [73] 4-9-6 (3*) D Harrison (12) *in tch, rdn 3 fs out, one pace*..............(14 to 1 op 12 to 1) 6
1586[5] ATLANTIC WAY [55] 5-8-5 M Roberts (2) *hdwy 4 fs out, drvn and effrt o'r 2 furlongs out, eased whn btn ins last*...................(11 to 1 op 8 to 1 tchd 12 to 1) 7
857[9] AUDE LA BELLE (Fr) [64] 5-9-0 Pat Eddery (11) *beh, effrt 3 fs out, sn no imprsn*..... (10 to 1 op 8 to 1 tchd 11 to 1) 8
1669[3] PROSEQUENDO (USA) [65] 6-8-8 (7*) D Wright (10) *nvr plcd to chal*..............(12 to 1 op 10 to 1 tchd 14 to 1) 9
1605[4] PEACH BRANDY [43] 4-7-7 N Adams (18) *prmnt till wknd 3 fs out*...........................(33 to 1 op 20 to 1) 10
1688[3] JADIDH [45] 5-7-9 G Bardwell (6) *beh fnl 5 fs.* ....(16 to 1 op 14 to 1) 11
1173[9] RAGAMUFFIN ROMEO [63] 4-8-13 Paul Eddery (9) *al beh.* ....(50 to 1 op 33 to 1) 12
1430 BELAFONTE [55] 6-8-5 A Tucker (5) *effrt hfwy, wknd 5 fs out*..............................(20 to 1 op 16 to 1) 13
1276[4] RIMOUSKI [43] 5-7-7 J Quinn (15) *beh most of way.* ....(50 to 1 tchd 66 to 1) 14
1607[2] TIGER SHOOT [56] 6-8-6 J Lowe (13) *chsd ldrs till wknd quickly 6 fs out*.............. (12 to 1 op 10 to 1) 15
1700* NORSTOCK [54] 6-8-4 R Price (3) *led aftr one furlong till hdd a m out, wknd quickly*...... (20 to 1 tchd 25 to 1) 16
1669[8] ELEGANT KING (Ire) [65] 4-9-1 S Whitworth (8) *led one furlong, beh frm hfwy*............(25 to 1 op 20 to 1) 17
1430 WHERE ARE WE [44] 7-7-8[4] (3*) B Doyle (16) *al beh.* ....(100 to 1) 18

Dist: 2½l, sht-hd, 1½l, 1½l, 2½l, 1½l, ½l, 15l, 1½l, 2½l. 3m 36.38s. a 11.38s (18 Ran).
SR: 32/54/33/38/37/41/21/29/15/ (Pride Of Britain Limited), L G Cottrell

1841 Grand Met Handicap Class B (0-105 3-y-o) £16,962 5f................ (3:00)

1057* LOCH PATRICK [80] 7-13 A McGlone (6) *slwly into strd and outpcd, hdwy and swtchd o'r one furlong out, str run ins to ld last strides*.... (15 to 2 op 6 to 1 tchd 8 to 1) 1
1449[6] LAUREL DELIGHT [84] 8-3 G Carter (3) *led, rdn fnl furlong, ct last strds*............(15 to 2 op 11 to 2 tchd 8 to 1) 2
1147* WALK THE BEAT [78] 7-11 A Tucker (2) *slwly into strd, sn reco'red, hdwy fnl furlong, kpt on cl hme.* ....(10 to 1 tchd 12 to 1) 3
1718 ANOTHER JADE [81] 7-7 (7*) D Wright (7) *hdwy o'r one furlong out, ran on*..... (5 to 1 op 7 to 1 tchd 9 to 1) 4
1337[6] SIMPLY SOOTY [80] 7-13 J Lowe (5) *outpcd, rdn 2 fs out, kpt on*.................... (11 to 2 op 5 to 1 tchd 9 to 2) 5
1258* PLAY HEVER GOLF [89] 8-8 D Holland (10) *chsd ldrs till wknd fnl furlong*..................(10 to 1 op 8 to 1) 6
1213* TRUE PRECISION [84] 8-3 L Charnock (8) *effrt to press ldrs 2 fs out, wknd o'r one furlong out.* ....(9 to 2 fav op 7 to 2) 7
1171[6] WHERE'S THE DANCE [75] 7-8[4] (3*) B Doyle (11) *al outpcd.* ....(25 to 1 tchd 33 to 1) 8
993[2] SABRE RATTLER [102] 9-7 Pat Eddery (4) *trkd ldrs till fdd o'r one furlong out*..... (9 to 1 op 8 to 1 tchd 10 to 1) 9
1760[2] PLUM FIRST [74] (bl) 7-7 N Adams (1) *early speed.* (16 to 1) 10
1449 ANSELLMAN [92] (bl) 8-11 J Reid (9) *effrt hfwy, sn btn.* ....(14 to 1 op 16 to 1 tchd 12 to 1) 11

Dist: Sht-hd, 1½l, 2½l, ¾l, ½l, ½l, 1l, ¾l, 2l, ¾l. 1m 3.91s. a 3.61s (11 Ran).
SR: 58/61/49/42/38/45/38/25/49/ (Miss E M L Coller), L J Holt

1842 Southern Comfort Maiden Stakes Class D (3-y-o) £10,416 1m..... (3:35)

459[4] WESTERN CAPE (USA) 9-0 Pat Eddery (2) *trkd ldrs, led one and a half fs out, readily.* ....(11 to 10 on op 6 to 4 on tchd Evens) 1
1311[3] TOCHAR BAN (USA) 8-9 W Carson (5) *ran on frm o'r 2 fs out, kpt on fnl furlong, no ch wth wnr.* ....(9 to 2 op 5 to 2 tchd 5 to 1) 2
1448 CANASKA STAR (bl) 9-0 A Munro (1) *chsd ldr till led 4 fs out, hdd and outpcd one and a half furlongs out.* ....(5 to 1 op 3 to 1 tchd 6 to 1) 3
352[6] RANI (Ire) 8-9 M Roberts (4) *broke wl, sn beh and nvr dngrs*..................(11 to 2 op 12 to 1 tchd 14 to 1) 4
1429[7] MIROSWAKI (USA) 9-0 D Holland (3) *sn led, hdd 4 fs out, wknd 3 furlongs out*..............(16 to 1 op 10 to 1) 5

Dist: 2½l, 1½l, 8l, ¾l. 1m 45.74s. a 6.24s (5 Ran).
SR: 48/35/35/6/9/ (K Abdulla), R Charlton

1843 Churchill Conditions Stakes Class B (3-y-o) £11,005 1½m............(4:10)

1364* WHITE MUZZLE 9-1 (4ex) J Reid (1) *broke wl sn clr, shaken up whn chlgd fnl furlong, kpt on well.* ....(4 to 1 on op 9 to 2 on tchd 7 to 2 on) 1
1364[5] RIGHT WIN (Ire) 9-3 T Quinn (2) *missed break and lost several ls strt, trkd wnr, hdwy 3 fs out, drvn and str chal fnl furlong, no extr.* ....(6 to 1 op 7 to 2 tchd 13 to 2) 2
SCOTTISH PEAK (Ire) 8-11 W R Swinburn (3) *missed break, al in 3rd, improved 6 fs out, rdn and btn ins fnl 3 furlongs*.......................... (8 to 1 op 10 to 1) 3

Dist: Nk, 8l. 2m 41.38s. a 13.18s (3 Ran).
SR: 11/12/-/ (Luciano Gaucci), P W Chapple-Hyam

1844 EBF Halifax Maiden Fillies Stakes Class D (2-y-o) £8,041 6f........(4:40)

1393[2] MARAGON 8-11 W Carson (4) *made virtually all, pushed alng and styd on ins last.* ....(100 to 30 op 7 to 2 tchd 5 to 1) 1
TAGHAREED (USA) 8-11 R Hills (1) *sn pressing wnr, ev ch frm o'r 2 fs out, shaken up fnl furlong, not quicken cl hme*.........(7 to 4 fav op 5 to 4 on tchd 15 to 8) 2
RED RITA (Ire) 8-11 A Munro (5) *chsd ldrs, drvn frm 2 fs out, kpt on wl fnl furlong.* ....(15 to 2 op 7 to 1 tchd 10 to 1) 3
1660[3] DOUCE MAISON (Ire) 8-11 S Whitworth (3) *in tch, pushed alng 2 and a half fs out, sn outpcd.* ....(8 to 1 op 10 to 1 tchd 12 to 1) 4
SCARLET DIVA 8-11 L Dettori (2) *slwly into strd, pushed alng o'r 2 fs out, sn btn.* (4 to 1 op 5 to 2 tchd 9 to 2) 5

Dist: ½l, nk, 6l, 2½l. 1m 19.95s. a 6.55s (5 Ran).
SR: 20/18/17/-/-/ (The Hon I V Matthews), R J R Williams

1845 Levy Board Rated Class B Handicap (0-105 4-y-o and up) £6,187 1¼m (5:10)

1346* ALDERBROOK [87] 4-8-8 Paul Eddery (1) *al chasing ldrs, led jst ins fnl 2 fs, idled in frnt and drvn final furlong, ran on wl*.......................... (11 to 4 op 7 to 4) 1
1663* RAMBO'S HALL [100] 8-9-7 W R Swinburn (6) *prmnt, outpcd 4 fs out, hdwy frm 2 furlongs out, styd on.* ....(9 to 2 op 4 to 1 tchd 7 to 2) 2
HIGHBROOK (USA) [86] 5-8-7 P Robinson (2) *led aftr one furlong, hdd jst ins fnl 2 fs, styd on same pace.* ....(16 to 1 op 14 to 1 tchd 20 to 1) 3
1450 RISK MASTER [93] 4-9-0 R Hills (5) *beh. hdwy o'r 2 fs out, styd on fnl furlong*.....(13 to 2 op 6 to 1 tchd 8 to 1) 4
1450[3] TALENT (USA) [86] (v) 5-8-7 A Munro (3) *led one furlong, rcd wide, still in tch, rdn and one pace frm o'r 2 fs out.* ....(6 to 1 op 10 to 1) 5
1021[4] ROCKAWHILE (Ire) [92] 4-8-13 Pat Eddery (4) *chsd ldrs, rdn 2 fs out, sn btn*..... (5 to 2 fav op 7 to 4 tchd 11 to 4) 6

Dist: 2l, nk, hd, sht-hd, 6l. 2m 12.17s. a 8.47s (6 Ran).
SR: 44/53/38/44/36/30/ (E Pick), Mrs J Cecil

AYR (good to soft)
Saturday June 19th
Going Correction: PLUS 0.65 sec. per fur.

1846 Belleisle Median Auction Maiden Stakes Class E (2-y-o) £2,549 6f (2:15)

1401[2] CELESTIAL RUMOUR (Ire) 9-0 K Darley (9) *prmnt, quickened to ld jst ins fnl furlong, ran on wl.* ....(6 to 4 on op Evens) 1
ANITA'S LOVE (Ire) 8-9 J Carroll (8) *in tch, styd on wl fnl 2 fs*..............................(8 to 1 op 6 to 1) 2
1536[2] ENCORE M'LADY (Ire) 8-9 S Perks (3) *led aftr one furlong till hdd jst ins fnl furlong, sn btn*.... (5 to 1 op 7 to 2) 3
1632[5] NO MEAN CITY (Ire) 9-0 A Mackay (7) *led one furlong, prmnt till wknd 2 out*....(6 to 1 op 4 to 1 tchd 7 to 1) 4
1497[9] FEARLESS WONDER 8-9 (5*) Darren Moffatt (10) *nvr trble ldrs*...................(16 to 1 op 12 to 1 tchd 20 to 1) 5
ALL IN THE MIND 9-0 T Williams (4) *beh, some late hdwy, nvr dngrs*..........................(40 to 1 op 16 to 1) 6
THUNDERBIRD TWO (Ire) 8-7 (7*) C Teague (11) *nvr dngrs.* ....(50 to 1 op 25 to 1) 7
CHANTRY BEATH 9-0 D Nicholls (1) *al beh.* ....(40 to 1 op 25 to 1) 8
FOUR OF SPADES 8-11 (3*) S D Williams (6) *sn beh.* ....(25 to 1 op 16 to 1) 9
STRATHTORE DREAM (Ire) 8-9 B Raymond (12) *chsd ldrs to hfwy, sn beh*..............(50 to 1 op 25 to 1) 10
MISS PIGALLE 8-9 G Duffield (5) *cl up till wknd quickly o'r 2 fs out*..........(16 to 1 op 12 to 1 tchd 25 to 1) 11

Dist: 3½l, hd, 6l, 3l, 1l, 1l, nk, 1l, hd, 3l. 1m 18.22s. a 7.32s (11 Ran).
SR: 32/13/12/-/-/-/ (P D Savill), M H Easterby

1847 Doonfoot Limited Stakes Class F (3-y-o and up) £2,623 1m 7f........(2:45)

1283* FUNNY CHOICE (Ire) 3-8-3³ (3*) S D Williams (6) *in tch, hdwy 5 fs out, led o'r 2 out, hld on wl und pres.* ....(5 to 1 op 4 to 1) 1
1681⁵ LEGION OF HONOUR 5-9-5 (7*) V Halliday (2) *trkd ldrs, effrt 3 fs out, rdn 2 out, styd on wl und pres.* ....(11 to 2 op 9 to 2) 2
1531⁷ PURITAN (Can) 4-9-12 G Duffield (3) *trkd ldr, led o'r 3 fs out, hdd over 2 out, wknd over one out*... (3 to 1 jt-fav) 3
453⁸ BRIDGE PLAYER 6-9-2 (5*) Darren Moffatt (8) *slwly into strd, hld up, gd hdwy 4 fs out, chlgd o'r 2 out, sn rdn and wknd*........................(16 to 1 op 20 to 1) 4
1601² MENTALASANYTHIN 4-9-12 A Mackay (4) *led till hdd o'r 3 fs out, sn wknd*.....................(4 to 1 op 7 to 2) 5
TRONCHETTO (Ire) 4-9-12 B Raymond (7) *beh, some hdwy 5 fs out, wknd 4 out.* (10 to 1 op 12 to 1 tchd 16 to 1) 6
427⁶ MYSTIC MEMORY 4-9-7 K Darley (5) *beh, effrt 4 fs out, sn wknd*....................(3 to 1 jt-fav tchd 100 to 30) 7
1601³ MINGUS (USA) 6-9-12 D Nicholls (9) *prmnt till wknd o'r 3 fs out*.............................(33 to 1 op 25 to 1) 8
Dist: ½l, 4l, ½l, 20l, sht-hd, 8l, 3l. 3m 31.86s. (8 Ran).
SR: -/14/10/4/-/ (Lt-Col W L Monteith), P Monteith

1848 High Speed Production Sprint Handicap Class D (0-80 3-y-o) £3,095 5f ....(3:15)

1740⁴ PRINCIPAL PLAYER (USA) [54] (bl) 7-11 F Norton (3) *cl up, rdn and slightly outpcd hfwy, kpt on wl und pres to ld ins fnl furlong*.......(12 to 1 op 10 to 1 tchd 14 to 1) 1
1518* SHADOW JURY [75] 9-4 K Darley (5) *made most till hdd and no extr ins fnl furlong.* ....(13 to 8 on op 5 to 4 on tchd 11 to 10 on) 2
899⁹ SCORED AGAIN [55] 7-12 A Mackay (2) *hld up in tch, pld hrd, hdwy hfwy, ev ch o'r one furlong out, sn rdn and one pace*.............................(16 to 1 op 10 to 1) 3
1633⁵ TWO MOVES IN FRONT (Ire) [78] 9-7 J Carroll (4) *cl up till wknd 2 fs out*........... (2 to 1 op 6 to 4 tchd 9 to 4) 4
1518⁴ SELVOLE [50] 7-2 (5*) Darren Moffatt (1) *prmnt, rdn hfwy, sn btn*..............................(66 to 1 op 50 to 1) 5
Dist: 1½l, 1l, 3l, 3½l. 1m 3.94s. a 5.84s (5 Ran).
SR: 31/46/22/33/-/ (Mrs Jean Neilson), P Monteith

1849 Williams De Broe Handicap Class E (0-70 3-y-o and up) £2,941 7f.... (3:45)

1282⁸ YOUNG VALENTINE [49] 4-8-13 B Raymond (8) *hld up, gd hdwy o'r one furlong out, led ins fnl furlong, ran on wl*...............................(20 to 1 op 14 to 1) 1
1325⁵ SIR ARTHUR HOBBS [54] 6-9-1 (3*) N Kennedy (6) *chsd ldrs, led one furlong out, hdd and no extr ins fnl furlong.* ....(5 to 1 op 4 to 1) 2
1811* LOMBARD SHIPS [53] (bl) 6-8-10 (7*,7ex) W Hawksley (7) *hld up, steady hdwy 3 fs out, ev ch one out, no extr ins fnl furlong*.............(7 to 4 fav op 6 to 4 tchd 15 to 8) 3
1194⁷ ROYAL COMEDIAN [40] 4-8-4 F Norton (3) *prmnt, rdn o'r 2 fs out, kpt on fnl furlong*........(10 to 1 tchd 12 to 1) 4
4744a⁸ CRESELLY [55] 6-9-5 K Darley (1) *led till hdd one furlong out, fdd*...........................(8 to 1 tchd 10 to 1) 5
1540⁴ ASHGORE [65] 3-9-6 T Williams (5) *chsd ldrs till wknd 2 fs out, tld off*...........................(7 to 2 op 3 to 1) 6
1799⁷ ALWAYS RISKY [54] 3-8-9 J Carroll (4) *in tch till wknd 2 fs out, tld off*........(11 to 1 op 10 to 1 tchd 12 to 1) 7
Dist: 1½l, sht-hd, hd, 1l, 20l, 1l. 1m 34.25s. a 10.25s (7 Ran).
SR: 14/14/5/-/10/-/-/ (The PBT Group), R M Whitaker

1850 Roman Warrior Shield Maiden Class D (3-y-o and up) £3,348 7f.......(4:15)

1285⁶ HUNTERS OF BRORA (Ire) 3-8-7 J Carroll (3) *in tch, hdwy o'r one furlong out, styd on wl to ld cl hme.* ....(14 to 1 op 10 to 1 tchd 16 to 1) 1
1616² DESERT VENUS 3-8-7 B Raymond (6) *hld up, steady hdwy o'r 2 fs out, led jst ins fnl furlong, hdd and no extr cl hme.* (7 to 4 on op 2 to 1 on tchd 13 to 8 on and 6 to 4 on) 2
1136³ NICHODOULA 3-8-7 G Duffield (1) *hld up, effrt whn not much room and swtchd 2 fs out, kpt on fnl furlong, not trble ldrs*...............(5 to 2 op 3 to 1 tchd 9 to 4) 3
MILLEMAY 3-8-7 A Mackay (7) *chsd ldrs, ev ch 2 fs out, kpt on same pace*.....................(66 to 1 op 33 to 1) 4
GRUMPY'S GRAIN (Ire) 3-8-12 K Darley (5) *beh till ran on wl fnl furlong, nrst finish*........(14 to 1 op 10 to 1) 5
1178⁹ MAJOR JACK 3-8-9 (3*) S D Williams (2) *trkd ldr, led wl o'r 2 fs out till hdd and wknd quickly jst ins fnl furlong.* ....(66 to 1 op 33 to 1) 6
MIDDLEHAM CASTLE 4-9-7 T Williams (4) *led till hdd wl o'r 2 fs out, wknd over one out.* ....(40 to 1 op 16 to 1 tchd 50 to 1) 7
Dist: Nk, 4l, 1½l, ½l, 1½l, 3½l. 1m 34.42s. a 10.42s (7 Ran).
SR: 5/4/-/-/ (Robert Gibbons), J D Bethell

1851 Longhill Maiden Fillies Stakes Class D (3-y-o) £3,231 1m...............(4:45)

1482⁴ ABBRAAK (USA) 8-11 B Raymond (4) *hld up in tch, steady hdwy to ld one furlong out, ran on strly.* ....(7 to 4 tchd 9 to 4) 1
1285⁴ BILOELA 8-11 K Darley (5) *trkd ldrs, led 3 fs out, hdd one out, sn btn*.........(5 to 4 fav op 6 to 4 tchd 7 to 4) 2
1595⁴ AZOLA (Ire) 8-11 F Norton (1) *in tch, pushed alng hfwy, effrt whn crrd rght o'r 2 fs out, kpt on same pace.* ....(7 to 2 op 3 to 1) 3
1463⁸ GROGFRYN 8-8 (3*) S D Williams (6) *led till hdd 3 fs out, swtchd rght and sn wknd*........(16 to 1 op 10 to 1) 4
1285⁷ SUSPECT 8-11 A Mackay (3) *chsd ldrs, rdn 3 fs out, sn wknd*...........................(20 to 1 tchd 33 to 1) 5
KEEN AND CLEAN (Ire) 8-6 (5*) Darren Moffatt (2) *dwlt, in tch till outpcd o'r 2 fs out*..........(33 to 1 op 25 to 1) 6
Dist: 5l, ¾l, 12l, 3½l, 3½l. 1m 46.12s. a 8.42s (6 Ran).
SR: 49/34/32/ (Nasser Abdullah), B Hanbury

1852 Snodgrass Apprentice Handicap Class G (0-70 3-y-o) £2,346 1m..(5:15)

1181³ GOLD DESIRE [39] 7-8¹ J Marshall (10) *prmnt, led o'r 2 fs out, ran on wl*...................(5 to 1 tchd 11 to 2) 1
963⁸ FORT VALLY [59] (bl) 8-11 (3*) G Parkin (3) *in tch, hdwy und pres 2 fs out, chalg whn hng lft o'r one out, kpt on towards finish*...................(16 to 1 op 14 to 1) 2
1178⁶ I REMEMBER YOU (Ire) [66] 9-7 H Bastiman (9) *cl up, chlgd 2 fs out, ev ch till no extr entering fnl furlong.* (12 to 1) 3
1600⁸ RUNRIG (Ire) [48] 8-0 (3*) R Havlin (5) *chsd ldrs till wknd 2 fs out*.................(9 to 2 op 4 to 1 tchd 5 to 1) 4
1417⁹ WONDERFUL YEARS (USA) [50] 8-5 V Halliday (7) *hld up, rdn 3 fs out, styd on same pace.* (7 to 2 fav tchd 9 to 2) 5
1424⁴ VIKING WATERS [52] 8-2 (5*) J Dennis (2) *in tch, effrt o'r 2 fs out, one pace*........(6 to 1 op 7 to 1 tchd 11 to 2) 6
1271⁷ MR ABBOT [44] 7-6 (7*) W Hawksley (8) *nvr dngrs.* ....(14 to 1 op 12 to 1) 7
1630⁷ SEVERE STORM [40] 7-4 (5*) C Teague (11) *chsd ldrs till wknd o'r 2 fs out*..............................(50 to 1) 8
883 ALBEIT [40] 7-6 (3*) Claire Balding (1) *led till hdd and wknd o'r 2 fs out*..................(6 to 1 tchd 7 to 1) 9
1419⁵ LETTERMORE [38] 7-2 (5*) M Baird (4) *beh, some hdwy 4 out, wknd o'r 2 out*......(6 to 1 op 9 to 2 tchd 7 to 1) 10
1160⁸ HIGH ROMANCE [51] 8-1 (5*) S Copp (6) *al beh.* ....(14 to 1 op 10 to 1) 11
Dist: 2l, nk, 5l, 2l, 2½l, 3½l, 1l, 4l, 2½l, sht-hd. 1m 48.19s. a 10.49s (11 Ran).
SR: 1/15/21/-/-/-/ (Mel Brittain), M Brittain

GOWRAN PARK (IRE) (good to yielding) Saturday June 19th

1853 Coolmore Race (3-y-o) £3,450 1m ....(2:30)

1512⁵ ARABIC TREASURE (USA) 9-2 M J Kinane (3) (10 to 9 on) 1
940⁴ KARINIYD (Ire) 9-0 J P Murtagh (2)...............(7 to 4) 2
787⁵ RELENTLESS BOY (Ire) 8-12 S Craine (4).........(20 to 1) 3
1575⁵ ST MARTHA (Ire) 8-9 C Roche (1).................(5 to 1) 4
Dist: ½l, 1l, 20l. 1m 48.30s. (4 Ran).
(Raymond J Rooney), D K Weld

1854 Ballyshaun (E.B.F.) Fillies Maiden (2-y-o) £3,795 6f.................. (3:00)

MEMORIES (Ire) 9-0 N G McCullagh (7).......... (10 to 1) 1
AL NAAYY 9-0 W J Supple (5)................(2 to 1 fav) 2
1442³ LUDDEN LADY (Ire) 8-8 (6*) J J Behan (11).........(7 to 1) 3
CONFIDENCE BOOST (USA) 9-0 M J Kinane (10) (15 to 2) 4
1567⁴ SUSIE SUNSHINE (Ire) 9-0 J P Murtagh (1)........ (6 to 1) 5
1571⁶ VALID VICTRESS (Ire) 9-0 R Hughes (8)............ (12 to 1) 6
BACK FROM HEAVEN (Ire) 9-0 K J Manning (4)... (12 to 1) 7
1332⁸ BENAZIR LADY (Ire) 8-8 (6*) J A Heffernan (2).....(20 to 1) 8
1571⁵ AVONDALE FOREST (Ire) 9-0 S Craine (6)........... (6 to 1) 9
NANCYS WOOD (Ire) 8-10 (4*) P Carberry (3)..... (33 to 1) 10
PASTELLE 9-0 P Shanahan (9)..................(20 to 1) 11
Dist: Sht-hd, 5l, hd, nk. 1m 17.50s. (11 Ran).
(J Turley), J G Burns

1855 Kilkenny City Vintners (E.B.F.) Maiden (3-y-o and up) £3,795 7f.........(3:30)

1443² DAFTARI (Ire) (bl) 3-9-0 J P Murtagh (3)......(11 to 10 fav) 1
STRATEGIC TIMING (Ire) 3-8-11 M J Kinane (10)... (6 to 1) 2
666⁵ ELIZABETH'S PET (Ire) 3-8-11 R Hughes (5)....... (3 to 1) 3
MY KERRY DANCER (USA) 3-9-0 S Craine (4).... (14 to 1) 4
1443⁸ WHAT A PLEASURE (Ire) 3-9-0 W J Supple (8).... (10 to 1) 5
1445³ JUNORIUS (Ire) 4-9-9 P Shanahan (9)...........(10 to 1) 6
OCEAN BLUE (Ire) 3-8-11 D Manning (6)........... (10 to 1) 7
1573⁸ ARROGANT LADY 3-8-11 P V Gilson (2)......... (16 to 1) 8
1568⁷ GEALLAINNBAN (Ire) 3-9-0 E A Leonard (1).......(50 to 1) 9
MADAME MINISTER (USA) 3-8-11 W J O'Connor (7) ....(10 to 1) su
Dist: 1l, 2½l, 6l, ¾l. 1m 38.40s. (10 Ran).
(H H Aga Khan), John M Oxx

1856 Morris Oil Premium Petrol Handicap (3-y-o and up) £3,450 1m....... (4:30)

1569* WANDERING THOUGHTS (Ire) [-] 4-7-12 (2*,7ex) D G O'Shea (6)......................................(2 to 1 fav) 1
1569² THATCHING CRAFT (Ire) [-] 4-9-2 W J Supple (4)..(10 to 1) 2

1549[4] MISS MISTLETOES (Ire) [-] 3-8-9 S Craine (7) . . . . . (10 to 1) 3
1513* NUNIVAK (USA) [-] 5-8-5 (6*,4ex) R V Skelly (1) . . . . . (8 to 1) 4
1611* SEEK THE FAITH (USA) [-] (bl) 4-9-6 (5ex) M J Kinane (9) . . . . . (9 to 4) 5
1644[2] DESERT CALM (Ire) [-] 4-9-1 (6*) B J Walsh (3) . . . . (10 to 1) 6
1164[5] MUSWELL BROOK (Ire) [-] 3-7-5 (8*) B A Hunter (8) (20 to 1) 7
1645[4] BASIE NOBLE [-] (bl) 4-8-13 N G McCullagh (2) . . . (10 to 1) 8
4685a MAID OF VISION (Ire) [-] 4-9-3 J P Murtagh (5) . . . . (14 to 1) 9
Dist: Nk, 2l, 7l, 6l. 1m 47.70s. (9 Ran).
(W Mythen), A P O'Brien

LINGFIELD (good to soft)
Saturday June 19th
Going Correction: PLUS 0.05 sec. per fur.

1857 Springfield Maiden Auction Stakes Class D (2-y-o) £3,406 5f. . . . . (6:55)

CHAMPAGNE GIRL 8-9 T Sprake (11) *led aftr 2 fs, pushed clr fnl furlong, readily.* . . . . (8 to 1 op 6 to 1) 1
RED CLOUD (Ire) 8-9 P Robinson (5) *slwly away, bustled alng hfwy, gd hdwy wl o'r one furlong out, ran on, improve.* . . . . (12 to 1 op 6 to 1) 2
1602[2] SOLO TICKET 9-0 J Reid (3) *led 2 fs, styd hndy and ev ch o'r one furlong out, no extr ins last.* . . . . (11 to 10 on tchd Evens and 5 to 4 on) 3
ROCKETEER (Ire) 8-7 (7*) Kim McDonnell (6) *chsd ldrs, rdn 2 fs out, styd on wl ins last.* . . . . (20 to 1 op 12 to 1) 4
EWAR EMPRESS (Ire) 8-6 (3*) B Doyle (9) *beh and sn rdn alng, ran green and wndrd wl o'r one furlong out, kpt on ins last, nvr nrr.* . . . . (17 to 2 op 6 to 1 tchd 9 to 1 and 10 to 1) 5
454 BLURRED IMAGE (Ire) 9-0 L Dettori (2) *prmnt till rdn and wknd fnl furlong.* . . . . (8 to 1 op 10 to 1 tchd 12 to 1) 6
DRAGON BOLD (Ire) 9-0 C Avery (8) *sn rdn alng, nvr able to chal.* . . . . (25 to 1 op 12 to 1) 7
1403 ANSELLADY 8-9 W Carson (7) *prmnt till rdn 2 fs out, sn btn.* . . . . (15 to 2 op 7 to 1 tchd 10 to 1) 8
1602[9] SWEET CAROLINE 8-2 (7*) G Forster (4) *speed to hfwy.* . . . . (20 to 1 op 16 to 1 tchd 25 to 1) 9
1241[7] CHARISMA GIRL 8-9 T Quinn (1) *speed on outsd till wknd 2 fs out.* . . . . . . (25 to 1 op 14 to 1 tchd 33 to 1) 10
ANOTHER DREAM (Ire) 9-0 B Rouse (10) *slwly away, outpcd.* . . . . . . (25 to 1 op 14 to 1 tchd 33 to 1) 11
Dist: 2l, 1l, nk, hd, hd, 2l, sht-hd, 2l, 5l, 12l. 1m 1.52s. a 4.62s (11 Ran).
SR: 8/-/1/-/-/-/ (Mrs P J Makin), P J Makin

1858 IPC Weeklies Group Handicap Class E (0-70 3-y-o and up) £2,780 1¼m (7:25)

1309[2] PRESTON GUILD (Ire) [53] 3-7-13 D Biggs (1) *al hndy, led wl o'r 2 fs out, clr fnl furlong, easily.* . . . . (7 to 2 op 3 to 1 tchd 4 to 1) 1
1409* MR TATE (Ire) [60] 4-9-4 T Quinn (8) *nvr far away, prmsg chal o'r 2 fs out, no extr appr last.* . . . . (5 to 4 on op 11 to 8 tchd 6 to 4) 2
1663[5] VANBOROUGH LAD [57] 4-9-1 J Reid (3) *chsd ldrs, came wide and ev ch o'r 2 fs out, kpt on ins last.* . . . . (15 to 2 op 8 to 1 tchd 11 to 2 and 8 to 1) 3
1389* ROCK THE BARNEY (Ire) [53] 4-8-11 B Rouse (4) *hld up in tch, hdwy on ins 3 fs out, ran on same pace.* . . . . (9 to 1 op 7 to 1 tchd 10 to 1 and 11 to 1) 4
GO FORUM [40] 8-7-12 S O'Gorman (7) *hld up and wl beh till rdn and some hdwy fnl 2 and a half fs, not a dngr.* . . . . (66 to 1 op 20 to 1 tchd 100 to 1) 5
1274 IKHTIRAA (USA) [55] 3-8-1 W Carson (5) *bustled alng to ld till hdd wl o'r 2 fs out, sn wknd.* . . . . (15 to 2 op 7 to 1 tchd 6 to 1 and 8 to 1) 6
1282[7] SCORCHER (Ire) [50] 3-7-8[1] (3*) B Doyle (2) *chsd ldr till wknd 3 fs out.* . . . . . . (50 to 1 op 20 to 1 tchd 100 to 1) 7
Dist: 3l, ½l, 5l, 4l, 4l. 2m 12.59s. a 7.59s (7 Ran).
SR: 14/27/23/9/ (Lady Matthews), R J R Williams

1859 Saffron Limited Stakes Class D (0-75 3-y-o) £3,465 7f. . . . . (8:25)

1697[3] PRAIRIE GROVE 9-0 W Carson (6) *chsd ldr, niggled alng hfwy, str run to ld ins last, cmftbly.* . . . . (5 to 2 fav op 4 to 1) 1
1455[4] SECOND CHANCE (Ire) 9-0 L Dettori (1) *al hndy, rdn 2 fs out, kpt on ins last.* . . . . (5 to 1 op 6 to 1) 2
1455[2] MISS GORGEOUS (Ire) 8-6 (3*) Emma O'Gorman (5) *led till wknd and hdd ins fnl furlong.* . . . . (11 to 4 op 5 to 2 tchd 3 to 1) 3
1408[3] FINAL FRONTIER (Ire) 9-0 T Quinn (4) *chsd ldrs, rdn o'r 2 fs out, not quicken.* . . . . . . (11 to 4 op 6 to 4 tchd 3 to 1) 4
1588 SIR THOMAS BEECHAM 9-0 B Rouse (2) *took keen hold, in tch till wknd 2 fs out.* . . . . (33 to 1 op 25 to 1 tchd 50 to 1 and 66 to 1) 5
1408[7] WALNUT BURL (Ire) 9-0 J Reid (3) *hld up, some hdwy o'r 2 fs out, sn btn.* . . . . (13 to 2 op 6 to 1 tchd 7 to 1) 6
1496[9] LANZAMAR 8-2 (7*) C Hawksley (7) *missed break, al beh.* . . . . (66 to 1 op 50 to 1 tchd 100 to 1) 7
Dist: 1l, ½l, 5l, 2l, 2l, 12l. 1m 25.65s. a 4.95s (7 Ran).
SR: 31/28/21/11/5/-/-/ (Giles Gleadell), R Hannon

1860 Summer Handicap Class D (3-y-o and up) £4,045 5f. . . . . (8:55)

1560[3] MISS VAXETTE [76] 4-9-5 (7*) M Humphries (8) *chsd ldrs, str run to ld o'r one furlong out, sn clr.* (4 to 1 tchd 7 to 2) 1
1560[4] PEERAGE PRINCE [66] (bl) 4-8-9 (7*) G Forster (6) *al hndy, ev ch o'r one furlong out, unbl to quicken.* . . . . (9 to 1 op 8 to 1 tchd 10 to 1) 2
1473* BORN TO BE [76] 4-9-12 T Quinn (3) *prmnt till rdn and no extr o'r one furlong out.* . . . . (13 to 2 op 9 to 2 tchd 7 to 1) 3
1492 SHADES OF JADE [48] 5-7-12 S O'Gorman (5) *beh till styd on fnl one and a half fs, nvr nrr.* . . . . (12 to 1) 4
1492* LITTLE SABOTEUR [69] 4-9-5 T Sprake (1) *in tch on outsd, effrt 2 fs out, sn btn.* . . . . (4 to 1 op 7 to 2) 5
DREAM OF TOMORROW [56] 5-8-6[1] B Rouse (4) *nvr able to chal.* . . . . (16 to 1 op 12 to 1) 6
1714[2] PURBECK CENTENARY [62] 3-8-5 Paul Eddery (7) *led till hdd o'r one furlong out, wknd quickly.* . . . . (5 to 2 fav op 3 to 1) 7
SEAMERE [72] 10-9-3 (5*) A Procter (2) *prmnt till wknd wl o'r one furlong out.* . . (20 to 1 op 16 to 1 tchd 25 to 1) 8
Dist: 2l, 5l, 1½l, 2½l, nk, nk, 6l. 59.94s. a 3.04s (8 Ran).
SR: 56/38/28/-/5/ (Vax Appliances Ltd), J L Spearing

LINGFIELD (A.W) (std)
Saturday June 19th
Going Correction: MINUS 0.45 sec. per fur.

1861 Choicest Maiden Handicap Class G Amateur Riders (0-70 3-y-o and up) £2,574 1¼m. . . . . (6:25)

1642[4] HILLSDOWN BOY (Ire) [49] 3-10-7 (5*) Mr T Cuff (7) *nvr far away, rdn alng wl o'r 2 fs out, str run fnl furlong to ld nr finish.* . . . . (20 to 1 op 16 to 1) 1
724 JULIASDARKINVADER [45] 3-10-3 (5*) Mr K Goble (14) *al hndy, led wl o'r 2 fs out, ct nr finish.* . . . . (12 to 1 tchd 14 to 1 and 16 to 1) 2
1340[5] BILJAN (USA) [65] 3-11-9 (5*) Miss M Clark (3) *led till hdd wl o'r 2 fs out, sn rdn and unbl to quicken.* . . . . (8 to 1 op 7 to 1 tchd 9 to 1) 3
1351[4] STALLED (Ire) [62] 3-11-11 Mr P Macewan (4) *chsd ldg bunch, hdwy on ins 2 fs out, no extr fnl furlong.* . . . . (9 to 2 jt-fav op 6 to 1) 4
1417[5] LEGAL ARTIST (Ire) [48] 3-10-11 Mrs L Pearce (8) *chsd ldrs till not much room and wknd o'r 2 fs out.* . . . . (6 to 1 op 5 to 1 tchd 13 to 2) 5
279[7] SINGING DETECTIVE [25] (v) 6-9-9 (5*) Miss Elaine Mills (5) *chsd ldg bunch till wknd 4 fs out.* . . . . (33 to 1 op 25 to 1 tchd 50 to 1) 6
1488[8] CHILTERN HUNDREDS (USA) [52] 3-10-10 (5*) Mrs J Musson (9) *beh till moderate hdwy fnl 2 and a half fs, nvr nrr.* . . . . (20 to 1 op 16 to 1) 7
420 DECIDING BID [20] 7-9-4 (5*) Miss D Pomeroy (6) *nvr able to chal.* . . . . (33 to 1) 8
1745[3] WOLF POWER (Ire) [57] 3-11-6 Mrs M Cowdrey (13) *missed break, wl beh till steady hdwy frm hfwy, wknd fnl 2 fs.* . . . . (5 to 1 op 4 to 1 tchd 6 to 1) 9
1690[9] M'BEBE [45] 3-10-8 Miss E Johnson Houghton (2) *hld up in midfield, rdn o'r 3 fs out, no imprsn.* . . . . (10 to 1 op 8 to 1 tchd 11 to 1) 10
1237 LOBELIA (Ire) [42] 3-10-0 (5*) Mrs J Naughton (1) *al rear div.* . . . . (33 to 1) 11
1353[4] WRITTEN AGREEMENT [28] 5-9-12 (5*) Mrs C Peacock (11) *al beh.* . . . . (16 to 1 op 14 to 1) 12
LADY POLY [33] 5-10-3 (5*) Miss S Watkins (12) *al beh.* . . . . (50 to 1 tchd 66 to 1) 13
1612[2] SHORT ENCOUNTER [43] 6-10-13 (5*) Miss T Bracegirdle (10) *beh thrght and pld up o'r one furlong out, lme.* . . . . (9 to 2 jt-fav op 7 to 2) pu
Dist: ½l, 1½l, 1l, 8l, ¾l, 2½l, sht-hd, 1½l, 2l, 2l. 2m 8.85s. a 5.65s (14 Ran).
SR: 24/19/36/31/1/-/ (Mrs S R Crowe), S Dow

1862 Knightway Promotions Handicap Class D (0-80 3-y-o and up) £3,084 1 ½m. . . . . (7:55)

1605 FACT OR FICTION [50] (bl) 7-9-6 A Clark (2) *wth ldr, led o'r 2 fs out, sn clr, hld on gmely ins last.* . . . . (25 to 1 op 14 to 1) 1
1731[3] NASEER (USA) [45] 4-9-1 J Reid (5) *chsd ldg pair, rdn o'r 2 fs out, styd on wl ins last.* . . . . (4 to 1 op 7 to 2 tchd 9 to 2) 2
1699* ONE OFF THE RAIL (USA) [73] 3-10-0 B Rouse (6) *led till rdn and hdd o'r 2 fs out, sn no extr.* . . . . (9 to 4 jt-fav op 7 to 4 tchd 5 to 2) 3
1699[2] DAY OF HISTORY (Ire) [45] 4-9-1 D Biggs (4) *in tch till rdn alng and lost pl o'r 4 fs out, no further dngr.* (9 to 4 jt-fav op 5 to 2 tchd 2 to 1) 4
1699[4] MY SPARKLING RING [24] 7-7-8[4] (3*) B Doyle (3) *al beh.* . . . . (25 to 1 op 14 to 1) 5
1129[6] NATIVE CHIEFTAN [58] (e/s) 4-10-0 T Quinn (1) *al beh.* . . . . (7 to 2 op 5 to 1 tchd 6 to 1) 6

Dist: ½l, 10l, 8l, 1½l, sht-hd. 2m 33.00s. a 3.70s (6 Ran).
SR: 15/9/2/ (Miss Brooke Sanders), Miss B Sanders

REDCAR (firm)
Saturday June 19th
Going Correction: MINUS 0.30 sec. per fur. (races 1,2,3,5,6,7), MINUS 0.55 (4)

1863 Liverton Selling Stakes Class G (2-y-o) £2,070 7f.................. (1:45)

OOH AH CANTONA 8-11 A Culhane (16) *chsd ldrs, hdwy to ld o'r one furlong out, hng lft and pushed out ins last.* ....(12 to 1 op 8 to 1 tchd 14 to 1) 1
1590⁴ PASSION SUNDAY 8-11 M Birch (15) *al frnt rnk, chlgd 2 fs out, rdn and kpt on ins last.* ....(6 to 4 on op Evens tchd 5 to 4) 2
GREEK NIGHT OUT (Ire) 8-6 Dean McKeown (13) *nvr far away, rdn and edgd lft appr fnl furlong, kpt on same pace*.............................. (8 to 1 op 6 to 1) 3
1598⁴ WILLWIN 8-6 J Fortune (14) *al hndy, led o'r 2 fs out till over one out, one pace ins last*......(7 to 1 op 6 to 1) 4
1135 ZIGGYS BOY 8-11 G Hind (6) *slwly into strd, beh and sn pushed alng, hdwy o'r one furlong out, ran on, nvr nrr*............................ (16 to 1 op 12 to 1) 5
1759 WINGS AHEAD 8-11 J Fanning (3) *beh, pushed alng to improve o'r 2 fs out, not quicken ins last.* ....(16 to 1 op 12 to 1) 6
SNUGFIT ANNIE 8-6 N Connorton (12) *trkd ldrs gng wl, shaken up o'r 2 fs out, sn drpd out, eased.* ....(33 to 1 op 20 to 1) 7
1355⁶ LUNAR RHAPSODY 8-3 (3*) S Maloney (11) *mid-div, drvn alng 3 fs out, one pace frm 2 out*.... (12 to 1 op 8 to 1) 8
COVER POINT (Ire) 8-11 T Lucas (8) *missed break, beh and sn outpcd, ran on fnl furlong, nvr dngrs.* ....(14 to 1 op 10 to 1) 9
1272 STEANARD BOY 8-11 R Cochrane (7) *beh, rdn alng hfwy, not pace to chal*..................(14 to 1 op 10 to 1) 10
1758 PHIL THE TILL (bl) 8-11 Dale Gibson (9) *chsd ldrs, rdn alng 3 fs out, wknd 2 out*..................(20 to 1 op 16 to 1) 11
1519⁷ XAMDIVAD (Ire) (bl) 7-13 (7*) J Tate (1) *wth ldr, rdn and wknd o'r 2 fs out*..................(14 to 1 op 10 to 1) 12
1245 AGGIES DREAM 8-8 (3*) J Weaver (10) *led till o'r 2 fs out, sn wknd*..................(25 to 1 op 20 to 1) 13
969³ NORBECK (Ire) (bl) 8-11 S Morris (4) *dwlt, beh, rdn and wknd hfwy*..................(12 to 1 op 10 to 1) 14
1499⁷ TEN TIMES TANGO 8-6 S Webster (2) *keen hold in rear, rdn aftr 3 fs, sn lost tch*.......... (33 to 1 op 20 to 1) 15
Dist: ½l, 3½l, nk, 2½l, 1l, 2l, 1½l, 2l, 1½l, sht-hd. 1m 24.80s. a 3.00s (15 Ran).
SR: 21/19/3/2/-/-/ (R M Whitaker), R M Whitaker

1864 Staithes Maiden Stakes Class D (3-y-o and up) £3,318 1¾m 19yds......(2:20)

1678³ CARA'S PRIDE 3-7-13 Dale Gibson (1) *al hndy, pushed alng 4 fs out, led o'r one out, drvn along, hld on wl ins last*................(16 to 1 tchd 14 to 1 and 20 to 1) 1
1603² DARZEE 3-8-5¹ R Cochrane (7) *chsd ldrs, rdn alng 4 fs out, hdwy 2 out, ran on wl fnl furlong, jst hld.* ....(2 to 1 on op 11 to 8 on tchd 5 to 4 on) 2
1430⁶ ALYDUNCAN (USA) 3-8-4 K Fallon (3) *led, clr o'r 3 fs out, hdd over one out, not quicken ins last.* ....(4 to 1 op 3 to 1 tchd 9 to 2) 3
NOUVELLE CUISINE 5-9-2 J Fanning (5) *unruly strt, hld up in tch, rdn to improve fnl 2 fs, short of room and swtchd, not quicken ins last*.......(33 to 1 op 14 to 1) 4
TRY N' FLY (Ire) 3-8-4 Dean McKeown (4) *dwlt, keen hold in rear, shrtlvd effrt on outsd o'r 3 fs out, fdd over 2 out*............................ (50 to 1 op 25 to 1) 5
1224² THE LAUGHING LORD 7-9-7 M Birch (6) *hld up, hdwy to dispute ld aftr 6 fs, wknd o'r 3 out.* (6 to 1 op 11 to 2) 6
Dist: Hd, 1½l, sht-hd, 8l, 7l. 3m 3.80s. a 7.30s (6 Ran).
(Greenland Park Ltd), P Calver

1865 Rothmans Royals North South Challenge Series Handicap Class D (0-80 4-y-o and up) £3,785 7f......... (2:50)

1658³ ARABAT [62] 6-9-8 K Fallon (8) *beh, rdn alng hfwy, improved o'r one furlong out, str run to ld nr finish.* ....(10 to 1 op 8 to 1) 1
1721⁹ GRANITTON BAY [64] (v) 6-9-10 A Culhane (1) *chsd ldrs, led wl o'r one furlong out till hdd nr finish*...... (14 to 1) 2
1782⁷ PRINCE BELFORT [62] 5-9-1 (7*) J Tate (5) *trkd ldrs, drvn alng o'r 2 fs out, one pace ins last.* ....(12 to 1 tchd 14 to 1) 3
1782* BALLAD DANCER [60] 8-9-6 (5ex) G Hind (6) *in tch on ins, effrt and rdn o'r 2 fs out, not quicken inside last.* ....(5 to 1 jt-fav op 9 to 2) 4
1193⁵ SARTIGILA [63] 4-9-9 R Cochrane (11) *slwly into strd, beh, hdwy o'r 2 fs out, not much room over one out, not quicken ins last*..................(7 to 1) 5
1588⁶ ASTERIX [51] (v) 5-8-8 (3*) J Weaver (4) *dwlt, beh, improved hfwy, ev ch on outsd o'r one furlong out, no extr ins last*..................(10 to 1 op 12 to 1 tchd 9 to 1) 6
1591⁹ CLAUDIA MISS [57] 6-9-3 Dean McKeown (10) *hld up rear, shaken up 3 fs out, nvr able to chal.* (9 to 1 op 10 to 1) 7
1591⁶ SUPREME BOY [53] 4-8-13 M Birch (2) *chsd ldrs on outsd, improved and ev ch o'r one furlong out, wknd.* ....(5 to 1 jt-fav tchd 9 to 2) 8
1658* LEGEND DULAC (Ire) [55] 4-9-1 M Tebbutt (3) *wth ldr, led o'r 2 fs out till wl over one out, sn btn.* ....(11 to 2 op 5 to 1) 9
ROAR ON TOUR [56] 4-9-2 J Fanning (9) *beh, bustled alng hfwy, nvr a factor*..................(16 to 1 op 14 to 1) 10
1766 BOY MARTIN [63] 4-9-9 J Fortune (12) *sn outpcd, nvr on terms*..................(16 to 1 op 20 to 1) 11
1397 ANGELS ANSWER (Ire) [56] 4-8-13 (3*) S Maloney (7) *made most till hdd and rdn o'r 2 fs out, sn btn.* ....(12 to 1 op 10 to 1) 12
Dist: Nk, 1l, ½l, nk, 2l, 1½l, ½l, nk, 6l, 2l. 1m 23.90s. a 2.10s (12 Ran).
SR: 45/46/41/37/39/21/22/16/17/ (Mrs H Wane), Martyn Wane

1866 Surfachem Lady Amateur Riders' Maiden Handicap Class G (0-70 3-y-o and up) £3,027 1m..............(3:25)

LET'S GET LOST [70] 4-11-0 (7*) Mrs M Haggas (9) *hld up, hdwy o'r 2 fs out, ran on to ld ins last, kpt on wl.* ....(10 to 1) 1
1421⁷ JOMOVE [35] 4-9-0 Mrs M Cowdrey (12) *in tch, led o'r one furlong out, hdd ins last, kpt on.* ....(12 to 1 op 10 to 1 tchd 14 to 1) 2
1307 ESSAYEFFSEE [44] 4-9-9 Miss J Winter (4) *in tch, effrt 2 fs out, not quicken ins last*.......... (14 to 1 op 12 to 1) 3
1185³ SUDDEN SPIN [58] 3-9-13 Miss I Diana W Jones (6) *nvr far away, led 3 fs out till o'r one out, no extr ins last.* ....(7 to 1 op 5 to 1) 4
1421² MASTER OFTHE HOUSE [47] 7-9-12 Mrs L Pearce (2) *hld up, hdwy o'r one furlong out, kpt on, nvr dngrs.* ....(7 to 4 fav op 3 to 1) 5
1434⁵ LORD LAMBSON [42] 4-9-7 Mrs A Farrell (16) *mid-div, effrt and rdn o'r 2 fs out, kpt on ins last.* (7 to 1 op 6 to 1) 6
1520⁷ THE DANDY DON (Ire) [47] 4-9-5 (7*) Miss M Carson (1) *in tch, improved and ev ch o'r 2 fs out, one pace over one out*..................(14 to 1) 7
1498⁶ MUMMYS ROCKET [43] (bl) 4-9-8 Mrs J Crossley (11) *beh, swtchd lft hfwy, sn chasing ldrs, fdd o'r one furlong out*.............................. (10 to 1 op 7 to 1) 8
CRESTWOOD LAD (USA) [52] 4-9-10 (7*) Miss A Yardley (8) *trkd ldrs, rdn o'r 3 fs out, wknd over one out.* ....(33 to 1 op 20 to 1) 9
1419 MURASIL (USA) [37] 4-9-2 Miss P Robson (14) *cl up, led o'r 4 fs out to 3 out, wknd*..................(20 to 1) 10
1421⁵ FUTURE FAME (USA) [40] 4-8-12 (7*) Mrs D Wilkinson (10) *dwlt, outpcd*..................(14 to 1 tchd 16 to 1) 11
1419⁹ CROMER'S EXPRESS [37] 4-8-9 (7*) Miss S Judge (13) *beh, drpd away hfwy*..................(33 to 1 op 25 to 1) 12
1498⁸ HYDROPIC [37] 6-9-2⁹ (7*) Miss R Clark (15) *chsd ldrs to hfwy, rdn and sn wknd*........... (50 to 1 op 33 to 1) 13
1729³ ALMOSTAUTOMATIC (Ire) [60] 4-10-8 (3*) Miss A Purdy (5) *led till o'r 4 fs out, wknd quickly, tld off.* ....(20 to 1 tchd 25 to 1) 14
1627³ B B GLEN [47] 3-8-13⁴ (7*) Mrs L Morris (7) *missed break, wndrd hfwy, tld off*..................(10 to 1) 15
WALTON MELODY [35] 6-8-7 (7*) Miss T Ager (3) *beh, lost tch hfwy, tld off*..................(50 to 1) 16
Dist: 1l, 1½l, 1l, 1½l, 2½l, 1½l, ½l, ¾l, 2l, 2½l. 1m 37.00s. a 2.10s (16 Ran).
SR: 38/-/4/5/-/-/ (P A Leonard), W J Haggas

1867 Ronaldshay Handicap Class C (0-90 3-y-o and up) £4,709 1¼m...... (3:55)

1346³ VALLANCE [76] 5-9-10 M Birch (4) *led or dsptd ld, led o'r 4 fs out, edgd lft frm 2 out, drvn clr appr last.* ....(5 to 2 tchd 3 to 1) 1
1720⁶ ROYAL CITIZEN (Ire) [70] 4-9-4 K Fallon (5) *hld up last, effrt 3 fs out, chsd wnr 2 out, not quicken ins last.* ....(20 to 1 op 16 to 1) 2
1330* NAIF (USA) [78] 3-9-0 R Cochrane (2) *patiently rdn, effrt and not clr run o'r 2 fs out, no extr over one out.* ....(Evens fav op 5 to 4 tchd 11 to 10 on) 3
1520² JUBRAN (USA) [68] 7-9-2 Dean McKeown (1) *led or dsptd ld till o'r 4 fs out, sn drvn alng, not quicken wl over one out*..................(13 to 2 op 5 to 1) 4
1422* I'M A DREAMER (Ire) [70] 3-8-6 Dale Gibson (3) *trkd ldg pair, pushed alng 4 fs out, wknd wl o'r one out.* ....(9 to 2 op 4 to 1 tchd 5 to 1) 5
Dist: 3l, 2l, ½l, 3½l. 2m 4.00s. a 2.80s (5 Ran).
SR: 52/40/32/33/16/ (Mrs P W Harris), P W Harris

1868 Forty Acre Maiden Stakes Class D (3-y-o and up) £3,494 1m.......... (4:30)

1239² TEJ SINGH (USA) 3-8-9 R Cochrane (4) *made all, rdn o'r 2 fs out, clr appr last, easily*........ (7 to 4 tchd 2 to 1) 1
1275⁷ BROCTUNE BAY 4-9-5 M Birch (5) *hld up in tch, swtchd o'r 2 fs out, kpt on ins last, not rch wnr.* ....(10 to 1 op 8 to 1 tchd 11 to 1) 2
1616⁵ SIMAAT (USA) 3-8-4 G Hind (2) *slwly into strd, chsd ldrs, effrt and rdn 3 fs out, ran green, eased whn btn o'r one out*............. (11 to 8 on op 5 to 4 on tchd Evens) 3

TINA'S DOMAIN 3-8-4 J Fortune (3) *trkd wnr, rdn o'r 2 fs out, sn wknd*.......................(12 to 1 op 8 to 1) 4
Dist: 3½l, 6l, 2½l. 1m 38.80s. a 3.90s (4 Ran).
SR: 1/ (Sheikh Mohammed), L M Cumani

1869 Ugthorpe Rating Related Maiden Stakes Class D (0-75 3-y-o) £3,084 6f ....(5:00)

1396^{5} BALIANA 8-9 K Fallon (2) *in tch, rdn alng hfwy, ran on to ld one furlong out, ridden clr*........(5 to 1 op 9 to 2) 1
1597^{2} PERSIAN CHARMER (Ire) (bl) 9-0 R Cochrane (4) *al prmnt, rdn hfwy, led briefly appr fnl furlong, no extr ins last*. .... (11 to 8 on op 5 to 4 on tchd Evens) 2
1196^{3} HOY-LIEGH-RAG 9-0 Dean McKeown (3) *led, rdn 2 fs out, hdd appr last, not quicken*.......... (4 to 1 op 3 to 1) 3
836 LANCASTER PILOT 9-0 A Culhane (5) *chsd ldrs, rdn hfwy, wknd o'r one furlong out*...........(10 to 1 op 9 to 1) 4
1327^{5} OSCAR THE SECOND (Ire) 9-0 J Fanning (1) *slwly into strd, hld up, rdn alng o'r one furlong out, no imprsn*. .... (14 to 1 op 12 to 1) 5
Dist: 2l, 5l, 1½l, 2l. 1m 12.30s. a 2.60s (5 Ran).
SR: 7/4/ (Purple Silks), C B B Booth

SOUTHWELL (A.W) (std)
Saturday June 19th
Going Correction: MINUS 0.20 sec. per fur.

1870 East Midlands Electricity Maiden Auction Stakes Class E (2-y-o) £1,534 5f ....(6:35)

1317^{2} PARADISE NEWS 8-2 (7*) D McCabe (4) *chsd ldrs, outpcd and rdn alng hfwy, hdwy o'r one furlong out, ran on strly ins last to ld on line*............(7 to 2 op 3 to 1) 1
1602^{5} MOMENT OF GLORY (Ire) 9-0 W Woods (3) *cl up, led 2 fs out, sn rdn, ct on line*.................. (5 to 2 op 2 to 1) 2
1324 STEPHENSONS ROCKET 9-0 J Carroll (1) *cl up, rdn 2 fs out, ev ch till no extr nr finish*. ....(9 to 4 fav op 5 to 2 tchd 11 to 4) 3
1561^{6} STUDFORD GIRL (bl) 8-9 T Lucas (5) *led to 2 fs out, sn rdn, wknd one out*...........................(10 to 1 op 8 to 1) 4
1583^{6} LIFE'S TOO SHORT (Ire) 8-9 W Hood (2) *slwly away, outpcd*.................................. (4 to 1 op 5 to 1) 5
Dist: Sht-hd, ½l, 3½l, 2½l. 1m 0.80s. a 2.90s (5 Ran).
SR: 17/21/19/-/-/ (Mrs F E Bravery), G C Bravery

1871 East Midlands Electricity Limited Stakes Class E (0-70 3-y-o and up) £1,534 6f...................... (7:05)

1502* HIGHBORN (Ire) 4-9-4 G Hind (5) *made all, rdn clr o'r 2 fs out, styd on strly ins last*........ (5 to 4 fav op 7 to 4) 1
429^{2} QUINSIGIMOND 3-8-5 G Duffield (2) *al chasing wnr, rdn 2 fs out, ev ch ins last, no extr nr finish*. ....(3 to 1 op 2 to 1) 2
1721^{7} AFRICAN CHIMES 6-8-11 (7*) D McCabe (1) *beh, hdwy on ins hfwy, effrt 2 fs out, sn rdn, styd on inside last*. ....(5 to 2 op 4 to 1 tchd 9 to 2) 3
1358^{2} APPEALING TIMES (USA) 4-9-4 S Wood (4) *in tch, rdn alng hfwy, sn wknd*...........................(7 to 1 op 5 to 1) 4
1677^{6} MAID WELCOME (bl) 6-8-13 Dean McKeown (3) *chsd ldg pair, rdn and wknd 2 and a half fs out*. ....(16 to 1 op 14 to 1) 5
Dist: 1½l, ¾l, 8l, 2½l. 1m 14.90s. a 1.50s (5 Ran).
SR: 50/31/41/9/-/ (Yorkshire Racing Club Owners Group 1990), P S Felgate

1872 East Midlands Electricity Handicap Class D (0-80 3-y-o) £3,055 1½m (7:35)

1629* RUNAWAY PETE (USA) [75] 9-0 (7*) T G McLaughlin (2) *dsptd ld, led 5 fs out, clr 2 and a half out, easily*. .... (7 to 4 fav op Evens tchd 2 to 1) 1
1673* CHARLIE BIGTIME [65] 8-8 (3*) J Weaver (4) *hld up in tch, hdwy 4 fs out, chsd wnr and rdn frm 2 out, no imprsn*. .... (2 to 1 tchd 9 to 4 and 7 to 4) 2
1309^{6} MAJOR TRIUMPH (Ire) [59] 8-5 G Duffield (3) *trkd ldrs, effrt 5 fs out, rdn 3 out, sn one pace*.......(9 to 2 op 6 to 1) 3
1534^{5} MULLED ALE (Ire) [55] 8-1^{3} W Woods (1) *dsptd ld, rdn 5 fs out, sn wknd*........ (12 to 1 op 10 to 1 tchd 14 to 1) 4
1501^{4} PRECUSSION [62] 8-8 R Price (3) *trkd ldrs to hfwy, sn pushed alng, beh fnl 3 fs*. ....(9 to 2 op 4 to 1 tchd 5 to 1) 5
Dist: 8l, 8l, 5l, 2½l. 2m 36.90s. a 3.00s (5 Ran).
SR: 53/27/5/-/-/ (Thomas T S Liang), P F I Cole

1873 First National Bank Selling Handicap Stakes Class G (0-60 3-y-o and up) £1,380 2m..................... (8:05)

226^{9} DANCING DAYS [27] (v) 7-7-13 (7*) J Tate (7) *trkd ldrs, hdwy 4 fs out, rdn to ld one and a half out, ran on gmely ins last*...(8 to 1) 1
973^{5} SULUK (USA) [38] 8-9-3 S Perks (9) *led, rdn 3 fs out, hdd one and a half out, kpt on wl*.......(4 to 1 op 3 to 1) 2
1281^{4} NOTED STRAIN (Ire) [49] 5-10-0 J Carroll (2) *mid-div, hdwy 5 fs out, effrt and ev ch 2 out, sn rdn, wknd entering last*..(100 to 30 fav op 7 to 2 tchd 4 to 1 and 3 to 1) 3
1453 RESISTING (USA) [22] (bl) 5-7-8 (7*) D McCabe (8) *beh, styd on fnl 3 fs, nvr dngrs*..............(25 to 1 op 20 to 1) 4
1276^{6} SELDOM IN [35] 7-9-0 Dean McKeown (3) *in tch, hdwy 6 fs out, chlgd 3 out, sn rdn, wknd 2 out*. (7 to 2 op 5 to 2) 5
4776a^{9} SPANISH WHISPER [26] 6-8-5 G Duffield (4) *cl up, rdn 4 fs out, sn wknd*...........(11 to 2 op 5 to 1 tchd 7 to 1) 6
1562 LADY RANDOLPH [28] (v) 4-8-7 M Wood (5) *cl up, rdn and wknd o'r 4 fs out*..................(20 to 1 op 16 to 1) 7
1702^{4} PREMIER BLUES (Fr) [42] (bl) 3-8-2 N Adams (1) *chsd ldrs, rdn 6 fs out, sn wknd*...(13 to 2 op 6 to 1 tchd 7 to 1) 8
1659 PERMANENTLY PINK [22] 7-8-1 W Woods (6) *hld up, some hdwy 6 fs out, sn btn*.............................(25 to 1) 9
Dist: ½l, 5l, 1½l, 10l, 2½l, 8l, 2l, sht-hd. 3m 43.90s. a 17.40s (9 Ran).
(R Flegg), J Parkes

1874 Fibresand Handicap Class E (0-70 3-y-o and up) £1,576 6f............. (8:35)

1675^{3} RED FAN (Ire) [67] (bl) 3-9-10 N Connorton (2) *cl up, led aftr one furlong, hrd rdn frm 2 out, styd on ins last*. ....(7 to 1 op 6 to 1 tchd 8 to 1) 1
1618^{5} FAMILY ROSE [35] 4-8-0 A Munro (9) *led one furlong, cl up, rdn 2 fs out, ev ch till no extr ins last*. ....(16 to 1 op 14 to 1) 2
1701^{5} BASSIO (Bel) [46] (h) 4-8-11 W Hood (1) *beh, styd on wl fnl 2 fs, nrst finish*.........(9 to 1 op 8 to 1 tchd 10 to 1) 3
1677^{3} MISS WHITTINGHAM (Ire) [56] 3-8-13 J Carroll (6) *chsd ldrs, hdwy 3 fs out, sn rdn, kpt on one pace frm 2 out*. ....(5 to 4 fav op 3 to 1) 4
1655^{2} KILDEE LAD [55] 3-8-12 N Adams (8) *chsd ldrs, effrt hfwy, sn rdn, wknd 2 fs out*...............(4 to 1 op 11 to 4) 5
1356^{4} MELODIC DRIVE [52] 3-8-9 G Hind (5) *nvr rch ldrs*. ....(11 to 1 op 10 to 1 tchd 12 to 1) 6
1480 COMPANY CASH [41] (bl) 5-8-6 J Fanning (3) *dwlt, al rear*. .... (10 to 1 op 8 to 1) 7
882 ANDY JACK [47] 4-8-9 (3*) J Weaver (4) *chsd ldrs, rdn hfwy, sn wknd*...........................(20 to 1 op 16 to 1) 8
1674 SALLY'S SON [56] (bl) 7-9-7 S Wood (7) *in tch, wide strt, sn rdn and lost pl, beh whn crashed through rls one furlong out, dead*...................... (9 to 1 op 7 to 1) ro
Dist: 1l, 1l, 3l, 2½l, nk, 5l, 5l. 1m 16.50s. a 3.10s (9 Ran).
SR: 24/-/3/-/-/-/ (Joe L Allbritton), J W Watts

1875 Lynne Coldron Anniversary Handicap Class E (0-70 3-y-o) £1,548 7f... (9:05)

1675^{8} ROSE FLYER (Ire) [56] 8-3 (7*) D McCabe (6) *made all, rdn clr 3 fs out, hld on wl fnl furlong*. (11 to 1 op 10 to 1) 1
1701^{7} KINGSTON BROWN [65] (v) 9-2 (3*) J Weaver (2) *chsd ldrs, effrt 3 fs out, sn rdn, styd on und pres ins last, not rch wnr*.....................(15 to 2 op 6 to 1 tchd 8 to 1) 2
1703^{2} DANCE TO ORDER (Ire) [67] 9-7 G Duffield (10) *chsd ldrs, rdn 3 fs out, styd on fnl furlong*. ....(9 to 4 fav op 11 to 4 tchd 7 to 2) 3
1737^{6} MONASTIC FLIGHT (Ire) [50] 8-4 J Fortune (8) *chsd wnr, rdn 4 fs out, wknd appr last*. .... (11 to 2 op 6 to 1 tchd 9 to 2) 4
1656^{8} NORTHERN JUDY (Ire) [43] 7-9^{3} (5*) A Garth (7) *slwly away, beh, styd on fnl 2 fs, nvr dngrs*.... (20 to 1 op 16 to 1) 5
862^{4} NORTHERN BLUFF [60] (v) 9-0 N Connorton (3) *prmnt, rdn 3 fs out, sn wknd*.................(6 to 1 op 5 to 1) 6
228^{5} PYTCHLEY DAWN [50] 8-4^{1} J Carroll (9) *chsd ldrs, rdn 3 fs out, sn wknd*...........(4 to 1 op 6 to 1 tchd 9 to 1) 7
PLATINUM VENTURE [63] 9-3 W Woods (1) *outpcd, sn rdn alng, al beh*.........(14 to 1 op 16 to 1 tchd 20 to 1) 8
1631^{6} JOTRA [44] 7-12 N Carlisle (5) *al rear*. (14 to 1 op 10 to 1) 9
1058 ON GOLDEN POND (Ire) [56] 8-10 A Munro (4) *sn outpcd, rdn alng, al beh*......................(8 to 1 op 7 to 1) 10
Dist: 1½l, ¾l, 2½l, 3½l, ¾l, 5l, 2½l, 3l, 4l. 1m 30.20s. a 4.10s (10 Ran).
SR: 14/18/18/-/-/-/ (A M Packaging Ltd), M C Chapman

WARWICK (good to soft)
Saturday June 19th
Going Correction: PLUS 0.20 sec. per fur. (races 1,2,3,4,5), MINUS 0.10 (6)

1876 Ferndale Apprentice Handicap Class E (0-80 3-y-o and up) £2,758 7f.. (6:15)

1701^{3} ON Y VA (USA) [55] 6-8-1 (8*) Sarah Thompson (1) *hdwy 2 fs out, led ins last, ran on wl*...........(7 to 1 op 6 to 1) 1
1530^{3} CEE-JAY-AY [70] 6-9-2 (8*) P Roberts (5) *slwly away, hdwy on ins entering strt, ev ch inside fnl furlong, unbl to quicken*..........(100 to 30 fav op 3 to 1 tchd 7 to 2) 2
1487^{4} JUST A STEP [60] 7-9-0 D Gibbs (3) *led till hdd and no extr ins fnl furlong*.......... (7 to 1 op 6 to 1 tchd 8 to 1) 3
1623* PRINCE ROONEY (Ire) [62] 5-9-2 P McCabe (4) *in rear, prog on outsd appr fnl furlong, not rch ldrs*. ....(11 to 2 op 7 to 2) 4
1588^{2} OLD COMRADES [56] 6-8-10 Mark Denaro (2) *cl up, ev ch ins last, no extr*..................... (11 to 2 op 5 to 1) 5

1707 BUDDY'S FRIEND (Ire) [57] 5-8-11 G Mitchell (9) *chsd ldr, wknd one and a half fs out*........(20 to 1 op 12 to 1) 6
1686² MUSTAHIL (Ire) [62] 4-8-11 (5*) R Waterfield (7) *al beh*. ....(11 to 2 op 5 to 1 tchd 13 to 2) 7
1663⁶ WAKI GOLD (USA) [66] 6-9-0 (6*) R Painter (6) *chsd ldrs, rdn o'r 2 fs out, wknd wl over one out*. ....(7 to 1 op 6 to 1 tchd 8 to 1) 8
1138⁹ GARTH [66] 5-8-12 (8*) L Aspell (8) *effrt o'r 2 fs out, sn btn*. ....(12 to 1 op 10 to 1) 9
Dist: 1½l, ½l, 1l, sht-hd, 4l, ½l, 2l, 2½l. 1m 28.90s. a 5.10s (9 Ran).
SR: 40/50/38/37/30/19/22/20/12/ (Marriott Stables Limited), R J R Williams

1877 Tote/Racing Post Ten To Follow Maiden Auction Stakes Class F (2-y-o) £2,070 7f...................... (6:45)

1211 ORANGE PLACE (Ire) 9-0 M Hills (11) *made all, rdn o'r one furlong out, kpt on wl*...............(6 to 1 op 5 to 2) 1
1602³ NONIOS (Ire) 9-0 M Roberts (5) *al handily plcd, rdn o'r one furlong out, ran on ins last, not rch wnr*. .... (11 to 4 op 7 to 2 tchd 4 to 1) 2
1481⁶ ASKING FOR ACES 8-9 J Quinn (13) *al cl up, ev ch 2 fs out, not quicken appr fnl furlong*......(16 to 1 op 10 to 1) 3
INDEFENCE (Ire) 9-0 D Holland (4) *al chasing ldrs, kpt on same pace last 2 fs*...................(10 to 1 op 6 to 1) 4
1119³ ROSE OF GLENN 8-4 (5*) Stephen Davies (3) *trkd frnt rnk, no imprsn last 2 fs*................................ (20 to 1) 5
GINGERBIRD (Ire) 8-9 W Ryan (8) *nrst finish*. ....(5 to 2 fav op 2 to 1 tchd 3 to 1) 6
1602⁴ MR MYSTICAL (Ire) 9-0 A McGlone (7) *chsd ldrs, no prog last 2 fs*................ (11 to 2 op 5 to 1 tchd 6 to 1) 7
FAIRFIELD DANCER 8-9 J Williams (10) *nvr nr to chal*. ....(33 to 1) 8
1263⁵ BURES (Ire) 8-7 (7*) S Mulvey (9) *nvr rchd ldrs*. ....(20 to 1 op 12 to 1) 9
1499 BILLPOSTER (Ire) 8-9 Alex Greaves (12) *nvr dngrs*. ....(25 to 1 op 16 to 1) 10
GAELIC RISK 8-7 (7*) P McCabe (2) *slwly away, al in rear*. ....(25 to 1 op 20 to 1) 11
830³ CAPITAL LADY (Ire) 8-6 (3*) D Harrison (15) *beh fnl 2 fs*. ....(25 to 1 op 20 to 1) 12
1131⁷ PRINCE DANZIG (Ire) 9-0 C Rutter (14) *pressed ldrs to hfwy, tld off*.......................(10 to 1 op 6 to 1) 13
CHELSEA LADY (Ire) 8-2 (7*) G Mitchell (1) *slwly into strd, al in rear, tld off*..................(33 to 1 op 25 to 1) 14
LAC DE GRAS (Ire) 9-0 G Bardwell (6) *tld off*......(33 to 1) 15
Dist: 2l, 2l, 2½l, ½l, 3l, sht-hd, hd, 3½l, 2½l, ½l. 1m 31.00s. a 7.20s (15 Ran).
SR: 13/7/-/-/-/-/ (Archer Van & Truck Hire Ltd), M Bell

1878 Victoria Mews Handicap Class D (0-80 3-y-o and up) £3,289 1¼m 169yds ....(7:15)

1409⁸ ATHAR (Ire) [61] 4-9-3 J Williams (7) *trkd ldg grp, led ins fnl furlong, ran on wl*...... (9 to 2 op 4 to 1 tchd 5 to 1) 1
1409⁹ WESTFIELD MOVES (Ire) [56] 5-8-12 J Quinn (9) *hld up, improved hfwy, led 3 fs out, hdd and not quicken ins last*....................(13 to 2 op 6 to 1 tchd 7 to 1) 2
1604⁸ HAROLDON (Ire) [68] 4-9-10 W Ryan (1) *settled in rear, prog 2 fs out, styd on ins last*......(14 to 1 op 12 to 1) 3
1626⁷ LADY LACEY [46] (v) 6-8-2 Dale Gibson (8) *no real prog last 2 fs*.................................(11 to 2 op 5 to 1) 4
LIGHT HAND [72] 7-9-7 (7*) S Mulvey (5) *wtd wth, smooth prog hfwy, no imprsn last 2 fs*...(3 to 1 fav op 9 to 2) 5
1231⁷ PRINCESS HAIFA (USA) [77] 3-9-5 M Roberts (4) *led one furlong, pushed alng hfwy, hrd rdn and ev ch one and a half fs out, eased whn btn ins last*. ....(7 to 2 op 5 to 2 tchd 4 to 1) 6
1498⁹ ACHELOUS [49] (bl) 6-8-5 D Holland (6) *led aftr one furlong, hdd 3 fs out, eased whn btn one out*. ....(15 to 2 op 6 to 1) 7
1414 RADIO CAROLINE [38] 5-7-8 J Lowe (3) *beh frm hfwy, tld off*.................................(25 to 1 op 20 to 1) 8
ANNABEL'S BABY (Ire) [50] 4-8-6 R Perham (2) *wl plcd to hfwy, tld off fnl 3 fs*..................(33 to 1 op 25 to 1) 9
Dist: 1½l, 1l, 2½l, ½l, 6l, 5l, 8l, 15l. 2m 22.80s. a 10.00s (9 Ran).
SR: 25/17/27/-/25/4/ (J W Buxton), R J Baker

1879 Warwick Oaks Conditions Stakes Class D (3-y-o and up) £3,835 1¼m 169yds..................... (7:45)

1587* LYPHARD'S DELTA (USA) 3-8-8 W Ryan (1) *trkd ldr, led one and a half fs out, rdn out*. ....(11 to 4 on op 5 to 2 on tchd 2 to 1 on) 1
PEARLY MIST (Ire) 3-8-6 M Roberts (2) *led, rdn 2 fs out, sn hdd, kpt on wl*.......... (8 to 1 op 7 to 1 tchd 9 to 1) 2
LILLE HAMMER 3-8-6 R Cochrane (3) *hld up, shaken up ins last 2 fs, no imprsn*..............(3 to 1 op 5 to 2) 3
Dist: ½l, 2½l. 2m 23.10s. a 10.30s (3 Ran).
SR: 13/10/5/ (S Khaled), H R A Cecil

1880 Ashorne Selling Handicap Stakes Class G (0-60 3-y-o and up) £1,380 1 ½m 115yds.................... (8:15)

1702* JALORE [45] 4-9-0 M Tebbutt (9) *wtd wth, smooth prog 4 fs out, led jst ins fnl furlong, readily*. (11 to 2 op 5 to 1) 1
GIORDANO (Ire) [54] 3-8-7 J Williams (3) *al wl plcd, ev ch one and a half fs out, unbl to quicken*. ....(9 to 2 op 10 to 1) 2
DIAMOND WEDDING (USA) [58] (bl) 4-9-13 M Roberts (5) *hld up and beh, hdwy 4 fs out, not clr run and swtchd lft o'r one out, kpt on one pace*........(10 to 1 op 7 to 1) 3
1268 EASTERN MAGIC [39] (bl) 5-8-8 R Cochrane (2) *al cl up, led ins last 2 fs, hdd and not quicken last 200 yards*. ....(6 to 1 op 5 to 1) 4
618 NOBLE SOCIETY [45] 5-9-0 R Perham (4) *hld up in rear, improved 3 fs out, nvr rch ldrs*.....(33 to 1 op 20 to 1) 5
1353 GEE DOUBLE YOU [33] 7-7-9 (7*) D Wright (12) *prog hfwy, lost pl 4 fs out*........(20 to 1 op 16 to 1 tchd 25 to 1) 6
1346 ASSEMBLY DANCER [50] 6-9-5 G Bardwell (6) *led till hdd ins last 2 fs, sn btn*................(25 to 1 op 20 to 1) 7
1237⁴ LOCH DUICH [54] 7-9-2 (7*) S Drowne (11) *pld hrd, cl up till wknd one and a half fs out*..........(9 to 1 op 6 to 1) 8
1477³ MRS SNUGGS (Ire) [59] 3-8-5 (7*) S Mulvey (1) *nvr a factor*. ....(4 to 1 fav tchd 5 to 1) 9
1562⁶ WINGED WHISPER (USA) [37] 4-8-6 W Ryan (8) *sn chasing ldr, wknd rpdly 2 fs out*......... (12 to 1 tchd 14 to 1) 10
WILTOSKI [44] (bl) 5-8-13 Dale Gibson (7) *cl up, rdn hfwy, wknd o'r 4 fs out*..................(14 to 1 op 12 to 1) 11
1281 SEASIDE MINSTREL [37] 5-8-6 J Lowe (10) *al in rear, tld off*...........................(33 to 1 op 20 to 1) 12
1389 SUMMER FLOWER [51] 3-8-4 D Holland (13) *prog 7 fs out, lost pl o'r 4 furlongs out, tld off*. ....(10 to 1 op 8 to 1 tchd 11 to 1) 13
Dist: 2l, 2½l, ½l, 7l, 3½l, nk, hd, 1½l, nk, 5l. 2m 50.50s. a 12.60s (13 Ran).
SR: -/-/3/-/-/-/ (Miss Jane Southall), R Hollinshead

1881 Henley In Arden Handicap Class E (0-70 3-y-o and up) £2,978 5f.... (8:45)

1492⁶ BRIGHT PARAGON (Ire) [45] 4-8-6 J Quinn (2) *trkd ldrs, rdn appr fnl furlong, sstnd chal to ld final strds*. ....(10 to 1 op 6 to 1) 1
862⁸ UMBRIA [42] 4-8-3² R Perham (10) *swrvd rght strt, improved hfwy, led ins fnl furlong, hdd last strds*. ....(5 to 1 op 5 to 2 tchd 11 to 2) 2
1696⁶ CASTLE MAID [33] 6-7-8¹ J Lowe (7) *beh and niggled alng, swtchd ins and gd hdwy appr fnl furlong, ran on*. ....(12 to 1 op 10 to 1 tchd 14 to 1) 3
1537⁸ MANOR ADVENTURE [62] 3-8-9 (7*) S Sanders (5) *al chasing ldrs, swtchd rght entering fnl furlong, kpt on*. ....(14 to 1 op 10 to 1) 4
1052⁹ TOMMY TEMPEST [50] 4-8-4 (7*) P McCabe (6) *led o'r 3 fs out, hdd and not quicken ins last*. ....(8 to 1 op 10 to 1 tchd 7 to 1) 5
1492 THE NOBLE OAK (Ire) [61] 5-9-1 (7*) Gina Faulkner (3) *wth ldrs, ev ch 2 fs out, not quicken appr fnl furlong*. ....(11 to 2 op 4 to 1) 6
1473⁶ MARTINA [67] 5-9-11 (3*) D Harrison (9) *chsd ldrs to hfwy*. ....(9 to 2 fav op 4 to 1 tchd 5 to 1) 7
1505* MOVING IMAGE (Ire) [61] 3-9-1 C Dwyer (1) *led o'r one furlong, wknd 2 fs out*.............(11 to 2 op 4 to 1) 8
Dist: Sht-hd, ½l, 1l, hd, ½l, 2½l, 3½l. 1m 0.60s. a 2.40s (8 Ran).
SR: 34/30/19/37/31/40/36/9/ (D C G Cooper), H J Collingridge

DORTMUND (GER) (good) Sunday June 20th

1882 Grosser Preis der Dortmunder Wirtschaft (Group 3) (3-y-o and up) £29,592 1m 1f..........................(3:45)

1217³ KARINGA BAY 6-9-6 B Rouse, *led 2 fs out, sn clr, cmftbly*. 1
1084² LE JARDIN (Ger) 5-9-4 A Tylicki, *beh, ran on fnl 2 fs, no imprsn on wnr*.. 2
IRON FIGHTER (Ger) 4-9-6 R Hillis, *dsptd ld o'r 5 fs, led 4 furlongs out to 2 out, one pace*...................... 3
1084 YOUNG MOON 7-9-6 M Santos, *mid-div, nvr dngrs*...... 4
4683a* MINING TYCOON (Ire) 4-9-4 K Woodburn, *dsptd ld o'r 5 fs, sn wknd*.. 5
MEERWIND (Ger) 4-9-4 L Mader, *al in rear*.............. 6
1125² LASKO (Ger) 3-8-1 A Best, *nvr plcd to chal*............ 7
Dist: 1 ¾l, 1 ¼l, ¾l, nk, 1½l, hd. 1m 46.70s. (7 Ran).
(K Higson), G L Moore

FREUDENAU (ATA) (good) Sunday June 20th

1883 Internationale Standard Meile (3-y-o and up) £5,217 1m..............(2:40)

1398⁴ LUCKY GUEST 6-9-11 L Piggott,........................ 1
RYAN'S GIFT (USA) 7-9-9 P Kallai,...................... 2
1084 REZON (Su) 5-9-4,... 3
Dist: 1½l, nk, ½l, 7l. 1m 38.00s. (10 Ran).
(Windflower Overseas Holdings Inc), J L Dunlop

1884 Casinos-Austria-Preis Osterreichisches Derby (3-y-o) £6,387 1½m ....(4:00)

1471³ ZIMZALABIM 9-0 D Holland, ... 1
MAZATENANGO (Ger) 9-0 D Ilic, ... 2
KARTHAGO (Ire) 9-0 3
MISSED FLIGHT 9-0 0
Dist: 7l, 3l, 1½l, 4l. 2m 28.60s. (16 Ran).
(Mrs M Schneider), B W Hills

SAN SIRO (ITY) (good to firm) Sunday June 20th

1885 Premio Malpensa (Maiden) 2yo £5,603 7f. .... (1:30)

1481⁴ PARNASO (Ire) 8-11 T Quinn, ... 1
MEDITERRANEO 8-11 W Carson, ... 2
ELBURZ (Ity) 8-11 E Botti, ... 3
BARACCA (Ire) 8-11 F Jovine, ... 6
Dist: ¾l, 2l, 4½l, nose, ½l, 1½l, nk, 3l, sht-hd, 11l. 1m 30.00s. (11 Ran).
(G Mazza), P A Kelleway

1886 Premio Bimbi (Listed) 2yo Colts & Fillies £8,876 5f. .... (1:55)

FUMO DI LONDRA (Ire) 2-8-11 W Carson, ... 1
1045⁵ IL CARAVAGGIO (Ire) 2-8-11 M Kinane, ... 2
1221³ LONDON KID (Ire) 2-8-11 S Dettori, ... 3
GOLD GATOR (USA) 2-8-11 M Latorre, ... 4
VENISE (Ity) 2-8-11 5
Dist: 5½l, 1l, 2l, 1l. 58.50s. (5 Ran).
(Gerecon Italia), J L Dunlop

1887 Premio d'Estate (Listed) 3yo £20,173 1m. .... (3:15)

1363² SMARGINATO (Ire) 8-8 W Carson, ... 1
4703a FUTURBALLA 8-8 M Kinane, *fnshd second, disqualified and plcd 5th*.. 2D
GOLDEN KABBUBY (USA) 8-8 M Latorre, *fnshd 3rd, plcd second*.. 2
958³ IOMMELLI (Ire) 8-8 T Quinn, *fnshd 4th, plcd 3rd*.......... 3
1363³ MAORI (Ity) 8-8 , *fnshd 5th, plcd 4th*........................ 4
SUPER ACTOR (USA) 8-8 6
DOLCE SORRISO (Ire) 8-8 7
Dist: 4½l, 1½l, 2½l, nose, 2½l, hd. 1m 39.60s. (7 Ran).
(Gerecon Italia), J L Dunlop

1888 Gran Premio di Milano (Group 1) 3yo+ Colts & Fillies £147,932 1½m... (4:20)

1217* PLATINI (Ger) 4-9-6 M Rimmer, *hld up 4th strt, hdwy on outsd to ld 2 and a half fs out, all out*................ 1
407⁹ PETIT LOUP (USA) 4-9-6 W R Swinburn, *trkd ldr til led 3 fs out, hdd 2 and a half furlongs out, hrd rdn, ran on wl*. 2
1085² GUADO D'ANNIBALE (Ire) 4-9-6 F Jovine, *last strt, kpt on fnl one and a half fs, took 3rd pl cl hme*.............. 3
1291³ DARIYOUN (USA) 5-9-6 F Head, *rcd in 3rd, effrt on ins 2 fs out, ev ch till wknd inside fnl furlong*.............. 4
1085⁸ GREEN SENOR (USA) 5-9-6 B Jovine, *7th strt, btn wl o'r 2 fs out*.. 5
1364³ MR RICHARD (Ire) 3-8-6 M Kinane, *set slow pace til hdd and wknd 3 fs out*.. 6
1124⁴ SHARP COUNSEL (Fr) 4-9-6 D Boeuf, *mid-div, cl 5th strt, one pace fnl 2 fs*.. 7
4727a⁶ SNURGE 6-9-6 T Quinn, *prmnt early, 6th strt, wknd 2 fs out*.. 8
Dist: Sht-nk, 2l, ½l, ½l, 2½l, 1½l, 2l. 2m 31.70s. (8 Ran).
(Stall Steigenberger), Bruno Schuetz

EDINBURGH (good) Monday June 21st

Going Correction: PLUS 0.25 sec. per fur. (race 1), MINUS 0.05 (2,3,4,5,6)

1889 Craigleith Claiming Stakes Class F (2-y-o) £2,365 5f. .... (2:30)

1759² LUCKY FOURTEEN 9-4 D Nicholls (5) *made all, clr o'r one furlong out, rdn and ran on wl ins last.*
..........................(4 to 1 op 3 to 1 tchd 9 to 2) 1
1519⁶ RED GRIT (Ire) (bl) 8-1 J Lowe (3) *al prmnt, rdn 2 fs out, kpt on ins last*........................ (50 to 1 op 25 to 1) 2
1739⁸ FADE AWAY (Ire) (bl) 8-1 K Darley (9) *dwlt, gd hdwy hfwy, rdn 2 fs out and edgd rght appr last, one pace.*
.... (50 to 1 op 25 to 1) 3
1759⁵ BRAMCOTE CENTURY 7-12² (3*) S Maloney (2) *prmnt, rdn 2 fs out, sn one pace*................(11 to 1 op 8 to 1) 4
1598⁶ IBERIAN MAGIC (Ire) 9-0 N Connorton (8) *slwly into strd, hdwy hfwy, sn rdn, one pace fnl 2 fs.*
.... (16 to 1 op 10 to 1) 5
1519⁵ SALTPETRE (Ire) 8-8 S Webster (7) *cl up, rdn hfwy, sn wknd*.. (20 to 1) 6
1245* THE FERNHILL FLYER (Ire) 8-11 J Carroll (1) *in tch, rdn hfwy and sn btn.*
.............(11 to 8 on op 6 to 4 on tchd 6 to 5 on) 7
1598⁵ FORREST MASTER (Ire) (v) 9-0 J Fanning (6) *cl up till rdn and wknd hfwy*..................(12 to 1 op 7 to 1) 8
1519⁴ PEASAN 8-10 A Mackay (4) *outpcd and beh frm hfwy.*
.... (33 to 1 op 25 to 1) 9
Dist: 2l, 2½l, 1l, 2½l, 1½l, 1½l, 1l, 8l. 1m 2.90s. a 5.10s (9 Ran).
SR: 27/2/-/-/-/-/ (Ian W Glenton), D W Chapman

1890 Yvonne Murray M.B.E. Handicap Class E (0-70 3-y-o and up) £2,805 1m 7f 16yds. .... (3:00)

1593⁷ CONTINUITY [55] 4-8-12 (3*) J Weaver (7) *hld up and beh, hdwy on bit 3 fs out, effrt and swtchd to ld ins last, rdn and ran on*..........................(10 to 1 op 7 to 1) 1
1738* OUR AISLING [72] 5-9-13 (5*,4ex) O Pears (1) *hld up and beh, hdwy 5 fs out, effrt o'r 2 out, sn rdn, led one and a half out till hdd and no extr ins last.*
....(7 to 4 tchd 9 to 4) 2
1654* KAYARTIS [51] 4-8-11 J Lowe (5) *hld up in tch, hdwy 5 fs out, effrt on outer 3 out, sn rdn and ev ch till no extr ins last*.....(13 to 8 fav op 7 to 4 tchd 6 to 4 and 2 to 1) 3
1738³ GREY COMMANDER [34] (v) 5-7-8¹ A Mackay (3) *in tch, hdwy 4 fs out, effrt and led briefly 2 out, wknd entering last*..............................(25 to 1 op 20 to 1) 4
1738² ALPHA HELIX [33] (v) 10-7-7 J Fanning (6) *chsd ldrs till wknd 5 fs out*........................ (25 to 1 op 20 to 1) 5
1517* LORD ADVOCATE [44] (bl) 5-8-1 (3*) M Fenton (2) *cl up, effrt to chal 3 fs out and sn hrd rdn, wknd wl o'r one out.*
....(25 to 1 op 16 to 1) 6
BAY TERN (USA) [40] 7-7-12¹ (3*) S Maloney (4) *in tch, hdwy 4 fs out, rdn 3 out and sn wknd.*
.... (10 to 1 op 8 to 1) 7
1439⁴ SAN PIER NICETO [45] 6-8-5 G Duffield (8) *led, rdn 3 fs out, hdd and wknd 2 out*................(14 to 1 op 8 to 1) 8
Dist: 1l, 3l, nk, 8l, ¾l, 1½l, 5l. 3m 21.90s. a 9.90s (8 Ran).
SR: -/10/-/-/-/ (Mrs Stella Barclay), E J Alston

1891 Baxi Handicap Class E (Div I) (0-70 3-y-o) £2,739 7f 15yds. .... (3:30)

1675* YUNUS EMRE (Ire) [50] 8-5 (3*) M Fenton (6) *chsd ldr, sn pushed alng, rdn 3 fs out, hrd drvn and styd on und pres ins last to ld nr line.*
........(6 to 5 fav op 11 to 10 tchd Evens and 5 to 4) 1
1271⁶ BRAXTON BRAGG (Ire) [49] 8-7 G Duffield (2) *led, rdn 2 fs out, hrd drvn ins last, ct nr finish.*
..............................(9 to 2 op 5 to 1 tchd 7 to 1) 2
1464⁵ FLASHELLA (Ire) [60] 9-4 K Darley (4) *trkd ldrs, effrt and hdwy 2 fs out, rdn and ev ch whn not clr run entering last, swtchd and kpt on.*
.... (13 to 2 op 5 to 1 tchd 7 to 1) 3
1760⁹ KILLY'S FILLY [56] 9-0 J Carroll (3) *chsd ldrs, rdn and hdwy o'r 2 fs out, ev ch ins last, kpt on.*
..............................(100 to 30 op 2 to 1) 4
1271⁹ GLIMPSE OF HEAVEN [63] 9-7 A Culhane (5) *in tch, effrt o'r 2 fs out and ch till wknd appr fnl furlong.*
.... (10 to 1 op 7 to 1) 5
Dist: Hd, hd, sht-hd, 5l. 1m 31.50s. a 6.30s (5 Ran).
SR: -/-/2/-/-/ (Yucel Birol), M Bell

1892 Linlithgow Claiming Stakes Class F (3-y-o) £2,412 1m 16yds. .... (4:00)

1736³ NUTTY BROWN (v) 8-8 (5*) O Pears (2) *cl up, led hfwy, rdn alng o'r 2 fs out, kpt on ins last.*
..........................(9 to 4 op 2 to 1 tchd 5 to 2) 1
1596* DRUMDONNA (Ire) 8-8 J Carroll (4) *trkd ldrs, hdwy to chase wnr hfwy, rdn to chal 2 fs out, kpt on one pace fnl furlong*..........................(5 to 2 op 7 to 4) 2
1170⁶ FRIENDLY KNIGHT 8-13 K Darley (5) *in tch, effrt and hdwy 3 fs out, sn rdn and one pace*. (12 to 1 op 8 to 1) 3
1701⁹ LAND O'LAKES (Ire) 9-0 G Duffield (1) *led to hfwy, rdn 3 fs out, one pace*........(6 to 4 fav op 7 to 4 tchd 2 to 1) 4
OUR PRICE 8-11 J Fortune (3) *cl up till slpd bend aftr 3 fs and sn beh*........................(50 to 1 op 25 to 1) 5
Dist: 2l, 4l, 1l, 25l. 1m 44.20s. a 5.70s (5 Ran).
SR: 7/-/ (John Lawson-Brown), S G Norton

1893 Baxi Handicap Class E (Div II) (0-70 3-y-o) £2,725 7f 15yds. .... (4:30)

1658² DANCING DOMINO [61] 9-7 K Darley (4) *cl up, led on bit 2 fs out, hrd hld*...(5 to 1 on op 7 to 2 on tchd 3 to 1 on) 1
861 SAINTED SUE [37] 7-11 A Mackay (3) *led, rdn and hdd 2 fs out, kpt on, no ch wth wnr*........(50 to 1 op 33 to 1) 2
1735² MISSED THE BOAT (Ire) [54] 8-7 (7*) V Halliday (1) *steadied strt, hdwy hfwy, effrt and rdn o'r 2 fs out, edgd rght and sn one pace*.........(9 to 2 op 7 to 2 tchd 5 to 1) 3
1848⁵ SELVOLE [43] 8-3 J Fanning (2) *cl up 3 fs, sn outpcd.*
..............................(25 to 1 tchd 33 to 1) 4
Dist: 2½l, 2l, 10l. 1m 32.30s. a 7.10s (4 Ran).
(P D Savill), M H Easterby

1894 Firth Of Forth Apprentice Handicap Class G (0-70 3-y-o and up) £2,242 1m 3f 32yds........................(5:00)

LATVIAN [62] 6-9-7 J Weaver (1) *trkd ldrs, effrt and hdwy 3 fs out, led 2 out, rdn and kpt on wl ins last.* ....(8 to 1 op 7 to 1 tchd 10 to 1) 1
1521[3] JAZILAH (Fr) [69] 5-10-0 F Norton (3) *chsd ldrs, hdwy 4 fs out, rdn wl o'r 2 out, kpt on one pace.* ....(11 to 10 on op Evens tchd 11 to 10) 2
1600* RAPID MOVER [35] (bl) 6-7-8[1] N Kennedy (5) *cl up, rdn to ld 3 fs out, hdd 2 out, kpt on und pres ins last.* ....(20 to 1 op 16 to 1) 3
1476[4] SUPER BLUES [43] 6-7-11 (5*) V Halliday (4) *hld up, hdwy on outer 3 fs out, sn rdn and ch 2 furlongs out, wknd appr fnl furlong*..... (20 to 1 op 16 to 1 tchd 25 to 1) 4
1781[3] PRIME PAINTER [68] 3-8-8 (5*) L Aspell (8) *led, rdn and hdd 3 fs out, grad wknd*..................(5 to 1 op 4 to 1) 5
1521* TANODA [45] 7-7-13 (5*) J Marshall (6) *chsd ldrs, effrt and hdwy 3 fs out, ch 2 out, sn rdn and grad wknd.* ....(9 to 2 op 4 to 1 tchd 5 to 1) 6
1521[9] ASTURIAS [36] 10-7-9[6] (5*) G Mitchell (9) *al rear.* (33 to 1) 7
1738[4] BLACKDOWN [56] 6-9-1 S Maloney (7) *slwly away, hdwy to chase ldrs hfwy, effrt and rdn 3 fs out, sn wknd.* ....(16 to 1 op 14 to 1 tchd 20 to 1) 8
1099[7] TRI MY WAY (Ire) [49] 3-7-8[8] (7*) Claire West (2) *al rear.* ....(200 to 1) 9

Dist: 1½l, ¾l, 1l, nk, ½l, 12l, 15l, 1½l. 2m 25.50s. a 6.00s (9 Ran).
SR: 41/45/9/15/25/15/ (J P Seymour), R Allan

PONTEFRACT (good to firm)
Monday June 21st

Going Correction: MINUS 0.30 sec. per fur. (races 1,3,4,5), MINUS 0.45 (2,6,7)

1895 Tattersalls Maiden Auction Series Stakes Qualifier Class E (Div I) (2-y-o) £3,054 6f......................(2:45)

1211[5] KINGSWELL PRINCE (Ire) 8-8 T Quinn (1) *tucked away on ins, improved 2 fs out, led o'r one out, kpt on wl inside last*..................(3 to 1 op 5 to 2) 1
1189[2] CALL TO MIND (Ire) 8-7 M Birch (8) *pressed ldr, rdn o'r 2 fs out, ev ch over one out, kpt on same pace ins fnl furlong*........(9 to 2 op 4 to 1 tchd 5 to 1 and 11 to 2) 2
HASTY BANK 8-6 K Fallon (6) *sluggish strt, beh and sn pushed alng, hdwy appr strt, swtchd and styd on wl fnl furlong, prmsg*......(8 to 1 op 6 to 1 tchd 10 to 1) 3
1481[3] NORTHERN CELADON (Ire) 8-10 P Robinson (2) *nvr far away, nosed ahead briefly o'r one furlong out, one pace ins last*....................(2 to 1 fav op 9 to 4) 4
1598[3] WOODLAND WHISPER 8-3 M Roberts (7) *led til hdd o'r one furlong out, wknd ins last*.... (14 to 1 op 10 to 1) 5
1456[5] BERNIE'S SISTER (Ire) 7-8 (7*) D Wright (11) *beh, pushed alng hfwy, kpt on fnl furlong, no imprsn.* ....(11 to 1 op 10 to 1) 6
1561[7] LEGAL TRAIN 8-6 W Ryan (10) *chsd ldrs, rdn alng hfwy, wknd entering strt*....................(16 to 1) 7
1418[9] DANGEROUS SHADOW 8-1 Dale Gibson (4) *in tch, pushed alng entering strt, sn btn.* ....(20 to 1 op 16 to 1 tchd 25 to 1) 8
1263[3] JOE JAGGER (Ire) 8-7 L Dettori (5) *in tch, effrt appr strt, wknd o'r one furlong out*..............(13 to 2 op 6 to 1) 9
1189[4] OLYMPIC BID 8-3 G Carter (9) *beh, rdn alng hfwy, sn btn.* ....(20 to 1 op 14 to 1) 10
1555 ASTROLOGY 8-3 L Charnock (3) *towards rear, sn pushed alng, wknd quickly frm hfwy, tld off*..........(33 to 1) 11

Dist: 2l, 2l, nk, 2½l, 4l, sht-hd, ¾l, hd, 1l, 8l. 1m 16.20s. a 1.50s (11 Ran).
SR: 28/19/10/13/-/-/ (Stephen Crown), M R Channon

1896 Smeaton Selling Handicap Class G (0-60 3-y-o) £2,427 1½m 8yds... (3:15)

1493[3] ANN HILL (Ire) [45] 8-13 W Ryan (9) *hld up in rear, improved o'r 3 fs out, rdn to ld ins fnl furlong, ran on.* ....(6 to 4 fav op 3 to 1 tchd 7 to 2) 1
1479[3] TTYFRAN [53] 9-7 S Perks (1) *hld up in last pl, took clr order 7 fs out, effrt 3 out, led wl o'r one out, hdd ins last, no extr*....................(4 to 1 op 3 to 1) 2
1562 BAJAN AFFAIR [33] 7-12 (3*) D Harrison (3) *chsd ldrs, outpcd and rdn o'r 3 fs out, improved over one out, kpt on ins last*....................(20 to 1 op 16 to 1) 3
1477[5] NANCY (Ire) [43] (bl) 8-11 L Dettori (7) *set steady pace, quickened 5 fs out, hdd wl o'r one out, no extr.* ....(9 to 2 tchd 5 to 1) 4
1533[9] TAKE A FLYER (Ire) [40] 8-1 (7*) S Drowne (5) *pressed ldg bunch, effrt and rdn appr strt, sn one pace.* ....(4 to 1 op 3 to 1) 5
1557[4] PETITE JESS [40] 8-3 (5*) N Gwilliams (8) *nvr far away, ev ch 2 fs out, wknd o'r one out*..................(10 to 1) 6
1702[6] BONNY PRINCESS [33] (bl) 8-1 N Carlisle (2) *chsd ldrs, drvn alng 3 fs out, fdd*............ (14 to 1 op 16 to 1) 7
1074 KENTUCKY DREAMS [42] 8-10 R P Elliott (4) *slwly into strd, hld up in tch, effrt appr strt, sn btn.* ....(20 to 1 op 16 to 1) 8
1283[6] THE BRACKETEER [33] 8-1 J Quinn (6) *mid-div, rdn 6 fs out, lost tch o'r 3 out, tld off*..................(33 to 1) 9

Dist: 1½l, 3½l, 2½l, ½l, 2l, 1l, 6l, dist. 2m 42.40s. a 7.40s (9 Ran).
(A S Hill), R Hollinshead

1897 Tattersalls Maiden Auction Series Stakes Qualifier Class E (Div II) (2-y-o) £3,028 6f.....................(3:45)

1497[4] SECRET SERENADE 8-10 Dean McKeown (8) *nvr far away, rdn and hng lft o'r one furlong out, ran on wl fnl furlong to ld post*............ (2 to 1 fav op 5 to 2) 1
TWICE IN BUNDORAN (Ire) 7-10 (5*) L Newton (1) *led, shaken up entering strt, ct post*.....(5 to 1 op 4 to 1) 2
MILL FORCE 8-5 (5*) Darren Moffatt (11) *sluggish strt, beh and sn rdn, hdwy entering strt, hng lft and styd on strly, can improve*................(12 to 1 op 10 to 1) 3
1758[6] THREE OF HEARTS 8-1 N Adams (5) *pressed ldr, shaken up o'r 2 fs out, wknd over one out.* (12 to 1 op 10 to 1) 4
HEATHYARDS LADY (USA) 8-1 A McGlone (2) *beh, rdn to improve hfwy, one pace entering strt.* ....(12 to 1 op 10 to 1) 5
1475[5] BALLARD RING (Ire) 8-1 L Charnock (9) *in tch til rdn and wknd 2 fs out*.................... (33 to 1 op 25 to 1) 6
1715[8] BEDAZZLE 8-8 G Carter (10) *beh on outer, effrt o'r 2 fs out, sn btn and eased*........................(12 to 1) 7
1529[4] ASTRAC (Ire) 8-9 B Raymond (7) *chsd ldrs, rdn o'r 2 fs out, wknd over one out*..... (4 to 1 tchd 9 to 2 and 5 to 1) 8
TISA WASITEEN (Ire) 8-4 J Quinn (6) *beh and sn pushed alng, nvr on terms*.............. (12 to 1 op 10 to 1) 9
MURPHY'S GOLD (Ire) 8-6 M Birch (3) *dwlt, beh, rdn alng hfwy, wknd entering strt*...........(7 to 1 op 6 to 1) 10
AUNTIE FAY (Ire) 7-13 (3*) D Harrison (4) *dwlt, beh, sn pushed alng, wknd o'r 2 fs out*..... (11 to 1 op 8 to 1) 11

Dist: Hd, 2½l, 3½l, 1½l, 3½l, ½l, hd, 1l, ¾l, 2l. 1m 16.60s. a 1.90s (11 Ran).
SR: 22/12/11/-/-/-/ (Colin G R Booth), J A Glover

1898 Active Business Services Handicap Class D (0-80 3-y-o and up) £4,659 6f ....(4:15)

1563* SOBERING THOUGHTS [60] 7-9-1 N Adams (1) *wth ldr, led 2 fs out, hld on wl whn hrd pressed fnl furlong.* ....(3 to 1 fav op 5 to 2) 1
1494[9] SULLY'S CHOICE (USA) [44] (bl) 12-7-13 S Wood (4) *led til hdd 2 fs out, rdn and chlgd ins fnl furlong, no extr towards finish*................ (16 to 1 op 14 to 1) 2
1835[3] STATE FLYER [58] (v) 5-8-6 (7*) G Forster (5) *slwly into strd, beh, hdwy and came wide strt, ran on ins fnl furlong, nvr dngrs*.................. (5 to 1 tchd 11 to 2) 3
1480[5] PARFAIT AMOUR [60] 4-9-1 G Carter (2) *chsd ldrs, drvn alng o'r 2 fs out, kpt on same pace ins last.* ....(6 to 1 op 7 to 1) 4
1520 SAVAHRA SOUND [69] 8-9-10 B Raymond (3) *in tch, effrt and rdn entering strt, one pace ins fnl furlong.* ....(12 to 1) 5
1744[7] DANCE ON SIXPENCE [48] 5-8-3 J Quinn (10) *hld up, effrt and pushed alng 2 fs out, one pace o'r one out.* ....(7 to 1 op 10 to 1) 6
1588 SIR OLIVER (Ire) [54] 4-8-9 M Roberts (8) *dwlt, sn in tch, rdn entering strt, not quicken*....... (7 to 1 op 8 to 1) 7
1591 PIMSBOY [49] (bl) 6-8-1 (3*) D Harrison (9) *beh and sn pushed alng, no imprsn fnl 2 fs*....(16 to 1 op 14 to 1) 8
1618* YES [55] 5-8-10 L Dettori (7) *beh, rdn hfwy, drpd away quickly, virtually pld up entering strt, lme.* ....(4 to 1 tchd 9 to 2) 9

Dist: ½l, 1½l, hd, 1l, 1½l, 1l, 3l, dist. 1m 15.60s. a 0.90s (9 Ran).
SR: 47/29/37/38/43/16/18/1/-/ (W E Solomon), J L Eyre

1899 Spindrifter Conditions Stakes Class D (2-y-o) £3,687 6f................(4:45)

1615* SAWTID 8-2 (5*) C Hodgson (4) *hld up in tch, took clr order hfwy, rdn to ld ins fnl furlong, kpt on wl.* ....(7 to 4 fav tchd 2 to 1 and 13 to 8) 1
1381[6] MISS MAH-JONG 8-9 Dean McKeown (5) *wth ldr, led 2 fs out, hdd ins last, no extr.* ....(6 to 1 op 11 to 2 tchd 13 to 2) 2
1098[2] MONKEY MUSIC 8-10 G Carter (3) *beh, rdn alng hfwy, improved entering strt, ran on, no extr towards finish.* ....(7 to 1 op 11 to 2) 3
1759* TWO D'S 8-7 M Birch (2) *trkd ldrs, effrt and shaken up 2 fs out, sn btn*.................(3 to 1 tchd 7 to 2) 4
1565[4] BOLD ARISTOCRAT (Ire) 9-0 S Perks (1) *led til rdn and hdd 2 fs out, wknd o'r one out.* ....(3 to 1 op 5 to 2 tchd 100 to 30) 5

Dist: 1l, 2½l, 5l, ½l. 1m 16.70s. a 2.00s (5 Ran).
SR: 17/15/6/-/-/ (J B R Leisure Ltd), D Morris

1900 G.M.S. Ticket Handicap Class E (0-70 3-y-o and up) £3,236 1¼m 6yds (5:15)

1562* SILVER SAMURAI [59] 4-9-10 L Dettori (6) *in tch, rdn 4 fs out, ran on to ld o'r one out, sn clr, easily.* ....(6 to 1 tchd 7 to 1 and 11 to 2) 1

1521^{4} TELEPHUS [50] 4-9-1 B Raymond (11) *mid-div, cld 3 fs out, rdn and ran on ins last*............(7 to 1 tchd 8 to 1) 2

1601^{7} REEL OF TULLOCH (Ire) [43] 4-8-8 M Roberts (4) *in tch, sn pushed alng, effrt 3 fs out, swtchd and ran on ins fnl furlong*..........................(12 to 1 op 10 to 1) 3

1612^{4} CAL NORMA'S LADY (Ire) [47] 5-8-5 (7*) J Tate (1) *chsd ldr, led o'r 3 fs out, hdd over one out, no extr*......(12 to 1) 4

1612^{6} AMLAK (USA) [50] 4-9-1 J Quinn (16) *chsd ldrs, improved and ev ch o'r one furlong out, not quicken.* ....(11 to 2 fav tchd 6 to 1 and 13 to 2) 5

1307 VENTURE FOURTH [38] 4-8-3 S Wood (8) *hld up, smooth hdwy o'r 3 fs out, chlgd over one out, wknd ins last.* ....(25 to 1) 6

1521^{5} NOT YET [32] 9-7-11 N Carlisle (7) *beh til hdwy o'r 2 fs out, kpt on, nvr dngrs*..................(20 to 1 op 16 to 1) 7

1612^{9} MISTY GODDESS (Ire) [53] 5-9-4 W Ryan (14) *mid-div, drvn alng 3 fs out, one pace fnl quarter m.* ....(11 to 1 op 10 to 1 tchd 12 to 1) 8

1566^{2} PERSIAN FOUNTAIN (Ire) [65] 3-9-1 (3*) D Harrison (5) *mid-div, sn rdn and drpd rear, steady hdwy on bit fnl 2 fs, nvr dngrs*..........................(13 to 2 op 6 to 1) 9

1685* SINCLAIR LAD (Ire) [56] (bl) 5-9-0 (7*) S Drowne (10) *slwly into strd, sn reco'red and rcd midfield, drvn over 3 fs out, soon one pace*..............................(10 to 1) 10

4662a LODGING [30] (v) 6-7-9^{2} L Charnock (15) *beh, drvn alng hfwy, nvr able to chal*.........................(100 to 1) 11

1389^{6} NORMAN WARRIOR [41] 4-8-2^{1} (5*) C Hodgson (18) *chsd ldrs, rdn 3 fs out, btn entering strt.* (12 to 1 op 10 to 1) 12

1781 GAY MING [39] 4-7-13 (5*) A Garth (19) *beh, drvn alng 4 fs out, sn btn*..................................(25 to 1) 13

OLICANA (Ire) [50] 3-8-3 E Johnson (3) *steadied strt, rstrained in rear, nvr rchd chalg pos.* ....(14 to 1 op 12 to 1) 14

1761^{6} BIDWEAYA (USA) [38] 6-8-3 G Carter (17) *mid-div, drvn alng hfwy, sn btn*............................(20 to 1) 15

1112 JOSEPH'S WINE (Ire) [38] 4-8-3^{1} Dean McKeown (9) *slwly into strd, beh, rdn whn not clr run appr strt, sn btn.* ....(14 to 1 op 12 to 1) 16

1460^{8} EMPEROR ALEXANDER (Ire) [50] (bl) 5-8-12 (3*) S D Williams (2) *in tch, sn lost pl and rdn alng, no dngr fnl half m.* ....(14 to 1 tchd 16 to 1) 17

1257^{6} DOUBLE SHERRY [32] 4-7-4 (7*) M Baird (13) *chsd ldrs til rdn and wknd o'r 3 fs out*.....................(20 to 1) 18

TOMASHENKO [50] 4-9-1 M Birch (12) *took keen hold, sn led, hdd o'r 3 fs out, wknd quickly, tld off*.....(33 to 1) 19

Dist: 3l, 1l, 1l, 1½l, ½l, 3½l, 6l, 4l, 1½l, 1l. 2m 10.40s. a 2.20s (19 Ran).

SR: 43/28/19/21/21/8/-/4/-/ (J D Cable), Mrs V A Aconley

1901 July Maiden Stakes Class D (3-y-o) £3,640 1¼m 6yds.............. (5:45)

1581^{2} GRAEGOS (Ire) 9-0 W Ryan (3) *trkd ldr, improved to ld 2 fs out, sn clr, eased towards finish*.....(7 to 4 op 6 to 4) 1

1671^{7} VISHNU (USA) 9-0 A McGlone (2) *dwlt, trkd ldg pair, shaken up o'r 2 fs out, kpt on ins last, no ch wth wnr.* ....(5 to 1 tchd 11 to 2) 2

1469^{3} GREENBANK (USA) 9-0 L Dettori (1) *led til hdd 2 fs out, rdn and sn btn.* (11 to 10 on op 5 to 4 on tchd Evens) 3

1581^{7} SCOTTISH WEDDING 8-9 B Raymond (4) *hld up in last pl, rdn and lost tch o'r 3 fs out.* ....(40 to 1 op 25 to 1 tchd 50 to 1) 4

Dist: 1½l, 10l, 5l. 2m 12.00s. a 3.80s (4 Ran).

SR: 17/14/-/-/ (L Marinopoulos), H R A Cecil

WINDSOR (good) Monday June 21st

Going Correction: MINUS 0.25 sec. per fur.

1902 Chiswick Selling Handicap Class G (0-60 3-y-o and up) £2,010 1¼m 7yds ....(6:35)

1138 TAUNTING (Ire) [45] 5-9-3 R Cochrane (12) *midfield till gd hdwy o'r 2 fs out, ran on to ld nr finish.* ....(12 to 1 op 10 to 1) 1

1627^{4} MALZETA (Ire) [45] 3-7-12 (7*) D Wright (14) *hdwy o'r 2 fs out, kpt on wl ins last.* (9 to 1 op 6 to 1 tchd 10 to 1) 2

BENGAL TIGER (Ire) [44] (v) 5-9-2 D Holland (3) *sn led, hrd rdn frm 2 fs out, hdd nr finish*......(10 to 1 op 8 to 1) 3

1562^{7} MALINDI BAY [34] 5-8-6 J Reid (1) *prmnt, ev ch o'r one furlong out, one pace*.............(10 to 1 op 8 to 1) 4

1230^{9} EMERALD EARS [29] 4-8-1 T Sprake (19) *wl beh till ran on fnl 2 fs, nvr nrr*..................(33 to 1 op 20 to 1) 5

1238^{8} LONG FURLONG [40] 5-8-12 Paul Eddery (15) *chsd ldrs till rdn and no hdwy fnl one and a half fs.* ....(5 to 1 fav op 8 to 1) 6

1685^{4} DAZZLING FIRE (Ire) [47] 4-8-12 (7*) Kim McDonnell (13) *midfield, effrt 3 fs out, ran on same pace.* ....(10 to 1 op 8 to 1) 7

1799 DOTS DEE [33] 4-8-0^{2} (7*) Michael Bradley (22) *rear div till styd on fnl 2 fs, nvr nrr.* ....(11 to 1 op 8 to 1 tchd 12 to 1) 8

1685^{6} BEAT THE BAGMAN (Ire) [40] 3-8-0 C Avery (16) *nvr nrr.* ....(16 to 1 tchd 20 to 1) 9

1453^{8} LITTLE PARK [44] 4-8-11 (5*) Stephen Davies (11) *beh till hdwy 3 fs out, sn one pace*........(20 to 1 op 16 to 1) 10

919^{7} WITH GUSTO [39] 6-8-11 J Williams (9) *nvr able to chal.* ....(20 to 1 tchd 25 to 1) 11

1685^{8} DON'T GIVE UP [46] (bl) 5-9-4 W Newnes (2) *chsd ldrs, ev ch wl o'r one furlong out, wkng whn not much room ins last*..................(16 to 1 op 14 to 1) 12

1626^{8} LER CRU (Ire) [55] 4-9-13 T Williams (10) *trkd ldrs, niggled alng 4 fs out, sn btn*...............(20 to 1 op 14 to 1) 13

1659 GEORGE ROPER [50] 3-8-10 B Rouse (8) *chsd ldrs till wknd 3 fs out*....................(33 to 1 op 20 to 1) 14

1498 STANE STREET (Ire) [42] 5-9-0 A Munro (17) *nvr better than mid-div*..........................(20 to 1 op 16 to 1) 15

1623^{9} OSGATHORPE [32] 6-8-4 R Perham (20) *chsd ldg bunch till wknd o'r 2 fs out*..............(33 to 1 op 20 to 1) 16

35 BROUGHTON BLUES (Ire) [29] 5-8-1 S O'Gorman (5) *beh, some hdwy o'r 4 fs out, nvr nr to chal.* ....(16 to 1 op 14 to 1) 17

1681^{9} BAYIN (USA) [38] 4-8-10 A Clark (25) *al rear div.* ....(25 to 1 op 20 to 1) 18

1696^{8} SLY PROSPECT (USA) [42] 5-9-0 R Wernham (18) *midfield, shrtlvd effrt 3 fs out, sn wknd*.....(16 to 1 op 12 to 1) 19

1623^{7} COOCHIE [30] (bl) 4-8-2 S Dawson (23) *slwly away, al beh.* ....(25 to 1 op 20 to 1) 20

DONT BEAT THE BABY [33] 5-8-5 R Price (4) *chsd ldr till wknd wl o'r 2 fs out*..............................(33 to 1) 21

1496^{8} WHO'S TOM (Ire) [39] 3-7-13 D Biggs (21) *al beh.* ....(16 to 1 op 14 to 1 tchd 20 to 1) 22

678 SOLID (Ire) [44] 5-9-2 S Whitworth (6) *beh till shrtlvd effrt o'r 4 fs out, sn wknd*..........(14 to 1 tchd 16 to 1) 23

1453 BRUSH WOLF (USA) [27] 4-7-6 (7*) A Whelan (7) *midfield, some hdwy 3 fs out, wknd quickly*.............(33 to 1) 24

1674^{4} LIFE'S A BREEZE [43] 4-8-8 (7*) D McCabe (24) *al beh.* ....(8 to 1 op 7 to 1 tchd 9 to 1) 25

Dist: ¾l, nk, nk, 2l, 1½l, ¾l, sht-hd, 1½l, sht-hd, 1½l. 2m 7.00s. a 4.50s (25 Ran).

SR: 33/19/29/18/9/17/22/7/-/ (Brian Oxton), M Blanshard

1903 Heathrow Handicap Class E (0-70 3-y-o and up) £2,469 5f 217yds......(7:05)

1658^{5} GREAT HALL [56] 4-9-3 J Williams (9) *wl beh till rapid hdwy frm o'r one furlong out, str run to ld ins last, pushed clr*............(7 to 1 op 6 to 1 tchd 15 to 2) 1

1664^{4} MOGWAI (Ire) [55] (v) 4-9-2 D Holland (11) *al prmnt, led o'r one furlong out, hdd and no extr ins last.* ....(8 to 1 op 7 to 1 tchd 9 to 1) 2

1664* PALACEGATE GOLD (Ire) [54] 4-9-1 A Munro (6) *midfield and rdn alng till hdwy 2 fs out, sn ev ch, not quicken ins last*....(11 to 2 op 5 to 1 tchd 6 to 1 and 13 to 2) 3

1698^{3} ISLAND KNIGHT (Ire) [67] 4-10-0 D Biggs (13) *al prmnt, led wl o'r one furlong out, sn hdd and ran on same pace.* ....(10 to 1 op 8 to 1 tchd 12 to 1) 4

1821^{2} ZINBAQ [35] 7-7-10^{2} T Williams (4) *pushed alng to go pace till gd hdwy and not clr run o'r one furlong out, ran on ins last*.........(100 to 30 fav op 4 to 1 tchd 9 to 2) 5

1416^{6} TEE GEE JAY [59] (bl) 3-8-12 J Curant (10) *slwly away and sn rdn alng, beh till ran on fnl 2 fs, nvr nrr.* ....(10 to 1 op 8 to 1) 6

1487 TURTLE BEACH [50] 4-8-11 W Newnes (5) *trkd ldg bunch till wknd o'r one furlong out*......(33 to 1 op 25 to 1) 7

1257^{7} BATCHWORTH BOUND [44] 4-8-5 C Rutter (7) *chsd ldr till wknd o'r one furlong out.* ....(12 to 1 op 10 to 1 tchd 14 to 1) 8

1394^{6} LEIGH CROFTER [56] (v) 4-9-3 J Reid (3) *nvr rch ldrs.* ....(12 to 1 op 10 to 1 tchd 14 to 1) 9

113^{9} GEMINI BAY [45] (bl) 4-8-6 S Dawson (12) *led till hdd wl o'r one furlong out, wknd quickly*....(25 to 1 op 20 to 1) 10

1326^{7} MURPHY'S HOPE (Ire) [60] (bl) 3-8-13 Pat Eddery (1) *chsd ldg bunch, wkng whn not clr run o'r one furlong out, sn btn*..................(9 to 1 op 8 to 1 tchd 10 to 1) 11

1492^{4} JOE SUGDEN [49] 9-8-10 Paul Eddery (8) *prmnt till wknd 2 fs out*.......................(10 to 1 tchd 11 to 1) 12

1696 APACHEE FLOWER [47] 3-8-0^{2} R Price (2) *beh frm hfwy.* ....(66 to 1 op 50 to 1) 13

1059 LOOTING (USA) [33] 7-7-8 G Bardwell (14) *speed 2 fs, sn rdn and wknd*..........................(10 to 1 op 7 to 1) 14

Dist: 2l, hd, 2l, 2½l, ¾l, 1l, 2l, ½l, 1½l, 1l. 1m 11.60s. a 1.30s (14 Ran).

SR: 47/38/36/41/-/12/7/-/3/ (P D Cundell), P D Cundell

1904 Dataserv Conditions Stakes Class D (3-y-o) £5,190 1¼m 7yds........(7:35)

435[6] DECLASSIFIED (USA) 8-10 R Cochrane (1) *made all, jnd frm 3 fs out, hld on wl ins last.*
............(5 to 2 op 6 to 4 tchd 11 to 4 and 3 to 1) 1
980* GONE FOR A BURTON (Ire) 8-10 Pat Eddery (3) *trkd ldr thrght, pushed alng to chal fnl 3 fs, no extr ins last.*
..............................(2 to 1 on op 2 to 1 on) 2
1719 CHAIN DANCE (v) 8-5 J Williams (2) *reluctant to race, tried to pull herself up aftr 2 fs, continued, tld off.*
.............................(15 to 2 op 8 to 1 tchd 6 to 1) 3
Dist: 2l, dist. 2m 5.60s. a 3.10s (3 Ran).
SR: 40/36/-/ (Edward P Evans), L M Cumani

1905 EBF Robert Walters Median Auction Maiden Stakes Class D (2-y-o) £5,127 5f 217yds......................(8:05)

1640[2] BLUEGRASS PRINCE (Ire) 9-0 Pat Eddery (14) *al hndy gng wl, led o'r one furlong out, sn clr, imprsv.*
.... (Evens fav op 11 to 10 tchd 5 to 4) 1
SWITCH BLADE (Ire) 8-9 L Dettori (4) *al prmnt, ev ch o'r one furlong out, kpt on same pace, no chance wth wnr.*
.........(10 to 1 op 5 to 1 tchd 12 to 1 and 14 to 1) 2
1583[7] ADMIRALELLA 8-9 J Reid (16) *led till hdd o'r one furlong out, sn rdn and styd on same pace.*
.... (12 to 1 op 10 to 1 tchd 8 to 1) 3
1624[3] MILLICENT NORTH 8-9 J Williams (18) *hld up in midfield, gd hdwy 2 fs out, kpt on wl clsg stages, nvr nrr.*
..........................(11 to 2 op 10 to 1 tchd 12 to 1) 4
1091 ANOTHERONE TO NOTE 8-7 (7*) Mark Denaro (17) *chsd ldrs till rdn and not quicken o'r one furlong out.*
...................................(50 to 1 tchd 66 to 1) 5
MACIZO 9-0 C Avery (2) *slwly away, beh and rdn alng till styd on on fnl one and a half fs, nvr nrr.*
....(50 to 1 op 33 to 1) 6
1763[3] SWORDSMANSHIP 9-0 G Duffield (20) *broke wl and prmnt till wknd 2 fs out*......(6 to 1 op 4 to 1 tchd 13 to 2) 7
DANCING LAWYER 9-0 W Newnes (3) *chsd ldg bunch, slightly outpcd o'r 2 fs out, kpt on fnl furlong, no dngr.*
....(50 to 1 op 20 to 1) 8
MERLIN'S FIELD (Ire) 9-0 S Raymont (7) *beh till came wide and hdwy 2 fs out, nvr trbld ldrs.* (33 to 1 op 16 to 1) 9
1211 NOT THE NADGER 9-0 C Rutter (12) *slwly away, beh till some hdwy 2 fs out, nvr able to chal.*
....(50 to 1 op 33 to 1) 10
1481[8] NORISKI'MARINGER 9-0 Paul Eddery (15) *rdn alng in midfield hfwy, nvr a threat*..........(50 to 1 op 33 to 1) 11
1350 NO SPEECHES (Ire) 9-0 D Biggs (21) *sn rdn alng in midfield, nvr trbld ldrs*................(50 to 1 op 20 to 1) 12
AWS (Ire) 9-0 W Carson (9) *nvr nr to chal.*
........................(14 to 1 op 7 to 1 tchd 16 to 1) 13
CYCLONE (Ire) 8-7 (7*) S Mulvey (5) *slwly away, beh till shrtlvd effrt o'r 2 fs out, nvr a dngr.*
....(50 to 1 op 20 to 1) 14
ARALIYA 8-9 M Hills (6) *no show*.....(50 to 1 op 25 to 1) 15
1535[3] GINGERILLO 9-0 A Munro (10) *prmnt till wknd o'r 2 fs out.*
........................(20 to 1 op 14 to 1 tchd 25 to 1) 16
COURT JESTER 9-0 D Holland (13) *sn rdn alng to go pace, al towards rear*................... (16 to 1 op 6 to 1) 17
776 SPORTING START 9-0 N Adams (19) *slwly away, al beh.*
....(50 to 1 op 33 to 1) 18
1602 SEVEN UP CYD 8-9 R Cochrane (1) *prmnt on outsd till lost pl fnl one and a half fs, sn beh*.... (50 to 1 op 33 to 1) 19
1497[5] SUPER SYMPHONIC 9-0 P Robinson (11) *chsd ldg bunch to hfwy, sn wknd.*
.........(20 to 1 op 14 to 1 tchd 25 to 1 and 33 to 1) 20
MISS DENBIGH 8-9 B Rouse (8) *in tch on outsd till ran green o'r 2 fs out, sn wknd and tld off.*
........................(20 to 1 op 33 to 1 tchd 40 to 1) 21
Dist: 5l, nk, 1½l, 4l, 2l, ¾l, ¾l, ½l, nk, ½l. 1m 11.60s. a 1.30s (21 Ran).
SR: 44/19/18/12/1/-/ (Bezwell Fixings Limited), R Hannon

1906 Motorway Handicap Class E (0-70 3-y-o) £2,511 1m 3f 135yds......... (8:35)

1488[4] EUPHONIC [66] 9-7 L Dettori (8) *al hndy, ev ch frm o'r one furlong out, sstnd effrt to ld nr finish.*
....(9 to 2 tchd 6 to 1) 1
1534* GENERAL MOUKTAR [66] 9-7 M Roberts (4) *trkd ldr gng wl, led o'r 2 fs out, hrd rdn over one out, hdd nr finish.*
.... (Evens fav tchd 6 to 5 and 5 to 4) 2
1709[2] SUPREME MASTER [65] 9-6 Pat Eddery (6) *trkd ldrs till outpcd wl o'r 2 fs out, kpt on fnl furlong.*
........................(4 to 1 tchd 7 to 2 and 9 to 2) 3
1426[7] BROUGHTONS FORMULA [59] (bl) 8-7 (7*) D McCabe (3) *hld up in tch, rdn and effrt 3 fs out, styd on.*
....(12 to 1 op 8 to 1) 4
876 BOXBOY [54] 8-9 S Whitworth (1) *slwly into strd, hdwy 5 fs out, ev ch o'r one out, sn rdn and btn.*
....(20 to 1 op 16 to 1) 5
1605[6] DUTCH DEBUTANTE [55] 8-10 W Newnes (7) *slwly away, hld up in tch, rdn wl o'r 2 fs out, sn no imprsn.*
...........(15 to 2 op 8 to 1 tchd 9 to 1 and 6 to 1) 6
980 BARSLEY [49] 8-1 (3*) B Doyle (5) *set slow pace till hdd o'r 2 fs out, sn rdn and unbl to quicken.*
........................(50 to 1 op 33 to 1 tchd 66 to 1) 7
1606 MISTY JENNI (Ire) [62] 9-3 A Munro (2) *pld hrd in tch, rdn o'r 2 fs out, sn wknd*............. (14 to 1 op 10 to 1) 8
Dist: Hd, 5l, sht-hd, 2½l, ¾l, nk, 6l. 2m 32.50s. a 9.50s (8 Ran).
(Paul Stamp), I A Balding

1907 Pall Mall Rating Related Maiden Stakes Class F (0-65 3-y-o) £2,040 1m 67yds......................... (9:05)

1470[3] TONY'S MIST 9-0 Pat Eddery (5) *al hndy, led o'r 2 fs out, hrd rdn and hld on gmely ins last.*
.....................(5 to 2 fav op 3 to 1 tchd 9 to 4) 1
1338 STORM VENTURE (Ire) 9-0 M Tebbutt (2) *trkd ldg bunch, hdwy and not much room wl o'r one furlong out, sn ev ch, kpt on*..............(7 to 2 op 3 to 1 tchd 9 to 2) 2
1746[4] ITS UNBELIEVABLE 8-7 (7*) D Wright (10) *led till hdd o'r 2 fs out, sn rdn alng, rallied ins last.*
........................(9 to 2 op 6 to 1 tchd 7 to 1) 3
1504[2] MY HARVINSKI 8-9 (5*) Stephen Davies (7) *hld up, gd hdwy 2 fs out, kpt on ins last, nvr nrr*......(7 to 1 op 5 to 1) 4
1007[3] PYRRHIC DANCE 9-0 M Hills (8) *hld up in tch, hdwy o'r 2 fs out, sn ev ch, ran on one pace*.....(8 to 1 op 6 to 1) 5
1377[3] TAKE THE MICK 9-0 M Roberts (1) *sn pushed alng, wth ldrs, ev ch 2 fs out, wknd ins last.*
........................(16 to 1 op 14 to 1 tchd 20 to 1) 6
1504[3] MARATHIA (bl) 8-9 W Woods (4) *chsd ldg bunch till rdn o'r 3 fs out, sn wknd*...............(16 to 1 op 8 to 1) 7
1777[9] SYLVANIA (Ire) 9-0 A Munro (3) *sn pushed alng in rear, nvr able to chal*.......... (12 to 1 op 6 to 1 tchd 14 to 1) 8
1232 ARRAS ROYALE 9-0 N Adams (6) *beh, rdn o'r 4 fs out, no ch whn hmpd and uns rdr over one out.*
..................................(66 to 1 tchd 100 to 1) ur
1591[5] KHISAL (Can) 9-0 W Carson (9) *trkd ldrs on ins, rdn alng and some hdwy whn broke leg o'r 2 fs out, destroyed.*
........................(5 to 1 op 6 to 1 tchd 7 to 1) pu
Dist: ½l, ¾l, sht-hd, ¾l, ¾l, 1½l, 1l. 1m 46.00s. a 5.00s (10 Ran).
(Mrs Chris Harrington), R Hannon

LONGCHAMP (FR) (good)
Monday June 21st

1908 Prix de la Butte Mortemart (Listed) (4-y-o and up) £14,337 1m 110yds. . (3:25)

ZABAR 5-8-11 D Boeuf,.................................. 1
1243[2] ARCHANGE (USA) 4-8-11 F Head,......................... 2
1243[4] THEATRICIAN (USA) 4-8-11 E Saint-Martin,............... 3
629[4] PORTICO (USA) 4-8-11 G Guignard,...................... 4
430[3] KITWOOD (USA) 4-8-12 T Jarnet,........................ 5
1243[3] WHAT KATY DID (USA) 4-,.............................. 6
FIRST AMENDMENT (Fr) 4-,............................... 7
DARBAWAN (Ire) 4-,..................................... 8
SHANGOL DE PERSE (Fr) 4-,.............................. 9
Dist: 2½l, ½l, nose, 2½l, 2l, hd, nk, sht-hd. 1m 43.50s. a 0.70s (9 Ran).
SR: 67/59/57/56/-/-/ (Gerald Leigh), J E Pease

BRIGHTON (good to firm)
Tuesday June 22nd
Going Correction: MINUS 0.40 sec. per fur.

1909 Montpelier Selling Stakes Class G (2-y-o) £2,070 6f 209yds........... (2:00)

1391 DEMI-PLIE 8-11 L Dettori (3) *sn rdn alng, chsd ldrs, hrd ridden o'r 2 fs out, styd on wl to ld ins last.*
........................(13 to 2 op 5 to 1 tchd 10 to 1) 1
1624[7] FOREVER BLUSHING 8-6 T Williams (11) *al prmnt, led and wndrd o'r 2 fs out, hdd ins last, no extr.*
.... (5 to 1 op 7 to 2 tchd 11 to 2) 2
1391[8] LYING EYES 8-4 (7*) D McCabe (5) *wl beh early, hdwy whn hmpd well o'r one furlong out, swtchd rght and ran on strly ins last, unlucky.*
........................(9 to 2 op 7 to 2 tchd 5 to 1) 3
1234[5] BON TON 8-6 C Rutter (2) *in tch, chlgd o'r 2 fs out, wkng whn edgd lft wl over one out, ran on same pace.*
..................................(7 to 1 op 5 to 1 tchd 8 to 1) 4
1391 MOSS HOUSE (Ire) 8-11 J Reid (13) *led till o'r 2 fs out, sn rdn, not quicken appr last.*
........................(10 to 1 op 8 to 1 tchd 12 to 1) 5
1741 BIEN CUIT 8-3 (3*) D Harrison (4) *trkd ldrs, rdn o'r 2 fs out, sn one pace*.........(40 to 1 op 16 to 1 tchd 50 to 1) 6
1189[9] SPORT RACING CLUB 8-6 A Munro (7) *mid-div, rdn o'r 2 fs out, staying on one pace whn not much room appr last.*
....................(4 to 1 fav op 5 to 1 tchd 11 to 2) 7
1741[8] LITTLE LUKE (Ire) 8-4 (7*) S Drowne (10) *nvr able to chal.*
........................(40 to 1 op 14 to 1 tchd 50 to 1) 8
1660 SHEILOBLIGE 8-6 B Rouse (1) *chsd ldrs, rdn and wknd o'r 2 fs out*..........(25 to 1 op 20 to 1 tchd 33 to 1) 9
1741 BRIGHT VENUS 8-6 N Adams (12) *chsd ldrs to hfwy, sn lost pl*..............(40 to 1 op 16 to 1 tchd 50 to 1) 10
1774[6] WHO'S CRYING NOW 7-13 (7*) P McCabe (6) *chsd ldrs to hfwy, sn rdn and wknd*........... (13 to 2 op 6 to 1) 11
1413[8] BITE THE BULLET (v) 8-11 J Quinn (9) *al beh.*
........................(40 to 1 op 20 to 1 tchd 50 to 1) 12
Dist: ½l, 2l, ½l, 1½l, sht-hd, 2½l, 2½l, 1½l, sht-hd, ¾l. 1m 24.20s. a 4.20s (12 Ran).

(Mrs C A B St George), D R Loder

1910 Operatic Society Challenge Cup Maiden Stakes Class D (3-y-o) £3,260 1m 3f 196yds.................. (2:30)

1526^{5} TOP RANK 9-0 L Dettori (4) *made all, quickened o'r 2 fs out, pld wl clr appr last, eased nr finish.* ....(3 to 1 op 2 to 1 tchd 7 to 2) 1

SNOWDROP TREE 8-9 A Clark (5) *slwly into strd, hld up in tch, rdn o'r 3 fs out, kpt on fnl furlong, no ch wth wnr*..........................(7 to 2 op 5 to 1 tchd 3 to 1) 2

1349^{2} PHROSE 9-0 J Reid (2) *tucked in hndy, rdn o'r 4 fs out, styd on same pace*.......................... (2 to 1 fav tchd 5 to 2) 3

1603^{9} SUN GREBE (Ire) 8-9 B Rouse (1) *chsd ldr, rdn o'r 3 fs out, sn btn*..........................(7 to 1 op 7 to 2) 4

1581^{3} SOUL DREAM (USA) 8-9 B Raymond (3) *hld up in tch, ev ch o'r 3 fs out, sn rdn and wknd*..... (7 to 1 op 5 to 1) 5

Dist: 3l, 4l, 1½l, nk. 2m 29.30s. a 1.80s (5 Ran).
SR: 34/23/20/12/11/ (A McParland), M C Pipe

1911 Lewes Maiden Stakes Class D (3-y-o and up) £3,494 1m 1f 209yds.... (3:00)

842 SEREN QUEST 3-8-1 (3*) D Harrison (9) *in tch, rdn o'r 3 fs out, str run to ld ins last*........... (11 to 2 op 5 to 1) 1

646^{3} AL SENAFI (Ire) 3-8-9 R Cochrane (5) *al hndy, led o'r 2 fs out, hrd rdn, hdd and no extr ins last.* ....(6 to 4 fav op 2 to 1) 2

821^{4} DUKRAME 3-8-4 W Newnes (4) *chsd ldrs, rdn alng o'r 3 fs out, styd on fnl furlong.* ....(8 to 1 op 5 to 1 tchd 10 to 1) 3

1671^{3} LAILATI (USA) 3-8-4 B Raymond (6) *prmnt, ev ch 2 fs out, sn rdn, ran on one pace*..........................(4 to 1 op 7 to 4) 4

821^{3} ALASKAN PRINCESS (Ire) 3-8-4 A Munro (2) *pld hrd, led till o'r 2 fs out, sn btn*.......(4 to 1 op 3 to 1 tchd 9 to 2) 5

CALL ME BLUE 3-8-9 D Holland (7) *trkd ldr, ev ch 3 fs out, sn rdn, not quicken.* (50 to 1 op 33 to 1 tchd 66 to 1) 6

1816^{3} MAD CASANOVA (bl) 8-9-7 J Quinn (8) *mid-div, rdn and no hdwy fnl 3 fs*.........(33 to 1 op 20 to 1 tchd 50 to 1) 7

1617 BITRAN 3-8-9 J Reid (1) *slwly into strd, al rear.* ....(33 to 1 op 16 to 1 tchd 50 to 1) 8

1060^{9} FINDON ACADEMY (Ire) 3-8-9 B Rouse (3) *wl beh hfwy.* ....(100 to 1 op 66 to 1) 9

1311 BIJOU FIRE (NZ) 5-9-2 A Tucker (10) *al beh.* ....(100 to 1 op 66 to 1) 10

Dist: ½l, 3l, 2l, hd, nk, 2½l, 8l, 10l, 2l. 2m 0.60s. a 2.40s (10 Ran).
SR: 26/30/19/15/14/18/25/-/-/ (N M Stewart), R Akehurst

1912 Hailsham Fillies Handicap Class E (0-70 3-y-o and up) £3,235 7f 214yds ....(3:30)

1663^{2} SARAH-CLARE [59] 5-9-10 J Reid (4) *tucked away in mid-div, hdwy o'r 3 fs out, led wl over one out, styd on.* ....(6 to 1 op 4 to 1) 1

1586^{9} PLAY WITH ME (Ire) [68] 3-9-9 L Dettori (10) *hld up, rdn 3 fs out, styd on strly fnl furlong, nvr nrr.* ....(8 to 1 op 6 to 1 tchd 9 to 1) 2

1606^{3} PANCHELLITA (USA) [50] 4-9-1 B Rouse (1) *nvr far away, led briefly 2 fs out, ran on one pace.* ....(5 to 1 op 3 to 1 tchd 11 to 2) 3

1606* ANATROCCOLO [38] 6-8-3 D Holland (7) *led to 2 fs out, sn rdn, not quicken*.......................... (6 to 1 op 4 to 1) 4

1743^{9} ROSIETOES (USA) [48] 5-8-6 (7*) Mark Denaro (3) *chsd ldrs, wknd o'r 2 fs out*..........................(9 to 1 op 6 to 1) 5

1656^{2} MISS FASCINATION [62] 3-8-12 (5*) K Rutter (6) *trkd ldrs, rdn alng wl o'r 2 fs out, sn btn*... (4 to 1 fav op 6 to 1) 6

1399^{4} CLEAR LOOK [55] (bl) 3-8-10 A Munro (9) *in tch, wide hme turn, sn rdn and wknd.* (7 to 1 op 6 to 1 tchd 8 to 1) 7

1606^{5} FIABA [49] 5-9-0 J Quinn (8) *chsd ldrs, no hdwy fnl 3 fs.* ....(6 to 1 op 9 to 2 tchd 7 to 1) 8

1586^{8} BAYDON BELLE (USA) [58] (bl) 3-8-13 B Raymond (11) *prmnt till rdn and wknd o'r 3 fs out, sn wl beh.* ....(10 to 1 op 8 to 1 tchd 12 to 1) 9

771 TRUNDLEY WOOD [69] 3-9-7 (3*) D Harrison (2) *sn niggled alng, al struggling*..........................(20 to 1 op 14 to 1) 10

Dist: 1½l, 3l, sht-hd, 2½l, hd, 2l, nk, 10l, 7l. 1m 33.60s. a 1.20s (10 Ran).
SR: 44/38/21/8/10/13/-/3/-/ (Miss Clare Coyne), R Akehurst

1913 Palace Maiden Handicap Class E (0-70 3-y-o) £3,390 6f 209yds.... (4:00)

1528^{4} DESERT NOMAD [48] 8-0 A Munro (8) *al hndy, rdn alng o'r 3 fs out, hdwy to ld over one out, pushed clr.* ....(9 to 2 op 4 to 1 tchd 5 to 1) 1

1697^{7} MEDLAND (Ire) [49] 7-12 (3*) D Harrison (1) *trkd ldrs, effrt o'r 2 fs out, sn ev ch, not quicken ins last.* ....(10 to 1 op 7 to 1 tchd 12 to 1) 2

1522^{4} COALISLAND [69] 9-7 A Tucker (11) *trkd ldr, led o'r 2 fs out to over one out, sn no extr.* ....(9 to 1 op 8 to 1 tchd 12 to 1) 3

1354^{2} WITHOUT A FLAG (USA) [57] 8-9 R Cochrane (6) *chsd ldrs, rdn and effrt o'r 2 fs out, kpt on ins last.* .... (100 to 30 fav op 6 to 1 tchd 3 to 1) 4

1377^{9} EXPORT MONDIAL [62] 8-9 (5*) K Rutter (5) *beh, rdn and styd on fnl 2 fs, nvr nrr*.............(12 to 1 op 7 to 1) 5

1240^{5} SHARP IMP [42] (bl) 7-8 N Carlisle (4) *chsd ldrs, rdn wl o'r 2 fs out, some late hdwy, no dngr.* ....(7 to 1 op 5 to 1 tchd 15 to 2) 6

1353 BAEZA [42] (v) 7-8^{1} J Quinn (3) *wl beh, styd on fnl one and a half fs, nrst finish.* (20 to 1 op 33 to 1 tchd 50 to 1) 7

1606^{6} SWISS MOUNTAIN [51] (v) 8-3^{1} W Newnes (9) *led one furlong, hndy till rdn and wknd 2 out.* (10 to 1 op 8 to 1) 8

1008^{8} MARWELL MITZI [45] 7-11 T Williams (7) *nvr trble ldrs.* ....(14 to 1 op 12 to 1 tchd 16 to 1) 9

1354^{6} JULY BRIDE [54] (bl) 8-6 B Rouse (2) *slwly into strd, al beh.* ....(13 to 2 op 4 to 1 tchd 7 to 1) 10

1383^{7} SOPHISTICATED AIR [55] (v) 8-7 L Dettori (10) *slwly into strd, reco'red to ld aftr one furlong, hdd over 2 out, wknd quickly, eased whn btn*.....(8 to 1 tchd 10 to 1) 11

Dist: 2l, ½l, ½l, nk, 1½l, ½l, 2l, 2½l, 2l, 1½l. 1m 22.10s. a 2.10s (11 Ran).
SR: 13/8/26/12/16/-/ (Eurostrait Ltd), S Dow

1914 Marine Handicap Class D (0-80 3-y-o and up) £3,201 5f 213yds........(4:30)

603 SCOTS LAW [42] (bl) 6-7-10 J Quinn (5) *made all, put head in air frm hfwy, ran on wl fnl furlong.* ....(4 to 1 tchd 5 to 1) 1

1584* SURE LORD (Ire) [70] 4-9-10 R Cochrane (6) *trkd ldr, rdn to chal 2 fs out, no extr ins last.* ....(11 to 4 fav op 5 to 2 tchd 7 to 2) 2

1728^{2} FARMER JOCK [54] 11-8-8 B Raymond (1) *nvr far away, effrt o'r one furlong out, one pace ins last.* ....(6 to 1 op 5 to 1 tchd 13 to 2) 3

1470* DOMULLA [78] 3-9-3 (7*) L Carter (4) *chsd ldrs, rdn o'r 2 fs out, kpt on fnl furlong.* (5 to 1 op 3 to 1 tchd 11 to 2) 4

1144 SURREY RACING [70] 5-9-10 B Rouse (3) *slwly into strd, beh till some hdwy o'r 2 fs out, styd on, nvr nrr.* ....(9 to 2 op 4 to 1) 5

1470^{2} VILLAVINA [69] 3-9-1 A Munro (2) *chsd ldrs, rdn and wknd o'r 2 fs out*..........................(7 to 1 tchd 8 to 1) 6

1473^{5} GALLANT HOPE [48] 11-7-13 (3*) D Harrison (7) *prmnt, rdn alng hfwy, sn wknd*.............. (8 to 1 tchd 10 to 1) 7

Dist: 1½l, hd, 1l, 1½l, 3l, 7l. 1m 8.80s. a 0.40s (7 Ran).
SR: 26/48/31/43/37/16/-/ (Mrs R J Doorgachurn), R J O'Sullivan

MAISONS LAFFITTE (FR) (good)
Tuesday June 22nd

1915 Prix Nimbus (Listed) 3-y-o £14,337 1 ½m 110yds.................... (2:25)

RAINTRAP 8-9 T Jarnet, ... 1

1012^{4} DONDOOK (USA) 8-9 D Boeuf, ... 2

1364 VAL SAUVAGE 8-9 C Asmussen, ... 3

PRACER (USA), ... 4

1410^{4} LUCIO (Ire), ... 5

1410^{3} IS ME (Can), ... 6

BLACK HEART (Fr), ... 7

1648^{4} TENET (Fr), ... 8

955^{7} ANGIO (USA), ... 9

ABILA DES MOTTES (Fr), ... 10

561^{6} MOLESNES (USA), ... 11

Dist: 2½l, nk, 2½l, 2l, 1½l, 2½l, sht-nk, 6l, 4l. 2m 34.40s. b 0.10s (11 Ran).
SR: 59/54/53/-/-/-/ (K Abdulla), A Fabre

NEWBURY (good)
Tuesday June 22nd

Going Correction: MINUS 0.25 sec. per fur. (races 1,3,5), MINUS 0.20 (2,4,6)

1916 Meridian Mid-Summer Maiden Fillies Stakes Class D (2-y-o) £3,582 6f 8yds ....(6:30)

1403^{3} BRAARI (USA) 8-11 W Carson (3) *hld up in tch, hdwy whn bumped by runner-up appr fnl furlong, led ins last, pushed out*..............(7 to 2 op 3 to 1 tchd 5 to 1) 1

1660^{9} RAJMAPATA 8-11 Pat Eddery (13) *led, edgd lft and bumped wnr appr fnl furlong, hdd ins last, ran on.* ....(12 to 1 op 10 to 1 tchd 16 to 1) 2

1403^{2} FAYROOZ (USA) 8-11 A Munro (9) *in tch, rdn o'r 2 fs out, kpt on one pace ins last.* ....(2 to 1 fav tchd 5 to 2 and 7 to 4) 3

DAVANNE 8-11 C Rutter (6) *rear, rdn 2 fs out, hdwy ins last*.......... (7 to 1 op 8 to 1 tchd 5 to 1) 4

SANGARE (Ire) 8-11 R Cochrane (7) *slwly away, rear till hdwy o'r one furlong out, ran on ins last.* ....(20 to 1 op 16 to 1 tchd 25 to 1) 5

SOOLAIMON (Ire) 8-11 J Reid (1) *slwly away, hdwy hfwy, kpt on one pace ins fnl 2 fs*.......... (8 to 1 op 5 to 1) 6

SPOT PRIZE (USA) 8-11 J Williams (10) *chsd ldrs, outpcd appr fnl furlong*..... (20 to 1 op 10 to 1 tchd 25 to 1) 7

BRENTWOOD (Ire) 8-11 S Raymont (8) *slwly away, rdn hfwy, rear till some late hdwy.* ....(25 to 1 op 16 to 1 tchd 33 to 1) 8

1708^{5} BET A PLAN (Ire) 8-8 (3*) D Harrison (5) *mid-div, rdn o'r 2 fs out, no further hdwy.* ....(25 to 1 op 12 to 1 tchd 33 to 1) 9

LOCHBELLE 8-11 L Dettori (11) *slwly away, rdn hfwy, al beh.*..................... (7 to 1 op 4 to 1 tchd 8 to 1) 10
BE EXCITING (Ire) 8-11 W Newnes (12) *slwly away, rdn o'r 2 fs out, sn btn*............(33 to 1 op 16 to 1) 11
GWERNYMYNYDD 8-11 D Holland (14) *trkd ldrs, rdn wl o'r one furlong out, wknd*........(25 to 1 op 20 to 1) 12
1403 ZALAMERA 8-11 C Avery (2) *prmnt on outsd till rdn and wknd 2 fs out*..............................(33 to 1) 13
Dist: 1½l, ¾l, 1½l, nk, 1l, ½l, ¾l, 1l, sht-hd, hd. 1m 14.17s. a 2.47s (13 Ran).
SR: 18/12/9/3/2/-/ (Hamdan Al-Maktoum), B W Hills

1917 Newbury Racecourse Driving Range Handicap Class D (0-80 3-y-o) £4,175 1m 5f 61yds....................(7:00)

1582* DUSTY POINT (Ire) [74] 9-4 W R Swinburn (3) *trkd ldrs, hdwy o'r 2 fs out, nudged into ld one out, shaken up ins last, eased cl hme.*
................(11 to 10 on op 5 to 4 on tchd Evens) 1
1426* MR COPYFORCE [57] 7-8 (7*) Antoinette Armes (5) *led till o'r 4 fs out, short of room and swtchd rght appr last, ran on to go second cl hme.*
......................(100 to 30 op 4 to 1 tchd 3 to 1) 2
1690⁶ DODGY DANCER [55] 7-13¹ A Munro (4) *hld up, hdwy to ld o'r 3 fs out, hrd rdn and hdd one out, one pace ins last.*
............................(6 to 1 op 9 to 2 tchd 13 to 2) 3
1495⁵ GUESTWICK [77] 9-7 W Carson (1) *rear, nvr gng wl, lost tch 5 fs out*....................(10 to 1 op 7 to 1) 4
1423⁴ ROMALITO [62] 8-6² R Cochrane (2) *trkd ldr, led o'r 4 fs out till over 3 out, sn rdn, wknd quickly 2 out.*
....(12 to 1 op 8 to 1) 5
Dist: ½l, ½l, 15l, 1½l. 2m 51.75s. a 5.55s (5 Ran).
SR: 22/4/1/-/-/ (Abdullah Ali), B Hanbury

1918 Kingston Smith Handicap Class D (0-80 3-y-o and up) £4,240 5f 34yds ....(7:30)

1664⁷ SEA-DEER [56] 4-8-6 A Munro (5) *wtd wth in tch, swtchd and hng lft wl o'r one furlong out, hdwy and edgd rght ins last, drvn out to ld nr finish*..... (8 to 1 op 6 to 1) 1
1677² TRIOMING [52] 7-8-2 N Adams (1) *led one and a half fs, led wl o'r one out, rdn and ran on, ct cl hme.*
....(6 to 1 op 5 to 1) 2
1806 MACFARLANE [75] 5-9-6 (5*) J Tate (6) *wtd wth, rdn and hdwy whn short of room entering fnl furlong, no extr nr finish*......................... (7 to 2 fav op 5 to 2) 3
1584 ACARA (Ire) [50] (bl) 4-8-0 J Quinn (2) *chsd ldrs, hrd rdn o'r one furlong out, one pace ins last.* (6 to 1 tchd 7 to 1) 4
1881⁶ THE NOBLE OAK (Ire) [61] (v) 5-8-11 J Reid (4) *led aftr one and a half fs, rdn and hdd wl o'r one out, one pace.*
...............................(13 to 2 op 6 to 1 tchd 7 to 1) 5
1815⁹ BARBEZIEUX [47] 6-7-11 W Carson (3) *in tch, rdn wl o'r one furlong out, sn btn.*
..........................(5 to 1 op 9 to 2 tchd 11 to 2) 6
1127 BELLS OF LONGWICK [72] 4-9-8 T Williams (7) *al struggling*..(7 to 1 op 8 to 1) 7
Dist: Hd, 1½l, 2l, nk, 3½l, 4l. 1m 1.60s. a 1.30s (7 Ran).
SR: 40/35/52/19/29/1/10/ (P Cook), L J Holt

1919 Wimpey Hobbs Fillies' Handicap Class D (0-80 3-y-o and up) £4,695 1 ¼m 6yds...................... (8:00)

1351² MIDNIGHT HEIGHTS [80] 3-9-9 W Carson (12) *pld hrd early, trkd ldrs, rdn 2 fs out, led entering last, pushed out*..................... (13 to 2 op 6 to 1 tchd 7 to 1) 1
1409 YILDIZ [70] 4-9-11 D Holland (11) *trkd ldr, led aftr 4 fs, rdn and hdd entering last, one pace*... (16 to 1 op 14 to 1) 2
1684* LICORNE [75] 3-9-4 W Ryan (7) *hld up, rdn o'r 3 fs out, hdwy appr last, kpt on one pace.*
......................(11 to 4 fav op 9 to 4 tchd 3 to 1) 3
1483⁴ EXHIBIT AIR (Ire) [77] 3-9-6 Pat Eddery (1) *chsd ldrs, rdn o'r 3 fs out, one pace 2 out*.............. (8 to 1 op 6 to 1) 4
1586⁷ CRACKLING [47] 4-8-2 S Dawson (6) *chsd ldrs, rdn o'r 4 fs out, wknd wl over one out*..........(7 to 1 op 10 to 1) 5
1625² CUTLASS (Ire) [75] 3-9-4 L Dettori (10) *led 4 fs, wth ldr till wknd wl o'r one out*.....(8 to 1 op 6 to 1 tchd 9 to 1) 6
1592⁵ NO COMEBACKS [53] 5-8-5 (3*) J Weaver (8) *nvr on terms.*
....(8 to 1 op 6 to 1) 7
1656⁴ LA MENORQUINA (USA) [68] 3-8-11 R Cochrane (3) *middiv, no hdwy fnl 3 fs.* (14 to 1 op 10 to 1 tchd 16 to 1) 8
1626* TENDRESSE (Ire) [56] 5-8-6 (5*) J Tate (2) *al rear.*
....(10 to 1 op 6 to 1) 9
1357⁴ DORAZINE [67] 3-8-10 J Quinn (5) *al beh.*
......................(20 to 1 op 16 to 1 tchd 25 to 1) 10
855⁶ LAMU LADY (Ire) [75] 3-9-4 J Reid (4) *al beh, tld off.*
.......................(14 to 1 op 12 to 1 tchd 16 to 1) 11
THIMBALINA [38] 7-7-1¹ (7*) Sharon Millard (9) *slwly away, al rear, tld off*....................................(33 to 1) 12
Dist: 3l, 1½l, 3½l, 3l, hd, 1l, nk, 1½l, 3l, 15l. 2m 6.17s. a 3.17s (12 Ran).
SR: 57/53/43/38/14/29/17/19/16/ (Ettore Landi), J L Dunlop

1920 Wildhern Conditions Stakes Class C (2-y-o) £5,475 6f 8yds...........(8:30)

1456* FIRST TRUMP 8-12 M Hills (1) *wtd wth, hdwy to ld o'r 2 fs out, rdn out ins last*....(13 to 8 op 6 to 4 tchd 7 to 4) 1
1640* REPREHEND 8-12 R Cochrane (2) *hld up, hdwy to go second 2 fs out, ev ch entering last, edgd lft and no imprsn cl hme*................(11 to 10 fav op 5 to 4) 2
1381² SPORTING WARRIOR (Ire) 8-10 S Morris (4) *slwly into strd, pld hrd, led o'r 3 fs out till over 2 out, sn btn.*
....(7 to 1 op 5 to 1) 3
1317* MOUNT LEINSTER 8-10 J Williams (3) *led till o'r 3 fs out, rdn and wknd 2 out*..(9 to 1 op 10 to 1 tchd 12 to 1) 4
Dist: 1½l, 8l, ½l. 1m 12.96s. a 1.26s (4 Ran).
SR: 43/37/3/1/ (Mollers Racing), G Wragg

1921 Elizabeth Ferrigno Wedding Anniversary Conditions Stakes Class C (3-y-o and up) £4,760 1m 7yds.........(9:00)

1329² WAGON MASTER (Fr) 3-8-6 W Carson (5) *al in tch, rdn to ld o'r one furlong out, ran on ins last.*
..............................(3 to 1 op 2 to 1 tchd 7 to 2) 1
1435* UNDERWATER (USA) 4-9-2 Pat Eddery (1) *hld up, hdwy on outsd o'r 3 fs out, chlgd appr last, one pace ins.*
.......................(13 to 8 fav op 9 to 4 tchd 6 to 4) 2
1617* BLUE LION 3-8-6 M Hills (7) *hld up, hdwy o'r 2 fs out, several poss and not clr run ins fnl two, ran on cl hme.*
..............................(9 to 2 op 4 to 1 tchd 5 to 1) 3
729⁵ LOST SOLDIER (USA) 3-8-6 R Cochrane (6) *hld up rear, hdwy o'r 2 fs out, ran on wl ins last, nvr nrr.*
....(12 to 1 op 8 to 1) 4
1716* FROGMARCH (USA) 3-8-6 J Reid (4) *pld hrd, trkd ldr, rdn o'r 2 fs out, wkng whn hmpd appr last.*
..........................(7 to 1 op 5 to 1 tchd 8 to 1) 5
1298⁸ CORALS DREAM (Ire) 4-9-1 A Munro (2) *chsd ldrs, rdn o'r 2 fs out, wkng whn short of room appr last.*
....(33 to 1 tchd 25 to 1) 6
1559² PETO 4-9-2 W Ryan (3) *led, rdn 2 fs out, hdd one and a half out, wknd quickly ins last*...... (7 to 1 op 5 to 1) 7
Dist: 1½l, ½l, nk, 4l, 3½l, 1½l. 1m 37.26s. a 1.46s (7 Ran).
SR: 46/51/39/38/26/24/20/ (Hamdan Al-Maktoum), A C Stewart

SLIGO (IRE) (yielding to soft)
Tuesday June 22nd

1922 Queen Maeve Maiden (3-y-o) £2,245 6f 110yds........................ (6:30)

1513⁴ AULD STOCK (Ire) (bl) 8-11 J F Egan (2)........ (7 to 4 fav) 1
1649⁴ SCALP (Ire) 9-0 P V Gilson (1).................... (3 to 1) 2
1610³ MISS CARMELLA (Ire) 8-11 W J Supple (3).......... (5 to 2) 3
848⁶ LUCKY PRINCE (Ire) (bl) 9-0 M J Kinane (7)........ (9 to 2) 4
1445⁶ OICHE MHAITH 8-11 D Manning (6)............. (14 to 1) 5
Dist: Nk, 4l, sht-hd, 3l. 1m 32.30s. (5 Ran).
(Miss E Kiely), Patrick Joseph Flynn

1923 Sligo Park Hotel Handicap (0-70 3-y-o and up) £2,762 6f 110yds........(7:00)

1825² PILGRIM BAY (Ire) [-] 3-9-4 (2*,4ex) D G O'Shea (5) (4 to 1) 1
1795³ LADY PRESIDENT (Ire) [-] (bl) 4-9-5 S Craine (7).... (9 to 2) 2
1570 SOMERTON BOY (Ire) [-] 3-9-11 M J Kinane (10).. (10 to 1) 3
1333⁴ WHAT MAGIC (Ire) [-] 3-9-7 Joanna Morgan (4).... (14 to 1) 4
1385 BOLD MOLLY (Ire) [-] 4-7-13 (2*) R M Burke (6).... (14 to 1) 5
1433³ SARA MAURETTE (Ire) [-] 3-9-0 N Byrne (2)......... (9 to 1) 6
1645² HERMES GOLD (Ire) [-] 3-9-0 W J Supple (8)...... (13 to 2) 7
1293 SOUTHERN RULE [-] (bl) 6-7-12 J F Egan (3)..... (10 to 1) 8
1122 WESTERN FRONTIER (Ire) [-] 3-7-13 (6*) R V Skelly (9)
....(50 to 1) 9
1293 REASON TO BELIEVE (Ire) [-] 4-8-1 (8*) R T Fitzpatrick (12)
....(50 to 1) 10
1433² TAJANAMA (Ire) [-] 5-8-6 N G McCullagh (1) (100 to 30 fav) 11
1385³ FILL MY GLASS [-] 9-7-6 (4*) W J Smith (11)...... (16 to 1) 12
Dist: ½l, sht-hd, 2l, 1½l. 1m 31.90s. (12 Ran).
(Frank A McNulty), E J O'Grady

1924 Rosses Point Auction Race (2-y-o) £2,245 6f 110yds............... (7:30)

1104* BONNIE CRATHIE (Ire) 8-7 P V Gilson (1).........(11 to 2) 1
1332 SUMMERHILL SPECIAL (Ire) 8-5 Joanna Morgan (3)
....(20 to 1) 2
1432⁴ SOPHIE'S PET (Ire) 8-2 J F Egan (2).............. (12 to 1) 3
KING SANCHO (Ire) 8-5 M J Kinane (5)......... (7 to 4 fav) 4
896² CATCH A DREAM (Ire) 8-0 (2*) R M Burke (8)....... (2 to 1) 5
820³ PETER'S POWER (Ire) 8-2 (6*) R V Skelly (7)....... (8 to 1) 6
1643² OVERALL MAJORITY (Ire) 8-2 N G McCullagh (6)....(7 to 1) 7
1792⁸ GREENRIDGE COURT (Ire) 7-8 (8*) B A Hunter (4) (20 to 1) 8
Dist: Hd, 1½l, 1½l, 3½l. 1m 32.60s. (8 Ran).
(Mrs C Collins), C Collins

WARWICK (good)
Tuesday June 22nd
Going Correction: MINUS 0.30 sec. per fur. (race 1), MINUS 0.20 (2,3,4,5,6)

1925 Enterprise Inns Fillies' Handicap Class E (0-70 3-y-o and up) £3,125 5f ....(6:15)

1881[4] MANOR ADVENTURE [62] 3-9-7 J Fortune (10) *hdwy 2 fs out, led ins last, drvn out*......... (12 to 1 op 10 to 1) 1
1881[3] CASTLE MAID [30] 6-7-10 Dale Gibson (5) *hdwy o'r one furlong out, ran on strly nr finish*... (8 to 1 op 6 to 1) 2
1287[9] MY ABBEY [54] 4-9-6 K Fallon (7) *al cl up, ev ch one furlong out, ran on*.............. (16 to 1 op 12 to 1) 3
1740[2] TREVORSNINEPOINTS [54] 3-8-13 K Darley (3) *led till ins fnl furlong, hrd rdn, ran on*....(4 to 1 fav tchd 9 to 2) 4
1782[2] SIMMIE'S SPECIAL [57] 5-9-9 S Perks (12) *al prmnt, ev ch o'r one furlong out, not quicken*.....(7 to 1 op 6 to 1) 5
1589[2] NORDOORA (Ire) [39] 4-8-0 (5*) Darren Moffatt (11) *al prmnt, ev ch 2 fs out, one pace*.............(7 to 1 op 6 to 1) 6
1528[6] FLORAC (Ire) [57] 3-8-9 (7*) D Wright (6) *speed o'r 3 fs*. .... (11 to 2 op 4 to 1 tchd 6 to 1) 7
1560[8] FOLLOWMEGIRLS [57] 4-9-9 A Clark (9) *nvr nr to chal*. .... (20 to 1 op 16 to 1) 8
1419[7] DAL MISS [27] (bl) 6-7-7 J Fanning (13) *nvr nrr*. .... (50 to 1 op 33 to 1) 9
1352[6] BELTHORN [47] 4-8-13 G Bardwell (4) *chsd ldr till wknd 2 fs out*........................ (20 to 1 op 16 to 1) 10
1287 NILU (Ire) [53] 5-8-12 (7*) S Sanders (16) *outpcd*. ....(25 to 1 op 20 to 1) 11
1454[6] SING AS WE GO [44] 3-8-3 G Carter (2) *outpcd*... (25 to 1) 12
916 CAMINO A RONDA [32] 4-7-5 (7*) Kim McDonnell (15) *al beh*..............................(50 to 1 op 33 to 1) 13
1668[4] MELODYS DAUGHTER [53] (bl) 3-8-12 J Lowe (1) *prmnt 3 fs*...(8 to 1) 14
1240[8] MY FOXY LADY [45] 3-8-4 A Mackay (17) *prmnt to hfwy*. ....(16 to 1 tchd 20 to 1) 15
DAVAMAL [33] 4-7-13[3] (7*) Michael Bradley (8) *al tld off*. .... (100 to 1 op 33 to 1) 16

Dist: ½l, hd, hd, 3l, ½l, nk, ½l, sht-hd, 1½l, nk. 1m 0.00s. a 1.80s (16 Ran).
SR: 41/14/37/29/27/7/17/22/-/ (Mrs Julie Martin), B A McMahon

1926 Bass Special Maiden Auction Stakes Class D (2-y-o) £3,406 7f........(6:45)

OVERACT (Ire) 8-9 G Carter (1) *al prmnt, led o'r one furlong out, ran on wl*..................(4 to 1 op 2 to 1) 1
1324[9] MAJESTIC HEIGHTS (Ire) 9-0 K Darley (6) *rdn alng mid-div, styd on fnl 2 fs, nvr nrr*......................... (6 to 1) 2
922[7] GIGUE 8-9 G Duffield (2) *led till o'r one furlong out, ran on*..............................(3 to 1 fav op 7 to 2) 3
DIAMOND CROWN (Ire) 9-0 A Clark (5) *hdwy 3 fs out, hrd rdn o'r 2 out, sn wknd*...............(11 to 2 op 7 to 2) 4
1324 BELLROI (Ire) 9-0 P Robinson (3) *chsd ldr till wknd o'r 2 fs out*...........................(25 to 1 op 16 to 1) 5
DULFORD LAD 9-0 S Whitworth (9) *hdwy 3 fs out, nvr nr to chal*..(33 to 1) 6
1624[9] MELODY DANCER 9-0 S Perks (4) *dwlt, al beh*. ....(10 to 1 tchd 12 to 1) 7
1350 TALYGARN 9-0 A Mackay (10) *rdn alng, sn beh*. ....(33 to 1 op 25 to 1) 8
1499[3] TRENDY DANCER (Ire) 8-9 (5*) O Pears (7) *prmnt o'r 3 fs, sn wknd*.......................(11 to 2 op 4 to 1) 9
1355[4] NOORAN 9-0 J Carroll (8) *prmnt till wknd quickly o'r 2 fs out, tld off*........................(7 to 1 op 6 to 1) 10

Dist: 2l, 1½l, 3l, 3½l, 1½l, 3½l, 2l, 1½l, 20l. 1m 28.10s. a 4.30s (10 Ran).
SR: 10/9/-/-/-/-/ (Lady Hayward), D R Loder

1927 Carling Black Label Handicap Class D (0-80 3-y-o and up) £3,289 1m... (7:15)

1876[7] MUSTAHIL (Ire) [62] 4-9-4 J Lowe (5) *made virtually all, hld on wl und pres*................. (9 to 1 op 7 to 1) 1
1670[5] MR VINCENT [76] 3-9-1 (7*) B Russell (2) *hdwy on ins and hrd rdn o'r 2 fs out, ev ch inside fnl furlong, ran on*. ....(4 to 1 op 3 to 1 tchd 9 to 2) 2
1584[6] BAYSHAM (USA) [72] (bl) 7-10-0 R Price (1) *al prmnt, ev ch o'r one furlong out, ran on*.........(9 to 1 op 10 to 1) 3
1451[4] FOURFORFUN [80] 3-9-12 B Raymond (4) *al prmnt, hrd rdn 2 fs out, not quicken*. ....(11 to 4 fav op 5 to 2 tchd 3 to 1) 4
4680a[5] DIACO [58] 8-9-0 P Robinson (9) *beh till ran on wl fnl 2 fs*. ....(20 to 1 op 8 to 1) 5
1177 ZAMANAYN (Ire) [63] 5-9-5 M Wigham (3) *strted slwly, gd hdwy fnl 2 fs, nrst finish*.........(33 to 1 op 25 to 1) 6
1390[4] GREEN'S FAIR (Ire) [68] 3-9-0 G Duffield (6) *in tch till rdn and wknd o'r 2 fs out*..................(5 to 1 op 4 to 1) 7
1080[6] GENSERIC (Fr) [66] 3-8-12 R Hills (7) *rcd very wide, wth wnr till wknd 2 fs out*. (12 to 1 op 7 to 1 tchd 14 to 1) 8
1604 VAGANOVA (Ire) [69] 4-9-11 R Perham (8) *mid-div till wknd o'r 2 fs out*............................(12 to 1 op 6 to 1) 9

Dist: ½l, 1½l, 1½l, nk, sht-hd, 1½l, 2½l, 1½l. 1m 40.60s. a 3.80s (9 Ran).
SR: 23/25/26/19/6/10/ (Unity Farm Holiday Centre Ltd), R J Hodges

1928 Draught Bass Selling Stakes Class G (3-y-o and up) £1,380 1¼m 169yds ....(7:45)

1604 BARAHIN (Ire) 4-9-13 A Clark (2) *hdwy 5 fs out, led o'r 2 out, drvn out*......(3 to 1 jt-fav op 9 to 4 tchd 7 to 2) 1
1880[8] LOCH DUICH 7-9-6 (7*) S Drowne (13) *al prmnt, jnd wnr o'r 2 fs out, hrd rdn, ran on*.........(9 to 1 op 6 to 1) 2
1799[5] FLETCHER'S BOUNTY (Ire) 4-9-6 K Darley (14) *hdwy 4 fs out, ev ch blw dist, ran on one pace*.........(3 to 1 jt-fav tchd 7 to 2) 3
1657[3] IRON BARON (Ire) 4-9-13 S Perks (5) *al prmnt, ran on one pace fnl 2 fs*..........................(6 to 1 op 5 to 1) 4
1626 CLEAR LIGHT 6-9-13 M Wigham (11) *al prmnt, jnd ldr entering strt, ran wide, one pace*. (14 to 1 op 10 to 1) 5
1458[8] ALICANTE (bl) 6-8-13 (7*) D McCabe (12) *chsd ldrs, no hdwy fnl 3 fs*.................................(33 to 1) 6
621[6] DEVONIAN (USA) 4-9-6 R Perham (3) *al mid-div*. ....(14 to 1 op 12 to 1) 7
BLACK BEAN 3-8-6 G Carter (7) *nvr nrr*. ....(12 to 1 op 6 to 1) 8
FOURTIMELUCKY 4-9-1 A Tucker (15) *chsd ldr, led 4 fs out, hdd and wknd o'r 2 out*.......(50 to 1 op 33 to 1) 9
CHRIS'S GLEN 4-8-13 (7*) Michael Bradley (10) *al beh*. ....(50 to 1 op 33 to 1) 10
SOLAR KNIGHT 3-8-1 N Carlisle (6) *slwly into strd, outpcd*..................................(33 to 1 op 20 to 1) 11
1562[9] METTERNICH 8-9-13 P Robinson (8) *al wl beh*. ....(8 to 1 op 5 to 1) 12
1422[7] SWEETWATER MOON 3-8-1 J Fanning (4) *led till wknd 4 fs out*..................................(33 to 1 op 20 to 1) 13
RAPINSKI 4-8-13 (7*) K Pattinson (1) *prmnt 5 fs, sn wknd, tld off*..................................(50 to 1 op 33 to 1) 14
1685 FRANKIE GOODMAN (Ire) (bl) 3-8-6 G Bardwell (9) *strted slwly, tld off*.................................. (33 to 1) 15

Dist: 2l, 1½l, 3l, 4l, 7l, 4l, 5l, 6l, 1½l, 1½l. 2m 18.90s. a 6.10s (15 Ran).
SR: 31/27/17/18/10/-/ (Martin Hickey), R J O'Sullivan

1929 Mitchells & Butlers Handicap Class D (0-80 3-y-o and up) £3,406 1¾m 194yds ....(8:15)

1380[9] FARMER'S PET [67] 4-9-8 G Carter (10) *chsd ldr, led 7 fs out, quickened clr 3 out, easily*...... (9 to 1 op 7 to 1) 1
1752[8] CHAKALAK [63] 5-9-4 P Robinson (11) *outpcd and tld off a m out, gd hdwy fnl 3 fs, fnshd fst*.... (9 to 2 op 6 to 1) 2
1056[7] FAMOUS BEAUTY [41] 6-7-7[2] (5*) A Garth (6) *dwlt, hdwy 4 fs out, ran on one pace fnl 2 furlongs*. ....(33 to 1 op 20 to 1) 3
1702[3] ENFANT DU PARADIS (Ire) [38] 5-7-1[1] (7*) D Wright (9) *chsd ldrs, styd on one pace fnl 2 fs*......(12 to 1 op 10 to 1) 4
1752 FRENCH IVY (USA) [73] 6-10-0 K Fallon (3) *gd hdwy 4 fs out, chsd wnr 3 out, wknd one furlong out*. ....(7 to 1 op 12 to 1 tchd 14 to 1) 5
994 BLAZON OF TROY [55] 4-8-10 S Whitworth (1) *wth ldrs till wknd 3 fs out*..................................(25 to 1 op 16 to 1) 6
1491* PONDERING [66] (v) 3-8-3 G Duffield (5) *al beh*. ....(100 to 30 fav op 11 to 4 tchd 7 to 2) 7
2264 MR POPPLETON [54] 4-8-9 A Mackay (2) *prmnt ten fs, sn wknd*..................................(20 to 1 op 10 to 1) 8
1775* FIVE TO SEVEN (USA) [74] 4-9-10 (5*,4ex) O Pears (8) *led till 7 fs out, wknd 4 out*.................. (9 to 1 op 6 to 1) 9
1779[2] MR WOODCOCK [51] 8-8-6 K Darley (4) *some hdwy 6 fs out, sn wknd*...........(5 to 1 op 7 to 2 tchd 3 to 1) 10
1731* CORINTHIAN GOD (Ire) [38] 4-7-7 (4ex) G Bardwell (7) *prmnt ten fs, sn lost pl, tld off*..............(8 to 1 op 6 to 1) 11

Dist: 2½l, ½l, 3½l, nk, 8l, ¾l, 7l, 2½l, 12l, 10l. 3m 12.80s. a 4.50s (11 Ran).
SR: 33/26/3/-/30/4/-/-/11/ (D R Midwood), G A Pritchard-Gordon

1930 Tennents Maiden Handicap Stakes Class F (0-60 3-y-o and up) £2,070 1½m 115yds............ (8:45)

1686[6] ICE STRIKE (USA) [36] (v) 4-8-7 R Hills (10) *hdwy 3 fs out, led wl ins fnl furlong, all out*.......(14 to 1 op 8 to 1) 1
1417[4] TURFMANS VISION [58] 3-8-13 S Perks (6) *hdwy 4 fs out, led o'r one furlong out till wl ins last, ran on*. ....(6 to 1 op 5 to 1) 2
1409[7] VIAGGIO [40] 5-8-11 G Carter (8) *al prmnt, led o'r 2 fs out till over one out, not quicken*........ (7 to 2 tchd 3 to 1) 3
1700[3] DOC'S COAT [40] 8-8-11 C Rutter (9) *gd hdwy 2 fs out, styd on, nrst finish*......(3 to 1 fav op 11 to 4 tchd 7 to 2) 4
1659[9] YIMKIN BOOKRA [44] 5-9-1 G Duffield (11) *hdwy fnl 2 fs, nrst finish*..................................(33 to 1 op 25 to 1) 5
1055[5] MATHAL (USA) [53] 4-9-10 C Avery (5) *led, sn clr, hdd o'r 2 fs out, kpt on*..................................(14 to 1 op 10 to 1) 6
975 SUDANOR (Ire) [38] 4-8-9 J Lowe (2) *chsd ldrs, no hdwy fnl 2 fs*..................................(25 to 1 op 20 to 1) 7
1459[4] MENA [60] 3-8-8 (7*) G Forster (1) *prmnt till wknd o'r 2 fs out*..................................(5 to 1 op 4 to 1) 8
BILLY BUNTER [52] 4-9-2 (7*) C Hawksley (3) *al beh*. ....(12 to 1 op 7 to 1) 9
902[8] CHARIOTEER [40] 4-8-11 N Carlisle (7) *al beh*. ....(25 to 1 op 20 to 1) 10
645 SHADANZA (Ire) [43] 4-9-0 K Darley (12) *outpcd*. ....(33 to 1 op 20 to 1) 11
MY GRAIN [37] 4-8-8 S Whitworth (4) *prmnt till wknd quickly o'r 2 fs out*.................(16 to 1 op 12 to 1) 12
MAJOR RISK [36] 4-8-7 A Clark (13) *chsd ldr till wknd quickly o'r 3 fs out*..................(20 to 1 op 16 to 1) 13

Dist: Nk, 3l, nk, ¾l, 1½l, 1l, 2½l, 6l, nk, 5l. 2m 44.40s. a 6.50s (13 Ran).
SR: 3/8/-/-/1/7/ (C R Nelson), J W Hills

YARMOUTH (good to firm)
Tuesday June 22nd
Going Correction: MINUS 0.45 sec. per fur. (races 1,2,3), MINUS 0.35 (4,5,6)

1931 Tote Place Only Maiden Fillies Stakes Class D (3-y-o) £4,581 1m 3yds. .(2:15)

1278^{3} GOLDEN GUEST 8-11 L Piggott (9) *made all, quickened 2 fs out, sn drw clr, cmftbly*........(3 to 1 fav op 5 to 1) 1
1171^{4} CROIRE (Ire) 8-11 M Hills (4) *wth wnr, rdn 2 fs out, no imprsn fnl furlong*...... (9 to 2 op 7 to 2 tchd 9 to 4) 2
AL KATIRIYAH (Ire) (e/c) 8-11 W Carson (2) *hdwy 2 fs out, ran on wl fnl furlong*. ....(11 to 1 op 10 to 1 tchd 12 to 1) 3
999^{5} FROSTY MORNING 8-8 (3*) B Doyle (5) *wth ldrs, rdn 2 fs out, unbl to quicken*.....(9 to 2 op 8 to 1 tchd 4 to 1) 4
PIPERS POOL (Ire) 8-11 Paul Eddery (11) *hld up, hdwy o'r 2 fs out, one pace fnl furlong*........ (6 to 1 op 7 to 2) 5
DANCING TRALTHEE (Ire) 8-8 (3*) J Weaver (1) *hdwy fnl 2 fs, not rch ldrs*........ (11 to 1 op 5 to 1 tchd 12 to 1) 6
732^{9} ALLIGRAM (USA) 8-11 W R Swinburn (7) *chsd ldrs till wknd fnl 2 fs*...........(8 to 1 op 6 to 1 tchd 10 to 1) 7
ESSEX GIRL 8-11 M Tebbutt (12) *prmnt to hfwy, no hdwy fnl 3 fs*.............................(25 to 1 op 20 to 1) 8
1452^{3} SHAHAADA (USA) 8-11 R Hills (3) *beh most of way*. .... (20 to 1 op 12 to 1) 9
1454^{3} BALL GOWN 8-11 J Lowe (8) *mid-div till wknd o'r 2 fs out*..................(20 to 1 op 12 to 1 tchd 25 to 1) 10
TOCCO JEWEL 8-11 D Biggs (10) *chsd ldrs 6 fs, wknd rpdly*................................. (40 to 1 op 25 to 1) 11
SYLVIA MACUSHLA 8-11 S Whitworth (6) *beh hfwy, tld off*. .... (50 to 1 op 25 to 1) 12

Dist: 5l, 2½l, sht-hd, ½l, ¾l, 2l, 2½l, hd, ½l, nk. 1m 37.00s. a 1.20s (12 Ran).
SR: 25/10/2/1/-/-/ (Exors Of The Late Mrs V Hue-Williams), Mrs J Cecil

1932 Tote Placepot Handicap Class E (0-70 3-y-o and up) £3,106 7f 3yds.... (2:45)

1455^{5} TAJDID (Ire) [56] 3-8-9 R Hills (11) *made virtually all, rdn out fnl furlong*......................(9 to 1 op 8 to 1) 1
1830 ANNABELLE ROYALE [63] 7-9-11 Dean McKeown (8) *slight ld one furlong, wth wnr till rdn and unbl to quicken fnl furlong*......... (100 to 30 fav op 11 to 4 tchd 7 to 2) 2
1377^{2} GOOD IMAGE [55] 3-8-8 S Whitworth (6) *effrt hfwy, in tch 2 fs out, no extr und pres fnl furlong*. (6 to 1 op 5 to 1) 3
1641^{4} SHINING JEWEL [66] 6-10-0 L Piggott (7) *chsd ldrs, rdn 2 fs out, ran on one pace*................ (4 to 1 op 9 to 2) 4
1306^{9} GWEEK (Ire) [52] 3-8-5 P Robinson (3) *hld up, ran on fnl 2 fs, not rch ldrs*...................... (8 to 1 op 10 to 1) 5
1846^{6} YONGE TENDER [41] (bl) 6-8-3 J Curant (9) *ran on one pace fnl 2 fs*................................(14 to 1 op 12 to 1) 6
1618^{2} WALK THAT WALK [59] 4-9-0 (7*) K Pattinson (10) *prmnt for o'r 4 fs*.................................. (6 to 1 op 5 to 1) 7
881 ROCA MURADA (Ire) [55] 4-9-3 M Hills (2) *prmnt 4 fs, wknd quickly 2 out*........................(8 to 1 op 7 to 1) 8
1707^{8} NIGEL'S LUCKY GIRL [50] 5-8-12 M Tebbutt (3) *wth ldrs till lost pl 3 fs out*...........................(50 to 1 op 25 to 1) 9
1399 CUBIST (Ire) [62] 3-9-1 W R Swinburn (5) *beh hfwy*. ....(12 to 1 op 10 to 1) 10

Dist: 1½l, 2½l, 1½l, 1½l, ½l, nk, 2l, hd, 1½l. 1m 25.20s. a 2.00s (10 Ran).
SR: 18/29/4/19/-/-/4/-/-/ (Hamdan Al-Maktoum), H Thomson Jones

1933 Bet With The Tote Selling Stakes Class G (2-y-o) £2,427 5f 43yds. .(3:15)

1529^{9} KING RAT (Ire) 8-11 Dean McKeown (9) *made all, drw clr o'r one furlong out, cmftbly*. ....(7 to 4 fav op 9 to 4 tchd 5 to 2) 1
1536^{6} LUCY'S GOLD 8-6 D Biggs (7) *wth ldrs, ev ch 2 fs out, unbl to quicken*..................(10 to 1 op 8 to 1) 2
496^{7} FLAIR LADY 8-6 T Sprake (4) *wth ldrs, rdn o'r 2 fs out, no extr*......................(4 to 1 op 9 to 2 tchd 7 to 2) 3
1555^{4} MRS JOGGLEBURY 8-1 (5*) J Tate (10) *al prmnt, kpt on one pace fnl 2 fs*........(8 to 1 op 6 to 1 tchd 10 to 1) 4
CARLY'S SECRET 8-11 R Hills (11) *mid-div, rdn hfwy, no hdwy*................... (9 to 2 op 5 to 1 tchd 6 to 1) 5
1741 LITTLE HOOLIGAN 8-11 Paul Eddery (6) *kpt on one pace frm hfwy*........................(12 to 1 tchd 14 to 1) 6
1135^{8} EL COHETE 8-11 S Whitworth (2) *nvr trble ldrs*. ....(11 to 1 op 10 to 1 tchd 12 to 1) 7
FILCH 7-13 (7*) G Milligan (5) *speed 3 fs, sn lost pl*. ....(12 to 1 op 10 to 1 tchd 14 to 1) 8
1672^{5} MAZZA 8-6 G Duffield (8) *nvr nr to chal*. .... (16 to 1 op 10 to 1) 9
1555^{7} TITCH ON TIME 8-6 P Robinson (3) *nvr a factor, beh fnl 2 fs*.......................................(8 to 1 op 5 to 1) 10
1253^{7} MY SONG OF SONGS 8-6 M Hills (1) *beh hfwy*. .... (33 to 1 op 16 to 1) 11

Dist: 6l, ¾l, 1½l, ½l, 2l, 2½l, 1½l, hd, ½l, nk. 1m 1.50s. a 0.80s (11 Ran).
SR: 34/5/2/-/-/-/ (The 2nd Kingsley House Partnership), M Johnston

1934 Angela Richardson Memorial Handicap Class D (0-80 3-y-o and up) £3,590 1¼m 21yds.................... (3:45)

538 MUJAWAB [68] 3-8-8 R Hills (3) *chsd ldr, led o'r 2 fs out, styd on wl und pres*. (12 to 1 op 10 to 1 tchd 16 to 1) 1
1414^{6} RIVAL BID (USA) [64] 5-9-2 N Day (2) *hld up, effrt 2 fs out, styd on fnl furlong, unbl to quicken nr finish*. ....(6 to 1 op 4 to 1) 2
1409^{3} GILDERDALE [72] 11-9-10 M Hills (1) *hld up, styd on fnl 3 fs, not trble ldrs*.... (11 to 8 fav op 5 to 4 tchd 7 to 4) 3
1592^{6} SURREY DANCER [67] 5-9-5 L Piggott (4) *led till o'r 2 fs out, sn rdn and no extr*..............(2 to 1 op 5 to 2) 4
1581^{5} MUTAWALI (Ire) [67] 3-8-7 W Carson (5) *chsd ldrs, in tch 3 fs out, sn rdn and wknd*..............(8 to 1 op 6 to 1) 5

Dist: ¾l, 3½l, 3½l, 4l. 2m 5.70s. a 1.70s (5 Ran).
SR: 42/48/49/37/17/ (Hamdan Al-Maktoum), H Thomson Jones

1935 Tote Credit Maiden Stakes Class D (3-y-o) £4,269 1¾m 17yds......... (4:15)

1426^{2} SOLARTICA (USA) 8-9 P Robinson (6) *hld up, hdwy o'r 3 fs out, led over 2 out, clr appr last, eased*. ....(13 to 8 fav op 6 to 4 tchd 7 to 4) 1
1625^{5} FOINERY 8-9 G Duffield (3) *outpcd at hfwy, styd on wl fnl 2 fs, no ch wth wnr*.....(13 to 2 op 6 to 1 tchd 7 to 1) 2
1603^{4} ELBURG (Ire) 9-0 M Hills (1) *chsd ldrs, in tch 3 fs out, unbl to quicken*.............. (9 to 2 op 4 to 1 tchd 5 to 1) 3
1533^{3} POINT THE WAY (Ire) 8-9 Paul Eddery (5) *led till o'r 2 fs out, ran on one pace*................... (11 to 4 tchd 3 to 1) 4
1802 MOHAYA (USA) 9-0 W R Swinburn (4) *prmnt till wknd fnl 3 fs, eased whn btn o'r one furlong out*. ....(25 to 1 op 14 to 1) 5
1244^{2} OMIDJOY (Ire) 8-9 W Woods (2) *wth ldr till rdn and wknd o'r 3 fs out, sn btn*......(8 to 1 op 8 to 1 tchd 10 to 1) 6

Dist: 5l, sht-hd, 2½l, 15l, dist. 2m 59.60s. a 2.60s (6 Ran).
SR: 20/10/14/4/-/-/ (B E Nielsen), J R Fanshawe

1936 Tote Dual Forecast Handicap Class E (0-70 3-y-o) £2,846 1¾m 17yds. . (4:45)

1625^{6} ELA BILLANTE [70] 9-7 P Robinson (4) *3rd till effrt 3 fs out, led o'r 2 out, rdn out*... (3 to 1 tchd 7 to 2 and 4 to 1) 1
1613^{4} RUSTY REEL [56] 8-4 (3*) B Doyle (1) *hdwy o'r 3 fs out, str run fnl 2 furlongs, kpt on*.......... (11 to 2 op 5 to 1) 2
1613^{3} QAFFAL (USA) [67] 9-4 R Hills (2) *led till hdd o'r 2 fs out, wknd one furlong out*.........(5 to 2 fav tchd 11 to 4) 3
880 SIDE BAR [45] 7-10^{2} D Biggs (5) *chsd ldr till wknd o'r 2 fs out*................... (20 to 1 op 14 to 1 tchd 25 to 1) 4
1359* CAST THE LINE [70] 9-7 A McGlone (3) *hld up, styd on same pace fnl 3 fs*...................(3 to 1 tchd 11 to 4) 5
1491^{4} MANON LESCAUT [43] 7-1 (7*) Martin Dwyer (6) *rdn 4 fs out, no hdwy fnl 3 furlongs*.............. (8 to 1 op 6 to 1) 6

Dist: 1½l, 6l, 6l, hd, ½l. 3m 0.80s. a 3.80s (6 Ran).
SR: 20/3/2/ (Mrs James McAllister), J R Fanshawe

CARLISLE (good to firm)
Wednesday June 23rd
Going Correction: MINUS 0.40 sec. per fur. (races 1,2), MINUS 0.30 (3,4,5,6)

1937 Heads Nook Selling Stakes Class G (3-y-o and up) £2,637 5f 207yds. .(2:15)

1760^{6} FORTIS PAVIOR (Ire) 3-8-13 A Culhane (1) *drvn alng to go pace, improved hfwy, swtchd ins fnl furlong, ran on to ld last 50 yards*.......................(7 to 1 op 6 to 1) 1
SAMSON-AGONISTES 7-9-3 (7*) S Sanders (11) *led, clr o'r one furlong out, wknd and drifted lft ins last, ct last 50 yards*.............. (3 to 1 fav op 11 to 4 tchd 7 to 2) 2
1736^{2} OBSIDIAN GREY 6-9-5 (5*) O Pears (5) *nvr far away, rdn 2 fs out, kpt on same pace*..............(7 to 2 op 3 to 1) 3
1865 ANGELS ANSWER (Ire) 4-9-0 (5*) Darren Moffatt (4) *al hndy, effrt and drvn alng o'r one furlong out, no extr*. .... (14 to 1 op 12 to 1) 4
1159^{9} HAWAYMYSON (Ire) (bl) 3-8-13 K Fallon (2) *drvn alng to improve hfwy, hng rght o'r one furlong out, no imprsn*. ....(12 to 1) 5
1815^{2} LANGTONIAN 4-9-7 (3*) Emma O'Gorman (10) *speed for o'r 3 fs*................. (13 to 2 op 11 to 2 tchd 7 to 1) 6
614^{5} MIDLIN 3-8-8 J Carroll (7) *speed to press ldg bunch 3 fs, fdd*..(12 to 1) 7
1597^{6} MINSK 7-9-2 G Duffield (12) *speed for o'r 3 fs*. ....(25 to 1 op 20 to 1 tchd 33 to 1) 8
1698^{9} PRESS ONWARD 3-8-8 Dean McKeown (13) *str hold, effrt hfwy, btn 2 fs out*.................. (33 to 1 op 25 to 1) 9
1578 MANX MONARCH 3-8-8 J Lowe (8) *wth ldrs, feeling pace o'r 2 fs out, sn btn*.................(10 to 1 op 8 to 1) 10
253 PRETTY CHIC 4-9-7 N Connorton (6) *sn struggling*. ....(50 to 1) 11
1358 WABWOM 4-9-4 (3*) S D Williams (9) *early speed, wknd quickly hfwy, eased whn btn*................. (100 to 1) 12
2517 NOT ALL BLISS 5-9-2 S Wood (3) *al struggling, tld off aftr 2 fs*........................ (100 to 1 op 50 to 1) 13

Dist: ½l, 2½l, 1½l, ¾l, 4l, ½l, 1½l, ½l, ¾l, 10l. 1m 14.10s. a 1.10s (13 Ran).
SR: 29/38/28/17/8/3/ (D Gill), R M Whitaker

1938 Castle Carrock Handicap Class E (0-70 3-y-o and up) £3,261 5f 207yds ....(2:45)

1782[6] MASTER POKEY [55] 9-8-12 (7*) P Johnson (5) *patiently rdn, swtchd ins to improve hfwy, led o'r one furlong out, ran on gmely*.....(13 to 2 op 11 to 2 tchd 7 to 1) 1
1282* SAKHAROV [50] 4-9-0 G Duffield (1) *chsd ldg bunch, drvn through to chal fnl furlong, edgd rght, jst hld*. ....(5 to 2 fav op 11 to 4 tchd 3 to 1) 2
INVIGILATE [60] 4-9-10 L Charnock (10) *nvr far away, ev ch and drvn alng o'r one furlong out, one pace*. ....(20 to 1 op 16 to 1) 3
1760* FORMIDABLE LIZ [54] 3-8-10 (7ex) J Lowe (4) *pressed ldg 4, rdn 2 fs out, styd on same pace*. ....(100 to 30 op 5 to 2 tchd 7 to 2) 4
FARNDALE [41] 6-8-0 (5*) Darren Moffatt (11) *sluggish strt, sn reco'red, led over 2 fs out till over one out, no extr*. ....(33 to 1 op 20 to 1) 5
1589[3] MISS ARAGON [54] 5-8-13 (5*) O Pears (8) *chsd alng in midfield hfwy, effrt 2 fs out, nvr able to chal*. ....(7 to 2 op 9 to 2) 6
1520 MISS HOSTESS [29] (bl) 6-7-7 N Carlisle (7) *sn drvn alng to keep up, ran on ins fnl furlong, nvr nrr*. ....(50 to 1 op 33 to 1) 7
1578 KICK ON MAJESTIC (Ire) [33] (bl) 4-7-11 J Fanning (9) *sn struggling to keep up, nvr rch ldrs*. (14 to 1 op 10 to 1) 8
1480[8] ZINGER [29] 5-7-0 (7*) D Wright (3) *speed 4 fs*. ....(20 to 1 op 16 to 1) 9
800 SUPER ROCKY [64] 4-9-7 (7*) H Bastiman (12) *led till o'r 2 fs out, sn btn*.......................(25 to 1 op 12 to 1) 10
376[9] ACIDOSIS [40] 4-8-4 S Wood (2) *unruly strt, drvn alng on outsd hfwy, sn btn*..................(50 to 1 op 33 to 1) 11
Dist: Hd, 2½l, 1l, 2l, ½l, hd, 5l, ½l, nk. 1m 13.60s. a 0.60s (11 Ran).
SR: 45/39/39/21/8/19/ (Lady Manton), M W Easterby

1939 Tennents Handicap Class D (0-80 3-y-o and up) £3,525 6f 206yds......(3:15)

1721[6] DEBSY DO (USA) [72] 4-9-9 (5*) O Pears (7) *trkd ldg trio, led wl o'r one furlong out, ran on gmely*. (9 to 1 op 7 to 1) 1
1777[4] CAUSLEY [70] 8-9-12 M Birch (4) *chsd ldr, drvn ahead briefly wl o'r one furlong out, rallied und pres ins last*. ....(7 to 2 op 4 to 1) 2
1865[5] SARTIGILA [63] 4-8-12 (7*) J Marshall (6) *sluggish strt, chsd alng to improve last 2 fs, styd on*..............(6 to 1) 3
1865[2] GRANITTON BAY [64] (v) 6-9-6 A Culhane (5) *chsd ldg 4, outpcd and drvn alng hfwy, styd on und pres last 2 fs*. ....(3 to 1 jt-fav tchd 7 to 2) 4
1799[8] CHANTRY BELLINI [48] (bl) 4-8-4 N Carlisle (3) *last and niggled alng aftr 3 fs, styd on frm 2 out, nvr nrr*. ....(14 to 1 op 10 to 1) 5
1737[3] THORNTON GATE [67] (bl) 4-9-6 (3*) S Maloney (8) *led, jnd and drvn alng o'r 2 fs out, hdd wl over one out, sn btn*. ....(3 to 1 jt-fav tchd 11 to 4) 6
1520 VALLEY OF TIME (Fr) [40] 5-7-10 J Fanning (1) *pressed ldg pair, struggling to hold pl hfwy, sn btn*. ....(33 to 1 op 25 to 1) 7
317[7] COSTA VERDE [78] 3-9-11 K Darley (2) *in tch, feeling pace hfwy, tld off*......................(25 to 1 op 20 to 1) 8
Dist: ¾l, hd, 3l, ¾l, 1½l, 10l, 20l. 1m 27.40s. a 2.00s (8 Ran).
SR: 52/48/40/32/14/28/-/-/ (Lintscan Ltd (Corbett Bookmakers)), S G Norton

1940 Tennent's Lager Carlisle Bell Handicap Class D (0-80 3-y-o and up) £4,698 7f 214yds....................(3:45)

1743* QUEEN WARRIOR [56] 4-7-11 (7*,5ex) D Wright (6) *patiently rdn, prog last 2 fs, ran on to ld wl ins last*. ....(9 to 2 op 4 to 1 tchd 5 to 1) 1
1800[4] WHO'S TEF (Ire) [51] 5-7-12[2] (3*) S Maloney (7) *led early, styd hndy, led o'r one furlong out, hdd and not quicken wl ins last*..............................(12 to 1) 2
1730* SET THE FASHION [56] (v) 4-8-4 (5ex) Dean McKeown (8) *nvr far away, drw level und pres one furlong out, one pace whn not much room cl hme*..................(4 to 1 fav) 3
1591[4] SPANISH VERDICT [64] 6-8-5 (7*) C Teague (2) *sn led, hdd and drvn alng o'r one furlong out, rallied, one pace towards finish*......... (7 to 1 op 6 to 1 tchd 8 to 1) 4
1720[3] COOL LUKE (Ire) [79] 4-9-8 (5*) J Tate (4) *settled midfield, effrt and drvn alng last 2 fs, outpcd one out, rallied*. ....(14 to 1 op 12 to 1) 5
1737* LAWNSWOOD JUNIOR [68] 6-9-2 (5ex) K Darley (10) *wtd wth, drvn into midfield o'r 2 fs out, not much room entering last, styd on*. (9 to 2 op 8 to 1 tchd 10 to 1) 6
425[4] RINGLAND (USA) [79] 5-9-8 (5*) Darren Moffatt (9) *patiently rdn, effrt whn hng towards stands side last 2 fs, styd on*..(16 to 1) 7
1707* PRINCESS OF ORANGE [47] 4-7-9 J Lowe (13) *trkd ldg bunch, effrt hfwy, drvn alng whn not much room o'r one furlong out, kpt on*..............................(12 to 1) 8
1501* MOHICAN BRAVE (Ire) [65] 3-8-3 K Fallon (11) *settled to track ldg bunch, effrt on ins o'r 2 fs out, no imprsn*. ....(12 to 1 op 10 to 1) 9

1777* QUANTITY SURVEYOR [58] 4-8-6 (5ex) G Duffield (12) *dsptd ld, rdn o'r 2 fs out, no extr*. ....(11 to 1 op 8 to 1 tchd 12 to 1) 10
1800[6] SCOTTISH PARK [56] (v) 4-7-11 (7*) J Marshall (3) *nvr far away, drvn alng whn pace quickened o'r 2 fs out, sn btn*..(20 to 1 op 16 to 1) 11
1398 HAMADRYAD (Ire) [80] 5-9-9 (5*) O Pears (1) *pressed ldrs, feeling pace and drvn alng o'r 2 fs out, no extr*. ....(16 to 1 tchd 20 to 1) 12
1578[6] MARY MACBLAIN [45] (bl) 4-7-7 A Mackay (5) *sluggish strt, chsd alng to keep in tch hfwy, nvr dngrs*.....(100 to 1) 13
Dist: ½l, ¾l, 1l, nk, nk, 2½l, ½l, hd, 1½l, 1½l. 1m 39.50s. a 1.60s (13 Ran).
SR: 30/23/26/31/45/33/36/2/9/ (Christopher Spence), P T Walwyn

1941 Burgh Barony Races Commemoration Cup Limited Stakes Amateur Riders Class F (0-70 3-y-o and up) £2,646 1½m.........................(4:15)

1657[4] AZUREUS (Ire) 5-11-0 Mr S Swiers (6) *al gng wl, led o'r 4 fs out, sn clr, canter*..........(6 to 4 on tchd 5 to 4 on) 1
1847[8] MINGUS (USA) 6-11-0 Mrs M Cowdrey (5) *chsd ldg 4, styd on to chase wnr appr fnl furlong, no imprsn*. ....(10 to 1 op 8 to 1) 2
1890[6] LORD ADVOCATE (bl) 5-11-0 Miss P Robson (7) *nvr far away, drvn alng last 2 fs, one pace*. ....(16 to 1 tchd 20 to 1) 3
1900[7] NOT YET (v) 9-10-10 (4*) Mr J Weymes (8) *ran in snatches, styd on last 2 fs, nvr able to chal*. (20 to 1 op 16 to 1) 4
1498 THE KARAOKE KING (bl) 4-10-10 (4*) Mrs J Boggis (2) *sluggish strt, wl beh till some late hdwy, nvr dngrs*. ....(5 to 1 op 6 to 1) 5
CARLINGFORD (USA) 7-10-10 (4*) Mr R D Green (3) *chsd ldrs, effrt and wide entering strt, sn btn*. ....(6 to 1 op 5 to 1 tchd 8 to 1) 6
1781 COXANN (bl) 7-10-10 (4*) Mr E Tolhurst (1) *wth ldrs, struggling to hold pl entering strt, sn lost tch*. ....(33 to 1 op 25 to 1) 7
1676[7] HEIR OF EXCITEMENT (bl) 8-11-0 Mr R Hale (4) *led till o'r 4 fs out, sn tld off*...................(33 to 1 op 25 to 1) 8
Dist: 8l, 3l, 3l, 3l, 6l, sht-hd, 20l. 2m 34.50s. a 4.50s (8 Ran).
SR: 47/31/25/19/13/1/-/-/ (J C Murdoch), Mrs M Reveley

1942 Wetheral Rating Related Maiden Stakes Class F (0-60 3-y-o and up) £2,444 1¾m 32yds............. (4:45)

1359[5] FOLLINGWORTH GIRL (Ire) 3-7-13 (3*) S Maloney (2) *pld hrd, rdn and looked btn entering strt, crrd head high, led wl ins fnl furlong, kpt on*....... (8 to 1 op 5 to 1) 1
1594[6] WAKT 3-8-2 G Duffield (4) *led, drvn alng and hdd wl o'r one furlong out, led briefly entering last, rdn and no extr*.......................... (5 to 4 op Evens tchd 11 to 8) 2
1479[5] SHARE A MOMENT (Can) (bl) 3-8-7 S Perks (1) *al hndy, hrd drvn to ld wl o'r one furlong out, hdd and wknd quickly entering last*. ....(Evens fav tchd 11 to 10 and 11 to 10 on) 3
Dist: 1½l, 7l. 3m 9.60s. a 11.80s (3 Ran).
(John L Holdroyd), S G Norton

CHESTER (good)
Wednesday June 23rd
Going Correction: MINUS 0.40 sec. per fur.

1943 Tarvin Claiming Stakes Class D (3-y-o and up) £4,370 1¼m 75yds......(6:30)

1299[5] DEE RAFT (USA) 3-8-7 D Holland (5) *trkd ldr, led 4 fs out, rdn clr 2 out, easily*..........................(7 to 2) 1
1832 ROSE GLEN 7-8-5 A Mackay (4) *hld up, hdwy hfwy, effrt 3 fs out, sn rdn, kpt on frm 2 out, no ch wth wnr*. ....(7 to 2 op 3 to 1 tchd 4 to 1) 2
1562[5] FORMAESTRE (Ire) 3-7-0 (7*) D Wright (7) *chsd ldrs, rdn o'r 3 fs out, sn one pace*..............................(8 to 1) 3
1582[4] CIVIL LAW (Ire) (bl) 3-8-7 K Darley (6) *hld up beh, rdn alng hfwy, some hdwy und pres and not keen fnl 2 fs, nvr a factor*................................(3 to 1 fav op 5 to 2) 4
1459[5] BARSAL (Ire) 3-7-11 (5*) J Tate (2) *chsd ldrs, rdn 3 fs out, sn one pace*.......................(14 to 1 op 10 to 1) 5
1743 WHAT LOLA WANTS (Ire) 3-7-9 J Quinn (1) *in tch, pushed alng hfwy, sn wknd*.................(10 to 1 op 7 to 1) 6
1784[7] CIVIL ACTION (Ire) 3-8-12 A Culhane (3) *led, rdn and hdd 4 fs out, sn wknd*......... (6 to 1 op 5 to 1 tchd 7 to 1) 7
Dist: 5l, ¾l, 4l, 2½l, ¾l, 20l. 2m 12.40s. a 3.30s (7 Ran).
SR: 19/7/-/-/ (D O Pickering), B W Hills

1944 Farndon Maiden Fillies Stakes Class D (2-y-o) £3,548 5f 16yds........(7:00)

BETTYKIMVIC 8-11 K Fallon (4) *chsd ldrs, rdn and hdwy 2 fs out, not much room and swtchd entering last, ridden and styd on to ld nr line*..........(20 to 1 op 12 to 1) 1
1296[2] INDIAHRA 8-11 K Darley (1) *led to one furlong out, rdn and led ins last, ct nr line*. ....(13 to 8 on op 2 to 1 on tchd 6 to 4 on) 2

I'M YOUR LADY 8-11 J Fortune (3) *cl up, effrt 2 fs out, sn rdn, led one out, edgd rght and hdd ins last, no extr.* ....(13 to 2 op 10 to 1 tchd 6 to 1) 3
PROMISE FULFILLED (USA) 8-6 (5*) O Pears (5) *slwly away, outpcd, styd on fnl furlong*...(7 to 1 op 4 to 1) 4
DAILY STAR 8-11 J Carroll (6) *cl up, rdn and ev ch 2 fs out, wknd o'r one out*..................(4 to 1 op 11 to 4) 5
Dist: Sht-hd, 2½l, ½l, 2½l. 1m 2.05s. a 1.75s (5 Ran).
SR: 22/21/11/9/-/ (John Patrick Barry), E J Alston

1945 GMS Industrial Fasteners Rated Class B Handicap (0-95 3-y-o and up) £6,546 6f 18yds......................(7:30)

1786 STACK ROCK [95] 6-9-2 (5*) Stephen Davies (4) *chsd ldr, effrt to ld ins fnl furlong, rdn and ran on wl.* ....(13 to 2 op 6 to 1 tchd 7 to 1) 1
1806[4] GORINSKY (Ire) [81] 5-8-7 J Carroll (2) *led, rdn and hdd ins fnl furlong, rallied und pres nr finish.* ....(3 to 1 fav op 5 to 2) 2
1786 CRADLE DAYS [88] 4-9-0 D Holland (9) *chsd ldrs, rdn 2 fs out, kpt on one pace*... (15 to 2 op 7 to 1 tchd 8 to 1) 3
1680[9] MASTER OF PASSION [93] 4-9-2 (3*) N Kennedy (6) *chsd ldrs, rdn 2 fs out, sn one pace*..... (12 to 1 op 10 to 1) 4
1680[4] RED ROSEIN [85] 7-8-11 J Fortune (7) *outpcd, rdn alng hfwy, styd on und pres fnl 2 fs, not rch ldrs.* ....(9 to 2 op 7 to 2) 5
1402[5] HOPE HALL (Ire) [81] 5-8-7 A Culhane (3) *chsd ldrs, rdn o'r 2 fs out, sn wknd*..................(25 to 1 op 20 to 1) 6
1679[7] DRUM SERGEANT [81] (bl) 6-8-2 (5*) J Tate (8) *slwly away, beh, rdn hfwy, some hdwy fnl 2 fs, nvr dngrs.* ....(7 to 1 op 6 to 1) 7
1680 CRYSTAL JACK (Fr) [84] 5-8-10 Paul Eddery (1) *cl up whn hmpd aftr one furlong, not reco'r*....(9 to 2 op 4 to 1) 8
1721 THE AUCTION BIDDER [81] 6-8-7 K Darley (5) *sn outpcd.* ....(12 to 1) 9
Dist: Hd, 6l, 3½l, 1l, hd, nk, 5l, 1½l. 1m 12.78s. b 0.72s (9 Ran).
SR: 73/58/41/32/20/15/14/-/-/ (Castle Racing), E J Alston

1946 Deeside Handicap Class D (0-80 3-y-o and up) £5,374 1½m 66yds......(8:00)

1328[4] MAD MILITANT (Ire) [67] 4-10-0 K Darley (4) *in tch, hdwy 3 fs out, rdn to chal appr last, styd on und pres to ld nr line*..........................(3 to 1 tchd 7 to 2) 1
1661[5] FOOLS ERRAND (Ire) [68] 3-9-0 S Whitworth (3) *trkd ldr, led 4 fs out, rdn o'r one out, hdd nr finish.* ....(7 to 1 op 6 to 1) 2
1681[8] KILLICK [51] 5-8-12 J Quinn (2) *trkd ldrs, chlgd 3 fs out, ev ch till rdn and wknd entering last*... (4 to 1 op 7 to 2) 3
1351[3] CASHELL [71] 3-9-3 Paul Eddery (5) *set slow pace, hdd 4 fs out, sn one pace*........(4 to 1 op 3 to 1 tchd 9 to 2) 4
GREEN'S CASSATT (USA) [51] 5-8-12 R Lappin (6) *al rear.* ....(20 to 1 op 16 to 1) 5
1681[2] PHILGUN [66] 4-9-10 (3*) S Maloney (1) *trkd ldrs, rdn and outpcd o'r 3 fs out, no dngr aftr.* (5 to 2 fav op 9 to 4) 6
Dist: Sht-hd, 4l, ½l, hd, 2½l. 2m 43.10s. a 6.30s (6 Ran).
SR: 2/-/-/ (Mrs B Facchino), R Hollinshead

1947 Midsummer Handicap Class D (0-80 3-y-o) £4,919 7f 2yds........... (8:30)

1528* FAIRY STORY (Ire) [73] 9-4 D Holland (4) *made all, rdn clr 2 fs out, easily*..................(6 to 4 fav tchd 7 to 4) 1
1581[8] DIWALI DANCER [50] (bl) 7-9 A Mackay (2) *hld up in tch, hdwy on ins 3 fs out, rdn and chsd wnr frm 2 out, no imprsn*..............................(8 to 1 op 10 to 1) 2
1697[6] INDERAPUTERI [71] 8-9 (7*) D McCabe (3) *in tch, hdwy and rdn 3 fs out, kpt on one pace frm 2 out.* ....(13 to 2 op 5 to 1 tchd 7 to 1) 3
1312[8] BEZIQUE (USA) [68] (v) 8-13 J Carroll (1) *chsd wnr, rdn 3 fs out, sn wknd*..................(9 to 2 op 4 to 1) 4
1595[3] AL SHAATI (Fr) [66] 8-11 K Darley (6) *slwly away, sn in tch, rdn hfwy, soon btn*..................(7 to 2 op 5 to 2) 5
1485[9] ROYAL ROLLER (Ire) [76] 9-7 Paul Eddery (5) *cl up, rdn 3 fs out, sn wknd*..............................(8 to 1) 6
Dist: 5l, 3l, 2½l, 3½l, 2½l. 1m 26.38s. a 0.98s (6 Ran).
SR: 47/9/21/10/-/-/ (The Fairy Story Partnership), J W Hills

1948 Broxton Maiden Stakes Class D (3-y-o) £4,290 1m 7f 195yds........(9:00)

1603[5] TILTY (USA) 9-0 K Darley (1) *trkd ldr, pushed alng o'r 4 fs out, rdn 3 out, styd on und pres to ld ins last.* ....(6 to 4 on op 7 to 4 on tchd 11 to 8 on) 1
1690[3] KEDGE 9-0 D Holland (2) *set steady pace, quickened o'r 4 fs out, rdn 2 out, hdd and no extr ins last.* ....(7 to 4 op 6 to 4) 2
1495[6] DESERT LAUGHTER (Ire) 9-0 S Perks (3) *in tch, rdn o'r 4 fs out, sn beh*..................(6 to 1 op 10 to 1) 3
Dist: 1½l, 20l. 3m 34.80s. a 9.80s (3 Ran).
(Exors Of The Late Mr D F Cock), R Hannon

KEMPTON (good)
Wednesday June 23rd

Going Correction: MINUS 0.10 sec. per fur. (races 1,2,4,5), MINUS 0.30 (3,6)

1949 Richard Dallyn Maiden Stakes Class D (2-y-o) £3,494 7f................(6:45)

LOMAS (Ire) 9-0 A Munro (3) *handily plcd, shaken up to ld o'r one over out, quickened clr, easily.* ....(5 to 2 fav op 7 to 4 tchd 11 to 4) 1
1446[4] SILVER WEDGE (USA) 9-0 Pat Eddery (11) *made most of rng till o'r one furlong out, ran on same pace.* ....(3 to 1 tchd 5 to 2 and 100 to 30) 2
1456[2] THE FLYING PHANTOM 9-0 P Robinson (2) *pressed ldr, ev ch frm o'r 2 fs out till over one out, ran on same pace.* ....(7 to 1 op 5 to 1) 3
BONAIGUA (Ire) 9-0 R Hills (7) *slwly into strd, hdwy o'r 2 fs out, one pace ins fnl furlong*.... (16 to 1 op 10 to 1) 4
DONTFORGET INSIGHT (Ire) 9-0 C Rutter (4) *ldg grp, rdn and not quicken o'r one furlong out, kpt on gmely.* ....(16 to 1 op 10 to 1 tchd 20 to 1) 5
JEAN DE FLORETTE (USA) 9-0 L Dettori (5) *styd on frm 2 fs out, nvr nrr*..............................(33 to 1 op 20 to 1) 6
1666[3] SHARP TYCOON (Ire) 9-0 B Rouse (10) *chsd ldrs til wknd frm 2 out*..............................(7 to 1 op 5 to 1) 7
PLUNDER BAY (USA) 9-0 G Hind (13) *al outpcd.* ....(33 to 1 op 16 to 1) 8
1666[9] DEBLYN 9-0 W Newnes (6) *nvr nr to chal.* ....(50 to 1 op 33 to 1) 9
1456[6] MIAMI HURRICANE (Ire) 9-0 W R Swinburn (14) *slwly into strd, sn racing in mid-div, btn o'r 2 fs out.* ....(12 to 1 tchd 16 to 1) 10
738 STOMPIN 8-11 (3*) B Doyle (9) *nvr trbld frnt rnk.* ....(20 to 1 tchd 25 to 1) 11
SHERIDAN (Ire) 9-0 W Carson (8) *slwly into strd, sn wl beh*..............................(14 to 1 op 8 to 1) 12
1142[7] EMMA GRIMES (Ire) 8-9 S Raymont (1) *rcd on outsd and in tch til wknd o'r 2 fs out*.......... (50 to 1 op 33 to 1) 13
1324[7] GREENFINCH (Can) 9-0 J Reid (12) *mid-div and in tch whn hmpd 4 fs out, rdn and wknd o'r 2 out.* ....(14 to 1 op 12 to 1) 14
Dist: 6l, nk, 1½l, 1½l, 3½l, 4l, 1½l, sht-hd, hd, ¾l. 1m 26.31s. a 2.21s (14 Ran).
SR: 56/38/37/32/27/16/4/-/-/ (Fahd Salman), R Hannon

1950 Ilph Fillies' Conditions Stakes Class D (3-y-o) £3,318 1m...............(7:15)

522* ANDROMAQUE (USA) 8-12 Pat Eddery (6) *steadied strt, pushed alng 3 fs out, led wl o'r one out, styd on well.* ....(6 to 1 tchd 7 to 1) 1
1638[5] JETBEEAH (Ire) 8-12 W R Swinburn (10) *wl in tch, str run and swtchd rght o'r one furlong out, ran on nr finish, fnshd second, disqualified.* ....(9 to 1 op 7 to 1 tchd 10 to 1) 2D
1616* ETOSHA 8-12 M Hills (9) *trkd ldrs, led 2 fs out, sn hdd, one pace ins last, fnshd 3rd, plcd second.* ....(5 to 1 op 6 to 1) 2
1016[9] EAST LIBERTY (USA) 8-8 L Dettori (7) *beh, rdn alng 3 fs out, ran on last 2 furlongs, not quicken, fnshd 4th, plcd 3rd*.............. (25 to 1 op 16 to 1 tchd 33 to 1) 3
1638[8] ARUSHA (Ire) 8-12 J Williams (4) *beh, moderate prog last 2 fs, not rch ldrs, fnshd 5th, plcd 4th.* ....(25 to 1 op 14 to 1) 4
1415[3] KATIBA (USA) 8-12 W Carson (8) *settled in rear, moderate prog last 2 fs, fnshd 6th, plcd 5th.* ....(16 to 1 op 10 to 1 tchd 20 to 1) 5
999[2] HELVELLYN (USA) 8-8 W Ryan (1) *cl up, led aftr 3 fs, hdd 2 out, wkng whn badly hmpd and snatched up o'r one furlong out*.......... (10 to 1 op 8 to 1 tchd 12 to 1) 7
1454* PONDICHERRY (USA) 8-10 W Woods (5) *rcd in midfield till hfwy, sn lost pl*...... (16 to 1 op 10 to 1 tchd 20 to 1) 8
1452* LINK RIVER (USA) 8-12 G Hind (2) *cl up, ev ch 2 fs out, wkng whn hmpd o'r one out.* ....(15 to 8 fav op 7 to 4 tchd 2 to 1) 9
1231[2] KHUBZA 8-12 A McGlone (3) *led for 3 fs, wknd o'r 2 furlongs out*.......... (13 to 2 op 9 to 2 tchd 7 to 1) 10
Dist: ¾l, 3l, 1½l, 2½l, 2l, 10l, 2½l, 2½l, 1½l. 1m 38.40s. a 1.60s (10 Ran).
SR: 62/60/51/42/38/32/ (Dr Carlos E Stelling), R Charlton

1951 Taylor Walker Handicap Class E (0-70 3-y-o and up) £3,132 1½m...... (7:45)

674[8] MAHRAJAN [47] 9-8-6[1] R Cochrane (8) *rcd in rear, ran on o'r 3 fs out, led over one out, rdn out.* ....(11 to 2 op 9 to 2 tchd 6 to 1) 1
GROVE SERENDIPITY (Ire) [44] (bl) 5-8-3 W Carson (12) *slwly into strd, sn rdn alng in mid-div, ran on to ld und pres 2 out, soon hdd, no extr ins fnl furlong.* ....(11 to 2 op 7 to 2) 2
SALMONID [55] 7-9-0 W Newnes (11) *led til hdd 2 fs out, outpcd o'r one out*... (25 to 1 op 20 to 1 tchd 33 to 1) 3
1414[8] ADDICTED TO LOVE [62] (bl) 4-9-7 W R Swinburn (13) *handily plcd, outpcd o'r 2 fs out, kpt on ag'n ins fnl furlong.* ....(5 to 1 fav op 9 to 2 tchd 11 to 2) 4
1858[5] GO FORUM [41] 8-8-0[1] A Munro (7) *mid-div, jnd issue 3 out, ev ch 2 out, btn fnl furlong.* ....(8 to 1 op 7 to 1 tchd 10 to 1) 5

1657* BALADIYA [67] 6-9-7 (5*) C Hodgson (10) *handily plcd, rdn alng and one pace appr fnl furlong.*
.... (11 to 2 op 5 to 1 tchd 6 to 1) 6
EASY TOOMEY [41] 5-7-11 (3*) B Doyle (3) *beh til effrt 3 out, no imprsn on ldrs last 2 fs...* (50 to 1 tchd 66 to 1) 7
1669 VITAL CLUE (USA) [69] 6-10-0 D Biggs (14) *settled in mid-div, hrd rdn 4 out, wknd o'r 2 out.* (20 to 1 op 14 to 1) 8
1688^{8} CHARMED LIFE [47] 4-8-6 J Williams (6) *rear most of way.*
........................(25 to 1 tchd 33 to 1) 9
1607^{8} HALLOW FAIR [37] 8-7-10^{3} T Williams (2) *slwly away, beh til moderate effrt o'r 2 fs out, not rch ldrs.*
.... (25 to 1 op 20 to 1 tchd 33 to 1) 10
1659 JONBEL [34] 5-7-5^{5} (7*) C Hawksley (16) *wl in tch, rdn alng 4 fs out, sn btn.......*(25 to 1 op 50 to 1 tchd 66 to 1) 11
1605^{7} SIMPLY (Ire) [49] 4-8-8 L Dettori (5) *trkd ldg grp, rdn and wknd 3 fs out...........* (7 to 1 op 6 to 1 tchd 8 to 1) 12
1709^{4} ONE MORE POUND [51] 3-7-9^{2} A Tucker (1) *al rear grp, lost tch 4 out...........*(12 to 1 op 10 to 1 tchd 14 to 1) 13
1612^{7} BARBARY REEF (Ire) [35] 5-7-8 G Bardwell (15) *chsd ldrs til wknd und pres o'r 3 fs out.*
.... (14 to 1 op 12 to 1 tchd 16 to 1) 14
Dist: 2½l, 7l, 1½l, 2l, ¾l, 1½l, 1l, ½l, hd, 2½l. 2m 32.61s. a 1.61s (14 Ran).
SR: 40/32/29/33/8/32/3/29/6/ (Mrs F A Harris), C J Benstead

1952 LBC Newstalk 97.3 FM Gala Stakes Class A (Listed Race) (3-y-o and up) £11,452 1¼m.................. (8:15)

1748^{9} SPARTAN SHAREEF (Ire) 4-9-10 W R Swinburn (4) *trkd ldr, led 2 fs out, drvn out...* (15 to 2 op 5 to 1 tchd 9 to 1) 1
1347^{2} PORT LUCAYA (bl) 3-8-12 L Dettori (3) *wl in tch, rdn alng o'r 2 fs out, jnd ldr fnl furlong, ran on und pres, jst fld.*
....................(85 to 40 fav op 6 to 4 tchd 9 to 4) 2
1539^{3} SALATIN (USA) 3-8-9 R Hills (5) *handily plcd, kpt on one pace frm 2 fs out.....* (14 to 1 op 12 to 1 tchd 16 to 1) 3
1347^{4} FITZCARRALDO (USA) 3-8-9 R Cochrane (1) *hld up towards rear, rdn alng 2 fs out, styd on one pace ins fnl furlong................* (7 to 1 op 5 to 1 tchd 15 to 2) 4
1559* ST NINIAN 7-9-7 M Birch (6) *rcd in mid-div, rdn alng o'r 2 fs out, no imprsn on ldrs fnl furlong.*
....(8 to 1 tchd 10 to 1) 5
1472^{7} SILVER WISP (USA) 4-9-7 Pat Eddery (7) *steadied leaving stalls, hld up in rear, rdn o'r 2 fs out, not quicken und pres over one out.............* (8 to 1 tchd 10 to 1) 6
1525 BASHAYER (USA) 3-8-4 W Carson (2) *led til hdd 2 fs out, eased whn btn ins fnl furlong.......* (3 to 1 op 4 to 1) 7
Dist: Sht-hd, 2l, nk, ¾l, 2l, nk. 2m 7.07s. a 5.27s (7 Ran).
SR: 48/35/28/27/37/33/15/ (C T Olley), C E Brittain

1953 '1812' Overture Handicap Class D (0-80 3-y-o and up) £3,201 6f.... (8:45)

1587^{6} DANCING SPIRIT (Ire) [70] 3-9-0 L Dettori (6) *hld up in tch, ran on to ld one furlong out, drvn out.*
....(12 to 1 tchd 14 to 1) 1
1584 TRUTHFUL IMAGE [74] (bl) 4-9-12 D Biggs (8) *trkd ldrs, not clr run o'r 2 fs out, sstnd chal fnl furlong, jst fld.*
.... (8 to 1 op 7 to 1 tchd 10 to 1) 2
1744^{2} MERRYHILL MAID (Ire) [67] 5-9-5 R Cochrane (9) *led aftr one furlong, hdd one out, rallied und pres...*(9 to 2 jt-fav tchd 5 to 1 and 4 to 1) 3
1584^{2} JIGSAW BOY [76] 4-10-0 J Williams (1) *beh til ran on fnl furlong, fnshd strly..........*(9 to 2 jt-fav tchd 5 to 1) 4
1394^{3} ZEBOIM [70] (bl) 7-9-1 (7*) Kim McDonnell (2) *cld on ldrs hfwy, ev ch one furlong out, not quicken last 100 yards.................* (9 to 1 op 6 to 1 tchd 10 to 1) 5
1744* GREY CHARMER (Ire) [63] 4-9-1 (6ex) W Newnes (5) *outpcd til rdn and styd on o'r one furlong out, nrst finish.*
.... (13 to 2 op 7 to 1 tchd 8 to 1) 6
1744^{4} BELFORT RULER [66] 6-9-4 J Reid (10) *led for one furlong, rdn and wknd o'r one out.*
.... (14 to 1 op 8 to 1 tchd 16 to 1) 7
1835^{7} EDUCATED PET [71] 4-9-9 T Williams (4) *mid-div, rdn and outpcd frm 2 out.....* (12 to 1 op 10 to 1 tchd 14 to 1) 8
1698^{2} SYLVAN BREEZE [70] (v) 5-9-8 B Rouse (7) *pressed ldrs for o'r 4 fs, wknd.....................*(14 to 1 op 12 to 1) 9
1494^{5} DARUSSALAM [68] 6-9-6 Pat Eddery (3) *al outpcd.*
.... (11 to 2 op 5 to 1 tchd 6 to 1) 10
Dist: Hd, ½l, hd, 1l, ½l, 2½l, hd, 1½l, 3½l. 1m 13.21s. a 2.41s (10 Ran).
SR: 40/51/42/50/40/31/24/28/21/ (L H J Ward), R Hannon

1954 Fireworks Finale Handicap Class D (0-80 3-y-o and up) £3,318 7f.... (9:15)

1830^{4} BALLERINA BAY [65] (v) 5-9-5 Pat Eddery (5) *hld up in rear, sstnd run ins last 2 fs, led nr finish.*
.... (100 to 30 fav op 4 to 1 tchd 9 to 2) 1
1713^{3} WISHAM (USA) [75] 3-9-6 B Raymond (2) *handily plcd, rdn to ld ins fnl furlong, hdd nr line.....* (7 to 1 op 5 to 1) 2
1298^{4} ROSEATE LODGE [67] 7-9-7 L Dettori (10) *trkd ldrs, ev ch entering fnl furlong, styd on one pace.*
.... (10 to 1 op 8 to 1) 3
1721^{2} MY BEST VALENTINE [80] 3-9-11 W R Swinburn (11) *led for one furlong, chsd ldr, led o'r 2 out, hdd ins fnl furlong, kpt on wl..............* (6 to 1 op 9 to 2 tchd 13 to 2) 4
1658^{7} QUEEN OF SHANNON (Ire) [70] 5-9-10 M Tebbutt (4) *wl in tch, rdn and not quicken frm 2 fs out.*
.... (10 to 1 op 8 to 1 tchd 12 to 1) 5
1374^{4} STAR GODDESS (USA) [71] 4-9-11 B Rouse (8) *pld hrd, ldg grp, dsptd ld o'r 2 out till over one out, no extr.*
.... (11 to 2 op 10 to 1) 6
1707^{5} LORD ALFIE [44] 4-7-12 A McGlone (9) *pld hrd, effrt and hard rdn o'r 2 fs out, no imprsn on ldrs.*
.... (12 to 1 op 10 to 1 tchd 14 to 1) 7
1641^{6} KISSAVOS [48] 7-8-2 F Norton (1) *nvr better than mid-div.*
........................(7 to 1 op 5 to 1 tchd 8 to 1) 8
1667^{4} WHATEVER'S RIGHT (Ire) [57] 4-8-11 N Adams (7) *nvr nr to chal.................................* (12 to 1 op 8 to 1) 9
917 PRECIOUS WONDER [65] 4-9-5 T Williams (3) *rcd in mid-div, wknd appr last 3 fs..........* (33 to 1 op 20 to 1) 10
1215 SADDLEHOME (USA) [66] 4-9-6 G Hind (13) *slwly into strd, sn racing in mid-div, wknd 3 fs out.*
.... (33 to 1 op 25 to 1) 11
1394^{7} OUR RITA [74] 4-10-0 R Cochrane (6) *al beh.*
.... (12 to 1 op 10 to 1) 12
1623 SPANISH LOVE [41] 7-7-9 Dale Gibson (12) *led aftr one furlong till hdd o'r 2 out, drpd out quickly.*
.... (33 to 1 op 20 to 1) 13
Dist: Nk, 1½l, 2l, 2l, sht-hd, sht-hd, ½l, 1½l, 2½l, 1½l. 1m 26.83s. a 2.53s (13 Ran).
SR: 36/36/32/30/23/23/-/-/1/ (Mrs Carol Whitwood), D T Thom

SALISBURY (good)
Wednesday June 23rd

Going Correction: MINUS 0.25 sec. per fur. (races 1,2,3,5), MINUS 0.10 (4,6,7)

1955 EBF Weyhill Maiden Fillies' Stakes Class D (2-y-o) £3,817 5f........ (2:00)

1804^{8} JADE PET 8-11 J Reid (3) *alaways prmnt, chlgd one furlong out, led wl ins last, ran on well.*
.... (15 to 2 op 5 to 1 tchd 8 to 1) 1
1708^{2} ROBIN LAKE (Ire) 8-11 L Dettori (7) *cl up, led o'r 2 fs out till hdd wl ins last, ran on.........*(11 to 8 on op 11 to 8) 2
477^{4} ALZIANAH 8-8 (3*) D Harrison (12) *trkd ldrs, short of room appr fnl furlong, ran on one pace.*
....(5 to 1 op 5 to 1 tchd 7 to 2) 3
1660^{6} MARJORIE'S MEMORY (Ire) 8-11 W Ryan (10) *rstrained early, chsd ldrs kpt on one pace fnl 2 fs.*
.... (16 to 1 op 12 to 1 tchd 20 to 1) 4
CHILLY TIME 8-11 J Williams (4) *beh, pushed alng 2 fs out, ran on ins last, prmsg.*
.... (33 to 1 op 20 to 1 tchd 40 to 1) 5
NATURAL PATH 8-11 W Carson (11) *chsd ldrs till outpcd frm wl o'r one furlong out.*
.... (12 to 1 op 10 to 1 tchd 14 to 1) 6
MARJORIE'S ORCHID 8-11 D Holland (8) *sn pushed alng, nvr on terms..........* (16 to 1 op 8 to 1 tchd 20 to 1) 7
1229^{6} CHINA ROBIN 8-11 R Cochrane (9) *led til hdd o'r 2 fs out, wknd ins last.........* (25 to 1 op 12 to 1 tchd 33 to 1) 8
IT'S SO EASY 8-11 Paul Eddery (5) *chsd ldrs, rdn 2 two fs out, wknd...........* (20 to 1 op 12 to 1 tchd 25 to 1) 9
WIDE OUTSIDE (Ire) 8-11 B Rouse (6) *dwlt, al beh.*
.... (50 to 1 op 20 to 1) 10
MIRIAM 8-11 Pat Eddery (1) *outpcd.*
.... (10 to 1 op 12 to 1 tchd 14 to 1) 11
1158^{7} SILVER SLIPPER 8-4 (7*) D Gibbs (2) *slwly into strd, outpcd...............................* (50 to 1 op 20 to 1) 12
Dist: ½l, 1½l, 1½l, 2l, 2l, 1l, 2l, sht-hd, 2½l, 5l. 1m 2.29s. a 2.49s (12 Ran).
SR: 22/20/14/8/-/-/ (Geoffrey C Greenwood), R Hannon

1956 Martin Claiming Handicap Class G (0-80 3-y-o and up) £2,826 1m... (2:30)

1588^{4} WILD STRAWBERRY [50] 4-9-4 B Rouse (1) *rcd alone stands side to hfwy, made all, jst hld on......* (20 to 1) 1
1799* SOOTY TERN [45] 6-8-6 (7*) Mark Denaro (9) *led far side grp, ev ch ins fnl furlong, ran on.*
........................(9 to 2 fav op 7 to 1 tchd 4 to 1) 2
1707^{4} LORD OBERON (Ire) [47] (bl) 5-9-1 R Cochrane (11) *hld up in mid-div, hdwy 2 fs out, swtchd lft o'r one out, ran on wl und pres ins last......* (7 to 1 op 10 to 1 tchd 12 to 1) 3
1707^{2} DANCING BEAU (Ire) [52] 4-9-6 J Reid (14) *chsd ldrs, rdn o'r one furlong out, styd on one pace ins last.*
.... (10 to 1 op 8 to 1) 4
1320^{7} CHANDIGARH [52] 5-9-6 Dale Gibson (10) *al prmnt, hrd rdn 2 fs out, kpt on one pace.*
.... (16 to 1 op 14 to 1 tchd 20 to 1) 5
1734^{2} PRINCE RODNEY [60] 4-10-0 W Carson (7) *trkd ldrs, hrd rdn o'r one furlong out, no response.*
........................(8 to 1 op 7 to 1 tchd 9 to 1) 6
1527 SLEEPLINE FANTASY [48] 8-9-2 L Dettori (18) *trkd ldrs till wknd o'r one furlong out.*
.... (11 to 1 op 10 to 1 tchd 12 to 1) 7
1686^{4} SAREEN EXPRESS (Ire) [45] 5-8-13 A Tucker (6) *hld up in mid-div, rdn and outpcd fnl 2 fs.*
.... (12 to 1 op 10 to 1 tchd 14 to 1) 8

1578[2] ROLY WALLACE [55] (bl) 4-9-9 M Wigham (3) *co'red up in mid-div, effrt 2 fs out, sn outpcd.* ....(10 to 1 op 8 to 1 tchd 11 to 1) 9
158[8] BY ARRANGEMENT (Ire) [47] 4-9-1 Pat Eddery (8) *al beh.* ....(11 to 1 op 10 to 1 tchd 12 to 1) 10
1696[5] ELEGANT TOUCH [52] 4-9-3 (3*) D Harrison (17) *nvr on terms*........................(10 to 1 tchd 12 to 1) 11
1685[3] AMBASSADOR ROYALE (Ire) [60] 5-10-0 J Williams (15) *al beh*........................(25 to 1 op 20 to 1) 12
1743[8] MEXICAN DANCER [55] 4-9-2 (7*) S Drowne (4) *mid-div. effrt o'r 2 fs out, sn btn.* ....(14 to 1 op 10 to 1 tchd 16 to 1) 13
1414 MAPLE BAY (Ire) [44] (bl) 4-8-12 W Newnes (12) *beh frm hfwy*........................(33 to 1 tchd 50 to 1) 14
1606 NAVARESQUE [47] 8-9-1 A Munro (5) *al beh.* ....(14 to 1 op 10 to 1 tchd 16 to 1) 15
ABSOLUTELY HUMMING [43] 7-8-11 N Adams (13) *reared strt, al beh*..........(50 to 1 op 33 to 1 tchd 66 to 1) 16
1659[4] AEDEAN [45] 4-8-13 T Williams (2) *rcd alone centre, al prmnt till rdn and wknd o'r 2 fs out*..........(20 to 1) 17
1498 SAFE ARRIVAL (USA) [48] (bl) 5-8-11 (5*) C Hodgson (16) *cl up til wknd hfwy*....(20 to 1 op 16 to 1 tchd 25 to 1) 18

Dist: Nk, nk, 2½l, 2l, ½l, 2½l, ½l, nk, 2l, ¾l. 1m 43.00s. a 3.50s (18 Ran).
SR: 22/16/17/14/8/14/ (Mrs Dorothy Price), Mark Campion

1957 Alderholt Sprint Handicap Class D (0-85 3-y-o and up) £5,287 5f.... (3:00)

BALIGAY [73] 8-9-9 L Dettori (1) *dwlt, sn in tch, hdwy to ld entering fnl furlong, ran on wl.* ....(25 to 1 op 16 to 1 tchd 33 to 1) 1
1687 BALLASECRET [76] 5-9-12 J Reid (4) *cl up, led o'r 2 fs out till hdd entering last, rallied und pres.* ....(8 to 1 op 6 to 1) 2
1744[8] SIR JOEY (USA) [77] 4-9-13 J Williams (2) *beh, hdwy ins fnl furlong, ran on*........................(12 to 1 op 8 to 1) 3
1687* MISTER JOLSON [70] 4-9-6 W Carson (9) *trkd ldrs, rdn o'r 2 fs out, kpt on und pres ins last.* ....(13 to 2 op 6 to 1 tchd 7 to 1) 4
1782[4] VERY DICEY [71] 5-9-7 R Cochrane (8) *al prmnt, ev ch one furlong out, sn wknd*...(11 to 2 op 5 to 1 tchd 6 to 1) 5
1687[4] BELLSABANGING [71] 3-9-0 T Williams (6) *al prmnt, ev ch 2 fs out, sn btn*...........(7 to 1 op 6 to 1 tchd 8 to 1) 6
1485[7] BODARI [78] 4-9-11 (3*) D Harrison (10) *led til hdd o'r 2 fs out, wknd*..........(14 to 1 op 12 to 1 tchd 16 to 1) 7
1258[2] ARAGROVE [71] 3-9-0 A Munro (3) *nvr on terms.* ....(13 to 2 op 6 to 1 tchd 15 to 2) 8
1668[3] PALEY PRINCE (USA) [73] (v) 7-9-9 W R Swinburn (7) *al beh.* ....(7 to 1 op 6 to 1 tchd 8 to 1) 9
1687[2] FIVESEVENFIVEO [74] 5-9-10 Pat Eddery (5) *nvr gng wl, al beh*..................(9 to 2 fav op 4 to 1 tchd 5 to 1) 10

Dist: Sht-hd, 2½l, 3l, ½l, 2l, 2l, 3l, hd, 4l. 1m 1.32s. a 1.52s (10 Ran).
SR: 54/56/47/28/27/12/18/-/-/ (H G Carnell & Son Ltd), R J Hodges

1958 Gibbs Mew Bibury Cup Handicap Class C (0-95 3-y-o) £5,433 1½m (3:30)

1717* AZHAR [95] 9-7 W R Swinburn (5) *made all, clr hfwy, given breather 5 fs out, shaken up whn chlgd o'r one out, pushed out*.......... (8 to 1 op 11 to 2 tchd 10 to 1) 1
1093* BARON FERDINAND [92] 9-4 R Cochrane (3) *hld up in rear, hdwy o'r 2 fs, ev ch appr last, hrd rdn and not quicken.* ....(11 to 4 op 7 to 2) 2
1586* RANEEN ALWATAR [84] 8-7 (3*) J Weaver (8) *hld up, pld hrd and effrt o'r 3 fs out, styd on one pace* ....(15 to 2 op 6 to 1 tchd 8 to 1) 3
1585[2] CROMARTY [81] 8-7 W Ryan (2) *trkd ldrs, effrt o'r 4 fs, sn outpcd*..................(8 to 1 op 5 to 1 tchd 9 to 1) 4
1719[2] JACKPOT STAR [90] 9-2 W Carson (7) *hld up in tch, shrtlvd effrt o'r 3 fs out, sn outpcd.* ....(8 to 1 op 7 to 1 tchd 9 to 1) 5
1469* FABULOUS MTOTO [81] 8-7 Pat Eddery (4) *hld up in rear, shrtlvd effrt o'r 3 fs out*.........(13 to 8 fav op 5 to 2) 6
1483[6] BAY QUEEN [82] 8-5 (3*) M Fenton (6) *trkd ldrs, cld 5 fs out, hrd rdn o'r 2 out, sn btn*..........(20 to 1 op 14 to 1) 7
1785 DEVILRY [82] 8-8 Paul Eddery (1) *chsd wnr, cl up 5 fs, rdn and wknd 3 out tld off*........... (20 to 1 op 12 to 1) 8

Dist: Nk, 10l, 3l, 6l, 3l, ¾l, 15l. 2m 34.75s. a 2.75s (8 Ran).
SR: 68/64/36/27/24/9/8/-/ (Sheikh Ahmed Al Maktoum), M R Stoute

1959 Southampton Claiming Stakes Class E (2-y-o) £3,106 6f 212yds.......(4:00)

1666[8] LUGANO 8-10 Pat Eddery (11) *cl up, led hfwy, sn clr, very easily*........................ (6 to 4 fav op 2 to 1) 1
1119[7] HE SHALL REIGN 8-6 W Carson (13) *trkd ldrs, not much room o'r 2 fs out, chsd wnr frm over one furlong out, no imprsn*........................ (8 to 1 tchd 10 to 1) 2
LINK MILES 9-0 J Reid (6) *beh, hdwy o'r 2 fs out, better for race*........................ (9 to 1 op 5 to 1) 3
TSWANA (Ire) 8-10 L Dettori (4) *took keen hold, trkd ldrs, edgd rght o'r 2 fs out, sn one pace.* (10 to 1 op 14 to 1) 4
1119[8] RISKY AFFAIR 8-2 Paul Eddery (5) *mid-div, hdwy 2 fs put, sn one pace*..........(11 to 1 op 8 to 1 tchd 12 to 1) 5
1489 GRANBY BELL 8-7 (7*) Mark Denaro (2) *trkd ldrs, no hdwy frm o'r 2 fs out*.................... (50 to 1 op 25 to 1) 6
1877[7] MR MYSTICAL (Ire) 8-10 B Rouse (10) *al prmnt, not much room o'r 2 fs out, sn btn.* ....(10 to 1 op 12 to 1 tchd 16 to 1) 7
1741[5] AERIAL VIEW 8-4 T Sprake (1) *cl up, slightly hmpd 3 fs out, ev ch 2 out, wknd und pres*... (33 to 1 op 12 to 1) 8
949 INDIAN CASTLE (Ire) 8-10 W Newnes (14) *nvr on terms wth ldrs*........................(50 to 1 op 20 to 1) 9
1602 CURBRIDGE (Ire) 8-12 A McGlone (9) *beh, hdwy 2 fs out, sn btn*........................ (50 to 1 op 25 to 1) 10
LUCKY HELEN 8-1 C Rutter (7) *in tch, swtchd lft 3 fs out, sn btn*.............. (20 to 1 op 12 to 1 tchd 25 to 1) 11
1689[3] PRIMOST 8-4 J Williams (15) *trkd ldrs, hmpd o'r 4 fs out, wknd over 2 out*.......(15 to 2 op 5 to 1 tchd 8 to 1) 12
1071[7] MILLY'S PET 8-5 N Adams (12) *nvr plcd to chal.* ....(33 to 1 op 14 to 1) 13
1091 SILVER BRIEF 8-6 A Tucker (8) *led til hdd hfwy, hrd rdn and wndrd und pres, sn wknd*................(50 to 1) 14
IRONGAME 8-4 R Perham (3) *al beh.* ....(14 to 1 op 6 to 1 tchd 16 to 1) 15

Dist: 2l, 3½l, 2½l, 3l, ¾l, 1l, nk, nk, 1l, hd. 1m 31.33s. a 5.73s (15 Ran).
(Yahya Nasib), N A Callaghan

1960 Herbert And Gwen Blagrave Memorial Conditions Stakes Class D (3-y-o) £4,110 1¾m.................. (4:30)

1678* ALINOVA (USA) 8-7 W Ryan (1) *trkd ldr, led o'r 3 fs out, not extended.* ....(2 to 1 on tchd 7 to 4 on and 9 to 4 on) 1
1585[3] PAT OR ELSE 8-6[1] R Cochrane (5) *trkd ldg pair, not clr run wl o'r one furlong out, chsd wnr ins last, no imprsn*....................(7 to 1 op 6 to 1 tchd 8 to 1) 2
1594* TASSET (Can) 8-12 C Rutter (3) *hld up in cl tch, effrt and hng rght o'r 2 fs out, one pace und pres.* ....(7 to 1 op 6 to 1 tchd 8 to 1) 3
1154* RITTO 8-12 W R Swinburn (2) *hld up, pld out o'r 3 fs out, sn cld, eased whn btn over one out.* .... (13 to 2 op 5 to 1 tchd 7 to 1) 4
METER MAN 8-7 (3*) J Weaver (4) *whished tail, led til hdd o'r 3 fs out, sn wknd, unded pres.* ....(66 to 1 op 50 to 1 tchd 100 to 1) 5

Dist: 2l, 1½l, 15l, ¾l. 3m 12.01s. a 14.31s (5 Ran).
(Sheikh Mohammed), H R A Cecil

1961 Downton Maiden Handicap Class F (0-65 3-y-o and up) £3,517 1m 1f 209yds........................ (5:00)

1626[4] WAR REQUIEM (Ire) [47] 3-8-5 J Williams (3) *mid-div, cld 3 fs out, led wl o'r one out, ran on well* ....(7 to 1 op 6 to 1 tchd 5 to 1 and 8 to 1) 1
1429[9] RIVIERE ACTOR (USA) [65] 3-9-9 W Carson (17) *beh, rdn alng 3 fs out, hdwy o'r one out, stumbled ins last, kpt on und pres*........................ (6 to 1 tchd 7 to 1) 2
1586 GESNERA [30] 5-8-0 N Adams (14) *beh, hdwy o'r 3 fs out, styd on*........................(16 to 1 tchd 20 to 1) 3
1457 CONCINNITY (USA) [52] 4-9-8 A Munro (18) *beh, hdwy o'r 2 fs out, kpt on*........ (16 to 1 op 12 to 1 tchd 20 to 1) 4
1690[4] SMART DAISY [49] 3-8-7 L Dettori (9) *led til hdd wl o'r one furlong out, one pace.* (6 to 1 op 8 to 1 tchd 10 to 1) 5
1439[7] ALTERMEERA [47] 5-9-3 G Bardwell (2) *chsd ldrs, hrd rdn and ev ch o'r 2 fs out, wknd ins last.* ....(12 to 1 tchd 14 to 1) 6
992 JOLIS ABSENT [43] 3-8-1 D Biggs (10) *chsd ldrs, rdn and not much room 2 fs, one pace*..... (33 to 1 op 25 to 1) 7
1493[2] PISTOLS AT DAWN (USA) [58] 3-9-2 Pat Eddery (15) *mid-div, effrt and cl wl o'r 2 fs out, sn one pace.* ....(7 to 2 fav op 5 to 1) 8
1255[5] COMMANCHE CREEK [62] 3-9-6 R Cochrane (8) *beh, hrd rdn o'r 2 fs out, no hdwy.* .... (9 to 1 op 7 to 1 tchd 10 to 1) 9
1743 FULL SHILLING (USA) [51] 4-9-0 (7*) P McCabe (13) *nvr dngrs*........................ (33 to 1) 10+
1459[3] DESERT CHALLENGER (Ire) [60] 3-9-4 A McGlone (1) *al beh.* ....(10 to 1 op 7 to 1 tchd 11 to 1) 10+
1417[7] BRONZE MAQUETTE (Ire) [54] 3-8-5 (7*) T G McLaughlin (7) *chsd ldrs, wkng whn stumbled 4 fs out.* ....(16 to 1 op 12 to 1) 12
1316 BAULKING TOWERS [44] 3-8-2 A Tucker (12) *trkd ldrs til rdn and wknd 4 fs out*...........(33 to 1 op 20 to 1) 13
PEGGOTTY [30] 5-7-7 (7*) D O'Neill (11) *trkd ldrs til wknd o'r 4 fs out*........................(33 to 1) 14
771 LOOSE ZEUS (USA) [54] 4-9-3 (7*) S Mulvey (6) *trkd ldrs, wknd o'r 3 fs out, tld off*..........(33 to 1 op 20 to 1) 15
1696[7] WESSEX WARRIOR [37] (v) 7-8-7 T Williams (5) *trkd ldrs, came wide into strt, wknd o'r 3 fs out, tld off.* .... (33 to 1 op 20 to 1) 16

Dist: ¾l, 2½l, 1l, nk, 2l, sht-hd, nk, 1½l, sht-hd, dd-ht. 2m 9.58s. a 5.58s (16 Ran).
SR: 25/41/13/33/17/23/6/20/21/ (Whitcombe Manor Racing Stables Limited), G B Balding

WEXFORD (IRE) (good to yielding) Wednesday June 23rd

1962 Stanley Cooker (Fillies) Handicap (0-70 4-y-o and up) £2,762 1½m 170yds ....(7:30)

575^7 MARILYN (Ire) [-] 4-9-12 M J Kinane (7) ....(6 to 1) 1
CONCERT ORCHESTRA (Ire) [-] 4-7-6 (2*) D G O'Shea (13) ....(33 to 1) 2
1508^2 ZUHAL [-] 5-8-12 (6*) C Everard (4) ....(9 to 2) 3
SIMPLY MARILYN (Ire) [-] 4-9-6 (6*) J J Behan (10) (10 to 1) 4
1013^6 PREMIER LEAP (Ire) [-] 4-8-4 (8*) B Fenton (12).....(7 to 1) 5
1651^4 TOP GENERATION [-] 4-7-12 (4*) W J Smith (9) ... (16 to 1) 6
GRECIAN LADY (Ire) [-] 4-8-12 Joanna Morgan (11) (50 to 1) 7
1508^5 SERJITAK [-] 6-8-9 R Hughes (2).................(8 to 1) 8
1202^9 LAGRION (USA) [-] (bl) 4-9-10 N Byrne (5)........(14 to 1) 9
1651^7 WINTER DREAMS (Ire) [-] 4-8-12 W J Supple (15) (12 to 1) 10
1756* CRAZY GAIL [-] 6-9-5 J P Murtagh (8)..........(9 to 4 fav) 11
1797 KOI CORP [-] 9-7-11^4 (2*) R M Burke (14)........(33 to 1) 12
1757 GO DEAS [-] 6-7-13^1 (6*) J A Heffernan (3)........(14 to 1) 13
Dist: ½l, sht-hd, hd, ¾l. 2m 38.50s. (13 Ran).

(Kildare Racing Club), M A O'Toole

1963 Katie Pats Bar & Restaurant Maiden (3-y-o and up) £2,762 1½m 170yds ....(8:00)

1441^7 BIRTHPLACE (Ire) 3-9-0 M J Kinane (8)............(4 to 1) 1
1573^3 DAHLIA'S BEST (USA) (bl) 3-9-0 W J Supple (7) (5 to 2 fav) 2
1507^2 PLUM LICK (Ire) 3-8-11 C Roche (5)...............(5 to 1) 3
1441^9 DALKEY ISLAND (Ire) 3-9-0 D Hogan (4)...........(7 to 2) 4
1622^2 SCHMEICHEL (Ire) 3-9-0 N Byrne (3)................(9 to 2) 5
1466^4 DARK HYACINTH (Ire) 3-8-11 R Hughes (1).......(12 to 1) 6
1507^9 ROLANDS GIRL (Ire) 3-8-5 (6*) J A Heffernan (6)...(33 to 1) 7
1620^9 DESIGNED STEP (Ire) 4-9-12 Joanna Morgan (2)..(66 to 1) 8
Dist: 2½l, hd, 3l, 1½l. 2m 37.90s. (8 Ran).

(Sheikh Mohammed), John M Oxx

CARLISLE (firm)
Thursday June 24th

Going Correction: MINUS 0.40 sec. per fur. (races 1,2,3), MINUS 0.30 (4,5,7), MINUS 0.55 (6)

1964 Cumrew Selling Stakes Class G (2-y-o) £2,553 5f 207yds........... (2:00)

812^4 HARPO'S SPECIAL 8-11 K Fallon (1) *broke wl frm poor draw, feeling pace and drvn alng hfwy, str run to ld entering fnl furlong, ran on.* ....(11 to 4 fav op 7 to 2 tchd 4 to 1) 1
1739^5 SPRINGHEAD 7-13 (7*) J Marshall (10) *nvr far away, ev ch and drvn alng entering fnl furlong, kpt on.* .... (12 to 1 op 8 to 1) 2
SUSELJA (Ire) 8-6 S Whitworth (4) *sluggish strt, improved to join issue hfwy, ev ch o'r one furlong out, kpt on same pace.*......................(33 to 1 op 25 to 1) 3
1615^2 BADGER'S BEND 8-6 P Robinson (6) *co'red up in midfield, effrt and drvn alng last 2 fs, styd on one pace.* ....(7 to 2 op 3 to 1) 4
1759^7 SHARPISH WORDS (bl) 8-11 Dean McKeown (7) *last and outpcd hfwy, ran on appr fnl furlong, nvr nrr.* .... (33 to 1 op 25 to 1) 5
1863^6 WINGS AHEAD 8-11 J Fanning (12) *sluggish strt, weaved through frm hfwy, styd on finish.*..............(33 to 1) 6
1078^2 CARAPELLE 8-6 G Duffield (2) *broke wl to show speed in frnt rnk for o'r 4 fs, sn btn.*..........(8 to 1 op 5 to 1) 7
1590^7 GRECIAN GARDEN 8-8 (5*) O Pears (9) *dictated pace for o'r 2 fs, fdd und pres over one out.* (12 to 1 op 10 to 1) 8
1706 OUT OF FAVOUR (Ire) 8-11 K Darley (5) *pld hrd, pressed ldg bunch till wknd quickly 2 fs out...* (33 to 1 op 20 to 1) 9
1391^7 T O O MAMMA'S (Ire) 8-6 J Carroll (8) *speed on ins till wknd quickly last 2 fs.*................ (20 to 1 tchd 25 to 1) 10
1413^4 ROCKY TWO 8-11 A Mackay (13) *missed break, nvr able to reco'r.*................................ (10 to 1 tchd 8 to 1) 11
1774^4 IRISH PERFORMER 8-6 N Connorton (11) *sn drvn alng to go pace, nvr a threat.*...............(5 to 1 op 6 to 1) 12
SUPER TIMES 8-6 J Fortune (3) *speed to chase ldrs 4 fs, sn btn.*................................... (33 to 1 op 25 to 1) 13
Dist: ½l, sht-hd, 3l, 2l, nk, nk, 7l, 2l, 2l, nk. 1m 14.80s. a 1.80s (13 Ran).
SR: 13/6/5/-/-/-/ (O Soberg-Olsen), Mrs J R Ramsden

1965 BBC Radio Cumbria Fillies Claiming Stakes Class F (3-y-o and up) £2,579 5f 207yds...................... (2:30)

1871^2 QUINSIGIMOND 3-8-7 G Duffield (2) *broke smartly, nosed ahead o'r 2 fs out, drw clr ins last, easily.* ....(11 to 8 on op 6 to 4 on tchd 5 to 4 on) 1
1937 MANX MONARCH 3-7-8^2 (5*) A Garth (4) *chsd ldg quartet, effrt and drifted rght ins fnl furlong, not rch wnr.* ....(14 to 1 op 12 to 1) 2
1577* MAGICATION 3-7-10 (7*) Claire Balding (8) *settled in last pl, drvn alng to improve last 2 fs, ran on finish.* .... (11 to 4 op 3 to 1 tchd 5 to 2) 3
1937^8 MINSK 7-8-3 Dean McKeown (5) *settled midfield, effrt whn impeded appr fnl furlong, kpt on finish.* ....(33 to 1 op 20 to 1) 4
1360^5 SAMANTHAS JOY 3-7-9 A Mackay (3) *slight ld for o'r 3 fs, wknd appr last.*......................(9 to 1 op 8 to 1) 5
1232 GRUBBY 4-7-10 (7*) M Humphries (1) *wth ldrs, rdn o'r one furlong out, fdd.*.................(50 to 1 op 33 to 1) 6
1396^9 CANAZEI (v) 3-7-9 J Fanning (6) *pressed ldrs, rdn whn pace lifted last 2 fs, sn btn.*.......(100 to 1 op 50 to 1) 7
1851^4 GROGFRYN 3-8-5 J Carroll (7) *sluggish strt, nvr a serious threat.*...................................(14 to 1 op 8 to 1) 8
Dist: 3½l, 3l, 1l, ½l, 2l, 7l, 6l. 1m 13.60s. a 0.60s (8 Ran).
SR: 33/9/3/-/-/ (A E T Mines), Sir Mark Prescott

1966 Norweb 'Smart Heat' Handicap Class E (0-70 3-y-o) £2,950 5f......... (3:00)

1874^4 MISS WHITTINGHAM (Ire) [54] 8-10 J Carroll (4) *wtd wth, improved on outsd to ld o'r one furlong out, gng clr whn edgd rght ins last.*............ (6 to 1 op 11 to 2) 1
1760^3 GUSSIE FINK-NOTTLE (Ire) [59] (bl) 9-1 K Darley (5) *trkd ldrs, bustled alng to improve o'r one furlong out, styd on.*................................ (9 to 1 op 7 to 1) 2
1714^4 KIMBOLTON KORKER [56] 8-12 S Whitworth (2) *wth ldrs, squeezed for room o'r 2 fs out, rallied ins last.* ....(11 to 1 op 8 to 1) 3
1478^4 COCONUT JOHNNY [59] 9-1 J Fanning (7) *nvr far away, nosed ahead briefly wl o'r one furlong out, rdn and not quicken.*............................(4 to 1 op 7 to 2) 4
1376^2 CLOUDY REEF [56] 8-7 (5*) A Garth (8) *tucked away on ins, effrt and not much room frm hfwy, kpt on same pace.* ....(13 to 2 op 11 to 2) 5
1760 ANDRULA MOU [47] 8-3 L Charnock (3) *made most for o'r 3 fs, fdd und pres.*..................(33 to 1 op 25 to 1) 6
1455^7 IOLITE [65] 9-7 P Robinson (6) *drvn alng to chase ldrs for 3 fs, fdd.*.............. (5 to 1 op 8 to 1 tchd 10 to 1) 7
1589* LIDA'S DELIGHT (Ire) [61] 9-3 T Lucas (1) *wth ldrs, rdn to dispute ld 2 fs out, sn ridden and btn.* ....(7 to 2 fav op 3 to 1) 8
Dist: 3l, ½l, ¾l, 1½l, 2½l, 1½l, ¾l. 1m 0.80s. a 0.80s (8 Ran).
SR: 40/33/28/28/19/-/12/5/ (J W Barrett), J Berry

1967 UCB Films Cumberland Plate Handicap Class D (0-80 3-y-o and up) £7,115 1½m........................ (3:30)

1400^2 NORTHERN GRADUATE (USA) [71] 4-9-12 K Darley (6) *trkd ldr, led and kicked for hme entering strt, hld on wl ins fnl fs.*...........(3 to 1 jt-fav tchd 7 to 2 and 11 to 4) 1
1476* KINOKO [61] 5-9-2 G Duffield (1) *patiently rdn, chsd alng to improve 2 fs out, str chal last, jst hld.*....... (8 to 1) 2
1520^9 AMERICAN HERO [55] 5-8-10 K Fallon (8) *dictated pace, quickened hfwy, hdd entering strt, kpt on.* ....(20 to 1 op 13 to 1) 3
1764^2 FAIR FLYER (Ire) [57] 4-8-12 Dean McKeown (5) *nvr far away, effrt and drvn alng o'r 2 fs out, styd on same pace.*.............................(6 to 1 op 11 to 2) 4
1827* BIG PAT [64] 4-9-5 (5ex) M Wigham (2) *in tch, niggled alng to go pace hfwy, flttered und pres o'r 2 fs out, one pace.* ....(3 to 1 jt-fav op 11 to 4) 5
1847^2 LEGION OF HONOUR [64] 5-8-12 (7*) V Halliday (4) *trkd ldg quartet, rdn entering strt, no imprsn last 2 fs.* ....(6 to 1 op 5 to 1) 6
1630^3 ARGYLE CAVALIER (Ire) [67] 3-8-7 J Carroll (7) *co'red up on ins, feeling pace and drvn alng over 2 fs out, sn btn.* .... (8 to 1 op 10 to 1 tchd 11 to 1) 7
1764^8 IN THE MONEY (Ire) [70] 4-9-11 S Perks (3) *trkd ldg grp, rdn whn pace lifted entering strt, sn lost tch.* (33 to 1) 8
Dist: ¾l, 2l, nk, nk, 4l, 2l, 20l. 2m 32.10s. a 2.10s (8 Ran).
SR: 55/43/33/34/40/32/16/-/ (P D Savill), Mrs M Reveley

1968 Rayophane Handicap Class E (0-70 3-y-o) £3,390 7f 214yds......... (4:00)

TIME HONORED (USA) [57] 8-12 G Duffield (9) *al gng best, led wl o'r one furlong out, readily.* ....(9 to 4 fav op 3 to 1) 1
1799 CANNY LAD [51] (v) 8-6 K Fallon (7) *nvr far away, led briefly 2 fs out, not pace of wnr o'r last.* ....(16 to 1 op 20 to 1) 2
1705^2 MRS DAWSON [57] 8-7 (5*) O Pears (8) *settled to track ldg bunch, drvn through frm midfield fnl furlong, ran on.* ....(7 to 1 op 5 to 1) 3
1081 DAYTONA BEACH (Ire) [66] 9-7 K Darley (2) *patiently rdn, swtchd ins and shaken up last 2 fs, prmsg.* .... (11 to 1 op 7 to 1 tchd 12 to 1) 4
1099^8 NICKNAME [46] 7-10 (5*) Darren Moffatt (6) *al hndy, led o'r 3 fs out till hdd 2 out, no extr.* .... (12 to 1 op 7 to 1 tchd 14 to 1) 5
1455^8 DUKE OF BUDWORTH [58] 8-13 P Robinson (12) *nvr far away, rdn 2 fs out, not quicken...* (16 to 1 op 14 to 1) 6
1186 SIMPLY SUPERB [45] 8-0^7 (7*) C Munday (5) *chsd ldrs, feeling pace and drvn alng last 2 fs, one pace.* (50 to 1) 7
1675^2 PERSONIMUS [41] (bl) 7-10 N Carlisle (1) *in tch, chsd alng whn pace lifted hfwy, styd on, nvr nrr.* ....(7 to 1 op 6 to 1 tchd 8 to 1) 8

1606[7] GUANHUMARA [45] (v) 8-0 A Mackay (10) *slight ld till hdd o'r 3 fs out, fdd*........(11 to 2 op 4 to 1 tchd 3 to 1) 9
1737[7] FREDDIE JACK [40] (bl) 7-6 (3*) N Kennedy (4) *wth ldrs for o'r 5 fs, fdd*................(20 to 1 op 16 to 1) 10
1776[6] DESIRABLE MISS [44] (v) 7-13 J Fanning (11) *dsptd ld, edgd away frm fence o'r 2 fs out, sn btn*.............(10 to 1) 11
STEAL A MARCH [47] 8-2 L Charnock (3) *sluggish strt, imprvg whn hmpd and f o'r 2 fs out.*
..........(14 to 1 op 10 to 1) f
Dist: 5l, 1½l, ¾l, 1l, 1l, 1l, 1l, 3l, 1½l, 8l. 1m 40.10s. a 2.20s (12 Ran).
SR: 29/8/9/16/-/2/ (Pinnacle Racing Stable), Sir Mark Prescott

1969 Mirfield Lady Amateur Riders' Handicap Class G (0-70 3-y-o and up) £2,322 6f 206yds.....................(4:30)

1736[4] SHALABIA [57] 4-11-7 Miss L Perratt (9) *chsd clr ldr, quickened ahead o'r one furlong out, ran on strly.*
..............................(9 to 2 tchd 5 to 1) 1
1866[5] MASTER OFTHE HOUSE [47] 7-10-11 Mrs A Farrell (2) *patiently rdn, improved gng wl last 2 fs, ridden last, one pace*......................(5 to 2 fav op 9 to 4) 2
1675[7] DEAD CALM [58] 3-10-13 Miss Diana Jones (3) *sluggish strt, drvn alng to keep up, styd on last 2 fs, nvr nrr.*
..............................(6 to 1) 3
1179[6] DOUBLE THE STAKES (USA) [28] (bl) 4-9-6 Miss J Winter (7) *set str pace, clr till hdd o'r one furlong out, no extr.*
..............................(9 to 1 op 6 to 1) 4
1600[9] PAULINUS [37] 5-9-10 (5*) Miss M Carson (4) *missed break, drvn alng to improve frm off the pace last 2 fs, nrst finish*.............(66 to 1 op 25 to 1 tchd 100 to 1) 5+
1866 MURASIL (USA) [37] 4-10-1 Miss P Robson (10) *drvn alng to go pace, styd on last 2 fs, nvr dngrs*.......(10 to 1) 5+
1733[5] HERETICAL MISS [59] 3-10-9 (5*) Mrs J Boggis (8) *chsd ldg pair, rdn hfwy, no imprsn*.........(11 to 2 op 5 to 1) 7
LAZY RHYTHM (USA) [49] 7-10-8 (5*) Mrs C Hirst (6) *sluggish strt, chsd alng thrght, nvr dngrs.*
........(14 to 1 op 10 to 1 tchd 16 to 1 and 20 to 1) 8
1597[7] MARIAN EVANS [22] 6-9-0 Miss L Eaton (1) *chsd alng to keep up, nvr a factor*.............(25 to 1 op 33 to 1) 9
1052[6] VERRO (USA) [38] (bl) 6-9-11 (5*) Miss A Purdy (5) *struggling aftr 2 fs, nvr a threat*.............(14 to 1 op 10 to 1) 10
Dist: 3½l, 2½l, nk, 1½l, dd-ht, ¾l, 4l, 10l, 5l. 1m 28.30s. a 2.90s (10 Ran).
SR: 34/13/7/-/-/-/ (E A Brook), C Parker

1970 Carlisle Club Limited Stakes Class E (0-70 3-y-o and up) £2,743 7f 214yds..............................(5:00)

1736* LAUREL QUEEN (Ire) 5-9-2 J Carroll (2) *made all, hrd drvn to remain clr o'r one furlong out, kpt on.*
..............(9 to 2 on op 5 to 1 on tchd 4 to 1 on) 1
1521[6] MEDIA MESSENGER 4-9-7 K Fallon (3) *nvr far away, effrt and rdn 2 fs out, kpt on same pace.* (15 to 2 op 6 to 1) 2
1811[6] HAND ON HEART (Ire) 4-9-2 K Darley (1) *sluggish strt, effrt and came wide strt, rdn and btn 2 fs out.*
.....................(15 to 2 op 8 to 1 tchd 10 to 1) 3
Dist: 6l, 12l. 1m 41.30s. a 3.40s (3 Ran).
SR: 15/2/-/ (Laurel (Leisure) Limited), J Berry

LONGCHAMP (FR) (good to firm) Thursday June 24th

1971 La Coupe (Group 3) (4-y-o and up) £23,895 1¼m..................(2:55)

1411[3] D'ARROS (Ire) 4-8-11 C Asmussen (4) *rcd in 4th on ins, hdwy 2 fs out, led half a furlong out, cmftbly.* (72 to 10) 1
1366[6] MARILDO (Fr) 6-9-4 G Guignard (5) *led, quickened 2 fs out, hdd half a furlong out, kpt on*...............(77 to 10) 2
1366[5] DIESE (USA) 4-8-13 T Jarnet (1) *pld hrd, rcd in 3rd, rdn 2 fs out, ran on one pace*....................(23 to 10) 3
1366[4] HATOOF (USA) 4-9-1 W R Swinburn (3) *hld up, 5th strt, effrt o'r 2 fs out, unbl to quicken*............(5 to 3 on) 4
1411* FUNNY BABY (Fr) 5-8-11 A Badel (2) *trkd ldr till rdn and no hdwy 2 fs out*..........................(99 to 10) 5
Dist: 1l, ½l, sht-nk, hd. 2m 7.60s. a 5.50s (5 Ran).
SR: 42/47/41/42/37/ (S Niarchos), F Boutin

SALISBURY (good to firm (races 1,2,3,4,5,6), firm (7)) Thursday June 24th

Going Correction: MINUS 0.20 sec. per fur. (races 1,2,3,4,5,7), MINUS 0.30 (6)

1972 Shrewton Rating Related Maiden Stakes Class F (0-65 3-y-o) £2,489 6f 212yds........................(2:20)

1635[2] PERDITION (Ire) 8-6 (3*) D Harrison (5) *hdwy 2 fs out, led wl ins last, ran on*.........(7 to 2 op 3 to 1 tchd 4 to 1) 1
1635[4] NOBLE RISK 9-0 J Reid (7) *led, edgd lft and hdd wl ins fnl furlong, ran on*.....................(9 to 2 op 4 to 1) 2
1459[2] ALTA VICTORIA (Ire) 8-9 Pat Eddery (2) *hld up, ev ch o'r one furlong out, hng rght and wknd ins last.*
.....................(9 to 4 fav op 5 to 2 tchd 3 to 1) 3
1482[5] AKHLAK (Ire) 8-9 W Carson (6) *chsd ldr, rdn and wknd o'r one furlong out*..................(3 to 1 op 5 to 2) 4
1623 KINTWYN 9-0 T Williams (4) *prmnt till hrd rdn and wknd o'r one furlong out*...............(33 to 1 op 16 to 1) 5
1008 DOCTOR-J (Ire) 9-0 S Raymont (3) *chsd ldrs, hrd rdn 2 fs out, one pace*..................(33 to 1 op 14 to 1) 6
1623 NO GAIN 8-2 (7*) Kim McDonnell (8) *wl beh fnl 3 fs.*
...................................(33 to 1 op 16 to 1) 7
MIM 8-9 W Ryan (10) *al wl beh.*
.....................(12 to 1 op 16 to 1 tchd 20 to 1) 8
4766a WOODLANDS ELECTRIC 9-0 N Adams (1) *hmpd strt, nvr nr to chal*...................(50 to 1 op 33 to 1) 9
1627 BEYOND THE LIMIT 8-9 A Clark (9) *prmnt till wknd quickly 2 fs out*..................(33 to 1 op 25 to 1) 10
Dist: Hd, 2½l, 3l, nk, nk, 8l, ½l, ¾l, 1½l. 1m 28.35s. a 2.75s (10 Ran).
SR: 33/37/24/15/19/18/ (The Losers Owners Group), J W Hills

1973 Noel Cannon Memorial Trophy Handicap Class C (0-95 3-y-o and up) £5,482 1m...........................(2:50)

1730[2] NORTH ESK (USA) [63] 4-8-2 G Carter (6) *al prmnt, led ins fnl furlong, drvn out*...(13 to 2 op 5 to 1 tchd 7 to 1) 1
1407[2] MARASTANI (USA) [89] 3-9-4 J Reid (4) *second till led 2 fs out, hdd ins last, ran on.*
.............................(4 to 1 op 5 to 2 tchd 9 to 2) 2
1743[2] DEEVEE [54] 4-7-7 J Lowe (1) *hld up, hdwy 2 fs out, not quicken ins last*..................(7 to 2 tchd 4 to 1) 3
945 RAKIS (Ire) [87] 3-9-2 W Carson (5) *led for 6 fs, ev ch one furlong out, not quicken.*
.....................(14 to 1 op 20 to 1 tchd 12 to 1) 4
1407[5] TISSISAT (USA) [89] 4-10-0 L Dettori (2) *hld up on ins, effrt 2 fs out, not much room one out, not quicken.*
.................................(7 to 1 op 6 to 1) 5
1641* WAVE HILL [74] 4-8-13 W Ryan (7) *hld up in rear, effrt 2 fs out, not quicken fnl furlong*....(5 to 2 fav tchd 3 to 1) 6
1636[5] NOBLE PET [87] 4-9-12 A Munro (3) *prmnt till wknd o'r one furlong out*.......(7 to 1 op 6 to 1 tchd 15 to 2) 7
Dist: 1l, sht-hd, 1½l, hd, hd, 2½l. 1m 43.53s. a 4.03s (7 Ran).
SR: 4/17/-/9/20/4/9/ (Alan J Speyer), D A Wilson

1974 Hampshire Rated Stakes Class B Handicap (0-95 4-y-o and up) £6,187 1½m..........................(3:20)

1770* SOURCE OF LIGHT [97] 4-9-9 (3ex) Pat Eddery (2) *made all, shaken up one furlong out, quickened.*
.....................(11 to 8 fav op Evens tchd 6 to 4) 1
1711[4] OPERA GHOST [82] 7-8-8 Paul Eddery (6) *al prmnt, ev ch one furlong out, not quicken wth wnr.*
.....................(3 to 1 op 5 to 2 tchd 100 to 30) 2
1484[3] NIGHT CLUBBING (Ire) [89] 4-9-1 A Munro (3) *al prmnt, ev ch 2 fs out, ran on one pace*..........(5 to 1 op 9 to 2) 3
QUADRIREME [81] 4-8-7 J Reid (5) *chsd wnr to hfwy, brght wide o'r 3 fs out, one pace.*
.....................(8 to 1 tchd 10 to 1 and 7 to 1) 4
1206[3] BADIE (USA) [95] 4-9-7 W Carson (1) *al wl beh.*
.....................(16 to 1 op 10 to 1 tchd 20 to 1) 5
1484[6] SONG OF SIXPENCE (USA) [83] 9-8-9 L Dettori (4) *rdn 4 fs out, no response, tld off*........(10 to 1 tchd 12 to 1) 6
Dist: 2½l, 1l, 2½l, 15l, 10l. 2m 32.51s. a 0.51s (6 Ran).
SR: 80/60/65/52/36/4/ (K Abdulla), R Charlton

1975 Veuve Clicquot Champagne Conditions Stakes Class B (2-y-o) £11,246 6f 212yds......................(3:50)

1790[3] GOVERNOR GEORGE (USA) 8-12 L Dettori (3) *hld up in rear, quickened to ld o'r one furlong out, sn clr, easily.*
.................................(9 to 4 op 6 to 4) 1
BLAZE AWAY (USA) 8-10 M Hills (4) *wth ldr, ev ch o'r one furlong out, not quicken with wnr.*
.....................(8 to 1 op 5 to 1 tchd 11 to 1) 2
738[2] RIVER DEEP (USA) 8-10 A Munro (1) *al prmnt, led wl o'r one furlong out, sn head and not quicken.*
.............................(Evens fav op 11 to 10 on) 3
1666* VENTA DE POSSA (USA) 8-12 L Piggott (2) *led o'r 5 fs, wknd quickly*.....................(11 to 2 op 3 to 1) 4
Dist: 6l, sht-hd, 10l. 1m 28.03s. a 2.43s (4 Ran).
SR: 41/21/20/-/ (Lucayan Stud), R Hannon

1976 Carnarvon Challenge Cup Amateur Riders Limited Stakes Class F (0-70 3-y-o) £2,684 1m 1f 209yds.....(4:20)

1488* DUVEEN (Ire) 10-10 Mr G Lewis (4) *al prmnt, led o'r 2 fs out, hld on wl*..................(3 to 1 tchd 4 to 1) 1
1906[2] GENERAL MOUKTAR 10-10 Mrs M Cowdrey (5) *hld up, smooth hdwy 3 fs out, ev ch fnl furlong, ran on.*
.............(2 to 1 fav tchd 9 to 4 and 13 to 8) 2
1675[4] VELASCO (Ire) 10-10 Mr T Jenks (3) *led aftr one furlong till 6 fs out, styd on one pace fnl 2 furlongs.*
.........................(5 to 1 op 4 to 1 tchd 6 to 1) 3

1704* BEAUMONT (Ire) 10-10 Mrs L Pearce (8) *dwlt, hdwy fnl 2 fs, nvr nrr*........(6 to 1 op 9 to 2 tchd 13 to 2) 4
926[5] HALHAM TARN (Ire) 10-10 Mrs D Arbuthnot (9) *led 6 fs out till o'r 2 out*..........(10 to 1 op 8 to 1 tchd 12 to 1) 5
1115[5] GRAND APPLAUSE (Ire) 10-10 Miss J Allison (6) *dwlt, hdwy 3 fs out, wknd o'r one out.* ....(10 to 1 op 8 to 1 tchd 11 to 1) 6
1008[6] NIGHT EDITION 10-10 Mr T Cuff (7) *al beh.* ....(50 to 1 op 20 to 1) 7
1705[4] IRISH DOMINION 10-5 (5*) Miss S Rowe (1) *nrly uns rdr aftr one furlong, in tch till wknd o'r 2 out.* ....(50 to 1 op 16 to 1) 8
1659 CANDARELA 10-0 (5*) Miss H Stubbings (2) *rcd very wide, led one furlong, wknd 5 out*......(100 to 1 op 50 to 1) 9
Dist: Hd, 4l, hd, 2½l, 5l, 2l, 6l, 4l. 2m 12.57s. a 8.57s (9 Ran).
SR: 18/17/9/8/3/-/ (Mrs D Weatherby), M Bell

1977 London Entertains Concierges Fillies Handicap Class E (0-70 3-y-o and up) £3,054 6f...................... (4:50)

1584 NEITHER NOR [59] 4-9-11 G Carter (10) *al prmnt, led ins fnl furlong, ran on wl.* ....(11 to 2 op 7 to 1 tchd 8 to 1 and 5 to 1) 1
4673a POYLE AMBER [43] 4-8-6 (3*) D Harrison (13) *al prmnt, led o'r 2 fs out till ins last, not quicken.* ....(50 to 1 op 33 to 1) 2
1743 PRINCESS JESSICA [31] 6-7-11[7] (7*) D McCabe (4) *gd hdwy 2 fs out, nrst finish*.........(50 to 1 op 33 to 1) 3
1537[7] LADY SABO [60] (bl) 4-9-12 Paul Eddery (3) *gd hdwy fnl 2 fs, nvr nrr*..............(6 to 1 op 5 to 1 tchd 13 to 2) 4
881 FLYING WIND [43] (bl) 4-8-9 B Rouse (5) *hld up, hdwy 2 fs out, rdn and not quicken o'r one out.* ....(12 to 1 op 10 to 1 tchd 16 to 1) 5
1623[5] TEANARCO (Ire) [62] 5-10-0 J Williams (2) *hdwy fnl 2 fs, not rch ldrs*............................(9 to 1 op 6 to 1) 6
1714* CHAMPAGNE GRANDY [68] 3-9-12 Pat Eddery (9) *prmnt till wknd o'r one furlong out.* ....(5 to 2 fav op 3 to 1 tchd 7 to 2) 7
1817[5] BONITA BEE [50] (v) 3-8-8 J Reid (1) *led on outsd till o'r 2 fs out*.............................(16 to 1 op 12 to 1) 8
1373[5] SCARLET PRINCESS [42] 5-8-8 A Munro (7) *nvr nr to chal.* ....(10 to 1 op 8 to 1) 9
1537 FATHOM FIVE (Ire) [39] 4-8-5 R Price (11) *outpcd.* ....(25 to 1 op 14 to 1) 10
1744 MY RUBY RING [53] 6-9-5 T Williams (12) *wth ldrs till wknd quickly wl o'r one furlong out.* ....(13 to 2 op 8 to 1 tchd 6 to 1) 11
1376* KARUKERA [57] 3-9-1 L Dettori (8) *outpcd.* ....(10 to 1 op 7 to 1 tchd 11 to 1) 12
HULLO MARY DOLL [35] 4-8-1 N Adams (6) *strted slwly, reluctant to race, al wl beh.* ....(66 to 1 op 50 to 1 tchd 100 to 1) 13
Dist: 1l, 1½l, hd, 1½l, ¾l, 3l, sht-hd, 2l, nk, 2l. 1m 14.17s. a 1.67s (13 Ran).
SR: 42/22/4/32/9/25/11/-/-/ (T S M S Riley-Smith), D A Wilson

1978 Tisbury Conditions Stakes Class D (3-y-o) £4,012 6f 212yds........... (5:20)

1117[4] FACTUAL (USA) 9-0 Pat Eddery (9) *led 3 fs out, hld on wl.* ....(2 to 1 fav tchd 7 to 4) 1
1558[2] DRAMANICE (USA) 9-0 L Piggott (5) *hld up, steady hdwy on bit 2 fs out, ev ch ins last, rdn and no extr.* ....(100 to 30 op 4 to 1 tchd 9 to 2 and 3 to 1) 2
1320* ABSOLUTE MAGIC 9-0 M Hills (7) *hdwy on ins o'r 2 fs out, ev ch one out, not quicken*........(25 to 1 op 16 to 1) 3
1404[2] MAGIQUE ROND POINT (USA) 8-11 W Ryan (3) *stumbled badly strt, hdwy o'r 2 fs out, ev ch over one out, not quicken*..........(11 to 4 op 5 to 2) 4
1174[7] THUNDER RIVER (Ire) 9-0 D Holland (6) *led till 3 fs out, one pace*....................(8 to 1 op 7 to 1 tchd 9 to 1) 5
1040[5] FEATHER FACE 9-0 A Munro (2) *chsd ldrs 4 fs, wknd 2 out.* ....(50 to 1 op 25 to 1) 6
1710[3] HEATHFIELD (USA) 8-11 C Rutter (4) *prmnt o'r 4 fs.* ....(33 to 1 op 25 to 1 tchd 50 to 1) 7
GREEN'S BID 9-0 W Carson (10) *hld up, ev ch o'r 2 fs out, wknd quickly*..........(13 to 2 op 5 to 1 tchd 8 to 1) 8
DISKETTE 8-2 (3*) D Harrison (8) *in tch o'r 4 fs, tld off.* ....(33 to 1 op 25 to 1 tchd 40 to 1) 9
Dist: ½l, ¾l, 1l, 3½l, ¾l, ¾l, nk, 10l. 1m 27.32s. a 1.72s (9 Ran).
SR: 53/51/49/43/35/33/28/30/-/ (K Abdulla), B W Hills

SOUTHWELL (good to firm)
Thursday June 24th
Going Correction: MINUS 0.25 sec. per fur.

1979 Highgate Claiming Stakes Class F (3-y-o and up) £2,243 1½m........ (2:10)

1477* GOODBYE MILLIE 3-7-12 (3*) S Maloney (8) *in tch, hdwy 5 fs out, quickened to ld 2 and a half out and sn clr, very easily*...........(5 to 4 fav op 11 to 10 tchd 11 to 8) 1
1438* RISING TEMPO (Ire) 5-9-0 (7*) D Wright (3) *hld up, hdwy hfwy, chsd wnr fnl 2 fs, no imprsn*...(7 to 4 op 2 to 1) 2
1493[5] TRANQUIL LADY (Ire) 3-8-1 J Quinn (7) *hld up, hdwy o'r 4 fs out, styd on fnl 2, nvr dngrs*....(8 to 1 tchd 10 to 1) 3
1799 MANULEADER 4-8-7 (7*) C Hawksley (1) *mid-div, rdn alng hfwy, nvr dngrs*.....(20 to 1 op 16 to 1 tchd 25 to 1) 4
SASKIA'S HERO 6-9-2 G Bardwell (5) *chsd ldrs, hdwy 5 fs out, led briefly 3 out, sn hdd and wknd.* ....(11 to 1 op 10 to 1 tchd 12 to 1) 5
288 RESTLESS MINSTREL (USA) (bl) 4-8-12 (5*) C Hodgson (6) *led, hdd 3 fs out, sn wknd*..........(14 to 1 op 12 to 1) 6
1662[4] MAYDAY CALLING 3-8-0 (3*) M Fenton (4) *chsd ldr, rdn o'r 4 fs out and sn wknd*.................(8 to 1 op 6 to 1) 7
1674 NEVENTER (Fr) (bl) 4-9-1 S Webster (2) *very slwly away, pld hrd and sn wth field, al rear*...(33 to 1 op 25 to 1) 8
Dist: 10l, nk, 12l, nk, 1l, 8l, 4l. 2m 40.30s. a 6.30s (8 Ran).
(Lintscan Ltd (Corbett Bookmakers)), S G Norton

1980 Hopeful Selling Stakes Class G (3-y-o) £2,070 2m.................... (2:40)

1819[4] SHE KNEW THE RULES (Ire) 8-6 T Quinn (3) *chsd ldr, led 4 fs out, quickened clr 2 and a half out, ran on.* ....(6 to 1 op 7 to 1) 1
1771[5] WALSHAM WITCH 8-4 (5*) J Tate (5) *hld up, hdwy o'r 4 fs out, rdn to chase wnr fnl 2 furlongs, one pace.* ....(5 to 1 op 7 to 1 tchd 9 to 2) 2
338[4] WESTRAY (Fr) 8-11 J Quinn (2) *trkd ldrs, effrt and hdwy 4 fs out, sn ev ch, rdn 3 out, soon one pace.* ....(7 to 1 op 4 to 1) 3
1880[9] MRS SNUGGS (Ire) 8-2 (7*) S Mulvey (1) *hld up and beh, hdwy 6 fs out, rdn o'r 3 out, sn btn.* ...(13 to 8 on op 6 to 4 on tchd 11 to 10 and 6 to 5) 4
1873[8] PREMIER BLUES (Fr) (bl) 8-6 D Biggs (4) *led, hdd 4 fs out, sn wknd*..........................(9 to 1 op 4 to 1) 5
Dist: 2½l, 4l, 4l, 12l. 3m 44.40s. a 18.40s (5 Ran).
(Peter Jolliffe), M R Channon

1981 Springfield Handicap Class E (0-70 3-y-o and up) £3,287 7f......... (3:10)

MINDOMICA [49] 4-8-12 (3*) Emma O'Gorman (1) *trkd ldrs on inner gng wl, not clr run and swtchd wide o'r one furlong out, led ins last, cmftbly.* (16 to 1 op 14 to 1) 1
1502[2] SANDMOOR DENIM [56] 6-9-1 (7*) G Strange (4) *chsd ldrs, hdwy 3 fs out, effrt and rdn to chal wl o'r one out, kpt on one pace*.......................(9 to 2 op 7 to 2) 2
1520[3] MCA BELOW THE LINE [58] (v) 5-9-10 S Webster (7) *al cl up, rdn to ld wl o'r one furlong out, hdd and no extr ins last*.........(11 to 2 op 9 to 2 tchd 6 to 1) 3
1562[4] WORKINGFORPEANUTS (Ire) [40] 3-7-11 J Quinn (8) *in tch, rdn and outpcd hfwy, styd on und pres fnl 2 fs, nvr dngrs*..............(12 to 1 op 14 to 1 tchd 10 to 1) 4
1799 DANDY DESIRE [40] (bl) 4-8-6 G Bardwell (2) *beh and pushed alng, styd on fnl 2 fs, nvr dngrs.* ....(33 to 1 op 20 to 1) 5
1194[4] GLENFIELD GRETA [55] 5-9-7 F Norton (6) *chsd ldrs, rdn o'r 2 fs out, sn wknd*.................(9 to 2 op 4 to 1) 6
845[4] PICKLES [50] 5-9-2 Dale Gibson (3) *led, rdn 2 fs out, sn hdd and wknd*..... (7 to 2 fav op 4 to 1 tchd 9 to 2) 7
1286[9] SUSANNA'S SECRET [41] 6-8-4 (3*) S Maloney (9) *chsd ldrs, effrt on outer 3 fs out, rdn and wknd 2 out.* ....(9 to 2 op 4 to 1) 8
1560 CRECHE [57] (bl) 4-9-3[1] (7*) E Husband (5) *chsd ldrs till lost pl hfwy, sn beh*......(12 to 1 op 10 to 1 tchd 16 to 1) 9
Dist: 2½l, sht-hd, 1½l, nk, 6l, 1l, 4l, 15l. 1m 29.50s. a 2.50s (9 Ran).
SR: 37/36/37/5/13/10/2/-/-/ (N S Yong), W A O'Gorman

1982 Morgan Handicap Class D (0-80 3-y-o and up) £3,201 6f................ (3:40)

1835* MACS MAHARANEE [67] 6-9-11 (7ex) G Hind (5) *chsd ldrs, pushed alng and hdwy o'r 2 fs out, led one and a half out and sn clr, easily.* ....(9 to 4 fav op 2 to 1 tchd 5 to 2) 1
1859[3] MISS GORGEOUS (Ire) [74] (bl) 3-9-7 (3*) Emma O'Gorman (7) *cl up, led o'r 2 fs out, sn rdn and hdd one and a half out, no ch wth wnr*... (13 to 2 op 11 to 2 tchd 7 to 1) 2
1679[5] GONDO [65] (v) 6-9-2 (7*) D Wright (2) *beh till styd on wl fnl 2 fs*..........................(4 to 1 op 3 to 1) 3
1874* RED FAN (Ire) [73] (bl) 3-9-9 (7ex) M Birch (1) *dwlt, sn rdn, kpt on fnl 2 fs, nvr dngrs.* ....(9 to 2 op 4 to 1 tchd 5 to 1) 4
1379[4] LAST STRAW [41] 5-7-13 J Quinn (3) *chsd ldg pair, rdn o'r 2 fs out, sn wknd*....................(6 to 1 op 5 to 1) 5
1273[5] HERSHEBAR [64] (bl) 3-8-7 (7*) G Strange (4) *nvr rch ldrs.* ....(7 to 1 op 8 to 1 tchd 9 to 1 and 10 to 1) 6
1052[8] WE'RE ALL GAME [53] 4-8-6 (5*) C Hodgson (6) *led, rdn and hdd 2 fs out, sn wknd*..........(25 to 1 op 14 to 1) 7
Dist: 7l, ½l, ½l, 1l, 2½l, 4l. 1m 15.30s. a 1.30s (7 Ran).
SR: 55/26/23/21/ (John S Martin), P S Felgate

1983 Dr Abernethy Median Auction Maiden Stakes Class F (Div I) (2-y-o) £2,534 6f .... (4:10)

COTTEIR CHIEF (Ire) 9-0 A McGlone (2) *slwly into strd and beh, hdwy on outer hfwy, quickened to ld o'r one and a half fs out, sn clr*.....................(7 to 1 op 7 to 2) 1

CAPTAIN STARLIGHT (Ire) 8-11 (3*) M Fenton (4) *chsd ldrs, effrt and ev ch o'r 2 fs out, sn rdn and styd on ins last.* ......(7 to 1 op 7 to 2) 2
1763² NON VINTAGE (Ire) 9-0 M Birch (6) *trkd ldrs, hdwy to chal and ev ch 2 fs out, sn rdn and not quicken.* ......(5 to 4 on op 5 to 4 tchd 11 to 8 on) 3
1499² ACCESS ADVANTAGE 8-9 W Woods (3) *led, rdn hfwy, hdd wl o'r one and a half fs out, sn wknd.* ......(5 to 2 op 2 to 1 tchd 100 to 30) 4
SEMAH'S DREAM 8-9 A Proud (5) *cl up, rdn and ev ch 2 fs out, sn wknd.*......(33 to 1 op 20 to 1) 5
1071⁵ OVALWORLD 9-0 S Wood (1) *chsd ldrs till wknd quickly o'r 2 fs out*......(20 to 1 op 14 to 1) 6
Dist: 4l, sht-hd, 8l, hd, 3½l. 1m 17.40s. a 3.40s (6 Ran).
SR: 2/-/-/ (M & N Plant Ltd), M C Pipe

1984 Thornton Handicap Class E (0-70 3-y-o and up) £3,261 2m..............(4:40)

1731⁴ MONARDA [61] 6-9-10 T Quinn (4) *hld up and beh, hdwy 6 fs out, rdn to ld one and a half out, hrd drvn and held on wl ins last*......(4 to 1 tchd 9 to 2) 1
1564² ANGELICA PARK [47] 7-8-10 M Birch (3) *trkd ldrs till outpcd 5 fs out, rdn and styd on to chal appr fnl furlong, no extr nr finish.* (3 to 1 fav op 5 to 2 tchd 100 to 30) 2
1654⁵ ELITE REG [38] (bl) 4-8-1 A McGlone (7) *led, hdd o'r 5 fs out, sn rdn and cl up, ev ch over one out, no extr ins last*......(100 to 30 op 7 to 2 tchd 4 to 1) 3
1457⁵ BRIGGSMAID [52] 5-9-1 M Tebbutt (6) *trkd ldrs, hdwy 6 fs out, led 3 out, sn rdn and hdd one and a half out, soon wknd*......(7 to 2 op 5 to 2) 4
1533 BOOTIKIN [39] (bl) 5-8-2 J Quinn (2) *chsd ldr, led o'r 5 fs out till hdd 3 out and sn wknd*....(20 to 1 op 16 to 1) 5
1654⁴ MEDIA STAR [33] 8-7-10¹ F Norton (5) *hld up, effrt and some hdwy hfwy, sn btn*......(8 to 1 op 10 to 1) 6
SASKIA'S REPRIEVE [35] 9-7-12 G Bardwell (1) *hld up, effrt and some hdwy hfwy, wknd o'r 4 fs out.* ......(14 to 1 op 10 to 1) 7
Dist: ½l, 3½l, ½l, 7l, hd, nk. 3m 37.20s. a 11.20s (7 Ran).
(Fahd Salman), P F I Cole

1985 Dr Abernethy Median Auction Maiden Stakes Class F (Div II) (2-y-o) £2,511 6f ......(5:10)

DARREN BOY (Ire) 9-0 T Quinn (6) *cl up on outer, effrt to ld o'r 2 fs out, ran on wl ins last*... (11 to 8 on op 5 to 4) 1
BARBAROJA 9-0 M Birch (4) *beh, hdwy on outer hfwy, chsd wnr 2 fs out, sn rdn and kpt on.* ......(5 to 2 op 2 to 1 tchd 11 to 4) 2
1497⁸ STARSPORT (Ire) 8-11 (3*) J Weaver (3) *led 2 fs, cl up and ev ch o'r two furlongs out, sn rdn and wknd.* ......(12 to 1 op 6 to 1) 3
1706⁴ JUST HARRY 9-0 D Biggs (2) *chsd ldrs, effrt and hdwy 2 and a half fs out, sn rdn and btn*.... (5 to 1 op 5 to 2) 4
1561 STRADISHALL 9-0 J Quinn (5) *nvr dngrs.* ......(50 to 1 op 20 to 1) 5
1739³ ROSIE VALENTINE (v) 8-9 G Hind (1) *cl up, led aftr 2 fs till rdn and hdd o'r two furlongs out, sn wknd and eased.* ......(12 to 1 op 6 to 1) 6
Dist: 2l, 8l, 1½l, nk, 10l. 1m 16.10s. a 2.10s (6 Ran).
SR: 28/20/-/ (D F Allport), P F I Cole

THURLES (IRE) (good)
Thursday June 24th

1986 Summer Apprentice Maiden (4-y-o and up) £2,245 1¾m 150yds.....(7:00)

HANG A RIGHT 6-9-7 T P Treacy (6)......(12 to 1) 1
1756³ SHAYISTA 8-9-4 B Fenton (3)......(9 to 2) 2
DANCE OF WORDS (Ire) 4-9-4 R T Fitzpatrick (2)...(5 to 1) 3
BALLYHYLAND (Ire) 4-9-2 (2*) J Barcoe (8)......(12 to 1) 4
1756⁵ JUST ONE CANALETTO (bl) 5-9-7 P J Smullen (5) (14 to 1) 5
309⁷ ARCTIC WEATHER (Ire) 4-9-7 P O'Casey (1)...(10 to 9 on) 6
1141⁴ ROYAL OPTIMIST 9-9-2 (2*) A J Dempsey (9)......(14 to 1) 7
1295 CHARIKAR (Ire) 4-9-5 (2*) D J Casey (4)......(10 to 1) 8
DEB'S TURN (Ire) 4-9-7 D J O'Donohoe (10)......(25 to 1) 9
1295 DYEGETME (Ire) 4-9-4 A J Beale (7)......(20 to 1) ro
Dist: 1l, 8l, 6l, 1½l. 3m 8.60s. (1C Ran).
(Thomas Mullins), P Mullins

1987 Horse And Jockey Handicap (0-60 3-y-o and up) £2,245 1½m 110yds...(8:00)

1235⁷ THE MAN FROM COOKS (Ire) [-] 4-9-5 (6*) C Everard (13) ......(10 to 1) 1
1621⁴ DIAMOND CLUSTER [-] 3-7-7 (8*) R T Fitzpatrick (18) ......(8 to 1) 2
1553⁷ PULMICORT [-] 3-8-12 R Hughes (2)......(3 to 1 fav) 3
SPOUT HOUSE (Ire) [-] 4-9-5 (2*) R M Burke (16)..(10 to 1) 4
1757⁸ MISS DARCY (Ire) [-] 5-9-10 (4*) P Carberry (11)...(12 to 1) 5
1385⁹ MAN OF STRAW [-] 7-7-10 Joanna Morgan (17)...(14 to 1) 6
1797⁴ SHY GAL (Ire) [-] 5-8-8 N Byrne (10)......(20 to 1) 7
1794* BOBADIL (Ire) [-] 3-8-7 (8*,4ex) P J Smullen (14)...(11 to 2) 8
1794 BENGALI (Ire) [-] 3-8-7 W J Supple (7)......(20 to 1) 9
912⁷ GREEK CHIME (Ire) [-] 4-9-2 (10*) B D Grattan (4)..(14 to 1) 10
HUGH DANIELS [-] 5-7-6 (10*) J D Moore (1)......(16 to 1) 11
1621⁶ RIYADH DANCER (Ire) [-] 3-8-10 J F Egan (8)......(14 to 1) 12
SIR ALFRED (USA) [-] 8-8-3 (4*) W J Smith (9)......(33 to 1) 13
SHERAVISION (Ire) [-] 4-8-12 (8*) P O Casey (3)...(14 to 1) 14
TANAISTE (USA) [-] (bl) 4-8-6 (6*) J A Heffernan,...(16 to 1) 15
1139 MAZZARELLO (Ire) [-] 3-7-0³ (10*) J P Cornally (5) (25 to 1) 16
849 KINVARA LADY (Ire) [-] 4-7-9⁶ (6*) J J Behan (12)..(25 to 1) 17
Dist: 1l, 3l, hd, ½l. 2m 41.50s. (17 Ran).
(P Senezio), E J O'Grady

BATH (good to firm)
Friday June 25th

Going Correction: MINUS 0.25 sec. per fur. (races 1,3), MINUS 0.35 (2,4,5,6)

1988 Swainswick Maiden Fillies Stakes Class D (2-y-o) £3,728 5f 161yds (6:30)

1403⁴ KISSININTHEBACKROW (USA) 8-11 R Hills (3) *hld up, prog hfwy, rdn appr fnl furlong, ran on to ld nr finish.* ..(Evens fav op 11 to 10 tchd 5 to 4 and 11 to 10 on) 1
CALLABONNA 8-11 T Quinn (6) *al cl up, rdn to ld o'r 2 fs out, hdd close hme*......(16 to 1 op 8 to 1) 2
1393⁴ SWAGGER LADY 8-11 W Carson (2) *al chasing ldrs, kpt on same pace last 2 fs*......(10 to 1 op 5 to 1) 3
DELROB 8-11 S Whitworth (4) *strted slwly, hld up, steady hdwy appr fnl furlong, better for race.* ......(66 to 1 op 20 to 1) 4
1706³ MIDUSHI (USA) 8-11 G Hind (7) *nvr rchd ldrs.* ......(8 to 1 op 6 to 1 tchd 9 to 1) 5
1708⁴ SISTER SUSAN 8-11 L Dettori (1) *slwly into strd, sn reco'red, led over 3 fs out till over 2 out, soon btn.* ......(8 to 1 op 4 to 1 tchd 10 to 1) 6
1933³ FLAIR LADY 8-11 T Sprake (5) *led o'r 2 fs, wknd two furlongs out*......(20 to 1 op 16 to 1 tchd 33 to 1) 7
1091⁹ JULIA TONGA 8-11 N Adams (9) *chsd ldrs to hfwy, tld off.* ......(66 to 1 op 20 to 1) 8
Dist: Nk, 2½l, ¾l, ¾l, 1½l, 3l, 10l. 1m 12.40s. a 3.00s (8 Ran).
SR: 8/7/-/-/-/ (Christopher Wright), J W Hills

1989 Clifton Handicap Class D (0-80 3-y-o and up) £3,201 2m 1f 34yds..... (7:00)

1345⁴ PROVENCE [69] 6-9-6 G Hind (3) *hld up, took clr order 9 fs out, drvn alng to ld o'r 2 furlongs out, held on wl ins last*......(7 to 4 fav op 5 to 4) 1
1564 CHUCKLESTONE [62] 10-8-13 J Reid (2) *led till hdd and hrd rdn o'r 2 fs out, rnwd effrt and ev ch entering fnl furlong, no extr towards finish.* ......(5 to 2 op 3 to 1 tchd 7 to 2) 2
1752⁹ BARDOLPH (USA) [73] 6-9-10 T Quinn (1) *wtd wth, rdn and flt footed o'r 2 fs out, styd on same pace appr fnl furlong*......(2 to 1 op 6 to 4) 3
1688⁴ CAROLES CLOWN [42] 7-7-7 N Adams (4) *chsd ldr till snatched up 7 fs out, lost tch fnl 4 furlongs, tld off.* ......(9 to 1 op 7 to 1 tchd 10 to 1) 4
Dist: 1l, 1½l, dist. 3m 45.60s. a 1.60s (4 Ran).
SR: 30/22/31/-/ (Mrs P W Harris), P W Harris

1990 Mid-Summer Claiming Stakes Class F (3-y-o) £2,490 5f 11yds..........(7:30)

1714 CHARITY EXPRESS (Ire) 8-8 J Reid (9) *al frnt rnk, led appr fnl furlong, drvn clr.* ......(85 to 40 op 5 to 2 tchd 3 to 1 and 13 to 8) 1
974* SYLVAN STARLIGHT (v) 8-10 T Quinn (1) *led o'r one furlong, hrd drvn and ran on one pace fnl 2 fs.* ......(2 to 1 fav op 11 to 10 tchd 9 to 4) 2
1817⁸ DOUBLE BOUNCE 9-7 W Newnes (5) *outpcd till ran on fnl 2 fs, nrst finish*......(25 to 1 op 16 to 1) 3
1728⁵ TEE-EMM 8-10 (7*) L Carter (4) *slwly into strd, sn chasing ldrs, no imprsn last 2 fs.* ......(11 to 2 op 5 to 1 tchd 6 to 1) 4
428 KIMMY'S PRINCESS 8-6 L Dettori (2) *wth ldr, led hfwy till hdd and wknd o'r one furlong out.* ......(11 to 2 op 5 to 1 tchd 13 to 2) 5
1627 AMBIVALENTATTITUDE 8-5 N Adams (6) *pressed ldrs till hrd rdn and wknd hfwy*......(50 to 1 op 33 to 1) 6
1501⁵ LOWRIANNA (Ire) 8-6 S Whitworth (7) *nvr wnt pace.* ......(8 to 1 op 6 to 1 tchd 12 to 1) 7
1057 ASCOM PAGER (Ire) 8-8 N Carlisle (3) *al struggling.* ......(25 to 1 op 20 to 1 tchd 33 to 1) 8
1698 JEAN BRODIE 9-2 J Williams (8) *al in rear.* ......(50 to 1 op 20 to 1) 9
Dist: 3½l, 1½l, sht-hd, 3½l, 2l, 1½l, 1½l, 1½l. 1m 2.20s. a 1.70s (9 Ran).
SR: 35/23/28/23/-/-/ (C G Davey), D J S Cosgrove

1991 Charles Saunders Handicap Class E (0-70 3-y-o) £2,700 1m 5yds..... (8:00)

1309⁵ MR CUBE (Ire) [58] 8-9 T Quinn (5) *al handily plcd, nosed ahead entering fnl furlong, hld on.* ......(9 to 1 op 7 to 1 tchd 11 to 1) 1

1656^{7} LATEST FLAME (Ire) [60] 8-11 R Hills (3) *led till hdd a furlong out, kpt on wl.* .... (10 to 1 op 8 to 1 tchd 11 to 1) 2
1408^{6} CREDIT SQUEEZE [70] 9-7 D Holland (7) *prog 3 fs out, chlgd one out, not quicken last 100 yards.* .... (13 to 2 op 9 to 2 tchd 7 to 1) 3
1417^{8} STEVIE'S WONDER (Ire) [46] 7-7[1] (5*) N Gwilliams (2) *al chasing ldrs, styd on same pace last 2 fs.* .... (12 to 1 op 8 to 1) 4
1697^{9} GLEN MILLER [59] 8-10 L Dettori (1) *cl up, no imprsn last 2 fs.* ....(20 to 1 op 16 to 1 tchd 25 to 1) 5
1818^{3} STARLIGHT ROSE (Ire) [49] (v) 8-0 E Johnson (6) *dwlt, swtchd rght and effrt o'r 2 fs out, nvr able to chal.* ....(10 to 1 op 6 to 1 tchd 11 to 1) 6
1745^{5} SHALHOLME [46] 7-11 N Adams (4) *ldg grp, pushed alng 3 fs out, sn btn.* .... (10 to 1 op 20 to 1 tchd 33 to 1) 7
1626^{9} HOMEMAKER [58] (v) 8-9 J Williams (9) *beh, effrt o'r 2 fs out, nvr dngrs.* .... (10 to 1 op 7 to 1 tchd 11 to 1) 8
1703^{3} JIHAAD (USA) [61] 8-12 W Carson (12) *prmnt 2 fs, drpd rear hfwy, no dngr aftr.* (9 to 4 fav op 7 to 2 tchd 2 to 1) 9
1470^{8} WILL'S LEGACY [48] 7-13 T Sprake (10) *in tch, effrt and hng rght 2 fs out, sn btn.* ....(12 to 1 op 10 to 1) 10
1313^{9} WESTERN VALLEY [48] (v) 7-13 N Carlisle (8) *pressed ldr till wknd ins last 3 fs.* .... (50 to 1 op 33 to 1) 11
1312 KOA [60] (v) 8-11 J Reid (13) *al beh.*..(20 to 1 op 10 to 1) 12
606^{8} SQUIRE YORK [60] 8-11 G Hind (11) *took str hold, al in rear.* .... (25 to 1 op 20 to 1 tchd 33 to 1) 13
Dist: Sht-hd, ½l, 3l, ½l, nk, 2½l, nk, 7l, ½l, 1½l. 1m 40.40s. a 1.40s (13 Ran).
SR: 32/33/41/8/19/8/-/8/-/ (Mrs David Anderson), P F I Cole

1992 Hamswell Maiden Stakes Class D (3-y-o and up) £3,640 1m 5yds..... (8:30)

1746^{7} RUE REMBRANDT (USA) 3-8-11 R Hills (11) *led aftr 2 fs, hng rght und pres two furlongs out, styd on wl.* .... (16 to 1 op 8 to 1) 1
DESERT POWER 4-9-7 R Price (10) *chsd ldrs, swtchd rght 2 fs out, chlgd appr fnl furlong, no extr ins last.* .... (66 to 1 op 33 to 1) 2
100^{2} NYMPH ERRANT 3-8-6 T Quinn (7) *cl up, ev ch one and a half fs out, unbl to quicken.*........(7 to 1 op 20 to 1) 3
1663^{9} NOVA SPIRIT 5-9-2 J Williams (4) *wtd wth, improved gng wl 2 and a half fs out, kpt on clsg stages.* .... (66 to 1 op 33 to 1) 4
1027^{6} YOUNG PETOSKI 3-8-11 W Newnes (12) *pressed ldrs, btn o'r one furlong out, eased ins last.* .... (13 to 2 op 4 to 1 tchd 7 to 1) 5
1713^{2} PRIME OF LIFE (Ire) 3-8-11 S Raymont (9) *hld up in mid-field, no imprsn last 3 fs.* .... (5 to 4 fav op 6 to 4 on tchd 11 to 8) 6
1628^{6} MOUNTAIN REACH 3-8-11 C Avery (3) *slwly into strd, nvr rchd ldrs.*..........................(66 to 1 op 33 to 1) 7
1784^{3} LORD BOTHWELL (USA) 3-8-11 J Reid (8) *led 2 fs, lost pl two and a half furlongs out.* ....(7 to 2 op 3 to 1 tchd 4 to 1) 8
JACK GRAY 5-9-7 G Hind (6) *sn pushed alng, al struggling, tld off.*....................(66 to 1 op 33 to 1) 9
1587^{8} WADIA (USA) 3-8-6 W Carson (2) *wl plcd to hfwy, tld off.* .... (6 to 1 op 10 to 1 tchd 14 to 1) 10
1628^{7} BOY SOLDIER 3-8-6 (5*) N Gwilliams (1) *al in rear, tld off.* .... (66 to 1 op 33 to 1) 11
Dist: 1½l, 1½l, sht-hd, 2½l, 2l, 5l, 3l, 10l, 3½l, 1½l. 1m 40.60s. a 1.60s (11 Ran).
SR: 31/36/16/25/12/6/ (K Abdulla), G Harwood

1993 Grittleton Rating Related Maiden Fillies Stakes Class F (3-y-o) £2,385 1¼m 46yds.......................... (9:00)

1266^{7} SPARKY'S SONG 8-11 R Hills (7) *hld up in rear, hdwy 2 and a half fs out, led ins last, rdn out.* ....(11 to 1 op 12 to 1 tchd 14 to 1) 1
1399^{2} BOBBYSOXER 8-11 J Reid (5) *led one furlong, led ag'n entering strt, swshd tail, rdn appr fnl furlong, hdd and not quicken ins last.*.... (4 to 1 op 5 to 2 tchd 9 to 2) 2
1704^{2} SUSQUEHANNA DAYS (USA) 8-11 L Dettori (2) *al handily plcd, pushed alng 4 fs out, chlgd entering fnl furlong, btn whn not much room nr finish.* .... (85 to 40 fav op 2 to 1 tchd 11 to 4) 3
1690^{2} BUGLET 8-11 J Williams (4) *wtd wth, effrt 3 fs out, no real prog last 2 furlongs.*.... (11 to 4 op 3 to 1 tchd 9 to 4) 4
1309 SKY BURST 8-11 N Carlisle (9) *cl up till wknd ins last 3 fs.* .... (20 to 1 op 10 to 1) 5
1587 MY MINNIE 8-11 W Carson (1) *pld hrd, led aftr one furlong, hdd entering strt, btn o'r 2 out.* .... (7 to 1 op 10 to 1 tchd 13 to 2) 6
SIAN WYN 8-11 D Holland (3) *rcd keenly in midfield, beh last 3 fs.*........................(50 to 1 op 25 to 1) 7
1690^{8} IS SHE QUICK (bl) 8-11 R Price (6) *hld up, improved hfwy, fdd 3 fs out.*........................(50 to 1 op 33 to 1) 8
1500^{2} LEGAL RISK (v) 8-11 S Whitworth (8) *midfield whn hmpd hfwy, sn beh, tld off.*........(7 to 1 op 11 to 2) 9
Dist: 1½l, 1½l, 5l, 5l, hd, 3l, nk, 12l. 2m 10.40s. a 4.00s (9 Ran).
SR: 21/18/15/5/-/-/ (Mrs Annette Barwick), J W Hills

DUNDALK (IRE) (good to soft)

Friday June 25th

1994 Tallonstown E.B.F. Fillies Maiden (2-y-o) £3,107 7f 166yds........... (6:30)

1854^{6} VALID VICTRESS (Ire) 9-0 P Gilson (8)..............(5 to 1) 1
1650 FANCY BOOTS (Ire) 9-0 N G McCullagh (2)........(14 to 1) 2
SHEEN FALLS (Ire) 9-0 M J Kinane (3).........(2 to 1 fav) 3
SCHONBEIN (Ire) 9-0 W J Supple (6)..............(3 to 1) 4
1854^{8} BENAZIR LADY (Ire) 8-8 (6*) J A Heffernan (1).....(12 to 1) 5
1571^{7} YOUR VILLAGE (Ire) 9-0 K J Manning (9)..........(4 to 1) 6
BOARDWALKER (Ire) 9-0 S Craine (5)..............(5 to 1) 7
AVALIN (Ire) 9-0 P Lowry (11)...................(12 to 1) 8
1650^{7} FINAL OPERA (Ire) 9-0 J F Egan (10)...........(25 to 1) 9
CULLENSTOWN LADY (Ire) 8-12 (2*) R M Burke (4) (8 to 1) 10
Dist: 3½l, hd, 1l, ¾l. 1m 44.50s. (10 Ran).
(Marvin Malmuth), Liam Browne

1995 Castlebellingham Handicap (0-70 3-y-o) £2,245 1m 1f.................(7:00)

1569^{6} BOBROSS (Ire) [-] 9-0 (6*) J A Heffernan (2).......(14 to 1) 1
1923^{7} HERMES GOLD (Ire) [-] 9-0 W J Supple (9).......(10 to 1) 2
1574^{4} BRIGENSER (Ire) [-] (bl) 9-1 P Shanahan (8).........(7 to 1) 3
1793* FAIRYDEL (Ire) [-] 8-13 (8*,5ex) P J Smullen (11)....(10 to 1) 4
981^{6} GLANCE CARD (Ire) [-] (bl) 8-11 (6*) C Everard (3) ....(7 to 2 fav) 5
1386^{6} MAJESTIC PADDY (Ire) [-] 8-12 (4*) P Carberry (4) (12 to 1) 6
MY GOSSIP (Ire) [-] 8-3 N G McCullagh (10)........(20 to 1) 7
981^{4} CHAMPAGNE NIGHT (Fr) [-] 9-2 J F Egan (12)......(6 to 1) 8
1574^{3} RAFFERTY'S INNER (Ire) [-] 8-7 (8*) R T Fitzpatrick (7) ....(9 to 2) 9
1822^{7} NO DUNCE (Ire) [-] 9-6 R Hughes (13)...........(20 to 1) 10
1294^{3} ABEREDW (Ire) [-] 8-12 J P Murtagh (16)..........(6 to 1) 11
1825^{5} GIRARDELLI (Ire) [-] 8-1 (4*) W J Smith (5)........(20 to 1) 12
1574^{6} RICH LIFE (Ire) [-] (bl) 9-2 M J Kinane (6)..........(4 to 1) 13
TAJARIB (Ire) [-] 8-11 B Coogan (14)..............(16 to 1) 14
848^{8} BOLD NOT BEAT (Ire) [-] 8-9 (2*) R M Burke (1)....(14 to 1) 15
1574^{8} KENTUCKY BABY (Ire) [-] (bl) 9-4 N Byrne (15)....(14 to 1) 16
Dist: Nk, ½l, ½l, nk. 2m 6.50s. (16 Ran).
(Mrs P D McCreery), Peter McCreery

1996 Blackrock Handicap (0-70 3-y-o and up) £2,245 1m 5f............... (7:30)

851* CORONADO (Ire) [-] 5-10-2 R Hughes (8).........(11 to 4) 1
1651^{2} ISLAND VISION (Ire) [-] 3-8-3 W J Supple (3) (5 to 2 jt-fav) 2
1467^{6} CEDAR COURT (Ire) [-] (bl) 5-9-9 C F Swan (5)..... (6 to 1) 3
1757^{5} SIMPLY GRAND [-] 6-9-2 N Byrne (2)............(16 to 1) 4
790 CORAL SOUND (Ire) [-] 3-8-9 S Craine (4).........(8 to 1) 5
1468 WESBEST (Ire) [-] 4-9-10 N G McCullagh (6)......(14 to 1) 6
1576 GONE LIKE THE WIND [-] 6-7-7 Joanna Morgan (7) (33 to 1) 7
1576^{3} HACKETTS CROSS (Ire) [-] 5-8-12 (6*) C Everard (11) ....(5 to 2 jt-fav) 8
1651^{6} ST AIDAN (Ire) [-] 5-7-5 (2*) D G O'Shea (10)........(8 to 1) 9
TOAST AND HONEY (Ire) [-] 4-9-8 P V Gilson (9)..(14 to 1) 10
Dist: 1l, 5½l, 1l, ½l. 2m 59.30s. (10 Ran).
(Lord White Of Hull), M J Grassick

1997 County Maiden (3-y-o and up) £2,245 1 ½m........................... (8:00)

870^{5} VELMA (USA) 3-8-11 P Shanahan (3)............(10 to 1) 1
DAYADAN (Ire) 3-9-0 D Hogan (11)..............(10 to 1) 2
1292^{2} MOUSE BIRD (Ire) 3-9-0 M J Kinane (14).......(5 to 4 on) 3
1335^{3} SAFE CONDUCT (Ire) 3-9-0 J P Murtagh (13)...... (7 to 2) 4
1622^{3} TIGHT FIST (Ire) 3-9-0 N Byrne (10)..............(16 to 1) 5
1507^{8} QUIVAL (USA) 8-11 P V Gilson (5)...............(20 to 1) 6
790^{6} HAANEM 3-8-11 W J Supple (1)..................(8 to 1) 7
282^{9} LIMAHEIGHTS (Ire) 3-8-3 (8*) P J Smullen (15).... (50 to 1) 8
RED MICKS WIFE (Ire) 3-8-11 J F Egan (12)....... (33 to 1) 9
BASSETJA (Ire) 4-9-12 R Hughes (7).............(20 to 1) 10
PEACE IN THE PARK (Ire) 3-8-11 K J Manning (4) (12 to 1) 11
WONDERFUL SONG (USA) 3-9-0 S Craine (9).... (20 to 1) 12
1236^{8} PARTICULAR (Ire) 3-8-10 (4*) W J Smith (6).......(12 to 1) 13
1609^{6} ARCH-T-GLEN (Ire) 3-8-6 (8*) D M McCullagh (8)..(66 to 1) 14
870 MY SPECIAL GUEST (Ire) 3-8-11 B Coogan (2)....(12 to 1) 15
Dist: 1½l, 1l, 2½l, 3½l. 2m 48.20s. (15 Ran).
(Allen E Paulson), D K Weld

DONCASTER (good to firm)

Friday June 25th

Going Correction: MINUS 0.10 sec. per fur.

1998 'Margaret' Median Auction Maiden Stakes Class E (2-y-o) £2,560 7f (2:15)

1640^{3} BALLAH SHACK (USA) 9-0 Paul Eddery (4) *unruly at strt, nvr far away, drvn ahead o'r one out, all out.* ....(9 to 4 on op 6 to 4 on tchd 11 to 8 on) 1
HARDING 9-0 A Munro (10) *patiently rdn, effrt and not clr run o'r one furlong out, swtchd lft, fnshd wl.* ....(8 to 1 op 4 to 1) 2
1381 HIT THE CANVAS (USA) 9-0 K Darley (7) *patiently rdn, swtchd outsd to improve o'r one furlong out, ran on und pres.*............(12 to 1 op 10 to 1 tchd 14 to 1) 3

SAINT AUBURN 9-0 T Lucas (11) *wtd wth, not much room and swtchd outsd o'r one furlong out, kpt on same pace*..............................(20 to 1 op 16 to 1) 4
730⁵ PARISH WALK (Ire) 9-0 J Lowe (5) *dsptd ld, led o'r 2 fs out till over one out, rallied*...........(10 to 1 op 6 to 1) 5
1418 MISS MILLIPEDE 8-9 A Culhane (2) *nvr far away, effrt und pres o'r one furlong out, eased whn btn ins last.* ....(25 to 1 op 20 to 1) 6
1758⁴ PARISIAN LOVER 9-0 N Connorton (8) *took str hold, trkd ldrs, not much room hfwy, eased whn btn o'r one furlong out*...............(11 to 1 op 8 to 1) 7
1715⁹ DOUBLE DANCER 9-0 M Birch (9) *set steady pace till hdd o'r 2 fs out, no extr*................(25 to 1 op 16 to 1) 8
SKELTON PRINCESS (Ire) 8-9 W Ryan (3) *sluggish strt, improved on outsd hfwy, grad wknd o'r one furlong out*...............................(20 to 1 op 16 to 1) 9
CRANFIELD CHARGER 8-6 (3*) S Maloney (6) *missed break, nvr able to reco'r*..............(33 to 1 op 16 to 1) 10
BARNPARK 9-0 S Webster (1) *unruly in stalls, missed break, virtually pld up aftr one furlong, tld off.* ....(33 to 1 op 25 to 1) 11

Dist: ½l, sht-hd, 1½l, 1½l, 1½l, ¾l, 2l, 1½l, 7l, dist. 1m 29.65s. a 6.25s (11 Ran).

(Abdulla Al Khalifa), G Lewis

1999 Phurnacite Conditions Stakes Class D (2-y-o) £2,880 5f................(2:45)

1555* TINKER OSMASTON 8-7 J Curant (3) *sn last, improved on outsd hfwy, quickened ahead o'r one furlong out, sprinted clr*............(7 to 4 op 5 to 2 tchd 11 to 4) 1
AMBER VALLEY (USA) 8-10 A Culhane (5) *sluggish strt, reco'red gng wl aftr 2 fs, not clr run over one furlong out, swtchd, fnshd well.* (6 to 1 op 7 to 1 tchd 7 to 2) 2
1798⁷ MITSIS 8-10 A Mackay (1) *al hndy, nosed ahead briefly o'r one furlong out, rdn and not quicken.* ....(25 to 1 op 16 to 1) 3
1706⁸ LAUNE (Aus) 8-5 Paul Eddery (4) *broke smartly to ld for o'r 3 fs, sn rdn and no extr.* ....(13 to 8 fav op 6 to 4 tchd 7 to 4) 4
1672* HALI (Ire) (bl) 9-0 R Cochrane (2) *sluggish strt, reco'red to press ldr over 3 fs, fdd*...............(5 to 1 op 4 to 1) 5

Dist: 3½l, 2½l, 1½l, hd. 1m 0.95s. a 2.15s (5 Ran).
SR: 40/29/19/8/16/ (Mrs S Foster), C N Williams

2000 British Coal Stakes Handicap Class D (0-80 3-y-o and up) £5,120 1¼m 60yds ....(3:15)

1398⁹ DRUMMER HICKS [75] 4-9-10 Dean McKeown (6) *trkd ldr, shaken up to ld o'r one furlong out, styd on wl.* ....(7 to 4 op 9 to 4 tchd 5 to 2) 1
1783² EXPRESS GIFT [61] 4-8-10 K Darley (5) *patiently rdn, improved entering strt, ridden last 2 fs, kpt on same pace*..........................(13 to 8 fav tchd 7 to 4) 2
801 ATHERTON GREEN (Ire) [64] 3-7-13¹ (3*) S Maloney (2) *chsd ldg quartet, improved to fltter 2 fs out, faltered, kpt on one pace*...........................(11 to 1 op 8 to 1) 3
1836³ WANZA [63] 3-8-0 E Johnson (1) *dictated pace, quickened 6 ls clr hfwy, hdd and fdd o'r one furlong out.* ....(5 to 1 op 4 to 1) 4
DOCTOR ROY [53] 5-8-2 A Munro (4) *chsd ldg bunch, drvn alng to keep up entering strt, nvr on terms.* ....(16 to 1 op 12 to 1) 5
1559⁴ WRETS [71] 4-8-13 (7*) R Painter (3) *chsd ldg pair, rdn appr strt, sn lost tch*...............(8 to 1 op 6 to 1) 6

Dist: 2l, ½l, 2l, 12l, 8l. 2m 10.80s. a 4.10s (6 Ran).
SR: 58/40/30/25/3/5/ (Mrs N Napier), E Weymes

2001 Taunton Cider Fillies Stakes Handicap Class E (0-70 3-y-o and up) £2,560 7f ....(3:45)

1658⁴ ROYAL GIRL [54] 6-9-3 N Connorton (4) *nvr far away, drvn ahead o'r one furlong out, kpt on wl.* (8 to 1 op 7 to 1) 1
1453 KELLY'S KITE [32] 5-7-5³ (7*) C Hawksley (3) *trkd ldg bunch, drvn up on outsd last 2 fs, styd on*.....(14 to 1) 2
1898⁴ PARFAIT AMOUR [60] 4-9-9 A Munro (10) *al hndy, effrt and drvn alng last 2 fs, kpt on same pace*.......(8 to 1) 3
1490⁶ TRIANGLEPOINT (Ire) [60] 3-8-11 (3*) D Harrison (8) *speed to press ldrs thrght, not quicken fnl furlong*.....(10 to 1) 4
1658⁸ QUIET VICTORY [33] (bl) 6-7-10 F Norton (9) *pushed alng to go pace, weaved through last 2 fs, fnshd wl*.... (9 to 1) 5
1656⁵ NITOUCHE [66] 3-9-6 R Cochrane (13) *pressed ldrs, feeling pace whn not much room o'r one furlong out, rallied.* ....(4 to 1) 6
1157⁴ PRIMULA BAIRN [68] 3-9-8 K Fallon (12) *last and drvn alng hfwy, weaved through last 2 fs, nrst finish.* ....(13 to 2 op 7 to 1) 7
1341⁵ HEATHYARDS GEM [58] 3-8-12 W Ryan (11) *made most for o'r 4 fs, fdd*..............................(14 to 1) 8
1761⁷ TRACHELIUM [70] 3-9-10 A Culhane (6) *trkd ldrs, edgd lft und pres o'r one furlong out, sn btn*..........(33 to 1) 9
1589 SUPREME DESIRE [48] 5-8-11 S Webster (7) *sluggish strt, nvr able to reco'r*............................(33 to 1) 10
1591² BERNSTEIN BETTE [63] 7-9-12 J Fanning (1) *sluggish strt, reco'red to take clr order hfwy, wknd over one furlong out*...........................(9 to 4 fav op 5 to 2) 11
1402⁴ QUEEN OF THE QUORN [69] 3-9-9 K Darley (2) *broke wl, feeling pace whn squeezed out o'r one furlong out, sn btn*.......................................(9 to 1) 12

Dist: ½l, 1½l, 1½l, ¾l, ½l, 5l, ½l, 1½l, hd, 2l. 1m 26.88s. a 3.48s (12 Ran).
SR: 40/16/39/25/5/27/14/2/9/ (Miss S E Hall), Miss S E Hall

2002 C.I.S.W.O. Handicap Stakes Class C (0-95 3-y-o and up) £4,160 1¾m 132yds ....(4:15)

1752 TAROUDANT [71] 6-9-2 K Darley (1) *trkd ldr, led and kicked for hme entering strt, styd on wl last 2 fs.* ....(2 to 1 op 9 to 4 tchd 5 to 2) 1
1770⁸ SWORD MASTER [72] 4-9-3 N Day (2) *patiently rdn, loomed up to chal last 2 fs, no extr ins last.* ....(4 to 1 op 7 to 2) 2
1682⁸ PHARAMINEUX [83] 7-10-0 A Munro (3) *last and hld up, effrt on ins o'r 2 fs out, sn rdn and not quicken.* ....(7 to 4 fav op 13 to 8 tchd 15 to 8) 3
1586² ELAINE TULLY (Ire) [83] 5-10-0 Paul Eddery (4) *dictated pace, hdd entering strt, sn rdn and one pace.* ....(7 to 2 tchd 4 to 1) 4

Dist: 1½l, 6l, hd. 3m 13.10s. a 8.60s (4 Ran).
SR: 1/ (G A Farndon), Mrs M Reveley

2003 Spinal Injuries Association Conditions Stakes Class D (3-y-o) £2,880 1½m..........................(4:45)

1539* OLD PROVENCE 8-12 R Cochrane (2) *sluggish strt, reco'red to ld over 3 fs out, hdd over 2 out, rallied to lead appr last, gmely*....(9 to 2 op 4 to 1 tchd 5 to 1) 1
1581* TREMOLANDO (USA) 8-12 Pat Eddery (3) *trkd ldg pair, led o'r 2 fs out, hng lft and hdd appr fnl furlong, no extr.* ...... (13 to 8 jt-fav op 6 to 4 tchd 5 to 4 and 7 to 4) 2
1506⁴ RAPID REPEAT (Ire) 8-5 Paul Eddery (5) *al hndy, rdn o'r 2 fs out, sn outpcd*....................(7 to 1 tchd 8 to 1) 3
1275* REFUGIO 8-12 W Ryan (1) *last and outpcd aftr 4 fs, nvr able to trble ldrs*.................(8 to 1 tchd 9 to 1) 4
1751⁵ LINDON LIME (USA) 8-12 A Munro (4) *dictated pace till hdd o'r 3 fs out, wknd quickly last quarter m.* ....(13 to 8 jt-fav op 2 to 1 tchd 5 to 2) 5

Dist: 1½l, 6l, 4l, 1½l. 2m 32.80s. a 2.30s (5 Ran).
SR: 63/60/41/40/37/ (Sheikh Mohammed), L M Cumani

GOODWOOD (good to firm)
Friday June 25th

Going Correction: MINUS 0.05 sec. per fur. (races 1,2,4,6), MINUS 0.10 (3,5)

2004 Royal Horse Artillery Bicentenary Apprentice Handicap Class D (0-80 4-y-o and up) £3,231 7f......... (6:45)

1734³ DANCING SENSATION (USA) [44] 6-7-9 (3*) D Wright (2) *gng wl in 4th pl, shaken up to ld o'r one furlong out, pushed out*........(13 to 8 fav op 11 to 8 tchd 7 to 4) 1
1474⁷ MERLINS WISH (USA) [74] 4-9-9 (5*) Mark Denaro (7) *slwly into strd, led aftr one furlong till o'r one out, kpt on same pace*..........................(8 to 1 op 7 to 1) 2
1584⁹ MASNUN (USA) [74] 8-9-11 (3*) B Russell (3) *hld up rear, hdwy 3 fs out, rdn and one pace appr last.* ....(3 to 1 op 5 to 2 tchd 100 to 30) 3
1696⁴ FAIR ENCHANTRESS [46] (bl) 5-7-11 (3*) Kim McDonnell (1) *led one furlong, pressed ldr, ev ch o'r one out, no extr.* ....(8 to 1 op 7 to 1 tchd 9 to 1) 4
1623 CHRISTIAN WARRIOR [42] 4-7-10⁶ (3*) D McCabe (4) *hld up in 3rd, not much room o'r one furlong out, sn rdn and btn*..............(66 to 1 op 50 to 1 tchd 100 to 1) 5
1667⁸ TAKENHALL [62] 8-8-13 (3*) J Tate (6) *settled towards rear, rdn alng o'r 2 fs out, no imprsn on ldrs.* ....(7 to 2 tchd 4 to 1) 6

Dist: 1½l, ½l, 1½l, sht-hd, nk. 1m 28.66s. a 4.06s (6 Ran).
SR: 18/43/41/8/3/22/ (Chelgate Public Relations Ltd), R Akehurst

2005 FSI Claiming Stakes Class F (3-y-o) £2,880 1½m.................. (7:15)

1802⁵ HADDAAJ (Ire) 8-7 (5*) J Tate (4) *trkd ldr, led 3 fs out, pushed clr appr last, not extended.* ....(5 to 4 tchd 13 to 8) 1
1625 MY SET PEACE 8-0⁵ (7*) Mark Denaro (3) *strted slwly, sn pushed alng in rear, lost tch hfwy, rdn and ran on appr fnl furlong, not rch wnr.* ....(12 to 1 op 50 to 1 tchd 66 to 1) 2
1746³ EURYTHMIC 8-8 A McGlone (2) *steadied strt, settled in 3rd, pushed alng and hng rght o'r 3 fs out, no extr frm 2 out*............ (11 to 10 fav op 6 to 4 on tchd 6 to 5) 3
1709⁶ NOEPROB (USA) 7-12 D Biggs (1) *led to 3 fs out, wknd o'r one out*...............(5 to 1 op 14 to 1 tchd 16 to 1) 4

Dist: 2½l, 2½l, 1½l. 2m 44.98s. a 11.98s (4 Ran).
(Sheikh Ahmed Al Maktoum), B Hanbury

2006 EBF Goodwood Golf Club Maiden Stakes Class D (2-y-o) £3,582 6f (7:40)

BEAUTETE 8-11 (3*) J Weaver (7) *strted slwly, wl beh till ran on frm 2 fs out, rdn to ld ins last, styd on well.* .... (12 to 1 op 10 to 1 tchd 14 to 1) 1
BAGSHOT 9-0 A Munro (6) *ldg grp, led 2 fs out, ran green and hng rght, rdn and hdd ins last, no extr.* ....(13 to 8 on op 6 to 4 on tchd 2 to 1 on) 2
1660[8] BIRD OF TIME (Ire) 8-9 A McGlone (3) *wl plcd, rdn alng and outpcd appr fnl furlong.......* (5 to 1 tchd 6 to 1) 3
1523[5] KOONOONA LADY 8-9 Pat Eddery (5) *trkd ldrs, rdn 2 fs out, sn outpcd.........* (7 to 2 op 3 to 1 tchd 4 to 1) 4
NORTHERN BAILIWICK (Ire) 9-0 A Clark (2) *strted slwly, rear and rdn o'r 2 fs out, no hdwy appr last.* .... (50 to 1 op 20 to 1) 5
1063 EUROCHEM LAD (Ire) 9-0 B Rouse (4) *led 4 fs, wknd und pres and eased o'r one out.........*(25 to 1 op 14 to 1) 6
1523[9] REGAL RAMBLER (Can) 9-0 B Raymond (1) *speed to hfwy, sn drpd out...........* (12 to 1 op 8 to 1 tchd 14 to 1) 7

Dist: 1l, 4l, 1l, ½l, 3l, 8l. 1m 13.77s. a 3.37s (7 Ran).
SR: 21/17/-/-/ (D G Churston), S Dow

2007 St John Ambulance Selling Handicap Stakes Class G (0-60 3-y-o and up) £2,415 2m..................... (8:10)

TOUCHING TIMES [39] 5-8-13 B Raymond (8) *made all, wl clr aftr 4 fs, styd on ins last.........*(16 to 1 tchd 20 to 1) 1
1936[6] MANON LESCAUT [43] 3-7-12 J Quinn (12) *slwly into strd, hld up, ran on 3 fs out, rdn and kpt on ins last.* ....(14 to 1 tchd 16 to 1) 2
1880* JALORE [50] 4-9-10 (5ex) M Tebbutt (9) *slwly into strd, hld up, hdwy o'r 3 fs out, rdn and ran on appr last.* .... (5 to 1 op 4 to 1 tchd 11 to 2) 3
1627[7] EARLY TO RISE [43] 3-7-12 D Biggs (14) *hdwy to chase wnr o'r 3 fs out, rdn and no extr appr last.* .... (10 to 1 op 8 to 1 tchd 11 to 1) 4
1880[5] NOBLE SOCIETY [45] 5-9-5 B Rouse (11) *ran on und pres appr last 2 fs, not rch wnr.* .... (20 to 1 op 16 to 1 tchd 25 to 1) 5
1663[8] COMMANCHERO [44] 6-8-11 (7*) S Drowne (2) *slwly into strd, sn in tch, rdn and effrt o'r 3 fs out, one pace 2 out.* .... (9 to 1 op 7 to 1 tchd 11 to 1) 6
1861 WRITTEN AGREEMENT [22] 5-7-9[6] (7*) D McCabe (5) *wl plcd to 6 fs out, ran on frm 2 out.* .... (20 to 1 op 16 to 1 tchd 25 to 1) 7
1353* DR ZEVA [35] 7-8-2 (7*) D Wright (1) *hld up, improved 4 fs out, no hdwy o'r 2 out......................*(9 to 2 jt-fav op 7 to 2 tchd 5 to 1) 8
1862[2] NASEER (USA) [49] 4-9-9 A Munro (6) *effrt 4 fs out, rdn and no prog o'r 2 out...* (9 to 2 jt-fav op 4 to 1 tchd 5 to 1) 9
THUNDER BUG (USA) [40] 5-8-11 (3*) J Weaver (10) *hld up, cld und pres 3 fs out, no extr 2 out.* .... (14 to 1 op 10 to 1 tchd 16 to 1) 10
1702[2] QUALITAIR MEMORY (Ire) [33] 4-8-7 C Rutter (13) *chsd wnr aftr 4 fs, wknd o'r 3 out.............*(9 to 1 op 6 to 1) 11
1281[7] CHINAMAN [25] (bl) 4-7-13 G Bardwell (3) *slwly into strd, mid-div hfwy, wknd 5 fs out, tld off.* .... (25 to 1 op 20 to 1) 12
1669 APACHE PRINCE [50] 6-9-10 Pat Eddery (7) *trkd wnr 4 fs, drpd rear 6 out, tld off.* .... (10 to 1 op 12 to 1 tchd 14 to 1) 13
FANLIGHT [48] 5-9-8 Candy Morris (4) *in tch early, drpd rear 6 fs out, tld off, fnshd lme.* .... (25 to 1 op 14 to 1 tchd 33 to 1) 14

Dist: 1l, 1l, 3½l, nk, ¾l, ¾l, ½l, nk, 6l, 2½l. 3m 32.80s. a 8.80s (14 Ran).
SR: 3/-/11/-/-/-/ (M B Orpen-Palmer), R Rowe

2008 John Scott-Barrett Handicap Class D (0-85 3-y-o and up) £3,655 6f.... (8:40)

1584[8] HOW'S YER FATHER [75] 7-9-6 A Munro (1) *hld up towards rear, hdwy and swtchd rght 2 fs out, led last 50 yards, ran on..........................*(4 to 1 tchd 7 to 2) 1
1977* NEITHER NOR [66] 4-8-4 (7*,7ex) D McCabe (6) *pressed ldr, led ins fnl furlong, hdd and not quicken last 50 yards.* ....(11 to 4 fav op 5 to 2 tchd 3 to 1) 2
1066 FASCINATION WALTZ [71] 6-9-2 J Quinn (2) *hld up, bumped aftr 2 fs, jnd ldrs o'r one out, ev ch, not quicken last 100 yards.* (15 to 2 op 5 to 1 tchd 8 to 1) 3
1527[2] SO RHYTHMICAL [83] 9-10-0 Pat Eddery (5) *led till ins fnl furlong, sn wknd....* (3 to 1 op 5 to 2 tchd 100 to 30) 4
BOLD MEMORY [81] 4-9-12 B Raymond (3) *bumped aftr 2 fs, hld up, effrt two out, rdn and btn appr last.* ....(10 to 1 tchd 12 to 1) 5
1821[7] COPPERMILL LAD [48] 10-7-0 (7*) Iona Wands (7) *improved frm rear hfwy, lost pl entering last 2 fs.* .... (12 to 1 op 8 to 1 tchd 14 to 1) 6
1744 POETS COVE [76] 5-9-7 C Rutter (4) *slwly into strd, hld up, wknd quickly hfwy.* .... (16 to 1 op 20 to 1 tchd 25 to 1) 7
MILAGRO [81] 4-9-5 (7*) Mark Denaro (8) *prmnt on outsd till wknd and pld up hfwy, lme.* .... (12 to 1 op 10 to 1 tchd 14 to 1) pu

Dist: ¾l, nk, 2½l, 3½l, 3l, 12l. 1m 12.29s. a 1.89s (8 Ran).
SR: 56/44/48/50/34/ (Unity Farm Holiday Centre Ltd), R J Hodges

2009 Weald And Downland Museum Handicap Class D (0-80 3-y-o) £3,699 1m ....(9:10)

1817* PERSIANSKY (Ire) [62] 7-12 (5*,7ex) J Tate (2) *trkd ldr, led 3 fs out, rdn out ins last.* .... (100 to 30 op 3 to 1 tchd 9 to 2) 1
1808[2] JUST YOU DARE (Ire) [80] 9-7 Pat Eddery (7) *handily plcd, rdn alng o'r 3 fs out, cld on ldr over one out, not quicken nr finish...* (5 to 4 fav op Evens tchd 11 to 8) 2
1588 MARK'S CLUB (Ire) [60] (bl) 8-1 J Quinn (5) *settled in 4th, rdn and not quicken fnl 2 fs.* ....(9 to 2 op 6 to 1 tchd 4 to 1) 3
1617[7] DIVINE BOY [70] 8-11 D Biggs (1) *hld up, drpd rear hfwy, effrt 2 fs out, not rch ldrs.* .... (9 to 1 op 6 to 1 tchd 10 to 1) 4
CITY ROCKET [77] 9-4 A Munro (3) *led 5 fs, wknd o'r one out.................*(12 to 1 tchd 14 to 1 and 10 to 1) 5
1818* LOCHORE [64] 8-5 (7ex) A Tucker (6) *lost many ls strt, rdn alng in rear o'r 3 fs out, nvr on terms.* .... (9 to 1 op 9 to 2 tchd 10 to 1) 6

Dist: ½l, 5l, 1½l, ½l, 2½l. 1m 40.01s. a 2.81s (6 Ran).
SR: 41/57/22/27/32/11/ (Mrs J M Beeby), B Hanbury

LINGFIELD (good (race 1), good to firm (2,3))

Friday June 25th

Going Correction: PLUS 0.05 sec. per fur.

2010 Massey Wedding Maiden Stakes Class D (3-y-o) £3,494 1¼m..... (3:10)

1594[2] MOSCOW SEA (USA) 9-0 A McGlone (7) *trkd ldrs, rdn o'r 2 fs out, styd on to ld appr last, drvn out.* ....(7 to 4 on op 2 to 1 on tchd 9 to 4 on) 1
1344 PROTON 9-0 G Duffield (1) *led o'r 5 fs, sn outpcd, rallied and ev ch over one furlong out, no extr ins last, fnshd 2nd, plcd 3rd..........*(9 to 1 op 10 to 1 tchd 14 to 1) 2D
PYRAMIS PRINCE (Ire) 9-0 C Rutter (2) *trkd ldrs, rdn 3 out, rng on whn hmpd 2 fs out, rallied ins last, nvr nrr, fnshd 3rd, plcd 2nd...............* (40 to 1 op 20 to 1) 2
MODI (USA) 8-9 T Quinn (8) *trkd ldrs, shaken up and not quicken o'r 2 fs out, styd on appr fnl furlong, improve.* ....(8 to 1 op 9 to 1) 4
1603[3] LEEWA (Ire) 9-0 A Clark (5) *trkd ldr, led o'r 4 fs out and quickened clr, rdn over 2 out, hdd and wknd appr last.* ....(4 to 1 op 3 to 1 tchd 9 to 2 and 5 to 1) 5
1746 ROSE OF MEDINA 8-9 W Newnes (3) *rear, effrt 3 fs out, nvr nr to chal...........*(40 to 1 op 20 to 1) 6
1642[5] MISTROY 8-6 (3*) J Weaver (4) *hld up, rdn and no prog o'r 2 fs out...........................* (40 to 1 op 20 to 1) 7
FATHER'S JOY 8-9 T Williams (6) *sn beh, tld off fnl 3 fs.* ....(25 to 1 tchd 50 to 1) 8

Dist: ¾l, sht-hd, 2l, 2l, 2½l, ½l, dist. 2m 11.96s. a 6.96s (8 Ran).
SR: 35/33/32/23/24/14/13/-/ (Sheikh Mohammed), H R A Cecil

2011 Sunderland Handicap Class D (0-75 3-y-o) £3,582 6f................ (4:40)

1817[2] NO EXTRAS (Ire) [66] 8-7 B Rouse (13) *hld up, gd prog frm hfwy, led jst ins fnl furlong, sn clr, cmftbly.* ....(14 to 1 op 12 to 1) 1
1633[2] CHILLY BREEZE [68] 8-9 G Duffield (11) *led till jst ins fnl furlong, ran on one pace.* .... (100 to 30 op 8 to 1 tchd 3 to 1) 2
1698* PETERSFORD GIRL (Ire) [80] 9-0 (7*) D McCabe (14) *hld up beh, prog whn not clr run o'r 2 fs out, ran on ins last, nvr nrr..............*(3 to 1 fav op 7 to 2 tchd 4 to 1) 3
1826[2] GO FLIGHTLINE (Ire) [60] (v) 7-12 (3*) M Fenton (9) *cl up, effrt and rdn wl o'r one furlong out, one pace.* .... (9 to 1 op 8 to 1 tchd 11 to 1) 4
1503[2] PRINCE SONGLINE [58] 7-13 A McGlone (6) *beh, rdn and styd on fnl 2 fs, nvr rchd ldrs.* .... (10 to 1 op 7 to 1 tchd 12 to 1) 5
1451[7] SIMPLY FINESSE [78] 9-5 D Holland (7) *chsd ldrs and no prog fnl 2 fs.........................* (5 to 1 tchd 6 to 1) 6
1473[9] SOBER LAD (Ire) [71] (bl) 8-9 (3*) J Weaver (2) *prmnt o'r 4 fs, eased whn btn ins last.* (9 to 1 op 14 to 1 tchd 8 to 1) 7
1714[6] AHJAY [58] 7-13 C Rutter (1) *nvr on terms.* .... (25 to 1 op 20 to 1 tchd 33 to 1) 8
1744[3] HALLORINA [67] 8-8 G Bardwell (10) *chsd ldrs, rdn o'r 2 fs out, sn btn...........................* (8 to 1 op 5 to 1) 9
1667[9] CYPRIAN DANCER (USA) [79] 9-6 T Quinn (12) *prmnt o'r 3 fs, sn rdn and wknd..............*(12 to 1 tchd 10 to 1) 10
1633[6] STARDUST EXPRESS [59] 8-0 T Williams (3) *prmnt, rdn and wknd 2 fs out...............................* (20 to 1) 11
1833[6] MONTONE (Ire) [64] 8-5 Dale Gibson (8) *chsd ldrs, wknd 2 fs out...........................*(20 to 1 op 12 to 1) 12
1635[8] SELECTABLE [52] 7-7 N Adams (5) *al beh.........* (50 to 1) 13
1312 AVRIL ETOILE [53] (v) 7-8 C Avery (4) *speed on outsd 4 fs, sn wknd.................*(25 to 1 op 20 to 1 tchd 33 to 1) 14

Dist: 3l, 2½l, ¾l, 3l, 2l, ¾l, ¾l, 1½l, ¾l, hd. 1m 11.88s. a 2.88s (14 Ran).
SR: 41/31/33/10/-/8/ (K Higson), G L Moore

2012 Piebald Apprentice Handicap Class E (0-70 3-y-o and up) £2,950 1¼m (5:10)

1685⁹ PRECIOUS CAROLINE (Ire) [36] 5-7-10 D Griffiths (1) *made all, clr 5 fs out, unchlgd*.......... (8 to 1 tchd 10 to 1) 1
1858⁴ ROCK THE BARNEY (Ire) [53] 4-8-13 W Hollick (6) *chsd ldrs, moderate 4th strt, rdn to chase wnr 2 fs out, no imprsn ins last*.............(13 to 8 fav op 5 to 4 tchd 7 to 4) 2
1353 BRONZE RUNNER [33] (bl) 9-7-7 A Daly (4) *strted very slwly, beh till ran on fnl 3 fs, nvr nrr*. ....(9 to 2 op 7 to 1 tchd 8 to 1) 3
COMEDY RIVER [54] 6-9-0 (7ex) F Savage (5) *strted very slwly, beh, ran wide into strt, styd on fnl 2 fs, nvr dngrs*..............................(7 to 2 tchd 4 to 1) 4
1701⁸ WESSEX MILORD [33] 8-7-7 W Hawksley (3) *chsd ldrs, 3rd strt, no prog fnl 2 fs*...............(25 to 1 op 16 to 1) 5
1781 EVERSET (Fr) [50] 5-8-10 G Faulkner (2) *chsd wnr till wknd 2 fs out*...........................(10 to 1 op 6 to 1) 6
ACT OF UNION (Ire) [68] 4-10-0 M Payne (7) *rear, lost tch 5 fs out, ran wide strt, sn wl beh*.................(7 to 1) 7
Dist: 3l, 3l, 3½l, ½l, 1½l, 20l. 2m 14.16s. a 9.16s (7 Ran).
SR: -/6/-/-/ (P D Cundell), P D Cundell

LINGFIELD (A.W) (std)
Friday June 25th
Going Correction: MINUS 0.25 sec. per fur.

2013 Roan Claiming Stakes Class F (3-y-o) £2,534 7f...................... (2:40)

624⁴ DEVIOUS DANCER 8-10 (7*) D McCabe (5) *trkd ldrs, rdn to ld appr fnl furlong, styd on wl*. .... (13 to 2 op 5 to 1 tchd 7 to 1) 1
1486² PIRATES GOLD (Ire) 8-10 (7*) D Wright (2) *hld up beh, prog hfwy, ev ch appr fnl furlong, hrd rdn and not quicken, styd on ins last*...................(3 to 1 tchd 7 to 2) 2
1743⁷ DAILY SPORT DON 9-3 A McGlone (3) *trkd ldr, led o'r 3 fs out, rdn 2 out, hdd appr last, one pace*. ....(3 to 1 op 7 to 4 tchd 100 to 30 and 7 to 2) 3
1701² BICHETTE 8-10 B Rouse (1) *led, rdn and hdd o'r 3 fs out, sn btn*........................(6 to 4 fav op 11 to 10) 4
1416 RUANO (bl) 8-0 (7*) A Liggins (7) *chsd ldrs, rdn and wknd o'r 2 fs out*........................(50 to 1 op 20 to 1) 5
1233⁸ ARYAN VESPER (e/s) 8-7 T Quinn (6) *chsd ldrs, rdn and wknd o'r 2 fs out*..................(33 to 1 op 20 to 1) 6
1627 JAFETICA (v) 8-6 W Newnes (4) *last and rdn aftr 3 fs, sn wl beh*..........................(33 to 1 op 14 to 1) 7
Dist: ¾l, sht-hd, 10l, 7l, 2½l, 12l. 1m 25.84s. a 2.44s (7 Ran).
SR: 40/38/37/-/ (G J Bush), W G M Turner

2014 Calor Beer Dispense Handicap Class D (0-80 3-y-o) £3,055 1½m...... (3:40)

1862³ ONE OFF THE RAIL (USA) [73] 9-7 B Rouse (5) *prog 7 fs out, led o'r 5 out, hld on wl ins last*.....(4 to 1 tchd 9 to 2) 1
1613* ARCTIC GUEST (Ire) [55] 8-3 T Williams (1) *chsd wnr 5 out, sn rdn alng, styd on appr fnl furlong, no extr wl ins last*.............. (6 to 5 fav op 5 to 4 tchd 11 to 10) 2
1701⁶ BRAVE HERO (USA) [46] 7-8 Dale Gibson (3) *in tch, rdn 4 fs out, sn btn*..............(10 to 1 op 8 to 1 tchd 12 to 1) 3
1709* HEART OF SPAIN [68] 9-2 W Newnes (4) *trkd ldrs gng wl, rdn 4 fs out, grad wknd*............ (3 to 1 op 5 to 2) 4
1776⁴ CHOUETTE [54] 7-9 (7*) D Wright (2) *set gd pace o'r 6 fs, sn rdn and wknd*.......... (15 to 2 op 8 to 1 tchd 10 to 1) 5
Dist: ¾l, 15l, 1½l, 12l. 2m 33.54s. a 4.24s (5 Ran).
SR: 35/15/ (K Higson), A Moore

2015 Barlow Handling Limited Stakes Class D (0-75 4-y-o and up) £3,143 1m ....(4:10)

1659³ SYLVAN SABRE (Ire) 4-8-11 W Newnes (1) *chsd ldr 5 fs out, rdn 3 out, ran on wl fnl furlong to ld last strd*. ....(5 to 2 op 4 to 1) 1
403⁵ BATTLE COLOURS (Ire) 4-8-11 G Duffield (4) *led, rdn o'r one furlong out, ran on, hdd last strd*. .... (11 to 10 fav op 5 to 4 on tchd 6 to 5) 2
1777² AMENABLE 8-8-11 Alex Greaves (3) *settled off the pace, shaken up and effrt o'r 2 fs out, nvr nr to chal*. ....(3 to 1 op 2 to 1) 3
4673a ERIK ODIN 6-8-4 (7*) G Milligan (2) *chsd ldr 3 fs, sn rdn alng, wknd o'r 2 out*. (25 to 1 op 20 to 1 tchd 33 to 1) 4
Dist: Sht-hd, 4l, 15l. 1m 38.06s. a 1.86s (4 Ran).
SR: 39/38/26/-/ (Sir Wm Garthwaite), P Mitchell

NEWCASTLE (good to firm)
Friday June 25th
Going Correction: MINUS 0.25 sec. per fur. (races 1,2,3,6), MINUS 0.10 (4,5,7)

2016 Brandling Conditions Stakes Class D (2-y-o) £5,531 7f................(5:45)

1481* PERUSAL 8-13 M Hills (2) *al cl up, effrt 2 fs out, led o'r one out, rdn and ran on ins last*. (6 to 4 fav op 2 to 1) 1
1381³ BROCTUNE GOLD 9-1 K Fallon (4) *set slow pace, quickened aftr 2 and a half fs, rdn two out, hdd and one pace o'r one out*............. (9 to 2 op 7 to 2 tchd 5 to 1) 2
1461² OCHOS RIOS (Ire) 8-12 (3*) D Harrison (1) *hld up, hdwy hfwy, rdn and edgd lft 2 fs out, sn one pace*.... (2 to 1) 3
1227* DISTINCTIVE AIR 8-13 Dean McKeown (5) *cl up, rdn and outpcd hfwy, styd on ins last, nvr dngrs*. .... (14 to 1 op 12 to 1) 4
1536* WANDERING ANGEL 8-10 P Robinson (3) *chsd ldrs, rdn wl o'r 2 fs out, sn btn*..................(7 to 1 op 6 to 1) 5
Dist: 1½l, 2l, 5l, hd. 1m 28.91s. a 4.91s (5 Ran).
(The Winning Team), R Hannon

2017 Tyne Tees Television Apprentice Claiming Stakes Class E (3-y-o and up) £3,850 7f...................(6:15)

1591⁸ KUMMEL KING 5-8-8 (7*) S Knott (1) *led, hdd 2 fs out, sn rdn, styd on wl to ld ins last*........ (6 to 1 op 4 to 1) 1
1736⁷ KHALLOOF (Ire) 4-8-11 (5*) C Teague (4) *cl up, led 2 fs out, sn rdn and edgd lft, hdd wl ins last*. .... (20 to 1 op 14 to 1) 2
BOLD ANGEL 6-9-8 S Maloney (3) *pld hrd, trkd ldrs, rdn o'r 2 fs out, kpt on one pace*. ....(9 to 4 on op 2 to 1 on tchd 15 to 8 on) 3
1358⁵ UCKERBY MOOR 4-9-0 (5*) V Halliday (5) *cl up, ev ch 2 fs out, sn rdn and one pace appr fnl furlong*. ....(12 to 1 tchd 14 to 1) 4
1388 TRIBAT 3-8-3 D Harrison (2) *cl up till rdn and wknd quickly o'r 2 fs out*.................. (8 to 1 op 7 to 1) 5
Dist: 2½l, hd, 1l, 20l. 1m 27.09s. a 3.09s (5 Ran).
SR: 28/21/26/20/-/ (David Hall), E J Alston

2018 Northern Rock Gosforth Park Cup Handicap Stakes Class B (0-105 3-y-o and up) £16,050 5f..............(6:45)

KING'S SIGNET (USA) [91] 4-9-5 N Day (9) *rcd centre, hdwy o'r 2 fs out, rdn to ld entering last, ran on wl und pres*. .... (14 to 1 op 12 to 1) 1
1679 VERDE ALITALIA (Ire) [76] 4-8-4 M Hills (19) *sn cl up stands side, rdn and ev ch entering fnl furlong, no extr nr finish*........................... (6 to 1 fav op 5 to 1) 2
795 SATANK (USA) [100] 3-9-7 N Connorton (18) *o'rall ldr stands side, rdn one and a half fs out, hdd entering last, no extr nr finish*............. (20 to 1 op 25 to 1) 3
1019⁹ REGAL CHIMES [100] 4-9-7 (7*) S Sanders (10) *led centre, rdn and ev ch o'r one furlong out, kpt on ins last*. ....(20 to 1) 4
1860* MISS VAXETTE [83] 4-8-4 (7*,7ex) M Humphries (20) *chsd ldrs stands side, rdn and kpt on fnl furlong*. .... (10 to 1 op 9 to 1) 5
1806 CANTORIS [87] 7-9-1 R Cochrane (15) *dwlt and beh till styd on wl fnl 2 fs*..... (15 to 2 op 10 to 1 tchd 7 to 1) 6
1815* JUST BOB [75] 4-8-3 (7ex) J Fortune (17) *prmnt stands side, rdn 2 fs out, grad wknd*..................(16 to 1) 7
1945* STACK ROCK [102] 6-9-11 (5*,7ex) O Pears (5) *cl up far side, rdn and ev ch 2 fs out, wknd appr last*. .... (16 to 1 op 12 to 1) 8
1679* CATHERINES WELL [78] 10-8-6 T Lucas (12) *mid-div till styd on fnl 2 fs, nvr dngrs*. ....(13 to 2 op 10 to 1 tchd 6 to 1) 9
1679² NEVER IN THE RED [84] (bl) 5-8-12 J Carroll (14) *nvr rch ldrs*....................(9 to 1 op 8 to 1 tchd 10 to 1) 10
1835 PENNY HASSET [71] 5-7-13[1] K Darley (7) *beh far side till styd on appr fnl furlong, nvr dngrs*. .... (20 to 1 op 16 to 1) 11
1806 TERRHARS (Ire) [89] 5-9-3 R Perham (8) *chsd ldrs far side, rdn 2 fs out, wknd appr last*.................. (14 to 1) 12
1113⁴ SAINT EXPRESS [93] 3-9-0 A Culhane (2) *chsd ldrs far side, effrt and rdn 2 fs out, sn wknd*.................(33 to 1) 13
1679⁹ PALLIUM (Ire) [70] 5-7-12 J Lowe (4) *dwlt, some hdwy far side 2 fs out, sn wknd*...........................(33 to 1) 14
1449 RISTON LADY (Ire) [86] 3-8-4 (3*) D Harrison (6) *nvr rch ldrs*. .... (33 to 1 op 25 to 1) 15
1420* EAGER DEVA [88] 6-9-2 W Ryan (11) *nvr a factor*. .... (11 to 1 op 10 to 1) 16
1957⁵ VERY DICEY [71] (v) 5-7-13 F Norton (1) *cl up far side till rdn and wknd 2 fs out*..........(20 to 1 op 14 to 1) 17
1159² ANOTHER EPISODE (Ire) [83] 4-8-4 (7*) P Roberts (16) *gd speed centre 3 fs, sn wknd*........................ (33 to 1) 18
1806 SIZZLING SAGA (Ire) [98] 5-9-12 P Robinson (13) *slwly away, al rear*.................................(33 to 1) 19
1679 SIGAMA (USA) [78] 7-8-3 (3*) N Kennedy (3) *led far side 3 fs, sn wknd*............ (20 to 1 op 16 to 1 tchd 22 to 1) 20
Dist: 1l, sht-hd, 1l, 3l, nk, ¾l, hd, sht-hd, 1½l, 1½l. 59.11s. a 0.21s (20 Ran).
SR: 76/57/73/76/47/50/35/61/36/ (Sheikh Mohammed), J H M Gosden

2019 Dataform U.K. Handicap Class C (0-95 3-y-o) £7,700 1¼m 32yds....... (7:20)

1838* DARMSTADT (USA) [73] 8-8 (3ex) R Cochrane (3) *made all, quickened 4 fs out, shaken up entering last, ran on wl*. ....(5 to 2 on op 9 to 4 on tchd 11 to 4 on) 1

1579^{3} WORDSMITH (Ire) [69] 8-4 K Fallon (1) *hld up, hdwy to chase wnr o'r 2 fs out, sn rdn, kpt on one pace ins last.* ... (15 to 2 op 5 to 1 tchd 8 to 1) 2
1558^{5} AJALAN (Ire) [86] 9-7 W Ryan (2) *chsd wnr, effrt and rdn 3 fs out, kpt on one pace appr last*... (6 to 1 op 5 to 1) 3
1579^{5} JALCANTO [73] 8-8 K Darley (4) *trkd ldrs till slightly outpcd 3 fs out, nvr dngrs aftr, eased ins last.* ... (7 to 1 op 6 to 1) 4
Dist: 2l, 2l, 3½l. 2m 14.87s. a 8.37s (4 Ran).
SR: -/-/5/-/ (Sheikh Mohammed), J H M Gosden

2020 William Edwin Neesham Limited Stakes Class D (0-75 4-y-o and up) £3,800 1¼m 32yds............. (7:50)

1768^{5} WALKING THE PLANK 4-8-11 P Robinson (1) *trkd ldrs, hdwy o'r 2 fs out, rdn to ld ins fnl furlong, hld on.* ... (6 to 5 on op 7 to 4 on tchd 11 to 10 on) 1
619^{5} WELL APPOINTED (Ire) 4-8-11 A Proud (3) *hld up, gd hdwy on outer 3 fs out, ev ch entering last, sn rdn and styd on wl*... (6 to 1 op 4 to 1) 2
1781 WESTHOLME (USA) 5-8-8 (3*) S Maloney (2) *led, quickened clr hfwy, slpd entering strt, rdn 2 fs out, hdd ins last, no extr nr finish*... (6 to 4 op 5 to 2) 3
Dist: Hd, ½l. 2m 13.17s. a 6.67s (3 Ran).
SR: 20/19/18/ (Michael White), P T Walwyn

2021 Federation Brewery LCL Pils Lager Maiden Stakes Class D (2-y-o) £5,921 6f.............................. (8:20)

MISTER BAILEYS 9-0 Dean McKeown (2) *dwlt, sn chasing ldrs centre, effrt and hdwy o'r 2 fs out, led over one and a half furlongs out, soon clr, imprsv.* ... (5 to 1 op 5 to 2 tchd 6 to 1) 1
LEVEL SANDS (USA) 9-0 G Duffield (7) *chsd ldrs stands side, rdn and hdwy 2 fs out, edgd lft and styd on ins last, no ch wth wnr.* ... (5 to 4 fav op 2 to 1 tchd 11 to 10) 2
1739^{2} ASHKERNAZY (Ire) 8-9 A Mackay (1) *o'rall ldr centre, rdn 2 fs out, sn hdd and kpt on one pace.* (10 to 1 op 8 to 1) 3
1446^{7} ALPINE SKIER (Ire) 9-0 K Darley (10) *cl up stands side, rdn o'r 2 fs out and kpt on one pace*... (8 to 1 tchd 9 to 1) 4
PLEASURE TRICK (USA) 9-0 S Perks (4) *beh, hdwy hfwy, rdn to chase ldrs 2 fs out, eased ins last.* ... (14 to 1 op 8 to 1) 5
MIDNIGHT MAGPIE (Ire) 8-7 (7*) D Thomas (8) *chsd ldrs stands side, rdn 2 fs out, wkng whn hmpd appr last.* ... (33 to 1 op 20 to 1) 6
1418^{8} DURHAM DRAPES 8-9 M Birch (12) *in tch stands side, rdn and styd on fnl 2 fs*... (14 to 1 op 10 to 1) 7
1814^{6} NORTHGATE SYMPHONY 9-0 P Robinson (9) *nvr rchd ldrs*... (33 to 1 op 25 to 1) 8
1580^{6} STARICA (Ire) 8-9 R Cochrane (6) *chsd ldrs centre to hfwy, sn wknd*... (25 to 1 op 12 to 1) 9
1556^{4} IN MY LEAGUE (Ire) 9-0 M Hills (3) *chsd ldr, rdn o'r 2 fs out and sn wknd*... (10 to 1 op 7 to 1) 10
1561^{5} MONKEY'S WEDDING 9-0 J Carroll (13) *speed stands side o'r 3 fs, sn wknd*... (14 to 1 op 12 to 1) 11
1798^{2} CLOSE TO REALITY 9-0 K Fallon (5) *in tch, effrt and hdwy o'r 2 fs out, sn rdn and btn.* ... (7 to 1 op 8 to 1 tchd 10 to 1) 12
1846^{7} THUNDERBIRD TWO (Ire) 9-0 N Connorton (11) *in tch, rdn alng aftr 2 fs and sn lost pl, tld off fnl two furlongs.* ... (33 to 1 op 20 to 1) 13
Dist: 7l, 2½l, 2l, ½l, 2l, ¾l, 1½l, ½l, 2l, ½l. 1m 13.72s. a 1.72s (13 Ran).
SR: 36/8/-/-/-/-/ (G R Bailey Ltd (Baileys Horse Feeds)), M Johnston

2022 Dobson Peacock Handicap Class D (0-85 3-y-o and up) £7,440 1m... (8:50)

1225^{4} SO SO [80] 3-9-2 W Ryan (5) *chsd ldrs, hdwy 3 fs out, rdn to chal one and a half out, styd on und pres ins last to ld on line*... (10 to 1 tchd 12 to 1) 1
1474 BLOCKADE (USA) [74] 4-9-6 M Hills (8) *led, clr o'r 2 fs out and sn rdn, ct on line*... (3 to 1 fav tchd 7 to 2) 2
1617^{4} MAP OF STARS (USA) [78] 3-9-0 R Cochrane (7) *chsd ldrs, wide strt, rdn o'r 2 fs out, styd on wl ins last.* ... (4 to 1 op 3 to 1) 3
1338 JERVIA [82] 3-9-4 G Duffield (3) *chsd ldrs, wide strt, rdn o'r 2 fs out, styd on wl ins last*... (8 to 1 op 7 to 1) 4
1721^{5} JALMUSIQUE [80] 7-9-12 M Birch (2) *chsd ldr, slpd entering strt and sn lost pl*... (11 to 2 op 5 to 1) 5
1207* AITCH N'BEE [78] 10-9-10 K Darley (4) *al rear*... (6 to 1) 6
1721^{3} VELOCE (Ire) [61] 5-8-7 A Mackay (6) *hld up, hdwy whn slpd up entering strt*... (5 to 1 tchd 6 to 1) su
Dist: Sht-hd, sht-hd, ½l, 6l, 1½l. 1m 41.40s. a 2.40s (7 Ran).
SR: 54/57/50/52/42/35/-/ (Geoffrey Martin), T D Barron

NEWMARKET (JULY) (good)
Friday June 25th

Going Correction: MINUS 0.05 sec. per fur. (races 1,3,4), MINUS 0.20 (2,5,6)

2023 Crimestoppers Claiming Stakes Class D (3-y-o) £2,880 1¼m.......... (2:00)

KARACHI 8-6 (3*) B Doyle (2) *hld up, hdwy 2 fs out, led one out, edgd rght, drvn out*... (16 to 1 op 10 to 1) 1
1771* DON'T FORGET MARIE (Ire) 7-9 (7*) A Whelan (1) *chsd ldr, led o'r 2 fs out to one out, hng rght, not quicken.* ... (15 to 8 fav op 6 to 4 tchd 2 to 1) 2
1315^{7} RUFFLE 8-0 J Quinn (5) *chsd ldrs, ev ch 2 fs out, not clr run wl ins last*... (13 to 2 op 8 to 1 tchd 10 to 1) 3
1479^{4} SOLO CHARTER 8-13 P Robinson (11) *hld up, hdwy und pres o'r 2 fs out, styd on.* ... (15 to 2 op 6 to 1 tchd 8 to 1) 4
ZONK 8-9 M Wigham (7) *rdn alng fnl 2 fs, styd on, nvr nrr*... (33 to 1 op 20 to 1) 5
1829^{8} SABO'S EXPRESS 8-2 (7*) Sarah Thompson (4) *no hdwy fnl 3 fs*... (9 to 1 op 8 to 1 tchd 14 to 1) 6
980 IMAGERY 8-4 G Carter (8) *prmnt 7 fs, sn lost pl.* ... (33 to 1 op 16 to 1 tchd 40 to 1) 7
1500^{4} BLUE TRUMPET 8-5 W Woods (3) *nvr better than mid-div.* ... (14 to 1 op 10 to 1) 8
1524 FIVEOFIVE (Ire) 8-6 L Piggott (6) *chsd ldrs to hfwy, beh fnl 2 fs*... (7 to 2 op 5 to 2) 9
1617 YOSHAARIK (Ire) (bl) 8-5 B Raymond (10) *led till o'r 2 fs out, sn wknd*... (16 to 1 op 12 to 1) 10
Dist: 1½l, 1½l, 3½l, ½l, 2l, 5l, ¾l, 5l, hd. 2m 8.00s. a 5.80s (10 Ran).
SR: 32/22/17/23/18/14/ (Mrs J L Hislop), C E Brittain

2024 Merivale Moore Handicap Class C (0-90 3-y-o) £5,026 5f........... (2:30)

1740* CALL ME I'M BLUE (Ire) [80] 9-1 (8ex) L Piggott (2) *trkd ldrs, rdn to ld ins fnl furlong, ran on wl.* ... (9 to 4 fav op 5 to 2 tchd 11 to 4) 1
1826^{3} JULIET BRAVO [63] 7-12 W Carson (4) *led, rdn o'r one furlong out, hdd and no extr ins last.* ... (5 to 1 tchd 11 to 2) 2
634^{6} BOLD COUNTY [69] 8-4 R P Elliott (7) *effrt 2 fs out, rdn one out, kpt on*... (11 to 1 op 10 to 1 tchd 12 to 1) 3
1826* MY BONUS [78] 8-8 (5*) L Newton (1) *al prmnt, ev ch o'r one furlong out, not quicken.* ... (6 to 1 op 5 to 1 tchd 13 to 2) 4
1215 DAANIERA (Ire) [68] 8-3 J Quinn (5) *slwly into strd, nvr trble ldrs*... (11 to 1 op 16 to 1 tchd 20 to 1) 5
1841^{3} WALK THE BEAT [78] 8-13 A Tucker (6) *dwlt strt, nvr able to chal*... (4 to 1 op 3 to 1) 6
1233* TRENTESIMO (Ire) [86] 9-7 G Carter (3) *chsd ldrs, rdn and wknd quickly 2 fs out*... (5 to 1 tchd 11 to 2) 7
Dist: 1½l, 1l, 3l, 5l, 7l, 2l. 59.76s. a 1.06s (7 Ran).
SR: 60/37/39/36/6/-/-/ (Harsh (Tipping Gears)), N Tinkler

2025 Tartan International Handicap Class C (0-95 3-y-o and up) £7,245 1¼m (3:00)

1711* USAIDIT [74] 4-9-10 J Reid (5) *chsd ldrs, pld out to ld ins fnl furlong, pushed out*... (3 to 1 jt-fav op 7 to 2 tchd 4 to 1) 1
1204^{2} TOP CEES [83] 3-9-7 W Carson (3) *chsd ldr, ev ch fnl 2 fs, not quicken ins last*... (3 to 1 jt-fav op 5 to 2) 2
1770^{9} PORT SUNLIGHT (Ire) [70] 5-9-6 L Dettori (6) *led till ins fnl furlong, no extr*... (100 to 30 op 5 to 2 tchd 7 to 2) 3
1711^{3} BENTICO [52] 4-8-2 J Quinn (4) *hld up, hdwy 3 fs out, ev ch 2 out, sn rdn and btn.* ... (4 to 1 op 9 to 2 tchd 5 to 1 and 7 to 2) 4
1777^{6} JAHANGIR (Ire) [70] 4-9-6 L Piggott (1) *hld up, hdwy 3 fs out, ran on one pace frm 2 out.* ... (9 to 1 op 10 to 1 tchd 12 to 1) 5
ELANMATINA (Ire) [73] 4-9-9 W Woods (2) *al rear, no ch fnl 3 fs*... (16 to 1 op 25 to 1 tchd 33 to 1) 6
Dist: 1l, 2l, 5l, 2l, 20l. 2m 9.44s. a 7.24s (6 Ran).
SR: 33/28/23/-/9/-/ (Mrs Pauline Merrick), T G Mills

2026 Girdlestone Pumps Handicap Class D (0-80 4-y-o and up) £3,622 1½m (3:30)

1605^{5} AMAZON EXPRESS [65] 4-9-4 J Reid (6) *hld up, rdn alng 4 fs out, str run fnl furlong, led last strds.* ... (13 to 8 fav op 6 to 4 tchd 15 to 8) 1
1827^{4} MISS PIN UP [75] 4-10-0 D Biggs (5) *hld up, hdwy 3 fs out, led o'r one out, hrd rdn and no extr, hdd last strds.* ... (7 to 2 op 3 to 1 tchd 4 to 1) 2
1409 FREE MOVER (Ire) [74] 4-9-13 W Carson (1) *chsd ldrs, rdn 2 fs out, not quicken fnl furlong.* ... (5 to 1 op 9 to 2 tchd 11 to 2) 3
1268 TALOS (Ire) [69] 5-9-8 R Hills (2) *prmnt, ch 2 fs out, sn rdn and btn*... (7 to 1 op 14 to 1) 4
1380 WILKINS [66] 4-9-5 B Raymond (4) *trkd ldr, led o'r 2 fs out, hdd and btn over one out*... (12 to 1 op 6 to 1) 5
1840^{8} AUDE LA BELLE (Fr) [64] 5-9-3 L Dettori (3) *led till o'r 2 fs out, no ch frm two out.* (6 to 1 op 7 to 1 tchd 11 to 2) 6
Dist: Hd, 1½l, 2½l, 2l, 1l. 2m 33.61s. a 4.81s (6 Ran).
SR: 50/59/55/45/38/34/ (Mrs Jill Moss), R Akehurst

2027 Unicite Maiden Stakes Class D (2-y-o) £3,752 6f..................... (4:00)

1715[3] SAIHAT (Ire) 9-0 L Piggott (7) *made all, shaken up one furlong out, sn drw clr.*
...(11 to 8 on op 5 to 4 on tchd Evens and 6 to 4 on) 1
IN LIKE FLYNN 9-0 L Dettori (5) *squeezed out strt, hdwy hfwy, in tch 2 fs out, no ch wth wnr.*
.... (13 to 2 op 4 to 1 tchd 7 to 1) 2
1277[2] NAKITA 8-2 (7*) G Forster (2) *wth wnr 4 fs, wknd o'r one out*.................. (8 to 1 op 5 to 1 tchd 10 to 1) 3
MR DEVIOUS 9-0 J Reid (3) *kpt on fnl 2 fs, not trble ldrs.*
......................................(6 to 1 op 5 to 2) 4
DAKOTA BRAVE (Ire) 9-0 W Hood (6) *wnt lft strt, prmnt till rdn and btn o'r one furlong out.*
.... (20 to 1 op 12 to 1 tchd 33 to 1) 5
TITANIUM HONDA (Ire) 8-11 (3*) B Doyle (4) *speed 4 fs, sn rdn and lost pl*................. (12 to 1 tchd 14 to 1) 6
MENTMORE LAD 9-0 W Carson (1) *not go pace, tld off.*
.... (16 to 1 op 8 to 1 tchd 20 to 1) 7
Dist: 4l, ¾l, sht-hd, 3l, 8l, 4l. 1m 14.70s. a 3.00s (7 Ran).
SR: 16/-/-/-/ (Prince A A Faisal), Mrs J Cecil

2028 St Andrews Park Fillies Conditions Stakes Class D (3-y-o) £3,492 6f (4:30)

1415* CARRANITA (Ire) 8-9 (5*) Stephen Davies (2) *wth ldr, led jst ins fnl furlong, rdn out*............ (3 to 1 tchd 4 to 1) 1
1415[2] SHEILA'S SECRET (Ire) 9-4 J Reid (4) *led till jst ins fnl furlong, not quicken*... (9 to 1 op 8 to 1 tchd 10 to 1) 2
1338[8] MARGARET'S GIFT 9-2 G Carter (5) *effrt o'r one furlong out, kpt on ins last*..... (13 to 2 op 8 to 1 tchd 9 to 1) 3
428* TAALIF 9-0 R Hills (1) *speed 4 fs, sn rdn, no hdwy.*
.... (6 to 1 tchd 7 to 1) 4
1171* WAFFLE ON 9-0 B Raymond (3) *missed break, sn prmnt, rdn 2 fs out, soon btn*.......................... (Evens fav) 5
Dist: Nk, ¾l, 3½l, 6l. 1m 13.75s. a 2.05s (5 Ran).
SR: 35/38/33/17/-/ (Lamb Lane Associates), B Palling

CHEPSTOW (good to firm) Saturday June 26th
Going Correction: MINUS 0.40 sec. per fur.

2029 Woodpecker Handicap Class D (0-80 4-y-o and up) £3,377 1¼m 36yds (2:20)

1242[6] MARCHMAN [53] 8-8-2[2] Paul Eddery (6) *al prmnt, led o'r one furlong out, ran on wl*......... (7 to 2 tchd 4 to 1) 1
1820* BOOKCASE [72] 6-9-7 J Williams (4) *hdwy 3 fs out, ev ch o'r one out, not quicken*........ (11 to 4 fav op 2 to 1) 2
1768[9] COURAGEOUS KNIGHT [69] 4-9-4 R Perham (5) *al prmnt, led o'r 2 fs out till over one out, not quicken.*
......................................(5 to 1 op 3 to 1) 3
1878* ATHAR (Ire) [65] 4-9-0 S Dawson (3) *hdwy 3 fs out, one pace fnl 2 furlongs*............ (11 to 2 op 7 to 2) 4
4732a[7] VALIANT WORDS [50] 6-7-13 A Tucker (7) *led till o'r 2 fs out*.................... (7 to 1 op 5 to 1 tchd 10 to 1) 5
1663[7] IMA RED NECK (USA) [49] 4-7-12 S O'Gorman (8) *al beh.*
.... (12 to 1 op 14 to 1 tchd 25 to 1) 6
ROSE ELEGANCE [76] 4-9-6 (5*) V Slattery (1) *al beh.*
.... (16 to 1 op 12 to 1 tchd 20 to 1) 7
BLUE AEROPLANE [74] (bl) 5-9-5[1] (5*) D Meredith (2) *prmnt till wknd o'r 2 fs out*............. (33 to 1 op 14 to 1) 8
Dist: 1½l, ½l, 1½l, 3l, 2½l, 3l, ½l. 2m 5.60s. a 2.00s (8 Ran).
SR: 27/43/39/32/11/5/26/23/ (Mrs P M King), J S King

2030 EBF Median Auction Maiden Stakes Class E (2-y-o) £3,300 6f 16yds.. (2:50)

1624[2] RAMBOLD 8-9 R Perham (8) *made all, hld on wl.*
..........................(6 to 1 op 5 to 1 tchd 7 to 1) 1
JAREEF'S WAY (Ire) 9-0 S Raymont (6) *al prmnt, ev ch fnl fdurlong, ran on*.................... (6 to 1 op 3 to 1) 2
1529[2] GONE TO POT 9-0 A Clark (10) *rdn and outpcd o'r 3 fs out, styd on fnl 2 furlongs*........... (5 to 2 fav op 6 to 4) 3
RED TAR 9-0 C Rutter (9) *nrst finish.*
.... (20 to 1 op 25 to 1 tchd 14 to 1) 4
1350 CHILIGRAY 9-0 W Newnes (5) *outpcd till ran on fnl 2 fs.*
........................(8 to 1 op 5 to 1 tchd 9 to 1) 5
1265 ROBERO 8-9 (5*) O Pears (1) *speed 4 fs.*
.... (33 to 1 op 25 to 1) 6
1624 SPEEDY SNAPS IMAGE 8-7 (7*) Mark Denaro (3) *speed 4 fs.*
....(50 to 1) 7
1489[7] BRAVE EDGE 9-0 Paul Eddery (11) *hld up, ev ch 2 fs out, wknd quickly*...................... (3 to 1 op 9 to 2) 8
ANZUM 9-0 J Williams (2) *strted slwly, al beh*....(33 to 1) 9
1624[6] FAIRFIELD CHOICE 8-9 N Day (12) *al wl beh.*
..................................(20 to 1 tchd 25 to 1) 10
325[5] FORMIDABLE LASS 8-9 T Lang (7) *speed o'r 3 fs.*
.... (20 to 1 op 16 to 1) 11
Dist: ½l, 2l, 5l, 2l, ½l, ½l, 3½l, 8l, 2½l, 7l. 1m 11.90s. a 2.40s (11 Ran).
SR: -/2/-/-/-/-/ (Sydney Mason), T M Jones

2031 Rothmans Royals North South Challenge Series Handicap Class D (0-80 3-y-o and up) £3,687 1m 14yds.. (3:20)

1421* MOON SPIN [64] 4-9-2 Paul Eddery (6) *trkd ldrs, quickened to ld ins fnl furlong, sn clr.*
..............................(11 to 2 op 4 to 1 tchd 6 to 1) 1
1474 SALBYNG [54] (v) 5-8-6 S Raymont (3) *al prmnt, led one furlong out, swrvd lft and hdd ins fnl furlong.*
........................(3 to 1 fav op 9 to 2 tchd 5 to 1) 2
1686* BOLD ACRE [65] 3-8-2 (5*) Stephen Davies (5) *led til one furlong out, not quicken*...........(4 to 1 tchd 5 to 1) 3
1777[3] NORTHERN TRIAL (USA) [45] (v) 5-7-11 A Tucker (4) *chsd ldrs, one pace fnl 2 fs.*
.... (12 to 1 op 14 to 1 tchd 10 to 1) 4
1667[2] MARINE DIVER [76] 7-10-0 J Williams (1) *pld hrd, jnd ldrs aftr 3 fs, ev ch o'r one out, wknd fnl furlong.*
....(11 to 2 op 4 to 1) 5
1375[4] CLASS ATTRACTION (USA) [68] 4-9-1 (5*) O Pears (2) *wth ldr till wknd o'r 2 fs out*. (6 to 1 op 5 to 1 tchd 7 to 1) 6
1876* ON Y VA (USA) [58] 6-8-10 A Clark (7) *al beh.*
....(7 to 1 op 6 to 1) 7
1312[6] DON TOCINO [66] 3-8-8 W Newnes (8) *al beh.*
..........................(8 to 1 op 6 to 1 tchd 9 to 1) 8
Dist: 2l, nk, ¾l, 2l, 3l, 1½l, nk. 1m 35.90s. a 3.50s (8 Ran).
SR: 1/-/-/-/-/ (Mrs W R Hern), Major W R Hern

2032 Starling Maiden Fillies Stakes Class D (3-y-o) £3,611 7f 16yds..........(3:55)

1522[3] OARE SPARROW 8-11 Paul Eddery (10) *made all, all out.*
....(4 to 1 tchd 7 to 2) 1
SARENA LADY (Ire) 8-11 C Rutter (3) *hdwy 2 fs out, ev ch ins fnl furlong, ran on.* (9 to 2 op 7 to 2 tchd 5 to 1) 2
LADY SABINA 8-6 (5*) V Slattery (2) *dwlt, hdwy 2 fs out, ev ch one out, not quicken*........... (33 to 1 op 20 to 1) 3
1587 BELMONT PRINCESS (Ire) 8-11 N Adams (5) *hdwy 3 fs out, ev ch o'r one out, wknd fnl furlong.*
.... (50 to 1 op 33 to 1) 4
1482[6] KAPUCHKA (Ire) 8-6 (5*) Stephen Davies (1) *jnd wnr and ev ch o'r 2 fs out, wknd over one out.*
.... (4 to 1 tchd 9 to 2 and 7 to 2) 5
1616[9] SHERGRESS 8-11 J Williams (8) *chsd wnr till wknd o'r 2 fs out*................................ (12 to 1 op 33 to 1) 6
1698[8] PHARLING 8-11 N Day (7) *speed o'r 4 fs.*
.... (20 to 1 op 12 to 1) 7
STEP ON IT 8-11 S O'Gorman (4) *prmnt 4 fs.*
.... (66 to 1 op 50 to 1) 8
1470[6] EISHRELA 8-11 A Clark (9) *al wl beh.* (20 to 1 op 14 to 1) 9
Dist: Hd, 2l, 4l, nk, ½l, 3l, 2l, 2½l. 1m 23.20s. a 3.20s (9 Ran).
SR: 7/6/-/-/-/-/ (Mrs Henry Keswick), P T Walwyn

2033 Chaffinch Rating Related Maiden Stakes Class F (3-y-o) £2,434 5f 16yds ....(4:25)

1848[3] SCORED AGAIN 9-0 A Clark (2) *al prmnt, led o'r one furlong out, all out.*
...................(7 to 4 fav tchd 2 to 1 and 11 to 8) 1
1966[5] CLOUDY REEF 8-2 (7*) M Humphries (1) *al prmnt, ev ch fnl furlong, ran on*..................... (5 to 2 op 9 to 4) 2
1376[3] DONTDRESSFORDINNER 9-0 R Perham (5) *hdwy and hrd rdn o'r a furlong out, ran on ins fnl last.*
..........................(7 to 1 op 5 to 1 tchd 9 to 1) 3
1874[5] KILDEE LAD (v) 9-0 N Adams (3) *pld hrd, led till wknd quickly o'r a furlong out*........... (5 to 2 op 7 to 4) 4
1829 CAUGHT REDHANDED (Ire) 8-9 W Newnes (4) *dwlt, al wl beh*........................... (10 to 1 tchd 14 to 1) 5
Dist: Sht-hd, 1½l, 4l, 15l. 58.60s. a 1.60s (5 Ran).
SR: 28/22/21/5/-/ (The PBT Group), R M Whitaker

2034 Swallow Maiden Handicap Class F (3-y-o and up) £2,623 2¼m 33yds.. (5:00)

757[7] RICH PICKINGS [36] 4-9-1 R Perham (4) *hdwy aftr 4 fs, led 5 out, styd on wl.*
...........(17 to 2 op 7 to 1 tchd 10 to 1 and 8 to 1) 1
1688[6] ROYAL PRINT (Ire) [40] 4-9-5 N Day (7) *hdwy 6 fs out, jnd wnr 3 out, ev ch, not quicken ins last.*
..........................(4 to 1 op 3 to 1 tchd 9 to 2) 2
1564[9] UNDERWYCHWOOD (Ire) [35] 5-9-1 S Dawson (3) *hdwy 4 fs out, styd on one pace fnl 2 furlongs.*
.... (16 to 1 op 10 to 1) 3
1321[2] INTREPID LASS [44] 6-9-3 (7*) Antoinette Armes (5) *pld hrd, chsd ldr, lost pl 7 fs out, rallied o'r 2 out, styd on.*
..........................(7 to 2 op 2 to 1 tchd 4 to 1) 4
1930[4] DOC'S COAT [40] 8-9-6 C Rutter (1) *hdwy 4 fs out, hrd rdn 3 out, wknd o'r one furlong out.*
.........................(5 to 2 fav op 4 to 1 tchd 9 to 4) 5
1840 JADIDH [42] (bl) 5-9-8 W Newnes (2) *hdwy 6 fs out, wknd 3 out, tld off*........................... (4 to 1 op 7 to 2) 6
838[7] CRYSTAL STONE [48] 3-8-7 A Tucker (8) *led 6 fs out till 5 out, wknd 3 out, tld off.*
.... (16 to 1 op 10 to 1 tchd 20 to 1) 7
1092 THE GORROCK [35] (bl) 4-8-7 (7*) G Milligan (9) *rcd wide, led till wknd 6 fs out, tld off fnl 4 furlongs.*
.... (50 to 1 op 33 to 1) 8
Dist: 1l, 1½l, nk, 2½l, 20l, 7l, dist. 4m 0.00s. (8 Ran).
(Apollo Excellsior Racing), D R Tucker

CURRAGH (IRE) (good to yielding)
Saturday June 26th
Going Correction: MINUS 0.15 sec. per fur. (race 1), NIL (2,3,4,5,6,7)

2035 Dunnes Stores Ladies Derby (3-y-o and up) £6,400 1½m. . . . . (2:00)

807[5] AIYBAK (Ire) 5-10-7 Miss U Smith (12) . . . . (8 to 1) 1
943[5] TBAAREEH (USA) 3-10-2 Miss C Hutchinson (7) (5 to 1 jt-fav) 2
MUBADIR (USA) 5-11-1 Mrs A Ferris (14) . . . . (11 to 2) 3
1823[5] MAMOURA (Ire) 3-9-9 Miss L Robinson (9) . . . . (11 to 2) 4
KEPPOLS PRINCE 6-10-0 (2*) Miss O Glennon (1) (25 to 1) 5
1996[8] HACKETTS CROSS (Ire) 5-10-10 Miss J Lewis (10) (20 to 1) 6
1013 SENSE OF VALUE 4-11-1 Miss A H Marshall (6) . . . (11 to 1) 7
1202* TONY'S FEN 4-11-9 Mrs M Mullins (4) . . . . (5 to 1 jt-fav) 8
1797[2] LEGAL ADVISER 6-10-13 Miss C Rogers (11) . . . . . (16 to 1) 9
1822 SPECIAL OFFER (Ire) (bl) 3-9-3 Miss A Gilsenan (2) (14 to 1) 10
959 GREEN GLEN (USA) 4-10-12 Miss C E Hyde (13) . . (16 to 1) 11
NORDIC SUN (Ire) 5-10-10 Miss I Leahy (3) . . . . (7 to 1) 12
897[8] ORTHORHOMBUS 4-11-9 Miss M Olivefalk (8) . . . (25 to 1) 13
1576[5] RISING WATERS (Ire) 5-11-1 Mrs D McDonogh (5) (14 to 1) 14
Dist: 1½l, 2l, ½l, nk, 4l, 5l. 2m 35.00s. a 5.50s (14 Ran).
SR: 48/40/49/28/34/34/29/-/-/ (Michael W J Smurfit), D K Weld

2036 Waterford Crystal Fillies E.B.F. Maiden (3-y-o) £5,520 1½m. . . . . (2:30)

SOVIET CHOICE (Ire) 9-0 M J Kinane (1) . . . . (3 to 1) 1
UNCONDITIONAL (Fr) 9-0 N G McCullagh (5) . . . . . (12 to 1) 2
KADASSA (Ire) 9-0 J P Murtagh (3) . . . . (5 to 4 on) 3
1573[6] SEAWORTHY (Ire) 9-0 S Craine (2) . . . . (8 to 1) 4
1652[5] BAHNASA (Ire) 9-0 D Hogan (6) . . . . (15 to 2) 5
258 NORDIC SUCCESS (Ire) 9-0 C Roche (4) . . . . (12 to 1) 6
Dist: 1½l, 1½l, 2½l, 12l. 2m 36.20s. a 6.70s (6 Ran).
SR: 33/30/27/22/-/-/ (Moyglare Stud Farm), D K Weld

2037 Japanese Gardens E.B.F. Maiden (2-y-o) £5,244 6f. . . . . (3:00)

1197[2] TANGO TRIO (Ire) 9-0 D V Smith (4) . . . . (11 to 1) 1
1022[2] BASSMAAT (USA) 8-11 C Roche (6) . . . . (5 to 1) 2
1022[8] RIDGE POOL (Ire) 8-11 R Hughes (18) . . . . (10 to 1) 3
1550[2] UNDER SIEGE (Ire) 9-0 L Piggott (1) . . . . (Evens fav) 4
1332[5] PEACE ROLE (USA) 9-0 M J Kinane (17) . . . . (8 to 1) 5
ORANGE PLEASURE (USA) 8-11 W J O'Connor (3) (25 to 1) 6
1197[5] OPULENT 9-0 P V Gilson (9) . . . . (9 to 1) 7
1197[6] MOMENTS TO CARE (Ire) 8-11 N G McCullagh (2) (10 to 1) 8
MANAAFIS (Ire) 9-0 W J Supple (7) . . . . (10 to 1) 9
EUROFLOWER (Ire) 8-11 S Craine (5) . . . . (16 to 1) 10
GAINSBOROUGH'S BOY (Ire) 9-0 J P Murtagh (10) (12 to 1) 11
BETTER YET (Ire) 8-11 N Byrne (12) . . . . (25 to 1) 12
1824[5] DANCING BRIEF (Ire) 8-12 (2*) D G O'Shea (16) . . . (33 to 1) 13
ALKEN (Ire) 8-8 (6*) J A Heffernan (15) . . . . (14 to 1) 14
1792[3] NURMI (Ire) 9-0 J F Egan (8) . . . . (12 to 1) 15
ALBERTA DIAMOND 8-11 P Shanahan (11) . . . . (20 to 1) 16
MY TRIVET (Ire) 9-0 P Lowry (14) . . . . (20 to 1) 17
CROSS SWORDS (USA) 9-0 K J Manning (13) . . . . (20 to 1) 18
Dist: ¾l, 2½l, 1½l, 1l. 1m 13.10s. a 2.60s (18 Ran).
SR: 48/42/32/29/25/-/ (The Step Inn Racing Syndicate), Bernard Lawlor

2038 Independent Newspapers Pretty Polly Stakes (Group 2) (3-y-o and up) £26,250 1¼m. . . . . (3:30)

1048* TAKAROUNA (USA) 3-8-8 J P Murtagh (11) *hld up, str hold early, swtchd lft und 2 fs out, prog to ld last 50 yards.* . . . . (7 to 1) 1
MARKET BOOSTER (USA) 4-9-11 M J Kinane (5) *dsptd ld one furlong, wl plcd, prog to chal o'r 2 out, sn led and rdn, ct last 50 yards.* . . . . (9 to 2) 2
1200[3] DANSE ROYALE (Ire) 3-8-8 L Piggott (10) *trkd ldr, rdn one and a half fs out, not much room, some prog ins last, styd on one pace cl hme.* . . . . (9 to 2) 3
1198[6] SPECIAL PAGEANT (Ire) 3-8-8 K J Manning (6) *led till rdn and hdd 2 fs out, kpt on wl und pres.* . . . . (20 to 1) 4
1525[2] ROYAL BALLERINA (Ire) (bl) 3-8-8 W J O'Connor (1) *wl plcd, rdn 2 fs out, ran on ins last.* . . . . (5 to 2 fav) 5
1200 EUROSTORM (USA) 3-8-8 P V Gilson (8) *hld up, gd prog 4 fs out, rdn 2 out, bumped o'r one out, no extr.* . . (9 to 1) 6
1200[5] TARAKANA (USA) 3-8-8 R Hughes (3) *rear, prog 2 fs out, rdn one and a half out, kpt on.* . . . . (12 to 1) 7
1525[9] GISARNE (USA) 3-8-8 P Shanahan (9) *mid-div, rdn 2 fs out, some prog one out, wknd ins last.* . . . . (9 to 1) 8
1525[8] MARILLETTE (USA) 3-8-11 G Hind (4) *al rear, rdn 2 and a half fs out, not quicken.* . . . . (7 to 1) 9
1511[4] RIYOOM (USA) 3-8-8 C Roche (2) *mid-div, rdn 3 and a half fs out, sn wknd.* . . . . (12 to 1) 10
Dist: Nk, ½l, ½l, sht-hd, nk, 1½l. 2m 6.00s. a 3.20s (10 Ran).
SR: 62/78/60/59/58/57/54/-/-/ (H H Aga Khan), John M Oxx

2039 Drogheda Memorial Hospital Handicap (0-100 3-y-o and up) £6,400 1m . . . . (4:00)

1549[5] READY (Ire) [-] 3-9-1 W J Supple (12) . . . . (7 to 1) 1
1514[2] FAYDINI (Ire) [-] 4-9-4 (4*) P Carberry (7) . . . . (7 to 1) 2
1202[6] SWEET NASHA (Ire) [-] 4-9-1 P V Gilson (14) . . . . . . (14 to 1) 3
1553* TRYARRA (Ire) [-] 3-8-4 (4ex) N G McCullagh (2) . . . . (7 to 1) 4
1609* TAWAR (Ire) [-] 3-8-12 R Hughes (3) . . . . (7 to 2 fav) 5
1549[3] GLOWING VALUE (Ire) [-] (bl) 3-9-1 J P Murtagh (11) . . . . (10 to 1) 6
1611[5] SECOND REVOLUTION (Ire) [-] 4-8-11 C Roche (5) (8 to 1) 7
1856[5] SEEK THE FAITH (USA) [-] (bl) 4-8-13 (5ex) M J Kinane (1) . . . . (8 to 1) 8
1823* ALALJA (Ire) [-] 3-9-4 L Piggott (13) . . . . (5 to 1) 9
1440 TINA'S CHARM (Ire) [-] 4-8-1 (4*) W J Smith (4) . . . . (25 to 1) 10
1645[5] NORDIC SAINT (Ire) [-] 4-7-10 Joanna Morgan (9) (10 to 1) 11
WILD SURPRISE (Ire) [-] 5-8-5 (8*) R T Fitzpatrick (6) . . . . (20 to 1) 12
NATIVE PORTRAIT [-] 6-7-5 (2*) D G O'Shea (10) . . (25 to 1) 13
1445[7] YONOKA (Fr) [-] 4-8-3 J F Egan (8) . . . . (33 to 1) 14
Dist: ½l, 2l, sht-hd, nk, ¾l, sht-hd. 1m 41.40s. a 4.80s (14 Ran).
SR: 29/34/21/9/16/17/12/-/-/ (Mrs Anne Coughlan), Kevin Prendergast

2040 Camp Tower Handicap (0-100 3-y-o) £4,140 1m 3f. . . . . (4:30)

1823[2] KIROV PREMIERE [-] 9-2 C Roche (10) . . . . (4 to 1) 1
1963[2] DAHLIA'S BEST (USA) [-] 7-12 (8*) R T Fitzpatrick (4) . . . . (14 to 1) 2
1553[4] MICKS DELIGHT (Ire) [-] 8-7 R Hughes (8) . . . . (9 to 2) 3
1466[2] HOPESVILLE (Ire) [-] 8-2 W J Supple (9) . . . . (12 to 1) 4
1572[4] FLAME OF PERSIA (Ire) [-] 9-5 W J O'Connor (5) . . . (8 to 1) 5
1139[9] DARK SWAN (Ire) [-] 7-5 (2*) D G O'Shea (7) . . . . . . (20 to 1) 6
898[4] GENERAL CHAOS (Ire) [-] 8-6 P V Gilson (1) . . . . (9 to 1) 7
1334[8] TARTAN LADY (Ire) [-] 9-2 S Craine (6) . . . . (14 to 1) 8
1199 SHAIKALA (Ire) [-] (bl) 8-12 J P Murtagh (2) . . . . (11 to 1) 9
850[3] LUSTRINO (USA) [-] 8-12 M J Kinane (3) . . . . (2 to 1 fav) 10
Dist: 1l, 2l, 3l, ½l. 2m 22.70s. (10 Ran).
(John L Wood), J S Bolger

2041 Anna Livia Handicap (0-80 3-y-o and up) £4,140 1m 1f. . . . . (5:00)

1856* WANDERING THOUGHTS (Ire) [-] 4-8-4 (6*,9ex) J A Heffernan (4) . . . . (6 to 1) 1
1163* SAIBOT (USA) [-] 4-9-8 M J Kinane (15) . . . . (7 to 4 fav) 2
1385* TINERANA (Ire) [-] 3-8-8 L Piggott (11) . . . . (4 to 1) 3
1569[3] RASSETTE (Ire) [-] 3-7-9 Joanna Morgan (13) . . . . . (14 to 1) 4
1856[6] DESERT CALM (Ire) [-] 4-9-7 (6*) B J Walsh (16) . . . (20 to 1) 5
RATHBRIDES JOY [-] 6-8-9 W J Supple (6) . . . . (16 to 1) 6
851[4] MAY WE DANCE (Ire) [-] 4-8-1 (2*) D G O'Shea (3) (25 to 1) 7
1569 SIGHTSEER (Ire) [-] 4-7-12 J F Egan (12) . . . . (66 to 1) 8
1574[2] COOLRAIN LADY (Ire) [-] (bl) 3-8-8 S Craine (14) . . (10 to 1) 9
KEDWICK (Ire) [-] 4-9-9 N G McCullagh (5) . . . . (25 to 1) 10
1794[2] MAYFIELD PRINCE (Ire) [-] 4-9-6 (6*) B Bowens (7) (10 to 1) 11
1252[7] NO DIPLOMACY (Ire) [-] 4-8-6 L O'Shea (10) . . . . . . (50 to 1) 12
1106[8] TEXAS FRIDAY (Ire) [-] 3-8-0 (2*) R M Burke (2) . . . . (66 to 1) 13
996 SIR ALWAH (Ire) [-] 4-8-3 R So (8) . . . . (66 to 1) 14
1440 YOUR UNCLE STANLEY (Ire) [-] 4-8-11 C Roche (1) (25 to 1) 15
1386[3] ICEFLOW (Fr) [-] 3-8-7 P V Gilson (9) . . . . (12 to 1) 16
Dist: 1l, 1l, 2½l, 4l. 1m 52.60s. a 3.10s (16 Ran).
SR: 49/59/43/25/49/-/ (W Mythen), A P O'Brien

DONCASTER (good to firm)
Saturday June 26th
Going Correction: PLUS 0.15 sec. per fur.

2042 Bentley Selling Stakes Class G (2-y-o) £2,553 6f. (6:15)

1706[9] ALLLEGSNOBRAIN 8-11 D Holland (6) *made all, drvn alng to go clr appr fnl furlong, ran on wl.* . . . . (3 to 1 op 8 to 1 tchd 10 to 1) 1
1413[6] UP THE MARINERS (Ire) 8-1 (5*) J Tate (5) *broke smartly to press wnr thrght, drvn alng o'r one furlong out sn outpcd.* . . . . (33 to 1 op 25 to 1) 2
1413* LEFT STRANDED 8-11 Paul Eddery (11) *nvr far away, rdn last 2 fs, sn outpcd.* . . . . (2 to 1 on op 6 to 4 on tchd 11 to 8 on) 3
1741[4] REAL POPCORN (Ire) 8-6 J Carroll (1) *chsd ldrs, effrt on outsd o'r 2 fs out, one pace.* . . . . (10 to 1 op 4 to 1 tchd 11 to 1) 4
MYSTICAL MICKEY (Ire) 8-11 Dean McKeown (2) *chsd alng in midfield, ran green hfwy, rng on finish.* . . . . (25 to 1 op 14 to 1) 5
1758 KNAYTON LAD (Ire) 8-8 (3*) S Maloney (4) *reminders aftr strt, ran green hfwy, nvr dngrs.* . . . (33 to 1 op 20 to 1) 6
908 EXPRESS LINE 8-6 S Whitworth (9) *jinked lft leaving stalls, drvn alng to go pace, no imprsn.* . . . . (50 to 1 op 25 to 1) 7
GOODWINCOPLEY 8-4 (7*) C Munday (3) *impeded leaving stalls, nvr able to reco'r.* . . . . (50 to 1 op 25 to 1) 8
1863[7] SNUGFIT ANNIE 8-6 T Lucas (10) *sluggish strt, chsd ldr for o'r 3 fs, eased whn btn.* . . . . (12 to 1 op 4 to 1) 9
900[9] CLASSIC MISS (Ire) 8-6 F Norton (7) *sluggish strt, chsd alng and nvr a dngr.* . . . . (50 to 1 op 33 to 1) 10

CRACKLEY LANE 8-11 Alex Greaves (8) *squeezed out leaving stalls, nvr able to reco'r*....... (50 to 1 op 33 to 1) 11
Dist: 7l, hd, 6l, 3½l, ½l, 2½l, hd, ¾l, 3½l, 3l. 1m 16.42s. a 5.02s (11 Ran).
SR: 15/-/-/-/-/-/ (M Woodall), P D Evans

2043 Castle W.M.C. Stayers Handicap Class E (0-70 4-y-o and up) £3,366 1 ¾m 132yds.................... (6:45)

1321[8] WHITE RIVER [32] 7-7-9 A Mackay (5) *settled off the pace, plenty to do o'r 3 fs out, str run to ld last 50 yards.* .... (11 to 1 op 10 to 1) 1
1601[4] SHAFFIC (Fr) [55] 6-9-4 Dean McKeown (6) *wtd wth, took clr order aftr 6 fs, led o'r 3 out, hdd and rdn last 50 yards, no extr*..........................(11 to 2 op 4 to 1) 2
1654[2] QUALITAIR SOUND (Ire) [42] 5-8-5 P Robinson (9) *tucked away in midfield, drvn up to chal o'r 2 fs out, kpt on same pace*..........................(11 to 2 op 9 to 2) 3
1654[3] BILBERRY [44] 4-8-7 J Lowe (2) *settled gng wl, effrt and drvn alng o'r 2 fs out, styd on one pace.* .... (11 to 2 op 4 to 1) 4
1967[2] KINOKO [61] 5-9-5 (5*) A Garth (10) *patiently rdn, improved on outsd to chal o'r 2 fs out, ridden and one pace*..........................(5 to 1 fav tchd 11 to 2) 5
904[9] DUGGAN [45] 6-8-8 D Holland (12) *nvr far away, effrt and drvn alng last 3 fs, no imprsn*......(12 to 1 op 10 to 1) 6
1476[2] BOLD AMBITION [41] 5-8-4 F Norton (11) *trkd ldr, nosed ahead brifely o'r 2 fs out, fdd appr fnl furlong.* .... (11 to 1 op 10 to 1) 7
1702[8] FANATICAL (USA) [40] 7-8-0 (3*) S Maloney (8) *settled in rear, effrt entering strt, outpcd last 2 fs.* .... (20 to 1 op 14 to 1) 8
1336[9] HORIZON (Ire) [55] (bl) 5-9-4 S Whitworth (3) *dictated pace, quickened aftr 6 fs, hdd o'r 3 out, sn btn.* .... (11 to 1 op 10 to 1) 9
1531* JAMES IS SPECIAL (Ire) [53] 5-9-2 J Quinn (7) *trkd ldg bunch, effrt entering strt, fdd o'r 2 fs out*.......(6 to 1) 10
BRUSQUE (USA) [32] 9-7-2 (7*) Claire Balding (4) *wtd wth, effrt and drvn alng appr strt, nvr dngrs*.......(33 to 1) 11
1112 ESCAPE TALK [30] 6-7-1[1] (7*) D Wright (1) *trkd ldg pair, struggling to hold pl aftr 6 fs, sn lost tch*...... (66 to 1) 12
Dist: 2l, ½l, 2½l, ¾l, 4l, 2½l, 5l, 8l, 2½l, nk. 3m 15.80s. a 11.30s (12 Ran).
SR: -/9/-/-/7/-/ (C Thomas), D Haydn Jones

2044 EBF Lonsdale Maiden Fillies Stakes Class D (2-y-o) £3,622 7f........(7:15)

OUBECK BLUE 8-11 R Cochrane (1) *sluggish strt, reco'red hfwy, quickened ahead over 2 fs out, ran on strly fnl furlong*..........................(20 to 1 op 16 to 1) 1
NIGHT SNOW 8-11 M Hills (7) *dsptd ld, ev ch and drvn alng o'r 2 fs out, kpt on same pace.* (10 to 1 op 6 to 1) 2
SAMHEH (USA) 8-11 W Carson (5) *unruly in stalls, missed break, outpcd hfwy, not clr run o'r 2 out, nvr nrr.* ....(7 to 2 on op 9 to 4 on tchd 2 to 1 on) 3
1863[3] GREEK NIGHT OUT (Ire) 8-11 Dean McKeown (3) *slight ld for o'r 4 fs, kpt on same pace*......(10 to 1 tchd 8 to 1) 4
GILBOA 8-11 P Robinson (2) *pressed ldg trio, hrd at work o'r one furlong out, kpt on*......... (10 to 1 op 6 to 1) 5
CHILTERN SHOW 8-11 A Mackay (6) *sluggish strt, outpcd and drvn alng hfwy, no imprsn*... (33 to 1 op 20 to 1) 6
DANCING ANGEL 8-11 S Whitworth (4) *sluggish strt, struggling frm hfwy*...............(33 to 1 op 20 to 1) 7
Dist: 4l, 1l, ½l, nk, 4l, 8l. 1m 30.50s. a 7.10s (7 Ran).
SR: 6/-/-/-/ (Mrs A Birkett), E Weymes

2045 Yorkshire Post Handicap Class D (0-85 3-y-o and up) £3,882 1m... (7:45)

1398 BIG BLUE [71] 4-8-11 (3*) B Doyle (7) *chsd ldg quartet, effrt and edgd lft o'r 2 fs out, weaved through to ld last strd.* .... (7 to 1 op 11 to 2) 1
1730[5] LANGTRY LADY [72] (v) 7-9-1 R Cochrane (2) *patiently rdn, improved on ins last 2 fs, led cl hme, ct post.* ....(7 to 2 tchd 9 to 2) 2
1768 BUZZARDS BELLBUOY [72] 4-9-1 J Quinn (6) *nvr far away, drvn to draw level o'r one furlong out, one pace cl hme*............(3 to 1 fav tchd 11 to 4 and 7 to 2) 3
1900[5] AMLAK (USA) [50] 4-7-7 G Bardwell (3) *trkd ldr, hrd rdn to ld o'r one furlong out, hdd cl hme.* .... (7 to 2 op 6 to 1 tchd 13 to 2) 4
1777[7] GOLDEN CHIP (Ire) [73] 5-8-9 (7*) V Halliday (8) *tried to make all, quickened for hme o'r 3 fs out, hdd over one out, one pace*...... .... (7 to 1 op 11 to 2) 5
1592[7] LEAP IN THE DARK (Ire) [51] 4-7-8[1] J Lowe (4) *al hndy, hrd at work 2 fs out, one pace*........ (16 to 1 op 10 to 1) 6
1530[9] WILL OF STEEL [85] 4-10-0 Dean McKeown (1) *hld up and beh, swtchd outsd and shaken up o'r 3 fs out, nvr nr to chal*...................................... (7 to 1 op 11 to 2) 7
1939[8] COSTA VERDE [78] 3-8-6 (5*) A Garth (5) *chsd ldrs, hrd at work o'r 2 fs out, sn btn*.......... (16 to 1 op 14 to 1) 8
Dist: Hd, hd, ½l, 2½l, 1½l, 4l, 10l. 1m 44.36s. a 7.66s (8 Ran).
SR: 3/3/2/-/-/ (Mrs Celia Miller), C E Brittain

2046 Great Yorkshire Radio Rating Related Maiden Stakes Class D (3-y-o and up) £3,114 1¼m 60yds.............. (8:15)

584[7] SAFIR (USA) 3-8-9 W Carson (1) *made most, drvn alng to quicken o'r 2 fs out, hld on wl ins fnl furlong.* .... (11 to 4 op 7 to 2 tchd 2 to 1) 1
1617[3] EL GAHAR 3-8-9 W Ryan (4) *patiently rdn, pld outsd to chal appr fnl furlong, ridden and kpt on same pace.* ....(5 to 4 on op 6 to 4 on tchd Evens) 2
825[6] COMPLETE MADNESS 3-8-9 M Hills (2) *trkd ldr, rdn to draw level o'r one furlong out, kpt on und pres.* ....(3 to 1 op 9 to 4) 3
1340[4] SASSIVER (USA) 3-8-9 S Perks (3) *nvr far away, effrt and drvn alng 2 fs out, eased whn btn fnl furlong.* .... (16 to 1 op 20 to 1 tchd 14 to 1) 4
Dist: ½l, ¾l, 3½l. 2m 19.34s. a 12.64s (4 Ran).
(Hamdan Al-Maktoum), J L Dunlop

2047 Go Racing In Yorkshire Maiden Handicap Class E (0-70 3-y-o and up) £3,236 6f............................. (8:45)

1537[3] JOIN THE CLAN [45] 4-9-5 Dean McKeown (5) *confidently rdn, swtchd ins to improve o'r one furlong out, sn led, ran on strly*...................(7 to 2 fav tchd 3 to 1) 1
1696[3] HARCLIFF [54] (bl) 4-10-0 J Lowe (14) *sluggish strt, drvn into midfield hfwy, ran on und pres fnl furlong, nvr nrr*.................. (9 to 1 op 10 to 1 tchd 11 to 1) 2
1737 TUMBLING (USA) [40] 5-9-0 W Carson (13) *al hndy, led aftr one and a half fs till o'r one furlong out, one pace.* .... (11 to 1 op 8 to 1) 3
1419[2] SILVER STONE BOY [34] 5-8-8 S Webster (7) *al frnt rnk, gng wl hfwy, rdn and not quicken o'r one furlong out.* ....(9 to 1 op 7 to 1) 4
1419[8] COLMAR [36] (bl) 3-8-2 Dale Gibson (3) *settled midfield, swtchd outsd to improve o'r one furlong out, kpt on.* ....(33 to 1) 5
1273[6] RED ADMIRAL [52] 3-9-4 R Cochrane (2) *reared and nrly uns rdr leaving stalls, swtchd to improve last 2 fs, fnshd wl*.......................... (9 to 1 op 7 to 1) 6
1534[9] BLAKES BEAU [48] 3-9-0 M Birch (8) *pressed ldrs till wknd and eased o'r one furlong out.* .... (10 to 1 op 12 to 1 tchd 16 to 1) 7
1300[3] FLASHMAN [58] (bl) 3-9-10 S Perks (1) *wth ldrs, ev ch and drvn alng o'r one furlong out, no extr.* .... (11 to 1 op 8 to 1) 8
1577[3] MISS OFFIE [43] 3-8-4 (5*) A Garth (4) *missed break, steady hdwy last 2 fs, nvr nrr*........... (20 to 1 op 16 to 1) 9
1655[5] FRIENDLY SMILE [50] 3-8-11 (5*) J Tate (17) *chsd ldg bunch, effrt and swtchd outsd 2 fs out, no imprsn.* ....(11 to 1 op 12 to 1 tchd 14 to 1 and 10 to 1) 10
1674 JOELLISE [35] (bl) 3-8-1 L Charnock (16) *chsd ldrs to hfwy, sn btn*...(33 to 1) 11
1589 MISS BRIGHTSIDE [41] 5-9-1 D Holland (10) *led for one and a half fs, styd hndy till fdd o'r one out.* .... (10 to 1 op 8 to 1) 12
1740[3] THE FED [52] 3-9-4 A Culhane (11) *speed to chase ldrs 4 fs, sn btn*................ (11 to 2 op 5 to 1 tchd 6 to 1) 13
962 CIZARD (Ire) [35] 3-8-1 J Quinn (15) *beh and drvn alng hfwy, nvr a factor*..........................(33 to 1) 14
SHOTLEY AGAIN [46] 3-8-12 Alex Greaves (9) *chsd alng to go pace hfwy, nvr a dngr*......................(33 to 1) 15
1316 FAIRFORD [44] 4-9-4 J Carroll (6) *missed break, nvr able to reco'r*.. (25 to 1) 16
456 BLACK BOY (Ire) [44] (bl) 4-8-13 (5*) O Pears (12) *speed to hfwy, sn btn*......................(20 to 1 op 16 to 1) 17
Dist: 2l, 1½l, hd, ¾l, 2l, 1½l, nk, ½l, 1½l, nk. 1m 15.86s. a 4.46s (17 Ran).
SR: 35/36/16/9/-/8/-/7/-/ (J Redden), Mrs N Macauley

LINGFIELD (good to firm)
Saturday June 26th
Going Correction: MINUS 0.30 sec. per fur.

2048 Spinal Injuries Association Apprentice Handicap Class E (0-70 3-y-o and up) £2,534 1¾m................ (6:00)

1827[8] WESTERN DYNASTY [68] 7-9-11 (3*) P McCabe (10) *trkd ldrs, led 5 fs out, sn clr, easily.* ....(7 to 2 op 4 to 1 tchd 9 to 2) 1
1607[7] DISPUTED CALL (USA) [61] 4-8-11 (10*) M Henry (3) *led aftr one furlong till hdd 5 out, chsd wnr, one pace.* .... (12 to 1 op 10 to 1 tchd 14 to 1) 2
1752[2] DOYCE [62] 4-9-0 (8*) Sarah Thompson (9) *beh, hdwy o'r 2 fs out, styd on*..................(5 to 2 fav op 7 to 4) 3
1775[3] KOVALEVSKIA [33] 8-7-0[1] (8*) Sharon Millard (1) *beh, effrt o'r 2 fs out, styd on*.....(13 to 2 op 7 to 2 tchd 7 to 1) 4
1746 POETIC FORM (Ire) [50] 3-7-7 G Mitchell (2) *trkd ldrs, one pace fnl 3 fs*......................(14 to 1 op 12 to 1) 5
1772[3] MILIYEL [45] 4-8-0 (5*) J Dennis (6) *hld up in rear, rdn 3 fs out, no imprsn*.......................... (12 to 1 op 10 to 1) 6
420[7] ALICE'S MIRROR [40] 4-8-0 N Varley (4) *chsd ldrs till wknd o'r 3 fs out*.......................... (25 to 1 op 16 to 1) 7
1318[7] CHILD STAR (Fr) [49] 4-8-4 (5*) S McCarthy (5) *led one furlong, cl up til wknd o'r 2 out.* .... (14 to 1 op 10 to 1 tchd 16 to 1) 8

1820 MOLLY SPLASH [51] 6-8-3 (8*) Michael Hunt (7) *hld up in rear, rdn alng hfwy, nvr dngrs*.... (14 to 1 op 10 to 1) 9
1731[6] SHIRL [33] 4-7-2 (5*) C Teague (11) *beh, effrt hfwy, sn btn*. .... (8 to 1 op 10 to 1) 10
Dist: 6l, ½l, ¾l, ½l, ½l, 3½l, 8l, 3l, sht-hd. 3m 6.90s. a 11.90s (10 Ran).
(M F Kentish), M J Ryan

2049 Tattersalls Maiden Auction Series Stakes Qualifier Class E (2-y-o) £2,967 5f. .... (7:00)

1640[4] EIGHTEEN TWELVE 8-9 J Reid (6) *hld up in tch, effrt 2 fs out, quickened to ld ins last, ran on wl*. .... (Evens fav op 5 to 4) 1
1773[2] RESONANT 8-12 G Duffield (8) *cl up, led o'r 2 fs out, hdd ins last, ran on*........ (3 to 1 op 9 to 4) 2
1401[4] SPRING LOADED 8-6 T Quinn (9) *led til hdd o'r 2 fs out, one pace*........ (6 to 1 op 8 to 1 tchd 10 to 1) 3
PADDY'S RICE 8-6 A Munro (3) *chsd ldrs, outpcd 2 fs out, shaken up and kpt on wl fnl furlong*. .... (33 to 1 op 20 to 1) 4
1665[3] THORNY BISHOP 8-6 S O'Gorman (10) *chsd ldrs till outpcd frm 2 fs out*........ (33 to 1 op 25 to 1) 5
PACIOLI 8-6 J Williams (4) *nvr on terms*. .... (33 to 1 op 16 to 1) 6
1523[7] ZORAHAYDA (Fr) 8-5 B Rouse (5) *nvr on terms*. .... (40 to 1 op 50 to 1) 7
1403[8] ZOLICA 8-1 T Sprake (1) *in tch, rdn alng hfwy, sn outpcd*...... (15 to 2 op 10 to 1 tchd 12 to 1 and 7 to 1) 8
HARLEQUIN WALK (Ire) 8-1 A McGlone (2) *sn outpcd*. .... (50 to 1 op 33 to 1) 9
1481[9] SELHURSTPARK FLYER (Ire) 8-6 G Carter (7) *pld hrd, hld up in tch, lost action o'r 2 fs out, virtually pulled up*. .... (16 to 1 op 14 to 1 tchd 20 to 1) 10
Dist: ¾l, 4l, 3½l, 2l, 1l, hd, 2½l, 3½l, 30l. 58.66s. a 1.76s (10 Ran).
SR: 30/30/8/-/-/-/ (Mrs L M Davies), R Hannon

2050 Heinz Handicap Class D (0-80 3-y-o and up) £3,882 5f. .... (7:30)

1010[3] PRESS THE BELL [73] 3-9-9 G Carter (10) *made all, rdn out*........ (4 to 1 fav op 5 to 1) 1
1352[5] CALL TO THE BAR (Ire) [59] 4-9-2 A Clark (9) *chsd ldrs, hrd rdn o'r one furlong out, ran on ins last*. .... (6 to 1 op 5 to 1) 2
1918[2] TRIOMING [52] 7-8-9 N Adams (5) *al prmnt, rdn o'r one furlong out, kpt on*........ (11 to 2 op 5 to 1) 3
1881[7] MARTINA [64] (bl) 5-9-7 K Darley (1) *chsd ldrs, pushed alng hfwy, outpcd frm o'r one furlong out*. .... (12 to 1 op 10 to 1) 4
1903[4] ISLAND KNIGHT (Ire) [67] 4-9-10 G Duffield (2) *in tch, rdn alng 2 fs out, no imprsn*........ (7 to 1 op 10 to 1) 5
1860[4] SHADES OF JADE [44] 5-8-1 S O'Gorman (8) *slwly into strd, nvr wnt pace*........ (5 to 1 op 10 to 1) 6
1728[6] STOCKTINA [42] 6-7-13[1] T Sprake (3) *outpcd*. .... (14 to 1 op 12 to 1) 7
1874[8] ANDY JACK [46] (bl) 4-8-3[1] W Woods (4) *cl up til wknd 2 fs out*........ (50 to 1 op 33 to 1) 8
1728[3] SERIOUS HURRY [58] 5-9-1 T Quinn (7) *pushed alng in tch, beh frm hfwy*........ (7 to 1) 9
1918* SEA-DEER [63] 4-9-6 (7ex) A Munro (6) *hld up in rear, stumbled and uns rdr appr 2 fs out*. (6 to 1 op 5 to 1) ur
Dist: ¾l, 1½l, 4l, ¾l, 1l, ¾l, 1½l, 5l. 58.36s. a 1.46s (10 Ran).
SR: 50/40/27/23/23/-/ (Sydney Mason), J Berry

2051 Sporting Life Rating Related Maiden Stakes Class F (3-y-o and up) £2,562 2m. .... (8:30)

1861[3] BILJAN (USA) 3-8-5 T Quinn (3) *set slow pace, quickened 4 fs out, hdd and edgd rght ins last, hrd rdn to ld ag'n cl hme*........ (7 to 2 on op 7 to 2 tchd 3 to 1 on) 1
1880[7] ASSEMBLY DANCER 6-9-10 N Adams (2) *rcd in last pl, wnt second o'r 3 fs out, led ins last till hdd cl hme*. .... (14 to 1 op 12 to 1 tchd 16 to 1 and 20 to 1) 2
1700[2] CARFAX 8-9-10 W Newnes (1) *trkd wnr till outpcd frm o'r 3 fs out*........ (5 to 2 tchd 7 to 2) 3
Dist: Hd, 7l. 3m 55.21s. a 31.71s (3 Ran).
(Fahd Salman), P F I Cole

LINGFIELD (A.W) (std) Saturday June 26th

Going Correction: MINUS 0.25 sec. per fur.

2052 Heinz Soups Selling Handicap Class G (0-60 3-y-o and up) £2,432 1½m .... (6:30)

1902 WITH GUSTO [31] 6-8-12 J Williams (3) *sn rdn alng in rear, hdwy o'r 3 fs out, led 2 out, soon clr, easily*. .... (9 to 1 op 14 to 1 tchd 8 to 1) 1
1353[5] ROMANIAN (Ire) [43] 5-9-10 T Quinn (2) *rdn alng thrght, cld o'r 3 fs out, one pace appr 2 out*. .... (9 to 4 fav op 11 to 4 tchd 3 to 1) 2
1731[7] PIE HATCH (Ire) [47] 4-10-0 G Duffield (7) *sn shaken up to track ldrs, led 8 fs out, hdd 2 out, one pace*. .... (6 to 1 op 4 to 1) 3
2012[3] BRONZE RUNNER [18] (bl) 9-7-13 T Sprake (6) *trkd ldrs, rdn and one pace fnl 3 fs*........ (6 to 1 tchd 7 to 1) 4
1712[7] RED JACK (Ire) [27] 4-8-8 A McGlone (9) *pushed alng to chase ldrs, rdn and wknd 4 fs out*. .... (10 to 1 op 8 to 1 tchd 12 to 1) 5
1493* STAPLEFORD LASS [48] 3-9-0 W Woods (1) *slwly into strd, beh, rdn and btn o'r 3 fs out*........ (7 to 2 op 5 to 2) 6
1414 RUBY DAVIES [26] 7-8-7 R Street (5) *mid-div, hdwy to track ldrs hfwy, rdn 5 fs out, sn btn, tld off*. .... (10 to 1 op 20 to 1 tchd 25 to 1) 7
1902 OSGATHORPE [32] (v) 6-8-13 B Rouse (4) *led aftr one furlong, hdd 8 fs out, wknd 5 out, tld off*. .... (25 to 1 op 20 to 1) 8
1148 WEALTHYWOO [38] (bl) 3-8-4 A Munro (8) *rcd freely, led o'r one furlong, cl up til wknd over 4 out, tld off*. .... (33 to 1 op 20 to 1) 9
Dist: 7l, 1½l, 4l, 6l, 5l, 20l, 3½l, 2½l. 2m 34.00s. a 4.70s (9 Ran).
SR: 21/19/20/-/-/-/ (M D Brunton), K O Cunningham-Brown

2053 Silver Anniversary Claiming Stakes Class F (3-y-o and up) £2,521 1m (8:00)

737 KNOCK TO ENTER (USA) 5-9-5 J Williams (5) *in cl tch, led hfwy, quickened clr appr 2 fs out, not extended*. .... (5 to 4 fav op 6 to 4 tchd Evens and 6 to 4) 1
1414[4] OUR EDDIE (v) 4-8-9 T Quinn (4) *led aftr one furlong till hdd hfwy, ev ch 3 fs out, rdn and one pace frm 2 out*. .... (12 to 1 op 10 to 1 tchd 16 to 1) 2
1701* RAGING THUNDER (bl) 3-8-9 K Darley (3) *in tch, cld hfwy, outpcd appr 2 fs out, rallied und pres*. .... (2 to 1 op 6 to 4 tchd 9 to 4 and 5 to 2) 3+
1745[6] ABSOLUTELY FACT (USA) 3-8-0 G Duffield (2) *cl up, ev ch 3 fs out, one pace frm o'r 2 out*. .... (7 to 2 op 4 to 1 tchd 11 to 2) 3+
STARLIGHT FLYER (bl) 6-9-0 N Adams (1) *led one furlong, cl up, lost tch o'r 3 out, tld off*. .... (17 to 2 op 12 to 1 tchd 16 to 1 and 8 to 1) 5
Dist: 5l, 2½l, dd-ht, 10l. 1m 38.48s. a 2.28s (5 Ran).
SR: 41/16/8/-/-/ (R B Payne), M Williams

LONGCHAMP (FR) (firm) Saturday June 26th

2054 Prix de Malleret (Group 2) (3-y-o) £35,842 1½m. .... (2:30)

1525[5] WEMYSS BIGHT 9-0 T Jarnet (1) *second strt, led 2 fs out, ran on wl, imprsv*........ (6 to 5 fav) 1
1506[2] DIAMONAKA (Fr) 8-9 C Asmussen (5) *led till 2 fs out, hrd rdn and one pace ins last*........ (2 to 1) 2
BRIGHT MOUNTAIN (USA) 8-9 D Boeuf (2) *3rd strt, rdn 2 fs out, kpt on one pace*........ (39 to 10) 3
1722[4] CORRAZONA (USA) 8-9 O Doleuze (4) *4th strt, some late hdwy*........ (24 to 10) 4
1722 ACCOMMODATING (USA) 8-9 E Saint-Martin (3) *nvr dngrs*. .... (2 to 1) 5
Dist: 4l, 2l, ¾l, 1½l. 2m 28.00s. b 1.10s (5 Ran).
SR: 75/62/58/56/53/ (K Abdulla), A Fabre

2055 Prix de la Porte Maillot (Group 3) (3-y-o and up) £23,895 7f. .... (3:30)

1368[2] BORODISLEW (USA) 3-8-5 O Doleuze (3) *led, quickened 2 fs out, hrd rdn fnl furlong, ct nr line*........ (15 to 2) 1+
1086[5] NIDD (USA) 3-8-5 T Jarnet (5) *4th strt, rdn and hdwy 2 fs out, chlgd one out, ct nr line*........ (39 to 10) 1+
1723[2] SHANGHAI (USA) 4-9-2 C Asmussen (2) *5th strt, not clr run o'r 2 fs out and over one out, fnshd wl, jst fld*. .... (5 to 4 on) 3
1283[2] ACTEUR FRANCAIS (USA) 5-9-2 S Guillot (4) *3rd strt, ev ch ins fnl furlong, no extr cl hme*........ (39 to 10) 4
1289[3] CRACK REGIMENT (USA) 5-9-2 E Saint-Martin (1) *hld up and last strt, hdwy 2 fs out, no extr ins last*... (11 to 1) 5
1546[2] TRESOR DU MESNIL (Fr) 3-8-8 G Mosse (6) *second strt, rdn and wknd 2 fs out*........ (82 to 10) 6
Dist: Dd-ht, nose, 1l, ¾l, 6l. 1m 19.70s. a 0.20s (6 Ran).
SR: 57/57/67/64/62/36/ (John T L Jones Jr & K Abdulla), Mrs C Head & A Fabre

2056 Prix du Pont de Flandre (Handicap) (4-y-o and up) £21,505 1m 7f 110yds (4:00)

DOUBLE BLASH 4-8-12 F Head, ... 1
MANHATTAN RIVER (Fr) 5-8-13 J Guerin, ... 2
VERY KING (Ire) 5-8-8[1] E Legrix, ... 3
1809[9] SWEET GLOW (Fr) 6-9-4 G Mosse, *mid-div, cld hfwy, second strt, ev ch wl o'r one furlong out, sn rdn and wknd*. 9
Dist: Nk, 1l, ¾l, nose, sht-nk, sht-hd, 1l, 2½l, 2l. 3m 17.50s. a 1.00s (15 Ran).
SR: 42/42/36/44/ (Prince Y Saud), E Lellouche

NEWCASTLE (good (races 1,2), good to

firm (3,4,5,6,7,8))
Saturday June 26th
Going Correction: MINUS 0.40 sec. per fur. (races 1,3,5,8), PLUS 0.05 (2,4,6,7)

2057 International Spinal Research Trust Handicap Stakes Class E (0-65 3-y-o and up) £2,560 1m..............(1:30)

1799^{2} PRIDE OF PENDLE [47] 4-8-12 K Darley (9) *beh, swtchd ins and gd hdwy 2 and a half fs out, sn rdn and styd on strly inside last to ld last 100 yards*.........(7 to 1 co-fav op 6 to 1) 1

1260^{9} STRAW THATCH [47] 4-8-12 J Carroll (6) *chsd ldrs, hdwy 2 fs out, rdn to chal and not much room entering fnl furlong, ran on*.................. (33 to 1 op 25 to 1) 2

1707^{7} BALLYRANTER [44] (v) 4-8-9 J Quinn (4) *led, clr 2 and a half fs out, sn rdn, edgd rght, hdd and no extr ins last*. ....(20 to 1) 3

1566^{3} MAROWINS [46] 4-8-11 N Carlisle (18) *beh, rapid hdwy on outer 2 fs out, staying on whn hmpd ins last, kpt on*. ....(11 to 1 op 12 to 1 tchd 10 to 1) 4

1591 GUESSTIMATION (USA) [47] 4-8-12 G Bardwell (12) *al prmnt, rdn to chal 2 fs out, edgd rght, hmpd and wknd entering last*................................ (20 to 1) 5

1737^{4} LADY DONOGHUE (USA) [53] 4-9-4 L Dettori (10) *chsd ldrs, rdn 2 fs out, sn one pace*................ (7 to 1 co-fav) 6

1592 MAJAL (Ire) [61] 4-9-7 (5*) J Tate (5) *chsd ldr, rdn 2 fs out, sn one pace*..................... (25 to 1 op 20 to 1) 7

1783^{3} DELPIOMBO [63] 7-10-0 M Birch (16) *in tch, hdwy 3 fs, rdn 2 furlongs out and sn one pace*...... (9 to 1 op 8 to 1) 8

1737^{8} MALCESINE (Ire) [44] 4-8-9 J Fortune (20) *prmnt, effrt on outer and ev ch 2 fs out, sn rdn and wknd*. .... (16 to 1 op 14 to 1) 9

1981^{3} MCA BELOW THE LINE [58] (v) 5-9-9 S Webster (1) *beh, hdwy und pres fnl 2 fs, nvr rchd ldrs*. .... (12 to 1 op 9 to 1) 10

1520^{5} HABETA (USA) [62] (bl) 7-9-13 J Lowe (13) *al mid-div*. ....(7 to 1 co-fav op 6 to 1) 11

1832 BROWNED OFF [46] 4-8-11 K Fallon (2) *nvr a factor*. .... (33 to 1 op 25 to 1) 12

1578^{4} COOL ENOUGH [37] 12-8-2 A Mackay (11) *al beh*. .... (12 to 1 op 10 to 1) 13

1436^{7} MATTS BOY [49] 5-9-0 N Connorton (19) *al beh*. .... (11 to 1 op 12 to 1) 14

1865 ROAR ON TOUR [53] 4-8-13 (5*) Darren Moffatt (14) *chsd ldrs till rdn and wknd 3 fs out*.....(20 to 1 op 16 to 1) 15

1704^{5} CARLTON EXPRESS (Ire) [50] 3-8-5 L Charnock (3) *chsd ldrs to hfwy, sn lost pl*.......................... (33 to 1) 16

964 SIE AMATO (Ire) [36] 4-8-1 J Fanning (7) *cl up, rdn wl o'r 2 fs out and sn wknd*.................................. (25 to 1) 17

1705^{3} SHAMROCK DANCER (Ire) [48] 3-8-0 (3*) S Maloney (8) *mid-div, lost pl and beh fnl 3 fs*......(20 to 1 tchd 33 to 1) 18

1849* YOUNG VALENTINE [54] 4-9-5 B Raymond (17) *al beh*. ....(10 to 1) 19

1185^{5} INOVAR [50] 3-8-5 A Culhane (15) *al outpcd and beh*. .... (33 to 1 op 20 to 1) 20

Dist: ¾l, 1l, ¾l, hd, 2½l, hd, 1½l, 1l, hd, ½l. 1m 41.18s. a 2.18s (20 Ran).

SR: 17/15/9/9/9/7/14/11/-/ (W B Imison), P Calver

2058 'Happiness Is A Cigar Called Hamlet' Claiming Stakes Class D (2-y-o) £7,700 6f...................... (2:00)

1401* MR M-E-N (Ire) 8-11 J Carroll (10) *trkd ldrs gng wl, effrt and not much room one and a half fs out, swtchd and squeezed through to ld ins last, ran on*. ....(9 to 4 fav op 9 to 2) 1

1741* STAR SPEEDER (Ire) 7-13 J Lowe (3) *led, rdn 2 fs out, hdd ins last, kpt on*.......................(5 to 1 op 4 to 1) 2

1497* MOSAIC GOLD 8-6 N Connorton (5) *trkd ldrs, hdwy to chal 2 fs out, ev ch ins last, kpt on und pres*. ....(5 to 1 op 7 to 2) 3

1355* LEAP OF FAITH (Ire) (bl) 8-0 F Norton (4) *rdn and hdwy on outer hfwy, kpt on same pace fnl 2 fs*. .... (12 to 1 op 10 to 1) 4

1381^{5} CULSYTH FLYER 8-5 W Ryan (11) *beh, hdwy o'r 2 fs out, sn rdn and kpt on same pace ins last*. .... (16 to 1 op 14 to 1) 5

2021^{4} ALPINE SKIER (Ire) 8-6 K Darley (1) *cl up, rdn o'r 2 fs out, wkng whn hmpd one furlong out*. (14 to 1 op 12 to 1) 6

1665^{4} STRAPPED 7-12 J Quinn (8) *in tch, rdn o'r 2 fs out and sn btn*................................ (16 to 1 op 14 to 1) 7

1624* SECOND SIGHT (Ire) 8-11 M Birch (7) *dwlt, sn in tch, rdn and wknd 2 and a half fs out*........(5 to 1 op 4 to 1) 8

1499* GOLDEN GRAND 8-5 R Hills (2) *prmnt, rdn o'r 2 fs out and sn wknd*......................... (12 to 1 op 10 to 1) 9

NOT FOR JOE 8-0 D Harrison (6) *speed to hfwy, sn lost pl*. .... (25 to 1 op 20 to 1) 10

1889* LUCKY FOURTEEN 8-4 J Fortune (9) *cl up, rdn alng hfwy and sn wknd*.......................(7 to 1 op 6 to 1) 11

Dist: 1½l, 1½l, 1½l, nk, 1l, 2½l, 1l, ½l, 1l, 15l. 1m 15.51s. a 3.51s (11 Ran).

SR: 33/15/16/4/8/5/ (Manchester Evening News Ltd), J Berry

2059 Harcros Timber & Building Supplies Stayers Championship Series Qualifier Handicap Class D (0-80 3-y-o and up) £7,570 1½m 93yds..........(2:45)

1812^{4} CONTRACT ELITE (Ire) [58] 3-7-7 A Mackay (7) *hld up and beh, hdwy o'r 3 fs out, sn rdn, styd on ins last to ld nr line*............................(16 to 1 op 14 to 1) 1

831^{4} SUNDERLAND ECHO [65] 4-9-1 K Darley (4) *trkd ldrs, hdwy 4 fs out, effrt and rdn o'r 2 furlongs out, styd on to ld ins last, hdd nr line*. .... (11 to 4 op 9 to 4 tchd 3 to 1) 2

1398 WILSONIC [65] (v) 4-9-1 Dean McKeown (10) *in tch, hdwy o'r 3 fs out, effrt to chal one and a half furlongs out, sn rdn and ev ch ins last, kpt on*..... (20 to 1 op 16 to 1) 3

1967^{5} BIG PAT [60] 4-8-10 M Wigham (6) *chsd ldrs, hdwy to ld wl o'r 2 fs out, sn rdn, hdd and wknd ins last*. ....(9 to 2 tchd 5 to 1) 4

1593^{3} TRUBEN (USA) [76] 4-9-12 L Dettori (1) *hld up, hdwy o'r 4 fs out, rdn 2 furlongs out and styd on one pace*. ....(5 to 1 op 9 to 2) 5

1894^{4} SUPER BLUES [43] 6-7-7 N Carlisle (3) *beh, gd hdwy 4 fs out, effrt and ch 2 furlongs out, sn rdn and wknd*. .... (14 to 1 op 12 to 1) 6

1770 LYPHANTASTIC (USA) [72] 4-9-8 W Ryan (2) *set fst pace, rdn o'r 3 fs out, sn hdd and wknd quickly*. ....(9 to 4 fav op 3 to 1 tchd 2 to 1) 7

NATIVE CROWN (Ire) [44] 5-7-8^{1} J Lowe (5) *chsd ldr, rdn 3 fs out and sn btn*.................(50 to 1 op 33 to 1) 8

1464^{4} MUFID (USA) [63] 4-8-13 J Fanning (8) *in tch, rdn 4 fs out and sn wknd*................................ (20 to 1) 9

1654 GOLDEN ISLE [55] 9-8-5 J Quinn (9) *chsd ldrs, rdn and wknd wl o'r 3 fs out*...............(25 to 1 op 20 to 1) 10

Dist: Hd, sht-hd, 1½l, 1l, ½l, 3l, 10l, 2l, 8l. 2m 37.76s. a 0.06s (10 Ran).

SR: 28/49/48/40/54/20/43/-/10/ (Brian Whitelaw), C W Thornton

2060 Journal 'Good Morning' Handicap Class C (0-100 3-y-o and up) £12,232 7f ....(3:15)

1325^{3} TAWAFIJ (USA) [69] 4-7-11 J Fanning (8) *trkd ldrs gng wl, effrt 2 fs out, led entering fnl furlong, sn clr*. .... (16 to 1 op 14 to 1) 1

1768 PIQUANT [80] 6-8-5 (3*) D Harrison (9) *chsd ldrs, effrt and rdn 2 fs out, kpt on ins last*. .... (13 to 2 op 7 to 1 tchd 6 to 1) 2

1830* EN ATTENDANT (Fr) [88] 5-9-2 B Raymond (3) *in tch, effrt and hdwy on outer appr fnl furlong, sn rdn and styd on*.................................... (8 to 1 op 7 to 1) 3

1326* STORITHS (Ire) [90] 3-8-9 M Birch (15) *in tch, effrt on outer 2 fs out, sn rdn and ch, kpt on und pres ins last*. ....(10 to 1 tchd 12 to 1) 4

1768 HIGH PREMIUM [85] 5-8-13 K Fallon (4) *cl up, led 2 and a half fs out till rdn, hdd and wknd entering fnl furlong*. .... (10 to 1 op 8 to 1) 5

1153^{4} IHTIRAZ [91] 3-8-10 R Hills (14) *mid-div, gd hdwy 2 fs out, kpt on ins last*................ (20 to 1 op 16 to 1) 6

2022 VELOCE (Ire) [65] 5-7-7 A Mackay (13) *beh till styd on strly fnl furlong, nrst finish*...........................(16 to 1) 7

1636^{7} TAUFAN BLU (Ire) [98] (bl) 4-9-7 (5*) J Tate (5) *dwlt, hdwy on outer 2 fs out, sn rdn and kpt on same pace*. .... (20 to 1 op 14 to 1) 8

1402^{2} BOLD AMUSEMENT [88] 3-8-7 K Darley (1) *cl up, rdn o'r 2 fs out and sn wknd*.............(10 to 1 tchd 11 to 1) 9

1830^{7} MISS HAGGIS [74] 4-8-2^{1} D Holland (6) *al mid-div*. .... (10 to 1 op 8 to 1) 10

1017^{4} TARNSIDE ROSAL [74] 3-7-7 Dale Gibson (11) *chsd ldrs, rdn o'r 2 fs out and sn wknd*...... (20 to 1 op 16 to 1) 11

1876^{2} CEE-JAY-AY [70] 6-7-12 N Carlisle (10) *in tch, rdn 2 fs out, sn wknd*............(6 to 1 fav op 7 to 1 tchd 8 to 1) 12

1658^{6} FIGHTER SQUADRON [68] (bl) 4-7-5 (5*) Darren Moffatt (18) *in tch on outer, effrt 2 fs out, sn rdn and no hdwy*. ....(12 to 1) 13

1939^{6} THORNTON GATE [68] 4-7-10 J Lowe (7) *prmnt, rdn 3 fs out and sn wknd*.................(16 to 1 op 14 to 1) 14

1719^{4} PERSIAN REVIVAL (Fr) [84] 3-8-3^{4} J Fortune (2) *led, rdn hfwy, hdd 2 and a half fs out and wknd quickly*. ....(20 to 1) 15

PARLIAMENT PIECE [90] 7-9-4 L Dettori (12) *chsd ldrs, effrt and rdn hfwy, sn wknd*..........(16 to 1 op 14 to 1) 16

1835^{5} PETITE-D-ARGENT [85] 4-8-13 W Ryan (17) *cl up, rdn aftr 3 fs and sn wknd*.....(12 to 1 op 10 to 1 tchd 14 to 1) 17

Dist: 2l, sht-hd, ½l, 1l, nk, hd, nk, nk, 1l, ¾l. 1m 26.95s. a 2.95s (17 Ran).

SR: 44/49/56/47/48/44/26/58/38/ (Stephen Laidlaw), R Allan

2061 'Newcastle Brown Ale' Northumberland Plate Centenary Handicap Stakes Class B (3-y-o and up) £57,300 2m 19yds........................ (3:50)

1779* HIGHFLYING [73] 7-7-11 (3ex) J Fanning (20) *al prmnt, hdwy 4 fs out, led 3 furlongs out and sn clr, easily*. ....(7 to 1) 1

1752* BALASANI (Fr) [83] 7-8-7 (8ex) D Holland (4) *hld up and beh, hdwy 6 fs out, rdn o'r 2 furlongs out and styd on, no ch wth wnr*..............(11 to 2 fav tchd 6 to 1) 2
1840² BRANDON PRINCE (Ire) [81] (bl) 5-8-5¹ B Raymond (5) *in tch, hdwy o'r 4 fs out, rdn 3 furlongs out and kpt on one pace*.......................... (20 to 1) 3
1405² NOT IN DOUBT (USA) [91] 4-9-1 L Dettori (16) *mid-div, gd hdwy 5 fs out, rdn o'r 3 out and sn one pace.* ....(6 to 1 op 5 to 1) 4
1752 BUSTINETTA [78] 4-7-13 (3*) S Maloney (18) *beh, hdwy hfwy, rdn and plugged on one pace fnl 3 fs.* .... (33 to 1 op 20 to 1) 5
773³ CASTLE CAVALIER [90] 5-9-0 K Darley (6) *chsd ldrs, rdn 3 fs out and sn wknd*......(8 to 1 op 7 to 1 tchd 9 to 1) 6
1809⁶ STAR PLAYER [85] 7-8-2 (7*) D Wright (15) *hld up and beh, hdwy o'r 4 fs out, kpt on fnl 2, nvr dngrs*......(33 to 1) 7
1682⁴ SARAWAT [78] 5-8-2 J Lowe (2) *hld up and beh, slpd bend hfwy, styd on fnl 3 fs, nvr a factor.* ....(12 to 1 op 10 to 1 tchd 14 to 1) 8
LEMON'S MILL (USA) [75] 4-7-13 J Quinn (8) *nvr rchd ldrs.* .... (14 to 1 op 12 to 1) 9
1682³ KAISER WILHELM [86] 4-8-10 W Ryan (12) *hld up and beh, effrt and some hdwy 6 fs out, nvr a factor.* .... (20 to 1 op 16 to 1) 10
1682* QUICK RANSOM [88] 5-8-12 (3ex) Dean McKeown (11) *mid-div, pushed alng 5 fs out and sn btn, eased fnl 2 furlongs*..................(13 to 2 op 6 to 1 tchd 8 to 1) 11
1840⁶ HIERARCH (USA) [73] 4-7-9¹ (3*) D Harrison (10) *led, rdn alng 6 fs out, hdd 3 out and sn wknd.* ....(20 to 1 tchd 25 to 1) 12
1682⁷ SATIN LOVER [87] 5-8-11 L Charnock (13) *nvr a factor.* ....(14 to 1 tchd 16 to 1) 13
1345³ RODEO STAR (USA) [73] 7-7-11 N Carlisle (9) *chsd ldrs till rdn and wknd o'r 4 fs out*........ (14 to 1 op 10 to 1) 14
1484* WELSH MILL (Ire) [90] 4-9-0 (6ex) M Birch (17) *cl up, rdn 6 fs out, wknd 3 out*...................(14 to 1 op 10 to 1) 15
1809³ MISS PLUM [75] 4-7-13 G Bardwell (1) *in tch, rdn alng hfwy, wknd 6 fs out*..............(20 to 1 op 14 to 1) 16
1380³ MERRY NUTKIN [73] 7-7-11 Dale Gibson (7) *nvr a factor.* ....(33 to 1 op 25 to 1) 17
1669* MULL HOUSE [76] 6-8-0¹ (3ex) R Hills (19) *chsd ldrs, rdn o'r 5 fs out and sn wknd*........(20 to 1 tchd 25 to 1) 18
Dist: 7l, ¾l, 3½l, 1½l, 2½l, 4l, 1½l, 5l, 1l, 1½l. 3m 25.10s. b 0.90s (18 Ran).
SR: 28/31/27/33/18/27/18/9/1/ (B Batey), G M Moore

2062 Wynyard Classic Northumberland Sprint Trophy Class C Handicap Stakes (0-95 3-y-o and up) £11,842 6f ....(4:30)

1127* CASTLEREA LAD [82] 4-9-3 W Ryan (8) *in tch, gd hdwy 2 fs out, rdn to ld ins fnl furlong, readily.* ....(9 to 2 op 7 to 1 tchd 8 to 1) 1
1953⁸ EDUCATED PET [69] 4-8-4 Dean McKeown (6) *prmnt, hdwy 2 fs out, rdn to ld entering fnl furlong, hdd and no extr ins last*........................ (20 to 1 op 16 to 1) 2
1449⁸ FARFELU [93] (bl) 6-10-0 D Holland (9) *cl up, led hfwy till rdn and hdd entering fnl furlong, edgd rght and wknd.* ....(16 to 1 op 14 to 1) 3
1835² SEA DEVIL [79] 7-9-0 N Connorton (12) *chsd ldrs, rdn 2 fs out, kpt on ins last*.....(6 to 1 op 8 to 1 tchd 11 to 2) 4
1066 CALEMAN [77] 4-8-12 R Hills (11) *chsd ldrs, rdn 2 fs out, kpt on same pace*..................(16 to 1 op 12 to 1) 5
1806 AMRON [88] 6-9-9 N Carlisle (13) *mid-div, hdwy and rdn one and a half fs out, styd on.* ....(11 to 1 op 12 to 1 tchd 14 to 1) 6
1563² BLUE GRIT [68] 7-8-3 J Lowe (7) *beh, hdwy 2 fs out, sn rdn and kpt on ins last*.................(14 to 1 op 12 to 1) 7
1379² HOB GREEN [73] 4-8-8 K Fallon (3) *in tch on outer, effrt and hdwy 2 fs out, sn rdn, edgd rght and wknd.* ....(3 to 1 fav op 9 to 4) 8
1680⁶ RESOLUTE BAY [74] 7-8-9 A Culhane (1) *al mid-div.* .... (16 to 1 op 14 to 1) 9
1841⁷ TRUE PRECISION [84] 3-8-11 L Charnock (14) *hdwy whn not much room hfwy, swtchd and rdn 2 fs out, no imprsn*.. (12 to 1) 10
1945⁵ RED ROSEIN [85] 7-9-6 J Fortune (5) *hdwy on outer o'r 2 fs out, sn rdn and btn*... (10 to 1 op 8 to 1 tchd 11 to 1) 11
1945⁷ DRUM SERGEANT [81] (bl) 6-8-13 (3*) D Harrison (4) *chsd ldrs, rdn hfwy, wknd 2 fs out*......(16 to 1 op 14 to 1) 12
1835 FLASHY'S SON [60] 5-7-9⁷ (7*) J Marshall (16) *led to hfwy, sn wknd*........................ (25 to 1 op 20 to 1) 13
1982³ GONDO [65] 6-8-0 J Quinn (10) *cl up, ev ch 2 fs out, sn rdn and wknd*....................(16 to 1 op 14 to 1) 14
1815⁸ DIET [61] (v) 7-7-7 (3*) N Kennedy (15) *cl up, rdn hfwy, sn wknd*...........................(25 to 1 op 16 to 1) 15
1806⁹ DENSBEN [78] 9-8-13 L Dettori (2) *in tch to hfwy, sn rdn and lost pl*......................(14 to 1 op 16 to 1) 16
Dist: 2l, 1l, nk, ¾l, hd, nk, sht-hd, sht-hd, 2l, 2l. 1m 14.12s. a 2.12s (16 Ran).
SR: 67/46/66/51/46/56/35/39/39/ (Mrs Tess Graham), R Hollinshead

2063 EBF Hexham Maiden Stakes Class D (2-y-o) £3,720 5f.................(5:05)

SMART PET 8-9 N Connorton (4) *cl up, effrt 2 fs out and sn led, rdn and ran on ins last.* ....(9 to 1 op 6 to 1 tchd 10 to 1) 1
1529⁶ CAPTAIN CARAT 9-0 K Fallon (6) *in tch, effrt and hdwy 2 fs out, sn rdn and kpt on ins last*.... (9 to 1 op 6 to 1) 2
1773³ STELLOSO 9-0 L Dettori (3) *cl up, led aftr 2 fs till rdn and hdd one and a half out, sn one pace.* ....(11 to 8 fav op 5 to 4 tchd 6 to 4) 3
1272 DANTE'S RUBICON (Ire) 9-0 L Charnock (5) *chsd ldrs, rdn 2 fs out, kpt on one pace*...........(20 to 1 op 16 to 1) 4
ANTIGUAN SKY 9-0 Raymond Berry (2) *nvr rchd ldrs.* ....(25 to 1 op 14 to 1) 5
1706² THE HAPPY LOON (Ire) 9-0 B Raymond (7) *led 2 fs, sn rdn, wknd one and a half furlongs out.* ....(15 to 8 op 7 to 4 tchd 9 to 4) 6
433⁵ ARTA 9-0 A Culhane (1) *cl up on outer till rdn and wknd quickly 2 fs out*..................(10 to 1 tchd 11 to 1) 7
Dist: 1l, nk, 3l, 2½l, 2l, 10l. 1m 2.46s. a 3.56s (7 Ran).
SR: 29/30/29/17/7/-/-/ (Mrs George Ward), Miss S E Hall

2064 Earsdon Maiden Stakes Class D (3-y-o and up) £3,882 1m..............(5:35)

1064⁴ WAINWRIGHT (USA) 4-9-7 L Dettori (6) *trkd ldr, led 2 and a half fs out, sn clr, cmftbly.* ....(5 to 2 op 9 to 4 tchd 2 to 1) 1
1784⁵ BAMBURGH (USA) 3-8-11 B Raymond (3) *chsd ldrs, rdn 3 fs out, styd on ins last, no ch wth wnr.* ....(6 to 1 op 5 to 1) 2
1617² MITRAAS (USA) 3-8-11 R Hills (4) *led, rdn 3 fs out, hdd and one pace*.........(Evens fav op 11 to 10 tchd 11 to 8) 3
1762³ PHILNIC 3-8-4 (7*) J Marshall (11) *mid-div, hdwy 4 fs out, sn rdn and one pace*.............. (25 to 1 op 20 to 1) 4
1784⁹ LOWLANDS SCRIBE 3-8-6 S Webster (10) *beh, styd on fnl 2 fs, nvr dngrs*.................. (25 to 1 op 16 to 1) 5
1851⁵ SUSPECT 3-8-3 (3*) N Kennedy (7) *chsd ldrs, rdn o'r 3 fs out and sn wknd*..................(50 to 1 op 25 to 1) 6
1864⁶ THE LAUGHING LORD 7-9-7 M Birch (1) *al mid-div.* ....(16 to 1 op 10 to 1) 7
1850⁷ MIDDLEHAM CASTLE 4-9-7 R P Elliott (8) *al rear.* .... (50 to 1 op 25 to 1) 8
1595⁵ KEEP BATTLING 3-8-11 N Connorton (2) *al rear.* .... (33 to 1 op 20 to 1) 9
FORENZA 3-8-6 K Fallon (9) *al beh*...(25 to 1 op 16 to 1) 10
1424⁵ MUSTN'T GRUMBLE (Ire) 3-8-11 L Charnock (5) *slwly away, al beh*.......................(20 to 1 op 16 to 1) 11
BLAKENEY BOY 3-8-11 J Fanning (12) *chsd ldrs to hfwy, sn lost pl and beh*..............................(50 to 1) 12
Dist: 1½l, nk, 7l, ½l, 2½l, ½l, 2½l, 5l, 3l, 10l. 1m 41.50s. a 2.50s (12 Ran).
SR: 22/7/6/-/-/-/ (Sheikh Mohammed), J H M Gosden

NEWMARKET (JULY) (good to firm)
Saturday June 26th
Going Correction: MINUS 0.30 sec. per fur.

2065 Kings Head, Dullingham Claiming Stakes Class D (3-y-o) £3,915 1m (2:00)

1720⁷ KING PARIS (Ire) 9-4 M Hills (8) *hld up, steady prog frm hfwy, shaken up to ld o'r one out, styd on.* ....(7 to 4 fav op 6 to 4 on tchd 15 to 8) 1
1684² ANORAK (USA) 9-8 R Cochrane (9) *trkd ldrs, led o'r 2 out till over one out, rallied ins fnl furlong.* ....(7 to 2 op 7 to 1) 2
1829³ RUBY COOPER 8-3 W Carson (4) *ldg grp, rdn and not quicken appr fnl furlong, kpt on cl hme.* ....(6 to 1 op 8 to 1 tchd 9 to 1) 3
1641⁷ REGALSETT 9-8 J Reid (11) *led for o'r 2 fs, pressed ldrs, no extr appr fnl furlong*..............(10 to 1 op 7 to 1) 4
PLEASE SAY YES (Ire) 8-5¹ G Carter (7) *led o'r 5 fs out till over 2 out, one pace appr fnl furlong.* ....(40 to 1 op 33 to 1 tchd 50 to 1) 5
1358* JAKE THE PAKE (Ire) 8-10 T Quinn (1) *cl up, rdn alng 3 out, no prog frm 2 out*........(5 to 1 op 6 to 1 tchd 7 to 1) 6
RIVA ROCK 8-1 (7*) D McCabe (6) *strted slwly, al beh.* .... (20 to 1 op 12 to 1) 7
1617⁹ RUPERT'S REVENGE (Ire) 8-4 A Munro (2) *hld up in tch till wknd quickly hfwy, tld off.* ....(40 to 1 op 33 to 1 tchd 50 to 1) 8
1831 MARKETING MAN 8-3 (7*) G Forster (5) *chsd ldrs till wknd und pres hfwy, tld off*............................ (33 to 1) 9
1829 O SO NEET 8-12 P Robinson (10) *missed break, sn wl plcd, wknd o'r 3 out, tld off*..........(20 to 1 tchd 25 to 1) 10
Dist: ¾l, 1½l, 1½l, 2l, 8l, 3l, 4l, 10l, 15l. 1m 40.00s. a 2.10s (10 Ran).
SR: 37/39/15/29/6/-/ (Mrs Pauline Karpidas), M Bell

2066 Dom Ruinart Champagne Handicap Class C (0-90 3-y-o) £5,300 1m.. (2:30)

1464⁶ JURA FOREST [70] 8-5 A Munro (2) *hld up, hdwy o'r 2 out, str brst to ld last 100 yards*........(8 to 1 tchd 10 to 1) 1
1016³ TYCHONIC [75] 8-10 Pat Eddery (10) *hld up, cld on ldrs 2 out, led entering fnl furlong, hdd and not quicken last 100 yards*..............(15 to 8 fav op 9 to 4 tchd 5 to 2) 2
1595* NAFUTH (USA) [77] 8-12 W Carson (14) *mid-div, ran on o'r 2 out, styd on strly ins fnl furlong.* ....(10 to 1 tchd 12 to 1) 3

945^{6} NURYANDRA [77] 8-12 M Hills (6) *hld up, effrt and not much room appr fnl furlong, styd on nr finish.* ....(25 to 1 op 20 to 1) 4
1453* KARINSKA [59] 7-8^{8} (7*) D McCabe (7) *pressed ldrs, rdn and not quicken one out*.........(33 to 1 op 25 to 1) 5
1528^{2} PETONELLAJILL [76] 8-11 J Reid (13) *beh til ran on ins last 2 fs, nvr nrr*........(9 to 1 op 6 to 1 tchd 10 to 1) 6
1780^{6} KEYWAY (USA) [77] 8-12 G Duffield (12) *mid-div, pushed alng hfwy, one pace appr fnl furlong.* ....(16 to 1 op 14 to 1) 7
985^{4} SHARJAH (USA) [86] 9-7 P Robinson (9) *handily plcd til rdn and no prog 2 out*..........(20 to 1 tchd 25 to 1) 8
1808 KASSBAAN (USA) [74] 8-9 W R Swinburn (11) *beh til styd on frm 2 out, nvr nrr*. (12 to 1 op 10 to 1 tchd 14 to 1) 9
1255^{6} TOTALLY UNIQUE (USA) [61] (v) 7-10^{1} D Biggs (5) *made most of rng til hdd entering fnl furlong, wknd.* ....(20 to 1 tchd 25 to 1) 10
1868* TEJ SINGH (USA) [76] 8-11 R Cochrane (8) *pressed ldr til rdn and wknd o'r one out*.......(10 to 1 tchd 12 to 1) 11
1780^{7} CLIBURNEL NEWS (Ire) [71] 7-13 (7*) S Mulvey (4) *chsd ldrs for o'r 5 fs*........................(25 to 1 op 20 to 1) 12
1670^{6} TRIPPIANO [72] 8-7 A McGlone (1) *in tch early, rdn and beh aftr 3 fs, tld off*..................(9 to 1 op 8 to 1) 13
1424* ARID [78] (v) 8-13 T Quinn (3) *ldg grp til lost pl 3 out, tld off*..........(9 to 1 op 10 to 1 tchd 12 to 1) 14
Dist: 1½l, hd, 2l, sht-hd, nk, hd, 1½l, hd, nk, ½l. 1m 38.94s. a 1.04s (14 Ran).
SR: 39/39/40/34/15/31/31/35/22/ (Lord Vestey), J R Fanshawe

2067 Ewar Stud Empress Stakes Class A (Listed Race) (2-y-o) £10,290 6f (3:05)

1766^{2} SNIPE HALL 9-1 P Robinson (4) *wl in tch, led ins fnl furlong, hld on nr line*............(5 to 2 tchd 3 to 1) 1
1766^{8} ROHITA (Ire) 9-1 Pat Eddery (3) *hld up in rear, improved 2 fs out, swtchd rght one out, str brst to squeeze through nr finish, jst fld.* ....(15 to 8 fav op 7 to 4 tchd 13 to 8 and 2 to 1) 2
1428^{4} MICHELLE HICKS 8-8 M Hills (1) *cl up, led o'r 2 fs out, hdd ins fnl furlong, rallied und pres.* ....(9 to 2 op 6 to 1 tchd 13 to 2) 3
1660^{2} NORFOLK LAVENDER (Can) 8-8 A Munro (2) *trkd ldrs in tch, rdn and ran on same pace fnl furlong.* ....(10 to 1 op 14 to 1 tchd 16 to 1) 4
1766^{6} THREATENING 8-11 R Cochrane (8) *slwly into strd, effrt frm rear o'r one furlong out, nvr nrr.* ....(12 to 1 tchd 10 to 1 and 14 to 1) 5
1766^{9} NERA 8-8 W R Swinburn (5) *led for o'r 3 fs, wknd fnl furlong*.............(16 to 1 op 12 to 1 tchd 20 to 1) 6
1583^{3} PRIMA SILK 8-8 D Biggs (9) *handily plcd on outsd, effrt o'r 2 fs out, wknd fnl furlong*......(33 to 1 op 20 to 1) 7
1234* NSX 8-11 T Quinn (6) *cl up for o'r 3 fs, sn wknd, tld off.* ....(11 to 1 op 14 to 1 tchd 16 to 1) 8
2027^{3} NAKITA 8-8 G Carter (7) *chsd ldrs to hfwy, wknd quickly, virtually pld up ins last 2 fs, tld off.* ....(33 to 1 tchd 40 to 1) 9
Dist: Nk, sht-hd, 2l, 2½l, 2½l, nk, 12l, 5l. 1m 12.52s. a 0.82s (9 Ran).
SR: 49/48/40/32/25/12/11/-/-/ (Mrs R T Watson), J Wharton

2068 Van Geest Criterion Stakes Class A (Group 3) (3-y-o and up) £20,580 7f (3:35)

794^{6} INCHINOR 3-8-12 T Quinn (9) *ldg grp, rdn and ran on to ld last 100 yards*........(7 to 1 op 8 to 1 tchd 9 to 1) 1
1347* MISTLE CAT (USA) 3-8-7 W Woods (6) *pressed ldr, led 3 fs out, hdd entering fnl furlong, rallied nr line.* ....(13 to 2 op 6 to 1 tchd 7 to 1) 2
1747^{2} INNER CITY (Ire) 4-9-7 R Cochrane (1) *hld up towards rear, str run und pres to ld entering fnl furlong, hdd and not quicken last 100 yards.* ....(15 to 8 fav op 5 to 4 tchd 2 to 1) 3
750* SPLICE 4-8-13 W R Swinburn (2) *hld up beh, ran on 2 fs out, no imprsn on ldrs ins fnl furlong.* ....(15 to 2 op 8 to 1 tchd 10 to 1) 4
1786^{6} SILVER WIZARD (USA) 3-8-7 A Munro (7) *led for 4 fs, wknd appr fnl furlong*......(13 to 2 op 6 to 1 tchd 7 to 1) 5
1019^{6} SO FACTUAL (USA) 3-8-7 Pat Eddery (4) *in tch, effrt o'r 2 fs out, btn over one out*....(7 to 2 op 4 to 1 tchd 9 to 2) 6
1205^{3} SON PARDO 3-9-1 J Reid (5) *chsd ldrs for 6 fs, no extr.* ....(33 to 1 op 20 to 1) 7
LITTLE MUNCHKIN (Ire) 3-8-12 W Carson (3) *in tch for 5 fs, sn lost pl*..................................(33 to 1) 8
1830 EURO FESTIVAL 4-9-2 A McGlone (10) *slwly into strd, al outpcd, tld off*..................(66 to 1 op 50 to 1) 9
823^{2} TOOCANDO (Ire) 3-8-4 G Carter (8) *dwlt, al beh, tld off.* ....(16 to 1 tchd 20 to 1) 10
Dist: ½l, nk, 5l, 2l, nk, sht-hd, 7l, 10l, 1½l. 1m 23.56s. b 0.64s (10 Ran).
SR: 76/69/82/59/47/46/53/29/3/ (Sir Philip Oppenheimer), R Charlton

2069 Slip Anchor Maiden Stakes Class D (2-y-o) £3,720 7f.................. (4:10)

MR EUBANKS (USA) 9-0 R Cochrane (6) *hld up wl in tch, swtchd rght o'r one out, quickened to ld ins fnl furlong, pushed clr*....................(4 to 1 op 7 to 2) 1
1666^{4} ALJAWAB (USA) 9-0 W Carson (4) *ldg grp, hrd rdn 2 out, outpcd by wnr ins fnl furlong.* ....(5 to 2 fav op 9 to 4 tchd 11 to 4) 2
TANAH MERAH (Ire) 9-0 T Quinn (5) *led til o'r 2 out, styd on und pres nr finish*..............(7 to 2 tchd 9 to 2) 3
1489^{6} ROMAN REEL (USA) 9-0 B Rouse (9) *in tch, led o'r 2 out, hdd and outpcd ins fnl furlong.* ....(25 to 1 op 20 to 1 tchd 33 to 1) 4
DARING DESTINY 8-9 T Sprake (1) *pushed alng in mid-div hfwy, styd on stdly last 2 fs, better for race.* ....(33 to 1 op 25 to 1) 5
ARECIBO (Ire) 8-11 (3*) B Doyle (2) *dsptd ld for 5 fs, eased whn btn fnl furlong*..............(16 to 1 op 10 to 1) 6
JAFEICA (Ire) 9-0 J Reid (7) *slwly into strd, al outpcd.* ....(10 to 1 op 8 to 1 tchd 11 to 1) 7
CHASING SHADOWS (Ire) 9-0 Pat Eddery (3) *handily plcd for o'r 4 fs, better for race*.........(6 to 1 tchd 7 to 1) 8
1828^{4} CHIEF EXECUTIVE 9-0 W R Swinburn (8) *slwly into strd, al beh*..........(8 to 1 tchd 10 to 1) 9
Dist: 3½l, hd, 1½l, nk, 5l, ¾l, sht-hd, 8l. 1m 27.55s. a 3.35s (9 Ran).
SR: 18/7/6/1/-/-/ (Roldvale Limited), P A Kelleway

2070 ANC Fred Archer Stakes Class A (Listed Race) (4-y-o and up) £9,159 1½m (4:45)

1118^{2} BOBZAO (Ire) 4-9-1 J Reid (1) *steadied leaving stalls, hld up in rear, ran on 2 out, reminders to ld ins fnl furlong, styd on*..................(4 to 1 op 7 to 2 tchd 9 to 2) 1
426^{3} LUPESCU 5-8-10 G Carter (6) *hld up in 4th pl, rdn to ld 2 out, hdd und pres ins fnl furlong, ran on same pace.* ....(8 to 1 tchd 7 to 1) 2
1538* SONUS (Ire) 4-9-1 W R Swinburn (2) *trkd ldr, ev ch and not quicken o'r 2 out, kpt on one pace ins fnl furlong.* ....(5 to 4 on op 7 to 4 on) 3
ANCHORITE 4-8-11 M Hills (3) *led til 2 out, wknd ins fnl furlong*..............(20 to 1 op 16 to 1 tchd 25 to 1) 4
1538^{4} BOLOARDO 4-8-11 W Carson (4) *pld hrd early stages, settled in 3rd pl, wknd o'r 2 out, sn lost tch.* ....(9 to 2 op 4 to 1) 5
Dist: ¾l, 1½l, 3½l, 10l. 2m 30.72s. a 1.92s (5 Ran).
SR: 46/39/41/30/10/ (T G Mills), T G Mills

2071 National Horseracing Museum Maiden Apprentice Stakes Class E (3-y-o and up) £2,794 1¾m 175yds (5:15)

MY ROSSINI 4-9-2 (5*) C Hawksley (3) *made all, sn clr, hng lft to race far side hfwy, hld on last strds.* ....(7 to 1 op 6 to 1 tchd 9 to 1) 1
1816^{4} POPSI'S LEGACY 6-8-11 (5*) D Toole (6) *beh, ran on 3 out, cld on wnr ins fnl furlong, jst fld.* ....(16 to 1 op 20 to 1 tchd 25 to 1) 2
1625^{4} THREEMILESTONE (USA) 3-7-13 B Doyle (4) *settled in 3rd pl, ran on frm 2 out, not quicken ins fnl furlong.* ....(2 to 1 on op 7 to 4 on tchd 11 to 8 on) 3
876 SCARLET TUNIC (USA) 3-7-13 (5*) J Wilkinson (1) *wl plcd, one pace last 2 fs*..................(6 to 1 op 4 to 1) 4
1603 SPICE BOX (USA) 3-7-11 (7*) Martin Dwyer (2) *hld up, rdn alng to improve frm 2 fs out, no imprsn on wnr clsg stages*..........(5 to 1 op 9 to 2 tchd 11 to 2) 5
366^{9} RUPPLES 6-9-2 (5*) D McCabe (5) *chsd wnr til wknd quickly o'r 2 fs out, tld off*.......(33 to 1 tchd 50 to 1) 6
Dist: Sht-hd, ¾l, 1½l, ¾l, 20l. 3m 14.72s. a 8.72s (6 Ran).
(Mrs Cherry Eaton), P J Bevan

CURRAGH (IRE) (good to yielding (race 1), good to firm (2,3,4,5,6,7)) Sunday June 27th

2072 St. Brigid E.B.F. Maiden (2-y-o) £5,244 7f............................ (1:40)

GOTHIC DREAM (Ire) 8-11 M J Kinane (9).........(7 to 2) 1
1824^{2} OLIVER MESSEL (Ire) 9-0 W J Supple (1).........(14 to 1) 2
SPECS APPEAL (Ire) (bl) 9-0 K J Manning (5).....(16 to 1) 3
1924^{2} SUMMERHILL SPECIAL (Ire) 8-11 Joanna Morgan (7) ....(20 to 1) 4
1332^{9} DAYESS (USA) 9-0 P Shanahan (2)..............(20 to 1) 5
MOHAAJIR (USA) 9-0 C Roche (3)...........(11 to 8 on) 6
DOHERTY (Ire) 9-0 R Hughes (4)................(14 to 1) 7
LAKE KARIBA 9-0 P V Gilson (11)................(7 to 1) 8
1650^{9} THE PLAYER NOBLE (Ire) 8-6 (8*) D Leahy (10)....(33 to 1) 9
938^{5} VENICE (Ire) 9-0 J P Murtagh (6)................(12 to 1) 10
Dist: 1½l, sht-hd, ½l, 2½l. 1m 28.70s. a 5.50s (10 Ran).
SR: 15/13/12/7/2/-/ (Lady Clague), John M Oxx

2073 P.V.Doyle Memorial Scurry Handicap (0-110 3-y-o and up) £12,000 6f 63yds (2:10)

ROSIE'S MAC (Ire) [-] 4-8-5 N G McCullagh (2)....(20 to 1) 1
1050* CLASSICAL AFFAIR (Ire) [-] 4-8-5 (6*) R V Skelly (4) (6 to 1) 2
1786 NORDIC FOX (Ire) [-] (bl) 3-8-11 C Roche (3) (5 to 1 co-fav) 3
897^{6} TROPICAL [-] (bl) 3-9-2 M J Kinane (10).... (5 to 1 co-fav) 4

1569^{5} MACGILLYCUDDY (Ire) [-] 4-6-13 (8*) G M Moylan (8) ....(14 to 1) 5
1201 SUMY [-] (bl) 3-8-9 R Hughes (6) .... (10 to 1) 6
1551^{2} BRADAWN BREEVER (Ire) [-] (bl) 4-9-10 W J Supple (7) ....(5 to 1 co-fav) 7
1611^{8} WALLY WALLENSKY (Ire) [-] 3-7-7 L O'Shea (13) .. (25 to 1) 8
572 NORDIC OAK (Ire) [-] 5-8-1 (6*) J A Heffernan (11) (10 to 1) 9
1825^{4} BENE MERENTI (Ire) [-] (bl) 3-7-7 Joanna Morgan (5) ....(25 to 1) 10
1513^{7} COMMON BOND (Ire) [-] 3-7-5 (2*) D G O'Shea (9) (25 to 1) 11
270^{4} PERSIAN CREEK (Ire) [-] 4-9-4 K J Manning (15) .. (14 to 1) 12
1575^{4} MY-O-MY (Ire) [-] 3-8-1 W Carson (14) ....(8 to 1) 13
1795* MAGIC DON (Ire) [-] (bl) 4-7-4^{5} (8*,3ex) R T Fitzpatrick (12) ....(16 to 1) 14
1515^{8} CLANDOLLY (Ire) [-] 5-7-13 (4*) W J Smith (17) .... (16 to 1) 15
787 DESERT THUNDER (Ire) [-] (bl) 4-8-13 P Shanahan (16) ....(12 to 1) 16

Dist: ¾l, nk, 1l, 2l, nk, sht-hd. 1m 17.80s. a 3.30s (16 Ran).
SR: 25/28/27/28/-/12/26/-/-/ (Joseph Wall), D Hanley

2074 Sea World International Stakes (Group 2) (3-y-o and up) £26,250 1m ....(2:45)

1747* ALFLORA (Ire) 4-9-11 M J Kinane (1) *wl plcd, rdn 2 fs out, drifted lft whn rallying to ld fnl half furlong, ran on, fnshd 1st, pld second*.......... (9 to 2) 1D
1047^{6} IVORY FRONTIER (Ire) 3-8-9 C Roche (10) *wl plcd, hmpd whn chalg on ins fnl furlong, ran on, fnshd second, pld 1st*.......... (9 to 1) 1
1364 MASTER TRIBE (Ire) 3-8-9 P V Gilson (2) *mid-div till prog to ld 2 fs out, hdd fnl half furlong, kpt on*....... (12 to 1) 3
1747^{3} HAZAAM (USA) 4-9-5 W R Swinburn (4) *mid-div, rdn and some prog 2 fs out, kpt on*.......... (11 to 2) 4
1552* MALVERNICO (Ire) 5-9-5 K J Manning (6) *rear, styd on strt wthout rching ldrs*.......... (14 to 1) 5
1548* CULTURE VULTURE (USA) 4-9-8 T Quinn (3) *rear till prog on outsd 3 fs out, ev ch 2 out, wknd ins last*. (5 to 4 fav) 6
1447^{3} ZAAHI (USA) 4-9-5 R Hills (8) *wl plcd till rdn and wknd 2 fs out*.......... (11 to 2) 7
1201^{8} SHAHIK (USA) 3-8-9 W J Supple (5) *last into strt, swtchd outsd 2 fs out, no imprsn on ldrs*.......... (20 to 1) 8
1049^{5} IRISH MEMORY 4-9-5 S Craine (9) *led till hdd and wknd 2 fs out*.......... (14 to 1) 9

Dist: ¾l, hd, 1l, nk, hd, 1½l. 1m 39.00s. a 2.40s (9 Ran).
SR: 75/57/56/63/62/64/56/-/-/ (Peter J P Gleeson), J S Bolger

2075 John Roarty Mem. E.B.F Railway Stks (Group 3) (2-y-o) £13,125 6f..... (3:20)

1750^{2} POLISH LAUGHTER (USA) 8-10 W R Swinburn (7) *made all, clr one furlong out, eased cl hme*.......... (6 to 4 fav) 1
571* KLY GREEN 8-10 C Roche (6) *chsd wnr frm hfwy, kpt on*. ....(8 to 1) 2
938* BARTOK (Ire) 8-10 P V Gilson (8) *mid-div till styd on fnl 2 fs*.......... (13 to 2) 3
1509* LAKE COUNTRY (Ire) 8-7 L Piggott (5) *missed break, prog into 3rd 2 fs out, wknd cl hme*.......... (9 to 2) 4
1044* MARVIN'S FAITH (Ire) 8-10 Pat Eddery (2) *wl plcd, ev ch 2 fs out, sn wknd*.......... (12 to 1) 5
1045^{6} GENUINE BID (Ire) 8-10 J P Murtagh (4) *rear, rdn and wknd hfwy*.......... (40 to 1) 6
1550* MONTE MARIO (USA) 8-10 M J Kinane (3) *unruly in stalls, mid-div till rdn and wknd 2 fs out*.......... (7 to 2) 7
1824* ALZUMA (Ire) 8-10 J F Egan (1) *wl plcd till rdn and wknd o'r 2 fs out*.......... (12 to 1) 8

Dist: 1l, 1l, ¾l, 4l, ¾l, 1½l. 1m 15.80s. a 5.30s (8 Ran).
(Juma Humaid), B Hanbury

2076 The Budweiser Irish Derby (Group 1) (3-y-o) £342,500 1½m..........(4:00)

1448* COMMANDER IN CHIEF 9-0 Pat Eddery (4) *wl plcd, prog into second 4 fs out, quickened to ld o'r 2 out, styd on strly*.......... (7 to 4 on) 1
1544* HERNANDO (Fr) 9-0 C Asmussen (5) *wl plcd, prog into second o'r 2 fs out, rdn one out, kpt on well*.... (9 to 4) 2
1751^{4} FORESEE 9-0 J P Murtagh (9) *mid-div, prog into 4th 2 fs out, drifted rght one out, styd on*.......... (25 to 1) 3
1544^{5} REGENCY 9-0 W Carson (8) *led till o'r 2 fs out, wknd fnl furlong*.......... (10 to 1) 4
1512* MASSYAR (Ire) 9-0 M J Kinane (2) *mid-div till prog into 4th 3 fs out, rdn and wknd 2 out*.......... (10 to 1) 5
1369^{3} SHREWD IDEA 9-0 W J O'Connor (10) *wl plcd, rdn and btn whn hmpd 2 fs out*.......... (25 to 1) 6
1748^{7} VIA PARIGI (Ire) 9-0 K J Manning (7) *rear, some prog in strt, not rch ldrs*.......... (100 to 1) 7
1448 DESERT TEAM (USA) 9-0 C Roche (1) *wl plcd, hrd rdn and btn whn hmpd 2 fs out*.......... (25 to 1) 8
1292* PORTERSTOWN BOY (Ire) 9-0 P Shanahan (3) *al rear*. ....(150 to 1) 9
1572^{3} LORD BENTLEY 9-0 W R Swinburn (11) *mid-div till rdn and wknd 4 fs out*.......... (100 to 1) 10
1572^{5} SIRSAN (Ire) (bl) 9-0 R Hughes (6) *al rear*.......... (250 to 1) 11

Dist: ¾l, 3l, 5l, 2l, hd, ¾l, 2l, sht-hd, 2l, 7l. 2m 31.20s. a 1.70s (11 Ran).
SR: 83/81/75/65/61/60/58/54/53/ (K Abdulla), H R A Cecil

2077 Anheuser Bush Curragh Cup (Listed) (3-y-o and up) £15,750 1¾m.....(4:45)

1787^{6} VINTAGE CROP 6-9-10 M J Kinane (9) *trkd ldrs, short of room one and a half fs out, squeezed through to ld one out, ran on strly*.......... (11 to 10 fav) 1
1554^{2} BALLYKETT LADY (USA) 3-8-3 W Carson (6) *wl plcd, second strt, rdn 2 fs out, styd on well cl hme*....... (7 to 1) 2
1024* GARABAGH (Ire) 4-10-1 J P Murtagh (3) *led till rdn and hdd one furlong out, no extr*.......... (10 to 1) 3
1512^{3} SINISSIPI (USA) 3-8-11 R Hughes (7) *rear, prog into 5th o'r 3 fs out, styd on, not rch ldrs*.......... (5 to 2) 4
1554^{3} IMAD (USA) 3-8-6 W J Supple (8) *mid-div, pushed alng 6 fs out, styd on one pace*.......... (12 to 1) 5
STRONG CASE (Ire) 5-9-10 W R Swinburn (1) *rear, nvr rch ldrs*.......... (16 to 1) 6
SIMPLY GLORIOUS (Ire) 4-9-10 J D Eddery (10) *mid-div, rdn and wknd 3 fs out*.......... (20 to 1) 7
LORD NOBLE (Ire) 5-9-10 C Roche (4) *al rear*.... (16 to 1) 8
1770^{7} PHARFETCHED 4-9-7 L Piggott (5) *mid-div, prog into 4th hfwy, sn wknd*.......... (10 to 1) 9

Dist: 3½l, 2½l, 1½l, ½l, 2l, ¾l. 3m 4.90s. a 9.40s (9 Ran).
SR: 16/-/9/-/-/-/ (Michael W J Smurfit), D K Weld

2078 McGrath Fillies Handicap (0-105 3-y-o and up) £9,000 7f..............(5:20)

1646* PERNILLA (Ire) [-] 3-9-2 C Roche (6) .... (2 to 1 jt-fav) 1
1575* MILLIE'S CHOICE (Ire) [-] 4-9-6 W J Supple (9) .... (10 to 1) 2
1855^{3} ELIZABETH'S PET (Ire) [-] 3-7-7^{4} (4*) W J Smith (2) (16 to 1) 3
1575^{2} KINDNESS ITSELF (Ire) [-] 3-7-5 (2*) D G O'Shea (8) ....(2 to 1 jt-fav) 4
1199^{2} KAYFA (Ire) [-] 4-8-13 (4*) P Carberry (1) .... (10 to 1) 5
1823^{4} CHEVIOT AMBLE (Ire) [-] 5-9-4 (6*) J R Barry (7) .. (10 to 1) 6
1513^{3} ELEGANT BLOOM (Ire) [-] (bl) 3-7-13 W Carson (5) (9 to 2) 7
1515 LUTE AND LYRE (Ire) [-] 4-8-5 J F Egan (4) .... (20 to 1) 8
2039 TINA'S CHARM (Ire) [-] 4-7-4^{5} (8*) R T Fitzpatrick (3) (50 to 1) 9

Dist: ½l, hd, hd, nk, sht-hd, 2½l. 1m 27.90s. a 4.70s (9 Ran).
SR: 32/34/6/5/28/34/1/-/-/ (T F Brennan), J S Bolger

HAMBURG (GER) (soft)
Sunday June 27th

2079 Idee Hansa-Preis (Group 2) (3-y-o and up) £57,143 1m 3f.............. (3:45)

1042^{5} CARLTON (Ger) 4-9-4 A Tylicki, *made virtually all, hdd one out, rallied to rgn ld 50 yards*.......... 1
1217^{7} SUGUNAS (Ger) 5-9-4 A Boschert, *6th strt, str run to ld one furlong out, hdd and no extr cl hme*.......... 2
695^{6} CHESA PLANA 4-8-11 B Raymond, *wtd wth, ran on wl fnl 2 fs, nvr nrr*.......... 3
1042* EMBARCADERO (Ger) 5-9-4 A Best, *rcd in 3rd, kpt on till no extr fnl 100 yards*.......... 4
1323^{2} CAPTAIN HORATIUS (Ire) 4-9-6 J Reid, *rcd in 4th till lost pl trng into strt*.......... 5
1085^{6} APIS (Ger) 4-9-2 O Schick, *rcd in second, chlgd 2 fs out, no extr*.......... 6
INKOGNITO (Ger) 5-9-2 T Hellier, *al beh*.......... 7
1217^{4} SPORTIVO (USA) 4-9-2 A Helfenbein, *nvr nr to chal*...... 8
1217^{2} HONDO MONDO (Ire) 5-9-6 M Rimmer, *al rear*.......... 9
406^{8} FRISCOLINO (Ger) 5-9-2 L Mader, *al last*.......... 0

Dist: Nk, 1l, hd, nk, ½l, ¾l, sht-hd, 3l. 2m 23.30s. (10 Ran).

LONGCHAMP (FR) (firm)
Sunday June 27th

2080 Prix des Tuileries (Listed) (3-y-o) £14,337 1¼m................. (2:30)

1693* VIVIANA (USA) 8-9 T Jarnet, ... 1
ADORED SLEW (USA) 8-9 A Cruz, ... 2
PELAGIC 8-9 E Saint-Martin, ... 3
SARLIYA (Ire) 8-9 D Bonilla, ... 4

Dist: Hd, nk, 2½l, ¾l, 1l, 1½l, 6l, 5l. 2m 3.30s. a 1.20s (9 Ran).
SR: 53/52/51/46/ (K Abdulla), A Fabre

2081 Grand Prix de Paris (Group 1) (3-y-o) £179,211 1¼m................. (3:10)

1544 FORT WOOD (USA) (bl) 9-2 S Guillot (3) *led till hdd briefly jst und 2 fs out, ran on wl, just hld on*.......... (11 to 2) 1
1367^{2} BIGSTONE (Ire) 9-2 D Boeuf (2) *mid-div, 5th strt, hdwy 2 fs out, ran on wl, jst fld*.......... (36 to 10) 2
SIAM (USA) 9-2 E Saint-Martin (8) *last strt, rdn 2 fs out, fnshd fst*.......... (133 to 10) 3
1544^{2} DERNIER EMPEREUR (USA) 9-2 T Jarnet (6) *7th and ran wide strt, chlgd 2 fs out, ev ch one out, one pace*. ....(18 to 10 fav) 4
1748^{3} EMPEROR JONES (USA) 9-2 R Cochrane (5) *4th strt, led briefly jst und 2 fs out, sn one pace*.......... (11 to 2) 5
1367^{3} SEMILLON 9-2 A Badel (4) *8th strt, rdn and one pace 2 fs out*.......... (92 to 10) 6

1546* SHARMAN (USA) 9-2 L Dettori (9) *nvr able to chal.* ....(11 to 2) 7
1367* LE BALAFRE (Fr) 9-2 O Peslier (1) *3rd strt, ev ch o'r 2 fs out, wknd*................(7 to 2) 8
1544⁴ NEWTON'S LAW (Ire) 9-2 G Mosse (7) *second strt, ev ch 2 and a half fs out, rdn and wknd two out*.....(62 to 10) 9
Dist: Nose, ¾l, nk, ½l, 3l, 1½l, sht-hd, 1½l. 2m 1.60s. b 0.50s (9 Ran).
SR: 77/76/74/73/72/66/63/62/59/ (Sheikh Mohammed), A Fabre

2082 Prix Hubert de Chaudenay (Group 2) (3-y-o) £47,790 1m 7f........... (4:20)

1410* EPAPHOS (Ger) 8-11 E Legrix (4) *last strt, hdwy 2 fs out, led one out, ran on wl*................(5 to 2) 1
1769* INFRASONIC 8-11 T Jarnet (6) *4th strt, rdn 2 fs out, kpt on fnl furlong*................(5 to 4 on) 2
1648³ KARMOUSIL (USA) 8-11 G Mosse (3) *second strt, led 2 fs out, kpt on fnl furlong*................ (79 to 10) 3
1769² SILVERDALE (USA) 8-11 R Cochrane (2) *5th strt, rdn 2 fs out, kpt on, nvr dngrs*................(51 to 10) 4
HUSBAND (USA) 8-11 M Boutin (1) *3rd strt, rdn and wknd 2 fs out*................(99 to 10) 5
1410² KARAYOR (Fr) (bl) 8-11 G Dubroeucq (5) *led till 2 fs out, sn rdn and wknd quickly*................(13 to 1) 6
Dist: ½l, nose, 1l, 6l, 2½l. 3m 9.40s. b 0.60s (6 Ran).
SR: 58/57/56/55/49/46/ (E Wanke), P Bary

SAN SIRO (ITY) (good to firm)
Sunday June 27th

2083 Premio Nico E Vittorio Castellini (Listed) (4-y-o and up) £20,173 1¼m (3:30)

1427³ HALF A TICK (USA) 5-9-1 C Rutter,................ 1
1548⁷ CAPOLAGO (Ire) 6-9-1 S Dettori,................ 2+
BEACHWOOD (Fr) 4-9-1 A Marcialis,................ 2+
FUNAMBULE (Ire) 5-9-3 D Leblond,................ 4
Dist: 1½l, dd-ht, nose, ½l, nk, hd, 2l. 2m 4.70s. (8 Ran).
(C J Wates), P F I Cole

ATLANTIC CITY (USA) (firm)
Sunday June 27th

2084 Caesars International Handicap (Grade 2) (3-y-o and up) £198,675 1m 1f 110yds..........................

STAR OF COZZENE (USA) 5-8-8 J Santos,........ (5 to 2) 1
LURE (USA) 4-8-11 M Smith,................ (5 to 4 on) 2
FINDER'S CHOICE (USA) 8-8-2¹ W Guerra,...... (47 to 1) 3
VAL DES BOIS (Fr) 7-8-7 C Nakatani,...........(27 to 10) 4
ROCKET FUEL (USA) 6-8-1 D Miller Jr,...........(26 to 1) 5
MADE OF GOLD (USA) 4-8-1 Georgina Frost,.....(30 to 1) 6
DR ZOOM (USA) 5-7-12 C Lopez Jr,.............(32 to 1) 7
Dist: 1l, 9l, 2 ¼l, nk, 2 ¾l, 4l. 1m 53.20s. (7 Ran).
(J Siegel), F Boutin

HOLLYWOOD (USA) (firm)
Sunday June 27th

2085 Beverly Hills Handicap (Grade 1) (3-y-o and up) £119,338 1m 1f...........

4729a* FLAWLESSLY (USA) 5-8-11 C McCarron,..... (10 to 9 on) 1
JOLYPHA (USA) 4-8-9 K Desormeaux,.........(5 to 4 on) 2
PARTY CITED (USA) 4-8-5 P Valenzuela,........(98 to 10) 3
1695⁶ STEFF GRAF (Brz) 5-8-1 D Flores,................(27 to 1) 4
Dist: 9l, nose, 2l. 1m 47.00s. (4 Ran).
(Harbor View Farm), C Whittingham

HAMILTON (good)
Monday June 28th

Going Correction: MINUS 0.30 sec. per fur. (races 1,2,3,6), MINUS 0.20 (4,5)

2086 Wylies Ltd Claiming Stakes Class F (3-y-o and up) £2,040 1m 1f 36yds. .(7:00)

1811³ IMPERIAL BID (Fr) 5-9-4 Dean McKeown (8) *trkd ldrs, hdwy o'r 3 fs out, chlgd 2 out, led entering last, sn rdn, ran on*................(9 to 2 op 4 to 1 tchd 5 to 1) 1
1811² BARLEY CAKE 3-8-3⁵ R Hills (2) *hld up beh, hdwy o'r 2 fs out, rdn and ev ch ins last, kpt on*... (6 to 1 op 5 to 1) 2
1932⁵ GWEEK (Ire) 3-8-2 P Robinson (1) *hld up beh, hdwy 3 fs out, rdn o'r one out, kpt on*......(5 to 2 fav op 3 to 1) 3
1892² DRUMDONNA (Ire) 3-8-6 J Carroll (4) *chsd ldr, led o'r 3 fs out, rdn 2 out, hdd and wknd entering last.*................(6 to 1 op 9 to 2) 4
1674⁹ PERSIAN LION 4-9-0 Alex Greaves (9) *in tch, effrt and hdwy 4 fs out, sn rdn, one pace.* (200 to 1 op 100 to 1) 5
1902³ BENGAL TIGER (Ire) (v) 5-8-12 D Holland (6) *led, rdn 4 fs out, sn hdd and wknd*............ (7 to 2 tchd 9 to 2) 6

4764a THISONESFORALICE 5-9-1 (7*) S Mulvey (5) *hld up, hdwy on outsd o'r 4 fs out, rdn 2 out, sn btn*.......(33 to 1) 7
1811⁴ SAOIRSE (Ire) 5-9-3 K Darley (7) *chsd ldrs, rdn hfwy, sn wknd*................(10 to 1 op 7 to 1) 8
1166⁴ BAFFIE 4-8-11 A Mackay (3) *prmnt, rdn and wknd 4 fs out*................ (50 to 1 op 20 to 1) 9
Dist: ½l, 1½l, 1½l, 4l, 2l, 1½l, 3½l, 8l. 1m 56.80s. a 2.80s (9 Ran).
SR: 20/3/-/-/-/-/ (Lord Durham), Denys Smith

2087 Letheby & Christopher Galloping Gourmet Rating Related Maiden Fillies Stakes Class E (0-70 3-y-o) £2,259 1m 65yds......................(7:30)

1733² PRINCESS TATEUM (Ire) 8-11 P Robinson (6) *trkd ldrs, effrt and not much room o'r 2 fs out, squeezed through to ld one and a half out, sn rdn, edgd rght, ran on.*................(7 to 2 op 3 to 1 tchd 4 to 1) 1
1435² DIPLOMATIST 8-11 J Carroll (5) *trkd ldrs, hdwy on ins and not clr run one and a half fs out, swtchd entering last, ran on wl und pres.* (7 to 1 op 5 to 1 tchd 8 to 1) 2
1743 MIND THE ROOF (Ire) 8-11 R Hills (3) *trkd ldrs, hdwy on outsd 3 fs out, chlgd and ev ch appr last, sn rdn, wknd wl ins last*................(4 to 1) 3
1464² LANDRAIL (USA) 8-11 D Holland (4) *cl up, led hfwy, sn rdn, hdd one and a half fs out, wknd ins last.* ......(6 to 5 fav op 11 to 8 tchd 11 to 10 and 6 to 4) 4
1630⁸ CORNFLAKE 8-11 K Fallon (1) *cl up, chlgd 2 and a half fs out, sn rdn, hng rght and wknd o'r one out.*................(16 to 1 op 14 to 1) 5
1737 DUSKY DUCHESS (Ire) (v) 8-11 J Fanning (2) *led to hfwy, sn wknd*................(200 to 1 op 100 to 1) 6
Dist: ¾l, 1l, 1½l, 1½l, 8l. 1m 46.60s. a 2.60s (6 Ran).
SR: 21/19/16/11/6/-/ (J R Good), M R Channon

2088 Estee Lauder 'Spellbound' Handicap Class E (0-70 3-y-o and up) £2,448 1m 65yds........................ (8:00)

1847⁵ MENTALASANYTHIN [62] 4-9-10 A Mackay (8) *trkd ldrs, hdwy to ld o'r 3 fs out, rdn and ran on strly ins last.*................(5 to 1 tchd 8 to 1) 1
1919⁷ NO COMEBACKS [53] 5-9-1 K Fallon (1) *hld up, hdwy on ins o'r 2 fs out, sn chasing wnr, kpt on und pres.*................ (4 to 1 fav tchd 9 to 2) 2
1849⁵ CRESELLY [55] 6-9-3 Dean McKeown (5) *chsd ldrs, effrt 3 fs out, sn ev ch, one pace und pres frm 2 out.*................(9 to 2 op 4 to 1 tchd 5 to 1) 3
1634⁶ BOLD MELODY [47] 4-8-9 D Holland (6) *in tch, hdwy o'r 3 fs out, not much room 2 out, sn rdn, one pace.*................(8 to 1 op 7 to 1) 4
1900⁶ VENTURE FOURTH [38] (bl) 4-8-0 P Robinson (3) *hld up beh, hdwy on outsd o'r 2 fs out, sn rdn, no imprsn.*................(5 to 1 op 6 to 1) 5
1181² WHITE CREEK (Ire) [63] (v) 3-9-1 J Carroll (7) *chsd ldr, led hfwy, sn rdn, hdd o'r 3 fs out, wknd.* (5 to 1 op 7 to 2) 6
1811⁵ GOLD SURPRISE (Ire) [52] 4-9-0 J Fortune (2) *led to hfwy.*................ (10 to 1 op 7 to 1 tchd 11 to 1) 7
1850⁵ GRUMPY'S GRAIN (Ire) [57] 3-8-9 J Fanning (4) *chsd ldrs, rdn o'r 3 fs out, sn lost pl and beh.* (10 to 1 op 7 to 1) 8
Dist: 1l, 2½l, 1l, nk, 6l, 3½l, 12l. 1m 46.30s. a 2.30s (8 Ran).
SR: 38/26/20/9/-/ (Mrs M O'Donnell), A Bailey

2089 Westpoint Hotel Selling Stakes Class G (3-y-o) £1,520 5f 4yds.........(8:30)

1159⁶ CRACKER JACK (bl) 8-11 J Fanning (3) *trkd ldg pair, effrt 2 fs out, rdn to ld ins last, ran on.*................(9 to 2 op 6 to 1 tchd 7 to 1) 1
2047⁵ COLMAR (bl) 8-6 K Fallon (1) *chsd ldrs, reminders and swtchd o'r 2 fs out, kpt on und pres ins last.*................(3 to 1 op 7 to 2 tchd 4 to 1) 2
766⁴ CONVENIENT MOMENT 8-12 J Carroll (2) *led, rdn 2 fs out, hdd and wknd ins last*........(6 to 4 on op 9 to 4 on) 3
1937⁹ PRESS ONWARD 8-6 Dean McKeown (4) *chsd ldr, rdn 2 fs out, wknd appr last.* (16 to 1 op 10 to 1 tchd 20 to 1) 4
Dist: 3½l, nk, 1l. 1m 1.10s. a 2.80s (4 Ran).
SR: 21/2/7/-/ (T Fairhurst), T Fairhurst

2090 EBF West Of Scotland Womens Business Club Median Auction Maiden Stakes Class E (2-y-o) £2,259 5f 4yds ....(9:00)

1798⁴ CASPIAN GOLD 9-0 Dean McKeown (7) *al cl up, hdwy to ld 2 fs out, rdn and ran on gmely ins last.*................ (15 to 2 op 8 to 1 tchd 10 to 1) 1
1828³ THE MULTIYORKER (Ire) 8-9 P Robinson (2) *trkd ldrs gng wl, hdwy 2 fs out, swtchd and chlgd entering last, rdn and kpt on well*........ (9 to 4 op 2 to 1 tchd 5 to 2) 2
1632² TEETOTALLER (Ire) 9-0 J Carroll (3) *prmnt, ev ch 2 fs out, sn rdn, one pace fnl furlong*....(7 to 4 fav tchd 2 to 1) 3
18,4⁴ LEADING PRINCESS (Ire) 8-9 J Fanning (4) *prmnt, rdn and one pace fnl 2 fs*................(12 to 1 op 8 to 1) 4
1227⁶ SNAKE PLISSKEN (Ire) 9-0 A Mackay (6) *chsd ldrs, rdn 2 fs out, kpt on same pace.* .... (4 to 1 op 9 to 2 tchd 5 to 1 and 7 to 2) 5

BLAIN 9-0 J Fortune (1) *cl up, rdn and wknd 2 fs out.* .... (50 to 1 op 20 to 1) 6
1632[3] GREY TOPPA 8-9 K Fallon (5) *led, rdn and hdd 2 fs out, sn wknd.* .... (7 to 1 op 8 to 1 tchd 9 to 1) 7
Dist: Sht-hd, 2l, 1l, 1½l, 5l, ½l. 1m 0.50s. a 2.20s (7 Ran).
SR: 36/30/27/18/17/-/-/ (P Nabavi), M Johnston

2091 Flowerscene Dozen Red Roses Maiden Handicap Class E (0-70 3-y-o and up) £2,364 1½m 17yds. . . . . (9:30)

1733[3] BAYRAK (USA) [65] 3-8-13 R Hills (6) *chsd ldrs, hdwy on bit 2 fs out, sn led, rdn and ran on strly ins last.* ....(11 to 4 op 3 to 1 tchd 5 to 2 and 4 to 1) 1
1890[7] BAY TERN (USA) [40] 7-8-3 K Fallon (2) *cl up, led aftr 4 fs, rdn 3 out, hdd one and a half out, kpt on gmely ins last.* ....(12 to 1 tchd 14 to 1) 2
1880[3] DIAMOND WEDDING (USA) [60] (bl) 4-9-9 D Holland (3) *hld up, hdwy 3 fs out, rdn appr last, kpt on wl.* ....(9 to 2 tchd 5 to 1) 3
2059[3] WILSONIC [65] (bl) 4-10-0 Dean McKeown (7) *hld up, hdwy 3 fs out, chlgd 2 out, ev ch till no extr wl ins last.* ....(2 to 1 fav op 9 to 4 tchd 5 to 2) 4
1630[4] CHALLENGER ROW (Ire) [49] (bl) 3-7-11 J Fanning (5) *chsd ldrs, rdn 3 fs out, sn one pace.* ....(7 to 2 op 4 to 1 tchd 9 to 2) 5
1866[9] CRESTWOOD LAD (USA) [50] 4-8-13 K Darley (4) *led 4 fs, cl up till rdn and wknd 3 out.*........ (25 to 1 op 20 to 1) 6
1781[7] CHADWICK'S GINGER [39] 5-8-2 P Robinson (1) *hld up, hdwy on outsd 3 fs out, rdn and wknd 2 out.* ....(20 to 1 tchd 25 to 1) 7
Dist: ½l, hd, ½l, 2½l, ½l, 2½l. 2m 36.60s. a 3.60s (7 Ran).
SR: 27/16/35/39/3/18/2/ (Hamdan Al-Maktoum), A C Stewart

LIMERICK (IRE) (good)
Monday June 28th

2092 Bellevue Race (3-y-o and up) £2,245 1¼m. . . . . (5:30)

1510* FAMILY FORTUNE (Ire) 3-9-2 P V Gilson (4) .....(Evens fav) 1
1822* MADANIYYA (USA) 3-8-13 J P Murtagh (5) .... (5 to 2) 2
1553[3] VALONA (Ire) 3-8-13 K J Manning (3) ....(3 to 1) 3
1609[5] ATLANTIC ADIOS (Ire) (bl) 3-9-2 P Shanahan (1)...(10 to 1) 4
1622 VROOM VROOM (Ire) 3-8-6 J F Egan (6).......... (20 to 1) 5
Dist: 1l, 4l, 7l, 2½l. 2m 3.50s. (5 Ran).
(Mrs M V O'Brien), Charles O'Brien

2093 Aughinish Island Claiming Race (2-y-o) £2,245 7f. . . . . (6:00)

1197 ORANEDIN 8-13 P Shanahan (1) ....(100 to 30) 1
1432[2] ALSTOMERIA 8-10 P V Gilson (5) ....(2 to 1 fav) 2
SUAVE REDSKIN (Ire) 8-13 W J Supple (3) ....(4 to 1) 3
WINTER'S OVER 8-2 N G McCullagh (4)........... (7 to 1) 4
1442 BOLD EMIR 8-13 S Craine (2) ....(10 to 1) 5
SPEEDWELL BLUE (USA) 7-8 (2*) D G O'Shea (7) (10 to 1) 6
JENZSOPH (Ire) 7-6 (6*) P P Murphy (9)..........(12 to 1) 7
HAVE A CUT (Ire) 7-8 (4*) W J Smith (6)........... (33 to 1) 8
CLASSIC EMBLEM (Ire) 7-12 J F Egan (8)........ (10 to 1) 9
Dist: 1½l, 4l, ¾l, ½l. 1m 27.10s. (9 Ran).
(Mrs O O'Connor), Declan Gillespie

2094 Limerick Q.R. Handicap (0-60 4-y-o and up) £2,245 2m. . . . .(8:00)

1508[6] BUZZ ALONG [-] 7-11-3 (3*) Mr A R Coonan (15) . . (10 to 1) 1
PARTY GUEST [-] 6-11-0 (7*) Mr J P Fahey (17) .... (16 to 1) 2
SILENT JET [-] 12-11-11 (5*) Mr H F Cleary (8) ..... (12 to 1) 3
1163[8] SOPHISM (USA) [-] 4-12-5 Mr T M Walsh (10)........(4 to 1) 4
1467 BROWN TOP [-] 6-10-3 (7*) Mr G P FitzGerald (11) (14 to 1) 5
QUIET CITY [-] 6-10-8 (7*) Mr J T McNamara (2) ....(8 to 1) 6
1962 GO DEAS [-] 6-10-13 (7*) Miss F M Crowley (3).....(8 to 1) 7
852 WOODFIELD ROSE [-] 4-10-5 (7*) Miss S J Leahy (14) ....(25 to 1) 8
1987 KINVARA LADY (Ire) [-] 4-9-9 (7*) Mr P A Roche (5) (25 to 1) 9
TERZIA [-] 6-10-3 (7*) Mr T R Hughes (1) ....(9 to 4 fav) 10
CAT FIGHT [-] 6-9-12 (7*) Mr A Daly (9)............(16 to 1) 11
1987[6] MAN OF STRAW [-] 7-10-3 Mr S R Murphy (6)...... (7 to 1) 12
FROZEN FRIEND [-] 10-10-8 (7*) Miss A Sloane (4) (14 to 1) 13
1757 BLUEJACKET (Ire) [-] (bl) 5-11-1 (3*) Mr D Marnane (13) ....(7 to 1) 14
SPRING RITE [-] 6-9-7 (7*) Mrs K Walsh (7)........ (10 to 1) 15
Dist: 3l, 4½l, 2l, 4½l. 3m 26.80s. (15 Ran).
(W M Roper), W M Roper

NOTTINGHAM (good to firm)
Monday June 28th
Going Correction: NIL

2095 Grace Selling Handicap Class G (0-60 3-y-o) £2,742 1m 54yds. . . . . (2:15)

1534[8] HOT OFF THE PRESS [45] 9-2 J Reid (11) *led 2 fs, prmnt, jnd ldr 3 out, led wl o'r one out, rdn out.* ....(7 to 1 op 6 to 1) 1
1074[5] GLOWING PATH [45] (v) 9-2 R Cochrane (9) *hld up in-mid-div, rdn o'r 2 fs out, picked up bit entering last, str run on ins to go second nr finish.*.......(10 to 1 op 6 to 1) 2
1635[5] SUPERENSIS [47] 8-11 (7*) Kim McDonnell (12) *led aftr 2 fs till wl o'r one out, edgd rght, one pace ins last.* .... (12 to 1 op 10 to 1) 3
1674[3] IRISH ROOTS (Ire) [49] (v) 9-3 (3*) J Weaver (14) *hld up, hdwy on outsd 3 fs out, kpt on one pace ins fnl 2.* ....(14 to 1 op 16 to 1 tchd 12 to 1) 4
1866 B B GLEN [47] 8-13 (5*) C Hodgson (4) *slwly away, hdwy o'r 2 fs out, kpt on one pace*....... (16 to 1 op 10 to 1) 5
1627[6] NIGHTMARE LADY [33] 7-11 (7*) C Hawksley (17) *mid-div, hdwy on outsd o'r 2 fs out, nvr nrr*............(25 to 1) 6
1771[7] SUMMERS DREAM [34] 7-12 (7*) D Wright (5) *mid-div, one pace ins fnl 2 fs*......(33 to 1 op 20 to 1 tchd 40 to 1) 7
1703[6] NORLING (Ire) [43] 9-0 G Duffield (8) *chsd ldrs, rdn and wknd 2 fs out*...................... (6 to 1 op 7 to 1) 8
1271[4] WALID'S PRINCESS (Ire) [49] 9-6 J Quinn (3) *mid-div, no hdwy fnl 3 fs*........ (5 to 1 fav op 6 to 1 tchd 7 to 1) 9
1674[2] CORONA GOLD [48] (bl) 9-5 W Carson (15) *chsd ldrs, rdn and wknd wl o'r 2 fs out*............(10 to 1 op 4 to 1) 10+
1480 DON'T TELL JEAN [35] 8-1 (5*) Darren Moffatt (1) *chsd ldrs till wknd wl o'r 2 fs out*...........(25 to 1 op 20 to 1) 10+
1501[6] MONET MONET MONET [39] 8-10 N Carlisle (2) *beh, no imprsn frm hfwy*...................(25 to 1 op 20 to 1) 12
1817[7] LE COUTEAU [50] 9-7 T Quinn (6) *in tch to hfwy.* ....(10 to 1 op 8 to 1) 13
1913[7] BAEZA [40] (v) 8-11 G Carter (18) *beh hfwy.* ....(20 to 1 op 16 to 1) 14
1896[8] KENTUCKY DREAMS [42] 8-13 R P Elliott (7) *al beh.* .... (50 to 1 op 25 to 1) 15
1972[9] WOODLANDS ELECTRIC [35] 8-6 N Adams (10) *slwly away, al beh*......................(50 to 1 op 33 to 1) 16
899 MUSICAL TIMES [50] 9-7 L Dettori (13) *al beh, tld off.* .... (16 to 1 op 10 to 1) 17
872 STOCKFORCE [47] (bl) 9-4 W Newnes (16) *frnt rnk till wknd quickly o'r 3 fs out, sn tld off.* .... (20 to 1 op 33 to 1) 18
Dist: ¾l, 1l, 1½l, ¾l, hd, 1½l, nk, 1½l, 3l, dd-ht. 1m 45.30s. a 5.30s (18 Ran).
SR: 23/21/20/17/13/-/-/2/3/ (R M Whitaker), R M Whitaker

2096 Nottingham Evening Post Maiden Stakes Class D (2-y-o) £3,699 6f 15yds . . . .(2:45)

1131[8] UNBLEST 9-0 G Duffield (3) *hld up, shaken up to ld appr fnl furlong, quickened clr ins, imprsv.* ....(7 to 4 fav tchd 6 to 4 and 2 to 1) 1
1091[2] JACOB BOGDANI 9-0 T Quinn (1) *hld up in tch, led briefly wl o'r one furlong out, outpcd ins last.* ....(3 to 1 op 5 to 2 tchd 7 to 2) 2
1773[6] TANFIRION CHIEF 9-0 R P Elliott (5) *pld hrd, led aftr 2 fs till wl o'r one out, kpt on one pace*............ (25 to 1) 3
LADY PHYL 8-6 (3*) B Doyle (2) *hld up, ran on ins fnl furlong, nvr nrr*.. (33 to 1) 4
1905[6] MACIZO 9-0 J Reid (4) *prmnt, dsptd ld 2 fs out, rdn and wknd entering last*................(20 to 1 op 25 to 1) 5
1640 IMPERIAL TREATMENT 9-0 W Newnes (6) *prmnt till outpcd ins fnl 2 fs.* ....(7 to 1 op 12 to 1 tchd 16 to 1 and 6 to 1) 6
THEON (USA) 9-0 W Ryan (7) *hld up, effrt o'r 2 fs out, nvr nr to chal*..............(4 to 1 op 6 to 4 tchd 9 to 2) 7
1063 VERCINGETORIX (Ire) 9-0 Paul Eddery (8) *prmnt, rdn o'r 2 fs out, wknd quickly appr last*.... (33 to 1 op 14 to 1) 8
PAPPA'S PET 9-0 L Piggott (9) *led 2 fs, rdn two out, sn btn, eased*..................(13 to 2 op 4 to 1 tchd 7 to 1) 9
Dist: 5l, ¾l, sht-hd, ¾l, 2½l, 2½l, 3½l, 10l. 1m 14.40s. a 2.90s (9 Ran).
SR: 42/22/19/13/15/5/ (Lord Vestey), J R Fanshawe

2097 Usher Walker Maiden Stakes Class D (3-y-o and up) £3,757 1m 54yds (3:15)

1587[2] TAHDID 3-8-6 W Carson (13) *made all, stretched out wl whn chlgd o'r one furlong out, cmftbly.* ....(6 to 4 on op 5 to 4) 1
1713[7] DESERT TIME 3-8-11 W R Swinburn (10) *hld up in cl tch, hdwy on bit to chal 2 fs out, sn rdn, no imprsn, eased whn held ins last*........(5 to 1 op 7 to 2 tchd 6 to 1) 2
TOPESKI 3-8-6 T Sprake (7) *hld up, hdwy on ins o'r 3 fs out, outpcd inside fnl 2.* ....(12 to 1 op 20 to 1 tchd 25 to 1) 3
MO-ADDAB (Ire) 3-8-11 A McGlone (2) *hld up, hdwy 3 fs out, kpt on one pace ins fnl 2.* .... (14 to 1 op 8 to 1 tchd 16 to 1) 4
1931[8] ESSEX GIRL 3-8-6 L Dettori (8) *hld up, hdwy 3 fs out, one pace fnl 2*..........(20 to 1 op 12 to 1 tchd 25 to 1) 5
1617[5] BALI HERO (Ire) 3-8-11 Paul Eddery (5) *al abt same pl, rdn and no hdwy ins fnl 3 fs*.............(5 to 1 op 3 to 1) 6
1671[8] MONAZITE 3-8-11 G Carter (3) *trkd ldrs till wknd o'r 2 fs out*................................(25 to 1 op 14 to 1) 7
1039 JUPITER STAR 4-9-7 P D'Arcy (6) *pld hrd, chsd wnr till rdn 2 fs out, wknd quickly*....... (66 to 1 op 50 to 1) 8
AMOREM 3-8-11 W Newnes (9) *al rear.* ....(33 to 1 op 20 to 1) 9

1587 PADDINGTON GIRL (Ire) 3-8-6 W Ryan (12) *al beh.* ....(33 to 1 op 16 to 1) 10
DISSIDENT DANCER 4-9-7 T Wall (11) *chsd ldrs, rdn o'r 3 fs out, sn btn.*....(150 to 1 op 100 to 1 tchd 200 to 1) 11
DUNBAR 3-8-11 G Duffield (4) *al beh, tld off fnl 3 fs.* ....(25 to 1 op 16 to 1) 12
1729[4] GATHERING 4-9-7 N Adams (14) *pld hrd, prmnt till ran wide into strt, sn btn, tld off.*......(50 to 1 op 33 to 1) 13
SPIRIT OF DANCE 4-8-13 (3*) S D Williams (1) *slwly away, al beh, tld off.*..................(66 to 1 op 50 to 1) 14
Dist: 4l, 3½l, 5l, 1l, 1l, 10l, 1½l, ¾l, 2½l, 2l. 1m 43.70s. a 3.70s (14 Ran).
SR: 37/30/14/4/-/-/ (Hamdan Al-Maktoum), P T Walwyn

2098 Harland Simon Claiming Stakes Class F (3-y-o) £2,444 1m 1f 213yds... (3:45)

1838[4] BEST APPEARANCE (Ire) (bl) 8-11 W R Swinburn (1) *hld up, swtchd rght 2 fs out, led appr last, sn clr, easily.* ....(13 to 8 fav op Evens tchd 7 to 4) 1
1416[9] CONVOY (bl) 8-11 T Quinn (4) *led one furlong, led hfwy till o'r 3 out, led 2 out till appr last, outpcd.* ....(3 to 1 op 4 to 1 tchd 9 to 2) 2
1697 MARAT (USA) 9-1 W Newnes (3) *trkd ldrs, led o'r 3 fs out to 2 out, outpcd appr last.*...........................(5 to 1) 3
1675[6] DONTBETALKING (Ire) 8-6 J Quinn (2) *led aftr one furlong to hfwy, ev ch 2 out, one pace.*...... (9 to 2 op 6 to 1) 4
HAPPY TUPPENCE 7-12 N Adams (5) *al last, lost tch o'r 3 fs out, tld off.*..........(11 to 2 op 5 to 1 tchd 6 to 1) 5
Dist: 5l, 2½l, ¾l, 30l. 2m 13.30s. a 10.30s (5 Ran).
(Bezwell Fixings Limited), J G FitzGerald

2099 Canadian Pacific Newsprint Lady Amateur Riders' Handicap Class F (0-75 3-y-o and up) £2,623 1m 54yds ....(4:15)

1498[2] THUNDERING [33] 8-9-4[1] Miss Diana Jones (2) *hld up rear, short of room and pld out wide one and a half fs out, ran on strly to ld nr finish.*..................(10 to 1) 1
1659[6] PUSEY STREET BOY [38] 6-9-4 (5*) Mrs S Bosley (6) *al prmnt, led o'r 2 fs out, ran on ins last, hdd cl hme.* ....(10 to 1 op 8 to 1 tchd 12 to 1) 2
ROMOOSH [64] 4-11-0 (7*) Miss F Burke (4) *hld up in tch, swtchd rght wl o'r one furlong out, ran on one pace ins last.*..................(14 to 1 op 16 to 1 tchd 12 to 1) 3
1866[3] ESSAYEFFSEE [44] 4-10-1 Miss J Winter (7) *dsptd ld till o'r 4 fs out, one pace appr last.*.......... (6 to 1 op 9 to 2) 4
1891* YUNUS EMRE (Ire) [50] 3-9-4 (7*) Mrs L Lawson (8) *made most till o'r 4 fs out, wknd appr last.* ....(9 to 2 op 3 to 1 tchd 5 to 1) 5
1623[2] BILL MOON [54] 7-10-11 Miss J Feilden (5) *hld up, hdwy on outsd 2 fs out, outpcd entering last.* ....(9 to 2 op 7 to 2 tchd 5 to 1) 6
2015* SYLVAN SABRE (Ire) [62] (v) 4-11-5 Miss J Allison (1) *hld up in tch, wknd wl o'r one furlong out.* .... (5 to 1 op 4 to 1 tchd 11 to 2) 7
1204 SHAMGAAN (USA) [60] 3-10-7 Mrs M Cowdrey (3) *pld hrd, rcd on ins, led o'r 4 fs out till over 2 out, sn btn, eased.* ....(7 to 2 fav op 3 to 1 tchd 4 to 1) 8
Dist: Hd, 4l, 1½l, nk, 1½l, 7l, 1l. 1m 45.30s. a 5.30s (8 Ran).
SR: 25/29/43/18/13/22/9/-/ (Miss Victoria Jones), A W Jones

2100 Ferag-RMO Handicap Class D (0-80 3-y-o and up) £3,201 1m 1f 213yds ....(4:45)

1900* SILVER SAMURAI [66] 4-9-7 (7ex) L Dettori (1) *trkd ldr, cruised into ld o'r 4 fs out, hrd hld.* ....(Evens fav op 11 to 10 on tchd 6 to 4) 1
1604[6] TIFFANY'S CASE (Ire) [57] 4-8-12 R Cochrane (2) *pld hrd, hld up in last pl, hdwy to go second appr fnl furlong, no ch wth wnr.*......... (6 to 1 op 4 to 1 tchd 7 to 1) 2
1878[3] HAROLDON (Ire) [69] 4-9-10 W Ryan (3) *hld up, wnt second o'r 2 fs out, hrd rdn and wknd appr last.* ....(4 to 1 op 5 to 1 tchd 6 to 1 and 7 to 2) 3
1225[8] JADIRAH (USA) [68] 3-8-11 W Carson (4) *led to 4 fs out, btn 2 out, eased.*....................... (7 to 2 op 2 to 1) 4
Dist: 3½l, 4l, 12l. 2m 11.60s. a 8.60s (4 Ran).
SR: 21/5/9/-/ (J D Cable), Mrs V A Aconley

2101 Shadwell Stud Apprentice Series Handicap Class F (0-70 3-y-o and up) £2,511 1¾m 15yds............ (5:15)

1712[3] FULL QUIVER [39] (v) 8-8-3 D Wright (5) *hld up rear, hdwy 2 fs out, ran on und str pres to ld last strd.* ....(6 to 1 op 5 to 1) 1
1430 BALLY KNIGHT [52] 7-9-2 C Hodgson (4) *hld up rear gng cmftbly, hdwy to ld 2 fs out, hrd rdn ins last, ct last strd.*..................(7 to 1 op 6 to 1 tchd 8 to 1) 2
1764[5] PERSIAN SOLDIER [44] 6-8-8 Darren Moffatt (7) *pld hrd, led aftr 4 fs to 2 out, kpt on one pace.*... (9 to 2 op 4 to 1) 3
1752 WELSHMAN [60] 7-9-10 Stephen Davies (1) *prmnt, pushed alng hfwy, rdn and wknd appr fnl furlong.* ....(11 to 4 fav op 2 to 1) 4
1834* QUALITAIR RHYTHM (Ire) [59] (v) 5-9-6 (3*) G Mitchell (3) *hld up in tch, rdn o'r 2 fs out, sn btn.*.. (11 to 2 op 9 to 2) 5
1764[6] EXPLOSIVE SPEED (USA) [38] 5-8-2 J Marshall (2) *led 4 fs, in tch till wknd o'r 2 out.* ....(11 to 2 op 5 to 1 tchd 7 to 1) 6
1732[4] GLINT OF AYR [54] 3-8-1 Kim McDonnell (8) *mid-div, lost tch ins fnl 3 fs.*.....................(9 to 1 op 6 to 1) 7
1654[9] STATIA (Ire) [29] 5-7-4 (3*) Claire Balding (6) *rcd keenly, prmnt till wknd quickly o'r 3 fs out, tld off.* ....(40 to 1 op 33 to 1) 8
Dist: Sht-hd, 4l, 3½l, 3½l, 8l, 2½l. 3m 5.30s. a 7.40s (8 Ran).
SR: 15/27/11/20/12/ (Richard Parker), Mrs Barbara Waring

RIPON (good)
Monday June 28th
Going Correction: MINUS 0.25 sec. per fur.

2102 William Hill 'First For Debit' Maiden Auction Fillies Stakes Class E (2-y-o) £2,976 6f.................... (2:30)

1672[2] FLOATING TRIAL 8-11 J Carroll (5) *led, rdn 2 fs out, hdd entering last, rallied to ld towards finish.* ....(9 to 1 op 7 to 1) 1
SKY MUSIC 8-11 N Connorton (2) *al frnt rnk, improved to ld entering fnl furlong, hdd towards finish.* ....(8 to 1 tchd 9 to 1) 2
1418[5] ELLARUTH (Ire) 8-11 P Robinson (9) *mid-div, drvn to improve fnl 2 fs, kpt on ins last.* ....(13 to 2 op 9 to 1 tchd 10 to 1 and 6 to 1) 3
1897[5] HEATHYARDS LADY (USA) 8-11 K Darley (7) *pressed ldr, ev ch fnl 2 fs, no extr wl ins last.*..... (14 to 1 op 12 to 1) 4
2021[9] STARICA (Ire) (bl) 8-8 (3*) S Maloney (4) *in tch, drvn alng 2 fs out, styd on ins last.*...................... (20 to 1) 5
1418[4] ORIENTAL AIR (Ire) 8-11 A Culhane (6) *in tch, pushed alng hfwy, improved on outer o'r one furlong out, kpt on same pace ins last.*........................ (7 to 1 op 6 to 1) 6
1418[2] MICHELLISA 8-11 Dean McKeown (3) *nvr far away, effrt and rdn 2 fs out, wknd ins last.* ....(13 to 8 fav op 2 to 1 tchd 6 to 4) 7
1926[3] GIGUE 8-11 K Fallon (10) *pressed ldg bunch on outsd, drvn o'r 2 fs out, wknd appr last.*....(8 to 1 op 7 to 1) 8
DEER IN THE GLEN 8-11 Dale Gibson (8) *slwly into strd, beh and sn pushed alng, lost tch o'r 2 fs out.* ....(16 to 1 op 14 to 1) 9
KENTUCKY FLYER 8-11 L Charnock (1) *beh and sn outpcd, struggling hfwy, eased o'r one furlong out.* ....(14 to 1 op 12 to 1 tchd 10 to 1) 10
S'AMUSER 8-11 A Clark (11) *sluggish strt, nvr able to reco'r.*..................................(10 to 1 op 8 to 1) 11
Dist: ½l, ½l, sht-hd, 1l, ½l, sht-hd, 3l, 8l, 2½l, 2l. 1m 13.10s. a 2.50s (11 Ran).
SR: 17/15/13/12/8/6/5/-/-/ (David Fish), J Berry

2103 William Hill Selling Stakes Class G (2-y-o) £2,322 5f.................. (3:00)

ROCHE ABBEY (Ire) 8-6 Dean McKeown (4) *chsd ldrs, rdn alng 2 fs out, ran on to ld ins fnl furlong, edgd rght and ran on wl.*..........(2 to 1 fav op 3 to 1 tchd 7 to 4) 1
1739[4] FORBIDDEN MONKEY 8-6 J Carroll (8) *dwlt, beh and sn pushed alng, improved hfwy, kpt on ins fnl furlong.* ....(7 to 2 op 5 to 1) 2
1889[2] RED GRIT (Ire) (bl) 8-6 J Lowe (7) *led one furlong, styd hndy, rgned ld o'r one furlong out, hdd ins last, no extr.*..........................(8 to 1 op 6 to 1) 3
HENRY THE HAWK 8-11 S Webster (6) *chsd ldrs, effrt and rdn 2 fs out, one pace whn not much room wl ins fnl furlong.*..................(20 to 1 op 14 to 1) 4
RATTLESNAKE ANNIE 8-6 Dale Gibson (2) *beh and sn drvn alng, kpt on fnl furlong, nvr dngrs* (10 to 1 op 8 to 1) 5
1837[7] DOCTOR JAMES (Ire) (bl) 8-11 K Darley (9) *fractious at strt, chsd ldrs, led aftr one furlong, hdd o'r one furlong out, wknd quickly.*.................. (3 to 1 op 7 to 4) 6
INAMORATA 8-6 S Whitworth (3) *beh, rdn alng aftr 2 fs, no imprsn.*............................(7 to 1 op 5 to 1) 7
1889[6] SALTPETRE (Ire) 8-11 M Wigham (1) *sn beh, pushed alng and ran green thrght, nvr on terms.* ....(20 to 1 op 12 to 1) 8
Dist: 1l, sht-hd, 2l, 3l, 1½l, 1l, 2½l. 1m 1.30s. a 3.30s (8 Ran).
SR: 1/-/-/-/-/ (Stephen Philip Sage), M Johnston

2104 William Hill Freephone Maiden Fillies Handicap Class F (0-60 3-y-o and up) £3,052 1m 1f.................. (3:30)

HEAVY ROCK (Ire) [27] 4-8-5 (5*) L Newton (10) *made all, clr 3 fs out, sn pushed alng, hld on gmely cl hme.* ....(20 to 1 op 16 to 1 tchd 25 to 1) 1
1776[2] CLAIRIFICATION (Ire) [48] 3-9-6 P Robinson (13) *hld up, gd hdwy o'r 2 fs out, str run fnl furlong, jst held.* ....(13 to 2 op 6 to 1) 2
1940 MARY MACBLAIN [34] 4-9-3 J Carroll (16) *mid-div, improved on inner 3 fs out, ran on wl fnl furlong.* ....(12 to 1) 3
1866[8] MUMMYS ROCKET [40] (bl) 4-9-9 A Mackay (11) *nvr far away, drvn alng o'r 2 fs out, kpt on same pace ins last.* .... (10 to 1 op 8 to 1) 4

1578[5] DANCES WITH GOLD [42] (bl) 3-9-0 Dean McKeown (6) *keen hold in rear, not much room and swtchd o'r 2 fs out, wnt rght appr last, no extr*.......... (9 to 2 op 5 to 1) 5
SLUMBER THYME (Ire) [38] 4-9-7 K Fallon (5) *in tch, drvn alng entering strt, kpt on same pace fnl 2 fs*... (16 to 1) 6
907[6] BOLD LINE [46] 3-9-4 Dale Gibson (12) *keen hold in mid-div, effrt 4 fs out, nvr able to chal*. (10 to 1 op 9 to 1) 7
202[6] BATTUTA [41] 4-9-10 M Birch (1) *hld up in rear, pushed alng 4 fs out, not pace to chal*................ (20 to 1) 8
1616 SMOCKING [50] (bl) 3-9-8 F Norton (3) *sn chasing ldrs, effrt and rdn o'r 2 fs out, wknd over one furlong out*. .... (9 to 1 op 8 to 1 tchd 10 to 1) 9
1900 DOUBLE SHERRY [32] (v) 4-9-1 A Culhane (2) *hld up, rdn to improve 4 fs out, no imprsn fnl 2 furlongs*. .... (14 to 1 op 12 to 1) 10
1399[8] INNOCENT ABROAD (Den) [40] 3-8-12 S Perks (14) *chsd ldrs, rdn alng o'r 2 fs out, sn btn*. (12 to 1 op 10 to 1) 11
1852[9] ALBEIT [35] 3-8-7 N Connorton (4) *ala beh, nvr on terms*. .... (25 to 1 op 20 to 1) 12
1562 NEWGATESKY [25] (bl) 3-7-11 L Charnock (7) *in tch, rdn o'r 3 fs out, sn btn*.............................. (33 to 1) 13
724 KATIE EILEEN (USA) [52] 3-9-10 A Clark (15) *chsd ldrs, drvn alng 4 fs out, sn wknd*.......... (4 to 1 fav op 6 to 1) 14
1735[3] CONTRAC COUNTESS (Ire) [47] 3-9-5 J Fortune (8) *chsd ldrs, rdn alng 4 fs out, grad lost pl*. (10 to 1 op 9 to 1) 15
PERSIAN MELODY (Ire) [51] 3-9-9 K Darley (9) *sluggish strt and veered lft, beh, lost tch o'r 3 fs out*. ....(9 to 1 op 7 to 1) 16

Dist: Hd, sht-hd, 5l, 1½l, ½l, 2½l, ½l, 1l, 2½l, ¾l. 1m 53.40s. a 2.40s (16 Ran).

SR: 26/35/31/22/8/13/2/6/1/ (Mrs C Tribe), D J S Cosgrove

2105 William Hill Handicap Class D (0-80 3-y-o) £3,406 6f................ (4:00)

OUBECK [60] 8-1 Dale Gibson (1) *nvr far away, rdn to improve o'r one furlong out, led ins last kpt on wl*. ....(10 to 1 tchd 9 to 1) 1
1833[4] HEART BROKEN [65] (bl) 8-6 K Fallon (2) *al prmnt, ev ch frm hfwy, no extr und pres ins fnl furlong*......(5 to 1) 2
1563[4] PINE RIDGE LAD (Ire) [61] 7-11 (5*) J Tate (7) *pressed ldrs, sn outpcd and drvn alng hfwy, kpt on fnl furlong, nvr dngrs*............... (7 to 2 fav op 3 to 1 tchd 4 to 1) 3
1356[5] LARN FORT [52] 7-7 J Fanning (6) *chsd ldrs, rdn hfwy, improved o'r one furlong out, kpt on*. (5 to 1 op 6 to 1) 4
1631[5] DAYJUZ (Ire) [52] (bl) 7-6[2] (3*) N Kennedy (4) *led til hdd ins fnl furlong, no extr*.............. (12 to 1 op 16 to 1) 5
1848* PRINCIPAL PLAYER (USA) [58] (bl) 7-13 F Norton (9) *chsd ldrs, drvn o'r 2 fs out, outpcd over one furlong out*. ....(4 to 1) 6
1679 BENZOE (Ire) [80] 9-7 T Lucas (8) *beh on outer, shaken up o'r 2 fs out, nvr rch ldrs*...........(6 to 1 tchd 7 to 1) 7
2045[8] COSTA VERDE [78] 9-0 (5*) A Garth (5) *beh, drvn aftr 2 fs, lost tch frm hfwy*................................(25 to 1) 8
1760 HELLO HOBSON'S (Ire) [65] 8-6 Dean McKeown (3) *missed break, tld off thrght*................(6 to 1 op 9 to 2) 9

Dist: 2l, 1l, ½l, 1½l, 3½l, 6l, 15l, dist. 1m 11.70s. a 1.10s (9 Ran).

SR: 35/32/24/13/7/-/ (Mrs A Birkett), E Weymes

2106 William Hill 'First For Prices' Claiming Stakes Class F (3-y-o and up) £2,684 6f ....(4:30)

1801 PALACEGATE TOUCH (bl) 3-8-13 L Charnock (1) *made all, clr 2 fs out, ran on gmely ins last*...(5 to 1 tchd 9 to 2) 1
1965[2] MANX MONARCH 3-7-8[6] (5*) A Garth (3) *chsd ldrs, outpcd and rdn hfwy, improved and swtchd rght o'r one furlong out, kpt on, not rch wnr*....(14 to 1 tchd 16 to 1) 2
1835[9] FINJAN 6-9-0 (7*) V Halliday (7) *in tch, rdn hfwy, not quicken ins fnl furlong*.............(3 to 1 op 5 to 2) 3
2017[3] BOLD ANGEL 6-9-7 M Birch (4) *nvr far away, shaken up o'r one furlong out, kpt on same pace*. ....(9 to 2 op 3 to 1) 4
1945[8] CRYSTAL JACK (Fr) 5-9-7 B Raymond (2) *chsd ldrs, drvn alng hfwy, wknd ins last*. ....(7 to 4 fav op 2 to 1 tchd 9 to 4) 5
1865 BOY MARTIN 4-8-9 J Fortune (5) *in tch, sn pushed alng, wknd wl o'r one furlong out*.......(14 to 1 op 12 to 1) 6
1560 ROCK SONG (Ire) 4-8-6 (3*) N Kennedy (6) *beh, drvn alng hfwy, sn lost tch*........................(50 to 1 op 33 to 1) 7

Dist: 1½l, 1l, nk, 4l, 3½l, 15l. 1m 11.50s. a 0.90s (7 Ran).

SR: 51/26/49/48/32/6/-/ (Palacegate Corporation Ltd), J Berry

2107 Levy Board Handicap Class E (0-70 3-y-o) £3,158 1½m 60yds....... (5:00)

838[5] MOUSSAHIM (USA) [64] (v) 9-7 B Raymond (5) *nvr far away, improved to ld 3 fs out, clr o'r 2 furlongs out, styd on strly*........... (6 to 1 op 5 to 1 tchd 13 to 2) 1
1836[2] DUPLICATE [64] 9-7 M Birch (2) *settled mid-div, took clr order entering strt, chsd wnr o'r 2 fs out, kpt on, no imprsn*..(7 to 2 op 3 to 1) 2
1630* HAZARD A GUESS (Ire) [61] 9-4 K Fallon (3) *hld up and beh, swtchd ins 4 fs out, sn pushed alng, ran on o'r 2 furlongs out, no extr inside last*. ....(6 to 4 fav op 7 to 4 tchd 15 to 8) 3
1423[6] AMIARGE [54] 8-11 M Wigham (7) *led til hdd o'r 3 fs out, sn drvn alng, wknd over one furlong out*. ....(11 to 1 op 12 to 1) 4
1836[4] MERRY MERMAID [46] 8-3 L Charnock (6) *pressed ldrs, drvn o'r 3 fs out, sn one pace*. ....(9 to 1 op 8 to 1 tchd 10 to 1) 5
1180[4] SIR EDWARD HENRY (Ire) [47] 8-4 R Lappin (1) *rear early, improved to track ldrs aftr 3 fs, ev ch o'r three out, wknd over 2 out*...(14 to 1) 6
1477[4] ON BROADWAY [58] 9-1 J Fortune (9) *dwlt, hld up, shaken up o'r 3 fs out, no imprsn*.........(14 to 1 op 12 to 1) 7
1154[6] NEVER SO BRAVE [54] 8-11 N Connorton (8) *settled mid-div, rdn 4 fs out, not pace to chal*. (16 to 1 op 33 to 1) 8
1802 HIGH CHAIR [47] 8-4 Dale Gibson (11) *hld up in rear, pushed alng o'r 2 fs out, sn btn*................(33 to 1) 9
864[6] KARIB [60] 9-0 (3*) S Maloney (10) *slwly into strd, sn in tch, last pl appr strt, wknd o'r 3 fs out*........(20 to 1) 10
1275 RESTRAINT [50] 8-7 F Norton (4) *keen hold, chsd ldrs, took clr order aftr 4 fs, rdn o'r 3 furlongs out, eased whn btn fnl 2 furlongs*..........................(20 to 1) 11

Dist: 3l, 2½l, 3½l, 8l, 2½l, hd, hd, 1l, ¾l, 12l. 2m 41.40s. a 6.40s (11 Ran).

SR: 12/6/-/-/-/-/ (Maktoum Al Maktoum), M R Stoute

2108 William Hill 'Action Line' Limited Stakes Class F (0-60 4-y-o and up) £2,807 1½m 60yds............. (5:30)

2059[4] BIG PAT 4-9-0 M Wigham (1) *chsd ldr, effrt o'r 2 fs out, led over one furlong out, edgd rght, forged clr ins last*. ....(13 to 8 fav op 6 to 4) 1
1586[6] MAY HILLS LEGACY (Ire) 4-8-9 M Birch (2) *led, quickened appr strt, rdn o'r 2 fs out, hdd over one furlong out, no extr*..............(13 to 2 op 7 to 1 tchd 6 to 1) 2
1392[4] HILLZAH (USA) 5-8-8[1] (7*) H Bastiman (7) *hld up, outpcd and rdn entering strt, improved o'r one furlong out, kpt on, nvr dngrs*..................(9 to 2 tchd 5 to 1) 3
1605[8] ROUSITTO 5-8-7 (7*) J Dennis (5) *hld up, pushed alng o'r 3 fs out, not quicken fnl 2 furlongs*.... (4 to 1 op 7 to 2) 4
1268 BRESIL (USA) 4-9-0 S Whitworth (4) *hld up, rdn to improve 3 fs out, wknd o'r one furlong out*. ....(6 to 1 op 7 to 1 tchd 8 to 1) 5
1321 IZITALLWORTHIT 4-8-6 (3*) N Kennedy (3) *hld up in tch, rdn o'r 3 fs out, nvr trble ldrs*................(33 to 1) 6
CARROLLS MARC (Ire) 5-9-0 Dale Gibson (6) *chsd ldg 2, rdn alng o'r 3 fs out, wknd two out*. ....(14 to 1 op 12 to 1) 7

Dist: 5l, 1l, nk, 3l, nk, 8l. 2m 42.80s. a 7.80s (7 Ran).

(Burton Park Country Club), J Pearce

WINDSOR (firm (race 1), good (2,3,4,5,6)) Monday June 28th

Going Correction: MINUS 0.45 sec. per fur. (races 1,3,5), MINUS 0.10 (2,4,6)

2109 Montrose Selling Stakes Class G (3-y-o and up) £1,772 1m 67yds.... (6:40)

1928* BARAHIN (Ire) 4-9-8 L Piggott (16) *in tch, ran on frm hfwy, rdn 2 out, led wl ins fnl furlong*. ....(7 to 2 op 3 to 1 tchd 4 to 1) 1
1696[9] SHALOU (bl) 4-9-8 L Dettori (4) *trkd ldrs, led o'r 4 fs out till hdd wl ins fnl furlong*. ....(14 to 1 op 10 to 1 tchd 16 to 1) 2
1690 QUEENS CONTRACTOR (bl) 3-8-7 T Quinn (14) *wl plcd, rdn and not quicken appr fnl furlong, rallied nr line*. ....(14 to 1 op 10 to 1 tchd 16 to 1) 3
1876[8] WAKI GOLD (USA) 6-9-8 Pat Eddery (13) *ldg grp, rdn and not quicken 2 fs out, styd on nr finish*. ....(2 to 1 fav op 9 to 4 tchd 11 to 4) 4
1304[8] PREMIER DANCE (v) 6-9-8 J Williams (18) *hld up, effrt appr last 2 fs, kpt on und pres ins fnl furlong*. ....(20 to 1 op 14 to 1 tchd 25 to 1) 5
1631[8] CREAGMHOR 3-8-7 C Rutter (11) *improved o'r 2 fs out, rdn and ran on one pace fnl furlong*. ....(33 to 1 op 20 to 1) 6
1956 ELEGANT TOUCH (bl) 4-8-10 (7*) R Painter (6) *hld up, improved o'r 2 fs out, one pace appr fnl furlong*. ....(14 to 1 op 10 to 1 tchd 16 to 1) 7
1928[7] DEVONIAN (USA) 4-9-3 R Perham (2) *ran on last 2 fs, nrst at finish*..........(33 to 1 op 20 to 1 tchd 40 to 1) 8
1696 HIGHEST PRAISE (USA) 10-9-8 M Hills (8) *mid-div, effrt o'r 2 fs out, no imprsn on ldrs fnl furlong*. ....(33 to 1 op 14 to 1) 9
1685 YOUNG JAMES 5-9-3 A Tucker (9) *nvr better than fnl placing*.............(33 to 1 op 20 to 1 tchd 40 to 1) 10
1715[5] GIN AND ORANGE 7-9-8 W Newnes (1) *mid-div most of way*....................(16 to 1 op 14 to 1 tchd 12 to 1) 11
1928 RAPINSKI 4-8-10 (7*) K Pattinson (15) *shrtlvd o'r 2 fs out, sn btn*.............................(33 to 1 op 20 to 1) 12
MAN OF THE SEASON (USA) 4-9-3 J Reid (3) *wl plcd til o'r 2 fs out*..................(10 to 1 op 12 to 1 tchd 8 to 1) 13
1623[6] GOTT'S DESIRE (bl) 7-9-8 B Rouse (12) *led for o'r 3 fs, wknd over 2 out*..........................(12 to 1 op 8 to 1) 14
ONE-O-EIGHT 3-8-2 A McGlone (10) *nvr able to chal*. ....(33 to 1 op 20 to 1 tchd 40 to 1) 15

SUKEY TAWDRY (bl) 7-9-3 N Adams (17) *nvr dngrs.* ....(33 to 1 op 20 to 1) 16
754 IBSEN 5-9-3 S Dawson (7) *nvr on terms.* ....(5 to 1 op 4 to 1 tchd 7 to 2 and 11 to 2) 17
Dist: ¾l, hd, 1l, sht-hd, 2l, 2½l, ¾l, 5l, 2l, sht-hd. 1m 44.80s. a 3.80s (17 Ran).
(Martin Hickey), R J O'Sullivan

2110 Reading University Turf Club Handicap Class E (0-70 3-y-o and up) £2,532 5f 217yds......................(7:10)

1821[5] HARRY'S COMING [52] 9-8-13 M Hills (15) *trkd ldrs, rdn to ld o'r one furlong out, styd on wl*....(6 to 1 op 8 to 1) 1
1881* BRIGHT PARAGON (Ire) [47] 4-8-8 J Quinn (1) *ldg grp, ev ch o'r one furlong out, ran on wl nr finish.* ....(8 to 1 op 6 to 1 tchd 9 to 1) 2
1267 SPECTACLE JIM [41] 4-8-2 N Adams (3) *wl plcd, ev ch o'r one furlong out, rdn and styd on nr line.* ....(33 to 1 tchd 40 to 1) 3
659 RICKY'S TORNADO (Ire) [62] 4-9-4 (5*) A Procter (13) *handily plcd, rdn o'r one furlong out, rallied clsg stages.* ....(16 to 1 op 20 to 1 tchd 25 to 1) 4
1903* GREAT HALL [63] 4-9-10 (7ex) J Williams (8) *hld up, ran on and not clr run o'r one furlong out, fnshd wl.* ....(100 to 30 fav op 5 to 2 tchd 7 to 2) 5
1408 RACING TELEGRAPH [59] 3-8-12 T Quinn (7) *steadied leaving stalls, outpcd till ran on last 2 fs, fnshd wl.* ....(8 to 1 op 6 to 1) 6
1209 COCKERHAM RANGER [62] (bl) 3-9-1 L Piggott (14) *hld up to hfwy, ran on 2 fs out, rdn and not quicken one out* ....(7 to 1 tchd 8 to 1) 7
1744[5] PHARAOH'S DANCER [67] 6-10-0 J Reid (12) *wl in tch, one pace appr fnl furlong*... (9 to 2 op 6 to 1 tchd 7 to 1) 8
600 MISS PRECOCIOUS [34] 5-7-9[2] A Tucker (11) *made most of rng for o'r 4 fs, not extr*.........(20 to 1 tchd 25 to 1) 9
1860[6] DREAM OF TOMORROW [50] 5-8-11 B Rouse (10) *nvr nrr.* .... (33 to 1 op 20 to 1) 10
ALLEZ BIANCO [60] 3-8-13 G Carter (2) *outpcd most of way*.............................. (33 to 1 op 16 to 1) 11
SCREECH [56] 3-8-9 W Newnes (9) *nvr dngrs.* ....(33 to 1 tchd 40 to 1) 12
1560 GANESHAYA [46] (bl) 4-8-4 (3*) D Harrison (5) *ldg grp, ev ch 2 fs out till btn o'r one out*.........(16 to 1 op 20 to 1) 13
1282[5] LORINS GOLD [61] 3-9-0 A McGlone (6) *in tch for 4 fs, wknd*..............................(14 to 1 op 12 to 1) 14
1903 GEMINI BAY [45] (bl) 4-8-6 S Dawson (4) *ldg grp til rdn and wknd o'r 2 fs out*.....(33 to 1 op 25 to 1 tchd 40 to 1) 15
Dist: 1l, sht-hd, sht-hd, hd, 1l, ½l, nk, 3l, 2½l, sht-hd. 1m 12.60s. a 2.30s (15 Ran).
SR: 41/32/25/45/45/29/30/42/-/ (Mrs D A Wetherall), R J Hodges

2111 Piper Champagne And Raffles Nightclub Handicap Class D (0-80 3-y-o and up) £3,622 1m 3f 135yds........ (7:40)

1951* MAHRAJAN [53] 9-8-2[2] (5ex) T Quinn (2) *hld up, steady hdwy o'r 3 fs out, led 2 out, clr fnl furlong, easily.* ....(6 to 5 on op 13 to 8 on tchd 11 to 10 on) 1
1430[7] INCHCAILLOCH (Ire) [71] 4-9-6 Paul Eddery (4) *led aftr one furlong, hdd 2 out, outpcd appr fnl furlong.* ....(7 to 2 op 5 to 1) 2
1346 THEMEDA [47] 4-7-10[3] (3*) D Harrison (1) *led for one furlong, trkd ldr till o'r 2 out, rdn and no extr.* ....(12 to 1 tchd 14 to 1) 3
2029[4] ATHAR (Ire) [65] 4-9-0 J Williams (5) *settled in 4th pl, hdwy four fs out, rdn and wknd 2 out.* ....(4 to 1 op 3 to 1 tchd 9 to 2) 4
ROMANSH [75] 4-9-10 J Reid (3) *settled in 3rd pl til lost pos o'r 4 fs out, sn lost tch, tld off.* (16 to 1 op 14 to 1) 5
Dist: 2l, hd, 2½l, 20l. 2m 28.10s. a 5.10s (5 Ran).
(Mrs F A Harris), C J Benstead

2112 Carr Kitkat Engineering Fillies Conditions Stakes Class D (2-y-o) £3,622 5f 217yds........................ (8:10)

1660* PALANA (USA) 8-12 L Dettori (1) *hld up in 4th pl, ran on frm hfwy, hrd rdn o'r one furlong out, led last strds.* ....(11 to 10 fav tchd Evens and 5 to 4) 1
1119* MAZEEKA (Ire) 8-12 T Quinn (2) *steadied strt, improved frm rear hfwy, ev ch ins fnl furlong, jst fld.* ....(15 to 8 op 7 to 4 tchd 9 to 4) 2
1009* BEARALL (Ire) 8-12 B Rouse (4) *led, rdn alng 2 fs out, hdd und pres last strds*..... (11 to 2 op 7 to 2 tchd 6 to 1) 3
1708[3] URSULINE 8-3 (5*) Stephen Davies (3) *settled in 3rd pl, rdn and wknd o'r 2 fs out, sn lost tch.* ....(15 to 2 op 5 to 1 tchd 8 to 1) 4
1350[5] HUMMINBIRDPRINCESS 8-8 N Adams (5) *chsd ldr, rdn and outpcd 2 fs out, wknd quickly.* ....(40 to 1 op 20 to 1 tchd 50 to 1) 5
Dist: Sht-hd, sht-hd, 12l, 8l. 1m 13.40s. a 3.10s (5 Ran).
SR: 24/23/22/-/-/ (George Strawbridge), I A Balding

2113 Greenacre Limited Stakes Class F (0-65 3-y-o and up) £2,302 1¼m 7yds ....(8:40)

1268[8] WASSL THIS THEN (Ire) 4-9-1 T Quinn (2) *sn chasing ldr, rdn to ld 2 fs out, drvn out.* ....(10 to 1 op 8 to 1 tchd 11 to 1) 1
1120[2] WAKIL (Ire) 4-9-6 N Carlisle (6) *al ldg grp, hrd rdn frm 2 out, ev ch ins fnl furlong, kpt on.* (11 to 2 op 11 to 4) 2
1490[8] MA BELLA LUNA 4-9-1 J Reid (13) *in tch, rdn to cl on ldrs 2 fs out, one pace ins fnl furlong.* ....(9 to 2 fav op 6 to 1 tchd 13 to 2) 3
990 ROMOLA NIJINSKY 5-9-1 L Piggott (10) *led til hdd 2 fs out, ran on same pace*........(7 to 1 op 6 to 1 tchd 8 to 1) 4
917[4] COMANCHE COMPANION 3-8-0 (3*) D Harrison (3) *hld up, effrt und pres on outsd o'r 2 fs out, not quicken over one out*............................ (5 to 1 op 7 to 2) 5
663 LEGAL EMBRACE (Can) 4-9-1 A Clark (9) *in tch in mid-div, rdn and one pace frm 2 fs out.* ....(9 to 1 op 10 to 1 tchd 12 to 1) 6
1743[3] VANROY (v) 9-9-6 L Dettori (5) *no imprsn on ldrs frm 2 fs out*.........(6 to 1 op 7 to 1 tchd 9 to 1 and 11 to 2) 7
1709[3] SWEET ROMEO 3-8-8 T Williams (11) *ldg grp til rdn and lost pl 2 fs out*..........(13 to 2 op 7 to 1 tchd 8 to 1) 8
1586 MISTY VIEW 4-9-1 R Price (14) *nvr able to chal.* ....(14 to 1 op 16 to 1 tchd 20 to 1) 9
1469[6] MELLERIO 3-8-8 Paul Eddery (8) *trkd ldrs for 7 fs.* ....(20 to 1 op 12 to 1 tchd 25 to 1) 10
834 IRISH GROOM (bl) 6-9-6 J Williams (1) *nvr on terms.* ....(33 to 1 op 20 to 1 tchd 40 to 1) 11
1711[9] RAPPORTEUR (USA) 7-9-6 W Newnes (12) *ldg grp til wknd 3 fs out*..........................(16 to 1 tchd 25 to 1) 12
1409 SLICK CHERRY 6-9-1 G Carter (7) *al outpcd towards rear.* ....(33 to 1 op 20 to 1 tchd 50 to 1) 13
1743 DUTY SERGEANT (Ire) 4-9-6 Pat Eddery (4) *slwly into strd, al outpcd*............(25 to 1 op 20 to 1 tchd 33 to 1) 14
Dist: ½l, 2½l, 1½l, ¾l, 2½l, 1½l, 1l, 3l, 2½l, 2l. 2m 4.80s. a 2.30s (14 Ran).
SR: 33/37/27/24/10/17/19/5/6/ (Mrs Josephine Carter), D W P Arbuthnot

2114 Woodland Maiden Auction Stakes Class F (2-y-o) £2,075 5f 10yds.. (9:10)

1814[5] WELSH MIST 8-9 W Woods (2) *chsd ldr, rdn to ld o'r one furlong out, jst hld on*...(5 to 1 op 4 to 1 tchd 7 to 1) 1
MAZENTRE FORWARD (Ire) 9-0 Pat Eddery (7) *strted slwly, rear till swtchd lft and ran on 2 fs out, edgd rght und pres ins fnl furlong, jst fld.* ....(5 to 2 op 2 to 1 tchd 7 to 2) 2
1499[5] LOVESCAPE 8-9 A Clark (8) *wl plcd, rdn and not quicken o'r one furlong out*................(20 to 1 op 10 to 1) 3
477[5] LIGHTNING BELLE 8-9 J Reid (1) *ldg grp, effrt 2 fs out, btn whn squeezed for room ins fnl furlong.* ....(9 to 4 fav op 7 to 2 tchd 2 to 1) 4
1689[2] ARKADY (Ire) 9-0 T Quinn (5) *led for o'r 3 fs, sn btn.* .... (5 to 2 op 5 to 4 tchd 11 to 4) 5
MIDSEAS 9-0 J Williams (6) *nvr gng pace of frnt rnk.* .... (50 to 1 op 20 to 1) 6
RADIANT DANCER 8-9 L Dettori (4) *broke wl, outpcd frm hfwy*................ (20 to 1 op 10 to 1 tchd 25 to 1) 7
SCREWBALL ANACONDA 9-0 W Newnes (3) *al outpcd.* ....(50 to 1 op 20 to 1) 8
Dist: Sht-hd, 3l, 1l, 2l, 1l, 5l, 1½l. 1m 1.60s. a 2.60s (8 Ran).
SR: 33/37/20/16/13/9/-/-/ (P Asquith), R Boss

CHEPSTOW (firm)
Tuesday June 29th

Going Correction: MINUS 0.15 sec. per fur. (races 1,2,3,4), MINUS 0.25 (5,6,7)

2115 Lion's Lodge Handicap Class E (0-70 3-y-o and up) £2,835 2¼m 33yds (2:00)

1752[7] MARDOOD [53] 8-9-5 J Williams (6) *hld up, hdwy o'r 3 fs out, rdn to ld appr fnl furlong, eased nr finish, cmftbly.* ....(7 to 4 fav op 2 to 1) 1
1989[2] CHUCKLESTONE [62] 10-10-0 T Quinn (4) *led, rdn 2 fs out, hdd appr fnl furlong, rallied gmely ins*.........(5 to 2) 2
1268[5] CHAMBROS [57] 6-9-9 R Cochrane (3) *hld up, wnt second 4 fs out, chlgd 2 out, rdn and one pace fnl furlong.* ....(5 to 2 op 2 to 1) 3
1688[7] PERFORATE [35] (bl) 4-8-0 A McGlone (5) *hld up early, hdwy to dispute second frm hfwy, styd prmnt till wknd 3 fs out*.............................(12 to 1 op 8 to 1) 4
1457[8] ARFEY (Ire) [54] 4-9-5 W Carson (2) *pld hrd early, trkd ldr for 7 fs, styd in tch, rdn 3 out, sn btn.* ....(10 to 1 tchd 11 to 1) 5
1840 ELEGANT KING (Ire) [60] 4-9-4 (7*) G McGrath (1) *sddl slpd sn aftr strt, wnt second after 7 fs, rdn 5 out, wknd o'r 3 out, tld off*...........................(25 to 1 op 16 to 1) 6
Dist: Nk, 3l, 10l, 2l, 15l. 3m 59.50s. (6 Ran).
(J C Fretwell), P Leach

2116 Cowbridge Conditions Stakes Class D (3-y-o) £3,377 1¼m 36yds.......(2:30)

1785 ALJAZZAF 9-0 W R Swinburn (5) *trkd ldr aftr 2 fs, led o'r two out, rdn clr entering last*....... (11 to 4 op 3 to 1) 1
755[3] DOUBLE BASS (USA) 9-4 W Ryan (3) *led 1st furlong, steadied in mid-div, hdwy o'r 2 fs out, styd on one pace*..............................(5 to 2 fav op 3 to 1) 2

1879[3] LILLE HAMMER 8-13 R Cochrane (2) *hld up in rear, hdwy hfwy, kpt on one pace fnl 2 fs*...... (11 to 2 op 4 to 1) 3
FRONTIER FLIGHT (USA) 9-4 Pat Eddery (4) *led aftr one furlong, rdn and hdd o'r 2 out, wknd appr last.* .... (11 to 4 op 9 to 4 tchd 100 to 30) 4
DAKAR RALLY 9-4 A McGlone (1) *beh, pushed alng frm hfwy, nvr got into race*.................(13 to 2 op 7 to 2) 5
Dist: 4l, 4l, 1½l, 4l. 2m 6.00s. a 2.40s (5 Ran).
SR: 61/57/44/46/38/ (Mohamed Obaida), C E Brittain

2117 NPI Maiden Stakes Class D (3-y-o) £3,611 1¼m 36yds............. (3:00)

1671[5] EL JUBAIL (Ire) 9-0 W Ryan (4) *led till hdd wl o'r 2 fs out, rdn to ld appr last, drvn out*........(13 to 2 op 4 to 1) 1
1831[2] KITHANGA (Ire) 8-9 R Cochrane (10) *wtd wth in tch, smooth hdwy to ld o'r 2 fs out, rdn and hdd appr last, kpt on ins*........................ (6 to 4 on op Evens) 2
1671[4] PISH KESH 8-9 A Clark (8) *nvr far away, outpcd 2 fs out, kpt on*.............................. (10 to 1 op 6 to 1) 3
PRINCESS SIOUX 8-9 B Raymond (7) *towards rear till hdwy o'r 2 fs out, styd on, nvr nrr*. (20 to 1 op 16 to 1) 4
LANKRIDGE 9-0 B Procter (9) *slwly away, beh till hdwy ins fnl 2 fs, nvr nrr*..................(33 to 1 op 16 to 1) 5
1315[8] CHARLOTTE DUNDAS 8-9 J Carroll (5) *trkd wnr till rdn o'r 2 fs out, wknd wl over one out*......(12 to 1 op 7 to 1) 6
1534[4] BOLTROSE 9-0 N Carlisle (2) *nvr on terms.* .... (50 to 1 op 33 to 1 tchd 66 to 1) 7
1746[6] CLIFTON GAME 9-0 J Lowe (6) *chsd ldrs till wknd o'r 2 fs out*................. (33 to 1 op 20 to 1 tchd 50 to 1) 8
1068 SIMPLY A HERO (Ire) 9-0 J Williams (11) *al beh.* .... (25 to 1 op 16 to 1 tchd 33 to 1) 9
1816[2] MORSTOCK 9-0 W Carson (3) *chsd ldrs till wknd o'r 3 fs out*.................. (13 to 2 op 14 to 1 tchd 6 to 1) 10
FLOATING ISLAND 8-9 W R Swinburn (1) *al in rear.* .... (10 to 1 op 6 to 1) 11
Dist: ½l, 4l, 2½l, 1½l, ½l, 6l, sht-hd, 2½l, 3l, 4l. 2m 7.30s. a 3.70s (11 Ran).
SR: 48/42/34/29/31/25/18/17/12/ (Prince A A Faisal), H R A Cecil

2118 Middle Lodge Handicap Class D (0-85 3-y-o) £3,703 1¼m 36yds....... (3:30)

1732* INDIAN FLASH (Ire) [60] 8-3 W Carson (1) *made most till hdd o'r 2 fs out, hrd rdn, led one out, edgd rght, all out.* .... (5 to 4 fav tchd 11 to 8 and 11 to 10) 1
1486* QUICK SILVER BOY [63] 8-1 (5*) Stephen Davies (2) *rcd keenly, trkd wnr, dsptd ld frm 4 fs out, edgd lft appr last, crrd rght, no extr nr finish.* .... (5 to 2 op 2 to 1 tchd 11 to 4) 2
1808 SHARAAR (USA) [78] 9-7 M Hills (3) *hld up, hdwy to take narrow ld o'r 2 fs out, rdn and hdd one out, one pace.* ....(2 to 1 op 5 to 4) 3
Dist: ½l, 2l. 2m 8.80s. a 5.20s (3 Ran).
SR: 22/24/35/ (Vijay Mallya), R Guest

2119 Bream Claiming Stakes Class F (2-y-o) £2,644 6f 16yds............ (4:00)

1774* BROOKHEAD LADY 7-12 (3*) S Maloney (4) *trkd ldrs, al gng wl, quickened to ld o'r 2 fs out, pushed clr ins last.* .... (5 to 4 fav tchd Evens and 11 to 8) 1
1158* MY LIFETIME LADY (Ire) 7-13 W Carson (2) *trkd ldrs, rdn to chase wnr ins fnl 2 fs.* ....(13 to 8 op 7 to 4 tchd 2 to 1 and 6 to 4) 2
1741[2] LITTLE EMMELINE 7-9 N Carlisle (6) *led till hdd o'r 2 fs out, one pace aftr*...........(11 to 2 op 7 to 1 tchd 5 to 1) 3
1391[4] NORTHERN STARLIGHT 8-0 J Lowe (3) *prmnt, rdn o'r 2 fs out, sn btn*....................................... (12 to 1) 4
GIPSY KID 7-6[5] (7*) C Hawksley (1) *slwly away, al outpcd.* .... (20 to 1 op 8 to 1) 5
1909[5] MOSS HOUSE (Ire) 7-7 (7*) Wendy Jones (5) *speed to hfwy, sn beh*.................................... (12 to 1 op 7 to 1) 6
Dist: 6l, 2l, 2½l, ¾l, 5l. 1m 11.00s. a 1.50s (6 Ran).
SR: 27/1/-/ (J E Abbey), P D Evans

2120 Summer Selling Stakes Class G (3-y-o) £2,385 1m 14yds........... (4:30)

1271 MAASTRICHT 9-0 M Hills (1) *came o'r to stands side, made all, hrd rdn appr fnl furlong, edgd lft, all out.* ....(7 to 1 op 5 to 1) 1
1344 RACHELLY 8-9 R Perham (9) *al prmnt, rdn o'r 2 fs out, ran on wl to snatch second cl hme*........ (3 to 1 op 2 to 1) 2
LADY BROKER 8-9 A Mackay (11) *hld up in tch, hdwy hfwy, hrd rdn to hold ev ch ins fnl furlong, no extr cl hme*...................................(9 to 4 fav op 6 to 1) 3
1628[2] NIGELS PROSPECT 9-0 J Williams (5) *mid-div, rdn 2 fs out, ran on ins last, nvr nrr.* .... (13 to 2 op 5 to 1 tchd 7 to 1) 4
RAGAZZO (Ire) 9-0 L Charnock (7) *al prmnt, hrd rdn and outpcd appr fnl furlong*..............(50 to 1 op 33 to 1) 5
1913[8] SWISS MOUNTAIN (bl) 8-9 W Ryan (8) *prmnt, hng lft in early stages, hrd rdn and ev ch 2 fs out, wknd appr last*..........................(9 to 2 op 4 to 1 tchd 7 to 2) 6
WEST END GIRL 8-9 J Carroll (10) *trkd wnr till wknd wl o'r one furlong out*...................(50 to 1 op 33 to 1) 7
1090 PRINCESS SHAWNEE 8-9 S Whitworth (3) *al beh.* .... (50 to 1 op 25 to 1) 8

1627 WHYALLA RAIN 8-9 S Perks (4) *hld up, effrt 3 fs out, sn btn*.................................(33 to 1 op 20 to 1) 9
1817[9] KUTAN (Ire) (bl) 9-0 A Tucker (6) *slwly away, al struggling in rear*...................(16 to 1 op 12 to 1 tchd 20 to 1) 10
FLASH OF JOY 8-4 (5*) Stephen Davies (2) *speed till wknd 3 fs out*..........................(25 to 1 op 20 to 1 tchd 33 to 1) 11
Dist: Nk, hd, 3l, nk, 1½l, 2½l, 6l, 2l, 5l, 1½l. 1m 35.80s. a 3.40s (11 Ran).
SR: 19/13/12/8/7/-/ (P A Deal), W J Haggas

2121 Levy Board Seventh Handicap Class E (0-70 3-y-o and up) £3,300 7f 16yds ....(5:00)

1954[7] LORD ALFIE [44] 4-8-4 S Whitworth (16) *in tch on stand side, hdwy appr fnl furlong, ran on strly to ld nr finish*..................................(14 to 1 op 12 to 1) 1
1932[3] GOOD IMAGE [55] 3-8-6 Pat Eddery (10) *al frnt rnk, hrd rdn to ld one furlong out, kpt on, hdd on line.* ....(15 to 2 op 8 to 1) 2
1903[5] ZINBAQ [36] 7-7-10 D Biggs (17) *al prmnt stand side, led 2 fs out, hdd one out, ran on, no extr nr finish.* ....(5 to 1 fav op 6 to 1 tchd 4 to 1) 3
1734[4] CHARMED KNAVE [55] 8-9-1 T Williams (13) *hld up, gd hdwy o'r 2 fs out, ran on, one pace ins last.* ....(6 to 1 op 9 to 2) 4
714 FAILAND [37] 6-7-11 A Tucker (12) *chsd ldrs stand side, no imprsn ins fnl 2 fs*............................. (33 to 1) 5
1876[5] OLD COMRADES [55] 6-8-8 (7*) Mark Denaro (2) *hld up, hdwy hfwy, rdn 2 fs out, not quicken appr last.* .... (14 to 1 op 10 to 1) 6
1604[4] WILL SOON [57] 4-9-3 R Cochrane (1) *al prmnt far side, led hfwy, hdd 2 fs out, edgd lft and fdd appr last.* ....(6 to 1 tchd 11 to 2) 7
1912[4] ANATROCCOLO [38] 6-7-12 W Carson (3) *led to hfwy, rdn 2 fs out, sn btn*........................(11 to 1 op 8 to 1) 8
1876[9] GARTH [63] (v) 5-9-2 (7*) L Aspell (6) *chsd ldrs till wknd 2 fs out*.................................(25 to 1 op 20 to 1) 9
1696[2] AQUADO [35] 4-7-9 N Carlisle (15) *prmnt stand side till fdd fnl 2 fs*..........................(11 to 1 op 14 to 1) 10
1697 GREENWICH CHALENGE [56] 3-8-7 E Johnson (7) *slwly away, nvr nr to chal*..................................(33 to 1) 11
1258[5] HAWAYAH (Ire) [70] 3-9-7 J Williams (5) *outpcd thrght.* ....(20 to 1 tchd 16 to 1) 12
1354[3] CHEREN BOY [33] 4-7-7 A Mackay (14) *nvr on terms.* ....(33 to 1) 13
1588[5] CEE-EN-CEE [60] (bl) 9-9-6 T Quinn (4) *prmnt on outsd, rdn hfwy, sn btn*.................... (12 to 1 tchd 10 to 1) 14
1729[2] HALBERT [66] 4-9-12 A McGlone (9) *outpcd thrght.* .... (16 to 1 op 12 to 1) 15
BELLA BAMBOLA (Ire) [46] 3-7-11 L Charnock (8) *speed for 5 fs, sn wknd*................................ (25 to 1 op 33 to 1) 16
1286 DESERT SPLENDOUR [57] 5-9-3 J Lowe (11) *in tch till wknd sn aftr hfwy*...................... (25 to 1 op 33 to 1) 17
Dist: Nk, ½l, 2½l, 1l, 2l, 1l, 1l, sht-hd, 1l, sht-hd. 1m 22.10s. a 2.10s (17 Ran).
SR: 32/33/21/32/11/23/22/-/24/ (K C Gomm), B J Meehan

FOLKESTONE (good to firm)
Tuesday June 29th
Going Correction: NIL (races 1,3,5), MINUS 0.10 (2,4), MINUS 0.20 (6)

2122 Coomes Handicap Class E (0-70 3-y-o) £2,976 6f 189yds............... (1:45)

1698[7] JALIB (Ire) [51] 8-12 R Hills (1) *chsd ldr till rdn alng o'r one out, rallied to ld last strds.* ....(13 to 8 fav op 5 to 4 tchd 7 to 4) 1
1697 NEWINGTON BUTTS (Ire) [60] 9-7 J Reid (3) *settled in 3rd pl, shaken up to ld o'r one out, hdd und pres last strds.* ....(5 to 2 tchd 3 to 1) 2
1408 DANCING DIAMOND (Ire) [51] 8-5 (7*) S Mulvey (4) *hld up in rear, cld on ldrs frm 2 out, ev ch, not quicken fnl 100 yards*........................(11 to 4 op 5 to 2 tchd 3 to 1) 3
1664[8] KRAYYAN DAWN [51] 8-12 S Dawson (2) *led til hdd o'r one out, no extr*.................................(6 to 1 op 7 to 2) 4
Dist: Hd, 1l, 3l. 1m 28.20s. a 7.30s (4 Ran).
(Hamdan Al-Maktoum), C J Benstead

2123 Coomes Maiden Auction Stakes Class F (2-y-o) £2,713 6f............... (2:15)

1905[3] ADMIRALELLA 8-9 J Reid (1) *cl up, rdn alng 2 out, led und pres ins fnl furlong, styd on.* .... (11 to 8 fav op 6 to 4 tchd 13 to 8 and 5 to 4) 1
1536[3] QUEEN'S TRUST 8-9 L Dettori (5) *handily plcd, slight advantage o'r 2 out, rdn and hdd ins fnl furlong, ran on*............................. (9 to 2 op 4 to 1 tchd 6 to 1) 2
1602[8] CANDI DAS (Ire) 8-6 (3*) D Harrison (9) *wl in tch, jnd ldrs and ev ch 2 out, rdn and outpcd ins fnl furlong.* ....(7 to 1 op 4 to 1) 3
1602[7] CHARLIES DREAM (Ire) 8-9 T Sprake (10) *led for o'r 3 fs, one pace ins fnl furlong.* .... (12 to 1 op 7 to 1 tchd 16 to 1) 4

ROBBY (Ire) 9-0 C Rutter (2) *slwly into strd, mid-div, effrt 2 out, one pace fnl furlong.* .... (25 to 1 op 12 to 1 tchd 33 to 1) 5
HONEST WOMAN 8-9 Paul Eddery (6) *rcd in mid-div, reminder hfwy, styd on one pace frm 2 out.* .... (25 to 1 op 14 to 1) 6
COME GO 8-9 R Hills (7) *slwly into strd, sn chasing frnt rnk, no extr ins last 2 fs.*........... (12 to 1 op 4 to 1) 7
1602 ROYAL INTERPRETER 8-11 (3*) J Weaver (4) *swtchd rght and effrt 2 out, not rch ldrs fnl furlong.* .... (10 to 1 op 5 to 2 tchd 12 to 1) 8
ABACUSAM 9-0 N Adams (3) *sn wl outpcd, tld off.* .... (25 to 1 op 12 to 1 tchd 33 to 1) 9
WILL GLOW 9-0 W Newnes (8) *in tch on outsd til wknd quickly hfwy, tld off whn pld up and dismounted ins fnl furlong*..................... (12 to 1 tchd 16 to 1) pu

Dist: Nk, 2½l, 2l, nk, nk, ¾l, 3l, 12l. 1m 15.70s. a 4.70s (10 Ran).
(George Mortimer), J Akehurst

2124 Coomes Maiden Handicap Class F (0-65 3-y-o and up) £2,898 1m 7f 92yds ....(2:45)

1134[7] BRANSBY ROAD (Ire) [47] 3-8-9 J Reid (5) *hld up, led o'r 2 out, rdn clr over one out.* (3 to 1 op 7 to 2 tchd 4 to 1) 1
1930[5] YIMKIN BOOKRA [44] 5-9-10 L Dettori (2) *led til hdd 6 out, ev ch o'r 2 out, rdn and one pace appr fnl furlong.* .... (6 to 1 op 4 to 1 tchd 13 to 2) 2
1517[3] POST IMPRESSIONIST (Ire) [47] (bl) 4-9-13 M Wigham (3) *cld on ldr aftr 4 fs, led 6 furlongs out, hdd o'r 2 out, sn rdn and btn*........... (15 to 8 fav op 6 to 4 tchd 2 to 1) 3
1426 CAROJANGO [49] 3-8-8 (3*) M Fenton (4) *chsd ldrs till lost tch o'r 6 out, tld off*..................... (10 to 1 op 5 to 1) 4
1819[2] GALACTIC FURY [56] 3-9-4 M Tebbutt (1) *hld up, wl in tch in 4th pl whn f o'r four fs out*........(3 to 1 op 4 to 1) f

Dist: 5l, 5l, 20l. 3m 27.90s. a 9.40s (5 Ran).
SR: 1/11/9/-/-/ (A D Spence), R Akehurst

2125 Coomes Selling Stakes Class G (2-y-o) £2,070 5f................. (3:15)

1279[5] OLD HOOK (Ire) 8-8 (3*) B Doyle (3) *trkd ldrs, rdn and ran on o'r one out, led ins fnl furlong, kpt on strly.* .... (20 to 1 op 10 to 1 tchd 25 to 1) 1
1741[3] WINDOW DISPLAY 8-11 Paul Eddery (6) *sn ldg grp, rdn to ld wl o'r one out, hdd and one pace ins fnl furlong.* ....(6 to 5 on op 5 to 4 on tchd Evens) 2
READY-FREDDIE 8-11 T Sprake (2) *chsd frnt rnk, hrd rdn and styd on one pace o'r one out.* (10 to 1 tchd 12 to 1) 3
1741[7] LADY RISKY 8-6 J Reid (7) *made most of rng for o'r 3 fs, fdd ins fnl furlong*.................. (4 to 1 op 9 to 4) 4
715 TERMITE 8-6 N Adams (4) *nvr better than mid-div.* .... (40 to 1 op 20 to 1 tchd 50 to 1) 5
1857 CHARISMA GIRL 8-6 C Rutter (8) *outpcd hfwy.* ....(5 to 1 tchd 7 to 1) 6
MUSIC PRINCESS 7-13 (7*) B Russell (1) *slwly into strd, al outpcd*................(20 to 1 op 8 to 1 tchd 33 to 1) 7
1602 CRAFTY CRICKETER 8-11 S Dawson (5) *speed to hfwy, sn lost pl*............. (33 to 1 op 10 to 1 tchd 50 to 1) 8
1741 THE SPIVE (bl) 8-11 G Bardwell (9) *edgd rght leaving stalls, cl up til wknd hfwy.* .... (40 to 1 op 14 to 1 tchd 50 to 1) 9

Dist: 1½l, 2½l, 1½l, 2l, 1½l, nk, 3l, 1½l. 1m 1.50s. a 2.90s (9 Ran).
SR: 29/23/13/2/-/-/ (Mrs A Smith), Allan Smith

2126 Coomes Handicap Class E (0-70 3-y-o and up) £3,080 1½m........... (3:45)

1770 MOONLIGHT QUEST [69] 5-10-0 L Dettori (2) *handily plcd, rdn and ran on o'r one out, led last strd.* .....(9 to 2 jt-fav op 8 to 1 tchd 10 to 1) 1
4679a[3] SNOW BLIZZARD [53] 5-8-12 J Reid (7) *set str pace, clr 2 out, rdn and hdd last strd*..... (9 to 2 jt-fav op 3 to 1) 2
1731[5] ROCQUAINE BAY [38] 6-7-11 C Rutter (9) *hld up, improved 3 out, rdn and styd on ins fnl furlong.* .... (10 to 1 op 7 to 1) 3
1862* FACT OR FICTION [47] (bl) 7-8-6 W Newnes (4) *chsd ldr til one out, no extr und pres.* .... (5 to 1 tchd 4 to 1 and 11 to 2) 4
1712[5] RAGTIME SONG [41] 4-8-0 N Adams (10) *ldg grp, rdn and btn wl o'r one out*..............(14 to 1 op 10 to 1) 5
1712[8] TAYLORS PRINCE [54] (v) 6-8-13 J Quinn (8) *chsd ldrs for ten fs, no extr*.......... (6 to 1 op 4 to 1 tchd 13 to 2) 6
1951[5] GO FORUM [38] 8-7-4 (7*) D Wright (1) *beh most of way.* .... (9 to 1 op 6 to 1 tchd 10 to 1) 7
1659[7] LUCKY NOIRE [50] 5-8-2 (7*) Gaye Harwood (3) *al towards rear*..................................(16 to 1 op 10 to 1) 8
1781[6] CATHOS (Fr) [44] 8-8-3 B Rouse (6) *mid-div, effrt 3 out, no imprsn last 2 fs*...........................(7 to 1 op 5 to 1) 9
1242[7] CHECKPOINT CHARLIE [50] 8-8-6 (3*) M Fenton (5) *hdwy frm rear o'r 3 out, wknd last 2 fs*.... (14 to 1 op 7 to 1) 10

Dist: Sht-hd, 1½l, ½l, 3l, hd, 2½l, sht-hd, ½l, 2½l. 2m 37.40s. a 6.90s (10 Ran).
SR: 45/28/10/18/6/18/-/8/1/ (Mrs John Lamb), B Hanbury

2127 Coomes Amateur Riders' Handicap Stakes Class G (0-70 3-y-o and up) £2,070 1m 1f 149yds............ (4:15)

KELIMUTU [33] 4-9-11 Mrs L Pearce (8) *mid-div, prog 2 out, sstnd run centre of course to ld last 100 yards, sn clr*..................... (6 to 1 op 14 to 1) 1
1699[6] DON'T DROP BOMBS (USA) [40] (v) 4-10-4 Miss J Feilden (10) *clr ldr til rdn and wknd fnl furlong, hdd last 100 yards*..................... (7 to 1 op 6 to 1 tchd 8 to 1) 2
1353[7] BARCHAM [35] 6-9-13 Miss D Jones (5) *styd on frm rear 2 out, nrst at finish*.... (12 to 1 op 14 to 1 tchd 16 to 1) 3
1453 MISS MAGENTA (Ire) [29] 5-9-3 (4*) Mr S Quilty (11) *hdwy 3 out, styd on one pace approachng fnl furlong.* .... (20 to 1 op 12 to 1 tchd 25 to 1) 4
1902 BROUGHTON BLUES (Ire) [29] (bl) 5-9-3 (4*) Mrs J Musson (14) *wl plcd, chsd ldr 3 out, rdn and no extr o'r one out.* .... (9 to 1 op 5 to 1 tchd 10 to 1) 5
1956 AEDEAN [45] 4-10-5 (4*) Mr M Ayres (9) *nvr nrr.* .... (11 to 1 op 8 to 1 tchd 12 to 1) 6
1861[2] JULIASDARKINVADER [52] 3-10-0 (4*) Mr K Goble (13) *wl plcd til rdn and wknd frm 2 out.* ....(9 to 2 op 4 to 1 tchd 6 to 1) 7
HALEIM [42] 6-10-2 (4*) Miss D Pomeroy (7) *nvr nr to chal.* .... (33 to 1 op 25 to 1) 8
1820[6] ALBERT [50] 6-11-0 Mrs D Arbuthnot (2) *nvr rchd ldrs.* ....(7 to 2 fav op 9 to 4) 9
1902[5] EMERALD EARS [29] 4-9-3 (4*) Miss E Mills (6) *outpcd most of way*..........................(16 to 1 op 14 to 1) 10
1698 UTRILLO (USA) [46] 4-10-6 (4*) Mr C Curley (4) *al outpcd.* .... (14 to 1 op 10 to 1) 11
1316[7] KALOKAGATHOS [33] 4-9-7 (4*) Mrs S Williams (12) *effrt 4 out, wknd last 2 fs*.... (11 to 1 op 8 to 1 tchd 12 to 1) 12
1862[6] NATIVE CHIEFTAN [64] 4-11-10 (4*) Mr T Cuff (3) *chsd ldr til 3 out, sn lost pl*...................(10 to 1 op 8 to 1) 13
1659 SUPREME OPTIMIST [29] (bl) 9-9-3 (4*) Mrs C Peacock (15) *wl plcd til wknd o'r 2 out.* .... (33 to 1 op 25 to 1 tchd 50 to 1) 14

Dist: 6l, ½l, 1l, 1½l, nk, 1½l, 1l, nk, hd, 3l. 2m 3.50s. a 5.90s (14 Ran).
SR: 32/28/22/10/11/26/ (James Furlong), J Pearce

CATTERICK (good to firm)
Wednesday June 30th

Going Correction: MINUS 0.20 sec. per fur. (races 1,5), MINUS 0.40 (2,3,4,6)

2128 Greta Bridge Selling Stakes Class G (2-y-o) £2,448 5f............... (2:10)

1837[5] LADY SHERIFF 8-6 T Lucas (7) *chsd ldrs, effrt one and a half fs out, sn rdn, edgd lft and styd on to ld wl ins last.* ....(2 to 1 fav op 6 to 4 tchd 9 to 4) 1
1889[3] FADE AWAY (Ire) (bl) 8-6 K Darley (3) *led aftr one furlong, rdn one and a half out, hdd and no extr wl ins last.* ....(6 to 1 tchd 8 to 1) 2
1590[9] SPRING STAR 8-6 L Charnock (4) *led one furlong, cl up till rdn and one pace one and a half fs out*...... (50 to 1) 3
886[8] CHEEKY CHAPPY 8-11 Alex Greaves (1) *dwlt, sn chasing ldrs, effrt and rdn 2 fs out, soon one pace.* .... (11 to 2 op 5 to 1 tchd 7 to 1) 4
1933[4] MRS JOGGLEBURY 8-1 (5*) J Tate (8) *prmnt, rdn alng hfwy, sn wknd*.........(8 to 1 op 7 to 1 tchd 9 to 1) 5
1615[4] RED QUEEN (Ire) 8-6 J Fortune (6) *al rear.* .... (16 to 1 op 12 to 1) 6
1739[6] ME NEITHER (bl) 8-6 J Carroll (2) *slwly into strd and sn rdn alng, al rear*..................(5 to 2 tchd 3 to 1) 7
1863 NORBECK (Ire) (bl) 8-11 S Morris (5) *slwly away and beh, stumbled and hng badly lft 2 fs out, pld up o'r one furlong out*.................. (20 to 1 op 14 to 1) pu

Dist: 1½l, 3l, nk, 2½l, 3l, hd. 1m 0.30s. a 2.80s (8 Ran).
SR: 16/10/-/2/-/ (E J Mangan), M W Easterby

2129 Staindrop Median Auction Maiden Stakes Class F (2-y-o) £2,758 7f (2:40)

1245[2] JACKSON HOUSE 9-0 K Fallon (6) *chsd ldr, effrt 2 fs out, rdn to ld entering last, hng lft, ran on, fnshd 1st, plcd second*............................ (8 to 1 op 4 to 1) 1D
1182[4] MOKAITE 8-2 (7*) J Marshall (2) *led, rdn 2 fs out, hdd entering fnl furlong, bumped wl ins last, no extr, fnshd second, plcd 1st*.................. (14 to 1 op 8 to 1) 1
1877[6] GINGERBIRD (Ire) 8-9 W Ryan (10) *slwly away, hdwy and wide strt, rdn fnl 2 fs and kpt on one pace.* .... (5 to 4 on op 6 to 4 tchd 2 to 1) 3
1998[5] PARISH WALK (Ire) 9-0 K Darley (9) *in tch, hdwy and wide strt, rdn 2 fs out, sn one paced*...... (6 to 1 op 5 to 1) 4
1983[2] CAPTAIN STARLIGHT (Ire) 8-11 (3*) M Fenton (4) *chsd ldrs, rdn o'r 2 fs out, sn wknd*........... (5 to 1 op 5 to 2) 5
1863 STEANARD BOY 9-0 J Fanning (8) *in tch, rdn 2 and a half fs out, no imprsn*................. (66 to 1 op 33 to 1) 6
BEX BOY (Ire) 9-0 T Lucas (12) *slwly away and beh till some late hdwy*........... (33 to 1 op 16 to 1) 7
BOLLIN NEIL 9-0 M Birch (13) *chsd ldrs, hdwy and wide strt, rdn o'r 2 fs out, sn btn*...... (25 to 1 op 12 to 1) 8
MUSICAL MARCH 8-9 Dean McKeown (3) *mid-div till wknd 2 fs out*.................... (33 to 1 op 16 to 1) 9
WAKE UP TO REALITY 8-9 R Lappin (5) *al rear.* .... (66 to 1 op 33 to 1) 10

1774⁹ KOHIMA BOY 9-0 J Carroll (7) *cl up till lost pl whn jmpd path aftr one and a half fs, sn prmnt till wknd 2 furlongs out*.......................... (25 to 1 op 16 to 1) 11
LOCHON 9-0 S Webster (11) *al rear*. (100 to 1 op 50 to 1) 12
2042 CRACKLEY LANE 9-0 Alex Greaves (1) *chsd ldrs, rdn 2 and a half fs out, sn wknd*............(100 to 1 op 50 to 1) 13
Dist: 1½l, 2l, 5l, 3l, 4l, hd, 1½l, 1½l, 1½l, nk. 1m 27.10s. a 4.10s (13 Ran).
(The Bridge Club), M D Hammond

2130 Northern Echo Handicap Class E (0-70 3-y-o) £2,950 1½m 44yds....... (3:10)

1832⁹ HASTA LA VISTA [38] (bl) 7-12 L Charnock (9) *chsd ldr, led 5 fs out, rdn fnl 2 furlongs and ran on wl*. ....(8 to 1 op 7 to 1) 1
1896² TTYFRAN [53] 8-13 J Carroll (6) *trkd ldrs, hdwy to chase wnr 4 fs out, rdn to chal 2 furlongs out, sn hrd drvn and ev ch till no extr*.............................. (5 to 1) 2
459 MONSIEUR DUPONT (Ire) [59] 9-5 G Duffield (3) *al prmnt, rdn 3 fs out, kpt on one pace*.........(5 to 1 op 9 to 2) 3
1875⁴ MONASTIC FLIGHT (Ire) [49] 8-9 J Fortune (1) *in tch, hdwy 4 fs out, rdn o'r 2 furlongs out, sn one pace*. .... (17 to 2 op 7 to 1 tchd 9 to 1) 4
1737⁵ THE PREMIER EXPRES [60] 9-1 (5*) O Pears (8) *hld up and beh, hdwy 4 fs out, rdn 2 furlongs out, no imprsn*. .... (16 to 1 op 12 to 1) 5
507* EFIZIA [61] 9-7 K Darley (10) *mid-div, effrt 5 fs out, rdn 2 furlongs out, sn wknd*.......................(4 to 1 jt-fav tchd 9 to 2 and 5 to 1) 6
1557³ HO-JOE (Ire) [54] 9-0 K Fallon (5) *hld up and beh, effrt and some hdwy 5 fs out, nvr dngrs*..................(8 to 1) 7
1540⁷ SPECIAL RISK (Ire) [51] 8-8 (3*) M Fenton (2) *in tch, effrt and hdwy 4 fs out, sn rdn and wknd 2 and a half furlongs out*...................... (16 to 1 op 12 to 1) 8
1146 LOCK TIGHT (USA) [55] 9-1 A Culhane (7) *al rear, pushed alng hfwy and sn btn*. ....(4 to 1 jt-fav op 7 to 2 tchd 9 to 2) 9
1813³ SANTA STELLAR [52] 8-12 Dean McKeown (4) *led, hdd 5 fs out, sn wknd*.....................(33 to 1 op 20 to 1) 10
Dist: ½l, 2l, 3½l, 4l, 1½l, 1½l, 8l, ½l, 2l. 2m 36.60s. a 1.60s (10 Ran).
SR: 19/33/35/18/21/19/9/-/-/ (K Hodgson), M W Easterby

2131 Aysgarth Claiming Stakes Class F (3-y-o and up) £2,660 1½m 44yds.. (3:40)

1864⁵ TRY N' FLY (Ire) 3-8-8 K Darley (2) *made all, rdn o'r 2 fs out, ran on wl*............................(3 to 1 op 5 to 2) 1
1642* MADAM GYMCRAK 3-8-8 Julie Bowker (1) *hld up in tch, smooth hdwy 3 fs out, rdn one and a half furlongs out, edgd lft and not quicken ins last*. ....(13 to 8 on op 2 to 1 on tchd 6 to 4 on) 2
1784 GOLDEN SAVANNAH 3-8-5 T Lucas (4) *hld up and beh, some hdwy 3 fs out, sn rdn and one pace*. ....(6 to 1 op 5 to 1) 3
1813² CAROUSEL MAGIC 3-8-4 Dean McKeown (3) *trkd ldr, rdn o'r 3 fs out, sn wknd*...............(12 to 1 op 8 to 1) 4
Dist: 1l, 10l, 2½l. 2m 43.60s. a 8.60s (4 Ran).
(P Caplan), Mrs M Reveley

2132 'Phu Tho' Handicap Class D (0-80 3-y-o) £3,084 5f.................... (4:10)

2047 THE FED [52] (v) 7-12³ (3*) S Maloney (3) *chsd ldrs, effrt to ld 2 fs out, sn clr*................ (14 to 1 op 10 to 1) 1
1518² COVENT GARDEN GIRL [62] (bl) 8-1 (7*) C Munday (5) *beh, hdwy 2 fs out, sn rdn and kpt on ins last, no ch wth wnr*.................................(5 to 1 op 4 to 1) 2
1848² SHADOW JURY [75] 9-7 K Darley (4) *chsd ldr, rdn 2 fs out and sn one pace*.......................(3 to 1 op 5 to 2) 3
2024³ BOLD COUNTY [69] 9-1 R P Elliott (2) *pld hrd, in tch, rdn hfwy, sn one pace*.. (2 to 1 fav op 9 to 4 tchd 5 to 2) 4
1966⁴ COCONUT JOHNNY [59] (bl) 8-5 J Fanning (6) *chsd ldrs, rdn 2 fs out, sn btn*.... (11 to 2 op 6 to 1 tchd 13 to 2) 5
1801⁶ FIRST PLAY [67] 8-13 J Carroll (1) *led, rdn and hdd 2 fs out, sn wknd*..........................(6 to 1 tchd 8 to 1) 6
Dist: 2½l, 1½l, 3½l, 1½l, nk. 59.00s. a 1.50s (6 Ran).
SR: 34/34/41/21/5/12/ (F E Downes), R M Whitaker

2133 Cotherstone Rating Related Maiden Fillies Stakes Class F (0-60 3-y-o) £2,467 7f...................... (4:40)

1496⁴ VILAMAR (Ire) 8-11 K Fallon (4) *hld up, smooth hdwy o'r 2 fs out, led one and a half out, edgd rght and rdn clr entering fnl furlong*............(10 to 1 tchd 12 to 1) 1
1850³ NICHODOULA 8-11 G Duffield (2) *trkd ldrs, hdwy and wide strt, rdn 2 fs out, kpt on one pace*. ....(6 to 4 on op 5 to 4 on tchd 6 to 5 on) 2
1630⁹ SUNRISE MORNING (USA) 8-11 M Birch (6) *chsd ldr, rdn 2 fs out, sn one pace*...... (8 to 1 op 6 to 1 tchd 9 to 1) 3
1891³ FLASHELLA (Ire) 8-11 J Carroll (5) *prmnt, rdn 3 fs out, sn one pace*.............. (7 to 2 op 2 to 1 tchd 4 to 1) 4
1761⁴ LAMSONETTI 8-11 Dean McKeown (3) *led, rdn o'r 2 fs out, hdd one and a half furlongs out, sn wknd*. .... (8 to 1 op 14 to 1) 5
Dist: 3l, hd, 2l, 2½l. 1m 25.70s. a 2.70s (5 Ran).
SR: 15/6/5/-/-/ (Pleasant Racing Club), E J Alston

EPSOM (firm)
Wednesday June 30th
Going Correction: MINUS 0.35 sec. per fur.

2134 Richard Littlejohn Rating Related Maiden Stakes Class E (0-70 3-y-o) £2,976 1¼m 18yds............ (6:35)

1976⁵ HALHAM TARN (Ire) 9-0 J Williams (3) *hld up in rear, hdwy 4 fs out, chsd ldr o'r 2 out, led last strds*. .... (5 to 1 tchd 6 to 1 and 9 to 2) 1
1581⁴ LT WELSH (USA) (v) 9-0 L Dettori (6) *in tch, led 3 out, rdn fnl furlong, hdd nr line*. (9 to 2 op 4 to 1 tchd 5 to 1) 2
1713⁵ CLEVER MINSTREL (USA) 9-0 R Hills (4) *hld up in rear, hdwy 3 out, one pace last 2 fs*. ....(7 to 1 op 5 to 1 tchd 8 to 1) 3
1776³ EYE WITNESS (Ire) 8-9 T Quinn (5) *pressed ldr, ev ch whn squeezed for room on rls 3 out, wknd last 2 fs*. ....(15 to 8 fav op 6 to 4 tchd 2 to 1) 4
1907³ ITS UNBELIEVABLE 8-7 (7*) D Wright (2) *sn led, hdd 3 fs out, soon btn*...........(9 to 1 op 7 to 1 tchd 10 to 1) 5
1859⁵ SIR THOMAS BEECHAM 9-0 B Rouse (7) *ldg grp, dsptd ld 3 fs out, sn rdn and outpcd*. ....(33 to 1 op 20 to 1 tchd 40 to 1) 6
1469⁴ ICE REBEL 9-0 W Newnes (1) *settled in mid-div, beh 4 fs out, lost tch frm 3 out*. (11 to 2 op 5 to 1 tchd 6 to 1) 7
Dist: Hd, 7l, 1½l, 4l, 1l, ¾l. 2m 7.75s. a 3.45s (7 Ran).
SR: 31/30/16/8/5/3/1/ (Lady Dundas), D R C Elsworth

2135 Epsom And Ewell Handicap Class C (0-90 3-y-o) £5,253 1½m 10yds.. (7:10)

1917² MR COPYFORCE [57] 7-7 N Adams (7) *chsd ldr, led 2 out, rdn clr fnl furlong*...............(3 to 1 fav op 5 to 2) 1
1946² FOOLS ERRAND (Ire) [68] 8-4 T Quinn (3) *settled in 3rd pl, rdn alng frm 3 out, outpcd ins last 2 fs*. ....(5 to 1 op 7 to 2) 2
1910* TOP RANK [77] 8-13 (4ex) L Dettori (4) *led til hdd 2 fs out, sn rdn and one pace*................(4 to 1 op 5 to 2) 3
1827² SATIN DANCER [83] 9-5 J Reid (2) *settled in 4th pl, rdn and effrt 3 fs out, swtchd lft o'r one out, ran on same pace*................(100 to 30 op 5 to 1 tchd 3 to 1) 4
KIMBERLEY BOY [82] 9-4 D Holland (6) *hld up in rear, improved 3 fs out, outpcd o'r one out*. ....(14 to 1 op 8 to 1) 5
678* GENERAL CHASE [68] 7-13 (5*) Stephen Davies (1) *prog frm rear o'r 5 fs out, chlgd on ins and ev ch 3 out, sn rdn and btn*................(7 to 1 op 5 to 1 tchd 8 to 1) 6
1558⁴ TAAHHUB (Ire) [85] 9-7 R Hills (8) *hld up in 5th pl, effrt 4 fs out, rdn and wknd 3 out*. ....(16 to 1 op 14 to 1 tchd 20 to 1) 7
Dist: 3l, hd, sht-hd. 2m 36.89s. a 1.39s (7 Ran).
SR: 23/28/36/41/ (Copyforce Ltd), Miss B Sanders

2136 LBC Newstalk 97.3 FM Handicap Class C (0-95 3-y-o and up) £5,775 7f ....(7:40)

1806⁷ ECHO-LOGICAL [85] 4-9-5 K Darley (4) *towards rear, cld on ldrs 3 fs out, ran on o'r one out, led nr finish*. .... (15 to 2 op 6 to 1 tchd 8 to 1) 1
1636³ ROCKY WATERS (USA) [94] 4-10-0 B Rouse (2) *beh til ran on 3 out, led o'r one furlong out, rdn and hdd nr finish*. .... (7 to 1 op 5 to 1 tchd 15 to 2) 2
1667⁶ YOURS BY RIGHT [83] 3-8-8 L Dettori (7) *wl in tch, effrt o'r 2 out, styd on ins fnl furlong*. ....(8 to 1 op 7 to 1 tchd 9 to 1) 3
1636⁸ PRENONAMOSS [79] 5-8-13 R Price (10) *ran on 3 fs out, not quicken appr fnl furlong*. ....(10 to 1 op 8 to 1 tchd 12 to 1) 4
1730⁴ HELIOS [76] 5-8-10 J Reid (6) *hld up towards rear, styd on last 2 fs, not rch ldrs*. ....(11 to 2 fav op 8 to 1 tchd 9 to 1) 5
2008² NEITHER NOR [65] 4-7-10 (3*,6ex) D Harrison (8) *hld up in rear, pld out to chal wl o'r 2 out, kpt on one pace fnl furlong*...........(6 to 1 op 5 to 1 tchd 13 to 2) 6
1830⁹ CONFRONTER [74] (v) 4-8-8 T Quinn (9) *trkd ldg grp, losing pl whn squeezed for room on outsd wl o'r 2 fs out*. ....(12 to 1 tchd 14 to 1) 7
1768 CLAYBANK (USA) [76] 4-8-10 D Holland (5) *chsd ldrs for o'r 4 fs*................. (16 to 1 op 14 to 1 tchd 20 to 1) 8
1859² SECOND CHANCE (Ire) [72] 3-7-4 (7*) D Wright (11) *settled towards rear, rdn 3 fs out, nvr on terms*. .... (14 to 1 op 12 to 1 tchd 16 to 1) 9
1697⁸ MITHI AL GAMAR (USA) [72] 3-7-11 A McGlone (1) *led til hdd and wknd wl o'r 2 fs out*. .... (10 to 1 op 8 to 1 tchd 11 to 1) 10
1485* RUNNING GLIMPSE (Ire) [82] 5-9-2 W Newnes (12) *ldg grp, led 2 fs out til o'r one out, sn wknd*. .... (15 to 2 op 6 to 1 tchd 8 to 1) 11
1744⁶ INVOCATION [69] 6-8-3 N Adams (3) *handily plcd, led wl o'r 2 fs out, sn hdd and wknd*. .... (14 to 1 op 10 to 1 tchd 16 to 1) 12
Dist: Nk, nk, 1½l, hd, 1l, 2½l, sht-hd, 1l, nk, nk. 1m 21.30s. a 0.90s (12 Ran).

SR: 55/63/42/42/38/24/25/26/10/ (P D Savill), R Hannon

2137 EBF Tattenham Maiden Stakes Class D (2-y-o) £3,557 5f.............(8:10)

1131[6] BASKERVILLE 9-0 J Reid (9) *handily plcd, shaken up to ld o'r one furlong out, pushed clr*....(6 to 1 op 7 to 1) 1
1788[7] DOLLAR GAMBLE (Ire) 9-0 K Darley (4) *wl in tch, not much room and swtchd rght o'r one furlong out, ran on nr line*..............(100 to 30 op 9 to 4 tchd 7 to 2) 2
1234[4] BOLD GEM 8-9 B Raymond (3) *pressed ldrs, ev ch one furlong out, rdn and no extr clsg stages.* ....(9 to 2 op 4 to 1 tchd 5 to 1) 3
2006[6] EUROCHEM LAD (Ire) (bl) 9-0 B Rouse (7) *led til hdd o'r one furlong out, styd on same pace.* ....(14 to 1 op 10 to 1 tchd 16 to 1) 4
1279[6] KERRIE-JO 8-9 R Hills (5) *not too wl away, sn chasing ldrs, rdn and not quicken o'r one furlong out.* ....(14 to 1 op 12 to 1 tchd 16 to 1) 5
DOMINO QUEEN (Ire) 8-9 L Dettori (6) *wl in tch, rdn and no extr appr fnl furlong, better for race.* (6 to 1 op 4 to 1) 6
1640[6] SOUTHERN RIDGE 9-0 J Williams (8) *strted slwly, al outpcd*.....(11 to 4 fav op 5 to 2 tchd 9 to 4 and 3 to 1) 7
DAVIDS DIAMOND 8-9 T Quinn (1) *sn outpcd.* ....(25 to 1 op 20 to 1) 8
BILLY CRUNCHEON 9-0 A Tucker (10) *slwly into strd, al outpcd*..........(25 to 1 op 20 to 1 tchd 33 to 1) 9

Dist: 3l, hd, 1l, hd, 5l, ¾l, 2½l, 1½l. 56.40s. a 1.70s (9 Ran).
SR: 31/19/13/14/8/-/ (Exors Of The Late Mrs J de Rothschild), R F Johnson Houghton

2138 Burgh Heath Claiming Stakes Class E (3-y-o) £3,785 1m 114yds....... (8:40)

1670[4] THE EXECUTOR 9-7 J Reid (6) *mid-div, pushed alng 3 fs out, ran on to ld o'r one out, pushed clr.* ....(9 to 2 op 4 to 1 tchd 5 to 1) 1
2053[3] RAGING THUNDER (bl) 9-4 K Darley (5) *handily plcd, led 2 fs out, hdd and not quicken o'r one out.* ....(6 to 1 tchd 7 to 1) 2
1943* DEE RAFT (USA) 9-2 D Holland (1) *mid-div, rdn and hdwy 3 out, one pace last 2 fs.* ....(7 to 2 fav op 7 to 4 tchd 4 to 1) 3
2065[4] REGALSETT 9-2 L Dettori (2) *led til 2 fs out, rdn and no extr*......................(5 to 1 tchd 6 to 1) 4
1039[3] CONSPICUOUS (Ire) 9-7 T Quinn (7) *wl plcd til rdn and one pace appr last 2 fs*.................(5 to 1 tchd 6 to 1) 5
1522[6] MISS COPYFORCE 9-2 W Newnes (10) *al beh.* ....(25 to 1 op 20 to 1 tchd 33 to 1) 6
1829[6] SALLY OF THE ALLEY 8-5 B Rouse (3) *outpcd thrght.* ....(25 to 1 op 16 to 1 tchd 33 to 1) 7
927 DELAY NO MORE 8-2 (7*) D Wright (9) *pressed ldr til lost pl quickly 3 fs out*..... (33 to 1 op 25 to 1 tchd 40 to 1) 8

Dist: 3l, 1l, ½l, 2½l, 8l, 3½l, 4l. 1m 43.39s. a 1.39s (8 Ran).
SR: 42/30/25/23/20/ (Exors Of The Late Mrs J de Rothschild), R F Johnson Houghton

2139 Epsom Downs Handicap Class D (0-80 3-y-o and up) £3,427 6f......... (9:10)

1957[2] BALLASECRET [76] 5-9-8 (5*) D Meredith (2) *made all, styd on wl ins fnl furlong*................ (9 to 2 op 9 to 4) 1
1730[3] SHIKARI'S SON [77] 6-10-0 P Robinson (6) *hld up in rear, rdn and ran on o'r one furlong out, fnshd wl.* ....(4 to 1 op 7 to 2 tchd 9 to 2) 2
1954[6] STAR GODDESS (USA) [71] 4-9-8 B Rouse (3) *chsd wnr, ev ch one furlong out, rdn and not quicken.* ....(8 to 1 op 7 to 1) 3
1744 FACE NORTH (Ire) [65] 5-9-2 T Quinn (5) *hld up in 5th pl, rdn alng hfwy, one pace appr fnl furlong.* ....(7 to 4 fav op 9 to 4 tchd 5 to 2) 4
1903[2] MOGWAI (Ire) [55] (v) 4-8-6 D Holland (1) *settled in 3rd pl, not much room 2 out, no extr fnl furlong.* ....(9 to 2 op 5 to 1 tchd 4 to 1) 5
606[6] PERSIAN GUSHER (Ire) [66] 3-8-9 L Dettori (4) *mid-div, rdn and no prog o'r 2 fs out*..........(8 to 1 tchd 10 to 1) 6

Dist: ½l, ½l, 1½l, hd, 7l. 1m 8.53s. a 0.63s (6 Ran).
SR: 58/57/49/37/26/1/ (R J Adams), R Dickin

GOWRAN PARK (IRE) (good)
Wednesday June 30th

2140 Bagenalstown Fillies Maiden (3-y-o and up) £2,762 1m 1f........... (6:00)

CENTER MORICHES (Ire) 3-9-0 C Roche (6)....... (6 to 1) 1
1510[2] KUDDAM (Ire) 3-9-0 P Shanahan (17).......... (5 to 4 on) 2
1796[7] LADY NOBLE (Ire) 3-9-0 J F Egan (14)........... (10 to 1) 3
1796[6] JU JU'S GIRL (Ire) 3-8-8 (6*) J A Heffernan (15).....(8 to 1) 4
1466[3] TEBRE (USA) (bl) 3-9-0 W J Supple (4)........... (10 to 1) 5
1855[7] OCEAN BLUE (Ire) 3-9-0 P V Gilson (2)........... (14 to 1) 6
1796[8] FESTIVAL GIRL (Ire) 3-9-0 R Hughes (7).......... (12 to 1) 7
SHPEEL (Ire) 3-9-0 D V Smith (9)................ (20 to 1) 8
1445[8] PEARL DAWN (Ire) 3-9-0 B Coogan (10).......... (20 to 1) 9
1610[5] PERSIAN GEM (Ire) 3-9-0 J D Eddery (11)........ (15 to 2) 10
1568[4] BLACK PIPER (Ire) 3-8-8 (6*) J J Behan (5)....... (12 to 1) 11
1507 ATSUKO (Ire) 3-9-0 S Craine (8)................ (14 to 1) 12
SILVER JAR (Ire) 3-9-0 N G McCullagh (12)....... (20 to 1) 13
1649 LADY GLOW (Ire) (bl) 3-9-0 D Hogan (16)......... (14 to 1) 14
1333[9] MISS MARESE (Ire) 3-9-0 K J Manning (13)....... (16 to 1) 15

Dist: 1l, 2½l, 3½l, hd. 2m 0.30s. (15 Ran).
(J R Banahan), J R Banahan

2141 June Handicap (0-65 3-y-o and up) £2,762 1m..................... (6:25)

1645[3] LORD GLENVARA (Ire) [-] 5-8-12 (4*) P Carberry (11) (8 to 1) 1
1644* RIENROE (Ire) [-] 4-10-2 P Shanahan (3)..... (9 to 2 jt-fav) 2
1621[3] TOUCHDOWN [-] 6-9-9 R Hughes (7)............. (7 to 1) 3
1569[4] RUSTIC-ORT (Ire) [-] (bl) 5-9-0 N G McCullagh (9) (9 to 2 jt-fav) 4
598[5] SISTER CARMEL (Ire) [-] 3-8-12 K J Manning (10) (20 to 1) 5
1995[4] FAIRYDEL (Ire) [-] 3-9-1 (8*,7ex) P J Smullen (6).... (8 to 1) 6
1622[4] TAUTEN (Ire) [-] 3-9-4 S Craine (8)............... (12 to 1) 7
TOMBARA (Ire) [-] 5-9-11 B Coogan (12).......... (14 to 1) 8
SON OF TEMPO (Ire) [-] 4-8-6 P V Gilson (16)..... (16 to 1) 9
1440[4] RETURN JOURNEY (Ire) [-] 4-9-4 (10*) J F Clarke (2) ....(12 to 1) 10
1757[6] TENCA (Ire) [-] 3-9-2 J P Murtagh (1)............ (14 to 1) 11
1385 SPECIAL SECRET (Ire) [-] 5-7-11 (4*) W J Smith (4) (20 to 1) 12
1995[8] CHAMPAGNE NIGHT (Fr) [-] 3-9-2 (2*) K H Ting (14) (12 to 1) 13
D'ORIOLA (Ire) [-] 3-8-7 J F Egan (13)........... (20 to 1) 14
981[5] PHILIP PATRICK (Ire) [-] 3-8-10 (6*) J J Behan (5).. (25 to 1) 15
1385[8] PERCY LANE (Ire) [-] 3-8-13 W J O'Connor (15).... (8 to 1) 16

Dist: Sht-hd, 1l, 1½l, ½l. 1m 40.60s. (16 Ran).
(P J P O'Connor), D P Kelly

2142 Carrolls Festival Handicap (0-70 3-y-o and up) £3,452 1m 1f 130yds.... (6:50)

1622[6] TRILLICK (Ire) [-] 3-9-0 J P Murtagh (8)............ (12 to 1) 1
1644[5] ALBERTA ROSE (Ire) [-] 4-9-5 (6*) J R Barry (17).... (6 to 1) 2
MEJEVE [-] 5-9-6 R Hughes (3).................. (14 to 1) 3
2041[6] RATHBRIDES JOY [-] 6-9-1 (6*) J A Heffernan (7) (4 to 1 fav) 4
2039 YONOKA (Fr) [-] 4-9-6 (8*) K M So (2)............. (20 to 1) 5
1962[2] CONCERT ORCHESTRA (Ire) [-] 4-7-7 (2*) D G O'Shea, ...(9 to 1) 6
1651* VICOSA (Ire) [-] 4-7-13[1] (2*) R M Burke (5)......... (7 to 1) 7
1466[6] EGALITE (Ire) [-] 3-7-10 (8*) R T Fitzpatrick,....... (16 to 1) 8
1202 PHARELLA [-] 5-9-1 (8*) B Fenton (9).............. (14 to 1) 9
1651[8] THE BOWER (Ire) [-] 4-7-7[3] (10*) P M Donohue (13) (16 to 1) 10
1553[8] RUPERT THE GREAT (Ire) [-] 3-9-1 (4*) P Carberry (1) ....(10 to 1) 11
1757* CALL MY GUEST (Ire) [-] 3-9-4 (3ex) W J Supple (12) ....(10 to 1) 12
1995* BOBROSS (Ire) [-] 3-9-3 (6*) R V Skelly (4).......... (9 to 1) 13
NORDIC SOUND (Ire) [-] 4-8-11 (8*) M W Martin (6) (14 to 1) 14
1251[3] ANSEO (Ire) [-] 4-9-2 C Roche (15)................ (7 to 1) 15
1235 PURPLE EMPEROR (Fr) [-] 4-10-0 S Craine (14)...(20 to 1) 16
1569[8] SOLAR FLASH (Ire) [-] 4-8-0 N G McCullagh (10).. (14 to 1) 17

Dist: 1l, ½l, 1½l, 1l. 2m 4.70s. (17 Ran).
(Fergus McGirr), A P O'Brien

2143 Kilkenny City Q.R. Handicap (0-80 4-y-o and up) £2,762 2m............ (8:30)

2035[5] KEPPOLS PRINCE [-] 6-9-11 (7*) Miss O Glennon (14) ....(6 to 1) 1
1467* PADASHPAN (USA) [-] 4-11-10 (5*) Mrs J M Mullins (2) ....(7 to 2) 2
1576[7] PERSIAN HAZE (Ire) [-] 4-11-3 (7*) Mr P R Lenihan (13) ....(14 to 1) 3
TRY A BRANDY [-] 11-10-6 (5*) Mr H F Cleary (1).. (12 to 1) 4
1752[6] MRS BARTON (Ire) [-] 5-11-3 (7*) Mr E Norris (4) (5 to 2 fav) 5
2094[7] GO DEAS [-] 6-9-11 (7*) Miss F Crowley (12)...... (12 to 1) 6
1468[6] NANARCH (USA) [-] 9-11-5 (7*) Mr J A Nash (9).... (10 to 1) 7
1962 CRAZY GAIL [-] 6-11-5 Mr A P O'Brien (8)........ (8 to 1) 8
1996[3] CEDAR COURT (Ire) [-] (bl) 5-11-10 Mr S R Murphy (6) ....(8 to 1) 9
4685a ENQELAAB (USA) [-] 5-12-3 (3*) Mr D Marnane (10) (14 to 1) 10
EVER SO BOLD [-] 6-10-10 (3*) Mrs S McCarthy (11) ....(20 to 1) 11
ACTION DANCER [-] 7-10-0 (7*) Mrs K Walsh (3).. (25 to 1) 12
SWEET DOWNS [-] 12-10-0 Mr M McNaulty (15).. (20 to 1) 13
807 MUNSIF (Fr) [-] 6-11-5 Mr P Fenton (5)........... (14 to 1) 14
2989 SIMPLY SWIFT [-] 6-11-3 Mr T Mullins (7).......... (9 to 1) 15

Dist: 8l, 10l, hd. 3m 37.90s. (15 Ran).
(John Houghton), John Houghton

LONGCHAMP (FR) (firm)
Wednesday June 30th
Going Correction: PLUS 0.10 sec. per fur.

2144 Prix du Bois (Group 3) (2-y-o) £23,895 5f.......................... (2:25)

PORTO VARAS (USA) (bl) 8-9 F Head (1) *slwly away, beh till hdwy 2 and a half fs out, led o'r one out, ran on wl.* ....(76 to 10) 1
BRAVE NOTE (Ire) 8-9 C Asmussen (2) *mid-div till hdwy one and a half fs out, fnshd wl*.............. (23 to 10) 2

1692* FOXHOUND (USA) 8-9 T Jarnet (5) *trkd ldr, chlgd 2 fs out, kpt on one pace*..........(5 to 3 on) 3
TELLURIUM (USA) 8-9 O Peslier (3) *in tch, effrt 2 fs out, one pace*..........(9 to 1) 4
FILHA DO AR (USA) 8-9 G Mosse (6) *nvr plcd to chal.* ....(23 to 10) 5
MY SIN (Ire) 8-9 O Doleuze (4) *led till jnd 2 fs out, hdd one and a half out, sn wknd*..........(11 to 1) 6
Dist: ½l, sht-hd, ¾l, 2½l, 2l. 58.00s. a 2.50s (6 Ran).
SR: 55/53/52/49/39/31/ (N I Della Rocchetta), F Boutin

SAN SIRO (ITY) (firm)
Wednesday June 30th

2145 Premio Villoresi (2-y-o) £5,603 6f ....(2:20)

ASHOKA 8-11 M Esposito,.......... 1
GUNNI (Ire) 8-11 M Tellini,.......... 2
SURIS (Ire) 8-11 S Soto, *slwly away, ran on 2 fs out, no extr ins last*.......... 3
Dist: Hd, nk, 5l, 10l, ½l. 1m 12.30s. (6 Ran).
(M Nicolai), F Gnesi

2146 Premio Cadenabbia (3-y-o) £4,483 1 ¼m..........(4:10)

NOXE (Ity) 8-12 M Planard,.......... 1
PISONE (Ity) 8-12 F Jovine,.......... 2
GLAMOUR AND GLORY (Ire) 8-12 S Soto,.......... 3
CRODARSHAAN (Ire) 8-11 L Sorrentino, *chsd ldrs in 5th, ev ch 2 fs out, eased fnl furlong*.......... 9
Dist: 1l, hd, nk, 1½l, 2½l, hd, 2l, 7l, hd, 6l. 2m 10.30s. (12 Ran).
(Razza Padana), R Discepolo

WARWICK (firm)
Wednesday June 30th
Going Correction: MINUS 0.30 sec. per fur.

2147 EBF Royal Maiden Stakes Class D (2-y-o) £3,377 5f..........(2:20)

1955 MIRIAM 8-9 D Holland (5) *made all, shaken up one furlong out, pushed out*..........(3 to 1 fav op 4 to 1) 1
1905 SPORTING START 9-0 N Adams (1) *broke wl, cl up, kpt on one pace ins fnl furlong*..........(20 to 1 op 16 to 1) 2
1905[5] ANOTHERONE TO NOTE 8-7 (7*) Mark Denaro (4) *cl up, rdn and ev ch o'r one furlong out, one pace ins last.* ....(7 to 2 op 2 to 1 tchd 4 to 1) 3
BELLEMINETTE (Ire) 8-9 J Williams (2) *missed break, beh, hdwy o'r one furlong out, nvr on terms.* ....(4 to 1 op 8 to 1) 4
1773[5] BANDITA 8-9 R Perham (6) *cl up til wknd o'r 2 fs out.* ....(4 to 1 op 3 to 1) 5
COVENTRY KID 9-0 G Carter (3) *outpcd, tld off.* ....(4 to 1 op 6 to 4) 6
Dist: 2l, ¾l, 5l, 5l, 10l. 1m 0.60s. a 2.40s (6 Ran).
SR: 17/14/11/ (Miss Amanda Whitehead), M J Fetherston-Godley

2148 Hazy Days Rating Related Maiden Stakes Class E (0-70 3-y-o and up) £2,950 1½m 115yds..........(2:50)

1838[2] HATTA RIVER (USA) (bl) 3-8-8 W R Swinburn (3) *made all, shaken up and wnt clr 2 fs out, sn rdn alng, eased cl hme*..........(2 to 1 fav tchd 9 to 4) 1
1684[3] ARMENIAN COFFEE (Ire) 3-8-8 G Carter (5) *trkd wnr till lost pl one m out, chsd winner fnl 3 fs, hrd rdn o'r 2 out, no imprsn*..........(3 to 1 op 9 to 4) 2
1625[8] ARAADH (USA) 3-8-3 N Carlisle (4) *in cl tch till rdn alng and one pace o'r 3 fs out.* (3 to 1 op 2 to 1 tchd 7 to 2) 3
1831 HOPEFUL PROSPECT 3-8-4[1] A Clark (2) *sn beh, nvr on terms*..........(16 to 1 op 14 to 1 tchd 20 to 1) 4
1802[7] PERO 3-8-8 D Holland (1) *slwly into strd, beh, cld one m out, sn pushed alng, hrd rdn 5 fs out, wknd o'r 3 out.* ....(7 to 2 op 3 to 1) 5
Dist: 3½l, 4l, 7l, 3½l. 2m 41.70s. a 3.80s (5 Ran).
SR: 19/12/ (Sheikh Ahmed Al Maktoum), Major W R Hern

2149 Nattrass Giles Handicap Class E (0-70 3-y-o and up) £3,002 1¼m 169yds..........(3:20)

1961* WAR REQUIEM (Ire) [52] 3-8-9 (5ex) J Williams (3) *trkd ldrs, hdwy to ld appr fnl furlong, jst hld on.* ....(6 to 1 op 11 to 2) 1+
1627[5] JUNCTION TWENTYTWO [50] 3-8-7 T Quinn (1) *prmnt, pushed alng o'r 2 fs out, ran on wl und pres ins fnl furlong, jst got up*..........(12 to 1 tchd 10 to 1) 1+
1832[2] EDGE OF DARKNESS [54] 4-9-8 (3*) D Harrison (4) *chsd ldrs, hdwy o'r 2 fs out, kpt on*.....(11 to 2 tchd 6 to 1) 3
1827 SEEK THE PEARL [68] 3-9-11 W R Swinburn (8) *hld up, effrt whn hmpd o'r one furlong out, rdn and kpt on ins last.* ....(7 to 1 op 9 to 2) 4
1626[5] CELIA BRADY [49] 5-9-6 C Rutter (11) *hld up, hdwy o'r 2 fs out, ev ch over one out, one pace.* ....(15 to 2 op 6 to 1 tchd 8 to 1) 5
1946[3] KILLICK [51] 5-9-8 A Mackay (12) *mid-div, effrt and one pace fnl 2 fs*..........(5 to 1 fav op 7 to 1) 6
1453 RED KITE [49] 4-9-6 G Carter (10) *cl up, ev ch appr fnl furlong, one pace*..........(14 to 1) 7
2012* PRECIOUS CAROLINE (Ire) [36] 5-8-7 J Lowe (5) *led til hdd appr fnl furlong, wknd.* ....(6 to 1 op 11 to 2 tchd 9 to 2) 8
1902[6] LONG FURLONG [40] 5-8-11 N Adams (7) *beh, hdwy o'r 2 fs out, not clr run on ins fnl furlong.* ....(12 to 1 tchd 14 to 1) 9
1880 WINGED WHISPER (USA) [35] 4-8-1 (5*) A Garth (9) *nvr better than mid-div*..........(25 to 1) 10
MELANCOLIA [43] 7-8-11 (3*) S D Williams (2) *hld up, al beh*..........(33 to 1 op 20 to 1) 11
1878[8] RADIO CAROLINE [28] (bl) 5-7-13 A Tucker (6) *strted slwly, al beh*..........(33 to 1 op 25 to 1) 12
Dist: Dd-ht, 1½l, 1l, nk, ½l. 2m 16.50s. a 3.70s (12 Ran).
SR: 26/24/39/37/31/32/ (Whitcombe Manor Racing Stables Limited & C G Major), G B Balding & C D Broad

2150 Harcros Timber & Building Supplies Stayers Championship Series Handicap Qualifier Class E (0-70 3-y-o and up) £2,898 2m 20yds..........(3:50)

1840[9] PROSEQUENDO (USA) [63] 6-9-10 A Clark (5) *wtd wth, cld o'r 5 fs out, led blw 2 out, quickened clr appr last, easily*..........(9 to 4 fav op 2 to 1) 1
1984[4] BRIGGSMAID [52] 5-8-13 W R Swinburn (2) *wtd wth, cld o'r 4 fs out, one pace frm 2 out.* ....(11 to 4 op 2 to 1 tchd 3 to 1) 2
1607[5] SINGING REPLY (USA) [35] 5-7-10 T Williams (3) *trkd ldr, led 5 fs out, rdn alng o'r 3 out, hdd blw 2 out, wknd.* ....(5 to 1 op 4 to 1) 3
1900 GAY MING [35] 4-7-7[2] (5*) A Garth (6) *hld up in tch, reminders o'r 6 fs out, sn outpcd.* ....(10 to 1 op 8 to 1 tchd 12 to 1) 4
1654[6] COST EFFECTIVE [32] 6-7-7 G Bardwell (4) *trkd ldrs, pushed alng o'r 6 fs out, sn outpcd.* (7 to 2 op 3 to 1) 5
1495[7] PAPER DAYS [51] 3-7-7 N Adams (1) *led til hdd o'r 5 fs out, wknd, tld off*..........(5 to 1 op 7 to 2) 6
Dist: 5l, 4l, ¾l, sht-hd, 15l. 3m 29.80s. a 4.30s (6 Ran).
SR: 19/3/-/ (J Daniels), M Dixon

2151 Warwick Festival Claiming Stakes Class F (3-y-o) £2,243 7f..........(4:20)

1780[4] UMBUBUZI (USA) 9-3 S Perks (11) *cl up, led 2 fs out, rdn out*..........(5 to 1 op 7 to 2) 1
1965* QUINSIGIMOND 8-12 T Quinn (6) *chsd ldrs, rdn alng and cld o'r 2 fs out, hng lft and one pace ins last.* ....(11 to 10 fav op 5 to 4 on) 2
1425[8] ANUSHA 8-10 G Carter (9) *trkd ldrs, hrd rdn o'r one furlong out, one pace*..........(4 to 1 op 2 to 1) 3
1932 CUBIST (Ire) 8-8 D Holland (4) *hld up beh ldrs, kpt on one pace fnl 2 fs*..........(8 to 1 op 5 to 1) 4
2047[9] MISS OFFIE 7-11 (5*) A Garth (2) *chsd ldrs, came wide into strt, sn one pace*.....(10 to 1 op 16 to 1 tchd 20 to 1) 5
1705[9] BLAKENEY'S DOUBLE (Ire) 8-6 (3*) S D Williams (8) *trkd ldrs till rdn and wknd o'r 2 fs out*..........(50 to 1) 6
1628 NANQUIDNO 7-13 G Bardwell (7) *chsd ldrs till wknd o'r 2 fs out*..........(33 to 1) 7
1390[7] TODDEN 8-0 (7*) S Mulvey (3) *mid-div, rdn and outpcd o'r 2 fs out*..........(20 to 1 op 12 to 1) 8
1685 KENNINGTON PROTON 8-0 N Adams (10) *led til hdd 2 fs out, wknd quickly*..........(50 to 1) 9
1628[8] RISKY TUESDAY 8-4 R Price (1) *al beh*..........(33 to 1) 10
1705[8] HONEYMOON DAWN (v) 7-12 A Mackay (5) *rstrained strt, al beh*..........(33 to 1) 11
Dist: 1½l, ¾l, 3l, 2l, 6l, 1½l, nk, 2½l, 4l, sht-hd. 1m 26.20s. a 2.40s (11 Ran).
SR: 36/26/22/11/-/-/ (F H Lee), F H Lee

2152 Syd Mercer Handicap Class D (0-80 3-y-o and up) £3,201 1½m 115yds..........(4:50)

1764* PRINCE HANNIBAL [79] 6-10-0 G Carter (6) *trkd ldg pair, led o'r one furlong out, rdn out*....(3 to 1 tchd 4 to 1) 1
1813* LAKE POOPO (Ire) [71] 3-8-4 D Holland (3) *trkd ldr, ev ch entering fnl furlong, rallied und pres.* ....(7 to 2 op 3 to 1 tchd 4 to 1) 2
1974[4] QUADRIREME [73] 4-9-1 (7*) D McCabe (5) *trkd ldg trio, outpcd o'r 3 fs out, hrd rdn over 2 out, kpt on.* ....(5 to 2 fav op 9 to 4 tchd 2 to 1) 3
1607[4] INCOLA [54] 7-7-10 (7*) Antoinette Armes (4) *led, quickened o'r 3 fs out, hdd over one out, one pace.* ....(7 to 2 op 9 to 4) 4
1929[8] MR POPPLETON [54] 4-8-3 A Mackay (1) *al beh.* ....(16 to 1 op 12 to 1 tchd 20 to 1) 5
1321 BEAU QUEST [54] (bl) 6-8-3 J Lowe (2) *beh, effrt o'r 2 fs out, btn quickly*..........(10 to 1 tchd 14 to 1) 6
Dist: ¾l, 1½l, ¾l, 6l, 2½l. 2m 42.70s. a 4.80s (6 Ran).
SR: 29/3/18/ (D R Hunnisett), J L Dunlop

YARMOUTH (firm)
Wednesday June 30th
Going Correction: MINUS 0.55 sec. per fur.

2153 Jellicoe Maiden Stakes Class D (2-y-o) £4,464 6f 3yds.............. (2:30)

IJLAL (Ire) 9-0 R Hills (1) *nvr far away, nosed ahead wl o'r one furlong out, drifted lft ins last, jst lasted, fnshd 1st, plcd second*.......... (5 to 1 op 11 to 4 tchd 11 to 2) 1D
KUTBEYA (USA) 8-9 W Carson (3) *sluggish strt, improved on outsd hfwy, chalg whn crrd lft ins fnl furlong, jst hld, fnshd second, awarded race*. .... (5 to 1 op 8 to 1 tchd 10 to 1) 1
1706[6] SHFNAK (Ire) 9-0 M Hills (5) *made most till hdd and rdn wl o'r one furlong out, kpt on same pace*. .... (14 to 1 op 10 to 1) 3
OCEAN PARK 9-0 R Cochrane (9) *patiently rdn, shaken up to improve last 2 fs, ran on finish*. ....(3 to 1 op 4 to 1 tchd 6 to 1 and 11 to 4) 4
PARROT CAGE 8-9 (5*) K Rutter (7) *co'red up on ins, effrt and ev ch over one furlong out, sn rdn and one pace*. .... (25 to 1 op 12 to 1) 5
1706 WIZARD KING 9-0 C Nutter (8) *steadied strt, swtchd outsd to improve o'r 2 fs out, sn rdn and outpcd*. .... (11 to 1 op 20 to 1 tchd 7 to 1) 6
JUBILEE ROYALE (Ire) 9-0 P Robinson (6) *settled midfield, effrt and swtchd outsd 2 fs out, sn rdn and btn*. .... (20 to 1 op 14 to 1 tchd 25 to 1) 7
BRYAN ROBSON (USA) 9-0 Pat Eddery (4) *broke smartly to dispute ld for o'r 4 fs, sn rdn and btn*. ....(5 to 2 fav op 6 to 4) 8
Dist: Sht-hd, 2½l, hd, 2l, 8l, ½l, 1½l. 1m 12.20s. a 1.20s (8 Ran).
SR: 10/4/-/-/-/ (Hamdan Al-Maktoum), D Morley

2154 Fastolff Selling Stakes Class G (3-y-o) £2,364 7f 3yds.................. (3:00)

1875[2] KINGSTON BROWN (v) 9-5 L Dettori (10) *made all, shaken up to go clr o'r 2 fs out, eased finish*. (4 to 1 op 7 to 2) 1
2065[5] PLEASE SAY YES (Ire) 8-7 (7*) G Forster (9) *tucked away in midfield, improved to chase wnr appr fnl furlong, fnshd wl*............... (9 to 2 op 7 to 2 tchd 5 to 1) 2
1829[5] EASTERN GLOW 8-9 W Woods (11) *co'red up beh ldrs, effrt and drvn alng over one furlong out, one pace*. ....(9 to 1 op 5 to 1) 3
1829 ASCOM PAGER TOO 8-9 Paul Eddery (8) *trkd ldg pair, edgd lft und pres o'r one furlong out, no extr*. .... (33 to 1 op 20 to 1) 4
1147[8] PATONG BEACH 8-9 R Hills (2) *al hndy, hrd at work o'r one furlong out, no extr*. ....(7 to 2 fav op 3 to 1 tchd 4 to 1) 5
1817[3] COVEN MOON (v) 8-9 J Quinn (4) *chsd ldg trio, feeling pace and drvn alng 2 fs out, sn btn*. ....(5 to 1 op 7 to 1 tchd 8 to 1) 6
DARING KING 9-0 W Hood (3) *trkd ldg bunch, hrd at work whn pace lifted o'r 2 fs out, sn btn*. .... (20 to 1 op 14 to 1 tchd 25 to 1) 7
1829[7] OUR SHADEE (USA) (bl) 9-0 M Wigham (5) *chsd ldg half-dozen for o'r 4 fs, sn btn*............(14 to 1 op 8 to 1) 8
1931 TOCCO JEWEL 8-9 D Biggs (6) *sluggish strt, drvn alng hfwy, nvr a threat*............... (33 to 1 op 16 to 1) 9
1937[7] MIDLIN 8-9 R Cochrane (1) *sluggish strt, nvr able to reco'r*............................(25 to 1 op 12 to 1) 10
1354[7] CASHABLE (v) 9-0 Pat Eddery (7) *took str hold, effrt on outsd o'r 2 fs out, sn lost tch*......(16 to 1 op 8 to 1) 11
Dist: ¾l, 3½l, hd, 2½l, 1½l, 2½l, ¾l, 2l, 1l, 1½l. 1m 24.10s. a 0.90s (11 Ran).
SR: 34/27/11/10/2/-/ (H E Lhendup Dorji), D R Loder

2155 EBF Maritime Museum Maiden Stakes Class D (2-y-o) £4,113 7f 3yds... (3:30)

1949[3] THE FLYING PHANTOM 9-0 P Robinson (4) *made all, drvn alng o'r one furlong out, drw clr wl ins last*. (5 to 4 jt-fav op 7 to 4 tchd 11 to 10) 1
BUMAAN (Ire) 9-0 R Hills (3) *nvr far away, drvn up to fltter o'r one furlong out, not quicken ins last*. ....(5 to 4 jt-fav op Evens tchd 11 to 8) 2
1895[6] BERNIE'S SISTER (Ire) 8-9 L Piggott (1) *rcd wide, shwd up wl for o'r 4 fs, fdd*....(16 to 1 op 25 to 1 tchd 14 to 1) 3
1119[6] SON OF HADEER 9-0 J Quinn (5) *chsd ldg trio thrght, feeling pace and rdn hfwy, no imprsn*. .... (40 to 1 op 20 to 1) 4
READY MONEY RILEY 9-0 Pat Eddery (2) *nvr gng pace, al tld off*......................(8 to 1 op 5 to 1 tchd 9 to 1) 5
Dist: 7l, 12l, 4l, 15l. 1m 23.30s. a 0.10s (5 Ran).
SR: 41/20/ (P H Betts (Holdings) Ltd), M H Tompkins

2156 South Walsham Handicap Class D (0-80 3-y-o and up) £3,655 1m 3yds .... (4:00)

1597* AJDAYT (USA) [77] 3-9-7 S Whitworth (5) *co'red up beh ldrs, swtchd outsd to improve over 2 fs out, kpt on wl to ld post*.......... (7 to 2 co-fav op 4 to 1 tchd 9 to 2) 1
1932[4] SHINING JEWEL [66] 6-9-6 L Piggott (6) *tried to make all, kidded alng entering fnl furlong, edgd lft and ct post*. ....(9 to 1 op 6 to 1 tchd 10 to 1) 2
1932[2] ANNABELLE ROYALE [60] 7-9-0 L Dettori (3) *wl plcd stands side, drvn alng o'r one furlong out, kpt on gmely*. ...... (7 to 2 co-fav op 4 to 1 tchd 9 to 2 and 3 to 1) 3
1973[6] WAVE HILL [74] 4-10-0 J Reid (2) *co'red up in midfield, swtchd for room over one furlong out, ran on und pres*. ....(7 to 1 op 6 to 1 tchd 8 to 1) 4
1830 AMADEUS AES [69] 4-9-4 (5*) C Hodgson (4) *al chasing ldrs, effrt and drvn alng last 2 fs, styd on*. ....(20 to 1 op 12 to 1) 5
1390* MISTY SILKS [67] 3-8-11 P Robinson (9) *last and drvn alng hfwy, some hdwy last 2 fs, nvr nrr*. (10 to 1 op 7 to 1) 7
1641[3] THEMAAM [56] 4-8-10 Pat Eddery (7) *wth ldrs for o'r 5 fs, fdd und pres*............................(11 to 1 op 7 to 1) 8
1069[3] ALBEMINE (USA) [68] 4-9-8 Paul Eddery (1) *pressed ldg trio, drvn alng whn pace lifted o'r 2 fs out, no extr*. ....(7 to 2 co-fav op 4 to 1 tchd 9 to 2) 9+
COUNTERCHECK (Ire) [51] 4-8-5 W Woods (8) *chsd ldg bunch, hrd at work o'r 2 fs out, sn btn*. ....(33 to 1 op 20 to 1) 9+
Dist: Sht-hd, 1l, ½l, nk, 3l, 1½l, sht-hd, 6l. 1m 36.80s. a 1.00s (9 Ran).
SR: 26/24/15/27/21/-/-/5/-/ (Sheikh Ahmed Al Maktoum), A C Stewart

2157 Sturdee Apprentice Limited Stakes Class G (3-y-o and up) £2,301 5f 43yds ....(4:30)

1728[4] TREASURE TIME (Ire) 4-8-13 (3*) K Rutter (4) *made all, hrd pressed ins fnl furlong, hld on grimly*. ....(7 to 1 op 5 to 1) 1
2050[4] MARTINA 5-8-11 (5*) B Russell (8) *squeezed out strt, improved into midfield hfwy, str chal fnl furlong, jst hld*............ (11 to 4 fav op 5 to 2 tchd 100 to 30) 2
1618[3] SPRING HIGH (bl) 6-8-11 (5*) C Scally (9) *sluggish strt, drvn alng to improve o'r one furlong out, ran on*. ....(4 to 1 op 5 to 1 tchd 6 to 1) 3
1677[7] EVER SO LONELY (bl) 4-8-9 (7*) W Hollick (3) *nvr far away, hrd at work o'r one furlong out, no extr pace*. ....(12 to 1 op 8 to 1) 4
1782 SIR TASKER (v) 5-9-7 B Doyle (1) *al hndy, ev ch and drvn alng 2 fs out, not quicken*..........(6 to 1 op 9 to 2) 5
1903 JOE SUGDEN 9-9-2 (5*) Debbie Biggs (10) *broke wl to show speed stands side for o'r 3 fs, no extr*. ....(12 to 1 op 8 to 1) 6
1932[7] WALK THAT WALK (v) 4-8-11 (5*) K Pattinson (6) *sluggish strt, some hdwy last 2 fs, nvr dngrs*. ....(6 to 1 op 5 to 1 tchd 7 to 1) 7
CUDDLY DATE 3-8-4 (5*) S Eiffert (7) *chsd alng in midfield, not pace of ldrs*..... (20 to 1 op 14 to 1 tchd 25 to 1) 8
1492 SKI CAPTAIN 9-9-2 (5*) L Carter (5) *reminders leaving stalls, chsd ldrs 3 fs, sn btn*. ....(16 to 1 op 20 to 1 tchd 14 to 1) 9
1782[8] LINCSTONE BOY (Ire) (bl) 5-9-2 (5*) P McCabe (2) *chsd alng beh ldg trio, no imprsn frm hfwy*. (20 to 1 op 16 to 1) 10
Dist: Hd, 1½l, 2½l, ½l, hd, 3½l, 1l, 1l, 1½l. 1m 0.80s. a 0.10s (10 Ran).
SR: 42/41/35/25/28/27/8/-/5/ (Chiltern Hills Racing Club), J White

2158 Ormesby Handicap Class D (0-80 3-y-o) £3,655 1¾m 17yds........... (5:00)

1827[3] MY PATRIARCH [77] 9-4 W Carson (2) *trkd ldr, drvn to nose ahead 2 fs out, edgd lft appr last, all out*. ....(11 to 10 on op 7 to 4) 1
1299[2] BOHEMIAN CROWN (USA) [79] 9-6 Pat Eddery (4) *dictated pace, hdd o'r 2 fs out, rallied, jst hld*. ....(7 to 2 op 5 to 2 tchd 4 to 1) 2
1936* ELA BILLANTE [74] 9-1 (4ex) P Robinson (1) *trkd ldg trio, drvn alng whn pace quickened o'r 2 fs out, sn outpcd*. ....(5 to 1 op 9 to 2 tchd 6 to 1) 3
1785[5] MARROS MILL [80] (v) 9-7 M Hills (3) *chsd ldg pair, hrd at work entering strt, outpcd last 2 fs*...(9 to 2 op 3 to 1) 4
Dist: ½l, 12l, 8l. 3m 3.00s. a 6.00s (4 Ran).
(Peter S Winfield), J L Dunlop

BRIGHTON (firm)
Thursday July 1st
Going Correction: MINUS 0.50 sec. per fur.

2159 EBF Median Auction Maiden Stakes Class E (2-y-o) £3,132 6f 209yds (2:20)

1877[2] NONIOS (Ire) (v) 9-0 W Newnes (3) *made all, quickened clr 3 fs out, unchlgd*............(9 to 2 on op 4 to 1 on) 1
2006[5] NORTHERN BAILIWICK (Ire) 9-0 N Adams (4) *al outpcd, rdn hfwy, no imprsn*................... (9 to 2 op 3 to 1) 2
Won by 3l. 1m 21.80s. a 1.80s (2 Ran).
SR: 21/12/ (J P Fleming), B J Meehan

2160 Rock Gardens Claiming Stakes Class G (3-y-o and up) £2,070 6f 209yds ....(2:50)

1730[6] CAPE PIGEON (USA) (bl) 8-9-1 D Holland (7) *pressed ldr, shaken up to ld o'r one furlong out, not extended.* ....(2 to 1 on op 7 to 4 on) 1
1527 ACROSS THE BAY (v) 6-8-13 J Reid (1) *in tch, sn pushed alng, styd on und pres appr fnl furlong, not rch wnr.* ....(13 to 2 op 6 to 1 tchd 8 to 1) 2
1628[3] CALISAR 3-8-9 T Sprake (4) *wl plcd, rdn alng hfwy, one pace fnl 2 fs*....(13 to 2 op 4 to 1 tchd 8 to 1) 3
JIM CANTLE 3-8-6 W Newnes (6) *led till rdn and hdd o'r one furlong out, sn btn.* ....(66 to 1 op 33 to 1 tchd 100 to 1) 4
1816[9] AUNT ADA 4-8-8 A Clark (5) *outpcd.* ....(50 to 1 op 20 to 1 tchd 66 to 1) 5
1817[6] POCONO KNIGHT (bl) 3-8-7 B Rouse (3) *nvr gng pace of ldrs*..................(14 to 1 op 10 to 1 tchd 16 to 1) 6
Dist: 2½l, 3l, 1l, 2l, 20l. 1m 21.40s. a 1.40s (6 Ran).
SR: 28/18/5/ (E J S Gadsden), L G Cottrell

2161 Joe Blanks Memorial Challenge Cup Handicap Class D (0-80 3-y-o and up) £3,348 7f 214yds................ (3:20)

1973[3] DEEVEE [55] 4-8-12 P Robinson (2) *hld up rear, str run und pres appr fnl furlong, led last strd.* ....(7 to 4 fav op 6 to 4 tchd 15 to 8) 1
1686[7] PRECIOUS AIR (Ire) [51] 5-8-8 B Rouse (3) *hld up, led 2 fs out, hdd und pres last strd*.........(3 to 1 op 7 to 2) 2
1474[9] KINGCHIP BOY [53] 4-8-10 D Biggs (1) *hld up, rdn and swtchd lft o'r one furlong out, outpcd ins last, fnshd 3rd, disqualified*........ (7 to 2 op 9 to 2 tchd 5 to 1) 3D
1830[2] HOPEFUL BID (Ire) [67] (bl) 4-9-10 J Reid (4) *chsd ldr, led o'r 3 fs out to 2 out, wkng whn not much room over one out, fnshd 4th, plcd 3rd.* ....(11 to 4 op 5 to 2 tchd 3 to 1) 3
539[7] LYN'S RETURN (Ire) [55] 4-8-5 (7*) G Rothwell (5) *led for o'r 4 fs, wkng whn hmpd over one out, fnshd 5th, plcd fourth*....................(20 to 1 op 14 to 1) 4
Dist: Sht-hd, 6l, 4l, 6l. 1m 33.40s. a 1.00s (5 Ran).
SR: 23/18/2/4/-/ (D Turner), C J Benstead

2162 Kingston Selling Handicap Class G (0-60 3-y-o and up) £2,406 1m 3f 196yds........................ (3:50)

1832[7] SEA PADDY [47] 5-8-13 (7*) H Bastiman (2) *rapid prog to ld o'r 2 fs out, rdn clr appr last.* ....(9 to 2 op 5 to 1 tchd 6 to 1) 1
1902[9] BEAT THE BAGMAN (Ire) [40] 3-8-0 N Adams (1) *hdwy 3 fs out, ran on und pres fnl furlong, no imprsn on wnr.* ....(20 to 1 op 10 to 1) 2
1900[3] REEL OF TULLOCH (Ire) [43] 4-9-2 D Biggs (3) *mid-div, cld on ldr 3 fs out, not quicken o'r one out.* ....(9 to 2 op 5 to 1) 3
2007 CHINAMAN [25] (bl) 4-7-12 A Tucker (12) *ldg grp, rdn and wknd frm 2 fs out*..............(33 to 1 op 20 to 1) 4
1951[3] SALMONID [55] 7-10-0 W Newnes (11) *led till o'r 2 fs out, sn wknd*..........(10 to 1 op 6 to 1 tchd 12 to 1) 5
1902[4] MALINDI BAY [34] 5-8-7 J Reid (4) *mid-div, effrt und pres 4 fs out, btn o'r 2 out*......(8 to 1 op 6 to 1 tchd 9 to 1) 6
1961[7] JOLIS ABSENT [43] 3-8-3 P Robinson (8) *rear most of way.* ....(4 to 1 fav op 5 to 1 tchd 6 to 1) 7
1731[2] PRINCESS EVITA (Fr) [39] 4-8-12 W Carson (6) *al rear.* ....(9 to 2 op 4 to 1) 8
278[3] ELIZA WOODING [32] (v) 5-8-5 D Holland (5) *beh last 3 fs.* ....(14 to 1 op 8 to 1) 9
159[3] KENYATTA (USA) [37] 4-8-10 B Rouse (7) *hmpd strt, sn wl beh*..................(14 to 1 op 12 to 1 tchd 16 to 1) 10
1896[6] PETITE JESS [40] 3-7-9 (5*) N Gwilliams (10) *ldg grp, chsd ldr hfwy, wknd quickly o'r 2 fs out.* ....(20 to 1 op 12 to 1 tchd 25 to 1) 11
1928[5] CLEAR LIGHT [40] (v) 6-8-13 M Wigham (9) *sn rdn alng to chase ldr, wknd hfwy, tld off.* ....(13 to 2 op 12 to 1 tchd 14 to 1) 12
Dist: 3½l, 1½l, 6l, 1½l, 1½l, 10l, 2l, ½l, ¾l, 2l. 2m 29.50s. a 2.00s (12 Ran).
SR: 26/-/12/-/9/-/ (Greg Lancaster), R Bastiman

2163 Pevensey Handicap Class E (0-70 3-y-o) £2,976 1m 1f 209yds......... (4:20)

1709[5] ALDERNEY PRINCE (USA) [70] 9-0 (7*) T G McLaughlin (3) *hld up, rdn and ran on o'r 2 fs out, led ins last, styd on wl*....................(13 to 2 op 5 to 1 tchd 7 to 1) 1
934 MUHTASHIM (Ire) [55] 8-6 D Holland (8) *pressed ldrs, led 3 fs out till o'r one out, rallied nr line.* ....(16 to 1 op 14 to 1 tchd 20 to 1) 2
1991[4] STEVIE'S WONDER (Ire) [46] 7-7[1] (5*) N Gwilliams (7) *led to 3 fs out, led o'r one out, sn hdd, no extr.* ....(6 to 1 op 5 to 1) 3
1606[8] SEDGY'S SISTER [54] 8-0 (5*) Stephen Davies (2) *beh, styd on last 2 fs, nrst finish*........... (20 to 1 op 14 to 1) 4
1851[3] AZOLA (Ire) [63] 9-0 B Raymond (1) *ldg grp, rdn and wknd wl o'r one furlong out*..............(5 to 1 op 9 to 2) 5
1776* SO SAUCY [51] 7-13 (3*) B Doyle (6) *mid-div, rdn alng 3 fs out, wknd 2 out.* (3 to 1 fav op 11 to 4 tchd 100 to 30) 6
1623 BLOWING (USA) [55] 7-13 (7*) Gaye Harwood (9) *trkd ldrs, lost pl o'r 2 fs out*................ (20 to 1 op 16 to 1) 7
2001[6] NITOUCHE [66] 9-3 J Reid (5) *hld up rear, effrt und pres o'r 2 fs out, wknd over one out*......(5 to 1 op 6 to 1) 8
1703[4] KAWASIR (Can) [45] (v) 7-10 W Carson (4) *hld up rear, rdn alng o'r 3 fs out, sn lost tch, tld off*...(7 to 2 op 5 to 1) 9
Dist: 1½l, hd, 6l, sht-hd, nk, 3½l, 1l, dist. 1m 59.50s. a 1.30s (9 Ran).
SR: 44/26/16/12/20/7/4/13/-/ (Fahd Salman), P F I Cole

2164 Preston Park Limited Stakes Class F (0-60 3-y-o and up) £2,243 6f 209yds ....(4:50)

1913* DESERT NOMAD 3-8-8 B Raymond (2) *chsd ldr, led 2 fs out, drvn out, jst hld on.* ....(10 to 1 op 8 to 1 tchd 11 to 1) 1
2011* NO EXTRAS (Ire) 3-8-13 B Rouse (7) *hdwy hfwy, wth wnr o'r one furlong out, jst fld*..... (6 to 4 fav op 11 to 10) 2
1927[5] DIACO 8-9-7 P Robinson (3) *str hold, in tch, not quicken und pres 2 fs out, kpt on fnl furlong.* ....(12 to 1 op 8 to 1) 3
1932* TAJDID (Ire) 3-8-13 W Carson (1) *led to 2 fs out, no extr.* ....(9 to 4 op 5 to 2 tchd 3 to 1 and 2 to 1) 4
DANNY BLUE (Ire) 3-8-13 D Holland (4) *trkd ldrs, rdn alng o'r 2 fs out, sn wknd.* (25 to 1 op 14 to 1 tchd 33 to 1) 5
1377[8] SHARP GAZELLE 3-8-8 W Newnes (6) *effrt und pres 3 fs out, wknd last 2 furlongs.* ....(40 to 1 op 33 to 1 tchd 50 to 1) 6
1735* FRANCIA 3-8-8 J Reid (5) *settled mid-div, rdn alng hfwy, wknd o'r 2 fs out*..................(13 to 2 op 5 to 1) 7
1623[8] CASHMIRIANA (Ire) 4-8-11 (5*) N Gwilliams (8) *outpcd.* ....(25 to 1 op 14 to 1 tchd 33 to 1) 8
1587[9] LITTLE MISS RIBOT 3-8-1 (7*) B Russell (9) *beh hfwy.* ....(40 to 1 op 25 to 1 tchd 50 to 1) 9
Dist: Sht-hd, 5l, 1½l, 5l, hd, 2½l, ½l, 4l. 1m 20.40s. a 0.40s (9 Ran).
SR: 36/40/33/20/5/-/ (Eurostrait Ltd), S Dow

CATTERICK (good to firm)
Thursday July 1st
Going Correction: MINUS 0.40 sec. per fur.

2165 Silver Birch Selling Stakes Class G (3-y-o and up) £2,364 5f 212yds.... (2:00)

1937[2] SAMSON-AGONISTES 7-9-7 J Fortune (6) *pressed ldr, led entering strt, clr o'r one furlong out, rdn out.* ....(6 to 4 on op 11 to 10 on tchd Evens) 1
1599[2] MURRAY'S MAZDA (Ire) 4-9-7 J Carroll (3) *chsd ldrs, drvn entering strt, kpt on fnl furlong, no ch wth wnr.* ....(4 to 1 op 5 to 2) 2
1736[6] SENSE OF PRIORITY 4-9-7 K Darley (8) *in tch, rdn to improve entering strt, kpt on fnl furlong, nvr dngrs.* ....(6 to 1 tchd 7 to 1) 3
1799[9] BREEZE AWAY 4-9-2 A Culhane (5) *chsd ldrs, drvn alng 2 fs out, kpt on same pace.* (8 to 1 op 7 to 1 tchd 9 to 1) 4
2017[5] TRIBAT 3-7-13 (3*) S Maloney (7) *dwlt, beh, rdn to improve entering strt, kpt on ins last, nrst finish.* ....(25 to 1 op 20 to 1) 5
1969[5] MURASIL (USA) (v) 4-9-0 K Fallon (2) *chsd ldrs, drvn o'r 2 fs out, btn over one out*..............(40 to 1 op 16 to 1) 6
1034 SNEEK (bl) 5-8-9 (5*) O Pears (4) *slwly into strd, beh, rdn appr strt, nvr able to chal*......(200 to 1 op 100 to 1) 7
1937[4] ANGELS ANSWER (Ire) 4-8-11 (5*) Darren Moffatt (1) *led till hdd entering strt, sn rdn and wknd.* (12 to 1 op 6 to 1) 8
861 JOVIAL KATE (USA) 6-9-2 G Hind (9) *beh on outer, rdn appr strt, sn lost tch*.............. (33 to 1 op 20 to 1) 9
Dist: 3l, 1½l, 2l, ½l, 2l, 1½l, ½l, 2l. 1m 11.50s. a 0.50s (9 Ran).
SR: 49/37/31/18/2/6/ (J B Wilcox), B A McMahon

2166 Old Oak Handicap Class E (0-70 4-y-o and up) £2,794 1m 7f 177yds.... (2:30)

1941[2] MINGUS (USA) [40] 6-9-1 K Fallon (4) *settled chasing grp, pushed alng to improve entering strt, quickened betw horses wl ins fnl furlong to ld cl hme*..........(6 to 1) 1
1890[3] KAYARTIS [51] 4-9-12 J Lowe (6) *rcd keenly, hld up, improved o'r 4 fs out, led over 3 out, sn rdn, ran on wl fnl 2 furlongs, ct cl hme.* ....(5 to 4 fav op Evens tchd 11 to 8) 2
2043[3] QUALITAIR SOUND (Ire) [42] 5-9-3 L Charnock (3) *hld up in last pl, took clr order o'r 4 fs out, ev ch fnl 2 furlongs, no extr wl ins last*..... (3 to 1 op 11 to 4 tchd 7 to 2) 3
1890[4] GREY COMMANDER [30] 5-8-5 A Mackay (2) *chsd clr ldr, outpcd and drvn alng o'r 5 fs out, kpt on same pace entering strt*.................. (5 to 1 op 9 to 2) 4
1890[5] ALPHA HELIX [30] (v) 10-8-5 J Fanning (1) *prmnt chasing grp, rdn o'r 4 fs out, sn drpd rear, kpt on ag'n over one furlong out, nvr dngrs*..........................(12 to 1) 5
1984[5] BOOTIKIN [39] (bl) 5-9-0 J Carroll (5) *led and sn clr, hdd o'r 3 fs out, grad wknd*.............(20 to 1 tchd 25 to 1) 6
Dist: Nk, ¾l, 3l, nk, 3l. 3m 30.80s. a 9.30s (6 Ran).
(A Antonelli), R F Fisher

2167 Tattersalls Maiden Auction Series Stakes Qualifier Class D (2-y-o) £3,289 7f.............................(3:00)

1895² CALL TO MIND (Ire) 8-7 M Birch (4) *trkd ldrs, effrt and drvn alng 2 fs out, drifted lft fnl furlong, ran on to ld cl hme*..............(11 to 10 on op 5 to 4 on tchd Evens) 1
PRIZEFIGHTER 8-13 K Darley (5) *tried to make all, shaken up 2 fs out, ran on wl, hdd cl hme.* (13 to 2 op 5 to 1) 2
1810² DIAMOND FRONTIER (Ire) 8-10 J Carroll (3) *dsptd ld, rdn 2 fs out, no extr ins last*... (7 to 2 op 3 to 1 tchd 5 to 1) 3
NEW INN 8-6 Dean McKeown (7) *chsd ldrs on outer, pushed alng appr strt, came wide, kpt on same pace ins fnl furlong*..........................(14 to 1 op 8 to 1) 4
1870⁴ STUDFORD GIRL 8-1 L Charnock (8) *in tch, rdn 3 fs out, wknd o'r one out*..................(16 to 1 op 14 to 1) 5
MON ROUGE (Ire) 8-6 A Mackay (6) *missed break, beh, rdn and wknd appr strt*................(14 to 1 op 10 to 2) 6
GUYLAIN 8-9 Dale Gibson (2) *missed break, sn outpcd and rdn, nvr on terms*..................(14 to 1 op 10 to 1) 7
Dist: Nk, 2l, 5l, 3½l, sht-hd, 6l. 1m 26.90s. a 3.90s (7 Ran).
(G Graham), M H Easterby

2168 Rambling Rose Handicap Class D (0-80 3-y-o) £3,406 7f........... (3:30)

1675⁵ NORTH ARDAR [56] 8-4 Dean McKeown (1) *made all, jnd 3 fs out, drvn alng 2 out, ran on wl fnl furlong.*
....(4 to 1 op 3 to 1) 1
1799⁴ PUBLIC WAY (Ire) [54] 8-2 J Lowe (2) *in tch, effrt and rdn entering strt, ran on wl ins last.*
..........................(7 to 2 op 3 to 1 tchd 4 to 1) 2
1893³ MISSED THE BOAT (Ire) [54] (bl) 8-2 K Darley (3) *dwlt, beh, niggled alng o'r 3 fs out, imprvg whn not clr run one out, kpt on same pace.* (10 to 1 op 8 to 1 tchd 12 to 1) 3
1891² BRAXTON BRAGG (Ire) [49] 7-11 J Fanning (4) *pressed ldr, chlgd 3 fs out, rdn entering strt, no extr o'r one out.*
...........................(2 to 1 fav op 5 to 2 tchd 11 to 4) 4
1579⁶ MHEMEANLES [73] 9-4 (3*) S Maloney (5) *chsd ldrs, improved and ev ch o'r 2 fs out, shaken up and not quicken wl over one out*............. (7 to 2 op 2 to 1) 5
Dist: Nk, 1½l, ½l, ¾l. 1m 25.60s. a 2.60s (5 Ran).
SR: 9/6/1/-/16/ (L Webster), M Johnston

2169 Weeping Willow Rating Related Maiden Stakes Class D (0-75 3-y-o) £3,231 1m 5f 175yds............ (4:00)

1784⁶ SMUGGLER'S POINT (USA) 9-0 J Carroll (2) *cl up, led aftr 3 fs, hdd after 6 furlongs, chlgd entering strt, rdn to ld one out, edgd lft and ran on wl.*
..............(13 to 8 on op 7 to 4 on tchd 6 to 4 on) 1
1772² MEANT TO BE 8-6 (3*) J Weaver (3) *led 3 fs, styd hndy, rgned ld aftr 6 furlongs, rdn entering strt, hdd one out, no extr*..............................(6 to 4 op 5 to 4) 2
RUSHALONG 9-0 T Lucas (1) *in tch, drvn alng 5 fs out, sn btn, eased entering strt, tld off.*
.................(16 to 1 op 14 to 1 tchd 20 to 1) 3
Dist: 1½l, 30l. 2m 58.60s. a 3.10s (3 Ran).
SR: 14/6/-/ (Sheikh Mohammed), J H M Gosden

2170 Spreading Chestnut Handicap Class E (0-70 3-y-o) £2,950 5f 212yds.... (4:30)

1599⁷ SECOND COLOURS (USA) [56] 9-1 K Darley (2) *prmnt, led aftr a furlong and a half, rdn and kpt on strly fnl 2 fs.*
..................(5 to 2 op 15 to 8 tchd 11 to 4) 1
1760⁴ MY GODSON [62] 9-2 (5*) O Pears (4) *in tch, effrt entering strt, edgd lft fnl 2 fs, kpt on, not rch wnr.*
....(8 to 1 op 9 to 2) 2
1966* MISS WHITTINGHAM (Ire) [61] 9-6 (7ex) J Carroll (3) *in tch, effrt and swtchd ins wl o'r one furlong out, not quicken inside last.* (13 to 8 fav op 2 to 1 tchd 6 to 4) 3
2011⁵ PRINCE SONGLINE [58] 9-3 A Mackay (5) *dwlt, beh, not much room 2 fs out, rdn and no imprsn.*
....(4 to 1 op 7 to 2) 4
1850⁶ MAJOR JACK [54] 8-10 (3*) S D Williams (7) *beh, drvn alng entering strt, kpt on fnl furlong, nvr dngrs.*
...................................(50 to 1 op 33 to 1) 5
1833⁹ MASTER PECKITT [41] 8-0 J Fanning (1) *led a furlong and a half, styd hndy, rdn and wknd o'r 2 fs out.* (33 to 1) 6
1762⁴ SELFISH LADY [43] 8-2 J Lowe (6) *chsd ldrs, effrt and rdn entering strt, wknd o'r one furlong out.*
...................(14 to 1 op 10 to 1 tchd 20 to 1) 7
Dist: 1½l, sht-hd, 3l, sht-hd, 6l, 5l. 1m 12.30s. a 1.30s (7 Ran).
SR: 27/27/25/10/5/-/-/ (P D Savill), Mrs M Reveley

EVRY (FR) (good)
Thursday July 1st

2171 Prix Pelleas (Listed) (3-y-o) £14,337 1 ¼m.......................... (3:05)

1648² JACKDIDI (Fr) 8-12 D Boeuf,.................................... 1
696⁶ FASTNESS (Ire) 9-2 F Head,.. 2
INTERVALLO (USA) 8-12 C Asmussen,.................... 3
431⁴ ASTAIR (Fr) 8-12 G Mosse,.................................... 4
Dist: Nose, 1½l, nose, nk, ¾l, 1l, 1½l. 2m 5.57s. a 1.57s (8 Ran).
SR: 62/65/58/57/ (M Benillouche), E Lellouche

HAYDOCK (good)
Thursday July 1st

Going Correction: MINUS 0.15 sec. per fur. (races 1,3,4,6), MINUS 0.10 (2,5)

2172 Halewood Apprentices Handicap Class E (0-80 3-y-o and up) £2,717 7f 30yds......................... (6:35)

2060⁷ VELOCE (Ire) [61] 5-8-9 D Wright (1) *al in tch gng wl, led well o'r one furlong out, ran on, cmftbly.*
....(3 to 1 op 11 to 4) 1
1734* SILKY SIREN [70] 4-8-13 (5*) R Painter (6) *pld hrd, hld up, hdwy to chase wnr ins fnl 2 fs, no imprsn.*
....................(7 to 4 fav op 6 to 4 tchd 15 to 8) 2
1939⁵ CHANTRY BELLINI [47] (bl) 4-7-6 (3*) Claire Balding (4) *rear, hdwy whn short of room and hmpd on ins wl o'r one furlong out, pld wide, ran on*......(16 to 1 op 14 to 1) 3
1939³ SARTIGILA [62] 4-8-10 J Marshall (5) *al beh, rdn hfwy, nvr got into race*......................... (5 to 1 op 4 to 1) 4
1761* LEAVE IT TO LIB [61] 6-8-9 J Tate (3) *led till wl o'r one furlong out, wknd*...... (7 to 2 op 4 to 1 tchd 9 to 2) 5
2106³ FINJAN [80] 6-10-0 V Halliday (2) *chsd ldr, rdn 2 fs out, hng lft, sn btn*......... (9 to 1 op 8 to 1 tchd 10 to 1) 6
Dist: 1½l, 2l, 2½l, hd, 5l. 1m 31.38s. a 4.18s (6 Ran).
SR: 16/20/-/ (Maximo Gonzalez), A Bailey

2173 George Fordham Handicap Class D (0-80 3-y-o and up) £3,111 6f.... (7:05)

1397⁴ DOKKHA OYSTON (Ire) [68] 5-9-8 J Carroll (7) *nvr far away, led wl o'r one furlong out, ran on strly.*
.... (12 to 1 op 10 to 1) 1
1865⁴ BALLAD DANCER [59] 8-8-13 M Birch (9) *wtd wth, hdwy o'r one furlong out, ran on, not rch wnr.*
....(8 to 1 op 7 to 1) 2
1898* SOBERING THOUGHTS [67] 7-9-2 (5*,7ex) O Pears (10) *led to 2 fs out, ran on one pace ins last.* (6 to 1 op 5 to 1) 3
1898² SULLY'S CHOICE (USA) [44] (bl) 12-7-7 (5*) Darren Moffatt (8) *trkd ldr, led briefly 2 fs out, rdn and edgd lft ins last.*
....(8 to 1) 4
2062² EDUCATED PET [69] 4-9-9 T Williams (5) *hld up in tch, rdn 2 fs out, no hdwy*.............. (3 to 1 fav op 11 to 4) 5
2062⁹ RESOLUTE BAY [74] 7-10-0 A Culhane (4) *slwly away, rdn o'r one furlong out, nvr nr to chal.*
....(12 to 1 tchd 14 to 1) 6
1938⁶ MISS ARAGON [54] 5-8-5 (3*) S Maloney (6) *slwly away, nvr on terms*.....................................(14 to 1) 7
1865⁶ ASTERIX [49] (v) 5-8-0 (3*) J Weaver (2) *speed far side, rdn 2 fs out, eased whn btn*............................(10 to 1) 8
1938³ INVIGILATE [60] 4-9-0 L Charnock (1) *speed far side to hfwy, rdn and eased whn btn*...... (9 to 1 op 7 to 1) 9
1914² SURE LORD (Ire) [70] 4-9-10 M Roberts (3) *speed far side, wknd quickly wl o'r one furlong out, eased.*
....(9 to 2 op 7 to 2) 10
Dist: 2l, 1½l, ½l, 3½l, nk, 1l, 2l, 8l, ½l. 1m 13.84s. a 2.24s (10 Ran).
SR: 51/34/36/11/22/26/2/-/-/ (Murray Grubb), J Berry

2174 Haydock Park July Trophy Stakes Class A formerly Saab Great Britain July Trophy Stakes (Listed Race) (3-y-o) £10,308 1m 3f 200yds....... (7:35)

1751² WINGED VICTORY (USA) 8-10 W R Swinburn (4) *trkd ldr, shaken up to ld o'r 2 fs out, pushed out.*
.............................(2 to 1 on tchd 7 to 4 on) 1
1904* DECLASSIFIED (USA) 8-13 R Cochrane (1) *led till o'r 2 fs out, rdn and ran on*................(7 to 1 op 5 to 1) 2
1603* EDBAYSAAN (Ire) 8-10 W Ryan (2) *al same pl, kpt on one pace ins fnl 2 fs*..................(5 to 1 tchd 9 to 2) 3
REVERE (Ire) 8-10 T Quinn (3) *hld up last, rdn 4 fs out, no hdwy*.............................(7 to 1 tchd 6 to 1) 4
Dist: 1½l, 3½l, 10l. 2m 30.84s. a 1.04s (4 Ran).
SR: 68/68/58/38/ (Pin Oak Stable), J H M Gosden

2175 Northwich Claiming Stakes Class F (3-y-o and up) £2,479 1m 30yds.... (8:05)

1849³ LOMBARD SHIPS (bl) 6-8-12 A Mackay (7) *hld up rear, hdwy o'r 3 fs out, led 2 out, pushed clr, easily.*
...............................(2 to 1 fav op 7 to 4) 1
1940⁸ PRINCESS OF ORANGE 4-8-11 (3*) S Maloney (2) *reared strt, rear till hdwy 3 fs out, squeezed through to chase wnr ins fnl 2*..............(8 to 1 tchd 10 to 1) 2
4663a VANART 4-9-6 S Webster (3) *hld up on ins, hdwy und pres whn short of room o'r 2 fs out, rdn, ran on to go 3rd cl hme*..............................(20 to 1 op 16 to 1) 3
2088⁶ WHITE CREEK (Ire) (v) 3-9-2 J Carroll (5) *nvr far away, led 3 fs out, rdn and hdd 2 out, one pace.* (5 to 1 op 4 to 1) 4
1832⁸ GREY ANCONA (Ire) (v) 4-8-12 L Charnock (9) *led to 3 fs out, no imprsn frm 2 out*..........................(25 to 1) 5
1849² SIR ARTHUR HOBBS 6-9-5 R Lappin (4) *mid-div, effrt 3 fs out, one pace aftr*..... (9 to 4 op 11 to 4 tchd 3 to 1) 6

1969[8] LAZY RHYTHM (USA) 7-8-8 (5*) O Pears (10) *trkd ldrs on outsd, wknd o'r 2 fs out*............(8 to 1 op 7 to 1) 7
1375 ARCTIC LINE (v) 5-8-11 (3*) J Weaver (8) *rear, effrt on outsd 3 fs out, sn btn*........................ (33 to 1) 8
1161[9] TINA MEENA LISA 4-8-10[1] C Dwyer (11) *trkd ldr to hfwy, sn beh*..................................(33 to 1 op 25 to 1) 9
COASTAL EXPRESS 4-9-9 K Darley (1) *prmnt to hfwy*. ....(12 to 1 tchd 14 to 1) 10
TOMMY TRUNGLE 3-8-11 W Ryan (6) *al beh, sn tld off*. ....(33 to 1 op 25 to 1) 11
Dist: 3l, 5l, ½l, 1½l, 1½l, 2½l, 1l, 2½l, 5l, 30l. 1m 44.86s. a 4.26s (11 Ran).
SR: 16/9/-/-/-/-/ (Mrs D M Mitchell), A Bailey

2176 Summer Selling Stakes Class F (2-y-o) £2,451 6f.................. (8:35)

1964[2] SPRINGHEAD 7-13 (7*) J Marshall (5) *trkd ldr, led o'r 2 fs out, pushed clr ins last, cmftbly*....(7 to 2 tchd 4 to 1) 1
1598[2] TURTLE ROCK 8-11 K Darley (7) *chsd ldrs, hrd rdn to press wnr appr fnl furlong, no extr final stages*. ....(5 to 4 on op 5 to 4) 2
1763[4] LAUREL ROMEO (Ire) 8-11 J Carroll (4) *speed to hfwy, no hdwy fnl 2 fs*......................(13 to 2 op 11 to 2) 3
1863 AGGIES DREAM 8-8 (3*) J Weaver (2) *outpcd, nvr got into race*..................................(33 to 1 op 25 to 1) 4
1413[3] MR BLOBBY (Ire) (bl) 8-11 L Charnock (1) *led till o'r 2 fs out, rdn and hng rght, sn btn*............(7 to 1 op 6 to 1) 5
1555 SILVERISTE (Ire) 8-11 T Quinn (8) *outpcd*.........(33 to 1) 6
GOVERNOR'S BAY 8-4 (7*) D Wright (6) *slwly away, al beh*. ....(33 to 1) 7
Dist: 1½l, 6l, 15l, 6l, 3l, 3l. 1m 15.47s. a 3.87s (7 Ran).
SR: 3/2/-/-/ (The Bridge Club), M D Hammond

2177 Runcorn Handicap Class D (0-80 3-y-o) £3,160 1¾m.................. (9:05)

2005* HADDAAJ (Ire) [73] 9-2 (3ex) M Roberts (3) *trkd ldr to hfwy, styd in cl tch, led 3 fs out, ran on whn chlgd 2 out, pushed out*........................(7 to 2 op 3 to 1) 1
1935* SOLARTICA (USA) [75] 9-4 (3ex) W R Swinburn (2) *hld up, hdwy on bit to chal 2 fs out, sn rdn, no imprsn ins last*. ....(13 to 8 on tchd 6 to 4 on and 7 to 4 on) 2
1827[7] SOUL EMPEROR [78] 9-7 T Quinn (1) *hld up, wide back strt, second hfwy, ev ch 3 fs out till wknd wl o'r one out*....................................(11 to 2 op 4 to 1) 3
1894[5] PRIME PAINTER [68] 8-5[1] (7*) L Aspell (4) *led to 3 fs out, sn outpcd*.................................(10 to 1 op 8 to 1) 4
Dist: 2½l, 7l, hd. 3m 5.20s. a 7.70s (4 Ran).
SR: 4/1/-/-/ (Sheikh Ahmed Al Maktoum), B Hanbury

NOTTINGHAM (good to firm)
Thursday July 1st
Going Correction: NIL (races 1,4,5,6), MINUS 0.05 (2,3)

2178 Ladies First Selling Handicap Class G (0-60 3-y-o and up) £2,162 1¾m 15yds ....(6:20)

1654 BALZINO (USA) [49] 4-9-11 K Fallon (5) *hld up and beh, steady hdwy 5 fs out, effrt and led o'r one and a half out, sn clr*..............(13 to 2 op 4 to 1 tchd 7 to 1) 1
1930[3] VIAGGIO [40] (v) 5-9-2 L Dettori (7) *chsd ldrs, gd hdwy 5 fs out, effrt and ev ch 2 out, sn rdn and one pace*. ....(7 to 2 op 5 to 2) 2
1702[5] MUST BE MAGICAL (USA) [24] 5-8-0[1] G Carter (4) *in tch, effrt 3 fs out, sn rdn and styd on und pres fnl 2 furlongs*...........................(14 to 1 tchd 16 to 1) 3
1984[6] MEDIA STAR [32] 8-8-8 Alex Greaves (12) *chsd ldr, rdn to ld briefly 2 fs out, sn one pace*.....(12 to 1 op 10 to 1) 4
1900 LODGING [28] (v) 6-8-4 G Hind (14) *led, rdn o'r 3 fs out, hdd 2 out and grad wknd*.....................(33 to 1) 5
2007[3] JALORE [52] 4-10-0 G Duffield (10) *hld up and beh, hdwy 5 fs out, rdn 3 out, hng lft and sn btn*. ....(11 to 4 fav op 4 to 1 tchd 9 to 2) 6
KINTARO [49] 5-9-11 J Williams (9) *hld up and beh, hdwy hfwy, rdn alng 4 fs out, sn one pace*. ....(10 to 1 op 6 to 1) 7
1896[4] NANCY (Ire) [43] (bl) 3-8-4 Dale Gibson (3) *al mid-div*. ....(14 to 1 op 10 to 1) 8
1896[3] BAJAN AFFAIR [33] 3-7-8 E Johnson (1) *prmnt, rdn o'r 4 fs out, sn wknd*..........(9 to 1 op 6 to 1 tchd 10 to 1) 9
1562[8] ABSOLUTLEY FOXED [29] (bl) 4-7-13[1] (7*) S Sanders (11) *chsd ldrs, rdn 4 fs out, wknd wl o'r 2 out*. ....(33 to 1 op 20 to 1) 10
710 GREEN'S SEAGO (USA) [49] 5-9-11 J Quinn (2) *mid-div, hdwy hfwy, rdn o'r 4 fs out, sn wknd*. ....(33 to 1 op 14 to 1) 11
1951[7] EASY TOOMEY [41] 5-9-3 Pat Eddery (8) *al beh*. ....(10 to 1 op 7 to 1) 12
1979[4] MANULEADER [43] 4-8-12 (7*) C Hawksley (6) *chsd ldrs to hfwy, sn lost pl and beh*...........(25 to 1 op 16 to 1) 13
Dist: 5l, 3½l, ¾l, sht-hd, ½l, 4l, 2l, 2l, 2½l, 8l. 3m 10.10s. a 12.20s (13 Ran).
(Exors Of The Late Mr K E Wheldon), Mrs J R Ramsden

2179 Silk Stockings Maiden Auction Stakes Class D (2-y-o) £3,348 6f 15yds. .(6:50)

1715[7] ABSOLUTELY FAYRE 9-0 Paul Eddery (10) *made all, rdn and ran on wl fnl furlong*. ....(4 to 1 op 5 to 1 tchd 6 to 1) 1
CAPTAIN SCARLET (Ire) 9-0 S Whitworth (3) *chsd ldrs, effrt and edgd rght fnl furlong, sn rdn and styd on wl ins last*...............................(20 to 1 op 12 to 1) 2
1905[9] MERLIN'S FIELD (Ire) 9-0 A McGlone (5) *al cl up, rdn 2 fs out, ev ch ins last, kpt on*. ....(10 to 1 op 8 to 1 tchd 12 to 1) 3
1324[6] SCHNOZZLE (Ire) 9-0 L Dettori (1) *chsd ldrs, effrt and ev ch 2 fs out, sn rdn, edgd rght and wknd*.........(2 to 1 jt-fav op 9 to 2 tchd 11 to 2) 4
1535[5] UN PARFUM DE FEMME (Ire) 9-0 G Bardwell (4) *in tch, rdn alng and outpcd hfwy, styd on fnl furlong*. ....(33 to 1 op 20 to 1) 5
SOMMERSBY (Ire) 9-0 R Hills (7) *trkd ldrs, effrt and rdn 2 fs out, hmpd o'r one out, no ch aftr*..........(2 to 1 jt-fav op 6 to 4) 6
ARCTIC DIAMOND 9-0 K Fallon (2) *beh, hdwy 2 fs out, kpt on*..................................(20 to 1 op 14 to 1) 7
RUNIC SYMBOL 9-0 J Quinn (6) *chsd ldrs, rdn 2 fs out, sn wknd*...................(6 to 1 op 5 to 1 tchd 9 to 2) 8
STOREY'S GATE (Ire) 9-0 G Duffield (8) *al outpcd and beh*. ....(7 to 1 op 3 to 1 tchd 8 to 1) 9
Dist: Hd, ½l, 3½l, ¾l, 1l, hd, ½l, 4l. 1m 14.50s. a 3.00s (9 Ran).
SR: 34/33/31/17/14/10/9/7/-/ (The Bloodstock Brothers), P W Harris

2180 'Pretty Woman' Claiming Stakes Class F (2-y-o) £2,087 5f 13yds.. (7:20)

1774[2] CLARET BUMBLE 8-3 T Sprake (3) *cl up, led on bit ins last, cmftbly*. (7 to 4 on op 11 to 8 on tchd 5 to 4 on) 1
1964 ROCKY TWO 8-3 (7*) S Sanders (1) *cl up, effrt and rdn appr fnl furlong, kpt on*. ....(16 to 1 op 14 to 1 tchd 20 to 1) 2
2058 LUCKY FOURTEEN 9-5 J Fanning (6) *led, rdn wl o'r one furlong out, hdd and no extr ins last*. (6 to 1 op 9 to 2) 3
1798 CREEK VALLEY 8-10 K Fallon (2) *ran green and outpcd hfwy, styd on appr fnl furlong, better for race*. ....(14 to 1 op 10 to 1) 4
1475[4] BOLD TIME MONKEY 8-6 G Carter (5) *slwly into strd and sn rdn alng to chase ldrs, hng lft 2 fs out and soon wknd*................................(5 to 1 tchd 9 to 2) 5
SPORTSGUIDE'S GIRL 7-11 (3*) B Doyle (4) *slwly away, al outpcd and beh*....................(14 to 1 op 10 to 1) 6
Dist: ½l, 2l, 5l, 6l, ¾l. 1m 4.00s. a 5.80s (6 Ran).
(Mrs P J Makin), P J Makin

2181 Gem AM Handicap Class E (0-70 3-y-o) £2,892 1m 54yds.............(7:50)

2009* PERSIANSKY (Ire) [69] 9-10 (7ex) L Dettori (6) *al prmnt, hdwy on bit to chase ldr 3 fs out, sn led and quickened clr, cmftbly*........... (2 to 1 op 9 to 4 tchd 11 to 4) 1
836 IJAB (Can) [66] 9-7 R Hills (1) *chsd ldrs and sn rdn alng, hdwy o'r 2 fs out, styd on und pres fnl furlong, no ch wth wnr*...............................(14 to 1 op 12 to 1) 2
1991[2] LATEST FLAME (Ire) [60] 9-1 Pat Eddery (5) *al prmnt, effrt o'r 2 fs out, sn rdn and one pace*. ....(7 to 4 fav op 13 to 8 tchd 2 to 1) 3
1330[7] MOVE SMARTLY (Ire) [60] 9-1 S Perks (4) *hdwy hfwy, sn rdn, styd on one pace fnl 2 fs*.......(12 to 1 op 8 to 1) 4
1968[3] MRS DAWSON [57] 8-12 A Proud (7) *cl up, hdwy to ld 4 fs out, rdn 3 furlongs out, sn hdd and grad wknd*. ....(7 to 1 op 6 to 1 tchd 8 to 1) 5
1771[4] PREMIER STAR [59] 8-11 (3*) M Fenton (3) *nvr rch ldrs*. ....(11 to 1 op 8 to 1 tchd 12 to 1) 6
1351[8] EXCESS BAGGAGE (Ire) [51] 8-6 J Williams (8) *sn led, rdn and hdd 4 fs out, soon wknd*....... (8 to 1 op 16 to 1) 7
1803[4] ALMONTY (Ire) [54] 8-9 G Carter (2) *al rear*. ....(25 to 1 op 20 to 1) 8
Dist: 3l, 4l, ½l, 2½l, 1l, 12l, ½l. 1m 47.10s. a 7.10s (8 Ran).
SR: 3/-/-/-/-/ (Mrs J M Beeby), B Hanbury

2182 Mardi Gras Limited Stakes Class F (0-60 3-y-o) £2,313 1m 1f 213yds (8:20)

1399[3] SHIRLEY ROSE 8-9 Dean McKeown (4) *al prmnt, hdwy to ld 3 fs out, sn rdn, hrd drvn and swshd tail fnl furlong, styd on*.................. (6 to 1 op 7 to 1 tchd 8 to 1) 1
1880[2] GIORDANO (Ire) 9-0 J Williams (2) *in tch, hdwy 4 fs out, rdn to chal appr fnl furlong, kpt on same pace*. ....(10 to 1 tchd 12 to 1) 2
1812* HYDE'S HAPPY HOUR 9-0 Pat Eddery (1) *cl up, led o'r 4 fs out, rdn and hdd 3 out, wknd over one out*. ....(9 to 2 tchd 6 to 1) 3
1872[3] MAJOR TRIUMPH (Ire) 8-9 L Dettori (8) *hld up and beh, hdwy 3 fs out, sn rdn and one pace*. ....(16 to 1 op 14 to 1) 4
1968* TIME HONORED (USA) 9-0 G Duffield (3) *in tch, pushed alng and hdwy o'r 3 fs out, rdn 2 out, sn hrd drvn and btn*...........(6 to 4 on op 7 to 4 on tchd 2 to 1 on) 5
338[5] BADAWI (Fr) 8-7 (7*) G Forster (5) *led, rdn and hdd o'r 4 fs out, sn wknd*...........................(33 to 1 op 20 to 1) 6

1784 THATCHED (Ire) 9-0 N Day (6) *chsd ldrs, rdn o'r 3 fs out, sn wknd*...............(14 to 1 op 25 to 1 tchd 33 to 1) 7
1686[8] SOVIET EXPRESS 9-0 Paul Eddery (7) *cl up, rdn 3 fs out, wknd o'r 2 out*...................(14 to 1 op 10 to 1) 8
Dist: 1½l, 3l, nk, 4l, 12l, 2l, 3l. 2m 11.10s. a 8.10s (8 Ran).
SR: 14/16/10/4/1/ (Greenland Park Ltd), M Johnston

2183 Midlands Ladies Racing Club Maiden Handicap Class E (0-70 3-y-o and up) £2,825 1m 1f 213yds............(8:50)

1781[9] INFERRING [40] 5-8-12 Dean McKeown (1) *chsd ldg pair, hdwy to ld o'r 3 fs out and rdn clr, styd on.* ....(9 to 1 op 7 to 1 tchd 10 to 1) 1
1866 HYDROPIC [28] 6-8-0 J Fanning (8) *al cl up, led 4 fs out, sn rdn and hdd, kpt on*...............(20 to 1 tchd 33 to 1) 2
1875 ON GOLDEN POND (Ire) [53] 3-9-0 L Dettori (7) *hld up in tch, hdwy o'r 4 fs out, rdn 3 out and sn one pace.* ....(5 to 1 op 7 to 1 tchd 8 to 1) 3
1961[4] CONCINNITY (USA) [52] 4-9-10 A McGlone (2) *in tch, effrt and some hdwy 4 fs out, sn rdn and btn.* ....(2 to 1 fav op 9 to 4 tchd 5 to 2) 4
1907[5] PYRRHIC DANCE [56] 3-9-3 R Hills (4) *chsd ldrs, rdn o'r 3 fs out, sn wknd*....... (5 to 2 op 15 to 8 tchd 2 to 1) 5
1626 SMART TEACHER (USA) [43] 3-8-4 N Adams (3) *nvr a factor*..(7 to 1) 6
1866 CROMER'S EXPRESS [33] 4-8-5 G Hind (6) *al beh.* ....(33 to 1 op 20 to 1) 7
4773a[9] IGNITED [37] 3-7-12 N Carlisle (5) *led, rdn and hdd 4 fs out, wknd quickly*... (20 to 1 op 16 to 1 tchd 25 to 1) 8
Dist: 3½l, 3½l, 7l, 6l, 1½l, 1½l, dist. 2m 11.60s. a 8.60s (8 Ran).
SR: 12/-/-/-/-/ (Mrs Terence A M Cockram), J S Wainwright

TIPPERARY (IRE) (good)
Thursday July 1st

2184 Glen Maiden (3-y-o and up) £2,762 7f ....(6:00)

1333 DOREG (Ire) 3-9-0 J P Murtagh (16)..................(16 to 1) 1
1765 GOODNIGHT KISS 3-8-11 P Shanahan (12).... (5 to 2 on) 2
1796[2] BELLISSI (Ire) 3-8-11 K J Manning (7)............(10 to 1) 3
3117 ROUNDWOOD ROSE (Ire) 3-8-11 W J O'Connor (13) ....(14 to 1) 4
1793[4] ARZAAQ (USA) (bl) 3-9-0 W J Supple (14)........ (12 to 1) 5
CRYSTAL SHIP (Ire) 3-8-11 P V Gilson (10)........ (3 to 1) 6
1855 MADAME MINISTER (USA) 3-8-9 (2*) D G O'Shea (11) ....(14 to 1) 7
1333 CAN'T RECALL (USA) 3-8-11 E McCabe (1)...... (20 to 1) 8
CARNAZAR (Ire) 3-8-11 N Byrne (5)................(20 to 1) 9
1855[6] JUNORIUS (Ire) 4-9-8 S Craine (4)................(25 to 1) 10
1610 DOZING WIZZ (Ire) 3-8-11 G Curran (2).......... (20 to 1) 11
1610[8] DONTKISSTHEJOCKEY (Ire) 3-8-11 Joanna Morgan (5) ....(25 to 1) 12
1106 WHISKEY HALL (Ire) (bl) 4-9-4 (4*) P Carberry (15) (33 to 1) 13
Dist: 3l, 1½l, 2l, ½l. 1m 32.20s. (13 Ran).
(Patrick F Headon), Declan Gillespie

2185 Low Low (C & G) Maiden (3-y-o) £4,142 1m 1f..........................(6:30)

TADJIK (USA) 9-0 J P Murtagh (6)................ (5 to 2) 1
1510[5] MONOPOLY MONEY (Ire) 9-0 P V Gilson (2)......... (9 to 2) 2
1441[4] SHEER OPULANCE (Ire) (bl) 9-0 P Shanahan (7) (7 to 4 fav) 3
311 CALIANDAK (Ire) 9-0 D Hogan (1)..................(12 to 1) 4
RED GLITTER (USA) 9-0 W J O'Connor (4)..........(8 to 1) 5
DANCEALOT (Ire) 8-12 (2*) D G O'Shea (5)....... (14 to 1) 6
1236[7] FALCARRAGH (Ire) 9-0 J F Egan (8)..............(14 to 1) 7
SOUTHERN REVIEW (Ire) 9-0 W J Supple (3)...... (8 to 1) 8
944[6] DANAMORE (Ire) 9-0 S Craine (9)...................(8 to 1) 9
Dist: Nk, 1l, nk, 2l. 1m 57.60s. (9 Ran).
(H H Aga Khan), John M Oxx

2186 Roscrea Handicap (0-80 3-y-o and up) £2,762 1½m................... (7:00)

1757[2] LYPHARD ABU (Ire) [-] 5-9-1 C Roche (8)...... (7 to 4 fav) 1
959[3] ANGAREB (Ire) [-] 4-8-7 P V Gilson (1)............(6 to 1) 2
1987[8] BOBADIL (Ire) [-] 3-7-10 (2*,5ex) D G O'Shea (4)....(9 to 1) 3
1962[4] SIMPLY MARILYN (Ire) [-] 4-9-2 S Craine (2)........(6 to 1) 4
1139[6] LAKE OF LOUGHREA (Ire) [-] 3-7-3 (8*) R T Fitzpatrick (9) ....(14 to 1) 5
MITAH (Ire) [-] 5-8-13 R Hughes (3)............. (14 to 1) 6
1794[6] SHARASTAMINA (USA) [-] (bl) 4-9-4 N G McCullagh (6) ....(5 to 1) 7
807[8] OFTEN AHEAD (Ire) [-] 5-9-10 J P Murtagh (5).....(15 to 2) 8
1466* DRIFT APART (Ire) [-] 3-8-13 W J O'Connor (7)..... (6 to 1) 9
Dist: ½l, 3½l, ½l, hd. 2m 37.50s. (9 Ran).
(D Bernie), J S Bolger

2187 Tipperary Sprint Race (Listed) (3-y-o and up) £8,627 5f...............(7:30)

2073* ROSIE'S MAC (Ire) 4-9-2 N G McCullagh (9) *mid-div, prog on outsd one furlong out, led last strds*.......(12 to 1) 1
1023[7] SOVEREIGN GRACE (Ire) 4-8-13 J P Murtagh (6) *led, rdn o'r one furlong out, hdd last strds*................(16 to 1) 2
1551[6] DAWNSIO (Ire) 3-8-12 R Hughes (5) *trkd ldrs, chlgd o'r one furlong out, ev ch ins last, kpt on*.......... (7 to 4 fav) 3
2073[7] BRADAWN BREEVER (Ire) (bl) 4-9-2 W J Supple (7) *chsd ldr, rdn and wknd o'r one furlong out*..............(9 to 4) 4
2078* PERNILLA (Ire) 3-9-0 C Roche (1) *wl plcd, rdn and wknd 2 fs out*...(7 to 2) 5
1551[7] DIAMONDS GALORE (Can) (bl) 8-9-7 P Shanahan (4) *mid-div, rdn and wknd 2 fs out*..................(11 to 1) 6
2073 CLANDOLLY (Ire) 5-8-13 D V Smith (8) *wl plcd to hfwy, sn wknd*.. (16 to 1) 7
573[8] PREPONDERANCE (Ire) 3-8-7 W J O'Connor (3) *mid-div, wknd 2 fs out*.................................(10 to 1) 8
Dist: Sht-hd, ½l, 1½l, hd. 56.80s. (8 Ran).
(Joseph Wall), D Hanley

2188 Monard E.B.F. Fillies Maiden (2-y-o) £3,797 5f..................... (8:00)

1197[8] MAHASEAL (USA) 9-0 W J Supple (5).............(7 to 1) 1
AINE'S PET (Ire) 8-10 (4*) P Carberry (8)............(10 to 1) 2
SOLAR ATTRACTION (Ire) 9-0 J P Murtagh (6).. (Evens fav) 3
SNOWING 9-0 S Craine (7)........................ (9 to 2) 4
INSUPERABLE (Ire) 9-0 N G McCullagh (4)....... (10 to 1) 5
GENEVIEVE FLEUR (Ire) 8-12 (2*) D G O'Shea (3)..(20 to 1) 6
1567[5] LAXEY LEAP (Ire) 9-0 K J Manning (1)............(12 to 1) 7
1854 PASTELLE (bl) 9-0 P Shanahan (2)..................(7 to 1) 8
Dist: Sht-hd, 1½l, nk, 1l. 59.10s. (8 Ran).
(Hamdan Al Maktoum), Kevin Prendergast

YARMOUTH (firm)
Thursday July 1st
Going Correction: MINUS 0.55 sec. per fur.

2189 Happisburgh Maiden Stakes Class D (3-y-o and up) £4,776 1m 3f 101yds ....(2:10)

1533[4] RAHIL (Ire) 3-8-9 R Hills (9) *enterprisingly rdn, made all, 6 ls clr till tired fnl furlong, jst lasted* (5 to 2 op 4 to 1) 1
PRINCE OF ANDROS (USA) 3-8-9 L Dettori (5) *tucked away in midfield, improved und pres o'r 2 fs out, fnshd strly.* ....(10 to 1 op 8 to 1 tchd 12 to 1) 2
662[8] USK THE WAY 3-8-4 W Ryan (7) *settled midfield, improved und pres 3 fs out, fnshd strly.* ....(5 to 4 fav op 6 to 4 tchd 11 to 10) 3
1831[7] RUSSIAN EMPIRE 3-8-9 M Roberts (2) *chsd clr, rdn whn pace lifted o'r 3 fs out, rallied, squeezed out cl hme.* ....(6 to 1 op 7 to 2) 4
DOVER PATROL (Ire) 3-8-9 A McGlone (6) *trkd ldg half dozen, rdn entering strt, nvr able to chal.* ....(10 to 1 op 5 to 1 tchd 12 to 1) 5
1831 COMFORTABLE 3-8-2 (7*) S Mulvey (4) *steadied strt, last strt, sn drvn alng, nvr dngrs.* ....(40 to 1 op 25 to 1 tchd 50 to 1) 6
1617 HATTA SUNSHINE (USA) 3-8-9 Paul Eddery (1) *trkd ldg trio, feeling pace and lost grnd o'r 3 fs out, sn btn.* ....(20 to 1 op 10 to 1) 7
1642[2] PRETTY BABY 3-8-4 M Hills (3) *pressed ldg pair till fdd und pres o'r 3 fs out.* (16 to 1 op 10 to 1 tchd 20 to 1) 8
Dist: Sht-hd, sht-hd, 1½l, 10l, 1½l, 10l, 2l. 2m 23.10s. b 0.40s (8 Ran).
SR: 36/35/29/31/11/8/-/-/ (Hamdan Al-Maktoum), H Thomson Jones

2190 High Steward Claiming Stakes Class F (3-y-o and up) £2,579 1m 3yds.. (2:40)

2156[2] SHINING JEWEL 6-9-5 L Piggott (6) *made all, drvn alng to go clr ins fnl furlong, kpt on.* ....(Evens fav op 7 to 4 tchd 2 to 1 and 5 to 4 on) 1
1829[2] STRIKE-A-POSE 3-8-1 J Quinn (2) *settled gng wl, improved to chal appr fnl furlong, ran on und pres.* ....(7 to 4 op 2 to 1 tchd 11 to 4 and 6 to 4) 2
1453 POP TO STANS 4-9-1 Alex Greaves (8) *chsd ldrs, improved stands side to flttr appr fnl furlong, kpt on one pace.* ....(20 to 1 op 8 to 1) 3
1829[4] YFOOL 3-8-1 R Hills (4) *nvr far away, effrt und pres o'r 2 fs out, one pace*.................. (4 to 1 op 2 to 1) 4
1658[9] COSMIC STAR (bl) 3-8-1 W Woods (3) *chsd ldg bunch, rdn o'r 2 fs out, no imprsn*............(20 to 1 op 10 to 1) 5
1696 J'ARRIVE (v) 4-8-3[2] (5*) C Hodgson (5) *wl plcd stands side for o'r 5 fs, fdd*...................(50 to 1 op 20 to 1) 6
1607 GREY WATCH 3-8-3 Paul Eddery (7) *chsd ldrs stands side, struggling to hold pl o'r 2 fs out, sn btn.* ....(50 to 1 op 20 to 1) 7
2023 YOSHAARIK (Ire) 3-8-2 M Roberts (1) *struggling to keep up hfwy, tld off*...................... (20 to 1 op 10 to 1) 8
Dist: 1l, ½l, 1½l, 5l, 6l, 3l, 4l. 1m 36.40s. a 0.60s (8 Ran).
SR: 30/9/21/2/-/ (D W Rolt), Mrs L Piggott

2191 Fred Armstrong Handicap Class E (0-70 3-y-o and up) £2,769 6f 3yds ....(3:10)

1096[9] ELTON LEDGER (Ire) [55] (bl) 4-9-2 Paul Eddery (4) *confidently rdn, quickened ahead o'r one furlong out, ran on wl.*..........(6 to 1 op 5 to 1 tchd 7 to 1) 1
1871[3] AFRICAN CHIMES [65] 6-9-12 L Dettori (6) *tried to make all, hdd and rdn o'r one furlong out, no extr.*..........(7 to 2 op 3 to 1 tchd 4 to 1) 2
1563 MARTINOSKY [67] 7-10-0 W R Swinburn (5) *chsd alng to keep up, styd on appr fnl furlong, nvr nrr.*..........(5 to 2 fav op 9 to 4 tchd 11 to 4) 3
1841[8] WHERE'S THE DANCE [69] 3-9-9 M Roberts (2) *chsd alng on outsd, effrt 2 fs out, kpt on same pace.*..........(4 to 1 op 9 to 2 tchd 5 to 1) 4
2157[3] SPRING HIGH [53] (bl) 6-8-7 (7*) C Scally (3) *broke wl to press ldr, rdn o'r one furlong out, kpt on.*..........(3 to 1 op 5 to 2 tchd 100 to 30) 5
761[9] AZRAG (Ire) [59] 3-8-13 R Hills (1) *struggling to go pace aftr 2 fs, tld off*..........(16 to 1 op 12 to 1) 6
Dist: 2½l, 1½l, ¾l, nk, 25l. 1m 10.90s. b 0.10s (6 Ran).
SR: 38/38/34/26/16/-/ (A A Scott), A A Scott

2192 Dunston Selling Stakes Class G (2-y-o) £2,259 6f 3yds.............(3:40)

1916[9] BET A PLAN (Ire) 8-6 Paul Eddery (5) *dsptd ld, drvn alng to pull away appr fnl furlong, ran on wl.*..........(5 to 4 on tchd 11 to 10 on) 1
1602 NORTHERN STORM (Ire) 8-11 W Woods (1) *dsptd ld, drvn alng last 2 fs, not quicken ins last*... (7 to 1 op 5 to 1) 2
1741 CLASSICAL DON (Ire) 8-11 L Dettori (3) *al hndy, rdn 2 fs out, kpt on same pace*.......... (8 to 1 tchd 11 to 1) 3
1926[4] DIAMOND CROWN (Ire) 8-11 T Quinn (2) *nvr far away, edgd lft und pres o'r 2 fs out, no imprsn.*..........(11 to 4 op 2 to 1) 4
Dist: 3l, 2l, ½l. 1m 12.60s. a 1.60s (4 Ran).
(Planflow (Leasing) Ltd), G Lewis

2193 Loddon Fillies' Handicap Class D (0-80 3-y-o and up) £3,590 7f 3yds..........(4:10)

1982[2] MISS GORGEOUS (Ire) [73] 3-9-9 (3*) Emma O'Gorman (3) *made all, reminders o'r 2 fs out, hld on grimly und hands and heels cl hme*..........(7 to 2 op 3 to 1) 1
1713* QUAVER (USA) [74] 3-9-13 M Roberts (2) *sluggish strt, hrd drvn to reco'r hfwy, ev ch fnl furlong, jst hld.*..........(7 to 4 on tchd 2 to 1 on and 13 to 8 on) 2
1761[5] DALALAH [67] 3-9-6 R Hills (1) *al hndy, hrd rdn to chal ins fnl furlong, ran on*..........(7 to 1 op 5 to 1) 3
1981[6] GLENFIELD GRETA [55] (bl) 5-9-2 W Ryan (4) *co'red up on ins, flttered over one furlong out, kpt on cl hme.*..........(12 to 1 op 7 to 1) 4
Dist: Hd, nk, ½l. 1m 23.80s. a 0.60s (4 Ran).
SR: 45/45/37/31/ (Thomas R Capehart), W A O'Gorman

2194 Hemsby Conditions Stakes Class C (3-y-o and up) £4,761 7f 3yds......(4:40)

1447[7] TIK FA (USA) (v) 4-9-9 W R Swinburn (3) *patiently rdn, ridden to weave through ins fnl furlong, got up on post*..........(5 to 1 op 7 to 2 tchd 11 to 2) 1+
1765 PEMBROKE (USA) 3-8-12 M Roberts (5) *trkd ldg pair, nosed ahead o'r one furlong out, rdn and ct post.*..........(9 to 4 fav op 6 to 4 tchd 11 to 8 and 5 to 2) 1+
1768 SPANISH STORM (Ire) (bl) 4-9-1 W Woods (4) *trkd to make all, hdd o'r one furlong out, rallied.*..........(14 to 1 op 10 to 1 tchd 16 to 1) 3
1765[9] ROGER THE BUTLER (Ire) 3-8-6 M Hills (1) *nvr far away, effrt und pres o'r one furlong out, kpt on same pace.*..........(9 to 1 op 8 to 1 tchd 10 to 1) 4
1710[2] LEE ARTISTE 5-8-9 T Quinn (2) *last and niggled alng hfwy, responded 2 fs out, one pace ins fnl furlong.*..........(7 to 2 op 11 to 4 tchd 4 to 1) 5
1636[2] BRIGADE 4-9-2 L Dettori (6) *trkd ldr, ev ch hfwy, wknd und pres appr fnl furlong.*..........(7 to 2 op 6 to 1 tchd 7 to 1) 6
Dist: Dd-ht, 1½l, ¾l, 2l, 6l. 1m 22.70s. b 0.50s (6 Ran).
SR: 59/48/46/35/32/21/ (Abdullah Ali & Sheikh Mohammed), B Hanbury & J H M Gosden

2195 Hickling Amateur Riders' Handicap Class G (0-70 3-y-o and up) £2,343 1¼m 21yds....................(5:10)

1685[2] OVERPOWER [56] 9-11-1[4] (5*) Mr M Jenkins (1) *patiently rdn, steady hdwy on ins to ld inside fnl furlong, ran on*..........(7 to 2 op 3 to 1 tchd 4 to 1) 1
1676[3] SUGEMAR [53] 7-10-8 (5*) Mr M Chapman (3) *led till hdd o'r 3 fs out, rallied to ld ag'n over 2, headed ins last, one pace*..........(6 to 1 op 5 to 1) 2
294 LOTS OF LUCK [61] 10-11-7 Mrs L Pearce (8) *wtd wth, brght wide to improve o'r 2 fs out, wndrd fnl furlong, swtchd last 50 yards, not quicken.*..........(11 to 4 fav op 7 to 4 tchd 3 to 1) 3
2104* HEAVY ROCK (Ire) [32] 4-9-6 (5ex) Mr G Lewis (6) *al hndy, led o'r 3 fs out till over 2 furlongs out, kpt on same pace.*..........(7 to 2 op 5 to 2) 4
1969[7] HERETICAL MISS [55] 3-9-13 (5*) Mrs J Boggis (2) *nvr far away, rdn o'r 2 fs out, not quicken.* (12 to 1 op 8 to 1) 5
1659[8] THRESHFIELD (USA) [55] 7-10-10 (5*) Mr C Curley (4) *trkd ldg bunch, drvn alng o'r 2 fs out, no imprsn.*..........(6 to 1 op 4 to 1) 6
2513 DIGGER DOYLE [59] 4-11-0 (5*) Mr V Lukaniuk (5) *al wl plcd, feeling pace and lost grnd o'r 2 fs out, tld off.*..........(12 to 1 op 10 to 1 tchd 14 to 1) 7
SHAURNI GIRL [37] 5-9-6 (5*) Miss H Webster (9) *wth ldrs for o'r 5 fs, tld off*..........(33 to 1 op 20 to 1) 8
Dist: 1l, 2½l, 3l, 1½l, ¾l, 20l, 4l. 2m 8.80s. a 4.80s (8 Ran).
SR: 27/22/25/-/-/8/-/-/ (M P Bowring), M H Tompkins

BEVERLEY (good to firm)
Friday July 2nd
Going Correction: MINUS 0.25 sec. per fur.

2196 Norwood Rating Related Maiden Stakes Class F (0-65 3-y-o) £2,460 2m 35yds..........................(6:45)

1423[2] MONDRAGON 9-0 J Lowe (3) *patiently rdn, brght wide to ld o'r one furlong out, ran on wl.* (2 to 1 fav op 5 to 4) 1
1942[2] WAKT 8-9 G Duffield (6) *trkd ldg pair, effrt und pres o'r one furlong out, styd on same pace ins last.*..........(17 to 2 op 6 to 1 tchd 9 to 1) 2
1772[5] ARC BRIGHT (Ire) 9-0 L Dettori (5) *chsd ldr, led appr strt till o'r one furlong out, one pace*...(11 to 2 op 7 to 1) 3
1936[2] RUSTY REEL 9-0 Dean McKeown (2) *wtd wth, chlgd 2 fs out, rdn and no extr fnl furlong*..........(5 to 2) 4
1423[3] VAIGLY SUNTHYME 9-0 S Morris (4) *chsd ldg trio, effrt und pres 2 fs out, not quicken*..... (11 to 2 op 5 to 1) 5
1735[4] ST ALZINA (Ire) 9-0 V Smith (1) *led, clr till wknd and hdd appr strt, tld off*..........(25 to 1 op 20 to 1) 6
Dist: 2l, sht-hd, 2½l, 4l, dist. 3m 39.40s. a 10.40s (6 Ran).
(Skeltools Ltd), Mrs M Reveley

2197 Pocklington Selling Handicap Class G (0-60 3-y-o and up) £2,938 7f 100yds..............................(7:10)

2001[3] PARFAIT AMOUR [60] 4-10-0 A Munro (8) *wtd wth, not clr run and swtchd ins 2 fs out, ran on to ld inside last, drvn out*..........(5 to 1) 1
2057[9] MALCESINE (Ire) [44] 4-8-12 J Fortune (5) *al hndy, ev ch and rdn 2 fs out, kpt on nr finish*... (7 to 1 op 6 to 1) 2
2057 COOL ENOUGH [37] 12-8-5 K Fallon (4) *patiently rdn, staying on whn not clr run o'r one furlong out, swtchd outsd, ran on*..........(6 to 1 tchd 13 to 2) 3
1932[9] NIGEL'S LUCKY GIRL [50] 5-9-4 J Lowe (6) *nvr far away, led briefly ins fnl furlong, one pace.* (4 to 1 op 8 to 1) 4
2104[6] SLUMBER THYME (Ire) [38] 4-8-6 J Fanning (12) *led early, hndy till rdn and not quicken appr fnl furlong.*..........(10 to 1 tchd 11 to 1) 5
1937[3] OBSIDIAN GREY [56] 6-9-5 (5*) O Pears (11) *al hndy, led o'r one furlong out, hdd and no extr ins last.*..........(5 to 1 op 4 to 1) 6
1578 JUST-GO-AGAIN [44] (bl) 4-8-12 L Charnock (13) *squeezed out strt, drvn alng to chase ldrs hfwy, no imprsn.*..........(33 to 1) 7
1737[2] ROUTING [49] 5-9-3 Dean McKeown (7) *steadied strt, brght wide and drvn alng hfwy, nvr rch ldrs.*..........(7 to 2 fav tchd 4 to 1) 8
1760 GATE OF HEAVEN [33] (v) 3-7-2 (5*) Darren Moffatt (9) *sn led, set str pace till hdd and wknd o'r one furlong out.*..........(25 to 1 op 20 to 1) 9
1965[6] GRUBBY [26] 4-7-8[7] (7*) M Humphries (2) *chsd ldrs for o'r 5 fs, sn btn*..........(20 to 1) 10
1979[8] NEVENTER (Fr) [51] 4-9-5 V Smith (10) *missed break, nvr a dngr*..........(33 to 1 op 25 to 1) 11
1898[8] PIMSBOY [49] (bl) 6-9-3 J Carroll (3) *chsd ldrs for o'r 4 fs, sn btn*..........(14 to 1) 12
VITAL VOLTAGE (Ire) [33] 4-8-1 S Morris (1) *in tch 5 fs, sn btn*..........(33 to 1) 13
Dist: 1l, hd, 2l, 1½l, hd, 1½l, 3½l, ¾l, 5l, ¾l. 1m 33.00s. a 2.70s (13 Ran).
SR: 45/26/18/25/8/25/8/2/-/ (R M Whitaker), R M Whitaker

2198 Tryton Yorkshire Pudding Handicap Class D (0-85 3-y-o and up) £7,700 1m 100yds..........................(7:35)

1981[2] SANDMOOR DENIM [56] 6-8-5 S Webster (11) *co'red up in midfield, rdn and not much room 2 fs out, led ins last, ran on*..........(10 to 1) 1
1604[5] NOBBY BARNES [57] 4-8-6 G Carter (8) *settled off the pace, swtchd outsd to improve und pres o'r one furlong out, fnshd wl*..........(7 to 1 op 6 to 1) 2
1800* SOVEREIGN PAGE (USA) [71] 4-9-1 (5*) J Tate (5) *al hndy, drvn alng to ld briefly fnl furlong, kpt on same pace.*..........(4 to 1 jt-fav tchd 9 to 2) 3
1940[2] WHO'S TEF (Ire) [51] 5-7-11 (3*) S Maloney (10) *trkd ldg pair, hrd drvn to draw level entering fnl furlong, not quicken cl hme*.......... (4 to 1 jt-fav op 7 to 2) 4
1939[2] CAUSLEY [70] 8-9-5 L Dettori (9) *led, jnd and drvn alng o'r one furlong out, hdd and no extr ins last*... (6 to 1) 5

2045[2] LANGTRY LADY [72] (v) 7-9-7 M Hills (1) *settled off the pace, effrt and bustled alng o'r 2 fs out, nvr able to chal*..............................(7 to 1 op 6 to 1) 6
1940[6] LAWNSWOOD JUNIOR [69] 6-8-11 (7*) M Humphries (6) *sluggish strt, drvn alng hfwy, nvr dngrs.* ....(8 to 1 op 7 to 1) 7
1839[3] FABRIANA [84] 3-9-10 D Holland (3) *wth ldrs, hrd drvn whn pace quickened o'r one furlong out, sn btn.* ....(12 to 1 op 14 to 1) 8
1830[6] SYLVAN (Ire) [77] (v) 4-9-12 G Duffield (7) *chsd ldrs for o'r 5 fs, sn btn*..............................(14 to 1 op 12 to 1) 9
1867[2] ROYAL CITIZEN (Ire) [73] 4-9-8 K Fallon (2) *struggling hfwy, nvr a factor*..............................(16 to 1) 10
Dist: ¾l, sht-hd, 1½l, 1l, 1½l, 2l, 1l, 2l. 1m 46.30s. a 3.50s (10 Ran).
SR: 7/6/19/-/10/7/-/1/-/ (E H Lunness), S R Bowring

2199 Tryton 'Toad In The Hole' Maiden Stakes Class D (2-y-o) £3,377 5f (8:05)

KNAYTON LASS 8-9 T Lucas (3) *tucked away beh ldrs, swtchd outsd to improve o'r one furlong out, led ins last, quickened clr*..............................(11 to 1 op 10 to 1) 1
1837[2] LUCIUS LOCKET (Ire) 9-0 J Carroll (5) *trkd ldr, led o'r one furlong out, edgd rght and hdd ins last, no extr.* .....(6 to 5 on op 5 to 4 on tchd 11 to 8 on and 11 to 10 on) 2
BRITANNIA MILLS 8-2 (7*) D McCabe (8) *drvn into midfield hfwy, styd on fnl furlong, nvr nrr.* ....(20 to 1 tchd 25 to 1) 3
1846[9] FOUR OF SPADES 8-11 (3*) S D Williams (6) *drvn alng to go pace, und pres last 2 fs, nvr rch ldrs.* ....(12 to 1 op 10 to 1 tchd 14 to 1) 4
LUCKY MESSAGE (USA) 8-9 G Duffield (1) *veered lft strt, ran green, nvr dngrs*..............................(4 to 1 op 5 to 2) 5
1461[9] WARTHILL WHISPERS 8-9 M Wigham (7) *led till hdd and wknd quickly o'r one furlong out.* (9 to 2 tchd 5 to 1) 6
1877 CAPITAL LADY (Ire) 8-9 J Fortune (2) *chsd ldg pair, fdd und pres o'r one furlong out*..............................(16 to 1 op 12 to 1) 7
MERISSA 8-9 L Charnock (4) *missed break, al struggling, tld off*..............................(16 to 1 op 14 to 1) 8
Dist: 5l, 2l, 5l, 2l, 1½l, 2½l, 7l. 1m 3.20s. a 1.50s (8 Ran).
SR: 40/25/12/-/-/ (Mrs J M Davenport), M W Easterby

2200 Jackson Catering Conditions Stakes Class C (2-y-o) £4,232 5f........(8:35)

1653* MILD REBUKE 8-7 M Hills (7) *tucked away gng wl, not clr run and swtchd 2 fs out, led o'r one out, easily.* ....(2 to 1 fav op 9 to 4 tchd 7 to 4) 1
1804[5] ROYAL INSIGNIA 8-12 A Munro (8) *led, drvn alng and hdd o'r one furlong out, no ch wth wnr.* ....(4 to 1 op 9 to 2 tchd 5 to 1) 2
1899[2] MISS MAH-JONG 8-5 Dean McKeown (9) *chsd alng to dispute ld, kpt on same pace ins fnl furlong.* ....(6 to 1 tchd 8 to 1) 3
1461[4] MISTER BLOY 8-12 J Carroll (5) *chsd ldg trio, drvn alng whn bumped 2 fs out, one pace.* ....(10 to 1 op 8 to 1 tchd 11 to 1) 4
1561* INDIAN CRYSTAL 8-5 G Duffield (6) *sluggish strt, last and outpcd hfwy, nvr nrr*...(11 to 2 op 5 to 1 tchd 6 to 1) 5
1082* KANGRA VALLEY 8-7 K Fallon (4) *early speed, drvn alng 2 fs out, sn btn*..............................(20 to 1 op 14 to 1) 6
1804[6] BANDON CASTLE (Ire) 8-12 J Fortune (2) *speed on outsd till wknd quickly 2 fs out.* ....(4 to 1 op 3 to 1 tchd 9 to 2) 7
Dist: 2l, 2l, 2l, 2l, 6l, ½l. 1m 4.40s. a 2.70s (7 Ran).
SR: 14/11/-/-/ (P D Player), D R Loder

2201 Craven Park Handicap Class E (0-70 3-y-o and up) £2,846 1m 3f 216yds ....(9:05)

1321[4] ALLMOSA [48] 4-9-11 D Holland (9) *chsd ldr, drvn to ld entering strt, styd on strly fnl furlong*..........(5 to 1) 1
1564[6] LUKS AKURA [34] (bl) 5-8-11 Dean McKeown (2) *set str pace, hdd and drvn alng entering strt, kpt on same pace fnl furlong*..............................(5 to 1 tchd 11 to 2) 2
2059[6] SUPER BLUES [43] 6-9-6 L Dettori (4) *drvn up to track ldg pair hfwy, effrt o'r one furlong out, one pace.* (11 to 2) 3
1593[6] EIRE LEATH-SCEAL [51] 6-10-0 M Wigham (5) *chsd ldg 6, hrd rdn o'r 2 fs out, no imprsn*..............................(11 to 2) 4
349[8] BALAAT (USA) [39] 5-8-9 (7*) D McCabe (8) *chsd ldg pair, hrd rdn o'r 2 fs out, nvr nrr*....... (33 to 1 op 25 to 1) 5
1438[5] REACH FOR GLORY [38] 4-9-1 A Culhane (7) *trkd ldg 4, effrt and not much room entering strt, sn btn.* (12 to 1) 6
1930* ICE STRIKE (USA) [42] (v) 4-9-5 (6ex) M Hills (6) *chsd ldrs, hrd drvn entering strt, sn btn.* (9 to 2 jt-fav op 7 to 2) 7
2043 ESCAPE TALK [27] 6-8-4 N Connorton (3) *sluggish strt, nvr a threat*..............................(25 to 1 op 50 to 1) 8
1738[5] YOUNG GEORGE [40] (v) 6-9-3 J Lowe (1) *trkd ldrs, und pres entering strt, wknd quickly*.............(9 to 2 jt-fav op 4 to 1) 9
Dist: 4l, ½l, 2½l, 2l, ½l, 7l, ¾l, 7l. 2m 35.90s. a 4.90s (9 Ran).
SR: 31/10/18/21/-/-/ (The Durdans Four (Ii) Two), T J Naughton

HAYDOCK (good) Friday July 2nd

Going Correction: MINUS 0.20 sec. per fur. (races 1,3,4,6), PLUS 0.10 (2,5)

2202 Steve Donoghue Maiden Stakes Class D (3-y-o) £3,707 7f 30yds........(2:15)

FIRST VEIL 8-9 J Williams (8) *al in tch, led appr fnl furlong, ran on, cleverly*..............................(6 to 1 op 7 to 2) 1
1954[2] WISHAM (USA) 8-9 (5*) J Tate (14) *hld up towards rear, hdwy 2 fs out, chlgd appr last, ran on und pres.* ....(6 to 1 op 4 to 1) 2
1698[4] JAAZIM (bl) 9-0 W Ryan (4) *mid-div, rdn 2 fs out, short of room appr last, ran on ins.* ....(9 to 1 op 8 to 1 tchd 10 to 1) 3
950[5] SO INTREPID (Ire) 9-0 M Birch (7) *trkd ldrs, rdn wl o'r one furlong out, one pace aftr*.........(16 to 1 op 12 to 1) 4
1808 GREEN KILT 9-0 J Carroll (5) *led till hdd o'r one furlong out, sn btn*..............................(6 to 1 op 9 to 2) 5
1713[6] THRIVING 8-9 K Fallon (2) *trkd ldrs, rdn 2 fs out, no extr.* ....(14 to 1 op 10 to 1) 6
AWESTRIKE (USA) 9-0 Paul Eddery (3) *chsd ldrs till wknd wl o'r one furlong out*..............(10 to 1 op 7 to 1) 7
1629[4] QUARRELLING 9-0 S Perks (13) *al towards rear.* ....(33 to 1 op 20 to 1) 8
NO CONTRACT (USA) 9-0 M Hills (9) *al towards rear.* ....(8 to 1 op 6 to 1) 9
2064 MUSTN'T GRUMBLE (Ire) 9-0 L Charnock (1) *slwly away, effrt on outsd 3 fs out, sn btn*.... (25 to 1 tchd 33 to 1) 10
AQUILETTA 8-9 A Culhane (12) *chsd ldr, shaken up 2 fs out, wknd quickly*..............(9 to 4 fav op 5 to 1) 11
1616[6] FUCHU 8-9 A Clark (6) *al beh*........(14 to 1 op 20 to 1) 12
1851[6] KEEN AND CLEAN (Ire) 8-4 (5*) Darren Moffatt (11) *al beh.* ....(33 to 1 op 25 to 1) 13
ZAJKO (USA) 9-0 L Dettori (10) *in tch to hfwy, sn rdn, eased whn btn*.................... (6 to 1 op 4 to 1) 14
Dist: Nk, 3½l, 1½l, 2½l, 2l, hd, 5l, 2½l, 6l, 1l. 1m 31.59s. a 4.39s (14 Ran).
SR: 7/11/-/-/-/-/ (Raymond Tooth), D R C Elsworth

2203 Baxi Solo Maiden Auction Stakes Class D (2-y-o) £3,127 6f........(2:45)

2027[4] MR DEVIOUS 9-0 L Dettori (3) *sn trkd ldr, rdn to ld wl o'r one furlong out, ran on.* .... (5 to 4 on tchd 11 to 8 on and 11 to 10 on) 1
CHASTIZE (Ire) 9-0 W Ryan (2) *rcd on outsd, hdwy o'r one furlong out, ran on, not rch wnr.* ....(17 to 2 op 5 to 1 tchd 9 to 1) 2
MISS SPRINGTIME 8-9 C Nutter (6) *led aftr one furlong, hdd wl o'r one out, one pace ins*.... (7 to 2 op 4 to 1) 3
1870[3] STEPHENSONS ROCKET 9-0 J Carroll (1) *led 1st furlong, prmnt till wknd wl o'r one out*.....(11 to 2 op 4 to 1) 4
VANESSA ROSE 8-9 A Mackay (5) *slwly away, nvr on terms*................ (10 to 1 op 7 to 1 tchd 12 to 1) 5
1689[4] DOCKYARD DORA 8-9 M Wigham (4) *rcd alone far side, eased whn btn o'r one furlong out.* (14 to 1 op 10 to 1) 6
Dist: 1½l, sht-hd, 5l, 2l, 6l. 1m 16.75s. a 5.15s (6 Ran).
SR: 9/3/-/ (Theobalds Stud), R Hannon

2204 Peter Walker Brewery Handicap Class D (0-85 4-y-o and up) £3,493 1¾m ....(3:20)

1827[5] DISCORD [72] 7-9-5 L Dettori (4) *hld up in rear, hdwy o'r 3 fs out, led 2 out, drvn out.* ....(11 to 4 op 5 to 2 tchd 3 to 1) 1
1336[4] CHIEF MINISTER (Ire) [70] (bl) 4-9-3 K Fallon (2) *hld up in tch, rdn to press wnr ins fnl 2 fs, ran on, eased whn btn cl hme*..............................(5 to 2 fav op 7 to 4) 2
1129[7] DIME BAG [72] 4-9-5 D Holland (5) *trkd ldr, led o'r 3 fs out, hdd 2 out, hrd rdn, wknd ins last*.... (3 to 1 op 7 to 2) 3
1336[2] WHITE WILLOW [77] 4-9-10 M Birch (3) *rcd mid-div, rdn and ev ch 2 fs out, sn btn.* ....(100 to 30 op 3 to 1 tchd 7 to 2) 4
2007[5] NOBLE SOCIETY [46] 5-7-7 A Mackay (1) *led till hdd o'r 3 fs out, rdn, sn wknd, eased*....... (25 to 1 tchd 33 to 1) 5
Dist: 1l, 2½l, 3l, 12l. 3m 2.92s. a 5.42s (5 Ran).
SR: 23/19/16/15/-/ (Yoshio Asakawa), Lord Huntingdon

2205 Frank Wootton Claiming Stakes Class E (3-y-o) £2,745 1m 3f 200yds... (3:55)

2023[2] DON'T FORGET MARIE (Ire) 8-1 (7*) A Whelan (1) *set steady pace, quickened o'r 2 fs out, edgd lft ins last, fnshd 1st, plcd second*..................(6 to 4 on op 2 to 1 on) 1D
1943[4] CIVIL LAW (Ire) (v) 9-7 L Dettori (2) *hld up, hdwy 2 fs out, hmpd and snatched up ins last, not reco'r, fnshd second, plcd 1st*.........(11 to 8 op 6 to 4 tchd 13 to 8) 1
2175 TOMMY TRUNGLE 8-13 W Ryan (3) *trkd ldr aftr 5 fs, chlgd 4 out, wknd rpdly 2 out, tld off*.... (20 to 1 op 14 to 1) 3
Dist: 3½l, 25l. 2m 49.00s. a 19.20s (3 Ran).
(Mrs B Facchino), R Hollinshead

2206 Pennine Conditions Stakes Class D (3-y-o and up) £3,571 6f........... (4:25)

1747[5] CATRAIL (USA) 3-9-6 J Carroll (1) *slwly into strd, sn in tch and gng wl, led appr fnl furlong, quickened clr.* ....(11 to 10 on op 5 to 4 on tchd Evens) 1
2062* CASTLEREA LAD 4-10-0 W Ryan (5) *hld up, hdwy 2 fs out, ran on to go second ins last*..........(5 to 1 op 4 to 1) 2
2018[3] SATANK (USA) 3-9-0 N Connorton (3) *led till hdd appr fnl furlong, outpcd*...................(11 to 4 op 2 to 1) 3
1718 ELLE SHAPED (Ire) 3-9-8 D Holland (4) *trkd ldr, rdn 2 fs out, sn outpcd*...................(16 to 1 op 12 to 1) 4
1302[6] JADE CITY 3-9-0 L Charnock (8) *al outpcd.* ....(33 to 1 op 20 to 1) 5
1806 WATHIK (USA) 3-9-2 N Carlisle (6) *al beh.* ....(10 to 1 op 7 to 1) 6
2060 PERSIAN REVIVAL (Fr) (bl) 3-8-10 M Birch (2) *swrvd lft strt, rcd alone far side, in tch for 4 fs, eased.* ....(20 to 1 op 14 to 1) 7

Dist: 5l, 3½l, ½l, hd, 5l, 8l. 1m 13.82s. a 2.22s (7 Ran).
SR: 74/62/34/40/31/13/-/ (Sheikh Mohammed), J H M Gosden

2207 Freddy Fox Fillies Handicap Class D (0-80 3-y-o and up) £3,610 1m 3f 200yds....................... (4:55)

1919[3] LICORNE [75] 3-9-2 W Ryan (1) *hld up, hdwy 4 fs out, wnt second o'r 2 out, hrd rdn to ld wl ins last, battled on gmely*...................(6 to 4 fav op 7 to 4) 1
1770 SHADOWS OF SILVER [74] 5-10-0 M Birch (7) *led, strly rdn 2 fs out, hdd wl ins last, rallied gmely nr finish.* ....(20 to 1 op 16 to 1) 2
1929[3] FAMOUS BEAUTY [41] 6-7-7[3] (5*) A Garth (4) *slwly away, hld up in rear, hdwy o'r 2 fs out, ran on one pace.* ....(9 to 1 op 10 to 1 tchd 12 to 1) 3
1836* SILKY HEIGHTS (Ire) [61] 3-8-2 N Connorton (6) *hld up in tch, styd on one pace fnl 2 fs.* ....(5 to 1 op 4 to 1 tchd 11 to 2) 4
1802[3] DUNNELLON [77] 3-9-4 M Hills (2) *nvr far away, rdn and hdwy o'r 2 fs out, wknd ins last*..... (7 to 1 op 6 to 1) 5
1776[5] IBTIKAR (USA) [52] (v) 3-7-7 A Mackay (3) *prmnt, rdn o'r 3 fs out, wknd stdly*..................(20 to 1 op 16 to 1) 6
1488[2] ALYAKKH (Ire) [74] 3-9-1 N Carlisle (8) *trkd ldr till rdn o'r 4 fs out, wknd over 3 out*..............(6 to 1 op 6 to 1) 7
1979* GOODBYE MILLIE [68] 3-8-4 (5*,5ex) O Pears (5) *in tch, hdwy to chase ldr o'r 4 fs out, rdn and wknd over 2 out.* ....(7 to 1 op 5 to 1) 8

Dist: Hd, 3½l, nk, 3½l, 1½l, 1½l, 2l. 2m 32.97s. a 3.17s (8 Ran).
SR: 46/57/17/23/32/4/23/13/ (Lord Howard de Walden), H R A Cecil

LONGCHAMP (FR) (soft (race 1), heavy (2)) Friday July 2nd

Going Correction: PLUS 0.20 sec. per fur. (race 1), NIL (2)

2208 Prix de Saint-Patrick (Listed) (3-y-o) £14,337 1m.................. (2:50)

LYNTON (USA) 8-9 T Jarnet,.................... 1
TRUE BEARING (USA) 8-9 F Head,.................... 2
853[4] EMBROS (USA) 8-9 E Saint-Martin,.................... 3
867[7] HURTEVENT (Fr) 8-9 D Boeuf,.................... 4

Dist: ¾l, ¾l, 1l, hd, ¾l, nk, 2l. 1m 41.80s. a 4.30s (8 Ran).
SR: 55/53/51/48/ (K Abdulla), A Fabre

SANDOWN (good to firm) Friday July 2nd

Going Correction: PLUS 0.15 sec. per fur. (races 1,3,4,5), MINUS 0.10 (2,6)

2209 Price Waterhouse Conditions Stakes Class C (2-y-o) £4,435 7f 16yds..(2:00)

1949* LOMAS (Ire) 8-12 A Munro (4) *beh, hdwy frm 3 fs out, ran on und pres appr last to ld cl hme.* ....(9 to 4 on op 3 to 1 on tchd 2 to 1 on) 1
1598* BRAILLE (Ire) 8-10 Dean McKeown (2) *led one and a half fs, chsd ldr, led 2 out, rdn fnl furlong, ct cl hme.* ....(9 to 4 op 5 to 2 tchd 3 to 1) 2
1895* KINGSWELL PRINCE (Ire) 8-10 T Quinn (1) *pld hrd, led aftr one and a half fs to 2 out, styd on one pace.* ....(10 to 1 op 6 to 1 tchd 12 to 1) 3
1828[8] WOODS VENTURE (Ire) (bl) 8-10 W Woods (3) *chsd ldrs, rdn 2 fs out, wknd one and a half out.* (66 to 1 op 20 to 1) 4

Dist: 1½l, 2½l, 10l. 1m 32.48s. a 5.98s (4 Ran).
SR: 24/17/9/-/ (Fahd Salman), R Hannon

2210 Wharf Dragon Stakes Class A (Listed Race) (2-y-o) £10,113 5f 6yds....(2:30)

1766[3] ELRAFA AH (USA) 8-7 R Hills (6) *trkd ldr, drvn alng o'r one furlong out, styd on wl to ld fnl 100 yards.* ....(5 to 2 fav op 2 to 1 tchd 11 to 4) 1
1788[5] YA MALAK 8-12 R Cochrane (2) *led, drvn alng frm one and a half fs out, hdd and no extr fnl 100 yards.* ....(100 to 30 op 9 to 2 tchd 3 to 1) 2

1804* GREAT DEEDS 8-12 T Quinn (3) *outpcd, rdn alng hfwy, styd on fnl furlong, not rch ldrs.* ....(11 to 4 op 2 to 1 tchd 3 to 1) 3
1804[2] BID FOR BLUE 8-12 L Piggott (5) *chsd ldrs, rdn 2 fs out, styd on same pace*...............(7 to 1 op 6 to 1) 4
1535* SWEET DECISION (Ire) 8-7 J Reid (1) *prmnt till outpcd fnl 2 fs*..............................(25 to 1 op 16 to 1) 5
1665* BALANDRA BAY (Ire) 8-12 Pat Eddery (4) *speed to hfwy.* ....(7 to 1 op 8 to 1 tchd 9 to 1) 6

Dist: Nk, 2½l, ½l, 2½l, 4l. 1m 1.34s. a 1.84s (6 Ran).
SR: 46/50/40/38/23/12/ (Hamdan Al-Maktoum), H Thomson Jones

2211 Royal Hong Kong Jockey Club Trophy Handicap Class B Guaranteed minimum value £80000 (0-110 3-y-o and up) £45,950 1¼m 7yds.......... (3:05)

1887* SMARGINATO (Ire) [98] 3-8-10 (4ex) G Carter (16) *beh, hdwy 3 fs out, ran on wl to ld ins last, drvn out.* ....(12 to 1 tchd 14 to 1) 1
1719* RIVER NORTH (Ire) [94] 3-8-6 (4ex) K Darley (5) *beh, drvn and hdwy o'r 2 fs out, styd on fnl furlong, not rch wnr.* ....(3 to 1 fav tchd 4 to 1) 2
1638[3] DANA SPRINGS (Ire) [81] 3-7-7 G Bardwell (9) *beh, drvn and hdwy o'r 2 fs out, ran on strly ins last.* ....(12 to 1 op 10 to 1 tchd 14 to 1) 3
1768[3] PHILIDOR [84] 4-8-7 R Cochrane (13) *in tch, rdn and ev ch one furlong out, one pace.* ....(13 to 2 op 6 to 1 tchd 7 to 1) 4
1768[2] ROYAL SEATON [85] 4-8-8 Pat Eddery (14) *chsd ldrs, led o'r 2 fs out till ins last, sn outpcd*....(14 to 1 tchd 16 to 1) 5
1711[7] CAMDEN'S RANSOM (USA) [74] 6-7-11 Dale Gibson (17) *beh, drvn and hdwy on rls o'r 2 fs out, styd on one pace fnl furlong*..........(20 to 1 op 16 to 1 tchd 25 to 1) 6
1143[2] CHATHAM ISLAND [71] 5-7-8[4] (3*) B Doyle (10) *led till o'r 2 fs out, wknd fnl furlong*..........(25 to 1 op 33 to 1) 7
1768[4] DOUBLE FLUTTER [77] 4-8-0 J Quinn (6) *sn prmnt, rdn o'r 2 fs out, wknd appr last*.......... (16 to 1 tchd 20 to 1) 8
1064[5] PELORUS [80] 8-7-10 (7*) Antoinette Armes (11) *slwly away, beh, pld wide o'r 3 fs out, sn rdn, no imprsn.* ....(33 to 1) 9
1808* SHOW FAITH (Ire) [85] 3-7-11 (4ex) W Carson (1) *beh, rdn 3 fs out, no prog*.......... (5 to 1 op 9 to 2 tchd 11 to 2) 10
1711[5] BARFORD LAD [79] (v) 6-8-2 A Munro (15) *beh, drvn 3 fs out, no imprsn frm 2 out*..........(33 to 1 op 25 to 1) 11
1805[3] HIGHLAND DRESS [103] 4-9-12 M Roberts (2) *hdwy to chase ldrs 5 fs out, wknd o'r 2 out.* (7 to 1 tchd 8 to 1) 12
2064* WAINWRIGHT (USA) [84] 4-8-7 (4ex) J Reid (12) *chsd ldrs till wknd 2 and a half fs out*.......(14 to 1 op 10 to 1) 13
1720[8] GREEK GOLD (Ire) [74] 4-7-11 F Norton (8) *prmnt 7 fs.* ....(40 to 1 op 33 to 1 tchd 50 to 1) 14
1682[2] DREAMS END [83] 5-8-6 G Hind (3) *chsd ldrs, rdn 3 fs out, in tch till wknd quickly one and a half out*....(20 to 1) 15
LAP OF LUXURY [85] 4-8-8 N Day (4) *effrt 3 fs out, sn wknd*..............................(33 to 1 op 25 to 1) 16
1667* FAWZ (Ire) [78] 4-8-1 (4ex) R Hills (7) *prmnt 6 fs.* ....(25 to 1 op 20 to 1) 17

Dist: 1½l, 1½l, sht-hd, 2½l, 2½l, ½l, 3l, ¾l, 3l, 3l. 2m 7.38s. a 3.48s (17 Ran).
SR: 76/69/53/66/62/46/42/42/43/ (Gerecon Italia), J L Dunlop

2212 Sino Group Trophy Handicap Class C (0-95 3-y-o) £7,425 7f 16yds..... (3:35)

1833* FIELD OF VISION (Ire) [69] 8-5 T Williams (6) *in tch, drvn to ld ins fnl furlong, ran on wl.* ....(8 to 1 op 10 to 1 tchd 11 to 1) 1
1338[5] PRINCESS KRIS [78] 9-0 Pat Eddery (13) *beh, hdwy and not much room o'r 2 fs out, edgd lft ins fnl two, ran on, not rch wnr*.............................(6 to 1 tchd 7 to 1) 2
2136[9] SECOND CHANCE (Ire) [72] 8-8 M Roberts (16) *led till ins fnl furlong, no extr*..............(20 to 1 op 16 to 1) 3
1954[4] MY BEST VALENTINE [79] 9-1 F Norton (14) *in tch, rdn and kpt on fnl 2 fs*......................(12 to 1 tchd 14 to 1) 4
1239[6] OK BERTIE [76] 8-7 (5*) C Hodgson (4) *drvn and hdwy o'r 2 fs out, kpt on ins last*............(20 to 1 tchd 25 to 1) 5
1818[4] PRINCELY FAVOUR (Ire) [78] 9-0 W Carson (12) *pressed ldrs, rdn 2 fs out, wknd fnl furlong*... (12 to 1 tchd 14 to 1) 6
1483[7] TOP PET (Ire) [79] 9-1 R Cochrane (10) *chsd ldrs, rdn 2 fs out, wknd appr last*..............(14 to 1 op 10 to 1) 7
1808[9] DIGPAST (Ire) [78] 9-0 Dean McKeown (9) *beh, ran on fnl 2 fs, nrst finish*.......... (8 to 1 op 7 to 1 tchd 9 to 1) 8
1841[5] SIMPLY SOOTY [78] 9-0 J Reid (15) *sn tracking ldrs, still wl th whn hmpd ins fnl 2 fs, not reco'r.* ....(20 to 1 op 16 to 1) 9
491[5] KELLY MAC [70] 8-6 J Quinn (2) *nvr rch ldrs.* ....(25 to 1 tchd 33 to 1) 10
1947* FAIRY STORY (Ire) [78] 9-0 (5ex) R Hills (3) *prmnt, rdn and effrt 2 fs out, wknd o'r one out.* ....(7 to 2 fav op 4 to 1 tchd 9 to 2) 11
1801[3] BALLON [71] 8-4 (3*) B Doyle (7) *in tch 4 fs.* ....(16 to 1 tchd 20 to 1) 12
1978[7] HEATHFIELD (USA) [85] 9-0 (7*) T G McLaughlin (1) *nvr rch ldrs*..............................(33 to 1 op 25 to 1) 13
1859[6] WALNUT BURL (Ire) [68] 8-4 N Adams (8) *slwly into strd, al beh*..............................(20 to 1 op 16 to 1) 14
1408[2] PAIR OF JACKS (Ire) [75] 8-11 W Woods (11) *chsd ldrs 4 fs.* ....(12 to 1 op 10 to 1) 15

945⁴ ABLE CHOICE (Ire) [78] 9-0 L Piggott (5) *beh, lost tch 4 fs out*..............................(12 to 1 tchd 14 to 1) 16
Dist: 1½l, 1½l, ½l, 2½l, 1½l, nk, ¾l, hd, 3½l, ½l. 1m 30.46s. a 3.96s (16 Ran).
SR: 47/51/40/45/34/31/31/28/27/ (R W Huggins), M Johnston

2213 Sha Tin Claiming Stakes Class E (3-y-o) £3,532 1¾m................ (4:05)

1819* SUMMER WIND (Ire) 7-9 (3*) B Doyle (4) *made all, drvn and styd on wl fnl 2 fs*....................(9 to 2 op 4 to 1) 1
1784⁴ TRIPLE 8-11 Pat Eddery (1) *hdwy to chse wnr aftr 6 fs, rdn o'r 2 out, no imprsn*.... (11 to 10 fav op 5 to 4 on) 2
1417³ RECORD LOVER (Ire) 8-5 M Roberts (5) *chsd ldrs, drvn and effrt 3 fs out, no imprsn fnl furlong*. ....(8 to 1 op 7 to 1 tchd 9 to 1) 3
1479² FLAMING MIRACLE (Ire) (bl) 8-5 W Carson (3) *chsd ldrs, lost pl hfwy, rdn and one pace frm 2 fs out*. ....(9 to 2 op 4 to 1 tchd 5 to 1) 4
1935⁶ OMIDJOY (Ire) 8-2¹ W Woods (2) *beh, effrt 3 fs out, sn btn*. ....(8 to 1 op 7 to 1 tchd 9 to 1) 5
1662⁷ WILL HYDE 7-13 N Adams (6) *chsd wnr 6 fs, prmnt till wknd o'r 2 out*......(40 to 1 op 20 to 1 tchd 50 to 1) 6
Dist: 3½l, 1½l, 1½l, 5l, ½l. 3m 12.10s. a 17.80s (6 Ran).
(Ray Richards), D R C Elsworth

2214 Year of the Rooster Handicap Class E (0-70 3-y-o) £3,610 5f 6yds...... (4:40)

1606 STORMY HEIGHTS [53] (bl) 8-4 M Roberts (1) *hdwy hfwy, drvn to ld ins fnl furlong, styd on*. ....(12 to 1 tchd 10 to 1) 1
2164² NO EXTRAS (Ire) [66] 9-3 (6ex) B Rouse (4) *hdwy 2 fs out, ran on ins last, not pace of wnr*. ....(11 to 4 fav tchd 100 to 30) 2
1801⁴ FIRST OPTION [70] 9-7 K Darley (3) *pressed ldr, slight ld ins fnl 2 fs, hdd inside last, not quicken*. ....(6 to 1 op 5 to 1) 3
1966² GUSSIE FINK-NOTTLE (Ire) [58] (bl) 8-9 L Piggott (10) *led till ins fnl 2 fs, styd pressing ldrs till inside last*. ....(5 to 1 op 6 to 1 tchd 7 to 1) 4
1881⁸ MOVING IMAGE (Ire) [59] 8-10 C Dwyer (9) *outpcd, drvn and ran on appr fnl furlong*.......(14 to 1 op 12 to 1) 5
1990* CHARITY EXPRESS (Ire) [68] 9-0 (5*,6ex) L Newton (6) *in tch, rdn 2 fs out, sn wknd*...(7 to 1 op 6 to 1 tchd 15 to 2) 6
1977⁷ CHAMPAGNE GRANDY [68] 9-5 Pat Eddery (7) *outpcd*. .... (6 to 1 op 9 to 2 tchd 13 to 2) 7
2024⁵ DAANIERA (Ire) [68] (bl) 9-5 J Quinn (2) *slwly into strd, outpcd*..........................(25 to 1 op 20 to 1) 8
1740⁷ COMET WHIRLPOOL (Ire) [50] (bl) 8-1 R Price (8) *speed to hfwy*................ (16 to 1 op 12 to 1 tchd 20 to 1) 9
1728* KENSWORTH LADY [52] 8-3 N Adams (5) *slwly into strd, outpcd*.................(7 to 1 op 6 to 1 tchd 15 to 2) 10
Dist: 2½l, 1½l, nk, 2l, 1½l, ¾l, ¾l, sht-hd, 5l. 1m 2.30s. a 2.80s (10 Ran).
SR: 24/27/25/12/5/8/5/2/-/ (Miss Elizabeth Colver), J R Jenkins

SOUTHWELL (A.W) (std)
Friday July 2nd
Going Correction: MINUS 0.30 sec. per fur. (race 1), NIL (2,3,4,5,6)

2215 Ash Apprentice Handicap Stakes Class G (0-70 4-y-o and up) £2,070 5f ....(2:40)

1589⁷ KALAR [40] (bl) 4-8-1 (5*) Claire Balding (1) *made all, clr 2 fs out, rdn and edgd rght appr last, hld on*. ....(6 to 1 op 5 to 1) 1
1677* SUPERLATIVEMAXIMUS (Ire) [62] 5-10-0 J Weaver (5) *chsd wnr, rdn appr fnl furlong, ran on wl nr finish*. ....(2 to 1 fav op 7 to 4 tchd 5 to 2) 2
1874² FAMILY ROSE [37] 4-8-3 Stephen Davies (3) *al prmnt, ev ch entering fnl furlong, not quicken*.... (6 to 1 op 5 to 1) 3
1918⁶ BARBEZIEUX [47] 6-8-10 (3*) D McCabe (2) *in tch and pushed alng hfwy, sn rdn and kpt on fnl furlong*. .... (10 to 1 op 8 to 1) 4
1815³ LOFT BOY [57] 10-9-5³ (7*) Clare Byrnes (9) *outpcd and hng badly lft hfwy, some late hdwy*. .... (10 to 1 op 7 to 1) 5
1937⁶ LANGTONIAN [53] (bl) 4-9-5 Emma O'Gorman (8) *al rear*. ....(9 to 2 op 4 to 1) 6
1925 NILU (Ire) [53] 5-9-2 (3*) S Sanders (6) *chsd ldrs, rdn hfwy and sn wknd*................................(12 to 1) 7
1925 CAMINO A RONDA [31] 4-7-7¹ (5*) P McCabe (7) *chsd ldrs to hfwy, sn lost pl*.................(33 to 1 op 25 to 1) 8
1982⁷ WE'RE ALL GAME [53] 4-9-5 S D Williams (4) *stumbled strt, sn chasing ldrs, rdn and wknd 2 fs out*. .... (12 to 1 op 16 to 1 tchd 20 to 1) 9
Dist: ½l, 1½l, ¾l, 3½l, ½l, 1½l, 1½l, 2l. 59.60s. a 1.70s (9 Ran).
SR: 28/48/17/24/20/14/8/-/-/ (E Stockdale), D W Chapman

2216 East Midlands Electricity Claiming Stakes Class F (2-y-o) £2,243 7f (3:10)

1497⁶ EXTRA BONUS 8-11 (3*) J Weaver (8) *trkd ldrs, hdwy on outer to chal 2 fs out, rdn to ld and hng lft appr last, eased nr finish*................................ (7 to 1) 1
1959² HE SHALL REIGN 8-6 W Newnes (5) *chsd ldrs, effrt and ev ch whn hmpd appr fnl furlong, swtchd and ran on wl nr finish*................ (9 to 4 fav op 6 to 4) 2
1774³ RITA'S JOY 7-13 T Sprake (1) *led, rdn 2 fs out, hdd appr last, kpt on*............ (9 to 2 op 5 to 1 tchd 6 to 1) 3
1211⁹ MEMORABLE 9-0 P Robinson (3) *beh till styd on fnl 2 fs, not rch ldrs*.................. (6 to 1 op 5 to 1) 4
1895 OLYMPIC BID 8-4 (3*) Emma O'Gorman (2) *cl up, rdn o'r 2 fs out, sn wknd*.................. (16 to 1 op 14 to 1) 5
1245⁶ STORM 7-7 (7*) D Wright (4) *cl up till rdn and wknd 3 fs out*.......................... (14 to 1 op 12 to 1) 6
1905⁷ SWORDSMANSHIP 9-0 G Duffield (9) *cl up, rdn 3 fs out, sn btn*......................(7 to 2 tchd 4 to 1) 7
1909⁷ SPORT RACING CLUB 7-12 J Lowe (7) *al rear*....(14 to 1) 8
1983⁵ SEMAH'S DREAM 8-5 A Proud (6) *al rear*. ....(25 to 1 op 20 to 1) 9
Dist: Nk, ¾l, 8l, nk, hd, 1½l, 3l, 1l. 1m 31.50s. a 5.40s (9 Ran).
SR: 19/10/1/-/-/-/ (Induna Racing Partners), C F Wall

2217 J. Rothchild Handicap Class E (0-70 3-y-o and up) £2,847 7f......... (3:40)

1147 MUSIC DANCER [50] 4-8-11 G Duffield (9) *prmnt, hdwy and rdn 2 fs out, styd on und pres ins last to ld on line*. ....(7 to 1) 1
1696* PENNY BANGER (Ire) [54] 3-8-7 J Fanning (2) *chsd ldg pair, hdwy 3 fs out, rdn o'r 2 out, styd on to ld wl ins last, hdd on line*....................(2 to 1 fav tchd 9 to 4) 2
1875* ROSE FLYER (Ire) [62] 3-8-8 (7*) D McCabe (4) *led, quickened clr hfwy, rdn 2 fs out, wknd and hdd ins last*. ....(7 to 2 op 100 to 30) 3
1238⁹ SEA PRODIGY [38] 4-7-13 T Sprake (1) *chsd ldrs, rdn 3 fs out, sn one pace*..............................(20 to 1) 4
1588 MASTER REACH [44] (bl) 4-8-5 S Whitworth (3) *chsd ldr, rdn o'r 2 fs out, sn wknd*.......... (6 to 1 op 5 to 1) 5
1674* ROCKY BAY [36] 4-7-11 J Lowe (8) *chsd ldrs, rdn 3 fs out, sn wknd*.......................... (13 to 2 op 6 to 1) 6
1871⁴ APPEALING TIMES (USA) [67] 4-9-7 (7*) Claire Balding (7) *al beh*..................................(10 to 1 op 7 to 1) 7
1938⁸ KICK ON MAJESTIC (Ire) [40] 4-7-8 (7*) D Wright (6) *al outpcd and beh*..................(14 to 1 op 12 to 1) 8
Dist: Hd, 2l, 5l, hd, 2½l, 6l, 2l. 1m 30.20s. a 4.10s (8 Ran).
SR: 36/31/33/2/7/-/4/-/ (John Purcell), R C Spicer

2218 Elm Selling Stakes Class G (3-y-o and up) £2,070 1½m................ (4:10)

1676⁴ SMILES AHEAD 5-9-3 (7*) C Hawksley (6) *chsd ldrs and sn pushed alng, rdn hfwy, styd on to ld appr fnl furlong, ran on gmely*..........(13 to 2 op 6 to 1 tchd 7 to 1) 1
1657⁶ SCOTTISH BALL 4-9-2 G Duffield (7) *chsd ldr, rdn 3 fs out, hrd drvn and ev ch ins last, kpt on*. (6 to 1 op 9 to 2) 2
1809 INTRICACY 5-9-5 W Newnes (5) *hdwy to chase ldrs hfwy, effrt and rdn o'r 2 fs out, kpt on same pace*. (9 to 4 jt-fav op 9 to 2) 3
1900 EMPEROR ALEXANDER (Ire) (bl) 5-9-7 (3*) S D Williams (3) *set gd pace, quickened clr 4 fs out, rdn o'r 2 out, wknd and hdd appr last*.....(13 to 2 op 6 to 1 tchd 7 to 1) 4
1627⁸ FLYING AMY 3-8-3 T Sprake (4) *beh, steady hdwy 5 fs out, rdn 3 out and sn wknd*............(20 to 1 op 16 to 1) 5
1732⁵ MISS PIMPERNEL 3-8-0 (3*) J Weaver (2) *in tch, rdn alng 5 fs out, sn wknd and wl beh frm 2 out*. ....(9 to 4 jt-fav op 11 to 10) 6
1928 SOLAR KNIGHT 3-8-3 A Tucker (1) *chsd ldrs 4 fs, sn lost pl and wl beh*................................. (20 to 1) 7
Dist: Hd, 2l, 8l, 7l, 15l, 1½l. 2m 42.00s. a 8.10s (7 Ran).
SR: 29/20/19/8/ (J V Mills), P J Bevan

2219 East Midlands Electricity Maiden Stakes Class D (3-y-o and up) £3,348 6f ....(4:45)

ALJAZ 3-8-11 (3*) J Weaver (9) *chsd ldrs, hdwy 2 and a half fs out, quickened to ld wl ins last, pushed clr*. ....(9 to 2 op 3 to 1) 1
1673³ SURAGON 3-8-11 (3*) S D Williams (8) *led, rdn 2 fs out, hdd and no extr wl ins last*. (9 to 1 op 8 to 1 tchd 12 to 1) 2
1057⁷ CHEAT (USA) 3-9-0 K Fallon (5) *chsd ldr, rdn to chal 2 fs out, ev ch till no extr wl ins last*. .... (13 to 2 op 4 to 1 tchd 7 to 1) 3
NEVER SURE (Ire) 3-8-9 T Quinn (6) *cl up, rdn o'r 2 and a half fs out, sn wknd*. ....(11 to 10 fav op 6 to 4 tchd 7 to 4) 4
397 SWINGING TICH 4-8-9 (7*) S Sanders (10) *in tch, effrt 2 and a half fs out, sn rdn and no imprsn*.......(14 to 1) 5
1668⁶ PRAIRIE DAWN 4-9-2 W Newnes (1) *nvr a factor*. (33 to 1) 6
1617 CUT FINE 3-8-9 P Robinson (2) *chsd ldrs to hfwy, sn wknd*........................ (13 to 2 op 4 to 1) 7
SLOE BRANDY 3-8-9 G Duffield (7) *very slwly away, al outpcd and wl beh*............... (10 to 1 op 7 to 1) 8
1762⁵ PRINCE PALACIO 3-9-0 S Morris (3) *al outpcd and wl beh*. ....(16 to 1) 9
1239⁹ DYNAMIC GEORGE 3-9-0 S Whitworth (4) *al outpcd and wl beh*.......................... (20 to 1 op 16 to 1) 10
Dist: 3½l, hd, 5l, 2½l, 8l, 2½l, 3l, 4l, 6l. 1m 16.30s. a 2.90s (10 Ran).
SR: 42/28/27/2/-/-/ (Ron Dawson), Miss Gay Kelleway

2220 Oak Handicap Class D (0-80 3-y-o) £3,318 1m....................(5:15)

1729* GRAN SENORUM (USA) [76] 9-6 A Munro (5) *chsd ldg pair, effrt and hdwy 2 fs out, rdn to ld appr last, ran on gmely*..........(4 to 1 op 3 to 1 tchd 9 to 2) 1
2066^{7} KEYWAY (USA) [77] 9-7 G Duffield (3) *led, rdn 2 fs out, hdd appr last, kpt on.* ....(Evens fav op 5 to 2 tchd 11 to 10 on) 2
1872^{2} CHARLIE BIGTIME [64] 8-5 (3*) J Weaver (2) *trkd ldrs, hdwy on inner 2 fs out, rdn and ev ch whn not much room appr last, kpt on*......................(4 to 1 op 3 to 1) 3
1940^{9} MOHICAN BRAVE (Ire) [72] 9-2 K Fallon (6) *chsd ldrs, effrt and hdwy 2 fs out, sn rdn and kpt on fnl furlong.* ....(5 to 1 tchd 6 to 1) 4
1705* MYSILV [65] 8-9 P Robinson (4) *cl up, ev ch o'r 2 fs out, sn rdn and wknd*......................(7 to 1 op 9 to 2) 5
1503^{6} DON'T BE SAKI (Ire) [49] 7-1^{1} (7*) D Wright (7) *al rear.* ....(20 to 1 op 14 to 1) 6

Dist: ¾l, ¾l, nk, 7l, 15l. 1m 43.00s. a 4.00s (6 Ran).
SR: 46/45/30/37/9/-/ (Fahd Salman), P F I Cole

WEXFORD (IRE) (good to firm)
Friday July 2nd

2221 Ferrycarrig Hotel Claiming Race (3-y-o) £2,762 1½m 170yds........(7:30)

NURSE MAID (Ire) 7-10 (2*) D G O'Shea (11).......(5 to 2) 1
1755^{3} ASSERT STAR 7-11 (6*) J A Heffernan (12).....(7 to 4 fav) 2
1250^{5} DUCHESS AFFAIR (Ire) 7-7^{1} (4*) W J Smith (7)....(20 to 1) 3
1755^{2} MILLERS MILL (Ire) 8-5 W J Supple (3)...........(11 to 2) 4
1252^{9} ROOTSMAN (Ire) 8-3 J F Egan (6)...............(8 to 1) 5
1652^{6} SHARP AT SIX (Ire) (bl) 7-13 (6*) K M Chin (10).....(8 to 1) 6
2142^{8} EGALITE (Ire) 7-8 (6*) R V Skelly (2)................(8 to 1) 7
BLYTHE (Arg) 7-3^{1} (8*) R T Fitzpatrick (5)..........(8 to 1) 8
CATCH ME STARSKY (Ire) 7-11 (2*) R M Burke (9) (12 to 1) 9
MR KOZINSKI (Ire) 8-13 K J Manning (4).........(14 to 1) 10
1107^{6} STEADY DEAR (Ire) 7-12 Joanna Morgan (1)......(10 to 1) 11

Dist: Nk, 4½l, 3l, 11l. 2m 35.60s. (11 Ran).
(The B B Horse Racing Club), M J P O'Brien

2222 Nicky Rackard Memorial Maiden (4-y-o and up) £3,452 2m..........(8:30)

MIA GEORGINA (Ire) 4-9-11 K J Manning (4)....(5 to 2 on) 1
BULLANGUERO (Ire) (bl) 4-9-6 (8*) D M McCullagh (2) ....(7 to 2) 2
1987 SHERAVISION (Ire) 4-9-3 (8*) P O Casey (5).......(14 to 1) 3
1576 AFAWI (Ire) 5-10-0 N Byrne (3)..................(25 to 1) 4
SAHCHAIN (Ire) 5-9-9 (2*) R M Burke (1)...........(9 to 1) 5

Dist: 4l, 3l, 1½l, dist. 3m 45.60s. (5 Ran).
(Ms Patricia Reddy), J S Bolger

BATH (firm)
Saturday July 3rd

Going Correction: MINUS 0.40 sec. per fur. (races 1,4,5,6), MINUS 0.30 (2,3)

2223 Francasal Selling Handicap Class G (0-60 3-y-o and up) £2,343 2m 1f 34yds ....(2:20)

QUIET RIOT [39] 11-9-10 R Price (9) *lost pl 6 fs out, hdwy 4 out, led o'r 2 out, ran on wl.* ....(10 to 1 op 8 to 1 tchd 12 to 1) 1
1902 STANE STREET (Ire) [37] 5-9-8 W Woods (3) *chsd ldr, ev ch 2 fs out, ran on one pace.* ....(16 to 1 op 8 to 1 tchd 20 to 1) 2
LITTLE BIG [38] 6-9-9 J Williams (10) *wl beh till gd hdwy fnl 2 fs*..................(100 to 30 jt-fav op 11 to 4) 3
1902^{8} DOTS DEE [32] 4-9-3 N Adams (7) *hdwy 6 fs out, jnd ldrs o'r 2 out, sn wknd*..................(5 to 1 op 3 to 1) 4
2150^{4} GAY MING [33] 4-8-11 (7*) J Dennis (1) *drpd rear and rdn appr strt, hdwy fnl 2 fs*.................(100 to 30 jt-fav op 3 to 1 tchd 7 to 2) 5
2034^{8} THE GORROCK [27] (bl) 4-8-12 A Tucker (2) *led till wknd o'r 2 fs out*..........(40 to 1 op 20 to 1 tchd 50 to 1) 6
4697a^{9} SWIFT REVENGE [34] 3-8-2 J Quinn (5) *hdwy 6 fs out, wknd 3 out*..........(11 to 1 op 8 to 1 tchd 12 to 1) 7
1700^{4} QUALITAIR IDOL [39] 4-9-3 (7*) Marie Plowright (8) *pld hrd, jnd ldrs a m out, wknd o'r 2 fs out.* ....(14 to 1 tchd 16 to 1) 8
1840 WHERE ARE WE [38] (v) 7-9-9 A Clark (4) *prmnt till wknd o'r 3 fs out*..........(7 to 1 op 16 to 1 tchd 13 to 2) 9

Dist: 5l, 3½l, 3l, 4l, 2½l, ½l, 2½l, ¾l. 3m 53.40s. a 9.40s (9 Ran).
(Ms M Horan), J White

2224 Weston Maiden Auction Stakes Class E (2-y-o) £2,957 5f 161yds.......(2:50)

2067^{7} PRIMA SILK 8-9 D Biggs (1) *al prmnt, led 2 fs out, sn clr, cmftbly*........................(6 to 4 fav op 9 to 4) 1
1877^{3} ASKING FOR ACES 8-9 J Williams (7) *hdwy 2 fs out, ran on fnl furlong, no ch wth wnr*........(5 to 1 tchd 7 to 1) 2
1988^{4} DELROB 8-9 S Whitworth (4) *al prmnt, crrd rght o'r a furlong out, not quicken.* ....(5 to 2 op 9 to 4 tchd 2 to 1 and 11 to 4) 3
PETITJEAN (Ire) 8-7 (7*) T G McLaughlin (6) *chsd ldr, led o'r 2 fs out, sn hdd, edgd rght over one out, one pace.* ....(17 to 2 op 4 to 1 tchd 10 to 1) 4
2049^{5} THORNY BISHOP 9-0 S O'Gorman (3) *led till wknd o'r 2 fs out*..................(25 to 1 op 20 to 1 tchd 33 to 1) 5
HENRY'S LUCK 9-0 J Quinn (2) *strted slwly, al wl beh.* ....(11 to 2 op 5 to 2) 6

Dist: 2½l, 2l, ½l, 10l, 10l. 1m 12.30s. a 2.90s (6 Ran).
SR: 3/-/-/ (Three Ply Racing), M J Ryan

2225 Little Somerford Limited Stakes Class F (0-65 3-y-o and up) £2,539 5f 161yds ....(3:25)

1821^{8} SAMSOLOM 5-9-0 J Quinn (6) *al prmnt, led wl o'r one furlong out, quickened clr.* ....(100 to 30 op 3 to 1 tchd 11 to 4 and 7 to 2) 1
1981* MINDOMICA 4-8-6 (3*) Emma O'Gorman (2) *dwlt, gd hdwy on ins 2 fs out, hmpd o'r one out, ran on inside fnl furlong*..........(5 to 2 fav op 2 to 1 tchd 11 to 4) 2
1914^{3} FARMER JOCK 11-9-0 A Clark (8) *hdwy 2 fs out, not quicken fnl furlong*..................(8 to 1 op 5 to 1) 3
1865^{8} SUPREME BOY 4-9-0 N Adams (1) *al prmnt, one pace fnl 2 fs*......................(7 to 1 op 8 to 1 tchd 10 to 1) 4
1925 BELTHORN 4-8-9 S O'Gorman (5) *led 2 fs, wknd two furlongs out*..........(25 to 1 op 16 to 1 tchd 33 to 1) 5
1348 HONEY SEEKER 4-9-0 S Whitworth (7) *nvr nr to chal.* ....(4 to 1 op 5 to 2 tchd 5 to 1) 6
1319^{9} LYNDON'S LINNET 5-9-0 A McGlone (4) *led aftr 2 fs, hdd and edgd rght wl o'r one out, edged lft, wknd fnl furlong*..........................(12 to 1 tchd 16 to 1) 7
NOT SO GENEROUS (Ire) 3-8-2 T Sprake (3) *beh most of way*..................(8 to 1 op 10 to 1 tchd 12 to 1) 8

Dist: 4l, 2½l, 1½l, 4l, 2l, 1½l, sht-hd. 1m 10.60s. a 1.20s (8 Ran).
SR: 42/21/16/10/-/ (The Hammond Partnership), P Howling

2226 McKinnon & Clarke Claiming Handicap Class F (0-70 3-y-o and up) £2,686 1m 5yds......................(3:55)

893^{7} DAM CERTAIN (Ire) [48] 4-8-10 A McGlone (12) *hdwy 3 fs out, led o'r one out, ran on wl*......(12 to 1 op 8 to 1) 1
1912^{7} CLEAR LOOK [52] 3-7-13^{1} (7*) T G McLaughlin (1) *led till o'r one furlong out, not quicken*...............(9 to 2 jt-fav op 6 to 1 tchd 8 to 1) 2
1902 DON'T GIVE UP [42] (bl) 5-8-4 R Price (11) *wl beh till ran on fnl 2 fs*................(12 to 1 op 8 to 1 tchd 14 to 1) 3
1927* MUSTAHIL (Ire) [66] 4-9-7 (7*) S Drowne (10) *chsd ldrs, rdn alng o'r 4 fs out, ran on one pace*...........(9 to 2 jt-fav op 3 to 1) 4
1961 FULL SHILLING (USA) [45] 4-8-0 (7*) P McCabe (2) *chsd ldr, ev ch 2 fs out, one pace.* ....(11 to 1 op 16 to 1 tchd 10 to 1) 5
1902 LER CRU (Ire) [51] 4-8-13 T Williams (6) *dwlt, wl beh till styd on fnl 2 fs*....................(8 to 1 op 25 to 1) 6
1956^{8} SAREEN EXPRESS (Ire) [43] 5-7-12 (7*) S McCarthy (4) *al midfield, effrt o'r 2 fs out, no hdwy*. (11 to 2 op 3 to 1) 7
1956^{7} SLEEPLINE FANTASY [45] 8-8-7 W Woods (7) *hdwy on ins 3 fs out, rdn and wknd 2 out.* ....(9 to 1 op 6 to 1 tchd 10 to 1) 8
1623 MARSH WARBLER [35] 5-7-11 N Adams (8) *prmnt till wknd quickly o'r 2 fs out*..........(12 to 1 op 6 to 1) 9
1976^{8} IRISH DOMINION [58] 3-8-11 A Tucker (9) *outpcd.* ....(16 to 1 op 12 to 1 tchd 33 to 1) 10
1623^{3} COURTING NEWMARKET [43] 5-8-5^{1} S Whitworth (3) *prmnt till wknd o'r 2 fs out*.....(6 to 1 op 9 to 2 tchd 7 to 1) 11

Dist: 2½l, 1½l, ¾l, ½l, 1½l, sht-hd, 10l, 1½l, 1½l, ½l. 1m 40.30s. a 1.30s (11 Ran).
SR: 29/16/10/32/9/10/1/-/-/ (Starling O'Toole), R Ingram

2227 St John Ambulance Maiden Stakes Class D (3-y-o) £3,611 1m 3f 144yds ....(4:25)

NORTHERN BOUND (Ire) 9-0 A Clark (5) *al prmnt, led o'r 2 fs out, drvn out*.......(7 to 1 op 8 to 1 tchd 12 to 1) 1
1603^{7} CYRUS THE BOLD (Ire) 9-0 W Woods (4) *al prmnt, ev ch 2 fs out, ran on one pace*..............(8 to 1 op 4 to 1) 2
1831^{3} MIDNIGHT POSTCARD (Fr) 8-9 A McGlone (1) *chsd ldrs, rdn and outpcd o'r 3 fs out, styd on fnl 2 furlongs.* ....(15 to 8 on op 5 to 2 on tchd 7 to 4 on) 3
1911^{5} ALASKAN PRINCESS (Ire) 8-2 (7*) T G McLaughlin (8) *led till wknd o'r 2 fs out*....................(6 to 1 op 9 to 2) 4
1993^{9} LEGAL RISK (v) 8-9 S Whitworth (2) *al beh.* ....(12 to 1 op 8 to 1 tchd 14 to 1) 5
185^{6} ROWLANDSONS GOLD (Ire) 8-9 A Tucker (6) *al beh.* ....(40 to 1 op 20 to 1 tchd 50 to 1) 6
KAHILI GINGER 8-9 D Biggs (3) *rapid hdwy one m out, wknd quickly 5 fs out, tld off.* ....(40 to 1 op 20 to 1 tchd 50 to 1) 7

Dist: 4l, 5l, 10l, 4l, 1l, dist. 2m 28.20s. a 1.20s (7 Ran).
SR: 41/33/18/-/ (Sheikh Ahmed Al Maktoum), Major W R Hern

2228 Kenneth Robertson Handicap Class D (0-80 3-y-o) £3,143 1m 5f 22yds. .(4:55)

1603^{6} HILL OF DREAMS [75] 9-7 S O'Gorman (2) *chsd ldrs, rdn and outpcd 2 fs out, swtchd and rallied ins fnl furlong, led cl hme*.........................(11 to 2 op 5 to 1) 1
1400^{5} HARLESTONE BROOK [68] 9-0 A McGlone (4) *al prmnt, led o'r 2 fs out till nr finish*......... (100 to 30 op 11 to 4) 2
1662* LUNAR RISK [62] 8-8 W Woods (3) *stumbled badly aftr 2 fs, sn prmnt, jnd ldr and ev ch o'r one out, no extr nr finish*..............................(7 to 2 op 11 to 4) 3
1872* RUNAWAY PETE (USA) [75] 9-0 (7*) T G McLaughlin (1) *led aftr 3 fs till o'r 2 out, hrd rdn and rallied one out, wknd nr finish*..................... (6 to 5 fav op 7 to 4) 4
1690^{5} GALEJADE [49] 7-9^{1} A Tucker (5) *led till ran very wide aftr 3 fs, sn wl beh*........(12 to 1 op 6 to 1 tchd 14 to 1) 5

Dist: ½l, hd, 2l, 4l. 2m 54.80s. a 6.50s (5 Ran).

(Paul Mellon), I A Balding

BEVERLEY (firm)
Saturday July 3rd
Going Correction: MINUS 0.05 sec. per fur. (races 1,2,3,5,6,7), MINUS 0.10 (4)

2229 Lair Gate Selling Stakes Class G (2-y-o) £2,665 7f 100yds........... (1:55)

1909* DEMI-PLIE (v) 9-4 W Carson (7) *made virtually all, hrd pressed last 2 fs, hld on grimly*.......(7 to 2 op 9 to 2) 1
1964^{7} CARAPELLE 8-6 M Birch (2) *settled off the pace, gd hdwy to draw level fnl furlong, ran on*. .... (7 to 1 op 8 to 1 tchd 10 to 1) 2
1964^{9} OUT OF FAVOUR (Ire) 8-11 G Hind (8) *took str hold, settled into midfield hfwy, ran on wl finish*. .... (33 to 1 op 20 to 1) 3
1263^{9} JUST BILL 8-11 S Webster (13) *nvr far away, ev ch and rdn o'r one furlong out, not quicken*. ....(12 to 1 tchd 14 to 1) 4
1909^{3} LYING EYES 8-6 (7*) D McCabe (6) *settled off the pace, swtchd outsd to improve last 2 fs, one pace*. .... (9 to 4 fav tchd 5 to 2) 5
1964^{6} WINGS AHEAD 8-11 J Fanning (9) *al tracking ldrs, rdn o'r 2 fs out, no extr*...... (11 to 1 op 10 to 1 tchd 12 to 1) 6
1964^{5} SHARPISH WORDS (bl) 8-11 Dean McKeown (12) *chsd ldrs, effrt whn not much room and swrvd o'r 2 fs out, no imprsn*..................................(5 to 1 op 8 to 1) 7
1763 SONIC (Ire) 8-11 T Lucas (11) *chsd alng in midfield, effrt on ins 2 fs out, eased whn btn*. .... (20 to 1 op 16 to 1 tchd 25 to 1) 8
2042^{6} KNAYTON LAD (Ire) (bl) 8-11 L Charnock (10) *took keen hold, effrt and hrd drvn hfwy, no imprsn*. .... (25 to 1 op 20 to 1) 9
2042^{4} REAL POPCORN (Ire) 8-6 J Fortune (5) *broke wl to dispute ld, rdn and wknd quickly 2 fs out*. (10 to 1 op 9 to 1) 10
1828 LONE RISK 8-4 (7*) G Forster (4) *dsptd ld, rdn 2 fs out, sn btn*..................................(12 to 1 tchd 10 to 1) 11
1758^{8} STORM LEADER 8-11 M Wigham (1) *chsd ldrs, rdn whn bumped o'r 2 fs out, sn btn*...................(20 to 1) 12
1590 JACQUI'S STAR (Ire) (bl) 8-8 (3*) D Harrison (3) *al beh, tld off*..(33 to 1) 13

Dist: Hd, 1½l, 2½l, 1½l, 1l, nk, 1l, 4l, 7l, 2l. 1m 35.80s. a 5.50s (13 Ran).

SR: 16/3/3/-/-/-/ (Mrs C A B St George), D R Loder

2230 Jacksons Bakery Handicap Class D (0-80 3-y-o and up) £4,347 5f.... (2:30)

1925^{6} NORDOORA (Ire) [42] 4-7-2 (5*) Darren Moffatt (2) *made all, clr 2 fs out, kpt on strly*. .... (9 to 1 op 7 to 1 tchd 10 to 1) 1
1835 METAL BOYS [77] 6-9-11 (3*) D Harrison (9) *tucked away on ins, effrt and bustled alng o'r one furlong out, kpt on same pace*.......................(6 to 1 op 9 to 2) 2
2173^{3} SOBERING THOUGHTS [64] 7-8-8 (7*) G Forster (8) *nvr far away, rdn and edgd lft o'r one furlong out, kpt on*. .... (100 to 30 op 4 to 1 tchd 9 to 2) 3
2018 PALLIUM (Ire) [67] 5-9-4 K Fallon (6) *chsd ldrs, improved und pres o'r one furlong out, styd on*. .... (8 to 1 op 10 to 1 tchd 11 to 1) 4
1589^{6} HERE COMES A STAR [64] 5-9-1 S Morris (7) *trkd ldrs, effrt and drvn alng o'r one furlong out, styd on*. .... (13 to 2 op 6 to 1 tchd 7 to 1) 5
2018^{9} CATHERINES WELL [77] 10-10-0 T Lucas (3) *trkd ldrs, not much room o'r one furlong out, shaken up fnl furlong, one pace*............................ (6 to 1 op 5 to 1) 6
1835^{6} HEAVEN-LIEGH-GREY [66] 5-9-3 W Carson (5) *sluggish strt, nvr able to reco'r*. .... (3 to 1 fav op 5 to 2 tchd 100 to 30) 7
1537 FILICAIA [51] (v) 7-8-2 Kim Tinkler (1) *sluggish strt, nvr a factor*............................(33 to 1 op 25 to 1) 8
1420 ANOTHER LANE [72] (bl) 6-9-9 W Newnes (4) *wth ldrs, rdn aftr 3 fs, fdd*.....................(25 to 1 tchd 33 to 1) 9

Dist: 2l, 1l, hd, 1l, 2l, 2½l, 1½l, 1½l. 1m 3.90s. a 2.20s (9 Ran).

SR: 30/57/40/42/35/40/19/-/13/ (David C Young), J L Harris

2231 Millers Maiden Stakes Class D (3-y-o) £3,850 5f..................... (3:00)

1655^{7} EL ARZ 9-0 W Hood (7) *co'red up beh ldrs, weaved through to ld ins fnl furlong, drvn out*.........(5 to 1) 1
PENNY FAN 8-9 W Newnes (8) *nvr far away, led o'r one furlong out till ins last, kpt on same pace*...(2 to 1 fav) 2
951 SCENT OF POWER 9-0 N Carlisle (2) *missed break, improved frm off the pace last 2 fs, fnshd wl*..(16 to 1) 3
1826^{4} NEWBURY COAT 9-0 W Carson (1) *chsd ldg quartet, effrt und str pres one furlong out, not quicken*...... (3 to 1) 4
CALAMANCO 8-9 S Webster (4) *al hndy, ran green o'r one furlong out, grad wknd*......................(8 to 1) 5
168^{7} RYDAL WATER 8-9 Dean McKeown (5) *sluggish strt, outpcd and struggling hfwy, nvr nr to chal*...... (14 to 1) 6
1760 SHE'S A BREEZE (bl) 8-9 M Birch (3) *struggling to keep up aftr one furlong, nvr a factor*................. (33 to 1) 7
1655^{4} HUMBER'S SUPREME (Ire) (bl) 8-6 (3*) D Harrison (9) *dsptd ld for o'r 3 fs, fdd*..............................(5 to 1) 8
BENOSO 9-0 M Wigham (6) *unruly in stalls, missed break, al outpcd*...................................(8 to 1) 9
1869^{5} OSCAR THE SECOND (Ire) (v) 9-0 J Fanning (11) *dsptd ld for o'r 3 fs, sn rdn and btn*......................... (12 to 1) 10

Dist: ½l, 1½l, ½l, 3½l, 6l, 1½l, sht-hd, 1l, 3l. 1m 6.00s. a 4.30s (10 Ran).

SR: 9/2/1/-/-/-/ (Nagy Azar), J W Payne

2232 Hull Mitsubishi Centre Lady Amateur Riders' Handicap Class F (0-70 3-y-o and up) £2,758 1m 1f 207yds.... (3:30)

1800^{3} TOUCH ABOVE [47] 7-9-7 Mrs A Farrell (4) *al gng best, led wl o'r 2 fs out, pushed clr fnl furlong, readily*. ....(11 to 8 fav op 7 to 4) 1
1781* SCENIC DANCER [51] 5-9-6 (5*) Miss L Hide (6) *steadied strt, effrt and swtchd lft o'r 2 fs out, styd on fnl furlong*................................ (5 to 2 op 2 to 1) 2
BRILLIANT [68] 5-11-0 Mrs L Pearce (1) *wtd wth, improved to fltter o'r one furlong out, rdn and not quicken*. ....(3 to 1) 3
1781 BREEZED WELL [49] 7-9-9^{9} (5*) Mrs H Noonan (8) *nvr far away, led entering strt till wl o'r 2 fs out, no extr*. ....(14 to 1 op 10 to 1) 4
A GENTLEMAN TWO [40] 7-8-8^{1} (7*) Miss M Carson (7) *pressed ldrs, rdn whn pace lifted o'r 2 fs out, sn btn*. ....(20 to 1 op 25 to 1) 5
2175^{7} LAZY RHYTHM (USA) [47] 7-9-3^{3} (7*) Mrs C Hirst (5) *al hndy, led appr strt till entering straight, sn rdn and no extr*..................................(16 to 1 op 12 to 1) 6
1937 NOT ALL BLISS [37] 5-8-11^{9} (5*) Miss A Deniel (2) *wth ldr, came very wide strt, sn lost tch*...(100 to 1 op 50 to 1) 7
288 THE METROPOLE (Ire) [33] 4-8-0 (7*) Miss S Judge (3) *led till rcd very wide and hdd appr strt, sn lost tch*...(50 to 1) 8

Dist: 4l, 1½l, 2½l, 5l, 1½l, 12l, ½l. 2m 7.60s. a 6.20s (8 Ran).

SR: 35/31/45/21/2/6/-/-/ (Mrs J Hazell), T D Barron

2233 Golden Grain Handicap Class C (0-90 3-y-o) £4,962 1m 100yds........ (4:00)

1733* ROYAL INTERVAL [74] 7-12 (7*) D McCabe (1) *al hndy, led and quickened o'r one furlong out, kpt on wl*. ....(7 to 1 tchd 8 to 1) 1
1808^{6} RIBHI (USA) [90] 9-7 W Carson (6) *co'red up on ins, not clr run and swtchd appr fnl furlong, ran on und pres*. ....(6 to 4 fav op 5 to 2) 2
1762* KNIGHT OF SHALOT (Ire) [80] 8-6 (5*) Stephen Davies (4) *settled gng wl, led well o'r one furlong out, sn hdd, kpt on same pace*.......................(6 to 1 op 9 to 2) 3
1968^{4} DAYTONA BEACH (Ire) [66] 7-11 L Charnock (3) *settled off the pace, improved gng wl 2 fs out, swtchd lft and rght ins last, one pace*...................(8 to 1 op 5 to 1) 4
1459* MUTAKALLAM (USA) [71] 8-2 N Carlisle (2) *set gd pace till hdd wl o'r one furlong out, no extr*. (6 to 1 op 9 to 2) 5
1716^{4} QUEENS CONSUL (Ire) [71] 7-13 (3*) D Harrison (5) *pressed ldg trio, feeling pace and drvn alng 2 fs out, no extr*. ....(6 to 1 tchd 7 to 1) 6
1496^{7} NORTHERN CHIEF [62] 7-7 J Lowe (7) *chsd ldg quartet till fdd und pres last 2 fs*..................(8 to 1 op 7 to 1) 7

Dist: ½l, 2l, 1½l, 1½l, 1½l, sht-hd. 1m 45.20s. a 2.40s (7 Ran).

SR: 48/62/46/27/27/22/12/ (G L Barker), W G M Turner

2234 Boothferry Park Fillies Conditions Stakes Class D (2-y-o) £3,114 7f 100yds......................... (4:30)

1926* OVERACT (Ire) 8-12 W Carson (1) *nvr far away, rdn last 2 fs, ran on grimly to ld last 50 yards*. .... (5 to 4 fav op 11 to 10 tchd Evens) 1
1303^{2} LAMBENT 8-12 W Newnes (5) *tried to make all, hrd pressed o'r one furlong out, ct last 50 yards*. ....(3 to 1 op 9 to 4) 2
1580^{4} PHYLIAN 8-8 M Birch (2) *wth ldr, ev ch and drvn alng last 2 fs, kpt on same pace*. (9 to 1 op 8 to 1 tchd 10 to 1) 3
2067^{8} NSX 8-12 G Hind (4) *tucked away on ins, not clr run frm o'r one furlong out, unlucky*........ (3 to 1 op 5 to 1) 4

AVONDALE ROSE 8-5 (3*) D Harrison (3) *steadied strt, effrt and ran green hfwy, eased whn btn.* .... (14 to 1 op 12 to 1 tchd 16 to 1) 5
730 BOLDANDPRETTY 8-8 M Wigham (6) *chsd ldg quartet, struggling hfwy, sn lost tch.*...... (20 to 1 op 16 to 1) 6
Dist: ¾l, 1½l, hd, 7l, 6l. 1m 36.30s. a 6.00s (6 Ran).
SR: 2/-/-/ (Lady Hayward), D R Loder

2235 Walkington Hayride Handicap Class D (0-70 3-y-o and up) £3,687 2m 35yds ....(5:00)

1155[4] MY DESIRE [69] 5-9-6 (5*) Darren Moffatt (3) *trkd ldg bunch, niggled alng aftr 5 fs, styd on wl to ld appr fnl furlong, sn clr.*...... (100 to 30 op 3 to 1 tchd 7 to 2) 1
KING WILLIAM [44] 8-8-0 J Lowe (6) *settled gng wl, improved on bit to ld entering strt, hdd o'r one furlong out, no extr.*....................(2 to 1 fav op 9 to 4) 2
1873* DANCING DAYS [38] (v) 7-7-8[1] J Fanning (7) *trkd ldg bunch, led briefly appr strt, rdn and one pace last 2 fs.* .... (14 to 1 op 12 to 1) 3
1779[4] BOLD ELECT [61] 5-9-3 M Wigham (5) *trkd ldg quartet, feeling pace and rdn o'r 2 fs out, sn outpcd.* ....(5 to 1 tchd 11 to 2) 4
1847[3] PURITAN (Can) [63] 4-9-5 L Charnock (4) *pressed ldr, niggled alng frm hfwy, wknd quickly entering strt, tld off.* ....(9 to 2 op 4 to 1) 5
1929[9] FIVE TO SEVEN (USA) [68] 4-9-5 (5*) O Pears (2) *trkd ldg pair, wknd quickly entering strt, tld off.* ....(7 to 1 op 6 to 1) 6
1816[7] FOREST STAR (USA) [54] 4-8-5 (5*) Stephen Davies (1) *led till hdd and wknd quickly appr strt, tld off.* .... (16 to 1 op 20 to 1) 7
Dist: 4l, 5l, 2l, 15l, hd, 25l. 3m 35.50s. a 6.50s (7 Ran).
SR: 38/9/-/19/6/10/-/ (Miss Jane Spensley), Mrs M Reveley

HAYDOCK (good)
Saturday July 3rd
Going Correction: NIL (races 1,3,4), PLUS 0.20 (2,5,6)

2236 Shadwell Stud Apprentice Series Handicap Class E (0-80 3-y-o and up) £3,551 1¼m 120yds............ (2:00)

1637[4] MIDYAN BLUE (Ire) [67] 3-8-3 J Tate (6) *trkd ldg pair, hdwy 4 fs out, effrt to chal 3 furlongs out, sn led and forged clr.*........................ (11 to 2 op 5 to 1) 1
2000* DRUMMER HICKS [80] 4-10-0 C Hodgson (7) *in tch, hdwy o'r 3 fs out, chsd wnr 2 furlongs out, sn rdn and one pace.*..........................(5 to 2 fav op 2 to 1) 2
1981[7] PICKLES [48] 5-7-10 B Doyle (2) *slwly away and beh, hdwy 4 fs out, rdn o'r 2 furlongs out and styd on one pace.*...........................(8 to 1 tchd 9 to 1) 3
SHABANAZ [75] 8-9-9 O Pears (3) *hld up, hdwy 4 fs out, rdn to chase wnr 2 furlongs out, wknd appr fnl furlong.*................... (7 to 1 op 6 to 1 tchd 8 to 1) 4
2088[2] NO COMEBACKS [48] 5-7-10 D Wright (1) *dwlt, al rear.* ....(9 to 2 op 4 to 1) 5
1832* COMMON COUNCIL [61] 4-8-9 J Marshall (4) *cl up, led aftr 3 fs, rdn three furlongs out, sn hdd and wknd.* ....(7 to 2 tchd 4 to 1) 6
1320[9] RUBY VISION (Ire) [45] 4-7-7 Claire Balding (8) *led 3 fs, cl up till rdn and wknd 4 furlongs out*............. (33 to 1) 7
Dist: 10l, 2l, nk, 8l, nk, 5l. 2m 15.96s. a 4.96s (7 Ran).
SR: 39/44/8/34/-/3/-/ (Keith H Palmer), J M P Eustace

2237 Edward Symmons & Partners Handicap Class C (0-100 3-y-o) £4,978 6f ....(2:35)

1718[4] LOOK WHO'S HERE (Ire) [97] 8-11 (7*) S Sanders (10) *cl up, effrt to ld ins last, rdn, edgd lft and hld on.* ....(6 to 1 op 4 to 1) 1
1765 RUSTIC CRAFT (Ire) [96] 9-3 R Cochrane (2) *hld up and beh, hdwy 2 fs out, rdn and styd on strly ins last.* ....(10 to 1 tchd 12 to 1) 2
2018 SAINT EXPRESS [90] 8-11 A Culhane (5) *chsd ldrs, swtchd and hdwy to ld one and a half fs out, sn rdn, hdd and no extr ins last.*.............................. (14 to 1) 3
1718[8] SOUTHERN MEMORIES (Ire) [87] 8-8 L Piggott (6) *trkd ldrs, effrt and hdwy on outer 2 fs out, sn ev ch rdn and wknd ins last.*..........................(11 to 4 fav op 9 to 2) 4
1718[9] CYNIC [85] 8-6[1] J Reid (3) *al prmnt, ev ch one and a half fs out, sn rdn, edgd rght and wknd.* (8 to 1 op 7 to 1) 5
1614[4] SHARP PROSPECT [80] 8-1 Paul Eddery (7) *chsd ldrs, rdn 2 fs out and sn wknd.*.............. (14 to 1 op 12 to 1) 6
1801[2] THE SHARP BIDDER (Ire) [79] 8-0 G Carter (4) *hld up, hdwy on outer o'r 2 fs out, sn rdn and wknd over one furlong out.*.................... (8 to 1 op 7 to 1 tchd 9 to 1) 7
542[4] ABTAAL [89] 8-10 R Hills (9) *led till hdd one and a half fs out and sn wknd.*...................(15 to 2 op 6 to 1) 8
1835[4] PRESS GALLERY [86] 8-7 D Holland (8) *cl up, rdn 2 fs out, wkng whn hmpd o'r one furlong out.* .... (9 to 1 op 7 to 1 tchd 10 to 1) 9

1532* CELESTIAL KEY (USA) [100] 9-2 (5*) O Pears (1) *cl up on outer, rdn hfwy, wknd o'r 2 fs out.*.. (6 to 1 op 9 to 2) 10
Dist: Sht-hd, 1½l, 3½l, 3l, 2l, 1l, 1½l, sht-hd, 12l. 1m 14.92s. a 3.32s (10 Ran).
SR: 62/60/48/31/17/4/-/3/-/ (S L Edwards), B A McMahon

2238 Lancashire Oaks Class A (Group 3) (3-y-o and up) £18,930 1m 3f 200yds (3:05)

1638* RAINBOW LAKE 3-8-4 W Ryan (1) *trkd ldrs gng wl, hdwy 2 fs out, shaken up to ld appr fnl furlong, sn clr, easily.* ....(11 to 8 fav op 5 to 4 tchd 6 to 4) 1
1789[3] TALENTED 3-8-4 J Carroll (7) *trkd ldrs, hdwy o'r 3 fs out, led 2 and a half furlongs out and sn rdn, hdd appr fnl furlong and one pace.*............ (12 to 1 op 9 to 1) 2
1842[4] RANI (Ire) 3-8-4 B Doyle (9) *hld up, hdwy on outer 3 fs out, rdn 2 furlongs out, kpt on ins last.*..........(33 to 1) 3
2070[2] LUPESCU 5-9-3 G Carter (2) *hld up in tch, effrt on inner 3 fs out, sn rdn and not much 2 furlongs out, kpt on one pace.*.............................. (9 to 1 op 6 to 1) 4
1269[2] ANNE BONNY 4-9-3 R Hills (3) *chsd ldr, ev ch 3 fs out, sn rdn and one pace.*... (14 to 1 op 12 to 1 tchd 16 to 1) 5
1030* ATHENS BELLE (Ire) 3-8-4 S Raymont (8) *hld up, hdwy on outer 4 fs out and sn ev ch, rdn o'r 2 furlongs out and one pace.*.................(7 to 1 op 6 to 1 tchd 8 to 1) 6
1462* ANNA OF SAXONY 4-9-3 J Reid (5) *hld up, hdwy o'r 3 fs out, sn rdn and one pace.*..........(10 to 1 op 8 to 1) 7
1789[2] IVIZA (Ire) 3-8-4 Paul Eddery (6) *led, rdn 3 fs out, sn hdd and btn.*.......................... (6 to 1 op 9 to 2) 8
Dist: 7l, nk, nk, ½l, 1l, nk, ½l. 2m 33.44s. a 3.64s (8 Ran).
SR: 54/40/39/51/50/35/47/33/ (K Abdulla), H R A Cecil

2239 195th Year of the Old Newton Cup Handicap Class B (0-110 3-y-o and up) £17,506 1m 3f 200yds...........(3:35)

1770 GLIDE PATH (USA) [74] 4-8-2 R Hills (5) *hld up, gd hdwy 4 fs out, effrt 2 furlongs out and sn led, rdn out.* .... (20 to 1 op 14 to 1) 1
2061* HIGHFLYING [85] 7-8-8 (5*) J Tate (1) *sn chasing ldrs, hdwy to chal 4 fs out, rdn and led briefly 2 furlongs out, soon hdd, kpt on wl und pres.* (5 to 1 tchd 11 to 2) 2
1770[2] TURGENEV (Ire) [98] 4-9-12 D Holland (3) *hld up and beh, hdwy on outer 3 fs out, sn rdn and kpt on one pace fnl 2 furlongs.*........................ (8 to 1 op 7 to 1) 3
1785* LEARMONT (USA) [86] 3-8-1 J Carroll (11) *mid-div, hdwy o'r 4 fs out, rdn 2 and a half furlongs out, kpt on one pace.*......................... (9 to 4 fav op 11 to 4) 4
1770 OH SO RISKY [95] 6-9-9 R Cochrane (10) *hld up, steady hdwy 3 fs out, rdn and one pace fnl 2 furlongs.* (16 to 1) 5
1917* DUSTY POINT (Ire) [79] 3-7-1 (7*) Antoinette Armes (4) *beh and sn pushed alng, swtchd wide o'r 2 fs out and styd on wl ins last, nrst finish.*..........(11 to 2 op 9 to 2) 6
1526* SUN OF SPRING [85] 3-8-0 Paul Eddery (2) *chsd ldrs, rdn 3 fs out, wknd 2 furlongs out.*.........(10 to 1 op 9 to 1) 7
1484[2] DUKE OF EUROLINK [100] 4-9-11 (3*) J Weaver (7) *in tch, effrt and hdwy o'r 3 fs out, sn rdn and one pace fnl 2 furlongs.*................................ (6 to 1 op 11 to 2) 8
2091[4] WILSONIC [67] (v) 4-7-2 (7*) D Wright (8) *cl up, rdn 4 fs out, wknd and btn whn not much room 2 furlongs out.* ....(33 to 1) 9
1770[3] BLACKPATCH HILL [85] 4-8-13 G Carter (6) *prmnt, led 4 fs out, sn rdn, hdd 2 furlongs out and soon wknd.* ....(11 to 2) 10
1450* FIELDRIDGE [84] 4-8-12 J Reid (9) *led, hdd 4 fs out and sn wknd.*..........................(16 to 1 op 14 to 1) 11
Dist: 2l, 2½l, hd, ¾l, hd, 4l, 3½l, ½l, sht-hd, 15l. 2m 32.73s. a 2.93s (11 Ran).
SR: 59/66/74/48/68/38/36/57/23/ (The Jampot Partnership), J W Hills

2240 EBF July Maiden Fillies Stakes Class D (2-y-o) £3,993 6f.............(4:05)

1706[5] KISSING COUSIN (Ire) 8-11 W Ryan (6) *made all, rdn 2 fs out and edgd rght, edged lft ins last, hld on.* ....(8 to 1 op 5 to 1 tchd 9 to 1) 1
SUAAD (Ire) 8-11 R Hills (7) *chsd ldrs, effrt o'r one furlong out and ev ch whn not clr run and swtchd ins last, styd on nr finish.*........................(7 to 1 op 5 to 1) 2
MANHATTAN SUNSET (USA) 8-11 J Reid (8) *in tch, rdn 2 fs out, styd on ins last.*...............(7 to 1 op 4 to 1) 3
984[5] NORDICO PRINCESS 8-11 S Perks (3) *cl up, hdwy and ev ch o'r one furlong out, sn rdn and no extr ins last.* .... (20 to 1 op 16 to 1) 4
WILD PLANET (USA) 8-11 Paul Eddery (1) *in tch, effrt on outer 2 fs out, sn rdn and kpt on one pace.* ....(5 to 1 op 7 to 2) 5
PLAYING TRICKS 8-11 R Cochrane (4) *beh, hdwy o'r 2 fs out, sn one pace.*.............. (20 to 1 op 12 to 1) 6
2067[3] MICHELLE HICKS 8-8 (3*) M Fenton (5) *cl up, pushed alng hfwy, rdn o'r 2 fs out and and sn btn.* ....(5 to 4 on op 6 to 4) 7
1857[5] EWAR EMPRESS (Ire) 8-8 (3*) B Doyle (9) *cl up till rdn 2 fs out and wknd.*....................(16 to 1 op 10 to 1) 8
MY GALLERY (Ire) 8-11 L Piggott (2) *dwlt, al beh.* .... (8 to 1 op 12 to 1) 9
Dist: ½l, 1l, hd, 1l, 1l, 3½l, 1½l, 15l. 1m 15.84s. a 4.24s (9 Ran).
SR: 36/34/30/29/25/21/7/1/-/ (Sheikh Mohammed), H R A Cecil

2241 Houghton Green Handicap Class E (0-70 3-y-o and up) £2,883 5f.... (4:35)

2062 GONDO [63] (v) 6-9-0 (7*) S Knott (3) *cl up, led 2 fs out and rdn clr, wknd ins last, jst hld on*.....(6 to 1 op 5 to 1) 1
$4783a^{7}$ JUCEA [54] 4-8-12 Paul Eddery (7) *beh, hdwy 2 fs out, rdn fnl furlong and ran on strly nr finish*. ....(25 to 1 op 16 to 1) 2
2157^{4} EVER SO LONELY [56] 4-8-7 (7*) W Hollick (12) *cl up, ev ch o'r one furlong out, sn rdn and kpt on*..........(8 to 1) 3
1494^{4} LANGUEDOC [65] 6-9-9 J Carroll (8) *trkd ldrs, effrt and hdwy o'r one furlong out, styd on ins last*. ....(6 to 1 op 5 to 1 tchd 13 to 2) 4
1379^{7} LUCEDEO [69] 9-9-6 (7*) M Humphries (2) *slwly away and swtchd to stands rls, gd hdwy 2 fs out, not clr run and switched lft entering last, styd on*. (10 to 1 op 8 to 1) 5
2047^{4} SILVER STONE BOY [35] 5-7-7 G Bardwell (5) *chsd ldr, rdn and ran on fnl furlong*. (6 to 1 op 8 to 1 tchd 9 to 1) 6
1925^{5} SIMMIE'S SPECIAL [59] 5-9-3 W Ryan (11) *led, rdn and hdd 2 fs out, sn btn*............(4 to 1 fav tchd 9 to 2) 7
1982^{5} LAST STRAW [39] 5-7-4 (7*) Claire Balding (6) *cl up, rdn 2 fs out and sn wknd*..................(14 to 1 op 12 to 1) 8
1835 ABSOLUTION [62] 9-9-6 N Connorton (10) *cl up 3 fs, sn wknd*..........................(8 to 1 tchd 10 to 1) 9
1860^{8} SEAMERE [67] (bl) 10-9-4 (7*) D Wright (9) *nvr a factor*. ....(10 to 1 op 8 to 1) 10
CONSULATE [52] 7-8-3 (7*) J Edmunds (1) *nvr rch ldrs*. ....(16 to 1 op 14 to 1) 11
COAT OF DREAMS [42] 4-8-0 S Dawson (4) *cl up 3 fs, sn wknd*......................................(33 to 1) 12

Dist: Nk, 1l, ½l, hd, nk, sht-hd, 1½l, 1½l, ¾l, 5l. 1m 2.84s. a 4.04s (12 Ran).
SR: 46/36/34/41/44/9/32/6/23/ (Mrs Helen O'Brien), E J Alston

HAMBURG (GER) (good)
Saturday July 3rd

2242 Holsten-Trophy (Group 3) (3-y-o and up) £48,980 6f..................(3:35)

1465^{4} ROBIN DES PINS (USA) 5-9-6 C Asmussen, *hld up, 4th strt, str run on outsd to ld one and a half fs out, unchlgd*.. 1
1646^{5} NIGHT JAR 6-9-0 K Woodburn, *wtd wth, prog on outsd 2 fs out, no ch with wnr*.................................. 2
MORE WIND (Ger) 7-9-2 A Tylicki, *led till hdd one and a half fs out*.. 3
MONTEPULCIANO (USA) 4-9-4 G Bocskai, *rcd in 3rd, cl up 2 fs out, unbl to quicken*.................................. 4
594^{6} TI ZINO (Fr) 3-8-7 M Hofer, *trkd ldr, rdn and no extr 2 fs out*.. 5
NIGHT MELODY (Ire) 3-8-7 K Darley, *hld up, hdwy 3 fs out, sn rdn and btn*... 6
FLEET FOR EUROPE 4-9-4 A Bond, *al beh*.............. 7

Dist: 4½l, 1½l, hd, ¾l, 1l, 2l. 1m 9.70s. (7 Ran).
(S S Niarchos), F Boutin

HOLLYWOOD (USA) (firm)
Saturday July 3rd

2243 Hollywood Gold Cup (Grade 1) (3-y-o and up) £273,179 1¼m..............

BEST PAL (USA) 5-8-9 C Black,............(11 to 10 fav) 1
146^{2} BERTRANDO (USA) 4-8-6 A Solis,................(7 to 2) 2
146^{3} MAJOR IMPACT (USA) 4-8-1 G Stevens,..........(84 to 10) 3
MARQUETRY (USA) 6-8-6 K Desormeaux,.........(7 to 2) 4
1541^{5} MISSIONARY RIDGE 6-8-3 C Nakatani,............(7 to 2) 5
671* LATIN AMERICAN (USA) 5-8-5 E Delahoussaye, (48 to 10) 6
CAMPO MARZIO (Chi) 5-7-11 J Garcia,..........(29 to 1) 7
1331* ROUGH HABIT (NZ) 7-8-5 M Dittman,.........(116 to 10) 8
LOTTERY WINNER (USA) 4-8-2 C McCarron,....(146 to 1) 9
POTRILLON (Arg) 5-8-3 L Pincay Jr,.............(19 to 1) 10

Dist: 2½l, 5½l, nk, nose, 4½l, 6l, ¾l, 2l, 6l. 2m 0.00s. (10 Ran).
(Golden Eagle Farm), I Jory

NAAS (IRE) (good)
Saturday July 3rd

Going Correction: MINUS 0.05 sec. per fur. (races 1,5), MINUS 0.20 (2,3,4,6)

2244 Main Street EBF Fillies Maiden (2-y-o) £3,795 6f...................... (2:00)

2037^{3} RIDGE POOL (Ire) 8-11 R Hughes (10).........(5 to 4 fav) 1
1509^{4} GO MILLIE (Ire) 8-11 W J Supple (3).............. (4 to 1) 2
1104^{5} ASTRADANE (Ire) 8-11 J F Egan (5)..............(16 to 1) 3
SAFKANA (Ire) 8-11 J P Murtagh (7)...............(7 to 2) 4
896^{8} MON PANACHE (Ire) 8-11 N G McCullagh (9)..... (16 to 1) 5
PRINCESS SHERA (Ire) 8-11 W J O'Connor (8)....(11 to 1) 6
1854^{5} SUSIE SUNSHINE (Ire) 8-5 (6*) J A Heffernan (1)...(10 to 1) 7
JENNY JINGLE (Ire) 8-11 K J Manning (6)........ (16 to 1) 8
1994^{8} AVALIN (Ire) 8-11 P Lowry (2)................... (20 to 1) 9
2037 EUROFLOWER (Ire) 8-11 S Craine (12)...........(14 to 1) 10
USTER (Ire) 8-9 (2*) R M Burke (11)..............(14 to 1) 11

Dist: 2½l, ½l, 1½l, 3½l. 1m 13.20s. a 3.70s (11 Ran).
SR: 17/7/5/-/-/-/ (H E The President Of Ireland), M J Grassick

2245 Prosperous Handicap (0-105 3-y-o and up) £6,900 1m 3f.............. (2:30)

1025^{2} NASSAU [-] 6-8-0 (4*) W J Smith (4)..............(7 to 2) 1
2035^{2} TBAAREEH (USA) [-] 3-7-11 (6*) J A Heffernan (3) ....(2 to 1 fav) 2
2035^{8} TONY'S FEN [-] 4-9-1 W J Supple (1)............. (9 to 2) 3
2039^{9} ALALJA (Ire) [-] 3-8-4 J F Egan (5).................. (5 to 1) 4
1514 DOMINO'S RING (Ire) [-] (bl) 4-8-3 N G McCullagh (2) ....(14 to 1) 5
1552^{8} PRE-EMINENT [-] 6-9-13 P Shanahan (6).........(10 to 1) 6

Dist: Nk, hd, 4l, 2½l. 2m 20.70s. a 4.20s (6 Ran).
SR: 26/24/35/16/10/-/ (Michael W J Smurfit), D K Weld

2246 Owenstown Stud FF Tuthill EBF Race (2-y-o) £5,175 7f.................(3:00)

305* COIS NA TINE (Ire) 9-2 C Roche (7)........... (2 to 1 fav) 1
2075^{6} GENUINE BID (Ire) 8-12 (4*) P Carberry (6).........(7 to 1) 2
1650* LA BERTA (Ire) 8-13 W J O'Connor (3).............(4 to 1) 3
1792* MY RAGAMUFFIN (Ire) 8-13 J P Murtagh (4).......(7 to 1) 4
BETTER FOLLY (Ire) 8-6 W J Supple (5)........... (10 to 1) 5
1550^{5} QUASIMODO (Ire) 8-3 (6*) R V Skelly (1)............(5 to 1) 6
OVERSEAS TRANSFER (Ire) 8-9 P Shanahan (2)... (5 to 1) 7

Dist: 5½l, 1l, hd, 3½l. 1m 25.30s. a 2.70s (7 Ran).
SR: 40/23/17/16/ (Niall Quinn), J S Bolger

2247 Sallins EBF Race (3-y-o and up) £3,450 1m...............................(3:30)

670^{6} ORMSBY (Ire) 4-9-5 P Shanahan (8)............. (14 to 1) 1
2035^{3} MUBADIR (USA) 5-9-1 (4*) P Carberry (9)..........(8 to 1) 2
2074^{8} SHAHIK (USA) 3-8-10 W J Supple (3)..............(5 to 1) 3
ENDSONG (USA) 3-8-7 C Roche (10).................(5 to 1) 4
1646^{6} DARK REEF 3-9-3 J P Murtagh (4)...................(8 to 1) 5
1568* ABEL TASMAN (USA) 3-8-13 P V Gilson (2).... (3 to 1 fav) 6
1856^{2} THATCHING CRAFT (Ire) 4-9-5 W J O'Connor (7)..(14 to 1) 7
2039^{6} GLOWING VALUE (Ire) (bl) 3-8-4 (6*) J J Behan (6) (12 to 1) 8
1549* LEGAL FLAIR (Ire) 3-9-3 R Hughes (1)...............(9 to 2) 9
1622* GOODIES TWO STEP (Ire) 3-8-13 N G McCullagh (5) ....(25 to 1) 10

Dist: Nk, sht-hd, 4l, sht-hd. 1m 37.60s. a 1.80s (10 Ran).
SR: 54/53/43/28/37/-/ (Peter Wetzel), D K Weld

2248 Furness Handicap (0-80 3-y-o and up) £2,760 6f..................... (3:55)

1922^{5} OICHE MHAITH [-] (bl) 3-8-8 R Hughes (14).......(12 to 1) 1
1856^{4} NUNIVAK (USA) [-] 5-9-0 (6*) R V Skelly (11)....... (7 to 1) 2
1923* PILGRIM BAY (Ire) [-] 3-9-0 (2*,3ex) D G O'Shea (5) ....(9 to 2 fav) 3
1795^{6} MASTER WORK [-] (bl) 5-7-9 Joanna Morgan (6)... (7 to 1) 4
1619^{7} FAIRY BRIDE (Ire) [-] 3-7-9 (6*) J J Behan (16).....(33 to 1) 5
1795^{8} FASTAFLOW (Ire) [-] 3-8-7 W J Supple (8)..........(10 to 1) 6
1795 TORCH SINGER [-] 3-7-7 (8*) J J Mullins (19).....(33 to 1) 7
1795^{5} AFTERGLOW (Ire) [-] (bl) 4-8-6 L O'Shea (15).......(9 to 1) 8
1553 DRESS DANCE (Ire) [-] 3-8-9 A J Nolan (2).........(33 to 1) 9
2073 BENE MERENTI (Ire) [-] (bl) 3-9-4 K J Manning (4) (12 to 1) 10
666 CISEAUX (USA) [-] (bl) 4-10-0 P Shanahan (1)...... (6 to 1) 11
1293 SALLUSTAR [-] (bl) 8-9-2 J P Murtagh (10)..........(8 to 1) 12
1825* FOREST [-] 3-9-4 (3ex) S Craine (17)...............(13 to 2) 13
1620 LOWLACK [-] 3-8-6 D V Smith (7)................(20 to 1) 14
1620 BELLE OF DREAMS (Ire) [-] 5-7-8^{2} (4*) W J Smith (12) ....(20 to 1) 15
EVOCATIVE (Ire) [-] 4-8-11 J F Egan (3)............(33 to 1) 16
280 SANDCHORUS (Ire) [-] (bl) 3-8-0 (8*) G Coogan (9) (20 to 1) 17
1105 EILEENS HOPE (Ire) [-] 3-8-4 (10*) T M Finn (18)...(33 to 1) 18

Dist: ¾l, 1½l, nk, ½l. 1m 11.60s. a 2.10s (18 Ran).
SR: 46/55/45/23/27/-/ (Mrs J Costelloe), Declan Gillespie

2249 Virginia EBF Maiden (3-y-o and up) £3,450 1¼m................... (4:30)

550^{9} BLAZING SPECTACLE (Ire) 3-8-9 P Shanahan (15) (8 to 1) 1
KHALYANI (Ire) 3-8-9 J P Murtagh (8)............... (3 to 1) 2
PLATINUM EMPIRE (USA) 3-8-9 P V Gilson (6).....(8 to 1) 3
1236^{3} GLAMOROUS BRIDE (Fr) 3-8-6 W J Supple (12) (9 to 4 fav) 4
1855^{4} MY KERRY DANCER (USA) 3-8-9 S Craine (7)..... (6 to 1) 5
ENIMDEE (Ire) 3-8-6 J F Egan (4)...................(12 to 1) 6
790^{7} LADIES GALLERY (Ire) 3-8-4 (2*) R M Burke (16)... (8 to 1) 7
1333 NURSES RUN (Ire) 3-8-6 J D Eddery (14).........(33 to 1) 8
KEPPOLS HARRIER (Ire) 3-8-9 A J Nolan (3)......(50 to 1) 9
1048 SELUNE (Fr) 3-8-6 N G McCullagh (9)...............(12 to 1) 10
QUIET CONFIDENCE (Ire) 3-8-6 W J O'Connor (10) (10 to 1) 11
1997^{8} LIMAHEIGHTS (Ire) 3-7-12 (8*) P J Smullen (1).... (20 to 1) 12
1755^{5} GARDENVALE VIC (Ire) 3-8-9 K J Manning (5).....(16 to 1) 13
1649 SIMPLE DANCER (Ire) 3-8-9 R Hughes (2)..........(50 to 1) 14
1796^{5} CRISSY (Ire) 3-8-4 (2*) D G O'Shea (13).......... (12 to 1) 15
848^{5} PENNY A DAY (Ire) 3-8-9 C Roche (11)............(12 to 1) 16

Dist: ½l, 2½l, 3l, 2l. 2m 11.30s. a 7.30s (16 Ran).
SR: 2/1/-/-/-/-/ (Moyglare Stud Farm), D K Weld

SANDOWN (good to firm)
Saturday July 3rd

Going Correction: PLUS 0.05 sec. per fur. (races 1,2,4,5,7), NIL (3,6)

2250 EBF Full Moon Maiden Stakes Class D (2-y-o) £4,182 7f 16yds..........(2:15)

1949[2] SILVER WEDGE (USA) 9-0 Pat Eddery (6) *trkd ldr, led o'r 3 fs out, rdn out*...... (100 to 30 op 3 to 1 tchd 5 to 1) 1
1640[9] BLAIR CASTLE (Ire) 9-0 L Dettori (10) *trkd ldrs, kpt on wl fnl 2 fs*.................(9 to 2 op 4 to 1 tchd 13 to 2) 2
1828[7] DANGER POINT 9-0 A Munro (9) *chsd ldrs, lost pl aftr 2 fs, hdwy o'r 3 out, hrd rdn over one out, kpt on.* ....(8 to 1 op 7 to 1 tchd 9 to 1) 3
1828[5] SANS ECOCIDE 9-0 G Duffield (8) *mid-div, outpcd 2 fs out, hrd rdn o'r one out, styd on.* ....(12 to 1 op 8 to 1 tchd 14 to 1) 4
687 CALLING (USA) 9-0 M Hills (11) *chsd ldrs, rdn o'r 2 fs out, wknd over one out*............... (50 to 1 op 33 to 1) 5
KHAMASEEN 9-0 M J Kinane (2) *strted slwly, beh, rdn and hdwy o'r 2 fs out, styd on, nrst finish.* .... (5 to 2 fav op 9 to 4 tchd 7 to 4 and 11 to 4) 6
ONE WILD OAT 8-9 M Roberts (4) *trkd ldrs, rdn o'r 2 fs out, wknd appr last*...(10 to 1 op 6 to 1 tchd 12 to 1) 7
LIMOSA 8-9 P Robinson (3) *strted slwly, nvr on terms.* ....(25 to 1 op 20 to 1 tchd 33 to 1) 8
LAKE PARVA 9-0 N Day (5) *chsd ldrs, sn pushed alng, rdn and ran green o'r 2 fs out, soon btn.* ....(12 to 1 op 5 to 1 tchd 14 to 1) 9
730 DOWN D ISLANDS 9-0 R Perham (1) *al beh.* ....(25 to 1 op 16 to 1) 10
1905[8] DANCING LAWYER 9-0 B Rouse (7) *rstrained strt, hld up in rear, nvr plcd to chal*..........(50 to 1 op 20 to 1) 11
1536[5] LEGENDARY LADY 8-9 F Norton (12) *led til hdd o'r 3 fs out, wknd quickly*..............(50 to 1 op 25 to 1) 12

Dist: 1l, sht-hd, 7l, hd, nk, sht-hd, 1½l, nk, ¾l, 7l. 1m 31.03s. a 4.53s (12 Ran).
SR: 37/34/33/12/11/10/4/-/3/ (Mrs Shirley Robins), G Lewis

2251 Commonwealth Handicap Class C (0-90 3-y-o and up) £5,550 2m 78yds ....(2:45)

967[3] ASIAN PUNTER (Ire) [66] 4-8-11 (7*) N Varley (3) *hld up beh, hdwy o'r 2 fs out, edgd rght and led one furlong out, pushed out*..........................(6 to 1 op 9 to 2) 1
1840[5] GREEN LANE (USA) [66] 5-9-4 A Munro (5) *chsd ldrs, rdn o'r 2 fs out, short of room on ins appr last, swtchd lft and ran on wl fnl furlong*.... (4 to 1 jt-fav tchd 9 to 2) 2
1772* HOOSIE [71] 3-8-6 M Roberts (4) *led til hdd one furlong out, no extr*..........(15 to 2 op 8 to 1 tchd 10 to 1) 3
1827[6] ROSGILL [62] 7-9-0 P Robinson (2) *trkd ldrs, hng rght o'r 2 fs out, one pace*..................(12 to 1 op 10 to 1) 4
1809[7] STAR QUEST [70] (v) 6-9-8 M J Kinane (1) *beh, rdn o'r 3 fs out, no imprsn*..........(14 to 1 op 12 to 1 tchd 16 to 1) 5
1688[2] SPECTACULAR DAWN [76] 4-10-0 Pat Eddery (6) *trkd ldr, rdn 3 fs out, one pace whn hmpd and snatched up appr fnl furlong*..............(9 to 2 op 4 to 1 tchd 5 to 1) 6
1752[5] SNOW BOARD [76] (bl) 4-10-0 G Duffield (7) *wtd wth, cld 5 fs out, rdn and btn 3 out*.......(4 to 1 jt-fav op 5 to 2) 7
2150[2] BRIGGSMAID [49] 5-7-12 (3*) N Kennedy (8) *hld up beh, effrt o'r 3 fs out, btn quickly.* .... (13 to 2 op 7 to 1 tchd 8 to 1) 8

Dist: Nk, 1½l, ¾l, 3l, 6l, 5l, 2½l. 3m 38.23s. a 9.23s (8 Ran).
SR: 20/19/5/11/16/16/11/-/ (Rory C Leader), A Hide

2252 Advanced Micro Devices Sprint Stakes Class A (Listed Race) (3-y-o and up) £14,005 5f 6yds.........(3:20)

1465[3] LOCHSONG 5-8-12 L Dettori (7) *made all, clr o'r one furlong out, unchlgd.* (85 to 40 op 2 to 1 tchd 5 to 2) 1
1807[6] BUNTY BOO 4-8-12 A Mackay (2) *outpcd, beh, hdwy o'r one furlong out, ran on wl, no ch wth wnr.* ....(11 to 1 op 8 to 1 tchd 12 to 1) 2
1614* LUCKY PARKES 3-8-6 Pat Eddery (3) *led chasing grp, hrd rdn 2 fs out, one pace.* ....(7 to 4 fav op 13 to 8 tchd 11 to 8) 3
1679[6] MEDAILLE D'OR (v) 5-9-7 A Munro (1) *chsd ldrs, hrd rdn o'r one furlong out, no imprsn*...(20 to 1 tchd 22 to 1) 4
1680[5] BOLD LEZ 6-9-3 M Roberts (5) *chsd ldrs till outpcd fnl 2 fs*.............................(10 to 1 op 12 to 1) 5
1806[8] BRANSTON ABBY (Ire) 4-8-12 G Duffield (4) *al beh.* ....(5 to 1 tchd 11 to 2) 6
1718* ARADANZA 3-8-11 M J Kinane (6) *pushed alng thrght, in tch till outpcd frm hfwy*.........(20 to 1 tchd 25 to 1) 7

Dist: 4l, 2l, 2l, 1½l, 2½l, hd. 1m 0.32s. a 0.82s (7 Ran).
SR: 82/66/52/59/49/34/32/ (J C Smith), I A Balding

2253 Coral-Eclipse Stakes Class A (Group 1) (3-y-o and up) £147,760 1¼m 7yds ....(4:05)

1472* OPERA HOUSE 5-9-7 M J Kinane (2) *trkd ldrs, cld o'r 2 fs out, led one and a half out, rdn out, jst hld on.* ....(9 to 2 op 5 to 1 tchd 11 to 2) 1
1366[2] MISIL (USA) 5-9-7 L Dettori (8) *chsd ldrs, rdn alng o'r 3 fs out, hdwy und pres 2 out, ran on wl fnl furlong, jst fld.* ....(25 to 1 op 20 to 1 tchd 33 to 1) 2
1448 TENBY 3-8-10 Pat Eddery (6) *trkd ldg pair, pushed alng o'r 5 fs out, outpcd over one out, rallied und pres, kpt on wl*.............................(11 to 4 op 2 to 1) 3
1882* KARINGA BAY 6-9-7 B Rouse (3) *trkd ldr, led o'r 2 fs out till hdd one and a half out, one pace.* ....(40 to 1 op 33 to 1) 4
1448[5] BARATHEA (Ire) 3-8-10 M Roberts (7) *hld up, took keen hold, hdwy to hold ev ch 2 fs out, shaken up and one pace appr last*............... (5 to 2 fav tchd 11 to 4) 5
1366* ARCANGUES (USA) 5-9-7 T Jarnet (1) *hld up in last pl, effrt o'r 2 fs out, not pace to chal.* ....(11 to 2 op 5 to 1 tchd 6 to 1) 6
1472[2] ENVIRONMENT FRIEND 5-9-7 G Duffield (5) *hld up, effrt and outpcd frm o'r 2 fs out.* ....(13 to 2 op 8 to 1 tchd 9 to 1) 7
1085* GREAT PALM (USA) 4-9-7 A Munro (4) *led till hdd o'r 2 fs out, wknd*.......................(16 to 1 tchd 20 to 1) 8

Dist: Sht-hd, 1½l, 3l, nk, ¾l, 5l, 2l. 2m 6.25s. a 2.35s (8 Ran).
SR: 89/88/74/79/67/76/66/62/ (Sheikh Mohammed), M R Stoute

2254 Sandown Rated Class B Handicap (0-100 3-y-o and up) £12,822 1m 14yds ....(4:40)

1471* PETER DAVIES (USA) [99] 5-9-7 L Dettori (9) *hld up, smooth hdwy 2 fs out, shaken up and quickened to ld ins last, cmftbly*.................... (100 to 30 fav op 5 to 1) 1
1845[5] TALENT (USA) [85] (v) 5-8-7 A Munro (6) *trkd ldr, led o'r 3 fs out till hdd and no extr ins last.* ....(5 to 1 op 6 to 1 tchd 13 to 2) 2
1768 GYMCRAK PREMIERE [98] 5-9-6 J Williams (4) *hld up beh, smooth hdwy o'r one furlong out, ran on wl fnl furlong*..............................(6 to 1 op 4 to 1) 3
1021 HOST (Ire) [85] 4-8-7 M J Kinane (7) *trkd ldrs, pushed alng o'r 2 fs out, sn one pace*.........(12 to 1 tchd 10 to 1) 4
1719[6] NOYAN [90] 3-8-3 G Duffield (8) *led til hdd o'r 3 fs out, no extr*.......................(16 to 1 tchd 20 to 1) 5
1636[6] LAW COMMISSION [97] 3-8-10 Pat Eddery (2) *hld up in rear, hdwy o'r 2 fs out, wknd appr last.* ....(10 to 1 tchd 11 to 1) 6
1559[3] KRISTIANSTAD [91] 4-8-13 M Roberts (5) *hld up beh, rdn o'r 2 fs out, no imprsn*.............. (6 to 1 op 5 to 1) 7
1638[7] NO RESERVATIONS (Ire) [86] 3-7-13 F Norton (10) *trkd ldrs, pushed alng 3 fs out, wknd appr last.* ....(10 to 1 tchd 8 to 1) 8
1768 NASHVILLE BLUES (Ire) [87] 4-8-9 M Hills (1) *strted slwly, hld up beh, shrtlvd effrt o'r 2 fs out.* (6 to 1 op 4 to 1) 9
2053[5] STARLIGHT FLYER [90] (bl) 6-8-12 A Mackay (3) *prmnt till wknd o'r 2 fs out*.....(25 to 1 op 33 to 1 tchd 40 to 1) 10

Dist: 2l, hd, 3l, 2½l, 5l, 3l, ¾l, ½l, ¾l. 1m 41.28s. a 2.18s (10 Ran).
SR: 80/60/72/50/38/30/24/8/16/ (Lucayan Stud), D R Loder

2255 Victoria Amateur Turf Club Handicap Class C (0-95 3-y-o and up) £5,758 5f 6yds......................... (5:15)

1478[3] MAGIC ORB [72] 3-8-5 A Mackay (6) *mid-div, hdwy o'r one furlong out to ld wl ins last, ran on well.* ....(16 to 1 op 14 to 1 tchd 20 to 1) 1
1584[7] PADDY CHALK [86] 7-9-11 A Munro (1) *beh, hdwy o'r one furlong out, ran on wl und pres*....(8 to 1 tchd 9 to 1) 2
1945[3] CRADLE DAYS [85] 4-9-10 M Roberts (8) *chsd ldrs gng wl, hdwy to ld ins fnl furlong, sn hdd and no extr.* ....(4 to 1 fav op 5 to 1) 3
2008[3] FASCINATION WALTZ [71] 6-8-10 J Quinn (7) *mid-div, cld 2 fs out, drifted rght and one pace und pres ins last.* ....(10 to 1 op 8 to 1 tchd 12 to 1) 4
1957[7] BODARI [74] 4-8-13 B Rouse (11) *cld up, ev ch entering fnl furlong, one pace*.... (16 to 1 op 14 to 1 tchd 20 to 1) 5
1860[3] BORN TO BE [76] 4-9-1 J Williams (5) *beh, hdwy hfwy, rdn and one pace frm o'r one furlong out.* ....(12 to 1 op 10 to 1 tchd 14 to 1) 6
2136 RUNNING GLIMPSE (Ire) [82] 5-9-0 (7*) B Russell (13) *al prmnt, led o'r one furlong out till ins last, wknd.* ....(12 to 1 op 10 to 1) 7
1835[7] FOOD OF LOVE [75] 5-9-0 P Robinson (9) *led til hdd o'r one furlong out, wknd ins last.* ....(14 to 1 op 12 to 1 tchd 16 to 1) 8
1806 AUGHFAD [83] 7-9-8 T Rogers (10) *chsd ldrs till wknd 2 fs out*..........(16 to 1 op 14 to 1 tchd 20 to 1) 9
2011[7] SOBER LAD (Ire) [69] (v) 3-8-2[1] G Duffield (4) *wth ldr, ev ch o'r one furlong out, wknd quickly.* ....(16 to 1 op 12 to 1 tchd 20 to 1) 10
1953[3] MERRYHILL MAID (Ire) [68] 5-8-7 M J Kinane (2) *outpcd.* ....(6 to 1 tchd 13 to 2) 11
2018[6] CANTORIS [85] 7-9-10 Pat Eddery (12) *outpcd.* ....(9 to 2 tchd 5 to 1) 12
1449 OLIFANTSFONTEIN [81] (bl) 5-9-6 L Dettori (3) *chsd ldrs till outpcd frm hfwy*............ (10 to 1 tchd 12 to 1) 13

Dist: ¾l, 1l, ¾l, 1l, nk, hd, 2l, nk, ¾l, ¾l. 1m 1.94s. a 2.44s (13 Ran).
SR: 42/59/54/37/36/37/42/27/34/ (M Olden), J L Spearing

2256 Spinal Injuries Association Handicap Class D (0-80 3-y-o and up) £4,201 1m 3f 91yds.......................(5:45)

1827 LOBILIO (USA) [65] (v) 4-8-13 M Roberts (6) *made all, kicked for hme 3 fs out, clr o'r one out, ran on wl* ....(5 to 1 op 11 to 2) 1
1711[8] KNOCK KNOCK [80] 8-10-0 L Dettori (3) *hld up, cld o'r 2 fs out, chsd wnr fnl furlong, eased whn no imprsn close hme*..................(11 to 4 op 9 to 4 tchd 3 to 1) 2
1764[3] AMBIGUOUSLY REGAL (USA) [79] 4-9-13 G Duffield (1) *trkd wnr, hrd rdn and one pace frm o'r one furlong out.* ....(7 to 2 op 3 to 1 tchd 11 to 4 and 4 to 1) 3
2026[2] MISS PIN UP [77] 4-9-11 Pat Eddery (2) *trkd ldrs, rdn 2 fs out, one pace*....................(9 to 4 fav op 2 to 1) 4
2126[9] CATHOS (Fr) [45] 8-7-7 A Mackay (4) *hld up in tch, pushed alng 3 fs out, wknd 2 out*..........(25 to 1 op 16 to 1) 5
BROOKS EXPRESS (Fr) [46] 4-7-8[1] J Quinn (5) *al beh.* ....(20 to 1 op 10 to 1) 6

Dist: 5l, 1½l, 2½l, 7l, 7l. 2m 28.49s. a 8.49s (6 Ran).
SR: 20/25/21/14/-/-/ (The Dowager Lady Beaverbrook), C E Brittain

SAN SIRO (ITY) (good)
Saturday July 3rd

2257 Premio Giuseppe de Montel (Listed) (2-y-o) £20,173 7f 110yds....... (3:00)

1543* SPAGHETTI WESTERN (Ire) 8-13 A Cruz, *rcd in 4th, led one and a half fs out, ran on wl*.......................... 1
CHOCOLUNE (Ity) 8-13 S Dettori,....................... 2
POLIUTO (Ire) 8-13 F Jovine,............................ 3
DANZIG TOUCH (USA) 8-13 V Mezzatesta,............... 4
1725[2] EL TEL (Fr) 8-13 T Quinn, *dsptd ld till led strt, hdd 2 fs out, wknd*... 6

Dist: ¾l, hd, 5½l, 2½l, ½l, 12l. 1m 36.80s. (7 Ran).
(Gerecon Italia), J L Dunlop

2258 Premio Gino Montovani (Listed) (2-y-o) £20,173 7f 110yds.......... (4:30)

1726* WHATCOMBE (USA) 8-9 T Quinn, *trkd ldr till led 2 fs out, ran on wl, cmftbly*.................................. 1
KARPACKA (Ire) 8-9 S Dettori,.......................... 2
1726[2] ALPRIDE (Ire) 8-9 P Perlanti,............................ 3
1361[4] SUSPIRIA (Ire) 8-9 A Cruz, *hld up in rear, some late prog, nvr nrr*... 4

Dist: 2l, 2l, 2l, 2l, nk, ½l, 5l, dist. 1m 35.60s. (10 Ran).
(Fahd Salman), P F I Cole

HAMBURG (GER) (firm)
Sunday July 4th

2259 BMW Deutsches Derby (Group 1) (3-y-o) £122,449 1½m............. (5:00)

1724[7] LANDO (Ger) 9-2 A Tylicki, *hld up, hdwy o'r 3 fs out, 7th strt, led 150 yards out, ran on wl*...........(235 to 10) 1
1369* MONSUN (Ger) 9-2 P Schiergen, *hdwy 4 fs out, second strt, led 2 out till 150 yards out, ran on*.........(8 to 1) 2
1724[2] STERNKONIG (Ire) 9-2 M Hofer, *al prmnt, 3rd strt, one pace fnl 2 fs*.......................... (36 to 10 fav) 3
1369[2] KOMTUR (USA) 9-2 K Woodburn, *trkd ldr, led o'r 4 fs out, hdd 2 out, wknd and hng lft one out*..........(10 to 1) 4
1724[5] CONCEPCION (Ger) 9-2 A Boschert, *hdwy fnl 2 fs, nrst finish*.......................................(18 to 1) 5
1724[3] ALTER ADEL 9-2 M Kinane, *hdwy fnl 2 fs, nrst finish.* ....(78 to 10) 6
PAETRO (Ger) 9-2 W Newnes, *hdwy o'r 4 fs out, kpt on one pace fnl 2 furlongs*..................... (68 to 10) 7
1724* KORNADO 9-2 A Best, *nvr rch chalg pos*.......(47 to 10) 8
1395* ARKONA (Ger) 9-2 O Schick, *prmnt, 5th strt, sn wknd.* ....(11 to 1) 9
1637* DARECLIFF (USA) 9-2 J Reid, *6th strt, sn btn*.... (48 to 1) 0
1448[7] REDENHAM (USA) 9-2 T Quinn, *trkd ldrs till wknd 5 fs out*...(39 to 1) 0
1843[3] SCOTTISH PEAK (Ire) 9-2 B Raymond, *al rear*.... (74 to 1) 0
1395[4] ELACATA (Ger) 9-2 M Rimmer, *al rear*...........(65 to 1) 0
LAW'S ANSWER (Ire) 9-2 R Hughes, *nvr dngrs*... (65 to 1) 0
THAGUS (Ger) 9-2 L Dettori, *hdwy 5 fs out, 4th strt, wknd 2 out*...(24 to 1) 0
LAMBADA (Ger) 9-2 L Piggott, *nvr better plcd*....(11 to 1) 0
MAGICAL RIVER (USA) 9-2 L Pyritz, *al rear*.......(18 to 1) 0
FRANCESCOLI (USA) 9-2 T Hellier, *beh fnl 2 fs*... (21 to 1) 0
DARK CANYON 9-2 H Horwart, *led for o'r 7 fs*....(92 to 1) 0

Dist: 1½l, 1 ¾l, 1l, ¾l, hd, ½l, nk, 3½l, 1 ¾l, ½l. 2m 26.80s. (19 Ran).
(Gestut Haus Ittlingen), H Jentzsch

SAN SIRO (ITY) (good to firm)
Sunday July 4th

2260 Premio Primi Passi (Group 3) (2-y-o) £28,591 6f..................... (4:30)

1647* FRED BONGUSTO (Ire) 8-11 B Jovine, *rcd in 3rd, led one and a half fs out, jst hld on*.......................... 1
1886* FUMO DI LONDRA (Ire) 8-11 W Carson, *rcd in second, ev ch one and a half fs out, ran on wl fnl furlong, jst fld.* 2
1221[2] BLINDING SPEED 8-11 M Latorre, *mid-div, one paced o'r 2 fs out*.. 3
LATE PARADE (Ire) 8-11 Jacqueline Freda, *led and sn clr, wknd one and a half fs out*.......................... 4
LUROCC (Ity) 8-11 M Pasquale, *outpcd*................. 5

Dist: Sht-hd, 3l, 3½l, dist. 1m 10.70s. (5 Ran).
(Scuderia Super King), R Brogi

ST-CLOUD (FR) (good)
Sunday July 4th

2261 Grand Prix de Saint-Cloud (Group 1) (3-y-o and up) £179,211 1½m....(2:05)

1472[4] USER FRIENDLY 4-9-5 G Duffield (5) *made all, ran on wl fnl 2 fs, cmftbly*........................(24 to 10 fav) 1
1472[3] APPLE TREE (Fr) 4-9-8 T Jarnet (3) *5th strt, rdn 2 fs out, kpt on wl*....................................(28 to 10) 2
1694[2] MODHISH (Ire) 4-9-8 S Guillot (4) *3rd strt, took second und 2 fs out, no extr cl hme*......................(42 to 10) 3
1448[3] BLUES TRAVELLER (Ire) 3-8-9 D Holland (8) *second strt, drpd back 3rd und 2 fs out, no extr fnl furlong.* (18 to 1) 4
1217 DEAR DOCTOR (Fr) 6-9-8 C Asmussen (2) *hld up, 7th strt, rdn 2 and a half fs out, one pace*..............(55 to 10) 5
1694[3] VERT AMANDE (Fr) 5-9-8 D Boeuf (6) *al abt same pl.* ....(45 to 10) 6
1219* DADARISSIME (Fr) 4-9-8 F Head (1) *nvr nr to chal.* ....(13 to 1) 7
1694[4] POLYTAIN (Fr) 4-9-8 G Mosse (7) *4th strt, rdn and wknd o'r 2 fs out*...................................(13 to 1) 8

Dist: 1½l, ½l, 1l, ½l, 1l, ¾l, 5l. 2m 28.50s. b 1.50s (8 Ran).
SR: 84/84/83/68/80/78/76/66/ (W J Gredley), C E Brittain

BELMONT PARK (USA) (firm)
Sunday July 4th

2262 Suburban Handicap (Grade 1) (3-y-o and up) £119,205 1¼m...............

1541[4] DEVIL HIS DUE (USA) 4-8-9 H McCauley,... (18 to 10 fav) 1
PURE RUMOR (USA) 4-7-12 R Davis,...........(74 to 10) 2
1541* WEST BY WEST (USA) 4-8-4 J-L Samyn,....... (27 to 10) 3
FANATIC BOY (Arg) 6-8-2 J Santos,............. (86 to 10) 4
JACKSONPORT (USA) 4-7-11 J Chavez,.........(27 to 1) 5
1541[2] VALLEY CROSSING (USA) 5-8-0 Julie Krone,......(7 to 2) 6
NORTHERN TREND (USA) 5-7-13 A Toribio,...... (39 to 1) 7
SUNNY SUNRISE (USA) 6-8-5 M Smith,.......... (11 to 1) 8

Dist: 1½l, ¾l, 2l, hd, 1½l, 6l, 1½l. 2m 1.25s. (8 Ran).
(Lion Crest Stable), H A Jerkens

OSTEND (BEL) (firm)
Sunday July 4th

2263 Prix Prosper Decloedt (4-y-o and up) £4,970 1¼m.................. (3:05)

1336[5] POINCIANA 4-8-7 R Cuylle, *hld up, hdwy o'r one furlong out, led 100 yards out, cmftbly*....................... 1
BLENDED 4-9-11 I Ferguson,............................ 2
MANIANA (Ire) 4-8-7 P Massage,........................ 3

Dist: ¾l, 3½l, ½l, ¾l. 2m 1.90s. (7 Ran).
(Bob Lalemant), R Hannon

EDINBURGH (good to firm)
Monday July 5th
Going Correction: MINUS 0.35 sec. per fur. (race 1), MINUS 0.30 (2,3,4,5,6)

2264 Rambling River Amateur Riders Handicap Class G (0-70 3-y-o and up) £2,304 5f...................... (2:15)

2173* DOKKHA OYSTON (Ire) [75] 5-12-0 (7ex) Miss Diana Jones (2) *dwlt, hdwy centre 2 fs out, styd on strly to ld ins last.* ....(5 to 1 op 7 to 2) 1
1623 RELENTLESS PURSUIT (Ire) [67] 5-11-1 (5*) Mrs J Chapple-Hyam (4) *cl up stands side, hdwy 2 fs out, rdn appr last, kpt on*............................ (12 to 1 op 8 to 1) 2
KABCAST [47] (bl) 8-9-9 (5*) Miss R Clark (9) *clr o'rall ldr far side, rdn over one furlong out, hdd and wknd ins last*............................. (16 to 1 tchd 20 to 1) 3
2105[6] PRINCIPAL PLAYER (USA) [58] (v) 3-10-5 Miss J Thurlow (1) *cl up stands side, effrt 2 fs out, sn rdn, kpt on ins last.* ....(9 to 1 op 6 to 1) 4

2215* KALAR [47] (bl) 4-10-0 Mrs L Pearce (6) *cl up centre, rdn hfwy, hng rght, wknd*............(7 to 2 fav op 3 to 1) 5
1841 PLUM FIRST [70] 3-10-12 (5*) Miss A Bycroft (3) *led stands side grp, rdn 2 fs out, sn btn*......(7 to 1 tchd 8 to 1) 6
1815^4 BEST EFFORT [51] 7-10-4 Miss P Robson (5) *chsd ldrs, effrt 2 fs out, sn rdn and btn*.........(4 to 1 op 3 to 1) 7
1740^8 SENSABO [39] 3-9-0 Mrs A Farrell (8) *speed 3 fs, sn wknd*. ....(20 to 1 tchd 25 to 1) 8
1815^5 BRAVE MELODY [33] 7-8-9 (5*) Miss J Bond (7) *prmnt, rdn and wknd 2 fs out*.................................(16 to 1) 9
Dist: 1l, 1½l, hd, 2½l, 1½l, hd, ¾l, ½l. 1m 0.40s. a 2.60s (9 Ran).
SR: 55/43/17/21/6/17/3/-/-/ (Murray Grubb), J Berry

2265 Holyrood Claiming Stakes Class F (3-y-o and up) £2,353 1m 7f 16yds. .(2:45)

1941^3 LORD ADVOCATE (v) 5-8-9 (7*) N Varley (2) *made all, rdn o'r 2 fs out, styd on gmely ins last*. ....(9 to 4 op 2 to 1 tchd 7 to 4) 1
2124^3 POST IMPRESSIONIST (Ire) (bl) 4-9-1 K Darley (4) *hld up, hdwy whn hmpd o'r 4 fs out, sn pushed alng, chlgd 2 out, ev ch and rdn ins last, not run on*. ....(5 to 4 fav tchd 6 to 4) 2
2166^5 ALPHA HELIX (v) 10-9-0 J Fanning (1) *cl up, effrt and ev ch o'r 2 fs out, sn rdn, wknd appr last*. (9 to 2 tchd 5 to 1) 3
1738^6 JOHN NAMAN (Ire) 4-8-11 (3*) S D Williams (3) *cl up, stumbled o'r 4 fs out, effrt and ch 2 out, sn rdn and btn*. ....(11 to 2 op 4 to 1 tchd 6 to 1) 4
Dist: ¾l, 5l, 8l. 3m 27.10s. a 15.10s (4 Ran).
(F Jestin), T Craig

2266 Everest Limited Stakes Class F (0-60 3-y-o) £2,395 1m 3f 32yds........(3:15)

2182* SHIRLEY ROSE 8-9 Dean McKeown (5) *trkd ldrs, hdwy 3 fs out, sn led, rdn and ran on wl frm 2 out*. ....(11 to 10 fav op 5 to 4 tchd Evens and 11 to 8) 1
1704^3 APACHE SQUAW 8-9 N Connorton (2) *in tch, hdwy 4 fs out, effrt 2 out, rdn to chal entering last, sn one pace*. ....(2 to 1) 2
888^6 KISS IN THE DARK 8-9 J Fanning (1) *prmnt, effrt and ev ch o'r 2 fs out, sn rdn, one pace ins last*. (5 to 1 op 7 to 2) 3
2064^6 SUSPECT 8-6 (3*) N Kennedy (4) *led 3 fs, cl up, rdn o'r three out, wknd 2 out*.................................(16 to 1) 4
2088^8 GRUMPY'S GRAIN (Ire) 9-0 K Darley (3) *in tch, hdwy to ld aftr 3 fs, rdn three out, sn hdd and wknd*. ....(16 to 1 op 12 to 1) 5
Dist: 2½l, nk, 3l, 1½l. 2m 29.30s. a 9.80s (5 Ran).
(Greenland Park Ltd), M Johnston

2267 Watsonians F.C. Handicap Class D (0-80 3-y-o and up) £2,981 1½m 31yds ....(3:45)

1894* LATVIAN [66] 6-9-3 (3*) J Weaver (3) *trkd ldg pair, hdwy 2 fs out, effrt and rdn to ld entering last, ran on*. ....(11 to 8 tchd 6 to 4) 1
1967* NORTHERN GRADUATE (USA) [73] 4-9-13 K Darley (2) *led to hfwy, rdn o'r 2 fs out, ev ch till one pace ins last*. ....(13 to 8 on op 6 to 4 on tchd 11 to 8 on) 2
2059^8 NATIVE CROWN (Ire) [40] 5-7-8^3 (3*) N Kennedy (1) *cl up pulling hrd, led hfwy, quickened clr o'r 3 fs out, sn rdn, hdd and no extr ins last*..........(20 to 1 op 14 to 1) 3
Dist: 2l, 1½l. 2m 38.20s. a 5.40s (3 Ran).
SR: 15/18/-/ (J P Seymour), R Allan

2268 Wallyford Selling Stakes Class G (2-y-o) £2,164 7f 15yds............. (4:15)

1863^2 PASSION SUNDAY 8-11 K Darley (2) *led, rdn 2 fs out, styd on und pres ins last*...............(5 to 4 fav op 6 to 4) 1
2129* MOKAITE 8-4 (7*) J Marshall (4) *cl up, ev ch 2 fs out, sn rdn, no extr wl ins last*.............. (2 to 1 op 7 to 4) 2
1863^4 WILLWIN 8-6 J Fortune (1) *trkd ldg pair, pushed alng and wide strt, sn no imprsn*. (9 to 1 op 8 to 1 tchd 10 to 1) 3
1895^5 WOODLAND WHISPER 8-6 Dean McKeown (3) *in tch till ran wide strt, sn beh*................(7 to 2 tchd 4 to 1) 4
Dist: 1½l, 5l, 3l. 1m 31.40s. a 6.20s (4 Ran).
(P D Savill), M H Easterby

2269 Dunbar Handicap Class F (0-70 3-y-o and up) £2,479 7f 15yds.........(4:45)

2088^3 CRESELLY [55] 6-8-11 (3*) J Weaver (4) *chsd ldr, hdwy to ld o'r 2 fs out, rdn appr last, ran on wl*. ....(7 to 2 op 4 to 1 tchd 3 to 1) 1
2197^8 ROUTING [49] 5-8-1 (7*) J Marshall (8) *hdwy to chase ldrs hfwy, rdn to chal appr fnl furlong, no extr ins last*. ....(8 to 1 op 5 to 1) 2
1893* DANCING DOMINO [65] 3-9-2 K Darley (7) *chsd ldrs, hdwy on outsd 2 fs out, sn rdn and ev ch, kpt on same pace ins last*............ (Evens fav op 6 to 4 tchd 13 to 8) 3
2198^7 LAWNSWOOD JUNIOR [68] 6-9-13 G Hind (3) *hld up, hdwy o'r 3 fs out, rdn and one pace frm 2 out*. .... (11 to 2 op 4 to 1 tchd 6 to 1) 4
1938^7 MISS HOSTESS [35] (h,bl) 6-7-8^4 (3*) N Kennedy (5) *hld up, effrt and wide strt, not rch ldrs*....(50 to 1 op 33 to 1) 5

1939^7 VALLEY OF TIME (Fr) [36] 5-7-4^2 (7*) N Varley (1) *sn clr, hdd and wknd o'r 2 fs out*............(20 to 1 op 16 to 1) 6
2011 STARDUST EXPRESS [54] 3-8-5 Dean McKeown (6) *in tch, rdn and wknd 3 fs out*. ....(10 to 1 op 8 to 1 tchd 12 to 1) 7
2086^9 BAFFIE [39] 4-7-12^7 (7*) G Forster (2) *prmnt to hfwy, sn wknd*..................................(50 to 1 op 33 to 1) 8
Dist: 1½l, nk, 2l, 3½l, 1½l, 1l, 1l. 1m 27.50s. a 2.30s (8 Ran).
SR: 34/23/30/35/-/ (Derek Young), R Allan

LEICESTER (good to firm)
Monday July 5th
Going Correction: NIL (races 1,2,5,7), MINUS 0.30 (3,4,6,8)

2270 Scraptoft Handicap Class D (0-80 3-y-o and up) £3,552 7f 9yds..........(2:00)

1830 SUPEROO [65] (bl) 7-9-5 Pat Eddery (5) *hld up in mid-div, pushed alng and hdwy one and a half fs out, led one out, ran on wl*.......... (5 to 1 op 7 to 2 tchd 11 to 2) 1
1970* LAUREL QUEEN (Ire) [67] 5-9-7 J Carroll (8) *led til hdd one furlong out, ran on*. ....(9 to 2 fav op 5 to 1 tchd 11 to 2) 2
2100^2 TIFFANY'S CASE (Ire) [57] 4-8-11 R Cochrane (11) *hld up, hdwy 2 fs out, ran on one pace und pres ins last*. ....(9 to 1 op 8 to 1 tchd 10 to 1) 3
1588^9 ALNASRIC PETE (USA) [46] 7-8-0 G Carter (1) *hld up, hdwy 2 fs out, kpt on*. ....(12 to 1 op 14 to 1 tchd 16 to 1 and 10 to 1) 4
1865^9 LEGEND DULAC (Ire) [55] 4-8-9 P Robinson (6) *cl up, one pace fnl 2 fs*...........................(12 to 1 tchd 14 to 1) 5
2001 BERNSTEIN BETTE [62] 7-9-2 J Williams (3) *beh, hdwy o'r one furlong out, styd on*. ....(13 to 2 op 6 to 1 tchd 7 to 1) 6
2066^5 KARINSKA [60] 3-7-13 (7*) D McCabe (9) *cl up til wknd o'r one furlong out*..................... (7 to 1 op 6 to 1) 7
1914^5 SURREY RACING [68] 5-9-8 B Rouse (4) *trkd ldrs, rdn 2 fs out, wknd*..............................(7 to 1 op 6 to 1) 8
1907^8 SYLVANIA (Ire) [56] (v) 3-8-2 A Munro (2) *chsd ldrs till outpcd hfwy*........................(20 to 1 op 16 to 1) 9
2121* LORD ALFIE [47] 4-8-1 (5ex) J Quinn (7) *took keen hold, in cl tch till wknd 2 fs out*.............(8 to 1 op 6 to 1) 10
NORTHERN RAINBOW [74] 5-10-0 D Biggs (10) *prmnt, rdn o'r 2 fs out, sn btn, tld off*.......... (25 to 1 op 20 to 1) 11
Dist: Nk, ½l, nk, 2l, 1½l, 2l, 1½l, 1l, sht-hd, 20l. 1m 25.70s. a 3.80s (11 Ran).
SR: 48/49/37/25/28/30/14/25/2/ (Mrs P A Garner), J Sutcliffe

2271 Sutton Selling Stakes Class G (2-y-o) £2,469 5f 218yds................ (2:30)

1959 PRIMOST 8-11 J Williams (3) *beh, hdwy blw 2 fs out, hng rght frm o'r one out, ran on to ld cl hme*. ....(3 to 1 fav op 5 to 2) 1
1758^9 CAPTAIN TAFFY (bl) 8-11 K Fallon (6) *cl up, led one and a half fs out till hdd close hme*. ....(9 to 1 op 12 to 1 tchd 14 to 1) 2
2103^2 FORBIDDEN MONKEY 8-6 J Carroll (5) *prmnt, rdn o'r 2 fs out, ev ch over one out, one pace*.... (4 to 1 op 7 to 2) 3
1877^5 ROSE OF GLENN 8-1 (5*) Stephen Davies (4) *prmnt, rdn alng hfwy, sn one pace*...............(6 to 1 op 5 to 1) 4
2125^3 READY-FREDDIE 8-11 T Sprake (11) *al prmnt, ev ch 2 fs out, wknd ins fnl furlong*.............. (10 to 1 op 7 to 1) 5
FELIZ (Ire) 8-6 P Robinson (2) *sn outpcd, hdwy o'r one furlong out, ran on*................ (20 to 1 op 8 to 1) 6
1108^7 CARNEGIE BLUE 8-6 A Munro (8) *pld hrd, trkd ldrs, lost pl appr hfwy, no dngr aftr*............(12 to 1 op 8 to 1) 7
VAN DIEMEN'S LAD (Ire) 8-11 Paul Eddery (7) *dwlt, sn rdn alng in rear, nvr on terms*........... (9 to 2 op 5 to 2) 8
1909^9 SHEILOBLIGE 8-6 B Rouse (10) *prmnt till wknd 2 fs out*. ....(25 to 1 op 14 to 1) 9
1877 CHELSEA LADY (Ire) 7-13 (7*) G Mitchell (1) *sn outpcd, cld hfwy, wknd one furlong out*..... (16 to 1 op 12 to 1) 10
1909^2 FOREVER BLUSHING 8-6 T Williams (9) *led til hdd one and a half fs out, wknd quickly*.........(8 to 1 op 6 to 1) 11
Dist: ½l, 2½l, 1½l, nk, 1½l, hd, 2l, 4l, hd, ½l. 1m 15.30s. a 4.90s (11 Ran).
(Kevan R Kynaston), M Williams

2272 Baxi Solo Handicap Class D (0-80 3-y-o) £3,882 1m 3f 183yds......... (3:00)

1934* MUJAWAB [73] 9-5 W Carson (6) *led chasing grp, led wl o'r 2 fs out, styd on well*....... (11 to 10 fav op 7 to 4) 1
1917^5 ROMALITO [56] 7-13 (3*) D Harrison (2) *hld up in rear, rdn and cld o'r 2 fs out, chsd wnr fnl furlong, kpt on*. ....(14 to 1 op 12 to 1) 2
1906^4 BROUGHTONS FORMULA [57] 7-10 (7*) D McCabe (3) *prmnt in chasing grp, cld 3 fs out, one pace frm 2 out*. .... (7 to 1 op 11 to 2) 3
1586^3 HARD TASK [75] 9-7 Paul Eddery (4) *cl up in chasing grp, rdn o'r 2 fs out, one pace*............ (8 to 1 op 7 to 1) 4
1910^3 PHROSE [73] 9-0 (5*) Stephen Davies (7) *led, sn wl clr, hdd well o'r 2 fs out, no extr*........... (14 to 1 op 12 to 1) 5
584^6 FOREVER SHINEING [73] 9-5 R Cochrane (5) *hld up beh, effrt 2 fs out, btn o'r one out*.........(9 to 1 op 6 to 1) 6

1917[3] DODGY DANCER [55] 8-1 A Munro (1) *hld up in rear, smooth hdwy to hold ev ch 3 fs out, sn rdn and btn.* ....(3 to 1 op 7 to 2) 7
Dist: ½l, 5l, ½l, nk, nk, 1l. 2m 34.70s. a 6.20s (7 Ran).
SR: 8/-/-/-/ (Hamdan Al-Maktoum), H Thomson Jones

2273 Appleby Claiming Stakes Class F (3-y-o and up) £3,076 1m 1f 218yds (3:30)

2113[9] MISTY VIEW 4-8-10 (5*) K Rutter (15) *sn pushed alng in rear, hdwy 3 fs out, led ins last, ran on wl.* ....(12 to 1 op 10 to 1) 1
2108[4] ROUSITTO 5-8-12 W Ryan (4) *beh, hdwy o'r one furlong out, kpt on und pres*..........(6 to 1 tchd 13 to 2) 2
2098* BEST APPEARANCE (Ire) (bl) 3-8-7 K Fallon (16) *chsd ldrs, hdwy to ld one and a half fs out, hdd ins last, no extr.* ....(5 to 1 op 4 to 1) 3
1746 BORROWED AND BLUE 3-8-0 A Munro (3) *mid-div, rdn o'r 3 fs out, kpt on wl und pres*..........(20 to 1 op 16 to 1) 4
2109[4] WAKI GOLD (USA) 6-8-12 W Carson (14) *led one furlong, chsd ldr, led o'r 3 fs out till hdd one and a half out, no extr*..........(6 to 1 op 9 to 2) 5
2064[8] MIDDLEHAM CASTLE 4-9-10 T Williams (8) *beh, hdwy 3 fs out, styd on*..........(25 to 1 op 20 to 1) 6
1961[9] COMMANCHE CREEK (bl) 3-8-13 R Cochrane (12) *trkd ldrs, rdn o'r 2 fs out, one pace.* ....(7 to 1 op 10 to 1 tchd 12 to 1) 7
2109[5] PREMIER DANCE (v) 6-8-10 J Williams (9) *beh, styd on fnl 2 fs*..........(14 to 1 op 12 to 1) 8
1603[8] BERING ISLAND (USA) 3-8-13 Pat Eddery (11) *trkd ldrs, hrd rdn 2 fs out, one pace.* ....(4 to 1 fav op 7 to 2 tchd 5 to 2) 9
2023[6] SABO'S EXPRESS 3-7-12 (7*) Sarah Thompson (7) *nvr better than mid-div*..........(12 to 1 tchd 14 to 1) 10
1878[9] ANNABEL'S BABY (Ire) 4-8-7 G Carter (13) *al beh.* ....(33 to 1 op 25 to 1) 11
2013[5] RUANO (bl) 3-8-2[1] W Woods (2) *strted slwly, al beh.* ....(50 to 1 op 33 to 1) 12
2052[7] RUBY DAVIES 7-8-5 N Adams (5) *trkd ldrs till rdn and wknd o'r 2 fs out*..........(33 to 1) 13
CLAR DUBH (Ire) 3-7-11 (7*) G Mitchell (10) *mid-div till wknd o'r 2 fs out*..........(33 to 1) 14
WHIMSICAL NOTION 3-7-11 (7*) D Wright (1) *took keen hold, led aftr one furlong, hdd o'r 3 fs out, wknd, tld off*..........(50 to 1 op 33 to 1) 15
Dist: ¾l, sht-hd, 1l, sht-hd, ½l, sht-hd, nk, 1½l, ¾l, 20l. 2m 6.80s. a 3.90s (15 Ran).
SR: 32/27/21/12/23/34/22/18/18/ (M R Pascall), J White

2274 Wigston Maiden Auction Stakes Class F (2-y-o) £2,905 7f 9yds.........(4:00)

1602 HAM N'EGGS 9-0 Pat Eddery (1) *wth ldr, led 3 fs out, pushed alng and ran on wl, not extended.* ....(11 to 4 fav op 5 to 2 tchd 3 to 1) 1
1877[4] INDEFENCE (Ire) 9-0 D Holland (6) *wtd wth, cld aftr 3 fs, kpt on wl frm 2 furlongs out.* ....(9 to 1 op 7 to 1 tchd 10 to 1) 2
1983[3] NON VINTAGE (Ire) (bl) 9-0 M Birch (11) *wtd wth beh, hdwy ins fnl furlong, fnshd wl*..........(8 to 1 op 6 to 1) 3
1949[7] SHARP TYCOON (Ire) 9-0 W Newnes (7) *chsd ldrs, rdn 2 fs out, kpt on wl fnl furlong*..........(9 to 2 op 7 to 2) 4
1877 PRINCE DANZIG (Ire) (bl) 9-0 J Reid (9) *mid-div, hdwy 2 fs out, sn one pace*..........(10 to 1 op 7 to 1) 5
1964[3] SUSELJA (Ire) 8-9 S Whitworth (4) *trkd ldrs, rdn and outpcd 2 fs out, kpt on ins last*..........(9 to 1 op 5 to 1) 6
1758[5] HEATHYARDS CRUSADE (Ire) 9-0 W Ryan (12) *rcd freely, led til hdd 3 fs out, btn o'r one out, eased*..........(20 to 1) 7
2027[5] DAKOTA BRAVE (Ire) 8-11 (3*) D Harrison (10) *took keen hold, trkd ldrs, swtchd rght 2 fs out, btn o'r one out.* ....(7 to 1 tchd 8 to 1) 8
2044[6] CHILTERN SHOW 8-9 A Mackay (3) *cl up til wknd 2 fs out.* ....(20 to 1 tchd 25 to 1) 9
POLAR CAP 9-0 G Duffield (8) *al beh.* ....(12 to 1 tchd 10 to 1) 10
DOMINANT PARTNER 9-0 R Cochrane (13) *in tch, rdn alng hfwy, sn outpcd*..........(14 to 1 op 12 to 1) 11
1885[6] BARACCA (Ire) 9-0 L Dettori (14) *trkd ldrs till wknd o'r 2 fs out*..........(8 to 1 op 7 to 1) 12
1863[9] COVER POINT (Ire) 9-0 T Lucas (5) *al beh.* ....(20 to 1 op 14 to 1) 13
Dist: ¾l, ¾l, sht-hd, 3l, 2l, 1½l, nk, sht-hd, 2½l, 3l. 1m 27.90s. a 6.00s (13 Ran).
SR: 10/8/6/5/-/-/ (Peter Hammond), R Hannon

2275 Mountsorrel Maiden Stakes Class D (Div I) (3-y-o and up) £3,406 1m 1f 218yds.......................(4:30)

RIVER BOYNE (USA) 3-8-10 Pat Eddery (11) *hld up towards rear, smooth hdwy o'r 2 fs out, led over one out, rdn and ran on wl*..........(5 to 2 fav tchd 7 to 4) 1
1027[9] TESHAMI (USA) 3-8-10 M Roberts (7) *hld up in mid-div, rdn o'r 2 fs out, kpt on wl fnl furlong.* ....(5 to 1 op 11 to 4) 2
1911[2] AL SENAFI (Ire) 3-8-10 R Cochrane (4) *trkd ldrs, led o'r 2 fs out till hdd over one out, kpt on.* ....(3 to 1 tchd 7 to 2 and 4 to 1) 3
CHUMMY'S PAL (USA) 3-8-10 J Reid (1) *chsd ldrs, outpcd o'r one furlong out, kpt on ins last*..(5 to 1 op 4 to 1) 4
1594[3] RASAYEL (USA) 3-8-0 (5*) J Tate (5) *trkd ldrs, led o'r 3 fs out till over 2 out, wknd.* ....(8 to 1 op 10 to 1 tchd 12 to 1) 5
SILVER SEA (Ire) 3-8-5 A Munro (9) *trkd ldrs, rdn o'r 3 fs out, sn outpcd*..........(16 to 1 op 12 to 1) 6
1784 KAHLO 3-8-5 T Lucas (3) *dwlt, al beh.* ....(50 to 1 op 25 to 1) 7
1784[8] FATAL SHOCK 3-8-5 J Lowe (6) *led til hdd 7 fs out, wknd 3 out*..........(25 to 1 op 20 to 1 tchd 50 to 1) 8
1831[9] SHIP'S TWINE (Ire) 3-8-5 Paul Eddery (2) *cl up, led 7 fs out till hdd o'r 3 out, sn btn*..........(14 to 1 op 8 to 1) 9
2097[9] AMOREM 3-8-10 W Newnes (10) *hld up, al beh.* ....(33 to 1 op 25 to 1) 10
QUEST FOR THE BEST 4-9-2 D Holland (8) *beh, effrt 3 fs out, sn btn, tld off*..........(25 to 1 op 10 to 1) 11
Dist: 1½l, nk, 7l, ½l, 1½l, 8l, 1½l, 1½l, 3½l, 12l. 2m 6.80s. a 3.90s (11 Ran).
SR: 27/24/23/9/3/-/ (K Abdulla), G Harwood

2276 Burton Handicap Class E (0-70 3-y-o and up) £2,820 5f 218yds........(5:00)

2047* JOIN THE CLAN [53] 4-9-3 L Dettori (6) *hld up, hdwy o'r one furlong out, squeezed through on ins cl hme.* ....(7 to 2 op 9 to 2) 1
2110[5] GREAT HALL [63] 4-9-13 J Williams (2) *hld up beh, hdwy blw 2 fs out, str run fnl furlong, jst fld.* ....(5 to 1 op 4 to 1) 2
2011[2] CHILLY BREEZE [67] 3-9-10 G Duffield (8) *led, rdn o'r one furlong out, ct cl hme*..........(9 to 2 op 5 to 1) 3
1938* MASTER POKEY [60] 9-9-3 (7*) P Johnson (4) *wtd wth, hdwy ins fnl furlong, fnshd wl*..........(10 to 1 op 9 to 2) 4
2173[9] INVIGILATE [60] 4-9-10 K Fallon (1) *cl up, rdn 2 fs out, ev ch entering last, one pace*..........(14 to 1 op 12 to 1) 5
2050[5] ISLAND KNIGHT (Ire) [64] 4-10-0 L Piggott (5) *cl up til wknd o'r one furlong out*..........(8 to 1 op 7 to 1) 6
2191* ELTON LEDGER (Ire) [62] (bl) 4-9-12 (7ex) B Raymond (7) *took keen hold, cl up till wknd appr fnl furlong.* ....(11 to 4 fav op 9 to 4) 7
1760[5] HALL BANK COTTAGE [45] 3-8-2 T Williams (3) *slwly into strd, rdn alng hfwy, no imprsn fnl 2 fs*..........(14 to 1) 8
Dist: Hd, 1½l, ½l, nk, ¾l, ½l, ¾l. 1m 13.80s. a 3.40s (8 Ran).
SR: 35/44/35/33/32/33/29/2/ (J Redden), Mrs N Macauley

2277 Mountsorrel Maiden Stakes Class D (Div II) (0-70 3-y-o and up) £3,377 1m 1f 218yds.......................(5:30)

1784[2] GONE TROPPO 3-8-10 W Ryan (8) *cl up, led one and a half fs out, sn quickened clr.* ....(11 to 10 on op Evens tchd 5 to 4 on) 1
DRAGON'S TEETH (Ire) 3-8-10 R Cochrane (1) *led til hdd one and a half fs out, one pace.* ....(6 to 1 op 5 to 1 tchd 8 to 1) 2
EMMA WOODFORD 3-8-5 N Adams (6) *trkd ldrs, cld 3 fs out, ev ch o'r 2 out, one pace*..........(33 to 1 op 20 to 1) 3
1716[3] SCOTSMAN (Ire) 3-8-10 M Roberts (4) *cl up, ev ch 3 fs out, one pace appr 2 out*..........(7 to 2 op 3 to 1) 4
ADMIRAL'S WELL (Ire) 3-8-10 L Dettori (10) *beh, styd on fnl 2 fs, nrst finish*..........(12 to 1 op 7 to 2) 5
1803[2] RAFIF (USA) 3-8-5 W Carson (2) *pld hrd, beh, styd on fnl 2 fs, nrst finish*..........(8 to 1 op 6 to 1) 6
COOL SECRETARY (USA) 3-8-5 W Woods (9) *al beh.* ....(20 to 1 op 10 to 1) 7
1992[7] MOUNTAIN REACH 3-8-10 A McGlone (3) *al beh.* ....(50 to 1 op 25 to 1) 8
2010[6] ROSE OF MEDINA 3-8-5 M Birch (7) *mid-div til wknd 3 fs out*..........(25 to 1 op 20 to 1) 9
TARROCK 3-8-10 B Procter (5) *unruly strt, missed break, reminder aftr 3 fs, sn hdwy to chase ldrs, till drpd out three furlongs out*..........(33 to 1 op 20 to 1) 10
Dist: 10l, 1l, 1½l, 3l, 2½l, 8l, 1½l, nk, 3½l. 2m 7.70s. a 4.80s (10 Ran).
SR: 18/-/-/-/-/ (L Marinopoulos), H R A Cecil

RIPON (good (races 1,3), good to firm (2,4,5,6))

Monday July 5th

Going Correction: MINUS 0.15 sec. per fur. (races 1,3), MINUS 0.10 (2,4,5,6)

2278 Skellgate Maiden Auction Fillies' Stakes Class F (2-y-o) £2,820 5f (7:00)

1897[2] TWICE IN BUNDORAN (Ire) 8-6 (5*) L Newton (1) *made all, shaken up 2 fs out, sn clr, easily.* ....(11 to 8 on op 6 to 4 on tchd 5 to 4 on) 1
1944[5] DAILY STAR 8-11 J Carroll (5) *nvr far away, drvn alng 2 fs out, kpt on same pace fnl furlong*..(8 to 1 op 13 to 2) 2
1229[5] COLNE VALLEY 8-11 B Raymond (7) *in tch, improved on outer o'r one furlong out, rdn and not quicken ins last.* ....(14 to 1 op 12 to 1) 3

2114[3] LOVESCAPE 8-11 A Clark (4) *pressed ldrs, drvn alng hfwy, no extr o'r one furlong out.* .... (11 to 2 op 5 to 1 tchd 6 to 1) 4
1837[6] OAKLEY MANOR 8-11 J Lowe (3) *in tch on inner, rdn alng o'r 2 fs out, fdd*.................... (12 to 1 op 10 to 1) 5
MISS FREEBIE (Ire) 8-11 J O'Reilly (6) *slwly into strd, beh and sn outpcd, effrt hfwy, not rch ldrs*........ (14 to 1) 6
ANGELIC DANCER 8-8 (3*) S D Williams (8) *wnt rght strt, beh, effrt on outer and rdn hfwy, btn and eased o'r one furlong out*.......... (8 to 1 op 10 to 1 tchd 12 to 1) 7
GLENLYON DUCHESS 8-11 J Fanning (2) *chsd ldrs, sn pushed alng, wknd quickly frm hfwy, tld off.* .... (14 to 1 op 12 to 1) 8
Dist: 3½l, ½l, 3l, 3l, hd, 6l, 12l. 1m 0.30s. a 2.30s (8 Ran).
SR: 36/22/20/8/-/ (Crazy Horse Bloodstock II), D J S Cosgrove

2279 St Agnesgate Claiming Stakes Class F (3-y-o) £2,924 1m...............(7:25)

1780[3] SILVERLOCKS 8-7 N Connorton (5) *keen hold, pressed ldrs, improved to chal o'r one furlong out, led ins last, ran on strly*......................(13 to 8 op 11 to 8) 1
2086[4] DRUMDONNA (Ire) 7-11 L Charnock (1) *led, jnd o'r one furlong out, hdd ins last, no extr*.... (9 to 1 op 8 to 1) 2
1760 BLUE RADIANCE 7-9 J Fanning (2) *chsd ldrs, drvn alng o'r 2 fs out, not clr run over one out, one pace ins last.* ....(14 to 1 op 12 to 1 tchd 16 to 1) 3
2065* KING PARIS (Ire) 8-9 (3*) M Fenton (6) *chsd ldrs, pushed alng o'r 3 fs out, some hdwy und pres over 2 out, one pace appr last*...(11 to 10 on op 11 to 10 tchd 6 to 5) 4
1979[3] TRANQUIL LADY (Ire) 8-1 J Quinn (4) *pressed ldr, drvn alng 3 fs out, wknd fnl 2*.......... (20 to 1 op 16 to 1) 5
1803[5] CHARLOTTES BILLO (bl) 8-0 K Darley (3) *slwly away, sn reco'red to join pack, drvn alng over 3 fs out, soon btn, tld off*.. (33 to 1) 6
2047 CIZARD (Ire) 7-8 J Lowe (7) *hld up, rdn alng o'r 3 fs out, sn lost tch, tld off*.................................... (50 to 1) 7
Dist: 2½l, 1½l, 2l, 5l, 10l, 5l. 1m 40.80s. a 2.50s (7 Ran).
SR: 44/26/19/30/4/-/-/ (Miss Betty Duxbury), Miss S E Hall

2280 Singer & Friedlander Handicap Class D (0-80 3-y-o) £3,720 6f......... (7:50)

2105[3] PINE RIDGE LAD (Ire) [61] 8-9 (5*) J Tate (4) *led, hdd o'r one furlong out, rallied to rgn ld entering fnl furlong, edgd lft and drvn out*......................(9 to 2 op 4 to 1) 1
2105* OUBECK [67] 9-6 (7ex) Dale Gibson (5) *in tch, smooth hdwy to ld o'r one furlong out, hdd entering last, no extr*......................(13 to 8 fav op 18 to 11 on) 2
2011[4] GO FLIGHTLINE (Ire) [59] 8-9 (3*) M Fenton (1) *wth ldr on ins, ev ch o'r 2 fs out, no extr appr last.* ....(4 to 1 tchd 7 to 2) 3
1833[7] BIRCHWOOD SUN [68] 9-7 J Lowe (6) *beh ldg grp, drvn alng hfwy, kpt on fnl furlong, nvr able to chal*. (8 to 1) 4
1937* FORTIS PAVIOR (Ire) [58] 8-11 A Culhane (2) *wth ldrs, drvn alng o'r 2 fs out, wknd wl over one out.* ....(9 to 2 op 4 to 1) 5
1421 ADMISSION (Ire) [45] 7-12 J Quinn (3) *chsd ldrs till rdn and wknd o'r 2 fs out*...................(25 to 1 op 20 to 1) 6
Dist: 2l, 4l, ½l, 2l, ½l. 1m 13.60s. a 3.00s (6 Ran).
SR: 22/20/-/3/-/-/ (Whitestonecliffe Racing Partnership), B Beasley

2281 National Medical Agency Handicap Class E (0-70 3-y-o) £2,924 1½m 60yds ....(8:20)

1948[3] DESERT LAUGHTER (Ire) [39] 7-10 J Quinn (4) *trkd ldr, outpcd and rdn 4 fs out, improved o'r 2 out, sstnd run to ld cl hme*.........................(10 to 1 op 20 to 1) 1
1934[5] MUTAWALI (Ire) [61] 9-4 K Darley (3) *set steady pace, quickened 4 fs out, rdn 2 out, hdd cl hme.* (4 to 1 op 7 to 2) 2
2107* MOUSSAHIM (USA) [70] (v) 9-13 (6ex) B Raymond (2) *hld up in last pl, effrt and hdwy o'r 3 fs out, ev ch 2 out, edgd rght and not quicken fnl furlong.* ....(2 to 1 on op 9 to 4 on) 3
1930[8] MENA [57] 8-7 (7*) G Forster (1) *chsd ldg pair, rdn o'r 3 fs out, lost tch over 2 out, tld off*....... (8 to 1 op 7 to 1) 4
Dist: ½l, 1½l, 20l. 2m 44.70s. a 9.70s (4 Ran).
(H S Yates), R Hollinshead

2282 St Marygate Selling Stakes Class G (3-y-o and up) £2,280 2m....... (8:50)

2178[6] JALORE 4-9-10 K Darley (5) *hld up in tch, effrt o'r 2 fs out, ran on to ld ins last, pushed clr.* ....(15 to 8 op 6 to 4 tchd 2 to 1) 1
1890[8] SAN PIER NICETO 6-9-10 Dean McKeown (3) *trkd ldr, led 4 fs out, rdn 2 out, hdd ins last, no extr.* ....(4 to 1 op 7 to 2 tchd 9 to 2) 2
2052[3] PIE HATCH (Ire) 4-9-5 G Duffield (4) *steadied strt, hld up in last pl, effrt on outer 3 fs out, sn pushed alng, not quicken appr last*........... (11 to 10 fav op 13 to 8) 3
1156[6] RUN MILADY 5-9-5 D Wilkinson (2) *chsd ldg pair, drvn alng 3 fs out, lost tch fnl 2 furlongs.* ....(14 to 1 op 12 to 1) 4
POLDER 7-9-10 A Clark (1) *led til hdd 4 fs out, sn drvn alng, wknd 2 out*............................ (12 to 1) 5
Dist: 2½l, 2l, 6l, 2l. 3m 42.30s. a 17.30s (5 Ran).
(Mrs J Coathup), R Hollinshead

2283 Kirkgate Handicap Class E (0-70 4-y-o and up) £3,054 1m.............(9:20)

1284 SHANNON EXPRESS [44] 6-8-3 Julie Bowker (4) *made all, clr o'r 2 fs out, shaken up, ran on wl fnl furlong.* ....(14 to 1) 1
2057* PRIDE OF PENDLE [53] 4-8-12 K Darley (2) *hld up, effrt 3 fs out, styd on strly fnl furlong, jst held.* .... (11 to 4 fav op 3 to 1 tchd 100 to 30) 2
2057[2] STRAW THATCH [51] 4-8-7 (3*) J Weaver (3) *chsd ldrs, effrt and rdn o'r 2 fs out, ran on wl fnl furlong.* ....(5 to 1 op 9 to 2) 3
2057 HABETA (USA) [60] (bl) 7-9-5 G Duffield (5) *tucked away on ins, effrt and shaken up o'r 2 fs out, kpt on inside last, nvr dngrs*......................(100 to 30 op 7 to 2) 4
1970[2] MEDIA MESSENGER [56] 4-9-1 K Fallon (7) *trkd ldr, rdn o'r 3 fs out, edgd rght one out, one pace.* ....(11 to 1 op 10 to 1) 5
2104[4] MUMMYS ROCKET [40] (bl) 4-7-13 A Mackay (1) *in tch, effrt 3 fs out, hmpd one out, one pace.* ....(11 to 1 op 10 to 1 tchd 12 to 1) 6
1578 PREMIER MAJOR (Ire) [35] (bl) 4-7-8[1] L Charnock (6) *in tch, effrt o'r 2 fs out, not quicken over one out.* ....(12 to 1 tchd 10 to 1) 7
1800[8] ASHDREN [69] 6-10-0 S Perks (9) *hld up, shaken up 2 fs out, nvr nr to chal*..................(8 to 1 op 7 to 1) 8
1927[6] ZAMANAYN (Ire) [63] 5-9-8 M Wigham (8) *sluggish strt, drvn alng 4 fs out, al beh*..........(11 to 1 op 10 to 1) 9
1800[9] SUNTAN (Fr) [59] (bl) 4-9-4 A Culhane (10) *chsd ldrs, drvn alng entering strt, one pace whn severely hmpd one furlong out, virtually pld up*..................(25 to 1) 10
Dist: Nk, hd, 4l, hd, ½l, 1l, 3l, ¾l, 25l. 1m 43.00s. a 4.70s (10 Ran).
SR: 7/15/12/9/4/-/-/3/-/ (R Cottam), E J Alston

ROSCOMMON (IRE) (good) Monday July 5th

2284 Four Mile House EBF (C&G) Maiden (2-y-o) £3,107 7f................(6:30)

1650[2] CORLEONIE (Ire) (bl) 9-0 W J Supple (5)...........(5 to 1) 1
869[7] PAUGIM (Ire) 9-0 M J Kinane (6)..................(6 to 1) 2
1824[4] VIVA VICTOR (Ire) 8-8 (6*) J J Behan (14).......... (8 to 1) 3
1792[2] DON'T KNOW (Ire) 9-0 K J Manning (13).......(5 to 4 fav) 4
CONCEPT HOUSE (Ire) 9-0 N Byrne (10).......... (20 to 1) 5
EUPHORIC (Ire) 9-0 J P Murtagh (9)............ (10 to 1) 6
1044[8] WHEREWILITALL END (Ire) 9-0 D Manning (3).....(12 to 1) 7
BOBSTAR DANCER (Ire) 8-6 (8*) B J Halligan (1).. (25 to 1) 8
SALTONIC (Ire) 9-0 S Craine (11).................. (7 to 1) 9
ARTFULNESS (Ire) 9-0 W J O'Connor (12)........ (10 to 1) 10
2093[5] BOLD EMIR 8-6 (8*) J J Stack (7)................(20 to 1) 11
SOUND MAN JIMACK (Ire) 8-4 (10*) J J Byrne (8) (20 to 1) 12
Dist: Sht-hd, sht-hd, ½l, 4l. 1m 33.30s. (12 Ran).
(Mrs Isobel Foley), Kevin Prendergast

2285 Lenabane Maiden (3-y-o and up) £2,245 7f...................... (7:00)

DINESEN 3-9-0 R Hughes,.......................... (Evens fav) 1
1922[3] MISS CARMELLA (Ire) 3-8-11 W J Supple (11).... (12 to 1) 2
2184[3] BELLISSI (Ire) 3-8-11 K J Manning (8)...............(6 to 1) 3
1922[2] SCALP (Ire) 3-9-0 W J O'Connor (1)................(9 to 1) 4
1855[8] ARROGANT LADY 3-8-3 (8*) J J Mullins (12)......(33 to 1) 5
870 MOONLIGHT PARTNER (Ire) 3-8-11 J P Murtagh (6) ....(20 to 1) 6
1995[6] MAJESTIC PADDY (Ire) 3-8-8 (6*) J A Heffernan (3) (20 to 1) 7
1793[2] RETICENT BRIDE (Ire) (bl) 3-8-11 M J Kinane (13) ....(100 to 30) 8
1793[5] BUTTERNUT (Ire) 3-8-11 N G McCullagh (15)..... (25 to 1) 9
2140[9] PEARL DAWN (Ire) 3-8-11 B Coogan (7)..........(33 to 1) 10
1443[5] ASTA MADERA (Ire) 3-8-11 J F Egan (4)..........(10 to 1) 11
704[3] PERSIAN RENDEZVOUS (Ire) 3-9-0 P V Gilson (5) (20 to 1) 12
1649 NORDIC GLARE (Ire) 3-9-0 C Roche (10)..........(20 to 1) 13
2184[9] CARNAZAR (Ire) 3-8-11 N Byrne (2)...............(20 to 1) 14
1333[6] LHOTSE (Ire) 3-8-11 S Craine (9).................(14 to 1) 15
Dist: 2½l, 1l, ½l, 1l. 1m 32.70s. (15 Ran).
(William J Betz), D Hanley

2286 M.Cooney & Sons Handicap (0-80 3-y-o and up) £2,762 1¼m.......... (7:30)

2039[3] SWEET NASHA (Ire) [-] 4-10-0 P V Gilson (2).... (7 to 2 fav) 1
2041[9] COOLRAIN LADY (Ire) [-] 3-8-8 S Craine (7)........(8 to 1) 2
2040[4] HOPESVILLE (Ire) [-] 3-8-10 J P Murtagh (10)...... (8 to 1) 3
1235[8] COMMAND 'N CONTROL [-] 4-8-5 (6*) J J Behan (6) ....(14 to 1) 4
1996[2] ISLAND VISION (Ire) [-] 3-7-13 W J Supple (8)....... (4 to 1) 5
1123 TRES JOUR (Ire) [-] 3-7-9 (2*) D G O'Shea (1)...... (20 to 1) 6
2041[7] MAY WE DANCE (Ire) [-] 4-7-9 (8*) R T Fitzpatrick (12) ....(16 to 1) 7
1553 TOPSEYS TIPPLE (Ire) [-] 3-8-11 (6*) R V Skelly (3) (14 to 1) 8
2142 SOLAR FLASH (Ire) [-] 4-7-1 (6*) P P Murphy (11)..(20 to 1) 9
NOORAJO (Ire) [-] 4-9-3 C Roche (9)..............(10 to 1) 10

1962[7] GRECIAN LADY (Ire) [-] 4-8-1 Joanna Morgan (5)..(16 to 1) 11
1292[6] MANGANS HILL (Ire) [-] 3-7-13 (4*) W J Smith (13) (12 to 1) 12
1611 PRECISE TIMING [-] (bl) 5-9-7 M J Kinane (4)......(6 to 1) pu
Dist: 1l, 2l, 1½l, 2½l. 2m 12.10s. (13 Ran).
(N Stassen), Joseph M Canty

2287 Ballybeg Maiden (3-y-o) £2,245 1½m ....(8:00)

1573[5] SHIRLEY'S DELIGHT (Ire) 8-11 R Hughes (8)......(12 to 1) 1
1997[3] MOUSE BIRD (Ire) 9-0 J P Murtagh (18)...........(9 to 2) 2
2036[2] UNCONDITIONAL (Fr) 8-11 N G McCullagh (16) (5 to 2 fav) 3
2040[2] DAHLIA'S BEST (USA) 9-0 W J Supple (1).........(7 to 1) 4
944[5] ALYREINA (USA) 8-11 C Roche (2)................(7 to 1) 5
2040 LUSTRINO (USA) 9-0 M J Kinane (13)..............(4 to 1) 6
1997[6] QUIVAL (USA) 8-5 (6*) J J Behan (10)............(14 to 1) 7
1335[6] TURNER PRIZE (Ire) 9-0 S Craine (14)............(10 to 1) 8
1997[9] RED MICKS WIFE (Ire) 8-11 J F Egan (5).........(16 to 1) 9
1997 ARCH-T-GLEN (Ire) 8-6 (8*) D M McCullagh (15)...(66 to 1) 10
1466[7] RYE HILL QUEEN (Ire) 8-5 (6*) R V Skelly (11).....(66 to 1) 11
1122[9] DANCING VISION (Ire) 8-6 (8*) B Fenton (7).......(50 to 1) 12
1574[7] CARAVELLE LAD (Ire) 9-0 P V Gilson (9)..........(20 to 1) 13
1139 MONTEJUSTICE (Ire) 8-11 N Byrne (17)..........(33 to 1) 14
1014[2] KIDAMIYA (Ire) 8-5 (6*) J A Heffernan (12).........(12 to 1) 15
870 CREHELP EXPRESS (Ire) 8-5 (6*) B Bowens (6)...(33 to 1) 16
Dist: Nk, sht-hd, sht-hd, ½l. 2m 40.50s. (16 Ran).
(Liam Doherty), Noel Meade

WINDSOR (good to firm)
Monday July 5th
Going Correction: MINUS 0.15 sec. per fur. (races 1,5), MINUS 0.30 (2,3,4,6)

2288 National Association Of Boys' Clubs Apprentice Selling Handicap Class G (0-60 3-y-o) £1,590 5f 217yds.... (6:35)

2095[8] NORLING (Ire) [43] 8-5 (5*) P Rose (2) *hld up in tch, ran on 2 fs out, led last 50 yards*.......(9 to 2 jt-fav op 7 to 2) 1
1913 SOPHISTICATED AIR [50] (bl) 9-0 (3*) D Griffiths (8) *wth ldrs, led 3 fs out, hng lft o'r one out, hdd fnl 50 yards.* ....(11 to 2 op 7 to 2 tchd 6 to 1) 2
1826[5] THE ORDINARY GIRL (Ire) [51] (v) 9-4 R Painter (9) *trkd ldrs, ev ch frm 2 fs out, not quicken nr finish.* ....(6 to 1 tchd 7 to 1) 3
2011 AVRIL ETOILE [48] 8-7 (8*) Iona Wands (7) *outpcd till ran on ins last 2 fs, nrst finish.* (9 to 1 op 5 to 1 tchd 10 to 1) 4
1714[8] PERFECT PASSION [44] 8-10[2] (3*) Rachel Bridger (10) *reared strt, sn mid-div, not clr run and swtchd rght o'r one furlong out, styd on.* ....(8 to 1 op 7 to 1 tchd 10 to 1) 5
1925 SING AS WE GO [40] 8-7 J Dennis (6) *led to hfwy, one pace appr fnl furlong*.....(10 to 1 op 12 to 1 tchd 14 to 1) 6
1972[6] DOCTOR-J (Ire) [54] (v) 9-7 J O'Dwyer (1) *slwly into strd, nvr better than mid-div*...................(9 to 2 jt-fav op 7 to 2 tchd 11 to 2) 7
2052[9] WEALTHYWOO [39] (bl) 8-6 K Pattinson (5) *effrt on outsd hfwy, not quicken ins last 2 fs.* ....(14 to 1 op 12 to 1 tchd 16 to 1) 8
2095 WOODLANDS ELECTRIC [35] 7-11 (5*) L Suthern (11) *wth ldrs for o'r 3 fs*...................(50 to 1 op 33 to 1) 9
2095 STOCKFORCE [47] 8-9 (5*) D O'Neill (4) *outpcd.* ....(25 to 1 op 20 to 1 tchd 33 to 1) 10
1714[7] BUCKSKI ECHO [43] (bl) 8-10 D Toole (3) *speed for o'r 2 fs, sn drpd rear*........... (9 to 1 op 6 to 1 tchd 10 to 1) 11
Dist: Nk, 1l, ¾l, 1l, hd, 1½l, 2l, 2½l, 3l, 5l. 1m 14.70s. a 4.40s (11 Ran).
(S Pedersen), N Tinkler

2289 Henry Cooper Handicap Class E (0-70 3-y-o and up) £2,595 1¼m 7yds (7:05)

2025[4] BENTICO [48] 4-8-13 Pat Eddery (4) *made all, pushed alng o'r 2 fs out, rdn clr appr last, eased.* ....(2 to 1 fav tchd 7 to 4) 1
1713[8] WELL SUITED [70] 3-9-10 J Reid (7) *str hdwy frm rear o'r 3 fs out, rdn and not quicken 2 out.* ....(12 to 1 op 10 to 1 tchd 14 to 1) 2
1820[9] SANTANA LADY (Ire) [56] 4-9-7 W Newnes (12) *chsd ldr, one pace last 2 fs*........................(10 to 1 op 12 to 1) 3
1956[4] DANCING BEAU (Ire) [52] 4-9-3 M Roberts (6) *hld up in mid-div, effrt o'r 2 fs out, not rch wnr.* ....(11 to 2 op 5 to 1 tchd 13 to 2) 4
2175[9] TINA MEENA LISA [28] 4-7-7 E Johnson (2) *ldg grp, rdn and no extr frm 2 fs out*...(10 to 1 op 20 to 1 tchd 33 to 1) 5
1930 MY GRAIN [35] 4-8-0 N Carlisle (11) *mid-div, no hdwy appr last 2 fs*.......................(33 to 1 op 20 to 1) 6
1902* TAUNTING (Ire) [49] 5-9-0 R Cochrane (3) *nvr nrr.* ....(13 to 2 op 6 to 1 tchd 15 to 2) 7
1320[3] RED COTTON [68] 3-9-8 Paul Eddery (10) *mid-div, wknd 3 fs out*.................(13 to 2 op 5 to 1 tchd 7 to 1) 8
2029[5] VALIANT WORDS [47] 6-8-12 A Munro (9) *chsd ldrs 7 fs, wknd*...............(15 to 2 op 7 to 1 tchd 8 to 1) 9
1659[5] BROWN CARPET [28] (bl) 6-7-1[1] (7*) D Wright (1) *rear, rdn alng 3 fs out, nvr on terms.* ....(12 to 1 op 10 to 1 tchd 16 to 1) 10

1746 TREBLE LASS [48] 3-8-2[1] D Holland (5) *wl plcd till wknd o'r 2 fs out*.......................(33 to 1 op 20 to 1) 11
2012[6] EVERSET (Fr) [41] 5-7-13 (7*) D McCabe (8) *al beh.* ....(33 to 1 op 20 to 1) 12
Dist: 2½l, sht-hd, 2½l, 2½l, 1l, 1½l, nk, 2l, 1½l, 8l. 2m 5.80s. a 3.30s (12 Ran).
SR: 36/42/38/29/-/5/16/23/9/ (Mark Christofi), M A Jarvis

2290 Harry Carpenter Conditions Stakes Class D (3-y-o) £3,947 1¼m 7yds (7:35)

1921[3] BLUE LION 9-0 M Roberts (3) *rcd in 3rd, pushed alng o'r 3 fs out, led over one out, cleverly*............(11 to 8 jt-fav op Evens tchd 6 to 4) 1
ICY SOUTH (USA) 9-0 L Dettori (6) *made most till appr fnl furlong, kpt on*....... (12 to 1 op 8 to 1 tchd 14 to 1) 2
1751[6] YELTSIN 9-0 Pat Eddery (1) *trkd ldr, ev ch 3 fs out, rdn and wknd 2 out*...........................(11 to 8 jt-fav op 6 to 4 tchd 7 to 4 and 5 to 4) 3
1383* SAVOY TRUFFLE (Fr) 8-9 W Ryan (2) *hld up in 5th, rdn alng and outpcd frm 3 fs out.* ....(7 to 1 op 6 to 1 tchd 9 to 1) 4
WEAVER BIRD 8-5 C Rutter (4) *hld up rear, rdn and outpcd 3 fs out*.......(25 to 1 op 20 to 1 tchd 33 to 1) 5
COMME D'HABITUDE (USA) 8-0 (5*) N Gwilliams (5) *settled in 4th till wknd o'r 2 fs out*........ (50 to 1 op 25 to 1) 6
Dist: 2l, 1½l, 3l, 2½l, 2l. 2m 4.20s. a 1.70s (6 Ran).
SR: 53/49/46/35/26/22/ (Sheikh Ahmed Bin Saeed Al Maktoum), G Wragg

2291 Bernard Hart Handicap Class E (0-70 3-y-o and up) £2,658 1m 67yds.. (8:05)

1956* WILD STRAWBERRY [55] 4-9-0 B Rouse (14) *made virtually all, rdn alng and styd on gmely ins fnl furlong.* ....(9 to 1 op 6 to 1) 1
1907[4] MY HARVINSKI [62] 3-8-12 D Holland (7) *hdwy o'r 3 fs out, rdn and not quicken ins last.* ....(6 to 1 op 4 to 1 tchd 7 to 1) 2
2099[2] PUSEY STREET BOY [38] 6-7-11 W Carson (11) *chsd wnr most of way, not quicken und pres fnl furlong.* ....(11 to 2 op 6 to 1 tchd 13 to 2) 3
1120 JOLTO [40] 4-7-10 (3*) B Doyle (15) *rear till ran on und pres o'r 2 fs out, no extr wl ins last.* (25 to 1 op 20 to 1) 4
681 HENBURY HALL (Ire) [49] 5-8-8 F Norton (13) *in tch in mid-div, kpt on one pace frm 2 fs out*...(25 to 1 op 16 to 1) 5
2109[2] SHALOU [41] 4-8-0 A Munro (12) *ldg grp, rdn and no extr ins last 2 fs.* (15 to 2 op 8 to 1 tchd 9 to 1 and 7 to 1) 6
1212[5] LIVONIAN [70] 3-9-6 M Roberts (1) *sn pushed alng into mid-div, lost pl bef hfwy, ran on fnl 2 fs*. ...(5 to 1 co-fav op 3 to 1 tchd 11 to 2) 7
1932[6] YONGE TENDER [39] (bl) 6-7-11[2] (3*) D Harrison (2) *nvr better than mid-div.* (12 to 1 op 14 to 1 tchd 16 to 1) 8
2127[6] AEDEAN [42] 4-8-1 T Williams (4) *hdwy frm rear on outsd 3 fs out, no prog from 2 out*......... (25 to 1 op 16 to 1) 9
1912* SARAH-CLARE [65] 5-9-10 J Reid (16) *ldg grp till wknd wl o'r one furlong out*.........(5 to 1 co-fav tchd 11 to 2) 10
1907* TONY'S MIST [65] 3-9-1 Pat Eddery (6) *wl plcd till lost pos o'r 2 fs out*..................(5 to 1 co-fav op 7 to 2) 11
1956 ABSOLUTELY HUMMING [42] 7-8-1[3] R Price (9) *al beh.* ....(50 to 1) 12
1707 BLAKE'S TREASURE [34] (bl) 6-7-7 N Carlisle (5) *nvr trble ldrs*..........................(50 to 1 op 33 to 1) 13
1991 WILL'S LEGACY [44] (bl) 3-7-8[1] N Adams (3) *mid-div till lost tch quickly o'r 2 fs out*..........(14 to 1 tchd 12 to 1) 14
Dist: ¾l, 1l, 2l, 2½l, nk, 1l, 2l, ¾l, nk, 1½l. 1m 44.00s. a 3.00s (14 Ran).
SR: 18/14/-/-/-/-/1/-/-/ (Copyforce Ltd), Miss B Sanders

2292 Frankie Vaughan Conditions Stakes Class D (2-y-o) £3,785 5f 217yds (8:35)

1804 ROXANIAN (Ire) 9-0 D Holland (4) *led aftr one furlong, wndrd lft o'r 2 out, swrvd rght and hdd one out, rdn to ld last 100 yards*........(9 to 1 op 9 to 2 tchd 10 to 1) 1
1565[2] INTERNATIONAL STAR (Ire) 8-6 (3*) Emma O'Gorman (8) *hdwy hfwy, lft in ld o'r one furlong out, rdn and hdd last 100 yards, no extr*............ (8 to 1 tchd 9 to 1) 2
2112[2] MAZEEKA (Ire) 8-9 Pat Eddery (7) *led one furlong, pressed ldrs, ev ch one out, no extr nr line.* ....(5 to 2 op 9 to 4 tchd 11 to 4) 3
2058[8] SECOND SIGHT (Ire) 8-12 M Roberts (3) *settled rear, rdn alng hfwy, styd on ins last 2 fs.* ....(16 to 1 op 10 to 1 tchd 20 to 1) 4
2016* PERUSAL 9-2 J Reid (1) *chsd ldrs, rdn alng 2 fs out, not quicken fnl furlong.* ....(13 to 8 fav op 7 to 4 tchd 2 to 1) 5
1689* CABCHARGE PRINCESS (Ire) 8-7 P Robinson (2) *in tch till wknd 2 fs out*........... (8 to 1 op 6 to 1 tchd 9 to 1) 6
1773* DANCES WITH RISK 8-9 G Hind (6) *ldg grp 4 fs.* ....(14 to 1 op 10 to 1 tchd 16 to 1) 7
2096[4] LADY PHYL 8-2 (3*) B Doyle (5) *strted slwly, al beh, tld off.* ....(8 to 1 op 14 to 1) 8
Dist: 1l, 1½l, 1l, 1l, 2½l, 3l, 12l. 1m 12.30s. a 2.00s (8 Ran).
SR: 42/33/27/26/26/7/-/-/ (Mrs Elaine Mitchell), M J Heaton-Ellis

2293 Ilia Kodicek Rating Related Maiden Stakes Class D (0-75 3-y-o) £3,172 1m 67yds.......................... (9:05)

602[3] SCORCHED AIR 8-9 M Hills (6) *hdwy frm rear and swtchd lft o'r 2 fs out, rdn to ld wl over one out, hld on.* ....(7 to 2 tchd 9 to 2) 1
1746[5] AJMAAN (USA) 9-0 M Roberts (1) *hld up last, ran on o'r 2 fs out, ev ch entering last, not quicken last 100 yards.* ....(6 to 1 op 3 to 1 tchd 13 to 2) 2
1972[2] NOBLE RISK 9-0 Pat Eddery (2) *led to hfwy, kpt on fnl furlong*................(11 to 4 op 2 to 1 tchd 3 to 1) 3
1616[4] CHAPKA (Ire) 8-9 L Piggott (3) *hld up rear, hdwy on outsd o'r 2 fs out, not quicken over one out.* ....(2 to 1 fav op 5 to 2) 4
MAWAYED (USA) 9-0 W Carson (4) *pressed ldr, led hfwy till wl o'r one out, sn wknd*........ (6 to 1 tchd 7 to 1) 5
BERGLIOT 8-9 R Perham (5) *rcd in 3rd till lost pl o'r 2 fs out*.................. (33 to 1 op 20 to 1 tchd 40 to 1) 6
Dist: 1l, 1½l, 1½l, 2l, 6l. 1m 45.80s. a 4.80s (6 Ran).
(Michael Wauchope), J W Hills

BELLEWSTOWN (IRE) (good to firm)
Tuesday July 6th

2294 Kilsharvan EBF Maiden (2-y-o) £3,107 5f.............................(5:30)

2037 NURMI (Ire) 9-0 J F Egan (6)..................... (10 to 1) 1
1104[2] ROYAL THIMBLE (Ire) 8-11 A J Nolan (7).......... (13 to 2) 2
1792[5] SPRING FORCE (Ire) (bl) 9-0 J P Murtagh (1) (4 to 1 co-fav) 3
LYDIA MC (Ire) 8-5 (6*) B J Walsh (5)................ (6 to 1) 4
2037[6] ORANGE PLEASURE (USA) 8-11 W J O'Connor (8) .... (4 to 1 co-fav) 5
2188[8] PASTELLE 8-3 (8*) D J O'Donohoe (9)............. (14 to 1) 6
1924[6] PETER'S POWER (Ire) 9-0 S Craine (12).......... (12 to 1) 7
SOCIAL GATHERING (Ire) 8-11 R Hughes (11).... (12 to 1) 8
BLACKROCK HERO (Ire) 9-0 P Shanahan (10)...... (14 to 1) 9
1924[5] CATCH A DREAM (Ire) 8-9 (2*) R M Burke (3) (4 to 1 co-fav) 10
COOLAGOWN DOME (Ire) 8-5 (6*) J J Behan (4).. (20 to 1) 11
1792[4] DASHING DANCER (Ire) (bl) 9-0 B Coogan (2).....(14 to 1) 12
Dist: 1½l, 2l, hd, 2½l. 59.50s. (12 Ran).
(Mrs Anna Doyle), Patrick Joseph Flynn

2295 Maurice McAuley Memorial Maiden (3-y-o and up) £2,762 5f.........(6:30)

1515[5] KILLEEN STAR (Ire) 3-9-0 R Hughes (1)....... (10 to 9 on) 1
2285 ASTA MADERA (Ire) 3-8-11 J F Egan (8)........... (5 to 1) 2
1795 FIVE LITTLE GIRLS (Ire) 3-8-11 K J Manning (6).... (7 to 1) 3
1622[8] INISHMOT (Ire) 3-8-11 N G McCullagh (7)........ (9 to 1) 4
1619[6] WHY ME LINDA (Ire) 4-9-3 J P Murtagh (4)......... (7 to 1) 5
2248 EILEENS HOPE (Ire) (bl) 3-8-11 P V Gilson (3)..... (10 to 1) 6
1822[6] PERSIAN LIGHT (Ire) 3-8-11 P Shanahan (5)...... (12 to 1) 7
1620[6] SORRECA (Ire) 4-8-11 (6*) J A Heffernan (2)....... (20 to 1) 8
Dist: ¾l, 4l, nk, 2l. 58.50s. (8 Ran).
(R Fabrizius), M J Grassick

2296 Oldbridge Concrete Handicap (0-80 3-y-o and up) £2,762 1¾m..... (7:00)

2186[2] ANGAREB (Ire) [-] 4-8-7 P V Gilson (5).......... (2 to 1 fav) 1
1996[6] WESBEST (Ire) [-] 4-9-1 N G McCullagh (2)......... (9 to 2) 2
PYLON SPARKS [-] (bl) 8-9-9 J P Murtagh (3)....... (14 to 1) 3
2186[5] LAKE OF LOUGHREA (Ire) [-] (bl) 3-7-3[2] (8*) R T Fitzpatrick (7) ....(9 to 1) 4
1467[9] UPPINGHAM [-] 7-7-11 (6*) J A Heffernan (9)..... (10 to 1) 5
1013[5] AQUINAS [-] 7-7-8 Joanna Morgan (1)............ (8 to 1) 6
1468[9] THATCH AND GOLD (Ire) [-] 5-9-8 (6*) J R Barry (4) (13 to 2) 7
2143 SWEET DOWNS [-] 12-7-1 (6*) P P Murphy (8)...... (25 to 1) 8
1757[4] MILLMOUNT (Ire) [-] (bl) 3-7-12 (4*) W J Smith (6)..(13 to 2) 9
Dist: 4½l, ½l, 4l, 14l. 3m 2.90s. (9 Ran).
(Lone Star Syndicate), M Halford

2297 Murphy Sand And Gravel Handicap (0-80 3-y-o and up) £2,935 1m... (8:00)

HAPPY ROVER [-] 8-10-0 J P Murtagh (14)........ (7 to 1) 1
2141[4] RUSTIC-ORT (Ire) [-] (bl) 5-7-10 (4*) W J Smith (9) (13 to 2) 2
1922* AULD STOCK (Ire) [-] (bl) 3-9-1 J F Egan (1)........(8 to 1) 3
1995 NO DUNCE (Ire) [-] 3-8-9 R Hughes (11)............(14 to 1) 4
1611[7] BARNAGEERA BOY (Ire) [-] 4-7-8 (8*) B J Halligan (15) ....(12 to 1) 5
2041[8] SIGHTSEER (Ire) [-] 4-7-4 (6*) P P Murphy (10).... (20 to 1) 6
1570[7] DAHAR'S LOVE (USA) [-] 4-7-2 (10*) J P Cornally (6) ....(10 to 1) 7
819[7] VLADIVOSTOK [-] 3-8-0 (8*) K M So (12)........... (20 to 1) 8
HOLIWAY STAR (Ire) [-] (bl) 3-8-9 (2*) K H Ting (16) (10 to 1) 9
2141 PHILIP PATRICK (Ire) [-] (bl) 3-8-1 (2*) D G O'Shea (4) ....(20 to 1) 10
1620[4] BUSINESS CENTRE (Ire) [-] 3-7-9 Joanna Morgan (13) ....(14 to 1) 11
2041 YOUR UNCLE STANLEY (Ire) [-] 4-8-6 (6*) J J Behan (2) ....(20 to 1) 12
1574* BIZANA (Ire) [-] 3-9-1 S Craine (7)..................(5 to 1) 13
1995[9] RAFFERTY'S INNER (Ire) [-] 3-7-12 (8*) R T Fitzpatrick (8) ....(6 to 1) bd
1645* SANS CERIPH (Ire) [-] 3-9-5 W J O'Connor (3)..(9 to 2 fav) su
868 ARDGILLIAN (Ire) [-] 3-8-12 N G McCullagh (5).... (12 to 1) pu
Dist: 1l, 4½l, 2½l, ¾l. 1m 36.50s. (16 Ran).
(Mrs E McMahon), F Dunne

MAISONS-LAFFITTE (FR) (good)
Tuesday July 6th

2298 Prix Messidor (Group 3) (3-y-o and up) £23,895 1m.................... (2:55)

FANMORE (USA) 5-9-2 T Jarnet (1) *trkd ldr, effrt o'r 2 fs out, led over one out, ran on wl*...........(10 to 9 on) 1
1367[7] CAESOUR (USA) 3-8-7 C Asmussen (4) *rcd in 3rd, effrt on outsd one and a half fs out, ran on strly ins last, jst fld.* ....(19 to 10) 2
1908* ZABAR 5-9-2 A Cruz (3) *led till o'r one furlong out, kpt on gmely*..............................(62 to 10) 3
920[4] TAKE RISKS (Fr) 4-9-6 G Mosse (2) *slwly away, al beh.* ....(26 to 10) 4
Dist: Sht-nk, ½l, 4½l. 1m 36.30s. a 1.60s (4 Ran).
SR: 72/62/69/59/ (K Abdulla), A Fabre

NEWMARKET (JULY) (good to firm)
Tuesday July 6th

Going Correction: MINUS 0.45 sec. per fur. (races 1,2,3,4,5,6), MINUS 0.55 (7)

2299 Eastern Electricity Maiden Stakes Class D (2-y-o) £4,854 7f........(2:00)

COLONEL COLLINS (USA) 9-0 J Reid (3) *nvr far away, niggled alng hfwy, led wl o'r one furlong out, quickened, imprsv*..........(11 to 4 op 2 to 1 tchd 4 to 1) 1
1666[2] POTENTATE (USA) 9-0 A Munro (11) *al hndy, drvn alng whn pace quickened o'r one furlong out, kpt on, no ch wth wnr*............... (5 to 1 op 7 to 2 tchd 11 to 2) 2
SOUTHERN POWER (Ire) 9-0 L Dettori (2) *tucked away on ins, ev ch and drvn alng 2 fs out, kpt on, better for race.* ....(10 to 1 op 7 to 1 tchd 5 to 1 and 12 to 1) 3
WILD INVADER (USA) 9-0 Pat Eddery (7) *led for o'r 5 fs, drvn alng appr last, no extr*....(7 to 4 fav tchd 9 to 4) 4
SAWLAJAN (USA) 9-0 W Carson (4) *missed break, last hfwy, swtchd outsd to improve 2 fs out, prmsg.* ....(14 to 1 op 7 to 1 tchd 16 to 1) 5
1131[5] ROISIN CLOVER 8-9 R Cochrane (5) *niggled alng to go pace aftr 2 fs, nvr rch ldrs.* ....(20 to 1 op 16 to 1 tchd 25 to 1) 6
1905 COURT JESTER 9-0 D Holland (10) *speed on outsd till wknd wl o'r one furlong out.* ....(40 to 1 op 20 to 1 tchd 50 to 1) 7
NAJM ALMAYDAAN (USA) 9-0 M Roberts (1) *wth ldrs, pushed alng and lost grnd hfwy, eased whn btn 2 fs out*...............................(14 to 1 op 5 to 1) 8
CLIFTON BEAT (USA) 9-0 M Hills (9) *sluggish strt, hdwy to track ldrs hfwy, wknd o'r one furlong out.* ....(50 to 1 op 20 to 1) 9
MASURI KABISA (USA) 8-9 J Quinn (6) *chsd alng to keep up, nvr a factor*....................(33 to 1 tchd 50 to 1) 10
1706 ZOES PET 8-9 G Bardwell (8) *reminders leaving stalls, struggling to go pace hfwy, tld off.* (50 to 1 op 33 to 1) 11
Dist: 7l, ¾l, nk, 5l, 3½l, 2½l, 1½l, hd, 5l, 25l. 1m 25.49s. a 1.29s (11 Ran).
SR: 33/12/10/9/-/-/ (R E Sangster), P W Chapple-Hyam

2300 H & K Commissions Handicap Class D (0-80 3-y-o and up) £8,285 1m... (2:35)

1641[2] SAIFAN [69] (bl) 4-9-0 (5*) C Hodgson (17) *trkd ldrs, drvn ahead entering fnl furlong, ran on wl.* ....(25 to 1 op 16 to 1) 1
1830[8] BRAVURA [77] 4-9-13 N Day (8) *settled off the pace, weaved through last 2 fs, fnshd wl.* ....(50 to 1 op 33 to 1) 2
1954* BALLERINA BAY [69] (v) 5-9-5 Pat Eddery (13) *patiently rdn, hdwy to chal appr fnl furlong, not quicken last 100 yards*.............. (9 to 1 op 8 to 1 tchd 10 to 1) 3
2022[2] BLOCKADE (USA) [76] 4-9-12 M Hills (9) *led, quickened hfwy, hdd and no extr entering fnl furlong.* ....(8 to 1 fav op 6 to 1) 4
1768[7] JADE VALE [77] 4-9-10 (3*) D Harrison (6) *chsd ldrs, improved o'r one furlong out, fnshd wl.* ....(9 to 1 op 10 to 1 tchd 11 to 1 and 8 to 1) 5
2161[3] HOPEFUL BID (Ire) [67] (bl) 4-9-3 J Reid (4) *settled midfield, drvn alng o'r one furlong out, ran on.* ....(20 to 1 op 16 to 1 tchd 25 to 1) 6
1612[3] TALENTED TING (Ire) [58] 4-8-8 N Carlisle (14) *wth ldrs till fdd und pres last 2 fs.* (20 to 1 op 16 to 1 tchd 25 to 1) 7
2065[2] ANORAK (USA) [78] 3-9-5 R Cochrane (7) *beh, styd on last 2 fs, nrst finish*......(20 to 1 op 16 to 1 tchd 25 to 1) 8
1954[8] KISSAVOS [46] 7-7-10 F Norton (2) *co'red up on ins, not much room over 2 fs out, ran on finish.* ....(20 to 1 tchd 33 to 1) 9
1927[2] MR VINCENT [79] 3-9-6 B Raymond (10) *wth ldrs, drvn alng to hold pl last 2 fs, fdd*...... (25 to 1 op 16 to 1) 10
2031* MOON SPIN [71] 4-9-7 Paul Eddery (1) *settled midfield, not much room o'r 2 fs out, nvr able to chal.* ....(9 to 1 op 8 to 1 tchd 10 to 1) 11

978[4] BLUE FLAG (USA) [69] 4-9-5 L Piggott (18) *al hndy, feeling pace and rdn o'r one furlong out, no extr.* ....(16 to 1 op 14 to 1 tchd 20 to 1) 12+
2045* BIG BLUE [73] 4-9-9 M Roberts (3) *co'red up on ins, not clr run over 3 fs out, styd on, nvr nrr.* ....(12 to 1 op 10 to 1 tchd 14 to 1) 12+
1612[8] LEXUS (Ire) [48] 5-7-12 D Biggs (5) *struggling hfwy, nvr a factor*........................(20 to 1 tchd 25 to 1) 14
1973* NORTH ESK (USA) [67] 4-9-3 G Carter (11) *chsd alng to keep up, nvr threatened ldrs*..................(12 to 1) 15
DODGY [59] (v) 6-8-9 A Munro (15) *chsd ldr, drvn alng wl o'r one furlong out, fdd*........ (33 to 1 tchd 50 to 1) 16
1592* SELF EXPRESSION [62] 5-8-12 L Dettori (12) *sluggish strt, swtchd outsd and some hdwy o'r 2 fs out, nvr dngrs.* .... (9 to 1 op 8 to 1 tchd 10 to 1) 17
2087[2] DIPLOMATIST [67] 3-8-8 W Carson (16) *speed to press ldrs for o'r 5 fs, fdd*...............(12 to 1 op 10 to 1) 18
1743[6] FOOLISH TOUCH [43] (v) 11-7-7 J Quinn (19) *sluggish strt, effrt on outsd o'r 2 fs out, nvr dngrs.* ....(25 to 1 tchd 33 to 1) 19

Dist: 1l, 1½l, ½l, nk, nk, ½l, 1½l, ½l, hd, 1½l. 1m 37.76s. b 0.14s (19 Ran).
SR: 53/58/45/50/50/30/28/34/18/ (Mrs Rosalie Hawes), D Morris

2301 Hillsdown Cherry Hinton Stakes Class A (Group 3) (2-y-o) £15,845 6f... (3:05)

1639* LEMON SOUFFLE 8-9 L Piggott (8) *confidently rdn, hdwy to ld o'r one furlong out, readily.* .... (5 to 4 fav op 11 to 10 on tchd 11 to 8) 1
1844[3] RED RITA (Ire) 8-9 R Cochrane (6) *nvr far away, drw level o'r one furlong out, kpt on same pace.* ....(25 to 1 op 20 to 1 tchd 33 to 1) 2
2067[2] ROHITA (Ire) 8-9 Pat Eddery (1) *steadied strt, drvn alng to improve on outsd last 2 fs, drifted lft ins last, one pace.* .... (9 to 4 op 5 to 2 tchd 11 to 4) 3
2067* SNIPE HALL 8-12 P Robinson (7) *chsd ldrs, effrt whn not much room ins fnl furlong, swtchd outsd, nvr nrr.* .... (8 to 1 op 6 to 1 tchd 10 to 1) 4
1766[7] DOUBLE DOWN 8-9 L Dettori (5) *made most for o'r 4 fs, rdn and no extr*......(14 to 1 op 12 to 1 tchd 16 to 1) 5
1916* BRAARI (USA) 8-9 W Carson (2) *tucked away on ins, ev ch hfwy, fdd o'r one furlong out*..... (14 to 1 op 10 to 1) 6
1790[4] IZZA 8-9 M Roberts (3) *wth ldrs, feeling pace o'r one furlong out, eased whn btn.* ....(16 to 1 op 20 to 1 tchd 14 to 1) 7
1708* WINSOME WOOSTER 8-9 W R Swinburn (4) *pressed ldg pair, hrd drvn o'r one furlong out, sn btn.* ....(50 to 1 op 25 to 1 tchd 66 to 1) 8

Dist: 1½l, ¾l, 1½l, nk, 2l, ¾l, 6l. 1m 12.63s. a 0.93s (8 Ran).
SR: 22/16/13/10/6/ (Lord Carnarvon), R Hannon

2302 Princess Of Wales's Stakes Class A (Group 2) (3-y-o and up) £38,046 1½m ....(3:40)

2076[8] DESERT TEAM (USA) 3-8-1 W Carson (7) *nvr far away, hrd rdn whn pace quickened last 3 fs, ran on gmely to ld cl hme*...............................(10 to 1 op 12 to 1) 1
1748[6] YOUNG BUSTER (Ire) 5-9-0 M Hills (2) *led, steadied hfwy, quickened last 3 fs, rdn and ct cl hme.* .... (16 to 1 op 14 to 1) 2
1805[2] RED BISHOP (USA) 5-9-0 M Roberts (6) *patiently rdn, improved on outsd to chal o'r one furlong out, ran on same pace*..........................(3 to 1 op 9 to 4) 3
1805* JEUNE 4-9-3 R Cochrane (3) *last and hld up, effrt and swtchd ins o'r one furlong out, not quicken last 100 yards*.............. (5 to 2 fav op 2 to 1 tchd 11 to 4) 4
1805[4] SAPIENCE 7-9-3 L Dettori (4) *al hndy, drw level hfwy, hrd drvn o'r one furlong out, fdd*.... (10 to 1 tchd 14 to 1) 5
1472[6] ZINAAD 4-9-3 W R Swinburn (5) *al hndy, drvn alng and ev ch 2 fs out, outpcd fnl furlong*...... (7 to 2 op 5 to 1) 6
1888[8] SNURGE 6-9-5 Pat Eddery (1) *nvr far away, jnd ldg pair hfwy, fdd o'r one furlong out.* .... (10 to 1 op 8 to 1 tchd 11 to 1) 7

Dist: Nk, 2l, ¾l, 2½l, ¾l, 2½l. 2m 26.70s. b 2.10s (7 Ran).
SR: 54/66/62/63/58/56/53/ (Maktoum Al Maktoum), J S Bolger

2303 Hamilton Rated Class B Handicap (0-100 3-y-o) £7,981 6f.......... (4:10)

2060[4] STORITHS (Ire) [91] 8-12 W R Swinburn (11) *patiently rdn, improved on outsd o'r one furlong out, ran on gmely to ld last strds*........... (7 to 1 op 6 to 1 tchd 15 to 2) 1
2028[2] SHEILA'S SECRET (Ire) [91] 8-12 J Reid (10) *al wl plcd, led o'r one furlong out, rdn and ct last strds*...... (10 to 1) 2
2062 TRUE PRECISION [86] 8-7 A Munro (4) *led for o'r one furlong, feeling pace and lost grnd 2 out, rallied ins last*.. (12 to 1) 3
1718[2] TROON [91] 8-12 L Piggott (2) *chsd alng hfwy, not much room till weaved through ins fnl furlong, ran on.* ....(5 to 1 tchd 11 to 2) 4
1841* LOCH PATRICK [86] 8-7 A McGlone (9) *nvr far away, effrt und pres o'r one furlong out, kpt on same pace.* ....(4 to 1 fav op 9 to 2 tchd 5 to 1) 5
1718[3] ABERGELE [88] 8-9 K Fallon (6) *chsd ldrs, feeling pace and rdn alng hfwy, kpt on fnl furlong, nrst finish.* .... (13 to 2 op 5 to 1 tchd 7 to 1) 6
2106* PALACEGATE TOUCH [86] (bl) 8-7 (3ex) J Carroll (12) *led aftr one and a half fs till o'r one out, fdd.* ....(16 to 1 tchd 20 to 1) 7
1718[5] YOUNG ERN [96] 9-3 M Roberts (3) *drvn alng to keep in tch hfwy, not pace to trble ldrs*..... (10 to 1 op 8 to 1) 8
1718[6] HEAVENLY RISK [86] 8-7 Pat Eddery (7) *wtd wth, improved wl o'r one furlong out, kpt on, nvr nrr.* ....(15 to 2 op 7 to 1 tchd 8 to 1) 9
1786 BRIGG FAIR [100] 9-7 L Dettori (8) *in tch, drvn alng hfwy, nvr able to rch ldrs*................(25 to 1 op 16 to 1) 10
DARK EYED LADY (Ire) [90] 8-11 R Price (5) *speed to chase ldg 4 for o'r four fs, fdd*........................ (33 to 1) 11
1213 YAKIN (USA) [86] 8-7 W Carson (1) *speed frnt rnk till fdd o'r one furlong out*.............(20 to 1 op 16 to 1) 12

Dist: Nk, 1½l, ¾l, hd, 1½l, 4l, ¾l, 2l, 2l, 2½l. 1m 11.24s. b 0.46s (12 Ran).
SR: 53/52/41/43/37/33/15/22/4/ (Mrs M Irwin), J W Watts

2304 Chesterfield Fillies Rated Class B Handicap (0-100 3-y-o) £7,967 7f (4:45)

1761[2] TOLEDO QUEEN (Ire) [82] 8-7 J Reid (5) *al hndy, jnd ldr 2 fs out, led jst ins last, hld on.* .... (12 to 1 op 10 to 1 tchd 14 to 1) 1
1765[6] MITHL AL HAWA [96] 9-7 W R Swinburn (7) *nvr far away, chlgd und pres o'r one furlong out, ran on, jst fld.* ....(7 to 1 op 10 to 1 tchd 11 to 1) 2
1174[8] FELUCCA [96] 9-7 Pat Eddery (4) *patiently rdn, imprvg whn not much room o'r one furlong out, wweaved through ins last, fnshd wl.* .... (4 to 1 op 11 to 4 tchd 9 to 2) 3
1780[8] SPARK (Ire) [82] 8-7 A Munro (6) *set modest pace, jnd and quickened 2 fs out, hdd jst ins last, kpt on.* .... (33 to 1 op 25 to 1) 4
1839* BARBOUKH [89] 9-0 L Dettori (3) *settled midfield, effrt und pres o'r one furlong out, ran on.* ....(11 to 4 fav op 5 to 2 tchd 9 to 4) 5
2028[3] MARGARET'S GIFT [87] 8-12 J Carroll (11) *nvr far away, ev ch and drvn alng o'r one furlong out, not quicken last 100 yards*............ (16 to 1 op 14 to 1 tchd 20 to 1) 6
1451* NORTHERN BIRD [85] 8-10 D Holland (2) *tucked away beh ldrs, effrt o'r one furlong out, kpt on.* .... (15 to 2 op 5 to 1 tchd 8 to 1) 7
1616[3] TRAPEZIUM [82] 8-7 M Roberts (8) *pld hrd, ev ch and drvn alng o'r one furlong out, kpt on same pace.* .... (12 to 1 op 10 to 1 tchd 14 to 1) 8
AMIRATI (USA) [88] 8-13 B Raymond (10) *trkd ldrs, effrt and drvn alng o'r one furlong out, not quicken ins last.* .... (33 to 1 op 20 to 1) 9
1839[4] ANEESATI [94] 9-2 (3*) B Doyle (1) *wth ldr, hrd drvn o'r one furlong out, no extr*.........(16 to 1 op 14 to 1) 10
1451[8] MOON OVER MIAMI [86] 8-11 W Newnes (9) *str hold, swtchd outsd to improve last 2 fs, not pace to chal.* .... (10 to 1 op 8 to 1 tchd 12 to 1) 11

Dist: Sht-hd, nk, ½l, nk, ¾l, sht-hd, nk, 1½l, hd, 2l. 1m 25.72s. a 1.52s (11 Ran).
SR: 23/36/35/19/25/21/18/14/15/ (R E Sangster), P W Chapple-Hyam

2305 Soham Handicap Class D (0-80 3-y-o and up) £4,464 5f...............(5:15)

1679 NED'S BONANZA [70] 4-9-6 Pat Eddery (8) *al wl plcd, led well o'r one furlong out, kpt on well nr finish.* .... (6 to 1 op 5 to 1 tchd 13 to 2) 1
1000 PAGEBOY [60] 4-8-10 R Cochrane (7) *nvr far away, hrd drvn o'r one furlong out, ran on wl last 50 yards.* ....(10 to 1 tchd 12 to 1) 2
2110[2] BRIGHT PARAGON (Ire) [47] 4-7-11 J Quinn (4) *settled midfield, rdn to improve o'r one furlong out, kpt on wl.* ....(7 to 1 tchd 8 to 1) 3
2018[2] VERDE ALITALIA (Ire) [78] 4-10-0 W Carson (2) *led for o'r 3 fs, rdn and not quicken wl ins last.* ....(11 to 8 fav op 5 to 4 tchd 13 to 8) 4
1860[2] PEERAGE PRINCE [66] (bl) 4-9-2 L Piggott (9) *pressed ldrs, drvn alng wl o'r one furlong out, one pace.* ....(8 to 1 op 6 to 1 tchd 9 to 1) 5
1806 ALLTHRUTHENIGHT (Ire) [78] 4-10-0 J Reid (10) *steadied strt, effrt and niggled alng o'r one furlong out, not quicken*..........................(14 to 1 tchd 16 to 1) 6
2050[9] SERIOUS HURRY [56] 5-8-6 W Newnes (5) *pressed ldrs, wknd appr fnl furlong*........... (20 to 1 op 16 to 1) 7
2132[4] BOLD COUNTY [68] 3-8-12 R P Elliott (6) *chsd alng and edgd lft hfwy, ran on, nvr nrr.* .... (10 to 1 op 8 to 1 tchd 12 to 1) 8
2050[7] STOCKTINA [43] 6-7-7 N Carlisle (3) *chsd ldrs, drvn alng last 2 fs, no imprsn*...............(20 to 1 op 14 to 1) 9
1815[8] GEMINI FIRE [58] 9-8-8 D Biggs (1) *bolted gng to post, tld off aftr 2 fs*........................(33 to 1 op 25 to 1) 10

Dist: ¾l, sht-hd, 1l, 1½l, 1l, 1½l, nk, 4l, dist. 58.52s. b 0.18s (10 Ran).
SR: 55/42/28/55/37/45/17/22/-/ (Ned Jones), M Dods

PONTEFRACT (firm)
Tuesday July 6th
Going Correction: MINUS 0.35 sec. per fur.

2306 York And Westminster Apprentice Series Round Two Handicap Class F (0-70 3-y-o and up) £2,562 1½m 8yds ....(2:20)

1161 EIGHTANDAHALF (Ire) [47] 4-9-2 D Wright (2) *led aftr one and a half fs, made rst, clr frm hfwy, drvn out, unchlgd*..................(8 to 1 tchd 9 to 1) 1
2130* HASTA LA VISTA [45] (bl) 3-8-1 (7ex) G Parkin (3) *led one and a half fs then chsd wnr, shrtlvd effrt 3 furlongs out, sn no further imprsn*......(7 to 4 op 5 to 4 tchd 15 to 8) 2
2207³ FAMOUS BEAUTY [44] 6-8-8 (5*) L Aspell (5) *dwlt, hld up, some hdwy 5 fs out, sn one pace.* ....(11 to 8 fav op 7 to 4 tchd 5 to 4) 3
1847⁶ TRONCHETTO (Ire) [59] (bl) 4-10-0 J Tate (1) *in tch till rdn hfwy, sn wknd, tld off.* ....(5 to 1 op 4 to 1 tchd 13 to 2 and 7 to 1) 4
BLAKES REACH [55] 3-8-4 (7*) Claire West (4) *in tch till sddl slpd aftr 4 fs, sn last, tld off.* (66 to 1 op 33 to 1) 5

Dist: 8l, 2½l, dist, 12l. 2m 38.80s. a 3.80s (5 Ran).
SR: 22/-/ (Mick Burrowes), G R Oldroyd

2307 Bradley Selling Stakes Class G (3-y-o) £2,217 1¼m 6yds.............. (2:50)

1399⁵ SCOFFERA 8-6 Kim Tinkler (6) *sn led, hrd rdn frm o'r one furlong out, jnd on post*............(8 to 1 op 7 to 1) 1+
2086² BARLEY CAKE 8-6 J Fanning (5) *hld up in tch, took clr order o'r 3 fs out, sstnd chal fnl furlong to dead-heat on post*........................(11 to 10 fav op 5 to 4) 1+
1896* ANN HILL (Ire) 8-11 W Ryan (1) *rstrained strt and patiently rdn, hdwy o'r 2 fs out, ran on one pace fnl furlong*.............................(7 to 2 op 5 to 2) 3
SEA-AYR (Ire) 8-3 (3*) J Weaver (2) *took keen hold, trkd ldr, rdn wl o'r 2 fs out, sn no extr.* ....(16 to 1 op 20 to 1 tchd 25 to 1) 4
136⁷ QUICK VICTORY 8-6 M Wigham (4) *handily plcd till rdn o'r 3 fs out, sn wknd*.............. (50 to 1 op 33 to 1) 5
2064 FORENZA 8-6 K Darley (3) *took keen hold, hld up in tch till drpd last wl o'r 2 fs out, sn well beh.* ....(7 to 2 tchd 4 to 1) 6

Dist: Dd-ht, 4l, 15l, ½l, 8l. 2m 16.50s. a 8.30s (6 Ran).
(Mrs Christine Cawley & W J Dobson), N Tinkler & T Fairhurst

2308 King Richard III Handicap Class E (0-70 3-y-o and up) £3,080 1m 4yds ....(3:20)

1940⁴ SPANISH VERDICT [64] 6-10-0 N Connorton (3) *nvr far away, rdn wl o'r one furlong out, str run to ld ins last 100 yards*..............(7 to 1 op 6 to 1 tchd 8 to 1) 1
902⁷ PATIENCE PLEASE [53] 4-9-0 (3*) S Maloney (11) *chsd ldrs, effrt on outsd frm 3 fs out, rdn and kpt on wl ins last.* ....(14 to 1 op 12 to 1) 2
2099³ ROMOOSH [64] 4-9-7 (7*) G Forster (9) *cl up, rdn and slightly outpcd o'r 2 fs out, came wide strt, ran on strly ins last*............. (12 to 1 op 10 to 1 tchd 14 to 1) 3
1956⁹ ROLY WALLACE [53] (bl) 4-9-3 M Wigham (14) *slwly into strd, beh till gd hdwy wl o'r one furlong out, ran on, nrst finish*........................ (14 to 1 op 10 to 1) 4
2057⁴ MAROWINS [46] 4-8-5 (5*) Stephen Davies (10) *beh, rdn wl o'r 2 fs out, ran on fnl furlong, nvr nrr.* ....(11 to 2 op 6 to 1 tchd 7 to 1) 5
2138² RAGING THUNDER [62] (bl) 3-9-3 K Darley (12) *al hndy, led wl o'r 2 fs out, hdd and wknd last 100 yards.* ....(5 to 1 fav tchd 4 to 1) 6
2197³ COOL ENOUGH [35] 12-7-13 J Lowe (8) *hld up an beh till ran on fnl one and a half fs, not rch ldrs.* ....(6 to 1 tchd 7 to 1) 7
1498 FALCONS DAWN [47] 6-8-11 G Duffield (4) *wl beh early, some hdwy fnl one and a half fs, no dngr.* .... (14 to 1 op 10 to 1) 8
1900 BIDWEAYA (USA) [32] 6-7-10 N Adams (13) *nvr better than mid-div*..................................(25 to 1) 9
2113 IRISH GROOM [39] (bl) 6-7-12 (5*) A Garth (6) *settled mid-field, rdn o'r 3 fs out, sn wknd*.....(20 to 1 op 16 to 1) 10
CAN CAN CHARLIE [58] 3-8-13 Dean McKeown (2) *chsd ldrs till wknd o'r 3 fs out*..........(20 to 1 op 14 to 1) 11
1913³ COALISLAND [69] 3-9-7 (3*) J Weaver (5) *sn prmnt, led o'r 3 fs out till hdd over 2 out, soon wknd and eased whn btn*.............................. (14 to 1 op 10 to 1) 12
1947² DIWALI DANCER [50] (bl) 3-8-5 A Mackay (7) *slwly away, al towards rear*........................(10 to 1 op 8 to 1) 13
2001⁹ TRACHELIUM [64] 3-9-5 A Culhane (1) *led till hdd o'r 3 fs out, stdly wknd and no ch whn slightly hmpd ins last.* ....(12 to 1 op 20 to 1 tchd 25 to 1) 14

Dist: ½l, sht-hd, hd, ½l, ½l, 3½l, 2l, 1½l, ¾l, hd. 1m 44.80s. a 2.70s (14 Ran).
SR: 32/19/29/17/8/13/ (Cox & Allen (Kendal) Ltd), Denys Smith

2309 Nyquist Handicap Class D (0-80 3-y-o and up) £4,308 6f.................(3:50)

1938⁴ FORMIDABLE LIZ [54] 3-8-3 G Duffield (1) *broke wl, made virtually all, rdn and flashed tail ins fnl furlong, jst hld on*.............................(10 to 1 op 8 to 1) 1
2060 MISS HAGGIS [72] 4-10-0 W Woods (6) *wtd wth, gd hdwy betw horses o'r one furlong out, hrd rdn and ran on wl ins last, jst fld*....................(7 to 1 tchd 8 to 1) 2
2173² BALLAD DANCER [59] 8-9-1 M Birch (5) *chsd ldrs, rdn o'r 2 fs out, kpt on same pace ins last.* (5 to 1 fav op 4 to 1) 3
2062⁷ BLUE GRIT [68] 7-9-10 J Lowe (7) *chsd ldg bunch, rdn o'r 2 fs out, kpt on fnl furlong*.......... (6 to 1 op 5 to 1) 4
1865³ PRINCE BELFORT [61] 5-9-3 N Adams (9) *al hndy, ev ch o'r one furlong out, unbl to quicken.* ....(6 to 1 tchd 11 to 2) 5
1898⁵ SAVAHRA SOUND [68] 8-9-5 (5*) O Pears (8) *prmnt, ev ch o'r 2 fs out, wknd appr last*........(12 to 1 op 10 to 1) 6
2173⁴ SULLY'S CHOICE (USA) [46] (bl) 12-8-2 K Darley (4) *dsptd early ld, rdn o'r 2 out, wkng whn hmpd appr fnl furlong*................... (17 to 2 op 8 to 1 tchd 9 to 1) 7
1898³ STATE FLYER [60] (v) 5-8-9 (7*) G Forster (2) *sn rdn alng in rear, nvr able to chal*............ (8 to 1 tchd 10 to 1) 8
1589 PRECENTOR [51] (bl) 7-8-7 Dean McKeown (3) *beh, some hdwy whn not much room wl o'r one furlong out, sn no dngr*........................... (8 to 1 tchd 10 to 1) 9
1286³ CELESTINE [62] 4-9-4 J Fanning (10) *chsd ldrs till wknd o'r 2 fs out*........................(10 to 1 op 8 to 1) 10

Dist: Hd, 2½l, nk, 1l, 3½l, hd, 1½l, 5l, 3l. 1m 15.40s. a 0.70s (10 Ran).
SR: 33/57/34/42/31/24/1/9/-/ (J Johnson), M D Hammond

2310 Tanshelf Maiden Stakes Class D (3-y-o and up) £3,757 1½m 8yds... (4:20)

1901² VISHNU (USA) 3-8-8 W Ryan (6) *al hndy, pushed alng to ld o'r 2 fs out, ran on strly.* (6 to 4 jt-fav tchd 13 to 8) 1
842⁴ BAWAETH (USA) 3-8-3 K Darley (2) *chsd ldrs, rdn and hdwy o'r 2 fs out, chlgd last, unbl to quicken.* (6 to 4 jt-fav op 11 to 8 tchd 5 to 4) 2
1769⁸ BLUE GROTTO (Ire) 3-8-8 G Duffield (10) *led till hdd o'r 2 fs out, wknd quickly appr last*...... (5 to 1 tchd 11 to 2) 3
2010⁷ MISTROY 3-8-1¹ (3*) J Weaver (4) *chsd ldrs till rdn and wknd o'r 2 fs out*...................(25 to 1 op 16 to 1) 4
1864⁴ NOUVELLE CUISINE 5-9-2 J Fanning (5) *pld hrd, wth ldrs till rdn and wknd quickly o'r 2 fs out.* ....(14 to 1 op 16 to 1 tchd 20 to 1) 5
2047 FAIRFORD 4-9-7 N Adams (8) *slwly into strd, sn beh, moderate hdwy o'r 2 fs out, no dngr.* ....(100 to 1 op 50 to 1) 6
2131³ GOLDEN SAVANNAH 3-8-8 T Lucas (1) *pld hrd early and rstrained, bustled alng wl o'r 2 fs out, nvr a threat.* ....(50 to 1 op 33 to 1) 7
COUREUR 4-9-7 Dean McKeown (9) *slwly away, niggled alng hfwy, shrtlvd effrt 3 fs out, sn wl beh.* ....(100 to 1 op 50 to 1) 8
1594⁷ WORLD WITHOUT END (USA) 4-9-2 (5*) O Pears (7) *took keen hold, settled midfield early, wl beh frm hfwy.* ....(100 to 1 op 50 to 1) 9
2131⁴ CAROUSEL MAGIC 3-8-8 S Perks (11) *al in rear.* ....(100 to 1 op 33 to 1) 10

Dist: 1l, 10l, 8l, 1l, 7l, 12l, sht-hd, 2l, 8l. 2m 35.70s. a 0.70s (10 Ran).
SR: 45/38/23/2/13/4/ (Lord Howard de Walden), H R A Cecil

2311 Monkhill Limited Stakes Class E (0-70 3-y-o and up) £2,950 1¼m 6yds (4:55)

1907² STORM VENTURE (Ire) 3-8-10 G Duffield (4) *trkd ldr, shaken up and quickened clr o'r 2 fs out, unchlgd.* .... (13 to 2 op 5 to 1 tchd 7 to 1) 1
1934² RIVAL BID (USA) 5-9-7 W Ryan (1) *hld up, hdwy gng wl o'r 2 fs out, not pace of wnr.* ....(5 to 2 tchd 9 to 4 and 11 to 4) 2
1894² JAZILAH (Fr) 5-9-7 K Darley (6) *chsd ldr, rdn o'r 3 fs out, ran on one pace*.... (13 to 8 fav op 7 to 4 tchd 6 to 4) 3
1875⁸ PLATINUM VENTURE 3-8-10 W Woods (2) *chsd ldrs, rdn o'r 2 fs out, sn wknd*...........................(33 to 1) 4
2009⁶ LOCHORE 3-8-10 Dean McKeown (7) *slwly away, hld up and beh, some hdwy o'r 3 furlong out, nvr able to chal.* .... (10 to 1 op 8 to 1) 5
1654⁸ LABURNUM 5-9-4 (3*) J Weaver (5) *led till hdd o'r 2 fs out, sn btn*.................. (5 to 1 op 9 to 2 tchd 11 to 2) 6
DEXTER CHIEF 4-9-0 (7*) T Fuggle (3) *hld up, pushed alng o'r 3 fs out, no hdwy.* (25 to 1 op 14 to 1 tchd 33 to 1) 7

Dist: 5l, 1½l, 7l, ½l, 2l, 12l. 2m 10.60s. a 2.40s (7 Ran).
SR: 37/38/35/10/9/16/-/ (Venture Racing Ltd), W Jarvis

2312 Baghill Maiden Handicap Class E (0-70 3-y-o and up) £3,002 5f.... (5:25)

2105⁵ DAYJUZ (Ire) [52] (bl) 3-9-0 S Perks (13) *made all, clr o'r one furlong out, cmftbly*............ (14 to 1 op 12 to 1) 1
1938⁵ FARNDALE [41] 6-8-9 G Duffield (9) *wth ldr, rdn 2 fs out, not look keen and ran on one pace frm last.* .... (11 to 2 op 9 to 2) 2
2214⁴ GUSSIE FINK-NOTTLE (Ire) [58] (bl) 3-9-6 K Darley (12) *chsd ldrs, rdn wl o'r one furlong out, unbl to quicken.* ....(9 to 2 fav tchd 5 to 1) 3
2033² CLOUDY REEF [50] 3-8-5 (7*) M Humphries (10) *chsd ldrs, rdn o'r 2 fs out, no extr*........................ (6 to 1) 4
2047 JOELLISE [31] (v) 3-7-2² (7*) Claire Balding (11) *slwly into strd, beh till ran on wl fnl one and a half fs, nvr nrr.* .... (33 to 1 op 25 to 1) 5

DOUBLE SHIFT [60] 4-9-7 (7*) D Wright (6) *pld hrd in mid-field till styd on fnl one and a half fs, not a dngr,*..... 6
1327^{3} DISCO BOY [57] 3-9-5 J Fortune (8) *sn hrd drvn to go pace, nvr able to chal*........(9 to 1 op 8 to 1 tchd 10 to 1) 7
882 BLYTON STAR (Ire) [42] 5-8-10 S Webster (5) *sn rdn alng in rear, nvr a dngr*..................(16 to 1 op 12 to 1) 8
1937 PRETTY CHIC [38] 4-8-6 N Connorton (1) *outpcd*. ....(20 to 1 op 50 to 1) 9
1760 CUMBRIAN CALYPSO [49] (bl) 3-8-11 M Birch (3) *al beh*. ....(20 to 1 op 14 to 1) 10
1966^{6} ANDRULA MOU [42] 3-8-4 L Charnock (7) *chsd ldrs to hfwy, sn rdn and wknd*..........(20 to 1 op 16 to 1) 11
2121 AQUADO [35] (bl) 4-8-1^{1} (3*) J Weaver (4) *al beh*. ....(8 to 1 op 7 to 1) 12
2047 MISS BRIGHTSIDE [40] (bl) 5-8-8 N Adams (2) *stumbled and uns rdr leaving stalls*. ....(17 to 2 op 7 to 1 tchd 9 to 1) ur

Dist: 2½l, 1l, ½l, sht-hd, 1½l, 3l, 1l, ½l, ½l, ¾l. 1m 2.40s. a 1.20s (13 Ran).
SR: 41/26/33/23/3/32/11/-/-/ (P Asquith), F H Lee

BATH (firm)
Wednesday July 7th
Going Correction: MINUS 0.30 sec. per fur.

2313 Calculating Claiming Stakes Class F (3-y-o) £2,434 1m 3f 144yds..... (2:15)

1491^{8} MR GENEAOLOGY (USA) (bl) 9-5 W Newnes (5) *strted slwly, hdwy 6 fs out, shaken up to ld o'r one out, cmftbly*............(7 to 4 fav op 9 to 4 tchd 11 to 4) 1
2098^{2} CONVOY (bl) 8-9 K Darley (4) *al prmnt, led 2 fs out till o'r one out, one pace*.....................(7 to 1 op 4 to 1) 2
2183^{3} ON GOLDEN POND (Ire) 9-0 C Rutter (2) *led 6 fs out till 2 out, sn wknd*..........(3 to 1 op 11 to 4 tchd 9 to 4) 3
2005^{2} MY SET PEACE 8-7 (7*) Mark Denaro (3) *lost tch 5 fs out, tld off*................................(4 to 1 op 3 to 1) 4
JACKAREW BOY 8-9 G Duffield (6) *led one furlong, wknd 5 fs out, tld off*..................(9 to 1 op 4 to 1) 5
1635^{9} NATASHA NORTH 8-2 N Adams (1) *dwlt, pld hrd, led aftr one furlong till ran very wide 6 out, sn tld off*. ....(20 to 1 op 14 to 1) 6

Dist: 3½l, 3½l, 25l, 1l, dist. 2m 31.40s. a 4.40s (6 Ran).
SR: 26/9/7/ (Mrs P A White), J White

2314 Limpley Stoke Conditions Stakes Class D (3 & 4-y-o) £3,318 1m 3f 144yds ....(2:50)

URGENT REQUEST (Ire) 3-8-10 K Darley (2) *made all, easily*.......................(15 to 8 op 6 to 4 tchd 9 to 4) 1
2116^{2} DOUBLE BASS (USA) 3-8-10 A McGlone (3) *chsd wnr, hrd rdn and ev ch 2 fs out, not quicken*. ....(11 to 10 on op 5 to 4 tchd 5 to 4 on) 2
2117^{3} PISH KESH 3-8-3^{2} A Clark (4) *hld up, ev ch o'r 3 fs out, one pace fnl 2 furlongs*.................(11 to 1 op 5 to 1) 3
SEAMA (USA) 3-8-5 G Duffield (1) *prmnt till wknd and eased 3 fs out*......... (11 to 2 op 6 to 1 tchd 8 to 1) 4
1685^{7} TOUT DE VAL 4-8-13 R Perham (5) *al last*. ....(100 to 1 op 33 to 1) 5

Dist: 4l, 4l, 8l, 12l. 2m 27.40s. a 0.40s (5 Ran).
SR: 57/49/34/20/4/ (K Abdulla), B W Hills

2315 Baxi Handicap Class D (0-80 3-y-o and up) £3,289 1¼m 46yds..........(3:25)

1934^{3} GILDERDALE [70] 11-9-10 J Williams (5) *al prmnt, led o'r one furlong out, drvn out*. ....(2 to 1 fav op 9 to 4 tchd 5 to 2) 1
55^{9} TIGER CLAW (USA) [45] 7-7-13 A McGlone (2) *al prmnt, hrd rdn o'r one furlong out, ran on ins last*. ....(20 to 1 op 12 to 1) 2
1145^{3} THALEROS [79] 3-9-8 A Clark (7) *al prmnt, led 3 fs out till o'r one out, ran on*..... (4 to 1 op 7 to 2 tchd 9 to 2) 3
1919 LAMU LADY (Ire) [70] 3-8-8 (5*) Stephen Davies (4) *hdwy o'r 2 fs out, ev ch over one out, ran on*. (12 to 1 op 10 to 1) 4
2046* SAFIR (USA) [79] 3-9-8 G Duffield (8) *led till 3 fs out, ran on one pace*............(3 to 1 op 5 to 2 tchd 100 to 30) 5
2149^{9} LONG FURLONG [39] (v) 5-7-7 N Adams (6) *hdwy on outsd o'r 2 fs out, hrd rdn over one out, one pace*. ....(16 to 1 op 12 to 1) 6
1919 DORAZINE [65] 3-8-1 (7*) D McCabe (3) *in tch till wknd 2 fs out*..............................(11 to 2 op 10 to 1) 7
1928^{2} LOCH DUICH [55] 7-8-2 (7*) S Drowne (1) *beh fnl 3 fs*. ....(8 to 1 op 10 to 1 tchd 12 to 1) 8

Dist: 1½l, sht-hd, nk, 1½l, hd, 1½l, 3l. 2m 8.90s. a 2.50s (8 Ran).
SR: 54/26/48/38/44/14/26/21/ (Abbott Racing Partners), J W Hills

2316 EBF Evershot Maiden Stakes Class D (2-y-o) £4,378 5f 161yds.........(3:55)

2096^{2} JACOB BOGDANI 9-0 C Rutter (2) *al prmnt, led wl o'r one furlong out, ran on well*............(9 to 2 op 4 to 1) 1
2021^{3} ASHKERNAZY (Ire) 8-9 K Darley (6) *led 4 fs, ran on*. ....(12 to 1 op 14 to 1) 2
1131 ARABOYBILL 9-0 A Clark (1) *hdwy o'r 2 fs out, hrd rdn over one out, ran on*..........................(33 to 1) 3
1142^{2} HADDIAH 8-9 G Duffield (11) *al prmnt, hrd rdn o'r one furlong out, not quicken*. ....(6 to 5 on op 11 to 10 tchd 5 to 4 on) 4
HELLO IRELAND 8-9 T Sprake (7) *dwlt, hdwy o'r 2 fs out, not clr over one out, better for race*. (10 to 1 op 7 to 1) 5
1988^{6} SISTER SUSAN 8-2 (7*) D Gibbs (3) *chsd ldrs, no hdwy fnl 2 fs*..............................(14 to 1 op 10 to 1) 6
SHARP SPRING 9-0 W Newnes (4) *nvr nr to chal*. ....(33 to 1 op 25 to 1) 7
1955^{5} CHILLY TIME 8-9 J Williams (8) *some hdwy 2 fs out, sn wknd*..........................(8 to 1 op 6 to 1) 8
2058^{7} STRAPPED 8-9 A Mackay (10) *speed 3 fs*. ....(20 to 1 tchd 25 to 1) 9
TAILCOAT (USA) 9-0 M Perrett (9) *mid-div till fdd fnl 2 fs*. ....(9 to 2 op 4 to 1 tchd 5 to 1) 10
DREAM MISSY 8-9 R Perham (5) *speed 3 fs*. ....(33 to 1 op 25 to 1) 11

Dist: 3½l, sht-hd, ¾l, 3½l, ¾l, 2l, ½l, ½l, 2½l, ¾l. 1m 12.20s. a 2.80s (11 Ran).
SR: 10/-/-/-/-/-/ (Richard Green (Fine Paintings)), P F I Cole

2317 Acton Turville Maiden Handicap Class E (0-70 3-y-o and up) £2,884 2m 1f 34yds........................(4:25)

2048^{6} MILIYEL [43] 4-8-13 (7*) D McCabe (3) *lost pl o'r 4 fs out, rallied and swtchd outsd over one out, styd on to ld wl ins fnl furlong*...............(6 to 1 op 9 to 2) 1
1930^{7} SUDANOR (Ire) [36] 4-8-13 A Mackay (4) *led till wl ins fnl furlong*..........................(25 to 1 op 12 to 1) 2
1732^{3} SWIFT SPRING (Fr) [54] 3-8-7 (7*) T G McLaughlin (2) *al prmnt, ran on one pace fnl 2 fs*..... (7 to 2 op 3 to 1) 3
2034^{2} ROYAL PRINT (Ire) [43] 4-9-6 N Day (6) *hdwy 5 fs out, ev ch o'r 2 out, hrd rdn, wknd fnl furlong*. ....(7 to 4 fav tchd 13 to 8) 4
OK CORRAL (USA) [47] (bl) 6-9-10 R Price (5) *chsd ldr till outpcd 3 fs out*......... (5 to 1 op 6 to 1 tchd 7 to 1) 5
265^{6} FLASH OF STRAW (Ire) [41] (v) 4-9-4 S Whitworth (8) *chsd ldrs, hrd rdn o'r 2 fs out, no response*. ....(9 to 1 op 6 to 1) 6
2109 YOUNG JAMES [28] 5-8-5 J Williams (1) *lost tch 4 fs out, tld off*..............................(20 to 1 op 12 to 1) 7
C D SHAREPLAN (USA) [60] 3-8-13 (7*) R Painter (7) *al wl beh, tld off*........................(12 to 1 op 8 to 1) 8

Dist: 1½l, 2l, 3½l, 2l, 5l, 8l, nk. 3m 52.30s. a 8.30s (8 Ran).
(Ron Dawson), Miss Gay Kelleway

2318 Saltford Apprentice Handicap Class G (0-70 3-y-o and up) £2,364 5f 11yds ....(5:00)

2050^{3} TRIOMING [54] 7-8-10 (3*) R Painter (2) *made all, ran on wl*..............................(2 to 1 fav op 5 to 2) 1
2110^{4} RICKY'S TORNADO (Ire) [62] 4-9-1 (6*) Tracey Purseglove (1) *wth wnr o'r 3 fs, not quicken*... (5 to 2 tchd 100 to 30) 2
2241^{5} LUCEDEO [69] 9-9-9 (5*) L Aspell (5) *hdwy 2 fs out, no extr fnl furlong*............(11 to 4 op 5 to 2 tchd 3 to 1) 3
1821^{6} UNVEILED [53] (bl) 5-8-12 S Mulvey (4) *prmnt 4 fs*. ....(4 to 1 tchd 7 to 2) 4
2001^{8} HEATHYARDS GEM [54] 3-7-11 (10*) F Savage (6) *unruly in stalls, swrvd rght strt, al beh*....... (9 to 1 op 7 to 1) 5
1623 GREEN'S STUBBS [34] 6-7-6^{6} (7*) L Suthern (3) *al beh*. .... (25 to 1 op 20 to 1 tchd 33 to 1) 6

Dist: 4l, 1l, 1½l, 3l, ½l. 1m 2.20s. a 1.70s (6 Ran).
SR: 35/27/30/8/-/-/ (A A King), A P Jones

BELLEWSTOWN (IRE) (good to firm)
Wednesday July 7th

2319 Tattersalls Auction Race (2-y-o) £2,935 1m.................... (5:30)

2072^{4} SUMMERHILL SPECIAL (Ire) 8-5 Joanna Morgan (5) ....(3 to 1 fav) 1
2246^{6} QUASIMODO (Ire) (bl) 8-5 P V Gilson (1)...........(4 to 1) 2
WAQAR (Ire) 7-13 (6*) J A Heffernan (16)......... (20 to 1) 3
2072^{9} THE PLAYER NOBLE (Ire) 8-5 (6*) S Chin (4)...... (20 to 1) 4
938^{8} MONMOUTH PARK 8-6 (2*) R M Burke (3)........(12 to 1) 5
1387^{2} SALLY'S TRUST (Ire) 9-0 K J Manning (2).........(14 to 1) 6
2244^{9} AVALIN (Ire) 8-2 P Lowry (6)....................(20 to 1) 7
1332 BAKER HILL (Ire) 8-4 (4*) W J Smith (14)..........(20 to 1) 8
EOINS LAD (Ire) 8-5 D V Smith (7)............... (16 to 1) 9
1994^{2} FANCY BOOTS (Ire) 8-5 N G McCullagh (10).......(7 to 1) 10
INISHMANN (Ire) 8-5 J F Egan (9).................(14 to 1) 11
2093^{3} SUAVE REDSKIN (Ire) 8-11 (6*) B J Walsh (12)......(6 to 1) 12
786^{7} MUSICAL BANKER (bl) 8-11 S Craine (13).........(5 to 1) 13
ATTYMON (Ire) 8-0 (2*) D G O'Shea (8)........... (20 to 1) 14

Dist: 2l, 3½l, 1l, 5l. 1m 38.20s. (14 Ran).
(P Beirne), P Beirne

2320 Ashbourne House Hotel Maiden (3-y-o and up) £2,762 1m.............(6:00)

1855^{5} WHAT A PLEASURE (Ire) 3-8-8 (6*) B J Walsh (1)... (8 to 1) 1
1048 STATE PRINCESS (Ire) 3-8-11 R Hughes (7).......(16 to 1) 2
LIBRAN ROCK (Ire) 3-9-0 N G McCullagh (2).......(7 to 2) 3
2141^{5} SISTER CARMEL (Ire) 3-8-11 K J Manning (3)......(8 to 1) 4

1385[5] BOLERO DANCER (Ire) 5-9-5 (4*) P Carberry (6) . . . (20 to 1) 5
2140[2] KUDDAM (Ire) (bl) 3-8-11 P Shanahan (4) . . . . (6 to 4 on) 6
868 JOHNS DANCER (Ire) 4-9-9 J F Egan (5) . . . . (33 to 1) 7
Dist: 1½l, ½l, 1l, ¾l. 1m 39.60s. (7 Ran).
(Mrs Kevin Prendergast), Kevin Prendergast

2321 Carrolls Festival Handicap (Div I) (0-70 3-y-o and up) £2,935 1m. . . (6:30)

2142[3] MEJEVE [-] 5-9-6 S Craine (12) . . . . (7 to 2 fav) 1
2141[8] TOMBARA (Ire) [-] 5-9-8 B Coogan (5) . . . . (13 to 2) 2
1513[6] GIFT OF PEACE (Ire) [-] 3-9-5 J P Murtagh (3) . . . . . . (9 to 2) 3
1294[8] VOUVRAY (Ire) [-] 3-8-7 Joanna Morgan (2) . . . . (16 to 1) 4
1793[7] ANOTHER FLYER (Ire) [-] 3-7-8 (2*) R M Burke (6) . . (50 to 1) 5
2142[5] YONOKA (Fr) [-] 4-9-6 (8*) K M So (4) . . . . (10 to 1) 6
2041[4] RASSETTE (Ire) [-] 3-8-10 K J Manning (9) . . . . (9 to 2) 7
1923[6] SARA MAURETTE (Ire) [-] 3-9-0 N Byrne (1) . . . . (7 to 1) 8
1923[9] WESTERN FRONTIER (Ire) [-] 3-8-5 P V Gilson (13) (20 to 1) 9
2142 RUPERT THE GREAT (Ire) [-] 3-9-7 R Hughes (10) (14 to 1) 10
BOB'S GIRL (Ire) [-] 4-7-8 (6*) P P Murphy (11) . . . . (25 to 1) 11
1996[7] GONE LIKE THE WIND [-] 6-7-7 A J Nolan (8) . . . . . (25 to 1) 12
2141 D'ORIOLA (Ire) [-] (bl) 3-8-5 J F Egan (7) . . . . (20 to 1) 13
2143 EVER SO BOLD [-] 6-8-8 (6*) J J Behan (15) . . . . . . (20 to 1) su
Dist: 4l, 1l, hd, 1l. 1m 38.80s. (14 Ran).
(Mrs M Cahill), B V Kelly

2322 Carrolls Festival Handicap (Div II) (0-70 3-y-o and up) £2,935 1m. . . (7:00)

2142 THE BOWER (Ire) [-] (bl) 4-8-1 (2*) R M Burke (6) . . (14 to 1) 1
996[6] TINCO PALENO [-] 9-9-3 P V Gilson (2) . . . . (11 to 1) 2
2142[2] ALBERTA ROSE (Ire) [-] 4-9-8 (6*) J R Barry (5) (9 to 4 jt-fav) 3
1385[7] TIGNES (Ire) [-] 5-8-13 R Hughes (1) . . . . (9 to 1) 4
1923[4] WHAT MAGIC (Ire) [-] 3-9-10 J F Egan (13) . . . . (10 to 1) 5
ICANSEEFORMILES (Ire) [-] 5-8-8 P Lowry (11) . . . (20 to 1) 6
2297[7] DAHAR'S LOVE (USA) [-] 4-8-6 (6*) B J Walsh (15) . . (8 to 1) 7
1995[5] GLANCE CARD (Ire) [-] 3-9-6 J P Murtagh (12) (9 to 4 jt-fav) 8
2094 BLUEJACKET (Ire) [-] (bl) 5-8-0 (6*) J J Behan (8) . . (12 to 1) 9
2141[7] TAUTEN (Ire) [-] 3-9-5 S Craine (10) . . . . (14 to 1) 10
1996[9] ST AIDAN (Ire) [-] 5-7-10 (2*) D G O'Shea (7) . . . . . . (10 to 1) 11
1755[6] DIGNIFIED (Ire) [-] (bl) 3-9-1 (4*) W J Smith (14) . . . . (14 to 1) 12
1649 WILLY THE WEAVER (Ire) [-] 3-8-6 D V Smith (9) . . . . (20 to 1) 13
1651[9] PICK'N HILL (Ire) [-] 5-6-13 (8*) B J Halligan (3) . . . . (20 to 1) su
Dist: 1½l, 1l, 5½l, ½l. 1m 38.30s. (14 Ran).
(Mrs C Collins), C Collins

2323 Anglo Printers Handicap (0-75 3-y-o and up) £2,762 5f. . . . . (8:00)

2248[8] AFTERGLOW (Ire) [-] (bl) 4-8-11 L O'Shea (12) . . . . (16 to 1) 1
1923[2] LADY PRESIDENT (Ire) [-] (bl) 4-8-10 (6*) R V Skelly (7) . . . . (3 to 1 fav) 2
1923[8] SOUTHERN RULE [-] (bl) 6-7-9 Joanna Morgan (16) (8 to 1) 3
1023 RECOLLECTION (Ire) [-] (bl) 4-8-12 (8*) B J Halligan (5) . . . . (12 to 1) 4
2248[3] PILGRIM BAY (Ire) [-] 3-9-6 (2*,2ex) D G O'Shea (6) (11 to 2) 5
1515* SHOOT THE DEALER (Ire) [-] 3-9-3 (8*) G Coogan (10) . . . . (5 to 1) 6
1251[6] FANTANTE (Ire) [-] 4-8-11 P V Gilson (4) . . . . (10 to 1) 7
1645[8] JARGONEL (Ire) [-] 3-8-13 N Byrne (2) . . . . (25 to 1) 8
849 ALSHOU (Ire) [-] (bl) 4-8-10 (6*) B Bowens (3) . . . . . (16 to 1) 9
1611[4] SAMOT (Ire) [-] (bl) 3-9-1 (6*) J R Barry (13) . . . . (12 to 1) 10
1923 REASON TO BELIEVE (Ire) [-] 4-8-0 (6*) J J Behan (9) . . . . (33 to 1) 11
1825[3] SHRAGRADDY LASS (Ire) [-] 3-8-12 N G McCullagh (14) . . . . (4 to 1) 12
1515 NEVER WRONG [-] 6-9-12 B Coogan (8) . . . . (16 to 1) 13
1570[8] SPEED DEMON [-] 3-8-1[1] P Lowry . . . . (20 to 1) 14
Dist: Sht-hd, nk, 1l, sht-hd. 59.00s. (14 Ran).
(Mrs Jessica Magnier), C P Magnier

2324 Bellewstown Inn (QR) Race (4-y-o and up) £2,762 1¾m. . . . . (8:30)

2035[6] HACKETTS CROSS (Ire) 5-10-11 (7*) Mr J A Nash (5) (7 to 1) 1
1986* HANG A RIGHT 6-11-5 Mr T Mullins (15) . . . . (6 to 1) 2
1996* CORONADO (Ire) 5-11-2 (3*) Mr R Neylon (13) . . (5 to 4 on) 3
1467 FESTIVAL DREAMS 8-11-0 Mr J P Durkan (4) . . . . . (10 to 1) 4
852[9] PRINCE YAZA 6-10-7 (7*) Mr A K Wyse (14) . . . . (9 to 1) 5
1822 GILT DIMENSION 6-10-9 (5*) Mrs J M Mullins (16) (10 to 1) 6
1013 SOUND PERFORMANCE (Ire) 4-10-11 (7*) Ms L Robinson (1) . . . . (20 to 1) 7
851[6] THIS IS MY LIFE (Ire) 4-11-0 Mr J P Dempsey (12) (20 to 1) 8
HERBERT LODGE (Ire) 4-10-9 (5*) Mr P M Kelly (7) (20 to 1) 9
851 GLAD'S NIGHT (Ire) 4-10-8 (3*) Mrs M Mullins (3) . . (25 to 1) 10
1467[5] CARES OF TOMORROW 6-10-7 (7*) Mr J A Hayes (2) . . . . (8 to 1) 11
STRAWTALDI (Ire) 5-10-7 (7*) Mr J D O'Connell (17) (66 to 1) 12
MILL BELLE (Ire) 4-10-11 Mr M McNulty (9) . . . . (25 to 1) 13
SWEET JENNY (Ire) 4-10-4 (7*) Miss F Loughran (8) (25 to 1) 14
1576 TALINGANA (Ire) 4-10-11 Mr S R Murphy (10) . . . . . (10 to 1) 15
Dist: Nk, 2l, 4½l, 3½l. 3m 6.70s. (15 Ran).
(F Heffernan), Noel T Chance

KEMPTON (good)
Wednesday July 7th

Going Correction: NIL (races 1,5), MINUS 0.25 (2,3,4,6)

2325 EBF Bull And Bear Median Auction Maiden Stakes Class E (2-y-o) £3,444 6f. . . . . (6:30)

1446[5] PETER ROWLEY 9-0 J Reid (12) *wth ldr, rdn to ld o'r one furlong out, styd on wl fnl 100 yards.* . . . . (12 to 1 op 10 to 1 tchd 14 to 1) 1
2006[2] BAGSHOT 9-0 A Munro (17) *ldg grp, ev ch fnl furlong, not quicken last 100 yards.* . . . .(13 to 8 fav op 6 to 4 tchd 11 to 8) 2
1640[5] DUELLO 9-0 J Quinn (18) *handily plcd, rdn alng and not quicken o'r one furlong out, styd on clsg stages.* . . . . (4 to 1 op 5 to 1) 3
MALINGERER 8-9 N Carlisle (19) *led for o'r 4 fs, wknd.* . . . . (33 to 1 tchd 50 to 1) 4
GLITTERAZZI 9-0 J Williams (15) *ran on frm 2 fs out, nrst finish.* . . . . (20 to 1 op 10 to 1) 5
1773[8] TOTON LAD 9-0 M Wigham (13) *wl plcd, rdn and not quicken appr fnl furlong.* . . . . (40 to 1 op 33 to 1 tchd 50 to 1) 6
2137[3] BOLD GEM 8-6 (3*) B Doyle (11) *trkd ldrs, one pace ins last 2 fs.* . . . . (20 to 1 op 12 to 1) 7
SAGASAN 9-0 A Clark (9) *in tch, rdn and btn o'r one furlong out.* . . . . (40 to 1 op 25 to 1 tchd 50 to 1) 8
BOOKWORM 8-11 (3*) J Weaver (1) *slwly into strd, nvr nrr.* . . . . (33 to 1 op 20 to 1) 9
1905[2] SWITCH BLADE (Ire) 8-9 L Dettori (4) *mid-div, no hdwy appr fnl furlong.* . . . . . . (13 to 2 op 5 to 1 tchd 7 to 1) 10
1773[4] KNIGHTRIDER 9-0 R Perham (3) *nvr better than mid-div.* . . . . (33 to 1 op 25 to 1) 11
WINGS OF HORAGE (Ire) 9-0 R Cochrane (16) *slwly into strd, outpcd.* . . . . (40 to 1 op 25 to 1 tchd 50 to 1) 12
LOVE OF THE NORTH (Ire) 9-0 M Perrett (14) *slwly into strd, al rear.* . . . . (20 to 1 op 10 to 1) 13
1916 ZALAMERA 8-9 A McGlone (2) *outpcd.* . . . . (40 to 1 op 33 to 1 tchd 50 to 1) 14
2030[5] CHILIGRAY 9-0 W Newnes (8) *al beh.* (33 to 1 op 20 to 1) 15
PANDROP 8-9 S O'Gorman (10) *slwly into strd, sn pushed alng, nvr dngrs.* . . . . (33 to 1 op 20 to 1) 16
NAME THE TUNE 9-0 B Rouse (6) *ldg grp till lost pl 2 fs out.* . . . . (40 to 1 op 25 to 1) 17
1905 GINGERILLO 8-9 (5*) N Gwilliams (7) *al rear.* . . . . (40 to 1 op 25 to 1 tchd 50 to 1) 18
Dist: ¾l, 2l, 2l, 2l, ½l, hd, 2l, 3½l, sht-hd, ¾l. 1m 13.90s. a 3.10s (18 Ran).
SR: 38/35/27/14/11/9/3/-/-/ (Mrs P Jubert), R Hannon

2326 Futures And Options Rating Related Maiden Stakes Class E (0-70 3-y-o) £2,742 1¾m 92yds. . . . . (7:00)

2071[4] SCARLET TUNIC (USA) 9-0 W R Swinburn (4) *settled in 3rd, pushed alng aftr one m, led o'r one furlong out, drvn out.* . . . . (7 to 1 op 5 to 1 tchd 8 to 1) 1
1961[2] RIVIERE ACTOR (USA) 9-0 W Carson (3) *pushed alng in 4th aftr four fs, ran on und pres 2 out, styd on one pace ins last.* . . . . (7 to 4 fav op 6 to 4 tchd 15 to 8) 2
2169[2] MEANT TO BE 8-9 L Dettori (2) *chsd ldr, led o'r 4 fs out, hdd und pres over one out, sn btn.* . . . . (11 to 4 op 3 to 1 tchd 7 to 2 and 5 to 2) 3
1597[3] SARANGANI BAY (USA) 9-0 J Reid (1) *hld up last, rdn and effrt o'r 3 fs out, wknd over 2 out.* . . . (5 to 1 op 7 to 1) 4
1077[3] ROSE NOBLE (USA) 8-9 Pat Eddery (5) *led till o'r 4 fs out, wknd 2 out.* . . . . (7 to 1 tchd 8 to 1) 5
Dist: 1½l, 8l, 2l, 7l. 3m 9.43s. (5 Ran).
(The Queen), Lord Huntingdon

2327 GRE Properties Handicap Class E (0-70 4-y-o and up) £3,444 7f. . . . (7:30)

1912[3] PANCHELLITA (USA) [50] 4-8-9 B Rouse (12) *made virtually all, rdn and styd on wl nr line.* . . . . (10 to 1 tchd 11 to 1) 1
1956[6] PRINCE RODNEY [61] 4-9-6 M Roberts (5) *in tch, sstnd run frm o'r 2 fs out, kpt on same pace ins last.* . . . . (10 to 1) 2
1480[2] FACE THE FUTURE [60] 4-9-5 W R Swinburn (4) *hdwy frm rear o'r 2 fs out, styd on ins fnl furlong.* . . . . (15 to 2 op 6 to 1 tchd 8 to 1) 3
2121[4] CHARMED KNAVE [55] 8-9-0 T Williams (13) *trkd ldrs, rdn and not quicken 2 fs out, styd on wl nr finish.* . . . . (9 to 1 op 8 to 1 tchd 10 to 1) 4+
1130[4] COURT MINSTREL [56] 4-9-1 C Avery (7) *hld up in rear, not much room o'r 2 fs out, swtchd lft one out, fnshd fst.* . . . . (11 to 1 op 7 to 1) 4+
CHICARD [44] 4-8-3 D Holland (6) *al wl plcd, rdn and not quicken 2 fs out, kpt on one pace nr finish.* . . . . (9 to 1 op 12 to 1 tchd 8 to 1) 6
2161 KINGCHIP BOY [53] 4-8-12 D Biggs (11) *ldg grp, rdn alng 2 fs out, no extr ins last.* . . (8 to 1 op 7 to 1 tchd 9 to 1) 7
1954[3] ROSEATE LODGE [67] 7-9-12 Pat Eddery (16) *hld up beh, str run on ins frm 2 fs out, eased whn btn fnl 100 yards.* . . . . (13 to 2 fav op 8 to 1) 8
2156[3] ANNABELLE ROYALE [66] 7-9-11 L Dettori (3) *improved hfwy, effrt und pres o'r 2 fs out, eased whn btn ins last.* . . . . (8 to 1 tchd 7 to 1 and 9 to 1) 9

1914[7] GALLANT HOPE [46] (bl) 11-8-5 J Quinn (8) *mid-div, rdn and effrt 2 fs out, no imprsn*.................(33 to 1) 10
1912[5] ROSIETOES (USA) [45] 5-7-11 (7*) Mark Denaro (9) *nvr better than mid-div*.... (16 to 1 tchd 20 to 1 and 14 to 1) 11
756 BROADWAY RUCKUS (Can) [50] (v) 4-8-9 J Williams (14) *nvr nr to chal*...................... (33 to 1 tchd 40 to 1) 12
2121 CEE-EN-CEE [60] (bl) 9-9-5 A Tucker (15) *in tch, rdn and no hdwy o'r 2 fs out*.....(25 to 1 op 20 to 1 tchd 33 to 1) 13
ABSO [65] 5-9-10 J Reid (1) *in tch on outsd to hfwy, sn wknd*............................(25 to 1 op 20 to 1) 14
1097 BEATLE SONG [54] (v) 5-8-13 R Cochrane (18) *handily plcd till rdn and wknd wl o'r one furlong out*. .... (9 to 1 op 10 to 1 tchd 12 to 1) 15
2012[7] ACT OF UNION (Ire) [65] 4-9-10 W Newnes (17) *outpcd*. .... (33 to 1 op 50 to 1) 16
4681a KIRRIEMUIR [47] 5-8-6 N Carlisle (10) *cl up till wknd wl o'r 2 fs out*......................... (33 to 1 op 25 to 1) 17
249 AIN'TLIFELIKETHAT [54] 6-8-13 Paul Eddery (2) *sn wl beh*. .... (33 to 1 op 25 to 1) 18

Dist: 1l, sht-hd, sht-hd, dd-ht, nk, 1½l, ½l, sht-hd, ½l, 1l. 1m 26.32s. a 2.22s (18 Ran).

SR: 35/43/41/35/36/23/27/39/37/ (C J Pennick), G L Moore

2328 Economist Handicap Class C (0-90 3-y-o and up) £5,005 1¼m...... (8:00)

1383[2] NASSMA (Ire) [82] 3-9-1 M Roberts (6) *in tch, rdn to ld one furlong out, drw clr*...........(4 to 1 jt-fav op 6 to 1) 1
1800[2] AKKAZAO (Ire) [71] 5-9-1 J Reid (4) *hld up, led 3 fs out to one out, one pace*. (4 to 1 jt-fav op 9 to 2 tchd 7 to 2) 2
1604* PENNY DROPS [73] 4-9-0 (3*) D Harrison (10) *hld up rear, ran on appr fnl furlong, fnshd strly*. ....(5 to 1 op 9 to 2 tchd 6 to 1) 3
1958[8] DEVILRY [77] (bl) 3-8-10 Paul Eddery (1) *hld up rear, ran on und pres 3 fs out, one pace appr last*. .... (9 to 1 op 12 to 1 tchd 8 to 1) 4
1820[7] MOVE A MINUTE (USA) [67] 4-8-8[2] (5*) A Procter (3) *hld up rear, nvr rch frnt rnk*..............(9 to 1 op 7 to 1) 5
1867* VALLANCE [84] 5-10-0 W R Swinburn (2) *trkd ldr, led o'r 4 fs out to 3 out, wknd and eased fnl furlong*. ....(6 to 1 op 5 to 1 tchd 7 to 1) 6
2113[6] LEGAL EMBRACE (Can) [63] 4-8-7 A Clark (8) *trkd ldrs, not quicken o'r 2 fs out, sn btn*. .... (20 to 1 op 14 to 1 tchd 25 to 1) 7
1594[4] MISS RITA [66] 4-8-10 M Wigham (9) *hld up rear, nvr able to chal*..........................(20 to 1 op 12 to 1) 8
1145[6] TICKERTY'S GIFT [78] 3-8-11 B Rouse (7) *wl plcd till wknd 3 fs out*......................... (16 to 1 op 10 to 1) 9
BAGALINO (USA) [85] 3-9-4 Pat Eddery (5) *led to 4 fs out, sn wknd and eased*........(7 to 1 op 6 to 1 tchd 8 to 1) 10

Dist: 2½l, sht-hd, 4l, sht-hd, 2l, 1l, nk, nk, 3l. 2m 4.71s. a 2.91s (10 Ran).

SR: 47/42/43/28/28/41/18/20/20/ (Sheikh Ahmed Bin Saeed Al Maktoum), J R Fanshawe

2329 LBC Newstalk 97.3 FM Claiming Stakes Class E (3-y-o and up) £3,028 6f ....(8:30)

2053* KNOCK TO ENTER (USA) 5-9-1 J Williams (9) *hdwy hfwy, led o'r one furlong out, rdn clr*..... (11 to 2 op 5 to 1) 1
1348[9] EASY LINE 10-8-2 (7*) Michael Denaro (4) *outpcd to hfwy, str run wl o'r one furlong out, fnshd well*. ....(8 to 1 tchd 10 to 1) 2
2018 SIZZLING SAGA (Ire) 5-9-6 R Cochrane (2) *chsd ldrs, ev ch o'r one furlong out, ran on same pace*. .... (15 to 2 op 5 to 1 tchd 8 to 1) 3
2004[2] MERLINS WISH (USA) 4-8-12 Pat Eddery (3) *slwly into strd, improved 2 fs out, not quicken fnl furlong*. ....(7 to 2 op 7 to 1) 4
1953[9] SYLVAN BREEZE (v) 5-8-5 W Newnes (7) *trkd ldr, led o'r 2 fs out till hdd and wknd over one out*. .... (16 to 1 op 20 to 1 tchd 25 to 1) 5
1992[9] JACK GRAY 5-8-9 A Mackay (8) *outpcd*. .... (100 to 1 op 66 to 1) 6
1148 PAT POINDESTRES 3-8-2 A Clark (10) *led till o'r 2 fs out, wknd over one out*. (50 to 1 op 33 to 1 tchd 100 to 1) 7
1527 SHARPTINO 4-8-5 L Dettori (1) *in tch till lost pl and eased hfwy*............... (25 to 1 op 20 to 1 tchd 50 to 1) 8
1487[9] DISTANT DYNASTY 3-7-13 J Quinn (6) *early speed, outpcd hfwy*.........................(66 to 1 tchd 100 to 1) 9

Dist: 2l, 1l, 1l, 1½l, 8l, 1l, 1½l, 5l. 1m 12.57s. a 1.77s (9 Ran).

SR: 66/52/59/47/34/6/ (R B Payne), M Williams

2330 City Evening Handicap Class D (0-80 3-y-o and up) £3,582 1m........ (9:00)

978[7] SINGERS IMAGE [53] 4-8-4[1] J Williams (4) *hld up, hdwy o'r 2 fs out, led one out, jst held on*. (16 to 1 tchd 20 to 1) 1
1956[3] LORD OBERON (Ire) [50] (v) 5-8-1 M Roberts (9) *in tch, jnd wnr one furlong out, ev ch und pres, jst fld*. .... (4 to 1 op 5 to 1 tchd 11 to 2) 2
1768 TROOPING (Ire) [73] 4-9-10 W Carson (3) *wl plcd, rdn and ev ch appr fnl furlong, not quicken*. (9 to 2 op 6 to 1) 3
2022[6] AITCH N'BEE [76] 10-9-13 L Dettori (2) *hld up rear, ran on o'r one furlong out, fnshd wl*.....(12 to 1 op 10 to 1) 4
2181* PERSIANSKY (Ire) [74] 3-9-2 (5ex) B Raymond (10) *trkd ldr, led o'r 3 fs out to one out, no extr*. ....(11 to 4 fav tchd 5 to 2 and 3 to 1) 5
1829[9] WAHEM (Ire) [63] 3-8-2 (3*) B Doyle (7) *led till o'r 3 fs out, wknd fnl furlong*................ (12 to 1 op 14 to 1) 6
2009[4] DIVINE BOY [68] 3-8-10 D Biggs (1) *hld up rear, not pace to chal frm 2 fs out*............. (16 to 1 tchd 20 to 1) 7
2031[2] SALBYNG [55] (v) 5-8-6 D Holland (5) *handily plcd, rdn and wknd o'r one furlong out*.....(5 to 1 tchd 6 to 1) 8
2065[3] RUBY COOPER [56] 3-7-12 J Quinn (6) *mid-div, rdn and wknd o'r 2 fs out*..................(20 to 1 op 14 to 1) 9
1744[9] SWIFT ROMANCE (Ire) [51] 5-8-2 A Mackay (11) *mid-div, improved hfwy, wknd quickly wl o'r one furlong out*. ....(8 to 1 tchd 7 to 1) 10
1927[9] VAGANOVA (Ire) [64] 4-9-1 R Perham (8) *al beh*. ....(25 to 1 op 16 to 1) 11

Dist: Sht-hd, 2l, sht-hd, 2½l, ¾l, nk, 2l, ½l, 1l, 1l. 1m 38.95s. a 1.95s (11 Ran).

SR: 31/27/44/46/27/14/18/8/-/ (Miss B Swire), G B Balding

NEWMARKET (JULY) (good to firm) Wednesday July 7th

Going Correction: MINUS 0.20 sec. per fur. (races 1,4,5,6), MINUS 0.30 (2,3,7)

2331 Ellesmere Selling Stakes Class E (2-y-o) £4,776 7f.................. (2:00)

1666[7] HEATHCLIFF (Ire) 8-13 D Holland (4) *led aftr one furlong, hrd pressed entering last, hld on gmely cl hme*. ....(7 to 1 tchd 15 to 2) 1
1959[3] LINK MILES 9-3 J Reid (3) *nvr far away, rousted alng o'r one furlong out, fnshd wl*.........(7 to 2 tchd 4 to 1) 2
1499[4] MISTER BEAT 8-13 K Fallon (2) *tucked away on ins, drvn through to chal inside fnl furlong, kpt on*. ....(10 to 1 tchd 8 to 1) 3
2058[4] LEAP OF FAITH (Ire) (bl) 8-8 L Dettori (11) *led one furlong, hndy and ev ch till rdn and not quicken fnl furlong*. .... (11 to 2 op 5 to 1 tchd 6 to 1) 4
1660[5] FOREST LOCH 8-1 (7*) D Wright (7) *chsd ldrs, rdn to improve o'r one furlong out, not pace to chal*. ....(11 to 4 fav tchd 3 to 1) 5
2044[4] GREEK NIGHT OUT (Ire) 8-12 Dean McKeown (12) *trkd ldg 4, effrt whn edgd lft o'r one furlong out, no extr*. .... (10 to 1 op 8 to 1 tchd 11 to 1) 6
1959[7] MR MYSTICAL (Ire) 8-13 B Rouse (10) *wth ldrs, edgd lft und pres o'r one furlong out, sn outpcd*. .... (14 to 1 op 12 to 1 tchd 16 to 1) 7
2274 DOMINANT PARTNER 8-13 R Cochrane (8) *settled midfield, feeling pace hfwy, styd on, nvr able to chal*. ....(25 to 1) 8
2155[5] READY MONEY RILEY 8-13 W Ryan (15) *sluggish strt, wl beh till styd on fnl furlong*...................(33 to 1) 9
EASY D'OR 9-0 (3*) M Fenton (9) *sluggish strt, nvr wnt pace*...(25 to 1) 10
1602 LORD WELLINGTON (Ire) 8-13 G Hind (1) *settled midfield, effrt and drvn alng o'r 2 fs out, no imprsn*.....(33 to 1) 11
LITTLE BID (USA) 8-8 B Raymond (14) *missed break, al struggling*......................(12 to 1 tchd 14 to 1) 12
1959[9] INDIAN CASTLE (Ire) 8-13 Pat Eddery (13) *pressed ldg pair 5 fs, wknd quickly*............................ (25 to 1) 13
1051[2] SHUTTLECOCK (bl) 8-13 L Piggott (6) *chsd ldg trio till wknd and eased last 2 fs*..........(9 to 1 tchd 10 to 1) 14

Dist: ½l, sht-hd, 1½l, 1½l, 2½l, ¾l, 6l, sht-hd, ¾l, 1½l. 1m 28.03s. a 3.83s (14 Ran).

SR: 21/23/18/8/3/-/ (Mrs J M Corbett), B W Hills

2332 More O'Ferrall Plc Maiden Stakes Class D (3-y-o) £4,893 1¼m..... (2:35)

SABREHILL (USA) 9-0 Pat Eddery (3) *al hndy, led o'r 3 fs out, quickened away appr last, easily*. .... (15 to 2 op 3 to 1 tchd 8 to 1) 1
1716[2] LACOTTE (Ire) 9-0 M Roberts (12) *tucked away in midfield, effrt and drvn alng o'r 2 fs out, drifted lft fnl furlong, no imprsn*. (5 to 2 fav tchd 3 to 1 and 9 to 4) 2
1831[5] PEACHES POLLY 8-9 Paul Eddery (8) *settled midfield, drvn alng to improve last 2 fs, ran on finish*. .... (14 to 1 op 12 to 1 tchd 16 to 1) 3
ASPECT (USA) 9-0 A Munro (16) *patiently rdn, improved frm midfield last 2 fs, styd on, nvr nrr*. .... (25 to 1 op 20 to 1) 4
2010 PROTON 9-0 L Piggott (9) *led, hdd and drvn alng o'r 3 fs out, fdd last 2*.......(16 to 1 op 14 to 1 tchd 20 to 1) 5
RUMPUS (Ire) 8-9 R Cochrane (14) *nvr far away, ev ch o'r 3 fs out, rdn and outpcd frm 2 out*. .... (6 to 1 tchd 8 to 1 and 11 to 2) 6
1831[4] MAMARA REEF 8-4 (5*) C Hodgson (7) *tucked away in midfield, effrt and drvn alng o'r 2 fs out, sn outpcd*. .... (20 to 1 op 14 to 1 tchd 25 to 1) 7
1454[4] TREAD CAREFULLY 8-9 W R Swinburn (4) *chsd ldg bunch, rdn o'r 2 fs out, sn btn*. .... (20 to 1 op 14 to 1 tchd 25 to 1) 8
1831 WANNABE 8-6 (3*) J Weaver (5) *pressed ldg 5, chsd alng whn pace quickened o'r 2 fs out, sn btn*. .... (50 to 1 op 33 to 1) 9

QUILLON 9-0 W Ryan (13) *wth ldrs, rdn o'r 2 fs out, fdd.* ....(14 to 1 op 8 to 1 tchd 16 to 1) 10
AWAY GIRL 8-9 D Holland (17) *missed break, steady hdwy frm off the pace last 2 fs, fnshd wl.* (50 to 1 op 33 to 1) 11
1176[3] ALASAD 9-0 W Carson (6) *trkd ldrs, lost grnd whn pace quickened o'r 2 fs out, sn btn.* ....(13 to 2 op 7 to 1 tchd 8 to 1) 12
1931[6] DANCING TRALTHEE (Ire) 8-2 (7*) Jo Hunnam (1) *prmnt on outsd till fdd o'r 2 fs out*..........(33 to 1 op 20 to 1) 13
BEND SABLE (Ire) 9-0 Dean McKeown (15) *str hold, shaken up to improve hfwy, nvr plcd to chal.* ....(50 to 1 op 33 to 1) 14
MICHAELA MIA (USA) 8-9 L Dettori (11) *tucked away in midfield, fdd whn pace quickened o'r 2 fs out.* ....(12 to 1 op 6 to 1) 15
2010[2] PYRAMIS PRINCE (Ire) 9-0 J Reid (2) *pressed ldg 6 for one m, fdd*..............(16 to 1 op 14 to 1 tchd 20 to 1) 16
2023[5] ZONK 9-0 M Wigham (10) *sluggish strt, nvr a factor.* ....(50 to 1 op 33 to 1) 17
1216[4] ERCKULE 8-11 (3*) B Doyle (18) *drvn alng virtually thrght, nvr a dngr*... (20 to 1 op 16 to 1 tchd 25 to 1) 18
Dist: 5l, 3l, 5l, sht-hd, 2l, ¾l, ¾l, hd, 2l, hd. 2m 2.59s. a 0.39s (18 Ran).
SR: 66/56/45/40/39/30/28/26/25/ (Sheikh Mohammed), H R A Cecil

2333 H.E. Limited Duke Of Cambridge Handicap Class B (0-105 3-y-o) £20,387 1¼m.................. (3:10)

1879* LYPHARD'S DELTA (USA) [80] 8-5 W Ryan (19) *tucked away gng wl, not clr run, swtchd o'r one furlong out, weaved through to ld last 100 yards, ran on*.........(7 to 1 jt-fav op 5 to 1 tchd 15 to 2) 1
1911* SEREN QUEST [78] 8-0 (3*) D Harrison (15) *co'red up beh ldrs, drvn through to ld ins fnl furlong, hdd last 100 yards, kpt on*........(14 to 1 op 12 to 1 tchd 16 to 1) 2
2022[3] MAP OF STARS (USA) [80] 8-5 M Roberts (1) *nvr far away, drvn up to chal o'r one furlong out, kpt on same pace.* ....(16 to 1 op 14 to 1) 3
2066[8] SHARJAH (USA) [84] 8-9 P Robinson (14) *al hndy, led wl o'r one furlong out till appr last, one pace.* ....(20 to 1 tchd 25 to 1) 4
1338[7] DUTOSKY [73] 7-12 G Bardwell (9) *trkd ldrs, drvn up on outsd to ld briefly appr fnl furlong, no extr*... (25 to 1) 5
1314[4] SPIN DOCTOR (Ire) [89] 9-0 R Cochrane (17) *al hndy, ev ch and drvn alng 2 fs out, not quicken.* ....(16 to 1 op 14 to 1) 6
1579* NESSUN DORMA [81] 8-6 M Hills (21) *patiently rdn, weaved through frm midfield last 2 fs, ran on.* ....(8 to 1 tchd 9 to 1) 7
2066[9] KASSBAAN (USA) [73] 7-12 J Quinn (22) *nvr far away, drvn alng whn pace quickened 2 fs out, no extr.* ....(25 to 1 op 20 to 1 tchd 33 to 1) 8
1784* GEORGE DILLINGHAM [90] 9-1 W R Swinburn (6) *wth ldrs, rdn whn pace lifted 2 fs out, no extr.* ....(16 to 1 op 14 to 1) 9
1976* DUVEEN (Ire) [70] 7-2 (7*) D Wright (18) *settled off the pace, shaken up to improve last 2 fs, ran on.* ....(12 to 1 tchd 14 to 1) 10
1919* MIDNIGHT HEIGHTS [86] 8-11 L Piggott (4) *prmnt on outsd till fdd last 2 fs.* (7 to 1 jt-fav op 10 to 1 tchd 12 to 1) 11
1839[2] FORTHWITH [84] 8-9 D Holland (16) *in tch, drvn alng whn pace quickened o'r 2 fs out, no imprsn.* ....(16 to 1 tchd 20 to 1 and 14 to 1) 12
1785[6] LYFORD CAY (Ire) [88] 8-13 J Reid (13) *hmpd and checked aftr 2 fs, nvr able to trble ldrs*....(16 to 1 tchd 20 to 1) 13
1842* WESTERN CAPE (USA) [96] 9-7 Pat Eddery (2) *wth ldrs, feeling pace and drvn alng o'r 2 fs out, grad wknd.* ....(12 to 1 op 10 to 1) 14
2066[3] NAFUTH (USA) [81] 8-6 W Carson (8) *squeezed for room and snatched up aftr 2 fs, not reco'r.* ....(16 to 1 tchd 20 to 1) 15
1638[4] SEASONAL SPLENDOUR (Ire) [90] 9-1 D Biggs (5) *wth ldrs till fdd und pres last 2 fs*.........(20 to 1 tchd 25 to 1) 16
2022[4] JERVIA [83] 8-8 A Munro (11) *chsd ldrs almost one m, fdd.* ....(25 to 1 tchd 33 to 1) 17
1670[8] DANNY BOY [81] 8-6 B Raymond (7) *led till hdd and wknd wl o'r one furlong out*............... (33 to 1) 18
987[5] PAMZIG (USA) [90] 9-1 Paul Eddery (12) *unruly at strt, nvr a threat*...............(25 to 1 tchd 33 to 1) 19
1761[3] SPICE AND SUGAR [69] 7-8 N Carlisle (10) *keen hold, in tch for o'r 5 fs*...............(50 to 1 tchd 66 to 1) 20
989 ERICOLIN (Ire) [80] 8-2 (3*) B Doyle (20) *chsd ldrs to hfwy, wknd quickly o'r 2 fs out*....... (25 to 1 tchd 33 to 1) 21
1670* BRANDONHURST [83] 8-8 L Dettori (3) *in tch for o'r 5 fs, fdd*...............(16 to 1 tchd 20 to 1) 22
Dist: Hd, 2½l, hd, nk, 2½l, sht-hd, ½l, ½l, ½l, ¾l. 2m 2.68s. a 0.48s (22 Ran).
SR: 56/53/50/53/41/52/43/34/50/ (S Khaled), H R A Cecil

2334 Falmouth Stakes Class A (Group 2) (3-y-o and up) £38,483 1m......... (3:40)

749[2] NICHE 3-8-6 L Piggott (2) *made virtually all, quickened clr o'r 2 fs out, styd on wl ins last.* ....(13 to 8 fav op 7 to 4) 1
DANCING BLOOM (Ire) 3-8-6 W Carson (6) *nvr far away, drvn alng to chase wnr last 2 fs, kpt on.* ....(16 to 1 op 14 to 1 tchd 20 to 1) 2
2074[6] CULTURE VULTURE (USA) 4-9-7 Pat Eddery (1) *settled midfield, effrt and drvn alng o'r 2 fs out, styd on same pace*...............(13 to 2 op 5 to 1 tchd 7 to 1) 3
1747[7] FEMININE WILES (Ire) 4-9-1 J Reid (5) *nvr far away, feeling pace and drvn alng o'r 2 fs out, not quicken.* ....(12 to 1 op 14 to 1) 4
INFORMATRICE (USA) 3-8-6 M Roberts (7) *al wl plcd, rdn o'r 2 fs out, no extr*...............(14 to 1 op 12 to 1) 5
1404[5] MYSTIC GODDESS (USA) 3-8-6 L Dettori (8) *trkd ldrs, effrt and bustled alng o'r 2 fs out, fdd.* ....(25 to 1 op 20 to 1 tchd 33 to 1) 6
1768[6] TENDER MOMENT (Ire) 5-9-1 B Doyle (4) *last and niggled alng hfwy, nvr a threat*...............(100 to 1 op 66 to 1) 7
1222[5] ANCESTRAL DANCER 3-8-9 M Hills (10) *settled midfield, effrt and drvn alng o'r 2 fs out, sn btn.* ....(20 to 1 op 16 to 1 tchd 25 to 1) 8
1767[4] NICER (Ire) 3-8-12 D Holland (11) *swrvd strt, in tch aftr 2 fs, outpcd o'r two out, sn btn.* ....(8 to 1 op 5 to 1 tchd 9 to 1) 9
1767[3] ZARANI SIDI ANNA (USA) (v) 3-8-6 W R Swinburn (9) *reared strt, rcd wide to chase wnr hfwy, wknd and eased o'r one furlong out*......... (4 to 1 op 7 to 2 tchd 9 to 2) 10
1767[5] SUMOTO 3-8-6 Paul Eddery (3) *in tch, feeling pace and drvn alng hfwy, nvr dngrs*...... (14 to 1 tchd 16 to 1) 11
Dist: 3½l, 3l, hd, 5l, 2l, 1½l, 8l, 3l, 2½l, 2l. 1m 37.08s. b 0.82s (11 Ran).
SR: 80/69/75/68/44/38/42/12/6/ (Lord Carnarvon), R Hannon

2335 SBJ Group July Stakes Class A (Group 3) (2-y-o) £15,555 6f..... (4:10)

1920* FIRST TRUMP 8-10 M Hills (3) *nvr far away, feeling pace and drvn alng o'r 2 fs out, rallied gmely to ld last 50 yards*...............(9 to 2 op 3 to 1) 1
1828* FAST EDDY 8-10 L Dettori (2) *al hndy, drvn ahead appr fnl furlong, hdd last 50 yards, kpt on.* ....(12 to 1 op 8 to 1) 2
1639[2] PRINCE BABAR 8-10 W Carson (4) *steadied strt, niggled alng to go pace hfwy, swtchd ins o'r one out, ran on.* ....(20 to 1 op 16 to 1 tchd 25 to 1) 3
1788* TURTLE ISLAND (Ire) 9-1 J Reid (5) *hmpd and checked strt, reco'red hfwy, rdn and kpt on same pace fnl furlong.* ....(5 to 4 on op Evens) 4
1750[3] WAJIBA RIVA (Ire) 8-10 Pat Eddery (6) *wth ldr, led hfwy till appr fnl furlong, one pace*...............(4 to 1 op 5 to 2) 5
1828[6] ALANEES 8-10 W R Swinburn (1) *led to hfwy, wknd quickly wl o'r one furlong out*.....(66 to 1 op 33 to 1) 6
Dist: ½l, 1½l, 1l, ½l, 8l. 1m 12.97s. a 1.27s (6 Ran).
SR: 47/45/39/40/33/1/ (Mollers Racing), G Wragg

2336 Princess Maiden Fillies Stakes Class D (2-y-o) £4,581 5f.............. (4:45)

PROPHECY (Ire) 8-11 Pat Eddery (1) *al hndy, led 2 fs out, kpt on strly fnl furlong.* (6 to 1 op 4 to 1 tchd 7 to 1) 1
REDRESS (USA) 8-11 A Munro (9) *sluggish strt, ran green and bustled alng, gd hdwy o'r one furlong out, prmsg.* ....(13 to 2 op 5 to 1 tchd 7 to 1) 2
PETULA 8-11 M Hills (7) *sluggish strt, chsd alng to improve frm off the pace last 2 fs, improve.* ....(14 to 1 tchd 20 to 1) 3
EN CACHETTE (Ire) 8-11 J Reid (8) *al hndy, led briefly o'r 2 fs out, rdn and no extr fnl furlong.* ....(3 to 1 fav op 4 to 1 tchd 11 to 4) 4
1944[3] I'M YOUR LADY 8-11 L Dettori (10) *settled aftr fst break, improved o'r one furlong out, ran on finish.* ....(20 to 1 tchd 25 to 1) 5
1955[3] ALZIANAH 8-8 (3*) D Harrison (4) *nvr far away, drw level o'r 2 fs out, no extr fnl furlong*......(8 to 1 op 10 to 1) 6
1916[2] RAJMAPATA 8-11 W Carson (5) *made most till o'r 2 fs out, fdd*.................... (9 to 2 op 4 to 1 tchd 5 to 1) 7
1790[5] L'ETAT C'EST MOI (USA) 8-11 W R Swinburn (3) *dsptd ld to hfwy, fdd appr fnl furlong*........(14 to 1 op 12 to 1) 8
EXOTIC FOREST 8-11 Paul Eddery (6) *trkd ldrs, feeling pace and rdn 2 fs out, fdd*.........(33 to 1 op 25 to 1) 9
UNBEKNOWNST (USA) 8-11 R Cochrane (11) *sluggish strt, nvr a threat*...........(8 to 1 op 4 to 1 tchd 10 to 1) 10
DAME PROSPECT 8-11 B Raymond (2) *missed break, not reco'r*...............(25 to 1 op 20 to 1 tchd 33 to 1) 11
Dist: ½l, ½l, 2½l, nk, 1½l, 3½l, ¾l, 6l, ¾l. 1m 0.15s. a 1.45s (11 Ran).
SR: 48/46/44/34/33/27/13/10/-/ (K Abdulla), J H M Gosden

2337 Reg Day Memorial Handicap Class D (0-80 3-y-o and up) £5,435 2m 24yds ....(5:15)

1752 ROSINA MAE [71] 4-9-8 Dean McKeown (9) *nvr far away, rdn o'r 3 fs out, rallied gmely to ld appr finish.* ....(6 to 1 op 9 to 2 tchd 13 to 2) 1
2061 MULL HOUSE [75] 6-9-12 W R Swinburn (7) *al hndy, feeling pace and drvn alng o'r 3 fs out, rallied to ld appr last, jst ct*............ (8 to 1 op 7 to 1 tchd 9 to 1) 2
1948* TILTY (USA) [66] 3-8-0 M Roberts (5) *settled midfield, outpcd and drvn alng o'r 3 fs out, str run fnl furlong, fnshd wl*...............(9 to 2 op 4 to 1 tchd 11 to 2) 3
1929* FARMER'S PET [75] 4-9-12 G Carter (1) *led, hdd and rdn appr fnl furlong, no extr.* ....(7 to 1 op 9 to 2 tchd 8 to 1) 4

2178* BALZINO (USA) [53] 4-8-4 (4ex) K Fallon (4) *patiently rdn, hdwy to join ldrs o'r 3 fs out, hng lft over one out, btn whn hmpd ins last.* (7 to 2 fav op 5 to 1 tchd 11 to 2) 5
2251⁴ ROSGILL [62] 7-8-13 P Robinson (2) *shwd up wl in frnt rnk till fdd o'r 2 fs out.* (10 to 1 op 8 to 1 tchd 12 to 1) 6
2048² DISPUTED CALL (USA) [63] 4-9-0 D Holland (3) *pressed ldrs, rdn o'r 2 fs out, sn btn.* .... (16 to 1 op 12 to 1 tchd 20 to 1) 7
2026⁶ AUDE LA BELLE (Fr) [59] 5-8-10 Pat Eddery (6) *wtd wth, effrt and drvn alng o'r 3 fs out, sn outpcd.* ....(5 to 1 op 9 to 2 tchd 7 to 2) 8
1840 RAGAMUFFIN ROMEO [60] 4-8-11 Paul Eddery (8) *trkd ldrs, feeling pace and drvn alng o'r 3 fs out, sn btn.* .... (33 to 1 op 25 to 1 tchd 50 to 1) 9
Dist: ½l, nk, 3½l, 6l, 5l, ½l, ¾l, ¾l. 3m 24.35s. a 1.35s (9 Ran).
SR: 47/50/23/45/17/21/21/15/14/ (Greenland Park Ltd), Lord Huntingdon

REDCAR (firm)
Wednesday July 7th
Going Correction: MINUS 0.35 sec. per fur. (races 1,2,5), MINUS 0.20 (3,4,6)

2338 Newcastle United Claiming Stakes Class F (3-y-o) £1,900 7f........ (6:45)

2154* KINGSTON BROWN (v) 8-13 M Hills (2) *made all, quickened 2 fs out, ran on fnl furlong.* ....(11 to 8 fav op 5 to 4) 1
2168⁴ BRAXTON BRAGG (Ire) 8-5 M Birch (5) *al prmnt, effrt to chase wnr 2 fs out, rdn and kpt on same pace fnl furlong*............. (9 to 1 op 8 to 1 tchd 11 to 1) 2
1186⁷ BRIGHT GEM 8-0 J Fanning (8) *in tch, rdn o'r 2 fs out, kpt on ins last, nvr dngrs*...............(12 to 1 op 9 to 1) 3
2064⁹ KEEP BATTLING 9-3 S Webster (1) *prmnt, rdn o'r 2 fs out, sn wknd*.......................................(33 to 1) 4
2133* VILAMAR (Ire) 8-8 N Connorton (6) *pld hrd in tch, rdn o'r 2 fs, sn btn*............................(9 to 4 op 7 to 4) 5
2175⁴ WHITE CREEK (Ire) (v) 9-3 J Carroll (7) *hld up, pushed alng hfwy, sn rdn and nvr a factor*...... (11 to 2 op 5 to 1) 6
1060 TASSAGH BRIDGE (Ire) 7-10 J Lowe (3) *in tch, effrt and hdwy on outer o'r 2 fs out, sn rdn and wknd.* .... (16 to 1 op 10 to 1) 7
1577⁶ STATE TACOMA 8-6 L Charnock (4) *al rear, tld off fnl 2 fs.* .... (40 to 1 op 33 to 1) 8
Dist: 1½l, 3½l, 1l, 2l, 1½l, 3½l, 15l. 1m 23.90s. a 2.10s (8 Ran).
SR: 31/18/2/16/1/5/-/-/ (H E Lhendup Dorji), D R Loder

2339 Fairfield Industries International Challenge Handicap Class D (0-80 3-y-o and up) £3,655 7f................ (7:10)

2001* ROYAL GIRL [58] 6-9-3 N Connorton (1) *prmnt, chsd ldr hfwy, rdn to ld ins last, hld on.* ....(7 to 2 op 3 to 1 tchd 4 to 1) 1
1833² TAJDIF (USA) [77] 3-10-0 M Hills (6) *hld up, hdwy 2 fs out, rdn and ev ch ins last, jst fld*.....(7 to 4 fav op 2 to 1) 2
1641⁸ SUPER BENZ [61] 7-9-6 J Fanning (2) *led, rdn 2 fs out, hdd and no extr ins last*............... (7 to 1 op 11 to 2) 3
1866² JOMOVE [37] 4-7-10 J Lowe (5) *hld up, effrt and hdwy o'r 2 fs out, rdn and kpt on one pace ins last.* ....(7 to 2 op 3 to 1 tchd 4 to 1) 4
2001⁵ QUIET VICTORY [37] (bl) 6-7-10³ F Norton (3) *chsd ldr till outpcd hfwy, styd on ins last*.......(10 to 1 op 8 to 1) 5
1865* ARABAT [66] 6-9-11 J Carroll (4) *dwlt, gd hdwy 2 fs out, sn ev ch, rdn and wknd entering fnl furlong.* .... (15 to 2 op 6 to 1 tchd 8 to 1) 6
Dist: Sht-hd, 1½l, ¾l, 2l, ½l. 1m 23.80s. a 2.00s (6 Ran).
SR: 36/46/33/7/1/28/ (Miss S E Hall), Miss S E Hall

2340 Middlesbrough Football Club Apprentice Selling Handicap Class G (0-60 3-y-o) £1,992 1¾m 19yds....... (7:40)

1980³ WESTRAY (Fr) [50] 9-7 J Tate (3) *trkd ldr, hdwy to ld 4 fs out, sn clr, eased fnl furlong, unchlgd.* .... (11 to 8 fav op 11 to 10 tchd 6 to 4) 1
838⁶ DANGER BABY [37] 8-8 D Wright (1) *hld up, rdn alng 5 fs out, plugged on one pace to take second ins last, no ch wth wnr*............................ (2 to 1 op 7 to 4) 2
1896⁷ BONNY PRINCESS [32] (v) 7-10 (7*) K Sked (4) *led and sn clr, rdn and hdd 4 fs out, grad wknd.* ....(11 to 2 op 5 to 1 tchd 6 to 1) 3
1980⁵ PREMIER BLUES (Fr) [42] 8-8 (5*) Sarah Thompson (2) *hld up, rdn 5 fs out, sn wl beh.* .... (6 to 1 tchd 11 to 2 and 13 to 2) 4
Dist: 6l, 3l, 15l. 3m 7.70s. a 11.20s (4 Ran).
(M Redditt), Dr J D Scargill

2341 Redcar Motor Company Handicap Class E (0-70 3-y-o) £2,343 1¼m (8:10)

2163⁶ SO SAUCY [51] 8-11 K Fallon (9) *made all, rdn 2 fs out, styd on strly*....... (3 to 1 fav op 11 to 4 tchd 5 to 2) 1
2130⁶ EFIZIA [61] 9-7 K Darley (5) *trkd ldrs, chsd wnr hfwy, effrt to chal 2 fs out, sn rdn and ev ch, wknd entering last.* ....(6 to 1 op 5 to 1) 2
2281⁴ MENA [57] 9-3 Dean McKeown (3) *hld up, hdwy 3 fs out, styd on und pres fnl 2 furlongs, nvr dngrs.* ....(10 to 1 tchd 12 to 1) 3
1832⁴ RAQS ASSAYF [49] 8-9 A Culhane (7) *chsd ldrs, rdn 3 fs out, sn one pace*...................(7 to 2 op 11 to 4) 4
1852* GOLD DESIRE [45] 8-5 J Carroll (1) *mid-div, hdwy to chase ldrs 4 fs out, sn rdn and one pace*............. (5 to 1) 5
1852⁷ MR ABBOT [40] 8-0 J Lowe (6) *al rear.* (16 to 1 op 8 to 1) 6
1283⁵ JENDORCET [46] 8-6 J Fanning (4) *nvr rch ldrs.* .... (16 to 1 op 14 to 1) 7
PINKERTON'S SILVER [51] 8-11 M Birch (8) *prmnt, rdn hfwy, sn wknd*.................... (12 to 1 op 8 to 1) 8
1356⁶ BROOMHOUSE LADY [53] 8-6 (7*) M Baird (2) *chsd ldrs, rdn and wknd 4 fs out*.............(16 to 1 op 10 to 1) 9
Dist: 2½l, 3l, 1½l, ½l, 1½l, 1½l, 1½l, 1½l. 2m 5.70s. a 4.50s (9 Ran).
SR: 32/37/27/16/11/3/6/8/7/ (L H J Ward), B J Meehan

2342 Darlington Maiden Auction Stakes Class F (2-y-o) £1,900 5f........ (8:40)

1814² CERTIFICATE-X 8-9 Dean McKeown (4) *cl up, leed aftr one furlong, rdn clr 2fs out, easily*... (5 to 4 fav op 6 to 4) 1
HICKLETON LADY (Ire) 8-9 K Darley (6) *hld up, hdwy hfwy, styd on ins last, better for race*......... (10 to 1) 2
1895⁷ LEGAL TRAIN 9-0 J Lowe (3) *led one furlong, cl up till ridde nad one pace 2 fs out*...........................(5 to 1) 3
908⁹ RICH HARMONY 9-0 Dale Gibson (8) *chsd ldrs, rdn 2 fs out, sn one paced*...................................(6 to 1) 4
1203⁶ DEMON DANCER (Ire) 9-0 N Connorton (2) *in toucnb, rdn hfwy sn wknd*..................................(5 to 1) 5
DUNSLOW ROAD 8-9 M Birch (7) *al rear.* .... (12 to 1 op 10 to 1) 6
MONKEY BOY (Ire) 9-0 J Carroll (1) *slwly away, al beh.* ....(8 to 1 op 7 to 1) 7
Dist: 3l, nk, ½l, 7l, 1½l, 10l. 58.00s. a 1.30s (7 Ran).
SR: 34/22/26/24/ (The 2nd Kingsley House Partnership), M Johnston

2343 Sunderland Handicap Class E (0-70 3-y-o and up) £2,385 1m 5f 135yds ....(9:10)

1847⁷ MYSTIC MEMORY [57] 4-8-13 (5*) Darren Moffatt (6) *set slow pace till jnd hfwy, rdn and hdd o'r 2 and a half fs out, styd on to ld ins last, ran on wl und pres.* ....(7 to 1 op 5 to 1) 1
2014² ARCTIC GUEST (Ire) [51] 3-7-11 J Fanning (1) *trkd ldg pair, took clr order 4 fs out, rdn and outpcd 3 out, styd on wl und pres ins last*..............(5 to 4 fav tchd 11 to 8) 2
1173 LOOKINGFORARAINBOW (Ire) [55] 5-9-2 N Connorton (7) *trkd ldrs, took clr order 4 fs out, rapid hdwy to ld 2 and a half out, sn clr, rdn, hdd no extr ins last.* ....(4 to 1 op 7 to 2 tchd 9 to 2) 3
2166⁴ GREY COMMANDER [33] 5-7-8¹ L Charnock (5) *trkd ldr, quickened to dispute ld hfwy, rdn 3 fs out, sn one paced*.......................(10 to 1 tchd 11 to 1) 4
2201⁹ YOUNG GEORGE [42] 6-8-3 J Lowe (2) *hld up and beh, outpcd o'r 4 fs out, nvr a factor*................ (6 to 1) 5
2166* MINGUS (USA) [47] 6-8-8 (5ex) K Fallon (4) *hld up and beh, outpcd o'r 4 fs out, nvr a factor*.....(11 to 2 op 9 to 2) 6
Dist: Nk, 2l, 8l, 6l, 2½l. 3m 8.70s. a 18.80s (6 Ran).
(Carnoustie Racing Club Ltd), Mrs M Reveley

BELLEWSTOWN (IRE) (firm)
Thursday July 8th

2344 Shallon E.B.F. Maiden (2-y-o) £3,107 1m..........................(5:30)

2072² OLIVER MESSEL (Ire) 9-0 W J Supple (1) ....(2 to 1 on) 1
2072 VENICE (Ire) 9-0 J P Murtagh (2)..................(10 to 1) 2
ONE DAY LATE 8-11 N G McCullagh (3)...........(10 to 1) 3
MALT LEAF (Ire) 8-5 (6*) J A Heffernan (4).........(10 to 1) 4
1994³ SHEEN FALLS (Ire) 8-11 P Shanahan (5)...........(4 to 1) 5
Dist: 4½l, 4½l, 6l, 5l. 1m 38.70s. (5 Ran).
(Mrs Catherine McNulty), Kevin Prendergast

2345 Heineken Handicap (0-90 4-y-o and up) £4,292 1m.................(6:30)

2041⁵ DESERT CALM (Ire) [-] 4-9-5 (6*) B J Walsh (10).... (9 to 2) 1
2297* HAPPY ROVER [-] 8-10-0 (5ex) J P Murtagh (7) (9 to 4 fav) 2
2297⁵ BARNAGEERA BOY (Ire) [-] 4-7-12¹ N G McCullagh (2) ....(12 to 1) 3
2322² TINCO PALENO [-] 9-7-10 (2*) R M Burke (1)......(13 to 2) 4
2041 NO DIPLOMACY (Ire) [-] 4-7-10 (6*) J J Behan (5)..(20 to 1) 5
2248² NUNIVAK (USA) [-] 5-8-13 W J Supple (3).........(7 to 2) 6
LAST EMPEROR (USA) [-] 6-8-5 P Shanahan (9).. (12 to 1) 7
2297⁶ SIGHTSEER (Ire) [-] 4-7-1 (6*) P P Murphy (8)..... (14 to 1) 8
2142 PURPLE EMPEROR (Fr) [-] 4-8-12 S Craine (6).... (16 to 1) 9
1794⁴ BRACKLOON BOY (Ire) [-] 4-8-9 P V Gilson (4).... (10 to 1) 10
Dist: 1l, 1l, ¾l, 2½l. 1m 36.90s. (10 Ran).
(Mrs C McNulty), Kevin Prendergast

2346 Derek Plant Race (3-y-o and up) £2,762 1¾m.......................... (8:00)

1997[4] SAFE CONDUCT (Ire) 3-9-0 J P Murtagh (3)........ (6 to 4) 1
2287[4] DAHLIA'S BEST (USA) 3-9-0 W J Supple (4).....(5 to 4 fav) 2
1755[7] TROPICAL LAKE (Ire) 3-8-11 S Craine (2)..........(20 to 1) 3
2041 KEDWICK (Ire) 4-10-1 N G McCullagh (5)..........(5 to 1) 4
1986[5] JUST ONE CANALETTO 5-9-7 (8*) T P Treacy (1)..(14 to 1) 5
753 AT YOUR SERVICE (Ire) 4-10-1 K F O'Brien (7).....(10 to 1) 6
Dist: Nk, 5l, 2l, 8l. 3m 8.30s. (6 Ran).
(F Dunne), F Dunne

CHEPSTOW (good to firm) Thursday July 8th

Going Correction: MINUS 0.05 sec. per fur. (races 1,2,3), MINUS 0.30 (4,5,6)

2347 Lysaght Amateur Riders Handicap Class G (0-70 3-y-o and up) £2,574 1½m 23yds..................... (6:30)

2201* ALLMOSA [53] 4-11-11 (5*,5ex) Mrs J Naughton (3) *sn trkd ldr, led 5 fs out, pushed out fnl furlong.*
.... (13 to 2 op 4 to 1 tchd 7 to 1) 1
2127[3] BARCHAM [35] 6-10-12 Miss Diana Jones (10) *nvr far away, outpcd 3 fs out, styd on wl fnl furlong.*
........................(5 to 1 op 7 to 1 tchd 9 to 2) 2
2043[6] DUGGAN [43] 6-11-1 (5*) Mr W McLaughlin (2) *hld up in rear, hdwy on outsd o'r 2 fs, one pace ins last.*
.... (7 to 1 op 8 to 1 tchd 10 to 1) 3
2043[8] FANATICAL (USA) [36] (bl) 7-10-8 (5*) Miss S Farrant (6) *hld up, hdwy 4 fs out, chsd wnr 2 furlongs out till found little ins last*...................... (14 to 1 op 10 to 1) 4
1941[5] THE KARAOKE KING [48] (bl) 4-11-6 (5*) Mrs J Boggis (5) *hld up in mid-div, hdwy o'r 3 fs out, one pace fnl 2.*
.................................(9 to 1 op 6 to 1) 5
1781[2] MYSTERIOUS MAID (USA) [44] 6-11-7 Mrs L Pearce (9) *prmnt till one pace fnl 3 fs*.... (4 to 1 fav tchd 11 to 2) 6
2232[2] SCENIC DANCER [51] 5-11-9 (5*) Miss L Hide (7) *hld up, no hdwy fnl 3 fs*..................(11 to 2 op 7 to 2) 7
1861* HILLSDOWN BOY (Ire) [49] 3-10-8 (5*) Mr T Cuff (4) *chsd ldrs till wknd o'r 2 fs out*....(9 to 1 op 6 to 1 tchd 10 to 1) 8
2149[8] PRECIOUS CAROLINE (Ire) [41] 5-11-4 Mrs D Arbuthnot (12) *hld up, hdwy hfwy, wknd quickly o'r 2 fs out.*
.... (14 to 1 op 10 to 1) 9
2007[7] WRITTEN AGREEMENT [25] 5-9-11 (5*) Mrs C Peacock (13) *led for 7 fs, wknd o'r 3 out*.........(33 to 1 op 20 to 1) 10
1600[6] MEESON CODE [24] 6-9-10 (5*) Mr V Lukaniuk (1) *slwly away, sn in tch, rdn 4 fs out, soon btn.*
.... (50 to 1 op 20 to 1) 11
HELLO SAM [29] 10-10-1 (5*) Miss A Purdy (8) *slwly away, al beh, tld off fnl 4 fs*............ (25 to 1 op 20 to 1) 12
SNICKERSNEE [39] 5-10-11 (5*) Miss J Southcombe (11) *prmnt to hfwy, tld off*............(33 to 1 op 20 to 1) 13
Dist: 1l, 2½l, hd, 3l, 1½l, 2l, 2l, 1l, ¾l, ¾l. 2m 42.10s. a 10.60s (13 Ran).
SR: 32/12/15/7/13/6/9/-/-/ (The Durdans Four (Ii) Two), T J Naughton

2348 Welsh Brewers Handicap Class D (0-80 3-y-o and up) £3,231 1¼m 36yds ....(7:00)

1858[2] MR TATE (Ire) [61] 4-9-5 J Reid (8) *trkd ldr, led o'r 2 fs out, edgd lft appr last, rdn out.*
..............(13 to 8 fav op 7 to 4 tchd 2 to 1) 1
1820[8] SCOTTISH BAMBI [65] 5-9-9 R Perham (4) *hld up in tch, rdn to go second o'r 2 fs out, edgd lft appr last, no imprsn ins*............................ (8 to 1 op 6 to 1) 2
2029[3] COURAGEOUS KNIGHT [69] 4-9-13 L Dettori (6) *hld up, hdwy o'r 2 fs out, hrd rdn appr last, ran on one pace.*
..................................(8 to 1 op 6 to 1) 3
1919[9] TENDRESSE (Ire) [53] 5-8-4 (7*) D McCabe (3) *hld up in rear, hdwy on outsd 2 fs out, not rch ldrs.*
..................................(7 to 1 op 4 to 1) 4
1781[4] SAINT CIEL (USA) [67] 5-9-4 (7*) Michael Denaro (1) *al abt same pl, no hdwy fnl 2 fs*...........(10 to 1 op 7 to 1) 5
1627* WHO'S THE BEST (Ire) [49] 3-7-10 J Quinn (2) *chsd ldrs, rdn o'r 3 fs out, one pace aftr.*
.... (8 to 1 op 10 to 1 tchd 7 to 1) 6
2100[3] HAROLDON (Ire) [69] 4-9-8 (5*) Stephen Davies (5) *slwly away, effrt o'r 3 fs out, nvr nr to chal.*
..................(16 to 1 op 10 to 1 tchd 20 to 1) 7
2113[4] ROMOLA NIJINSKY [62] 5-9-6 L Piggott (7) *led till hdd o'r 2 fs out, sn wknd, eased*..............(11 to 2 op 8 to 1) 8
Dist: 1½l, ¾l, 3l, 2½l, nk, sht-hd, 2½l. 2m 9.20s. a 5.60s (8 Ran).
SR: 44/45/47/25/34/4/34/22/ (John Falvey), R Akehurst

2349 Welsh Riband Conditions Stakes Class B formerly the Welsh Derby Stakes (3-y-o and up) £9,146 1½m 23yds.......................... (7:30)

MACK THE KNIFE (bl) 4-9-4 L Piggott (3) *sn led, drw clr 2 fs out, eased ins, unchlgd.*
.... (6 to 4 on tchd 11 to 8 on and 13 to 8 on) 1
2070[4] ANCHORITE 4-9-5 Pat Eddery (2) *led briefly, sn hdd, trkd wnr, rdn o'r 3 fs out, lost tch 2 out.*
.... (13 to 8 op 11 to 8 tchd 7 to 4) 2
2108* BIG PAT 4-9-6 L Dettori (1) *al last, lost tch fnl half m.*
......................................(10 to 1 op 12 to 1) 3
Dist: 10l, 30l. 2m 35.70s. a 4.20s (3 Ran).
SR: 56/37/-/ (Sir John Astor), Major W R Hern

2350 Alveston Maiden Handicap Class E (0-70 3-y-o and up) £3,276 7f 16yds ....(8:00)

2047[3] TUMBLING (USA) [40] 5-8-2 A Munro (2) *in rear on outsd, gd hdwy o'r 2 fs out, led appr last, ran on.*
....................................(8 to 1 op 5 to 1) 1
CASTING SHADOWS [46] 4-8-8 D Holland (3) *hld up, short of room o'r 2 fs out, hdwy appr last, no imprsn ins.*
.... (15 to 2 op 5 to 1 tchd 8 to 1) 2
1898[7] SIR OLIVER (Ire) [50] 4-8-12 J Williams (5) *hld up in rear, hdwy o'r one furlong out, ran on, nvr nrr.*
....................................(7 to 1 op 4 to 1) 3
2057[5] GUESSTIMATION (USA) [47] 4-8-9 G Bardwell (7) *al prmnt, wnt second appr fnl furlong, wknd ins.*
.........................(9 to 2 op 7 to 1 tchd 8 to 1) 4
2127 KALOKAGATHOS [33] 4-7-9 J Quinn (1) *wl in rear on outsd, hdwy o'r one furlong out, nvr nrr.*
.... (14 to 1 op 10 to 1) 5
2031[6] CLASS ATTRACTION (USA) [65] 4-9-13 M Perrett (9) *chsd ldrs, rdn 2 fs out, no extr*............ (8 to 1 op 5 to 1) 6
2004[5] CHRISTIAN WARRIOR [42] 4-7-11 (7*) D McCabe (13) *led, clr 2 fs out, wknd and hdd appr last.*
.... (25 to 1 op 16 to 1) 7
2012[5] WESSEX MILORD [31] 8-7-3[3] (7*) Claire Balding (4) *slwly away, effrt 2 fs out, nvr nr to chal.* (33 to 1 op 20 to 1) 8
1977 HULLO MARY DOLL [32] 4-7-8[1] Dale Gibson (12) *speed to o'r hfwy*.............................. (66 to 1 op 50 to 1) 9
2121 CHEREN BOY [31] (v) 4-7-7 N Adams (8) *prmnt on outsd till wknd o'r 2 fs out*.............. (25 to 1 op 20 to 1) 10
VIS-A-VIS [40] 4-8-2 R Price (10) *speed to hfwy, wknd quickly, tld off*......................(33 to 1 op 12 to 1) 11
2164[8] CASHMIRIANA (Ire) [53] 4-9-1 C Rutter (11) *chsd ldrs, wknd o'r 2 fs out, stumbled and broke leg one and a half out, destroyed*........................ (16 to 1 tchd 20 to 1) ur
2121[2] GOOD IMAGE [54] 3-8-8 Pat Eddery (6) *chsd ldr to 3 fs out, pld up lme aftr 2 out.*
.....................(13 to 8 fav op 9 to 4 tchd 11 to 4) pu
Dist: 1½l, ¾l, 4l, 2½l, nk, 1½l, ½l, ¾l, 2l, 20l. 1m 22.90s. a 2.90s (13 Ran).
SR: 13/14/16/1/-/10/ (Robert Gibbons), J D Bethell

2351 Maple Conditions Stakes Class D (3 & 4-y-o) £3,494 7f 16yds.......... (8:30)

1638[6] LACERTA (Ire) 3-8-6[1] J Reid (4) *hld up in tch, smooth hdwy to ld o'r 2 fs out, pushed clr ins last.*
....................................(2 to 1 op 6 to 4) 1
2060[9] BOLD AMUSEMENT 3-8-12 K Darley (6) *chsd ldrs, hrd rdn to go second appr fnl furlong, ran on.*
....................................(7 to 4 fav op 2 to 1) 2
DIXIELAND MELODY (USA) 3-8-12 W R Swinburn (7) *led till hdd o'r 2 fs out, one pace appr last.* (15 to 8 op 2 to 1) 3
1315[9] DASHING MARCH 4-8-11 J Williams (2) *nvr on terms*
...................................(80 to 1 op 50 to 1) 4
CASTLE-VIEW 3-8-3 D Holland (1) *outpcd thrght.*
.....................(50 to 1 op 20 to 1 tchd 66 to 1) 5
GREAT PLOVER 3-8-8 J Quinn (3) *slwly away, al beh.*
.....................(50 to 1 op 25 to 1 tchd 66 to 1) 6
1375 CHEEKY TUNE 4-9-2 R Price (5) *chsd ldr to hfwy, wknd quickly 2 fs out*.................. (100 to 1 op 20 to 1) 7
1278[9] SUEENA 3-8-0[4] (7*) S Drowne (8) *outpcd frm strt, tld off.*
.... (100 to 1 op 33 to 1) 8
Dist: 4l, 2l, 10l, 2½l, 2l, nk, 15l. 1m 23.20s. a 3.20s (8 Ran).
SR: 12/6/-/-/-/ (R E Sangster), P W Chapple-Hyam

2352 Fleur De Lys Handicap Class E (0-70 3-y-o and up) £2,957 5f 16yds... (9:00)

1903[8] BATCHWORTH BOUND [40] 4-7-13 C Rutter (7) *al prmnt, rdn to ld one and a half fs out, drvn out.*
.....................(16 to 1 op 10 to 1 tchd 20 to 1) 1
2157* TREASURE TIME (Ire) [59] 4-8-13 (5*) K Rutter (10) *led till hdd one and a half fs out, rallied ins last.*
.............................(7 to 2 fav tchd 11 to 4) 2
1925[2] CASTLE MAID [34] 6-7-7 J Quinn (9) *mid-div, hdwy 2 fs out, ran on ins last*...................(9 to 2 op 6 to 1) 3
2318[3] LUCEDEO [69] 9-10-0 L Dettori (8) *slwly away, hdwy 2 fs out, kpt on one pace ins last.*
.... (13 to 2 op 6 to 1 tchd 15 to 2) 4
1881[5] TOMMY TEMPEST [49] 4-8-8 D Holland (5) *in frnt rnk till wknd wl o'r one furlong out*...... (8 to 1 tchd 10 to 1) 5
2214 KENSWORTH LADY [52] 3-8-2 (3*) D Harrison (6) *unruly bef strt, reared up leaving stalls, nvr nr to chal.*
.... (12 to 1 op 8 to 1) 6
2110[9] MISS PRECOCIOUS [36] (v) 5-7-9[2] A Tucker (1) *prmnt on outsd, rdn o'r 2 fs out, sn btn*......(25 to 1 op 16 to 1) 7
1744 IRON KING [59] 7-9-4 K Darley (4) *hld up, effrt o'r 2 fs out, wknd appr last*.....................(10 to 1 op 8 to 1) 8

1096 GRAND TIME [39] 4-7-12 G Bardwell (2) *outpcd, al struggling in rear*............(12 to 1 op 6 to 1) 9
2173[8] ASTERIX [49] 5-8-8 N Adams (3) *al in rear on outsd.*
..........................(14 to 1 op 10 to 1) 10
1309 OCTOBER BREW (USA) [60] 3-8-13 M Perrett (11) *outpcd frm strt*..............(12 to 1 op 8 to 1 tchd 14 to 1) 11
Dist: Nk, 2l, nk, 4l, 2l, hd, hd, 3l, hd, 6l. 58.60s. a 1.60s (11 Ran).
SR: 23/41/8/42/6/-/-/6/-/ (Mrs Diana Price), S Mellor

NOTTINGHAM (good to firm)
Thursday July 8th
Going Correction: MINUS 0.10 sec. per fur. (races 1,2,3,6), NIL (4,5)

2353 'Young At Heart' Selling Handicap Class G (0-60 3-y-o and up) £2,784 1m 1f 213yds.....................(2:20)

2052[4] BRONZE RUNNER [28] (bl) 9-8-0 T Sprake (6) *nvr far away, led o'r 2 fs out, hng lft over one out, rdn out.*
..........................(14 to 1 op 8 to 1) 1
1588[3] MAI PEN RAI [37] (v) 5-8-9 J Quinn (3) *in tch, improved and ev ch fnl furlong, not quicken towards finish.*
..........................(6 to 1 op 5 to 1 tchd 7 to 1) 2
1941[4] NOT YET [31] 9-8-3 D Holland (11) *beh, improved fnl 2 fs, ran on finish*..........................(16 to 1 op 8 to 1) 3
2029[6] IMA RED NECK (USA) [44] 4-9-2 A McGlone (13) *in tch, drvn alng to improve 4 fs out, kpt on und pres ins last.*
..........................(6 to 4 on op 3 to 1) 4
2149 WINGED WHISPER (USA) [35] 4-8-0 (7*) D McCabe (5) *al prmnt, chlgd o'r 2 fs out, not quicken fnl furlong.*
..........................(33 to 1) 5
1880[4] EASTERN MAGIC [40] (bl) 5-8-12 Paul Eddery (15) *mid-div, drvn alng 3 fs out, swtchd and styd on fnl furlong.*
..........................(10 to 1 op 7 to 1) 6
2201[6] REACH FOR GLORY [38] (v) 4-8-3 (7*) G Parkin (7) *mid-div, sn pushed alng and lost pl, improved on inner o'r 2 fs out, kpt on towards finish, nvr dngrs.*
..........................(20 to 1 op 8 to 1) 7
2109 IBSEN [45] 5-9-3 R Perham (17) *hld up, shaken up and steady hdwy fnl 2 fs, nvr plcd to chal.*
..........................(5 to 1 op 4 to 1 tchd 6 to 1) 8
2162[5] SALMONID [56] 7-9-7 (7*) D O'Neill (8) *led till o'r 2 fs out, no extr*..........................(14 to 1 op 8 to 1) 9
4678a EIRAS MOOD [50] 4-9-3 (5*) Stephen Davies (1) *beh, effrt and rdn on outsd 3 fs out, not pace to chal.*
..........................(10 to 1 op 8 to 1) 10
2197[7] JUST-GO-AGAIN [44] (bl) 4-9-2 B Raymond (16) *in tch, pushed alng 3 fs out, wknd*........(33 to 1 op 20 to 1) 11
2178 ABSOLUTLEY FOXED [29] 4-7-13[1] (3*) S Maloney (10) *beh, rdn alng 4 fs out, no imprsn*.......(33 to 1 op 25 to 1) 12
1702 ELECTROJET [21] 5-7-7 N Adams (12) *beh, drvn alng entering strt, nvr on terms*.........(33 to 1 op 20 to 1) 13
2107[5] MERRY MERMAID [46] 3-8-7 L Charnock (4) *hld up, rdn alng 3 fs out, sn btn*..............(14 to 1 op 8 to 1) 14
2109[6] CREAGMHOR [49] 3-8-10 J Lowe (2) *slwly into strd, al struggling*..........................(25 to 1) 15
1596[2] BOLD FLASH [50] 3-8-4 (7*) J Gracey (9) *chsd ldrs, rdn alng o'r 2 fs out, wknd quickly*..... (12 to 1 op 7 to 1) 16
Dist: ¾l, sht-hd, ½l, 2l, hd, 1½l, ½l, 3l, 7l, sht-hd. 2m 8.60s. a 5.60s (16 Ran).
SR: 20/27/20/32/19/23/18/24/29/ (Austin Stroud & Co Ltd), S Mellor

2354 Post Office Handicap Class E (0-70 3-y-o and up) £3,002 1m 1f 213yds..............................(2:55)

1900[8] MISTY GODDESS (Ire) [48] 5-8-13 (5*) K Rutter (4) *pressed ldrs, not clr run 2 fs out and appr last, swtchd and quickened to ld ins last, kpt on wl.*
..........................(11 to 2 op 5 to 1 tchd 6 to 1) 1
1566[5] SHARQUIN [42] 6-8-12 M Wigham (7) *pressed ldg bunch, drvn alng entering strt, improved und pres 2 fs out, ev ch one furlong out, kpt on*..........(10 to 1 op 8 to 1) 2
1900[2] TELEPHUS [52] 4-9-8 J Lowe (9) *pressed ldg grp, hdwy o'r 2 fs out, led over one furlong out, hdd ins last, no extr.*
..................(4 to 1 jt-fav op 7 to 2 tchd 9 to 2) 3
AFFA [51] 4-9-7 S Whitworth (1) *mid-div, rdn alng to improve o'r 2 fs out, ev ch one furlong out, sn one pace.*
..........................(16 to 1 op 10 to 1) 4
2000[3] ATHERTON GREEN (Ire) [65] 3-9-7 (3*) S D Williams (2) *chsd ldrs, drvn alng 3 fs out, not much room and swtchd ins o'r one furlong out, one pace inside last*.....(4 to 1 jt-fav tchd 9 to 2 and 5 to 1) 5
1946[5] GREEN'S CASSATT (USA) [50] 5-9-3 (3*) S Maloney (5) *beh, drvn 3 fs out, kpt on fnl furlong, nvr dngrs.*
..........................(6 to 1 op 7 to 1) 6
1781 BRECKENBROUGH LAD [41] 6-8-11 B Raymond (3) *hld up, pushed alng 4 furlong sout, nvr able to chal.*
..........................(25 to 1 op 20 to 1) 7
1981[5] DANDY DESIRE [37] (bl) 4-8-7 J Williams (6) *beh, drvn alng 3 fs out, not rch ldrs*.........(14 to 1 tchd 16 to 1) 8
2183* INFERRING [45] 5-9-1 (5ex) L Charnock (10) *nvr far away, chlgd o'r 3 fs out, wknd wl over one furlong out.*
..........................(7 to 1 op 5 to 1) 9

2108[5] BRESIL (USA) [58] 4-10-0 R Hills (11) *trkd ldrs, improved to ld 3 furlong out, hdd o'r one furlong out, wknd quickly*..........................(16 to 1 op 14 to 1) 10
1910[4] SUN GREBE (Ire) [66] (bl) 3-9-11 Paul Eddery (8) *set gd pace, hdd 3 fs out, sn btn*................(10 to 1 op 6 to 1) 11
Dist: 1½l, hd, 3l, 1½l, 2l, 1½l, 1½l, nk, 1½l, 5l. 2m 9.20s. a 6.20s (11 Ran).
SR: 32/23/32/25/25/17/5/-/5/ (J R Good), M A Jarvis

2355 Awebb Electrical Network Handicap Class D (0-80 3-y-o) £3,289 1¾m 15yds..............................(3:25)

2158* MY PATRIARCH [81] 9-11 (4ex) Paul Eddery (3) *trkd ldg pair gng wl, improved to ld 2 fs out, sn clr, very easily.*
..................(11 to 10 on op Evens tchd 11 to 10) 1
2051* BILJAN (USA) [65] 8-9 J Carroll (2) *trkd ldr, outpcd and drvn alng 3 fs out, kpt on fnl furlong, no ch wth wnr.*
..........................(6 to 1 op 4 to 1) 2
1917[4] GUESTWICK [72] 9-2 B Raymond (1) *hld up in tch, outpcd 3 fs out, shaken up and kpt on fnl furlong, nvr dngrs.*
..........................(16 to 1 op 14 to 1) 3
1930[2] TURFMANS VISION [62] 8-6 S Perks (5) *hld up in last pl, rdn alng 3 fs out, nvr able to chal*....(9 to 2 op 7 to 2) 4
1935[2] FOINERY [71] 9-1 R Hills (4) *led, hdd 2 fs out, sn rdn and btn*..........................(4 to 1 op 7 to 2) 5
Dist: 4l, 2½l, 1l, ¾l. 3m 8.20s. a 10.30s (5 Ran).
(Peter S Winfield), J L Dunlop

2356 Help The Aged Claiming Stakes Class F (2-y-o) £2,422 6f 15yds........(4:00)

2176[3] LAUREL ROMEO (Ire) 9-0 J Carroll (5) *chsd ldrs, effrt and rdn o'r 2 fs out, ran on fnl furlong to ld cl hme.*
..................(11 to 2 op 4 to 1 tchd 6 to 1) 1
2058[5] CULSYTH FLYER 9-3 Paul Eddery (4) *led, shaken up o'r one furlong out, hdd and no extr cl hme.*
..................(11 to 8 fav op Evens tchd 6 to 4) 2
2049[6] PACIOLI 8-6 J Williams (2) *in tch, ran green and sn pushed alng, swtchd outsd hfwy, ran on to chal wl ins fnl furlong, no extr last strds.*
..................(13 to 8 op 5 to 2 tchd 6 to 4) 3
1985[6] ROSIE VALENTINE 8-5 D Holland (3) *pressed ldr, shaken up hfwy, wknd o'r one furlong out.* (9 to 1 op 9 to 2) 4
2103[7] INAMORATA 7-7 J Lowe (1) *wnt lft ldg stalls, sn in tch and ran green, lost touch o'r one furlong out.*
..........................(25 to 1 op 12 to 1) 5
Dist: Nk, hd, 2l, 10l. 1m 17.00s. a 5.50s (5 Ran).
(Laurel (Leisure) Limited), J Berry

2357 EBF Maiden Fillies' Stakes Class D (2-y-o) £4,342 6f 15yds............(4:30)

TRICORNE 8-11 T Sprake (2) *hld up, swtchd and improved on bit 2 fs out, quickened to ld ins last, sn clr, easily*..........................(14 to 1 op 8 to 1) 1
PLACITANA (USA) 8-11 N Adams (7) *pressed ldg grp, swtchd to improve o'r one furlong out, kpt on ins last, not rch wnr*..........................(33 to 1 op 20 to 1) 2
1403[9] MONAASSABAAT (USA) 8-11 B Raymond (5) *nvr far away, led wl o'r one furlong out, hdd ins last, one pace.*
..........................(Evens fav op 3 to 1) 3
MEHTHAAF (USA) 8-11 R Hills (1) *in tch on outer, effrt and rdn 2 fs out, not quicken ins last*.....(9 to 1 op 5 to 1) 4
SO SEDULOUS (USA) 8-11 Paul Eddery (4) *in tch, rdn alng 2 fs out, one pace appr last.*
..................(11 to 8 op 5 to 4 on tchd 6 to 4) 5
WAVELET 8-11 D Holland (8) *trkd ldrs, rdn hfwy, no extr fnl 2 fs*..........................(14 to 1 op 6 to 1) 6
2292[8] LADY PHYL 8-11 S Whitworth (6) *sn led, rdn and hdd wl o'r one furlong out, fdd*.............(33 to 1 op 20 to 1) 7
2006[4] KOONOONA LADY 8-11 J Lowe (3) *chsd ldrs, rdn and lost tch o'r 2 fs out*..................(33 to 1 op 20 to 1) 8
RANKAIDADE 8-11 S Perks (9) *dwlt, beh, drpd away frm hfwy*..........................(33 to 1 op 20 to 1) 9
Dist: 2½l, ½l, ½l, ¾l, 3½l, ½l, 4l, nk. 1m 14.90s. a 3.40s (9 Ran).
SR: 29/19/17/15/12/-/ (S P Tindall), R Charlton

2358 Active Life Apprentice Maiden Handicap Class G (0-70 3-y-o and up) £2,301 1m 54yds......................(5:00)

1661[4] SILVER GROOM (Ire) [52] 3-8-12[1] (8*) G McGrath (5) *in tch, improved and hng lft o'r one furlong out, chlgd ins last, led cl hme*..... (11 to 4 fav op 9 to 2 tchd 5 to 1) 1
1861[4] STALLED (Ire) [54] 3-9-7 P McCabe (7) *hld up, rdn to improve 3 fs out, ran on strly fnl furlong, jst fld.*
..........................(5 to 1 op 9 to 2) 2
2031[4] NORTHERN TRIAL (USA) [45] (v) 5-9-7 G Mitchell (4) *keen hold, hld up in tch, effrt 3 fs out, ran on to ld ins last, hdd cl hme*............(13 to 2 op 5 to 1 tchd 7 to 1) 3
1993[6] MY MINNIE [53] 3-9-6 S Mulvey (10) *beh, plenty to do and drvn alng 3 fs out, gd hdwy o'r one out, fnshd strly.*
..........................(11 to 1 op 16 to 1) 4
1673[2] TEJANO GOLD (USA) [55] 3-8-12 (10*) A Daly (1) *chsd ldr, rdn 3 fs out, kpt on same pace fnl furlong.*
..........................(10 to 1 op 7 to 1) 5

1303 QUEEN OF DREAMS [31] 5-8-2 (5*) G Milligan (3) *chsd ldrs gng wl, effrt o'r one furlong out, sn ev ch, no extr last 100 yards*..........................(7 to 1 op 6 to 1) 6
17308 NATCHEZ TRACE [52] (v) 4-9-6 (8*) D Griffiths (9) *beh, rdn alng 3 fs out, ran on ins last, nvr dngrs.*
.... (14 to 1 op 6 to 1) 7
16569 MOST SIOUXTABLE [52] 3-8-9 (10*) G Mills (6) *chsd ldrs, effrt o'r 2 fs out, not quicken ins last.*
.................................(14 to 1 op 12 to 1) 8
19937 SIAN WYN [40] 3-8-2 (5*) M Baird (8) *keen hold, nvr far away, effrt 3 fs out, wknd 2 out.* (20 to 1 tchd 25 to 1) 9
9347 FESTIN [60] (bl) 3-9-3 (10*) C Adamson (2) *sn led, clr entering strt, hdd ins last, drpd away quickly.*
.................................(11 to 1 op 7 to 1) 10

Dist: Sht-hd, nk, 1½l, sht-hd, nk, ½l, 1½l, 2½l, nk. 1m 48.20s. a 8.20s (10 Ran).
(L Fust), A P Jarvis

NEWMARKET (JULY) (good to firm)
Thursday July 8th
Going Correction: MINUS 0.15 sec. per fur. (races 1,3,4,5,6), MINUS 0.25 (2)

2359 Child & Co. Superlative Stakes Class A (Listed Race) (2-y-o) £9,189 7f (2:00)

BAL HARBOUR 8-11 Pat Eddery (2) *co'red up on ins, swtchd outsd to improve over 2 fs out, led last 100 yards, ran on*..(7 to 4 tchd 9 to 4) 1
SHEPTON MALLET (Ire) 8-11 J Reid (1) *patiently rdn, quickened to ld wl o'r one furlong out, hdd last 100 yards, prmsg*..........(13 to 2 op 4 to 1 tchd 10 to 1) 2
1975* GOVERNOR GEORGE (USA) 9-2 L Dettori (5) *pld hrd, swtchd outsd and effrt o'r one furlong out, sn rdn and outpcd*.............(5 to 4 fav tchd Evens and 11 to 8) 3
2069* MR EUBANKS (USA) 8-11 R Cochrane (4) *settled to track ldr, lost grnd whn pace quickened o'r one furlong out, no extr*................(13 to 2 op 9 to 2 tchd 7 to 1) 4
1804 PAPAGAYOS (Ire) 8-11 M Roberts (3) *led till wl o'r one furlong out, eased whn btn ins last.*
.... (40 to 1 op 20 to 1 tchd 50 to 1) 5

Dist: Nk, 5l, 2l, 2½l. 1m 29.26s. a 5.06s (5 Ran).
SR: 5/4/ (K Abdulla), H R A Cecil

2360 Bahrain Trophy Class A (Listed Race) (3-y-o) £9,594 1¾m 175yds......(2:35)

17695 SPRING TO ACTION 8-10 L Dettori (2) *tucked away gng wl, led o'r 2 fs out, cleverly.*
.... (5 to 1 op 6 to 1 tchd 13 to 2) 1
17244 TIOMAN ISLAND 8-10 J Reid (4) *pld hrd to hfwy, swtchd outsd to draw level o'r 2 fs out, kpt on wl*....(7 to 2 jt-fav op 3 to 1 tchd 4 to 1) 2
17896 MAGICAL RETREAT (USA) 8-10 D Biggs (1) *nvr far away, led briefly o'r 2 fs out, kpt on wl nr finish.*
.... (25 to 1 op 16 to 1 tchd 33 to 1) 3
2116* ALJAZZAF 8-10 W R Swinburn (3) *al wl plcd, ev ch o'r one furlong out, kpt on same pace.*
.... (13 to 2 op 8 to 1 tchd 6 to 1) 4
20824 SILVERDALE (USA) 8-10 M Roberts (6) *al hndy, ev ch and drvn alng o'r 2 fs out, not quicken ins last*...(7 to 2 jt-fav op 11 to 4 tchd 4 to 1) 5
20033 RAPID REPEAT (Ire) (v) 8-5 P Robinson (8) *pressed ldrs, effrt o'r 2 fs out, sn rdn and one pace.*
.... (25 to 1 op 14 to 1 tchd 33 to 1) 6
17694 SAINT KEYNE 8-10 Pat Eddery (5) *led till wl o'r 2 fs out, wknd*................(11 to 2 op 9 to 2 tchd 6 to 1) 7
17693 KASSAB 8-10 W Carson (7) *unruly stalls, wl plcd on ins till rdn o'r 3 fs out, virtually pld up over one out.*
.... (13 to 2 op 5 to 1 tchd 7 to 1) 8

Dist: Nk, 1½l, 1l, 1l, nk, 2l, dist. 3m 6.07s. a 0.07s (8 Ran).
SR: 58/57/54/52/50/44/45/-/ (The Queen), I A Balding

2361 TNT Aviation Handicap Class C (0-95 3-y-o) £10,275 1m...............(3:05)

18085 BEAUCHAMP HERO [80] 8-7 N Carlisle (3) *co'red up on ins, chalg whn hmpd inside fnl furlong, swtchd and ran on to ld cl hme*..........(14 to 1 op 12 to 1 tchd 16 to 1) 1
15243 SHAMAM (USA) [87] 9-0 P Robinson (9) *al hndy, led o'r 2 fs out, drifted lft and hdd ins last, rallied cl hme.*
.................................(20 to 1 tchd 25 to 1) 2
20662 TYCHONIC [80] 8-7 Pat Eddery (1) *tucked away on ins, drvn alng and swtchd o'r 2 fs out, ran on to ld inside last, ct cl hme*...... (6 to 1 fav op 5 to 1 tchd 13 to 2) 3
1808 EASY ACCESS (Ire) [89] 9-2 G Carter (8) *rdn alng to go pace, improved on outsd last 2 fs, styd on.*
.... (33 to 1 op 25 to 1) 4
13022 CHATOYANT [89] 9-2 M Hills (12) *nvr far away, ev ch and bustled alng o'r 2 fs out, kpt on same pace.*
.... (14 to 1 op 12 to 1) 5
20192 WORDSMITH (Ire) [69] 7-10 D Biggs (4) *trkd ldrs, effrt and not much room o'r 2 fs out, not quicken.*
.... (14 to 1 op 12 to 1 tchd 16 to 1) 6
19732 MARASTANI (USA) [90] 9-3 J Reid (13) *nvr far away, feeling pace and drvn alng o'r 2 fs out, no extr.*
.... (12 to 1 op 10 to 1 tchd 14 to 1) 7
19785 THUNDER RIVER (Ire) [94] 9-7 A Munro (2) *wl plcd on ins, hrd drvn o'r 2 fs out, fdd*..........(33 to 1 op 25 to 1) 8
1808 CONEYBURY (Ire) [88] 9-1 R Cochrane (14) *trkd ldrs, effrt and drvn alng o'r 2 fs out, not quicken.*
.... (10 to 1 op 12 to 1 tchd 14 to 1) 9
1808 MECKLENBURG (Ire) [86] 8-13 M Roberts (15) *beh and niggled alng aftr 3 fs, shrtlvd effrt on outsd o'r 2 out, no imprsn*..........................(8 to 1 op 6 to 1) 10
16675 VAYAVAIG [81] 8-8 W R Swinburn (16) *chsd ldrs for o'r 5 fs.*
.................................(14 to 1 tchd 16 to 1) 11
13023 STAR MANAGER (USA) [87] 8-7 (7*) T G McLaughlin (17) *beh and drvn alng most of way.*
.... (20 to 1 op 16 to 1 tchd 25 to 1) 12
2022* SO SO [83] 8-10 W Newnes (10) *chsd alng in mid-div hfwy, nvr a threat*.................................(14 to 1) 13
1931* GOLDEN GUEST [86] 8-13 L Piggott (5) *co'red up beh ldrs, effrt and not much room over one furlong out, nvr able to chal*.... (9 to 1 op 10 to 1 tchd 12 to 1 and 8 to 1) 14
1808 WOODHAUNTER (USA) [81] 8-8 W Ryan (11) *beh and drvn alng, nvr a factor*.................. (25 to 1 tchd 33 to 1) 15
19503 EAST LIBERTY (USA) [80] 8-7 L Dettori (7) *settled mid-div, feeling pace o'r 2 fs out, sn btn*.... (12 to 1 op 10 to 1) 16
19734 RAKIS (Ire) [86] 8-13 W Carson (6) *pressed ldrs, bustled alng whn hmpd o'r 2 fs out, eased when btn.*
.................................(14 to 1 tchd 16 to 1) 17

Dist: ¾l, sht-hd, 3l, 1½l, 4l, hd, 2½l, 1l, 1½l, 1l. 1m 40.55s. a 2.65s (17 Ran).
SR: 35/40/32/32/27/-/15/11/2/ (E Penser), J L Dunlop

2362 July Cup Class A (Group 1) (3-y-o and up) £106,365 6f.................(3:40)

17868 HAMAS (Ire) 4-9-6 W Carson (9) *rcd wide, led appr hfwy, quickened clr frm 2 fs out, easily.* (33 to 1 op 25 to 1) 1
1786* COLLEGE CHAPEL 3-8-13 L Piggott (1) *al hndy, bustled alng o'r 2 fs out, styd on, no ch wth wnr.*
.... (9 to 4 fav op 3 to 1 tchd 100 to 30) 2
9548 ZIETEN (USA) 3-8-13 T Jarnet (12) *beh and pushed alng hfwy, styd on last 2 fs, nvr nrr*.....(4 to 1 tchd 9 to 2) 3
17862 KEEN HUNTER (USA) 6-9-6 M Roberts (8) *bustled alng to go pace, improved on outsd last 2 fs, nvr nrr.*
.... (5 to 1 op 4 to 1 tchd 11 to 2) 4
5125 MARINA PARK 3-8-10 Dean McKeown (7) *trkd ldrs, effrt and drvn alng o'r 2 fs out, one pace.*
.... (12 to 1 op 10 to 1 tchd 14 to 1) 5
17869 FYLDE FLYER 4-9-6 G Carter (4) *nvr far away, drvn alng o'r 2 fs out, not quicken*.......... (50 to 1 tchd 66 to 1) 6
1807* ELBIO (v) 6-9-6 Pat Eddery (3) *chsd alng beh ldrs, kpt on last 2 fs, no imprsn*...... (4 to 1 op 3 to 1 tchd 9 to 2) 7
20685 SILVER WIZARD (USA) (bl) 3-8-13 A Munro (11) *beh and bustled alng hfwy, nvr able to rch chalg pos.*
.................................(20 to 1 tchd 25 to 1) 8
5805 BASIM (USA) 3-8-13 C Roche (2) *dsptd ld for o'r 3 fs, fdd und pres*..........................(12 to 1 op 10 to 1) 9
16142 MIDHISH 3-8-13 W R Swinburn (5) *chsd ldrs, hrd drvn o'r 2 fs out, no imprsn*..... (25 to 1 op 33 to 1 tchd 40 to 1) 10
18074 FREDDIE LLOYD (USA) 4-9-6 J Reid (6) *slight ld till appr hfwy, drvn alng o'r 2 fs out, fdd*...(33 to 1 op 25 to 1) 11
14066 ARTISTIC REEF 4-9-6 R Cochrane (10) *chsd ldrs till wknd quickly o'r 2 fs out*..............(100 to 1 op 66 to 1) 12

Dist: 3l, ¾l, nk, 1½l, ½l, 1½l, nk, 1½l, 2½l, sht-hd. 1m 13.08s. a 1.38s (12 Ran).
SR: 60/41/38/44/28/36/30/22/16/ (Hamdan Al-Maktoum), P T Walwyn

2363 Ladbroke Bunbury Cup Handicap Class B (0-105 3-y-o and up) £25,050 7f ....(4:10)

20603 EN ATTENDANT (Fr) [90] 5-9-4 L Piggott (4) *patiently rdn, hdwy into midfield hfwy, swtchd ins to ld o'r one furlong out, drvn out.*
.... (14 to 1 op 16 to 1 tchd 20 to 1) 1
2172* VELOCE (Ire) [65] 5-7-7 A Mackay (14) *chsd alng to improve frm midfield hfwy, swtchd ins fnl furlong, ran on wl.*
.... (20 to 1 op 25 to 1) 2
14074 DRESS SENSE (Ire) [89] 4-9-3 M Roberts (25) *settled gng wl, hdwy to ld 2 fs out, hdd o'r one out, rdn and not quicken fnl furlong.*
.................(7 to 1 fav op 12 to 1 tchd 6 to 1) 3
2060* TAWAFIJ (USA) [77] 4-8-5 J Fanning (27) *trkd ldrs, chlgd appr fnl furlong, kpt on same pace last 100 yards.*
.... (11 to 1 op 10 to 1 tchd 12 to 1) 4
1830 HERORA (Ire) [86] 4-8-7 (7*) D Wright (7) *co'red up in midfield, effrt and drvn alng over 2 fs out, styd on.*
.................................(25 to 1 tchd 33 to 1) 5
18303 RISE UP SINGING [69] (bl) 5-7-11 J Quinn (12) *al hndy, drvn alng o'r 2 fs out, one pace.* (14 to 1 tchd 16 to 1) 6
1806 MASTER PLANNER [89] 4-9-3 D Biggs (17) *settled midfield, improved und pres o'r 2 fs out, one pace.*
.................................(20 to 1 tchd 22 to 1) 7
18305 HIGHLAND MAGIC (Ire) [83] 5-8-11 C Rutter (3) *sluggish strt, styd on last 2 fs, nrst finish*...(16 to 1 op 14 to 1) 8
17479 POWERFUL EDGE [100] 4-10-0 L Dettori (21) *nvr far away, feeling pace and drvn alng o'r 2 fs out, no extr.*
.................................(20 to 1 tchd 25 to 1) 9+

1172 KAYVEE [94] 4-9-8 W R Swinburn (18) *chsd alng in midfield, effrt o'r 2 fs out, not pace to chal*........(20 to 1) 9+

2136^{5} HELIOS [76] 5-8-4 G Carter (10) *drvn alng to improve last 2 fs, nrst finish*.........(33 to 1 tchd 40 to 1) 11

1680^{3} VENTURE CAPITALIST [92] (bl) 4-9-6 Pat Eddery (26) *missed break, beh till ran on appr fnl furlong, nvr nrr.* ....(14 to 1 op 20 to 1) 12

2212* FIELD OF VISION (Ire) [77] 3-7-11 (8ex) T Williams (23) *pushed alng to go pace, effrt hfwy, nvr able to chal.* ....(14 to 1) 13

1830 SATRAP (Ire) [82] 5-8-10 R Cochrane (13) *drvn alng in midfield hfwy, not pace of ldrs*.... (50 to 1 op 66 to 1) 14

1806 BEWARE OF AGENTS [89] 4-9-3 Dean McKeown (24) *reared strt, nvr able to rch chalg pos*.................(33 to 1) 15

1768 BAND ON THE RUN [97] 6-9-4 (7*) S Sanders (9) *chsd ldrs for o'r 4 fs, fdd*.....................(33 to 1 op 25 to 1) 16

2060^{5} HIGH PREMIUM [85] 5-8-13 K Fallon (8) *chsd ldrs, hrd drvn o'r 2 fs out, fdd*..................(16 to 1 op 14 to 1) 17

2194^{3} SPANISH STORM (Ire) [90] (bl) 4-9-4 W Woods (22) *made most to 2 fs out, fdd*............. (20 to 1 tchd 25 to 1) 18

465^{5} ADWICK PARK [81] 5-8-6 (3*) M Fenton (15) *beh and drvn alng, nvr a dngr*.................................(33 to 1) 19

2136^{2} ROCKY WATERS (USA) [94] 4-9-8 B Rouse (5) *chsd alng to keep up hfwy, fdd 2 fs out*....... (16 to 1 tchd 14 to 1) 20

1636* CROFT VALLEY [95] 6-9-9 J Reid (16) *speed 5 fs.* ....(10 to 1 tchd 12 to 1) 21

1806^{6} HARD TO FIGURE [95] 7-9-9 W Carson (19) *chsd alng hfwy, sn outpcd*.... (16 to 1 tchd 14 to 1 and 20 to 1) 22

1973^{7} NOBLE PET [85] 4-8-13 A Munro (11) *in tch, effrt and drvn alng hfwy, fdd*..................................(25 to 1) 23

2136^{7} CONFRONTER [74] 4-7-13 (3*) D Harrison (2) *chsd alng far side, struggling last 2 fs*.........................(33 to 1) 24

1808 ERTLON [78] 3-7-9 (3*) B Doyle (20) *drvn alng hfwy, sn btn*..(33 to 1) 25

2283^{8} ASHDREN [69] 6-7-11 G Bardwell (6) *early speed, fdd o'r 2 fs out*..............................(33 to 1 op 25 to 1) 26

2139^{2} SHIKARI'S SON [77] 6-8-5 P Robinson (1) *chsd alng aftr 3 fs, rdn and btn 2 out*.............. (20 to 1 op 25 to 1) 27

Dist: Nk, 1½l, 1½l, 2l, ½l, 1½l, ½l, 3½l, dd-ht, 2l. 1m 25.07s. a 0.87s (27 Ran).

SR: 75/49/68/51/54/35/50/42/48/ (Mrs B Newton), B Hanbury

2364 EBF Fulbourn Maiden Stakes Class D (2-y-o) £5,572 6f.................(4:45)

MAGNASONIC (USA) 9-0 Pat Eddery (4) *al hndy, led o'r 2 fs out, drifted lft ins last, ran on strly.* ....(13 to 8 fav op 9 to 4 tchd 5 to 2) 1

ALLEZ CYRANO (Ire) 9-0 M Hills (14) *nvr far away, drvn alng o'r one furlong out, ran on, prmsg.* ....(6 to 1 op 4 to 1 tchd 3 to 1 and 13 to 2) 2

LAFTAH (USA) 9-0 M Roberts (5) *led centre grp till o'r 2 fs out, no extr fnl furlong.* .... (11 to 2 op 5 to 1 tchd 6 to 1) 3

BATTLING BLUE 9-0 W R Swinburn (3) *tucked away beh ldrs, improved o'r one furlong out, ran on, improve.* .... (16 to 1 op 12 to 1 tchd 20 to 1) 4

DIESAN (USA) 9-0 L Dettori (10) *sluggish strt, hdwy last 2 fs, ran on*............... (8 to 1 op 5 to 1 tchd 9 to 1) 5

FAAL MARIO (USA) 9-0 A Munro (7) *trkd ldrs, effrt and pushed alng o'r one furlong out, kpt on same pace.* .... (14 to 1 op 12 to 1 tchd 20 to 1) 6

FAIRY HEIGHTS (Ire) 8-9 W Ryan (8) *unruly stalls, sluggish strt, swtchd outsd to improve last 2 fs, ran on.* .... (50 to 1 op 25 to 1) 7

BIG SQUEEZE (USA) 9-0 D Biggs (11) *pressed ldrs 4 fs, no imprsn ins last*................. (33 to 1 tchd 50 to 1) 8

2069^{6} ARECIBO (Ire) 8-11 (3*) B Doyle (1) *chsd ldrs, feeling pace and bustled alng 2 fs out, not quicken.* .... (33 to 1 op 20 to 1) 9

DAHIYAH (USA) 9-0 W Carson (12) *settled midfield, bustled alng hfwy, improved o'r one furlong out, eased whn btn ins last*.........(6 to 1 op 5 to 1 tchd 8 to 1) 10

1456^{8} STORM REGENT 9-0 W Woods (9) *chsd ldrs, wknd 2 fs out*.............................. (50 to 1 op 33 to 1) 11

1523^{8} JEYPORE JO 9-0 R Cochrane (13) *chsd ldrs 4 fs.* .... (33 to 1 op 16 to 1) 12

544^{3} RAPIER POINT (Ire) 9-0 Dean McKeown (2) *rcd alone far side, led hfwy, hdd o'r 2 fs out, eased whn btn.* .... (25 to 1 op 14 to 1) 13

1955 WIDE OUTSIDE (Ire) 8-9 B Rouse (6) *chsd ldrs, wknd last 2 fs*...................(50 to 1 op 33 to 1 tchd 66 to 1) 14

Dist: 4l, ¾l, ¾l, ½l, 1½l, hd, ½l, hd, 2½l, nk. 1m 15.35s. a 3.65s (14 Ran).

SR: 9/-/-/-/-/-/ (K Abdulla), R Charlton

REDCAR (firm)
Thursday July 8th

Going Correction: MINUS 0.65 sec. per fur. (races 1,2,6), MINUS 0.20 (3,4,5)

2365 Jolly Sailor Selling Handicap Stakes Class G (0-60 3-y-o) £2,070 5f... (2:10)

1925^{4} TREVORSNINEPOINTS [55] 9-7 K Darley (5) *made all, hng lft frm hfwy, ran on strly*....... (11 to 8 fav op 6 to 4) 1

1833^{8} MILBANK CHALLENGER [54] 9-6 M Birch (8) *broke wl and prmnt stands side, rdn 2 fs out, kpt on ins last.* ....(9 to 1 op 6 to 1) 2

1505^{5} OUR MICA [48] (bl) 9-0 G Duffield (6) *al prmnt, rdn 2 fs out, kpt on same pace*..................(8 to 1 op 6 to 1) 3

1925 MELODYS DAUGHTER [50] (bl) 9-2 F Norton (11) *al prmnt stands side, ev ch o'r one furlong out, unbl to quicken.* .... (12 to 1 op 10 to 1) 4

1990^{5} KIMMY'S PRINCESS [40] 8-6 A Clark (10) *prmnt, ev ch hfwy, wknd o'r one furlong out*.....................(8 to 1) 5

1965^{5} SAMANTHAS JOY [47] 8-13 J Fortune (4) *chsd ldrs, rdn alng hfwy, stdly wknd*............(14 to 1 op 12 to 1) 6

2047 SHOTLEY AGAIN [40] 8-6 Alex Greaves (9) *outpcd til moderate hdwy 2 fs out, nvr a dngr*.....(50 to 1 op 33 to 1) 7

1937^{5} HAWAYMYSON (Ire) [53] 9-2 (3*) J Weaver (3) *sn rdn alng, nvr able to chal*...................... (8 to 1 op 6 to 1) 8

2089* CRACKER JACK [50] (bl) 8-9 (7*,7ex) J Marshall (1) *al beh,* ....(9 to 1 op 7 to 1) 9

1159^{8} THE CUT [32] (v) 7-5 (7*) N Varley (7) *al outpcd and beh.* ....(50 to 1 op 33 to 1) 10

2170^{6} MASTER PECKITT [41] (bl) 8-2 (5*) J Tate (2) *sn rdn alng and wl beh*...............................(25 to 1 op 20 to 1) 11

Dist: 1l, hd, 2½l, 2½l, hd, 3l, 1½l, ¾l, 1l, 4l. 57.20s. a 0.50s (11 Ran).

SR: 32/27/20/12/-/-/ (T S Child), Mrs M Reveley

2366 St John Ambulance Rating Related Maiden Stakes Class E (0-70 3-y-o) £2,821 7f...................... (2:45)

1836^{8} DUKE OF DREAMS 9-0 K Darley (1) *midfield till hdwy o'r 2 fs out, pld wide to chal over one out, led ins last and styd on wl*........................ (20 to 1 op 14 to 1) 1

741^{6} SKY WISH 9-0 N Connorton (5) *wth ldr, led o'r one furlong out, hdd and no extr ins last*.....................(7 to 1) 2

2133^{2} NICHODOULA 8-9 G Duffield (7) *sn scrubbed alng and prmnt, ev ch o'r one furlong out, no extr ins last.* ....(3 to 1 fav op 5 to 2) 3

1866^{4} SUDDEN SPIN (v) 9-0 J Fortune (3) *led till hdd o'r one furlong out, sn rdn and unbl to quicken*....... (4 to 1) 4

2164^{5} DANNY BLUE (Ire) 9-0 Gay Kelleway (8) *beh till some hdwy hfwy, nvr able to chal*...............(4 to 1 op 5 to 1) 5

1891^{5} GLIMPSE OF HEAVEN 8-9 A Culhane (2) *prmnt, rdn o'r 2 fs out, wknd quickly appr fnl furlong.* (9 to 1 op 7 to 1) 6

1396^{3} MOLLY BRAZEN 8-9 M Birch (6) *prmnt to hfwy, sn wknd.* ....(5 to 1 op 9 to 2) 7

1968^{7} SIMPLY SUPERB 9-0 T Lucas (4) *al struggling.* ....(50 to 1 op 33 to 1) 8

Dist: ½l, 1l, 1½l, 3½l, 5l, 5l, 1l. 1m 22.90s. a 1.10s (8 Ran).

SR: 15/13/5/5/-/ (Miss E Shepherd), Mrs M Reveley

2367 Evening Gazette Handicap Class D (0-80 4-y-o and up) £3,427 1¼m (3:15)

1941* AZUREUS (Ire) [70] 5-9-6 K Darley (1) *tucked away, checked on turn 6 fs out and sn pushed alng, styd on wl to ld one out, ran on*................ (5 to 4 fav op Evens) 1

1820^{3} KNOWTH (Ire) [69] 4-9-5 A Clark (4) *trkd ldr, led wl o'r 2 fs out, hdd one out, sn no extr.* ....(9 to 4 op 2 to 1 tchd 5 to 2) 2

2236^{6} COMMON COUNCIL [61] (v) 4-8-4 (7*) J Marshall (3) *led, quickened o'r 4 fs out, hdd wl over 2 out, sn btn.* .... (13 to 2 op 5 to 1 tchd 7 to 1) 3

2020^{2} WELL APPOINTED (Ire) [74] 4-9-10 M Birch (2) *hld up, pushed alng 4 fs out, nvr a threat*... (5 to 1 op 4 to 1) 4

Dist: 2l, 4l, 12l. 2m 4.80s. a 3.60s (4 Ran).

SR: 50/45/29/18/ (J C Murdoch), Mrs M Reveley

2368 Sea Pigeon Handicap Class D (0-80 3-y-o and up) £3,114 2m 4yds... (3:50)

2002* TAROUDANT [74] 6-10-0 K Darley (4) *al hndy gng wl, led o'r 3 fs out, shaken up well over one out, styd on cmftbly*....(11 to 8 op 5 to 4 tchd 6 to 4 and 13 to 8) 1

1989* PROVENCE [71] 6-9-11 G Hind (3) *led till hdd o'r 3 fs out, sn rdn alng, rallied fnl furlong, kpt on.* ....(6 to 5 fav op 5 to 4 tchd 11 to 10) 2

1041^{6} DOMINANT SERENADE [50] 4-7-11 (7*) J Marshall (1) *trkd ldr, rdn o'r 3 fs out still ev ch over one out, one pace.* .... (11 to 2 op 5 to 1) 3

1847^{4} BRIDGE PLAYER [42] 6-7-5 (5*) Darren Moffatt (2) *hld up in last pl, short lived effrt o'r 4 fs out, sn wknd.* ....(14 to 1 op 12 to 1 tchd 16 to 1) 4

Dist: Nk, 1½l, 15l. 3m 32.20s. a 9.20s (4 Ran).

(G A Farndon), Mrs M Reveley

2369 Red Cross Handicap Class E (0-70 3-y-o and up) £3,054 1m 1f..........(4:20)

2232* TOUCH ABOVE [51] 7-8-11 (7*,4ex) V Halliday (1) *nvr far away, hdwy o'r 4 fs out, sn ev ch, led one out, ran on.* ....(9 to 4 jt-fav op 6 to 4) 1

1969^{2} MASTER OFTHE HOUSE [46] 7-8-6 (7*) J Marshall (4) *chsd ldrs, led 3 fs out till hdd one out, not quicken.* ....(5 to 1 tchd 6 to 1) 2

1737 WAAZA (USA) [50] (bl) 4-8-12 (5*) O Pears (5) *hld up and beh till styd on fnl 2 fs, nrst finish.* (14 to 1 op 12 to 1) 3

2088⁵ VENTURE FOURTH [35] 4-8-2 S Wood (2) *hld up and beh, some hdwy o'r 3 fs out, nvr able to chal.* ....(8 to 1 op 7 to 1) 4
2017⁴ UCKERBY MOOR [52] 4-9-5 S Webster (3) *led till hdd 3 fs out, stdly wknd*......(20 to 1 op 12 to 1 tchd 25 to 1) 5
1969³ DEAD CALM [56] 3-8-10 (3*) J Weaver (8) *hld up, short lived effrt o'r 4 fs out, kpt on same pace.* ....(10 to 1 op 7 to 1) 6
2217⁸ KICK ON MAJESTIC (Ire) [31] 4-7-12 Julie Bowker (7) *wth ldr, ev ch 4 fs out, sn lost pl.* ....(25 to 1 op 20 to 1 tchd 33 to 1) 7
1832³ KAGRAM QUEEN [57] 5-9-10 K Darley (6) *in tch, hdwy whn stumbled 5 fs out, sn pushed alng and lost touch, eased fnl 2 furlongs*........(9 to 4 jt-fav tchd 2 to 1 and 5 to 2) 8
Dist: 1½l, 3½l, 2½l, 1½l, 3½l, nk, dist. 1m 52.20s. a 3.70s (8 Ran).
SR: 22/12/6/-/-/ (Mrs J Hazell), T D Barron

2370 EBF Mermaid Maiden Stakes Class D (2-y-o) £4,207 5f................(4:55)

2049 SELHURSTPARK FLYER (Ire) 9-0 J Fortune (4) *made virtually all, rdn out fnl furlong*.....(11 to 1 op 10 to 1) 1
DANCE FOCUS 9-0 T Ives (6) *chsd ldrs, shaken up wl o'r one furlong out, swtchd lft and kpt on ins last.* ....(7 to 2 op 6 to 4) 2
1798⁶ HELLABY 9-0 K Darley (5) *chsd ldrs, effrt o'r one furlong out, not quicken ins last*.........(14 to 1 op 12 to 1) 3
2049² RESONANT 9-0 G Duffield (7) *al prmnt, rdn wl o'r one furlong out, no extr.* ....(Evens fav op 11 to 10 tchd 6 to 5) 4
1798⁵ ELUNED MAY 8-9 A Culhane (3) *prmnt till rdn and wknd wl o'r one furlong out.* (11 to 2 op 5 to 1 tchd 6 to 1) 5
GRANGE DANCER (Ire) 8-4 (5*) Darren Moffatt (2) *sn rdn alng and outpcd*........(33 to 1 tchd 50 to 1) 6
1763⁹ WOODTONG (bl) 9-0 S Webster (1), *dived lft leaving stalls, sn outpcd and beh*........(33 to 1 op 20 to 1) 7
Dist: 1½l, hd, 2½l, 4l, 6l, hd. 57.10s. a 0.40s (7 Ran).
SR: 27/21/20/10/ (Chris Deuters), J Berry

CHESTER (good)
Friday July 9th
Going Correction: NIL (races 1,2), PLUS 0.15 (3,4,5,6)

2371 Watergate Apprentice Handicap Class E (0-70 3-y-o and up) £2,860 7f 122yds ....(6:30)

2121⁷ WILL SOON [57] 4-8-6 (10*) S Drake (8) *made all, drvn out, ran on gmely*........(8 to 1 op 7 to 1) 1
2175* LOMBARD SHIPS [66] (bl) 6-9-1 (10*,7ex) W Hollick (5) *mid-div, rdn and styd on appr fnl furlong, no ch wth wnr.* ....(11 to 2 op 4 to 1 tchd 6 to 1) 2
1943³ FORMAESTRE (Ire) [46] 3-7-3 (7*) F Savage (3) *chsd ldr, shaken up o'r 2 out, kpt on same pace.* ....(8 to 1 tchd 6 to 1) 3
1866⁷ THE DANDY DON (Ire) [44] 4-7-9 (8*) C Teague (4) *towards rear, drvn alng 4 out, kpt on one pace ins fnl furlong.* ....(12 to 1 op 10 to 1) 4
2060 CEE-JAY-AY [69] 6-9-6 (8*) P Roberts (7) *strted slwly, beh, kpt on one pace frm o'r one out.* ....(3 to 1 fav op 4 to 1 tchd 5 to 2) 5
2017* KUMMEL KING [54] 5-8-5 (8*) S Knott (9) *wth ldr til rdn and wknd hfwy*........(5 to 1 op 4 to 1) 6
2099⁵ YUNUS EMRE (Ire) [51] 3-7-9 (6*) J O'Dwyer (6) *towards rear, rdn and effrt appr 2 out, sn btn.* (6 to 1 op 4 to 1) 7
2127⁸ HALEIM [42] 6-7-10 (5*) D Griffiths (1) *cl up til rdn and wknd 3 out*........(33 to 1 op 20 to 1) 8
1247⁹ PANTHER (Ire) [66] 3-8-9 (7*) W Hawksley (2) *al beh, lost tch 2 out*........(12 to 1 op 6 to 1) 9
Dist: 3l, 2l, sht-hd, 1l, 4l, 2½l, ¾l, 12l. 1m 36.55s. a 4.55s (9 Ran).
SR: 34/34/-/5/27/-/ (Henry Candy), H Candy

2372 Henry Gee Claiming Stakes Class E (3-y-o and up) £3,460 1½m 66yds (7:00)

2059⁵ TRUBEN (USA) 4-8-13 L Dettori (3) *trkd ldr, led o'r 4 out, styd on gmely*.....(6 to 5 on op 6 to 4 on tchd Evens) 1
2205* CIVIL LAW (Ire) (v) 3-8-5 M Roberts (1) *hld up in tch, drvn alng 3 out, ran on wl ins fnl furlong, not rch wnr.* ....(4 to 1) 2
2205 DON'T FORGET MARIE (Ire) 3-7-7 (5*) D Wright (5) *pld hrd, chsd ldr, drvn alng and outpcd 4 out, kpt on ins fnl furlong*........(3 to 1 tchd 11 to 4 and 100 to 30) 3
1901⁴ SCOTTISH WEDDING 3-7-12 L Charnock (4) *set slow pace, hdd o'r 4 out, rallied over 2 out, no extr ins fnl furlong.* ....(14 to 1 tchd 16 to 1) 4
2289⁵ TINA MEENA LISA 4-8-0 (7*) C Hawksley (2) *strted very slwly, al in rear*.....(25 to 1 op 16 to 1 tchd 33 to 1) 5
Dist: 1l, 1l, hd, 8l. 2m 49.09s. a 12.29s (5 Ran).
(Lucayan Stud), D R Loder

2373 Harcros Timber & Building Supplies Stayers Championship Series Handicap Qualifier Class C (0-90 3-y-o and up) £4,980 1½m 66yds.........(7:30)

2126* MOONLIGHT QUEST [74] 5-9-12 (5ex) L Dettori (7) *chsd ldr, shaken up to ld o'r one out, ran on strly.* ....(8 to 1 op 7 to 1) 1
1711⁶ ALMAMZAR (USA) [85] 3-9-10 Paul Eddery (2) *led til hdd o'r one out, sn rdn, kpt on*............(10 to 1 op 8 to 1) 2
1946* MAD MILITANT (Ire) [71] 4-9-9 K Darley (8) *hld up in tch, shaken up o'r 2 out, ran on ins fnl furlong.* ....(6 to 1 op 8 to 1) 3
1979² RISING TEMPO (Ire) [67] 5-8-12 (7*) N Varley (6) *in tch, drvn alng and lost pl hfwy, styd on ag'n frm 2 out.* (33 to 1) 4
2019* DARMSTADT (USA) [79] 3-9-4 M Roberts (1) *chsd ldrs, effrt and rdn o'r 2 out, no extr entering fnl furlong, eased whn btn*.......(11 to 10 on op 5 to 4 on tchd Evens) 5
2059* CONTRACT ELITE (Ire) [62] 3-8-1 A Mackay (5) *in rear, rdn o'r 3 fs out, sn btn*.......(8 to 1 op 7 to 1 tchd 9 to 1) 6
1275⁵ MOUNT FUJI [75] 3-9-0 M Hills (4) *towards rear, hdwy hfwy, chsd ldr 4 out, rdn and wknd o'r 2 out.* ....(11 to 1 op 10 to 1) 7
2149⁶ KILLICK [51] 5-7-12 (5*) D Wright (3) *dwlt, sn in tch, drvn alng and wknd 4 out*........(8 to 1 op 12 to 1) 8
Dist: 3½l, 1½l, ½l, ½l, 20l, ½l, 30l. 2m 44.14s. a 7.34s (8 Ran).
SR: 57/48/44/39/37/ (Mrs John Lamb), B Hanbury

2374 EBF Aldford Maiden Stakes Class D (2-y-o) £4,272 5f 16yds..........(8:00)

2096⁸ VERCINGETORIX (Ire) 9-0 Paul Eddery (1) *made all, ran wide entering strt, rdn and quickened o'r one out, hld on gmely*...........(10 to 1 op 16 to 1 tchd 20 to 1) 1
1456⁴ YAWARA 8-9 M Roberts (7) *badly outpcd and beh, hdwy on ins appr fnl furlong, swtchd outsd and fnshd wl inside last*.........(7 to 4 fav op 6 to 4 tchd 15 to 8) 2
2063³ STELLOSO 9-0 L Dettori (4) *chsd ldr, rdn wide entering strt, kpt on same pace*..............(4 to 1 op 3 to 1) 3
859⁴ DINOT (Ire) 9-0 S Perks (2) *in tch, rdn alng hfwy, sn outpcd*.............(12 to 1 op 10 to 1 tchd 14 to 1) 4
1846² ANITA'S LOVE (Ire) 8-9 J Carroll (5) *in tch, drvn alng hfwy, sn btn*........(9 to 2 op 4 to 1) 5
1296⁴ LANCASHIRE LIFE (Ire) 9-0 K Fallon (3) *chsd ldrs, rdn entering strt, wknd one out*.....(14 to 1 tchd 16 to 1) 6
BASHFUL BRAVE 9-0 M Hills (6) *in tch til rdn and wknd o'r one out*........(6 to 1 op 4 to 1) 7
Dist: Nk, 5l, 1½l, 2l, 1½l, 6l. 1m 4.84s. a 4.54s (7 Ran).
SR: 24/18/3/-/ (Lord Hartington), G Lewis

2375 Red Deer Handicap Class C (0-95 3-y-o) £5,452 5f 16yds..............(8:30)

2237³ SAINT EXPRESS [90] 9-7 A Culhane (4) *struggled to go early pace, hdwy appr fnl furlong, ran on to ld wl ins last, all out*........(13 to 2 op 6 to 1) 1
2237⁷ THE SHARP BIDDER (Ire) [79] 8-10 K Darley (3) *outpcd and wl beh, ran on strly ins fnl furlong, edgd rght cl hme, jst fld*........(11 to 1 op 10 to 1) 2
2024* CALL ME I'M BLUE (Ire) [86] 9-3 L Piggott (5) *struggled to go early pace, rdn to chal appr fnl furlong, sn ev ch, no extr and not much room cl hme*......(5 to 2 op 2 to 1) 3
1841² LAUREL DELIGHT [87] 9-4 L Dettori (1) *led till wl ins fnl furlong, wknd*.......(2 to 1 fav op 9 to 4 tchd 5 to 2) 4
1860⁷ PURBECK CENTENARY [63] 7-8¹ J Quinn (2) *chsd ldrs, rdn and edgd rght entering fnl furlong, wknd*......(8 to 1) 5
2050* PRESS THE BELL [80] 8-11 J Carroll (6) *wth ldr till wknd and hmpd entering fnl furlong.* ....(4 to 1 op 7 to 2 tchd 9 to 2) 6
Dist: Hd, nk, 3l, ½l, 6l. 1m 3.33s. a 3.03s (6 Ran).
SR: 61/49/55/44/18/11/ (M G St Quinton), R M Whitaker

2376 Cardinal Puff Conditions Stakes Class C (4-y-o and up) £4,965 1¼m 75yds ....(9:00)

1768 TAPIS ROUGE (Ire) 4-8-11 M Roberts (1) *chsd ldr, led 3 out, ran on strly appr fnl furlong, sn clr, eased cl hme.* ....(7 to 4 fav op 6 to 4) 1
1748 YOUNG SENOR (USA) 4-9-4 M Hills (4) *hld up in tch, took clr order 6 out, chsd ldr frm 3 out, shaken up to chal entering strt, rdn and no extr ins last.* ....(15 to 8 op 6 to 4 tchd 2 to 1) 2
1952⁵ ST NINIAN 7-9-1 M Birch (2) *trkd ldr, rdn entering strt, kpt on fnl furlong*........(7 to 2 op 3 to 1) 3
1462² BOLD PURSUIT (Ire) 4-8-12 K Fallon (3) *in tch til rdn and outpcd frm 2 out*........(8 to 1 op 12 to 1) 4
2071* MY ROSSINI 4-8-4 (7*) C Hawksley (5) *led til shaken up and hdd 3 out, sn wknd*........(12 to 1 op 25 to 1) 5
Dist: 3½l, ¾l, 2l, 5l. 2m 13.37s. a 4.27s (5 Ran).
SR: 70/70/65/58/47/ (Sheikh Mohammed), H R A Cecil

LINGFIELD (good to firm)
Friday July 9th
Going Correction: PLUS 0.15 sec. per fur.

2377 London & Edinburgh Selling Stakes Class G (2-y-o) £2,544 5f........(2:45)

2042[3] LEFT STRANDED 9-2 K Darley (12) *made virtually all, rdn 2 fs out, jst hld on*......(5 to 1 op 5 to 2 tchd 11 to 2) 1
1519* PALACEGATE JO (Ire) (v) 8-8 (3*) J Weaver (8) *strted slwly, beh, effrt and not clr run 2 fs out, swtchd and ran on strly ins last, jst fld*..............(9 to 4 fav op 2 to 1) 2
1742[6] RANDOM 8-6 W Newnes (11) *led briefly 4 out, pressed wnr aftr till no extr appr fnl furlong*. (8 to 1 op 7 to 2) 3
1583[9] MIGHTY KINGDOM (Ire) (bl) 7-13 (7*) B Russell (4) *beh and sn rdn alng, styd on fnl 2 fs, nvr nrr*. ....(5 to 1 op 8 to 1 tchd 10 to 1 and 9 to 2) 4
2125[6] CHARISMA GIRL (v) 8-6 Dean McKeown (7) *prmnt 3 fs, sn rdn and btn*..............(20 to 1 op 12 to 1) 5
2125[2] WINDOW DISPLAY (v) 9-2 R Cochrane (1) *rcd centre, speed 3 fs, sn btn*............(11 to 2 op 7 to 2 tchd 7 to 1) 6
ON THE WING AGAIN 8-6 N Adams (5) *strted slwly, prog hfwy to chase ldg pair, wknd wl o'r one furlong out*. ....(20 to 1 op 12 to 1) 7
LOUGH KEY LADY (Ire) 8-1 (5*) Stephen Davies (13) *al beh*. ....(33 to 1 op 20 to 1) 8
1933[2] LUCY'S GOLD 8-6 D Biggs (9) *prmnt to hfwy, sn wknd*. ....(9 to 2 op 14 to 1 tchd 16 to 1) 9
2271[9] SHEILOBLIGE (bl) 8-6 B Rouse (6) *speed to hfwy, wknd 2 fs out*..........................(20 to 1 tchd 16 to 1) 10
2192[2] NORTHERN STORM (Ire) (bl) 8-11 W Woods (2) *rcd centre, nvr on terms*.........(14 to 1 op 10 to 1 tchd 16 to 1) 11
MADAM FRASCATI (Ire) 7-13 (7*) G Forster (3) *rcd centre, al wl beh*..........................(25 to 1 op 12 to 1) 12
Dist: ¾l, 3l, ½l, 3l, 1l, ¾l, ¾l, ½l, 2l, 2½l. 1m 1.57s. a 4.67s (12 Ran).
SR: 24/16/-/-/-/-/ (P D Savill), G Lewis

2378 Al Amead Fillies Handicap Class E (0-70 3-y-o and up) £3,131 6f.... (4:20)

1977 MY RUBY RING [49] 6-9-1 T Williams (9) *trkd ldrs, led one furlong out, drvn out*....(8 to 1 op 6 to 1 tchd 9 to 1) 1
1977[2] POYLE AMBER [45] 4-8-8 (3*) D Harrison (8) *led till a furlong out, ran on und pres ins last*....(5 to 1 op 3 to 1) 2
2276* JOIN THE CLAN [60] 4-9-12 (7ex) Dean McKeown (10) *hld up, effrt whn stumbled o'r 2 fs out, ran on wl ins last, nrst finish*....... (100 to 30 fav op 2 to 1 tchd 7 to 2) 3
2024[2] JULIET BRAVO [64] 3-9-9 K Darley (6) *trkd ldrs till not quicken appr fnl furlong, eased whn btn*. ....(9 to 2 op 7 to 2) 4
2170[7] SELFISH LADY [43] 3-8-2 G Hind (11) *chsd ldrs, rdn o'r 2 fs out, no real imprsn aftr*. ....(25 to 1 op 20 to 1 tchd 33 to 1) 5
1821[3] FAY'S SONG (Ire) [58] 5-9-3 (7*) L Carter (4) *prmnt til wknd and eased one furlong out, dismounted aftr finish*. ....(9 to 2 tchd 6 to 1) 6
1977[3] PRINCESS JESSICA [35] 6-7-8 (7*) B Russell (3) *chsd ldrs, rdn and wknd 2 fs out*. ....(10 to 1 op 8 to 1 tchd 12 to 1) 7
1977[8] BONITA BEE [44] 3-8-3 N Adams (2) *slwly into strd, rcd centre, al beh*. ....(16 to 1 op 14 to 1 tchd 20 to 1 and 25 to 1) 8
2164[9] LITTLE MISS RIBOT [52] 3-8-4 (7*) D McCabe (5) *strted slwly, chsd alng to keep in tch, wknd 2 fs out*. ....(11 to 1 op 6 to 1 tchd 12 to 1) 9
1966[7] IOLITE [61] (bl) 3-9-6 R Cochrane (7) *prmnt till rdn and wknd rpdly hfwy, sn tld off*. ....(12 to 1 op 10 to 1 tchd 14 to 1) 10
Dist: Hd, 3½l, 3½l, ¾l, 1½l, nk, 2l, 1l, 20l. 1m 13.36s. a 4.36s (10 Ran).
SR: 32/27/28/11/-/3/ (Mrs Marion Wickham), D R Laing

2379 Ashurst Limited Stakes Class D (0-75 3-y-o) £3,289 7f 140yds......... (4:50)

2212[3] SECOND CHANCE (Ire) 9-0 W Newnes (3) *made all, rdn wl o'r one furlong out, ran on well*. ....(7 to 2 tchd 4 to 1 and 3 to 1) 1
2060 TARNSIDE ROSAL 8-9 K Darley (4) *strted slwly, hld up, prog 2 fs out, chlgd appr last, unbl to quicken*. ....(3 to 1 op 2 to 1 tchd 7 to 2) 2
1780[2] AWESTRUCK 9-0 N Day (5) *trkd ldrs, rdn o'r 3 fs out, styd on same pace*......(5 to 2 fav tchd 3 to 1 and 9 to 4) 3
2212 PAIR OF JACKS (Ire) 9-0 W Woods (1) *pressed wnr, rdn 3 fs out, sn wknd*..........(9 to 1 op 4 to 1 tchd 10 to 1) 4
2139[6] PERSIAN GUSHER (Ire) 8-11 (3*) J Weaver (6) *hld up, effrt 2 fs out, sn wknd*.......(14 to 1 op 6 to 1 tchd 16 to 1) 5
2202[3] JAAZIM (bl) 9-0 A McGlone (2) *trkd ldrs gng wl, rdn 2 fs out, found nil*..........(4 to 1 op 5 to 2 tchd 5 to 1) 6
Dist: 1l, 2l, 8l, ½l, 2l. 1m 33.86s. a 5.56s (6 Ran).
SR: 34/26/25/1/-/-/ (Down And Outs Racing), P Mitchell

LINGFIELD (A.W) (std)
Friday July 9th
Going Correction: MINUS 0.30 sec. per fur.

2380 Tauber Claiming Stakes Class F (3-y-o and up) £2,556 5f..............(2:15)

1326[8] LUCAYAN TREASURE (v) 3-9-0 K Darley (7) *chsd ldrs, effrt 2 fs out, ran on wl to ld ins last, sn clr*. ....(5 to 2 fav op 3 to 1) 1
2157[5] SIR TASKER 5-9-2 R Cochrane (4) *led 3 fs out, rdn wl o'r one out, hdd and no extr ins last*.... (7 to 1 op 5 to 1) 2
1981[9] CRECHE (bl) 4-9-3 (7*) E Husband (5) *al prmnt, rdn and ev ch ins fnl furlong, wknd nr finish*. ....(11 to 2 op 7 to 2 tchd 6 to 1) 3
1316 SUMMER EXPRESS 4-8-6 Alex Greaves (1) *led for one furlong, rdn and btn o'r 2 out, kpt on ag'n ins last*. ....(25 to 1 op 20 to 1) 4
2018 VERY DICEY 5-9-0 W Woods (2) *led 4 fs out to 3 out, wknd wl o'r one out*..........(9 to 2 op 3 to 1 tchd 5 to 1) 5
2157[2] MARTINA 5-8-2 (7*) B Russell (6) *al struggling*. ....(11 to 4 op 3 to 1 tchd 7 to 2) 6
1000 TINO TERE 4-8-13 (3*) J Weaver (3) *strted slwly, al last and beh*..............(6 to 1 op 5 to 1 tchd 13 to 2) 7
Dist: 2½l, 1l, 3l, 1½l, 2l, 8l. 59.44s. a 1.24s (7 Ran).
SR: 45/37/41/11/13/-/-/ (H E Lhendup Dorji), D R Loder

2381 Aegon Equestrian Handicap Class D (0-80 3-y-o and up) £3,231 1½m (3:20)

2014* ONE OFF THE RAIL (USA) [73] 3-9-10 B Rouse (5) *wtd wth, prog to ld o'r 5 fs out, sn clr, eased appr fnl furlong, unchlgd*..........................(3 to 1 op 2 to 1) 1
1699[7] MODESTO (USA) [49] 5-8-13 R Cochrane (1) *led one furlong, rdn and outpcd hfwy, styd on ag'n fnl 3 fs, took second nr finish*..................(8 to 1 op 6 to 1) 2
2126[4] FACT OR FICTION [56] (bl) 7-9-6 W Newnes (2) *led aftr one furlong till o'r 5 out, chsd wnr after, nvr any imprsn, lost second cl hme*..........................(5 to 2 jt-fav tchd 11 to 4 and 9 to 4) 3
1919[5] CRACKLING [42] 4-8-3 (3*) D Harrison (4) *hld up, outpcd o'r 5 fs out, no ch aftr*......................(5 to 2 jt-fav op 7 to 2 tchd 9 to 4) 4
1488[7] SECRET ASSIGNMENT (USA) [68] 3-9-5 D Biggs (3) *chsd ldrs, rdn aftr 4 fs, wknd four out, sn tld off*. ....(14 to 1 op 10 to 1) 5
1862[5] MY SPARKLING RING [33] (bl) 7-7-11[4] T Williams (7) *prmnt till rdn and wknd 7 fs out, tld off fnl 3 furlongs*. ....(20 to 1 op 14 to 1) 6
1931 BALL GOWN [59] 3-8-10 Dean McKeown (6) *strted slwly, al beh, tld off hfwy*......(7 to 1 op 10 to 1 tchd 12 to 1) 7
Dist: 2l, ¾l, 20l, 15l, 25l, 10l. 2m 34.00s. a 4.70s (7 Ran).
SR: 27/12/17/-/ (K Higson), A Moore

2382 Jardine Insurance Brokers Handicap Class D (0-80 3-y-o and up) £3,201 7f ....(3:50)

2139[3] STAR GODDESS (USA) [69] 4-9-5 B Rouse (5) *keen hold, prmnt, led appr fnl furlong, hrd rdn and jst hld on*. ....(9 to 4 fav tchd 2 to 1 and 5 to 2) 1
2136 INVOCATION [78] 6-10-0 N Adams (4) *prmnt, led o'r 2 out, hdd appr fnl furlong, swshd tail and not quicken last strds*..................(6 to 1 op 5 to 1 tchd 7 to 1) 2
2193* MISS GORGEOUS (Ire) [80] 3-9-5 (3*,5ex) Emma O'Gorman (3) *led, rdn 3 fs out, sn hdd, kpt on one pace*.... (5 to 2) 3
1701[4] SARUM [54] 7-8-4 C Rutter (1) *rear, rdn 4 fs out, kpt on one pace*..................(9 to 2 op 4 to 1 tchd 7 to 2) 4
2013[3] DAILY SPORT DON [62] 3-8-4 A McGlone (2) *rear, rdn 3 fs out, kpt on one pace*... (7 to 2 op 5 to 2 tchd 4 to 1) 5
Dist: Sht-hd, 2l, ½l, ½l. 1m 25.43s. a 2.03s (5 Ran).
SR: 43/51/39/19/17/ (K Higson), G L Moore

WARWICK (good)
Friday July 9th
Going Correction: PLUS 0.10 sec. per fur. (races 1,2,3,4,6), MINUS 0.25 (5)

2383 Hateley Apprentice Rating Related Maiden Stakes Class F (3-y-o and up) £2,243 1m.................... (2:30)

1993[3] SUSQUEHANNA DAYS (USA) 3-8-0 (7*) Martin Dwyer (8) *pressed ldrs, led 3 out, rdn clr wl o'r one out, eased*. ....(100 to 30 op 7 to 2 tchd 4 to 1) 1
2182[2] GIORDANO (Ire) 3-8-7 (5*) G Milligan (3) *ran on frm rear 2 out, chsd wnr appr fnl furlong, no imprsn*. ....(7 to 2 op 4 to 1) 2
1635[3] SWEET DISORDER (Ire) 3-8-7 D Wright (2) *wl in tch, rdn and outpcd last 2 fs*. ....(11 to 4 fav op 5 to 2 tchd 3 to 1) 3
1954[9] WHATEVER'S RIGHT (Ire) 4-9-7 C Hawksley (1) *strted slwly, improved 3 out, one pace last 2 fs*... (10 to 1 op 8 to 1) 4
1422[4] ABSALOM'S PILLAR 3-8-7 (5*) P Johnson (6) *nvr rchd chalg pos*............(11 to 1 op 8 to 1 tchd 12 to 1) 5
1913[5] EXPORT MONDIAL 3-8-12 J Tate (5) *wl plcd til wknd 2 out*. ....(5 to 1 op 4 to 1) 6
1976[9] CANDARELA 3-8-7 J D Smith (4) *sn prmnt, led o'r 4 out, hdd 3 out, ran wide entering strt, outpcd last 2 fs*. ....(40 to 1 op 33 to 1) 7
1354 JELLYROLL BLUES (v) 4-9-2 N Varley (7) *led for o'r 3 fs, wknd quickly, tld off last 2 furlongs*. ....(66 to 1 op 50 to 1) 8
Dist: 3½l, 4l, sht-hd, 8l, 1½l, 1½l, 25l. 1m 41.50s. a 4.70s (8 Ran).
SR: 34/28/11/24/-/ (Paul Mellon), I A Balding

2384 McCoist Selling Handicap Stakes Class G (0-60 3-y-o and up) £2,070 1m ....(3:00)

2318[6] GREEN'S STUBBS [25] (v) 6-7-13 N Carlisle (17) *hld up, str run o'r one out, led last 100 yards.* (33 to 1 op 14 to 1) 1
1902 COOCHIE [26] (bl) 4-8-0 S Dawson (10) *slwly into strd, ran on o'r one out, styd on nr finish.* ....(16 to 1 op 20 to 1 tchd 33 to 1) 2
2053[2] OUR EDDIE [39] (v) 4-8-13 T Quinn (14) *led 5 out till rdn and hdd last 100 yards, ran on.* (4 to 1 fav tchd 9 to 2) 3
1237[7] MASTER BEVELED [52] 3-8-12 (5*) C Hodgson (3) *hld up, ran on last 2 fs, one pace fnl 100 yards.* ....(12 to 1 op 8 to 1) 4
1743 COOL COQUELIN (Ire) [35] 5-8-6 (3*) B Doyle (1) *hdwy o'r 2 out, rdn and not quicken over one out.* ....(25 to 1 tchd 33 to 1) 5
1902 LITTLE PARK [40] 4-9-0 Paul Eddery (20) *rcd wide, pressed ldrs, ev ch frm o'r 2 out till over one out, no extr.* ....(10 to 1 op 12 to 1 tchd 8 to 1) 6
2095[3] SUPERENSIS [47] 3-8-5 (7*) Kim McDonnell (11) *in tch, ran on one pace frm 2 out.* (13 to 2 op 5 to 1 tchd 7 to 1) 7
1685 SIMON ELLIS (Ire) [35] 4-8-4 (5*) D Wright (4) *slwly into strd, hdwy o'r 2 out, one pace appr fnl furlong.* ....(25 to 1 op 20 to 1) 8
1902 BRUSH WOLF (USA) [20] 4-7-8[7] (7*) A Whelan (18) *wtd wth in rear, effrt ins last 2 fs, no imprsn on ldrs inside fnl furlong.*..................(50 to 1 op 25 to 1) 9
1991[7] SHALHOLME [43] 3-8-8 J Williams (2) *nvr dngrs.* ....(8 to 1 op 6 to 1) 10
2109[7] ELEGANT TOUCH [50] (bl) 4-9-10 M Perrett (13) *hld up in rear, effrt o'r 2 out, not nr to chal...* (8 to 1 op 5 to 1) 11
278 TAMASHA [30] (v) 4-8-4 G Bardwell (12) *chsd ldrs for o'r 6 fs.*..................(12 to 1 op 6 to 1 tchd 14 to 1) 12
1913[6] SHARP IMP [39] (bl) 3-7-13 (5*) J Tate (7) *wl plcd for 6 fs.* ....(11 to 1 op 8 to 1) 13
2109 GOTT'S DESIRE [42] (bl) 7-9-2 M Wigham (6) *wl plcd, not much room o'r 3 out, wknd over 2 out.* ....(9 to 1 op 7 to 1 tchd 10 to 1) 14
2283[6] MUMMYS ROCKET [40] (bl) 4-9-0 A Mackay (21) *chsd ldrs for o'r 5 fs*..................(7 to 1 op 6 to 1 tchd 8 to 1) 15
2065[8] RUPERT'S REVENGE (Ire) [55] 3-9-6 W Hood (19) *nvr on terms*..................(20 to 1 op 14 to 1) 16
2165[9] JOVIAL KATE (USA) [39] (bl) 6-8-13 B Raymond (8) *led for 3 fs, hmpd and wknd o'r three out.* (25 to 1 op 16 to 1) 17
1938 ACIDOSIS [35] 4-8-9 J Fortune (5) *prmnt for 3 fs, lost pl quickly, tld off*..................(50 to 1 op 25 to 1) 18

Dist: 1l, ½l, 2½l, 1l, 2½l, ¾l, nk, nk, hd, ½l. 1m 41.90s. a 5.10s (18 Ran).
SR: 21/19/30/26/15/12/8/4/-/ (A Barrow), A Barrow

2385 Pioneer Mixconcrete Claiming Stakes Class G (2-y-o) £2,070 7f........(3:30)

1926[6] DULFORD LAD 8-8 S Whitworth (5) *hld up towards rear, not clr run hfwy, str brst appr fnl furlong, led last strds*..................(20 to 1 op 10 to 1) 1
WESTERN FLEET (USA) 8-12 T Quinn (3) *hld up, hdwy and pushed alng 3 out, led one out, hdd last strds.* ....(5 to 1 op 3 to 1) 2
1959[4] TSWANA (Ire) 8-9 B Raymond (8) *cld on ldr hfwy, slight advantage 2 out till one out, rallied und pres.* ....(11 to 4 op 5 to 2 tchd 3 to 1) 3
2102[8] GIGUE 8-2 Paul Eddery (4) *sn pushed alng in mid-div, effrt und pres o'r one out, ran on one pace.* ....(9 to 4 fav op 5 to 2) 4
1985[3] STARSPORT (Ire) 8-11 J Fortune (6) *ldg grp til outpcd 3 out, rallied und pres o'r one out, not quicken.* ....(7 to 1 tchd 8 to 1) 5
1897[9] TISA WASITEEN (Ire) 7-13 (5*) L Newton (2) *led for 5 fs, sn btn*..................(8 to 1 op 7 to 1) 6
1905 ARALIYA 8-5 J Williams (7) *al outpcd, lost tch 3 out, tld off*..................(25 to 1 op 16 to 1) 7

Dist: Sht-hd, nk, 2½l, sht-hd, 4l, 15l. 1m 30.10s. a 6.30s (7 Ran).
SR: 10/13/9/-/2/-/-/ (Hammy Racing), B R Millman

2386 Baxi Solo Handicap Class E (0-70 4-y-o and up) £3,054 1¾m 194yds...(4:00)

1984* MONARDA [63] 6-10-0 T Quinn (1) *rcd wide, hdwy to ld 3 out, shaken up and styd on wl fnl furlong.* ....(3 to 1 op 5 to 2 tchd 100 to 30) 1
JAWANI (Ire) [50] 5-9-1 B Raymond (7) *hld up, led 6 out, rdn and hdd 3 out, not quicken ins last 2 fs.* ....(11 to 2 op 4 to 1) 2
2115[6] ELEGANT KING (Ire) [60] 4-9-4 (7*) G McGrath (2) *led, sn clr, hdd 6 out, outpcd fnl 3 fs.* ....(20 to 1 op 10 to 1 tchd 25 to 1) 3
2111[3] THEMEDA [47] 4-8-12 Paul Eddery (5) *chsd ldr, dsptd ld 6 out, wknd o'r 3 out*..................(11 to 2 op 9 to 2) 4
1873[5] SELDOM IN [30] 7-7-9 A Mackay (3) *wl plcd til rdn and wknd 5 out*..................(13 to 2 op 3 to 1) 5
2115[4] PERFORATE [35] 4-8-0 G Bardwell (4) *beh, rdn alng hfwy, sn tld off*.......... (12 to 1 op 10 to 1 tchd 14 to 1) 6
1951[2] GROVE SERENDIPITY (Ire) [48] (bl) 5-8-13 M Perrett (6) *hld up in rear, hdwy into 3rd pl whn pld up lme 3 out, fractured off-hind pastern, destroyed.* ....(6 to 4 fav op 7 to 4) pu

Dist: 2l, 12l, 7l, 8l, 25l. 3m 17.00s. a 8.70s (7 Ran).
SR: 42/27/25/5/ (Fahd Salman), P F I Cole

2387 Renown Handicap Class D (0-80 3-y-o and up) £3,260 5f...............(4:30)

2126[6] RHYTHMIC DANCER [70] 5-9-10 A Mackay (6) *led, hdd o'r one out, rdn to rgn advantage wl ins fnl furlong, all out*.................. (7 to 2 op 5 to 2 tchd 4 to 1) 1
JESS REBEC [51] 5-8-5 N Carlisle (1) *hld up, cld on ldr frm 2 out, slight ld o'r one out, hdd wl ins fnl furlong, no extr on line*.......... (11 to 2 op 9 to 2 tchd 6 to 1) 2
2352[3] CASTLE MAID [40] 6-7-8[1] Dale Gibson (4) *beh, rdn alng 2 out, styd on ins fnl furlong.* ....(4 to 1 op 5 to 2 tchd 9 to 2) 3
1957[8] ARAGROVE [70] 3-9-4 T Quinn (7) *pld hrd and hld up, pushed alng frm hfwy, not quicken appr fnl furlong.* ....(3 to 1 fav tchd 7 to 2) 4
1000 PETRACO (Ire) [71] 5-9-11 Paul Eddery (2) *chsd ldr for o'r 3 fs, sn btn*..................(7 to 1 op 6 to 1) 5
2214[8] DAANIERA (Ire) [65] (bl) 3-8-13 A Clark (3) *strted slwly, sn pressing ldrs, rdn and outpcd o'r one out.* .... (14 to 1 op 8 to 1) 6

Dist: Nk, 2½l, ½l, hd, ¾l. 1m 0.00s. a 1.80s (6 Ran).
SR: 49/29/8/30/36/21/ (Mrs Robert Heathcote), J L Spearing

2388 McPherson Maiden Handicap Stakes Class F (0-65 3-y-o and up) £2,243 1¼m 169yds.................... (5:00)

1861[5] LEGAL ARTIST (Ire) [46] 3-8-9 B Raymond (9) *hld up, shaken up and hdwy 2 out, led and edgd rght ins fnl furlong, styd on wl*..................(14 to 10 op 10 to 1) 1
2130[2] TTYFRAN [57] 3-9-6 T Quinn (5) *hdwy on outsd 5 out, led o'r one out, not much room and hdd ins fnl furlong, swtchd lft and ran on...* (7 to 2 op 3 to 1 tchd 4 to 1) 2
1993[5] SKY BURST [44] 3-8-7 N Carlisle (7) *handily plcd, ev ch o'r one out, rdn and slightly hmpd ins fnl furlong, no extr.* ....(14 to 1 tchd 16 to 1) 3
2104[2] CLAIRIFICATION (Ire) [48] 3-8-11 J Williams (10) *hld up, improved frm hfwy, led 2 out, hdd o'r one out, one pace*..................(9 to 4 fav op 2 to 1 tchd 7 to 4) 4
2183[2] HYDROPIC [28] 6-8-3 Dale Gibson (4) *trkd ldr, led o'r 5 out to 2 out, styd on same pace*.......... (10 to 1 op 7 to 1) 5
2223[4] DOTS DEE [32] 4-8-0 (7*) Michael Bradley (2) *dwlt, pushed alng frm hfwy, one pace last 2 fs*.....(9 to 1 op 7 to 1) 6
678 YAAKUM [47] 4-9-3 (5*) L Newton (1) *led til hdd o'r 5 out, rallied 2 out, wknd over one out.* ....(4 to 1 op 12 to 1 tchd 14 to 1) 7
2101[7] GLINT OF AYR [54] 3-9-3 A Clark (6) *hld up, cld on ldrs hfwy, wknd o'r 3 out.* ....(20 to 1 op 12 to 1 tchd 25 to 1) 8
1838[3] TWO LUMPS [65] 3-10-0 S O'Gorman (8) *chsd ldrs til rdn and wknd fnl 4 fs*.................. (12 to 1 op 7 to 1) 9
1943[6] WHAT LOLA WANTS (Ire) [45] 3-8-8 A Mackay (3) *sn beh, pld up aftr 4 fs, broke hind leg, destroyed.* .... (16 to 1 op 8 to 1) pu

Dist: 2l, ½l, 1l, ¾l, 2l, 2½l, 6l, 4l. 2m 22.70s. a 9.90s (10 Ran).
SR: 7/14/-/2/-/-/2/-/-/ (Tony Briam), N A Graham

YORK (good)
Friday July 9th

Going Correction: MINUS 0.05 sec. per fur. (races 1,4,6), MINUS 0.25 (2,3,5,7)

2389 Black Duck Conditions Stakes Class C (2-y-o) £5,346 6f................(2:00)

1788[2] GOLD LAND (USA) 9-2 A Munro (4) *trkd ldrs, hdwy on bit hfwy, led o'r 2 fs out, shaken up and ran on ins last.* .... (7 to 4 on tchd 13 to 8 on and 15 to 8 on) 1
1999[2] AMBER VALLEY (USA) 8-10 W Carson (3) *led, hdd o'r 2 fs out, sn rdn and kpt on.* .... (6 to 1 tchd 5 to 1 and 13 to 2) 2
2027* SAIHAT (Ire) 8-12 L Piggott (1) *cl up, rdn o'r 2 fs out, sn one pace*.................. (4 to 1 op 3 to 1) 3
2049* EIGHTEEN TWELVE 8-10 J Reid (2) *cl up, rdn o'r 2 fs out, sn one pace*.................. (10 to 1 op 8 to 1) 4
2096[3] TANFIRION CHIEF 8-10 R P Elliott (5) *sn outpcd and beh.* ....(50 to 1 op 33 to 1) 5

Dist: 1½l, 4l, 1l, 12l. 1m 12.72s. a 2.72s (5 Ran).
SR: 42/30/16/10/-/ (Fahd Salman), P F I Cole

2390 Monks Cross Conditions Stakes Class B (3-y-o and up) £7,034 7f 202yds (2:35)

1786 THOURIOS 4-9-5 W Carson (7) *made all, quickened 2 fs out, rdn and ran on wl fnl furlong.* ....(9 to 4 op 7 to 4 tchd 5 to 2) 1
2194* TIK FA (USA) (v) 4-9-9 W R Swinburn (1) *hld up, hdwy on outsd 2 and a half fs out, rdn to chlgd entering last, kpt on*.................. (6 to 1 op 5 to 1 tchd 13 to 2) 2

2174[4] REVERE (Ire) 3-8-6 A Munro (3) *chsd ldg pair till outpcd and lost pl 3 fs out, styd on und pres appr last.* ....(14 to 1 op 10 to 1) 3
1347[6] RAPID SUCCESS (USA) 3-8-10 L Piggott (4) *chsd ldg pair, effrt and ev ch o'r 2 fs out, sn rdn, wknd appr last.* ....(16 to 1 tchd 20 to 1) 4
596[7] MELLOTTIE 8-9-11 J Lowe (5) *hld up and beh, effrt and headay 2 and a half fs out, sn rdn and no imprsn.* ....(2 to 1 fav op 7 to 4) 5
1850* HUNTERS OF BRORA (Ire) 3-8-3 J Carroll (2) *hld up, effrt and hdwy on inner o'r 2 fs out, sn rdn and wknd wl over one furlong out*.............. (50 to 1 op 33 to 1) 6
2068[7] SON PARDO 3-8-12 J Reid (6) *mid-div, effrt and hdwy 3 fs out, sn ev ch, rdn and wknd wl o'r one furlong out.* ....(13 to 2 op 6 to 1 tchd 7 to 1) 7

Dist: 1½l, 2½l, 1½l, 2½l, 1½l, 1l. 1m 36.69s. a 0.39s (7 Ran).
SR: 69/68/43/42/49/22/28/ (Athos Christodoulou), G Harwood

2391 Ralph Country Homes Handicap Class C (0-90 3-y-o and up) £7,512 7f 202yds ....(3:10)

1768[8] FOREVER DIAMONDS [81] 6-9-7 M Birch (1) *beh, swtchd ins and hdwy 2 and a half fs out, rdn to ld inside last, jinked 100 yards out, kpt on*.... (11 to 2 fav op 5 to 1) 1
2045[3] BUZZARDS BELLBUOY [73] (v) 4-8-13 J Quinn (3) *al prmnt, effrt to chal appr fnl furlong, sn rdn and led briefly entering last, kpt on wl und pres*...............(7 to 1) 2
2045[5] GOLDEN CHIP (Ire) [70] 5-8-10 Pat Eddery (7) *led, rdn 2 fs out, hdd entering last, not quicken.* (9 to 1 op 8 to 1) 3
1867[4] JUBRAN (USA) [67] 7-8-7 M Roberts (12) *in tch, hdwy o'r 2 fs out, sn rdn and one pace*....... (7 to 1 tchd 15 to 2) 4
2025[5] JAHANGIR (Ire) [69] 4-8-9 L Piggott (4) *in tch, effrt 2 fs out, sn rdn and one pace*.......... (10 to 1 op 12 to 1) 5
2057[7] MAJAL (Ire) [59] 4-7-13 L Charnock (8) *cl up, rdn 2 fs out, grad wknd*... (25 to 1) 6
1721[4] BLOW DRY (Ire) [80] 3-8-11 A Culhane (2) *hld up, hdwy on inner whn hmpd 2 and a half fs out, styd on und pres appr last*..............(6 to 1 op 9 to 2 tchd 13 to 2) 7
MBULWA [54] 7-7-8 J Fanning (13) *cl up, rdn o'r 2 fs, grad wknd*.. (33 to 1) 8
2283[9] ZAMANAYN (Ire) [63] 5-8-3 K Fallon (5) *slwly away, al rear.* ....(33 to 1) 9
2022[5] JALMUSIQUE [78] 7-9-1 (3*) S Maloney (11) *cl up, ev ch o'r 2 fs out, sn rdn and wknd*........... (9 to 1 op 7 to 1) 10
2000[5] DOCTOR ROY [53] 5-7-7 J Lowe (9) *al rear*.......(33 to 1) 11
2060 PARLIAMENT PIECE [88] 7-9-9 (5*) Darren Moffatt (6) *in tch, rdn 3 fs out, sn wknd*..............(12 to 1 op 8 to 1) 12
1768 DOUBLE ECHO (Ire) [74] 5-9-0 W Carson (10) *in tch, rdn 3 fs out, sn wknd*...................(7 to 1 tchd 15 to 2) 13

Dist: ½l, 3½l, 4l, sht-hd, 1½l, 1½l, 5l, 2½l, 2l, nk. 1m 37.18s. a 0.88s (13 Ran).
SR: 64/54/40/25/26/11/18/-/-/ (Mrs J B Russell), M H Easterby

2392 Gordon Morley Memorial Handicap Class C (0-90 3-y-o and up) £7,700 5f ....(3:40)

2018[5] MISS VAXETTE [82] 4-8-13 (7*) M Humphries (10) *in tch, hdwy 2 fs out, rdn and styd on strly ins last to led nr line*.................................(10 to 1 op 8 to 1) 1
1806 ASHTINA [82] 8-9-6 J Quinn (5) *prmnt, rdn to chal entering fnl furlong, led briefly nr finish, ct near line.* ....(14 to 1 op 12 to 1) 2
1449[5] POYLE GEORGE [90] 8-9-9 (5*) A Procter (2) *prmnt, hdwy and rdn to ld appr fnl furlong, hdd and no extr nr finish*..............................(14 to 1 op 12 to 1) 3
1560* EWALD (Ire) [70] 5-8-8 L Dettori (3) *al prmnt, effrt and ev ch appr fnl furlong, sn rdn and no extr ins last.* ....(7 to 1 tchd 15 to 2) 4
2241[7] SIMMIE'S SPECIAL [59] (bl) 5-7-8[2] (5*) A Garth (4) *mid-div, hdwy 2 fs out, styd on ins last*................ (16 to 1) 5
1860[5] LITTLE SABOTEUR [68] 4-8-6 A Munro (15) *mid-div, rdn 2 fs out, styd on ins last*.............(12 to 1 op 10 to 1) 6
2230[7] HEAVEN-LIEGH-GREY [66] 5-8-4 J Carroll (7) *chsd ldrs, rdn 2 fs out, kpt on one pace*........................... (8 to 1) 7
2241[4] LANGUEDOC [65] 6-8-3 L Charnock (14) *nvr rch ldrs.* ....(16 to 1 op 14 to 1 tchd 20 to 1) 8
2062 DRUM SERGEANT [79] (bl) 6-9-3 M Roberts (9) *nvr rch ldrs.* ....(11 to 1 op 10 to 1) 9
1679[8] BEAU VENTURE (USA) [85] 5-9-9 S Perks (1) *cl up till rdn and wknd 2 fs out*...............(16 to 1 op 14 to 1) 10
1420[6] SINGING STAR [69] 7-8-0 (7*) Claire Balding (13) *dwlt, al rear*......................................(20 to 1 op 16 to 1) 11
2230[6] CATHERINES WELL [77] 10-9-1 T Lucas (8) *dwlt, al rear.* ....(11 to 1 op 10 to 1 tchd 12 to 1) 12
986[7] GILT THRONE [85] 6-9-2 (7*) S Mulvey (11) *al rear.* ....(20 to 1 op 16 to 1) 13
2305* NED'S BONANZA [77] 4-9-1 (7ex) Pat Eddery (12) *chsd ldr, rdn 2 fs out, sn wknd*........... (4 to 1 fav op 5 to 1) 14
2255[8] FOOD OF LOVE [75] 5-8-13 J Reid (16) *nvr rch ldrs.* ....(20 to 1 op 14 to 1) 15
2018 SIGAMA (USA) [76] 7-9-0 R Lappin (6) *led and clr, rdn 2 fs out, hng rght, hdd and wknd appr fnl furlong.* ....(20 to 1 op 16 to 1) 16

Dist: Nk, ½l, hd, 1l, hd, ¾l, 1½l, hd, hd, sht-hd. 59.17s. a 1.87s (16 Ran).
SR: 64/63/69/48/33/41/36/29/42/ (Vax Appliances Ltd), J L Spearing

2393 Foss Rated Class B Handicap (0-105 3-y-o) £6,373 1m 3f 195yds......(4:10)

1719[3] KEY TO MY HEART (Ire) [89] 8-7 K Fallon (4) *hld up, hdwy 2 and a half fs out, effrt to led entering last, rdn and ran on*.......................(15 to 2 op 7 to 1 tchd 8 to 1) 1
2025[2] TOP CEES [89] 8-7 W R Swinburn (3) *chsd ldrs, effrt 2 fs out, rdn to ld one and half furlongs out, hdd entering last, kpt on*..........................(4 to 1 tchd 9 to 2) 2
1958* AZHAR [103] 9-7 M Roberts (2) *led, rdn 2 fs out, sn hdd and one pace appr last*.............(3 to 1 op 5 to 2) 3
2003[5] LINDON LIME (USA) [99] 8-10 (7*) T G McLaughlin (1) *chsd ldr, rdn o'r 2 fs out and sn wknd.* ....(3 to 1 op 5 to 2 tchd 100 to 30 and 7 to 2) 4
1785[3] MASTER CHARLIE [94] 8-12 L Dettori (5) *chsd ldrs, effrt 2 and a half fs out, sn rdn and btn, eased.* ....(5 to 2 fav op 3 to 1 tchd 9 to 4) 5

Dist: 1l, 4l, 6l, 25l. 2m 29.26s. a 1.26s (5 Ran).
SR: 50/48/54/38/-/ (Mrs Maureen Pickering), D Moffatt

2394 Petergate Maiden Fillies Stakes Class D (2-y-o) £4,152 6f 214yds.......(4:40)

1916[3] FAYROOZ (USA) 8-11 A Munro (5) *made virtually all, rdn 2 fs out, ran on*...... (15 to 8 fav op 7 to 4 tchd 2 to 1) 1
1916[8] BRENTWOOD (Ire) 8-11 Pat Eddery (1) *ran green, chsd ldrs, pushed alng and hdwy o'r 2 fs out, rdn to chal appr fnl furlong, one pace ins last.* ....(3 to 1 tchd 11 to 4) 2
EARTH CHARTER 8-11 M Roberts (2) *cl up, ev ch o'r 2 fs out, sn rdn and wknd*............... (6 to 1 op 4 to 1) 3
SABAYIK (Ire) 8-11 R Hills (3) *chsd ldrs, effrt 3 fs out, rdn and wknd 2 furlongs out.* ....(100 to 30 op 5 to 2 tchd 7 to 2) 4
1810[7] GLIDINGONBY (Ire) 8-11 W R Swinburn (4) *dwlt, sn cl up, rdn 3 fs out, soon wknd*.............. (10 to 1 op 8 to 1) 5

Dist: 3l, 7l, 3½l, 5l. 1m 26.51s. a 4.81s (5 Ran).
SR: 20/11/ (Fahd Salman), P F I Cole

2395 Levy Board Rated Class B Handicap (0-95 4-y-o and up) £6,233 1m 3f 195yds.......................... (5:10)

1682[6] CRYSTAL CROSS (USA) [81] 4-8-9 L Dettori (5) *chsd ldrs, swtchd and effrt 2 fs out, sn rdn, styd on to ld ins last.* ....(6 to 1 op 4 to 1) 1
2256[3] AMBIGUOUSLY REGAL (USA) [79] 4-8-7 G Duffield (2) *chsd ldr, hdwy to chal 3 fs out, rdn to ld appr fnl furlong, hdd and not quicken ins last.* ....(100 to 30 op 7 to 2 tchd 4 to 1) 2
2061 WELSH MILL (Ire) [93] 4-9-7 L Piggott (4) *jnd 3 fs out, rdn and hdd appr last, grad wknd*.......(5 to 1 op 5 to 2) 3
1974[2] OPERA GHOST [84] 7-8-12 W R Swinburn (3) *hld up and beh, hdwy o'r 3 fs out, rdn 2 furlongs out, one pace appr last*......................(5 to 4 fav op 15 to 8) 4+
VIARDOT (Ire) [87] 4-9-1 M Birch (1) *in tch, rdn 2 fs out, kpt on one pace*.......................(10 to 1 op 7 to 1) 4+
1752 JUSTICE (Fr) [80] 5-8-8 M Roberts (6) *in tch till rdn and wknd 3 fs out*...................(16 to 1 op 10 to 1) 6

Dist: 2l, 1½l, dd-ht, ¾l, 20l. 2m 31.08s. a 3.08s (6 Ran).
SR: 34/28/39/30/31/-/ (Urs E Schwarzenbach), I A Balding

CHESTER (soft)
Saturday July 10th
Going Correction: PLUS 0.35 sec. per fur.

2396 Eccleston Claiming Stakes Class E (3-y-o and up) £4,500 7f 2yds...... (2:20)

2106[4] BOLD ANGEL 6-9-0 K Fallon (8) *bustled alng to go early pace, hdwy hfwy, led one furlong out, drw clr.* ....(7 to 2 co-fav op 5 to 2) 1
1921[6] CORALS DREAM (Ire) 4-9-8 W Woods (1) *chsd ldg pair, ev ch and rdn o'r one furlong out, not quicken.* (7 to 2 co-fav op 4 to 1) 2
2198[5] CAUSLEY 8-8-9 (7*) S Sanders (6) *dsptd ld, rdn o'r one furlong out, no extr*..........................(7 to 2 co-fav op 4 to 1 tchd 3 to 1) 3
1017 BOLD SEVEN (Ire) 3-7-12 (3*) N Kennedy (7) *missed break, chsd alng to improve last 2 fs, no imprsn.* ....(7 to 1 op 8 to 1) 4
1527 TYRIAN PURPLE (Ire) 5-9-0 D Holland (4) *set str pace, rdn and hdd one furlong out, fdd*................(10 to 1) 5
1657[9] ABALENE 4-9-0 J Quinn (3) *sluggish strt, drvn alng to go pace, nvr dngrs*................ (50 to 1 op 33 to 1) 6
2121 DESERT SPLENDOUR 5-8-8 J Lowe (9) *missed break, not reco'r*..................(20 to 1 op 12 to 1) 7
2212 HEATHFIELD (USA) 3-9-2 T Quinn (2) *drvn alng and sn outpcd, nvr a threat*............(6 to 1 op 5 to 1) 8
1875[6] NORTHERN BLUFF (v) 3-8-0 A Mackay (5) *early speed, drvn alng and lost grnd hfwy, sn lost tch.* ....(14 to 1 op 12 to 1) 9

Dist: 4l, hd, 5l, sht-hd, 12l, 3½l, 1½l, 10l. 1m 31.98s. a 6.58s (9 Ran).
SR: 38/34/27/-/9/-/ (A M Wragg), M H Easterby

2397 Chester Summer Handicap Class D (0-80 3-y-o and up) £7,096 2¼m 117yds ....(2:50)

2061 MISS PLUM [75] 4-10-0 J Carroll (6) *patiently rdn, smooth hdwy to ld o'r 4 fs out, brght wide strt, styd on gmely.* ....(9 to 2 op 4 to 1 tchd 5 to 1) 1
1890^{2} OUR AISLING [75] 5-9-9 (5*) O Pears (4) *trkd ldr, given breather hfwy, rallied to draw level o'r one furlong out, one pace*......................(7 to 2 tchd 4 to 1) 2
2101^{4} WELSHMAN [58] 7-8-11 J Quinn (1) *dictated pace till hdd o'r 4 fs out, sn outpcd*................(7 to 4 fav op 6 to 4) 3
1989^{3} BARDOLPH (USA) [70] 6-9-9 T Quinn (2) *settled gng wl, moved up to join ldr hfwy, fdd last 3 fs.* ....(3 to 1 op 5 to 2) 4
1345 HUNTING GROUND [44] (bl) 5-7-11 A Mackay (3) *trkd ldg trio, rdn fnl circuit, lost tch last 4 fs.* ....(9 to 1 op 10 to 1 tchd 11 to 1) 5
Dist: 2l, 10l, 6l, 5l. 4m 28.66s. a 29.16s (Flag start) (5 Ran).
(Lucayan Stud), D R Loder

2398 Cheshire Yeomanry Handicap Class D (0-80 3-y-o and up) £7,512 1¼m 75yds ....(3:20)

2100* SILVER SAMURAI [72] 4-9-9 J Lowe (6) *settled gng wl, shaken up to ld 2 fs out, smoothly.* ....(3 to 1 fav op 5 to 2 tchd 7 to 2) 1
2354^{6} GREEN'S CASSATT (USA) [50] 5-8-1 R Lappin (4) *patiently rdn, improved o'r 2 fs out, styd on, no ch wth wnr.* ....(25 to 1 op 14 to 1) 2
1851^{2} BILOELA [63] 3-8-3 K Fallon (1) *wth ldrs, led o'r 3 fs out, hdd 2 furlongs out, kpt on same pace.* ....(15 to 2 op 8 to 1 tchd 7 to 1) 3
2088* MENTALASANYTHIN [65] 4-9-2 A Mackay (10) *trkd ldrs, improved last 2 fs, no imprsn ins last.* ....(8 to 1 tchd 7 to 1) 4
1785 BEAUMAN [74] 3-9-0 T Quinn (9) *trkd ldrs, feeling pace o'r 3 fs out, wknd appr fnl furlong*.....(10 to 1 op 9 to 1) 5
1816* MISS SHAGRA (USA) [78] 3-9-4 D Holland (7) *nvr far away, hrd at work o'r 3 fs out, fdd.* ....(4 to 1 op 9 to 2 tchd 5 to 1) 6
1476^{3} BIGWHEEL BILL (Ire) [73] (bl) 4-9-10 J Carroll (2) *led till hdd o'r 3 fs out, rallied, not quicken appr fnl furlong.* ....(8 to 1 op 7 to 1 tchd 10 to 1) 7
1579^{8} CUTTHROAT KID (Ire) [57] 3-7-8 (3*) N Kennedy (3) *last and chsd alng most of way, nvr a threat.* ....(25 to 1 op 20 to 1) 8
1579^{2} SPRING FLYER (Ire) [61] 3-8-1 F Norton (5) *wth ldrs, feeling pace o'r 3 fs out, eased whn btn fnl furlong.* ....(9 to 1 op 8 to 1) 9
2289^{7} TAUNTING (Ire) [49] 5-8-0 J Quinn (11) *chsd ldrs, hrd at work o'r 4 fs out, sn btn*..........(12 to 1 op 10 to 1) 10
1005* NAHLATI (Ire) [60] 3-8-0 G Bardwell (8) *trkd ldg pair, drvn alng and lost grnd o'r 3 fs out, tld off.* ....(8 to 1 op 6 to 1) 11
Dist: 5l, nk, 3l, 2l, 2l, 7l, 2½l, 4l, 2½l, 3½l. 2m 21.32s. a 12.22s (11 Ran).
SR: 23/-/-/-/-/-/ (J D Cable), Mrs V A Aconley

2399 City Wall Conditions Stakes Class B (3-y-o and up) £9,681 5f 16yds...(3:50)

2018^{8} STACK ROCK 6-9-5 K Fallon (8) *pressed ldg pair, drvn alng fnl furlong, ran on gmely*..... (13 to 2 op 5 to 1) 1
1551^{3} PALACEGATE EPISODE (Ire) 3-8-13 J Carroll (3) *tried to make all, hdd fnl furlong, kpt on same pace.* ....(4 to 1 op 7 to 2 tchd 9 to 2) 2
2252^{2} BUNTY BOO 4-8-13 A Mackay (1) *wth ldr, hrd at work o'r one furlong out, no extr.* ....(9 to 4 fav op 5 to 2 tchd 11 to 4) 3
1807^{5} EL YASAF (Ire) 5-9-4 D Holland (7) *chsd alng to go pace hfwy, improved last 2 fs, nvr nrr*....(3 to 1 op 11 to 4) 4
511^{7} SILCA-CISA 4-8-12 T Quinn (4) *drvn alng and outpcd hfwy, nvr a factor*...................(9 to 1 op 8 to 1) 5
2018^{4} REGAL CHIMES 4-9-5 S Sanders (6) *drvn alng and sn outpcd, nvr a threat*...............(9 to 1 op 7 to 1) 6
2206^{4} ELLE SHAPED (Ire) 3-9-0 O Pears (5) *sluggish strt, al struggling*......................(14 to 1 op 12 to 1) 7
PEPERONATA (Ire) 3-8-3 J Lowe (2) *sn struggling and outpcd, nvr a factor*..............(25 to 1 op 20 to 1) 8
Dist: 2l, 5l, 2½l, 10l, ¾l, 1½l, 2½l. 1m 3.41s. a 3.11s (8 Ran).
SR: 78/64/44/39/-/ (Castle Racing), E J Alston

2400 Retail Advertising Services Conditions Stakes Class D (2-y-o) £5,192 5f 16yds........................ (4:20)

1437^{3} STIMULANT 8-9 T Quinn (7) *made virtually all, quickened clr fnl furlong, readily.* ....(9 to 2 fav op 7 to 2 tchd 5 to 1) 1
2240^{4} NORDICO PRINCESS 8-5 S Perks (1) *chsd ldrs, drvn through on ins last 2 fs, ran on wl*... (8 to 1 op 6 to 1) 2
1590* RANDONNEUR (Ire) 8-5 G Hind (3) *al wl plcd, ev ch and drvn alng o'r one furlong out, not quicken.* ....(6 to 1 op 4 to 1) 3
1739* PLAINSONG 8-5 K Fallon (2) *chsd alng to improve frm midfield appr fnl furlong, fnshd wl.* (7 to 1 op 5 to 1) 4
2240^{9} MY GALLERY (Ire) 8-5 A Mackay (5) *al chasing ldrs, drvn alng o'r 2 fs out, one pace*.........(33 to 1 op 25 to 1) 5
1461^{7} HILTONS TRAVEL (Ire) 8-10 S Webster (11) *bustled alng in midfield, styd on last 2 fs, nvr nrr.* (20 to 1 op 16 to 1) 6
1529* ALLWIGHT THEN (Ire) 9-0 R Lappin (8) *trkd ldrs gng wl, effrt and not much room last 2 fs, eased whn btn ins last*.....................................(7 to 1 op 8 to 1) 7
1742^{2} ANTONIA'S FOLLY 8-9 J Carroll (9) *speed for 3 fs, fdd.* ....(7 to 1 op 8 to 1) 8
1798* MISTER PISTE (Ire) 8-12 D Holland (10) *broke wl, sn rdn, fdd frm hfwy*.........................(13 to 2 op 7 to 1) 9
HONG KONG FUTURE (Ire) 8-7 (3*) S D Williams (6) *missed break, nvr able to reco'r*..........(33 to 1 op 25 to 1) 10
2063* SMART PET 8-9 J Lowe (12) *rdn to hfwy, nvr a factor.* ....(11 to 2 op 6 to 1 tchd 5 to 1) 11
Dist: 5l, hd, ½l, 2½l, 1l, 1l, 2½l, 10l, 2l, nk. 1m 5.65s. a 5.35s (11 Ran).
SR: 23/-/-/-/-/-/ (Lord Derby), J W Watts

2401 Alice Hawthorn Maiden Fillies Stakes Class D (3-y-o) £4,435 7f 122yds (4:50)

1931^{2} CROIRE (Ire) 8-11 F Norton (5) *nvr far away, led 2 fs out, hdd briefly one out, ran on strly last 100 yards.* ....(11 to 8 fav op 6 to 4 tchd 7 to 4) 1
1285^{8} CITY TIMES (Ire) (bl) 8-4 (7*) S Sanders (4) *al hndy, drw level o'r one furlong out, kpt on und pres.* ....(16 to 1 op 12 to 1) 2
2219^{4} NEVER SURE (Ire) 8-11 T Quinn (8) *nvr far away, drw level o'r one furlong out, sn rdn, rallied towards finish.* ....(6 to 1 tchd 7 to 1) 3
KOSATA (Ire) 8-11 D Holland (3) *sluggish strt, prog to ld briefly one furlong out, no extr last 100 yards.* ....(9 to 2 op 3 to 1) 4
ANNYBAN 8-11 S Perks (6) *frnt rnk till wknd and eased fnl furlong, improve*..............(50 to 1 op 25 to 1) 5
2191^{4} WHERE'S THE DANCE 8-11 J Quinn (7) *pressed ldrs for o'r 4 fs, fdd*...........................(7 to 1 op 6 to 1) 6
2032^{4} BELMONT PRINCESS (Ire) 8-11 J Lowe (1) *tried to make all, hdd 2 fs out, sn btn.* ....(16 to 1 op 33 to 1 tchd 50 to 1) 7
WAZEERAH (USA) 8-11 G Hind (2) *lost many ls strt, nvr able to reco'r*...........................(9 to 2 op 4 to 1) 8
Dist: ¾l, ¾l, ½l, 5l, 6l, 5l, 5l. 1m 41.36s. a 9.36s (8 Ran).
(Exors Of The Late Sir Robin McAlpine), G Wragg

CURRAGH (IRE) (yielding)
Saturday July 10th

Going Correction: PLUS 0.35 sec. per fur. (races 1,4,5,6,7), PLUS 0.10 (2,3)

2402 Lagan (E.B.F.) Maiden (2-y-o) £5,244 7f.............................(2:15)

2072^{3} SPECS APPEAL (Ire) (bl) 9-0 C Roche (6)..........(5 to 1) 1
2037 GAINSBOROUGH'S BOY (Ire) 9-0 J P Murtagh (8) (12 to 1) 2
2037^{9} MANAAFIS (Ire) 9-0 W J Supple (2)...............(8 to 1) 3
MARCONI (Ire) 9-0 L Piggott (5)...............(6 to 4 fav) 4
1571^{4} ALJAWZA (USA) 8-11 M J Kinane (1).............(2 to 1) 5
RAZIDA (Ire) 8-11 K J Manning (3)...............(14 to 1) 6
2037^{7} OPULENT 9-0 P V Gilson (9).....................(8 to 1) 7
LOVELY DEISE (Ire) 8-11 R Hughes (10)..........(14 to 1) 8
REGAL ACCESS (USA) 9-0 S Craine (7)..........(10 to 1) 9
CHART BUSTER 8-11 P Shanahan (4)..............(14 to 1) 10
Dist: Sht-hd, 3½l, sht-hd, ½l. 1m 30.40s. a 7.20s (10 Ran).
SR: 29/28/17/16/11/-/ (Mrs J S Bolger), J S Bolger

2403 Shernazar (E.B.F.) Curragh Stakes (Group 3) (2-y-o) £14,375 5f..... (2:45)

1567* EICHTERCUA (Ire) 8-7 J F Egan (3) *led, rdn o'r 2 fs out, hdd over one out, sn rgned ld, kpt on*..................(14 to 1) 1
1788^{4} LONG GALLERY (Ire) 8-10 M J Kinane (6) *wl plcd for o'r one and a half fs, rdn 2 out, prog fnl furlong*.......(9 to 2) 2
1804 THE PUZZLER (Ire) 8-10 Pat Eddery (1) *str hold early, trkd ldr, swtchd rght hfwy to ld o'r one furlong out, sn hdd and wknd*....................................(6 to 4 fav) 3
1571^{9} PEACE TOKEN (Ire) 8-7 B Coogan (7) *wl plcd, dsptd ld 2 fs out, sn wknd*...................................(10 to 1) 4
2037^{2} BASSMAAT (USA) 8-7 C Roche (4) *wl plcd, rdn o'r 2 fs out, sn lost pl*..(7 to 2) 5
THE BREADMAN (Ire) 8-10 S Craine (2) *strted slwly, rear, little room 2 fs out, not quicken*..................(10 to 1) 6
1643* WAVE THE WAND (Ire) 8-10 W J Supple (5) *wnt rght strt, rdn and some prog 2 fs out, sn wknd*........... (8 to 1) 7
Dist: 2½l, ½l, nk, 1l. 1m 0.70s. a 2.40s (7 Ran).
SR: 55/48/46/42/38/-/-/ (Mrs P H O'Sullivan), K O'Sullivan

2404 Emirates Airline Scurry Handicap (0-105 3-y-o and up) £5,770 6f 63yds ....(3:15)

2073^{3} NORDIC FOX (Ire) [-] 3-9-5 C Roche (2).........(3 to 1 fav) 1
2073^{2} CLASSICAL AFFAIR (Ire) [-] 4-8-12 (6*) R V Skelly (3) (7 to 2) 2
2073^{4} TROPICAL [-] (bl) 3-9-10 M J Kinane (10)..........(6 to 1) 3

2073^{9} NORDIC OAK (Ire) [-] (bl) 5-9-0 K J Manning (6) ... (12 to 1) 4
1823^{3} SABAYA (USA) [-] 3-8-12 W J Supple (7) ....(13 to 2) 5
2073^{6} SUMY [-] (bl) 3-9-3 M Roberts (8) ....(7 to 1) 6
2073 MAGIC DON (Ire) [-] 4-7-2 (8*) R T Fitzpatrick (4) .. (14 to 1) 7
1201 CAURSELLE (Ire) [-] 4-8-6 (8*) P J Smullen (9) .....(16 to 1) 8
1551^{9} LEADING TIME (Fr) [-] 4-9-6 (6*) J A Heffernan (5) (20 to 1) 9
2078^{8} LUTE AND LYRE (Ire) [-] (bl) 4-8-9 L Piggott (1) .... (14 to 1) 10
Dist: ½l, ¾l, hd, 1l. 1m 18.10s. a 3.60s (10 Ran).
SR: 46/43/46/35/29/-/ (Mrs Catherine Shubotham), J S Bolger

2405 Kildangan Stud Irish Oaks (Group 1) (3-y-o) £113,000 1½m. ....(3:55)

2054* WEMYSS BIGHT 9-0 Pat Eddery (8) *hld up, swtchd lft ins fnl 2 fs, prog to ld jst inside last, kpt on.* .... (9 to 2) 1
2038^{5} ROYAL BALLERINA (Ire) 9-0 W J Supple (5) *mid-div, prog 3 fs out to ld one and a half out, hdd jst ins last, kpt on.* ....(12 to 1) 2
1525^{3} OAKMEAD (Ire) 9-0 J Reid (9) *wl plcd, rdn to track ldr 2 and a half fs out, kpt on fnl furlong.* .... (15 to 2) 3
1525* INTREPIDITY 9-0 M Roberts (4) *hld up, rdn 5 fs out, styd on fnl furlong.* .... (11 to 10 fav) 4
2038^{3} DANSE ROYALE (Ire) 9-0 L Piggott (2) *trkd ldr, led 3 fs out, rdn and hdd one and half out, wknd ins last.* (11 to 1) 5
2077^{2} BALLYKETT LADY (USA) 9-0 C Roche (3) *hld up, prog on outsd 4 fs out, kpt on strt.* .... (40 to 1) 6
2038^{4} SPECIAL PAGEANT (Ire) 9-0 K J Manning (7) *rear, rdn o'r 2 fs out, some prog, sn no extr.* .... (33 to 1) 7
2038* TAKAROUNA (USA) 9-0 M J Kinane (10) *hld up, smooth prog 2 fs out, sn rdn, wknd one out.* .... (8 to 1) 8
2038^{6} EUROSTORM (USA) 9-0 P V Gilson (6) *wl plcd, rdn to chal 2 fs out, sn wknd.* .... (33 to 1) 9
1525 ALOUETTE 9-0 S Craine (1) *wl plcd, rdn 4 fs out, sn wknd.* ....(66 to 1) 10
2040^{5} FLAME OF PERSIA (Ire) 9-0 R Hughes (11) *led till rdn and hdd 3 fs out, sn wknd.* ....(100 to 1) 11
Dist: ½l, 4l, sht-hd, 2½l, 2l, nk, ¾l, 1l, 7l, 14l. 2m 35.80s. a 6.30s (11 Ran).
SR: 79/78/70/69/64/60/59/57/55/ (K Abdulla), A Fabre

2406 Ford Maverick Handicap (0-90 3-y-o) £3,795 1m. .... (4:30)

2297 BIZANA (Ire) [-] 8-6 R Hughes (9) .... (10 to 1) 1
1610* SAFAYN (USA) [-] 8-9 M J Kinane (5) .... (11 to 8 fav) 2
1856^{3} MISS MISTLETOES (Ire) [-] 8-8 S Craine (2) ....(5 to 1) 3
1652^{2} FLORA WOOD (Ire) [-] 8-5 W J Supple (8) ....(6 to 1) 4
1755* SAINT HILDA (Ire) [-] 7-12 N G McCullagh (3) ....(9 to 1) 5
307 NORDIC UNION (Ire) [-] 7-9 (6*) J A Heffernan (1) .. (10 to 1) 6
2248* OICHE MHAITH [-] (bl) 7-7 (8*,6ex) R T Fitzpatrick (7) (7 to 1) 7
1553^{6} SIR SLAVES [-] 9-0 P Shanahan (6) ....(16 to 1) 8
FAIRY FANTASY (Ire) [-] 7-8 (2*) D G O'Shea (4) ... (20 to 1) 9
Dist: Hd, 1l, 1l, 3l. 1m 42.40s. a 5.80s (9 Ran).
SR: 47/49/45/39/23/-/ (Breffni Syndicate), Noel Meade

2407 Minstrel Stakes (Listed) (3-y-o and up) £8,625 1m. .... (5:00)

1200^{8} ASEMA (USA) 3-8-11 M J Kinane (3) *hld up, prog to ld jst ins fnl furlong, quickened clr.* .... (11 to 8 fav) 1
2074^{5} MALVERNICO (Ire) 5-9-6 K J Manning (1) *wl plcd, prog to ld one and a half fs out, sn hdd, no extr.* .... (7 to 1) 2
2076^{7} VIA PARIGI (Ire) 3-8-8 C Roche (5) *trkd ldr, rdn 3 fs out, kpt on fnl furlong.* .... (3 to 1) 3
2074^{9} IRISH MEMORY 4-9-3 S Craine (6) *led, rdn 3 fs out, hdd one and a half out, wknd.* ....(12 to 1) 4
2187^{4} BRADAWN BREEVER (Ire) (bl) 4-9-3 W J Supple (2) *wl plcd, rdn 2 fs out, not quicken.* ....(14 to 1) 5
NICEA (Ire) 3-8-5 R Hughes (4) *al rear, rdn 3 fs out, not quicken.* .... (4 to 1) 6
Dist: 2l, ½l, nk, ½l. 1m 41.00s. a 4.40s (6 Ran).
SR: 72/75/61/69/67/-/ (Allen E Paulson), D K Weld

2408 Ragusa Stud Handicap (0-100 3-y-o and up) £6,900 1¾m. ....(5:30)

1507* SHAIYBARA (Ire) [-] 3-8-4 M J Kinane (2) ...... (5 to 4 fav) 1
2186^{4} SIMPLY MARILYN (Ire) [-] 4-7-9 (6*) J J Behan (9) .. (10 to 1) 2
1468^{5} MASAI WARRIOR [-] 6-8-8 (2*) R M Burke (3) ..... (10 to 1) 3
GENERAL IDEA [-] 8-8-5 P Shanahan (6) .... (20 to 1) 4
SUPER FLAME (Can) [-] 6-9-6 J P Murtagh (5) .... (12 to 1) 5
2296^{5} UPPINGHAM [-] 7-7-1 (6*) P P Murphy (7) .... (20 to 1) 6
2077^{5} IMAD (USA) [-] 3-8-2 W J Supple (10) ....(9 to 2) 7
PENNINE TUNE (Ire) [-] 4-8-13 C Roche (1) .... (7 to 1) 8
895^{8} NEMURO (USA) [-] 5-10-0 C F Swan (8) .... (33 to 1) 9
1809^{4} CURRENCY BASKET (Ire) [-] 4-9-6 R Hughes (4) ... (8 to 1) 10
Dist: 2l, 1l, 5l, 3½l. 3m 7.00s. a 11.50s (10 Ran).
SR: 24/17/24/9/17/-/ (H H Aga Khan), John M Oxx

EVRY (FR) (good)
Saturday July 10th

2409 Prix Chloe (Group 3) (3-y-o) £23,895 1m. ....(3:35)

1765^{7} HOLLY GOLIGHTLY 8-9 A Cruz (5) *al prmnt, 3rd strt, led 2 fs out till ct on line.* .... (30 to 1) 1+
1722^{7} ROUQUETTE 8-9 A Badel (2) *hld up, 9th strt, hdwy on ins 2 fs out, ran on wl to line.* .... (56 to 10) 1+
1722 FRESHER 8-9 O Benoist (9) *hld up, 8 strt, hdwy fnl 2 fs, ran on.* .... (36 to 1) 3
DIS MOI TOUT (Fr) 8-9 O Peslier (3) *4th strt, ev ch 2 fs out, ran on one pace o'r one out.* ....(22 to 1) 4
1368^{3} POLLY'S WIKA (USA) 8-9 E Saint-Martin (4) *trkd ldr, ev ch 2 fs out, no extr ins last.* .... (20 to 1) 5
1545^{3} SHOWGUM (Fr) 8-9 A Junk (10) *nvr able to chal.* (22 to 1) 6
1722^{2} BAYA (USA) 8-9 T Jarnet (8) *6th and not much room strt, rdn and one pace wl o'r one furlong out.* ... (2 to 1 on) 7
SHAMSIYA (USA) 8-9 G Mosse (6) *strted slwly, last strt, hdwy and badly baulked wl o'r one furlong out, not rcvr.* ....(56 to 10) 8
1753* HAWK BEAUTY (USA) 8-9 C Asmussen (7) *7th strt, rdn and btn 2 fs out.* ....(71 to 10) 9
1722 GAIRSIC (Fr) 8-9 G Benoit (1) *led for 6 fs.* .... (56 to 10) 10
Dist: Dd-ht, 2l, sht-nk, hd, sht-hd, 1½l, nk, 2l, 15l. 1m 38.59s. a 1.19s (10 Ran).
SR: 65/65/59/58/57/56/51/50/44/ (Victor Behrens & T Attias), R Hannon & Mme M Bollack-Badel

LINGFIELD (good)
Saturday July 10th

Going Correction: NIL (races 1,3,4,5,7), MINUS 0.10 (2,6)

2410 Godstone Maiden Stakes Class D (Div I) (3-y-o) £3,465 7f. .... (2:30)

1762^{2} DAGNY JUEL (USA) 8-9 W Newnes (10) *led till hdd 4 fs out, led ag'n o'r one out, pushed out.* ....(2 to 1 fav op 5 to 4 tchd 9 to 4) 1
1239^{8} THE LITTLE FERRET 9-0 B Rouse (5) *trkd ldrs, rdn and ran on wl ins fnl furlong.* .... (100 to 30 op 7 to 2 tchd 9 to 2) 2
1765 FRIENDLY BRAVE (USA) 8-9 (5*) N Gwilliams (1) *wth ldr, rcd freely, led 4 fs out to o'r one out, one pace.* ....(3 to 1 op 7 to 2 tchd 5 to 2) 3
CHUMMY'S SAGA 9-0 Dean McKeown (3) *chsd ldrs, rdn and styd on one pace fnl 2 fs.* .....(8 to 1 tchd 12 to 1) 4
FOOT-BEAT 8-2 (7*) Antoinette Armes (7) *cl up till outpcd o'r 3 fs out.* .... (33 to 1 op 14 to 1) 5
BRECKLAND (Ire) 8-11 (3*) J Weaver (8) *outpcd, ran on fnl 2 fs, nrst finish.* ....(50 to 1 op 20 to 1) 6
1522^{5} HOME SAFE 9-0 M Hills (2) *chsd ldrs, shaken up o'r 2 fs out, wknd over one out.* .... (16 to 1 op 14 to 1 tchd 20 to 1) 7
BIRD TROUBLE (Ire) 9-0 C Avery (6) *outpcd aftr 3 fs, hrd rdn three out, no imprsn.* .... (50 to 1 op 25 to 1) 8
JACKSONS BAY 9-0 M Perrett (4) *ran green in mid-div till wknd o'r 3 fs out.* ....(14 to 1 op 10 to 1 tchd 20 to 1) 9
JOAN'S GIFT 8-9 T Williams (9) *strted slwly, al beh.* .... (50 to 1 op 33 to 1) 10
ARABIAN SHADES 8-9 S O'Gorman (11) *outpcd, tld off.* .... (33 to 1 op 25 to 1) 11
Dist: ¾l, 1l, 3l, 5l, 6l, nk, 5l, 3½l, 1l, 20l. 1m 24.12s. a 3.42s (11 Ran).
SR: 44/47/44/35/15/2/1/-/-/ (Miss K Rausing), J L Dunlop

2411 Bakers Lane Selling Handicap Class G (0-60 3-y-o) £2,713 1¼m. ..... (3:00)

1961^{5} SMART DAISY [48] 8-13 S O'Gorman (9) *hld up, smooth hdwy hfwy, led appr 2 fs out, easily.* ....(3 to 1 fav op 9 to 4 tchd 7 to 2) 1
1732^{2} HAVEN OF LOVE (Ire) [56] 9-0 (7*) J D Smith (8) *beh, sn pushed alng, hdwy hfwy, hrd rdn o'r one out, one pace.* .... (7 to 2 op 7 to 1 tchd 8 to 1) 2
2109^{3} QUEENS CONTRACTOR [44] (bl) 8-4 (5*) D McCabe (1) *led till hdd appr 2 fs out, one pace und pres.* ....(4 to 1 op 5 to 2) 3
2095^{6} NIGHTMARE LADY [31] 7-5^{2} (7*) C Hawksley (6) *strted slwly, outpcd in rear, hdwy o'r 2 fs out, styd on wl.* .... (12 to 1 op 6 to 1) 4
2127^{7} JULIASDARKINVADER [49] 9-0 Candy Morris (5) *beh, hdwy o'r one furlong out, nrst finish.* .... (14 to 1 op 8 to 1) 5
MAC TOMB [29] 7-3 (5*) D Wright (2) *beh, hrd rdn 3 fs out, nvr nr to chal.* ....(33 to 1 op 20 to 1) 6
2160^{6} POCONO KNIGHT [45] 8-10 C Avery (10) *chsd ldrs, pushed alng 6 fs out, btn 3 out.* .... (20 to 1 op 14 to 1 tchd 25 to 1) 7
1802^{9} MINTEEN [54] 9-0 (5*) K Rutter (4) *trkd ldrs till wknd o'r 3 fs out.* ....(7 to 1 op 10 to 1 tchd 6 to 1) 8
1642^{7} MISS RIBBONS [40] 8-5 T Williams (7) *trkd ldrs, rdn 2 fs out, btn quickly.* .... (25 to 1 op 16 to 1 tchd 33 to 1) 9
2182^{6} BADAWI (Fr) [48] 8-13 Dean McKeown (11) *chsd ldrs, hrd rdn o'r 5 fs out, wknd over 3 out.* .... (10 to 1 op 7 to 1 tchd 12 to 1) 10
2130^{8} SPECIAL RISK (Ire) [46] (bl) 8-11 M Hills (3) *wth ldr till wknd o'r 4 fs out.* .... (12 to 1 op 7 to 1) 11
Dist: 4l, 2l, 3l, 2l, 1½l, 6l, 3½l, 2l, 12l, 6l. 2m 11.01s. a 6.01s (11 Ran).
SR: 29/29/13/-/8/-/ (Robert Jenkinson), I A Balding

2412 Bet With The Tote Nursery Class C (2-y-o) £5,970 6f. .... (3:30)

2030* RAMBOLD [-] 8-9 T Williams (10) *wth ldrs, reminder hfwy, led o'r one furlong out, rdn out.* (10 to 1 tchd 12 to 1) 1
2159* NONIOS (Ire) [-] 9-2 W Newnes (1) *trkd ldrs, hrd rdn and ev ch one furlong out, kpt on one pace.* ....(14 to 1 op 10 to 1 tchd 16 to 1) 2
2192* BET A PLAN (Ire) [-] 7-10 (5*) D Wright (9) *sn pushed alng in rear, hrd rdn 2 fs out, ran on ins last.* ....(4 to 1 op 9 to 2 tchd 5 to 1 and 7 to 2) 3
2224[2] ASKING FOR ACES [-] 8-0 (7*) B Russell (2) *in tch, hdwy and ev ch o'r 2 fs out, sn hng lft and one pace.* ....(25 to 1 op 14 to 1) 4
1624[4] WICKLOW BOY (Ire) [-] 8-5 (7*) A Whelan (8) *al prmnt, rdn 2 fs out, one pace*......(12 to 1 op 10 to 1 tchd 14 to 1) 5
1742[3] FOLLY FINNESSE [-] 8-7 A Tucker (6) *outpcd till ran on wl fnl furlong*..........(10 to 1 op 8 to 1 tchd 12 to 1) 6
1933* KING RAT (Ire) [-] 8-11 Dean McKeown (4) *led till hdd o'r one furlong out, wknd.* (6 to 1 op 7 to 1 tchd 9 to 1) 7
2119* BROOKHEAD LADY [-] 9-7 W R Swinburn (5) *hld up beh ldrs, effrt 2 fs out, sn btn.* ....(13 to 2 op 6 to 1 tchd 7 to 1) 8
2090[2] THE MULTIYORKER (Ire) [-] 8-2[3] (3*) J Weaver (7) *cl up till wknd hfwy, sddl slpd.* ....(15 to 8 fav op 6 to 4 tchd 2 to 1) 9
2137[4] EUROCHEM LAD (Ire) [-] 9-1 B Rouse (3) *rcd freely, cl up till wknd appr 2 fs out.* ....(25 to 1 op 16 to 1 tchd 33 to 1) 10

Dist: 2½l, ¾l, sht-hd, hd, nk, 3l, 2l, 6l, 8l. 1m 13.17s. a 4.17s (10 Ran).
SR: 12/9/-/-/-/-/ (Sydney Mason), T M Jones

2413 Champagne Jacquart Silver Trophy Rated Class A Handicap (Listed Race) (0-105 3-y-o and up) £10,446 7f 140yds ....(4:00)

2363 CROFT VALLEY [95] 6-8-13 Dean McKeown (6) *sn led, hdd one and a half fs out, rallied ins last, led post.* ....(11 to 2 op 9 to 2 tchd 6 to 1) 1
1002 LITTLE BEAN [99] (bl) 4-9-3 M Hills (4) *chsd ldrs, hdwy to ld one and a half fs out, not run on and hdd post.* ....(11 to 2 op 9 to 2) 2
1002[8] MIZAAYA [100] 4-9-4 W R Swinburn (7) *trkd ldrs, ev ch 2 fs out, one pace appr last*............(5 to 1 tchd 6 to 1) 3
1921[2] UNDERWATER (USA) [100] 4-9-4 T Sprake (2) *outpcd hfwy, hdwy o'r 2 fs out, styd on, not pace to chal.* ....(9 to 2 op 7 to 2 tchd 5 to 1) 4
2363 ROCKY WATERS (USA) [96] 4-9-0 B Rouse (9) *in tch, effrt o'r 2 fs out, not pace to chal.* ....(9 to 1 op 6 to 1 tchd 10 to 1) 5
2194[6] BRIGADE [94] 4-8-12 J Weaver (8) *wth wnr, rdn o'r 3 fs out, ev ch 2 out, btn over one out.* (7 to 2 fav op 5 to 1) 6
2363 HELIOS [89] 5-8-7 A Tucker (5) *cl up, niggled alng o'r 4 fs out, hrd rdn and btn 2 out*..........(40 to 1 op 25 to 1) 7
2254[7] KRISTIANSTAD [89] (bl) 4-8-7 W Newnes (3) *rcd freely, cl up till wknd o'r 2 fs out*..........(16 to 1 op 12 to 1) 8
1407* PAY HOMAGE [103] 5-9-7 S O'Gorman (1) *beh, lost tch o'r 3 fs out, tld off*..........(5 to 1 op 9 to 2 tchd 11 to 2) 9

Dist: Sht-hd, 1l, 1l, 4l, ¾l, 2½l, 5l, 8l. 1m 31.73s. a 3.43s (9 Ran).
SR: 48/51/49/46/30/26/13/-/-/ (Miss Vivian Pratt), R Akehurst

2414 Surrey Conditions Stakes Class D (2-y-o) £3,201 7f.................. (4:30)

1877* ORANGE PLACE (Ire) 8-11 M Hills (2) *cl up, led o'r 4 fs out, shaken up over one out, sn clr.* ....(5 to 2 op 7 to 4 tchd 11 to 4) 1
2210[6] BALANDRA BAY (Ire) 9-1 W R Swinburn (6) *cl up, pushed alng o'r 2 fs out, hrd rdn and one pace appr last.* ....(5 to 2 op 11 to 4) 2
1489[3] TIMELY EXAMPLE (USA) 8-4 (7*) T G McLaughlin (4) *in cl tch, pushed alng o'r 2 fs out, kpt on wl.* ....(15 to 8 fav op 7 to 4 tchd 9 to 4) 3
2240[8] EWAR EMPRESS (Ire) 8-6 W Newnes (3) *pld hrd, in tch, effrt o'r 2 fs out, btn quickly*.......(20 to 1 op 8 to 1) 4
2027[7] MENTMORE LAD 8-11 B Rouse (5) *led till hdd o'r 4 fs out, wknd over 2 out, tld off.* ....(8 to 1 op 12 to 1 tchd 14 to 1) 5

Dist: 2l, hd, 7l, 12l. 1m 25.77s. a 5.07s (5 Ran).
SR: 21/19/14/-/-/ (Archer Van & Truck Hire Ltd), M Bell

2415 Redhill Handicap Class E (0-70 3-y-o and up) £3,131 1¾m............(5:00)

2150[3] SINGING REPLY (USA) [31] 5-8-1 T Sprake (9) *hld up in rear grp, hdwy o'r 7 fs out, led over 2 out, sn clr, easily.* ....(5 to 1 co-fav op 9 to 2) 1
1607[6] SUMMER PAGEANT [69] 3-9-10 W R Swinburn (2) *trkd ldrs, led o'r 5 fs out till hdd over 2 out, one pace.* (5 to 1 co-fav op 4 to 1) 2
2256[5] CATHOS (Fr) [39] 8-8-9 B Rouse (1) *hld up beh, hdwy o'r 3 fs out, styd on one pace.* ....(10 to 1 op 8 to 1 tchd 7 to 1) 3
2048[7] ALICE'S MIRROR [36] 4-8-6 A Tucker (6) *chsd ldrs, styd on und pres fnl 2 fs*..................(33 to 1 op 20 to 1) 4
2007* TOUCHING TIMES [50] 5-9-6 M Perrett (8) *al prmnt, rdn and one pace appr 2 fs out.* (5 to 1 co-fav tchd 6 to 1) 5
2007[8] DR ZEVA [35] 7-8-0 (5*) D Wright (11) *beh, styd on fnl 2 fs, nvr nrr*............... (13 to 2 op 6 to 1 tchd 7 to 1) 6
2126[7] GO FORUM [34] 8-8-4 M Hills (4) *in tch, cld o'r 5 fs out, gng wl, rdn and btn quickly over 2 furlongs out.* ....(7 to 1 op 5 to 1 tchd 8 to 1) 7
2126[5] RAGTIME SONG [39] 4-8-9 N Adams (10) *al beh.* ....(10 to 1 op 8 to 1 tchd 12 to 1) 8
1669 SARAZAR (USA) [50] 4-9-6 W Newnes (5) *beh, rdn alng hfwy, no response*......(11 to 2 op 5 to 1 tchd 6 to 1) 9
2007 APACHE PRINCE [44] (bl) 6-9-0 T Williams (7) *trkd ldrs, drvn 6 fs out, sn btn.* (25 to 1 op 20 to 1 tchd 33 to 1) 10
1911 BIJOU FIRE (NZ) [47] 5-9-0 (3*) J Weaver (3) *led till hdd o'r 5 fs out, wknd quickly, tld off*......(16 to 1 op 20 to 1) 11

Dist: 3l, 1l, 1½l, ½l, 1½l, 15l, 8l, 6l, 2l, dist. 3m 8.93s. a 13.93s (11 Ran).
(Mrs K Oseman), R J Price

2416 Godstone Maiden Stakes Class D (Div II) (3-y-o) £3,435 7f............. (5:30)

2202[2] WISHAM (USA) 9-0 M Hills (4) *al prmnt, quickened to ld appr fnl furlong, cmftbly*....(6 to 4 jt-fav tchd 13 to 8) 1
2097[2] DESERT TIME 9-0 W R Swinburn (9) *trkd ldr, ev ch appr fnl furlong, kpt on und pres*..............(6 to 4 jt-fav op 5 to 4 tchd 13 to 8) 2
950 DAWALIB (USA) 9-0 R Price (10) *led till hdd appr fnl furlong, one pace*...... (7 to 1 op 5 to 1 tchd 8 to 1) 3
662 IMPECCABLE TASTE 8-2 (7*) J D Smith (2) *in tch, rdn 2 fs out, one pace*..............(50 to 1 op 33 to 1) 4
2202[7] AWESTRIKE (USA) 9-0 W Newnes (3) *trkd ldrs till wknd 2 fs out*...........................(12 to 1 op 8 to 1) 5
1972[5] KINTWYN 9-0 T Williams (5) *cl up, rdn 2 fs out, wknd o'r one out*...........................(25 to 1 op 16 to 1) 6
JIMMY HIMSELF 9-0 T Sprake (6) *beh frm hfwy.* ....(50 to 1 op 33 to 1) 7
BUY BY NIGHT 8-6 (3*) J Weaver (7) *strted slwly, nvr on terms*..........................(100 to 1 op 33 to 1) 8
ARABIAN CASTLE 9-0 M Perrett (8) *in cl tch till rdn and wknd o'r 2 fs out*...............(100 to 1 op 33 to 1) 9
1992 BOY SOLDIER 8-9 (5*) N Gwilliams (1) *in tch to hfwy.* ....(66 to 1 op 33 to 1) 10

Dist: 3l, ¾l, 5l, ¾l, 10l, hd, sht-hd, ½l, 8l. 1m 25.46s. a 4.76s (10 Ran).
SR: 29/20/18/-/1/-/ (P G Goulandris), B Hanbury

SALISBURY (good to firm)
Saturday July 10th

Going Correction: PLUS 0.10 sec. per fur. (races 1,2,3,5), MINUS 0.05 (4), MINUS 0.15 (6)

2417 Myrobella Maiden Auction Stakes Class F (2-y-o) £2,534 6f........ (1:55)

2067[9] NAKITA 8-2 (7*) G Forster (1) *hdwy o'r 2 fs out, led wl over one out, sn clr*..........(5 to 2 op 9 to 4 tchd 11 to 4) 1
1857[6] BLURRED IMAGE (Ire) 9-0 W Carson (9) *led o'r 4 fs, hng badly lft fnl furlong, not quicken.* ....(2 to 1 fav tchd 5 to 2) 2
2224[6] HENRY'S LUCK 9-0 R Hills (3) *hdwy 2 fs out, ran on ins last*.............................(12 to 1 op 7 to 1) 3
1877[8] FAIRFIELD DANCER 8-9 J Williams (6) *prmnt early, not hold pl, gd hdwy o'r one furlong out, ran on.* ....(16 to 1 op 10 to 1) 4
2114[7] RADIANT DANCER 8-9 R Perham (4) *al prmnt, no hdwy fnl 2 fs*.......................(50 to 1 op 20 to 1) 5
2058 NOT FOR JOE 9-0 A Clark (8) *chsd ldr, grad wknd fnl 2 fs.* ....(12 to 1 op 10 to 1 tchd 14 to 1) 6
1211 MYSTERY MOON 8-9 N Adams (2) *strted slwly, sn prmnt, wknd 2 fs out*........(10 to 1 op 8 to 1 tchd 12 to 1) 7
2123[3] CANDI DAS (Ire) 8-9 Paul Eddery (5) *prmnt 4 fs.* ....(7 to 2 op 9 to 2 tchd 5 to 1) 8
299 GENERAL FAIRFAX (Ire) 9-0 C Rutter (7) *al wl beh.* ....(50 to 1 op 25 to 1) 9

Dist: 3½l, nk, sht-hd, 3½l, 2½l, 3l, 1½l, 4l. 1m 17.90s. a 5.40s (9 Ran).
(Theobalds Stud), C N Allen

2418 Owen Tudor Handicap Class D (0-80 3-y-o and up) £3,850 6f......... (2:25)

2139* BALLASECRET [80] 5-9-9 (5*) D Meredith (7) *made all, ran on wl*..................(15 to 2 op 6 to 1 tchd 8 to 1) 1
1953[2] TRUTHFUL IMAGE [76] (bl) 4-9-3 (7*) P McCabe (5) *hld up, hdwy and wnt rght o'r 2 fs out, ev ch ins last, swtchd lft, ran on*......(6 to 1 jt-fav tchd 7 to 1 and 11 to 2) 2
1957* BALIGAY [77] 8-9-11 Paul Eddery (2) *gd hdwy o'r 2 fs out, ev ch over one out, not quicken*...(8 to 1 tchd 10 to 1) 3
2004[3] MASNUN (USA) [74] 8-9-8 A Clark (13) *prmnt whn badly hmpd o'r 2 fs out, gd late hdwy*.....(8 to 1 op 6 to 1) 4
1927[3] BAYSHAM (USA) [72] (bl) 7-9-1 (5*) Stephen Davies (6) *chsd ldrs, rdn and not quicken o'r one furlong out.* ....(6 to 1 jt-fav tchd 7 to 1 and 15 to 2) 5
1953[6] GREY CHARMER (Ire) [62] 4-8-10 S Whitworth (9) *nrst finish*..................................(11 to 1 op 8 to 1) 6
1953* DANCING SPIRIT (Ire) [73] 3-9-0 R Hills (4) *no hdwy fnl 2 fs.* ....(8 to 1 op 6 to 1) 7
1744 AROOM [73] 3-9-0 W Carson (12) *sn beh.* ....(7 to 1 op 6 to 1 tchd 8 to 1) 8
1821* CAROMISH (USA) [60] 6-8-8 N Adams (8) *speed 3 fs, wkng whn hmpd o'r 2 out*.... (7 to 1 op 6 to 1 tchd 8 to 1) 9

1377[7] JEREMIAHS BOY [54] (bl) 3-7-9 S Dawson (1) *beh fnl 3 fs.* ....(20 to 1 op 14 to 1 tchd 25 to 1) 10
1703[5] AL MOULOUKI [77] 3-9-4 W Hood (11) *reared up strt, al wl beh*..................(14 to 1 op 10 to 1 tchd 16 to 1) 11
945 ROYAL DEED (USA) [73] (v) 3-9-0 R Perham (10) *whipped round sn aftr strt, refused to race, took no part.* ....(33 to 1 op 16 to 1) I
Dist: 1½l, 3½l, 2½l, nk, nk, ½l, 1½l, ½l, 8l, 2l. 1m 15.60s. a 3.10s (12 Ran).
SR: 64/54/41/28/25/14/16/10/2/ (R J Adams), R Dickin

2419 EBF Queenpot Maiden Stakes Class D (2-y-o) £4,597 6f 212yds.........(2:55)

HARVEST MOUSE 9-0 S Raymont (10) *strted slwly, steadway hdwy 3 fs out, not clr run 2 furlongs out, quickened to ld wl ins last, ran on.* ....(3 to 1 op 5 to 2 tchd 9 to 4) 1
1489[8] DUTY TIME 9-0 J Williams (3) *wl beh till gd hdwy fnl 2 fs.* ....(33 to 1 op 20 to 1 tchd 40 to 1) 2
LAXFORD BRIDGE 9-0 Paul Eddery (11) *al prmnt, led o'r 2 fs out till wl ins last.* (10 to 1 op 14 to 1 tchd 33 to 1) 3
2069[7] JAFEICA (Ire) 9-0 R Perham (8) *chsd ldrs, ran on one pace fnl 2 fs.*.............................(33 to 1 op 14 to 1) 4
1949[4] BONAIGUA (Ire) 9-0 R Hills (1) *dwlt, sn prmnt, ev ch o'r one furlong out, not quicken.* ....(11 to 8 fav op 2 to 1 tchd 9 to 4 and 5 to 4) 5
INZAR 8-9 (5*) Stephen Davies (6) *led o'r 4 fs.* ....(15 to 2 op 4 to 1 tchd 8 to 1) 6
1497[7] KILLING TIME 9-0 W Carson (4) *no hdwy fnl 2 fs.* ....(8 to 1 op 12 to 1 tchd 16 to 1) 7
2069[3] TANAH MERAH (Ire) 9-0 C Rutter (5) *prmnt 5 fs.* ....(4 to 1 op 7 to 2 tchd 5 to 1) 8
1949[8] PLUNDER BAY (USA) 9-0 S Whitworth (9) *wth ldr till wknd o'r 2 fs out*..........(33 to 1 op 20 to 1 tchd 40 to 1) 9
TOWER GREEN 9-0 A Clark (2) *al beh.* ....(25 to 1 op 12 to 1) 10
1959[6] GRANBY BELL 8-7 (7*) Mark Denaro (7) *prmnt 4 fs.* ....(50 to 1 op 33 to 1 tchd 66 to 1) 11
Dist: Nk, nk, 3½l, 1½l, 5l, hd, nk, 3l, ¾l, 8l. 1m 30.66s. a 5.06s (11 Ran).
SR: 35/34/33/22/17/2/1/-/-/ (The Lady Vestey), R Charlton

2420 Crested Lark Handicap Class D (0-80 4-y-o and up) £3,557 1½m...... (3:25)

1929[6] BLAZON OF TROY [52] 4-8-5 S Whitworth (6) *al prmnt, led 3 fs out, sn clr, ran on wl.* ....(12 to 1 op 10 to 1 tchd 14 to 1) 1
2026* AMAZON EXPRESS [66] 4-9-5 W Carson (1) *lost pl and hrd rdn o'r 5 fs out, sn wl beh, gd hdwy fnl 2 furlongs, not rch wnr*.........(11 to 10 fav op 6 to 4 tchd 7 to 4) 2
2111[2] INCHCAILLOCH (Ire) [71] 4-9-10 Paul Eddery (5) *second till led 6 fs out, hdd 3 out, ran on one pace.* ....(6 to 1 op 5 to 1 tchd 13 to 2) 3
1607[9] ACROBATE (USA) [59] 4-8-12 J Williams (3) *wl beh till gd hdwy fnl 2 fs*.......................(7 to 1 op 5 to 1) 4
2273[5] WAKI GOLD (USA) [60] 6-8-13 R Hills (2) *led 6 fs, ev ch 3 out, one pace*..........................(10 to 1 op 7 to 1) 5
1626 TIME FOR A FLUTTER [57] (bl) 4-8-10 R Perham (4) *in tch till wknd 3 fs out*.....(33 to 1 op 20 to 1 tchd 40 to 1) 6
1992[4] NOVA SPIRIT [59] 5-8-12 M Wigham (3) *beh fnl 4 fs.* ....(16 to 1 op 14 to 1 tchd 20 to 1) 7
2048* WESTERN DYNASTY [75] 7-9-7 (7*) P McCabe (7) *beh fnl 4 fs, eased o'r 2 out*.................... (11 to 2 op 7 to 2) 8
Dist: 3½l, 1½l, ½l, ¾l, 5l, 1½l, 8l. 2m 36.90s. a 4.90s (8 Ran).
SR: 36/43/45/32/31/18/17/17/ (David F Wilson), T Thomson Jones

2421 Fair Trial Handicap Class D (0-80 3-y-o) £4,532 1m...................(3:55)

2156* AJDAYT (USA) [80] 9-7 S Whitworth (10) *al prmnt, rdn 2 fs out, ran on wl to ld last strd.* ....(7 to 2 fav op 3 to 1 tchd 11 to 4) 1
1992* RUE REMBRANDT (USA) [69] 8-10 Paul Eddery (11) *second till led o'r 3 fs out, hrd rdn ins fnl furlong, hdd post.* ....(13 to 2 op 5 to 1 tchd 7 to 1) 2
1991* MR CUBE (Ire) [61] 7-11 (5*) Stephen Davies (8) *al prmnt, ev ch 2 fs out, ran on one pace.* ....(9 to 1 op 8 to 1 tchd 10 to 1) 3
2156[7] MISTY SILKS [64] 8-5 S Raymont (9) *chsd ldrs, one pace fnl 2 fs*.................... (9 to 2 op 8 to 1 tchd 10 to 1) 4
2117 MORSTOCK [67] 8-1 (7*) S Drowne (2) *hld up, effrt 2 fs out, ran on one pace*....................(20 to 1 op 12 to 1) 5
2087* PRINCESS TATEUM (Ire) [68] 8-9 C Rutter (6) *chsd ldrs, no hdwy fnl 2 fs*.......................(12 to 1 op 6 to 1) 6
1991[3] CREDIT SQUEEZE [71] 8-12 R Hills (5) *rdn o'r 2 fs out, no extr appr fnl furlong.* (11 to 1 op 8 to 1 tchd 12 to 1) 7
2121 HAWAYAH (Ire) [67] 8-8 M Wigham (4) *wl beh till some late hdwy*..........(20 to 1 op 12 to 1 tchd 25 to 1) 8
1642[3] HE'S A KING (USA) [77] 9-4 J Williams (3) *no hdwy fnl 3 fs.* ....(14 to 1 op 12 to 1) 9
1991[5] GLEN MILLER [57] 7-12 E Johnson (1) *beh fnl 3 fs.* ....(25 to 1 op 14 to 1 tchd 33 to 1) 10
1859* PRAIRIE GROVE [74] 9-1 W Carson (7) *badly hmpd o'r 4 fs out, not rcvr*.......... (4 to 1 tchd 5 to 1 and 7 to 2) 11
1906[8] MISTY JENNI (Ire) [57] 7-12 S Dawson (12) *led o'r 4 fs, wknd quickly*..........................(20 to 1 op 8 to 1) 12
Dist: Sht-hd, 3l, 5l, 1½l, nk, ¾l, nk, ½l, 7l, 3½l. 1m 44.23s. a 4.73s (12 Ran).
SR: 48/36/19/7/5/5/6/1/9/ (Sheikh Ahmed Al Maktoum), A C Stewart

2422 Felstead Amateur Riders Limited Stakes Class G (0-65 3-y-o and up) £2,364 1¾m.................. (4:25)

1426[8] HIGH SUMMER 3-9-5 Miss Diana Jones (6) *al prmnt, led 3 fs out, edgd lft, jst hld on*....................(7 to 2 co-fav op 5 to 1 tchd 11 to 2 and 100 to 30) 1
2115* MARDOOD 8-10-3 (3*) Miss L Horsey (5) *hdwy 3 fs out, str run fnl furlong, jst fld*.......................(7 to 2 co-fav op 5 to 2 tchd 4 to 1) 2
2386* MONARDA 6-10-3 (3*) Miss M Clark (4) *hdwy 4 fs out, ev ch fnl 2 furlongs, edgd lft, ran on*..............(7 to 2 co-fav op 9 to 4 tchd 4 to 1) 3
2347[5] THE KARAOKE KING (bl) 4-10-3 (3*) Mrs J Boggis (7) *hdwy a m out, ev ch 3 fs out, ran on one pace.* ....(10 to 1 tchd 12 to 1) 4
2337[7] DISPUTED CALL (USA) 4-10-6 Mr C Vigors (9) *al prmnt, led o'r 4 fs out till 3 out, grad wknd*....(5 to 1 tchd 7 to 1) 5
1861[6] SINGING DETECTIVE (v) 6-10-3 (3*) Miss Elaine Mills (1) *led till wknd o'r 4 fs out*.............. (66 to 1 op 33 to 1) 6
BACK TO FORM 8-10-3 (3*) Mrs C Price (3) *wl beh fnl 6 fs.* ....(66 to 1 op 33 to 1) 7
TRUST DEED (USA) 5-10-3 (3*) Mr K Santana (11) *beh and hrd rdn 4 fs out, no responce.* ....(40 to 1 op 25 to 1 tchd 50 to 1) 8
FORTUNE STAR (Ire) 4-10-3 (3*) Miss M Bridger (10) *prmnt 7 fs*..........................(20 to 1 op 10 to 1) 9
COINAGE (bl) 10-10-6 Miss E Johnson Houghton (8) *beh whn slpd up 7 fs out*.............. (66 to 1 op 25 to 1) su
1779[5] JULFAAR (USA) 6-10-6 Mrs L Pearce (2) *beh whn slpd up o'r 7 fs out*............ (9 to 2 op 5 to 1 tchd 13 to 2) su
Dist: Sht-hd, nk, 6l, 3l, 8l, 4l, 6l, 7l. 3m 3.39s. a 5.69s (Flag start) (11 Ran).
SR: 27/41/40/28/22/6/ (The Queen), Lord Huntingdon

SOUTHWELL (A.W) (std)
Saturday July 10th

Going Correction: MINUS 0.10 sec. per fur. (race 1), PLUS 0.10 (2,3,4,5,6)

2423 Emperor Claiming Stakes Class F (2-y-o) £2,070 5f.................(6:30)

1926[9] TRENDY DANCER (Ire) 8-10 R Cochrane (8) *made all, rdn wl o'r one furlong out, kpt on well ins last.* ....(100 to 30 op 3 to 1 tchd 7 to 2) 1
1889[7] THE FERNHILL FLYER (Ire) (v) 8-10 J Carroll (3) *chsd wnr, rdn 2 fs out, ev ch entering last, kpt on.* ....(11 to 10 on op 11 to 10 tchd 6 to 5) 2
2128[4] CHEEKY CHAPPY 8-6 Alex Greaves (7) *al prmnt, swtchd and effrt 2 fs out, sn rdn and one pace.* ....(8 to 1 tchd 10 to 1) 3
1499[9] BESSIE'S WILL 7-8[1] A Mackay (5) *in tch, hdwy 2 fs out, kpt on one pace ins last*.......... (33 to 1 op 25 to 1) 4
2216[8] SPORT RACING CLUB 8-2[5] K Fallon (1) *hmpd strt, hdwy o'r 2 fs out, sn rdn and one pace*...(16 to 1 op 12 to 1) 5
2128[5] MRS JOGGLEBURY 7-12 (5*) J Tate (4) *chsd ldrs, rdn 2 fs out, sn wknd*....................(14 to 1 tchd 16 to 1) 6
ADMIRING 8-4 G Duffield (9) *slwly away, al beh.* ....(6 to 1 op 7 to 2) 7
WENLOCK LADY 8-0 (5*) A Garth (6) *slwly away, al beh.* ....(40 to 1 op 20 to 1 tchd 50 to 1) 8
SUZY LLOYD 7-8 (7*) Claire Balding (2) *wnt lft strt, chsd ldrs till wknd quickly 2 fs out.* ....(20 to 1 op 12 to 1 tchd 25 to 1) 9
Dist: 1½l, 2l, 3l, 2l, ¾l, 2½l, 15l, 12l. 1m 0.40s. a 2.50s (9 Ran).
SR: 36/30/18/-/-/-/ (P G Manning), S G Norton

2424 Butterfly Rating Related Maiden Stakes Class E (0-70 3-y-o) £2,217 6f ....(7:00)

2105[2] HEART BROKEN 8-9 K Fallon (4) *chsd ldg pair, hdwy hfwy, chlgd 2 fs out, sn led and clr, easily.* ....(5 to 4 on tchd Evens) 1
2219[2] SURAGON 8-11 (3*) S D Williams (5) *cl up, led o'r 3 fs out, rdn 2 out, sn hdd and one pace*.... (3 to 1 tchd 5 to 2) 2
1655[6] ROYAL MUSIC 9-0 J Carroll (1) *led, rdn and hdd o'r 3 fs out, sn wknd*....................(10 to 1 tchd 12 to 1) 3
2110 ALLEZ BIANCO 8-9 R Cochrane (6) *chsd ldrs, rdn hfwy, sn wknd*..............(11 to 1 op 8 to 1 tchd 12 to 1) 4
2047 FRIENDLY SMILE 8-9 G Duffield (3) *slwly into strd, al beh.* ....(9 to 1 op 8 to 1) 5
1376[7] LAID BACK BEN 8-9 (5*) A Garth (2) *al beh.* ....(12 to 1 op 8 to 1 tchd 14 to 1) 6
Dist: 8l, 5l, 2½l, 5l, 3l. 1m 16.70s. a 3.30s (6 Ran).
SR: 41/14/-/ (J G FitzGerald), J G FitzGerald

2425 Gaswarm Homes Fillies Handicap Class E (0-70 3-y-o) £2,406 7f... (7:30)

2217[2] PENNY BANGER (Ire) [57] 9-2 Dean McKeown (10) *chsd ldrs, rdn 2 fs out, styd on ins last to ld nr finish.* ....(9 to 4 fav op 5 to 2 tchd 11 to 4) 1

2217[3] ROSE FLYER (Ire) [62] 9-2 (5*) D McCabe (5) *led 2 fs, cl up, led o'r two out, sn hrd rdn, hdd and no extr nr finish.* ....(6 to 1 op 4 to 1) 2
1740[5] FINAL OAK [44] 8-3[1] G Duffield (6) *chsd ldg pair, rdn o'r 2 fs out, ev ch till one pace fnl furlong.* ....(7 to 1 tchd 8 to 1) 3
2318[5] HEATHYARDS GEM [54] 8-13 R Cochrane (2) *cl up, led aftr 2 fs till rdn and hdd o'r two out, wknd.* ....(8 to 1 op 7 to 1) 4
1981[4] WORKINGFORPEANUTS (Ire) [38] 7-11 J Lowe (3) *beh, rdn alng o'r 3 fs out, styd on und pres ins last, nvr dngrs.* ....(4 to 1 op 5 to 1) 5
2098[4] DONTBETALKING (Ire) [40] 7-13 J Quinn (1) *chsd ldrs, rdn alng hfwy, sn one pace*........(10 to 1 op 7 to 1) 6
1675[9] EASY TOUCH [42] 8-1 A Mackay (8) *in tch, rdn hfwy, wide strt, sn wknd*........ (33 to 1 op 25 to 1) 7
1705[6] RIVER FIRE (Ire) [45] 8-4 K Fallon (7) *al rear.* .... (25 to 1 op 16 to 1) 8
1852[6] VIKING WATERS [48] (bl) 8-2 (5*) J Tate (9) *slwly into strd, hdwy to chase ldrs hfwy, sn rdn, wknd o'r 2 fs out.* ....(8 to 1 tchd 7 to 1) 9
2220[6] DON'T BE SAKI (Ire) [42] 8-1 A Proud (4) *al rear.* ....(14 to 1 tchd 16 to 1) 10

Dist: ½l, 1½l, 1½l, ¾l, ¾l, 8l, 2½l, 2l, 2½l. 1m 32.00s. a 5.90s (10 Ran).
SR: 24/27/4/9/-/-/ (R W Huggins), M Johnston

2426 Derry Building Services Limited Stakes Class F (0-60 3-y-o and up) £2,070 1m.................... (8:00)

2095 CORONA GOLD (bl,e/s) 3-8-12 K Fallon (8) *cl up, chlgd 2 fs out, rdn to ld appr one out, hdd ins last, rallied to lead on line*........(14 to 1 op 10 to 1) 1
2031[7] ON Y VA (USA) 6-8-9 (7*) Sarah Thompson (3) *chsd ldrs, hdwy o'r 2 fs out, rdn to ld ins last, hdd on line.* ....(3 to 1 tchd 7 to 2) 2
2193[4] GLENFIELD GRETA (bl) 5-9-2 F Norton (4) *led, rdn 2 fs out, hdd and wknd appr last*........(8 to 1 op 6 to 1) 3
1490[2] CAPTAIN MARMALADE 4-9-7 L Dettori (1) *hld up, hdwy 2 fs out, sn rdn, kpt on one pace.* ....(7 to 4 fav op 5 to 2 tchd 6 to 4) 4
2218[4] EMPEROR ALEXANDER (Ire) (bl) 5-9-4 (3*) S D Williams (2) *in rear and pushed alng, some hdwy und pres fnl 2 fs, nvr dngrs*........(12 to 1 op 10 to 1) 5
2181[5] MRS DAWSON 3-8-7 J Carroll (5) *slwly into strd and beh, hdwy und pres 2 fs out, sn btn*..... (5 to 1 tchd 4 to 1) 6
2175[2] PRINCESS OF ORANGE 4-9-2 S Webster (7) *chsd ldrs till rdn and wknd o'r 2 fs out*........(7 to 1 op 6 to 1) 7
1273 CRAIGIE BOY 3-8-12 Alex Greaves (6) *in tch, rdn o'r 2 fs out, sn wknd*........ (20 to 1 op 12 to 1 tchd 25 to 1) 8

Dist: Hd, 3½l, nk, 2½l, 4l, 2l, 5l. 1m 46.00s. a 7.00s (8 Ran).
SR: 5/8/-/1/-/ (T J FitzGerald), J G FitzGerald

2427 Roger Johnstone And Partners Handicap Stakes Class E (0-70 3-y-o and up) £2,427 1½m................ (8:30)

1840[4] SHUJAN (USA) [65] 4-10-0 L Dettori (7) *led aftr 2 fs, sn clr, rdn frm two out, styd on gmely ins last.* ....(13 to 8 fav op 9 to 4) 1
1676* PHARLY DANCER [61] 4-9-10 Dean McKeown (5) *prmnt, chsd wnr aftr 4 fs, rdn 3 out, kpt on.* ....(11 to 4 tchd 3 to 1) 2
2195[2] SUGEMAR [58] 7-9-2 (5*) D McCabe (8) *chsd ldrs, rdn 4 fs out, kpt on one pace*... (6 to 1 op 5 to 1 tchd 13 to 2) 3
2108[6] IZITALLWORTHIT [31] 4-7-8[4] (3*) N Kennedy (9) *in tch, hdwy 5 fs out, rdn 3 out, sn one pace.* .... (25 to 1 op 12 to 1) 4
1840[7] ATLANTIC WAY [54] 5-9-3 J Quinn (6) *mid-div, hdwy 5 fs out, sn rdn, wknd 3 out*........ (4 to 1 op 3 to 1) 5
2166[3] QUALITAIR SOUND (Ire) [52] 5-9-1 K Fallon (2) *hld up, hdwy hfwy, rdn 4 fs out, sn btn*........(9 to 1 op 8 to 1) 6
1600[5] GAILY DANCE [31] 5-7-8[1] N Carlisle (1) *chsd ldrs, rdn hfwy, sn wknd, tld off*........ (33 to 1 op 25 to 1) 7
1438[9] REAPERS REWARD [31] 5-7-8[6] (5*) A Garth (3) *slwly away, al beh, tld off fnl 5 fs*........(50 to 1 op 33 to 1) 8
MY GIRL FRIDAY [31] 4-7-8[1] J Fanning (4) *led 2 fs, rdn and wknd quickly aftr 4 furlongs, sn tld off.* .... (10 to 1 op 33 to 1) 9

Dist: 1½l, 6l, 2l, 15l, 7l, dist, 20l. 2m 40.90s. a 7.00s (9 Ran).
SR: 56/49/34/3/-/-/ (M J Polglase), R W Armstrong

2428 Chinese Handicap Class E (0-70 4-y-o and up) £2,259 6f.............. (9:00)

1938[2] SAKHAROV [43] 4-8-1 P Robinson (1) *trkd ldrs, hdwy 2 fs out, led appr last, sn rdn, styd on.* ....(Evens fav op 11 to 10 tchd 5 to 4) 1
1394[8] CHOIR PRACTICE [62] (bl,e/s) 6-9-6 C Rutter (5) *slwly into strd and beh, hdwy on ins 2 fs out, rdn to chal inside last, no extr*........(8 to 1 op 6 to 1) 2
1502[3] LORD NASKRA (USA) [51] (bl) 4-8-6 (3*) Emma O'Gorman (7) *hld up, hdwy on outsd o'r 2 fs out, sn rdn, kpt on ins last*........ (6 to 1 tchd 7 to 1) 3
2215[3] FAMILY ROSE [38] 4-7-10 J Lowe (6) *chsd ldrs, rdn o'r 2 fs out, sn wknd*........(4 to 1 op 6 to 1 tchd 7 to 1) 4
2191[2] AFRICAN CHIMES [70] 6-10-0 S Webster (3) *beh and rdn alng, effrt o'r 2 fs out, no hdwy*......(7 to 1 op 5 to 1) 5
2309[6] SAVAHRA SOUND [70] (v) 8-9-9 (5*) O Pears (4) *cl up, effrt to ld o'r 2 fs out, sn rdn, hdd and wknd over one out.* ....(10 to 1 op 6 to 1) 6
2197 GRUBBY [36] 4-7-8[6] (5*) A Garth (2) *led, rdn 3 fs out, hdd and wknd o'r 2 out*........(25 to 1 op 20 to 1) 7

Dist: 1½l, 1½l, 4l, 3l, 3½l, 3½l. 1m 17.90s. a 4.50s (7 Ran).
SR: 9/22/5/-/ (J R Good), M A Jarvis

YORK (good to firm)
Saturday July 10th

Going Correction: MINUS 0.05 sec. per fur. (races 1,6,7), MINUS 0.25 (2,3,4,5)

2429 Jervaulx Median Auction Maiden Stakes Class E (2-y-o) £4,142 6f (2:00)

2114[2] MAZENTRE FORWARD (Ire) 9-0 L Dettori (8) *made all, shaken up o'r one furlong out, pushed clr ins last, easily*........(11 to 4 fav op 2 to 1) 1
1998[4] SAINT AUBURN 9-0 T Lucas (5) *al frnt rnk, edgd lft and outpcd 2 fs out, rallied and ev ch appr last, no extr.* ....(7 to 1) 2
1985[2] BARBAROJA 9-0 M Birch (11) *chsd ldrs on ins, shaken up o'r 2 fs out, outpcd over one out, kpt on inside last, nvr nrr*........(7 to 2 op 4 to 1 tchd 9 to 2) 3
BOLD TIMING 8-9 G Duffield (9) *slwly into strd, beh, shaken up hfwy, not clr run o'r 2 fs out, improved and swtchd over one out, kpt on ins last.* (8 to 1 op 6 to 1) 4
JUDGE DREAD 9-0 R Cochrane (7) *nvr far away, rdn and ev ch wl o'r one furlong out, wknd*...(8 to 1 op 6 to 1) 5
1897[6] BALLARD RING (Ire) 8-9 L Charnock (10) *pressed ldg grp, pushed alng aftr 2 fs, swtchd outsd two out, kpt on, no imprsn*........(33 to 1 op 20 to 1) 6
1846[8] CHANTRY BEATH 9-0 N Carlisle (6) *chsd ldrs, bustled alng o'r 2 fs out, fdd*........(33 to 1 op 25 to 1) 7
SEMINOLE WIND 9-0 W Ryan (13) *missed break, beh, shaken up to improve o'r 2 fs out, not clr run and swtchd over one out, nrst finish, improve.* ....(25 to 1 op 20 to 1) 8
1598[8] MOLLINSBURN (Ire) 8-7 (7*) N Varley (2) *dwlt, sn in tch on outsd, pushed alng hfwy, wknd*...(50 to 1 op 25 to 1) 9
1759[6] TYPOGRAPHER (Ire) 9-0 J Fanning (12) *beh, drvn alng o'r 2 fs out, nvr able to chal*........ (33 to 1 op 25 to 1) 10
1401[8] SALVOR (Ire) 9-0 Dale Gibson (1) *ressed ldrs, rdn alng 3 fs out, wknd*........ (25 to 1 op 20 to 1) 11
SHARONE 8-9 N Connorton (3) *pressed ldg bunch, ran green, fdd hfwy*........ (10 to 1) 12
STAR PERFORMER (Ire) 9-0 K Darley (4) *beh and sn pushed alng, nvr on terms*..... (13 to 2 op 4 to 1 tchd 7 to 1) 13

Dist: 3l, 2l, ¾l, 1½l, 3½l, 1½l, hd, 1½l, 3½l, 3l. 1m 14.18s. a 4.18s (13 Ran).
SR: 10/-/-/-/-/-/ (The Winning Team), R Hannon

2430 Friargate Conditions Stakes Class C (2-y-o) £4,517 6f 214yds.........(2:35)

1905* BLUEGRASS PRINCE (Ire) 8-12 L Dettori (6) *chsd ldrs gng wl, shaken up to ld o'r one furlong out, hng lft, hdd briefly ins last, ran on well nr finish.* ....(11 to 4 op 3 to 1 tchd 7 to 2 and 5 to 2) 1
1277* CLASSIC SKY (Ire) 8-10 W Ryan (7) *hld up, hdwy o'r 2 fs out, rdn to ld briefly ins last, no extr cl hme.* ....(8 to 1 tchd 9 to 1) 2
1790[2] TIME STAR (USA) 8-10 A Munro (1) *reluctant to enter stalls, chsd ldrs on ins, drvn alng wl o'r 2 fs out, not quicken over one out*........ (2 to 1 fav op 6 to 4) 3
1975[2] BLAZE AWAY (USA) 8-10 R Cochrane (4) *dwlt, sn tracking ldrs, effrt and rdn 2 fs out, outpcd appr last.* ....(11 to 2 op 3 to 1) 4
1863* OOH AH CANTONA 8-10 A Culhane (3) *hld up, pushed alng 3 fs out, nvr able to chal*......(16 to 1 op 14 to 1) 5
2016[2] BROCTUNE GOLD 8-12 K Darley (2) *sn led, rdn o'r 2 fs out, hdd over one out, fdd*........ (8 to 1 op 7 to 1) 6
2155* THE FLYING PHANTOM 8-12 P Robinson (5) *trkd ldr, rdn alng 3 fs out, wknd 2 out.* .... (11 to 2 op 5 to 1 tchd 6 to 1) 7
2016[4] DISTINCTIVE AIR 8-10 G Duffield (8) *chsd ldrs on outsd, rdn alng entering strt, wknd 3 fs out*........(25 to 1) 8

Dist: Nk, 6l, 1½l, 5l, ½l, ¾l, 2l. 1m 23.89s. a 2.19s (8 Ran).
SR: 39/36/18/13/-/ (Bezwell Fixings Limited), R Hannon

2431 John Smith's Bitter Handicap Class C (0-90 3-y-o and up) £6,212 6f 214yds ....(3:10)

1777[8] DUNE RIVER [63] 4-8-1 G Carter (5) *made all, shaken up o'r 2 fs out, hld on gmely ins last*... (6 to 1 op 13 to 2) 1
2230[3] SOBERING THOUGHTS [63] 7-7-10 (5*) J Tate (11) *pressed ldr, rdn o'r 2 fs out, ev ch ins last, kpt on same pace nr finish*........(7 to 1 op 8 to 1) 2
2212[4] MY BEST VALENTINE [79] 3-8-9 M Birch (9) *pressed ldrs, effrt 3 fs out, improved and ev ch ins last, no extr nr finish*........(9 to 2 fav tchd 5 to 1) 3

2197* PARFAIT AMOUR [63] 4-8-1 A Munro (3) *al hndy, pushed alng o'r 2 fs out, kpt on same pace ins last.* ....(10 to 1 op 8 to 1) 4
2237[4] SOUTHERN MEMORIES (Ire) [85] 3-9-1 L Dettori (4) *trkd ldr, effrt and rdn alng o'r 2 fs out, one pace ins last.* ....(13 to 2 op 5 to 1) 5
2136[4] PRENONAMOSS [78] 5-9-2 R Cochrane (6) *in tch, effrt and drvn alng o'r 2 fs out, not quicken over one out.* ....(13 to 2 op 5 to 1) 6
1768 LITTLE ROUSILLON [65] 5-7-10 (7*) Kim McDonnell (10) *hld up on outsd, pushed alng to improve 3 fs out, no imprsn o'r one out*....................(12 to 1 op 8 to 1) 7
2062[4] SEA DEVIL [79] 7-9-3 N Connorton (2) *chsd ldrs on ins, rdn alng o'r 2 fs out, btn over one out*...(13 to 2 op 5 to 1) 8
2068[9] EURO FESTIVAL [87] 4-9-8 (3*) D Harrison (8) *hld up, rdn and not clr run o'r 2 fs out, swtchd and not pace to chal*....................(14 to 1 op 12 to 1) 9
BRAVEBOY [72] 5-8-7 (3*) B Doyle (1) *hld up on ins, drvn alng 3 fs out, nvr on terms*....................(25 to 1) 10
1869* BALIANA [73] 3-8-3 A Culhane (7) *hld up, drvn alng o'r 3 fs out, sn btn*....................(11 to 1 op 8 to 1) 11

Dist: 1l, hd, 1½l, 1½l, sht-hd, ¾l, 1½l, 6l, 4l, 2½l. 1m 23.93s. a 2.23s (11 Ran).

SR: 27/24/31/18/27/27/12/21/11/ (E R W Stanley), D R Loder

2432 Foster's Silver Cup Rated Class A Handicap (Listed Race) (0-105 3-y-o and up) £9,559 1m 7f 195yds.... (3:40)

2061[3] BRANDON PRINCE (Ire) [89] (bl) 5-8-7 L Dettori (3) *trkd ldg pair, swtchd o'r 3 fs out, led over 2 out, sn rdn, styd on wl fnl furlong*..... (2 to 1 jt-fav op 9 to 4 tchd 5 to 2) 1
2061 KAISER WILHELM [89] 4-8-7 W Ryan (2) *hld up last, improved 3 fs out, ev ch and rdn o'r one out, one pace und pres ins last*....(11 to 4 op 3 to 1 tchd 100 to 30) 2
2070[5] BOLOARDO [103] 4-9-7 B Doyle (1) *pressed ldr, led o'r 3 fs out till over 2 out, rdn and sn lost tch.* ....(6 to 1 op 4 to 1) 3
1769[6] ACANTHUS (Ire) [96] (bl) 3-7-11[1] A McGlone (4) *led, shaken up entering strt, hdd o'r 3 fs out, wknd wl over 2 out.* ....(2 to 1 jt-fav op 6 to 4) 4

Dist: 1½l, 15l, 2½l. 3m 24.18s. a 3.18s (4 Ran).

SR: 21/19/18/-/ (R P B Michaelson), I A Balding

2433 John Smith's Magnet Cup Handicap Class B (0-110 3-y-o and up) £34,141 1¼m 85yds.................... (4:15)

1958[2] BARON FERDINAND [92] 3-8-9 R Cochrane (1) *in tch, led 2 fs out, edgd rght, styd on strly ins last*.......(4 to 1 jt-fav op 3 to 1) 1
1768 KING ATHELSTAN (USA) [96] 5-9-10 L Dettori (8) *nvr far away, chlgd 2 fs out, rdn and kpt on same pace ins last.* ....(16 to 1 op 14 to 1) 2
2311[3] JAZILAH (Fr) [69] 5-7-11 J Fanning (3) *dsptd ld, led 3 fs out to 2 out, rdn and kpt on ins last*... (16 to 1 op 14 to 1) 3
2211[7] CHATHAM ISLAND [68] 5-7-7 (3*) B Doyle (7) *dsptd ld, drvn alng 3 fs out, kpt on same pace o'r one out.* ....(10 to 1 op 12 to 1) 4
1681[6] REDSTELLA (USA) [84] (v) 4-8-12 M Birch (9) *hld up last, rdn to improve o'r 3 fs out, swtchd rght 2 out, styd on finish, nvr dngrs*....................(25 to 1 op 20 to 1) 5
2236[4] SHABANAZ [75] 8-8-3 K Darley (5) *hld up, pushed alng appr strt, swtchd ins, improved o'r 2 fs out, ran on inside last*....................(10 to 1 tchd 9 to 1) 6
1866* LET'S GET LOST [70] 4-7-12 A Munro (10) *chsd ldrs, niggled alng appr strt, drvn o'r 3 fs out, not quicken fnl 2.* ....(13 to 2 op 6 to 1 tchd 7 to 1) 7
1525 GROVE DAFFODIL (Ire) [94] (v) 3-8-4 (7*) S Mulvey (4) *slwly into strd, improved into midfield aftr 4 fs, drvn alng 3 out, sn one pace*....................(25 to 1 tchd 20 to 1) 8
1845[3] HIGHBROOK (USA) [81] 5-8-9 P Robinson (13) *hld up, drvn alng entering strt, not pace to chal*..........(4 to 1 jt-fav op 9 to 2 tchd 5 to 1) 9
2020[3] WESTHOLME (USA) [69] 5-7-10[2] (3*) S Maloney (11) *hld up, hmpd and stumbled aftr 3 fs, drvn alng o'r three out, no imprsn*....................(12 to 1) 10
1450[2] ROSE ALTO [89] 5-9-3 G Duffield (12) *settled midfield, drvn alng 4 fs out, btn 3 out*............(8 to 1 tchd 10 to 1) 11
1940[7] RINGLAND (USA) [79] 5-8-2 (5*) Darren Moffatt (6) *tucked away on ins, niggled alng appr strt, effrt and drvn along 4 fs out, nvr a factor*...... (25 to 1 tchd 33 to 1) 12
1770[4] LAST EMBRACE (Ire) [83] 4-8-8 (3*) D Harrison (14) *dwlt, hld up, drvn alng entering strt, lost tch fnl 3 fs.* ....(13 to 2 op 5 to 1 tchd 7 to 1) 13

Dist: 1½l, 1½l, 1½l, 2l, nk, 2½l, ¾l, 4l, 1½l, 2½l. 2m 8.50s. a 0.50s (13 Ran).

SR: 64/76/46/42/54/44/34/45/35/ (Exors Of The Late Mrs J de Rothschild), R Charlton

2434 Webster's Green Label Best Handicap Class C (0-90 3-y-o and up) £6,264 6f ....(4:45)

1806 EVERGLADES (Ire) [85] 5-9-9 R Cochrane (5) *tucked away beh ldrs, effrt and swtchd outsd 2 fs out, ran on to ld wl ins last*..........................(4 to 1 fav op 7 to 1) 1
2276[4] MASTER POKEY [60] 9-7-12 L Charnock (10) *pressed ldrs, effrt and wnt lft o'r one furlong out, hng rght entering last, kpt on strly, fnshd second, disqualified.* ....(12 to 1 op 10 to 1) 2D
2008* HOW'S YER FATHER [79] 7-9-3 A Munro (19) *in tch on ins, effrt 2 fs out, kpt on strly last, fnshd 3rd, plcd second.* ....(10 to 1) 2
1945[2] GORINSKY (Ire) [84] 5-9-8 G Carter (3) *led, rdn 2 fs out, hdd wl ins last, no extr, fnshd 4th, plcd 3rd.* ....(7 to 1 tchd 8 to 1) 3
1806[2] CUMBRIAN WALTZER [90] 8-10-0 M Birch (15) *hld up beh, not clr run o'r one furlong out, squeezing through whn hmpd entering last, kpt on wl, fnshd 5th, plcd 4th.* ....(6 to 1 op 5 to 1) 4
2309[5] PRINCE BELFORT [61] (bl) 5-7-10[2] (5*) J Tate (14) *chsd ldrs, effrt and rdn 2 fs out, crrd rght entering last, no extr, fnshd 6th, plcd 5th*.............. (16 to 1 tchd 20 to 1) 5
2276[5] INVIGILATE [58] 4-7-10 Dale Gibson (11) *beh, sn pushed alng, improved on ins 2 fs out, kpt on wl one out, nrst finish*....................(20 to 1) 7
2173[5] EDUCATED PET [71] 4-8-9 K Darley (1) *prmnt, drvn alng o'r 2 fs out, not quicken frm one out*...........(12 to 1) 8
1953[5] ZEBOIM [69] (bl) 7-8-0 (7*) Kim McDonnell (8) *cl up, hmpd aftr one and a half fs, sn drvn alng, one pace frm 2 out.* ....(20 to 1) 9
2309 CELESTINE [62] (v) 4-8-0 J Fanning (16) *in tch on ins, pushed alng hfwy, hmpd entering fnl furlong, not reco'r*....................(33 to 1 op 25 to 1) 10
2062 RED ROSEIN [83] 7-9-7 J Fortune (18) *slwly into strd, beh, drvn to improve hfwy, wknd ins fnl furlong*...(12 to 1) 11
2060 PETITE-D-ARGENT [83] 4-9-7 P Robinson (17) *pressed ldrs, effrt o'r 2 fs out, hng lft and wknd over one out.* ....(16 to 1 op 20 to 1 tchd 14 to 1) 12
2173[6] RESOLUTE BAY [70] (v) 7-8-8 A Culhane (4) *chsd ldrs, hmpd aftr one furlong, drvn alng hfwy, wknd.* ....(20 to 1) 13
2173[7] MISS ARAGON [55] 5-7-7 N Carlisle (13) *in tch, effrt and drvn alng o'r 2 fs out, one pace whn hmpd and snatched up entering last*....................(33 to 1) 14
1806 BERTIE WOOSTER [80] 10-9-4 W Ryan (7) *beh, pushed alng hfwy, nvr rch ldrs*.......... (12 to 1 op 10 to 1) 15
1806 SAGEBRUSH ROLLER [84] 5-9-8 G Duffield (6) *sn beh, nvr plcd to chal*....................(16 to 1) 16
2264[6] PLUM FIRST [70] (bl) 3-7-12 (3*) S Maloney (9) *chsd ldrs, bumped aftr one and a half fs, sn pushed alng, wknd hfwy, eased*.................... (25 to 1) 17
2230[8] FILICAIA [55] (v) 7-7-7 Kim Tinkler (12) *dwlt, beh, pushed alng hfwy, nvr wnt pace*....................(50 to 1) 18
2062[5] CALEMAN [76] (bl) 4-9-0 L Dettori (2) *chsd ldrs, hmpd aftr one and a half fs, rdn and wknd quickly hfwy, eased fnl 2, tld off*............(17 to 2 op 8 to 1 tchd 9 to 1) 19

Dist: 1½l, sht-hd, sht-hd, 1½l, hd, 1½l, 1½l, nk, ½l, nk. 1m 11.64s. a 1.64s (19 Ran).

SR: 71/40/58/62/62/32/23/30/27/ (Miss Sophie Oppenheimer), R Charlton

2435 Fishergate Nursery Class C (2-y-o) £5,253 5f.................... (5:15)

1766 NIGHTITUDE [-] 9-5 W Ryan (1) *nvr far away, led o'r one furlong out, hld on gmely whn hrd pressed ins last.* ....(20 to 1 op 14 to 1) 1
2067[6] NERA [-] 9-3 L Dettori (3) *in tch, effrt o'r 2 fs out, chlgd ins last, ran on wl, jst fld*....................(100 to 30 jt-fav op 3 to 1 tchd 7 to 2) 2
1303[3] DANCE OF THE SWANS (Ire) [-] 8-11 Dale Gibson (4) *chsd ldrs, ev ch o'r one furlong out, not quicken ins last.* ....(5 to 1 op 9 to 2) 3
2200[2] ROYAL INSIGNIA [-] 9-4 (3*) M Fenton (2) *led till o'r one furlong out, sn btn*..................(7 to 1 op 6 to 1) 4
1837[3] CHILIOLA [-] 7-10[1] (3*) S Maloney (8) *prmnt stands side till rdn and wknd fnl 2 fs*...... (100 to 30 jt-fav op 4 to 1) 5
1168[3] JIMMY THE SKUNK (Ire) [-] 9-0 G Carter (7) *in tch, improved hfwy, sn rdn alng, outpcd o'r one furlong out*....................(5 to 1) 6
2200[5] INDIAN CRYSTAL [-] 8-5 A Munro (5) *nvr far away, rdn alng hfwy, wknd o'r one furlong out*..........(5 to 1) 7
2180[3] LUCKY FOURTEEN [-] 8-5 N Carlisle (6) *chsd ldrs, lost pl aftr 2 fs, sn btn*.........(15 to 2 op 8 to 1 tchd 7 to 1) 8

Dist: Sht-hd, 3l, 1½l, 3l, nk, 3l, 6l. 1m 0.37s. a 3.07s (8 Ran).

SR: 39/36/18/22/-/2/-/-/ (Miss Gloria Abbey), M J Heaton-Ellis

HOPPEGARTEN (GER) (soft)
Sunday July 11th

2436 Berlin Brandenburg-Trophy der Landesbank Berlin (Group 3) (3-y-o and up) £89,796 1m.................... (3:45)

1395[2] QUEBRADA (Ire) 3-8-1 P Schiergen, *3rd strt, led 2 and a half fs out, ran on wl*.................... 1
1747[6] ALHIJAZ 4-9-6 W Carson, *6th strt, rdn 2 fs out, squeezed through ins fnl furlong, fnshd second, relegated to 4th.* 2D
1747[4] SWING LOW 4-9-6 R Cochrane, *hld up, hdwy fnl 2 fs, nrst finish, fnshd 3rd, awarded second*.................... 2

953² NASR ALLAH (USA) 3-8-5 A Starke, *5th strt, second 2 fs out, wkng whn hmpd ins fnl furlong, fnshd 4th, plcd 3rd* ... 3
1084⁴ AUTOCRACY (Ire) 4-9-6 W Newnes, *4th strt, one pace fnl 2 fs* ... 5
1748⁵ ENHARMONIC (USA) 6-9-6 L Dettori, *nvr able to chal* ... 6
1882⁴ YOUNG MOON 7-9-6 J McLaughlin, *second strt, sn wknd.* 7
1084 KONIGSLOWE 4-9-6 Paul Eddery, *al rear* ... 8
LITRON (Ger) 4-9-6 L Pyritz, *led for 5 and a half fs, wknd quickly* ... 9
Dist: ¾l, ¾l, nk, 4½l, 3l, 8l, 2l, dist. 1m 39.80s. (9 Ran).
(Gestut Fahrhof), H Jentzsch

LE LION D'ANGERS (FR) (good to soft)
Sunday July 11th

2437 Prix du Fonds European de L'Elevage (Listed) (4-y-o and up) £35,842 1¼m ... (1:30)

1748² URBAN SEA (USA) 4-9-1 C Asmussen, ... 1
2083* HALF A TICK (USA) 5-9-1 T Quinn, *mid-div, not much room strt, ran on wl fnl 2 fs* ... 2
1971⁵ FUNNY BABY (Fr) 5-9-1 A Badel, ... 3
Dist: 2l, nose, 1½l, sht-hd, 2½l, 2½l, 1l, 2½l. (Time not taken) (14 Ran).
(David Tsui), J Lesbordes

TURIN (ITY) (soft)
Sunday July 11th

2438 Premio Veio (2-y-o) £6,724 7f 110yds ... (1:00)

STANCE (USA) 8-5 S Dettori, ... 1
1810* KEZIO RUFO (Ire) 8-7 G Carter, *led one furlong out till cl hme* ... 2
BOLD DEPUTY (USA) 8-7 M Planard, ... 3
Dist: ¾l, nk, ¾l, 2l, 1½l, 1 ¼l, 4l, ¾l. 1m 35.80s. (9 Ran).
(G Verricelli), G Verricelli

2439 St Leger Italiano (Group 3) (3-y-o) £40,015 1¾m 110yds ... (4:00)

PAY ME BACK (Ire) 9-2 S Dettori, *rcd in 3rd, chlgd o'r 2 fs out, led fnl 150 yards, drvn out* ... 1
1547* DI GIACOMO 9-2 G Carter, *led aftr one furlong till 150 yards out* ... 2
GIANANI 9-2 M Pasquale, *led for one furlong, second strt, chlgd 3 out, kpt on one pace* ... 3
LUCKY BOSS (Ire) 9-2 G Bietolini, *al last* ... 4
Dist: ½l, 3 ¼l, 8l. 3m 15.40s. (4 Ran).
(Scuderia Pidienne), G Verricelli

BELMONT PARK (USA) (firm)
Sunday July 11th

2440 Coaching Club American Oaks (Grade 1) (3-y-o) £99,338 1¼m ...

935* SKY BEAUTY (USA) 8-9 M Smith, ... (10 to 1 on) 1
570⁴ FUTURE PRETENSE (USA) 8-9 H McCauley, ... (14 to 1) 2
935⁴ SILKY FEATHER (USA) 8-9 R Migliore, ... (21 to 1) 3
762* DISPUTE (USA) 8-9 J D Bailey, ... (42 to 10) 4
STANDARD EQUIPMENT (USA) 8-9 C Antley, ... (14 to 1) 5
Dist: ½l, 2l, 3l, 12l. 2m 1.56s. (5 Ran).
(Georgia E Hofmann), H A Jerkens

HOLLYWOOD (USA) (firm)
Sunday July 11th

2441 Hollywood Oaks (Grade 1) (3-y-o) £86,358 1m 1f ...

HOLLYWOOD WILDCAT (USA) 8-9 E Delahoussaye, ... (17 to 1) 1
4792a⁷ FIT TO LEAD (USA) 8-9 C McCarron, ... (83 to 10) 2
ADORYDAR (USA) 8-9 G Almeida, ... (58 to 10) 3
4792a² PASSING VICE (USA) 8-9 K Desormeaux, ... (69 to 10) 4
LIKEABLE STYLE (USA) 8-9 G Stevens, ... (10 to 7 on) 5
ADDED ASSET (USA) 8-9 P Valenzuela, ... (28 to 1) 6
SWAZI'S MOMENT (USA) 8-9 C Nakatani, ... (15 to 2) 7
NORTENA (USA) 8-9 D Flores, ... (66 to 1) 8
FONDLY REMEMBERED (USA) 8-9 L Pincay Jr, ... (64 to 1) 9
Dist: 1 ¾l, 6½l, nose, ½l, 2½l, 1 ¾l, 5½l, 13l. 1m 48.40s. (9 Ran).
(I & Marjorie Cowan), N Drysdale

WOODBINE (CAN) (firm)
Sunday July 11th

2442 Queen's Plate (Grade 1) (3-y-o) £113,264 1¼m ...

PETESKI (Can) 9-0 C Perret, ... 1
CHEERY KNIGHT (Can) 9-0 D Seymour, ... 2
JANROFFOLE (Can) 9-0 M Walls, ... 3
FLASHY REGENT (Can) 9-0 S Hawley, ... 4
EXPLOSIVE RED (Can) 9-0 M Larsen, ... 5
CIRCULATING (Can) 9-0 R Dos Ramos, ... 6
REGENT RUNNER (Can) 9-0 D Clark, ... 7
CORPORATE REVENUE (Can) 9-0 D David, ... 8
BRIARTIC STAR (Can) 9-0 R Platts, ... 9
FLEETWARD (Can) 9-0 T Kabel, ... 0
IMPERIAL BANDIT (Can) 9-0 R Landry, ... 0
Dist: 6l, 1 ¼l, nose, 2l, 8l, 2½l, 3½l, 2l, 2 ¾l, nose. 2m 4.20s. (11 Ran).
(Earle I Mack), R Attfield

BEVERLEY (good to firm)
Monday July 12th

Going Correction: MINUS 0.20 sec. per fur. (races 1,2,3,5,6), NIL (4)

2443 Pocklington Selling Stakes Class G (3-y-o) £1,660 1m 3f 216yds ... (6:45)

2130⁷ HO-JOE (Ire) 8-11 Julie Bowker (5) *chsd clr ldr aftr 3 fs, drvn alng entering strt, ran on to ld o'r one furlong out, sn clear* ... (3 to 1 op 5 to 2 tchd 7 to 2) 1
1942³ SHARE A MOMENT (Can) 8-11 W Ryan (1) *hld up, shaken up 4 fs out, kpt on to go second ins fnl furlong, no ch wth wnr* ... (9 to 4 fav op 5 to 2 tchd 11 to 4) 2
1980² WALSHAM WITCH 8-8 (5*) J Tate (2) *pressed ldr, led aftr 2 fs, sn wl clr, hdd o'r one furlong out, hng rght and soon btn* ... (3 to 1 op 4 to 1) 3
1968⁶ DUKE OF BUDWORTH 8-11 P Robinson (6) *hld up in last pl, shaken up appr strt, nvr able to chal.* ... (3 to 1 op 5 to 2) 4
2104 INNOCENT ABROAD (Den) 8-6 S Perks (3) *hld up, drvn alng o'r 4 fs out, no imprsn entering strt* ... (10 to 1) 5
2205³ TOMMY TRUNGLE (v) 8-11 F Norton (4) *led 2 fs, sn lost pl, drvn 5 furlongs out, soon wknd, tld off entering strt.* ... (25 to 1 op 20 to 1) 6
Dist: 6l, 3½l, 5l, sht-hd, 20l. 2m 37.80s. a 6.80s (6 Ran).
SR: 5/-/-/ (S Ho), J M Carr

2444 I. J. Blakey Haulage Handicap Class D (0-80 3-y-o and up) £3,492 1m 1f 207yds ... (7:10)

2149⁴ SEEK THE PEARL [68] 3-9-6 P Robinson (1) *in tch, improved entering strt to ld o'r one furlong out, rdn clr ins last* ... (3 to 1 op 5 to 2) 1
2138³ DEE RAFT (USA) [66] 3-9-4 D Holland (5) *led and sn clr, hdd o'r a furlong out, kpt on same pace.* ... (15 to 8 fav op 6 to 4 tchd 2 to 1) 2
2354² SHARQUIN [42] 6-8-5 J Carroll (6) *chsd ldr, effrt and pushed alng o'r 2 fs out, not quicken appr last.* ... (5 to 1 tchd 6 to 1) 3
1637⁵ DREAMS ARE FREE (Ire) [76] 3-10-0 W Ryan (3) *nvr far away, effrt and ev ch 2 fs out, sn no extr.* ... (4 to 1 op 3 to 1) 4
2308⁸ FALCONS DAWN [47] 6-8-10 S Perks (4) *hld up, effrt and rdn o'r 2 fs out, no imprsn* ... (10 to 1 op 8 to 1) 5
2104 DOUBLE SHERRY [30] 4-7-7 J O'Reilly (2) *al beh, lost tch entering strt, tld off* ... (20 to 1) 6
Dist: 5l, ¾l, 4l, 7l, 7l. 2m 5.80s. a 4.40s (6 Ran).
SR: 42/30/15/30/-/-/ (Cheveley Park Stud), J R Fanshawe

2445 Westwood Amateur Handicap Class G (0-70 3-y-o and up) £2,574 7f 100yds ... (7:35)

2283² PRIDE OF PENDLE [53] 4-10-7 Mrs A Farrell (12) *confidently rdn in rear, gd hdwy 2 fs out, wl timed run fnl furlong to ld nr finish.* ... (5 to 2 fav op 7 to 2 tchd 9 to 4) 1
2291³ PUSEY STREET BOY [40] 6-9-3 (5*) Mrs S Bosley (8) *chsd ldr, led o'r 2 fs out, sn shaken up, hdd nr finish.* ... (11 to 1 op 7 to 1) 2
2308² PATIENCE PLEASE [53] 4-10-7 Mrs G Rees (7) *nvr far away, chlgd 2 fs out, not quicken ins last.* ... (7 to 1 op 5 to 1) 3
2057⁶ LADY DONOGHUE (USA) [51] 4-10-5 Mr M Buckley (17) *hld up, improved entering strt, styd on wl fnl furlong.* ... (7 to 1 op 6 to 1) 4
1095 LADY OF SHADOWS [42] 3-8-11 (5*) Mr T Cuff (19) *settled midfield, improved fnl 2 fs, nrst finish.* ... (33 to 1 op 25 to 1) 5
919⁴ MAY SQUARE (Ire) [37] 5-8-12 (7*) Mr C Appleby (1) *beh, ran wide strt, hdwy 2 fs out, hng rght ins last, no extr.* ... (20 to 1 op 14 to 1) 6
1207⁶ BOLD HABIT [67] 8-11-7 Mrs L Pearce (18) *hld up in rear, hdwy fnl 2 fs, kpt on wl, nrst finish.* (9 to 1 op 7 to 1) 7

2232^{4} BREEZED WELL [45] 7-9-9^{1} (5*) Mrs H Noonan (13) *mid-div, effrt 2 fs out, not quicken*......... (16 to 1 op 14 to 1) 8
2283^{7} PREMIER MAJOR (Ire) [35] 4-9-3^{8} (5*) Mrs D Kettlewell (10) *chsd ldrs, pushed alng entering strt, not clr run and swtchd 2 fs out, sn rdn and kpt on same pace.* .... (20 to 1 op 14 to 1) 9
2099* THUNDERING [36] 8-9-4 Miss Diana Jones (16) *mid-div, pushed alng o'r 2 fs out, no imprsn.* (8 to 1 op 7 to 1) 10
2127^{2} DON'T DROP BOMBS (USA) [40] (v) 4-9-8 Miss J Feilden (3) *beh, effrt and came wide strt, one pace o'r one out.* .... (14 to 1 op 10 to 1) 11
2369^{6} DEAD CALM [56] (bl) 3-10-2 Mrs J Crossley (9) *chsd ldrs, chlgd o'r 2 fs out, wknd over one furlong out.* .... (16 to 1 op 12 to 1) 12
971^{9} DIAMOND INTHE DARK (USA) [53] 5-10-2 (5*) Miss L Hide (5) *mid-div, pushed alng entering strt, sn one pace.* .... (20 to 1) 13
1898^{6} DANCE ON SIXPENCE [46] 5-9-9 (5*) Mr P Close (2) *hld up, effrt on outer entering strt, hmpd and wknd a furlong out*.............................. (14 to 1 op 10 to 1) 14
1969^{5} PAULINUS [34] 5-8-10^{1} (7*) Miss M Carson (15) *beh, rdn entering strt, sn btn*........ (33 to 1 op 25 to 1) 15
2232^{7} NOT ALL BLISS [32] 5-8-10^{1} (5*) Miss A Deniel (11) *chsd ldrs on ins, rdn alng 3 fs out, sn btn*.............. (100 to 1) 16
1866 ALMOSTAUTOMATIC (Ire) [55] 4-10-4 (5*) Miss A Purdy (14) *led til hdd o'r 2 fs out, wknd quickly*......... (33 to 1) 17
1866 WALTON MELODY [32] 6-8-7 (7*) Miss T Ager (4) *slwly into strd, al struggling in rear*.................... (100 to 1) 18
AMY'S STAR [33] 7-9-1^{8} (7*) Mr M Haigh (6) *chsd ldrs, pushed alng appr strt, sn lost tch*........... (100 to 1) 19
Dist: ½l, ¾l, 1½l, 3l, ½l, ½l, hd, ½l, ½l, 2½l. 1m 34.40s. a 4.10s (19 Ran).
SR: 37/22/33/26/-/1/29/6/-/ (W B Imison), P Calver

2446 East Yorkshire Glazing Claiming Stakes Class F (2-y-o) £2,777 5f (8:05)

2119^{2} MY LIFETIME LADY (Ire) 8-5^{1} S Perks (6) *made all, rdn 2 fs out, veered badly lft ins fnl furlong, kpt on wl.* .... (7 to 4 fav tchd 13 to 8) 1
2128* LADY SHERIFF 8-9 T Lucas (2) *beh and sn outpcd, hdwy and swtchd o'r one furlong out, kpt on ins last.* .... (7 to 2 tchd 4 to 1) 2
2203^{6} DOCKYARD DORA 8-2 P Robinson (8) *nvr far away, drvn alng 2 fs out, not quicken ins last*.. (6 to 1 op 11 to 2) 3
2199^{8} MERISSA 8-0 K Darley (3) *hmpd strt, sn outpcd in rear, gd hdwy o'r one furlong out, edgd rght and no extr entering last*.......................................(20 to 1) 4
2102* FLOATING TRIAL 8-5 J Carroll (1) *wth ldr, ev ch and rdn 2 fs out, edgd lft and sn btn*.......... (3 to 1 op 5 to 2) 5
1889^{4} BRAMCOTE CENTURY 7-12 F Norton (7) *in tch, pushed alng to improve hfwy, one pace whn hmpd and snatched up entering last furlong.* (16 to 1 op 12 to 1) 6
2042 CLASSIC MISS (Ire) 7-11^{1} (3*) B Doyle (4) *unruly strt, al struggling in rear*.............................(33 to 1) 7
2128 NORBECK (Ire) 8-3 S Morris (5) *chsd ldrs, pushed alng hfwy, wknd o'r one furlong out*... (33 to 1 op 25 to 1) 8
Dist: 2l, hd, 4l, 1l, hd, 5l, 1½l. 1m 4.90s. a 3.20s (8 Ran).
SR: 27/23/15/-/-/ (Lifetime U K Ltd), R Hollinshead

2447 Birthright Stakes Maidens Class D (2-y-o) £2,880 7f 100yds........... (8:35)

HIGHLAND LEGEND (USA) 8-9 W Ryan (2) *hld up in cl tch, took closer order entering strt, led o'r one furlong out, quickened clr ins last.* ....(11 to 8 on op 6 to 4 on tchd 7 to 4 on) 1
KIYAS 9-0 R Hills (5) *trkd ldg pair, not clr run o'r 2 fs out, quickened betw horses to chal appr last, edgd lft, one pace*.. .... (6 to 4 op 5 to 4 tchd 7 to 4) 2
1998^{8} DOUBLE DANCER 9-0 M Birch (4) *led, rdn alng entering strt, hdd o'r one furlong out, no extr.* .... (12 to 1 op 8 to 1) 3
395^{9} LADY SWIFT 8-4 (5*) A Garth (3) *trkd ldr, chlgd hfwy, rdn and wknd o'r one furlong out, eased ins last.* .... (25 to 1 op 20 to 1) 4
Dist: 2½l, 3l, 6l. 1m 38.20s. a 7.90s (4 Ran).
(Angus Dundee Ltd), H R A Cecil

2448 Hull Maiden Handicap Class E (0-70 3-y-o) £2,511 1m 3f 216yds...... (9:05)

2162^{7} JOLIS ABSENT [39] 7-7 G Bardwell (3) *chsd ldrs, rdn 5 fs out, outpcd 3 furlongs out, improved o'r one out, str run ins last to ld towards finish*..... (9 to 2 op 3 to 1) 1
2148^{2} ARMENIAN COFFEE (Ire) [67] (bl) 9-7 W Ryan (2) *sn led, hdd and rdn o'r one furlong out, rallied to rgn ld ins last, headed towards finish.* .... (6 to 4 fav op 13 to 8 tchd 7 to 4 and 11 to 8) 2
2266^{2} APACHE SQUAW [60] 9-0 N Connorton (4) *early ldr, styd hndy, chlgd entering strt, led o'r one furlong out, hdd ins last, one pace*....................... (9 to 2 op 3 to 1) 3
2341^{6} MR ABBOT [40] 7-3 (5*) Darren Moffatt (6) *keen hold, rstrained in rear, pushed alng to improve o'r 3 fs out, kpt on same pace fnl 2 furlongs.* .... (8 to 1 op 7 to 1 tchd 10 to 1) 4

2107^{4} AMIARGE [54] 8-8 P Robinson (5) *hld up in rear, effrt and rdn entering strt, sn btn.* .... (13 to 2 op 6 to 1 tchd 7 to 1) 5
2107 KARIB [56] (bl) 8-10 K Darley (1) *chsd ldrs, rdn o'r 3 fs out, sn btn, tld off*.................(14 to 1 op 12 to 1) 6
Dist: 1l, 2½l, 4l, 12l, 15l. 2m 37.00s. a 6.00s (6 Ran).
SR: -/21/9/ (Peter Hart), M J Ryan

DUNDALK (IRE) (firm)
Monday July 12th

2449 Drumcar Maiden (3-y-o) £2,245 1½m ....(6:00)

2249^{3} PLATINUM EMPIRE (USA) 9-0 P V Gilson (3) (11 to 10 fav) 1
2036^{3} KADASSA (Ire) 8-11 J P Murtagh (1).............. (5 to 4) 2
GLENGARRY BONNET (Ire) 8-11 N Byrne (2)..... (14 to 1) 3
2036^{5} BAHNASA (Ire) 8-11 D Hogan (4)............... (10 to 1) 4
2287^{9} RED MICKS WIFE (Ire) 8-11 W J Supple (6)....... (10 to 1) 5
1107^{7} BIT OF A THING (Ire) 8-10 (4*) W J Smith (5)...... (20 to 1) 6
Dist: 6l, 7l, 1l, 13l. 2m 35.80s. (6 Ran).
(Mrs M V O'Brien), Charles O'Brien

2450 Omeath Claiming Race (2-y-o) £2,245 7f 166yds.....................(6:30)

2093^{6} SPEEDWELL BLUE (USA) (bl) 7-7^{1} (4*) W J Smith (8) (8 to 1) 1
2244^{5} MON PANACHE (Ire) 8-6 P Shanahan (2).......... (4 to 1) 2
2093^{2} ALSTOMERIA 8-10 P V Gilson (5)............(11 to 8 fav) 3
2319 SUAVE REDSKIN (Ire) 8-13 W J Supple (6).........(6 to 1) 4
2093^{4} WINTER'S OVER 8-0 (2*) D J O'Shea (1)...........(7 to 1) 5
2093^{7} JENZSOPH (Ire) 7-12 A J Nolan (7)............... (25 to 1) 6
1994^{9} FINAL OPERA (Ire) 7-10 Joanna Morgan (4).......(25 to 1) 7
1387^{3} CAN BUT DREAM (Ire) 8-4 (2*) R M Burke (3)..... (10 to 1) 8
Dist: Nk, 4l, hd, 2½l. 1m 39.80s. (8 Ran).
(M Benacerraf), D K Weld

2451 Mullaharlin Handicap (0-75 3-y-o and up) £2,245 7f 166yds............(7:00)

2345^{4} TINCO PALENO [-] 9-8-5 (2*) R M Burke (14)......(11 to 2) 1
2285^{2} MISS CARMELLA (Ire) [-] 3-8-10 W J Supple (7) (2 to 1 fav) 2
2321 RUPERT THE GREAT (Ire) [-] 3-8-11 (4*) P Carberry (11) ....(20 to 1) 3
2143 MUNSIF (Fr) [-] 6-8-13 P V Gilson (12)............(14 to 1) 4
PRINCIPLE MUSIC (USA) [-] 5-10-0 P Shanahan (5) (10 to 1) 5
1651^{5} ARDLEA HOUSE (Ire) [-] 4-7-8 Joanna Morgan (9).. (7 to 1) 6
1620^{5} CAMEY'S CHOICE (Ire) [-] 3-7-7 (4*) W J Smith (3) (16 to 1) 7
1995 ABEREDW (Ire) [-] 3-8-4 (2*) D G O'Shea (8)........(8 to 1) 8
SKELLIG [-] 7-9-6 D Hogan (13)...................(10 to 1) 9
2141^{6} FAIRYDEL (Ire) [-] 3-8-7 (8*) P J Smullen (1)........ (6 to 1) 10
2248 BENE MERENTI (Ire) [-] (bl) 3-9-3 J P Murtagh (2)..(16 to 1) 11
1574 MISS TWIN PEAKS (Ire) [-] 3-8-7 (10*) T Hagger (4) (10 to 1) 12
2248 EVOCATIVE (Ire) [-] 4-8-13 D V Smith (6)..........(25 to 1) 13
2322 PICK'N HILL (Ire) [-] 5-7-0^{1} (8*) B J Halligan (10)... (33 to 1) 14
Dist: 1l, 2½l, ½l, 4l. 1m 37.00s. (14 Ran).
(Mrs Julia Harley), J C Harley

2452 Collon Race (3-y-o and up) £2,245 1m 1f............................ (7:30)

1853^{3} RELENTLESS BOY (Ire) 3-8-13 (4*) P Carberry (3).. (6 to 4) 1
2322^{5} WHAT MAGIC (Ire) 3-8-3 (4*) W J Smith (7).........(7 to 1) 2
2247^{8} GLOWING VALUE (Ire) (bl) 3-8-10 J P Murtagh (8) ....(11 to 8 fav) 3
2247 GOODIES TWO STEP (Ire) 3-9-3 W J Supple (6)....(7 to 1) 4
PAKED (Ire) 3-8-7 D V Smith (4)................. (40 to 1) 5
1164^{8} CAROLINA RUA (USA) 3-7-13 (8*) G Coogan (1)...(25 to 1) 6
SKEAF (Ire) 3-8-10 B Coogan (2)................. (10 to 1) 7
Dist: ½l, 2l, 10l, 9l. 1m 59.80s. (7 Ran).
(Mrs Sarah Hughes), Edward Lynam

EDINBURGH (good to firm)
Monday July 12th
Going Correction: MINUS 0.20 sec. per fur.

2453 EBF Prestonpans Median Auction Maiden Stakes Class E (2-y-o) £2,932 7f 15yds.......................(2:15)

2167^{2} PRIZEFIGHTER 9-0 K Darley (3) *settled gng wl, led o'r 2 fs out, ran green and edgd lft, drvn out.* .... (11 to 8 on op 5 to 4 tchd 6 to 4) 1
2155^{2} BUMAAN (Ire) 9-0 R Hills (4) *patiently rdn, pld outsd to chal last 2 fs, crowded, ran on wl*.... (9 to 4 op 6 to 4) 2
2229^{6} WINGS AHEAD 9-0 N Connorton (2) *nvr far away, effrt und pres o'r 2 fs out, one pace fnl furlong.* .... (66 to 1 op 50 to 1) 3
1897^{7} BEDAZZLE 9-0 G Duffield (1) *led till o'r 2 fs out, fdd appr last*........................(33 to 1 op 20 to 1) 4
2129 JACKSON HOUSE 9-0 K Fallon (5) *wtd wth, swtchd outsd 3 fs out, hng lft, sn rdn and btn.* .... (4 to 1 op 3 to 1 tchd 11 to 4) 5
Dist: ½l, 6l, 2½l, 8l. 1m 30.40s. a 5.20s (5 Ran).
SR: 1/-/ (P D Savill), T D Barron

2454 Dunbar Claiming Stakes Class F (3-y-o and up) £2,549 7f 15yds..... (2:45)

2160² ACROSS THE BAY (v) 6-9-0 G Duffield (5) *steadied aftr one and a half fs, drvn through on ins appr last, ran on to ld last 50 yards*.........(2 to 1 op 7 to 4 tchd 9 to 4) 1
1631⁷ ROSE GEM (Ire) 4-9-1 K Fallon (7) *made most, clr entering strt, jnd 2 fs out, hdd and one pace last 50 yards*. ....(11 to 1 op 7 to 1) 2
2338* KINGSTON BROWN (v) 3-8-13 (3*) J Weaver (4) *chsd ldr, drvn up to draw level 2 fs out, wndrd, sn rdn and no extr*..........(11 to 10 fav op 5 to 4 tchd 11 to 8) 3
2154² PLEASE SAY YES (Ire) 3-8-1 (7*) G Forster (6) *pld hrd to hfwy, effrt on outsd 2 fs out, kpt on*. (5 to 1 op 4 to 1) 4
1981⁸ SUSANNA'S SECRET 6-9-1 (5*) O Pears (1) *nvr far away, effrt und pres 2 fs out, ran on same pace*. ....(33 to 1 op 12 to 1) 5
2338³ BRIGHT GEM 3-8-3 J Fanning (3) *trkd ldg 4, swtchd ins o'r one furlong out, ran on*.......... (33 to 1 op 12 to 1) 6
1893² SAINTED SUE 3-7-13 J Quinn (2) *chsd ldrs, feeling pace o'r 3 fs out, sn lost tch*............(33 to 1 op 20 to 1) 7

Dist: 1½l, 1½l, sht-hd, nk, hd, 20l. 1m 28.60s. a 3.40s (7 Ran).

SR: 28/24/20/11/22/4/-/ (J A Redmond), S Dow

2455 Newbattle Selling Handicap Class G (0-60 3-y-o and up) £2,274 1m 7f 16yds ....(3:15)

2235³ DANCING DAYS [31] (v) 7-8-7 Dean McKeown (5) *settled in tch, improved und pres o'r 2 fs out, ran on gmely to ld cl hme*................(3 to 1 fav tchd 5 to 2 and 7 to 2) 1
2162³ REEL OF TULLOCH (Ire) [42] 4-9-4 K Darley (3) *patiently rdn, improved to ld o'r 2 fs out, drvn alng fnl furlong, jst ct*............................(4 to 1 tchd 9 to 2) 2
1676⁵ ANAR (Ire) [37] (v) 4-8-8 (5*) O Pears (4) *ran in snatches, swtchd outsd and rallied last 2 fs, ran on*. ....(9 to 2 op 4 to 1) 3
2232⁵ A GENTLEMAN TWO [36] 7-8-12 J Fortune (2) *settled off the pace, improved und pres to chal appr fnl furlong, kpt on same pace*................(33 to 1 op 12 to 1) 4
2265³ ALPHA HELIX [26] (v) 10-8-2 J Fanning (6) *chsd clr ldr aftr 2 fs, led o'r 3 out till over two out, one pace*. ....(5 to 1 tchd 11 to 2) 5
1894⁸ BLACKDOWN [52] 6-10-0 K Fallon (1) *wtd wth, swtchd outsd to improve o'r 2 fs out, rdn and no extr appr last*. ....(16 to 1 op 10 to 1) 6
1600⁷ BE THE BEST [35] 5-8-11 L Charnock (8) *chsd ldrs, struggling entering strt, tld off*......... (14 to 1 op 6 to 1) 7
2265* LORD ADVOCATE [46] (v) 5-9-5 (3*,5ex) N Kennedy (7) *led 2 fs, hndy till outpcd o'r two out, sn btn*. ....(7 to 1 op 5 to 1) 8
BELFORT PRINCE [33] 6-8-6 (3*) J Weaver (9) *dashed up to ld aftr 2 fs, clr till wknd and hdd o'r two out, tld off*. ....(25 to 1 op 33 to 1 tchd 50 to 1) 9

Dist: Hd, nk, 1l, 2½l, 8l, 15l, 2l, dist. 3m 20.50s. a 8.50s (9 Ran).

(R Flegg), J Parkes

2456 Le Garcon d'Or Handicap Class E (0-70 3-y-o and up) £2,787 5f.... (3:45)

2241⁹ ABSOLUTION [58] 9-8-13 (3*) J Weaver (3) *sn beh, swtchd outsd and hdwy hfwy, led o'r one furlong out, ran on wl*................................(7 to 1 tchd 8 to 1) 1
2365* TREVORSNINEPOINTS [62] (v) 3-9-0 (7ex) K Darley (4) *chsd alng to improve into midfield hfwy, effrt und pres o'r one furlong out, ran on*............ (4 to 1 op 3 to 1) 2
2392⁴ EWALD (Ire) [70] 5-10-0 Dean McKeown (7) *made most, hdd and drvn alng o'r one furlong out, kpt on same pace*. ....(6 to 5 fav op 11 to 8) 3
1589⁸ BRISAS [35] (v) 6-7-7 J Fanning (8) *pressed ldg pair, hrd drvn o'r one furlong out, not quicken*. .... (25 to 1 op 16 to 1) 4
2215⁶ LANGTONIAN [52] (bl) 4-8-10 Alex Greaves (6) *chsd alng to go early pace, improved 2 fs out, kpt on und pres*. .... (9 to 1 op 7 to 1 tchd 10 to 1) 5
2264⁴ PRINCIPAL PLAYER (USA) [58] 3-8-5 (5*) O Pears (5) *sluggish strt, rdn alng thrght, kpt on ins fnl furlong*. ....(9 to 1 op 7 to 1) 6
2264⁹ BRAVE MELODY [36] 7-7-8¹ L Charnock (1) *nvr far away, ev ch on outsd hfwy, rdn and btn appr fnl furlong*. .... (50 to 1 op 20 to 1) 7
1782 LE CHIC [47] 7-8-5 K Fallon (2) *speed till fdd und pres o'r one furlong out*................(15 to 2 tchd 8 to 1) 8

Dist: 2½l, hd, 1½l, ¾l, ½l, 1½l, 6l. 59.90s. a 2.10s (8 Ran).

SR: 40/28/41/-/14/12/-/-/ (M F Hyman), M P Naughton

2457 George Boyd Fillies Handicap Class E (0-70 3-y-o and up) £2,871 1½m 31yds ....(4:15)

1779³ SALU [48] 4-8-10 G Duffield (3) *patiently rdn, hdwy entering strt, led wl o'r one furlong out, sn clr*. .... (11 to 4 op 3 to 1 tchd 7 to 2) 1
2239⁹ WILSONIC [65] (v) 4-9-13 Dean McKeown (5) *trkd ldr, reminder aftr one furlong, led o'r 2 out, hng rght and hdd wl over one out, sn btn*. .... (5 to 2 op 9 to 4 tchd 11 to 4) 2
2195⁴ HEAVY ROCK (Ire) [32] 4-7-8⁵ (5*) L Newton (4) *led till o'r 2 fs out, hmpd and swtchd wl over one out, one pace*. .... (11 to 2 op 3 to 1 tchd 6 to 1) 3
2266⁴ SUSPECT [55] 3-8-1 (3*) N Kennedy (1) *trkd ldg pair, drvn alng whn pace quickened o'r 3 fs out, sn btn*. ....(25 to 1 op 14 to 1) 4
2266³ KISS IN THE DARK [53] 3-8-2 K Darley (2) *nvr far away, drvn alng to hold pl entering strt, rdn and btn 3 fs out*. ....(9 to 4 fav op 2 to 1) 5

Dist: 8l, 6l, 7l, 3½l. 2m 37.90s. a 5.10s (5 Ran).

SR: 21/22/ (W N Lumley), J Etherington

2458 Bridge Of Steel Limited Stakes Class E (0-70 3-y-o and up) £2,821 1m 3f 32yds........................ (4:45)

2189* RAHIL (Ire) 3-8-12 R Hills (1) *made all, quickened clr o'r 2 fs out, rdn and swshd tail over one out, jst hld on*. ....(9 to 4 op 2 to 1) 1
2367* AZUREUS (Ire) 5-9-10 K Darley (5) *wtd wth, hrd drvn to improve o'r 2 fs out, str run ins last, jst fld*. ....(6 to 4 fav op 5 to 4 tchd 7 to 4) 2
2087⁵ CORNFLAKE 3-8-7 K Fallon (4) *trkd ldg pair, hrd drvn whn pace quickened o'r 2 fs out, one pace*. .... (50 to 1 op 25 to 1) 3
1613² MOIDART 3-8-7 G Duffield (2) *trkd wnr, feeling pace and hrd drvn o'r 2 fs out, sn btn*. .... (2 to 1 tchd 9 to 4 and 7 to 4) 4
1894³ RAPID MOVER 6-9-10 S McCann (3) *trkd ldrs, lot grnd whn pace quickened o'r 2 fs out, tld off*....... (66 to 1) 5

Dist: Nk, 10l, 1½l, 12l. 2m 24.20s. a 4.70s (5 Ran).

SR: 29/40/3/-/-/ (Hamdan Al-Maktoum), H Thomson Jones

2459 Mill Hill Handicap Class E (0-70 3-y-o and up) £2,857 1m 16yds....... (5:15)

2057³ BALLYRANTER [46] (v) 4-8-10 J Quinn (3) *al hndy, drvn ahead o'r 2 fs out, styd on strly*. .... (11 to 2 op 5 to 1 tchd 6 to 1) 1
2086* IMPERIAL BID (Fr) [64] 5-10-0 K Fallon (12) *patiently rdn, hdwy to chal last 2 fs, kpt on und pres cl hme*. .... (6 to 1 op 5 to 1 tchd 13 to 2) 2
2269² ROUTING [47] 5-8-4 (7*) J Marshall (5) *missed break, chsd alng to improve o'r 2 fs out, styd on und pres fnl furlong*................ (11 to 2 op 5 to 1 tchd 6 to 1) 3
2269* CRESELLY [58] 6-9-5 (3*,5ex) J Weaver (7) *led till o'r 2 fs out, rdn and kpt on same pace*... (4 to 1 fav op 7 to 2) 4
2197² MALCESINE (Ire) [45] 4-8-9 J Fortune (10) *nvr far away, swtchd outsd and hrd drvn o'r 2 fs out, not quicken*. .... (8 to 1 op 7 to 1 tchd 10 to 1) 5
2308⁹ BIDWEAYA (USA) [32] 6-7-4¹ (7*) C Teague (9) *sluggish strt, hdwy frm off the pace last 2 fs, ran on*. .... (20 to 1 op 16 to 1) 6
2289⁴ DANCING BEAU (Ire) [52] 4-9-2 G Duffield (8) *chsd ldrs, drvn alng o'r 2 fs out, no imprsn*. ....(5 to 1 op 9 to 2 tchd 6 to 1) 7
GRINNELL [56] 3-8-11 J Fanning (4) *beh and pushed alng hfwy, nvr nr to chal*................(14 to 1 tchd 16 to 1) 8
2086⁷ THISONESFORALICE [41] 5-7-12 (7*) S Mulvey (2) *drvn alng to go pace hfwy, nvr a factor*. (16 to 1 op 12 to 1) 9
2269⁵ MISS HOSTESS [37] (bl) 6-8-1⁸ S McCann (1) *pressed ldrs, effrt und pres 3 fs out, fdd*.........(50 to 1 op 33 to 1) 10
1421 HIZEEM [30] (v) 7-7-8¹ L Charnock (11) *beh and pushed alng hfwy, nvr a threat*.......... (50 to 1 op 33 to 1) 11

Dist: Nk, 2l, hd, 3l, ½l, sht-hd, ¾l, 2½l, sht-hd, 12l. 1m 41.50s. a 3.00s (11 Ran).

SR: 27/44/21/31/9/-/13/6/-/ (P J Byrnes), H J Collingridge

KILLARNEY (IRE) (good to yielding) Monday July 12th

2460 Cahernane/White Gates Hotel Maiden (3-y-o) £3,452 1½m............. (6:00)

2249² KHALYANI (Ire) 9-0 M J Kinane (4)..............(5 to 2 on) 1
1963³ PLUM LICK (Ire) 8-11 K J Manning (2).................(7 to 2) 2
NORDIC THORN (Ire) 8-8 (6*) J A Heffernan (1).....(10 to 1) 3
2287⁸ TURNER PRIZE (Ire) 9-0 S Craine (3)...............(10 to 1) 4
2287 ARCH-T-GLEN (Ire) 8-6 (8*) D M McCullagh (6).... (33 to 1) 5
2185⁵ RED GLITTER (USA) 9-0 C Roche (5)............ (11 to 1) 6

Dist: Nk, 5½l, 1½l, 15l. 2m 46.20s. (6 Ran).

(H H Aga Khan), John M Oxx

2461 Heineken Handicap (0-90 4-y-o and up) £6,902 1½m................ (6:30)

2039 NATIVE PORTRAIT [-] 6-7-2 (6*) P P Murphy (7).... (8 to 1) 1
2245⁵ DOMINO'S RING (Ire) [-] (bl) 4-9-5 R Hughes (6)....(20 to 1) 2
1511⁷ EBONY AND IVORY (Ire) [-] 4-9-8 (6*) B J Walsh (1) (10 to 1) 3
2186* LYPHARD ABU (Ire) [-] 5-8-12 (5ex) C Roche (8)..... (3 to 1) 4
2245* NASSAU [-] 6-9-10 (4ex) M J Kinane (9)....... (2 to 1 fav) 5

2286[4] COMMAND 'N CONTROL [-] 4-7-10 (6*) J J Behan (4) ....(12 to 1) 6
2296* ANGAREB (Ire) [-] 4-8-3 (6ex) J F Egan (10) .... (6 to 1) 7
1468 ALL YOURS (Ire) [-] 4-7-13[1] (6*) J A Heffernan (5) .. (25 to 1) 8
2296[2] WESBEST (Ire) [-] 4-8-3 N G McCullagh (11) .... (7 to 1) 9
FARAGHAN (Ire) [-] 4-9-5 (6*) C Everard (2) .... (20 to 1) 10
NEXT TYCOON (Ire) [-] 5-9-12 K J Manning (3) .... (12 to 1) 11
Dist: 1l, 2l, sht-hd, hd. 2m 46.60s. (11 Ran).
(M J Corbett), M J Corbett

2462 Kerry E.B.F. Maiden (2-y-o) £3,797 1m 100yds........................ (7:00)

2284[2] PAUGIM (Ire) (bl) 9-0 M J Kinane (3).......... (13 to 8 on) 1
MISS NUTWOOD (Ire) 8-11 N G McCullagh (1) .... (20 to 1) 2
1854[3] LUDDEN LADY (Ire) 8-5 (6*) J J Behan (9) ....(9 to 2) 3
1854[7] BACK FROM HEAVEN (Ire) 8-11 C Roche (5) ....(8 to 1) 4
2319 MUSICAL BANKER 9-0 S Craine (2) .... (8 to 1) 5
MAIN REFRAIN (Ire) 9-0 J F Egan (4) .... (7 to 1) 6
2284 ARTFULNESS (Ire) 8-8 (6*) B J Walsh (8) .... (14 to 1) 7
1643[4] OVER THE MAIGUE (Ire) 8-3 (8*) B Fenton (7) ..... (20 to 1) 8
2093[8] HAVE A CUT (Ire) 8-11 R Hughes (6) .... (20 to 1) 9
Dist: ½l, 2½l, 1½l, 9l. 1m 52.80s. (9 Ran).
(T J Monaghan), D K Weld

2463 Munster Joinery/East Avenue Handicap (0-80 3-y-o and up) £3,797 1m 100yds........................ (7:30)

2247[7] THATCHING CRAFT (Ire) [-] 4-9-6 (6*) J J Behan (2) (9 to 2) 1
2141[2] RIENROE (Ire) [-] 4-9-0 M J Kinane (9) ....(11 to 8 fav) 2
1794[7] FLORAL STREET [-] 4-9-5 R Hughes (3) .... (12 to 1) 3
2142[9] PHARELLA [-] 5-8-6 (6*) P P Murphy (5) .... (10 to 1) 4
1443* OVERCAST (Ire) [-] 3-9-0 C Roche (8) .... (13 to 2) 5
SONG OF THE WOODS [-] 4-9-4 (8*) R T Fitzpatrick (1) ....(33 to 1) 6
1794[5] RAIN RITE (Ire) [-] 4-8-12 (8*) B Fenton (7) .... (8 to 1) 7
2142* TRILLICK (Ire) [-] 3-8-3 (6*,4ex) J A Heffernan (6) ... (7 to 1) 8
2248 FOREST [-] 3-9-0 S Craine (10) ....(8 to 1) 9
2297 YOUR UNCLE STANLEY (Ire) [-] 4-8-9 J F Egan (4) (16 to 1) 10
Dist: 12l, 5l, nk, 6l. 1m 48.10s. (10 Ran).
(Hugh McMahon), Hugh McMahon

SOUTHWELL (good to firm)
Monday July 12th
Going Correction: MINUS 0.35 sec. per fur.

2464 Weston Maiden Stakes Class D (3-y-o) £3,669 1½m.................. (2:00)

2189[2] PRINCE OF ANDROS (USA) 9-0 L Dettori (7) *trkd ldrs, hdwy on bit 3 fs out, led o'r 2 out, rdn and ran on wl ins last*.....(11 to 8 fav op 6 to 4 tchd 2 to 1 and 5 to 4) 1
KERKURA (USA) 8-9 A McGlone (3) *trkd ldrs, hdwy 3 fs out, effrt to chal appr fnl furlong and sn ev ch, rdn and kpt on*.............................. (8 to 1 op 4 to 1) 2
2227[2] CYRUS THE BOLD (Ire) 9-0 D Holland (9) *hld up, hdwy hfwy, rdn o'r 2 fs out and kpt on one pace.* ....(6 to 1 op 5 to 1 tchd 7 to 1) 3
1842[5] MIROSWAKI (USA) 9-0 Paul Eddery (4) *in tch, hdwy 3 fs out, sn rdn and styd on same pace*........... (12 to 1) 4
2071[3] THREEMILESTONE (USA) 8-4 (5*) C Hodgson (1) *cl up, led aftr 3 fs, rdn three out, sn hdd and wknd 2 out.* ....(8 to 1 op 6 to 1) 5
2189[3] USK THE WAY 8-9 W Ryan (10) *cl up, rdn alng 5 fs out, wknd wl o'r 2 out*......................(5 to 2 tchd 7 to 2) 6
1831 MR BEAN 8-11 (3*) D Harrison (8) *in tch, effrt 5 fs out, sn rdn and btn*.............................(25 to 1 op 20 to 1) 7
MYNYOSS 9-0 J Carroll (11) *slwly into strd, some hdwy 5 fs out, sn wknd*........................ (20 to 1 op 14 to 1) 8
2065 O SO NEET 9-0 P Robinson (6) *al rear.* .... (33 to 1 op 20 to 1) 9
1859 BECKY'S GIRL 8-9 A Mackay (2) *led 3 fs, rdn and lost pl hfwy, tld off fnl 4 furlongs*....... (100 to 1 op 33 to 1) 10
JARIN ROSE (Ire) 8-4 (5*) J Tate (5) *prmnt 5 fs, sn rdn and lost pl, tld off fnl 4 furlongs*...... (100 to 1 op 33 to 1) 11
Dist: ½l, 5l, 3½l, nk, 10l, 7l, 12l, 1½l, dist, 6l. 2m 35.80s. a 1.80s (11 Ran).
SR: 40/34/29/22/16/-/ (Lucayan Stud), D R Loder

2465 Worfield Selling Stakes Class G (2-y-o) £2,070 7f.................. (2:30)

2229[2] CARAPELLE 8-6 M Birch (7) *steadied strt and beh, gd hdwy 2 fs out, led one and a half out, sn clr.* .... (9 to 4 fav op 7 to 2 tchd 4 to 1 and 9 to 2) 1
2278[6] MISS FREEBIE (Ire) 8-6 A Culhane (4) *chsd ldrs, rdn o'r 2 fs out, styd on ins last*........................... (12 to 1) 2
2331[7] MR MYSTICAL (Ire) (v) 8-11 A McGlone (5) *led, rdn o'r 2 fs out, hdd one and a half out and sn one pace.* ....(9 to 2 op 2 to 1 tchd 5 to 1) 3
HILL FARM DANCER 8-6 D Holland (3) *cl up, rdn 2 and a half fs out, sn one pace*.......... (16 to 1 op 14 to 1) 4
BANG IN TROUBLE (Ire) 8-11 L Dettori (6) *cl up, effrt and ev ch o'r 2 fs out, sn rdn and wknd over one out.* ....(7 to 1 op 5 to 1) 5

1899[4] TWO D'S 8-7 (3*) S Maloney (1) *slwly into strd and beh till styd on fnl 2 fs, nvr dngrs*.......... (4 to 1 op 11 to 4) 6
2216[6] STORM 8-11 A Mackay (2) *cl up, rdn o'r 2 fs out and grad wknd*............................(16 to 1 op 20 to 1) 7
1959 LUCKY HELEN 8-6 C Rutter (9) *nvr rchd ldrs.* ....(20 to 1 op 16 to 1 tchd 25 to 1) 8
2176[5] MR BLOBBY (Ire) 8-11 J Carroll (8) *cl up on outer, rdn 3 fs out and sn wknd*.....................(5 to 1 op 7 to 2) 9
Dist: 10l, 3l, nk, 5l, ¾l, 5l, 1½l, 1½l. 1m 29.70s. a 2.70s (9 Ran).
SR: 15/-/-/-/-/-/ (C A Webster), M H Easterby

2466 July Claiming Stakes Class F (4-y-o and up) £2,243 6f.............. (3:00)

1977[4] LADY SABO 4-8-1[1] Paul Eddery (6) *chsd ldg pair, hdwy o'r 2 fs out, rdn to ld appr fnl furlong, pushed out.* ....(13 to 8 on op 6 to 4 on tchd 5 to 4 on) 1
2276[6] ISLAND KNIGHT (Ire) 4-9-0 P Robinson (3) *led one furlong, cl up till led o'r 2 out, sn rdn, hdd and not quicken appr last*................................ (3 to 1 op 5 to 2) 2
1589 STRIP CARTOON (Ire) (bl) 5-8-10 (7*) G Strange (4) *in tch, rdn o'r 2 fs out, kpt on one pace*.... (10 to 1 op 7 to 1) 3
2165[8] ANGELS ANSWER (Ire) 4-8-1 (5*) Darren Moffatt (5) *chsd ldrs, effrt o'r 2 fs out, sn rdn and one pace.* .... (10 to 1 op 6 to 1) 4
1230[8] BLUE POINT (Ire) 4-7-9 (5*) D Wright (2) *nvr rchd ldrs.* .... (33 to 1 op 25 to 1) 5
1961 LOOSE ZEUS (USA) (bl) 4-8-9 S Webster (1) *led aftr one furlong till rdn and hdd o'r 2 out, sn wknd.* .... (10 to 1 op 8 to 1) 6
Dist: 2½l, 3l, nk, 6l, 6l. 1m 14.80s. a 0.80s (6 Ran).
SR: 29/32/23/11/-/-/ (Cronk Thoroughbred Racing Ltd), G Lewis

2467 Pattingham Handicap Class E (0-70 4-y-o and up) £3,002 2m........ (3:30)

2388[7] YAAKUM [47] (v) 4-8-5 L Dettori (1) *trkd ldrs gng wl, hdwy 4 fs out, effrt to ld on bit entering fnl furlong, ran on, cmftbly*.............(14 to 1 op 12 to 1 tchd 16 to 1) 1
1984[2] ANGELICA PARK [47] (bl) 7-8-5 M Birch (2) *cl up, led hfwy, rdn 2 out, hdd and no extr entering fnl furlong.* .... (11 to 4 op 9 to 4) 2+
2337[8] AUDE LA BELLE (Fr) [59] 5-9-3 A Mackay (5) *slwly away and beh, hdwy 4 fs out, rdn o'r 2 out, styd on ins last.* ....(9 to 2 op 7 to 2) 2+
2043[2] SHAFFIC (Fr) [58] 6-9-2 J Carroll (7) *in tch, rdn alng hfwy, hdwy und pres 4 out, wknd fnl 2 fs.* ....(9 to 4 fav op 2 to 1) 4
2178[2] VIAGGIO [41] 5-7-13 G Bardwell (8) *chsd ldrs, hdwy 4 fs out, sn rdn and wknd o'r 2 out.* ....(11 to 2 op 5 to 1 tchd 6 to 1) 5
2343[6] MINGUS (USA) [45] 6-8-3 Paul Eddery (3) *trkd ldrs, rdn alng 5 fs out and sn btn*...........(7 to 1 tchd 8 to 1) 6
2178[7] KINTARO [49] 5-8-7 D Holland (4) *led to hfwy, sn lost pl and beh*.......... (16 to 1 op 12 to 1 tchd 20 to 1) 7
Dist: 1l, dd-ht, 2½l, 10l, 2l, 25l. 3m 34.80s. a 8.80s (7 Ran).
(S Whittle), J E Banks

2468 Aldersley Handicap Class D (0-80 3-y-o and up) £3,289 7f............ (4:00)

2060 THORNTON GATE [66] 4-9-7 (3*) S Maloney (1) *made most, rdn 2 fs out, styd on wl ins last*..... (8 to 1 op 7 to 1) 1
2198* SANDMOOR DENIM [62] 6-9-6 S Webster (2) *chsd ldrs, rdn 2 fs out, styd on ins last.* (9 to 2 op 4 to 1 tchd 5 to 1) 2
2428[5] AFRICAN CHIMES [66] 6-9-10 M Perrett (4) *hld up, hdwy 2 fs out, sn rdn and styd on ins last*... (8 to 1 op 7 to 1) 3
2225[2] MINDOMICA [55] 4-8-10 (3*) Emma O'Gorman (5) *hld up, hdwy and wide strt, effrt and ev ch entering fnl furlong, sn rdn and wknd ins last*..(2 to 1 fav op 5 to 2) 4
2280* PINE RIDGE LAD (Ire) [65] 3-8-10 (5*,5ex) J Tate (6) *cl up, ev ch 2 fs out, sn rdn and wknd.* .... (11 to 2 op 4 to 1 tchd 6 to 1) 5
2164* DESERT NOMAD [62] 3-8-12 B Raymond (3) *chsd ldg pair, effrt and rdn 2 fs out, sn wknd*..... (7 to 2 op 3 to 1) 6
Dist: 1½l, ¾l, sht-hd, 1½l, 2½l. 1m 28.80s. a 1.80s (6 Ran).
SR: 46/37/39/27/24/13/ (T H Bennett), M H Easterby

2469 Whitmore Reans Apprentice Handicap Stakes Class G (0-70 3-y-o) £2,070 6f ....(4:30)

2170[3] MISS WHITTINGHAM (Ire) [61] 8-4 (8*) P Roberts (3) *cl up, hdwy on inner o'r 2 fs out, sn led, rdn and ran on fnl furlong*..........................(9 to 4 fav op 6 to 4) 1
2105[4] LARN FORT [52] 8-3 P McCabe (5) *cl up, rdn 2 fs out and ev ch, kpt on ins last*... (7 to 2 op 9 to 4 tchd 4 to 1) 2
1982[6] HERSHEBAR [62] (bl) 8-5 (8*) G Strange (2) *hld up, hdwy o'r 2 fs out, sn rdn and kpt on.* ....(9 to 2 op 7 to 2 tchd 5 to 1) 3
1326[9] HOTARIA [70] 9-4 (3*) G Parkin (1) *led, rdn 2 fs out, sn hdd and wknd appr last*................ (5 to 2 op 3 to 1) 4
1160 GIRL NEXT DOOR [54] 8-5 Mark Denaro (4) *chsd ldrs, rdn o'r 2 fs out and sn wknd.* .... (15 to 2 op 4 to 1 tchd 8 to 1) 5
Dist: 1½l, ¾l, 2½l, 3½l. 1m 15.70s. a 1.70s (5 Ran).
SR: 22/7/14/12/-/ (J W Barrett), J Berry

2470 Levy Board Seventh Handicap Class E (0-70 3-y-o and up) £2,322 1½m (5:00)

2353⁴ IMA RED NECK (USA) [44] (v) 4-9-7 A McGlone (4) *hld up, hdwy on bit 3 fs out, effrt to ld o'r one out, cmftbly.* ....(9 to 4 op 5 to 4 tchd 5 to 2) 1
2101³ PERSIAN SOLDIER [44] 6-9-2 (5*) Darren Moffatt (2) *led, rdn 2 fs out, hdd and one pace appr last.* ....(Evens fav op Evens) 2
2235⁷ FOREST STAR (USA) [47] 4-9-10 D Holland (5) *prmnt, hdwy to chase ldr 4 out, rdn 3 out, one pace fnl 2 fs.* ....(9 to 2 op 6 to 1 tchd 7 to 1) 3
2201⁸ ESCAPE TALK [22] 6-7-13 G Bardwell (1) *chsd ldrs, rdn o'r 5 fs out, sn lost pl*....(16 to 1 op 10 to 1) 4
2071⁶ RUPPLES [20] 6-7-11 E Johnson (3) *chsd ldr till rdn and wknd o'r 4 fs out*....(14 to 1 op 10 to 1) 5

Dist: 1½l, 7l, 12l, 10l. 2m 38.30s. a 4.30s (5 Ran).
SR: 22/19/8/-/-/ (Mrs J E Ward), J S Moore

WINDSOR (good to firm)
Monday July 12th

Going Correction: MINUS 0.10 sec. per fur. (races 1,4,5), MINUS 0.25 (2,3,6)

2471 Spur Selling Handicap Class G (0-60 3-y-o and up) £1,786 1m 3f 135yds ....(6:30)

2353* BRONZE RUNNER [33] (bl) 9-8-7 (5ex) T Sprake (14) *al in tch, pushed alng o'r 2 fs out, ran on to ld appr last, kpt on*....(12 to 1 op 6 to 1 tchd 14 to 1) 1
2273⁸ PREMIER DANCE [40] 6-9-0 B Rouse (11) *rear till hdwy 3 fs out, swtchd rght o'r one out, ran on strly ins last.* ....(7 to 1 op 6 to 1 tchd 8 to 1) 2
BONDAID [39] 9-8-13 R Price (3) *prmnt, led o'r 4 fs out till appr last, one pace*...(25 to 1 op 14 to 1 tchd 33 to 1) 3
2052² ROMANIAN (Ire) [40] 5-9-0 T Quinn (15) *in tch, one pace fnl 2 fs*....(7 to 1 op 6 to 1 tchd 8 to 1) 4
2052* WITH GUSTO [35] 6-8-9 J Williams (13) *hld up on outsd, kpt on ins fnl 3 fs, nvr nr to chal.* ....(8 to 1 op 6 to 1 tchd 9 to 1) 5
2289 BROWN CARPET [27] (bl) 6-8-1 T Williams (6) *led 2 fs, in tch, rdn 3 out, one pace.* ....(9 to 1 op 10 to 1 tchd 7 to 1) 6
1930⁹ BILLY BUNTER [50] 4-9-10 V Smith (10) *rcd on outsd, hdwy hfwy, rdn 3 fs out, not pace to chal*....(6 to 1 jt-fav op 8 to 1 tchd 12 to 1) 7
1873³ NOTED STRAIN (Ire) [49] 5-9-9 Pat Eddery (16) *al abt same pl, rdn 3 fs out, no hdwy.* ....(13 to 2 op 5 to 1 tchd 7 to 1) 8
2162² BEAT THE BAGMAN (Ire) [40] 3-8-1 N Adams (2) *beh, some hdwy ins fnl 3 fs*....(10 to 1 op 8 to 1 tchd 12 to 1) 9
1902² MALZETA (Ire) [47] 3-8-8 W Newnes (9) *al mid-div.* ....(6 to 1 jt-fav op 7 to 2) 10
MABTHUL (USA) [42] 5-9-2 A Clark (8) *chsd ldrs till wknd 3 fs out*....(33 to 1) 11
2127⁵ BROUGHTON BLUES (Ire) [22] 5-7-9⁴ (5*) D McCabe (18) *hld up, effrt 3 fs out, sn btn.* ....(10 to 1 op 8 to 1 tchd 14 to 1) 12
2109 GIN AND ORANGE [50] 7-9-10 S Whitworth (19) *al rear.* ....(16 to 1 op 12 to 1) 13
2057 SHAMROCK DANCER (Ire) [42] 3-8-3 A Munro (12) *al beh.* ....(14 to 1 op 12 to 1) 14
2162⁴ CHINAMAN [20] (bl) 4-7-8 A Tucker (7) *al beh.* ....(33 to 1 op 20 to 1) 15
2223⁹ WHERE ARE WE [31] 7-8-5 M Hills (1) *al beh.* ....(16 to 1 op 12 to 1 tchd 20 to 1) 16
1907 ARRAS ROYALE [39] 3-7-7 (7*) N Varley (17) *led aftr 2 fs to 4 out, wknd quickly*....(33 to 1) 17
4716a CANBRACK (Ire) [27] 4-8-1 Dale Gibson (4) *al beh.* (33 to 1) 18
210 MARIOLINO [28] 6-7-9 (7*) Antoinette Armes (20) *al beh.* ....(33 to 1 op 16 to 1) 19

Dist: Hd, 1½l, 3½l, ¾l, 1l, 1½l, 1½l, 1l, ½l, 1½l. 2m 30.00s. a 7.00s (19 Ran).
SR: 12/18/14/8/1/-/11/7/-/ (Austin Stroud & Co Ltd), S Mellor

2472 EBF Median Auction Maiden Stakes Class E (2-y-o) £3,003 5f 10yds. . (6:55)

1788⁸ CRAGGANMORE 9-0 M Hills (8) *in tch, hdwy hfwy, rdn to ld appr fnl furlong, ran on wl.* ....(7 to 4 op 9 to 4 tchd 5 to 2) 1
2027² IN LIKE FLYNN 9-0 L Piggott (4) *made most till appr fnl furlong, ran on.* ....(13 to 8 fav op 6 to 4 tchd 11 to 8 and 7 to 4) 2
2096⁵ MACIZO 9-0 A Munro (2) *nvr far away, hrd rdn and ev ch one and a half fs out, kpt on.* ....(16 to 1 op 12 to 1 tchd 20 to 1) 3
1583⁸ KERAMIC 8-9 J Williams (7) *dsptd ld, ev ch o'r one furlong out, one pace ins last*....(16 to 1 op 8 to 1) 4
CALL ME GRAHAM 9-0 B Rouse (5) *slwly into strd, sn chasing ldrs, rdn and wknd appr fnl furlong.* ....(14 to 1 op 10 to 1 tchd 16 to 1) 5
MICHAELMAS PARK (Ire) 9-0 T Quinn (10) *sn rdn alng, in tch 3 fs*.... (16 to 1 op 12 to 1 tchd 20 to 1) 6
1265 QUEEN'S ADMIRAL 9-0 L Dettori (9) *speed 3 fs.* ....(20 to 1 op 12 to 1) 7
POLHYMNIA 8-9 R Cochrane (6) *slwly into strd, nvr got into race*....(12 to 1 op 6 to 1) 8
MIRENTIA 8-2 (7*) N Varley (1) *outpcd.* ....(10 to 1 op 8 to 1 tchd 14 to 1) 9
ROCKSTINE (Ire) 8-9 W Newnes (3) *slwly away, al beh.* ....(33 to 1 op 25 to 1) 10
1857 ANOTHER DREAM (Ire) 9-0 S O'Gorman (11) *sn outpcd.* ....(33 to 1 op 20 to 1) 11

Dist: 2l, hd, nk, 6l, ¾l, nk, nk, 5l, 2½l, 3l. 1m 0.60s. a 1.60s (11 Ran).
SR: 43/35/34/28/9/6/5/-/-/ (A Stoddard), J W Hills

2473 Nimble Fillies Conditions Stakes Class D (2-y-o) £4,425 5f 217yds (7:20)

1766⁴ VELVET MOON (Ire) 8-13 A Munro (1) *pushed alng frm strt, led appr fnl furlong, drvn out.* ....(6 to 4 on op 7 to 4 on tchd 11 to 8 on) 1
2058² STAR SPEEDER (Ire) 8-4 (5*) D Wright (5) *made most till appr fnl furlong, hrd rdn and edgd lft ins.* ....(12 to 1 op 8 to 1) 2
1683⁴ ELECTION SPECIAL 8-13 R Cochrane (3) *outpcd, sn rdn, ran on fnl furlong, nvr nrr*....(6 to 1 tchd 8 to 1) 3
2112³ BEARALL (Ire) 8-13 B Rouse (2) *in tch till outpcd appr fnl furlong*....(9 to 2 op 3 to 1 tchd 11 to 2) 4
2224* PRIMA SILK 8-11 L Dettori (4) *dsptd ld till hrd rdn and wknd quickly o'r one furlong out.* ....(9 to 1 op 7 to 1 tchd 10 to 1) 5
1265 CARLTON CROWN (USA) 8-9 S Whitworth (6) *al beh, tld off hfwy*.... (66 to 1 op 33 to 1) 6

Dist: 1l, 2½l, nk, 2½l, 20l. 1m 12.20s. a 1.90s (6 Ran).
SR: 31/23/17/16/4/-/ (Fahd Salman), P F I Cole

2474 Woodland Handicap Class D (0-80 3-y-o and up) £3,947 1¼m 7yds. . . . . (7:50)

2289* BENTICO [54] 4-8-5¹ (5ex) Pat Eddery (4) *made all, shaken up 2 fs out, ran on wl, cmftbly.* ....(5 to 2 fav op 2 to 1 tchd 11 to 4) 1
2311* STORM VENTURE (Ire) [70] 3-8-10 (5ex) L Dettori (7) *mid-div, hdwy to chase ldr ins fnl 3 fs.* (3 to 1 tchd 7 to 2) 2
2315² TIGER CLAW (USA) [45] 7-7-10 J Lowe (8) *hld up in tch on ins, ran on one pace fnl 2 fs*.... (10 to 1 op 12 to 1) 3
2113* WASSL THIS THEN (Ire) [63] 4-9-0 T Quinn (9) *trkd ldrs, rdn o'r 2 fs out, one pace*.... (6 to 1 op 4 to 1) 4
1743⁴ CALL THE BUREAU [61] 4-8-12 M Roberts (10) *beh, some hdwy o'r 2 fs out, nvr dngrs*.... (10 to 1 tchd 12 to 1) 5
2029² BOOKCASE [73] 6-9-10 J Williams (3) *hld up in tch, hmpd on bend aftr 5 fs, nvr got into race after.* ....(10 to 1 op 8 to 1 tchd 12 to 1) 6
1745* WARM SPELL [70] 3-8-10 B Rouse (2) *in tch, rdn 3 fs out, wknd 2 out*....(9 to 1 op 7 to 1 tchd 10 to 1) 7
1712² SWIFT SILVER [60] 6-8-11 R Cochrane (5) *rcd on outsd, effrt whn bumped 3 fs out, eased when btn.* ....(13 to 2 op 7 to 1 tchd 8 to 1 and 6 to 1) 8
756 EXCLUSION [70] 4-9-7 W Newnes (1) *chsd wnr till wknd 3 fs out*....(20 to 1 op 16 to 1 tchd 25 to 1) 9
TORGHIA [60] 6-8-11 Dale Gibson (6) *al beh*.... (33 to 1) 10

Dist: 2l, 2l, 2½l, sht-hd, 3½l, ½l, 1½l, nk, ¾l. 2m 6.50s. a 4.00s (10 Ran).
SR: 41/42/24/37/34/39/24/22/31/ (Mark Christofi), M A Jarvis

2475 Storacall Handicap Class D (0-80 3-y-o and up) £3,850 1m 67yds. . . . . . . (8:20)

1940* QUEEN WARRIOR [62] 4-9-1 Pat Eddery (6) *hld up, rapid hdwy o'r 3 fs out, led over 2 out, eased nr finish, cmftbly*....(9 to 4 fav tchd 100 to 30) 1
2113² WAKIL (Ire) [67] 4-9-6 A Munro (4) *trkd ldrs, kpt on one pace ins fnl 2 fs*.... (4 to 1 op 9 to 4) 2
1940³ SET THE FASHION [58] (v) 4-8-8 (3*) D Harrison (2) *hld up, hdwy 3 fs out, sn rdn, kpt on one pace.* ....(3 to 1 tchd 100 to 30) 3
2156⁹ COUNTERCHECK (Ire) [47] 4-8-0 N Carlisle (8) *chsd ldrs, no imprsn fnl 2 fs*.... (25 to 1 op 16 to 1 tchd 33 to 1) 4
1768 GRAND VITESSE (Ire) [71] 4-9-10 M Roberts (5) *hld up rear, styd on fnl 2 fs, nvr dngrs.* ....(9 to 1 op 8 to 1 tchd 7 to 1 and 10 to 1) 5
DOSSERI [41] 5-7-8 J Lowe (9) *trkd ldr, led 3 fs out, sn hdd, no extr.* ....(10 to 1 op 14 to 1 tchd 20 to 1 and 9 to 1) 6
2291* WILD STRAWBERRY [60] 4-8-13 (5ex) B Rouse (3) *led to 3 fs out, wknd quickly, tld off*....(9 to 2 tchd 5 to 1) 7
2029⁸ BLUE AEROPLANE [70] (bl) 5-9-9 M Perrett (1) *al beh, tld off hfwy*.... (40 to 1 op 33 to 1 tchd 50 to 1) 8
2110 DREAM OF TOMORROW [45] 5-7-12 S Dawson (7) *pld hrd, chsd ldrs to hfwy, sn beh, tld off.* ....(40 to 1 op 33 to 1 tchd 50 to 1) 9

Dist: 1½l, ½l, 3l, ¾l, sht-hd, 10l, 12l, 20l. 1m 43.80s. a 2.80s (9 Ran).
SR: 47/47/36/16/38/7/ (Christopher Spence), P T Walwyn

2476 Rosemead Handicap Class E (0-70 3-y-o) £2,490 5f 217yds. . . . . (8:50)

2154⁸ OUR SHADEE (USA) [52] (bl) 8-7 M Wigham (9) *slwly into strd, rear till hdwy 2 fs out, ran on wl to ld ins last.* .... (14 to 1 op 12 to 1 tchd 16 to 1) 1

2288^{4} AVRIL ETOILE [48] 7-10 (7*) Iona Wands (7) *al prmnt, rdn to ld 2 fs out, edgd lft and hdd ins last, kpt on.* .... (16 to 1 op 12 to 1 tchd 20 to 1) 2
1903^{6} TEE GEE JAY [54] (bl) 8-9 J Curant (1) *rear, hdwy whn short of room 2 fs out, ran on ins last.* .... (100 to 30 op 4 to 1 tchd 9 to 2) 3
2013^{2} PIRATES GOLD (Ire) [62] 9-3 T Quinn (12) *beh, ran on ins fnl 2 fs, nvr nrr*......... (5 to 1 op 6 to 1 tchd 8 to 1) 4
2132^{2} COVENT GARDEN GIRL [62] 9-3 L Dettori (6) *sn chsd alng, no imprsn ins fnl 2 fs*........... (5 to 2 fav op 2 to 1) 5
2293^{6} BERGLIOT [50] 8-5 R Perham (4) *led to 2 fs out, one pace.* .... (16 to 1 op 12 to 1) 6
2011^{9} HALLORINA [66] 9-7 Pat Eddery (3) *rcd on outsd, effrt 2 fs out, eased whn btn*................(11 to 2 op 7 to 2) 7
1232^{7} SALVATORE GIULIANO [47] 8-2 J Lowe (10) *in tch till wknd 2 fs out*........................ (20 to 1 op 10 to 1) 8
2110 SCREECH [51] 8-6 W Newnes (8) *wth ldr to hfwy, rdn and wknd 2 fs out*.................... (25 to 1 op 16 to 1) 9
1^{7} ANOTHER KINGDOM [52] 8-7 A Clark (11) *al beh.* .... (16 to 1 op 12 to 1 tchd 20 to 1) 10
1352 HARD ROCK MINER [46] 8-1 N Adams (2) *speed on outsd to hfwy*................ (40 to 1 op 33 to 1 tchd 50 to 1) 11
1503^{5} RED LEADER (Ire) [63] 8-11 (7*) T G McLaughlin (5) *outpcd hfwy*................ (10 to 1 op 7 to 1 tchd 12 to 1) 12

Dist: Nk, 2½l, nk, 1½l, ½l, 5l, 1l, ¾l, 1½l, nk. 1m 12.20s. a 1.90s (12 Ran).
SR: 25/20/16/23/17/3/ (K T Ivory), K T Ivory

BEVERLEY (firm)
Tuesday July 13th

Going Correction: MINUS 0.05 sec. per fur. (races 1,2,3,4), MINUS 0.25 (5,6)

2477 Electrolux Handicap Class D (0-80 3-y-o and up) £3,114 2m 35yds......(2:30)

1929^{2} CHAKALAK [70] 5-9-8 T Quinn (3) *trkd ldr, rdn 2 fs out, hdwy to ld appr last, ran on wl und pres.* .... (7 to 2 op 11 to 4) 1
2235* MY DESIRE [75] 5-9-8 (5*) Darren Moffatt (1) *trkd ldg pair, hdwy 3 fs out, rdn 2 out, chlgd and ev ch ins last, kpt on nr finish*..................(9 to 4 jt-fav op 2 to 1) 2
2235^{2} KING WILLIAM [45] 8-7-11 J Lowe (4) *hld up, hdwy o'r 2 fs out, effrt and hng rght over one out, one pace.* ....(9 to 4 jt-fav op 11 to 4) 3
2251^{6} SPECTACULAR DAWN [76] 4-10-0 W Carson (2) *set steady pace, quickened hfwy and 5 fs out, rdn o'r 2 out, hdd and wknd appr last*............... (11 to 4 op 9 to 4) 4

Dist: Nk, 3½l, sht-hd. 3m 41.60s. a 12.60s (4 Ran).
(P F Chakko), S Dow

2478 Sharp Claiming Stakes Class E (3-y-o) £3,114 7f 100yds............... (3:00)

2279* SILVERLOCKS 8-8 N Connorton (1) *stumbled strt, cl up, effrt 2 fs out, led entering last, cmftbly.* .... (7 to 4 on tchd 13 to 8 on) 1
2151* UMBUBUZI (USA) 8-6 S Perks (2) *trkd ldr, hdwy to ld 2 fs out, sn rdn, hdd and not quicken entering last.* ....(7 to 2 tchd 4 to 1) 2
2013* DEVIOUS DANCER 8-0 (5*) D McCabe (4) *led, rdn o'r 2 fs out, sn hdd, wknd ins last*..........(6 to 1 op 5 to 1) 3
2106^{2} MANX MONARCH 7-8^{5} (5*) A Garth (3) *cl up, rdn o'r 2 fs out, wknd appr last*................(14 to 1 op 8 to 1) 4

Dist: 1½l, 1½l, 1½l. 1m 34.80s. a 4.50s (4 Ran).
SR: 21/14/8/-/ (Miss Betty Duxbury), Miss S E Hall

2479 Comet Handicap Class C (0-100 3-y-o) £4,540 7f 100yds............. (3:30)

2097* TAHDID [79] 8-4 W Carson (3) *made all, quickened o'r 2 fs out, rdn and ran on fnl furlong.* .... (11 to 10 fav op 6 to 4 tchd 13 to 8) 1
2363 FIELD OF VISION (Ire) [76] 8-1 G Duffield (5) *hld up, effrt on ins 2 fs out, rdn and styd on inside last.* ....(4 to 1 op 7 to 2) 2
2303^{8} YOUNG ERN [96] 9-7 T Quinn (2) *hld up beh, hdwy on outsd o'r 2 fs out, rdn and ev ch appr last, kpt on one pace*.................. (6 to 1 op 5 to 1 tchd 13 to 2) 3
1808 YAQTHAN (Ire) [85] 8-10 R Hills (4) *chsd ldr, rdn and ev ch 2 fs out, wknd entering last*....... (6 to 1 tchd 13 to 2) 4
2220* GRAN SENORUM (USA) [79] 7-13^{2} (7*) T G McLaughlin (1) *slwly away, hdwy to chase ldrs hfwy, effrt and ev ch 2 fs out, sn rdn, wknd appr last*....... (5 to 1 op 4 to 1) 5

Dist: ¾l, 2l, hd, 1½l. 1m 34.30s. a 4.00s (5 Ran).
SR: 24/19/33/21/10/ (Hamdan Al-Maktoum), P T Walwyn

2480 Pace Handicap Class E (0-70 3-y-o) £3,377 1m 100yds.............. (4:00)

2183^{6} SMART TEACHER (USA) [41] 8-2^{4} G Duffield (7) *made all, quickened 2 fs out, sn clr, ran on wl.* (12 to 1 op 7 to 1) 1
2047^{8} FLASHMAN [56] 9-3 S Perks (4) *beh, hdwy 2 fs out, styd on ins last, no ch wth wnr*........(14 to 1 op 12 to 1) 2
2366* DUKE OF DREAMS [59] 9-6 (6ex) T Quinn (10) *chsd ldrs, hdwy on ins 2 fs out, sn rdn, one pace fnl furlong.* .... (100 to 30 fav op 3 to 1 tchd 7 to 2) 3
2104^{5} DANCES WITH GOLD [39] (bl) 8-0 J Lowe (8) *dwlt, beh, hdwy hfwy, rdn and hng rght 2 fs out, kpt on one pace.* .... (13 to 2 op 6 to 1) 4
1836^{6} MISSA BREVIS (USA) [60] (bl) 9-7 M Roberts (2) *in tch, hdwy o'r 2 fs out, sn rdn, wknd appr last.* ....(5 to 1 op 7 to 1) 5
2398^{8} CUTTHROAT KID (Ire) [57] (bl) 9-4 K Darley (3) *hld up, hdwy hfwy, sn rdn, btn 2 fs out*......... (12 to 1 op 10 to 1) 6
2270^{7} KARINSKA [60] 9-2 (5*) D McCabe (6) *chsd wnr, rdn 2 fs out, wknd*........... (6 to 1 op 11 to 2 tchd 13 to 2) 7
2095* HOT OFF THE PRESS [49] 8-10 A Culhane (5) *chsd ldrs, rdn 3 fs out, sn btn*.................. (13 to 2 op 6 to 1) 8
2233^{7} NORTHERN CHIEF [59] 9-6 M Birch (1) *cl up on outsd, rdn 3 fs out, sn wknd*.................. (8 to 1 op 7 to 1) 9

Dist: 5l, ¾l, 2½l, 2½l, ¾l, hd, ¾l, 5l. 1m 46.20s. a 3.40s (9 Ran).
SR: 31/31/32/4/17/12/14/1/-/ (Triple Crowners III), P W Harris

2481 Toshiba Claiming Handicap Class G (0-60 3-y-o and up) £3,582 5f.... (4:30)

2312 AQUADO [33] 4-8-1 W Carson (9) *chsd ldrs, rdn and hdwy appr fnl furlong, styd on to ld wl ins last*..... (10 to 1) 1
1631* MISS SIHAM (Ire) [44] 4-8-5 (7*) Claire Balding (14) *led, rdn appr fnl furlong, hdd and no extr wl ins last.* ....(7 to 1 tchd 6 to 1) 2
2241^{8} LAST STRAW [37] 5-8-5 G Duffield (11) *chsd ldrs, effrt and ev ch entering fnl furlong, sn rdn, not quicken.* ....(8 to 1 op 6 to 1) 3
2230* NORDOORA (Ire) [48] 4-8-11 (5*) Darren Moffatt (3) *cl up, rdn wl o'r one furlong out, sn one pace.* ....(5 to 1 op 4 to 1) 4
1464^{9} SHALAKO [43] 3-8-0 (5*) A Garth (12) *beh, styd on fnl 2 fs, nvr dngrs*.................(16 to 1 op 14 to 1) 5
2309^{3} BALLAD DANCER [60] 8-10-0 M Birch (4) *beh, hdwy 2 fs out, kpt on fnl furlong, not rch ldrs.* ....(7 to 1 op 6 to 1 tchd 8 to 1) 6
2001 SUPREME DESIRE [46] 5-9-0 S Webster (7) *al mid-div.* .... (16 to 1 op 20 to 1) 7
2197^{9} GATE OF HEAVEN [32] (bl) 3-7-8^{1} L Charnock (2) *wnt lft strt, chsd ldrs on outsd till rdn and wknd 2 fs out.* ....(25 to 1) 8
MISS LIMELIGHT [26] 4-7-8 J Lowe (1) *crrd lft strt, sn beh.* ....(33 to 1) 9
2312 ANDRULA MOU [43] (bl) 3-8-5^{1} T Lucas (8) *chsd ldrs 3 fs, sn wknd*.. (20 to 1) 10
2151^{9} KENNINGTON PROTON [31] (bl) 3-7-7 N Carlisle (5) *al beh.* ....(33 to 1) 11
1945 DOESYOUDOES [45] 4-8-8 (5*) O Pears (6) *al beh.* .... (20 to 1 op 16 to 1) 12
2384 ACIDOSIS [35] (bl) 4-8-3 K Darley (10) *cl up to hfwy, sn rdn, wknd quickly*...........................(33 to 1) 13

Dist: 1½l, 1½l, 3½l, 4l, 1l, nk, 1½l, 4l, nk, ¾l. 1m 3.50s. a 1.80s (13 Ran).
SR: 26/31/18/15/-/7/ (Gallagher Materials Ltd), N A Callaghan

2482 Sony Maiden Stakes Class D (2-y-o) £3,318 5f..................... (5:00)

2316^{2} ASHKERNAZY (Ire) 8-9 K Darley (3) *led, rdn and hdd entering fnl furlong, rallied und pres to ld on line.* ....(5 to 2 op 3 to 1 tchd 7 to 2) 1
2199^{5} LUCKY MESSAGE (USA) 8-9 T Quinn (6) *chsd ldrs, hdwy to chal appr fnl furlong, sn rdn, led entering last, hdd on line*..................(11 to 1 op 10 to 1 tchd 12 to 1) 2
JETHOU (Ire) 9-0 M Roberts (1) *unruly, led to strt, dwlt, sn chasing ldrs, effrt 2 fs out, soon rdn and btn.* ....(11 to 8 on op 2 to 1 on tchd 5 to 4 on) 3
2229^{8} SONIC (Ire) 9-0 T Lucas (4) *beh, some hdwy fnl 2 fs, nvr a factor*..(20 to 1) 4
2199^{3} BRITANNIA MILLS 8-4 (5*) D McCabe (2) *chsd wnr, rdn 2 fs out, sn wknd*......................(10 to 1 op 8 to 1) 5
THE ARDINGLY FAIR (Ire) 9-0 L Charnock (5) *chsd ldrs 3 fs, sn wknd*....................................(16 to 1) 6

Dist: Hd, 2½l, 7l, 7l, 1½l. 1m 3.60s. a 1.90s (6 Ran).
SR: 32/31/26/ (Paul Sharkey), J L Spearing

DOWN ROYAL (IRE) (good to firm)
Tuesday July 13th

2483 K.P.M.G. Peat Marwick Maiden (3-y-o and up) £1,380 7f..............(2:20)

2078^{3} ELIZABETH'S PET (Ire) 3-8-10 L Piggott (1).....(5 to 4 on) 1
2285^{8} RETICENT BRIDE (Ire) 3-8-10 M J Kinane (2).......(7 to 2) 2
1649^{8} MARY'S CASE (Ire) 3-8-13 C Roche (4)............ (25 to 1) 3
1619^{2} MARKIEVICZ (Ire) 3-8-10 R Hughes (3)............(7 to 4) 4

Dist: 2l, ½l, 2l. (Time not taken) (4 Ran).
(Mrs D A Breen), E P Harty

2484 Eastwood Irelands Leading Bookmaker Handicap (0-65 3-y-o and up) £1,380 1½m 68yds............. (3:10)

2035^{7} SENSE OF VALUE [-] 4-9-8 N G McCullagh (15).... (5 to 1) 1
1962 WINTER DREAMS (Ire) [-] 4-9-2 R Hughes (12)..... (7 to 1) 2
1995 RICH LIFE (Ire) [-] (bl) 3-8-13 M J Kinane (9)........(4 to 1) 3
2286^{5} ISLAND VISION (Ire) [-] 3-8-7 (6*) B J Walsh (8) (9 to 4 fav) 4

1139^{8} REGAL PRETENDER (Ire) [-] 3-7-8 (6*) R V Skelly (1) (14 to 1) 5
1987^{7} SHY GAL (Ire) [-] 5-7-12 (2*) R M Burke (2)........(14 to 1) 6
2322 ST AIDAN (Ire) [-] 5-7-10 (2*) D G O'Shea (4)......(14 to 1) 7
2141 TENCA (Ire) [-] 3-8-9 (4*) P Carberry (6)............(6 to 1) 8
2222^{3} SHERAVISION (Ire) [-] 4-8-7 (8*) P O Casey (11)....(16 to 1) 9
1295^{7} COUNTESS PAHLEN (Ire) [-] 4-7-9 (8*) R T Fitzpatrick (10) ....(20 to 1) 10
2287 CREHELP EXPRESS (Ire) [-] 3-8-5 (6*) B Bowens (13) ....(16 to 1) 11
2320^{5} BOLERO DANCER (Ire) [-] (bl) 5-8-11 L O'Shea (7) (12 to 1) 12
LEAVING CERT [-] 6-7-9^{3} (8*) P J Smullen (3)......(12 to 1) 13
706^{6} MUMMYS BEST [-] 7-9-0 (6*) J A Heffernan (5)....(20 to 1) 14
DUSTSCREEN (USA) [-] 9-8-10 P Lowry (14)......(10 to 1) 15
Dist: 2½l, sht-hd, 3l, 6l. (Time not taken) (15 Ran).
(F Dunne), F Dunne

2485 Ulster Harp Derby Handicap (0-100 3-y-o) £11,050 1½m 68yds...... (3:40)

2040* KIROV PREMIERE [-] 9-4 C Roche (4)..........(6 to 4 fav) 1
2221* NURSE MAID (Ire) [-] 7-5 (2*) D G O'Shea (1)......(20 to 1) 2
1853^{2} KARINIYD (Ire) [-] (bl) 9-7 M J Kinane (6)...........(9 to 4) 3
2076 SIRSAN (Ire) [-] 8-7 R Hughes (5)................(12 to 1) 4
1483^{2} ECU DE FRANCE (Ire) [-] 9-1 L Piggott (2)..........(5 to 2) 5
2092^{4} ATLANTIC ADIOS (Ire) [-] (bl) 7-11 (8*) D J O'Donohoe (3) ....(25 to 1) 6
Dist: Hd, 2½l, 1l, hd. (Time not taken) (6 Ran).
(John L Wood), J S Bolger

2486 Maid Of Mournes (C&G) EBF Maiden (2-y-o) £2,415 7f................(4:05)

1442^{4} GIULIO ROMANO (Ire) 9-0 C Roche (3)............(7 to 4) 1
UNBUCKLE (Ire) 9-0 M J Kinane (1)............(5 to 4 on) 2
2344^{2} VENICE (Ire) 9-0 R Hughes (4)....................(9 to 2) 3
1792^{7} MAJESTIC MAN (Ire) 8-8 (6*) J A Heffernan (2)....(16 to 1) 4
Dist: 2l, 1½l, sht-hd. (Time not taken) (4 Ran).
(T F Brennan), J S Bolger

2487 Tattersalls Auction Race (2-y-o) £1,380 7f...................... (4:35)

1924^{4} KING SANCHO (Ire) 8-5 M J Kinane (5)........(7 to 4 fav) 1
2294^{2} ROYAL THIMBLE (Ire) 8-5 A J Nolan (10)...........(3 to 1) 2
2319^{8} BAKER HILL (Ire) 7-12 (10*) D Cullen Jnr (6).......(20 to 1) 3
MASCOT 8-2 L O'Shea (2).......................(14 to 1) 4
2246^{4} MY RAGAMUFFIN (Ire) 8-12 N G McCullagh (3)....(5 to 2) 5
SAWDUST (Ire) 7-10 (6*) R V Skelly (7)............(16 to 1) 6
MEGAN'S DREAM (Ire) 8-5 P Lowry (4)..........(14 to 1) 7
1994^{5} BENAZIR LADY (Ire) 7-8 (8*) R T Fitzpatrick (1)....(14 to 1) 8
ISLAND ROCK (Ire) 7-11^{1} (6*) J A Heffernan (9).....(7 to 1) 9
Dist: 2l, 1l, 1l, 9l. (Time not taken) (9 Ran).
(Dr Jerome Torsney), E J O'Grady

EVRY (FR) (good)
Tuesday July 13th

2488 Prix de Ris-Orangis (Group 3) (3-y-o and up) £23,895 6f..............(3:00)

1791* THREE FOR FANTASY (Ire) 3-8-6 O Peslier (3) *chsd ldrs, hdwy o'r one furlong out, led jst und one and a half out, ran on wl*..........(31 to 10) 1
1043* NEW EUROPE 3-8-6 L Mader (4) *trkd ldr, rdn 2 fs out, rallied cl hme*..........(11 to 1) 2
1220^{4} DANAKAL (USA) 3-8-9 G Mosse (2) *broke wl, led aftr one furlong till tired well ins last*..........(4 to 1) 3
1791^{4} CHARME SLAVE (Fr) (bl) 5-9-0 E Legrix (5) *hld up, rdn 2 fs out, kpt on, nvr nrr*..........(11 to 1) 4
1791^{2} SOMERSHAM (USA) 3-8-9 T Jarnet (7) *rcd in 4th, rdn 2 fs out, one pace*..........(51 to 10) 5
1011^{5} DREAM TALK (bl) 6-9-4 N Jeanpierre (1) *broke wl, ev ch 2 fs out, sn one pace*..........(17 to 1) 6
2055* NIDD (USA) 3-9-0 Pat Eddery (6) *mid-div till rdn and wknd 2 fs out*..........(6 to 5 fav) 7
Dist: Nk, sht-hd, 1l, 1½l, 2l, nk. 1m 11.19s. a 0.89s (7 Ran).
SR: 62/61/63/64/53/54/49/ (Anne de Contades), N Clement

FOLKESTONE (good to firm)
Tuesday July 13th

Going Correction: MINUS 0.30 sec. per fur. (races 1,2,3,4,7), MINUS 0.40 (5,6)

2489 Sunley Estates Handicap Class E (0-70 3-y-o) £3,054 1m 1f 149yds (1:45)

2272^{7} DODGY DANCER [56] 8-7^{1} S Whitworth (2) *hld up last, prog 2 fs out, pld out entering last, styd on strly to ld nr finish*..........(7 to 2 op 9 to 4) 1
2358* SILVER GROOM (Ire) [52] 8-3 J Quinn (3) *settled 3rd, effrt 2 fs out, rdn to ld appr last, hdd nr finish*..........(2 to 1 fav op 5 to 4 tchd 9 to 4) 2
1911^{6} CALL ME BLUE [70] 9-7 D Holland (4) *led till rdn and hdd appr fnl furlong, kpt on one pace*..........(7 to 2 op 3 to 1 tchd 9 to 2) 3
2163^{3} STEVIE'S WONDER (Ire) [47] 7-12 T Williams (1) *pressed ldr till rdn and not quicken 2 fs out, eased whn btn*..........(5 to 2 tchd 3 to 1) 4
Dist: ½l, 1½l, 4l. 2m 3.20s. a 5.60s (4 Ran).
SR: 8/2/22/-/ (T W Langley), M R Channon

2490 P & O European Ferries Handicap Class E (0-70 4-y-o and up) £2,847 1m 1f 149yds......................(2:15)

CASE FOR THE CROWN (USA) [39] 6-8-10 L Dettori (4) *keen hold, trkd ldr, quickened to ld ins fnl furlong, cleverly*..........(9 to 4 fav op 2 to 1) 1
1862^{4} DAY OF HISTORY (Ire) [53] 4-9-3 (7*) J D Smith (3) *trkd ldr, effrt to ld wl o'r one furlong out, hdd ins last, ran on*..........(9 to 2 op 3 to 1 tchd 5 to 1) 2
2127^{9} ALBERT [49] 6-9-6 G Carter (5) *led till hdd and not quicken wl o'r one furlong out*..........(7 to 2 op 5 to 2 tchd 4 to 1) 3
1699^{4} NORTHERN CONQUEROR (Ire) [48] 5-9-5 D Holland (1) *settled 4th, rdn and no prog 2 fs out*..........(3 to 1 op 2 to 1 tchd 7 to 2) 4
2226^{3} DON'T GIVE UP [41] (bl) 5-8-12 R Price (2) *last, chsd alng 3 fs out, sn no prog*......(5 to 1 op 4 to 1 tchd 8 to 1) 5
Dist: Hd, 3½l, 1½l, ½l. 2m 6.20s. a 8.60s (5 Ran).
(Mrs B J Curley), B J Curley

2491 Infocheck Group Barnardos Benefit Fillies' Handicap Class E (0-70 3-y-o and up) £3,106 6f 189yds........(2:45)

2197^{4} NIGEL'S LUCKY GIRL [47] 5-9-1 J Quinn (8) *chsd ldr, rdn to ld appr fnl furlong, edgd rght ins last, styd on*..........(14 to 1 op 12 to 1 tchd 16 to 1) 1
2121^{8} ANATROCCOLO [36] 6-8-4 W Newnes (2) *sn led and clr, rdn and hdd appr fnl furlong, btn whn hmpd ins last*..........(8 to 1 op 5 to 1) 2
1977^{5} FLYING WIND [41] 4-8-9 B Rouse (1) *prog to chase ldrs aftr 2 fs, ev ch two out, rdn and not quicken, ran on ag'n cl hme*..........(7 to 1 op 8 to 1) 3
1947^{3} INDERAPUTERI [68] 3-10-0 A Munro (10) *chsd ldrs, rdn and styd on appr fnl furlong, nrst finish*..........(15 to 2 op 4 to 1 tchd 8 to 1) 4
2122^{2} NEWINGTON BUTTS (Ire) [60] 3-9-6 J Reid (5) *chsd ldrs, sn rdn alng, no prog fnl 2 fs*..........(11 to 2 op 7 to 2 tchd 6 to 1) 5
2226* DAM CERTAIN (Ire) [55] 4-9-9 A McGlone (9) *al same pl, rdn and no prog 2 fs out*..........(11 to 2 op 5 to 2) 6
2270^{3} TIFFANY'S CASE (Ire) [54] 4-9-8 R Cochrane (3) *al same pl, rdn and no prog 2 fs out*..........(5 to 2 fav tchd 9 to 4 and 11 to 4) 7
2212 BALLON [68] 3-9-11 (3*) B Doyle (6) *last and outpcd, styd on appr fnl furlong, nvr dngrs*..........(12 to 1 op 8 to 1 tchd 14 to 1) 8
2318^{4} UNVEILED [53] 5-9-7 M Hills (4) *al beh*. (14 to 1 op 8 to 1) 9
Dist: 1½l, hd, 1½l, 2l, ¾l, sht-hd, hd, 5l. 1m 23.30s. a 2.40s (9 Ran).
SR: 33/17/21/35/21/22/20/25/3/ (N P Greening), R Harris

2492 EBF John Holman & Sons Ltd Median Auction Maiden Stakes Class E (2-y-o) £3,239 6f 189yds.............. (3:15)

1418^{3} FOOTSTEPS (Ire) 8-9 A Munro (13) *made all, hrd rdn o'r one furlong out, ran on wl*..........(9 to 2 op 9 to 4 tchd 5 to 1) 1
BRIERLEY 8-9 L Dettori (2) *trkd wnr aftr 3 fs, ev ch wl o'r one out, hrd rdn and unbl to quicken*..........(10 to 1 tchd 8 to 1 and 12 to 1) 2
1350^{8} BANDAR PERAK (v) 9-0 G Carter (7) *cl up and sn pushed alng, outpcd hfwy, hrd rdn 2 fs out, styd on*..........(33 to 1 op 20 to 1) 3
2250 DANCING LAWYER 9-0 W Newnes (8) *prmnt till rdn and one pace o'r 2 fs out*..........(12 to 1 tchd 25 to 1) 4
ZUNO NOELYN 8-9 Paul Eddery (6) *chsd ldrs and sn pushed alng, one pace fnl 2 fs*......(11 to 4 op 7 to 2) 5
2240^{6} PLAYING TRICKS 8-9 R Cochrane (5) *mid-div, outpcd hfwy, ran on appr fnl furlong, nrst finish*..........(2 to 1 fav tchd 5 to 2) 6
1624^{8} SHERIFF 9-0 M Hills (3) *rear till modest late prog, nvr dngrs*..........(9 to 1 op 7 to 1 tchd 10 to 1) 7
YOUNG AT HEART (Ire) 9-0 J Reid (11) *ran green, beh, nvr nrr*..........(33 to 1 op 20 to 1) 8
MISS TEMERITY 8-9 N Adams (4) *slwly away, al rear*..........(25 to 1 op 10 to 1) 9
2044^{7} DANCING ANGEL 8-6 (3*) B Doyle (9) *prmnt till wknd 3 fs out*..........(50 to 1 op 20 to 1) 10
2153^{5} PARROT CAGE 9-0 P Robinson (10) *chsd ldrs, badly hmpd o'r 3 fs out, not rcvr*...(12 to 1 op 6 to 1 tchd 14 to 1) 11
2112^{5} HUMMINBIRDPRINCESS 8-9 B Rouse (12) *al beh*..........(33 to 1 op 16 to 1 tchd 50 to 1) 12
1905 MISS DENBIGH 8-9 D Holland (1) *al beh, tld off fnl 2 fs*..........(50 to 1 op 16 to 1) 13
Dist: 3l, 2l, hd, 5l, hd, 3l, 4l, 1½l, ½l, 1½l. 1m 24.50s. a 3.60s (13 Ran).
SR: 8/-/-/-/-/-/ (Fahd Salman), P F I Cole

2493 Waltons & Morse Selling Stakes Class G (2-y-o) £2,070 6f.............(3:45)

1988[7] FLAIR LADY 8-6 T Sprake (4) *trkd ldrs gng wl, led o'r 2 fs out, rdn out ins last*................(5 to 1 op 4 to 1) 1
1741[9] CA IRA (Ire) 8-6 J Williams (2) *co'red up beh ldrs, not clr run over one furlong out, squeezed through ins last, not quicken last 50 yards.*
........................(9 to 2 op 5 to 1 tchd 6 to 1) 2
1774[7] CURTIS THE FIRST 8-11 W Newnes (6) *reminder aftr 2 fs, al prmnt, ev ch one furlong out, not quicken.*
....................................(4 to 1 op 3 to 1) 3
1933[7] EL COHETE 8-8 (3*) B Doyle (7) *wth ldrs on outsd, rdn o'r 2 fs out, wknd ins last.* (12 to 1 op 8 to 1 tchd 14 to 1) 4
2159[2] NORTHERN BAILIWICK (Ire) 8-11 N Adams (3) *sn chsd alng, wth ldr o'r 3 fs, wknd*...... (2 to 1 fav op 3 to 1) 5
2006[7] REGAL RAMBLER (Can) (bl) 8-11 Paul Eddery (5) *reminders leaving stalls, led till o'r 2 fs out, wknd rpdly.*
.........................(5 to 1 op 7 to 2 tchd 6 to 1) 6
RAGTIME GIRL 8-0[1] (7*) S Drowne (1) *strted slwly, al tld off*...................(14 to 1 op 8 to 1 tchd 16 to 1) 7

Dist: 1l, 1l, 3l, nk, 5l, 12l. 1m 14.00s. a 3.00s (7 Ran).

(Mrs M S Teversham), W G M Turner

2494 Barnardos Day Limited Stakes Class F (0-65 3-y-o and up) £2,243 6f.. (4:15)

2139[4] FACE NORTH (Ire) 5-9-7 J Reid (5) *trkd ldrs gng easily, led wl o'r one furlong out, ran on well.*
.....................(7 to 4 fav op 9 to 4 tchd 5 to 2) 1
ABERLADY 3-8-9 P Robinson (7) *led for o'r 4 fs, shaken up and unbl to quicken*....(11 to 2 op 4 to 1 tchd 6 to 1) 2
2378* MY RUBY RING 6-9-2 T Williams (6) *cl up, hrd rdn appr fnl furlong, ran on one pace.*
.........................(4 to 1 op 3 to 1 tchd 5 to 1) 3
2110* HARRY'S COMING 9-9-7 M Hills (2) *settled rear, rdn o'r 2 fs out, styd on, nvr nrr.* (13 to 2 op 3 to 1 tchd 7 to 1) 4
1954 SADDLEHOME (USA) 4-9-7 A Munro (3) *prmnt till wknd wl o'r one furlong out*...(20 to 1 op 10 to 1 tchd 25 to 1) 5
1858[7] SCORCHER (Ire) 3-8-11 (3*) B Doyle (4) *cl up, rdn hfwy, sn btn*.................. (25 to 1 op 12 to 1 tchd 33 to 1) 6
2318[2] RICKY'S TORNADO (Ire) 4-9-7 J Williams (1) *wth ldr till rdn and wknd 2 fs out*.......(9 to 2 op 3 to 1 tchd 5 to 1) 7

Dist: 1½l, 1½l, nk, 2l, 4l, hd. 1m 11.50s. a 0.50s (7 Ran).

SR: 49/31/32/36/28/5/11/ (Normandy Developments (London)), R Akehurst

2495 Barnardos Day Handicap Class E (0-70 3-y-o) £2,847 1m 7f 92yds..(4:45)

2343[2] ARCTIC GUEST (Ire) [51] 9-7 Dean McKeown (4) *keen hold, trkd ldrs, led 3 fs out, rdn and hng lft appr last, styd on wl*..................(2 to 1 fav op 6 to 4 tchd 5 to 2) 1
2007[2] MANON LESCAUT [46] 9-2 J Quinn (5) *trkd ldrs, rdn 3 fs out, ran on ins last, nrst finish*.... (10 to 1 op 11 to 2) 2
2340* WESTRAY (Fr) [50] 9-1 (5*) J Tate (7) *settled last, prog hfwy, ev ch appr fnl furlong, not quicken.*
.......................(15 to 2 op 4 to 1 tchd 8 to 1) 3
2341* SO SAUCY [53] 9-9 (3ex) K Fallon (3) *led till tried to run out bend aftr 5 fs, beh after, modest late prog.*
.........................(5 to 2 op 3 to 1 tchd 4 to 1) 4
2048[5] POETIC FORM (Ire) [48] 9-4 R Cochrane (2) *hld up in tch, rdn and wknd 4 fs out.*
.....................(10 to 1 op 8 to 1 tchd 16 to 1) 5
2124* BRANSBY ROAD (Ire) [51] 9-7 J Reid (6) *lft in ld aftr 5 fs, hdd and wknd 3 out*....(11 to 4 op 5 to 2 tchd 3 to 1) 6
2227[6] ROWLANDSONS GOLD (Ire) [43] 8-13 A Munro (1) *trkd ldr till nrly crrd out bend aftr 5 fs, drpd rear, not reco'r.*
.....................(20 to 1 op 12 to 1 tchd 33 to 1) 7

Dist: ¾l, hd, 10l, 6l, nk, 2½l. 3m 26.40s. a 7.90s (7 Ran).

(The Fairyhouse 1992 Partnership), M Johnston

KILLARNEY (IRE) (yielding to soft)
Tuesday July 13th

2496 Shannon Great Southern Fillies Handicap (0-75 3-y-o) £3,452 1m 3f... (7:00)

1514[7] GLENBRACK [-] 9-1 (6*) J R Barry (2)............. (3 to 1) 1
2286 MANGANS HILL (Ire) [-] 8-9 (6*) P P Murphy (5)....(10 to 1) 2
1431[3] L-WAY FIRST (Ire) [-] 8-0 (8*) G M Moylan (4).......(14 to 1) 3
1755[8] WICKLOW WAY (Ire) [-] 9-3 W J Supple (9).........(7 to 1) 4
1995[7] MY GOSSIP (Ire) [-] 7-11 (4*) W J Smith (7).........(5 to 1) 5
1568[6] TRIBAL MEMORIES (Ire) [-] 7-10 (6*) J J Behan (3) (12 to 1) 6
2322 DIGNIFIED (Ire) [-] 9-0 P Shanahan (6)............(10 to 1) 7
2221[7] EGALITE (Ire) [-] (bl) 8-4 J F Egan (1)...............(12 to 1) 8
2286[2] COOLRAIN LADY (Ire) [-] 9-6 S Craine (8)...... (6 to 4 fav) 9

Dist: 6l, sht-hd, ¾l, 5l. 2m 44.00s. (9 Ran).

(John Bernard O'Connor), Patrick Joseph Flynn

2497 Corrib Great Southern Maiden (3-y-o and up) £3,452 1m 100yds...... (7:30)

1796[4] SUEKAR (Ire) 3-8-11 J P Murtagh (5)...........(Evens fav) 1
PETOFI 3-9-0 P Shanahan (3).........................(5 to 1) 2
2140[4] JU JU'S GIRL (Ire) 3-8-11 K J Manning (1)........(11 to 4) 3
2185[8] SOUTHERN REVIEW (Ire) 3-9-0 W J Supple (7)... (10 to 1) 4
2322 TAUTEN (Ire) 3-8-11 S Craine (2)................ (10 to 1) 5
2140 SILVER JAR (Ire) 3-8-5 (6*) J J Behan (8)......... (10 to 1) 6
CELTICCARO (Ire) 5-9-9 J F Egan (6).............. (40 to 1) 7

Dist: 1½l, 6l, 7l, 2½l. 1m 55.10s. (7 Ran).

(T J Monaghan), John M Oxx

2498 Eyre Square Great Southern Handicap (0-70 4-y-o and up) £3,452 1¾m ....(8:00)

851 STEEL MIRROR [-] 4-8-12 P V Gilson (11)....(9 to 2 jt-fav) 1
2035 GREEN GLEN (USA) [-] (bl) 4-10-0 S Craine (6).....(6 to 1) 2
SWIFT PAL [-] 8-6-13 (8*) G M Moylan (5).........(14 to 1) 3D
2142[6] CONCERT ORCHESTRA (Ire) [-] 4-7-8 Joanna Morgan (10)
....(5 to 1) 3
1468 TIME IS UP (Ire) [-] 4-8-13 (4*) W J Smith (7)...... (10 to 1) 4
1987 HUGH DANIELS [-] 5-6-12[1] (10*) J D Moore (4)....(14 to 1) 5
1987 SIR ALFRED (USA) [-] 8-7-13[4] J F Egan (8)....... (25 to 1) 6
4685a MORNING SARGE [-] 5-9-6 (6*) J J Behan (2)...... (8 to 1) 7
1962[8] SERJITAK [-] 6-8-9 J P Murtagh (1)..........(9 to 2 jt-fav) 8
1756[4] LACKOTWINE (Ire) [-] 4-8-9 W J Supple (9)....... (5 to 1) 9
OH JACKO [-] 6-8-1 (6*) P P Murphy (3).......... (12 to 1) 10

Dist: 2l, 4½l, 2½l, 10l. 3m 51.10s. (11 Ran).

(Mrs M Halford), M Halford

LEICESTER (good)
Tuesday July 13th

Going Correction: MINUS 0.35 sec. per fur.

2499 Blaby Selling Stakes Class G (3-y-o) £2,511 1m 8yds................ (6:30)

2097[5] ESSEX GIRL 8-6 L Dettori (6) *nvr far away, led o'r 2 fs out, forged clr ins fnl furlong, cmftbly.*
.... (13 to 8 fav op 7 to 4 tchd 9 to 4 and 6 to 4) 1
2095[5] B B GLEN 8-2[1] (5*) C Hodgson (4) *trkd ldrs, drvn alng to improve last 2 fs, styd on, not rch wnr.*
....(9 to 1 op 4 to 1) 2
2190[5] COSMIC STAR (bl) 8-11 W Woods (5) *led aftr one and a half fs, hng badly lft und pres o'r one furlong out, kpt on*................................ (20 to 1 op 16 to 1) 3
2154[4] ASCOM PAGER TOO 8-6 A Clark (2) *settled midfield, imprvg whn crrd badly lft o'r one furlong out, swtchd, one pace*............................. (25 to 1 op 16 to 1) 4
1911[8] BITRAN 8-11 P Robinson (7) *steadied strt, drvn alng to go pace hfwy, kpt on, nvr nr to chal*...(16 to 1 op 8 to 1) 5
1175[4] FILOU FILANT (Fr) 8-11 S Whitworth (11) *tucked away in midfield, effrt and drvn alng o'r 2 fs out, no imprsn.*
.... (11 to 2 op 3 to 1 tchd 6 to 1) 6
2154[9] TOCCO JEWEL 7-13 (7*) P McCabe (3) *chsd alng in midfield, no imprsn last 2 fs*..........(50 to 1 op 25 to 1) 7
2151[6] BLAKENEY'S DOUBLE (Ire) 8-8 (3*) S D Williams (9) *jinked lft strt, drvn alng to keep up, nvr a threat.*
....(50 to 1 op 33 to 1) 8
2134[6] SIR THOMAS BEECHAM 8-11 B Raymond (16) *chsd alng to go pace, some hdwy last 2 fs, nvr dngrs.*
.....................................(16 to 1 tchd 25 to 1) 9
1705[5] A BADGE TOO FAR (Ire) (v) 8-6 G Bardwell (14) *sn rdn alng to keep in tch, nvr a threat.*
.... (11 to 1 op 8 to 1 tchd 12 to 1) 10
1662[6] SLIVOVITZ 8-11 W Ryan (12) *broke wl to show gd speed in frnt rnk till wknd o'r 2 fs out.*
..........................(8 to 1 op 7 to 1 tchd 9 to 1) 11
LITTLE OSBORNE (Ire) (bl) 8-6 M Hills (8) *led for one and a half fs, styd hndy till fdd o'r 2 furlongs out, eased whn btn*................................ (12 to 1 op 33 to 1) 12
2023[8] BLUE TRUMPET (v) 8-11 Dale Gibson (10) *chsd alng to go pace, nvr a factor*................(33 to 1 op 20 to 1) 13
2109 ONE-O-EIGHT 8-6 A McGlone (13) *sn drvn alng, nvr a factor*..............................(50 to 1 op 33 to 1) 14
2151 RISKY TUESDAY 8-6 R Price (1) *al wl outpcd.*
....(50 to 1 op 33 to 1) 15
2273 WHIMSICAL NOTION 8-6 G Hind (15) *wl plcd far side till wknd und pres o'r 2 fs out*.................... (50 to 1) 16

Dist: 2½l, 1l, 3½l, 6l, 1l, 1½l, 2½l, ½l, 1½l, 2½l. 1m 39.00s. a 3.90s (16 Ran).

(Lucayan Stud), D R Loder

2500 Radio Leicester Nursery Class E (2-y-o) £2,406 5f 2yds............ (7:00)

1955[4] MARJORIE'S MEMORY (Ire) [-] 9-6 J Reid (1) *slightly hmpd and checked strt, improved gng wl hfwy, led appr fnl furlong, drvn out*...... (17 to 2 op 6 to 1 tchd 9 to 1) 1
2278[3] COLNE VALLEY [-] (bl) 8-1 M Roberts (3) *broke smartly to make most till appr fnl furlong, rallied gmely cl hme.*
..........................(6 to 1 op 7 to 1 tchd 9 to 1) 2
2200[4] MISTER BLOY [-] 9-7 J Carroll (7) *sluggish strt, chsd alng hfwy, kpt on wl fnl furlong, nvr nrr.* (8 to 1 op 7 to 1) 3
2137[5] KERRIE-JO [-] 8-10 R Hills (4) *gd speed centre, feeling pace and rdn o'r one furlong out, no extr.*
.... (16 to 1 op 14 to 1 tchd 20 to 1) 4
2090* CASPIAN GOLD [-] 8-7 Dean McKeown (5) *wth ldrs far side, rdn to ld briefly hfwy, no extr fnl furlong.*
....(5 to 2 tchd 11 to 4) 5
1561[3] GAELIC STAR (Ire) [-] 8-7 W Ryan (6) *chsd ldrs, feeling pace and bustled alng 2 fs out, eased whn btn fnl furlong.*
.... (13 to 2 op 4 to 1) 6

2180[2] ROCKY TWO [-] 8-12 L Dettori (8) *chsd alng beh ldg bunch, feeling pace 2 fs out, eased whn btn ins last.* ....(12 to 1 op 10 to 1) 7
1778[6] INDIAN DREAMER [-] 8-6 G Duffield (2) *wnt lft strt, quickly reco'red, hrd at work 2 fs out, sn btn.* ....(2 to 1 fav op 9 to 4 tchd 5 to 2) 8
Dist: Hd, 5l, 1½l, 4l, ¾l, 1½l, ½l. 1m 0.30s. a 1.60s (8 Ran).
SR: 39/19/19/2/-/ (F J Sainsbury), M J Heaton-Ellis

2501 Uppingham Handicap Class D (0-80 3-y-o and up) £3,435 1m 3f 183yds ....(7:30)

1770 MUCH SOUGHT AFTER [74] 4-10-0 G Duffield (9) *tucked away on ins, led o'r 2 fs out, hrd pressed fnl furlong, gmely*..................(13 to 2 op 5 to 1 tchd 7 to 1) 1
2272[2] ROMALITO [56] 3-7-10[2] (3*) D Harrison (7) *chsd ldg 6, not much room o'r 3 fs out, drvn through to chal fnl furlong, jst hld*........................(5 to 1 op 4 to 1) 2
1868[2] BROCTUNE BAY [67] 4-9-7 L Dettori (5) *nvr far away, hrd drvn o'r 2 fs out, kpt on same pace fnl furlong.* ....(9 to 2 tchd 7 to 2) 3
2113 RAPPORTEUR (USA) [57] 7-8-11 W Newnes (10) *tried to make all, hdd and rdn o'r 2 fs out, one pace.* ....(16 to 1 op 14 to 1) 4
2273[2] ROUSITTO [54] 5-8-8 W Ryan (8) *patiently rdn, broke wide to improve last 3 fs, kpt on, nvr able to chal.* ....(7 to 2 fav op 5 to 2) 5
4760a[9] SHARP TOP [53] 5-8-0 (7*) P McCabe (6) *trkd ldg bunch, hrd drvn whn pace lifted o'r 2 fs out, no imprsn.* ....(14 to 1 op 10 to 1) 6
1858[3] VANBOROUGH LAD [57] 4-8-11 J Reid (4) *al hndy, hrd drvn whn pace quickened o'r 2 fs out, fdd.* ....(9 to 1 op 8 to 1 tchd 11 to 1 and 7 to 1) 7
2010[5] LEEWA (Ire) [74] 3-9-1 M Roberts (3) *rcd wide, wth ldrs for o'r a m, fnshd tld off*..............(9 to 2 op 4 to 1) 8
Dist: ¾l, 3½l, 1l, 1½l, 4l, 3½l, 20l. 2m 36.20s. a 7.70s (8 Ran).
(The MSA Partnership), D Morley

2502 Tattersalls Maiden Auction Series Stakes Qualifier Class D (2-y-o) £3,699 7f 9yds....................... (8:00)

1926[2] MAJESTIC HEIGHTS (Ire) 8-10 L Dettori (2) *chsd alng on outsd, improved to ld o'r one furlong out, ran on wl.* ....(7 to 1 op 4 to 1) 1
1897[3] MILL FORCE 8-10 K Darley (14) *nvr far away, shaken up hfwy, led briefly o'r one furlong out, ran green, kpt on.* ....(7 to 2 fav op 5 to 2 tchd 4 to 1) 2
2274[2] INDEFENCE (Ire) 8-6 D Holland (1) *rcd wide, ran in snatches, kpt on wl ins fnl furlong, nvr nrr.* ....(4 to 1 op 3 to 1 tchd 9 to 2) 3
2179[3] MERLIN'S FIELD (Ire) 8-12 A McGlone (13) *al hndy, led hfwy till o'r one furlong out, kpt on same pace.* ....(7 to 1 op 5 to 1 tchd 8 to 1) 4
FABULOUS PRINCESS (Ire) 8-6 M Roberts (5) *sluggish strt, steady hdwy whn not much room fnl furlong, nvr nrr.* ....(25 to 1 op 14 to 1) 5
2114[6] MIDSEAS 8-8 J Reid (11) *led to hfwy, drvn alng o'r one furlong out, no extr*..........(33 to 1 op 20 to 1) 6
2167[6] MON ROUGE (Ire) 8-6 W Woods (9) *broke wl to show gd speed for o'r 5 fs*...................(25 to 1 op 20 to 1) 7
2030[6] ROBERO 8-7 (5*) O Pears (12) *trkd ldg bunch, effrt and drvn alng o'r 2 fs out, no imprsn*...(40 to 1 op 20 to 1) 8
2102[3] ELLARUTH (Ire) 8-1 P Robinson (6) *rcd freely in midfield, pushed alng 2 fs out, sn btn.* ....(8 to 1 op 7 to 1 tchd 10 to 1) 9
2331 LORD WELLINGTON (Ire) 8-7 G Hind (7) *settled midfield, hrd at work hfwy,. sn btn*.........(40 to 1 op 33 to 1) 10
BLAAZIING JOE (Ire) 8-10 T Quinn (3) *rdn alng 3 out, nvr a factor*..................(13 to 2 op 7 to 1 tchd 5 to 1) 11
2123[5] ROBBY (Ire) 8-6 Dean McKeown (15) *chsd ldrs far side for 5 fs, fdd*.............................(20 to 1 op 12 to 1) 12
SEA SPOUSE 8-7 (3*) D Harrison (4) *steadied strt, nvr a threat*..............................(40 to 1 op 33 to 1) 13
HEIGHT OF DECORUM 8-6 S Whitworth (8) *broke wl to chase ldrs for o'r 4 fs, fdd.* ....(20 to 1 op 25 to 1 tchd 33 to 1) 14
CHEERFUL GROOM (Ire) 8-6 J Fanning (10) *very slwly away, improved rpdly hfwy, wknd jst as quickly.* ....(40 to 1 op 33 to 1) 15
Dist: 2l, hd, nk, 3½l, 1½l, ½l, 2½l, 3½l, 1l, ¾l. 1m 26.60s. a 4.70s (15 Ran).
(Mrs C A Hawkings), R Hannon

2503 Cardinal Wolsey Handicap Class E (0-70 3-y-o) £2,929 7f 9yds..... (8:30)

2308 DIWALI DANCER [50] (bl) 8-6 F Norton (1) *al ldg trio, drvn alng o'r 2 fs out, ran on grimly to ld post.* ....(10 to 1 op 8 to 1) 1
2276[8] HALL BANK COTTAGE [46] (bl) 8-2 J Fanning (3) *al hndy, led hfwy, drvn 3 ls clr fnl furlong, ct post.* ....(11 to 1 op 8 to 1) 2
1377[6] SEASON'S STAR [51] 8-7 S Dawson (4) *led to hfwy, outpcd and drvn alng 2 fs out, rallied gmely fnl furlong.* ....(10 to 1 op 8 to 1) 3
1972* PERDITION (Ire) [64] 9-3 (3*) D Harrison (6) *steadied strt, effrt and bustled alng hfwy, not pace to chal.* ....(9 to 4 op 13 to 8 tchd 5 to 2) 4
2233[4] DAYTONA BEACH (Ire) [65] 9-7 K Darley (2) *co'red up in midfield, ran lazily and drvn alng hfwy, nvr able to chal*..........................(2 to 1 fav op 3 to 1) 5
2212 WALNUT BURL (Ire) [63] 9-5 J Reid (7) *chsd ldg quartet, hrd drvn 2 fs out, sn outpcd*.........(9 to 2 op 7 to 2) 6
Dist: Sht-hd, hd, 4l, 3l, nk. 1m 26.30s. a 4.40s (6 Ran).
(Mrs Ann Case), A Bailey

2504 Glebe Rating Related Maiden Fillies' Stakes Class E (0-70 3-y-o) £2,238 5f 2yds......................... (9:00)

2288[3] THE ORDINARY GIRL (Ire) (v) 8-11 J Reid (8) *rcd far side, nvr far away, drvn ahead o'r one furlong out, jst lasted*.........................(11 to 2 op 4 to 1) 1
1618[4] BREAKFAST BOOGIE 8-11 L Dettori (3) *trkd ldrs, hrd drvn and plenty to do 2 fs out, ran on ins last, jst fld.* ....(11 to 8 on op 7 to 4 on tchd 5 to 4 on) 2
2312[4] CLOUDY REEF 8-4 (7*) M Humphries (5) *al hndy, led hfwy till o'r one furlong out, rdn but not quicken last 100 yards*..........................(3 to 1 tchd 9 to 2) 3
2288[5] PERFECT PASSION 8-8[4] (7*) Rachel Bridger (4) *dsptd ld to hfwy, feeling pace o'r one furlong out, sn outpcd.* ....(33 to 1 op 16 to 1) 4
SICILY OAK 8-11 W Newnes (6) *drvn alng in midfield hfwy, sn struggling*..............(20 to 1 op 10 to 1) 5
2032[9] EISHRELA 8-11 D Holland (1) *broke wl to ld to hfwy, fdd und pres last 2 fs*..............(50 to 1 tchd 33 to 1) 6
2151[7] NANQUIDNO 8-11 G Bardwell (7) *chsd ldrs, hrd drvn hfwy, sn struggling*..............(50 to 1 op 33 to 1) 7
2095 MUSICAL TIMES 8-11 Dean McKeown (2) *chsd ldrs to hfwy, sn rdn and btn*............(25 to 1 op 20 to 1) 8
Dist: Hd, 1½l, 6l, 6l, 2l, ¾l, 5l. 1m 1.00s. a 2.30s (8 Ran).
SR: 16/15/9/-/-/ (M Mac Carthy), T Casey

CATTERICK (good)
Wednesday July 14th
Going Correction: MINUS 0.10 sec. per fur.

2505 Huddersfield Selling Stakes Class G (2-y-o) £2,406 7f................(2:30)

2167[4] NEW INN 8-11 W R Swinburn (8) *trkd ldrs, rdn to ld one furlong out, ran on wl*..............(5 to 1 op 3 to 1) 1
2229[5] LYING EYES 8-4 (7*) P McCabe (13) *dsptd ld, led 4 fs out, rdn 2 out, hdd one out, kpt on.* ....(8 to 1 op 7 to 1 tchd 9 to 1) 2
1561[4] BENEFICIARY 8-6 M Birch (12) *trkd ldrs, effrt o'r 2 fs out, kpt on same pace*.............(6 to 4 fav op 2 to 1) 3
2268[4] WOODLAND WHISPER 8-6 W Ryan (7) *mid-div, kpt on fnl 2 fs, not trble ldrs*..... (8 to 1 op 7 to 1 tchd 10 to 1) 4
2229[4] JUST BILL 8-11 S Webster (9) *beh, styd on fnl 2 fs, not trble ldrs*...........................(10 to 1 op 7 to 1) 5
1078[7] SURPRISE BREEZE 8-11 A Culhane (11) *nvr dngrs.* ....(9 to 1 op 8 to 1 tchd 10 to 1) 6
2128[3] SPRING STAR 8-3 (3*) J Weaver (2) *led to 4 fs out, wknd o'r 2 out*............(20 to 1 op 16 to 1 tchd 25 to 1) 7
2447[4] LADY SWIFT 8-1 (5*) A Garth (5) *al beh.* ....(25 to 1 op 20 to 1) 8
2167[7] GUYLAIN (v) 8-11 Dale Gibson (3) *in tch till wknd 3 fs out.* ....(33 to 1 op 25 to 1) 9
2271[8] VAN DIEMEN'S LAD (Ire) 8-11 Paul Eddery (6) *chsd ldrs, sn drvn alng, wknd o'r 2 fs out*..................(20 to 1) 10
1272[8] HIGHFIELD LAD 8-11 J Fanning (1) *strted slwly, al beh.* ....(14 to 1 op 12 to 1) 11
2129 WAKE UP TO REALITY 8-6 R Lappin (4) *al beh, tld off.* ....(100 to 1 op 50 to 1) 12
1877 BILLPOSTER (Ire) (bl) 8-6 J Carroll (10) *prmnt, broke leg and pld up aftr one and a half fs, destroyed.* ....(33 to 1 op 25 to 1) pu
Dist: 3l, 4l, 1½l, 2½l, 1l, 2l, 3l, 2l, 7l, 6l. 1m 27.70s. a 4.70s (13 Ran).
SR: 16/7/-/-/-/ (Mrs Christine Sharratt), E Weymes

2506 Wakefield Handicap Class E (0-70 4-y-o and up) £2,898 1½m 44yds.... (3:00)

2108[7] CARROLLS MARC (Ire) [53] 5-9-2 Dale Gibson (8) *hld up, hdwy o'r 2 fs out, styd on wl to ld ins last.* ....(14 to 1 op 12 to 1) 1
2343* MYSTIC MEMORY [60] 4-9-4 (5*,3ex) Darren Moffatt (3) *chsd ldrs, pushed alng 4 fs out, hdwy o'r 2 out, ev ch one out, no extr fnl furlong*.....................(7 to 2 tchd 4 to 1) 2
1400[6] HOT PUNCH [35] 4-7-12 J Fanning (1) *cl up, led 3 fs out till hdd and no extr ins last*..........(14 to 1 op 16 to 1) 3
2347[3] DUGGAN [43] 6-8-3 (3*) J Weaver (5) *hld up, effrt 3 fs out, kpt on fnl furlong*...................(9 to 2 op 4 to 1) 4
2029* MARCHMAN [57] 8-9-6 Paul Eddery (7) *in tch, effrt 2 fs out, ev ch one out, wknd fnl furlong*...... (3 to 1 fav) 5
2201[4] EIRE LEATH-SCEAL [49] 6-8-12 J Carroll (6) *led to 3 fs out, wknd 2 out*...........................(11 to 2 op 6 to 1) 6
302 MADAGANS GREY [63] 5-9-12 W Woods (2) *prmnt, dsptd ld o'r 3 fs out, wknd 2 out*........ (16 to 1 op 12 to 1) 7

2201[3] SUPER BLUES [42] 6-8-5 W Ryan (4) *in tch, dsptd ld o'r 3 fs out, ev ch 2 out, sn rdn and wknd.* .... (13 to 2 op 6 to 1) 8
Dist: 1½l, sht-hd, sht-hd, 3½l, 3½l, 3l, 1½l. 2m 42.50s. a 7.50s (8 Ran).
SR: 15/19/-/-/7/ (P I P Electrics Limited), P C Haslam

2507 Dewsbury Maiden Stakes Class D (3-y-o and up) £3,348 1m 5f 175yds (3:30)

2189[5] DOVER PATROL (Ire) 3-8-6 W Ryan (7) *in tch, quickened to ld o'r 2 fs out, styd on wl.* .... (11 to 4 op 3 to 1 tchd 7 to 2) 1
1625[3] NAWAHIL 3-8-1 R Hills (3) *led till o'r 2 fs out, kpt on, no ch wth wnr.*......................(2 to 1 fav op 7 to 4) 2
2332 MICHAELA MIA (USA) 3-8-2[4] (3*) J Weaver (5) *hld up, hdwy 3 fs out, rdn o'r one out, kpt on same pace.* ....(4 to 1 op 3 to 1) 3
ASLAN (Ire) 5-9-7 W R Swinburn (4) *cl up, effrt o'r 2 fs out, sn btn.*.............................(6 to 1 op 5 to 1) 4
2117[6] CHARLOTTE DUNDAS 3-8-2[1] J Carroll (6) *chsd ldrs, pushed alng o'r 3 fs out, wknd over 2 out.* ....(6 to 1 op 4 to 1 tchd 7 to 1) 5
2310[8] COUREUR 4-9-7 D Wilkinson (2) *chsd ldrs, wknd 3 fs out.* ....(100 to 1) 6
2273[6] MIDDLEHAM CASTLE 4-9-7 Paul Eddery (1) *al beh.* ....(20 to 1 op 16 to 1 tchd 25 to 1) 7
Dist: 7l, ¾l, 8l, 3½l, 10l, ½l. 3m 5.60s. a 10.10s (7 Ran).
(L B Holliday), H R A Cecil

2508 Halifax Fillies' Handicap Class D (0-80 3-y-o and up) £3,114 5f 212yds.. (4:00)

2418[2] TRUTHFUL IMAGE [76] (bl) 4-9-3 (7*) P McCabe (1) *trkd ldrs, led entering fnl furlong, ran on wl.* ....(Evens fav op 5 to 4 on) 1
SHE'S SMART [80] 5-10-0 M Birch (2) *led till entering fnl furlong, no extr*..................(16 to 1 op 12 to 1) 2
2466[4] ANGELS ANSWER (Ire) [49] 4-7-6 (5*) Darren Moffatt (3) *in tch, ev ch 2 fs out, sn rdn and one pace.* ....(7 to 1 op 6 to 1) 3
1850[2] DESERT VENUS [72] 3-8-13 W R Swinburn (5) *in tch, effrt 2 fs out, sn btn*..........(5 to 2 tchd 9 to 4 and 11 to 4) 4
2133[3] SUNRISE MORNING (USA) [56] (bl) 3-7-11 F Norton (4) *chsd ldr till wknd 2 fs out*................(5 to 1 op 4 to 1) 5
Dist: 3l, 1½l, 2½l, 3½l. 1m 12.90s. a 1.90s (5 Ran).
SR: 60/52/15/21/-/ (P E Axon), M J Ryan

2509 Leyburn Limited Stakes Class D (0-75 4-y-o and up) £3,199 7f......... (4:30)

2270[2] LAUREL QUEEN (Ire) 5-8-9 J Carroll (1) *made all, clr 2 fs out, easily*.....................(6 to 5 on op 5 to 4 on) 1
2198[9] SYLVAN (Ire) (v) 4-8-9 W R Swinburn (3) *in tch, chsd wnr aftr 2 fs, rdn two out, no imprsn*.............. (5 to 4) 2
4789a[7] GENTLE HERO (USA) 7-8-7 (7*) I Jardine (2) *chsd wnr 2 fs, outpcd hfwy, sn beh*.............. (12 to 1 op 10 to 1) 3
Dist: 8l, 6l. 1m 27.80s. a 4.80s (3 Ran).
SR: 13/-/-/ (Laurel (Leisure) Limited), J Berry

2510 Leeds Handicap Class E (0-70 3-y-o and up) £3,106 5f...............(5:00)

2365[3] OUR MICA [48] (bl) 3-8-4 J Carroll (1) *cl up, led hfwy, wnt rght 2 fs out, ran on wl fnl furlong, cmftbly.* ....(4 to 1 op 3 to 1) 1
2312[3] GUSSIE FINK-NOTTLE (Ire) [58] (bl) 3-9-0 W Ryan (7) *prmnt, rdn o'r one furlong out, kpt on, no ch wth wnr.* ....(4 to 1 tchd 9 to 2) 2
2380[2] SIR TASKER [60] 5-9-8 Paul Eddery (8) *chsd ldrs, rdn 2 fs out, kpt on same pace.* ....(7 to 2 fav op 3 to 1 tchd 4 to 1) 3
2264[3] KABCAST [47] (bl) 8-8-9 S Wood (6) *led to hfwy, hmpd 2 fs out, sn btn*.........................(4 to 1 op 3 to 1) 4
1801[8] SABO SONG [68] (bl) 3-9-10 S Webster (5) *dwlt, nvr dngrs.* .... (9 to 1 op 8 to 1 tchd 10 to 1) 5
2305 GEMINI FIRE [58] 9-9-3 (3*) J Weaver (4) *sn beh.* ....(14 to 1 op 20 to 1) 6
2481[5] SHALAKO [43] 3-7-8 (5*) A Garth (2) *dwlt, al beh.* ....(25 to 1 op 16 to 1) 7
1740 WHISPERDALES [56] 3-8-12 S Morris (3) *sn beh, tld off.* .... (25 to 1 op 20 to 1) 8
Dist: 2½l, 2½l, 1½l, 2l, 2½l, 2l, 10l. 59.90s. a 2.40s (8 Ran).
SR: 32/32/30/11/18/4/-/-/ (Mike Dodds), J Berry

DOWN ROYAL (IRE) (good to yielding) Wednesday July 14th

2511 Smirnoff Handicap (0-65 3-y-o and up) £1,380 5f...................... (6:30)

2323[7] FANTANTE (Ire) [-] 4-9-6 P V Gilson (6)............ (5 to 1) 1
1923 FILL MY GLASS [-] 9-7-12 (4*) W J Smith (2)........(12 to 1) 2
2323* AFTERGLOW (Ire) [-] (bl) 4-9-9 (3ex) L O'Shea (5) (5 to 2 jt-fav) 3
2295[5] WHY ME LINDA (Ire) [-] 4-9-10 D Manning (9)..... (10 to 1) 4
2323[3] SOUTHERN RULE [-] (bl) 6-8-4 Joanna Morgan (4) ....(5 to 2 jt-fav) 5
2295[8] SORRECA (Ire) [-] (bl) 4-8-11 R Hughes (1)........(20 to 1) 6
1619[4] NEWYORK CONNECTION (Ire) [-] 3-8-2 (10*) D Cullen Jnr (3) ....(14 to 1) 7
2248 BELLE OF DREAMS (Ire) [-] (bl) 5-8-4 (6*) B Bowens (7) ....(8 to 1) 8
2295[3] FIVE LITTLE GIRLS (Ire) [-] 3-9-5 K J Manning (8)...(7 to 1) 9
Dist: ¾l, 2l, ½l, sht-hd. (Time not taken) (9 Ran).
(Mrs C Collins), C Collins

2512 Baileys Ladies Fashion Series (3-y-o and up) £1,380 1¾m............(7:00)

1997* VELMA (USA) 3-9-2 Miss U Smyth (7)..........(9 to 4 on) 1
1962[6] TOP GENERATION 4-9-7 (2*) Miss T Cunningham (4) ....(10 to 1) 2
1997 BASSETJA (Ire) 4-9-7 (2*) Miss M Savage (2).......(9 to 2) 3
2324[7] SOUND PERFORMANCE (Ire) 4-10-8[3] Miss L Robinson (8) ....(14 to 1) 4
LUCK OF A LADY (Ire) 4-9-9 Miss A Sloane (5)....(16 to 1) 5
1797[5] MISSED OPPORTUNITY (Ire) 5-9-10 (2*) Miss W Oakes (3) ....(33 to 1) 6
PERSIAN GLEN (bl) 6-9-12 Miss H McCourt (1)... (25 to 1) 7
1443 BELLE O' THE BAY (Ire) 4-9-11[4] (2*) Miss J Cox (6) (33 to 1) 8
LITTLE MOON 4-9-9 Miss S D Blair (9)...........(25 to 1) 9
Dist: 4l, 1l, 3l, ½l. (Time not taken) (9 Ran).
(Allen E Paulson), D K Weld

2513 Gilbey's Ulster Oaks Handicap (0-90 3-y-o and up) £3,450 1¼m...... (7:30)

2405 FLAME OF PERSIA (Ire) [-] 3-9-3 R Hughes (4).. (6 to 4 on) 1
2286 GRECIAN LADY (Ire) [-] 4-7-7 Joanna Morgan (2)..(25 to 1) 2
2451 MISS TWIN PEAKS (Ire) [-] 3-7-13 (2*) R M Burke (6) (7 to 1) 3
2041 ICEFLOW (Fr) [-] 3-7-8[1] (6*) R V Skelly (7)..........(5 to 1) 4
1987[5] MISS DARCY (Ire) [-] 5-7-9 (4*) W J Smith (1).......(7 to 1) 5
HAVIN' A BALL (Ire) [-] 4-7-9 (8*) B J Halligan (5)...(20 to 1) 6
Dist: 2l, hd, 3½l, ¾l. (Time not taken) (6 Ran).
(E Flynn), Michael Kauntze

2514 Budweiser Handicap (0-65 3-y-o and up) £1,380 7f..................(8:00)

2297[2] RUSTIC-ORT (Ire) [-] (bl) 5-9-5 R Hughes (2)....(3 to 1 fav) 1
2345[5] NO DIPLOMACY (Ire) [-] 4-9-5 (4*) P Carberry (11) (14 to 1) 2
2322[4] TIGNES (Ire) [-] 5-9-4 K J Manning (13)............(6 to 1) 3
1651 LOVE OF ERIN (Ire) [-] 4-7-7 L O'Shea (10)....... (25 to 1) 4
2321[8] SARA MAURETTE (Ire) [-] 3-9-9 N Byrne (4)........(5 to 1) 5
2248[6] FASTAFLOW (Ire) [-] 3-9-1 (6*) B J Walsh (15)...... (6 to 1) 6
2345[8] SIGHTSEER (Ire) [-] 4-8-5 (10*) D A O'Sullivan (16) (14 to 1) 7
NABEEL (USA) [-] 7-9-9 (4*) W J Smith (8)........ (16 to 1) 8
2248[7] TORCH SINGER [-] 3-9-1 P V Gilson (7)...........(7 to 1) 9
1995 GIRARDELLI (Ire) [-] 3-8-4 (8*) P J Smullen (9).....(16 to 1) 10
2141 PERCY LANE (Ire) [-] 3-9-0 (6*) B Bowens (6)..... (10 to 1) 11
2321[4] VOUVRAY (Ire) [-] 3-9-2 Joanna Morgan (12)..... (10 to 1) 12
2323 SPEED DEMON [-] 3-8-10 P Lowry (14).......... (25 to 1) 13
Dist: 2l, 1½l, 1l, sht-hd. (Time not taken) (13 Ran).
(J Kennedy), Edward Lynam

KILLARNEY (IRE) (soft) Wednesday July 14th

2515 Murphys Irish Stout Maiden (4-y-o and up) £3,450 1¾m................(4:00)

BIG MATT (Ire) 5-9-0 C Roche (5)..................(9 to 4) 1
2077[6] STRONG CASE (Ire) 5-9-0 S Craine (3).........(7 to 4 on) 2
CAN'T THINK WHAT 6-8-5 (6*) J J Behan (2).......(5 to 1) 3
BACK DOOR JOHNNY 7-9-0 J F Egan (4)........(10 to 1) 4
VALLEY TUFF (Ire) 5-9-0 B Coogan (1)...........(40 to 1) 5
Dist: ½l, 15l, 25l, dist. 3m 39.80s. (5 Ran).
(J McKeon), P Burke

2516 Muckross Park Hotel Claiming Race (3-y-o and up) £3,450 1m 3f..... (4:30)

2346[3] TROPICAL LAKE (Ire) 3-7-1 (6*) P P Murphy (6)....(13 to 2) 1
1995[2] HERMES GOLD (Ire) 3-7-13 W J Supple (4).... (5 to 4 fav) 2
2221[4] MILLERS MILL (Ire) 3-8-0 (2*) D G O'Shea (7)...... (3 to 1) 3
2346[6] AT YOUR SERVICE (Ire) 4-8-6 (6*) J J Behan (9)... (12 to 1) 4
2406[9] FAIRY FANTASY (Ire) 3-7-3 (8*) R T Fitzpatrick (11)..(9 to 1) 5
2094[5] BROWN TOP 6-8-10 S Craine (3)................(12 to 1) 6
1755 ANIMATE (Ire) 3-7-3 (8*) G M Moylan (8)..........(14 to 1) 7
2221[6] SHARP AT SIX (Ire) (bl) 3-7-12 J F Egan (10)....... (10 to 1) 8
Dist: Hd, 10l, 1l, 2½l. 2m 39.70s. (8 Ran).
(Mrs E Irwin), T Stack

2517 Carrolls Festival Handicap (0-70 3-y-o and up) £3,450 1m 3f........... (5:00)

1987[3] PULMICORT [-] (bl) 3-8-6 M J Kinane (2).......... (4 to 1) 1
2142 CALL MY GUEST (Ire) [-] 3-9-2 W J Supple (1)..... (5 to 1) 2
2461[6] COMMAND 'N CONTROL [-] 4-9-2 (6*) J J Behan (13) ....(7 to 1) 3
1621* TWO MAGPIES [-] 6-7-12 J F Egan (10)........... (5 to 1) 4
2040[6] DARK SWAN (Ire) [-] 3-8-9 (2*) D G O'Shea (11)... (10 to 1) 5

1962[5] PREMIER LEAP (Ire) [-] 4-8-3 (8*) B Fenton (12).....(5 to 1) 6
2496[2] MANGANS HILL (Ire) [-] 3-8-7 (6*) P P Murphy (8)..(14 to 1) 7
1822[3] TRANQUIL BEAUTY (Ire) [-] 4-9-1 (6*) C Everard (7) ....(7 to 2 fav) 8
CARBON FIVE (Ire) [-] 4-8-0[2] (6*) J A Heffernan (6) (20 to 1) 9
Dist: 5l, 2½l, 1l, 4l. 2m 40.00s. (9 Ran).
(Mrs Nuala Cribbin), M Halford

2518 Star Seafoods Fillies Maiden (3-y-o and up) £3,450 1m 3f........... (5:30)

PARNALA (USA) 3-9-0 M J Kinane (3)..........(11 to 8 on) 1
2297[4] NO DUNCE (Ire) 3-9-0 J P Murtagh (9)........... (10 to 1) 2
2140[3] LADY NOBLE (Ire) 3-9-0 J F Egan (6)..............(6 to 1) 3
2036[4] SEAWORTHY (Ire) 3-9-0 S Craine (2)..............(7 to 2) 4
2140[6] OCEAN BLUE (Ire) 3-9-0 P Shanahan (5).......... (14 to 1) 5
2140 BLACK PIPER (Ire) 3-8-8 (6*) J A Heffernan (7)..... (8 to 1) 6
SYGNE OF RICHES (Ire) 3-8-12 (2*) D G O'Shea (1) (33 to 1) pu
Dist: 3l, 6l, 6l, 2½l. 2m 41.00s. (7 Ran).
(H H Aga Khan), John M Oxx

SANDOWN (soft)
Wednesday July 14th
Going Correction: PLUS 0.30 sec. per fur. (race 1), PLUS 0.60 (2,3,4,5), PLUS 0.40 (6)

2519 'Ahead Of The Field' Maiden Auction Stakes Class D (2-y-o) £3,415 5f 6yds ....(6:25)

2364[4] BATTLING BLUE 9-0 Pat Eddery (5) *pressed ldr, drvn hfwy, hrd driven to ld ins last, rdn out.* .... (5 to 4 on op 9 to 4 on tchd 11 to 10 on) 1
2370[2] DANCE FOCUS 9-0 T Ives (2) *led, shaken up o'r one furlong out, hdd ins last, kpt on, no extr cl hme.* .... (2 to 1 op 5 to 2 tchd 11 to 4) 2
1689[5] MAJOR SUCCESS (Ire) 9-0 D Holland (1) *chsd ldrs, outpcd frm 2 fs out*....................... (16 to 1 op 10 to 1) 3
2147[2] SPORTING START 9-0 N Adams (4) *nvr gng pace.* .... (20 to 1 op 14 to 1 tchd 25 to 1) 4
WHITE LADY 8-9 W Carson (3) *slwly into strd, al wl beh.* .... (10 to 1 op 7 to 1) 5
Dist: Nk, 8l, hd, 12l. 1m 4.04s. a 4.54s (5 Ran).
SR: 39/38/6/5/-/ (David Thompson), R Hannon

2520 Harpers & Queen Selling Handicap Class F (0-60 3-y-o and up) £3,311 1m 1f...............................(6:55)

1878[4] LADY LACEY [45] (v) 6-9-6 J Williams (2) *hdwy 3 fs out, led one and a half out, sn clr, easily*.....(8 to 1 op 7 to 1) 1
2369[3] WAAZA (USA) [50] (bl) 4-9-8 (3*) D Harrison (3) *chsd ldrs, led 3 fs out, rdn 2 out, hdd one and a half out, styd on same pace*.............. (12 to 1 op 8 to 1 tchd 14 to 1) 2
2289[9] VALIANT WORDS [47] (bl) 6-9-8 T Quinn (8) *prmnt, led 5 fs out to 3 out, styd on same pace*...... (9 to 1 op 6 to 1) 3
1900 NORMAN WARRIOR [37] (v) 4-8-7 (5*) C Hodgson (13) *chsd ldrs, rdn and kpt on same pace fnl 2 fs.* .... (12 to 1 op 10 to 1 tchd 14 to 1) 4
1008[5] BILLYBACK [53] 3-9-4 W Carson (12) *drvn and hdwy 3 fs out, one pace frm 2 out*............ (8 to 1 op 10 to 1) 5
2226[6] LER CRU (Ire) [48] 4-9-9 T Williams (16) *chsd ldrs, outpcd 5 fs out, drvn and effrt o'r 2 out, no imprsn.* ....(5 to 1 fav op 14 to 1 tchd 9 to 2) 6
1097 RED SOMBRERO [39] 4-9-0 A Clark (11) *beh, drvn and some prog appr fnl 2 fs*..........................(33 to 1) 7
2001[2] KELLY'S KITE [38] 5-8-13 J Quinn (14) *in tch, wknd o'r 2 fs out*..(9 to 1 op 6 to 1) 8
2163[7] BLOWING (USA) [50] 3-9-1 M Perrett (17) *chsd ldrs till wknd 3 fs out*........ (16 to 1 op 14 to 1 tchd 20 to 1) 9
1861[7] CHILTERN HUNDREDS (USA) [45] 3-8-10 J Reid (9) *al beh.* .... (16 to 1 op 14 to 1 tchd 20 to 1) 10
2308[4] ROLY WALLACE [53] (bl) 4-10-0 D Biggs (1) *nvr rch ldrs.* .... (12 to 1 op 10 to 1) 11
2113 SLICK CHERRY [34] 6-8-6 (3*) B Doyle (15) *prmnt till wknd 3 fs out*............. (16 to 1 op 14 to 1 tchd 20 to 1) 12
2181[7] EXCESS BAGGAGE (Ire) [45] 3-8-10 Pat Eddery (6) *rcd wide, led aftr 2 fs to 5 out, wknd 3 out.* ....(8 to 1 op 7 to 1 tchd 9 to 1) 13
2291[5] HENBURY HALL (Ire) [49] 5-9-10 W Newnes (7) *led 2 fs, prmnt till wknd o'r 3 out.* .... (16 to 1 op 14 to 1 tchd 20 to 1) 14
2160[5] AUNT ADA [45] 4-9-6 L Dettori (10) *chsd ldrs till wknd rpdly o'r 3 fs out*..... (12 to 1 op 10 to 1 tchd 14 to 1) 15
2291 ABSOLUTELY HUMMING [39] (bl) 7-9-0 N Adams (18) *slwly away, al beh*.. (33 to 1) 16
Dist: 12l, 1l, ¾l, nk, 2½l, 2½l, 1l, 5l, 5l, hd. 2m 2.13s. a 10.93s (16 Ran).
SR: 23/4/-/-/-/-/ (Mrs K L Perrin), G B Balding

2521 Jennifer's Diary Handicap Class D (0-80 4-y-o and up) £4,713 1¾m (7:25)

2026[3] FREE MOVER (Ire) [74] 4-9-8 W Carson (8) *beh, drvn 3 fs out, led one and a half out, styd on wl.* ....(5 to 1 tchd 11 to 2) 1
2101[2] BALLY KNIGHT [55] 7-8-2[4] (5*) C Hodgson (7) *hld up rear, hdwy o'r 3 fs out, led 2 and a half out to one and a half out, one pace*.......... (11 to 2 op 7 to 2 tchd 6 to 1) 2
2002[2] SWORD MASTER [73] 4-9-7 W R Swinburn (5) *chsd ldr, led 3 and a half fs out to 2 and a half out, drvn and one pace und pres*..... (7 to 2 jt-fav op 3 to 1 tchd 4 to 1) 3
2256* LOBILIO (USA) [71] (v) 4-9-5 B Marcus (6) *chsd ldrs, rdn 3 fs out, no imprsn*.......................... (4 to 1 op 3 to 1) 4
2043 JAMES IS SPECIAL (Ire) [50] 5-7-12 J Quinn (9) *beh, hdwy o'r 3 fs out, wknd one and a half out.* ....(7 to 2 jt-fav op 5 to 1) 5
1911[7] MAD CASANOVA [67] (bl) 8-8-10 (5*) D McCabe (1) *in tch till wknd 2 fs out*.....................(8 to 1 tchd 10 to 1) 6
2111[5] ROMANSH [71] 4-9-5 J Reid (2) *str hold, led to 3 and a half fs out, wknd rpdly*..........(25 to 1 tchd 33 to 1) 7
Dist: 3½l, ½l, 3l, 4l, 2½l, 20l. 3m 13.72s. a 19.42s (7 Ran).
(Chesa Racing), N A Graham

2522 Town And County Pommery Handicap Class D (0-85 3-y-o) £5,015 7f 16yds ....(7:55)

1927[4] FOURFORFUN [80] 8-9 (7*) Mark Denaro (9) *hdwy 3 fs out, led jst ins fnl furlong, ran on wl.* .... (12 to 1 op 8 to 1 tchd 14 to 1) 1
2011[6] SIMPLY FINESSE [77] 8-13 T Quinn (8) *led o'r 4 fs out, drvn alng over 2 out, hdd jst ins last, styd on.* ....(8 to 1 tchd 9 to 1) 2
1806 CHILI HEIGHTS [81] 9-3 L Dettori (4) *hdwy o'r 2 fs out, ran on fnl furlong, not rch ldrs.* ....(11 to 2 fav op 8 to 1 tchd 5 to 1) 3
2212[5] OK BERTIE [74] 8-5 (5*) C Hodgson (12) *hdwy o'r 2 fs out, ran on fnl furlong*... (12 to 1 op 10 to 1 tchd 14 to 1) 4
PLUCK [78] 9-0 Pat Eddery (10) *trkd ldrs, gng wl 2 fs out, fdd fnl furlong*.........(6 to 1 op 9 to 2 tchd 13 to 2) 5
1718 SPECIAL ONE [71] 8-7 D Holland (13) *beh, drvn and hdwy o'r 2 fs out, kpt on fnl furlong*.....(20 to 1 op 14 to 1) 6
2379* SECOND CHANCE (Ire) [77] 8-13 (5ex) W Newnes (5) *chsd ldrs till wknd ins fnl 2 fs.* .... (10 to 1 op 8 to 1 tchd 12 to 1) 7
259[3] ERLKING (Ire) [72] 8-8 A Munro (2) *hdwy 4 fs out, btn whn hmpd o'r one out*..................(16 to 1 op 14 to 1) 8
2009[5] CITY ROCKET [76] 8-12 W R Swinburn (16) *led till o'r 4 fs out, fdd ins fnl 2*............... (16 to 1 tchd 20 to 1) 9
2212[9] SIMPLY SOOTY [77] 8-13 J Lowe (1) *beh, rdn o'r 2 fs out, no imprsn*........... (11 to 1 op 14 to 1 tchd 10 to 1) 10
2135[7] TAAHHUB (Ire) [75] (bl) 8-11 W Carson (14) *in tch early, beh fnl 4 fs*................ (7 to 1 op 6 to 1 tchd 8 to 1) 11
2363 ERTLON [78] 9-0 B Marcus (11) *effrt 3 fs out, wknd 2 out.* .... (20 to 1 op 16 to 1 tchd 25 to 1) 12
1833[3] BOLD THATCHER [70] 8-6 F Norton (6) *prmnt for o'r 3 fs.* .... (15 to 2 op 10 to 1 tchd 7 to 1) 13
2136[3] YOURS BY RIGHT [85] 9-2 (5*) D McCabe (7) *chsd ldrs till wknd 3 fs out*.....................(10 to 1 tchd 12 to 1) 14
4747a[5] PISTOL (Ire) [80] 8-13 (3*) D Harrison (3) *beh most of way, tld off*..(50 to 1 op 33 to 1) 15
Dist: ½l, 6l, hd, 3l, 1l, nk, 1l, 1½l, ¾l, 3l. 1m 33.73s. a 7.23s (15 Ran).
SR: 56/51/37/29/24/14/19/11/10/ (Mrs R F Knipe), R Hannon

2523 'Smart Insider' Claiming Stakes Class E (3-y-o) £3,246 1¼m 7yds...... (8:25)

1961[8] PISTOLS AT DAWN (USA) 8-6 J Reid (11) *trkd ldrs, led one and a half fs out, rdn out.* .... (11 to 2 op 5 to 1 tchd 6 to 1) 1
2273[9] BERING ISLAND (USA) 8-5 Pat Eddery (1) *chsd ldrs, led 3 fs out, rdn 2 out, hdd one and a half out, not quicken und pres*...................(4 to 1 op 3 to 1 tchd 9 to 2) 2
1827 CHIAPPUCCI (Ire) (v) 8-13 W R Swinburn (3) *hdwy 4 fs out, chsd ldrs frm 2 out, no imprsn.* .... (6 to 1 op 10 to 1 tchd 12 to 1) 3
1504[4] WOLLBOLL 8-11 T Sprake (9) *beh, styd on ins fnl 2 fs.* .... (33 to 1 op 25 to 1) 4
AMAZING AIR (USA) 8-7 J Williams (2) *wl beh till shaken up 3 fs out, some prog frm 2 out*....(14 to 1 op 10 to 1) 5
1993* SPARKY'S SONG 7-11 (3*) D Harrison (6) *beh, hdwy 3 fs out, rdn 2 out, wknd o'r one out.* .... (3 to 1 fav op 2 to 1 tchd 100 to 30) 6
1771[3] FORMAL AFFAIR 8-0 D Biggs (4) *chsd ldrs till wknd 2 fs out*..(9 to 2 op 7 to 2) 7
2134[5] ITS UNBELIEVABLE 8-5 (5*) D Wright (8) *led, styd far side strt, hdd 3 fs out, btn 2 out.* .... (10 to 1 op 7 to 1 tchd 12 to 1) 8
1906[7] BARSLEY 7-12 (3*) B Doyle (7) *in tch till wknd 3 fs out.* .... (33 to 1 op 25 to 1) 9
2471 ARRAS ROYALE 8-0 N Adams (10) *prmnt 6 fs, tld off.* ....(50 to 1) 10
Dist: ½l, 2½l, 6l, 1½l, 1½l, 2l, 3½l, 8l, 20l. 2m 15.89s. a 11.99s (10 Ran).
SR: 32/30/33/19/12/2/-/1/-/ (G Howard-Spink), R Hannon

2524 LBC Newstalk 97.3 FM Handicap Class D (0-80 4-y-o and up) £4,622 5f 6yds........................ (8:55)

1918[7] BELLS OF LONGWICK [66] 4-9-0 T Williams (3) *hdwy hfwy, led one furlong out, drvn clr.* .... (11 to 1 op 12 to 1 tchd 10 to 1) 1

2418* BALLASECRET [86] 5-10-1 (5*,6ex) D Meredith (10) *prmnt, led o'r 2 fs out till over one out, kpt on.*
.... (15 to 2 op 6 to 1 tchd 8 to 1) 2
2255^{5} BODARI [73] 4-9-7 D Holland (2) *pressed ldrs, led o'r one furlong out to one out, not quicken ins last.*
....................(4 to 1 fav op 3 to 1 tchd 9 to 2) 3
2050 SEA-DEER [59] 4-8-7 A Munro (7) *beh and outpcd, hdwy fnl furlong, ran on*.....(9 to 1 op 8 to 1 tchd 10 to 1) 4
2230^{2} METAL BOYS [78] 6-9-9 (3*) D Harrison (6) *chsd ldrs, one pace fnl furlong*.........(8 to 1 op 7 to 1 tchd 9 to 1) 5
2110^{3} SPECTACLE JIM [45] 4-7-7 N Adams (9) *hdwy o'r one furlong out, styd on fnl furlong.*
.......................(25 to 1 op 20 to 1 tchd 33 to 1) 6
1473 LOVE RETURNED [76] 6-9-10 M Tebbutt (13) *prmnt till wknd appr fnl furlong*..........(20 to 1 op 16 to 1) 7
2318* TRIOMING [54] 7-8-2 A Clark (5) *chsd ldrs for o'r 3 fs.*
....................................(8 to 1 op 9 to 2) 8
2157^{6} JOE SUGDEN [47] 9-7-9 J Lowe (8) *slwly into strd, effrt hfwy, wknd ins fnl 2 fs.*
.....................(12 to 1 op 16 to 1 tchd 20 to 1) 9
1957^{4} MISTER JOLSON [70] 4-8-11 (7*) S Drowne (1) *speed 3 fs.*
....................................(7 to 1 tchd 8 to 1) 10
1806 LORD HIGH ADMIRAL (Can) [77] 5-9-11 T Quinn (4) *led till o'r 2 fs out, sn wknd*..............(7 to 1 tchd 8 to 1) 11
2327 AIN'TLIFELIKETHAT [54] (bl) 6-8-2 F Norton (12) *slwly into strd, al beh*...................... (33 to 1 op 25 to 1) 12

Dist: 2l, ¾l, ¾l, sht-hd, 3½l, 1l, 2l, ¾l, 1½l, 2l. 1m 4.22s. a 4.72s (12 Ran).
SR: 46/58/42/25/43/-/23/-/-/ (Mrs Marion Wickham), D R Laing

SOUTHWELL (A.W) (std)
Wednesday July 14th
Going Correction: PLUS 0.10 sec. per fur.

2525 Chelsea Handicap Class E (0-70 3-y-o and up) £3,209 1m.............(2:15)

2057 SIE AMATO (Ire) [47] 4-8-13 J Fortune (5) *led 2 fs, cl up, pushed alng 3 furlongs out, effrt to chal o'r one furlong out, rdn ins last, led nr line.*
.....................(20 to 1 op 14 to 1 tchd 25 to 1) 1
1968^{2} CANNY LAD [49] (bl,e/s) 3-8-6 K Fallon (7) *cl up, led aftr 2 fs, rdn appr fnl furlong, hdd nr finish.*
................................(17 to 2 op 6 to 1) 2
2045^{4} AMLAK (USA) [50] (v) 4-8-11 (5*) J Tate (4) *in tch, hdwy 2 and a half fs out, effrt and ev ch appr fnl furlong, sn rdn, hng lft and one pace.*
.............................(5 to 1 op 4 to 1 tchd 6 to 1) 3
2220^{3} CHARLIE BIGTIME [64] 3-9-7 A Munro (6) *mid-div, hdwy 3 fs out, sn rdn and styd on one pace.* (9 to 2 op 4 to 1) 4
2217^{4} SEA PRODIGY [34] (bl) 4-8-0 T Sprake (9) *prmnt, rdn 2 fs out, grad wknd.*
.........(10 to 1 op 14 to 1 tchd 16 to 1 and 8 to 1) 5
1591 HERBRAND (Ire) [37] (bl) 4-8-0 (3*) S Maloney (1) *chsd ldrs, rdn 2 and a half fs out, sn wknd*...(20 to 1 op 12 to 1) 6
2300^{3} BALLERINA BAY [61] (v) 5-9-13 G Duffield (8) *dwlt, nvr rchd ldrs*...(3 to 1 fav op 5 to 2 tchd 100 to 30 and 7 to 2) 7
2217* MUSIC DANCER [54] 4-9-6 L Dettori (2) *chsd ldrs, rdn o'r 2 fs out, sn wknd*....................(9 to 2 tchd 5 to 1) 8
2065^{6} JAKE THE PAKE (Ire) [70] 3-9-13 T Quinn (3) *nvr rchd ldrs.*
...............................(10 to 1 op 6 to 1) 9
2086^{5} PERSIAN LION [30] 4-7-10 L Charnock (10) *cl up, rdn 3 fs out, sn wknd*.................................(33 to 1) 10

Dist: Hd, 2½l, ¾l, 6l, 1½l, ½l, 1½l, 7l, 2l. 1m 45.10s. a 6.10s (10 Ran).
SR: 20/12/14/17/-/-/ (Red Rose Partnership), Capt J Wilson

2526 Mayfair Selling Stakes Class G (2-y-o) £2,070 6f...................... (2:45)

2016^{5} WANDERING ANGEL 8-12 L Dettori (5) *cl up gng wl, led on bit 2 fs out, easily*....(6 to 5 fav op 5 to 4 tchd 6 to 4) 1
2423^{2} THE FERNHILL FLYER (Ire) (v) 8-12 G Carter (7) *sn chasing ldrs, effrt and hdwy o'r 2 fs out, rdn and kpt on appr fnl furlong, no ch wth wnr.*
.... (5 to 1 op 7 to 2 tchd 11 to 2) 2
2042^{9} SNUGFIT ANNIE 8-6 T Lucas (2) *chsd ldrs, rdn 2 fs out, styd on fnl furlong*..................(16 to 1 op 14 to 1) 3
1555^{6} LADY WESTBURY (Ire) 8-6 T Sprake (6) *steadied strt, hdwy hfwy, rdn 2 fs out, kpt on one pace.*
....................(14 to 1 op 12 to 1 tchd 16 to 1) 4
586^{4} STEADFAST ELITE (Ire) 8-12 K Darley (4) *led, rdn and hdd 2 fs out, sn wknd*..................... (7 to 1 op 5 to 1) 5
GRETELS PET 8-6 L Charnock (8) *beh, wide strt, some late hdwy*..................................(20 to 1 op 14 to 1) 6
2271^{2} CAPTAIN TAFFY (bl,e/s) 8-11 K Fallon (9) *al beh.*
.................................(5 to 1 op 4 to 1) 7
2042^{8} GOODWINCOPLEY 8-8 (3*) S Maloney (1) *slwly into strd, al beh*....................................(33 to 1) 8
1583 BELLAROY 8-1 (5*) Stephen Davies (3) *cl up, rdn 3 fs out, sn wknd*...................(33 to 1 op 20 to 1) 9

Dist: 2½l, 1l, 4l, 6l, 1l, 8l, 1l, ½l. 1m 18.50s. a 5.10s (9 Ran).
SR: 8/-/-/-/-/-/ (Mrs P T Fenwick), D R Loder

2527 Allott & Lomax Handicap Class D (0-80 3-y-o and up) £3,026 6f......... (3:15)

2113^{8} SWEET ROMEO [57] 3-8-3 Dean McKeown (1) *made all, rdn clr a furlong and a half out, eased nr finish.*
.... (4 to 1 tchd 9 to 2 and 5 to 1) 1
2269^{7} STARDUST EXPRESS [68] 3-9-0 T Williams (2) *cl up, rdn 2 fs out, kpt on one pace*............(12 to 1 op 7 to 1) 2
2428^{2} CHOIR PRACTICE [62] (bl,e/s) 6-9-1 C Rutter (3) *slwly away and beh, rdn alng hfwy, styd on fnl 2 fs, nvr dngrs.*
..................................(9 to 4 op 6 to 4) 3
1871* HIGHBORN (Ire) [75] 4-10-0 G Hind (4) *chsd ldg pair, rdn o'r 2 fs out, sn wknd*...........(11 to 8 fav op 6 to 4) 4
2206^{5} JADE CITY [80] 3-9-12 L Charnock (5) *slwly away, al beh.*
..................................(8 to 1 op 4 to 1) 5

Dist: 3½l, 1½l, 4l, 8l. 1m 16.40s. a 3.00s (5 Ran).
SR: 41/38/33/30/-/ (The Fairyhouse 1992 Partnership), M Johnston

2528 East Midlands Electricity Plc Maiden Stakes Class D (2-y-o) £3,201 7f (3:45)

715^{3} HIGHLY FASHIONABLE (Ire) 8-9 T Quinn (5) *chsd ldrs, hdwy to ld o'r 2 fs out, pushed clr appr last, eased nr finish*..............................(11 to 4 op 2 to 1) 1
2044^{2} NIGHT SNOW 8-9 M Hills (3) *cl up, led aftr 2 fs, rdn and hdd o'r two furlongs out, kpt on.*
..............(7 to 4 fav op 2 to 1 tchd 5 to 2) 2
1949^{6} JEAN DE FLORETTE (USA) 9-0 L Dettori (6) *chsd ldrs, pushed alng hfwy, some hdwy 2 fs out, sn one pace.*
..................................(3 to 1 op 7 to 2) 3
1624^{5} MOCKINGBIRD 8-6 (3*) D Harrison (1) *chsd ldrs, rdn 2 and a half fs out, nvr dngrs.* (4 to 1 op 9 to 2 tchd 5 to 1) 4
1926 NOORAN 9-0 G Carter (4) *led 2 fs, cl up till rdn and wknd o'r two furlongs out*......................... (20 to 1) 5
ROSSALL POINT 8-11 (3*) S Maloney (2) *slwly away, al rear*...........................(10 to 1 op 7 to 1) 6

Dist: 3l, 4l, 4l, 8l, 5l. 1m 32.00s. a 5.90s (6 Ran).
SR: 17/8/1/ (Stephen Crown), P F I Cole

2529 Provident Mutual Claiming Stakes Class F (3-y-o) £2,243 1½m..... (4:15)

2207^{8} GOODBYE MILLIE 8-6 (5*) O Pears (5) *trkd ldrs, hdwy to ld o'r 2 fs out, edgd lft, rdn and ran on wl fnl furlong.*
(5 to 4 on op 6 to 4 on tchd 6 to 5 on and 11 to 10 on) 1
2086^{3} GWEEK (Ire) 8-4 P Robinson (2) *trkd ldrs, hdwy and rdn o'r 2 fs out, kpt on und pres ins last.* (8 to 1 op 6 to 1) 2
980 CRIMINAL RECORD (USA) (v) 9-3 A Munro (6) *trkd ldr, effrt 3 fs out and sn ev ch, rdn 2 furlongs out, soon one pace.*
.............................(12 to 1 op 6 to 1) 3
2219^{8} SLOE BRANDY 8-4 G Duffield (1) *in tch, rdn o'r 4 fs out, plugged on one pace.* (7 to 1 op 12 to 1 tchd 14 to 1) 4
2052^{6} STAPLEFORD LASS 8-2 (3*) D Harrison (7) *in tch, rdn o'r 4 fs out, sn wknd*........... (13 to 2 op 6 to 1 tchd 7 to 1) 5
2443^{2} SHARE A MOMENT (Can) 8-9 K Darley (4) *led, drvn 3 fs out, hdd o'r 2 furlongs out, sn wknd*..... (7 to 1 op 6 to 1) 6
1746 FORGE GOLD 8-10 (7*) C Hawksley (3) *sn beh and rdn alng, tld off frm hfwy*............ (40 to 1 op 33 to 1) 7

Dist: Nk, 6l, 5l, 4l, 15l, 8l. 2m 43.00s. a 9.10s (7 Ran).
SR: 18/10/11/-/ (Lintscan Ltd (Corbett Bookmakers)), S G Norton

2530 Battersea Handicap Class E (0-70 4-y-o and up) £3,028 1½m.......... (4:45)

2427* SHUJAN (USA) [70] 4-10-1 (5ex) L Dettori (3) *cl up, led aftr 2 fs, clr 7 furlongs out, eased fnl furlong, unchlgd.*
.... (5 to 4 on op 6 to 4 on tchd 11 to 10 on) 1
1832 GREAT ORATION (Ire) [38] 4-7-11 L Charnock (7) *chsd ldrs, rdn and hdwy 5 fs out, styd on und pres fnl 2 furlongs, no ch wth wnr*.......(20 to 1 op 16 to 1 tchd 25 to 1) 2
456 MODEST HOPE (USA) [69] 6-10-0 Alex Greaves (6) *hdwy to chase wnr hfwy, rdn 4 fs out, plugged on one pace.*
...............................(11 to 2 op 4 to 1) 3
2218* SMILES AHEAD [60] (v) 5-8-12 (7*) C Hawksley (5) *cl up till rdn hfwy and sn wknd*.............(11 to 2 op 5 to 1) 4
1873^{2} SULUK (USA) [38] 8-7-11 J Quinn (2) *in tch, rdn hfwy, sn wknd*.................(5 to 1 op 9 to 2 tchd 11 to 2) 5
DESPERATE MAN [53] 4-8-12 G Duffield (4) *sn outpcd and wl beh, tld off frm hfwy*..........................(50 to 1) 6
1578 MELTONBY [49] 4-8-8 Kim Tinkler (1) *led 2 fs, sn pushed alng, lost pl aftr 5 furlongs, tld off.* (50 to 1 op 33 to 1) 7

Dist: 4l, 1½l, 5l, 3½l, 15l, 5l. 2m 41.70s. a 7.80s (7 Ran).
SR: 49/9/37/18/ (M J Polglase), R W Armstrong

ST-CLOUD (FR) (good to soft)
Wednesday July 14th
Going Correction: PLUS 0.15 sec. per fur.

2531 Prix Eugene Adam (Group 2) (3-y-o) £47,790 1¼m.................. (2:55)

1765^{5} REVELATION (Ire) 8-11 A Cruz (5) *3rd strt, effrt 2 fs out, led one and a half out, ran on wl, imprsv*.......(119 to 10) 1
696^{3} TALLOIRES (USA) 8-11 T Jarnet (8) *6th strt, effrt 2 fs out, quickened one and a half out, ran on wl, not rch wnr.*
....(28 to 10) 2
2081^{3} SIAM (USA) 8-11 C Asmussen (7) *bumped 3 fs out, 8th strt, not clr run 2 out, nrst finish*...............(8 to 5 fav) 3

1448[9] FATHERLAND (Ire) (bl) 8-11 L Piggott (1) *al mid-div, 5th strt, rdn and hdwy 2 fs out, lost 3rd on line*.....(5 to 2) 4
1544[8] SIN KIANG (Fr) 8-11 G Mosse (9) *al prmnt, second strt, led 2 out till one and a half out, no extr*.........(87 to 10) 5
955[3] SAWASDEE (Fr) 8-11 J Boisnard (6) *pld hrd early, last strt, some late prog*..(14 to 1) 6
1149[3] SISMART (Fr) 8-11 S Guillot (4) *nvr dngrs*.......(28 to 10) 7
1367[8] RANGER (Fr) 8-11 D Boeuf (2) *led till rdn and wknd 2 fs out*..(16 to 1) 8
HIGHEST SWEEP (Fr) 8-11 E Legrix (3) *al prmnt, 3rd strt, rdn and wknd quickly 2 fs out*..................(25 to 1) 9
Dist: 2l, 2l, sht-hd, 1l, 2l, ½l, ½l, 5l. 2m 7.60s. a 3.60s (9 Ran).
SR: 76/72/68/67/65/61/60/59/49/ (Cheveley Park Stud), R Hannon

YARMOUTH (good to firm (races 1,2,3), good (4,5,6))
Wednesday July 14th
Going Correction: MINUS 0.20 sec. per fur.

2532 Anglian Racing Club Handicap Class E (0-70 3-y-o and up) £3,172 6f 3yds ....(6:35)

2225* SAMSOLOM [68] 5-10-0 K Darley (3) *settled gng wl, quickened ahead entering fnl furlong, drvn out*. ....(6 to 1 op 11 to 2 tchd 7 to 1) 1
2099[6] BILL MOON [52] 7-8-5 (7*) Michael Denaro (6) *co'red up in midfield, swtchd through to improve fnl furlong, ran on wl*.................... (6 to 1 op 5 to 1 tchd 7 to 1) 2
2157[7] WALK THAT WALK [58] 4-8-11 (7*) K Pattinson (7) *nvr far away, feeling pace and rdn 2 fs out, rallied ins last*. ....(10 to 1 tchd 14 to 1) 3
2110[6] RACING TELEGRAPH [59] 3-8-12 M Wigham (5) *steadied strt, bustled alng to go pace hfwy, kpt on, nvr nrr*. ....(3 to 1 tchd 5 to 2 and 7 to 2) 4
2305[2] PAGEBOY [60] 4-9-6 R Cochrane (4) *tried to make all, hdd entering fnl furlong, fdd*. ....(15 to 8 fav op 7 to 4 tchd 9 to 4) 5
700 HONEY VISION [42] (bl) 4-8-2 G Bardwell (8) *chsd alng in midfield hfwy, nvr able to chal*....(33 to 1 op 20 to 1) 6
2291[9] AEDEAN [42] (bl) 4-8-2 E Johnson (1) *rcd wide, in tch for o'r 4 fs, sn btn*....................(50 to 1 op 20 to 1) 7
2428[3] LORD NASKRA (USA) [51] (v) 4-8-8 (3*) Emma O'Gorman (2) *sluggish strt, last thrght, nvr dngrs*. ....(12 to 1 op 10 to 1 tchd 14 to 1) 8
Dist: Nk, 1½l, 3l, 2l, nk, 6l, 3l. 1m 13.00s. a 2.00s (8 Ran).
SR: 50/33/33/15/15/ (The Hammond Partnership), P Howling

2533 Harrison Selling Stakes Class G (2-y-o) £2,385 7f 3yds............. (7:05)

1955 SILVER SLIPPER 8-6 M Roberts (3) *nvr far away, hrd drvn o'r 2 fs out, swtchd fnl furlong, led on line*. ....(7 to 2 tchd 9 to 2) 1
2268* PASSION SUNDAY 8-11 K Darley (5) *led, hrd pressed ins fnl furlong, ct on line*..........(2 to 1 on op 6 to 4 on) 2
1933[8] FILCH (v) 7-13 (7*) G Milligan (4) *wth wnr, hrd drvn o'r one furlong out, kpt on same pace*.....(16 to 1 op 12 to 1) 3
2155[3] BERNIE'S SISTER (Ire) 7-13 (7*) G Forster (1) *settled gng wl, cruised up on outsd 2 fs out, rdn and not run on*. ....(13 to 2 op 4 to 1) 4
2331 LITTLE BID (USA) 8-1 (5*) J Tate (2) *chsd ldg quartet, effrt and drvn alng 2 fs out, wknd ins last*. ....(8 to 1 op 6 to 1) 5
Dist: Sht-hd, 2l, nk, 1½l. 1m 27.80s. a 4.60s (5 Ran).
SR: 2/6/ (S M Threadwell), R Hannon

2534 Applegate Fillies' Handicap Class E (0-70 3-y-o) £3,158 1m 3yds..... (7:35)

1991[6] STARLIGHT ROSE (Ire) [50] 8-3 E Johnson (6) *sluggish strt, reco'red to join issue aftr 2 fs, str run fnl furlong, edgd lft, led last 50 yards*................(8 to 1 tchd 9 to 1) 1
2193[3] DALALAH [66] 9-5 R Hills (1) *settled gng wl, led on bit 2 fs out, hrd drvn fnl furlong, ct last 50 yards*. ....(3 to 1 op 5 to 2) 2
1776[8] ROCK THE BOAT [58] 8-11 K Darley (8) *last and hld up, swtchd outsd to chal wl o'r one furlong out, rdn and not quicken*.......................... (7 to 1 tchd 8 to 1) 3
1816[5] CRYSTAL REAY [65] 9-4 R Cochrane (2) *settled to track ldrs, drvn alng whn pace lifted 2 fs out, no extr*. ....(11 to 4 fav op 3 to 1) 4
1803* ASTERN (USA) [68] 9-7 M Roberts (5) *tucked away, hrd drvn whn pace quickened 2 fs out, no extr*. ....(7 to 2 op 3 to 1) 5
2190[7] GREY WATCH [40] (bl) 7-7 N Carlisle (4) *nvr far away, feeling pace and drvn alng o'r 2 fs out, fdd*. .... (25 to 1 op 33 to 1) 6
2330[9] RUBY COOPER [56] 8-9 N Day (7) *trkd ldg pair for o'r 4 fs, wknd und pres over one furlong out*. .... (10 to 1 op 8 to 1 tchd 11 to 1) 7
Dist: ½l, 4l, sht-hd, sht-hd, 5l, sht-hd. 1m 41.50s. a 5.70s (7 Ran).
(B Thomas), C A Horgan

2535 S.E.S Instrumentation Median Auction Maiden Stakes Class E (2-y-o) £3,158 6f 3yds........................(8:05)

POLISH ADMIRAL 9-0 N Day (3) *made all, hrd pressed and swshd tail fnl furlong, kpt on grimly last 50 yards*. ....(4 to 1 op 5 to 1 tchd 7 to 1) 1
2336[3] PETULA 8-9 M Hills (2) *wtd wth, swtchd outsd to chal entering fnl furlong, not quicken last 50 yards*. ....(6 to 4 on op 2 to 1 on tchd 5 to 2 on) 2
BRADWELL (Ire) 8-2 (7*) S Mulvey (1) *nvr far away, effrt and drvn alng o'r one furlong out, one pace*. ....(7 to 1 op 5 to 1) 3
HERR TRIGGER 9-0 R Cochrane (4) *wth wnr, hrd drvn o'r one furlong out, no extr*. ....(10 to 1 op 8 to 1 tchd 14 to 1) 4
TIN VENTURE 9-0 W Woods (6) *steadied strt, improved gng wl hfwy, rdn and fdd o'r one furlong out*. .... (12 to 1 op 10 to 1) 5
1277[5] TEXANNE (Bel) 8-9 Paul Smith (5) *trkd ldrs, feeling pace and drvn alng 2 fs out, fdd*. ....(16 to 1 op 10 to 1 tchd 20 to 1) 6
Dist: 1l, 4l, 1½l, 4l, 1½l. 1m 13.80s. a 2.80s (6 Ran).
SR: 20/11/-/ (Walter Grubmuller), C F Wall

2536 Courthouse Claiming Stakes Class F (3-y-o and up) £2,660 2m....... (8:35)

1004[6] MISTRESS BEE (USA) 4-9-5 R Hills (6) *dictated pace, quickened up entering strt, kpt on strly ins fnl furlong*. ....(14 to 1 op 12 to 1 tchd 16 to 1) 1
2265[2] POST IMPRESSIONIST (Ire) 4-9-4 R Cochrane (4) *al hndy, drvn up to chal o'r one furlong out, not go past*. ....(11 to 4 op 3 to 1) 2
2223* QUIET RIOT 11-9-5 R Price (5) *trkd ldg quartet, lft fltfooted whn pace quickened o'r 3 fs out, styd on one pace fnl furlong*.....................(9 to 2 op 7 to 2) 3
2007[4] EARLY TO RISE 3-8-0 (7*) J D Smith (3) *nvr far away, ev ch and drvn alng o'r 3 fs out, btn over one out*. ....(6 to 1 tchd 13 to 2) 4
2422 JULFAAR (USA) 6-9-10 K Darley (2) *last and hld up, effrt entering strt, rdn and btn 3 fs out*. ....(5 to 4 fav tchd 13 to 8) 5
2109 RAPINSKI 4-9-8 T Wall (1) *trkd ldg trio, hrd drvn o'r 3 fs out, tld off*..........................(33 to 1 op 25 to 1) 6
Dist: ¾l, 7l, 2½l, 4l, 20l. 3m 35.50s. (6 Ran).
(D R Stoddart), D Morley

2537 Horning Handicap Class E (0-70 3-y-o and up) £3,054 1¼m 21yds......(9:05)

2333 DUVEEN (Ire) [70] 3-9-3 (3*) M Fenton (1) *nvr far away, wndrd und pres o'r 3 fs out, rallied to ld wl over one out, gmely*.........(3 to 1 jt-fav op 5 to 2 tchd 7 to 2) 1
1936[5] CAST THE LINE [66] 3-9-2 M Roberts (4) *al hndy, led 3 fs out till wl o'r one out, rallied*. ....(7 to 1 op 6 to 1 tchd 8 to 1) 2
2195* OVERPOWER [61] 9-9-1 (7*) S Mulvey (5) *steadied strt, drvn alng to improve last 3 fs, staying on finish*. ....(9 to 2 op 4 to 1 tchd 5 to 1) 3
1934[4] SURREY DANCER [63] 5-9-10 B Raymond (2) *tucked away, effrt and squeezed for room o'r 3 fs out, styd on ins last*.........(3 to 1 jt-fav op 11 to 4 tchd 100 to 30) 4
1566[7] MISTER BLAKE [53] (bl) 3-8-2[2] (3*) Emma O'Gorman (6) *set modest pace, quickened entering strt, hdd 3 fs out, no extr*............................(14 to 1 tchd 16 to 1) 5
2300[7] TALENTED TING (Ire) [58] 4-9-5 N Carlisle (3) *took keen hold, effrt and drvn alng o'r 3 fs out, fdd over one out*. ....(7 to 2 op 5 to 2) 6
Dist: Nk, 1l, nk, 8l, 12l. 2m 8.50s. a 4.50s (6 Ran).
SR: 41/36/40/41/4/-/ (Mrs D Weatherby), M Bell

CATTERICK (good to soft)
Thursday July 15th
Going Correction: PLUS 0.15 sec. per fur.

2538 'A' One Apprentice Claiming Stakes Class F (3-y-o) £2,377 1m 5f 175yds ....(2:10)

2313* MR GENEAOLOGY (USA) (bl) 9-4 K Rutter (1) *nvr far away, niggled alng 4 fs out, effrt and rdn 2 out, led ins last, sn clr*.......... (6 to 4 on op 11 to 8 on tchd 5 to 4 on) 1
2131* TRY N' FLY (Ire) 9-1 Darren Moffatt (3) *sn led, shaken up entering strt, hdd ins last, no'extr*....(6 to 4 op Evens) 2
1278[8] MAGIC FAN (Ire) 8-1 (7*) Carol Davison (4) *hld up, outpcd o'r 4 fs out, shaken up over 2 out, not pace to chal*. .... (50 to 1 op 25 to 1) 3
LIME JUICE 8-2[1] (5*) S Copp (2) *missed break, beh, took clr order aftr 5 fs, rdn alng 4 out, btn whn hng badly rght entering strt, tld off*. ....(12 to 1 op 8 to 1 tchd 14 to 1) 4
Dist: 2½l, 10l, 20l. 3m 14.50s. a 19.00s (4 Ran).
(Mrs P A White), J White

2539 Tunstall Nursery Class E (2-y-o) £3,183 7f........................ (2:40)

2216* EXTRA BONUS [-] 9-4 (3*) J Weaver (3) *dwlt, hld up, rdn to improve entering strt, sstnd run to ld wl ins fnl furlong.* ....(9 to 1 op 8 to 1) 1
2021 CLOSE TO REALITY [-] 9-0 K Fallon (5) *led, rdn alng entering strt, clr whn hng rght o'r one furlong out, hdd wl ins last, not quicken*............. (16 to 1 op 14 to 1) 2
2069[9] CHIEF EXECUTIVE [-] 8-6 J Reid (11) *in tch, hmpd bend o'r 2 fs out, rdn and kpt on same pace fnl furlong.* ....(3 to 1 jt-fav op 6 to 4) 3
1758[3] KOMPLICITY [-] 8-9 N Connorton (8) *in tch, effrt and drvn alng 2 fs out, one pace appr last.* (12 to 1 tchd 10 to 1) 4
1758* OVIDEO [-] 8-12 G Duffield (4) *nvr far away, rdn alng entering strt, one pace o'r one furlong out*...(3 to 1 jt-fav op 9 to 2 tchd 5 to 1) 5
1810[4] BLASTER BATES (USA) [-] 9-5 Alex Greaves (7) *beh, pushed alng entering strt, kpt on fnl furlong, nvr able to chal.* .... (16 to 1 op 10 to 1) 6
1763* IMPOSING GROOM (Ire) [-] 9-2 B Raymond (13) *mid-div, sn pushed alng, rdn and one pace fnl 2 fs.* ....(5 to 1 op 4 to 1) 7
1810[5] GOLDEN STAR (Ire) [-] 9-4 J Fanning (6) *hld up, rdn alng entering strt, nvr on terms*...................(16 to 1) 8
1998[7] PARISIAN LOVER [-] 8-10 K Darley (1) *sn wth ldr, drvn alng entering strt, grad wknd.* ....(10 to 1 tchd 8 to 1 and 12 to 1) 9
1964* HARPO'S SPECIAL [-] 8-9 (7*) D Thomas (10) *hld up in rear, shaken up entering strt, nvr nr to chal.* ....(9 to 1 op 8 to 1) 10
1519[3] WESTCOAST [-] 7-13 J Lowe (12) *mid-div, pushed alng appr strt, lost tch 2 fs out*.....................(20 to 1) 11

Dist: 1½l, 3l, ½l, 4l, 2l, nk, 1½l, hd, nk, 6l. 1m 29.00s. a 6.00s (11 Ran).
SR: 33/21/4/5/-/-/ (Induna Racing Partners), C F Wall

2540 Grove Selling Handicap Class G (0-60 3-y-o) £2,574 7f................ (3:10)

2151[4] CUBIST (Ire) [55] (bl) 9-7 B Raymond (9) *nvr far away, chlgd entering strt, sn led, pushed out ins fnl furlong.* ....(5 to 1 tchd 11 to 2) 1
2478[4] MANX MONARCH [46] 8-7 (5*) A Garth (4) *dwlt, beh, rdn to improve entering strt, edgd rght appr last, no extr fnl 100 yards*...........................(5 to 1 op 4 to 1) 2
2288* NORLING (Ire) [40] 8-6 L Charnock (10) *prmnt, led aftr 2 fs, rdn entering strt, sn hdd, not quicken.* ....(11 to 4 fav op 7 to 4) 3
1760[6] MAKE MINE A DOUBLE [42] 8-8 N Connorton (2) *in tch, effrt and rdn 2 fs out, swtchd entering last, no extr.* ....(6 to 1 op 5 to 1) 4
1735[5] BROOKLANDS EXPRESS [43] 8-9 J Carroll (8) *led 2 fs, hmpd aftr 3 furlongs, drvn appr strt, wknd fnl two furlongs*............(14 to 1 op 10 to 1 tchd 16 to 1) 5
2365[7] SHOTLEY AGAIN [40] 8-3 (3*) S Maloney (6) *chsd ldrs, effrt and drvn alng o'r 3 fs out, wknd 2 out.* .... (33 to 1 op 25 to 1) 6
2338[2] BRAXTON BRAGG (Ire) [48] 9-0 G Duffield (1) *wth ldrs, rdn alng appr strt, wknd wl o'r one furlong out.* ....(4 to 1 tchd 9 to 2) 7
2095[4] IRISH ROOTS (Ire) [47] 8-6 (7*) Ruth Coulter (5) *beh, pushed alng o'r 3 fs out, sn lost tch, tld off*...(7 to 1 op 5 to 1) 8
2279[7] CIZARD (Ire) [29] 7-9[1] J Lowe (3) *mid-div, outpcd hfwy, lost tch appr strt, tld off*.......(33 to 1 op 25 to 1) 9

Dist: 1½l, 5l, nk, 4l, 1½l, 1l, 10l, ½l. 1m 28.80s. a 5.80s (9 Ran).
SR: 35/21/-/1/-/-/ (Lord Hartington), D Morley

2541 Wood House Maiden Stakes Class D (Div I) (2-y-o) £3,231 5f 212yds.. (3:40)

WEST QUEST (Can) 9-0 A Munro (6) *nvr far away, rdn alng wl o'r one furlong out, ran on to ld entering last, kpt on well*..........(5 to 4 on op Evens tchd 5 to 4) 1
1988[2] CALLABONNA 8-9 G Duffield (3) *pressed ldr, led aftr 2 fs, rdn entering strt, hng lft o'r one out, hdd entering last, no extr*............................(3 to 1 op 11 to 8) 2
2021[6] MIDNIGHT MAGPIE (Ire) 9-0 K Fallon (4) *in tch, effrt 2 fs out, kpt on fnl furlong, no extr towards finish.* ....(12 to 1 op 8 to 1 tchd 14 to 1) 3
DOUBLE SIXTEEN 8-7 (7*) D Thomas (1) *dwlt, beh, improved entering strt, styd on fnl furlong, nrst finish, prmsg*.................................(25 to 1 op 20 to 1) 4
RACING BRENDA 8-9 L Charnock (7) *chsd ldrs, pushed alng aftr 2 fs, one pace o'r one furlong out.* .... (33 to 1 op 25 to 1) 5
2090[6] BLAIN 9-0 J Carroll (8) *in tch, effrt and rdn alng 2 fs out, wknd entering last*..................(25 to 1 op 20 to 1) 6
2342[4] RICH HARMONY 9-0 Dean McKeown (5) *led 2 fs, styd hndy, drvn appr strt, wknd two furlongs out.* ....(10 to 1 op 12 to 1 tchd 14 to 1) 7
PRINCESS CARMEN (Ire) 8-4 (5*) C Hodgson (9) *slwly into strd, beh, pushed alng hfwy, no imprsn.* .... (16 to 1 op 8 to 1) 8
1158 MARBLE 8-9 N Connorton (2) *missed break, al struggling in rear, tld off fnl 2 fs*............ (50 to 1 op 33 to 1) 9

Dist: 1½l, 1½l, sht-hd, 1½l, 2l, 1l, 6l, 12l. 1m 16.20s. a 5.20s (9 Ran).
SR: 14/3/2/1/-/-/ (Fahd Salman), P F I Cole

2542 Wood House Maiden Stakes Class D (Div II) (2-y-o) £3,231 5f 212yds..(4:10)

1944[4] PROMISE FULFILLED (USA) 8-9 J Fortune (1) *dwlt, sn reco'red and led, rdn 2 fs out, hld on gmely, hrd pressed fnl furlong*..........................(7 to 1 op 6 to 1) 1
1895[4] NORTHERN CELADON (Ire) 9-0 B Raymond (4) *pressed ldr, chlgd o'r one furlong out, no extr towards finish.* ....(5 to 1 op 6 to 1) 2
1916[6] SOOLAIMON (Ire) 8-9 J Reid (2) *nvr far away, pushed alng entering strt, one pace appr last.* ....(6 to 5 fav op 6 to 4 tchd 11 to 10) 3
2179[7] ARCTIC DIAMOND 9-0 K Fallon (9) *in tch, pushed alng hfwy, kpt on same pace fnl 2 fs*....(16 to 1 op 12 to 1) 4
BEECHFIELD FLYER 9-0 J Carroll (8) *cl up, rdn alng 2 fs out, sn btn*..........(14 to 1 op 10 to 1 tchd 16 to 1) 5
INSIDER TRADER 9-0 A Munro (3) *chsd ldrs, pushed alng entering strt, grad wknd*.......... (12 to 1 op 6 to 1) 6
673[2] LADY HIGHFIELD 8-9 M Tebbutt (5) *bolted to post, beh, rdn alng hfwy, sn btn*................(5 to 1 op 4 to 1) 7
BROWLEA LYNDENE 8-4 (5*) Darren Moffatt (7) *reared in stalls, sn outpcd and beh, struggling frm hfwy.* .... (40 to 1 op 25 to 1) 8
2153[6] WIZARD KING 9-0 G Duffield (6) *hmpd and snatched up sn aftr strt, beh, shaken up entering strt, nvr a factor.* .... (16 to 1 op 12 to 1) 9

Dist: ½l, 3l, 5l, 3½l, 1½l, 7l, ½l, sht-hd. 1m 15.70s. a 4.70s (9 Ran).
SR: 19/22/5/-/-/-/ (G G Ashton), S G Norton

2543 Cataractonium Handicap Class D (0-80 3-y-o and up) £3,377 7f.... (4:45)

2057 MCA BELOW THE LINE [58] (v) 5-9-0 S Webster (1) *nvr far away, led hfwy, drvn alng 2 fs out, ran on wl ins last.* .... (12 to 1 op 10 to 1) 1
2339[3] SUPER BENZ [61] 7-9-3 J Fortune (6) *led to hfwy, styd upsides, rdn and ev ch o'r one furlong out, not quicken ins last*............................(13 to 2 op 5 to 1) 2
2168* NORTH ARDAR [58] 3-8-6 Dean McKeown (8) *chsd ldrs, outpcd 3 fs out, improved o'r one out, not quicken ins last*.................................. (6 to 1 op 9 to 2) 3
2132[5] COCONUT JOHNNY [56] 3-8-4 J Fanning (2) *trkd ldrs, drvn alng entering strt, one pace o'r one furlong out.* .... (14 to 1 op 10 to 1) 4
2168[2] PUBLIC WAY (Ire) [55] 3-8-3 J Lowe (5) *in tch, rdn to improve entering strt, btn o'r one furlong out.* .... (13 to 2 op 6 to 1) 5
1799[3] DREAM CARRIER (Ire) [55] 5-8-4 (7*) V Halliday (7) *beh, drvn alng 4 fs out, no imprsn entering strt.* ....(5 to 1 op 11 to 2 tchd 6 to 1) 6
2233[3] KNIGHT OF SHALOT (Ire) [80] 3-10-0 J Reid (4) *hld up, took clr order hfwy, rdn o'r 2 fs out, sn btn.* ....(5 to 2 fav tchd 3 to 1) 7
2172[5] LEAVE IT TO LIB [60] 6-8-11 (5*) J Tate (9) *dwlt, swtchd lft strt, jnd issue aftr 3 fs, rcd alng far side entering strt, lost tch 2 out, eased*................ (6 to 1 op 9 to 2) 8

Dist: 1l, 2l, 2½l, 1½l, 3l, 3l, 10l. 1m 29.00s. a 6.00s (8 Ran).
SR: 26/26/9/-/-/ (Mrs A Harker), W L Barker

CHEPSTOW (good to soft (race 1), soft (2,3,4,5,6)) Thursday July 15th

Going Correction: PLUS 0.90 sec. per fur. (races 1,2,4), PLUS 0.55 (3,5,6)

2544 Alderney Apprentice Handicap Class G (0-70 3-y-o and up) £2,469 1½m 23yds.......................... (6:30)

1840 RIMOUSKI [33] 5-8-3 D Wright (9) *hld up in rear, hdwy o'r 3 fs out, led 2 out, shaken up ins last, cleverly.* ....(13 to 2 op 7 to 1 tchd 10 to 1) 1
2108[3] HILLZAH (USA) [54] 5-9-10 H Bastiman (6) *hld up in rear, hdwy 4 fs out, pressed wnr ins fnl 2 furlongs.* ....(4 to 1 tchd 9 to 2) 2
2306[3] FAMOUS BEAUTY [48] 6-8-13 (5*) L Aspell (2) *slwly away, hld up, hdwy on outsd 3 fs out, not pace to chal.* ....(7 to 2 fav op 3 to 1) 3
2223[3] LITTLE BIG [38] 6-8-8 T G McLaughlin (8) *rcd keenly, led o'r 4 fs out, hdd 2 out, rdn and wknd ins last.* ....(6 to 1 op 9 to 2) 4
1902[7] DAZZLING FIRE (Ire) [44] 4-9-0 Kim McDonnell (4) *led till o'r 4 fs out, wknd 2 out*.... (7 to 1 op 5 to 1 tchd 15 to 2) 5
2273 ANNABEL'S BABY (Ire) [40] 4-8-5 (5*) Wendy Jones (5) *pld hrd, trkd ldr till o'r hfwy, btn over 3 fs out.* .... (33 to 1 op 20 to 1) 6
2126[8] LUCKY NOIRE [45] 5-8-10 (5*) P Houghton (1) *chsd ldrs till wknd 3 fs out.* ....(5 to 1 op 4 to 1 tchd 9 to 2 and 7 to 2) 7
2310[6] FAIRFORD [44] 4-9-0 N Varley (7) *mid-div, lost tch 3 fs out.* .... (16 to 1 op 12 to 1) 8
876 MOST EQUAL [58] 3-9-1 S Drowne (3) *al beh, tld off fnl 3 fs*...............................(16 to 1 op 10 to 1) 9

Dist: Sht-hd, 4l, 3l, 3½l, sht-hd, 8l, 2½l, 12l. 2m 50.10s. a 18.60s (9 Ran).
SR: 11/31/17/1/-/-/ (John Steventon), B R Cambridge

2545 Mumbles Rating Related Maiden Stakes Class D (3-y-o) £3,172 1¼m 36yds. . . . . (7:00)

JOHNS ACT (USA) 9-0 J Williams (4) *hld up in rear, hdwy o'r 2 fs out, strly rdn to ld wl ins last.* . . . . (6 to 1 tchd 9 to 1) 1

2046[3] COMPLETE MADNESS 9-0 D Holland (1) *led aftr one furlong, hdd 5 out, led ag'n wl o'r 3 out, sn rdn till wknd and ct well ins last.*..... (9 to 4 op 2 to 1 tchd 5 to 2) 2

2333[3] MAP OF STARS (USA) 9-0 M Roberts (6) *hld up, pushed alng o'r 4 fs out, rdn and ev ch 2 out, wknd appr last.* . . . . (6 to 4 on op 2 to 1 on) 3

1776[9] GLEAM OF GOLD (bl) 8-9 M Perrett (3) *led for one furlong, led ag'n 5 out, hdd wl o'r 3 out, rdn and sn btn, tld off.* . . . . (33 to 1 op 20 to 1) 4

Dist: 1l, 6l, dist. 2m 18.30s. a 14.70s (4 Ran).
SR: 45/43/31/-/ (Brian Ching), D Haydn Jones

2546 Sark Maiden Auction Stakes Class E (2-y-o) £2,982 6f 16yds. . . . . (7:30)

1790[7] CHICKAWICKA (Ire) 9-0 S Whitworth (2) *hld up in tch, hdwy to ld appr fnl furlong, drvn out.* . . . .(5 to 2 fav op 6 to 4 tchd 11 to 4) 1

1229[4] HEVER GOLF ROSE 8-9 D Holland (7) *hld up, hdwy 2 fs out, rdn and swtchd lft appr last, ran on ins.* . . . .(9 to 2 op 6 to 1 tchd 7 to 2) 2

2274[5] PRINCE DANZIG (Ire) (bl) 9-0 J Reid (3) *slwly away, rdn hfwy, styd on ins fnl furlong, nvr dngrs.* . . . . (16 to 1 op 12 to 1 tchd 20 to 1) 3

AL JINN 9-0 R Cochrane (1) *al prmnt on outsd, ev ch one and a half fs out, no extr ins.*...... (10 to 1 op 5 to 1) 4

399[4] JASARI (Ire) 9-0 T Quinn (5) *al prmnt, led briefly wl o'r one furlong out, fdd ins.*... (5 to 1 op 4 to 1 tchd 13 to 2) 5

2179[8] RUNIC SYMBOL 9-0 L Dettori (10) *led aftr 2 fs, rdn and hdd two out, sn btn.*.......... (8 to 1 op 11 to 2) 6

QUEENS COTTAGE (Ire) 8-9 M Roberts (4) *al prmnt, led briefly 2 fs out, wkng whn bumped appr last.* . . . . (25 to 1 op 20 to 1) 7

922 PETITE BIJOU 8-4 (5*) D Wright (6) *pld hrd, speed to o'r hfwy.*..........................(20 to 1 tchd 50 to 1) 8

2224[3] DELROB 8-9 J Williams (9) *hld up, effrt o'r 2 fs out, wkng whn hng lft appr last.*.............(6 to 1 tchd 5 to 1) 9

2250 LEGENDARY LADY 8-9 A Munro (11) *outpcd thrght.* . . . . (16 to 1 op 14 to 1 tchd 20 to 1) 10

2123[9] ABACUSAM 9-0 A McGlone (8) *led for 2 fs, wknd quickly hfwy, tld off.*...................... (66 to 1 op 20 to 1) 11

Dist: 1l, 3½l, ¾l, 1½l, 1l, 2½l, 3l, ¾l, 3l, 8l. 1m 16.20s. a 6.70s (11 Ran).
SR: 32/23/14/11/5/1/ (Merthyr Tydfil Car Auction Limited), B R Millman

2547 Sir Gordon Richards Handicap Class D (0-80 3-y-o) £3,348 2m 49yds. . (8:00)

1929[7] PONDERING [64] (v) 8-13 A Munro (3) *trkd ldr, led o'r 4 fs out, clr 2 out, very easily.* . . . . (6 to 1 op 9 to 2 tchd 13 to 2) 1

1372[2] KADASTROF (Fr) [72] 9-7 J Reid (4) *trkd ldrs, chsd wnr fnl 3 fs.*.................................. (11 to 2 op 7 to 2) 2

2337[3] TILTY (USA) [66] 9-1 M Roberts (5) *hld up, rdn o'r 5 fs out, no imprsn fnl 3 furlongs.* . . . .(6 to 4 fav op 5 to 4 tchd 13 to 8) 3

2150[6] PAPER DAYS [44] 7-2 (5*) D Wright (1) *hld up in rear, hdwy 5 fs out, rdn o'r 3 out, one pace.*...(12 to 1 op 10 to 1) 4

1785[4] ALLESCA [72] 9-7 N Adams (2) *al in rear, struggling frm hfwy.*....................................(7 to 2 op 3 to 1) 5

2196[3] ARC BRIGHT (Ire) [53] 8-2 J Quinn (6) *led till hdd o'r 4 fs out, rdn and sn btn, virtually pld up ins last.* . . . . (17 to 2 op 7 to 1 tchd 9 to 1) 6

Dist: 4l, 2½l, 2½l, 7l, 15l. 3m 48.20s. a 21.20s (Flag start) (6 Ran).
SR: 33/37/28/3/24/-/ (M C Pipe), M C Pipe

2548 University And Literary Club Handicap Class E (0-70 3-y-o and up) £3,153 7f 16yds. . . . . (8:30)

2327[2] PRINCE RODNEY [61] 4-9-1 (7*) Mark Denaro (8) *led aftr 2 fs, pushed out ins last.*....... (11 to 2 jt-fav op 5 to 1) 1

1954 SPANISH LOVE [38] 7-7-13 J Quinn (7) *hld up, hdwy o'r 2 fs out, ran on wl to go second ins last.* . . . .(8 to 1 tchd 12 to 1) 2

1903[3] PALACEGATE GOLD (Ire) [54] 4-9-1 A Munro (5) *led for 2 fs, styd prmnt, rallied and ran on fnl furlong.* . . . . (8 to 1 op 7 to 1 tchd 10 to 1) 3

GREAT HAND [46] 7-8-7[1] J Reid (12) *slwly away, hld up in rear, hdwy hfwy, kpt on ins fnl 2 fs.* . . . . (20 to 1 op 12 to 1) 4

1179[5] KINNEGAD KID [37] 4-7-12[2] A McGlone (13) *chsd ldrs, hdwy o'r 2 fs out, rdn and no extr entering last.* . . . .(10 to 1 op 20 to 1 tchd 33 to 1) 5

1953 DARUSSALAM [63] 6-9-5 (5*) A Procter (9) *al prmnt, chsd wnr hfwy till wknd approachiang fnl furlong.* . . . . (16 to 1 op 10 to 1) 6

1907[6] TAKE THE MICK [56] (bl) 3-8-9 R Perham (6) *chsd ldrs, no hdwy ins fnl 2 fs.*...... (9 to 1 op 7 to 1 tchd 10 to 1) 7

2226[7] SAREEN EXPRESS (Ire) [41] 5-8-2 C Rutter (2) *rcd on outsd, nvr nr to chal.*........................ (7 to 1 op 9 to 2) 8

2121[3] ZINBAQ [39] 7-8-0[1] P Robinson (4) *in tch till wknd 2 fs out.* . . . .(11 to 2 jt-fav op 4 to 1) 9

2121[5] FAILAND [35] 6-7-10 A Tucker (3) *prmnt till wknd quickly 2 fs out.*................... (16 to 1 op 10 to 1) 10

4731a[6] CANADIAN CAPERS [55] 4-9-2 S Whitworth (1) *speed on outsd to hfwy.*....................(20 to 1 op 14 to 1) 11

WOODLANDS LEGEND [38] 4-7-13 N Adams (11) *al in rear.* . . . . (50 to 1 op 33 to 1) 12

2421[8] HAWAYAH (Ire) [67] 3-9-6 M Wigham (14) *hld up, al in rear.* . . . . (16 to 1 op 8 to 1) 13

2227[5] LEGAL RISK [60] (v) 3-8-13 J Williams (10) *al beh.* . . . . (16 to 1 op 12 to 1) 14

Dist: ¾l, sht-hd, 2½l, sht-hd, ¾l, ½l, 1½l, 1½l, 5l, 2½l. 1m 28.10s. a 8.10s (14 Ran).
SR: 44/19/34/18/8/32/15/3/-/ (G A Bosley), R Hannon

2549 Lundy Island Handicap Class E (0-70 3-y-o and up) £2,957 5f 16yds. . . (9:00)

1881[2] UMBRIA [44] 4-8-6 T Quinn (4) *slwly into strd, hdwy 2 fs out, strly rdn to ld ins last, sn clr.* . . . . (9 to 4 fav tchd 11 to 4) 1

2352* BATCHWORTH BOUND [47] 4-8-9 (7ex) C Rutter (6) *al prmnt, led wl o'r one furlong out, rdn and hdd ins last, no extr.*................(13 to 2 op 5 to 1 tchd 7 to 1) 2

1977[9] SCARLET PRINCESS [40] 5-8-2 A Munro (5) *chsd ldrs, rdn and outpcd fnl furlong.*............ (8 to 1 tchd 7 to 1) 3

2378[2] POYLE AMBER [45] 4-8-4 (3*) D Harrison (11) *al frnt rnk, rdn and no extr entering fnl furlong.* . . . .(9 to 2 op 3 to 1 tchd 5 to 1) 4

1903[7] TURTLE BEACH [46] 4-8-8 J Reid (9) *al abt same pl, no hdwy appr fnl furlong.* . . . . (14 to 1 op 20 to 1 tchd 12 to 1) 5

2327 GALLANT HOPE [46] (bl) 11-8-3 (5*) D McCabe (8) *rdn hfwy, nvr nr to chal.*....................(16 to 1 op 12 to 1) 6

2352[5] TOMMY TEMPEST [49] 4-8-11 D Holland (3) *outpcd frm hfwy.*....................................(8 to 1 op 5 to 1) 7

2305[9] STOCKTINA [39] 6-7-12 (3*) B Doyle (7) *prmnt, led briefly 2 fs out, hng lft, wknd quickly.*..... (14 to 1 op 10 to 1) 8

1977 FATHOM FIVE (Ire) [42] 4-8-4[4] J Williams (10) *hld up in rear, nvr on terms.*.........(14 to 1 op 12 to 1 tchd 16 to 1) 9

2241 SEAMERE [62] (bl) 10-9-5 (5*) D Wright (2) *led till hdd 2 fs out, wknd quickly, eased ins last.* . . . . (12 to 1 tchd 10 to 1 and 14 to 1) 10

Dist: 2½l, ½l, 1l, 2½l, 1½l, ½l, 2½l, 3l, ¾l. 1m 2.60s. a 5.60s (10 Ran).
SR: 35/28/19/20/11/5/6/-/-/ (S Kay), R Akehurst

HAMILTON (good (races 1,2,3,4), good to soft (5,6))

Thursday July 15th

Going Correction: MINUS 0.10 sec. per fur.

2550 Rutherglen Selling Stakes Class G (3-y-o and up) £1,716 1m 65yds. . . . (6:45)

1210 MISSY-S (Ire) 4-9-2 L Charnock (4) *cl up, led aftr one and a half fs, styd on wl fnl furlong.*..... (12 to 1 op 8 to 1) 1

2279[2] DRUMDONNA (Ire) 3-8-7 Dale Gibson (1) *trkd ldrs, effrt o'r 2 out, ev ch over one out, rdn and kpt on same pace.* . . . .(9 to 4 op 3 to 1) 2

1939[4] GRANITTON BAY (v) 6-9-7 A Culhane (8) *chsd ldrs, drvn alng o'r 3 out, kpt on same pace.* . . . . (5 to 4 fav op Evens tchd 11 to 8) 3

2353 CREAGMHOR (bl) 3-8-12 Paul Eddery (7) *led one and a half fs, cl up, rdn o'r 2 out, ev ch till wknd entering fnl furlong.*............................ (12 to 1 tchd 14 to 1) 4+

2371[3] FORMAESTRE (Ire) 3-8-2 (5*) O Pears (5) *in tch, effrt 3 out, sn rdn and one pace.*....(5 to 1 op 6 to 1 tchd 7 to 1) 4+

1970[3] HAND ON HEART (Ire) 4-8-13 (3*) S D Williams (3) *hld up in tch, effrt o'r 3 out, sn rdn and btn.* (33 to 1 op 20 to 1) 6

FUNNY ROSE 3-8-7 K Darley (2) *slwly into strd, al beh, lost tch fnl 3 fs, tld off.*...........(66 to 1 op 50 to 1) 7

Dist: 4l, 2l, 1½l, dd-ht, ¾l, 25l. 1m 48.00s. a 4.00s (7 Ran).
SR: 30/9/17/3/-/5/-/ (B J Llewellyn), D Burchell

2551 Glengoyne Single Highland Malt Scotch Whisky Handicap Class D (0-80 3-y-o) £3,552 1m 1f 36yds. . . . . . . (7:15)

2273[3] BEST APPEARANCE (Ire) [63] (bl) 8-10 K Fallon (7) *dwlt, hld up in tch, outpcd o'r 3 out, styd on strly frm 2 out to ld ins fnl furlong.*......... (8 to 1 op 6 to 1 tchd 9 to 1) 1

1867[5] I'M A DREAMER (Ire) [65] 8-12 D Gibson (6) *in tch, outpcd o'r 3 fs out, styd on wl frm 2 out to chal ins last, no extr towards finish.*.......................... (8 to 1 op 7 to 1) 2

2341[2] EFIZIA [59] 8-6 K Darley (5) *trkd ldrs, slightly outpcd o'r 3 fs out, hdwy to ld over one out, hdd and no extr ins last.*.................................. (3 to 1 fav op 9 to 4) 3

2031[3] BOLD ACRE [66] 8-13 R Price (4) *ld till hdd 7 fs out, cl up, rdn 2 out, ev ch one out, no extr.*.... (9 to 2 op 4 to 1) 4

2107^6 SIR EDWARD HENRY (Ire) [46] (bl) 7-7 A Mackay (3) *hld up in tch, hdwy to track ldrs 5 fs out, outpcd o'r 3 out, styd on fnl furlong*..........(10 to 1 op 7 to 1) 5
2379^3 AWESTRUCK [74] 9-7 G Duffield (2) *cl up, led 7 fs out till hdd o'r one out, wknd fnl furlong*... (9 to 2 op 4 to 1) 6
2182^3 HYDE'S HAPPY HOUR [58] 8-5 L Charnock (1) *prmnt till wknd 2 fs out*....................... (6 to 1 op 5 to 1) 7
Dist: ¾l, 1½l, 1l, 1½l, 1l, 7l. 1m 59.40s. a 5.40s (7 Ran).
SR: 1/1/-/-/ (Bezwell Fixings Limited), J G FitzGerald

2552 Burnbank Claiming Stakes Class F (2-y-o) £1,952 6f 5yds............. (7:45)

2180* CLARET BUMBLE 8-4 G Duffield (2) *pld hrd early, led aftr one furlong, rdn and ran on wl fnl furlong.* ....(9 to 2 op 7 to 2) 1
2042* ALLLEGSNOBRAIN 9-0 Paul Eddery (3) *pld hrd early, in tch, effrt o'r one furlong out, sn rdn, no imprsn.* ....(7 to 4 op 9 to 4) 2
1846* CELESTIAL RUMOUR (Ire) 9-0 K Darley (1) *set slow pace one furlong, trkd wnr, rdn o'r one out, sn btn.* .... (11 to 10 on op 6 to 4 on tchd Evens) 3
Dist: 3½l, 2l. 1m 15.70s. a 5.00s (3 Ran).
(S A B Dinsmore), P C Haslam

2553 Penrose Hill Handicap Class E (0-70 3-y-o and up) £2,427 6f 5yds.... (8:15)

2062 DIET [60] (v) 7-9-1 (7*) R Havlin (5) *made all, strly pressed fnl 2 fs, styd on wl*......(6 to 1 op 4 to 1 tchd 7 to 1) 1
2469* MISS WHITTINGHAM (Ire) [61] 3-9-2 J Carroll (1) *trkd ldrs, chlgd 2 fs out, sn rdn, ev ch till no extr cl hme.* ....(4 to 1 op 7 to 2) 2
1185^6 PEEDIE PEAT [60] 3-9-1 M Birch (4) *in tch, effrt o'r 2 out, kpt on wl und pres fnl furlong*...(10 to 1 tchd 14 to 1) 3
2170* SECOND COLOURS (USA) [61] 3-9-2 K Darley (3) *chsd ldrs, rdn 2 fs out, kpt on same pace, btn whn slightly hmpd cl hme*.......... (100 to 30 fav op 2 to 1 tchd 7 to 2) 4
2170^2 MY GODSON [62] 3-8-12 (5*) O Pears (8) *chsd ldrs, effrt o'r 2 fs out, one paced*................(7 to 2 tchd 4 to 1) 5
2339^6 ARABAT [66] 6-10-0 K Fallon (2) *sn beh.* ....(8 to 1 op 6 to 1 tchd 9 to 1) 6
2434 FILICAIA [46] (v) 7-8-8 Kim Tinkler (9) *cl up, rdn o'r 2 fs out, fdd*.............................. (25 to 1 op 16 to 1) 7
Dist: ½l, ¾l, 1l, 1½l, 3½l, 2l. 1m 13.80s. a 3.10s (7 Ran).
SR: 34/26/22/19/14/11/-/ (Mrs M S J Clydesdale), Miss L A Perratt

2554 Westwood Maiden Auction Stakes Class F (2-y-o) £1,970 5f 4yds... (8:45)

1401^7 ONCE MORE FOR LUCK (Ire) 9-0 K Darley (11) *mid-div, str run fnl furlong to ld cl hme.* .... (100 to 30 op 2 to 1 tchd 7 to 2) 1
1897^4 THREE OF HEARTS 8-9 J Fortune (12) *chsd ldrs, rdn hfwy, chlgd ins fnl furlong, no extr cl hme.* ....(16 to 1 tchd 20 to 1) 2
2049^3 SPRING LOADED 9-0 Dean McKeown (5) *trkd ldrs, led o'r one furlong out, hdd and no extr cl hme.* ....(9 to 2 op 3 to 1) 3
2331^3 MISTER BEAT 9-0 K Fallon (9) *al chasing ldrs, kpt on fnl furlong*................ (8 to 1 op 6 to 1 tchd 9 to 1) 4
2199^2 LUCIUS LOCKET (Ire) 9-0 J Carroll (4) *cl up till wknd fnl furlong*..........................(3 to 1 fav op 4 to 1) 5
2063^5 ANTIGUAN SKY 9-0 Dale Gibson (10) *nvr trbld ldrs.* .... (10 to 1 op 8 to 1) 6
343^5 GOOD SPIRITS 8-9 M Birch (7) *sn beh, some late hdwy, nvr nrr*.......................... (66 to 1 op 33 to 1) 7
MONSIEUR BLEU 9-0 J Fanning (3) *nvr dngrs.* .... (33 to 1 op 20 to 1) 8
2400 HONG KONG FUTURE (Ire) 8-11 (3*) S D Williams (8) *led till hdd o'r one furlong out, sn wknd.* (25 to 1 op 20 to 1) 9
MISS KATIE LOUISE 8-9 J Lowe (13) *chsd ldrs to hfwy.* .... (20 to 1 op 16 to 1 tchd 25 to 1) 10
2278^8 GLENLYON DUCHESS 8-2 (7*) R Havlin (6) *in tch till wknd 2 fs out*............................ (66 to 1 op 33 to 1) 11
2190^4 CREEK VALLEY 9-0 Raymond Berry (2) *al beh.* ....(12 to 1 op 20 to 1 tchd 25 to 1 and 10 to 1) 12
MR TOWSER 9-0 G Duffield (1) *sn wl beh.* ....(33 to 1 tchd 50 to 1) 13
Dist: ¾l, sht-hd, 1½l, 4l, 1½l, 3½l, ¾l, hd, 1½l, 7l. 1m 1.30s. a 3.00s (13 Ran).
SR: 30/22/26/20/4/-/ (C C Buckley), Mrs M Reveley

2555 Glasgow Fair Handicap Class E (0-70 3-y-o) £2,469 1m 3f 16yds....... (9:15)

2118* INDIAN FLASH (Ire) [62] 9-7 K Darley (4) *led 2 fs, led 3 out, hrd pressed fnl furlong, jst hld on.* .... (5 to 4 fav op Evens tchd 11 to 8) 1
1630^5 MILNGAVIE (Ire) [43] 8-2 J Fanning (2) *trkd ldrs, chlgd 3 fs out, kpt on wl last, jst fld.* .... (9 to 4 op 5 to 2 tchd 11 to 4) 2
2130^5 THE PREMIER EXPRES [58] 9-3 R Lappin (1) *prmnt, effrt 3 fs out, kpt on wl towards finish*....(5 to 1 tchd 9 to 2) 3
1674 MY BALLYBOY [57] 9-2 A Mackay (5) *beh frm hfwy, some late hdwy, nvr dngrs*...................(25 to 1 op 16 to 1) 4
1596^3 BARDIA [40] 7-13 Kim Tinkler (6) *dwlt, al beh.* .... (11 to 1 op 10 to 1 tchd 12 to 1) 5
BOHEMIAN QUEEN [48] 8-7 J Lowe (3) *beh frm hfwy.* .... (12 to 1 op 14 to 1 tchd 16 to 1) 6
2064 BLAKENEY BOY [38] 7-6 (5*) Darren Moffatt (7) *led aftr 2 fs till hdd 3 out, sn wknd*........ (33 to 1 tchd 50 to 1) 7
Dist: Hd, nk, 10l, 1½l, 3½l, nk. 2m 26.80s. a 6.80s (7 Ran).
SR: 28/8/22/1/ (Vijay Mallya), R Guest

KILLARNEY (IRE) (heavy) Thursday July 15th

2556 Killarney Racegoers Handicap (0-65 3-y-o and up) £3,450 1m 100yds (4:00)

2142 ANSEO (Ire) [-] 4-9-5 C Roche (4)................(7 to 1) 1
1855^9 GEALLAINNBAN (Ire) [-] 3-9-0 E A Leonard (2).... (33 to 1) 2
1755^9 DUNANY ROSE (Ire) [-] 3-8-12 N G McCullagh (5) (25 to 1) 3
2141^3 TOUCHDOWN [-] 6-9-9 R Hughes (13)........ (5 to 2 fav) 4
1610^4 BRAZEN ANGEL (Ire) [-] 3-8-12 (6*) J R Barry (3)... (9 to 2) 5
1574 ALDENA (Ire) [-] 3-8-4 D Manning (1).............(25 to 1) 6
2248^5 FAIRY BRIDE (Ire) [-] 3-8-5 (6*) J J Behan (11).....(10 to 1) 7
1440^7 NORDIC MINE (Ire) [-] (bl) 3-8-12 K J Manning (8)..(10 to 1) 8
2322^6 ICANSEEFORMILES (Ire) [-] 5-8-8 P Lowry (7).....(10 to 1) 9
1621^2 FURTHER NOTICE (Ire) [-] 4-7-11 (2*) R M Burke (12) (5 to 1) 10
2321^2 TOMBARA (Ire) [-] 5-9-11 B Coogan (9)............(6 to 1) 11
1923 TAJANAMA (Ire) [-] 5-8-10 S Craine (10)...........(8 to 1) 12
1620^8 SHESOMETHINGELSE (Ire) [-] 3-7-12 (6*) J A Heffernan (6) ....(25 to 1) 13
Dist: 1½l, 2½l, sht-hd, 10l. 1m 55.10s. (13 Ran).
(L Thompson), E J O'Grady

2557 Dawn Milk Run Handicap (0-85 3-y-o and up) £5,520 2m 1f........... (4:30)

1508* LET IT RIDE (Ire) [-] 4-8-5 (6*) J J Behan (1)........ (8 to 1) 1
2460^2 PLUM LICK (Ire) [-] 3-8-7 C Roche (4).............. (5 to 2) 2
2143^6 GO DEAS [-] 6-7-5 (2*) D G O'Shea (3)........... (12 to 1) 3
1141* SOLBA (USA) [-] 4-9-4 J P Murtagh (5)........ (5 to 4 fav) 4
1334^4 BLUE DIANA (Ire) [-] 3-8-9 J F Egan (6)............(5 to 1) 5
NAMELOC [-] 9-9-12 M J Kinane (2).............. (7 to 1) 6
Dist: 3l, 3½l, 5½l, dist. 4m 18.10s. (6 Ran).
(J S Gutkin), E J O'Grady

2558 Dunnes Stores Ladies Fashion Series (3-y-o and up) £3,700 1½m.....(5:00)

1963* BIRTHPLACE (Ire) 3-9-8^3 Miss L Robinson (2)...(7 to 4 on) 1
1140^5 PRINTOUT (Ire) 3-8-11 Miss A Gilsenan (3)........ (5 to 1) 2
1987^4 SPOUT HOUSE (Ire) 4-9-5 (2*) Miss E Purcell (1)....(5 to 2) 3
Dist: Nk, ½l. 3m 6.70s. (3 Ran).
(Sheikh Mohammed), John M Oxx

SANDOWN (soft) Thursday July 15th

Going Correction: PLUS 0.60 sec. per fur. (races 1,3,4,5,6), PLUS 0.35 (2)

2559 EBF Raynes Park Maiden Stakes Class D (2-y-o) £4,084 7f 16yds..(2:20)

BUDE 9-0 Pat Eddery (3) *made all, shaken up and quickened entering fnl furlong, not extended.* .... (15 to 8 on op 5 to 2 on tchd 13 to 8 on) 1
1949 SHERIDAN (Ire) 9-0 W Carson (4) *trkd wnr, jnd issue 3 out, rdn and not quicken ins fnl furlong.* .... (12 to 1 op 10 to 1 tchd 14 to 1) 2
WISHING (USA) 9-0 L Dettori (5) *mid-div, effrt o'r 3 out, sn outpcd*................(5 to 1 op 7 to 2 tchd 11 to 2) 3
DALWOOD 9-0 M Roberts (1) *slwly into strd, settled in 3rd pl, rdn and outpcd last 3 fs*.......(12 to 1 op 10 to 1) 4
RICH MISS 8-9 W Newnes (7) *nvr gng pace of ldrs.* .... (50 to 1 op 33 to 1) 5
RANA SANGA 9-0 L Piggott (6) *settled in mid-div, pushed alng and outpcd frm 3 out, eased appr fnl furlong.* ....(8 to 1 op 6 to 1 tchd 9 to 1) 6
LOOSE CHANGE 8-9 B Rouse (2) *drpd rear aftr 2 fs.* .... (50 to 1 op 33 to 1) 7
Dist: 1l, 10l, 1l, 12l, hd, 2l. 1m 37.00s. a 10.50s (7 Ran).
SR: 6/3/-/-/ (K Abdulla), H R A Cecil

2560 Baxi Solo Handicap Class D (0-80 3-y-o) £4,143 5f 6yds............... (2:50)

2214^2 NO EXTRAS (Ire) [73] 9-2 B Rouse (2) *hld up beh, ran on o'r one out, led last 100 yards, styd on wl.* .... (13 to 2 op 11 to 2 tchd 7 to 1) 1
1714^5 TUSCAN DAWN [69] 8-12 T Quinn (5) *led til hdd und pres fnl 100 yards*...................... (8 to 1 tchd 9 to 1) 2
2231^4 NEWBURY COAT [66] (bl) 8-9 W Carson (4) *chsd ldr til one out, rallied und pres*... (9 to 1 op 8 to 1 tchd 10 to 1) 3
1667^7 CATHERINEOFARAGON [78] 9-7 J Williams (6) *ldg grp, rdn and outpcd appr fnl furlong.* (6 to 1 jt-fav tchd 7 to 1) 4
2214* STORMY HEIGHTS [62] (bl) 8-5 M Roberts (13) *handily plcd in mid-div, rdn and not quicken appr fnl furlong.* .... (13 to 2 op 9 to 2 tchd 7 to 1) 5

2280[3] GO FLIGHTLINE (Ire) [59] 8-2 G Bardwell (10) *nvr on terms.* ....(8 to 1 op 7 to 1 tchd 9 to 1) 6
2011[8] AHJAY [54] 7-11 J Quinn (1) *outpcd most of way.* ....(12 to 1 op 10 to 1 tchd 14 to 1) 7
2157[8] CUDDLY DATE [53] 7-3 (7*) Kim McDonnell (7) *ldg grp til lost pos o'r one out.*....................(40 to 1 op 33 to 1) 8
2231* EL ARZ [72] 9-1 R Cochrane (9) *mid-div to hfwy, sn btn.* ....(11 to 1 op 10 to 1 tchd 12 to 1) 9
1655* PUTOUT [74] (bl) 9-3 D Biggs (12) *pressed ldrs til wknd o'r one out.*.........(6 to 1 jt-fav op 11 to 2 tchd 13 to 2) 10
691[5] JOBIE [75] 9-4 M Hills (3) *hld up, rdn alng hfwy, sn outpcd.*..............(10 to 1 op 12 to 1 tchd 14 to 1) 11
Dist: 2l, 1l, 3l, ¾l, 3l, hd, hd, 1½l, hd, 2l. 1m 3.88s. a 4.38s (11 Ran).
SR: 49/37/30/30/11/-/-/-/1/ (K Higson), G L Moore

2561 Harcros Stayers Handicap Qualifier Class C (0-90 3-y-o) £4,879 1¾m (3:25)

2239[6] DUSTY POINT (Ire) [79] 9-2 W R Swinburn (3) *prog hfwy, led 3 out, shaken up o'r one out, pushed clr.* ....(9 to 4 fav tchd 5 to 2 and 2 to 1) 1
2272* MUJAWAB [77] 9-0 (4ex) R Hills (4) *hld up in rear, pushed alng 5 out, rdn to chase wnr last 2 fs, no imprsn.* ....(8 to 1 op 5 to 1) 2
1625* HAUNTED WOOD (USA) [82] 9-5 M Roberts (5) *sn tracking ldr, led 4 out till 3 out, wknd appr fnl furlong.* ....(7 to 2 op 3 to 1 tchd 4 to 1) 3
2251[3] HOOSIE [73] 8-10 B Marcus (2) *wl in tch, ev ch 3 out, wknd frm 2 out.*........(11 to 2 op 6 to 1 tchd 7 to 1) 4
2135* MR COPYFORCE [64] 8-1 W Carson (1) *led til 4 out, rallied and ev ch 3 out, sn btn.* (13 to 2 op 6 to 1 tchd 7 to 1) 5
1906* EUPHONIC [71] 8-8 L Dettori (6) *hld up beh, improved 6 out, ev ch 3 out, wknd quickly, tld off.* ....(6 to 1 op 5 to 1 tchd 13 to 2) 6
Dist: 4l, 5l, 2l, 8l, 30l. 3m 14.23s. a 19.93s (6 Ran).
(Abdullah Ali), B Hanbury

2562 Milcars Fillies' Conditions Stakes Class B (2-y-o) £7,700 7f 16yds. .(4:00)

NEWS AND ECHO (USA) 8-11 W R Swinburn (2) *hld up in rear, rdn and ran on o'r one out, led nr line.* ....(12 to 1 tchd 16 to 1) 1
2234* OVERACT (Ire) 9-1 L Dettori (1) *cld on ldrs hfwy, rdn to ld o'r one out, hdd nr finish.*........(11 to 4 tchd 7 to 2) 2
1339* A SMOOTH ONE (Ire) 8-13 Pat Eddery (3) *chsd ldr, ev ch frm o'r 2 out, hrd rdn and not quicken nr line.* ....(6 to 4 fav tchd 13 to 8 and 11 to 8) 3
2112* PALANA (USA) 9-1 M Hills (4) *hld up, jnd ldrs o'r 2 out, ev ch entering fnl furlong, wknd final 100 yards.* ....(9 to 2 op 11 to 4 tchd 5 to 1) 4
2044* OUBECK BLUE 8-13 R Cochrane (5) *sn led, hdd und pres o'r one out, wknd quickly.* ....(11 to 2 op 5 to 1 tchd 9 to 2 and 6 to 1) 5
Dist: Nk, 1l, 3½l, 3l. 1m 38.17s. a 11.67s (5 Ran).
(Roldvale Limited), P A Kelleway

2563 Heathrow Maiden Stakes Class D (3-y-o and up) £3,766 1m 14yds. . . . (4:35)

2275[2] TESHAMI (USA) 3-8-12 M Roberts (9) *wl plcd, led 3 out, drw clr fnl furlong easily.* ......(100 to 30 fav op 5 to 2 tchd 2 to 1 and 7 to 2) 1
1839[5] BOBBIE DEE 3-8-7 Pat Eddery (2) *mid-div, ran on o'r 2 out, chsd wnr und pres appr fnl furlong, not quicken.* ....(7 to 2 tchd 9 to 2) 2
2117[5] LANKRIDGE 3-8-12 L Piggott (14) *led for one furlong, trkd ldr, ev ch frm 3 out, no extr appr fnl furlong.* ....(14 to 1 op 12 to 1 tchd 16 to 1) 3
1931[3] AL KATIRIYAH (Ire) (e/c) 3-8-7 W Carson (10) *hld up towards rear, ran on fnl furlong, nrst at line.* ....(9 to 1 op 7 to 1 tchd 10 to 1) 4
1344[8] FUNNY HILARIOUS (USA) 3-8-7 T Quinn (15) *wl in tch, ev ch 3 out, wknd last 2 fs.* ....(12 to 1 op 6 to 1 tchd 14 to 1) 5
2064[3] MITRAAS (USA) 3-8-12 R Hills (7) *settled towards rear, effrt o'r 2 out, not rch ldrs fnl furlong.* ....(11 to 2 op 4 to 1 tchd 6 to 1) 6
MISWAKI DANCER (USA) 3-8-12 W R Swinburn (3) *nvr nrr.* ....(12 to 1 op 10 to 1 tchd 14 to 1) 7
WELSH HERITAGE (Ire) 3-8-4 (3*) D Harrison (6) *nvr better than mid-div.*....... (14 to 1 op 12 to 1 tchd 16 to 1) 8
DUBAI SUMMER 3-8-12 P Robinson (4) *al towards rear.* ....(16 to 1 op 14 to 1 tchd 20 to 1) 9
2202 FUCHU 3-8-7 B Marcus (16) *led aftr one furlong, hdd 3 out, wknd 2 out.*.....(20 to 1 op 16 to 1 tchd 25 to 1) 10
423[4] CHAMPAGNE 'N ROSES 3-8-7 L Dettori (12) *ldg grp, ev ch frm 3 out, wknd quickly o'r one out.* ....(11 to 1 op 10 to 1 tchd 12 to 1) 11
2097[6] BALI HERO (Ire) 3-8-12 M Hills (11) *midfield til drpd rear last 3 fs.*............(14 to 1 op 10 to 1 tchd 16 to 1) 12
2275 AMOREM 3-8-12 W Newnes (1) *pressed ldrs til wknd o'r 3 out.*..........................(50 to 1 op 25 to 1) 13
BROUGHTONS TURMOIL 4-9-7 R Cochrane (8) *in tch til lost pl o'r 2 out.*..................(33 to 1 op 25 to 1) 14
582 SULA MOON 3-8-7 J Williams (13) *al beh, tld off fnl 3 fs.* ....(50 to 1 op 33 to 1) 15
Dist: 3l, 3l, 5l, ½l, ½l, nk, hd, 4l, 1l, sht-hd. 1m 47.05s. a 7.95s (15 Ran).
SR: 50/36/32/12/10/13/12/6/-/ (Sheikh Mohammed), J H M Gosden

2564 CPM Field Marketing Apprentice Handicap Class E (0-70 3-y-o and up) £2,851 1¼m 7yds. . . . . (5:10)

2025[3] PORT SUNLIGHT (Ire) [69] 5-9-4 (10*) D O'Neill (2) *hld up, hdwy o'r 2 out, not clr run and swtchd rght to ld jst over one out, pushed clear.* ....(3 to 1 fav op 7 to 2 tchd 4 to 1) 1
1712[4] JADE GREEN [62] 4-8-11 (10*) C Webb (1) *hld up in rear, improved o'r 3 out, ev ch one out, not quicken.* ....(5 to 1 op 4 to 1 tchd 11 to 2) 2
2300 LEXUS (Ire) [48] 5-8-0[1] (8*) Sarah Thompson (5) *led for 2 fs, lost pl aftr 4 furlongs, styd on ag'n fnl furlong.* ....(9 to 1 op 7 to 1 tchd 10 to 1) 3
2149* WAR REQUIEM (Ire) [55] 3-7-13[1] (5*) D Griffiths (4) *led aftr 2 fs, hdd o'r one out, no extr.* ....(13 to 2 op 5 to 1 tchd 7 to 1) 4
1961[6] ALTERMEERA [45] 5-8-4 G Parkin (7) *rear til cld on ldr 6 out, dsptd ld 2 out, rdn and btn o'r one out.* ....(10 to 1 op 14 to 1 tchd 16 to 1) 5
1919 THIMBALINA [34] 7-7-0[1] (8*) Sharon Millard (9) *in tch, rdn and no hdwy last 2 fs.* (9 to 1 op 8 to 1 tchd 10 to 1) 6
2149* JUNCTION TWENTYTWO [53] 3-7-10 (5*) G Milligan (6) *drpd rear aftr 4 fs, lost tch last 3 furlongs.* ....(11 to 2 op 5 to 1 tchd 6 to 1) 7
2109* BARAHIN (Ire) [62] 4-9-7 D Gibbs (8) *pressed ldrs til wknd o'r 3 out, sn lost tch.*................ (8 to 1 op 6 to 1) 8
Dist: 2l, 1½l, 1½l, ¾l, 2½l, 12l, 4l. 2m 17.66s. a 13.76s (8 Ran).
SR: 36/25/8/1/-/ (Mrs C J Powell), R Hannon

HAMILTON (soft)
Friday July 16th

Going Correction: PLUS 0.15 sec. per fur. (races 1,2,3), PLUS 0.05 (4,5,6)

2565 Sunday Mail Handicap Class E (0-70 3-y-o and up) £2,343 1½m 17yds (6:45)

2059[2] SUNDERLAND ECHO [68] 4-9-12 K Darley (1) *cl up, slight ld o'r 4 out, hrd pressed over one out, styd on wl und pres fnl furlong.* ....(11 to 4 on op 2 to 1 on tchd 3 to 1 on) 1
2458[5] RAPID MOVER [35] (bl) 6-7-7 A Mackay (3) *in tch, hdwy o'r 3 out, dsptd ld over one out, no extr ins fnl furlong.* ....(4 to 1 op 3 to 1) 2
2059[9] MUFID (USA) [58] 4-8-13 (3*) J Weaver (2) *led 2 fs, prmnt, chlgd o'r 4 out, rdn over two out, sn btn.* ....(25 to 1 op 8 to 1) 3
2267[3] NATIVE CROWN (Ire) [40] 5-7-9[2] (5*) A Garth (4) *in tch, effrt 4 out, no hdwy*......................(14 to 1 op 8 to 1) 4
2043 BRUSQUE (USA) [35] 9-7-7 Kim Tinkler (5) *led aftr 2 fs till hdd o'r 4 out, wknd over 3 out*... (20 to 1 tchd 33 to 1) 5
Dist: ¾l, 7l, 3l, 7l. 2m 40.80s. a 7.80s (5 Ran).
SR: 52/17/26/2/-/ (Northeast Press Limited), Mrs M Reveley

2566 Clyde Claiming Stakes Class F (3-y-o and up) £2,005 1m 3f 16yds. . . . . (7:15)

1783[4] AEGAEN LADY 4-8-9 (3*) J Weaver (6) *hld up in tch, steady hdwy to ld jst ins fnl furlong, ran on.*.......(2 to 1 fav) 1
1783[6] LE TEMERAIRE 7-9-3 Kim Tinkler (1) *led till hdd jst ins fnl furlong, no extr und pres.*............(4 to 1 op 7 to 2) 2
2279[3] BLUE RADIANCE 3-7-10 J Fanning (4) *trkd ldrs, chlgd wl o'r one out, ev ch till wknd fnl furlong.* ....(9 to 2 op 4 to 1 tchd 5 to 1) 3
LORLANNE 3-8-5 T Williams (2) *dwlt, hld up, effrt 3 out, no hdwy*......................(33 to 1 op 10 to 1) 4
1493[4] PALACEGATE SUNSET (bl) 3-8-1 (7*) P Roberts (7) *prmnt till wknd o'r 2 out*.......(6 to 1 op 4 to 1 tchd 7 to 1) 5
2265[4] JOHN NAMAN (Ire) 4-8-9 A Mackay (5) *in tch, rdn 3 out, sn btn*.................(16 to 1 op 10 to 1 tchd 20 to 1) 6
1892[3] FRIENDLY KNIGHT 3-8-1 K Darley (3) *in tch till wknd o'r 2 out*..........................(14 to 1 op 8 to 1) 7
Dist: 1½l, 2½l, 8l, nk, 8l, ½l. 2m 28.20s. a 8.20s (7 Ran).
SR: 33/35/9/2/4/-/-/ (D H Blackwood), J Etherington

2567 Letheby & Christopher Handicap Class D (0-80 4-y-o and up) £3,260 1m 65yds. . . . . (7:45)

2000[2] EXPRESS GIFT [64] 4-8-12 K Darley (4) *trkd ldr, slight ld 3 out, hrd pressed one out, styd on wl.* .... (2 to 1 fav op 9 to 4 tchd 5 to 2 and 15 to 8) 1
2369[2] MASTER OFTHE HOUSE [46] 7-7-8 L Charnock (3) *hld up, smooth hdwy to dispute ld one out, sn rdn and no extr.* ....(11 to 1 op 7 to 1) 2
824[9] HIGH LOW (USA) [78] 5-9-12 N Day (1) *led till hdd 3 out, ev ch till wknd entering fnl furlong.* ....(100 to 30 op 3 to 1 tchd 7 to 2) 3

2283[3] STRAW THATCH [51] 4-7-13 T Williams (5) *in tch, effrt 3 out, one paced*................(5 to 2 tchd 11 to 4) 4
2308* SPANISH VERDICT [69] 6-9-3 (5ex) N Connorton (2) *trkd ldrs, effrt 3 out, sn btn.* (6 to 1 op 5 to 1 tchd 8 to 1) 5
Dist: 1½l, 1½l, 1½l, 2½l. 1m 49.10s. a 5.10s (5 Ran).
SR: 40/17/44/12/22/ (M W Horner, H Young, And D S Arnold), Mrs M Reveley

2568 Carousel Snowball Selling Stakes Class G (3-y-o and up) £1,674 6f 5yds ....(8:15)

2165[2] MURRAY'S MAZDA (Ire) 4-9-7 J Carroll (1) *trkd ldrs, dsptd ld o'r 2 out till found extr und pres fnl furlong.* ....(6 to 4 on tchd 11 to 8 on) 1
1618[6] MU-ARRIK (v) 5-9-0 (7*) P Houghton (4) *cl up, dsptd ld gng wl o'r 2 out till no extr fnl furlong.* ....(20 to 1 op 10 to 1 tchd 25 to 1) 2
1228[4] AYR RAIDER (v) 6-9-7 J Fanning (2) *trkd ldr, swtchd o'r 2 out, rdn over one out, no imprsn*.....(7 to 2 op 4 to 1) 3
2197[6] OBSIDIAN GREY 6-9-7 G Duffield (5) *led till hdd o'r 2 out, sn wknd*..(7 to 2) 4
Dist: ½l, 4l, 1½l. 1m 14.70s. a 4.00s (4 Ran).
SR: 33/31/15/9/ (Murray Grubb), J Berry

2569 Joe Punter Nursery Class E (2-y-o) £2,280 6f 5yds.................. (8:45)

1580* BELLA PARKES [-] 9-0 J Carroll (4) *made all, rdn and ran on strly fnl 2 fs*.................(2 to 1 fav tchd 9 to 4) 1
2176[2] TURTLE ROCK [-] 8-10 K Darley (1) *dwlt, hld up, smooth hdwy hfwy, effrt 2 out, kpt on wl, no ch wth wnr.* ....(11 to 4 op 3 to 1 tchd 5 to 2) 2
2200[3] MISS MAH-JONG [-] 9-7 Dean McKeown (2) *chsd ldrs, pushed alng hfwy, one paced.* ....(5 to 1 op 4 to 1 tchd 11 to 2) 3
2090[7] GREY TOPPA [-] 7-11[1] F Norton (5) *prmnt, rdn o'r 2 out, sn wknd*..................(7 to 1 op 9 to 2 tchd 8 to 1) 4
1895[8] DANGEROUS SHADOW [-] 8-7 J Fanning (6) *in tch, ev ch o'r 2 out, sn rdn and wknd.* ....(13 to 2 op 4 to 1 tchd 8 to 1) 5
2268[2] MOKAITE [-] 8-11 (7*) J Marshall (3) *wth ldr till wknd o'r 2 out*....................................(11 to 1 op 6 to 1) 6
Dist: 3½l, 5l, 6l, nk, 5l. 1m 14.40s. a 3.70s (6 Ran).
SR: 32/14/5/ (Joseph Heler), J Berry

2570 Ginestri Ice Cream Maiden Handicap Class E (0-70 3-y-o and up) £2,301 5f 4yds........................... (9:15)

2312[5] JOELLISE [28] (v) 3-7-13 (7*) Claire Balding (3) *trkd ldr, led o'r one out, hng rght, ran on wl.* ....(2 to 1 tchd 13 to 8 and 9 to 4) 1
2120 FLASH OF JOY [31] 3-8-9 R Price (1) *led, rdn 2 out, hdd o'r one out, sn btn.* ....(5 to 1 op 4 to 1 tchd 6 to 1 and 7 to 1) 2
2312[2] FARNDALE [41] 6-9-10 G Duffield (2) *dwlt, sn in tch, effrt o'r one out, soon rdn and no imprsn.* .... (11 to 8 on op 5 to 4 on tchd Evens) 3
Dist: 3½l, nk. 1m 3.00s. a 4.70s (3 Ran).
SR: 3/-/6/ (Jackson Construction Co Ltd), J Balding

NEWBURY (good)
Friday July 16th
Going Correction: PLUS 0.20 sec. per fur. (races 1,4,5,7), MINUS 0.05 (2,3,6)

2571 EBF Ecchinswell Maiden Stakes Class D (2-y-o) £4,760 6f 8yds.........(2:00)

BAROSSA VALLEY (Ire) 9-0 J Reid (8) *trkd ldrs, al gng wl, led ins fnl 2 fs, pushed out, cmftbly.* ....(5 to 4 fav op 6 to 4) 1
2030[2] JAREEF'S WAY (Ire) 9-0 Pat Eddery (17) *trkd ldr, led briefly 2 fs out, ran on one pace.* ....(4 to 1 op 5 to 2 tchd 9 to 2) 2
1844[5] SCARLET DIVA 8-9 L Dettori (9) *chsd ldrs, rdn 2 fs out, ran on one pace*.........(14 to 1 op 10 to 1 tchd 16 to 1) 3
2325[5] GLITTERAZZI 9-0 J Williams (6) *trkd ldrs, rdn 2 fs out, kpt on*...................(10 to 1 op 6 to 1 tchd 11 to 1) 4
ART TATUM (Ire) 9-0 R Hills (1) *rear, rcd on outsd, styd on aftr 2 fs out*..............(33 to 1 op 16 to 1) 5
1640 WILDFIRE (Swi) 9-0 A Munro (11) *mid-div, kpt on ins fnl 2 fs*...................(14 to 1 op 10 to 1 tchd 16 to 1) 6
2316[3] ARABOYBILL 9-0 A Clark (12) *mid-div, pushed alng hfwy, kpt on one pace*..................(33 to 1 op 16 to 1) 7
1640 TANBIH 9-0 W Carson (15) *beh, sn pushed alng, ran on ins fnl furlong, nvr nrr.* ....(20 to 1 op 12 to 1 tchd 25 to 1) 8
PLATINI (Ire) 9-0 M Roberts (2) *rcd on outsd, nvr dngrs.* ....(12 to 1 op 8 to 1) 9
PERSONAL PRIDE (Ire) 9-0 R Cochrane (14) *mid-div, nvr nr to chal*...............................(16 to 1 op 10 to 1) 10
1905[4] MILLICENT NORTH 8-9 Paul Eddery (4) *led to 2 fs out, wknd*................(16 to 1 op 10 to 1 tchd 20 to 1) 11
IOLANI 8-9 S Raymont (7) *slwly away, effrt hfwy, eased whn btn*..........................(20 to 1 op 14 to 1) 12
1497 VEDO NUDO 9-0 P Robinson (5) *trkd ldrs, rdn o'r 2 fs out, sn btn*...........................(50 to 1 op 20 to 1) 13
SPARKLING ROBERTA 8-9 N Adams (13) *outpcd.* ....(66 to 1 op 33 to 1 tchd 100 to 1) 14
WAAFED (USA) 9-0 W R Swinburn (10) *mid-div, rdn hfwy, eased whn btn*........................(14 to 1 op 6 to 1) 15
AIRSPEED FLYER (USA) 9-0 R Perham (3) *speed on outsd to hfwy*............................(33 to 1 op 16 to 1) 16
SEE MY GUEST (Fr) 8-9 S Dawson (16) *very slwly away, tld off hfwy*.........(66 to 1 op 33 to 1 tchd 100 to 1) 17
Dist: 2l, ¾l, ½l, 1l, hd, ¾l, 1½l, hd, 1l, sht-hd. 1m 16.16s. a 4.46s (17 Ran).
SR: 35/27/19/22/18/17/14/8/7/ (R E Sangster), P W Chapple-Hyam

2572 Watermill Conditions Stakes Class B (3-y-o and up) £7,034 7f 64yds...(2:30)

2390* THOURIOS 4-9-6 W R Swinburn (2) *made all, rdn o'r one furlong out, ran on gmely*..........(7 to 2 op 5 to 2) 1
GABR 3-8-9 W Carson (11) *hld up rear, hdwy 2 fs out, ran on to go second ins last, no imprsn cl hme.* ....(10 to 1 tchd 12 to 1) 2
1765[8] HUMAM (Ire) 3-8-9 R Hills (8) *al prmnt, ev ch 2 fs out, no extr ins last*..........(10 to 1 op 8 to 1 tchd 11 to 1) 3
2068[8] LITTLE MUNCHKIN (Ire) 3-8-9 D Holland (4) *hld up, hrd rdn and hdwy o'r 2 fs out, ran on ins last.* ....(20 to 1 op 16 to 1 tchd 25 to 1) 4
2202* FIRST VEIL 3-8-4 J Williams (10) *wtd wth in tch, no imprsn fnl 2 fs*..............(10 to 1 op 7 to 1 tchd 11 to 1) 5
2304[3] FELUCCA 3-8-4 Pat Eddery (7) *hld up, rdn 2 fs out, not pace to chal*........(15 to 8 fav op 2 to 1 tchd 7 to 4) 6
2194* PEMBROKE (USA) 3-8-13 M Roberts (9) *hld up, effrt o'r 2 fs out, wknd ins last*................(9 to 1 op 6 to 1) 7
2390[7] SON PARDO 3-8-13 J Reid (6) *hld up, rdn o'r 2 fs out, nvr dngrs*................(16 to 1 op 12 to 1 tchd 20 to 1) 8
1208[6] SUNDAY'S HILL 4-9-3 R Cochrane (3) *trkd wnr, rdn o'r 2 fs out, wknd*............(33 to 1 op 25 to 1 tchd 50 to 1) 9
1109* CAVATINA 3-8-4 S D Williams (1) *pld hrd, chsd ldrs, rdn o'r 2 fs out, wknd quickly appr last*...(33 to 1 op 20 to 1) 10
1213[8] CARBON STEEL (Ire) 3-8-7 Paul Eddery (5) *hld up rear, al beh*.......................(33 to 1 op 25 to 1 tchd 50 to 1) 11
Dist: ½l, 1½l, 3l, 2½l, 1½l, nk, 1l, 4l, 4l, 5l. 1m 28.76s. a 1.46s (11 Ran).
SR: 79/66/61/52/39/34/42/39/31/ (Athos Christodoulou), G Harwood

2573 Planning Consultancy Handicap Class C (0-90 3-y-o and up) £4,889 2m (3:00)

2251[5] STAR QUEST [70] 6-9-9 L Dettori (2) *chsd ldr, rdn and hdwy o'r one furlong out, led last 100 yards, ran on.* ....(13 to 2 op 7 to 1 tchd 6 to 1) 1
2034[4] INTREPID LASS [45] 6-7-5 (7*) Antoinette Armes (4) *led, sn clr, rdn appr last, hdd last 100 yards, no extr.* ....(4 to 1 tchd 5 to 1) 2
2337[2] MULL HOUSE [75] 6-10-0 W R Swinburn (1) *chsd ldrs, lost pl o'r 4 fs out, rdn to go 3rd wl over one out.* ....(15 to 8 fav op 6 to 4 tchd 2 to 1) 3
2204[5] NOBLE SOCIETY [40] 5-7-7 N Adams (3) *hld up, effrt o'r 3 fs out, wknd 2 out*................(16 to 1 op 10 to 1) 4
2026[4] TALOS (Ire) [67] 5-9-6 D Holland (5) *hld up rear, effrt 3 fs out, nvr on terms*...................(2 to 1 op 7 to 4) 5
Dist: 1½l, 12l, 2½l, nk. 3m 33.48s. a 7.48s (5 Ran).
SR: 26/-/17/-/5/ (David Morris), J R Jenkins

2574 Hackwood Stakes Class A (Listed Race) (3-y-o and up) £11,034 6f 8yds ....(3:30)

2206* CATRAIL (USA) 3-8-8 M Roberts (9) *hld up in tch, rdn to ld one furlong out, eased nr finish.* ....(6 to 5 on op Evens tchd 11 to 10) 1
2362 MIDHISH 3-8-8 W R Swinburn (3) *trkd ldr, led 2 fs out to one out, kpt on*...... (14 to 1 op 16 to 1 tchd 25 to 1) 2
1786[4] MONTENDRE 6-9-4 J Reid (7) *nvr far away, hdwy appr fnl furlong, ran on ins*...........(9 to 2 tchd 11 to 2) 3
2303 BRIGG FAIR 3-8-8 R Perham (8) *in tch till outpcd hfwy, ran on strly ins fnl furlong.* .... (50 to 1 op 33 to 1 tchd 66 to 1) 4
2068[4] SPLICE 4-8-13 Pat Eddery (1) *beh, rdn wl o'r one furlong out, ran on, nvr dngrs*...(7 to 1 op 6 to 1 tchd 8 to 1) 5
1786 RAIN BROTHER (USA) 3-8-12 D Holland (6) *led to 2 fs out, sn rdn, no extr*................. (20 to 1 tchd 25 to 1) 6
2237* LOOK WHO'S HERE (Ire) 3-8-12 L Dettori (4) *rear but in tch, no hdwy ins fnl 2 fs*.............. (20 to 1 op 12 to 1) 7
1337[4] STAR FAMILY FRIEND (Ire) 3-8-7 P Robinson (2) *speed till wknd 2 fs out*.......(50 to 1 op 33 to 1 tchd 66 to 1) 8
2237[2] RUSTIC CRAFT (Ire) 3-8-8 R Cochrane (5) *in tch till wknd appr fnl furlong*..................(8 to 1 tchd 9 to 1) 9
2252[7] ARADANZA 3-8-8 Paul Eddery (10) *in tch till wknd wl o'r one furlong out*................ (20 to 1 tchd 16 to 1) 10
2028* CARRANITA (Ire) 3-8-3 A Clark (11) *slwly away, rdn to be in tch, wknd o'r 2 fs out*........................ (33 to 1) 11
Dist: ¾l, ¾l, hd, 1½l, 3l, nk, 2l, 3½l, 2½l, 2½l. 1m 13.94s. a 2.24s (11 Ran).
SR: 73/70/77/66/65/52/51/38/25/ (Sheikh Mohammed), J H M Gosden

2575 Chattis Hill Maiden Fillies' Stakes Class D (2-y-o) £3,497 5f 34yds..(4:00)

1916[7] SPOT PRIZE (USA) 8-11 R Cochrane (5) *hld up, squeezed through to ld jst ins fnl furlong, ran on*.....(4 to 1 co-fav op 3 to 1) 1
2336[5] I'M YOUR LADY 8-11 L Dettori (8) *trkd ldr, ev ch whn wnt lft entering fnl furlong, one pace ins last*...(4 to 1 co-fav op 5 to 2) 2
LITTLE BEAUT 8-11 M Roberts (2) *outpcd early, pushed alng frm hfwy, ran on ins fnl furlong, nvr nrr*. .... (12 to 1 op 8 to 1) 3
ANN'S PEARL (Ire) 8-11 W R Swinburn (1) *prmnt on outsd, led one and a half fs out, hng rght and hdd jst ins last, wknd*.................. (9 to 2 op 4 to 1 tchd 6 to 1) 4
ASDAF (USA) 8-11 W Carson (6) *outpcd, nvr on terms*. ....(4 to 1 co-fav op 3 to 1 tchd 9 to 2) 5
1955[7] MARJORIE'S ORCHID 8-11 D Holland (4) *led till one and a half fs out, btn whn hmpd entering last, eased*. ....(7 to 1 op 6 to 1 tchd 8 to 1) 6
MALAGA 8-11 A Munro (7) *played up bef strt, nvr on terms*.................. (13 to 2 op 3 to 1 tchd 7 to 1) 7
Dist: 1l, 1½l, ¾l, 4l, 6l, hd. 1m 5.58s. a 5.28s (7 Ran).
SR: 12/8/2/-/ (J C Smith), D R C Elsworth

2576 Whitehorse Handicap Class D (0-80 3-y-o) £3,752 1¼m 6yds........ (4:30)

2333[5] DUTOSKY [73] 9-0 R Cochrane (1) *al prmnt, led one and a half fs out, edgd rght und pres ins last*...(100 to 30 jt-fav op 5 to 2 tchd 7 to 2) 1
1912[2] PLAY WITH ME (Ire) [72] 8-13 L Dettori (8) *pld hrd early, trkd ldr, led o'r 2 fs out to one and a half out, rdn and ran on ins last*......... (5 to 1 op 7 to 2 tchd 11 to 2) 2
873[6] GOLD TASSEL [60] 8-1 M Roberts (2) *hld up, rdn and hdwy o'r 2 fs out, ev ch entering last, kpt on*. .... (12 to 1 op 10 to 1) 3
1586 MATARIS [63] 8-4 W Carson (6) *led till o'r 2 fs out, eased whn btn ins last*................. (14 to 1 op 12 to 1) 4
2383* SUSQUEHANNA DAYS (USA) [60] 7-8 (7*) Martin Dwyer (4) *in tch, rdn o'r 2 fs out, one pace*..............(100 to 30 jt-fav op 4 to 1 tchd 9 to 2 and 3 to 1) 5
1991[8] HOMEMAKER [56] 7-11 N Adams (7) *hld up, nvr on terms*. .... (12 to 1 op 10 to 1) 6
1115[6] NEMEA (USA) [75] 9-2 Pat Eddery (9) *hld up, rdn 3 fs out, nvr on terms*........... (15 to 2 op 7 to 1 tchd 8 to 1) 7
1958[7] BAY QUEEN [80] 9-4 (3*) M Fenton (5) *hld up in tch, rdn o'r 3 fs out, wknd over 2 out*..................................(8 to 1) 8
1972[8] MIM [54] 7-9 S Dawson (3) *al beh, tld off fnl 2 fs*. .... (33 to 1 op 25 to 1) 9
Dist: ¾l, hd, 3½l, 3½l, 1½l, nk, 7l, dist. 2m 9.34s. a 6.34s (9 Ran).
SR: 32/29/16/12/2/-/13/4/-/ (Lord Matthews), R J R Williams

2577 Levy Board Handicap Class D (0-80 3-y-o and up) £3,611 7f......... (5:00)

2066 ARID [77] 3-9-7 M Roberts (10) *nvr far away, rdn to ld appr fnl furlong, jst hld on*........(11 to 1 op 10 to 1) 1
1977[6] TEANARCO (Ire) [59] 5-8-10 L Dettori (4) *al prmnt, hrd rdn fnl furlong, pressed wnr to line*. .... (7 to 1 op 5 to 1 tchd 15 to 2) 2
2491[7] TIFFANY'S CASE (Ire) [57] 4-8-8 E Johnson (7) *rcd on outsd, hdwy appr fnl furlong, ran on*. .... (9 to 1 op 8 to 1 tchd 10 to 1) 3
2293[3] NOBLE RISK [68] 3-8-12 W R Swinburn (1) *led till hdd appr fnl furlong, rallied ins*...............(8 to 1 op 10 to 1) 4
2350* TUMBLING (USA) [45] 5-7-10 (5ex) W Carson (8) *hld up, hdwy appr fnl furlong, ran on, nvr nrr*.....(11 to 2 jt-fav op 5 to 1 tchd 6 to 1) 5
2270* SUPEROO [70] (bl) 7-9-7 (5ex) Pat Eddery (6) *pld hrd, hld up, hdwy o'r one furlong out, short of room ins last, no extr*.....................(7 to 1 op 6 to 1 tchd 15 to 2) 6
1954[5] QUEEN OF SHANNON (Ire) [68] 5-9-5 M Tebbutt (11) *in tch, rdn 2 fs out, one pace*............ (9 to 1 op 10 to 1) 7
2327[4] COURT MINSTREL [56] 4-8-7 J Reid (12) *hld up, no hdwy fnl 2 fs*........... (11 to 2 jt-fav op 5 to 1 tchd 6 to 1) 8
2172[2] SILKY SIREN [71] 4-9-8 S Whitworth (5) *hld up, hdwy hfwy, wkng whn short of room ins fnl furlong*. ....(7 to 1 op 6 to 1) 9
1698[5] UNIFICATION (Ire) [49] 4-8-0 N Adams (9) *hld up, al beh*. .... (20 to 1 op 16 to 1) 10
2327 BROADWAY RUCKUS (Can) [52] (v) 4-8-3[2] J Williams (13) *chsd ldrs till wknd 2 fs out*..........................(33 to 1) 11
STEPPIN HIGH [61] 3-8-5 A Munro (2) *al beh*. .... (20 to 1 op 14 to 1) 12
Dist: Sht-hd, ¾l, hd, hd, 1½l, nk, 2½l, ¾l, 4l, 3½l. 1m 30.53s. a 6.43s (12 Ran).
SR: 32/20/16/19/2/22/19/-/12/ (Sheikh Mohammed), J H M Gosden

NEWMARKET (JULY) (good to soft)
Friday July 16th
Going Correction: PLUS 0.55 sec. per fur. (races 1,3,5,6), PLUS 0.40 (2,4)

2578 Yellow Label Claiming Stakes Class E (3-y-o) £3,080 1m..............(6:30)

WATER GYPSY 8-9 D Holland (6) *hld up, improved 3 fs out, led o'r one out, rdn out*. .... (14 to 1 op 6 to 1 tchd 20 to 1) 1
2190[2] STRIKE-A-POSE 7-12 (3*) D Harrison (3) *wl plcd, ev ch 2 fs out, not quicken ins last*...... (9 to 4 fav tchd 5 to 2) 2
2300[8] ANORAK (USA) 9-4 R Cochrane (10) *hld up rear, hdwy o'r 2 fs out, ran on one pace fnl furlong*. .... (11 to 4 op 2 to 1 tchd 3 to 1) 3
2095[9] WALID'S PRINCESS (Ire) 8-1[2] A Munro (2) *trkd ldr, led 3 fs out till o'r one out, sn btn*. .... (14 to 1 op 10 to 1 tchd 16 to 1) 4
2279[4] KING PARIS (Ire) 9-3 (3*) M Fenton (5) *hld up, cld on ldrs o'r 2 fs out, sn rdn, wknd fnl furlong*. ....(3 to 1 tchd 100 to 30) 5
2065[7] RIVA ROCK 8-4[1] (7*) G Faulkner (11) *strted slwly, beh most of way*..........................(50 to 1 op 25 to 1) 6
2411[9] MISS RIBBONS 7-6 (7*) Kim McDonnell (4) *led to 3 fs out, wknd 2 out*...................... (50 to 1 op 33 to 1) 7
EASTERN CHARLY (Bel) 8-7 (7*) S Eiffert (9) *chsd ldrs 6 fs, rdn and weakend quickly o'r one out*. .... (33 to 1 op 12 to 1) 8
MISTER FORUM 8-10 Pat Eddery (7) *reluctant to race, sn tld off, pld up hfwy, dismounted*. .... (12 to 1 op 6 to 1 tchd 14 to 1) pu
Dist: 1½l, 1½l, 4l, 3½l, ¾l, 3½l, 12l. 1m 47.02s. a 9.12s (9 Ran).
SR: 24/11/23/-/2/-/ (John B Sunley), M J Heaton-Ellis

2579 St Petersburg Conditions Stakes Class C (3-y-o and up) £4,761 1½m ....(7:00)

579[3] ALWAYS FRIENDLY 5-9-0 A Munro (4) *hld up rear, hdwy 5 fs out, led o'r one out, edgd rght ins last, rdn out*. .... (100 to 30 op 3 to 1 tchd 7 to 2) 1
2070[3] SONUS (Ire) 4-9-9 M Roberts (5) *chsd ldr, led briefly 2 fs out, rdn and rallied ins last, no extr nr line*. .... (100 to 30 op 5 to 2 tchd 7 to 2) 2
2349* MACK THE KNIFE (bl) 4-9-9 L Piggott (2) *led till rdn and hdd 2 fs out, wknd o'r one out*. (3 to 1 fav tchd 4 to 1) 3
1952[4] FITZCARRALDO (USA) 3-8-6[2] R Cochrane (3) *in tch till rdn and wknd 4 fs out, sn lost touch*. .... (9 to 1 op 12 to 1 tchd 8 to 1) 4
1746* TEEN JAY 3-8-4 M Hills (1) *trkd ldrs till rdn and lost tch 4 fs out*.................(14 to 1 op 12 to 1 tchd 16 to 1) 5
2238[3] RANI (Ire) 3-7-13 W Carson (6) *wl plcd till pushed alng and drpd rear 6 fs out*............... (4 to 1 op 3 to 1) 6
Dist: 2l, 8l, 3½l, 10l, 7l. 2m 36.23s. a 7.43s (6 Ran).
SR: 74/79/63/39/17/-/ (Fahd Salman), H Candy

2580 Nicole Ponsardin Maiden Stakes Class D (3-y-o and up) £3,687 6f (7:30)

2202[4] SO INTREPID (Ire) 3-9-0 Paul Eddery (9) *steadied strt, improved hfwy, led 2 fs out, shaken up and styd on strly*.................(10 to 1 op 8 to 1 tchd 12 to 1) 1
2304[8] TRAPEZIUM 3-8-9 M Roberts (8) *hld up, jnd wnr 2 fs out, ev ch frm o'r one out, not quicken nr finish*. ....(4 to 1 op 7 to 2 tchd 9 to 2) 2
2202 AQUILETTA 3-8-9 T Quinn (6) *hld up rear, str brst and swtchd lft 2 fs out, one pace fnl furlong*. .... (12 to 1 op 10 to 1 tchd 14 to 1) 3
2351[4] DASHING MARCH 4-9-1 J Williams (10) *slwly into strd, beh till styd on ins last 2 fs, not rch ldrs*. .... (40 to 1 op 33 to 1 tchd 50 to 1) 4
872 AGHAR (Ire) 3-9-0 L Piggott (11) *hld up rear, moderate prog fnl 2 fs*........................(10 to 1 tchd 12 to 1) 5
1616[7] PRINCESS HAYLEY 3-8-9 R Cochrane (5) *chsd ldrs, styd on one pace frm 2 fs out*.............. (14 to 1 op 10 to 1) 6
2231[2] PENNY FAN 3-8-9 A Munro (1) *in tch for o'r 3 fs, no extr*. ....(8 to 1 op 6 to 1 tchd 9 to 1) 7
PISTON (Ire) 3-9-0 W R Swinburn (4) *led to 2 fs out, sn btn*. .... (6 to 1 op 5 to 1 tchd 13 to 2) 8
CIRCLE OF CHALK (Fr) 3-8-9 Pat Eddery (13) *ldg grp till lost pl 2 fs out*....... (5 to 2 fav op 7 to 2 tchd 4 to 1) 9
PRIMOCELLE 3-8-2 (7*) Sarah Holland (7) *in tch in mid-div, wknd 2 fs out*........ (40 to 1 op 20 to 1 tchd 50 to 1) 10
FASHION QUEEN 3-8-9 B Raymond (2) *pressed ldrs for o'r 3 fs*.................. (25 to 1 op 14 to 1 tchd 33 to 1) 11
SUNNYVIEW LAD 3-9-0 N Carlisle (3) *cl up till wknd o'r 2 fs out*................................ (40 to 1 op 33 to 1) 12
2202 ZAJKO (USA) (v) 3-9-0 L Dettori (12) *in tch to hfwy, lost touch quickly, tld off*............ (14 to 1 op 10 to 1) 13
Dist: ¾l, 4l, 2½l, ¾l, ¾l, 2l, 6l, 2l, ¾l, nk. 1m 17.53s. a 5.83s (13 Ran).
SR: 49/41/25/21/17/9/1/-/-/ (Mrs P W Harris), P W Harris

2581 Prix De La Grande Dame Handicap Class C (0-95 4-y-o and up) £5,162 1¼m.......................... (8:00)

2025* USAIDIT [78] 4-8-13 J Reid (7) *hld up gng wl in mid-div, shaken up to ld entering fnl furlong, rdn out*. .... (100 to 30 fav op 3 to 1 tchd 7 to 2) 1
1919[2] YILDIZ [71] 4-8-6 Pat Eddery (1) *ldg grp, rdn to ld briefly o'r one furlong out, kpt on one pace*. .... (15 to 2 op 6 to 1 tchd 8 to 1) 2

1064 BOLD STROKE [78] 4-8-13 W Carson (9) *led aftr one furlong, clr till hdd o'r one furlong out, ran on same pace.* ....(10 to 1 op 8 to 1 tchd 12 to 1) 3
2211 WAINWRIGHT (USA) [80] 4-9-1 M Roberts (8) *hld up rear, hdwy o'r 2 fs out, not trble ldrs appr last.* ....(9 to 1 op 7 to 1 tchd 10 to 1) 4
2211 BARFORD LAD [73] 6-8-8 A Munro (2) *settled mid-div, rdn and no prog o'r 2 fs out.* (9 to 1 op 8 to 1 tchd 10 to 1) 5
1845* ALDERBROOK [93] 4-10-0 Paul Eddery (12) *ldg grp till wknd ins last 2 fs*...... (4 to 1 tchd 7 to 2 and 9 to 2) 6
2211 DREAMS END [82] 5-9-3 G Hind (6) *effrt frm rear 3 fs out, no imprsn on ldrs*...............(12 to 1 tchd 14 to 1) 7
1878[5] LIGHT HAND [72] 7-8-7 P Robinson (10) *trkd ldg grp, wknd o'r 2 fs out*.........(12 to 1 op 10 to 1 tchd 14 to 1) 8
632[5] CANNY CHRONICLE [78] 5-8-6 (7*) S Mulvey (4) *strted slwly, beh most of way*...........(33 to 1 op 20 to 1) 9
1720[2] TOP SHIEL [79] 5-9-0 R Cochrane (5) *al rear.* ....(6 to 1 op 11 to 2) 10
2254 STARLIGHT FLYER [86] (bl) 6-9-7 L Dettori (11) *led one furlong, chsd ldr till rdn and wknd quickly o'r 3 out, tld off*...............(33 to 1 op 50 to 1 tchd 66 to 1) 11

Dist: 2l, ½l, 6l, ½l, 3½l, 2½l, 4l, 4l, 1½l, 15l. 2m 10.07s. a 7.87s (11 Ran).
SR: 60/49/55/45/37/50/34/16/14/ (Mrs Pauline Merrick), T G Mills

2582 Clicquot Rose Handicap Class D (0-80 3-y-o and up) £3,720 6f......... (8:30)

1932[8] ROCA MURADA (Ire) [52] 4-8-7 P Robinson (3) *wl plcd, rdn to ld one furlong out, jst hld on*.....(8 to 1 op 5 to 1) 1
1806 BLUE TOPAZE [73] 5-10-0 J Williams (8) *hld up last, ran on ins fnl 2 fs, fnshd strly.* (7 to 1 op 6 to 1 tchd 8 to 1) 2
2532[4] RACING TELEGRAPH [59] 3-8-8 M Wigham (9) *led aftr 2 fs, hdd two out, kpt on und pres nr finish.* ....(8 to 1 op 6 to 1) 3
2255 MERRYHILL MAID (Ire) [68] 5-9-9 R Cochrane (5) *led 2 fs, led two out to one out, no extr.* ....(9 to 1 op 8 to 1 tchd 10 to 1) 4
2305[3] BRIGHT PARAGON (Ire) [47] 4-8-2 J Quinn (1) *handily plcd, rdn and not quicken frm 2 fs out.* ....(3 to 1 fav op 11 to 4 tchd 7 to 2) 5
2309[4] BLUE GRIT [68] 7-9-4 (5*) J Tate (6) *chsd ldrs 4 fs.* ....(6 to 1 op 5 to 1 tchd 13 to 2) 6
2136[8] CLAYBANK (USA) [73] 4-10-0 W Carson (7) *settled rear, rdn alng o'r 2 fs out, not trble ldrs*....... (6 to 1 op 5 to 1) 7
2191[3] MARTINOSKY [66] 7-9-7 W R Swinburn (2) *in tch in mid-div, rdn o'r 2 fs out, wknd appr last.* ....(11 to 2 op 5 to 1 tchd 6 to 1) 8

Dist: Hd, 1½l, 1l, ¾l, 3l, 4l, ¾l. 1m 18.11s. a 6.41s (8 Ran).
SR: 31/51/25/36/12/21/10/-/ (Tim Corby), M J Ryan

2583 Widow Maiden Fillies' Stakes Class D (2-y-o) £3,915 7f................(9:00)

2364[7] FAIRY HEIGHTS (Ire) 8-11 Pat Eddery (1) *steadied strt, hld up, hdwy to ld o'r 2 fs out, rdn clr fnl furlong.* ....(100 to 30 op 5 to 2 tchd 7 to 2) 1
LA QUICA 8-11 T Quinn (2) *cl up, outpcd 2 fs out, styd on ins last.* (13 to 8 fav op 6 to 4 tchd 5 to 4 and 7 to 4) 2
SONG OF YEARS (Ire) 8-11 R Hills (6) *hld up rear, ev ch 2 fs out, not quicken appr last, wknd.* (16 to 1 op 12 to 1) 3
JANGADA 8-11 W Carson (5) *pressed ldr, rdn and outpcd o'r 2 fs out, styd on clsg stages.* ....(9 to 2 op 10 to 1 tchd 12 to 1 and 4 to 1) 4
EDWINA (Ire) 8-11 M Hills (3) *chsd ldrs till rdn and outpcd 2 fs out*............. (14 to 1 op 12 to 1 tchd 16 to 1) 5
RARE BIRD (USA) 8-11 M Roberts (4) *led till o'r 2 fs out, sn btn, eased fnl furlong*... (3 to 1 op 9 to 4 tchd 7 to 2) 6

Dist: 3½l, 1l, 1l, 6l, ¾l. 1m 33.84s. a 9.64s (6 Ran).
SR: 10/-/-/ (Frank W Golding), N A Callaghan

SOUTHWELL (A.W) (std)
Friday July 16th

Going Correction: MINUS 0.15 sec. per fur. (race 1), PLUS 0.05 (2,3,4,5,6,7)

2584 Emperor Handicap Class E (0-70 3-y-o and up) £3,131 5f...............(2:20)

2214[9] COMET WHIRLPOOL (Ire) [56] (bl) 3-9-3 J Quinn (1) *trkd ldrs, hdwy 2 fs out, effrt to ld ins last, ran on.* ....(10 to 1 op 7 to 1) 1
2191[5] SPRING HIGH [60] (bl) 6-9-12 M Wigham (8) *al cl up stands rail, rdn and ev ch appr fnl furlong, kpt on ins last.* ....(8 to 1 op 6 to 1) 2
2089[3] CONVENIENT MOMENT [55] 3-9-2 G Carter (2) *cl up, led aftr 2 fs, rdn o'r one out, hdd and no extr ins last.* ....(9 to 1 op 5 to 1) 3
2215[7] NILU (Ire) [50] 5-9-2 T Quinn (7) *led 2 fs, cl up, rdn fnl two furlongs, kpt on ins last*..........................(16 to 1) 4
2428[4] FAMILY ROSE [38] (v) 4-8-1 (3*) D Harrison (10) *al cl up stands rls, ev ch 2 fs out, sn rdn and not quicken entering last*........... (5 to 1 op 9 to 2 tchd 6 to 1) 5
2387[2] JESS REBEC [51] 5-9-3 N Carlisle (6) *steadied strt, swtchd lft, hdwy 2 fs out, rdn and kpt on ins last.* ....(4 to 1 op 11 to 4) 6
2214[5] MOVING IMAGE (Ire) [54] 3-9-1 C Dwyer (3) *chsd ldrs, ev ch 2 fs out, sn rdn and wknd appr fnl furlong.* ....(7 to 2 fav op 5 to 1 tchd 3 to 1) 7
1677[5] NO QUARTER GIVEN [59] 8-9-11 G Hind (5) *chsd ldrs, rdn 2 fs out, sn wknd*....... (9 to 1 op 8 to 1 tchd 10 to 1) 8
2312[9] PRETTY CHIC [45] 4-8-6 (5*) O Pears (4) *cl up to hfwy, sn rdn and lost pl*.............................. (16 to 1) 9
2215[9] WE'RE ALL GAME [45] (v) 4-8-8 (3*) N Kennedy (9) *dwlt, sn chasing ldrs, hdwy 2 fs out, ev ch, rdn and wknd quickly o'r one furlong out.* ....(14 to 1 op 20 to 1 tchd 10 to 1) 10

Dist: 1l, ½l, ½l, hd, nk, 1l, 1½l, 1l, ½l. 1m 0.50s. a 2.60s (10 Ran).
SR: 36/41/29/27/14/26/20/24/6/ (Colin W Anderton), Pat Mitchell

2585 KPMG Peat Marwick Selling Handicap Stakes Class G (0-60 3-y-o and up) £2,070 1½m.................. (2:50)

495 FIRST FLING (Ire) [40] 4-9-2 G Hind (8) *hld up and beh, hdwy hfwy, rdn 2 fs out, styd on to ld ins last.* ....(8 to 1 op 7 to 1) 1
2178[3] MUST BE MAGICAL (USA) [39] 5-9-1 G Carter (10) *mid-div, hdwy hfwy, rdn to chal 2 fs out, kpt on ins last.* ....(7 to 2 tchd 9 to 2) 2
2455[3] ANAR (Ire) [40] (v) 4-8-11 (5*) O Pears (6) *chsd ldrs, led o'r 4 fs out, rdn 2 out, hdd and wknd ins last.* ....(5 to 1 op 9 to 2) 3
AT PEACE [37] 7-8-13 R Price (9) *hld up and beh, hdwy hfwy, rdn o'r 2 fs out, sn one pace.* ....(5 to 2 fav tchd 4 to 1) 4
2178 GREEN'S SEAGO (USA) [43] 5-9-5 J Quinn (5) *chsd ldrs, rdn o'r 4 fs out, sn wknd*......................(16 to 1) 5
1873[6] SPANISH WHISPER [26] 6-7-11 (5*) D Wright (3) *chsd ldrs, rdn alng hfwy, wknd o'r 4 fs out.* ....(16 to 1 op 12 to 1 tchd 20 to 1) 6
709[6] MR WISHING WELL [38] (e/s) 7-9-0 T Quinn (11) *hld up and beh, hdwy hfwy, rdn o'r 2 fs out, sn wknd.* ....(6 to 1 op 5 to 1) 7
2530[5] SULUK (USA) [38] 8-9-0 S Perks (7) *hld up, rdn alng hfwy, nvr a factor*............ (6 to 1 tchd 11 to 2) 8
2197 NEVENTER (Fr) [52] 4-10-0 V Smith (2) *cl up, rdn 5 4longs out, sn wknd*...................(33 to 1 op 20 to 1) 9
2149 MELANCOLIA [38] (bl) 7-9-0 J Fortune (1) *led, rdn and hdd o'r 4 fs out, sn wknd*.....(6 to 1 op 3 to 1 tchd 7 to 1) 10

Dist: 1½l, 1½l, 7l, 10l, ¾l, 8l, 7l, 7l, 15l. 2m 41.50s. a 7.60s (10 Ran).
SR: 32/28/26/9/-/-/ (A C Edwards), Dr J D Scargill

2586 Latham Midland Caberboard Prize Maiden Auction Stakes Class F (2-y-o) £2,243 6f...................... (3:20)

2274[7] HEATHYARDS CRUSADE (Ire) 9-0 S Perks (7) *al prmnt, effrt to chal 2 fs out, rdn o'r one out, styd on ins last to ld nr line*..........................(10 to 1 op 6 to 1) 1
2199[4] FOUR OF SPADES 9-0 J Fortune (9) *led, rdn o'r one furlong out, hdd and no extr nr line.* ....(12 to 1 tchd 14 to 1) 2
1895[3] HASTY BANK 9-0 M Birch (4) *in tch, hdwy on outer 2 fs out, sn ev ch, rdn and not quicken ins last.* ... (5 to 4 fav op Evens tchd 11 to 10 on and 11 to 8) 3
2274[8] DAKOTA BRAVE (Ire) 8-11 (3*) D Harrison (3) *chsd ldrs, rdn 2 fs out, kpt on one pace.* ....(100 to 30 op 3 to 1 tchd 9 to 2 and 5 to 1) 4
SEDIMENTARY 8-9 (5*) C Hodgson (2) *slwly away and beh till styd on fnl 2 fs, nvr dngrs*........(9 to 1 op 5 to 2) 5
1983[6] OVALWORLD 8-9 (5*) O Pears (6) *cl up, rdn o'r 2 fs out, wknd over one out*................(33 to 1 op 20 to 1) 6
2180[5] BOLD TIME MONKEY 8-9 G Carter (1) *cl up on inner, rdn o'r 2 fs out, sn wknd*.............. (10 to 1 op 7 to 1) 7
BAROSKI 9-0 J Quinn (5) *stumbled strt, al beh.* ....(33 to 1 op 25 to 1) 8
OZZIE JONES 8-9 (5*) D McCabe (8) *sn outpcd and beh.* ....(33 to 1 op 20 to 1) 9

Dist: Sht-hd, 1½l, ½l, 8l, ½l, 6l, 1l, 2l. 1m 17.90s. a 4.50s (9 Ran).
SR: 16/15/9/7/-/-/ (L A Morgan), R Hollinshead

2587 Garbos Nightclub Rating Related Maiden Stakes Class E (3-y-o) £2,821 2m............................(3:50)

2372[4] SCOTTISH WEDDING 8-4 (5*) O Pears (2) *trkd ldrs gng wl, hdwy o'r 3 fs out, led on bit 2 out, clr appr last, unchlgd*............................(4 to 1 op 5 to 1) 1
2213[4] FLAMING MIRACLE (Ire) 9-0 T Quinn (7) *chsd ldr, led 4 fs out, sn rdn, hdd 2 out, wknd appr last.* ....(9 to 4 fav op 7 to 4 tchd 5 to 2) 2
2355[4] TURFMANS VISION 9-0 S Perks (1) *in tch, rdn 6 fs out and lost touch, plodded on one pace fnl 4 furlongs.* ....(4 to 1 op 3 to 1) 3
2317[8] C D SHAREPLAN (USA) 9-0 G Carter (4) *chsd ldrs, rdn hfwy, sn lost pl and beh*.........(10 to 1 op 8 to 1) 4
1477[2] MOUNTAIN WILLOW 8-9 J Lowe (6) *chsd ldg pair, rdn 6 fs out, sn wl beh*....... (11 to 4 op 5 to 2 tchd 3 to 1) 5
1054 DOOGAREY 9-0 R Price (5) *led, rdn and hdd 4 fs out, wknd quickly*....................(25 to 1 op 20 to 1) 6

Dist: 20l, 25l, 3½l, 1l, 15l. 3m 42.50s. a 16.00s (6 Ran).
(J Asquith), S G Norton

2588 Thompson Jewitt International Claiming Stakes Class F (2-y-o) £2,243 7f ....(4:20)

2229* DEMI-PLIE (v) 8-9 G Carter (5) *chsd ldrs, rdn alng 3 fs out, hdwy on inner to chal 2 out, styd on und pres to ld entering last.* ....(11 to 10 on op Evens tchd 5 to 4 and 11 to 8) 1
2377[6] WINDOW DISPLAY 8-7 T Quinn (3) *chsd ldrs, hdwy to ld 2 fs out, sn rdn, hdd and not quicken entering last.* ....(9 to 1 op 10 to 1 tchd 8 to 1) 2
1909[6] BIEN CUIT 7-12[3] (3*) D Harrison (9) *in tch, rdn o'r 2 fs out, styd on ins last.*..................(16 to 1 op 10 to 1) 3
2423* TRENDY DANCER (Ire) 8-8 (5*) O Pears (1) *cl up, led aftr 3 fs till 2 out, sn rdn and wknd.* ....(7 to 2 op 4 to 1 tchd 3 to 1) 4
1774[5] FINISHING KIND (v) 8-2 J Quinn (7) *in tch, rdn o'r 2 fs out, sn one pace*..................(20 to 1 op 16 to 1) 5
2533[2] PASSION SUNDAY 9-7 M Birch (6) *chsd ldrs, rdn 2 and a half fs out, sn one pace*..............(7 to 1 op 7 to 2) 6
2216[5] OLYMPIC BID 8-6 J Fortune (2) *cl up, rdn o'r 2 fs out, sn wknd*..................(16 to 1 op 12 to 1) 7
2229 LONE RISK (bl) 7-12 (7*) G Forster (4) *led 3 fs, cl up till rdn and wknd quickly o'r 2 out*........(33 to 1 op 25 to 1) 8
STAR TRAVELLER 8-11 M Wigham (8) *slwly away, al beh.* ....(20 to 1 op 14 to 1) 9

Dist: 2l, 1½l, 6l, 3l, ½l, ¾l, 12l, 10l. 1m 30.90s. a 4.80s (9 Ran).
SR: 28/20/6/3/-/-/ (Mrs C A B St George), D R Loder

2589 Red Admiral Limited Stakes Class E (0-70 3-y-o) £3,131 1m..........(4:50)

2289[8] RED COTTON 8-9 P D'Arcy (4) *unruly strt, made all, clr fnl 2 fs, easily*.....................(7 to 4 op 11 to 10) 1
2525[4] CHARLIE BIGTIME (v) 8-9 (5*) D McCabe (1) *slwly into strd, sn pushed alng, hdwy hfwy, chsd wnr fnl 2 fs, no imprsn*............(6 to 4 on op 5 to 4 on tchd Evens) 2
1874[6] MELODIC DRIVE 9-0 G Hind (2) *chsd ldrs, effrt o'r 2 fs out, sn rdn and one pace*....(9 to 1 op 8 to 1 tchd 10 to 1) 3
1875[5] NORTHERN JUDY (Ire) 8-9 S Perks (3) *chsd wnr to hfwy, sn one pace*..........................(12 to 1 op 10 to 1) 4

Dist: 7l, 2l, hd. 1m 44.30s. a 5.30s (4 Ran).
SR: 22/6/-/-/ (Lord Weinstock), M R Stoute

2590 Levy Board Handicap Class E (0-70 3-y-o and up) £3,365 7f..........(5:20)

2426[3] GLENFIELD GRETA [53] (bl) 5-9-2 G Hind (7) *cl up, led 2 and a half fs out, rdn clr and ran on*............(7 to 2 co-fav op 9 to 4) 1
1874[3] BASSIO (Bel) [46] (h) 4-8-9 W Hood (3) *chsd ldrs, rdn and hmpd 3 fs out, swtchd and ran on wl fnl 2, not rch wnr.* ....(9 to 2 op 4 to 1 tchd 5 to 1) 2
1776[7] NELLIE'S GAMBLE [68] 3-9-10 T Quinn (2) *mid-div, hdwy hfwy, chsd wnr fnl 2 fs, kpt on one pace*....(7 to 2 co-fav op 4 to 1) 3
1817[4] BROUGHTON'S PORT [61] 3-8-12 (5*) D McCabe (5) *beh till styd on fnl 2 fs, nrst finish*....(7 to 2 co-fav op 3 to 1) 4
971 SWYNFORD FLYER [31] 4-7-8[4] (3*) N Kennedy (8) *chsd ldrs, rdn and edgd lft 3 fs out, sn one pace*.........(20 to 1) 5
1969 VERRO (USA) [31] (bl) 6-7-8[1] J Lowe (1) *al rear.* ....(14 to 1 op 16 to 1) 6
2106[7] ROCK SONG (Ire) [40] 4-7-12 (5*) D Wright (4) *dwlt, al rear.* ....(14 to 1 op 20 to 1) 7
2354[8] DANDY DESIRE [37] (bl) 4-8-0 J Quinn (6) *led, rdn and hdd 2 and a half fs out, wknd quickly.* ....(7 to 1 op 8 to 1 tchd 13 to 2) 8

Dist: 2l, hd, ¾l, 1½l, 8l, hd, 4l. 1m 31.30s. a 5.20s (8 Ran).
SR: 29/16/30/21/-/ (S M Grey), P S Felgate

THIRSK (good)
Friday July 16th
Going Correction: MINUS 0.20 sec. per fur. (races 1,2,3,6,7), MINUS 0.30 (4,5)

2591 Hutton Wandesley Handicap Class D (0-80 3-y-o and up) £3,260 1½m (2:10)

2470[2] PERSIAN SOLDIER [44] 6-8-8 K Fallon (2) *made all, shaken up 2 fs out, styd on strly ins last*....(11 to 2 op 5 to 1) 1
2427[2] PHARLY DANCER [59] 4-9-9 Dean McKeown (5) *nvr far away, rdn and ev ch frm 2 fs out, not quicken ins last.* ....(3 to 1 fav tchd 100 to 30) 2
2000[4] WANZA [60] 3-8-12 G Duffield (7) *took keen hold early, pressed ldr, ev ch and drvn alng appr 2 fs out, not quicken o'r one out*.... (13 to 2 op 6 to 1 tchd 7 to 1) 3
2501[5] ROUSITTO [54] 5-9-4 W Ryan (4) *hld up in rear, rdn to improve 2 fs out, no imprsn ins last.* (4 to 1 op 9 to 2) 4
2043[5] KINOKO [61] 5-9-11 K Darley (6) *hld up in rear, rdn to improve appr strt, not pace to chal fnl 2 fs*.....(4 to 1) 5
2444[3] SHARQUIN [42] 6-8-6 J Carroll (1) *hld up in tch, pushed alng 2 fs out, sn btn*..................................(8 to 1) 6
2057 ROAR ON TOUR [49] 4-8-8 (5*) Darren Moffatt (3) *chsd ldrs, pushed alng hfwy, btn entering strt*..........(14 to 1) 7

Dist: 2l, 3l, 2½l, 1½l, 3½l, 3½l. 2m 34.70s. a 4.50s (7 Ran).
SR: 25/36/19/20/24/-/-/ (Norman Firth), Mrs M Reveley

2592 Westow Conditions Stakes Class D (2-y-o) £3,231 7f..................(2:40)

2240* KISSING COUSIN (Ire) 8-9 W Ryan (4) *made all, quickened wl o'r one furlong out, drw clr ins last.* ....(6 to 4 fav op 7 to 4 tchd 2 to 1) 1
2414* ORANGE PLACE (Ire) 9-0 M Hills (2) *took keen hold, trkd ldr, effrt and rdn 2 fs out, one pace appr last.* ....(85 to 40 op 2 to 1 tchd 7 to 4 and 9 to 4) 2
2234[2] LAMBENT 8-9 W Newnes (3) *trkd ldg pair, drvn alng entering strt, sn outpcd, kpt on und pres ins fnl furlong, nvr dngrs*...... (6 to 1 op 11 to 2 tchd 13 to 2) 3
1959* LUGANO 8-12 K Darley (1) *slwly into strd, hld up in last pl, ran slightly wide entering strt, rdn and sn btn, eased*...........................(100 to 30 op 9 to 4) 4

Dist: 6l, nk, 8l. 1m 25.60s. a 2.80s (4 Ran).
SR: 32/19/13/-/ (Sheikh Mohammed), H R A Cecil

2593 Ness Selling Handicap Class G (0-60 3-y-o) £2,721 1m...............(3:10)

1872[4] MULLED ALE (Ire) [48] 9-7 G Duffield (1) *tucked away on ins, effrt 2 fs out, not much room and swtchd inside last, ran on strly to ld on line.* ....(7 to 2 op 4 to 1 tchd 9 to 2) 1
2540[2] MANX MONARCH [46] 9-0 (5*) A Garth (3) *hld up in rear, effrt and swtchd outsd 2 fs out, ran on wl fnl furlong, jst held*..................(2 to 1 fav op 7 to 4) 2
2104 ALBEIT [29] 8-2 J Fanning (4) *in tch, improved to ld 2 fs out, edgd lft fnl one and a half furlongs, ct on line.* ....(14 to 1 op 12 to 1 tchd 16 to 1) 3
2095[7] SUMMERS DREAM [32] 8-5 K Fallon (6) *hld up, improved appr 2 fs out, rdn and not quicken ins last.* ....(10 to 1 op 8 to 1) 4
2104[7] BOLD LINE [42] 9-1 Dean McKeown (2) *taken early to post, missed break, beh, effrt and drvn alng o'r 2 fs out, no imprsn*..................(9 to 2 op 4 to 1 tchd 5 to 1) 5
1102[5] QUESSONG [38] 8-11 R Lappin (7) *trkd ldrs, ev ch 2 fs out, rdn and sn btn*.........(8 to 1 op 7 to 1 tchd 9 to 1) 6
2089[4] PRESS ONWARD [33] 8-6 T Williams (8) *rcd keenly, prmnt, led aftr 2 fs, hdd two furlongs out, sn btn*..... (10 to 1) 7
2095 DON'T TELL JEAN [32] (bl) 8-5 L Charnock (5) *led 2 fs, styd hndy, drvn alng entering strt, sn lost tch, eased o'r one furlong out*...................... (16 to 1 op 12 to 1) 8

Dist: Sht-hd, sht-hd, 2l, 3l, 3l, 7l, 5l. 1m 39.70s. a 3.80s (8 Ran).
SR: 26/23/5/2/3/ (W J Bridge), C F Wall

2594 Back A Winner By Train-Tote Handicap Class D (0-80 3-y-o and up) £3,348 6f...............................(3:40)

2392 CATHERINES WELL [77] 10-10-0 T Lucas (8) *trkd ldrs gng wl, effrt o'r one furlong out, led ins last, hng lft, pushed out*.............(11 to 2 op 5 to 1 tchd 6 to 1) 1
2062 DENSBEN [76] 9-9-13 K Fallon (9) *beh and sn outpcd, imprvg whn hmpd and swtchd o'r one furlong out, not clr run and switched ins last, styd on strly.* ....(4 to 1 fav tchd 9 to 2) 2
2309[7] SULLY'S CHOICE (USA) [45] (bl) 12-7-10 S Wood (3) *dsptd ld, hdd ins fnl furlong, no extr*...... (9 to 1 op 8 to 1) 3
2434 PLUM FIRST [70] (bl) 3-8-12 (3*) S Maloney (4) *dsptd ld, rdn o'r one furlong out, not quicken wl ins last.* ....(12 to 1 tchd 10 to 1) 4
2434[7] INVIGILATE [58] 4-8-9 Dale Gibson (1) *beh and sn pushed alng, not clr run 2 fs out, swtchd ins, kpt on inside last, nvr dngrs*..........................(5 to 1 op 9 to 2) 5
1563[7] SLADES HILL [63] 6-9-0 W Ryan (2) *pressed ldrs, not clr run 2 fs out and appr fnl furlong, swtchd and not quicken ins last*...............(5 to 1 tchd 9 to 2) 6
2305[8] BOLD COUNTY [67] 3-8-12 Dean McKeown (7) *hmpd strt, pressed ldg grp, rdn o'r 2 fs out, not quicken ins last.* ....(7 to 1) 7
1801 EGG [62] 3-8-7 T Williams (6) *hmpd strt, beh and sn pushed alng, kpt on fnl furlong, nvr able to chal.* ....(9 to 1 op 7 to 1 tchd 10 to 1) 8
2510[5] SABO SONG [68] 3-8-13 S Webster (5) *frnt rnk, rdn 2 fs out, sn btn*...................... (12 to 1 tchd 14 to 1) 9

Dist: ½l, ½l, hd, nk, sht-hd, 1l, ¾l, 7l. 1m 11.10s. a 1.10s (9 Ran).
SR: 56/53/20/38/31/35/29/21/-/ (K Hodgson), M W Easterby

2595 EBF Westhorpe Maiden Fillies Stakes Class D (2-y-o) £4,449 6f........(4:10)

POTSCLOSE 8-11 Dean McKeown (2) *pressed ldrs, improved to draw level o'r one furlong out, ran green and wndrd ins last, led last strd.* .... (10 to 1 op 8 to 1 tchd 11 to 1) 1
2240[3] MANHATTAN SUNSET (USA) 8-6 (5*) Stephen Davies (4) *trkd ldrs, improved to ld o'r one furlong out, sn jnd, ran on wl, hdd last strd.* ....(11 to 4 on op 9 to 4 on tchd 2 to 1 on) 2
1844[4] DOUCE MAISON (Ire) 8-8 (3*) B Doyle (3) *chsd ldrs, effrt on outer o'r 2 fs out, not quicken over one out.* ....(4 to 1 op 3 to 1) 3

2429^{6} BALLARD RING (Ire) 8-11 N Connorton (5) *nvr far away, shaken up o'r 2 fs out, wknd over one out*.....(33 to 1) 4
1272 DAUNTLESS FORT 8-11 L Charnock (6) *led till hdd o'r one furlong out, sn btn*..........(50 to 1 op 40 to 1) 5
2129^{9} MUSICAL MARCH 8-11 W Newnes (1) *prmnt, drvn alng hfwy, wknd quickly o'r one furlong out*........(20 to 1) 6
Dist: Hd, 3½l, 1½l, 1l, 8l. 1m 12.50s. a 2.50s (6 Ran).
SR: 11/10/-/ (Duke Of Roxburghe), M Johnston

2596 Thirsk Licensed Traders Maiden Stakes Class D (3-y-o) £3,552 7f (4:40)

1344^{5} PIXTON (Ire) 9-0 G Duffield (1) *chsd ldrs, effrt and rdn o'r 2 fs out, edgd lft and led over one out, ran on wl ins last*. ....(5 to 4 on op 9 to 4 on) 1
2097^{4} MO-ADDAB (Ire) 9-0 A McGlone (9) *beh, rdn entering strt, improved o'r one furlong out, fnshd wl*. ....(7 to 4 op 11 to 4 tchd 6 to 4) 2
MISS RITZ 8-9 Dale Gibson (4) *dwlt, beh, improved to chase ldrs o'r 2 fs out, rdn and kpt on same pace ins last*..(33 to 1) 3
DUELETTA 8-9 W Newnes (3) *in tch, effrt on ins 2 fs out, swtchd o'r one out, one pace inside last*. ....(33 to 1 op 20 to 1) 4
1388^{9} WARM TOES 8-9 Dean McKeown (2) *led till hdd o'r one furlong out, fdd ins last*..........................(25 to 1) 5
1931 SYLVIA MACUSHLA 8-6 (3*) B Doyle (8) *dwlt, beh, pushed alng appr strt, no imprsn fnl 2 fs*. (50 to 1 op 33 to 1) 6
1566 GRANDERISE (Ire) 9-0 L Charnock (6) *chsd ldrs, rdn o'r 2 fs out, sn btn*.........................(50 to 1 op 33 to 1) 7
2416^{7} JIMMY HIMSELF 9-0 T Sprake (7) *beh, came wide strt, edgd rght and sn btn*..............(50 to 1 op 33 to 1) 8
2219^{7} CUT FINE 8-9 J Carroll (5) *wth ldr till rdn and wknd quickly wl o'r one furlong out*.....(16 to 1 op 14 to 1) 9
Dist: ¾l, 2½l, nk, ½l, 4l, ½l, 1l, 1l. 1m 26.70s. a 3.90s (9 Ran).
SR: 21/19/6/5/3/-/ (Mrs J Yarnold), Mrs J Cecil

2597 Levy Board Apprentice Handicap Class E (0-70 3-y-o and up) £2,924 1m ....(5:10)

YOUNG JASON [40] 10-8-7 (5*) J Dennis (4) *hld up in rear, effrt and swtchd o'r one furlong out, led ins last, kpt on wl*..(12 to 1 op 10 to 1) 1
1956^{2} SOOTY TERN [49] 6-9-7 Mark Denaro (6) *led, hdd o'r 2 fs out, rallied to rgn ld one out, headed last 100 yards, kpt on same pace*..................(2 to 1 fav op 7 to 4) 2
934^{5} BRACKENTHWAITE [51] 3-8-5 (10*) Kimberley Hart (1) *tucked away on ins, effrt and rdn o'r 2 fs out, ev ch one out, not quicken*..........................(10 to 1 op 8 to 1) 3
2099^{4} ESSAYEFFSEE [43] 4-8-7 (8*) S Copp (8) *took keen hold, nvr far away, rdn o'r one furlong out, one pace ins last*..(11 to 2 op 9 to 2) 4
2354 BRESIL (USA) [52] 4-9-2 (8*) G McGrath (7) *pressed ldg grp, sddl slpd hfwy, rdn o'r 2 fs out, one pace appr last*. ....(5 to 1 op 10 to 1) 5
2172^{3} CHANTRY BELLINI [46] (bl) 4-8-8 (10*) G Mills (3) *dwlt, sn chasing ldrs, improved to ld o'r 2 fs out, hdd one out, soon btn*..............(6 to 1 op 9 to 2 tchd 13 to 2) 6
2425^{9} VIKING WATERS [48] 3-8-12 R Havlin (2) *trkd ldrs, chlgd o'r 2 fs out, rdn and wknd quickly over one out*. ....(25 to 1 op 20 to 1) 7
1852^{2} FORT VALLY [59] (bl) 3-9-9 G Parkin (5) *missed break, beh, rdn entering strt, wknd 2 fs out*......(8 to 1 op 6 to 1) 8
Dist: 1l, ¾l, 2l, ¾l, 1l, 10l, 1½l. 1m 39.20s. a 3.30s (8 Ran).
SR: 25/31/23/17/24/15/-/-/ (Mrs Gillian Lee), F H Lee

AYR (good)
Saturday July 17th

Going Correction: PLUS 0.15 sec. per fur. (races 1,2,4,5,6), NIL (3)

2598 St Quivox Maiden Stakes Class D (3-y-o and up) £3,494 1¼m........ (2:20)

1992^{2} DESERT POWER 4-9-7 L Charnock (7) *led aftr 3 fs, rdn and ran on wl frm 2 out*. (5 to 2 op 7 to 4 tchd 3 to 1) 1
2277^{5} ADMIRAL'S WELL (Ire) 3-8-11 J Carroll (5) *dwlt, sn in tch, effrt 3 fs out, ev ch o'r one out, kpt on, no imprsn on wnr*.................(5 to 4 fav tchd Evens and 11 to 8) 2
2202^{8} QUARRELLING 3-8-11 K Darley (4) *trkd ldrs, pushed alng o'r 3 fs out, kpt on fnl furlong*..... (7 to 1 tchd 6 to 1) 3
2064^{4} PHILNIC 3-8-4 (7*) J Marshall (2) *beh, effrt o'r 3 fs out, kpt on same pace*............(8 to 1 op 6 to 1 tchd 9 to 1) 4
2275^{7} KAHLO 3-8-6 M Birch (6) *led 3 fs, chsd wnr till wknd 2 out*..................(16 to 1 op 10 to 1 tchd 20 to 1) 5
1594^{5} QUARTZ HILL (USA) 4-9-2 (5*) J Tate (1) *prmnt till wknd 2 fs out, eased whn btn fnl furlong*. (50 to 1 op 16 to 1) 6
2266^{5} GRUMPY'S GRAIN (Ire) (v) 3-8-11 J Fortune (3) *al beh, lost tch 3 fs out*........................(50 to 1 op 20 to 1) 7
Dist: 1½l, 3½l, 1l, ½l, 12l, 3l. 2m 14.62s. a 9.62s (7 Ran).
SR: 26/13/6/4/ (Rhys Thomas Williams), D Burchell

2599 Campbeltown Claiming Stakes Class F (3-y-o and up) £2,467 1m 5f 13yds ....(2:50)

1847* FUNNY CHOICE (Ire) 3-8-3 (3*) S D Williams (4) *cl up, rdn 2 fs out, led one out, styd on*. ....(11 to 10 on op 5 to 4 on tchd Evens) 1
2310^{5} NOUVELLE CUISINE 5-8-11 (5*) J Tate (2) *chsd ldr, led 3 fs out to one out, no extr*...............(7 to 4 op 7 to 4) 2
2086^{8} SAOIRSE (Ire) 5-8-7 (5*) Darren Moffatt (1) *hld up, pushed alng 6 fs out, hdwy to join ldrs 3 out, ev ch o'r one out, no extr fnl furlong*..................(14 to 1 op 7 to 1) 3
HOD-MOD (Ire) 3-8-6 A Mackay (3) *led to 3 fs out, wknd quickly, tld off*.........(9 to 1 op 7 to 1 tchd 10 to 1) 4
Dist: 1l, hd, dist. 2m 57.95s. a 11.95s (4 Ran).
(Lt-Col W L Monteith), P Monteith

2600 Tote Bookmakers Sprint Trophy Handicap Class C (0-90 3-y-o and up) £11,452 6f...................... (3:20)

2062^{8} HOB GREEN [72] 4-8-10 K Fallon (1) *dwlt, beh, steady hdwy hfwy, led entering fnl furlong, ran on wl*. ....(13 to 2 op 5 to 1 tchd 7 to 1) 1
1801* FOR THE PRESENT [80] 3-8-12 K Darley (7) *trkd ldrs, led wl o'r one furlong out till entering last, no extr*. ....(17 to 2 op 7 to 1 tchd 9 to 1) 2
2434^{4} CUMBRIAN WALTZER [90] 8-10-0 M Birch (8) *trkd ldrs, lost pl hfwy, styd on und pres fnl 2 fs*............(7 to 2 jt-fav op 9 to 2 tchd 5 to 1) 3
2264* DOKKHA OYSTON (Ire) [79] 5-9-3 J Carroll (4) *dwlt, sn in tch, effrt o'r 2 fs out, kpt on same pace*. ....(7 to 1 op 6 to 1 tchd 8 to 1) 4
2481^{6} BALLAD DANCER [60] 8-7-12 T Williams (10) *chsd ldrs, rdn 2 fs out, no hdwy*..........................(10 to 1) 5
2230^{4} PALLIUM (Ire) [66] 5-8-4 A Culhane (5) *prmnt till wknd 2 fs out*.................................(16 to 1 op 14 to 1) 6
2363^{2} VELOCE (Ire) [70] 5-8-8 A Mackay (6) *prmnt till wknd 2 fs out*...........(7 to 2 jt-fav op 4 to 1 tchd 5 to 1) 7
2553* DIET [60] (v) 7-7-12 F Norton (9) *led till wl o'r one furlong out, sn wknd*...................(12 to 1 op 10 to 1) 8
2434 RED ROSEIN [82] 7-9-6 J Fortune (11) *hld up, effrt whn not clr run o'r one furlong out, sn btn*.........(25 to 1) 9
2553^{4} SECOND COLOURS (USA) [61] 3-7-2 (5*) Darren Moffatt (3) *prmnt till wknd 2 fs out*...........(8 to 1 tchd 10 to 1) 10
2392^{8} LANGUEDOC [64] 6-8-2 L Charnock (2) *chsd ldrs till wknd 2 fs out*...........................(14 to 1 tchd 16 to 1) 11
Dist: 2½l, ½l, 2l, ½l, 4l, ½l, 1½l, sht-hd, 3l, 1½l. 1m 12.85s. a 1.95s (11 Ran).
SR: 57/49/63/44/23/13/15/-/20/ (P A Leonard), Mrs J R Ramsden

2601 Rothmans Royals North South Challenge Series Handicap Class C (0-90 3-y-o and up) £5,015 1m........ (3:50)

2398^{4} MENTALASANYTHIN [65] 4-8-9 A Mackay (8) *chsd ldrs, effrt o'r 2 fs out, styd on wl to ld ins last*. ....(5 to 1 op 9 to 2 tchd 6 to 1) 1
2363 HIGH PREMIUM [84] 5-10-0 K Fallon (7) *cl up, dsptd ld o'r 2 fs till no extr wl ins last*. ....(11 to 2 op 5 to 1 tchd 6 to 1) 2
2551^{4} BOLD ACRE [66] 3-8-2 L Charnock (2) *led till ins fnl furlong, no extr*.......................(7 to 1 tchd 8 to 1) 3
2391 JALMUSIQUE [74] 7-9-4 M Birch (3) *steadied strt, hld up, some hdwy 3 fs out, no extr fnl furlong*. ....(12 to 1 op 10 to 1) 4
2175^{6} SIR ARTHUR HOBBS [55] 6-7-10 (3*) N Kennedy (6) *prmnt till wknd o'r one furlong out*...... (12 to 1 op 10 to 1) 5
2045^{7} WILL OF STEEL [83] 4-9-13 J Carroll (4) *in tch, effrt o'r 2 fs out, no hdwy*.................. (10 to 1 op 8 to 1) 6
2433 RINGLAND (USA) [74] 5-8-13 (5*) Darren Moffatt (5) *nvr dngrs*...........................(7 to 1 tchd 8 to 1) 7
1768 INDIAN SLAVE (Ire) [70] 5-9-0 K Darley (9) *chsd ldrs till wknd 2 fs out*........(5 to 2 fav op 11 to 4 tchd 3 to 1) 8
Dist: ¾l, ¾l, 2l, sht-hd, 1½l, 1l, 1½l. 1m 42.05s. a 4.35s (8 Ran).
SR: 47/64/36/46/26/49/37/28/ (Mrs M O'Donnell), A Bailey

2602 Bute Selling Handicap Class G (0-60 3-y-o) £2,469 7f................ (4:20)

1829 ADAMPARIS [42] (bl) 8-3 T Williams (1) *hld up, hdwy o'r 2 fs out, styd on wl to ld nr finish*. ....(8 to 1 op 6 to 1 tchd 10 to 1) 1
1968^{5} NICKNAME [44] 8-5 K Fallon (4) *cl up, led aftr 3 fs till hdd and no extr nr finish*.............. (5 to 1 tchd 6 to 1) 2
2168^{3} MISSED THE BOAT (Ire) [52] (bl) 8-13 K Darley (5) *hld up, steady hdwy 3 fs out, rdn 2 out, kpt on same pace*. ....(9 to 2 op 4 to 1) 3
1869^{4} LANCASTER PILOT [60] (v) 9-7 A Culhane (8) *chsd ldrs, ev ch 2 fs out, one pace*..............(10 to 1 op 7 to 1) 4
1965^{3} MAGICATION [55] 8-9 (7*) Claire Balding (6) *slwly into strd, beh, some hdwy fnl 3 fs, not rch ldrs*. (9 to 2 op 7 to 2) 5
1399 EVAHART [33] 7-8 (7*) J Marshall (2) *prmnt till wknd 2 fs out*..............................(33 to 1 op 20 to 1) 6
2550^{2} DRUMDONNA (Ire) [55] 9-2 J Carroll (10) *chsd ldrs, ev ch o'r 2 fs out, sn wknd, tld off*. ....(2 to 1 fav op 7 to 4 tchd 5 to 2) 7
1968 FREDDIE JACK [35] (bl) 7-7 (3*) N Kennedy (3) *slwly into strd, al beh, tld off*... (25 to 1 op 20 to 1 tchd 33 to 1) 8

2570[2] FLASH OF JOY [33] 7-8[1] L Charnock (7) *led 3 fs, sn wknd, tld off*..........................(33 to 1 op 20 to 1) 9
Dist: ¾l, 3l, 3½l, ¾l, 1l, 15l, 1½l, 4l. 1m 29.50s. a 5.50s (9 Ran).
SR: 22/22/21/18/11/-/ (Invoshire Ltd), G A Pritchard-Gordon

2603 EBF Millport Median Auction Maiden Stakes Class E (2-y-o) £3,020 7f (4:50)

1580[2] CUT THE RED TAPE (Ire) 8-9 T Williams (1) *trkd ldr, led 2 fs out, ran on wl fnl furlong.* (11 to 8 on op 11 to 8 on) 1
2021[7] DURHAM DRAPES 8-9 M Birch (5) *chsd ldrs, effrt o'r 2 fs out, kpt on wl fnl furlong.* ....(10 to 1 op 7 to 1 tchd 11 to 1 and 14 to 1) 2
1763[7] GLORIETTE 8-9 K Fallon (8) *led to 2 fs out, one pace.* ....(8 to 1 op 7 to 1 tchd 9 to 1) 3
2167[3] DIAMOND FRONTIER (Ire) 9-0 J Carroll (3) *chsd ldrs, effrt o'r 2 fs out, one pace*..............(7 to 2 tchd 4 to 1) 4
1846 STRATHTORE DREAM (Ire) 8-9 F Norton (4) *beh, hdwy 3 fs out, rdn 2 out, wknd fnl furlong*...(33 to 1 op 25 to 1) 5
CRISTAL SPRINGS 8-9 J Fortune (2) *slwly into strd, sn in tch, effrt 3 fs out, wknd 2 out.* ....(10 to 1 op 8 to 1 tchd 11 to 1) 6
1846[6] ALL IN THE MIND 9-0 K Darley (7) *beh, effrt 3 fs out, sn btn*..................(11 to 1 op 12 to 1 tchd 14 to 1) 7
AUCKLAND CASTLE 8-7 (7*) C Teague (6) *al beh.* ....(50 to 1 op 20 to 1) 8
Dist: 3½l, ½l, 3½l, ¾l, 6l, 5l, 2½l. 1m 30.92s. a 6.92s (8 Ran).
SR: 7/-/-/-/-/ (Julian Clopet And Partners), M Johnston

LEOPARDSTOWN (IRE) (good to firm)
Saturday July 17th
Going Correction: PLUS 0.10 sec. per fur. (races 1,2), MINUS 0.20 (3,4,5,6)

2604 Oatlands Handicap (0-90 3-y-o) £3,105 6f............................ (2:00)

2323[5] PILGRIM BAY (Ire) [-] 8-1 (2*) R M Burke (9)........(9 to 2) 1
2285[6] MOONLIGHT PARTNER (Ire) [-] 8-9 C Roche (6)...(14 to 1) 2
2451 BENE MERENTI (Ire) [-] (bl) 7-11 (6*) R V Skelly (1) (16 to 1) 3
2078[4] KINDNESS ITSELF (Ire) [-] (bl) 9-3 J P Murtagh (3) ....(9 to 4 fav) 4
2039* READY (Ire) [-] 9-6 (6*) B J Walsh (7)..............(7 to 2) 5
2078[7] ELEGANT BLOOM (Ire) [-] (bl) 9-2 M J Kinane (2)... (3 to 1) 6
2323[8] JARGONEL (Ire) [-] 7-6 (2*) D G O'Shea (8)........(20 to 1) 7
2297[9] HOLIWAY STAR (Ire) [-] (bl) 8-2 J F Egan (5)........(20 to 1) 8
2323 SHRAGRADDY LASS (Ire) [-] 7-1 (6*) J J Behan (4) (10 to 1) 9
Dist: ¾l, sht-hd, 1½l, 2l. 1m 14.30s. a 2.80s (9 Ran).
SR: 45/48/41/49/50/-/ (Frank A McNulty), E J O'Grady

2605 David Crowley Rochestown EBF Stakes (Listed) (2-y-o) £8,625 6f (2:30)

2246* COIS NA TINE (Ire) 8-10 C Roche (5) *dsptd ld till rdn to go clr 2 fs out, hdd entering last, rallied, led last strd.* ....(6 to 4 fav) 1
1571[3] COMMON RUMPUS (Ire) 8-7 J P Murtagh (7) *trkd ldrs, rdn o'r 2 fs out, prog to ld entering last, ct last strd.* (10 to 1) 2
269* CITY NIGHTS (Ire) 8-10 M J Kinane (2) *trkd ldrs, rdn 2 fs out, ran on ins last*..........................(6 to 1) 3
1750[4] SHARP PHASE (Ire) 8-10 P V Gilson (6) *dsptd ld to 2 fs out, short of room one out, wknd*...............(100 to 30) 4
2246[5] BETTER FOLLY (Ire) 8-7 W J Supple (3) *hld up, rdn 2 fs out, ran on ins last*..........................(20 to 1) 5
2284[3] VIVA VICTOR (Ire) 8-10 J J Behan (1) *wl plcd, rdn 2 fs out, wknd fnl furlong*..........................(16 to 1) 6
2244* RIDGE POOL (Ire) 8-7 R Hughes (4) *hld up, wknd bef hfwy, sn pld up, broke hip*..........................(7 to 2) pu
Dist: Sht-hd, 2l, 1½l, 1l. 1m 14.10s. a 2.60s (7 Ran).
SR: 56/52/47/41/34/-/-/ (Niall Quinn), J S Bolger

2606 Kileview Construction Ballycorus Stakes (Listed) (3-y-o and up) £8,625 7f ....(3:00)

2078[5] KAYFA (Ire) 4-8-13 P Carberry (5) *made all, rdn and quickened o'r 2 fs out, kpt on*......................(16 to 1) 1
2247[5] DARK REEF 3-9-0 J P Murtagh (8) *strted slwly, rdn 3 fs out, ran on strly fnl furlong*..........................(14 to 1) 2
2074[3] MASTER TRIBE (Ire) 3-9-0 P V Gilson (7) *wl plcd, rdn 2 and a half fs out, not quicken till ran on ins last.* ....(5 to 4 fav) 3
1047 UNUSUAL HEAT (USA) 3-9-5 M J Kinane (4) *rear, rdn 2 fs out, ran on strly fnl furlong, short of room cl hme.* ....(6 to 1) 4
2078[6] CHEVIOT AMBLE (Ire) 5-8-13 J F Egan (3) *trkd ldr, rdn 3 fs out, wknd ins last*..........................(7 to 1) 5
2404* NORDIC FOX (Ire) 3-9-2 C Roche (9) *trkd ldr, rdn 2 and a half fs out, wknd ins last*..........................(13 to 2) 6
2073 PERSIAN CREEK (Ire) 4-9-2 K J Manning (6) *mid-div, rdn o'r 2 fs out, some prog one and a half out, kpt on.* ....(20 to 1) 7
1445* LOCK'S HEATH (Can) 3-9-8 R Hughes (1) *wl plcd, rdn 2 fs out, short of room one and a half out, eased ins last.* ....(6 to 1) 8
897[7] EL ZORRO DORADO (Ire) 3-8-9 S Craine (2) *hld up, short of room one and a half fs out and ag'n ins last.* (16 to 1) 9
2247[3] SHAHIK (USA) 3-8-9 W J Supple (10) *wl plcd, rdn 2 fs out, wknd one out*..........................(8 to 1) 10
Dist: ½l, sht-hd, ¾l, 1l. 1m 28.50s. a 3.10s (10 Ran).
SR: 32/31/30/33/24/-/ (Vincent Loughnane), Noel Meade

2607 Conroy E.B.F. Race (3-y-o and up) £4,830 1½m.................. (3:30)

2247[2] MUBADIR (USA) 5-9-3 (4*) P Carberry (5)..........(6 to 1) 1
2407[3] VIA PARIGI (Ire) 3-8-9 C Roche (2)............(5 to 4 on) 2
1572[2] SEMPLE STADIUM (Ire) 3-9-2 P V Gilson (1)........ (4 to 1) 3
1202 POLLYS GLOW (Ire) 4-9-5 (6*) C Everard (4)...... (20 to 1) 4
2076[9] PORTERSTOWN BOY (Ire) 3-9-4 M J Kinane (3)....(7 to 2) 5
Dist: 1l, 3l, 7l, 12l. 2m 32.30s. a 1.30s (5 Ran).
SR: 70/56/57/52/21/ (Liam Keating), Noel Meade

2608 Golden Pages 25th Anniversary Handicap (0-110 3-y-o and up) £16,600 1m 1f ....(4:00)

2245[6] PRE-EMINENT [-] (bl) 6-9-7 M J Kinane (9).........(9 to 2) 1
2345* DESERT CALM (Ire) [-] 4-7-8 (8*,6ex) R T Fitzpatrick (5) ....(12 to 1) 2
1768 APPROACH THE BENCH (Ire) [-] 5-9-4 (6*) C Everard (2) ....(3 to 1 fav) 3
2039[2] FAYDINI (Ire) [-] 4-8-7 S Craine (8)................(11 to 2) 4
2245[3] TONY'S FEN [-] 4-8-9 W J Supple (1)............(8 to 1) 5
1199[8] GALLARDINI (Ire) [-] 4-8-7 P V Gilson (7).......... (12 to 1) 6
1552 BE MY HOPE (Ire) [-] 4-8-11 R Hughes (4)......... (10 to 1) 7
1768 SALMON EILE (Ire) [-] 5-9-8 J P Murtagh (3)....... (9 to 2) 8
GARBONI (USA) [-] 4-7-10 (4*) W J Smith (6)......(20 to 1) 9
Dist: 2½l, hd, 1l, ½l. 1m 51.60s. a 1.10s (9 Ran).
SR: 63/36/57/37/37/-/ (Michael W J Smurfit), D K Weld

2609 Clarmallagh E.B.F. Maiden (3-y-o and up) £3,450 1¼m................(4:30)

KRISDALINE (USA) 3-8-7 M J Kinane (3).......(7 to 4 on) 1
1573[2] ROYAL VISION (Ire) 4-9-6 K J Manning (8).........(9 to 2) 2
2184[6] CRYSTAL SHIP (Ire) 3-8-7 P V Gilson (1)..........(10 to 1) 3
SHARKASHKA (Ire) 3-8-7 D Hogan (5)...............(14 to 1) 4
1048[5] KYRENIA 3-8-7 J P Murtagh (6)..................(7 to 1) 5
1335[2] NA-AMMAH (Ire) 3-8-7 W J Supple (4)...............(9 to 1) 6
2249 QUIET CONFIDENCE (Ire) 3-8-7 R Hughes (10)... (33 to 1) 7
BETTER GOODS (Ire) 3-8-7 N G McCullagh (7)....(25 to 1) 8
2185[9] DANAMORE (Ire) 3-8-10 S Craine (9)..............(33 to 1) 9
Dist: 1l, 2½l, 2½l, ¾l. 2m 8.20s. a 3.50s (9 Ran).
SR: 38/49/31/26/24/-/ (Sheikh Mohammed), John M Oxx

LINGFIELD (good to soft)
Saturday July 17th
Going Correction: NIL

2610 Worth Selling Stakes Class G (2-y-o) £2,499 5f..................... (6:30)

2292[7] DANCES WITH RISK 8-13 G Hind (11) *made all, clr 2 fs out, shaken up appr last, ran on wl.* .... (13 to 8 fav op Evens tchd 7 to 4) 1
1689[6] SPORTING HEIR (Ire) (bl) 8-11 R Perham (8) *chsd ldrs, rdn o'r 2 fs out, ran on appr last, no ch wth wnr.* ....(33 to 1 op 20 to 1) 2
1640[8] FIRST SHOT 8-11 M Perrett (10) *chsd ldrs, rdn hfwy, styd on one pace*............(7 to 4 op 5 to 2 tchd 3 to 1) 3
2274[9] CHILTERN SHOW 8-6 A Tucker (9) *outpcd and hrd rdn hfwy, no imprsn on ldrs aftr*.....(5 to 1 tchd 3 to 1) 4
1959 SILVER BRIEF 8-11 A McGlone (7) *outpcd and hrd rdn aftr 2 fs, kpt on appr last, nvr dngrs*... (33 to 1 op 20 to 1) 5
2377[7] ON THE WING AGAIN 8-6 N Adams (4) *chsd wnr, rdn and hng lft wl o'r one furlong out, wknd.* .... (7 to 1 op 6 to 1 tchd 10 to 1) 6
2125[7] MUSIC PRINCESS 7-13 (7*) B Russell (6) *sn rdn alng, al beh*..................(33 to 1 op 20 to 1) 7
2472[7] QUEEN'S ADMIRAL 8-6 (5*) D Wright (2) *rcd centre, nvr on terms*..................(20 to 1 op 10 to 1) 8
2125[8] CRAFTY CRICKETER 8-11 S Dawson (3) *rcd centre, nvr on terms*..................(33 to 1 op 25 to 1) 9
2125[5] TERMITE 8-6 B Rouse (1) *rcd centre, al beh.* ....(33 to 1 op 12 to 1) 10
Dist: 2l, 3½l, 4l, 1l, ¾l, 2½l, hd, ½l, nk. 1m 0.29s. a 3.39s (10 Ran).
SR: 31/21/7/-/-/-/ (Roldvale Limited), G Lewis

2611 Pulborough Handicap Class E (0-70 3-y-o) £2,782 2m.............. (7:00)

2213* SUMMER WIND (Ire) [61] 8-9 (3*) B Doyle (7) *made all, rdn o'r one furlong out, ran on wl*....... (7 to 2 op 9 to 4) 1
2290[6] COMME D'HABITUDE (USA) [74] 9-11 M Roberts (3) *keen hold, cl up, hrd rdn to chase wnr o'r 2 fs out, ev ch over one out, wknd ins last.* .... (10 to 1 op 8 to 1 tchd 12 to 1) 2
2196[2] WAKT [52] 8-3 W Carson (6) *wtd wth, effrt o'r 3 fs out, sn rdn and not quicken, styd on ins last.* ....(3 to 1 tchd 100 to 30) 3

2495[2] MANON LESCAUT [43] 7-3 (5*) D Wright (4) *settled last, effrt o'r 3 fs out, sn rdn, wknd over one out, fnshd 4th, disqualified*........................ (3 to 1 tchd 7 to 2) 4D
2355[2] BILJAN (USA) [62] 8-13 A Munro (2) *chsd wnr 3 fs and ag'n 5 out, rdn and wknd o'r 2 out, fnshd 5th, plcd 4th.* ......(85 to 40 fav op 11 to 4 tchd 3 to 1 and 2 to 1) 4
2313[4] MY SET PEACE [42] 7-4[4] (7*) A Whelan (5) *chsd wnr aftr 3 fs, wknd 5 out, fnshd 6th, plcd 5th.* (25 to 1 op 14 to 1) 5
Dist: 3½l, nk, 3½l, 3l, 7l. 3m 36.22s. a 12.72s (6 Ran).
(Ray Richards), D R C Elsworth

2612 East Grinstead Handicap Class D (0-80 3-y-o and up) £4,012 7f 140yds ....(8:00)

2004* DANCING SENSATION (USA) [48] 6-7-13 (5*) D Wright (6) *trkd ldrs, prog to ld o'r 2 fs out, drw clr appr last, cmftbly*.........................(3 to 1 fav op 9 to 4) 1
2031[8] DON TOCINO [62] 3-8-10 W Carson (5) *wth ldr, ev ch 2 fs out, sn rdn and one pace.* ....(11 to 1 op 8 to 1 tchd 12 to 1) 2
2270[4] ALNASRIC PETE (USA) [46] 7-8-2 G Carter (4) *hld up in tch, effrt o'r 2 fs out, sn rdn and not quicken.* ....(7 to 2 op 4 to 1 tchd 6 to 1) 3
1487[8] JUST JAMIE [56] 3-8-4 W Newnes (7) *cl up, rdn 3 fs out, sn btn*.................................(6 to 1 op 5 to 1) 4
2300 DODGY [57] (v) 6-8-13 M Perrett (2) *prmnt till rdn and wknd 2 fs out*....................... (7 to 1 op 8 to 1) 5
2212[8] DIGPAST (Ire) [75] 3-9-9 A McGlone (3) *led till hdd and wknd rpdly o'r 2 fs out*...................(5 to 1 op 4 to 1) 6
2212 ABLE CHOICE (Ire) [76] 3-9-10 M Roberts (1) *rcd centre, in tch, rdn hfwy, sn wknd.* (5 to 1 op 7 to 1 tchd 8 to 1) 7
Dist: 3l, 5l, ¾l, 2½l, 4l, 2l. 1m 34.18s. a 5.88s (7 Ran).
SR: 2/-/-/-/ (Chelgate Public Relations Ltd), R Akehurst

LINGFIELD (A.W) (std)
Saturday July 17th
Going Correction: MINUS 0.20 sec. per fur.

2613 Arundel Apprentice Maiden Handicap Class F (0-70 3-y-o and up) £2,660 1 ¼m.......................... (6:00)

2411[5] JULIASDARKINVADER [49] 3-8-6 (5*) L Carter (7) *rcd wide, in tch, led 4 fs out, rdn clr o'r 2 out, styd on.* .... (13 to 2 op 6 to 1 tchd 7 to 1) 1
2384[3] OUR EDDIE [55] (v) 4-9-6 (7*) F Savage (5) *cl up, rdn to chase wnr 2 fs out, styd on, nvr able to chal*....(7 to 2) 2
1907[7] MARATHIA [58] (v) 3-8-10 (10*) A Liggins (4) *prmnt, led briefly o'r 4 fs out, not quicken frm 2 out.* ....(16 to 1 tchd 20 to 1) 3
1913[4] WITHOUT A FLAG (USA) [61] 3-9-1 (8*) Michael Hunt (1) *chsd ldrs, outpcd o'r 3 fs out, kpt on und pres frm 2 out.* ....(9 to 2 op 4 to 1 tchd 5 to 1) 4
2499[9] SIR THOMAS BEECHAM [59] (e/s) 3-8-13 (8*) A Martinez (2) *stumbled strt, nvr gng wl, beh hfwy.* ....(16 to 1 tchd 20 to 1) 5
2358[2] STALLED (Ire) [62] (v) 3-9-10 G Mitchell (8) *slwly away, al beh, no ch fnl 4 fs*..................(7 to 4 fav tchd 2 to 1) 6
1733[4] SHARRO [57] 3-9-0 (5*) J Dennis (6) *led till o'r 4 fs out, wknd*.............................. (11 to 2 tchd 6 to 1) 7
Dist: 1l, 2½l, 3l, 4l, 3l, 2½l. 2m 9.16s. a 5.96s (7 Ran).
SR: 17/31/19/16/6/3/-/ (Mike Culling), A Moore

2614 Sevenoaks Limited Stakes Class D (0-75 3-y-o and up) £3,084 1¼m (7:30)

2099[7] SYLVAN SABRE (Ire) (v) 4-9-7 W Newnes (4) *trkd ldrs, rdn o'r 4 fs out, led wl over one out, hld on well.* ....(7 to 1 op 5 to 1) 1
2420[5] WAKI GOLD (USA) 6-9-7 G Carter (3) *led 7 fs out to 5 out, led 3 out till wl o'r one out, hrd rdn and rallied ins last.* .... (10 to 1 op 8 to 1) 2
2381* ONE OFF THE RAIL (USA) 3-8-11 B Rouse (1) *led 3 fs, led ag'n 5 out, hdd and wknd three out.* ....(Evens fav tchd 5 to 4 and 11 to 10 on) 3
2020* WALKING THE PLANK 4-9-7 P Robinson (2) *outpcd and rdn aftr 3 fs, beh after*..............(3 to 1 op 2 to 1) 4
1745[4] LAVENDER COTTAGE 3-8-6 M Roberts (5) *nvr gng wl, al beh, tld off fnl 3 fs*.......(6 to 1 op 5 to 1 tchd 8 to 1) 5
Dist: ½l, 12l, nk, 30l. 2m 7.35s. a 4.15s (5 Ran).
SR: 46/45/11/20/-/ (Sir Wm Garthwaite), P Mitchell

2615 Ashurst Handicap Class E (0-70 3-y-o) £2,709 1½m.................. (8:30)

2134* HALHAM TARN (Ire) [56] 8-11 J Williams (4) *settled last, prog 4 fs out, rdn to ld o'r one out, ran on wl.* .... (5 to 4 fav tchd 13 to 8) 1
2411* SMART DAISY [55] 8-10 B Rouse (5) *cl up, led 4 fs out, rdn and hdd o'r one out, one pace.* .... (11 to 4 op 5 to 2 tchd 3 to 1) 2
1935[4] POINT THE WAY (Ire) [66] 9-7 Paul Eddery (3) *led till pushed alng and hdd 4 fs out, wknd 2 out*... (3 to 1 op 7 to 2) 3
1906[5] BOXBOY [42] 7-6 (5*) D Wright (2) *settled 4th, outpcd four fs out, no ch aftr*......(11 to 2 op 4 to 1 tchd 6 to 1) 4
2023[7] IMAGERY [47] 8-2 A McGlone (1) *pressed ldr till rdn and wknd o'r 4 fs out, sn tld off*........(20 to 1 op 12 to 1) 5
Dist: 5l, 6l, 6l, 20l. 2m 35.37s. a 6.07s (5 Ran).
SR: 12/1/ (Lady Dundas), D R C Elsworth

NEWBURY (good)
Saturday July 17th
Going Correction: PLUS 0.25 sec. per fur. (races 1,3,4,5,7), NIL (2,6)

2616 Mtoto Donnington Castle Conditions Stakes Class B (2-y-o) £8,031 7f (1:30)

2430[2] CLASSIC SKY (Ire) 8-10 W R Swinburn (5) *hld up rear, hdwy on outsd 2 fs out, ran on to ld ins last.* .... (2 to 1 op 13 to 8 tchd 5 to 2) 1
CULT HERO (Can) 8-10 J Reid (1) *trkd ldr, led o'r 2 fs out, hdd and no extr ins last*...........(11 to 2 op 3 to 1) 2
2021* MISTER BAILEYS 8-12 Dean McKeown (4) *hld up beh ldrs, shut in on rls frm o'r 2 fs out, swtchd lft ins last, ran on, unlucky*.......... (11 to 10 fav op 7 to 4 tchd 2 to 1) 3
2325* PETER ROWLEY 8-10 M Roberts (2) *led till o'r 2 fs out, lost pl, ran on ins last*.....(11 to 1 op 8 to 1 tchd 12 to 1) 4
1985* DARREN BOY (Ire) 8-10 T Quinn (3) *hld up, hdwy 2 fs out, wknd ins last*..................... (14 to 1 op 8 to 1) 5
Dist: ½l, sht-hd, 1l, 2l. 1m 31.28s. a 7.18s (5 Ran).
SR: 15/13/14/9/3/ (Saeed Suhail), B Hanbury

2617 Harcros Timber & Building Supplies Stayers Championship Series Handicap Qualifier Class C (0-90 3-y-o and up) £7,668 1m 5f 61yds......... (2:00)

2204* DISCORD [76] 7-9-0 M Roberts (1) *slwly away, settled rear, al gng wl, hdwy o'r 2 fs out, led appr last, pushed out, cmftbly*.....(5 to 1 jt-fav tchd 11 to 2 and 9 to 2) 1
473[7] FLIGHT LIEUTENANT (USA) [79] 4-9-3 R Perham (4) *hld up rear, rdn o'r 4 fs out, hdwy over 2 out, ran on ins last.* .... (20 to 1 op 16 to 1) 2
1067[2] LEAGUE LEADER (Ire) [82] 3-8-7 W R Swinburn (10) *prmnt, led 3 fs out till appr last, kpt on one pace.* .... (13 to 2 op 6 to 1 tchd 7 to 1) 3
2373* MOONLIGHT QUEST [80] 5-9-4 M Hills (3) *wtd wth on ins, styd on fnl 2 fs, nvr nr to chal.* .... (13 to 2 op 6 to 1 tchd 7 to 1) 4
1028[5] MILLION IN MIND (Ire) [86] 4-9-10 W Newnes (7) *led to 3 fs out, rdn and wknd o'r one out.* ....(14 to 1 op 12 to 1 tchd 16 to 1) 5
2420[8] WESTERN DYNASTY [75] 7-8-6 (7*) P McCabe (13) *sn trkd ldr, prmnt till wknd o'r 2 fs out.* (14 to 1 tchd 16 to 1) 6
1946[6] PHILGUN [65] 4-8-3 Dale Gibson (6) *settled mid-div, rdn 3 fs out, one pace aftr*.............(14 to 1 tchd 16 to 1) 7
2420[2] AMAZON EXPRESS [66] 4-8-4 T Quinn (2) *nvr far away, rdn and ev ch 2 fs out, wknd quickly appr last.* ....(5 to 1 jt-fav tchd 11 to 2 and 9 to 2) 8
CASTORET [87] 7-9-8 (3*) D Harrison (12) *hld up rear, effrt 3 fs out, wknd wl o'r one out*...... (16 to 1 op 14 to 1) 9
1770[5] DURSHAN (USA) [81] 4-9-5 A Munro (5) *mid-div, rdn o'r 3 fs out, nvr on terms.* (12 to 1 op 10 to 1 tchd 14 to 1) 10
2061[6] CASTLE CAVALIER [90] 5-10-0 J Reid (8) *pld hrd, prmnt, ev ch o'r 3 fs out, wknd over 2 out.* .... (6 to 1 op 9 to 2 tchd 13 to 2) 11
1809 REQUESTED [76] 6-9-0 M Perrett (11) *prmnt, rdn 5 fs out, wknd 4 out, tld off*.................. (14 to 1 tchd 16 to 1) 12
MILZIG (USA) [90] 4-9-9 (5*) A Procter (9) *al rear, lost tch o'r 4 fs out, tld off*................. (25 to 1 tchd 33 to 1) 13
Dist: 1½l, 1l, 3½l, 4l, ½l, nk, nk, 1½l, 1½l, hd. 2m 50.31s. a 4.11s (13 Ran).
SR: 59/59/47/51/49/37/26/26/44/ (Yoshio Asakawa), Lord Huntingdon

2618 Weatherbys And Sales Super Sprint Trophy Class B (2-y-o) £56,912 5f 34yds.......................... (2:30)

1766* RISKY 8-10 W R Swinburn (14) *al prmnt, led hfwy, shaken up and ran on ins fnl furlong.* (11 to 8 on op 6 to 4 on tchd 7 to 4 on and 5 to 4 on) 1
1766 POMMES FRITES (Ire) 8-7 L Piggott (10) *hld up in tch, strly rdn and hdwy appr fnl furlong, kpt on.* ....(20 to 1 tchd 33 to 1) 2
2335[4] TURTLE ISLAND (Ire) 9-7 J Reid (15) *outpcd and rear, rdn and ran on strly fnl furlong, nvr nrr.* .... (9 to 2 op 7 to 2 tchd 11 to 2) 3
2114* WELSH MIST 7-13 M Roberts (5) *prmnt in centre, outpcd entering fnl furlong*........... (20 to 1 tchd 25 to 1) 4
2292* ROXANIAN (Ire) 8-7 D Holland (9) *chsd ldrs, outpcd hfwy, rdn and styd on ins last.* .... (16 to 1 op 20 to 1 tchd 33 to 1) 5
KING RAMBO 8-5 S Perks (12) *rear, strly rdn frm hfwy, ran on ins fnl 2 fs, nvr nrr*.......(100 to 1 op 66 to 1) 6
1203* STRAIGHT ARROW 8-6 A Munro (3) *mid-div, styd on appr fnl furlong, nvr nrr*................. (16 to 1 op 14 to 1) 7
2210[4] BID FOR BLUE 9-0 Paul Eddery (8) *broke wl, led briefly aftr 2 fs, wknd o'r one out*.........(33 to 1 op 25 to 1) 8
1828[2] ANZIO (Ire) 8-4 N Day (16) *sn rdn alng, not pace to chal.* .... (33 to 1 op 25 to 1) 9

1999* TINKER OSMASTON 7-13 J Curant (4) *prmnt far side till wknd o'r one furlong out*..........(10 to 1 op 8 to 1) 10
2359⁵ PAPAGAYOS (Ire) 8-10 B Marcus (2) *rcd on outsd, nvr on terms*............................(66 to 1 op 50 to 1) 11
2006³ BIRD OF TIME (Ire) 8-5 T Quinn (1) *al beh.* ....(66 to 1 tchd 100 to 1) 12
1742* ISABELLA SHARP 8-6 M Hills (11) *led 2 fs, wknd two out.* ....(20 to 1 op 25 to 1 tchd 33 to 1) 13
1788⁶ HIGH DOMAIN (Ire) 8-6 A Clark (13) *outpcd.* ....(25 to 1 tchd 33 to 1) 14
1828⁹ MARCH OF TIME (bl) 8-4 Dean McKeown (6) *outpcd.* ....(100 to 1) 15
2147* MIRIAM 8-3 J Weaver (7) *outpcd*.....(66 to 1 op 50 to 1) 16

Dist: 1l, sht-hd, 2l, 2½l, ½l, nk, 1l, nk, nk, 1l. 1m 4.06s. a 3.76s (16 Ran).
SR: 47/40/53/23/21/17/17/21/10/ (Roldvale Limited), R Hannon

2619 Manton Rose Bowl Stakes Class A (Listed Race) (2-y-o) £11,575 6f 8yds ....(3:00)

1790* STATE PERFORMER (USA) 9-2 J Reid (1) *made all, canter.* ....(7 to 1 on op 11 to 2 on) 1
2325² BAGSHOT 8-11 A Munro (2) *chsd wnr, rdn o'r one furlong out, no imprsn*....................(11 to 2 op 7 to 2) 2

Won by 3½l. 1m 18.32s. a 6.62s (2 Ran).
SR: -/-/ (R E Sangster), P W Chapple-Hyam

2620 Shrivenham Handicap Class C (0-90 3-y-o and up) £4,532 5f 34yds... (3:30)

2392³ POYLE GEORGE [90] 8-9-9 (5*) A Procter (2) *wtd wth, rdn and hdwy 2 fs out, led appr last, ran on.* ....(9 to 2 fav op 11 to 4 tchd 5 to 1) 1
2303⁹ HEAVENLY RISK [85] 3-8-11 (7*) Mark Denaro (5) *slwly into strd, beh whn short of room and swtchd rght appr fnl furlong, ran on strly ins last.* ....(7 to 1 tchd 8 to 1 and 13 to 2) 2
2255⁷ RUNNING GLIMPSE (Ire) [82] 5-9-6 M Roberts (3) *chsd ldrs, outpcd 2 fs out, kpt on ins last*.....(7 to 1 tchd 8 to 1) 3
2380⁶ MARTINA [60] 5-7-5 (7*) C Hawksley (4) *nvr far away, hdwy o'r one furlong out, no extr ins last*......(8 to 1) 4
2165* SAMSON-AGONISTES [77] 7-9-1 T Quinn (8) *led till hdd and wknd appr fnl furlong*..........(5 to 1 op 9 to 2) 5
2255⁹ AUGHFAD [81] (v) 7-9-5 J Reid (6) *frnt rnk, ev ch 2 fs out, wknd entering last*...................(5 to 1 tchd 11 to 2) 6
2018 EAGER DEVA [88] 6-9-12 L Piggott (1) *speed on outsd till wknd o'r one furlong out*............(5 to 1 op 6 to 1) 7
BANGLES [82] 3-8-12 (3*) D Harrison (7) *speed till wknd wl o'r one furlong out*....................(7 to 1 op 10 to 1) 8
2225⁵ BELTHORN [55] 4-7-7 N Carlisle (9) *slwly away, nvr got into race*...........................(50 to 1 op 33 to 1) 9

Dist: ½l, 1½l, 1½l, ½l, ¾l, ½l, 2l, ¾l. 1m 3.88s. a 3.58s (9 Ran).
SR: 69/57/53/25/40/41/46/27/2/ (Cecil Wiggins), D R C Elsworth

2621 Arlington International Racecourse Stakes Class A (Listed Race) (3-y-o and up) £11,355 1¼m 6yds......(4:00)

2332* SABREHILL (USA) 3-8-6 M Roberts (2) *rcd keenly in 3rd pl, short of room and pld out 3 fs out, led 2 out, sn clr, fnshd 1st, disqualified.* ....(13 to 8 fav op 7 to 4 tchd 2 to 1) 1D
2070* BOBZAO (Ire) 4-9-10 T Quinn (3) *hld up, cl 4th whn slightly bumped 3 fs out, ran on to go second ins last, fnshd second, plcd 1st*..............(14 to 1 op 10 to 1) 1
1952² PORT LUCAYA (bl) 3-9-0 Pat Eddery (4) *sn trkd ldr, ev ch 3 fs out to 2 out, one pace aftr, fnshd 3rd, plcd second.* ....(7 to 2 op 9 to 2) 2
2302² YOUNG BUSTER (Ire) 5-9-10 M Hills (5) *led to 2 fs out, one pace aftr, fnshd 4th, plcd 3rd.* ....(6 to 1 op 5 to 1 tchd 13 to 2) 3
1448 PLANETARY ASPECT (USA) 3-8-6 J Reid (1) *al last, rdn o'r 3 fs out, no hdwy, fnshd 5th, plcd 4th.* ....(7 to 2 op 5 to 2 tchd 4 to 1) 4

Dist: 4l, 1½l, hd, 3l. 2m 5.43s. a 2.43s (5 Ran).
SR: 68/78/65/74/50/ (T G Mills), T G Mills

2622 Levy Board Seventh Handicap Class C (0-90 3-y-o and up) £5,380 1m (4:30)

2330² LORD OBERON (Ire) [54] (v) 5-8-0 M Roberts (7) *hld up, al gng wl, hdwy to ld ins fnl furlong, sn clr.* ....(9 to 2 op 4 to 1) 1
1068⁷ SEA SIREN [67] 3-8-5 W Newnes (4) *led till rdn and hdd ins fnl furlong, outpcd*.......... (12 to 1 tchd 14 to 1) 2
1808⁷ WALI (USA) [85] 3-9-9 Pat Eddery (3) *chsd ldrs, rdn 2 fs out, one pace aftr*........(5 to 2 fav op 4 to 1 tchd 9 to 4) 3
2361⁴ EASY ACCESS (Ire) [88] 3-9-5 (7*) Mark Denaro (2) *trkd ldrs, rdn 2 fs out, outpcd entering last.* ....(7 to 1 op 6 to 1 tchd 8 to 1) 4
2211⁸ DOUBLE FLUTTER [77] 4-9-9 A Munro (6) *chsd ldrs, rdn and wknd o'r one furlong out*....... (9 to 1 op 8 to 1) 5
2156⁴ WAVE HILL [73] 4-9-5 M Perrett (10) *hld up, effrt o'r 2 fs out, one pace ins last*...(6 to 1 op 5 to 1 tchd 13 to 2) 6
1579⁹ EXPO MONDIAL (Ire) [82] 3-9-6 M Hills (5) *in tch till wknd o'r 2 fs out*...........(25 to 1 op 20 to 1 tchd 33 to 1) 7
1402³ CARELAMAN [89] 3-9-13 J Reid (1) *mid-div, wknd o'r 2 fs out*...................(8 to 1 op 6 to 1 tchd 9 to 1) 8
2330⁴ AITCH N'BEE [76] 10-9-8 T Quinn (8) *al beh.* ....(13 to 2 op 5 to 1 tchd 7 to 1) 9
404⁴ SUIVEZ [80] 3-9-4 B Marcus (9) *rcd alone stands side, in cl tch till rdn and wknd 3 fs out*....(20 to 1 tchd 25 to 1) 10

Dist: 4l, 3½l, ¾l, 1½l, 3½l, 3½l, 1½l, nk, 2l. 1m 41.63s. a 4.53s (10 Ran).
SR: 48/41/48/49/41/26/16/18/12/ (Mrs A Quinn), J Akehurst

NEWMARKET (JULY) (good to soft)
Saturday July 17th
Going Correction: PLUS 0.25 sec. per fur. (races 1,2,3,4,5), PLUS 0.10 (6,7)

2623 Food Brokers Dr Pepper Conditions Stakes Class D (3-y-o) £4,542 1¼m ....(2:15)

1404³ INSTANT AFFAIR (USA) 8-11 W Carson (2) *settled in 3rd, ran on 3 fs out, hrd rdn to ld ins last, all out.* (3 to 1 co-fav op 5 to 2) 1
SURPRISE SURPRISE 8-4 (7*) Antoinette Armes (3) *chsd ldr, led o'r 2 fs out, rdn and hdd ins last, kpt on.* ....(12 to 1 op 20 to 1 tchd 25 to 1) 2
1831* IMAGINARY (Ire) 9-1 Pat Eddery (6) *hld up rear, prog o'r 3 fs out, ev ch und pres wl ins last, not quicken cl hme.* ....(3 to 1 co-fav op 5 to 2 tchd 7 to 2) 3
1802* MOONSHINE LAKE 9-1 A McGlone (8) *slwly into strd, hdwy frm rear 3 fs out, rdn and no imprsn on ldrs appr last*.................(12 to 1 op 10 to 1 tchd 14 to 1) 4
1950⁴ ARUSHA (Ire) 9-1 J Williams (5) *rcd in 4th pl til lost pos 5 fs out*.................................(14 to 1 op 10 to 1) 5
1347⁷ URRY URRY URRY 8-13 R Cochrane (7) *mid-div to hfwy, sn lost tch, tld off*....(25 to 1 op 20 to 1 tchd 33 to 1) 6
2334⁵ INFORMATRICE (USA) 8-11 W Ryan (9) *clr ldr till hdd o'r 2 fs out, sn wknd, tld off*....... (3 to 1 co-fav op 7 to 4) 7
1671⁶ MENHAAD (Ire) 8-11 S Whitworth (1) *al beh, tld off.* ....(33 to 1 op 25 to 1) 8
2117 FLOATING ISLAND 8-11 P Robinson (4) *al rear, tld off.* ....(50 to 1 op 33 to 1) 9

Dist: Hd, nk, 10l, 3l, 15l, nk, 2½l, 1½l. 2m 8.61s. a 6.41s (9 Ran).
SR: 58/57/60/40/34/2/ (Athos Christodoulou), P F I Cole

2624 Invesco Handicap Class D (0-80 3-y-o and up) £4,620 1m.............(2:45)

2161* DEEVEE [60] 4-8-10 P Robinson (1) *hld up, hdwy frm rear 3 fs out, led o'r one out, rdn clr.* ....(6 to 1 op 5 to 1 tchd 13 to 2) 1
2300⁴ BLOCKADE (USA) [76] 4-9-9 (3*) M Fenton (10) *led centre of course, hdd o'r one furlong out, styd on same pace.* ....(5 to 1 op 4 to 1) 2
EDEN'S CLOSE [69] 4-8-12 (7*) S Mulvey (5) *wl plcd, str chal 2 fs out, rdn and one pace fnl furlong.* ....(33 to 1 op 20 to 1) 3
2383⁴ WHATEVER'S RIGHT (Ire) [55] 4-8-5 L Dettori (9) *mid-div, cld on ldrs o'r 2 fs out, not quicken ins last.* ....(8 to 1 op 12 to 1) 4
2300 NORTH ESK (USA) [66] 4-9-2 G Carter (6) *chsd ldr centre of course, not quicken appr fnl furlong.* ....(6 to 1 op 5 to 1 tchd 13 to 2) 5
2156⁸ THEMAAM [53] 4-8-3 W Ryan (3) *mid-div, effrt o'r 2 fs out, sn rdn and btn*.......(12 to 1 op 10 to 1 tchd 14 to 1) 6
LA BAMBA [75] 7-9-11 W Hood (8) *slwly into strd, al rear.* ....(25 to 1 op 16 to 1) 7
2363⁶ RISE UP SINGING [66] (bl) 5-9-2 R Cochrane (7) *rcd alone far side, cl up till wknd frm 2 fs out* ....(7 to 2 fav tchd 4 to 1) 8
2416³ DAWALIB (USA) [73] 3-9-1 W Carson (4) *mid-div, effrt and rdn o'r 2 fs out, wknd over one out.* ....(13 to 2 op 6 to 1 tchd 7 to 1) 9
2330⁷ DIVINE BOY [65] 3-8-7 D Biggs (2) *steadied strt, al beh.* ....(12 to 1 op 14 to 1 tchd 16 to 1) 10

Dist: 2l, sht-hd, ¾l, ½l, 8l, 3½l, hd, 3½l, ¾l. 1m 43.51s. a 5.61s (10 Ran).
SR: 42/52/44/28/37/-/11/1/-/ (D Turner), C J Benstead

2625 Chemist Brokers Salon Selectives Rated Class B Handicap (0-100 4-y-o and up) £7,015 1¾m 175yds.....(3:15)

2239⁵ OH SO RISKY [94] 6-9-1 J Williams (3) *lost grnd strt, rear till ran on 3 fs out, rdn to ld wl ins last.* ....(15 to 8 op 7 to 4 tchd 13 to 8 and 2 to 1) 1
2395* CRYSTAL CROSS (USA) [86] 4-8-7 L Dettori (1) *set moderate early pace, quickened aftr 5 fs, rdn and hdd wl ins last.* ....(Evens fav op 11 to 10 tchd 5 to 4) 2
1065⁵ MICHELOZZO (USA) [100] 7-9-0 (7*) D Gibbs (2) *chsd ldr, pushed alng o'r 4 fs out, outpcd 3 out, tld off.* ....(4 to 1 op 3 to 1 tchd 9 to 2) 3

Dist: ½l, 25l. 3m 22.91s. a 16.91s (3 Ran).
(The Oh So Risky Syndicate), D R C Elsworth

2626 Primula Maiden Stakes Class D (2-y-o) £3,850 6f.................. (3:45)

2364[5] DIESAN (USA) 9-0 W Carson (4) *cl up, led aftr 2 fs till o'r one out, shaken up to ld ins last, ran on.* ....(Evens fav op 6 to 4 on tchd 11 to 10) 1
PAONIC (Ire) 9-0 R Cochrane (9) *handily plcd, slight advantage o'r one furlong out, hdd and not quicken last 100 yards*.........(10 to 1 op 8 to 1 tchd 12 to 1) 2
FRIENDLY CHAMP (Ire) 9-0 R Price (3) *cld on ldrs o'r 2 fs out, ev ch appr last, styd on same pace nr finish.* ....(6 to 1 op 4 to 1) 3
DYNAMIC DELUXE (USA) 9-0 L Dettori (7) *trkd ldrs, rdn and one pace frm 2 fs out*............(5 to 1 op 7 to 2) 4
BILLIE GREY 8-9 G Hind (5) *dwlt, nvr nr to chal.* ....(20 to 1 tchd 33 to 1) 5
SECUNDUS (Ire) 8-11 (3*) B Doyle (8) *slwly into strd, al outpcd*...............(33 to 1 op 20 to 1 tchd 40 to 1) 6
2325[6] TOTON LAD 9-0 P Robinson (6) *led 2 fs, wknd two out.* ....(25 to 1 op 20 to 1 tchd 33 to 1) 7
DESERT PRESIDENT 9-0 W R Swinburn (1) *rdn alng and outpcd frm hfwy*...... (13 to 2 op 5 to 1 tchd 8 to 1) 8
Dist: ½l, ¾l, 4l, 2l, 4l, 5l, 6l. 1m 15.97s. a 4.27s (8 Ran).
SR: 45/43/40/24/11/ (Sheikh Ahmed Al Maktoum), J H M Gosden

2627 Food Brokers Trophy Rated Stakes Class B Handicap (0-100 3-y-o) £16,657 1m.................. (4:15)

2361* BEAUCHAMP HERO [87] 8-10 W Carson (1) *ldg grp, led and quickened clr entering fnl furlong, styd on strly.* ....(11 to 4 op 2 to 1 tchd 3 to 1) 1
1921[4] LOST SOLDIER (USA) [98] 9-7 R Cochrane (4) *hld up, hdwy 3 fs out, led 2 out till entering last, ran on same pace.* ....(7 to 1 op 6 to 1 tchd 8 to 1) 2
2066* JURA FOREST [84] 8-7 P Robinson (3) *hld up rear, str run appr fnl furlong, not rch wnr.* ....(5 to 1 op 6 to 1 tchd 7 to 1) 3
1808[4] MUJAAZAFAH (USA) [86] 8-9 D Holland (6) *wl in tch, rdn and not much room 2 fs out, styd on one pace ins last.* ....(9 to 4 fav op 11 to 4) 4
2416* WISHAM (USA) [84] 8-7 W Ryan (2) *pld hrd in mid-div, effrt 2 fs out, btn ins last.* ....(13 to 2 op 6 to 1 tchd 7 to 1) 5
2254[5] NOYAN [86] 8-6 (3*) M Fenton (9) *led to 2 fs out, wknd o'r one out*............................(10 to 1 op 12 to 1) 6
2254[6] LAW COMMISSION [93] 9-2 J Williams (8) *chsd ldr 6 fs, lost tch o'r one out*.......(16 to 1 op 12 to 1 tchd 20 to 1) 7
Dist: 3l, hd, sht-hd, 2½l, ½l, 7l. 1m 42.35s. a 4.45s (7 Ran).
SR: 59/61/46/47/37/37/23/ (E Penser), J L Dunlop

2628 Food Brokers - Fisherman's Friend Handicap Class C (0-100 3-y-o and up) £5,253 5f...................... (4:45)

2392* MISS VAXETTE [85] 4-8-13 (7*) M Humphries (6) *handily plcd, shaken up to ld ins fnl furlong, ran on wl.* ....(5 to 1 co-fav op 9 to 2) 1
1982* MACS MAHARANEE [81] 6-9-2 G Hind (3) *pressed ldr, led o'r one furlong out till ins last, not quicken.* ....(13 to 2 op 5 to 1) 2
2363[7] MASTER PLANNER [86] 4-9-7 D Biggs (1) *ldg grp, rdn and outpcd fnl furlong*..... (11 to 2 op 5 to 1 tchd 6 to 1) 3
2305[5] PEERAGE PRINCE [65] (bl) 4-7-11[4] (7*) G Forster (5) *hdwy frm rear o'r 2 fs out, no imprsn on ldrs ins last.* ....(8 to 1 op 10 to 1) 4
2434[8] EDUCATED PET [70] 4-8-5 Dean McKeown (8) *wl in tch, rdn and not extr o'r one furlong out*........(5 to 1 co-fav tchd 11 to 2 and 9 to 2) 5
2392 GILT THRONE [81] 6-9-2 P Robinson (2) *outpcd thrght.* ....(14 to 1 op 10 to 1 tchd 16 to 1) 6
2062[3] FARFELU [93] (bl) 6-10-0 W Carson (7) *led for o'r 3 fs, sn btn*.................... (6 to 1 op 5 to 1 tchd 13 to 2) 7
1614[3] STEPANOV (USA) [95] 3-9-11 L Dettori (4) *rcd in mid-div, rdn and not quicken 2 fs out, eased whn btn fnl furlong*..........................(5 to 1 co-fav op 4 to 1) 8
Dist: 1l, 2½l, 3½l, ¾l, 1l, 1½l, 3l. 1m 1.10s. a 2.40s (8 Ran).
SR: 68/60/55/20/22/29/35/20/ (Vax Appliances Ltd), J L Spearing

2629 Chemist Brokers Evenflo Conditions Stakes Class D (2-y-o) £4,009 5f (5:15)

1653* MOSCOW ROAD 9-0 W R Swinburn (3) *made all, rdn and kpt on wl ins fnl furlong.* ....(5 to 2 op 11 to 4 tchd 3 to 1 and 9 to 4) 1
718[7] CARRIE KOOL 8-5 W Woods (4) *rcd in 3rd pl, str chal appr fnl furlong, not quicken last 100 yards.* .... (20 to 1 op 16 to 1 tchd 25 to 1) 2
2435[2] NERA 8-6[1] L Dettori (1) *outpcd in 4th pl, reminder hfwy, effrt one one furlong out, not rch wnr.* ....(Evens fav op 13 to 8 on tchd 11 to 8) 3
1899* SAWTID 8-4 (5*) C Hodgson (5) *slightly hmpd strt, sn outpcd*..................(9 to 2 op 6 to 1 tchd 4 to 1) 4
1142[4] DON'T BE KOI (Ire) 8-5 Dean McKeown (2) *pressed wnr till rdn and wknd o'r one out*.............. (6 to 1 op 8 to 1) 5
Dist: 2½l, 2l, 4l, 1½l. 1m 1.83s. a 3.13s (5 Ran).
SR: 47/28/21/8/-/ (G C Sampson), R Hannon

RIPON (good)

Saturday July 17th

Going Correction: MINUS 0.10 sec. per fur. (races 1,5), MINUS 0.15 (2,3,4,6)

2630 EBF Yorkshire Childrens Hospital Trust Maiden Stakes Class D (2-y-o) £4,127 5f..................... (2:35)

2336[6] ALZIANAH 8-9 G Duffield (1) *made all, rdn appr fnl furlong, ran on wl*.................(5 to 4 fav op 13 to 8) 1
1798[3] GENERAL GUBBINS 9-0 R Hills (4) *al cl up, ev ch appr fnl furlong, rdn and ran on*.............(8 to 1 op 7 to 1) 2
2137[6] DOMINO QUEEN (Ire) 8-9 J Quinn (9) *al prmnt, ev ch 2 fs out, sn rdn and one pace appr last*..(8 to 1 op 6 to 1) 3
2278[2] DAILY STAR 8-9 J Fanning (10) *mid-div and pushed alng, hdwy and rdn 2 fs out, styd on ins last, nvr dngrs.* ....(13 to 2 op 6 to 1 tchd 7 to 1) 4
2129[8] BOLLIN NEIL 8-11 (3*) S Maloney (5) *outpcd and beh till styd on fnl 2 fs*...................(20 to 1 op 14 to 1) 5
FEATHERSTONE LANE 9-0 S Webster (2) *outpcd and beh, sn pushed alng, styd on und pres fnl furlong.* ....(33 to 1 op 25 to 1) 6
2374[6] LANCASHIRE LIFE (Ire) 8-9 (5*) Stephen Davies (3) *cl up to hfwy, sn rdn and wknd*..........(14 to 1 op 16 to 1) 7
BOLD SIXTEEN (USA) 8-9 B Raymond (8) *cl up, rdn hfwy, sn wknd*...............(13 to 2 op 5 to 1 tchd 7 to 1) 8
HILL REEF (Fr) 9-0 Raymond Berry (6) *dwlt, al outpcd and beh*...................................(16 to 1 op 12 to 1) 9
2129 CRACKLEY LANE 9-0 T Lucas (7) *slwly into strd, al outpcd and beh*...................... (40 to 1 op 25 to 1) 10
Dist: ½l, 3l, 3l, 1½l, 1½l, 1l, 1½l, 3½l, 15l. 1m 0.60s. a 2.60s (10 Ran).
SR: 33/36/19/7/6/-/ (Sheikh Amin Dahlawi), G A Pritchard-Gordon

2631 Geoffrey Guest Selling Stakes Class G (3-y-o and up) £2,570 1m..... (3:05)

2307* SCOFFERA 3-8-8 Kim Tinkler (14) *made all, rdn 2 fs out, ran on wl fnl furlong*................(8 to 1 op 7 to 1) 1
1777[5] SALDA 4-9-7 B Raymond (4) *trkd ldrs, hdwy 3 fs out, effrt 2 out, sn rdn, kpt on one pace ins last.* ....(9 to 4 fav op 2 to 1 tchd 5 to 2) 2
2175[3] VANART 4-9-2 S Webster (11) *al prmnt, rdn 2 fs out and sn one pace*.........................(6 to 1 tchd 13 to 2) 3
2057 MATTS BOY (v) 5-9-7 N Connorton (10) *hld up and beh, hdwy o'r 2 fs out, rdn appr last, styd on one pace.* ....(6 to 1 op 5 to 1) 4
YEVEED (Ire) 3-8-5 (3*) S Maloney (9) *beh, hdwy on inner 3 fs out, sn rdn and one pace*...........(7 to 1 op 5 to 1) 5
MY LINDIANNE 6-8-11 J Fanning (2) *slwly into strd, hdwy on outer o'r 3 fs out, sn rdn, wknd 2 furlongs out.* .... (50 to 1 op 33 to 1) 6
2369[5] UCKERBY MOOR 4-8-9 (7*) V Halliday (5) *prmnt, rdn 3 fs out, sn wknd*...................(12 to 1 op 10 to 1) 7
1799 DEPUTY TIM 10-9-0 (7*) H Bastiman (7) *in tch, rdn o'r 3 fs out, sn btn*..........(25 to 1 op 20 to 1 tchd 33 to 1) 8
2283 SUNTAN (Fr) (bl) 4-9-7 J Quinn (8) *nvr rchd ldrs.* ....(8 to 1 op 7 to 1) 9
4695a HABEEBITTI NADIA 3-8-3 J Lowe (12) *nvr better than mid-div*..................................(33 to 1 op 25 to 1) 10
2097 DUNBAR 3-8-8 G Duffield (1) *slwly away, al rear.* .... (16 to 1 op 25 to 1 tchd 33 to 1) 11
2169[3] RUSHALONG (bl) 3-8-8 T Lucas (13) *chsd ldrs till rdn and wknd o'r 3 fs out*.....(16 to 1 op 33 to 1 tchd 14 to 1) 12
2165[7] SNEEK (bl) 5-8-11 (5*) O Pears (3) *chsd ldrs, rdn and wknd o'r 3 fs out*......................................(33 to 1) 13
2197 VITAL VOLTAGE (Ire) 4-9-2 S Morris (6) *al rear.* ....(25 to 1 tchd 33 to 1) 14
Dist: 1½l, 5l, hd, 8l, 3½l, 1½l, 3l, nk, 1½l, 1l. 1m 41.40s. a 3.10s (14 Ran).
SR: 30/38/18/22/-/-/ (Mrs Christine Cawley), N Tinkler

2632 Eversheds Hepworth & Chadwick Bell-Ringer Handicap Class C (0-95 3-y-o and up) £7,505 1½m 60yds (3:35)

2373[5] DARMSTADT (USA) [77] 3-8-7 G Duffield (8) *al prmnt, effrt and hdwy 3 fs out, rdn to ld 2 furlongs out, edgd rght and kpt on und pres ins last*... (2 to 1 fav tchd 5 to 2) 1
2236[2] DRUMMER HICKS [80] 4-9-8 M Tebbutt (5) *in tch, hdwy and pushed alng o'r 3 out, effrt to chal 2 fs out, sn rdn and kpt on ins last*.................(11 to 2 op 5 to 1) 2
2373[2] ALMAMZAR (USA) [86] 3-9-2 R Hills (3) *cl up, led hfwy, rdn 3 fs out, hdd 2 out, kpt on und pres ins last.* ....(9 to 2 op 4 to 1) 3
1818* BLUE BLAZER [83] 3-8-13 B Raymond (4) *trkd ldrs, effrt 3 fs out, rdn 2 out, kpt on one pace*...(13 to 2 op 6 to 1) 4
1802[6] BLUE LAWS (Ire) [72] 3-8-2 J Fanning (6) *al prmnt, rdn 3 fs out, kpt on one pace*... (9 to 1 op 10 to 1 tchd 8 to 1) 5
PEANUTS PET [52] 8-7-8[1] J Quinn (2) *beh till styd on fnl 2 fs, nvr a factor*.................(33 to 1 op 25 to 1) 6
2591[5] KINOKO [61] 5-7-12 (5*) A Garth (9) *al mid-div.* ....(14 to 1 op 16 to 1) 7
2395[4] VIARDOT (Ire) [86] 4-10-0 J Lowe (7) *beh, pushed alng hfwy, some hdwy o'r 3 fs out, sn wknd*.........(7 to 1) 8
2398[7] BIGWHEEL BILL (Ire) [69] (bl) 4-8-11 N Connorton (10) *led to hfwy, cl up till rdn 4 fs out, sn wknd.* ....(10 to 1 tchd 9 to 1) 9

LORD HASTIE (USA) [76] 5-8-13 (5*) O Pears (1) *mid-div, hdwy on outer 5 fs out, rdn 3 out, sn wknd*....(16 to 1) 10
Dist: ½l, 1½l, ¾l, 1l, 10l, ½l, 1l, 6l, 15l. 2m 38.90s. a 3.90s (10 Ran).
SR: 36/50/41/36/23/-/3/26/-/ (Sheikh Mohammed), J H M Gosden

2633 Air UK Handicap Stakes Class D (0-80 3-y-o and up) £3,850 1¼m...... (4:05)

2391³ GOLDEN CHIP (Ire) [70] 5-9-10 G Duffield (1) *made all, rdn wl o'r one furlong out, ran on gmely ins last.* ....(5 to 1 tchd 11 to 2) 1
2391⁴ JUBRAN (USA) [64] 7-9-4 R Hills (8) *al prmnt, effrt to chase ldr 2 fs out, sn rdn and kpt on wl.* ....(4 to 1 fav tchd 9 to 2) 2
2232³ BRILLIANT [67] 5-9-7 M Wigham (2) *in tch, hdwy and rdn 3 fs out, sn outpcd, styd on ins last*.............. (6 to 1) 3
1940 SCOTTISH PARK [56] 4-8-10 B Raymond (9) *chsd ldrs, effrt and hdwy o'r 2 fs out, rdn wl over one out, sn one pace.* ....(16 to 1 op 14 to 1) 4
2308⁵ MAROWINS [46] 4-8-0 J Quinn (7) *hld up, hdwy 4 fs out, rdn wl o'r 2 out, sn one pace.* ....(9 to 2 op 4 to 1 tchd 5 to 1) 5
2555³ THE PREMIER EXPRES [58] 3-8-2 R Lappin (3) *cl up, rdn 3 fs out, grad wknd fnl 2 furlongs*.............. (14 to 1) 6
2354³ TELEPHUS [54] 4-8-8 J Lowe (4) *beh, rdn hfwy, nvr a factor*.................(11 to 2 tchd 5 to 1) 7
2168⁵ MHEMEANLES [70] 3-8-11 (3*) S Maloney (6) *al rear.* ....(15 to 2 op 7 to 1 tchd 8 to 1) 8
1460⁴ RED INDIAN [40] 7-7-8 J Fanning (5) *hld up and beh, effrt and some hdwy 3 fs out, sn rdn and wknd.* ....(10 to 1 tchd 9 to 1) 9
Dist: ¾l, 6l, sht-hd, ¾l, ½l, 1½l, ½l, 12l. 2m 8.10s. a 4.10s (9 Ran).
SR: 54/46/37/25/13/14/17/22/-/ (A H Jackson), A P Stringer

2634 Hartwell Motor Contracts Maiden Handicap Stakes Class E (0-70 3-y-o and up) £3,210 6f................(4:35)

2366⁴ SUDDEN SPIN [57] (v) 3-9-7 (7*) P Roberts (3) *made virtually all, rdn o'r one furlong out, ran on wl ins last.* ....(6 to 1 op 5 to 1) 1
2365² MILBANK CHALLENGER [55] 3-9-12 G Duffield (2) *al cl up, effrt to chal 2 fs out, ev ch till rdn and not quicken ins last*.............. (5 to 2 fav op 3 to 1) 2
2241⁶ SILVER STONE BOY [33] 5-8-10 S Webster (8) *al prmnt, effrt 2 fs out, sn hrd rdn, edgd rght appr last, one pace.* ....(4 to 1 op 7 to 2 tchd 9 to 2) 3
2288² SOPHISTICATED AIR [53] (v) 3-9-10 S O'Gorman (7) *dwlt, sn chasing ldrs, effrt and ev ch 2 fs out, rdn and btn whn bumped entering last*....(4 to 1 op 7 to 2 tchd 9 to 2) 4
2154⁶ COVEN MOON [48] 3-9-5 J Quinn (4) *dwlt, outpcd and beh till styd on fnl 2 fs, nvr dngrs*........(7 to 1 op 6 to 1) 5
2231 OSCAR THE SECOND (Ire) [47] 3-9-4 M Tebbutt (1) *in tch, rdn alng hfwy, kpt on same pace.* (16 to 1 op 14 to 1) 6
2280⁶ ADMISSION (Ire) [42] 3-8-13 N Connorton (5) *prmnt, rdn and hng rght hfwy, sn wknd and beh.* ....(16 to 1 op 14 to 1) 7
1162⁴ SMITH N'ALLAN [50] 3-9-2 (5*) O Pears (6) *in tch, rdn alng hfwy, wknd 2 fs out*....................(14 to 1) 8
2510⁷ SHALAKO [43] 3-8-9 (5*) A Garth (9) *prmnt on outer, sn rdn and hng rght hfwy, wknd*..........(20 to 1 op 16 to 1) 9
Dist: 1l, 1½l, 2½l, 3l, 1½l, 3½l, 1½l, 6l. 1m 13.90s. a 3.30s (9 Ran).
SR: 36/30/8/12/-/-/-/ (Countess Of Lonsdale), J Berry

2635 CSI Rating Related Maiden Stakes Class E (0-70 3-y-o) £3,210 1m 1f (5:05)

2291⁷ LIVONIAN 9-0 G Duffield (5) *trkd ldg pair, hdwy to join ldr 3 fs out, led one and a half out, rdn ins last, hld on.* ....(11 to 8 fav op 6 to 4) 1
2134² LT WELSH (USA) (v) 9-0 S O'Gorman (6) *chsd ldr, not much room 2 fs out, swtchd and rdn appr fnl furlong, styd on ins last*..............(11 to 4 op 9 to 4 tchd 3 to 1) 2
2181² IJAB (Can) 9-0 R Hills (1) *led, rdn 2 fs out, hdd appr fnl furlong, sn wknd*...................(9 to 2 op 7 to 2) 3
2398³ BILOELA 8-9 J Quinn (7) *in tch, effrt and rdn 3 fs out, wknd wl o'r one out*.....(4 to 1 op 7 to 2 tchd 9 to 2) 4
2107⁸ NEVER SO BRAVE 9-0 N Connorton (4) *hld up, effrt and hdwy 4 fs out, sn rdn and wknd*...(16 to 1 op 12 to 1) 5
590⁶ BREAKING HEARTS (Ire) 8-9 J Fanning (3) *in tch, effrt and hdwy on outer 4 fs out, sn rdn and btn 3 out.* ....(16 to 1 op 12 to 1) 6
Dist: Hd, 3½l, 5l, 12l, 3l. 1m 54.90s. a 3.90s (6 Ran).
SR: 21/20/9/ (Sheikh Mohammed), J H M Gosden

SOUTHWELL (good)
Saturday July 17th
Going Correction: MINUS 0.15 sec. per fur.

2636 Stirrup Handicap Class E (0-700 3-y-o and up) £2,448 6f...............(6:15)

1734⁵ QUICK STEEL [51] (bl) 5-8-10 (7*) S Mulvey (1) *slwly away, beh til rapid hdwy 2 fs out, rdn to ld nr finish.* ....(8 to 1 tchd 7 to 1) 1
2468⁴ MINDOMICA [55] 4-9-4 (3*) Emma O'Gorman (8) *beh, hdwy aftr 4 fs, led o'r one out til hdd nr finish.* ....(3 to 1 fav op 6 to 1 tchd 13 to 2) 2
2425² ROSE FLYER (Ire) [57] 3-8-12 (5*) D McCabe (6) *led for 3 fs, trkd ldr til led ag'n 2 out, sn hdd and not quicken.* ....(7 to 1 op 6 to 1) 3
2481* AQUADO [40] 4-8-6 (7ex) S Whitworth (10) *beh, gd hdwy to chase ldr aftr 4 fs, not quicken o'r one out.* ....(6 to 1 op 4 to 1) 4
2466³ STRIP CARTOON (Ire) [56] (bl) 5-9-1 (7*) G Strange (4) *chsd ldrs, rdn and no imprsn o'r 2 fs out.* (13 to 2 op 6 to 1) 5
2288⁷ DOCTOR-J (Ire) [52] 3-8-12 S Raymont (5) *chsd ldrs til one pace fnl 2 fs*....................(10 to 1 op 7 to 1) 6
2241 COAT OF DREAMS [40] 4-7-13 (7*) J Bramhill (9) *beh, one pace fnl 3 fs*....................(20 to 1 op 14 to 1) 7
2276⁷ ELTON LEDGER (Ire) [62] (bl) 4-10-0 B Raymond (2) *prmnt, led aftr 3 fs, hdd three out, sn wknd.* (7 to 1 op 5 to 1) 8
2280⁴ BIRCHWOOD SUN [67] 3-9-13 J Lowe (3) *beh aftr 2 fs.* ....(9 to 1 op 8 to 1) 9
1631³ CHOICE LOT [36] (bl) 6-8-2 Julie Bowker (7) *prmnt for 3 fs, wknd quickly, beh o'r 2 out*....... (16 to 1 op 10 to 1) 10
Dist: ¾l, 5l, 2l, hd, ½l, 1½l, 2½l, 8l, 3l. 1m 16.30s. a 2.30s (10 Ran).
SR: 39/40/16/-/12/-/ (Quicksteel Ltd), T P McGovern

2637 Hames & Boden Fillies Selling Stakes Class G (2-y-o) £1,380 6f........(6:45)

2042² UP THE MARINERS (Ire) 8-6 (5*) K Rutter (7) *made all, rdn and styd on wl whn chlgd ins fnl furlong, all out.* ....(11 to 2 op 9 to 2) 1
2268³ WILLWIN 8-8 (3*) Emma O'Gorman (2) *bolted bef strt, hld up, 5th strt, rdn to chal 2 fs out, swtchd ins last, jst fld.* ....(10 to 1 op 8 to 1) 2
2123⁶ HONEST WOMAN 8-6 (5*) D McCabe (4) *chsd ldr, ev chnance 3 fs out, one pace fnl furlong.* ....(4 to 1 op 3 to 1) 3
2167⁵ STUDFORD GIRL 8-11 T Lucas (1) *chsd ldrs, 4th strt, rdn and no imprsn ins fnl 2 fs*.......... (11 to 2 op 9 to 2) 4
2216⁹ SEMAH'S DREAM (bl) 8-11 A Proud (3) *beh, pushed alng o'r 3 fs out, kpt on one pace*..... (25 to 1 tchd 33 to 1) 5
2278⁵ OAKLEY MANOR 8-11 J Lowe (8) *trkd ldr, 3rd strt, wknd o'r one furlong out*................(9 to 2 op 3 to 1) 6
2229 REAL POPCORN (Ire) 8-11 G Duffield (5) *pressed ldr, second strt, wknd quickly fnl 2 fs*.....(8 to 1 op 10 to 1) 7
708⁸ CRUISING CHICK 8-6 (5*) O Pears (6) *beh, pushed alng aftr 2 fs, no imprsn*.............. (25 to 1 tchd 33 to 1) 8
2271⁴ ROSE OF GLENN 8-6 (5*) Stephen Davies (9) *hld up, sn rdn alng, beh o'r 3 fs out.* (7 to 2 fav op 9 to 2 tchd 5 to 1) 9
Dist: Nk, 2l, 1½l, ¾l, 4l, 4l, 2½l. 1m 17.70s. a 3.70s (9 Ran).
SR: 5/4/-/-/-/-/ (The Mariners Partnership), C Smith

2638 N.P.T. Plant Maiden Handicap Class D (0-75 3-y-o and up) £3,465 7f.... (7:15)

2358³ NORTHERN TRIAL (USA) [45] (v) 5-8-13 T Sprake (3) *hld up and beh, hdwy o'r 2 fs out, 6th strt, rdn to ld wl ins fnl furlong, drvn out*....... (5 to 1 op 4 to 1 tchd 7 to 2) 1
2047⁷ BLAKES BEAU [44] (bl) 3-8-2 (3*) S Maloney (6) *hld up, hdwy 3 fs out, 3rd strt, led one out til hdd ins last, not quicken.* (7 to 4 fav op 4 to 1 tchd 9 to 2 and 5 to 4) 2
884³ NOBLE MEASURE (Ire) [48] (bl) 3-8-3¹ (7*) G Strange (10) *hld up, 5th strt, styd on wl ins fnl 2 fs, one pace.* ....(14 to 1 op 10 to 1 tchd 16 to 1) 3
2350⁷ CHRISTIAN WARRIOR [38] (v) 4-8-1 (5*) D McCabe (8) *led til hdd o'r one furlong out, not quicken.* ....(25 to 1 op 16 to 1) 4
2181⁶ PREMIER STAR [54] (bl) 3-8-12 (3*) M Fenton (4) *chsd ldrs, 4th strt, no imprsn ins fnl 2 fs.* ....(4 to 1 op 6 to 1 tchd 7 to 1) 5
2308 COALISLAND [67] 3-9-9 (5*) N Gwilliams (7) *prmnt til lost pl aftr 2 fs, rdn and styd on one pace fnl two furlongs.* ....(14 to 1 op 8 to 1) 6
2426⁸ CRAIGIE BOY [55] 3-9-2 G Duffield (1) *last and outpcd aftr 3 fs, styd on fnl 2 furlongs, no imprsn.* ....(33 to 1 op 20 to 1) 7
VIRGINIA COTTAGE [36] 4-7-11 (7*) J Bramhill (2) *beh aftr 3 fs, no imprsn fnl 2 furlongs*........(33 to 1 op 20 to 1) 8
2358 FESTIN [56] (bl) 3-9-0 (3*) J Weaver (5) *pressed ldr, second strt, wknd quickly fnl 2 fs*..........(7 to 1 op 4 to 1) 9
2293⁵ MAWAYED (USA) [65] 3-9-12 R Hills (9) *prmnt 4 fs, wknd quickly*............... (11 to 2 op 7 to 2 tchd 3 to 1) 10
Dist: 1½l, 1½l, 3l, hd, 1½l, 2l, 2l, 2½l, 1½l. 1m 30.90s. a 3.90s (10 Ran).
SR: 25/12/11/-/7/15/ (Elias Gale Racing), K R Burke

2639 Saddle Claiming Stakes Class F (3-y-o and up) £2,070 7f...............(7:45)

2329³ SIZZLING SAGA (Ire) 5-9-7 R Cochrane (8) *hld up, hdwy 3 fs out, 3rd strt, led o'r one out, sn drw clr.* ....(11 to 8 on op Evens) 1
2434 CELESTINE (v) 4-8-10 J Fanning (5) *led aftr one furlong til hdd o'r one out, not quicken.* ....(11 to 2 op 5 to 1 tchd 6 to 1) 2
2434 RESOLUTE BAY 7-9-7 A Culhane (3) *hld up, 6th strt, rdn and styd on ins fnl furlong, not rch 1st 2.* ....(8 to 1 op 6 to 1) 3+

828[7] GALLERY ARTIST (Ire) 5-8-2 (7*) S Eiffert (2) *chsd ldrs, 4th and ev ch strt, sn rdn and one pace.* ....(14 to 1 op 10 to 1) 3+
2380[4] SUMMER EXPRESS 4-8-7 Alex Greaves (4) *led one furlong, pressed ldr, second strt, wknd ins fnl 2 fs.* ....(20 to 1 op 16 to 1) 5
2120[6] SWISS MOUNTAIN 3-7-9 J Lowe (6) *beh, styd on fnl 2 fs, one pace*....(20 to 1 op 16 to 1) 6
2532[8] LORD NASKRA (USA) 4-8-8 (3*) Emma O'Gorman (1) *nvr rchd ldrs, one pace fnl 3 fs*....(12 to 1 op 10 to 1) 7
376[7] MOST SURPRISING (Ire) 4-8-10 B Raymond (7) *pressed ldrs aftr 2 fs, 5th strt, sn wknd*....(20 to 1 op 16 to 1) 8
2329[6] JACK GRAY 5-9-5 A Mackay (9) *chsd ldrs, 7th strt, wknd quickly, tld off fnl 2 fs*....(33 to 1) 9

Dist: 3½l, 2½l, dd-ht, 1½l, 6l, 2½l, 3l, dist. 1m 29.50s. a 2.50s (9 Ran).
SR: 53/31/34/22/15/-/ (J David Abell), J Wharton

2640 Girth Handicap Class E (0-70 3-y-o) £2,301 2m.... (8:15)

2354 SUN GREBE (Ire) [63] 9-7 B Raymond (4) *hld up, cld on ldrs 5 fs out, 3rd strt, led 2 out, drvn clr.* ....(6 to 1 op 5 to 1 tchd 13 to 2) 1
2207[6] IBTIKAR (USA) [49] (v) 8-7 R Hills (1) *trkd ldg trio, second strt, led briefly 2 fs out, sn hdd, rdn and one pace.* ....(4 to 1 op 7 to 2 tchd 9 to 2) 2
1942* FOLLINGWORTH GIRL (Ire) [53] 8-6 (5*) O Pears (5) *led aftr 3 furlong til hdd o'r 2 out, rdn and not quicken.* ....(2 to 1 fav op 9 to 4) 3
2443[3] WALSHAM WITCH [51] 8-4 (5*) K Rutter (2) *hld up, pressed ldr 6 fs out, 4th strt, wknd quickly, tld off fnl furlong.* ....(6 to 1 op 4 to 1) 4
2281* DESERT LAUGHTER (Ire) [45] 8-3 J Quinn (3) *led for 3 fs, wknd quickly 5 out, 5th strt, tld off fnl 2 furlongs.* ....(5 to 2 tchd 9 to 4) 5

Dist: 7l, ½l, 25l, 6l. 3m 44.10s. a 18.10s (5 Ran).
(Sir Thomas Pilkington), J L Dunlop

2641 Bridle Handicap Class E (0-70 3-y-o and up) £2,742 1¼m.... (8:45)

2354* MISTY GODDESS (Ire) [53] 5-8-11 (5*) K Rutter (1) *hld up and beh, rapid hdwy to ld o'r one furlong out, styd on wl*....(5 to 1 op 4 to 1 tchd 3 to 1) 1
1858* PRESTON GUILD (Ire) [60] 3-8-13 R Cochrane (3) *trkd ldrs, 5th strt, rdn and styd on ins fnl 2 fs, not quicken.* ....(9 to 4 fav op 5 to 2 tchd 3 to 1) 2
2427[3] SUGEMAR [54] 7-8-12 (5*) D McCabe (15) *beh, rdn and styd on wl fnl 2 fs, kpt on nr finish.* (12 to 1 op 10 to 1) 3
2348[5] SAINT CIEL (USA) [64] 5-9-6 (7*) Michael Denaro (14) *beh, rapid hdwy ins fnl 2 fs, styd on nr finish.* ....(12 to 1 op 8 to 1) 4
2391[6] MAJAL (Ire) [55] 4-9-4 Dean McKeown (13) *prmnt, led o'r 6 fs out til hdd appr fnl furlong.* ....(9 to 1 op 10 to 1 tchd 12 to 1) 5
2391 DOCTOR ROY [48] 5-8-11 Alex Greaves (4) *prmnt aftr 4 fs, 6th strt, one pace*....(16 to 1 op 20 to 1 tchd 14 to 1) 6
2332 BEND SABLE (Ire) [66] 3-9-5 Dale Gibson (11) *hld up, hdwy aftr 6 fs, second strt, sn btn.* ....(3 to 1 op 7 to 1 tchd 10 to 1) 7
243[6] KRONPRINZ (Ire) [31] 5-7-8[1] N Carlisle (5) *beh til styd on fnl 4 fs, one pace*....(33 to 1) 8
FLYING DOWN TO RIO (Ire) [39] 5-7-11 (5*) A Garth (12) *beh, chsd ldrs aftr 6 fs, no imprsn fnl 3 furlongs*....(33 to 1) 9
1707[6] VICTOR ROMEO [32] 4-7-9 A Mackay (6) *prmnt 6 fs, beh fnl 3 furlongs*....(33 to 1) 10
4740a[7] STAR RAGE (Ire) [43] 3-7-10 J Quinn (8) *chsd ldr, ev ch 3 fs out, sn wknd*....(33 to 1) 11
2104[3] MARY MACBLAIN [38] 4-7-13[1] (3*) S Maloney (2) *al beh.* ....(12 to 1 op 7 to 1) 12
9[7] MEL'S ROSE [58] 8-9-7 J Lowe (9) *chsd ldrs for 6 fs, beh fnl 3 furlongs*....(33 to 1) 13
2149[7] RED KITE [49] 4-8-12 G Duffield (7) *led for o'r 6 fs, sn wknd*....(16 to 1 op 14 to 1) 14
1416 JAMANE [49] 3-8-2 J Fanning (10) *al beh*....(33 to 1) 15

Dist: 2l, ¾l, nk, hd, 1½l, ¾l, ½l, 2l, ½l, 5l. 2m 12.60s. (15 Ran).
(J R Good), M A Jarvis

SAN SIRO (ITY) (good)
Saturday July 17th

2642 Premio Bielmonte Maiden (C & G) (2-y-o) £5,603 1m.... (2:50)

1885[2] MEDITERRANEO 8-11 A Cruz, *rcd in 3rd, led 3 fs out, sn wnt clr, unchlgd*.... 1
SALSIR 8-11 M Esposito,.... 2
MOUTHEFRINGE (Ire) 8-11 G Verricelli,.... 3
SAPORE DI SALE 8-11 A Parravani, *al in rear, nvr able to chal*.... 0

Dist: 9l, 1l, 5l, nk, 1l, 1½l, 1l, ¾l, 7l, ½l. 1m 43.30s. (15 Ran).
(Gerecon Italia), J L Dunlop

BRATISLAVA (CZE) (good to firm)
Sunday July 18th

2643 Slovenske Derby (3-y-o) £6,851 1½m.... (4:15)

1884* ZIMZALABIM 9-0 L Piggott, *hld up, hdwy to ld 3 fs out, sn clr, very easily*.... 1
MANHATTAN PROJECT 9-0 P Piatkowski,.... 2
FAUST (Su) 9-0 T Vana,.... 3
WHITE MOON 9-0 J Korpas,.... 4
ARKENDALE DIAMOND (USA) 9-0 J Bojko,.... 5
REMBO (Su) 9-0 -,.... 6
BOLD PROSPECT 9-0 A Petrlik,.... 7
GIUSEPPE 9-0 Z Lindovsky,.... 8
VIZUM 9-0 Mr L Sara,.... 9
DHAHRAN 9-0 B Koteles,.... 0
DEMBINSZKY 9-0 P Kallai,.... 0
ELIMINATOR 9-0 D Andres,.... 0

Dist: 8l, 11l, 13l, 6l, 1l, 2½l, 2l, 4l, 4l, 2½l. 2m 33.14s. (12 Ran).
(Mrs M Schneider), B W Hills

FRANKFURT (GER) (good)
Sunday July 18th

2644 Ammerschlager Frankfurt-Pokal (Group 3) (3-y-o and up) £28,571 1¼m.... (3:50)

1882[3] IRON FIGHTER (Ger) 4-9-1 R Hillis, *mid-div, cl thired strt, led one and a half fs out, ran on wl*.... 1
2079[8] SPORTIVO (USA) 4-9-1 A Helfenbein, *wtd wth, 7th strt, str run to take second cl hme*.... 2
1217[6] TWIST AND TURN 4-9-3 W R Swinburn, *rcd in second, led 2 fs out, hdd and one paced frm one and a half furlongs out*.... 3
1748 LUCKY LINDY (Ire) 4-9-5 B Rouse, *ran in snatches, 4th strt, ev ch one furlong out, no extr cl hme*.... 4
SAN FRANZISCO (Ger) 6-8-10 G Huber, *hld up in mid-div, ran on wl clsg stages*.... 5
1125[3] AMARANT (Ger) 3-8-0 A Best, *cl 3rd to 4 fs out, lost pl on turn, ran on one pace fnl 2 furlongs*.... 6
2079[7] INKOGNITO (Ger) 5-9-1 T Hellier, *nvr nrr*.... 7
TIMELY THREAT (USA) 3-8-1[1] M Hofer, *set str pace to 2 fs outs, sn wknd*.... 8
KFAAF (Ire) 6-9-3 D Wildman, *al beh*.... 9
LEOPOLDO (Ger) 5-8-10 A Tylicki, *al beh*.... 0
536[4] EXTRA POINT 3-8-1[1] E Saint-Martin, *prmnt, 4th 3 fs out, wknd*.... 0
DIAMOND OF ZURICH (Ger) 4-8-13 J P Murtagh, *al in rear.* 0

Dist: 1½l, nk, sht-hd, hd, 1l, 1 ¼l, 2l, 2l. 2m 5.84s. (12 Ran).
(V Storckmann), H Steinmetz

HOLLYWOOD (USA) (firm)
Sunday July 18th

2645 Vanity Handicap (Grade 1) (3-y-o and up) £109,271 1m 1f....

1695[3] RE TOSS (Arg) 6-8-3[1] E Delahoussaye,....(36 to 10) 1
1695* PASEANA (Arg) 6-9-0 C McCarron,....(10 to 7 on) 2
1695[4] GUIZA (USA) 6-8-2[1] K Desormeaux,....(121 to 10) 3
MISS HIGH BLADE (USA) 5-8-1 G Stevens,....(135 to 10) 4
1695[2] BOLD WINDY (USA) 4-8-2 C Black,....(17 to 2) 5
560[7] SOUTHERN TRUCE (USA) 5-8-3 C Nakatani,....(145 to 10) 6
VIEILLE VIGNE (Fr) 6-8-1 J Steiner,....(68 to 1) 7
SAROS ON THE TOWN (USA) 4-8-1[1] D Flores,....(12 to 1) ur

Dist: 1 ¼l, 2 ¼l, 3l, 1 ¼l, 5½l, 5½l. 1m 47.80s. (8 Ran).
(A & L Risdon), H Moreno

MAISONS-LAFFITTE (FR) (soft)
Sunday July 18th
Going Correction: NIL (race 1), PLUS 0.25 (2)

2646 Prix Barteux (Group 3) (3-y-o) £23,895 1m 7f 110yds.... (3:05)

1915* RAINTRAP 8-8 Pat Eddery (6) *hld up, 4th strt, led one and a half fs out, pushed out, ran on wl*....(10 to 7 on) 1
SVANDA (Fr) 8-8 R Laplanche (1) *3rd strt, chlgd 2 fs out, ev ch one and a half furlong out, kpt on one pace.* ....(105 to 10) 2
BACOUCHE (Fr) 8-8 O Poirier (4) *led till one and a half fs out*....(19 to 1) 3
1915[2] DONDOOK (USA) (bl) 8-8 D Boeuf (2) *hld up, last strt, hdwy 2 fs out, kpt on same pace one and a half furlongs out*....(27 to 10) 4
1915[4] PRACER (USA) 8-5 T Jarnet (3) *pld hrd early, 5th strt, effrt 2 fs out, nvr able to chal*....(15 to 2) 5
KERKI (USA) 8-8 C Asmussen (5) *second strt, rdn and wknd wl o'r 2 fs out*....(57 to 10) 6

Dist: 2l, sht-hd, nk, 1l, 4l. 3m 21.50s. a 8.50s (6 Ran).
SR: 9/7/6/5/1/-/ (K Abdulla), A Fabre

2647 Prix Robert Papin (Group 2) (2-y-o) £41,816 5f 110yds.............. (3:55)

PSYCHOBABBLE (Ire) 8-11 C Asmussen (4) *trkd ldrs, hdwy o'r 2 fs out, led two out, ran on wl*....(6 to 5 fav) 1
2075[4] LAKE COUNTRY (Ire) 8-9 E Legrix (1) *al cl up, ev ch 2 fs out, ran on one pace o'r one out*..................(29 to 1) 2
FAR MIST (Fr) 8-9 O Peslier (5) *hld up, hdwy 2 fs out, ran on one pace fnl furlong*..................(24 to 1) 3
2144[2] BRAVE NOTE (Ire) 8-11 J Reid (6) *ev ch 2 fs out, one pace appr fnl furlong*................................(5 to 1) 4
2144* PORTO VARAS (USA) (bl) 8-11 F Head (2) *hld up, effrt 2 fs out, one pace o'r one out*......................(7 to 2) 5
BLUE BURGEE (USA) 8-9 D Boeuf (3) *led till 2 fs out.* ....(57 to 10) 6
ANGEL OF THE NIGHT (USA) 8-11 B Jovine (7) *cl up till rdn and wknd 2 fs out*...................................(5 to 1) 7
ROI D'O (Fr) 8-11 T Jarnet (8) *in tch for o'r 3 fs*... (10 to 1) 8
Dist: 2l, nk, nk, 1½l, hd, 2½l, 1l. 1m 6.80s. a 3.10s (8 Ran).
SR: 63/53/52/53/47/44/36/32/ (S Niarchos), Miss C Head

NAPLES (ITY) (good to firm)
Sunday July 18th

2648 Premio FIA Breeders' Cup (Listed) (2-y-o fillies) £20,173 7f 110yds.... (7:30)

2240[7] MICHELLE HICKS 8-8 T Quinn, *trkd ldrs, cld up 2 fs out, led one and a half out, quickened clr one out, ran on wl*.. 1
2258[4] SUSPIRIA (Ire) 8-8 A Cruz,.............................. 2
SOPRAN ARMONY (Ire) 8-8 M Esposito,.................. 3
2258* WHATCOMBE (USA) 8-10 A Munro, *mid-div, ev ch o'r one furlong out, wknd fnl furlong*........................ 4
BODINIYEH (Ire) 8-8 V Mezzatesta,......................... 5
MAREMMA MIA (Ity) 8-8 L Dettori,.......................... 6
1571[2] DANISH (Ire) 8-8 W J Supple, *al rear*...................... 7
CERIGNOLA (Ire) 8-8 F Sparapano,......................... 8
Dist: 2½l, 1½l, ¾l, 3½l, 2l, ¾l, 3½l. 1m 29.00s. (8 Ran).
(Paul M Hicks), M Bell

2649 Premio FIA European Breeders' Fund (Listed) (2-y-o colts) £20,173 7f 110yds ....(8:20)

1725* TORRISMONDO (USA) 8-8 T Quinn, *midfield, slpd bend, prog o'r 2 fs out, led one and a half out, easily*........ 1
LEAR WHITE (USA) 8-8 M Pasquale,........................ 2
2260[3] BLINDING SPEED 8-8 Jacqueline Freda,.................. 3
SECRELLY (USA) 8-8 V Mezzatesta,......................... 4
SUGARLAND EXPRESS (Ire) 8-8 A Cruz,................... 5
1647[3] CASTEL RUNDEGG (Ity) 8-8 A Sauli,...................... 6
RAS (Ity) 8-8 D Zarroli,.. 7
STONY BEST (Ire) 8-8 S Morales,............................ 8
TARGET WINNER (Ire) 8-8 A Corniani,..................... 9
DOMINION POWER 8-8 A Luongo,............................ 10
BISCUITER (Ire) 8-8 B Jovine,............................... pu
Dist: 2l, nk, ¾l, ¾l, ½l, 1½l, 2½l, 3½l, 2l. 1m 30.40s. (11 Ran).
(Lord Portman), P F I Cole

2650 Gran Premio Citta di Napoli (Group 3) (3-y-o and up) £29,049 1¼m..........

1952* SPARTAN SHAREEF (Ire) 4-8-13 L Dettori, *al cl up, 4th strt, rdn o'r 2 fs out, led fnl strds*........................ 1
692[3] TAFF'S ACRE (Ire) 4-8-13 A Cruz, *sn tracking ldr, second strt, led 100 yards out, ct last strds*....................... 2
1548[2] PROSPECTIVE RULER (USA) 5-9-2 D Holland, *led till 100 yards out*.. 3
593[3] ANOTHER BOB (USA) 5-8-13 Jacqueline Freda, *squeezed for room 5 fs out, 5th strt, styd on fnl 2 furlongs, nrst finish*.. 4
1727[2] DAMA GRANDE 4-8-9 M Pasquale, *3rd strt, no extr fnl 2 fs*.. 5
SAGAL WELLS 6-8-13 T Quinn, *6th strt, chlgd o'r one furlong out, sn btn*.. 6
GOLDEN FORZANDO 4-8-13 A Munro, *nvr a factor*....... 7
958[4] STEVE LUCKY (Ire) 3-8-3 M Esposito, *reared stalls, al rear*. 8
Dist: Sht-hd, ½l, ½l, 3½l, 3l, 4l, dist. 2m 3.20s. (8 Ran).
(C T Olley), C E Brittain

AYR (good)
Monday July 19th

Going Correction: MINUS 0.15 sec. per fur. (races 1,2,3), NIL (4,5,6,7)

2651 Tam O'Shanter Claiming Stakes Class F (3-y-o) £2,489 6f.............. (2:00)

2396[4] BOLD SEVEN (Ire) 8-12 S Perks (5) *trkd ldrs, swtchd wl o'r one out, ran on well to ld ins fnl furlong.* ....(11 to 2 op 4 to 1) 1
2303[7] PALACEGATE TOUCH (bl) 9-7 G Carter (4) *led, hng lft 2 out, hdd ins fnl furlong, no extr*... (9 to 4 on op 6 to 4 on) 2
2469[2] LARN FORT 8-9 J Fanning (7) *cl up till outpcd hfwy, styd on fnl furlong*.....................(12 to 1 op 8 to 1) 3
2338[5] VILAMAR (Ire) 8-8 K Fallon (2) *trkd ldrs, effrt 2 fs out, sn rdn and btn*...........................(5 to 1 op 7 to 1) 4
2202 KEEN AND CLEAN (Ire) 8-11 (5*) Darren Moffatt (3) *al beh.* ....(50 to 1 tchd 66 to 1) 5
BALLY ROBERT 8-10 (3*) J Weaver (1) *al beh.* ....(66 to 1 op 50 to 1) 6
Dist: 2l, 2½l, 1l, 2l, 6l. 1m 13.49s. a 2.59s (6 Ran).
SR: 28/29/7/2/2/-/ (F H Lee), F H Lee

2652 Garry Owen Cup Nursery Class D (2-y-o) £3,566 6f.................. (2:30)

2364 STORM REGENT [-] 8-7 W Woods (5) *hld up, steady hdwy to ld o'r one furlong out, edgd rght, styd on.* ....(4 to 1 op 3 to 1 tchd 9 to 2) 1
1846[4] NO MEAN CITY (Ire) [-] (bl) 9-6 A Mackay (2) *led till hdd o'r one furlong out, kpt on wl fnl furlong.* ....(8 to 1 op 6 to 1 tchd 9 to 1) 2
2430[8] DISTINCTIVE AIR [-] (bl) 9-7 L Dettori (4) *al prmnt, not clr run fnl furlong, kpt on.* (15 to 2 op 5 to 1 tchd 8 to 1) 3
2216[2] HE SHALL REIGN [-] 9-2 T Williams (6) *beh, hdwy 2 fs out, ch entering fnl furlong, no extr.* ....(13 to 2 op 5 to 1 tchd 7 to 1) 4
2102[5] STARICA (Ire) [-] (bl) 7-11 (5*) Darren Moffatt (1) *in tch, sn pushed alng, no hdwy und pres fnl furlong.* ....(4 to 1 op 5 to 1) 5
2176* SPRINGHEAD [-] 8-4 (7*) J Marshall (3) *chsd ldr till wknd wl o'r one furlong out, lost tch fnl furlong, tld off.* ....(9 to 4 fav op 2 to 1 tchd 5 to 2) 6
Dist: ½l, ½l, 1½l, ¾l, 12l. 1m 14.59s. a 3.69s (6 Ran).
SR: 1/12/11/ (The Storm Syndicate), S P C Woods

2653 Daily Record Handicap Class E (0-70 3-y-o and up) £3,452 5f......... (3:00)

2241* GONDO [68] (v) 6-9-7 (7*) S Knott (3) *chsd ldr, led 2 fs out, ran on wl*..........(100 to 30 op 11 to 4 tchd 7 to 2) 1
2456* ABSOLUTION [65] 9-9-8 (3*,7ex) J Weaver (4) *in tch, rdn wl o'r one furlong out, styd on, no imprsn on wnr.* ....(5 to 2 tchd 9 to 4 and 11 to 4) 2
2434[5] PRINCE BELFORT [61] (bl) 5-9-7 L Dettori (5) *chsd ldrs, rdn 2 fs out, one pace*........... (9 to 4 fav tchd 3 to 1) 3
2241 CONSULATE [52] 7-8-5 (7*) Claire Balding (2) *in tch, effrt 2 fs out, hng lft and no hdwy*...... (12 to 1 op 10 to 1) 4
2312* DAYJUZ (Ire) [59] (bl) 3-9-0 S Perks (1) *led till hdd 2 out, fdd*.................................. (9 to 2 op 7 to 2) 5
Dist: 2½l, 1l, 2l, 3l. 1m 0.62s. a 2.52s (5 Ran).
SR: 49/36/28/11/1/ (Mrs Helen O'Brien), E J Alston

2654 Tennents Scottish Classic Class A (Group 3) (3-y-o and up) £20,058 1¼m ....(3:30)

2211[2] RIVER NORTH (Ire) 3-8-6 K Darley (7) *hld up, hdwy 3 fs out, led o'r one out, ran on wl, eased cl hme.* ....(100 to 30 op 3 to 1 tchd 7 to 2 and 4 to 1) 1
1538[2] ONLY ROYALE (Ire) 4-8-13 R Cochrane (3) *in tch, effrt o'r 2 fs out, ran on wl fnl furlong.* ....(5 to 1 tchd 6 to 1 and 7 to 1) 2
2290* BLUE LION 3-8-6 M Roberts (1) *trkd ldrs, slight ld 2 fs out, sn hdd, kpt on same pace*.................. (5 to 2 fav) 3
1952[3] SALATIN (USA) 3-8-6 W Carson (5) *hld up, hdwy o'r 2 fs out, kpt on wl fnl furlong*..................(25 to 1) 4
1538[3] SHUAILAAN (USA) 4-9-2 R Hills (10) *prmnt, chlgd o'r 2 fs out, sn rdn and one pace.* ....(13 to 2 op 6 to 1 tchd 7 to 1) 5
2247* ORMSBY (Ire) 4-9-2 M J Kinane (4) *in tch, effrt 3 fs out, no real hdwy*.....................(14 to 1 op 12 to 1) 6
1065[3] LINPAC WEST 7-9-5 B Raymond (9) *cl up, dsptd ld hfwy till wknd 2 out*..................................(12 to 1) 7
525[9] BREAK BREAD (USA) 4-9-5 J Reid (8) *mid-div, effrt 3 fs out, sn btn*.....................(20 to 1 op 16 to 1) 8
2390[5] MELLOTTIE 8-9-2 J Lowe (6) *hld up, effrt o'r 2 fs out, no hdwy*.....................(14 to 1 op 10 to 1) 9
2290[2] ICY SOUTH (USA) 3-8-6 L Dettori (2) *led or dsptd ld till hdd 2 out, sn wknd*......(11 to 1 op 14 to 1 tchd 10 to 1) 10
Dist: Nk, 1½l, hd, 2l, nk, 1½l, 1l, hd, 1l. 2m 8.12s. a 3.12s (10 Ran).
SR: 61/67/57/56/62/61/61/59/55/ (P D Savill), Lady Herries

2655 Tennent Trophy Rated Class B Handicap (0-95 3-y-o and up) £6,016 1m 7f ....(4:00)

2432* BRANDON PRINCE (Ire) [88] (bl) 5-9-7 L Dettori (3) *hld up gng wl, gd hdwy o'r 2 furlong sout, led entering fnl furlong, easily*......(3 to 1 fav op 7 to 2 tchd 4 to 1) 1
AAHSAYLAD [75] (bl) 7-8-3 (5*) K Rutter (2) *in tch, lost pl and rdn 4 fs out, hdwy 3 out, kpt on fnl furlong, no ch wth wnr*...(6 to 1) 2
1960[4] RITTO [77] 3-7-9[2] W Carson (6) *pld hrd early, led aftr 2 fs till hdd entering fnl furlong, sn btn.* ....(6 to 1 tchd 11 to 2) 3

1809[8] GOOD HAND (USA) [87] 7-9-6 N Connorton (4) *in tch, pushed alng 5 out, rdn 3 out, styd on same pace.* ....(8 to 1 tchd 7 to 1) 4
2368* TAROUDANT [78] 6-8-11 K Darley (5) *trkd ldrs, effrt 3 fs out, kpt on same pace*..............(9 to 2 op 3 to 1) 5
2372* TRUBEN (USA) [75] 4-8-5 (3*) J Weaver (7) *led 2 fs, trkd ldr till wknd quickly o'r two furlongs out, tld off.* ....(16 to 1 op 14 to 1 tchd 20 to 1) 6
2061[8] SARAWAT [76] 5-8-9 J Fanning (1) *trkd ldrs, rdn 3 out, sn wknd, tld off*.........................(7 to 2 op 3 to 1) 7
Dist: 2l, ¾l, ½l, 2½l, 12l, 2l. 3m 18.46s. a 5.96s (7 Ran).
SR: 47/32/17/41/29/14/13/ (R P B Michaelson), I A Balding

2656 Daily Record Claiming Stakes Class F (4-y-o and up) £2,668 7f.........(4:30)

2396[2] CORALS DREAM (Ire) 4-9-7 W Woods (2) *chsd clr ldrs, led wl o'r one furlong out, styd on well.* ....(4 to 1 op 9 to 2 tchd 5 to 1) 1
2371[2] LOMBARD SHIPS (bl) 6-8-2 A Mackay (6) *in tch, hdwy 3 fs out, chsd wnr o'r one out, kpt on, no imprsn.* .... (7 to 4 fav op 2 to 1 tchd 9 to 4 and 5 to 2) 2
2431[4] PARFAIT AMOUR 4-8-8 A Culhane (8) *in tch, hdwy 3 fs out, kpt on fnl furlong*..........................(6 to 1 op 9 to 2) 3
2454* ACROSS THE BAY (v) 6-8-11 K Darley (5) *beh, styd on fnl 3 fs, not rch ldrs*.......................(8 to 1 op 5 to 1) 4
1969* SHALABIA 4-8-1 (5*) Darren Moffatt (4) *led or dsptd ld till hdd wl o'r one furlong, fdd*..........(6 to 1 op 5 to 1) 5
2392[9] DRUM SERGEANT 6-9-3 M Roberts (7) *nvr nr ldrs.* ....(7 to 1 op 6 to 1) 6
1138 CHANCE REPORT 5-8-0[2] R Lappin (1) *al beh.* ....(100 to 1 op 50 to 1) 7
2550[6] HAND ON HEART (Ire) (v) 4-8-5[4] (3*) S D Williams (9) *wth ldr till wknd quickly 2 fs out*.........(100 to 1 op 50 to 1) 8
2311[7] DEXTER CHIEF 4-8-8 (5*) K Rutter (3) *in tch till wknd 3 fs out*..................................(33 to 1 op 20 to 1) 9
Dist: 1l, 1½l, 1½l, 1½l, 6l, 3½l, 1½l, ½l. 1m 27.48s. a 3.48s (9 Ran).
SR: 54/32/33/31/21/14/ (Mrs C Hamson), C F Wall

2657 Western House Handicap Class C (0-95 3-y-o and up) £4,920 7f.... (5:00)

2600[7] VELOCE (Ire) [70] 5-8-11 A Mackay (4) *hld up, hdwy 3 out, led one out, ran on wl.* (11 to 2 op 9 to 2 tchd 6 to 1) 1
2391 PARLIAMENT PIECE [83] 7-9-10 K Darley (5) *led till hdd one out, kpt on wl*....................(25 to 1 op 12 to 1) 2
2363[4] TAWAFIJ (USA) [77] 4-9-1 (3*) J Weaver (8) *mid-div, steady hdwy to chal entering fnl furlong, sn rdn and one pace*.............................. (9 to 2 op 4 to 1) 3
2396* BOLD ANGEL [78] 6-9-5 M Birch (6) *hld up, pushed alng 3 out, kpt on wl fnl furlong*.........................(9 to 2) 4
2434 SAGEBRUSH ROLLER [82] 5-9-9 B Raymond (3) *hld up, effrt o'r 2 fs out, kpt on wl fnl furlong.* .... (16 to 1 op 10 to 1) 5
2391[7] BLOW DRY (Ire) [76] 3-8-10 W Carson (9) *cl up, dsptd ld 3 fs out, till wknd fnl furlong*............(5 to 1 op 7 to 2) 6
2304* TOLEDO QUEEN (Ire) [85] 3-9-5 J Reid (7) *chsd ldrs, effrt 3 fs out, wknd wl o'r one out.* ....(3 to 1 fav op 4 to 1 tchd 5 to 1) 7
1737[9] GANT BLEU (Fr) [57] 6-7-12 J Fanning (2) *dwlt, sn in tch, effrt 3 fs out, wknd entering fnl furlong.* ....(20 to 1 tchd 25 to 1) 8
2304[4] SPARK (Ire) [82] 3-9-2 L Dettori (1) *chsd ldrs till wknd 2 fs out*..................................(9 to 1 op 7 to 1) 9
Dist: 1½l, hd, hd, hd, 2l, ½l, 2l, 5l. 1m 27.80s. a 3.80s (9 Ran).
SR: 40/48/41/41/44/25/32/5/8/ (Maximo Gonzalez), A Bailey

BATH (good)
Monday July 19th

Going Correction: MINUS 0.25 sec. per fur. (races 1,5,6), MINUS 0.10 (2,3,4)

2658 Knockdown Selling Handicap Class G (0-60 3-y-o and up) £2,511 1m 5f 22yds ....(2:15)

2347[4] FANATICAL (USA) [36] (bl) 7-9-1 W Newnes (8) *hld up in rear, hdwy o'r 6 fs out, led ins last, ran on.* ....(9 to 2 op 5 to 1 tchd 11 to 2) 1
2471[5] WITH GUSTO [35] 6-9-0 J Williams (1) *beh, hdwy o'r 3 fs out, styd on.* ....(9 to 2 op 5 to 1 tchd 11 to 2 and 4 to 1) 2
2223[5] GAY MING [31] 4-8-5 (5*) A Garth (12) *beh, hdwy o'r 3 fs out, styd on*......................(12 to 1 op 10 to 1) 3
2282[3] PIE HATCH (Ire) [38] (v) 4-9-3 G Duffield (13) *al hndy, led o'r 5 fs out, hdd and no extr ins last.* ....(7 to 2 fav op 11 to 4) 4
2388[6] DOTS DEE [28] 4-8-0 (7*) Mark Denaro (7) *mid-div, effrt and styd on fnl 2 fs*................(7 to 1 op 10 to 1) 5
2317[6] FLASH OF STRAW (Ire) [36] (v) 4-9-1 S Whitworth (10) *al prmnt, rdn and ev ch 3 fs out, sn btn.* ....(12 to 1 op 8 to 1) 6
2314[5] TOUT DE VAL [30] 4-8-9 R Perham (11) *chsd ldrs, effrt 5 fs out, no imprsn*....................(25 to 1 op 20 to 1) 7

2223[8] QUALITAIR IDOL [32] 4-8-11 F Norton (2) *mid-div, rdn and no hdwy fnl 3 fs*..............(25 to 1 op 20 to 1) 8
SEE NOW [45] 8-9-10 J Quinn (3) *al beh.* ....(50 to 1 tchd 66 to 1) 9
2034[7] CRYSTAL STONE [43] 3-8-9 A Tucker (5) *chsd ldrs till wknd o'r 5 fs out*...............(25 to 1 op 16 to 1) 10
2113 MELLERIO [57] (bl) 3-9-9 Paul Eddery (9) *al beh.* ....(6 to 1 op 4 to 1) 11
4797a[9] SILLY HABIT (USA) [32] (v) 7-8-11 Dale Gibson (6) *prmnt till rdn alng 5 fs out, sn btn*..........(25 to 1 op 16 to 1) 12
2223[6] THE GORROCK [24] (bl) 4-7-10 (7*) Kim McDonnell (4) *led, sn clr, hdd o'r 5 fs out, wknd, tld off.* ....(33 to 1 op 50 to 1 tchd 66 to 1) 13
Dist: 1½l, nk, 2½l, 7l, ½l, 8l, ¾l, sht-hd, 1½l, 3l. 2m 52.40s. a 4.10s (13 Ran).
SR: 28/24/19/21/-/4/ (Duckhaven Stud), R J Baker

2659 Melksham Maiden Stakes Class D (2-y-o) £3,523 5f 11yds............ (2:45)

1899[3] MONKEY MUSIC (bl) 9-0 J Carroll (1) *tardy strt, sn led, made rst, rdn out*.......(9 to 2 op 6 to 1 tchd 4 to 1) 1
1999[4] LAUNE (Aus) 8-9 Paul Eddery (8) *bolted to strt, chsd ldrs, cld 2 fs out, rdn one out, kpt on wl*...(7 to 1 op 5 to 1) 2
NOBLE SPIRIT (Ire) 9-0 Pat Eddery (3) *al prmnt, pld out to chal appr fnl furlong, ran on one pace, eased cl hme, improve*.......................... (3 to 1 fav op 7 to 4) 3
2316[8] CHILLY TIME 8-9 J Williams (7) *beh, rdn and hdwy o'r one furlong out, ran on*...................(9 to 2 op 8 to 1) 4
2356[3] PACIOLI 9-0 M Wigham (9) *missed break, beh till ran on appr fnl furlong, nrst finish*........(10 to 1 op 8 to 1) 5
1355[3] GREENSON (Ire) 9-0 T Quinn (11) *cl up, pushed alng 2 fs out, wknd appr last*...............(12 to 1 op 8 to 1) 6
SARMATIAN (USA) 9-0 G Duffield (10) *nvr on terms.* .... (10 to 1 op 5 to 1) 7
2472[5] CALL ME GRAHAM 9-0 B Rouse (2) *prmnt, pushed alng 2 fs out, wknd appr last*..............(6 to 1 tchd 7 to 1) 8
969[6] COLONEL SINCLAIR (Ire) 9-0 W Ryan (5) *led one furlong, cl up till rdn and wknd appr last*.... (50 to 1 op 33 to 1) 9
2472 ROCKSTINE (Ire) 8-9 W Newnes (6) *outpcd.* .... (50 to 1 op 25 to 1) 10
HIGHLAND BONNIE 8-9 A Clark (4) *outpcd.* .... (50 to 1 op 33 to 1) 11
Dist: 1l, nk, 2½l, 2l, 4l, 1½l, ¾l, sht-hd, ½l, 1l. 1m 4.40s. a 3.90s (11 Ran).
SR: 12/3/7/-/-/-/ (The Monkey Racing Club Limited), J Berry

2660 Tote Computer Handicap Class C (0-90 3-y-o) £4,565 5f 11yds..... (3:15)

2387[4] ARAGROVE [69] 8-4[1] W Newnes (1) *in tch, hdwy 2 fs out, led appr last, ran on wl.* .... (6 to 1 tchd 8 to 1 and 11 to 2) 1
2375[3] CALL ME I'M BLUE (Ire) [86] 9-2 (5*) O Pears (8) *cl up, led o'r 2 fs out till hdd appr last, one pace.* ....(2 to 1 fav op 6 to 4) 2
2375[2] THE SHARP BIDDER (Ire) [80] 9-1 W Ryan (2) *beh, hdwy o'r one furlong out, kpt on und pres ins last.* ....(4 to 1 op 7 to 2 tchd 9 to 2) 3
2375[5] PURBECK CENTENARY [60] 7-9 J Quinn (7) *led till hdd o'r 2 fs out, wknd ins last*.............(11 to 1 op 7 to 1) 4
2024[4] MY BONUS [80] 8-10 (5*) L Newton (5) *trkd ldrs, rdn and ev ch o'r one furlong out, wknd ins last.* .... (10 to 1 op 7 to 1) 5
2033[3] DONTDRESSFORDINNER [58] 7-2 (5*) D Wright (3) *nvr on terms*..............................(25 to 1 op 20 to 1) 6
2024[7] TRENTESIMO (Ire) [80] 9-1 J Carroll (6) *chsd ldrs, rdn hfwy, sn btn*.............................(5 to 1 op 7 to 2) 7
2418 JEREMIAHS BOY [58] 7-7 N Adams (4) *al beh.* ....(14 to 1 op 25 to 1 tchd 12 to 1) 8
Dist: 2½l, 2l, 1½l, nk, 1l, 1½l, 1½l. 1m 2.40s. a 1.90s (8 Ran).
SR: 42/49/35/9/28/2/18/-/ (K F Khan), L J Holt

2661 Cotswold Conditions Stakes Class D (3-y-o) £3,201 5f 11yds..........(3:45)

2252[3] LUCKY PARKES 9-3 J Carroll (4) *made all, shaken up and quickened clr appr fnl furlong, eased cl hme.* .... (7 to 2 on tchd 3 to 1 on) 1
2303 DARK EYED LADY (Ire) 8-5 T Quinn (3) *wth wnr, rdn alng 2 fs out, outpcd appr last*............ (13 to 2 op 5 to 1) 2
2219* ALJAZ 9-0 Pat Eddery (5) *broke wl, sn outpcd, rdn o'r one furlong out, ran on ins last*.........(13 to 2 op 5 to 1) 3
2401[7] BELMONT PRINCESS (Ire) 8-5 N Adams (2) *sn chsd ldg pair til wknd appr fnl furlong*......... (33 to 1 op 20 to 1) 4
1990[9] JEAN BRODIE 8-5 T Lang (1) *reared strt, outpcd.* .... (66 to 1 op 50 to 1) 5
Dist: 5l, hd, 6l, 8l. 1m 1.90s. a 1.40s (5 Ran).
SR: 65/33/41/8/-/ (Joseph Heler), J Berry

2662 St John Ambulance Handicap Class E (0-70 3-y-o and up) £3,080 2m 1f 34yds ....(4:15)

2115[2] CHUCKLESTONE [61] 10-10-0 T Quinn (3) *trkd ldr, rdn alng 6 fs out, led 4 out, ridden out.* ....(9 to 2 op 6 to 1 tchd 13 to 2 and 4 to 1) 1
2415* SINGING REPLY (USA) [35] 5-8-2 T Sprake (1) *al prmnt, ev ch 2 fs out, kpt on*... (4 to 1 fav op 9 to 2 tchd 7 to 2) 2

2397[3] WELSHMAN [57] 7-9-10 J Quinn (11) *al prmnt, ev ch 2 fs out, one pace*......... (13 to 2 op 6 to 1 tchd 7 to 1) 3
2347* ALLMOSA [57] 4-9-10 D Holland (4) *hld up beh, hdwy blw 3 fs out, styd on*.................(13 to 2 op 7 to 1) 4
2317* MILIYEL [45] 4-8-7 (5*) D McCabe (5) *mid-div, styd on fnl 2 fs*..............................(8 to 1 tchd 17 to 2) 5
2034* RICH PICKINGS [42] 4-8-9 R Perham (12) *mid-div, cld o'r 5 fs out, sn rdn and styd on one pace.*
..................................(12 to 1 op 11 to 1) 6
1752 PATROCLUS [45] 8-8-12 Paul Eddery (8) *beh, effrt 6 fs out, nvr on terms*..........................(9 to 1 op 8 to 1) 7
2124[2] YIMKIN BOOKRA [43] 5-8-10 J Carroll (7) *beh, hdwy 6 fs out, sn hrd rdn, wknd o'r 3 out*....(16 to 1 op 14 to 1) 8
2422[8] TRUST DEED (USA) [40] 5-8-7 F Norton (2) *al beh.*
..................................(50 to 1 op 33 to 1) 9
2317[2] SUDANOR (Ire) [36] 4-7-12 (5*) D Wright (10) *led till hdd 4 fs out, wknd*.......................(12 to 1 op 10 to 1) 10
2223[2] STANE STREET (Ire) [38] 5-8-5 G Duffield (13) *trkd ldrs till rdn and wknd 4 fs out*.......................(20 to 1) 11
2347 SNICKERSNEE [35] 5-7-9 (7*) Antoinette Armes (6) *al beh.*
.....................(40 to 1 op 33 to 1 tchd 50 to 1) 12
2282[5] POLDER [40] 7-8-7 A Clark (9) *chsd ldrs till wknd o'r 6 fs out*..............................(50 to 1 op 33 to 1) 13

Dist: 1½l, 2l, nk, nk, sht-hd, 10l, 1½l, 3l, 6l, 3l. 3m 51.90s. a 7.90s (13 Ran).
(Mark O'Connor), J S King

2663 Mendip Handicap Class D (0-80 3-y-o and up) £3,318 1m 5yds.........(4:45)

2300 MOON SPIN [70] 4-9-10 Paul Eddery (3) *trkd ldrs gng wl, hrd rdn o'r one furlong out, ran on well und pres to ld cl hme*............................(11 to 2 op 6 to 1) 1
2421[2] RUE REMBRANDT (USA) [75] 3-9-7 Pat Eddery (10) *trkd ldr, led 3 fs out, hrd rdn ins last, hdd cl hme.*
..................................(15 to 8 fav op 5 to 2) 2
2293[2] AJMAAN (USA) [71] 3-9-3 S Whitworth (7) *hld up, rdn alng 3 fs out, ran on wl fnl furlong*....... (7 to 1 op 5 to 1) 3
2330* SINGERS IMAGE [58] 4-8-12 J Williams (8) *hld up beh, hdwy o'r 2 fs out, nvr nr to chal*... (5 to 1 tchd 6 to 1) 4
2638* NORTHERN TRIAL (USA) [52] (v) 5-8-6 (7ex) T Sprake (6) *strted slwly, beh, cld o'r 3 fs out, wknd appr last.*
..................................(16 to 1 op 10 to 1) 5
2418[5] BAYSHAM (USA) [71] 7-9-11 R Price (4) *trkd ldrs, ev ch 2 fs out, wknd appr last*..............(16 to 1 op 10 to 1) 6
2138[4] REGALSETT [69] 3-9-1 T Quinn (2) *led til hdd 3 fs out, wknd*..............................(14 to 1 op 10 to 1) 7
2226[4] MUSTAHIL (Ire) [65] 4-9-5 R Perham (1) *trkd ldrs, rdn and wknd 3 fs out*......... (12 to 1 op 8 to 1 tchd 14 to 1) 8
2291[2] MY HARVINSKI [66] 3-8-12 D Holland (5) *al beh.*
..................................(10 to 1 op 8 to 1) 9
1956 MEXICAN DANCER [52] 4-8-6 J Quinn (9) *beh frm hfwy.*
..................................(33 to 1 op 14 to 1) 10

Dist: 1½l, 5l, ¾l, sht-hd, 2l, ¾l, 1l, ¾l, 3½l. 1m 40.70s. a 1.70s (10 Ran).
SR: 55/47/28/21/14/27/15/16/7/ (Mrs W R Hern), Major W R Hern

BALLINROBE (IRE) (good (race 1), good to soft (2,3,4)) Monday July 19th

2664 George Moore Corruna Handicap (0-70 3-y-o and up) £2,245 1¼m (6:00)

1294[4] SLIGHTLY SCRUFFY (Ire) [-] 3-9-5 P V Gilson (4) ... (9 to 2) 1
2286[9] SOLAR FLASH (Ire) [-] 4-7-12 N G McCullagh (2) .. (12 to 1) 2
487[4] ONOMATOPOEIA (Ire) [-] 3-9-1 J F Egan (1)........(4 to 1) 3
1757[3] THE BERUKI (Ire) [-] 3-8-11 (6*) P P Murphy (6) (3 to 1 fav) 4
BEAU BEAUCHAMP [-] 6-9-7 (4*) P Carberry (5) ....(8 to 1) 5
848 ROCKY (Ire) [-] 3-7-11 (4*) W J Smith (8) ....(5 to 1) 6
2286[6] TRES JOUR (Ire) [-] 3-8-4 (2*) D G O'Shea (7)..... (10 to 1) 7
2463[8] TRILLICK (Ire) [-] 3-9-6 J P Murtagh (9)............(6 to 1) 8
2286[7] MAY WE DANCE (Ire) [-] (bl) 4-9-0 R Hughes (3)... (10 to 1) 9

Dist: 4l, 5½l, 2l, 2l. 2m 17.80s. (9 Ran).
(Leung Yiu Nin), Daniel J Murphy

2665 Lough Apprentice Handicap (0-60 4-y-o and up) £2,245 1¼m.......... (6:30)

2322* THE BOWER (Ire) [-] (bl) 4-8-9 (4*,8ex) P M Donohue (7)
..................................(9 to 2) 1
2346[5] JUST ONE CANALETTO [-] 5-9-4 J R Barry (2).... (14 to 1) 2
2142[7] VICOSA (Ire) [-] 4-8-6 (2*) P J Smullen (6)...... (7 to 2 fav) 3
1513 ACCELL (Ire) [-] 4-9-8 (2*) R T Fitzpatrick (1)....... (8 to 1) 4
2451[4] MUNSIF (Fr) [-] 6-9-9 R V Skelly (10)............... (4 to 1) 5
1621[5] MR GERAN (Ire) [-] 4-9-2 J J Behan (9)...............(7 to 1) 6
2498[9] LACKOTWINE (Ire) [-] 4-9-0 (4*) J F Clarke (4).....(12 to 1) 7
SPECIAL CORNER (Ire) [-] 5-9-3 P P Murphy (5)...(12 to 1) 8
1644[6] SIMPLY PHRASED (Ire) [-] (bl) 4-8-7 (4*) A P Colgan (3)
..................................(20 to 1) 9
2484[7] ST AIDAN (Ire) [-] 5-7-13 (4*) D A O'Sullivan (8).... (10 to 1) su

Dist: 1½l, ½l, 4l, ¾l. 2m 19.10s. (10 Ran).
(Mrs C Collins), C Collins

2666 Fort E.B.F. Maiden (2-y-o) £3,107 6f ....(7:30)

1924[3] SOPHIE'S PET (Ire) 8-11 J F Egan (6)............. (4 to 1) 1
2487[2] ROYAL THIMBLE (Ire) 8-11 A J Nolan (10)....(7 to 2 jt-fav) 2
2188[5] INSUPERABLE (Ire) 8-11 N G McCullagh (2)..(7 to 2 jt-fav) 3
1643[3] BRUGATTI (Ire) 8-11 J P Murtagh (11)..............(6 to 1) 4
2294[7] PETER'S POWER (Ire) (bl) 9-0 P V Gilson (7)...... (12 to 1) 5
BUTLER BRENNAN (Ire) 9-0 W J Supple (5)........ (10 to 1) 6
2294[9] BLACKROCK HERO (Ire) 9-0 B Coogan (4)....... (14 to 1) 7
FRISKY MISS (Ire) 8-11 D Hogan (13)............(20 to 1) 8
305[8] ASTRO REEF (Ire) 8-4 (10*) A P Colgan (12).......(20 to 1) 9
2284 SOUND MAN JIMACK (Ire) (bl) 9-0 P Shanahan (1) (12 to 1) 10
2402[8] LOVELY DEISE (Ire) 8-11 R Hughes (9)........... (10 to 1) 11
2294 COOLAGOWN DOME (Ire) 8-5 (6*) J J Behan (3).. (20 to 1) 12

Dist: 4l, 2l, hd, ½l. (Time not taken) (12 Ran).
(Mrs C Grassick), M J Grassick

2667 Corrib Claiming Race (3-y-o and up) £2,245 6f...................... (8:00)

2184 JUNORIUS (Ire) 4-8-8 S Craine (5)................(7 to 1) 1
2321[6] YONOKA (Fr) (bl) 4-8-2 N G McCullagh (2).........(7 to 1) 2
2285[5] ARROGANT LADY (bl) 3-6-13 (8*) J J Mullins (4) (9 to 2 jt-fav) 3
705[2] ELLE A TED (Ire) 3-7-9 (2*) D G O'Shea (8)...........(6 to 1) 4
2285 PEARL DAWN (Ire) 3-7-3 (8*) R T Fitzpatrick (9)... (16 to 1) 5
1822[5] MYRO BALANNE (Ire) 3-7-7 (4*) W J Smith (7).... (16 to 1) 6
258 TEGEMEZA (Ire) 3-8-1 (2*) R M Burke (13)..........(5 to 1) 7
2514[6] FASTAFLOW (Ire) (bl) 3-8-1 W J Supple (11).. (9 to 2 jt-fav) 8
1649 DAIRINE'S DELIGHT (Ire) 3-7-13 J F Egan (12).... (20 to 1) 9
2511[6] SORRECA (Ire) 4-7-7 (6*) P P Murphy (1).......... (20 to 1) 10
2285 PERSIAN RENDEZVOUS (Ire) 3-7-4 (6*) J J Behan (10)
..................................(6 to 1) 11
1294[9] SILVER SHARP (Ire) 3-7-10 Joanna Morgan (6).... (10 to 1) 12

Dist: Hd, 2l, ¾l, ¾l. 1m 16.00s. (12 Ran).
(Mrs G Hourigan), G T Hourigan

WINDSOR (good) Monday July 19th

Going Correction: MINUS 0.20 sec. per fur. (races 1,4), PLUS 0.10 (2,3,5,6)

2668 Burning Bush Selling Stakes Class G (2-y-o) £1,702 5f 217yds.........(6:20)

2331[4] LEAP OF FAITH (Ire) (v) 8-11 W R Swinburn (7) *made virtually all, shaken up and styd on ins fnl furlong.*
.... (2 to 1 fav op 9 to 4 tchd 5 to 2 and 7 to 4) 1
2417[6] NOT FOR JOE 8-11 W Newnes (9) *gd prog on outsd 2 fs out, styd on one pace ins fnl furlong.*
..................................(20 to 1 op 16 to 1) 2
2377[4] MIGHTY KINGDOM (Ire) (bl) 8-6 B Rouse (2) *pressed ldr, ev ch o'r one furlong out, not quicken ins fnl furlong.*
..................................(8 to 1 tchd 10 to 1) 3
1933[6] LITTLE HOOLIGAN 8-11 C Rutter (1) *jnd ldrs hfwy, rdn and no extr one furlong out.*
.....................(16 to 1 op 20 to 1 tchd 12 to 1) 4
2119[4] NORTHERN STARLIGHT 8-11 N Adams (12) *wl in tch, one pace fnl 2 fs*.......................(20 to 1 op 12 to 1) 5
2377[5] CHARISMA GIRL (v) 7-13 (7*) A Martinez (3) *trkd frnt rnk, rdn and not quicken o'r one furlong out.*
..................................(33 to 1 op 16 to 1) 6
2493[2] CA IRA (Ire) 8-6 J Williams (8) *wl plcd for o'r 4 fs.*
.... (13 to 2 op 7 to 1 tchd 5 to 1) 7
PAGODA 8-6 A Munro (15) *chsd ldrs, wknd o'r one furlong out*......................(14 to 1 op 8 to 1) 8
BIRD OF THE WIND 8-6 W Ryan (4) *outpcd.*
..................................(16 to 1 op 14 to 1) 9
2137[8] DAVIDS DIAMOND 8-6 N Day (6) *al rear grp.*
..................................(33 to 1 op 20 to 1) 10
1798[9] CELESTIAL DANCE 8-6 G Carter (11) *sn pushed alng in rear, nvr on terms*.............(12 to 1 op 10 to 1) 11
2417[3] HENRY'S LUCK 8-11 S Whitworth (16) *slwly into strd, al beh*.................................. (5 to 1 op 5 to 2) 12
2042[7] EXPRESS LINE (bl) 8-3 (3*) B Doyle (13) *cl up for o'r 3 fs, wknd quickly*............................... (33 to 1) 13
2271 CHELSEA LADY (Ire) 8-6 Dale Gibson (10) *nvr rch frnt rnk.*
..................................(33 to 1 op 20 to 1) 14
715 FAST BEAT 8-6 A McGlone (5) *ldg grp til lost pl frm 2 out.*
..................................(33 to 1 op 20 to 1) 15
2316[6] SISTER SUSAN 8-6 Pat Eddery (14) *squeezed out at strt, sn tld off*..............(5 to 1 op 4 to 1 tchd 11 to 2) 16

Dist: ¾l, 1½l, 3½l, nk, 5l, 4l, ½l, 3l, 1½l, 4l. 1m 13.10s. a 2.80s (16 Ran).
SR: 17/14/3/-/-/-/ (R M Stevenson), D R Loder

2669 Windsor Handicap Class E (0-70 3-y-o and up) £2,700 1m 3f 135yds.... (6:45)

2523* PISTOLS AT DAWN (USA) [61] 3-8-8 (5ex) Pat Eddery (5) *prog o'r 2 fs out, str run to ld last 25 yards.*
..................................(9 to 2 op 6 to 1) 1
2111* MAHRAJAN [57] 9-9-2 T Quinn (9) *gd prog 3 fs out, led o'r one out, hdd last 25 yards, rallied und pres.*
.... (4 to 1 fav op 7 to 2 tchd 9 to 2 and 5 to 1) 2
2386[4] THEMEDA [43] 4-8-2 Dale Gibson (7) *trkd ldrs, and kpt on one pace last 2 fs*................ (16 to 1 tchd 14 to 1) 3
2101* FULL QUIVER [43] (v) 8-7-11 (5*) D Wright (13) *in tch, gd hdwy o'r 2 fs out, edgd slightly lft and not quicken over one out*.............(10 to 1 tchd 12 to 1 and 9 to 1) 4

2149^{3} EDGE OF DARKNESS [54] 4-8-10 (3*) D Harrison (2) *wl plcd, one appr fnl furlong*.............. (10 to 1 op 8 to 1) 5
415^{4} SPANISH REFUGE [56] 3-8-3 A Munro (17) *handily plcd, kpt on one pace frm 2 fs out*....... (16 to 1 op 14 to 1) 6
2272^{3} BROUGHTONS FORMULA [57] 3-7-13 (5*) D McCabe (20) *hld up, styd on last 2 fs, nvr nrr*... (12 to 1 op 10 to 1) 7
1872^{5} PRECUSSION [56] 3-8-3 R Price (4) *mid-div, ran on to ld 4 fs out, hdd and no extr o'r one out*........... (20 to 1) 8
2152^{4} INCOLA [54] 7-8-6 (7*) Antoinette Armes (16) *mid-div most of way*................................ (11 to 2 op 7 to 1) 9
2474^{3} TIGER CLAW (USA) [47] 7-8-6 M Hills (14) *wl plcd til wknd o'r 3 fs out*.......... (9 to 1 op 8 to 1 tchd 10 to 1) 10
2111^{4} ATHAR (Ire) [63] 4-9-8 J Williams (3) *effrt 4 fs out, no extr ins last 2 furlongs*............... (14 to 1 tchd 16 to 1) 11
2615^{4} BOXBOY [51] 3-7-12 J Quinn (6) *nvr trble frnt rnk*. .... (33 to 1 op 20 to 1) 12
1143 EVERY ONE A GEM [43] 6-8-2 N Adams (1) *nvr nr ldrs*. .... (33 to 1) 13
1951^{8} VITAL CLUE (USA) [69] 6-10-0 D Biggs (19) *in tch til wknd o'r 3 fs out*....................... (33 to 1 op 25 to 1) 14
1704^{4} CALIBRATE [61] 3-8-8 W Newnes (18) *chsd ldr till wknd o'r 3 fs out*...................... (20 to 1 op 16 to 1) 15
1929 CORINTHIAN GOD (Ire) [35] 4-7-8 G Bardwell (15) *rdn alng and drpd rear frm hfwy*............ (16 to 1 op 14 to 1) 16
2195^{6} THRESHFIELD (USA) [50] 7-8-9 W Ryan (11) *cl up til lost pl o'r 3 fs out*. (7 to 1 op 5 to 1 tchd 8 to 1 and 10 to 1) 17
OOZLEM (Ire) [58] 4-9-3 B Rouse (12) *nvr dngrs*. .... (25 to 1 op 16 to 1) 18
975 STAR MINSTREL (Ire) [56] 3-8-3^{1} A Clark (8) *cld on ldrs hfwy, wknd 2 out*.................. (33 to 1 op 25 to 1) 19
2415 BIJOU FIRE (NZ) [39] 5-7-12 A McGlone (10) *led til hdd and wknd 4 fs out*................................ (33 to 1) 20

Dist: Nk, 1½l, 1½l, nk, nk, sht-hd, ½l, nk, ½l, 1½l. 2m 30.10s. a 7.10s (20 Ran).

SR: 35/42/25/22/32/21/21/19/28/ (G Howard-Spink), R Hannon

2670 Iron Blue Claiming Stakes Class F (3-y-o and up) £1,828 1m 67yds.... (7:10)

2329^{4} MERLINS WISH (USA) 4-9-4 Pat Eddery (16) *trkd ldrs, led o'r 2 fs out, rdn clr, not extended ins fnl furlong*. .... (3 to 1 op 5 to 2 tchd 7 to 2) 1
2113^{7} VANROY (v) 9-9-0 S Whitworth (9) *prog 3 fs out, styd on one pace appr fnl furlong*. .... (7 to 1 op 4 to 1 tchd 8 to 1) 2
2367^{4} WELL APPOINTED (Ire) (v) 4-9-4 R Cochrane (10) *handily plcd, ev ch o'r 2 fs out, not quicken over one out*. .... (8 to 1 op 6 to 1) 3
1912^{8} FIABA 5-8-5 J Quinn (11) *wl plcd, no extr appr fnl furlong* .... (14 to 1 op 20 to 1) 4
1035^{5} CHAFF 6-8-4^{2} (5*) C Hodgson (1) *trkd ldrs, outpcd frm 2 fs out*................................ (33 to 1) 5
2270 NORTHERN RAINBOW 5-9-0 Dale Gibson (4) *mid-div, effrt o'r 2 fs out, no imprsn on ldrs fnl furlong*. .... (14 to 1 op 12 to 1) 6
2127 EMERALD EARS 4-8-2 T Sprake (21) *pld hrd, styd on last 2 fs, nvr nrr*.......... (16 to 1 op 14 to 1 tchd 20 to 1) 7
ELTARA 3-8-7 A Munro (15) *prog frm rear last 2 fs*. .... (20 to 1 op 16 to 1) 8
2350^{6} CLASS ATTRACTION (USA) 4-8-9 M Perrett (5) *ldg grp til wknd 2 fs out*. ....(7 to 1 op 8 to 1 tchd 10 to 1 and 6 to 1) 9
2217^{6} ROCKY BAY 4-8-5 J Williams (2) *led aftr 3 fs, hdd and wknd o'r 2 out*................................ (20 to 1) 10
AMY COME HOME 3-8-7 G Carter (17) *slwly into strd, nvr better than mid-div*............ (33 to 1 op 25 to 1) 11
2471 MABTHUL (USA) (v) 5-8-8 W Ryan (14) *nvr better than fnl placing*................................ (33 to 1) 12
155^{6} MASRUR (USA) 4-9-2 A Clark (20) *nvr rch chalg pos*. .... (33 to 1) 13
2471 CANBRACK (Ire) 4-8-10 R Price (7) *chsd ldrs for o'r 5 fs*. .... (33 to 1) 14
2328^{4} DEVILRY (bl) 3-8-11 Paul Eddery (8) *mid-div, hrd rdn 3 fs out, sn btn*.......... (9 to 4 fav op 5 to 2 tchd 2 to 1) 15
1954 PRECIOUS WONDER 4-8-9 (7*) S Drowne (19) *in tch til rdn and no prog frm 3 out*............ (16 to 1 op 14 to 1) 16
2351^{5} CASTLE-VIEW 3-8-3 D Holland (13) *al towards rear*. .... (33 to 1) 17
2351^{6} GREAT PLOVER 3-8-2 F Norton (3) *al beh*........ (33 to 1) 18
2109 MAN OF THE SEASON (USA) 4-8-9 T Quinn (18) *chsd ldrs to hfwy*.......................... (14 to 1 op 10 to 1) 19
2011 SELECTABLE 3-7-10 N Adams (12) *al beh, tld off*. (33 to 1) 20
SHROPSHIRE BLUE 3-7-9^{1} S Dawson (6) *led for 3 fs, wknd o'r three out, tld off*. (16 to 1 op 14 to 1 tchd 20 to 1) 21

Dist: 2½l, 4l, ¾l, ¾l, 1l, ¾l, hd, 6l, 1½l, 1½l. 1m 46.50s. a 5.50s (21 Ran).

SR: 34/22/14/-/-/3/ (J A Lazzari), R Hannon

2671 Thames Handicap Class D (0-80 3-y-o and up) £3,785 5f 217yds........ (7:40)

2255^{4} FASCINATION WALTZ [71] 6-9-6 G Carter (7) *hld up, str brst to ld appr fnl furlong, quickened clr*. .... (11 to 2 op 5 to 1 tchd 6 to 1) 1
2524^{4} SEA-DEER [59] 4-8-8 A Munro (1) *wl plcd, slight advantage 2 fs out, hdd o'r one out, kpt on same pace*. ....(13 to 2 op 6 to 1 tchd 7 to 1 and 8 to 1) 2
2494^{4} HARRY'S COMING [57] 9-8-6 M Hills (3) *mid-div, ran on appr fnl furlong, styd on nr finish*. .... (6 to 1 tchd 7 to 1 and 8 to 1) 3
2327^{3} FACE THE FUTURE [61] 4-8-10 W R Swinburn (8) *trkd ldrs, rdn and not quicken o'r one furlong out*. .... (4 to 1 fav tchd 9 to 2) 4
2418 AL MOULOUKI [77] 3-9-6 R Cochrane (2) *hld up beh, ran on fnl furlong, nrst finish*. .... (12 to 1 op 10 to 1 tchd 14 to 1) 5
2008^{5} BOLD MEMORY [78] 4-9-13 Pat Eddery (9) *ldg grp, ev ch o'r 2 fs out, outpcd over one out*. .... (6 to 1 op 5 to 1 tchd 13 to 2) 6
2524^{6} SPECTACLE JIM [44] 4-7-7 N Adams (11) *pressed ldrs, ev ch o'r 2 fs out, fdd*................ (20 to 1 op 16 to 1) 7
2008^{6} COPPERMILL LAD [44] 10-7-0 (7*) Iona Wands (12) *outpcd most of way*...................... (14 to 1 tchd 16 to 1) 8
1918^{4} ACARA (Ire) [48] (bl) 4-7-11 J Quinn (10) *led for o'r 3 fs, no extr*................. (10 to 1 op 8 to 1 tchd 11 to 1) 9
2418 ROYAL DEED (USA) [73] 3-9-2 R Perham (4) *wl plcd, led o'r 2 fs out, sn hdd, wknd fnl furlong*. (50 to 1 op 33 to 1) 10
RAINBOW FLEET [58] 5-8-7 Paul Eddery (5) *rear most of way*............... (25 to 1 op 20 to 1 tchd 33 to 1) 11
1957 FIVESEVENFIVEO [74] 5-9-2 (7*) S Drowne (13) *mid-div, rdn and no prog frm 2 fs out*............ (10 to 1 op 8 to 1) 12
2050^{6} SHADES OF JADE [44] 5-7-7 G Bardwell (6) *effrt frm rear hfwy, sn btn*................ (20 to 1 tchd 25 to 1) 13

Dist: 2½l, hd, 3l, 2l, hd, nk, 1½l, nk, hd, 4l. 1m 11.80s. a 1.50s (13 Ran).

SR: 52/30/27/19/21/27/ (Fred A Havercroft), D Shaw

2672 Eton Limited Stakes Class D (0-80 3-y-o) £3,980 1m 67yds............. (8:10)

2522* FOURFORFUN 9-0 B Raymond (5) *settled in 3rd pl, sstnd run frm 2 fs out, led nr line*. ....(9 to 4 op 7 to 4 tchd 5 to 2) 1
2138* THE EXECUTOR 9-0 J Reid (7) *chsd ldr, led and edgd lft und pres one furlong out, hdd last strds*. ....(2 to 1 fav op 9 to 4 tchd 5 to 2) 2
2293* SCORCHED AIR 8-9 M Hills (3) *led, quickened o'r 3 fs out, hdd one furlong out, ran one one pace*. .... (11 to 2 op 5 to 1 tchd 6 to 1) 3
1278* SUNTARA (Ire) 8-9 D Holland (1) *hld up beh, pushed alng o'r 2 fs out, styd on one pace fnl furlong*. ....(9 to 2 op 7 to 2 tchd 5 to 1) 4
1808 HADEER'S DANCE 9-0 R Price (6) *mid-div, pushed alng hfwy, wknd o'r 2 fs out*........... (14 to 1 op 10 to 1) 5
747^{7} NABJELSEDR 9-0 R Hills (2) *hld up in rear, shaken up and no imprsn on ldrs frm 2 fs out*. (20 to 1 op 12 to 1) 6
1808 ABERDEEN HEATHER 9-0 J Williams (4) *mid-div til rdn and wknd o'r 2 fs out*...........(12 to 1 tchd 14 to 1) 7

Dist: Sht-hd, 1½l, ½l, 5l, 7l, 1l. 1m 48.80s. a 7.80s (7 Ran).

(Mrs R F Knipe), R Hannon

2673 Agars Plough Handicap Class E (0-70 3-y-o and up) £2,784 1¼m 7yds (8:40)

2474* BENTICO [59] 4-9-3 (7ex) Pat Eddery (3) *made all, shaken up o'r 2 fs out, rdn and styd on fnl furlong*. ....(5 to 4 fav op 6 to 4 tchd 7 to 4) 1
2289^{3} SANTANA LADY (Ire) [56] 4-9-0 W Newnes (2) *chsd wnr most of way, rdn and not quicken frm 2 fs out*. .... (11 to 2 op 13 to 2 tchd 7 to 1) 2
1956^{5} CHANDIGARH [50] 5-8-8 R Cochrane (6) *beh til hdwy 3 fs out, nrst at line*...... (20 to 1 op 14 to 1 tchd 25 to 1) 3
2471^{6} BROWN CARPET [35] (bl) 6-7-2 (5*) D Wright (8) *trkd ldrs, rdn and one pace frm 2 fs out*......(25 to 1 op 20 to 1) 4
2014^{4} HEART OF SPAIN [61] 3-8-9 W R Swinburn (15) *handily plcd, kpt on und pres last 2 fs*. ....(11 to 1 op 10 to 1 tchd 12 to 1 and 14 to 1) 5
2354^{4} AFFA [49] 4-8-7 S Whitworth (9) *effrt frm rear 3 fs out, styd on ins last 2 furlongs*. (12 to 1 op 8 to 1 tchd 14 to 1) 6
2328^{5} MOVE A MINUTE (USA) [67] 4-9-11 J Williams (4) *wl plcd, rdn and no extr frm 2 fs out*. .... (7 to 1 op 6 to 1 tchd 8 to 1 and 9 to 1) 7
2183^{4} CONCINNITY (USA) [50] 4-8-8 A Munro (1) *rcd in mid-div most of way, no hdwy last 3 fs*.....(25 to 1 op 14 to 1) 8
2291^{4} JOLTO [40] 4-7-12 J Quinn (11) *effrt frm rear o'r 3 fs out, wknd over 2 out*.................. (16 to 1 op 12 to 1) 9
2353 EIRAS MOOD [47] 4-8-5 A Clark (12) *mid-div, no prog frm 3 fs out*............................ (33 to 1 op 20 to 1) 10
402^{4} EL VOLADOR [65] 6-9-9 W Ryan (10) *hdwy frm rear appr hfwy, btn o'r 2 fs out*................ (9 to 1 op 7 to 1) 11
2012^{2} ROCK THE BARNEY (Ire) [53] 4-8-11 B Rouse (5) *effrt frm rear, o'r 3 fs out, no prog und pres last 2 furlongs*. .... (14 to 1 op 10 to 1 tchd 16 to 1) 12
4805a^{8} PIPERS REEL [54] 3-7-13 (3*) D Harrison (13) *stumbled leaving stalls, sn tracking ldrs, eased whn btn o'r 2 fs out*................ (20 to 1 op 14 to 1 tchd 25 to 1) 13
1114^{7} WOODMANS STAR [52] 3-8-0 F Norton (14) *al beh*. .... (66 to 1 op 50 to 1) 14
2371^{8} HALEIM [35] 6-7-7 N Adams (7) *beh whn broke foreleg and uns rdr o'r 2 fs out, destroyed*..... (66 to 1 op 50 to 1) ur

Dist: 1½l, 2l, nk, 1½l, 1l, 2l, 1½l, hd, nk, 1½l. 2m 10.80s. a 8.30s (15 Ran).

SR: 30/24/14/-/11/7/21/1/-/ (Mark Christofi), M A Jarvis

BALLINROBE (IRE) (good)

Tuesday July 20th

2674 Bank Of Ireland Ballinrobe Maiden (3-y-o and up) £2,935 6f. . . . . (7:00)

2667^5 PEARL DAWN (Ire) 3-8-5 (6*) J J Behan (1) . . . .(16 to 1) 1
639^7 KILTIMONY 3-8-3 (8*) J J Mullins (6) . . . . (9 to 1) 2
2285^4 SCALP (Ire) 3-9-0 P V Gilson (7) . . . . (5 to 2) 3
RUNNING GREAT (Ire) 3-8-11 S Craine (5) . . . .(9 to 1) 4
2483^2 RETICENT BRIDE (Ire) (bl) 3-8-11 M J Kinane (9) (6 to 4 fav) 5
2184^4 ROUNDWOOD ROSE (Ire) 3-8-11 P Shanahan (8) . . (4 to 1) 6
OMESMACJOY (Ire) 3-9-0 N G McCullagh (4) . . . . .(33 to 1) 7
Dist: 2l, 2l, 1l, 5l. 1m 16.10s. (7 Ran).
(Mrs M Chance), Noel T Chance

2675 Mayo GAA Supporters 5000 Sweeps Handicap (0-75 3-y-o and up) £3,452 6f . . . .(7:30)

2323^2 LADY PRESIDENT (Ire) [-] (bl) 4-8-7 (6*) J J Behan (4) . . . .(11 to 10 fav) 1
1923^5 BOLD MOLLY (Ire) [-] 4-7-3 (6*) P P Murphy (2) . . . .(10 to 1) 2
1795^2 MUGNANO [-] 7-8-10 (6*) B J Walsh (3) . . . . (6 to 1) 3
2297^3 AULD STOCK (Ire) [-] (bl) 3-9-2 (6*) J R Barry (1) . . . (11 to 4) 4
2463^9 FOREST [-] 3-9-7 S Craine (5) . . . .(6 to 1) 5
705^6 SLEET (Ire) [-] 3-8-9 (8*) P M Donohue (6) . . . .(12 to 1) 6
Dist: 1½l, hd, 2l, 1l. 1m 15.90s. (6 Ran).
(Yoshiki Akazawa), Patrick Prendergast

2676 Bernard And Tommy Joyce Memorial Maiden (3-y-o and up) £2,935 1¾m . . . .(8:00)

1997^2 DAYADAN (Ire) 3-9-0 M J Kinane (8) . . . . (6 to 4 on) 1
1467^7 CAMDEN BUZZ (Ire) 5-9-5 (6*) T P Treacy (6) . . . .(5 to 2) 2
SACULORE (Ire) 5-10-0 N G McCullagh (1) . . . . (16 to 1) 3
2249 GARDENVALE VIC (Ire) 3-9-0 S Craine (2) . . . . (16 to 1) 4
2460^6 RED GLITTER (USA) 3-8-8 (6*) J J Behan (5) . . . . (12 to 1) 5
982^7 HAIL TO HOME (Ire) 3-8-5 (6*) P P Murphy (4) . . . . .(33 to 1) 6
MRS RUMPOLE (Ire) 4-9-5 (6*) B Bowens (3) . . . .(7 to 1) 7
488 TANHONEY (Ire) 3-8-11 P Shanahan (7) . . . . (40 to 1) 8
Dist: Hd, 15l, 11l, 7l. 3m 15.70s. (8 Ran).
(H H Aga Khan), John M Oxx

2677 Lough Mask Handicap (0-75 3-y-o) £2,245 1¼m. . . . . (8:30)

2286^3 HOPESVILLE (Ire) [-] 8-12 (6*) B J Walsh (11) . . . .(5 to 1) 1
1334^5 VINEY (USA) [-] (bl) 9-7 M J Kinane (3) . . . .(5 to 1) 2
1963^4 DALKEY ISLAND (Ire) [-] 8-13 (6*) J J Behan (9) . . . . .(9 to 1) 3
TERN DANCER (Ire) [-] (bl) 8-7 N G McCullagh (2) (20 to 1) 4
1995 TAJARIB (Ire) [-] (bl) 7-13 (8*) G Coogan (8) . . . . (33 to 1) 5
2249 SIMPLE DANCER (Ire) [-] 7-4 (6*) P P Murphy (10) . . (4 to 1) 6
2321^9 WESTERN FRONTIER (Ire) [-] 7-12 Joanna Morgan (1) . . . .(25 to 1) 7
2287 CARAVELLE LAD (Ire) [-] 8-8 P V Gilson (5) . . . . (14 to 1) 8
1649 CLANFLUTHER (Ire) [-] 8-0 (2*) D G O'Shea (4) . . . . (25 to 1) 9
1995^3 BRIGENSER (Ire) [-] (bl) 8-13 P Shanahan (6) . . . (7 to 4 fav) 10
KILDERRY (Ire) [-] 7-9^2 A J Nolan (7) . . . . (33 to 1) 11
Dist: 4l, nk, 1½l, hd. 2m 18.70s. (11 Ran).
(Mrs J M Ryan), A P O'Brien

EDINBURGH (good)
Tuesday July 20th
Going Correction: MINUS 0.10 sec. per fur. (races 1,2,3,4,6), MINUS 0.25 (5)

2678 Musselburgh Links Apprentice Handicap Class G (0-70 4-y-o and up) £2,232 1½m 31yds. (2:00)

2367^3 COMMON COUNCIL [57] (v) 4-9-1 J Marshall (7) *made all, hrd pressed entering fnl furlong, hld on wl.* . . . . (15 to 2 op 6 to 1 tchd 8 to 1) 1
2353^3 NOT YET [36] 9-7-8^1 M Humphries (5) *prmnt, dsptd ld entering fnl furlong, no extr towards finish.* . . . .(8 to 1 op 7 to 1) 2
BATABANOO [66] 4-9-5 (5*) C Teague (2) *hld up, hdwy o'r 3 fs out, rdn 2 out, swtchd and ran on wl fnl furlong.* . . . .(3 to 1 fav op 5 to 2) 3
2565^2 RAPID MOVER [36] (bl) 6-7-8 N Varley (8) *chsd ldr, chlgd entering fnl furlong, wknd towards finish.* . . . .(9 to 2 op 4 to 1 tchd 5 to 1) 4
2506^4 DUGGAN [43] 6-8-1 Claire Balding (4) *trkd ldrs, effrt 3 fs out, sn rdn, kpt on same pace.* . . . . .(4 to 1 tchd 9 to 2) 5
2162* SEA PADDY [52] 5-8-10 H Bastiman (1) *hld up, effrt 3 fs out, sn hrd rdn, kpt on same pace.* . . . .(100 to 30 op 3 to 1 tchd 7 to 2) 6
78 BORING (USA) [59] 4-9-3^1 (7*) J Williams (6) *in tch till wknd 4 fs out, tld off.* . . . . (33 to 1 tchd 50 to 1) 7
PUBLIC APPEAL [70] 4-9-9 (5*) P Roberts (3) *chsd ldrs till wknd 3 fs out, tld off.* . . . .(100 to 1 op 66 to 1) 8
Dist: Sht-hd, 1½l, hd, 2l, 1½l, 15l, 2½l. 2m 42.10s. a 9.30s (8 Ran).
SR: -/-/1/-/-/ (Mrs E E Newbould), M D Hammond

2679 Braids Claiming Stakes Class F (2-y-o) £2,200 7f 15yds. . . . . (2:30)

2505^5 JUST BILL 8-9 S Webster (1) *chsd ldr, rdn to ld jst ins fnl furlong, kpt on wl.* . . . . .(7 to 2 tchd 4 to 1 and 9 to 2) 1
2569^6 MOKAITE 8-9 (7*) J Marshall (2) *led till jst ins fnl furlong, rdn and no extr.* . . . .(9 to 4 fav op 7 to 4) 2
2453^3 WINGS AHEAD 8-8 (5*) O Pears (6) *hld up, hdwy 2 fs out, ran on fnl furlong, nrst finish.* . . . .(9 to 2 op 5 to 1 tchd 6 to 1) 3
2588^7 OLYMPIC BID 9-2 J Carroll (7) *in tch, effrt o'r 3 fs out, sn rdn, kpt on same pace.* . . . . (8 to 1 tchd 9 to 1 and 10 to 1) 4
2465^4 HILL FARM DANCER 8-8 K Darley (5) *in tch till wknd o'r 2 fs out.* . . . . (4 to 1 op 7 to 2 tchd 9 to 2) 5
1895 ASTROLOGY 8-4 Kim Tinkler (4) *beh hfwy.* . . . . (25 to 1 op 33 to 1) 6
1773^9 DEAR MADAM 9-2 J Fortune (3) *chsd ldrs till wknd o'r 2 fs out.* . . . . (33 to 1 op 25 to 1) 7
Dist: 2l, 1½l, 1½l, 6l, 1½l, 1½l. 1m 29.30s. a 4.10s (7 Ran).
SR: 23/24/16/14/ (W H Turner), J Etherington

2680 Gullane Handicap Class D (0-80 3-y-o and up) £3,062 1m 16yds. . . . . . . (3:00)

2459^3 ROUTING [49] 5-8-1 (7*) J Marshall (4) *slwly into strd, sn tracking ldrs, stumbled o'r 3 fs out, soon led, styd on wl fnl furlong.* . . . .(4 to 1 op 7 to 2) 1
2269^4 LAWNSWOOD JUNIOR [66] 6-9-11 K Darley (5) *hld up, hdwy 3 fs out, chsd wnr fnl 2 furlongs, rdn entering final furlong, no imprsn.* . . . .(11 to 4 fav op 3 to 1 tchd 5 to 2) 2
2639^2 CELESTINE [59] (v) 4-9-4 J Fanning (3) *slight ld till hdd o'r 3 fs out, remained cl up, one pace fnl 2 furlongs.* . . . . (8 to 1 op 6 to 1 tchd 9 to 1 and 10 to 1) 3
2283^5 MEDIA MESSENGER [55] 4-9-0 K Fallon (6) *in tch, effrt 3 fs out, kpt on same pace.* . . . . (16 to 1 op 10 to 1) 4
2220^2 KEYWAY (USA) [77] 3-10-0 G Duffield (2) *wth ldr till hfwy, one pace fnl 3 fs, eased whn btn ins last.* . . . .(7 to 2 op 3 to 1) 5
2088^4 BOLD MELODY [44] 4-8-3 J Carroll (1) *in tch, rdn 3 fs out, sn btn.* . . . . (7 to 2 tchd 4 to 1) 6
Dist: 1l, 1½l, 1½l, 2½l, ½l. 1m 42.00s. a 3.50s (6 Ran).
SR: 30/44/32/23/29/2/ (Mrs M A Doohan), M D Hammond

2681 Luftness Rating Related Maiden Fillies' Stakes Class E (0-70 3-y-o) £2,795 1m 16yds. . . . .(3:30)

1587^5 SINGER ON THE ROOF (v) 8-11 K Darley (3) *trkd ldr, led o'r 3 fs out, sn clr, easily.* (7 to 2 on op 4 to 1 on tchd 3 to 1 on and 10 to 3 on) 1
1852^4 RUNRIG (Ire) 8-11 J Fanning (2) *in tch, chsd wnr 3 fs out, no imprsn.* . . . .(7 to 2 tchd 3 to 1 and 4 to 1) 2
1191^8 GOLDMIRE 8-11 K Fallon (1) *led till o'r 3 fs out, sn btn.* . . . . (14 to 1 op 10 to 1) 3
Dist: 10l, 6l. 1m 43.70s. a 5.20s (3 Ran).
SR: 7/-/-/ (J C Smith), I A Balding

2682 Vogrie Park Selling Handicap Class G (0-60 3-y-o and up) £2,242 5f. . . . (4:00)

2481^2 MISS SIHAM (Ire) [44] 4-8-10 (7*) Claire Balding (5) *led far side aftr 2 fs, all out.* . . . .(9 to 4 fav op 11 to 4 tchd 3 to 1) 1
2510^4 KABCAST [47] (bl) 8-9-6 S Wood (4) *led stands side, no extr cl hme.* . . . . (7 to 2 op 3 to 1 tchd 4 to 1) 2
2508^3 ANGELS ANSWER (Ire) [49] 4-9-8 K Darley (3) *chsd ldr stands side, kpt on fnl furlong.* . . . .(8 to 1 op 6 to 1 tchd 9 to 1) 3
2215^4 BARBEZIEUX [47] 6-8-13 (7*) V Halliday (10) *chsd ldrs, kpt on fnl furlong.* . . . .(8 to 1 op 7 to 1 tchd 9 to 1 and 10 to 1) 4
2456^5 LANGTONIAN [52] (bl) 4-9-8 (3*) Emma O'Gorman (8) *in tch, kpt on fnl furlong, not trble ldrs.* . . . . .(8 to 1 op 6 to 1) 5
1893^4 SELVOLE [36] 3-7-13 (5*) Darren Moffatt (2) *chsd ldrs till wknd 2 fs out.* . . . . (20 to 1 op 25 to 1 tchd 33 to 1) 6
2456^7 BRAVE MELODY [28] 7-8-1 Julie Bowker (6) *led far side for 2 fs, wknd two out.* . . . . (20 to 1 op 14 to 1) 7
2456^4 BRISAS [34] (v) 6-8-7 J Fanning (9) *chsd ldrs till wknd o'r one furlong out.* . . . .(6 to 1 tchd 7 to 1) 8
2445 PAULINUS [34] (v) 5-8-0 (7*) C Teague (7) *sn beh.* . . . . (66 to 1 op 50 to 1) 9
2445 NOT ALL BLISS [28] 5-7-11^3 (7*) C Munday (1) *beh hfwy.* . . . . (100 to 1 op 66 to 1) 10
Dist: Sht-hd, ½l, sht-hd, 2l, 2½l, hd, nk, 3l, nk. 1m 0.30s. a 2.50s (10 Ran).
SR: 28/30/30/27/24/-/ (Ardsley Racing), J Balding

2683 Muirfield Handicap Class E (0-70 3-y-o and up) £2,832 1m 7f 16yds. . . . . (4:30)

2397^5 HUNTING GROUND [39] (bl) 5-9-1 A Mackay (9) *in tch, led 2 fs out, sn clr.* . . . .(8 to 1 tchd 10 to 1) 1
2251^8 BRIGGSMAID [52] 5-10-0 M Tebbutt (7) *hld up, steady hdwy to chal 2 fs out, sn rdn and one pace.* . . . .(6 to 1 op 5 to 1) 2

2455^{5} ALPHA HELIX [28] (v) 10-8-4 J Fanning (8) *beh, hdwy o'r 3 fs out, kpt on same pace fnl 2 furlongs.* ....(9 to 1 op 7 to 1 tchd 10 to 1) 3
2565^{4} NATIVE CROWN (Ire) [40] 5-9-2 N Connorton (2) *trkd ldrs, led 3 fs out till 2 out, one pace*..........(14 to 1) 4
2368^{4} BRIDGE PLAYER [35] 6-8-6 (5*) Darren Moffatt (3) *chsd ldrs, one pace 2 fs out*..........(11 to 2 op 9 to 2 tchd 6 to 1) 5
2467^{6} MINGUS (USA) [45] 6-9-7 K Fallon (5) *nvr nr ldrs.* ....(10 to 1 op 8 to 1 tchd 11 to 1) 6
SEXY MOVER [30] 6-8-6 S Webster (6) *led till hfwy, grad lost pl*..........(33 to 1 op 16 to 1) 7
2275^{8} FATAL SHOCK [50] 3-8-11 J Lowe (10) *trkd ldrs, drvn alng 7 fs out, wknd o'r 3 out.* ....(7 to 1 op 6 to 1 tchd 8 to 1 and 9 to 1) 8
2306^{4} TRONCHETTO (Ire) [52] 4-10-0 K Darley (1) *prmnt till wknd o'r 2 fs out*..........(25 to 1 op 16 to 1 tchd 33 to 1) 9
2495^{3} WESTRAY (Fr) [52] 3-8-13 G Duffield (4) *cl up, led hfwy till 3 fs out, sn wknd*..........(6 to 4 fav op 5 to 2) 10
Dist: 8l, 2½l, 1l, 1½l, nk, 4l, 1½l, 3½l, 10l. 3m 23.60s. a 11.60s (10 Ran).
(Esprit de Corps Racing), A Bailey

FOLKESTONE (good to firm)
Tuesday July 20th
Going Correction: NIL (races 1,2), MINUS 0.15 (3,4,5,6)

2684 Bridge Selling Handicap Class G (0-60 3-y-o and up) £2,595 1m 1f 149yds ....(1:45)

2471^{3} BONDAID [39] 9-9-0 R Price (7) *rcd in 3rd, led wl o'r 2 fs out, sn clr*..........(13 to 2 op 10 to 1 tchd 6 to 1) 1
2288 BUCKSKI ECHO [40] 3-8-5 R Perham (12) *ldg grp, outpcd last 2 fs*..........(25 to 1 op 20 to 1 tchd 33 to 1) 2
2520^{2} WAAZA (USA) [49] (bl) 4-9-7 (3*) D Harrison (4) *cld on ldrs o'r 3 fs out, not quicken 2 out*..........(6 to 1 op 9 to 2) 3
2490^{4} NORTHERN CONQUEROR (Ire) [48] 5-9-9 D Holland (10) *mid-div, styd on one pace 2 fs out*....(8 to 1 op 7 to 1) 4
4707a MEDBOURNE (Ire) [32] 4-8-0 (7*) P McCabe (6) *led aftr one furlong till wl o'r 2 out, no extr*....(33 to 1 op 25 to 1) 5
2127^{4} MISS MAGENTA (Ire) [23] 5-7-5 (7*) C Hawksley (8) *styd on last 2 fs, not rch ldrs.* (12 to 1 op 10 to 1 tchd 14 to 1) 6
2520^{6} LER CRU (Ire) [48] 4-9-9 T Williams (1) *beh, effrt 3 fs out, no imprsn*..........(5 to 1 op 3 to 1) 7
2213^{5} OMIDJOY (Ire) [54] 3-9-5 W Woods (11) *nvr nr to chal.* ....(5 to 1 op 6 to 1 tchd 7 to 1) 8
2471* BRONZE RUNNER [37] (bl) 9-8-12 (5ex) T Sprake (3) *in tch till outpcd last 3 fs*...(9 to 2 fav op 7 to 2 tchd 5 to 1) 9
2384^{4} MASTER BEVELED [50] (v) 3-8-10 (5*) C Hodgson (9) *led one furlong, chsd ldr till wknd o'r 2 fs out.* ....(12 to 1 op 8 to 1) 10
2384* GREEN'S STUBBS [30] (v) 6-8-5 N Carlisle (5) *strted slwly, al beh*..........(10 to 1) 11
1913 JULY BRIDE [52] 3-9-3 B Rouse (2) *al beh.* ....(9 to 1 op 6 to 1 tchd 10 to 1) 12
Dist: 7l, nk, 3½l, 1½l, 1½l, hd, 4l, 5l, 1½l, 4l. 2m 4.80s. a 7.20s (12 Ran).
SR: 28/5/23/15/-/-/ (A J Allright), J White

2685 Storagetek Disk Maker Challenge Cup Fillies' Handicap Class E (0-70 3-y-o and up) £3,366 1½m..........(2:15)

1993^{2} BOBBYSOXER [64] 3-9-3 Pat Eddery (2) *handily plcd, led 5 fs out, rdn clr o'r one out, styd on*... (9 to 2 op 7 to 2) 1
2448* JOLIS ABSENT [40] 3-7-7 (4ex) G Bardwell (4) *prmnt till lost pl hfwy, ran on frm rear o'r one furlong out, fnshd strly*..........(100 to 30 fav op 9 to 4 tchd 4 to 1) 2
1321 PRINCESS ERMYN [43] 4-8-8 A Clark (3) *chsd ldr to hfwy, rdn o'r 3 fs out, kpt on one pace over one out.* ....(16 to 1 op 20 to 1 tchd 25 to 1) 3
879^{6} GILBERT'S GIRL [34] 6-7-13 J Quinn (6) *in tch, cld 3 fs out, not quicken appr last*... (7 to 1 op 6 to 1 tchd 9 to 1) 4
1746 MISS MICHELLE [47] 3-8-0^{2} T Sprake (8) *cld on ldrs 3 fs out, rdn and no hdwy o'r one out.* ....(33 to 1 op 20 to 1 tchd 40 to 1) 5
2126^{3} ROCQUAINE BAY [39] 6-8-4 C Rutter (7) *styd on one pace appr fnl furlong, no ch wth wnr*.....(9 to 2 op 4 to 1) 6
2315^{4} LAMU LADY (Ire) [70] 3-9-9 J Reid (9) *ldg grp till wknd wl o'r one furlong out*..........(5 to 1 op 5 to 2) 7
2474 TORGHIA [60] 6-9-11 Dale Gibson (1) *sn tracking ldrs, rdn and lost pl ins last 2 fs*..........(33 to 1 op 12 to 1) 8
2544^{7} LUCKY NOIRE [45] 5-8-10 M Perrett (5) *outpcd till effrt o'r 2 fs out, no imprsn*..........(20 to 1 op 8 to 1) 9
2014^{5} CHOUETTE [52] 3-8-5 W Newnes (10) *led 7 fs, drpd out quickly, tld off*..........(20 to 1 op 12 to 1) 10
Dist: 1½l, 4l, ¾l, 1½l, ½l, 1½l, ½l, 4l, 20l. 2m 40.80s. a 10.30s (10 Ran).
(P G Goulandris), J L Dunlop

2686 Godfrey Evans Rating Related Maiden Stakes Class E (0-70 3-y-o and up) £3,054 6f..........(2:45)

2329^{5} SYLVAN BREEZE (v) 5-9-3 W Newnes (2) *edgd rght strt, made all, pushed alng 2 fs out, styd on ins last.* ....(6 to 1 op 10 to 1) 1
2466^{2} ISLAND KNIGHT (Ire) 4-9-3 P Robinson (1) *hld up, cld on ldrs o'r one furlong out, not quicken ins last.* ....(9 to 2 op 7 to 2 tchd 5 to 1) 2
1914^{6} VILLAVINA 3-7-13 (7*) A Martinez (10) *jnd ldrs hfwy, ev ch wl o'r one furlong out, styd on same pace.* ....(6 to 1 op 4 to 1) 3
2212 KELLY MAC 3-8-11 Paul Eddery (4) *pressed ldrs, rdn and no extr appr fnl furlong.* ....(100 to 30 op 5 to 2 tchd 7 to 2) 4
2381^{5} SECRET ASSIGNMENT (USA) (bl) 3-8-11 D Biggs (6) *in tch for o'r 4 fs, ran on one pace.* ....(16 to 1 op 8 to 1 tchd 20 to 1) 5
2121 HALBERT 4-9-3 J Reid (7) *wl plcd till wknd o'r one furlong out*..........(10 to 1 op 7 to 1 tchd 12 to 1) 6
2378^{7} PRINCESS JESSICA 6-8-7 (5*) D McCabe (3) *outpcd.* ....(33 to 1 op 16 to 1) 7
2231^{3} SCENT OF POWER 3-8-11 Pat Eddery (8) *prmnt for o'r 3 fs, sn wknd*..........(5 to 2 fav op 7 to 2 tchd 9 to 2) 8
2445 ALMOSTAUTOMATIC (Ire) 4-9-3 G Bardwell (9) *speed to hfwy, wknd quickly and lost tch.* (33 to 1 op 20 to 1) 9
Dist: ¾l, 1½l, 1½l, ¾l, 2l, 3½l, 3l, 8l. 1m 14.20s. a 3.20s (9 Ran).
SR: 21/18/1/-/-/-/ (Mrs R A Johnson), P Mitchell

2687 Brickhouse Maiden Auction Stakes Class F (2-y-o) £2,243 6f..........(3:15)

2417^{2} BLURRED IMAGE (Ire) 9-0 Pat Eddery (1) *hld up, led 2 fs out, edgd rght o'r one out, pushed out.* ....(6 to 4 on tchd 7 to 4 on and 11 to 8 on) 1
CINNAMON SPRINGS (Ire) 8-9 P Robinson (4) *beh, rdn alng o'r 2 fs out, styd on one pace ins last.* ....(12 to 1 op 5 to 1) 2
2385^{4} GIGUE 8-9 Paul Eddery (7) *pressed ldrs, ev ch 2 fs out, outpcd fnl furlong.* ....(4 to 1 op 5 to 1 tchd 6 to 1 and 7 to 2) 3
2049^{9} HARLEQUIN WALK (Ire) 8-9 G Bardwell (3) *pushed alng hfwy, nvr trble frnt rnk*..........(50 to 1 op 25 to 1) 4
2114^{8} SCREWBALL ANACONDA 9-0 W Newnes (6) *cld on ldrs hfwy, ev ch 2 fs out, wknd o'r one out.* ....(33 to 1 op 25 to 1 tchd 50 to 1) 5
2325 WINGS OF HORAGE (Ire) 9-0 R Cochrane (2) *led 4 fs, sn btn.* ....(7 to 1 op 8 to 1 tchd 12 to 1) 6
COUPLES 8-9 B Rouse (5) *lost tch hfwy, tld off.* ....(12 to 1 op 6 to 1) 7
Dist: 2l, 3½l, nk, 5l, ¾l, 20l. 1m 15.00s. a 4.00s (7 Ran).
SR: 2/-/-/-/ (N Ahamad), R Hannon

2688 Leslie Ames Memorial Handicap Class E (0-70 3-y-o and up) £3,002 5f ....(3:45)

2549^{2} BATCHWORTH BOUND [45] 4-8-8 C Rutter (2) *hld up, swtchd rght and ran on 2 fs out, led o'r one out, pushed out, cleverly*..........(13 to 8 fav op 5 to 4 tchd 7 to 4) 1
1566 SPLASH OF SALT (Ire) [65] 3-9-9 D Holland (6) *hld up, rdn alng o'r 2 fs out, not much room over one out, styd on.* ....(11 to 1 op 7 to 1 tchd 12 to 1) 2
2504* THE ORDINARY GIRL (Ire) [57] (v) 3-9-1 (5ex) J Reid (3) *led till o'r one furlong out, ran on same pace.* ....(13 to 2 op 9 to 2 tchd 7 to 1) 3
1267 GOODY FOUR SHOES [52] 5-8-8 (7*) B Russell (5) *in tch on outsd, effrt o'r one furlong out, not quicken ins last.* ....(3 to 1 op 7 to 2 tchd 4 to 1) 4
1373 CONISTON LAKE (Ire) [58] 4-9-7 B Rouse (1) *outpcd most of way*..........(25 to 1 op 12 to 1) 5
2524^{8} TRIOMING [61] 7-9-10 Pat Eddery (4) *pressed ldr, ev ch 2 fs out, wknd and eased o'r one out.* ....(4 to 1 tchd 7 to 2 and 9 to 2) 6
Dist: 1½l, sht-hd, nk, 7l, 10l. 1m 0.90s. a 2.30s (6 Ran).
SR: 33/42/33/32/10/-/ (Mrs Diana Price), S Mellor

2689 Ruckinge Nursery Class E (2-y-o) £2,950 5f..........(4:15)

1446^{8} PRINCE AZZAAN (Ire) [-] 9-6 Pat Eddery (7) *hld up, ran on 2 fs out, led o'r one out, quickened clr, easily.* ....(5 to 4 on op Evens tchd 5 to 4) 1
2325^{7} BOLD GEM [-] 9-2 B Raymond (2) *hld up rear, ran on und pres wl o'r one furlong out, no imprsn on wnr fnl furlong*..........(11 to 2 op 4 to 1 tchd 7 to 1) 2
1391^{2} RISKIE THINGS [-] 8-1 (7*) Mark Denaro (3) *wth ldr, slight ld 2 fs out till hdd and outpcd o'r one out.* ....(11 to 2 op 4 to 1) 3
1742^{5} MADAME GREGOIRE [-] 8-11 (5*) J Tate (4) *led to 2 fs out, outpcd o'r one out*..........(14 to 1 op 10 to 1) 4
1959^{5} RISKY AFFAIR [-] (bl) 8-4 Paul Eddery (5) *cl up, ev ch 2 fs out, no extr*..........(7 to 1 tchd 15 to 2) 5
1905 SUPER SYMPHONIC [-] (v) 9-7 P Robinson (8) *rcd centre, al outpcd*..........(25 to 1 op 10 to 1 tchd 33 to 1) 6
2412 EUROCHEM LAD (Ire) [-] (bl) 9-4 B Rouse (6) *prmnt centre till wknd 2 fs out, eased.* ....(25 to 1 op 12 to 1 tchd 33 to 1) 7
Dist: 2½l, 3l, 5l, 2½l, 1½l, hd. 1m 1.20s. a 2.60s (7 Ran).
SR: 39/25/5/-/ (K Al-Said), N A Callaghan

ST-CLOUD (FR) (good)

Tuesday July 20th
Going Correction: PLUS 0.10 sec. per fur.

2690 **Prix Minerve (Group 3) (3-y-o) £23,895 1½m.......................... (3:00)**

1722⁵ BRIGHT MOON (USA) (bl) 8-9 T Jarnet (2) *5th strt, rdn 2 fs out, rapid prog ins last, led on line*........ (10 to 7 on) 1
2080² ADORED SLEW (USA) 8-9 A Cruz (3) *second strt, rdn to ld 2 fs out, hrd ridden ins last, ct on line*........... (7 to 1) 2
2054³ BRIGHT MOUNTAIN (USA) 8-9 D Boeuf (1) *4th strt, effrt 2 fs out, one pace fnl furlong*.................... (10 to 7 on) 3
RIVE (USA) 8-9 C Asmussen (4) *last strt, some hdwy fnl furlong, nvr plcd to chal*...................... (11 to 2) 4
1222³ ZAFFERA (USA) 8-9 G Mosse (6) *led till hdd and wknd 2 fs out*.. (53 to 10) 5
KINDERGARTEN 9-0 S Guillot (5) *3rd strt, effrt and ev ch 2 fs out, wknd one and a half out*............ (31 to 10) 6
Dist: Sht-hd, 2½l, 2l, ½l, ½l. 2m 35.60s. a 5.60s (6 Ran).
SR: 51/50/45/41/40/44/ (Daniel Wildenstein), A Fabre

WEXFORD (IRE) (good)
Tuesday July 20th

2691 **Tuskar House Maiden (3-y-o and up) £2,762 1½m 170yds............ (7:00)**

1335⁴ ERZADJAN (Ire) 3-9-0 J P Murtagh (8).......... (5 to 4 on) 1
2249⁸ NURSES RUN (Ire) 3-8-11 J F Egan (1)............(16 to 1) 2
2460³ NORDIC THORN (Ire) 3-9-0 K J Manning (7)....... (7 to 2) 3
ROYAL ANTELOPE (Fr) 3-8-11 D Hogan (5).......(13 to 2) 4
1997 PARTICULAR (Ire) 3-8-10 (4*) W J Smith (4)........(16 to 1) 5
2285⁷ MAJESTIC PADDY (Ire) 3-8-10 (4*) P Carberry (6)..(20 to 1) 6
VERIFIED (Ire) 3-8-11 R Hughes (3)................ (8 to 1) 7
1963⁷ ROLANDS GIRL (Ire) 3-8-11 R J Supple (9)....... (33 to 1) 8
SAGE PRINCE (Ire) 3-8-8 (6*) J A Heffernan (2)....(20 to 1) 9
Dist: 4l, sht-hd, 4l, ½l. 2m 53.60s. (9 Ran).
(H H Aga Khan), John M Oxx

2692 **Equip Handicap (0-65 3-y-o and up) £2,762 1½m 170yds............ (7:30)**

2221² ASSERT STAR [-] 3-8-13 J P Murtagh,..........(9 to 4 fav) 1
2321⁷ RASSETTE (Ire) [-] 3-8-11 K J Manning (6).......... (9 to 1) 2
1987⁹ BENGALI (Ire) [-] 3-7-13 W J Supple (9)............ (12 to 1) 3
MORNING NURSE (Ire) [-] 4-9-7 T Horgan (10)..... (20 to 1) 4
NORTHMAID (Ire) [-] (bl) 4-9-7 (6*) J A Heffernan (8) (16 to 1) 5
2345⁷ LAST EMPEROR (USA) [-] 6-9-1 (10*) A P Colgan (13) .... (14 to 1) 6
1996 TOAST AND HONEY (Ire) [-] 4-10-3 (6*) C Everard (3) .... (16 to 1) 7
1962 KOI CORP [-] 9-7-12 (2*) R M Burke (7)............(20 to 1) 8
2513⁵ MISS DARCY (Ire) [-] 5-9-5 (4*) P Carberry (15).....(10 to 1) 9
2249 LIMAHEIGHTS (Ire) [-] 3-8-7 (8*) P J Smullen (11)....(9 to 1) 10
1987² DIAMOND CLUSTER [-] (bl) 3-7-8 (8*) R T Fitzpatrick (1) .... (6 to 1) 11
2484⁵ REGAL PRETENDER (Ire) [-] 3-7-9¹ (6*) R V Skelly (4) (8 to 1) 12
2094⁹ KINVARA LADY (Ire) [-] 4-7-7 L O'Shea (12)........(20 to 1) 13
2484² WINTER DREAMS (Ire) [-] 4-9-3 R Hughes (5)....... (7 to 1) 14
2322⁹ BLUEJACKET (Ire) [-] 5-8-3 J F Egan (2)...........(12 to 1) 15
Dist: 2½l, nk, 2l, 6l. 2m 45.90s. (15 Ran).
(Ms M Hogan), A P O'Brien

2693 **Gorey Q.R. Handicap (0-65 3-y-o and up) £2,245 2m..................(8:00)**

309⁸ PAGET [-] 6-10-9 (7*) Mr A K Wyse (3)..........(6 to 4 fav) 1
1987 GREEK CHIME (Ire) [-] 4-11-6 (3*) Mr D Marnane (4) (12 to 1) 2
1987 RIYADH DANCER (Ire) [-] 3-9-11 (7*) Mr E Norris (7) (14 to 1) 3
2143⁹ CEDAR COURT (Ire) [-] 5-11-11 (7*) Mr G O'Leary (12) .... (10 to 1) 4
298⁷ MARIAN YEAR [-] 7-9-13 (7*) Mr P A Roche (5).....(14 to 1) 5
2498⁶ SIR ALFRED (USA) [-] 8-9-11 (7*) Mr T Murphy (6) (20 to 1) 6
2296⁸ SWEET DOWNS [-] 12-10-1 (5*) Mr D McGoona (8) (25 to 1) 7
1986² SHAYISTA [-] 8-11-13 (3*) Mr R O'Neill (10)......... (5 to 1) 8
2498⁸ SERJITAK [-] 6-11-1 (3*) Mrs S McCarthy (13)....... (6 to 1) 9
2287 RYE HILL QUEEN (Ire) [-] 3-9-11 (7*) Mr G R Ryan (2) .... (16 to 1) 10
2557³ GO DEAS [-] 6-10-1 (7*) Miss F M Crowley (9)....... (7 to 1) 11
2498 SWIFT PAL [-] 8-9-13² (7*) Mr R J Foley (1)..........(6 to 1) su
790 ONODI (Ire) [-] 3-9-11 (7*) Mr M Hyland (11).........(33 to 1) pu
Dist: Hd, 1l, nk, 6l. 3m 44.20s. (13 Ran).
(A P Wyse), A Redmond

DONCASTER (good)
Wednesday July 21st
Going Correction: MINUS 0.15 sec. per fur. (races 1,3,4), MINUS 0.25 (2,5,6)

2694 **Vaux Samson Selling Stakes Class F (3,4,5-y-o) £2,758 1½m......... (2:30)**

2536² POST IMPRESSIONIST (Ire) 4-9-2 L Dettori (4) *pressed ldr, led o'r 3 fs out, clr 2 out, jnd over one out, ran on gmely*. ....(5 to 2 tchd 11 to 4) 1
2307³ ANN HILL (Ire) 3-8-8 W Ryan (6) *steadied strt, patiently rdn, hdwy entering strt, swtchd o'r 3 fs out, level over one out, jst hld*.................. (2 to 1 fav op 7 to 4) 2
1662⁵ RAVENSPUR (Ire) 3-8-9 M Roberts (7) *pressed ldrs, pushed alng o'r 6 fs out, effrt and rdn 3 out, not quicken 2 out*. .... (7 to 2 op 11 to 4 tchd 4 to 1) 3
2178⁹ BAJAN AFFAIR 3-8-4 Dean McKeown (3) *trkd ldrs, rdn alng o'r 3 fs out, hng lft over 2 out, sn btn*. .... (20 to 1 op 16 to 1) 4
2104⁸ BATTUTA 4-8-11 (5*) D Wright (9) *led till o'r 3 fs out, sn rdn alng, wknd 2 out*..........................(9 to 1 op 16 to 1) 5
1979⁶ RESTLESS MINSTREL (USA) (v) 4-9-7 J Quinn (8) *in tch, drvn alng o'r 2 fs out, sn btn*. .... (12 to 1 op 10 to 1 tchd 14 to 1) 6
2366⁸ SIMPLY SUPERB 3-8-9 T Lucas (1) *hld up, rdn to improve 3 fs out, not pace to chal*........... (33 to 1 op 20 to 1) 7
MANULIFE 4-9-7 A Clark (2) *hld up, drvn alng o'r 3 fs out, fdd*.............................. (20 to 1 op 16 to 1) 8
1305⁹ TEN HIGH (Ire) 4-9-2 N Connorton (10) *hld up rear, drpd away and eased o'r 2 fs out*....... (33 to 1 op 25 to 1) 9
769⁶ GHYLLDALE (v) 5-8-13 (7*) H Bastiman (5) *nvr far away, pushed alng hfwy, wknd entering strt, sn lost tch, eased*.............(16 to 1 op 14 to 1 tchd 20 to 1) 10
Dist: Hd, 8l, 1½l, 1½l, 10l, ½l, 1l, 20l, 2½l. 2m 35.76s. a 5.26s (10 Ran).
SR: 31/22/7/-/8/-/ (David Cahal), J L Harris

2695 **Tattersalls Maiden Auction Series Fillies Stakes Qualifier Class D (2-y-o) £3,377 7f...................... (3:00)**

2546² HEVER GOLF ROSE 8-5 Paul Eddery (11) *made virtually all, shaken up 2 fs out, ran on wl fnl furlong*. ....(3 to 1 tchd 7 to 2) 1
TASHLA 8-7 L Dettori (12) *pressed ldrs on ins, squeezed through o'r one furlong out, ev ch fnl furlong, no extr nr finish*............... (9 to 2 op 5 to 2 tchd 5 to 1) 2
1660⁷ ROSE CIEL (Ire) 8-3 M Roberts (5) *beh, drvn aftr 2 fs, improved two out, kpt on ins last, nvr dngrs*. .... (12 to 1 op 8 to 1) 3
MUMTAZ FLYPAST 8-8 M Birch (2) *beh, weaved through 2 fs out, kpt on ins last, improve*.... (14 to 1 op 10 to 1) 4
2595⁴ BALLARD RING (Ire) 8-3 N Connorton (7) *in tch, effrt and not clr run o'r one furlong out, not quicken ins last*. .... (20 to 1 op 16 to 1) 5
1758² GLENVALLY 8-3 J Fortune (1) *trkd ldrs on outsd, rdn fnl 2 fs, one pace*..........(12 to 1 op 14 to 1 tchd 10 to 1) 6
RED DANCER 8-5 (3*) M Fenton (3) *dwlt, beh, effrt on outsd o'r 2 fs out, one pace over one out*. .... (10 to 1 op 8 to 1) 7
1556⁷ TAUFELIANE 8-4 Dean McKeown (4) *wth ldrs, rdn o'r 2 fs out, wknd*.............................. (33 to 1 op 20 to 1) 8
1944² INDIAHRA 8-6 K Darley (9) *pressed ldrs, effrt and shaken up o'r 2 fs out, no imprsn whn not much room wl ins last*................ (9 to 4 fav op 5 to 2 tchd 7 to 2) 9
812⁹ YO (Ire) 8-9 W R Swinburn (8) *wth ldrs, rdn o'r 2 fs out, bumped over one out, sn btn*. .... (11 to 1 op 10 to 1 tchd 16 to 1) 10
2502⁵ FABULOUS PRINCESS (Ire) 8-8 T Quinn (10) *tucked away beh ldrs, shaken up o'r 2 fs out, fdd*. ....(7 to 1 op 5 to 1 tchd 8 to 1) 11
2492⁹ MISS TEMERITY 8-5 N Adams (6) *bumped strt, beh and sn rdn, nvr on terms*................ (33 to 1 op 20 to 1) 12
Dist: ½l, 1½l, 1l, 4l, ½l, ½l, 1½l, 1l, hd, hd. 1m 27.66s. a 4.26s (12 Ran).
SR: 1/1/-/-/-/-/ (R A Popely), T J Naughton

2696 **Wards Sheffield Best Bitter Handicap Class D (0-85 3-y-o and up) £4,542 1 ¼m 60yds.................... (3:30)**

2266* SHIRLEY ROSE [62] 3-8-5 Dean McKeown (5) *led, shaken up o'r 2 fs out, hmpd over one out, ran on gmely ins last*................................(13 to 2 op 6 to 1) 1
2267* LATVIAN [70] 6-9-6 (3*) J Weaver (8) *trkd ldrs, rdn o'r 3 fs out, outpcd over 2 out, improved fnl furlong, kpt on wl nr finish*..............(6 to 1 op 5 to 1 tchd 13 to 2) 2
2398⁵ BEAUMAN [67] (bl) 3-8-10 T Quinn (2) *keen hold, al hndy, effrt fnl 2 fs, ev ch ins last, no extr nr finish*. .... (10 to 1 op 12 to 1) 3
1800⁵ SUPERTOP [63] 5-9-2 Paul Eddery (7) *in tch, outpcd o'r 2 fs out, sn rdn alng, ran on ins last, nvr dngrs*. .... (11 to 2 op 5 to 1) 4
2551* BEST APPEARANCE (Ire) [64] (bl) 3-8-7 (4ex) K Fallon (9) *slwly into strd, hld up, rdn alng 4 fs out, imprvg whn swtchd rght ins last, kpt on nr finish*. ....(6 to 1 op 5 to 1) 5
2300 SELF EXPRESSION [60] 5-8-13 M Roberts (4) *hld up rear, pushed alng to improve 3 fs out, one pace ins last*. ....(7 to 2 fav op 5 to 1 tchd 11 to 2) 6
2458² AZUREUS (Ire) [75] 5-10-0 K Darley (6) *hld up in tch, improved o'r 2 fs out, ev ch over one out, not quicken ins last*............... (13 to 2 op 6 to 1 tchd 7 to 1) 7
2181⁴ MOVE SMARTLY (Ire) [57] 3-8-0 P Robinson (1) *tucked away on ins, shaken up whn not much room fnl 2 fs, wknd last 100 yards*............................ (16 to 1) 8

2107[2] DUPLICATE [67] 3-8-10 M Birch (10) *hld up, pushed alng entering strt, btn o'r 2 fs out*........(8 to 1 op 7 to 1) 9
ROBENKO (USA) [72] 4-9-11 L Dettori (3) *nvr far away, rdn alng 3 fs out, wknd wl o'r one out, eased.* ....(20 to 1 op 14 to 1) 10
Dist: ¾l, sht-hd, 1½l, ½l, 1l, sht-hd, ¾l, 6l, 1½l. 2m 14.84s. a 8.14s (10 Ran).
SR: -/10/-/-/-/-/7/-/-/ (Greenland Park Ltd), M Johnston

2697 'In Honour Of Country Life Inns' Fillies' Handicap Class D (0-85 3-y-o) £4,077 1m.................... (4:00)

2361 EAST LIBERTY (USA) [80] 9-7 L Dettori (3) *trkd ldrs gng wl, not clr run and swtchd o'r 2 fs out, hng lft and led appr last, ran on well*..........(13 to 2 op 6 to 1) 1
1482[3] SEROTINA (Ire) [65] 8-6 T Quinn (4) *hld up rear, swtchd 3 fs out, hdwy and hng lft o'r one out, ev ch fnl furlong, one pace last 50 yards*......................(9 to 2 jt-fav op 5 to 1 tchd 11 to 2) 2
2401* CROIRE (Ire) [75] 9-2 Paul Eddery (2) *nvr far away, squeezed through ins to ld o'r 2 fs out, hdd appr last, no extr*..............................(5 to 1 tchd 11 to 2) 3
1931[4] FROSTY MORNING [70] 8-11 M Roberts (1) *led till o'r 2 fs out, kpt on same pace appr last.* ....(13 to 2 op 6 to 1 tchd 7 to 1) 4
1312[9] SPRING SUNRISE [61] 8-2 F Norton (11) *sn beh, swtchd ins 3 fs out, kpt on fnl furlong, nvr dngrs.* ....(14 to 1 op 12 to 1) 5
1670[3] DON'T JUMP (Ire) [75] 9-2 P Robinson (9) *nvr far away, effrt and rdn o'r 2 fs out, wknd wl over one out.* ....(6 to 1 tchd 13 to 2) 6
1801[9] ROYAL DIVA [64] 8-5 N Connorton (5) *mid-div, not much room 3 fs out, no imprsn frm 2 out.* (25 to 1 op 20 to 1) 7
2401[2] CITY TIMES (Ire) [60] (bl) 8-1 K Darley (6) *tucked away beh ldrs, not clr run and swtchd o'r 2 fs out, nvr able to chal*..........................(9 to 2 jt-fav op 4 to 1) 8
2333 SPICE AND SUGAR [66] 8-7 J Carroll (8) *trkd ldrs on outsd, pushed alng 4 fs out, btn o'r 2 out.* (10 to 1 op 8 to 1) 9
683 KENNEDYS PRIMA [70] 8-11 J Fortune (7) *trkd ldrs, rdn o'r 3 fs out, wknd 2 out*..............(20 to 1 op 16 to 1) 10
Dist: ¾l, 2l, 5l, ½l, 1l, 3l, 1½l, ¾l, 2½l. 1m 40.18s. a 3.48s (10 Ran).
SR: 37/20/24/4/-/4/ (Paul Mellon), I A Balding

2698 Baxi Solo Conditions Stakes Class D (3-y-o and up) £3,523 6f.........(4:30)

1231[4] SIWAAYIB 3-8-6[1] W R Swinburn (3) *dwlt, hld up, effrt on outsd 2 fs out, ran on to ld ins last, kpt on wl.* ....(6 to 1 tchd 13 to 2) 1
REALITIES (USA) 3-8-8 W Carson (7) *pressed ldr, led o'r 2 fs out, sn rdn, hdd ins last, kpt on same pace.* ....(7 to 4 fav op 3 to 1) 2
2329* KNOCK TO ENTER (USA) 5-9-2 J Williams (6) *pressed ldrs, effrt and rdn 2 fs out, one pace ins last.* ....(4 to 1 tchd 9 to 2) 3
2574[4] BRIGG FAIR 3-9-2 R Perham (5) *handily plcd, improved and ev ch fnl 2 fs, rdn and no extr ins last.* ....(2 to 1 op 5 to 4) 4
HICKORY BLUE 3-8-3 (5*) O Pears (2) *keen hold, trkd ldrs, outpcd o'r 2 fs out, kpt on ins last, nvr dngrs.* ....(25 to 1 op 20 to 1) 5
2231[5] CALAMANCO 3-8-4[1] S Webster (1) *led, shaken up hfwy, hdd o'r 2 fs out, not quicken*.......(33 to 1 op 25 to 1) 6
Dist: Nk, ½l, 2l, 2l, ¾l. 1m 13.89s. a 2.49s (6 Ran).
SR: 12/13/19/11/-/-/ (Maktoum Al Maktoum), A A Scott

2699 Marcrist Diamond Handicap Class E (0-70 3-y-o) £3,002 5f........... (5:00)

2214[6] CHARITY EXPRESS (Ire) [62] 9-3 D Biggs (5) *tucked away beh ldrs, effrt o'r one furlong out, sstnd run fnl furlong to ld nr finish*.....................(12 to 1 op 10 to 1) 1
2504[3] CLOUDY REEF [49] 7-11 (7*) M Humphries (9) *pressed ldrs, improved to ld o'r one furlong out, hdd and no extr nr finish*.................................(7 to 1 op 6 to 1) 2
2424[2] SURAGON [60] 9-1 J Williams (2) *beh, not clr run o'r 2 fs out, kpt on ins last, broke leg aftr line, destroyed.* ....(14 to 1 op 12 to 1) 3
2001[7] PRIMULA BAIRN [66] 9-7 K Fallon (6) *handily plcd, rdn hfwy, ev ch 2 fs out, not quicken ins last.* ....(8 to 1 tchd 10 to 1) 4
2456[2] TREVORSNINEPOINTS [60] (v) 9-1 J Fortune (11) *nvr far away, ev ch and rdn hfwy, kpt on same pace appr last.* ....(5 to 2 fav op 3 to 1) 5
1966[8] LIDA'S DELIGHT (Ire) [60] 9-1 T Lucas (8) *led till o'r one furlong out, not quicken*.......... (12 to 1 op 8 to 1) 6
1762[7] FORDALLIA [38] 7-7 J Quinn (3) *beh, shaken up 2 fs out, kpt on ins last, nvr dngrs*..........................(33 to 1) 7
2132* THE FED [64] (v) 9-2 (3*) S Maloney (1) *in tch on outsd, effrt and rdn hfwy, btn and eased o'r one furlong out.* ....(15 to 2 op 7 to 1 tchd 6 to 1 and 8 to 1) 8
2312[7] DISCO BOY [57] 8-12 T Quinn (4) *frnt rnk, rdn hfwy, wknd and eased o'r one furlong out.* ....(14 to 1 op 12 to 1) 9
1744 VISIMOTION (USA) [63] 9-4 W R Swinburn (10) *prmnt stands rail, rdn alng o'r 2 fs out, sn btn.* ....(8 to 1 op 6 to 1) 10
Dist: Nk, 2½l, hd, ¾l, ½l, nk, 3½l, 2l, 2l. 1m 0.90s. a 2.10s (10 Ran).
SR: 36/22/23/28/19/17/-/6/-/ (C G Davey), D J S Cosgrove

NAAS (IRE) (good to yielding) Wednesday July 21st

Going Correction: PLUS 0.30 sec. per fur.

2700 Abbey Street EBF Maiden (3-y-o and up) £3,452 5f.................. (5:30)

1105 MISS ANITA (Ire) (bl) 3-8-8 R Hughes (10).........(10 to 1) 1
2497[4] SOUTHERN REVIEW (Ire) (bl) 3-8-11 W J Supple (6) (6 to 1) 2
2285 NORDIC GLARE (Ire) 3-8-4[1] (8*) T E Durcan (9)....(10 to 1) 3
RIFLEBIRD (Ire) 3-8-8 P Shanahan (2).............(8 to 1) 4
2497[2] PETOFI (bl) 3-8-11 M J Kinane (1).............(6 to 4 fav) 5
BLACKTRENCH LADY (Ire) 5-8-13 J P Murtagh (8) (9 to 4) 6
BOSSY PATRICIA (Ire) 3-8-8 D V Smith (4).........(14 to 1) 7
1164 I'M NO LADY (Ire) 3-8-8 N Byrne (7).............(50 to 1) 8
2184 DOZING WIZZ (Ire) 3-8-6 (2*) R M Burke (3).......(50 to 1) 9
2285 CARNAZAR (Ire) 3-8-0[2] (10*) K M Byrne (5).......(14 to 1) 10
Dist: 1½l, 1½l, ¾l, 2½l. 1m 2.00s. a 4.00s (10 Ran).
SR: 44/41/35/29/22/-/ (Mrs Marion Hendron), Edward Lynam

2701 Jasmine EBF Maiden (2-y-o) £3,797 7f ....(6:00)

2462[4] BACK FROM HEAVEN (Ire) 8-11 C Roche (8)......(13 to 2) 1
2319[2] QUASIMODO (Ire) (bl) 9-0 R Hughes (7)...........(10 to 1) 2
2486[2] UNBUCKLE (Ire) 9-0 M J Kinane (17)..........(9 to 4 fav) 3
1824[3] BEAUCHAMP IMPERIAL 9-0 P Shanahan (2)..... (11 to 2) 4
869[2] SEE YOU (Ire) 9-0 W J Supple (5).................(5 to 1) 5
1650[3] METROELLA (Ire) 8-11 J P Murtagh (1)..............(9 to 1) 6
2244[6] PRINCESS SHERA (Ire) 8-5 (6*) J A Heffernan (18)..(7 to 1) 7
2344[4] MALT LEAF (Ire) 8-11 K J Manning (6)............(16 to 1) 8
LEO'S FRIEND (Ire) 9-0 M G Cleary (13)...........(50 to 1) 9
896 I HAVE A DREAM (Ire) 9-0 D V Smith,............(16 to 1) 10
2462[6] MAIN REFRAIN (Ire) 9-0 J F Egan (16)..............(14 to 1) 11
HABBI (Ire) 8-11 S Craine (10)...................(16 to 1) 12
ZARA ZAREEN (Ire) 9-0 N G McCullagh (14)...... (33 to 1) 13
INNOVATIVE (Ire) 9-0 D Hogan (3).................(20 to 1) 14
1854 NANCYS WOOD (Ire) 8-5 (6*) J J Behan (9)........ (25 to 1) 15
CAIRNBRAE (Ire) 8-6 (8*) T J Daly (12)............(12 to 1) 16
INCHINTAGGART 9-0 P V Gilson (11)...............(12 to 1) 17
SEAPARK LADY (Ire) 8-9 (2*) R M Burke (4).......(25 to 1) 18
Dist: 2½l, ¾l, 2l, 2½l. 1m 28.50s. a 5.90s (18 Ran).
SR: 40/35/33/27/19/-/ (Benners Hotel Syndicate), J S Bolger

2702 Mary Street Fillies Handicap (0-85 3-y-o and up) £2,762 1¼m.......... (7:00)

2092[2] MADANIYYA (USA) [-] 3-9-3 (6*) C Everard (6)...... (6 to 1) 1
2036* SOVIET CHOICE (Ire) [-] 3-9-10 M J Kinane (4)..... (3 to 1) 2
2461[4] LYPHARD ABU (Ire) [-] (bl) 5-9-3 (8*) M W Martin (2) (10 to 1) 3
2485[2] NURSE MAID (Ire) [-] 3-8-3 (2*) D G O'Shea (12) (11 to 4 fav) 4
1294* LA CENERENTOLA (Ire) [-] 3-8-13 (4*) P Carberry (9) (6 to 1) 5
2406[6] NORDIC UNION (Ire) [-] 3-8-13 C Roche (3)..........(10 to 1) 6
2140[5] TEBRE (USA) [-] (bl) 3-8-12 W J Supple (8)....... (14 to 1) 7
1997[7] HAANEM [-] 3-8-2 (6*) B J Walsh (11)............ (14 to 1) 8
2186[3] BOBADIL (Ire) [-] 3-7-11 (8*) P J Smullen (5).........(8 to 1) 9
2078[9] TINA'S CHARM (Ire) [-] 4-9-3 (4*) W J Smith (10)...(33 to 1) 10
1995 KENTUCKY BABY (Ire) [-] (bl) 3-8-7[1] S Craine (1)..(12 to 1) 11
Dist: 1l, ½l, 4½l, hd. 2m 14.10s. a 10.10s (11 Ran).
SR: 38/37/37/8/19/-/ (H H Aga Khan), John M Oxx

2703 Athgoe Apprentice Race (3-y-o and up) £2,762 1m..................(7:30)

BRATA (USA) 3-8-1 (6*) D J O'Donohoe (1).........(7 to 1) 1
1200 ADOLESCENCE (Ire) 3-8-7 R M Burke (11).... (10 to 9 on) 2
2483[4] MARKIEVICZ (Ire) 3-8-1 (6*) G M Moylan (5)...... (10 to 1) 3
2451[2] MISS CARMELLA (Ire) 3-8-3 (4*) B J Walsh (3)..... (6 to 1) 4
2497* SUEKAR (Ire) 3-9-0 D G O'Shea (6)...............(5 to 1) 5
2320[2] STATE PRINCESS (Ire) 3-8-3 (4*) P P Murphy (4)...(14 to 1) 6
SUTTONIAN (Ire) 4-8-7 (8*) J J Byrne (8)..........(14 to 1) 7
2513[4] ICEFLOW (Fr) 3-7-13 (8*) D J Casey (10)............(12 to 1) 8
2609[8] BETTER GOODS (Ire) 3-8-3 (4*) J A Heffernan (7)..(16 to 1) 9
1793[3] TORC MOUNTAIN (Ire) 3-8-6 (4*) R V Skelly (2)....(12 to 1) 10
TEAK ROAD (Ire) 3-8-8 (2*) P Carberry (9)......... (33 to 1) 11
Dist: ½l, 1½l, ¾l, 3l. 1m 41.20s. a 5.40s (11 Ran).
SR: 48/46/41/39/37/-/ (Allen E Paulson), D K Weld

2704 Mile Mill Nursery (2-y-o) £2,762 6f ....(8:00)

2605[6] VIVA VICTOR (Ire) [-] 7-7[3] (6*) J J Behan (3)........(7 to 2) 1
2486* GIULIO ROMANO (Ire) [-] 7-13 (6*) J A Heffernan (1) (11 to 2) 2
2319* SUMMERHILL SPECIAL (Ire) [-] 8-3 (3ex) Joanna Morgan (4) ....(9 to 2) 3
1442* DILIGENT DODGER (Ire) [-] 8-4 W J Supple (6) (11 to 4 fav) 4
1924* BONNIE CRATHIE (Ire) [-] 8-1 (2*) R M Burke (2)..... (5 to 1) 5
2487[5] MY RAGAMUFFIN (Ire) [-] 8-3 N G McCullagh (7).. (10 to 1) 6
1608[3] GALLIC VICTORY (Ire) [-] 7-3 (6*) P P Murphy (5).. (12 to 1) 7
Dist: 2l, sht-hd, 2½l, 1l. 1m 14.00s. a 4.50s (7 Ran).
SR: 28/29/26/17/12/-/-/ (Marvin Malmuth), Liam Browne

REDCAR (good to firm)
Wednesday July 21st
Going Correction: MINUS 0.15 sec. per fur. (races 1,2,3,6), NIL (4,5)

2705 Macmillan Nurses Appeal Selling Stakes Class G (2-y-o) £1,553 7f (6:30)

2505 HIGHFIELD LAD 8-11 J Fanning (3) *in tch on outer, rdn and hdwy 2 fs out, styd on to ld entering fnl furlong, kpt on*..............(50 to 1 op 25 to 1) 1
2505³ BENEFICIARY 8-6 M Birch (9) *cl up, led aftr 2 fs, rdn wl o'r one furlong out, hdd and no extr entering last.*..............(5 to 2 tchd 11 to 4) 2
2446⁶ BRAMCOTE CENTURY 8-6 J Lowe (11) *hld up, hdwy o'r 2 fs out, rdn and ev ch appr last, sn one paced.*..............(20 to 1 op 16 to 1) 3
2492⁷ SHERIFF 8-11 R Hills (8) *in tch, hdwy hfwy, effrt to chal and ev ch o'r one furlong out, sn rdn and one paced.*..............(4 to 1 tchd 9 to 2) 4
2229³ OUT OF FAVOUR (Ire) 8-11 K Darley (1) *sn cl up, ev ch 2 fs out, soon rdn and btn.*..............(7 to 4 fav op 11 to 8 tchd 2 to 1) 5
2229⁷ SHARPISH WORDS (bl) 8-11 S Webster (5) *in tch, outpcd and lost pl hfwy, sn hrd rdn, styd on ins last.*..............(8 to 1 op 7 to 1 tchd 9 to 1) 6
2129⁶ STEANARD BOY 8-6 (5*) J Tate (6) *nvr rch ldrs.*..............(25 to 1 op 20 to 1) 7
2539 WESTCOAST 8-11 N Connorton (7) *cl up, rdn 2 and a half fs out, sn wknd*..............(50 to 1 op 33 to 1) 8
1814⁷ PARIS SYMPHONY (Ire) 8-11 J Carroll (4) *hld up, gd hdwy on outer 3 fs out, ev ch 2 out, sn rdn and wknd, eased ins last*..............(9 to 1 op 7 to 1) 9
2505 VAN DIEMEN'S LAD (Ire) 8-11 Dean McKeown (10) *al rear.*..............(50 to 1 op 33 to 1) 10
708 DUCHESS DAISY 8-6 Kim Tinkler (2) *led 2 fs, lost pl hfwy, sn wl beh*..............(50 to 1) 11
Dist: 1l, 1½l, 2l, 3½l, 1l, 3½l, hd, ¾l, 1l, 20l. 1m 27.70s. a 5.90s (11 Ran).
(Mrs P J Garthwaite), T Fairhurst

2706 Cheveley Park Stud Median Auction Maiden Stakes Class D (2-y-o) £3,200 6f.............................(6:55)

1844² TAGHAREED (USA) 8-9 R Hills (8) *made all, clr wl o'r one furlong out, easily.*..............(2 to 1 on op 7 to 4 on tchd 13 to 8 on) 1
2482² LUCKY MESSAGE (USA) 8-9 W Ryan (13) *chsd ldrs, rdn o'r 2 fs out, styd on ins last, no ch wth wnr.*..............(8 to 1 tchd 9 to 1) 2
2482³ JETHOU (Ire) 9-0 N Connorton (5) *cl up, rdn 2 fs out, sn one paced*..............(8 to 1 op 7 to 1 tchd 9 to 1) 3
SUSHI BAR (Ire) 9-0 K Darley (4) *mid-div till styd on fnl 2 fs, nrst finish*..............(33 to 1 op 20 to 1) 4
NORTHWISE (Ire) 8-9 Dean McKeown (7) *prmnt, rdn and one paced fnl 2 fs*..............(11 to 1 op 8 to 1) 5
2586⁶ OVALWORLD 9-0 S Wood (6) *chsd ldrs, rdn o'r 2 fs out, sn one paced*..............(100 to 1) 6+
1227 CURIE CRUSADER (Ire) 9-0 J Carroll (12) *al chasing ldrs, rdn 2 fs out, sn one paced*..............(50 to 1 op 33 to 1) 6+
2274⁶ SUSELJA (Ire) 8-9 J Fortune (17) *beh, rdn and hdwy 2 fs out, styd on ins last*..............(25 to 1) 8
PRIMUM TEMPUS 8-9 M Birch (1) *in tch, rdn o'r 2 fs out, sn wknd*..............(33 to 1 op 20 to 1) 9
830⁷ ANOTHER GOVERNOR 9-0 T Lucas (16) *nvr a factor.*..............(50 to 1 op 33 to 1) 10
2129 LOCHON 9-0 S Webster (9) *cl up, rdn hfwy, grad wknd.*..............(100 to 1 op 50 to 1) 11
TILLY OWL 8-4 (5*) O Pears (14) *chsd ldrs, rdn hfwy, sn wknd*..............(33 to 1 op 25 to 1) 12
2541⁴ DOUBLE SIXTEEN 9-0 K Fallon (10) *nvr rch ldrs.*..............(11 to 1 op 8 to 1) 13
SINBAD 9-0 J Lowe (11) *slwly away, al beh.*..............(100 to 1 op 50 to 1) 14
2446⁴ MERISSA 8-9 C Dwyer (15) *al rear*..............(33 to 1) 15
UNCLE DOUG 8-9 (5*) Darren Moffatt (3) *al rear, beh frm hfwy*..............(50 to 1) 16
Dist: 3½l, 1½l, 6l, 1l, hd, dd-ht, 1l, ¾l, 1½l, ½l. 1m 11.70s. a 2.00s (16 Ran).
SR: 37/23/22/-/-/-/ (Hamdan Al-Maktoum), H Thomson Jones

2707 Safeway Stakes Handicap Class E (0-70 3-y-o and up) £3,200 6f....(7:25)

2600⁵ BALLAD DANCER [60] 8-9-12 M Birch (2) *cl up, led o'r 3 fs out, quickened clr appr last, easily.*..............(100 to 30 op 3 to 1 tchd 7 to 2) 1
1891⁴ KILLY'S FILLY [55] 3-9-1 J Carroll (3) *cl up, rdn o'r 2 fs out, kpt on one pace*..............(7 to 2 op 3 to 1 tchd 4 to 1) 2
1782⁵ ROCK OPERA (Ire) [54] 5-9-6 K Fallon (6) *outpcd and beh, swtchd rght 2 fs out, styd on und pres ins last.*..............(5 to 1 op 4 to 1) 3
2594⁵ INVIGILATE [58] 4-9-10 K Darley (8) *dwlt, sn in tch, hdwy o'r 2 fs out, soon rdn and one pace.*..............(5 to 2 fav op 9 to 4) 4
1740⁶ LUCKY MILL [44] (bl) 3-8-4 R Lappin (7) *sn prmnt, rdn o'r 2 fs out, soon btn*..............(10 to 1 tchd 12 to 1) 5
2384 JOVIAL KATE (USA) [35] 6-8-1 S Wood (5) *led 2 and a half fs, sn rdn and wknd o'r two out*..............(33 to 1 op 25 to 1) 6
2553⁷ FILICAIA [46] 7-8-12 Kim Tinkler (1) *al rear.*..............(33 to 1 op 25 to 1) 7
1736⁵ CLEDESCHAMPS [44] 4-8-10 S Morris (4) *cl up, rdn o'r 2 fs out, sn wknd*..............(12 to 1 op 8 to 1 tchd 14 to 1) 8
Dist: 4l, hd, 1½l, 1½l, 2½l, 1l, hd. 1m 12.20s. a 2.50s (8 Ran).
SR: 44/17/21/19/-/ (W B Imison), P Calver

2708 'Barbour Jacket' Limited Stakes Class D (0-80 3-y-o) £3,200 1¼m.....(7:55)

1464* SOLOMON'S DANCER (USA) 9-0 Dean McKeown (3) *pld hrd, trkd ldrs, hdwy 3 fs out, rdn one and a half out, hng lft, led entering last, ran on*..............(11 to 4 op 3 to 1) 1
2315⁵ SAFIR (USA) 9-0 R Hills (4) *trkd ldr, hdwy o'r 4 fs out, sn led, rdn one and a half out, hdd entering last, no extr.*..............(9 to 4 op 2 to 1 tchd 5 to 2) 2
2576⁸ BAY QUEEN 8-6 (3*) M Fenton (1) *trkd ldg pair, hdwy 3 fs out, sn pushed alng, swtchd and ev ch o'r one out, kpt on und pres*..............(9 to 2 op 7 to 2) 3
1154⁴ BARRATRY 9-0 W Ryan (5) *led, jnd o'r 4 fs out, sn rdn and hdd, wknd wl over 2 out.*..............(13 to 8 fav op 7 to 4 tchd 2 to 1) 4
Dist: 1½l, hd, 7l. 2m 6.80s. a 5.60s (4 Ran).
SR: 44/41/35/26/ (D D Hart), W W Haigh

2709 Federation Brewery LCL Pils Lager Claiming Stakes Class G (3-y-o and up) £2,070 2m 4yds.............(8:25)

2467² ANGELICA PARK (v) 7-9-2 J Quinn (4) *chsd ldr, effrt to ld 3 fs out, sn clr, styd on*..............(11 to 8 fav op 7 to 4) 1
2235⁵ PURITAN (Can) 4-9-12 Kim Tinkler (3) *hld up and beh, pushed alng hfwy, hdwy 5 fs out, chsd wnr fnl 2 furlongs, no imprsn*..............(100 to 30 op 3 to 1 tchd 7 to 2) 2
1491⁷ WORKING TITLE (Ire) 3-8-10 W Ryan (2) *chsd ldg pair, rdn o'r 6 fs out, styd on one pace fnl 3 furlongs.*..............(8 to 1 op 7 to 1) 3
2455⁴ A GENTLEMAN TWO 7-8-11 (5*) O Pears (5) *hld up, effrt and rdn 5 fs out, nvr rch ldrs*..............(10 to 1 op 7 to 1) 4
2536* MISTRESS BEE (USA) 4-9-7 R Hills (1) *led, rdn o'r 3 fs out, sn ridden and wknd quickly*..............(3 to 1 op 5 to 2) 5
2340³ BONNY PRINCESS (v) 3-7-7 J Lowe (6) *al rear.*..............(33 to 1 op 16 to 1) 6
Dist: 2½l, 10l, 6l, 4l, 8l. 3m 30.10s. a 7.10s (6 Ran).
SR: 31/38/12/12/13/-/ (Parkers Of Peterborough Plc), J Wharton

2710 Cleveland Potash Maiden Handicap Stakes Class D (0-80 3-y-o and up) £2,880 7f.....................(8:55)

2421 GLEN MILLER [52] (bl) 3-9-6 Dean McKeown (1) *made all, rdn o'r one furlong out, ran on ins last.*..............(5 to 1 op 4 to 1) 1
2339⁴ JOMOVE [36] 4-8-11 K Darley (5) *in tch, hdwy hfwy, effrt 2 fs out, rdn to chal entering fnl furlong, no extr nr finish*..............(5 to 4 fav op 11 to 8) 2
2358⁷ NATCHEZ TRACE [49] (v) 4-9-10 W Ryan (6) *in tch, effrt o'r 2 fs out, sn rdn and one pace*..............(3 to 1 tchd 7 to 2) 3
SYKE LANE [33] 4-8-8 A Culhane (4) *cl up till rdn and wknd 2 fs out*..............(14 to 1 op 12 to 1 tchd 16 to 1) 4
2634³ SILVER STONE BOY [33] 5-8-8 S Webster (3) *chsd wnr, rdn alng hfwy, wknd o'r 2 fs out*..............(4 to 1 op 3 to 1) 5
Dist: 1l, 3l, 3l, nk. 1m 25.70s. a 3.90s (5 Ran).
SR: 32/20/24/-/-/ (Mrs John Etherton), J W Payne

SANDOWN (good to firm (race 1), good (2,3,4,5,6))
Wednesday July 21st
Going Correction: MINUS 0.10 sec. per fur. (race 1), PLUS 0.10 (2,3,4,5,6)

2711 'Wednesday Club' Claiming Stakes Class E (3-y-o) £3,109 5f 6yds...(6:20)

2560* NO EXTRAS (Ire) 9-1 B Rouse (4) *ran on o'r 2 fs out, led last 100 yards, cleverly.*..............(11 to 8 on op 6 to 4 on tchd 5 to 4 on) 1
2255 SOBER LAD (Ire) (v) 8-9 Pat Eddery (6) *led to last 100 yards, styd on gmely*..............(7 to 2 op 3 to 1 tchd 4 to 1) 2
2634⁴ SOPHISTICATED AIR (bl) 8-0 S O'Gorman (7) *ldg grp, rdn appr fnl furlong, rallied und pres nr line.*..............(12 to 1 op 8 to 1) 3
1470⁵ CHILI LADY 8-0 T Sprake (8) *wth ldr, rdn and one pace appr fnl furlong*..............(20 to 1 op 14 to 1) 4
1320 MARCHMAIN 8-5 G Carter (3) *slwly into strd, effrt o'r 2 fs out, no imprsn ins last.*..............(20 to 1 op 14 to 1 tchd 25 to 1) 5
1977 KARUKERA 7-2 (7*) Kim McDonnell (1) *outpcd and pushed alng hfwy, nvr nr to chal.*..............(10 to 1 op 8 to 1 tchd 6 to 1) 6

RIVER REFUGE 8-2 Dale Gibson (2) *wl plcd till wknd 2 fs out*.................(20 to 1 op 14 to 1 tchd 25 to 1) 7
2231⁹ BENOSO 7-9³ (7*) Elizabeth Turner (5) *sn outpcd, tld off hfwy*.............................(50 to 1 op 25 to 1) 8
Dist: ½l, sht-hd, 1l, 1½l, ¾l, 2l, 20l. 1m 1.78s. a 2.28s (8 Ran).
SR: 45/37/27/23/22/9/8/-/ (K Higson), G L Moore

2712 Pacemaker & Thoroughbred Breeder Racing Schools Apprentice Handicap Class E (0-70 3-y-o) £3,018 1m 14yds ....(6:45)

2113⁵ COMANCHE COMPANION [61] 9-2 A Garth (11) *wl plcd, ran on to ld 2 fs out, clr fnl furlong*.....................(9 to 2 fav op 4 to 1 tchd 5 to 1) 1
1912⁶ MISS FASCINATION [60] 9-1 K Rutter (10) *in tch, hdwy to chase wnr appr fnl furlong, no imprsn*.......................(7 to 1 op 6 to 1 tchd 15 to 2) 2
2311⁵ LOCHORE [60] 9-1 S Drowne (2) *beh till rdn and styd on appr fnl furlong, not trble wnr*....(14 to 1 op 10 to 1) 3
2001⁴ TRIANGLEPOINT (Ire) [58] 8-13 D Harrison (3) *hdwy frm rear o'r one furlong out, nrst finish*. (7 to 1 op 6 to 1) 4
2291 TONY'S MIST [65] 9-6 Mark Denaro (12) *styd on last 2 fs, not rch ldrs*...............................(10 to 1) 5
2182⁷ THATCHED (Ire) [47] 7-13 (3*) Sally Radford-Howes (4) *chsd ldrs to 3 fs out, sn rdn, no extr*...(20 to 1 tchd 25 to 1) 6
2499 SLIVOVITZ [57] (bl) 8-12 Stephen Davies (1) *chsd ldr, led 3 fs out to 2 out, wknd one out*........(16 to 1 op 12 to 1) 7
2612⁴ JUST JAMIE [56] 8-8 (3*) S Drake (15) *nvr better than mid-div*.................(16 to 1 op 12 to 1 tchd 20 to 1) 8
2347⁸ HILLSDOWN BOY (Ire) [46] 7-12 (3*) A Martinez (7) *mid-div, rdn and effrt o'r 2 fs out, sn btn*... (14 to 1 op 10 to 1) 9
2098³ MARAT (USA) [49] 8-4 Kim McDonnell (13) *al beh*.................................(25 to 1 op 20 to 1) 10
2066 CLIBURNEL NEWS (Ire) [66] 9-7 S Mulvey (14) *nvr on terms*...(12 to 1) 11
1947⁴ BEZIQUE (USA) [65] 9-6 J Weaver (9) *wl plcd till wknd 2 fs out*.................(7 to 1 op 6 to 1 tchd 15 to 2) 12
1913² MEDLAND (Ire) [50] 8-2 (3*) L Carter (6) *led to 3 fs out, wknd quickly*...............(9 to 1 op 7 to 1 tchd 10 to 1) 13
2416⁹ ARABIAN CASTLE [49] 8-1 (3*) S McCarthy (8) *al beh, tld off*...(33 to 1) 14
1607 RISK PROOF [49] 8-3² (3*) P Rose (5) *beh whn sddl slpd and uns rdr 4 fs out*..............(20 to 1 op 16 to 1) ur
Dist: 5l, 2l, 5l, 1½l, 3½l, 2l, 4l, ½l, 2l, ¾l. 1m 43.64s. a 4.54s (15 Ran).
SR: 46/30/24/7/9/-/ (Drofmor Racing), T J Naughton

2713 Farebrother Handicap Class C (0-90 3-y-o and up) £5,602 1¾m...... (7:15)

2530* SHUJAN (USA) [72] 4-9-7 (4ex) L Dettori (7) *sn clr, jnd one furlong out, rdn and hld on last strd*.........................(4 to 1 op 7 to 2 tchd 9 to 2) 1+
2177* HADDAAJ (Ire) [75] 3-8-10 M Roberts (6) *chsd wnr, cl up one furlong out, sstnd chal to dead-heat last strd*....................(15 to 8 fav op 7 to 4 tchd 2 to 1) 1+
2501⁶ SHARP TOP [53] 5-7-9 (7*) P McCabe (3) *outpcd till hdwy o'r 3 fs out, styd on frm 2 out, not rch ldrs*.....................................(12 to 1 tchd 14 to 1) 3
2470* IMA RED NECK (USA) [50] (v) 4-7-13 (4ex) A McGlone (2) *improved to dispute second pl hfwy, rdn and btn o'r 2 fs out*.................(9 to 1 op 6 to 1) 4
2523² BERING ISLAND (USA) [60] 3-7-4 (5*) D Wright (5) *beh till effrt 3 fs out, no prog 2 out*.........................(9 to 2 op 3 to 1 tchd 5 to 1) 5
IRISH STAMP (Ire) [75] 4-9-10 W Carson (4) *al wl beh, tld off*..............................(12 to 1 tchd 14 to 1) 6
Dist: Dd-ht, 15l, ½l, 15l, 10l. 3m 2.57s. a 8.27s (6 Ran).
SR: 38/27/-/ (M J Polglase & Sheikh Ahmed Al Maktoum), R W Armstrong & B Hanbury

2714 Travis Perkins Maiden Stakes Class D (2-y-o) £3,649 7f 16yds..........(7:45)

NIJO 9-0 G Carter (11) *mid-div, ran on 2 fs out, led o'r one out, pushed clr*..................(7 to 2 fav op 6 to 1) 1
ZUBOON (USA) 9-0 W Carson (7) *hld up rear, ran on 2 fs out, chsd wnr fnl furlong, no imprsn*.......................(5 to 1 op 3 to 1 tchd 11 to 2) 2
MEELAAD (Ire) 9-0 M Roberts (1) *pressed ldr, led o'r 2 fs out till hdd and outpcd over one out*. (8 to 1 op 6 to 1) 3
PRIVY COUNCIL (USA) 9-0 L Dettori (4) *handily plcd, effrt 3 fs out, rdn and one pace 2 out*.........................(4 to 1 op 3 to 1 tchd 9 to 2) 4
2299⁶ ROISIN CLOVER 8-9 A McGlone (10) *led till o'r 2 fs out, wknd fnl furlong*................(10 to 1 tchd 11 to 1) 5
IDLE HOUND (USA) 9-0 Pat Eddery (6) *beh till effrt last 2 fs, not rch ldrs*. (9 to 2 op 7 to 2 tchd 3 to 1 and 5 to 1) 6
1949 GREENFINCH (Can) 9-0 T Quinn (3) *mid-div till rdn and no prog 3 fs out*......................(10 to 1 op 8 to 1) 7
2528³ JEAN DE FLORETTE (USA) 9-0 W R Swinburn (8) *in 3rd pl till wknd und pres o'r 2 fs out*...... (8 to 1 op 12 to 1) 8
2316 DREAM MISSY 8-9 R Perham (2) *al beh*.................................(33 to 1 tchd 40 to 1) 9
Dist: 6l, 4l, 1l, 2½l, 3l, nk, 1l, 3½l. 1m 31.10s. a 4.60s (9 Ran).
SR: 42/24/12/9/-/-/ (Sheikh Ahmed Bin Saeed Al Maktoum), G A Pritchard-Gordon

2715 Surrey Racing Handicap Class D (0-80 3-y-o and up) £4,690 7f 16yds... (8:15)

2136⁶ NEITHER NOR [66] 4-9-8 G Carter (7) *handily plcd gng wl, led entering fnl furlong, pushed out*.......................(6 to 1 op 5 to 1 tchd 13 to 2) 1
2590⁴ BROUGHTON'S PORT [61] 3-8-10 J Reid (6) *trkd ldr, led o'r 2 fs out till entering last, kpt on wl*.........................(5 to 1 op 6 to 1 tchd 9 to 2) 2
917 DUCKEY FUZZ [50] 5-8-6 A McGlone (8) *al ldg grp, rdn o'r one furlong out, not quicken ins last*.....................(16 to 1 op 14 to 1 tchd 20 to 1) 3
1485⁸ ASSIGNMENT [72] 7-10-0 T Williams (3) *hld up rear, hrd rdn to cl on ldrs o'r one furlong out, no extr last 100 yards*.................(16 to 1 op 12 to 1 tchd 20 to 1) 4
2421 PRAIRIE GROVE [74] 3-9-2 (7*) Mark Denaro (2) *not much room o'r 2 fs out, hdwy over one out, styd on*......................(4 to 1 fav op 9 to 2 tchd 7 to 2) 5
SAAFEND [72] 5-10-0 W R Swinburn (9) *hld up rear, not clr run o'r 2 fs out and over one out, nrst finish*......................................(14 to 1 op 12 to 1) 6
2548⁸ SAREEN EXPRESS (Ire) [41] 5-7-11 C Rutter (5) *mid-div, rdn alng and one pace last 2 fs*.....................(12 to 1 op 10 to 1 tchd 14 to 1) 7
2431 BRAVEBOY [69] 5-9-11 M Roberts (4) *ldg grp till wknd o'r one furlong out*..................(20 to 1 op 16 to 1) 8
760⁷ AFFIDARE (Ire) [58] 4-9-0 D Holland (10) *hld up, effrt o'r 2 fs out, no extr appr last*.....................(16 to 1 op 14 to 1 tchd 20 to 1) 9
2212⁷ TOP PET (Ire) [76] 3-9-11 T Quinn (11) *led till o'r 2 fs out, wknd over one out*..................(7 to 1 op 5 to 1) 10
1744 DOMICKSKY [65] 5-9-7 W Carson (1) *hld up rear, not clr run ins last 2 fs, no imprsn on ldrs*... (6 to 1 op 5 to 1) 11
Dist: ¾l, 1½l, nk, 1½l, ½l, 3l, ½l, ½l, 2½l, 3½l. 1m 31.83s. a 5.33s (11 Ran).
SR: 39/25/16/37/27/30/-/16/3/ (T S M S Riley-Smith), D A Wilson

2716 LBC Newstalk 97.3 FM Rating Related Maiden Fillies' Stakes Class D (0-75 3-y-o) £3,434 1¼m 7yds........ (8:45)

2277⁶ RAFIF (USA) 8-11 W Carson (9) *in tch, rdn alng o'r 2 fs out, ran on fnl furlong, led last strds*.........................(7 to 1 op 5 to 1 tchd 8 to 1) 1
2300 DIPLOMATIST 8-11 J Reid (3) *chsd ldrs, led o'r 2 fs out, hrd rdn fnl furlong, hdd on line*.........................(7 to 1 op 6 to 1 tchd 8 to 1) 2
1383⁴ CORAL GEM 8-11 M Roberts (7) *pld hrd, jnd ldr 7 fs out, led 3 out till o'r 2 out, one pace ins last*.........................(4 to 1 tchd 11 to 2) 3
1946⁴ CASHELL 8-11 L Dettori (10) *handily plcd, rdn alng o'r 2 fs out, no extr fnl furlong*.........................(8 to 1 op 7 to 1 tchd 9 to 1) 4
1961 BRONZE MAQUETTE (Ire) 8-11 E Johnson (5) *sn pushed alng in last pl, improved 2 fs out, no imprsn on ldrs fnl furlong*.................(50 to 1 op 33 to 1 tchd 66 to 1) 5
2275⁵ RASAYEL (USA) 8-11 W R Swinburn (4) *wl plcd till rdn and no hdwy appr fnl furlong*.........................(8 to 1 op 6 to 1 tchd 9 to 1) 6
1684⁴ SAKURA QUEEN (Ire) 8-11 W Woods (2) *beh aftr 2 fs, effrt o'r two out, nvr nrr*..............(20 to 1 op 14 to 1) 7
1469² SING A RAINBOW (Ire) 8-11 Pat Eddery (1) *beh aftr 4 fs, not dngrs after*........(7 to 4 fav tchd 2 to 1 and 13 to 8) 8
2314³ PISH KESH 8-11 A Clark (6) *led to 3 fs out, sn wknd*.......................(9 to 1 op 6 to 1 tchd 10 to 1) 9
1482⁷ HAZY KAY (Ire) 8-11 D Biggs (8) *beh and rdn alng aftr 3 fs*.....................(20 to 1 op 16 to 1 tchd 25 to 1) 10
Dist: Hd, 2½l, ¾l, nk, 3l, 6l, 3½l, 2l, 4l. 2m 10.48s. a 6.58s (10 Ran).
SR: 41/40/35/33/32/26/14/7/3/ (Hamdan Al-Maktoum), A C Stewart

YARMOUTH (good)
Wednesday July 21st

Going Correction: MINUS 0.20 sec. per fur. (races 1,2,3,4), MINUS 0.25 (5,6)

2717 Scratby Handicap Class D (0-75 3-y-o and up) £3,915 7f 3yds..........(2:15)

2582* ROCA MURADA (Ire) [58] 4-8-10 (7*,6ex) P McCabe (11) *settled gng wl, nosed ahead on bit 3 fs out, idled in frnt, rdn out*............................(13 to 2 op 5 to 1) 1
2391⁵ JAHANGIR (Ire) [66] 4-9-11 B Raymond (7) *patiently rdn, quickened up to chal entering fnl furlong, kpt on wl*.......................(9 to 1 op 7 to 1 tchd 10 to 1) 2
2532² BILL MOON [52] 7-8-4 (7*) Michael Denaro (1) *al hndy, led briefly o'r 3 fs out, not quicken fnl furlong*...(5 to 1 op 4 to 1) 3
2426⁴ CAPTAIN MARMALADE [54] 4-8-8 (5*) K Rutter (5) *sticky strt, swtchd outsd to improve hfwy, kpt on und pres fnl furlong*................(8 to 1 op 7 to 1 tchd 9 to 1) 4
2190* SHINING JEWEL [68] 6-9-13 L Piggott (9) *nvr far away, drw level o'r 2 fs out, no extr ins last*........(9 to 2 jt-fav op 4 to 1 tchd 7 to 2) 5

2476[3] TEE GEE JAY [54] (bl) 3-8-3 (3*) D Harrison (10) *missed break, chsd alng hfwy, no imprsn*...........(9 to 2 jt-fav op 6 to 1 tchd 7 to 1) 6
2537[5] MISTER BLAKE [53] (bl) 3-8-3[1] (3*) Emma O'Gorman (6) *wth ldrs, niggled alng hfwy, fdd o'r one furlong out.* ....(33 to 1 op 16 to 1 tchd 40 to 1) 7
2373[7] MOUNT FUJI [70] 3-9-8 M Hills (3) *trkd ldg bunch, effrt and rdn alng hfwy, sn outpcd*......(10 to 1 op 7 to 1) 8
2164[4] TAJDID (Ire) [61] 3-8-13 R Hills (4) *wth ldr, hrd rdn o'r 2 fs out, edgd lft, wknd quickly*..........(6 to 1 op 4 to 1) 9
SABOTEUR [37] 9-7-10[3] A Mackay (2) *slight ld to hfwy, wknd rpdly last 2 fs*...............(50 to 1 op 20 to 1) 10
Dist: Hd, 2l, nk, 3l, sht-hd, 5l, 2½l, 4l, 15l. 1m 27.00s. a 3.80s (10 Ran).
SR: 25/32/12/13/18/-/ (Tim Corby), M J Ryan

2718 Elizabeth Simpson Selling Stakes Class G (2-y-o) £2,448 7f 3yds...(2:45)

2519[3] MAJOR SUCCESS (Ire) 8-11 D Holland (1) *enterprisingly rdn, rcd alone far side, clr thrght, ran on.* ....(6 to 1 op 4 to 1 tchd 7 to 1) 1
1870[2] MOMENT OF GLORY (Ire) 8-11 R Cochrane (4) *chsd alng wth main grp, styd on appr fnl furlong, nrst finish.* ....(6 to 4 fav op 11 to 10 tchd 7 to 4) 2
PAT'S SPLENDOUR 8-3[2] (5*) C Hodgson (9) *settled wth chasing bunch, led that grp o'r 2 fs out, drifted lft fnl furlong, no extr*.......(14 to 1 op 8 to 1 tchd 16 to 1) 3
2502 ROBBY (Ire) 8-11 A Munro (10) *drvn alng wth stands side bunch, styd on fnl furlong, nvr nrr*. (14 to 1 op 8 to 1) 4
2533[5] LITTLE BID (USA) 8-6 M Hills (6) *bustled alng to improve stands side hfwy, no imprsn appr fnl furlong.* ....(16 to 1 op 20 to 1) 5
2377 NORTHERN STORM (Ire) 8-11 W Woods (11) *chsd alng wth main grp, struggling last 2 fs*......(33 to 1 op 20 to 1) 6
2119[6] MOSS HOUSE (Ire) 8-11 B Marcus (7) *outpcd and drvn alng most of way, nvr a threat.* ....(12 to 1 op 8 to 1 tchd 14 to 1) 7
1909[4] BON TON 8-6 C Rutter (3) *trkd main bunch, effrt hfwy, nvr dngrs*..............(8 to 1 op 7 to 1 tchd 12 to 1) 8
2465[7] STORM (bl) 8-11 G Hind (8) *drvn alng to go pace hfwy, nvr dngrs*...............(33 to 1 tchd 40 to 1) 9
2533[3] FILCH (v) 8-6 L Piggott (5) *led main grp to hfwy, wknd rpdly, eased o'r one furlong out*.... (11 to 2 op 6 to 1) 10
2336 DAME PROSPECT 8-6 B Raymond (2) *rdn alng the whole way, nvr a factor*................ (12 to 1 op 7 to 1) 11
1741 MR GORDON BENNETT 8-11 T Williams (12) *sluggish strt, reco'red to ld main grp hfwy, hdd over 2 out, sn lost tch*.............................. (50 to 1 op 25 to 1) 12
Dist: 4l, sht-hd, 2l, 6l, nk, 10l, 3½l, 2l, 3l, ½l. 1m 26.70s. a 3.50s (12 Ran).
SR: 24/12/6/5/-/-/ (W J Gredley), B W Hills

2719 Beauchamp Maiden Handicap Class E (0-70 3-y-o and up) £3,002 6f 3yds ....(3:15)

2350[3] SIR OLIVER (Ire) [50] 4-9-2 A Munro (4) *nvr far away, effrt and edgd lft o'r one furlong out, led last 100 yards, jst hld on*.................. (7 to 1 op 5 to 1 tchd 8 to 1) 1
2047[6] RED ADMIRAL [52] 3-8-12 R Cochrane (6) *tried to make all, hdd last 100 yards, rallied gmely.* .... (11 to 2 op 4 to 1 tchd 6 to 1) 2
2350[4] GUESSTIMATION (USA) [45] (bl) 4-8-11 G Bardwell (10) *chsd alng to improve frm off the pace last 2 fs, ran on und pres, nrst finish*..................(8 to 1 op 6 to 1) 3
2383[6] EXPORT MONDIAL [56] (bl) 3-9-2 M Tebbutt (11) *rcd stands side, drvn up to join issue hfwy, not quicken ins fnl furlong*...............(14 to 1 op 8 to 1 tchd 16 to 1) 4
1463[4] CLANROCK [61] 3-9-7 A Culhane (5) *nvr far away, rdn to draw level o'r 2 fs out, fdd fnl furlong.* .... (15 to 2 op 6 to 1) 5
2424[5] FRIENDLY SMILE [47] 3-8-2 (5*) K Rutter (9) *chsd alng to improve stands side o'r 2 fs out, not pace to chal.* .... (14 to 1 op 10 to 1 tchd 16 to 1) 6
2560[7] AHJAY [54] 3-9-0 M Wigham (2) *trkd ldrs centre, feeling pace and rdn 2 fs out, sn btn*......(5 to 1 tchd 12 to 1) 7
2686[2] ISLAND KNIGHT (Ire) [62] 4-10-0 L Piggott (1) *settled gng wl, effrt and shaken up 2 fs out, fdd.* ....(11 to 2 op 5 to 1 tchd 6 to 1) 8
2338[7] TASSAGH BRIDGE (Ire) [40] 3-8-0 A Mackay (8) *outpcd and drvn alng, nvr able to rch ldrs*.................... (33 to 1) 9
2503[2] HALL BANK COTTAGE [43] (bl) 3-8-3 T Williams (3) *sluggish strt, drvn up on outsd hfwy, rdn and found nothing.* ....(4 to 1 fav tchd 3 to 1 and 9 to 2) 10
2122[4] KRAYYAN DAWN [46] 3-8-6 S Dawson (7) *sluggish strt, drvn alng most of way, nvr able to chal*....... (20 to 1) 11
Dist: Sht-hd, 2l, 3l, ¾l, dd-ht, ¾l, ¾l, ¾l, 4l, nk. 1m 13.50s. a 2.50s (11 Ran).
SR: 28/23/14/7/9/-/-/10/-/ (Ms S A Joyner), R J Hodges

2720 EBF Medler Maiden Stakes Class D (2-y-o) £4,191 5f 43yds..........(3:45)

2519[2] DANCE FOCUS 9-0 Pat Eddery (7) *made most, hrd pressed appr fnl furlong, hld on grimly cl hme.* ....(11 to 8 on op Evens) 1
INGOZI 8-9 M Hills (8) *sluggish strt, swtchd outsd to improve hfwy, ran on strly fnl furlong, prmsg.* .... (11 to 4 op 6 to 4 tchd 3 to 1) 2
IRADAH (USA) 8-9 R Hills (9) *patiently rdn, shaken up to draw level appr fnl furlong, ran green, can improve.* ....(7 to 1 op 5 to 1 tchd 8 to 1) 3
793 TONDRES (USA) 9-0 B Marcus (1) *wth wnr, hrd drvn whn pace quickened o'r one furlong out, sn btn.* .... (20 to 1 op 10 to 1) 4
2535[4] HERR TRIGGER 9-0 L Piggott (6) *early speed, pushed alng hfwy, btn 2 fs out*....(12 to 1 op 10 to 1 tchd 14 to 1) 5
MISTER O'GRADY (Ire) 9-0 R Cochrane (5) *chsd alng to go pace hfwy, sn lost tch*...............(50 to 1 op 25 to 1) 6
TONE CONTROL 9-0 W Woods (4) *sluggish strt, struggling to go pace hfwy, sn lost tch.* (20 to 1 op 10 to 1) 7
2414[5] MENTMORE LAD 9-0 G Hind (2) *speed to hfwy, lost tch last 2 fs*.................................(50 to 1 op 33 to 1) 8
Dist: Hd, hd, 4l, 12l, 1l, sht-hd, 15l. 1m 2.50s. a 1.80s (8 Ran).
SR: 43/37/36/25/-/ (N S Yong), W A O'Gorman

2721 Lydia Eva Claiming Stakes Class F (3-y-o) £2,399 2¼m 51yds......... (4:15)

2340[2] DANGER BABY 8-3 G Duffield (4) *settled aftr 2 fs, improved and edgd lft o'r 3 furlongs out, led over one out, styd on*.......... (14 to 1 op 16 to 1 tchd 12 to 1) 1
2495[7] ROWLANDSONS GOLD (Ire) 7-13 (3*) B Doyle (3) *led till hdd ten fs out, struggling to hold pl o'r 3 out, rallied fnl furlong*...............(25 to 1 op 12 to 1 tchd 33 to 1) 2
2547* PONDERING (v) 9-7 A Munro (1) *settled gng wl, led ten fs out, quickened entering strt, hdd and rdn o'r one out, sn btn*........(7 to 4 on tchd 6 to 4 on and 2 to 1 on) 3
1980* SHE KNEW THE RULES (Ire) 8-2 C Rutter (2) *wth ldrs for a m, struggling appr strt, tld off.* ....(2 to 1 op 7 to 4 tchd 6 to 4) 4
Dist: 3½l, 3½l, 20l. 4m 6.90s. a 5.90s (4 Ran).
(David S Blake), Bob Jones

2722 Caister Handicap Class D (0-80 3-y-o and up) £3,687 1¼m 21yds......(4:45)

2398[6] MISS SHAGRA (USA) [70] 3-8-13 B Raymond (5) *set out to make all, hdd and drvn alng o'r 2 fs out, rallied to ld last 50 yards*............ (7 to 2 op 4 to 1 tchd 3 to 1) 1
2433[7] LET'S GET LOST [71] 4-9-10 L Piggott (2) *al hndy, nosed ahead o'r 2 fs out, hrd drvn fnl furlong, ct last 50 yards.* ....(9 to 4 fav tchd 5 to 2 and 2 to 1) 2
2300 BIG BLUE [72] 4-9-8 (3*) B Doyle (1) *nvr far away, hrd drvn o'r 2 fs out, swtchd outsd fnl furlong, ran on.* ....(9 to 2 op 4 to 1) 3
2198[3] SOVEREIGN PAGE (USA) [75] 4-10-0 M Hills (4) *al hndy, rdn to draw level o'r one furlong out, kpt on same pace.* ....(3 to 1 op 2 to 1) 4
2202[6] THRIVING [63] 3-8-6 A Munro (3) *took keen hold, effrt entering strt, rdn and one pace last 2 fs.* .... (11 to 1 op 8 to 1 tchd 12 to 1) 5
Dist: Nk, 1½l, ½l, 2½l. 2m 8.00s. a 4.00s (5 Ran).
SR: 34/44/42/44/17/ (Maktoum Al Maktoum), M R Stoute

BRIGHTON (good to firm)
Thursday July 22nd
Going Correction: MINUS 0.30 sec. per fur.

2723 Blackmantle Handicap Class E (0-70 3-y-o and up) £2,898 5f 213yds.. (2:30)

2225[3] FARMER JOCK [54] 11-10-0 J Reid (8) *hld up in rear, prog hfwy, led o'r one out, pushed out.* ....(9 to 2 op 4 to 1 tchd 5 to 1) 1
2494[3] MY RUBY RING [54] 6-10-0 T Williams (2) *handily plcd, led o'r 2 out till over one out, not quicken nr finish.* ....(11 to 4 fav op 5 to 2 tchd 3 to 1) 2
2636[4] AQUADO [40] 4-9-0 (7ex) Pat Eddery (5) *hld up in rear, not much room and ran on o'r 2 out, eased whn btn ins fnl furlong*..................................(7 to 2 tchd 3 to 1) 3
2549[3] SCARLET PRINCESS [40] 5-9-0 A Munro (6) *chsd ldrs, outpcd 2 out, grad wknd*..........(5 to 1 tchd 11 to 2) 4
2350 VIS-A-VIS [35] 4-8-9 R Price (7) *in tch, no prog last 2 fs.* ....(66 to 1 op 33 to 1) 5
CONE LANE [35] 7-8-2 (7*) B Russell (1) *pressed ldrs to hfwy, sn lost pl*.................... (66 to 1 op 33 to 1) 6
1914* SCOTS LAW [48] (bl) 6-9-8 D Biggs (9) *led aftr 2 fs, hdd o'r two out, wknd over one out*..........(4 to 1 op 3 to 1) 7
BLUE TAIL [50] 5-9-3 (7*) S Drowne (4) *outpcd most of way.* .... (66 to 1 op 33 to 1) 8
RESTORE [45] (v) 10-9-5 W Newnes (3) *led for 2 fs, wknd o'r two out*..........................(25 to 1 op 14 to 1) 9
Dist: ¾l, 6l, 1l, 3l, sht-hd, nk, ½l, sht-hd. 1m 10.40s. a 2.00s (9 Ran).
SR: 38/35/-/-/-/-/ (S Thompson), Mrs N Macauley

2724 Raggetts Selling Stakes Class G (3-y-o) £2,070 6f 209yds.......... (3:00)

2005[4] NOEPROB (USA) 8-2 (7*) J D Smith (11) *towards rear, ran on o'r one out, styd on to ld nr line.* ....(11 to 1 op 10 to 1 tchd 12 to 1) 1
1972[3] ALTA VICTORIA (Ire) 8-9 Pat Eddery (15) *wl plcd, led 3 out, rdn o'r one out, hdd last few strds*........(100 to 30 jt-fav op 2 to 1 tchd 4 to 1) 2

2476 RED LEADER (Ire) 9-0 A Clark (10) *prog 3 out, rdn and not quicken ins fnl furlong*.............(16 to 1 op 8 to 1) 3
1528⁹ PONTEVECCHIO MODA 8-9 J Reid (12) *hdwy on outsd 2 out, kpt on one pace fnl furlong.* ....(9 to 2 tchd 4 to 1 and 5 to 1) 4
2384⁷ SUPERENSIS 9-0 A Munro (13) *mid-div, effrt o'r 2 out, rdn and not quicken fnl furlong.* ....(16 to 1 op 14 to 1 tchd 20 to 1) 5
2120 KUTAN (Ire) 9-0 A Tucker (16) *hdwy frm rear last 2 fs, no imprsn on ldrs*.......(33 to 1 op 25 to 1 tchd 50 to 1) 6
2164⁶ SHARP GAZELLE 8-9 W Newnes (5) *rcd in mid-div, no extr frm 2 out*...........................(20 to 1 op 12 to 1) 7
2160³ CALISAR 9-0 T Sprake (2) *chsd frnt rnk til lost pos o'r 2 out, kpt on ag'n fnl furlong*.........(7 to 1 op 5 to 1) 8
2639⁶ SWISS MOUNTAIN (v) 8-9 T Williams (6) *led til 3 out, wknd ins last 2 fs*.......................(33 to 1 op 16 to 1) 9
2445⁵ LADY OF SHADOWS 8-2 (7*) A Martinez (8) *chsd ldrs, wknd o'r one out*..........(20 to 1 op 14 to 1 tchd 25 to 1) 10
BAN RI (Ire) 8-9 A McGlone (7) *wl plcd for well o'r 4 fs.* ....(25 to 1 op 16 to 1) 11
QUE TEE AH 8-2 (7*) G Rothwell (14) *outpcd.* ....(33 to 1 op 20 to 1 tchd 50 to 1) 12
1902 GEORGE ROPER 9-0 B Rouse (18) *speed to hfwy.* ....(25 to 1 op 16 to 1) 13
INDIAN FIRE 9-0 D Biggs (9) *strted slwly, al beh.* ....(33 to 1 op 20 to 1) 14
2410⁸ BIRD TROUBLE (Ire) 9-0 C Avery (3) *outpcd frm hfwy.* ....(33 to 1) 15
2540* CUBIST (Ire) (bl) 8-9 B Raymond (17) *rcd on wide outsd, no imprsn on ldrs appr last 2 fs*.............(100 to 30 jt-fav op 9 to 2 tchd 3 to 1) 16
2160⁴ JIM CANTLE 9-0 R Perham (1) *wth ldrs til wknd o'r 2 out, badly hmpd and uns rdr over one out.* ....(20 to 1 op 8 to 1) ur

Dist: ½l, 2l, ¾l, hd, 2l, hd, nk, 3l, 2l, 2l. 1m 22.70s. a 2.70s (17 Ran).

SR: 23/21/20/13/17/11/5/9/-/ (R M Cyzer), C A Cyzer

2725 Chippendale Maiden Stakes Class D (3-y-o and up) £3,494 7f 214yds..(3:30)

1027³ EL DUCO (USA) 3-8-9 Pat Eddery (8) *made all, quickened clr ins fnl furlong, very easily.* ....(2 to 1 on op 7 to 4 on tchd 13 to 8 on) 1
2202⁵ GREEN KILT 3-8-9 A Munro (5) *hdwy 4 out, rdn and kpt on one pace fnl furlong*................(13 to 2 op 5 to 1) 2
2410² THE LITTLE FERRET 3-8-9 B Rouse (4) *chsd wnr frm hfwy, rdn and wknd fnl furlong.* ....(7 to 2 op 4 to 1 tchd 5 to 1) 3
CUFF LINK (Ire) 3-8-9 J Reid (3) *mid-div, not pace to chal frm 2 out*........................(8 to 1 tchd 10 to 1) 4
2120⁵ RAGAZZO (Ire) 3-8-9 B Raymond (1) *chsd ldrs til rdn and outpcd o'r 2 out*...................(50 to 1 op 25 to 1) 5
1698⁶ GARRY'S CHOICE 4-9-7 N Adams (2) *beh most of way.* ....(40 to 1 op 20 to 1) 6
2120⁷ WEST END GIRL 3-8-4 A McGlone (6) *chsd ldrs till wknd o'r 3 out*...........................(66 to 1 op 33 to 1) 7
THARIF 5-9-0 (7*) Antoinette Armes (7) *slwly into strd, sn prmnt, drpd rear frm hfwy, tld off.* (66 to 1 op 33 to 1) 8

Dist: 3½l, 3l, 1½l, 6l, 3l, 8l, 15l. 1m 34.80s. a 2.40s (8 Ran).

SR: 23/12/3/-/-/ (K Abdulla), R Charlton

2726 Beau Brummel Claiming Stakes Class F (3-y-o) £2,243 1m 1f 209yds... (4:00)

2523⁷ FORMAL AFFAIR 8-1 (7*) J D Smith (7) *ran on 4 out, led o'r 2 out, rdn and styd on wl ins fnl furlong.* ....(4 to 1 op 3 to 1) 1
1528⁸ FANFOLD (Ire) 8-6 W Newnes (4) *hld up, rdn alng o'r 2 out, cld on wnr over one out, not quicken ins fnl furlong*..................(9 to 4 fav op 6 to 4 tchd 5 to 2) 2
2529⁴ SLOE BRANDY 8-5¹ Pat Eddery (5) *wl plcd, slight advantage o'r 3 out, hdd over 2 out, btn appr fnl furlong.* ....(4 to 1 op 9 to 2 tchd 5 to 1) 3
2489⁴ STEVIE'S WONDER (Ire) 8-13 T Williams (6) *led for 3 fs, trkd ldr til lost pl o'r three out, wknd over 2 out.* ....(11 to 2 op 7 to 2 tchd 6 to 1) 4
2464⁷ MR BEAN (v) 8-11 J Reid (1) *chsd ldrs for 7 fs, no extr.* ....(9 to 2 op 12 to 1) 5
1491 DO BE WARE 8-1 A McGlone (3) *sn outpcd in rear, tld off.* ....(40 to 1 op 33 to 1 tchd 50 to 1) 6
2411⁷ POCONO KNIGHT (v) 8-7 C Avery (8) *led aftr 3 fs, hdd and wknd o'r three out, tld off.* ....(25 to 1 op 16 to 1 tchd 33 to 1) 7
2578 MISTER FORUM 8-9 B Rouse (2) *al outpcd in rear, tld off frm hfwy*...(33 to 1) 8

Dist: 1½l, 7l, 1l, ½l, 15l, 10l, 10l. 2m 2.80s. a 4.60s (8 Ran).

SR: 18/13/-/4/1/ (R M Cyzer), C A Cyzer

2727 Brighton Summer Challenge Cup Handicap Class D (0-80 3-y-o and up) £3,084 1m 3f 196yds............(4:30)

2343³ LOOKINGFORARAINBOW (Ire) [57] 5-9-9 N Day (7) *mid-div, ran on to ld 3 out, quickened clr, easily.* ....(11 to 2 op 9 to 2) 1
1951⁴ ADDICTED TO LOVE [62] (bl) 4-10-0 Pat Eddery (6) *drpd rear hfwy, ran on 3 out, rdn and styd on fnl furlong, not rch wnr*............(4 to 1 op 3 to 1 tchd 9 to 2) 2
1146⁹ TEMPLE KNIGHT [60] 4-9-5 (7*) J D Smith (4) *hdwy frm 3 out to dispute ld 4 out, outpcd last 2 fs.* ....(8 to 1 op 7 to 1 tchd 9 to 1) 3
2415⁸ RAGTIME SONG [34] 4-8-0 N Adams (5) *chsd ldr, led 4 out til 3 out, outpcd 2 out*...........(12 to 1 tchd 10 to 1) 4
2148* HATTA RIVER (USA) [72] (bl) 3-9-12 A Clark (3) *led til hdd 4 out, sn lost pl*.......(7 to 4 fav op 6 to 4 tchd 2 to 1) 5
2163⁴ SEDGY'S SISTER [48] 3-7-12¹ (5*) Stephen Davies (2) *chsd ldrs til wknd o'r 3 out, eased whn btn last 2 fs.* ....(13 to 2 op 14 to 1) 6
2161⁴ LYN'S RETURN (Ire) [54] 4-9-6 A Tucker (1) *settled in rear til shrtlvd effrt hfwy, sn wknd.* ....(8 to 1 op 7 to 1 tchd 9 to 1) 7

Dist: 5l, 1½l, 8l, 10l, 8l, 10l. 2m 31.30s. a 3.80s (7 Ran).

SR: 35/30/25/-/ (B M Saumtally), Bob Jones

2728 Fitzherbert Handicap Class E (0-70 3-y-o and up) £2,898 5f 59yds... (5:00)

1957⁶ BELLSABANGING [68] 3-10-0 T Williams (2) *hld up, hdwy 2 out, led entering fnl furlong, quickened, pushed out and styd on*....................(9 to 4 fav op 7 to 4) 1
2352⁶ KENSWORTH LADY [50] 3-8-10 N Adams (6) *hld up, rdn and str run appr fnl furlong, no extr last 50 yards.* ....(6 to 1 op 5 to 1) 2
2329⁷ PAT POINDESTRES [47] 3-8-7 A Clark (5) *led til hdd entering fnl furlong, sn outpcd.* ....(4 to 1 op 3 to 1 tchd 5 to 1) 3
1871⁵ MAID WELCOME [56] (bl) 6-9-7 J Reid (7) *chsd ldrs, no hdwy ins last 2 fs*.......(6 to 1 op 8 to 1 tchd 9 to 1) 4
1990⁴ TEE-EMM [54] 3-9-0 W Newnes (1) *pressed ldr til wknd o'r one out*..............(12 to 1 op 8 to 1 tchd 14 to 1) 5
2121 BELLA BAMBOLA (Ire) [42] 3-8-2 D Biggs (3) *al outpcd.* ....(33 to 1 op 20 to 1 tchd 50 to 1) 6
2378⁴ JULIET BRAVO [63] 3-9-9 A Munro (4) *lost many ls leaving stalls, virtually took no part.* ....(3 to 1 op 5 to 2 tchd 100 to 30) 7

Dist: 2l, 1½l, 3l, 4l, 2½l, 12l. 1m 2.50s. a 2.40s (7 Ran).
SR: 35/9/-/2/ (Mrs Marion Wickham), D R Laing

DONCASTER (good to firm)
Thursday July 22nd
Going Correction: MINUS 0.20 sec. per fur.

2729 Close Consumer Amateur Handicap Class F (0-80 3-y-o and up) £2,637 2m 110yds........................(6:20)

2337⁴ FARMER'S PET [74] 4-11-9 (5*) Mr P Pritchard-Gordon (18) *wth ldr, led hfwy, shaken up fnl 2 fs, styd on strly.* ....(6 to 1 jt-fav tchd 13 to 2) 1
2662⁴ ALLMOSA [57] 4-10-6 (5*) Mrs J Naughton (2) *nvr far away, effrt o'r 2 fs out, kpt on ins last*.............(6 to 1 jt-fav tchd 5 to 1) 2
2347² BARCHAM [39] 6-9-7 Miss Diana Jones (16) *tucked away on ins, improved hfwy, hmpd o'r 2 fs out, swtchd rght over one out, styd on wl*.......................(8 to 1) 3
2422⁴ THE KARAOKE KING [48] (bl) 4-9-11 (5*) Mrs J Boggis (11) *settled midfield, pushed alng 4 fs out, sn no room, kpt on frm 2 out, nrst finish*.....................(12 to 1) 4
901⁴ PINISI [39] 8-9-7 Mrs A Farrell (5) *nvr far away, effrt and rdn o'r 3 fs out, not quicken appr last*........(20 to 1) 5
2477³ KING WILLIAM [45] 8-9-8 (5*) Miss T Spearing (17) *dwlt, hld up rear, pushed alng entering strt, styd on fnl 2 fs, nvr dngrs*..(8 to 1) 6
2585⁷ MR WISHING WELL [39] 7-9-2 (5*) Mr T Cuff (3) *hld up, effrt entering strt, styd on fnl 2 fs, nrst finish*...... (25 to 1) 7
2306* EIGHTANDAHALF (Ire) [56] 4-10-5 (5*) Miss A Deniel (7) *led to hfwy, styd hndy, rdn 3 fs out, wknd o'r one out.* ....(10 to 1 op 8 to 1 tchd 12 to 1) 8
2587* SCOTTISH WEDDING [60] 3-9-12 (3ex) Mrs J Crossley (10) *hld up, effrt on ins o'r 3 fs out, nvr able to chal.* ....(13 to 2 op 5 to 1) 9
2071² POPSI'S LEGACY [60] 6-11-0 Miss Y Haynes (13) *mid-div, lost pl hfwy, wide and effrt entering strt, hng lft fnl 2 fs, no imprsn*........................(9 to 1 op 8 to 1) 10
2347 WRITTEN AGREEMENT [39] 5-9-2 (5*) Mrs C Peacock (12) *mid-div, pushed alng entering strt, one pace o'r 2 fs out*..(33 to 1) 11
2662⁶ RICH PICKINGS [42] 4-9-5 (5*) Miss S Rowe (4) *mid-div, rdn to cl entering strt, wknd o'r 2 fs out.* ....(16 to 1 op 10 to 1) 12
2347⁶ MYSTERIOUS MAID (USA) [43] 6-9-11 Mrs L Pearce (15) *beh, styd on fnl 2 fs, nrst finish*.....(10 to 1 op 8 to 1) 13
TOUCH 'N' PASS [40] 5-9-8⁶ (5*) Mrs S Easterby (6) *chsd ldrs, lost pl aftr 4 fs, no dngr after*.............(50 to 1) 14
1772⁶ FAIRWAYS ON TARGET [60] 7-11-0 Mr M Buckley (1) *chsd ldrs, rdn o'r 3 fs out, wknd 2 out*...(12 to 1 op 10 to 1) 15
2353⁵ WINGED WHISPER (USA) [39] 4-9-2 (5*) Mrs W Pickering (9) *keen hold, in tch, pushed alng appr strt, btn 3 fs out.* ....(33 to 1) 16

CLWYD LODGE [39] 6-9-2 (5*) Miss S Higgins (8) *slwly into strd, al struggling, tld off*..........(50 to 1) 17
WASHINGTON RED [42] 4-9-10³ Mr G Lewis (14) *beh, lost tch hfwy, tld off*..........(50 to 1) 18
Dist: 1l, nk, 3l, hd, ½l, 3½l, 1½l, 5l, ½l, sht-hd. 3m 38.09s. a 8.09s (18 Ran).
SR: 28/10/-/-/-/-/ (D R Midwood), G A Pritchard-Gordon

2730 Doncaster Stallholders Conditions Stakes Class C (2-y-o) £4,421 6f (6:45)

2096* UNBLEST 8-12 G Duffield (3) *trkd ldr, led o'r 2 fs out, edgd lft, strode out wl ins last*..........(6 to 4 op 5 to 4) 1
1556* TORCH ROUGE 8-12 D Holland (8) *swtchd lft strt, hld up in tch, cld hfwy, chlgd 2 fs out, kpt on same pace ins last*..........(5 to 4 fav tchd 11 to 8) 2
THREE IN ONE 8-10 W R Swinburn (7) *in tch gng wl, rdn 2 fs out, kpt on ins last, no ch wth 1st two.*..........(6 to 1 op 11 to 2) 3
1437⁴ LEGATEE 8-6¹ R Cochrane (5) *hld up last, pushed alng hfwy, outpcd fnl 2 fs*..........(16 to 1 op 14 to 1) 4
1778⁴ RAVEN'S RETURN (Ire) 8-12 S Perks (2) *led, edgd lft frm hfwy, hdd o'r 2 fs out, rdn and sn btn.*..........(25 to 1 op 20 to 1) 5
1837* TAKADOU (Ire) 8-12 P Robinson (4) *keen hold, chsd ldrs, rdn o'r 2 fs out, fdd*..........(10 to 1 op 8 to 1) 6
Dist: ¾l, 4l, 3½l, nk, 1½l. 1m 14.88s. a 3.48s (6 Ran).
SR: 4/1/-/ (Lord Vestey), J R Fanshawe

2731 'Dazzling Doncaster Markets' Handicap Class D (0-85 3-y-o) £4,542 6f (7:10)

1633⁷ ALASIB [73] 9-0 L Dettori (6) *pressed ldr, led hfwy, shaken up o'r one furlong out, styd on wl*...(8 to 1 op 7 to 1) 1
2660³ THE SHARP BIDDER (Ire) [80] 9-7 K Darley (5) *pressed ldrs, effrt and rdn o'r one furlong out, ev ch ins last, not quicken last 50 yards*..........(6 to 1) 2
1300* TRINITY HALL [62] 8-3 D Holland (3) *slwly away, improved on outsd 2 fs out, kpt on same pace ins last.*..........(13 to 2 op 6 to 1 tchd 7 to 1) 3
2468⁵ PINE RIDGE LAD (Ire) [66] 8-2 (5*) J Tate (7) *led, rdn and hdd hfwy, sn outpcd, kpt on ins fnl furlong.*..........(6 to 1 op 11 to 2) 4
1848⁴ TWO MOVES IN FRONT (Ire) [77] 9-4 G Carter (4) *nvr far away, rdn o'r 2 fs out, no extr inaide last.*..........(11 to 2 op 5 to 1) 5
1780⁵ WILLSHE GAN [77] 9-4 W Carson (1) *trkd ldrs on outsd, ev ch hfwy, one pace ins fnl furlong*...(9 to 1 op 10 to 1) 6
1801⁵ RAIN SPLASH [72] 8-6 (7*) Claire Balding (9) *sn beh, pushed alng hfwy, not clr run ins fnl furlong, swtchd lft, no imprsn*..........(10 to 1 op 8 to 1) 7
2431 BALIANA [73] 9-0 A Culhane (2) *trkd ldrs, rdn alng bef hfwy, not quicken appr last*..........(12 to 1) 8
2280² OUBECK [67] 8-8 Dale Gibson (8) *pressed ldrs, lost action hfwy, swtchd lft o'r one furlong out, sn drvn alng, edgd rght and wknd ins last.*..........(100 to 30 fav op 3 to 1 tchd 7 to 2) 9
Dist: 1½l, 1½l, ¾l, sht-hd, hd, ½l, 1½l, 2l. 1m 13.09s. a 1.69s (9 Ran).
SR: 42/43/19/20/30/29/22/17/3/ (A Foustok), W Jarvis

2732 'Come To Doncaster Markets' Conditions Stakes Class D (3-y-o and up) £3,850 7f (7:40)

2363⁹ POWERFUL EDGE 4-9-0 L Dettori (7) *al gng best, pressed ldrs, quickened to ld one furlong out, shaken up, styd on strly*..........(5 to 4 fav op 2 to 1) 1
1680⁸ DOUBLE BLUE 4-9-2 Dean McKeown (3) *wth ldr, led o'r 3 fs out to one out, hng rght, no extr, fnshd second, disqualified*..........(8 to 1) 2D
1950² ETOSHA 3-8-6 M Hills (6) *hld up, effrt 2 fs out, hmpd ins last, no extr, fnshd 3rd, plcd second.*..........(5 to 1 tchd 4 to 1 and 11 to 2) 2
1978³ ABSOLUTE MAGIC 3-8-11 W Carson (5) *pressed ldrs, swtchd lft hfwy, sn drvn alng, not quicken appr fnl furlong, fnshd 4th, plcd 3rd*..........(11 to 2 op 7 to 2) 3
1231⁸ SHAMISEN 3-8-2 B Marcus (8) *chsd ldrs, rdn o'r 2 fs out, staying on whn hmpd and snatched up ins last, not rcvr, fnshd 5th, plcd 4th*..........(16 to 1 tchd 14 to 1) 4
DESERT GREEN (Fr) 4-9-0 P D'Arcy (4) *slwly into strd, sn in tch, effrt o'r 2 fs out, not quicken, fnshd 6th, plcd 5th*..........(11 to 2 op 3 to 1) 5
2431⁹ EURO FESTIVAL 4-9-2 W R Swinburn (9) *hld up on ins, effrt o'r 2 fs out, not rch ldrs*..........(20 to 1 op 16 to 1) 7
2572⁹ SUNDAY'S HILL 4-9-4 (3*) D Harrison (1) *led till rdn and hdd o'r 3 fs out, wknd*..........(14 to 1) 8
2028⁴ TAALIF 3-8-6 R Hills (2) *chsd ldrs, ev ch hfwy, wknd o'r 2 fs out*..........(16 to 1 op 14 to 1) 9
Dist: 2½l, 2½l, 2½l, hd, 1l, 4l, 4l, 5l. 1m 24.42s. a 1.02s (9 Ran).
SR: 64/58/40/37/27/36/26/19/-/ (J C Smith), I A Balding

2733 Wards Thorne Best Bitter Handicap Class E (0-70 3-y-o and up) £3,236 7f (8:10)

2057 BROWNED OFF [42] 4-8-7 M Hills (7) *hld up, hdwy and weaved through o'r one furlong out, led ins last, kpt on wl*..........(25 to 1 op 16 to 1) 1
2270⁵ LEGEND DULAC (Ire) [53] 4-9-4 P Robinson (14) *handily plcd, led o'r 2 fs out till ins last, no extr.*..........(12 to 1 tchd 14 to 1) 2
2445³ PATIENCE PLEASE [54] 4-9-2 (3*) S Maloney (15) *nvr far away, rdn to improve on ins o'r one furlong out, kpt on same pace wl inside last*..........(13 to 2 op 8 to 1) 3
2308⁷ COOL ENOUGH [35] 12-8-0 K Darley (3) *hld up, not clr run o'r one furlong out, ran on ins last.*..........(14 to 1 op 12 to 1) 4
2491* NIGEL'S LUCKY GIRL [52] 5-9-3 (5ex) J Quinn (1) *in tch, drvn alng o'r 2 fs out, kpt on same pace ins last.*..........(10 to 1 op 8 to 1) 5
2548* PRINCE RODNEY [67] 4-9-11 (7*,5ex) Mark Denaro (9) *nvr far away, chlgd o'r 2 fs out, rdn over one out, one pace ins last*..........(9 to 1 op 8 to 1) 6
1849⁴ ROYAL COMEDIAN [41] 4-8-6 G Carter (10) *chsd ldrs, rdn alng o'r 2 fs out, crrd lft over one out, one pace.*..........(16 to 1) 7
2475⁴ COUNTERCHECK (Ire) [47] 4-8-12 L Dettori (12) *pressed ldrs, drvn o'r 2 fs out, btn over one out.*..........(9 to 1 op 8 to 1) 8
2236³ PICKLES [46] 5-8-11 R Cochrane (8) *dwlt, hld up, drvn alng hfwy, nvr able to chal.*..........(7 to 1 op 8 to 1 tchd 13 to 2) 9
2543² SUPER BENZ [61] 7-9-12 J Fortune (6) *dsptd ld, drvn o'r 2 fs out, wknd wl over one out*..........(9 to 1 op 8 to 1) 10
2480* SMART TEACHER (USA) [44] 3-8-2² (5ex) G Duffield (11) *narrow ld till o'r 2 fs out, sn drpd away.*..........(9 to 4 fav tchd 5 to 2 and 2 to 1) 11
DARIKA LAD [51] 5-9-2 W R Swinburn (5) *dwlt, beh, rdn hfwy, sn btn, eased fnl furlong*....(25 to 1 op 20 to 1) 12
2339⁵ QUIET VICTORY [32] (bl) 6-7-11⁴ (3*) D Harrison (4) *hmpd strt, beh, rdn hfwy, no imprsn*..........(16 to 1) 13
1210⁶ JOKIST [50] 10-8-8 (7*) S Jones (2) *beh, pushed alng hfwy, nvr on terms*..........(16 to 1 tchd 20 to 1) 14
Dist: 1l, ½l, 1l, hd, 2½l, hd, 2l, ½l, ½l, 1l. 1m 25.84s. a 2.44s (14 Ran).
SR: 35/43/42/20/36/43/16/16/13/ (J E Swiers), Mrs J R Ramsden

2734 Doncaster Corn Exchange Limited Stakes Class E (0-70 4-y-o and up) £2,950 6f (8:40)

2532* SAMSOLOM 5-9-0 K Darley (3) *hld up last, improved on bit o'r 2 fs out, led over one out, shaken up, drw clr ins last*..........(9 to 4 fav op 2 to 1 tchd 5 to 2) 1
2434⁹ ZEBOIM (bl) 7-8-7 (7*) Kim McDonnell (6) *pressed ldrs, effrt and shaken up o'r 2 fs out, ev ch over one out, not quicken ins last*..........(5 to 1 op 4 to 1) 2
2653³ PRINCE BELFORT 5-8-9 (5*) O Pears (1) *led, shaken up o'r 2 fs out, hdd over one out, wknd ins last.*..........(6 to 1 op 4 to 1 tchd 7 to 1) 3
2582⁴ MERRYHILL MAID (Ire) 5-8-9 R Cochrane (5) *pressed ldr, rdn alng hfwy, btn wl o'r one furlong out.*..........(5 to 2 op 3 to 1 tchd 7 to 2) 4
2548⁶ DARUSSALAM 6-8-9 W Carson (2) *chsd ldrs, rdn o'r 2 fs out, fdd*..........(9 to 2 op 4 to 1 tchd 5 to 1) 5
1159³ ARC LAMP 7-9-0 J Fortune (4) *trkd ldrs, drvn alng hfwy, wknd 2 fs out*..........(12 to 1 op 10 to 1 tchd 14 to 1) 6
Dist: 4l, nk, 5l, 4l, 2l. 1m 12.72s. a 1.32s (6 Ran).
SR: 50/34/33/8/-/-/ (The Hammond Partnership), P Howling

HAMILTON (good to firm)
Thursday July 22nd
Going Correction: MINUS 0.30 sec. per fur.

2735 Wallace Quinn, Barrachnie Handicap Class D (0-80 3-y-o and up) £3,720 1m 5f 9yds (2:10)

2267² NORTHERN GRADUATE (USA) [73] 4-10-0 K Darley (3) *cl up, pushed alng 5 fs out, led 2 out, sn rdn and styd on wl.*..........(7 to 2 jt-fav op 5 to 2 tchd 4 to 1) 1
2457² WILSONIC [65] (v) 4-9-6 Dean McKeown (4) *led till hdd 6 fs out, led ag'n 4 out, headed 2 out, kpt on wl.*..........(10 to 1 op 6 to 1) 2
2683² BRIGGSMAID [52] 5-8-7 M Tebbutt (5) *in tch, pushed alng 5 fs out, styd on same pace frm 3 out.*..........(9 to 2 op 4 to 1 tchd 5 to 1) 3
2521⁵ JAMES IS SPECIAL (Ire) [50] 5-8-5 J Quinn (6) *hld up, outpcd 5 out, hdwy fnl 2 fs, nvr dngrs.*..........(9 to 2 op 5 to 1) 4
2043⁴ BILBERRY [44] 4-7-13 J Lowe (2) *trkd ldrs, pushed alng 5 out, no hdwy*..........(7 to 2 jt-fav op 3 to 1) 5
2601* MENTALASANYTHIN [69] 4-9-10 (4ex) A Mackay (1) *hld up, quickened to ld 6 out, hdd 4 out, weakend o'r 2 out.*..........(4 to 1 tchd 9 to 2 and 5 to 1) 6
Dist: 1l, 2l, ¾l, 1½l, 7l. 2m 52.80s. a 6.80s (6 Ran).
SR: 7/-/-/ (P D Savill), Mrs M Reveley

2736 Corehouse Claiming Stakes Class F (3-y-o) £2,579 1m 65yds (2:40)

1900 OLICANA (Ire) 7-9 (7*) J Marshall (3) *hld up, hdwy 4 out, styd on wl to ld ins fnl furlong*.... (16 to 1 op 12 to 1) 1

2454[4] PLEASE SAY YES (Ire) 8-1 (7*) V Halliday (2) *prmnt, slight ld o'r 2 fs out, hdd ins fnl furlong, kpt on wl.* ....(9 to 2 op 7 to 2) 2

2307* BARLEY CAKE 7-11 J Fanning (4) *hld up, hdwy o'r 2 fs out, ev ch fnl furlong no extr towards finish.* ....(5 to 2 fav op 9 to 4 tchd 11 to 4) 3

2478[3] DEVIOUS DANCER 8-9 (5*) D McCabe (8) *trkd ldrs, chlgd o'r one furlong out, no extr ins fnl furlong.* ....(3 to 1 op 7 to 2 tchd 4 to 1) 4

2555[4] MY BALLYBOY 8-0 A Mackay (6) *cl up, dsptd ld o'r 2 fs out, sn rdn and one pace*.... (8 to 1 op 6 to 1) 5

1630[6] VELVET HEART (Ire) 8-5 K Darley (1) *hld up, hdwy o'r 4 fs out, wknd 2 out*.... (12 to 1 op 6 to 1 tchd 14 to 1) 6

1868[4] TINA'S DOMAIN 8-5 J Carroll (5) *in tch, rdn o'r 2 fs out, sn btn*.... (25 to 1 op 20 to 1) 7

1968 DESIRABLE MISS (v) 8-1 J Lowe (7) *led till hdd o'r 2 fs out, sn wknd*.... (14 to 1 op 12 to 1) 8

Dist: Nk, hd, 2l, 2½l, 15l, hd, 2½l. 1m 47.40s. a 3.40s (8 Ran).
SR: -/5/-/4/-/ (Ecudawn), M D Hammond

2737 I.M.I. Yorkshire Fittings Maiden Handicap Class F (0-65 3-y-o and up) £3,071 1m 65yds.... (3:10)

1928[3] FLETCHER'S BOUNTY (Ire) [44] (v) 4-9-6 K Darley (4) *hld up, steady hdwy 4 fs out, led ins fnl furlong, ran on wl.* .... (6 to 1 tchd 7 to 1 and 15 to 2) 1

2480[4] DANCES WITH GOLD [39] (bl) 3-8-7 Dean McKeown (12) *slwly into strd, sn in tch, effrt 3 out, ev ch one out, no extr ins fnl furlong*.... (10 to 1 op 8 to 1 tchd 11 to 1) 2

4690a MAGNETIC POINT (USA) [47] 4-9-9 J Carroll (13) *cl up, led o'r 4 fs till hdd and no extr ins fnl furlong.* ....(8 to 1 op 7 to 1) 3

2525 PERSIAN LION [30] 4-8-6 Alex Greaves (11) *in tch, effrt 3 fs out, kpt on wl fnl furlong*.... (40 to 1 tchd 50 to 1) 4

2388[5] HYDROPIC [26] 6-8-2 S Wood (10) *chsd ldrs, effrt o'r 2 fs out, ch entering fnl furlong, kpt on*.... (10 to 1) 5

2525[2] CANNY LAD [49] (v) 3-9-3 K Fallon (2) *prmnt, ev ch o'r one furlong out, btn whn not much room fnl furlong.* ....(5 to 1 fav op 4 to 1) 6

2593[6] QUESSONG [38] (v) 3-8-6 R Lappin (8) *prmnt till wknd o'r 2 fs out*.... (25 to 1 op 16 to 1) 7

2371[4] THE DANDY DON (Ire) [44] 4-9-6 J Lowe (1) *nvr dngrs.* .... (10 to 1 op 8 to 1) 8

2596[7] GRANDERISE (Ire) [44] 3-8-12 M Birch (9) *led till hdd o'r 4 fs out, sn wknd*.... (20 to 1 op 33 to 1) 9

2369[4] VENTURE FOURTH [32] 4-8-8 J Quinn (7) *prmnt will wknd 2 out*.... (8 to 1 op 7 to 1 tchd 9 to 1 and 10 to 1) 10

2553[3] PEEDIE PEAT [60] 3-9-9 (5*) O Pears (6) *al beh.* .... (10 to 1 op 7 to 1 tchd 11 to 1) 11

2459[9] THISONESFORALICE [41] 5-9-3 J Fanning (3) *beh, hdwy to chase ldrs o'r 5 fs out, wknd over 2 out.* ....(14 to 1 op 12 to 1 tchd 16 to 1 and 20 to 1) 12

2341[4] RAQS ASSAYF [45] 3-8-13 A Culhane (5) *beh frm hfwy, tld off*.... (8 to 1 op 7 to 1) 13

Dist: 2l, nk, ½l, nk, 2l, 6l, 3½l, 1½l, 3l, 1½l. 1m 46.60s. a 2.60s (13 Ran).
SR: 30/11/26/7/2/11/ (P Willis), Mrs M Reveley

2738 Arthur Balding Handicap Class E (0-70 3-y-o and up) £3,080 6f 5yds.... (3:40)

2553[2] MISS WHITTINGHAM (Ire) [61] 3-8-12 (7*) P Roberts (3) *chsd ldr, led o'r 2 fs out, cmftbly.* ....(6 to 5 on op Evens tchd 11 to 10 and 5 to 4 on) 1

2264[7] BEST EFFORT [50] 7-9-0 K Fallon (4) *in tch, effrt o'r 2 fs out, chsd wnr over one furlong out, kpt on, no imprsn.* ....(6 to 1 tchd 7 to 1) 2

2568[3] AYR RAIDER [60] (v) 6-9-10 J Fanning (5) *in tch, rdn hfwy, no hdwy*.... (6 to 1 op 5 to 1) 3+

2570* JOELLISE [38] (v) 3-7-3 (7*,7ex) Claire Balding (2) *hld up, effrt o'r 2 fs out, kpt on same pace*... (8 to 1 op 6 to 1) 3+

2600[8] DIET [67] (v) 7-9-10 (7*,7ex) R Havlin (1) *led till hdd o'r 2 fs out, fdd*.... (9 to 2 op 3 to 1) 5

Dist: 2l, 1½l, ½l, 2l. 1m 12.10s. a 1.40s (5 Ran).
SR: 41/28/32/2/29/ (J W Barrett), J Berry

2739 Lee Selling Stakes Class F (2-y-o) £2,691 5f 4yds.... (4:10)

2435[6] JIMMY THE SKUNK (Ire) 9-2 J Carroll (4) *made all, rdn fnl furlong, hld on wl.* ....(Evens fav op 11 to 10 on tchd 5 to 4) 1

2554[3] SPRING LOADED 8-11 Dean McKeown (5) *cl up, rdn o'r one furlong out, kpt on fnl furlong.* ....(11 to 8 op 13 to 8 tchd 7 to 4 and 5 to 4) 2

1759 NOSMO KING (Ire) (bl) 8-11 K Darley (3) *al chasing ldrs, kpt on und pres fnl furlong.* .... (20 to 1 tchd 25 to 1 and 33 to 1) 3

2103[4] HENRY THE HAWK 8-11 S Webster (1) *chsd ldrs, outpcd hfwy, styd on und pres fnl furlong.* (14 to 1 op 8 to 1) 4

2429 SALVOR (Ire) (v) 8-11 J Lowe (2) *al beh, lost tch hfwy.* .... (10 to 1 op 12 to 1) 5

Dist: ¾l, ¾l, nk, 10l. 1m 0.80s. a 2.50s (5 Ran).
SR: 22/14/11/10/-/ (J David Abell), J Berry

2740 Craignethan Maiden Handicap Class F (0-60 3-y-o and up) £3,004 1m 3f 16yds.... (4:40)

2551[5] SIR EDWARD HENRY (Ire) [45] (bl) 3-8-10 R Lappin (6) *trkd ldrs, chlgd o'r one furlong out, led ins fnl furlong, kpt on wl*.... (10 to 1 op 8 to 1 tchd 12 to 1) 1

2458[3] CORNFLAKE [45] 3-8-10 K Fallon (8) *trkd ldrs, effrt o'r 2 fs out, ev ch entering fnl furlong, kpt on wl.* ....(4 to 1 tchd 9 to 2) 2

1929 MR WOODCOCK [48] 8-9-10 J Carroll (7) *led till hdd ins fnl furlong, kpt on same pace.* .... (3 to 1 tchd 100 to 9 and 7 to 2) 3

2530[2] GREAT ORATION (Ire) [38] 4-9-0 A Mackay (3) *hld up, effrt o'r 3 fs out, styd on wl fnl furlong.* (10 to 1 op 8 to 1) 4

2358[8] MOST SIOUXTABLE [48] 3-8-13 J Fanning (4) *in tch, effrt 3 fs out, no hdwy*.... (8 to 1 op 6 to 1) 5

1601[6] DON'T CRY [27] 5-8-3 Kim Tinkler (1) *al beh*.... (20 to 1) 6

2091[2] BAY TERN (USA) [42] 7-9-4 M Birch (2) *wth ldr till weakend o'r 2 fs out*.... (11 to 4 fav op 7 to 2) 7

2383[5] ABSALOM'S PILLAR [56] 3-9-7 J Lowe (5) *in tch till wknd 2 out*.... (20 to 1 op 12 to 1) 8

Dist: ½l, ½l, sht-hd, 8l, 3l, 4l, 7l. 2m 23.00s. a 3.00s (8 Ran).
SR: 33/32/45/34/17/1/8/-/ (Peter Barr), F H Lee

TIPPERARY (IRE) (good)
Thursday July 22nd

2741 Westair Aviation (Fillies) Handicap (0-85 3-y-o) £3,452 7f.... (5:30)

2483* ELIZABETH'S PET (Ire) [-] 9-5 M J Kinane (2)... (3 to 1 fav) 1
2406[4] FLORA WOOD (Ire) [-] (bl) 8-13 W J Supple (6).... (4 to 1) 2
2514[9] TORCH SINGER [-] 7-1 (6*) P P Murphy (3).... (20 to 1) 3
1515[9] PETITE EPAULETTE [-] 9-1 (4*) P Carberry (1).... (14 to 1) 4
2406[3] MISS MISTLETOES (Ire) [-] 9-2 S Craine (4).... (7 to 2) 5
2556[3] DUNANY ROSE (Ire) [-] 7-11 N G McCullagh (9)... (10 to 1) 6
2406[7] OICHE MHAITH [-] (bl) 8-9 J P Murtagh (7).... (8 to 1) 7
2463[5] OVERCAST (Ire) [-] 8-7 (6*) J J Behan (5).... (8 to 1) 8
2297 SANS CERIPH (Ire) [-] 9-4 R Hughes (8).... (5 to 1) 9
Dist: 1½l, hd, 1l, 1l. 1m 34.10s. (9 Ran).
(Mrs D A Breen), E P Harty

2742 Rear Cross E.B.F. Fillies Maiden (2-y-o) £3,797 7f.... (6:00)

TIMINIYA (Ire) 9-0 R Hughes (3).... (8 to 1) 1
1509[3] DANCING AT LUNASA (Ire) 9-0 J P Murtagh (16)... (7 to 2) 2
SARANGA (Ire) 9-0 D Hogan (8).... (12 to 1) 3
1854[2] AL NAAYY 9-0 W J Supple (15).... (5 to 4 fav) 4
2402 CHART BUSTER 9-0 M J Kinane (11).... (8 to 1) 5
DANITA (Ire) 9-0 C Roche (13).... (5 to 1) 6
NEWPORT MADAM (Ire) 8-8 (6*) J J Behan (14)... (10 to 1) 7
1608[6] ZOE BAIRD 8-6 (8*) B Fenton (1).... (14 to 1) 8
KRAYYALEI (Ire) 9-0 S Craine (10).... (10 to 1) 9
2037 ALBERTA DIAMOND 9-0 P Shanahan (7).... (20 to 1) 10
MAKE THAT CALL (Ire) 9-0 P V Gilson (12).... (12 to 1) 11
LADY SAPIEN (Ire) 9-0 N G McCullagh (2).... (33 to 1) 12
COOLOWEN FLASH (Ire) 8-8 (6*) J A Heffernan (6) (33 to 1) 13
SMART ROSIE (Ire) 9-0 D V Smith (9).... (33 to 1) 14
2244[8] JENNY JINGLE (Ire) 9-0 K J Manning (5).... (16 to 1) 15
Dist: 1l, ¾l, sht-hd, 1½l. 1m 34.70s. (15 Ran).
(H H Aga Khan), John M Oxx

2743 Cappawhite Maiden (3-y-o) £2,762 1m 1f.... (6:30)

1796[3] BRAVE RAIDER (Ire) 9-0 M J Kinane (2).... (4 to 1) 1
2249[5] MY KERRY DANCER (USA) 9-0 S Craine (10).... (5 to 1) 2
2247[4] ENDSONG (USA) 8-11 C Roche (9).... (7 to 4 on) 3
2140[8] SHPEEL (Ire) 8-11 P Shanahan (1).... (33 to 1) 4
2609[7] QUIET CONFIDENCE (Ire) 8-11 R Hughes (3).... (16 to 1) 5
2497[3] JU JU'S GIRL (Ire) 8-11 K J Manning (4).... (10 to 1) 6
2185[6] DANCEALOT (Ire) 8-8 (6*) J J Behan (11).... (16 to 1) 7
LADYS BID (Ire) 8-11 J F Egan (6).... (12 to 1) 8
2516[7] ANIMATE (Ire) 8-3 (8*) J J Stack (7).... (25 to 1) 9
2249 CRISSY (Ire) 8-11 N G McCullagh (8).... (20 to 1) 10
1997 MY SPECIAL GUEST (Ire) 8-11 B Coogan (5).... (25 to 1) 11
Dist: Nk, ¾l, 2½l, ¾l. 1m 53.60s. (11 Ran).
(Moyglare Stud Farm), D K Weld

2744 Aer Rianta Shannon Challenge Race (Listed) (3-y-o and up) £8,627 1¾m.... (7:00)

2408* SHAIYBARA (Ire) 3-8-7 J P Murtagh (6) *mid-div, prog 4 fs out, quickened to ld o'r one out, styd on*.... (11 to 4) 1

2405[6] BALLYKETT LADY (USA) 3-8-7 C Roche (3) *led, rdn 2 fs out, hdd o'r one out, kpt on*.... (5 to 2 fav) 2

JUDICIAL FIELD (Ire) 4-9-10 P Shanahan (5) *trkd ldr, rdn and lost pl 4 fs out, kpt on ag'n r-in*.... (16 to 1) 3

2518* PARNALA (USA) 3-8-7 D Hogan (1) *mid-div, styd on one pace*.... (12 to 1) 4

2143[8] CRAZY GAIL 6-9-7 W J Supple (2) *rear, some prog 4 fs out, kpt on one pace r-in*.... (25 to 1) 5

895* SLEET SKIER 6-10-1 M J Kinane (8) *hld up, rdn and no imprsn 3 fs out*..........(100 to 30) 6
2077^{3} GARABAGH (Ire) 4-10-1 R Hughes (4) *wl plcd, prog to track ldr 6 fs out, rdn 3 out, sn wknd*..........(5 to 1) 7
309^{6} SANNDILA (Ire) 5-9-7 M Duffy (7) *al rear*..........(14 to 1) 8
Dist: 1½l, 7l, 1½l, 4l. 2m 56.90s. (8 Ran).
(H H Aga Khan), John M Oxx

2745 Muskerry E.B.F. Race (2-y-o) £4,142 5f ....(7:30)

1886^{2} IL CARAVAGGIO (Ire) (bl) 9-7 M J Kinane (2)..........(5 to 2) 1
2075^{2} KLY GREEN 9-7 C Roche (6)..........(6 to 4 on) 2
2294^{4} LYDIA MC (Ire) 8-11 W J Supple (1)..........(10 to 1) 3
1332^{4} STAGE LEFT EVEN (Ire) 9-0 S Craine (4)..........(11 to 2) 4
2403^{7} WAVE THE WAND (Ire) 9-7 R Hughes (3)..........(10 to 1) 5
1442^{6} MONICA'S CHOICE (Ire) 9-0 K J Manning (5)..........(20 to 1) 6
DACANI STAR (Ire) 8-11 P Shanahan (8)..........(11 to 2) 7
Dist: 2l, 1½l, hd, 8l. 59.20s. (7 Ran).
(Andrea Schiavi), D K Weld

YARMOUTH (good)
Thursday July 22nd
Going Correction: MINUS 0.05 sec. per fur. (races 1,2,3,4), MINUS 0.20 (5,6)

2746 North Walsham Handicap Class C (0-95 3-y-o) £5,047 6f 3yds..........(2:20)

2237^{9} PRESS GALLERY [84] 9-1 P Robinson (8) *patiently rdn, quickened to ld o'r one furlong out, ran on strly.* ....(8 to 1 op 7 to 1) 1
CAPE WEAVER [90] 9-7 L Dettori (9) *chsd alng to go pace, hdwy und pres last 2 fs, ran on wl.* ....(4 to 1 tchd 11 to 2) 2
HUFFA (USA) [85] 9-2 M Hills (7) *nvr far away, effrt and drvn alng 2 fs out, kpt on same pace ins last.* ....(10 to 1 op 8 to 1) 3
2469^{4} HOTARIA [70] 8-1 N Carlisle (3) *led centre grp for o'r 4 fs, rdn and one pace last 100 yards*..........(16 to 1 op 14 to 1) 4
1213 PRINCESS OBERON (Ire) [82] 8-10 (3*) M Fenton (6) *chsd alng to improve frm midfield 2 fs out, styd on finish.* ....(8 to 1 op 7 to 1 tchd 9 to 1) 5
2494^{2} ABERLADY [65] 7-10 G Bardwell (5) *frnt rnk in centre, feeling pace and rdn 2 fs out, no extr.* ....(7 to 2 fav op 3 to 1 tchd 4 to 1) 6
2237^{8} ABTAAL [86] (bl) 9-3 R Hills (1) *rcd alone far side, speed 4 fs, eased whn btn*..........(8 to 1 op 6 to 1) 7
1718 GREENLET (Ire) [81] 8-12 W R Swinburn (4) *sluggish strt, nvr gng pace, eased last 2 fs*..........(4 to 1 op 3 to 1) 8
Dist: 2½l, ¾l, ¾l, 1½l, 8l, 1½l, 4l. 1m 13.80s. a 2.80s (8 Ran).
SR: 39/35/27/9/15/ (Lord Howard de Walden), Mrs J Cecil

2747 Golden Mile Selling Handicap Class G (0-60 3-y-o and up) £2,826 1m 3yds ....(2:50)

2291^{8} YONGE TENDER [37] (bl) 6-8-8 (3*) D Harrison (1) *wth ldr far side, led o'r 2 fs out, drvn clr, all out.* ....(6 to 1 fav op 8 to 1 tchd 10 to 1) 1
2445^{6} MAY SQUARE (Ire) [37] 5-8-11 W Ryan (10) *chsd ldrs, improved hfwy, styd on to ld stands grp ins fnl furlong, ran on*..........(12 to 1 op 10 to 1 tchd 14 to 1) 2
2384^{6} LITTLE PARK [37] 4-8-11 P Robinson (19) *pressed ldrs, led stands side grp o'r one furlong out till ins last, one pace*..........(16 to 1 op 10 to 1 tchd 20 to 1) 3
2004^{4} FAIR ENCHANTRESS [44] (bl) 5-9-4 D Holland (18) *chsd stands side grp, effrt 2 fs out, not quicken.* ....(8 to 1 tchd 9 to 1) 4
2631^{8} DEPUTY TIM [39] 10-8-9^{3} (7*) H Bastiman (12) *nvr far away, feeling pace and drvn alng 2 fs out, no extr.* ....(20 to 1 op 14 to 1 tchd 25 to 1) 5
2499^{4} ASCOM PAGER TOO [43] 3-8-9 W R Swinburn (4) *speed stands side 6 fs, fdd*..........(14 to 1 op 10 to 1) 6
2590^{2} BASSIO (Bel) [42] (h) 4-9-2 W Hood (14) *sluggish strt, improved centre last 2 fs, nvr nrr*..........(7 to 1 op 6 to 1) 7
2215^{8} CAMINO A RONDA [27] 4-7-9^{1} (7*) P McCabe (16) *led stands side grp, clr hfwy, hdd and wknd o'r one furlong out*..........(33 to 1 op 20 to 1) 8
2525^{3} AMLAK (USA) [50] (v) 4-9-10 L Dettori (2) *led far side till o'r 2 fs out, wknd quickly*. (13 to 2 op 5 to 1 tchd 7 to 1) 9
2520^{4} NORMAN WARRIOR [37] (v) 4-8-6 (5*) C Hodgson (7) *frnt rnk for o'r 5 fs, fdd*..........(12 to 1 op 8 to 1 tchd 14 to 1) 10
2520^{8} KELLY'S KITE [38] 5-8-5 (7*) C Hawksley (17) *sluggish strt, some hdwy last 2 fs, nvr nrr*..........(8 to 1 op 6 to 1) 11
2585 MELANCOLIA [38] (bl) 7-8-9 (3*) S D Williams (15) *chsd stands side grp for o'r 5 fs, fdd*..........(14 to 1 op 20 to 1) 12
2466^{5} BLUE POINT (Ire) [28] (bl) 4-8-2 G Hind (8) *chsd alng in midfield hfwy, sn lost tch*..........(33 to 1 op 20 to 1) 13
2291^{6} SHALOU [44] 4-9-4 M Hills (11) *chsd ldrs to hfwy, sn btn.* ....(7 to 1 op 10 to 1 tchd 6 to 1) 14
238^{6} FIRST HOME [30] 6-7-11 (7*) Kim McDonnell (9) *outpcd.* ....(33 to 1 op 20 to 1) 15
2499^{3} COSMIC STAR [50] (v) 3-9-2 W Woods (13) *wth ldrs, feeling pace o'r 2 fs out, sn lost tch*..........(7 to 1 tchd 8 to 1) 16
2232^{6} LAZY RHYTHM (USA) [45] 7-9-5 F Norton (3) *reared strt, not reco'r*..........(20 to 1 op 14 to 1) 17
2104^{9} SMOCKING [46] 3-8-5 (7*) Elizabeth Turner (6) *sluggish strt, nvr a factor*..........(33 to 1 op 20 to 1) 18
2443^{4} DUKE OF BUDWORTH [55] (v) 3-9-0 (7*) S Mulvey (5) *unruly in stalls, sn drvn alng, tld off last 3 fs.* ....(25 to 1 op 14 to 1) 19
Dist: 1l, hd, 4l, 5l, 5l, 1½l, 1l, 2l, 1½l, ¾l. 1m 39.80s. a 4.00s (19 Ran).
SR: 31/28/27/22/2/-/ (C N Williams), C N Williams

2748 EBF Scroby Sands Maiden Fillies Stakes Class D (2-y-o) £4,308 7f 3yds ....(3:20)

2240^{2} SUAAD (Ire) 8-11 R Hills (5) *pld hrd, led aftr 2 and a half fs, tacked lft to race centre, ran on strly fnl furlong.* (7 to 4 on op 11 to 8 on tchd 5 to 4 on and 2 to 1 on) 1
MISS RINJANI 8-11 M Hills (2) *nvr far away, str chal o'r one furlong out, kpt on same pace.* ....(2 to 1 op 11 to 8 tchd 9 to 4) 2
2541^{8} PRINCESS CARMEN (Ire) 8-11 L Dettori (1) *led 2 and a half fs, feeling pace and rdn o'r one out, no extr.* ....(14 to 1 op 10 to 1) 3
CHILDREN'S CHOICE (Ire) 8-11 P Robinson (3) *niggled alng and drifted rght to stands side hfwy, sn outpcd.* ....(20 to 1 op 16 to 1 tchd 25 to 1) 4
Dist: 1½l, 6l, 12l. 1m 28.80s. a 5.60s (4 Ran).
SR: 8/3/-/-/ (Hamdan Al-Maktoum), H Thomson Jones

2749 Acle Maiden Stakes Class D (3-y-o) £3,850 7f 3yds..........(3:50)

2563 FUCHU 8-6 (3*) B Doyle (15) *co'red up gng wl, drvn to ld ins fnl furlong, gmely*..........(33 to 1 op 20 to 1) 1
MAKIN (USA) 9-0 W Carson (8) *led till drvn alng and hdd ins fnl furlong, rallied*..........(4 to 1 op 7 to 4) 2
ARVOLA 8-9 W R Swinburn (14) *sluggish strt, hdwy o'r 2 fs out, ran green, fnshd wl.* ....(11 to 2 op 9 to 2 tchd 6 to 1) 3
2563^{9} DUBAI SUMMER 9-0 P Robinson (9) *prressed ldg pair, hrd drvn o'r one furlong out, not quicken.* ....(20 to 1 op 14 to 1 tchd 25 to 1) 4
NUMUTHEJ (USA) 8-9 R Hills (12) *trkd ldrs, hdwy last 2 fs, ran on*..........(9 to 1 op 10 to 1 tchd 12 to 1) 5
AWESOME VENTURE 8-11 (3*) J Weaver (6) *speed on outsd for o'r 5 fs, no extr*..........(25 to 1 op 20 to 1 tchd 33 to 1) 6
2580 ZAJKO (USA) 9-0 G Hind (16) *wth ldrs, feeling pace and drvn alng o'r one furlong out, fdd.* (33 to 1 op 20 to 1) 7
1308^{5} GRANVILLE CORNER 9-0 N Carlisle (10) *settled midfield, feeling pace and rdn hfwy, nvr able to chal.* ....(50 to 1 op 25 to 1) 8
821 MISS KINABALU 8-9 M Hills (7) *wl plcd for o'r 5 fs, sn btn.* ....(8 to 1 op 12 to 1 tchd 16 to 1) 9
PACIFIC POWER 9-0 D Holland (4) *sluggish strt, not reco'r*..........(25 to 1 op 16 to 1) 10
VARELITO (Ire) (bl) 8-11 (3*) Emma O'Gorman (2) *hmpd and crrd lft strt, not reco'r*..........(33 to 1 op 20 to 1) 11
PEA FORTY FIVE 8-9 S Whitworth (3) *swrvd lft strt, nvr a factor*..........(66 to 1 op 50 to 1) 12
2563 CHAMPAGNE 'N ROSES 8-9 L Dettori (11) *wth ldrs, drvn alng whn pace quickened o'r 2 fs out, fdd.* ....(8 to 1 op 12 to 1 tchd 16 to 1) 13
Dist: Nk, hd, 4l, 2½l, nk, 3½l, 3½l, 2½l, 4l, 5l. 1m 27.00s. a 3.80s (13 Ran).
SR: 33/37/31/24/11/15/4/-/-/ (C E Brittain), C E Brittain

2750 City Of Norwich Claiming Stakes Class F (3-y-o and up) £2,601 1m 3f 101yds..........(4:20)

1951^{6} BALADIYA 6-8-10 (5*) C Hodgson (1) *made all, quickened appr strt, drw clr approaching fnl furlong.* ....(5 to 2 op 2 to 1 tchd 11 to 4) 1
2537^{3} OVERPOWER 9-9-0 P Robinson (4) *tucked away on ins, improved to track wnr o'r 2 fs out, no imprsn inside last*..........(11 to 8 fav op 2 to 1) 2
2471 GIN AND ORANGE 7-9-0 S Whitworth (5) *co'red up on ins, improved over 2 fs out, styd on same pace inside last.* ....(20 to 1 op 12 to 1) 3
2544^{2} HILLZAH (USA) 5-8-13 (7*) H Bastiman (6) *patiently rdn, brght wide to improve entering strt, edgd lft last 2 fs, one pace*..........(4 to 1 op 3 to 1) 4
WORTHY MEMORIES 4-9-5 N Carlisle (9) *trkd ldg 4, lost grnd whn pace quickened entering strt, sn btn.* ....(14 to 1 op 10 to 1) 5
1928^{8} BLACK BEAN 3-8-0 (3*) B Doyle (7) *in tch, und pres entering strt, fdd o'r 2 fs out*..........(14 to 1 op 7 to 1) 6
MERCERS MAGIC (Ire) (v) 5-9-0^{2} T Wall (8) *trkd wnr, feeling pace and lost grnd entering strt, sn btn.* ....(50 to 1 op 25 to 1) 7
PEARLED (USA) 6-8-12 M Wigham (2) *chsd ldg pair till appr strt, tld off*..........(50 to 1 op 25 to 1) 8
2536^{6} RAPINSKI 4-8-9 (7*) K Pattinson (3) *pressed ldrs, struggling appr strt, sn tld off*..........(50 to 1 op 33 to 1) 9
Dist: 6l, 1½l, nk, 10l, 4l, 6l, 3½l, dist. 2m 27.00s. a 3.50s (9 Ran).
SR: 43/30/27/32/11/-/ (Mrs Rosalie Hawes), D Morris

2751 Belton Maiden Handicap Class D (0-75 3-y-o and up) £3,817 1¾m 17yds (4:50)

2130^{3} MONSIEUR DUPONT (Ire) [59] 3-7-10^{1} (3*) D Harrison (6) *settled gng wl, led 3 fs out, hrd pressed appr last, gmely*............... (6 to 4 fav op 2 to 1 tchd 9 to 4) 1
2196^{4} RUSTY REEL [55] 3-7-8 G Bardwell (4) *nvr far away, drw level und pres o'r one furlong out, edgd lft, no extr cl hme*.................................(12 to 1 op 10 to 1) 2
2326^{2} RIVIERE ACTOR (USA) [71] 3-8-10 W Ryan (1) *al hndy, ev ch whn idled o'r one furlong out, swtchd ins last, kpt on*.................(5 to 1 op 4 to 1 tchd 11 to 2) 3
1840 PEACH BRANDY [41] 4-7-8^{1} N Carlisle (2) *led, quickened appr strt, hdd 3 fs out, kpt on same pace.* .... (14 to 1 op 8 to 1) 4
1827^{9} DEDUCE [75] 4-10-0 M Hills (9) *patiently rdn, hdwy to chal o'r 3 fs out, ridden and not quicken 2 out.* ....(9 to 2 op 5 to 1 tchd 6 to 1 and 4 to 1) 5
2281^{2} MUTAWALI (Ire) [65] 3-8-4 W Carson (8) *trkd ldrs gng wl, effrt on outsd o'r 3 fs out, rdn and no imprsn.* ....(8 to 1 tchd 10 to 1) 6
2091^{3} DIAMOND WEDDING (USA) [61] 4-8-11 (3*) B Doyle (7) *chsd ldrs, drvn alng whn pace quickened in strt, nvr able to chal*.....................................(8 to 1 op 3 to 1) 7
2178 EASY TOOMEY [40] 5-7-0 (7*) Kim McDonnell (5) *trkd ldrs, effrt and drvn alng 3 fs out, sn outpcd.* .... (50 to 1 op 33 to 1) 8
2328^{8} MISS RITA [63] 4-9-2 M Wigham (3) *sluggish strt, lost grnd appr strt, tld off*...................(8 to 1 tchd 10 to 1) 9

Dist: ¾l, 1½l, hd, 2½l, 1l, 1½l, 6l, dist. 3m 5.40s. a 8.40s (9 Ran).
(Wafic Said), B W Hills

ASCOT (good)
Friday July 23rd
Going Correction: MINUS 0.05 sec. per fur. (races 1,4,6,7), MINUS 0.15 (2,3,5)

2752 Cranbourne Chase Maiden Stakes Class D (3-y-o) £11,053 1¼m....(2:00)

PETER QUINCE 9-0 W Ryan (16) *chsd ldrs, shaken up to ld appr fnl furlong, quickened clr, cmftbly.* ....(10 to 1 op 8 to 1 tchd 14 to 1) 1
2332^{2} LACOTTE (Ire) 9-0 M Roberts (14) *cl up, led appr 2 fs out till approaching one out, one pace whn swrvd lft ins last*.................................(13 to 8 on op 5 to 4) 2
1802^{2} TREE OF LIFE 8-9 R Cochrane (5) *sn led, hdd appr 2 fs out, one pace*..............................(8 to 1 op 4 to 1) 3
KESTON POND (Ire) 9-0 L Dettori (10) *beh, hdwy o'r 3 fs out, one pace 2 out*...(25 to 1 op 33 to 1 tchd 50 to 1) 4
2416^{5} AWESTRIKE (USA) 9-0 Paul Eddery (8) *trkd ldrs, pushed alng entering strt, wknd o'r one furlong out.* .... (33 to 1 op 20 to 1) 5
MEAVY 8-9 D Harrison (12) *mid-div, effrt and hdwy o'r 3 fs out, sn one pace*... (25 to 1 op 16 to 1 tchd 33 to 1) 6
1344^{7} PARANGO (USA) 9-0 B Marcus (13) *cl up, pushed alng o'r 3 fs out, sn outpcd*... (25 to 1 op 14 to 1 tchd 33 to 1) 7
2416^{4} IMPECCABLE TASTE 8-9 J Reid (1) *sn in tch, effrt and no hdwy fnl 3 fs*............................(33 to 1 op 20 to 1) 8
1831 ROYAL BALLET (Ire) 8-9 A McGlone (11) *mid-div, rdn o'r 3 fs out, sn btn*........................(33 to 1 op 20 to 1) 9
1429^{8} INTENTION (USA) 9-0 W Newnes (7) *al beh.* .... (33 to 1 op 25 to 1) 10
1992^{6} PRIME OF LIFE (Ire) 9-0 D Holland (2) *mid-div, rdn o'r 3 fs out, sn btn*..............................(8 to 1 op 9 to 2) 11
RIZ BIZ (USA) 8-9 M Hills (4) *missed break, al beh.* .... (33 to 1 op 20 to 1) 12
4755a VILLAGE GREEN (Fr) 9-0 M Perrett (9) *cl up, wknd quickly o'r 3 fs out*............................(33 to 1 op 20 to 1) 13
CAMBARA 8-9 P D'Arcy (6) *al rear.* ....(16 to 1 op 12 to 1 tchd 20 to 1) 14
2563^{4} AL KATIRIYAH (Ire) (e/c) 8-9 W Carson (15) *beh, hdwy o'r 6 fs out, wknd over 4 out, tld off, virtually pld up.* ....(8 to 1 op 7 to 1 tchd 6 to 1) 15

Dist: 3l, 4l, 3l, 5l, 3l, hd, 2½l, hd, 8l, 3l. 2m 6.94s. a 3.24s (15 Ran).
SR: 63/57/44/43/33/22/26/16/15/ (Lord Howard de Walden), H R A Cecil

2753 Palan Rated Class B Handicap (0-100 3-y-o and up) £9,279 5f......... (2:30)

2399^{6} REGAL CHIMES [100] 4-9-7 L Dettori (2) *made all, pushed alng and ran on wl fnl furlong.* ....(9 to 1 op 8 to 1 tchd 10 to 1) 1
2392^{2} ASHTINA [86] 8-8-7 J Quinn (3) *cl up, hrd rdn and ev ch ins fnl furlong, no extr close hme.* ....(100 to 30 op 4 to 1 tchd 3 to 1) 2
1841^{9} SABRE RATTLER [100] 3-9-2 W Carson (10) *rcd alone centre, al prmnt, one pace frm o'r one furlong out.* ....(9 to 1 op 8 to 1 tchd 10 to 1) 3
2255 CANTORIS [86] 7-8-7 D Holland (9) *outpcd till ran on ins fnl furlong*............(9 to 1 op 8 to 1 tchd 10 to 1) 4
2392 BEAU VENTURE (USA) [86] (bl) 5-8-4 (3*) N Kennedy (1) *trkd ldrs, wknd appr fnl furlong.* ....(16 to 1 op 14 to 1 tchd 20 to 1) 5
2620^{3} RUNNING GLIMPSE (Ire) [86] 5-8-7 M Roberts (7) *in tch, pushed alng hfwy, sn hrd rdn, not pace to chal.* ....(9 to 1 op 7 to 1 tchd 10 to 1) 6
2018 TERRHARS (Ire) [87] 5-8-3 (5*) D McCabe (11) *outpcd, nvr on terms*.................(9 to 1 op 8 to 1 tchd 10 to 1) 7
2255^{6} BORN TO BE [86] 4-8-0 (7*) A Martinez (6) *trkd ldrs till wknd o'r one furlong out.* ....(33 to 1 op 25 to 1 tchd 40 to 1) 8
2524* BELLS OF LONGWICK [86] 4-8-7 (3ex) T Williams (4) *prmnt, hrd rdn 2 fs out, sn btn*.......................... (33 to 1) 9
2628* MISS VAXETTE [88] 4-8-2 (7*,3ex) M Humphries (8) *pld hrd, rstrained rear, sn outpcd.* ....(3 to 1 fav op 5 to 2 tchd 100 to 30) 10
891^{9} BIT OF A LARK [96] 5-9-3 S Perks (5) *prmnt till wknd 2 fs out*.....................(25 to 1 op 20 to 1 tchd 33 to 1) 11

Dist: ½l, 2½l, 1½l, sht-hd, hd, 1½l, 3½l, 1½l, 1l, 2l. 1m 0.93s. a 0.63s (11 Ran).
SR: 79/63/62/47/46/45/40/25/19/ (Michael Sturgess), B A McMahon

2754 Virginia Water Maiden Stakes Class D Sponsored by Mrs H. J. Heinz (2-y-o) £9,961 6f...................... (3:00)

GLATISANT 8-11 M Hills (2) *made all, shaken up appr fnl furlong, quickened clr, imprsv.* ....(11 to 10 on op 11 to 10) 1
BLUE SIREN 8-11 R Cochrane (7) *cl up, rdn and ev ch 2 fs out, outpcd appr last*....(7 to 1 op 4 to 1 tchd 8 to 1) 2
LEOPARDESS (Ire) 8-11 M Roberts (4) *trkd ldrs, pushed alng o'r 2 fs out, kpt on fnl furlong.* ....(16 to 1 op 12 to 1 tchd 20 to 1) 3
TAKREEM (USA) 8-11 W Carson (1) *slwly into strd, outpcd, hdwy o'r one furlong out, one pace ins last.* ....(7 to 1 op 4 to 1 tchd 8 to 1) 4
SUPER GODDESS (Ire) 8-11 D Holland (6) *chsd ldrs, shaken up 2 fs out, wknd o'r one out.* ....(15 to 2 op 9 to 2 tchd 8 to 1) 5
CADENABBIA (USA) 8-11 J Reid (5) *trkd ldrs, pushed alng hfwy, wknd 2 fs out.* (14 to 1 op 10 to 1 tchd 16 to 1) 6
ROSY LYDGATE 8-11 Paul Eddery (3) *keen hold, in tch till outpcd frm 2 fs out*...(20 to 1 op 16 to 1 tchd 25 to 1) 7
PIZZAZZ 8-11 L Dettori (8) *in tch, rdn and flashed tail o'r 2 fs out, sn btn*........(10 to 1 op 8 to 1 tchd 12 to 1) 8

Dist: 5l, 1½l, hd, 7l, 1l, 2l, 5l. 1m 16.64s. a 3.24s (8 Ran).
SR: 14/-/-/-/-/ (Sir Philip Oppenheimer), G Wragg

2755 Brown Jack Handicap Class D (0-80 3-y-o and up) £12,330 2m 45yds (3:30)

1669^{7} BOLD RESOLUTION (Ire) [50] 5-7-12 M Roberts (3) *hld up in mid-div, hdwy o'r 2 fs out, led over one out, sn clr.* .... (5 to 1 fav) 1
2617 REQUESTED [76] 6-9-10 M Perrett (9) *beh, hdwy o'r 2 fs out, styd on wl*.......(16 to 1 op 14 to 1 tchd 20 to 1) 2
2477* CHAKALAK [68] 5-8-13 (3*,3ex) D Harrison (13) *chsd ldrs, swtchd lft 2 fs out, led briefly one and a half out, one pace*...................(13 to 2 op 6 to 1 tchd 7 to 1) 3
2251* ASIAN PUNTER (Ire) [72] 4-8-13 (7*) N Varley (10) *beh, hdwy on ins 5 fs out, led o'r 3 out to one and a half out, one pace*.....................(7 to 1 op 6 to 1 tchd 8 to 1) 4
2662* CHUCKLESTONE [64] 10-8-12 (3ex) N Day (8) *trkd ldrs, rdn alng 4 fs out, one pace*..(8 to 1 op 7 to 1 tchd 9 to 1) 5
2048^{3} DOYCE [63] 4-8-11 R Cochrane (6) *hld up beh, hdwy o'r 2 fs out, nrst finish*...... (7 to 1 op 6 to 1 tchd 15 to 2) 6
2617^{8} AMAZON EXPRESS [66] 4-9-0 A McGlone (1) *hld up rear, hdwy o'r 5 fs out, hrd rdn 2 out, no response.* ....(12 to 1 op 8 to 1 tchd 14 to 1) 7
2573* STAR QUEST [73] 6-9-7 (3ex) L Dettori (7) *beh, effrt on ins o'r 3 fs out, wknd over 2 out*.........(8 to 1 op 7 to 1) 8
2521* FREE MOVER (Ire) [77] 4-9-11 (3ex) W Carson (4) *trkd ldrs till lost pl o'r 4 fs out*...............(6 to 1 tchd 8 to 1) 9
2048^{8} CHILD STAR (Fr) [46] 4-7-8^{8} (7*) S McCarthy (12) *trkd ldr, led 5 fs out till o'r 3 out, wknd.* ....(33 to 1 op 25 to 1 tchd 40 to 1) 10
2547^{2} KADASTROF (Fr) [72] 3-8-4 S Dawson (2) *trkd ldrs, rdn and wknd o'r 3 fs out*.................(14 to 1 op 12 to 1) 11
2002^{4} ELAINE TULLY (Ire) [80] 5-10-0 J Reid (5) *led to 5 fs out, btn whn hmpd and snatched up 2 out.* (16 to 1 op 14 to 1) 12

Dist: 3l, nk, 4l, 1½l, 3½l, 1l, 5l, 2½l, ¾l, 8l. 3m 33.55s. a 8.55s (12 Ran).
SR: -/13/4/4/-/-/ (R M Cyzer), C A Cyzer

2756 EBF Sandwich Maiden Stakes Class D (2-y-o) £10,052 7f...............(4:05)

IONIO (USA) 9-0 B Marcus (2) *trkd ldrs, led o'r one furlong out, rdn and ran on wl.* ....(10 to 1 op 8 to 1 tchd 12 to 1) 1
2299^{3} SOUTHERN POWER (Ire) 9-0 L Dettori (5) *dsptd ld, led o'r 3 fs out, rdn and hdd over one out, one pace.* ....(6 to 5 fav op Evens tchd 11 to 8) 2
FITZROVIAN (Ire) 9-0 M Roberts (1) *led till o'r 3 fs out, shaken up 2 out, no extr.* ....(15 to 8 op 7 to 4 tchd 6 to 4 and 2 to 1) 3
HOBART 9-0 R Cochrane (4) *in tch till outpcd 2 fs out.* ....(20 to 1 op 14 to 1 tchd 25 to 1) 4
MUWAFIK 9-0 W Carson (3) *ran green, sn outpcd, nvr on terms*..................(11 to 2 op 7 to 2 tchd 6 to 1) 5

Dist: 2l, 3½l, 8l, 4l. 1m 30.25s. a 3.95s (5 Ran).
SR: 25/19/8/-/-/ (The Dowager Lady Beaverbrook), C E Brittain

2757 Chester Apprentice Handicap Class E (0-90 3-y-o and up) £4,542 1m... (4:35)

2390⁴ RAPID SUCCESS (USA) [90] 3-9-8 (6*) A Procter (7) *led till appr 2 fs out, rallied to ld cl hme.* ....(6 to 1 op 7 to 1 tchd 8 to 1) 1
2333⁸ KASSBAAN (USA) [71] 3-8-3 (6*) J Tate (10) *trkd ldrs, led appr 2 fs out, strd shortened and hdd cl hme.* ....(7 to 1 op 9 to 2 tchd 8 to 1) 2
2520* LADY LACEY [50] (v) 6-7-7 (3*,5ex) N Varley (11) *chsd ldrs, hdwy blw 2 fs out, kpt on wl fnl furlong.* ....(9 to 4 fav op 7 to 2 tchd 4 to 1) 3
1242 MON PETITNAMOUR (Ire) [47] 4-7-2 (5*) M Baird (13) *slwly into strd, sn reco'red to chase ldrs, styd on one pace fnl 2 fs.*........(33 to 1 tchd 40 to 1) 4
1686⁵ PROUD BRIGADIER (Ire) [57] 5-8-0 (3*) P McCabe (3) *sn pushed alng in mid-div, hrd rdn o'r 2 fs out, kpt on.* ....(8 to 1 op 7 to 1 tchd 9 to 1) 5
2121⁶ OLD COMRADES [53] 6-7-10 (3*) D McCabe (4) *beh, hdwy o'r one furlong out, styd on, nrst finish.* ....(9 to 1 op 7 to 1) 6
2333 DANNY BOY [75] (bl) 3-8-5 (8*) Mark Denaro (9) *trkd ldrs till wknd appr fnl furlong*........(7 to 1 op 6 to 1) 7
2363 NOBLE PET [82] 4-9-4 (10*) C Webb (1) *sn outpcd, nvr on terms*........(12 to 1 tchd 14 to 1) 8
2029⁷ ROSE ELEGANCE [71] 4-9-0 (3*) V Slattery (12) *beh, rdn alng o'r 3 fs out, no imprsn*........(16 to 1 tchd 20 to 1) 9
2431⁷ LITTLE ROUSILLON [62] 5-8-2 (6*) Kim McDonnell (8) *trkd ldrs till wknd o'r one furlong out.* ....(12 to 1 op 10 to 1 tchd 14 to 1) 10
690 SALBUS [86] 3-9-2 (8*) A Martinez (6) *al beh.* ....(25 to 1 op 20 to 1) 11
2121⁹ GARTH [60] (v) 5-8-0 (6*) M Humphries (5) *al beh.* ....(20 to 1 op 16 to 1) 12
2391⁹ ZAMANAYN (Ire) [60] 5-8-3 (3*) T G McLaughlin (2) *al beh.* ....(33 to 1) 13
Dist: Hd, hd, 4l, 1½l, 1½l, hd, 1l, 6l, 1½l, 1½l. 1m 43.50s. a 4.00s (13 Ran).
SR: 48/28/14/-/4/-/8/20/-/ (Yoshiki Akazawa), D R C Elsworth

2758 Balmoral Handicap Class C (0-90 3-y-o) £8,805 1¼m................. (5:10)

2010* MOSCOW SEA (USA) [81] 8-12 M Roberts (9) *trkd ldr, led appr 2 fs out, rdn and ran on wl.* ....(7 to 1 op 6 to 1 tchd 8 to 1) 1
2333 BRANDONHURST [80] 8-11 L Dettori (7) *mid-div, hdwy 2 fs out, ev ch ins last, ran on.* ....(8 to 1 op 10 to 1 tchd 11 to 1) 2
2333⁹ GEORGE DILLINGHAM [87] 9-4 Paul Eddery (10) *beh, rdn and hdwy o'r 2 fs out, kpt on und pres ins last.* ....(11 to 1 op 10 to 1 tchd 14 to 1) 3
2333 NAFUTH (USA) [81] 8-12 W Carson (15) *trkd ldrs, rdn 2 fs out, wknd ins last*........(14 to 1 op 12 to 1) 4
2135⁵ KIMBERLEY BOY [77] 8-8 D Holland (13) *beh, styd on und pres fnl 2 fs, nrst finish.* ....(12 to 1 op 8 to 1 tchd 14 to 1) 5
2019³ AJALAN (Ire) [83] 8-9 (5*) J Tate (5) *beh, rdn o'r 2 fs out, nrst finish*........(16 to 1 op 12 to 1) 6
1921⁵ FROGMARCH (USA) [90] 9-7 J Reid (1) *beh, hdwy o'r one furlong out, nvr nrr*........(14 to 1 op 12 to 1) 7
2289² WELL SUITED [71] 8-2¹ B Marcus (8) *mid-div, rdn alng thrght, no hdwy fnl 3 fs.* ....(11 to 2 op 6 to 1 tchd 7 to 1) 8
2236* MIDYAN BLUE (Ire) [75] 8-6 R Cochrane (2) *nvr on terms.* ....(11 to 4 fav op 7 to 2 tchd 9 to 2) 9
2066⁴ NURYANDRA [78] 8-9 M Hills (16) *trkd ldrs, wknd wl o'r one furlong out*........(12 to 1 op 10 to 1) 10
2361 RAKIS (Ire) [84] 9-1 J Williams (11) *rcd freely, led till appr 2 fs out, wknd*........(33 to 1 op 20 to 1) 11
2272⁶ FOREVER SHINEING [72] 8-0 (3*) D Harrison (14) *rear, hrd rdn o'r 2 fs out, no imprsn.* ....(25 to 1 op 20 to 1 tchd 33 to 1) 12
1976⁴ BEAUMONT (Ire) [67] 7-12 A McGlone (3) *trkd ldg pair till wknd o'r 3 fs out*......(14 to 1 op 8 to 1 tchd 16 to 1) 13
2351³ DIXIELAND MELODY (USA) [85] 9-2 B Raymond (6) *chsd ldrs, wknd 3 fs out*... (11 to 1 op 10 to 1 tchd 12 to 1) 14
2379⁴ PAIR OF JACKS (Ire) [70] 8-1 C Rutter (12) *al beh.* ....(33 to 1 op 20 to 1) 15
Dist: Nk, 3l, 1½l, hd, ¾l, hd, 2l, nk, nk, 3½l. 2m 8.45s. a 4.75s (15 Ran).
SR: 46/44/45/36/31/35/41/18/21/ (Sheikh Mohammed), H R A Cecil

AYR (good to firm)
Friday July 23rd
Going Correction: MINUS 0.30 sec. per fur. (races 1,2), NIL (3,4,5,6)

2759 EBF Safari Maiden Fillies' Stakes Class D (2-y-o) £4,125 6f........(6:20)

2429⁴ BOLD TIMING 8-11 K Darley (1) *made virtually all, rdn and quickened clr one and a half fs out, easily.* ....(5 to 4 op Evens) 1
2595² MANHATTAN SUNSET (USA) 8-6 (5*) Stephen Davies (2) *chsd wnr and sn pushed alng, rdn o'r 2 fs out, soon one pace*........(6 to 4 on op 5 to 4 on) 2
1846 MISS PIGALLE 8-4 (7*) R Havlin (3) *in tch till rdn and wknd o'r 2 fs out*........(33 to 1 op 25 to 1) 3
Dist: 7l, 4l. 1m 13.67s. a 2.77s (3 Ran).
SR: 6/-/-/ (Clearview Partnership), Mrs M Reveley

2760 Liz Claiborne Maiden Handicap Class E (0-70 3-y-o and up) £2,148 5f.. (6:50)

2634² MILBANK CHALLENGER [55] 3-9-9 (3*) S Maloney (6) *chsd ldrs, hdwy 2 fs out, rdn to ld entering last, kpt on.* ....(5 to 4 fav tchd 11 to 8) 1
2707⁵ LUCKY MILL [44] (bl) 3-9-1 R Lappin (3) *chsd ldrs, hdwy 2 fs out, led one and a half out, edgd rght, hdd and no extr entering last*........(5 to 1) 2
2510² GUSSIE FINK-NOTTLE (Ire) [57] (bl) 3-10-0 K Darley (5) *led, rdn 2 fs out, sn hdd, ev ch till not much room and no extr ins last*........(11 to 4 op 2 to 1 tchd 3 to 1) 3
2682⁹ PAULINUS [34] 5-8-10 L Charnock (1) *dwlt and beh, hdwy hfwy, sn rdn and styd on wl fnl furlong.* ....(50 to 1 op 16 to 1 tchd 66 to 1) 4
2133⁵ LAMSONETTI [51] 3-9-8 A Culhane (2) *dwlt, hdwy to chase ldrs hfwy, sn rdn, wknd appr fnl furlong.* ....(10 to 1 op 5 to 1) 5
2424³ ROYAL MUSIC [50] 3-9-7 J Fortune (4) *prmnt, rdn hfwy, sn wknd*........(12 to 1 op 5 to 1) 6
Dist: 2½l, hd, sht-hd, 3½l, 1½l. 1m 0.39s. a 2.29s (6 Ran).
SR: 36/15/27/8/6/-/ (Milbank Foods Ltd), M H Easterby

2761 Ayrshire Post Chatline Claiming Stakes Class F (3-y-o and up) £1,813 1m 5f 13yds....................(7:20)

2455⁶ BLACKDOWN 6-9-3 K Darley (4) *in tch, hdwy 5 fs out, effrt to ld 2 out, rdn clr appr last.* ....(5 to 4 jt-fav tchd 11 to 8) 1
FLING IN SPRING 7-9-7 A Mackay (1) *trkd ldr till rdn alng and outpcd 4 fs out, styd on und pres ins last.* ....(66 to 1 op 20 to 1 tchd 100 to 1) 2
2445⁹ PREMIER MAJOR (Ire) 4-8-12 L Charnock (2) *hld up, gd hdwy 3 fs out, ev ch 2 out, sn rdn and one pace appr last*........(4 to 1 op 7 to 1 tchd 8 to 1 and 10 to 1) 3
2566⁵ PALACEGATE SUNSET (bl) 3-8-8 J Fortune (3) *set steady pace, quickened o'r 3 fs out, sn rdn, hdd 2 out, wknd appr last*......(5 to 4 jt-fav op 5 to 4 on tchd 11 to 8) 4
Dist: 4l, 1½l, 1l. 3m 2.33s. a 16.33s (4 Ran).
(Thomas Dyer), T Dyer

2762 Frasercard Gold Handicap Class D (0-80 4-y-o and up) £3,021 7f.... (7:50)

2468* THORNTON GATE [69] 4-9-10 (3*,3ex) S Maloney (4) *trkd ldr, effrt 2 fs out, led one out, rdn and ran on wl.* ....(100 to 30 op 5 to 2 tchd 7 to 2) 1
2633* GOLDEN CHIP (Ire) [73] 5-10-3 (3ex) K Darley (1) *led, quickened 2 fs out, rdn and hdd one out, rallied ins last.* ....(2 to 1 fav op 9 to 4 tchd 7 to 4) 2
2680* ROUTING [52] 5-8-3 (7*,3ex) J Marshall (2) *pld hrd, chsd ldrs, hdwy to chal 2 fs out, sn rdn and ev ch, kpt on ins last*........(7 to 2 op 3 to 1 tchd 4 to 1) 3
2057 YOUNG VALENTINE [54] 4-8-12 A Culhane (3) *hld up in tch, effrt and hdwy on inner 2 fs out, sn rdn and one pace fnl furlong*........(10 to 1 op 7 to 1) 4
2656² LOMBARD SHIPS [66] (bl) 6-9-10 A Mackay (5) *chsd ldrs, rdn o'r 2 fs out, sn wknd*........(5 to 1 tchd 11 to 2) 5
Dist: ½l, hd, 3l, 1l. 1m 28.17s. a 4.17s (5 Ran).
SR: 50/52/30/23/32/ (T H Bennett), M H Easterby

2763 West Sound Radio Ladykiller Selling Stakes Class G (3-y-o and up) £1,855 1 ¼m......................... (8:20)

2597⁴ ESSAYEFFSEE 4-8-13 K Darley (3) *hld up in tch, hdwy 3 fs out, led 2 out, rdn clr appr last, kpt on.* ....(5 to 2 on tchd 9 to 4 on) 1
2736⁵ MY BALLYBOY 3-8-3 A Mackay (1) *led, rdn o'r 2 fs out, sn hdd, styd on und pres ins last*....... (9 to 4 op 7 to 4) 2
2464⁸ MYNYOSS 3-8-3 J Fortune (2) *trkd ldr, effrt to chal 2 fs out, sn rdn and ev ch till wknd entering last.* ....(20 to 1 op 14 to 1) 3
Dist: 1l, 2½l. 2m 13.79s. a 8.79s (3 Ran).
SR: 11/-/-/ (Mrs S D Murray), Mrs M Reveley

2764 Bernshaw Handicap Class E (0-70 3-y-o) £2,305 1m.................. (8:50)

2269³ DANCING DOMINO [65] 9-7 K Darley (1) *trkd ldrs, effrt and hdwy 2 fs out, not much room and swtchd o'r one out, quickened to ld ins last*........(5 to 2 jt-fav op 11 to 4 tchd 3 to 1) 1
2202 MUSTN'T GRUMBLE (Ire) [50] 8-6 L Charnock (7) *trkd ldrs, smooth hdwy 3 fs out, led one and a half out, sn rdn, hdd and not quicken ins last*..(5 to 2 jt-fav op 4 to 1) 2

2597³ BRACKENTHWAITE [51] 8-0 (7*) V Halliday (5) *beh on inner, rdn o'r 3 fs out, swtchd wide 2 out, styd on wl appr last.* ....(4 to 1 op 5 to 2 tchd 9 to 2) 3
2480² FLASHMAN [56] 8-12 R Lappin (4) *hld up, gd hdwy o'r 2 fs out, sn ev ch, rdn and one pace appr last.* ....(6 to 1 op 5 to 1) 4
2341⁵ GOLD DESIRE [43] 7-12² (3*) S Maloney (6) *cl up, led wl o'r 2 fs out, rdn and hdd appr last, sn wknd.* ....(12 to 1 op 6 to 1) 5
2503* DIWALI DANCER [53] (bl) 8-9 (5ex) F Norton (3) *led, rdn 3 fs out, sn hdd, grad wknd*.......... (8 to 1 op 5 to 1) 6
2459⁸ GRINNELL [56] 8-12 J Fortune (2) *chsd ldrs, rdn 3 fs out, sn wknd*..........................(20 to 1 op 10 to 1) 7
Dist: 2½l, 1½l, 1½l, nk, sht-hd, 3½l. 1m 42.54s. a 4.84s (7 Ran).
SR: 34/11/7/7/-/2/-/ (P D Savill), M H Easterby

CARLISLE (good)
Friday July 23rd

Going Correction: MINUS 0.25 sec. per fur. (races 1,2), MINUS 0.05 (3,4,5,6)

2765 Graham Commercials Ltd Selling Handicap Class G (0-60 3-y-o) £2,553 5f 207yds......................(2:20)

2540³ NORLING (Ire) [46] 8-10 L Charnock (7) *made all, shaken up and edgd lft 2 fs out, drvn, ran on gmely whn hrd pressed fnl furlong.* (9 to 4 fav op 5 to 2 tchd 11 to 4) 1
2280⁵ FORTIS PAVIOR (Ire) [57] 9-7 A Culhane (3) *chsd ldrs, effrt and rdn entering strt, chlgd appr fnl furlong, no extr wl ins last*..........................(11 to 4 op 5 to 2) 2
2540⁶ SHOTLEY AGAIN [34] 7-12 F Norton (6) *trkd ldr, hrd drvn hfwy, ev ch o'r one furlong out, sn one paced.* ....(14 to 1 tchd 12 to 1) 3
2593³ ALBEIT [29] 7-7 A Mackay (5) *trkd ldrs, effrt and swtchd ins 2 fs out, not quicken appr last.* (11 to 4 op 5 to 2) 4
2540⁹ CIZARD (Ire) [29] 7-2 (5*) Darren Moffatt (2) *hld up in last pl, effrt and came wide strt, nvr able to chal.* ....(50 to 1 op 33 to 1) 5
609⁷ SUPREME SOVIET [48] 8-12 K Darley (4) *tucked away on ins, shaken up o'r 2 fs out, sn btn.* (16 to 1 op 14 to 1) 6
2365⁹ CRACKER JACK [49] (bl) 8-13 J Fanning (1) *keen hold, handily plcd, pushed alng entering strt, fdd.* ....(13 to 2 op 6 to 1 tchd 7 to 1) 7
Dist: ½l, 3½l, ½l, 8l, ½l, 2l. 1m 15.30s. a 2.30s (7 Ran).
SR: 20/29/-/-/ (S Pedersen), N Tinkler

2766 Chas Kendall Maiden Auction Stakes Class D (2-y-o) £3,172 5f........(2:50)

ISLAND MAGIC 8-7 (7*) D Thomas (9) *dwlt, sn reco'red to chase ldrs, not clr over one furlong out, swtchd ins last, ran on to ld nr finish*..............(12 to 1 op 10 to 1) 1
908³ RAFFERTY'S RULES (Ire) 9-0 K Fallon (1) *prmnt, shaken up hfwy, chlgd o'r one furlong out, led ins last, hdd nr finish*.............(7 to 4 fav op 13 to 8 tchd 5 to 4) 2
2203⁴ STEPHENSONS ROCKET 9-0 J Carroll (2) *wth ldr, led o'r 2 fs out, hdd ins last, no extr.* ....(15 to 2 op 6 to 1 tchd 8 to 1) 3
BEATS WORKING 9-0 A Mackay (7) *slwly into strd, beh, improved 2 fs out, kpt on, nvr able to chal.* ....(20 to 1 op 14 to 1) 4
MONIS (Ire) 9-0 S Whitworth (5) *sluggish strt, beh, pushed alng entering strt, nvr able to chal*...(3 to 1 op 5 to 1) 5
2554² THREE OF HEARTS 8-9 J Fortune (6) *led, hdd o'r 2 fs out, rdn and rallied, wknd fnl furlong.* ....(9 to 2 op 7 to 2 tchd 5 to 1) 6
1263⁶ PORTITE SOPHIE 8-9 K Darley (8) *chsd ldrs on ins, drvn alng entering strt, sn outpcd.* ....(10 to 1 op 8 to 1 tchd 12 to 1) 7
RISKY GIFT 9-0 L Charnock (3) *in tch, rdn o'r 2 fs out, sn btn*..........................(12 to 1 op 7 to 1) 8
DROP THE DONKEY 8-9 M Birch (4) *sn beh and pushed alng, lost tch entering strt*.........(33 to 1 op 20 to 1) 9
Dist: Nk, 1½l, 2½l, 2½l, ½l, 7l, 1½l, ½l. 1m 2.00s. a 2.00s (9 Ran).
SR: 35/34/28/18/8/1/ (M R Charlton), Mrs J R Ramsden

2767 Holiday Club Pontin's Handicap Class D (0-80 3-y-o and up) £3,655 1½m ....(3:20)

2565* SUNDERLAND ECHO [70] 4-10-1 (5ex) K Darley (6) *trkd ldr, led 4 fs out, drvn alng entering strt, forged clr.* ....(5 to 2 fav op 2 to 1) 1
2457* SALU [53] 4-8-12 (5ex) M Birch (2) *hld up in rear, took clr order 6 fs out, kpt on entering strt, not rch wnr.* ....(3 to 1 op 4 to 1) 2
1894⁶ TANODA [43] 7-8-2 A Mackay (5) *mid-div, drvn alng o'r 4 fs out, improved und pres over 2 out, styd on, nvr dngrs*..........................(7 to 1 op 6 to 1) 3
1864* CARA'S PRIDE [71] 3-9-4 Dale Gibson (3) *keen hold, pressed ldrs, pushed alng o'r 4 fs out, btn entering strt.* ....(11 to 2 op 9 to 2) 4
2591³ WANZA [60] 3-8-7 K Fallon (7) *trkd ldg pair, rdn o'r 3 fs out, wknd und pres entering strt.* (14 to 1 op 12 to 1) 5
2310⁴ MISTROY [58] 3-8-2 (3*) J Weaver (4) *led till hdd 4 fs out, sn drvn alng, btn entering strt*....... (14 to 1 op 12 to 1) 6
2373⁴ RISING TEMPO (Ire) [65] 5-9-5 (5*) D Wright (1) *hld up, feeling pace and drvn alng 5 fs out, nvr a factor.* ....(8 to 1 op 5 to 1) 7
1190⁵ DEB'S BALL [59] 7-9-4 J Fanning (8) *hld up, outpcd and rdn 4 fs out, sn btn*.................. (8 to 1 op 7 to 1) 8
Dist: 4l, 4l, 2½l, 3½l, 5l, 6l, 1½l. 2m 35.50s. a 5.50s (8 Ran).
SR: 54/29/11/22/4/ (Northeast Press Limited), Mrs M Reveley

2768 Scania Cumbria Distributors Champion Apprentice Handicap Class E (0-70 3-y-o and up) £3,080 7f 214yds ....(3:50)

2459⁶ BIDWEAYA (USA) [28] 6-7-9 (3*) D Wright (3) *pressed ldrs, drvn alng o'r 3 fs out, sstnd run to ld ins fnl furlong, kpt on wl*.............. (4 to 1 op 5 to 1 tchd 7 to 2) 1
2597* YOUNG JASON [45] 10-8-10 (5*,5ex) J Dennis (4) *hld up in rear, improved entering strt, kpt on fnl furlong, not rch wnr*.......................... (3 to 1 jt-fav op 5 to 2) 2
2426* CORONA GOLD [48] (bl,e/s) 3-8-10 F Norton (8) *pressed ldg pair, effrt and ev ch entering strt, chlgd ins last, one pace last 75 yards*.................. (4 to 1 op 7 to 2) 3
2198⁴ WHO'S TEF (Ire) [54] 5-9-10 S Maloney (7) *led, shaken up entering strt, hdd ins fnl furlong, no extr*....(3 to 1 jt-fav op 5 to 2 tchd 7 to 2) 4
2088⁷ GOLD SURPRISE (Ire) [48] 4-8-11 (7*) M Proctor (1) *hld up, improved 2 fs out, kpt on ins last, nvr dngrs.* ....(6 to 1 op 9 to 2) 5
2369⁷ KICK ON MAJESTIC (Ire) [27] 4-7-11 Darren Moffatt (5) *chsd ldrs, pushed alng o'r 3 fs out, wknd entering strt.* ....(10 to 1 op 8 to 1 tchd 12 to 1) 6
ROSCOMMON JOE (Ire) [50] 3-8-12 S D Williams (6) *wth ldr, drvn alng o'r 3 fs out, lost tch entering strt, tld off.* ....(20 to 1 op 14 to 1) 7
2306⁵ BLAKES REACH [47] 3-8-2 (7*) Claire West (2) *rcd wide, hld up, struggling frm hfwy, tld off*... (50 to 1 op 16 to 1) 8
Dist: 1½l, hd, 1½l, sht-hd, 15l, 8l, 8l. 1m 43.30s. a 5.40s (8 Ran).
SR: -/9/3/12/5/ (Jeff Slaney), J L Eyre

2769 Scania Trucks Claiming Stakes Class F (3-y-o) £2,601 6f 206yds.......(4:20)

2338⁶ WHITE CREEK (Ire) (v) 8-9 (7*) P Roberts (8) *tucked away on ins, effrt entering strt, edgd lft appr fnl furlong, led entering last, ran on wl.* ....(7 to 2 op 5 to 1 tchd 11 to 2) 1
2593⁵ BOLD LINE (bl) 7-11 Dale Gibson (4) *prmnt, led aftr 2 fs, hdd o'r two out, not clr run one out, swtchd ins last, styd on*.......................... (10 to 1 op 8 to 1) 2
2001 QUEEN OF THE QUORN 8-11 G Hind (2) *led 2 fs, styd hndy, rgned ld o'r two furlongs out, hdd entering last, one pace*.......................... (9 to 4 fav op 5 to 2) 3
2736* OLICANA (Ire) 8-2 (7*) J Marshall (7) *rdr lost irons strt, in tch, improved hfwy, ev ch 2 fs out, one pace ins last.* ....(4 to 1 op 5 to 2 tchd 9 to 2) 4
RUPERT COURT 7-10 (7*) Kimberley Hart (6) *keen hold, beh, hdwy hfwy, rdn entering strt, one pace.* ....(16 to 1 op 14 to 1) 5
2454⁶ BRIGHT GEM 8-5 J Fanning (3) *chsd ldrs, rdn alng entering strt, btn o'r one furlong out*......(9 to 1 op 8 to 1) 6
2445 DEAD CALM (bl) 8-9 (3*) J Weaver (1) *chsd ldrs, drvn alng o'r 3 fs out, ran wide strt, one pace fnl 2 furlongs.* ....(8 to 1 op 7 to 1) 7
TIL FRIDAY 8-6 F Norton (5) *beh, tld off hfwy, ran on entering strt, nvr dngrs*......... (20 to 1 op 16 to 1) 8
2279⁶ CHARLOTTES BILLO (bl) 8-5 L Charnock (10) *beh, rdn alng hfwy, lost tch entering strt, tld off.* (33 to 1 op 25 to 1) 9
ROBRO (bl) 8-5 R Lappin (9) *slwly into strd, al beh, tld off frm hfwy*..........................(33 to 1) 10
Dist: 1l, 1½l, 1l, 2½l, nk, ¾l, 5l, 5l, 10l. 1m 31.10s. a 5.70s (10 Ran).
SR: 11/-/-/-/-/-/ (J K Brown), J Berry

2770 Borderway Mart Limited Stakes Class D (3-y-o) £3,730 6f 206yds.......(4:50)

2382³ MISS GORGEOUS (Ire) 8-9 F Norton (1) *made all, sn clr, shaken up entering strt, styd on wl.* ....(6 to 5 op Evens tchd 5 to 4) 1
2330⁵ PERSIANSKY (Ire) 8-11 (3*) J Weaver (3) *chsd clr ldr, rdn to improve o'r 3 fs out, wndrd appr last, one pace.* .... (11 to 10 on op 5 to 4 on tchd Evens) 2
2543⁴ COCONUT JOHNNY 8-11 (3*) S D Williams (2) *chsd ldg pair, outpcd aftr 2 fs, rdn entering strt, nvr able to chal*..........................(7 to 1 op 5 to 1) 3
Dist: 2l, 7l. 1m 29.30s. a 3.90s (3 Ran).
SR: 31/30/9/ (Thomas R Capehart), W A O'Gorman

MAISONS-LAFFITTE (FR) (good)
Friday July 23rd

2771 Prix Maurice de Nieuil (Group 2) (3-y-o and up) £47,790 1½m 110yds....(2:55)

1694* SERRANT (USA) 5-9-6 T Jarnet (4) *hld up, 5th strt, hdwy 2 fs out, led one and a half out, ran on wl.* (23 to 10 fav) 1
1888[2] PETIT LOUP (USA) 4-9-8 W Swinburn (5) *led till one and a half fs out, hrd rdn, ran on gmely*............(7 to 2) 2
1648* TURNERS HILL 3-8-5 Pat Eddery (2) *trkd ldr, second strt, ev ch 2 fs out, no extr ins last*.............. (36 to 10) 3
DJAIS (Fr) 4-9-2 A S Cruz (1) *3rd strt, kpt on wl*. (104 to 1) 4
1915[3] VAL SAUVAGE 3-8-5 C Asmussen (3) *hld up, last strt, effrt 2 fs out, nvr able to chal*.......................(64 to 10) 5
1291[2] GRAND FLOTILLA (USA) 6-9-2 D Boeuf (6) *4th strt, rdn and wknd 2 fs out*..................................(71 to 10) 6
Dist: ¾l, ½l, hd, 2l, 1l. 2m 41.00s. (6 Ran).
(D Wildenstein), A Fabre

PONTEFRACT (good to firm)
Friday July 23rd
Going Correction: MINUS 0.30 sec. per fur. (races 1,4,6), MINUS 0.35 (2,3,5)

2772 Jack Berry Appeal Claiming Stakes Class F (2-y-o) £2,574 6f........ (6:45)

2356[2] CULSYTH FLYER 8-9 W Ryan (6) *chsd ldrs, hdwy 2 fs out, led jst ins last, ran on wl.* ....(5 to 1 op 4 to 1 tchd 6 to 1) 1
2505[6] SURPRISE BREEZE 7-13 T Williams (8) *prmnt, chlgd one furlong out, kpt on ins last, no imprsn on wnr.* ....(12 to 1 op 10 to 1) 2
2526[7] CAPTAIN TAFFY (bl) 8-5 K Fallon (11) *cl up, slight ld one furlong out, sn hdd and no extr*...................(14 to 1) 3
BOLD ALEX 8-2 (5*) O Pears (4) *hld up in tch, hdwy fnl 2 fs, nrst finish*..................... (20 to 1 op 16 to 1) 4
2412[8] BROOKHEAD LADY 8-6 Dean McKeown (7) *cl up, chlgd o'r one furlong out, wknd ins last*....(Evens fav op 5 to 4) 5
2446[5] FLOATING TRIAL 8-4 J Carroll (2) *led to one furlong out, sn btn*.................... (6 to 1 op 7 to 1 tchd 8 to 1) 6
MINIBAR 7-11 J Quinn (3) *slwly into strd, nvr nr to chal.* ....(16 to 1 op 14 to 1) 7
2389[5] TANFIRION CHIEF 9-0 R P Elliott (10) *nvr dngrs.* ....(8 to 1 op 7 to 1) 8
1959 MILLY'S PET 8-1 N Adams (5) *slwly into strd,nvr dngrs.* ....(33 to 1 op 20 to 1) 9
1763 BESCABY GIRL 8-3 N Connorton (1) *nvr dngrs.* ....(20 to 1 op 16 to 1) 10
1897 MURPHY'S GOLD (Ire) 8-7 M Birch (9) *beh most of way.* ....(33 to 1 op 25 to 1) 11
1798 GALLIC GENT 8-7 T Lucas (12) *chsd ldrs till wknd o'r 2 fs out*.................................(20 to 1 op 16 to 1) 12
Dist: 2l, 1l, ¾l, 1l, 1l, 3l, 1½l, 2l, ¾l, 7l. 1m 18.00s. a 3.30s (12 Ran).
(W Cully), R Hollinshead

2773 Yorkshire Television Handicap Class E (0-70 3-y-o) £2,679 1½m 8yds (7:10)

2388[2] TTYFRAN [58] 8-12 S Perks (3) *hld up, hdwy o'r 2 fs out, led one out, ran on wl*......................(7 to 2 co-fav tchd 4 to 1 and 3 to 1) 1
2361[6] WORDSMITH (Ire) [67] 9-7 K Fallon (7) *in tch, not clr run 2 fs out till swtchd one out, ran on wl, not rch wnr.* ....(7 to 2 co-fav op 5 to 2) 2
2555[2] MILNGAVIE (Ire) [43] 7-11 J Fanning (8) *trkd ldrs, led 3 fs out to one out, one pace*...... (7 to 2 co-fav op 3 to 1) 3
2315[7] DORAZINE [61] 9-1 J Quinn (4) *trkd ldrs, effrt 2 fs out, chlgd entering last, sn rdn and btn.* (8 to 1 op 7 to 1) 4
2117[7] BOLTROSE [57] 8-11 N Adams (11) *beh, hdwy to chase ldrs 5 fs out, kpt on same pace 2 out.* ....(14 to 1 op 12 to 1) 5
1068 ELEGANT HUSSAR [64] (v) 9-4 M Birch (10) *led to 3 fs out, wknd 2 out*......................(8 to 1 tchd 9 to 1) 6
2279[5] TRANQUIL LADY (Ire) [55] 8-2 (7*) S Knott (5) *in tch till wknd 3 fs out*..................... (14 to 1 op 12 to 1) 7
1259[3] MOONSHINE DANCER [47] 7-10 (5*) Darren Moffatt (9) *chsd ldrrs till wknd o'r 2 fs out*.......... (10 to 1 op 8 to 1) 8
2448[5] AMIARGE [54] (v) 8-8 J Carroll (2) *cl up till wknd o'r 2 fs out*.............................. (14 to 1 op 12 to 1) 9
Dist: 1l, 1½l, ½l, 5l, 8l, 1l, 6l, 1½l. 2m 41.50s. a 6.50s (9 Ran).
(Mrs C E Collinson), F H Lee

2774 Wakefield Shirt Group Handicap Class D (0-80 3-y-o and up) £3,687 1¼m 6yds ....(7:35)

2530[3] MODEST HOPE (USA) [53] 6-8-1 Alex Greaves (3) *hld up, hdwy on ins 2 fs out, led inside last, ran on wl.* ....(16 to 1 tchd 20 to 1) 1
2398* SILVER SAMURAI [80] 4-10-0 L Dettori (9) *trkd ldrs, hdwy to chal entering fnl furlong, sn rdn, kpt on same pace.* ....(15 to 8 fav op 7 to 4) 2
2354[5] ATHERTON GREEN (Ire) [63] 3-8-1 J Quinn (7) *in tch, hdwy to ld o'r one furlong out, hdd and no extr ins last.* ....(10 to 1 op 8 to 1) 3
2696[6] SELF EXPRESSION [60] 5-8-8 K Fallon (6) *mid-div, effrt o'r 2 fs out, kpt on same pace.* ....(13 to 2 op 6 to 1 tchd 7 to 1) 4
2433 WESTHOLME (USA) [68] 5-9-2 M Birch (5) *trkd ldr, effrt 2 fs out, one pace*..................(10 to 1 tchd 11 to 1) 5
1681[7] GOLDEN TORQUE [64] 6-8-6[1] (7*) H Bastiman (1) *hld up, effrt o'r 2 fs out, no hdwy*.........(20 to 1 tchd 25 to 1) 6
1928[4] IRON BARON (Ire) [46] 4-7-8[1] J Fanning (8) *dwlt, beh, some late hdwy, nvr dngrs*.............(20 to 1 op 16 to 1) 7
2537[4] SURREY DANCER [63] (bl) 5-8-11 B Raymond (4) *led till o'r one furlong out, sn wknd*.......... (7 to 2 op 11 to 2) 8
2348[4] TENDRESSE (Ire) [52] 5-8-0 M Roberts (10) *hld up, effrt 3 fs out, no hdwy*...................... (11 to 2 op 5 to 1) 9
2567* EXPRESS GIFT [70] 4-8-13 (5*,6ex) Darren Moffatt (2) *prmnt, rdn 2 fs out, sn wknd*.............(7 to 1 tchd 8 to 1) 10
Dist: ½l, hd, 4l, sht-hd, 1½l, 1½l, 1l, 2½l, 3l. 2m 12.90s. a 4.70s (10 Ran).
SR: 5/31/3/2/9/2/ (J McManamon), B Richmond

2775 Red Shirt Night Claiming Stakes Class F (3-y-o and up) £2,490 1m 4yds (8:05)

2095[2] GLOWING PATH (v) 3-8-5 M Roberts (2) *hld up, efort o'r 2 fs out, ran on strly to ld cl hme.* ....(11 to 2 op 6 to 1 tchd 7 to 1) 1
2396[3] CAUSLEY 8-9-4 B Raymond (12) *led, clr 2 fs out, hdd and no extr cl hme*......(13 to 8 fav op 7 to 4 tchd 2 to 1) 2
2478[2] UMBUBUZI (USA) 3-8-11 S Perks (5) *prmnt, kpt on same pace fnl 2 fs*..........................(7 to 2 op 3 to 1) 3
2445 DIAMOND INTHE DARK (USA) (v) 5-8-7 (5*) O Pears (11) *chsd ldrs, one pace fnl 2 fs*...................(16 to 1) 4
2371[6] KUMMEL KING 5-8-2 (7*) S Knott (8) *chsd ldrs, one pace fnl 2 fs*..........................(10 to 1 op 8 to 1) 5
1425[9] NO SUBMISSION (USA) 7-9-5 S Wood (3) *chsd ldrs, pushed alng 3 fs out, no hdwy*.......(5 to 1 op 4 to 1) 6
1477[7] ASTRAC TRIO (USA) 3-8-6 K Fallon (1) *nvr dngrs.* ....(33 to 1 op 25 to 1) 7
2578[6] RIVA ROCK 3-8-6 A McGlone (6) *slwly into strd, nvr dngrs*.............................(14 to 1 op 12 to 1) 8
292 MISS EL ARAB (Ire) 5-8-5 Dean McKeown (4) *chsd ldrs till wknd 2 fs out*.................................(25 to 1) 9
2540[8] IRISH ROOTS (Ire) 3-7-10 (7*) Ruth Coulter (7) *prmnt till wknd 2 fs out*.................................(16 to 1) 10
JASPER ONE 3-8-2 N Connorton (10) *al beh.* ....(33 to 1 op 20 to 1) 11
PETAL'S JARRED 3-8-0 J Quinn (9) *al beh.* ....(12 to 1 op 10 to 1) 12
Dist: ½l, 7l, 2½l, sht-hd, hd, ¾l, 3½l, ¾l, 8l, 1½l. 1m 44.50s. a 2.40s (12 Ran).
SR: 19/30/2/-/-/-/ (C John Hill), C J Hill

2776 St John Ambulance Maiden Stakes Class D (3-y-o) £3,816 1½m 8yds (8:35)

TRAMMEL 9-0 A McGlone (2) *hld up, hdwy 4 fs out, led entering last, styd on wl*...........(10 to 1 op 8 to 1) 1
2332 ALASAD 9-0 R Hills (8) *trkd ldrs, led o'r one furlong out, sn hdd, no extr*....................(7 to 1 tchd 8 to 1) 2
2332 QUILLON 9-0 W Ryan (9) *trkd ldrs, chlgd o'r one furlong out, kpt on same pace*..............(13 to 2 op 5 to 1) 3
1802[8] EDITHMEAD (Ire) 8-9 S Whitworth (3) *hld up, hdwy 3 fs out, styd on wl fnl furlong, not rch ldrs.* ....(33 to 1 op 20 to 1) 4
1879[2] PEARLY MIST (Ire) 8-9 B Marcus (4) *prmnt, effrt o'r 2 fs out, kpt on same pace*.............. (9 to 2 op 4 to 1) 5
2332[8] TREAD CAREFULLY 8-9 L Dettori (6) *mid-div, effrt o'r 2 fs out, sn btn*..........(9 to 1 op 6 to 1 tchd 11 to 1) 6
1176 COMBELLINO 9-0 N Adams (14) *in tch, effrt 3 fs out, sn btn*..................................(50 to 1 op 25 to 1) 7
DARK DEN (USA) 9-0 Paul Eddery (13) *trkd ldr, ev ch 2 fs out, sn rdn and wknd*.............. (9 to 2 op 4 to 1) 8
1785[8] YAHMI (Ire) 9-0 M Roberts (7) *led till o'r one furlong out, sn wknd*............(9 to 4 fav op 5 to 2 tchd 3 to 1) 9
985[5] COLORFUL AMBITION 9-0 C Dwyer (10) *prmnt till wknd o'r 2 fs out*..........(14 to 1 op 10 to 1 tchd 16 to 1) 10
2046[4] SASSIVER (USA) 9-0 S Perks (5) *slwly into strd, al beh.* ....(20 to 1 op 16 to 1) 11
230[3] SOLOMAN SPRINGS (USA) 8-9 (5*) O Pears (12) *al beh.* ....(16 to 1 tchd 20 to 1) 12
2275[6] SILVER SEA (Ire) 8-9 B Raymond (1) *chsd ldrs, wknd 4 fs out*.................................(20 to 1 op 14 to 1) 13
1581[6] HAYDON BRIDGE (Ire) 9-0 M Birch (11) *in tch till wknd 3 fs out*..................(16 to 1 op 20 to 1 tchd 33 to 1) 14
Dist: 1l, nk, 3½l, 2½l, 10l, nk, 3½l, nk, 8l, 4l. 2m 35.70s. a 0.70s (14 Ran).
SR: 51/49/48/36/31/11/15/8/7/ (K Abdulla), H R A Cecil

2777 International Spinal Research Trust Handicap Class D (0-80 3-y-o and up) £3,435 5f....................... (9:05)

1925[3] MY ABBEY [55] 4-8-6 K Fallon (2) *chsd ldrs, led jst ins fnl furlong, ran on strly*...............(13 to 2 op 5 to 1) 1
1925* MANOR ADVENTURE [66] 3-8-12 L Dettori (9) *in tch, hdwy 2 fs out, styd on wl fnl furlong*... (7 to 2 fav op 4 to 1) 2
2653[5] DAYJUZ (Ire) [59] (bl) 3-8-5 Paul Eddery (5) *led till jst ins fnl furlong, no extr*.....................(13 to 2 op 6 to 1) 3
2380[5] VERY DICEY [71] 5-9-8 J Carroll (3) *prmnt, ev ch o'r one furlong out, one pace*...............(7 to 1 op 5 to 1) 4
2434 MISS ARAGON [52] 5-8-3 Dean McKeown (10) *in tch, kpt on fnl furlong, not trble ldrs.* ....(9 to 1 op 10 to 1 tchd 8 to 1) 5

2230[9] ANOTHER LANE [70] (bl) 6-9-7 M Birch (4) *nvr dngrs.* ....(25 to 1 op 20 to 1) 6
2018[7] JUST BOB [73] 4-9-3 (7*) M Proctor (1) *dwlt, nvr dngrs.* ....(7 to 1 op 6 to 1) 7
2392[5] SIMMIE'S SPECIAL [59] 5-8-5 (5*) A Garth (8) *prmnt till wknd o'r one furlong out*...........(8 to 1 op 6 to 1) 8
2628[5] EDUCATED PET [70] (bl) 4-9-7 T Williams (6) *cl up till wknd 2 fs out*..................(9 to 2 op 5 to 1) 9
1815[7] SO SUPERB [60] (bl) 4-8-11 S Webster (7) *al beh.* (14 to 1) 10
Dist: 3l, nk, 1½l, sht-hd, 1½l, 1½l, 1½l, 1½l, 1l. 1m 2.30s. a 1.10s (10 Ran).
SR: 40/34/26/37/17/29/26/6/11/ (Abbey Racing), E J Alston

TIPPERARY (IRE) (good to yielding) Friday July 23rd

2778 Monard E.B.F. (C & G) Maiden (2-y-o) £3,797 7f..................... (5:30)

VIA CONDOTTI (Ire) 9-0 C Roche (3)..............(4 to 1) 1
2402[2] GAINSBOROUGH'S BOY (Ire) 9-0 M J Kinane (10) ....(7 to 4 on) 2
2072[7] DOHERTY (Ire) 9-0 R Hughes (4)...............(10 to 1) 3
2284[4] DON'T KNOW (Ire) 9-0 K J Manning (6)...........(7 to 1) 4
RUDI'S PRIDE (Ire) 9-0 J F Egan (5)...............(8 to 1) 5
MULMUS (Ire) 9-0 S Craine (8)...............(12 to 1) 6
1509[7] PEARL OF ORIENT (Ire) 8-12 (2*) R M Burke (1)... (25 to 1) 7
FINAL REMINDER (Ire) 9-0 P Shanahan (9).......(10 to 1) 8
POSE AND CAMPAIGN (Ire) 9-0 J P Murtagh (7)...(10 to 1) 9
Dist: 2½l, ½l, 2l, 5l. 1m 33.60s. (9 Ran).
(D H W Dobson), J S Bolger

2779 Silvermines Race (3-y-o and up) £2,762 7f..................... (6:00)

2184* DOREG (Ire) 3-9-4 J P Murtagh (7)................(5 to 1) 1
2606[8] LOCK'S HEATH (Can) 3-9-1 M J Kinane (4).....(Evens fav) 2
2247[6] ABEL TASMAN (USA) 3-9-7 P V Gilson (2).........(5 to 1) 3
572 UKUD (USA) 3-8-11 S Craine (1)..................(8 to 1) 4
2073 COMMON BOND (Ire) 3-8-7 (8*) B Fenton (5).....(20 to 1) 5
2285[3] BELLISSI (Ire) 3-8-3 (8*) P J Smullen (9)..........(10 to 1) 6
2452[3] GLOWING VALUE (Ire) 3-8-8 (6*) J A Heffernan (6) (10 to 1) 7
2452[4] GOODIES TWO STEP (Ire) 3-9-4 N G McCullagh (8) (25 to 1) 8
Dist: 2l, 2l, 1l, 3½l. 1m 32.90s. (8 Ran).
(Patrick F Headon), Declan Gillespie

2780 Galbally Handicap (0-85 3-y-o and up) £2,762 5f..................... (6:30)

2073[5] MACGILLYCUDDY (Ire) [-] (bl) 4-8-9 (6*) J J Behan (11) ....(9 to 2) 1
2404[7] MAGIC DON (Ire) [-] (bl) 4-8-7 (8*) R T Fitzpatrick (1) (10 to 1) 2
2073 MY-O-MY (Ire) [-] 3-9-9 S Craine (2)..............(8 to 1) 3
2323[4] RECOLLECTION (Ire) [-] (bl) 4-8-7 N G McCullagh (4) ....(11 to 1) 4
1825[7] IBDA [-] 3-8-4 (6*) B J Walsh (5)..................(11 to 1) 5
2667* JUNORIUS (Ire) [-] 4-8-13 (6*,5ex) J A Heffernan (10) (8 to 1) 6
1795 MEMSAHB [-] (bl) 4-9-6 M J Kinane (8)........(4 to 1 fav) 7
2323[6] SHOOT THE DEALER (Ire) [-] 3-8-13 C Roche (6)..(11 to 2) 8
2404 LUTE AND LYRE (Ire) [-] (bl) 4-9-3 (6*) C Everard (7) (8 to 1) 9
4684a SAND OR STONE (Ire) [-] 5-9-10 D V Smith (3)....(14 to 1) 10
2604[7] JARGONEL (Ire) [-] (bl) 3-7-13 (2*) D G O'Shea (9) (16 to 1) 11
Dist: ½l, nk, 3l, 1l. 58.60s. (11 Ran).
(Mrs Rita Hale), Patrick Prendergast

2781 Milestone Fillies Maiden (3-y-o) £2,762 1½m.................. (7:00)

2609[4] SHARKASHKA (Ire) 9-0 J P Murtagh (9)........(9 to 4 fav) 1
2287[5] ALYREINA (USA) 9-0 C Roche (2)..................(7 to 1) 2
MAGIC FEELING (Ire) 8-12 (2*) D G O'Shea (4)....(12 to 1) 3
2287[3] UNCONDITIONAL (Fr) 9-0 N G McCullagh (8)......(6 to 1) 4
PUSH THE BUTTON (Ire) 9-0 M J Kinane (12)........(5 to 1) 5
790[3] ANDANTE (Ire) 8-12 (2*) R M Burke (7)...........(11 to 2) 6
1507 NEW LOVE (Ire) 8-10 (4*) W J Smith (5)...........(25 to 1) 7
1822[2] UP SHE FLEW (USA) 9-0 R Hughes (10)...........(7 to 1) 8
MISS MAYTHORN (Ire) 9-0 J F Egan (6)...........(12 to 1) 9
2449[3] GLENGARRY BONNET (Ire) 9-0 N Byrne (13).....(12 to 1) 10
982[6] DO-TELL-ME (Ire) 8-8 (6*) R V Skelly (3)..........(33 to 1) 11
2518 SYGNE OF RICHES (Ire) 8-8 (6*) J A Heffernan (1) (25 to 1) ur
Dist: 4l, 1½l, 3l, 4½l. 2m 37.50s. (12 Ran).
(Lady Clague), John M Oxx

2782 Knockaney Handicap (0-80 3-y-o and up) £2,762 1m 1f.............. (7:30)

2451[3] RUPERT THE GREAT (Ire) [-] (bl) 3-8-7 R Hughes (7) (5 to 1) 1
2463[7] RAIN RITE (Ire) [-] 4-9-6 J P Murtagh (2)...........(8 to 1) 2
2741[2] FLORA WOOD (Ire) [-] (bl) 3-9-0 S Craine (3)....(2 to 1 fav) 3
DARCY'S THATCHER [-] 9-9-8 M J Kinane (9)....(10 to 1) 4
4686a VLADIMIR'S WAY (Ire) [-] (bl) 4-9-0 J F Egan (1).... (7 to 1) 5
2141 RETURN JOURNEY (Ire) [-] 4-8-10 (2*) R M Burke (4) (7 to 1) 6
308 SHIRWAN (Ire) [-] 4-9-4 (6*) C Everard (8).........(14 to 1) 7
MILLENIUM LASS (Ire) [-] 5-7-10[1] (6*) J A Heffernan (6) ....(8 to 1) 8
2665[4] ACCELL (Ire) [-] 4-8-3 (2*) D G O'Shea (5)..........(7 to 2) 9
Dist: 1l, 2l, sht-hd, 3½l. 1m 54.60s. (9 Ran).
(H Cheung), Noel Meade

YARMOUTH (good) Friday July 23rd

Going Correction: MINUS 0.20 sec. per fur.

2783 Star Handicap Class D (0-80 3-y-o) £3,494 1m 3f 101yds............ (2:10)

2023* KARACHI [64] 8-5 (3*) B Doyle (1) *wtd wth, improved o'r one furlong out, rdr tangled whip in reins, rallied to ld post*........................(7 to 2 co-fav tchd 4 to 1) 1
2523[3] CHIAPPUCCI (Ire) [59] (v) 8-3 P Robinson (5) *al hndy, quickened to ld o'r one furlong out, ran on, jst ct.* ....(7 to 2 co-fav op 5 to 2) 2
2495[4] SO SAUCY [56] 8-0 A Tucker (2) *tried to make all, hdd and drvn alng o'r one furlong out, sn outpcd.* ....(9 to 2 op 7 to 2 tchd 5 to 1) 3
2341[3] MENA [54] 7-12 N Carlisle (7) *last and hld up, effrt and drvn alng o'r 3 fs out, not pace to chal.* ....(16 to 1 op 10 to 1 tchd 20 to 1) 4
2555* INDIAN FLASH (Ire) [67] 8-11 (5ex) W Woods (6) *trkd ldr, nosed ahead briefly o'r one furlong out, rdn and wknd ins last*..............................(4 to 1 op 3 to 1) 5
2228[3] LUNAR RISK [62] 8-6 A Munro (3) *trkd ldg quartet, rdn o'r 2 fs out, sn btn*..............(7 to 2 co-fav op 4 to 1) 6
Dist: Sht-hd, 4l, 1½l, ¾l, 7l. 2m 27.40s. a 3.90s (6 Ran).
SR: 32/26/15/10/21/2/ (Mrs J L Hislop), C E Brittain

2784 Burlington Selling Handicap Class G (0-60 3-y-o) £2,448 1¼m 21yds.. (2:40)

2520[5] BILLYBACK [53] 9-5 D Biggs (4) *patiently rdn, drvn ahead o'r one furlong out, kpt on und pres.* ....(4 to 1 op 7 to 2 tchd 11 to 4 and 9 to 2) 1
1836[7] NOMADIC FIRE [55] 9-7 M Tebbutt (6) *wtd wth, bustled alng to chal ins fnl furlong, jst hld.* ....(9 to 2 op 4 to 1 tchd 5 to 1) 2
2411 BADAWI (Fr) [38] (bl) 8-4 N Carlisle (1) *co'red up on ins, effrt and rdn 2 fs out, styd on*..........(14 to 1 op 12 to 1) 3
2411[4] NIGHTMARE LADY [30] 7-3 (7*) C Hawksley (2) *nvr far away, led o'r 2 fs out till over one out, one pace.* ....(9 to 1 op 6 to 1 tchd 10 to 1) 4
2499[2] B B GLEN [45] 8-6 (5*) C Hodgson (5) *co'red up beh ldrs, swtchd outsd 2 fs out, one pace.* ....(2 to 1 fav op 7 to 4 tchd 5 to 2 and 11 to 4) 5
1709[7] BURNING COST [49] 9-1 P Robinson (7) *led aftr 2 fs till o'r two out, rdn and no extr*..........(7 to 2 tchd 4 to 1) 6
2523[9] BARSLEY [45] 8-8 (3*) B Doyle (3) *led for 2 fs, styd hndy till wknd und pres o'r two out, tld off.* ....(16 to 1 op 10 to 1 tchd 20 to 1) 7
Dist: Nk, ¾l, 1½l, nk, 2l, dist. 2m 9.50s. a 5.50s (7 Ran).
SR: 30/31/12/1/15/15/-/ (M J Ryan), M J Ryan

2785 Tattersalls Maiden Auction Series Stakes Qualifier Class D (2-y-o) £3,465 7f 3yds........................ (3:10)

PERSIAN ELITE (Ire) 8-8 T Quinn (1) *al hndy, drvn to nose ahead o'r one furlong out, hld on grimly last 50 yards.* ....(9 to 2 op 5 to 2 tchd 5 to 1 and 11 to 2) 1
2502[3] INDEFENCE (Ire) 8-6 Dean McKeown (7) *wth ldr, led appr hfwy, continually edgd lft, hdd o'r one out, rallied.* ....(100 to 30 fav op 5 to 2 tchd 7 to 2) 2
I FEAR NOTHING 8-9 G Carter (2) *tucked away beh ldrs, ev ch o'r one furlong out, hng lft, no extr.* ....(9 to 2 op 5 to 2) 3
2250[5] CALLING (USA) 8-13 A Munro (9) *led till hdd appr hfwy, drvn alng last 2 fs, styd on one pace.* ....(7 to 1 op 5 to 1 tchd 8 to 1) 4
PENNINE PINK (Ire) 8-6 G Duffield (3) *nvr far away, drvn alng last 2 fs, kpt on same pace*.....(10 to 1 op 8 to 1) 5
WALSHAM WHISPER (Ire) 8-1 P Robinson (5) *steadied strt, effrt and pushed alng hfwy, ran on fnl furlong.* ....(12 to 1 op 10 to 1 tchd 14 to 1) 6
VLAMINCK (Ire) 8-13 R Hills (4) *steadied strt, shaken up o'r 2 fs out, nvr plcd to chal.* ....(7 to 1 op 5 to 1 tchd 8 to 1) 7
DOM PENNION 8-9 W Woods (8) *trkd ldg trio, feeling pace and drvn alng 2 fs out, sn btn*...... (5 to 1 op 7 to 1) 8
2153[7] JUBILEE ROYALE (Ire) 7-13 (7*) S Mulvey (6) *chsd alng in midfield hfwy, sn lost tch*........ (25 to 1 op 14 to 1) 9
Dist: Sht-hd, 3l, 1½l, nk, nk, 2l, 3l, 6l. 1m 27.20s. a 4.00s (9 Ran).
SR: 13/10/4/3/-/-/ (Elite Racing Club), P F I Cole

2786 Carlton Nursery Class D (2-y-o) £3,523 7f 3yds........................ (3:40)

2412[9] THE MULTIYORKER (Ire) [-] 8-7 P Robinson (8) *steadied strt, gd hdwy to ld on outsd o'r one furlong out, swshd tail and hng rght, kpt on.* ....(5 to 2 fav op 5 to 4 tchd 11 to 4) 1
2331* HEATHCLIFF (Ire) [-] 9-5 M Wigham (9) *al hndy, rdn to nose ahead 2 fs out, hdd o'r one out, kpt on same pace.* .... (11 to 2 op 9 to 2 tchd 6 to 1) 2

1169[5] ERRIS BOY [-] 8-6 A Clark (10) *nvr far away, ev ch and drvn alng o'r 2 fs out, kpt on same pace.* .... (12 to 1 op 8 to 1 tchd 14 to 1) 3
2153[3] SHFNAK (Ire) [-] 9-0 R Hills (2) *trkd ldrs, effrt and drvn alng last 2 fs, kpt on one pace.* .... (6 to 1 op 5 to 1 tchd 7 to 1) 4
2539[4] KOMPLICITY [-] 8-9 G Duffield (7) *rcd freely in midfield, hng lft last 2 fs, no imprsn.*........ (6 to 1 op 5 to 1) 5
865[3] MR ROUGH [-] 8-3 (5*) C Hodgson (3) *led till hdd 2 fs out, grad wknd.*........ (11 to 2 op 9 to 2 tchd 6 to 1) 6
1665[5] BENFLEET [-] 8-8 N Carlisle (1) *wth ldr, feeling pace and rdn 2 fs out, fdd.*........ (16 to 1 op 7 to 1 tchd 20 to 1) 7
2316[9] STRAPPED [-] 7-13 (7*) Antoinette Armes (6) *speed on outsd for 5 fs, fdd.*........ (25 to 1 op 14 to 1 tchd 33 to 1) 8
2192[3] CLASSICAL DON (Ire) [-] 7-12 (3*) B Doyle (4) *co'red up, effrt hfwy, wknd und pres 2 fs out.* .... (14 to 1 op 8 to 1 tchd 16 to 1) 9

Dist: 1l, ¾l, 3½l, 1l, 2l, 1½l, hd, ½l. 1m 27.80s. a 4.60s (9 Ran).
SR: 3/12/-/-/-/-/ (Multiyork Ltd), M H Tompkins

2787 Furzedown Maiden Stakes Class D (3-y-o and up) £3,525 5f 43yds..... (4:10)

2560[3] NEWBURY COAT (bl) 3-8-9 G Duffield (7) *made all, quickened clr o'r 2 fs out, unchlgd.* .... (4 to 1 op 9 to 2 tchd 11 to 2) 1
DESERT CHAMP (USA) 4-9-0 G Carter (1) *rcd wide, effrt and ran green last 2 fs, no imprsn.* .... (11 to 1 op 9 to 2 tchd 12 to 1) 2
2580[8] PISTON (Ire) 3-8-9 T Quinn (4) *chsd ldg pair thrght, outpcd 2 fs out, staying on finish.* .... (9 to 4 fav op 5 to 4 tchd 5 to 2) 3
2379[6] JAAZIM (bl) 3-8-9 R Hills (5) *broke wl to dispute ld for 2 fs, drvn alng o'r one out, one pace.* .... (7 to 2 op 3 to 1 tchd 4 to 1) 4
LADY HONDA (Ire) 3-8-1 (3*) B Doyle (6) *reared strt, improved frm off the pace last 2 fs, fnshd wl.* .... (12 to 1 op 8 to 1) 5
1655[3] OLYMPIA 3-8-4 J Lowe (2) *chsd alng to keep up appr hfwy, not pace to chal.*........ (4 to 1 op 5 to 2) 6
2711[8] BENOSO 3-8-2 (7*) Elizabeth Turner (3) *sluggish strt, nvr able to reco'r.*........ (50 to 1 op 33 to 1) 7

Dist: 2½l, 2½l, 3½l, 2½l, 7l, 1½l. 1m 2.50s. a 1.80s (7 Ran).
SR: 38/33/18/4/ (John R Goddard), M McCormack

2788 Chateau Handicap Class E (0-70 3-y-o and up) £2,898 5f 43yds......... (4:40)

1782[9] MEESON TIMES [40] 5-7-13 N Carlisle (9) *chsd alng stands side, quickened ahead o'r one furlong out, ran on wl.* .... (14 to 1 op 12 to 1 tchd 16 to 1) 1
2582[5] BRIGHT PARAGON (Ire) [48] 4-8-7 J Quinn (8) *sluggish strt, chsd alng to improve hfwy, kpt on wl ins fnl furlong.* .... (9 to 2 op 4 to 1 tchd 5 to 1) 2
2157[9] SKI CAPTAIN [47] 9-8-6 D Biggs (7) *drvn alng stands side, ev ch hfwy, kpt on fnl furlong.*........ (16 to 1 op 10 to 1) 3
2584[2] SPRING HIGH [53] (bl) 6-8-12 M Wigham (5) *nvr far away, ev ch 2 fs out, one pace.* (4 to 1 tchd 9 to 2 and 5 to 1) 4
2504[2] BREAKFAST BOOGIE [63] 3-9-3 G Duffield (4) *trkd ldr on outer, rdn 2 fs out, one pace.* .... (6 to 1 op 5 to 1 tchd 7 to 1) 5
2352[2] TREASURE TIME (Ire) [63] 4-9-3 (5*) K Rutter (1) *made most on outsd for o'r 3 fs, no extr.* .... (9 to 2 op 7 to 2 tchd 5 to 1) 6
2241[2] JUCEA [57] 4-9-2 J Lowe (2) *chsd alng beh ldrs, ev ch 2 fs out, fdd.*........ (7 to 2 fav op 3 to 1 tchd 4 to 1) 7
2524[9] JOE SUGDEN [47] 9-8-6 A Clark (3) *shwd up wl on outsd for 3 fs, sn btn.*........ (10 to 1 op 7 to 1) 8

Dist: 1½l, ¾l, ½l, ½l, sht-hd, 2l, 6l. 1m 2.50s. a 1.80s (8 Ran).
SR: 28/30/26/30/33/37/23/-/ (Charles Castle), R Bastiman

ASCOT (good)
Saturday July 24th
Going Correction: PLUS 0.40 sec. per fur.

2789 Colenso Diamond Conditions Stakes Ladies Class C (3-y-o and up) £6,316 1m........................... (2:00)

1950* ANDROMAQUE (USA) 3-9-3 Mrs M Cowdrey (15) *hld up in tch, prog and edgd rght 2 out, led ins fnl furlong, ran on strly.*........ (9 to 4 jt-fav op 2 to 1 tchd 5 to 2) 1
2405[7] SPECIAL PAGEANT (Ire) 3-9-3 Mrs L Pearce (2) *prmnt, led 4 fs out, rdn 2 out, hdd and one pace ins last.* (9 to 4 jt-fav op 5 to 2) 2
2421[7] CREDIT SQUEEZE 3-9-8 Miss E Johnson Houghton (13) *settled mid-div, swtchd wide and effrt 2 fs out, ran on wl ins last, nvr nrr.* (50 to 1 op 33 to 1 tchd 100 to 1) 3
2525[7] BALLERINA BAY (v) 5-9-11 Miss Diana Jones (10) *chsd ldrs, effrt whn not clr run 2 fs out, ran on ins last, nrst finish.*........ (50 to 1 op 33 to 1 tchd 66 to 1) 4
2478* SILVERLOCKS 3-9-3 Mrs A Farrell (12) *prmnt, hrd rdn and one pace fnl 2 fs.*........ (14 to 1) 5
1636 AMAZE 4-10-2 Miss J Winter (8) *chsd ldrs, hmpd o'r 3 out, styd on one pace fnl 2 fs.* .... (14 to 1 op 12 to 1 tchd 16 to 1) 6
1710* NEW CAPRICORN (USA) 3-9-8 Mrs G Jarvis (6) *prmnt, ev ch o'r 2 out, hng rght und pres and wknd appr fnl furlong.*........ (7 to 2 tchd 4 to 1) 7
2490[5] DON'T GIVE UP (bl) 5-9-13 (3*) Miss V Haigh (3) *beh till ran on ins fnl furlong, nvr dngrs.*... (200 to 1 op 150 to 1) 8
2308[3] ROMOOSH 4-9-8 (3*) Miss F Burke (16) *prmnt, led 5 fs out till 4 out, wknd 2 out.* .... (66 to 1 op 50 to 1 tchd 100 to 1) 9
2582[8] MARTINOSKY 7-10-2 Miss M Clark (7) *rear, ran wide entering strt, effrt o'r 2 fs out, sn wknd.* .... (66 to 1 op 50 to 1 tchd 100 to 1) 10
497* THOUSLA ROCK (Ire) 4-9-13 (3*) Mrs J Chapple-Hyam (11) *al rear, rdn and no prog o'r 2 fs out.* .... (8 to 1 tchd 10 to 1) 11
2445[2] PUSEY STREET BOY 6-10-2 Mrs S Bosley (5) *led 3 fs, wknd rpdly 2 out.*........ (50 to 1 tchd 66 to 1) 12
LAMBOURN RAJA 7-10-2 Mrs J Wilkinson (4) *al beh, tld off fnl 3 fs.*........ (200 to 1 op 150 to 1) 13
2422[9] FORTUNE STAR (Ire) 4-9-13 (3*) Miss M Bridger (9) *sn rdn alng, al beh, tld off fnl 3 fs.*........ (200 to 1 op 150 to 1) 14
1262[4] DICKINS (bl) 3-9-2 (3*) Miss Elaine Mills (1) *al wl beh, tld off hfwy.*........ (200 to 1 op 150 to 1) 15

Dist: 3l, 1½l, 1½l, hd, 3l, 3½l, 2½l, hd, 1½l, ½l. 1m 45.64s. a 6.14s (15 Ran).
SR: 59/50/50/48/39/43/24/24/18/ (Dr Carlos E Stelling), R Charlton

2790 Princess Margaret Stakes Class A (Group 3) (2-y-o) £22,464 6f..... (2:35)

2562[3] A SMOOTH ONE (Ire) 8-8 J Reid (1) *al prmnt, rdn 2 fs out, ran on strly ins last to ld nr finish.* .... (12 to 1 tchd 14 to 1) 1
2200* MILD REBUKE 8-8 L Dettori (3) *trkd ldrs, prog and rdn 2 fs out, ev ch wl ins last, ran on.* .... (15 to 2 op 8 to 1 tchd 9 to 1) 2+
2301[2] RED RITA (Ire) 8-8 R Cochrane (6) *prmnt, led o'r 3 fs out, rdn and hdd over one out, ev ch wl ins last, ran on.* .... (100 to 30 op 3 to 1 tchd 7 to 2) 2+
2210[3] GREAT DEEDS 8-8 T Quinn (5) *trkd ldrs, rdn to ld o'r one furlong out, edgd rght ins last, hdd nr finish.* .... (6 to 1 tchd 13 to 2 and 7 to 1) 4
2336* PROPHECY (Ire) 8-8 Pat Eddery (4) *hld up, prog and bumped wl o'r 2 fs out, hrd rdn and ev ch well ins last, no extr nr finish.*........ (9 to 2 op 3 to 1) 5
2357* TRICORNE 8-8 W R Swinburn (2) *hld up, pld wide and effrt wl o'r 2 out, rdn and ev ch whn not clr run ins fnl furlong, not rcvr.*........ (9 to 4 fav op 5 to 2) 6
738[4] MISS AMY LOU (Ire) 8-8 W Carson (7) *led o'r 2 fs, wknd rpdly two out, tld off.*........ (33 to 1 op 25 to 1) 7

Dist: ¾l, dd-ht, nk, nk, ¾l, dist. 1m 18.24s. a 4.84s (7 Ran).
SR: 45/42/42/41/40/37/-/ (Bob Lalemant), R Hannon

2791 King George VI And Queen Elizabeth Diamond Stakes Class A (Group 1) (3-y-o and up) £270,259 1½m...... (3:20)

2253* OPERA HOUSE 5-9-7 M Roberts (2) *trkd ldrs gng wl, prog to ld 2 fs out, hrd rdn appr last, ran on well.* .... (8 to 1 op 7 to 1 tchd 9 to 1) 1
1843* WHITE MUZZLE 3-8-9 J Reid (10) *settled mid-div, prog 3 out, rdn and ran on fnl 2 fs, unbl to chal.* .... (9 to 1 op 7 to 1 tchd 10 to 1) 2
2076* COMMANDER IN CHIEF 3-8-9 Pat Eddery (5) *trkd ldrs gng wl, led o'r 2 fs out, sn rdn and hdd, ran on one pace.* .... (7 to 4 fav op 6 to 4 tchd 15 to 8) 3
2261* USER FRIENDLY 4-9-4 G Duffield (4) *led till o'r 2 fs out, sn rdn and btn.*........ (11 to 4 tchd 5 to 2 and 3 to 1) 4
1787* DRUM TAPS (USA) 7-9-7 L Dettori (7) *prmnt, chsd ldr o'r 5 fs out to 3 out, hrd rdn and one pace.* .... (20 to 1 op 25 to 1) 5
2253[7] ENVIRONMENT FRIEND 5-9-7 Paul Eddery (1) *hld up in tch, effrt and hrd rdn 3 fs out, no imprsn on ldrs.* .... (40 to 1 op 33 to 1 tchd 50 to 1) 6
2302* DESERT TEAM (USA) 3-8-9 C Roche (6) *chsd ldr o'r 4 fs, lost pl and rdn 5 out, rallied 3 out, sn wknd.* .... (66 to 1 op 33 to 1) 7
2253[3] TENBY 3-8-9 W Carson (3) *chsd ldr o'r 7 fs out till over 5 out, rdn and btn wl over 3 out.*.... (8 to 1 tchd 9 to 1) 8
2302[4] JEUNE 4-9-7 R Cochrane (8) *steadied strt, hld up in tch, effrt and rdn 3 fs out, sn wknd.* (50 to 1 tchd 66 to 1) 9
1888* PLATINI (Ger) 4-9-7 M Rimmer (9) *al rear, rdn and wknd o'r 2 fs out.*........ (14 to 1 op 10 to 1 tchd 16 to 1) 10

Dist: 1½l, sht-hd, 10l, nk, 1½l, 2½l, ½l, 2½l, 4l. 2m 33.94s. a 5.74s (10 Ran).
SR: 98/83/82/71/73/70/53/52/59/ (Sheikh Mohammed), M R Stoute

2792 EBF Granville Maiden Stakes Class D (2-y-o) £10,867 6f.............. (4:00)

GRAND LODGE (USA) 9-0 L Dettori (2) *trkd ldrs gng easily, quickened to ld one furlong out, sn clr, imprsv.* .... (11 to 4 fav op Evens tchd 3 to 1) 1
MAJESTIC EAGLE (Ire) 9-0 M Hills (3) *trkd ldr, led hfwy, rdn and hdd one furlong out, ran on one pace.* .... (7 to 2 op 5 to 1) 2
TOM MORGAN 9-0 R Cochrane (4) *slwly into strd, prog frm rear hfwy, rdn and styd on one pace fnl 2 fs.* .... (16 to 1 op 10 to 1 tchd 20 to 1) 3

CEDEZ LE PASSAGE (Fr) 9-0 M Roberts (1) *led to hfwy, sn rdn and one pace*...... (6 to 1 op 5 to 1 tchd 7 to 1) 4
INNISHOWEN (USA) 9-0 Pat Eddery (5) *ran green, beh till styd on ins fnl furlong, nvr dngrs*. .... (5 to 1 op 9 to 2 tchd 11 to 2) 5
GOBSMACKED (USA) 9-0 W R Swinburn (6) *trkd ldrs, rdn o'r 2 fs out, sn wknd*. (15 to 2 op 10 to 1 tchd 12 to 1) 6
SOZZLED 9-0 D Holland (7) *swrvd leaving stalls, al rear, beh fnl 2 fs*......................... (6 to 1 op 7 to 2) 7
Dist: 6l, 1½l, 3½l, 2½l, 2l, 1½l. 1m 17.78s. a 4.38s (7 Ran).
SR: 60/36/30/16/6/-/-/ (Lord Howard de Walden), W Jarvis

2793 Sandringham Rated Class B Handicap (0-105 3-y-o and up) £9,768 1¼m (4:30)

1398 MUHAYAA (USA) [97] 4-9-3 W R Swinburn (5) *trkd ldr, led 2 fs out, rdn out*...................... (7 to 1 tchd 6 to 1) 1
2003² TREMOLANDO (USA) [100] 3-8-10 Pat Eddery (7) *led till 2 fs out, rdn and ev ch ins last, unbl to quicken*. .... (5 to 4 fav op Evens tchd 11 to 8) 2
736³ TOMOS [100] 3-8-10 M Roberts (1) *prmnt, rdn 2 fs out, styd on one pace*............... (12 to 1 tchd 14 to 1) 3
2238⁴ LUPESCU [101] 5-9-7 L Dettori (3) *trkd ldrs, rdn 2 fs out, one pace*............... (5 to 1 op 6 to 1 tchd 9 to 2) 4
1845⁴ RISK MASTER [93] 4-8-13 D Holland (2) *strted slwly, hld up last, effrt o'r 2 fs out, btn whn not clr run over one out*.............................(10 to 1 tchd 12 to 1) 5
2413² LITTLE BEAN [101] 4-9-7 M Hills (6) *hld up, effrt 3 fs out, sn rdn and no imprsn, wknd ins last*. .... (7 to 1 op 6 to 1 tchd 15 to 2) 6
1717⁶ PHARLY STORY [87] 5-8-7 R Cochrane (4) *trkd ldrs till wknd rpdly 2 fs out*.............(10 to 1 tchd 12 to 1) 7
Dist: 1½l, 2½l, nk, ¾l, ¾l, 15l. 2m 12.40s. a 8.70s (7 Ran).
SR: 56/46/41/51/41/47/3/ (Maktoum Al Maktoum), A A Scott

2794 Crocker Bulteel Handicap Class B (0-105 3-y-o and up) £11,940 1m (5:00)

824³ DAWNING STREET (Ire) [90] 5-9-4 Pat Eddery (12) *beh, detached last o'r 3 fs out, swtchd outsd and rapid prog aftr, str run ins last to ld fnl strd*............. (10 to 1) 1
2328³ PENNY DROPS [75] 4-8-0 (3*) D Harrison (9) *prmnt, led wl o'r 2 fs out, rdn and ran on appr last, hdd fnl strd*. ....(5 to 1 fav op 8 to 1) 2
2622* LORD OBERON (Ire) [66] (v) 5-7-8 J Quinn (11) *mid-div, prog 2 fs out, rdn and ev ch ins last, unbl to quicken*. ....(6 to 1 op 9 to 2) 3
2233² RIBHI (USA) [95] 3-9-1 W Carson (15) *hld up beh, bumped o'r 2 out, gd prog appr fnl furlong, nrst finish*. .... (12 to 1 op 10 to 1 tchd 14 to 1) 4
1820² GOOGLY [70] 4-7-12 G Bardwell (1) *chsd ldrs, rdn and lost pl hfwy, styd on wl ag'n appr fnl furlong*. .... (14 to 1 op 16 to 1 tchd 20 to 1) 5
2300² BRAVURA [81] 4-8-9 W R Swinburn (7) *trkd ldrs, prog 2 out, chsd ldr briefly one furlong out, sn no extr*. .... (14 to 1 op 12 to 1) 6
2622⁵ DOUBLE FLUTTER [75] 4-8-3 C Rutter (4) *chsd ldrs, lost pl hfwy, hrd rdn and styd on ag'n appr fnl furlong*. .... (20 to 1 op 16 to 1 tchd 25 to 1) 7
1973⁵ TISSISAT (USA) [88] 4-9-2 L Dettori (16) *mid-div, effrt o'r 2 out, rdn and wknd ins fnl furlong*. ....(15 to 2 op 8 to 1 tchd 9 to 1 and 7 to 1) 8
1021 PERFAY (USA) [84] 5-8-12 R Cochrane (13) *prmnt till rdn and wknd o'r one furlong out*..... (33 to 1 op 25 to 1) 9
2581⁴ WAINWRIGHT (USA) [78] 4-8-6 M Roberts (14) *mid-div, effrt o'r 2 fs out, wknd appr last*. .... (11 to 1 op 12 to 1 tchd 10 to 1) 10
2300⁵ JADE VALE [77] 4-8-5 M Hills (17) *keen hold, chsd ldrs, effrt o'r 2 fs out, sn rdn and wknd*. ....(10 to 1 tchd 11 to 1) 11
2211 LAP OF LUXURY [82] 4-8-10 N Day (3) *led o'r 5 fs, sn wknd*. .... (12 to 1 op 10 to 1 tchd 14 to 1) 12
1537⁵ LOUISVILLE BELLE (Ire) [66] 4-7-8¹ R Street (8) *beh, squeezed out o'r 2 fs out, no ch aftr*........... (33 to 1) 13
2363 BAND ON THE RUN [94] (bl) 6-9-8 T Quinn (6) *prmnt 5 fs, sn wknd*..................(20 to 1 op 16 to 1 tchd 25 to 1) 14
2031⁵ MARINE DIVER [74] 7-8-2 Paul Eddery (5) *strted very slwly, effrt into mid-div whn hmpd hfwy, sn wknd*. .... (16 to 1 op 14 to 1 tchd 20 to 1) 15
1800⁷ LEIF THE LUCKY (USA) [75] 4-8-3 J Williams (10) *al rear, bumped and f o'r 2 fs out*........ (16 to 1 tchd 20 to 1) f
Dist: Sht-hd, ¾l, ¾l, 2½l, hd, nk, 3½l, 4l, 3l, ¾l. 1m 45.53s. a 6.53s (16 Ran).
SR: 54/38/27/46/21/31/24/26/10/ (Windflower Overseas Holdings Inc), J L Dunlop

2795 Blacknest Handicap Class C (0-90 3-y-o and up) £7,505 1½m.......... (5:30)

1770 WHITECHAPEL (USA) [74] 5-9-4 W R Swinburn (1) *trkd ldrs, led o'r 2 fs out, rdn and ran on wl*. .... (7 to 2 op 11 to 4 tchd 4 to 1) 1
2328* NASSMA (Ire) [88] 3-9-6 M Roberts (7) *prmnt, rdn o'r 2 fs out, chsd wnr appr last, nvr able to chal*. .... (7 to 2 op 11 to 4 tchd 4 to 1) 2
1976² GENERAL MOUKTAR [67] 3-7-13 W Carson (3) *prmnt, led o'r 5 fs out till over 2 out, rdn and one pace*. .... (3 to 1 fav op 11 to 4 tchd 100 to 30) 3
2328 BAGALINO (USA) [80] 3-8-12 Pat Eddery (4) *led till o'r 5 fs out, sn hrd rdn and lost pl, styd on ag'n ins last*. ....(5 to 1 tchd 11 to 2) 4
2474⁶ BOOKCASE [72] 6-9-2 J Williams (2) *hld up, lost tch 4 fs out, ran on o'r 2 out, nvr nrr*.... (12 to 1 tchd 14 to 1) 5
2617² FLIGHT LIEUTENANT (USA) [84] 4-10-0 J Reid (5) *trkd ldrs, rdn o'r 2 fs out, wknd appr last*. .... (13 to 2 op 5 to 1 tchd 7 to 1) 6
2002³ PHARAMINEUX [80] 7-9-10 T Quinn (6) *hld up, rdn and lost tch 4 fs out, sn tld off*. .... (14 to 1 op 10 to 1 tchd 16 to 1) 7
Dist: 2½l, 1½l, 2½l, 1l, ½l, 25l. 2m 41.22s. a 13.02s (7 Ran).
SR: 22/19/-/3/5/16/-/ (The Queen), Lord Huntingdon

AYR (good to firm) Saturday July 24th

Going Correction: MINUS 0.10 sec. per fur. (races 1,4,5,6), MINUS 0.25 (2,3)

2796 EBF Cambusdoon Maiden Stakes Class D (2-y-o) £3,881 7f........(2:10)

1715⁴ MAKE A NOTE (USA) 9-0 K Darley (3) *chsd ldrs, pushed alng 3 fs out, hdwy and rdn to ld appr last, hng lft, ran on*.........................(11 to 4 on op 2 to 1 on) 1
2250⁷ ONE WILD OAT 8-9 K Fallon (2) *led one furlong, cl up, ev ch appr fnl furlong, kpt on und pres*. .... (11 to 2 op 7 to 2 tchd 6 to 1) 2
MAURANGI 9-0 J Fortune (7) *trkd ldg pair, hdwy 3 fs out, ev ch 2 out, sn rdn and edgd lft, kpt on ins last*. .... (33 to 1 op 20 to 1) 3
2610⁴ CHILTERN SHOW 8-9 A Mackay (4) *led aftr one furlong, rdn 2 out, hdd o'r one furlong and one pace*. .... (14 to 1 op 10 to 1) 4
2541⁵ RACING BRENDA 8-9 L Charnock (1) *chsd ldrs, rdn o'r 2 fs out, sn one pace*...................(14 to 1 op 7 to 1) 5
2539⁶ BLASTER BATES (USA) 9-0 Alex Greaves (6) *in tch, chsd alng hfwy, sn wknd*.............(16 to 1 op 14 to 1) 6
2429⁹ MOLLINSBURN (Ire) 8-7 (7*) N Varley (5) *dwlt, sn wl beh, tld off hfwy*........................(33 to 1 op 25 to 1) 7
Dist: 2l, 1½l, ½l, 6l, 2½l, 20l. 1m 28.92s. a 4.92s (7 Ran).
SR: 16/5/5/-/ (P D Savill), R Hannon

2797 Star Form Claiming Stakes Class F (3-y-o and up) £2,575 6f........... (2:40)

2568* MURRAY'S MAZDA (Ire) 4-9-1 (7*) P Roberts (7) *cl up, led hfwy, rdn 2 fs out, edgd rght ins last, kpt on*... (3 to 1) 1
2656⁶ DRUM SERGEANT (bl) 6-9-9 (3*) J Weaver (4) *chsd ldrs, hdwy 2 fs out, sn rdn and kpt on one pace*. ....(5 to 2 op 2 to 1) 2
2594⁴ PLUM FIRST (bl) 3-8-13 (3*) S Maloney (2) *led to hfwy, sn rdn, one pace fnl 2 fs*........... (9 to 4 fav op 5 to 2) 3
2106⁶ BOY MARTIN 4-8-5 (7*) M Proctor (1) *in tch till outpcd hfwy, kpt on und pres fnl 2 fs*..... (14 to 1 op 10 to 1) 4
2456⁶ PRINCIPAL PLAYER (USA) (v) 3-8-12 A Mackay (5) *cl up, ev ch 2 and a half fs out, sn rdn and wknd*. .... (10 to 1 op 8 to 1) 5
2682³ ANGELS ANSWER (Ire) 4-8-13 K Darley (8) *chsd ldrs, rdn o'r 2 fs and sn wknd*............. (14 to 1 op 10 to 1) 6
Dist: 2½l, 1l, 1l, hd, 6l. 1m 13.32s. a 2.42s (6 Ran).
SR: 30/24/10/2/1/-/ (Murray Grubb), J Berry

2798 Bridgestone/Firestone Handicap Class D (0-80 3-y-o and up) £3,468 6f ....(3:10)

2594² DENSBEN [78] 9-10-0 K Fallon (1) *hld up, pushed alng hfwy, swtchd outsd and hdwy 2 fs out, sn rdn to styd on to ld ins last*...............(3 to 1 fav op 5 to 2) 1
2657* VELOCE (Ire) [77] 5-9-13 (7ex) A Mackay (3) *beh, hdwy o'r 2 fs out, sn rdn, styd on ins last*....... (5 to 1 op 4 to 1) 2
2434 MASTER POKEY [62] 9-8-12 K Darley (7) *cl up, led one and a half fs out, sn rdn, hdd and not quicken ins last*. ....(100 to 30 op 7 to 2) 3
2738⁵ DIET [64] (v) 7-8-7 (7*) R Havlin (6) *led, rdn and hdd one and a half fs out, kpt on und pres*. (20 to 1 op 12 to 1) 4
2594⁶ SLADES HILL [62] 6-8-12 J Fortune (4) *cl up, effrt one and a half fs out and sn ev ch, rdn and wknd ins last*. ....(6 to 1 tchd 7 to 1) 5
2738² BEST EFFORT [50] 7-8-0 G Hind (5) *chsd ldrs, rdn o'r 2 fs out, kpt on one pace fnl furlong*...(12 to 1 op 10 to 1) 6
2653* GONDO [75] (v) 6-9-4 (7*,7ex) S Knott (2) *cl up to hfwy, sn rdn and wknd*.....................(7 to 2 tchd 4 to 1) 7
Dist: Nk, 1l, hd, nk, nk, 7l. 1m 12.15s. a 1.25s (7 Ran).
SR: 59/57/38/39/36/23/20/ (Mrs Janet M Pike), Denys Smith

2799 Daily Star Handicap Class E (0-70 4-y-o and up) £2,853 1m............(3:40)

2597² SOOTY TERN [49] 6-8-5 (3*) J Weaver (5) *led, rdn 2 fs out and sn hdd, styd on und pres to ld ins last, ran on*. ....(9 to 4 fav op 5 to 2) 1
2641⁵ MAJAL (Ire) [55] 4-9-0 L Charnock (6) *trkd wnr, effrt 2 fs out and sn led, rdn and hdd ins last, no extr*. .... (12 to 1 op 8 to 1) 2

2656[8] HAND ON HEART (Ire) [44] (v) 4-8-0 (3*) S Maloney (9) *hld up and beh, gd hdwy 2 fs out, rdn and ran on strly ins last.* .... (50 to 1 op 33 to 1) 3
2567[2] MASTER OFTHE HOUSE [48] 7-8-0 (7*) J Marshall (1) *hld up, hdwy o'r 2 fs out, sn rdn and kpt on one pace.* ....(6 to 1) 4
2543[6] DREAM CARRIER (Ire) [52] 5-8-4 (7*) V Halliday (7) *in tch, effrt and hdwy 3 fs out, rdn 2 out and one pace.* .... (9 to 1 op 7 to 1 tchd 10 to 1) 5
2426[7] PRINCESS OF ORANGE [52] 4-8-4 (7*) N Varley (4) *hld up, hdwy hfwy, rdn 3 fs out, sn wknd.* (20 to 1 op 12 to 1) 6
2735[6] MENTALASANYTHIN [69] 4-10-0 A Mackay (8) *chsd ldrs, effrt and rdn 3 fs out, sn btn*.........(7 to 2 op 9 to 2) 7
2641[6] DOCTOR ROY [46] 5-8-5 Alex Greaves (2) *al rear.* ....(8 to 1 op 7 to 1) 8
2283* SHANNON EXPRESS [49] 6-8-8 Julie Bowker (3) *chsd ldrs, rdn 3 fs out, sn wknd*...............(6 to 1 op 5 to 1) 9
Dist: ¾l, hd, 1½l, 1l, 3l, sht-hd, 1l, 4l. 1m 40.89s. a 3.19s (9 Ran).
SR: 34/38/26/25/26/17/33/7/-/ (J M Bradley), J M Bradley

2800 Ailsa Craig Selling Handicap Class F (0-60 3-y-o and up) £2,623 1m 7f 16yds ....(4:10)

2455[2] REEL OF TULLOCH (Ire) [41] 4-9-6 K Darley (5) *hld up, hdwy o'r 3 fs out and sn drvn alng, styd on wl fnl 2 furlongs to ld well ins last.* .... (9 to 4 fav op 5 to 2 tchd 11 to 4 and 3 to 1) 1
2658[4] PIE HATCH (Ire) [38] (bl) 4-9-3 G Hind (8) *trkd ldrs, led aftr 7 fs and sn clr, rdn one and a half out, hdd and no extr wl ins last*..........................(7 to 1 op 6 to 1) 2
2091[5] CHALLENGER ROW (Ire) [48] 3-8-9 (3*) S Maloney (3) *hld up, rdn alng hfwy, hrd drvn and kpt on one pace fnl 3 fs*.................................(9 to 2 op 5 to 1) 3
2178[8] NANCY (Ire) [40] (bl) 3-8-4 L Charnock (2) *chsd ldrs, rdn o'r 3 fs out, one pace*................. (20 to 1 op 14 to 1) 4
2683[3] ALPHA HELIX [26] (v) 10-8-5 J Fortune (9) *beh, hdwy 4 fs out, sn drvn alng, nvr dngrs.* .... (10 to 1 op 8 to 1 tchd 11 to 1) 5
2455* DANCING DAYS [37] (v) 7-8-13 (3*) J Weaver (7) *prmnt, rdn 3 fs out, sn wknd*.....................(5 to 1 op 4 to 1) 6
2282[2] SAN PIER NICETO [45] (v) 6-9-3 (7*) J Marshall (6) *prmnt, rdn 3 fs out, sn wknd*......................(6 to 1 op 5 to 1) 7
2455[8] LORD ADVOCATE [42] (v) 5-9-0 (7*) N Varley (1) *led 7 fs, rdn 6 out, sn wknd*...................(16 to 1 op 10 to 1) 8
Dist: ¾l, 10l, 2½l, 1l, 2½l, 3l, 7l. 3m 19.12s. a 6.62s (8 Ran).
SR: 25/20/5/-/-/2/7/-/ (Darren Croft), P C Haslam

2801 Scottish Racing Club Scots Wha'hae Handicap For Amateur Riders Class E (0-80 3-y-o and up) £2,787 1m 5f 13yds ....(4:40)

2061 MERRY NUTKIN [73] 7-11-5 Mr M Buckley (4) *al prmnt, effrt to ld o'r 2 fs out, rdn and ran on wl fnl furlong.* .... (10 to 1 op 5 to 1) 1
1288* GREY POWER [66] 6-10-12 Mr S Swiers (5) *hld up and beh, gd hdwy o'r 2 fs out, effrt and rdn appr fnl furlong, sn ev ch, kpt on.* ....(7 to 2 op 4 to 1 tchd 9 to 2 and 3 to 1) 2
2521[3] SWORD MASTER [73] 4-11-5 Miss D J Jones (8) *al prmnt, effrt and hdwy to chal 2 fs out, sn hrd rdn, one pace ins last*.............................. (5 to 2 fav op 11 to 4) 3
2735[3] BRIGGSMAID [52] 5-9-12 Mr J Rees (7) *hld up and beh, hdwy o'r 2 fs out, sn rdn and kpt on one pace.* ....(5 to 1 op 6 to 1 tchd 9 to 2) 4
1967[6] LEGION OF HONOUR [64] 5-10-10 Miss P Robson (6) *chsd ldrs, hdwy 3 fs out, effrt and ev ch 2 out, rdn and wknd appr last*..............(11 to 1 op 8 to 1 tchd 12 to 1) 5
2368[3] DOMINANT SERENADE [47] 4-9-7 Mr C Bonner (2) *led, rdn and hdd o'r 2 fs out, sn wknd.* ....(7 to 2 op 4 to 1 tchd 9 to 2) 6
2655[6] TRUBEN (USA) [75] 4-11-7 Miss L Perratt (3) *mid-div, hdwy 4 fs out, rdn 3 out, grad wknd*..... (14 to 1 op 12 to 1) 7
2599[4] HOD-MOD (Ire) [55] 3-9-2 Miss S Chittenden (1) *in tch, wide strt, rdn 3 fs out, sn wknd.* ....(16 to 1 op 12 to 1 tchd 20 to 1) 8
Dist: Nk, ¾l, 1½l, ½l, 4l, 30l. 2m 56.95s. a 10.95s (8 Ran).
SR: 10/2/7/-/-/ (Robert F S Newall), Mrs M Reveley

BELMONT PARK (USA) (firm)
Saturday July 24th

2802 Top Flight Handicap (Grade 1) (3-y-o and up) £59,603 1m 1f...............

1691[3] YOU'D BE SURPRISED (USA) 4-8-0 J Bailey,..... (26 to 10) 1
560[2] LOOIE CAPOTE (USA) 4-8-3 M Smith,............ (8 to 1) 2
1184[2] SHARED INTEREST (USA) 5-8-2[1] J Santos,....... (7 to 1) 3
FORTUNATE FAITH (USA) 3-7-10[1] J R Velazquez,.. (5 to 1) 4
1691[2] DEPUTATION (USA) 4-8-5 Julie Krone,......... (Evens fav) 5
SPINNING ROUND (USA) 4-8-1 J Chavez,......... (19 to 1) 6
1691[5] QUEEN OF TRIUMPH (USA) 4-8-2[2] C Perret,..... (22 to 1) 7
Dist: Hd, 2½l, 2l, 1½l, nk, 18l. 1m 48.82s. (7 Ran).
(Rokeby Stables), M Miller

EVRY (FR) (good)
Saturday July 24th

2803 Prix Daphnis (Group 3) (3-y-o) £23,895 1m 1f..........................(4:10)

2171[4] ASTAIR (Fr) 8-9 G Mosse (1) *3rd strt, led one and a half fs out, ran on wl*.......................................(76 to 10) 1
2081[5] EMPEROR JONES (USA) 8-12 B Raymond (4) *trkd ldr, led one and a half fs out till fnl 110 yards, kpt on.* (34 to 10) 2
2171[2] FASTNESS (Ire) 8-9 F Head (8) *in rear and 9th strt, hdwy 2 fs out, nrst finish*...............................(74 to 10) 3
2068[2] MISTLE CAT (USA) 8-9 W Woods (2) *led till one and a half fs out, unbl to quicken fnl furlong*..............(76 to 10) 4
2531[8] RANGER (Fr) 8-12 W Mongil (5) *nvr able to chal.* (20 to 1) 5
2171* JACKDIDI (Fr) 8-9 D Boeuf (10) *nvr able to chal.* (95 to 10) 6
953[5] GLORIEUX DANCER (Fr) 8-12 O Poirier (7) *nvr on terms.* ....(45 to 1) 7
2298[2] CAESOUR (USA) 8-9 C Asmussen (11) *mid-div, 4th strt, rdn 2 fs out, wknd one and a half out*........(33 to 10) 8
2208* LYNTON (USA) 8-9 T Jarnet (3) *nvr nrr*..... (27 to 10 fav) 9
DIODEME (Fr) 8-9 G Guignard (9) *al rear*.......... (37 to 1) 10
Dist: ¾l, nk, nk, ¾l, nk, sht-nk, 1½l, 2l, 5l. 1m 48.40s. b 2.90s (10 Ran).
SR: 71/72/68/67/68/64/66/60/56/ (Marquesa de Moratalla), A de Royer-Dupre

LEOPARDSTOWN (IRE) (good to firm (races 1,2), good (3,4,5,6,7))
Saturday July 24th

Going Correction: NIL (races 1,2), MINUS 0.10 (3,4,5,6,7)

2804 Glenalua Two Year Old EBF Maiden £5,244 6f...................... (2:15)

LOW KEY AFFAIR (USA) 8-11 M J Kinane (1)..(11 to 8 fav) 1
MASAWA (Ire) 8-11 J P Murtagh (6)................(9 to 4) 2
1432[5] SLICK DEALER (Ire) 8-10 (4*) P Carberry (8).......(16 to 1) 3
2402[3] MANAAFIS (Ire) 9-0 S Craine (4).................(6 to 1) 4
QUINTILIANI (Ire) 9-0 J F Egan (13).............(16 to 1) 5
CELESTIAL PLAIN (Ire) 8-11 P Shanahan (10).....(10 to 1) 6
2666[8] FRISKY MISS (Ire) 8-11 D Hogan (9)..............(25 to 1) 7
ROSE BUNCH 9-0 P V Gilson (3)....................(14 to 1) 8
2037 BETTER YET (Ire) 8-11 N Byrne (11)...............(25 to 1) 9
2402[6] RAZIDA (Ire) 8-11 K J Manning (7)..................(8 to 1) 10
2284[6] EUPHORIC (Ire) 9-0 N G McCullagh (5)...........(10 to 1) 11
2188[6] GENEVIEVE FLEUR (Ire) 8-9 (2*) D G O'Shea (2)...(20 to 1) 12
IMPOSING TIME 8-10 (4*) W J Smith (12).........(33 to 1) 13
Dist: 1l, ¾l, 1½l, 2½l. 1m 14.70s. a 3.20s (13 Ran).
SR: 33/29/29/23/13/-/ (Moyglare Stud Farm), D K Weld

2805 Belgrave Stakes (Listed) (3-y-o and up) £8,625 6f...................(2:40)

2404[3] TROPICAL (bl) 3-9-0 M J Kinane (9) *trkd ldr, led o'r one furlong out, ran on strly*...................(7 to 2 fav) 1
2606[7] PERSIAN CREEK (Ire) 4-9-2 J F Egan (3) *rear, prog o'r one furlong out, ran on und pres ins last*..........(20 to 1) 2
1646[2] DASHING COLOURS (Ire) 4-9-4 P Shanahan (7) *hld up, not much room one and a half fs out, quickened ins last, kpt on*...(10 to 1) 3
2187[5] PERNILLA (Ire) 3-9-0 K J Manning (4) *wl plcd till weakend o'r one furlong out*...............................(7 to 1) 4
1047[9] MYSTERIOUS WAYS (Ire) (bl) 3-8-10 P V Gilson (8) *led till rdn and hdd o'r one furlong out*..............(9 to 2) 5
2187* ROSIE'S MAC (Ire) 4-9-7 N G McCullagh (5) *hld up, prog to chal 2 fs out, wknd o'r one out*...................(10 to 1) 6
2187[3] DAWNSIO (Ire) 3-8-12 J P Murtagh (6) *trkd ldrs, rdn and wknd one and a half fs out, eased fnl furlong.* (9 to 2) 7
1201 UP AND AT 'EM 3-9-3 B Coogan (1) *wl plcd, rdn one and a half fs out, sn wknd*...............................(9 to 2) 8
2407[5] BRADAWN BREEVER (Ire) (bl) 4-9-2 S Craine (2) *wl plcd, rdn and wknd o'r one furlong out*...............(7 to 1) 9
Dist: ¾l, sht-hd, 2½l, hd. 1m 13.50s. a 2.00s (9 Ran).
SR: 60/59/60/46/41/-/ (The Sussex Stud Limited), D K Weld

2806 Strathmore Handicap (0-80 3-y-o and up) £3,105 7f...................(3:05)

1645[6] DOBIE (USA) [-] 5-9-7 M J Kinane (9).......(4 to 1 co-fav) 1
2039 NORDIC SAINT (Ire) [-] 4-8-9 (6*) J A Heffernan (8)..(6 to 1) 2
2604[3] BENE MERENTI (Ire) [-] (bl) 3-8-7 (6*) R V Skelly (6) ....(4 to 1 co-fav) 3
2320* WHAT A PLEASURE (Ire) [-] 3-8-4 (6*) B J Walsh (5) (5 to 1) 4
2451[8] ABEREDW (Ire) [-] 3-8-0 (2*) D G O'Shea (1)...... (10 to 1) 5
1569 INAUGURATION (Ire) [-] 4-8-3 (6*) J J Behan (7).... (16 to 1) 6
2073[8] WALLY WALLENSKY (Ire) [-] 3-9-1 (4*) P Carberry (10) ....(4 to 1 co-fav) 7
2248 SALLUSTAR [-] (bl) 8-8-11 J P Murtagh (4)..........(6 to 1) 8
2248[9] DRESS DANCE (Ire) [-] (bl) 3-8-4 A J Nolan (3)..... (25 to 1) 9
2514 VOUVRAY (Ire) [-] 3-7-12 Joanna Morgan (2)....... (25 to 1) 10
Dist: 1l, 3½l, nk, 1½l. 1m 30.20s. a 4.80s (10 Ran).
SR: 25/16/3/-/-/-/ (Michael Watt), D K Weld

2807 Orby EBF Stakes (Listed) (2-y-o) £8,775 7f.................... (3:35)

2075³ BARTOK (Ire) 8-11 P V Gilson (2) *str hold early, trkd ldr, prog to ld one furlong out, quickened clr*...... (6 to 4) 1
2605³ CITY NIGHTS (Ire) 8-11 M J Kinane (1) *led to one furlong out, hmpd entering last, wknd*............. (Evens fav) 2
2246² GENUINE BID (Ire) 8-11 J P Murtagh (4) *al rear, rdn hfwy, sn btn*.. (14 to 1) 3
2402* SPECS APPEAL (Ire) (bl) 8-11 K J Manning (3) *trkd ldr, prog to ld appr 3 fs out, broke both frnt legs and came dwn, destroyed*.................................... (5 to 1) su
Dist: 2½l, 4l. 1m 30.80s. a 5.40s (4 Ran).
SR: 5/ (Mrs G W Jennings), C Collins

2808 Obelisk Handicap (0-95 3-y-o and up) £6,900 1¼m.................. (4:00)

1514⁹ SKIPO (USA) [-] (bl) 3-8-10 M J Kinane (6)...... (5 to 2 fav) 1
2346² DAHLIA'S BEST (USA) [-] 3-7-8 (8*) R T Fitzpatrick (5) .... (5 to 1) 2
2039⁴ TRYARRA (Ire) [-] 3-8-3 N G McCullagh (2)......... (7 to 2) 3
2039⁷ SECOND REVOLUTION (Ire) [-] 4-8-3 (6*) J A Heffernan (4) .... (6 to 1) 4
2485³ KARINIYD (Ire) [-] (bl) 3-9-4 J P Murtagh (3)........ (7 to 2) 5
HE'S A FLYER [-] (bl) 9-7-10² (2*) R M Burke (7)... (16 to 1) 6
KHAZARI (USA) [-] 5-8-7 (2*) D G O'Shea (1)...... (12 to 1) 7
Dist: 1½l, nk, 4l, 4½l. 2m 8.00s. a 3.30s (7 Ran).
SR: 53/42/42/40/40/-/-/ (Allen E Paulson), D K Weld

2809 Ballycullen Stakes (Listed) (3-y-o and up) £8,625 1m 1f.............. (4:30)

2608* PRE-EMINENT (bl) 6-10-0 M J Kinane (6) *made all, rdn 2 and a half fs out, kpt on und str pres ins last*... (2 to 1) 1
1552⁴ BALLYKETT PRINCE (Ire) (bl) 5-9-6 K J Manning (2) *trkd ldr, prog to dispute ld one furlong out, sn no extr*... (4 to 1) 2
2038⁷ TARAKANA (USA) 3-8-10 J P Murtagh (1) *trkd ldrs, prog o'r 2 fs out, not much room, swtchd rght over one out, ran on*....................................... (7 to 4 fav) 3
1853* ARABIC TREASURE (USA) 3-9-1 P Shanahan (3) *hld up, prog one furlong out, ran on strly, jst fld*..... (12 to 1) 4
2247⁹ LEGAL FLAIR (Ire) 3-8-13 P V Gilson (4) *trkd ldrs, not quicken ins last*.................................. (10 to 1) 5
Dist: Sht-hd, sht-hd, sht-hd, 1l. 1m 58.10s. a 7.60s (5 Ran).
(Michael W J Smurfit), D K Weld

2810 Mapis EBF Maiden (3-y-o and up) £3,450 1m.................... (5:00)

2040⁷ GENERAL CHAOS (Ire) 3-9-0 P V Gilson (4)........ (5 to 2) 1
RENEWED DYNASTY (USA) 3-9-0 M J Kinane (2) .... (11 to 8 on) 2
2140⁷ FESTIVAL GIRL (Ire) 3-8-11 N G McCullagh (3).... (12 to 1) 3
2609⁵ KYRENIA 3-8-11 J P Murtagh (8)................. (7 to 2) 4
1441 INDIGENT (Ire) 3-8-11 S Craine (7)............... (14 to 1) 5
2452⁵ PAKED (Ire) 3-8-11 D V Smith (6)................. (33 to 1) 6
Dist: 1½l, 4½l, 2½l, 2½l. 1m 43.30s. a 5.30s (6 Ran).
SR: 9/4/-/ (J N Anthony), C Collins

NEWCASTLE (good to firm) Saturday July 24th

Going Correction: MINUS 0.10 sec. per fur. (races 1,2,3,4), MINUS 0.20 (5,6)

2811 Renacare Jackie Milburn Memorial Apprentice Handicap Class F (0-80 3-y-o and up) £2,444 7f......... (2:15)

2567⁵ SPANISH VERDICT [66] 6-9-2 (5*) C Teague (4) *led, hdd entering fnl furlong, kpt on wl to ld ag'n cl hme.* .... (5 to 1 tchd 9 to 2) 1
2339² TAJDIF (USA) [80] 3-10-0 J Tate (2) *hld up, smooth hdwy to ld entering fnl furlong, hdd and no extr cl hme.* .... (9 to 4 fav op 5 to 2 tchd 11 to 4 and 2 to 1) 2
2339* ROYAL GIRL [62] 6-9-3 T G McLaughlin (6) *prmnt, ev ch o'r one furlong out, kpt on same pace*... (4 to 1 op 3 to 1) 3
2597⁶ CHANTRY BELLINI [44] (bl) 4-7-13 D Wright (3) *in tch, rdn o'r one furlong out, no hdwy*....... (9 to 1 op 8 to 1) 4
2425* PENNY BANGER (Ire) [59] 3-8-7 D McCabe (5) *in tch, rdn o'r one furlong out, no hdwy*..... (5 to 1 tchd 11 to 2) 5
2582⁶ BLUE GRIT [66] 7-9-7 A Procter (1) *in tch, rdn o'r one furlong out, sn wknd*................................ (6 to 1) 6
2509³ GENTLE HERO (USA) [67] 7-9-1 (7*) I Jardine (7) *wth wnr till wknd 3 fs out*.................................. (20 to 1) 7
Dist: Nk, 3l, 3½l, 1½l, 7l, 7l. 1m 27.62s. a 3.62s (7 Ran).
SR: 42/48/28/-/ (Cox & Allen (Kendal) Ltd), Denys Smith

2812 Fresenius Fillies Conditions Stakes Class D (2-y-o) £3,525 7f........ (2:45)

2473² STAR SPEEDER (Ire) 8-4 (5*) D Wright (3) *set slow pace, quickened hfwy, hdd o'r 2 fs out, rdn to ld ag'n entering fnl furlong, all out*............. (7 to 2 op 3 to 1) 1
2234⁴ NSX 8-13 P Robinson (4) *pld hrd early, cl up, slight ld o'r 2 out, hdd entering fnl furlong, kpt on wl.* .... (11 to 2 op 6 to 1 tchd 5 to 1) 2
1766⁵ QUEENBIRD 9-5 W Ryan (1) *cl up, dsptd ld o'r 2 fs out, ev ch till no extr close hme.* ....(7 to 4 on tchd 2 to 1 on and 13 to 8 on) 3
2562⁵ OUBECK BLUE 8-13 M Tebbutt (2) *hld up, lost tch hfwy, styd on wl fnl furlong*.............. (12 to 1 op 8 to 1) 4
Dist: Hd, hd, 2½l. 1m 34.07s. a 10.07s (4 Ran).
(Giles W Pritchard-Gordon), G Lewis

2813 Rambling River Handicap Class C (0-95 3-y-o and up) £7,505 5f.... (3:15)

2524⁷ LOVE RETURNED [72] 6-8-13 M Tebbutt (12) *hld up, gd hdwy o'r 2 fs out, led over one out, ran on wl.* .... (10 to 1 op 12 to 1) 1
2392 SINGING STAR [65] 7-7-13 (7*) Claire Balding (1) *hld up far side, gd hdwy o'r one furlong out, kpt on wl fnl furlong*............................ (14 to 1 op 16 to 1) 2
2230⁵ HERE COMES A STAR [62] 5-8-3 A Clark (13) *hld up, not much room and hmpd o'r one furlong out, str run fnl furlong, nrst finish*.............................. (10 to 1) 3
2392 NED'S BONANZA [74] 4-9-1 J Lowe (11) *chsd ldrs, slightly hmpd jst ins fnl furlong, kpt on*..... (7 to 1 op 6 to 1) 4
2510³ SIR TASKER [59] 5-8-0² P Robinson (4) *led far side, one pace fnl furlong*................ (14 to 1 op 12 to 1) 5
2620⁷ EAGER DEVA [87] 6-10-0 W Ryan (9) *made most stand side till hdd o'r one furlong out, sn btn*........... (12 to 1) 6
2600⁶ PALLIUM (Ire) [64] 5-8-5 A Culhane (6) *in tch, no hdwy fnl 2 fs*.................................. (14 to 1 tchd 12 to 1) 7
2594* CATHERINES WELL [81] 10-9-8 T Lucas (3) *dwlt, sn in tch far side, no hdwy fnl 2 fs.* .... (15 to 2 op 7 to 1 tchd 8 to 1) 8
2653² ABSOLUTION [65] 9-8-3 (3*) M Fenton (2) *chsd ldrs far side till wknd 2 fs out*............. (7 to 1 tchd 15 to 2) 9
2508² SHE'S SMART [80] 5-9-7 M Birch (5) *cl up till wknd 2 fs out*.................(9 to 2 fav op 13 to 2 tchd 4 to 1) 10
2707* BALLAD DANCER [66] 8-8-7 (7ex) J Fanning (7) *chsd ldrs to hfwy, sn wknd*..................... (8 to 1 op 7 to 1) 11
654⁴ NIFTY FIFTY (Ire) [75] 4-9-2 J Carroll (8) *chsd ldrs till wknd 2 fs out*.. (16 to 1) 12
2456³ EWALD (Ire) [70] 5-8-11 T Williams (10) *dsptd ld till wknd wl o'r one furlong out, btn whn hmpd jst ins fnl furlong*............................ (7 to 1 op 6 to 1) 13
Dist: ¾l, sht-hd, 2l, 1½l, 2l, 1½l, sht-hd, sht-hd, ½l, 1½l. 1m 1.37s. a 2.47s (13 Ran).
SR: 40/30/26/30/9/29/-/16/-/ (J M Ratcliffe), W Jarvis

2814 Fastnet Claiming Stakes Class G (2-y-o) £2,364 5f.................. (3:45)

2569⁵ DANGEROUS SHADOW 7-13 (5*) Darren Moffatt (8) *in tch, rdn and hdwy o'r one furlong out, led ins fnl furlong, ran on wl*.......... (12 to 1 tchd 10 to 1 and 14 to 1) 1
2446² LADY SHERIFF 8-10 T Lucas (4) *cl up, led hfwy, hng lft, hdd ins fnl furlong, no extr*........ (4 to 1 tchd 7 to 2) 2
2446³ DOCKYARD DORA (bl) 8-2 P Robinson (10) *trkd ldrs, not clr run o'r one furlong out, kpt on fnl furlong.* .... (13 to 2 op 6 to 1 tchd 7 to 1) 3
2342² HICKLETON LADY (Ire) 8-4 W Ryan (9) *beh, styd on fnl 2 fs, not rch ldrs*....... (15 to 8 fav op 2 to 1 tchd 7 to 4) 4
2423⁵ SPORT RACING CLUB (bl) 7-11⁶ (5*) D McCabe (5) *chsd ldrs, rdn wl o'r one furlong out, sn btn*........ (25 to 1) 5
1082 TILQUHILLIE ROSE 7-10³ (7*) C Munday (6) *slwly into strd, beh till some late hdwy, nvr dngrs.* (16 to 1 op 12 to 1) 6
2554⁵ LUCIUS LOCKET (Ire) (bl) 8-11 J Carroll (3) *cl up, rdn 2 fs out, wknd entering fnl furlong*...... (5 to 1 op 4 to 1) 7
SECONDS AWAY 8-11 J Fanning (2) *sn beh.* .... (25 to 1 op 14 to 1) 8
2103³ RED GRIT (Ire) (v) 8-2 J Lowe (7) *led to hfwy, sn wknd.* ....(9 to 1 op 8 to 1) 9
Dist: 1½l, 2½l, 2l, ½l, 2½l, ½l, nk, 3½l. 1m 2.65s. a 3.75s (9 Ran).
SR: 5/5/-/-/-/-/ (Prime Maintenance), Mrs M Reveley

2815 1993 Great North British Transplant Games Handicap Stakes Class C (0-90 3-y-o and up) £4,160 1¼m 32yds (4:15)

2361 MECKLENBURG (Ire) [82] 3-9-9 W Ryan (1) *hld up, smooth hdwy to ld o'r 2 fs out, sn clr, very easily.* ....(5 to 4 fav op 6 to 4 tchd 7 to 4) 1
2470³ FOREST STAR (USA) [44] (v) 4-7-9 J Lowe (6) *in tch, effrt o'r 3 fs out, rdn over one out, kpt on same pace*... (12 to 1) 2
2507⁷ MIDDLEHAM CASTLE [50] 4-8-1 T Williams (3) *chsd ldr, led 6 fs out, hdd o'r 2 out, kpt on same pace.* .... (6 to 1 tchd 7 to 1 and 11 to 2) 3
ARAK (USA) [73] 5-9-10 A Culhane (5) *trkd ldrs, effrt 3 fs out, rdn wl o'r one out, kpt on same pace.* ....(9 to 1 op 7 to 1) 4
2177³ SOUL EMPEROR [72] 3-8-10 (3*) M Fenton (4) *led till hdd 6 fs out, wknd 4 out, tld off*.......... (3 to 1 op 5 to 2) 5
Dist: 5l, 1l, 1½l, dist. 2m 9.29s. a 2.79s (5 Ran).
SR: 61/23/27/47/-/ (Sheikh Mohammed), H R A Cecil

2816 Rothmans Royals North South Challenge Series Handicap Class D (0-80

3-y-o and up) £3,687 1m. . . . . (4:45)

AVISHAYES (USA) [49] 6-7-13 J Fanning (6) *hld up, hdwy 3 fs out, led o'r one out, ran on wl.* . . . . (9 to 1 op 7 to 1 tchd 10 to 1) 1
2445* PRIDE OF PENDLE [58] 4-8-8 W Ryan (4) *hld up, hdwy o'r 2 fs out, ran on wl fnl furlong, not rch wnr.* . . . . (3 to 1 fav op 7 to 2 tchd 9 to 2) 2
771⁶ WELLINGTON ROCK (USA) [76] 4-9-12 P Robinson (9) *led aftr 2 fs till hdd o'r one out, kpt on same pace.* . . . . (8 to 1 tchd 9 to 1) 3
2601⁴ JALMUSIQUE [73] 7-9-9 M Birch (10) *hld up, smooth hdwy 3 fs out, rdn 2 out, one pace.* . . . . (4 to 1 op 5 to 1) 4
2459² IMPERIAL BID (Fr) [67] 5-9-3 A Clark (8) *chsd ldrs, effrt 2 fs out, one pace.* . . . . (11 to 2 op 9 to 2) 5
2391⁸ MBULWA [51] 7-7-10 (5*) J Tate (7) *trkd ldrs, no hdwy fnl 2 fs.* . . . . (16 to 1 op 14 to 1) 6
2491⁴ INDERAPUTERI [66] 3-8-3 (5*) D McCabe (2) *in tch, outpcd wl o'r 2 fs out, styd on fnl furlong.* . . . . (10 to 1) 7
2431² SOBERING THOUGHTS [65] 7-8-10 (5*) O Pears (3) *prmnt till wknd 2 fs out.* . . . . (9 to 1 op 7 to 1 tchd 10 to 1) 8
2220⁴ MOHICAN BRAVE (Ire) [62] 3-8-4 A Culhane (1) *led 2 fs, cl up, chlgd two out, wknd quickly entering fnl furlong.* . . . . (10 to 1 op 12 to 1) 9
2283⁴ HABETA (USA) [60] (bl) 7-8-10 J Lowe (5) *hld up, effrt o'r 2 fs out, no hdwy.* . . . . (8 to 1 op 7 to 1) 10
Dist: 1l, 3½l, ½l, nk, 1½l, 1l, hd, ½l, hd. 1m 41.02s. a 2.02s (10 Ran).
SR: 31/37/44/39/32/11/15/21/8/ (P Davidson-Brown), Mrs M Reveley

SOUTHWELL (good)
Saturday July 24th
Going Correction: MINUS 0.20 sec. per fur.

2817 EBF Gooseberry Maiden Stakes Class D (Div I) (2-y-o) £4,092 6f. . . . . (2:25)

2374³ STELLOSO 9-0 G Carter (3) *made all, quickened last 2 fs, hld on gmely.* . . . . (7 to 2 op 9 to 2) 1
1916⁵ SANGARE (Ire) 8-9 A McGlone (8) *al hndy, str chal fnl furlong, jst hld.* . . . (6 to 5 on op 11 to 8 on tchd Evens) 2
AMIDST 8-9 Dean McKeown (9) *missed break, hdwy on outsd last 2 fs, one pace last 50 yards.* (5 to 1 op 7 to 2) 3
543⁹ BALI WARRIOR (Ire) 9-0 R Hills (7) *tucked away on ins, effrt and rdn o'r one furlong out, kpt on one pace.* . . . . (16 to 1 op 14 to 1) 4
2364 WIDE OUTSIDE (Ire) 8-9 B Rouse (2) *co'red up on ins, effrt and rdn 2 fs out, no extr.* . . . . (20 to 1 op 33 to 1) 5
2542⁶ INSIDER TRADER 9-0 A Munro (5) *pressed wnr, rdn 2 fs out, fdd.* . . . . (16 to 1 op 12 to 1) 6
SKIPTAMALOO 8-9 F Norton (6) *slwly away, hdwy last 2 fs, nrst finish.* . . . . (33 to 1) 7
1759 TOOGOODFORYOU 9-0 M Wigham (1) *sluggish strt, not reco'r.* . . . . (33 to 1) 8
Dist: Hd, 1½l, 1½l, 1l, 1l, 2l, 12l. 1m 16.90s. a 2.90s (8 Ran).
SR: 18/12/6/5/-/ (Davie Wong), D R Loder

2818 EBF Gooseberry Maiden Stakes Class D (Div II) (2-y-o) £4,092 6f. . . . . . . (2:55)

2400² NORDICO PRINCESS 8-9 S Perks (3) *made virtually all, hrd pressed fnl furlong, hld on gmely.* . . . . (5 to 4 on op 5 to 4 tchd 6 to 4) 1
730 LUNAR MISSION (Ire) 8-7 (7*) S Mulvey (2) *patiently rdn, swtchd ins and shaken up o'r one furlong out, fnshd strly.* . . . . (12 to 1 op 6 to 1) 2
2316⁵ HELLO IRELAND 8-9 T Sprake (8) *nvr far away, rdn to chal ins fnl furlong, kpt on.* . . . . (5 to 1 op 5 to 2) 3
2370³ HELLABY 9-0 N Connorton (1) *al hndy, rdn to chal o'r one furlong out, not quicken.* . . . . (13 to 2 op 6 to 1 tchd 7 to 1) 4
1598⁷ SING SONG BLUES 9-0 G Carter (4) *trkd ldrs, effrt on ins o'r 2 fs out, outpcd fnl furlong.* . . . (16 to 1 op 10 to 1) 5
673 TIMBER BROKER 9-0 W Newnes (7) *drvn alng in frnt rnk, wide strt, fdd 2 fs out.* . . . . (25 to 1 op 20 to 1) 6
GALAXY RAIN 9-0 T Wall (5) *last and drvn alng, nvr wnt pace.* . . . . (16 to 1 op 14 to 1) 7
SUNDAY RISK 9-0 A Munro (6) *trkd ldrs for o'r 3 fs, sn btn.* . . . . (12 to 1 op 6 to 1) 8
Dist: Sht-hd, hd, 3½l, 4l, 6l, sht-hd, 6l. 1m 17.50s. a 3.50s (8 Ran).
SR: 1/5/-/-/-/ (J D Graham), R Hollinshead

2819 Tayberry Selling Stakes Class G (2-y-o) £2,070 7f. . . . . (3:25)

2325 LOVE OF THE NORTH (Ire) 8-11 R Hills (4) *nvr far away, drvn to ld o'r one furlong out, hld on gmely.* . . . . (7 to 2 fav op 3 to 1 tchd 4 to 1) 1
2668 CELESTIAL DANCE 8-6 G Carter (6) *chsd alng to go pace, weaved through fnl furlong, edgd lft, fnshd wl.* . . . . (9 to 1 op 10 to 1 tchd 8 to 1) 2
2465² MISS FREEBIE (Ire) 8-1 (5*) Stephen Davies (10) *chsd alng in midfield, improved to chal o'r one furlong out, not quicken cl hme.* . . . . (9 to 2 op 7 to 2) 3
2493⁵ NORTHERN BAILIWICK (Ire) (bl) 8-11 M Wigham (7) *al hndy, ev ch and drvn alng o'r one furlong out, one pace.* . . . . (13 to 2 op 9 to 2 tchd 7 to 1) 4
WARWICK WARRIOR (Ire) 8-11 Dean McKeown (1) *wth ldr, led o'r 3 fs out till over one out, fdd.* (9 to 1 op 8 to 1) 5
2637⁵ SEMAH'S DREAM (bl) 8-6 A McGlone (3) *drvn alng to keep up hfwy, effrt o'r 2 fs out, no imprsn.* . . . . (10 to 1 op 12 to 1 tchd 14 to 1 and 8 to 1) 6
1583 LEGAL CONQUEST 8-6 W Newnes (5) *broke wl, struggling to go pace aftr 2 fs, sn lost tch.* . . . . (6 to 1) 7
2180⁶ SPORTSGUIDE'S GIRL 8-3 (3*) B Doyle (9) *led till o'r 3 fs out, fdd und pres.* . . . . (14 to 1 op 12 to 1) 8
2417⁹ GENERAL FAIRFAX (Ire) (bl) 8-11 A Munro (8) *struggling to keep up hfwy, tld off.* . . . . (8 to 1 op 14 to 1) 9
Dist: Hd, 1½l, hd, 12l, 1½l, 10l, 1½l, 2½l. 1m 31.40s. a 4.40s (9 Ran).
SR: 10/4/-/3/-/-/ (J H Richmond-Watson), G Harwood

2820 Strawberry Handicap Class D (0-80 3-y-o) £3,435 1¼m. . . . . (3:55)

2641² PRESTON GUILD (Ire) [61] 8-7 D Biggs (1) *made most, hdd briefly o'r one furlong out and ins last, rallied gmely.* . . . . (9 to 4 fav op 2 to 1 tchd 5 to 2) 1
926* MANILA BAY (USA) [75] 9-7 A Munro (3) *patiently rdn, led briefly o'r one furlong out and ins last, jst hld.* . . . . (4 to 1 tchd 5 to 1) 2
2135⁶ GENERAL CHASE [64] 8-5 (5*) Stephen Davies (7) *al hndy, drvn alng last 2 fs, ran on strly nr finish.* . . . . (15 to 2 op 6 to 1 tchd 8 to 1) 3
2328⁹ TICKERTY'S GIFT [71] 9-3 B Rouse (4) *wth ldr, rdn 2 fs out, not quicken fnl furlong.* . . . . (6 to 1 op 8 to 1 tchd 11 to 2) 4
2383² GIORDANO (Ire) [62] 8-8 Dean McKeown (5) *trkd ldg trio, ev ch and rdn 2 fs out, one pace.* . . . . (6 to 1 op 7 to 1) 5
2308 CAN CAN CHARLIE [55] 8-1 R P Elliott (6) *trkd ldrs, effrt and drvn alng appr strt, sn lost tch.* (9 to 1 op 8 to 1) 6
2635³ IJAB (Can) [65] 8-11 R Hills (2) *wl plcd, effrt and hrd drvn 2 fs out, wknd quickly.* . . . . (6 to 1 op 11 to 2 tchd 7 to 1 and 5 to 1) 7
Dist: Sht-hd, hd, 2½l, hd, 10l, 1½l. 2m 12.50s. (7 Ran).
(Lady Matthews), R J R Williams

2821 Raspberry Limited Stakes Class E (0-70 3-y-o and up) £3,054 6f. . . . (4:25)

2509* LAUREL QUEEN (Ire) 5-9-2 G Carter (3) *made all, quickened hfwy, kpt on strly fnl furlong.* . . . . (Evens fav tchd 5 to 4 on) 1
2636² MINDOMICA 4-8-13 (3*) Emma O'Gorman (2) *trkd wnr, effrt and bustled alng o'r one furlong out, no imprsn.* . . . . (5 to 1 tchd 6 to 1) 2
2276³ CHILLY BREEZE 3-8-5 (5*) K Rutter (1) *sluggish strt, brght wide to improve rpdly o'r one furlong out, kpt on, nvr nrr.* . . . . (9 to 4 op 2 to 1 tchd 5 to 2) 3
2219⁵ SWINGING TICH 4-9-2 T Wall (4) *sluggish strt, drvn into midfield hfwy, not quicken o'r one furlong out.* . . . . (25 to 1 op 20 to 1) 4
KIMBERLEY PARK 5-9-2 A Munro (5) *trkd ldg pair, rdn o'r one furlong out, no extr.* . . . . (11 to 1 op 8 to 1 tchd 12 to 1) 5
2638³ NOBLE MEASURE (Ire) (bl) 3-8-8 (7*) G Strange (6) *chsd ldg 4, struggling 2 fs out, sn btn.* . . . . . (25 to 1 op 20 to 1) 6
Dist: 2½l, 2l, 2½l, nk, 3½l. 1m 15.50s. a 1.50s (6 Ran).
SR: 48/38/24/20/19/4/ (Laurel (Leisure) Limited), J Berry

2822 Blackberry Claiming Stakes Class F (3 & 4-y-o) £2,243 1½m. . . . . (4:55)

2372² CIVIL LAW (Ire) (v) 3-9-1 S Perks (3) *wtd wth, rdn appr strt, rallied to ld o'r one furlong out, drvn clr.* . . . . (11 to 10 on op Evens) 1
FORGETFUL 4-8-13 R Price (5) *led till o'r 4 fs out, rallied und pres, one pace ins last.* . . . . (8 to 1 op 7 to 1) 2
2538² TRY N' FLY (Ire) 3-9-1 A Munro (6) *al hndy, led o'r 4 fs out, rdn and hdd over one out, no extr.* . . . (9 to 4 op 6 to 4) 3
2544⁶ ANNABEL'S BABY (Ire) 4-9-0 M Wigham (2) *settled midfield, hdwy last 2 fs, nvr plcd to chal.* . . . . (20 to 1 op 16 to 1) 4
2162 KENYATTA (USA) 4-8-13 B Rouse (4) *chsd ldrs, feeling pace hfwy, nvr a threat.* . . . . (9 to 1 op 7 to 1 tchd 10 to 1) 5
2353 ABSOLUTLEY FOXED (bl) 4-8-8 G Carter (1) *trkd ldg pair, lost grnd whn pace quickened appr strt, sn btn.* . . . . (40 to 1 op 20 to 1) 6
1562 HATAAL (Ire) 4-8-3 (5*) Stephen Davies (7) *sn outpcd and drvn alng, al beh.* . . . . (50 to 1 op 33 to 1) 7
Dist: 4l, hd, 5l, 7l, hd, 5l. 2m 41.60s. a 7.60s (7 Ran).
SR: 1/-/-/-/ (Mrs B Facchino), R Hollinshead

2823 Loganberry Maiden Handicap Class E (0-70 3-y-o and up) £3,106 1½m (5:25)

2506⁸ SUPER BLUES [40] 6-9-0 W Newnes (7) *led, quickened entering strt, styd on wl.* . . . . (7 to 2 op 9 to 2) 1
2148³ ARAADH (USA) [60] 3-9-8 R Hills (2) *nvr far away, effrt und pres last 2 fs, hng lft, no imprsn ins last.* . . . . (5 to 2 op 2 to 1 tchd 11 to 4) 2
1600 INVISIBLE ARMOUR [33] (bl) 4-8-7 Dale Gibson (3) *trkd ldg trio, ev ch entering strt, rdn and no extr o'r one furlong out.* . . . . (8 to 1 op 14 to 1) 3

2057 INOVAR [39] 3-8-1 G Carter (4) *pressed ldg pair, rdn entering strt, sn outpcd*................ (33 to 1 op 25 to 1) 4
2470^{5} RUPPLES [19] 6-7-7 S Wood (1) *in tch, struggling to keep up entering strt, sn btn*..................... (33 to 1) 5
2448^{3} APACHE SQUAW [57] 3-9-5 N Connorton (5) *wtd wth, improved to go hndy entering strt, sn rdn and btn.* ....(2 to 1 fav op 7 to 4 tchd 9 to 4) 6
2587^{5} MOUNTAIN WILLOW [62] (v) 3-9-10 Dean McKeown (6) *chsd ldg 5 till fdd und pres appr strt.* .... (6 to 1 op 5 to 1 tchd 13 to 2) 7
Dist: 2½l, 2½l, 8l, 2l, 4l, 6l. 2m 41.10s. a 7.10s (7 Ran).
SR: 5/8/-/-/ (W H Clarke), T D Barron

SOUTHWELL (A.W) (std)
Saturday July 24th
Going Correction: MINUS 0.05 sec. per fur.

2824 Vodka Handicap Class E (0-70 3-y-o and up) £2,448 7f...............(6:20)

2327^{*} PANCHELLITA (USA) [53] 4-9-2 B Rouse (5) *made all, drvn alng last 2 fs, kpt on wl*..............(4 to 1 op 7 to 2) 1
2589^{*} RED COTTON [62] 3-9-4 P D'Arcy (4) *al hndy, ev ch and drvn alng last 2 fs, kpt on same pace.* ....(5 to 2 fav op 9 to 4 tchd 11 to 4) 2
2425^{3} FINAL OAK [43] 3-7-13 A Mackay (2) *al wl plcd, effrt and drvn alng 2 fs out, one pace ins last.* (9 to 1 op 8 to 1) 3
2426^{2} ON Y VA (USA) [57] 6-8-13 (7*) Sarah Thompson (9) *nvr far away, hrd drvn 2 fs out, one pace.* (4 to 1 tchd 9 to 2) 4
2585^{9} NEVENTER (Fr) [43] 4-8-6 R Price (7) *chsd ldrs, rdn hfwy, btn 2 fs out*........................(33 to 1 op 25 to 1) 5
2270^{6} BERNSTEIN BETTE [60] 7-9-9 G Hind (1) *sluggish strt, drvn alng, fdd last 2 fs*..................... (7 to 1 op 8 to 1) 6
2590^{6} VERRO (USA) [31] (bl) 6-7-8^{1} Dale Gibson (3) *sluggish strt, al struggling*......................(20 to 1 op 16 to 1) 7
2590^{3} NELLIE'S GAMBLE [68] 3-9-10 A Munro (6) *trkd ldg 6, struggling o'r 2 fs out, sn btn*........ (8 to 1 op 6 to 1) 8
2525^{9} JAKE THE PAKE (Ire) [65] (bl) 3-9-7 G Carter (8) *struggling hfwy, sn lost tch*...............................(10 to 1) 9
Dist: ½l, 2l, ½l, 8l, nk, 4l, 3½l, 7l. 1m 30.20s. a 4.10s (9 Ran).
SR: 35/35/10/29/-/7/ (C J Pennick), G L Moore

2825 East Midlands Electricity Plc Nottingham Selling Stakes Class G (0-70 2-y-o) £2,070 6f................ (6:50)

2610^{2} SPORTING HEIR (Ire) (bl) 8-11 M Wigham (5) *made virtually all, drvn clr last 2 fs, kpt on strly*.... (6 to 1 op 9 to 2) 1
2588^{2} WINDOW DISPLAY 9-0 S Whitworth (2) *nvr far away, chsd wnr und pres last 2 fs, no imprsn.* .... (15 to 8 fav op 9 to 4 tchd 5 to 2 and 7 to 4) 2
2423^{4} BESSIE'S WILL 8-6 A Mackay (1) *last and drvn alng, hdwy centre last 2 fs, swshd tail, nvr nrr.* ....(25 to 1 op 20 to 1 tchd 33 to 1) 3
2049^{7} ZORAHAYDA (Fr) 8-6 B Rouse (4) *chsd ldg trio, effrt and drvn alng centre last 2 fs, one pace.* .... (7 to 1 op 8 to 1 tchd 10 to 1) 4
1391^{9} STORM HEIGHTS 8-6 A Munro (7) *broke wl, struggling to keep up aftr 2 fs, sn btn*......... (10 to 1 tchd 11 to 1) 5
2526^{4} LADY WESTBURY (Ire) 8-6 T Sprake (6) *pressed ldrs, rdn 2 fs out, sn btn*........................(6 to 1 op 8 to 1) 6
2526^{2} THE FERNHILL FLYER (Ire) (v) 8-9 J Carroll (3) *squeezed out aftr one and a half fs, hrd drvn hfwy, wknd quickly.* ....(2 to 1 op 6 to 4) 7
Dist: 4l, hd, 2½l, 4l, 3l, 6l. 1m 18.30s. a 4.90s (7 Ran).
(Sporting Partners), M D I Usher

2826 Folks That Live On The Hill Median Auction Maiden Stakes Class F (2-y-o) £2,070 7f...................... (7:20)

2429^{3} BARBAROJA 9-0 K Fallon (11) *al wl plcd, led jst o'r 3 fs out, kpt on strly to go clr ins last.* (7 to 4 fav op 3 to 1) 1
1998^{3} HIT THE CANVAS (USA) 9-0 K Darley (12) *al hndy, feeling pace and drvn alng 2 fs out, styd on ins last.* ....(7 to 2 op 5 to 2 tchd 4 to 1) 2
2069^{4} ROMAN REEL (USA) 9-0 B Rouse (3) *wl plcd, ev ch o'r 2 fs out, no extr ins last*.... (9 to 2 op 7 to 2 tchd 11 to 2) 3
A MILLION WATTS 9-0 N Connorton (10) *patiently rdn, shaken up to improve o'r one furlong out, prmsg.* ....(14 to 1 op 12 to 1) 4
2626^{6} SECUNDUS (Ire) 8-11 (3*) B Doyle (9) *chsd alng to go pace, styd on last 2 fs, nvr nrr*..........(12 to 1 op 10 to 1) 5
2586^{8} BAROSKI 9-0 Dean McKeown (4) *struggling to go pace aftr 2 fs, styd on frm two out, nvr nrr*......... (33 to 1) 6
922^{6} FRANKLY MY DEAR (bl) 9-0 J Carroll (1) *wth ldrs for o'r 5 fs, fdd*...............................(12 to 1 op 16 to 1) 7
2030^{4} RED TAR 9-0 W Newnes (6) *drvn alng to keep up hfwy, nvr a factor*.........................(12 to 1 op 8 to 1) 8
AMORET (Ire) 8-9 G Duffield (8) *sluggish strt, not reco'r.* ....(10 to 1 op 7 to 1) 9
2234^{6} BOLDANDPRETTY 8-9 M Wigham (5) *led till jst o'r 3 fs out, fdd*..(33 to 1) 10
2482^{4} SONIC (Ire) 9-0 T Lucas (7) *in tch to hfwy, sn btn.* .... (25 to 1 op 20 to 1) 11

1998 CRANFIELD CHARGER 8-9 C Dwyer (2) *sluggish strt, struggling hfwy*............................(33 to 1) 12
Dist: 5l, 1l, 7l, 1½l, 5l, 3l, nk, 2½l, 3½l, 1½l. 1m 31.20s. a 5.10s (12 Ran).
SR: 18/3/-/-/-/-/ (Marquesa de Moratalla), J G FitzGerald

2827 Garbos Nightclub Handicap Class E (0-70 3-y-o and up) £2,574 1½m (7:50)

2396^{6} ABALENE [49] 4-8-7 W Newnes (2) *slight ld to hfwy, rallied to lead wl o'r one furlong out, styd on well.* .... (20 to 1 op 12 to 1) 1
2213^{3} RECORD LOVER (Ire) [60] 3-8-6 A Munro (10) *nvr far away, led hfwy, rdn and hdd wl o'r one furlong out, one pace.* ....(5 to 1 tchd 9 to 2) 2
973 DASHING FELLOW (Ire) [45] 5-7-10 (7*) G Milligan (6) *al hndy, rdn last 3 fs, no imprsn*..... (25 to 1 op 20 to 1) 3
2585^{*} FIRST FLING (Ire) [47] 4-8-5 G Hind (7) *settled midfield, drvn alng whn pace quickened last 4 fs, no imprsn.* ....(9 to 2 tchd 5 to 1) 4
2591^{2} PHARLY DANCER [69] 4-9-13 Dean McKeown (1) *edgy bef race, trkd ldrs, effrt and rdn o'r 3 fs out, sn ridden.* ....(100 to 30 fav op 5 to 2 tchd 7 to 2) 5
2530^{7} MELTONBY [36] 4-7-8^{1} Kim Tinkler (8) *dsptd ld for o'r 4 fs, lost tch appr strt*.................(25 to 1 op 20 to 1) 6
2641^{8} KRONPRINZ (Ire) [35] 5-7-7 S Wood (9) *chsd ldrs to hfwy, tld off*...................................(16 to 1 op 12 to 1) 7
2615^{2} SMART DAISY [57] 3-8-3 B Rouse (3) *settled midfield, struggling hfwy, tld off*............ (7 to 2 op 11 to 2) 8
2152^{5} MR POPPLETON [55] 4-8-13 A Mackay (5) *struggling most of way, tld off*...................... (6 to 1 tchd 7 to 1) 9
2428^{7} GRUBBY [36] 4-7-8^{6} (5*) A Garth (4) *bolted gng to post, tld off hfwy*.......................... (33 to 1 op 20 to 1) 10
Dist: 1½l, 8l, 5l, 5l, 12l, 1½l, 10l, 20l, 8l. 2m 38.70s. a 4.80s (10 Ran).
SR: 39/35/16/8/20/-/ (S Taberner), J Mackie

2828 East Midlands Electricity Plc Rating Related Maiden Stakes Class F (0-60 3-y-o and up) £2,070 1½m...... (8:20)

2529^{3} CRIMINAL RECORD (USA) (v) 3-8-9 A Munro (7) *trkd ldrs, drvn to ld appr strt, hld on gmely fnl furlong.* ....(5 to 2 op 2 to 1 tchd 3 to 1) 1
2589^{4} NORTHERN JUDY (Ire) 3-7-13 (5*) A Garth (4) *trkd ldrs, effrt o'r one furlong out, rdn and not go past.* ....(10 to 1 tchd 12 to 1) 2
JURIS PRUDENCE (Ire) 5-9-2 G Duffield (6) *al hndy, hrd drvn last 2 fs, one pace*.................. (9 to 1 op 8 to 1) 3
HAVE A NIGHTCAP 4-9-7 Dean McKeown (1) *led till appr strt, wknd frm 2 fs out*...........(14 to 1 tchd 16 to 1) 4
2530^{6} DESPERATE MAN 4-9-7 J Carroll (2) *wth ldrs till wknd quickly entering strt*..................................(33 to 1) 5
2277^{9} ROSE OF MEDINA 3-8-4 W Newnes (8) *rcd wide, in tch to strt, sn lost touch*....... (8 to 1 op 7 to 1 tchd 9 to 1) 6
2273^{4} BORROWED AND BLUE 3-8-4 N Day (3) *last and drvn alng hfwy, nvr a factor.* ....(5 to 4 fav op 11 to 8 tchd 11 to 10) 7
NICHOLAS STAR 4-9-7 T Wall (5) *unruly strt, struggling hfwy, tld off*.......................................(33 to 1) 8
Dist: Hd, 8l, 5l, 15l, 2½l, 5l, dist. 2m 43.40s. a 9.50s (8 Ran).
(M L Oberstein), Lord Huntingdon

2829 Gin Handicap Class E (0-70 3-y-o and up) £2,343 5f...................(8:50)

2636^{5} STRIP CARTOON (Ire) [51] 5-8-2 (7*) G Strange (2) *rcd far side, improved to ld o'r one furlong out, forged clr.* ....(6 to 1 op 5 to 1) 1
2476^{5} COVENT GARDEN GIRL [62] 3-9-1 T Lucas (1) *broke wl, crossed to stands side to ld aftr 2 fs, hdd o'r one out, no extr*.................................. (7 to 1 tchd 8 to 1) 2
2584^{*} COMET WHIRLPOOL (Ire) [60] (bl) 3-8-13 J Quinn (4) *nvr far away, rdn o'r one furlong out, one pace.* ....(6 to 1 op 5 to 1) 3
2584^{3} CONVENIENT MOMENT [55] 3-8-8 J Carroll (8) *wl plcd stands side, drvn alng o'r one furlong out, no extr.* .... (5 to 1 jt-fav tchd 11 to 2) 4
2392 FOOD OF LOVE [70] 5-10-0 A Munro (3) *chsd alng in midfield, no imprsn appr fnl furlong.* .... (14 to 1 op 12 to 1) 5
1096^{8} COBBLERS HILL [56] 4-9-0 T Lang (6) *chsd ldrs, hrd drvn last 2 fs, not pace to chal.* .... (9 to 1 op 12 to 1 tchd 14 to 1) 6
2481^{3} LAST STRAW [45] 5-7-10 (7*) Claire Balding (7) *drvn alng beh ldrs, no imprsn last 2 fs.* .... (13 to 2 op 7 to 1 tchd 8 to 1) 7
2481 ANDRULA MOU [40] 3-7-7 S Wood (10) *chsd ldrs to hfwy, fdd*...................................... (33 to 1 op 16 to 1) 8
2594^{7} BOLD COUNTY [65] 3-9-4 Dean McKeown (5) *sluggish strt, not reco'r*............. (9 to 1 op 7 to 1 tchd 10 to 1) 9
2481^{4} NORDOORA (Ire) [35] 4-7-7 A Mackay (9) *unruly strt, led on stands side 2 fs, wknd quickly two out*....(5 to 1 jt-fav op 11 to 4) 10
Dist: 2½l, 1½l, 2l, ½l, nk, 2l, 4l, 2½l, 1l. 1m 0.40s. a 2.50s (10 Ran).
SR: 40/36/28/15/33/18/ (Mrs Irene Pryce), S R Bowring

VELIEFENDI (TUR) (firm)

Saturday July 24th

2830 Topkapi Trophy (3-y-o and up) £39,735 1m........................... (2:30)

SOUTHERN DANCER 6-9-6 M Cilgin, *hld up in rear, hdwy 2 fs out, led fnl 50 yards, ran on wl*.................. 1
1883* LUCKY GUEST 6-9-6 L Piggott, *rcd in 4th, swtchd 2 fs out, led briefly ins fnl furlong, no extr final 50 yards*....... 2
ABBAS (Tur) 5-9-6 S Akdi, *trkd ldr till rdn to ld one and a half fs out, hdd ins fnl furlong, kpt on*............... 3
PROGAY 7-9-6 H Karatas,.................................. 4
2627[6] NOYAN 3-8-11 E Cankilic, *led till one and a half fs out*... 5
ABREK 3-8-11 A Ozdeniz,................................ 6
Dist: ½l, ½l, ½l, 1½l, 3l. 1m 35.30s. (6 Ran).
(S Tokdemir), O Kandur

WARWICK (good) Saturday July 24th

Going Correction: PLUS 0.05 sec. per fur.

2831 St Pauls Handicap Class E (3-y-o and up) £2,831 6f.................. (6:10)

2387[5] PETRACO (Ire) [69] 5-9-11 (3*) S D Williams (6) *made virtually all, rdn appr fnl furlong, styd on wl nr finish.* ....(9 to 2 op 5 to 1 tchd 4 to 1) 1
2636* QUICK STEEL [57] (bl) 5-8-9 (7*) S Mulvey (7) *trkd ldrs, rdn and not quicken o'r one furlong out, ran on cl hme.* ....(6 to 4 op Evens) 2
1961 PEGGOTTY [34] 5-7-4[4] (7*) A Whelan (5) *slwly into strd, sn pushed alng towards rear, improved o'r 2 fs out, rallied wl ins fnl furlong*..............(66 to 1 op 25 to 1) 3
2418[9] CAROMISH (USA) [60] 6-9-5 N Adams (2) *pressed wnr, ev ch appr fnl furlong, no extr last 100 yards.* ....(11 to 8 fav op 5 to 4 tchd 13 to 8) 4
2499[8] BLAKENEY'S DOUBLE (Ire) [42] 3-7-9[2] A Tucker (3) *slwly into strd, nvr on terms.* ....(16 to 1 op 25 to 1 tchd 33 to 1) 5
EVER SO SHARP [34] 10-7-7[7] (7*) C Hawksley (1) *sn wl outpcd*...........................(66 to 1 op 25 to 1) 6
Dist: 1l, sht-hd, nk, 3½l, 5l. 1m 15.90s. a 4.20s (6 Ran).
SR: 36/20/1/21/-/-/ (B W Hampson), N A Smith

2832 Yarnolds Of Stratford Handicap Class D (0-80 3-y-o) £3,260 7f......... (6:40)

2382[5] DAILY SPORT DON [62] 8-7 A McGlone (7) *made all, hrd rdn o'r one out, kpt on wl last 100 yards.* ....(10 to 1 op 6 to 1) 1
2548 HAWAYAH (Ire) [63] 8-8 M Perrett (5) *hld up in rear, improved o'r 2 out, swtchd rght over one out, hng lft and ran on last 100 yards.* ....(8 to 1 op 10 to 1 tchd 11 to 1) 2
2543[3] NORTH ARDAR [58] 8-3 T Williams (6) *cl up, rdn and not quicken appr fnl furlong*..............(11 to 2 op 5 to 1) 3
2212[6] PRINCELY FAVOUR (Ire) [76] 9-7 S Raymont (3) *hld up in mid-div, rdn and one pace frm 2 fs out.* ....(13 to 2 op 7 to 2 tchd 7 to 1) 4
2522[6] SPECIAL ONE [68] 8-13 D Holland (8) *ldg grp, rdn alng and no extr ins last 2 fs.* ....(7 to 2 op 4 to 1 tchd 3 to 1 and 4 to 1) 5
2522[9] CITY ROCKET [73] 9-1 (3*) D Harrison (9) *beh and pushed alng hfwy, no imprsn on ldrs frm 2 fs out.* ....(12 to 1 op 8 to 1 tchd 14 to 1) 6
2560 JOBIE [70] 9-1 M Hills (4) *effrt hfwy, no prog last 2 fs.* ....(12 to 1 op 10 to 1 tchd 16 to 1) 7
2681* SINGER ON THE ROOF [74] (v) 9-5 (5ex) L Dettori (1) *wl in tch til btn o'r 2 fs out.* ....(3 to 1 fav op 5 to 2 tchd 100 to 30) 8
2288[9] WOODLANDS ELECTRIC [49] (v) 7-8[1] N Adams (2) *pld hrd and fld to settle, al beh*............(66 to 1 op 50 to 1) 9
2122[3] DANCING DIAMOND (Ire) [48] 7-7 N Carlisle (10) *speed to hfwy, sn wknd*.........(9 to 1 op 8 to 1 tchd 11 to 1) 10
Dist: 2l, sht-hd, 2l, 1½l, 2½l, 2l, 2l, 4l, 4l. 1m 28.80s. a 5.00s (10 Ran).
SR: 24/19/13/25/12/9/ (Roldvale Limited), R Hannon

2833 Waterside Selling Handicap Stakes Class G (0-60 3-y-o) £1,380 1¼m 169yds....................... (7:10)

2384 SHALHOLME [39] 8-10 M Hills (5) *hld up in 4th pl, lost pos o'r 2 fs out, ran on und pres over one out, led and edgd lft ins fnl furlong*................(11 to 2 op 6 to 1) 1
2289 TREBLE LASS [42] 8-13 L Dettori (7) *rcd in 3rd pl, led o'r 3 fs out, hrd rdn and hdd ins fnl furlong.* ....(14 to 1 op 12 to 1 tchd 16 to 1) 2
2411[3] QUEENS CONTRACTOR [42] 8-13 D Holland (2) *chsd ldr til outpcd 3 fs out, rdn and styd on ag'n appr fnl furlong.* ....(6 to 4 fav op 7 to 4) 3
2411[6] MAC TOMB [25] 7-10 N Adams (4) *hld up, pushed alng to improve hfwy, wth ldr o'r 2 fs out till wknd ins fnl furlong*............................(12 to 1 op 8 to 1) 4
2223[7] SWIFT REVENGE [28] 7-8 (5*) D Wright (3) *slwly into strd, pushed alng in rear hfwy, styd on one pace last 2 fs.* ....(16 to 1 op 14 to 1) 5
1880 SUMMER FLOWER [46] (bl) 9-0 (3*) S D Williams (1) *hld in rear, effrt o'r 3 fs out, no prog last 2 furlongs.* ....(20 to 1 op 14 to 1) 6
2120[4] NIGELS PROSPECT [50] 9-7 J Williams (8) *rdn to take clr order hfwy, effrt 4 fs out, btn o'r 2 out.* ....(11 to 2 op 4 to 1) 7
2130 SANTA STELLAR [46] (bl) 9-3 T Williams (6) *clr ldr til wknd and hdd o'r 3 fs out*.................(5 to 1 op 7 to 2) 8
Dist: 1½l, 1½l, ½l, 1½l, 10l, 4l, 7l. 2m 24.20s. a 11.40s (8 Ran).
(Mrs M Palmer), P G Murphy

2834 Mary Arden Handicap Class E (0-70 3-y-o and up) £2,978 1¼m 169yds ....(7:40)

2388* LEGAL ARTIST (Ire) [50] 3-8-3 A McGlone (13) *dsptd 3rd pl, outpcd 2 fs out, str run und pres to ld last strds.* ....(7 to 1 op 6 to 1) 1
2474[8] SWIFT SILVER [57] 6-9-7 J Reid (6) *led till o'r 3 fs out, led ag'n entering last 2 furlongs, hdd on line.* ....(5 to 1 op 4 to 1 tchd 6 to 1) 2
2134[3] CLEVER MINSTREL (USA) [68] 3-9-7 M Perrett (14) *chsd ldr, led o'r 3 fs out, hdd entering last 2, not quicken und pres ins fnl furlong*................(8 to 1 op 7 to 1) 3
1951 HALLOW FAIR [32] 8-7-10[1] T Williams (9) *in tch, rdn and effrt o'r one furlong out, not quicken ins fnl furlong.* ....(20 to 1 tchd 25 to 1) 4
2308 IRISH GROOM [34] 6-7-6[1] (7*) C Hawksley (10) *hld up, hdwy hfwy, sn rdn alng, styd on one pace last 2 fs.* ....(14 to 1 op 20 to 1) 5
2398[2] GREEN'S CASSATT (USA) [50] 5-9-0 R Lappin (5) *rcd in mid-div, rdn and no prog frm 2 fs out.* ....(8 to 1 op 6 to 1) 6
4709a[8] STEPPE CLOSER [50] 3-8-0 (3*) D Harrison (11) *mid-div, cld on ldrs 4 fs out, no extr ins last 2 furlongs.* ....(16 to 1 op 12 to 1) 7
2576[6] HOMEMAKER [50] (v) 3-8-3 N Adams (7) *mid-div, effrt 5 fs out, wknd o'r 2 out*..............(14 to 1 op 12 to 1) 8
2475[6] DOSSERI [39] 5-8-3 D Biggs (12) *beh, effrt o'r 4 fs out, no prog last 2 furlongs*.................. (12 to 1 op 7 to 1) 9
2525[5] SEA PRODIGY [30] (bl) 4-7-3 (5*) D Wright (2) *beh most of way*............................ (33 to 1 op 25 to 1) 10
1951 ONE MORE POUND [46] 3-7-13 A Tucker (8) *al rear grp.* ....(33 to 1) 11
1414 RARE OCCURANCE [41] 3-7-8[1] N Carlisle (1) *beh thrght.* ....(50 to 1) 12
2474[5] CALL THE BUREAU [60] 4-9-10 D Holland (3) *al beh.* ....(15 to 2 op 7 to 1 tchd 8 to 1) 13
2100[4] JADIRAH (USA) [66] 3-9-5 L Dettori (4) *dsptd 3rd pl til lost pos 3 fs out, eased whn btn last 2 furlongs.* ....(7 to 2 fav op 7 to 1) 14
Dist: Hd, 3l, sht-hd, 1½l, nk, nk, 3l, ¾l, ¾l, 4l. 2m 22.10s. a 9.30s (14 Ran).
SR: -/18/12/-/-/-/ (Tony Briam), N A Graham

2835 Potterton Myson Interpart Conditions Stakes Class D (4-y-o and up) £3,451 1½m 115yds.................... (8:10)

2579[3] MACK THE KNIFE (bl) 4-9-5 W R Swinburn (2) *chsd ldr, led o'r 3 fs out, quickened clr 2 out, pushed out, eased nr line*.............................(11 to 8 op 11 to 10) 1
1787 ALLEGAN (USA) 4-9-5 Pat Eddery (1) *set str pace, rdn and hdd o'r 3 fs out, outpcd 2 out, rallied ins fnl furlong, no extr nr line.* (6 to 4 on tchd 11 to 8 on and 5 to 4 on) 2
2376[5] MY ROSSINI 4-8-3 (7*) C Hawksley (3) *slwly into strd, al wl outpcd, sn lost tch*............... (20 to 1 op 14 to 1) 3
Dist: 1l, 15l. 2m 42.40s. a 4.50s (3 Ran).
SR: 66/64/25/ (Sir John Astor), Major W R Hern

2836 Stratford Festival Maiden Auction Stakes Class F (2-y-o) £2,070 7f (8:40)

PAVAKA (v) 9-0 L Dettori (5) *led for o'r 2 fs, ran on to ld ag'n nr finish*...........(4 to 1 op 9 to 4 tchd 9 to 2) 1
2385[2] WESTERN FLEET (USA) 9-0 Pat Eddery (6) *led o'r 4 fs out, hrd rdn and hdd nr line.* ....(5 to 4 on op 11 to 10 tchd 5 to 4) 2
2603[6] CRISTAL SPRINGS 8-9 W R Swinburn (3) *al wl plcd, rdn and styd on ins fnl furlong*......(12 to 1 tchd 14 to 1) 3
2123[4] CHARLIES DREAM (Ire) 8-9 D Holland (7) *pressed ldrs, ev ch und pres ins fnl furlong, no extr last few yards.* ....(7 to 1 op 10 to 1 tchd 13 to 2) 4
1926[7] MELODY DANCER 9-0 S Perks (8) *trkd frnt rnk, one pace last 2 fs*............(16 to 1 op 14 to 1 tchd 20 to 1) 5
2571 SPARKLING ROBERTA 8-9 N Adams (4) *hld up towards rear, outpcd frm o'r 2 fs out*......(20 to 1 tchd 33 to 1) 6
TECHNICOLORED 8-9 A McGlone (2) *strted slwly, nvr rchd frnt rnk*...........................(7 to 1 op 7 to 2) 7
2502 HEIGHT OF DECORUM 9-0 J Williams (1) *rcd in mid-div, wknd 2 fs out*......................... (40 to 1 op 25 to 1) 8
RINUS MASTER (Ire) 9-0 M Perrett (9) *strted slwly, al outpcd, tld off*..................(50 to 1 op 33 to 1) 9
Dist: Hd, ¾l, ¾l, 4l, 1½l, ½l, 1½l, 20l. 1m 31.10s. a 7.30s (9 Ran).
(Michael Worth), D R Loder

DUSSELDORF (GER) (soft)
Sunday July 25th

2837 Preis der Privatbankiers Merck, Finck & Co (Group 1) (3-y-o and up) £81,633 1½m. . . . . (3:45)

2259^{8} KORNADO 3-8-6 M Rimmer, *rcd in second, chlgd one and a half fs out, led one out, cmftbly*. 1
2079^{3} CHESA PLANA 4-9-3 M Hoffer, *led, hrd rdn one and a half fs out, hdd one out, ran on one pace*. 2
1124^{8} PROTEKTOR (Ger) 4-9-7 T Hellier, *nvr better plcd*. 3
2259^{6} ALTER ADEL 3-8-6 A Best, *al last*. 4
Dist: 2½l, 5l, 1l. 2m 40.10s. (4 Ran).
(Stall Granum), Bruno Schuetz

MONMOUTH PARK (USA) (firm)
Sunday July 25th

2838 Philip H Iselin Handicap (Grade 1) (3-y-o and up) £198,675 1m 1f. . . . .

2262^{6} VALLEY CROSSING (USA) 5-8-1 C Antley, ... (43 to 10) 1
2262* DEVIL HIS DUE (USA) 4-8-11 H McCauley, ... (21 to 10) 2
2243^{2} BERTRANDO (USA) 4-8-7 A Solis, ... (10 to 9 on) 3
SCUDAN (USA) 4-8-0^{2} N Santagata, ... (44 to 1) 4
STALWARS (USA) 8-8-2 J Diaz, ... (44 to 1) 5
SNAPPY LANDING (USA) 4-7-13 R Davis, ... (21 to 1) 6
PISTOLS AND ROSES (USA) 4-8-4 H Castillo Jr, (73 to 10) 7
BERKLEY FITZ (USA) 4-7-12 J Bravo, ... (30 to 1) 8
Dist: Hd, 2 ¼l, 8l, ½l, 18l, 4l, hd. 1m 49.20s. (8 Ran).

VELIEFENDI (TUR) (firm)
Sunday July 25th

2839 Bosphorous Trophy (Group 2) (3-y-o and up) £39,735 1½m. . . . .(2:30)

2076^{6} SHREWD IDEA 3-8-10 M Roberts, *prog to go second 7 fs out, jnd ldr 3 out, hrd rdn, ran on to ld strd stride*. 1
COLON (Ger) 4-9-6 A Boschert, *led till ct last strd*. 2
GOLDEN HAWK 3-8-10 L Piggott, *hld up, some prog fnl 3 fs, nvr rch ldrs*. 3
1219^{5} DOWN THE FLAG (USA) 6-9-7 S Akdi, ... 4
LALA 4-9-6 M Cilgin, ... 5
SARISAKA 4-9-6 A Ozdeniz, ... 6
Dist: Nose, 5l, 4l. 2m 31.14s. (6 Ran).
(Saeed Manana), M Kauntze

GALWAY (IRE) (soft)
Monday July 26th

2840 GPT Industrial Properties (C&G) EBF Maiden (2-y-o) £5,522 7f. . . . . (6:10)

MUSICAL INSIGHT (Ire) 9-0 J P Murtagh (10) . . . . . . (9 to 4) 1
2037^{5} PEACE ROLE (USA) 9-0 M J Kinane (12) . . . . (Evens fav) 2
CASHEL MARKET (Ire) 9-0 C Roche (8) . . . . (4 to 1) 3
1567^{6} EAS GEIPTINE 8-8 (6*) R V Skelly (2) . . . .(20 to 1) 4
BOB BARNES (Ire) 8-8 (6*) J A Heffernan (3) . . . . . . (14 to 1) 5
STELFOX (Ire) 9-0 P V Gilson (5) . . . .(10 to 1) 6
SINGING DANCER (Ire) 8-10^{2} (6*) C Everard (6) . . . (10 to 1) 7
RING-A-RUAN (Ire) 9-0 J F Egan (7) . . . . (10 to 1) 8
BERGERACONHOLIDAY (Ire) 9-0 N G McCullagh (1) . . . . (20 to 1) 9
1432^{6} TREJOLY PIGEONS (Ire) 9-0 D Manning (11) . . . . . .(25 to 1) 10
Dist: 1½l, 2l, 6l, 3l. 1m 36.10s. (10 Ran).
(Lady Clague), John M Oxx

2841 GPT Galway Q.R. Handicap (0-100 4-y-o and up) £10,052 2m. . . . .(6:50)

1468* SHANKORAK [-] 6-9-13 (7*) Mr D J Kavanagh (4) . .(13 to 2) 1
2143^{2} PADASHPAN (USA) [-] 4-10-2 (5*) Mrs J M Mullins (13) . . . . (13 to 2) 2
2461^{3} EBONY AND IVORY (Ire) [-] 4-11-5 (7*) Mr A K Wyse (11) . . . . (12 to 1) 3
2035 RISING WATERS (Ire) [-] 5-10-9 (7*) Mrs D McDonogh (3) . . . . (20 to 1) 4
2461* NATIVE PORTRAIT [-] 6-10-3^{3} (6ex) Mr P Fenton (5) (8 to 1) 5
2408 CURRENCY BASKET (Ire) [-] 4-11-9 Mr A J Martin (7) . . . . (12 to 1) 6
2693^{8} SHAYISTA [-] 8-9-11 (3*) Mr R O'Neill (9) . . . .(20 to 1) 7
2408^{9} NEMURO (USA) [-] (bl) 5-11-5 (7*) Mr G J Harford (10) . . . . (33 to 1) 8
LIFE SAVER (Ire) [-] 4-10-0 Mr S R Murphy (8) . . . . .(13 to 2) 9
1809* RISZARD (USA) [-] 4-12-7 Mr A P O'Brien (16) . . . . . (14 to 1) 10
2035* AIYBAK (Ire) [-] 5-11-4 (5*) Mr J A Nash (12) . . . . (6 to 1 fav) 11
2143^{5} MRS BARTON (Ire) [-] 5-9-9 (7*) Mr E Norris (6) . . . .(10 to 1) 12
2324* HACKETTS CROSS (Ire) [-] 5-10-4 (3*) Mr A R Coonan (1) . . . . (10 to 1) 13
2296^{3} PYLON SPARKS [-] (bl) 8-10-11 Mr J P Dempsey (15) . . . . (16 to 1) 14
2693^{7} SWEET DOWNS [-] 12-9-9 (5*) Mr D McGoona (2) (100 to 1) 15
2324^{2} HANG A RIGHT [-] 6-10-0 (7*) Mr P A Roche (17) . . (10 to 1) 16
Dist: Nk, ½l, 2½l, 6l. 3m 57.30s. (16 Ran).
(E J O'Mahony), Francis Berry

2842 GPT Van & Truck Rentals Handicap (0-70 3-y-o and up) £3,797 1½m (7:25)

912^{3} FONTANAYS (Ire) [-] 5-9-1 S Craine (16) . . . . (10 to 1) 1
2517^{2} CALL MY GUEST (Ire) [-] 3-8-10 (6*) B J Walsh (2) (10 to 1) 2
2484* SENSE OF VALUE [-] 4-9-9 (5ex) J P Murtagh (18) . . (8 to 1) 3
2517^{6} PREMIER LEAP (Ire) [-] 4-8-3 (8*) B Fenton (4) . . . . .(12 to 1) 4
2498^{2} GREEN GLEN (USA) [-] (bl) 4-10-0 C F Swan (6) . . .(12 to 1) 5
2665^{2} JUST ONE CANALETTO [-] 5-8-3 (6*) J J Behan (17) . . . . (14 to 1) 6
2693^{2} GREEK CHIME (Ire) [-] 4-8-10 (4*) P Carberry (15) (12 to 1) 7
2516^{3} MILLERS MILL (Ire) [-] 3-8-6 (6*) R V Skelly (11) . . . (20 to 1) 8
2664^{4} THE BERUKI (Ire) [-] 3-8-13 P Shanahan (7) . . . .(12 to 1) 9
2461^{9} WESBEST (Ire) [-] 4-9-11 N G McCullagh (10) . . . . . (16 to 1) 10
2558^{3} SPOUT HOUSE (Ire) [-] 4-8-10 (2*) R M Burke (14) . . (5 to 1) 11
2702^{9} BOBADIL (Ire) [-] 3-8-1 (8*) P J Smullen (9) . . . .(14 to 1) 12
2517^{5} DARK SWAN (Ire) [-] 3-8-9 (2*) D G O'Shea (13) . . . (20 to 1) 13
1822^{9} STEEL CHIMES (Ire) [-] (bl) 4-9-5 M J Kinane (12) . . .(8 to 1) 14
2692 REGAL PRETENDER (Ire) [-] 3-7-9 Joanna Morgan (3) . . . . (25 to 1) 15
1335^{7} HIND VISION (Ire) [-] 3-8-12 J F Egan (8) . . . . (12 to 1) 16
BOZO BAILEY [-] 3-7-7 A J Nolan (5) . . . . (33 to 1) 17
2286 NOORAJO (Ire) [-] 4-10-0 C Roche (1) . . . .(14 to 1) 18
2222^{5} SAHCHAIN (Ire) [-] 5-7-6 (6*) P P Murphy (19) . . . . . (33 to 1) 19
2517* PULMICORT [-] (bl) 3-9-0 (8ex) P V Gilson (20) . .(9 to 2 fav) su
Dist: 2½l, 2½l, 1l, nk. 2m 53.80s. (20 Ran).
(E A Mac Redmond), B V Kelly

2843 GPT DIY Fillies Maiden (3-y-o and up) £3,797 7f. (8:00)

2249^{7} LADIES GALLERY (Ire) 3-9-0 P V Gilson (5) . . . . (4 to 1) 1
2184^{2} GOODNIGHT KISS (bl) 3-9-0 M J Kinane (1) . . . . (5 to 4 on) 2
2497^{6} SILVER JAR (Ire) 3-8-8 (6*) J J Behan (10) . . . . (20 to 1) 3
LOOK NONCHALANT (Ire) 4-9-3 (4*) P Carberry (9) (40 to 1) 4
SHY TEACHER (Ire) 3-9-0 N Byrne (4) . . . .(33 to 1) 5
AURLIANO (Ire) 3-9-0 D V Smith (7) . . . .(25 to 1) 6
1610^{7} FAX ME NOW (Ire) 3-9-0 J F Egan (3) . . . . (20 to 1) 7
2604^{2} MOONLIGHT PARTNER (Ire) 3-9-0 C Roche (6) . . . . (7 to 2) 8
1622^{7} OUT OF STEP (Ire) 4-9-7 K J Manning (8) . . . .(50 to 1) 9
Dist: ¾l, 3l, 1½l, 1l. 1m 38.20s. (9 Ran).
(Donal O'Buachalla), C Collins

LINGFIELD (good)
Monday July 26th
Going Correction: MINUS 0.45 sec. per fur.

2844 Jacksbridge Maiden Auction Stakes Class F (2-y-o) £2,735 7f. . . . . (2:00)

2129^{3} GINGERBIRD (Ire) 8-9 W Ryan (6) *trkd ldr, rdn o'r one furlong out, led ins last, styd on.* (11 to 4 tchd 3 to 1) 1
2331^{2} LINK MILES 9-0 J Reid (2) *led, tacked o'r to stands rail, rdn and hdd ins fnl furlong, no extr.* . . . . (6 to 4 fav tchd 5 to 4) 2
SYABAS (Ire) 9-0 T Quinn (8) *prmnt, swtchd outsd o'r one furlong out, ran on ins last.* . . . . (8 to 1 op 12 to 1 tchd 14 to 1) 3
1949 EMMA GRIMES (Ire) 8-9 S Raymont (10) *mid-div and out of tch, shaken up and styd on fnl 2 fs, nvr nrr.* . . . . (33 to 1 op 20 to 1) 4
2492^{8} YOUNG AT HEART (Ire) 9-0 G Carter (3) *chsd ldrs centre, rdn o'r 2 fs out, no prog*. . . . . (25 to 1 op 20 to 1) 5
1985^{5} STRADISHALL 9-0 N Day (13) *chsd ldrs, rdn and no prog o'r 2 fs out*. . . . .(20 to 1 op 14 to 1 tchd 33 to 1) 6
COMEONUP 9-0 A McGlone (1) *wl beh, moderate late prog, nvr dngrs*. . . . . (16 to 1 op 10 to 1) 7
1959 CURBRIDGE (Ire) 9-0 B Rouse (4) *chsd ldrs, rdn and wknd o'r 2 fs out*. (25 to 1 op 20 to 1) 8
TROPICAL VISTA 8-9 C Rutter (9) *al beh.* . . . . (33 to 1 op 25 to 1) 9
HOODLUM 8-7 (7*) S Eiffert (11) *al wl beh*. . . . . . . (20 to 1) 10
MILAIRIOUS (Ire) 9-0 G Duffield (7) *al wl beh.* . . . . (7 to 1 op 4 to 1) 11
877^{9} SOUTHDOWN GIRL 8-2 (7*) S Drowne (12) *mid-div, wknd hfwy*. . . . . (16 to 1 op 12 to 1 tchd 20 to 1) 12
HELLO MAMA 8-9 W Carson (5) *ran green, al beh.* . . . . (12 to 1 op 10 to 1) 13
Dist: ½l, ¾l, 3l, 2l, 4l, 1l, 2l, 3½l, nk, 4l. 1m 24.63s. a 3.93s (13 Ran).
(A S Reid), H R A Cecil

2845 Horley Conditions Stakes Class D (2-y-o) £3,377 6f. . . . . (3:00)

2364^{8} BIG SQUEEZE (USA) 8-10 D Biggs (9) *al prmnt, rdn o'r one furlong out, ran on wl to ld last strd.* . . . . (6 to 1 op 5 to 1 tchd 13 to 2) 1

2535* POLISH ADMIRAL 8-12 N Day (1) *trkd ldrs, led wl o'r one furlong out, hrd rdn and wndrd entering last, hdd fnl strd*......... (4 to 1 op 7 to 2 tchd 9 to 2 and 5 to 1) 2
2472* CRAGGANMORE 8-12 D Holland (4) *hld up in tch, led o'r 2 fs out till wl over one out, not quicken nr finish*. .... (11 to 4 fav op 5 to 2 tchd 100 to 30) 3+
2153* KUTBEYA (USA) 8-9 W Carson (7) *trkd ldrs, effrt on stand rail o'r 2 fs out, ev ch over one out, not quicken*. ....(7 to 2 op 7 to 1) 3+
2147³ ANOTHERONE TO NOTE 8-3 (7*) Mark Denaro (2) *keen hold, prmnt, rdn and ev ch o'r one furlong out, one pace*.............................. (50 to 1 op 33 to 1) 5
1857* CHAMPAGNE GIRL 8-9 T Sprake (8) *led o'r 3 fs, sn rdn and btn*............... (10 to 1 op 6 to 1 tchd 12 to 1) 6
2364⁹ ARECIBO (Ire) 8-10 W Ryan (6) *slwly into strd, beh till styd on ins fnl furlong, nvr dngrs*. .... (14 to 1 op 10 to 1 tchd 16 to 1) 7
2203* MR DEVIOUS 9-0 J Reid (3) *trkd ldrs, pushed alng hfwy, sn btn*............. (11 to 1 op 7 to 1 tchd 12 to 1) 8
1169* SIGANCA 8-5 G Duffield (5) *beh, rdn hfwy, no prog*. .... (12 to 1 op 8 to 1) 9
Dist: Sht-hd, 1½l, dd-ht, 1½l, 3l, ¾l, ½l, 2l. 1m 11.54s. a 2.54s (9 Ran).
(R M Cyzer), C A Cyzer

2846 Nicholson Graham & Jones Handicap Class D (0-80 3-y-o and up) £3,231 5f ....(4:00)

2560² TUSCAN DAWN [69] 3-9-4 G Carter (4) *made all, clr 2 fs out, eased ins last, unchlgd*......... (5 to 1 op 3 to 1) 1
2671² SEA-DEER [58] 4-8-12 A Munro (7) *outpcd in mid-div till ran on wl appr fnl furlong, no ch wth wnr*. ....(3 to 1 fav op 7 to 2) 2
2753⁹ BELLS OF LONGWICK [73] 4-9-6 (7*) T G McLaughlin (8) *chsd ldrs, rdn 2 fs out, styd on one pace*. .... (4 to 1 tchd 9 to 2 and 5 to 1) 3
2392 SIGAMA (USA) [74] 7-9-11 (3*) N Kennedy (2) *chsd wnr till wknd appr fnl furlong*. (13 to 2 op 5 to 1 tchd 7 to 1) 4
1918⁵ THE NOBLE OAK (Ire) [59] (v) 5-8-13 J Reid (3) *chsd ldrs, rdn and no prog 2 fs out, eased whn btn*. .... (6 to 1 op 5 to 1 tchd 13 to 2) 5
2549⁸ STOCKTINA [42] 6-7-10⁶ (3*) B Doyle (5) *sn rdn alng, beh till styd on fnl furlong, no dngr*... (20 to 1 op 14 to 1) 6
2549⁵ TURTLE BEACH [42] (v) 4-7-10 N Adams (6) *hld up beh, rdn hfwy, no prog*...................(12 to 1 op 8 to 1) 7
2476⁶ BERGLIOT [47] 3-7-5 (5*) D Wright (9) *chsd ldrs, rdn and wknd 2 fs out*......................... (8 to 1 op 7 to 1) 8
2110 LORINS GOLD [57] 3-8-6 A McGlone (1) *al beh*. .... (16 to 1 op 14 to 1 tchd 20 to 1) 9
Dist: 1½l, 3½l, 2½l, 1½l, ¾l, 1l, hd, 8l. 57.34s. a 0.44s (9 Ran).
SR: 50/38/39/30/9/-/ (Miss Antonia Taverner), J Berry

2847 Levy Board Fillies' Handicap Class E (0-70 3-y-o and up) £3,287 1¼m (5:00)

2108² MAY HILLS LEGACY (Ire) [50] 4-9-4 T Quinn (12) *chsd ldr, led wl o'r 2 fs out, drvn out*. .... (13 to 2 op 5 to 1 tchd 7 to 1) 1
2475⁷ WILD STRAWBERRY [60] 4-10-0 B Rouse (8) *led one furlong, prmnt aftr, rdn 3 fs out, ran on ins last, nrst finish*.................(8 to 1 op 6 to 1 tchd 9 to 1) 2
2673² SANTANA LADY (Ire) [56] 4-9-10 W Newnes (7) *chsd ldrs, effrt and rdn wl o'r 2 fs out, ran on one pace ins last*. ....(7 to 2 op 3 to 1) 3
2685⁹ LUCKY NOIRE [39] 5-8-1¹ (7*) Gaye Harwood (2) *hld up beh, brght very wide strt, prog fnl 2 fs, not rch ldrs*. ....(16 to 1 tchd 14 to 1) 4
2757⁴ MON PETITNAMOUR (Ire) [37] 4-8-0 (5*) D Wright (11) *chsd ldrs, rdn o'r 2 fs out, styd on one pace*. ....(8 to 1 op 5 to 1) 5
2576³ GOLD TASSEL [60] 3-9-4 W Carson (6) *mid-div, pushed alng o'r 4 fs out, kpt on one pace over 2 out*. ....(11 to 4 fav op 3 to 1 tchd 7 to 2) 6
2347⁹ PRECIOUS CAROLINE (Ire) [37] 5-8-5 D Biggs (4) *rear, rdn 3 out, no prog fnl 2 fs*. (10 to 1 op 12 to 1 tchd 14 to 1) 7
2457³ HEAVY ROCK (Ire) [32] 4-7-9 (5*) L Newton (10) *dwlt, led aftr one furlong, sn clr, rdn and hdd wl o'r 2 fs out, wknd*.............................. (12 to 1 op 8 to 1) 8
2685 CHOUETTE [52] 3-8-10 J Reid (5) *hld up rear, effrt and brght wide strt, sn no prog*. .... (25 to 1 op 20 to 1 tchd 33 to 1) 9
2670⁷ EMERALD EARS [32] 4-8-0⁵ T Sprake (3) *taken dwn early, hld up rear, prog 4 fs out, rdn and wknd 2 out*. ....(14 to 1 tchd 16 to 1) 10
1612 BELLATRIX [36] 5-8-1 (3*) B Doyle (1) *hld up beh, effrt o'r 3 fs out, sn wknd*.................. (14 to 1 op 10 to 1) 11
921 SUPPER WITH SUSIE [40] 3-7-12 F Norton (9) *mid-div, lost pl 4 fs out, sn beh*.................. (20 to 1 op 14 to 1) 12
Dist: ¾l, ½l, 2½l, ½l, 1½l, 3½l, ¾l, 1l, 1½l, 2l. 2m 8.96s. a 3.96s (12 Ran).
SR: 19/27/22/-/-/7/ (Exors Of The Late Mrs G P Williams), D W P Arbuthnot

LINGFIELD (A.W) (std)
Monday July 26th
Going Correction: MINUS 0.25 sec. per fur.

2848 John Rogerson Memorial Handicap Class D (0-60 3-y-o and up) £3,143 6f ....(2:30)

2508* TRUTHFUL IMAGE [66] (bl) 4-9-1 D Biggs (4) *chsd alng beh ldrs, rdn and prog o'r one furlong out, led wl ins last, ran on well*. .... (5 to 4 on tchd 11 to 10 on and 11 to 8 on) 1
2382* STAR GODDESS (USA) [71] 4-9-6 B Rouse (5) *led one furlong, led ag'n hfwy till hdd and not quicken wl ins last, eased whn btn*. ....(100 to 30 op 5 to 2 tchd 7 to 2 and 4 to 1) 2
2723³ AQUADO [44] 4-7-2 (5*) D Wright (1) *sn outpcd and rdn alng, styd on wl appr fnl furlong, nrst finish*. .... (10 to 1 op 8 to 1 tchd 12 to 1) 3
2382² INVOCATION [79] 6-10-0 N Adams (2) *led aftr one furlong till hfwy, wth ldr after till not quicken appr last*. .... (100 to 30 op 5 to 2 tchd 7 to 2) 4
Dist: 2½l, hd, 3l. 1m 13.74s. a 2.94s (4 Ran).
SR: 12/7/-/2/ (P E Axon), M J Ryan

2849 Origin Technology In Business Selling Stakes Class F (3-y-o and up) £2,489 1¼m.................. (3:30)

2564⁸ BARAHIN (Ire) 4-9-10 A Clark (2) *trkd ldrs, prog 4 out, led wl o'r one furlong out, sn clr, cmftbly*. ....(6 to 1 op 4 to 1) 1
2226⁵ FULL SHILLING (USA) 4-9-5 T Sprake (8) *trkd ldrs, prog 4 out, ev ch 2 fs out, hrd rdn and one pace*. .... (20 to 1 op 16 to 1 tchd 25 to 1) 2
2520 EXCESS BAGGAGE (Ire) 3-9-0 W Ryan (6) *hld up last, prog o'r 3 fs out, ran on ins last, not rch ldrs*......(9 to 4 jt-fav op 5 to 2 tchd 3 to 1) 3
2684* BONDAID 9-9-10 R Price (4) *prmnt, led o'r 4 fs out till wl over one out, wknd*..........................(9 to 4 jt-fav op 7 to 4 tchd 5 to 2) 4
2527³ CHOIR PRACTICE (bl,e/s) 6-9-10 C Rutter (7) *pld hrd and hld up, effrt 3 fs out, nvr nr to chal*. (7 to 1 op 5 to 1) 5
2613² OUR EDDIE (v) 4-9-5 W Newnes (3) *prmnt, led o'r 5 fs out till over 4 out, hrd rdn and wknd*.... (7 to 2 op 9 to 2) 6
2351⁷ CHEEKY TUNE 4-9-5 T Quinn (5) *trkd ldrs, rdn 4 fs out, wknd rpdly*.................... (33 to 1 tchd 50 to 1) 7
2313⁵ JACKAREW BOY 3-8-9 G Duffield (1) *led o'r 4 fs, wknd rpdly, sn tld off*......(16 to 1 op 12 to 1 tchd 20 to 1) 8
Dist: 6l, 3l, nk, 5l, 2l, 25l, 15l. 2m 8.24s. a 5.04s (8 Ran).
SR: 35/18/7/16/6/ (Martin Hickey), R J O'Sullivan

2850 Dormansland Maiden Handicap Class F (0-65 3-y-o and up) £2,422 1m 5f ....(4:30)

2613⁵ SIR THOMAS BEECHAM [52] (e/s) 3-9-3 T Quinn (2) *hld up last, prog and pushed alng 4 fs out, styd on wl to ld appr last, sn clr*......(12 to 1 op 10 to 1 tchd 14 to 1) 1
2536⁴ EARLY TO RISE [40] 3-8-5 D Biggs (1) *hld up in tch, prog to ld wl o'r 2 fs out, rdn and hdd appr last, one pace*. ....(3 to 1 op 7 to 4) 2
2673⁸ CONCINNITY (USA) [50] 4-10-0 A Munro (5) *trkd ldrs, led 4 fs out till wl o'r 2 out, hrd rdn and one pace*. ....(4 to 1 op 3 to 1 tchd 9 to 2) 3
2662⁸ YIMKIN BOOKRA [39] 5-9-3 G Duffield (4) *trkd ldr, led 5 fs out till 4 out, sn rdn and btn*............... (5 to 2 fav) 4
1936⁴ SIDE BAR [40] 3-8-5 G Carter (3) *in tch till wknd 4 fs out*. ....(4 to 1 op 7 to 2 tchd 9 to 2) 5
2422⁶ SINGING DETECTIVE [25] (v) 6-8-3 T Sprake (6) *led to 5 fs out, sn wknd*......... (7 to 1 op 12 to 1 tchd 13 to 2) 6
Dist: 4l, 2l, 5l, 7l, 6l. 2m 48.84s. a 5.84s (6 Ran).
SR: 12/-/11/ (Mrs Heather Chakko), S Dow

NEWCASTLE (good to firm)
Monday July 26th
Going Correction: NIL (races 1,2,3,4,5), MINUS 0.25 (6,7)

2851 Federation Brewery 'Medallion Lager' Handicap Class E (0-70 3-y-o) £2,950 6f ....(2:15)

1849⁶ ASHGORE [64] 9-6 T Williams (2) *made all, shaken up o'r 2 fs out, ran on wl*........ (9 to 2 op 4 to 1 tchd 5 to 1) 1
2636⁹ BIRCHWOOD SUN [65] (bl) 9-7 J Lowe (6) *beh, sn pushed alng, hdwy fnl 2 fs, nrst finish*..... (10 to 1 op 7 to 1) 2
2476* OUR SHADEE (USA) [57] (bl) 8-13 M Wigham (4) *prmnt, ev ch 2 fs out, kpt on same pace*........ (4 to 1 op 7 to 2) 3
2634* SUDDEN SPIN [62] (v) 8-11 (7*) P Roberts (3) *chsd ldr, wknd 2 fs out*. (15 to 8 fav op 2 to 1 tchd 9 to 4 and 7 to 4) 4
2308 TRACHELIUM [57] 8-13 K Darley (5) *in tch, no hdwy fnl 2 fs*.................................. (9 to 1 op 6 to 1) 5
2699⁶ LIDA'S DELIGHT (Ire) [60] 9-2 T Lucas (1) *reared strt, sn in tch, wknd 2 fs out*.................(11 to 2 op 4 to 1) 6
Dist: 3l, sht-hd, 1½l, 3½l, 5l. 1m 15.12s. a 3.12s (6 Ran).
SR: 44/33/24/23/4/-/ (Harvey Ashworth), M Johnston

2852 Federation Brewery High Level Brown Ale Claiming Stakes Class G (2-y-o) £2,406 6f. . . . .(2:45)

2541[3] MIDNIGHT MAGPIE (Ire) 8-4 K Fallon (2) *trkd ldr, led one furlong out, pushed out.* . . . .(11 to 10 on op 11 to 8 on tchd Evens) 1
2356* LAUREL ROMEO (Ire) 8-7 J Carroll (1) *set slow pace, quickened 2 fs out, hdd one out, no extr*. . (2 to 1 op 7 to 4) 2
1774 SWEET WHISPER 8-4 K Darley (3) *cl up 3rd, effrt 2 fs out, not clr run and snatched up one out, not reco'r.* . . . .(9 to 2 op 4 to 1 tchd 5 to 1) 3
Dist: ½l, 1l. 1m 22.64s. a 10.64s (3 Ran).
(O Soberg-Olsen), Mrs J R Ramsden

2853 Federation Brewery L.C.L. Pils Lager Beeswing Stakes Class A (Group 3) (3-y-o and up) £20,940 7f. . . . .(3:15)

1765[4] EUROLINK THUNDER 3-8-7 R Cochrane (7) *hld up, hdwy to ld wl o'r one furlong out, held on well und pres.* . . . .(5 to 1 op 7 to 1 tchd 8 to 1) 1
1117* HALF TERM (USA) 3-8-7 L Dettori (3) *trkd ldrs, led 2 fs out, sn hdd, kpt on wl und pres fnl furlong*. . . . . (9 to 4 fav) 2
2376[2] YOUNG SENOR (USA) (bl) 4-9-0 M Hills (6) *dwlt, hld up, hdwy o'r 2 fs out, chlgd over one out, ev ch ins last, no extr und pres*. (8 to 1 tchd 9 to 1) 3
1205[8] SOOTY SWIFT (Ire) 3-8-4 B Marcus (9) *chsd ldrs, one pace fnl 2 fs*. . . . .(66 to 1 op 50 to 1) 4
2572* THOURIOS 4-9-0 R Hills (8) *made most to 2 fs out, sn btn.* . . . .(7 to 2 op 11 to 4 tchd 5 to 2) 5
2390[2] TIK FA (USA) (v) 4-9-0 W R Swinburn (5) *in tch, rdn o'r 2 fs out, no hdwy*. . . . .(8 to 1 op 7 to 1) 6
1747[8] CALLING COLLECT (USA) 4-9-2 J Carroll (4) *in tch till wknd o'r 2 fs out*. . . . . (10 to 1 tchd 11 to 1) 7
2572[8] SON PARDO (bl) 3-8-11 K Darley (1) *wth ldr till wknd 2 fs out*. . . . .(25 to 1) 8
1978* FACTUAL (USA) 3-8-7 Pat Eddery (2) *in tch, rdn alng hfwy, sn beh*. . . . .(8 to 1 op 6 to 1) 9
Dist: Sht-hd, 1l, 7l, 2½l, ½l, sht-hd, 1l, 6l. 1m 25.93s. a 1.93s (9 Ran).
SR: 64/63/67/36/38/36/37/29/7/ (Eurolink Group Plc), J L Dunlop

2854 Federation Brewery Special Ale Rated Class B Handicap For Harry Peacock Memorial Challenge Cup (0-95 3-y-o and up) £6,616 7f. . . . (3:45)

2060[6] IHTIRAZ [91] 3-8-13 R Hills (9) *hld up, swtchd lft and hdwy o'r one furlong out, led ins last, ran on wl.* . . . .(7 to 1 tchd 6 to 1) 1
2363 BEWARE OF AGENTS [86] 4-9-1 M Hills (7) *beh, hdwy o'r one furlong out, kpt on wl nr finish.* . . . .(20 to 1 tchd 25 to 1) 2
2363[9] KAYVEE [92] 4-9-7 W R Swinburn (10) *mid-div, hdwy to ld jst ins fnl furlong, sn hdd, no extr.* . . . .(12 to 1 tchd 14 to 1) 3
2060[2] PIQUANT [82] 6-8-11 Pat Eddery (6) *beh, hdwy whn not much room o'r one furlong out, styd on wl nr finish.* . . . .(4 to 1 jt-fav op 9 to 2 tchd 5 to 1) 4
2413[6] BRIGADE [92] 4-9-7 L Dettori (1) *prmnt, chlgd one furlong out, no extr ins last.* (12 to 1 op 10 to 1 tchd 14 to 1) 5
2363[5] HERORA (Ire) [83] 4-8-12 B Raymond (8) *trkd ldrs, chlgd one furlong out, sn rdn and one pace.* . . . .(7 to 1 op 6 to 1) 6
2732 DOUBLE BLUE [92] 4-9-7 T Williams (12) *led till jst ins fnl furlong, sn btn*. . . . .(8 to 1 op 7 to 1) 7
2600[3] CUMBRIAN WALTZER [89] 8-9-4 M Birch (4) *mid-div, effrt o'r one out, no hdwy*. . . . .(7 to 1 op 6 to 1) 8
2303[6] ABERGELE [87] 3-8-9 K Fallon (11) *chsd ldrs, ev ch o'r one furlong out, wknd fnl furlong*. . . . . . . (9 to 1 op 8 to 1) 9
2657[2] PARLIAMENT PIECE [83] (v) 7-8-12 K Darley (2) *cl up till wknd quickly o'r one furlong out, tld off*. . . .(4 to 1 jt-fav tchd 7 to 2 and 9 to 2) 10
2601[6] WILL OF STEEL [81] 4-8-10 J Carroll (5) *al beh, tld off.* . . . .(16 to 1) 11
Dist: 1½l, hd, nk, 2l, sht-hd, ½l, ¾l, 1½l, 15l, 1½l. 1m 26.73s. a 2.73s (11 Ran).
SR: 58/55/60/49/53/43/50/45/31/ (Hamdan Al-Maktoum), H Thomson Jones

2855 Federation Brewery Best Scotch Conditions Stakes Class C (3-y-o and up) £4,769 5f. . . . . (4:15)

2661* LUCKY PARKES 3-9-0 J Carroll (3) *chsd ldr, led one furlong out, ran on wl*. . . . . (Evens fav op 6 to 5 on) 1
2399* STACK ROCK 6-9-0 (5*) Stephen Davies (2) *led to one furlong out, kpt on*. . . . .(5 to 4 op 11 to 8) 2
2375* SAINT EXPRESS 3-9-0 A Culhane (1) *in tch, effrt 2 fs out, rdn entering last, no imprsn.* . . . .(7 to 1 op 6 to 1 tchd 8 to 1) 3
Dist: 2l, 3l. 1m 0.34s. a 1.44s (3 Ran).
SR: 71/68/51/ (Joseph Heler), J Berry

2856 Martini Bianco Summer Handicap Class E (0-70 3-y-o and up) £2,976 1 ¼m 32yds. (4:45)

2551[3] EFIZIA [61] 3-9-8 K Darley (3) *trkd ldr, quickened to ld entering fnl furlong, cmftbly.* . . . .(11 to 10 on op 11 to 8 on) 1
2520 ROLY WALLACE [53] (bl) 4-9-10 M Wigham (1) *in tch, effrt and chsd wnr fnl furlong, no imprsn.* . . . . (11 to 4 op 5 to 2 tchd 3 to 1) 2
1764[7] TOUR LEADER (NZ) [53] 4-9-10 B Raymond (2) *set slow pace, shaken up 3 fs out, hdd entering last, sn btn.* . . . .(5 to 2 op 7 to 2) 3
Dist: 2l, ½l. 2m 25.47s. a 18.97s (3 Ran).
(Mrs H I S Calzini), Mrs M Reveley

2857 Harcros Timber & Building Supplies Stayers Championship Series Handicap Qualifier Class D (0-80 3-y-o and up) £3,655 1½m 93yds. . . . .(5:15)

2735* NORTHERN GRADUATE (USA) [76] 4-10-1 (3ex) K Darley (5) *prmnt, chsd ldr frm hfwy, led o'r 2 fs out, rdn over one out, styd on wl, jst hld on.* . . . . (3 to 1 op 7 to 4 tchd 100 to 30) 1
2061 HIERARCH (USA) [70] 4-9-9 Pat Eddery (2) *hld up, effrt o'r 2 fs out, rdn over one out, styd on wl, jst held.* . . . . (2 to 1 fav tchd 5 to 2) 2
2506[2] MYSTIC MEMORY [63] 4-8-11 (5*) Darren Moffatt (3) *led 2 fs, prmnt, kpt on same pace frm two out.* . . . . (13 to 2 op 7 to 1) 3
ROBERTY LEA [65] 5-9-4 M Birch (1) *hld up, effrt 3 fs out, no hdwy*. . . . . (7 to 1 tchd 13 to 2) 4
2281[3] MOUSSAHIM (USA) [70] (v) 3-8-11 W R Swinburn (4) *led aftr 2 fs till o'r two out, sn wknd.* . . . . (100 to 30 op 7 to 2 tchd 4 to 1) 5
Dist: Hd, 5l, 2l, 7l. 2m 40.89s. a 3.19s (5 Ran).
SR: 52/45/28/26/5/ (P D Savill), Mrs M Reveley

SOUTHWELL (good (races 1,2), good to firm (3,4,5,6))
Monday July 26th
Going Correction: MINUS 0.50 sec. per fur.

2858 Nutcracker Suite Apprentice Claiming Stakes Class G (3-y-o and up) £1,725 1 ¼m. . . . . (6:25)

2750[2] OVERPOWER 9-8-9 (10*) J Gotobed (2) *al prmnt, effrt and hdwy to ld one furlong out, kpt on.* . . . .(7 to 4 on op 2 to 1 on tchd 13 to 8 on) 1
2398 TAUNTING (Ire) 5-8-12 (5*) S McCarthy (6) *led, rdn 2 fs out, hdd one furlong out, kpt on.* . . . . (13 to 2 op 6 to 1 tchd 7 to 1) 2
GREENACRES STAR 3-8-0 (8*) J Bramhill (1) *chsd ldrs, hdwy 3 fs out, sn rdn, kpt on ins last*. . . . .(33 to 1) 3
2154[5] PATONG BEACH 3-7-6 (10*) M Henry (3) *dwlt, hdwy hfwy, effrt o'r 2 fs out and sn rdn, kpt on und pres ins last.* . . . .(5 to 1 tchd 6 to 1) 4
2354[7] BRECKENBROUGH LAD 6-8-3 (10*) Kimberley Hart (5) *hld up, hdwy hfwy, effrt to chal and ev ch appr fnl furlong, no extr ins last*. . . . .(14 to 1) 5
2641[9] FLYING DOWN TO RIO (Ire) 5-8-12 (5*) L Aspell (7) *prmnt, chsd ldr hfwy till rdn o'r 2 fs out, sn wknd*. . . . (33 to 1) 6
2175[8] ARCTIC LINE 5-9-3 D Gibbs (8) *mid-div, effrt and some hdwy 4 fs out, nvr dngrs*. . . . .(50 to 1) 7
2165[6] MURASIL (USA) 4-8-5 (10*) I Jardine (10) *al rear*. (20 to 1) 8
1928 CHRIS'S GLEN 4-8-12 (5*) A Whelan (4) *al rear*. . . (50 to 1) 9
2670 SHROPSHIRE BLUE 3-7-9 (5*) M Baird (9) *chsd ldrs pulling hrd, sddl slpd aftr 2 fs and sn lost pl, tld off fnl 4 furlongs*. . . . .(14 to 1) 10
Dist: Nk, ½l, hd, ½l, 8l, 2½l, 2½l, 1½l. 2m 13.90s. (10 Ran).
(M P Bowring), M H Tompkins

2859 Giselle Maiden Handicap Stakes Class F (0-60 3-y-o and up) £2,070 1 ¼m. . . . . (6:55)

2716[5] BRONZE MAQUETTE (Ire) [50] 3-9-4 E Johnson (11) *hld up and beh, steady hdwy hfwy, effrt to chal 2 fs out, sn rdn, led ins last, kpt on*. . . . . . . (4 to 1 fav tchd 5 to 1) 1
2480[6] CUTTHROAT KID (Ire) [49] (bl) 3-9-3 G Hind (2) *mid-div, gd hdwy hfwy, effrt 2 fs out and sn led, hrd rdn and hdd ins last, kpt on*. . . . . . .(8 to 1 op 12 to 1 tchd 14 to 1) 2
1969[4] DOUBLE THE STAKES (USA) [26] 4-8-4 G Bardwell (13) *hld up and beh, steady hdwy hfwy, ev ch appr fnl furlong, sn rdn and kpt on one pace*. . . . . . (14 to 1 op 12 to 1) 3
2411 SPECIAL RISK (Ire) [35] 3-8-0 (3*) M Fenton (10) *mid-div, hdwy o'r 3 fs out, rdn 2 furlongs out, kpt on one pace.* . . . .(16 to 1) 4
2326[5] ROSE NOBLE (USA) [60] 3-10-0 G Duffield (12) *chsd ldr, rdn o'r 2 fs out, sn wknd.* (8 to 1 tchd 10 to 1 and 7 to 1) 5

2641 MARY MACBLAIN [36] 4-9-0 A Munro (3) *beh, hdwy 3 fs out, kpt on fnl 2 furlongs, not rch ldrs.* ....(8 to 1 op 6 to 1) 6
2737[5] HYDROPIC [26] (bl) 6-8-4 J Fanning (6) *led, rdn 3 fs out, hdd 2 furlongs out, sn wknd.*........(8 to 1) 7
1743 FAIRY WISHER (Ire) [35] 4-8-13 J Lowe (8) *chsd ldrs, rdn alng hfwy, no hdwy.*........(20 to 1) 8
2358[9] SIAN WYN [36] 3-8-4 G Carter (4) *nvr a factor*....(20 to 1) 9
2425[8] RIVER FIRE (Ire) [45] (bl) 3-8-13 J Quinn (5) *al rear.* ....(33 to 1 op 25 to 1) 10
2197[5] SLUMBER THYME (Ire) [35] 4-8-13 K Fallon (14) *nvr rchd ldrs.*........(10 to 1 tchd 11 to 1) 11
2425[7] EASY TOUCH [45] 3-8-13 A Mackay (9) *al rear.* ....(33 to 1 op 25 to 1) 12
2183[5] PYRRHIC DANCE [56] (bl) 3-9-10 D Holland (15) *chsd ldrs, rdn alng hfwy, wknd 4 fs out.*.......(7 to 1 op 6 to 1) 13
2130[4] MONASTIC FLIGHT (Ire) [48] 3-9-2 J Fortune (7) *chsd ldrs, rdn o'r 4 fs out, sn wknd.*........(7 to 1) 14

Dist: Hd, 2l, 1½l, 3l, 2½l, 2½l, ½l, 1½l, ½l, 3½l. 2m 10.00s. (14 Ran).
(O G Flynn), B J McMath

2860 Romeo & Juliet Selling Handicap Stakes Class G (0-60 3-y-o and up) £1,725 1m 3f.................. (7:25)

2427[4] IZITALLWORTHIT [29] 4-8-3[1] G Carter (8) *dwlt, sn chasing ldrs, hdwy 3 fs out, quickened to ld appr last, ran on.* ....(5 to 1 op 7 to 1) 1
2471[2] PREMIER DANCE [44] 6-9-4 A Mackay (4) *hld up, hdwy 3 fs out, rdn 2 furlongs out, styd on ins last.* ....(7 to 2 op 11 to 4) 2
2678[2] NOT YET [34] 9-8-8 D Holland (7) *cl up, effrt o'r 2 fs out, ev ch till not quicken and rdn entering last.* ....(7 to 4 fav op 9 to 4) 3
2536[5] JULFAAR (USA) [50] 6-9-10 G Bardwell (2) *hld up, hdwy o'r 3 fs out, rdn and ch one and a half furlongs out, sn one pace.*........(9 to 1 op 8 to 1 tchd 10 to 1) 4
2471 BROUGHTON BLUES (Ire) [21] (bl) 5-7-9[1] J Quinn (6) *led, rdn 3 fs out, hdd o'r one furlong out, sn wknd.* (12 to 1) 5
2520[7] RED SOMBRERO [35] 4-8-9 A Munro (3) *chsd ldrs, rdn o'r 2 fs out, one pace appr last.*........(10 to 1 op 8 to 1) 6
2162[6] MALINDI BAY [28] 5-8-2 J Lowe (5) *hld up, hdwy 4 fs out, effrt o'r 2 furlongs out, sn rdn and ch till wknd ins last.* ....(10 to 1 op 9 to 1) 7
2585[5] GREEN'S SEAGO (USA) [43] 5-9-3 W Woods (1) *chsd ldrs, rdn alng 5 fs out and sn lost pl.*... (25 to 1 op 20 to 1) 8

Dist: 1½l, 2l, 2½l, ½l, hd, ¾l, 12l. 2m 25.40s. a 3.60s (8 Ran).
SR: -/10/-/7/-/ (Brian Trotman), J Mackie

2861 Swan Lake Handicap Class D (0-80 3-y-o and up) £3,201 6f......... (7:55)

2309[2] MISS HAGGIS [76] 4-9-12 W Woods (3) *trkd ldrs, hdwy 2 fs out, sn led, quickened clr entering last.* ....(9 to 2 op 5 to 1 tchd 11 to 2) 1
2527* SWEET ROMEO [57] 3-8-1 T Williams (1) *outpcd and sn pushed alng, hdwy 3 fs out, styd on und pres ins last.* ....(5 to 2 fav op 9 to 4) 2
2309* FORMIDABLE LIZ [59] 3-8-3 G Duffield (2) *cl up, effrt 2 fs out and sn ev ch, rdn and one pace entering last.* ....(11 to 2 op 5 to 1) 3
2352 ASTERIX [47] 5-7-11 J Lowe (5) *beh and outpcd, effrt and wide strt, styd on und pres fnl 2 fs, nrst finish.* ....(25 to 1 op 16 to 1) 4
2584[4] NILU (Ire) [48] 5-7-12 A Mackay (4) *cl up, ev ch 2 fs out, sn rdn and wknd entering last.* ....(11 to 1 op 12 to 1 tchd 10 to 1) 5
2738* MISS WHITTINGHAM (Ire) [70] 3-8-7 (7*,7ex) P Roberts (8) *sn led, rdn 2 fs out, hdd and wknd o'r one furlong out.* ....(6 to 1 op 5 to 1) 6
2636[3] ROSE FLYER (Ire) [54] 3-7-12 S Wood (7) *cl up, rdn o'r 2 fs out, wknd over one furlong out.* ....(10 to 1 op 12 to 1 tchd 14 to 1) 7
2671* FASCINATION WALTZ [78] 6-10-0 (7ex) G Carter (6) *dwlt, effrt and wide strt, sn rdn and wknd wl o'r one furlong out.*........(9 to 2 tchd 5 to 1) 8

Dist: 1½l, sht-hd, 2l, 1l, 3l, 1½l, hd. 1m 13.90s. b 0.10s (8 Ran).
SR: 54/23/24/10/7/11/-/18/ (P Asquith), R Boss

2862 EBF Firebird Median Auction Maiden Stakes Class E (2-y-o) £3,676 7f (8:25)

1211[8] PERSIAN AFFAIR (Ire) 8-11 (3*) M Fenton (7) *made virtually all, rdn 2 fs out, ran on gmely ins last.* ....(6 to 1 tchd 7 to 1 and 5 to 1) 1
2571[7] ARABOYBILL 9-0 K Fallon (6) *beh, gd hdwy o'r 2 fs out, rdn and ran on wl ins last.*........(10 to 1 tchd 8 to 1) 2
2147[4] BELLEMINETTE (Ire) 8-9 A Mackay (13) *beh, hdwy 2 fs out, rdn and ran on strly ins last.*....(12 to 1 tchd 14 to 1) 3
RUBY ESTATE (Ire) 8-9 J Quinn (14) *beh, gd hdwy on outer 2 fs out, rdn and styd on wl ins last.* ....(33 to 1 op 20 to 1) 4
2429[8] SEMINOLE WIND 9-0 T Williams (4) *beh, hdwy 2 fs out, rdn and styd on wl last.*........(20 to 1 op 16 to 1) 5
2559[4] DALWOOD 9-0 R Hills (12) *chsd ldrs, rdn 2 fs out, one pace entering last.*........(7 to 1 op 4 to 1) 6
SALOME'S DANCE 8-9 G Duffield (2) *dwlt and beh till styd on fnl 2 fs.*........(12 to 1 op 8 to 1) 7
2429[7] CHANTRY BEATH 9-0 J Fanning (5) *in tch, outpcd hfwy, styd on fnl 2 fs.*........(25 to 1 op 20 to 1) 8
1916 GWERNYMYNYDD 8-9 D Holland (15) *nvr rchd ldrs.* ....(12 to 1 op 7 to 1) 9
2465[5] BANG IN TROUBLE (Ire) 9-0 K Darley (10) *wth wnr, rdn 2 and a half fs out, sn wknd.*........(33 to 1) 10
2030[9] ANZUM 9-0 G Carter (1) *nvr rchd ldrs.* ....(50 to 1 op 33 to 1) 11
1998[2] HARDING 9-0 A Munro (9) *chsd ldrs, sn rdn alng, wknd 3 fs out.*........(6 to 5 fav op 5 to 4 tchd 13 to 8) 12
2342[5] DEMON DANCER (Ire) 9-0 N Connorton (11) *chsd ldrs, rdn 3 fs out, sn wknd.*........(25 to 1) 13
2706[6] OVALWORLD 8-9 (5*) O Pears (3) *al rear.*........(33 to 1) 14
2234[5] AVONDALE ROSE 8-9 J Fortune (8) *cl up, rdn 3 fs out, sn wknd.*........(25 to 1 op 16 to 1) 15

Dist: ½l, hd, ½l, ½l, ½l, 3l, ¾l, ½l, 1½l, 2½l. 1m 29.20s. a 2.20s (15 Ran).
SR: 15/13/7/5/8/6/ (R D A Kelly), M Bell

2863 Sleeping Beauty Handicap Class E (0-70 3-y-o and up) £2,364 7f.... (8:55)

2425[5] WORKINGFORPEANUTS (Ire) [38] (v) 3-7-7 J Lowe (4) *slwly into strd and beh, sn pushed alng, hdwy on outer 2 and a half fs out, styd on wl to ld entering last.* ....(8 to 1 tchd 10 to 1) 1
2428[6] SAVAHRA SOUND [66] 8-10-0 S Webster (7) *in tch, smooth hdwy 2 fs out, ev ch entering last, sn rdn and kpt on.* ....(12 to 1 op 14 to 1) 2
2503[5] DAYTONA BEACH (Ire) [63] 3-9-4 K Darley (2) *chsd ldrs, hmpd 3 fs out, hdwy on inner 2 furlongs out, ev ch entering last, not quicken.* ....(7 to 1 op 8 to 1 tchd 13 to 2) 3
274 JUVENARA [43] 7-8-4[2] (3*) S D Williams (1) *beh, gd hdwy on inner 2 fs out, rdn and ran on fnl furlong*.....(20 to 1) 4
2527[2] STARDUST EXPRESS [50] 3-8-5 T Williams (3) *led, rdn 2 fs out, hdd entering last, sn wknd.*... (6 to 1 op 11 to 2) 5
2717[7] MISTER BLAKE [48] 3-8-3[3] (3*) Emma O'Gorman (6) *hld up, hdwy o'r 2 fs out, sn rdn, kpt on ins last.*..... (12 to 1) 6
2445 DANCE ON SIXPENCE [44] 5-8-6 J Quinn (9) *in tch, effrt and rdn 2 fs out, sn one pace.*....... (7 to 1 op 5 to 1) 7
2503[3] SEASON'S STAR [53] (v) 3-8-8 S Dawson (5) *chsd ldrs, rdn 2 fs out and ev ch till wknd one furlong out.* ....(5 to 1 fav tchd 9 to 2) 8
2657[8] GANT BLEU (Fr) [57] 6-9-5 A Culhane (8) *prmnt, effrt and hdwy to chal 2 fs out, ev ch till wknd appr last.* ....(6 to 1 op 11 to 2) 9
2602[8] FREDDIE JACK [38] 3-7-7 G Bardwell (10) *slwly away, sn cl up, rdn 2 fs out, ev ch till wknd entering last.* ....(25 to 1 op 33 to 1) 10
2371[7] YUNUS EMRE (Ire) [50] 3-8-2 (3*) M Fenton (11) *chsd ldrs, rdn alng 3 fs out, wknd o'r 2 furlongs out.* ....(8 to 1 op 7 to 1) 11

Dist: 2½l, 1½l, nk, 2½l, ¾l, hd, nk, ½l, nk, ½l. 1m 28.30s. a 1.30s (11 Ran).
SR: 7/34/19/5/-/-/-/-/5/ (Julian Graves Ltd), C A Smith

WINDSOR (good)
Monday July 26th
Going Correction: NIL (races 1,2,4,6), MINUS 0.30 (3,5)

2864 Castle Limited Stakes Class F (0-65 3-y-o) £2,005 1m 67yds......... (6:10)

2764* DANCING DOMINO 9-0 W Ryan (4) *sn tracking 1st 2, shaken up to ld o'r one furlong out, kpt up to work nr finish.*.....(13 to 8 on op 5 to 4 on tchd 11 to 10 on) 1
2712[5] TONY'S MIST 9-0 J Reid (1) *led, rdn alng 2 fs out, hdd o'r one out, styd on same pace.*.........(9 to 2 op 7 to 2) 2
2503[4] PERDITION (Ire) 8-6 (3*) D Harrison (6) *hld up rear, improved hfwy, jnd ldrs o'r 2 fs out, sn rdn and outpcd.* ....(9 to 2 op 3 to 1) 3
1912 TRUNDLEY WOOD 8-9 N Carlisle (5) *steadied strt, hld up rear, cld on ldrs 3 fs out, rdn and wknd frm 2 out.* ....(14 to 1 op 8 to 1) 4
2613* JULIASDARKINVADER 9-0 Candy Morris (2) *chsd ldr till rdn and wknd 2 fs out.* ....(25 to 1 op 20 to 1 tchd 33 to 1) 5
2138[8] DELAY NO MORE 9-0 W Newnes (3) *pld hrd, in tch, rdn and wknd 3 fs out, tld off.*.....(50 to 1 op 33 to 1) 6

Dist: ¾l, 6l, 3½l, 2l, 20l. 1m 46.90s. a 5.90s (6 Ran).
SR: 12/10/-/ (P D Savill), M H Easterby

2865 Royal Star And Garter Claiming Stakes Class F (3-y-o and up) £1,674 1m 3f 135yds................. (6:40)

2658[2] WITH GUSTO 6-9-3 T Quinn (7) *hld up rear, hdwy o'r 3 fs out, hrd rdn to ld wl ins last.* ....(9 to 2 op 6 to 1 tchd 7 to 1) 1
2501[7] VANBOROUGH LAD 4-9-4 J Reid (3) *mid-div, hdwy 4 fs out, led 2 out, hdd und pres wl ins last.* ....(9 to 2 op 3 to 1 tchd 5 to 1) 2

2330 SWIFT ROMANCE (Ire) 5-9-5 S Whitworth (6) *slwly into strd, hdwy frm rear o'r 3 fs out, ev ch 2 out, not quicken ins last*..............................(9 to 1 op 6 to 1) 3
2544[5] DAZZLING FIRE (Ire) 4-8-5 (7*) Kim McDonnell (2) *trkd ldr, led o'r 3 fs out to 2 out, no extr*....(10 to 1 tchd 8 to 1) 4
2656[9] DEXTER CHIEF 4-8-10 (5*) K Rutter (10) *wl plcd till rdn and outpcd last 2 fs*.........(11 to 2 op 5 to 1 tchd 6 to 1) 5
WEDNESDAYS AUCTION (Ire) 5-9-7 M Perrett (4) *in tch, rdn and outpcd appr last 2 fs*..........(33 to 1 op 20 to 1) 6+
2273[7] COMMANCHE CREEK (bl) 3-8-7 R Cochrane (5) *set str pace, hdd and wknd o'r 3 fs out.*
.... (2 to 1 fav op 7 to 4 tchd 6 to 4 and 9 to 4) 6+
MOYMET 7-9-3 T Sprake (8) *nvr rch frnt rnk.*
.................................(33 to 1 op 14 to 1) 8
1746 MORAN BRIG 3-8-3 S O'Gorman (9) *al beh.*
.................................(20 to 1 op 12 to 1) 9
2109 SUKEY TAWDRY (bl) 7-8-9 N Adams (1) *chsd ldrs till wknd quickly 5 fs out, tld off*.........(50 to 1 op 33 to 1) 10
Dist: Nk, 1l, 1½l, 12l, sht-hd, dd-ht, 3½l, 10l, 30l. 2m 30.60s. a 7.60s (10 Ran).
SR: 27/27/26/16/-/-/ (M D Brunton), K O Cunningham-Brown

2866 Tattersalls Maiden Auction Series Stakes Qualifier Class E (2-y-o) £3,416 5f 217yds......................(7:10)

2535[2] PETULA 8-6 M Hills (17) *made all, quickened ins fnl furlong, cmftbly.*
.......(11 to 10 fav op 5 to 4 tchd 11 to 8 and Evens) 1
ONE ON ONE 8-2 N Day (15) *trkd ldrs, cld on wnr 2 fs out, one pace ins last*.....(16 to 1 op 12 to 1 tchd 20 to 1) 2
922[3] OBVIOUS RISK 8-6 J Reid (4) *hdwy 2 fs out, rdn and not quicken ins last*........(11 to 2 op 4 to 1 tchd 6 to 1) 3
1602 ELEVATOR SHAFT (Ire) 8-6 T Quinn (11) *ldg grp, rdn and outpcd appr fnl furlong.*
...........(8 to 1 op 14 to 1 tchd 16 to 1 and 6 to 1) 4
2179[5] UN PARFUM DE FEMME (Ire) 8-9 L Dettori (1) *in tch on outsd, no hdwy ins last 2 fs.*
.....................(16 to 1 op 10 to 1 tchd 20 to 1) 5
908[2] PERSIAN HERITAGE 8-11 R Cochrane (14) *ldg grp, outpcd o'r one furlong out*......(6 to 1 op 4 to 1 tchd 8 to 1) 6
2546[7] QUEENS COTTAGE (Ire) 8-1 Dale Gibson (12) *wl plcd till rdn and no extr 2 fs out*..........(33 to 1 op 16 to 1) 7
2049[4] PADDY'S RICE 8-6 Paul Eddery (9) *speed 4 fs.*
.................................(16 to 1 op 6 to 1) 8
979[5] VICEROY RULER 8-11 S Whitworth (7) *swtchd to outsd and styd on frm 2 fs out*..........(20 to 1 op 14 to 1) 9
CHITA RIVERA 8-9 T Sprake (3) *outpcd most of way.*
.................................(20 to 1 op 7 to 1) 10
HIGH HOLME 8-6 A McGlone (5) *slwly into strd, effrt o'r 2 fs out, not rch frnt rnk*...........(33 to 1 op 20 to 1) 11
2472[6] MICHAELMAS PARK (Ire) 8-3 (7*) B Russell (2) *speed on outsd for o'r 3 fs*..............(20 to 1 op 12 to 1) 12
1905 NOT THE NADGER 8-11 C Rutter (8) *nvr nr to chal.*
.................................(33 to 1 op 20 to 1) 13
2325 NAME THE TUNE 8-6 B Rouse (16) *speed to hfwy.*
.................................(33 to 1 op 20 to 1) 14
ONLY FOOLS 8-7 J Williams (10) *nvr on terms.*
.................................(33 to 1 op 12 to 1) 15
HEALTHY RISK 8-6 N Adams (13) *outpcd.*
.................................(33 to 1 op 20 to 1) 16
1708[6] DANCING ROSINA (Ire) 8-5 W Newnes (6) *slwly into strd, al outpcd, tld off*.................(33 to 1 op 16 to 1) 17
Dist: 2l, nk, 8l, 2½l, ½l, 2½l, 1½l, 1l, ¾l, 1l. 1m 11.00s. a 0.70s (17 Ran).
SR: 42/30/33/1/-/-/ (M A Khan), M Bell

2867 Royal Borough Handicap Class D (0-80 3-y-o and up) £3,557 1¼m 7yds ....(7:40)

2669* PISTOLS AT DAWN (USA) [61] 3-8-12 (5ex) J Reid (2) *trkd ldr, rdn alng 2 fs out, found extr to ld last strds.*
...................(7 to 4 jt-fav op 6 to 4 tchd 15 to 8) 1
2673* BENTICO [68] 4-10-1 (5ex) Pat Eddery (4) *led, rdn alng o'r one furlong out, hdd last strds*...............(7 to 4 jt-fav op 6 to 4 tchd 11 to 8 and 15 to 8) 2
2564[4] WAR REQUIEM (Ire) [55] 3-8-6 J Williams (1) *hld up rear, improved 3 fs out, not quicken o'r one out.*
.........................(7 to 2 op 5 to 2 tchd 4 to 1) 3
1346 REGAL AURA (Ire) [71] 3-9-8 M Perrett (3) *rcd keenly in 3rd, pushed alng o'r 3 fs out, one pace 2 out.*
......................(7 to 1 tchd 8 to 1 and 6 to 1) 4
Dist: Hd, 6l, 3½l. 2m 10.40s. a 7.90s (4 Ran).
SR: 19/35/-/9/ (G Howard-Spink), R Hannon

2868 Long Walk Handicap Class E (0-70 3-y-o and up) £2,532 5f 217yds......(8:10)

2671[7] SPECTACLE JIM [41] (bl) 4-8-1 N Adams (11) *hdwy frm rear o'r one furlong out, str brst to ld nr finish.*
....................(12 to 1 op 14 to 1 tchd 20 to 1) 1
2549[4] POYLE AMBER [48] 4-8-5 (3*) D Harrison (1) *wth ldrs, led o'r one furlong out, hdd und pres nr finish.*
......................(6 to 1 op 5 to 1 tchd 13 to 2) 2
2327 CEE-EN-CEE [57] (v) 9-9-3 A Tucker (4) *ldg grp, ev ch o'r one furlong out, no extr wl ins last.*
..............................(12 to 1 tchd 16 to 1) 3
2671[3] HARRY'S COMING [57] 9-9-3 M Hills (3) *hld up, ran on 2 fs out, ev ch one out, kpt on same pace.*
..........................(5 to 1 tchd 6 to 1) 4
2584[7] MOVING IMAGE (Ire) [56] 3-8-10 C Dwyer (2) *in tch, rdn alng and one pace appr fnl furlong.*
.................................(14 to 1 op 10 to 1) 5
2378[6] FAY'S SONG (Ire) [58] 5-9-4 T Quinn (9) *mid-div most of way, one pace last 2 fs.* (13 to 2 op 6 to 1 tchd 7 to 1) 6
2418[6] GREY CHARMER (Ire) [62] 4-9-8 W Newnes (5) *nvr rch frnt rnk*...................(7 to 1 op 6 to 1 tchd 8 to 1) 7
2225[6] HONEY SEEKER [64] 4-9-10 S Whitworth (13) *chsd ldrs 4 fs.*
.................................(14 to 1 op 12 to 1) 8
BALLYHAYS (Ire) [59] 4-8-12 (7*) L Carter (6) *slwly into strd, nvr on terms*.................(25 to 1 op 16 to 1) 9
1687[3] LETSBEONESTABOUTIT [68] (bl) 7-10-0 L Dettori (7) *pressed ldr, led 2 fs out till o'r one out, sn wknd.*
..............................(7 to 1 tchd 9 to 1) 10
2524 MISTER JOLSON [68] 4-9-7 (7*) S Drowne (8) *mid-div, no hdwy last 2 fs*........(14 to 1 op 12 to 1 tchd 16 to 1) 11
2327[6] CHICARD [44] 4-8-4 Paul Eddery (12) *led 4 fs, sn btn.*
.......................(4 to 1 fav op 5 to 1 tchd 7 to 2) 12
990 ALPHONSO [59] 4-9-5 J Williams (10) *outpcd.*
.................................(25 to 1 op 16 to 1) 13
Dist: ½l, 3½l, 1l, 2l, ½l, 2l, 1½l, ½l, 2l, hd. 1m 11.50s. a 1.20s (13 Ran).
SR: 27/32/27/23/8/14/10/6/-/ (J J Harrow), J O'Donoghue

2869 Great Park Handicap Class E (0-70 3-y-o and up) £2,232 1m 67yds..(8:40)

2673[4] BROWN CARPET [27] (bl) 6-7-2 (5*) D Wright (9) *in tch, ran on to ld und pres 2 fs out, styd on ins last.*
.......................(13 to 2 op 5 to 1 tchd 7 to 1) 1
2715[3] DUCKEY FUZZ [50] 5-9-2 Paul Eddery (6) *prog 3 fs out, ev ch ins last, not quicken nr finish.*
..........................(5 to 1 op 9 to 2 tchd 4 to 1) 2
2161[2] PRECIOUS AIR (Ire) [55] 5-9-7 B Rouse (14) *hld up in tch, cld 2 fs out, one pace ins last.*
.......................(5 to 1 op 6 to 1 tchd 13 to 2) 3
2548[4] GREAT HAND [45] 7-8-11 J Reid (7) *hld up in mid-div, cld on ldrs frm 3 fs out, one pace appr last.*
.......................(13 to 2 op 9 to 2 tchd 7 to 1) 4
2597[5] BRESIL (USA) [52] 4-9-4 Pat Eddery (2) *ldg grp, led o'r 4 fs out to 2 out, no extr*..............(9 to 2 fav op 7 to 2) 5
2789[8] DON'T GIVE UP [39] (bl) 5-8-5 D Biggs (13) *slwly into strd, beh till styd on last 2 fs.*
....................(16 to 1 op 14 to 1 tchd 20 to 1) 6
2138[7] SALLY OF THE ALLEY [43] 3-8-1 C Rutter (5) *in tch, effrt o'r 2 fs out, not rch frnt rnk*..........(14 to 1 op 10 to 1) 7
2663[4] SINGERS IMAGE [58] 4-9-10 J Williams (3) *rear, effrt 3 fs out, no imprsn last 2 furlongs.*
......................(7 to 1 op 5 to 1 tchd 15 to 2) 8
2548[5] KINNEGAD KID [35] 4-8-1 A McGlone (15) *slwly into strd, beh most of way*......(11 to 1 op 7 to 1 tchd 12 to 1) 9
2548 WOODLANDS LEGEND [35] 4-8-1 F Norton (12) *al rear.*
.................................(50 to 1 tchd 66 to 1) 10
2641 RED KITE [43] 4-8-9 M Hills (8) *chsd ldrs aftr 3 fs, wknd o'r 2 out*............................(12 to 1 tchd 14 to 1) 11
2273 CLAR DUBH (Ire) [37] 3-7-9 N Adams (1) *al rear.*
....................(16 to 1 op 20 to 1 tchd 25 to 1) 12
WEEKDAY CROSS (Ire) [39] 5-8-5 S Whitworth (4) *mid-div, improved hfwy, wknd o'r 2 fs out.*
.....................(40 to 1 op 33 to 1 tchd 50 to 1) 13
1238 LAST APPEARANCE [35] 4-8-1 Dale Gibson (10) *led till o'r 4 fs out, sn wknd*..............................(50 to 1) 14
Dist: ¾l, 3l, sht-hd, 2l, 2l, 1l, nk, 1½l, 8l, hd. 1m 46.30s. a 5.30s (14 Ran).
SR: -/21/17/6/7/-/-/3/-/ (R Del Rosario), C A Horgan

BEVERLEY (good to firm)
Tuesday July 27th
Going Correction: NIL (races 1,2,5,6), PLUS 0.10 (3,7), MINUS 0.30 (4)

2870 Ladygate Selling Handicap Class G (0-60 3-y-o) £2,534 1m 3f 216yds (2:10)

2773[3] MILNGAVIE (Ire) [45] 9-2 Dean McKeown (7) *al wl plcd, brght wide to ld o'r 2 fs out, styd on well.*
.....................(100 to 30 op 3 to 1 tchd 7 to 2) 1
2448[4] MR ABBOT [37] 8-8 J Lowe (1) *patiently rdn, last strt, gd hdwy to chal o'r one furlong out, ridden and no extr.*
.................................(8 to 1 op 6 to 1) 2
2219[9] PRINCE PALACIO [35] 8-6 N Connorton (5) *settled midfield, drvn up to improve last 2 fs, styd on one pace.*
.........................(5 to 1 op 6 to 1 tchd 4 to 1) 3
2593[4] SUMMERS DREAM [31] 7-13 (3*) S Maloney (6) *trkd ldg bunch, rdn to fltter o'r one furlong out, one pace.*
.................................(20 to 1 op 16 to 1) 4
2520 CHILTERN HUNDREDS (USA) [40] 8-6 (5*) D McCabe (10) *co'red up on ins, short of room over 2 fs out, swtchd lft fnl furlong, one pace*..............................(16 to 1) 5
2694[2] ANN HILL (Ire) [50] 9-0 (7*) M Humphries (8) *trkd ldrs, effrt whn squeezed out o'r 2 fs out, rdn and no response.*
.......................(5 to 2 fav tchd 9 to 4 and 3 to 1) 6
2773[8] MOONSHINE DANCER [47] 9-4 K Darley (3) *trkd ldrs, hrd at work 2 fs out, no imprsn*..........(8 to 1 op 7 to 1) 7

2800[3] CHALLENGER ROW (Ire) [48] (bl) 9-5 M Birch (9) *dictated pace, hdd entering strt, sn btn.*.....(11 to 2 op 5 to 1) 8
2602[6] EVAHART [30] 7-9[1] (7*) J Marshall (4) *rcd freely in frnt rnk, led briefly entering strt, fdd*.......(14 to 1 op 12 to 1) 9
Dist: 3l, nk, sht-hd, 1½l, 1½l, 3l, ½l, ¾l. 2m 39.50s. a 8.50s (9 Ran).
SR: 17/3/-/-/1/8/ (A S Robertson), M Johnston

2871 Max Jaffa Memorial Handicap Class E (0-70 3-y-o and up) £3,377 1m 3f 216yds........................ (2:40)

2678[3] BATABANOO [66] 4-10-0 K Darley (5) *patiently rdn, drvn through to ld ins fnl furlong, ran on.* ....(7 to 4 fav op 11 to 8) 1
1967[4] FAIR FLYER (Ire) [54] 4-9-2 Dean McKeown (2) *tried to make all, quickened entering strt, hdd ins fnl furlong, one pace.*.............................. (4 to 1 op 7 to 2) 2
SCALP 'EM (Ire) [32] 5-7-8[1] L Charnock (3) *fly jmpd leaving stalls, sn reco'red, ev ch over one furlong out, one pace.* .... (20 to 1 op 16 to 1) 3
2678[6] SEA PADDY [55] 5-8-10 (7*) H Bastiman (6) *nvr far away, drvn alng o'r 2 fs out, not quicken.* (13 to 2 op 5 to 1) 4
2544[3] FAMOUS BEAUTY [44] 6-7-13 (7*) J Dennis (1) *trkd ldrs, feeling pace entering strt, rdn and btn o'r 2 fs out.* .... (12 to 1 op 10 to 1) 5
2235[4] BOLD ELECT [58] 5-9-6 M Wigham (4) *trkd ldg trio, hrd at work whn pace quickened o'r 2 fs out, sn btn.* .... (85 to 40 op 7 to 2 tchd 2 to 1) 6
Dist: ¾l, 3½l, 7l, sht-hd, 3l. 2m 37.40s. a 6.40s (6 Ran).
SR: 50/36/7/16/4/12/ (P D Savill), Mrs M Reveley

2872 'Go Racing In Yorkshire' Claiming Stakes Class F (3-y-o and up) £2,623 5f .... (3:05)

2777[6] ANOTHER LANE 6-8-13 M Birch (2) *sluggish strt, steady hdwy and not clr run o'r one furlong out, quickened through to ld last 50 yards, ran on.* .... (10 to 1 op 12 to 1 tchd 14 to 1) 1
2797[2] DRUM SERGEANT (bl) 6-9-1 (3*) J Weaver (10) *nvr far away, rdn to draw level ins fnl furlong, kpt on.* ....(3 to 1 tchd 7 to 2) 2
GIPSY FIDDLER 5-9-10 Dean McKeown (5) *tried to make all, rdn and hdd last 50 yards, no extr.* ....(4 to 1 op 3 to 1) 3
2524[5] METAL BOYS 6-9-11 (3*) D Harrison (8) *settled midfield, swtchd outsd o'r one furlong out, effrt ins last, ran on.* .... (4 to 1 tchd 7 to 2 and 9 to 2) 4
2225[8] NOT SO GENEROUS (Ire) 3-8-6 T Sprake (1) *trkd ldrs, drvn alng o'r one furlong out, rallied towards finish.* ....(14 to 1 tchd 16 to 1) 5
2288[6] SING AS WE GO 3-7-10 N Carlisle (7) *nvr far away, effrt and not much room hfwy, rallied ins last.*.... (33 to 1) 6
VICTORIAS PASSION 3-8-7 (3*) S D Williams (3) *sluggish strt, last and struggling till ran on wl fnl furlong.* .... (33 to 1 op 25 to 1) 7
2620[5] SAMSON-AGONISTES 7-8-13 (7*) S Sanders (6) *wth ldr, feeling pace and drvn alng o'r one furlong out, no extr.* ....(5 to 2 fav op 9 to 4 tchd 2 to 1) 8
2481[9] MISS LIMELIGHT 4-8-4[1] S Webster (4) *chsd ldrs, hrd rdn 2 fs out, fdd*........................ (33 to 1 op 25 to 1) 9
Dist: 1l, ½l, nk, hd, ½l, sht-hd, 1l, 8l. 1m 4.80s. a 3.10s (9 Ran).
SR: 47/48/52/55/32/20/33/39/-/ (Mrs E Harris), J Wharton

2873 Timeform Ladies For Dorothy Laird Trophy Handicap Class F (3-y-o and up) £2,758 1m 1f 207yds........ (3:35)

2489* DODGY DANCER [59] 3-9-9 Lorna Vincent (7) *trkd ldrs, improved to ld o'r one furlong out, ran on wl.* .... (6 to 1 op 11 to 2 tchd 13 to 2) 1
FATHER DAN (Ire) [40] 4-9-0 Gay Kelleway (5) *al hndy, led entering strt till o'r one furlong out, kpt on same pace.* ....(33 to 1) 2
2066 TEJ SINGH (USA) [74] 3-10-10 Mrs S Cumani (4) *patiently rdn, shaken up to improve o'r one furlong out, fnshd strly*................. (11 to 2 op 5 to 1 tchd 6 to 1) 3
2445[4] LADY DONOGHUE (USA) [51] 4-9-8 (3*) Wendy Jones (10) *trkd ldg trio, ev ch and drvn alng 2 fs out, one pace.* .... (13 to 2 op 6 to 1) 4
2369* TOUCH ABOVE [54] 7-10-0 Mrs A Farrell (9) *patiently rdn, hmpd and checked hfwy, not much room on ins whn ridden o'r 2 fs out, no imprsn*..... (3 to 1 tchd 7 to 2) 5
2127* KELIMUTU [41] 4-9-1 Mrs L Pearce (2) *taken gingerly to post, wtd wth, brght wide to improve o'r 2 fs out, no extr*......................... (11 to 4 fav op 2 to 1) 6
2348[8] ROMOLA NIJINSKY [59] 5-10-5 Miss Diana Jones (6) *wth ldrs for almost a m, fdd*............(9 to 1 op 10 to 1) 7
2614[4] WALKING THE PLANK [75] (v) 4-11-2 (5*) Mrs A Turner (8) *dictated pace till hdd entering strt, fdd o'r 2 fs out.* .... (10 to 1 op 8 to 1) 8
1247[5] TINSASHE (Ire) [50] 3-8-9 (5*) Miss I Foustok (3) *chsd alng to keep up hfwy, nvr a factor*........ (20 to 1 op 14 to 1) 9
2520 HENBURY HALL (Ire) [43] (v) 5-9-3 Ann Stokell (1) *wth ldrs, hrd at work o'r 2 fs out, fdd*.................(33 to 1) 10
Dist: 1½l, sht-hd, 1½l, 6l, 1l, ¾l, 1l, 10l, 1l. 2m 5.80s. a 4.40s (10 Ran).
SR: 35/23/46/30/21/6/22/36/-/ (T W Langley), M R Channon

2874 Holderness Pony Club Fillies' Handicap Class D (3-y-o and up) £3,590 1m 100yds........................ (4:05)

2499* ESSEX GIRL [58] 3-8-9 K Darley (5) *led early, styd hndy till led ag'n und pres entering fnl furlong, jst hld on.* .... (5 to 4 fav tchd 11 to 8) 1
2421[4] MISTY SILKS [62] 3-8-10 (3*) J Weaver (2) *last and hld up, rapid hdwy appr fnl furlong, jst fld.* .... (4 to 1 op 5 to 1 tchd 11 to 2) 2
2534[5] ASTERN (USA) [68] 3-9-5 G Hind (1) *made most, jnd and rdn 2 fs out, hdd and not quicken entering fnl furlong.* ....(7 to 1 op 6 to 1) 3
2633[3] BRILLIANT [65] 5-9-10 M Wigham (4) *trkd ldg trio, feeling pace and drvn alng last 2 fs, no extr.* (7 to 2 op 3 to 1) 4
2635[4] BILOELA [62] 3-8-13 K Fallon (3) *al hndy, drw level 2 fs out, fdd fnl furlong*.. .... (7 to 1 op 6 to 1) 5
Dist: Sht-hd, 2l, 2½l, ¾l. 1m 48.00s. a 5.20s (5 Ran).
SR: 17/20/20/17/4/ (Lucayan Stud), D R Loder

2875 EBF Minster Moorgate Maiden Stakes Class D (2-y-o) £4,199 7f 100yds (4:35)

2714[4] PRIVY COUNCIL (USA) 9-0 K Darley (7) *settled to track ldg trio, swtchd outsd o'r one furlong out, kpt on to ld post*............... (11 to 8 fav op 2 to 1 tchd 9 to 4) 1
WAZIN (USA) 9-0 N Carlisle (6) *nvr far away, drvn through to ld o'r one furlong out, wknd and ct post.* ....(7 to 2 op 2 to 1) 2
WINN'S PRIDE (Ire) 9-0 S Perks (4) *tucked away, chsd alng to improve last 2 fs, styd on.* .... (14 to 1 op 10 to 1 tchd 16 to 1) 3
ELFLAA (Ire) 9-0 M Tebbutt (3) *sluggish strt, effrt whn squeezed for room 2 fs out, ran on finish.* .... (5 to 1 op 4 to 1 tchd 11 to 2) 4
MHEANMETOO 9-0 M Birch (5) *patiently rdn, effrt and squeezed for room 2 fs out, ran green, rallied.* .... (15 to 2 op 8 to 1 tchd 7 to 1) 5
2429 SHARONE 8-9 N Connorton (8) *led till hdd and no extr o'r one furlong out*...... (16 to 1 op 10 to 1 tchd 20 to 1) 6
DANCING REBEL (Ire) 9-0 K Fallon (1) *wl outpcd and drvn alng hfwy, styd on last 2 fs, nvr nrr.* (10 to 1 op 7 to 1) 7
2447[3] DOUBLE DANCER 9-0 L Charnock (2) *trkd ldr, drvn alng and hmpd 2 fs out, sn btn*........(8 to 1 tchd 12 to 1) 8
Dist: Sht-hd, 2l, 1l, 1l, 1½l, 1½l, 5l. 1m 36.10s. a 5.80s (8 Ran).
SR: 13/12/6/3/-/ (Davie Wong), D R Loder

2876 Family Day Maiden Auction Stakes Class E (2-y-o) £3,054 5f........ (5:05)

HANNAH'S MUSIC 8-9 Dean McKeown (5) *nvr far away, drvn ahead ins fnl furlong, gng clr whn edgd rght last 50 yards*....................................(16 to 1) 1
2021 MONKEY'S WEDDING (bl) 9-0 K Darley (10) *nvr far away, ev ch whn wndrd und pres fnl furlong, rallied.* .... (14 to 1 op 10 to 1) 2
2586[3] HASTY BANK 9-0 M Birch (9) *sluggish strt, improved hfwy, ev ch fnl furlong, kpt on*..... (8 to 1 op 5 to 1) 3
2618[6] KING RAMBO 9-0 S Perks (12) *tried to make all, veered lft fnl furlong, hdd and no extr last 50 yards.* .... (5 to 4 on op 6 to 4 on) 4
MR BERGERAC (Ire) 8-11 (3*) J Weaver (6) *tucked away in midfield, imprvg whn not much room entering fnl furlong, kpt on*.....................(16 to 1 op 12 to 1) 5
PETRINA BAY 8-9 A Culhane (4) *chsd ldrs, swtchd ins and not much room fnl furlong, nvr nrr.* .... (25 to 1 op 14 to 1) 6
2659[6] GREENSON (Ire) 9-0 C Rutter (2) *chsd alng to go pace, styd on fnl furlong, nvr nrr*............ (10 to 1 op 8 to 1) 7
2063[4] DANTE'S RUBICON (Ire) 9-0 L Charnock (1) *rcd freely, jnd ldr aftr one furlong, fdd o'r one furlong out*...(16 to 1) 8
2542[4] ARCTIC DIAMOND 9-0 K Fallon (11) *sn last, shaken up and steady hdwy last 2 fs, nvr plcd to chal.* .... (12 to 1 op 8 to 1) 9
2342[3] LEGAL TRAIN 9-0 S Webster (13) *drvn alng on ins, effrt hfwy, sn outpcd*...............(10 to 1 op 8 to 1) 10
1561 MAZINA 8-2 (7*) J Marshall (3) *chsd alng to keep up hfwy, no imprsn*........................(33 to 1 op 20 to 1) 11
2526[3] SNUGFIT ANNIE 8-9 T Lucas (7) *speed to chase ldrs to hfwy, sn btn*...................... (20 to 1 op 14 to 1) 12
Dist: 1l, 1l, nk, 1l, ½l, 1l, 1½l, hd, 7l, 1l. 1m 5.40s. a 3.70s (12 Ran).
SR: 31/32/28/27/23/16/17/11/10/ (Pat FitzGerald), P C Haslam

GALWAY (IRE) (soft)
Tuesday July 27th

2877 McDonogh Fertilizer (C&G) Maiden (3-y-o and up) £4,142 7f........... (5:35)

1333[5] GLACIAL ARCTIC (USA) 3-9-0 M J Kinane (5)......(2 to 1) 1
2185[2] MONOPOLY MONEY (Ire) 3-9-0 P V Gilson (7)..(7 to 4 fav) 2
1510[3] BOTHSIDESNOW (Ire) 3-9-0 R Hughes (2).........(4 to 1) 3
TALES OF HEARSAY (Ger) 3-9-0 N G McCullagh (1) (4 to 1) 4
2703 TORC MOUNTAIN (Ire) (bl) 3-9-0 W J Supple (6)...(14 to 1) 5
2497[7] CELTICCARO (Ire) 5-9-7 J F Egan (3)........... (66 to 1) 6

2703 TEAK ROAD (Ire) 3-8-10 (4*) S Craine (4) .... (50 to 1) 7
Dist: 2½l, hd, 3½l, 3l. 1m 39.10s. (7 Ran).
(Andrea Schiavi), D K Weld

2878 McDonogh Handicap (0-110 3-y-o and up) £16,752 1m 100yds. .... (6:50)

2608^7 BE MY HOPE (Ire) [-] 4-8-13 N G McCullagh (7) ... (16 to 1) 1
2041* WANDERING THOUGHTS (Ire) [-] 4-7-5 (2*) D G O'Shea (1) .... (5 to 1 jt-fav) 2
2806^7 WALLY WALLENSKY (Ire) [-] 3-7-7 Joanna Morgan (13) .... (25 to 1) 3
1717^3 LOKI (Ire) [-] 5-7-13 (8*) D J O'Donohoe (6) .... (10 to 1) 4
2608^8 SALMON EILE (Ire) [-] 5-9-10 J P Murtagh (4) ..... (10 to 1) 5
2078^2 MILLIE'S CHOICE (Ire) [-] 4-8-12 (6*) B J Walsh (14) (10 to 1) 6
1334^7 NEVER BACK DOWN (Ire) [-] 3-7-6^4 (6*) J J Behan (9) .... (12 to 1) 7
2809^5 LEGAL FLAIR (Ire) [-] 3-8-2 W J Supple (5) .... (9 to 1) 8
2654^6 ORMSBY (Ire) [-] 4-9-5 M J Kinane (17) .... (8 to 1) 9
GODS EXPRESS (Ire) [-] 5-7-11 (2*) R M Burke (3) (25 to 1) 10
2608^6 GALLARDINI (Ire) [-] 4-8-9 K J Manning (10) ...... (20 to 1) 11
2606* KAYFA (Ire) [-] 4-8-11 (4*,2ex) P Carberry (2) .... (8 to 1) 12
2809^2 BALLYKETT PRINCE (Ire) [-] (bl) 5-9-7 C Roche (16) .... (5 to 1 jt-fav) 13
2606^5 CHEVIOT AMBLE (Ire) [-] 5-9-6 J F Egan (15) ..... (12 to 1) 14
2452* RELENTLESS BOY (Ire) [-] 3-7-11 (4*) W J Smith (12) .... (20 to 1) 15
2035 ORTHORHOMBUS [-] (bl) 4-8-9 S Craine (8) ...... (50 to 1) 16
Dist: Nk, nk, nk, 1½l, 6l, 8l. 1m 55.80s. (16 Ran).
(K M Griffin), D Hanley

2879 Albatros Suregrass Handicap (0-75 3-y-o and up) £3,797 7f. .... (7:25)

2463^2 RIENROE (Ire) [-] 4-9-8 M J Kinane (12) .... (2 to 1 fav) 1
2322^8 GLANCE CARD (Ire) [-] (bl) 3-8-11 P Shanahan (5) .. (8 to 1) 2
2675^2 BOLD MOLLY (Ire) [-] 4-7-3 (6*) P P Murphy (15) .... (8 to 1) 3
PAKOL (Ire) [-] 4-8-12 (4*) W J Smith (3) .... (50 to 1) 4
2556 TAJANAMA (Ire) [-] 5-8-0 D V Smith (9) .... (14 to 1) 5
2780* MACGILLYCUDDY (Ire) [-] 4-9-10 (6*,5ex) J J Behan (8) .... (7 to 1) 6
2321^3 GIFT OF PEACE (Ire) [-] 3-8-12 J P Murtagh (13) .... (8 to 1) 7
2511^5 SOUTHERN RULE [-] 6-7-8 Joanna Morgan (18) .. (14 to 1) 8
1444 SHESLOOKINATME (Ire) [-] 4-7-10 (2*) R M Burke (6) .... (33 to 1) 9
2295^4 INISHMOT (Ire) [-] 3-8-5 (6*) R V Skelly, ... (14 to 1) 10
2806^2 NORDIC SAINT (Ire) [-] 4-9-5 C Roche (4) .... (5 to 1) 11
599 DONMIR LOVEBIRD (Ire) [-] (bl) 3-8-0 W J Supple (10) .... (33 to 1) 12
2677^7 WESTERN FRONTIER (Ire) [-] 3-7-8 (2*) D G O'Shea (7) .... (16 to 1) 13
2221^8 BLYTHE (Arg) [-] (bl) 3-8-0 N G McCullagh (11) .... (14 to 1) 14
Dist: 5½l, 3½l, 2l, 1l. 1m 39.00s. (14 Ran).
(Ovidstown Investments Ltd), D K Weld

2880 McDonogh Feeds E.B.F. Maiden Fillies Race (2-y-o) £5,522 7f. ..... (8:00)

1022^3 ASTRONAVE (Ire) 9-0 M J Kinane (4) .... (11 to 8 fav) 1
IRRESTIBLE LADY (Ire) 9-0 C Roche (12) .... (3 to 1) 2
ZORINA 9-0 J P Murtagh (9) .... (5 to 2) 3
AXLENO (Ire) 9-0 J F Egan (8) .... (33 to 1) 4
SEANEE SQUAW 9-0 B Coogan (1) .... (20 to 1) 5
FOOLISH FLIGHT (Ire) 9-0 P V Gilson (13) .... (12 to 1) 6
NOREASTER (Ire) 9-0 K J Manning (11) .... (50 to 1) 7
REBEL DANCER (Ire) 9-0 S Craine (7) .... (50 to 1) 8
2742 JENNY JINGLE (Ire) 9-0 R Hughes (2) .... (50 to 1) 9
2666 LOVELY DEISE (Ire) 9-0 D Manning (5) .... (33 to 1) 10
2462^8 OVER THE MAIGUE (Ire) 8-8 (6*) P P Murphy (6) (100 to 1) 11
2188^2 AINE'S PET (Ire) 8-10 (4*) P Carberry (3) .... (10 to 1) 12
Dist: 1½l, 2½l, 2½l, 3½l. 1m 42.10s. (12 Ran).
(Andrea Schiavi), D K Weld

2881 McDonogh Timber Handicap (0-80 3-y-o and up) £3,797 2m. .... (8:35)

1468^3 CLIVEDEN GAIL (Ire) [-] 4-10-0 M J Kinane (9) ...... (3 to 1) 1
2692* ASSERT STAR [-] 3-8-0 (6ex) W J Supple (13) .. (9 to 4 fav) 2
2484^4 ISLAND VISION (Ire) [-] 3-7-4^3 (8*) R T Fitzpatrick (11) (8 to 1) 3
2408^3 MASAI WARRIOR [-] 6-9-10 C F Swan (3) .... (10 to 1) 4
2461^7 ANGAREB (Ire) [-] 4-8-13 P V Gilson (7) .... (14 to 1) 5
1996^5 CORAL SOUND (Ire) [-] 3-7-7 Joanna Morgan (8) .. (12 to 1) 6
1962* MARILYN (Ire) [-] 4-8-12 (6*) J J Behan (12) .... (8 to 1) 7
2557^5 BLUE DIANA (Ire) [-] 3-8-9 J F Egan (10) .... (14 to 1) 8
2186^6 MITAH (Ire) [-] 5-8-13 R Hughes (5) .... (12 to 1) 9
2287 KIDAMIYA (Ire) [-] 3-7-6 (2*) D G O'Shea (1) .... (16 to 1) 10
2512^2 TOP GENERATION [-] 4-7-1 (6*) P P Murphy (2) ... (16 to 1) 11
2222* MIA GEORGINA (Ire) [-] 4-9-0 K J Manning (4) ...... (8 to 1) pu
Dist: 2l, 9l, 2½l, 15l. 4m 4.40s. (12 Ran).
(Inte Thoroughbred Breeders Inc), D K Weld

GOODWOOD (good to soft)
Tuesday July 27th
Going Correction: PLUS 0.45 sec. per fur.

2882 Citroen Xantia Handicap Class D (0-85 3-y-o and up) £8,480 1m. .... (2:30)

2712* COMANCHE COMPANION [61] 3-7-9 (5*) A Garth (17) *made virtually all, clr o'r one furlong out, ran on wl.* .... (5 to 1 fav tchd 6 to 1) 1
2327^7 KINGCHIP BOY [51] (v) 4-7-12 A Tucker (12) *al prmnt, rdn alng 2 fs out, edgd lft und pres ins last, no extr.* .... (25 to 1 op 16 to 1) 2
2198^2 NOBBY BARNES [61] 4-8-8 G Carter (19) *chsd ldrs, rdn to chal 2 fs out, kpt on wl und pres..*(20 to 1 op 14 to 1) 3
2612* DANCING SENSATION (USA) [54] 6-7-10 (5*) D Wright (6) *beh, hdwy wl o'r one furlong out, ran on well.* .... (7 to 1 tchd 8 to 1) 4
2624^3 EDEN'S CLOSE [70] 4-9-3 P Robinson (11) *mid-div, rdn alng 2 fs out, styd on.* .... (25 to 1 op 16 to 1) 5
2489^2 SILVER GROOM (Ire) [54] 3-7-7 N Adams (10) *chsd ldrs, rdn 3 fs out, one pace fnl furlong* ...... (33 to 1 op 20 to 1) 6
2624^4 WHATEVER'S RIGHT (Ire) [55] 4-8-2 D Holland (5) *beh, hdwy o'r 2 fs out, ran on und pres.* ..... (33 to 1 op 20 to 1) 7
2361 VAYAVAIG [79] 3-9-4 W R Swinburn (20) *in tch, effrt 2 fs out, sn no imprsn, eased whn btn cl hme.* .... (16 to 1 tchd 25 to 1) 8
2624* DEEVEE [66] 4-8-13 G Duffield (8) *beh, effrt o'r 2 fs out, nvr on terms.* .... (8 to 1 tchd 9 to 1) 9
2715^6 SAAFEND [72] 5-9-5 L Dettori (15) *trkd ldrs, rdn o'r 2 fs out, sn btn.* .... (11 to 1 op 12 to 1 tchd 10 to 1) 10+
2330^3 TROOPING (Ire) [73] 4-9-6 W Carson (4) *hld up, hrd rdn o'r 2 fs out, sn btn.* .... (12 to 1 tchd 20 to 1) 10+
2577^8 COURT MINSTREL [57] 4-8-4 A Munro (1) *beh, effrt on outsd o'r 2 fs out, no imprsn.* .... (20 to 1 op 16 to 1 tchd 25 to 1) 12
2577^3 TIFFANY'S CASE (Ire) [57] 4-8-4 E Johnson (18) *slwly into strd, al beh.* .... (14 to 1 op 12 to 1 tchd 9 to 1) 13
2391^2 BUZZARDS BELLBUOY [77] (v) 4-9-10 J Quinn (16) *trkd ldrs till wknd o'r one furlong out.* .... (25 to 1 op 16 to 1 tchd 33 to 1) 14
2624 DIVINE BOY [62] 3-8-1 D Biggs (9) *beh, pushed alng 4 fs out, no imprsn.* .... (25 to 1 tchd 33 to 1) 15
2300^6 HOPEFUL BID (Ire) [65] (bl) 4-8-12 J Reid (14) *mid-div, slightly hmpd o'r 4 fs out, sn no imprsn.* .... (16 to 1 op 14 to 1 tchd 20 to 1) 16
2004^6 TAKENHALL [60] 8-8-7 F Norton (13) *al beh.* .... (20 to 1 op 16 to 1) 17
2631^2 SALDA [63] 4-8-10 B Raymond (2) *mid-div, pushed alng o'r 3 fs out, wknd over 2 out.* ...... (33 to 1 op 20 to 1) 18
2612^6 DIGPAST (Ire) [70] 3-8-9 T Quinn (3) *mid-div, rdn 3 fs out, wknd wl o'r one out.* .... (16 to 1 op 14 to 1) 19
2211 FAWZ (Ire) [76] 4-9-9 R Hills (7) *trkd wnr, pushed alng 3 fs out, sn wknd.* .... (25 to 1 op 20 to 1) 20
Dist: 1½l, nk, ½l, nk, hd, 1½l, nk, 1½l, nk, dd-ht. 1m 44.13s. a 6.93s (20 Ran).
SR: 36/29/38/29/44/19/23/38/28/ (Drofmor Racing), T J Naughton

2883 Gordon Stakes Class A (Group 3) (3-y-o) £19,884 1½m. .... (3:10)

1843^2 RIGHT WIN (Ire) 8-10 J Reid (9) *trkd ldrs, led appr 2 fs out, rdn clr ins last.* ....(3 to 1 fav op 5 to 2 tchd 7 to 2) 1
1448 SHAREEK (USA) 8-10 W R Swinburn (5) *set steady pace till hdd hfwy, cl up, ran on wl fnl furlong.* .... (20 to 1) 2
1751* BENEFICIAL 9-1 M Hills (4) *wtd wth in cl tch, closed to hold ev ch 2 fs out, sn one pace.* .... (4 to 1 tchd 9 to 2 and 7 to 2) 3
1751^3 AZZILFI 8-10 W Carson (7) *took keen hold early, cl up, hrd rdn wl o'r one furlong out, not quicken.* .... (9 to 2 op 5 to 1) 4
1749^2 NEEDLE GUN (Ire) 8-10 Pat Eddery (3) *cl up, led hfwy till hdd appr 2 fs out, no extr.* .... (7 to 2 op 5 to 2) 5
1512^4 MAJORITY (Ire) 8-10 D Holland (8) *hld up in tch, rdn 2 fs out, not pace to chal.* (25 to 1 op 20 to 1 tchd 40 to 1) 6
2332^3 PEACHES POLLY 8-7 G Duffield (1) *hld up in tch, outpcd wl o'r 2 fs out, ran on ins last.* .... (50 to 1 op 33 to 1) 7
2360^2 TIOMAN ISLAND 8-10 T Quinn (6) *hld up in tch, pushed alng 3 fs out, btn quickly 2 out.* .... (13 to 2 op 6 to 1 tchd 8 to 1) 8
Dist: 2½l, sht-hd, hd, 3½l, 1½l, 3½l, ¾l. 2m 42.26s. a 9.26s (8 Ran).
SR: 57/52/56/50/43/40/30/31/ (Conal Kavanagh), R Hannon

2884 William Hill Cup Handicap Class B (4-y-o and up) £39,168 1¼m. ..... (3:45)

2367^2 KNOWTH (Ire) [69] 4-7-2 (5*) D Wright (5) *hld up beh, smooth hdwy 3 fs out, rdn to ld ins last, edgd lft, fnshd 1st, plcd second.* .... (16 to 1 tchd 20 to 1) 1D
2433 ROSE ALTO [89] 5-8-13 G Duffield (8) *hld up, hdwy o'r 2 fs out, led over one out, hdd and crrd lft ins last, fnshd second, awarded race.* .... (25 to 1 op 16 to 1) 1
2433^6 SHABANAZ [75] 8-7-8 (5*) Stephen Davies (6) *hld up in mid-div, ran on frm o'r one furlong out, no extr ins last.* .... (11 to 1 op 6 to 1 tchd 12 to 1) 3
2564* PORT SUNLIGHT (Ire) [69] 5-7-7 N Adams (1) *hld up in rear, hdwy o'r 2 fs out, ev ch over one out, one pace entering last.* .... (4 to 1 fav op 6 to 1 tchd 7 to 2) 4
1768 EFHARISTO [88] (v) 4-8-12 B Marcus (13) *trkd ldrs, led 7 fs out till hdd o'r one out, wknd.* .... (20 to 1 op 16 to 1) 5

2581² YILDIZ [71] 4-7-9 W Carson (12) *beh, cld hfwy, rdn alng 3 fs out, sn hrd ridden and no imprsn.* .... (11 to 2 op 6 to 1 tchd 7 to 1) 6
2256² KNOCK KNOCK [80] 8-8-4 L Dettori (4) *beh, hdwy on outsd o'r 2 fs out, wknd one out.* .... (14 to 1 op 12 to 1 tchd 16 to 1) 7
2311² RIVAL BID (USA) [69] 5-7-7 J Quinn (9) *al prmnt, rdn and ev ch o'r 2 fs out, sn btn*............ (25 to 1 tchd 33 to 1) 8
2254² TALENT (USA) [84] (v) 5-8-8 A Munro (10) *led till hdd 7 fs out, cl up till wknd o'r 2 out.* .... (12 to 1 op 10 to 1 tchd 14 to 1) 9
1450 THE POWER OF ONE [70] 4-7-8 A Mackay (11) *chsd ldrs till wknd o'r 2 fs out*................ (50 to 1 tchd 66 to 1) 10
2391 DOUBLE ECHO (Ire) [74] 5-7-12 T Williams (7) *trkd ldrs, effrt o'r 2 fs out, btn quickly*.......(33 to 1 op 25 to 1) 11
2433² KING ATHELSTAN (USA) [92] 5-9-2 B Raymond (3) *trkd ldrs, rdn alng o'r 5 fs out, btn whn squeezed out over 2 out.* ....(5 to 1 op 3 to 1) 12
2376* TAPIS ROUGE (Ire) [104] 4-10-0 (4ex) Pat Eddery (2) *rcd wide, cl up till wknd o'r 4 fs out, tld off.* .... (6 to 1 op 5 to 1 tchd 13 to 2) 13
Dist: ¾l, ¾l, 1½l, 2l, nk, 7l, 1l, 2½l, ¾l, 7l. 2m 12.48s. a 6.98s (13 Ran).
SR: 54/72/56/47/62/44/39/26/36/ (T & J Vestey), J R Fanshawe

2885 Oak Tree Stakes Class A (Listed Race) (3-y-o and up) £13,702 7f (4:15)

2304 MOON OVER MIAMI 3-8-7 J Reid (10) *hld up, hmpd o'r 5 fs out, hdwy wl over one out, ran on to ld ins last, rdn out*.......................(33 to 1 tchd 40 to 1) 1
1174⁶ ARJUZAH (Ire) 3-8-7 W Carson (7) *cl up, led one and a half fs out till hdd ins last, hrd rdn and no extr.* ....(7 to 1 op 6 to 1) 2
1765³ ABBEY'S GAL 3-8-7 L Dettori (8) *chsd ldrs, squeezed out o'r one furlong out, swtchd lft and ran on strly ins last, unlucky*............(11 to 8 fav op 7 to 4 tchd 5 to 4) 3
QUEEN'S VIEW (Fr) 3-8-7 R Cochrane (12) *hld up, hdwy 2 fs out, kpt on one pace*............(7 to 1 tchd 9 to 1) 4
2334⁶ MYSTIC GODDESS (USA) 3-8-7 T Quinn (1) *trkd ldrs, tacked across to stands side entering strt, ev ch 2 fs out, wknd ins last*........ (14 to 1 op 12 to 1 tchd 16 to 1) 5
746² MATILA (Ire) 3-8-7 R Hills (9) *hld up, hdwy o'r 2 fs out, sn ev ch, wknd, better for race.* .... (9 to 1 op 7 to 1 tchd 10 to 1) 6
2304⁶ MARGARET'S GIFT 3-8-7 J Carroll (2) *in tch, pushed alng 2 fs out, rdn and wknd o'r one out.* .... (33 to 1 op 25 to 1 tchd 40 to 1) 7
1978⁴ MAGIQUE ROND POINT (USA) 3-8-7 W Ryan (4) *led till hdd one and a half fs out, wknd*..... (10 to 1 tchd 12 to 1) 8
2304² MITHL AL HAWA 3-8-7 W R Swinburn (3) *trkd ldrs, ev ch 2 fs out, wknd*.......... (6 to 1 op 9 to 2 tchd 13 to 2) 9
2334⁷ TENDER MOMENT (Ire) 5-9-0 B Doyle (6) *beh, pld out and cld 2 fs out, sn btn*..........(33 to 1 tchd 40 to 1) 10
POKER CHIP 3-8-7 M Hills (5) *chsd ldrs till wknd 2 fs out.* .... (10 to 1 tchd 12 to 1 and 14 to 1) 11
Dist: Hd, ½l, 1l, 5l, 1½l, 2l, nk, 3½l, 2l, nk. 1m 30.24s. a 5.64s (11 Ran).
SR: 56/55/53/50/35/30/24/23/12/ (Barry J Ross), C James

2886 Ralph Hubbard Memorial Nursery Handicap Class C (2-y-o) £5,526 5f ....(4:45)

2370* SELHURSTPARK FLYER (Ire) [-] 7-12 W Carson (4) *made all, shaken up o'r one furlong out, ran on wl.* ....(7 to 2 fav tchd 4 to 1) 1
2123* ADMIRALELLA [-] 8-0 (5*) D Wright (8) *slwly into strd, outpcd, rdn and hdwy o'r one furlong out, kpt on wl fnl furlong*..........(14 to 1 op 8 to 1 tchd 16 to 1) 2
2689² BOLD GEM [-] 7-9 (3*) B Doyle (1) *al prmnt, hrd rdn o'r one furlong out, kpt on*... (10 to 1 op 7 to 1 tchd 11 to 1) 3
2364 RAPIER POINT (Ire) [-] 8-10 R Cochrane (12) *strted slwly, beh, rdn alng o'r one furlong out, ran on ins last.* .... (11 to 1 op 10 to 1 tchd 12 to 1) 4
2400⁷ ALLWIGHT THEN (Ire) [-] 8-10 Paul Eddery (3) *trkd wnr gng wl, ev ch o'r one furlong out, sn wknd.* .... (14 to 1 op 12 to 1 tchd 16 to 1) 5
2292⁶ CABCHARGE PRINCESS (Ire) [-] 8-3 P Robinson (6) *chsd ldrs, not clr run and lost pl 2 fs out, shaken up and kpt on ins last*....................... (14 to 1 op 10 to 1) 6
1955* JADE PET [-] 9-7 J Reid (7) *beh, hdwy 2 fs out, wknd one out*..................(14 to 1 op 12 to 1 tchd 16 to 1) 7
2500² COLNE VALLEY [-] (bl) 7-9 J Quinn (10) *rdn and wknd o'r one furlong out*........ (9 to 1 op 7 to 1 tchd 10 to 1) 8
2610* DANCES WITH RISK [-] 7-5 (7*) C Hawksley (9) *prmnt, pushed alng hfwy, wknd entering last.* ....(9 to 2 op 4 to 1 tchd 5 to 1) 9
2292³ MAZEEKA (Ire) [-] 8-13 T Quinn (5) *sn rdn alng, trkd ldrs till wknd 2 fs out*...................(11 to 1 op 7 to 1) 10
2301⁸ WINSOME WOOSTER [-] 9-6 Pat Eddery (2) *chsd ldrs, rdn alng 2 fs out, eased whn btn appr last.* .... (11 to 1 op 8 to 1 tchd 12 to 1) 11
2435³ DANCE OF THE SWANS (Ire) [-] 8-8 Dale Gibson (13) *strted slwly, outpcd*................. (8 to 1 op 10 to 1) 12
Dist: 1½l, nk, 2½l, 1½l, nk, hd, 2½l, sht-hd, 1l, ¾l. 1m 1.82s. a 5.02s (12 Ran).
SR: 29/30/22/24/18/10/27/-/-/ (Chris Deuters), J Berry

2887 EBF New Ham Maiden Fillies Stakes Class D (2-y-o) £5,390 7f........(5:20)

AVERTI (USA) 8-11 Pat Eddery (1) *hld up beh, hdwy on outsd 2 fs out, quickened to ld entering last, rdn out.* ....(9 to 4 fav op 11 to 10 tchd 5 to 2) 1
ARECIBA (USA) 8-11 J Reid (10) *cl up, led 2 fs out till hdd ins last, no extr*.......... (5 to 1 op 5 to 2 tchd 11 to 2) 2
2357² PLACITANA (USA) 8-11 W R Swinburn (3) *mid-div, rdn and hdwy 2 fs out, kpt on wl.* ....(14 to 1 op 16 to 1 tchd 20 to 1 and 25 to 1) 3
1916 LOCHBELLE 8-11 L Dettori (8) *cl up, pushed alng 3 fs out, one pace o'r one out*...............(14 to 1 op 8 to 1) 4
SLIP A COIN 8-11 W Ryan (7) *beh, hdwy o'r one furlong out, styd on, nrst finish*............(50 to 1 op 33 to 1) 5
1142³ DIAMOND PARK (Ire) 8-11 B Raymond (2) *beh, hdwy o'r one furlong out, styd on nrst finish.* .... (10 to 1 tchd 12 to 1 and 14 to 1) 6
2492² BRIERLEY 8-11 W Newnes (12) *sn led, hdd 2 fs out, wknd.* .... (33 to 1 op 20 to 1 tchd 50 to 1) 7
BALMAHA 8-11 M Hills (11) *chsd ldrs till wknd 2 fs out.* .... (50 to 1 op 25 to 1 tchd 66 to 1) 8
BERMUDA LADY (USA) 8-11 Paul Eddery (6) *strted slwly, al beh*................ (33 to 1 op 25 to 1 tchd 50 to 1) 9
2067⁴ NORFOLK LAVENDER (Can) 8-11 A Munro (5) *cl up till wknd quickly 2 fs out*... (3 to 1 op 7 to 1 tchd 8 to 1) 10
AZHAAR (USA) 8-11 W Carson (4) *broke wl, chsd ldrs, rdn o'r 3 fs out, sn btn*.....(10 to 1 op 8 to 1 tchd 12 to 1) 11
CINDY'S STAR (Ire) 8-11 D Holland (9) *trkd ldrs, effrt 3 fs out, sn wknd*....... (50 to 1 op 33 to 1 tchd 66 to 1) 12
Dist: ¾l, hd, 3l, 5l, nk, 1½l, ¾l, 1½l, nk, hd. 1m 31.83s. a 7.23s (12 Ran).
SR: 36/34/33/24/9/8/3/1/-/ (K Abdulla), H R A Cecil

CATTERICK (good to firm)
Wednesday July 28th
Going Correction: MINUS 0.20 sec. per fur. (races 1,2,3,4,5), MINUS 0.05 (6)

2888 Courage Top Selling Stakes Class G (3,4,5-y-o) £2,343 1m 5f 175yds..(2:20)

2443* HO-JOE (Ire) 3-8-10 Julie Bowker (5) *made all, clr o'r one out, hld on wl fnl furlong*........... (7 to 4 op 5 to 4) 1
2800* REEL OF TULLOCH (Ire) 4-9-10 K Darley (1) *chsd wnr till outpcd o'r 3 out, kpt on und pres fnl 2 fs.* ....(11 to 8 fav op 6 to 4 tchd 7 to 4) 2
2658³ GAY MING 4-9-0 (5*) A Garth (4) *hld up, pushed alng 4 fs out, kpt on fnl 2 furlongs, nrst finish.* ....(7 to 1 op 6 to 1) 3
2585³ ANAR (Ire) 4-9-5 (5*) O Pears (2) *prmnt, chlgd o'r 2 fs out, sn rdn and btn*...................(11 to 2 op 4 to 1) 4
2763³ MYNYOSS 3-8-10 G Carter (3) *in tch till outpcd 5 fs out, tld off*.............................(25 to 1 op 20 to 1) 5
Dist: ¾l, ½l, ¾l, 30l. 3m 7.20s. a 11.70s (5 Ran).
(S Ho), J M Carr

2889 Group 4 Handicap Class E (0-70 3-y-o and up) £2,950 7f..............(2:50)

2832³ NORTH ARDAR [58] 3-9-3 T Williams (4) *chsd ldrs, effrt o'r 2 fs out, led entering fnl furlong, kpt on wl.* .... (3 to 1 fav tchd 7 to 2) 1
2593² MANX MONARCH [49] 3-8-3 (5*) A Garth (6) *beh, hdwy o'r 2 fs out, rdn over one out, styd on, nrst finish.* ....(4 to 1 tchd 9 to 2) 2
2165³ SENSE OF PRIORITY [62] 4-10-0 K Darley (7) *chsd ldr o'r 2 fs out, hdd entering fnl furlong, no extr.* .... (5 to 1 op 4 to 1 tchd 6 to 1) 3
2454² ROSE GEM (Ire) [56] 4-9-3 (5*) O Pears (3) *led till hdd o'r 2 out, kpt on same pace fnl furlong*....(5 to 1 op 4 to 1) 4
590* CICERONE [64] 3-9-9 G Hind (5) *in tch, no hdwy fnl 2 fs.* ....(8 to 1 op 6 to 1) 5
2444⁵ FALCONS DAWN [40] (v) 6-8-6 J Lowe (2) *al beh.* ....(7 to 1 tchd 9 to 1) 6
2707⁸ CLEDESCHAMPS [44] 4-8-10 S Morris (1) *beh frm hfwy, tld off*............. (14 to 1 op 12 to 1 tchd 16 to 1) 7
Dist: 2½l, 1l, 1½l, 1½l, 2½l, 20l. 1m 25.90s. a 2.90s (7 Ran).
SR: 39/22/39/28/24/-/-/ (L Webster), M Johnston

2890 BT Emergency Planning Conditions Stakes Class D (2-y-o) £3,348 7f (3:25)

2389³ SAIHAT (Ire) 9-1 B Raymond (3) *trkd ldr, pushed alng 3 out, led ins fnl furlong, all out.* .... (6 to 5 fav op Evens tchd 5 to 4) 1
2505* NEW INN 8-11 J Fanning (2) *in tch, effrt o'r 2 fs out, ev ch ins last, no extr cl hme.* (9 to 1 op 7 to 1 tchd 10 to 1) 2
1897* SECRET SERENADE 8-13 K Darley (1) *slwly into strd, beh, hdwy o'r 2 out, slightly hmpd over one out, kpt on wl towards finish*......... (5 to 1 op 4 to 1 tchd 11 to 2) 3
1565⁵ TOP SHOW (Ire) 8-12 (3*) J Weaver (6) *led till hdd ins fnl furlong, no extr*................... (50 to 1 op 20 to 1) 4
2058³ MOSAIC GOLD 9-1 N Connorton (4) *trkd ldrs, effrt o'r 2 fs out, edgd rght over one out, swtchd jst ins fnl furlong, kpt on same pace*.................. (5 to 1 tchd 9 to 2) 5

2595* POTSCLOSE 8-10 T Williams (5) *in tch till wknd o'r 2 fs out*..................................(5 to 1 op 9 to 2) 6
Dist: Hd, nk, 1½l, sht-hd, 8l. 1m 26.10s. a 3.10s (6 Ran).
SR: 34/29/30/27/26/-/ (Prince A A Faisal), Mrs J Cecil

2891 Serco Limited Invitation Handicap Class D (0-80 3-y-o and up) £3,703 1m 5f 175yds......................(4:00)

2043⁷ BOLD AMBITION [41] (v) 6-7-7 J Lowe (3) *trkd ldr, quickened to ld 2 fs out, styd on wl und pres.* ....(11 to 2 op 3 to 1) 1
2694* POST IMPRESSIONIST (Ire) [51] 4-8-3 (4ex) K Darley (1) *led till hdd 2 fs out, styd on wl und pres.* ....(5 to 2 tchd 3 to 1) 2
2397² OUR AISLING [76] 5-9-9 (5*) O Pears (2) *hld up in tch, effrt 2 fs out, sn rdn and no imprsn.* ....(13 to 8 on tchd 7 to 4 on) 3
Dist: Nk, 2½l. 3m 13.00s. a 17.50s (3 Ran).
(T Kersey), T Kersey

2892 Wots In Store Claiming Stakes Class F (3-y-o and up) £2,709 7f.........(4:30)

2639* SIZZLING SAGA (Ire) 5-9-9 K Darley (1) *chsd ldrs, led o'r one furlong out, ran on wl.* (5 to 2 on tchd 9 to 4 on) 1
2651² PALACEGATE TOUCH (v) 3-8-13 G Carter (2) *led till hdd o'r one furlong out, kpt on same pace.* (7 to 2 op 11 to 4) 2
2568⁴ OBSIDIAN GREY 6-8-9 (5*) O Pears (6) *chsd ldrs, outpcd o'r 2 fs out, no dngr aftr.* ....(10 to 1 op 9 to 1 tchd 11 to 1) 3
DO TELL 3-8-4² (3*) S D Williams (4) *beh, some late hdwy und pres, nvr dngrs.*..........................(100 to 1) 4
NOT EARSAY 3-7-7 J Fanning (5) *cl up till wknd o'r 2 fs out*..................................(33 to 1 op 25 to 1) 5
Dist: 1l, 4l, 1l, 6l. 1m 25.40s. a 2.40s (5 Ran).
SR: 52/39/28/16/-/ (J David Abell), J Wharton

2893 Northern Upholstery Maiden Handicap Class E (0-70 3-y-o and up) £2,847 5f..................................(5:00)

2760³ GUSSIE FINK-NOTTLE (Ire) [57] (bl) 3-9-10 K Darley (2) *trkd ldr, led hfwy, pushed out*.... (11 to 10 fav tchd 6 to 5) 1
2699² CLOUDY REEF [49] 3-8-9 (7*) M Humphries (3) *in tch, sn pushed alng, chsd wnr fnl 2 fs, no imprsn*...... (5 to 4) 2
2760⁶ ROYAL MUSIC [50] (bl) 3-9-3 G Carter (1) *led to hfwy, sn wknd*.................. (6 to 1 op 11 to 2 tchd 7 to 1) 3
Dist: 3½l, 6l. 1m 0.70s. a 3.20s (3 Ran).
SR: 41/19/-/ (Mrs S Sturman), T D Barron

EPSOM (good)
Wednesday July 28th
Going Correction: MINUS 0.40 sec. per fur.

2894 Warren Apprentice Handicap Class E (0-75 4-y-o and up) £3,752 1¼m 18yds..................................(6:10)

2348* MR TATE (Ire) [66] 4-9-0 (5*) L Carter (4) *trkd ldrs, 3rd strt, effrt o'r 2 fs out, rdn and edgd lft ins last, led nr finish.* ....(15 to 8 fav op 7 to 4) 1
2641* MISTY GODDESS (Ire) [58] 5-8-11 K Rutter (2) *wtd wth, 5th strt, pushed alng and prog to ld 2 fs out, ran on, hdd nr finish*..................................(2 to 1 tchd 7 to 4) 2
2685⁴ GILBERT'S GIRL [40] 6-7-4 (3*) N Varley (3) *led till rdn and hdd 2 fs out, ev ch one out, btn whn hmpd ins last.* ....(11 to 1 op 8 to 1 tchd 12 to 1) 3
1974⁶ SONG OF SIXPENCE (USA) [75] 9-9-7 (7*) C Scudder (6) *hld up, 6th strt, no imprsn on ldrs fnl 2 fs.* ....(13 to 2 op 6 to 1 tchd 8 to 1) 4
SAKIL (Ire) [42] 5-7-9⁶ (5*) A Martinez (1) *drpd beh hfwy, last strt, ran on ins fnl furlong, nvr dngrs.* ....(33 to 1 op 20 to 1) 5
2564⁶ THIMBALINA [40] 7-7-2 (5*) Sharon Millard (7) *sddl slpd sn aftr strt, trkd ldr after 3 fs till wknd wl o'r 2 out.* ....(20 to 1 op 12 to 1) 6
2490³ ALBERT [47] 6-8-0 J Tate (5) *trkd ldr 3 fs, 4th strt, sn lost pl*..................................(11 to 2 op 4 to 1) 7
Dist: Hd, 2½l, 4l, sht-hd, 2½l, ¾l. 2m 11.54s. a 7.24s (7 Ran).
(John Falvey), R Akehurst

2895 EBF Walton Median Auction Maiden Fillies Stakes Class D (2-y-o) £3,590 6f..................................(6:40)

2575³ LITTLE BEAUT 8-11 W Woods (1) *trkd ldrs on ins, swtchd 2 fs out, ran on wl to ld inside last, cmftbly.* ....(11 to 4 op 7 to 4 tchd 3 to 1) 1
GOOD FETCH 8-11 T Quinn (3) *pressed ldr, rdn to ld appr fnl furlong, hdd and no extr ins last.* (6 to 1 op 4 to 1) 2
2336⁷ RAJMAPATA 8-11 Pat Eddery (2) *led till rdn and hdd o'r one furlong out, not quicken.* ....(6 to 4 fav op 7 to 4 tchd 2 to 1) 3
2357⁷ LADY PHYL 8-8 (3*) B Doyle (5) *cl up, ran wide entering strt, rdn and one pace fnl 2 fs.* ....(12 to 1 op 10 to 1 tchd 14 to 1) 4
2668⁶ CHARISMA GIRL 8-11 Dean McKeown (9) *chsd ldrs, ran wide entering strt, sn no prog.* ....(40 to 1 op 33 to 1 tchd 50 to 1) 5
2492⁵ ZUNO NOELYN 8-11 Paul Eddery (4) *cl up, ran wide entering strt, rdn and wknd appr fnl furlong.* ....(13 to 2 op 6 to 1 tchd 7 to 1) 6
INFRA BLUE (Ire) 8-11 B Marcus (7) *outpcd.* ....(16 to 1 op 10 to 1) 7
Dist: 1½l, 2l, 2l, 2l, 2l, 2½l. 1m 10.43s. a 2.53s (7 Ran).
(Victor Sujanani), S P C Woods

2896 Olympic Handicap Class D (0-80 3-y-o and up) £4,624 5f...............(7:10)

2305⁶ ALLTHRUTHENIGHT (Ire) [75] 4-9-10 J Reid (2) *hld up, prog hfwy, hrd rdn to ld ins fnl furlong, ran on wl.* ....(6 to 1 op 5 to 1) 1
2392⁶ LITTLE SABOTEUR [68] 4-9-3 Pat Eddery (3) *al prmnt, hrd rdn and ev ch ins fnl furlong, ran on one pace.* ....(4 to 1 op 7 to 2 tchd 9 to 2) 2
2018 ANOTHER EPISODE (Ire) [74] 4-9-2 (7*) P Roberts (1) *led till ins fnl furlong, no extr.* (13 to 2 op 7 to 1 tchd 8 to 1) 3
2688² SPLASH OF SALT (Ire) [65] 3-8-9 D Holland (6) *sn beh, rdn o'r 2 fs out, ran on strly ins last, nrst finish.* ....(5 to 1 tchd 11 to 2) 4
2671 SHADES OF JADE [44] 5-7-7 G Bardwell (7) *wth ldr till rdn and one pace fnl 2 fs*.............. (20 to 1 op 14 to 1) 5
2788³ SKI CAPTAIN [47] 9-7-10 D Biggs (4) *sn outpcd and rdn alng, nvr dngrs*.................. (14 to 1 op 10 to 1) 6
2549* UMBRIA [50] 4-7-13 S Dawson (5) *dwlt, last and sn rdn alng, nvr rch ldrs*...(13 to 8 fav op 5 to 4 tchd 7 to 4) 7
2846⁶ STOCKTINA [44] 6-7-7 N Carlisle (8) *prmnt, rdn and wknd hfwy*..................................(25 to 1 op 16 to 1) 8
Dist: 1l, sht-hd, nk, 1½l, ¾l, nk, 2l. 55.54s. a 0.84s (8 Ran).
SR: 53/42/47/32/10/10/12/-/ (G Steinberg), L J Holt

2897 Ring & Brymer Handicap Class E (0-70 3-y-o and up) £4,737 7f......... (7:40)

1821⁴ MR NEVERMIND (Ire) [60] 3-9-1 B Rouse (3) *trkd ldrs gng easily, led 2 fs out, sn clr, rdn out.* ....(9 to 1 op 10 to 1 tchd 12 to 1) 1
2163⁸ NITOUCHE [64] 3-9-0 (5*) J Tate (10) *sn rdn alng, mid-div till ran on fnl 2 fs, no ch wth wnr.* ....(12 to 1 op 10 to 1 tchd 14 to 1) 2
2747* YONGE TENDER [43] (bl) 6-8-2 (3*,6ex) D Harrison (5) *rear, rdn o'r 2 fs out, ran on appr last, nvr nrr.* ....(8 to 1 op 6 to 1) 3
2639³ RESOLUTE BAY [65] (v) 7-9-13 J Reid (6) *beh, brght wide and ran on fnl 2 fs, nvr dngrs*........(8 to 1 op 9 to 1) 4
2396⁵ TYRIAN PURPLE (Ire) [61] 5-9-6 (3*) B Doyle (9) *chsd ldrs, rdn and one pace fnl 2 fs*.........(7 to 1 tchd 8 to 1) 5
2491² ANATROCCOLO [38] 6-8-0 N Carlisle (7) *prmnt, rdn o'r 2 fs out, wknd ins last*..................(12 to 1 op 8 to 1) 6
2548⁹ ZINBAQ [37] 7-7-13 S Dawson (15) *mid-div, effrt 3 fs out, sn no imprsn*..........................(10 to 1 op 8 to 1) 7
1927⁷ GREEN'S FAIR (Ire) [67] (v) 3-9-8 M Hills (4) *led to 2 fs out, wknd*..................................(10 to 1 op 8 to 1) 8
2811⁵ PENNY BANGER (Ire) [59] 3-9-0 Dean McKeown (2) *last till some hdwy fnl 2 fs, nvr nr to chal*.............(8 to 1) 9
2548³ PALACEGATE GOLD (Ire) [56] 4-9-4 Pat Eddery (1) *hld up in tch, rdn and no prog o'r 2 fs out.* ....(11 to 2 fav tchd 6 to 1) 10
2577 UNIFICATION (Ire) [46] 4-8-8 T Quinn (12) *mid-div till rdn and wknd o'r 2 fs out.* ....(11 to 1 op 10 to 1 tchd 12 to 1) 11
2686³ VILLAVINA [67] 3-9-8 Paul Eddery (13) *al wl in rear.* ....(10 to 1 op 8 to 1) 12
2532⁶ HONEY VISION [36] (bl) 4-7-12 G Bardwell (11) *chsd ldrs, hrd rdn and wknd 3 fs out*........ (33 to 1 op 16 to 1) 13
Dist: 2l, 1½l, ½l, 1½l, 1l, 1l, hd, ½l, 2l, 2l. 1m 21.91s. a 1.51s (13 Ran).
SR: 36/34/15/35/26/-/-/18/8/ (K Higson), G L Moore

2898 LBC Newstalk 97.3 FM Claiming Stakes Class G (3-y-o) £2,950 1m 114yds.......................... (8:10)

2726* FORMAL AFFAIR 8-1 (7*) J D Smith (1) *al prmnt, pushed alng 2 fs out, ran on strly ins last to ld nr finish.* ....(11 to 2 op 4 to 1) 1
2726² FANFOLD (Ire) 8-4 T Quinn (12) *prmnt, rdn to ld o'r one furlong out, ran on, hdd nr finish.* ....(5 to 1 op 9 to 2 tchd 11 to 2) 2
2726⁴ STEVIE'S WONDER (Ire) 8-4 (5*) N Gwilliams (6) *pressed ldr, led 2 fs out, hdd and one pace appr last.* ....(25 to 1 op 20 to 1) 3
2578² STRIKE-A-POSE 7-13 (3*) D Harrison (3) *chsd ldrs, rdn and prog o'r 2 fs out, styd on one pace appr last.* ....(5 to 1 op 4 to 1 tchd 11 to 2) 4
2670 DEVILRY (bl) 8-13 Paul Eddery (4) *mid-div, rdn and prog 3 furlong out, staying on but btn whn not clr run appr last*..........................(3 to 1 jt-fav op 5 to 1 tchd 6 to 1) 5
2724* NOEPROB (USA) 8-6 Pat Eddery (2) *led to 2 fs out, wknd.* ....(13 to 2 op 7 to 1 tchd 6 to 1 and 15 to 2) 6

2499⁶ FILOU FILANT (Fr) 8-4 (3*) B Doyle (7) *chsd ldrs, rdn and hng rght strt, sn btn*............ (20 to 1 op 12 to 1) 7
2499 LITTLE OSBORNE (Ire) 8-4 M Hills (5) *al beh*. .... (25 to 1 op 16 to 1) 8
2578* WATER GYPSY 9-2 D Holland (8) *chsd ldrs till rdn and wknd 3 fs out*.............. (3 to 1 jt-fav tchd 7 to 2) 9
1817 DOUBLE DEALING (Ire) (bl) 8-5 A Tucker (10) *strted slwly, al beh*................................ (33 to 1 op 20 to 1) 10
2410⁷ HOME SAFE 9-3 Dean McKeown (11) *strted slwly, al beh*. .... (33 to 1 op 20 to 1) 11
2712 RISK PROOF 8-5 D Biggs (9) *sn rdn alng, al beh*. .... (33 to 1 op 25 to 1) 12

Dist: ½l, 1½l, ½l, 2l, 3½l, 1l, 8l, ¾l, ¾l, 12l. 1m 43.74s. a 1.74s (12 Ran).
SR: 17/11/11/2/7/-/ (R M Cyzer), C A Cyzer

2899 Lonsdale Limited Stakes Class F (0-65 3-y-o and up) £2,950 1¼m 18yds (8:40)

2685* BOBBYSOXER 3-8-6 Pat Eddery (4) *hld up, effrt 3 fs out, hrd rdn ins fnl furlong to ld last strd*. ....(7 to 4 fav op 6 to 4 tchd 2 to 1) 1
2696* SHIRLEY ROSE 3-8-6 Dean McKeown (1) *led, rdn 2 fs out, ran on, hdd last strd*.................. (9 to 4 op 7 to 4) 2
2561⁵ MR COPYFORCE 3-8-11 W Newnes (3) *trkd ldr, rdn 3 fs out, ev ch appr last, one pace*...... (7 to 2 tchd 4 to 1) 3
2207⁴ SILKY HEIGHTS (Ire) 3-8-6 J Reid (2) *trkd ldrs, rdn and not quicken appr fnl furlong*. ....(7 to 2 op 4 to 1 tchd 3 to 1) 4

Dist: Sht-hd, 3½l, 2l. 2m 7.11s. a 2.81s (4 Ran).
SR: 24/23/21/12/ (P G Goulandris), J L Dunlop

GALWAY (IRE) (yielding)
Wednesday July 28th

2900 Digital DECnet Handicap (0-75 4-y-o and up) £4,140 2m..............(3:00)

4685a⁸ LOSHIAN (Ire) [-] 4-9-8 J P Murtagh (9)........ (9 to 4 fav) 1
1622⁵ NORDIC RACE [-] 6-8-11 S Craine (5)............(12 to 1) 2
1986³ DANCE OF WORDS (Ire) [-] 4-8-13 J F Egan (1)... (10 to 1) 3
2498⁴ TIME IS UP (Ire) [-] 4-8-9 (4*) W J Smith (7)....... (14 to 1) 4
1794⁸ OPEN MARKET (USA) [-] 4-10-0 M J Kinane (8).... (5 to 1) 5
2498* STEEL MIRROR [-] 4-8-13 (5ex) P V Gilson (6)......(4 to 1) 6
852⁶ AEGEAN FANFARE (Ire) [-] 4-9-3 R Hughes (10)... (10 to 1) 7
2664⁵ BEAU BEAUCHAMP [-] 6-9-1 (4*) P Carberry (4)....(7 to 2) 8
KLICKITAT [-] (bl) 6-7-5 (2*) D G O'Shea (2)....... (16 to 1) 9

Dist: 7l, 6l, hd, ½l. 3m 43.80s. (Flag start) (9 Ran).
(Mrs Anna Foxe), A P O'Brien

2901 Digital All-In-1 Handicap (0-70 3-y-o and up) £4,140 1m 100yds...... (4:25)

2321* MEJEVE [-] 5-10-0 S Craine (15)...............(12 to 1) 1
981² PHASE IN [-] 3-9-1 M J Kinane (7)............. (9 to 4 fav) 2
2321 BOB'S GIRL (Ire) [-] 4-7-7⁴ (6*) J J Behan (9)..... (25 to 1) 3
2094 SPRING RITE [-] (bl) 6-7-1 (6*) P P Murphy (2).....(33 to 1) 4
2141* LORD GLENVARA (Ire) [-] 5-9-2 W J Supple (17)....(5 to 1) 5
2484 BOLERO DANCER (Ire) [-] 5-8-8 L O'Shea (14)..... (20 to 1) 6
2664² SOLAR FLASH (Ire) [-] 4-7-9 (2*) D G O'Shea (4)....(10 to 1) 7
2322³ ALBERTA ROSE (Ire) [-] 4-9-6 (6*) J R Barry (3).... (11 to 2) 8
2692⁴ MORNING NURSE (Ire) [-] 4-9-3 K J Manning (10) (14 to 1) 9
2676³ SACULORE (Ire) [-] 5-9-10 N G McCullagh (8).....(14 to 1) 10
2452² WHAT MAGIC (Ire) [-] 3-9-2 (4*) W J Smith (12)..... (9 to 1) 11
ZORIA (Ire) [-] 5-9-0 (4*) P Carberry (16)........ (12 to 1) 12
2556⁴ TOUCHDOWN [-] 6-9-6 R Hughes (6)............. (6 to 1) 13
2184 DONTKISSTHEJOCKEY (Ire) [-] 3-7-7 Joanna Morgan (5) ....(20 to 1) 14
2664⁷ TRES JOUR (Ire) [-] (bl) 3-8-7 P Shanahan (11).... (20 to 1) 15

Dist: 1l, 1l, sht-hd, ½l. 1m 52.00s. (15 Ran).
(Mrs M Cahill), B V Kelly

2902 Digital Decstation Maiden (Q.R) (3-y-o and up) £4,140 1½m...........(5:00)

2287⁶ LUSTRINO (USA) (bl) 3-10-6 (5*) Mr J A Nash (2).... (9 to 2) 1
2518² NO DUNCE (Ire) 3-10-3 (5*) Mrs S McCarthy (7).... (9 to 2) 2
2249⁹ KEPPOLS HARRIER (Ire) 3-10-4 (7*) Mr B Foster (9) (33 to 1) 3
CHANCERY QUEEN (Ire) 4-11-6 Mr A P O'Brien (16) ....(5 to 2 fav) 4
SPLENDID KING (Ire) 3-10-4 (7*) Mr S P Hennessy (1) ....(12 to 1) 5
2287 DANCING VISION (Ire) 3-10-4 (7*) Mr G P FitzGerald (4) ....(33 to 1) 6
2609⁹ DANAMORE (Ire) 3-10-4 (7*) Mr K Whelan (14)..... (16 to 1) 7
SWALLOWS NEST 6-11-2 (7*) Mr D A Harney (12) (16 to 1) 8
1756² SIR SOOJE (Ire) 4-11-9 Mr P Fenton (15).......... (10 to 1) 9
2691⁷ VERIFIED (Ire) 3-10-1 (7*) Mr G R Ryan (6)........ (16 to 1) 10
941⁸ L'EQUIPE (Ire) 3-10-8 (3*) Mr D Marname (13)...... (7 to 2) 11
282 GOLDEN SPHINX (Ire) 3-10-1 (7*) Miss W Fox (3)..(50 to 1) 12
2094 CAT FIGHT 6-10-13 (7*) Mr A Daly (8)............ (66 to 1) 13
2674⁷ OMESMACJOY (Ire) 3-10-4 (7*) Mr P A Roche (5)..(25 to 1) 14
RISKY GALORE 3-10-4 (7*) Miss F M Crowley (10) (12 to 1) 15

Dist: 8l, hd, nk, 1l. 2m 47.40s. (15 Ran).
(Mrs Michael Watt), D K Weld

2903 Digital Alpha Maiden (3-y-o and up) £4,140 1m 100yds.............. (5:30)

LOUGHMOGUE (Ire) 3-8-11 J P Murtagh (5)...... (10 to 1) 1
2877³ BOTHSIDESNOW (Ire) 3-9-0 R Hughes (2)..........(7 to 2) 2
2185³ SHEER OPULANCE (Ire) 3-9-0 M J Kinane (3)...(Evens fav) 3
2516² HERMES GOLD (Ire) 3-8-11 W J Supple (6)........ (9 to 1) 4
2703⁸ ICEFLOW (Fr) (bl) 3-8-11 P V Gilson (4)...........(14 to 1) 5
2743² MY KERRY DANCER (USA) 3-9-0 S Craine (7)..... (9 to 4) 6
2743⁸ LADYS BID (Ire) 3-8-11 J F Egan (1)............ (33 to 1) 7

Dist: 1l, 1½l, ¾l, 4l. 1m 52.80s. (7 Ran).
(Mrs H McParland), F Flood

GOODWOOD (good to soft)
Wednesday July 28th

Going Correction: PLUS 0.25 sec. per fur. (races 1,2,4), PLUS 0.15 (3,5,6)

2904 Country Club Hotels Goodwood Handicap Class C (0-90 3-y-o and up) £10,672 2½m.................. (2:30)

2655² AAHSAYLAD [75] (bl) 7-9-8 J Williams (4) *hld up rear, pushed alng and ran on 3 fs out, hrd rdn to ld ins last*. .... (4 to 1 jt-fav tchd 9 to 2) 1
2251² GREEN LANE (USA) [70] 5-9-3 T Quinn (1) *handily plcd, hrd rdn to ld o'r one furlong out, hdd and one pace ins last*.................. (9 to 2 tchd 5 to 1 and 4 to 1) 2
2617⁶ WESTERN DYNASTY [72] 7-8-12 (7*) P McCabe (2) *wl plcd, chsd ldr o'r 6 fs out, led over 2 out till over one out, sn btn*................ (16 to 1 op 14 to 1 tchd 20 to 1) 3
2397* MISS PLUM [81] 4-10-0 L Dettori (8) *hld up rear, prog 4 fs out, rdn 3 out, wknd o'r one out*............(4 to 1 jt-fav tchd 9 to 2) 4
2204² CHIEF MINISTER (Ire) [72] (v) 4-9-5 K Fallon (10) *hld up, hdwy o'r 4 fs out, wknd 3 out*..... (5 to 1 tchd 11 to 2) 5
2415⁵ TOUCHING TIMES [46] 5-7-7 N Carlisle (6) *led aftr one furlong, clr after 5 fs, wknd and hdd o'r 2 out*. ....(16 to 1 tchd 20 to 1) 6
2755³ CHAKALAK [70] 5-9-3 L Piggott (7) *mid-div, rdn alng and wknd one m out, tld off*. .... (13 to 2 op 8 to 1 tchd 9 to 1) 7
1864³ ALYDUNCAN (USA) [72] 3-8-0 W Carson (5) *led one furlong, chsd ldr till o'r 6 out, sn wknd*. .... (10 to 1 op 7 to 1) 8
2662⁷ PATROCLUS [47] 8-7-8¹ S Dawson (9) *settled rear, lost tch 7 fs out, tld off*...... (40 to 1 op 25 to 1 tchd 50 to 1) 9

Dist: 1½l, 4l, 10l, 12l, 1½l, 20l, 12l, ½l. 4m 25.57s. a 11.57s (Flag start) (9 Ran).
SR: 42/35/33/32/11/-/ (Ms M Horan), J White

2905 Sussex Stakes Class A (Group 1) (3-y-o and up) £79,700 1m......... (3:10)

2081² BIGSTONE (Ire) 3-8-13 D Boeuf (5) *mid-div, not clr run o'r 2 fs out, led over one out, wndrd lft und pres last 100 yards*...............(14 to 1 op 12 to 1 tchd 16 to 1) 1
749* SAYYEDATI 3-8-10 W R Swinburn (9) *hld up rear, swtchd lft 2 fs out, ran on fnl furlong, not quicken nr finish*. .... (11 to 1 op 8 to 1) 2
2068* INCHINOR 3-8-13 L Dettori (3) *mid-div, pushed alng o'r 2 fs out, ev ch over one out, no extr*....(5 to 1 op 6 to 1) 3
2334³ CULTURE VULTURE (USA) 4-9-4 T Quinn (4) *hdwy frm rear 3 fs out, ev ch o'r one out, ran on one pace*. .... (28 to 1 op 25 to 1 tchd 33 to 1) 4
2436 ALHIJAZ 4-9-7 W Carson (2) *settled mid-div, pushed alng o'r 2 fs out, one pace appr last*... (20 to 1 tchd 33 to 1) 5
2074 ALFLORA (Ire) 4-9-7 B Marcus (8) *ldg grp, led briefly wl o'r one furlong out, wknd ins last*. .... (16 to 1 op 14 to 1 tchd 20 to 1) 6
794* ZAFONIC (USA) 3-8-13 Pat Eddery (10) *hld up towards rear, pushed alng hfwy, effrt and rdn o'r 2 fs out, no imprsn on ldrs*.....(6 to 5 on op 5 to 4 on tchd Evens) 7
954⁹ TINNERS WAY (USA) 3-8-13 Paul Eddery (1) *led till wl o'r one furlong out, lost pl quickly*....(66 to 1 op 33 to 1) 8
1765* ARDKINGLASS 3-8-13 W Ryan (6) *trkd ldrs till wknd o'r one furlong out*...... (12 to 1 op 8 to 1 tchd 14 to 1) 9
2068³ INNER CITY (Ire) 4-9-7 R Cochrane (7) *hld up rear, rdn and wknd o'r 2 fs out, sn lost tch*. .... (11 to 1 op 8 to 1 tchd 12 to 1) 10

Dist: 1½l, 2½l, 1½l, ½l, ¾l, 1½l, 5l, hd, 12l. 1m 40.19s. a 2.99s (10 Ran).
SR: 84/76/71/71/72/70/57/42/41/ (Daniel Wildenstein), E Lellouche

2906 Richmond Stakes Class A (Group 2) (2-y-o) £29,005 6f..............(3:45)

2335* FIRST TRUMP 8-11 M Hills (1) *rcd in 3rd pl, led o'r 2 fs out, rdn over one out, drvn out*. .... (100 to 30 op 2 to 1 tchd 7 to 2) 1
1750* STONEHATCH (USA) 8-11 J Reid (5) *cld on ldr 2 fs out, ev ch, rdn and not quicken wl ins last*. .... (13 to 8 on op 11 to 8 on tchd 5 to 4 on) 2
2260² FUMO DI LONDRA (Ire) 8-11 W Carson (2) *pld hrd, led aftr one furlong till o'r 2 out, outpcd ins last*. .... (10 to 1 op 14 to 1 tchd 16 to 1) 3

2359[3] GOVERNOR GEORGE (USA) 8-11 L Dettori (3) *slwly into strd, rdn alng hfwy, nvr rch ldrs.* ....(10 to 1 op 7 to 1 tchd 11 to 1) 4
2209[2] BRAILLE (Ire) 8-11 Dean McKeown (4) *led one furlong, wth ldr till rdn and wknd 2 out.* ....(20 to 1 op 25 to 1 tchd 16 to 1) 5
Dist: ½l, 5l, 3l, ¾l. 1m 12.69s. a 2.29s (5 Ran).
SR: 69/67/47/35/32/ (Mollers Racing), G Wragg

2907 Tote Gold Trophy Handicap Class B (0-105 3-y-o) £33,630 1½m..... (4:15)

2211[3] DANA SPRINGS (Ire) [89] 8-11 L Dettori (14) *in tch, not much room o'r 2 fs out, sstnd run und pres to ld nr line.* ....(10 to 1 op 8 to 1 tchd 12 to 1) 1
2333[6] SPIN DOCTOR (Ire) [88] 8-10 R Cochrane (2) *hld up rear, ran on o'r 2 fs out, led ins last, hdd nr line.* ....(16 to 1 op 14 to 1 tchd 20 to 1) 2
1904[2] GONE FOR A BURTON (Ire) [88] 8-10 L Piggott (6) *hld up rear, cld on ldrs frm 2 fs out, ev ch ins last, no extr close hme*..............(14 to 1 tchd 16 to 1 and 12 to 1) 3
2333[2] SEREN QUEST [84] 8-6 T Quinn (12) *hld up, prog o'r 2 fs out, led over one out till wknd and not much room ins last*....................(15 to 2 op 7 to 1 tchd 8 to 1) 4
2617[3] LEAGUE LEADER (Ire) [85] 8-7 C Asmussen (17) *mid-div, rdn and not quicken o'r 2 fs out, styd on fnl furlong.* ....(10 to 1 tchd 12 to 1) 5
2174[3] EDBAYSAAN (Ire) [92] 9-0 W Ryan (8) *in tch, not much room o'r 2 fs out, not quicken over one out.* ....(11 to 1 op 12 to 1 tchd 14 to 1 and 10 to 1) 6
2135[4] SATIN DANCER [83] (bl) 8-5 M Hills (15) *hdwy and not much room o'r 2 fs out, effrt over one out, not rch frnt rnk*....................(25 to 1 tchd 33 to 1) 7
1785[2] PISTOL RIVER (Ire) [94] 9-2 J Reid (1) *sn mid-div, rdn and not quicken last 2 fs.* ....(6 to 1 fav tchd 7 to 1 and 5 to 1) 8
2563[3] LANKRIDGE [79] 8-1 W Carson (3) *slwly into strd, sn hndy, one pace frm 2 fs out.* ....(14 to 1 op 12 to 1 tchd 16 to 1) 9
2632* DARMSTADT (USA) [81] 8-3 D Holland (13) *led 2 fs, led 3 out, hdd and wknd o'r one out.* ....(9 to 1 op 7 to 1 tchd 10 to 1) 10
1785 CIRCUS COLOURS [77] 7-13 A McGlone (5) *wl plcd, led briefly o'r 3 fs out, wknd 2 out.* ....(16 to 1 op 14 to 1 tchd 20 to 1) 11
2393[2] TOP CEES [93] 9-1 Paul Eddery (9) *nvr on terms.* ....(33 to 1 op 25 to 1) 12
2332 ERCKULE [73] 7-9[3] (3*) B Doyle (11) *mid-div till drpd rear last 2 fs*..............(25 to 1 op 33 to 1 tchd 40 to 1) 13
2545[2] COMPLETE MADNESS [77] 7-13 F Norton (7) *led aftr 2 fs, hdd and wknd o'r 3 out*.........(33 to 1 tchd 50 to 1) 14
2561* DUSTY POINT (Ire) [86] 8-8 W R Swinburn (4) *settled mid-div, wknd wl o'r 2 fs out.* ....(13 to 2 op 8 to 1 tchd 6 to 1) 15
2390[3] REVERE (Ire) [89] 8-11 A Munro (10) *jmpd path and drpd rear aftr 3 fs*....................(7 to 1 op 6 to 1) 16
Dist: Nk, ½l, 1½l, ½l, sht-hd, 2l, 3l, sht-hd, 1½l, 3½l. 2m 41.55s. a 8.55s (16 Ran).
SR: 41/39/38/31/31/37/24/29/13/ (G Howard-Spink), R Hannon

2908 Charlton Mill Handicap Class C (0-90 3-y-o) £5,162 5f................ (4:45)

2660[2] CALL ME I'M BLUE (Ire) [86] 9-4 L Piggott (4) *ldg grp, rdn to ld ins fnl furlong, kpt on.* ....(6 to 1 op 11 to 2 tchd 13 to 2) 1
2303[5] LOCH PATRICK [85] 9-3 A McGlone (3) *beh till ran on appr fnl furlong, fnshd wl.* ....(7 to 2 fav op 4 to 1 tchd 9 to 2) 2
1136[2] BALLET SHOES (Ire) [75] 8-7[1] W R Swinburn (5) *hld up, cld on ldrs o'r one furlong out, styd on wl nr line.* ....(8 to 1 op 10 to 1 tchd 11 to 1) 3
2375[6] PRESS THE BELL [80] 8-12 J Carroll (9) *slwly into strd, sn led, hrd rdn and hdd ins fnl furlong.* ....(16 to 1 op 14 to 1 tchd 20 to 1) 4
1841[4] ANOTHER JADE [80] 8-12 Pat Eddery (11) *trkd ldrs on outsd, effrt und pres o'r one furlong out, no extr.* ....(13 to 2 op 5 to 1) 5
2699[8] THE FED [64] (v) 7-10 D Biggs (8) *pressed ldr, rdn and not quicken entering fnl furlong.* ....(20 to 1 op 14 to 1 tchd 25 to 1) 6
2560[4] CATHERINEOFARAGON [75] 8-7 J Williams (2) *beh till styd on fnl furlong, nvr nrr*.............(11 to 2 op 9 to 2) 7
2560[6] GO FLIGHTLINE (Ire) [61] 7-7 G Bardwell (6) *rdn to cl on ldrs 2 fs out, one pace ins last*.........(12 to 1 op 10 to 1) 8
2728[7] JULIET BRAVO [63] 7-9 W Carson (7) *ldg grp, rdn and wknd entering fnl furlong.* ....(11 to 1 op 8 to 1 tchd 12 to 1) 9
2560 PUTOUT [70] (v) 8-2 R Hills (1) *in tch to hfwy, wknd quickly*..............(8 to 1 op 10 to 1 tchd 12 to 1) 10
Dist: 1l, hd, 1½l, 1½l, hd, ½l, hd, 2l, 5l. 1m 0.01s. a 3.21s (10 Ran).
SR: 55/50/39/38/32/15/24/9/3/ (Harsh (Tipping Gears)), N Tinkler

2909 EBF Findon Maiden Stakes Class D (2-y-o) £5,162 6f................. (5:20)

ELECTRIFY (USA) 9-0 Pat Eddery (4) *trkd ldrs, rdn to ld last 100 yards, styd on wl.* ....(5 to 4 fav op 11 to 10 tchd Evens) 1
1715[2] JAZEEL (USA) 9-0 W Carson (1) *made most till hdd last 100 yards, kpt on und pres.* (9 to 4 op 3 to 1 tchd 7 to 2) 2
2240[5] WILD PLANET (USA) 8-9 C Asmussen (8) *hld up, shaken up and ran on o'r one furlong out, kpt on nr finish, better for race*..........(8 to 1 op 6 to 1 tchd 9 to 1) 3
2336[4] EN CACHETTE (Ire) 8-9 J Reid (7) *trkd ldrs, ev ch 2 fs out, rdn and no extr ins last.* ....(10 to 1 op 7 to 1 tchd 11 to 1) 4
PERYLLYS 8-9 W Newnes (5) *slwly into strd, beh till styd on fnl furlong, nrst finish.* ....(66 to 1 op 50 to 1 tchd 100 to 1) 5
GALLANT SPIRIT (Ire) 9-0 L Dettori (2) *slwly into strd, sn wl plcd, rdn and wknd o'r one furlong out.* ....(20 to 1 op 12 to 1) 6
1296[3] ROOFTOP FLYER (Ire) 9-0 W R Swinburn (9) *ldg grp till wknd o'r one furlong out.* ....(16 to 1 op 14 to 1 tchd 20 to 1) 7
2603[4] DIAMOND FRONTIER (Ire) 9-0 J Carroll (11) *slwly into strd, nvr rch frnt rnk*..................(50 to 1 op 20 to 1) 8
2546[6] RUNIC SYMBOL 9-0 R Cochrane (12) *outpcd.* ....(66 to 1 op 33 to 1 tchd 100 to 1) 9
2224[5] THORNY BISHOP (bl) 9-0 G Bardwell (3) *pld hrd, not settle, outpcd hfwy*..................(66 to 1 tchd 100 to 1) 10
2559[7] LOOSE CHANGE 8-9 B Rouse (10) *cl up till wknd quickly 2 fs out*..........(66 to 1 op 50 to 1 tchd 100 to 1) 11
Dist: ½l, 1½l, hd, 3½l, ¾l, 1l, 7l, ½l, 3l, nk. 1m 14.20s. a 3.80s (11 Ran).
SR: 42/40/29/28/14/16/12/-/-/ (K Abdulla), H R A Cecil

LEICESTER (good)
Wednesday July 28th

Going Correction: MINUS 0.05 sec. per fur. (races 1,2,3,6), PLUS 0.10 (4,5)

2910 Coplow Handicap Class E (0-70 3-y-o and up) £3,080 5f 2yds..........(6:25)

2813[3] HERE COMES A STAR [62] 5-9-10 A Clark (4) *hld up, rdn and gd hdwy appr fnl furlong, ran on to ld ins last, all out*................(11 to 4 fav op 3 to 1 tchd 7 to 2) 1
2688* BATCHWORTH BOUND [51] 4-8-13 (5ex) C Rutter (2) *hld up in tch, ran on strly fnl furlong, jst fld.* ....(4 to 1 op 3 to 1) 2
2734[6] ARC LAMP [58] 7-9-6 J Fortune (10) *al prmnt, led hfwy, hrd rdn and hdd ins fnl furlong, no extr nr finish.* ....(16 to 1 op 10 to 1) 3
2661[4] BELMONT PRINCESS (Ire) [54] 3-8-6 (5*) Stephen Davies (1) *pld hrd, al in tch on stands side, ran on fnl furlong.* ....(20 to 1) 4
1925[8] FOLLOWMEGIRLS [55] 4-9-3 K Fallon (3) *wtd wth, ran on ins fnl furlong, nvr nrr*...........(16 to 1 op 13 to 1) 5
2225[7] LYNDON'S LINNET [58] 5-9-3 (3*) J Weaver (8) *nvr far away, rdn and ran on fnl furlong*............(14 to 1) 6
1494 ADMIRALS REALM [56] 4-9-4 A Mackay (5) *in tch till wknd entering fnl furlong*..............(16 to 1 op 12 to 1) 7
2723* FARMER JOCK [59] 11-9-7 (5ex) G Duffield (9) *prmnt, rdn 2 fs out, sn btn*....................(6 to 1) 8
2728[2] KENSWORTH LADY [50] 3-8-7 N Adams (7) *reared up leaving stalls, nvr got into race*........(11 to 2 op 6 to 1) 9
2416[6] KINTWYN [54] 3-8-11 T Williams (6) *led to hfwy, stdly wknd*....................(10 to 1 op 8 to 1) 10
Dist: Nk, 1½l, sht-hd, nk, hd, 3l, 1½l, ½l, 1l. 1m 1.70s. a 3.00s (10 Ran).
SR: 45/33/34/24/29/31/17/14/-/ (Mrs June Goodridge), J M Carr

2911 Molyneux Selling Stakes Class G (2-y-o) £2,742 5f 218yds........... (6:55)

KATHANNA 8-3 (3*) J Weaver (12) *hld up, hdwy 2 fs out, ran on strly and squeezed through to ld one out, rdn out*....................(8 to 1 op 10 to 1) 1
2271* PRIMOST 8-11 (5*) D Wright (11) *al in tch, hrd rdn o'r one furlong out, ran on*.................(3 to 1 op 5 to 2) 2
2554[6] ANTIGUAN SKY 8-11 K Fallon (4) *slwly into strd, hdwy wl o'r one furlong out, ran on ins last.* ....(5 to 2 fav tchd 3 to 1 and 100 to 30) 3
2502 CHEERFUL GROOM (Ire) 8-13[2] T Wall (2) *trkd ldr, led hfwy, rdn and hdd one furlong out, one pace.* ....(25 to 1 op 20 to 1) 4
1254[3] BURMA STAR 8-6 N Adams (8) *chsd ldrs, kpt on one pace ins fnl 2 fs*....................(8 to 1 op 5 to 1) 5
2493* FLAIR LADY 8-11 T Sprake (13) *in frnt rnk till rdn and wknd appr fnl furlong*............. (9 to 1 op 7 to 1) 6
JOBISDUN 8-11 S O'Gorman (6) *al mid-div, pushed alng frm hfwy, nvr dngrs*....................(33 to 1) 7
2546[8] PETITE BIJOU 8-6 A Mackay (3) *led to hfwy, wknd 2 fs out*....................(20 to 1 op 14 to 1) 8
2718[8] BON TON (v) 8-6 S Whitworth (10) *in tch till wknd 2 fs out.* ....(12 to 1 op 8 to 1) 9
2588[9] STAR TRAVELLER 8-11 M Wigham (9) *al towards rear.* ....(33 to 1 op 25 to 1) 10
2493[7] RAGTIME GIRL 8-0[1] (7*) S Drowne (1) *swrvd lft strt, al beh.* ....(33 to 1 op 20 to 1) 11

949[6] MISS IGLOO 8-6 J Quinn (7) *speed to hfwy.* .... (12 to 1 op 8 to 1) 12
2472 ANOTHER DREAM (Ire) 8-11 T Williams (5) *sn rdn alng, al beh.* ....(33 to 1) 13
Dist: 1½l, 1½l, nk, 3l, 2l, 2l, ¾l, 1½l, 6l, hd. 1m 15.50s. a 5.10s (13 Ran).
(T H Stuart D Egan J Murphy), B Palling

2912 Rutland Handicap Class D (0-80 3-y-o and up) £3,817 1m 8yds.........(7:25)

2421[9] HE'S A KING (USA) [74] 3-9-7 L Dettori (1) *made all, shaken up whn pressed o'r one furlong out, ran on wl.* ....(7 to 2 op 5 to 1) 1
2421[3] MR CUBE (Ire) [61] 3-8-1 (7*) T G McLaughlin (3) *hld up in tch, wnt second o'r 2 fs out, chlgd appr fnl furlong, one pace ins last.*................ (7 to 4 fav tchd 2 to 1) 2
2719[7] AHJAY [50] 3-7-11 J Quinn (2) *pld hrd, chsd wnr for most of 1st 5 fs, rdn and outpcd o'r one out.* ....(8 to 1 op 6 to 1) 3
2499[7] TOCCO JEWEL [46] 3-7-2 (5*) D Wright (5) *hld up, rdn 3 fs out, no further hdwy...*(15 to 2 op 4 to 1 tchd 8 to 1) 4
2749* FUCHU [66] 3-8-13 (5ex) G Duffield (6) *hld up, ev ch whn rdn o'r 2 fs out, sn btn.*...............(2 to 1 op 7 to 4) 5
Dist: 1½l, 5l, 2½l, 6l, 1l. 1m 41.00s. a 5.90s (5 Ran).
SR: 12/-/ (Lady Swaythling), J L Dunlop

2913 Thistleton Gap Handicap Class D (0-80 3-y-o and up) £3,687 1m 3f 183yds ....(7:55)

2501* MUCH SOUGHT AFTER [78] 4-9-12 G Duffield (4) *al prmnt and gng wl, trkd ldr frm hfwy, led o'r 2 fs out, rdn appr last, ran on.*........................(3 to 1 tchd 7 to 2) 1
1840 TIGER SHOOT [55] 6-8-3 J Lowe (2) *trkd ldr to hfwy, pushed alng frm 4 fs out, styd on to go second appr fnl furlong.*........................ (4 to 1 op 7 to 2) 2
2617[4] MOONLIGHT QUEST [80] 5-10-0 L Dettori (3) *wtd wth, rdn 3 fs out, kpt on one pace ins fnl 2 furlongs.* ....(5 to 2 fav op 2 to 1) 3
1878[2] WESTFIELD MOVES (Ire) [58] 5-8-6 J Quinn (7) *in tch, rdn o'r 2 fs out, one pace aftr*............ (6 to 1 op 5 to 1) 4
2420[3] INCHCAILLOCH (Ire) [70] 4-9-4 B Raymond (6) *led till hdd o'r 2 fs out, sn btn*.....(5 to 1 op 6 to 1 tchd 7 to 1) 5
HOME FROM THE HILL (Ire) [80] 3-8-13 (3*) M Fenton (1) *hld up, rdn 3 fs out, no hdwy.*........ (20 to 1 op 16 to 1) 6
451[5] APOLLO DE ORIENTE [57] 3-7-7 N Adams (5) *slwly away, sn wl beh, tld off.*................(100 to 1 op 50 to 1) 7
Dist: 1½l, 3½l, hd, 7l, 1½l, dist. 2m 35.20s. a 6.70s (7 Ran).
SR: 57/31/49/26/24/19/-/ (The MSA Partnership), D Morley

2914 Rothley Claiming Stakes Class F (3-y-o) £2,301 1m 1f 218yds........(8:25)

2314[4] SEAMA (USA) 8-12 A Munro (7) *trkd ldr, led o'r 3 fs out, drvn alng ins fnl 2 furlongs.* ....(11 to 8 fav op 11 to 10 tchd Evens) 1
2523[6] SPARKY'S SONG 8-8 R Hills (5) *hld up, hdwy o'r 3 fs out, rdn and ran on one pace fnl 2 furlongs.* ....(2 to 1 tchd 9 to 4) 2
4717a BLOWEDIFIKNOW 8-9 J Williams (4) *pld hrd, nvr out of 1st 3, ran on one pace fnl 2 fs.*........ (16 to 1 op 12 to 1) 3
2566[3] BLUE RADIANCE (v) 8-0 J Fanning (2) *pld hrd, led till hdd o'r 3 fs out, wknd 2 out.* (4 to 1 op 5 to 1 tchd 11 to 2) 4
COBBS CROSS 8-6 (3*) N Kennedy (1) *hld up, effrt o'r 3 fs out, sn btn.*............................(50 to 1 op 33 to 1) 5
2529[7] FORGE GOLD 8-13 J Quinn (3) *al beh, no ch fnl 4 fs.* ....(33 to 1) 6
2775 PETAL'S JARRED 8-3[1] K Fallon (6) *beh, hdwy 4 fs out, rdn 3 out, sn btn and eased, tld off....* (25 to 1 op 16 to 1) 7
Dist: 3l, sht-hd, 8l, 1½l, ½l, 25l. 2m 11.60s. a 8.70s (7 Ran).
SR: 21/11/11/-/ (Fahd Salman), Sir Mark Prescott

2915 Tom Cribb Limited Stakes Class F (0-65 3-y-o and up) £2,637 7f 9yds ....(8:55)

2327[4] CHARMED KNAVE 8-9-7 T Williams (4) *al travelling wl stands side, rdn to ld appr fnl furlong, ran on well.* .... (12 to 1 op 10 to 1) 1
2864* DANCING DOMINO 3-9-0 K Darley (1) *hld up in tch, rdn wl o'r one furlong out, ran on ins last, no imprsn.* ....(15 to 8 fav op 7 to 4 tchd 2 to 1) 2
2656[3] PARFAIT AMOUR 4-9-2 A Culhane (7) *nvr far away far side, led briefly one and a half fs out, rdn and ran on one pace.*........................ (6 to 1 op 5 to 1) 3
2172[4] SARTIGILA 4-9-2 G Duffield (3) *slwly away, steadied in rear, gd hdwy appr fnl furlong, ran on, nvr nrr.* ....(6 to 1 tchd 13 to 2) 4
2327[9] ANNABELLE ROYALE 7-9-7 L Dettori (6) *led till hdd one and a half fs out, ran on one pace...* (4 to 1 op 5 to 1) 5
2716 HAZY KAY (Ire) 3-8-9 A Munro (2) *prmnt till rdn and wknd 2 fs out.*............................(12 to 1 op 8 to 1) 6
2824[6] BERNSTEIN BETTE 7-9-2 J Williams (5) *in tch till rdn and outpcd fnl 2 fs.*..(6 to 1) 7
2190[3] POP TO STANS 4-9-7 Alex Greaves (8) *prmnt till wknd o'r 2 fs out.*............................ (25 to 1 op 20 to 1) 8
Dist: 1½l, ½l, ¾l, ½l, 3½l, 4l, 4l. 1m 27.10s. a 5.20s (8 Ran).
SR: 24/12/12/10/13/ (Mrs M E Olsson), D R Laing

SOUTHWELL (A.W) (std)
Wednesday July 28th
Going Correction: PLUS 0.10 sec. per fur.

2916 Hera Maiden Auction Stakes Class F (2-y-o) £2,534 6f................(2:10)

2554[4] MISTER BEAT 9-0 L Charnock (3) *fst away, made all, drvn clr last 2 fs, ran on.*............. (Evens fav op 2 to 1) 1
2687[2] CINNAMON SPRINGS (Ire) 8-9 P Robinson (2) *chsd wnr thrght, rdn o'r one furlong out, kpt on same pace.* ....(3 to 1 op 9 to 4) 2
343[4] JOYRIDER 8-11 (3*) M Fenton (1) *drvn alng to show gd speed for o'r 4 fs, no extr.*.......... (13 to 2 op 5 to 1) 3
2546[9] DELROB 8-9 A Mackay (6) *nvr far away, feeling pace and drvn alng 2 fs out, not quicken......* (7 to 1 op 5 to 1) 4
2706 DOUBLE SIXTEEN 9-0 M Wigham (4) *last away, chsd alng all the way, nvr nr to chal.* ....(9 to 2 op 4 to 1 tchd 5 to 1) 5
2659[9] COLONEL SINCLAIR (Ire) 9-0 S Perks (7) *chsd alng and sn outpcd, nvr a factor*...............(25 to 1 op 20 to 1) 6
Dist: 1½l, 3½l, 3l, 10l, 1l. 1m 17.50s. a 4.10s (6 Ran).
SR: 30/19/10/ (P Asquith), J G FitzGerald

2917 Apollo Selling Stakes Class G (2-y-o) £2,448 7f...................... (2:40)

2689[6] SUPER SYMPHONIC 8-11 P Robinson (3) *made all, quickened wl clr last 2 fs, easily.* ....(11 to 4 op 5 to 2 tchd 3 to 1 and 7 to 2) 1
2819[4] NORTHERN BAILIWICK (Ire) (bl) 8-11 M Wigham (8) *chsd alng beh ldrs, improved frm off the pace o'r one furlong out, nvr nrr.*...........(5 to 1 op 4 to 1 tchd 11 to 2) 2
2679* JUST BILL 9-0 S Webster (4) *unruly in stalls, chsd wnr most of way, fdd fnl furlong.*........(4 to 1 op 3 to 1) 3
2526[5] STEADFAST ELITE (Ire) 8-9 G Duffield (5) *al hndy, feeling pace and drvn alng o'r 2 fs out, no extr.* ....(7 to 4 fav op 3 to 1) 4
2637[8] CRUISING CHICK 8-6 J Fortune (11) *nvr far away, hrd at work o'r 2 fs out, one pace*.................... (25 to 1) 5
MISS TUT (Ire) 8-6 T Sprake (7) *sn struggling, nvr able to rch ldrs.*............................(33 to 1 op 25 to 1) 6
2679[5] HILL FARM DANCER 8-1 (5*) D Wright (1) *chsd ldrs for o'r 4 fs, wknd quickly.*.............................. (12 to 1) 7
1926[8] TALYGARN (v) 8-11 A Mackay (10) *bolted a full circuit bef race, al struggling.*............. (20 to 1 op 16 to 1) 8
THATCHED ROOF (Ire) 8-6 T Lucas (6) *edgy bef race, drvn alng to keep in tch, btn hfwy.*......(10 to 1 op 7 to 1) 9
1863 PHIL THE TILL (bl) 8-11 Dale Gibson (2) *drvn alng in midfield hfwy, sn lost tch.*............(33 to 1 op 25 to 1) 10
WARWICK WHISPER (Ire) 8-11 N Day (9) *unruly gng to post, refused to race, took no part.* (10 to 1 op 8 to 1) I
Dist: 12l, ½l, 1½l, ¾l, 3l, sht-hd, 2l, 8l, 5l. 1m 32.10s. a 6.00s (11 Ran).
SR: 18/-/-/-/-/ (Jack Maxwell), M H Tompkins

2918 Gloucestershire Coal Merchants Rating Related Maiden Stakes Class E (0-70 3-y-o and up) £2,821 7f.... (3:15)

2719[8] ISLAND KNIGHT (Ire) 4-9-7 P Robinson (6) *confidently rdn, cruised ahead o'r one furlong out, idled, ridden out.* ....(11 to 10 on op 11 to 10) 1
2598[4] PHILNIC 3-9-0 G Duffield (2) *wth ldr, led hfwy, kicked for hme 2 fs out, hdd o'r one out, one pace.* ....(7 to 2 op 3 to 1) 2
951 SAXON MAGIC 3-8-9 J Quinn (1) *last and drvn alng, styd on und pres o'r one furlong out, nvr nr to chal.* ....(5 to 1 op 9 to 2) 3
2719[4] EXPORT MONDIAL 3-9-0 M Tebbutt (5) *led till hdd hfwy, drvn alng o'r 2 fs out, sn outpcd.....* (4 to 1 op 7 to 2) 4
2638[8] VIRGINIA COTTAGE 4-9-2 J Fortune (7) *trkd ldg pair, hrd at work and lost grnd hfwy, sn btn.*.......... (16 to 1) 5
Dist: 2½l, 8l, 2½l, 6l. 1m 32.10s. a 6.00s (5 Ran).
SR: 28/13/ (Knight Group), M J Ryan

2919 K P H Industrial Services Ltd-BS5750 Achievement Day Handicap Class E (0-70 3-y-o and up) £2,950 6f.... (3:50)

2425[4] HEATHYARDS GEM [51] 3-8-10 S Perks (5) *sluggish strt, drvn alng to improve on outsd 2 fs out, kpt on to ld last 50 yards.*.....................(5 to 1 op 9 to 2) 1
2861[3] FORMIDABLE LIZ [59] 3-9-4 G Duffield (2) *nvr far away, drvn ahead o'r one furlong out, ct last 50 yards.* .... (2 to 1 jt-fav op 7 to 4) 2
2590* GLENFIELD GRETA [59] (bl) 5-9-5 (5*) D Wright (4) *last and drvn alng, improved on ins 2 fs out, kpt on same pace inside last.*.................. (2 to 1 jt-fav op 9 to 4) 3
2829[3] COMET WHIRLPOOL (Ire) [60] (bl) 3-9-5 J Quinn (3) *pushed alng in midfield, improved to fltter o'r one furlong out, kpt on same pace.*..................(4 to 1 op 7 to 2) 4
2707[6] JOVIAL KATE (USA) [47] 6-8-12 J Fortune (7) *broke wl, feeling pace and drvn alng hfwy, no imprsn last 2 fs.* ....(5 to 1 op 8 to 1) 5

2831[5] BLAKENEY'S DOUBLE (Ire) [40] (bl) 3-7-8 (5*) L Newton (6) *led aftr one furlong, drvn clr o'r 2 fs out, hdd over one out, sn btn*........................(16 to 1 op 14 to 1) 6

2829[8] ANDRULA MOU [36] 3-7-9 L Charnock (1) *led one furlong, chsd alng to hold pl hfwy, fdd wl o'r one furlong out.* ....(25 to 1) 7

Dist: ½l, 2½l, nk, 8l, ½l, 2½l. 1m 17.60s. a 4.20s (7 Ran).
SR: 24/30/26/20/ (Mrs B L Morgan), R Hollinshead

2920 Paris Handicap Class E (0-70 3-y-o and up) £2,976 1m..............(4:20)

2475[3] SET THE FASHION [48] (v) 4-8-8 (3*) D Harrison (8) *al gng wl, led o'r 2 fs out, quickened, easily.* ....(11 to 10 fav op 7 to 4) 1

2747[2] MAY SQUARE (Ire) [34] 5-7-11 J Quinn (10) *took keen hold, improved to draw level 2 fs out, not pace of wnr.* ....(4 to 1 tchd 5 to 1) 2

2775[4] DIAMOND INTHE DARK (USA) [50] (v) 5-8-13 Alex Greaves (5) *chsd alng in midfield, kpt on und pres last 2 fs, one pace*..(14 to 1) 3

2525* SIE AMATO (Ire) [51] 4-9-0 J Fortune (9) *led early, styd hndy till rdn and no extr o'r one furlong out.* ....(8 to 1 op 7 to 1) 4

1626 GALLANT JACK (Ire) [54] 4-9-3 A Mackay (6) *chsd alng in midfield, kpt on same pace last 2 fs.* ....(20 to 1 op 16 to 1) 5

1940 QUANTITY SURVEYOR [65] 4-10-0 G Duffield (7) *settled midfield, hrd at work hfwy, nvr able to chal.* ....(11 to 1 op 6 to 1) 6

2747[7] BASSIO (Bel) [47] (h) 4-8-10 W Hood (3) *settled off the pace, nvr trble ldrs*.........................(10 to 1 op 9 to 1) 7

2590[5] SWYNFORD FLYER [30] 4-7-6[2] (3*) N Kennedy (4) *drvn alng to go pace, nvr a threat*.......................(20 to 1) 8

2300 FOOLISH TOUCH [44] 11-8-2 (5*) D McCabe (1) *outpcd and drvn alng thrght*..........................(7 to 1 op 5 to 1) 9

2086[8] BENGAL TIGER (Ire) [45] (v) 5-8-8 M Wigham (2) *sn led, hdd o'r 2 fs out, wknd quickly*..........(6 to 1 op 12 to 1) 10

Dist: 5l, 3½l, 3l, nk, 1½l, 4l, 1½l, 2½l, 2½l. 1m 42.70s. a 3.70s (10 Ran).
SR: 53/24/29/21/23/29/ (The Queen), Lord Huntingdon

2921 Aries Handicap Class E (0-70 3-y-o and up) £2,898 1½m............(4:50)

2306[2] HASTA LA VISTA [47] (bl) 3-7-7 L Charnock (3) *wth ldr, led o'r 5 fs out, kicked clr entering strt, unchlgd.* .... (11 to 4 op 2 to 1) 1

2348[7] HAROLDON (Ire) [65] 4-9-4 (5*) Stephen Davies (5) *lft many ls strt, pld hrd and improved hfwy, styd on, no ch wth wnr*................. (85 to 40 op 11 to 4 tchd 2 to 1) 2

2152[6] BEAU QUEST [48] (bl) 6-8-1 (5*) D Wright (4) *chsd alng to go pace hfwy, some hdwy last 2 fs, nvr dngrs.* ....(4 to 1 op 9 to 2 tchd 5 to 1) 3

2678* COMMON COUNCIL [67] (v) 4-9-4 (7*) J Marshall (2) *led till hdd o'r 5 fs out, wknd quickly entering strt, eased.* ....(7 to 4 fav op 6 to 4) 4

2747 FIRST HOME [35] 6-7-0 (7*) Kim McDonnell (1) *in tch, struggling hfwy, tld off*.................. (20 to 1 op 16 to 1) 5

Dist: 12l, 8l, 2l, 30l. 2m 41.80s. a 7.90s (5 Ran).
SR: 12/18/ (K Hodgson), M W Easterby

GALWAY (IRE) (yielding)
Thursday July 29th

2922 Guinness Handicap (0-80 3-y-o) £4,140 1m 100yds.....................(4:25)

2702[5] LA CENERENTOLA (Ire) [-] 8-11 (4*) P Carberry (5)..(6 to 1) 1
2406[2] SAFAYN (USA) [-] (bl) 9-8 M J Kinane (3)..... (7 to 4 jt-fav) 2
2878[3] WALLY WALLENSKY (Ire) [-] 9-4 S Craine (7) (7 to 4 jt-fav) 3
2677 BRIGENSER (Ire) [-] (bl) 8-7 P Shanahan (4).........(8 to 1) 4
2604[8] HOLIWAY STAR (Ire) [-] 8-11 W J Supple (6)....... (14 to 1) 5
2675[4] AULD STOCK (Ire) [-] 9-2 J F Egan (2).............(13 to 2) 6
2702 KENTUCKY BABY (Ire) [-] (bl) 8-0 (4*) W J Smith (8) (14 to 1) 7

Dist: Sht-hd, nk, 1l, 1l. 1m 56.60s. (7 Ran).
(Mrs Maureen Hunt), Noel Meade

2923 Smithwicks Handicap (0-80 3-y-o and up) £4,140 1½m................(5:30)

2287* SHIRLEY'S DELIGHT (Ire) [-] 3-8-11 (4*) P Carberry (1) ....(11 to 4) 1
2041[2] SAIBOT (USA) [-] 4-9-13 M J Kinane (9)........ (Evens fav) 2
2513[2] GRECIAN LADY (Ire) [-] 4-7-13 Joanna Morgan (4) (16 to 1) 3
1025* FERRYCARRIG HOTEL (Ire) [-] 4-8-9 (6*) J A Heffernan (6) ....(4 to 1) 4
2498[7] MORNING SARGE [-] 5-8-12 (6*) J J Behan (2)....(14 to 1) 5
2496[4] WICKLOW WAY (Ire) [-] 3-8-7 W J Supple (7)......(10 to 1) 6
2781[9] MISS MAYTHORN (Ire) [-] 3-8-11 J F Egan (5)......(16 to 1) 7
2513[6] HAVIN' A BALL (Ire) [-] 4-8-6 (8*) B J Halligan (3)...(33 to 1) 8

Dist: Sht-hd, 3l, 4½l, 4l. 2m 50.80s. (8 Ran).
(Liam Doherty), Noel Meade

GOODWOOD (good to soft)
Thursday July 29th

Going Correction: PLUS 0.55 sec. per fur. (races 1,2,3,5,7), PLUS 0.50 (4,6)

2924 Lanson Champagne Vintage Stakes Class A (Group 3) (2-y-o) £19,680 7f ....(2:30)

2616[3] MISTER BAILEYS 8-11 Dean McKeown (2) *cl up, al gng wl, led o'r 2 fs out, pushed clr, not extended.* ....(13 to 8 fav op 7 to 4 tchd 6 to 4) 1

2335[3] PRINCE BABAR 8-11 L Dettori (3) *trkd ldrs, chsd wnr frm o'r one furlong out, kpt on, no imprsn.* ....(4 to 1 op 5 to 1) 2

2209* LOMAS (Ire) 8-11 A Munro (7) *led, pushed alng 3 fs out, hdd o'r 2 out, one pace.* (3 to 1 op 5 to 2 tchd 7 to 2) 3

2616* CLASSIC SKY (Ire) 8-11 W R Swinburn (5) *wtd wth in tch, effrt o'r 2 fs out, sn one pace, eased ins last.* ....(6 to 1 op 7 to 2) 4

2359[4] MR EUBANKS (USA) 8-11 J Reid (6) *cl up, ev ch o'r 2 fs out, sn wknd*........(20 to 1 op 12 to 1 tchd 25 to 1) 5

2006* BEAUTETE 8-11 L Piggott (4) *al beh, lost tch 3 fs out, tld off*.............................(14 to 1 tchd 20 to 1) 6

Dist: 2½l, 1½l, 6l, 1½l, 6l. 1m 31.42s. a 6.82s (6 Ran).
SR: 52/44/39/21/16/-/ (G R Bailey Ltd (Baileys Horse Feeds)), M Johnston

2925 Tiffany Goodwood Cup Class A (Group 3) (3-y-o and up) £27,200 2m ....(3:10)

2579[2] SONUS (Ire) (v) 4-9-3 Pat Eddery (7) *hld up beh, rdn alng and hdwy o'r 2 fs out, shaken up to ld wl ins last, cleverly*.................(4 to 1 op 7 to 4 tchd 9 to 2) 1

1787[2] ASSESSOR (Ire) 4-9-7 T Quinn (6) *trkd ldrs, cld hfwy, led o'r 2 fs out till wl ins last, no extr.* .... (6 to 4 fav op 13 to 8 tchd 7 to 4 and 5 to 4) 2

1787[5] ARCADIAN HEIGHTS 5-9-3 L Dettori (1) *trkd ldrs, led o'r 3 fs out till over 2 out, one pace*..... (14 to 1 op 12 to 1) 3

2238[5] ANNE BONNY 4-8-11 W R Swinburn (4) *hld up beh ldrs, hrd rdn o'r 2 fs out, one pace.* .... (25 to 1 op 16 to 1 tchd 33 to 1) 4

2061[4] NOT IN DOUBT (USA) 4-9-0 J Reid (5) *cl up, outpcd o'r 2 fs out, kpt on*......... (14 to 1 op 12 to 1 tchd 16 to 1) 5

1809[2] JACK BUTTON (Ire) 4-9-0 N Day (2) *chsd ldrs, pushed alng o'r 5 fs out, outpcd over 3 out, kpt on und pres ins last.* .... (14 to 1 op 20 to 1 tchd 25 to 1) 6

2360[3] MAGICAL RETREAT (USA) 3-7-12 D Biggs (9) *chsd ldrs, pushed alng 5 fs out, wknd o'r 2 out.* .... (10 to 1 op 12 to 1 tchd 14 to 1) 7

1787[7] DARU (USA) (v) 4-9-0 R Cochrane (3) *hld up beh, effrt o'r 2 fs out, no response*...(14 to 1 op 10 to 1 tchd 16 to 1) 8

2439[2] DI GIACOMO 3-7-12 W Carson (8) *sn led, hdd o'r 3 fs out, wknd quickly, tld off*..............(9 to 1 op 16 to 1) 9

Dist: 1l, 4l, 2l, sht-hd, 2l, 2l, nk, 15l. 3m 35.36s. a 11.36s (9 Ran).
SR: 77/80/72/64/66/64/46/61/30/ (Sheikh Mohammed), J H M Gosden

2926 Schweppes Golden Mile Handicap Class B (3-y-o and up) £65,422 1m ....(3:45)

2211[4] PHILIDOR [86] 4-8-4 (3*) N Kennedy (13) *chsd ldrs, hdwy 2 fs out, ran on to ld last strd.* ....(13 to 2 op 7 to 1 tchd 8 to 1) 1

2627[2] LOST SOLDIER (USA) [98] 3-8-11 R Cochrane (12) *hld up beh, rapid hdwy o'r one furlong out, ran on strly ins last, jst fld*.......................(16 to 1 tchd 20 to 1) 2

2211 SHOW FAITH (Ire) [92] 3-8-5 Pat Eddery (6) *hld up rear, rapid hdwy o'r 2 fs out, led over one out, ct last strd.* ....(8 to 1 op 7 to 1 tchd 10 to 1) 3

2758[7] FROGMARCH (USA) [90] 3-8-3 R Hills (3) *beh, hdwy o'r 2 fs out, ran on*......... (33 to 1 op 25 to 1 tchd 40 to 1) 4

2304[7] NORTHERN BIRD [85] 3-7-12 D Biggs (11) *chsd ldrs, kpt on one pace und pres frm o'r one furlong out.* .... (20 to 1 op 16 to 1 tchd 25 to 1) 5

2371[5] CEE-JAY-AY [72] 6-7-7 L Charnock (18) *slwly into strd, sn reco'red to mid-div, kpt on wl und pres fnl furlong.* ....(50 to 1 op 33 to 1) 6

1808 NORFOLK HERO [86] 3-7-13 A Munro (19) *prmnt, ev ch o'r 2 fs out, sn hrd rdn, wknd ins last.* ....(33 to 1 tchd 40 to 1) 7

2794[7] DOUBLE FLUTTER [78] 4-7-13 C Rutter (4) *beh, rdn and hdwy o'r one furlong out, kpt on wl.* ....(33 to 1 tchd 40 to 1) 8

2624[2] BLOCKADE (USA) [76] 4-7-8 (3*) D Harrison (17) *led till o'r one furlong out, wknd.* ....(10 to 1 op 8 to 1 tchd 11 to 1) 9

2391* FOREVER DIAMONDS [84] 6-8-5 (3ex) M Birch (16) *chsd ldrs, rdn o'r 2 fs out, btn over one out.* ....(10 to 1 tchd 12 to 1) 10

2413[9] PAY HOMAGE [103] 5-9-10 M Hills (9) *hld up rear, shrtlvd effrt o'r 2 fs out*.................. (25 to 1 op 20 to 1) 11

1015[4] STONEY VALLEY [93] 3-8-6 J Reid (20) *trkd ldrs, ch o'r 2 fs out, wknd over one out*...........(16 to 1 op 14 to 1) 12

2475* QUEEN WARRIOR [72] 4-7-2 (5*) D Wright (14) *trkd ldrs, rdn alng o'r 2 fs out, sn wknd*......................(20 to 1) 13

2431[6] PRENONAMOSS [79] 5-8-0 F Norton (7) *al beh.* .... (40 to 1 op 33 to 1 tchd 50 to 1) 14

2885[3] ABBEY'S GAL [102] 3-9-1 W R Swinburn (1) *al beh.* .... (9 to 1 op 8 to 1 tchd 10 to 1) 15
1720[4] CUMBRIAN CHALLENGE (Ire) [94] 4-8-12 (3*) S Maloney (5) *trkd ldrs, wknd o'r 2 fs out.* .... (20 to 1 op 16 to 1 tchd 25 to 1) 16
2361[2] SHAMAM (USA) [87] 3-8-0 W Carson (8) *al beh.* .... (9 to 1 op 12 to 1 tchd 8 to 1) 17
2254* PETER DAVIES (USA) [106] 5-9-13 (7ex) L Dettori (10) *chsd ldrs, wknd quickly o'r 2 fs out.* ....(5 to 1 fav op 9 to 2 tchd 11 to 2) 18
2212 FAIRY STORY (Ire) [83] 3-7-8[1] (3*) B Doyle (15) *cl up, styd alone far rail entering strt, wknd o'r 2 fs out.* .... (33 to 1 op 25 to 1) 19
Dist: Sht-hd, sht-hd, 2l, nk, hd, ¾l, hd, ¾l, ½l, nk. 1m 42.97s. a 5.77s (19 Ran).
SR: 72/75/68/60/54/48/52/51/47/ (J C Smith), J M P Eustace

2927 King George Stakes Class A (Group 3) (3-y-o and up) £21,060 5f........(4:15)

2252* LOCHSONG 5-8-11 L Dettori (5) *made virtually all, ran on gmely ins fnl furlong.* ....(13 to 8 fav tchd 7 to 4 and 6 to 4) 1
1807[3] PARIS HOUSE 4-9-8 J Carroll (3) *wth wnr, rdn o'r 2 fs out, ev ch whn wndrd und pres ins last, no extr cl hme.* .... (9 to 2 op 5 to 1 tchd 11 to 2) 2
2362[4] KEEN HUNTER (USA) 6-9-10 W R Swinburn (7) *beh, hdwy o'r one furlong out, kpt on und pres.* ....(4 to 1 op 3 to 1 tchd 9 to 2) 3
2362[5] MARINA PARK 3-8-11 Dean McKeown (4) *pushed alng thrght, chsd ldrs, not pace to chal frm o'r one furlong out.*.......................... (9 to 1 op 7 to 1 tchd 10 to 1) 4
2399[3] BUNTY BOO 4-8-11 A Munro (10) *outpcd, hdwy o'r one furlong out, nrst finish.* .... (33 to 1 op 25 to 1 tchd 50 to 1) 5
1019 BLYTON LAD 7-9-0 S Webster (1) *prmnt till wknd 2 fs out.* ....(16 to 1) 6
2399[4] EL YASAF (Ire) 5-9-0 Pat Eddery (9) *outpcd.* .... (20 to 1 op 25 to 1 tchd 33 to 1) 7
2362 ARTISTIC REEF 4-9-0 T Quinn (2) *speed to hfwy.* .... (50 to 1 op 66 to 1) 8
2187[2] SOVEREIGN GRACE (Ire) 4-8-11 J Murtagh (8) *chsd ldrs, rdn o'r 2 fs out, sn btn.* ....(50 to 1 op 33 to 1 tchd 100 to 1) 9
1786[5] GARAH 4-8-11 R Cochrane (11) *nvr gng pace, al beh.* .... (10 to 1 op 8 to 1 tchd 11 to 1) 10
2362 FREDDIE LLOYD (USA) 4-9-5 J Reid (6) *cl up to hfwy, wknd quickly*.................... (25 to 1 tchd 33 to 1) 11
Dist: Hd, nk, 2½l, ½l, nk, 1l, ½l, 1½l, sht-hd, nk. 1m 0.20s. a 3.40s (11 Ran).
SR: 79/89/90/67/65/67/63/61/52/ (J C Smith), I A Balding

2928 Kinrara Handicap Class C (0-90 3-y-o) £5,845 7f....................... (4:45)

2671[5] AL MOULOUKI [77] 8-10 R Cochrane (15) *reared strt, beh, rapid hdwy o'r one furlong out, led ins last, ran on wl.* .... (9 to 1 op 7 to 1 tchd 11 to 1) 1
2479[2] FIELD OF VISION (Ire) [78] 8-11 T Williams (4) *beh, pushed alng o'r 3 fs out, hdwy to ld over one out, hdd ins last, one pace*............(9 to 1 op 8 to 1 tchd 10 to 1) 2
2390[6] HUNTERS OF BRORA (Ire) [73] 8-6 A Munro (5) *beh, hdwy o'r one furlong out, styd on.* ....(7 to 1 op 6 to 1 tchd 8 to 1) 3
2522[3] CHILI HEIGHTS [79] 8-12 J Williams (9) *beh, hdwy o'r one furlong out, nrst finish*...............(10 to 1 tchd 11 to 1) 4
2522[7] SECOND CHANCE (Ire) [75] 8-8 W Newnes (6) *trkd ldrs, rdn 2 fs out, one pace*.... (16 to 1 op 14 to 1 tchd 20 to 1) 5
2468[6] DESERT NOMAD [60] 7-2 (5*) D Wright (11) *trkd ldrs, rdn o'r 2 fs out, sn btn*....(16 to 1 op 14 to 1 tchd 20 to 1) 6
2476[7] HALLORINA [64] 7-11 G Bardwell (7) *pushed alng thrght, nvr better than mid-div*.........(20 to 1 tchd 25 to 1) 7
1808 EMBANKMENT (Ire) [88] 9-0 (7*) Mark Denaro (10) *nvr better than mid-div*.................. (12 to 1 tchd 14 to 1) 8
2577* ARID [80] 8-13 L Dettori (12) *cl up, led on bit 3 fs out, hdd o'r one out, wknd quickly.* .... (6 to 1 op 5 to 1 tchd 13 to 2) 9
2725[3] THE LITTLE FERRET [75] 8-8 B Rouse (14) *led 2 fs, cl up till wknd o'r two furlongs out.* ....(14 to 1 op 12 to 1 tchd 16 to 1) 10
2543[7] KNIGHT OF SHALOT (Ire) [78] 8-6 (5*) Stephen Davies (3) *chsd ldrs, effrt 3 fs out, sn btn*.....(14 to 1 op 12 to 1) 11
2522[2] SIMPLY FINESSE [80] 8-13 T Quinn (8) *cl up, led aftr 2 fs to 3 out, btn quickly.* .... (100 to 30 fav op 4 to 1 tchd 3 to 1) 12
2503[6] WALNUT BURL (Ire) [60] 7-7 N Adams (2) *strted slwly, al beh*.................(25 to 1 op 20 to 1 tchd 33 to 1) 13
Dist: 1½l, 1½l, ½l, 4l, nk, hd, 1l, 4l, 8l, 2l. 1m 31.61s. a 7.01s (13 Ran).
SR: 49/45/35/39/23/7/10/31/11/ (G Jabre), J W Payne

2929 Lavant Nursery Handicap Class C (2-y-o) £5,481 6f................. (5:20)

2374* VERCINGETORIX (Ire) [-] 8-10 Paul Eddery (1) *outpcd, rdn and hdwy hfwy, led ins fnl furlong, pushed out.* ....(7 to 2 jt-fav op 5 to 2 tchd 4 to 1) 1
2571 MILLICENT NORTH [-] 8-9 J Williams (3) *trkd ldrs, led o'r one furlong out till ins last, ran on.* ....(6 to 1 op 4 to 1 tchd 7 to 1) 2
1778[2] BEST KEPT SECRET [-] 9-7 J Carroll (2) *chsd ldrs, lost pl hfwy, kpt on ins fnl furlong*...................(7 to 2 jt-fav op 4 to 1 tchd 3 to 1) 3
2539[3] CHIEF EXECUTIVE [-] 7-9 (3*) D Harrison (7) *cl up, led o'r 3 fs out till over one out, wknd.* .... (6 to 1 op 5 to 1 tchd 13 to 2) 4
1446[6] CONNECT (Ire) [-] 8-9 B Rouse (4) *trkd ldrs for o'r 4 fs.* ....(6 to 1 op 7 to 1) 5
2325 KNIGHTRIDER [-] 8-5 T Quinn (11) *trkd ldrs to hfwy.* ....(11 to 1 op 10 to 1 tchd 12 to 1) 6
2325 GINGERILLO [-] (bl) 7-4 (5*) D Wright (6) *led till o'r 3 fs out, sn wknd*..........(33 to 1 op 25 to 1 tchd 50 to 1) 7
2689[3] RISKIE THINGS [-] 7-3[3] (7*) E Greehy (10) *outpcd.* ....(8 to 1 tchd 10 to 1) 8
2472[3] MACIZO [-] 9-1 A Munro (9) *outpcd, tld off.* ....(12 to 1 op 10 to 1 tchd 14 to 1) 9
Dist: 1½l, 3½l, ½l, 2l, 2½l, 6l, ¾l, 2½l, 10l. 1m 16.07s. a 5.67s (9 Ran).
SR: 43/36/34/9/10/-/ (Lord Hartington), G Lewis

2930 Drawing Room Handicap Class D (0-80 3-y-o and up) £5,708 1m 1f (5:50)

2794[5] GOOGLY [70] 4-9-6 J Reid (12) *al prmnt, led ins fnl furlong, ran on wl*................(3 to 1 fav op 4 to 1) 1
2757[3] LADY LACEY [54] (v) 6-7-11 (7*) N Varley (10) *mid-div early, in ld o'r 2 fs out, hdd and no extr ins last.* ....(4 to 1 op 7 to 2 tchd 9 to 2) 2
2211[6] CAMDEN'S RANSOM (USA) [71] 6-9-4 (3*) B Doyle (6) *beh, ran on ins fnl furlong, nrst finish.* (8 to 1 tchd 10 to 1) 3
2348[3] COURAGEOUS KNIGHT [70] 4-9-6 W R Swinburn (7) *beh, hdwy o'r 2 fs out, nrst finish.* ....(12 to 1 op 10 to 1 tchd 14 to 1) 4
2820[4] TICKERTY'S GIFT [71] (bl) 3-8-12 B Rouse (9) *nvr far away, ev ch o'r 2 fs out, wknd.* ....(16 to 1 op 12 to 1 tchd 20 to 1) 5
2567[3] HIGH LOW (USA) [78] 5-9-7 (7*) S Giles (5) *chasing ldrs whn hrd rdn o'r 2 fs out, sn btn.* (14 to 1 tchd 16 to 1) 6
2834[6] GREEN'S CASSATT (USA) [50] 5-8-0 R Lappin (3) *trkd ldrs till wknd o'r 2 fs out*.............. (33 to 1 op 20 to 1) 7
2672[3] SCORCHED AIR [73] 3-9-0 M Hills (1) *ev ch o'r 2 fs out, sn wknd*.................(8 to 1 op 7 to 1 tchd 10 to 1) 8
2624[5] NORTH ESK (USA) [66] 4-9-2 A Munro (11) *hld up, hrd rdn o'r 2 fs out, no imprsn.* ....(12 to 1 op 10 to 1 tchd 14 to 1) 9
829 GLISSO (Ire) [52] 3-7-7 N Adams (13) *wth early ldr, beh o'r 2 fs out, tld off*.......(16 to 1 op 14 to 1 tchd 20 to 1) 10
2233* ROYAL INTERVAL [80] 3-9-2 (5*) D McCabe (2) *early ldr, beh o'r 2 fs out, tld off.* (10 to 1 op 8 to 1 tchd 11 to 1) 11
2672[5] HADEER'S DANCE [75] 3-9-2 L Piggott (4) *tracking ldrs 2 fs out, sn btn, tld off*.......(8 to 1 op 6 to 1 tchd 9 to 1) 12
Dist: Sht-hd, 1l, 4l, 3½l, nk, 3½l, sht-hd, ½l, 20l, 1l. 2m 1.70s. a 9.70s (12 Ran).
SR: 35/18/33/24/9/24/-/2/3/ (A G Lansley), W G R Wightman

HAMILTON (good to firm)
Thursday July 29th
Going Correction: MINUS 0.45 sec. per fur. (races 1,2,6), MINUS 0.30 (3,4,5)

2931 Bonnington Selling Stakes Class G (3-y-o and up) £1,646 1m 1f 36yds. .(6:30)

2670[6] NORTHERN RAINBOW 5-9-0 Dale Gibson (5) *slwly into strd, sn chasing ldrs, rdn 2 fs out, rdr lost whip ins last, styd on wl to dead-heat on line.* (7 to 4 fav op 6 to 4) 1+
2680[6] BOLD MELODY 4-8-13 (3*) J Weaver (1) *trkd ldr, led o'r 4 fs out, rdn 2 out, jst hld on*.............(5 to 1 op 4 to 1) 1+
2747 LAZY RHYTHM (USA) 7-9-2 (5*) O Pears (6) *hld up rear, pushed alng 5 fs out, rdn o'r 3 out, not rch ldrs.* ....(25 to 1 op 16 to 1) 3
2602[7] DRUMDONNA (Ire) 3-8-7 J Fortune (2) *led till o'r 4 fs out, wknd 3 out*........................(6 to 1 op 5 to 1) 4
2769[4] OLICANA (Ire) 3-8-5 (7*) J Marshall (4) *hld up, rdn 3 fs out, sn btn*.......................(15 to 8 op 5 to 2 tchd 7 to 4) 5
2768[8] BLAKES REACH 3-8-0 (5*) Darren Moffatt (3) *chsd ldrs, outpcd o'r 5 fs out, beh whn swrvd lft over 3 out.* ....(100 to 1 op 50 to 1) 6
Dist: Dd-ht, 8l, 3l, 2l, 6l. 1m 58.60s. a 4.60s (6 Ran).
(Ms K Valentini & W J Whitaker), I Campbell & P C Haslam

2932 Halt Bar Lobey Dosser El Fideldo Handicap Class E (0-70 3-y-o and up) £2,574 1m 65yds.............. (7:00)

2537[6] TALENTED TING (Ire) [55] (v) 4-9-7 (3*) J Weaver (7) *made all, clr whn wnt lft o'r one furlong out, styd on wl.* ....(8 to 1 op 7 to 1 tchd 9 to 1) 1
2236[5] NO COMEBACKS [53] 5-9-8 K Fallon (1) *beh, hdwy to chase wnr o'r one furlong out, no imprsn fnl furlong.* ....(6 to 1 tchd 8 to 1) 2
2768* BIDWEAYA (USA) [28] 6-7-11 J Fanning (8) *chsd ldrs, kpt on same pace fnl 2 fs*...... (3 to 1 op 5 to 2 tchd 9 to 4) 3

2601[5] SIR ARTHUR HOBBS [54] 6-9-9 S Perks (6) *beh, effrt 4 fs out, not rch ldrs*....................(10 to 1 op 7 to 1) 4
2737* FLETCHER'S BOUNTY (Ire) [49] (v) 4-9-4 (5ex) K Darley (3) *beh, effrt o'r 3 fs out, nvr dngrs.* ....(11 to 4 fav op 5 to 2 tchd 3 to 1) 5
2737[2] DANCES WITH GOLD [38] (bl) 3-7-13 Dale Gibson (2) *cl up till wknd o'r 3 fs out*....................(6 to 1 op 4 to 1) 6
2540[7] BRAXTON BRAGG (Ire) [47] (bl) 3-8-1 (7*) J Marshall (5) *prmnt till wknd o'r 2 fs out.* ....(8 to 1 op 10 to 1 tchd 12 to 1) 7
2555[7] BLAKENEY BOY [33] 3-7-3 (5*) Darren Moffatt (4) *chsd ldrs till wknd 5 fs out*....................(100 to 1) 8
Dist: 8l, 3½l, 4l, 3l, 8l, 5l, 1½l. 1m 45.00s. a 1.00s (8 Ran).
SR: 39/13/-/-/-/ (Martin Wickens), P C Haslam

2933 Hyndford Claiming Stakes Class F (2-y-o) £2,005 6f 5yds............. (7:30)

2705[2] BENEFICIARY 8-3[1] K Fallon (3) *trkd ldr, led o'r one furlong out, rdn entering last, hld on wl.* ....(5 to 2 op 2 to 1) 1
2814[4] HICKLETON LADY (Ire) 8-8 K Darley (2) *slwly into strd, beh, swtchd o'r 2 fs out, styd on wl und pres fnl furlong, not rch wnr*....................(7 to 4 fav op 9 to 4) 2
2739[4] HENRY THE HAWK 8-6 (3*) J Weaver (1) *al prmnt, rdn 2 fs out, kpt on same pace*.......... (5 to 1 tchd 11 to 2) 3
2739[3] NOSMO KING (Ire) (bl) 8-13 J Fortune (6) *led till o'r one furlong out, wknd fnl furlong*....... (6 to 1 op 5 to 1) 4
2637[6] OAKLEY MANOR 8-0 J Fanning (5) *prmnt, rdn o'r 2 fs out, wknd over one out*.............. (16 to 1 op 12 to 1) 5
2668 CHELSEA LADY (Ire) 7-12 Dale Gibson (4) *beh hfwy.* ....(10 to 1 op 5 to 1) 6
Dist: 1l, 3l, 2½l, 7l, 5l. 1m 13.50s. a 2.80s (6 Ran).
(Reg Griffin), M H Easterby

2934 Orbiston Handicap Class E (0-70 3-y-o) £2,385 6f 5yds............... (8:00)

1540[6] PEACEFULL REPLY (USA) [58] 9-0 S Perks (2) *cl up, led one furlong out, ran on wl*............ (8 to 1 op 10 to 1) 1
2861[2] SWEET ROMEO [57] 8-13 K Darley (8) *slight ld to one furlong out, no extr.* ....(11 to 8 fav op 6 to 4 tchd 13 to 8) 2
2851[2] BIRCHWOOD SUN [65] (bl) 9-4 (3*) J Weaver (6) *beh till styd on wl fnl 2 fs, nrst finish*........... (8 to 1 op 6 to 1) 3
2707[2] KILLY'S FILLY [55] 8-11 J Fortune (7) *slwly into strd, sn prmnt, ev ch 2 fs out, soon rdn and btn.* ....(11 to 2 op 5 to 1 tchd 6 to 1) 4
2737 PEEDIE PEAT [60] (v) 9-2 K Fallon (1) *in tch, effrt hfwy, no hdwy*....................(10 to 1 op 6 to 1) 5
1966[3] KIMBOLTON KORKER [54] 8-3 (7*) Claire Balding (4) *prmnt till wknd 2 fs out*......(13 to 2 op 6 to 1 tchd 7 to 1) 6
2769[2] BOLD LINE [38] (bl) 7-8[1] Dale Gibson (9) *prmnt till wknd 2 fs out*.................. (6 to 1 op 9 to 2 tchd 7 to 1) 7
Dist: 1½l, 1½l, 1l, 1½l, 1½l, 1l. 1m 12.10s. a 1.40s (7 Ran).
SR: 36/29/31/17/16/4/-/ (Peter Barr), F H Lee

2935 Gaetan Billiard Champagne Apprentice Handicap Class G (0-70 4-y-o and up) £1,970 5f 4yds..............(8:30)

2532[5] PAGEBOY [60] 4-8-13 (7*) C Adamson (2) *cl up, led ins fnl furlong, ran on wl*...... (9 to 2 op 6 to 1 tchd 7 to 1) 1
2813[7] PALLIUM (Ire) [64] 5-9-10 V Halliday (5) *al prmnt, chlgd ins fnl furlong, no extr nr finish*.....(10 to 1 tchd 8 to 1) 2
2788* MEESON TIMES [47] 5-8-7 (7ex) H Bastiman (4) *prmnt, outpcd hfwy, hdwy o'r one furlong out, ev ch ins last, no extr*.................... (4 to 1 fav tchd 9 to 2) 3
2734[3] PRINCE BELFORT [61] 5-9-7 J Tate (6) *led till ins fnl furlong, no extr*....................(5 to 1 op 7 to 1) 4
2215[5] LOFT BOY [57] 10-8-10 (7*) K Sked (1) *beh till styd on fnl furlong, not trble ldrs*............(20 to 1 op 16 to 1) 5
2798[4] DIET [64] (v) 7-9-5 (5*) L Aspell (3) *cl up till wknd o'r one furlong out*.................... (7 to 1 op 6 to 1) 6
2682[4] BARBEZIEUX [47] 6-8-7 J Marshall (9) *beh, hdwy to chase ldrs o'r one furlong out, wknd ins last.* ....(9 to 1 op 10 to 1) 7
2797* MURRAY'S MAZDA (Ire) [72] 4-10-1 (3*,7ex) P Roberts (7) *chsd ldrs till wknd o'r one furlong out.* ....(11 to 2 op 5 to 1 tchd 6 to 1) 8
Dist: ½l, ½l, ¾l, 2l, ¾l, sht-hd, 2l. 1m 0.00s. a 1.70s (8 Ran).
SR: 42/44/25/36/24/28/10/27/ (Lord Scarsdale), P C Haslam

2936 Wallace Limited Stakes Class E (0-70 3-y-o and up) £2,394 1½m 17yds (9:00)

2767* SUNDERLAND ECHO 4-9-10 K Darley (3) *made all, shaken up o'r 2 fs out, styd on wl fnl furlong.* ....(5 to 1 on op 6 to 1 on) 1
2566* AEGAEN LADY 4-9-2 (3*) J Weaver (2) *trkd wnr, effrt entering fnl furlong, kpt on, no imprsn.* ....(4 to 1 op 7 to 2 tchd 9 to 2) 2
Won by 1l. 2m 38.40s. a 5.40s (2 Ran).
SR: 2/-/ (Northeast Press Limited), Mrs M Reveley

SALISBURY (good)

Thursday July 29th
Going Correction: MINUS 0.10 sec. per fur. (races 1,5,6), MINUS 0.30 (2,3,4)

2937 Newnham Maiden Stakes Class D (3-y-o and up) £3,728 1½m........ (6:15)

ALKHAFJI 4-9-7 W Ryan (6) *hld up in tch on outsd, steady hdwy 4 fs out, led o'r one out, sn clr.* ....(5 to 4 on op 9 to 4) 1
BAG OF TRICKS (Ire) 3-8-9 Pat Eddery (12) *slwly into strd, sn trkd ldrs, led o'r 2 fs out, hdd over one out, one pace.* ....(6 to 1 op 5 to 1 tchd 9 to 1) 2
1746[2] LAMBAST 3-8-4 W Carson (5) *pld hrd, trkd ldrs, rdn o'r 2 fs out, styd on one pace.* ....(7 to 2 tchd 11 to 2 and 3 to 1) 3
2071[5] SPICE BOX (USA) 3-8-9 T Sprake (1) *trkd ldrs, pushed alng frm hfwy, kpt on one pace fnl 3 fs.* ....(20 to 1 op 10 to 1) 4
2489[3] CALL ME BLUE 3-8-9 D Holland (14) *trkd ldrs till wknd 2 fs out*.................. (12 to 1 op 8 to 1 tchd 16 to 1) 5
2275[4] CHUMMY'S PAL (USA) 3-8-9 S Dawson (9) *led to hfwy, styd in tch till wknd 2 fs out, eased.* ....(9 to 1 op 5 to 1 tchd 10 to 1) 6
2332[7] MAMARA REEF 3-8-4 A McGlone (7) *hld up in rear, rdn 5 fs out, no hdwy fnl 3*.............. (12 to 1 op 6 to 1) 7
2623[8] MENHAAD (Ire) 3-8-4 S Whitworth (11) *chsd ldrs early, no ch frm hfwy*.................. (33 to 1 op 20 to 1) 8
2277[3] EMMA WOODFORD 3-7-11 (7*) B Russell (2) *pld hrd, led hfwy, hdd o'r 2 fs out, wknd quickly.* ....(11 to 1 op 5 to 1 tchd 12 to 1) 9
2716[9] PISH KESH 3-8-4 A Clark (4) *pld hrd, prmnt to hfwy, sn beh, tld off*..........(20 to 1 op 14 to 1 tchd 25 to 1) 10
EUSTATIA 3-8-4 C Rutter (13) *al beh, tld off.* ....(50 to 1 op 33 to 1) 11
PUSHY WOMAN 4-9-2 R Perham (3) *al beh, tld off.* ....(100 to 1 op 50 to 1) 12
2670 GREAT PLOVER 3-8-9 F Norton (10) *al beh, tld off.* ....(100 to 1 op 50 to 1) 13
Dist: 4l, 2½l, 3l, 4l, 2½l, ¾l, ½l, ¾l, 15l, 10l. 2m 35.56s. a 3.56s (13 Ran).
SR: 59/39/29/28/20/15/8/7/5/ (Prince A A Faisal), H R A Cecil

2938 Robinson Handicap Class E (0-70 3-y-o) £3,366 1m...................(6:45)

STAY WITH ME BABY [60] 8-10[4] (5*) A Procter (12) *styd alone on far side, led entering fnl furlong, drvn out.* ....(14 to 1 op 12 to 1 tchd 16 to 1) 1
2686[5] SECRET ASSIGNMENT (USA) [60] 8-11 D Biggs (10) *al prmnt, led o'r 2 fs out, hrd rdn and hdd entering last, ran on*.................... (10 to 1 tchd 12 to 1) 2
2358[4] MY MINNIE [51] 8-2 T Sprake (1) *hld up, hdwy frm hfwy, one pace ins fnl 2 fs*..............(4 to 1 tchd 9 to 2) 3
2563 BALI HERO (Ire) [68] (bl) 9-5 R Hills (6) *slwly into strd, mid-div, hdwy und pres o'r 2 fs out, nvr nr to chal.* ....(10 to 1 op 7 to 1) 4
2548[7] TAKE THE MICK [53] 8-4 C Rutter (3) *slwly away, nvr nr to chal*............ (11 to 1 op 7 to 1 tchd 12 to 1) 5
1903 MURPHY'S HOPE (Ire) [57] 8-8 D Holland (11) *hld up in tch, no hdwy fnl 2 fs*..................(16 to 1 op 14 to 1) 6
2612[2] DON TOCINO [62] 8-13 L Dettori (9) *prmnt till rdn and wknd o'r 2 fs out*.................. (5 to 1 tchd 11 to 2) 7
2697[5] SPRING SUNRISE [61] 8-12 R Cochrane (5) *in tch for 5 fs, sn beh*.............. (12 to 1 op 10 to 1 tchd 14 to 1) 8
2622[2] SEA SIREN [70] 9-7 W Newnes (7) *led till hng lft and hdd wl o'r 2 fs out, sn btn.* ....(7 to 2 fav op 3 to 1 tchd 4 to 1) 9
2544[9] MOST EQUAL [50] 8-1 F Norton (4) *in tch till wknd 3 fs out.* ....(25 to 1 op 20 to 1) 10
759 BAYFAN (Ire) [53] 8-4 A McGlone (8) *trkd ldr to hfwy, drpd out quickly*.................. (25 to 1 op 16 to 1) 11
2122* JALIB (Ire) [51] 8-2 W Carson (2) *al beh.* ....(11 to 2 op 6 to 1 tchd 5 to 1) 12
Dist: Hd, 5l, ¾l, 3½l, 2l, 2l, nk, 6l, 5l, 2½l. 1m 43.09s. a 3.59s (12 Ran).
SR: 7/6/-/-/-/-/ (Adept (80) Ltd), D R C Elsworth

2939 Downing Claiming Stakes Class F (3-y-o) £2,780 6f.................. (7:15)

1991 WESTERN VALLEY 7-12 (3*) B Doyle (6) *al prmnt, led o'r one furlong out, drvn out*........ (33 to 1 op 20 to 1) 1
2832[4] PRINCELY FAVOUR (Ire) (bl) 9-4 Pat Eddery (2) *led till hdd o'r one furlong out, ran on und pres.* ....(2 to 1 fav op 5 to 2 tchd 7 to 4) 2
2746[5] PRINCESS OBERON (Ire) 8-11 L Dettori (10) *rcd prmntly far side, ev ch entering fnl furlong, no imprsn nr finish.* ....(11 to 4 op 9 to 4 tchd 3 to 1) 3
2623[6] URRY URRY URRY 8-5 W Carson (7) *in tch till outpcd ins fnl 2 fs*....................(7 to 2 op 3 to 1) 4
2711[4] CHILI LADY 8-7 T Sprake (9) *in frnt rnk till wknd o'r 2 fs out*....................(9 to 1 op 7 to 1) 5
1990[3] DOUBLE BOUNCE 9-4 W Newnes (12) *al mid-div, nvr nr to chal*....................(12 to 1 op 10 to 1) 6
2636[6] DOCTOR-J (Ire) 8-6 S Raymont (13) *chsd ldrs, rdn hfwy, sn btn*.................. (25 to 1 op 20 to 1) 7

1990[6] AMBIVALENTATTITUDE 8-2 F Norton (5) *al beh.* .... (66 to 1 op 50 to 1) 8
1278[5] SENOR L'AMOUR 8-10 A McGlone (1) *al beh.* .... (33 to 1 op 20 to 1) 9
1588 JEWEL THIEF 8-8 J Williams (11) *al beh.* .... (20 to 1 op 12 to 1) 10
2580 PRIMOCELLE 8-6 (7*) M Handley (14) *al beh.* .... (25 to 1 op 20 to 1) 11
2476 ANOTHER KINGDOM 8-9 A Clark (4) *outpcd thrght.* .... (33 to 1 op 20 to 1) 12
DOT THE DOMINO 7-9 (5*) D Wright (3) *slwly away, al beh.* .... (50 to 1 op 20 to 1) 13
Dist: ½l, 1½l, 6l, 1½l, 4l, 2½l, 2l, ½l, 2l, ¾l. 1m 13.74s. a 1.24s (13 Ran).
SR: 26/41/28/-/-/-/ (M D Brunton), K O Cunningham-Brown

2940 Magdalene Fillies' Handicap Class D (0-80 3-y-o and up) £4,012 6f 212yds ....(7:45)

2715* NEITHER NOR [72] 4-9-10 (6ex) G Carter (7) *hld up in tch, rdn o'r 2 fs out, ran on strly to ld wl ins last.* ....(6 to 1 op 5 to 1 tchd 7 to 1) 1
2491[5] NEWINGTON BUTTS (Ire) [58] 3-7-10 (7*) B Russell (3) *al prmnt, led o'r 2 fs out, hng lft und pres, strtened entering last, edgd rght and hdd ins, no extr.* .... (10 to 1 op 8 to 1) 2
2577[2] TEANARCO (Ire) [61] 5-8-13 L Dettori (2) *hld up on stands side, hdwy 2 fs out, hrd rdn, kpt on one pace ins last.* .... (5 to 2 fav tchd 7 to 2) 3
1604[7] POLAR STORM (Ire) [72] 3-9-3 J Reid (13) *al prmnt far side, one pace appr fnl furlong.* .... (11 to 2 op 7 to 1 tchd 5 to 1) 4
2577[7] QUEEN OF SHANNON (Ire) [66] 5-9-4 M Tebbutt (10) *hld up, rdn 2 fs out, kpt on one pace fnl furlong.* ....(6 to 1 op 5 to 1 tchd 7 to 1) 5
1956 NAVARESQUE [45] 8-7-11 F Norton (9) *led till hdd o'r 2 fs out, eased whn btn fnl furlong....* (20 to 1 op 14 to 1) 6
2066[6] PETONELLAJILL [76] 3-9-7 Pat Eddery (12) *hld up in tch, hdwy hfwy, fdd o'r one out.* .... (7 to 2 op 9 to 2 tchd 11 to 2) 7
990 KYRENIA GAME [65] 3-8-10 S O'Gorman (11) *slwly away and wl beh till some hdwy o'r 2 fs out, nvr dngrs.* .... (33 to 1 op 25 to 1 tchd 50 to 1) 8
2548 CANADIAN CAPERS [52] 4-8-4 S Whitworth (1) *al beh.* .... (25 to 1 op 16 to 1) 9
2577 BROADWAY RUCKUS (Can) [47] (v) 4-7-13 T Williams (5) *gd speed to hfwy, sn beh.* .... (33 to 1 op 20 to 1) 10
1968[9] GUANHUMARA [48] (v) 3-7-2 (5*) D Wright (4) *prmnt till wknd o'r 2 fs out.* ....(33 to 1 op 20 to 1) 11
2660[5] MY BONUS [80] 3-9-11 D Biggs (8) *al beh.* .... (16 to 1 op 14 to 1) 12
2548[2] SPANISH LOVE [42] 7-7-8[1] J Quinn (6) *al beh.* .... (10 to 1 op 8 to 1) 13
Dist: 1½l, 1l, 2½l, hd, 1½l, ¾l, 2l, hd, sht-hd, 5l. 1m 27.74s. a 2.14s (13 Ran).
SR: 46/20/27/23/23/-/19/2/-/ (T S M S Riley-Smith), D A Wilson

2941 Trinity Conditions Stakes Class D (3-y-o and up) £3,850 1m 1f 209yds (8:15)

2464* PRINCE OF ANDROS (USA) 3-8-12 L Dettori (1) *hld up in tch, smooth hdwy to ld o'r 2 fs out, rdn appr last, ran on, cmftbly.* .... (9 to 1 op 8 to 1 tchd 10 to 1) 1
2275* RIVER BOYNE (USA) 3-8-12 Pat Eddery (5) *hld up towards rear, hdwy on outsd 3 fs out, rdn appr last, ran on.* ....(7 to 4 jt-fav op 5 to 2 tchd 11 to 4) 2
1845[6] ROCKAWHILE (Ire) 4-9-3 W Ryan (7) *hld up in rear, hdwy 3 fs out, ev ch appr fnl furlong, one pace ins.* ....(6 to 1 op 4 to 1) 3
1200 AJFAN (USA) 3-8-3 R Hills (4) *trkd ldrs, ev ch whn short of room one furlong out, one pace aftr.* ....(7 to 4 jt-fav op Evens) 4
1958[5] JACKPOT STAR 3-8-12 J Reid (3) *trkd ldr till wknd ins fnl 2 fs.* .... (25 to 1 op 12 to 1) 5
2227* NORTHERN BOUND (Ire) 3-8-12 A Clark (2) *led, rdn 4 fs out, hdd o'r 2 out, sn btn.* .... (16 to 1) 6
2623[5] ARUSHA (Ire) (bl) 3-8-7 W Carson (8) *hld up in rear, rdn frm hfwy, beh fnl 3 fs.* .... (16 to 1 op 12 to 1) 7
2116[4] FRONTIER FLIGHT (USA) 3-8-8 G Carter (6) *pld hrd in mid-div, rdn o'r 3 fs out, sn btn.* .... (25 to 1 op 12 to 1) 8
Dist: 2½l, ¾l, 2l, 5l, 2l, 8l, ¾l. 2m 7.77s. a 3.77s (8 Ran).
SR: 50/45/48/30/29/25/4/3/ (Lucayan Stud), D R Loder

2942 Pembroke Handicap Class E (0-70 3-y-o and up) £3,236 1½m.......... (8:45)

1906[3] SUPREME MASTER [62] 3-8-9 L Dettori (8) *al gng wl, hdwy o'r 2 fs out, led well over one out, pushed out.* .... (5 to 2 fav op 3 to 1 tchd 7 to 2 and 9 to 4) 1
2685[6] ROCQUAINE BAY [39] 6-7-12 C Rutter (2) *hld up, steady hdwy 3 fs out, hrd rdn to run on ins fnl furlong.* .... (14 to 1 op 12 to 1) 2
2420[4] ACROBATE (USA) [57] (bl) 4-9-2 W Carson (6) *nvr far away, took narrow ld 3 fs out, hdd wl o'r one out, ran on und pres.* ....(3 to 1 op 6 to 1) 3
2669[4] FULL QUIVER [43] (v) 8-7-11 (5*) D Wright (13) *hld up, hdwy 3 fs out, rdn and ran on wl ins fnl 2 furlongs.* .... (10 to 1 op 8 to 1) 4
2669 CORINTHIAN GOD (Ire) [35] 4-7-8 J Quinn (3) *mid-div, rdn 3 fs out, wknd appr last.* ....(20 to 1 op 16 to 1) 5
2678[5] DUGGAN [46] 6-8-5[2] R Cochrane (14) *hld up, hdwy 4 fs out, rdn o'r 2 out, one pace.* ....(11 to 1 op 8 to 1 tchd 12 to 1) 6
2669 VITAL CLUE (USA) [69] 6-10-0 D Biggs (7) *al mid-div, no hdwy fnl 3 fs.* ....(33 to 1 op 20 to 1) 7
2523[4] WOLLBOLL [52] 3-7-13 T Sprake (12) *chsd ldrs, rdn and wknd wl o'r 2 fs out.* .... (12 to 1 op 8 to 1) 8
2669[9] INCOLA [54] 7-8-6 (7*) Antoinette Armes (1) *mid-div, wl beh fnl 3 fs.* .... (14 to 1 op 10 to 1) 9
2669[3] THEMEDA [43] 4-7-13 (3*) D Harrison (10) *trkd ldr, led briefly o'r 3 fs out, rdn and sn btn.* .... (4 to 1 tchd 11 to 2 and 7 to 2) 10
1392[8] KASHAN (Ire) [52] 5-8-11 J Williams (11) *al beh.* .... (50 to 1 op 33 to 1) 11
2669 BOXBOY [48] 3-7-9 S Dawson (4) *al beh.* ....(20 to 1 tchd 25 to 1) 12
2353[9] SALMONID [51] 7-8-3 (7*) A Lakeman (5) *sn trkd ldr, wknd quickly 3 fs out.* .... (33 to 1 op 20 to 1) 13
2686[9] ALMOSTAUTOMATIC (Ire) [50] 4-8-9 M Tebbutt (9) *led, sn clr, hdd 3 fs out, wknd quickly, tld off.* .... (33 to 1) 14
Dist: ¾l, nk, nk, 8l, ¾l, sht-hd, ½l, 1½l, 5l, 3½l. 2m 36.36s. a 4.36s (14 Ran).
SR: 39/26/43/28/4/13/35/5/16/ (Harry W Hopgood), R Hannon

YARMOUTH (good)
Thursday July 29th
Going Correction: PLUS 0.10 sec. per fur.

2943 Bradwell Claiming Stakes Class E (3-y-o) £2,742 1¾m 17yds......... (2:10)

2716[6] RASAYEL (USA) 7-12 J Quinn (4) *patiently rdn, drvn ahead wl o'r 2 out, styd on well to go clr fnl furlong.* .... (15 to 8 on op 2 to 1 on tchd 9 to 4 on and 7 to 4 on) 1
1613[6] UME RIVER (Ire) 8-3 P Robinson (1) *trkd ldr, led o'r 3 fs out till wl over 2 out, rdn and no extr pace.* .... (11 to 4 op 5 to 2 tchd 3 to 1) 2
1772[4] NAAWY 8-0 (5*) K Rutter (2) *pressed ldg pair, feeling pace o'r 3 fs out, sn struggling.* .... (9 to 1 op 5 to 1 tchd 10 to 1) 3
2784[7] BARSLEY 8-2[1] G Duffield (3) *set modest pace, quickened up appr strt, hdd and wknd o'r 3 fs out.......* (25 to 1) 4
Dist: 6l, 7l, sht-hd. 3m 11.20s. a 14.20s (4 Ran).
(Saeed Suhail), B Hanbury

2944 Wroxham Handicap Class E (0-70 3-y-o and up) £3,002 7f 3yds........ (2:40)

2717* ROCA MURADA (Ire) [61] 4-9-0 (7*,5ex) P McCabe (4) *settled midfield, shaken up to improve hfwy, led wl o'r one furlong out, ran on well.* ....(7 to 2 op 3 to 1) 1
2602* ADAMPARIS [47] (bl) 3-8-0 P Robinson (1) *co'red up in midfield, drvn up on outsd to draw level over one furlong out, kpt on same pace.* .... (14 to 1 op 8 to 1) 2
2717[2] JAHANGIR (Ire) [66] 4-9-12 B Raymond (3) *niggled alng in midfield, improved to flter o'r one furlong out, rdn and found little.* .... (5 to 2 fav op 2 to 1) 3
2459* BALLYRANTER [50] (v) 4-8-10 J Quinn (9) *chsd alng to go pace, improved frm midfield o'r one furlong out, nvr nrr.* ....(13 to 2 op 5 to 1) 4
2170[4] PRINCE SONGLINE [55] (bl) 3-8-8 W Woods (8) *chsd ldg trio, feeling pace 2 fs out, sn btn.* .... (9 to 1 op 8 to 1 tchd 10 to 1) 5
2717[9] TAJDID (Ire) [61] (bl) 3-9-0 N Carlisle (6) *led aftr one furlong till wl o'r one out, fdd.* (9 to 1 op 7 to 1 tchd 10 to 1) 6
2710* GLEN MILLER [57] (bl) 3-8-10 (5ex) G Duffield (5) *trkd ldrs, drvn alng whn pace lifted 2 fs out, sn btn.* ....(7 to 1 op 6 to 1) 7
2445[7] BOLD HABIT [65] 8-9-11 M Wigham (7) *sluggish strt, nvr a factor.* ....(12 to 1 op 8 to 1) 8
2717 SABOTEUR [34] 9-7-8[1] A Mackay (2) *broke wl to ld for one furlong, fdd und pres 2 out.* ....(33 to 1 op 25 to 1) 9
Dist: 2l, 3½l, 3½l, 5l, ¾l, 8l, 3l, 4l. 1m 28.80s. a 5.60s (9 Ran).
SR: 34/7/22/-/-/-/ (Tim Corby), M J Ryan

2945 Keith Tuck Final Fling Handicap Class D (0-75 3-y-o and up) £3,395 6f 3yds ....(3:05)

2832[7] JOBIE [70] 3-9-10 W Woods (5) *tacked o'r to ld on stands side, made all, pushed out.* ....(9 to 2 op 6 to 1 tchd 7 to 2) 1
2378[3] JOIN THE CLAN [57] 4-9-3 G Duffield (3) *drvn alng to keep up, str chal fnl furlong, edgd lft, one pace.* .... (6 to 4 fav tchd 2 to 1) 2
2788[4] SPRING HIGH [53] (bl) 6-8-13 M Wigham (2) *gd speed centre, hrd drvn o'r 2 fs out, no extr.....*(9 to 2 op 3 to 1) 3
2734[2] ZEBOIM [68] (bl) 7-9-7 (7*) Kim McDonnell (1) *gd speed on outsd, drvn alng o'r one furlong out, sn btn.* .... (5 to 1 op 7 to 2 tchd 11 to 2) 4
2636[8] ELTON LEDGER (Ire) [61] 4-9-7 B Raymond (4) *nvr far away, effrt and drvn alng o'r one furlong out, no extr.* ....(9 to 2 op 3 to 1) 5
Dist: 1l, 8l, ¾l, hd. 1m 15.00s. a 4.00s (5 Ran).
SR: 42/31/-/7/-/ (J A Redmond), W J Haggas

2946 Marina Leisure Centre Selling Stakes Class G (2-y-o) £2,259 6f 3yds...(3:35)

2423[7] ADMIRING 8-3 (3*) M Fenton (3) *led for o'r a furlong, styd upsides till rgned ld over one out, drvn out.* ....(13 to 1 op 7 to 1 tchd 14 to 1) 1
2748[3] PRINCESS CARMEN (Ire) 8-6 B Raymond (2) *al hndy, str chal appr fnl furlong, kpt on*................(3 to 1 jt-fav op 5 to 2 tchd 4 to 1) 2
1523[6] GRANMAS DELIGHT 8-6 W Woods (6) *trkd ldrs, tacked o'r to stands side hfwy, not quicken over one furlong out.* ....(3 to 1 jt-fav op 7 to 2 tchd 4 to 1) 3
2637[3] HONEST WOMAN 8-6 A Mackay (4) *steadied strt, drvn into midfield o'r 2 fs out, kpt on, no imprsn.* ....(8 to 1 op 5 to 1) 4
2417[8] CANDI DAS (Ire) (bl) 8-6 G Duffield (5) *bustled alng in midfield, some hdwy last 2 fs, nvr able to chal.* ....(6 to 1 op 4 to 1) 5
2668 DAVIDS DIAMOND (v) 8-6 P Robinson (7) *wnt freely to post, steadied strt, struggling hfwy, no imprsn.* .... (8 to 1 op 20 to 1 tchd 25 to 1) 6
2271[3] FORBIDDEN MONKEY (bl) 8-6 G Carter (1) *chsd ldrs on outsd, hrd drvn 2 fs out, no response.* ....(7 to 2 op 5 to 2 tchd 4 to 1) 7
POOR WILLY 8-4 (7*) S Jones (8) *led aftr one and a half fs till o'r one out, sn btn*............(16 to 1 op 10 to 1) 8
Dist: ½l, 3l, 2½l, 1l, 2½l, hd, 2l. 1m 16.80s. a 5.80s (8 Ran).
(Friendly Society), M Bell

2947 Cotman Fillies Conditions Stakes Class D (2-y-o) £4,347 5f 43yds..(4:05)

1804[7] EVENING FALLS 9-0 G Hind (4) *made all, quickened to go clr o'r one furlong out, easily*.......(14 to 1 op 6 to 1) 1
2400[3] RANDONNEUR (Ire) 8-10 J Quinn (1) *al hndy, hrd drvn o'r one furlong out, no ch wth wnr*.....(4 to 1 op 5 to 1) 2
2629[2] CARRIE KOOL 8-12 W Woods (7) *crrd rght strt, nvr far away, staying on whn drifted lft fnl furlong, one pace.* ....(6 to 1 op 3 to 1) 3
2435* NIGHTITUDE 9-2 B Raymond (3) *pressed ldrs, hrd drvn last 2 fs, not quicken.* .... (5 to 4 fav tchd 6 to 4 and Evens) 4
2400[8] ANTONIA'S FOLLY 9-0 G Carter (5) *niggled alng in midfield, effrt 2 fs out, unbl to quicken.* (12 to 1 op 6 to 1) 5
2630* ALZIANAH (v) 9-0 G Duffield (6) *jinked rght strt, struggling whn pace lifted hfwy, fdd o'r one furlong out.* .... (5 to 1 op 4 to 1 tchd 13 to 2) 6
Dist: 7l, nk, 2l, ¾l, 1½l. 1m 5.00s. a 4.30s (6 Ran).
SR: 25/-/-/ (Mrs Carol J Welch), J L Spearing

2948 Carnival Handicap Class E (0-70 3-y-o and up) £2,846 1¼m 21yds......(4:35)

1812[2] DARING PAST [56] (bl) 3-9-3 G Duffield (2) *settled midfield, drvn alng to improve o'r one furlong out, ran on to ld last strds*................................(7 to 1 op 6 to 1) 1
2859* BRONZE MAQUETTE (Ire) [55] 3-9-2 (5ex) E Johnson (1) *last and hld up, improved und pres appr fnl furlong, ev ch last 50 yards, ran on*.................................(4 to 1) 2
2311[4] PLATINUM VENTURE [56] 3-9-3 W Woods (6) *made most, hdd o'r 2 fs out, rallied to ld ag'n ins last, headed cl hme*................................(20 to 1 op 12 to 1) 3
2774* MODEST HOPE (USA) [58] 6-10-1 (5ex) Alex Greaves (4) *settled gng wl, quickened up to ld o'r one furlong out, hdd and wknd ins last*............(4 to 1 tchd 9 to 2) 4
2784* BILLYBACK [57] 3-8-11 (7*,5ex) P McCabe (3) *co'red up on ins, swtchd to chal inside fnl furlong, wknd last 50 yards*...............................(5 to 1 op 5 to 2) 5
2669[8] PRECUSSION [56] (bl) 3-9-3 R Price (7) *al hndy, hrd drvn o'r 3 fs out, btn 2 out*................ (9 to 1 op 5 to 1) 6
RIVE-JUMELLE (Ire) [50] 5-9-4 (3*) M Fenton (5) *settled to track ldrs, feeling pace o'r 2 fs out, no extr.* .... (9 to 1 op 10 to 1 tchd 8 to 1) 7
2126[6] TAYLORS PRINCE [52] (v) 6-9-9 J Quinn (8) *nvr far away, led o'r 2 fs til one out, wknd quickly.* ....(3 to 1 fav op 4 to 1) 8
Dist: Hd, hd, 3½l, sht-hd, 2l, 6l, 4l. 2m 12.10s. a 8.10s (8 Ran).
SR: 32/30/30/35/23/18/10/4/ (Keith Sturgis), R Boss

EDINBURGH (good to firm)
Friday July 30th
Going Correction: MINUS 0.25 sec. per fur. (races 1,3), MINUS 0.10 (2,4,5,6)

2949 Stockbroker's Claiming Stakes Class F (2-y-o) £1,903 5f..............(6:30)

449[4] MAD ABOUT MEN 8-8 J Carroll (2) *in tch, hdwy to ld wl o'r one furlong out, all out.* (5 to 1 op 6 to 1 tchd 4 to 1) 1
2759[3] MISS PIGALLE 9-2 Dale Gibson (7) *beh, styd on wl fnl 2 fs, not rch wnr*......................(20 to 1 op 14 to 1) 2
2423[3] CHEEKY CHAPPY 9-3 Alex Greaves (8) *wth ldrs, ev ch o'r one furlong out, kpt on*......................(10 to 1) 3
2814[8] SECONDS AWAY 9-7 K Darley (4) *trkd ldrs, kpt on same pace fnl 2 fs*......................(16 to 1 op 14 to 1) 4
2772[3] CAPTAIN TAFFY (v) 8-13 L Charnock (6) *made most till wl o'r one furlong out, kpt on same pace.* ....(13 to 8 fav op 6 to 4 tchd 7 to 4) 5
2271[5] READY-FREDDIE 8-10 (3*) J Weaver (1) *prmnt till wknd entering fnl furlong*................(9 to 2 op 7 to 2) 6
2814[9] RED GRIT (Ire) (bl) 8-12 J Lowe (3) *dsptd ld till wknd o'r one furlong out*..................(12 to 1 op 8 to 1) 7
2637[2] WILLWIN 8-8 J Fortune (5) *cl up till wknd 2 fs out.* ....(7 to 1 op 4 to 1) 8
Dist: Nk, ¾l, 1½l, sht-hd, 1½l, 3l, 1½l. 1m 1.30s. a 3.50s (8 Ran).
SR: -/6/4/2/-/ (Manchester Evening News Ltd), J Berry

2950 Bell Lawrie/Brewin Dolphin Marriage Handicap Class E (0-70 3-y-o and up) £2,284 1m 7f 16yds.............(7:00)

2683* HUNTING GROUND [42] (bl) 5-9-11 (3ex) G Duffield (2) *trkd ldrs, led o'r 4 fs out, styd on strly fnl furlong.* ....(11 to 10 on op Evens) 1
2043* WHITE RIVER [38] 7-9-7 J Lowe (4) *in tch, hdwy 4 fs out, chsd wnr frm 2 out, no imprsn*.......(9 to 2 op 5 to 1) 2
2683[4] NATIVE CROWN (Ire) [34] 5-9-3 N Connorton (3) *in tch, hdwy 3 fs out, one pace 2 out.* .... (11 to 1 op 8 to 1 tchd 12 to 1) 3
2888[2] REEL OF TULLOCH (Ire) [44] 4-9-13 (3ex) K Darley (1) *in tch, lost pl o'r 4 fs out, kpt on und pres frm 2 out, nvr dngrs.* ....(7 to 2 op 4 to 1 tchd 9 to 2) 4
2506[3] HOT PUNCH [37] 4-9-6 Dale Gibson (5) *prmnt, rdn 3 fs out, one pace*.........................(16 to 1 op 12 to 1) 5
WHATCOMESNATURALLY (USA) [35] 4-8-11 (7*) J Marshall (6) *led till o'r 4 fs out, wknd over 2 out.* .... (20 to 1 op 14 to 1) 6
2800[5] ALPHA HELIX [26] (v) 10-8-9 J Fanning (7) *al beh.* ....(20 to 1 op 16 to 1) 7
Dist: 2½l, 1½l, ½l, 2½l, 3½l, 6l. 3m 24.50s. a 12.50s (7 Ran).
(Esprit de Corps Racing), A Bailey

2951 Bell Lawrie White Handicap Class E (0-70 3-y-o and up) £2,232 5f.... (7:30)

1938 SUPER ROCKY [60] 4-8-13 (7*) H Bastiman (2) *chsd ldrs, pushed alng hfwy, led ins fnl furlong, ran on wl.* ....(7 to 2 op 4 to 1) 1
2682[2] KABCAST [45] (bl) 8-8-5 J Fanning (5) *led till ins fnl furlong, no extr*................(5 to 2 co-fav op 2 to 1) 2
2813[9] ABSOLUTION [65] 9-9-8 (3*) J Weaver (1) *in tch, rdn 2 fs out, no hdwy*.....(5 to 2 co-fav op 2 to 1 tchd 3 to 1) 3
2510* OUR MICA [53] (bl) 3-8-8 J Carroll (4) *chsd ldr till wknd wl o'r one furlong out*.......... (5 to 2 co-fav op 2 to 1) 4
Dist: 2l, 2½l, 1½l. 59.50s. a 1.70s (4 Ran).
SR: 47/24/34/11/ (I B Barker), R Bastiman

2952 BLW Discretionary Portfolio Management Selling Stakes Class G (2-y-o) £1,871 7f 15yds................ (8:00)

2679[2] MOKAITE 8-6 (7*) J Marshall (1) *made all, clr one furlong out, jst hld on*...... (2 to 1 fav op 6 to 4 tchd 9 to 4) 1
2331 SHUTTLECOCK 8-11 K Darley (2) *prmnt till outpcd hfwy, hdwy o'r 2 fs out, styd on wl und pres fnl furlong, jst fld*...............................(9 to 4 op 3 to 1 tchd 2 to 1) 2
2554[8] MONSIEUR BLEU 8-11 J Fanning (3) *in tch, outpcd hfwy, styd on fnl 2 fs, nrst finish.* .... (11 to 1 op 8 to 1 tchd 14 to 1) 3
2825[3] BESSIE'S WILL 8-6 J Carroll (4) *chsd ldrs, outpcd hfwy, styd on fnl 2 fs, not rch lders*...... (10 to 1 op 4 to 1) 4
2705[3] BRAMCOTE CENTURY 8-6 J Lowe (5) *pld hrd early, sn chasing wnr, wknd o'r 2 fs out.* .... (5 to 2 op 2 to 1 tchd 11 to 4) 5
Dist: Nk, 3l, 2l, 10l. 1m 31.90s. a 6.70s (5 Ran).
(The Bridge Club), M D Hammond

2953 Investment Trust Management Service Rating Related Maiden Stakes Class F (0-60 3-y-o) £2,113 1m 16yds ....(8:30)

2163[5] AZOLA (Ire) (v) 8-9 K Darley (5) *chsd ldrs, rdn to ld ins fnl furlong, ran on wl.* (13 to 8 fav op 7 to 4 tchd 2 to 1) 1
2366[3] NICHODOULA 8-9 G Duffield (2) *cl up, led aftr 2 fs till ins last, no extr*...................... (4 to 1 tchd 9 to 2) 2
2764[2] MUSTN'T GRUMBLE (Ire) 9-0 Kim Tinkler (1) *dwlt, hld up beh, hdwy o'r 2 fs out, rdn over one out, ran on wl.* ....(7 to 2 op 5 to 2 tchd 5 to 1) 3
2133[4] FLASHELLA (Ire) 8-9 J Carroll (8) *led 2 fs, chsd ldr, rdn o'r two furlongs out, kpt on same pace.* .... (15 to 2 op 6 to 1 tchd 8 to 1) 4
2736[2] PLEASE SAY YES (Ire) 8-7 (7*) V Halliday (9) *beh, hdwy 3 fs out, one pace 2 out*................ (7 to 1 op 5 to 1) 5
2338[4] KEEP BATTLING 9-0 J Fanning (3) *in tch, effrt 3 fs out, sn btn*...................... (12 to 1 op 10 to 1) 6
2634[8] SMITH N'ALLAN 9-0 J Fortune (4) *prmnt till wknd 3 fs out.* ....(25 to 1 tchd 33 to 1) 7
2548 LEGAL RISK 8-9 J Lowe (7) *sn beh.* .... (11 to 1 op 10 to 1 tchd 12 to 1) 8
Dist: 2l, 1l, 2½l, 1½l, 3l, 7l, ¾l. 1m 42.20s. a 3.70s (8 Ran).
SR: 28/22/24/11/11/2/-/-/ (E J Loder), D R Loder

2954 BLW PEP Taxbreak Handicap Class E (0-70 3-y-o and up) £2,316 1m 16yds ....(9:00)

2543[8] LEAVE IT TO LIB [59] 6-9-1 (5*) J Tate (3) *led one furlong, wth ldr, led o'r 2 out, hld on wl.* ....(3 to 1 op 11 to 4 tchd 100 to 30) 1
2680[2] LAWNSWOOD JUNIOR [66] 6-9-13 K Darley (4) *hld up, effrta nd swtchd o'r 2 fs out, kpt on wl fnl furlong, not rch wnr.*............................(2 to 1 fav op 5 to 2) 2
1520[8] SKOLERN [36] 9-7-11 J Fanning (1) *in tch, effrt o'r 2 fs out, kpt on fnl furlong*..................(25 to 1 op 16 to 1) 3
2459[4] CRESELLY [58] 6-9-2 (3*) J Weaver (2) *chsd ldrs, effrt o'r 2 fs out, sn rdn, kpt on fnl furlong.* ....(100 to 30 op 3 to 1 tchd 7 to 2) 4
2762[3] ROUTING [54] 5-8-8 (7*,5ex) J Marshall (5) *slight ld aftr one furlong till o'r 2 out, wknd fnl furlong.* ....(7 to 2 tchd 4 to 1) 5
2769* WHITE CREEK (Ire) [61] (v) 3-9-0 (5ex) J Carroll (6) *beh hfwy.* ....(11 to 1 op 8 to 1) 6
Dist: 1l, ½l, sht-hd, 1½l, 4l. 1m 41.90s. a 3.40s (6 Ran).
SR: 43/47/15/36/27/14/ (Mrs C Calver), P Calver

GALWAY (IRE) (good to yielding) Friday July 30th

2955 Guinness Extra Stout Handicap (0-105 3-y-o and up) £6,902 1½m...... (5:50)

2608[9] GARBONI (USA) [-] 4-8-11 M J Kinane (3).......... (2 to 1) 1
2040[3] MICKS DELIGHT (Ire) [-] 3-7-8 Joanna Morgan (1).. (3 to 1) 2
2077[4] SINISSIPI (USA) [-] 3-9-2 J P Murtagh (6)....... (7 to 4 fav) 3
2923[5] MORNING SARGE [-] 5-7-8[5] (6*) J J Behan (2).... (16 to 1) 4
997* DESERT WISH [-] 3-7-12 (6*) J A Heffernan (4)..... (5 to 1) 5
Dist: 1½l, sht-hd, 4l, 3l. 2m 41.90s. (5 Ran).
(Raymond J Rooney), D K Weld

2956 Smithwicks Maiden (3-y-o and up) £4,142 1½m................... (7:05)

2781[2] ALYREINA (USA) (bl) 3-8-11 K J Manning (9)....... (7 to 2) 1
RETURN AGAIN (Ire) 3-8-11 R Hughes (5)........ (16 to 1) 2
2808[2] DAHLIA'S BEST (USA) 3-9-0 W J Supple (10)...... (9 to 4) 3
2781[3] MAGIC FEELING (Ire) 3-8-11 J P Murtagh (1)... (7 to 4 fav) 4
GLENSTAL FLAGSHIP (Ire) 3-8-8 (6*) J A Heffernan (6) ....(20 to 1) 5
2249[6] ENIMDEE (Ire) 3-8-11 J F Egan (4)............... (9 to 1) 6
2676[4] GARDENVALE VIC (Ire) 3-9-0 S Craine (3)........ (20 to 1) 7
2676[6] HAIL TO HOME (Ire) 3-8-5 (6*) P P Murphy (8).... (100 to 1) 8
RUNNING SLIPPER (Ire) 3-8-6 (8*) P J Smullen (7) (25 to 1) 9
2902 OMESMACJOY (Ire) 3-9-0 N G McCullagh (2).... (100 to 1) 10
Dist: 4l, 1l, 3l, nk. 2m 41.70s. (Flag start) (10 Ran).
(J David Brillembourg), J S Bolger

2957 Harp Lager Handicap (0-90 3-y-o and up) £4,142 1m 100yds.......... (7:40)

2286* SWEET NASHA (Ire) [-] 4-9-7 P V Gilson (8)........ (6 to 1) 1
2878[2] WANDERING THOUGHTS (Ire) [-] 4-8-5 W J Supple (1) ....(5 to 4 fav) 2
1202 PRIVATE GUY (Ire) [-] (bl) 4-9-11 M J Kinane (11)... (7 to 1) 3
2345 BRACKLOON BOY (Ire) [-] 4-7-9 (6*) R V Skelly (10) (20 to 1) 4
2779[8] GOODIES TWO STEP (Ire) [-] 3-8-7 N G McCullagh (9) ....(33 to 1) 5
2406* BIZANA (Ire) [-] 3-8-9 R Hughes (3)................ (7 to 1) 6
2878 GALLARDINI (Ire) [-] 4-10-0 K J Manning (7)....... (14 to 1) 7
2463* THATCHING CRAFT (Ire) [-] 4-9-7 (6*,12ex) C Everard (6) ....(9 to 2) 8
2142 BOBROSS (Ire) [-] 3-7-11 (6*) J A Heffernan (5).... (20 to 1) 9
2463[4] PHARELLA [-] 5-7-6 (6*) P P Murphy (2)........... (20 to 1) 10
Dist: Nk, 1½l, nk, 1l. 4m 48.70s. (10 Ran).
(N Stassen), Joseph M Canty

2958 Arthur's Race (4-y-o and up) £4,142 1m........................... (8:10)

PERSIAN TACTICS (bl) 4-9-5 M J Kinane (7)....... (5 to 2) 1
2408[2] SIMPLY MARILYN (Ire) 4-8-10 (6*) J J Behan (6)..... (6 to 1) 2
2408[5] SUPER FLAME (Can) 6-9-5 J P Murtagh (10)........ (7 to 2) 3
2744[5] CRAZY GAIL 6-9-2 W J Supple (9)................... (8 to 1) 4
2609[2] ROYAL VISION (Ire) 4-9-0 K J Manning (3)..... (7 to 4 fav) 5
ROSSMANAGHER (Ire) 4-9-0 S Craine (4)......... (16 to 1) 6
2516[4] AT YOUR SERVICE (Ire) 4-8-10 (4*) P Carberry (12) (14 to 1) 7
2512[5] LUCK OF A LADY (Ire) 4-8-5 (6*) J A Heffernan (11) (25 to 1) 8
1295 RIYASHA (Ire) 5-8-11 J F Egan (5)................. (50 to 1) 9
Dist: 3l, 2l, nk, 20l. 3m 14.00s. (9 Ran).
(Michael W J Smurfit), D K Weld

2959 Carlsberg Auction Race (2-y-o) £4,142 7f................................ (8:40)

2778[3] DOHERTY (Ire) 8-5 M J Kinane (4)............ (10 to 9 on) 1
NORTHERN FRONTIER (Ire) 7-13 (6*) J A Heffernan (5) ....(6 to 1) 2
NEVER TOLD (Ire) 8-0 (2*) R M Burke (8)........... (7 to 1) 3
2701[5] SEE YOU (Ire) (bl) 8-5 W J Supple (7)............... (3 to 1) 4
LADY COUNSEL (Ire) 8-5 N G McCullagh (1)...... (10 to 1) 5
2462[7] ARTFULNESS (Ire) 8-8 (6*) J J Behan (6)......... (20 to 1) 6
2487[9] ISLAND ROCK (Ire) 7-8 (8*) B A Hunter (2)........ (16 to 1) 7
Dist: 2l, 2l, 8l, 2½l. 1m 31.50s. (7 Ran).
(Mrs Helen Walsh), T M Walsh

GOODWOOD (good to soft) Friday July 30th

Going Correction: PLUS 0.45 sec. per fur. (races 1,6), PLUS 0.55 (2,3,4,5,7)

2960 Molecomb Stakes Class A (Group 3) (2-y-o) £19,680 5f.............. (2:30)

2618* RISKY 8-12 W R Swinburn (3) *hld up in cl tch, shaken up to ld o'r one furlong out, sn clr, cmftbly.* ....(9 to 4 on op 11 to 4 on tchd 2 to 1 on) 1
1804[3] IMPERIAL BAILIWICK (Ire) 8-7 J Williams (2) *in cl tch till outpcd hfwy, ran on wl fnl furlong.* ....(40 to 1 op 33 to 1 tchd 50 to 1) 2
2618 ISABELLA SHARP 8-7 M Hills (1) *led one furlong, trkd ldr, shaken up appr 2 out, one pace.* ....(40 to 1 op 25 to 1 tchd 50 to 1) 3
2629* MOSCOW ROAD 8-12 T Quinn (4) *led aftr one furlong till o'r one out, sn hrd rdn, wknd ins last.* ....(9 to 2 op 4 to 1 tchd 5 to 1) 4
SWEET TEMPTATION (Ire) 8-7 J Reid (5) *swrvd rght strt, nvr on terms*............ (6 to 1 op 9 to 2 tchd 7 to 1) 5
Dist: 3½l, ¾l, 4l, 2½l. 1m 0.77s. a 3.97s (5 Ran).
SR: 64/45/42/31/16/ (Roldvale Limited), R Hannon

2961 Leslie And Godwin Spitfire Handicap Class B (0-110 3-y-o) £34,605 1¼m ....(3:10)

2333 WESTERN CAPE (USA) [92] 8-12 Pat Eddery (18) *hld up beh, hdwy on ins o'r 3 fs out, hrd rdn over one out, squeezed through to ld inside last, ran on wl.* ....(14 to 1 tchd 16 to 1) 1
2333 MIDNIGHT HEIGHTS [85] 8-5 A Munro (19) *al prmnt, hrd rdn o'r 2 fs out, ev ch ins last, no extr und pres cl hme.* ....(14 to 1 op 16 to 1 tchd 20 to 1 and 12 to 1) 2
2275[3] AL SENAFI (Ire) [85] 8-5 R Cochrane (14) *beh, hdwy 2 fs out, ran on wl fnl furlong.* ....(12 to 1 op 14 to 1 tchd 16 to 1) 3
1952[7] BASHAYER (USA) [101] 9-7 W Carson (17) *prmnt, led o'r 3 fs out till over one out, rallied ins last, wknd cl hme.* ....(25 to 1 op 16 to 1) 4
2563* TESHAMI (USA) [91] 8-11 W R Swinburn (1) *hld up beh ldrs, hdwy on bit o'r 3 fs out, rdn to ld over one out till hdd and wknd ins last*..............(3 to 1 fav tchd 7 to 2) 5
2304[5] BARBOUKH [89] 8-9 L Dettori (9) *hld up beh, hdwy centre 2 fs out, kpt on*........(9 to 1 op 10 to 1 tchd 12 to 1) 6
2333 LYFORD CAY (Ire) [85] 8-0 (5*) Stephen Davies (6) *beh, hdwy o'r one furlong out, nrst finish.* ....(20 to 1 op 16 to 1 tchd 25 to 1) 7
2563[2] BOBBIE DEE [79] 7-10 (3*) D Harrison (13) *hld up beh, rdn 3 fs out, hdwy 2 out, no prog entering last.* ....(20 to 1 op 16 to 1) 8
1808[3] BRIGANTE DI CIELO [93] 8-13 T Quinn (8) *prmnt, ev ch wl o'r one furlong out, hrd rdn and wknd appr last.* ....(14 to 1 op 12 to 1 tchd 16 to 1) 9
2537* DUVEEN (Ire) [73] 7-7 A Mackay (5) *beh, pushed alng o'r 5 fs out, hdwy wl over 2 out, btn over one out.* ....(16 to 1 op 14 to 1 tchd 20 to 1) 10
2758[9] MIDYAN BLUE (Ire) [75] 7-6 (3*) N Kennedy (10) *al beh.* ....(12 to 1 op 14 to 1 tchd 20 to 1) 11
2576* DUTOSKY [76] 7-10 G Bardwell (2) *trkd ldrs, effrt o'r 2 fs out, sn btn*..........(25 to 1 op 16 to 1 tchd 33 to 1) 12
2474[2] STORM VENTURE (Ire) [75] 7-9 J Quinn (16) *chsd ldrs, wknd 3 fs out*........(20 to 1 op 16 to 1 tchd 25 to 1) 13
2757* RAPID SUCCESS (USA) [90] 8-7 (3*) B Doyle (7) *cl up, wknd quickly 3 fs out*................ (20 to 1 op 14 to 1) 14
2277* GONE TROPPO [87] 8-7 W Ryan (11) *chsd ldrs, rdn 3 fs out, sn btn*............................(9 to 1 op 8 to 1) 15
2421* AJDAYT (USA) [87] 8-7 S Whitworth (4) *hld up rear, nvr on terms*................(16 to 1 op 12 to 1 tchd 20 to 1) 16
2622[3] WALI (USA) [85] 8-5 R Hills (15) *al beh.* ....(25 to 1 tchd 33 to 1) 17
2732[4] SHAMISEN [88] 8-8 B Marcus (12) *led till o'r 3 fs out, wknd quickly*................ (50 to 1 op 33 to 1) 18
Dist: Nk, 1l, ½l, ¾l, 1l, hd, nk, 1l, ½l, 2l. 2m 13.82s. a 8.32s (18 Ran).
SR: 70/62/60/75/63/59/54/47/59/ (K Abdulla), R Charlton

2962 Schroders Glorious Rated Class A Handicap (Listed Race) (0-105 4-y-o and up) £22,784 1½m...........(3:45)

2581* USAIDIT [91] 4-8-7 J Reid (5) *hld up beh, hdwy 3 fs out, rdn to ld ins last, ran on wl.* ....(7 to 1 op 8 to 1 tchd 10 to 1) 1
2793* MUHAYAA (USA) [97] 4-8-13 W R Swinburn (8) *trkd ldrs, led o'r 3 fs out till over one out, rallied to ld briefly ins last, ran on, fnshd lme*..... (11 to 2 op 9 to 2 tchd 6 to 1) 2

1974* SOURCE OF LIGHT [102] 4-9-4 Pat Eddery (11) *hld up mid-div, hdwy 2 fs out, led o'r one out till ins last, sn one pace*..........................(3 to 1 fav op 4 to 1) 3
2238⁷ ANNA OF SAXONY [104] 4-9-6 W Carson (12) *hld up beh, hdwy on ins whn snatched up o'r 3 fs out, sn swtchd lft, headway over one out, one pace.* ....(20 to 1 op 16 to 1) 4
2239⁸ DUKE OF EUROLINK [98] 4-9-0 R Cochrane (1) *hld up, cld o'r 2 fs out, sn one pace.* ....(12 to 1 op 10 to 1 tchd 14 to 1) 5
2437² HALF A TICK (USA) [105] 5-9-7 T Quinn (3) *hld up rear, hdwy o'r 2 fs out, one pace over one out.* ....(8 to 1 tchd 10 to 1) 6
2239³ TURGENEV (Ire) [98] 4-9-0 D Holland (13) *mid-div, cld 3 fs out, wknd und pres wl o'r one out.* (11 to 2 op 9 to 2) 7
1974³ NIGHT CLUBBING (Ire) [91] 4-8-7 L Dettori (2) *prmnt, rcd centre entering strt, ev ch 2 fs out, wknd.* ....(12 to 1 tchd 14 to 1) 8
390³ CASPIAN TERN (USA) [91] 4-8-7 A Munro (10) *prmnt, rdn and wknd 2 fs out*....(16 to 1 op 14 to 1 tchd 20 to 1) 9
2617⁹ CASTORET [91] 7-8-7 D Harrison (4) *al beh.* .... (20 to 1 op 16 to 1) 10
2395³ WELSH MILL (Ire) [92] 4-8-8 L Piggott (7) *led, rcd centre entering strt, hdd o'r 3 fs out, sn wknd und pres, tld off.* ....(12 to 1) 11
2349² ANCHORITE [95] 4-8-11 R Hills (6) *trkd ldr, wknd quickly o'r 3 fs out, tld off*..................(33 to 1 op 25 to 1) 12
Dist: 1l, 1½l, ½l, ¾l, hd, 5l, 1½l, ¾l, ½l, 20l. 2m 42.30s. a 9.30s (12 Ran).
SR: 66/70/72/73/65/71/54/44/42/ (Mrs Pauline Merrick), T G Mills

2963 Seeboard Rated Class B Handicap (0-95 3-y-o) £10,203 1¾m....... (4:15)

2116³ LILLE HAMMER [80] 8-13 R Cochrane (3) *hld up beh, hdwy on ins o'r 3 fs, hrd rdn over one out, ran on strly to ld wl inside last.* ....(9 to 1 op 12 to 1 tchd 14 to 1 and 8 to 1) 1
2177² SOLARTICA (USA) [75] 8-8 L Dettori (4) *chsd ldrs, led 2 fs out till wl ins last, ran on.* ....(15 to 2 op 7 to 1 tchd 8 to 1) 2
2355* MY PATRIARCH [88] 9-7 W Carson (9) *hld up beh, effrt and not clr run on ins o'r 2 fs out, pld out over one out, ran on wl*.................. (15 to 2 op 7 to 1 tchd 8 to 1) 3
1495* SHYNON [79] 8-12 P Robinson (1) *led to 2 fs out, sn outpcd*.................... (7 to 1 op 6 to 1 tchd 8 to 1) 4
1960* ALINOVA (USA) [88] 9-7 Pat Eddery (12) *cl up, ev ch 2 fs out, sn wknd*......(7 to 4 fav tchd 13 to 8 and 2 to 1) 5
2611² COMME D'HABITUDE (USA) [75] 8-8 J Reid (5) *trkd ldrs till lost pl o'r 4 fs out, cld 3 out, sn one pace.* ....(20 to 1 op 16 to 1 tchd 25 to 1) 6
2632⁴ BLUE BLAZER [82] (bl) 9-1 W Ryan (7) *beh, cld 3 fs out, btn 2 out*.................(11 to 1 op 12 to 1 tchd 10 to 1) 7
2228* HILL OF DREAMS [76] 8-9 M Hills (2) *trkd ldrs till wknd 2 fs out*.................(14 to 1 op 12 to 1 tchd 16 to 1) 8
2758 FOREVER SHINEING [74] 8-4 (3*) D Harrison (8) *mid-div, effrt o'r 3 fs out, sn btn*............(50 to 1 op 33 to 1) 9
1960³ TASSET (Can) [80] 8-13 T Quinn (10) *trkd ldrs, pushed alng o'r 5 fs out, hrd rdn 3 out, wknd quickly.* ....(14 to 1 op 12 to 1 tchd 16 to 1) 10
2333 SEASONAL SPLENDOUR (Ire) [86] 8-12 (7*) J D Smith (11) *al beh*............................ (12 to 1 tchd 16 to 1) 11
2272⁵ PHROSE [74] 8-2 (5*) Stephen Davies (6) *trkd ldrs till wknd 5 fs out, tld off*................(50 to 1 op 33 to 1) 12
Dist: 2l, 3l, 5l, 2½l, ½l, hd, 2l, 10l, 2½l, ¾l. 3m 9.14s. a 11.84s (12 Ran).
SR: 58/49/56/37/41/27/33/23/1/ (Baron Edouard de Rothschild), L M Cumani

2964 EBF Selsey Maiden Stakes Class D (2-y-o) £5,481 7f.................. (4:45)

ESCARPMENT (USA) 9-0 J Reid (11) *hld up, pld out and hdwy o'r one furlong out, str run to ld last strd.* ....(3 to 1 op 9 to 2) 1
2559³ WISHING (USA) 9-0 W R Swinburn (12) *trkd ldrs, rdn to ld ins fnl furlong, ct last strd.* .... (12 to 1 op 8 to 1 tchd 14 to 1) 2
2299⁵ SAWLAJAN (USA) 9-0 W Carson (2) *led, rdn and hdd ins fnl furlong, no extr*.................(9 to 1 op 5 to 1) 3
2250² BLAIR CASTLE (Ire) 9-0 L Dettori (10) *chsd ldrs, ev ch o'r one furlong out, sn one pace.* .... (6 to 1 op 5 to 1 tchd 13 to 2) 4
2419⁹ PLUNDER BAY (USA) 9-0 S Whitworth (8) *cl up, ev ch 2 fs out, wknd*..........................(50 to 1 op 33 to 1) 5
2299⁴ WILD INVADER (USA) 9-0 Pat Eddery (9) *hld up in rear, hdwy o'r 2 fs out, btn over one out.* ....(13 to 8 fav op 5 to 4 tchd 7 to 4) 6
BRAVE PATRIARCH (Ire) 9-0 T Quinn (6) *chsd ldrs, pushed alng hfwy, sn btn*....(33 to 1 op 16 to 1 tchd 50 to 1) 7
HADI (Ire) 9-0 B Marcus (4) *cl up till wknd 2 fs out.* ....(25 to 1 op 14 to 1 tchd 50 to 1) 8
NOTHING TO WEAR 9-0 M Hills (7) *beh, hdwy to track ldrs 3 fs out, wknd o'r one out*.......(25 to 1 tchd 50 to 1) 9
VILLAGE EAGLE (Fr) 9-0 R Cochrane (5) *al beh.* ....(33 to 1 op 20 to 1 tchd 50 to 1) 10
PRINCELY GAIT 9-0 D Biggs (3) *hdwy to track ldrs aftr 2 fs, ev ch 3 out, wknd*.............(20 to 1 op 10 to 1) 11
BEYOND THE STARS 9-0 J Williams (1) *al beh, tld off.* ....(66 to 1 op 33 to 1 tchd 100 to 1) 12
Dist: Sht-hd, 1½l, 3l, 4l, 3l, 2l, ½l, hd, 1½l, 3l. 1m 31.74s. a 7.14s (12 Ran).
SR: 51/50/45/36/24/15/9/7/6/ (R E Sangster), P W Chapple-Hyam

2965 Chichester City Handicap Class C (0-90 3-y-o and up) £5,026 5f.... (5:20)

2524³ BODARI [73] 4-9-0 D Holland (1) *cl up, led o'r one furlong out, rdn out*...........(11 to 4 op 5 to 2 tchd 3 to 1) 1
2620⁶ AUGHFAD [79] (v) 7-9-6 J Reid (5) *outpcd, hdwy whn hng rght o'r one furlong out, ran on ins last, jst fld.* ....(5 to 2 fav op 9 to 4 tchd 11 to 4) 2
2753⁸ BORN TO BE [75] 4-8-13 (3*) D Harrison (3) *cl up, ev ch ins fnl furlong, no extr close hme.* ....(8 to 1 op 7 to 1 tchd 9 to 1) 3
2018 NEVER IN THE RED [83] (bl) 5-9-10 L Piggott (4) *led till o'r one furlong out, wknd.* (7 to 2 tchd 3 to 1 and 4 to 1) 4
2418³ BALIGAY [77] 8-9-4 A Munro (2) *outpcd.* ....(4 to 1 op 7 to 2 tchd 9 to 2) 5
Dist: Nk, sht-hd, 3½l, 5l. 1m 1.75s. a 4.95s (5 Ran).
SR: 46/51/46/40/14/ (R J Thomas), D A Wilson

2966 Heyshott Apprentice Handicap Class E (0-90 4-y-o and up) £5,117 7f.. (5:50)

2869² DUCKEY FUZZ [51] 5-7-4 (3*) D Wright (2) *trkd ldg pair, led o'r one furlong out, ran on wl und pres.* ....(3 to 1 op 9 to 4 tchd 7 to 2) 1
2882³ NOBBY BARNES [61] 4-8-3 F Norton (4) *hld up in last pl, smooth hdwy 2 fs out, shaken up and ev ch ins last, no extr cl hme*......... (9 to 4 fav op 5 to 2 tchd 11 to 4) 2
2577⁹ SILKY SIREN [71] 4-8-13 D Harrison (1) *in cl tch, rdn 2 fs out, one pace ins last*...(7 to 2 op 11 to 4 tchd 4 to 1) 3
2582⁷ CLAYBANK (USA) [68] 4-8-5 (5*) S McCarthy (5) *led till o'r one furlong out, one pace*..........(8 to 1 tchd 9 to 1) 4
2656* CORALS DREAM (Ire) [88] 4-9-13 (3*,6ex) S Mulvey (3) *rcd freely, trkd ldr, ev ch 2 fs out, wknd quickly.* ....(9 to 2 op 5 to 1) 5
Dist: Nk, 3l, sht-hd, 7l. 1m 32.54s. a 7.94s (5 Ran).
SR: 18/27/28/24/23/ (Mrs W M Faletti), R M Flower

NEWMARKET (JULY) (good)
Friday July 30th
Going Correction: MINUS 0.35 sec. per fur. (races 1,2,3,5), MINUS 0.15 (4,6)

2967 Side Hill Apprentice Selling Handicap Class E (0-60 3-y-o) £2,872 5f... (6:15)

2504⁴ PERFECT PASSION [42] 8-1 (3*) Antoinette Armes (1) *wl plcd centre, nosed ahead hfwy, hrd pressed fnl furlong, ran on well*................(6 to 1 op 5 to 1 tchd 13 to 2) 1
2476² AVRIL ETOILE [51] 8-6 (7*) Iona Wands (5) *nvr far away, ev ch fnl furlong, ran on und pres*......(4 to 1 op 7 to 2) 2
2033⁴ KILDEE LAD [53] 8-10 (5*) R Painter (7) *trkd ldrs, effrt and crrd lft o'r one furlong out, rallied und pres.* ....(9 to 2 op 7 to 1 tchd 4 to 1) 3
2684 MASTER BEVELED [50] (v) 8-12 S D Williams (3) *al hndy, chalg whn squeezed out o'r one furlong out, kpt on wl towards finish*........(10 to 1 op 7 to 1 tchd 11 to 1) 4
2777³ DAYJUZ (Ire) [59] (bl) 9-7 N Kennedy (2) *broke smartly, crossed o'r to ld on stands side, hdd hfwy, drifted lft over one out, fdd*... (2 to 1 fav op 6 to 4 tchd 9 to 4) 5
1341⁶ FOLLY VISION (Ire) [57] 9-0 (5*) A Lakeman (4) *sluggish strt, chsd alng hfwy, nvr able to chal*....(10 to 1 op 8 to 1) 6
720⁹ BARASSIE [39] 7-10 (5*) Sharon Millard (6) *chsd ldg bunch, struggling to keep up hfwy, nvr dngrs.* ....(20 to 1 op 16 to 1) 7
Dist: ½l, hd, sht-hd, 2l, 7l, 2½l. 1m 0.16s. a 1.46s (7 Ran).
SR: 26/33/34/30/31/1/-/ (N Bryce-Smith), J J Bridger

2968 EBF Dexa'tex Maiden Stakes Class D (2-y-o) £5,088 7f................(6:45)

CONCORDIAL (USA) 9-0 Pat Eddery (12) *patiently rdn, quickened ahead jst o'r 2 fs out, shaken up fnl furlong, ran on wl*...(5 to 1 op 3 to 1 tchd 6 to 1 and 13 to 2) 1
LOVING LEGACY 8-9 R Hills (10) *wtd wth, quickened up to draw level ins fnl furlong, ran on same pace.* .... (16 to 1 op 10 to 1) 2
NICOLOTTE 9-0 M Hills (9) *settled midfield, improved to ld briefly 3 fs out, not quicken fnl furlong.* ....(9 to 4 fav op 4 to 1 tchd 7 to 4) 3
OVERBURY (Ire) 9-0 L Dettori (2) *settled gng wl, ev ch o'r one furlong out, not quicken fnl furlong.* ....(3 to 1 tchd 9 to 4 and 100 to 30) 4
KING'S THEATRE (Ire) 9-0 W Ryan (1) *nvr far away, effrt on outsd last 2 fs, kpt on one pace*... (8 to 1 op 4 to 1) 5
2559⁶ RANA SANGA 9-0 G Carter (4) *made most in centre for 5 fs, grad wknd.* ....(16 to 1 op 12 to 1 tchd 20 to 1 and 25 to 1) 6
ERHAAB (USA) 9-0 W Carson (8) *chsd alng to go pace hfwy, kpt on wl last 2 fs, nrst finish.* ....(14 to 1 op 10 to 1 tchd 16 to 1) 7

RUPAN 9-0 B Raymond (7) *sluggish strt, steady hdwy frm off the pace last 2 fs, can improve.* (33 to 1 op 16 to 1) 8
SEEING RED 8-9 P D'Arcy (3) *trkd ldrs, ev ch hfwy, fdd appr fnl furlong*..... (25 to 1 op 16 to 1 tchd 33 to 1) 9
KING CURAN (USA) 9-0 T Quinn (17) *gd speed stands' side for o'r 4 fs, fdd.* ....(25 to 1 op 20 to 1 tchd 33 to 1 and 50 to 1) 10
2571 WAAFED (USA) 9-0 W R Swinburn (6) *drvn alng thrght, nvr able to rch ldrs*..................(33 to 1 op 16 to 1) 11
RAGSAT AL OMOR (Ire) 9-0 P Robinson (16) *broke wl to show gd speed in frnt rnk for o'r 4 fs, fdd.* ....(14 to 1 tchd 20 to 1 and 25 to 1) 12
2546⁴ AL JINN 9-0 R Cochrane (11) *chsd ldg bunch, effrt hfwy, fdd last 2 fs*..................(33 to 1 op 14 to 1) 13
SOUTH EASTERN FRED 9-0 V Smith (18) *steadied strt, pushed alng hfwy, nvr a threat.* ....(33 to 1 op 16 to 1 tchd 50 to 1) 14
DANCING CLOWN 9-0 S Whitworth (13) *steadied strt, shaken up hfwy, nvr a threat*..... (33 to 1 op 20 to 1) 15
LITTLE GENT (Ire) 8-7 (7*) L Carter (15) *pushed alng to chase ldg bunch for o'r 4 fs, fdd*... (33 to 1 op 20 to 1) 16
PEARL DAISY 8-9 N Carlisle (5) *struggling aftr 2 fs, tld off.* ....(33 to 1 op 25 to 1 tchd 50 to 1) 17

Dist: 1l, 1½l, 3½l, 2l, sht-hd, 1l, 1l, sht-hd, hd, 2l. 1m 26.44s. a 2.24s (17 Ran).
SR: 30/22/22/11/5/4/1/-/-/ (K Abdulla), R Charlton

2969 Vardy Continental Handicap Class C (0-90 3-y-o and up) £6,472 6f.... (7:15)

2628³ MASTER PLANNER [84] 4-9-7 (7*) J D Smith (8) *wth ldr, led o'r 2 fs out, cooly rdn fnl furlong, hld on wl.* ....(7 to 2 fav op 3 to 1 tchd 4 to 1) 1
2494* FACE NORTH (Ire) [66] 5-8-10 T Quinn (4) *tucked away beh ldrs, str chal ins fnl furlong, jst hld.* ....(9 to 2 op 5 to 1 tchd 11 to 2) 2
2434 BERTIE WOOSTER [77] 10-9-7 L Dettori (7) *nvr far away, effrt and drvn alng last 2 fs, kpt on same pace.* ....(13 to 2 op 6 to 1 tchd 7 to 1 and 8 to 1) 3
2060 FIGHTER SQUADRON [66] (bl) 4-8-7 (3*) S D Williams (6) *patiently rdn, pushed up to flter o'r one furlong out, kpt on same pace*..................(12 to 1) 4
2861⁸ FASCINATION WALTZ [78] 6-9-8 (7ex) G Carter (10) *sluggish strt, swtchd ins to improve last 2 fs, styd on same pace.* ....(11 to 1 op 10 to 1 tchd 12 to 1) 5
2434 CALEMAN [75] 4-9-5 Pat Eddery (9) *al chasing ldrs, hrd at work last 2 fs, not pace to chal.* ....(7 to 1 op 6 to 1 tchd 8 to 1) 6
2255* MAGIC ORB [77] 3-9-1 A Mackay (1) *al chasing ldrs, effrt und pres o'r 2 fs out, no imprsn.* ....(6 to 1 op 5 to 1 tchd 13 to 2) 7
2106⁵ CRYSTAL JACK (Fr) [77] (v) 5-9-7 S Perks (3) *broke fst to ld for o'r 3 fs, fdd ins fnl furlong*..... (20 to 1 op 14 to 1) 8
2329² EASY LINE [81] 10-9-4 (7*) Michael Denaro (5) *in tch, hrd at work last 2 fs, not pace to chal*..... (13 to 2 op 6 to 1) 9
492⁹ ABIGAILS BOY (Hol) [56] 4-8-0 J Quinn (2) *sluggish strt, chsd alng thrght, no imprsn*..................(33 to 1) 10

Dist: Sht-hd, 2½l, nk, nk, 1l, ½l, 2l, 2½l, 2½l. 1m 12.05s. a 0.35s (10 Ran).
SR: 65/46/47/35/46/39/33/31/25/ (R M Cyzer), C A Cyzer

2970 Travis Perkins Handicap Class E (0-70 3-y-o and up) £4,272 1¼m...... (7:45)

2348² SCOTTISH BAMBI [67] 5-10-0 R Perham (7) *patiently rdn, drvn through to ld wl ins fnl furlong, ran on well.* ....(11 to 2 op 6 to 1 tchd 13 to 2) 1
2490* CASE FOR THE CROWN (USA) [45] 6-8-6 L Dettori (11) *made most till wl ins fnl furlong, rallied, not quicken cl hme.* ....(5 to 4 fav op 6 to 4 tchd 15 to 8) 2
2874⁴ BRILLIANT [65] 5-9-12 M Wigham (9) *co'red up in midfield, brst through to chal wl ins fnl furlong, fnshd well.* ....(11 to 1 op 8 to 1 tchd 12 to 1) 3
2564⁵ ALTERMEERA [43] (v) 5-7-13 (5*) D Wright (10) *patiently rdn, improved entering fnl furlong, fnshd wl.* ....(16 to 1 op 14 to 1 tchd 20 to 1) 4
2673⁶ AFFA [47] (v) 4-8-8 S Whitworth (3) *trkd ldrs, nosed ahead briefly appr fnl furlong, one pace cl hme.* ....(12 to 1 op 10 to 1 tchd 14 to 1) 5
2727³ TEMPLE KNIGHT [60] 4-9-0 (7*) J D Smith (5) *rcd wide, nvr far away, drvn alng o'r one furlong out, not quicken.* ....(14 to 1 op 10 to 1 tchd 16 to 1) 6
2589² CHARLIE BIGTIME [63] 3-9-0 T Quinn (6) *nvr far away, ev ch and rdn o'r one furlong out, no extr.* ....(8 to 1 tchd 10 to 1) 7
2564³ LEXUS (Ire) [46] 5-8-0 (7*) Sarah Thompson (4) *wth ldrs, hrd at work o'r 2 fs out, fdd.* ....(7 to 1 tchd 15 to 2 and 8 to 1) 8
2641 MEL'S ROSE [52] 8-8-13 G Hind (12) *tucked away on ins, feeling pace o'r 3 fs out, sn btn.* ....(20 to 1 op 16 to 1 tchd 33 to 1) 9
2673 WOODMANS STAR [52] 3-8-0 (3*) N Kennedy (2) *rcd freely in frnt rnk till wknd und pres last 3 fs.* ....(33 to 1 tchd 50 to 1) 10
2696⁸ MOVE SMARTLY (Ire) [57] 3-8-8 S Perks (1) *trkd ldrs, lost grnd whn pace quickened o'r 2 fs out, sn btn.* ....(12 to 1 op 10 to 1 tchd 14 to 1) 11
2256⁶ BROOKS EXPRESS (Fr) [40] 4-8-1 J Quinn (8) *co'red up on ins, hrd at work over 3 fs out, sn btn.* ....(14 to 1 op 12 to 1 tchd 16 to 1 and 20 to 1) 12

Dist: Nk, sht-hd, sht-hd, sht-hd, 2l, 1½l, 7l, 3½l, 1½l, 4l. 2m 7.13s. a 4.93s (12 Ran).
SR: 50/27/46/23/26/35/25/4/3/ (William J Kelly), R Hannon

2971 Bunbury Fillies' Conditions Stakes Class D (3-y-o and up) £4,503 6f (8:15)

2698* SIWAAYIB 3-9-0 W R Swinburn (4) *patiently rdn, quickened up to ld ins fnl furlong, ran on strly.* ....(2 to 1 fav op 7 to 4 tchd 9 to 4) 1
2303² SHEILA'S SECRET (Ire) 3-9-2 T Quinn (1) *nvr far away, nosed ahead briefly one furlong out, kpt on same pace.* ....(5 to 2 op 4 to 1) 2
2303 YAKIN (USA) 3-8-8 R Hills (2) *al hndy, ev ch last 2 fs, ran on same pace*..................(20 to 1 op 14 to 1) 3
2011³ PETERSFORD GIRL (Ire) 3-8-12 L Dettori (5) *tucked away, ev ch and drvn alng last 2 fs, one pace.* ....(10 to 1 tchd 12 to 1) 4
2620⁸ BANGLES 3-8-12 B Raymond (7) *broke smartly to ld for 5 fs, grad wknd*..................(8 to 1 op 12 to 1) 5
2351* LACERTA (Ire) 3-8-12 J Reid (8) *wth ldrs, ev ch 2 fs out, not quicken fnl furlong*.................. (6 to 1 op 5 to 1) 6
1415⁴ BROCKTON DANCER 3-8-12 L Piggott (3) *shwd up wl on outsd for o'r 4 fs, fdd*.... (6 to 1 op 7 to 1 tchd 8 to 1) 7
2574 CARRANITA (Ire) 3-8-11 (5*) Stephen Davies (6) *sluggish strt, reco'red to join issue aftr a furlong, wknd quickly over 2 fs*..................(8 to 1 op 7 to 1 tchd 9 to 1) 8

Dist: 1½l, ½l, nk, nk, ¾l, 2l, 6l. 1m 12.99s. a 1.29s (8 Ran).
SR: 32/28/18/21/20/17/9/-/ (Maktoum Al Maktoum), A A Scott

2972 Running Gap Handicap Class E (0-70 3-y-o) £4,142 1½m.............. (8:45)

2415² SUMMER PAGEANT [68] 9-5 W R Swinburn (4) *led aftr 2 fs, made rst, kpt on strly fnl furlong*... (10 to 1 op 8 to 1) 1
2507² NAWAHIL [67] 9-4 W Carson (16) *led for 2 fs, styd hndy, rnwd effrt fnl furlong, kpt on.* ....(5 to 1 op 6 to 1 tchd 9 to 2) 2
2464⁴ MIROSWAKI (USA) [70] 9-7 Paul Eddery (10) *trkd ldg bunch, rdn to improve last 2 fs, styd on same pace.* ....(20 to 1 tchd 25 to 1) 3
2773² WORDSMITH (Ire) [67] 9-4 K Fallon (9) *patiently rdn, improved into midfield o'r 2 fs out, kpt on same pace ins last*.................. (3 to 1 fav op 5 to 1 tchd 11 to 2) 4
2501² ROMALITO [59] 8-10 R Cochrane (15) *wtd off the pace, styd on wl last 2 fs, fnshd well.* ....(6 to 1 op 5 to 1 tchd 7 to 1) 5
2870* MILNGAVIE (Ire) [49] 8-0 (4ex) T Williams (5) *al pressing ldrs, feeling pace o'r 2 fs out, not quicken.* ....(10 to 1 op 8 to 1 tchd 11 to 1) 6
2669⁷ BROUGHTONS FORMULA [56] (bl) 8-2 (5*) D McCabe (2) *tucked away in midfield, effrt aftr a m, styd on same pace*..................(12 to 1 tchd 14 to 1) 7
1613⁵ PUGET DANCER (USA) [55] (v) 8-3 (3*) M Fenton (7) *steadied strt, dashed up on outsd last 3 fs, one pace.* ....(16 to 1 op 14 to 1) 8
2464⁶ USK THE WAY [64] 9-1 W Ryan (12) *wth ldrs, drvn alng 2 fs out, grad wknd*....... (6 to 1 op 9 to 2 tchd 13 to 2) 9
2783⁴ MENA [50] 8-1 N Carlisle (1) *co'red up beh ldrs, effrt aftr a m, outpcd last 2 fs*..................(16 to 1 op 14 to 1) 10
602 ACCESS FESTIVALS [48] 7-13 J Quinn (13) *chsd ldrs for o'r a m, rdn, no extr*..................(33 to 1) 11
2277⁸ MOUNTAIN REACH [50] 8-1 C Avery (8) *in tch, feeling pace aftr a m, sn struggling*..................(33 to 1) 12
2273 SABO'S EXPRESS [50] 8-1 D Biggs (14) *settled midfield, effrt entering strt, fdd o'r 2 fs out.* ....(12 to 1 op 14 to 1 tchd 16 to 1) 13
1812⁵ SILVER STANDARD [56] 8-7 Pat Eddery (3) *pressed ldrs till wknd quickly last 3 fs*.......... (10 to 1 tchd 8 to 1) 14
2332 ZONK [49] 8-0 G Bardwell (11) *wth ldrs for a m, wknd quickly*..................(14 to 1 tchd 16 to 1) 15
1613⁷ MOUJEEB (USA) [64] 8-8 (7*) P McCabe (6) *trkd ldg bunch till wknd quickly o'r 2 fs out*...... (33 to 1 op 20 to 1) 16

Dist: ¾l, 2l, 2½l, 1l, 3l, ¾l, 1½l, 1l, 1½l, ½l. 2m 33.64s. a 4.84s (16 Ran).
SR: 39/36/35/27/17/1/6/2/9/ (Cheveley Park Stud), J R Fanshawe

THIRSK (firm)
Friday July 30th

Going Correction: MINUS 0.15 sec. per fur. (races 1,4,5,6), MINUS 0.40 (2,3)

2973 Golden Fleece Claiming Stakes Class F (2-y-o) £2,601 7f.............. (2:15)

2430⁵ OOH AH CANTONA 8-11 A Culhane (3) *nvr far away, shaken up to ld appr 2 fs out, forged clr ins last.* ....(7 to 2 tchd 3 to 1) 1
2552³ CELESTIAL RUMOUR (Ire) 8-11 K Darley (5) *tucked away on ins, effrt and swtchd o'r 2 fs out, kpt on inside last, no ch wth wnr*.......... (5 to 2 op 3 to 1 tchd 7 to 2) 2
BOJOLLY 8-4 W Newnes (9) *slwly into strd, sn pushed alng to keep up, ran on wl fnl 2 fs, can improve.* ....(12 to 1 op 14 to 1) 3

2826[9] AMORET (Ire) 8-3 G Duffield (8) *trkd ldrs on outer, pushed alng entering strt, unbl to quicken fnl 2 fs.* ....(12 to 1 tchd 14 to 1) 4
2603[8] AUCKLAND CASTLE 8-9 N Connorton (2) *led aftr a furlong, shaken up entering strt, hdd appr 2 fs out, grad wknd*......................(33 to 1 op 25 to 1) 5
1189[8] DRAGON MAN 8-7 Dean McKeown (11) *beh, pushed alng entering strt, sn swtchd, kpt on fnl furlong, nvr able to chal*..(12 to 1) 6
2588[5] FINISHING KIND 7-12 J Lowe (4) *made most one furlong, styd upsides, pushed alng entering strt, wknd fnl 2 fs.* ....(20 to 1) 7
2542[8] BROWLEA LYNDENE 7-9 (5*) Darren Moffatt (7) *pressed ldrs, bustled alng hfwy, wknd o'r 2 fs out, tld off.* ....(33 to 1) 8
PLUM DENNIS 8-9 Alex Greaves (1) *sluggish strt, al struggling in rear, tld off*...............(33 to 1 op 25 to 1) 9
2588* DEMI-PLIE (v) 8-7 G Carter (6) *mid-div, outpcd and drvn alng appr strt, fdd, tld off.* ....(2 to 1 fav op 11 to 8 tchd 9 to 4) 10
804 PRINCE SKYBURD 8-7 M Birch (10) *rcd rear, pushed alng entering strt, sn lost tch, tld off*..............(33 to 1) 11
Dist: 6l, 2l, 3½l, ½l, 2½l, 1½l, 8l, 1l, nk, 8l. 1m 26.60s. a 3.80s (11 Ran).
SR: 24/6/-/-/-/- (E Wilkinson), R M Whitaker

2974 Lewis Geipel Memorial Challenge Cup Nursery Class D (2-y-o) £3,640 6f ....(2:50)

2539[2] CLOSE TO REALITY [-] 9-2 K Fallon (10) *dwlt, beh, improved o'r one furlong out, ran on and swtchd ins last, led cl hme*......................(8 to 1 op 7 to 1) 1
2446* MY LIFETIME LADY (Ire) [-] 8-10 S Perks (8) *nvr far away, rdn alng 2 fs out, led ins last, edgd lft, hdd nr finish.* ....(7 to 1 tchd 8 to 1) 2
2552* CLARET BUMBLE [-] 8-11 G Duffield (11) *keen hold, co'red up beh ldrs, not much room hfwy, swtchd to improve over one furlong out, ev ch ins last, no extr.* ....(9 to 4 fav op 2 to 1 tchd 5 to 2) 3
2890[4] TOP SHOW (Ire) [-] 9-0 (3*) J Weaver (1) *tacked o'r to stands side leaving stalls, led, hdd ins last, no extr.* ....(11 to 1 op 10 to 1 tchd 12 to 1) 4
2412[2] NONIOS (Ire) [-] 9-7 W Newnes (4) *pressed ldg grp, rdn alng and not much room 2 fs out, one pace fnl furlong.* ....(8 to 1 op 7 to 1) 5
2539[8] GOLDEN STAR (Ire) [-] 8-6 J Fanning (5) *chsd ldrs, drvn alng hfwy, not quicken wl o'r one furlong out.* (14 to 1) 6
2482* ASHKERNAZY (Ire) [-] 8-11 K Darley (3) *cl up on outer, drvn alng o'r 2 fs out, not quicken, eased ins fnl furlong.* ....(7 to 1 op 8 to 1 tchd 6 to 1) 7
1999[5] HALI (Ire) [-] 8-9 Dean McKeown (2) *co'red up on outer, effrt and rdn 2 fs out, sn btn*...... (16 to 1 op 14 to 1) 8
2435[8] LUCKY FOURTEEN [-] 9-1 A McGlone (7) *taken early to post, chsd ldrs, hrd at work hfwy, btn 2 fs out.* ....(16 to 1 op 12 to 1) 9
2554 CREEK VALLEY [-] 7-12 (3*) S Maloney (9) *sluggish strt, nvr able to reco'r*...................(14 to 1 tchd 12 to 1) 10
2539 HARPO'S SPECIAL [-] 7-12 (5*) Darren Moffatt (6) *beh, shaken up hfwy, nvr on terms.* ....(11 to 1 op 12 to 1 tchd 14 to 1) 11
Dist: Nk, 1l, nk, 5l, nk, nk, 3l, 1½l, 1½l, 3l. 1m 10.80s. a 0.80s (11 Ran).
SR: 38/31/28/33/17/1/5/-/-/ (Mrs B D Southam), Mrs J R Ramsden

2975 Go Racing In Yorkshire Handicap Class D (0-80 3-y-o and up) £3,377 6f ....(3:25)

2172[6] FINJAN [76] 6-9-7 (3*) J Weaver (7) *tucked away beh ldrs, rdn to ld entering fnl furlong, edgd lft and styd on wl.* ....(16 to 1 op 14 to 1) 1
2798[5] SLADES HILL [62] 6-8-10 K Darley (6) *trkd ldrs, rdn to chal a furlong out, no extr wl ins last*............(4 to 1 jt-fav op 5 to 1) 2
2777[8] SIMMIE'S SPECIAL [59] (bl) 5-8-2 (5*) A Garth (4) *dsptd ld, wnt on 2 fs out, edgd rght, hdd entering last, edged lft and no extr*......................... (9 to 1 op 8 to 1) 3
2798[3] MASTER POKEY [62] 9-8-10 T Lucas (8) *co'red up beh ldrs, effrt and swtchd over one furlong out, not quicken ins last*..............................(4 to 1 jt-fav op 5 to 2) 4
2851* ASHGORE [71] 3-8-13 (7ex) Dean McKeown (2) *dsptd ld, drvn alng 2 fs out, one pace*......(5 to 1 tchd 11 to 2) 5
2527[5] JADE CITY [80] 3-9-8 K Fallon (5) *beh, outpcd hfwy, ran on fnl furlong, nrst finish*........(14 to 1 op 12 to 1) 6
2594[3] SULLY'S CHOICE (USA) [45] (bl) 12-7-7 S Wood (3) *nvr far away, drvn alng hfwy, one pace o'r one furlong out.* ....(9 to 1 op 10 to 1) 7
2105[8] COSTA VERDE [68] 3-8-10 A Culhane (10) *sn beh and outpcd, no imprsn fnl 2 fs*............(25 to 1 op 33 to 1) 8
2707[3] ROCK OPERA (Ire) [55] 5-8-3[1] G Duffield (9) *bumped leaving stalls, sn outpcd and drvn alng, nvr able to chal.* ....(13 to 2 op 6 to 1 tchd 7 to 1) 9
2813 BALLAD DANCER [66] 8-9-0 (7ex) M Birch (1) *chsd ldrs on outer, rdn o'r 2 fs out, grad wknd*....(8 to 1 op 6 to 1) 10
Dist: 1l, ½l, 2½l, 1l, 1½l, ¾l, 2½l, hd, 2l. 1m 10.40s. a 0.40s (10 Ran).
SR: 54/36/31/24/23/26/-/1/-/ (Mrs R Olivier), Martyn Wane

2976 Stokesley Rating Related Maiden Stakes Class D (0-80 3-y-o) £3,199 7f ....(3:55)

2832[6] CITY ROCKET 9-0 B Raymond (1) *made all, shaken up whn hrd pressed 2 fs out, pushed clr ins last.* ....(3 to 1 op 5 to 2) 1
2725[2] GREEN KILT 9-0 Dean McKeown (3) *pressed ldr, improved to chal 2 fs out, rdn and not quicken fnl furlong.* ....(11 to 4 on tchd 5 to 2 on) 2
2934[7] BOLD LINE (bl) 8-9 K Darley (2) *dwlt, trkd ldg pair, shaken up entering strt, drpd away o'r one furlong out.* .... (12 to 1 op 10 to 1) 3
Dist: 4l, 7l. 1m 25.80s. a 3.00s (3 Ran).
SR: 39/27/1/ (Mrs C R Walford), P J Makin

2977 Peter Bell Memorial Fillies' Handicap Class E (0-70 3-y-o and up) £3,313 1½m.......................... (4:25)

2823* SUPER BLUES [45] 6-8-13 (5ex) W Newnes (1) *trkd ldg pair, swtchd outsd to ld on bit appr fnl furlong, sn shaken up, hng lft ins last, eased towards finish.* ....(100 to 30 op 7 to 2 tchd 4 to 1) 1
2495* ARCTIC GUEST (Ire) [55] 3-8-11 Dean McKeown (2) *pressed ldr, rdn to ld o'r 2 fs out, hdd appr last, one pace und pres*..............(11 to 8 fav op 11 to 10 tchd 6 to 4) 2
1603 KINCHENJUNGA [68] 3-9-10 A McGlone (5) *hld up in cl tch, outpcd and pushed alng leaving back strt, no dngr fnl 2 fs*................................(3 to 1 op 9 to 4) 3
1077[4] BLUSHING BARADA (USA) [64] 3-9-6 B Raymond (4) *set gd clip, hdd o'r 2 fs out, sn btn.* ....(5 to 1 op 4 to 1 tchd 11 to 2) 4
Dist: ¾l, 12l, 1½l. 2m 34.20s. a 4.00s (4 Ran).
SR: 41/37/26/19/ (W H Clarke), T D Barron

2978 Cowesby Apprentice Maiden Handicap Class F (0-75 3-y-o and up) £2,601 1m.......................... (4:55)

1947[6] ROYAL ROLLER (Ire) [72] 3-10-0 G Forster (3) *patiently rdn, smooth hdwy entering strt, led 2 fs out, clr whn hng badly lft ins fnl furlong*.......... (5 to 1 tchd 11 to 2) 1
2765[4] ALBEIT [37] 3-7-5[3] (5*) C Teague (6) *beh, outpcd and rdn hfwy, ran on fnl 2 fs, wnt second on line, nvr dngrs.* ....(10 to 1 op 8 to 1) 2
2694[7] SIMPLY SUPERB [45] (bl) 3-8-1 C Munday (1) *cl up, hmpd aftr one furlong, led entering strt, hdd 2 fs out, drvn and one pace ins last*..........(20 to 1 op 16 to 1) 3
2737[6] CANNY LAD [49] (bl) 3-8-5 D McCabe (8) *swtchd to ins rail leaving stalls, led, hdd entering strt, rallied and ev ch o'r one out, no extr inside last*...... (5 to 1 op 9 to 2) 4
2889[2] MANX MONARCH [49] 3-8-5 M Humphries (7) *nvr far away, rdn alng 2 fs out, one pace.* ....(100 to 30 op 3 to 1 tchd 7 to 2) 5
2710[2] JOMOVE [36] 4-8-0 N Varley (4) *sluggish strt, beh, rdn to improve o'r 2 fs out, no imprsn.* ....(85 to 40 fav op 2 to 1 tchd 9 to 4) 6
2858[8] MURASIL (USA) [34] (v) 4-7-5 (7*) F Savage (5) *pressed ldr, rdn alng appr strt, wknd o'r 2 fs out.* ....(16 to 1 op 12 to 1) 7
2597[8] FORT VALLY [56] 3-8-9 (3*) G Parkin (2) *in tch on inner, badly hmpd bend entering strt, sn lost touch.* ....(10 to 1 op 8 to 1) 8
Dist: 3l, sht-hd, sht-hd, 3l, 2½l, 5l, 3l. 1m 39.50s. a 3.60s (8 Ran).
SR: 42/-/5/8/-/ (J N Oliver), P J McBride

VICHY (FR) (good to soft) Friday July 30th

2979 Grand Prix de Vichy (Group 3) (3-y-o and up) £29,869 1¼m...........(3:30)

1971[2] MARILDO (Fr) (bl) 6-9-9 G Guignard (10) *al prmnt, second strt, chlgd one and a half fs out, led ins last, ran on wl.* 1
1124[6] OUMNAZ (Fr) 4-9-2 R Laplanche (8) *hld up in mid-div, prog one and a half fs out, took second on line*........ 2
VINCENZO (Ger) 4-9-2 C Asmussen (6) *led till one furlong out, no extr*.. 3
2531[6] SAWASDEE (Fr) 3-8-7 W Mongil (9) *mid-div, hdwy 2 fs out, ev ch one out, one pace*.................................. 4
2012 FAY WRAY (Fr) 3-8-4 G Elorriaga-Santos (2) *rear till some late prog, nvr plcd to chal*.............................. 5
2261[8] POLYTAIN (Fr) 4-9-2 G Mosse (1) *4th strt, chlgd 2 fs out, sn btn*... 6
1411[2] COMPOTA (Fr) 4-8-13 O Peslier (7) *3rd strt, ev ch 2 fs out, one pace*.. 7
2437[3] FUNNY BABY (Fr) 5-9-2 A Badel (5) *in tch till 2 fs out*..... 8
DICTIONARY (Ire) 3-8-7 M Boutin (3) *al rear*............. 9
2771[5] VAL SAUVAGE 3-8-7 E Saint-Martin (4) *mid-div till wknd 2 fs out*.. 10
Dist: 2½l, nose, 1l, ½l, 1½l, 1l, 3l, 5l, ¾l. 2m 2.30s. (10 Ran).
(D Smaga), D Smaga

DEAUVILLE (FR) (soft)
Saturday July 31st
Going Correction: PLUS 0.40 sec. per fur. (races 1,2), NIL (3)

2980 Prix Yacowlef (Listed) (2-y-o) £14,337 6f. . . . . (2:00)

ETERNAL REVE (USA) 9-0 C Asmussen, ... 1
KEY OF LUCK (USA) 9-2 F Head, ... 2
CELTIC ARMS (Fr) 9-2 E Saint-Martin, ... 3
LA GRANDE CASCADE (USA) 9-0 M Boutin, ... 4
Dist: Nose, hd, ½l. 1m 15.90s. a 7.50s (4 Ran).
(Mrs Lucy Young Boutin), F Boutin

2981 Prix d'Astarte (Group 3) (3-y-o and up) £35,842 1m. . . . . (3:00)

1545* SKI PARADISE (USA) 3-8-7 S Guillot (9) *rear early, rdn 2 fs out, chlgd one and a half out, led und one out, ran on.* . . . . (28 to 10) 1
2409³ FRESHER 3-8-7 F Head (6) *rear, rdn 2 fs out, chlgd one and a half out, ev ch ran on*. . . . (11 to 1) 2
1767² ELIZABETH BAY (USA) 3-8-7 T Jarnet (7) *mid-div, led und 2 fs out till under one out, ran on*. . . . (14 to 10 fav) 3
2409* HOLLY GOLIGHTLY 3-8-7 C Asmussen (5) *rcd in second, one pace 2 fs out, ran on fnl furlong, fnshd wl*. (15 to 1) 4
1088³ BALLINAMALLARD (USA) 4-9-0 O Peslier (2) *in rear, rdn o'r 2 fs out, nrst finish*. . . . (13 to 1) 5
VERVEINE (USA) 4-9-0 D Boeuf (3) *al mid-div, kpt on fnl 2 fs*. . . . (45 to 10) 6
2409* ROUQUETTE 3-8-7 A Badel (1) *nvr dngrs*. . . . (93 to 10) 7
273³ KENBU (Fr) 4-9-0 E Saint-Martin (11) *nvr able to chal*. . . . (21 to 1) 8
2334⁸ ANCESTRAL DANCER 3-8-11 G Mosse (8) *prmnt till rdn and wknd 2 fs out*. . . . (20 to 1) 9
2409⁶ SHOWGUM (Fr) 3-8-7 A Junk (10) *mid-div till outpcd 2 fs out*. . . . (37 to 1) 0
2409 GAIRSIC (Fr) 3-8-7 G Benoit (4) *led till und 2 fs out, sn wknd*. . . . (35 to 1) 0
Dist: ½l, sht-hd, nk, nk, sht-nk, 1½l, nk, 4l, 1½l. 1m 39.40s. a 4.40s (11 Ran).
SR: 75/73/72/71/77/76/64/70/55/ (Zenya Yoshida), A Fabre

GALWAY (IRE) (good to yielding)
Saturday July 31st

2982 Jockeys Association E.B.F. Maiden (2-y-o) £6,210 1m 100yds. . . . . (3:00)

2462² MISS NUTWOOD (Ire) 8-11 P Shanahan (4) . . . . (6 to 1) 1
ACROSS THE TRACKS (Ire) 8-9 (2*) D G O'Shea (13) . . . . (20 to 1) 2
2072⁵ DAYESS (USA) 9-0 M J Kinane (7) . . . . (9 to 4) 3
2284⁵ CONCEPT HOUSE (Ire) 9-0 N Byrne (5) . . . . (20 to 1) 4
1197³ CLIFDON FOG (Ire) 9-0 K J Manning (12) . . . . (Evens fav) 5
2840⁵ BOB BARNES (Ire) 9-0 J P Murtagh (3) . . . . (10 to 1) 6
2840⁴ EAS GEIPTINE 8-8 (6*) R V Skelly (2) . . . . (20 to 1) 7
2742 MAKE THAT CALL (Ire) 8-11 P V Gilson (6) . . . . (12 to 1) 8
2486⁴ MAJESTIC MAN (Ire) 8-8 (6*) J A Heffernan (8) . . . . (33 to 1) 9
DUGORT STRAND (Ire) 8-8 (6*) B Bowens (10) . . . . (20 to 1) 10
ACTION LAD (Ire) 9-0 S Craine (11) . . . . (20 to 1) 11
Dist: 11l, 1l, ¾l, 1l. 1m 52.40s. (11 Ran).
(Joseph G Murphy), Joseph G Murphy

2983 Oranmore Dairies Fresh Cream Nursery Handicap (2-y-o) £3,795 7f. . .(3:30)

2294³ SPRING FORCE (Ire) [-] 9-1 W J Supple (7) . . . . (12 to 1) 1
2093* ORANEDIN [-] 9-1 (4*) P Carberry (8) . . . . (12 to 1) 2
1387* SHIOWEN (Ire) [-] 8-10 M J Kinane (6) . . . . (5 to 4 fav) 3
2450² MON PANACHE (Ire) [-] 8-6 R Hughes (9) . . . . (11 to 2) 4
2704³ SUMMERHILL SPECIAL (Ire) [-] 9-3 J P Murtagh (2) (5 to 2) 5
2462³ LUDDEN LADY (Ire) [-] 8-13 S Craine (4) . . . . (10 to 1) 6
2742⁸ ZOE BAIRD [-] 7-11 (8*) B Fenton (5) . . . . (10 to 1) 7
2704⁵ BONNIE CRATHIE (Ire) [-] 9-3 P V Gilson (1) . . . . (8 to 1) 8
2319⁶ SALLY'S TRUST (Ire) [-] 7-10 (6*) J J Behan (3) . . . . (16 to 1) 9
Dist: Nk, 2l, ½l, 1l. 1m 38.00s. (9 Ran).
(Mrs Patrick Prendergast), Patrick Prendergast

2984 Oranmore Light Milk Handicap (0-85 3-y-o) £3,795 1½m. . . . . (4:00)

2249* BLAZING SPECTACLE (Ire) [-] 9-2 M J Kinane (10) . . . . (10 to 9 on) 1
2923* SHIRLEY'S DELIGHT (Ire) [-] 9-0 (4*,5ex) P Carberry (7) . . . . (3 to 1) 2
2092³ VALONA (Ire) [-] 9-4 K J Manning (9) . . . . (3 to 1) 3
2842⁹ THE BERUKI (Ire) [-] 8-3 P Shanahan (6) . . . . (12 to 1) 4
2406⁵ SAINT HILDA (Ire) [-] 8-3 W J Supple (4) . . . . (12 to 1) 5
2842⁸ MILLERS MILL (Ire) [-] 7-10 (6*) R V Skelly (2) . . . . (14 to 1) 6
2676⁸ TANHONEY (Ire) [-] 7-3 (6*) P P Murphy (5) . . . . (50 to 1) 7
1292⁴ MAN OF ARRAN (Ire) [-] 8-11 (2*) R M Burke (3) . . . (10 to 1) 8
2484 CREHELP EXPRESS (Ire) [-] 7-10 (2*) D G O'Shea (1) . . . . (33 to 1) 9
Dist: 2l, 1½l, 3½l, 11l. 2m 39.80s. (9 Ran).
(Moyglare Stud Farm), D K Weld

GOODWOOD (good to soft)
Saturday July 31st
Going Correction: PLUS 0.25 sec. per fur. (races 1,2,4,5,7), PLUS 0.50 (3,6)

2985 Vodapage Conditions Stakes Class B (3-y-o) £6,918 1m. . . . .(2:00)

2572² GABR 8-12 W Carson (2) *hld up 4th, cld on ldr o'r 2 fs out, shaken up to ld last 100 yards.* . . . . (11 to 10 on op Evens tchd 5 to 4 and 5 to 4 on) 1
1364 VISTO SI STAMPI (Ire) 8-12 T Quinn (1) *led till rdn and hdd last 100 yards, rallied und pres.* . . . . (15 to 2 op 7 to 1 tchd 8 to 1) 2
2623³ IMAGINARY (Ire) 8-7 W Ryan (3) *in 5th pl, cld on ldrs 3 fs out, sn pushed alng, outpcd appr last.* . . . . (4 to 1 op 3 to 1) 3
2579⁴ FITZCARRALDO (USA) 8-10 R Cochrane (5) *chsd ldr till o'r 2 fs out, sn rdn and one pace*. . . . (4 to 1 op 11 to 4) 4
2752 VILLAGE GREEN (Fr) 8-10 J Reid (4) *in 3rd pl till wknd o'r 2 fs out*. . . . (100 to 1 op 50 to 1) 5
GENTLEMAN SID 8-10 J Lowe (6) *lost many ls strt, al tld off*. . . . (100 to 1 op 66 to 1 tchd 150 to 1) 6
Dist: Nk, 6l, hd, 4l, 30l. 1m 41.76s. a 4.56s (6 Ran).
SR: 60/59/36/38/26/-/ (Hamdan Al-Maktoum), R W Armstrong

2986 Vodafone Nassau Stakes Class A (Group 2) (3-y-o and up) £51,550 1¼m . . . . (2:40)

2333* LYPHARD'S DELTA (USA) 3-8-6 W Ryan (4) *mid-div, ran on 3 fs out, led wl o'r one out, rdn and edgd lft ins last, styd on*. . . . (10 to 1 tchd 14 to 1) 1
2654² ONLY ROYALE (Ire) 4-9-2 R Cochrane (7) *hld up rear, ran on 3 fs out, rdn to chal 2 out, not quicken ins last.* . . . . (5 to 1 op 9 to 2 tchd 11 to 2) 2
1525⁴ SUEBOOG (Ire) 3-8-6 W R Swinburn (9) *hld up mid-div, not much room and swtchd lft o'r 2 fs out, switched rght and ran on ins last.* (7 to 2 fav tchd 4 to 1 and 3 to 1) 3
2334⁴ FEMININE WILES (Ire) 4-9-2 J Reid (1) *settled in 3rd, rdn and not quicken 2 fs out, one pace fnl furlong.* . . . . (20 to 1 op 16 to 1 tchd 25 to 1) 4
2038⁹ MARILLETTE (USA) 3-8-6 L Piggott (5) *hld up last, ran on and short of room 2 fs out, no imprsn on ldrs ins last.* . . . . (8 to 1 tchd 9 to 1) 5
2334² DANCING BLOOM (Ire) 3-8-6 L Dettori (6) *handily plcd, squeezed for room and checked 2 fs out, no extr appr last*. . . . (4 to 1 op 3 to 1) 6
2623* INSTANT AFFAIR (USA) 3-8-6 T Quinn (3) *pushed alng and effrt frm rear 3 fs out, no prog 2 out.* . . . . (25 to 1 op 20 to 1 tchd 33 to 1) 7
1030⁶ LOVE OF SILVER (USA) 3-8-6 G Duffield (8) *chsd ldr, led 3 fs out till wl o'r one out, wknd.* . . . . (25 to 1 op 20 to 1 tchd 33 to 1) 8
1789* THAWAKIB (Ire) 3-8-9 W Carson (2) *led to 3 fs out, wknd 2 out*. . . . (4 to 1 op 3 to 1) 9
Dist: 1½l, ¾l, 2½l, ¾l, 2l, ¾l, 1l, 8l. 2m 11.93s. a 6.43s (9 Ran).
SR: 53/60/48/53/41/37/35/33/20/ (S Khaled), H R A Cecil

2987 Vodac Stewards' Cup Handicap Class B (3-y-o and up) £48,250 6f. . . . . (3:15)

2018* KING'S SIGNET (USA) [98] 4-9-10 (7ex) W Carson (21) *chsd ldrs, led wl o'r one furlong out, sn clr, cmftbly.* . . . . (16 to 1 op 14 to 1) 1
2363 HARD TO FIGURE [95] 7-9-7 R Cochrane (6) *beh to hfwy, ran on 2 fs out, fnshd wl*. . . . (20 to 1 tchd 25 to 1) 2
2434² HOW'S YER FATHER [75] 7-8-1 F Norton (13) *ran on last 2 fs, styd on one pace ins last.* . . . . (10 to 1 co-fav op 14 to 1 tchd 16 to 1) 3
1945⁴ MASTER OF PASSION [93] 4-9-5 M Tebbutt (28) *trkd frnt rnk, rdn and one pace fnl furlong.* (66 to 1 op 50 to 1) 4
2363 VENTURE CAPITALIST [92] (bl) 4-9-4 K Darley (7) *hdwy o'r one furlong out, ran on*. . . . (25 to 1 op 20 to 1) 5
2008⁴ SO RHYTHMICAL [83] 9-8-9 G Bardwell (4) *hdwy last 2 fs, not rch wnr*. . . . (33 to 1 tchd 40 to 1) 6
2582² BLUE TOPAZE [73] 5-7-13 A Mackay (5) *hdwy frm 2 fs out, nvr nrr*. . . . (16 to 1 op 20 to 1) 7
2434³ GORINSKY (Ire) [81] 5-8-7 J Carroll (25) *led hfwy till wl o'r one furlong out, wknd*. . . . (20 to 1 tchd 16 to 1) 8
1806³ ARABELLAJILL [91] 4-9-3 L Dettori (29) *in tch, rdn and one pace 2 fs out*. . . . (10 to 1 co-fav op 12 to 1) 9
1953⁴ JIGSAW BOY [77] 4-8-3¹ J Williams (27) *hld up, effrt o'r one furlong out, nrst finish*. . . . (12 to 1 tchd 14 to 1) 10
2255² PADDY CHALK [86] 7-8-12 A Munro (9) *chsd ldrs for o'r 4 fs*. . . . (16 to 1 op 25 to 1) 11
1213 GARNOCK VALLEY [92] 3-8-12 W R Swinburn (14) *ldg grp till wknd o'r one furlong out*. . . . (33 to 1) 12
2777⁹ EDUCATED PET [69] 4-7-8² (3*) B Doyle (15) *speed for o'r 3 fs*. . . . (50 to 1 op 40 to 1) 13
2418⁴ MASNUN (USA) [74] 8-8-0 D Biggs (22) *nvr better than mid-div*. . . . (25 to 1 tchd 33 to 1) 14

2821^{5} KIMBERLEY PARK [67] 5-7-5^{5} (7*) N Varley (24) *nvr rch ldrs.* ...(66 to 1 tchd 100 to 1) 15
2303^{3} TRUE PRECISION [84] 3-8-4 L Charnock (18) *speed 4 fs.* ...(20 to 1) 16
2303^{4} TROON [91] (bl) 3-8-11 L Piggott (3) *in tch in mid-div, no hdwy last 2 fs*...(14 to 1 op 16 to 1 tchd 12 to 1) 17
2524^{2} BALLASECRET [76] 5-8-2 J Lowe (16) *led to hfwy, wknd 2 fs out*...(10 to 1 co-fav tchd 9 to 1) 18
2848^{4} INVOCATION [69] 6-7-9 S Dawson (2) *nvr nr to chal.* ...(66 to 1 op 50 to 1 tchd 100 to 1) 19
2753^{7} TERRHARS (Ire) [89] (bl) 5-9-1 R Perham (8) *nvr on terms.* ...(40 to 1 op 50 to 1) 20
2206^{2} CASTLEREA LAD [87] 4-8-13 (5ex) W Ryan (10) *mid-div, no hdwy 2 fs out*...(14 to 1 op 12 to 1) 21
2062^{6} AMRON [88] 6-9-0 N Carlisle (20) *in tch 4 fs*... (33 to 1) 22
1806* NAGIDA [89] 4-8-12 (3*) J Weaver (1) *nvr on terms.* ...(10 to 1 co-fav tchd 11 to 1) 23
2734^{4} MERRYHILL MAID (Ire) [69] 5-7-4 (5*) D Wright (30) *speed to hfwy*...(66 to 1) 24
2753^{2} ASHTINA [82] 8-8-8 J Quinn (11) *pressed ldrs till wknd 2 fs out*...(16 to 1) 25
1337^{5} LORD OLIVIER (Ire) [104] 3-9-5 (5*) K Rutter (12) *wl plcd to hfwy*...(50 to 1 tchd 66 to 1) 26
1957^{3} SIR JOEY (USA) [77] 4-8-3 N Adams (23) *nvr trble ldrs.* ...(33 to 1 tchd 40 to 1) 27
2753^{6} RUNNING GLIMPSE (Ire) [82] 5-8-8 W Newnes (19) *in tch to hfwy*...(33 to 1) 28
2868 LETSBEONESTABOUTIT [68] (bl) 7-7-8 A Tucker (17) *al beh.* ...(66 to 1 tchd 100 to 1) 29

Dist: 1½l, nk, 1½l, hd, hd, hd, hd, hd, 1l, hd. 1m 15.00s. a 4.60s (29 Ran).
SR: 78/69/48/60/58/48/37/44/53/ (Sheikh Mohammed), J H M Gosden

2988 Vodata Nursery Handicap Class C (2-y-o) £5,663 7f... (3:45)

2058^{6} ALPINE SKIER (Ire) [-] 8-9 K Darley (5) *pressed ldrs, led 2 fs out till entering last, led last 100 yards, styd on.* ...(12 to 1 op 10 to 1 tchd 14 to 1) 1
2539* EXTRA BONUS [-] 9-3 (3*) J Weaver (12) *hld up in tch, swtchd lft 2 fs out, slight ld entering last, sn hdd, rallied nr line*...(7 to 2 jt-fav tchd 9 to 2) 2
2546^{5} JASARI (Ire) [-] 8-7 J Reid (3) *chsd ldrs, rdn and kpt on one pace frm 2 fs out*...(10 to 1 op 12 to 1) 3
2274^{4} SHARP TYCOON (Ire) [-] 8-8 W R Swinburn (6) *handily plcd, led briefly o'r 2 fs out, outpcd over one out.* ...(14 to 1 op 10 to 1) 4
2786^{8} STRAPPED [-] 7-7 N Adams (2) *hld up in tch, rdn and no extr 2 fs out*...(33 to 1 op 16 to 1) 5
2419^{2} DUTY TIME [-] 8-9 W Carson (8) *rdn alng and styd on last 2 fs, nvr nrr*...(7 to 2 jt-fav tchd 3 to 1) 6
2546^{3} PRINCE DANZIG (Ire) [-] (v) 8-2 A Munro (4) *mid-div, no hdwy appr last 2 fs.* (14 to 1 op 10 to 1 tchd 16 to 1) 7
2412* RAMBOLD [-] 9-0 R Perham (10) *led till o'r 2 fs out, wknd over one out*... (9 to 1 op 8 to 1 tchd 11 to 1) 8
2292^{4} SECOND SIGHT (Ire) [-] 9-7 G Duffield (7) *beh and pushed alng 3 fs out, nvr on terms.* ...(14 to 1 op 8 to 1 tchd 16 to 1) 9
2772* CULSYTH FLYER [-] 8-8 W Ryan (9) *al beh.* ...(11 to 1 op 10 to 1 tchd 12 to 1) 10
2412^{3} BET A PLAN (Ire) [-] 7-8 (5*) D Wright (1) *chsd ldrs, wknd o'r 2 fs out*...(7 to 1 op 6 to 1 tchd 8 to 1) 11
2357^{8} KOONOONA LADY [-] 7-13 J Lowe (11) *mid-div, rdn and wknd 3 fs out*...(25 to 1 op 14 to 1) 12

Dist: Hd, 1l, 3½l, 3l, ½l, 1½l, sht-hd, hd, sht-hd, 2l. 1m 31.74s. a 7.14s (12 Ran).
SR: 14/24/8/-/-/-/ (P D Savill), R Hannon

2989 Turf Club Claiming Stakes Class D (3-y-o and up) £5,526 1m... (4:15)

2475^{5} GRAND VITESSE (Ire) 4-8-6 (7*) D Gibbs (5) *led aftr one furlong, shaken up 2 out, kpt on strly.* ...(6 to 1 op 5 to 1 tchd 7 to 1) 1
2138^{5} CONSPICUOUS (Ire) 3-8-4 A Munro (3) *wl plcd, chsd wnr frm 3 fs out, one pace ins last*... (7 to 1 tchd 8 to 1) 2
2671^{6} BOLD MEMORY 4-8-8 J Reid (6) *hld up in tch, squeezed for room o'r 2 fs out, styd on fnl furlong.* ...(8 to 1 op 7 to 1) 3
2015^{2} BATTLE COLOURS (Ire) 4-8-11 G Duffield (9) *wl plcd, rdn alng 3 fs out, no extr 2 out.* ...(9 to 2 op 7 to 2 tchd 5 to 1) 4
2847^{5} MON PETITNAMOUR (Ire) 4-8-6 L Charnock (8) *hld up rear, rdn and no hdwy o'r 2 fs out*... (50 to 1 op 33 to 1) 5
1092^{4} PREROGATIVE 3-8-4 L Dettori (1) *mid-div, rdn alng 3 fs out, sn btn*... (4 to 1 fav op 3 to 1 tchd 9 to 2) 6
1703* MONSIGNOR PAT (USA) 3-9-0 W Ryan (7) *led one furlong, chsd wnr to 3 out, wknd 2 out*... (9 to 2 op 3 to 1) 7
2944^{3} JAHANGIR (Ire) 4-9-4 L Piggott (4) *hld up rear, rdn and swtchd lft 3 fs out, not rch ldrs.* ...(5 to 1 op 6 to 1 tchd 7 to 1) 8
DANCING MISS (Ire) 4-8-1 C Avery (2) *hld up rear, rdn alng o'r 3 fs out, no hdwy*... (50 to 1 op 33 to 1) 9

Dist: 2½l, hd, 4l, 1l, hd, 8l, 6l, 4l. 1m 42.22s. a 5.02s (9 Ran).
SR: 54/37/40/31/23/20/6/-/-/ (Robert Whitworth), R Hannon

2990 Surplice Maiden Stakes Class D (2-y-o) £5,754 6f... (4:45)

STAR TALENT (USA) 9-0 R Cochrane (13) *rear, hdwy 2 fs out, shaken up to ld last 100 yards, cleverly.* ...(6 to 1 op 4 to 1 tchd 13 to 2) 1
ALAFLAK (Ire) 9-0 W Carson (1) *wl plcd, led one furlong out, hdd and not quicken last 100 yards.* ...(100 to 30 fav op 7 to 2 tchd 5 to 1 and 3 to 1) 2
DEVOTEE 8-9 G Duffield (7) *cl up, led 2 fs out to one out, edgd lft und pres ins last.* ...(12 to 1 op 10 to 1 tchd 14 to 1) 3
VARSAVIA (USA) 8-9 W R Swinburn (2) *in tch, hdwy and not much room o'r one furlong out, swtchd lft, hmpd and snatched up ins last.* ...(13 to 2 op 5 to 1 tchd 8 to 1) 4
NORDANCE PRINCE (Ire) 9-0 K Darley (10) *slwly into strd, beh till styd on appr fnl furlong*... (33 to 1 op 20 to 1) 5
RISKY TU 8-9 Gay Kelleway (4) *in tch, rdn and outpcd hfwy*...(14 to 1 op 8 to 1) 6
ROBSERA (Ire) 9-0 J Reid (5) *led to hfwy, wknd 2 fs out.* ...(14 to 1 op 10 to 1) 7
PARTY SEASON 9-0 D Biggs (11) *slwly into strd, mid-div, no hdwy 2 fs out*...(14 to 1 op 10 to 1) 8
MONRUSH (Ire) 8-11 (3*) J Weaver (14) *outpcd.* ...(25 to 1 op 20 to 1 tchd 33 to 1) 9
KENTAVRUS WAY (Ire) 9-0 S Raymont (8) *cl up, led 3 fs out to 2 out, wknd o'r one out*... (10 to 1 op 9 to 2) 10
THE LONE DANCER 9-0 L Dettori (12) *settled mid-div, no hdwy last 2 fs*...(6 to 1 op 5 to 1) 11
PRESENTLY 8-6 (3*) M Fenton (9) *outpcd.* ...(14 to 1 op 8 to 1) 12
EL BAILADOR (Ire) 9-0 A Munro (3) *slwly into strd, outpcd.* ...(20 to 1 tchd 25 to 1) 13
MAJOR ROWAN 9-0 C Avery (6) *slwly into strd, outpcd.* ...(50 to 1 op 33 to 1) 14

Dist: 1½l, 1½l, 2½l, 4l, ¾l, 1l, nk, sht-hd, hd, 1½l. 1m 15.63s. a 5.23s (14 Ran).
SR: 55/49/38/28/17/9/10/9/8/ (J C Smith), D R C Elsworth

2991 Trundle Handicap Class C (0-80 3-y-o and up) £5,208 1½m... (5:20)

2490^{2} DAY OF HISTORY (Ire) [55] 4-8-9 D Biggs (3) *hld up, pushed alng 3 fs out, rdn 2 out, led nr finish.* ...(9 to 2 op 5 to 1 tchd 4 to 1) 1
2158^{4} MARROS MILL [76] (v) 3-9-1 (3*) M Fenton (6) *handily plcd, rdn to ld last 100 yards, hdd nr line.* ...(13 to 2 op 5 to 1 tchd 7 to 1) 2
2135^{2} FOOLS ERRAND (Ire) [71] 3-8-13 J Reid (1) *trkd ldr, slight ld one furlong out, hdd and no extr last 100 yards.* ...(11 to 2 op 9 to 2 tchd 6 to 1) 3
2795^{5} BOOKCASE [70] 6-9-10 J Williams (2) *hld up rear, rdn alng and not much room o'r one furlong out, styd on nr finish*... (9 to 2 op 5 to 1 tchd 11 to 2 and 4 to 1) 4
2722* MISS SHAGRA (USA) [73] 3-9-1 W R Swinburn (5) *led till hdd und pres one furlong out, sn wknd*...(7 to 2 jt-fav op 3 to 1) 5
2420* BLAZON OF TROY [57] 4-8-11 K Darley (4) *wl plcd till rdn alng and drpd rear o'r 4 fs out, tld off.* ...(7 to 2 jt-fav op 5 to 2 tchd 4 to 1) 6

Dist: ¾l, ¾l, nk, 2l, 20l. 2m 44.03s. a 11.03s (6 Ran).
SR: 15/22/15/25/12/-/ (R M Cyzer), C A Cyzer

NEWMARKET (JULY) (good)
Saturday July 31st
Going Correction: MINUS 0.40 sec. per fur.

2992 Jif Lemon Amateur Riders' Handicap Class E (0-80 4-y-o and up) £3,106 1½m... (2:15)

2632^{8} VIARDOT (Ire) [80] 4-12-0 Mr M Buckley (11) *tucked away on ins, took wrong course aftr 4 fs, wnt back, quickened to ld wl inside last, ran on*... (11 to 2 op 4 to 1) 1
2729^{4} THE KARAOKE KING [48] (bl) 4-9-5 (5*) Mrs J Boggis (14) *keen hold, took wrong course aftr 4 fs, wnt back, ev ch ins last, kpt on*...(7 to 1 op 8 to 1 tchd 10 to 1) 2
2347^{7} SCENIC DANCER [49] 5-9-6 (5*) Miss L Hide (12) *trkd ldrs, took wrong course aftr 4 fs, wnt back to ld, shaken up and hdd wl ins last, no extr*... (11 to 2 op 9 to 2) 3
2761* BLACKDOWN [49] 6-9-11 Miss A Harwood (3) *trkd ldrs, took wrong course aftr 4 fs, wnt back, ev ch till outpcd fnl furlong*...(10 to 1 op 8 to 1 tchd 12 to 1) 4
2789 LAMBOURN RAJA [71] 7-11-5^{17} (5*) Mr K Tork (4) *took wrong course aftr 4 fs, pld up*... (50 to 1 op 33 to 1) pu
2581 STARLIGHT FLYER [75] (bl) 6-11-4 (5*) Mr T Waters (1) *took wrong course aftr 4 fs, pld up*... (50 to 1 op 33 to 1) pu
2685^{8} TORGHIA [53] 6-9-10 (5*) Miss M Sandercock (9) *led till took wrong course aftr 4 fs, pld up.* (33 to 1 op 25 to 1) pu
2729^{3} BARCHAM [45] 6-9-7 Mrs P Nash (8) *took wrong course aftr 4 fs, pld up*...(4 to 1 fav op 5 to 1) pu
2834^{2} SWIFT SILVER [60] 6-10-3 (5*) Mrs J Musson (10) *took wrong course aftr 4 fs, pld up*...(6 to 1 op 9 to 2) pu
2506^{7} MADAGANS GREY [61] 5-10-9 Mrs L Pearce (5) *took wrong course aftr 4 fs, pld up.* (9 to 1 op 5 to 1 tchd 10 to 1) pu
2789 FORTUNE STAR (Ire) [55] 4-9-12 (5*) Miss M Bridger (7) *took wrong course aftr 4 fs, pld up*... (33 to 1 op 20 to 1) pu

674 EVERSO IRISH [46] 4-9-8[6] (5*) Mr W McLaughlin (2) *took wrong course aftr 4 fs, pld up*..... (33 to 1 op 25 to 1) pu
KHALIDI (Ire) [75] 4-11-4 (5*) Miss E Gandolfo (6) *took wrong course aftr 4 fs, pld up*.......... (12 to 1 op 8 to 1) pu
2420[6] TIME FOR A FLUTTER [53] (bl) 4-10-1[6] (5*) Mr E James (13) *took wrong course aftr 4 fs, pld up*. (25 to 1 op 20 to 1) pu
Dist: ½l, sht-hd, 15l. 2m 38.35s. a 9.55s (14 Ran).
(Mrs H North), Mrs M Reveley

2993 Robinson's Fruit Drinks Claiming Stakes Class E (3-y-o) £2,924 7f (2:45)

2522[4] OK BERTIE 8-6 (5*) C Hodgson (8) *patiently rdn, quickened through on ins to ld fnl furlong, jst lasted.* ....(11 to 4 op 5 to 2 tchd 3 to 1) 1
1587[4] COMMON LAW (Ire) 9-2 Pat Eddery (5) *tried to make all, hdd ins fnl furlong, rallied, jst fld.* ....(2 to 1 fav op 11 to 4 tchd 3 to 1) 2
2712 CLIBURNEL NEWS (Ire) 8-2 P Robinson (3) *trkd ldg trio, ev ch and drvn alng 2 fs out, outpcd fnl furlong.* .... (15 to 2 op 10 to 1 tchd 7 to 1) 3
2717[6] TEE GEE JAY (v) 7-11 (3*) D Harrison (9) *tucked away on ins, ev ch and rdn o'r one furlong out, one pace.* ....(8 to 1 op 7 to 1) 4
2939[2] PRINCELY FAVOUR (Ire) 9-5 M Hills (2) *gd speed on outsd till fdd und pres entering fnl furlong.* ....(11 to 2 op 9 to 2) 5
2749 PACIFIC POWER 8-7 Emma O'Gorman (4) *sluggish strt, reco'red to track ldrs hfwy, rdn and btn over 2 fs out.* .... (16 to 1 op 14 to 1) 6+
2154[3] EASTERN GLOW 8-2[2] W Woods (6) *wth ldr, feeling pace 2 fs out, fdd fnl furlong.* ....(25 to 1 op 16 to 1 tchd 33 to 1) 6+
2578[4] WALID'S PRINCESS (Ire) 7-8 Dale Gibson (1) *sluggish strt, reco'red to race in tch hfwy, fdd wl over one furlong out*.................................... (10 to 1 op 8 to 1) 8
2011 MONTONE (Ire) 9-1 G Carter (7) *tucked away beh ldrs, effrt hfwy, outpcd last 2 fs*........ (16 to 1 op 14 to 1) 9
Dist: Sht-hd, 5l, hd, 4l, 2½l, dd-ht, sht-hd, ¾l. 1m 25.59s. a 1.39s (9 Ran).
SR: 34/38/9/6/13/-/ (Peter Newman), D Morris

2994 EBF Colman's Mustard Maiden Stakes Class D (2-y-o) £4,425 6f (3:20)

FOREST GAZELLE (USA) 9-0 Pat Eddery (1) *confidently rdn, quickened up to ld entering fnl furlong, drvn out.* ....(11 to 10 on op 5 to 4 tchd 6 to 4) 1
ATAARED (USA) 9-0 B Raymond (2) *tried to make all, hdd entering fnl furlong, kpt on wl.* .... (11 to 1 op 6 to 1 tchd 12 to 1) 2
OWINGTON 9-0 M Hills (6) *patiently rdn, shaken up to improve o'r one furlong out, one ot note.* ....(5 to 2 op 2 to 1 tchd 100 to 30 and 7 to 2) 3
1131 CALYPSO MONARCH (Ire) 9-0 W Woods (3) *shaped wl on outsd for o'r 4 fs, grad wknd*....... (16 to 1 op 7 to 1) 4
STORM SHIP (Ire) 9-0 G Carter (11) *wl plcd on ins, drw level hfwy, rdn and not quicken o'r one furlong out.* .... (25 to 1 op 14 to 1) 5
KNAVE'S ASH (USA) 9-0 Paul Eddery (4) *patiently rdn, ran green and edgd lft 2 fs out, rng on finish.* .... (12 to 1 op 7 to 1 tchd 14 to 1) 6
MILLION LIGHTS (Ire) 8-9 A Clark (8) *settled midfield, chsd alng whn pace lifted last 2 fs, one pace.* .... (16 to 1 op 12 to 1 tchd 20 to 1) 7
2336[9] EXOTIC FOREST 8-9 P Robinson (9) *took keen hold, pressed ldrs for 4 fs, fdd.* .... (20 to 1 op 12 to 1 tchd 25 to 1) 8
UNCLE BILL 9-0 B Marcus (5) *settled midfield, effrt whn baulked o'r 2 fs out, sn btn*........ (25 to 1 op 16 to 1) 9
STEADY RISK 9-0 S Whitworth (10) *trkd ldg bunch, shaken up hfwy, nvr plcd to chal*. (50 to 1 op 20 to 1) 10
WORLD TRAVELLER 8-11 (3*) Emma O'Gorman (7) *sluggish strt, improved on ins hfwy, sn rdn and btn.* .... (33 to 1 op 20 to 1) 11
Dist: ½l, 3½l, ¾l, 3½l, 2l, hd, 3½l, 4l, 2l, 4l. 1m 12.56s. a 0.86s (11 Ran).
SR: 35/33/19/16/2/-/ (K Abdulla), R Charlton

2995 Robinsons Barley Water Handicap Class D (0-80 3-y-o) £4,308 1m.. (3:50)

2757[2] KASSBAAN (USA) [75] 9-7 B Raymond (4) *patiently rdn, shaken up to ld entering fnl furlong, drvn clr.* ....(7 to 2 tchd 4 to 1) 1
2663[3] AJMAAN (USA) [71] 9-3 S Whitworth (5) *al wl plcd, led and quickened o'r one furlong out, hdd entering last, one pace*................................ (7 to 1 op 6 to 1) 2
2715[5] PRAIRIE GROVE [72] 9-4 Pat Eddery (3) *nvr far away, effrt and drvn alng o'r one furlong out, kpt on same pace.* .... (11 to 4 fav tchd 3 to 1) 3
2383[3] SWEET DISORDER (Ire) [59] 8-2 (3*) D Harrison (1) *settled on outsd, effrt and bustled alng last 2 fs, not quicken.* ....(10 to 1) 4
2680[5] KEYWAY (USA) [74] 9-6 C Nutter (2) *led for o'r 6 fs, wknd und pres last 100 yards*......................... (10 to 1) 5
2578[5] KING PARIS (Ire) [75] 9-7 M Hills (7) *tucked away on ins, effrt and bustled alng o'r 2 fs out, not pace to chal.* ....(5 to 1) 6

2418[8] AROOM [68] 9-0 P Robinson (8) *sluggish strt, chsd alng to race in tch hfwy, no imprsn*...... (9 to 1 tchd 10 to 1) 7
921[2] OCARA (USA) [67] 8-13 G Carter (6) *bolted gng to post, pld hrd till wknd quickly o'r 2 fs out*.....(7 to 1 op 6 to 1) 8
Dist: 2½l, 2½l, ½l, 1l, 3½l, 1½l, 4l. 1m 39.20s. a 1.30s (8 Ran).
SR: 40/28/21/6/18/8/-/-/ (Maktoum Al Maktoum), A A Scott

2996 Tenth Running Of The Colman's Of Norwich Class C Nursery (2-y-o) £20,225 6f..................... (4:20)

2695* HEVER GOLF ROSE [73] 8-1 Paul Eddery (11) *al hndy, led wl o'r one furlong out, ran on strly.* ....(8 to 1 tchd 10 to 1) 1
2618[7] STRAIGHT ARROW [-] 9-1 (3*) D Harrison (18) *co'red up on ins, drvn alng to improve over one furlong out, kpt on same pace*........... (12 to 1 op 10 to 1 tchd 14 to 1) 2
2786* THE MULTIYORKER (Ire) [-] 7-7 Dale Gibson (3) *trkd ldg bunch, drvn through to improve fnl furlong, ran on.* ....(12 to 1) 3
2812* STAR SPEEDER (Ire) [-] 8-6 (7*) B Russell (14) *chsd alng to improve frm midfield last 2 fs, ran on und pres.* .... (16 to 1 op 14 to 1) 4
2569* BELLA PARKES [-] 8-6 G Carter (10) *al frnt rnk, drvn alng o'r one furlong out, no extr.* ....(5 to 1 op 6 to 1 tchd 7 to 1) 5
2137[2] DOLLAR GAMBLE (Ire) [-] 8-2 B Marcus (13) *chsd ldg bunch, improved und pres o'r one furlong out, no imprsn*............................ (14 to 1 op 10 to 1) 6
2618[9] ANZIO (Ire) [-] 8-12 M Hills (2) *shwd up wl on outsd till fdd und pres entering fnl furlong.* .... (12 to 1 op 10 to 1 tchd 14 to 1) 7
2618 MIRIAM [-] 7-10 (5*) J Tate (12) *broke wl to dispute ld for 4 fs, no extr*..................(50 to 1 tchd 66 to 1) 8
2689* PRINCE AZZAAN (Ire) [-] 8-8 Pat Eddery (6) *sluggish strt, drvn into midfield hfwy, kpt on, not pace to chal.* ....(11 to 4 fav op 3 to 1 tchd 7 to 2) 9
2618 TINKER OSMASTON [-] 8-8 J Curant (7) *chsd alng towards outsd, effrt o'r 2 fs out, not rch ldrs*........... (12 to 1) 10
2552[2] ALLLEGSNOBRAIN [-] 8-2[1] D Holland (1) *made most for o'r 4 fs, wknd fnl furlong*........... (10 to 1 tchd 12 to 1) 11
2209[3] KINGSWELL PRINCE (Ire) [-] 8-12 S Whitworth (15) *chsd ldrs for o'r 3 fs, fdd*.................. (14 to 1 op 16 to 1) 12
718[8] TUTU SIXTYSIX [-] 7-10 (3*) N Kennedy (9) *drvn alng in midfield hfwy, not pace of ldrs*.... (16 to 1 op 14 to 1) 13
2720* DANCE FOCUS [-] 8-13 (3*) Emma O'Gorman (8) *speed to chase ldrs for o'r 4 fs, fdd*........................(20 to 1) 14
2016[3] OCHOS RIOS (Ire) [-] 9-2 (5*) Stephen Davies (16) *bustled alng to keep up aftr 2 fs, nvr a threat.* ....(25 to 1 tchd 33 to 1) 15
2786[5] KOMPLICITY [-] 7-7 E Johnson (17) *chsd ldg bunch to hfwy, sn btn*.................. (50 to 1 op 33 to 1) 16
2629[4] SAWTID [-] 8-3 A Clark (4) *bustled alng to go pace, nvr a factor*..........................(12 to 1 op 16 to 1) 17
2652[3] DISTINCTIVE AIR [-] (bl) 8-3 P Robinson (5) *chsd alng hfwy, nvr a threat*.................................. (25 to 1) 18
Dist: 1½l, ¾l, 1½l, sht-hd, 1½l, 2½l, 1½l, 1l, hd, 1½l. 1m 11.61s. b 0.09s (18 Ran).
SR: 41/52/24/38/30/20/20/3/6/ (R A Popely), T J Naughton

2997 Ladbroke Handicap Class C (0-90 3-y-o and up) £6,264 1¼m.......... (4:50)

2333 FORTHWITH [84] 3-9-4 T Quinn (4) *patiently rdn, quickened up on outsd to ld 2 fs out, ran on stronly.* ....(14 to 1 tchd 16 to 1) 1
2333[7] NESSUN DORMA [80] 3-9-0 M Hills (2) *settled gng wl, swtchd to chal entering fnl furlong, rdn and not quicken cl hme*.................... (9 to 2 tchd 5 to 1) 2
2333[4] SHARJAH (USA) [86] 3-9-6 P Robinson (1) *wtd wth, shaken up to chal entering fnl furlong, not quicken towards finish*..............(4 to 1 op 3 to 1 tchd 9 to 2) 3
2239[7] SUN OF SPRING [81] 3-9-1 Paul Eddery (3) *pressed ldrs, hrd drvn o'r 2 fs out, not quicken.* ....(15 to 2 op 7 to 1 tchd 8 to 1) 4
1661[3] MISBELIEF [72] 3-8-6 G Carter (6) *trkd ldg pair, drvn alng whn pace quickened last 2 fs, one pace.* ....(100 to 30 op 4 to 1 tchd 11 to 4) 5
2632[2] DRUMMER HICKS [83] 4-9-13 M Tebbutt (5) *unruly at strt, settled to track ldrs, outpcd o'r 2 fs out, nvr able to chal*..............................(7 to 1 tchd 8 to 1) 6
1483* SCULLER (USA) [85] 3-9-5 Pat Eddery (7) *led till hdd and rdn 2 fs out, eased whn btn ins last.* ....(11 to 4 fav op 3 to 1 tchd 7 to 2) 7
Dist: 1l, hd, 2l, hd, 6l, nk. 2m 2.93s. a 0.73s (7 Ran).
SR: 57/51/56/47/37/46/37/ (L H J Ward), J W Hills

2998 Colman's Sauces Conditions Stakes Class C (2-y-o) £4,314 7f........(5:25)

1715* CARMOT 9-1 T Quinn (3) *al hndy, drvn ahead o'r one furlong out, gng clr whn drifted lft.* ....(5 to 4 fav op 11 to 10) 1
2626* DIESAN (USA) 9-1 B Raymond (6) *rcd freely, led aftr 3 fs till o'r one furlong out, not pace of wnr.* .... (3 to 1 op 11 to 4 tchd 7 to 2) 2

2616^{4} PETER ROWLEY 8-11 Pat Eddery (7) *tucked away on ins, drw level o'r one furlong out, kpt on same pace.* .... (3 to 1 op 5 to 2 tchd 100 to 30) 3
2179* ABSOLUTELY FAYRE 9-1 Paul Eddery (2) *led for 3 fs, rallied to ld ag'n briefly o'r one furlong out, no extr.* .... (8 to 1 op 14 to 1 tchd 16 to 1) 4
2720^{4} TONDRES (USA) (v) 8-11 B Marcus (4) *pressed ldrs, feeling pace and drvn alng 2 fs out, sn btn.* .... (14 to 1 tchd 20 to 1) 5
2438^{2} KEZIO RUFO (Ire) 9-1 M Wigham (5) *struggling to go pace hfwy, nvr a factor*............... (20 to 1 op 16 to 1) 6

Dist: 6l, sht-hd, 1l, 5l, 2l. 1m 25.28s. a 1.08s (6 Ran).
SR: 43/25/20/21/2/-/ (Sheikh Mohammed), P F I Cole

SARATOGA (USA) (firm)
Saturday July 31st

2999 Test Stakes (Grade 1) (3-y-o) £59,603 7f..................................

MISSED THE STORM (USA) 8-2 M Smith,......... (5 to 2) 1
MISS INDY ANNA (Can) 8-2 E Maple,.........(10 to 9 on) 2
935^{2} EDUCATED RISK (USA) 8-2 J D Bailey,......... (29 to 10) 3
TRUE AFFAIR (USA) 8-9 J Velasquez,...........(78 to 10) 4
FIGHTING JET (USA) 8-4 C Bisond,............. (23 to 1) 5

Dist: Hd, 8l, 2l, 1l. 1m 22.12s. (5 Ran).
(Pin Oak Farm), W Mott

THIRSK (firm)
Saturday July 31st

Going Correction: MINUS 0.50 sec. per fur. (races 1,2,3,7), MINUS 0.30 (4,5,6)

3000 Topcliffe Fillies' Conditions Stakes Class C (2-y-o) £4,266 6f........(2:20)

2542* PROMISE FULFILLED (USA) 8-8 (5*) O Pears (4) *made virtually all, rdn o'r one out, drw clr fnl furlong.* .... (100 to 30 op 3 to 1) 1
2400^{4} PLAINSONG 8-11 K Fallon (5) *wth ldr, effrt wl o'r one out, kpt on same pace*.......(7 to 2 tchd 3 to 1 and 4 to 1) 2
2199* KNAYTON LASS 8-13 T Lucas (3) *trkd ldrs, effrt wl o'r one out, ran on ins fnl furlong*.......(7 to 4 fav op 5 to 4) 3
2695^{9} INDIAHRA 8-11 S Perks (1) *cl up, effrt wl o'r one out, sn btn*.................... (9 to 2 op 6 to 1 tchd 7 to 1) 4
2400 SMART PET 8-13 N Connorton (2) *trkd ldrs, effrt wl o'r one out, sn btn*.................... (8 to 1 tchd 9 to 1) 5

Dist: 3l, ½l, ¾l, 2l. 1m 11.10s. a 1.10s (5 Ran).
SR: 17/3/3/-/-/ (G G Ashton), S G Norton

3001 EBF Sutton Maiden Stakes Class D (2-y-o) £4,270 5f................. (2:50)

2766^{4} BEATS WORKING 9-0 K Fallon (13) *in tch, quickened to ld ins fnl furlong, sn clr, cmftbly*......(11 to 2 op 5 to 1) 1
2630^{2} GENERAL GUBBINS 8-9 (5*) O Pears (4) *cl up, led 2 out, hdd ins fnl furlong, no extr.* .... (5 to 1 tchd 11 to 2 and 9 to 2) 2
1556^{6} PALACEGATE JACK (Ire) 9-0 J Fortune (1) *chsd ldrs, ev ch entering fnl furlong, kpt on same pace.* .... (4 to 1 fav op 5 to 1 tchd 7 to 2) 3
1739^{7} BOLLIN MARY 8-9 M Birch (5) *led till hdd 2 out, kpt on same pace*.........................(16 to 1 op 12 to 1) 4
2630^{9} HILL REEF (Fr) 8-7 (7*) D Thomas (11) *in tch, kpt on wl fnl furlong, not trble ldrs*.........................(20 to 1) 5
2630^{3} DOMINO QUEEN (Ire) 8-9 N Day (9) *stumbled strt, prmnt, ev ch o'r one out, wknd fnl furlong.* ....(7 to 1 tchd 8 to 1) 6
K-REG 9-0 J Fanning (12) *dwlt, beh till styd on fnl 2 fs, nvr dngrs*.........................(16 to 1 op 12 to 1) 7
1418 AJNAS (Ire) 8-9 R Hills (6) *chsd ldrs till wknd o'r one out.* ....(5 to 1 op 4 to 1) 8
MILLIE'S DREAM 8-9 S Perks (8) *mid-div, effrt 2 out, sn btn*.............................. (16 to 1 op 14 to 1) 9
2817^{4} BALI WARRIOR (Ire) 9-0 N Connorton (10) *al beh.* ....(7 to 1 op 6 to 1) 10
2706 MERISSA 8-9 T Lucas (2) *nvr better than mid-div.* ....(20 to 1) 11
2554^{9} HONG KONG FUTURE (Ire) 8-11 (3*) S D Williams (3) *mid-div, rdn hfwy, sn wknd*.....................(25 to 1) 12
2618 MARCH OF TIME (bl) 9-0 A McGlone (7) *al beh.* .... (16 to 1 op 14 to 1) 13

Dist: 2½l, ½l, sht-hd, 1½l, hd, 3½l, 1l, hd, 1l, 1½l. 58.10s. a 0.90s (13 Ran).
SR: 32/22/20/14/13/7/ (M R Charlton), Mrs J R Ramsden

3002 Coopers & Lybrand Selling Handicap Ladies Class F (0-60 3-y-o and up) £3,125 6f...................... (3:25)

2861^{4} ASTERIX [47] 5-10-13 (5*) Mrs D McHale (15) *trkd ldrs, effrt and swtchd o'r one out, led ins fnl furlong, wnt lft, hld on wl und pres*..................... (6 to 1 op 7 to 1) 1
2560^{8} CUDDLY DATE [48] 3-10-13 Miss Diana Jones (1) *led till hdd ins fnl furlong, no extr*...................... (16 to 1) 2
2760^{4} PAULINUS [31] 5-9-9 (7*) Miss M Carson (7) *in tch, effrt 2 out, chalg whn crrd lft ins fnl furlong, no extr towards finish*..........................(16 to 1 op 14 to 1) 3
2639^{5} SUMMER EXPRESS [50] 4-11-0 (7*) Miss C Spearing (16) *chsd ldrs, effrt 2 out, kpt on fnl furlong.* .... (11 to 1 op 14 to 1 tchd 10 to 1) 4
2769^{7} DEAD CALM [50] (v) 3-11-1 Mrs J Crossley (8) *slwly into strd, beh till styd on wl und pres fnl 2 fs, nrst finish.* ....(12 to 1) 5
2127 SUPREME OPTIMIST [20] (bl) 9-8-13^{1} (7*) Mrs C Peacock (18) *chsd ldrs, effrt 2 out, kpt on fnl furlong*... (25 to 1) 6
2602^{3} MISSED THE BOAT (Ire) [50] (bl) 3-10-8 (7*) Miss F Burke (11) *chsd ldrs, rdn 2 out, kpt on same pace.* ....(9 to 1 op 7 to 1) 7
2682^{8} BRISAS [31] (v) 6-9-11 (5*) Miss D J Jones (14) *cl up till wknd o'r one out*....................(8 to 1 op 7 to 1) 8
2978^{5} MANX MONARCH [49] 3-10-9 (5*) Miss T Spearing (4) *nvr trbld ldrs*..............(8 to 1 tchd 9 to 1 and 7 to 1) 9
2775^{9} MISS EL ARAB (Ire) [42] 5-10-8 (5*) Miss A Deniel (2) *chsd ldrs, rdn hfwy, sn btn*.......... (25 to 1 tchd 33 to 1) 10
2639^{9} JACK GRAY [47] 5-10-13 (5*) Mrs S Bosley (13) *al beh.* ....(25 to 1) 11
2935^{7} BARBEZIEUX [46] 6-10-10 (7*) Mrs C Dods (10) *al beh.* ....(8 to 1 op 6 to 1) 12
2682 NOT ALL BLISS [24] 5-9-2 (7*) Miss A Armitage (17) *sn beh.* ....(50 to 1) 13
2682^{7} BRAVE MELODY [26] 7-9-4 (7*) Miss J Bond (5) *al beh.* .... (16 to 1 op 14 to 1) 14
2768^{6} KICK ON MAJESTIC (Ire) [20] (bl) 4-8-12 (7*) Miss A Bycroft (6) *strted slwly, al beh*............(16 to 1 op 14 to 1) 15
2827 GRUBBY [26] 4-9-11 Mrs G Rees (12) *sn beh.* .... (25 to 1 op 20 to 1) 16
2597^{7} VIKING WATERS [41] 3-10-1 (5*) Mrs D Kettlewell (3) *rcd wide, in tch till wknd 2 out*.................. (25 to 1) 17
2975^{7} SULLY'S CHOICE (USA) [45] (bl) 12-10-9 (7*) Miss R Clark (9) *reluctant to race and strted very slwly, wl tld off till styd on fnl 2 fs*...............(5 to 1 fav tchd 11 to 2) 18

Dist: ¾l, hd, hd, nk, nk, nk, 3½l, 1l, sht-hd, 1l. 1m 12.00s. a 2.00s (18 Ran).
SR: 32/24/12/30/23/-/21/-/2/ (Clifton Hunt), J M Bradley

3003 Barclays Bank Handicap Class D (0-80 3-y-o and up) £4,386 1½m...... (4:00)

2591* PERSIAN SOLDIER [46] 6-7-8 J Fanning (1) *made all, clr 2 out, pushed out*................ (7 to 4 fav op 5 to 2) 1
2767^{2} SALU [53] 4-7-12 (3*) S Maloney (7) *beh, pushed alng 4 out, hdwy o'r 2 out, styd on wl towards finish*...... (9 to 2) 2
2207^{2} SHADOWS OF SILVER [80] 5-10-0 M Birch (3) *chsd ldr, one pace fnl 2 fs*.......................... (5 to 1 op 9 to 2) 3
1439^{3} FIRST BID [64] 6-8-12 A Culhane (2) *chsd ldrs, effrt 3 out, wknd 2 out*.......................(11 to 2 op 9 to 2) 4
2632^{7} KINOKO [56] 5-7-13 (5*) A Garth (4) *al beh, outpcd 4 out, no dngr aftr*...........................(8 to 1 op 7 to 1) 5
2506* CARROLLS MARC (Ire) [59] 5-8-0 (7*) C Adamson (6) *chsd ldrs, effrt 3 out, wknd quickly 2 out.* (6 to 1 op 5 to 1) 6

Dist: ½l, 3½l, 5l, 6l, 4l. 2m 31.70s. a 1.50s (6 Ran).
SR: 29/35/55/29/9/4/ (Norman Firth), Mrs M Reveley

3004 Silver Cross Handicap Class D (0-80 3-y-o and up) £4,581 1m........ (4:30)

2799* SOOTY TERN [53] 6-7-13^{1} (7*) Mark Denaro (11) *trkd ldrs, led one out, ran on wl*.............(11 to 2 op 6 to 1) 1
2775^{2} CAUSLEY [71] 8-9-9 M Birch (10) *led till hdd one out, kpt on*.................... (13 to 2 op 7 to 1 tchd 6 to 1) 2
2816^{2} PRIDE OF PENDLE [62] 4-9-0 G Hind (4) *beh, steady hdwy hfwy, chalg whn not much room entering fnl furlong, kpt on*.........................(3 to 1 fav tchd 11 to 4) 3
2543* MCA BELOW THE LINE [63] (v) 5-9-1 S Webster (2) *beh till styd on wl und pres fnl 2 fs, not rch ldrs.* .... (10 to 1 op 8 to 1 tchd 11 to 1) 4
2762* THORNTON GATE [72] 4-9-7 (3*) S Maloney (9) *trkd ldrs, effrt 2 out, kpt on same pl*.......... (11 to 2 op 6 to 1) 5
2680^{3} CELESTINE [57] (v) 4-8-9 J Fanning (3) *chsd ldr, chlgd o'r one out, wknd fnl furlong.* .... (12 to 1 op 10 to 1 tchd 14 to 1) 6
2863^{2} SAVAHRA SOUND [66] 8-9-4 N Day (13) *prmnt till wknd entering fnl furlong*........................ (10 to 1) 7
2863^{9} GANT BLEU (Fr) [55] 6-8-7 A Culhane (7) *hld up, steady hdwy to track ldrs 2 out, wknd entering last.* ....(14 to 1 op 12 to 1) 8
2799^{5} DREAM CARRIER (Ire) [50] 5-7-9 (7*) Kimberley Hart (8) *beh, hdwy 3 out, wknd o'r one out*..... (14 to 1 op 12 to 1) 9
2657^{6} BLOW DRY (Ire) [74] 3-9-4 S Perks (6) *mid-div, effrt whn not much room o'r one out, sn btn.* .... (15 to 2 op 7 to 1 tchd 8 to 1) 10
2638^{7} CRAIGIE BOY [51] 3-7-9 S Wood (5) *mid-div till wknd 3 out, tld off*............................... (33 to 1) 11
2975^{8} COSTA VERDE [68] 3-8-7 (5*) A Garth (12) *prmnt till wknd 3 out, tld off*...................(33 to 1 op 25 to 1) 12
4211a* BOLDVILLE BASH (Ire) [71] 3-8-8 (7*) V Halliday (1) *strted slwly, al beh, tld off.* (14 to 1 op 12 to 1 tchd 16 to 1) 13

Dist: 2½l, 1½l, 1l, nk, hd, 2l, sht-hd, 1½l, sht-hd, 15l. 1m 38.00s. a 2.10s (13 Ran).
SR: 24/34/20/18/26/10/13/1/-/ (J M Bradley), J M Bradley

3005 Yorkshire Television Maiden Stakes Class D (3-y-o and up) £3,699 1m (5:00)

2046[2] EL GAHAR 3-8-11 A McGlone (3) *trkd ldrs, chlgd on bit 2 out, shaken up to ld entering fnl furlong, sn clr, cmftbly*.......(2 to 1 op 5 to 2) 1
STORM CANYON (Ire) 3-8-11 G Hind (1) *slwly into strd, sn led, rdn o'r one out, hdd entering fnl furlong, soon btn.* .... (15 to 8 on op 3 to 1 on tchd 13 to 8 on) 2
2032[6] SHERGRESS 3-8-6 K Fallon (7) *hld up, styd on wl fnl 2 fs, nrst finish*.......(25 to 1) 3
PROMITTO 3-8-6 J Fortune (4) *trkd ldrs, effrt 2 out, kpt on same pace*.......(25 to 1 op 33 to 1) 4
2401[5] ANNYBAN 3-8-6 S Perks (2) *chsd ldr till wknd 2 out.* .... (20 to 1 op 33 to 1) 5
WAWEEWAWOO (Ire) 5-8-9 (5*) Darren Moffatt (5) *in tch till wknd o'r 3 out*....... (66 to 1 op 50 to 1) 6
RICHER SPIRIT 4-8-11 (3*) S D Williams (6) *in tch till wknd quickly o'r 2 out*.......(66 to 1 tchd 100 to 1) 7

Dist: 3½l, 3l, 1l, 8l, 2l, 8l. 1m 39.00s. a 3.10s (7 Ran).
SR: 15/4/-/-/ (Prince A A Faisal), H R A Cecil

3006 Directors Trophy Maiden Handicap Class E (0-70 3-y-o and up) £2,976 6f (5:30)

2225[4] SUPREME BOY [51] 4-9-8 G Hind (1) *made all, ran on wl fnl furlong*.......(13 to 2 op 11 to 2 tchd 7 to 1) 1
2697 KENNEDYS PRIMA [63] 3-10-0 J Fortune (8) *in tch, hdwy to track ldrs hfwy, rdn o'r one out, no imprsn on wnr.* .... (5 to 1 tchd 11 to 2 and 6 to 1) 2
2765[3] SHOTLEY AGAIN [31] 3-7-10 J Fanning (9) *wth ldr till o'r one out, kpt on same pace*....... (8 to 1) 3
2821[6] NOBLE MEASURE (Ire) [48] (bl) 3-8-6 (7*) G Strange (6) *beh till styd on fnl 2 fs, not rch ldrs*....(12 to 1 op 10 to 1) 4
2638[2] BLAKES BEAU [46] (bl) 3-8-11 M Birch (2) *trkd ldrs, rdn wl o'r one out, sn btn.* (7 to 2 fav op 3 to 1 tchd 11 to 4) 5
2638[4] CHRISTIAN WARRIOR [35] (v) 4-8-6 K Fallon (5) *nvr dngrs.* ....(8 to 1 tchd 7 to 1) 6
2710[5] SILVER STONE BOY [33] (v) 5-8-4 S Webster (7) *chsd ldrs, rdn o'r 2 out, sn btn*....... (6 to 1) 7
2584[9] PRETTY CHIC [31] 4-8-2 N Connorton (3) *al beh*...(20 to 1) 8
2719 HALL BANK COTTAGE [47] (bl) 3-8-12 T Williams (4) *dwlt, rdn to stay in tch, wknd o'r 2 out*...(11 to 2 op 9 to 2) 9

Dist: 1½l, ½l, 1½l, 2½l, 1½l, 1l, 2l, 2l. 1m 10.60s. a 0.60s (9 Ran).
SR: 36/36/2/13/1/-/ (The Superlatives), P W Harris

WINDSOR (good to firm (races 1,2,4,6), good (3,5))
Saturday July 31st
Going Correction: MINUS 0.10 sec. per fur. (races 1,2,4,6), MINUS 0.55 (3,5)

3007 Fosters Selling Handicap Class G (0-60 3-y-o and up) £1,954 1m 67yds (6:00)

2548 FAILAND [32] 6-8-10 A Mackay (19) *led to 3 fs out, led 2 out, hld on wl*.......(33 to 1 op 20 to 1) 1
2684[3] WAAZA (USA) [49] (bl) 4-9-10 (3*) D Harrison (7) *mid-div, prog o'r 2 fs out, ev ch wl ins last, no extr nr finish.* ....(6 to 1 tchd 13 to 2) 2
2747 SHALOU [40] (bl) 4-9-4 J Quinn (1) *prmnt, led 3 fs out to 2 out, ev ch ins last, no extr.* .... (13 to 2 op 5 to 1 tchd 7 to 1) 3
2154[7] DARING KING [48] 3-9-4 W Hood (17) *mid-div, prog o'r 2 fs out, ran on ins last, nvr nrr.* ....(16 to 1 op 12 to 1 tchd 20 to 1) 4
2869[6] DON'T GIVE UP [39] (bl) 5-9-3 W Newnes (10) *wl beh till prog o'r 2 fs out, ran on ins last, nvr nrr.* .... (4 to 1 fav op 6 to 1 tchd 7 to 1 and 7 to 2) 5
2724 GEORGE ROPER [41] (bl) 3-8-11 B Rouse (9) *prmnt, not clr run 2 fs out, styd on one pace ins last.* ....(11 to 1 op 12 to 1 tchd 10 to 1) 6
2520 ABSOLUTELY HUMMING [32] 7-8-10 R Price (14) *prmnt, rdn o'r 3 fs out, styd on one pace*.......(33 to 1) 7
SUNLEY SPARKLE [43] 5-9-7 W Woods (8) *rear till gd prog fnl 2 fs, nvr nrr*....... (20 to 1 op 12 to 1) 8
2724 BAN RI (Ire) [45] 3-9-1 S Dawson (18) *hld up and wl beh, prog fnl 2 fs, nrst finish*....... (33 to 1 op 20 to 1) 9
2550[4] CREAGMHOR [47] 3-9-3 C Rutter (13) *chsd ldrs, kpt on one pace fnl 2 fs*.......(20 to 1 op 12 to 1) 10
2471 MALZETA (Ire) [47] 3-8-12 (5*) D Wright (2) *prmnt, rdn and wknd 2 fs out*....... (7 to 1 op 4 to 1) 11
DAVE'S LASS [40] 4-9-4 T Wilson (16) *mid-div, nvr dngrs.* .... (25 to 1 op 14 to 1) 12
2684 GREEN'S STUBBS [28] (v) 6-8-6 N Carlisle (12) *nvr dngrs.* ....(8 to 1 op 6 to 1) 13
2684 JULY BRIDE [48] 3-9-4 A Morris (15) *chsd ldrs till wknd 3 fs out*....... (16 to 1 op 10 to 1 tchd 20 to 1) 14
2824[7] VERRO (USA) [35] (bl) 6-8-13 G Bardwell (21) *prmnt till rdn and wknd 3 fs out*....(25 to 1 op 20 to 1 tchd 33 to 1) 15
2520 AUNT ADA [38] 4-8-11 (5*) A Procter (3) *nvr dngrs.* .... (12 to 1 op 10 to 1 tchd 14 to 1) 16
1426 ESERIE DE CORES (USA) [44] (bl) 3-8-9 (5*) C Hodgson (6) *beh, hrd rdn o'r 3 fs out, no prog*... (12 to 1 op 8 to 1) 17
417 CAVALIER PRINCE (Ire) [42] 3-8-12 J Lowe (20) *al wl beh.* .... (14 to 1 op 7 to 1 tchd 16 to 1) 18
2686[7] PRINCESS JESSICA [35] 6-8-6 (7*) S Drowne (5) *al beh.* .... (16 to 1 op 12 to 1) 19
MY BOY BUSTER [36] 4-8-7 (7*) B Russell (11) *mid-div, prog and hrd rdn o'r 3 fs out, sn wknd.* .... (33 to 1 op 12 to 1) 20
2109[8] DEVONIAN (USA) [44] 4-9-8 R Perham (4) *beh fnl 3 fs.* .... (25 to 1 op 12 to 1) 21

Dist: Nk, 1l, sht-hd, ½l, ½l, ½l, ½l, hd, sht-hd, 6l. 1m 46.70s. a 5.70s (21 Ran).
SR: -/14/2/1/-/-/ (Ms Tessa Hartwell), R Brotherton

3008 Courage Master Plan Conditions Stakes Class D (4-y-o and up) £3,294 1m 67yds....... (6:30)

1921[7] PETO 4-8-12 W Ryan (1) *led 5 fs, hrd rdn to ld ins last, edgd lft, hld on.* .... (6 to 5 on op 11 to 8 on tchd 11 to 10 on) 1
2363 SPANISH STORM (Ire) (bl) 4-8-12 W Woods (2) *trkd ldr, led 2 fs out till ins last, not quicken nr finish.* ....(3 to 1 op 5 to 2 tchd 100 to 30) 2
2413[5] ROCKY WATERS (USA) 4-9-2 B Rouse (3) *pld hrd, hld up, prog to ld 3 fs out, hdd and wknd 2 out.* .... (5 to 2 op 9 to 4 tchd 11 to 4) 3

Dist: Nk, 12l. 1m 45.60s. a 4.60s (3 Ran).
SR: 17/16/-/ (Sheikh Mohammed), H R A Cecil

3009 EBF Molson Special Dry Median Auction Maiden Stakes Class E (2-y-o) £2,826 5f 217yds....... (7:00)

2492[4] DANCING LAWYER 9-0 A Munro (5) *made all, edgd lft frm o'r one furlong out,hld on.* .... (10 to 1 tchd 12 to 1 and 8 to 1) 1
1804[9] ARZ (USA) 9-0 R Hills (12) *trkd ldrs, rdn to chal appr fnl furlong, edgd lft and no extr ins last.* ....(2 to 1 fav op 5 to 2 tchd 3 to 1) 2
1265 ROYALE FIGURINE (Ire) 8-9 C Rutter (7) *dwlt, sn prmnt, rdn hfwy, ev ch ins fnl furlong, no extr.* .... (33 to 1 op 20 to 1) 3
FROMAGE 8-9 W Ryan (9) *prog to join ldrs hfwy, ev ch whn not much room ins fnl furlong, not reco'r.* ....(20 to 1 op 14 to 1 tchd 33 to 1) 4
LADY WILLIAMS (Ire) 8-6 (3*) D Harrison (18) *mid-div, ran on appr fnl furlong, nrst finish*.....(14 to 1 op 7 to 1) 5
2659[4] CHILLY TIME 8-9 J Williams (2) *prmnt, ev ch appr fnl furlong, wknd ins last.* .... (12 to 1 op 14 to 1 tchd 20 to 1) 6
1773[7] ARAFARAZ 9-0 C Avery (6) *mid-div, kpt on one pace fnl 2 fs, nvr dngrs*....... (33 to 1 op 20 to 1) 7
2695 YO (Ire) 8-9 D Biggs (17) *nvr nrr.* .... (25 to 1 op 20 to 1 tchd 33 to 1) 8
1905 AWS (Ire) 9-0 W Carson (8) *prmnt, wkng whn hmpd appr fnl furlong*.......(12 to 1 op 6 to 1) 9
GAY DEVIL 9-0 Pat Eddery (14) *prmnt till wknd wl o'r one furlong out*....... (9 to 2 op 3 to 1 tchd 5 to 1) 10
SIMPLY A SEQUEL (Ire) 9-0 G Duffield (4) *wl beh, some prog fnl 2 fs, nvr dngrs*..... (11 to 2 op 8 to 1 tchd 12 to 1) 11
HIGH SWINGER 9-0 B Rouse (15) *strted slwly, wl beh till some late prog, nvr dngrs.* ....(20 to 1 op 12 to 1 tchd 25 to 1) 12
1905 NORISKI'MARINGER 9-0 L Dettori (16) *nvr dngrs.* .... (25 to 1 op 14 to 1) 13
2030[7] SPEEDY SNAPS IMAGE 9-0 G Bardwell (3) *al rear.* .... (33 to 1 op 20 to 1) 14
2836[8] HEIGHT OF DECORUM 9-0 S Whitworth (19) *prmnt till wknd aftr hfwy*.......(33 to 1 op 20 to 1) 15
2826[8] RED TAR 9-0 W Newnes (1) *prmnt till rdn and wknd wl o'r 2 fs out*....... (25 to 1 op 14 to 1) 16
2720[5] HERR TRIGGER 9-0 R Cochrane (11) *al beh.* .... (12 to 1 op 10 to 1 tchd 14 to 1) 17
1378[4] AQUA VIVA (v) 9-0 A Geran (10) *strted slwly, al beh.* .... (20 to 1 op 12 to 1 tchd 25 to 1) 18
MANDEVILLE GEORGE 9-0 L Piggott (13) *al beh, tld off fnl 2 fs*....... (13 to 2 op 5 to 1 tchd 8 to 1) 19

Dist: ½l, 1½l, nk, 1½l, 1½l, 5l, 1½l, ¾l, 1½l, nk. 1m 11.40s. a 1.10s (19 Ran).
SR: 12/10/-/-/-/-/ (Vintage Services Limited), B J Meehan

3010 Courage Beer Company Handicap Class D (0-80 3-y-o and up) £3,492 1m 3f 135yds....... (7:30)

2795[4] BAGALINO (USA) [77] 3-9-5 Pat Eddery (5) *made all, rdn wl o'r 2 fs out, hld on gmely*...... (11 to 8 fav op 5 to 2) 1
2727[2] ADDICTED TO LOVE [59] 4-8-13 W R Swinburn (2) *hld up, prog 4 fs out, rdn to chal ins last, no extr cl hme.* .... (11 to 2 op 5 to 1) 2
2581[5] BARFORD LAD [70] 6-9-10 L Dettori (3) *trkd ldrs, prog and ev ch appr fnl furlong, wknd ins last.* .... (11 to 2 op 4 to 1 tchd 6 to 1) 3
2669[2] MAHRAJAN [61] 9-9-1 T Quinn (8) *hld up beh, prog o'r 3 fs out, ev ch appr last, wknd.* .... (3 to 1 op 9 to 4 tchd 100 to 30) 4

2474[4] WASSL THIS THEN (Ire) [63] 4-8-10 (7*) T G McLaughlin (1) *chsd wnr, rdn o'r 3 fs out, wknd 2 out.* .... (11 to 2 op 7 to 2 tchd 6 to 1) 5
BO KNOWS BEST (Ire) [64] 4-9-4 B Rouse (7) *prmnt, rdn and wknd o'r 3 fs out.* .... (12 to 1 op 10 to 1 tchd 14 to 1) 6
WINGS OF FREEDOM (Ire) [52] 5-8-6 T Wilson (6) *keen hold, rear, lost tch o'r 3 fs out*..........(20 to 1 op 12 to 1) 7
2669 EVERY ONE A GEM [40] 6-7-8 N Adams (4) *strted slwly, al beh*......................................(33 to 1 op 20 to 1) 8
Dist: Nk, 2l, ½l, 7l, 8l, 2½l, 6l. 2m 28.40s. a 5.40s (8 Ran).
SR: 40/33/40/30/18/3/-/-/ (K Abdulla), R Charlton

3011 Wadworth 6X Handicap Class E (0-70 3-y-o and up) £2,929 5f 10yds... (8:00)

2846[5] THE NOBLE OAK (Ire) [59] (bl) 5-9-3 G Duffield (9) *rdn thrght, made all, jst hld on.* .... (15 to 2 op 8 to 1 tchd 10 to 1) 1
2387[3] CASTLE MAID [35] 6-7-7 J Lowe (6) *chsd ldrs, rdn and prog o'r one furlong out, ran on ins last, jst fld.* .... (9 to 1 op 8 to 1 tchd 10 to 1) 2
2831* PETRACO (Ire) [73] 5-9-10 (7*) T G McLaughlin (5) *prmnt, hrd rdn and not quicken o'r one furlong out, ran on ins last*.................................(9 to 1 op 5 to 1) 3
2628[4] PEERAGE PRINCE [65] (bl) 4-9-9 R Cochrane (2) *prmnt, hrd rdn 2 fs out, ran on one pace.* .... (13 to 2 op 5 to 1 tchd 7 to 1) 4
2699* CHARITY EXPRESS (Ire) [68] 3-9-7 D Biggs (12) *cl up, rdn and styd on one pace fnl 2 fs.* ....(7 to 1 op 6 to 1 tchd 8 to 1) 5
AGWA [38] 4-7-10 F Norton (7) *sn rdn alng, prmnt till outpcd hfwy, styd on ins fnl furlong.* (9 to 2 op 8 to 1) 6
2734[5] DARUSSALAM [57] (bl) 6-9-1 W Carson (3) *rear, swtchd lft and ran on appr fnl furlong, nvr nrr.* ....(7 to 2 fav op 5 to 1 tchd 11 to 2) 7
2688[3] THE ORDINARY GIRL (Ire) [55] (v) 3-8-8 J Reid (11) *trkd ldrs gng easily, not clr run fnl 2 fs, eased whn btn.* .... (9 to 2 op 5 to 1 tchd 11 to 2) 8
2728[3] PAT POINDESTRES [50] 3-8-3[5] A Clark (4) *prog frm rear hfwy, rdn 2 fs out, wknd appr last.* .... (11 to 1 op 7 to 1 tchd 12 to 1) 9
2476[9] SCREECH [45] 3-7-12 Dale Gibson (8) *speed to hfwy, sn wknd*.................................(25 to 1 op 20 to 1) 10
2723[8] BLUE TAIL [45] 5-7-13[3] (7*) S Drowne (1) *al wl beh.* .... (33 to 1 op 25 to 1 tchd 50 to 1) 11
2351[8] SUEENA [42] 3-7-9 J Quinn (10) *al wl beh.* ....(33 to 1 tchd 50 to 1) 12
Dist: Sht-hd, ¾l, ½l, nk, ½l, 1l, ½l, ¾l, 5l, 3l. 59.50s. a 0.50s (12 Ran).
SR: 38/13/48/38/35/8/23/14/6/ (M McCormack), M McCormack

3012 John Smith's Maiden Stakes Class D (3-y-o and up) £4,079 1¼m 7yds (8:30)

1842[2] TOCHAR BAN (USA) 3-8-3 (3*) B Doyle (24) *al prmnt, led 2 fs out, sn clr, jst hld on.* ....(11 to 4 fav op 4 to 1 tchd 5 to 2) 1
777* WINTER FOREST (USA) 3-8-11 W Ryan (13) *beh, rapid prog 2 fs out, ran on strly ins last, jst fld.* ....(7 to 2 op 2 to 1 tchd 4 to 1) 2
DANISH FORT 3-8-11 C Rutter (15) *rear, prog 2 fs out, ran on ins last, nvr nrr*...(16 to 1 op 14 to 1 tchd 20 to 1) 3
1789[7] REINE DE NEIGE 3-8-6 W R Swinburn (17) *led 6 fs out to 2 out, wknd appr last*.................(7 to 2 op 6 to 1) 4
2332[9] WANNABE 3-8-6 R Cochrane (9) *prmnt till wknd wl o'r one furlong out*..................(7 to 1 op 20 to 1) 5
CITTERN 3-8-11 A Clark (23) *prog and swtchd lft 3 fs out, styd on same pace*................(25 to 1 op 20 to 1) 6
2332 PYRAMIS PRINCE (Ire) 3-8-11 J Reid (4) *prog whn crrd lft 3 fs out, wknd appr last.* .... (20 to 1 op 14 to 1 tchd 25 to 1) 7
751[9] KARSHI 3-8-11 G Duffield (14) *prmnt, wknd 2 fs out.* .... (16 to 1 op 10 to 1) 8
2332[5] PROTON 3-8-11 B Rouse (7) *prmnt, ev ch o'r 2 fs out, sn wknd*..........(12 to 1 op 20 to 1 tchd 25 to 1) 9
DANDONG 3-8-11 Pat Eddery (20) *hld up beh, last aftr 4 fs, prog frm 3 out, nvr plcd to chal.* ....(7 to 1 op 4 to 1 tchd 8 to 1) 10
2752 RIZ BIZ (USA) 3-8-3 (3*) M Fenton (2) *nvr nrr.* .... (20 to 1 op 14 to 1) 11
2332 AWAY GIRL 3-8-3 (3*) D Harrison (18) *beh till moderate late prog, nvr nrr*...............................(33 to 1) 12
2522 PISTOL (Ire) 3-8-11 W Woods (22) *mid-div, no prog fnl 2 fs.* .... (25 to 1 op 20 to 1 tchd 33 to 1) 13
1992 WADIA (USA) 3-8-6 R Hills (5) *chsd ldrs till wknd 3 fs out.* .... (33 to 1 op 14 to 1) 14
2670[8] ELTARA 3-8-6 A Munro (11) *nvr dngrs.* .... (25 to 1 op 14 to 1) 15
ELEGANT JADE 3-8-6 W Newnes (25) *nvr dngrs.* .... (33 to 1 op 20 to 1) 16
2670 AMY COME HOME 3-8-6 J Williams (6) *nvr dngrs.* (33 to 1) 17
TOKYO 3-8-6 P D'Arcy (16) *prmnt till wknd wl o'r 3 fs out.* .... (25 to 1 op 14 to 1) 18
COLIN MUSET 3-8-11 L Dettori (21) *prog to chase ldrs o'r 3 fs out, sn no imprsn, eased.* .... (12 to 1 op 7 to 1 tchd 14 to 1) 19
2563 BROUGHTONS TURMOIL 4-9-7 A Mackay (8) *led 4 fs, wknd 3 out*...................(33 to 1 op 20 to 1) 20
FIDA (Ire) 3-8-6 W Carson (3) *wl beh hfwy.* .... (10 to 1 op 8 to 1 tchd 12 to 1) 21
SILK ISLAND 3-8-11 G Hind (10) *prmnt 3 fs, sn beh.* .... (25 to 1 op 16 to 1) 22
TEOROMA 3-8-11 J Quinn (1) *strted slwly, al wl beh.* .... (25 to 1 op 20 to 1) 23
DAJAM 3-8-1 (5*) Stephen Davies (19) *al beh*..... (33 to 1) 24
WHITE CITY 3-8-11 Dale Gibson (12) *beh whn pld up 2 fs out, broke leg, destroyed*..........................(33 to 1) pu
Dist: Hd, 2l, 2½l, 2½l, ½l, ¾l, 5l, ½l, 2l, 3½l. 2m 5.90s. a 3.40s (25 Ran).
SR: 48/52/48/38/33/37/35/25/24/ (D R C Elsworth), D R C Elsworth

COLOGNE (GER) (good to soft)
Sunday August 1st

3013 Ostermann-Pokal (Group 3) (3-y-o and up) £24,490 1m.................(4:10)

2644[8] TIMELY THREAT (USA) 3-8-5 N Grant, *al prmnt, led 2 fs out, drvn out*.. 1
1724[9] TROPICAL KING (Ger) 3-8-5 M Rimmer, *hld up in rear, rdn 2 fs out, ran on wl ins fnl furlong*.......................... 2
LITTLE TOO MUCH (Ire) 3-8-1 K Darley, *mid-div, ran on fnl furlong, nvr dngrs*.. 3
1724[8] IROKESE (Ger) 3-8-5 A Helfenbein, *mid-div, ran on fnl furlong, nvr dngrs*.. 4
1084[5] BANNIER (Ger) 6-9-3 T Hellier, *al mid-div*.............. 5
INDIAN LAKE 4-9-3 P Schiergen, *prmnt till wknd fnl furlong*.. 6
2436[5] AUTOCRACY (Ire) 4-8-13 W Newnes, *nvr able to chal*..... 7
2436[7] YOUNG MOON 7-9-5 T Manning, *led till hdd and wknd 2 fs out*.. 8
2644[6] AMARANT (Ger) 3-8-5 J Lowe, *al beh*.................. 9
Dist: ½l, 2l, hd, 2l, 4l, 1l, hd. 1m 38.83s. (9 Ran).

DEAUVILLE (FR) (soft)
Sunday August 1st
Going Correction: PLUS 0.40 sec. per fur.

3014 Prix de Cabourg (Group 3) (2-y-o) £23,895 6f.................... (2:00)

COUP DE GENIE (USA) 8-8 C Asmussen, *al cl up, led one furlong out, pushed out, ran on wl*.........(2 to 1 fav) 1
2144[3] FOXHOUND (USA) 8-11 T Jarnet, *mid-div, outpcd o'r one furlong out, ran on ag'n fnl furlong*.........(34 to 10) 2
GREEN TUNE (USA) 8-11 O Doleuze, *rear till hdwy 2 fs out, fnshd wl*...............................(21 to 10) 3
2260* FRED BONGUSTO (Ire) 9-2 E Legrix, *trkd ldr, chlgd 2 fs out, no extr ins fnl furlong*................. (89 to 10) 4
2144[4] TELLURIUM (USA) 8-11 F Head, *dwlt, rear till prog 2 fs out, no extr fnl furlong*....................... (20 to 1) 5
2144[5] FILHA DO AR (USA) 8-8 E Saint-Martin, *beh till some hdwy fnl 2 fs, nvr able to chal*.......................(35 to 1) 6
CELLA (Ire) 8-8 A Badel, *led till wknd quickly one furlong out*...(66 to 10) 7
2647[7] ANGEL OF THE NIGHT (USA) 8-11 D Boeuf, *prmnt, ev ch 2 fs out, rdn and btn one out*.................. (12 to 1) 8
Dist: 2l, nose, ½l, ¾l, ½l, 2l, 4l. 1m 12.40s. a 4.00s (8 Ran).
SR: 62/57/56/59/51/46/38/25/ (S S Niarchos), F Boutin

3015 Prix Maurice de Gheest (Group 2) (3-y-o and up) £47,790 6f 110yds... (3:05)

2362[2] COLLEGE CHAPEL 3-9-0 L Piggott (13) *hld up last, hdwy o'r 2 fs out, led one out, ran on wl*........... (33 to 10) 1
2488[3] DANAKAL (USA) 3-8-9 G Mosse (6) *mid-div, not clr run 2 fs out, hdwy ins fnl furlong, fnshd wl*...... (69 to 10) 2
1765[2] MATELOT (USA) 3-8-9 D Boeuf (4) *al cl up, not clr run 2 fs out, fnshd wl*........................(19 to 10 co-fav) 3
1807[2] WOLFHOUND (USA) 4-9-0 Pat Eddery (3) *led till one furlong out, ran on one pace*............(19 to 10 co-fav) 4
2362[3] ZIETEN (USA) 3-8-9 T Jarnet (9) *trkd ldr, effrt 2 fs out, one pace o'r one out*................. (19 to 10 co-fav) 5
2055[5] CRACK REGIMENT (USA) 5-9-0 E Saint-Martin (12) *mid-div, hdwy 2 fs out, ran on one pace*...............(44 to 1) 6
2242* ROBIN DES PINS (USA) 5-9-4 C Asmussen (7) *mid-div, not clr run 2 fs out, not pace to chal ins fnl furlong.* ....(64 to 10) 7
2055* BORODISLEW (USA) 3-8-6 O Doleuze (2) *prmnt till 2 fs out*...(11 to 1) 8
2574[9] RUSTIC CRAFT (Ire) 3-8-9 F Head (10) *prmnt till fdd 2 fs out*...(83 to 1) 9
2055[4] ACTEUR FRANCAIS (USA) 5-9-0 S Guillot (14) *prmnt, effrt 2 fs out, sn one pace*...............................(28 to 1) 0
2488[4] CHARME SLAVE (Fr) (bl) 5-9-0 E Legrix (5) *mid-div till wknd fnl 2 fs*...............................(20 to 1) 0
1365* SECRET THING (USA) 4-9-4 V Mezzatesta (1) *mid-div, beh 2 fs out*...(37 to 1) 0
2074[4] HAZAAM (USA) 4-9-0 Paul Eddery (8) *dwlt, cl up hfwy, btn o'r 2 fs out*...........................(19 to 10 co-fav) 0

1723^{3} GOTHLAND (Fr) 4-9-0 O Peslier (11) *nvr nrr than mid-div.* ....(22 to 1) 0
Dist: 1l, nk, nk, hd, sht-nk, ¾l, 1l, 1½l, ½l, 1½l. 1m 18.30s. a 3.30s (14 Ran).
SR: 86/77/76/80/74/78/79/63/60/ (Red Nab Racing Ltd), M V O'Brien

LINGFIELD (good)
Sunday August 1st
Going Correction: MINUS 0.30 sec. per fur.

3016 EBF Tulsa Maiden Stakes Class D (2-y-o) £6,116 6f.................. (2:40)

AVERTI (Ire) 9-0 T Quinn (7) *trkd ldrs gng wl, led 2 fs out, sn clr, easily*.. 1
2030^{8} BRAVE EDGE 9-0 W Carson (12) *in tch, short of room appr fnl furlong, ran on ins*................................ 2
2559^{5} RICH MISS 8-9 A Clark (9) *outpcd early, styd on ins fnl 2 fs*.. 3
2137^{9} BILLY CRUNCHEON 9-0 A Tucker (10) *led to 2 fs out, sn outpcd*.. 4
2502^{6} MIDSEAS 9-0 J Williams (8) *chsd ldrs till wknd hfwy*..... 5
BLAZING HONDA (Ire) 9-0 B Marcus (4) *slwly away, some late hdwy, nvr dngrs*.. 6
1955^{8} CHINA ROBIN 8-9 L Dettori (5) *al rear*.......................... 7
2447^{2} KIYAS 9-0 R Hills (3) *chsd ldr till wknd 2 fs out*............ 8
1706 CRETAN GIFT 9-0 M Hills (6) *slwly away, al beh*.......... 9
FATALIST 9-0 G Duffield (1) *slwly into strd, sn in tch on outsd, lost touch o'r 2 fs out*.................................. 10
Dist: 4l, 5l, 3l, hd, nk, ¾l, 1l, 3½l, hd. 1m 10.74s. a 1.74s (10 Ran).
SR: 29/13/-/-/-/-/ (D J Deer), W R Muir

3017 Charlie Chester Club Handicap Class C (0-90 3-y-o and up) £6,067 7f 140yds ....(3:05)

2479* TAHDID [83] 3-9-10 W Carson (9) *led aftr 2 fs, rdn appr last, hld on gmely*.. 1
2928^{2} FIELD OF VISION (Ire) [78] 3-9-5 T Williams (8) *nvr far away, jnd wnr one furlong out, edgd lft and no extr cl hme*.. 2
2789^{4} BALLERINA BAY [70] (v) 5-9-4 L Dettori (6) *hld up rear, hdwy o'r one furlong out, ran on ins*................. 3
2431^{3} MY BEST VALENTINE [81] 3-9-8 F Norton (3) *hld up, hdwy 2 fs out, hrd rdn and no extr ins last*................ 4
2928^{5} SECOND CHANCE (Ire) [75] 3-9-2 M Hills (7) *frnt rnk till rdn and wknd entering fnl furlong*.................... 5
2156^{5} AMADEUS AES [68] 4-8-11 (5*) C Hodgson (12) *led 2 fs, no hdwy frm two out*.. 6
2915^{5} ANNABELLE ROYALE [63] 7-8-11 N Adams (13) *mid-diviion, one pace fnl 2 fs*.................................... 7
2328^{2} AKKAZAO (Ire) [73] 5-9-2 (5*) N Gwilliams (1) *in tch on outsd, wknd 2 fs out*.. 8
2757 SALBUS [80] 3-9-7 T Quinn (10) *al beh*......................... 9
2715^{8} BRAVEBOY [65] 5-8-13 B Marcus (2) *prmnt far side to hfwy*.. 10
4745a^{2} POLEDEN (USA) [66] 3-8-7 G Duffield (5) *al beh*............ 11
Dist: Hd, 1½l, nk, 1½l, ¾l, 1l, sht-hd, 5l, nk, 5l. 1m 29.63s. a 1.33s (11 Ran).
SR: 55/49/43/46/35/33/25/34/19/ (Hamdan Al-Maktoum), P T Walwyn

3018 Sunday Express Handicap Class D (0-80 3-y-o and up) £4,935 1m 3f 106yds.......................... (3:55)

1093^{7} MOSHAAJIR (USA) [73] 3-9-2 (5*) K Rutter (5) *hld up rear, hdwy on outsd 2 fs out, styd on to ld wl ins last*...... 1
2474^{7} WARM SPELL [69] 3-9-3 B Rouse (7) *nvr far away, rdn o'r 2 fs out, kpt on to go second cl hme*...................... 2
2501^{4} RAPPORTEUR (USA) [55] 7-8-10 (3*) D Harrison (6) *trkd ldr, led 3 fs out, rdn entering last, wknd and hdd wl ins*... 3
2942^{5} CORINTHIAN GOD (Ire) [36] 4-7-8^{1} J Quinn (2) *chsd ldrs, rdn 3 fs out, one pace 2 out*........................... 4
2521^{4} LOBILIO (USA) [69] (v) 4-9-13 B Marcus (4) *led to 3 fs out, one pace*.. 5
2669 OOZLEM (Ire) [52] 4-8-10 A McGlone (3) *al beh, lost tch 4 fs out*... 6
Dist: ¾l, nk, 3l, ½l, 15l. 2m 28.38s. a 4.18s (6 Ran).
SR: 31/25/20/-/27/-/ (Steve MacDonald), C Smith

LINGFIELD (A.W) (std)
Sunday August 1st
Going Correction: MINUS 0.30 sec. per fur.

3019 Tripleprint Handicap Class C (0-90 3-y-o and up) £7,440 1¼m..... (3:30)

1612^{5} LOWAWATHA [62] 5-8-3 (5*) C Hodgson (3) *prmnt early, lost pl on bend aftr 2 fs, rdn and hdwy 4 out, led o'r two out, drvn clr, easily*.. 1
2433^{4} CHATHAM ISLAND [71] 5-9-3 B Marcus (5) *hld up rear, rdn hfwy, styd on frm 2 fs out, no ch wth wnr*............ 2
2315* GILDERDALE [82] 11-10-0 M Hills (7) *nvr far away, one pace fnl 2 fs*.. 3
2672^{7} ABERDEEN HEATHER [89] 3-9-12 J Williams (1) *hld up rear, some hdwy 3 fs out, nvr nr to chal*.............. 4
2696^{4} SUPERTOP [62] 5-8-5 (3*) D Harrison (2) *al mid-div*....... 5
2614^{3} ONE OFF THE RAIL (USA) [78] 3-9-1 B Rouse (4) *sn trkd ldr, led hfwy till o'r 2 fs out, soon outpcd*................ 6
2381^{2} MODESTO (USA) [50] 5-7-10 N Carlisle (8) *trkd ldrs till drpd out hfwy*... 7
2614* SYLVAN SABRE (Ire) [75] (v) 4-9-7 L Dettori (6) *chsd ldrs till wknd o'r 3 fs out*... 8
2762^{2} GOLDEN CHIP (Ire) [68] 5-9-0 G Duffield (9) *led to hfwy, sn beh*.. 9
Dist: 3l, 5l, 3½l, 4l, 1½l, nk, ½l, 1½l. 2m 5.01s. a 1.81s (9 Ran).
SR: 46/49/50/41/15/19/-/23/13/ (N Lunn), D Morris

3020 Tote Sunday Selling Stakes Class E (3-y-o and up) £4,854 7f.........(4:20)

2380* LUCAYAN TREASURE (v) 3-9-4 L Dettori (12) *hld up, al gng wl, hdwy to ld entering fnl furlong, sn clr, cmftbly*.... 1
475 WILD AND LOOSE 5-9-3 (7*) Tracey Purseglove (15) *rcd outsd, ran on ins fnl 2 fs, nvr nrr*.............................. 2
2584^{5} FAMILY ROSE 4-9-4 G Duffield (6) *trkd ldr, ev ch entering fnl furlong, one pace*.. 3
2300^{9} KISSAVOS 7-9-10 J Williams (3) *beh, hdwy 2 fs out, kpt on, nvr nrr*.. 4
2897^{5} TYRIAN PURPLE (Ire) 5-9-5 (5*) A Garth (1) *led till entering fnl furlong, no extr*.. 5
2379^{5} PERSIAN GUSHER (Ire) (e/s) 3-9-1 (3*) J Weaver (2) *prmnt, one pace fnl furlong*.. 6
2724^{3} RED LEADER (Ire) 3-9-4 T Quinn (7) *hld up, effrt o'r 2 fs out, wknd appr last*.. 7
2466* LADY SABO 4-9-2 (3*) D Harrison (11) *nvr gng pace*....... 8
2670^{4} FIABA 5-8-12 (7*) T G McLaughlin (14) *al beh*............. 9
2723^{6} CONE LANE 7-9-3 (7*) B Russell (9) *outpcd*................ 10
2849^{3} EXCESS BAGGAGE (Ire) (bl) 3-9-4 M Hills (5) *al beh*....... 11
2688^{5} CONISTON LAKE (Ire) 4-9-10 B Rouse (4) *al beh*........ 12
2747^{8} CAMINO A RONDA 4-8-6 (7*) P McCabe (13) *chsd ldrs till wknd quickly wl o'r one furlong out*........................ 13
Dist: 3l, ½l, ¾l, sht-hd, sht-hd, 3l, 2l, sht-hd, ½l, 2½l. 1m 26.05s. a 2.65s (13 Ran).
SR: 33/30/22/26/25/18/9/4/3/ (H E Lhendup Dorji), D R Loder

3021 Crawley Warren Handicap Class E (0-70 3-y-o and up) £3,882 2m... (4:45)

2827^{2} RECORD LOVER (Ire) [65] 3-9-5 L Dettori (4) *settled mid-div gng wl, wnt second 3 fs out, led appr last, easily*....... 1
2865* WITH GUSTO [44] 6-8-13 (4ex) G Duffield (8) *mid-div, ran on frm 3 fs out, wnt second on line*......................... 2
2386^{2} JAWANI (Ire) [53] 5-9-8 J Quinn (6) *hld up, hdwy to ld o'r 5 fs out, rdn and hdd over one out, one pace*........... 3
2727^{4} RAGTIME SONG [28] 4-7-11 N Adams (2) *chsd ldrs, rdn and one pace fnl 2 fs*... 4
BAHRAIN QUEEN (Ire) [40] 5-8-4 (5*) K Rutter (7) *rear, styd on one pace fnl 3 fs*.. 5
2729^{7} MR WISHING WELL [33] 7-8-2^{3} (3*) J Weaver (9) *hld up rear, effrt 3 fs out, wknd 2 out*............................ 6
2415^{6} DR ZEVA [41] 7-8-5 (5*) D Wright (10) *hld up rear, some hdwy 3 fs out, nvr got into race*.......................... 7
2381^{3} FACT OR FICTION [56] (bl) 7-9-11 A Clark (3) *pld hrd, in tch till wknd o'r 3 fs out*... 8
2611* SUMMER WIND (Ire) [66] 3-9-1 (5*) A Procter (1) *led till o'r 5 fs out, sn wknd*.. 9
4742a GHOSTLY GLOW [49] 4-9-4 T Quinn (5) *chsd ldr, rdn o'r 4 fs out, wknd over 3 out*.................................... 10
Dist: 3½l, sht-hd, 3l, 1l, 6l, 12l, 2½l, 7l, 15l. 3m 27.22s. a 5.22s (10 Ran).
SR: 5/-/3/-/-/-/ (M L Oberstein), Lord Huntingdon

MUNICH (GER) (soft)
Sunday August 1st

3022 Bayerisches Zuchtrennen (Group 1) (3-y-o and up) £114,286 1¼m....(3:20)

2038^{2} MARKET BOOSTER (USA) 4-9-2 M Kinane, *trkd ldr gng wl, chlgd 2 fs out, led one out, ran on well*................. 1
2259^{4} KOMTUR (USA) 3-8-7 K Woodburn, *led till hdd one furlong out, kpt on gmely*.. 2
2079^{9} HONDO MONDO (Ire) 5-9-6 M Hofer, *hld up in last, ran on wl fnl 3 fs*.. 3
1748^{4} GEORGE AUGUSTUS (USA) 5-9-6 J Reid, *hld up, 6th strt, not much room 2 fs out, swtchd one and a half out, ran on wl*.. 4
2079^{6} APIS (Ger) 4-9-6 O Schick, *rcd in 3rd, one pace 2 fs out.* 5
2803^{7} GLORIEUX DANCER (Fr) 3-8-7 O Poirier, *prmnt till 2 fs out.* 6
2644^{4} LUCKY LINDY (Ire) 4-9-6 R Cochrane, *rcd in 4th, rdn and btn 3 fs out*.. 7
Dist: 1 ¾l, 2l, ¾l, ½l, nk, 3l. 2m 8.97s. (7 Ran).
(Moyglare Stud Farms Ltd), D K Weld

3023 Grosser Waldemar Zeitelhack Grosser Sprint Preis (Listed) (3-y-o and up) £14,286 6f 110yds..... (4:35)

2252^{6} BRANSTON ABBY (Ire) 4-9-6 J Reid,............................ 1
FANTOMAS (Ger) 5-9-13 K Woodburn,........................ 2
CATALAN (USA) 4-9-0 G Schadler,.............................. 3
2644^{9} KFAAF (Ire) 6-9-6 D Wildman,.................................. 4

Dist: 1 ¼l, 7l, nk, hd, 3½l. 1m 19.09s. (7 Ran).
(J David Abell), M Johnston

OSTEND (BEL) (firm)
Sunday August 1st

3024 Prix Chevalier de Stuers-Ladbroke (3-y-o and up) £11,928 1m.........(3:05)

MARITHEUS (Fr) 4-8-11 I Ferguson,.................... 1
EGOISTE (USA) 3-8-3 P Massage,...................... 2
2722[3] BIG BLUE 4-8-11 B Doyle, *hld up, ran on fnl 2 fs, nrst finish*.. 3
Dist: 1l, ¾l, ¾l, 2l. (Time not taken) (8 Ran).
(Haras du Tribury), R Crepon

LEOPARDSTOWN (IRE) (good)
Monday August 2nd

3025 Silverpark EBF Maiden (3-y-o and up) £3,450 1m.................... (2:30)

2609[3] CRYSTAL SHIP (Ire) 3-8-11 L Piggott (1)...........(2 to 1) 1
ALBERTAZZI (Ire) 3-9-0 K J Manning (5)...........(6 to 1) 2
2703[4] MISS CARMELLA (Ire) 3-8-11 W J Supple (3)...... (7 to 1) 3
870[2] CREATIVE CRAFT (USA) (bl) 3-8-11 M J Kinane (2) ....(6 to 4 fav) 4
SARAKARTA (USA) 3-8-11 D Hogan (4)........... (9 to 2) 5
Dist: ¾l, 3l, 1l, 15l. 1m 44.50s. a 6.50s (5 Ran).
(Mrs M V O'Brien), Charles O'Brien

3026 Newtownpark Nursery (2-y-o) £3,450 6f............................(3:00)

2704[4] DILIGENT DODGER (Ire) [-] 8-9 W J Supple (5)..... (5 to 1) 1
2403[3] THE PUZZLER (Ire) [-] 9-7 P V Gilson (4).... (3 to 1 co-fav) 2
2983[2] ORANEDIN [-] 8-10 S Craine (2)................. (5 to 1) 3
2487* KING SANCHO (Ire) [-] 8-7 R Hughes (1).... (3 to 1 co-fav) 4
2462* PAUGIM (Ire) [-] (bl) 8-12 M J Kinane (6).....(3 to 1 co-fav) 5
2487[3] BAKER HILL (Ire) [-] 7-12 (6*) J J Behan (3)....... (16 to 1) 6
Dist: 1½l, 1½l, 2½l, 4½l. 1m 13.80s. a 2.30s (6 Ran).
SR: 37/43/26/13/-/-/ (Mrs D M Donohoe), Kevin Prendergast

3027 Joe McGrath Handicap (0-110 3-y-o and up) £10,250 6f..............(3:30)

2404[2] CLASSICAL AFFAIR (Ire) [-] 4-8-7 (6*) J J Behan (4) (5 to 1) 1
2404[4] NORDIC OAK (Ire) [-] (bl) 5-8-6 W J Supple (1).... (10 to 1) 2
2187[6] DIAMONDS GALORE (Can) [-] 8-9-10 M J Kinane (7) (8 to 1) 3
2606[9] EL ZORRO DORADO (Ire) [-] (bl) 3-8-4 R Hughes (6) (12 to 1) 4
2779[4] UKUD (USA) [-] 3-7-3 (8*) R T Fitzpatrick (9).......(14 to 1) 5
2805[2] PERSIAN CREEK (Ire) [-] 4-8-13 K J Manning (10) ....(5 to 2 fav) 6
2805[5] MYSTERIOUS WAYS (Ire) [-] 3-8-11 L Piggott (8)... (5 to 1) 7
2604* PILGRIM BAY (Ire) [-] 3-7-5 (2*) D G O'Shea (5)......(9 to 2) 8
2780 SAND OR STONE (Ire) [-] 5-8-0 A J Nolan (3)......(25 to 1) 9
2878 ORTHORHOMBUS [-] (bl) 4-8-9 S Craine (2)......(25 to 1) 10
Dist: Nk, nk, nk, ½l. 1m 12.80s. a 1.30s (10 Ran).
SR: 61/53/70/49/40/-/ (Paul Farrell), T M Walsh

3028 Donnybrook Handicap (0-75 3-y-o and up) £4,140 1¼m................(4:00)

2901[2] PHASE IN [-] 3-8-7 M J Kinane (16)........... (5 to 2 fav) 1
2923[4] FERRYCARRIG HOTEL (Ire) [-] 4-9-3 P V Gilson (13) (6 to 1) 2
1025 THE BURSER [-] 7-9-7 (6*) C Everard (14)........ (16 to 1) 3
2517[3] COMMAND 'N CONTROL [-] 4-8-7 (6*) J J Behan (8) (8 to 1) 4
2677* HOPESVILLE (Ire) [-] 3-9-1 (6*,6ex) T P Treacy (6)...(6 to 1) 5
2041 SIR ALWAH (Ire) [-] 4-7-7 (8*) R T Fitzpatrick (7).... (33 to 1) 6
1163[7] LAKE HOTEL (Ire) [-] 4-9-0 D Hogan (15)......... (16 to 1) 7
2806[4] WHAT A PLEASURE (Ire) [-] 3-8-2 (10*) I Browne (12) ....(12 to 1) 8
2782[5] VLADIMIR'S WAY (Ire) [-] (bl) 4-9-4 W J Supple (10) (12 to 1) 9
2142[4] RATHBRIDES JOY [-] (bl) 6-8-8 (4*) W J Smith (9)...(7 to 1) 10
NORDIC BEE (Ire) [-] 4-8-13 K J Manning (11).....(16 to 1) 11
2514[2] NO DIPLOMACY (Ire) [-] 4-8-9 R Hughes (3)....... (8 to 1) 12
2808[6] HE'S A FLYER [-] 9-8-13 (2*) R M Burke (4)....... (20 to 1) 13
2297 PHILIP PATRICK (Ire) [-] 3-7-13 (2*) D G O'Shea (1) (33 to 1) 14
2677[3] DALKEY ISLAND (Ire) [-] 3-9-2 L Piggott (5)........ (7 to 1) 15
Dist: 1½l, ½l, 2½l, ½l. 2m 8.20s. a 3.50s (15 Ran).
SR: 48/55/64/45/52/-/ (Michael Hilary Burke), D K Weld

3029 Brownstown Stud Stakes (Listed) (3-y-o and up) £8,625 1m.......... (4:30)

2405[9] EUROSTORM (USA) 3-8-10 P V Gilson (4) *mid-div, prog 2 fs out, styd on strly ins last to ld on line*...... (3 to 1 fav) 1
2789[2] SPECIAL PAGEANT (Ire) 3-8-10 K J Manning (7) *led, quickened 2 ls clr two fs out, rdn, kpt on, hdd on line.* ....(10 to 3) 2
2805[3] DASHING COLOURS (Ire) 4-9-8 J C Deegan (2) *mid-div, prog 2 fs out, styd on strly ins last*............ (6 to 1) 3
1200 CHANZI (USA) (bl) 3-9-1 R Hughes (1) *wl plcd, rdn 2 fs out, slightly hmpd one out, kpt on*................(10 to 1) 4
2843[2] GOODNIGHT KISS (bl) 3-8-10 M J Kinane (5) *hld up, prog 3 fs out, ev ch 2 out, no extr ins last*.............(4 to 1) 5
2741* ELIZABETH'S PET (Ire) 3-8-10 L Piggott (10) *wl plcd, prog to track ldr 3 fs out, rdn and wknd ins last*....(10 to 1) 6
2404[5] SABAYA (USA) 3-8-10 W J Supple (6) *hld up, rdn and kpt on one pace in strt*..........................(8 to 1) 7
2879* RIENROE (Ire) 4-9-3 W J Smith (8) *al in rear*.....(16 to 1) 8
1511 OENOTHERA (Ire) 3-8-10 S Craine (9) *al in rear*...(12 to 1) 9
1552[9] WINNING HEART (bl) 6-9-3 N Byrne (3) *trkd ldr, rdn and lost pl 3 fs out, wknd*......................... (20 to 1) 10
Dist: Sht-hd, ¾l, 3l, 1l. 1m 40.70s. a 2.70s (10 Ran).
SR: 44/43/53/37/29/-/ (Mrs G W Jennings), C Collins

3030 Dargle EBF Maiden (2-y-o) £5,244 7f...............................(5:00)

ZAVALETA (Ire) 8-11 K J Manning (11).............(9 to 2) 1
FLAG FEN (USA) 9-0 M J Kinane (10).......... (5 to 4 on) 2
2605[5] BETTER FOLLY (Ire) 8-11 W J Supple (4).......... (8 to 1) 3
LEGAL AIM (Ire) 9-0 S Craine (7)..................(8 to 1) 4
2701[2] QUASIMODO (Ire) (bl) 9-0 R Hughes (5)........... (8 to 1) 5
2804[8] ROSE BUNCH 9-0 P V Gilson (2)................(14 to 1) 6
JACQUIMO (Ire) 9-0 D Hogan (3)................(16 to 1) 7
LESLEY'S ANGEL (Ire) 9-0 P Lowry (8)...........(16 to 1) 8
RAHAL (Ire) 9-0 D V Smith (9)...................(14 to 1) 9
2701[6] METROELLA (Ire) 8-11 N Byrne (1).............. (12 to 1) 10
EMELIA'S PET (Ire) 9-0 J F Egan (6)..............(25 to 1) 11
Dist: 2l, 2l, nk, 1l. 1m 32.60s. a 7.20s (11 Ran).
(Mrs Catherine Shubotham), J S Bolger

RIPON (good to firm)
Monday August 2nd

Going Correction: MINUS 0.20 sec. per fur. (races 1,2,4), MINUS 0.15 (3,5,6)

3031 EBF Trampoline Maiden Stakes Class D (2-y-o) £4,485 6f.............(2:30)

SOLAR WAGON (USA) 9-0 Pat Eddery (1) *made all, drw clr frm 2 fs out, easily*.................. (2 to 1 op Evens) 1
MADLY SHARP 9-0 G Duffield (6) *beh, styd on fnl 2 fs, no ch wth wnr*...................... (14 to 1 op 10 to 1) 2
STAR JAZZ (Ire) 8-9 Paul Eddery (2) *in tch, kpt on fnl 2 fs.* .... (11 to 1 op 7 to 1 tchd 12 to 1) 3
2730[3] THREE IN ONE 9-0 W R Swinburn (9) *prmnt, rdn 2 fs out, sn btn*.........(5 to 4 fav op 2 to 1 tchd 9 to 4) 4
2542[5] BEECHFIELD FLYER 9-0 J Carroll (4) *cl up till squeezed out aftr 2 fs, no dngr after.* .... (20 to 1 op 16 to 1 tchd 25 to 1) 5
2706[4] SUSHI BAR (Ire) 9-0 K Darley (8) *nvr nr ldrs.* .... (12 to 1 op 8 to 1) 6
2630[5] BOLLIN NEIL 9-0 M Birch (3) *wth ldr till wknd 2 fs out.* .... (25 to 1 op 16 to 1) 7
2630[6] FEATHERSTONE LANE 9-0 S Webster (7) *early speed, beh hfwy*........................... (50 to 1 op 33 to 1) 8
TRIBUNE 9-0 T Williams (5) *outpcd and reminders, al beh.* .... (16 to 1 op 14 to 1 tchd 20 to 1) 9
Dist: 7l, nk, hd, 5l, ½l, 2l, 1l, 1½l. 1m 12.70s. a 2.10s (9 Ran).
SR: 34/6/-/4/-/-/ (K Abdulla), R Charlton

3032 Bouncing Castle Selling Handicap Class G (0-60 3-y-o and up) £2,658 5f...............................(3:00)

2620[4] MARTINA [58] 5-9-12 Pat Eddery (4) *chsd ldrs, ran on wl to ld well ins fnl furlong*......... (13 to 8 fav op 5 to 2) 1
3002[8] BRISAS [31] (v) 6-7-13 J Fanning (5) *al prmnt, chlgd ins fnl furlong, no extr nr finish.* .... (12 to 1 op 10 to 1 tchd 14 to 1) 2
2549[7] TOMMY TEMPEST [47] (bl) 4-8-8 (7*) P McCabe (2) *led till wl ins fnl furlong, no extr*.................. (12 to 1) 3
2821[4] SWINGING TICH [46] 4-9-0 L Dettori (3) *chsd ldrs, kpt on wl fnl furlong*.............................. (10 to 1) 4
2682* MISS SIHAM (Ire) [45] 4-8-6 (7*) Claire Balding (7) *prmnt, kpt on fnl furlong*...................(6 to 1 op 9 to 2) 5
2770[3] COCONUT JOHNNY [55] (bl) 3-9-5 W Newnes (13) *dsptd ld far side, kpt on fnl furlong.* .... (10 to 1 op 8 to 1 tchd 12 to 1) 6
2264[5] KALAR [46] (bl) 4-9-0 S Wood (11) *led far side grp, kpt on same pace fnl furlong*........... (14 to 1 op 10 to 1) 7
2312 MISS BRIGHTSIDE [40] (bl) 5-8-8 S Webster (12) *rcd far side, not trble ldrs*................(16 to 1 op 14 to 1) 8
3002 BARBEZIEUX [46] 6-8-7 (7*) V Halliday (14) *dwlt, swtchd to stands side, styd on fnl 2 fs, not rch ldrs.* .... (16 to 1 op 10 to 1) 9
2549 SEAMERE [58] (bl) 10-9-12 J Lowe (9) *nvr dngrs.* ....(10 to 1 tchd 12 to 1) 10
2760[2] LUCKY MILL [43] (v) 3-8-7 R Lappin (16) *rcd far side, chsd ldrs till wknd o'r one furlong out.* (14 to 1 op 10 to 1) 11
2919[5] JOVIAL KATE (USA) [29] 6-7-11 T Williams (8) *rcd centre, in tch till wknd o'r one furlong out*.............(25 to 1) 12
2829[4] CONVENIENT MOMENT [54] 3-9-4 J Carroll (15) *rcd far side, chsd ldrs till wknd 2 fs out*.... (12 to 1 op 8 to 1) 13
1599[6] NORTH OF WATFORD [46] 8-9-0 K Fallon (6) *beh hfwy.* .... (14 to 1 op 12 to 1) 14

2510[8] WHISPERDALES [50] 3-9-0 S Morris (1) *beh hfwy.* ....(33 to 1 op 25 to 1) 15
2504[5] SICILY OAK [50] 3-9-0 G Duffield (10) *sn beh.* ....(20 to 1 op 16 to 1) 16
Dist: Nk, 1½l, nk, nk, 2l, hd, hd, sht-hd, 1½l, 4l. 1m 0.20s. a 2.20s (16 Ran).
SR: 48/20/30/28/26/24/18/11/16/ (Laurel (Leisure) Limited), G Lewis

3033 'Go Racing In Yorkshire' Handicap Class E (0-70 3-y-o and up) £3,557 1 ½m 60yds...................... (3:30)

2871[2] FAIR FLYER (Ire) [54] 4-8-12 R P Elliott (5) *hld up, effrt whn not clr run o'r 2 fs out, several poss, swtchd ins and styd on und pres to ld on line*..... (4 to 1 tchd 9 to 2) 1
2501[3] BROCTUNE BAY [66] 4-9-10 K Darley (4) *led aftr 2 fs, shaken up 3 out, kpt on wl, ct on line.* ....(11 to 4 fav op 5 to 2 tchd 3 to 1) 2
2591[4] ROUSITTO [49] 5-8-7 W Ryan (7) *hld up, effrt o'r 2 fs out, ev ch ins last, no extr nr finish*..............(4 to 1) 3
2633[2] JUBRAN (USA) [68] 7-9-12 J Carroll (3) *sn tracking ldr, rdn o'r 2 fs out, ev ch ins last, no extr nr finish.* ....(9 to 2 op 4 to 1) 4
2632 LORD HASTIE (USA) [70] 5-9-9 (5*) O Pears (2) *led one furlong, in tch, rdn 2 out, one pace.* (7 to 1 op 10 to 1) 5
1416[8] KINTAVI [52] 3-7-13 J Fanning (1) *led aftr one furlong, hdd one furlong later, trkd ldrs, effrt 2 out, sn btn.* ....(12 to 1 op 10 to 1) 6
2891* BOLD AMBITION [40] (v) 6-7-12 (5ex) J Lowe (6) *trkd ldrs, effrt o'r 2 fs out, btn whn hmpd entering last.* ....(8 to 1 op 7 to 1) 7
Dist: Hd, ¾l, hd, 3l, 2l, ½l. 2m 42.60s. a 7.60s (7 Ran).
SR: 4/15/-/14/10/-/-/ (William Provan Hunter), M Johnston

3034 Armstrong Memorial Challenge Cup Rated Class B Handicap (0-95 3-y-o and up) £6,720 6f................(4:00)

2434* EVERGLADES (Ire) [91] 5-9-7 Pat Eddery (2) *sn tracking ldr, rdn o'r one furlong out, led ins last, kpt on wl.* .... (Evens fav op 5 to 4 tchd 6 to 4) 1
2434 PETITE-D-ARGENT [81] 4-8-11 J Carroll (1) *led till ins fnl furlong, kpt on wl*...........(20 to 1 op 16 to 1) 2
2732[7] EURO FESTIVAL [80] 4-8-10 W R Swinburn (4) *trkd ldrs, effrt 2 fs out, kpt on same pace*.... (16 to 1 op 14 to 1) 3
2975* FINJAN [79] 6-8-9 (3ex) J Weaver (3) *trkd ldrs, effrt 2 fs out, kpt on same pace*.............. (8 to 1 tchd 9 to 1) 4
2657[5] SAGEBRUSH ROLLER [82] 5-8-12 G Duffield (7) *hld up, styd on wl fnl 2 fs, nrst finish*..... (25 to 1 op 20 to 1) 5
2753[5] BEAU VENTURE (USA) [82] 5-8-12 S Perks (9) *in tch, effrt 2 fs out, no hdwy*.................. (14 to 1 tchd 16 to 1) 6
2861* MISS HAGGIS [79] 4-8-9 (3ex) W Woods (10) *hld up, effrt 2 fs out, no hdwy*.......... (6 to 1 op 11 to 2 tchd 13 to 2) 7
2854[8] CUMBRIAN WALTZER [89] 8-9-5 M Birch (8) *chsd ldrs till wknd 2 fs out*.......... (6 to 1 op 5 to 1 tchd 13 to 2) 8
2798* DENSBEN [81] 9-8-11 K Fallon (6) *beh, pushed alng hfwy, no hdwy*..................... (8 to 1 op 7 to 1) 9
1945[9] THE AUCTION BIDDER [79] 6-8-9 W Ryan (5) *in tch, effrt 2 fs out, sn btn*................................. (20 to 1) 10
Dist: Nk, 3l, hd, 4l, 1½l, 2l, 1½l, 2½l, 2½l. 1m 11.90s. a 1.30s (10 Ran).
SR: 57/46/33/31/18/12/1/5/-/ (Miss Sophie Oppenheimer), R Charlton

3035 See-Saw Claiming Stakes Class F (3-y-o and up) £2,831 1¼m......... (4:30)

2816[5] IMPERIAL BID (Fr) 5-9-5 K Fallon (5) *in tch, hdwy 3 fs out, slight ld jst ins last, hld on wl*.....(5 to 1 tchd 11 to 2) 1
2696[7] AZUREUS (Ire) 5-9-10 K Darley (7) *hld up, hdwy 3 fs out, rdn to chal one out, no extr ins last.* ....(15 to 8 fav op 7 to 4 tchd 2 to 1) 2
2815[4] ARAK (USA) 5-9-5 A Culhane (3) *chsd ldr, led o'r 3 fs out till jst ins last, kpt on*............... (3 to 1 op 11 to 4) 3
2696[5] BEST APPEARANCE (Ire) (bl) 3-9-1 W R Swinburn (1) *trkd ldrs, rdn 2 furlong out, one pace.* ....(9 to 2 op 4 to 1 tchd 5 to 1) 4
719 INFANTRY GLEN 3-8-10 M Birch (8) *hld up, effrt 2 fs out, no hdwy*................................ (33 to 1) 5
2775[6] NO SUBMISSION (USA) 7-9-2 (5*) O Pears (4) *led till o'r 3 fs out, fdd*..............(17 to 2 op 8 to 1 tchd 9 to 1) 6
2678[7] BORING (USA) 4-8-12 (7*) I Jardine (6) *in tch, effrt 3 fs out, sn btn*...........................(25 to 1 tchd 33 to 1) 7
1836[9] RAGGERTY (Ire) 3-9-1 W Newnes (2) *prmnt to hfwy, sn lost tch, tld off*................................ (16 to 1) 8
Dist: Nk, nk, 5l, 2l, 1½l, 8l, 20l. 2m 8.20s. a 4.20s (8 Ran).
SR: 48/52/46/32/23/31/13/-/ (Lord Durham), Denys Smith

3036 Tommy Shedden Challenge Trophy Handicap Stakes Class C (0-90 3-y-o) £5,344 1m 1f.................. (5:00)

2789[5] SILVERLOCKS [78] 9-0 N Connorton (9) *trkd ldrs, not clr run 2 fs out, swtchd o'r one out, ran on wl to ld ins last.* ....(5 to 1 tchd 11 to 2) 1
2333 JERVIA [80] 9-2 G Duffield (8) *trkd ldrs, chlgd o'r one furlong out, ev ch ins last, kpt on.* (10 to 1 op 8 to 1) 2
2361 GOLDEN GUEST [83] 9-5 L Dettori (2) *led till ins fnl furlong, no extr*........................ (8 to 1 op 7 to 1) 3
2545[3] MAP OF STARS (USA) [83] 9-5 Pat Eddery (10) *chsd ldr, chlgd o'r one furlong out, ev ch till wknd ins last.* ....(3 to 1 fav op 9 to 4 tchd 100 to 30) 4
2398[9] SPRING FLYER (Ire) [59] 7-4 (5*) D Wright (1) *in tch, hdwy o'r 3 fs out, rdn over 2 out, kpt on same pace.* .... (9 to 1 op 10 to 1 tchd 12 to 1) 5
2416[2] DESERT TIME [76] 8-12 W R Swinburn (7) *in tch, hdwy 4 fs out, not much room 2 out, wknd fnl furlong.* ....(4 to 1 op 6 to 1 tchd 13 to 2) 6
2290[4] SAVOY TRUFFLE (Fr) [85] 9-7 W Ryan (5) *hld up, effrt 3 fs out, no hdwy*..................(7 to 2 tchd 4 to 1) 7
2361 SO SO [82] 9-4 W Newnes (4) *hld up, effrt and swtchd 3 fs out, sn rdn and btn*..................(10 to 1) 8
MAM'ZELLE ANGOT [62] 7-12 Dale Gibson (6) *al beh.* ....(33 to 1 op 25 to 1) 9
468 HARPOON LOUIE (USA) [80] 9-2 K Darley (3) *mid-div, wknd o'r 3 fs out*..............(16 to 1 op 14 to 1) 10
Dist: 1½l, 1l, 1½l, 2½l, 4l, 1½l, 6l, 7l, 1½l. 1m 53.70s. a 2.70s (10 Ran).
SR: 39/36/36/31/-/4/ (Miss Betty Duxbury), Miss S E Hall

TIPPERARY (IRE) (good to yielding) Monday August 2nd

3037 Greenane Race (3-y-o and up) £2,760 1½m.......................... (2:30)

2691* ERZADJAN (Ire) 3-8-12 J P Murtagh (5)..........(3 to 1) 1
1609[3] SHAWGATNY (USA) 3-8-3 (6*) J A Heffernan (1).... (5 to 1) 2
3884a* INK BY THE DRUM (USA) 5-9-9 T Horgan (3)..... (12 to 1) 3
2408[7] IMAD (USA) 3-8-6 (6*) B J Walsh (2)..............(11 to 2) 4
2512* VELMA (USA) 3-8-12 P Shanahan (6)........(11 to 10 fav) 5
2485[4] SIRSAN (Ire) 3-8-12 N G McCullagh (4)............(9 to 1) 6
Dist: ¾l, 3l, ½l, 4l. 2m 46.40s. (6 Ran).
(H H Aga Khan), John M Oxx

3038 Carrintwohill (Fillies) Handicap (0-90 3-y-o and up) £4,140 1½m...... (3:00)

2035[4] MAMOURA (Ire) [-] 3-9-1 J P Murtagh (3)........... (7 to 2) 1
2702[2] SOVIET CHOICE (Ire) [-] 3-8-9 P Shanahan (1).. (Evens fav) 2
2702[3] LYPHARD ABU (Ire) [-] (bl) 5-8-6 (6*) J A Heffernan (2) (5 to 1) 3
1046[2] LADY TYONE (Ire) [-] 3-8-6 N G McCullagh (6).... (11 to 2) 4
2702[7] TEBRE (USA) [-] (bl) 3-7-11 L O'Shea (7)..........(12 to 1) 5
1962[9] LAGRION (USA) [-] (bl) 4-8-1 Joanna Morgan (4).. (16 to 1) 6
2140* CENTER MORICHES (Ire) [-] 3-8-1 (6*) R V Skelly (9) (9 to 1) 7
2692[9] MISS DARCY (Ire) [-] 5-7-3 (8*) G M Moylan (8)....(16 to 1) 8
Dist: Hd, ½l, 3½l, hd. 2m 48.70s. (8 Ran).
(H H Aga Khan), John M Oxx

3039 August EBF Maiden (2-y-o) £3,795 5f ....(3:30)

KERAKA (USA) 8-11 J P Murtagh (11).......... (5 to 4 fav) 1
MISS KRISTIN (Ire) 8-5 (6*) J A Heffernan (1)........ (4 to 1) 2
2745[4] STAGE LEFT EVEN (Ire) 8-10 (4*) P Carberry (7).... (9 to 2) 3
2804[4] MANAAFIS (Ire) 8-8 (6*) B J Walsh (2)............ (6 to 1) 4
2188[3] SOLAR ATTRACTION (Ire) 8-11 D Manning (10)..... (6 to 1) 5
2246[7] OVERSEAS TRANSFER (Ire) 9-0 P Shanahan (5).. (10 to 1) 6
JOYFUL MUSIC (Ire) 8-3 (8*) B Fenton (12)........ (25 to 1) 7
2742 COOLOWEN FLASH (Ire) 8-11 Joanna Morgan (13) (16 to 1) 8
FINAL EXHIBIT (Ire) 8-3 (8*) T Durcan (4)..........(20 to 1) 9
PETERS BIRD (Ire) 8-8 (6*) R V Skelly (3).......... (20 to 1) 10
2244[3] ASTRADANE (Ire) (bl) 8-11 N G McCullagh (6)..... (10 to 1) 11
INDIAN EXPRESS 8-11 B Coogan (8)............. (12 to 1) 12
BILLY BUZZ (Ire) 8-3 (8*) J A Hunter (9).............(16 to 1) 13
Dist: Sht-hd, 1½l, hd, 4l. 56.70s. (13 Ran).
(H H Aga Khan), John M Oxx

3040 Galteemore Race (3-y-o and up) £2,760 5f...................... (4:00)

2295[2] ASTA MADERA (Ire) 3-8-8 N G McCullagh (2)...(5 to 2 fav) 1
1795[9] CARRIG STAR (Ire) 4-8-11 (4*) P Carberry (3).......(4 to 1) 2
2700[6] BLACKTRENCH LADY (Ire) 5-8-12 J P Murtagh (5) (6 to 1) 3
2700[3] NORDIC GLARE (Ire) 3-8-3 (8*) T Durcan (1)........ (4 to 1) 4
2674[4] RUNNING GREAT (Ire) 3-8-8 J D Eddery (4).........(4 to 1) 5
2700[4] RIFLEBIRD (Ire) 3-8-8 P Shanahan (6)..............(5 to 1) 6
1610 BRASS BUTTON (Ire) 3-8-2 (6*) R V Skelly (7)..... (20 to 1) 7
Dist: ¾l, 1½l, 2½l, ½l. 57.30s. (7 Ran).
(J E Mulhern), J E Mulhern

BRIGHTON (firm) Tuesday August 3rd

Going Correction: MINUS 0.15 sec. per fur.

3041 Alfriston Maiden Stakes Class D (2-y-o) £4,127 5f 59yds........... (2:00)

2659[2] LAUNE (Aus) 8-9 Paul Eddery (1) *hld up beh, hdwy and squeezed through one and a half fs out, led one out, sn clr*................(10 to 1 op 7 to 1 tchd 12 to 1) 1
2618 BIRD OF TIME (Ire) 8-9 T Quinn (5) *led till hdd one furlong out, no extr*......................(12 to 1 op 6 to 1) 2

2542[2] NORTHERN CELADON (Ire) 9-0 P Robinson (2) *trkd ldrs, shaken up and one pace frm o'r one furlong out.* ....(9 to 2 op 5 to 1 tchd 6 to 1) 3
1428[5] HELLO MISTER 9-0 J Williams (7) *wth ldr, ev ch 2 fs out, one pace*.......................... (25 to 1 tchd 33 to 1) 4
LADY VENDETTA (USA) 8-9 J Reid (3) *strted slwly, nvr on terms*.............................. (20 to 1 op 7 to 1) 5
2575[6] MARJORIE'S ORCHID 8-9 L Dettori (6) *cl up, pushed alng o'r 2 fs out, wknd over one out*......(12 to 1 op 6 to 1) 6
2720[3] IRADAH (USA) 8-9 R Hills (4) *trkd ldrs till squeezed out and out paced one and a half fs out, eased whn btn.* ....(13 to 8 on op 5 to 4 on) 7

Dist: 3l, 1½l, nk, 3l, ¾l, 1½l. 1m 3.00s. a 2.90s (7 Ran).
SR: 21/9/8/7/ (Lord Howard de Walden), Mrs J Cecil

3042 Town Hall Handicap Class E (0-70 3-y-o and up) £3,080 7f 214yds..... (2:30)

2330[6] WAHEM (Ire) [60] 3-9-5 B Marcus (7) *led 3 fs, cl up, chlgd and edgd lft und pres one out, sn led, ran on wl.* ....(15 to 2 op 8 to 1 tchd 7 to 1) 1
2882[2] KINGCHIP BOY [51] (v) 4-9-3 D Biggs (6) *cl up, led 5 fs out, quickened 2 out, hdd ins last, one pace.* ....(5 to 2 fav op 2 to 1) 2
2164[3] DIACO [58] 8-9-10 P Robinson (4) *hld up beh ldrs, took keen hold, one pace und pres fnl 2 fs.* ....(9 to 1 op 7 to 1 tchd 10 to 1) 3
2757[6] OLD COMRADES [51] 6-9-3 J Reid (3) *wtd wth, cld hfwy, hrd rdn 2 fs out, one pace.* ....(6 to 1 op 4 to 1 tchd 13 to 2) 4+
2869[3] PRECIOUS AIR (Ire) [55] 5-9-7 B Rouse (5) *trkd ldrs, pld out and effrt 2 fs out, sn one pace.* ....(11 to 2 op 5 to 1 tchd 13 to 2) 4+
2673 PIPERS REEL [49] 3-8-5 (3*) D Harrison (10) *cl up, pushed alng o'r 3 fs out, sn wknd.* ....(9 to 1 op 8 to 1 tchd 12 to 1) 6
2327 ROSIETOES (USA) [42] 5-8-8 N Carlisle (9) *hld up, short lived effrt o'r 2 fs out*.............(14 to 1 op 10 to 1) 7
2940[6] NAVARESQUE [45] 8-8-11 J Williams (8) *cl up till wknd o'r 3 furlons out*.....................(14 to 1 op 8 to 1) 8
2524 AIN'TLIFELIKETHAT [47] (bl) 6-8-13 Paul Eddery (1) *al beh.* ....(12 to 1 op 10 to 1) 9
2110 GEMINI BAY [37] 4-8-3 S Dawson (2) *al beh, tld off.* ....(66 to 1 op 50 to 1) 10

Dist: 2l, ¾l, 1½l, dd-ht, 3l, 5l, 1l, 4l, 25l. 1m 35.60s. a 3.20s (10 Ran).
SR: 39/31/36/24/28/6/ (C E Brittain), C E Brittain

3043 Downs Selling Stakes Class G (3-y-o and up) £2,070 1m 1f 209yds.... (3:00)

2858* OVERPOWER 9-9-7 P Robinson (1) *hld up in cl tch, pld out wl o'r one furlong out, led ins last, ran on well.* ....(13 to 8 op 5 to 4) 1
2849* BARAHIN (Ire) 4-9-7 A Clark (2) *took keen hold, cl up, led 2 fs out till hdd ins last, ran on.* (11 to 10 fav op 6 to 4) 2
2858[2] TAUNTING (Ire) 5-9-7 R Cochrane (5) *led till hdd 2 fs out, hrd rdn and one pace.* (9 to 2 tchd 5 to 1 and 4 to 1) 3
2673 EIRAS MOOD 4-8-11 (5*) Stephen Davies (4) *cl up, pushed alng o'r 3 fs out, ev ch 2 out, sn outpcd.* ....(25 to 1 op 10 to 1 tchd 33 to 1) 4
SALAR'S SPIRIT 7-9-2 (5*) D McCabe (3) *in tch till wknd 4 fs out*..............................(66 to 1 op 33 to 1) 5

Dist: Nk, 3½l, 3½l, 3l. 2m 7.40s. a 9.20s (5 Ran).
(M P Bowring), M H Tompkins

3044 Duke Of Norfolk Memorial Handicap Class D (0-80 3-y-o) £5,848 1m 3f 196yds........................ (3:30)

2228[4] RUNAWAY PETE (USA) [74] 9-6 T Quinn (1) *wth ldr, outpcd o'r 4 fs out, rdn and ran on frm wl over one furlong out, led ins last, styd on well.* ....(11 to 2 op 4 to 1 tchd 6 to 1) 1
2537[2] CAST THE LINE [67] 8-13 A McGlone (4) *trkd ldg pair, led appr 3 fs out till hdd ins last, no extr.* ....(7 to 2 tchd 4 to 1) 2
2899[3] MR COPYFORCE [62] 8-8 W Newnes (2) *set steady pace, hdd appr 3 fs out, one pace und pres.* ....(5 to 2 fav op 11 to 4 tchd 3 to 1) 3
2561[6] EUPHONIC [68] 9-0 L Dettori (5) *trkd ldrs, cld o'r 5 fs out, rdn and ev ch 2 out, one pace*.....(11 to 4 tchd 3 to 1) 4
2495[6] BRANSBY ROAD (Ire) [47] 7-2 (5*) D Wright (3) *in tch, outpcd o'r 4 fs out, pld out and rdn 3 out, not pace to chal.* ....(12 to 1 op 8 to 1 tchd 14 to 1) 5
2333 ERICOLIN (Ire) [75] 9-7 B Marcus (6) *strted very slow and lost many ls, al beh*.... (9 to 1 op 8 to 1 tchd 10 to 1) 6

Dist: 2l, ¾l, hd, ¾l, 12l. 2m 31.40s. a 3.90s (6 Ran).
SR: 49/38/31/36/13/17/ (Thomas T S Liang), P F I Cole

3045 Withdean Handicap Class D (0-80 3-y-o) £3,143 1m 1f 209yds......... (4:00)

2277[2] DRAGON'S TEETH (Ire) [77] 9-7 R Cochrane (5) *cl up, reminder 3 fs out, sn led, drvn out ins last.* ....(Evens fav op 5 to 4 on tchd 11 to 10) 1
2421[6] PRINCESS TATEUM (Ire) [66] 8-10 P Robinson (1) *hld up, effrt o'r 2 fs out, styd on ins last*.....(7 to 2 op 2 to 1) 2
2864[5] JULIASDARKINVADER [49] 7-0 (7*) Kim McDonnell (2) *cl up, ev ch 3 fs out, sn one pace.* ....(14 to 1 op 7 to 1 tchd 16 to 1) 3
2398 NAHLATI (Ire) [56] 7-11 (3*) B Doyle (3) *led till hdd 2 and a half fs out, wndrd und pres, wknd ins last.* ....(11 to 4 op 5 to 2 tchd 3 to 1) 4

Dist: 5l, 1l, 2l. 2m 3.70s. a 5.50s (4 Ran).
SR: 37/16/-/-/ (Lord Weinstock), L M Cumani

3046 South Coast Claiming Stakes Class E (3-y-o and up) £2,924 6f 209yds. .(4:30)

2724[7] SHARP GAZELLE 3-7-12 (5*) Stephen Davies (3) *made all, pushed alng o'r 2 fs out, drvn out.* (33 to 1 op 10 to 1) 1
2686[6] HALBERT 4-8-11 (7*) D O'Neill (4) *cl up, hrd rdn and edgd lft o'r one furlong out, kpt on*...... (10 to 1 op 5 to 1) 2
2160* CAPE PIGEON (USA) 8-9-1 J Reid (1) *cl up, rdn 2 fs out, not clr run and one pace frm o'r one out.* ....(6 to 1 on op 4 to 1 on) 3
1233[3] FIVE ISLANDS 3-8-13 T Quinn (2) *hld up in cl tch, effrt 2 fs out, not much room and one pace ins last.* ....(10 to 1 op 6 to 1) 4

Dist: ½l, 1l, ¾l. 1m 24.20s. a 4.20s (4 Ran).
SR: 10/23/17/13/ (M Pattimore), B Smart

3047 Levy Board Maiden Handicap Class F (0-60 3-y-o and up) £2,758 6f 209yds ....(5:00)

2712 MEDLAND (Ire) [45] 3-8-4 (3*) D Harrison (3) *mid-div, sn rdn, pld out wl o'r one furlong out, ran on und pres to ld ins last*...... (11 to 2 jt-fav op 4 to 1 tchd 6 to 1) 1
2915[6] HAZY KAY (Ire) [55] (bl) 3-9-3 Gay Kelleway (7) *beh, rdn and hdwy 2 fs out, ran on wl fnl furlong.* ....(11 to 1 op 8 to 1 tchd 12 to 1) 2
2181[8] ALMONTY (Ire) [44] (bl) 3-8-1 (5*) N Gwilliams (14) *trkd ldrs, ev ch ins fnl furlong, no extr cl hme.* ....(12 to 1 tchd 20 to 1) 3
2724 LADY OF SHADOWS [39] 3-8-1 F Norton (9) *trkd ldrs, led briefly ins fnl furlong, ran on*..... (20 to 1 op 12 to 1) 4
2638[9] FESTIN [51] (bl) 3-8-13 R Cochrane (2) *trkd ldrs, rdn and not quicken 2 fs out, ran on ins last.* ....(6 to 1 tchd 8 to 1) 5
2733[8] COUNTERCHECK (Ire) [44] 4-8-12 N Day (16) *chsd ldrs, hrd rdn o'r one furlong out, ev ch ins last, wknd cl hme.* ....(9 to 1 op 6 to 1) 6
2832[9] WOODLANDS ELECTRIC [31] (v) 3-7-4[4] (7*) M Baird (1) *beh till styd on ins fnl furlong, nrst finish.* ....(66 to 1 op 50 to 1) 7
2723[5] VIS-A-VIS [28] 4-7-3 (7*) N Varley (5) *trkd ldrs till wknd ins fnl furlong*..........(16 to 1 op 20 to 1 tchd 33 to 1) 8
2226[2] CLEAR LOOK [54] 3-9-2 T Quinn (6) *made most, hrd rdn o'r one furlong out, hdd ins last, wknd.* ....(11 to 2 jt-fav op 5 to 1) 9
2831[3] PEGGOTTY [39] 5-8-0 (7*) A Whelan (8) *chsd ldrs till wknd o'r 2 fs out*...........(11 to 1 op 7 to 1 tchd 12 to 1) 10
2312[6] DOUBLE SHIFT [58] 4-9-12 S Whitworth (15) *chsd ldrs, wkng whn slightly hmpd 2 fs out*... (10 to 1 op 7 to 1) 11
2724[5] SUPERENSIS [50] (v) 3-8-12 W Newnes (13) *wth ldr, wkng whn squeezed out o'r one furlong out.* ....(11 to 1 op 10 to 1 tchd 12 to 1) 12
2897 UNIFICATION (Ire) [46] 4-8-7 (7*) L Carter (4) *al beh.* ....(14 to 1 op 8 to 1 tchd 16 to 1) 13
2476 HARD ROCK MINER [39] 3-8-1 N Adams (11) *al beh.* ....(33 to 1 tchd 50 to 1) 14
2864[6] DELAY NO MORE [44] 3-8-6 Paul Eddery (12) *al beh.* ....(33 to 1 op 20 to 1) 15

Dist: Nk, nk, hd, ¾l, hd, 2½l, 1l, nk, 2l, 5l. 1m 23.40s. a 3.40s (15 Ran).
SR: 26/35/23/17/27/25/-/-/17/ (G A Jackman), D A Wilson

DEAUVILLE (FR) (good to soft)
Tuesday August 3rd
Going Correction: PLUS 0.40 sec. per fur.

3048 Prix des Yearlings (Listed) (2-y-o) £14,337 7f..................... (2:55)

BARODET (USA) 8-11 T Jarnet, ... 1
NEC PLUS ULTRA (Fr) 8-11 G Mosse, ... 2
IGUASSU (Fr) 8-8 E Legrix, ... 3
FLAGNY (Fr) 8-8 F Head, ... 4

Dist: ¾l, 2½l, ½l, 2½l, ½l, 1½l, ½l, ¾l. 1m 27.90s. a 5.90s (9 Ran).
SR: 51/49/38/36/ (P de Moussac), A Fabre

NOTTINGHAM (good to firm)
Tuesday August 3rd
Going Correction: MINUS 0.20 sec. per fur. (races 1,2,5,6), MINUS 0.10 (3,4)

3049 Rome Selling Handicap Class G (0-60 3-y-o) £2,057 1¾m 15yds....... (6:00)

2850[5] SIDE BAR [40] (bl) 8-9 A Tucker (7) *trkd ldrs, hdwy to ld 3 fs out and edgd rght, rdn 2 furlongs out, styd on wl ins last*..................(11 to 1 op 8 to 1 tchd 12 to 1) 1

2870[6] ANN HILL (Ire) [52] 9-7 W Ryan (3) *hld up and beh, gd hdwy 3 fs out, chsd wnr and rdn o'r one furlong out, kpt on one pace*........(5 to 1 op 4 to 1 tchd 11 to 2) 2

2850[2] EARLY TO RISE [40] 8-9 D Biggs (6) *hld up, hdwy o'r 3 fs out, sn rdn alng and kpt on one pace fnl 2 furlongs.* ....(4 to 1 jt-fav op 3 to 1) 3

2694[4] BAJAN AFFAIR [34] 8-0 (3*) N Kennedy (4) *led 2 fs, chsd ldr till chlgd 3 out, sn rdn and wknd appr fnl furlong.* ....(16 to 1 op 14 to 1) 4

2228[5] GALEJADE [48] 9-3 J Williams (5) *pld hrd, led aftr 2 fs, rdn and hdd 3 furlongs out, grad wknd.* (9 to 2 op 5 to 1) 5

2784[3] BADAWI (Fr) [37] (bl) 8-6 N Carlisle (1) *hld up, effrt and rdn alng o'r 3 fs out, nvr a factor*..(4 to 1 jt-fav op 5 to 1) 6

2833[4] MAC TOMB [24] 7-7 C Avery (8) *chsd ldrs, rdn 3 fs out, sn one pace*............(12 to 1 op 20 to 1 tchd 25 to 1) 7

2833[5] SWIFT REVENGE [25] 7-3 (5*) D Wright (9) *hld up, effrt and some hdwy 4 fs out, sn rdn and wknd.* ....(8 to 1 op 7 to 1) 8

2107[9] HIGH CHAIR [44] 8-13 Dale Gibson (2) *cl up, rdn o'r 3 fs out, sn btn*...........(10 to 1 op 7 to 1 tchd 12 to 1) 9

Dist: 2l, 5l, 1l, 1½l, nk, 2l, 1l, 2l. 3m 7.20s. a 9.30s (9 Ran).

(P J Flavin), M J Ryan

3050 Dublin Limited Stakes Class F (0-65 3-y-o and up) £2,332 1m 54yds.. (6:30)

2550* MISSY-S (Ire) 4-8-9 (5*) V Slattery (4) *made all, clr 3 fs out, rdn and ran on wl fnl 2 furlongs.* ....(7 to 1 op 5 to 1 tchd 8 to 1) 1

2426[6] MRS DAWSON 3-8-7 Pat Eddery (3) *trkd ldg pair, effrt and hdwy o'r 2 fs out, sn rdn, styd on ins last, not rch wnr*..............................(12 to 1 op 10 to 1) 2

213[3] KRYPTOS (USA) 3-8-7 W R Swinburn (1) *chsd ldrs, rdn and outpcd o'r 2 fs out, styd on wl und pres ins last.* ....(5 to 1 op 3 to 1) 3

2863[3] DAYTONA BEACH (Ire) (v) 3-8-12 K Darley (2) *hld up, hdwy and not much room o'r 2 fs out, sn rdn, wknd appr last.* ....(4 to 1 tchd 5 to 1) 4

2697[8] CITY TIMES (Ire) (bl) 3-8-0 (7*) S Sanders (6) *chsd wnr, rdn and wknd wl o'r 2 fs out*..................(9 to 1 op 5 to 1) 5

2832[2] HAWAYAH (Ire) 3-8-7 L Dettori (7) *trkd ldrs, effrt 3 fs out, sn rdn and btn*...... (7 to 4 fav op 9 to 4 tchd 5 to 2) 6

2834[5] IRISH GROOM 6-8-12 (7*) C Hawksley (8) *nvr a factor.* ....(50 to 1 op 33 to 1) 7

2764[4] FLASHMAN 3-8-12 S Perks (5) *al rear.* .... (10 to 1 op 8 to 1 tchd 11 to 1) 8

Dist: ¾l, ½l, 3l, hd, 4l, hd, 3l. 1m 44.10s. a 4.10s (8 Ran).

SR: 14/5/3/-/-/ (B J Llewellyn), D Burchell

3051 Tote Nottingham Stewards Cup Handicap Class D (0-85 3-y-o and up) £3,882 6f 15yds....................... (7:00)

2522[5] PLUCK [77] 3-9-3 Pat Eddery (8) *hld up, hdwy and not clr run one and a half fs out, swtchd and squeezed through wl ins last to ld nr finish.* ....(15 to 8 fav op 7 to 4 tchd 9 to 4) 1

2975 BALLAD DANCER [68] 8-8-13 M Birch (3) *hld up, pushed alng and hdwy 2 fs out, str run to ld wl ins last, hdd nr finish*............................(25 to 1 op 16 to 1) 2

2731* ALASIB [78] 3-9-4 L Dettori (9) *al cl up, ev ch ins fnl furlong, not quicken nr finish*.......(7 to 1 op 5 to 1) 3

2965[2] AUGHFAD [79] (v) 7-9-10 J Reid (5) *cl up, hmpd aftr one furlong, effrt to ld one furlong out, sn rdn, hdd wl ins last*..............................(7 to 1 op 5 to 1) 4

2276[2] GREAT HALL [66] 4-8-11 J Williams (4) *beh, swtchd outsd and hdwy 2 fs out, sn rdn and kpt on ins last.* ....(7 to 1 op 8 to 1 tchd 6 to 1) 5

2628[2] MACS MAHARANEE [83] 6-9-9 (5*) D Wright (11) *mid-div, rdn alng hfwy, kpt on ins last.* .... (13 to 2 op 7 to 1 tchd 6 to 1) 6

3011[3] PETRACO (Ire) [73] 5-9-1 (3*) S D Williams (1) *led, rdn 2 fs out, sn hdd and wknd ins last*.....(14 to 1 op 12 to 1) 7

2731[7] RAIN SPLASH [71] 3-8-4 (7*) Claire Balding (6) *nvr rch ldrs.* .... (25 to 1 op 16 to 1) 8

2379[2] TARNSIDE ROSAL [71] 3-8-11 J Carroll (10) *slwly away, gd hdwy on outer hfwy, effrt to chal 2 fs out, sn rdn and wknd*............................(14 to 1 op 10 to 1) 9

2777[7] JUST BOB [72] 4-9-3 J Fortune (2) *chsd ldrs, effrt to chal 2 fs out, sn rdn and wknd*..........(20 to 1 op 16 to 1) 10

2777[2] MANOR ADVENTURE [66] 3-8-6 A Mackay (7) *cl up, ev ch o'r 2 fs out, sn rdn and wknd*......(9 to 1 op 10 to 1) 11

Dist: Nk, hd, ¾l, nk, 2½l, hd, 1½l, 1l, 2l, 2l. 1m 13.50s. a 2.00s (11 Ran).

SR: 51/46/50/53/39/46/35/22/18/ (Lord Derby), R Charlton

3052 Paris Maiden Auction Fillies' Stakes Class F (2-y-o) £2,257 6f 15yds.. (7:30)

2866[2] ONE ON ONE 8-11 M Hills (11) *made all, quickened 2 fs out, sn clr*........(11 to 8 fav op 11 to 10 tchd 7 to 4) 1

1263[7] LADY-BO-K 8-11 W R Swinburn (10) *in tch, hdwy to chase wnr 2 fs out, sn rdn and not quicken appr last.* .... (25 to 1 op 20 to 1 tchd 33 to 1) 2

776[8] CRYSTAL MAGIC 8-11 Pat Eddery (9) *prmnt till outpcd and lost pl hfwy, hdwy 2 fs out, sn rdn and hng badly, eased ins last*..........(2 to 1 op 5 to 2 tchd 13 to 8) 3

2695[5] BALLARD RING (Ire) 8-11 N Connorton (2) *chsd ldrs, rdn 2 fs out, edgd rght and kpt on one pace*........(33 to 1) 4

2630[4] DAILY STAR 8-11 J Carroll (3) *cl up, rdn and wknd 2 fs out.* ....(14 to 1 op 10 to 1 tchd 16 to 1) 5

2687[3] GIGUE 8-11 J Reid (1) *cl up, rdn o'r 2 fs out, sn wknd.* ....(20 to 1 op 10 to 1) 6

PURSUIT OF GLORY 8-11 D Biggs (8) *stumbled strt, hdwy hfwy, sn rdn, no imprsn*.........(5 to 1 tchd 13 to 2) 7

2706[8] SUSELJA (Ire) 8-11 J Fortune (5) *cl up, rdn hfwy and sn wknd*..............(25 to 1 op 20 to 1 tchd 33 to 1) 8

1998[9] SKELTON PRINCESS (Ire) 8-11 W Ryan (4) *al rear.* ....(33 to 1 op 20 to 1) 9

2668[7] CA IRA (Ire) 8-11 L Dettori (6) *cl up till rdn hfwy, sn wknd.* ....(50 to 1) 10

Dist: 2½l, 3l, nk, 3l, ½l, 2l, 8l, 5l, 8l. 1m 14.50s. a 3.00s (10 Ran).

SR: 25/15/3/2/-/-/ (Cheveley Park Stud), W J Haggas

3053 London Rating Related Maiden Stakes Class E (0-70 3-y-o) £2,579 1m 1f 213yds........................ (8:00)

2635[2] LT WELSH (USA) (v) 9-0 L Dettori (8) *hld up, smooth hdwy 4 fs out, rdn one and a half out, styd on wl to ld ins last.* ....(7 to 4 fav tchd 6 to 4 and 15 to 8) 1

2758[8] WELL SUITED 9-0 J Reid (6) *prmnt, effrt to chal 2 fs out, rdn and ev ch entering last, kpt on one pace.* .... (5 to 2 op 9 to 4 tchd 11 to 4) 2

1426 LEAR KING (USA) 9-0 W R Swinburn (5) *cl up, hdwy to ld 3 fs out, sn rdn, hdd and not quicken ins last.* .... (4 to 1 op 5 to 1 tchd 11 to 2) 3

1312 GREEN CHILI 8-9 M Hills (2) *hld up, pld hrd, hdwy and not clr run o'r 2 fs out, sn rdn, one paced.* ....(14 to 1 op 8 to 1) 4

2773[6] ELEGANT HUSSAR (v) 9-0 M Birch (4) *led, rdn and hdd 3 fs out, sn wknd*..........................(14 to 1 op 12 to 1) 5

2421[5] MORSTOCK 9-0 J Williams (9) *beh, effrt 3 fs out, sn rdn, no hdwy*..........................(9 to 1 op 7 to 1) 6

2801[8] HOD-MOD (Ire) 9-0 A Mackay (3) *chsd ldrs, rdn 3 fs out, sn wknd*.................................. (50 to 1) 7

2972 MOUJEEB (USA) 8-7 (7*) P McCabe (7) *al rear.* .... (25 to 1 op 16 to 1) 8

SUPER SCENARIO 9-0 R Perham (1) *cl up, rdn 4 fs out, wknd 3 out, sn beh*.................................. (66 to 1) 9

Dist: 2l, sht-hd, 6l, ¾l, 3l, 5l, 2l, 8l. 2m 6.30s. a 3.30s (9 Ran).

SR: 47/43/42/25/28/22/12/8/-/ (George Strawbridge), I A Balding

3054 Brussels Handicap Class D (0-80 3-y-o) £3,435 1m 54yds............. (8:30)

2576[5] SUSQUEHANNA DAYS (USA) [61] 8-8 L Dettori (5) *led 2 fs, cl up, rdn to chal two out, styd on to ld entering last, kpt on gmely*..........................(7 to 2 op 3 to 1) 1

2522 ERTLON [74] 9-7 M Birch (4) *hld up, hdwy on inner 3 fs out, effrt and not clr run one and a half out, swtchd and rdn to chal ins last, kpt on.* .... (9 to 1 op 5 to 1 tchd 10 to 1) 2

2631* SCOFFERA [61] 8-8 Kim Tinkler (6) *led aftr 2 fs, rdn two and a half out, sn hdd and no extr ins last.* ....(11 to 2 op 4 to 1) 3

2757[7] DANNY BOY [72] 9-5 J Reid (1) *trkd ldg pair, effrt 3 fs out, rdn 2 out, sn one paced.* .... (100 to 30 fav op 5 to 2 tchd 7 to 2) 4

2136 MITHI AL GAMAR (USA) [69] 9-2 W R Swinburn (7) *in tch, smooth hdwy on outer 3 fs out, ev ch 2 out, sn rdn, wknd entering last*.................. (4 to 1 op 7 to 2) 5

2775[3] UMBUBUZI (USA) [70] 9-3 S Perks (3) *chsd ldrs, rdn o'r 2 fs out, sn wknd*..........(9 to 2 op 5 to 1 tchd 13 to 2) 6

Dist: ½l, 2l, 1½l, 2l, 4l. 1m 42.80s. a 2.80s (6 Ran).

SR: 27/38/19/25/16/5/ (Paul Mellon), I A Balding

REDCAR (good to firm)
Tuesday August 3rd

Going Correction: MINUS 0.40 sec. per fur.

3055 Sapphire Selling Stakes Class F (3-y-o and up) £2,243 1m 1f........... (2:15)

2566[2] LE TEMERAIRE 7-9-5 Kim Tinkler (8) *made all, hld on wl fnl furlong*.............(9 to 2 op 7 to 2 tchd 5 to 1) 1

1271[2] AMERIGUE 3-8-1 (5*) J Tate (1) *prmnt, effrt 3 out, styd on wl fnl furlong, not rch wnr.* .... (5 to 1 op 4 to 1 tchd 11 to 2) 2

2768[2] YOUNG JASON 10-9-2 (3*) N Kennedy (4) *hld up, gd hdwy o'r 2 out, styd on wl fnl furlong, nrst finish.* ....(4 to 1 tchd 9 to 2) 3

MAJOR IVOR 8-9-5 K Darley (9) *hld up, hdwy 4 out, rdn o'r 2 out, kpt on same pace*.........(9 to 2 op 7 to 2) 4

2454[5] SUSANNA'S SECRET 6-9-2 (3*) O Pears (5) *in tch, effrt 3 out, sn rdn and one paced.* .... (20 to 1 op 16 to 1 tchd 25 to 1) 5

2736[3] BARLEY CAKE 3-8-6 J Fanning (3) *mid-div, effrt 3 out, rdn 2 out, one paced*...............(3 to 1 fav op 11 to 4) 6

2856[2] ROLY WALLACE (bl) 4-9-5 M Wigham (7) *slwly into strd, sn chasing ldrs, rdn and wknd o'r 2 out.* (6 to 1 op 5 to 1) 7
962 CREAM OF THE CROP (Ire) 5-9-2 (3*) S D Williams (2) *chsd ldr till wknd quickly o'r 2 out, tld off.* (100 to 1) 8
WITHOUT LEAVE 4-9-5 N Connorton (6) *slwly into strd, beh whn ran wide 5 out, sn tld off.* (100 to 1) 9
Dist: ½l, 2l, 2l, nk, 2½l, 2½l, 15l, 10l. 1m 54.40s. a 5.90s (9 Ran).
(Dave Douglas), N Tinkler

3056 Harcros Timber & Building Supplies Stayers Championship Series Handicap Qualifier Class E (0-70 3-y-o and up) £3,132 1¾m 19yds..........(2:45)

2729[8] EIGHTANDAHALF (Ire) [59] 4-9-10 J Fortune (5) *in tch, steady hdwy to ld 2 out, sn clr, eased fnl furlong.* (12 to 1 op 10 to 1 tchd 14 to 1) 1
2196* MONDRAGON [68] 3-9-6 J Lowe (3) *beh, hdwy 5 out, styd on to take second ins fnl furlong, not rch wnr.* (5 to 1 jt-fav op 9 to 2) 2
2201[2] LUKS AKURA [34] (v) 5-7-13 T Williams (1) *led, sn clr, hdd 2 out, no extr.* (5 to 1 jt-fav tchd 11 to 2) 3
2729 FAIRWAYS ON TARGET [56] 7-9-7 K Darley (9) *in tch till outpcd hfwy, styd on fnl 3 fs, nvr dngrs.* (20 to 1 op 16 to 1) 4
2888[3] GAY MING [34] 4-7-8 (5*) A Garth (4) *beh, styd on fnl 3 fs, not trble ldrs.* (9 to 1 op 7 to 1) 5
2735[5] BILBERRY [40] 4-8-5 J Carroll (7) *prmnt, stumbled badly aftr 2 fs, chsd ldr o'r 4 out till over two out.* (11 to 2 op 5 to 1 tchd 6 to 1) 6
2178[4] MEDIA STAR [30] 8-7-9 L Charnock (8) *beh, effrt 4 out, no hdwy.* (20 to 1) 7
2343[5] YOUNG GEORGE [37] (bl) 6-8-2 J Fanning (6) *nvr nr ldrs.* (16 to 1 op 12 to 1) 8
2632[6] PEANUTS PET [46] 8-8-11 K Fallon (11) *al beh.* (8 to 1 tchd 10 to 1) 9
2860[4] JULFAAR (USA) [50] 6-9-1 G Bardwell (10) *chsd ldrs till wknd 4 out.* (9 to 1 op 8 to 1) 10
2767[4] CARA'S PRIDE [67] 3-9-5 Dale Gibson (2) *chsd clr ldr till wknd o'r 4 out.* (13 to 2 op 5 to 1) 11
Dist: 3½l, 1½l, 2l, 1½l, 1½l, 8l, 8l, 6l, 3½l, 3l. 3m 4.80s. a 8.30s (11 Ran).
(Mick Burrowes), B Beasley

3057 Ruby Amateur Riders' Handicap Class F (0-70 4-y-o and up) £2,735 7f ....(3:15)

2789 PUSEY STREET BOY [43] 6-9-13 (7*) Mrs S Bosley (6) *trkd ldrs, led ins fnl furlong, kpt on wl.* (10 to 1 op 8 to 1) 1
2568[2] MU-ARRIK [50] 5-10-13 Mr R Hale (4) *slight ld till hdd ins fnl furlong, no extr.* (15 to 2 op 7 to 1 tchd 8 to 1) 2
PRINCESS MAXINE (Ire) [55] 4-11-4 Mr M Buckley (5) *al prmnt, chlgd o'r one out, ev ch till no extr ins fnl furlong.* (100 to 30 fav op 7 to 2) 3
2717[3] BILL MOON [54] 7-11-3 Miss J Feilden (12) *beh, hdwy hfwy, ev ch 2 out, kpt on same pace.* (6 to 1 tchd 11 to 2) 4
3002[3] PAULINUS [31] 5-9-1 (7*) Miss M Carson (3) *chsd ldrs, ev ch o'r one out, kpt on same pace.* (16 to 1 op 12 to 1) 5
636 AFFORDABLE [55] 5-11-4 Miss Diana Jones (1) *trkd ldrs, effrt 2 out, one paced.* (16 to 1 op 14 to 1) 6
2747 KELLY'S KITE [35] 5-9-5 (7*) Mr P Close (2) *slwly into strd, in tch, kpt on und pres fnl 2 fs.* (20 to 1 op 14 to 1) 7
2656[5] SHALABIA [61] 4-11-10 Mr D Parker (7) *mid-div, no hdwy fnl 2 fs.* (12 to 1 op 10 to 1) 8
2719[3] GUESSTIMATION (USA) [44] (bl) 4-10-7 Mrs L Pearce (14) *trkd ldrs, ev ch o'r one out, sn rdn and wknd.* (6 to 1 op 11 to 2 tchd 13 to 2) 9
2975[9] ROCK OPERA (Ire) [53] 5-11-2 Mrs M Cowdrey (10) *nvr dngrs.* (20 to 1 op 14 to 1) 10
2733[3] PATIENCE PLEASE [55] 4-10-11 (7*) Mrs S Easterby (9) *cl up till wknd 2 out.* (13 to 2 op 6 to 1 tchd 7 to 1) 11
2897[4] RESOLUTE BAY [65] (v) 7-12-0 Mr S Whitaker (8) *in tch, effrt 2 out, sn hrd rdn and btn.* (10 to 1 op 8 to 1) 12
3002 KICK ON MAJESTIC (Ire) [30] (bl) 4-9-0 (7*) Miss A Bycroft (11) *sn beh.* (66 to 1) 13
2183[7] CROMER'S EXPRESS [30] 4-9-0 (7*) Mrs D Wilkinson (13) *slwly into strd, swtchd lft aftr 2 fs, al beh.* (100 to 1) 14
Dist: 1l, ¾l, 1½l, ½l, 1½l, 1l, ½l, nk, nk, sht-hd. 1m 24.70s. a 2.90s (14 Ran).
SR: 35/39/42/36/11/30/7/31/13/ (M A Wilkins), J R Bosley

3058 G + H McGill Handicap Class D (0-75 4-y-o and up) £3,557 1m........(3:45)

2774[4] SELF EXPRESSION [57] 5-8-10 (7*) D Thomas (6) *hld up, hdwy o'r one out, ran on wl to ld cl hme.* (7 to 1 op 6 to 1 tchd 8 to 1) 1
2811* SPANISH VERDICT [68] 6-9-7 (7*) C Teague (3) *cl up, led o'r 3 out, kpt on wl fnl furlong, ct close hme.* (15 to 2 op 7 to 1 tchd 8 to 1) 2
2799[2] MAJAL (Ire) [57] 4-9-3 L Charnock (7) *trkd ldrs, effrt 2 out, ev ch one out, no extr.* (10 to 1 op 8 to 1) 3
2816[6] MBULWA [48] 7-8-3 (5*) J Tate (2) *led till hdd o'r 3 out, rdn 2 out, kpt on same pace.* (4 to 1 op 9 to 2) 4
2799[3] HAND ON HEART (Ire) [46] (v) 4-8-3 (3*) S Maloney (9) *hld up, effrt 2 out, styd on und pres fnl furlong, nrst finish.* (12 to 1 op 10 to 1 tchd 14 to 1) 5
2816* AVISHAYES (USA) [55] 6-9-1 K Darley (5) *dwlt, hld up, effrt and swtchd wl o'r one out, kpt on same pace.* (6 to 5 fav op 5 to 4) 6
2631[3] VANART [48] 4-8-8 S Webster (8) *prmnt till wknd 2 out.* (20 to 1 op 16 to 1) 7
2811[4] CHANTRY BELLINI [41] (bl) 4-8-1 J Fanning (1) *mid-div, rdn 2 out, sn wknd.* (16 to 1 op 14 to 1) 8
1307 MARTINI EXECUTIVE [54] (bl) 5-9-0 K Fallon (4) *mid-div, pushed alng hfwy, wknd 2 out.* (20 to 1 op 16 to 1) 9
Dist: Nk, 1½l, sht-hd, 1l, sht-hd, 4l, 1½l, nk. 1m 36.70s. a 1.80s (9 Ran).
SR: 28/38/22/12/7/15/ (Jonathan Ramsden), Mrs J R Ramsden

3059 Emerald Limited Stakes Class F (0-65 3-y-o) £2,556 5f................(4:15)

2699[5] TREVORSNINEPOINTS 8-9 K Darley (4) *swtchd lft strt, made all, rcd alone far side frm hfwy, ran on wl.* (3 to 1 op 11 to 4 tchd 100 to 30) 1
2851[6] LIDA'S DELIGHT (Ire) 8-7 (7*) P Johnson (5) *sn pushed alng, kpt on wl to take second entering fnl furlong, no ch wth wnr.* (14 to 1 tchd 20 to 1) 2
2711[2] SOBER LAD (Ire) (v) 9-0 J Carroll (3) *in tch, rdn 2 out, one paced.* (15 to 8 fav op 7 to 4 tchd 2 to 1) 3
2967[5] DAYJUZ (Ire) (h,bl) 9-0 S Perks (6) *led main grp till no extr entering fnl furlong.* (11 to 2 op 5 to 1 tchd 6 to 1) 4
2699[9] DISCO BOY (bl) 9-0 A Mackay (2) *in tch till wknd entering fnl furlong.* (14 to 1 op 12 to 1) 5
2829[9] BOLD COUNTY 8-9 T Williams (1) *sn pushed alng, beh frm hfwy.* (3 to 1 op 11 to 4) 6
Dist: 2½l, ½l, 1½l, nk, 6l. 58.00s. a 1.30s (6 Ran).
SR: 29/24/22/16/15/-/ (T S Child), Mrs M Reveley

3060 Opal Limited Stakes Class E (0-65 3-y-o and up) £3,106 6f.............(4:45)

2151[2] QUINSIGIMOND 3-8-9 M Birch (9) *prmnt, chsd ldr frm 3 out, led entering fnl furlong, ran on wl.* (5 to 1 op 4 to 1) 1
2889[3] SENSE OF PRIORITY (v) 4-9-5 K Darley (7) *led till hdd entering fnl furlong, no extr.* (16 to 1 op 12 to 1 tchd 20 to 1) 2
2934* PEACEFULL REPLY (USA) 3-9-0 S Perks (10) *in tch, effrt o'r 2 out, hrd rdn over one out, kpt on fnl furlong.* (7 to 1 op 5 to 1 tchd 8 to 1) 3
2811[3] ROYAL GIRL 6-9-0 N Connorton (11) *in tch, effrt 3 out, kpt on fnl furlong, not rch ldrs.* (5 to 1 op 4 to 1 tchd 11 to 2) 4
2934[3] BIRCHWOOD SUN (bl) 3-9-0 J Weaver (1) *beh till styd on wl fnl 2 fs, nrst finish.* (14 to 1 op 12 to 1) 5
2975[5] ASHGORE 3-9-0 T Williams (8) *in tch, rdn hfwy, no hdwy.* (11 to 2 op 9 to 2) 6
2553[6] ARABAT 6-9-5 K Fallon (4) *beh till some late hdwy, not trble ldrs.* (16 to 1 op 14 to 1) 7
2851[3] OUR SHADEE (USA) (bl) 3-9-0 M Wigham (2) *chsd ldrs till wknd 3 out.* (25 to 1 op 16 to 1) 8
2724[2] ALTA VICTORIA (Ire) 3-8-6 (3*) O Pears (6) *chsd ldr till wknd 3 out.* (12 to 1 op 10 to 1) 9
2811[7] GENTLE HERO (USA) 7-8-12 (7*) I Jardine (3) *al beh.* (25 to 1 op 16 to 1) 10
2105[9] HELLO HOBSON'S (Ire) (bl) 3-8-9 A Culhane (5) *in tch till wknd 3 out.* (11 to 4 fav op 5 to 1 tchd 5 to 2) 11
Dist: 1½l, ½l, 2½l, ¾l, 3l, 1½l, 1½l, 1½l, 2l, 6l. 1m 10.10s. a 0.40s (11 Ran).
SR: 40/44/37/27/23/12/11/-/-/ (A E T Mines), Sir Mark Prescott

ROSCOMMON (IRE) (yielding)
Tuesday August 3rd

3061 International Reunion Claiming Race (3-y-o and up) £2,245 1½m......(6:30)

2692[7] TOAST AND HONEY (Ire) 4-8-13 (6*) C Everard (9) (12 to 1) 1
2782[4] DARCY'S THATCHER 9-9-4 M J Kinane (3).... (9 to 4 fav) 2
2903[4] HERMES GOLD (Ire) 3-8-0 W J Supple (1)......... (3 to 1) 3
2841 PYLON SPARKS (bl) 8-9-6 J P Murtagh (7)........ (8 to 1) 4
2902[5] SPLENDID KING (Ire) 3-9-3 S Craine (4)........... (7 to 1) 5
2221[5] ROOTSMAN (Ire) 3-7-11 (8*) G M Moylan (10)..... (20 to 1) 6
1652[4] TOUCHING MOMENT (Ire) 3-8-7 P V Gilson (5).....(6 to 1) 7
2496[7] DIGNIFIED (Ire) (bl) 3-7-10 (4*) W J Smith (8)...... (16 to 1) 8
2515[5] VALLEY TUFF (Ire) 5-9-0 B Coogan (2)........... (33 to 1) 9
NOUKTAIYA (Fr) 3-7-12 (6*) J A Heffernan (6)..... (10 to 1) 10
Dist: Nk, 1½l, hd, ½l. 2m 46.40s. (10 Ran).
(K Crow), Patrick Martin

3062 Roscommon (Fillies) Maiden (3-y-o) £2,762 1¼m.................. (7:00)

LIMBO LADY (USA) 8-8 (6*) J J Behan (10)........ (8 to 1) 1
2249[4] GLAMOROUS BRIDE (Fr) 9-0 W J Supple (11)..(6 to 4 fav) 2
2743[4] SHPEEL (Ire) 9-0 P Shanahan (4)................. (8 to 1) 3
2743[9] ANIMATE (Ire) 9-0 S Craine (8)................. (25 to 1) 4
NORDIC ABU (Ire) 8-6 (8*) T E Durcan (5)........(12 to 1) 5
2743[5] QUIET CONFIDENCE (Ire) 8-10 (4*) P Carberry (9).. (8 to 1) 6
2518[3] LADY NOBLE (Ire) 9-0 J F Egan (2)............... (9 to 1) 7
2956[8] HAIL TO HOME (Ire) 9-0 N G McCullagh (6).......(33 to 1) 8
2810[3] FESTIVAL GIRL (Ire) 9-0 R Hughes (1)............ (4 to 1) 9
TROPICAL DESERT (Ire) 8-8 (6*) P P Murphy (3)...(25 to 1) 10

2743 CRISSY (Ire) 9-0 K J Manning (7)................(25 to 1) 11
Dist: ½l, 2l, 6l, 1l. 2m 19.90s. (11 Ran).
(John Muldoon), P Aspell

3063 O'Gara Royal Hotel Handicap (0-80 3-y-o and up) £2,935 2m........ (7:30)

2186[8] OFTEN AHEAD (Ire) [-] 5-9-6 P V Gilson (1)........ (7 to 1) 1
2346* SAFE CONDUCT (Ire) [-] 3-9-1 J P Murtagh (9).....(7 to 1) 2
2296[9] MILLMOUNT (Ire) [-] (bl) 3-8-0 (4*) W J Smith (8)...(16 to 1) 3
2143[7] NANARCH (USA) [-] 9-9-2 W J Supple (7)..........(10 to 1) 4
2900* LOSHIAN (Ire) [-] 4-9-8 (6*,10ex) J A Heffernan (5) (Evens fav) 5
2693 RYE HILL QUEEN (Ire) [-] 3-7-5 (2*) D G O'Shea (11) (50 to 1) 6
2496[3] L-WAY FIRST (Ire) [-] 3-6-13 (8*) G M Moylan (4)...(25 to 1) 7
2842[7] GREEK CHIME (Ire) [-] 4-8-6 J F Egan (3).........(14 to 1) 8
2900[7] AEGEAN FANFARE (Ire) [-] 4-8-13 R Hughes (6)...(14 to 1) 9
852[2] SYLVIA FOX [-] 6-9-1 M J Kinane (2)..............(11 to 2) 10
2036[6] NORDIC SUCCESS (Ire) [-] 3-7-12 (2*) R M Burke (12)
....(25 to 1) 11
Dist: Nk, 1½l, 4l, ½l. 3m 51.50s. (11 Ran).
(N Stassen), Joseph M Canty

3064 Castlerea E.B.F. Race (2-y-o) £3,107 7f ....(8:30)

2778[2] GAINSBOROUGH'S BOY (Ire) (bl) 8-10 M J Kinane (1)
....(Evens fav) 1
2701* BACK FROM HEAVEN (Ire) 8-13 K J Manning (4)... (5 to 2) 2
571[9] YAHTHAB (Ire) 8-10 W J Supple (3)...............(5 to 2) 3
STRANGFORD LOUGH (Ire) 8-10 P Shanahan (2) (20 to 1) 4
Dist: ¾l, 3l, 6l. 1m 37.90s. (4 Ran).
(Lady Clague), John M Oxx

BRIGHTON (firm)
Wednesday August 4th
Going Correction: MINUS 0.30 sec. per fur.

3065 Black Rock Conditions Stakes Class D (3-y-o and up) £3,406 6f 209yds. .(2:00)

2732* POWERFUL EDGE 4-9-4 L Dettori (5) *wtd wth, prog 2 fs out, shaken up to ld appr last, pushed out.*
..................................(5 to 4 on tchd Evens) 1
2572[7] PEMBROKE (USA) 3-9-6 Pat Eddery (3) *wtd wth, effrt and cld o'r one furlong out, chlgd ins last, al hld.*
..................................(5 to 2 tchd 9 to 4) 2
2854[7] DOUBLE BLUE 4-9-2 T Williams (1) *chsd ldr, hrd rdn o'r 2 fs out, ev ch appr last, one pace*....(5 to 1 tchd 6 to 1) 3
3008[3] ROCKY WATERS (USA) 4-9-6 B Rouse (4) *set fst pace till hdd and wknd appr fnl furlong*.... (10 to 1 op 8 to 1) 4
2563 SULA MOON 3-8-3 J Quinn (2) *strted slwly, sn rdn alng, al beh*........................... (150 to 1 op 100 to 1) 5
Dist: Nk, 2l, 3½l, 25l. 1m 20.90s. a 0.90s (5 Ran).
SR: 59/60/50/43/-/ (J C Smith), I A Balding

3066 Goring Selling Handicap Stakes Class G (0-60 3-y-o and up) £2,070 1m 3f 196yds........................ (2:30)

2800[2] PIE HATCH (Ire) [40] (bl) 4-9-4 G Duffield (2) *dwlt, sn trkd ldrs, led o'r 6 fs out, rdn appr last, ran on wl.*
......................(5 to 2 fav op 7 to 2 tchd 4 to 1) 1
2658* FANATICAL (USA) [43] (bl) 7-9-7 W Newnes (9) *cl up, trkd wnr frm hfwy, rdn 2 fs out, not quicken.*
.........................(9 to 2 op 7 to 2 tchd 5 to 1) 2
1956 BY ARRANGEMENT (Ire) [45] 4-9-9 L Dettori (4) *prmnt, chsd ldg pair 4 fs out, hrd rdn and no imprsn frm 3 out.*
.... (16 to 1 op 7 to 1) 3
2658[6] FLASH OF STRAW (Ire) [32] (bl) 4-8-10 S Whitworth (5) *beh, hrd rdn and kpt on one pace fnl 3 fs.*
.... (10 to 1 op 6 to 1) 4
2865[6] WEDNESDAYS AUCTION (Ire) [45] 5-9-2 (7*) T G McLaughlin (1) *beh, hrd rdn and kpt on one pace fnl 2 fs.*
.......................(10 to 1 op 14 to 1 tchd 20 to 1) 5
2048[9] MOLLY SPLASH [46] 6-9-3 (7*) J D Smith (8) *in tch 7 fs, sn lost pl*............................(9 to 2 tchd 5 to 1) 6
2662 STANE STREET (Ire) [30] 5-8-8 J Reid (3) *led for o'r 5 fs, wknd*.............................(9 to 1 op 10 to 1) 7
1712[9] APRIL CITY [45] 4-9-9 D Holland (6) *rear, rdn hfwy, wknd o'r 3 fs out*........................ (12 to 1 op 7 to 1) 8
2415[7] GO FORUM [29] 8-8-7 Pat Eddery (7) *in tch, effrt o'r 3 fs out, sn no imprsn, eased whn btn.*
.........................(9 to 2 op 4 to 1 tchd 5 to 1) 9
Dist: 2½l, 8l, 1½l, ½l, 3½l, 8l, 3l, 5l. 2m 32.50s. a 5.00s (9 Ran).
SR: 18/16/2/-/-/-/ (Miss Elizabeth Aldous), Sir Mark Prescott

3067 Brighton Challenge Cup Handicap Class C (0-95 4-y-o and up) £5,588 1m 3f 196yds........................ (3:00)

2239* GLIDE PATH (USA) [81] 4-9-10 M Hills (4) *trkd ldrs, shaken up to ld 2 fs out, sn clr, eased ins last.*
.... (3 to 1 fav op 9 to 4 tchd 100 to 30) 1
2239 BLACKPATCH HILL [84] 4-9-13 W Carson (7) *keen hold, trkd ldr, led 3 fs out to 2 out, no ch wth wnr.*
.........................(6 to 1 op 5 to 1 tchd 7 to 1) 2
2727* LOOKINGFORARAINBOW (Ire) [59] 5-8-2 J Quinn (2) *hld up in tch, effrt o'r 2 fs out, ran on one pace.*
.........................(4 to 1 op 7 to 2 tchd 9 to 2) 3
2617 DURSHAN (USA) [78] 4-9-7 J Reid (5) *led to 3 fs out, rdn and one pace*..................... (12 to 1 op 16 to 1) 4
2625[2] CRYSTAL CROSS (USA) [85] 4-10-0 L Dettori (3) *in tch, pushed alng 4 fs out, btn o'r 2 out.*
........................(11 to 2 op 5 to 1 tchd 6 to 1) 5
2795[7] PHARAMINEUX [77] 7-9-6 T Quinn (6) *hld up, prog 4 fs out, sn rdn and btn*...........(7 to 2 op 4 to 1 tchd 5 to 1) 6
2239 FIELDRIDGE [82] 4-9-11 Pat Eddery (1) *keen hold, trkd ldrs till rdn and wknd o'r 2 fs out*........(9 to 1 op 8 to 1) 7
Dist: 2l, 2l, ¾l, 3½l, nk, 6l. 2m 31.50s. a 4.00s (7 Ran).
SR: 34/33/4/21/21/12/5/ (The Jampot Partnership), J W Hills

3068 Stanmer Claiming Stakes Class F (3-y-o) £2,243 7f 214yds........... (3:30)

2928 THE LITTLE FERRET 9-7 B Rouse (1) *made all, clr one furlong out, ran on wl.*
....................(100 to 30 op 5 to 2 tchd 7 to 2) 1
2724[4] PONTEVECCHIO MODA 8-0 W Carson (7) *keen hold, trkd ldrs, rdn o'r 2 fs out, ran on ins last, no ch wth wnr.*
.........................(3 to 1 op 7 to 4 tchd 7 to 2) 2
3007[9] BAN RI (Ire) 7-10 T Williams (5) *keen hold, trkd ldrs, rdn o'r 2 fs out, styd on one pace*.....(10 to 1 tchd 14 to 1) 3
2366[5] DANNY BLUE (Ire) (bl) 8-11 A Munro (2) *chsd wnr, rdn and one pace fnl 2 fs*........(11 to 2 op 8 to 1 tchd 9 to 2) 4
2023[9] FIVEOFIVE (Ire) 8-4 Pat Eddery (4) *hld up, effrt whn not clr run appr fnl furlong, no ch aftr.*
....................(2 to 1 fav op 9 to 4 tchd 5 to 2) 5
SEATTLE AFFAIR (Ire) 8-10 A Clark (8) *chsd ldrs till rdn and wknd o'r 3 fs out*.....(20 to 1 op 10 to 1 tchd 25 to 1) 6
1861 LOBELIA (Ire) 7-5 (5*) D Wright (6) *dwlt, chsd ldrs till wknd rpdly hfwy*....................... (33 to 1 op 16 to 1) 7
Dist: 3l, 1l, hd, 2l, 8l, 25l. 1m 35.90s. a 3.50s (7 Ran).
SR: 19/-/-/-/ (K Higson), R Hannon

3069 Jimmy Heal Memorial Trophy Nursery Handicap Class D (2-y-o) £3,660 5f 59yds......................... (4:00)

2886* SELHURSTPARK FLYER (Ire) [-] 8-13 (7ex) W Carson (3) *led one furlong, pushed alng hfwy, led appr last, sn clr, cmftbly*........(6 to 4 on op 7 to 4 on tchd 5 to 4 on) 1
2500* MARJORIE'S MEMORY (Ire) [-] 9-7 J Reid (1) *hld up, effrt and rdn wl o'r one furlong out, one pace.*
.................................(2 to 1 tchd 6 to 4) 2
1837[4] JUST GREENWICH [-] (bl) 8-0 A Munro (2) *led aftr one furlong, clr hfwy, hdd and wknd appr last.*
.........................(9 to 2 op 5 to 1 tchd 6 to 1) 3
Dist: 4l, 2½l. 1m 2.20s. a 2.10s (3 Ran).
SR: 26/18/-/ (Chris Deuters), J Berry

3070 Hassocks Handicap Class D (0-80 3-y-o) £3,231 6f 209yds............. (4:30)

2912[3] AHJAY [48] 7-9 J Quinn (2) *hld up last, prog to ld one furlong out, held on wl*............(10 to 1 op 12 to 1) 1
2897* MR NEVERMIND (Ire) [66] 8-13 (6ex) B Rouse (5) *wtd wth, prog 2 fs out, ev ch ins last, no extr nr finish.*
..............................(5 to 2 fav op 2 to 1) 2
2638[6] COALISLAND [64] (bl) 8-11 J Weaver (1) *chsd ldr, hrd rdn 2 fs out, ev ch appr last, not quicken, eased whn btn.*
.................(10 to 1 tchd 9 to 1 and 12 to 1) 3
2770* MISS GORGEOUS (Ire) [74] 9-4 (3*) Emma O'Gorman (6) *set fst pace till hdd and wknd one furlong out.*
..................................(5 to 1 op 4 to 1) 4
1859[4] FINAL FRONTIER (Ire) [72] 9-5 T Quinn (7) *chsd ldrs, rdn o'r 2 fs out, sn btn*.......... (4 to 1 op 9 to 2 tchd 6 to 1) 5
2832* DAILY SPORT DON [67] 9-0 A McGlone (4) *chsd ldrs, rdn and wknd 3 fs out*.......................(7 to 1 op 5 to 1) 6
2787[3] PISTON (Ire) [72] 9-5 B Raymond (3) *chsd ldrs, rdn and wknd wl o'r 2 fs out*.....(7 to 2 op 4 to 1 tchd 9 to 2) 7
Dist: ½l, 6l, 3l, 1½l, 6l, 1l. 1m 21.50s. a 1.50s (7 Ran).
SR: 27/43/23/24/17/-/-/ (R J Thomas), D A Wilson

FAIRYHOUSE (IRE) (good to firm)
Wednesday August 4th

3071 Ratoath EBF Fillies Maiden (2-y-o) £3,797 7f..................... (5:30)

2742[7] NEWPORT MADAM (Ire) 9-0 S Craine (8).........(12 to 1) 1
2402[5] ALJAWZA (USA) 9-0 M J Kinane (7)...............(3 to 1) 2
2804 RAZIDA (Ire) 9-0 K J Manning (17)...............(10 to 1) 3
ICY TUNDRA 9-0 R Hughes (14)...................(7 to 1) 4
CLARADANE (Ire) 9-0 J P Murtagh (18)........ (7 to 4 fav) 5
SHEER STYLE (Ire) 8-10 (4*) P Carberry (15)...... (14 to 1) 6
2982[8] MAKE THAT CALL (Ire) 9-0 P V Gilson (13).........(33 to 1) 7
2880[4] AXLENO (Ire) 9-0 J F Egan (6)....................(6 to 1) 8
SENDER VICTORIOUS (Ire) 8-8 (6*) J J Behan (2)..(14 to 1) 9
2742 SMART ROSIE (Ire) 9-0 D V Smith (9)............. (40 to 1) 10
FAYR DILLY (Ire) 8-8 (6*) R V Skelly (10)........... (25 to 1) 11
1994[4] SCHONBEIN (Ire) 9-0 W J Supple (1)..............(10 to 1) 12
DREAMS OF SUMMER (Ire) 9-0 P Shanahan (11)..(16 to 1) 13

MONTEGO BAY (Ire) 9-0 J C Deegan (16)........ (20 to 1) 14
2804 GENEVIEVE FLEUR (Ire) 8-12 (2*) D G O'Shea (12) (25 to 1) 15
GROUND ATTACK (Ire) 9-0 N G McCullagh (3).... (25 to 1) 16
REMAIN ANONYMOUS (Ire) 8-4 (10*) D A O'Sullivan (4) ....(33 to 1) 17
1792[9] COUNTESS OUNAVARRA (Ire) 9-0 J D Eddery (5) (20 to 1) 18
Dist: 1l, sht-hd, 1l, 1½l. 1m 27.88s. (18 Ran).

(Mrs Anna Doyle), Liam Browne

3072 Platinum Race (Listed) (3-y-o and up) £8,627 1m.................... (6:00)

2878 KAYFA (Ire) 4-9-5 P Carberry (5) *made all, quickened whn chlgd one and a half fs out, jst hld on*.........(8 to 1) 1
2878[6] MILLIE'S CHOICE (Ire) 4-9-0 W J Supple (1) *rear till str brst to chal 2 fs out, jst fld*..........................(6 to 1) 2
2606[6] NORDIC FOX (Ire) 3-8-10 K J Manning (6) *trkd ldrs till prog to chal 2 fs out, rdn and kpt on*................ (5 to 1) 3
2809[4] ARABIC TREASURE (USA) (bl) 3-8-10 M J Kinane (4) *trkd ldrs, not much room entering strt, rdn and wknd one furlong out*.................................. (5 to 4 fav) 4
1808 COLOUR PARTY (USA) 3-8-10 R Hughes (2)........ (14 to 1) 5
2878[5] SALMON EILE (Ire) 5-9-8 J P Murtagh (3) *rdn in rear 2 fs out, styd on cl hme*.......................... (7 to 2) 6
Dist: Sht-hd, nk, 2l, 1l. 1m 42.90s. (6 Ran).

(Vincent Loughnane), Noel Meade

3073 Tattersalls Auction Race (2-y-o) £3,452 7f...................... (6:30)

1044[7] ZIRAVELLO (Ire) 9-3 M J Kinane (7)............... (7 to 1) 1
2319[3] WAQAR (Ire) 8-5 P Shanahan (22)................. (8 to 1) 2
2959[2] NORTHERN FRONTIER (Ire) 7-13 (6*) J A Heffernan (15) .... (5 to 2 fav) 3
2487[4] MASCOT 8-2 J F Egan (10).......................... (12 to 1) 4
3030[5] QUASIMODO (Ire) (bl) 8-5 P V Gilson (21).........(11 to 2) 5
1045[7] TRIMBLEMILL (Ire) 8-11 B Coogan (2)............(8 to 1) 6
SEAFORTH (Ire) 8-11 R Hughes (20)............... (14 to 1) 7
2319[7] AVALIN (Ire) 8-2 P Lowry (18)..................... (25 to 1) 8
2666[6] BUTLER BRENNAN (Ire) 8-3 (2*) R M Burke (14)...(12 to 1) 9
2745[3] LYDIA MC (Ire) 8-8 W J Supple (3)................ (6 to 1) 10
PERFECT CADENCE (Ire) 8-0 (2*) D G O'Shea (9)..(20 to 1) 11
2319 INISHMANN (Ire) 8-5 J C Deegan (12).............. (33 to 1) 12
2666[2] ROYAL THIMBLE (Ire) 8-2 A J Nolan (5)........... (8 to 1) 13
2701 NANCYS WOOD (Ire) 7-8 (8*) R T Fitzpatrick (11).. (40 to 1) 14
2840[8] RING-A-RUAN (Ire) 9-3 K J Manning (13).........(20 to 1) 15
2701 I HAVE A DREAM (Ire) 8-8 D V Smith (19).......... (20 to 1) 16
DR LEUNT (Ire) 7-13 (6*) R V Skelly (23).......... (25 to 1) 17
2487[6] SAWDUST (Ire) 8-2 Joanna Morgan (8).............. (16 to 1) 18
2294[8] SOCIAL GATHERING (Ire) 8-5 (6*) J J Behan (17).. (20 to 1) 19
2487[8] BENAZIR LADY (Ire) 7-10 (6*) P P Murphy (1)..... (20 to 1) 20
2487[7] MEGAN'S DREAM (Ire) 8-1 (4*) W J Smith (4)..... (25 to 1) 21
JINGLING SILVER (Ire) 7-11 (8*) J J Mullins (16)... (12 to 1) 22
1924[8] GREENRIDGE COURT (Ire) 7-9[1] (8*) B A Hunter (6) (50 to 1) 23
Dist: 3l, hd, ¾l, 1l. 1m 27.90s. (23 Ran).

(Andrea Schiavi), D K Weld

3074 Rathbeggan Maiden (3-y-o and up) £2,762 7f...................... (7:00)

1855[2] STRATEGIC TIMING (Ire) (bl) 3-8-11 M J Kinane (4) ....(7 to 4 on) 1
2248 LOWLACK (bl) 3-8-11 N G McCullagh (6).........(20 to 1) 2
1236 SKERRIES BELL 3-8-11 P V Gilson (10)........... (10 to 1) 3
2879 NORDIC SAINT (Ire) 4-9-0 (6*) J A Heffernan (5)... (13 to 2) 4
2667[7] TEGEMEZA (Ire) 3-8-9 (2*) R M Burke (8).......... (12 to 1) 5
2700[7] BOSSY PATRICIA (Ire) 3-8-11 D V Smith (1).......(50 to 1) 6
2843[4] LOOK NONCHALANT (Ire) 4-8-13 (4*) P Carberry (3) ....(13 to 2) 7
2903[7] LADYS BID (Ire) 3-8-11 J F Egan (11)............ (20 to 1) 8
2810[6] PAKED (Ire) 3-8-7 (4*) W J Smith (12)..............(66 to 1) 9
2700[8] I'M NO LADY (Ire) 3-8-11 N Byrne (13)........... (66 to 1) 10
ELEGANT NORA (Ire) 3-8-5 (6*) B J Walsh (7)..... (25 to 1) 11
2667[4] ELLE A TED (Ire) 3-8-11 R Hughes (2)............. (8 to 1) 12
2902 VERIFIED (Ire) 3-8-11 J P Murtagh (9).............(20 to 1) 13
Dist: 1½l, sht-hd, sht-hd, 5½l. 1m 27.60s. (13 Ran).

(Moyglare Stud Farm), D K Weld

3075 Horseshow Handicap (0-85 3-y-o) £2,762 1m...................... (7:30)

1549[2] SUAVE GROOM (Ire) [-] (bl) 9-4 M J Kinane (3)..... (4 to 1) 1
2810* GENERAL CHAOS (Ire) [-] 9-1 (3ex) P V Gilson (4).. (4 to 1) 2
2664* SLIGHTLY SCRUFFY (Ire) [-] (bl) 8-9 (5ex) J C Deegan (5) ....(8 to 1) 3
2922[3] WALLY WALLENSKY (Ire) [-] 8-9 (4*) P Carberry (9) ....(11 to 4 fav) 4
2780[5] IBDA [-] 8-8 W J Supple (8)......................... (16 to 1) 5
2140 MISS MARESE (Ire) [-] (bl) 7-9 (6*) R V Skelly (10).. (25 to 1) 6
2903[5] ICEFLOW (Fr) [-] (bl) 8-3 J F Egan (7)............. (14 to 1) 7
1574[9] VERITABLE GALLERY (Ire) [-] 7-12[2] N G McCullagh (6) ....(8 to 1) 8
KAR OR [-] 9-5 R Hughes (1)......................... (12 to 1) 9
2587 SOUNDPROOF (Ire) [-] 8-11 (6*) J J Behan (2).....(10 to 1) 10
Dist: 1l, 1l, 1½l, 2½l. 1m 42.80s. (10 Ran).

(Dr Anne J F Gillespie), D K Weld

3076 Derrinstown Apprentice Series Handicap (0-75 3-y-o and up) £3,797 1m 1f .... (8:00)

2957[2] WANDERING THOUGHTS (Ire) [-] 4-9-6 (4*) J R Barry (6) .... (13 to 8 fav) 1
2451* TINCO PALENO [-] 9-9-4 R M Burke (7)........... (7 to 1) 2
2665* THE BOWER (Ire) [-] (bl) 4-8-0 (6*,4ex) P M Donohue (21) ....(5 to 1) 3
2841 HANG A RIGHT [-] 6-9-9 (4*) T P Treacy (15)...... (16 to 1) 4
2322[7] DAHAR'S LOVE (USA) [-] (bl) 4-7-8 (8*) J P Cornally (17) ....(10 to 1) 5
2901[6] BOLERO DANCER (Ire) [-] 5-8-1 (4*) P P Murphy (16) ....(20 to 1) 6
BLUES COMPOSER (Ire) [-] 4-8-5 (4*) B J Walsh (5) (12 to 1) 7
2957[4] BRACKLOON BOY (Ire) [-] 4-9-2 (4*) R V Skelly (9)..(8 to 1) 8
2556[6] ALDENA (Ire) [-] 3-7-8 D G O'Shea (19)............(33 to 1) 9
2517[4] TWO MAGPIES [-] (bl) 6-7-4 (6*) G M Moylan (12)...(8 to 1) 10
2451[6] ARDLEA HOUSE (Ire) [-] 4-7-6[3] (4*) J J Behan (13) (10 to 1) 11
2665[3] VICOSA (Ire) [-] 4-7-10[5] (6*) P J Smullen (3)........ (7 to 1) 12
870[8] GLAS AGUS OR (Ire) [-] 3-8-13 (2*) J A Heffernan (10) ....(10 to 1) 13
2141 CHAMPAGNE NIGHT (Fr) [-] 3-8-6 (6*) B Fenton (18) ....(20 to 1) 14
2741[3] TORCH SINGER [-] 3-7-11 (6*) J J Mullins (4)...... (12 to 1) 15
2692 WINTER DREAMS (Ire) [-] 4-8-2 (8*) T Hagger (20) (14 to 1) 16
ELEGANT ISLE [-] 9-9-6 (2*) W J Smith (1)........ (25 to 1) 17
1651[3] SUTTON CENTENARY (Ire) [-] 5-7-4 (6*) B J Halligan (14) ....(14 to 1) 18
Dist: ¾l, 3l, 3l, 1l. 1m 54.90s. (18 Ran).

(W Mythen), A P O'Brien

3077 Greenpark Maiden (Q.R.) (3-y-o and up) £2,762 1m 5f............... (8:30)

FERRAGOSTO (Ire) 4-11-8 Mr P Fenton (2)....... (13 to 8) 1
EASTER SIXTEEN 7-11-3 (5*) Mr J A Nash (7).....(10 to 1) 2
1963[6] DARK HYACINTH (Ire) (bl) 3-10-4 (3*) Mr R Naylon (6) ....(10 to 1) 3
LEAD ME LEAD MENOT (USA) 4-11-0 (5*) Mr D Valentine (4) ....(8 to 1) 4
COMBINE CALL 6-11-8 Mr T Mullins (1)..........(10 to 1) 5
2324 CARES OF TOMORROW 6-11-1 (7*) Mr F Cooper (8) ....(12 to 1) 6
WALK RITE BACK (Ire) 4-11-1 (7*) Mr J A Hayes (5) (10 to 1) 7
LEAP INTO SPRING (Ire) 4-11-8 Mr A P O'Brien (3) .... (6 to 4 fav) 8
THE GREY NEWT (Ire) 4-11-1 (7*) Mr A K Wyse (12) (25 to 1) 9
KAWA-KAWA 6-10-12 (7*) Mr J M Collier (15)..... (33 to 1) 10
2693[6] SIR ALFRED (USA) 8-11-1 (7*) Mr G Kingston (9).. (25 to 1) 11
2958[8] LUCK OF A LADY (Ire) 4-11-9[11] (7*) Mr I McCathy (11) ....(33 to 1) 12
ARI'S FASHION 8-10-12 (7*) Mr B M Cash (13)....(33 to 1) 13
ROYAL OUTING (Ire) 4-11-1 (7*) Miss A L Moore (10) ....(25 to 1) 14
2324 GLAD'S NIGHT (Ire) 4-11-0 (5*) Mrs J M Mullins (14) (20 to 1) pu
Dist: 1l, 4l, 5l, 5l. 2m 51.40s. (15 Ran).

(D H W Dobson), J S Bolger

KEMPTON (good)
Wednesday August 4th
Going Correction: MINUS 0.30 sec. per fur.

3078 LBC Newstalk 97.3 FM Apprentice Handicap Class F (0-70 3-y-o and up) £3,054 1½m.................. (6:00)

2685[3] PRINCESS ERMYN [42] 4-8-3 (3*) B Russell (10) *made all, pushed out fnl furlong, jst hld on*. .... (14 to 1 op 16 to 1 tchd 20 to 1) 1
2942* SUPREME MASTER [65] 3-8-13 (5*,3ex) Mark Denaro (9) *mid-div, ran on o'r 2 fs out, sstnd chal fnl furlong, jst fld*.................. (9 to 2 fav op 4 to 1 tchd 5 to 1) 2
2834[4] HALLOW FAIR [32] 8-7-10[1] F Norton (5) *slwly into strd, hdwy o'r 4 fs out, kpt on one pace frm 2 out*. .... (20 to 1 op 12 to 1 tchd 33 to 1) 3
2733[9] PICKLES [43] 5-8-7 B Doyle (1) *steadied strt, hdwy 4 fs out, rdn and not quicken appr last*. (8 to 1 op 6 to 1) 4
2755 CHILD STAR (Fr) [44] 4-8-3 (5*) S McCarthy (15) *in 3rd to 2 fs out, no extr und pres*..............(20 to 1 op 14 to 1) 5
2669[6] SPANISH REFUGE [56] 3-8-9 D Harrison (4) *mid-div, effrt o'r 2 fs out, not rch ldrs*..............(6 to 1 op 9 to 2) 6
1951 SIMPLY (Ire) [44] 4-8-3 (5*) L Carter (7) *pressed wnr till wknd 2 fs out*........... (13 to 2 op 9 to 2 tchd 7 to 1) 7
2942[7] VITAL CLUE (USA) [64] 6-9-9 (5*) D Gibbs (3) *in tch till lost pl o'r 4 fs out*........ (16 to 1 op 20 to 1 tchd 33 to 1) 8
2615* HALHAM TARN (Ire) [70] 3-9-4 (5*) Tracey Purseglove (8) *improved o'r 4 fs out, effrt und pres over 2 out, btn appr last*.................. (6 to 1 op 9 to 2 tchd 7 to 1) 9
MAGSOOD [44] 8-8-5 (3*) J D Smith (14) *slwly into strd, reco'red to race mid-div, no prog frm 3 fs out*. .... (50 to 1 op 33 to 1 tchd 66 to 1) 10
2415[3] CATHOS (Fr) [36] 8-7-9 (5*) Sharon Millard (6) *slwly into strd, al rear*.......................... (14 to 1 op 8 to 1) 11

2544* RIMOUSKI [37] 5-8-1 D Wright (12) *slwly into strd, nvr rch ldrs*..........(12 to 1 op 8 to 1) 12
2383[7] CANDARELA [42] 3-7-9[2] N Gwilliams (13) *ldg grp till wknd wl o'r 2 fs out*..........(33 to 1 tchd 50 to 1) 13
2972[7] BROUGHTONS FORMULA [57] 3-8-7 (3*) D McCabe (11) *al beh*..........(16 to 1 op 12 to 1) 14
Dist: Hd, 3½l, 1½l, 1½l, 4l, 1½l, hd, 3l, 1½l, sht-hd. 2m 33.90s. a 2.90s (14 Ran).
SR: 27/38/9/17/15/8/4/23/12/ (J Daniels), M Dixon

3079 EBF Rivermead Maiden Stakes Class D (2-y-o) £4,413 7f..........(6:30)

2453[2] BUMAAN (Ire) 9-0 R Hills (13) *made virtually all, rdn out and styd on ins fnl furlong.*..........(15 to 2 op 6 to 1 tchd 8 to 1) 1
STASH THE CASH (Ire) 9-0 S Raymont (4) *pressed wnr most of way, rdn and not quicken wl ins fnl furlong.*..........(20 to 1 op 16 to 1 tchd 25 to 1) 2
2419[5] BONAIGUA (Ire) 9-0 M Hills (2) *hld up in tch, rdn alng o'r 2 fs out, not quicken ins last.*..........(11 to 1 op 10 to 1 tchd 14 to 1) 3
2325[3] DUELLO 9-0 L Dettori (7) *handily plcd, chlgd and not much room wl o'r one furlong out, swtchd rght and not quicken*..........(10 to 1 op 8 to 1) 4
2419[3] LAXFORD BRIDGE 9-0 Paul Eddery (12) *sn pushed alng in mid-div, cld o'r 2 fs out, styd on ins last.*..........(3 to 1 fav op 7 to 2 tchd 4 to 1) 5
2862[2] ARABOYBILL 9-0 A Clark (3) *trkd ldrs, outpcd appr fnl furlong*..........(25 to 1 op 20 to 1) 6
WATER BARON (USA) 9-0 A Munro (16) *ldg grp till wknd 3 fs out*..........(25 to 1 op 20 to 1) 7
SUPERLATIVECASTING 9-0 T Williams (10) *in tch, rdn alng hfwy, btn o'r 2 fs out*..........(33 to 1 op 25 to 1) 8
EXPLORE MONDIAL (Ire) 9-0 R Cochrane (15) *mid-div most of way*..........(14 to 1 tchd 16 to 1) 9
2571[5] ART TATUM (Ire) 9-0 Pat Eddery (14) *pressed ldrs till lost pl o'r 3 fs out*..........(7 to 2 tchd 5 to 2) 10
SWINGING SIXTIES (Ire) 9-0 Candy Morris (9) *settled mid-div, no hdwy appr last 2 fs*..........(33 to 1 op 25 to 1) 11
PETITE MEMORIES (USA) 8-9 J Reid (11) *sn pushed alng in rear, nvr on terms*....(12 to 1 op 25 to 1 tchd 33 to 1) 12
PRISCIAN'S HEAD 9-0 G Duffield (1) *slwly into strd, mid-div, pushed alng hfwy, wknd wl o'r 2 fs out.*..........(7 to 1 op 9 to 2) 13
TOMMY COOPER 8-9 (5*) D Wright (5) *slwly into strd, beh most of way*..........(33 to 1 op 25 to 1) 14
TAMMUZ 9-0 W R Swinburn (8) *al beh.*..........(14 to 1 op 12 to 1) 15
PATRICE 9-0 W Newnes (6) *slwly into strd, al beh, tld off.*..........(25 to 1 op 16 to 1 tchd 33 to 1) 16
Dist: ½l, 1½l, nk, nk, 3l, 2½l, ¾l, 1l, 1l, hd. 1m 26.67s. a 2.57s (16 Ran).
SR: 30/28/23/22/21/12/4/2/-/ (Hamdan Al-Maktoum), H Thomson Jones

3080 Premier Markets Handicap Class C (0-90 3-y-o) £5,089 7f..........(7:00)

1841[6] PLAY HEVER GOLF [89] 9-6 D Holland (11) *made all, quickened clr 2 fs out, hrd rdn and hld on nr line.*..........(12 to 1 op 10 to 1) 1
2928* AL MOULOUKI [80] 8-11 (5ex) R Cochrane (12) *hld up in mid-div, hdwy 2 fs out, rdn o'r one out, str run nr finish, jst fld*......(3 to 1 fav op 11 to 4 tchd 5 to 2) 2
1375[6] BELFRY GREEN (Ire) [70] 8-1 R Hills (6) *hld up last, hdwy o'r 2 fs out, rdn and ran on ins last.* (8 to 1 op 12 to 1) 3
1978[9] DISKETTE [73] 8-1 (3*) D Harrison (9) *settled rear, hdwy o'r 2 fs out, styd on ins last*..........(20 to 1 op 14 to 1) 4
1978[6] FEATHER FACE [80] 8-11 W Newnes (10) *trkd wnr, rdn and outpcd 2 fs out, wknd ins last.* (14 to 1 op 8 to 1) 5
2686[4] KELLY MAC [63] 7-8[1] J Quinn (7) *presed ldrs, rdn and wknd wl o'r one furlong out*.....(14 to 1 tchd 16 to 1) 6
2711* NO EXTRAS (Ire) [79] 8-10 B Rouse (8) *pld hrd, hld up rear, nvr nr ldrs*..........(6 to 1 op 5 to 1 tchd 13 to 2) 7
2431[5] SOUTHERN MEMORIES (Ire) [83] 9-0 Pat Eddery (1) *al rear.*..........(7 to 1 op 6 to 1 tchd 8 to 1) 8
2746[2] CAPE WEAVER [90] 9-7 L Dettori (2) *settled mid-div, rdn o'r 2 fs out, sn btn*..........(9 to 2 op 4 to 1 tchd 5 to 1) 9
1329[5] HILARY GERRARD (USA) [82] 8-13 G Duffield (3) *slwly into strd, sn reco'red, prmnt till wknd wl over 2 fs out.*..........(11 to 1 op 10 to 1 tchd 14 to 1) 10
Dist: Hd, 1l, 1½l, ½l, 2l, 2l, 1l, 1l, sht-hd. 1m 25.83s. a 1.53s (10 Ran).
SR: 52/42/29/27/32/9/19/20/24/ (R A Popely), T J Naughton

3081 Ladbroke Racing Commentary 0891 222111 Handicap Class E (0-70 3-y-o and up) £3,557 5f..........(7:30)

2846[2] SEA-DEER [59] 4-9-5 A Munro (2) *hld up, hdwy wl o'r one furlong out, led last 150 yards, jst held on.*..........(100 to 30 fav op 3 to 1 tchd 7 to 2) 1
3011[4] PEERAGE PRINCE [65] (bl) 4-9-11 R Cochrane (1) *hld up rear, ran on o'r one furlong out, fnshd strly, jst fld.*..........(7 to 1 op 6 to 1 tchd 8 to 1) 2
2699 VISIMOTION (USA) [59] 3-9-1 W R Swinburn (6) *led one furlong, led o'r one out, hdd and not quicken last 150 yards*..........(10 to 1 op 8 to 1) 3
2910[6] LYNDON'S LINNET [58] 5-9-4 J Weaver (3) *squeezed for room leaving stalls, hdwy and edgd rght und pres wl o'r one furlong out, no imprsn ins last.*..........(11 to 1 op 7 to 1 tchd 12 to 1) 4
2788[8] JOE SUGDEN [45] 9-8-5 W Newnes (8) *chsd ldrs for o'r 3 fs, no extr*..........(14 to 1 tchd 20 to 1) 5
2945* JOBIE [73] 3-10-1 (6ex) W Woods (9) *beh, rdn and effrt whn hmpd o'r one furlong out, not rcvr.*..........(7 to 2 op 3 to 1 tchd 4 to 1) 6
1267 LOVE LEGEND [68] (v) 8-9-9 (5*) A Procter (7) *slwly into strd, swtchd rght hfwy, squeezed for room o'r one furlong out, no extr*..........(10 to 1 tchd 11 to 1) 7
2896[5] SHADES OF JADE [38] 5-7-12 G Bardwell (5) *led aftr one furlong till o'r one out, sn btn.*..........(13 to 2 op 8 to 1 tchd 6 to 1) 8
1492 TEMPLE FORTUNE (USA) [65] 4-9-11 L Dettori (4) *cl up till wknd wl o'r one furlong out.*..........(12 to 1 op 10 to 1 tchd 14 to 1) 9
Dist: Sht-hd, ¾l, 2½l, ½l, hd, hd, nk, 4l. 59.99s. a 1.79s (9 Ran).
SR: 39/44/31/24/9/32/30/-/10/ (P Cook), L J Holt

3082 Lyde Green Nursery Class D (2-y-o) £3,720 6f..........(8:00)

2895[4] LADY PHYL [-] 8-6 (3*) B Doyle (9) *hld up, hdwy and swtchd rght o'r one furlong out, not much room and switched lft ins last, led nr finish*...(8 to 1 op 14 to 1) 1
2929* VERCINGETORIX (Ire) [-] 9-8 (5ex) Paul Eddery (11) *trkd ldrs, led appr fnl furlong, hdd and outpcd nr finish.*..........(5 to 2 fav op 2 to 1 tchd 11 to 4) 2
2786[4] SHFNAK (Ire) [-] (bl) 8-7 M Hills (8) *led till appr fnl furlong, outpcd last 100 yards*..........(14 to 1 op 12 to 1) 3
2528[4] MOCKINGBIRD [-] (v) 8-1 (3*) D Harrison (6) *chsd ldrs, pushed alng hfwy, effrt 2 fs out, no extr fnl furlong.*..........(20 to 1 op 14 to 1) 4
2886[2] ADMIRALELLA [-] 9-5 J Reid (10) *handily plcd, wkng whn hmpd o'r one furlong out.*..........(7 to 2 op 3 to 1 tchd 9 to 2) 5
2155[4] SON OF HADEER [-] 7-11 J Quinn (2) *strted slwly, al outpcd*..........(33 to 1) 6
2668* LEAP OF FAITH (Ire) [-] (v) 8-8 L Dettori (1) *in tch, pushed alng most of way, wknd 2 fs out.*..........(8 to 1 op 7 to 1 tchd 9 to 1) 7
2502[4] MERLIN'S FIELD (Ire) [-] 9-0 (7*) Mark Denaro (7) *rcd keenly and not clr run 1st furlong, pushed alng in mid-div till wknd 2 out*..........(10 to 1 op 8 to 1 tchd 11 to 1) 8
2652* STORM REGENT [-] 8-7 W Woods (3) *mid-div, pushed alng hfwy, no prog last 2 fs*...(6 to 1 op 5 to 1 tchd 7 to 1) 9
2836[4] CHARLIES DREAM (Ire) [-] 8-9 D Holland (4) *cl up till bumped and wknd o'r 2 fs out*.....(20 to 1 op 14 to 1) 10
Dist: ½l, 2½l, 3½l, hd, 2½l, ½l, ¾l, 2l, 3l. 1m 13.07s. a 2.27s (10 Ran).
SR: 14/25/-/-/-/-/ (Network Builders Ltd), B J Meehan

3083 'Looking For A Hurdler' Claiming Stakes Class F (3-y-o) £2,768 1¼m..........(8:30)

2914* SEAMA (USA) 8-11 A Munro (6) *made virtually all, styd on und pres to hold on last strds.*..........(11 to 10 fav op Evens tchd 6 to 5) 1
2663[7] REGALSETT 9-1 J Reid (3) *pld hrd, trkd wnr frm hfwy, hard rdn to dispute ld last 50 yards, jst fld.*..........(4 to 1 tchd 9 to 2) 2
2444[2] DEE RAFT (USA) 9-4 Pat Eddery (4) *chsd wnr frm hfwy, dsptd ld last 50 yards, no extr last strds.*..........(11 to 4 op 2 to 1 tchd 3 to 1) 3
1816[6] CHASE THE STARS 8-13 W Newnes (2) *hld up rear, effrt hfwy, rdn and outpcd last 3 fs*...(10 to 1 tchd 12 to 1) 4
2098[5] HAPPY TUPPENCE 8-2 J Quinn (7) *pld hrd, hld up, rdn and wknd 3 fs out*..........(20 to 1 op 10 to 1) 5
1628[9] WHATONE BELL 8-6 (7*) Mark Denaro (1) *mid-div, rdn and wknd o'r 3 fs out*....(66 to 1 op 33 to 1 tchd 100 to 1) 6
Dist: Sht-hd, sht-hd, 8l, 15l, 5l. 2m 7.01s. a 5.21s (6 Ran).
SR: 15/18/20/ (Fahd Salman), Sir Mark Prescott

NOTTINGHAM (good)
Wednesday August 4th

Going Correction: MINUS 0.20 sec. per fur. (races 1,2,3), MINUS 0.35 (4,5,6)

3084 Greasley Miners Welfare Selling Stakes Class G (2-y-o) £2,110 6f 15yds..........(6:15)

2668 SISTER SUSAN 8-6 W Ryan (6) *cl up, led hfwy, rdn clr appr last, ran on wl*..........(5 to 1 op 7 to 2) 1
2659[5] PACIOLI 8-11 J Williams (5) *al cl up, ev ch o'r one furlong out, sn rdn, one paced*..........(6 to 4 fav op 2 to 1) 2
2911[4] CHEERFUL GROOM (Ire) 8-11 G Hind (7) *mid-div, effrt and hdwy 2 fs out, sn rdn and one paced.*..........(11 to 2 op 4 to 1 tchd 6 to 1) 3
1741 WADDLE (Ire) 8-4 (7*) S Mulvey (3) *slwly into strd and beh, styd on und pres fnl 2 fs*..........(10 to 1 op 6 to 1) 4

2819⁵ WARWICK WARRIOR (Ire) 8-11 Dean McKeown (9) *cl up, led aftr 2 fs to hfwy, rdn two out, sn wknd.* ....(13 to 2 op 10 to 1 tchd 14 to 1) 5
2705⁹ PARIS SYMPHONY (Ire) 8-6 (5*) J Tate (8) *chsd ldrs, effrt and hdwy o'r 2 fs out, sn rdn, edgd rght, wknd appr last*.................................(11 to 1 op 7 to 1) 6
2772⁷ MINIBAR 8-6 N Connorton (2) *nvr rch ldrs.* ....(16 to 1 op 14 to 1) 7
POETIC FANCY 8-6 J Lowe (4) *dwlt, al rear.* ....(14 to 1 op 8 to 1) 8
2423⁶ MRS JOGGLEBURY 8-1 (5*) K Rutter (1) *led 2 fs, sn rdn alng, wknd wl o'r two out*.........(16 to 1 op 8 to 1) 9
WENLOCH LAD 8-12¹ T Wall (10) *dwlt, al beh*....(33 to 1) 10
Dist: 4l, 2½l, ¾l, 5l, ¾l, 1l, ½l, 3l, 2l. 1m 14.80s. a 3.30s (10 Ran).
SR: 2/-/-/-/-/-/ (T A Johnsey), R Hannon

3085 Rainworth Miners Welfare Handicap Class E (0-70 3-y-o and up) £2,238 5f 13yds......................... (6:45)

2829⁵ FOOD OF LOVE [70] 5-10-0 J Williams (6) *trkd ldrs gng wl, smooth hdwy 2 fs out, quickened to led entering last, sn clr*.................................(16 to 1 op 10 to 1) 1
2813² SINGING STAR [68] 7-9-5 (7*) Claire Balding (8) *hld up and beh, hdwy 2 fs out, styd on strly ins last, not rch wnr.* ....(11 to 2 op 7 to 2) 2
3011² CASTLE MAID [35] 6-7-7 J Lowe (9) *hld up, hdwy 2 fs out, sn rdn, styd on ins last*........(15 to 8 fav op 7 to 2) 3
1925⁹ DAL MISS [35] (bl) 6-7-5⁵ (7*) C Hawksley (4) *led till hdd and wknd entering last*.......................(50 to 1) 4
2813⁵ SIR TASKER [56] 5-9-0 P Robinson (5) *chsd ldrs, rdn 2 fs out, one pace appr last*..............(7 to 1 op 6 to 1) 5
2584⁶ JESS REBEC [54] 5-8-12 W Ryan (7) *beh, gd hdwy 2 fs out, staying on whn not clr run o'r one out, not rcvr.* ....(12 to 1 op 8 to 1) 6
2861⁵ NILU (Ire) [48] 5-8-6 A Mackay (1) *cl up, ev ch 2 fs out, sn rdn, wknd o'r one out*...........(14 to 1 op 10 to 1) 7
2935* PAGEBOY [60] 4-9-4 L Piggott (3) *cl up, ev ch 2 fs out, sn rdn and wknd appr last.* (3 to 1 op 9 to 4 tchd 7 to 2) 8
2910³ ARC LAMP [56] 7-9-0 J Fortune (2) *cl up, rdn and ev ch 2 fs out, wknd o'r one out*..............(7 to 1 op 5 to 1) 9
Dist: 2½l, 3l, sht-hd, 2½l, nk, 1½l, 1½l, ½l. 1m 0.30s. a 2.10s (9 Ran).
SR: 52/40/-/-/5/2/ (J David Abell), J Wharton

3086 Welbeck Colliery Welfare Claiming Stakes Class F (2-y-o) £2,219 5f 13yds .... (7:15)

2500⁷ ROCKY TWO 8-6 A Mackay (1) *al cl up, led 2 fs out, sn rdn, styd on gmely ins last*..........(8 to 1 op 6 to 1) 1
839⁷ IVA'S FLYER (Ire) 8-1 L Charnock (5) *dwlt, sn cl up, rdn 2 fs out, ev ch till no extr nr finish*.....(14 to 1 op 10 to 1) 2
2500⁶ GAELIC STAR (Ire) 8-4 W Ryan (8) *chsd ldrs, rdn and hdwy 2 fs out, styd on strly ins last*........(5 to 1 op 9 to 2) 3
NAPOLEON STAR (Ire) 8-10 J Williams (2) *in tch, effrt 2 fs out, sn rdn and styd on ins last*... (33 to 1 op 25 to 1) 4
2852³ SWEET WHISPER 8-5 G Hind (4) *chsd ldrs, rdn alng and hdwy whn not clr run one and a half fs out, ev ch when hmpd ins last, not reco'r*........ (9 to 4 fav tchd 5 to 2) 5
2818⁴ HELLABY 8-10 W Carson (6) *led, rdn and hdd 2 fs out, grad wknd*............(11 to 4 op 5 to 2 tchd 3 to 1) 6
2125* OLD HOOK (Ire) 8-9 (5*) K Rutter (7) *chsd ldrs, sn rdn alng, lost pl hfwy, soon beh*..............(8 to 1 op 4 to 1) 7
LUKES BROTHER (Ire) 8-10 K Fallon (9) *slwly into strd, ran green, al beh*.........(8 to 1 op 25 to 1 tchd 33 to 1) 8
Dist: Nk, hd, ½l, hd, ¾l, 5l, 2l. 1m 1.20s. a 3.00s (8 Ran).
SR: 12/6/8/12/6/8/-/-/ (R Thornhill), B A McMahon

3087 British Coal Handicap Class E (0-70 3-y-o and up) £2,959 2m 9yds... (7:45)

2950* HUNTING GROUND [51] (bl) 5-9-7 (6ex) A Mackay (9) *hld up, hdwy hfwy, effrt to ld 2 fs out, sn rdn, ran on gmely ins last*............(3 to 1 fav op 9 to 2 tchd 11 to 2) 1
2751⁴ PEACH BRANDY [40] 4-8-10 N Adams (2) *al cl up, chlgd 3 fs out, rdn to ld briefly o'r 2 out, sn hdd, ev ch, kpt on.* ....(14 to 1 op 10 to 1) 2
2458⁴ MOIDART [69] 3-9-10 P Robinson (6) *hld up, gd hdwy 6 fs out, rdn 2 out, styd on ins last*......(12 to 1 op 8 to 1) 3
2662² SINGING REPLY (USA) [36] 5-8-6 T Sprake (12) *hld up and beh, hdwy 6 fs out, rdn 2 out, kpt on, not rch ldrs.* ....(6 to 1) 4
2337⁵ BALZINO (USA) [51] 4-9-7 K Fallon (13) *hld up and beh, hdwy on inner 6 fs out, squeezed through and ev ch 2 out, sn rdn, wknd appr last*........ (13 to 2 op 6 to 1) 5
2611³ WAKT [52] 3-8-7 W Carson (1) *sn led, rdn 3 fs out, soon hdd, grad wknd*.......(9 to 1 op 8 to 1 tchd 10 to 1) 6
2386⁵ SELDOM IN [25] 7-7-9 J Fanning (7) *chsd ldrs, rdn and wknd 5 fs out*.......................(16 to 1 op 14 to 1) 7
2585² MUST BE MAGICAL (USA) [23] (bl) 5-7-7 J Lowe (3) *chsd ldrs, effrt o'r 3 fs out, sn rdn and one paced.* ....(16 to 1 op 14 to 1) 8
2355³ GUESTWICK [68] 3-9-9 B Raymond (14) *hld up and beh, effrt and some hdwy 5 fs out, not rach ldrs.* ....(11 to 1 op 8 to 1) 9
1948² KEDGE [59] 3-9-0 L Piggott (5) *prmnt, rdn 3 fs out, wknd 2 out*.................................(11 to 2 op 6 to 1) 10
2166⁶ BOOTIKIN [33] (bl) 5-8-3 L Charnock (10) *prmnt, rdn and wknd 4 fs out*.................................(33 to 1) 11
HIRAM B BIRDBATH [35] 7-8-5 Dale Gibson (11) *al beh.* ....(33 to 1) 12
2729⁵ PINISI [34] 8-8-4 J Williams (8) *in tch, rdn 6 fs out, sn wknd*................(11 to 1 op 12 to 1 tchd 10 to 1) 13
SPORTS VIEW [47] 4-8-10 (7*) S Drowne (4) *al rear.* ....(14 to 1 op 12 to 1) 14
Dist: Sht-hd, nk, 3½l, 1l, 2½l, 7l, 2½l, ¾l, nk, 5l. 3m 28.90s. a 4.70s (14 Ran).
SR: 4/-/5/-/-/-/ (Esprit de Corps Racing), A Bailey

3088 East Kirkby Miners Welfare Fillies' Handicap Class E (0-70 3-y-o and up) £2,892 1m 54yds............... (8:15)

2874² MISTY SILKS [62] 3-9-3 D Biggs (12) *chsd ldrs, hdwy on outer 3 fs out, rdn to ld appr last, edgd lft ins last and ran on wl*..............(11 to 2 op 5 to 1 tchd 6 to 1) 1
2712² MISS FASCINATION [60] 3-8-10 (5*) K Rutter (2) *trkd ldrs, effrt 3 fs out, led 2 out, sn rdn, hdd appr last, kpt on.* ....(3 to 1 fav op 5 to 1 tchd 9 to 4) 2
2164⁷ FRANCIA [57] 3-8-7 (5*) J Tate (1) *chsd ldr, effrt to chal 3 fs out, ev ch whn rdn and not quicken entering last.* ....(20 to 1 op 14 to 1) 3
2915³ PARFAIT AMOUR [63] 4-9-11 A Culhane (3) *chsd ldrs, effrt and hdwy 2 and a half fs out, sn rdn and kpt on one pace*.....................(9 to 1 op 7 to 1) 4
2863* WORKINGFORPEANUTS (Ire) [43] (v) 3-7-12 (5ex) J Lowe (9) *hld up and beh, hdwy 3 fs out, sn rdn and styd on ins last, not rch ldrs*...................(6 to 1 op 5 to 1) 5
2859 RIVER FIRE (Ire) [45] (bl) 3-8-0 N Adams (6) *chsd ldrs, hdwy to ld 3 fs out, sn rdn and hdd 2 out, grad wknd.* (33 to 1) 6
2882 TIFFANY'S CASE (Ire) [57] 4-9-5 E Johnson (11) *hld up in mid-div, effrt and hdwy 3 fs out, rdn 2 out, sn btn.* ....(9 to 1 op 7 to 1 tchd 10 to 1) 7
1061⁶ DANSEUSE FRANCAISE (Ire) [45] 3-8-0¹ K Darley (8) *in tch, effrt and rdn 3 fs out, sn one paced.* ....(25 to 1 op 14 to 1) 8
2425⁶ DONTBETALKING (Ire) [40] 3-7-9 J Fanning (4) *led, rdn and hdd 3 fs out, sn wknd*...............(20 to 1 op 14 to 1) 9
2931* BOLD MELODY [46] 4-8-8 (5ex) L Piggott (10) *nvr rch ldrs.* ....(7 to 1 op 9 to 2) 10
2580⁴ DASHING MARCH [66] 4-10-0 J Williams (7) *al rear.* ....(25 to 1 op 20 to 1) 11
2834 JADIRAH (USA) [65] (bl) 3-9-6 W Carson (5) *in tch, rdn o'r 4 fs out, sn wknd*.....................(13 to 2 op 8 to 1) 12
Dist: 1½l, 1l, ½l, 2½l, 1½l, ¾l, ½l, 4l, 1l, 3l. 1m 44.90s. a 4.90s (12 Ran).
(P E Axon), M J Ryan

3089 Clipstone Miners Welfare Handicap Class E (0-70 3-y-o and up) £2,847 1m 1f 213yds..................... (8:45)

2932* TALENTED TING (Ire) [60] (v) 4-9-13 (5ex) K Darley (9) *trkd ldr, hdwy to ld 3 fs out, sn clr, rdn appr fnl furlong, ran on wl*...........................(6 to 4 jt-fav op 5 to 4) 1
2506⁵ MARCHMAN [57] 8-9-10 B Raymond (3) *chsd ldrs, hdwy o'r 3 fs out, chased wnr one and a half out, sn rdn, kpt on*....................(6 to 1 op 9 to 2 tchd 13 to 2) 2
2641 VICTOR ROMEO [28] (v) 4-7-9 A Mackay (2) *beh, effrt 3 fs out, sn rdn, styd on fnl 2 furlongs, nvr dngrs.* (33 to 1) 3
ENCHANTED FLYER [27] 6-7-8 N Adams (6) *beh, styd on fnl 2 fs, nvr dngrs*............................(33 to 1) 4
2291 BLAKE'S TREASURE [26] (bl) 6-7-7 J Lowe (1) *sn led, rdn and hdd 3 fs out, soon wknd*.................(33 to 1) 5
1930 MAJOR RISK [34] 4-7-8 (7*) C Hawksley (4) *mid-div, effrt o'r 3 fs out, sn rdn, no hdwy*..................(20 to 1) 6
1093 ZAAHEYAH (USA) [62] 3-9-6 P Robinson (8) *chsd ldrs, rdn o'r 3 fs out, sn wknd*.............(10 to 1 op 7 to 1) 7
1900 TOMASHENKO [45] 4-8-9 (3*) S D Williams (5) *beh, hdwy o'r 4 fs out, sn rdn, wknd 3 out.* ....(25 to 1 op 33 to 1 tchd 50 to 1) 8
2970² CASE FOR THE CROWN (USA) [45] 6-8-12 L Piggott (7) *chsd ldg pair, rdn 3 fs out, sn btn*... (6 to 4 jt-fav op 7 to 4) 9
Dist: 2½l, 6l, 4l, 2l, hd, 8l, 5l, ¾l. 2m 6.50s. a 3.50s (9 Ran).
SR: 43/35/-/-/-/-/ (Martin Wickens), P C Haslam

PONTEFRACT (good)
Wednesday August 4th

Going Correction: MINUS 0.20 sec. per fur. (races 1,3,4,7), MINUS 0.30 (2,5,6)

3090 Hyde Sporting Promotions Ladies Handicap Class F (0-70 3-y-o and up) £2,954 1¼m 6yds.............. (2:50)

2847⁴ LUCKY NOIRE [39] 5-9-13 Miss A Harwood (8) *hld up, imprvg whn not much room o'r 2 fs out, ran on to ld appr last, kpt on wl*.... (9 to 2 op 5 to 1 tchd 11 to 2) 1
2789³ CREDIT SQUEEZE [70] 3-11-7 Miss E Johnson Houghton (3) *nvr far away, effrt and not much room o'r one furlong out, shaken up and styd on ins last.* ....(4 to 1 fav op 7 to 2) 2

2859[2] CUTTHROAT KID (Ire) [49] (v) 3-10-0 Mrs M Cowdrey (7) *early ldr, styd hndy, rdn to chal o'r one furlong out, hng lft and kpt on one pace ins last.* (9 to 2 op 7 to 2) 3
2445 THUNDERING [36] 8-9-10 Miss Diana Jones (2) *tucked away on inner, effrt entering strt, one pace.* .... (9 to 1 op 8 to 1 tchd 10 to 1) 4
2859[3] DOUBLE THE STAKES (USA) [26] 4-9-0 Mrs G Rees (12) *sn led, hdd aftr 3 fs, styd upsides, rgned ld o'r three furlongs out, headed appr last, no extr.* .... (12 to 1 op 10 to 1) 5
2445[8] BREEZED WELL [43] 7-10-3 Mrs H Noonan (5) *co'red up beh ldrs, rdn alng entering strt, sn btn.* .... (16 to 1 op 14 to 1) 6
2856[3] TOUR LEADER (NZ) [53] 4-10-13 Mrs A Farrell (10) *slwly into strd, beh, rdn to improve 4 fs out, no imprsn entering strt.* .... (14 to 1 op 16 to 1 tchd 20 to 1) 7
2931[3] LAZY RHYTHM (USA) [41] 7-9-12 (3*) Mrs C Hirst (9) *in tch on outer, took clr order 4 fs out, rdn and wknd entering strt.* .... (25 to 1 op 20 to 1) 8
1832[5] WEAVER GEORGE (Ire) [39] 3-9-3[2] (3*) Miss C Metcalfe (4) *cl up, led aftr 3 fs, hdd o'r three furlongs out, grad lost pl.* .... (25 to 1 op 20 to 1) 9
2709[6] BONNY PRINCESS [36] 3-9-1[4] (3*) Miss S Storey (1) *beh til rdn and wknd o'r 3 fs out.* .... (100 to 1 op 66 to 1) 10
365[5] KALKO [58] 4-11-1 (3*) Miss K Milligan (6) *beh til rdn alng and lost tch o'r 3 fs out.* .... (20 to 1 op 16 to 1) 11
2195[3] LOTS OF LUCK [60] 10-11-6 Mrs L Pearce (11) *mid-div, pushed alng appr strt, wknd quickly o'r one furlong out.* .... (11 to 2 op 5 to 1 tchd 6 to 1) 12
Dist: 1l, 2l, 1½l, 1l, 1½l, 5l, ¾l, 1l, 6l, nk. 2m 15.50s. a 7.30s (12 Ran).
SR: 20/40/15/8/-/10/10/-/-/ (Mrs Carol Harrison), G Harwood

3091 Featherstone Maiden Stakes Class D (2-y-o) £4,378 6f. .... (3:20)

2357[3] MONAASSABAAT (USA) 8-9 W R Swinburn (12) *nvr far away, led wl o'r one furlong out, pushed clr ins last.* .... (2 to 1 fav op 13 to 8) 1
SALSKA 8-9 Dean McKeown (5) *trkd ldrs, outpcd and drvn alng appr strt, kpt on ins fnl furlong.* .... (12 to 1 op 8 to 1) 2
2626[4] DYNAMIC DELUXE (USA) 9-0 R Cochrane (10) *led til hdd wl o'r one furlong out, rdn and no extr.* (5 to 1 op 4 to 1) 3
WINNING LINE 9-0 M Birch (11) *beh, shaken up and swtchd entering strt, styd on strly ins last, prmsg.* .... (25 to 1 op 16 to 1) 4
IN A MOMENT (USA) 9-0 J Fortune (8) *trkd ldrs, drvn alng appr strt, one pace.* .... (14 to 1 op 8 to 1) 5
2818[2] LUNAR MISSION (Ire) 9-0 K Darley (3) *wth ldr, ev ch entering strt, rdn and sn btn.* (9 to 4 op 5 to 2 tchd 3 to 1) 6
2374[4] DINOT (Ire) 9-0 S Perks (6) *pressed ldg grp, rdn alng hfwy, btn entering strt.* .... (14 to 1 op 12 to 1) 7
SNOWDON SLIGHTS 8-9 P Robinson (7) *sluggish strt, nvr able to reco'r.* .... (25 to 1 op 16 to 1) 8
2482[6] THE ARDINGLY FAIR (Ire) 9-0 L Charnock (9) *co'red up beh ldrs, pushed alng hfwy, sn lost tch.* .... (100 to 1 op 50 to 1) 9
Dist: 4l, nk, 1l, sht-hd, 3½l, 3l, 7l, 6l. 1m 16.90s. a 2.20s (9 Ran).
SR: 15/-/3/-/-/-/ (Maktoum Al Maktoum), M R Stoute

3092 Upton Claiming Stakes Class F (3-y-o) £2,611 1½m 8yds. .... (3:50)

2822* CIVIL LAW (Ire) 8-6 S Perks (2) *hld up in last pl, pushed alng 3 fs out, ran on entering strt to ld ins last, kpt on wl.* .... (7 to 4 op 6 to 4) 1
2773* TTYFRAN 8-6 Paul Eddery (3) *hld up in tch, improved to ld o'r one furlong out, hdd ins last, kpt on.* .... (11 to 10 on op 11 to 10) 2
2640[3] FOLLINGWORTH GIRL (Ire) 8-0 (3*) S Maloney (6) *cl up, led aftr 2 fs, drvn and hdd o'r 3 out, rallied and ev ch over one out, not quicken.* .... (13 to 2 op 6 to 1) 3
2775 JASPER ONE 8-4 N Connorton (5) *led 2 fs, trkd ldr, rgned ld o'r 3 out, hdd over one out, sn btn.* .... (50 to 1 op 33 to 1) 4
LARKSPUR LEGEND 8-5 J Fanning (1) *chsd ldg 2, rdn alng o'r 3 fs out, wknd entering strt.* ... (33 to 1 op 25 to 1) 5
2538[4] LIME JUICE 8-1 K Darley (4) *strted slwly, sn in tch, pushed alng 5 fs out, lost touch 4 out, eased, tld off.* .... (14 to 1 tchd 20 to 1) 6
Dist: ½l, 5l, 5l, 6l, dist. 2m 41.70s. a 6.70s (6 Ran).
SR: 1/-/-/ (Mrs B Facchino), R Hollinshead

3093 Parkside Innes & Leisure Handicap Class C (0-90 3-y-o and up) £5,071 1m 4yds. .... (4:20)

2794 LAP OF LUXURY [79] 4-9-7 N Day (4) *trkd ldg 2, effrt and rdn o'r two fs out, led over one out, kpt on wl.* .... (9 to 2 op 11 to 2) 1
2663* MOON SPIN [78] 4-9-6 Paul Eddery (1) *nvr far away, effrt whn no room appr strt, ran on to chal approaching last, one pace.* .... (7 to 4 fav op 2 to 1) 2
2212[2] PRINCESS KRIS [81] 3-9-2 W R Swinburn (2) *hld up, improved to join issue hfwy, led briefly o'r one furlong out, edgd rght and kpt on one pace.* (9 to 4 op 2 to 1) 3
2254[9] NASHVILLE BLUES (Ire) [83] 4-9-11 R Hills (5) *swtchd lft leaving stalls, pressed ldrs, effrt appr strt, chlgd approaching last, one pace.* .... (11 to 2 op 5 to 1) 4
1940 HAMADRYAD (Ire) [77] (v) 5-9-2 (3*) O Pears (3) *led til hdd o'r one furlong out, sn btn and eased.* .... (7 to 1 op 6 to 1 tchd 8 to 1) 5
Dist: 1l, 1l, ½l, 6l. 1m 47.30s. a 5.20s (5 Ran).
SR: 5/1/-/1/-/ (I C Hill-Wood), W Jarvis

3094 Chaplins Club Handicap Class E (0-70 3-y-o and up) £3,817 5f. .... (4:50)

2951[2] KABCAST [47] (bl) 8-8-5 S Wood (4) *made all, clr o'r one furlong out, eased towards finish.* .... (11 to 2 op 5 to 1 tchd 6 to 1) 1
2910[5] FOLLOWMEGIRLS [55] 4-8-13 K Fallon (7) *beh and sn pushed alng, improved on outer entering strt, kpt on ins last, no ch wth wnr.* .... (12 to 1 op 10 to 1) 2
2816[8] SOBERING THOUGHTS [65] 7-9-9 N Adams (10) *in tch on outer, pushed alng hfwy, one pace fnl furlong.* (6 to 1) 3
2600 SECOND COLOURS (USA) [60] 3-9-0 K Darley (1) *sn last and bustled alng, not clr run entering strt, swtchd and styd on strly fnl furlong, nrst finish.* .... (4 to 1 fav op 9 to 2) 4
974[4] MAGIC PEARL [70] 3-9-5 (5*) Stephen Davies (9) *chsd ldrs, rdn alng o'r 2 fs out, no extr over one out.* .... (20 to 1 op 14 to 1) 5
2910[7] ADMIRALS REALM [56] 4-9-0 A Mackay (3) *dwlt, sn pushed alng in rear, kpt on in strt, nvr dngrs.* .... (11 to 1 op 10 to 1) 6
2553[5] MY GODSON [62] (bl) 3-9-2 J Fortune (5) *chsd ldrs, pushed alng thrght, one pace fnl 2 fs.* .... (11 to 1 op 8 to 1) 7
2760* MILBANK CHALLENGER [60] 3-9-0 M Birch (6) *hld up towards rear, shaken up o'r one furlong out, kpt on, nvr nr to chal.* .... (9 to 2 tchd 4 to 1) 8
2570[3] FARNDALE [43] 6-8-1[2] P Robinson (2) *nvr far away, rdn alng hfwy, wknd entering strt.* ... (14 to 1 op 10 to 1) 9
2765* NORLING (Ire) [46] 3-8-0 L Charnock (8) *chsd ldrs, pushed alng hfwy, wknd entering strt.* ...... (6 to 1 op 9 to 2) 10
Dist: 1½l, 1l, ¾l, ½l, nk, ½l, nk, 3l, 3l. 1m 2.60s. a 1.40s (10 Ran).
SR: 33/35/41/29/37/26/26/23/-/ (Mrs M M Marshall), D W Chapman

3095 'Go Racing In Yorkshire' Claiming Stakes Class F (3-y-o) £2,635 5f (5:20)

2214[3] FIRST OPTION 8-9 K Darley (4) *reluctant to enter stalls, chsd ldg 2, ran on to ld a furlong out, kpt on wl.* .... (2 to 1 fav op 5 to 2) 1
2939[3] PRINCESS OBERON (Ire) 8-3 (3*) M Fenton (3) *pressed ldg grp, effrt and rdn o'r 2 fs out, swtchd and hng rght one out, kpt on.* .... (5 to 2 op 7 to 4) 2
2896[4] SPLASH OF SALT (Ire) 8-3 (5*) A Garth (1) *sn outpcd and beh, improved and edgd rght o'r one furlong out, kpt on ins last.* .... (4 to 1 op 7 to 2 tchd 9 to 2) 3
3032[6] COCONUT JOHNNY (bl) 8-3 J Fanning (2) *led, rdn entering strt, hdd one furlong out, no extr.* .... (9 to 1 op 12 to 1 tchd 14 to 1) 4
2660[7] TRENTESIMO (Ire) 8-10 J Carroll (7) *wth ldr, ev ch appr fnl furlong, fdd.* .... (5 to 1 op 4 to 1) 5
SAY SUNPAK 7-9 L Charnock (5) *unruly at strt, chsd ldrs, shaken up entering strt, sn btn.* ... (50 to 1 op 33 to 1) 6
2711[7] RIVER REFUGE 8-0 Dale Gibson (6) *pressed ldg grp, rdn hfwy, lost tch entering strt.* ...... (20 to 1 op 16 to 1) 7
Dist: ¾l, 3l, 2l, ¾l, 5l, 3l. 1m 2.20s. a 1.00s (7 Ran).
SR: 45/39/29/16/20/-/-/ (P D Savill), M H Easterby

3096 Ledstone Median Auction Maiden Stakes Class F (3-y-o) £2,954 1½m 8yds. .... (5:50)

2752[6] MEAVY 8-9 M Tebbutt (3) *made all, clr entering strt, shaken up and hng rght fnl furlong, kpt on wl.* .... (9 to 4 op 3 to 1) 1
HOME PARK (Ire) 9-0 P D'Arcy (1) *nvr far away, took clr order 3 fs out, shaken up entering strt, kpt on, not rch wnr.* .... (6 to 1 op 9 to 2 tchd 7 to 1) 2
TOMSK 9-0 N Day (4) *co'red up beh ldrs, rdn alng and lost pl hfwy, improved und pres appr strt, one pace ins last.* .... (7 to 1 op 6 to 1) 3
2937[4] SPICE BOX (USA) 9-0 S O'Gorman (5) *cl up, drvn alng o'r 3 fs out, wknd entering strt.* ...... (5 to 1 tchd 6 to 1) 4
2507[3] MICHAELA MIA (USA) 8-9 K Darley (7) *trkd ldrs, hrd at work 3 fs out, sn btn.* .... (2 to 1 fav op 11 to 8) 5
2834 RARE OCCURANCE 8-7 (7*) R Painter (6) *took keen hold early, in tch, pushed alng 4 fs out, wknd 3 out.* .... (100 to 1 op 50 to 1) 6
SHARP SENSATION 8-9 (5*) J Marshall (8) *pressed ldg grp, effrt and rdn alng 4 fs out, sn btn.* (66 to 1 op 20 to 1) 7
DANCE FEVER (Ire) 9-0 M Birch (2) *hld up, reminders hfwy, lost tch 4 fs out, eased and tld off.* ...... (20 to 1) 8
Dist: 2½l, 3½l, 10l, 4l, ½l, 5l, dist. 2m 38.00s. a 3.00s (8 Ran).
SR: 41/41/34/14/1/5/-/-/ (Lord & Lady Roborough), W Jarvis

BATH (good to firm)
Thursday August 5th

Going Correction: MINUS 0.30 sec. per fur. (races

1,5,6), MINUS 0.05 (2,3,4)

3097 Colerne Apprentice Handicap Class E (0-80 3-y-o) £2,835 2m 1f 34yds. .(2:10)

2783³ SO SAUCY [54] 8-10 B Doyle (6) *made all, pushed clr 2 fs out, easily*............. (5 to 1 op 4 to 1 tchd 6 to 1) 1
2751* MONSIEUR DUPONT (Ire) [65] 9-7 D Harrison (1) *hld up, hdwy to go second o'r 2 fs out, rdn and no imprsn.* ....(11 to 8 fav op 6 to 4 tchd 7 to 4) 2
2721* DANGER BABY [37] 7-7 N Kennedy (7) *hld up, hdwy to chase wnr 6 fs out, rdn and one pace frm o'r 2 out.* ....(100 to 30 op 3 to 1 tchd 5 to 2 and 7 to 2) 3
2721² ROWLANDSONS GOLD (Ire) [37] 7-4 (3*) N Varley (5) *chsd wnr to hfwy, rdn o'r 3 fs out, one pace aftr.* .... (12 to 1 op 8 to 1 tchd 14 to 1) 4
2709³ WORKING TITLE (Ire) [46] 7-13² (5*) Mark Denaro (3) *hmpd on bend aftr 7 fs, al beh, lost tch 4 furlongs out, eased one out, tld off*........(11 to 1 op 6 to 1 tchd 12 to 1) 5
2721⁴ SHE KNEW THE RULES (Ire) [49] 8-5 F Norton (4) *prmnt, chsd wnr frm hfwy to 6 fs out, stdly wknd, tld off.* .... (9 to 1 op 11 to 2) 6
1557⁶ MERCH FACH (Ire) [44] 8-0⁵ (3*) S Drowne (2) *al beh, tld off whn pld up o'r 4 fs out*........... (33 to 1 op 20 to 1) pu

Dist: 5l, 1½l, 2l, 15l, 12l. 3m 52.30s. a 8.30s (7 Ran).
(L H J Ward), B J Meehan

3098 Willesley Two Year Old Selling Stakes Class G £2,490 5f 11yds........ (2:40)

2119³ LITTLE EMMELINE 8-6 N Carlisle (6) *made all, rdn entering fnl furlong, hld on wl*...... (5 to 2 fav tchd 9 to 4) 1
2377³ RANDOM 8-6 W Newnes (8) *nvr far away, rdn to go second appr fnl furlong, ran on ins, no imprsn cl hme.* ....(9 to 2 op 4 to 1) 2
2844⁸ CURBRIDGE (Ire) 8-11 J Williams (2) *mid-div, rdn frm hfwy, ran on wl ins fnl furlong*....(16 to 1 op 10 to 1) 3
1241⁵ MONSIEUR PETONG 8-11 D Holland (12) *chsd ldrs, one pace entering fnl furlong.* ....(3 to 1 op 4 to 1 tchd 5 to 1) 4
1169⁴ THREEPENNY-BRIDGE 8-11 T Sprake (10) *chsd wnr till outpcd appr fnl furlong.* .... (12 to 1 op 8 to 1 tchd 14 to 1) 5
2911⁷ JOBISDUN 8-11 A Clark (9) *slwly away, some hdwy 2 fs out, nvr dngerous*.................(33 to 1 op 16 to 1) 6
2772⁹ MILLY'S PET 8-6 J Quinn (4) *al towards rear.* .... (20 to 1 op 12 to 1) 7
2668⁵ NORTHERN STARLIGHT 8-11 N Adams (11) *prmnt till wknd wl o'r one furlong out.* ....(13 to 2 op 5 to 1 tchd 7 to 1 and 8 to 1) 8
2911 RAGTIME GIRL 8-6 Paul Eddery (1) *slwly away, al beh.* .... (33 to 1 op 16 to 1) 9
2176⁴ AGGIES DREAM 8-4 (7*) Mark Denaro (3) *in tch to hfwy, rdn and sn btn*..................(33 to 1 op 20 to 1) 10
2493⁴ EL COHETE 8-11 R Hills (7) *prmnt till wknd quickly appr fnl furlong*..........(14 to 1 op 10 to 1 tchd 16 to 1) 11
HYMIE HALL 8-11 C Rutter (5) *slwly away, al outpcd.* ....(16 to 1 op 12 to 1 tchd 20 to 1) 12

Dist: Hd, 2½l, 2½l, sht-hd, 4l, ½l, 2l, 2l, 1l, ½l. 1m 4.80s. a 4.30s (12 Ran).
SR: 1/-/-/-/-/-/ (J K Morrish), L G Cottrell

3099 Whirlwind Sprint Handicap Class D (0-85 3-y-o and up) £3,435 5f 11yds ....(3:10)

2050² CALL TO THE BAR (Ire) [61] 4-8-9 A Clark (2) *al in tch, led o'r one furlong out, ran on strly.* .... (7 to 2 fav op 4 to 1 tchd 9 to 2 and 3 to 1) 1
2660* ARAGROVE [76] 3-9-6 W Newnes (3) *hld up in tch, hdwy to hold ev ch appr fnl furlong, rdn and kpt on ins.* ....(9 to 2 op 3 to 1) 2+
2728* BELLSABANGING [74] 3-9-4 T Williams (8) *al prmnt, led briefly one and a half fs out, ran on one pace.* ....(6 to 1 op 5 to 1) 2+
2987⁷ BLUE TOPAZE [76] 5-9-10 M Wigham (1) *slwly away, making hdwy whn short of room appr fnl furlong, kpt on ins*...................(11 to 2 op 9 to 2 tchd 6 to 1) 4
2327 BEATLE SONG [51] 5-7-13 N Carlisle (5) *beh, effrt one and a half fs out, ran on one pace.* .... (14 to 1 op 8 to 1 tchd 16 to 1) 5
2387* RHYTHMIC DANCER [74] 5-9-8 M Tebbutt (9) *prmnt till rdn and outpcd entering fnl furlong.* .... (5 to 1 op 9 to 2 tchd 11 to 2) 6
2620⁹ BELTHORN [46] 4-7-8¹ A Tucker (6) *slwly away, al towards rear*.......................(33 to 1 op 16 to 1) 7
2945³ SPRING HIGH [51] (bl) 6-7-13 G Bardwell (4) *rdn frm hfwy, beh fnl 2 fs*...............(13 to 2 op 7 to 1 tchd 8 to 1) 8
2688⁶ TRIOMING [59] 7-8-7 N Adams (7) *led till hdd one and a half fs out, wknd quickly, eased*...(12 to 1 op 10 to 1) 9

Dist: 1½l, dd-ht, 1l, 1½l, ¾l, 1½l, nk, 2l. 1m 3.00s. a 2.50s (9 Ran).
SR: 40/45/43/45/14/34/-/4/4/ (Trow Lane Farm), M McCormack

3100 August Claiming Stakes Class F (3-y-o and up) £2,854 5f 161yds........(3:40)

2872⁸ SAMSON-AGONISTES 7-9-1 T Quinn (2) *trkd ldr, led o'r 2 fs out, clr one out, eased nr finish*... (7 to 2 op 3 to 1) 1
2491⁹ UNVEILED 5-7-13¹ (7*) S Drowne (7) *rcd on outsd towards rear till hdwy hfwy, rdn and ran on strly to go second on line*.................(14 to 1 op 10 to 1 tchd 16 to 1) 2
1972⁷ NO GAIN 3-7-9 (7*) Kim McDonnell (9) *in rear till hdwy 2 fs out, ran on und pres ins last*...... (33 to 1 op 16 to 1) 3
2939 JEWEL THIEF (v) 3-8-9 J Williams (10) *hld up, hdwy 2 fs out, rdn and kpt on ins last*....... (33 to 1 op 20 to 1) 4
2848* TRUTHFUL IMAGE (bl) 4-8-10 (7*) P McCabe (6) *prmnt, ev ch and gng wl 2 fs out, wknd quickly entering last.* ....(6 to 4 on tchd 11 to 8 on and 5 to 4 on) 5
2494⁷ RICKY'S TORNADO (Ire) 4-8-12 (5*) A Procter (8) *trkd ldrs till wknd wl o'r one furlong out*.... (10 to 1 op 9 to 1) 6
2910 KINTWYN 3-8-9 T Williams (5) *slwly away, al beh.* .... (25 to 1 op 16 to 1) 7
2967⁴ MASTER BEVELED (bl) 3-8-2 (5*) Stephen Davies (4) *led till hdd o'r 2 fs out, drpd out quickly.* ....(14 to 1 op 12 to 1 tchd 16 to 1) 8
1696 SUI GENERIS (Ire) 3-8-2 J Quinn (1) *outpcd thrght.* ....(33 to 1) 9
2728⁶ BELLA BAMBOLA (Ire) 3-8-2 L Charnock (3) *speed for 2 fs, sn beh, tld off*......................(33 to 1 op 16 to 1) 10

Dist: 1½l, sht-hd, 1l, 2l, 1½l, 3½l, ¾l, 3l, 10l. 1m 12.30s. a 2.90s (10 Ran).
SR: 37/21/17/20/20/14/ (J B Wilcox), B A McMahon

3101 Be Hopeful Memorial Handicap Class D (0-75 3-y-o) £3,640 1m 5yds... (4:10)

2752⁵ AWESTRIKE (USA) [68] 9-2 Paul Eddery (6) *hld up, al gng wl, smooth hdwy to ld appr fnl furlong, sn clr, cmftbly.* ....(5 to 1 op 4 to 1) 1
2938* STAY WITH ME BABY [65] 8-8 (5*,5ex) A Procter (9) *al prmnt, ev ch one and a half fs out, kpt on one pace.* ....(9 to 2 op 4 to 1 tchd 5 to 1) 2
2882⁶ SILVER GROOM (Ire) [54] 8-2 J Quinn (2) *hld up, hdwy 4 fs out, kpt on one pace ins fnl 2*...... (7 to 1 op 11 to 2) 3
2764⁶ DIWALI DANCER [52] (bl) 8-0 F Norton (3) *slwly away, hld up in rear, hdwy on ins frm hfwy, swtchd rght o'r 2 out, one pace aftr*................(14 to 1 op 12 to 1) 4
2978* ROYAL ROLLER (Ire) [72] 8-13 (7*) G Forster (10) *rcd in tch on outsd, effrt o'r 2 fs out, one pace.* ....(3 to 1 fav op 9 to 2) 5
2867⁴ REGAL AURA (Ire) [71] (bl) 9-5 A Clark (7) *led till rdn and hdd one and a half fs out, sn btn*... (8 to 1 op 12 to 1) 6
2672⁴ SUNTARA (Ire) [73] 9-7 D Holland (8) *rcd on outsd, effrt 3 fs out, slightly hmpd sn aftr, wknd.* ....(13 to 2 op 6 to 1 tchd 8 to 1) 7
2725⁵ RAGAZZO (Ire) [50] 7-12 L Charnock (1) *chsd ldrs till rdn and wknd o'r 2 fs out.* ....(20 to 1 op 16 to 1 tchd 25 to 1) 8
2775* GLOWING PATH [66] (v) 9-0 M Hills (5) *in tch till outpcd 3 fs out*................................(7 to 1 op 5 to 1) 9
2534² DALALAH [71] 9-5 R Hills (4) *in tch early, beh frm hfwy.* ....(8 to 1 op 7 to 1) 10

Dist: 3½l, 1½l, sht-hd, ½l, 1½l, 1l, 1½l, ¾l, 6l. 1m 40.60s. a 1.60s (10 Ran).
SR: 42/28/12/9/27/21/20/-/6/ (George L Ohrstrom), Mrs J Cecil

3102 Silkwood Maiden Handicap Class E (0-70 3-y-o and up) £3,300 1¼m 46yds ....(4:40)

2815² FOREST STAR (USA) [45] (v) 4-8-3 (5*) Stephen Davies (14) *made virtually all, hrd rdn wl o'r one furlong out, styd on gmely ins*.......... (13 to 2 op 6 to 1 tchd 8 to 1) 1
2873⁹ TINSASHE (Ire) [48] 3-7-13 (3*) N Kennedy (6) *pld hrd early, nvr far off pace, rdn 2 fs out, ran on ins last.* .... (20 to 1 op 14 to 1 tchd 33 to 1) 2
1919⁶ CUTLASS (Ire) [70] 3-9-10 R Hills (5) *mid-div till outpcd o'r 3 fs out, ran on wl ins fnl 2.* ....(3 to 1 fav op 4 to 1 tchd 9 to 2) 3
2937⁵ CALL ME BLUE [70] 3-9-10 Paul Eddery (1) *trkd wnr, dsptd ld 2 fs out, no extr ins last.* .... (15 to 2 op 6 to 1 tchd 8 to 1) 4
2834⁷ STEPPE CLOSER [48] 3-7-13 (3*) D Harrison (10) *chsd ldrs, rdn o'r 2 fs out, kpt on one pace*..... (7 to 1 op 4 to 1) 5
2350² CASTING SHADOWS [48] 4-8-11 D Holland (9) *towards rear, hdwy o'r 2 fs out, nvr nrr.* ....(9 to 2 op 4 to 1 tchd 5 to 1) 6
2420⁷ NOVA SPIRIT [54] 5-9-3 J Williams (11) *in rear, some hdwy 3 fs out, nvr nr to chal*........................ (8 to 1) 7
2384² COOCHIE [30] (bl) 4-7-7 N Adams (12) *slwly away, hdwy hfwy, rdn and wknd o'r 2 fs out.* .... (11 to 1 op 8 to 1 tchd 12 to 1) 8
2350⁵ KALOKAGATHOS [30] 4-7-7 G Bardwell (13) *al in rear.* .... (14 to 1 op 8 to 1) 9
2849² FULL SHILLING (USA) [42] 4-8-5 T Sprake (2) *pld hrd, in cl tch till wknd o'r 2 fs out*...........(14 to 1 op 9 to 1) 10
1309 MY SISTER LUCY [40] 3-7-8¹ J Quinn (8) *mid-div, beh fnl 3 fs*..............................(33 to 1 op 20 to 1) 11
2859 PYRRHIC DANCE [56] 3-8-10 M Hills (3) *al beh.* .... (16 to 1 op 10 to 1) 12
WOODLANDS CROWN [30] 10-7-3³ (7*) N Varley (4) *sn beh, tld off fnl 3 fs*........ (50 to 1 op 33 to 1 tchd 66 to 1) 13

Dist: 1½l, ½l, ½l, ½l, ¾l, 1l, 3½l, 2l, nk, 1l. 2m 10.10s. a 3.70s (13 Ran).
SR: 26/17/38/37/14/21/25/-/-/ (J Naughton), Miss Gay Kelleway

BRIGHTON (good to firm)

Thursday August 5th
Going Correction: MINUS 0.20 sec. per fur.

3103 Ringmer Selling Stakes Class G (2-y-o) £2,070 5f 59yds. . . . . (2:00)

2895[5] CHARISMA GIRL 8-6 G Duffield (5) *prmnt, rdn hfwy, swtchd rght and ran on to ld wl ins fnl furlong, all out.* . . . . . (14 to 1 op 16 to 1 tchd 20 to 1) 1
2946[5] CANDI DAS (Ire) (bl) 7-13 (7*) Antoinette Armes (8) *chsd ldrs, gd prog appr fnl furlong, fnshd strly, nvr nrr.* . . . . . (14 to 1 op 12 to 1) 2
2949[6] READY-FREDDIE 8-6 (5*) D McCabe (4) *strted slwly, beh, prog on outer and edgd lft appr fnl furlong, ran on ins last, nrst finish.* . . . . . (12 to 1 op 10 to 1) 3
2886[9] DANCES WITH RISK 8-6 G Hind (9) *sn led, rdn o'r 2 fs out, hdd and wknd wl ins last.* . . . . . (11 to 10 on op 5 to 4 on tchd Evens) 4
2316[7] SHARP SPRING 8-6 (5*) K Rutter (6) *chsd ldrs, rdn and styd on one pace appr fnl furlong.* . . . . . (14 to 1 op 10 to 1 tchd 16 to 1) 5
1203[8] MACE EL REEM 8-6 M Roberts (13) *chsd ldr, rdn hfwy, ev ch appr fnl furlong, wknd.* . . . . . (16 to 1 op 12 to 1 tchd 20 to 1) 6
1009[5] PETRATHENE (bl) 8-6 J Reid (14) *strted slwly, sn chasing ldrs, rdn and not quicken appr fnl furlong.* . . . . . (10 to 1 op 7 to 1) 7
JUST A SINGLE (Ire) 8-11 A McGlone (1) *wl beh, rng on whn not clr run o'r one furlong out, styd on ins last, nvr nr to chal.* . . . . . (20 to 1 op 10 to 1) 8
2492 HUMMINBIRDPRINCESS 8-6 B Rouse (11) *chsd ldrs till wknd wl o'r one furlong out.* . . . . . (50 to 1 op 33 to 1) 9
2911[9] BON TON 8-6 S Whitworth (3) *al rear.* (33 to 1 op 25 to 1) 10
2610 TERMITE 8-6 R Perham (7) *prmnt, wkng whn not clr run wl o'r one furlong out.* . . . . . (50 to 1 op 33 to 1) 11
2814[5] SPORT RACING CLUB (bl) 8-6 A Munro (2) *cl up till wknd 2 fs out.* . . . . . (25 to 1 op 20 to 1) 12
2610[9] CRAFTY CRICKETER (bl) 8-11 S Dawson (10) *chsd ldrs, rdn and wknd sn aftr hfwy.* . . . . . (50 to 1 op 33 to 1) 13
2911[5] BURMA STAR 8-6 R Cochrane (12) *al last and wl beh.* . . . . . (10 to 1 op 7 to 1) 14
Dist: ¾l, ¾l, sht-hd, 1½l, ½l, nk, ½l, 3½l, 1l, nk. 1m 3.90s. a 3.80s (14 Ran).
(Clear Height Racing), S Dow

3104 Marina Maiden Auction Stakes Class D (2-y-o) £3,289 5f 213yds. . . . . . . (2:30)

AL BATTAR (USA) 9-0 R Cochrane (2) *dwlt, last till effrt o'r one out, ran on strly to ld wl ins fnl furlong, improve.* . . . . . (11 to 4 op 6 to 4 tchd 3 to 1) 1
2586[5] SEDIMENTARY 8-11 (3*) C Hodgson (5) *led, hrd rdn 2 fs out, hdd and no extr wl ins last.* . . . (33 to 1 op 10 to 1) 2
1211[3] NICE WELCOME 8-9 W Woods (4) *trkd ldrs gng easily, effrt o'r one furlong out, shaken up and found nil.* . . . . . (13 to 8 on op 5 to 4 on) 3
2668 HENRY'S LUCK 9-0 S Whitworth (1) *chsd ldr o'r 3 fs, sn hrd rdn and one pace.* . . . . . (12 to 1 tchd 16 to 1) 4
DOME PATROL 9-0 A Munro (3) *cl up till rdn and wknd o'r one furlong out.* . . . . . (10 to 1 op 6 to 1) 5
Dist: 1l, 1½l, 2l, 2l. 1m 12.20s. a 3.80s (5 Ran).
(Umm Qarn Racing), L M Cumani

3105 Brighton Sprint Handicap Class C (0-95 3-y-o and up) £6,264 5f 59yds . . . . (3:00)

2392[7] HEAVEN-LIEGH-GREY [64] 5-8-2 A Munro (1) *made all, rdn 2 fs out, clr appr last, jst hld on.* . . . (7 to 1 op 10 to 1) 1
2363 SHIKARI'S SON [80] 6-9-4 G Duffield (6) *strted slwly, hld up, prog on outsd wl o'r one furlong out, ran on strly ins last, jst fld.* . . . . . (5 to 1 op 9 to 2 tchd 11 to 2) 2
2628[7] FARFELU [90] 6-10-0 R Cochrane (4) *chsd wnr, rdn 2 fs out, kpt on one pace.* . . . . . (5 to 1 tchd 11 to 2) 3
2620[2] HEAVENLY RISK [88] 3-9-8 A McGlone (2) *beh and rdn alng, styd on frm o'r one furlong out, nvr nrr.* . . . . . (7 to 1 op 6 to 1 tchd 8 to 1) 4
2715[4] ASSIGNMENT [72] 7-8-10 S Whitworth (3) *rear and rdn alng, effrt 2 fs out, sn one pace.* . . . . (12 to 1 op 8 to 1) 5
2987 TERRHARS (Ire) [84] 5-9-8 R Perham (9) *cl up till rdn and wknd wl o'r one furlong out.* . . . . (16 to 1 tchd 14 to 1) 6
2969[6] CALEMAN [75] 4-8-13 W Woods (7) *prmnt 2 fs, sn rdn and outpcd.* . . . . . (20 to 1 op 12 to 1) 7
2987 RUNNING GLIMPSE (Ire) [81] 5-9-5 M Roberts (5) *prmnt till rdn and wknd 2 fs out.* . . . . . (11 to 1 op 8 to 1 tchd 12 to 1) 8
2305[4] VERDE ALITALIA (Ire) [78] 4-9-2 J Reid (8) *prmnt, rdn o'r 2 fs out, wknd rpdly.* (5 to 2 fav op 2 to 1 tchd 11 to 4) 9
Dist: Sht-hd, 4l, 2½l, 1l, 1l, 1l, 3½l, 7l. 1m 2.20s. a 2.10s (9 Ran).
SR: 25/40/34/18/2/10/ (Peter M Dodd), J Berry

3106 Cliftonville Rating Related Maiden Stakes Class F (3-y-o) £2,243 1m 3f 196yds. . . . . (3:30)

2752[8] IMPECCABLE TASTE 8-9 M Roberts (4) *prmnt, rdn to ld 3 fs out, styd on.* . . . (7 to 4 fav tchd 13 to 8 and 15 to 8) 1
2847[6] GOLD TASSEL 8-9 J Reid (5) *dwlt, hld up, prog o'r 3 fs out, ev ch 2 out, hrd rdn and not quicken.* . . . . . (9 to 4 op 6 to 4 tchd 5 to 2) 2
1111[7] RISPOTO 8-9 G Duffield (1) *hld up, prog 4 fs out, ev ch 2 out, not quicken, styd on ag'n ins last.* . . . . . (5 to 1 tchd 11 to 2) 3
2828[7] BORROWED AND BLUE 8-9 A Munro (6) *led to 3 fs out, sn outpcd, styd on ag'n ins last.* . . . . . (7 to 1 tchd 8 to 1 and 6 to 1) 4
2685[5] MISS MICHELLE 8-9 R Perham (3) *al rear, hrd rdn and wknd 3 fs out.* . . . . . (25 to 1 op 20 to 1 tchd 33 to 1) 5
2189[8] PRETTY BABY 8-9 R Cochrane (2) *prmnt, jnd ldr o'r 3 fs out, sn rdn and wknd rpdly.* . . . . . (9 to 1 op 6 to 1 tchd 10 to 1) 6
Dist: 1l, ¾l, nk, 12l, 7l. 2m 36.10s. a 8.60s (6 Ran).
(R M Cyzer), C A Cyzer

3107 Brighton Summer Handicap Class D (0-75 3-y-o and up) £3,172 1m 1f 209yds. . . . . (4:00)

2873[3] TEJ SINGH (USA) [74] 3-9-7 M Roberts (6) *keen hold, trkd ldrs, led 2 fs out, ran on wl.* . . . . . (11 to 8 fav op 7 to 4 tchd 2 to 1 and 5 to 4) 1
2930[4] COURAGEOUS KNIGHT [70] 4-9-5 (7*) D Gibbs (3) *last, chsd alng 4 fs out, ran on o'r 2 out, chased wnr ins last, nvr able to chal.* . . . . . (9 to 1 op 7 to 1 tchd 10 to 1) 2
2113[3] MA BELLA LUNA [61] 4-9-3 J Reid (5) *settled rear, effrt on outer o'r 2 fs out, sn rdn and not quicken.* . . . . . (7 to 2 op 5 to 2 tchd 4 to 1) 3
2445 DON'T DROP BOMBS (USA) [39] 4-7-9 S Dawson (4) *led till rdn and hdd 2 fs out, one pace.* . . . (20 to 1 op 14 to 1) 4
2669 TIGER CLAW (USA) [46] 7-8-2 A Munro (1) *prmnt, rdn 3 fs out, one pace.* . . . . . (6 to 1 op 8 to 1 tchd 9 to 1) 5
2491[3] FLYING WIND [42] 4-7-12 A Morris (2) *hld up, prog o'r 3 out, rdn and wknd 2 fs out.* . . . . . (14 to 1 op 12 to 1 tchd 16 to 1) 6
2120[2] RACHELLY [53] 3-8-0 A McGlone (7) *chsd ldr to 4 fs out, sn rdn and wknd.* . . . . . (8 to 1 op 5 to 1 tchd 10 to 1) 7
Dist: 2½l, 2l, 1l, 1l, 8l, 1½l. 2m 2.70s. a 4.50s (7 Ran).
SR: 42/42/29/5/10/-/-/ (Sheikh Mohammed), L M Cumani

3108 Edburton Maiden Handicap Class D (0-80 3-y-o and up) £3,114 5f 213yds . . . . (4:30)

2580[2] TRAPEZIUM [78] 3-10-0 M Roberts (2) *made all, clr o'r one furlong out, pushed out nr finish, cmftbly.* . . . . . (15 to 8 op 6 to 4 tchd 2 to 1) 1
2868[2] POYLE AMBER [48] 4-8-3 G Duffield (3) *al chasing wnr, hrd rdn 2 fs out, ran on one pace.* . . . . . (13 to 8 fav op 2 to 1) 2
2711[3] SOPHISTICATED AIR [54] 3-8-4 S O'Gorman (1) *cl up on ins, rdn 2 fs out, ran on one pace inside last.* . . . . . (4 to 1 tchd 9 to 2) 3
2897 VILLAVINA [62] 3-8-12 A Munro (4) *chsd ldrs till rdn and wknd 2 fs out.* . . . . . (13 to 2 op 6 to 1 tchd 7 to 1) 4
2613[7] SHARRO [65] 3-9-1 Gay Kelleway (5) *chsd ldrs till wknd rpdly o'r 2 fs out.* . . . . . (25 to 1 op 12 to 1) 5
Dist: 1l, sht-hd, 6l, 20l. 1m 10.10s. a 1.70s (5 Ran).
SR: 56/27/27/11/-/ (Sheikh Mohammed), L M Cumani

DEAUVILLE (FR) (good to soft)
Thursday August 5th
Going Correction: PLUS 0.40 sec. per fur.

3109 Prix de Thiberville (Listed) (3-y-o) £14,337 1½m 110yds. . . . . (3:15)

DABARA (Ire) 8-9 G Mosse, ... 1
2690[3] BRIGHT MOUNTAIN (USA) 8-9 D Boeuf, ... 2
JO KNOWS (USA) 8-9 D Bonilla, ... 3
RAINY SKY 8-9 Pat Eddery, ... 4
Dist: 1l, 1½l, sht-hd, sht-hd, hd, ¾l, 2l, 4l. 2m 48.10s. a 11.60s (9 Ran).
SR: 29/27/24/23/ (H H Aga Khan), A de Royer-Dupre

MALLOW (IRE) (good to firm)
Thursday August 5th

3110 Fermoy Nursery (2-y-o) £2,245 5f . . . . (6:00)

2403[4] PEACE TOKEN (Ire) [-] 8-13 (8*) G Coogan (6) . . (6 to 4 fav) 1
2188* MAHASEAL (USA) [-] 8-7 W J Supple (3) . . . . . (5 to 2) 2
3039 ASTRADANE (Ire) [-] 8-3 (6*) R V Skelly (2) . . . . . (9 to 1) 3
1608[4] EASTROP DANCER (Ire) [-] 7-8 (6*) J J Behan (4) . . . (6 to 1) 4
2704[7] GALLIC VICTORY (Ire) [-] (bl) 8-5[1] P Shanahan (1) . . (5 to 2) 5
Dist: Nk, 2½l, 5l, hd. 57.10s. (5 Ran).
(Mrs B Howard), J G Coogan

3111 Newmarket Maiden (3-y-o and up) £2,245 1m 1f. . . . . (7:00)

2700[5] PETOFI 3-9-0 M J Kinane (2) . . . . . (6 to 4) 1

2956^{3} DAHLIA'S BEST (USA) 3-9-0 W J Supple (4)....(5 to 4 fav) 2
2460^{4} TURNER PRIZE (Ire) (bl) 3-9-0 S Craine (3).........(6 to 1) 3
2843^{3} SILVER JAR (Ire) 3-8-5 (6*) J J Behan (1)...........(4 to 1) 4
Dist: 3l, 3l, 20l. 1m 53.10s. (4 Ran).
(Mrs S Khan), D K Weld

3112 Sugar Factory Handicap (0-70 3-y-o and up) £2,245 1m 1f........... (7:30)

2496^{5} MY GOSSIP (Ire) [-] 3-8-1 N G McCullagh (11)..(5 to 2 fav) 1
$4686a^{7}$ VISTAGE (Ire) [-] 5-9-10 J P Murtagh (2)..........(10 to 1) 2
1922^{4} LUCKY PRINCE (Ire) [-] 3-9-2 M J Kinane (5).......(4 to 1) 3
2901^{9} MORNING NURSE (Ire) [-] 4-8-12 (4*) P Carberry (10)
....(10 to 1) 4
2556^{8} NORDIC MINE (Ire) [-] 3-8-0 (6*) J A Heffernan (3) (14 to 1) 5
1794^{9} WARREN STREET (Ire) [-] 3-9-2 S Craine (9)......(10 to 1) 6
2692^{3} BENGALI (Ire) [-] 3-7-13[1] W J Supple (1)...........(5 to 1) 7
2141^{9} SON OF TEMPO (Ire) [-] 4-7-11 (2*) R M Burke (7) (14 to 1) 8
3040^{2} CARRIG STAR (Ire) [-] 4-9-1 (6*) J J Behan (6).....(10 to 1) 9
2556^{5} BRAZEN ANGEL (Ire) [-] 3-9-1 J F Egan (8)....... (6 to 1) 10
2677^{4} TERN DANCER (Ire) [-] (bl) 3-8-11 B Coogan (4).... (8 to 1) 11
Dist: 2l, 1l, sht-hd, 3l. 1m 53.20s. (11 Ran).
(N Stassen), Joseph M Canty

PONTEFRACT (good to soft (races 1,2), soft (3,4,5,6))

Thursday August 5th

Going Correction: PLUS 0.25 sec. per fur. (races 1,4,5), MINUS 0.05 (2,3,6)

3113 York & Westminster Apprentice Series Limited Stakes Round Three Class F (0-65 3-y-o) £2,807 1¼m 6yds ....(2:50)

2856* EFIZIA 8-4 (5*) S Copp (3) *trkd ldrs, hdwy 3 fs out, led entering last, pushed out*...........(3 to 1 op 5 to 2) 1
2873* DODGY DANCER 8-11 (3*) R Painter (6) *cl up, led 2 and a half fs out, quickened clr, rdn and hdd entering last, kpt on*.............................. (4 to 1 op 3 to 1) 2
2774^{3} ATHERTON GREEN (Ire) 9-0 G Parkin (2) *hld up, hdwy 3 fs out, effrt 2 out, sn rdn, styd on one pace.*
....(4 to 1 op 3 to 1) 3
2107^{3} HAZARD A GUESS (Ire) 8-9 (5*) D Thomas (4) *hld up beh, hdwy on ins o'r 2 fs out, sn rdn, styd on one pace.*
..................(5 to 2 fav op 3 to 1 tchd 7 to 2) 4
2696^{9} DUPLICATE 8-11 (3*) P Johnson (1) *cl up, rdn o'r 3 fs out, sn btn*...............................(5 to 1 op 4 to 1) 5
2104 NEWGATESKY 8-4 (5*) J Dennis (5) *led, rdn and hdd 2 and a half fs out, sn wknd*..........(100 to 1 op 50 to 1) 6
Dist: ¾l, 2½l, ¾l, 5l, 5l. 2m 21.60s. a 13.40s (6 Ran).
(Mrs H I S Calzini), Mrs M Reveley

3114 EBF Carleton Maiden Stakes Class D (2-y-o) £4,056 5f................(3:20)

2754^{2} BLUE SIREN 8-9 L Dettori (6) *made virtually all, quickened clr 2 fs out, easily*.....(6 to 4 on tchd 11 to 8 on) 1
2357^{9} RANKAIDADE 8-9 S Perks (7) *chsd ldrs, rdn 2 fs out, styd on ins last, no ch wth wnr*.........(14 to 1 op 16 to 1) 2
GILABTENI 8-9 B Raymond (2) *cl up, rdn o'r 2 fs out, sn one pace*...............(11 to 4 op 9 to 4 tchd 3 to 1) 3
PELAMIS 8-11 (3*) S D Williams (5) *cl up, rdn o'r 2 fs out, sn one pace*.........................(20 to 1 op 16 to 1) 4
2862 DEMON DANCER (Ire) 9-0 N Connorton (4) *cl up to hfwy, sn rdn, one pace*.......................(66 to 1 op 33 to 1) 5
SURPRISE GUEST (Ire) 9-0 Dean McKeown (3) *slwly away, beh till styd on fnl furlong, better for race.*
......................(16 to 1 op 12 to 1 tchd 20 to 1) 6
KILLY'S RAYNJA (Ire) 9-0 J Carroll (1) *outpcd.*
......................(16 to 1 op 10 to 1 tchd 20 to 1) 7
Dist: 8l, 1½l, nk, hd, nk, 3½l. 1m 5.00s. a 3.80s (7 Ran).
SR: 14/-/-/-/ (J C Smith), I A Balding

3115 Dianne Nursery Class D (2-y-o) £4,620 6f................................(3:50)

1653^{3} CYARNA QUINN (Ire) [71] 8-5 W Carson (4) *chsd ldrs, hdwy on outsd 2 fs out, sn rdn, styd on to ld ins last.*
..................................(7 to 1 op 12 to 1) 1
2906^{5} BRAILLE (Ire) [87] 9-7 Dean McKeown (6) *sn led, quickened o'r 2 fs out, rdn and hdd ins last, no extr.*
.................................(2 to 1 fav op 5 to 2) 2
2706^{2} LUCKY MESSAGE (USA) [67] 8-1 K Darley (2) *chsd ldrs, pushed alng 2 fs out, effrt and swtchd appr last, sn rdn, one pace*.......(100 to 30 op 3 to 1 tchd 7 to 2) 3
2929^{3} BEST KEPT SECRET [84] 9-4 J Carroll (1) *cl up, chlgd one and a half fs out, sn rdn and hng lft, wknd ins last.*
....(9 to 2 op 4 to 1) 4
2974^{2} MY LIFETIME LADY (Ire) [72] 8-6 S Perks (5) *cl up, rdn and edgd rght 2 fs out, wknd appr last*... (4 to 1 op 7 to 2) 5
1303^{4} WIXI (Ire) [77] 8-11 P Robinson (3) *dwlt, hdwy o'r 2 fs out, sn rdn and btn*.............(16 to 1 op 12 to 1) 6
Dist: ½l, 3l, ½l, nk, 10l. 1m 18.50s. a 3.80s (6 Ran).
SR: 9/23/-/6/-/-/ (M Quinn), M R Channon

3116 Jim Gundill Memorial Handicap Class D (0-80 3-y-o and up) £3,655 1½m 8yds ....(4:20)

2801^{2} GREY POWER [68] 6-9-6 K Darley (2) *trkd ldrs gong wl, hdwy to ld 3 fs out, wide strt, rdn clr appr last, ran on strly*............ (11 to 8 fav op 11 to 10 tchd 6 to 4) 1
2373^{6} CONTRACT ELITE (Ire) [59] 3-8-0 A Mackay (8) *cl up, led aftr 4 fs, rdn and hdd 3 out, kpt on onc pace und pres.*
........................(9 to 2 op 4 to 1 tchd 5 to 1) 2
2581^{9} CANNY CHRONICLE [70] 5-9-8 P Robinson (4) *hld up, hdwy 3 fs out, rdn 2 out, kpt on one pace.*
........................(9 to 2 op 4 to 1 tchd 5 to 1) 3
1781^{5} SHAMSHOM AL ARAB (Ire) [52] 5-7-13 (5*) Darren Moffatt (6) *led 4 fs, cl up, effrt 3 out, rdn o'r 2 out, sn btn.*
....(7 to 2 op 4 to 1) 4
SAMAIN (USA) [53] 6-8-2 (3*) S Maloney (3) *pld hrd, trkd ldrs, effrt o'r 3 fs out, ev ch till rdn and wknd over 2 out*.......... (9 to 1 op 8 to 1 tchd 10 to 1) 5
Dist: 6l, 3l, 7l, 10l. 2m 48.70s. a 13.70s (5 Ran).
(A Frame), Mrs M Reveley

3117 Ronnie Senior 65th Birthday Maiden Stakes Class D (3-y-o and up) £3,728 1m 4yds.......................(4:50)

2627^{4} MUJAAZAFAH (USA) 3-9-0 J Carroll (2) *mid-div, hdwy 3 fs out, sn rdn alng, shaken up 2 out, styd on wl und pres to ld well ins last*................(Evens fav op 6 to 4) 1
ICE POOL (USA) 3-8-9 W Ryan (15) *led, wide strt, quickened clr 2 fs out, rdn and hdd wl ins last.*
........................(9 to 2 op 4 to 1 tchd 5 to 1) 2
2749^{2} MAKIN (USA) 3-9-0 W Carson (1) *prmnt, chsd ldr 2 and a half fs out, sn rdn, kpt on one pace.* (7 to 1 op 9 to 2) 3
NORTHERN BRED (Ire) 3-9-0 J Weaver (5) *beh, hdwy 3 fs out, styd on wl frm 2 out, nrst finish.*
.............................(14 to 1 op 10 to 1) 4
LA SPEZIA 3-8-9 P Robinson (14) *in tch, effrt and rdn o'r 2 fs out, kpt on one pace*........... (20 to 1 op 16 to 1) 5
WEFY (USA) 3-9-0 B Raymond (9) *mid-div, hdwy 3 fs out, rdn and kpt on one pace frm 2 out.* (20 to 1 op 12 to 1) 6
2507^{4} ASLAN (Ire) 5-9-7 K Fallon (4) *beh, styd on fnl 3 fs, nvr dngrs*... (20 to 1) 7
2120^{3} LADY BROKER 3-8-9 A Mackay (13) *prmnt, rdn 3 fs out, wknd*.. (50 to 1) 8
2563^{7} MISWAKI DANCER (USA) 3-9-0 K Darley (3) *al mid-div.*
....(7 to 1 op 9 to 2) 9
2507^{6} COUREUR 4-9-7 Dean McKeown (12) *dwlt, hdwy to join ldrs hfwy, rdn o'r 2 fs out, sn wknd.*
.............................(100 to 1 op 66 to 1) 10
2598^{6} QUARTZ HILL (USA) 4-9-2 (5*) J Tate (8) *chsd ldrs, rdn o'r 3 fs out, sn wknd*..............................(100 to 1) 11
2858^{3} GREENACRES STAR 3-8-2 (7*) S Sanders (7) *chsd ldrs to hfwy, sn lost pl*................ (50 to 1 op 33 to 1) 12
1093 ROLLING WATERS 3-9-0 Dale Gibson (6) *al beh.*
.............................(100 to 1 op 66 to 1) 13
Dist: 1½l, 1½l, 2l, 3l, 4l, 1½l, ¾l, 1l, 2l, 1½l. 1m 47.20s. a 5.10s (13 Ran).
SR: 54/44/44/38/24/17/19/5/7/ (Sheikh Ahmed Al Maktoum), J H M Gosden

3118 August Fillies' Handicap Class E (0-70 3-y-o and up) £3,028 6f......... (5:20)

1193^{7} NORDAN RAIDER [60] 5-9-11 N Connorton (3) *trkd ldrs gng wl, hdwy and wide strt, led one and a half fs out, pushed clr ins last*........... (9 to 2 co-fav op 6 to 1) 1
3094^{2} FOLLOWMEGIRLS [55] 4-9-6 K Fallon (4) *chsd ldrs, effrt and wide strt, rdn and ev ch appr fnl furlong, sn one pace*.........................(9 to 2 co-fav op 7 to 2) 2
2934^{4} KILLY'S FILLY [55] 3-9-1 J Carroll (7) *led 2 fs, cl up, rdn two out, sn one pace*...................(13 to 2 op 5 to 1) 3
2821^{2} MINDOMICA [60] 4-9-8 (3*) Emma O'Gorman (8) *cl up, led aftr 2 fs, wide strt, sn rdn, hdd one and a half out, soon wknd*.........................(9 to 2 co-fav op 4 to 1) 4
3095^{3} SPLASH OF SALT (Ire) [63] 3-9-4 (5*) A Garth (6) *chsd ldrs, rdn o'r 2 fs out, sn btn*........ (9 to 2 co-fav op 3 to 1) 5
LOLA WANTS [58] 3-9-4 P Robinson (2) *dwlt, sn pushed alng, al beh*.......... (11 to 1 op 7 to 1 tchd 12 to 1) 6
2777^{5} MISS ARAGON [50] 5-9-1 L Dettori (5) *outpcd.* (9 to 2 co-fav op 5 to 1 tchd 11 to 2) 7
Dist: 2½l, 2l, 3l, 2l, 6l, 8l. 1m 17.70s. a 3.00s (7 Ran).
SR: 45/30/17/15/5/-/-/ (Miss J A Camacho), M J Camacho

HAYDOCK (soft)

Friday August 6th

Going Correction: PLUS 0.20 sec. per fur. (races 1,3,6), PLUS 0.25 (2,4,5)

3119 Bank Quay Handicap Class D (0-85 3-y-o and up) £3,668 1¼m 120yds ....(6:15)

2773^{4} DORAZINE [61] 3-8-3 D Holland (4) *set modest pace, quickened aftr 4 fs, hdd o'r 3 out, sn pushed alng, rallied to rgn ld ins last, kpt on wl*......... (14 to 1 op 10 to 1) 1

2641[4] SAINT CIEL (USA) [64] 5-8-9 (7*) Michael Denaro (7) *chsd ldg 3, drvn alng o'r 2 fs out, sn outpcd, ran on ins fnl furlong*.......... (15 to 2 op 7 to 1 tchd 8 to 1) 2
1967[7] ARGYLE CAVALIER (Ire) [63] 3-8-5 W Carson (1) *trkd ldrs, drvn alng 3 fs out, ev ch one out, no extr last 50 yards*. .... (11 to 2 op 5 to 1 tchd 6 to 1) 3
2884[3] SHABANAZ [74] 8-9-9 (3*) O Pears (5) *steadied strt, hld up in last, effrt and drvn alng o'r 2 fs out, ev ch fnl furlong, one pace last 100 yards*. .... (7 to 4 fav tchd 2 to 1) 4
2696[3] BEAUMAN [68] (bl) 3-8-10 T Quinn (6) *keen hold, nvr far away, improved goig wl to ld o'r 3 fs out, drvn alng over one out, hdd ins last, sn btn*. .... (5 to 1 op 9 to 2 tchd 11 to 2) 5
2564[2] JADE GREEN [60] 4-8-12 W R Swinburn (2) *patiently rdn, pushed alng 3 fs out, nvr able to chal*. ....(4 to 1 op 9 to 2) 6
2774[5] WESTHOLME (USA) [64] 5-8-13 (3*) S Maloney (3) *hld up, pushed alng to improve o'r 2 fs out, no imprsn fnl furlong*.......... (8 to 1 op 7 to 1) 7
Dist: ¾l, sht-hd, sht-hd, 1½l, hd, ¾l. 2m 24.97s. a 13.97s (7 Ran).
(C John Hill), C J Hill

3120 Tattersalls Maiden Auction Series Stakes Qualifier Class E (2-y-o) £2,851 5f.......... (6:45)

2766[3] STEPHENSONS ROCKET 8-9 T Quinn (7) *made all, shaken up o'r one furlong out, kpt on strly*. (11 to 4 op 3 to 1) 1
2123[2] QUEEN'S TRUST 8-2 W Carson (3) *nvr far away, drvn alng 2 fs out, kpt on same pace ins fnl furlong*. ....(15 to 8 fav op 5 to 4) 2
2766[6] THREE OF HEARTS 7-8 (7*) M Humphries (6) *beh and sn pushed alng, took clr order hfwy, kpt on same pace fnl furlong*.......... (8 to 1 op 7 to 1) 3
2866 HIGH HOLME 8-6 S Webster (5) *in tch, rdn alng hfwy, not quicken o'r one furlong out*.......... (20 to 1 op 16 to 1) 4
2876[5] MR BERGERAC (Ire) 8-6 J Weaver (4) *dwlt, beh, imprvg whn not clr run o'r one furlong out, rdn and sn btn*. .... (11 to 4 op 3 to 1) 5
2916[6] COLONEL SINCLAIR (Ire) 8-6 S Perks (2) *in tch on outsd, reminders o'r one furlong out, sn drpd away*. .... (33 to 1 op 25 to 1) 6
2554 MISS KATIE LOUISE 8-2[1] G Duffield (1) *prmnt, shaken up 2 fs out, sn btn*..........(16 to 1 op 25 to 1) 7
Dist: 1½l, 3l, 2½l, 6l, 1½l, 1l. 1m 3.51s. a 4.71s (7 Ran).
SR: 26/13/-/-/ (John Stephenson & Sons (Nelson) Ltd), J Berry

3121 John Stephenson & Sons Nelson Ltd Handicap Class D (0-80 3-y-o and up) £3,629 1m 3f 200yds.......... (7:15)

2857[4] ROBERTY LEA [65] 5-8-13 T Quinn (1) *made all, pushed alng 2 fs out, hld on gmely whn hrd pressed ins last*. .... (100 to 30 op 5 to 2 tchd 7 to 2) 1
2373[3] MAD MILITANT (Ire) [70] 4-9-4 W R Swinburn (4) *slwly into strd, patiently rdn, improved on bit 3 fs out, drvn 2 out, ev ch, edgd lft, no extr ins fnl furlong*. .... (5 to 1 op 9 to 2 tchd 11 to 2) 2
2913* MUCH SOUGHT AFTER [82] 4-10-2 (4ex) G Duffield (3) *in tch on ins, imprvg whn no room a furlong out, kpt on same pace*.......... (3 to 1 jt-fav op 5 to 2) 3
2801[5] LEGION OF HONOUR [61] 5-8-2 (7*) V Halliday (5) *patiently rdn, cld hfwy, ev ch 2 fs out, wknd ins last*. ....(6 to 1 tchd 7 to 1) 4
164[4] LARA'S BABY (Ire) [55] 5-8-3 D Holland (6) *trkd ldg pair, drvn alng to hold pl 3 fs out, grad wknd*. .... (20 to 1 op 16 to 1) 5
2576[2] PLAY WITH ME (Ire) [73] 3-8-10 W Carson (2) *keen hold, trkd ldr, pushed alng and outpcd entering strt, drvn and ev ch o'r 2 fs out, sn wknd*..........(3 to 1 jt-fav op 11 to 4 tchd 100 to 30) 6
Dist: 1½l, ¾l, nk, 15l, 3l. 2m 37.69s. a 7.89s (6 Ran).
SR: 44/46/56/34/-/-/ (Wentdale Const Ltd), Mrs M Reveley

3122 Manchester Evening News Conditions Stakes Class D (2-y-o) £3,551 6f (7:45)

JUST HAPPY (USA) 8-11 W R Swinburn (2) *dwlt, trkd ldrs gng wl, shaken up to ld ins fnl furlong, styd on strly*. ....(11 to 10 fav op 5 to 4 tchd 11 to 8 and Evens) 1
2766* ISLAND MAGIC 9-1 K Fallon (3) *trkd ldrs on ins, not clr run o'r one furlong out, swtchd outsd and effrt entering last, no extr last 50 yards*.......... (3 to 1 op 5 to 1) 2
2058* MR M-E-N (Ire) 9-5 J Carroll (1) *dwlt, sn pressing ldr, rdn to ld o'r one furlong out, hdd ins last, soon outpcd*. .... (13 to 8 op Evens tchd 7 to 4) 3
1899[5] BOLD ARISTOCRAT (Ire) 8-11 S Perks (4) *hng lft thrght, led, shaken up o'r 2 fs out, hdd over one out, sn btn*. .... (16 to 1 op 14 to 1 tchd 20 to 1) 4
Dist: 1½l, 5l, 1½l. 1m 16.65s. a 5.05s (4 Ran).
SR: 26/24/8/-/ (Maktoum Al Maktoum), M R Stoute

3123 Haydock Park Pony Club Claiming Stakes Class F (3-y-o) £2,465 6f (8:15)

2892[2] PALACEGATE TOUCH (bl) 9-3 J Carroll (1) *cl up, led aftr one furlong, sn wl clr, rdn out towards finish*. .... (6 to 4 op 11 to 10) 1
2872[6] SING AS WE GO 7-9 N Carlisle (3) *led a furlong, chsd clr ldr, drvn o'r 2 fs out, no imprsn*. .... (8 to 1 op 10 to 1 tchd 14 to 1) 2
2731[2] THE SHARP BIDDER (Ire) 9-7 W R Swinburn (2) *chsd ldg pair, drvn alng hfwy, not on terms*. .... (5 to 4 on op 11 to 10) 3
2749 PEA FORTY FIVE 8-5 J Weaver (4) *sluggish strt, al struggling in rear*.......... (16 to 1 op 33 to 1) 4
Dist: 12l, 7l, 7l. 1m 15.67s. a 4.07s (4 Ran).
SR: 52/ (Palacegate Corporation Ltd), J Berry

3124 Halewood Handicap Class E (0-70 3-y-o and up) £3,078 1m 30yds.......... (8:45)

2474[9] EXCLUSION [63] 4-10-0 W Newnes (7) *made all, pushed alng 3 fs out, kpt on wl fnl furlong*. (8 to 1 tchd 9 to 1) 1
2353[2] MAI PEN RAI [40] (v) 5-8-5 D Holland (5) *chsd ldg pair, drvn alng 3 fs out, ran on ins fnl furlong*..........(3 to 1 jt-fav op 4 to 1) 2
2633[5] MAROWINS [45] 4-8-10 K Fallon (1) *hld up, rdn to improve 4 fs out, not clr run 2 out, swtchd, styd on ins last, nvr dngrs*.......... (11 to 2 op 5 to 1) 3
2459[5] MALCESINE (Ire) [44] (v) 4-8-9 J Fortune (2) *pressed ldrs, drvn alng 3 fs out, not quicken o'r one out*. .... (10 to 1 op 8 to 1) 4
2920[9] FOOLISH TOUCH [40] 11-8-5 A Mackay (6) *dwlt, beh til styd on fnl furlong, nrst finish*. .... (15 to 2 op 12 to 1 tchd 7 to 1) 5
2577[5] TUMBLING (USA) [45] 5-8-10 W Carson (8) *hld up in tch, effrt on outer 2 fs out, no imprsn*..........(3 to 1 jt-fav op 9 to 4) 6
2824[4] ON Y VA (USA) [58] 6-9-2 (7*) Sarah Thompson (4) *keen hold, trkd ldr, ev ch o'r 2 fs out, shaken up and wknd over one out*..........(7 to 1 op 6 to 1 tchd 8 to 1) 7
2932[3] BIDWEAYA (USA) [33] 6-7-12 N Adams (3) *hld up, effrt and rdn o'r 2 fs out, sn btn*..........(7 to 1 op 5 to 1) 8
Dist: ½l, 3l, 2½l, 1½l, 2l, ¾l, 3½l. 1m 48.99s. a 8.39s (8 Ran).
SR: 13/-/-/-/-/ (T A F Frost), H Candy

NEWMARKET (JULY) (good to firm)
Friday August 6th

Going Correction: MINUS 0.05 sec. per fur. (races 1,4), MINUS 0.20 (2,3,5,6)

3125 Headland International Properties Handicap Class C (0-90 3-y-o and up) £5,754 2m 24yds.......... (6:00)

2755* BOLD RESOLUTION (Ire) [59] 5-8-2 M Roberts (3) *hld up, cld on ldrs o'r 3 fs out, shaken up to ld over one out, sn clr, eased*..........(5 to 2 fav tchd 9 to 4 and 11 to 4) 1
2337* ROSINA MAE [76] 4-9-5 Dean McKeown (13) *led aftr one furlong till after 6 fs, led o'r 2 out till over one out, one pace*.......... (15 to 2 op 6 to 1 tchd 8 to 1) 2
2368[2] PROVENCE [71] 6-9-0 Paul Eddery (15) *handily plcd, hrd rdn and one pace last 2 fs*. ....(8 to 1 op 6 to 1 tchd 9 to 1) 3
2755[8] STAR QUEST [73] 6-9-2 L Dettori (5) *cl up, led aftr 6 fs for one furlong, led o'r 2 out till over one out, no extr*. .... (20 to 1 op 16 to 1) 4
2801[3] SWORD MASTER [73] 4-9-2 N Day (11) *hld up mid-div, effrt 3 fs out, no hdwy ins last 2*.......... (16 to 1 op 9 to 1) 5
2576[7] NEMEA (USA) [72] 3-8-0[2] P Robinson (14) *beh, styd on last 2 fs, nrst finish*..........(16 to 1 op 14 to 1 tchd 20 to 1) 6
2655[4] GOOD HAND (USA) [85] 7-10-0 N Connorton (12) *hld up mid-div, rdn and drpd rear 5 fs out, no dngr aftr*. .... (11 to 1 op 8 to 1 tchd 12 to 1) 7
2573[3] MULL HOUSE [77] 6-9-6 L Piggott (7) *led one furlong, chsd ldrs till wknd o'r 3 fs out*. .... (9 to 1 op 8 to 1 tchd 10 to 1) 8
2713[6] IRISH STAMP (Ire) [70] 4-8-13 M Wigham (1) *hld up rear, nvr nr to chal*..........(50 to 1 op 20 to 1) 9
2751[2] RUSTY REEL [67] (v) 3-7-9[5] (3*) B Doyle (2) *effrt frm rear 4 fs out, rdn and no hdwy from 2 out*. .... (40 to 1 op 25 to 1) 10
2349[3] BIG PAT [61] 4-8-4 G Bardwell (10) *beh most of way*. .... (20 to 1 op 14 to 1) 11
2891[3] OUR AISLING [76] 5-9-5 Pat Eddery (4) *prmnt till drpd rear 5 fs out, swtchd lft and effrt o'r 3 out, eased whn btn last 2 furlongs*.......... (16 to 1 op 10 to 1) 12
2521[2] BALLY KNIGHT [59] 7-8-2[3] (3*) C Hodgson (9) *hld up rear, nvr on terms*..........(16 to 1 op 14 to 1 tchd 20 to 1) 13
2467* YAAKUM [53] (v) 4-7-10 J Quinn (6) *led aftr 7 fs, sn clr, hdd o'r 3 out, lost pl quickly*. .... (16 to 1 op 14 to 1 tchd 20 to 1) 14
Dist: 2½l, 2l, ¾l, 1½l, 1l, 3½l, 1½l, ¾l, ½l, 4l. 3m 26.99s. a 3.99s (14 Ran).
SR: 40/54/47/47/45/28/52/42/33/ (R M Cyzer), C A Cyzer

3126 Billingham Robinson Accountants Selling Stakes Class F (2-y-o) £3,106 7f.......... (6:30)

2533* SILVER SLIPPER 8-11 M Roberts (4) *handily plcd, rdn to ld appr fnl furlong, drvn out*........ (4 to 1 op 6 to 1) 1
2946² PRINCESS CARMEN (Ire) 8-6 Pat Eddery (6) *cl up, led o'r 2 fs out till appr last, rallied last 100 yards.* .... (11 to 4 fav tchd 7 to 2) 2
2786⁶ MR ROUGH 8-8 (3*) C Hodgson (11) *settled rear, rdn alng o'r 2 fs out, styd on ins last, nrst finish.* ....(9 to 2 op 7 to 2) 3
3084⁵ WARWICK WARRIOR (Ire) 8-11 L Piggott (8) *in tch, cld on ldrs 3 fs out, ev ch one out, wknd.* ....(16 to 1 op 12 to 1 tchd 20 to 1) 4
2668 EXPRESS LINE 8-6 R Hills (5) *unruly strt, beh till effrt 2 fs out, no imprsn on ldrs ins last.* (33 to 1 tchd 100 to 1) 5
1350 MR MORIARTY (Ire) 8-11 W Ryan (1) *in tch on outsd till rdn and btn o'r 2 fs out.* ....(25 to 1 op 16 to 1 tchd 33 to 1) 6
2331 EASY D'OR 8-8 (3*) M Fenton (12) *pressed ldrs, wknd und pres 2 fs out*..........(16 to 1 op 12 to 1 tchd 20 to 1) 7
2603³ GLORIETTE 8-6 W Woods (10) *led till o'r 2 fs out, wknd over one out*.................................(9 to 2 op 5 to 2) 8
1536⁴ SALT STONE (Ire) 8-6 P Robinson (2) *ldg grp till wknd o'r 2 fs out*.............................. (10 to 1 op 8 to 1) 9
ARIAN SPIRIT (Ire) 8-1 (5*) D McCabe (9) *strted slwly, al beh*.................. (20 to 1 op 6 to 1 tchd 25 to 1) 10
2844 HOODLUM 8-4 (7*) S Eiffert (3) *early pace, wknd hfwy.* .... (25 to 1 op 20 to 1 tchd 33 to 1) 11

Dist: 1½l, 1½l, 2l, 1½l, 1½l, 1½l, ½l, ¾l, 2½l, 1l. 1m 28.24s. a 4.04s (11 Ran).
SR: 15/5/5/-/-/-/ (S M Threadwell), R Hannon

3127 Bernard Lloyd Associates Handicap Class C (0-90 3-y-o and up) £5,253 6f ....(7:00)

2734* SAMSOLOM [74] 5-9-2 K Darley (4) *hld up, hdwy and not much room o'r 2 fs out, rdn to ld over one out, drvn out.* .... (13 to 2 op 7 to 1 tchd 6 to 1) 1
2944* ROCA MURADA (Ire) [68] 4-8-3 (7*,6ex) P McCabe (6) *hld up rear, ran on o'r 2 fs out, styd on und pres ins last.* .... (13 to 2 op 6 to 1 tchd 7 to 1) 2
2969* MASTER PLANNER [90] 4-9-11 (7*,6ex) J D Smith (10) *in tch, chlgd 2 fs out, not quicken o'r one out, styd on nr finish*.............. (6 to 1 fav tchd 5 to 1 and 7 to 1) 3
2661² DARK EYED LADY (Ire) [80] 3-9-3 L Dettori (8) *led till o'r one furlong out, ran on one pace.* ....(25 to 1 op 20 to 1 tchd 33 to 1) 4
2971⁴ PETERSFORD GIRL (Ire) [79] 3-9-2 J Reid (1) *in tch, jnd ldrs 2 fs out, ev ch till no extr last 100 yards.* ....(7 to 1 op 6 to 1) 5
2969⁴ FIGHTER SQUADRON [66] 4-8-5 (3*) S D Williams (11) *cl up, ev ch 2 fs out, one pace fnl furlong*............(12 to 1) 6
2987⁶ SO RHYTHMICAL [81] 9-9-9 Pat Eddery (7) *hld up, ran on o'r 2 fs out, no imprsn wl ins last*...(7 to 1 tchd 8 to 1) 7
2908⁵ ANOTHER JADE [80] 3-9-3 R Hills (9) *mid-div, no prog last 2 fs*.............................. (14 to 1 op 10 to 1) 8
2971⁵ BANGLES [78] 3-8-12 (3*) D Harrison (2) *cl up, ev ch 2 fs out, wknd o'r one out*............... (7 to 1 op 6 to 1) 9
WADERS DREAM (Ire) [73] 4-9-1 J Quinn (5) *wl plcd 4 fs, sn lost pl*..(33 to 1) 10
2255³ CRADLE DAYS [86] 4-10-0 M Roberts (3) *speed to hfwy.* .... (15 to 2 op 7 to 1 tchd 8 to 1) 11

Dist: ¾l, nk, sht-hd, ½l, nk, 2l, 3l, 2½l, 2½l, nk. 1m 12.80s. a 1.10s (11 Ran).
SR: 56/47/68/52/49/40/47/29/17/ (The Hammond Partnership), P Howling

3128 Venture Business Forms Claiming Stakes Class E (3-y-o and up) £3,525 1 ½m.......................... (7:30)

3035² AZUREUS (Ire) 5-10-0 K Darley (1) *hld up in 3rd, led o'r 2 fs out, pushed clr appr last*....... (5 to 4 fav op 13 to 8) 1
2970⁶ TEMPLE KNIGHT 4-9-11 Pat Eddery (3) *led 6 fs, ev ch o'r 2 out, rdn and outpcd appr last*........(3 to 1 op 7 to 2) 2
2943* RASAYEL (USA) 3-8-5 B Raymond (4) *rcd keenly, chsd ldr, led 6 fs out till o'r 2 out, sn lost tch*...(2 to 1 op 6 to 4) 3
2471⁷ BILLY BUNTER 4-8-9 (7*) C Hawksley (2) *steadied strt, hld up rear, pushed alng 4 fs out, no hdwy.* ....(10 to 1 tchd 14 to 1) 4

Dist: 3½l, 7l, 2l. 2m 37.54s. a 8.74s (4 Ran).
SR: 21/11/-/-/ (J C Murdoch), Mrs M Reveley

3129 Tudor Gate Hotel And Restaurant Nursery Class D (2-y-o) £5,049 7f ....(8:00)

2492* FOOTSTEPS (Ire) [73] 8-1 (7*) T G McLaughlin (10) *trkd ldr, led 3 fs out, rdn clr 2 out, hld on nr line*......(4 to 1 jt-fav op 6 to 1 tchd 13 to 2) 1
2826² HIT THE CANVAS (USA) [68] 8-3 K Darley (8) *wl plcd, rdn alng 2 fs out, chsd wnr fnl furlong, rallied cl hme.* ....(4 to 1 jt-fav op 9 to 4) 2
2866⁶ PERSIAN HERITAGE [76] 8-11 R Cochrane (4) *slwly into strd, beh till ran on ins last 2 fs, not rch wnr.* ....(8 to 1 tchd 9 to 1) 3
2786² HEATHCLIFF (Ire) [74] 8-9 M Wigham (5) *hld up rear, rdn to improve o'r 2 fs out, kpt on one pace ins last.* ....(6 to 1 tchd 7 to 1) 4
2786³ ERRIS BOY [61] 7-10¹ D Biggs (11) *ldg grp, rdn alng and not quicken frm 2 fs out*......... (12 to 1 tchd 14 to 1) 5
2435⁴ ROYAL INSIGNIA [86] 9-4 (3*) M Fenton (9) *led to 3 fs out, wknd wl o'r one out.* (16 to 1 op 12 to 1 tchd 20 to 1) 6
2875⁸ DOUBLE DANCER [64] (bl) 7-13 J Quinn (6) *mid-div till reminders and drpd rear hfwy, kpt on clsg stages.* ....(33 to 1 op 25 to 1) 7
2412⁵ WICKLOW BOY (Ire) [72] 8-7 Pat Eddery (7) *hld up mid-div, rdn and effrt o'r 2 fs out, btn appr last.* ....(15 to 2 op 8 to 1 tchd 7 to 1) 8
1804 SHEPHERD MARKET (Ire) [82] 9-3 L Piggott (2) *hld up rear, effrt and reminders 3 fs out, not rch ldrs.* ....(10 to 1 tchd 12 to 1) 9
2929⁵ CONNECT (Ire) [72] 8-7 B Rouse (3) *wl plcd till wknd 2 fs out*.................. (9 to 1 op 7 to 1 tchd 10 to 1) 10
1985⁴ JUST HARRY [61] 7-10 G Bardwell (1) *settled rear, hrd rdn hfwy, sn lost tch*..................(8 to 1 tchd 9 to 1) 11

Dist: Nk, 4l, 1½l, hd, 3½l, ¾l, 3l, 2½l, 2½l, 8l. 1m 26.45s. a 2.25s (11 Ran).
SR: 39/33/29/22/8/22/ (Fahd Salman), P F I Cole

3130 Carwin Maiden Stakes Class D (2-y-o) £3,980 7f..................... (8:30)

HAWKER HUNTER (USA) 9-0 A Munro (13) *led to 2 fs out, rallied to ld last strds.* ....(11 to 8 fav op 11 to 10 tchd Evens and 6 to 4) 1
2792⁵ INNISHOWEN (USA) 9-0 Pat Eddery (12) *pressed ldr, led 2 fs out till rdn and hdd last strds.* ....(7 to 2 op 6 to 1 tchd 7 to 1 and 3 to 1) 2
BULAXIE 8-9 M Hills (11) *ran on frm rear 2 fs out, ev ch wl ins last, jst fld*.................... (33 to 1 op 20 to 1) 3
LEAR DANCER (USA) 9-0 J Reid (6) *handily plcd, rdn and outpcd appr fnl furlong.* .... (11 to 1 op 6 to 1 tchd 12 to 1) 4
WAYFARERS WAY (USA) 9-0 L Dettori (1) *mid-div, effrt on outsd o'r 2 fs out, styd on one pace fnl furlong.* ....(16 to 1 op 14 to 1 tchd 20 to 1) 5
SHOOFK 9-0 M Roberts (2) *ldg grp, not quicken 2 fs out, styd on one pace fnl furlong*.....(14 to 1 tchd 20 to 1) 6
IRON GENT (USA) 9-0 B Raymond (14) *wl plcd, rdn and not quicken o'r one furlong out.* ....(16 to 1 op 12 to 1 tchd 20 to 1) 7
RORY 9-0 Paul Eddery (8) *slwly into strd, improved o'r 2 fs out, nrst finish*................. (14 to 1 op 20 to 1) 8
WEST BUOYANT (USA) 9-0 W Ryan (16) *chsd frnt rnk, rdn and no extr appr last 2 fs*.........(20 to 1 op 12 to 1) 9
SHERMAN (Ire) 9-0 R Hills (9) *ldg grp till rdn and wknd o'r 2 fs out*............... (9 to 1 op 7 to 1 tchd 12 to 1) 10
BALLYMORRIS (Ire) 9-0 B Rouse (15) *al beh.* ....(33 to 1 op 25 to 1 tchd 50 to 1) 11
FARAS ELNAAS 9-0 W Woods (10) *in tch for o'r 4 fs.* ....(12 to 1 op 6 to 1) 12
FOURTH OF JUNE (USA) 9-0 B Marcus (3) *slwly into strd, sn mid-div, wknd o'r 2 fs out.* ....(16 to 1 op 14 to 1 tchd 20 to 1) 13
ELSDON (Ire) 9-0 P Robinson (4) *slwly into strd, outpcd.* ....(33 to 1 op 25 to 1) 14
2968 DANCING CLOWN 9-0 K Darley (7) *al rear.* ....(33 to 1 op 25 to 1) 15
2720⁶ MISTER O'GRADY (Ire) 9-0 R Cochrane (5) *wl plcd till rdn and wknd 3 fs out*................(33 to 1 op 25 to 1) 16

Dist: Nk, sht-hd, 5l, ½l, sht-hd, nk, 3½l, nk, hd, hd. 1m 26.92s. a 2.72s (16 Ran).
SR: 38/37/31/21/19/18/17/6/5/ (Fahd Salman), P F I Cole

REDCAR (good to soft) Friday August 6th

Going Correction: MINUS 0.10 sec. per fur.

3131 Bedale Selling Stakes Class G (2-y-o) £2,532 6f...................... (2:30)

2933* BENEFICIARY 8-6 M Birch (2) *confidently rdn, trkd ldr, led o'r one furlong out, sn clr, cmftbly.* .... (Evens fav op 5 to 4 tchd 6 to 4) 1
2541⁹ MARBLE 8-1 (5*) Darren Moffatt (5) *in tch, styd on wl fnl 2 fs, not rch wnr*................... (20 to 1 tchd 25 to 1) 2
WALWORTH LADY 8-6 S Webster (7) *slwly into strd, beh till styd on und pres fnl 2 fs, faltered ins last, kpt on.* ....(12 to 1 op 10 to 1) 3
2772⁶ FLOATING TRIAL (v) 8-6 J Carroll (9) *led till o'r one furlong out, wknd ins last*..................(7 to 4 op 5 to 4) 4
SUPERHOO 8-11 Dean McKeown (6) *nvr trble ldrs.* ....(14 to 1 op 10 to 1) 5
1759⁸ ARKINDALE SPIRIT (Ire) 8-11 T Lucas (3) *in tch, effrt hfwy, no hdwy*.. (12 to 1) 6
2766⁸ RISKY GIFT 8-11 L Charnock (1) *chsd ldrs till wknd quickly wl o'r one furlong out*......(20 to 1 op 8 to 1) 7
2705⁸ WESTCOAST (bl) 8-11 W Newnes (8) *in tch till wknd o'r 2 fs out*.. (25 to 1) 8
TEE JAY BABY 8-6 J Fanning (4) *dwlt, al beh.* ....(33 to 1 op 25 to 1) 9

Dist: 3½l, 2½l, sht-hd, 2½l, 3½l, 6l, 12l, 6l. 1m 13.40s. a 3.70s (9 Ran).
SR: 6/-/-/-/-/-/ (Reg Griffin), M H Easterby

3132 Cleveland Maiden Stakes Class D (3-y-o and up) £3,494 7f........... (3:00)

2749^{6} AWESOME VENTURE 3-8-12 J Weaver (3) *trkd ldrs, hdwy 3 fs out, slight ld o'r one out, sn rdn, hdd wl ins last, led on line*..........(9 to 1 op 7 to 1) 1
991^{3} AUTUMNIS (USA) 3-8-12 Pat Eddery (5) *led till o'r one furlong out, styd on und pres to ld wl ins last, ct on line*..........(5 to 4 on op Evens) 2
2787^{2} DESERT CHAMP (USA) 4-9-4 B Raymond (2) *trkd ldrs, effrt o'r 2 fs out, kpt on same pace*.......(11 to 4 op 2 to 1) 3
2698^{6} CALAMANCO 3-8-7 S Webster (1) *beh, hdwy 3 fs out, kpt on wl fnl furlong, not trble ldrs*..........(33 to 1) 4
1308^{4} SOBA UP 3-8-7 M Birch (11) *prmnt till wknd o'r 2 fs out.*..........(50 to 1) 5
522^{4} WILLOW RIVER (Can) 3-8-7 G Hind (8) *chsd ldrs, rdn o'r 2 fs out, sn btn*..........(11 to 1 op 10 to 1) 6
2596^{4} DUELETTA 3-8-7 W Newnes (4) *nvr dngrs*........(20 to 1) 7
2596^{3} MISS RITZ 3-8-7 Dale Gibson (10) *in tch till wknd hfwy.*..........(20 to 1) 8
2231^{6} RYDAL WATER 3-8-7 Dean McKeown (9) *al beh*...(50 to 1) 9
DARAJAH (USA) 3-8-7 J Carroll (6) *chsd ldrs till wknd hfwy*..........(6 to 1) 10

Dist: Sht-hd, 5l, 1½l, 2½l, 1l, 6l, ½l, 7l, 8l. 1m 24.90s. a 3.10s (10 Ran).
SR: 41/40/31/15/7/4/ (Back Hill Bloodstock Ltd), J A R Toller

3133 Heritage Homes Nursery Handicap Class D (2-y-o) £3,687 5f........(3:30)

2377* LEFT STRANDED [73] 9-3 K Darley (3) *chsd ldr, rdn to ld o'r one furlong out, jst hld on.*..........(9 to 2 op 5 to 1 tchd 4 to 1) 1
2435^{5} CHILIOLA [64] 8-8 Pat Eddery (4) *in tch, rdn 2 fs out, hdwy whn hmpd one out, ran on wl und pres, jst fld.*..........(6 to 1 op 5 to 1) 2
2659* MONKEY MUSIC [71] (bl) 9-1 J Carroll (11) *in tch, pushed alng hfwy, ran on wl und pres fnl 2 fs, nrst finish.*..........(7 to 2 op 5 to 2) 3
2814^{2} LADY SHERIFF [70] 9-0 T Lucas (2) *trkd ldrs, chlgd o'r one furlong out, sn rdn, one pace*.......(11 to 2 op 7 to 1) 4
2342* CERTIFICATE-X [73] 9-3 Dean McKeown (9) *chsd ldrs, edgd lft one furlong out, no extr*.........(10 to 1 op 9 to 1) 5
2974^{3} CLARET BUMBLE [68] 8-12 G Duffield (8) *chsd ldrs, effrt 2 fs out, no hdwy*..........(3 to 1 fav op 4 to 1) 6
3001 MERISSA [52] 7-10 L Charnock (7) *beh, some late hdwy, not trble ldrs*..........(16 to 1 op 14 to 1) 7
2569^{4} GREY TOPPA [50] 7-8 J Lowe (10) *in tch, no hdwy fnl 2 fs.*..........(20 to 1 op 16 to 1) 8
2949^{3} CHEEKY CHAPPY [61] 8-5 Alex Greaves (6) *in tch, hdwy o'r one furlong out, wknd fnl furlong.*..........(11 to 1 op 10 to 1) 9
2818* NORDICO PRINCESS [77] 9-7 S Perks (1) *led till o'r one furlong out, sn btn*..........(14 to 1 op 10 to 1) 10
2541^{7} RICH HARMONY [66] (bl) 8-10 W Newnes (5) *beh, sn rdn, lost tch hfwy*..........(10 to 1) 11

Dist: Sht-hd, ½l, ¾l, hd, 2½l, hd, hd, ¾l, ¾l, 10l. 59.70s. a 3.00s (11 Ran).
SR: 33/23/28/24/26/11/ (P D Savill), G Lewis

3134 Pat Phoenix Handicap Class E (0-70 3-y-o and up) £3,236 1m 3f......(4:00)

3033^{3} ROUSITTO [49] 5-8-9 W R Swinburn (10) *hld up, hdwy o'r 3 fs out, chlgd, not much room and edgd lft ins last, ran on wl to ld nr finish*........(3 to 1 fav tchd 100 to 30) 1
3033^{4} JUBRAN (USA) [68] 7-10-0 J Carroll (9) *dwlt, sn in tch, jnd ldr hfwy, led 4 fs out, rdn 2 out, hdd and no extr nr finish*..........(5 to 1 op 4 to 1) 2
2799^{4} MASTER OFTHE HOUSE [47] 7-8-7 G Duffield (6) *hld up, hdwy 3 fs out, chlgd one out, bumped ins last, no extr.*..........(6 to 1 op 8 to 1) 3
2551^{2} I'M A DREAMER (Ire) [68] 3-9-4 Dale Gibson (2) *in tch, pushed alng 4 fs out, ev ch 2 out, kpt on*........(9 to 2) 4
2101^{8} STATIA (Ire) [33] 5-7-7 Kim Tinkler (1) *beh, styd on wl fnl 2 fs, not rch ldrs*..........(100 to 1) 5
3056^{8} YOUNG GEORGE [37] 6-7-11 J Lowe (4) *prmnt till outpcd o'r 3 out, no dngr aftr*..........(16 to 1 tchd 20 to 1) 6
2457^{5} KISS IN THE DARK [53] 3-8-3 J Fanning (8) *mid-div, effrt o'r 3 fs out, ev ch 2 out, sn wknd*....(12 to 1 op 8 to 1) 7
2740* SIR EDWARD HENRY (Ire) [47] (v) 3-7-11 N Carlisle (3) *led to 4 fs out, wknd*..........(9 to 2 op 7 to 2) 8
2591^{7} ROAR ON TOUR [41] 4-8-1^{2} K Darley (5) *prmnt till wknd hfwy, tld off*..........(8 to 1 op 7 to 1 tchd 9 to 1) 9

Dist: ½l, 1l, ½l, 6l, 2l, nk, 5l, 15l. 2m 24.20s. a 8.80s (9 Ran).
SR: -/14/-/1/-/-/ (J Pattison), R Hollinshead

3135 Old Raby Claiming Stakes Class F (3-y-o and up) £2,534 1¼m........(4:30)

2369^{8} KAGRAM QUEEN 5-8-13 K Darley (5) *chsd ldrs, effrt 3 fs out, led o'r one out, styd on wl.*..........(6 to 4 jt-fav op 11 to 10) 1
2633^{9} RED INDIAN 7-9-2 Dale Gibson (3) *in tch, effrt 3 fs out, ev ch entering last, no extr*..........(7 to 1 op 8 to 1) 2
3035^{6} NO SUBMISSION (USA) 7-9-6 S Wood (4) *led till o'r 3 fs out, kpt on wl fnl furlong.*..........(6 to 4 jt-fav op 5 to 4 tchd 13 to 8) 3
2859 SLUMBER THYME (Ire) (bl) 4-8-3 L Charnock (6) *trkd ldr, led o'r 3 fs out till over one out, sn btn.*..........(12 to 1 op 8 to 1 tchd 14 to 1) 4

2769^{8} TIL FRIDAY 3-8-10 J Lowe (1) *al beh, lost tch fnl 3 fs.*..........(10 to 1 op 7 to 1) 5
3005^{6} WAWEEWAWOO (Ire) 5-9-0 (5*) Darren Moffatt (2) *al beh, rdn o'r 3 fs out, sn lost tch*..........(50 to 1 op 33 to 1) 6

Dist: 2½l, sht-hd, 1l, 12l, 10l. 2m 10.30s. a 9.10s (6 Ran).
(Mrs E A Kettlewell), Mrs M Reveley

3136 Summer Season Fillies' Handicap Class D (0-80 3-y-o and up) £3,260 5f..........(5:00)

2813* LOVE RETURNED [78] 6-10-0 M Tebbutt (2) *trkd ldrs, led wl o'r one furlong out, ran on well.*..........(7 to 2 op 3 to 1 tchd 4 to 1) 1
2018 PENNY HASSET [68] 5-9-4 T Lucas (1) *chsd ldrs, rdn o'r one furlong out, kpt on, no ch wth wnr.*..........(11 to 4 fav op 7 to 2 tchd 4 to 1) 2
2813 SHE'S SMART [78] 5-10-0 M Birch (8) *in tch, swtchd lft aftr 2 fs, effrt two out, kpt on same pace.*..........(15 to 2 op 6 to 1 tchd 8 to 1) 3
2935^{3} MEESON TIMES [46] 5-7-10 N Carlisle (3) *beh, effrt 2 fs out, kpt on fnl furlong*..........(4 to 1 op 3 to 1) 4
1478^{6} LOCAL HEROINE [71] 3-9-3 J Carroll (5) *led till wl o'r one furlong out, sn btn*..........(12 to 1 op 8 to 1) 5
2975^{3} SIMMIE'S SPECIAL [58] (bl) 5-8-8 K Darley (6) *cl up till wknd o'r one furlong out*..........(4 to 1 op 7 to 2) 6
2813 NIFTY FIFTY (Ire) [70] 4-9-6 G Duffield (7) *chsd ldrs till wknd o'r one furlong out*..........(10 to 1 op 8 to 1) 7

Dist: 3l, 1½l, sht-hd, 1l, 1½l, 1l. 58.90s. a 2.20s (7 Ran).
SR: 60/38/42/9/26/11/19/ (J M Ratcliffe), W Jarvis

SOUTHWELL (good)
Friday August 6th
Going Correction: MINUS 0.20 sec. per fur.

3137 Starfish Maiden Stakes Class D (2-y-o) £4,699 7f..................(2:20)

2430^{4} BLAZE AWAY (USA) 9-0 L Dettori (6) *chsd ldrs, pushed alng and hdwy on outer 3 fs, led one and a half furlongs out, sn quickened clr, easily.*..........(6 to 4 on op 5 to 4 on) 1
2862^{4} RUBY ESTATE (Ire) 8-9 J Quinn (7) *in tch, hdwy 2 and a half fs out, effrt and rdn o'r one furlong out, styd on, no ch wth wnr*..........(7 to 1 op 5 to 1) 2
2817^{3} AMIDST 8-9 Paul Eddery (5) *led 2 fs, cl up till led o'r two furlongs out, sn rdn and hdd one and a half furlongs out, one pace*..........(7 to 1 op 5 to 1) 3
2844^{6} STRADISHALL (bl) 9-0 N Day (2) *chsd ldg pair, rdn 2 fs out and sn one pace*.... (14 to 1 op 25 to 1 tchd 33 to 1) 4
2153^{4} OCEAN PARK 9-0 R Cochrane (1) *cl up, led aftr 2 fs, till rdn and hdd o'r two furlongs out, sn wknd.*..........(7 to 2 op 5 to 2) 5
2385^{5} STARSPORT (Ire) (bl) 9-0 J Fortune (8) *chsd ldrs, till rdn 2 fs out, sn wknd*..........(33 to 1 op 25 to 1) 6
2994 WORLD TRAVELLER 8-11 (3*) Emma O'Gorman (4) *dwlt, sn in tch, rdn 3 fs out and soon wknd.* (40 to 1 op 33 to 1) 7
HARLESTONE FIRS 9-0 W Carson (3) *slwly away, outpace and sn tld off*..........(16 to 1 op 10 to 1) 8

Dist: 4l, 1½l, 2l, 2½l, 5l, 10l, 5l. 1m 29.20s. a 2.20s (8 Ran).
SR: 46/29/24/23/15/ (Paul Mellon), I A Balding

3138 Candy-Floss Selling Stakes Class G (3-y-o) £2,070 1¼m.............(2:50)

1852^{5} WONDERFUL YEARS (USA) 9-0 K Fallon (1) *led to hfwy, pushed alng to chase ldr, rdn 2 fs out, styd on ins last to ld nr line*........ (13 to 8 fav op 5 to 4 tchd 7 to 4) 1
2529^{6} SHARE A MOMENT (Can) 9-0 L Dettori (5) *prmnt, hdwy to ld hfwy and sn pushed clr, rdn one and a half fs out, wknd ins last and ct nr finish*...... (9 to 4 op 11 to 4) 2
2529^{5} STAPLEFORD LASS (bl) 8-12 W Woods (4) *hld up, hdwy hfwy, effrt 2 fs out, sn rdn and wknd entering fnl furlong*..........(7 to 4 op 5 to 4) 3
80 LADY MAGADI 8-9 A Mackay (3) *chsd ldrs, rdn alng hfwy, sn lost pl and beh fnl 4 fs*..........(66 to 1 op 50 to 1) 4
2914^{7} PETAL'S JARRED 8-9 M Wigham (2) *beh frm hfwy.*..........(20 to 1 op 16 to 1) 5

Dist: Hd, 10l, 4l, 8l. 2m 17.30s. (5 Ran).
(Milton Wong), Mrs J R Ramsden

3139 Bucket & Spade Handicap Class D (0-80 3-y-o and up) £3,348 1¼m (3:20)

2884^{8} RIVAL BID (USA) [68] 5-9-12 N Day (5) *trkd ldrs, smooth hdwy 3 fs out, effrt to ld one and a half furlongs out, sn clr*..........(9 to 2) 1
2873^{5} TOUCH ABOVE [54] 7-8-5 (7*) V Halliday (2) *hld up, hdwy 4 fs out, effrt and a rdn one and a half furlongs out, kpt on one pace*..........(7 to 1 op 13 to 2) 2
2708^{2} SAFIR (USA) [77] 3-9-12 W Carson (6) *hld up, pushed alng 5 fs out, hdwy o'r 2 furlongs out and sn rdn, kpt on und pres ins last*..........(5 to 1 tchd 11 to 2) 3
2458* RAHIL (Ire) [79] 3-10-0 R Hills (4) *led, rdn o'r 2 fs out, hdd one and a half furlongs out, grad wknd.*..........(4 to 1 fav tchd 9 to 2) 4

2940⁹ CANADIAN CAPERS [52] 4-8-10 S Whitworth (8) *mid-div, hdwy hfwy, rdn o'r 2 fs and sn one pace*...... (20 to 1) 5
2776 COLORFUL AMBITION [65] 3-9-0 Paul Eddery (7) *prmnt, rdn 3 fs out, wknd wl o'r one furlong out.* ....(6 to 1 tchd 13 to 2) 6
2978⁴ CANNY LAD [47] (v) 3-7-10 J Quinn (9) *chsd ldr, rdn 3 fs out, wknd wl o'r one furlong out.* ....(10 to 1 tchd 11 to 1) 7
2820* PRESTON GUILD (Ire) [64] 3-8-13 D Biggs (1) *chsd ldrs, rdn alng hfwy, lost pl 3 fs out and sn beh.* ....(9 to 2 op 4 to 1 tchd 5 to 1) 8
2940⁸ KYRENIA GAME [65] 3-9-0 S O'Gorman (3) *al wl beh, tld off fnl 4 fs*.......... (14 to 1) 9
Dist: 3½l, 1l, ¾l, 2½l, 8l, 3l, 6l, 5l. 2m 11.10s. (9 Ran).
(David Altham), M A Jarvis

3140 Sand Castle Handicap Class E (0-70 3-y-o and up) £3,235 7f......... (3:50)

2768³ CORONA GOLD [50] 3-8-6 K Fallon (5) *al prmnt, effrt hfwy, led 2 fs out, rdn clr*..........(9 to 2 op 3 to 1) 1
836⁴ WATERLORD (Ire) [64] 3-9-6 L Dettori (6) *led, rdn and hdd 2 fs out, kpt on one pace.* (5 to 1 op 9 to 2 tchd 11 to 2) 2
2762⁴ YOUNG VALENTINE [52] 4-9-0 A Culhane (1) *in tch, effrt on inner 2 fs out, sn rdn, styd on one pace ins last.* ....(5 to 1 op 4 to 1) 3
2920⁷ BASSIO (Bel) [39] (h) 4-8-1 D Biggs (3) *al prmnt, effrt and ev ch o'r 2 fs out, sn rdn and one pace.* .... (12 to 1 op 10 to 1) 4
2789 MARTINOSKY [64] 7-9-12 N Day (8) *chsd ldrs, effrt and rdn 2 fs out, sn one pace*..........(8 to 1 op 7 to 1) 5
2663⁵ NORTHERN TRIAL (USA) [51] (v) 5-8-13 T Sprake (7) *chsd ldrs, effrt and rdn 2 fs out, sn one pace.* ....(4 to 1 fav op 9 to 2 tchd 5 to 1) 6
2863⁶ MISTER BLAKE [48] 3-8-2¹ (3*) Emma O'Gorman (4) *mid-div, swtchd ins and hdwy o'r one and a half fs out, sn rdn and btn*..........(9 to 1 op 7 to 1) 7
2121 GREENWICH CHALENGE [53] 3-8-9 M Wigham (9) *al rear.* .... (25 to 1 op 20 to 1) 8
2264⁸ SENSABO [37] 3-7-7 G Bardwell (2) *al rear.* .... (16 to 1 op 33 to 1) 9
Dist: 5l, 1½l, sht-hd, ¾l, ½l, ¾l, 7l, 1½l. 1m 29.10s. a 2.10s (9 Ran).
SR: 40/39/28/14/37/22/11/-/- (T J FitzGerald), J G FitzGerald

3141 Sea Breeze Claiming Stakes Class F (2-y-o) £2,243 6f................(4:20)

2668⁴ LITTLE HOOLIGAN 8-1 C Rutter (3) *chsd ldrs, effrt 2 fs and sn rdn, staying on whn lft in ld wl ins last.* ....(7 to 1 op 6 to 1) 1
2637* UP THE MARINERS (Ire) 7-13² (5*) K Rutter (2) *cl up, rdn to ld one and a half fs out, sn clr, wndrd badly ins fnl furlong, wknd, hdd and not run on nr finish.* ....(5 to 2 op 2 to 1) 2
2825* SPORTING HEIR (Ire) (bl) 8-13 M Wigham (4) *led, rdn 2 fs out, sn hdd and wknd appr last.* .... (15 to 8 fav op 2 to 1 tchd 9 to 4 and 7 to 4) 3
2818⁵ SING SONG BLUES (bl) 8-7 J Fortune (6) *chsd ldrs, rdn o'r 2 fs out and sn btn*..... (7 to 2 op 3 to 1 tchd 4 to 1) 4
2533⁴ BERNIE'S SISTER (Ire) (v) 8-4 D Biggs (1) *beh, effrt and some hdwy 2 and a half fs out, sn rdn and wknd.* .... (11 to 2 op 6 to 1 tchd 13 to 2) 5
BLUEY 8-7 R P Elliott (5) *al outpcd and beh.* .... (40 to 1 op 20 to 1) 6
Dist: 1l, 5l, 8l, 5l, 12l. 1m 16.70s. a 2.70s (6 Ran).
SR: 9/6/-/ (A Kinghorn), M R Channon

3142 Deck-Chair Maiden Handicap Class E (0-70 3-y-o and up) £3,390 1½m (4:50)

2859⁸ FAIRY WISHER (Ire) [35] 4-7-3 (7*) N Varley (4) *chsd ldrs, hdwy hfwy, led 4 fs out, wide strt, sn rdn and ran on wl fnl 2 furlongs*..... (12 to 1 op 16 to 1 tchd 20 to 1) 1
2822⁴ ANNABEL'S BABY (Ire) [33] 4-7-8 N Adams (6) *hld up, hdwy hfwy, effrt 3 fs out and sn ev ch rdn and kpt on one pace fnl 2 furlongs*.......... (11 to 2 op 9 to 2) 2
2341⁸ PINKERTON'S SILVER [46] 3-7-10 D Biggs (2) *in tch, hdwy 4 fs out, rdn 3 furlongs out and sn one pace.* ....(9 to 1 op 7 to 1) 3
2992 EVERSO IRISH [37] 4-7-12 A Mackay (5) *led aftr one furlong, hdd hfwy, sn rdn and one pace fnl 4 fs.* ....(7 to 1 op 6 to 1) 4
4723a² DONIA (USA) [67] 4-10-0 A Munro (8) *chsd ldrs, led hfwy, sn rdn and hdd 4 fs out, wknd 2 and a half furlongs out*..........(13 to 8 fav op 3 to 1 tchd 7 to 2) 5
2107 RESTRAINT [46] 3-7-10 A Tucker (7) *hld up, hdwy hfwy, rdn o'r 3 fs out and sn wknd*..... (20 to 1 op 16 to 1) 6
3090⁷ TOUR LEADER (NZ) [53] (bl) 4-8-7 (7*) V Halliday (1) *hld up, hdwy to join ldrs hfwy, rdn o'r 3 fs out, and sn wknd.* ....(6 to 1 op 9 to 2) 7
2847⁹ CHOUETTE [43] 3-7-5³ (5*) D Wright (9) *slwly away, al beh.* .... (17 to 2 op 7 to 1 tchd 9 to 1) 8
2828⁴ HAVE A NIGHTCAP [40] 4-8-1 F Norton (3) *led one furlong, cl up till rdn and wknd hfwy, sn lost pl and beh.* .... (17 to 2 op 6 to 1 tchd 9 to 1) 9
Dist: 2l, 8l, 6l, 2½l, ¾l, 1l, 2l, 2l. 2m 38.50s. a 4.50s (9 Ran).
SR: 13/7/-/-/8/-/ (Miss M T Sheridan), M F Barraclough

AYR (soft)
Saturday August 7th
Going Correction: PLUS 0.80 sec. per fur. (races 1,2,3,4,5), PLUS 0.35 (6)

3143 Barassie Median Auction Maiden Stakes Class E (2-y-o) £3,011 7f (2:35)

2756⁴ HOBART 9-0 N Day (6) *in tch, hdwy to chase ldr 2 out, kpt on wl und pres to ld post.* ....(9 to 2 op 7 to 2 tchd 5 to 1) 1
2792³ TOM MORGAN 9-0 J Quinn (4) *pld hrd, cl up, led hfwy, rdn fnl furlong, ct post.* ....(6 to 4 on op 7 to 4 on tchd 11 to 8 on) 2
2603⁷ ALL IN THE MIND 8-7 (7*) K Sked (8) *cl up, ev ch 2 out, one pace*..........(66 to 1 op 33 to 1 tchd 100 to 1) 3
2862⁵ SEMINOLE WIND 9-0 T Williams (1) *in tch, effrt 3 out, kpt on same pace*..........(9 to 2 op 5 to 1 tchd 8 to 1) 4
2706 SINBAD 8-11 (3*) N Kennedy (2) *beh, effrt whn not clr 2 out, no hdwy aftr*..........(33 to 1 op 20 to 1) 5
1895⁹ JOE JAGGER (Ire) 8-9 (5*) J Marshall (3) *trkd ldrs, effrt 3 out, wknd 2 out*..........(25 to 1 op 16 to 1) 6
2706⁶ CURIE CRUSADER (Ire) 9-0 T Quinn (7) *led to hfwy, cl up till wknd o'r 2 out*..........(25 to 1 op 20 to 1) 7
2796⁷ MOLLINSBURN (Ire) 8-9 (5*) Darren Moffatt (5) *slwly into strd, al beh*..........(100 to 1 op 33 to 1) 8
2554⁷ GOOD SPIRITS 8-6 (3*) S D Williams (10) *in tch, effrt 3 out, wknd quickly 2 out*.......... (50 to 1 op 33 to 1) 9
Dist: Hd, 5l, 1½l, 3l, 1½l, 1½l, 8l, 3l. 1m 35.24s. a 11.24s (9 Ran).
SR: 15/14/-/-/-/-/ (Davie Wong), G C Bravery

3144 Old Prestwick Selling Handicap Class G (0-60 3-y-o) £2,379 7f......... (3:05)

3006³ SHOTLEY AGAIN [30] 7-9 J Quinn (1) *made most, kpt on wl fnl furlong*.......(100 to 30 fav op 5 to 1 tchd 6 to 1) 1
3002 VIKING WATERS [37] 7-13 (3*) N Kennedy (6) *trkd ldrs, chlgd 2 out, ev ch till no extr ins fnl furlong.* ....(8 to 1 op 7 to 1) 2
2634⁷ ADMISSION (Ire) [38] 7-12 (5*) J Marshall (7) *prmnt, rcd wide strt, ev ch 3 out, one pace.* ....(5 to 1 op 6 to 1 tchd 7 to 1) 3
3060⁹ ALTA VICTORIA (Ire) [56] 9-7 T Williams (9) *trkd ldrs, rcd wide strt, effrt 3 out, no imprsn.* .... (11 to 2 op 5 to 1 tchd 6 to 1) 4
2087⁶ DUSKY DUCHESS (Ire) [38] (v) 8-3¹ J Weaver (4) *in tch, rdn o'r 2 out, sn btn*.......... (20 to 1) 5
2775 IRISH ROOTS (Ire) [45] (bl) 8-3 (7*) Ruth Coulter (2) *dsptd ld till rdn and wknd 2 out*..........(14 to 1 op 8 to 1) 6
2388⁸ GLINT OF AYR [48] (bl) 8-13 T Quinn (8) *hld up, effrt 3 out, no hdwy*.......... (9 to 2 tchd 5 to 1) 7
1965⁷ CANAZEI [28] (v) 7-7 Kim Tinkler (3) *al beh.* .... (33 to 1 op 25 to 1) 8
3053⁷ HOD-MOD (Ire) [44] 8-9 N Day (5) *slwly into strd, sn pushed alng and wl beh, tld off.* .... (11 to 2 op 5 to 2 tchd 6 to 1) 9
Dist: 1½l, 5l, 1½l, 1½l, 1l, nk, 2½l, dist. 1m 33.60s. a 9.60s (9 Ran).
SR: 21/23/9/22/-/3/5/-/-/ (J A Swinburne), N Bycroft

3145 Fullerton Conditions Stakes Class D (2-y-o) £3,111 7f................(3:35)

2592³ LAMBENT 8-9 J Quinn (3) *led till hdd 2 out, rdn to ld ag'n ins fnl furlong, ran on wl*..........(7 to 1 op 5 to 1) 1
2714* NIJO 9-0 N Day (1) *trkd ldrs, led 2 out, rdn and hdd ins fnl furlong, sn btn*..........(3 to 1 on op 4 to 1 on) 2
2785* PERSIAN ELITE (Ire) 9-0 T Quinn (2) *hld up, effrt 3 out, no hdwy*..........(7 to 2 tchd 9 to 2) 3
2652⁵ STARICA (Ire) (bl) 8-5 J Weaver (4) *trkd ldr, chlgd o'r 2 out, sn rdn and wknd*..........(33 to 1 op 20 to 1) 4
Dist: 4l, 3l, 1l. 1m 34.82s. a 10.82s (4 Ran).
SR: 17/10/1/-/ (R L Heaton), E Weymes

3146 Gaetan Billard Champagne Handicap Class D (0-80 3-y-o and up) £3,225 1 ¼m......................... (4:05)

2567⁴ STRAW THATCH [52] 4-8-8 J Weaver (8) *hld up, hdwy whn not clr run o'r one furlong out, barged through to ld wl ins last, disqualified*..........(5 to 1 tchd 6 to 1) 1D
2118³ SHARAAR (USA) [77] 3-9-10 N Day (2) *led aftr 2 fs, rdn o'r two out, hdd wl ins fnl furlong, no extr, fnshd second, plcd 1st*.......... (5 to 1 op 4 to 1) 1
2797⁵ PRINCIPAL PLAYER (USA) [56] 3-7-12 (5*) J Marshall (7) *hld up, hdwy o'r 2 out, styd on same pace fnl furlong, fnshd 3rd, plcd second*.......... (20 to 1 op 16 to 1) 2
2799⁸ DOCTOR ROY [42] 5-7-7 (5*) Darren Moffatt (4) *chsd ldrs, outpcd 3 out, styd on fnl furlong, fnshd 4th, plcd 3rd.* ....(6 to 1 op 9 to 2 tchd 4 to 1) 3
2457⁴ SUSPECT [48] 3-7-6 (3*) N Kennedy (1) *led 2 fs, cl up, not clr run o'r one out, not rcvr, fnshd 5th, plcd 4th.* .... (16 to 1 op 12 to 1) 4
2543⁵ PUBLIC WAY (Ire) [58] 3-8-5⁴ T Quinn (6) *in tch, chlgd 2 out, rdn whn badly hmpd ins fnl furlong, fnshd 6th, plcd 5th*..........(12 to 1 op 8 to 1) 5

2740[2] CORNFLAKE [46] 3-7-7 J Quinn (5) *hld up, rdn to chal 2 fs out, sn wknd*........(2 to 1 fav op 3 to 1 tchd 7 to 2) 7
2815[3] MIDDLEHAM CASTLE [50] 4-8-6 T Williams (3) *prmnt till wknd 2 fs out*........................ (5 to 1 op 4 to 1) 8
Dist: 1l, ¾l, ½l, nk, ½l, ¾l, 10l. 2m 19.56s. a 14.56s (8 Ran).
SR: 28/42/19/13/9/18/4/-/ (Ali K Al Jafleh), W J Haggas

3147 Royal Troon Handicap Class E (0-70 3-y-o and up) £2,913 1m 7f...... (4:35)

2740[7] BAY TERN (USA) [39] 7-8-4[1] J Weaver (3) *made all, rdn 2 out, styd on wl*..........(6 to 1 op 5 to 1 tchd 7 to 1) 1
2972[6] MILNGAVIE (Ire) [48] 3-7-13 T Williams (4) *in tch, chsd wnr frm 4 out, ev ch 2 out, rdn and no imprsn.*
....................................(3 to 1 tchd 7 to 2) 2
2735[4] JAMES IS SPECIAL (Ire) [47] 5-8-12 J Quinn (2) *hld up, hdwy o'r 3 out, rdn 2 out, one pace.*
..............................(7 to 4 fav tchd 11 to 8) 3
2740[6] DON'T CRY [28] 5-7-7 Kim Tinkler (7) *chsd ldrs, lost pl hfwy, no dngr aftr*..................(33 to 1 op 16 to 1) 4
2683[5] BRIDGE PLAYER [29] 6-7-3 (5*) Darren Moffatt (5) *hld up, effrt 4 out, no hdwy*................ (3 to 1 tchd 5 to 2) 5
2683[8] FATAL SHOCK [43] 3-7-6[1] (3*) N Kennedy (6) *dwlt, sn prmnt, pushed alng 6 out, grad wknd frm 4 out.*
................................(20 to 1 op 12 to 1) 6
GROUSE-N-HEATHER [60] 4-9-8 (3*) S D Williams (1) *hld up, pushed alng 5 out, sn lost tch, tld off.*
................................(14 to 1 op 8 to 1) 7
Dist: 1½l, 3½l, 2l, ½l, nk, dist. 3m 30.35s. a 17.85s (7 Ran).
SR: 31/24/33/12/12/11/-/ (Thomas Dyer), T Dyer

3148 Belleisle Handicap Class D (0-80 3-y-o and up) £3,176 6f................(5:05)

2935[6] DIET [63] (v) 7-8-6 (5*) J Marshall (3) *made all, clr 2 out, wkng towards finish*............(5 to 1 op 4 to 1) 1
2594[8] EGG [58] 3-8-1 T Williams (4) *in tch, rdn hfwy, styd on wl fnl furlong*.................................. (4 to 1) 2
3060[7] ARABAT [64] (v) 6-8-12 T Quinn (1) *chsd wnr to hfwy, wkng whn swtchd o'r one out*....... (7 to 1 op 6 to 1) 3
2600[4] DOKKHA OYSTON (Ire) [78] 5-9-5 (7*) P Roberts (2) *dwlt, in tch, chsd wnr hfwy, till wknd entering fnl furlong.*
.... (Evens fav op 5 to 4 tchd 11 to 8) 4
2798[6] BEST EFFORT [50] 7-7-12 J Weaver (5) *hld up, effrt hfwy, sn btn*..................................(6 to 1 op 4 to 1) 5
Dist: Nk, 4l, ½l, 1½l. 1m 15.81s. a 4.91s (5 Ran).
SR: 41/30/25/37/3/ (Mrs M S J Clydesdale), Miss L A Perratt

DEAUVILLE (FR) (good)
Saturday August 7th
Going Correction: PLUS 0.25 sec. per fur.

3149 Prix de Psyche (Group 3) (3-y-o) £23,895 1¼m.................. (2:55)

2405[5] DANSE ROYALE (Ire) 8-11 L Piggott (4) *trkd ldrs, second strt, led one and a half fs out, ran on wl ins last, easily.*
....(23 to 10) 1
2080* VIVIANA (USA) 8-11 T Jarnet (1) *al prmnt, 3rd strt, rdn and ran on wl fnl furlong, no ch wth wnr*...(13 to 10 jt-fav) 2
SOUPLESSE (USA) 8-11 Pat Eddery (6) *mid-div, 7th strt, rdn 2 fs out, ran on ins last*............ (13 to 10 jt-fav) 3
1722[9] AUBE INDIENNE (Fr) 8-11 C Asmussen (8) *in rear, 8th strt, rdn 2 fs out, one pace fnl furlong*........... (62 to 10) 4
2238[6] ATHENS BELLE (Ire) 8-11 D Boeuf (7) *hld up last, some hdwy fnl furlong, nrst finish*.................... (13 to 1) 5
LOCHNAU LADY (Fr) 8-11 G Mosse (9) *led, rdn 2 fs out, hdd one and a half out, sn wknd*............. (14 to 1) 6
QUEEN OF LOVE (Ger) 8-11 E Legrix (3) *mid-div, 5th strt, one pace frm 2 fs out*.......................(20 to 1) 7
2690[6] KINDERGARTEN 8-11 S Guillot (5) *in rear, 6th strt, nvr able to chal*.....................................(7 to 1) 8
2054[5] ACCOMMODATING (USA) 8-11 E Saint-Martin (2) *4th strt, rdn and wknd 2 fs out*.............................(10 to 1) 9
Dist: 1½l, nk, 2½l, ¾l, nk, 1½l, ½l, ¾l. 2m 7.00s. a 5.30s (9 Ran).
SR: 69/66/65/60/58/57/54/53/51/ (Miss P F O'Kelly), M J Grassick

DEL MAR (USA) (firm)
Saturday August 7th

3150 Ramona Handicap (Grade 1) (3-y-o and up) £123,510 1m 1f..............

2085* FLAWLESSLY (USA) 5-8-13 C McCarron, ... (10 to 9 on) 1
HEART OF JOY (USA) 6-8-2 D Flores, ... (276 to 10) 2
4728a7 LET'S ELOPE (NZ) 6-8-6 P Valenzuela, ...(41 to 10) 3
2645* RE TOSS (Arg) 6-8-5 E Delahoussaye, ... (84 to 10) 4
KALITA MELODY 5-8-0 C Black, ...(466 to 10) 5
2085[2] JOLYPHA (USA) 4-8-9 K Desormeaux, ...(23 to 10) 6
PLEASANT BABY (USA) 4-8-0 G Stevens, ...(40 to 1) 7
Dist: 1l, 1l, ½l, 3l, 2 ¾l, 1½l. 1m 48.20s. (7 Ran).
(Harbor View Farm), C Whittingham

GROSSETO (ITY) (good to firm)
Saturday August 7th

3151 Premio Citta' di Grosseto (Listed) (3-y-o) £20,173 1m 165yds.............

2643* ZIMZALABIM 8-7 J-P Lopez, ... 1
1887 FUTURBALLA 8-7 S Bietolini, ... 2
1887[4] MAORI (Ity) 8-7 S Landi, ... 3
1887[6] SUPER ACTOR (USA) 8-7 L Sorrentino, ... 4
Dist: 2l, 2l, ½l, 2l, 15l, 4l, nk. 1m 45.00s. (8 Ran).
(Mrs M Schneider), B W Hills

HAYDOCK (soft)
Saturday August 7th
Going Correction: PLUS 0.30 sec. per fur.

3152 Harcros Timber & Building Supplies Stayers Championship Series Handicap Qualifier Class D (0-85 3-y-o and up) £6,320 1¾m................(2:00)

1582[3] CUMBRIAN RHAPSODY [70] 3-7-11 (3*) S Maloney (4) *patiently rdn, took clr order hfwy, led blw dist, ridden out*...(12 to 1) 1
2228[2] HARLESTONE BROOK [66] 3-7-10 W Carson (11) *al wl plcd, led 3 fs out to blw dist, kpt on und pres.*
........................(11 to 2 op 5 to 1 tchd 6 to 1) 2
2904[5] CHIEF MINISTER (Ire) [70] 4-8-13 D Holland (7) *trkd ldrs, effrt and hrd rdn 2 fs out, styd on.* (13 to 2 op 6 to 1) 3
2061[7] STAR PLAYER [83] 7-9-12 J Williams (3) *wl beh hfwy, styd on fnl 2 fs, nvr nrr*................ (16 to 1 op 12 to 1) 4
1958[4] CROMARTY [77] 3-8-7 A McGlone (5) *pressed ldr, rdn o'r 2 fs out, sn wknd*..................(3 to 1 fav op 7 to 2) 5
2713* SHUJAN (USA) [79] 4-9-8 J Reid (9) *led and sn wl clr, wknd o'r 3 fs out, soon hdd and btn*...... (11 to 2 op 9 to 2) 6
2617[7] PHILGUN [62] 4-8-5 J Carroll (2) *hld up, hdwy 6 fs out, shaken up o'r 2 furlongs out, sn btn.* (9 to 1 op 7 to 1) 7
2835[3] MY ROSSINI [66] 4-8-2 (7*) C Hawksley (12) *trkd ldrs, hrd rdn 3 fs out, sn wknd*..............................(16 to 1) 8
2992* VIARDOT (Ire) [82] 4-9-11 M Hills (8) *hld up in rear, effrt entering strt, wknd fnl 2 fs*.......... (7 to 1 op 5 to 1) 9
2395[4] OPERA GHOST [83] 7-9-12 P Robinson (10) *strted slwly, al in rear, tld off*..........................(10 to 1 op 8 to 1) 10
2750* BALADIYA [67] 6-8-7 (3*) C Hodgson (6) *chsd ldrs o'r 8 fs, sn rdn and wknd, tld off*.......... (14 to 1 op 12 to 1) 11
Dist: 2l, sht-hd, 7l, ½l, ½l, 4l, 1½l, 1½l, 12l, sht-hd. 3m 7.67s. a 10.17s (11 Ran).
SR: 26/18/34/33/13/27/2/3/23/ (Cumbrian Industrials Ltd), M H Easterby

3153 Coral Handicap Class B (0-100 3-y-o and up) £11,405 5f..............(2:30)

2987[8] GORINSKY (Ire) [84] 5-9-2 J Carroll (4) *smartly away, made all, clr o'r a furlong out, very easily.*
..............................(5 to 1 fav op 7 to 1) 1
2628[8] STEPANOV (USA) [91] 3-9-5 M Roberts (5) *al wl plcd, hrd rdn o'r a furlong out, one pace.*
.... (9 to 1 op 8 to 1 tchd 10 to 1) 2
1918[3] MACFARLANE [74] 5-8-6 F Norton (14) *hld up, hdwy o'r a furlong out, ran on strly fnl furlong.*
..............................(8 to 1 tchd 9 to 1) 3
1806[5] SIR HARRY HARDMAN [94] 5-9-12 S Perks (9) *trkd ldrs, kpt on und pres ins fnl furlong*..... (9 to 1 op 10 to 1) 4
1083[3] MISTERTOPOGIGO (Ire) [86] 3-9-0 W Carson (7) *hld up, hdwy o'r 2 fs out, sn rdn, ran on one pace.*
.................................(9 to 1 op 10 to 1) 5
1680* DOMINUET [95] 8-9-13 J Lowe (8) *beh and outpcd, swtchd lft o'r a furlong out, ran on*........(8 to 1 tchd 9 to 1) 6
2574[8] STAR FAMILY FRIEND (Ire) [93] 3-9-7 P Robinson (13) *beh, hdwy blw dist, ran on wl ins fnl furlong.*
...............................(16 to 1 op 14 to 1) 7
2698[5] HICKORY BLUE [75] 3-7-12 (5*) Stephen Davies (11) *pressed wnr, rdn o'r a furlong out, sn btn*.............(14 to 1) 8
2753[4] CANTORIS [82] 7-8-11 (3*) C Hodgson (10) *nvr a factor.*
...............................(13 to 2 op 6 to 1) 9
2798[7] GONDO [76] 6-8-8[2] J Reid (6) *chsd ldrs o'r 4 fs, sn outpcd.*
..............................(14 to 1 tchd 12 to 1) 10
2965* BODARI [76] 4-8-8 D Holland (12) *speed 3 fs.*
................................(8 to 1 tchd 9 to 1) 11
2987 SIR JOEY (USA) [75] 4-8-7 J Williams (1) *strted slwly, al beh*........................ (16 to 1 tchd 14 to 1) 12
2620* POYLE GEORGE [94] 8-9-7 (5*) A Procter (2) *speed on outsd o'r 3 fs, sn rdn and wknd.*
....................(13 to 2 op 10 to 1 tchd 6 to 1) 13
1019[8] ROCK SYMPHONY [100] 3-10-0 M Hills (3) *slwly into strd, sn outpcd and beh*.............................(16 to 1) 14
Dist: 2½l, sht-hd, hd, nk, sht-hd, hd, sht-hd, 1½l, nk, ½l. 1m 2.10s. a 3.30s (14 Ran).
SR: 66/59/45/64/51/63/56/37/42/ (William Robertson), J Berry

3154 Burtonwood Brewery Rose Of Lancaster Stakes Class A (Group 3) (3-y-o and up) £21,366 1¼m 120yds....(3:00)

KNIFEBOX (USA) 5-9-7 M Roberts (1) *made all, quickened clr fnl furlong, imprsv.* ....(11 to 10 fav op Evens tchd 5 to 4) 1
953 COLWAY ROCK (USA) 3-8-7 N Connorton (3) *wtd wth, hdwy to join wnr 3 fs out, sn rdn, ran on one pace.* ....(5 to 2 op 9 to 4 tchd 11 to 4) 2
2962[6] HALF A TICK (USA) 5-9-7 C Rutter (2) *chsd wnr, ev ch 3 fs out, squeezed for room 2 out, sn rdn and btn.* ....(9 to 4 op 2 to 1) 3
Dist: 5l, 2½l. 2m 19.70s. a 8.70s (3 Ran).
SR: 52/28/37/ (Sheikh Mohammed), J H M Gosden

3155 Rothmans Royals North South Challenge Series Handicap Class D (0-85 3-y-o and up) £5,897 7f 30yds... (3:30)

2254[8] NO RESERVATIONS (Ire) [81] 3-9-6 J Reid (4) *pressed ldr, shaken up to ld wl ins fnl furlong.* .... (9 to 1 op 8 to 1 tchd 10 to 1) 1
2775[5] KUMMEL KING [51] 5-7-5 (5*) D Wright (5) *led and sn clr, rdn o'r a furlong out, ct nr finish.* (16 to 1 op 14 to 1) 2
2657[4] BOLD ANGEL [78] 6-9-9 M Birch (8) *chsd ldrs, rdn to chal 2 fs out, one pace*...............................(4 to 1) 3
2794 MARINE DIVER [72] 7-9-3 J Williams (9) *dwlt, hld up and beh, hdwy o'r 2 fs out, not rch ldrs*...(9 to 1 op 8 to 1) 4
2926[6] CEE-JAY-AY [69] 6-9-0 J Carroll (7) *dwlt, beh, rdn 3 fs out, styd on ins fnl furlong, nvr nr to chal.* .... (7 to 2 fav tchd 4 to 1) 5
2363[8] HIGHLAND MAGIC (Ire) [83] 5-10-0 C Rutter (6) *hld up, effrt o'r 3 fs out, wknd fnl 2 furlongs.* .... (9 to 1 op 8 to 1 tchd 10 to 1) 6
3011[7] DARUSSALAM [55] (bl) 6-8-0 W Carson (1) *chsd ldrs, rdn and wknd 2 fs out*..................(9 to 1 op 8 to 1) 7
2715[2] BROUGHTON'S PORT [64] 3-8-3 M Roberts (3) *trkd ldrs, effrt and outpcd 3 fs out, sn btn.* ....(4 to 1 op 7 to 2 tchd 9 to 2) 8
2622[9] AITCH N'BEE [75] 10-9-6 A McGlone (2) *chsd ldrs, rdn o'r 2 fs out, sn wknd*................... (10 to 1 op 8 to 1) 9
Dist: Hd, 3½l, nk, 2l, 2l, hd, 6l, ¾l. 1m 32.78s. a 5.58s (9 Ran).
SR: 55/30/46/39/30/38/9/-/9/ (C W Sumner And Jim Short), R F Johnson Houghton

3156 EBF Hermitage Green Maiden Fillies' Stakes Class D (2-y-o) £4,110 6f (4:00)

2357[4] MEHTHAAF (USA) 8-11 W Carson (3) *al cl up, led o'r 2 fs out, quickened clr fnl furlong, very easily.* ....(2 to 1 op 5 to 2 tchd 3 to 1) 1
2575[5] ASDAF (USA) 8-11 M Hills (7) *chsd ldrs, rdn blw dist, kpt on fnl furlong, no ch wth wnr*...... (9 to 1 op 7 to 1) 2
2336[2] REDRESS (USA) 8-11 C Rutter (6) *slwly into strd, hdwy und pres o'r 2 fs out, not pace to chal.* .... (11 to 8 fav op 11 to 10 on tchd 6 to 4) 3
AS SHARP AS 8-11 D Holland (2) *dwlt, sn chasing ldrs, wknd wl o'r a furlong out*............ (9 to 1 op 6 to 1) 4
2325[4] MALINGERER 8-11 N Carlisle (4) *nvr plcd to chal.* ....(12 to 1 tchd 14 to 1) 5
2400[5] MY GALLERY (Ire) 8-6 (5*) D Wright (5) *led aftr a furlong till o'r 2 out, sn rdn and btn*.......... (16 to 1 op 14 to 1) 6
2535[3] BRADWELL (Ire) 8-11 P Robinson (1) *led a furlong, rdn and wknd hfwy, tld off*.......... (12 to 1 op 10 to 1) 7
Dist: 10l, 2½l, 1½l, 3½l, 2½l, 15l. 1m 15.21s. a 3.61s (7 Ran).
SR: 61/21/11/5/ (Hamdan Al-Maktoum), J L Dunlop

3157 Prescot Claiming Stakes Class F (3-y-o and up) £2,710 1¼m 120yds (4:30)

2774[8] SURREY DANCER 5-9-2 J Reid (2) *hld up gng wl, smooth hdwy 3 fs out, quickened to ld ins fnl furlong, readily.* ....(4 to 1 op 3 to 1 tchd 9 to 2) 1
2581[8] LIGHT HAND 7-8-12 P Robinson (5) *dwlt, hld up and beh, hdwy to ld entering fnl furlong, sn hdd, unbl to quicken*.............(7 to 4 fav op Evens tchd 2 to 1) 2
2673[3] CHANDIGARH 5-8-9 M Roberts (4) *al prmnt, led 2 fs out till o'r one out, sn rdn and wknd*............(12 to 1) 3
2613[4] WITHOUT A FLAG (USA) 3-8-13 W Carson (3) *trkd ldrs, rdn and wnt lft o'r a furlong out, sn wknd.* ....(10 to 1 tchd 8 to 1) 4
2372[3] DON'T FORGET MARIE (Ire) 3-7-7 (5*) D Wright (6) *led to 2 fs out, sn rdn, btn whn hmpd blw dist.* (4 to 1 op 5 to 1) 5
2631 DUNBAR 3-7-12 (3*) S Maloney (7) *chsd ldrs till wknd o'r 3 fs out, tld off*...............................(33 to 1) 6
BELGRAN (USA) 4-9-12 D Holland (1) *in tch, effrt to chal o'r 2 fs out, sn rdn and wknd, tld off.* ....(5 to 1 op 7 to 1 tchd 8 to 1) 7
Dist: 2½l, 5l, 1½l, 15l, 8l, 3l. 2m 21.29s. a 10.29s (7 Ran).
SR: 31/22/9/10/ (Cronk Thoroughbred Racing Ltd), B Hanbury

3158 Harvey Jones Rated Class B Handicap (0-95 3-y-o and up) £6,446 1m 30yds......................... (5:00)

2961[5] TESHAMI (USA) [91] 3-8-13 M Roberts (10) *hld up in tch, led on bit 2 fs out, sn clr, shaken up nr finish.* ....(11 to 10 on op 6 to 4) 1
2361[9] CONEYBURY (Ire) [86] 3-8-5 (3*) C Hodgson (4) *al cl up, ev ch 2 fs out, rdn and ran on ins fnl furlong.* .... (15 to 2 op 5 to 1 tchd 8 to 1) 2
2351[2] BOLD AMUSEMENT [86] 3-8-8 C Rutter (5) *led to 2 fs out, kpt on und pres fnl furlong*..................(14 to 1) 3
2672* FOURFORFUN [84] 3-7-13 (7*) A Whelan (9) *wtd wth in rear, hdwy o'r 2 fs out, nrst finish.* (7 to 1 tchd 6 to 1) 4
2793[5] RISK MASTER [91] 4-9-6 D Holland (6) *strted slwly, took clr order o'r 2 fs out, styd on und pres fnl furlong.* .... (9 to 1 op 10 to 1 tchd 8 to 1) 5
1021 AMAZING FEAT (Ire) [85] 4-9-0 J Reid (1) *hld up, effrt 3 fs out, wknd blw dist*............... (10 to 1 op 12 to 1) 6
2794[8] TISSISAT (USA) [86] 4-9-1 M Hills (7) *chsd ldrs, rdn o'r 2 fs out, sn wknd*......................(8 to 1 op 5 to 1) 7
2758[4] NAFUTH (USA) [79] 3-8-1 W Carson (3) *chsd ldrs, hrd rdn and wknd o'r a furlong out*....... (9 to 1 op 10 to 1) 8
2789[6] AMAZE [91] 4-9-6 A Clark (2) *hld up in rear, effrt 3 fs out, eased whn btn appr fnl furlong*... (14 to 1 op 12 to 1) 9
2926 CUMBRIAN CHALLENGE (Ire) [92] 4-9-7 M Birch (8) *cl up, ev ch 3 fs out, sn rdn and wknd, tld off*......... (12 to 1) 10
Dist: ¾l, hd, hd, 1½l, 3l, hd, nk, 5l, 10l. 1m 47.17s. a 6.57s (10 Ran).
SR: 38/31/30/27/36/21/21/6/10/ (Sheikh Mohammed), J H M Gosden

LEOPARDSTOWN (IRE) (good)
Saturday August 7th
Going Correction: PLUS 0.05 sec. per fur.

3159 Corrig EBF Maiden (2-y-o) £5,244 1m ....(2:10)

2880[3] ZORINA 8-11 M J Kinane (7)...................(13 to 8) 1
2880[2] IRRESTIBLE LADY (Ire) 8-11 C Roche (2).... (11 to 10 fav) 2
DANCING SUCCESS (USA) 9-0 S Craine (4)....... (8 to 1) 3
SHANKAR (Ire) 9-0 P V Gilson (1)................. (8 to 1) 4
SHOREWOOD (Ire) 9-0 J P Murtagh (3)............(5 to 1) 5
BUBBLY PROSPECT (USA) 9-0 K J Manning (6)...(12 to 1) 6
IAN MY BOY (Ire) 9-0 Joanna Morgan (5).........(33 to 1) 7
Dist: Sht-hd, 7l, 3l, ¾l. 1m 43.10s. a 5.10s (7 Ran).
SR: 27/26/8/-/ (Sheikh Mohammed), John M Oxx

3160 Kimmage Handicap (0-75 3-y-o and up) £3,105 7f...................(2:35)

2248 CISEAUX (USA) [-] 4-10-0 M J Kinane (13)..... (9 to 2 fav) 1
2514* RUSTIC-ORT (Ire) [-] (bl) 5-8-10 W R Swinburn (7) (13 to 2) 2
3028[8] WHAT A PLEASURE (Ire) [-] 3-8-10 (6*) B J Walsh (11) ....(12 to 1) 3
3076[2] TINCO PALENO [-] 9-8-13 (2*) R M Burke (2).......(6 to 1) 4
2345[3] BARNAGEERA BOY (Ire) [-] 4-8-7 N G McCullagh (6) ....(12 to 1) 5
2806[8] SALLUSTAR [-] (bl) 8-9-2 J P Murtagh (12).........(6 to 1) 6
2879[3] BOLD MOLLY (Ire) [-] 4-7-4 (6*) P P Murphy (10)...(12 to 1) 7
2514[3] TIGNES (Ire) [-] 5-8-2 J F Egan (5)................(10 to 1) 8
2297[8] VLADIVOSTOK [-] 3-8-13 J C Deegan (8).........(20 to 1) 9
2843[9] OUT OF STEP (Ire) [-] 4-7-0 (8*) G M Moylan (4)... (16 to 1) 10
2248[4] MASTER WORK [-] (bl) 5-7-11 A J Nolan (9)...... (15 to 2) 11
2514[4] LOVE OF ERIN (Ire) [-] (bl) 4-7-5 (2*) D G O'Shea (1) (33 to 1) 12
1649[5] BERESFORD LADY (Ire) [-] 3-8-8 P V Gilson (14)... (6 to 1) 13
2451 FAIRYDEL (Ire) [-] 3-8-10 (8*) P J Smullen (3)......(14 to 1) 14
Dist: 1½l, 2½l, hd, nk. 1m 33.00s. a 7.60s (14 Ran).
SR: 5/-/-/-/-/ (G Olivero), D K Weld

3161 Walshestown EBF Maiden (3-y-o) £3,450 6f...................... (3:00)

2674[2] KILTIMONY 8-11 P V Gilson (5)...................(5 to 1) 1
1649[2] GREAT CABARET (Ire) 9-0 M J Kinane (4)......(6 to 4 fav) 2
COUTURE DIAMANT (Ire) 8-9 (2*) R M Burke (3)...(16 to 1) 3
2877[5] TORC MOUNTAIN (Ire) (bl) 8-8 (6*) J J Behan (6)...(10 to 1) 4
OROVILLE 8-11 S Craine (2)...................... (6 to 1) 5
2806[3] BENE MERENTI (Ire) (bl) 9-0 J P Murtagh (1)....... (4 to 1) 6
2843[6] AURLIANO (Ire) 8-11 D J Smith (7)...............(20 to 1) 7
2700[2] SOUTHERN REVIEW (Ire) (bl) 9-0 W J Supple (8)... (6 to 1) 8
Dist: 1l, 1l, ¾l, nk. 1m 15.50s. a 4.00s (8 Ran).
SR: 23/22/15/15/11/ (Mrs C Collins), C Collins

3162 Phoenix Sprint Stakes (Group 3) (3-y-o and up) £14,375 6f..............(3:30)

2805* TROPICAL (bl) 3-8-11 M J Kinane (9) *trkd ldrs, prog to ld ins fnl furlong, cmftbly*.......................(4 to 1) 1
2574[3] MONTENDRE 6-9-1 P V Gilson (8) *hld up, prog appr fnl furlong, fnshd wl*..................................(5 to 1) 2
2574[2] MIDHISH 3-8-10 W R Swinburn (2) *wl plcd, led one and a half fs out till ins fnl furlong, rdn and kpt on.* (6 to 1) 3
3029[3] DASHING COLOURS (Ire) 4-8-12 P Shanahan (6) *rear, prog whn swtchd rght 2 fs out, ran on*.............. (10 to 1) 4
3072[3] NORDIC FOX (Ire) 3-8-10 K J Manning (7) *reear, styd on wl fnl furlong*.. (14 to 1) 5
2927[4] MARINA PARK 3-8-11 Dean McKeown (10) *prmnt, led 4 fs out to one and a half out, sn wknd*........(9 to 4 fav) 6
2407[2] MALVERNICO (Ire) 5-9-1 C Roche (3) *wl plcd, rdn and wknd o'r 2 fs out*..................................(9 to 1) 7
2805[8] UP AND AT 'EM (bl) 3-9-0 B Coogan (1) *swtchd rght to track ldrs, hmpd o'r 2 fs out, switched lft, rdn and no imprsn*.. (12 to 1) 8

2805[9] BRADAWN BREEVER (Ire) (bl) 4-9-1 W J Supple (5) *led 2 fs, rdn and wknd two out*........................(14 to 1) 9
2805[7] DAWNSIO (Ire) (bl) 3-8-7 J P Murtagh (4) *wl plcd, rdn and wknd 2 fs out*..............................(12 to 1) 10
Dist: 1l, hd, nk, 1l. 1m 12.80s. a 1.30s (10 Ran).
SR: 77/77/71/72/66/-/ (The Sussex Stud Limited), D K Weld

3163 Sandymount Handicap (0-105 3-y-o and up) £6,900 1½m............(4:00)

2405 ALOUETTE [-] 3-8-9 C Roche (5).................. (4 to 1) 1
2841[6] CURRENCY BASKET (Ire) [-] 4-8-9 J P Murtagh (1) (8 to 1) 2
2881[9] MITAH (Ire) [-] 5-7-1 (6*) P P Murphy (2)............ (20 to 1) 3
2076 LORD BENTLEY [-] 3-7-10 (6*) J A Heffernan (7)....(5 to 1) 4
COCKNEY LAD (Ire) [-] 4-7-7[6] (6*) J J Behan (3)... (25 to 1) 5
3038[4] LADY TYONE (Ire) [-] 3-7-7 Joanna Morgan (9).... (15 to 2) 6
2744[6] SLEET SKIER [-] 6-10-0 M J Kinane (8)........ (3 to 1 fav) 7
1140* SAFFRON CROCUS [-] (bl) 3-7-5 (2*) D G O'Shea (6) (7 to 2) 8
1552 NINJA DANCER (USA) [-] 4-9-9 P Shanahan (4)... (14 to 1) 9
Dist: 5½l, nk, 2l, 2½l. 2m 36.30s. a 5.30s (9 Ran).
SR: 48/37/20/25/11/-/ (Miss K Rausing), J S Bolger

3164 Rialto Handicap (0-80 3-y-o) £3,105 1¼m............................ (4:30)

2702* MADANIYYA (USA) [-] 9-5 (6*,4ex) C Everard (6) (9 to 4 fav) 1
2496[9] COOLRAIN LADY (Ire) [-] 8-8 (4*) P Carberry (7).... (6 to 1) 2
2808[3] TRYARRA (Ire) [-] 9-6 J P Murtagh (3).......... (100 to 30) 3
2923[6] WICKLOW WAY (Ire) [-] 8-7 W J Supple (1)....... (12 to 1) 4
2702[6] NORDIC UNION (Ire) [-] 8-8 C Roche (2)...........(12 to 1) 5
2677[2] VINEY (USA) [-] (bl) 9-1 M J Kinane (5)...............(4 to 1) 6
2297 RAFFERTY'S INNER (Ire) [-] 7-13 (8*) R T Fitzpatrick (8) ....(7 to 1) 7
2321[5] ANOTHER FLYER (Ire) [-] 7-9[4] (2*) R M Burke (4).. (20 to 1) 8
Dist: 1½l, ¾l, 2½l, ½l. 2m 14.90s. a 10.20s (8 Ran).
SR: 14/-/4/-/-/ (H H Aga Khan), John M Oxx

3165 Stepaside EBF Race (3-y-o and up) £3,795 1m.................... (5:00)

2606[3] MASTER TRIBE (Ire) 3-9-9 P V Gilson (4)....... (7 to 4 on) 1
2607* MUBADIR (USA) 5-9-10 (4*) P Carberry (3).........(4 to 1) 2
ANLACE 4-9-4 M J Kinane (1).......................(8 to 1) 3
1796* FAIRY LORE (Ire) 3-8-10 (6*) J J Behan (5).........(7 to 1) 4
574[5] RONDELLI (Ire) 3-9-0 C Roche (2)................ (13 to 2) 5
Dist: 1l, 2½l, ¾l, 2l. 1m 42.10s. a 4.10s (5 Ran).
SR: 54/56/38/34/26/ (Lord Harrington), C Collins

LINGFIELD (good to firm)
Saturday August 7th
Going Correction: MINUS 0.25 sec. per fur.

3166 Pier Median Auction Maiden Fillies' Stakes Class F (2-y-o) £2,700 6f (5:50)

2887[7] BRIERLEY 8-11 R Perham (4) *al prmnt, led wl o'r one furlong out, pushed out, cmftbly.* ....(7 to 1 tchd 10 to 1 and 12 to 1) 1
2895[3] RAJMAPATA 8-11 L Piggott (13) *led 2 fs, styd hndy, ev ch o'r one furlong out, not quicken.* ....(3 to 1 op 5 to 2 tchd 7 to 2) 2
MUSIC OF DANCE (Ire) 8-6 (5*) J Tate (15) *al prmnt, led aftr 2 fs, hdd wl o'r one out, sn rdn and one pace.* .... (12 to 1 op 33 to 1) 3
YO-CANDO (Ire) 8-6 (5*) L Newton (6) *prmnt, rdn o'r 2 fs out, wknd appr last*...............(33 to 1 op 20 to 1) 4
3009[4] FROMAGE 8-11 T Sprake (2) *chsd ldrs, effrt 2 fs out, kpt on one pace fnl furlong.* .... (9 to 1 op 5 to 1 tchd 10 to 1) 5
2374[2] YAWARA 8-8 (3*) B Doyle (5) *chsd ldg bunch, rdn alng appr hfwy, wknd o'r one furlong out.* ....(6 to 4 fav op 5 to 4 tchd 7 to 4) 6
3016[3] RICH MISS 8-11 B Rouse (14) *prmnt, rdn o'r 2 fs out, sn btn*........(9 to 1 op 7 to 1 tchd 10 to 1 and 11 to 1) 7
SPORTING STORY (Ire) 8-11 N Adams (8) *outpcd and beh till styd on fnl one and a half fs, nvr nrr.* .... (33 to 1 op 20 to 1) 8
2299 MASURI KABISA (USA) 8-12[1] V Smith (16) *nvr better than midfield*............ (16 to 1 op 10 to 1 tchd 20 to 1) 9
A SUITABLE GIRL 8-11 S Dawson (7) *sn rdn alng in midfield, ran green frm hfwy, no hdwy fnl 2 fs.* .... (33 to 1 op 20 to 1) 10
MY MOONA 8-11 A Tucker (10) *al rear div*....... (33 to 1) 11
1555[3] BUNNY RUN 8-4 (7*) L Carter (3) *al beh.* ....(33 to 1 op 20 to 1) 12
ALL THE JOYS 8-11 G Bardwell (1) *in tch on outsd, rdn hfwy, wknd*............................(33 to 1 op 20 to 1) 13
DAVID'S DREAM (Hol) 8-6 (5*) K Rutter (11) *al outpcd and wl beh*.................................... (33 to 1 op 20 to 1) 14
ESOTERIC (Ire) 8-11 S O'Gorman (12) *slwly away, outpcd.* .... (33 to 1 op 20 to 1) 15
Dist: 2l, ¾l, 1½l, hd, 2l, ½l, 3l, nk, 2½l, 3½l. 1m 11.31s. a 2.31s (15 Ran).
SR: 21/13/10/4/3/-/ (Mrs G S Forbes), B Smart

3167 South Coast Conditions Stakes Class D (2-y-o) £3,201 5f..............(6:50)

2886[7] JADE PET 8-9 L Piggott (2) *chsd ldg pair, led jst o'r one furlong out, shaken up, cmftbly.* ....(Evens fav tchd 11 to 10) 1
2618[5] ROXANIAN (Ire) 8-13 (5*) J Tate (4) *made most till hdd jst o'r one furlong out, sn rdn and not pace of wnr.* ....(11 to 10 op Evens tchd 6 to 5) 2
2500[4] KERRIE-JO 8-5 S Whitworth (3) *wth ldr till rdn and wknd wl o'r one furlong out.* .... (20 to 1 op 14 to 1 tchd 25 to 1) 3
2866 NAME THE TUNE 8-10 B Rouse (6) *sn beh, nvr plcd to chal*............... (66 to 1 op 50 to 1 tchd 100 to 1) 4
SWIFT NICK NEVISON 8-10 R Perham (5) *chsd ldrs, wndrd lft hfwy, sn rdn and wknd*....... (100 to 1 op 50 to 1) 5
CHARLIE CHARLIE 8-10 Candy Morris (1) *veered lft leaving stalls, al beh and outpcd.* .... (33 to 1 op 66 to 1 tchd 100 to 1) 6
Dist: 1½l, 4l, 4l, 3½l, 6l. 58.34s. a 1.44s (6 Ran).
SR: 41/44/15/4/-/-/ (Geoffrey C Greenwood), R Hannon

3168 Laurel Racing Club Handicap Class E (0-70 3-y-o and up) £3,076 6f.... (7:20)

2723[2] MY RUBY RING [58] 6-9-5 S Whitworth (15) *al wl plcd stands side, led o'r one furlong out, sn clr, readily.* ....(7 to 2 fav op 4 to 1 tchd 3 to 1) 1
2671 ROYAL DEED (USA) [67] 3-9-9 R Perham (3) *wnt prmnt aftr 2 fs, ev ch o'r one out, ran on one pace ins last.* .... (50 to 1 op 33 to 1) 2
2846[9] LORINS GOLD [53] (bl) 3-8-9 S Dawson (10) *led till hdd o'r one furlong out, kpt on same pace.* (25 to 1 op 20 to 1) 3
2939[6] DOUBLE BOUNCE [60] 3-8-11 (5*) K Rutter (9) *chsd ldr, ev ch o'r one furlong out, unbl to quicken.* .... (25 to 1 op 16 to 1) 4
2868[6] FAY'S SONG (Ire) [55] 5-8-9 (7*) L Carter (2) *prmnt, ev ch 2 fs out, wknd appr last.* (10 to 1 op 11 to 1 tchd 12 to 1) 5
2969 ABIGAILS BOY (Hol) [51] 4-8-12 G Hind (12) *midfield till styd on fnl furlong, nvr nrr*........ (33 to 1 op 20 to 1) 6
2897 PALACEGATE GOLD (Ire) [54] 4-9-1 A Munro (11) *chsd ldg bunch, rdn o'r 2 fs out, one pace.* .... (5 to 1 op 6 to 1 tchd 13 to 2) 7
2868[3] CEE-EN-CEE [56] (v) 9-9-3 A Tucker (16) *sn rdn alng stands side, in tch till wknd 2 fs out*......(5 to 1 tchd 11 to 2) 8
2868[9] BALLYHAYS (Ire) [55] 4-8-9 (7*) T Ashley (5) *nvr better than mid-div*.......................... (33 to 1 op 20 to 1) 9
1903[9] LEIGH CROFTER [54] 4-9-1 J Williams (6) *chsd ldrs in midfield till wknd 2 fs out*........ (25 to 1 op 14 to 1) 10
2868* SPECTACLE JIM [49] (bl) 4-8-10 N Adams (7) *slwly into strd and beh, rdn hfwy, nvr able to chal.* .... (11 to 1 op 7 to 1 tchd 12 to 1) 11
2868 MISTER JOLSON [67] 4-9-7 (7*) S Drowne (8) *panicked in stalls, slwly away, al beh*........ (20 to 1 op 14 to 1) 12
2939* WESTERN VALLEY [61] 3-9-0 (3*) B Doyle (14) *chsd ldrs till rdn and wknd o'r 2 fs out.* .... (8 to 1 op 7 to 1 tchd 10 to 1) 13
1911[9] FINDON ACADEMY (Ire) [55] 3-8-11 B Rouse (4) *rcd wide, midfield to hfwy, sn wknd.* .... (16 to 1 op 14 to 1 tchd 20 to 1) 14
2671 RAINBOW FLEET [56] 5-9-3 T Rogers (1) *rcd wide and prmnt 2 fs, wknd quickly.* .... (33 to 1 op 25 to 1 tchd 50 to 1) 15
1664[6] GALLOP TO GLORY [53] 3-8-2 (7*) A Martinez (13) *al beh.* .... (20 to 1 op 14 to 1) 16
Dist: 3½l, sht-hd, nk, hd, ¾l, 1l, 1l, 1½l, 2l, hd. 1m 10.93s. a 1.93s (16 Ran).
SR: 36/26/11/17/16/9/8/6/-/ (Mrs Marion Wickham), D R Laing

3169 Metropole Limited Stakes Class D (0-70 3-y-o and up) £3,611 7f.... (8:20)

2821* LAUREL QUEEN (Ire) 5-8-13 J Carroll (1) *made all, clr o'r 2 fs out, easily*.............(7 to 4 on tchd 6 to 4 on) 1
2915* CHARMED KNAVE 8-9-4 T Williams (5) *trkd ldr, rdn wl o'r 2 fs out, kpt on same pace.* .... (9 to 2 op 11 to 2 tchd 6 to 1) 2
3051[5] GREAT HALL 4-9-4 J Williams (4) *beh early, effrt o'r 2 fs out, sn rdn and not quicken.* .... (7 to 1 tchd 8 to 1 and 9 to 1) 3
2173 SURE LORD (Ire) 4-9-4 A Munro (3) *in tch till rdn and wknd 2 fs out*......... (8 to 1 op 7 to 1 tchd 10 to 1) 4
2270[8] SURREY RACING 5-9-4 B Rouse (6) *beh, rdn wl o'r 2 fs out, no imprsn*................. (12 to 1 tchd 16 to 1) 5
2673[9] JOLTO 4-9-4 S Whitworth (2) *chsd ldrs on outsd, rdn wl o'r 2 fs out, wknd*............. (50 to 1 tchd 100 to 1) 6
Dist: 4l, ¾l, 4l, 1½l, ½l. 1m 22.17s. a 1.47s (6 Ran).
SR: 51/44/42/30/25/23/ (Laurel (Leisure) Limited), J Berry

LINGFIELD (A.W) (std)
Saturday August 7th
Going Correction: MINUS 0.20 sec. per fur.

3170 Polegate Selling Handicap Class G (0-60 3-y-o) £2,011 1½m........ (6:20)

3049[3] EARLY TO RISE [40] 8-7 (7*) J D Smith (6) *made all, jnd o'r 2 fs out, drvn clr appr last.* ....(13 to 8 fav op 2 to 1 tchd 9 to 4) 1

2942 BOXBOY [37] 8-11 S Whitworth (4) *trkd ldr, rdn to chal o'r 2 fs out, wknd appr last*............(4 to 1 op 11 to 2) 2
2683 WESTRAY (Fr) [47] 9-2 (5*) K Rutter (3) *chsd ldrs, rdn o'r 3 fs out, no imprsn fnl 2*.... (5 to 2 op 6 to 4 tchd 11 to 4) 3
2870[5] CHILTERN HUNDREDS (USA) [47] 9-7 J Williams (5) *chsd ldrs, rdn o'r 3 fs out, sn wknd.* ....(6 to 1 op 9 to 2 tchd 7 to 1) 4
3007 ESERIE DE CORES (USA) [40] (bl) 9-0 N Adams (2) *wl beh frm hfwy, tld off*................ (14 to 1 tchd 16 to 1) 5
2943[4] BARSLEY [36] 8-5 (5*) J Tate (1) *al beh, tld off.* .... (20 to 1 op 14 to 1) 6
Dist: 3½l, 3l, 2l, 25l, 3½l. 2m 36.64s. a 7.34s (6 Ran).
SR: 3/-/-/ (R M Cyzer), C A Cyzer

3171 Gatwick Handicap Class E (0-70 3-y-o and up) £2,259 2m..............(7:50)

3021[4] RAGTIME SONG [28] 4-8-6 N Adams (7) *in tch, hdwy to ld 5 fs out, clr 2 out, eased nr finish.* ....(7 to 2 op 4 to 1 tchd 9 to 2) 1
2850* SIR THOMAS BEECHAM [56] (e/s) 3-8-12 (7*) A Martinez (4) *hld up in tch, effrt 4 fs out, sn chasing wnr, no imprsn fnl 2 furlongs*.......(13 to 8 fav op 7 to 4 tchd 2 to 1) 2
4817a[9] MISTER LAWSON [34] 7-8-12 J Williams (3) *wtd wth, beh till some hdwy 6 fs out, no imprsn fnl 3, nvr able to chal*.................. (9 to 1 op 8 to 1 tchd 10 to 1) 3
210[3] SERIOUS ACTION [42] 4-9-1 (5*) K Rutter (5) *trkd ldrs, rdn 5 fs out, sn btn*..........(7 to 4 op 6 to 4 tchd 15 to 8) 4
2869 LAST APPEARANCE [25] 4-7-10 (7*) Antoinette Armes (6) *wth ldr till wknd 5 fs out*.........(66 to 1 op 50 to 1) 5
2834 ONE MORE POUND [40] (bl) 3-8-3 A Tucker (2) *led till hdd 5 fs out, wknd quickly, tld off.* ....(25 to 1 op 16 to 1 tchd 33 to 1) 6
Dist: 4l, 12l, 1½l, 12l, dist. 3m 26.17s. a 4.17s (6 Ran).
SR: 18/27/8/14/-/-/ (Mrs Elizabeth Kiernan), A Moore

MERANO (ITY) (good)
Saturday August 7th

3172 Premio San Cassiano (2-y-o) £4,483 7f 110yds.......................(4:00)

CAZZUTO (Ire) 8-9 A Parravani, *hld up, hdwy 2 fs out, led one out, easily*.. 1
RANUSH (Ire) 8-9 P Perlanti,............................ 2
RAIN AGAIN (Ity) 8-9 P Yanez,............................ 3
Dist: 3l, 1½l, 3½l, 2l, ½l, 8l, 2l, ½l, hd. (Time not taken) (13 Ran).
(J L Dunlop), J Dunlop

NEWMARKET (JULY) (good to firm)
Saturday August 7th

Going Correction: MINUS 0.35 sec. per fur. (races 1,7), MINUS 0.25 (2,3,4,5,6)

3173 Montana Wines Maiden Stakes Class D (3-y-o and up) £3,915 1½m....(2:10)

2117[2] KITHANGA (Ire) 3-8-6[1] R Cochrane (14) *mid-div, ran on 3 fs out, led o'r one out, pushed clr.* ....(4 to 1 op 3 to 1 tchd 11 to 4) 1
2464[2] KERKURA (USA) 3-8-5 K Fallon (10) *hld up, prog o'r 3 fs out, ev ch 2 out, styd on one pace ins last.* ....(9 to 2 op 8 to 1) 2
2776[3] QUILLON 3-8-10 W Ryan (12) *pressed ldr, led 4 fs out till o'r one out, sn outpcd.* .... (100 to 30 fav op 5 to 2 tchd 4 to 1) 3
2776[2] ALASAD 3-8-10 R Hills (15) *trkd ldrs, ev ch 2 fs out, outpcd appr last*....... (5 to 1 op 7 to 2 tchd 11 to 2) 4
CLASSIC CABOOSE (USA) 3-8-3 (7*) Michael Denaro (7) *beh, styd on one pace last 2 fs.* ....(33 to 1 op 20 to 1 tchd 40 to 1) 5
1678[2] COLLIER BAY 3-8-10 L Dettori (8) *handily plcd, rdn and no hdwy ins last 2 fs*..............(8 to 1 tchd 10 to 1) 6
2937[2] BAG OF TRICKS (Ire) 3-8-10 A Munro (9) *led aftr one furlong to 4 out, eased whn btn 2 out.* .... (10 to 1 op 8 to 1 tchd 11 to 1) 7
1176[9] PRINCESS DAVID (USA) 3-8-5 G Bardwell (3) *chsd ldrs till wknd 3 fs out*..................... (25 to 1 op 16 to 1) 8
2189[4] RUSSIAN EMPIRE 3-8-10 B Raymond (6) *mid-div to hfwy, btn o'r 3 fs out*....... (25 to 1 op 16 to 1 tchd 33 to 1) 9
BALMORAL BELLE 3-8-6[1] M Esposito (11) *slwly into strd, effrt frm rear o'r 5 fs out, not rch frnt rnk.* ....(33 to 1 op 20 to 1) 10
SIANISKI 4-9-2 B Marcus (5) *led one furlong, pushed alng hfwy, wknd o'r 3 out*.............(33 to 1 op 25 to 1) 11
2750[5] WORTHY MEMORIES 4-9-2 W Woods (4) *beh, effrt and rdn o'r 3 fs out, no imprsn*.........(66 to 1 op 50 to 1) 12
3012 TEOROMA 3-8-10 G Hind (1) *beh, effrt on outsd hfwy, sn btn*................................ (66 to 1 op 50 to 1) 13
2523[5] AMAZING AIR (USA) 3-8-10 A Mackay (13) *al beh.* ....(50 to 1 op 33 to 1 tchd 66 to 1) 14
Dist: 3l, ¾l, 3½l, 8l, ½l, ½l, 3l, ¾l, 1½l, 2½l. 2m 28.88s. a 0.08s (14 Ran).
SR: 49/42/45/38/22/21/20/9/12/ (Fittocks Stud Limited), L M Cumani

3174 Brooks Of Norwich Claiming Stakes Class E (3-y-o and up) £3,132 7f (2:40)

2663[2] RUE REMBRANDT (USA) 3-9-0 R Hills (1) *made all, shaken up and styd on strly frm 2 fs out.* (7 to 4 fav op 5 to 2) 1
2995[6] KING PARIS (Ire) 3-8-6 (3*) M Fenton (2) *trkd wnr most of way, rdn and kpt on one pace last 2 fs.* ....(8 to 1 tchd 10 to 1) 2
2892* SIZZLING SAGA (Ire) 5-9-6 R Cochrane (8) *steadied strt, hld up in mid-div, improved o'r 2 fs out, no imprsn on wnr fnl furlong*.................... (2 to 1 op 9 to 4) 3
587[4] A PRAYER FOR WINGS 9-8-11 L Dettori (6) *hld up rear, swtchd rght and hdwy o'r 2 fs out, one pace appr last.* .... (5 to 2 op 5 to 4 tchd 11 to 4) 4
2915[8] POP TO STANS 4-8-10 B Raymond (7) *trkd ldrs till wknd last 2 fs*............................ (66 to 1 op 33 to 1) 5
2749[8] GRANVILLE CORNER 3-8-11 W Ryan (4) *steadied strt, hld up, rdn alng and not rch frnt rnk fnl 2 fs.* ....(50 to 1 tchd 66 to 1) 6
2578[8] EASTERN CHARLY (Bel) 3-8-3 G Hind (3) *ldg grp till wknd 2 fs out*.......................... (66 to 1 op 33 to 1) 7
BALLYGRIFFIN BELLE 4-8-8 N Adams (5) *in tch, rdn and wknd rpdly wl o'r 2 fs out*........ (66 to 1 op 50 to 1) 8
Dist: 1½l, 1l, 1½l, 10l, nk, 1½l, 7l. 1m 26.26s. a 2.06s (8 Ran).
SR: 43/33/41/27/-/ (K Abdulla), G Harwood

3175 Dickins Invitation Limited Handicap Class E (0-70 3-y-o and up) £3,396 1m ....(3:15)

2717[5] SHINING JEWEL [68] 6-10-7 Miss R Kierans (10) *cl up on outsd, led o'r 2 fs out, edgd rght ins last, hld on wl.* ....(11 to 2 op 6 to 1 tchd 13 to 2) 1
2762[5] LOMBARD SHIPS [63] 6-10-2 Miss Diana Jones (11) *hdwy frm rear o'r 2 fs out, jnd wnr ins last, not quicken nr line*.................................(9 to 1 op 7 to 1) 2
3057[4] BILL MOON [54] 7-9-7 Mrs M Cowdrey (2) *pld hrd, ldg grp, ev ch 2 fs out, edgd lft and not quicken appr last.* ....(4 to 1 jt-fav op 7 to 2 tchd 9 to 2) 3
2873[2] FATHER DAN (Ire) [47] 4-9-0 Miss I Weiner (7) *hld up in mid-div, improved o'r 2 fs out, styd on one pace ins last.* ....(10 to 1 tchd 11 to 1) 4
2948* DARING PAST [61] 3-9-7 Miss S Tarrou (3) *beh, rdn alng o'r 2 fs out, ran on ins last, nrst finish.* (7 to 1 op 6 to 1) 5
3002[5] DEAD CALM [54] (v) 3-9-0 Mrs A Farrell (4) *slwly into strd, settled mid-div, swtchd lft and not much room o'r one furlong out, no extr last 100 yards.* (14 to 1 op 12 to 1) 6
2882 TAKENHALL [59] 8-9-12 Miss K Neilson (6) *chsd ldrs, lost pl o'r 3 fs out, kpt on fnl furlong*...... (10 to 1 op 8 to 1) 7
2930[9] NORTH ESK (USA) [65] 4-10-4 Miss O Hulinska (8) *rear most of way, rdn and no imprsn appr last 2 fs.* .... (15 to 2 op 10 to 1 tchd 11 to 1) 8
2612[5] DODGY [52] (v) 6-9-5 Mrs D Arbuthnot (5) *led till o'r 2 fs out, sn btn*......................... (4 to 1 jt-fav op 3 to 1) 9
2384[5] COOL COQUELIN (Ire) [47] 5-9-0 Miss K Schlick (9) *trkd ldrs till wknd ins last 2 fs*............. (50 to 1 op 33 to 1) 10
2750[9] RAPINSKI [47] 4-9-0 Miss J Winter (1) *trkd ldrs 5 fs, wknd quickly*....................... (66 to 1 tchd 100 to 1) 11
Dist: Nk, 2l, sht-hd, nk, ¾l, 1l, 2½l, 4l, nk, 5l. 1m 40.85s. a 2.95s (11 Ran).
SR: 47/41/26/18/24/15/24/22/-/ (D W Rolt), Mrs L Piggott

3176 Columbus Sweet Solera Stakes Class A (Listed Race) (2-y-o) £9,594 7f (3:45)

2583* FAIRY HEIGHTS (Ire) 8-8 A Munro (3) *hld up in tch, hrd rdn and ran on o'r one furlong out, led last 100 yards, pushed out*..........................(7 to 2 op 5 to 1) 1
2706* TAGHAREED (USA) 8-8 R Hills (1) *cl up, led hfwy, hdd und pres wl ins fnl furlong, ran on.* (5 to 2 fav tchd 3 to 1) 2
2583[3] SONG OF YEARS (Ire) 8-8 B Raymond (2) *trkd ldg grp, rdn and styd on appr fnl furlong, not quicken last 100 yards*............................ (20 to 1 op 16 to 1) 3
2562[2] OVERACT (Ire) 8-8 L Dettori (7) *hld up in mid-div, rdn alng o'r 2 fs out, hmpd over one out, styd on one pace.* ....(5 to 1 op 7 to 2) 4
2301[7] IZZA 8-8 S Whitworth (4) *mid-div, not much room 2 fs out, effrt o'r one out, extr ins last*...... (14 to 1 op 12 to 1) 5
2575* SPOT PRIZE (USA) 8-8 R Cochrane (9) *hld up rear, ran on last 2 fs, nrst finish*... (14 to 1 op 8 to 1 tchd 16 to 1) 6
GREAT TRIVIALITY 8-8 B Marcus (8) *beh, ran on und pres o'r one furlong out, not rch wnr.* ....(20 to 1 op 12 to 1 tchd 25 to 1) 7
2812[3] QUEENBIRD 8-11 W Ryan (6) *cl up, rdn and bumped o'r one furlong out, lost pos ins last.* .... (11 to 2 op 3 to 1 tchd 6 to 1) 8
2603* CUT THE RED TAPE (Ire) 8-8 G Duffield (5) *led to hfwy, edgd rght and wknd appr fnl furlong*...(20 to 1 op 16 to 1) 9
2812[2] NSX 8-8 K Fallon (10) *hld up, effrt o'r 2 fs out, sn rdn alng, no imprsn on ldrs over one out.* ....(12 to 1 op 8 to 1) 10
Dist: ½l, 1½l, nk, hd, hd, nk, 1½l, 5l, 1½l. 1m 26.41s. a 2.21s (10 Ran).
SR: 35/33/28/27/26/25/24/22/4/ (Frank W Golding), N A Callaghan

3177 Brierley Investments Handicap Class B (0-105 3-y-o and up) £23,150 7f (4:20)

2363* EN ATTENDANT (Fr) [96] 5-9-12 W Ryan (17) *dwlt, beh till str run on outsd wl o'r one furlong out, led and hng lft entering last, sn clr.* (11 to 1 op 10 to 1 tchd 12 to 1) 1
2601⁸ INDIAN SLAVE (Ire) [68] 5-7-10¹ (3*) D Harrison (7) *pressed ldrs, ev ch o'r 2 fs out till over one out, kpt on gmely.* ....(12 to 1 tchd 14 to 1) 2
2854² BEWARE OF AGENTS [88] 4-9-4 R P Elliott (10) *slwly into strd, hdwy frm rear last 2 fs, styd on nr finish.* .... (16 to 1 op 14 to 1) 3
3093³ PRINCESS KRIS [82] 3-8-6¹ R Cochrane (6) *chsd ldg grp, styd on one pace frm 2 fs out*.....(14 to 1 tchd 16 to 1) 4
2969² FACE NORTH (Ire) [71] 5-7-10 (5*) B Russell (8) *cl up, led o'r 2 fs out, hdd and outpcd entering last.* ....(14 to 1 op 16 to 1 tchd 20 to 1) 5
2479³ YOUNG ERN [94] 3-8-11 (7*) Michael Denaro (4) *wl plcd, str chal 2 fs out, outpcd ins last*......(25 to 1 op 20 to 1) 6
2995* KASSBAAN (USA) [81] 3-8-5 B Raymond (16) *ran on frm rear o'r 2 fs out, ev ch over one out, no extr.* ....(4 to 1 fav op 11 to 2 tchd 6 to 1) 7
2926⁷ NORFOLK HERO [85] 3-8-9 A Munro (14) *mid-div, rdn and kpt on one pace last 2 fs*........ (12 to 1) 8
2966⁵ CORALS DREAM (Ire) [82] 4-8-12 W Woods (13) *chsd ldrs, ev ch und pres o'r 2 fs out, sn btn.* (33 to 1 op 25 to 1) 9
2811² TAJDIF (USA) [82] 3-8-6 S Whitworth (3) *mid-div, hdwy 2 fs out, not quicken fnl furlong*.....(14 to 1 tchd 12 to 1) 10
3127⁶ FIGHTER SQUADRON [65] (bl) 4-7-2 (7*) N Varley (15) *nvr on terms*........ (25 to 1 op 20 to 1) 11
2600* HOB GREEN [81] 4-8-11 K Fallon (18) *hld up rear, shrtlvd effrt o'r 2 fs out, nvr dngrs.* .... (11 to 2 op 9 to 2 tchd 6 to 1) 12
2798² VELOCE (Ire) [79] 5-8-9 A Mackay (5) *hld up, effrt o'r 2 fs out, not rch ldrs*........ (14 to 1 op 12 to 1) 13
2522 YOURS BY RIGHT [83] 3-8-7 G Duffield (1) *prmnt till lost pl hfwy*........(20 to 1 tchd 25 to 1) 14
2698² REALITIES (USA) [96] 3-9-6 L Dettori (9) *chsd ldrs 4 fs.* .... (11 to 1 op 12 to 1 tchd 10 to 1) 15
2206⁶ WATHIK (USA) [93] 3-9-3 R Hills (11) *in tch in mid-div, rdn and wknd 2 fs out*........ (33 to 1) 16
2926⁹ BLOCKADE (USA) [76] 4-8-3 (3*) M Fenton (2) *led till o'r 2 fs out, drpd out rpdly*.... (9 to 1 op 10 to 1 tchd 8 to 1) 17
Dist: 2½l, ¾l, nk, hd, ¾l, nk, ½l, sht-hd, sht-hd, 1½l. 1m 24.45s. a 0.25s (17 Ran).
SR: 82/46/64/51/45/60/46/48/50/ (Mrs B Newton), B Hanbury

3178 Fay, Richwhite Maiden Stakes Class D (3-y-o) £3,882 6f. . . . . (4:50)

3005² STORM CANYON (Ire) 9-0 L Dettori (8) *pld hrd early, jnd ldr hfwy, led o'r one furlong out, pushed clr, eased nr line*.....(11 to 8 fav op 7 to 4 tchd 2 to 1 and 5 to 4) 1
2908³ BALLET SHOES (Ire) 8-9 R Cochrane (1) *made most till o'r one furlong out, sn outpcd.* .... (11 to 4 op 7 to 4 tchd 3 to 1) 2
2580³ AQUILETTA 8-9 K Fallon (2) *trkd ldrs, rdn alng and one pace last 2 fs*........ (8 to 1 tchd 10 to 1) 3
JAWAAL 9-0 B Raymond (5) *edgd rght strt, chsd ldrs, outpcd appr fnl furlong.* (6 to 1 op 4 to 1 tchd 8 to 1) 4
2580⁷ PENNY FAN 8-9 A Munro (6) *edgd rght strt, pld hrd, speed til outpcd o'r 2 fs out.* (25 to 1 op 20 to 1 tchd 33 to 1) 5
FILL 8-9 R Hills (7) *squeezed for room strt, shaken up and no hdwy appr last 2 fs.* (5 to 1 op 8 to 1 tchd 10 to 1) 6
2032⁵ KAPUCHKA (Ire) 8-9 S Whitworth (3) *chsd ldrs 4 fs, sn btn.* .... (25 to 1 op 20 to 1 tchd 33 to 1) 7
2787⁵ LADY HONDA (Ire) 8-6 (3*) D Harrison (4) *wl plcd till wknd quickly hfwy, sn lost tch*........(25 to 1 op 20 to 1) 8
Dist: 2½l, 3l, 3l, ½l, ¾l, 1½l, 12l. 1m 12.38s. a 0.68s (8 Ran).
SR: 56/41/29/22/15/12/6/-/ (Sheikh Mohammed), J H M Gosden

3179 Auckland Handicap Class C (0-95 3-y-o and up) £4,793 1¼m. . . . . (5:20)

1802⁴ ARKAAN (USA) [80] 3-8-11 B Raymond (4) *mid-div, rdn and ran on 2 fs out, got up last strds.* ....(6 to 1 tchd 7 to 1) 1
2882⁵ EDEN'S CLOSE [70] 4-8-3 (7*) S Mulvey (5) *wl plcd, rdn to ld 2 fs out, hdd last strds.* ....(7 to 1 op 6 to 1 tchd 8 to 1) 2
2581⁷ DREAMS END [82] 5-9-8 R Cochrane (10) *hld up in mid-div, hmpd and lost pl entering last 2 fs, styd on wl nr finish*........(11 to 1 op 14 to 1 tchd 10 to 1) 3
2867² BENTICO [70] 4-8-10 W Ryan (3) *led till rdn and hdd entering last 2 fs, no extr last 100 yards.* ....(4 to 1 op 3 to 1 tchd 9 to 2) 4
2627³ JURA FOREST [84] 3-9-1 G Duffield (6) *hld up rear, hrd rdn frm 2 fs out, styd on one pace.* ....(5 to 2 fav tchd 11 to 2 and 9 to 4) 5
2696 ROBENKO (USA) [68] 4-8-8 L Dettori (7) *wl in tch, effrt und pres and edgd rght entering last 2 fs, one pace fnl furlong*........(20 to 1 op 16 to 1 tchd 25 to 1) 6
2992 SWIFT SILVER [60] 6-7-9 (5*) D McCabe (1) *hld up rear, effrt und pres 2 fs out, not rch frnt rnk.* .... (11 to 1 op 16 to 1) 7
2820² MANILA BAY (USA) [77] 3-8-8 A Munro (2) *settled rear, not rch ldrs last 2 fs*........(5 to 1 op 9 to 2 tchd 11 to 2) 8
2938² SECRET ASSIGNMENT (USA) [65] 3-7-10¹ D Biggs (8) *trkd ldr till lost pl frm 2 fs out*........(11 to 1 op 8 to 1) 9
DORSET DUKE [88] 6-10-0 R Hills (9) *al beh, lost tch last 2 fs*........(20 to 1 op 16 to 1) 10
Dist: Hd, 1½l, sht-hd, 1l, nk, nk, nk, ¾l, 10l. 2m 6.19s. a 3.99s (10 Ran).
SR: 22/20/29/16/19/11/2/9/-/ (Maktoum Al Maktoum), M R Stoute

REDCAR (good to soft)
Saturday August 7th
Going Correction: MINUS 0.15 sec. per fur.

3180 Staintondale Selling Stakes Class G (3-y-o and up) £2,070 7f. . . . . (2:15)

2892³ OBSIDIAN GREY 6-9-3 (3*) O Pears (8) *wth ldr, led aftr 3 fs, quickened clr o'r one furlong out, hng markedly lft and ran on wl*........(12 to 1 op 10 to 1) 1
2765² FORTIS PAVIOR (Ire) 3-9-0 A Culhane (2) *led 3 fs, styd hndy, drvn alng o'r 2 furlongs out, kpt on same pace ins last*........(6 to 1 op 5 to 1 tchd 7 to 1) 2
3055⁵ SUSANNA'S SECRET 6-9-6 Dale Gibson (9) *handily plcd, rdn alng 3 fs out, kpt on same pace ins fnl furlong.* .... (9 to 1 op 8 to 1 tchd 10 to 1) 3
2932⁵ FLETCHER'S BOUNTY (Ire) 4-9-6 J Fanning (5) *hld up in rear, pushed alng o'r 2 fs out, swtchd over one out, kpt on ins last*........ (10 to 1 op 8 to 1) 4
1990² SYLVAN STARLIGHT (v) 3-8-9 C Nutter (4) *trkd ldrs, effrt and drvn alng o'r 2 fs out, not quicken over one out.* ....(9 to 2 op 7 to 2 tchd 5 to 1) 5
2849⁵ CHOIR PRACTICE (bl) 6-9-6 M Tebbutt (11) *sluggish strt, swtchd lft, beh, pushed alng hfwy, improved o'r one furlong out, not pace to chal*........ (8 to 1 op 6 to 1) 6
3060 GENTLE HERO (USA) 7-9-6 Paul Eddery (1) *nvr far away, effrt and rdn o'r 2 furlong out, btn over one out, eased.* ....(8 to 1 op 7 to 1) 7
2656⁴ ACROSS THE BAY (v) 6-9-6 K Darley (3) *co'red up beh ldg bunch, pushed alng to improve 3 fs out, no imprsn.* ....(5 to 2 fav op 4 to 1) 8
1577⁴ COLFAX CLASSIC 3-8-9 D Biggs (7) *tucked away beh ldrs, not clr run o'r 2 fs out, rdn and sn btn.* .... (20 to 1 op 16 to 1) 9
2733 DARIKA LAD 5-9-6 J Fortune (10) *dwlt, swtchd lft strt, beh, rdn alng hfwy, nvr on terms.* (20 to 1 op 16 to 1) 10
FOR GOLD 3-8-9 W Newnes (6) *beh, outpcd and drvn alng aftr 3 fs, wndrd and sn lost tch.* .... (14 to 1 op 12 to 1) 11
Dist: 3l, ½l, 1½l, 2l, nk, hd, sht-hd, 2l, 8l, 2l. 1m 26.70s. a 4.90s (11 Ran).
SR: 17/2/6/1/-/-/ (Miss L C Siddall), Miss L C Siddall

3181 BonusPrint Fillies' Handicap Class D (0-80 3-y-o and up) £3,817 1¼m (2:45)

2847* MAY HILLS LEGACY (Ire) [53] 4-9-2 Paul Eddery (4) *set steady pace, quickened entering strt, shaken up and ran on strly fnl 2 fs*........(5 to 2 op 2 to 1) 1
2961 DUTOSKY [74] 3-10-0 D Biggs (1) *hld up in cl tch, effrt and rdn o'r 2 fs out, no extr ins fnl furlong.* (2 to 1 jt-fav tchd 9 to 4) 2
2930⁷ GREEN'S CASSATT (USA) [47] 5-8-5 (5*) A Garth (3) *trkd ldr, pushed alng o'r 3 fs out, sn outpcd, ran on ins fnl furlong, nvr dngrs*........ (7 to 1 op 6 to 1) 3
2874* ESSEX GIRL [63] 3-9-3 K Darley (2) *chsd ldg pair, shaken up to take clr order 3 fs out, drvn and no extr o'r one out*........ (2 to 1 jt-fav) 4
Dist: 2½l, 1½l, ¾l. 2m 12.30s. a 11.10s (4 Ran).
(Exors Of The Late Mrs G P Williams), D W P Arbuthnot

3182 Paul Daniels Handicap Class D (0-80 3-y-o and up) £5,340 1m. . . . . (3:20)

CROSSILLION [79] 5-10-0 Paul Eddery (6) *patiently rdn, took clr order 3 fs out, ran on to ld entering last, kpt on wl*........ (10 to 1 op 8 to 1) 1
3004* SOOTY TERN [61] 6-8-3 (7*) Mark Denaro (7) *led, shaken up o'r one furlong out, hdd one out, kpt on same pace ins last*........ (9 to 2 op 7 to 2) 2
3057³ PRINCESS MAXINE (Ire) [55] 4-8-4 Dale Gibson (4) *nvr far away, jnd issue hfwy, nosed ahead briefly one furlong out, sn btn*........(9 to 2 op 7 to 2) 3
3004³ PRIDE OF PENDLE [62] 4-8-11 W Newnes (1) *hld up, drvn to improve o'r 2 fs out, no extr ins last.* .....(4 to 1 jt-fav op 3 to 1) 4
3004⁶ CELESTINE [56] (v) 4-8-5 J Fanning (2) *pressed ldg grp, drvn alng hfwy, btn 2 furlong out.* .... (11 to 1 op 10 to 1 tchd 12 to 1) 5
3058³ MAJAL (Ire) [57] 4-8-6 L Charnock (3) *rcd keenly, wth ldr, reminders hfwy, wknd o'r 2 fs out*... (6 to 1 op 9 to 2) 6
BONUS POINT [60] 3-8-2 K Darley (5) *keen hold, trkd ldrs, drvn alng 3 furlong sout, sn outpcd*........(4 to 1 jt-fav op 6 to 1) 7
Dist: 2½l, 1l, nk, 8l, nk, 7l. 1m 37.90s. a 3.00s (7 Ran).
SR: 51/25/16/22/ (G Wragg), G Wragg

3183 Leigh-Ann Johns Median Auction Maiden Fillies' Stakes Class F (2-y-o) £2,243 5f. . . . . (3:50)

2575[4] ANN'S PEARL (Ire) 8-11 K Darley (9) *nvr far away, improved on bit to ld o'r one furlong out, sn clr, easily.* ....(11 to 8 on op Evens tchd 5 to 4) 1
2505[7] SPRING STAR 8-8 (3*) O Pears (4) *led a furlong and a half centre, styd hndy, drvn alng 2 fs out, edgd rght and kpt on und pres ins last.* (40 to 1 op 33 to 1 tchd 50 to 1) 2
CAPONATA (Ire) 8-11 J Fortune (8) *bumped leaving stalls, in tch centre, effrt and rdn 2 fs out, kpt on same pace ins last.*.................................(11 to 2 op 9 to 2) 3
2595[5] DAUNTLESS FORT 8-11 W Newnes (2) *led far side grp, rdn alng o'r 2 fs out, no ch wth centre group over one furlong out.*.........(25 to 1 op 20 to 1 tchd 33 to 1) 4
2102 KENTUCKY FLYER 8-11 L Charnock (1) *chsd ldr far side, rdn and one pace fnl 2 fs*..........................(33 to 1) 5
1475[3] KAYDARAJ 8-11 Paul Eddery (6) *led aftr a furlong and a half, rdn and hdd o'r one furlong out, sn btn.* .... (10 to 1 op 8 to 1) 6
1763[6] LEVEL EDGE 8-11 M Tebbutt (3) *sn pushed alng beh ldrs, swtchd to far side aftr 2 fs, soon drvn along, btn wl o'r one furlong out*.................. (14 to 1 op 12 to 1) 7
2876[6] PETRINA BAY 8-11 A Culhane (5) *chsd ldrs centre, drvn alng hfwy, fdd o'r one furlong out.* (11 to 2 op 9 to 2) 8
968[9] SHANNARA (Ire) 8-11 S Morris (7) *veered rght leaving stalls, pressed ldg grp centre, drvn alng hfwy, sn struggling, tld off*..................... (33 to 1 op 20 to 1) 9
MONKEY FACE 8-11 Dale Gibson (10) *missed break, sn wl beh and al struggling, tld off*................ (14 to 1) 10

Dist: 4l, ½l, 2½l, 2l, 1l, hd, 1l, 12l, 3l. 59.70s. a 3.00s (10 Ran).

SR: 22/6/4/-/-/-/ (Mrs Paul Levinson), P J Makin

3184 Levy Board Claiming Handicap Class E (0-70 3-y-o and up) £3,183 6f.. (4:15)

2869[9] KINNEGAD KID [33] 4-7-8[4] (5*) N Gwilliams (8) *tacked o'r to far side aftr a furlong, al hndy, improved to ld over one furlong out, sn clr, ran on wl ins last*......... (12 to 1) 1
2868[8] HONEY SEEKER [62] 4-9-10 K Darley (4) *dwlt, sn chasing ldrs, improved and hng lft o'r one furlong out, kpt on ins last, not rch wnr*.............(4 to 1 fav op 6 to 1) 2
2975[2] SLADES HILL [62] 6-9-7 (3*) O Pears (1) *in tch gng wl, effrt and rdn o'r one furlong out, not quicken ins last.* ....(5 to 1 op 4 to 1) 3
3002* ASTERIX [51] 5-8-6 (7*) Mark Denaro (6) *beh ldg grp, rdn to improve o'r 2 fs out, kpt on same pace ins fnl furlong.* ....(7 to 1 op 6 to 1) 4
3051[2] BALLAD DANCER [66] 8-10-0 W Newnes (7) *in tch, effrt and rdn alng o'r 2 fs out, not pace to chal.* ....(5 to 1 op 4 to 1) 5
2480[3] DUKE OF DREAMS [62] 3-9-5 Paul Eddery (9) *beh, shaken up and not much room 2 fs out, kpt on, nvr able to chal.* ....(8 to 1 op 7 to 1) 6
2600 LANGUEDOC [61] 6-9-9 L Charnock (2) *prmnt, swtchd to far side and led aftr a furlong, sn clr, hdd o'r one out, soon btn*..(8 to 1) 7
2651[3] LARN FORT [53] (v) 3-8-10 J Fanning (3) *chsd ldrs, rdn alng hfwy, fdd*..........................(12 to 1 op 10 to 1) 8
2934[2] SWEET ROMEO [59] 3-9-2 J Fortune (5) *led for a furlong, styd hndy, hrd drvn frm hfwy, sn btn.* ....(5 to 1 op 4 to 1) 9

Dist: 2½l, 1½l, 1l, 2l, sht-hd, ¾l, 3½l, ½l. 1m 11.90s. a 2.20s (9 Ran).

SR: 19/38/32/17/24/14/15/-/-/ (Mrs M T Morgan), R Ingram

3185 Go Racing In Yorkshire Apprentice Maiden Handicap Class F (0-70 3-y-o and up) £2,556 1m 1f........... (4:45)

2697[2] SEROTINA (Ire) [67] (bl) 3-10-0 D Gibbs (6) *patiently rdn, swtchd to improve o'r 3 fs out, led over one out, styd on strly*............ (11 to 8 fav op 5 to 4 tchd 6 to 4) 1
EDIREPUS [48] 5-8-9 (8*) S Copp (2) *rcd freely, in tch, improved to chal 2 fs out, not pace of wnr ins last.* ....(6 to 1 op 5 to 1) 2
1566[6] GYPSY CRYSTAL (USA) [34] 3-7-4 (5*) M Baird (5) *led 2 fs, styd hndy, outpcd and lost pl entering strt, ran on o'r one out, edgd lft and stayed on*......(6 to 1 op 4 to 1) 3
2384[9] BRUSH WOLF (USA) [24] 4-7-2 (5*) D Thomas (4) *keen hold, beh, squeezed through bend o'r 4 fs out, ev ch 2 out, one pace*..............................(20 to 1 op 12 to 1) 4
962 THROW AWAY LINE [40] 4-8-4 (5*) D Thomas (3) *tucked away on ins, improved to ld 3 fs out, hdd o'r one out, no extr*..................................(20 to 1 op 16 to 1) 5
2740[5] MOST SIOUXTABLE [44] 3-7-9 (10*) G Mills (1) *cl up, led aftr 2 fs, hdd o'r 3 out, rdn and sn btn*....(8 to 1 op 6 to 1) 6
2289[6] MY GRAIN [28] 4-7-11 Mark Denaro (8) *nvr far away, led briefly o'r 3 fs out, sn drvn alng, btn 2 furlongs out.* .... (11 to 2 op 4 to 1) 7
2678[8] PUBLIC APPEAL [58] 4-9-13 P Roberts (7) *in tch on outer, pushed alng wl o'r 3 fs out, sn lost touch, tld off.* .... (20 to 1 op 25 to 1) 8

Dist: 2½l, 1l, 3½l, ½l, ¾l, 10l, 12l. 1m 57.70s. a 9.20s (8 Ran).

(Lord & Lady Roborough), W Jarvis

3186 EBF Sinnington Maiden Fillies Stakes Class D (2-y-o) £4,306 7f........(5:15)

2748[2] MISS RINJANI 8-11 Paul Eddery (4) *trkd ldrs gng wl, improved to chal o'r one furlong out, rdn to ld well ins last, jst hld on.* ....(11 to 8 fav op 5 to 4 tchd Evens and 6 to 4) 1
BONNY BRIDE (Ire) 8-11 M Tebbutt (1) *slwly into strd, sn chasing ldrs, not clr run o'r 2 out, outpcd and rdn over one out, ran on strly ins last, jst fld.* ....(11 to 2 op 5 to 1 tchd 6 to 1) 2
2695[4] MUMTAZ FLYPAST 8-11 K Darley (3) *wth ldrs, definite advantage aftr 3 fs, jnd o'r one out, edgd lft, hdd wl ins last, no extr.* ....(11 to 4 op 3 to 1 tchd 7 to 2 and 5 to 2) 3
1683[5] MATISSE 8-11 Dale Gibson (2) *nvr far away, improved to chal o'r one furlong out, one pace ins last.* .... (20 to 1 op 14 to 1) 4
MONKEY WENCH (Ire) 8-11 J Fortune (7) *chsd ldrs, drvn alng aftr 3 fs, no imprsn fnl 2*.......(12 to 1 op 7 to 1) 5
SHIFTING MIST 8-11 C Nutter (5) *dsptd ld 3 fs, sn drvn alng, btn o'r 2 out*..................(10 to 1 op 7 to 1) 6
2973[3] BOJOLLY 8-11 A Culhane (6) *dsptd ld 3 fs, sn pushed alng, wknd o'r 2 out*....... (12 to 1 op 14 to 1 tchd 10 to 1) 7

Dist: Sht-hd, 1l, 3½l, 6l, 2l, nk. 1m 26.40s. a 4.60s (7 Ran).

SR: 12/11/8/-/ (J L C Pearce), G Wragg

SARATOGA (USA) (good)
Saturday August 7th

3187 Sword Dancer Handicap (Grade 1) (3-y-o and up) £79,470 1½m............

SPECTACULAR TIDE (USA) 4-8-0 Julie Krone, ...(43 to 10) 1
SQUARE CUT (USA) 4-7-13 J Bailey, ...(132 to 10) 2
DR KIERNAN (USA) 4-8-5 C Antley, ...(16 to 10 fav) 3
1370[4] REVASSER (USA) 4-7-10 P Day, ... (23 to 10) 4
FUTURIST (USA) 5-8-0 J Santos, ...(79 to 10) 5
ROYAL PAGEANT (USA) 4-7-8 C Bisono, ... (166 to 10) 6
1971* D'ARROS (Ire) 4-8-2 M Smith, ... (23 to 10) 7
MIO ROBERTINO (USA) 4-7-10 J Chavez, ...(38 to 1) 8
TRAMPOLI (USA) 4-7-13 J-L Samyn, ... (122 to 10) pu

Dist: 2 ¾l, ¾l, ½l, ½l, hd, 10l, 6l. 2m 30.39s. (9 Ran).

(Royal Lines Stable), S Hough

SOUTHWELL (A.W) (std)
Saturday August 7th

Going Correction: PLUS 0.20 sec. per fur. (race 1), PLUS 0.15 (2,3,4,5,6)

3188 Picasso Handicap Class E (0-70 3-y-o and up) £2,385 6f................(6:00)

2428* SAKHAROV [49] 4-9-4 P Robinson (6) *beh and sn pushed alng, wide strt and gd hdwy 2 fs out, rdn and styd on to ld wl ins last*...... (11 to 8 fav op 7 to 4 tchd 2 to 1) 1
2829[2] COVENT GARDEN GIRL [64] 3-10-0 T Lucas (4) *trkd ldg pair, effrt and hdwy 2 fs out, led o'r one out, sn rdn and hdd wl ins last*... (11 to 2 op 5 to 1 tchd 13 to 2) 2
2829* STRIP CARTOON (Ire) [58] 5-9-6 (7*) G Strange (1) *led, rdn 2 fs out, hdd o'r one out, kpt on und pres ins last.* ....(4 to 1 op 9 to 2) 3
646 LAURA [50] 4-9-5 B Crossley (2) *slwly into strd, sn chasing ldrs, rdn o'r 2 fs out and soon btn.* .... (12 to 1 op 8 to 1) 4
2584[8] NO QUARTER GIVEN [55] 8-9-10 J Lowe (7) *chsd ldrs, rdn 3 fs out and sn btn*........................(12 to 1 op 8 to 1) 5
2560[5] STORMY HEIGHTS [53] (bl) 3-9-3 S Perks (5) *pushed alng hfwy, nvr a factor*...........................(9 to 2 op 7 to 2) 6
2424[6] LAID BACK BEN [45] 3-8-4 (5*) Stephen Davies (3) *cl up till rdn and wknd quickly o'r 2 fs out.* (33 to 1 op 20 to 1) 7

Dist: 1½l, ½l, 5l, 1½l, 1½l, 4l. 1m 17.90s. a 4.50s (7 Ran).

SR: 38/42/39/11/10/-/-/ (J R Good), M A Jarvis

3189 Keeble Hawson Selling Stakes Class G (2-y-o) £1,725 7f..............(6:30)

2917[2] NORTHERN BAILIWICK (Ire) (bl) 8-11 M Wigham (10) *middiv, hdwy o'r 2 fs out, sn rdn, styd on und pres to ld wl ins last*............... (9 to 1 op 7 to 1 tchd 10 to 1) 1
2917[9] THATCHED ROOF (Ire) 7-13 (7*) C Munday (9) *al prmnt, effrt and led 2 fs out, rdn and hng lft appr fnl furlong, swrvd badly rght, hdd wl ins last.* (40 to 1 op 33 to 1) 2
2952[2] SHUTTLECOCK 8-6 (5*) Stephen Davies (1) *cl up, led aftr 3 fs till rdn and hdd 2 furlongs out, kpt on one pace appr last*.................................(11 to 2 op 6 to 1) 3
2786[7] BENFLEET 8-11 R Price (2) *in tch, effrt and not clr run 2 and a half fs out, swtchd wide and styd on strly ins last*................................(8 to 1 op 6 to 1) 4
2952[4] BESSIE'S WILL 8-6 A Mackay (8) *chsd ldrs, rdn 2 fs out, kpt on one pace appr last*.......(20 to 1 op 12 to 1) 5
2917* SUPER SYMPHONIC 9-2 P Robinson (12) *sn cl up, ev ch o'r 2 fs out, soon rdn and btn.* ....(11 to 10 on op 5 to 4 tchd 5 to 4 on) 6
2862 BANG IN TROUBLE (Ire) 8-11 S Perks (3) *chsd ldrs, rdn and hng lft 2 and a half fs out, sn btn.* .... (8 to 1 op 12 to 1 tchd 16 to 1) 7

MAKROY (Ire) 8-6 (5*) D Wright (5) *slwly into strd, nvr rch ldrs*..............................(50 to 1 op 33 to 1) 8
2876 SNUGFIT ANNIE 8-6 T Lucas (7) *led 3 fs, cl up till rdn and wknd quickly o'r 2 furlongs out*.... (12 to 1 op 7 to 1) 9
2668 FAST BEAT 8-6 B Crossley (11) *sn outpcd and beh*. .... (40 to 1 op 20 to 1) 10
2814^{6} TILQUHILLIE ROSE 8-7^{1} C Dwyer (6) *sn outpcd and wl beh*.................................(12 to 1 op 8 to 1) 11
2526^{8} GOODWINCOPLEY 8-7^{3} (7*) P Johnson (4) *sn outpcd and beh*..............................(50 to 1 op 33 to 1) 12
Dist: 1½l, 2½l, 1½l, 1½l, 2½l, 2½l, 7l, 1½l, 3½l, 2l. 1m 33.10s. a 7.00s (12 Ran).
SR: 8/-/-/-/-/-/ (Dr Ian R Shenkin), M D I Usher

3190 East Midlands Electricity Plc Handicap Class E (0-70 3-y-o and up) £2,406 7f.............................(7:00)

3020^{5} TYRIAN PURPLE (Ire) [61] (bl) 5-9-2 (3*) D Harrison (8) *sn led and clr, rdn 2 fs out, styd on gmely ins last*. .... (11 to 2 op 6 to 1) 1
2897^{9} PENNY BANGER (Ire) [61] 3-8-13 L Dettori (9) *chsd ldrs, hdwy to chal 2 fs out, sn rdn and ev ch till hrd drvn and no extr nr finish*..................(4 to 1 tchd 9 to 2) 2
2919^{3} GLENFIELD GRETA [59] (bl) 5-8-12 (5*) D Wright (6) *in tch, hdwy o'r 2 fs out, sn rdn and styd on ins last*. .... (11 to 2 op 9 to 2) 3
2848^{3} AQUADO [42] 4-8-0 A Mackay (7) *chsd ldrs, rdn o'r 2 fs out, kpt on one pace*.............. (11 to 1 op 9 to 1) 4
2525^{8} MUSIC DANCER [54] 4-8-12 G Duffield (1) *prmnt till hmpd and lost pl aftr one furlong, beh and wide strt, styd on fnl 2 fs, nrst finish*................(7 to 2 fav op 6 to 1) 5
3140^{4} BASSIO (Bel) [49] (h) 4-8-7^{4} W Hood (4) *mid-div, effrt and rdn hfwy, not rch ldrs*.............(12 to 1 op 10 to 1) 6
3004^{9} DREAM CARRIER (Ire) [70] 5-9-7 (7*) V Halliday (5) *sn wl beh, some hdwy fnl 2 fs, nvr dngrs*....(10 to 1 tchd 12 to 1) 7
2919* HEATHYARDS GEM [57] 3-8-9 S Perks (2) *al rear*. .... (13 to 2 op 5 to 1 tchd 7 to 1) 8
2978^{3} SIMPLY SUPERB [43] (bl) 3-7-9 L Charnock (3) *chsd ldr, rdn 3 fs out and sn wknd*. (11 to 1 op 10 to 1 tchd 12 to 1) 9
1505^{7} MANADEL [42] (bl) 3-7-8^{1} J Lowe (10) *chsd ldrs, rdn 3 fs out and sn wknd*.....(40 to 1 op 33 to 1 tchd 50 to 1) 10
Dist: Hd, 2½l, 2½l, hd, 7l, 2½l, hd, nk, 15l. 1m 31.70s. a 5.60s (10 Ran).
SR: 37/30/26/1/12/-/ (T O'Flaherty), T J Naughton

3191 Van Gogh Limited Stakes Class E (0-70 3-y-o and up) £2,794 1m... (7:30)

2995^{8} OCARA (USA) 3-8-9 L Dettori (3) *trkd ldrs, hdwy 3 fs out, led 2 out, sn clr*.................. (6 to 5 fav op 2 to 1) 1
2716^{7} SAKURA QUEEN (Ire) 3-8-9 W Woods (4) *chsd ldrs, hdwy 3 fs out, effrt and rdn 2 out, kpt on one pace*. .... (10 to 1 op 7 to 1) 2
2918* ISLAND KNIGHT (Ire) 4-9-7 P Robinson (1) *hld up, hdwy on inner 2 and a half fs out, sn rdn, one pace*. ....(11 to 8 op Evens tchd 6 to 4) 3
LEXIA 8-9-2 W Newnes (5) *led, rdn and hdd 2 fs out, sn wknd, wnt lme ins last*. .... (20 to 1 op 16 to 1 tchd 25 to 1) 4
2918^{2} PHILNIC 3-9-0 G Duffield (6) *chsd ldr, rdn alng aftr 3 fs, lost pl hfwy, sn beh*.... (13 to 2 op 5 to 1 tchd 7 to 1) 5
Dist: 2½l, 7l, 2½l, 15l. 1m 45.50s. a 6.50s (5 Ran).
SR: 16/8/ (Lucayan Stud), D R Loder

3192 Gainsborough Claiming Stakes Class E (3 & 4-y-o) £1,952 1m......... (8:00)

2816^{9} MOHICAN BRAVE (Ire) 3-8-9 K Fallon (9) *chsd ldrs on outer, hdwy and wide strt, led wl o'r one furlong out, sn rdn clr*.....................(11 to 4 op 7 to 2 tchd 5 to 2) 1
2993^{6} PACIFIC POWER 3-8-8 (3*) Emma O'Gorman (4) *slwly into strd, beh and pushed alng, wide strt, hdwy 2 fs out, styd on ins last, no ch wth wnr*. .... (14 to 1 tchd 16 to 1 and 20 to 1) 2
2670 ROCKY BAY 4-8-7 A Mackay (8) *beh and sn rdn alng, hdwy und pres 2 fs out, styd on wl fnl furlong, nrst finish*...............................(16 to 1 op 12 to 1) 3
2551^{6} AWESTRUCK 3-8-13 G Duffield (7) *chsd ldrs and rdn alng thrght, hdwy 2 fs out, sn hrd drvn and one pace*. ....(11 to 8 fav op 7 to 4 tchd 2 to 1) 4
732^{7} BY QUEEN (Ire) 3-8-10 M Wigham (2) *chsd ldrs, rdn 3 fs out, sn one pace*................. (25 to 1 op 20 to 1) 5
2747 COSMIC STAR (bl) 3-8-2 W Woods (5) *chsd ldrs, rdn and hdwy to ld 3 fs out, hdd wl o'r one out, sn wknd*. ....(16 to 1 op 12 to 1 tchd 20 to 1) 6
2833^{6} SUMMER FLOWER 3-7-5 (5*) D Wright (1) *sn outpcd and beh*.................................(25 to 1 op 20 to 1) 7
2870^{9} EVAHART 3-7-10 J Quinn (3) *led, rdn o'r 3 fs out, sn hdd and wknd*............................ (50 to 1 op 33 to 1) 8
1422^{6} GUV'NORS GIFT 3-8-1 (7*) S Mulvey (10) *chsd ldrs on outer, rdn alng hfwy, wknd o'r 2 and a half fs out*. ....(9 to 2 tchd 5 to 1) 9
2000^{6} WRETS (bl) 4-8-12 L Dettori (6) *cl up, rdn 3 fs out, sn wknd*...................................(7 to 1 op 6 to 1) 10
Dist: 5l, 1½l, ½l, 2l, 4l, 1½l, 3½l, 1½l, 12l. 1m 45.00s. a 6.00s (10 Ran).
SR: 23/10/1/5/-/-/ (J Dick), J G FitzGerald

3193 Turner Handicap Class E (0-70 3-y-o and up) £2,574 1½m............ (8:30)

2827^{3} DASHING FELLOW (Ire) [40] 5-8-0 J Quinn (10) *al prmnt, hdwy to ld 3 fs out, sn wl clr, eased ins last*....(14 to 1) 1
2860^{2} PREMIER DANCE [40] 6-8-0 A Mackay (12) *mid-div, hdwy o'r 4 fs out, rdn over 2 furlongs out and styd on, no ch wth wnr*.......................... (12 to 1 tchd 11 to 1) 2
2827* ABALENE [56] 4-9-2 W Newnes (13) *cl up, led aftr 2 fs, rdn and hdd 3 furlongs out, kpt on one pace*. ....(5 to 1 op 6 to 1 tchd 7 to 1) 3
2828* CRIMINAL RECORD (USA) [60] (v) 3-8-9 L Dettori (5) *in tch, hdwy 5 fs out, effrt and rdn 3 furlongs out, sn one pace*. ....(4 to 1 jt-fav op 7 to 1) 4
2948^{4} MODEST HOPE (USA) [68] 6-10-0 Alex Greaves (14) *beh, hdwy on inner 3 fs out, kpt on und pres fnl 2 furlongs, nvr dngrs*........................(12 to 1 op 9 to 1) 5
2921* HASTA LA VISTA [54] (bl) 3-8-3 L Charnock (8) *cl up, effrt and rdn 3 fs out, wknd 2 furlongs out*........(4 to 1 jt-fav op 3 to 1) 6
2970^{7} CHARLIE BIGTIME [63] 3-8-12 D Holland (7) *hld up and beh, hdwy o'r 4 fs out, rdn 3 out and no imprsn*. .... (12 to 1 op 8 to 1) 7
SAYMORE [59] 7-9-0 (5*) S Wynne (9) *al beh*. .... (33 to 1 op 25 to 1) 8
2529^{2} GWEEK (Ire) [53] 3-8-2 P Robinson (4) *beh, hdwy 5 fs out, rdn and wknd o'r 2 out*. .... (17 to 2 op 8 to 1 tchd 9 to 1) 9
2992 BARCHAM [35] 6-7-9 J Lowe (11) *prmnt till rdn and lost pl 5 fs out, sn beh*.........(5 to 1 op 6 to 1 tchd 13 to 2) 10
3003^{6} CARROLLS MARC (Ire) [53] 5-8-10 (3*) C Hodgson (6) *prmnt, rdn o'r 4 fs out and sn wknd*. (12 to 1 op 8 to 1) 11
2729^{9} SCOTTISH WEDDING [65] 3-8-11 (3*) O Pears (3) *prmnt till lost pl hfwy, sn beh*.................. (10 to 1 op 8 to 1) 12
2834 SEA PRODIGY [33] 4-7-3^{1} (5*) D Wright (1) *led 2 fs, sn lost pl and wl beh frm hfwy*..............(40 to 1 op 33 to 1) 13
Dist: 3l, 1½l, 1½l, 2l, 3l, ¾l, 8l, 1l, ½l, ½l. 2m 41.00s. a 7.10s (13 Ran).
SR: 33/27/40/30/45/14/21/12/-/ (Mrs Val Rapkins), Mrs L Piggott

DEAUVILLE (FR) (good)
Sunday August 8th
Going Correction: PLUS 0.20 sec. per fur.

3194 Prix de Pomone (Group 2) (3-y-o and up) £35,842 1m 5f 110yds....... (3:10)

2690* BRIGHT MOON (USA) (bl) 3-8-7 T Jarnet (7) *mid-div, 4th strt, led o'r one furlong out, sn clr, easily*. (19 to 10 jt-fav) 1
1472^{5} SPRING 4-9-2 W Carson (6) *rcd alone on ins, second strt, led 2 fs out till o'r one out, kpt on one pace*...(97 to 10) 2
2405^{3} OAKMEAD (Ire) 3-8-7 D Holland (2) *al prmnt, dsptd ld 5 fs out, 3rd strt, ran on one pace fnl furlong*. (19 to 10 jt-fav) 3
1787^{4} SOUGHT OUT (Ire) 5-9-2 G Mosse (3) *led or dsptd till 2 fs out, sn wknd*.................................(47 to 10) 4
1088^{4} HALESIA (USA) 4-9-2 D Boeuf (4) *nvr able to chal*. (12 to 1) 5
2579* ALWAYS FRIENDLY 5-9-2 W R Swinburn (1) *al rear*. ....(45 to 10) 6
1693^{3} VALLEY QUEST 3-8-7 F Head (5) *al last*..........(13 to 1) 7
Dist: 2½l, nk, 2l, sht-nk, nk, 10l. 2m 58.00s. a 9.00s (7 Ran).
SR: 30/34/24/29/28/27/-/ (Daniel Wildenstein), A Fabre

3195 Prix de la Calonne (Listed) (3-y-o) £14,337 1m.................... (4:20)

638^{4} BINT LARIAAF (USA) 9-2 W R Swinburn, ... 1
LOST PRAIRIE (USA) 8-11 T Jarnet, ... 2
2981 SHOWGUM (Fr) 9-2 A Junk, ... 3
2409^{8} SHAMSIYA (USA) 8-11 G Mosse, ... 4
Dist: 1½l, ½l, 2l, nk, 2½l, 1½l, ½l, ½l, 2½l. 1m 43.40s. a 8.40s (10 Ran).
(Maktoum Al Maktoum), Mrs C Head

HOPPEGARTEN (GER) (good to soft)
Sunday August 8th

3196 Grosser Preis von Berlin (Group 3) (3-y-o and up) £81,633 6f 110yds... (4:10)

1786 PIPS PRIDE 3-8-10 S Raymont, *made virtually all far side, clr one furlong out, rdn and kpt on wl fnl furlong*. 1
2436^{3} NASR ALLAH (USA) 3-8-10 A Starke, *trkd wnr, no extr fnl furlong*.. 2
2436* QUEBRADA (Ire) 3-8-6 P Schiergen, *led stands side, rdn and no extr fnl 2 fs*.. 3
SHARP PROD (USA) 3-8-10 L Piggott, *hdwy to chal 2 fs out, no extr ins last*.. 4
1786^{3} DOLPHIN STREET (Fr) 3-8-10 C Asmussen, *hld up, hdwy hfwy, one pace fnl 2 fs*.................................... 5
TAMANNA (USA) 3-8-6 G Hind, *nvr nrr*.................. 6
2885 POKER CHIP 3-8-10 R Cochrane, *al beh*................. 7
2488^{2} NEW EUROPE 3-8-6 L Mader, *speed for 3 fs*............. 8
TROGLIO 4-9-6 J Lowe, *nvr plcd to chal*................. 9

LUPULINA (USA) 3-8-6 Paul Eddery, *outpcd*.............. 10
Dist: 3l, ½l, 2½l, 2l, 3½l, 2l. 1m 16.10s. (10 Ran).
(Mrs V S Grant), R Hannon

LEOPARDSTOWN (IRE) (good)
Sunday August 8th

3197 Dunnes Stores Ladies Fashion Series (3-y-o and up) £3,450 1¼m......(2:10)

2781^{8} UP SHE FLEW (USA) 3-8-11 Mrs C Doyle (3)......(25 to 1) 1
3037^{2} SHAWGATNY (USA) 3-9-11^{8} Miss C Hutchinson (5) (11 to 4) 2
BONNIFER (Ire) 4-9-7 (2*) Miss C Cashman (2)....(33 to 1) 3
3037^{5} VELMA (USA) 3-9-6^{3} Miss U Smyth (6).........(100 to 30) 4+
2781* SHARKASHKA (Ire) 3-9-6^{3} Miss L Robinson (1) (5 to 4 on) 4+
2691^{2} NURSES RUN (Ire) 3-8-11 Miss A Sloane (4)......(14 to 1) 6
Dist: 1½l, 6l, hd, dd-ht. 2m 11.40s. a 6.70s (6 Ran).
SR: 25/36/22/18/18/-/ (F X Doyle), F X Doyle

3198 Mongey Communications EBF Maiden (3-y-o and up) £4,140 1½m ....(2:40)

TIGERSONG (USA) 3-9-0 M J Kinane (5)......(10 to 9 on) 1
2743^{3} ENDSONG (USA) 3-8-11 C Roche (6).............(2 to 1) 2
1335^{5} CARRICK PIKE (USA) (bl) 3-9-0 K J Manning (2)....(8 to 1) 3
2691^{4} ROYAL ANTELOPE (Fr) 3-8-11 J P Murtagh (4).....(5 to 1) 4
2676^{5} RED GLITTER (USA) 3-8-8 (6*) J J Behan (1)......(20 to 1) 5
TODDY MARK (Ire) 4-9-11 N Byrne (3)...........(33 to 1) 6
Dist: 4½l, 5½l, 2l, 1l. 2m 39.40s. a 8.40s (6 Ran).
SR: 10/-/-/ (Mrs A J F O'Reilly), D K Weld

3199 Ballyroan Stakes (Listed) (3-y-o and up) £8,625 1¼m................(3:10)

2608^{3} APPROACH THE BENCH (Ire) 5-9-5 J Reid (7) *mid-div, prog 2 fs out, quickened to ld wl ins last*......... (100 to 30) 1
2609* KRISDALINE (USA) 3-8-7 L Dettori (6) *trkd ldr, dsptd ld 2 fs out, led one out, hdd wl ins last*...............(8 to 1) 2
2878^{9} ORMSBY (Ire) 4-9-5 M J Kinane (4) *wl plcd, ev ch 2 fs out, rdn and styd on one pace*.....................(6 to 1) 3
3072^{4} ARABIC TREASURE (USA) 3-8-10 T Quinn (2) *hld up, prog 2 fs out, rdn and no extr ins last*.................(8 to 1) 4
3029^{2} SPECIAL PAGEANT (Ire) 3-8-7 C Roche (5) *led, jnd 2 fs out, hdd one out, wknd*........................(5 to 2 fav) 5
2809^{3} TARAKANA (USA) 3-8-7 W J Supple (3) *hld up, rdn 2 fs out, kpt on one pace*..............................(3 to 1) 6
Dist: ½l, ¾l, hd, nk. 2m 10.80s. a 6.10s (6 Ran).
SR: 39/26/36/26/22/-/ (J E Mulhern), J E Mulhern

3200 Heinz '57' Phoenix Stakes (Group 1) (2-y-o) £85,500 6f...............(3:45)

2618^{3} TURTLE ISLAND (Ire) 9-0 J Reid (5) *trkd ldr, dsptd ld 2 fs out, led o'r one out, styd on und pres cl hme*. ....(7 to 4 fav) 1
1571* LAS MENINAS (Ire) 8-11 S Craine (8) *mid-div, not much room 2 fs out, swtchd to chal one furlong out, styd on strly ins last*................................(10 to 1) 2
2335^{2} FAST EDDY 9-0 L Dettori (2) *mid-div, prog 2 fs out, slightly hmpd one furlong out, no extr ins last*. ....(11 to 4) 3
3039* KERAKA (USA) 8-11 J P Murtagh (3) *led, jnd 2 fs out, hdd o'r one out, slightly hmpd, wknd ins last*......(12 to 1) 4
2389* GOLD LAND (USA) 9-0 T R Quinn (1) *swrvd lft leaving stalls, prog 2 fs out, ev ch one out, wknd ins last*. ....(3 to 1) 5
2730^{6} TAKADOU (Ire) 9-0 D Harrison (7) *al rear*......... (20 to 1) 6
2745^{2} KLY GREEN 9-0 C Roche (6) *wl plcd, rdn 2 fs out, wknd o'r one out*................................(12 to 1) 7
2075^{7} MONTE MARIO (USA) (bl) 9-0 M J Kinane (9) *reared and lost grnd leaving stalls, al rear*...................(12 to 1) 8
2983^{6} LUDDEN LADY (Ire) 8-11 J J Behan (10) *prmnt early, lost pl 2 fs out*...................................(100 to 1) 9
Dist: ½l, 3½l, ½l, ¾l, 1½l, 2l, ¾l, hd. 1m 14.40s. a 2.90s (9 Ran).
SR: 36/31/20/15/15/9/1/-/-/ (R E Sangster), P W Chapple-Hyam

3201 Circle Paints Handicap (0-100 3-y-o and up) £6,900 5f...............(4:15)

2780^{3} MY-O-MY (Ire) [-] 3-8-12 S Craine (7)..............(6 to 1) 1
3027* CLASSICAL AFFAIR (Ire) [-] 4-9-8 (6*,3ex) J J Behan (5) .... (2 to 1 fav) 2
2741^{7} OICHE MHAITH [-] (bl) 3-7-5 (6*) P P Murphy (9)...(10 to 1) 3
3027^{2} NORDIC OAK (Ire) [-] (bl) 5-9-4 C Roche (2).......(11 to 4) 4
3040* ASTA MADERA (Ire) [-] 3-7-5 (2*) D G O'Shea (3)....(7 to 1) 5
2780^{7} MEMSAHB [-] (bl) 4-8-8 M J Kinane (8).............(7 to 1) 6
2780^{2} MAGIC DON (Ire) [-] (bl) 4-7-9 (8*) R T Fitzpatrick (6) (10 to 1) 7
2323 NEVER WRONG [-] (bl) 6-7-10 (2*) R M Burke (4)..(25 to 1) 8
2780^{8} SHOOT THE DEALER (Ire) [-] (bl) 3-7-8 (8*) G M Moylan (1) ....(12 to 1) 9
Dist: 2½l, 2l, hd, nk. 1m 0.40s. a 1.70s (9 Ran).
SR: 59/65/26/46/20/-/ (R E Sangster), T Stack

3202 Shankill Handicap (0-95 3-y-o and up) £4,140 1m 1f...................(4:45)

2957* SWEET NASHA (Ire) [-] 4-10-0 (5ex) J Reid (6)......(7 to 2) 1
2923^{2} SAIBOT (USA) [-] 4-9-2 M J Kinane (1)......... (Evens fav) 2
LOVELY ALI (Ire) [-] 4-7-13 (6*) J A Heffernan (4)...(16 to 1) 3
3029^{9} OENOTHERA (Ire) [-] (bl) 3-9-4 S Craine (5).......(10 to 1) 4
2345^{2} HAPPY ROVER [-] 8-9-12 J P Murtagh (8)..........(8 to 1) 5
3076* WANDERING THOUGHTS (Ire) [-] 4-8-12 (5ex) L Dettori (7) ....(7 to 2) 6
2957^{6} BIZANA (Ire) [-] 3-8-7 (4*) P Carberry (2)..........(14 to 1) 7
Dist: ¾l, ½l, 5l, ¾l. 1m 54.10s. a 3.60s (7 Ran).
SR: 53/39/26/24/30/-/-/ (N Stassen), Joseph M Canty

3203 Blackhorse EBF Maiden (2-y-o) £5,244 7f.............................(5:15)

MANNTARI (Ire) 9-0 J P Murtagh (4)...............(4 to 1) 1
2840^{2} PEACE ROLE (USA) 9-0 M J Kinane (7)............(2 to 1) 2
2742^{2} DANCING AT LUNASA (Ire) 8-11 L Dettori (8)..... (10 to 1) 3
2072^{6} MOHAAJIR (USA) 9-0 C Roche (3)............(5 to 4 fav) 4
2840^{7} SINGING DANCER (Ire) 8-10 (4*) P Carberry (2)... (25 to 1) 5
3030^{4} LEGAL AIM (Ire) 9-0 S Craine (6)...................(8 to 1) 6
NORDIC AIR (Ire) 9-0 K J Manning (1)............(20 to 1) 7
3073^{9} BUTLER BRENNAN (Ire) 9-0 W J Supple (5)...... (33 to 1) 8
Dist: 1l, 1l, ¾l, 4½l. 1m 31.20s. a 5.80s (8 Ran).
SR: 8/5/-/-/-/ (H H Aga Khan), John M Oxx

OSTEND (BEL) (good)
Sunday August 8th

3204 Prix du President et Madame Max Dugniolls (Handicap) (3-y-o and up) £14,911 1m 3f..................(3:05)

2884^{7} KNOCK KNOCK 8-9-11 S O'Gorman, *al prmnt, led 3 fs out, rdn o'r one out, ran on*.......................... 1
LAZY MOOD (Ire) 3-8-2 P Massage,...................... 2
ERROLL'S TEAM (Ire) 3-7-1 T Blaise,.................... 3
Dist: ½l, 1½l, hd, nk, 1l. (Time not taken) (11 Ran).
(G M Smart), I A Balding

DEL MAR (USA) (firm)
Sunday August 8th

3205 Eddie Read Handicap (Grade 1) (3-y-o and up) £121,689 1m 110yds.........

597* KOTASHAAN (Fr) 5-8-10 K Desormeaux,......(10 to 9 on) 1
LEGER CAT (Arg) 7-8-4 C Nakatani,.............. (3 to 1) 2
RAINBOW CORNER 4-8-1^{1} G Stevens,.........(33 to 10) 3
PATRIOTAKI (USA) 4-8-1^{2} C Black,.............. (16 to 1) 4
STARK SOUTH (USA) 5-8-2 R Romero,.......... (11 to 1) 5
L'EXPRESS (Chi) 4-8-1^{1} C McCarron,............(18 to 1) 6
Dist: 3l, ½l, nose, 1 ¾l, 9l. 1m 48.40s. (6 Ran).
(La Presle Farm), R Mandella

NEUSS (GER) (good)
Sunday August 8th

3206 Deutscher Buchmacher Stutenpreis von Neuss (Group 3) (3-y-o and up) £27,959 1¼m 110yds........... (3:45)

1395^{3} OSTWAHL (Ire) 3-8-5 A Bond, *mid-div, second strt, led o'r one furlong out, drvn out*........................... 1
2837^{2} CHESA PLANA 4-9-4 M Rimmer, *led till o'r one furlong out, ev ch fnl furlong, no extr cl hme*................... 2
1395^{6} SHINE SHARE (Ire) 3-8-5 A Helfenbein, *hld up in rear, fnshd fst fnl furlong, too much to do*................. 3
2259^{9} ARKONA (Ger) 3-8-9 O Schick, *mid-div, trkd ldrs strt, one pace o'r one furlong out*.......................... 4
2259 ELACATA (Ger) 3-8-5 M Hofer, *nvr better plcd*........... 5
2926^{8} DOUBLE FLUTTER 4-9-4 C Rutter, *second till wknd and sn btn strt*.. 6
2646^{5} PRACER (USA) 3-8-6 W Mongil, *mid-div, drpd rear o'r 3 fs out, tld off*.. 7
Dist: ½l, ¾l, 1½l, ¾l. 2m 10.44s. (7 Ran).
(Mrs B And Mrs M Schuluter), P Lautner

SARATOGA (USA) (firm)
Sunday August 8th

3207 Ballerina Stakes (Grade 1) (3-y-o and up) £45,775 7f.......................

2802^{6} SPINNING ROUND (USA) 4-8-7 J Chavez,........ (12 to 1) 1
NOVEMBER SNOW (USA) 4-8-7 C Antley,....(13 to 10 fav) 2
APELIA (Can) 4-8-10 L Attard,.................. (22 to 10) 3
1184^{6} NANNERL (USA) 6-8-7 J D Bailey,................(11 to 1) 4
2999* MISSED THE STORM (USA) 3-8-2 M Smith,......(34 to 10) 5

SANTA CATALINA (USA) 5-8-4 J Santos, ... (18 to 1) 6
LIZEALITY (USA) 4-8-4 Julie Krone, ... (23 to 1) 7
Dist: 2l, ½l, 2½l, nk, 2l, 13l. 1m 21.49s. (7 Ran).
(Kinsman Stud), J Baker

SAN SEBASTIAN (SPA) (good to firm) Sunday August 8th

3208 Premio Gobierno Vasco (Group 3) (3-y-o and up) £57,554 1m......... (1:00)

2436[6] ENHARMONIC (USA) 6-9-2 M Hills, *al prmnt, 5th strt, swtchd one and a half fs out, ran on strly to ld 50 yards out*......... 1
FERDI (Fr) 3-8-9 K Fallon, *al prmnt, rdn to ld appr fnl furlong, hdd and no extr final 50 yards*......... 2
POLICY MATTER (USA) 3-8-9 R Hills, *rear till hdwy o'r 2 fs out, nrst finish*......... 3
DON'T LEAVE ME (Fr) 4-9-2 K Darley, ... 4
PARTIPRAL (USA) 4-9-2 J Horcajada, ... 5
1908[4] PORTICO (USA) 4-9-2 P V Gilson, ... 6
MELODY SINGER 4-8-11 J-L Martinez, ... 7
CABALLO (Spa) 4-9-2 S Vidal, ... 8
TOTI-GUAY (Spa) 3-8-9 D Guillemin, ... 9
2171[3] INTERVALLO (USA) 3-8-9 C Piccioni, ... 0
DADY PINK (Fr) 3-8-9 J-A Machado, ... 0
FALUCHO (Ire) 4-9-2 F Gonzalez, ... 0
NAUPLION (Spa) 4-9-2 W Ryan, ... 0
Dist: Nk, 2½l, ½l, hd, ½l, 1½l. 1m 36.50s. (13 Ran).
(The Queen), Lord Huntingdon

LEICESTER (good to firm) Monday August 9th

Going Correction: MINUS 0.30 sec. per fur.

3209 EBF Captains Median Auction Maiden Fillies' Stakes Class D (2-y-o) £4,110 7f 9yds......... (6:00)

BALLERINA (Ire) 8-11 W R Swinburn (13) *hmpd strt, reco'red to join ldrs aftr 2 fs, led over one out, ran on strly*......... (5 to 1 op 9 to 4) 1
SHORTFALL 8-11 L Dettori (12) *chsd ldrs, improved und pres entering fnl furlong, styd on same pace.* .... (5 to 1 op 5 to 2) 2
2394[2] BRENTWOOD (Ire) 8-11 L Piggott (14) *wnt lft strt, nvr far away, rdn and not quicken fnl furlong.* .... (5 to 1 tchd 11 to 2) 3
2818[3] HELLO IRELAND 8-11 T Sprake (10) *al hndy, led o'r 2 fs out till over one out, rdn and one pace.* .... (10 to 1 op 6 to 1) 4
1580[3] CELTIC CEILIDH 8-11 J Williams (6) *sluggish strt, improved into midfield hfwy, styd on, nvr nrr.* .... (10 to 1 op 8 to 1) 5
2887 CINDY'S STAR (Ire) 8-11 W Woods (5) *led till o'r 2 fs out, fdd appr last*......... (40 to 1 op 33 to 1) 6
1916 BE EXCITING (Ire) 8-11 T Quinn (7) *in tch, drvn alng o'r 2 fs out, nvr able to chal*......... (100 to 30 fav op 5 to 1) 7
DELIVER (Ire) 8-11 D Holland (2) *al hndy, chlgd und pres o'r 2 fs out, wknd appr last*......... (10 to 1 op 5 to 1) 8
VALMARANA (USA) 8-11 R Hills (9) *chsd ldrs for o'r 4 fs, fdd*......... (25 to 1 op 20 to 1) 9
JEMIMA PUDDLEDUCK 8-11 R Price (11) *drvn alng in midfield, nvr a threat*......... (50 to 1 op 33 to 1) 10
2887[9] BERMUDA LADY (USA) 8-11 Paul Eddery (3) *sluggish strt, not reco'r*......... (33 to 1) 11
LADY SILK 8-11 A McGlone (1) *sluggish strt, nvr wnt pace*......... (16 to 1 op 14 to 1) 12
1774[8] DISH OF THE DAY (Ire) 8-11 C Rutter (8) *pressed ldrs for o'r 4 fs, sn wknd*......... (50 to 1 op 33 to 1) 13
HALL OF PEARLS 8-11 N Adams (4) *missed break, al beh.* .... (50 to 1 op 33 to 1) 14
Dist: 2l, 3l, hd, 5l, nk, ½l, sht-hd, 1½l, hd, 1l. 1m 25.00s. a 3.10s (14 Ran).
SR: 19/13/4/3/-/-/ (Lord Weinstock), M R Stoute

3210 Langham Selling Nursery Class G (2-y-o) £2,595 5f 218yds......... (6:30)

2876[7] GREENSON (Ire) [53] 9-1 T Quinn (3) *nvr far away, drvn to ld o'r one furlong out, ran on wl*. (7 to 4 fav op 5 to 2) 1
2974 HARPO'S SPECIAL [56] 9-4 M Wigham (1) *chsd ldrs, effrt on outsd o'r 2 fs out, edgd rght und pres, ran on.* .... (7 to 2 op 2 to 1) 2
2689[5] RISKY AFFAIR [50] (bl) 8-12 Paul Eddery (2) *chsd ldrs, improved und pres last 2 fs, no imprsn fnl furlong.* .... (5 to 1 op 3 to 1) 3
2718[6] NORTHERN STORM (Ire) [59] 9-7 W Woods (6) *led, edgd rght und pres and hdd o'r one furlong out, fdd ins last.* .... (14 to 1 op 10 to 1) 4
2199[7] CAPITAL LADY (Ire) [54] 9-2 J Quinn (4) *trkd ldr, effrt and drvn alng 2 fs out, no extr*......... (25 to 1 op 20 to 1) 5
2377[9] LUCY'S GOLD [51] 8-13 D Biggs (8) *trkd ldg trio, feeling pace whn not much room o'r one furlong out, sn btn.* .... (14 to 1 op 8 to 1) 6
1905 SEVEN UP CYD [56] 9-4 L Dettori (9) *tucked away on ins, chalg whn squeezed for room o'r one furlong out, eased when btn*......... (8 to 1 op 5 to 1 tchd 9 to 1) 7
2718 FILCH [56] 8-11 (7*) G Milligan (7) *unruly stalls, sluggish strt, al outpcd*......... (12 to 1 op 7 to 1 tchd 14 to 1) 8
Dist: ½l, 6l, sht-hd, 1l, hd, 8l, 6l. 1m 13.40s. a 3.00s (8 Ran).
SR: 5/6/-/-/-/ (Richard Green (Fine Paintings)), P F I Cole

3211 Batchelor Bowles Leicester Handicap Class D (0-80 3-y-o and up) £4,012 1m 1f 218yds......... (7:00)

2970* SCOTTISH BAMBI [70] 5-9-9 R Perham (7) *trkd ldg 6, hdwy to ld one furlong out, ran on wl*..... (6 to 1 op 5 to 1) 1
2708[4] BARRATRY [67] (bl) 3-8-11 A McGlone (10) *pressed ldrs, swtchd ins o'r one furlong out, ran on wl und pres.* .... (7 to 1 op 5 to 1 tchd 8 to 1) 2
2722[4] SOVEREIGN PAGE (USA) [74] 4-9-13 W R Swinburn (11) *al hndy, led o'r 2 fs out to one out, rdn and one pace.* .... (8 to 1 op 7 to 1 tchd 9 to 1) 3
2722[2] LET'S GET LOST [72] 4-9-11 L Piggott (5) *tld off appr strt, hdwy on ins last 2 fs, kpt on, nvr nrr.* ......(11 to 2 jt-fav op 6 to 1) 4
2913[4] WESTFIELD MOVES (Ire) [56] 5-8-9 J Quinn (3) *nvr far away, drvn alng o'r 2 fs out, no extr.* .... (12 to 1 op 10 to 1) 5
1711 RUTLAND WATER (USA) [63] 6-9-2 T Quinn (1) *settled beh ldrs, effrt and drvn alng 3 fs out, not pace to chal.* .... (7 to 1 op 9 to 2) 6
3012[7] PYRAMIS PRINCE (Ire) [75] 3-9-5 J Reid (9) *settled midfield, effrt and drvn alng o'r 2 fs out, not quicken.* .... (14 to 1 tchd 16 to 1) 7
2716* RAFIF (USA) [74] 3-9-4 W Carson (2) *trkd ldg 4, und pres o'r 2 fs out, sn btn*......... (11 to 2 jt-fav op 9 to 2) 8
2907 CIRCUS COLOURS [76] 3-9-6 L Dettori (8) *patiently rdn, improved into midfield hfwy, ridden alng o'r 2 fs out, sn btn*......... (6 to 1 op 8 to 1) 9
3017[7] ANNABELLE ROYALE [63] 7-9-2 N Adams (4) *in tch, chsd alng o'r 2 fs out, nvr able to chal.* .... (20 to 1 op 14 to 1 tchd 25 to 1) 10
1777 ANNACURRAGH (Ire) [40] 4-7-7 E Johnson (6) *led, clr entering strt, hdd o'r 2 fs out, eased whn btn appr last.* .... (40 to 1 op 33 to 1 tchd 50 to 1) 11
Dist: 1½l, nk, 5l, ½l, 3l, 1½l, 2l, nk, nk, 6l. 2m 5.20s. a 2.30s (11 Ran).
SR: 56/41/56/44/27/28/28/23/24/ (William J Kelly), R Hannon

3212 Evans Of Leicester Mercedes-Benz Limited Stakes Class F (0-65 3-y-o) £2,364 1m 3f 183yds......... (7:30)

2867* PISTOLS AT DAWN (USA) 9-0 J Reid (1) *al hndy, jnd ldr 2 fs out, ran on to ld last 100 yards, jst lasted.* .... (5 to 4 fav op Evens tchd 6 to 4) 1
2823[2] ARAADH (USA) 8-9 R Hills (3) *trkd ldg 4, str chal und pres fnl furlong, jst fld*......... (8 to 1 op 6 to 1 tchd 9 to 1) 2
1919[8] LA MENORQUINA (USA) 8-9 J Weaver (2) *co'red up on ins, effrt and not clr run over one furlong out, rallied last 100 yards*......... (8 to 1 op 4 to 1) 3
2972[5] ROMALITO 9-0 L Dettori (6) *pressed ldg trio, drvn alng last 2 fs, styd on*......... (4 to 1 op 3 to 1) 4
2783[5] INDIAN FLASH (Ire) 8-9 L Piggott (5) *led, quickened o'r 3 fs out, wknd and hdd last 100 yards.* .... (7 to 2 op 4 to 1 tchd 5 to 1) 5
2587[3] TURFMANS VISION 9-0 W R Swinburn (4) *patiently rdn, last strt, effrt 3 fs out, ridden and not run on.* .... (20 to 1 tchd 25 to 1) 6
Dist: Sht-hd, 1l, ¾l, ¾l, 5l. 2m 33.10s. a 4.60s (6 Ran).
SR: 19/13/11/14/7/2/ (G Howard-Spink), R Hannon

3213 Rearsby Claiming Stakes Class F (3-y-o) £2,385 7f 9yds......... (8:00)

2944[7] GLEN MILLER 8-12 L Dettori (6) *set modest pace, quickened hfwy, styd on strly to go clr fnl furlong.* .... (3 to 1 op 7 to 2 tchd 4 to 1) 1
2747[6] ASCOM PAGER TOO 8-13 J Quinn (1) *al hndy, drvn alng whn pace quickened last 2 fs, ran on same pace.* .... (33 to 1 tchd 50 to 1) 2
2993[6] EASTERN GLOW (bl) 8-3[2] W Woods (4) *steadied strt, improved hfwy, drvn alng last 2 fs, not pace to chal.* .... (14 to 1 op 10 to 1) 3
2711[6] KARUKERA 7-8 (7*) Kim McDonnell (2) *wtd wth, effrt and drvn alng last 2 fs, kpt on, nvr nrr.* .... (13 to 2 op 3 to 1 tchd 7 to 1) 4
2769[5] RUPERT COURT 8-6 T Quinn (5) *pld hrd, chsd ldrs for o'r 4 fs, not pace to chal*......... (12 to 1) 5
THE WEND 8-4 T Sprake (7) *settled on ins, drvn alng last 2 fs, no imprsn*...... (25 to 1 op 20 to 1 tchd 33 to 1) 6
2651* BOLD SEVEN (Ire) 8-13 (3*) N Kennedy (3) *steadied strt, pld hrd to hfwy, rdn and btn o'r 2 fs out.* .... (5 to 4 on op 11 to 10 tchd 6 to 5) 7
Dist: 3l, 1½l, hd, ½l, 1½l, ½l. 1m 26.40s. a 4.50s (7 Ran).
(Mrs John Etherton), J W Payne

3214 Institute Of Insurance Brokers Handicap Class D (0-80 3-y-o) £3,915 1m

8yds. .... (8:30)

2912* HE'S A KING (USA) [80] 9-7 L Dettori (6) *made all, hrd pressed entering fnl furlong, edgd rght, kpt on wl cl hme*................ (100 to 30 op 5 to 2 tchd 7 to 2) 1
2697[3] CROIRE (Ire) [73] 9-0 M Hills (2) *nvr far away, str chal entering fnl furlong, ran on wl.* (5 to 2 fav op 3 to 1) 2
2770[2] PERSIANSKY (Ire) [74] 9-1 W R Swinburn (1) *trkd ldg 4, effrt and rdn last 2 fs, kpt on same pace.* ....(7 to 2 op 3 to 1 tchd 9 to 2) 3
2939[4] URRY URRY URRY [73] 9-0 W Carson (5) *trkd ldrs, feeling pace o'r 2 fs out, no extr.* (5 to 1 op 4 to 1 tchd 6 to 1) 4
2577[4] NOBLE RISK [68] 8-9 J Reid (4) *trkd wnr, drvn alng o'r 2 fs out, sn btn*........................(11 to 2 op 5 to 1) 5
1709[8] THE SNOUT [60] 7-11[1] (5*) D McCabe (3) *in tch, drvn alng hfwy, sn struggling*.............. (16 to 1 op 12 to 1) 6

Dist: ¾l, 3l, 3½l, ½l, 2½l. 1m 36.40s. a 1.30s (6 Ran).
SR: 52/43/35/23/16/-/ (Lady Swaythling), J L Dunlop

THIRSK (good)
Monday August 9th

Going Correction: MINUS 0.05 sec. per fur. (races 1,6), PLUS 0.25 (2,3,4,5)

3215 EBF Bowncroft Median Auction Maiden Stakes Class E (2-y-o) £3,048 5f. .... (6:10)

3000[4] INDIAHRA 8-9 S Perks (8) *sn cl up, led o'r one out, hng lft fnl furlong, ran on wl.* (11 to 2 op 9 to 2 tchd 6 to 1) 1
2766[2] RAFFERTY'S RULES (Ire) 9-0 K Fallon (3) *in tch, effrt 2 out, swtchd o'r one out, kpt on*..........(4 to 1 op 5 to 1) 2
2626[2] PAONIC (Ire) 9-0 R Cochrane (1) *led aftr one furlong till hdd o'r one out, one paced.* .... (6 to 5 on op 6 to 4 on tchd 11 to 10 on) 3
2876[2] MONKEY'S WEDDING (bl) 9-0 J Carroll (9) *beh, kpt on frm hfwy, not trble ldrs*..........................(10 to 1) 4
3001[7] K-REG 9-0 K Darley (5) *beh till styd on fnl 2 fs, nrst finish.* .... (33 to 1 op 20 to 1) 5
2114[4] LIGHTNING BELLE 8-9 G Duffield (2) *chsd ldrs till wknd 2 out*................ (14 to 1 op 12 to 1 tchd 16 to 1) 6
2063[6] THE HAPPY LOON (Ire) 9-0 M Birch (6) *led one furlong, wknd hfwy*....................(12 to 1 tchd 14 to 1) 7
REGINA ALICIA 8-9 Dean McKeown (4) *al beh.* .... (20 to 1 op 16 to 1) 8
1082[5] FUSSY SIOUX 8-9 T Lucas (7) *cl up till wknd hfwy.* .... (40 to 1 op 33 to 1) 9

Dist: 2½l, hd, 5l, ¾l, 1½l, 3l, 1½l, hd. 59.90s. a 2.70s (9 Ran).
SR: 36/31/30/10/7/-/ (P J Lawton), R Hollinshead

3216 West Yorkshire Selling Handicap Class G (0-60 3-y-o and up) £2,763 1m .... (6:40)

3135[4] SLUMBER THYME (Ire) [31] (bl) 4-8-6 W Ryan (12) *beh, gd hdwy 3 out, led ins fnl furlong, ran on wl.* .... (14 to 1 op 12 to 1) 1
3002[9] MANX MONARCH [47] 3-8-10 (5*) A Garth (3) *in tch, steady hdwy to ld jst ins fnl furlong, sn hdd, kpt on.* .... (12 to 1 op 10 to 1) 2
3058[7] VANART [48] 4-9-9 S Webster (11) *in tch whn hmpd aftr 3 fs, kpt on wl fnl three furlongs, nrst finish.* .... (16 to 1 op 14 to 1) 3
2978[2] ALBEIT [33] 3-8-1 K Darley (15) *nvr far away, led o'r one out, sn hdd, one paced*............. (7 to 1 op 6 to 1) 4
2932[6] DANCES WITH GOLD [38] (bl) 3-8-6 Dean McKeown (8) *in tch whn hmpd aftr 3 fs, effrt three out, kpt on und pres fnl 2, not rch ldrs*.................. (14 to 1 op 10 to 1) 5
2976[3] BOLD LINE [39] (bl) 3-8-7 R Cochrane (10) *slwly into strd, hld up, hdwy 3 out, kpt on fnl furlong, not rch ldrs.* .... (12 to 1 op 14 to 1 tchd 16 to 1) 6
2733[4] COOL ENOUGH [35] 12-8-10 K Fallon (13) *beh, styd on fnl 3 fs, not rch ldrs*.........(5 to 1 op 6 to 1 tchd 7 to 1) 7
1284 GOLDEN ANCONA [27] 10-7-13 (3*) S Maloney (18) *mid-div, effrt 3 out, one paced*.............(25 to 1 op 20 to 1) 8
2710[4] SYKE LANE [31] 4-8-6 A Culhane (7) *trkd ldrs, led o'r 2 out, hdd over one out, sn btn*........ (16 to 1 op 20 to 1) 9
2954[3] SKOLERN [36] (v) 9-8-11 J Fanning (9) *trkd ldrs, effrt 3 out, ev ch 2 out, wknd o'r one out.* ....(11 to 2 op 6 to 1 tchd 7 to 1 and 8 to 1) 10
2540[4] MAKE MINE A DOUBLE [40] 3-8-8 N Connorton (4) *nvr far away, effrt 3 out, ev ch 2 out, sn rdn and wknd.* .... (14 to 1 op 12 to 1) 11
2932[4] SIR ARTHUR HOBBS [52] 6-9-13 R Lappin (17) *mid-div, effrt 3 out, wknd 2 out*.......................(10 to 1) 12
3007* FAILAND [35] 6-8-10 A Mackay (6) *dsptd ld till wknd o'r 2 out*..............................(9 to 1 op 7 to 1) 13
4679a[9] TOLL BOOTH [34] 4-8-9 Alex Greaves (2) *nvr dngrs.* ....(33 to 1) 14
2747[5] DEPUTY TIM [39] 10-8-8[1] (7*) H Bastiman (16) *nvr dngrs.* .... (20 to 1 op 16 to 1) 15
2540[5] BROOKLANDS EXPRESS [39] 3-8-7 J Carroll (5) *prmnt till wknd 3 out*..................................(20 to 1) 16
862 ROBIX (Ire) [46] 3-9-0 S Wood (1) *slight ld till hdd o'r 2 out, sn wknd*.......................... (25 to 1 op 20 to 1) 17
2897[3] YONGE TENDER [42] (bl) 6-9-3 B Raymond (14) *al beh, lost tch hfwy, tld off, fnshd lme.* ....(7 to 2 fav op 9 to 2 tchd 5 to 1) 18

Dist: 1½l, 1½l, 2l, hd, 2l, 2½l, 1½l, 3l, 1l, hd. 1m 42.20s. a 6.30s (18 Ran).
SR: 28/32/35/7/11/6/1/-/-/ (J W Searle), J G FitzGerald

3217 Yorkshire Pudding Conditions Stakes Class D (3-y-o) £3,552 1½m. .... (7:10)

2793[3] TOMOS 9-4 B Raymond (5) *made all, rdn 2 out, styd on wl*..................... (7 to 4 op 11 to 8 tchd 2 to 1) 1
AZILIAN (Ire) 9-4 Pat Eddery (4) *chsd ldr, rdn to chal 2 out, kpt on, no imprsn.* (6 to 4 fav op 11 to 8 tchd 5 to 4) 2
2310* VISHNU (USA) 9-6 W Ryan (2) *in tch, pushed alng 4 out, ch 2 out, sn rdn and btn.* .... (11 to 4 op 7 to 2 tchd 4 to 1) 3
2579[5] TEEN JAY 9-4 R Cochrane (1) *hld up, reminders 6 out, rdn o'r 3 out, no hdwy*.............. (14 to 1 op 12 to 1) 4
MAKENA 8-9 M Wood (3) *sn beh, lost tch 6 out, wl tld off.* .... (50 to 1 op 33 to 1) 5

Dist: 1½l, 6l, 7l, dist. 2m 37.60s. a 7.40s (5 Ran).
SR: 60/57/47/31/-/ (Saif Ali), D Morley

3218 Tattersalls Maiden Auction Series Stakes Qualifier Class E (2-y-o) £3,183 7f. .... (7:40)

2844[3] SYABAS (Ire) 8-8 Dean McKeown (5) *made all, ran on strly fnl 2 fs*..............(5 to 1 op 9 to 2 tchd 11 to 2) 1
2796[3] MAURANGI 8-7 J Fortune (7) *chsd ldrs, effrt 3 out, rdn 2 out, kpt on fnl furlong, no ch wth wnr.* ....(8 to 1 op 7 to 1) 2
1497 SANDMOOR CHAMBRAY 8-10 M Birch (10) *chsd ldr, effrt 3 out, rdn 2 out, kpt on same pace*..(20 to 1 op 16 to 1) 3
2695[2] TASHLA 8-5 K Darley (3) *mid-div, pushed alng 4 out, kpt on fnl 2 fs, not trble ldrs.* .... (11 to 10 on op 13 to 8 on tchd Evens) 4
2844 MILAIRIOUS (Ire) 8-6 R Cochrane (4) *chsd ldrs, effrt 3 out, wknd o'r one out*.... (16 to 1 op 10 to 1 tchd 20 to 1) 5
MANOLETE 8-6 J Carroll (11) *beh, some hdwy 3 out, one paced fnl 2 fs*....................... (33 to 1 op 25 to 1) 6
2274 BARACCA (Ire) 8-8 W Ryan (6) *beh, effrt whn hmpd 2 out, not trble ldrs*....................(25 to 1 op 14 to 1) 7
3009 SIMPLY A SEQUEL (Ire) 8-8 G Duffield (12) *sn beh.* .... (8 to 1 op 12 to 1) 8
2973[9] PLUM DENNIS 8-7 L Charnock (9) *sn beh.* .... (33 to 1 op 25 to 1) 9
2866[5] UN PARFUM DE FEMME (Ire) 8-9 G Bardwell (2) *mid-div, effrt 3 out, sn btn*...............(20 to 1 tchd 25 to 1) 10
YES TO THE BEST 8-6 J Fanning (1) *slwly into strd, al beh.* .... (33 to 1 op 25 to 1) 11
2129[4] PARISH WALK (Ire) 8-3 (3*) O Pears (8) *prmnt till wknd o'r 3 out*............................ (25 to 1 op 20 to 1) 12

Dist: 6l, 1l, ½l, 2½l, 1½l, ¾l, 1½l, sht-hd, 1l, 2½l. 1m 30.20s. a 7.40s (12 Ran).
SR: 9/-/-/-/-/-/ (S T Oon), S Dow

3219 Pickhill Handicap Class D (0-80 3-y-o) £3,465 1m. .... (8:10)

1867[3] NAIF (USA) [78] 9-7 R Cochrane (3) *dsptd ld to hfwy, remained cl up, led o'r 2 out, hrd rdn and edgd lft fnl furlong, styd on*....(2 to 1 fav op 5 to 2 tchd 11 to 4) 1
2824[2] RED COTTON [62] 8-5 P D'Arcy (5) *trkd ldrs, led hfwy, hdd o'r 2 out, rdn whn slightly hmpd fnl furlong, kpt on*............................. (6 to 1 op 9 to 2) 2
2749 CHAMPAGNE 'N ROSES [61] 8-4 J Carroll (12) *trkd ldrs, effrt o'r 2 out, ch over one out, kpt on same pace.* .... (12 to 1 op 8 to 1) 3
2993* OK BERTIE [72] 9-1 M Birch (4) *hld up in tch, hdwy to track ldrs 2 out, not clr run o'r one out, kpt on und pres towards finish*..................... (6 to 1 op 5 to 1) 4
2480[9] NORTHERN CHIEF [56] 7-11[1] (3*) S Maloney (2) *mid-div, rdn o'r 2 out, sn btn*...(7 to 1 op 10 to 1 tchd 12 to 1) 5
2889[5] CICERONE [62] 8-5 J Fortune (10) *in tch, rdn o'r 2 out, sn btn*............................. (12 to 1 op 10 to 1) 6
1656* STYLISH ROSE (Ire) [65] 8-8 J Lowe (6) *dsptd ld till fdd frm 3 out*...............................(10 to 1 op 8 to 1) 7
3060[5] BIRCHWOOD SUN [65] (bl) 8-8 S Webster (7) *dwlt, sn pushed alng, rdn 3 out, nvr dngrs.* (14 to 1 op 10 to 1) 8
2170[5] MAJOR JACK [50] 7-7 J Fanning (9) *beh, some hdwy 3 out, wknd 2 out*...................... (33 to 1 op 25 to 1) 9
3004 BOLDVILLE BASH (Ire) [66] 8-9 K Darley (1) *slightly hmpd 5 out, al beh*.......................(10 to 1 op 13 to 2) 10
2731[8] BALIANA [71] 9-0 K Fallon (8) *in tch till wknd 3 out.* ....(16 to 1) 11

Dist: 2l, nk, hd, 12l, 2½l, ¾l, nk, 1½l, 4l, ¾l. 1m 41.90s. a 6.00s (11 Ran).
SR: 47/25/23/33/-/-/ (Sultan Mohammed), L M Cumani

3220 Asenby Handicap Class D (0-80 3-y-o) £3,406 5f. .... (8:40)

2846* TUSCAN DAWN [78] 9-7 J Carroll (1) *swtchd rght strt, made all, ran on wl*..... (5 to 1 op 6 to 1 tchd 7 to 1) 1
2699[4] PRIMULA BAIRN [65] (v) 8-8 K Fallon (10) *chsd ldr, rdn o'r one out, kpt on*..................(6 to 1 tchd 13 to 2) 2
3011[5] CHARITY EXPRESS (Ire) [68] 8-11 D Biggs (13) *chsd ldrs, rdn 2 out, kpt on fnl furlong*.......(8 to 1 tchd 9 to 1) 3

2731[6] WILLSHE GAN [74] 9-3 Dean McKeown (12) *in tch, kpt on wl fnl 2 fs, not rch ldrs.* .... (9 to 1 op 10 to 1 tchd 11 to 1) 4
3153[8] HICKORY BLUE [75] 9-1 (3*) O Pears (11) *trkd ldrs, effrt entering fnl furlong, one paced*...... (8 to 1 op 7 to 1) 5
2975[6] JADE CITY [75] 9-4 M Birch (8) *nvr nr to chal.* .... (10 to 1 op 12 to 1) 6
2940 MY BONUS [77] 9-6 N Connorton (4) *beh till some late hdwy, nvr dngrs*........ (20 to 1 op 16 to 1) 7
2908[6] THE FED [61] (v) 8-4 A Culhane (7) *chsd ldrs, sn pushed alng, no hdwy fnl 2 fs*............ (14 to 1 op 12 to 1) 8
2105[7] BENZOE (Ire) [77] 9-6 T Lucas (5) *unruly in stalls, nvr dngrs*..................... (20 to 1) 9
2787* NEWBURY COAT [74] (bl) 9-3 G Duffield (14) *mid-div, effrt hfwy, wknd o'r one out.* .... (7 to 2 fav op 4 to 1 tchd 3 to 1 and 11 to 4) 10
2893* GUSSIE FINK-NOTTLE (Ire) [62] (bl) 8-5 W Ryan (3) *chsd ldrs to hfwy*.......................... (14 to 1 op 12 to 1) 11
2908[8] GO FLIGHTLINE (Ire) [57] (v) 8-0 G Bardwell (2) *chsd ldrs to hfwy*.......................... (12 to 1 op 10 to 1) 12
1982[4] RED FAN (Ire) [70] (bl) 8-13 J Lowe (9) *dwlt, al beh.* .... (14 to 1 op 12 to 1) 13
2132[3] SHADOW JURY [74] 9-3 K Darley (6) *unruly in stalls, al beh, tld off*........ (12 to 1 op 10 to 1) 14

Dist: 2l, ½l, hd, hd, 4l, 1l, nk, 1½l, sht-hd, 1½l. 59.40s. a 2.20s (14 Ran).
SR: 58/37/38/43/43/27/25/8/18/ (Miss Antonia Taverner), J Berry

WINDSOR (good to firm)
Monday August 9th

Going Correction: MINUS 0.10 sec. per fur. (races 1,4,5,6,7), MINUS 0.35 (2,3)

3221 Stratfieldsaye Selling Stakes Class G (3-y-o and up) £2,301 1m 3f 135yds ....(2:30)

1771[2] KIAWAH 3-8-4 (7*) N Varley (4) *steadied strt, prog frm rear 3 fs out, sstnd run to ld ins last.* (5 to 4 fav op 6 to 4) 1
2865[2] VANBOROUGH LAD 4-9-13 J Reid (3) *wl plcd, led 3 fs out, rdn alng 2 out, hdd and not quicken ins last.* .... (15 to 8 op 6 to 4 tchd 2 to 1) 2
2471[8] NOTED STRAIN (Ire) 5-9-13 Pat Eddery (2) *settled in mid-div, rdn and outpcd last 2 fs*....... (7 to 2 tchd 4 to 1) 3
2992 FORTUNE STAR (Ire) 4-9-6 (7*) Rachel Bridger (6) *trkd ldrs, rdn and wknd o'r 3 fs out.* .... (20 to 1 op 14 to 1 tchd 25 to 1) 4
2013[7] JAFETICA 3-8-8 W Newnes (1) *led to 3 fs out, sn btn.* .... (20 to 1 op 14 to 1 tchd 25 to 1) 5
PETITE JUNE (Ire) 3-8-3 (5*) N Gwilliams (7) *settled rear, lost tch 5 fs out, tld off.* .... (20 to 1 op 8 to 1 tchd 25 to 1) 6
3007[7] ABSOLUTELY HUMMING 7-9-13 R Price (5) *chsd ldr, wknd o'r 3 fs out, tld off*............ (40 to 1 op 16 to 1) 7

Dist: ½l, 12l, 1½l, 1l, 15l, sht-hd. 2m 30.90s. a 7.90s (7 Ran).
SR: 7/22/-/-/ (R S Field), J R Fanshawe

3222 Robert And Norah Wilmot Nursery Class E (2-y-o) £3,080 5f 217yds (3:00)

2718* MAJOR SUCCESS (Ire) [72] 8-13 D Holland (2) *led till hdd and swrvd lft o'r one furlong out, led und pres last 100 yards*.......... (9 to 1 op 7 to 1 tchd 10 to 1) 1
2996[9] PRINCE AZZAAN (Ire) [77] 9-4 Pat Eddery (11) *hld up, ran on o'r 2 fs out, led over one out, hdd and outpcd last 100 yards*.............. (5 to 4 fav op 6 to 4 tchd 15 to 8) 2
1277[3] ALCOVE [77] 9-4 L Dettori (7) *chsd ldrs, rdn and outpcd ins last 2 fs*............. (5 to 1 op 6 to 1 tchd 7 to 1) 3
2996 KINGSWELL PRINCE (Ire) [80] 9-7 T Quinn (4) *handily plcd, rdn and no extr 2 fs out.* .... (7 to 1 op 10 to 1 tchd 12 to 1) 4
2886[4] RAPIER POINT (Ire) [80] 9-7 J Weaver (1) *effrt o'r 2 fs out, rdn and btn over one out.* .... (12 to 1 op 10 to 1 tchd 14 to 1) 5
3009* DANCING LAWYER [74] 9-1 W Newnes (8) *wl plcd 4 fs, wknd*........................ (11 to 2 op 4 to 1) 6
2929[6] KNIGHTRIDER [64] 8-5 J Williams (6) *outpcd.* .... (16 to 1 tchd 20 to 1) 7
2886[6] CABCHARGE PRINCESS (Ire) [73] 9-0 P Robinson (10) *chsd ldrs till wknd o'r 2 fs out.* .... (9 to 1 op 10 to 1 tchd 12 to 1 and 8 to 1) 8
1535[2] BROUGHTONS PARTNER [60] 8-1 J Quinn (5) *al beh.* .... (20 to 1 op 14 to 1) 9
1279[3] SUN CHIEF (Ire) [69] 8-10 N Day (3) *outpcd.* .... (16 to 1 op 7 to 1 tchd 20 to 1) 10
2929[7] GINGERILLO [54] (bl) 7-9 Dale Gibson (9) *rear most of way.* .... (20 to 1 op 33 to 1) 11

Dist: 1l, 3l, nk, 2½l, 2½l, 1½l, 3l, 2l, 2l, hd. 1m 11.30s. a 1.00s (11 Ran).
SR: 37/38/26/28/18/2/ (W J Gredley), B W Hills

3223 Juniors Conditions Stakes Class D (2-y-o) £3,850 5f 217yds.......... (3:30)

3016* AVERTI (Ire) 9-0 T Quinn (1) *hld up, chsd ldr o'r 2 fs out, hrd rdn over one out, led wl ins last.* .... (Evens fav op 5 to 4 tchd 6 to 4) 1
2730[2] TORCH ROUGE 9-0 D Holland (6) *led till rdn and hdd wl ins fnl furlong*........ (15 to 8 op 6 to 4 tchd 2 to 1) 2
2519* BATTLING BLUE 9-0 Pat Eddery (3) *chsd ldr for o'r 3 fs, outpcd appr last*.......... (5 to 1 op 11 to 4) 3
2994[6] KNAVE'S ASH (USA) 8-10 M Roberts (2) *nvr gng pace of ldrs*..................(14 to 1 op 8 to 1 tchd 16 to 1) 4
2924[6] BEAUTETE 9-0 J Weaver (5) *prmnt 3 fs, sn wknd.* .... (16 to 1 op 10 to 1 tchd 20 to 1) 5
2123[8] ROYAL INTERPRETER 8-10 R Perham (4) *outpcd.* .... (66 to 1 op 25 to 1 tchd 100 to 1) 6

Dist: Hd, 8l, 3l, 3½l, 6l. 1m 10.80s. a 0.50s (6 Ran).
SR: 48/47/15/ (D J Deer), W R Muir

3224 Shadwell Stud Apprentice Series Handicap Class E (0-80 3-y-o and up) £3,131 1¼m 7yds.............. (4:00)

2847[3] SANTANA LADY (Ire) [58] 4-8-7 (5*) Ruth Coulter (7) *made all, styd on strly frm 2 fs out.* .... (4 to 1 op 5 to 1 tchd 11 to 2) 1
3019[3] GILDERDALE [74] 11-10-0 B Doyle (2) *ldg grp, chsd wnr o'r 4 fs out, not quicken 2 out*.......... (13 to 2 op 5 to 1) 2
2884[4] PORT SUNLIGHT (Ire) [70] 5-9-5 (5*) D O'Neill (8) *wl plcd, rdn to chal 2 fs out, no extr appr last.* .... (2 to 1 fav op 9 to 4 tchd 7 to 4) 3
3185 WINGS COVE [70] 3-9-1 J Tate (3) *hld up, cld on ldrs 3 fs out, outpcd ins last 2*.... (7 to 1 op 8 to 1 tchd 9 to 1) 4
2869* BROWN CARPET [39] (bl) 6-7-7 D Wright (5) *hdwy frm rear o'r 3 fs out, rdn and no imprsn 2 out.* .... (9 to 1 op 10 to 1 tchd 11 to 1) 5
2894[4] SONG OF SIXPENCE (USA) [70] 9-9-3 (7*) C Scudder (10) *settled rear, not rch ldrs fnl 3 fs*.... (10 to 1 op 8 to 1) 6
2684[9] BRONZE RUNNER [39] (bl) 9-7-0 (7*) A Daly (9) *mid-div, wknd o'r 2 fs out*................(16 to 1 op 14 to 1) 7
817[4] QAMOOS (Ire) [76] 3-9-0 (7*) Lisa Jacobs (1) *chsd wnr till lost pl o'r 4 fs out*.... (14 to 1 op 12 to 1 tchd 16 to 1) 8
2948[7] RIVE-JUMELLE (Ire) [47] 5-8-1 M Fenton (4) *shrtlvd effrt frm rear hfwy, wknd 3 fs out.* .... (9 to 1 op 10 to 1 tchd 8 to 1) 9
321[7] PIGALLE WONDER [48] (bl) 5-8-2 B Russell (6) *rear till shrtlvd effrt o'r 3 fs out, wknd over 2 out.* .... (10 to 1 tchd 12 to 1) 10

Dist: 4l, 1½l, 1½l, 2½l, 1½l, 2l, ½l, 6l, 3½l. 2m 8.30s. a 5.80s (10 Ran).
SR: 30/38/31/19/-/20/-/12/-/ (F J Sainsbury), M J Heaton-Ellis

3225 Andrew And Karen Reid Wedding Day Maiden Stakes Class D (3-y-o and up) £3,933 1m 67yds.............. (4:30)

3012[4] REINE DE NEIGE 3-8-9 W R Swinburn (21) *made all, shaken up to go wl clr o'r one furlong out, eased cl hme.* .... (11 to 4 op 3 to 1 tchd 9 to 2) 1
2985[5] VILLAGE GREEN (Fr) 3-8-11 (3*) B Doyle (4) *3rd, rdn to chase wnr o'r one furlong out, no imprsn.* .... (16 to 1 op 25 to 1 tchd 33 to 1) 2
2752 CAMBARA 3-8-9 W Carson (11) *trkd wnr, ev ch o'r 2 fs out, rdn and no extr over one out.* (20 to 1 op 12 to 1) 3
2749[3] ARVOLA 3-8-9 M Roberts (12) *hdwy 3 fs out, one pace 2 out*.................(15 to 8 fav op 6 to 4 tchd 9 to 4) 4
WORDS OF WISDOM (Ire) 3-9-0 W Newnes (10) *ran on fnl 2 fs, nrst finish*......................(25 to 1 tchd 33 to 1) 5
2725[4] CUFF LINK (Ire) 3-9-0 J Reid (5) *hdwy 3 fs out, not rch frnt rnk frm 2 out*......................(7 to 1 op 8 to 1) 6
2884 THE POWER OF ONE (bl) 4-9-7 A Tucker (6) *mid-div, no imprsn on ldrs frm 3 fs out*.........(50 to 1 op 20 to 1) 7
2563[8] WELSH HERITAGE (Ire) 3-8-6 (3*) D Harrison (8) *nvr nrr.* .... (16 to 1 op 10 to 1 tchd 20 to 1) 8
3012 SILK ISLAND 3-9-0 G Hind (15) *mid-div most of way.* .... (25 to 1 op 14 to 1 tchd 33 to 1) 9
REMEMBER THIS (Ire) 3-8-7 (7*) J D Smith (16) *effrt 3 fs out, no prog ins last 2*..............(25 to 1 op 12 to 1) 10
ROYAL MANOEVRE 3-8-9 (5*) Stephen Davies (13) *nvr better than mid-div*..... (20 to 1 op 10 to 1 tchd 25 to 1) 11
ON THE LEDGE (USA) 3-9-0 S Whitworth (19) *wl plcd 5 fs.* .... (16 to 1 op 8 to 1 tchd 20 to 1) 12
VALBRA 3-8-9 Pat Eddery (3) *nvr on terms.* .... (4 to 1 op 2 to 1 tchd 9 to 2) 13
3012 RIZ BIZ (USA) 3-8-9 M Hills (7) *rear most of way.* .... (33 to 1 op 25 to 1 tchd 40 to 1) 14
IVORY HUTCH 3-9-0 A Clark (20) *slwly into strd, al beh.* .... (50 to 1 op 25 to 1 tchd 66 to 1) 15
2416[8] BUY BY NIGHT 3-8-9 J Weaver (14) *nvr on terms.* .... (50 to 1 op 25 to 1) 16
2749[4] DUBAI SUMMER 3-9-0 N Day (2) *in tch till wknd appr last 2 fs*....................... (16 to 1 op 12 to 1) 17
2410 JOAN'S GIFT 3-8-9 T Williams (17) *nvr trble ldrs.* .... (50 to 1 op 33 to 1 tchd 66 to 1) 18
DIXIE DIAMOND 3-8-9 B Rouse (18) *in tch to hfwy.* .... (50 to 1 op 25 to 1) 19
2725[6] GARRY'S CHOICE 4-9-7 Dale Gibson (1) *handily plcd till wknd 3 fs out*........ (50 to 1 op 25 to 1 tchd 66 to 1) 20
CUCKMERE VENTURE 3-8-9 F Norton (9) *strted slwly, al beh, tld off, virtually pld up last 3 fs.* .... (33 to 1 op 25 to 1) 21

Dist: 2l, 1l, 3½l, 1l, ½l, 2l, ½l, 8l, 4l, 1½l. 1m 43.50s. a 2.50s (21 Ran).
SR: 45/44/36/25/27/25/26/12/-/ (Maktoum Al Maktoum), A A Scott

3226 Seniors Handicap Class E (0-70 3-y-o) £3,340 1m 67yds. . . . . (5:00)

7[5] KNOBBLEENEEZE [61] (v) 9-4 S Whitworth (3) *settled 3rd, rdn to ld o'r one furlong out, drvn out, jst hld on.* . . . . (16 to 1 op 12 to 1) 1
2733 SMART TEACHER (USA) [47] 8-4 G Hind (5) *led till hdd und pres o'r one furlong out, rallied nr line, jst fld.* . . . .(6 to 1 op 9 to 2) 2
2712[3] LOCHORE [59] 9-2 A Tucker (10) *strted slwly, beh till ran on o'r 2 fs out, fnshd strly.* . . . . (6 to 1 op 4 to 1 tchd 13 to 2) 3
2912[2] MR CUBE (Ire) [63] 8-13 (7*) T G McLaughlin (8) *trkd ldr, ev ch 2 fs out, rdn and outpcd o'r one out.* . . . . (3 to 1 fav tchd 7 to 2) 4
2938[6] MURPHY'S HOPE (Ire) [54] 8-11 M Roberts (7) *sn rdn alng, effrt appr last 2 fs, no imprsn on frnt rnk.* . . . . (12 to 1 op 8 to 1) 5
2013[4] BICHETTE [60] 9-3 B Rouse (9) *handily plcd, rdn to chal o'r 2 fs out, no extr*. . . . .(16 to 1 op 10 to 1) 6
2928 WALNUT BURL (Ire) [55] 8-12 J Reid (4) *hld up, hdwy thee fs out, btn ins last 2*. . . . .(8 to 1 tchd 9 to 1) 7
3179[9] SECRET ASSIGNMENT (USA) [64] 9-0 (7*) J D Smith (2) *nvr on terms*. . . . . (8 to 1 op 7 to 1 tchd 10 to 1) 8
2938 JALIB (Ire) [51] 8-8 T Williams (6) *sn beh.* . . . . (16 to 1 op 8 to 1) 9
2938[8] SPRING SUNRISE [56] (v) 8-13 F Norton (11) *hld up mid-div, rdn and no hdwy frm 3 fs out.* . . . . (8 to 1 op 14 to 1 tchd 16 to 1) 10
1972[4] AKHLAK (Ire) [58] 9-1 W Carson (1) *al rear.* . . . .(4 to 1 tchd 5 to 1) 11

Dist: Sht-hd, 3½l, ¾l, 4l, 2l, 5l, 6l, 3½l, 2l, ½l. 1m 45.00s. a 4.00s (11 Ran).
SR: 32/17/18/20/-/-/ (Anthony Andrews), M R Channon

3227 Swan Fillies' Conditions Stakes Class D (3-y-o and up) £3,318 1m 67yds . . . . (5:30)

749 STELLA MYSTIKA (USA) 3-8-11 M Roberts (1) *rcd keenly, made all, clr 4 fs out, pushed alng 2 out, not extended.* . . . .(11 to 8 fav op 6 to 4 tchd 7 to 4) 1
2732[2] ETOSHA 3-8-11 M Hills (3) *chsd wnr o'r 3 fs out, rdn 2 out, one pace appr last*. . . . . .(2 to 1 op 6 to 4 tchd 9 to 4) 2
2572[5] FIRST VEIL 3-8-11 W Carson (4) *hld up rear, hdwy o'r 2 fs out, rdn and not quicken appr last.* (11 to 4 op 7 to 2) 3
SELF ASSURED (Ire) 3-8-7 S Whitworth (2) *chsd wnr, lost pl o'r 3 fs out, drpd rear frm 2 out, eased clsg stages.* . . . . (15 to 2 op 4 to 1 tchd 8 to 1) 4

Dist: 2l, ½l, 10l. 1m 44.40s. a 3.40s (4 Ran).
SR: 34/28/26/-/ (Sheikh Mohammed), L M Cumani

BATH (good to firm) Tuesday August 10th

Going Correction: MINUS 0.35 sec. per fur. (races 1,4,5,6,7), MINUS 0.05 (2,3)

3228 August Selling Stakes Class G (3-y-o and up) £2,553 1m 5yds. . . . .(2:00)

HARVEST ROSE 4-8-5 A Clark (18) *beh till rapid hdwy 3 fs out, led one and a half furlongs out, clr ins last.* . . . . (66 to 1 op 33 to 1) 1
3046[3] CAPE PIGEON (USA) (bl) 8-9-1 D Holland (2) *led aftr one and a half fs, rdn 2 furlongs out, hdd one and a half furlongs out, outpcd*. . . . .(11 to 10 on op 6 to 4) 2
2938[5] TAKE THE MICK (bl) 3-8-5 C Rutter (17) *beh, rdn and hdwy o'r 2 fs out, ran on ins last*. . . . . (12 to 1 op 10 to 1) 3
3007[5] DON'T GIVE UP (bl) 5-9-1 W Newnes (6) *hdwy 3 fs out, drvn and styd on ins fnl 2 furlongs.* . . . .(10 to 1 tchd 14 to 1) 4
2670 MAN OF THE SEASON (USA) 4-8-10 J Reid (11) *led one and a half fs, styd chasing ldrs till wknd fnl furlong.* . . . . (20 to 1 op 14 to 1) 5
2953[8] LEGAL RISK (v) 3-8-0 A Mackay (3) *hdwy ins fnl 2 fs, kpt on final furlong*. . . . .(25 to 1 op 16 to 1) 6
2658[7] TOUT DE VAL 4-8-5 R Perham (12) *chsd ldrs, rdn 3 fs out, sn wknd*. . . . . (66 to 1 op 50 to 1) 7
1965[8] GROGFRYN 3-8-0 A Tucker (9) *nvr rchd ldrs*. . . . (50 to 1) 8
3007 GREEN'S STUBBS (v) 6-9-1 N Carlisle (16) *mid-div, rdn 3 fs, sn wknd*. . . . . (33 to 1 op 20 to 1) 9
DAWN POPPY 5-8-0[2] (7*) S Drowne (13) *nvr rchd ldrs.* . . . . (66 to 1 op 40 to 1) 10
2097 GATHERING 4-8-10 J Williams (5) *beh most of way.* . . . .(33 to 1) 11
2663 MEXICAN DANCER 4-8-10 K Darley (8) *chsd ldrs till hmpd aftr 3 fs, nvr dngrs after*. . . . .(8 to 1 op 5 to 1) 12
MING BLUE 4-7-13[1] (7*) Mark Denaro (7) *nvr better than mid-div*. . . . .(33 to 1 op 20 to 1) 13
3007[3] SHALOU (bl) 4-9-1 L Dettori (14) *chsd ldrs till wknd o'r 3 fs out*. . . . .(8 to 1 tchd 9 to 1) 14
TODAY'S FANCY 5-9-1 M Wigham (10) *sn beh.* . . . . (66 to 1 op 50 to 1) 15
2970 BROOKS EXPRESS (Fr) 4-8-10 T Quinn (4) *chsd ldrs 4 fs, sn wknd*. . . . .(12 to 1 op 9 to 1) 16
3083[5] HAPPY TUPPENCE 3-8-0 S Dawson (15) *sn wl beh.* . . . . (20 to 1 op 12 to 1) 17

Dist: 2½l, 3½l, 3½l, ¾l, 2½l, 2l, 1l, 6l, ½l, ¾l. 1m 40.80s. a 1.80s (17 Ran).
SR: 22/24/3/2/-/-/ (E A Badger), O O'Neill

3229 Luckington Limited Stakes Class F (0-60 3-y-o and up) £2,833 5f 11yds . . . . (2:30)

3032* MARTINA 5-9-2 Paul Eddery (16) *hdwy 2 fs out, str run to ld ins last, jst hld on*. . . . . (6 to 1 op 13 to 2) 1
3047 DOUBLE SHIFT 4-9-2 S Whitworth (1) *mid-div, hdwy 2 fs out, str run ins last, jst fld*. . . . . (16 to 1 op 10 to 1) 2
2746[6] ABERLADY 3-8-7 (5*) K Rutter (6) *pressed ldrs, led o'r one furlong out, hdd ins last, styd on same pace.* . . . .(6 to 1 tchd 7 to 1) 3
3059* TREVORSNINEPOINTS 3-8-12 K Darley (5) *led till hdd o'r one furlong out, rdn and found no extr.* . . . .(2 to 1 fav op 3 to 1) 4
2788[7] JUCEA 4-9-2 A Mackay (17) *beh and outpcd, gd hdwy o'r one furlong out, fnshd wl*. . . . . (20 to 1 op 10 to 1) 5
2660[8] JEREMIAHS BOY (bl) 3-9-3 J Williams (4) *styd on frm o'r one furlong out, nrst finish*. . . . .(20 to 1 op 8 to 1) 6
2910[8] FARMER JOCK 11-9-7 L Dettori (14) *kpt on fnl furlong, nrst finish*. . . . . (14 to 1 op 8 to 1) 7
3032 SEAMERE (bl) 10-9-2 (5*) D Wright (2) *chsd ldrs till wknd ins fnl 2 fs*. . . . . (20 to 1 op 14 to 1 tchd 25 to 1) 8
1627 AIR COMMAND (Bar) 3-8-10 (7*) S Drowne (7) *nvr rchd ldrs.* . . . . (66 to 1 op 33 to 1) 9
BEVELED EDGE 4-9-2 A Clark (18) *nvr gng pace of ldrs.* . . . . (66 to 1 op 25 to 1) 10
2945[5] ELTON LEDGER (Ire) 4-9-2 (5*) J Tate (11) *gd speed to wknd 2 fs out*. . . . . (14 to 1 op 10 to 1) 11
RAYS MEAD 5-9-2 C Avery (12) *nvr gng pace of ldrs.* . . . . (33 to 1 op 20 to 1) 12
3081[3] VISIMOTION (USA) (v) 3-9-3 D Holland (15) *pressed ldrs to hfwy*. . . . .(13 to 2 op 8 to 1 tchd 6 to 1) 13
2660[4] PURBECK CENTENARY 3-8-10 (7*) L Carter (10) *pressed ldrs to hfwy*. . . . . (14 to 1 op 12 to 1 tchd 16 to 1) 14
3011[8] THE ORDINARY GIRL (Ire) (v) 3-8-12 J Reid (8) *nvr plcd to chal*. . . . .(11 to 1 op 10 to 1 tchd 12 to 1) 15
3081[8] SHADES OF JADE 5-9-2 T Williams (20) *sn outpcd.* . . . . (33 to 1 op 20 to 1) 16
720 CLARE'S BOY 3-8-10 (7*) Mark Denaro (9) *sn outpcd.* . . . . (66 to 1 op 33 to 1) 17
2910[4] BELMONT PRINCESS (Ire) 3-8-7 (5*) Stephen Davies (13) *outpcd*. . . . .(16 to 1 op 10 to 1) 18
IT BITES (Ire) 3-8-12 S Dawson (3) *swrvd badly lft strt, al wl beh*. . . . . (66 to 1 op 33 to 1) 19

Dist: Sht-hd, ¾l, 2l, hd, 1½l, 1l, sht-hd, nk, 3½l, 2l. 1m 3.30s. a 2.80s (19 Ran).
SR: 41/40/33/25/28/23/23/22/17/ (Laurel (Leisure) Limited), G Lewis

3230 Tripleprint Maiden Fillies' Stakes Class D (2-y-o) £3,669 5f 11yds. .(3:00)

EHTFAAL (Ire) 8-11 R Hills (7) *al tracking ldrs, led one and a half fs out, kpt on wl*. . . . .(4 to 1 op 5 to 2) 1
2357[5] SO SEDULOUS (USA) 8-11 M Hills (5) *in tch, effrt whn hmpd one and a half fs out, rallied fnl furlong, fnshd wl*. . . . .(9 to 4 jt-fav op 7 to 4) 2
2990[3] DEVOTEE 8-11 Paul Eddery (11) *pressed ldrs, drvn o'r 2 fs out, ev ch one and a half furlongs out, styd on.* . . . .(9 to 4 jt-fav op 3 to 1 tchd 4 to 1) 3
1632[4] SHALBOURNE (USA) 8-11 J Reid (1) *pressed ldrs, ev ch one and a half fs out, not quicken fnl furlong.* . . . . (8 to 1 op 10 to 1) 4
VENUS VICTORIOUS (Ire) 8-11 J Williams (2) *effrt whn hmpd 3 fs out, kpt on wl appr fnl furlong*. . . . (33 to 1) 5
REASON TO DANCE 8-11 A Mackay (4) *outpcd, rdn 2 fs out, styd on wl fnl furlong*. . . . . (8 to 1 op 4 to 1) 6
1403 RAISA POINT 8-11 T Quinn (6) *chsd ldrs, led 2 fs out, hdd one and a half furlongs out, sn wknd*. . . . .(33 to 1) 7
2994[7] MILLION LIGHTS (Ire) 8-11 L Dettori (9) *chsd ldrs 3 fs.* . . . . (14 to 1 op 10 to 1) 8
SALANKA (Ire) 8-11 K Darley (12) *sn drvn alng, not pace to chal*. . . . . (12 to 1 op 8 to 1) 9
2412[6] FOLLY FINNESSE 8-11 S Whitworth (3) *led till hdd 2 fs out, sn wknd*. . . . . (25 to 1 op 16 to 1) 10
839 JANE HERRING 8-4 (7*) S Drowne (8) *outpcd.* . . . . (50 to 1 op 33 to 1) 11
NAWAFELL 8-6 (5*) J Tate (10) *outpcd.* . . . .(20 to 1 op 14 to 1) 12

Dist: 1½l, hd, 1l, nk, sht-hd, 1½l, hd, 1l, 3½l, 3l. 1m 2.80s. a 2.30s (12 Ran).
SR: 46/40/39/35/34/33/27/26/22/ (Hamdan Al-Maktoum), H Thomson Jones

3231 BBC Radio Bristol Handicap Class D (0-80 4-y-o and up) £3,201 2m 1f 34yds . . . . (3:30)

2477[4] SPECTACULAR DAWN [72] 4-9-9 J Reid (3) *made all, nudged alng frm 3 fs out, rdn ins last, hld on wl.* . . . .(7 to 1 op 6 to 1) 1
3125[5] SWORD MASTER [73] 4-9-10 N Day (5) *hld up, plenty to do 4 fs out, drvn and hdwy frm 3 furlongs out, chlgd one furlong out, no extr wl ins last.* (8 to 1 op 7 to 1) 2

2422[3] MONARDA [67] 6-9-4 T Quinn (7) *beh till hdwy hfwy, drvn and outpcd ins fnl 3 fs, styd on und pres ag'n final furlong*.......................(7 to 2 op 4 to 1) 3
2755[5] CHUCKLESTONE [64] 10-9-1 Paul Eddery (6) *chsd wnr, pushed alng frm ten fs out, wknd one furlong out*.
.......................(7 to 2 op 5 to 2) 4
3087* HUNTING GROUND [52] (bl) 5-8-3 (4ex) A Mackay (9) *beh, hdwy 5 fs out, rdn alng 3 furlongs out, wknd ins fnl 2 furlongs*.............(9 to 4 fav op 3 to 1 tchd 7 to 2) 5
1929[5] FRENCH IVY (USA) [72] 6-9-9 D Holland (4) *beh, styd on frm 4 fs out, wknd 2 furlongs out*.......(10 to 1 op 7 to 1) 6
CALGARY REDEYE [65] 6-9-2 J Williams (2) *chsd ldrs till wknd ins fnl 3 fs*.............................(10 to 1) 7
2729 RICH PICKINGS [42] 4-7-7 N Adams (1) *chsd ldrs till wknd 7 fs out, sn tld off*...................(20 to 1 op 12 to 1) 8
Dist: ¾l, 3l, ½l, 2½l, 2l, 8l, 30l. 3m 46.40s. a 2.40s (8 Ran).
SR: 25/24/15/11/-/14/-/-/ (Peter S Winfield), J L Dunlop

3232 Pennsylvania Claiming Stakes Class F (3-y-o) £2,434 1m 3f 144yds... (4:00)

3049[5] GALEJADE 8-5[1] J Williams (1) *missed break, pld hrd, chsd ldr aftr 2 fs, led two furlongs out, drvn and styd on wl well o'r one furlong out*.
.....................(10 to 1 op 8 to 1 tchd 12 to 1) 1
2673[5] HEART OF SPAIN 8-11 W Newnes (5) *trkd ldrs, hdwy 4 fs out, chlgd frm one and a half furlongs out till no extr wl ins last*........................(11 to 8 fav op 7 to 4) 2
2611[4] BILJAN (USA) 9-0 T Quinn (3) *led till 6 fs out, hdd 2 furlongs out, sn btn*.....(2 to 1 op 7 to 4 tchd 9 to 4) 3
2773[5] BOLTROSE (v) 8-11 N Adams (2) *missed break, drvn alng to stay in tch 6 fs out, btn 4 furlongs out*.
.....................................(12 to 1 op 8 to 1) 4
2833[8] SANTA STELLAR 7-13 Dale Gibson (4) *beh, rdn and drpd out 5 fs out*.......................(16 to 1 op 14 to 1) 5
2833* SHALHOLME 7-13 C Rutter (6) *pld hrd, steadied rear, hdwy 5 fs out, wknd quickly o'r 3 furlongs out*.
....(6 to 1 op 5 to 1) 6
Dist: Hd, 4l, 4l, 7l, 10l. 2m 29.50s. a 2.50s (6 Ran).
SR: 25/30/25/14/-/-/ (Mrs Judy Mihalop), D Haydn Jones

3233 Mile Maiden Handicap Class F (0-65 3-y-o and up) £2,959 1m 5yds... (4:30)

MISS CRUSTY [35] 5-8-3 N Adams (6) *in tch, hdwy 3 fs out, drvn to ld and edgd lft jst ins last, ran on*.
......................................(50 to 1 op 20 to 1) 1
3102[6] CASTING SHADOWS [48] 4-9-2 D Holland (17) *al in tch, led one and a half fs out, hdd and not much room jst ins last, kpt on*..........................(3 to 1 fav op 9 to 2) 2
2938[3] MY MINNIE [50] 3-8-11 T Sprake (1) *chsd ldrs, chlgd frm 2 fs out till not quicken ins last*.
.........................(9 to 2 op 7 to 1 tchd 8 to 1) 3
2384 SHARP IMP [36] 3-7-11 Dale Gibson (12) *hdwy o'r 2 fs out, drvn and styd on fnl furlong*....(20 to 1 op 10 to 1) 4
2722[5] THRIVING [59] 3-9-6 J Reid (11) *mid-div, pushed alng and hdwy 3 fs out, styd on same pace appr fnl furlong*.
......................................(11 to 2 op 7 to 2) 5
3047[8] VIS-A-VIS [28] 4-7-3 (7*) N Varley (5) *led till hdd one and a half fs out, sn outpcd*...........(20 to 1 op 16 to 1) 6
2384[8] SIMON ELLIS (Ire) [32] 4-8-0 T Williams (9) *mid-div, rdn and effrt 2 and a half fs out, sn wknd*. (20 to 1 op 12 to 1) 7
3046[2] HALBERT [60] 4-9-7 (7*) Wendy Jones (18) *beh, some prog appr fnl 2 fs*..........(11 to 1 op 8 to 1 tchd 12 to 1) 8
3047 SUPERENSIS [50] 3-8-11 W Newnes (3) *chsd ldrs o'r 5 fs*.
......................................(12 to 1 op 10 to 1) 9
2869[7] SALLY OF THE ALLEY [39] 3-8-0 C Rutter (10) *nvr gng pace of ldrs*..............................(10 to 1 op 6 to 1) 10
2859 EASY TOUCH [35] (v) 3-7-10 A Mackay (16) *slwly into strd, sn reco'red, wknd 3 fs out*.........(33 to 1 op 20 to 1) 11
2930 GLISSO (Ire) [45] 3-8-6 J Williams (15) *nvr better than mid-div*...................................(12 to 1 op 6 to 1) 12
2504[6] EISHRELA [35] 3-7-5 (5*) D Wright (2) *nvr dngrs*.
......................................(33 to 1 op 20 to 1) 13
2820[7] IJAB (Can) [62] (bl) 3-9-9 R Hills (4) *chsd ldrs till wknd 3 fs out*...................................(7 to 1 op 5 to 1) 14
2942 ALMOSTAUTOMATIC (Ire) [40] 4-8-8 N Day (14) *beh frm hfwy*...................................(50 to 1 op 20 to 1) 15
2226 IRISH DOMINION [54] (v) 3-9-1 R Perham (7) *uns rdr towards rear whn faltered and unseated rider 4 fs out*.
.....................(20 to 1 op 14 to 1 tchd 25 to 1) ur
1627 OLIVIA VAL [35] 3-7-10 N Carlisle (13) *sn beh, tld off whn pld up o'r 2 fs out*...................(20 to 1 op 10 to 1) pu
Dist: 1½l, hd, 1½l, nk, 2l, ¾l, 2l, hd, 1½l, nk. 1m 42.10s. a 3.10s (17 Ran).
SR: 1/9/3/-/6/-/ (M W Ash), O O'Neill

3234 Ashwick Apprentice Handicap Class E (0-65 3-y-o and up) £2,884 1m 5yds ....(5:00)

2920* SET THE FASHION [58] (v) 4-8-12 D Harrison (1) *rcd in 3rd till drvn to ld 2 fs out, styd on wl fnl furlong*.
...(11 to 10 on op Evens tchd 11 to 10 and 5 to 4 on) 1
2794 JADE VALE [74] 4-10-0 F Norton (3) *chsd ldr, drvn to chal 2 fs out, kpt on, not pace of wnr fnl furlong*.
....(9 to 4 op 5 to 4) 2
2479[5] GRAN SENORUM (USA) [77] (bl) 3-9-7 (3*) T G McLaughlin (4) *led till hdd 2 fs out, sn outpcd*.
..........................(7 to 2 op 3 to 1 tchd 4 to 1) 3
NOEL (Ire) [53] 4-8-7 D Wright (2) *4th most of way, lost tch fnl 3 fs*..........................(16 to 1 op 10 to 1) 4
Dist: 2l, 7l, 7l. 1m 40.00s. a 1.00s (4 Ran).
SR: 41/51/26/-/ (The Queen), Lord Huntingdon

CATTERICK (good)
Tuesday August 10th

Going Correction: PLUS 0.05 sec. per fur. (races 1,2,3,5,6), PLUS 0.15 (4)

3235 Tattersalls Bookmakers Selling Stakes Class G (2-y-o) £2,057 7f (6:00)

2996 KOMPLICITY 8-11 N Connorton (7) *trkd ldrs, led o'r 2 out, drvn clr*..................(9 to 2 op 8 to 1 tchd 9 to 1) 1
2588[6] PASSION SUNDAY 8-11 K Darley (9) *in tch, hdwy 4 out, rdn 2 fs out, kpt on same pace*.
.........(9 to 4 fav op 6 to 4 tchd 5 to 4 and 5 to 2) 2
2819[2] CELESTIAL DANCE 8-6 J Carroll (10) *chsd ldrs, kpt on fnl 2 fs*.................................(5 to 1 tchd 7 to 1) 3
2331[6] GREEK NIGHT OUT (Ire) 8-6 Dean McKeown (1) *wth ldr, led wl o'r 2 fs out, sn hdd, one pace*.
...........................(7 to 2 op 5 to 2 tchd 4 to 1) 4
2819[3] MISS FREEBIE (Ire) 8-6 A Culhane (12) *beh till styd on fnl 3 fs, nrst finish*......................(16 to 1 op 8 to 1) 5
2952[5] BRAMCOTE CENTURY 8-3 (3*) O Pears (11) *in tch, no hdwy fnl 3 fs*.......................(25 to 1 op 20 to 1) 6
2952[3] MONSIEUR BLEU 8-11 J Weaver (8) *in tch, effrt 3 fs out, sn btn*...................................(12 to 1 op 8 to 1) 7
2876 MAZINA 8-6 K Fallon (4) *slight ld till hdd o'r 2 fs out, sn wknd*..(33 to 1) 8
1519[2] MACAROON LADY 8-6 Alex Greaves (2) *sn beh*.
......................................(20 to 1 op 16 to 1) 9
3084[7] MINIBAR 8-3 (3*) S Maloney (13) *sn beh*..........(33 to 1) 10
2679[6] ASTROLOGY 8-6 Kim Tinkler (3) *sn beh*........(100 to 1) 11
UCKERBY LAD 8-11 S Webster (6) *dwlt, al beh*. (100 to 1) 12
2526[8] GRETELS PET (v) 8-6 L Charnock (5) *early speed, sn beh*.
....(33 to 1) 13
Dist: 2l, ½l, 1l, 2½l, 2l, 2½l, 5l, 1½l, 1l, 1½l. 1m 29.10s. a 6.10s (13 Ran).
SR: 11/5/-/-/-/-/ (Hole In The Wall Breeding-Racing), Bob Jones

3236 Abi And Ropers Caravan World Nursery Class E (2-y-o) £2,978 5f 212yds ....(6:25)

2739* JIMMY THE SKUNK (Ire) [72] 8-12 J Carroll (1) *chsd ldrs, slightly hmpd 3 out, led one out, all out*.
..............................(7 to 2 fav tchd 4 to 1) 1
2569[3] MISS MAH-JONG [75] 9-1 Dean McKeown (4) *al cl up, rdn o'r 2 fs out, no extr ins fnl furlong*.
.....................(12 to 1 op 10 to 1 tchd 14 to 1) 2
2916* MISTER BEAT [72] 8-9 (3*) O Pears (5) *trkd ldrs, ev ch o'r one out, hng lft ins fnl furlong, no extr*.
................................(5 to 1 tchd 11 to 2) 3
2974[4] TOP SHOW (Ire) [81] 9-7 J Weaver (2) *led till hdd one furlong out, kpt on same pace*......(9 to 1 op 8 to 1) 4
2668[3] MIGHTY KINGDOM (Ire) [55] (bl) 7-9 L Charnock (9) *sn beh and pushed alng, styd on fnl 2 fs, nrst finish*.
......................................(10 to 1 op 8 to 1) 5
3082[9] STORM REGENT [61] 8-1[1] W Woods (8) *beh, hdwy to chase ldrs hfwy, kpt on same pace frm 2 fs out*.
....(6 to 1 op 5 to 1) 6
2916[5] DOUBLE SIXTEEN [60] 7-11 (3*) S Maloney (6) *slwly into strd, nvr dngrs*.......................(11 to 2 op 9 to 2) 7
2974 CREEK VALLEY [54] 7-3 (5*) Darren Moffatt (7) *slwly into strd, nvr dngrs*.......................(20 to 1 op 16 to 1) 8
2739[2] SPRING LOADED [66] 8-6 K Darley (3) *chsd ldrs till wknd o'r 2 fs out*.............................(4 to 1 op 9 to 2) 9
2730[5] RAVEN'S RETURN (Ire) [78] 9-4 S Perks (10) *al beh*.
....(20 to 1) 10
Dist: Hd, ¾l, 1½l, nk, ½l, 1½l, hd, ½l, 3½l. 1m 16.00s. a 5.00s (10 Ran).
SR: 4/6/-/3/-/-/ (J David Abell), J Berry

3237 Charles Clinkard Fine Footwear Handicap Class E (0-70 3-y-o and up) £2,709 7f.......................(6:50)

2733[7] ROYAL COMEDIAN [39] 4-8-3[1] (3*) O Pears (5) *loose bef strt, made all, clr o'r 2 fs out, kpt on wl und pres*.
.....................(9 to 1 op 10 to 1 tchd 12 to 1) 1
3216[7] COOL ENOUGH [35] 12-7-12 (3*) S Maloney (1) *beh, kpt on wl und pres fnl 2 fs, not rch wnr*.
.....................(11 to 2 op 5 to 1 tchd 6 to 1) 2
3004[4] MCA BELOW THE LINE [62] (v) 5-10-0 S Webster (7) *sn pushed alng, chsd wnr aftr 3 fs, rdn o'r 2 out, no imprsn*.........(11 to 4 op 9 to 4 tchd 3 to 1) 3
2889* NORTH ARDAR [62] 3-9-8 Dean McKeown (4) *chsd wnr 3 fs, in tch, no hdwy fnl 2 furlongs*. (9 to 4 fav tchd 5 to 2) 4
3216[2] MANX MONARCH [47] 3-8-2 (5*) A Garth (2) *slwly into strd, beh, effrt hfwy, nvr trble ldrs*........(5 to 1 op 4 to 1) 5
3002[7] MISSED THE BOAT (Ire) [50] (bl) 3-8-10 K Darley (3) *in tch, rdn o'r 2 fs out, sn btn*. (6 to 1 tchd 7 to 1 and 11 to 2) 6

Dist: 1½l, 1½l, sht-hd, 1½l, sht-hd. 1m 27.90s. a 4.90s (6 Ran).
SR: 23/14/36/29/9/11/ (Fir Trading Ltd), B W Murray

3238 Northern Aggregates Claiming Stakes Class F (3-y-o and up) £2,301 5f (7:20)

2872³ GIPSY FIDDLER (v) 5-9-7 Dean McKeown (1) *slwly into strd, sn chasing ldrs, styd on wl to ld jst ins fnl furlong.* ....(7 to 4 fav op 5 to 4 tchd 15 to 8) 1
2872² DRUM SERGEANT (bl) 6-9-4 J Weaver (3) *in tch, pushed alng hfwy, styd on fnl furlong.* ....(4 to 1 op 3 to 1 tchd 9 to 2) 2
2510⁶ GEMINI FIRE 9-9-1 A Culhane (4) *slwly into strd, beh till styd on fnl furlong, nrst finish.* ....(40 to 1 op 33 to 1 tchd 50 to 1) 3
2896³ ANOTHER EPISODE (Ire) 4-8-8 (7*) P Roberts (2) *wth ldr, slight ld o'r one furlong out, hdd jst ins fnl furlong, sn btn*....................(2 to 1 op 5 to 2 tchd 11 to 4) 4
2846⁴ SIGAMA (USA) 7-8-11 (3*) N Kennedy (5) *slight ld till o'r one furlong out, wknd fnl furlong*...(4 to 1 op 5 to 1) 5
Dist: 1½l, sht-hd, 3½l, 1½l. 1m 1.20s. a 3.70s (5 Ran).
SR: 48/39/35/21/14/ (Mrs J A Beighton), J A Glover

3239 Thornton Stud Maiden Handicap Class E (0-70 3-y-o and up) £2,469 1m 7f 177yds......................(7:50)

2740³ MR WOODCOCK [48] 8-9-10 K Darley (5) *made all, clr o'r one furlong out, styd on wl*....................(3 to 1) 1
2871³ SCALP 'EM (Ire) [31] 5-8-7 L Charnock (9) *in tch, hdwy to track ldrs aftr 5 fs, chasing wnr whn hit rls 3 out, kpt on, no imprsn*......................(6 to 1 op 11 to 2) 2
3147⁴ DON'T CRY [22] 5-7-12 Kim Tinkler (7) *beh, hdwy 4 fs out, hrd rdn o'r one out, styd on*.................. (14 to 1) 3
2801⁶ DOMINANT SERENADE [44] 4-9-6 Dean McKeown (8) *prmnt, pushed alng 5 fs out, fdd frm 3 out.* ....(15 to 8 fav op 7 to 4 tchd 2 to 1) 4
2800⁴ NANCY (Ire) [37] (bl) 3-7-5 (7*) Claire Balding (1) *pld hrd early, trkd ldrs, effrt 3 fs out, rdn 2 out, sn btn.* .... (20 to 1 op 16 to 1) 5
2823³ INVISIBLE ARMOUR [32] 4-8-8 J Weaver (6) *prmnt till wknd o'r 3 fs out*.......(13 to 2 op 6 to 1 tchd 7 to 1) 6
2823⁷ MOUNTAIN WILLOW [54] 3-8-12 (3*) O Pears (2) *in tch, hdwy to chase ldrs aftr 6 fs, reminder 5 out, sn wknd, tld off*..........................(12 to 1 tchd 14 to 1) 7
2823⁴ INOVAR [35] 3-7-7 (3*) N Kennedy (3) *beh most of way, tld off*...............................(25 to 1 op 16 to 1) 8
HAUT-BRION (Ire) [35] 4-8-11 Alex Greaves (4) *slwly into strd, al beh, lost tch 6 out, wl tld off.* ....(50 to 1 op 33 to 1) 9
Dist: 6l, 1½l, 1l, 3l, 3½l, 20l, 10l, 25l. 3m 34.30s. a 12.80s (9 Ran).
(P A Tylor), Mrs M Reveley

3240 Okay-Buster Amateur Riders Handicap Class E (0-70 3-y-o and up) £2,110 1½m 44yds....................(8:20)

3171² SIR THOMAS BEECHAM [56] 3-11-0 Mr T Cuff (8) *in tch gng wl, steady hdwy to ld o'r one furlong out, pushed out.* ....(6 to 1 op 9 to 2) 1
3003⁴ FIRST BID [59] 6-12-0 Mr S Whitaker (2) *hld up in tch, hdwy 3 out, chsd wnr fnl furlong, rdn and no imprsn.* ....(2 to 1 fav op 3 to 1) 2
2859⁷ HYDROPIC [24] 6-9-2 (5*) Miss R Clark (5) *prmnt, outpcd 4 fs out, slightly hmpd 2 out, styd on.* ....(14 to 1 op 12 to 1) 3
3193 CARROLLS MARC (Ire) [53] 5-11-8 Mrs L Pearce (7) *beh, hdwy 4 fs out, styd on same pace fnl 2 furlongs.* ....(11 to 2 op 6 to 1 tchd 5 to 1) 4
740⁴ SRIVIJAYA [58] 6-11-13 Mr M Buckley (6) *led till hdd o'r one furlong out, sn btn.* .... (9 to 1 op 6 to 1 tchd 10 to 1) 5
VALIANT WARRIOR [50] 5-11-0 (5*) Miss Kate Milligan (1) *beh and styd on fnl 3 fs, not trble ldrs.* ....(25 to 1 tchd 33 to 1) 6
2860³ NOT YET [39] 9-10-8 Mr J Weymes (4) *chsd ldrs, effrt 3 fs out, no hdwy*.......................(8 to 1 op 7 to 1) 7
2942⁶ DUGGAN [41] 6-10-10 Mr W McLaughlin (3) *prmnt, chsd ldr o'r 2 fs out till wknd over one out.* .... (15 to 2 op 10 to 1 tchd 7 to 1) 8
3035⁷ BORING (USA) [55] 4-11-5 (5*) Miss S Storey (10) *nvr nr ldrs*..........................(25 to 1 op 20 to 1) 9
MARANDISA [37] 6-10-6 Mr R D Green (11) *prmnt till wknd o'r 2 fs out*......................(33 to 1 op 25 to 1) 10
2878 AS D'EBOLI (Fr) [40] 6-10-9 Mr C Bonner (9) *in tch till wknd o'r 3 fs out*......................(16 to 1 op 12 to 1) 11
3138² SHARE A MOMENT (Can) [49] 3-10-7 Miss J Southall (12) *al beh*..............................(14 to 1 op 8 to 1) 12
Dist: 2l, 2½l, 4l, 2l, 1l, nk, ¾l, 6l, nk, 6l. 2m 45.80s. a 10.80s (12 Ran).
SR: 26/36/-/17/18/8/ (Mrs Heather Chakko), S Dow

DEAUVILLE (FR) (good)
Tuesday August 10th
Going Correction: PLUS 0.20 sec. per fur.

3241 Prix de Reux (Listed) (3-y-o and up) £14,337 1½m 110yds........... (2:50)

2082⁵ HUSBAND (USA) 3-8-7 C Asmussen,.................... 1
SAMOURZAKAN (Ire) 4-9-2 G Mosse,.................... 2
1219³ NON PARTISAN (USA) 4-9-2 T Jarnet,.................... 3
2654⁷ LINPAC WEST 7-9-8 G Hind,.......................... 4
2646⁴ DONDOOK (USA) (bl) 3-8-7 D Boeuf,.................. 7
Dist: ¾l, ½l, ½l, sht-hd, ¾l, 1½l. 2m 47.60s. a 11.10s (7 Ran).
SR: 7/14/13/18/-/ (Mlle P Augustus), J Fellows

SLIGO (IRE) (soft)
Tuesday August 10th

3242 Lough Gill Maiden (3-y-o and up) £2,245 6f 110yds............... (6:00)

2703³ MARKIEVICZ (Ire) 3-8-3 (8*) G M Moylan (5) .. (3 to 1 jt-fav) 1
2674⁵ RETICENT BRIDE (Ire) 3-8-11 M J Kinane (3) (3 to 1 jt-fav) 2
3074³ SKERRIES BELL 3-8-11 P V Gilson (1)............ (9 to 2) 3
2323 SAMOT (Ire) (bl) 3-9-0 J F Egan (4)................(6 to 1) 4D
3040⁴ NORDIC GLARE (Ire) 3-8-6 (8*) T E Durcan (7)......(8 to 1) 4
2674³ SCALP (Ire) 3-9-0 W J Supple (8).................(7 to 2) 6
2879⁷ GIFT OF PEACE (Ire) (bl) 3-8-11 C Roche (2).......(6 to 1) 7
SHEBA'S PAL 6-9-2 D Manning (6).............. (33 to 1) 8
Dist: 1l, hd, 4½l, 4l. 1m 31.20s. (8 Ran).
(J Crowley), M J Grassick

3243 Lissadell EBF Maiden (2-y-o) £3,107 6f 110yds........................ (6:30)

2959³ NEVER TOLD (Ire) 8-11 P V Gilson (5)............(10 to 1) 1
2403⁶ THE BREADMAN (Ire) 9-0 S Craine (3).........(2 to 1 fav) 2
2840⁶ STELFOX (Ire) 8-12 (2*) R M Burke (12)...........(12 to 1) 3
2701 CAIRNBRAE (Ire) 9-0 J F Egan (4)................(25 to 1) 4
SALMON RIVER (USA) 9-0 N G McCullagh (2)..... (4 to 1) 5
3039⁹ FINAL EXHIBIT (Ire) 8-11 C Roche (15)...........(12 to 1) 6
2701⁸ MALT LEAF (Ire) 8-5 (6*) J A Heffernan (13)....... (14 to 1) 7
2880⁷ NOREASTER (Ire) 8-11 K J Manning (8)..........(10 to 1) 8
2244² GO MILLIE (Ire) 8-11 W J Supple (1)............. (3 to 1) 9
ALL SHOW (Ire) 8-4 (10*) D A O'Sullivan (14)......(25 to 1) 10
2344⁵ SHEEN FALLS (Ire) 8-11 M J Kinane (11)........... (8 to 1) 11
2284⁷ WHEREWILITALL END (Ire) 8-10 (4*) P Carberry (9) (16 to 1) 12
2880⁵ SEANEE SQUAW 8-11 B Coogan (6)..............(8 to 1) 13
BANZAI (Ire) 8-11 Joanna Morgan (7)............(25 to 1) 14
LIGNUMVITAE (Ire) 8-12 (2*) D J O'Shea (10)......(33 to 1) 15
Dist: 1l, 5½l, hd, 2½l. 1m 33.10s. (15 Ran).
(Mrs Geraldine Ryan), C Collins

3244 McSharry/Foley Handicap (0-70 3-y-o and up) £2,762 6f 110yds........(7:30)

2879⁹ SHESLOOKINATME (Ire) [-] 4-8-4 (2*) L M Burke (8) (20 to 1) 1
2297 BUSINESS CENTRE (Ire) [-] 3-8-11 J F Egan (5)... (16 to 1) 2
2667⁹ DAIRINE'S DELIGHT (Ire) [-] 3-7-4 (6*) P P Murphy (12) ....(33 to 1) 3
2511* FANTANTE (Ire) [-] 4-9-7 P V Gilson (10)............ (6 to 1) 4
2452⁶ CAROLINA RUA (USA) [-] 3-7-11 (4*) W J Smith (11) (14 to 1) 5
2675* LADY PRESIDENT (Ire) [-] (bl) 4-9-5 (6*) J J Behan (6) .... (7 to 4 fav) 6
2451⁷ CAMEY'S CHOICE (Ire) [-] (bl) 3-8-3 W J Supple (4) (10 to 1) 7
2295* KILLEEN STAR (Ire) [-] 3-9-12 M J Kinane (7).......(9 to 2) 8
SNATCH IT (Ire) [-] (bl) 3-7-12 N G McCullagh (13).. (8 to 1) 9
2675³ MUGNANO [-] 7-9-4 (6*) J A Heffernan (1).......... (5 to 1) 10
2667 SORRECA (Ire) [-] (bl) 4-7-9 (2*) D G O'Shea (2)... (20 to 1) 11
Dist: 1l, ¾l, 4l, nk. 1m 32.10s. (11 Ran).
(L T Reilly), L T Reilly

3245 Leguard QR Flat Race (4-y-o and up) £2,762 1½m................... (8:00)

2782⁷ SHIRWAN (Ire) 4-10-12 (5*) Mr G J Harford (7)......(9 to 4) 1
2901 SACULORE (Ire) 5-10-10 (7*) Mr A Daly (4)........(10 to 1) 2
2693⁴ CEDAR COURT (Ire) 5-11-0 (3*) Mr A R Coonan (6) ....(5 to 4 fav) 3
2512³ BASSETJA (Ire) 4-10-7 (7*) Mr P A Roche (1)....... (5 to 1) 4
CARA DEILISH (bl) 7-10-9 (5*) Mr J A Nash (5)....... (8 to 1) 5
3077 LUCK OF A LADY (Ire) 4-10-7 (7*) Mr B M Cash (3) (25 to 1) 6
912⁶ ALVATUR (Ire) 4-10-10 (7*) Mr D J Kavanagh (2)... (16 to 1) 7
2902 CAT FIGHT 6-10-7 (7*) Miss G Morgan (8)........ (33 to 1) 8
Dist: ½l, 4½l, 7l, 7l. 3m 15.70s. (8 Ran).
(Anthony Kennedy), Francis Ennis

YARMOUTH (good to firm)
Tuesday August 10th
Going Correction: MINUS 0.25 sec. per fur.

3246 Market Gates Claiming Stakes Class F (3-y-o) £2,601 1¼m 21yds.......(2:15)

2993³ CLIBURNEL NEWS (Ire) 8-2 P Robinson (8) *patiently rdn, dashed up on outsd to ld o'r one furlong out, styd on wl*.................. (8 to 1 op 7 to 1 tchd 10 to 1) 1

2865[6] COMMANCHE CREEK 8-11 R Cochrane (2) *al hndy, ev ch and rdn o'r one furlong out, edgd lft last 100 yards, one pace*..............................(12 to 1 op 8 to 1) 2
2381[7] BALL GOWN 8-0 J Lowe (1) *trkd ldg trio, ev ch and not much room fnl furlong, not quicken.* ....(20 to 1 op 10 to 1) 3
3055[6] BARLEY CAKE 7-10 J Fanning (4) *settled gng wl, prmsg effrt whn squeezed for room 2 fs out, rdn and one pace.* ....(4 to 1 op 7 to 2 tchd 9 to 2) 4
2914[2] SPARKY'S SONG 8-6 W Carson (10) *sluggish strt, improved into midfield entering strt, rdn and no extr o'r one furlong out.* (7 to 2 fav op 3 to 1 tchd 4 to 1) 5
2948[5] BILLYBACK 8-5 D Biggs (5) *nvr far away, ev ch and drvn alng o'r 2 fs out, rdn and not quicken.* ....(11 to 2 op 6 to 1 tchd 7 to 1) 6
1483[8] FASHIONABLE DANCER 8-2 (3*) B Doyle (6) *tongue-tied, crashed through rls gng to post, al hndy, led o'r 3 out till over one furlong out, sn btn.* ....(16 to 1 op 12 to 1 tchd 20 to 1) 7
2989[7] MONSIGNOR PAT (USA) 9-7 L Piggott (3) *dictated pace till hdd o'r 3 fs out, wknd and hng rght 2 furlongs out.* ....(5 to 1 op 5 to 2) 8
FRAGMENT (Ire) 8-11 W R Swinburn (7) *struggling to keep up aftr 3 fs, nvr a factor.* ....(20 to 1 op 12 to 1 tchd 25 to 1) 9
2828[6] ROSE OF MEDINA 7-5[2] (7*) C Hawksley (9) *chsd ldrs, brght wide entering strt, rdn and btn o'r 2 fs out.* ....(33 to 1 op 20 to 1) 10
Dist: 1l, 2l, 4l, 1½l, nk, 1½l, 4l, 7l, hd. 2m 8.40s. a 4.40s (10 Ran).
SR: 19/26/11/-/6/4/1/9/-/ (East Lancs Newspapers Readers Club), M H Tompkins

3247 Levy Board Maiden Handicap Class E (0-70 3-y-o and up) £3,209 7f 3yds ....(2:45)

2953[2] NICHODOULA [55] 3-9-1 G Duffield (7) *nvr far away, drw level last 3 fs, put head in air, rdn to ld last 50 yards.* ....(3 to 1 op 2 to 1 tchd 7 to 2) 1
3057[9] GUESSTIMATION (USA) [44] (bl) 4-8-10 G Bardwell (3) *al hndy, nosed ahead o'r 2 fs out, rdn ins fnl furlong, ct last 50 yards*.......................(8 to 1 op 6 to 1) 2
2697[4] FROSTY MORNING [67] 3-9-13 M Roberts (1) *tucked away on ins, ev ch and drvn alng 2 fs out, one pace.* .....(11 to 4 fav op 2 to 1 tchd 3 to 1 and 100 to 30) 3
2638 MAWAYED (USA) [60] 3-9-6 W Carson (2) *led early, styd hndy till rdn and no extr o'r one furlong out.* ....(7 to 1 op 9 to 2) 4
2912[4] TOCCO JEWEL [40] 3-8-0 D Biggs (8) *sluggish strt, bustled alng thrght, kpt on fnl furlong, nvr nrr.* ....(16 to 1 op 12 to 1) 5
128[8] DUNMAGLASS [35] 6-7-10 (5*) L Newton (6) *trkd ldrs, hrd at work whn pace quickened 2 fs out, no extr.* ....(6 to 1 op 6 to 1) 6
3047[2] HAZY KAY (Ire) [55] (bl) 3-9-1 Gay Kelleway (5) *al struggling to keep up, nvr a factor.* ....(6 to 1 op 7 to 2 tchd 13 to 2) 7
3020 CAMINO A RONDA [27] 4-7-0 (7*) Kim McDonnell (4) *made most for o'r 4 fs, fdd und pres*......(33 to 1 op 25 to 1) 8
2868 ALPHONSO [52] (bl) 4-9-4 R Cochrane (9) *trkd ldrs, feeling pace, drvn alng o'r 2 fs out, sn btn.* (20 to 1 op 12 to 1) 9
Dist: ¾l, 4l, nk, 1½l, 1½l, 3½l, 2½l, 1½l. 1m 27.10s. a 3.90s (9 Ran).
SR: 16/9/14/6/-/-/ (Hesmonds Stud), Sir Mark Prescott

3248 Hopton Holiday Village Fillies' Conditions Stakes Class D (2-y-o) £4,308 7f 3yds............................(3:15)

DANCE TO THE TOP 8-10 R Cochrane (1) *settled gong wl, quickened through to ld o'r one furlong out, pushed out*...................(10 to 1 op 6 to 1 tchd 11 to 1) 1
2887* AVERTI (USA) 9-0 Pat Eddery (4) *led early, styd upsides till rdn alng fnl furlong, not quicken cl hme.* ....(2 to 1 on op 7 to 4 on tchd 6 to 4 on) 2
2754[3] LEOPARDESS (Ire) 8-10 M Roberts (2) *made most for o'r 5 fs, rdn and not quicken fnl furlong.* ....(5 to 1 op 4 to 1 tchd 7 to 1) 3
2067[5] THREATENING 9-0 G Bardwell (7) *trkd ldg pair, ev ch and bustled alng o'r 2 fs out, one pace.* (16 to 1 op 10 to 1) 4
1988* KISSININTHEBACKROW (USA) 9-0 W Carson (3) *co'red up beh ldrs, effrt and drvn alng 2 fs out, sn outpcd.* ....(14 to 1 op 10 to 1 tchd 16 to 1) 5
SARIYAA 8-10 W R Swinburn (5) *swtchd ins and chsd alng hfwy, nvr rchd ldrs*................(12 to 1 op 8 to 1) 6
YAWATTA (Ire) 8-10 L Piggott (6) *steadied strt, niggled alng aftr 2 fs, nvr a threat*..........(33 to 1 op 16 to 1) 7
Dist: ½l, 3l, ½l, 2½l, 3½l, 7l. 1m 26.70s. a 3.50s (7 Ran).
SR: 17/19/6/8/ (Cheveley Park Stud), M R Stoute

3249 Holiday Playground Selling Handicap Class G (0-80 3 & 4-y-o) £2,637 1m 3yds............................(3:45)

2464[9] O SO NEET [45] 3-8-9 P Robinson (2) *last and outpcd hfwy, styd on grimly last 2 fs to ld cl hme.* ....(12 to 1 op 20 to 1 tchd 25 to 1) 1
1852 LETTERMORE [34] 3-7-12 J Lowe (4) *trkd ldg bunch, improved to ld 2 fs out, rdn and ct cl hme.* ....(14 to 1 op 12 to 1 tchd 16 to 1) 2
2898[7] FILOU FILANT (Fr) [47] 3-8-11 M Roberts (5) *tried to make all, clr hfwy, hdd 2 fs out, kpt on same pace*....(8 to 1) 3
2784[5] B B GLEN [48] 3-8-9 (3*) C Hodgson (7) *al hndy, veered lft und pres 2 fs out, one pace*.........(12 to 1 op 8 to 1) 4
2859[4] SPECIAL RISK (Ire) [33] 3-7-11 D Biggs (3) *broke wl to show gd speed in frnt rnk for o'r 6 fs, no extr.* ....(9 to 1 op 8 to 1 tchd 10 to 1) 5
2593* MULLED ALE (Ire) [53] 3-9-3 G Duffield (1) *chsd alng on ins, hrd at work 2 fs out, fdd*...........(7 to 1 op 11 to 2) 6
2341[7] JENDORCET [40] (v) 3-8-4 J Fanning (12) *chsd alng in midfield, no imprsn last 2 fs*.......(20 to 1 op 16 to 1) 7
2898[4] STRIKE-A-POSE [53] 3-9-3 L Piggott (11) *sn drvn alng to go pace, nvr a threat.* ....(11 to 4 fav op 7 to 2 tchd 4 to 1) 8
3068[2] PONTEVECCHIO MODA [55] (bl) 3-9-5 W Carson (9) *trkd ldrs, struggling to hold pl o'r 2 fs out, sn btn.* ....(11 to 2 op 9 to 2 tchd 6 to 1) 9
3047[5] FESTIN [51] 3-9-1 R Cochrane (13) *settled to track ldrs, struggling hfwy, eased whn btn*... (7 to 1 op 5 to 1) 10
2532[3] WALK THAT WALK [57] 4-10-0 T Wall (6) *chsd ldg bunch for o'r 4 fs, fdd*..........................(12 to 1 op 8 to 1) 11
2747[3] LITTLE PARK [40] 4-8-11 W R Swinburn (8) *gd speed on outsd for o'r 5 fs, fdd.* (10 to 1 op 8 to 1 tchd 11 to 1) 12
1902 WHO'S TOM (Ire) [32] 3-7-10 G Bardwell (14) *drvn alng to keep up hfwy, sn btn*..........(20 to 1 tchd 25 to 1) 13
2939 ANOTHER KINGDOM [40] 3-8-4 J Quinn (10) *chsd alng in midfield, struggling last 2 fs*.......(25 to 1 op 16 to 1) 14
Dist: Nk, 2½l, hd, 1½l, 6l, 1½l, 3½l, hd, 3½l, 2l. 1m 39.70s. a 3.90s (14 Ran).
SR: 7/-/-/-/-/-/ (Roalco Limited), M H Tompkins

3250 Manship Median Auction Maiden Stakes Class E (2-y-o) £3,080 6f 3yds ....(4:15)

2145[3] SURIS (Ire) 9-0 R Cochrane (4) *al hndy, quickened ahead o'r one furlong out, rdn out.* ....(15 to 8 op 7 to 4 tchd 9 to 4) 1
2862[6] DALWOOD 9-0 M Roberts (3) *dictated pace for o'r 4 fs, rallied und pres*........(6 to 1 op 5 to 1 tchd 8 to 1) 2
3016[2] BRAVE EDGE 9-0 W Carson (6) *rcd freely in frnt rnk, edgd lft und pres o'r one furlong out, found nothing.* ....(11 to 8 fav op 6 to 4 tchd 7 to 4) 3
1071[6] MILLRIDGE (Ire) 8-9 L Piggott (2) *co'red up on ins, effrt and shaken up 2 fs out, not pace to chal.* ....(12 to 1 tchd 16 to 1 and 20 to 1) 4
2785[7] VLAMINCK (Ire) 9-0 A McGlone (1) *tucked away on ins, feeling pace o'r 2 fs out, sn outpcd.* (10 to 1 op 5 to 1) 5
1905 CYCLONE (Ire) 9-0 P Robinson (5) *sluggish strt, last and niggled alng hfwy, sn lost tch, tld off.* ....(25 to 1 op 12 to 1) 6
Dist: ½l, 3l, 3½l, sht-hd, 20l. 1m 13.80s. a 2.80s (6 Ran).
SR: 14/12/-/ (Scuderia Rencati Srl), L M Cumani

3251 Filby Bridge Handicap Class E (0-70 3-y-o and up) £2,950 5f 43yds... (4:45)

3085[6] JESS REBEC [54] 5-9-1 J Quinn (7) *tucked away beh ldrs, brst through to ld ins fnl furlong, drvn out.* ....(11 to 1 op 7 to 1 tchd 12 to 1) 1
2821[3] CHILLY BREEZE [66] 3-9-9 G Duffield (4) *sluggish strt, swtchd outsd and drvn alng hfwy, ran on wl fnl furlong, nrst finish*.............. (3 to 1 fav tchd 7 to 2) 2
3188[6] STORMY HEIGHTS [62] (bl) 3-9-5 M Roberts (2) *co'red up on ins, drvn alng 2 fs out, kpt on wl towards finish.* ....(7 to 1 op 5 to 1) 3
3032[2] BRISAS [32] (v) 6-7-7 J Fanning (8) *al hndy, nosed ahead hfwy, wknd and hdd ins fnl furlong, no extr.* ....(6 to 1 tchd 7 to 1) 4
2951* SUPER ROCKY [67] 4-9-7 (7*) H Bastiman (9) *gd speed on outsd till rdn and fdd entering fnl furlong.* ....(4 to 1 op 7 to 2) 5
3081[5] JOE SUGDEN [45] 9-8-6 R Cochrane (3) *chsd ldrs, hrd at work hfwy, sn outpcd*..........(8 to 1 tchd 10 to 1) 6
2896[6] SKI CAPTAIN [45] 9-8-6 D Biggs (1) *slight ld to hfwy, fdd und pres wl o'r one furlong out*....(14 to 1 op 10 to 1) 7
3099[9] TRIOMING [59] 7-9-6 Pat Eddery (5) *dsptd ld till wknd and eased o'r one furlong out*..........(8 to 1 op 6 to 1) 8
2110[7] COCKERHAM RANGER [61] 3-9-4 W R Swinburn (6) *sn drvn alng to keep up, nvr a factor*...... (12 to 1 op 8 to 1) 9
Dist: Nk, ¾l, sht-hd, 3l, sht-hd, 1½l, 1l, nk. 1m 2.50s. a 1.80s (9 Ran).
SR: 39/46/39/12/35/12/6/16/13/ (Byron J Stokes), J E Banks

3252 East Coast Handicap Class D (0-80 3-y-o and up) £3,435 1¾m 17yds (5:15)

2729* FARMER'S PET [79] 4-10-0 W R Swinburn (1) *led till hdd o'r 3 fs out, rallied to ld ag'n 2 furlongs out, forged clr.* .... (13 to 2 op 5 to 1 tchd 7 to 1) 1
2561⁴ HOOSIE [71] 3-8-7 M Roberts (4) *settled gng wl, led on bit o'r 3 fs out, hdd and hng fire 2 furlongs out, not keen.* .... (11 to 2 op 6 to 1 tchd 13 to 2) 2
3056* EIGHTANDAHALF (Ire) [63] 4-8-12 (4ex) J Fortune (5) *settled midfield, drvn up to fltter 2 fs out, styd on same pace.* ....(5 to 1 op 4 to 1) 3
2801⁴ BRIGGSMAID [50] 5-7-13 W Carson (8) *patiently rdn, steady hdwy on ins o'r 3 fs out, kpt on, not pace to chal*.................. (4 to 1 op 5 to 1 tchd 11 to 2) 4
2963⁹ FOREVER SHINEING [69] 3-7-13¹ (7*) Sarah Thompson (3) *rcd freely and checked 1st bend, sn hndy, rdn and outpcd last 2 fs*...................(25 to 1 op 14 to 1) 5
2857* NORTHERN GRADUATE (USA) [79] 4-10-0 Pat Eddery (2) *trkd ldrs, hrd at work 3 fs out, sn lost pl.* ....(3 to 1 fav op 11 to 4 tchd 7 to 2) 6
2256⁴ MISS PIN UP [75] 4-9-10 D Biggs (7) *sluggish strt, struggling frm hfwy, tld off*.............(5 to 1 op 9 to 2) 7
Dist: 4l, 1½l, 1l, 6l, hd, dist. 3m 2.30s. a 5.30s (7 Ran).
SR: 26/-/-/-/ (D R Midwood), G A Pritchard-Gordon

BEVERLEY (good to firm)
Wednesday August 11th
Going Correction: PLUS 0.10 sec. per fur.

3253 Grape Lane Selling Stakes Class G (3-y-o and up) £2,490 5f........... (2:10)

3060² SENSE OF PRIORITY 4-9-4 K Darley (8) *hmpd aftr half a furlong and beh, hdwy hfwy, rdn o'r one out, kpt on wl und pres to ld last strd*.........(5 to 4 fav op 11 to 8) 1
2777⁴ VERY DICEY 5-9-4 J Carroll (1) *led, clr 2 out, kpt on wl fnl furlong, ct last strd*.....(5 to 2 op 2 to 1 tchd 3 to 1) 2
3085⁹ ARC LAMP 7-9-4 J Fortune (6) *chsd ldrs, sn pushed alng, styd on wl fnl furlong*..............(6 to 1 op 9 to 2) 3
2967³ KILDEE LAD 3-8-9 (5*) Stephen Davies (4) *chsd ldr, one pace frm 2 fs out*...................(8 to 1 op 7 to 1) 4
3032⁴ SWINGING TICH 4-8-13 A Mackay (2) *slwly into strd, nvr rch ldrs*................ (8 to 1 op 7 to 1 tchd 9 to 1) 5
3004 CRAIGIE BOY 3-9-0 G Duffield (5) *sn beh*.........(20 to 1) 6
206⁹ ANGEL'S WING 4-8-6 (7*) Marie Plowright (7) *chsd ldrs to hfwy, sn wknd*..................(50 to 1 op 25 to 1) 7
Dist: Sht-hd, 2½l, 3l, ½l, ½l, 7l. 1m 5.20s. a 3.50s (7 Ran).
SR: 44/43/33/17/14/13/-/ (P D Savill), M H Easterby

3254 Contrac Computer Supplies Nursery Class D (2-y-o) £4,142 5f........ (2:40)

3133* LEFT STRANDED [78] 9-3 (5ex) K Darley (11) *made all, ran on wl*.............(7 to 2 jt-fav op 9 to 2 tchd 5 to 1) 1
3000⁵ SMART PET [68] 8-7 N Connorton (3) *beh, hdwy hfwy, chsd wnr o'r one out, kpt on no imprsn fnl furlong.* ....(9 to 1 op 6 to 1) 2
3133² CHILIOLA [64] 8-0 (3*) S Maloney (6) *beh, hdwy to chase ldrs hfwy, kpt on same pace fnl furlong*......(7 to 2 jt-fav op 3 to 1 tchd 4 to 1) 3
381⁹ MUCKROSS PARK [54] 7-1¹ (7*) F Savage (2) *beh till styd on fnl 2 fs, not rch ldrs*...........(33 to 1 op 25 to 1) 4
2947² RANDONNEUR (Ire) [79] 9-4 J Weaver (7) *mid-div, kpt on same pace fnl 2 fs*.................(9 to 1 op 12 to 1) 5
2876⁹ ARCTIC DIAMOND [63] 8-2 K Fallon (8) *beh, hdwy 2 fs out, nvr nr to chal*.....................(13 to 2 op 5 to 1) 6
2200⁷ BANDON CASTLE (Ire) [82] 9-7 J Fortune (4) *chsd ldr till wknd o'r one furlong out*..........(16 to 1 op 12 to 1) 7
2949* MAD ABOUT MEN [59] 7-12 L Charnock (10) *chsd ldrs, effrt hfwy, wknd entering fnl furlong.* .... (13 to 2 op 6 to 1 tchd 7 to 1) 8
2730⁴ LEGATEE [78] 9-3 G Duffield (9) *mid-div till wknd 2 fs out.* .... (12 to 1 op 10 to 1) 9
3115* CYARNA QUINN (Ire) [76] 9-1 (5ex) P Robinson (5) *mid-div till wknd 2 out*.......................... (7 to 1 op 6 to 1) 10
2435⁷ INDIAN CRYSTAL [69] 8-8 Dean McKeown (1) *prmnt till wknd 2 out*.....................................(14 to 1) 11
Dist: 1½l, 2½l, ¾l, hd, 1½l, 3l, nk, 3½l, 2½l, 1½l. 1m 6.30s. a 4.60s (11 Ran).
SR: 21/5/-/-/2/-/ (P D Savill), G Lewis

3255 Charles Elsey Memorial Challenge Trophy Handicap Class D (0-80 3-y-o and up) £4,370 2m 35yds....... (3:10)

2640* SUN GREBE (Ire) [66] 3-8-1 K Darley (5) *hld up, hdwy 4 out, rdn o'r one out, led ins fnl furlong, all out.* ....(4 to 1 fav op 7 to 2) 1
2477² MY DESIRE [74] 5-9-5 (5*) Darren Moffatt (6) *hld up, hdwy on outsd o'r 2 out, rdn over one out, chlgd ins fnl furlong, no extr cl hme*........................(9 to 2) 2
2904⁷ CHAKALAK [68] 5-9-4 J Weaver (1) *chsd ldr, pushed alng 3 out, chlgd ins fnl furlong, no extr cl hme.* ....(9 to 2 op 4 to 1 tchd 5 to 1) 3
3033⁵ LORD HASTIE (USA) [70] 5-9-3 (3*) O Pears (4) *led, rdn o'r 2 fs out, hdd ins fnl furlong, sn btn*. (8 to 1 tchd 9 to 1) 4
3113⁴ HAZARD A GUESS (Ire) [63] 3-7-12 J Lowe (9) *hld up, hdwy o'r 2 fs out, one pace fnl furlong*....(13 to 2 op 6 to 1) 5
1890* CONTINUITY [61] 4-8-11 K Fallon (8) *in tch, effrt 3 fs out, no hdwy*...........................(9 to 1 op 8 to 1) 6
2158³ ELA BILLANTE [72] 3-8-7 P Robinson (2) *trkd ldrs, effrt 3 fs out, wknd 2 out*....................(9 to 1 op 8 to 1) 7
2729⁶ KING WILLIAM [43] 8-7-0 (7*) Antoinette Armes (3) *hld up, hdwy on outsd 4 fs out, wknd o'r 2 out.* ....(7 to 1 op 6 to 1) 8
2310³ BLUE GROTTO (Ire) [75] 3-8-10 G Duffield (7) *prmnt, rdn o'r 3 fs out, sn wknd*.................(14 to 1 op 12 to 1) 9
Dist: Hd, sht-hd, 1½l, ¾l, 7l, 6l, 6l, 1½l. 3m 45.50s. a 16.50s (9 Ran).
(Sir Thomas Pilkington), J L Dunlop

3256 Hull Daily Mail Handicap Class E (0-70 3-y-o) £3,936 1m 1f 207yds...... (3:40)

3113* EFIZIA [65] 9-4 K Darley (1) *in tch, steady hdwy to ld entering fnl furlong, drvn out.* ......(11 to 8 fav op 5 to 4 tchd 11 to 10 and 6 to 4) 1
2764³ BRACKENTHWAITE [51] 7-11 (7*) V Halliday (2) *hld up, hdwy o'r 3 fs out, rdn over one out, kpt on wl fnl furlong*..............(6 to 1 op 5 to 1 tchd 13 to 2) 2
3134⁴ I'M A DREAMER (Ire) [68] 9-7 Dean McKeown (4) *led till edgd lft and hdd entering fnl furlong, kpt on.* ....(5 to 1 tchd 11 to 2) 3
3045² PRINCESS TATEUM (Ire) [66] 9-5 P Robinson (7) *trkd ldr, not much room entering fnl furlong, kpt on same pace.* ....(6 to 1 op 5 to 1) 4
2758 BEAUMONT (Ire) [63] 9-2 G Duffield (6) *prmnt, chlgd 2 fs out, sn rdn and one pace.* .... (11 to 2 op 5 to 1 tchd 6 to 1) 5
2697⁷ ROYAL DIVA [58] 8-11 N Connorton (3) *in tch, effrt o'r 2 fs out, no hdwy*.................................(16 to 1) 6
2598⁵ KAHLO [59] 8-12 B Raymond (5) *mid-div till lost pl and beh hfwy, no dngr aftr*...........(12 to 1 op 10 to 1) 7
PANIC BUTTON (Ire) [48] 7-12 (3*) S Maloney (8) *pld hrd, hld up, rdn o'r 2 fs out, sn btn*.........(14 to 1 op 12 to 1) 8
Dist: Nk, 2l, 1l, ¾l, 1l, 6l, 3l. 2m 11.20s. a 9.80s (8 Ran).
SR: 16/1/14/10/5/ (Mrs H I S Calzini), Mrs M Reveley

3257 East Riding Yeomanry Challenge Trophy Amateur Riders Handicap Class E (0-80 3-y-o and up) £2,821 7f 100yds ....(4:10)

2459⁷ DANCING BEAU (Ire) [48] 4-9-3 (5*) Mr T Cuff (3) *beh, steady hdwy o'r 2 fs out, ran on strly to ld last strds.* .... (11 to 2 op 4 to 1) 1
2882 TROOPING (Ire) [71] 4-11-3 Miss A Harwood (1) *trkd ldrs, chlgd entering fnl furlong, sn rdn, no extr nr finish.* ....(7 to 2 op 3 to 1) 2
2873⁴ LADY DONOGHUE (USA) [50] 4-9-10 Mr M Buckley (7) *beh, gd hdwy 3 fs out, slight ld one out, ct last strds.* .... (11 to 2 op 5 to 1) 3
3004² CAUSLEY [73] 8-11-5 E McMahon (5) *led till hdd one furlong out, no extr.* ....(11 to 4 fav op 7 to 2 tchd 4 to 1) 4
3155⁹ AITCH N'BEE [75] 10-11-7 Mrs M Cowdrey (9) *nvr nr ldrs.* .... (13 to 2 op 5 to 1 tchd 7 to 1) 5
677⁸ MAINLY ME [58] 4-10-4 Mrs L Pearce (2) *mid-div till wknd 2 fs out*................(6 to 1 op 5 to 1 tchd 13 to 2) 6
2226 COURTING NEWMARKET [40] 5-9-0 Miss S A Billot (8) *chsd ldrs till wknd 2 fs out*............. (12 to 1 op 10 to 1) 7
3059² LIDA'S DELIGHT (Ire) [58] 3-9-12 Mrs A Farrell (6) *reared up and slwly into strd, al beh*...........................(10 to 1) 8
3002⁶ SUPREME OPTIMIST [40] (bl) 9-8-13⁶ (7*) Mrs C Peacock (4) *chsd ldr till wknd o'r 2 fs out*.......................... (50 to 1) 9
Dist: Nk, sht-hd, 2l, 6l, 7l, hd, 3½l, 4l. 1m 36.40s. a 6.10s (9 Ran).
SR: 28/50/28/45/29/-/ (Lennard Lazarus), S Dow

3258 Ladies Day Claiming Stakes Class E (3-y-o and up) £3,080 1m 100yds (4:40)

2989⁴ BATTLE COLOURS (Ire) 4-9-10 G Duffield (2) *trkd ldrs, led o'r 3 fs out, styd on wl*..............(3 to 1 op 9 to 4) 1
3175² LOMBARD SHIPS (bl) 6-8-9 A Mackay (1) *mid-div, hdwy to chase wnr o'r 2 fs out, kpt on, no imprsn.* ....(7 to 4 fav op 5 to 4) 2
2633⁴ SCOTTISH PARK 4-8-4 (5*) J Marshall (9) *in tch, hdwy 3 fs out, rdn 2 out, kpt on same pace.* .... (11 to 2 op 8 to 1 tchd 5 to 1) 3
3058⁵ HAND ON HEART (Ire) (v) 4-8-11 (3*) S Maloney (4) *in tch, effrt 3 fs out, kpt on same pace fnl 2 furlongs.* (12 to 1) 4
3053⁵ ELEGANT HUSSAR (v) 3-8-7 M Birch (8) *led till hdd o'r 3 fs out, fdd*...(8 to 1) 5
2892⁵ NOT EARSAY 3-7-8³ (5*) A Garth (5) *sn beh, some hdwy fnl 2 fs, not trble ldrs*...........................(33 to 1) 6
2873 HENBURY HALL (Ire) (v) 5-8-10 Ann Stokell (7) *cl up till wknd o'r 2 fs out*................................ (33 to 1) 7
2366² SKY WISH 3-8-11 N Connorton (6) *in tch till wknd o'r 2 fs out*..............................(7 to 1 tchd 15 to 2) 8
ABLE MCCLEOD 3-9-3 J Fanning (3) *dwlt, sn wl beh, tld off*.............(16 to 1 op 20 to 1 tchd 14 to 1) 9
Dist: 2½l, 2l, 1½l, 3l, 1l, 1½l, 2½l, dist. 1m 50.30s. a 7.50s (9 Ran).
SR: 10/-/-/-/-/-/ (Garth Insoll), Sir Mark Prescott

3259 Journal Maiden Stakes Class D (2-y-o) £3,819 7f 100yds............... (5:10)

CHARITY CRUSADER 8-9 (5*) Stephen Davies (9) *slwly into strd, mid-div, headay 2 fs out, edgd rght and led ins fnl furlong, all out*........ (9 to 1 op 8 to 1 tchd 10 to 1) 1
2968[8] RUPAN 9-0 W R Swinburn (15) *mid-div, hdwy o'r 2 fs out, ev ch ins fnl furlong, no extr*.......(6 to 1 tchd 8 to 1) 2
3079[3] BONAIGUA (Ire) 9-0 K Darley (14) *beh, styd on wl fnl 2 fs, nrst finish*........................(9 to 2 tchd 11 to 2) 3
2714[2] ZUBOON (USA) 9-0 R Hills (10) *nvr far away, effrt 2 fs out, ev ch ins fnl furlong, kpt on.*
.......................(3 to 1 fav op 7 to 2 tchd 4 to 1) 4
2964[4] BLAIR CASTLE (Ire) 9-0 S O'Gorman (13) *chsd ldrs, ev ch one furlong out, no extr*.............(7 to 1 op 9 to 2) 5
2364[6] FAAL MARIO (USA) 9-0 G Duffield (16) *made most till hdd ins fnl furlong, no extr.* (4 to 1 op 5 to 2 tchd 9 to 2) 6
2968 WAAFED (USA) (bl) 9-0 B Raymond (3) *chsd ldrs, ev ch one furlong out, wknd fnl furlong*................ (20 to 1) 7
THE CHAIRMAN (Ire) 9-0 S Perks (5) *mid-div, styd on fnl 2 fs, not rch ldrs*......... (9 to 1 op 8 to 1 tchd 10 to 1) 8
1227[8] RIVA'S BOOK (USA) 9-0 J Carroll (12) *beh, effrt o'r 2 fs out, kpt on fnl furlong*...............(50 to 1 op 33 to 1) 9
2419 TOWER GREEN 9-0 A Clark (8) *chsd ldrs, wkng whn hmpd ins fnl furlong*.................................(25 to 1) 10
2299[9] CLIFTON BEAT (USA) 9-0 K Fallon (11) *nvr trble ldrs.*
.... (33 to 1 op 25 to 1) 11
1602[6] KARSEAM (Ire) 9-0 N Connorton (7) *chaseed ldrs till wknd o'r one furlong out*...............(50 to 1 op 33 to 1) 12
3016 FATALIST 8-7 (7*) N Varley (1) *sn beh.* (33 to 1 op 16 to 1) 13
UNPREJUDICE 9-0 J Lowe (6) *in tch till wknd 2 fs out.*
.... (33 to 1 op 25 to 1) 14
2964[8] HADI (Ire) 9-0 Dean McKeown (2) *wth ldr till wknd quickly o'r 2 fs out*........................ (20 to 1 op 16 to 1) 15
IMPRESSIVE 9-0 M Birch (4) *al beh*..............(33 to 1) 16
RICH GLOW 9-0 Alex Greaves (17) *sn beh, tld off.*
.... (50 to 1 op 33 to 1) 17

Dist: ½l, hd, ¾l, hd, sht-hd, 1½l, hd, 1l, nk, 3½l. 1m 36.40s. a 6.10s (17 Ran).
SR: 20/18/17/15/14/13/8/7/4/ (Express Marie Curie Racing Club), P W Chapple-Hyam

SALISBURY (good to firm)
Wednesday August 11th

Going Correction: MINUS 0.20 sec. per fur. (races 1,2,3,4,5,6), MINUS 0.35 (7)

3260 EBF Sandown Maiden Stakes Class D (Div I) (2-y-o) £4,464 6f..........(2:20)

2792[2] MAJESTIC EAGLE (Ire) 9-0 M Hills (8) *trkd ldrs, led wl o'r one furlong out, sn clr, easily.*
..................(7 to 4 on op 11 to 10 on tchd Evens) 1
BAHRAIN STAR (USA) 8-9 W Carson (1) *led aftr one furlong, rdn and hdd wl o'r one out, one pace.*
.... (20 to 1 op 8 to 1) 2
2990 KENTAVRUS WAY (Ire) 9-0 S Raymont (9) *settled rear, prog hfwy, ran on appr fnl furlong, nvr nrr.*
.... (10 to 1 op 7 to 1) 3
2571[3] SCARLET DIVA 8-9 L Dettori (6) *trkd ldrs, swtchd lft o'r one furlong out, styd on one pace.*
......................(5 to 1 op 7 to 2 tchd 11 to 2) 4
TANDIA 8-9 A McGlone (3) *mid-div, styd on one pace fnl 2 fs, nvr dngrs*.........(20 to 1 op 25 to 1 tchd 33 to 1) 5
LIME STREET BLUES (Ire) 9-0 Pat Eddery (5) *cl up, rdn hfwy, sn btn, eased ins fnl furlong.* (10 to 1 op 7 to 1) 6
2250[9] LAKE PARVA 9-0 T Quinn (7) *led one furlong, wth ldr till rdn and edgd lft 2 out, sn wknd*... (20 to 1 op 10 to 1) 7
PERSIAN SAINT (Ire) 9-0 J Williams (2) *slwly into strd, pushed alng 4 fs out, al beh.*
.......................(16 to 1 op 12 to 1 tchd 20 to 1) 8
INDIAN TEMPLE 9-0 Paul Eddery (10) *sn rdn alng, al beh.*
.......................(40 to 1 op 25 to 1 tchd 50 to 1) 9
DRESSEDFORSUCCESS 8-9 N Adams (4) *strted slwly, al beh*..(50 to 1 op 25 to 1) 10

Dist: 6l, 1l, 2l, 1l, 1½l, sht-hd, 3l, 2l, 12l. 1m 14.71s. a 2.21s (10 Ran).
SR: 32/3/4/-/-/-/ (Garrett J Freyne), J W Hills

3261 H. S. Lester Memorial Challenge Cup Handicap Class D (0-80 3-y-o and up) £3,757 6f 212yds............... (2:50)

2882 COURT MINSTREL [55] 4-8-7 J Reid (3) *rear, rdn and prog wl o'r one furlong out, led ins last, ran on well.*
....(8 to 1 tchd 10 to 1) 1
2270 LORD ALFIE [48] 4-7-11 (3*) B Doyle (11) *mid-div, prog to ld appr fnl furlong, hdd ins last, ran on.*
.... (25 to 1 op 16 to 1) 2
3101* AWESTRIKE (USA) [75] 3-9-7 (7ex) Paul Eddery (12) *rear, rdn 3 fs out, ran on strly ins last, nvr nrr.*
....(5 to 2 fav op 9 to 2) 3
3169[5] SURREY RACING [65] 5-9-3 B Rouse (19) *chsd ldrs, prog and ev ch appr fnl furlong, not quicken.*
.... (16 to 1 op 12 to 1) 4
2032* OARE SPARROW [69] 3-9-1 R Cochrane (1) *chsd ldrs centre, rdn 2 fs out, ran on ins last, nrst finish.*
.... (20 to 1 op 14 to 1) 5
2577[6] SUPEROO [68] (bl) 7-9-6 Pat Eddery (16) *prmnt till fdd appr fnl furlong*...... (13 to 2 op 11 to 2 tchd 7 to 1) 6
2987 JIGSAW BOY [76] 4-10-0 J Williams (9) *mid-div, ran on appr fnl furlong, nrst finish.*
.......................(11 to 1 op 9 to 1 tchd 12 to 1) 7
3017[6] AMADEUS AES [68] (v) 4-9-3 (3*) C Hodgson (6) *prmnt centre, ev ch o'r one furlong out, one pace.*
.... (25 to 1 op 20 to 1) 8
3175[7] TAKENHALL [59] 8-8-11 F Norton (4) *beh till styd on appr fnl furlong, nvr nrr*.............. (16 to 1 op 12 to 1) 9
3054[2] ERTLON [74] 3-9-6 M Roberts (8) *chsd ldrs centre, kpt on one pace fnl 2 fs*.......................(12 to 1 op 10 to 1) 10
3139[5] CANADIAN CAPERS [48] (v) 4-8-0 C Rutter (5) *strted slwly, beh till styd on fnl 2 fs, nvr dngrs.* (33 to 1 op 25 to 1) 11
2663[6] BAYSHAM (USA) [69] (bl) 7-9-7 S Whitworth (18) *prmnt, led o'r 2 fs out till hdd and wknd appr last.*
.... (14 to 1 op 12 to 1) 12
2719* SIR OLIVER (Ire) [54] 4-8-6 W Carson (2) *nvr dngrs.*
.... (12 to 1 op 10 to 1) 13
2723[7] SCOTS LAW [48] (bl) 6-8-0 D Biggs (13) *led till o'r 2 fs out, sn wknd*..............................(20 to 1 op 16 to 1) 14
2969[3] BERTIE WOOSTER [76] 10-10-0 L Dettori (10) *rdn hfwy, al rear*..(14 to 1 op 12 to 1) 15
2789[9] ROMOOSH [65] 4-9-3 T Quinn (14) *prmnt, rdn 3 fs out, sn wknd*.......................................(20 to 1 op 14 to 1) 16
2670 MASRUR (USA) [60] 4-8-12 T Sprake (7) *al rear*... (50 to 1) 17
2008[7] POETS COVE [70] 5-9-8 W Newnes (15) *al beh*.... (33 to 1) 18
2612[3] ALNASRIC PETE (USA) [45] 7-7-11 J Quinn (17) *strted slwly, al beh*............................ (14 to 1 op 8 to 1) 19

Dist: 1l, 1½l, nk, ½l, 1½l, 1l, nk, sht-hd, ½l, 2l. 1m 27.66s. a 2.06s (19 Ran).
SR: 41/31/47/42/38/38/43/34/24/ (G W Knight), L J Holt

3262 Upavon Fillies Stakes Class A (Listed Race) (3-y-o and up) £9,586 1m 1f 209yds........................ (3:20)

2907* DANA SPRINGS (Ire) 3-8-5 L Dettori (8) *trkd ldrs, rdn to ld 2 fs out, hld on wl*...... (7 to 1 op 6 to 1 tchd 15 to 2) 1
2789* ANDROMAQUE (USA) 3-8-8 R Cochrane (2) *hld up mid-div, prog 2 fs out, ev ch ins last, no extr nr finish.*
.......................(3 to 1 op 11 to 4 tchd 7 to 2) 2
2925[7] MAGICAL RETREAT (USA) 3-8-13 D Biggs (4) *chsd ldr, rdn o'r 3 fs out, styd on one pace*...... (25 to 1 op 16 to 1) 3
2038[8] GISARNE (USA) 3-8-13 L Piggott (5) *settled mid-div, not clr run 2 fs out, swtchd lft and ran on ins last, not rch ldrs*..(6 to 1 op 8 to 1) 4
2986[7] INSTANT AFFAIR (USA) 3-8-5 T Quinn (9) *prmnt, rdn o'r 2 fs out, one pace*..................... (16 to 1 op 12 to 1) 5
2961[4] BASHAYER (USA) 3-8-8 W Carson (1) *rear, effrt and rdn o'r 2 fs out, kpt on one pace.*
.......................(9 to 4 fav op 5 to 2 tchd 11 to 4) 6
2961[6] BARBOUKH 3-8-13 J Reid (6) *strted slwly, last till effrt and rdn o'r 2 fs out, nvr able to chal*.......... (20 to 1) 7
2623[2] SURPRISE SURPRISE 3-8-5 W Newnes (10) *led to 2 fs out, wknd*..(10 to 1 op 9 to 1) 8
IVORY PALM (USA) 3-8-5 Pat Eddery (7) *beh, brief effrt o'r 2 fs out, sn btn*......................(9 to 1 op 6 to 1) 9
2986[8] LOVE OF SILVER (USA) 3-8-13 M Roberts (3) *beh, pushed alng o'r 3 fs out, no prog*.......... (25 to 1 op 20 to 1) 10

Dist: ½l, 1l, sht-hd, 2l, 2l, ¾l, 3l, 2l, 2l. 2m 5.65s. a 1.65s (10 Ran).
SR: 55/57/60/59/47/46/49/35/31/ (G Howard-Spink), R Hannon

3263 Violet Applin Challenge Cup Handicap Class D (0-80 3-y-o and up) £4,012 1½m.......................... (3:50)

2899* BOBBYSOXER [69] 3-8-9 Pat Eddery (5) *led 2 fs, led 4 out, drvn out*...........................(4 to 1 co-fav op 5 to 2) 1
2941[6] NORTHERN BOUND (Ire) [79] 3-9-5 M Roberts (3) *prmnt, rdn to chase wnr 3 fs out, ev ch ins last, unbl to quicken*.......................................(11 to 2 op 9 to 2) 2
2673 EL VOLADOR [62] 6-8-13 W Ryan (8) *hld up, prog 3 fs out, rdn and one pace appr last*... (4 to 1 co-fav op 6 to 1) 3
2963 TASSET (Can) [77] 3-9-3 T Quinn (7) *led aftr 2 fs till rdn and hdd 4 out, kpt on one pace.*
.......................(17 to 2 op 7 to 1 tchd 9 to 1) 4
2755 ELAINE TULLY (Ire) [77] 5-10-0 J Reid (6) *cl up till wknd o'r 2 fs out*.......................................(8 to 1 op 6 to 1) 5
1176[9] MUTAMANNI [73] 3-8-13 W Carson (1) *prog hfwy, sn pushed alng, swtchd lft 2 fs out, wknd.*
.......................(14 to 1 op 8 to 1 tchd 16 to 1) 6
2991[6] BLAZON OF TROY [56] 4-8-7 S Whitworth (2) *wtd wth, effrt and rdn o'r 2 fs out, sn wknd.*
.......................(11 to 1 op 10 to 1 tchd 12 to 1) 7
3053[2] WELL SUITED [70] 3-8-10 L Dettori (9) *chsd ldrs, rdn and wknd 4 fs out*..................(4 to 1 co-fav op 3 to 1) 8
2713[4] IMA RED NECK (USA) [50] (v) 4-8-1 A McGlone (4) *pld up lme aftr 3 fs, destroyed*........... (20 to 1 op 16 to 1) pu

Dist: ¾l, 3l, hd, 7l, ¾l, 5l, 7l. 2m 34.45s. a 2.45s (9 Ran).
SR: 46/54/42/45/42/25/9/-/-/ (P G Goulandris), J L Dunlop

3264 Bembridge Claiming Stakes Class F (2-y-o) £2,915 6f 212yds.........(4:20)

2250 DOWN D ISLANDS (bl) 9-5 Pat Eddery (1) *rcd centre, made all, rdn 2 fs out, ran on wl*....(5 to 1 jt-fav tchd 6 to 1) 1
2385* DULFORD LAD 9-1 S Whitworth (17) *prog hfwy, chsd wnr ins fnl 2 fs, ran on one pace*......... (6 to 1 op 7 to 2) 2

2689[4] MADAME GREGOIRE 8-7 R Cochrane (5) *rear, prog and swtchd lft 2 fs out, ran on ins last, nrst finish.* .... (13 to 2 op 6 to 1 tchd 7 to 1) 3
3098[8] NORTHERN STARLIGHT (v) 8-5 N Adams (18) *trcked ldrs, rdn 2 fs out, styd on one pace*..... (25 to 1 op 14 to 1) 4
2465[3] MR MYSTICAL (Ire) (v) 7-13 (7*) Mark Denaro (2) *mid-div, rdn and styd on frm 2 fs out, nvr nrr.* (9 to 1 op 6 to 1) 5
2911[2] PRIMOST 8-11 J Williams (14) *rear, rdn 3 fs out, styd on appr last, nvr nrr.* ....(5 to 1 jt-fav op 9 to 2 tchd 11 to 2) 6
3189* NORTHERN BAILIWICK (Ire) (bl) 8-11 M Wigham (12) *prmnt till rdn and wknd ins fnl 2 fs*....... (12 to 1 op 9 to 1) 7
3009 HIGH SWINGER 8-13 B Rouse (11) *chsd ldrs, no prog fnl 2 fs*.....................(10 to 1 op 12 to 1 tchd 8 to 1) 8
2844[9] TROPICAL VISTA 8-6 W Newnes (9) *chsd ldrs, no prog fnl 2 fs*...............................(33 to 1 op 25 to 1) 9
3052[6] GIGUE 8-4 M Roberts (10) *prmnt till wknd 2 fs out, eased whn btn*.............................. (8 to 1 op 6 to 1) 10
1741 AIR RAID 8-7 J Quinn (15) *strted slwly, beh, prog 2 fs out, nvr rch ldrs*........................(33 to 1 op 25 to 1) 11
3009 MANDEVILLE GEORGE 9-0 S Raymont (7) *prmnt for o'r 4 fs, sn wknd*........................ (16 to 1 op 12 to 1) 12
2714[9] DREAM MISSY 7-11 (5*) N Gwilliams (6) *chsd ldrs for o'r 4 fs, sn wknd*........................ (33 to 1 op 25 to 1) 13
3084[8] POETIC FANCY 8-4 W Ryan (8) *nvr dngrs.* .... (33 to 1 op 20 to 1) 14
3098 HYMIE HALL 8-5 C Rutter (13) *last and rdn aftr 3 fs, al beh*...................................(33 to 1 op 20 to 1) 15
2465[8] LUCKY HELEN (v) 8-2 D Biggs (16) *prmnt for o'r 4 fs, wknd rpdly*.................................(33 to 1 op 20 to 1) 16
2419 GRANBY BELL 8-12 (7*) D Gibbs (4) *beh hfwy.* .... (20 to 1 op 16 to 1) 17
2911 STAR TRAVELLER 8-6 (3*) C Hodgson (19) *al beh.* (33 to 1) 18
1624 CLANCY'S EXPRESS (bl) 9-2 (3*) M Fenton (3) *beh hfwy.* .... (33 to 1 op 25 to 1) 19

Dist: 1½l, 3½l, nk, 2½l, hd, ½l, 1½l, nk, nk, 1l. 1m 29.53s. a 3.93s (19 Ran).
SR: 25/16/-/-/-/-/ (R J Shannon), R Hannon

3265 EBF Sandown Maiden Stakes Class D (Div II) (2-y-o) £4,464 6f......... (4:50)

2909[3] WILD PLANET (USA) 8-9 R Cochrane (5) *made all, quickened clr hfwy, easily.* .... (6 to 5 on op 11 to 10 on tchd Evens) 1
ASTRAL WEEKS (Ire) 9-0 S Raymont (4) *rear, sn pushed alng, ran on fnl 2 fs, wnt second ins last, no ch wth wnr*...............................(20 to 1 op 8 to 1) 2
TOWERING TALENT (USA) 8-9 (5*) A Procter (6) *slwly into strd, sn tracking ldrs, prog to chase wnr wl o'r one furlong out, no imprsn.* (6 to 1 op 8 to 1 tchd 10 to 1) 3
2909[5] PERYLLYS 8-9 W Newnes (8) *chsd wnr, hrd rdn hfwy, wknd wl o'r one furlong out*....... (4 to 1 tchd 5 to 1) 4
PRINCE OF GAELS 9-0 C Rutter (7) *chsd ldrs, hrd rdn hfwy, wknd appr fnl furlong.* .... (20 to 1 op 14 to 1 tchd 25 to 1) 5
3079 SWINGING SIXTIES (Ire) 9-0 B Rouse (2) *chsd ldrs to hfwy, sn beh*...........................(33 to 1 op 25 to 1) 6
FERRYMAN (USA) 9-0 Pat Eddery (3) *hld up, nvr nr to chal*.................... (6 to 1 op 2 to 1 tchd 13 to 2) 7
3016[7] CHINA ROBIN 8-9 W Ryan (1) *strted slwly, beh hfwy.* ....(33 to 1 op 20 to 1) 8
ROUSAY 9-0 M Roberts (9) *unruly stalls, chsd ldrs till wknd rpdly o'r 2 fs out*........... (6 to 1 tchd 7 to 1) 9

Dist: 8l, 1½l, 3½l, 2l, 4l, 2l, 2l, ½l. 1m 14.94s. a 2.44s (9 Ran).
SR: 22/-/-/-/-/-/ (S S Niarchos), R Charlton

3266 Freshwater Handicap Class D (0-80 3-y-o and up) £3,492 5f......... (5:20)

2908[4] PRESS THE BELL [79] 3-9-3 (7*) P Roberts (3) *made all, rdn o'r one furlong out, jst hld on.* .....(100 to 30 fav op 5 to 1 tchd 11 to 2 and 3 to 1) 1
3080[7] NO EXTRAS (Ire) [79] 3-9-10 B Rouse (6) *squeezed strt, last till prog o'r one furlong out, fnshd strly, jst fld.* ....(5 to 1 op 4 to 1) 2
3153 BODARI [76] 4-9-11 R Cochrane (5) *pressed wnr, hrd rdn 2 fs out, ev ch ins last, no extr*........(11 to 2 op 9 to 2) 3
3099[2] BELLSABANGING [74] 3-9-5 T Williams (1) *chsd ldrs, rdn hfwy, kpt on one pace*..........................(7 to 2) 4
2910[9] KENSWORTH LADY [50] 3-7-9 N Adams (4) *chsd ldrs, rdn hfwy, btn o'r one furlong out*........(8 to 1 op 7 to 1) 5
2896* ALLTHRUTHENIGHT (Ire) [79] 4-10-0 W Newnes (7) *chsd ldrs till wknd one furlong out*.....(5 to 1 tchd 13 to 2) 6
2965[3] BORN TO BE [76] 4-9-11 W Ryan (2) *chsd ldrs for o'r 3 fs, eased whn btn*......... (6 to 1 op 5 to 1 tchd 13 to 2) 7

Dist: Sht-hd, ½l, 2l, 1½l, 3½l, 3l. 1m 0.88s. a 1.08s (7 Ran).
SR: 53/52/51/37/7/26/11/ (Sydney Mason), J Berry

SANDOWN (good to firm)
Wednesday August 11th
Going Correction: MINUS 0.05 sec. per fur.

3267 Clifton Reed Training Median Auction Maiden Stakes Class F (2-y-o) £3,598 5f 6yds......................... (5:50)

2996[6] DOLLAR GAMBLE (Ire) 9-0 T Quinn (2) *made virtually all, shaken up to go clr wl o'r one furlong out, eased nr finish*............(11 to 8 on op Evens tchd 6 to 4 on) 1
2571 VEDO NUDO 9-0 J Reid (6) *pressed wnr till rdn and outpcd wl o'r one furlong out.* ....(14 to 1 op 8 to 1 tchd 16 to 1) 2
SMOOTH HOUND 9-0 D Holland (1) *outpcd, ran on appr fnl furlong, no ch wth wnr*.......... (4 to 1 op 2 to 1) 3
2659[7] SARMATIAN (USA) 9-0 Jaki Houston (4) *slwly into strd, sn wl plcd, effrt und pres 2 fs out, outpcd appr last.* .... (16 to 1 op 12 to 1) 4
1857[8] ANSELLADY 8-9 W Carson (8) *sn outpcd.* ....(10 to 1 tchd 16 to 1) 5
2626[7] TOTON LAD 8-11 (3*) D Harrison (10) *mid-div, rdn alng and not quicken 2 fs out.* .... (20 to 1 op 16 to 1 tchd 25 to 1) 6
2826[7] FRANKLY MY DEAR 9-0 W Woods (3) *wl plcd for o'r 3 fs.* ....(20 to 1 op 10 to 1) 7
3001 MARCH OF TIME 9-0 A McGlone (5) *cl up till wknd quickly und pres 2 fs out.* ....(25 to 1 op 14 to 1 tchd 33 to 1) 8
BERG (Ire) 9-0 L Piggott (9) *strted slwly, pld up aftr 100 yards*.................. (8 to 1 op 4 to 1 tchd 9 to 1) pu

Dist: 4l, hd, hd, 1½l, hd, ¾l, 1½l. 1m 3.34s. a 3.84s (9 Ran).
SR: 18/2/1/-/-/-/ (J A Leek), R Hannon

3268 Sandown Exhibition Centre Conditions Stakes Class D (3-y-o and up) £4,201 1m 14yds................ (6:20)

MUHTARRAM (USA) 4-9-0 W Carson (1) *hld up, hdwy to ld and edgd rght wl o'r one furlong out, pushed clr.* .... (11 to 4 op 7 to 4 tchd 3 to 1) 1
2259 REDENHAM (USA) 3-8-9 L Dettori (8) *in tch, not much room 3 fs out, swtchd rght 2 out, ran on one pace fnl furlong*.................. (15 to 2 op 7 to 1 tchd 8 to 1) 2
1084 DARBONNE (USA) 3-8-8 M Roberts (4) *cld on ldrs 3 fs out, ev ch and not much room 2 out, not quicken.* .... (9 to 1 op 7 to 1 tchd 10 to 1) 3
3008[2] SPANISH STORM (Ire) (bl) 4-9-0 W Woods (2) *hld up rear, not clr run o'r 2 fs out, rdn and styd on ins last.* .... (16 to 1 op 14 to 1 tchd 20 to 1) 4
2621[4] PLANETARY ASPECT (USA) 3-8-11 J Reid (7) *rcd keenly, pressed ldrs till rdn and one pace appr fnl furlong.* ....(7 to 2 op 7 to 1 tchd 8 to 1) 5
2725* EL DUCO (USA) 3-8-11 Pat Eddery (6) *led aftr one furlong till wl o'r one out, sn outpcd, wknd clsg stages.* .... (9 to 4 fav tchd 5 to 2) 6
3117[9] MISWAKI DANCER (USA) 3-8-7 Paul Eddery (5) *outpcd.* .... (66 to 1 op 25 to 1) 7
1978[8] GREEN'S BID 3-8-11 T Quinn (3) *led one furlong, trkd ldr till wknd und pres 2 out, tld off*.....(14 to 1 op 8 to 1) 8

Dist: 2½l, hd, ¾l, ½l, sht-hd, 12l, 15l. 1m 41.73s. a 2.63s (8 Ran).
SR: 55/42/40/44/39/38/-/-/ (Hamdan Al-Maktoum), J H M Gosden

3269 Golf Club Handicap Class D (0-80 3-y-o and up) £4,474 1m 14yds......(6:50)

2882 SAAFEND [70] 5-9-4 Pat Eddery (7) *hld up rear, hdwy o'r 2 fs out, rdn over one out, quickened to ld last 100 yards, ran on*.................. (7 to 1 op 5 to 1 tchd 8 to 1) 1
2882[4] DANCING SENSATION (USA) [55] 6-7-12 (5*) D Wright (9) *cld on ldrs frm rear and bumped o'r 2 fs out, ev ch whn edgd rght und pres over one out, rallied nr line.* ....(11 to 2 jt-fav op 4 to 1) 2
3042[2] KINGCHIP BOY [54] (v) 4-8-2 D Biggs (10) *ran on and edgd lft o'r 2 fs out, hng left over one out, ran on same pace.* .... (17 to 2 op 8 to 1 tchd 9 to 1) 3
2156[9] ALBEMINE (USA) [66] 4-9-0 Paul Eddery (1) *led till ins fnl furlong, ran on same pace.* ....(20 to 1 op 16 to 1 tchd 25 to 1) 4
2897[2] NITOUCHE [66] 3-8-2 (5*) J Tate (5) *hld up, cld on ldrs o'r 2 fs out, not quicken ins last*........ (25 to 1 op 20 to 1) 5
2882[9] DEEVEE [66] 4-9-0 P Robinson (8) *hld up, hdwy frm rear last 2 fs, nrst finish*.... (9 to 1 op 7 to 1 tchd 10 to 1) 6
2995[3] PRAIRIE GROVE [70] 3-8-11 L Dettori (6) *in tch, effrt o'r 2 fs out, rdn and not quicken over one out.* .... (14 to 1 op 12 to 1 tchd 16 to 1) 7
3042* WAHEM (Ire) [65] 3-8-6 (5ex) M Roberts (14) *pressed ldrs till wknd und pres appr fnl furlong.* .... (6 to 1 op 5 to 1 tchd 13 to 2) 8
3017[8] AKKAZAO (Ire) [73] 5-9-7 J Reid (13) *hdwy and squeezed for room o'r 2 fs out, not rcvr*...............(11 to 2 jt-fav op 7 to 1 tchd 8 to 1) 9
2622[6] WAVE HILL [71] 4-8-12 (7*) T G McLaughlin (15) *hdwy on ins and not much room 3 fs out, one pace appr last.* ....(14 to 1 op 10 to 1 tchd 16 to 1) 10
2522[8] ERLKING (Ire) [69] 3-8-7 (3*) D Harrison (11) *ldg grp till lost pl 2 fs out*.........................(25 to 1 op 20 to 1) 11
2717[4] CAPTAIN MARMALADE [53] 4-8-1 A McGlone (2) *hld up, imprvg whn not clr run o'r 2 fs out, not rcvr.* ....(25 to 1 op 20 to 1 tchd 33 to 1) 12
3175* SHINING JEWEL [73] 6-9-7 (5ex) L Piggott (4) *pressed ldrs till wknd wl o'r one furlong out, eased whn btn.* ....(11 to 1 op 8 to 1 tchd 12 to 1) 13
2794[6] BRAVURA [80] 4-10-0 N Day (12) *al beh.* ....(14 to 1 op 12 to 1 tchd 16 to 1) 14

1604[9] DASWAKI (Can) [65] 5-8-13 A Morris (3) *jnd ldr aftr 2 fs, wknd quickly two out*..(25 to 1 op 14 to 1) 15
Dist: ½l, nk, ¾l, ¾l, 2½l, 3½l, 1l, sht-hd, 1l, 3½l. 1m 42.29s. a 3.19s (15 Ran).
SR: 50/33/31/41/32/31/17/9/23/ (J B R Leisure Ltd), J Sutcliffe

3270 LBC Newstalk 97.3 FM Handicap Class E (0-70 3-y-o and up) £3,582 5f 6yds.......................... (7:20)

3081[4] LYNDON'S LINNET [57] 5-9-3 J Weaver (5) *hld up, hdwy hfwy, led wl o'r one furlong out, pushed clr, cmftbly.* .... (5 to 1 op 9 to 2 tchd 11 to 2) 1
3006* SUPREME BOY [55] 4-9-1 G Hind (8) *wth ldr, led hfwy, hdd and outpcd appr fnl furlong.* ....(7 to 1 op 6 to 1 tchd 8 to 1) 2
2910[2] BATCHWORTH BOUND [54] 4-9-0 C Rutter (11) *ldg grp, rdn and outpcd appr fnl furlong*........(13 to 2 op 5 to 1) 3
3042 GEMINI BAY [37] (bl) 4-7-11 S Dawson (3) *outpcd till styd on fnl furlong, not rch wnr*.................... (33 to 1) 4
3081[2] PEERAGE PRINCE [65] (bl) 4-9-11 R Cochrane (1) *hld up, ran on ins last 2 fs, no imprsn*....(4 to 1 fav op 7 to 2) 5
2944[5] PRINCE SONGLINE [53] (v) 3-8-9 Pat Eddery (2) *hld up, effrt hfwy, nvr rch frnt rnk*..........(6 to 1 op 9 to 2) 6
3060[8] OUR SHADEE (USA) [57] (bl) 3-8-8 (5*) K Rutter (4) *led to hfwy, wknd o'r one furlong out.* (14 to 1 tchd 16 to 1) 7
1714 BELLE SOIREE [47] 3-7-12 (5*) B Russell (9) *mid-div, rdn and no imprsn last 2 fs*.......... (10 to 1 tchd 14 to 1) 8
3085[3] CASTLE MAID [37] 6-7-11 J Quinn (10) *nvr able to chal.* .... (10 to 1 op 8 to 1 tchd 11 to 1) 9
1502[6] TOFF SUNDAE [51] 3-8-7[1] M Tebbutt (12) *speed to hfwy, wknd quickly*.............................. (33 to 1) 10
3002[2] CUDDLY DATE [50] 3-8-6 L Piggott (6) *cl up for o'r 2 fs, sn lost pl*..................(9 to 1 op 8 to 1 tchd 10 to 1) 11
2387[6] DAANIERA (Ire) [62] (bl) 3-9-4 B Rouse (7) *strted slwly, al outpcd*.. (33 to 1) 12
Dist: 4l, 1½l, ¾l, hd, hd, 1½l, 3½l, 1l, 2½l, ½l. 1m 2.00s. a 2.50s (12 Ran).
SR: 48/30/23/3/30/13/11/-/-/ (J Bryan Smith), R Ingram

3271 Reid Minty Litigation Solicitors Handicap Class C (0-90 3-y-o and up) £5,106 1¾m.......................... (7:50)

2997[4] SUN OF SPRING [81] 3-9-2 M Roberts (4) *hld up, led on bridle o'r 2 fs out, pushed out, easily.* .... (11 to 2 op 7 to 1 tchd 15 to 2) 1
1669[5] ALQAIRAWAAN [57] 4-8-5 B Rouse (1) *wth ldrs, led 3 fs out till o'r 2 out, styd on same pace.* ....(5 to 2 fav op 9 to 2 tchd 5 to 1) 2
1593* CALL THE GUV'NOR [68] 4-9-2 W Ryan (7) *handily plcd, ev ch 2 fs out, no extr appr last*.........(7 to 2 op 3 to 1) 3
2972[3] MIROSWAKI (USA) [72] 3-8-7 Paul Eddery (3) *ldg grp, rdn and one pace frm 3 fs out*.........(8 to 1 tchd 10 to 1) 4
2913[2] TIGER SHOOT [56] 6-8-4 W Newnes (6) *led aftr 2 fs to 3 out, sn lost tch*.........(9 to 1 op 8 to 1 tchd 10 to 1) 5
2857[2] HIERARCH (USA) [72] 4-9-6 Pat Eddery (9) *beh most of way, lost tch frm 3 fs out.* .... (6 to 1 op 9 to 2 tchd 13 to 2) 6
HOLIDAY ISLAND [65] 4-8-13 S Whitworth (2) *nvr on terms.* .... (20 to 1 op 16 to 1 tchd 25 to 1) 7
3067[6] PHARAMINEUX [77] 7-9-11 T Quinn (5) *hld up rear, nvr rch ldrs*..................................(6 to 1 op 5 to 1) 8
2751[3] RIVIERE ACTOR (USA) [71] 3-8-6 W Carson (8) *led 2 fs, wknd o'r 3 out*......... (9 to 1 op 8 to 1 tchd 10 to 1) 9
Dist: 2l, nk, 3½l, 15l, ¾l, nk, 2½l, 3l. 2m 58.85s. a 4.55s (9 Ran).
SR: 50/35/45/29/-/10/2/9/-/ (Sheikh Mohammed), M R Stoute

3272 Reid Minty Libel & Slander Maiden Stakes Class D (3-y-o and up) £3,712 1 ¼m 7yds...................... (8:20)

DEL DEYA (Ire) 3-8-7 L Piggott (20) *steadied strt, hdwy frm rear 3 fs out, rdn o'r one out, hrd drvn to ld nr finish.* .... (14 to 1 op 12 to 1 tchd 16 to 1) 1
821[7] TAP ON AIR 3-8-7 D Holland (16) *ldg grp, rdn to ld 2 fs out, hrd ridden and hdd nr finish.* .... (11 to 1 op 12 to 1 tchd 16 to 1) 2
3012[2] WINTER FOREST (USA) 3-8-12 M Roberts (4) *mid-div, pushed alng 4 fs out, styd on one pace frm 2 out.* ....(5 to 4 fav op 7 to 4 tchd 11 to 10) 3
1275[2] LIKE THE SUN (USA) 3-8-7 W R Swinburn (11) *trkd frnt rnk, not much room o'r 2 fs out, rdn and not quicken appr last*.........................(8 to 1 op 12 to 1) 4
BOMBLET 3-8-7 J Reid (8) *effrt on outsd 4 fs out, one pace frm 2 out*...........................(50 to 1 op 33 to 1) 5
2332[6] RUMPUS (Ire) 3-8-7 R Cochrane (3) *led one furlong, chsd ldrs, one pace frm 2 out.* (8 to 1 op 6 to 1 tchd 9 to 1) 6
2752[4] KESTON POND (Ire) 3-8-12 L Dettori (17) *handily plcd, wth ldr 3 fs out till btn o'r one out.* .... (10 to 1 op 14 to 1 tchd 16 to 1) 7
2776[8] DARK DEN (USA) 3-8-12 Paul Eddery (14) *led aftr one furlong to 7 out, led 3 out to 2 out, wknd.* .... (50 to 1 op 20 to 1) 8
2963 SEASONAL SPLENDOUR (Ire) (bl) 3-8-7 D Biggs (19) *stumbled strt, effrt frm rear o'r 2 fs out, no imprsn appr last*...............(16 to 1 tchd 20 to 1 and 14 to 1) 9
2010[4] MODI (USA) 3-8-4 (3*) D Harrison (12) *mid-div, rdn alng o'r 3 fs out, nvr dngrs*................(33 to 1 op 20 to 1) 10
NAVAJO LOVE SONG (Ire) 3-8-7 B Procter (18) *prmsg run on ins o'r 3 fs out, wknd over one out.* ....(50 to 1 op 20 to 1) 11
2776[4] EDITHMEAD (Ire) 3-8-7 S Whitworth (13) *nvr nr to chal.* .... (20 to 1 op 16 to 1 tchd 25 to 1) 12
3117[7] ASLAN (Ire) 5-9-7 M Wigham (1) *rear most of way.* ....(33 to 1 tchd 50 to 1) 13
3012 DANDONG 3-8-12 Pat Eddery (7) *ldg grp, wide entering strt o'r 3 fs out, sn btn*............ (4 to 1 tchd 6 to 1) 14
3012 COLIN MUSET 3-8-12 G Hind (10) *chsd ldrs for o'r 7 fs.* ....(50 to 1 op 33 to 1) 15
3012 ELEGANT JADE 3-8-7 W Newnes (5) *al beh.* ....(50 to 1 op 20 to 1) 16
MAJBOOR YAFOOZ (USA) 3-8-12 B Crossley (2) *slwly into strd, rdn alng in rear most of way.* (50 to 1 op 20 to 1) 17
NAWAAYA (USA) 3-8-7 B Raymond (15) *led aftr 3 fs, hdd and wknd three out, tld off*........(50 to 1 op 25 to 1) 18
Dist: Hd, 4l, ¾l, 3½l, ½l, 1½l, ¾l, 2l, nk, ½l. 2m 7.22s. a 3.32s (18 Ran).
SR: 55/54/51/44/37/36/38/36/27/ (Sheikh Ahmed Al Maktoum), J H M Gosden

SLIGO (IRE) (heavy)
Wednesday August 11th

3273 Cleveragh Claiming Race (2-y-o) £2,243 6f 110yds............... (3:30)

2450[5] WINTER'S OVER 7-2 (8*) G M Moylan (9)..........(5 to 1) 1
786 CLANCY NOSSEL (Ire) 8-1 W J Supple (7).........(5 to 1) 2
2450[6] JENZSOPH (Ire) 7-10 A J Nolan (4)..................(14 to 1) 3
2983[4] MON PANACHE (Ire) 7-12 (6*) J A Heffernan (2) (Evens fav) 4
3071 REMAIN ANONYMOUS (Ire) (bl) 7-12 (4*) W J Smith (1) ....(12 to 1) 5
MEGLIO CHE POSSO (Ire) 7-10 L O'Shea (3)...... (6 to 1) 6
2701 SEAPARK LADY (Ire) 7-8 (6*) J J Behan (5)........(12 to 1) 7
NORTHERN FANCY (Ire) 7-11 (2*) D G O'Shea (8) (20 to 1) 8
305[9] DEARMISTERSHATTER (Ire) 8-5 Joanna Morgan (6) ....(12 to 1) 9
Dist: ¾l, 2½l, ½l, 5½l. 1m 39.40s. (9 Ran).
(Lord White Of Hull), M J Grassick

3274 Coolcullen Maiden (3-y-o and up) £2,243 1½m.................. (4:30)

2518[5] OCEAN BLUE (Ire) (bl) 3-8-7 (4*) P Carberry (1).....(7 to 2) 1
3038[5] TEBRE (USA) (bl) 3-8-11 W J Supple (5)...............(3 to 1) 2
3077[3] DARK HYACINTH (Ire) (bl) 3-8-11 N Byrne (4)...(9 to 4 fav) 3
SYDNEY SUSSEX (Ire) 3-8-8 (6*) J A Heffernan (3)..(5 to 2) 4
2902[7] DANAMORE (Ire) 3-9-0 S Craine (2)...............(11 to 2) 5
Dist: Sht-hd, 5½l, ½l, dist. 3m 32.60s. (5 Ran).
(Michael H Keogh), Declan Gillespie

3275 Heineken Handicap (0-75 3-y-o and up) £2,760 1½m................ (5:00)

2842[2] CALL MY GUEST (Ire) [-] 3-9-0 W J Supple (5)..... (3 to 1) 1
2842* FONTANAYS (Ire) [-] 5-9-3 (5ex) S Craine (6).... (5 to 4 on) 2
3063[7] L-WAY FIRST (Ire) [-] 3-8-0 (2*) D G O'Shea (3).... (10 to 1) 3
1514 MAXWELTON BRAES (Ire) [-] 4-9-12 C F Swan (4) (12 to 1) 4
2901[7] SOLAR FLASH (Ire) [-] 4-7-7 A J Nolan (2)......... (9 to 2) 5
Dist: 2l, ¾l, 15l, 12l. 3m 56.00s. (5 Ran).
(Bezwell Fixings Ltd), Kevin Prendergast

TRAMORE (IRE) (good (races 1,2), good to firm (3))
Wednesday August 11th

3276 Smithwicks QR Handicap (0-75 4-y-o and up) £3,652 2m............. (7:00)

3063[4] NANARCH (USA) [-] 9-11-5 (7*) Mr J Connolly (7)... (7 to 1) 1
298[5] RANDOM PRINCE [-] 9-10-0 Mr S R Murphy (11)... (6 to 1) 2
CLASS ACT [-] 7-9-11 (3*) Miss M Olivefalk (12)... (25 to 1) 3
2693* PAGET [-] 6-10-6 (7*) Mr A K Wyse (10)............(5 to 1) 4
3028[4] COMMAND 'N CONTROL [-] 4-11-0 (7*) Mr K Whelan (6) ....(11 to 2) 5
2841[7] SHAYISTA [-] 8-11-6 (3*) Mr R O'Neill (4)....... (4 to 1 fav) 6
1508[9] PALACE GEM [-] (bl) 6-10-9 (5*) Mr P J Casey (3).. (10 to 1) 7
1141 INDIANA GOLD (Ire) [-] 5-9-8[1] (7*) Miss W Fox (9)..(20 to 1) 8
2693[5] MARIAN YEAR [-] 7-9-7 (7*) Mr P A Roche (5)....... (8 to 1) 9
MISS MUSKY [-] 6-9-9[2] (7*) Mr M Hyland (8)...... (25 to 1) 10
852 ASTRA (Ire) [-] 4-10-13 (7*) Mr E Norris (1)........ (14 to 1) 11
Dist: Nk, sht-hd, hd, 1½l. 3m 46.00s. (11 Ran).
(Mrs Kevin Prendergast), Kevin Prendergast

3277 Shell Unleaded Handicap (0-60 3-y-o and up) £2,590 1¾m............ (7:30)

2296[4] LAKE OF LOUGHREA (Ire) [-] 3-8-7 (6*) B J Walsh (11) ....(8 to 1) 1
2901[4] SPRING RITE [-] (bl) 6-7-1 (6*) P P Murphy (4)....... (7 to 1) 2
2842[4] PREMIER LEAP (Ire) [-] 4-8-13 (8*) B Fenton (5).....(6 to 1) 3
3063[6] RYE HILL QUEEN (Ire) [-] 3-8-8 N G McCullagh (6) (16 to 1) 4

2693³ RIYADH DANCER (Ire) [-] 3-8-0 (8*) R T Fitzpatrick (3) ....(10 to 1) 5
2296⁶ AQUINAS [-] 7-8-10¹ R A Hennessy (8)............(7 to 1) 6
2556 FURTHER NOTICE (Ire) [-] 4-8-3 (2*) R M Burke (9) (14 to 1) 7
2512⁴ SOUND PERFORMANCE (Ire) [-] 4-9-8 (6*) R V Skelly (7) ....(16 to 1) 8
3063⁸ GREEK CHIME (Ire) [-] 4-9-6 (6*) T P Treacy (13)....(9 to 2) 9
2693⁹ SERJITAK [-] 6-8-13 (6*) J R Barry (12)............(8 to 1) 10
VALS CHOICE (Ire) [-] 4-8-5 (6*) B Bowens (2).....(25 to 1) 11
2498³ CONCERT ORCHESTRA (Ire) [-] 4-8-4 D V Smith (1) (8 to 1) 12
2092⁵ VROOM VROOM (Ire) [-] 3-7-12⁵ (8*) P J Smullen (14) ....(33 to 1) 13
2900² NORDIC RACE [-] 6-9-5 (6*) C Everard (10).....(7 to 2 fav) 14

Dist: 1l, 2l, 2l, sht-hd. 3m 6.80s. (14 Ran).

(Bezwell Fixings Ltd), Kevin Prendergast

3278 Curraghmore Maiden (3-y-o and up) £2,245 1m 1f..................(8:30)

2703⁶ STATE PRINCESS (Ire) 3-8-5 (6*) P P Murphy (6)....(5 to 1) 1
3025³ MISS CARMELLA (Ire) 3-8-5 (6*) B J Walsh (3).. (Evens fav) 2
3075⁷ ICEFLOW (Fr) (bl) 3-8-11 N G McCullagh (5).......(8 to 1) 3
2692⁸ KOI CORP 9-9-10⁴ J P Deegan (1)...............(20 to 1) 4
2703⁷ SUTTONIAN (Ire) 4-8-10 (10*) W J Walsh (2).......(3 to 1) 5
VALAMIR (Ire) 3-9-0 D Duggan (4)...............(14 to 1) 6

Dist: ½l, 1½l, 2½l, 6l. 2m 4.60s. (6 Ran).

(Sportsmans Inn Syndicate), D T Hughes

BEVERLEY (good)
Thursday August 12th

Going Correction: NIL (races 1,2,6), PLUS 0.10 (3,4,5)

3279 St John Ambulance Claiming Stakes Class E (2-y-o) £3,106 5f........(2:10)

2814* DANGEROUS SHADOW 7-10 (5*) Darren Moffatt (10) *outpcd and chsd alng hfwy, improved on ins to ld fnl furlong, veered lft, drvn out, fnshd 1st, plcd 3rd.* ....(6 to 4 fav tchd 13 to 8 and 11 to 8) 1D
3133⁴ LADY SHERIFF (bl) 8-9 T Lucas (2) *sn led, clr hfwy, rdn and hdd ins fnl furlong, hmpd cl hme, fnshd second, awarded race*..........(5 to 1 op 9 to 2 tchd 11 to 2) 1
2814⁷ LUCIUS LOCKET (Ire) 8-12 J Fortune (5) *chsd ldg pair, improved und pres to ld briefly ins fnl furlong, crowded and not quicken cl hme, fnshd 3rd, plcd second.* ....(14 to 1 op 8 to 1) 2
3086³ GAELIC STAR (Ire) 8-8 W Ryan (8) *chsd alng to keep up, gd hdwy appr fnl furlong, nrst finish.* ....(13 to 2 op 6 to 1 tchd 7 to 1) 4
3086⁶ HELLABY (bl) 8-4 K Darley (3) *chsd ldg trio, hrd at work 2 fs out, unbl to quicken.* (13 to 2 op 6 to 1 tchd 7 to 1) 5
2668⁸ PAGODA 8-2¹ G Duffield (7) *chsd clr ldr, drvn alng whn hmpd entering fnl furlong, no extr.* ....(15 to 2 op 11 to 2 tchd 8 to 1) 6
3254⁴ MUCKROSS PARK 8-3 J Weaver (9) *outpcd and drvn alng thrght, nvr a factor.* (16 to 1 op 14 to 1 tchd 20 to 1) 7
BOLD JOKER 8-8 K Fallon (6) *sn outpcd and drvn alng, al struggling*........................(33 to 1 op 20 to 1) 8
3098⁴ MONSIEUR PETONG 8-4 P Robinson (4) *veered lft leaving stalls, nvr wnt pace*... (12 to 1 op 6 to 1 tchd 14 to 1) 9
MATABUNGKAY 9-0 N Connorton (1) *backward, outpcd thrght, tld off*....................(33 to 1 op 20 to 1) 10

Dist: 1l, sht-hd, 2½l, 1l, hd, 7l, 2½l, 1½l, 2l. 1m 6.40s. a 4.70s (10 Ran).

(E J Mangan), M W Easterby

3280 Struthers & Carter Sprint Handicap Class D (0-80 3-y-o and up) £3,877 5f ....(2:40)

3094⁶ ADMIRALS REALM [52] 4-8-2 A Mackay (2) *nvr far away, quickened ahead one furlong out, ran on strly.* ....(16 to 1 op 12 to 1 tchd 20 to 1) 1
2910* HERE COMES A STAR [66] 5-9-2 A Clark (6) *patiently rdn, imprvg into midfield whn not clr run 2 fs out, swtchd and hmpd o'r one out, fnshd wl.* ....(13 to 2 op 11 to 2 tchd 7 to 1) 2
3004⁷ SAVAHRA SOUND [68] 8-9-4 S Webster (1) *chsd alng on outsd, effrt o'r one furlong out, styd on same pace.* ....(25 to 1 op 20 to 1) 3
3094* KABCAST [54] (bl) 8-8-4 (7ex) S Wood (11) *set gd pace, rdn and hdd one furlong out, no extr.* ....(5 to 1 fav op 9 to 2) 4
2872* ANOTHER LANE [70] 6-9-6 P Robinson (10) *bustled alng in midfield, improved on outisde appr fnl furlong, nrst finish*.......................(6 to 1 tchd 7 to 1) 5
2969⁸ CRYSTAL JACK (Fr) [74] (v) 5-9-10 S Perks (12) *broke wl to show speed for o'r 3 fs, no extr*................(12 to 1) 6
3184³ SLADES HILL [62] 6-8-12 K Darley (3) *bustled alng in midfield, effrt 2 fs out, not pace to chal.* ....(8 to 1 tchd 10 to 1) 7
2935² PALLIUM (Ire) [65] 5-9-1 K Fallon (7) *sluggish strt, imprvg on ins whn not clr run o'r one furlong out, not rcvr.* ....(7 to 1 tchd 8 to 1) 8
3085⁵ SIR TASKER [56] 5-8-1 (5*) Darren Moffatt (5) *chsd ldrs, hrd at work 2 fs out, fdd*..............(16 to 1 op 12 to 1) 9
3081⁷ LOVE LEGEND [68] (v) 8-8-13 (5*) A Procter (8) *wtd wth, effrt on ins whn hmpd o'r one furlong out, swtchd lft, nvr able to chal*..............................(12 to 1) 10
3136³ SHE'S SMART [78] 5-10-0 M Birch (13) *gd speed on ins for o'r 3 fs, fdd*..............(12 to 1 op 10 to 1) 11
3238² DRUM SERGEANT [76] (bl) 6-9-12 J Weaver (14) *chsd ldrs, effrt on ins whn not much room o'r one furlong out, eased when btn*....................(8 to 1 tchd 9 to 1) 12
2731⁹ OUBECK [66] 3-8-12 B Raymond (4) *settled midfield, drvn alng to go pace hfwy, btn 2 fs out*...(10 to 1 op 8 to 1) 13

Dist: 3½l, nk, hd, ½l, 1½l, nk, 1½l, sht-hd, 2l, 3½l. 1m 3.90s. a 2.20s (13 Ran).

SR: 44/44/45/30/44/42/29/26/16/ (P W Leslie), B A McMahon

3281 Lady Taverners Nursery Class D (2-y-o) £4,258 7f 100yds...........(3:10)

2274* HAM N'EGGS [73] 9-1 G Duffield (16) *made all, pushed alng to quicken last 2 fs, styd on stoutly.* ....(3 to 1 fav tchd 7 to 2 and 11 to 4) 1
3052⁴ BALLARD RING (Ire) [59] 8-1 J Fanning (6) *steadied strt, brght wide to improve o'r 2 fs out, kpt on wl, not rch wnr*...............................(14 to 1 op 16 to 1) 2
2167* CALL TO MIND (Ire) [77] 9-5 M Birch (5) *al hndy, ev ch and drvn alng 2 fs out, kpt on same pace.* ....(9 to 1 op 7 to 1 tchd 10 to 1) 3
2876³ HASTY BANK [59] 8-1 L Charnock (1) *nvr far away, ev ch and drvn alng last 2 fs, no extr*...... (4 to 1 op 7 to 2) 4
2772² SURPRISE BREEZE [55] 7-11 N Carlisle (4) *al wl plcd, drvn alng whn pace lifted 2 fs out, no extr.* ....(16 to 1 op 14 to 1) 5
2539⁵ OVIDEO [66] 8-8 J Lowe (11) *chsd alng in midfield, effrt o'r 2 fs out, no imprsn*.......... (10 to 1 tchd 12 to 1) 6
3141² UP THE MARINERS (Ire) [58] 8-0 A Mackay (14) *pressed wnr for o'r 4 fs, fdd*..................(16 to 1 op 14 to 1) 7
2695⁶ GLENVALLY [65] 8-7 P Robinson (8) *beh and drvn alng hfwy, some late hdwy, nvr dngrs.* (16 to 1 op 14 to 1) 8
1889⁸ FORREST MASTER (Ire) [53] 7-4 (5*) Darren Moffatt (2) *chsd ldg bunch, came wide to join issue o'r 2 fs out, fdd appr fnl furlong*........................(25 to 1 op 20 to 1) 9
1763⁵ JOHNNIE THE JOKER [60] 8-2 Dale Gibson (9) *chsd alng in midfield hfwy, not pace of ldrs.* (12 to 1 tchd 14 to 1) 10
3218 PARISH WALK (Ire) [62] 7-11 (7*) F Savage (3) *sn outpcd and drvn alng, nvr a factor*........................(20 to 1) 11
3141⁵ BERNIE'S SISTER (Ire) [58] 8-0 G Bardwell (7) *sluggish strt, struggling hfwy, nvr a factor*.....(25 to 1 op 16 to 1) 12
2852* MIDNIGHT MAGPIE (Ire) [64] 8-6 K Fallon (12) *unruly in stalls, drvn alng to keep in tch hfwy, sn btn.* ....(15 to 2 op 11 to 2 tchd 8 to 1) 13
3189 TILQUHILLIE ROSE [57] 7-11¹ (3*) S Maloney (15) *chsd ldg bunch for o'r 4 fs, fdd*........................(20 to 1) 14
2890² NEW INN [79] 9-7 W Ryan (13) *unruly in stalls, steadied strt, lost tch hfwy, tld off.* ....(10 to 1 tchd 11 to 1 and 12 to 1) 15

Dist: 2l, nk, 5l, 2½l, ½l, 1l, 1½l, ½l, 1½l, hd. 1m 36.00s. a 5.70s (15 Ran).

SR: 27/7/24/-/-/-/ (Peter Hammond), R Hannon

3282 Bog Trotter Handicap Class C (0-90 3-y-o and up) £5,089 1m 1f 207yds ....(3:40)

2708³ BAY QUEEN [75] 3-8-9 (3*) M Fenton (6) *patiently rdn, quickened up to ld o'r 2 fs out, forged clr.* ....(7 to 1 tchd 8 to 1) 1
3033* FAIR FLYER (Ire) [60] 4-8-6 (5ex) R P Elliott (3) *wtd wth, gd hdwy to take clr order o'r 2 fs out, styd on, not rch wnr.* ....(8 to 1 op 7 to 1) 2
2444* SEEK THE PEARL [76] 3-8-13 P Robinson (4) *tucked away in midfield, drvn through last 2 fs, styd on same pace.* ....(5 to 1 op 9 to 2 tchd 11 to 2) 3
3058⁴ MBULWA [48] 7-7-8 L Charnock (1) *dictated pace till hdd o'r 2 fs out, sn rdn and btn*....................(7 to 1) 4
1275 RAFTERS [75] 4-9-7 N Day (2) *trkd ldg trio, feeling pace o'r 2 fs out, sn rdn and no extr*.....(12 to 1 op 8 to 1) 5
2328⁶ VALLANCE [82] 5-9-9 (5*) J Tate (9) *wth ldr, drvn alng o'r 2 fs out, wknd quickly*.... (7 to 1 op 6 to 1 tchd 8 to 1) 6
3036² JERVIA [80] 3-9-3 G Duffield (5) *nvr far away, struggling whn pace lifted o'r 2 fs out, sn btn*... (9 to 1 op 7 to 1) 7
3010⁵ WASSL THIS THEN (Ire) [63] 4-8-9 K Darley (8) *co'red up on ins, hmpd by faller bend appr hfwy, sn lost tch.* ....(10 to 1 tchd 12 to 1) 8
2961⁷ LYFORD CAY (Ire) [83] (bl) 3-9-1 (5*) Stephen Davies (7) *steadied leaving stalls, clipped heels of rival and slpd up bend appr hfwy*............(9 to 4 fav op 7 to 2) su

Dist: 12l, sht-hd, 2l, sht-hd, 10l, nk, 12l. 2m 7.00s. a 5.60s (9 Ran).

SR: 52/22/28/5/31/18/6/-/-/ (B J Warren), M Bell

3283 Toll Gavel Selling Stakes Class E (3-y-o and up) £2,950 2m 35yds....(4:10)

2891² POST IMPRESSIONIST (Ire) 4-9-5 K Darley (3) *dsptd ld, crossed o'r to lead on stands side over 2 fs out, styd on wl ins last*..........(13 to 8 op 7 to 4 tchd 6 to 4) 1
2694³ RAVENSPUR (Ire) 3-8-5 J Weaver (2) *patiently rdn, improved gng wl o'r 2 fulrongs out, ridden and swshd tail, not keen*.......................(6 to 1 op 8 to 1) 2

2353^{7} REACH FOR GLORY 4-9-6 A Culhane (7) *trkd ldg quartet, ev ch and drvn alng last 2 fs, one pace.* .... (14 to 1 op 10 to 1 tchd 16 to 1) 3

2871^{5} FAMOUS BEAUTY 6-9-1 W Ryan (4) *settled gng wl, prmsg effrt 2 fs out, rdn and not run on.* .... (6 to 4 fav op 5 to 4 tchd 7 to 4) 4

1702 ALIZARI (USA) 4-9-6 S Webster (1) *pressed ldg pair, struggling to hold pl hfwy, sn lost tch.* (16 to 1 op 14 to 1) 5

3113^{6} NEWGATESKY 3-8-0 J Fanning (6) *slight ld till hdd o'r 2 fs out, wknd quickly*..................(25 to 1) 6

TRENTSIDE VALOUR (v) 8-9-1 (5*) K Rutter (5) *chsd ldg trio to hfwy, sn lost tch, tld off*...................(25 to 1) 7

Dist: 2l, ½l, 5l, 12l, 5l, dist. 3m 47.00s. a 18.00s (7 Ran).

(David Cahal), J L Harris

3284 EBF Routh Maiden Fillies' Stakes Class D (2-y-o) £3,913 5f........(4:40)

3086^{2} IVA'S FLYER (Ire) 8-11 L Charnock (1) *broke smartly, crossed o'r to stands side, made all, clr fnl furlong.* ....(5 to 1 op 7 to 2) 1

2817^{7} SKIPTAMALOO 8-11 P Robinson (6) *sluggish strt, bustled alng to improve hfwy, styd on, not rch wnr.* ....(14 to 1 tchd 16 to 1) 2

3114^{2} RANKAIDADE 8-11 S Perks (3) *chsd wnr, hrd at work last 2 fs, no extr*........................ (9 to 2 op 7 to 2) 3

2994^{8} EXOTIC FOREST 8-11 G Duffield (8) *chsd alng to improve frm off the pace last 2 fs, nvr nrr*....(11 to 2 op 5 to 1) 4

968^{6} TRYSAIL 8-11 K Darley (7) *outpcd and drvn alng hfwy, styd on last 2 fs, nvr nrr*............(8 to 1 op 5 to 1) 5

3156^{6} MY GALLERY (Ire) 8-11 A Mackay (5) *chsd alng to go pace aftr 3 fs, sn btn*........(5 to 1 op 9 to 2 tchd 11 to 2) 6

3001^{9} MILLIE'S DREAM 8-11 W Ryan (2) *early speed, struggling hfwy, sn btn*..................................(8 to 1) 7

2949^{2} MISS PIGALLE 8-11 J Fanning (4) *broke wl, drvn alng to hold pl hfwy, sn btn.* (7 to 2 fav op 4 to 1 tchd 9 to 2) 8

Dist: 2½l, ¾l, 2½l, 2l, 3½l, 1½l, 3l. 1m 6.00s. a 4.30s (8 Ran).
SR: 11/1/-/-/-/ (Mrs Iva Winton), J Berry

DEAUVILLE (FR) (good)
Thursday August 12th
Going Correction: PLUS 0.65 sec. per fur.

3285 Prix de Tourgeville (Listed) (3-y-o) £14,337 1m.................... (2:35)

BON POINT 8-11 T Jarnet,............................ 1

SANDCREEK (Ire) 8-11 D Boeuf,........................ 2

2208^{2} TRUE BEARING (USA) 8-11 F Head,..................... 3

1791^{3} BERINSFIELD 8-11 S Guillot,......................... 4

2627* BEAUCHAMP HERO 8-11 L Piggott,..................... 8

Dist: Sht-nk, 1½l, hd, 2½l, hd, 2½l, 2l, hd, 6l. 1m 42.30s. a 7.60s (10 Ran).
SR: 61/60/55/54/46/ (K Abdulla), A Fabre

SALISBURY (good)
Thursday August 12th
Going Correction: PLUS 0.20 sec. per fur. (races 1,2,4,5,6,7), PLUS 0.05 (3)

3286 Broad Chalke Maiden Fillies Stakes Class D (3-y-o) £3,523 6f 212yds (2:20)

752^{2} GHOST TREE (Ire) 8-11 M Roberts (12) *trkd ldrs, al gng wl, shaken up to ld ins fnl furlong, not extended.* ....(6 to 5 fav op 5 to 4 on tchd 5 to 4) 1

JASARAH (Ire) 8-11 W Carson (9) *cl up, led o'r 3 fs out till ins last, ran on wl*.....................(14 to 1 op 7 to 1) 2

2508^{4} DESERT VENUS 8-11 W R Swinburn (6) *chsd ldrs, hrd rdn o'r one furlong out, kpt on.* .... (14 to 1 op 8 to 1 tchd 16 to 1) 3

2993^{2} COMMON LAW (Ire) 8-11 Pat Eddery (5) *led till o'r 3 fs out, one pace*............(100 to 30 op 9 to 4 tchd 7 to 2). 4

2961^{8} BOBBIE DEE 8-11 W Newnes (1) *hld up beh ldrs, rdn and cld 2 fs out, sn one pace*...........(5 to 1 tchd 7 to 1) 5

POLAR MOON 8-11 A Munro (3) *keen hold early, trkd ldrs, rdn alng 2 fs out, outpcd*... (33 to 1 tchd 25 to 1) 6

2580^{9} CIRCLE OF CHALK (Fr) 8-11 S Raymont (11) *in tch, effrt 3 fs out, btn 2 out*.....(16 to 1 op 14 to 1 tchd 20 to 1) 7

3225 JOAN'S GIFT 8-11 T Williams (7) *sn beh, tld off.* .... (50 to 1 op 33 to 1 tchd 66 to 1) 8

2596^{9} CUT FINE 8-11 Paul Eddery (10) *cl up, hrd rdn 3 fs out, sn btn, tld off*..........(33 to 1 op 16 to 1 tchd 40 to 1) 9

TOUCHEE BOUCHEE 8-11 T Quinn (2) *trkd ldrs till wknd blw 3 fs out, tld off*...............(33 to 1 op 16 to 1) 10

MYJINKA 8-11 J Williams (8) *dwlt, al beh, tld off.* ....(100 to 1 op 33 to 1 tchd 150 to 1) 11

Dist: ¾l, 5l, ½l, 2l, 3l, hd, 15l, 5l, 2l, 20l. 1m 29.88s. a 4.28s (11 Ran).
SR: 54/52/37/35/29/20/19/-/-/ (Sheikh Mohammed), J H M Gosden

3287 Tattersalls Maiden Auction Series Stakes Qualifier Class E (2-y-o) £3,390 6f.. (2:50)

3052^{2} LADY-BO-K 8-2 R Hills (3) *al prmnt gng wl, led one and a half fs out, ran on well.* (9 to 1 op 6 to 1 tchd 10 to 1) 1

3031^{3} STAR JAZZ (Ire) 8-5 Paul Eddery (4) *al prmnt, led 3 fs out to one and a half out, no extr.* .... (11 to 2 op 4 to 1 tchd 6 to 1) 2

JAYANNPEE 8-9 L Dettori (6) *chsd ldrs, hdwy and ev ch appr fnl furlong, ran on one pace.* (11 to 2 op 9 to 2) 3

2571^{9} PLATINI (Ire) 8-11 M Roberts (17) *sn pushed alng in rear, rdn and hdwy 2 fs out, one pace ins last.* ....(15 to 2 op 6 to 1 tchd 8 to 1) 4

PRINCE OF ANITA (Ire) 8-13 D Holland (16) *beh, ran on fnl 2 fs, nvr nrr*........... (40 to 1 op 33 to 1 tchd 50 to 1) 5

PARTY LINE 8-6 A Munro (8) *hdwy 2 fs out, styd on.* ....(25 to 1 op 16 to 1 tchd 33 to 1) 6

2659^{3} NOBLE SPIRIT (Ire) 8-11 Pat Eddery (12) *chsd ldrs till wknd 2 fs out*...........................(6 to 1 tchd 8 to 1) 7

POLAR QUEST 8-8 J Carroll (9) *nvr dngrs.* ....(25 to 1 op 20 to 1) 8

3016^{5} MIDSEAS 8-8 J Reid (14) *trkd ldrs till wknd 2 fs out.* ....(33 to 1 op 25 to 1) 9

2895^{2} GOOD FETCH 8-2 T Quinn (11) *prmnt, ev ch 2 fs out, sn btn*..........................(4 to 1 fav op 3 to 1) 10

TRADE WIND 8-13 J Williams (18) *strted slwly, beh till moderate late prog*......................... (20 to 1) 11

2895^{7} INFRA BLUE (Ire) 8-2 (3*) D Harrison (7) *trkd ldrs, ev ch 2 fs out, sn btn*........................(25 to 1 op 20 to 1) 12

3104^{4} HENRY'S LUCK 8-8 S Whitworth (15) *sn tracking ldrs, ev ch 2 fs out, wknd*.........................(25 to 1 op 20 to 1) 13

FOOT TAPPER (Ire) 8-8 R Price (5) *al beh.* ....(40 to 1 op 33 to 1 tchd 50 to 1) 14

2571 SEE MY GUEST (Fr) 8-5 S Dawson (10) *nvr dngrs.* ....(50 to 1 tchd 66 to 1) 15

2916^{3} JOYRIDER 8-7 M Hills (13) *beh hfwy.* ....(16 to 1 op 8 to 1 tchd 20 to 1) 16

2817^{2} SANGARE (Ire) 8-8 W Carson (2) *al beh.* ....(8 to 1 op 6 to 1 tchd 9 to 1) 17

718^{6} NO WHAT I MEAN (Ire) 8-1 T Williams (1) *led to 3 fs out, wknd, tld off*....... (40 to 1 op 33 to 1 tchd 50 to 1) 18

Dist: ¾l, ¾l, 3l, ½l, ½l, ¾l, 1l, ¾l, sht-hd, 5l. 1m 17.74s. a 5.24s (18 Ran).
SR: 7/7/8/-/-/-/ (Ms Theresa McEvoy), Bob Jones

3288 Harcros Timber & Building Supplies Stayers Championship Series Handicap Qualifier Class E (0-70 3-y-o and up) £4,077 1¾m................ (3:20)

3021^{9} SUMMER WIND (Ire) [66] 3-8-11 R Cochrane (5) *led 2 fs, cl up, led o'r 3 out, rdn and styd on wl.* ....(11 to 1 op 10 to 1 tchd 12 to 1) 1

2422* HIGH SUMMER [67] 3-8-12 L Dettori (16) *trkd ldrs, rdn 2 fs out, kpt on*.............. (5 to 1 jt-fav op 7 to 1) 2

2729^{2} ALLMOSA [60] 4-9-4 Paul Eddery (3) *trkd ldrs, rdn and one pace fnl 2 fs*..........(10 to 1 op 7 to 1 tchd 11 to 1) 3

2865^{3} SWIFT ROMANCE (Ire) [49] 5-8-7 S Whitworth (9) *hld up, hdwy o'r 2 fs out, styd on*.......(14 to 1 tchd 16 to 1) 4

LAST CONQUEST (Ire) [63] 4-9-7 D Biggs (7) *trkd ldrs, rdn and one pace fnl 3 fs.* (25 to 1 op 20 to 1 tchd 33 to 1) 5

3066^{2} FANATICAL (USA) [46] 7-8-4 W Newnes (10) *hld up beh, hdwy o'r one furlong out, styd on.* ....(20 to 1 tchd 25 to 1) 6

2669^{5} EDGE OF DARKNESS [52] 4-8-7 (3*) D Harrison (4) *chsd ldrs, ch o'r 2 fs out, sn btn.* .... (11 to 1 op 10 to 1 tchd 12 to 1) 7

2950^{2} WHITE RIVER [40] 7-7-12 T Williams (15) *hdwy o'r 5 fs out, ch 2 out, rdn and wknd quickly*.... (10 to 1 op 8 to 1) 8

3087^{4} SINGING REPLY (USA) [36] 5-7-8 A Tucker (2) *beh, pushed alng and hdwy 5 fs out, hrd rdn 2 out, sn btn.* ....(12 to 1 op 10 to 1 tchd 14 to 1) 9

3010^{2} ADDICTED TO LOVE [62] (bl) 4-9-6 W R Swinburn (12) *hld up, hdwy o'r 4 fs out, wknd over 2 out, eased appr last.* .... (7 to 1 op 6 to 1 tchd 15 to 2) 10

3021^{2} WITH GUSTO [43] 6-8-1 W Carson (11) *hld up rear, effrt 5 fs out, no imprsn.* (5 to 1 jt-fav op 9 to 2 tchd 11 to 2) 11+

2662 SUDANOR (Ire) [35] 4-7-3[1] (5*) D Wright (17) *al rear.* ....(25 to 1 op 20 to 1) 11+

SHERINGA [70] 4-10-0 J Williams (1) *beh, effrt and hdwy 3 fs out, sn btn*.......................(25 to 1 op 20 to 1) 13

1951^{9} CHARMED LIFE [46] 4-8-4 N Adams (8) *al beh.* ....(11 to 1 op 8 to 1) 14

2727^{5} HATTA RIVER (USA) [70] (bl) 3-9-1 M Roberts (13) *led aftr 2 fs, rcd freely, hdd o'r 3 out, wknd quickly.* ....(12 to 1 op 8 to 1) 15

Dist: 4l, 2l, 2l, 2l, ½l, 2l, 4l, 1½l, 3½l, 4l. 3m 3.28s. a 5.58s (Flag start) (15 Ran).
SR: 48/41/43/28/38/20/22/2/-/ (Ray Richards), D R C Elsworth

3289 Whitchurch Conditions Stakes Class C (2-y-o) £5,402 6f 212yds.........(3:50)

2990* STAR TALENT (USA) 8-12 R Cochrane (3) *trkd ldr, pld out 2 fs out, quickened and sn led, pushed out.* ....(7 to 4 op 9 to 4) 1

2571* BAROSSA VALLEY (Ire) 8-12 J Reid (1) *hld up in tch, ev ch 2 fs out, shaken up and ran on same pace ins last.* .... (13 to 8 fav op 11 to 10 tchd 7 to 4) 2

1920^{2} REPREHEND 8-12 Pat Eddery (2) *led till blw 2 fs out, hrd rdn appr last, no extr*............ (9 to 4 op 7 to 4) 3

Dist: 1½l, nk. 1m 34.75s. a 9.15s (3 Ran).

(J C Smith), D R C Elsworth

3290 Tote Bookmakers Handicap Class C (0-90 3-y-o and up) £6,262 1m... (4:20)

2940[4] POLAR STORM (Ire) [70] 3-8-5 J Williams (1) *trkd ldrs, led o'r 2 fs out, ran on wl, cmftbly.* ...(9 to 1 op 8 to 1 tchd 10 to 1) 1
2622[8] CARELAMAN [85] 3-9-6 L Dettori (2) *hld up beh, hdwy 2 fs out, ran on, no imprsn on wnr ins last.* ...(8 to 1 op 10 to 1 tchd 12 to 1) 2
2930[3] CAMDEN'S RANSOM (USA) [73] 6-9-1 R Cochrane (3) *hld up beh, hdwy and not clr run o'r one furlong out, ran on ins last*...(7 to 1 op 8 to 1 tchd 10 to 1) 3
3093[2] MOON SPIN [78] 4-9-6 Paul Eddery (5) *hld up, not clr run o'r 2 fs out, hdwy over one out, one pace ins last.* ...(7 to 1 tchd 8 to 1) 4
2816[3] WELLINGTON ROCK (USA) [75] 4-9-3 W Newnes (11) *hld up beh ldrs, rdn o'r one furlong out, one pace.* ...(11 to 1 op 10 to 1 tchd 12 to 1) 5
2930[2] LADY LACEY [57] (v) 6-7-6 (7*) N Varley (4) *mid-div, rdn and hdwy o'r one furlong out, sn swtchd rght, one pace.* ...(6 to 1 op 5 to 1) 6
2961 AJDAYT (USA) [85] 3-9-6 M Roberts (8) *trkd ldrs, rdn 2 fs out, one pace*...(7 to 1 op 6 to 1 tchd 8 to 1) 7
2794[3] LORD OBERON (Ire) [69] (v) 5-8-11 T Quinn (9) *co'red up beh ldrs, ev ch 2 fs out, sn btn.* ...(11 to 2 fav op 5 to 1 tchd 6 to 1) 8
2966* DUCKEY FUZZ [56] 5-7-7 (5*) D Wright (12) *cl up, ev ch o'r 2 fs out, btn over one out*...(11 to 1 op 10 to 1) 9
3175[8] NORTH ESK (USA) [65] 4-8-7 A Munro (7) *cl up till wknd o'r 2 fs out*...(16 to 1 op 14 to 1) 10
1919[4] EXHIBIT AIR (Ire) [74] 3-8-9 Pat Eddery (6) *led till o'r 2 fs out, wknd*...(11 to 1 op 8 to 1) 11
2758 RAKIS (Ire) [81] 3-9-2 W Carson (13) *rcd alone far side, jnd main grp o'r 3 fs out, sn btn, tld off.* ...(20 to 1 op 14 to 1) 12

Dist: 2½l, 2l, nk, ½l, 2l, nk, 2l, 1½l, 1½l, 3½l. 1m 45.27s. a 5.77s (12 Ran).
SR: 28/35/24/28/23/-/19/4/-/ (Dexam International Limited), Lady Herries

3291 Amesbury Fillies Conditions Stakes Class D (3-y-o and up) £3,720 5f (4:50)

2927[5] BUNTY BOO 4-9-6 T Quinn (3) *trkd ldrs, hrd rdn o'r one furlong out, ran on to ld ins last.* ...(9 to 4 op 2 to 1 tchd 5 to 2) 1
2855* LUCKY PARKES 3-9-8 J Carroll (9) *cl up, led hfwy till ins fnl furlong, no extr.* (5 to 4 fav op 7 to 4 tchd 2 to 1) 2
2971[2] SHEILA'S SECRET (Ire) 3-9-4 J Reid (1) *cl up, evrey ch entering fnl furlong, one pace und pres.* ...(13 to 2 op 5 to 1) 3
2971[3] YAKIN (USA) 3-8-10 R Hills (6) *hld up beh, hdwy 2 fs out, styd on one pace*...(20 to 1 op 14 to 1) 4
2028[5] WAFFLE ON 3-9-0 W R Swinburn (2) *beh, ran on frm o'r one furlong out, nrst finish*...(7 to 1 op 8 to 1) 5
2753 MISS VAXETTE 4-9-5 (7*) M Humphries (7) *hld up, rdn to improve o'r 2 fs out, sn one pace*...(16 to 1 op 10 to 1) 6
2971[7] BROCKTON DANCER (bl) 3-8-7 (7*) Mark Denaro (8) *slwly into strd, nvr on terms.* ...(20 to 1 op 12 to 1 tchd 25 to 1) 7
1000 INHERENT MAGIC (Ire) 4-9-5 M Roberts (5) *trkd ldrs, pushed alng hfwy, btn 2 fs out, eased.* ...(25 to 1 op 14 to 1) 8
2522 SIMPLY SOOTY (bl) 3-9-0 S Whitworth (4) *led to hfwy, sn wknd*...(33 to 1 op 16 to 1 tchd 40 to 1) 9

Dist: 1l, nk, hd, hd, 2½l, 2l, ½l, 2l. 1m 2.67s. a 2.87s (9 Ran).
SR: 69/67/62/53/56/58/38/41/28/ (Mrs R C Mayall), B A McMahon

3292 Levy Board Handicap Class E (0-70 3-y-o and up) £3,287 6f......... (5:20)

3011[6] AGWA [38] 4-7-11 F Norton (1) *cl up, led hfwy, rdn out.* ...(9 to 2 op 7 to 2 tchd 5 to 1) 1
2671[4] FACE THE FUTURE [61] 4-9-6 W R Swinburn (8) *beh, hdwy 2 fs out, ran on ins last.* ...(7 to 2 fav op 9 to 2 tchd 5 to 1) 2
2995[7] AROOM [65] (bl) 3-9-5 W Carson (3) *prmnt, ev ch one furlong out, one pace*...(7 to 1 op 6 to 1) 3
3100[2] UNVEILED [51] 5-8-3 (7*) S Drowne (6) *mid-div, rdn o'r 2 fs out, hdwy over one out, kpt on und pres.* ...(15 to 2 op 8 to 1 tchd 9 to 1) 4
2868[4] HARRY'S COMING [57] 9-9-2 M Hills (10) *sn pushed alng, hdwy o'r one furlong out, one pace ins last.* ...(5 to 1 op 9 to 2) 5
2712[7] SLIVOVITZ [48] (bl) 3-8-2 M Roberts (7) *led to hfwy, wknd 2 fs out, eased ins last*...(8 to 1 tchd 10 to 1) 6
3020[2] WILD AND LOOSE [67] 5-9-5 (7*) Tracey Purseglove (5) *beh, hdwy o'r 2 fs out, btn over one out.* ...(12 to 1 op 10 to 1 tchd 14 to 1) 7
2938 BAYFAN (Ire) [43] (bl) 3-7-11 A McGlone (4) *chsd ldrs, rdn o'r 2 fs out, sn btn*...(50 to 1 op 33 to 1 tchd 66 to 1) 8
2549[6] GALLANT HOPE [41] (bl) 11-8-0 J Quinn (2) *chsd ldrs till wknd o'r 2 fs out*...(14 to 1 op 10 to 1) 9
2660[6] DONTDRESSFORDINNER [52] 3-8-1 (5*) D Wright (9) *mid-div, pushed alng hfwy, sn beh.* ...(20 to 1 op 16 to 1 tchd 25 to 1) 10

Dist: ¾l, ½l, ¾l, 2l, 3½l, 3l, 2l, nk, 6l. 1m 16.64s. a 4.14s (10 Ran).

SR: 24/44/41/29/27/-/11/-/-/ (I A Baker), R J O'Sullivan

TRAMORE (IRE) (good) Thursday August 12th

3293 Seaside Maiden (3-y-o and up) £2,275 1¾m......................... (5:30)

2902[2] NO DUNCE (Ire) 3-8-2 (6*) J J Behan (1)........(6 to 4 on) 1
1014[3] SUNSET CAFE (Ire) (bl) 3-8-4 (4*) W J Smith (5).... (6 to 1) 2
3076 WINTER DREAMS (Ire) 4-9-3 (4*) P Carberry (4).... (5 to 1) 3
2881 KIDAMIYA (Ire) (bl) 3-8-8 N G McCullagh (2)........(6 to 1) su

Dist: 6l, 25l. 3m 5.80s. (4 Ran).
(Mrs P Mullins), P Mullins

3294 Carrolls Festival Handicap (0-70 3-y-o and up) £2,935 1m 1f........... (7:30)

3112[4] MORNING NURSE (Ire) [-] 4-8-13 (4*) P Carberry (2) (10 to 1) 1
2463[3] FLORAL STREET [-] 4-9-7 (6*) C Everard (12)..... (10 to 1) 2
SCOTSMAN'S BAY (Ire) [-] 4-8-5 (6*) J J Behan (4) (10 to 1) 3
3160[3] WHAT A PLEASURE (Ire) [-] 3-9-0 (6*) B J Walsh (15) (5 to 1) 4
3112[2] VISTAGE (Ire) [-] 5-9-11 N Byrne (6)........ (100 to 30 fav) 5
2667[6] MYRO BALANNE (Ire) [-] 3-8-5 (4*) W J Smith (11) (20 to 1) 6
2901[8] ALBERTA ROSE (Ire) [-] 4-9-6 (6*) J R Barry (3)..... (6 to 1) 7
2842 DARK SWAN (Ire) [-] 3-9-0 (2*) D G O'Shea (13).... (14 to 1) 8
2677[8] CARAVELLE LAD (Ire) [-] 3-8-11 P V Gilson (7).... (14 to 1) 9
2702 TINA'S CHARM (Ire) [-] 4-9-4 (8*) R T Fitzpatrick (10) ...(25 to 1) 10
3076[9] ALDENA (Ire) [-] 3-7-11 Joanna Morgan (1)....... (20 to 1) 11
3028[9] VLADIMIR'S WAY (Ire) [-] 4-9-11 C F Swan (14)....(12 to 1) 12
3075[6] MISS MARESE (Ire) [-] (bl) 3-8-11 (6*) R V Skelly (8) (20 to 1) 13
3111[4] SILVER JAR (Ire) [-] 3-8-1 (8*) P J Smullen (9)..... (10 to 1) 14
3160[8] TIGNES (Ire) [-] 5-8-8 J F Egan (5)............... (10 to 1) 15

Dist: Sht-hd, nk, hd, 2l. 2m 1.10s. (15 Ran).
(Garrett J Freyne), Niall Madden

3295 Dunmore East Opportunity Maiden (4-y-o and up) £2,245 2m.......... (8:00)

2324[8] THIS IS MY LIFE (Ire) 4-8-11 (6*) C Everard (2)..(2 to 1 fav) 1
BRAVE HENRY 5-8-13 (4*) W J Smith (11)........(10 to 1) 2
2516[6] BROWN TOP 6-8-9 (8*) B Fenton (10)............(10 to 1) 3
RALPH SQUARE (bl) 5-8-9 (8*) R T Fitzpatrick (3)..(14 to 1) 4
SAD COMMENTARY 6-8-11 (6*) P P Murphy (7)...(12 to 1) 5
FIGHTING TALK (USA) 4-8-13 (4*) P Carberry (8)..(10 to 1) 6
MARYJO (Ire) 4-8-8 (6*) J J Behan (4)............(20 to 1) 7
KILCSEM EILE (Ire) 4-8-8 (6*) R V Skelly (13)......(14 to 1) 8
LORD GREYSTONES 6-9-3 D V Smith (9).......... (8 to 1) 9
2222[4] AFAWI (Ire) 5-9-3 N Byrne (12)................ (4 to 1) 10
3077 KAWA-KAWA 6-9-0 J F Egan (6)................(10 to 1) 11
CHUCK'S TREASURE (Ire) 4-8-9 (8*) P J Smullen (5) ...(12 to 1) 12
OZONE LASS (Ire) (bl) 5-8-8 (6*) B J Walsh (1).....(20 to 1) 13

Dist: 2l, ¾l, 2½l, 20l. 3m 45.70s. (13 Ran).
(P M Grace), E P Harty

3296 Portlaw Handicap (0-60 4-y-o and up) £2,245 1m 1f................... (8:30)

3076[3] THE BOWER (Ire) [-] (bl) 4-9-3 P V Gilson (7)....... (7 to 2) 1
3076[6] BOLERO DANCER (Ire) [-] 5-8-10 (6*) R V Skelly (9) (14 to 1) 2+
3076[7] BLUES COMPOSER (Ire) [-] 4-9-6 W J Supple (8) ...(7 to 4 fav) 2+
3160 OUT OF STEP (Ire) [-] 4-8-2 (6*) J J Behan (12).... (14 to 1) 4
2782[9] ACCELL (Ire) [-] 4-9-4 (4*) P Carberry (6).........(6 to 1) 5
3112[8] SON OF TEMPO (Ire) [-] 4-8-8 N G McCullagh (11) (12 to 1) 6
2842[6] JUST ONE CANALETTO [-] 5-8-13 (6*) C Everard (2) (7 to 1) 7
2556[9] ICANSEEFORMILES (Ire) [-] 5-8-2 (8*) R T Fitzpatrick (10) ...(16 to 1) 8
2511[4] WHY ME LINDA (Ire) [-] 4-9-10 D Manning (1)..... (14 to 1) 9
2484[9] SHERAVISION (Ire) [-] 4-9-4 D Duggan (5)......... (16 to 1) 10
2879[5] TAJANAMA (Ire) [-] 5-8-11 (4*) W J Smith (4)...... (10 to 1) 11
3242[8] SHEBA'S PAL [-] 6-8-10 N Byrne (3)............. (25 to 1) 12

Dist: 1l, dd-ht, 2l, ¾l. 2m 1.50s. (12 Ran).
(Mrs C Collins), C Collins

DUNDALK (IRE) (good) Friday August 13th

3297 Mullacrew Maiden (3-y-o) £2,245 7f 166yds.......................... (6:15)

CORTIJA PARK (Ire) 8-7 (4*) P Carberry (3).........(5 to 1) 1
2483[3] MARY'S CASE (Ire) 9-0 C Roche (6)...............(5 to 1) 2
2320[6] KUDDAM (Ire) 8-11 M J Kinane (4)............ (7 to 4 fav) 3
2779[6] BELLISSI (Ire) 8-3 (8*) P J Smullen (5)............. (9 to 2) 4
2903[6] MY KERRY DANCER (USA) 9-0 K J Manning (2)....(2 to 1) 5
BOSTON VIEW (Ire) 8-11 J P Murtagh (1).........(16 to 1) 6

Dist: Nk, sht-hd, ½l, 1l. 1m 39.40s. (6 Ran).
(Mrs J R Mullion), D T Hughes

3298 Omeath Handicap (0-65 3-y-o) £2,245 1m 1f.......................... (6:45)

3028* PHASE IN [-] 9-10 (5ex) M J Kinane (7).........(5 to 4 on) 1
3112* MY GOSSIP (Ire) [-] 8-11 (5ex) J P Murtagh (4).....(2 to 1) 2
3076 CHAMPAGNE NIGHT (Fr) [-] 8-11 (8*) P J Smullen (8) ....(12 to 1) 3
2806 VOUVRAY (Ire) [-] 8-6 (4*) P Carberry (5)..........(14 to 1) 4
1995 BOLD NOT BEAT (Ire) [-] 8-9 (2*) R M Burke (2)....(25 to 1) 5
2879 WESTERN FRONTIER (Ire) [-] 7-12 (6*) J A Heffernan (6) ....(20 to 1) 6
3164[8] ANOTHER FLYER (Ire) [-] 7-7 (8*) G M Moylan (1)..(25 to 1) 7
2320[4] SISTER CARMEL (Ire) [-] 8-13 K J Manning (3).....(7 to 1) 8
Dist: 1½l, 4l, ¾l, 12l. 2m 0.90s. (8 Ran).
(Michael Hilary Burke), D K Weld

3299 Rostrevor Maiden (3-y-o and up) £2,245 1½m.................. (7:15)

TROUBLE SHOOT (USA) 3-9-0 K J Manning (5)....(8 to 1) 1
2956[2] RETURN AGAIN (Ire) 3-8-11 J P Murtagh (6)....(Evens fav) 2
GARRAFITA (Ire) 3-8-11 C Roche (4)..............(9 to 2) 3
1441[6] PALAIYTA (Ire) 3-8-11 M J Kinane (1)..............(5 to 2) 4
CLASSY KAHYASI (Ire) 3-8-11 P Shanahan (2).....(8 to 1) 5
1467 PHARACH (Ire) 4-9-11 J Ely (3)...................(20 to 1) 6
Dist: 2l, 1l, 1l, 2l. 2m 42.90s. (6 Ran).
(Mrs Patricia Elia), D Hanley

3300 Knockbridge Race (3-y-o and up) £2,407 7f 166yds............... (8:15)

2779[2] LOCK'S HEATH (Can) 3-9-4 M J Kinane (3).....(7 to 4 on) 1
NORDIC QUEEN (Ire) 3-8-11 C Roche (1)..........(8 to 1) 2
2903[2] BOTHSIDESNOW (Ire) (bl) 3-8-10 (4*) P Carberry (2) (13 to 8) 3
Dist: 2l, 3l. 1m 40.20s. (3 Ran).
(Sheikh Mohammed), John M Oxx

FOLKESTONE (good to firm (races 1,2,3,4), good (5,6)) Friday August 13th

Going Correction: MINUS 0.15 sec. per fur. (races 1,2,4,6), MINUS 0.25 (3,5)

3301 John McCarthy Maiden Handicap Stakes Class F (0-60 3-y-o and up) £2,243 1m 1f 149yds............(1:45)

3102[2] TINSASHE (Ire) [42] 3-8-7 M Tebbutt (14) *al wl plcd, led 2 fs out, sn drw well clr, eased bef line.* ....(3 to 1 fav op 4 to 1 tchd 5 to 1) 1
3175[4] FATHER DAN (Ire) [40] 4-9-0 Gay Kelleway (6) *beh till ran on ins last 2 fs, no imprsn on wnr*..... (4 to 1 tchd 6 to 1) 2
3106[3] RISPOTO [58] 3-9-9 G Duffield (9) *hdwy frm rear o'r one furlong out, no ch wth wnr.* ....(9 to 1 op 6 to 1 tchd 10 to 1) 3
2882[7] WHATEVER'S RIGHT (Ire) [54] 4-10-0 B Rouse (8) *styd on last 2 fs, nrst finish*......(7 to 1 op 4 to 1 tchd 8 to 1) 4
2918[3] SAXON MAGIC [50] 3-9-1 J Quinn (10) *in tch, chsd wnr entering last 2 fs, sn outpcd, wknd clsg stages.* ....(16 to 1 op 10 to 1) 5
3090[3] CUTTHROAT KID (Ire) [53] (v) 3-9-4 K Darley (4) *in tch, rdn and effrt o'r 2 fs out, found no extr.* ....(6 to 1 op 9 to 2 tchd 7 to 1) 6
3047[6] COUNTERCHECK (Ire) [44] 4-9-4 N Carlisle (13) *ldg grp til lost pl o'r 2 fs out*..... (12 to 1 op 7 to 1 tchd 14 to 1) 7
2710[3] NATCHEZ TRACE [46] 4-9-6 S O'Gorman (3) *towards rear most of way*......... (11 to 1 op 10 to 1 tchd 12 to 1) 8
3142[8] CHOUETTE [42] (v) 3-8-7 W Newnes (7) *pressed ldrs til wknd 2 fs out*........(25 to 1 op 14 to 1 tchd 33 to 1) 9
2972 ACCESS FESTIVALS [46] 3-8-11 W Woods (1) *hrd rdn in mid-div o'r 2 fs out, not trble ldrs.* (25 to 1 op 12 to 1) 10
2784[4] NIGHTMARE LADY [30] 3-7-9 G Bardwell (5) *effrt und pres 3 fs out, wknd last 2.* (14 to 1 op 12 to 1 tchd 16 to 1) 11
2523 ARRAS ROYALE [35] 3-7-13[2] (3*) D Harrison (11) *made most of rng til hdd and wknd 2 fs out.* ....(50 to 1 op 25 to 1 tchd 66 to 1) 12
2712 ARABIAN CASTLE [40] (bl) 3-8-5 N Adams (12) *improved frm hfwy, rdn o'r 3 fs out, sn wknd.* ....(66 to 1 op 20 to 1) 13
Dist: 3½l, 4l, hd, 2½l, 1½l, 4l, hd, ¾l, 2l, 4l. 2m 3.60s. a 6.00s (13 Ran).
SR: 18/18/19/23/5/5/ (A Foustok), W Jarvis

3302 Douglas MacPherson Memorial Handicap Class E (0-70 3-y-o and up) £3,416 6f 189yds......................(2:15)

2824* PANCHELLITA (USA) [55] 4-9-4 B Rouse (7) *made all, quickened clr o'r one furlong out, styd on cl hme.* ....(9 to 4 fav op 5 to 2 tchd 11 to 4) 1
2897[7] ZINBAQ [35] 7-7-12 T Williams (3) *hdwy hfwy, rdn and styd on one pace pace appr fnl furlong.* ....(14 to 1 op 10 to 1) 2
3140[2] WATERLORD (Ire) [64] 3-9-7 Paul Eddery (5) *chsd wnr most of way, not quicken appr fnl furlong.* ....(7 to 1 op 5 to 1 tchd 8 to 1) 3
2816[7] INDERAPUTERI [65] 3-9-8 W Newnes (11) *snatched up aftr one furlong, styd on frm o'r 2 fs out, not rch wnr ins fnl furlong*...............(8 to 1 tchd 7 to 1 and 10 to 1) 4
2733 JOKIST [46] 10-8-9 M Tebbutt (10) *effrt o'r 2 fs out, nvr nrr*.......................(20 to 1 op 10 to 1) 5
2928[6] DESERT NOMAD [58] 3-9-1 G Duffield (8) *wl plcd, rdn and no extr appr fnl furlong*.............(6 to 1 op 8 to 1) 6
2733[5] NIGEL'S LUCKY GIRL [51] 5-9-0 J Quinn (2) *ldg grp til rdn and wknd o'r one furlong out.* ....(9 to 1 op 6 to 1 tchd 10 to 1) 7
2863 YUNUS EMRE (Ire) [48] 3-8-5 S Whitworth (9) *nvr better than mid-div*.......................(20 to 1 op 10 to 1) 8
2987 INVOCATION [65] 6-10-0 N Adams (1) *improved frm hfwy, rdn and not quicken 2 fs out.* ....(16 to 1 op 12 to 1 tchd 20 to 1) 9
3050[4] DAYTONA BEACH (Ire) [63] 3-9-6 K Darley (4) *slwly into strd, mid-div til wknd last 2 fs.* ....(10 to 1 op 7 to 1 tchd 12 to 1) 10
2719 KRAYYAN DAWN [41] 3-7-12 C Rutter (12) *slwly into strd, al beh*.......................(33 to 1 op 20 to 1) 11
2939 PRIMOCELLE [47] 3-7-11 (7*) Antoinette Armes (6) *slwly into strd, al towards rear.* ....(14 to 1 op 12 to 1 tchd 16 to 1) 12
2327 KIRRIEMUIR [44] 5-8-7 N Carlisle (14) *broke wl, hmpd and snatched up aftr one furlong, sn drpd rear.* ....(14 to 1 op 8 to 1 tchd 16 to 1) 13
Dist: 1½l, nk, ½l, ¾l, 1l, hd, 1½l, ¾l, 3l, 1½l. 1m 24.00s. a 3.10s (13 Ran).
SR: 41/16/38/37/22/25/23/9/30/ (C J Pennick), G L Moore

3303 St Loye's College Foundation Selling Stakes Class G (2-y-o) £2,070 6f (2:45)

3098[5] THREEPENNY-BRIDGE (bl) 8-11 T Sprake (8) *hdwy hfwy, led o'r one furlong out, styd on cl hme.* ....(33 to 1 op 12 to 1) 1
3141* LITTLE HOOLIGAN 8-11 C Rutter (5) *in tch, rdn alng o'r 2 fs out, ran on fnl furlong, no extr nr line.* ....(13 to 2 op 4 to 1 tchd 7 to 1) 2
2988 BET A PLAN (Ire) 8-6 Paul Eddery (6) *wth ldr, led o'r 2 fs out, hdd over one out, ran on same pace.* ....(9 to 4 op 3 to 1) 3
3103 SPORT RACING CLUB (bl) 8-6 W Newnes (7) *led for o'r 3 fs, outpcd und pres over one out*.....(33 to 1 op 14 to 1) 4
1640 KINGSCOURT JOHN-A (Ire) 8-11 N Adams (3) *outpcd til styd on clsg stages, nrst finish*.....(33 to 1 op 12 to 1) 5
3086[5] SWEET WHISPER 8-6 K Darley (1) *sn rdn alng in mid-div, no prog last 2 fs*............ (Evens fav tchd 11 to 8) 6
3098[3] CURBRIDGE (Ire) 8-11 B Rouse (2) *swtchd rght and effrt hfwy, wknd appr fnl furlong*.......(8 to 1 op 5 to 1) 7
2990 MAJOR ROWAN 8-11 C Avery (10) *slwly into strd, chsd ldrs for o'r 3 fs*.................(10 to 1 tchd 33 to 1) 8
2973[7] FINISHING KIND 8-6 G Duffield (11) *rcd alone far side, cl up for o'r 3 fs*..................(33 to 1 op 14 to 1) 9
PINATUBO 8-4 (7*) Antoinette Armes (9) *outpcd most of way*...........................(33 to 1 op 10 to 1) 10
PITIARA 8-3 (3*) D Harrison (4) *slwly into strd, outpcd hfwy*...........................(33 to 1 op 12 to 1) 11
Dist: Nk, 1½l, 3½l, 4l, hd, 2l, hd, hd, 8l, 1½l. 1m 14.20s. a 3.20s (11 Ran).
SR: 3/2/-/-/-/-/ (E Goody), W G M Turner

3304 London Friends Of St Loye's Claiming Stakes Class F (3-y-o) £2,243 1m 7f 92yds......................... (3:15)

1935[3] ELBURG (Ire) 9-7 K Darley (3) *chsd ldr, pushed alng 5 fs out, led entering last 2 furlongs, pushed clr, not extended*......................(11 to 4 on op 7 to 4 on) 1
3193[9] GWEEK (Ire) 8-6 P Robinson (2) *hld up in last pl, cld on ldrs 3 fs out, rdn and not quicken frm o'r one out.* ....(4 to 1 op 5 to 2) 2
2587[2] FLAMING MIRACLE (Ire) (bl) 9-7 C Rutter (4) *led til rdn and hdd entering last 2 fs, sn btn.* ....(7 to 1 op 5 to 1 tchd 8 to 1) 3
3049[8] SWIFT REVENGE 8-6 J Quinn (1) *settled in 3rd pl, pushed alng 5 fs out, outpcd appr last 2 furlongs.* ....(33 to 1 op 14 to 1) 4
Dist: 2l, 7l, 10l. 3m 27.20s. a 8.70s (4 Ran).
(Sheikh Mohammed), G Harwood

3305 H.K. Furniture Ltd Handicap Class E (0-70 3-y-o and up) £3,183 6f.... (3:45)

3168[5] FAY'S SONG (Ire) [55] 5-8-6 (7*) L Carter (3) *hld up in tch, str run o'r 2 fs out, led over one out, jst held on.* ....(11 to 2 op 4 to 1) 1
3292[5] HARRY'S COMING [57] 9-9-1 T Sprake (6) *prog frm 2 fs out, fnshd wl, jst fld*........ (7 to 1 op 6 to 1 tchd 8 to 1) 2
3108[2] POYLE AMBER [53] 4-8-8 (3*) D Harrison (1) *improved appr last 2 fs, ran on und pres fnl furlong, no extr cl hme.* ....(9 to 2 fav op 5 to 2 tchd 5 to 1) 3
2945[4] ZEBOIM [65] (bl) 7-9-2 (7*) Kim McDonnell (12) *pressed ldrs on outsd, ev ch frm 2 fs out, one pace ins fnl furlong.* .... (10 to 1 op 5 to 1) 4
2846[7] TURTLE BEACH [38] 4-7-3 (7*) Antoinette Armes (5) *made most of rng for o'r 4 fs, wknd.* ....(11 to 1 op 8 to 1 tchd 12 to 1) 5
2863[5] STARDUST EXPRESS [47] 3-8-0 T Williams (4) *cl up til rdn and wknd o'r one furlong out*...... (5 to 1 op 8 to 1) 6

2139[5] MOGWAI (Ire) [54] (v) 4-8-12 Paul Eddery (7) *trkd frnt rnk, rdn and not quicken o'r 2 fs out, wknd over one out.* ....(5 to 1 op 6 to 1 tchd 7 to 1) 7
2504[7] NANQUIDNO [40] 3-7-7 G Bardwell (9) *outpcd.* ....(33 to 1 op 20 to 1) 8
2534[7] RUBY COOPER [52] 3-8-5 J Quinn (10) *ldg grp for o'r 3 fs, wknd.*............................(16 to 1 op 12 to 1) 9
3168 GALLOP TO GLORY [53] 3-8-6 G Duffield (11) *outpcd.* ....(25 to 1 op 12 to 1) 10
2898 HOME SAFE [54] 3-8-7 S Whitworth (8) *ldg grp for 4 fs, lost pl quickly*............................(33 to 1 op 20 to 1) 11
1641[9] MAC'S FIGHTER [70] (bl) 8-10-0 F Norton (2) *hld up in rear, tld off hfwy, virtually pld up clsg stages.* ....(12 to 1 op 10 to 1 tchd 14 to 1) 12
Dist: Hd, nk, nk, 2l, 1l, 4l, 5l, 1l, 3l, sht-hd. 1m 12.60s. a 1.60s (12 Ran).
SR: 37/38/33/44/9/9/5/-/-/ (S Harper), R Akehurst

3306 Paul Cook Maiden Handicap Class E (0-70 3-y-o and up) £3,106 1½m (4:15)

3049[6] BADAWI (Fr) [39] (bl) 3-7-7 N Carlisle (7) *handily plcd, hrd rdn to ld ins fnl furlong, styd on nr finish.* ....(14 to 1 op 10 to 1 tchd 16 to 1) 1
3053[3] LEAR KING (USA) [69] 3-9-9 G Duffield (5) *rcd keenly in tch, rdn alng o'r 3 fs out, led und pres over one out, hdd and one pace last 100 yards.* ......(5 to 4 fav op Evens tchd 5 to 4 on and 11 to 8) 2
2521[6] MAD CASANOVA [63] (bl) 8-10-0 J Quinn (2) *hld up in rear, improved o'r 2 fs out, not much room appr fnl furlong, swtchd lft, ran on cl hme.* ....(8 to 1 op 7 to 1 tchd 10 to 1) 3
2134[7] ICE REBEL [59] 3-8-13 W Newnes (3) *led til hdd 5 fs out, styd on wl ag'n appr fnl furlong.* ....(11 to 2 op 9 to 2 tchd 6 to 1) 4
2751[6] MUTAWALI (Ire) [61] 3-9-1 S Whitworth (1) *wl plcd, led 5 fs out, sn drvn alng, hdd and wknd o'r one out.* ....(7 to 2 op 4 to 1 tchd 5 to 1) 5
739 UP ALL NIGHT [28] 4-7-7 G Bardwell (6) *rcd in mid-div til rdn and outpcd o'r 3 fs out.* ....(20 to 1 op 12 to 1 tchd 25 to 1) 6
3087 SPORTS VIEW [47] 4-8-12 Paul Eddery (4) *hld up in rear, effrt o'r 2 fs, wknd over one out.* ....(13 to 2 op 3 to 1 tchd 7 to 1) 7
Dist: 1½l, hd, 1l, 5l, 1½l, ½l. 2m 38.60s. a 8.10s (7 Ran).
SR: -/7/11/-/ (Mrs Julie Jones), C N Allen

HAYDOCK (soft)
Friday August 13th

Going Correction: PLUS 0.45 sec. per fur. (races 1,2,4,5,6), PLUS 0.40 (3)

3307 Sutton Apprentice Handicap Class F (0-80 3-y-o and up) £2,724 1m 3f 200yds........................ (5:45)

3181[3] GREEN'S CASSATT (USA) [47] 5-8-0 A Garth (1) *trkd ldrs, effrt o'r 3 fs out, styd on wl to ld ins last, ran on.* ....(12 to 1 op 10 to 1 tchd 14 to 1) 1
3211[5] WESTFIELD MOVES (Ire) [56] 5-8-6 (3*) C Hawksley (11) *nvr far away, drvn to ld o'r 3 fs out, hdd and rdn ins last, no extr*............................(10 to 1 tchd 11 to 1) 2
2750[4] HILLZAH (USA) [57] 5-8-8[1] (3*) H Bastiman (9) *sluggish strt, improved on outsd entering strt, ev ch o'r 2 fs out, one pace*............................(10 to 1 tchd 12 to 1) 3
2767[8] DEB'S BALL [53] 7-8-3 (3*) S Sanders (2) *steadied strt, improved frm off the pace last 3 fs, ran on finish.* ....(10 to 1 op 8 to 1) 4
2755 KADASTROF (Fr) [72] 3-8-7 (7*) Michelle Thomas (6) *trkd ldr, led entering strt till o'r 3 fs out, not quicken appr last*............................(14 to 1) 5
2936* SUNDERLAND ECHO [75] 4-10-0 Darren Moffatt (7) *al hndy, rdn to chal o'r 3 fs out, btn 2 out.* ....(7 to 4 fav op 6 to 4) 6
3134* ROUSITTO [54] 5-8-2 (5*,5ex) J Dennis (8) *sluggish strt, drvn alng to improve hfwy, no imprsn last 2 fs.* ....(4 to 1 op 5 to 1) 7
3157[5] DON'T FORGET MARIE (Ire) [58] 3-7-13[6] (7*) W Hawksley (10) *chsd ldg bunch, effrt entering strt, btn o'r 2 fs out.* ....(12 to 1 tchd 10 to 1) 8
238[3] BAHER (USA) [50] 4-7-10 (7*) Carol Davison (4) *pressed ldrs, ev ch till fdd o'r 2 fs out, tld off*....(16 to 1 op 14 to 1) 9
2632[9] BIGWHEEL BILL (Ire) [62] 4-9-1 Stephen Davies (5) *led till entering strt, wknd quickly o'r 2 fs out, eased.* ....(15 to 2 op 8 to 1 tchd 7 to 1) 10
2992 KHALIDI (Ire) [75] 4-10-0 V Slattery (12) *trkd ldrs, drvn alng entering strt, sn lost tch, tld off*.. (25 to 1 op 16 to 1) 11
Dist: 1½l, 2½l, 3½l, 1l, 1½l, 1½l, 20l, ½l, 12l, 2½l. 2m 40.66s. a 10.86s (11 Ran).
SR: 31/37/33/22/28/39/15/-/-/ (K K Baron), W M Brisbourne

3308 Knotty Ash Handicap Class E (0-70 3-y-o and up) £3,078 1¼m 120yds ....(6:15)

3019* LOWAWATHA [45] 5-8-2[2] (3*,4ex) C Hodgson (7) *nvr far away, led o'r 3 fs out till entering last, rallied to ld cl hme*............................(7 to 1 op 6 to 1) 1
3135[2] RED INDIAN [37] 7-7-9 Dale Gibson (10) *nvr far away, drvn alng to ld entering fnl furlong, hdd and no extr cl hme*....................(15 to 2 op 7 to 1 tchd 8 to 1) 2
2820[5] GIORDANO (Ire) [61] 3-8-6 (3*) S Maloney (12) *chsd ldg bunch, effrt and drvn alng o'r 2 fs out, staying on finish*... (11 to 1 op 12 to 1 tchd 14 to 1 and 10 to 1) 3
2932[2] NO COMEBACKS [53] 5-8-11 K Fallon (3) *sluggish strt, improved into midfield hfwy, ev ch and rdn o'r 2 fs out, one pace*............................(8 to 1 op 7 to 1) 4
3121[2] MAD MILITANT (Ire) [70] 4-10-0 K Darley (5) *trkd ldg bunch, bustled alng to improve o'r 3 fs out, not pace to chal.* ....(7 to 1 op 6 to 1 tchd 8 to 1) 5
2873[6] KELIMUTU [41] 4-7-13 J Lowe (6) *in tch, swtchd to stands side entering strt, ev ch till wknd 2 fs out*......(12 to 1) 6
3089[4] ENCHANTED FLYER [35] 6-7-2 (5*) Darren Moffatt (4) *beh and bustled alng hfwy, styd on last 2 fs, nvr nrr.* ....(33 to 1 op 25 to 1) 7
2774[6] GOLDEN TORQUE [61] 6-8-12 (7*) H Bastiman (1) *wtd wth, improved und pres o'r 3 fs out, fdd over one out.* ....(6 to 1 fav op 11 to 2 tchd 7 to 1) 8
2894[2] MISTY GODDESS (Ire) [60] 5-8-13 (5*) K Rutter (9) *fst away, settled, drvn alng entering strt, no imprsn.* ....(13 to 2 op 6 to 1 tchd 7 to 1) 9
3090[5] DOUBLE THE STAKES (USA) [35] 4-7-7[3] (3*) N Kennedy (14) *chsd ldg trio, drvn alng entering strt, btn o'r 2 fs out.* ....(20 to 1) 10
2858[6] FLYING DOWN TO RIO (Ire) [35] 5-7-2 (5*) D Wright (11) *chsd ldg bunch to strt, sn rdn and btn*..............(20 to 1) 11
3119* DORAZINE [67] 3-9-1 (4ex) D Holland (8) *wth ldr, led aftr 3 fs till o'r three out, fdd*............. (7 to 1 op 6 to 1) 12
3102* FOREST STAR (USA) [49] (v) 4-8-2 (5*,4ex) Stephen Davies (15) *led 3 fs, hndy till wknd und pres entering strt.* ....(10 to 1 op 8 to 1) 13
1943[7] CIVIL ACTION (Ire) [55] 3-8-3 E Johnson (2) *trkd clr ldg pair, drvn alng entering strt, sn lost tch.* ....(20 to 1 op 16 to 1) 14
2236[7] RUBY VISION (Ire) [36] 4-7-8[6] (5*) A Garth (13) *in tch, swtchd to stands side strt, sn tld off*..........(33 to 1) 15
Dist: ½l, 4l, 1½l, 6l, hd, sht-hd, ¾l, 2l, 2½l, 3½l. 2m 22.59s. a 11.59s (15 Ran).
SR: 20/11/17/16/21/-/-/8/3/ (N Lunn), D Morris

3309 Rainhill Nursery Class E (2-y-o) £2,851 5f............................ (6:45)

3215* INDIAHRA [77] 9-5 (6ex) S Perks (5) *settled gng wl, drvn ahead entering fnl furlong, kpt on well.* ....(6 to 1 op 11 to 2) 1
2917[4] STEADFAST ELITE (Ire) [51] 7-2 (5*) D Wright (9) *settled midfield, drvn alng to improve o'r one furlong out, ran on wl finish*........................(8 to 1 op 6 to 1) 2
3254[9] LEGATEE [78] 9-6 M Birch (8) *chsd alng to improve frm midfield last 2 fs, ran on*.........(25 to 1 op 20 to 1) 3
2996 ALLLEGSNOBRAIN [74] 9-2 D Holland (2) *al hndy, led o'r one furlong out till entering last, rdn and one pace.* ....(14 to 1 op 12 to 1) 4
3133[7] MERISSA [52] 7-3 (5*) Darren Moffatt (3) *sluggish strt, bustled alng to improve last 2 fs, ran on finish.* ....(14 to 1 op 12 to 1) 5
3120* STEPHENSONS ROCKET [77] 9-5 (6ex) J Carroll (6) *nvr far away, rdn and ev ch 2 fs out, not quicken.* ....(6 to 1 op 11 to 2) 6
2200[6] KANGRA VALLEY [71] 8-13 L Dettori (10) *led, clr aftr one furlong, hdd o'r one out, sn btn*.... (6 to 1 op 12 to 1) 7
1168[6] DUNDEELIN [59] 8-1 Dale Gibson (7) *speed 3 fs, no extr.* ....(25 to 1) 8
3001* BEATS WORKING [79] 9-7 K Fallon (4) *strted slwly, chsd alng to improve on ins hfwy, not clr run and snatched up o'r one furlong out, eased*......(4 to 1 op 11 to 4) 9
3254* LEFT STRANDED [79] 9-7 (6ex) K Darley (1) *pressed ldr, struggling to hold pl 2 fs out, sn btn.* ....(7 to 2 fav op 3 to 1) 10
Dist: 1l, ¾l, hd, sht-hd, 3½l, 6l, hd, 1l, hd. 1m 3.93s. a 5.13s (10 Ran).
SR: 42/12/36/31/8/19/ (P J Lawton), R Hollinshead

3310 Claude Harrison Memorial Challenge Trophy Handicap Class E (0-70 3-y-o and up) £2,965 1m 30yds....... (7:15)

2747 NORMAN WARRIOR [35] (bl) 4-8-3[1] J Carroll (2) *nvr far away, drvn to ld entering fnl furlong, hld on wl.* ....(16 to 1) 1
2638[5] PREMIER STAR [51] 3-8-12 L Dettori (13) *patiently rdn, improved frm midfield to draw level ins fnl furlong, jst fld*....................(7 to 1 op 8 to 1 tchd 9 to 1) 2
3124[2] MAI PEN RAI [40] (v) 5-8-8 D Holland (1) *settled gng wl, weaved through frm midfield o'r one furlong out, kpt on same pace*........(9 to 4 fav op 5 to 2 tchd 7 to 2) 3
2737 THISONESFORALICE [35] 5-8-3 J Lowe (12) *al hndy, rdn to ld o'r one furlong out, hdd entering last, one pace.* ....(20 to 1 op 16 to 1) 4
2940 BROADWAY RUCKUS (Can) [43] 4-8-6 (5*) Stephen Davies (5) *trkd ldg 6, drvn alng o'r 2 fs out, styd on same pace.* ....(20 to 1) 5

2920^{6} QUANTITY SURVEYOR [56] 4-9-10 M Birch (11) *nvr far away, drvn alng 2 fs out, no extr*.... (9 to 1 op 8 to 1) 6
3124^{4} MALCESINE (Ire) [44] (v) 4-8-12 J Fortune (10) *pressed ldrs, rdn o'r 2 fs out, sn btn*..........(10 to 1 op 8 to 1) 7
3055^{3} YOUNG JASON [47] 10-9-1 S Perks (4) *bustled alng and outpcd aftr 3 fs, nvr nr to chal*......(7 to 1 op 11 to 2) 8
3007 VERRO (USA) [31] 6-7-13 Dale Gibson (8) *chsd ldrs for o'r 5 fs, sn btn*.........................(33 to 1 op 25 to 1) 9
2631^{4} MATTS BOY [49] (v) 5-8-12 (5*) J Tate (6) *struggling aftr 3 fs, nvr nr to chal*.......................(8 to 1 tchd 9 to 1) 10
2863^{4} JUVENARA [45] 7-8-8 (5*) L Newton (7) *chsd ldr, rdn alng o'r 2 fs out, sn btn*............................(16 to 1) 11
2824^{8} NELLIE'S GAMBLE [46] 3-8-7 K Darley (3) *co'red up on ins, struggling to hold pl over 2 fs out, sn btn*. ....(8 to 1 op 10 to 1) 12
2799^{9} SHANNON EXPRESS [46] (v) 6-9-0 Julie Bowker (9) *led, quickened entering strt, hdd and wknd quickly o'r one furlong out*.........................(9 to 1 op 8 to 1) 13

Dist: Sht-hd, 2l, 1½l, sht-hd, 3½l, 6l, 1½l, hd, hd, 2l. 1m 50.14s. a 9.54s (13 Ran).
SR: 2/10/-/-/-/-/ (Mrs Patricia Lunn), D Morris

3311 Swan With Two Necks Selling Stakes Class F (3-y-o) £2,591 1m 30yds (7:45)

3101^{9} GLOWING PATH (v) 9-5 D Holland (8) *co'red up in midfield, swtchd to stands side to ld over one furlong out, ran on wl*...................(11 to 2 op 4 to 1 tchd 6 to 1) 1
3080^{6} KELLY MAC 9-0 L Dettori (1) *nvr far away, led 2 fs out till o'r one out, kpt on same pace*...(7 to 4 fav op 11 to 4) 2
3249^{4} B B GLEN 8-6 (3*) C Hodgson (3) *trkd ldrs, hrd rdn to chal o'r one furlong out, kpt on same pace*. ....(6 to 1 tchd 7 to 1) 3
3192^{9} GUV'NORS GIFT 8-7 (7*) S Mulvey (10) *patiently rdn, drw level o'r one furlong out, ridden and no extr*... (5 to 1) 4
2635^{6} BREAKING HEARTS (Ire) 8-9 K Darley (2) *al hndy, ev ch and rdn 2 fs out, not quicken*..................(14 to 1) 5
2724^{9} SWISS MOUNTAIN 8-4 (5*) Stephen Davies (5) *chsd ldrs, effrt and drvn alng 2 fs out, not pace to chal*. (20 to 1) 6
3055^{2} AMERIGUE 8-9 (5*) J Tate (12) *chsd ldg 4, feeling pace o'r 2 fs out, sn btn*....................(7 to 1 op 11 to 2) 7
2914^{5} COBBS CROSS 8-11 (3*) N Kennedy (9) *in tch, struggling to keep up hfwy, sn btn*........................(33 to 1) 8
2651^{4} VILAMAR (Ire) 9-0 K Fallon (6) *sluggish strt, chsd alng hfwy, nvr a threat*................(10 to 1 op 8 to 1) 9
2824^{3} FINAL OAK 8-9 A Mackay (4) *led aftr 2 fs, quickened clr entering strt, hdd two out, sn btn*. (14 to 1 op 12 to 1) 10
2366^{6} GLIMPSE OF HEAVEN 8-9 W Carson (7) *trkd ldg trio, hrd drvn o'r 2 fs out, sn btn*..............(7 to 1 op 6 to 1) 11
2863 FREDDIE JACK 9-0 R Lappin (11) *led 2 fs, lost grnd o'r two furlongs out, sn btn*..............(33 to 1 op 25 to 1) 12

Dist: 2½l, 1½l, 5l, 2½l, ¾l, 5l, 4l, 2½l, 2½l, 5l. 1m 50.20s. a 9.60s (12 Ran).
SR: 17/4/-/-/-/-/ (C John Hill), C J Hill

3312 Eccleston Fillies' Conditions Stakes Class D (3-y-o and up) £3,512 7f 30yds ....(8:15)

1950^{5} KATIBA (USA) 3-8-12 W Carson (2) *wtd wth, brght stands side to ld o'r one furlong out, drvn clr*. ....(7 to 2 op 3 to 1) 1
2971^{6} LACERTA (Ire) 3-8-7 (5*) Stephen Davies (3) *set steady pace, quickened hfwy, hdd o'r 2 fs out, rallied*. ....(9 to 4 op 3 to 1) 2
3050^{5} CITY TIMES (Ire) (bl) 3-8-1 (7*) S Sanders (6) *nvr far away, led o'r 2 fs out till over one out, one pace*. ....(25 to 1 op 33 to 1) 3
915* WINGED VICTORY (Ire) 3-9-2 L Dettori (1) *settled gng wl, effrt hfwy, rdn 2 fs out, sn btn*. (Evens fav op 6 to 4 on) 4
3117^{8} LADY BROKER 3-8-8 A Mackay (4) *trkd ldr, evry ch and rdn o'r 2 fs out, one pace*..........(33 to 1 op 50 to 1) 5

Dist: 2½l, nk, 2½l, ¾l. 1m 38.79s. a 11.59s (5 Ran).
(Hamdan Al-Maktoum), J L Dunlop

NEWBURY (good)
Friday August 13th

Going Correction: MINUS 0.15 sec. per fur. (races 1,4,5), MINUS 0.30 (2,3,6,7)

3313 Jack Colling Polar Jest Apprentice Handicap Class E (0-90 3-y-o and up) £3,600 6f 8yds................ (2:10)

3169^{3} GREAT HALL [66] (bl) 4-7-13 (5*) D Griffiths (8) *beh, rapid hdwy appr fnl furlong, ran on wl to ld nr finish*. ....(7 to 1 op 6 to 1) 1
1914^{4} DOMULLA [76] 3-8-6 (3*) B Russell (6) *outpcd early, hdwy 2 fs out, led appr last, kpt on, ct cl hme*. ....(9 to 1 op 7 to 1) 2
2264^{2} RELENTLESS PURSUIT (Ire) [67] 5-8-5 Stephen Davies (5) *hld up in tch, hdwy o'r one furlong out, ev ch ins last, one pace*..............(13 to 2 op 6 to 1 tchd 7 to 1) 3
2987^{9} ARABELLAJILL [90] 4-9-9 (5*) D Gibbs (4) *outpcd, hdwy appr fnl furlong, styd on*. ....(3 to 1 fav op 4 to 1 tchd 11 to 4) 4
2928^{4} CHILI HEIGHTS [78] 3-8-8 (3*) N Varley (10) *chsd ldrs, rdn 2 fs out, sn one pace*..................(7 to 1 tchd 8 to 1) 5
2418^{7} DANCING SPIRIT (Ire) [73] 3-8-1 (5*) Mark Denaro (7) *chsd ldrs, one pace fnl 2 fs*. (10 to 1 op 8 to 1 tchd 11 to 1) 6
2969^{5} FASCINATION WALTZ [77] 6-8-12 (3*) T G McLaughlin (1) *wnt lft strt, hdwy 2 fs out, no prog frm one and a half out*..................................(9 to 1 op 7 to 1) 7
2831^{4} CAROMISH (USA) [60] 6-7-7 (5*) G Milligan (3) *pressed ldrs, led o'r 2 fs out to one and a half out, sn wknd*. ....(9 to 1 op 6 to 1 tchd 10 to 1) 8
3127^{4} DARK EYED LADY (Ire) [80] 3-8-13 A Procter (9) *pressed ldrs for o'r 3 fs*.............(6 to 1 op 5 to 1 tchd 13 to 2) 9
3006^{6} CHRISTIAN WARRIOR [55] (v) 4-7-2 (5*) M Baird (2) *led to 2 and a half fs out, sn wknd*.......(50 to 1 tchd 66 to 1) 10

Dist: 1½l, ½l, sht-hd, 2½l, hd, ½l, ½l, 5l, 7l. 1m 12.83s. a 1.13s (10 Ran).
SR: 49/48/42/64/37/31/38/19/14/ (P D Cundell), P D Cundell

3314 Newbury Racecourse Chiropractic Clinic Handicap Class B (0-100 3-y-o) £8,480 1¼m 6yds............. (2:40)

2361^{5} CHATOYANT [88] 8-12 W R Swinburn (3) *in tch, hdwy o'r one furlong out, squeezed through to ld wl ins last*. ....(11 to 1 op 10 to 1 tchd 12 to 1) 1
2545* JOHNS ACT (USA) [80] 8-4 J Williams (7) *mid-div, hdwy 2 fs out, drvn and edgd rght ins last, ran on strly, jst fld*. ....(20 to 1 tchd 33 to 1) 2
2997^{3} SHARJAH (USA) [88] 8-12 M Roberts (4) *chsd ldrs, drvn to ld one furlong out, hdd and not quicken ins last*. ....(7 to 1 tchd 8 to 1) 3
2961^{9} BRIGANTE DI CIELO [93] 9-3 T Quinn (10) *beh, hdwy 3 fs out, led 2 out to one out, styd on same pace*. ....(12 to 1 tchd 10 to 1) 4
2961 RAPID SUCCESS (USA) [95] 9-0 (5*) A Procter (11) *led to 2 fs out, sn one pace*................(25 to 1 tchd 33 to 1) 5
2997^{2} NESSUN DORMA [82] 8-6 M Hills (6) *hdwy o'r 2 fs out, wknd appr last*.....................(9 to 1 op 8 to 1) 6
2961* WESTERN CAPE (USA) [97] 9-7 Pat Eddery (15) *beh, drvn alng o'r 3 fs out, effrt 2 out, wknd over one out*. ....(11 to 2 fav op 9 to 2 tchd 6 to 1) 7
932^{7} MARIUS (Ire) [70] 7-2^{1} (7*) N Varley (14) *beh, drvn alng 4 fs out, some prog frm 2 out*..........(20 to 1 op 16 to 1) 8
2941^{8} FRONTIER FLIGHT (USA) [85] 8-9 S Raymont (1) *chsd ldrs, ev ch 3 fs out, wknd 2 out*..........................(33 to 1) 9
2961 GONE TROPPO [84] 8-8 W Ryan (8) *chsd ldrs, rdn 2 fs out, wkng whn hmpd jst ins last*. ....(11 to 1 op 8 to 1 tchd 12 to 1) 10
2563^{6} MITRAAS (USA) [74] 7-12 W Carson (13) *chsd ldrs for o'r 6 fs*....................(10 to 1 op 8 to 1 tchd 11 to 1) 11
2783* KARACHI [71] 7-9^{5} (3*) B Doyle (12) *beh, nvr rch ldrs*. ....(14 to 1) 12
2758^{2} BRANDONHURST [84] (v) 8-8 L Dettori (5) *chsd ldrs for o'r 6 fs*..............................(9 to 1 op 8 to 1) 13
684 FORTENSKY (USA) [85] 8-9 R Cochrane (9) *hdwy into mid-div hfwy, wknd 3 fs out*. ....(13 to 2 op 6 to 1 tchd 7 to 1) 14
1670^{7} WYNONA (Ire) [81] (bl) 8-5 N Day (16) *beh fnl 5 fs*. ....(25 to 1 op 33 to 1) 15

Dist: Nk, ¾l, 1½l, hd, 4l, sht-hd, 2½l, ¾l, sht-hd, 2l. 2m 4.13s. a 1.13s (15 Ran).
SR: 57/48/54/56/57/36/50/18/31/ (Lord Derby), J W Watts

3315 Gardner Merchant Hungerford Stakes Class A (Group 3) (3-y-o and up) £25,110 7f 64yds.............. (3:10)

2905^{3} INCHINOR 3-8-11 L Dettori (2) *trkd ldrs, drvn fnl furlong, styd on gmely to ld last strds*. ....(2 to 1 fav op 7 to 4 tchd 85 to 40) 1
3015^{4} WOLFHOUND (USA) 4-9-8 M Roberts (4) *trkd ldrs, led jst ins fnl 2 fs, hrd rdn final furlong, ct last strds*. ....(4 to 1 op 5 to 1 tchd 6 to 1) 2
2436^{2} SWING LOW 4-9-5 L Piggott (8) *beh, plenty to do 3 fs out, styd on appr last, fnshd wl*. ....(11 to 1 op 10 to 1 tchd 12 to 1) 3
2985* GABR 3-8-8 W Carson (1) *chsd ldrs, led 2 and a half fs out till jst ins fnl two, outpcd final furlong*. ....(6 to 1 tchd 7 to 1) 4
2905^{9} ARDKINGLASS 3-8-11 W Ryan (9) *drvn and hdwy frm 3 fs out, no imprsn from 2 out*...........(9 to 1 op 6 to 1) 5
2574^{7} LOOK WHO'S HERE (Ire) 3-8-8 B Raymond (7) *chsd ldrs, no prog frm o'r 2 fs out*..............(33 to 1 tchd 40 to 1) 6
2971* SIWAAYIB 3-8-6^{1} W R Swinburn (12) *beh, some prog appr 2 fs out, no dngr*......(12 to 1 op 10 to 1 tchd 14 to 1) 7
3015 HAZAAM (USA) (v) 4-9-3 Pat Eddery (10) *mid-div, effrt o'r 2 fs out, sn btn*....... (11 to 1 op 10 to 1 tchd 12 to 1) 8
1532^{3} MOJAVE (v) 4-9-3 R Cochrane (6) *slwly away, al beh*. ....(25 to 1 op 20 to 1 tchd 33 to 1) 9
MOUNTAIN ASH 4-9-0 (3ex) D Holland (5) *led to 2 and a half fs out, sn wknd*. (14 to 1 op 12 to 1 tchd 16 to 1) 10
ADJMAL (Ire) 4-9-0 A Bond (3) *chsd ldrs for o'r 4 fs*. ....(50 to 1 op 33 to 1 tchd 66 to 1) 11
2885 TENDER MOMENT (Ire) 5-8-11 B Doyle (11) *al beh*. ....(100 to 1 op 66 to 1) 12
2853^{8} SON PARDO (bl) 3-8-13 T Quinn (13) *al beh*. ....(50 to 1 op 33 to 1 tchd 66 to 1) 13

Dist: Sht-hd, 2l, ½l, 1½l, 1½l, 2l, hd, 3½l, sht-hd, ¾l. 1m 26.28s. b 1.02s (13

Ran).
SR: 79/89/80/67/65/57/49/59/48/ (Sir Philip Oppenheimer), R Charlton

3316 Washington Singer Stakes Class A (Listed Race) (2-y-o) £8,629 7f...(3:40)

2299* COLONEL COLLINS (USA) 8-11 Pat Eddery (1) *made virtually all, came clr fnl 2 fs, easily.* ....(11 to 2 on op 9 to 2 on tchd 4 to 1 on) 1
THABIT (USA) 8-11 W Carson (4) *3rd till ran on to chase wnr o'r 2 fs out, kpt on, improve*....(13 to 2 op 6 to 1) 2
2964 VILLAGE EAGLE (Fr) 8-11 M Roberts (2) *chsd wnr till o'r 2 fs out, sn outpcd*.....(40 to 1 op 50 to 1 tchd 66 to 1) 3
BRANDON COURT (Ire) 8-11 L Dettori (3) *al last, lost tch fnl 3 fs*...............................(16 to 1 op 10 to 1) 4
Dist: 3½l, 5l, 7l. 1m 26.01s. a 1.91s (4 Ran).
SR: 53/42/27/6/ (R E Sangster), P W Chapple-Hyam

3317 K D Marketing Sellmore Maiden Fillies Stakes Class D (2-y-o) £4,305 6f 8yds.......................... (4:10)

2887² ARECIBA (USA) 8-11 D Holland (14) *made virtually all, hrd drvn fnl furlong, hld on gmely.* ....(5 to 2 fav tchd 9 to 4 and 11 to 4) 1
RAKLI 8-11 Pat Eddery (11) *settled mid-div, drvn 2 fs out, ran on to chal und pres fnl furlong, no extr cl hme.* ....(7 to 2 op 5 to 2 tchd 4 to 1) 2
2720² INGOZI 8-11 M Hills (13) *chsd ldrs, rdn and kpt on wl fnl furlong*................. (7 to 2 op 4 to 1 tchd 5 to 1) 3
RELATIVELY SPECIAL 8-11 R Cochrane (2) *sn frnt rnk, rdn o'r one furlong out, no extr ins last.* .... (11 to 2 op 6 to 1 tchd 5 to 1) 4
LYPHARD STREET (USA) 8-11 A Munro (4) *sn pressing ldrs, rdn o'r one furlong out, soon outpcd.* ....(16 to 1 op 14 to 1) 5
FAWAAKEH (USA) 8-11 R Hills (18) *chsd ldrs, rdn 2 fs out, wknd one out*.......(33 to 1 op 25 to 1 tchd 40 to 1) 6
2583⁵ EDWINA (Ire) 8-11 W R Swinburn (17) *chsd ldrs, rdn 2 fs out, wknd one and a half out*................(33 to 1) 7
2887⁶ DIAMOND PARK (Ire) 8-11 B Raymond (6) *broke wl, pressed wnr early, prmnt till wknd 2 fs out*..............(25 to 1) 8
TAFFETA SILK (USA) 8-11 L Dettori (9) *beh, hdwy hfwy, no imprsn frm o'r 2 fs out.* ....(33 to 1 op 25 to 1 tchd 50 to 1) 9
AWTAAR (USA) 8-11 W Carson (8) *nvr gng pace of ldrs.* ....(25 to 1 op 16 to 1) 10
BELLA RAGAZZA 8-11 S Raymont (12) *outpcd.* ....(50 to 1 op 25 to 1) 11
VIRGINIA WATER (USA) 8-11 S Dawson (1) *outpcd.* ....(50 to 1 op 33 to 1) 12
BROOKS MASQUERADE 8-11 M Roberts (15) *chsd ldrs 4 fs*..................(20 to 1 op 16 to 1 tchd 25 to 1) 13
1063 HIGHLAND WARNING 8-8 (3*) B Doyle (10) *sn outpcd.* ....(50 to 1 tchd 66 to 1) 14
KHAYA 8-11 W Ryan (16) *sn outpcd.* (50 to 1 op 25 to 1) 15
PAB'S CHOICE 8-11 A Clark (3) *outpcd.* ....(50 to 1 op 33 to 1) 16
BUNNY GEE 8-11 J Williams (7) *sn beh*..........(50 to 1) 17
Dist: Sht-hd, ¾l, 3l, sht-hd, 1l, 3l, 1½l, nk, ¾l, hd. 1m 13.26s. a 1.56s (17 Ran).
SR: 48/47/44/32/31/27/15/9/8/ (R E Sangster), P W Chapple-Hyam

3318 Mr Cotton Of Chichester Anniversary Conditions Stakes Class C (3-y-o) £4,396 1½m 5yds.............. (4:40)

2941* PRINCE OF ANDROS (USA) 9-1 L Dettori (6) *hld up rear, hdwy frm 4 fs out, rdn o'r one out, styd on to ld ins last, all out*..............(7 to 4 fav op 6 to 4 tchd 2 to 1) 1
1006² KUSAMBA (USA) 8-13 T Quinn (3) *led, rdn 2 fs out, hdd ins last, rallied gmely und pres, jst fld.* .... (10 to 1 op 8 to 1 tchd 12 to 1) 2
2117* EL JUBAIL (Ire) 8-13 W Ryan (5) *chsd ldrs, chlgd frm 2 fs out till outpcd ins last*..............(7 to 1 op 5 to 1) 3
1751⁸ SHAIBA (USA) 8-13 M Roberts (4) *beh, shaken up 3 fs out, moderate prog frm 2 out*........... (11 to 4 op 5 to 2) 4
2259 SCOTTISH PEAK (Ire) 8-11 W R Swinburn (1) *chsd ldrs, chlgd o'r 2 fs out, sn wknd*....... (16 to 1 op 12 to 1) 5
2776* TRAMMEL 8-13 Pat Eddery (7) *in tch, rdn 4 fs out, sn wknd*............................(3 to 1 tchd 7 to 2) 6
2985⁶ GENTLEMAN SID 8-11 J Williams (2) *in tch till wknd o'r 4 fs out*.............(100 to 1 op 50 to 1 tchd 150 to 1) 7
Dist: Sht-hd, 1l, 5l, nk, 6l, 25l. 2m 32.83s. a 3.23s (7 Ran).
SR: 33/30/28/18/15/5/-/ (Lucayan Stud), D R Loder

3319 Levy Board Handicap Class C (0-95 3-y-o and up) £4,878 2m........ (5:10)

3125* BOLD RESOLUTION (Ire) [64] 5-7-13 (5ex) M Roberts (1) *broke wl, steadied rear, hdwy 2 fs out, squeezed through to ld one out, cmftbly.* ....(11 to 8 fav op 6 to 4 tchd 13 to 8) 1
2507* DOVER PATROL (Ire) [85] 3-8-5 W Ryan (7) *mid-div, hdwy hfwy, str chal 2 fs out, outpcd ins last.* .... (11 to 2 op 4 to 1) 2
2432² KAISER WILHELM [85] 4-9-6 Pat Eddery (4) *made most to one furlong out, kpt on und pres*.... (8 to 1 op 6 to 1) 3
2755⁶ DOYCE [62] 4-7-11 W Carson (2) *sn chasing ldrs, drvn alng 3 fs out, styd on*............ (8 to 1 tchd 10 to 1) 4
2904² GREEN LANE (USA) [72] 5-8-7 T Quinn (3) *chsd ldrs, chlgd 3 fs out till outpcd approachin last.* (5 to 1 tchd 6 to 1) 5
2925⁶ JACK BUTTON (Ire) [93] 4-10-0 N Day (5) *prmnt till outpcd 7 fs out, one pace 3 out.* .... (12 to 1 op 10 to 1 tchd 14 to 1) 6
2904³ WESTERN DYNASTY [72] 7-8-7 L Dettori (8) *beh, hdwy on outsd o'r 3 fs out, wknd ins fnl 2.* .... (15 to 2 op 6 to 1 tchd 8 to 1) 7
MAESTROSO (Ire) [65] 4-8-0 A Tucker (6) *beh, lost tch 6 fs out, tld off*..........(25 to 1 op 20 to 1 tchd 33 to 1) 8
Dist: ½l, ½l, nk, hd, 1½l, 4l, dist. 3m 29.12s. a 3.12s (8 Ran).
SR: 6/11/25/1/10/29/4/-/ (R M Cyzer), C A Cyzer

SOUTHWELL (A.W) (std)
Friday August 13th
Going Correction: PLUS 0.20 sec. per fur. (races 1,3,4,5,6), NIL (2)

3320 Camelia Fillies' Handicap Class E (0-70 3-y-o and up) £3,157 1½m (2:20)

2899⁴ SILKY HEIGHTS (Ire) [60] 3-9-7 N Connorton (10) *chsd ldrs, hdwy 5 fs out, effrt 2 out and sn led, rdn clr appr last, ran on*............................ (8 to 1 op 7 to 1) 1
2827⁴ FIRST FLING (Ire) [47] 4-9-5 G Hind (4) *mid-div, hdwy 5 fs out, rdn 2 out, ran on ins last, not rch wnr.* ....(9 to 1 op 8 to 1) 2
2615³ POINT THE WAY (Ire) [65] (v) 3-9-9 (3*) N Kennedy (12) *led one furlong, cl up till led 4 fs out, rdn 2 out and sn hdd, one pace*............................ (6 to 1 op 4 to 1) 3
2631⁵ YEVEED (Ire) [47] 3-8-8 M Birch (8) *al prmnt, pushed alng 3 fs out, effrt and ev ch 2 out, sn rdn and one pace.* ....(9 to 2 fav op 6 to 1) 4
2747 MELANCOLIA [31] 7-7-12² (7*) Elizabeth Turner (2) *hld up and beh, hdwy o'r 4 fs out, styd on fnl 2 furlongs, not rch ldrs*.................................. (33 to 1) 5
2860* IZITALLWORTHIT [39] 4-8-6 (5*) D Wright (1) *mid-div, effrt 5 fs out, not rch ldrs*.................. (11 to 1 op 8 to 1) 6
3005⁵ ANNYBAN [49] 3-8-10 S Perks (5) *led aftr one furlong till hdd 4 fs out and sn wknd*........ (25 to 1 op 20 to 1) 7
2977³ KINCHENJUNGA [62] 3-9-9 A McGlone (7) *prmnt, rdn hfwy, wknd 4 fs out*..................(7 to 1 op 5 to 1) 8
2972⁸ PUGET DANCER (USA) [57] (v) 3-9-1 (3*) M Fenton (3) *chsd ldrs, rdn hfwy, sn lost pl and beh*....(8 to 1 op 6 to 1) 9
2894⁶ THIMBALINA [28] 7-7-9 (5*) D McCabe (6) *nvr a factor.* ....(7 to 1 op 6 to 1) 10
2847 SUPPER WITH SUSIE [34] 3-7-9² A Mackay (13) *mid-div, hdwy 5 fs out, sn rdn and wknd 3 out*........(33 to 1) 11
3083⁴ CHASE THE STARS [63] 3-9-3 (7*) J D Smith (9) *slwly into strd, rdn alng, al beh*..............(16 to 1 op 14 to 1) 12
NISHARA [22] 5-7-8¹ J Lowe (11) *al rear, wl beh fnl 4 fs.* .... (40 to 1 op 33 to 1) 13
Dist: 1½l, 3½l, sht-hd, 7l, 1½l, 1½l, 2l, 1l, 8l, 8l. 2m 43.20s. a 9.30s (13 Ran).
SR: 38/33/33/14/-/-/-/5/-/ (Bernard Bloom), M J Camacho

3321 Rambling Rose Selling Stakes Class G (2-y-o) £2,070 5f..............(2:50)

3131⁴ FLOATING TRIAL (v) 8-11 J Carroll (8) *made all, rdn and edgd lft fnl furlong, kpt on.* ....(7 to 2 fav op 3 to 1 tchd 4 to 1) 1
3183⁵ KENTUCKY FLYER 8-6 L Charnock (4) *al prmnt, rdn 2 fs out and ev ch, kpt on ins last*.....(33 to 1 op 25 to 1) 2
2916⁴ DELROB 8-6 A Mackay (1) *rcd far side, chsd ldrs, rdn 2 fs out, kpt on ins last*................(10 to 1 op 8 to 1) 3
3114⁴ PELAMIS 8-11 J Fortune (11) *chsd ldrs, rdn 2 fs out, styd on one pace*.................. (8 to 1 op 7 to 1) 4
3103³ READY-FREDDIE 8-6 (5*) D McCabe (6) *chsd ldrs centre, rdn 2 fs out, kpt on und pres ins last.* .... (12 to 1 op 10 to 1) 5
3069³ JUST GREENWICH (bl) 8-6 Dale Gibson (12) *cl up till rdn 2 fs out, sn wknd*.................. (9 to 2 op 4 to 1) 6
3141³ SPORTING HEIR (Ire) (bl) 9-2 M Wigham (9) *outpcd and beh till styd on und pres fnl 2 fs, nvr dngrs.* ....(9 to 2 op 4 to 1 tchd 5 to 1) 7
2817⁸ TOOGOODFORYOU 8-11 J Fanning (5) *nvr rch ldrs.* ....(33 to 1) 8
3131⁶ ARKINDALE SPIRIT (Ire) 8-11 T Lucas (3) *speed o'r 3 fs.* ....(16 to 1) 9
3133 RICH HARMONY 8-11 N Connorton (13) *al outpcd and beh*.................. (12 to 1 op 8 to 1) 10
2946⁸ POOR WILLY 8-4 (7*) S Jones (2) *al rear.* .... (12 to 1 op 10 to 1) 11
2423⁹ SUZY LLOYD 8-4¹ (3*) O Pears (7) *beh frm hfwy.* .... (25 to 1 op 33 to 1) 12
LADY FEATHERS 8-6 S Wood (10) *al outpcd and beh.* .... (33 to 1 op 25 to 1) 13
Dist: 1½l, 1½l, 1½l, 1½l, ½l, 2l, 3½l, nk, 1½l, 1½l. 1m 1.20s. a 3.30s (13 Ran).
SR: 31/20/14/13/7/-/2/-/-/ (David Fish), J Berry

3322 Langleys Insurance Claims Department Maiden Handicap Class E (0-70 3-y-o and up) £2,924 1¾m...... (3:20)

2495^{5} POETIC FORM (Ire) [40] (bl) 3-8-11 J Weaver (4) *sn led, pushed clr 3 fs out, rdn and styd on wl ins last.* ....(6 to 1 tchd 7 to 1) 1
3142^{2} ANNABEL'S BABY (Ire) [33] 4-9-3 M Wigham (8) *in tch, hdwy hfwy, effrt 3 fs out, sn rdn and styd on one pace fnl 2 furlongs*........(4 to 1 fav op 3 to 1 tchd 9 to 2) 2
2870^{3} PRINCE PALACIO [35] 3-8-6 N Connorton (5) *al prmnt, rdn 3 fs out, kpt on one pace fnl 2 furlongs.* ....(9 to 2 op 7 to 2) 3
2828^{3} JURIS PRUDENCE (Ire) [38] 5-9-8 J Fortune (1) *cl up, rdn 3 fs out, kpt on one pace*........(7 to 1) 4
2950^{6} WHATCOMESNATURALLY (USA) [32] 4-8-11 (5*) J Marshall (7) *prmnt till rdn hfwy, sn lost pl and beh.* ....(6 to 1 op 8 to 1 tchd 9 to 1) 5
2828^{2} NORTHERN JUDY (Ire) [53] 3-9-10 S Perks (2) *prmnt, effrt and rdn o'r 4 fs out, sn wknd*........(11 to 2 op 4 to 1) 6
2573^{4} NOBLE SOCIETY [38] 5-9-8 R Price (3) *al rear, beh frm hfwy*........(8 to 1 op 7 to 1) 7
2860^{6} RED SOMBRERO [34] 4-9-4 A Mackay (6) *al rear, beh frm hfwy*........(12 to 1) 8

Dist: 4l, 2½l, 1l, 20l, 7l, 12l, 10l. 3m 13.40s. a 13.40s (8 Ran).

(Trojan Racing), C Weedon

3323 Fuschia Handicap Class D (0-80 3-y-o and up) £3,318 6f...............(3:50)

2527^{4} HIGHBORN (Ire) [73] 4-10-0 G Hind (6) *cl up, led hfwy, rdn ins last and ran on wl*........(8 to 1 op 6 to 1) 1
2861^{6} MISS WHITTINGHAM (Ire) [56] 3-8-6 J Carroll (4) *hld up, hdwy hfwy, effrt 2 fs out, rdn to chal entering last, no extr nr finish*........(9 to 4 fav op 5 to 2 tchd 11 to 4) 2
3188^{2} COVENT GARDEN GIRL [64] 3-9-0 T Lucas (7) *led, hdd hfwy, cl up and ev ch till rdn and no extr ins last.* ....(5 to 1 op 4 to 1) 3
2475^{9} DREAM OF TOMORROW [50] 5-8-5 L Charnock (5) *chsd ldrs, rdn hfwy, kpt on one pace*........(33 to 1) 4
2661^{3} ALJAZ [78] 3-10-0 A Mackay (3) *hld up, wide strt and hdwy o'r 2 fs out, sn rdn and no imprsn.* ....(100 to 30 op 3 to 1 tchd 4 to 1) 5
2217^{7} APPEALING TIMES (USA) [65] 4-8-13 (7*) Claire Balding (8) *chsd ldrs, rdn 3 fs out, kpt on one pace.* ....(16 to 1 op 14 to 1) 6
3184^{9} SWEET ROMEO [64] 3-9-0 R P Elliott (2) *cl up till rdn hfwy, sn wknd*........(13 to 2 op 6 to 1) 7
1073^{4} WELLSY LAD (USA) [45] 6-8-0 S Wood (1) *dwlt, rdn hfwy, nvr dngrs*........(9 to 1 op 8 to 1 tchd 12 to 1) 8

Dist: ½l, 1½l, 4l, hd, 1½l, 5l, ½l. 1m 18.20s. a 4.80s (8 Ran).
SR: 42/18/20/-/17/3/-/-/ (Yorkshire Racing Club Owners Group 1990), P S Felgate

3324 Clematis Claiming Stakes Class F (3-y-o and up) £2,245 7f........... (4:20)

2380^{3} CRECHE (bl) 4-9-2^{2} (7*) E Husband (1) *dsptd ld till led aftr 2 fs, sn clr, rdn appr fnl furlong, kpt on ins last.* ....(5 to 2 op 6 to 4) 1
3192^{5} BY QUEEN (Ire) 3-8-3 (3*) M Fenton (5) *chsd ldrs, rdn 2 fs out, kpt on one pace*........(6 to 1 op 9 to 2) 2
AVIATOR'S DREAM 3-8-11 L Charnock (4) *dsptd ld for 2 fs, chsd wnr, rdn and one pace fnl two furlongs.* ....(11 to 1 op 14 to 1 tchd 16 to 1 and 10 to 1) 3
2550^{4} FORMAESTRE (Ire) 3-7-3 (7*) Claire Balding (2) *sn beh, rdn 3 fs out, styd on fnl 2 furlongs, nvr dngrs.* ....(6 to 4 fav op 13 to 8 tchd 7 to 4) 4
SEASIDE DREAMER 3-7-13 J O'Reilly (7) *sn outpcd, beh frm hfwy*........(33 to 1 op 25 to 1) 5
FLYING FASCINATION 5-8-12 T Wall (6) *very slwly away, sn tld off*........(33 to 1 op 25 to 1) 6
2589^{3} MELODIC DRIVE 3-8-7 G Hind (3) *dwlt, pld up lme aftr one furlong*........(7 to 1 op 6 to 1) pu

Dist: 4l, ¾l, hd, 20l, dist. 1m 31.70s. a 5.60s (7 Ran).
SR: 44/17/20/4/ (Brian Pollins), Mrs N Macauley

3325 Jasmine Handicap Class E (0-70 3-y-o and up) £3,054 1m.............(4:50)

2920^{5} GALLANT JACK (Ire) [52] 4-9-3 A Mackay (11) *slwly into strd, sn reco'red, led appr fnl furlong, styd on und pres*........(13 to 2 op 14 to 1) 1
2014^{3} BRAVE HERO (USA) [41] 3-7-13 D Biggs (3) *cl up till hmpd and lost pl aftr 3 fs, styd on strly fnl 2 furlongs, nrst finish*........(14 to 1 op 12 to 1) 2
2920^{2} MAY SQUARE (Ire) [36] 5-8-1^{1} G Hind (7) *trkd ldrs gng wl, led and quickened 3 fs out, hdd o'r one out, no extr.* ....(5 to 2 fav tchd 3 to 1) 3
2624^{6} THEMAAM [63] 4-10-0 A McGlone (1) *chsd ldrs, effrt and swtchd o'r one furlong out, styd on wl.* ....(13 to 2 op 6 to 1 tchd 8 to 1) 4
2970 WOODMANS STAR [42] 3-8-0^{2} R Price (10) *drvn alng and beh, hdwy entering strt, kpt on wl towards finish.* ....(16 to 1 op 25 to 1) 5
3124^{7} ON Y VA (USA) [55] 6-8-13 (7*) Sarah Thompson (8) *in tch till outpcd fnl 2 and a half fs*........(9 to 1 op 6 to 1) 6
2326^{4} SARANGANI BAY (USA) [66] 3-9-7 (3*) M Fenton (5) *cl up till rdn and wknd wl o'r one furlong out.* ....(8 to 1 op 11 to 2) 7
2898^{3} STEVIE'S WONDER (Ire) [57] 3-8-10 (5*) N Gwilliams (12) *sn rdn and beh, nvr dngrs*........(8 to 1 op 11 to 2) 8
3088^{9} DONTBETALKING (Ire) [36] 3-7-8 J Fanning (6) *pushed alng thrght, nvr trble ldrs*........(20 to 1) 9
2920^{8} SWYNFORD FLYER [29] 4-7-8^{1} L Charnock (2) *led till hdd 3 fs out, sn lost pl*........(33 to 1 op 25 to 1) 10
829^{9} SPORTING SPIRIT [45] 3-8-3 S Wood (9) *rdn hfwy, nvr dngrs*........(33 to 1 op 25 to 1) 11
2920^{4} SIE AMATO (Ire) [50] 4-9-1 J Fortune (4) *chsd ldrs till rdn and wknd o'r 3 fs out*........(10 to 1 op 8 to 1) 12

Dist: 1l, 2l, sht-hd, 1½l, 4l, 2l, 2½l, 3l, 8l, nk. 1m 45.50s. a 6.50s (12 Ran).
SR: 30/9/5/31/-/6/4/-/-/ (S Hunter), D Haydn Jones

TRAMORE (IRE) (good to firm)
Friday August 13th

3326 Noel Cummins Bookmaker (Fillies) Handicap (0-75 3-y-o and up) £2,762 1½m.......................... (6:00)

2958^{2} SIMPLY MARILYN (Ire) [-] 4-9-1 (6*) J J Behan (1) (2 to 1 fav) 1
1122^{4} ALIBAR'S PET (Ire) [-] 3-8-11 J F Egan (5)........ (11 to 1) 2
3163^{3} MITAH (Ire) [-] 5-9-0^{2} (6*) T P Treacy (6)........(9 to 2) 3
2923^{3} GRECIAN LADY (Ire) [-] 4-8-7 Joanna Morgan (2)... (6 to 1) 4
2558^{2} PRINTOUT (Ire) [-] 3-8-1 W J Supple (4)........ (8 to 1) 5
2881^{6} CORAL SOUND (Ire) [-] 3-7-11 (6*) R V Skelly (10) (10 to 1) 6
2702^{4} NURSE MAID (Ire) [-] 3-8-10 (2*) D G O'Shea (8).... (5 to 1) 7
3038^{6} LAGRION (USA) [-] (bl) 4-8-10 (6*) B J Walsh (7)... (12 to 1) 8
2513^{3} MISS TWIN PEAKS (Ire) [-] 3-9-0 P V Gilson (9)..... (6 to 1) 9
2517^{7} MANGANS HILL (Ire) [-] 3-8-3 (4*) W J Smith (3)... (14 to 1) 10

Dist: 2½l, ¾l, ½l, nk. 2m 31.90s. (10 Ran).

(Mrs St J O'Connell), Liam Browne

3327 Noel M. Griffin Memorial Handicap (0-85 3-y-o and up) £6,352 1m 1f (6:30)

3164^{3} TRYARRA (Ire) [-] 3-9-6 (4*) J J Behan (3).......... (5 to 1) 1
2922^{6} AULD STOCK (Ire) [-] 3-9-0 (6*) J R Barry (5)...... (10 to 1) 2
2901* MEJEVE [-] 5-9-12 (5ex) S Craine (10)........ (9 to 2) 3
3028^{3} THE BURSER [-] 7-9-7 (6*) C Everard (8)......... (11 to 2) 4
2782^{3} FLORA WOOD (Ire) [-] 3-9-5 W J Supple (7)........ (8 to 1) 5
3076^{4} HANG A RIGHT [-] 6-9-3 (6*) T P Treacy (2)........ (8 to 1) 6
2323^{9} ALSHOU (Ire) [-] 4-8-2 (8*) B Fenton (1)...........(10 to 1) 7
3075^{3} SLIGHTLY SCRUFFY (Ire) [-] 3-9-4 P V Gilson (4).. (10 to 1) 8
2922^{2} SAFAYN (USA) [-] (bl) 3-9-8 (4*) W J Smith (6)... (5 to 2 fav) 9
2901 WHAT MAGIC (Ire) [-] (bl) 3-9-4 D J Smith (11).....(14 to 1) 10

Dist: 1½l, ¾l, ¾l, 2l. 1m 59.90s. (10 Ran).

(Mrs K Doyle), A P O'Brien

3328 Metal Man Claiming Race (3-y-o and up) £2,245 1m 1f............... (7:30)

2667^{2} YONOKA (Fr) 4-8-6 P V Gilson (5)............... (7 to 1) 1
3276^{5} COMMAND 'N CONTROL 4-8-12 J F Egan (10).... (6 to 1) 2
LENANTO (Ire) 5-8-12 W J Supple (4)........... (7 to 1) 3
2514^{5} SARA MAURETTE (Ire) 3-7-10 (4*) W J Smith (9)....(8 to 1) 4
2879 INISHMOT (Ire) 3-7-6^{4} (8*) R T Fitzpatrick (3)......(14 to 1) 5
2324^{6} GILT DIMENSION (bl) 6-8-10 (4*) J J Behan (6).... (11 to 4) 6
3061^{2} DARCY'S THATCHER 9-8-10 S Craine (2)......(9 to 4 fav) 7
3242^{7} GIFT OF PEACE (Ire) 3-7-8 (2*) D G O'Shea (7)..... (8 to 1) 8
SHREWD MOVE 4-8-2 (6*) R V Skelly (8).......... (8 to 1) 9

Dist: Nk, 2l, sht-hd, 2½l. 1m 58.70s. (9 Ran).

(Miss E M Galvin), Daniel J Murphy

3329 T.J. Carroll & Co. Ltd. Opportunity Maiden (3-y-o) £2,935 1½m..... (8:30)

1649^{6} NORDICOLINI (Ire) 8-7 (4*) W J Smith (6).......... (3 to 1) 1
2702^{8} HAANEM 8-11 W J Supple (1)............... (9 to 4 jt-fav) 2
2956^{6} ENIMDEE (Ire) 8-11 J F Egan (4)............ (9 to 4 jt-fav) 3
2956^{7} GARDENVALE VIC (Ire) 8-10 (4*) J J Behan (3)..... (5 to 1) 4
2901 TRES JOUR (Ire) 8-11 P V Gilson (5)............. (12 to 1) 5
1236^{9} BOB THE YANK (Ire) 9-0 S Craine (2)............ (10 to 1) 6

Dist: ¾l, 2l, 1½l, ¾l. 2m 37.80s. (6 Ran).

(Ronald Arculli), D K Weld

CURRAGH (IRE) (yielding)
Saturday August 14th

Going Correction: PLUS 0.50 sec. per fur. (races 1,3,4,5,6), PLUS 0.40 (2,7)

3330 Baxi Solo Handicap (0-80 3-y-o and up) £4,155 6f.................. (2:00)

3160* CISEAUX (USA) [-] 4-10-3 (7ex) M J Kinane (9) (5 to 1 jt-fav) 1
1611^{3} MACQUARIE RIDGE (USA) [-] 5-8-1 W J Supple (7) ....(5 to 1 jt-fav) 2
3161^{6} BENE MERENTI (Ire) [-] (bl) 3-8-13 (6*) R V Skelly (8) (14 to 1) 3
3201^{5} ASTA MADERA (Ire) [-] 3-8-6 (4*) J J Behan (5).... (10 to 1) 4

3075^{4} WALLY WALLENSKY (Ire) [-] 3-9-2 (4*) P Carberry (13) ....(6 to 1) 5
3160 MASTER WORK [-] (bl) 5-7-5 (2*) D G O'Shea (10) (12 to 1) 6
CLONALEENAN [-] (bl) 4-7-9 Joanna Morgan (15) (12 to 1) 7
3040^{3} BLACKTRENCH LADY (Ire) [-] 5-9-1 J P Murtagh (6) ....(14 to 1) 8
2879^{8} SOUTHERN RULE [-] 6-7-8^{1} A J Nolan (16) ....(16 to 1) 9
3074^{4} NORDIC SAINT (Ire) [-] 4-8-13 (6*) J A Heffernan (4) (10 to 1) 10
NOBLE SAM (Ire) [-] 4-7-11 (2*) R M Burke (3) .....(50 to 1) 11
3201^{7} MAGIC DON (Ire) [-] (bl) 4-9-1 (8*) R T Fitzpatrick (1) (9 to 1) 12
2511^{2} FILL MY GLASS [-] 9-7-7^{4} (4*) W J Smith (11) .....(16 to 1) 13
3244^{4} FANTANTE (Ire) [-] (bl) 4-8-10 P V Gilson (17) ......(10 to 1) 14
3201^{3} OICHE MHAITH [-] (bl) 3-9-1 P Shanahan (12) ......(7 to 1) 15
2556^{2} GEALLAINNBAN (Ire) [-] 3-8-5 J F Egan (2) .... (20 to 1) 16
2780^{6} JUNORIUS (Ire) [-] 4-9-7 S Craine (14) .... (14 to 1) 17
Dist: ¾l, sht-hd, 4l, hd. 1m 16.40s. a 5.90s (17 Ran).
SR: 59/26/43/18/27/-/ (G Olivero), D K Weld

3331 Royal Whip Stakes (Group 3) (3-y-o and up) £11,500 1½m...........(2:30)

1511* RAYSEKA (Ire) 3-8-4 M J Kinane (1) *hld up, prog 4 fs out, quickened to ld 2 out, styd on strly*............(9 to 4) 1
2405^{2} ROYAL BALLERINA (Ire) 3-8-4 W J Supple (5) *mid-div, prog 3 fs out, ev ch 2 out, rdn and no extr one out, kpt on.* ....(5 to 4 on) 2
1770^{6} ARBUSHA (USA) 4-9-1 C Roche (3) *trkd ldr, prog 6 fs out, led 3 out to 2 out, kpt on*......................(5 to 1) 3
2607^{5} PORTERSTOWN BOY (Ire) (bl) 3-8-7 P Shanahan (4) *al rear, rdn 4 fs out, sn wknd*.........................(12 to 1) 4
895 DOWLAND (USA) 5-9-4 P V Gilson (2) *led, clr aftr 3 fs, hdd three out, sn wknd*..........................(14 to 1) 5
Dist: 2½l, 2l, 20l, 15l. 2m 35.90s. a 6.40s (5 Ran).
SR: 74/69/76/28/9/ (H H Aga Khan), John M Oxx

3332 Tattersalls Auction Race (2-y-o) £3,795 6f...................... (3:00)

2804^{3} SLICK DEALER (Ire) 8-5 P V Gilson (13) .... (4 to 1) 1
TONGABEZI (Ire) 7-12 (2*) R M Burke (9) .... (16 to 1) 2
3073* ZIRAVELLO (Ire) 9-3 M J Kinane (7) .... (13 to 8 fav) 3
820^{5} ABSOLUTE RULER (Ire) 8-7 C Roche (11) .... (14 to 1) 4
3064^{3} YAHTHAB (Ire) 9-3 W J Supple (8) .... (6 to 1) 5
3073 INISHMANN (Ire) 8-5 J F Egan (3) ....(20 to 1) 6
1608* CATWALKER (Ire) 9-3 J P Murtagh (12) ....(5 to 1) 7
APPEARANCE MONEY (Ire) 7-10 (4*) J J Behan (10) ....(14 to 1) 8
BRIEF RESPITE (Ire) 8-7 P Shanahan (2) .... (10 to 1) 9
1197 THE MARDYKE (Ire) 9-0 K J Manning (4) .... (16 to 1) 10
3273^{9} DEARMISTERSHATTER (Ire) 8-3 Joanna Morgan (5) ....(33 to 1) 11
3073 PERFECT CADENCE (Ire) 7-12 (2*) D G O'Shea (1) (12 to 1) 12
Dist: 2l, hd, ½l, hd. 1m 18.20s. a 7.70s (12 Ran).
(Mrs G Hourigan), G T Hourigan

3333 Desmond Stakes (Group 3) (3-y-o and up) £11,500 1m.................(3:30)

2407* ASEMA (USA) 3-8-12 M J Kinane (3) *wl plcd, quickened to ld one furlong out, styd on strly*............(6 to 4 fav) 1
2853* EUROLINK THUNDER 3-8-8 P Shanahan (2) *hld up, prog 2 fs out, ev ch one out, kpt on, no chance wth wnr.* ....(4 to 1) 2
2076^{5} MASSYAR (Ire) 3-9-1 J P Murtagh (7) *trkd ldr, rdn to ld 2 fs out, hdd one out, kpt on one pace*.............(2 to 1) 3
3072^{6} SALMON EILE (Ire) 5-9-1 S Craine (4) *led to 2 fs out, rdn and wknd ins last*.............................(10 to 1) 4
3162^{7} MALVERNICO (Ire) 5-9-1 C Roche (1) *trkd ldr, rdn and lost pl 2 fs out, kpt on clsg stages*...................(8 to 1) 5
2878* BE MY HOPE (Ire) 4-8-12 P V Gilson (5) *al rear, rdn and kpt on one pace fnl 2 fs*...........................(12 to 1) 6
3162^{9} BRADAWN BREEVER (Ire) (bl) 4-9-1 W J Supple (6) *al rear, rdn and wknd one furlong out*................(25 to 1) 7
Dist: 1l, nk, 2½l, ¾l. 1m 46.20s. a 9.60s (7 Ran).
SR: 14/7/13/5/3/-/-/ (Allen E Paulson), D K Weld

3334 Silken Thomas Handicap (0-100 3-y-o and up) £4,140 7f...............(4:00)

3027^{7} MYSTERIOUS WAYS (Ire) [-] 3-9-5 J P Murtagh (2) .... (6 to 4 fav) 1
3027^{5} UKUD (USA) [-] 3-8-3 W J Supple (5) ....(5 to 1) 2
2451^{9} SKELLIG [-] 7-7-7^{2} (4*) J J Behan (9) ....(14 to 1) 3
2806* DOBIE (USA) [-] 5-8-6 M J Kinane (6) ....(4 to 1) 4
1552^{7} CLASSIC MATCH (Ire) [-] 5-9-2 (4*) P Carberry (4) (14 to 1) 5
3165^{5} RONDELLI (Ire) [-] 3-9-6 C Roche (3) ....(13 to 2) 6
3072^{5} COLOUR PARTY (USA) [-] 3-9-8 P V Gilson (1) .....(9 to 1) 7
BOURREE [-] 5-7-12 J F Egan (7) ....(14 to 1) 8
895 LIFEWATCH VISION [-] 6-10-0 P Shanahan (8) .... (16 to 1) 9
Dist: 2½l, ¾l, sht-hd, 1l. 1m 30.40s. a 7.20s (9 Ran).
SR: 50/26/16/26/37/-/ (Mrs A Manning), M V O'Brien

3335 EBF Tyros Stakes (Listed) (2-y-o) £8,625 7f....................... (4:30)

MAJESTIC ROLE (Fr) 8-8 R M Burke (5) *mid-div, prog 2 fs out, dsptd ld ins last, styd on strly to lead cl hme.* ....(20 to 1) 1

2072* GOTHIC DREAM (Ire) 8-11 J P Murtagh (6) *mid-div, prog 2 fs out, dsptd ld one out, no extr cl hme*.........(5 to 2) 2
2778* VIA CONDOTTI (Ire) 8-11 C Roche (10) *trkd ldr, prog 2 fs out, dsptd ld one out, no extr ins last*..........(6 to 1) 3
2648^{7} DANISH (Ire) 8-11 P V Gilson (1) *trkd ldr, prog 2 fs out, dsptd ld one out, sn rdn and wknd*............(8 to 1) 4
2880* ASTRONAVE (Ire) 8-11 M J Kinane (9) *hld up, some prog 2 fs out, rdn one out, eased whn btn ins last*.... (6 to 4 fav) 5
3030* ZAVALETA (Ire) 8-11 K J Manning (7) *hld up, kpt on fnl 2 fs, not rch ldrs*...................................(8 to 1) 6
2778^{6} MULMUS (Ire) 8-11 S Craine (2) *rear, kpt on fnl 2 fs, not rch ldrs*.......................................(33 to 1) 7
3064* GAINSBOROUGH'S BOY (Ire) (bl) 8-11 P Carberry (8) *led, 6 ls clr hfwy, hdd one out, wknd quickly*....... (14 to 1) 8
3026* DILIGENT DODGER (Ire) 8-11 W J Supple (11) *al rear.* ....(14 to 1) 9
2983^{5} SUMMERHILL SPECIAL (Ire) 8-8 Joanna Morgan (3) *wl plcd, rdn and wknd 2 fs out*......................(20 to 1) 10
3073^{7} SEAFORTH (Ire) (bl) 8-11 J F Egan (4) *mid-div, rdn and wknd 2 fs out*...............................(25 to 1) 11
Dist: ¾l, 2l, ¾l, 3½l. 1m 31.40s. a 8.20s (11 Ran).
SR: 24/25/19/17/6/-/ (M Hagai), Michael Kauntze

3336 Robertstown Handicap (0-105 3-y-o and up) £6,900 2m..............(5:00)

2984^{2} SHIRLEY'S DELIGHT (Ire) [-] 3-7-10 (5ex) Joanna Morgan (9) ....(7 to 1) 1
2245^{2} TBAAREEH (USA) [-] 3-8-9 C Roche (10) .... (5 to 1) 2
2744^{4} PARNALA (USA) [-] 3-7-12 (2*) D G O'Shea (5) ..(3 to 1 fav) 3
1576^{2} DUHARRA (Ire) [-] (bl) 5-9-1 (4*) W J Smith (1) .....(12 to 1) 4
2881^{4} MASAI WARRIOR [-] 6-8-3 (2*) R M Burke (4) ...... (9 to 1) 5
2841 AIYBAK (Ire) [-] 5-9-2 M J Kinane (8) .... (5 to 1) 6
2608^{5} TONY'S FEN [-] 4-9-10 W J Supple (7) ....(10 to 1) 7
1576^{9} KAZKAR (Ire) [-] 5-8-0 J F Egan (6) ....(25 to 1) 8
2958^{3} SUPER FLAME (Can) [-] 6-9-2 J P Murtagh (3) ..... (8 to 1) 9
3037^{3} INK BY THE DRUM (USA) [-] 5-7-8^{5} (4*) J J Behan (2) (6 to 1) 10
Dist: 5l, 2½l, hd, 4½l. (Time not taken) (10 Ran).
(Liam Doherty), Noel Meade

DEAUVILLE (FR) (good)
Saturday August 14th

3337 Prix Guillaume d'Ornano (Group 2) (3-y-o) £35,842 1¼m.............. (3:00)

2081^{4} DERNIER EMPEREUR (USA) 8-12 S Guillot, *broke slwly, 4th strt, effrt and quickened 2 fs out, led one and a half furlongs out, ran on wl*.. 1
2803^{3} FASTNESS (Ire) 8-12 F Head, *pld hrd early, last strt, rdn 2 fs out, ran on wl, took second pl cl hme*.............. 2
JEUNE HOMME (USA) 8-12 C Asmussen, *5th strt, effrt 2 fs out, quickened to chal for ld one and a half furlongs out, kpt on*.. 3
2621^{2} PORT LUCAYA 8-12 G Mosse, *trkd ldr in second, second strt, rdn and ran on one pl fnl 2 fs*...................... 4
2076^{4} REGENCY 9-2 Pat Eddery, *led till heded one and a half fs out, wknd quickly*.. 5
1149^{2} IRISH PROSPECTOR (Fr) 8-12 E Legrix, *mid-div, 3rd strt, rdn and wknd 2 fs out*.............................. 6
Dist: 2½l, ½l, 1l, 3l, 6l. 2m 7.00s. a 5.30s (6 Ran).
SR: 45/40/39/37/35/19/ (Paul de Moussac), A Fabre

3338 Prix du Haras de la Huderie (Listed) (2-y-o) £14,337 7f...............(4:10)

SIGNE DIVIN (USA) 9-2 S Guillot, ... 1
SIMPLY TRICKY (USA) 9-2 , *fnshd 2nd, disq and plcd 6th.* 2D
LUNAFAIRY (Fr) 8-13 T Jarnet, *fnshd 3rd, plcd 2nd*....... 2
WEST MAN (USA) 8-12 M Boutin, *fnshd 4th, plcd 3rd*...... 3
Dist: 1l, hd, 2l, ½l, nose, 2½l, hd, 2l, ½l, sht-nk. 1m 24.50s. a 2.50s (11 Ran).
SR: 65/62/58/55/ (P de Moussac), A Fabre

LA TESTE DE BUCH (FR) (firm)
Saturday August 14th

3339 Criterium de Bequet (Listed) (2-y-o) £11,947 6f.................... (3:50)

2996^{2} STRAIGHT ARROW 8-9 D Harrison, ... 1
RIVER ARLY (Fr) 8-12 , ... 2
WARN ME (Fr) 8-9 P Julien, ... 3
2541^{2} CALLABONNA , ... 4
Dist: 2l, 2½l, 2½l, ½l. (Time not taken) (5 Ran).
(J R Bailey), Lord Huntingdon

LINGFIELD (good)
Saturday August 14th

Going Correction: MINUS 0.40 sec. per fur. (races 1,2,4), MINUS 0.35 (3,5)

3340 Blackberry Lane Apprentice Handicap Class G (0-70 3-y-o and up) £2,678 7f

140yds. . . . . (5:15)

917[8] MULCIBER [62] 5-9-5 (8*) P Houghton (7) *hld up, ran on 3 out, led ins fnl furlong, shaken up and kpt on nr line.* . . . .(5 to 1 op 4 to 1) 1
3070[6] DAILY SPORT DON [66] 3-9-2 (8*) D O'Neill (9) *made most of rng til hdd ins fnl furlong, styd on gmely.* . . . .(4 to 1 op 5 to 2) 2
2149[5] CELIA BRADY [46] 5-8-1 (10*) Sarah Holland (2) *styd on frm rear ins last 2 fs, not quicken last 100 yards.* . . . . (15 to 2 op 5 to 1 tchd 8 to 1) 3
3261 CANADIAN CAPERS [46] 4-8-5 (6*) R Painter (4) *beh til styd on frm 2 fs out, no imprsn on wnr.* . . . .(9 to 2 op 4 to 1 tchd 5 to 1) 4
906 GAMEFULL GOLD [39] 4-7-10 (8*) A Martinez (6) *chsd ldrs til drpd rear hfwy, kpt on ag'n clsg stages.* . . . .(20 to 1 op 33 to 1) 5
3213[2] ASCOM PAGER TOO [40] 3-7-7 (5*) D Toole (3) *in tch on outsd til lost pl o'r one furlong out.* . . . .(7 to 2 fav op 5 to 2 tchd 4 to 1) 6
2747[4] FAIR ENCHANTRESS [43] (bl) 5-8-5 (3*) J O'Dwyer (5) *wl plcd til beh hfwy.* . . . . (7 to 1 op 6 to 1) 7
2967[7] BARASSIE [36] 3-7-2[2] (8*) Sharon Millard (1) *ldg grp til wknd o'r 2 fs out.* . . . .(20 to 1 op 33 to 1) 8
2329[9] DISTANT DYNASTY [35] 3-7-2 (5*) Wendy Jones (8) *dsptd ld til o'r 2 fs out, sn btn.* . . . .(50 to 1 op 33 to 1) 9

Dist: Nk, 1l, 2½l, 4l, ½l, nk, 5l, 2½l. 1m 30.68s. a 2.38s (9 Ran).
SR: 31/27/11/3/-/-/ (Mrs Penny Treadwell), G Harwood

3341 Felcourt Rating Related Maiden Fillies' Stakes Class F (0-70 3-y-o) £2,143 7f 140yds. . . . . (6:10)

1181[4] LAKAB (USA) 8-11 R Hills (2) *wl plcd, led o'r 3 fs out, pushed clr appr fnl furlong, easily..* (8 to 1 op 6 to 1) 1
2580[6] PRINCESS HAYLEY 8-11 L Dettori (4) *in tch and sn pushed alng, cld on ldrs 3 fs out, one pace appr fnl furlong.* . . . . (11 to 8 fav op 6 to 4 tchd 7 to 4 and 5 to 4) 2
3005[3] SHERGRESS 8-11 J Quinn (6) *mid-div, outpcd hfwy, styd on fnl furlong, nrst finish.* . . . . . . (10 to 1 tchd 12 to 1) 3
2940[2] NEWINGTON BUTTS (Ire) 8-11 T Quinn (1) *uns rdr and bolted bef strt, hdwy hfwy, rdn and not quicken 2 fs out, eased ins fnl furlong.* . . . . (9 to 2 op 11 to 4 tchd 5 to 1) 4
2938[9] SEA SIREN 8-11 W Newnes (5) *led to hfwy, wknd o'r 2 fs out.* . . . . (9 to 2 op 5 to 1 tchd 4 to 1) 5
3108[4] VILLAVINA 8-11 D Biggs (3) *pressed ldr for 3 fs, wknd o'r 2 out.* . . . . (10 to 1 op 8 to 1 tchd 12 to 1) 6
2138[6] MISS COPYFORCE 8-4 (7*) Antoinette Armes (7) *slwly into strd, al outpcd, tld off.* . . . .(9 to 1 op 16 to 1 tchd 20 to 1 and 8 to 1) 7

Dist: 4l, 4l, sht-hd, 2l, ½l, 30l. 1m 30.09s. a 1.79s (7 Ran).
SR: 24/12/-/-/ (Hamdan Al-Maktoum), H Thomson Jones

3342 Anzani Handicap Class E (0-70 3-y-o and up) £2,574 1m 3f 106yds. . . . (6:40)

3018[3] RAPPORTEUR (USA) [55] 7-8-13 W Newnes (7) *handily plcd, quickened to ld o'r 4 fs out, rdn clr, eased nr finish.* . . . .(9 to 2 op 7 to 2 tchd 5 to 1) 1
1717[5] AREMEF (USA) [65] 4-9-9 Paul Eddery (4) *hld up in rear, improved 3 fs out, styd on into second pl fnl furlong, not rch wnr.* . . . . (8 to 1 op 7 to 1) 2
3157* SURREY DANCER [70] 5-10-0 W Ryan (10) *hld up in rear, hdwy o'r 4 fs out, rdn and one pace last 2 furlongs.* . . . .(5 to 1 op 7 to 2) 3
2992 TORGHIA [53] 6-8-11 T Quinn (1) *led for one furlong, ldg grp, chsd wnr o'r 4 out till wknd ins fnl furlong.* . . . . (33 to 1 op 20 to 1) 4
3066* PIE HATCH (Ire) [46] (bl) 4-8-4 R Hills (2) *strted slwly, cld on ldrs hfwy, not much room o'r 4 fs, no extr appr last 2 furlongs.* . . . .(3 to 1 fav tchd 5 to 2 and 7 to 2) 5
3078[7] SIMPLY (Ire) [43] 4-8-1 F Norton (6) *led aftr one furlong, hdd o'r 4 out, wknd over 2 out, tld off.* . . . . (13 to 2 op 4 to 1 tchd 7 to 1) 6
2751[9] MISS RITA [55] 4-8-13 L Dettori (9) *chsd ldrs til wknd o'r 3 fs, tld off.* . . . .(7 to 1 tchd 8 to 1) 7
2942 THEMEDA [43] (bl) 4-7-10 (5*) B Russell (8) *cl up til lost pl o'r 4 fs out, ran wide over 2 out, tld off.* . . . .(5 to 1 tchd 13 to 2) 8

Dist: 5l, ¾l, 1½l, 1½l, 15l, 15l, 1½l. 2m 25.99s. a 1.79s (8 Ran).
SR: 41/41/44/24/14/ (Richard Berenson), C C Elsey

3343 Felixstowe Limited Stakes Class E (3-y-o) £2,595 6f. . . . . (7:10)

2787[4] JAAZIM 9-0 R Hills (1) *rcd alone far side, definite ldr o'r 2 fs out, styd on strly.* . . . .(14 to 1 op 10 to 1) 1
2731[3] TRINITY HALL 8-9 D Holland (4) *beh till hdwy 2 fs out, led stand side grp ins fnl furlong, no imprsn on wnr nr finish.* . . . .(14 to 1 tchd 16 to 1) 2
3095* FIRST OPTION 9-0 K Darley (6) *hld up stand side, hdwy und pres o'r 2 fs out, not quicken ins last.* . . . .(11 to 8 fav op 7 to 4) 3
3251[2] CHILLY BREEZE 8-9 G Duffield (5) *prmnt, led stands side grp o'r 2 fs out, rdn and no extr ins last.* . . . .(4 to 1 op 6 to 1) 4
2214[7] CHAMPAGNE GRANDY 8-9 F Norton (3) *wl in tch stand side, one pace last 2 fs.* . . . .(16 to 1 op 12 to 1 tchd 20 to 1) 5
1162[2] DITTISHAM (USA) (bl) 8-9 L Dettori (7) *led stands side grp for o'r 3 fs, wknd.* . . . .(9 to 1 op 6 to 1 tchd 10 to 1) 6
3220[3] CHARITY EXPRESS (Ire) 8-9 D Biggs (2) *in tch stands side, no prog ins last 2 fs.* . . . .(12 to 1 op 7 to 1) 7
3006[2] KENNEDYS PRIMA 8-9 W Ryan (9) *mid-div stands side, shaken up hfwy, wknd 2 fs out.* . . . . (10 to 1 op 6 to 1) 8
1470[7] TARTIB (Ire) 9-0 T Quinn (8) *speed to hfwy stands side, sn lost pl, tld off.* . . . . (33 to 1 op 20 to 1) 9
3168[2] ROYAL DEED (USA) 8-9 M Tebbutt (10) *walked dwn to strt, whipped round leaving stalls, refused to race.* . . . . (10 to 1 op 8 to 1) I

Dist: 2½l, 1l, 2l, 3l, 1l, 5l, 5l, 15l. 1m 9.35s. a 0.35s (10 Ran).
SR: 45/30/31/18/6/2/ (Hamdan Al-Maktoum), Major W R Hern

3344 Twenty-one Today Rating Related Maiden Stakes Class E (0-70 3-y-o) £2,489 2m. (7:40)

2972[9] USK THE WAY 8-9 W Ryan (4) *made all, rdn alng 2 fs out, kpt on wl ins fnl furlong.* . . . . (7 to 1 op 5 to 1) 1
2991[3] FOOLS ERRAND (Ire) 9-0 T Quinn (1) *chsd wnr til o'r 4 fs out, cld up ag'n and ev ch 2 out, not quicken ins fnl furlong.* . . . .(2 to 1 fav op 7 to 4 tchd 9 to 4) 2
3125[6] NEMEA (USA) 8-9 R Hills (6) *hld up in rear, ran on o'r 3 fs out, not quicken appr fnl furlong, rallied nr line.* . . . .(9 to 4 op 2 to 1 tchd 5 to 2) 3
3087[9] GUESTWICK 9-0 B Raymond (5) *wl plcd, chsd wnr o'r 4 fs out til over 2 out, btn ins fnl furlong.* (7 to 2 op 5 to 1) 4
2776[7] COMBELLINO 9-0 N Adams (2) *in tch til rdn and wknd o'r 3 fs out.* . . . . (33 to 1 op 20 to 1) 5
3096[5] MICHAELA MIA (USA) 8-9 L Dettori (3) *hld up in rear, rdn alng o'r 3 fs out, no imprsn on ldrs.* . . . .(8 to 1 op 6 to 1 tchd 9 to 1) 6

Dist: 2½l, hd, 5l, 6l, 5l. 3m 35.16s. a 11.66s (6 Ran).
(Cliveden Stud), H R A Cecil

LINGFIELD (A.W) (std)
Saturday August 14th
Going Correction: MINUS 0.30 sec. per fur.

3345 Crockham Hill Selling Stakes Class G (2-y-o) £2,427 6f. . . . .(5:40)

3009 NORISKI'MARINGER 8-11 B Rouse (5) *made virtually all, rdn clr o'r 2 fs out, styd on cmftbly.* . . . . (7 to 2 op 11 to 2 tchd 3 to 1) 1
3103* CHARISMA GIRL (e/s) 8-13 D Biggs (3) *pressed ldrs til rdn and outpcd o'r 2 fs out.* . . . .(6 to 4 fav op 5 to 4 tchd 15 to 8 and 2 to 1) 2
3264 GIGUE 8-6 F Norton (2) *wl plcd, rdn and one pace appr last 2 fs.* . . . . (5 to 1 op 4 to 1) 3
1615[5] ROCKABYE BAILEYS 8-3 (3*) C Hodgson (8) *beh til ran on 2 fs out, styd on one pace fnl furlong.* . . . .(14 to 1 op 7 to 1 tchd 16 to 1) 4
2909 THORNY BISHOP (bl) 8-4 (7*) Antoinette Armes (7) *steadied leaving stalls, outpcd til effrt 2 fs out, ran on one pace fnl furlong.* . . . .(20 to 1 op 14 to 1) 5
3103[9] HUMMINBIRDPRINCESS 8-1 (5*) B Russell (4) *sn outpcd, rdn and lost tch hfwy.* . . . .(20 to 1 op 14 to 1) 6
1964[8] GRECIAN GARDEN 8-13 S Whitworth (6) *wth ldrs, rdn o'r 3 fs out, wknd and eased ins last 2 furlongs.* . . . . (17 to 2 op 8 to 1 tchd 9 to 1) 7
2911 MISS IGLOO (bl) 8-6 J Quinn (9) *sn outpcd, rdn and lost tch frm hfwy.* . . . .(9 to 1 op 6 to 1 tchd 10 to 1) 8

Dist: 5l, 1½l, 1l, ½l, 4l, nk, 20l. 1m 14.79s. a 3.99s (8 Ran).
(Roldvale Limited), G Lewis

3346 Saxby Handicap Class E (0-70 3-y-o and up) £2,427 1¼m. . . . .(8:10)

3193* DASHING FELLOW (Ire) [49] 5-9-7 J Quinn (4) *hld up in rear, pushed alng o'r 3 out, not much room over 2 out, rdn to ld wl ins fnl furlong.* . . . . (6 to 5 fav op Evens tchd 5 to 4) 1
1819[3] TROPICAL JUNGLE (USA) [59] 3-9-1 (7*) J D Smith (7) *chsd ldr, led o'r 3 fs out, hrd rdn over one out, hdd wl ins fnl furlong.* . . . . (9 to 2 op 5 to 1) 2
3045[3] JULIASDARKINVADER [53] 3-8-9 (7*) L Carter (6) *trkd ldrs aftr 3 fs, rdn and outpcd appr fnl furlong.* . . . .(9 to 1 op 7 to 1 tchd 10 to 1) 3
2712[9] HILLSDOWN BOY (Ire) [54] (e/s) 3-9-3 T Quinn (2) *in tch, rdn alng o'r 2 fs out, no imprsn on ldrs appr fnl furlong.* . . . . (9 to 1 op 6 to 1 tchd 10 to 1) 4
2827[8] SMART DAISY [52] 3-9-1 B Rouse (3) *pld hrd in tch till wknd o'r 3 fs out.* . . . .(5 to 1 op 11 to 2) 5
3020[9] FIABA [52] 5-9-5 (5*) B Russell (5) *rcd in rear, rdn alng hfwy, nvr on terms.* . . . .(33 to 1 op 20 to 1) 6
2834[9] DOSSERI [35] 5-8-7 D Biggs (1) *led til hdd o'r 3 fs out, wknd and eased wl over one out.* . . . .(8 to 1 op 10 to 1 tchd 12 to 1) 7

Dist: Nk, 5l, ½l, 10l, hd, 1l. 2m 7.27s. a 4.07s (7 Ran).
SR: 36/36/20/20/-/6/-/ (Mrs Val Rapkins), Mrs L Piggott

NEWBURY (good to firm)
Saturday August 14th
Going Correction: MINUS 0.30 sec. per fur.

3347 St Hugh's Stakes Class A (Listed) (2-y-o) £9,331 5f 34yds............ (2:00)

2866* PETULA 8-8 M Hills (7) *pressed ldrs, led o'r one furlong out, drvn out*...................... (8 to 1 tchd 9 to 1) 1
2400* STIMULANT 8-8 T Quinn (4) *led till appr fnl furlong, kpt on*.................... (15 to 2 op 7 to 1 tchd 8 to 1) 2
2790[6] TRICORNE 8-8 W R Swinburn (6) *hdwy 2 fs out, styd on same pace fnl furlong.* ....(100 to 30 op 3 to 1 tchd 7 to 2) 3
2790[2] MILD REBUKE 8-11 L Dettori (1) *chsd ldrs till outpcd o'r one furlong out*.......... (7 to 2 op 11 to 4) 4
2618[2] POMMES FRITES (Ire) 8-8 L Piggott (5) *pressed ldrs, lost pl 2 fs out, ran on ins last.* ....(9 to 4 fav tchd 5 to 2 and 2 to 1) 5
2301[5] DOUBLE DOWN 8-8 W Carson (2) *speed to hfwy.* ....(8 to 1 tchd 9 to 1) 6
2210[5] SWEET DECISION (Ire) 8-8 J Williams (3) *al rear, outpcd hfwy*............... (40 to 1 op 33 to 1 tchd 50 to 1) 7

Dist: 1½l, 1½l, 2½l, nk, 1½l, 2½l. 1m 0.61s. a 0.31s (7 Ran).
SR: 56/50/44/37/33/27/17/ (M A Khan), M Bell

3348 Stratton Handicap Class C (0-90 3-y-o and up) £5,247 5f 34yds.........(2:30)

3105* HEAVEN-LIEGH-GREY [69] 5-8-8 K Darley (5) *led half a furlong, frnt rnk till led appr last, hld on gmely.* .... (15 to 2 op 7 to 1 tchd 8 to 1) 1
2908[7] CATHERINEOFARAGON [73] 3-8-8 J Williams (7) *outpcd, plenty to do 2 fs out, shaken up and ran on fnl furlong, fnshd fst, jst fld*................ (20 to 1 tchd 25 to 1) 2
3099* CALL TO THE BAR (Ire) [67] 4-8-6 A Clark (9) *chsd ldrs, str chal appr fnl furlong, kpt on wl.* (10 to 1 tchd 12 to 1) 3
3105[6] TERRHARS (Ire) [82] 5-9-7 L Piggott (3) *beh, hdwy 2 fs out, ev ch jst ins last, not quicken*.... (16 to 1 tchd 20 to 1) 4
3127[8] ANOTHER JADE [78] 3-8-13 W R Swinburn (4) *hdwy to chase ldrs 2 fs out, kpt on fnl furlong.* ....(20 to 1 tchd 25 to 1) 5
3153[9] CANTORIS [81] 7-9-6 D Holland (1) *outpcd, rdn o'r one furlong out, ran on fnl furlong, fnshd wl.* .... (10 to 1 op 8 to 1) 6
2987 ASHTINA [89] 8-10-0 J Quinn (10) *chsd ldrs till outpcd fnl furlong*................ (14 to 1 op 10 to 1) 7
3051[4] AUGHFAD [81] (v) 7-9-6 W Newnes (12) *chsd ldrs till fdd fnl furlong*..................(14 to 1 op 12 to 1) 8
3085* FOOD OF LOVE [80] 5-9-5 M Roberts (14) *chsd ldrs till rdn and outpcd fnl 2 fs.* (7 to 1 fav op 6 to 1 tchd 8 to 1) 9
2846[3] BELLS OF LONGWICK [73] 4-8-12 S Whitworth (2) *hdwy 2 fs out, ev ch one out, wknd quickly.* .... (16 to 1 op 14 to 1 tchd 20 to 1) 10
3095[2] PRINCESS OBERON (Ire) [71] 3-8-6 M Hills (15) *speed stands side 3 fs*.......(11 to 1 op 12 to 1 tchd 14 to 1) 11
3136* LOVE RETURNED [87] 6-9-12 M Tebbutt (11) *outpcd, effrt hfwy, sn btn*........(9 to 1 op 7 to 1 tchd 10 to 1) 12
2987 PADDY CHALK [87] 7-9-12 A Munro (13) *outpcd.* ....(8 to 1 tchd 9 to 1) 13
3105[9] VERDE ALITALIA (Ire) [78] (bl) 4-9-3 W Carson (8) *led aftr half a furlong till appr fnl furlong, sn wknd.* ....(9 to 1 op 8 to 1 tchd 10 to 1) 14

Dist: Sht-hd, ½l, 1l, hd, ¾l, nk, ½l, nk, 1l, nk. 1m 0.78s. a 0.48s (14 Ran).
SR: 53/52/48/59/50/54/61/51/49/ (Peter M Dodd), J Berry

3349 Ibn Bey Geoffrey Freer Stakes Class A (Group 2) (3-y-o and up) £40,063 1m 5f 61yds......................... (3:00)

2883[4] AZZILFI 3-8-5 W Carson (4) *led to 2 and a half fs out, styd on wl und pres to ld ag'n ins last, hld on well.* (5 to 1) 1
2925[2] ASSESSOR (Ire) 4-9-9 T Quinn (5) *4th till hdwy to chase wnr four fs out, led 2 and a half out till ins last, kpt on wl*.. (5 to 1 op 4 to 1) 2
2925* SONUS (Ire) (v) 4-9-3 M Roberts (2) *5th till hdwy 3 fs out, rdn 2 out, styd on one pace fnl furlong.* ....(11 to 8 fav op 5 to 4 tchd 6 to 4) 3
2302[6] ZINAAD 4-9-6 W R Swinburn (1) *chsd wnr to 4 fs out, wknd ins fnl 2 furlongs*.................. (5 to 1 tchd 9 to 2) 4
1018[4] SHAMBO 6-9-6 L Dettori (3) *hdwy to chase ldrs 3 fs out, sn rdn, wknd o'r one out*............. (11 to 2 op 5 to 1) 5

Dist: Nk, 1l, 3l, 1l. 2m 56.75s. a 10.55s (5 Ran).
(Prince A A Faisal), J L Dunlop

3350 Eurolink Silver Trophy Rated Class B Handicap (0-100 3-y-o and up) £9,806 7f.............................. (3:30)

2854* IHTIRAZ [97] 3-9-0 R Hills (14) *in tch, quickened to ld ins fnl furlong, ran on wl.* (7 to 1 op 6 to 1 tchd 15 to 2) 1
2854[3] KAYVEE [93] 4-9-2 W R Swinburn (8) *beh, gd hdwy frm 2 fs out, str chal ins last, not pace of wnr.* ....(10 to 1 tchd 11 to 1) 2
3155* NO RESERVATIONS (Ire) [85] 3-8-2 D Holland (16) *al tracking ldrs, rdn and chlgd ins last, one pace.* ....(11 to 1 op 10 to 1 tchd 12 to 1) 3
2732[8] SUNDAY'S HILL [89] (bl) 4-8-12 J Quinn (3) *hdwy on outsd 2 fs out, led appr one out, hdd and outpcd ins last.* ....(33 to 1 tchd 40 to 1) 4
3065[4] ROCKY WATERS (USA) [90] 4-8-13 B Rouse (9) *pressed ldrs, ev ch o'r one furlong out, wknd fnl furlong.* .... (16 to 1 op 14 to 1) 5
2413* CROFT VALLEY [98] 6-9-7 T Quinn (13) *sn led, hdd o'r one furlong out, wknd ins last*...........(8 to 1 op 7 to 1) 6
3225[7] THE POWER OF ONE [84] (bl) 4-8-0 (7*) Kim McDonnell (2) *outpcd and pushed alng, hdwy frm 2 fs, nrst finish.* ....(100 to 1 op 66 to 1) 7
2928[8] EMBANKMENT (Ire) [86] 3-8-3 W Carson (10) *some prog fnl 2 fs, not a dngr*...... (14 to 1 op 12 to 1 tchd 16 to 1) 8
3177[6] YOUNG ERN [92] 3-8-9 W Ryan (12) *early speed, not a dngr frm hfwy*................. (14 to 1 tchd 16 to 1) 9
2987 TROON [89] 3-8-6 L Piggott (15) *chsd ldrs till wknd ins fnl 2 fs*..................................(12 to 1 op 14 to 1) 10
2627[5] WISHAM (USA) [84] 3-8-1 M Roberts (6) *drvn and effrt o'r 2 fs out, sn wknd*..................................(16 to 1) 11
COLOUR SERGEANT [87] 5-8-10 A Munro (1) *hdwy 3 fs out, wknd 2 out*......(11 to 1 op 10 to 1 tchd 12 to 1) 12
2627[7] LAW COMMISSION [89] 3-8-6 A Mackay (11) *stumbled strt, effrt hfwy, sn wknd*............ (25 to 1 tchd 33 to 1) 13
2854[5] BRIGADE [90] 4-8-13 K Darley (5) *early speed, sn outpcd.* ....(12 to 1 tchd 14 to 1) 14
3177[3] BEWARE OF AGENTS [88] 4-8-11 M Hills (7) *rdn and effrt hfwy, wknd o'r 2 fs out.* .... (15 to 2 op 7 to 1 tchd 9 to 1) 15
3065* POWERFUL EDGE [98] 4-9-7 L Dettori (4) *effrt to get in beh ldrs 2 fs out, sn btn.* (11 to 2 fav op 5 to 1 tchd 6 to 1) 16

Dist: 1½l, 1½l, sht-hd, 2½l, nk, nk, ¾l, nk, 3½l, hd. 1m 24.20s. a 0.10s (16 Ran).
SR: 67/64/45/54/47/54/39/33/38/ (Hamdan Al-Maktoum), H Thomson Jones

3351 Levy Board Nursery Class C (2-y-o) £4,920 7f 64yds................ (4:05)

2988[6] DUTY TIME [75] 8-10 W Carson (7) *broke wl, lost pl aftr one and a half fs and sn well beh, gd hdwy one and a half out, ran on well to ld last strds.* .... (100 to 30 fav op 7 to 2 tchd 4 to 1) 1
1988[5] MIDUSHI (USA) [70] 8-5 K Darley (2) *hdwy 3 fs out, chlgd one and a half out, led ins last, ct last strds.* .... (7 to 1 op 6 to 1 tchd 15 to 2) 2
2695[3] ROSE CIEL (Ire) [73] 8-8 M Roberts (4) *chsd ldrs, led o'r one furlong out till ins last, styd on*... (7 to 1 tchd 15 to 2) 3
3001 BALI WARRIOR (Ire) [64] 7-10 (3*) B Doyle (1) *prmnt, led 2 fs out till appr fnl furlong, kpt on.* .... (7 to 1 op 6 to 1 tchd 15 to 2) 4
2292[5] PERUSAL [86] 9-7 T Quinn (9) *chsd ldrs, rdn 3 fs out, styd on fnl furlong*.......................(7 to 1 op 6 to 1) 5
3129* FOOTSTEPS (Ire) [82] 8-10 (7*) T G McLaughlin (8) *prmnt, ev ch 2 fs out, wknd o'r one out.* .... (7 to 2 tchd 3 to 1 and 4 to 1) 6
2988[7] PRINCE DANZIG (Ire) [65] (v) 8-0 A Munro (3) *outpcd.* .... (20 to 1 op 16 to 1 tchd 25 to 1) 7
3129[4] HEATHCLIFF (Ire) [74] 8-9 D Holland (6) *led to 2 fs out, sn wknd*...................(10 to 1 op 8 to 1 tchd 12 to 1) 8
2668[2] NOT FOR JOE [65] 8-0 A McGlone (5) *beh, rdn alng 3 fs out, sn btn*..........(14 to 1 op 12 to 1 tchd 16 to 1) 9

Dist: Sht-hd, hd, ¾l, ½l, 7l, 1½l, nk, 6l. 1m 28.81s. a 1.51s (9 Ran).
SR: 41/35/37/26/46/21/-/7/-/ (Aubrey Ison), J L Dunlop

3352 EBF Yattendon Maiden Stakes Class D (2-y-o) £5,052 7f..............(4:35)

PENCADER (Ire) 9-0 D Holland (14) *trkd ldrs, led 2 fs out, pushed clr fnl furlong, cmftbly.* ....(6 to 4 on op 11 to 10) 1
HAWAJISS 8-9 W R Swinburn (15) *mid-div, hdwy to chase ldrs 2 fs out, ran on fnl furlong, not pace of wnr.* .... (8 to 1 op 6 to 1 tchd 10 to 1) 2
1324[8] PICCOLO 9-0 W Woods (22) *beh, hdwy o'r 2 fs out, ran on fnl furlong, no imprsn cl hme*......(66 to 1 op 33 to 1) 3
2756[2] SOUTHERN POWER (Ire) 9-0 L Dettori (10) *sn in tch, ev ch 2 fs out, kpt on*.......... (13 to 2 op 5 to 1 tchd 8 to 1) 4
LA RIVERAINE (USA) 8-9 M Hills (16) *mid-div, hdwy 2 fs out, ran on fnl furlong*...........(66 to 1 op 25 to 1) 5
2364 JEYPORE JO 8-7 (7*) D Gibbs (19) *pressed ldrs, styd on one pace fnl 2 fs*................(66 to 1 op 33 to 1) 6
GOLDEN ARROW (Ire) 9-0 S O'Gorman (20) *some prog fnl 2 fs, styd on*........................ (33 to 1 op 20 to 1) 7
UNCLE OSWALD 9-0 M Roberts (24) *beh till hdwy 2 and a half fs out, nrst finish*..............(25 to 1 op 20 to 1) 8
2826[5] SECUNDUS (Ire) 8-11 (3*) B Doyle (1) *chsd ldrs for o'r 4 fs, styd on same pace frm 2 out*...... (66 to 1 op 33 to 1) 9
FRAGRANT BELLE (USA) 8-9 J Williams (2) *chsd ldrs far side, no hdwy frm o'r 2 fs out*.....(33 to 1 op 16 to 1) 10
1666[5] MAKE A STAND 9-0 W Newnes (12) *mid-div, one pace frm o'r 2 fs out*................ (33 to 1 op 20 to 1) 11
2968[7] ERHAAB (USA) 9-0 W Carson (3) *chsd ldrs far side, no prog frm o'r 2 fs out*... (12 to 1 op 8 to 1 tchd 14 to 1) 12

SOVINISTA 8-9 A McGlone (11) *led to 2 fs out, sn btn.* ....(20 to 1 op 33 to 1 tchd 16 to 1) 13
BIRD ISLAND 9-0 C Avery (6) *chsd ldrs for o'r 4 fs.* ....(66 to 1 op 33 to 1) 14
MIGHTY FORUM 8-9 (5*) A Procter (13) *slwly into strd, outpcd most of way.* (25 to 1 op 20 to 1 tchd 33 to 1) 15
SCUD MISSILE (Ire) 9-0 K Darley (7) *outpcd, nvr dngrs.* ....(25 to 1 op 20 to 1 tchd 33 to 1) 16
SHIKAREE (Ire) 9-0 A Clark (8) *early speed, sn outpcd.* ....(50 to 1 op 20 to 1 tchd 100 to 1) 17
CASTLE COMBE (Ire) 8-9 (5*) Stephen Davies (9) *prmnt early, rdn and btn hfwy*..........(12 to 1 op 8 to 1) 18
CONVOY POINT (Ire) 9-0 Paul Eddery (23) *outpcd, al beh.* ....(33 to 1 op 20 to 1) 19
2502[8] ROBERO 9-0 A Munro (21) *sn outpcd.* ....(66 to 1 op 25 to 1) 20
RAVEN'S ROOST (Ire) 9-0 W Ryan (18) *nvr better than mid-div*....................(66 to 1 op 33 to 1) 21
PAMPERED GUEST (Ire) 9-0 L Piggott (17) *prmnt, ev ch 2 fs out, sn btn*....................(33 to 1 op 20 to 1) 22
2862[3] BELLEMINETTE (Ire) 8-9 A Mackay (25) *outpcd.* ....(50 to 1 op 33 to 1) 23
Dist: 2l, ½l, 1½l, 1l, ¾l, 1l, ½l, ¾l, ¾l, 1½l. 1m 25.80s. a 1.70s (23 Ran).
SR: 43/32/35/30/22/25/22/20/18/ (R E Sangster), P W Chapple-Hyam

3353 August Handicap Class C (0-100 3-y-o and up) £7,720 1½m 5yds.......(5:05)

2795[3] GENERAL MOUKTAR [67] 3-8-0 A McGlone (1) *in tch, smooth hdwy to track ldrs 2 fs out, led appr last, pushed out*....................(5 to 1 op 7 to 2) 1
3019[2] CHATHAM ISLAND [70] 5-8-11 (3*) B Doyle (7) *trkd ldrs gng wl, led 2 fs out, hdd appr last, styd on, not pace of wnr.* ....(13 to 2 op 7 to 1) 2
2163* ALDERNEY PRINCE (USA) [75] 3-8-3 (5*) Stephen Davies (4) *mid-div, hdwy 3 fs out, edgd lft ins fnl 2, ran on.* ....(10 to 1 tchd 12 to 1) 3
2930* GOOGLY [74] 4-9-4 G Bardwell (3) *beh, rdn 3 fs out, styd on fnl furlong, not rch ldrs*....... (11 to 2 tchd 6 to 1) 4
2795[6] FLIGHT LIEUTENANT (USA) [80] 4-9-10 W Carson (5) *beh, hdwy 3 fs out, sn one pace.* ....(9 to 2 fav op 4 to 1 tchd 5 to 1) 5
3003[3] SHADOWS OF SILVER [76] 5-9-6 A Mackay (11) *hdwy to chase ldrs 7 fs out, led 3 out to 2 out, sn wknd.* ....(8 to 1 tchd 10 to 1) 6
2907[7] SATIN DANCER [81] (bl) 3-9-0 K Darley (12) *beh, effrt o'r 3 fs out, sn wknd*....................(6 to 1 op 7 to 1) 7
2758[6] AJALAN (Ire) [81] 3-9-0 D Holland (9) *led aftr 3 fs to three out, wkng whn hmpd ins fnl 2*.................(7 to 1) 8
2913[6] HOME FROM THE HILL (Ire) [75] 3-8-8 M Hills (8) *led 3 fs, prmnt till wknd 2 and a half out, no ch whn hmpd ins fnl two*.............. (20 to 1 op 16 to 1 tchd 25 to 1) 9
3157[7] BELGRAN (USA) [72] 4-9-2 J Williams (2) *al beh, lost tch fnl 2 fs, fnshd lme*....... (10 to 1 op 20 to 1 tchd 25 to 1) 10
Dist: 1½l, nk, 1½l, 3½l, 1½l, 4l, 1½l, nk. 2m 31.28s. a 1.68s (10 Ran).
SR: 33/44/37/44/43/36/22/19/12/ (A S Helaissi), M C Pipe

RIPON (good)
Saturday August 14th

Going Correction: MINUS 0.05 sec. per fur. (races 1,4,6), MINUS 0.15 (2,3,5)

3354 Webb Seal Double Glazing Apprentice Handicap Stakes Class E (0-70 3-y-o and up) £2,880 6f..............(2:15)

3184[4] ASTERIX [51] 5-8-8 (3*) Mark Denaro (9) *nvr far away, drvn ahead wl ins fnl furlong, ran on*....(10 to 1 op 8 to 1) 1
3094[3] SOBERING THOUGHTS [64] 7-9-10 M Humphries (12) *tried to make all, wndrd fnl furlong, hdd and no extr towards finish*....................(8 to 1 tchd 9 to 1) 2
3184[7] LANGUEDOC [59] 6-9-0 (5*) D Thomas (16) *co'red up in midfield, drifted rght frm hfwy, not much room over one furlong out, kpt on*............ (14 to 1 op 12 to 1) 3
3118[3] KILLY'S FILLY [54] 3-8-2 (7*) P Fessey (1) *wl plcd stands side thrght, drvn alng fnl furlong, one pace.* ....(6 to 1 tchd 7 to 1 and 11 to 2) 4
3032[8] MISS BRIGHTSIDE [39] (bl) 5-7-8 (5*) M Baird (8) *chsd ldg bunch, not much room hfwy, brst through fnl furlong, ran on*....................(33 to 1 op 25 to 1) 5
3002[4] SUMMER EXPRESS [51] 4-8-4 (7*) L Suthern (6) *al chasing ldrs, effrt and drvn alng frm 2 fs out, one pace.* (12 to 1) 6
2915[4] SARTIGILA [61] 4-9-7 J Marshall (14) *nvr far away, drvn alng o'r one furlong out, no extr.* ....(8 to 1 op 7 to 1 tchd 9 to 1) 7
3136[2] PENNY HASSET [68] 5-9-9 (5*) P Johnson (10) *settled mid-field, effrt and rdn alng o'r one furlong out, no extr.* ....(5 to 1 fav tchd 11 to 2) 8
3180[7] GENTLE HERO (USA) [56] 7-8-9 (7*) I Jardine (13) *chsd alng on outsd, effrt 2 fs out, not quicken.* ....(33 to 1 op 20 to 1) 9
3118[7] MISS ARAGON [48] 5-8-8 C Hawksley (5) *missed break, improved into midfield hfwy, not clr run o'r one furlong out, nvr nrr*....................(14 to 1 op 12 to 1) 10

ETERNAL FLAME [63] 5-9-2 (7*) M Henry (15) *shwd up wl in frnt rnk for 4 fs, no extr*..........(33 to 1 op 20 to 1) 11
2731[4] PINE RIDGE LAD (Ire) [65] 3-9-6 S Mulvey (4) *broke wl to show gd speed in frnt rnk for o'r 4 fs, fdd.* ....(8 to 1 tchd 9 to 1) 12
3057[5] PAULINUS [33] 5-7-3[1] (5*) C Teague (11) *co'red up in mid-field, drvn alng hfwy, not pace to chal.* ....(14 to 1 op 12 to 1) 13
2636[7] COAT OF DREAMS [38] 4-7-7 (5*) C Adamson (7) *sn struggling to keep up, nvr a factor*......(25 to 1 op 20 to 1) 14
3036[9] MAM'ZELLE ANGOT [58] 3-8-6 (7*) J Gracey (2) *bolted gng to post, struggling aftr 2 fs, tld off*.............. (14 to 1) 15
Dist: ½l, ½l, 1½l, 1l, hd, hd, 1l, hd, sht-hd, 2½l. 1m 15.00s. a 4.40s (15 Ran).
SR: 3/14/7/-/-/-/ (Clifton Hunt), J M Bradley

3355 Wharfedale Selling Handicap Class G (0-60 3-y-o) £2,511 1¼m........ (2:45)

2353 MERRY MERMAID [43] 9-1 L Charnock (10) *nvr far away, squeezed through to ld o'r one furlong out, gng clr whn drifted rght, ran on, fnshd 1st, disqualified.* ....(7 to 1 op 5 to 1) 1D
3035[5] INFANTRY GLEN [47] (v) 9-5 G Duffield (6) *patiently rdn, swtchd ins and not clr run o'r 2 fs out, got through fnl furlong, ran on, fnshd second, awarded race.* ....(5 to 2 fav op 7 to 2) 1
2870[2] MR ABBOT [37] 8-9 J Lowe (9) *wtd wth, steady hdwy last 2 fs, rdn and kpt on same pace fnl furlong, fnshd 3rd plcd second*.................... (4 to 1 op 7 to 2) 2
2972 SABO'S EXPRESS [47] 9-5 R Cochrane (4) *led, hdd and rdn o'r one furlong out, no extr, fnshd 4th, plcd 3rd.* ....(4 to 1 tchd 7 to 2) 3
3249[7] JENDORCET [40] 8-12 K Fallon (1) *al hndy, ev ch and rdn 2 fs out, wkng whn squeezed for room appr last, fnshd 5th, plcd 4th*....................(14 to 1) 4
3157[6] DUNBAR [37] 8-9 N Connorton (13) *al hndy, ev ch 2 fs out, fdg whn squeezed for room appr last, fnshd 6th, plcd 5th*.................... (16 to 1 op 14 to 1) 5
3090 BONNY PRINCESS [23] 7-2 (7*) N Varley (12) *chsd ldg bunch, feeling pace and rdn o'r 2 fs out, no imprsn.* ....(20 to 1) 7
2538[3] MAGIC FAN (Ire) [40] 8-12 B Raymond (5) *trkd ldg bunch for o'r 5 fs, wknd*.................... (16 to 1) 8
2555[5] BARDIA [36] 8-8 Kim Tinkler (7) *settled off the pace, steady hdwy last 2 fs, nvr nrr*....................(20 to 1) 9
2736[6] VELVET HEART (Ire) [49] 9-7 E Johnson (2) *niggled alng to keep up, effrt on outsd hfwy, btn 2 fs out.* ....(7 to 1 op 6 to 1) 10
3144[5] DUSKY DUCHESS (Ire) [34] 8-1 (5*) Darren Moffatt (8) *trkd ldg 4, rdn 2 fs out, sn btn*.................... (20 to 1) 11
2353 BOLD FLASH [45] 9-3 Dale Gibson (11) *co'red up on ins, rdn alng hfwy, eased whn btn 2 fs out*........ (12 to 1) 12
2769[9] CHARLOTTES BILLO [38] (bl) 8-7 (3*) S Maloney (3) *wth ldrs 5 fs, eased whn btn*....................(20 to 1) 13
Dist: 1½l, 1½l, 2½l, 1½l, nk, sht-hd, 2½l, nk, ½l, 5l. 2m 10.90s. a 6.90s (13 Ran).
SR: 17/18/5/10/-/-/ (G R Platt), G R Oldroyd

3356 Crowther Homes Handicap Stakes Class D (0-80 3-y-o and up) £3,840 1½m 60yds.................... (3:15)

2272[4] HARD TASK [74] 3-9-6 J Carroll (15) *nvr far away, styd on to ld o'r one furlong out, drw clr.* (14 to 1 op 12 to 1) 1
3134[2] JUBRAN (USA) [70] 7-9-8 (5*) A Garth (4) *al hndy, led o'r 3 fs out till over one out, rdn and one pace*.....(10 to 1) 2
3113[5] DUPLICATE [63] 3-8-6 (3*) S Maloney (11) *tucked away in midfield, improved o'r 2 fs out, styd on fnl furlong.* .... (9 to 1 op 12 to 1 tchd 14 to 1) 3
3173[9] RUSSIAN EMPIRE [65] 3-8-11 R Cochrane (9) *trkd ldg bunch, effrt and drvn alng o'r 2 fs out, styd on same pace*....................(4 to 1 jt-fav op 7 to 2) 4
3116[3] CANNY CHRONICLE [68] 5-9-4 (7*) S Mulvey (14) *patiently rdn, gd hdwy on outsd o'r 3 fs out, no imprsn appr last.* ....(12 to 1) 5
2207[5] DUNNELLON [77] 3-9-9 B Raymond (12) *trkd ldg quartet, feeling pace and rdn o'r 3 fs out, fdd*.........(14 to 1) 6
3003[2] SALU [54] 4-8-11 G Duffield (2) *chsd ldg bunch, effrt and rdn o'r 2 fs out, sn outpcd*.....(4 to 1 jt-fav op 6 to 1) 7
FLOATING LINE [59] 5-9-2 A Culhane (5) *wth ldrs, hrd at work o'r 3 fs out, fdd*....................(33 to 1) 8
2970[3] BRILLIANT [65] 5-9-8 M Wigham (8) *al chasing ldrs, drvn alng frm 3 fs out, fdd*............ (7 to 1 tchd 15 to 2) 9
2871[4] SEA PADDY [52] 5-8-9 Dale Gibson (1) *sluggish strt, some hdwy hfwy, nvr able to chal*..... (16 to 1 op 12 to 1) 10
3056[9] PEANUTS PET [42] 8-7-10 (3*) N Kennedy (3) *trkd ldrs, drvn alng o'r 3 fs out, sn btn*....................(33 to 1) 11
3036 HARPOON LOUIE (USA) [76] 3-9-8 N Connorton (6) *beh, swtchd ins and some hdwy entering strt, nvr dngrs.* ....(16 to 1 op 14 to 1) 12
2776 HAYDON BRIDGE (Ire) [60] 3-8-1 (5*) J Tate (10) *chsd ldrs, feeling pace 3 fs out, fdd.* ....(10 to 1 op 8 to 1 tchd 11 to 1) 13
3003* PERSIAN SOLDIER [50] 6-8-7 K Fallon (7) *dictated pace till o'r 3 fs out, wkng whn swrvd into rls over 2 furlongs out, eased*....................(6 to 1 op 5 to 1) 14

ROLLING THE BONES (USA) [60] 4-9-0 (3*) M Fenton (13) *chsd alng and came wide strt, nvr a factor.* .... (33 to 1 op 25 to 1) 15
Dist: 6l, ¾l, 3l, 6l, 2l, ¾l, nk, 2l, 2½l, 1½l. 2m 39.60s. a 4.60s (15 Ran).
SR: 42/37/17/13/15/9/-/-/1/ (J W Rowles), R F Johnson Houghton

3357 Ripon Horn Blower Conditions Stakes Class C (2-y-o) £4,710 5f........(3:45)

2876* HANNAH'S MUSIC 8-5 G Duffield (1) *badly outpcd and drvn alng, gd hdwy and swtchd outsd appr fnl furlong, ran on to ld last 50 yards.* .... (17 to 2 op 8 to 1 tchd 10 to 1) 1
2845[3] CRAGGANMORE 8-10 R Cochrane (3) *chsd ldg trio, outpcd hfwy, ran on strly fnl furlong.* ....(9 to 2 op 4 to 1 tchd 5 to 1) 2
2960[3] ISABELLA SHARP 8-6 (3*) M Fenton (6) *dsptd ld, nosed ahead entering fnl furlong, ct last 50 yards....* (4 to 1) 3
3122[3] MR M-E-N (Ire) 9-0 J Carroll (2) *set gd pace till entering fnl furlong, rdn and no extr.......* (2 to 1 fav tchd 5 to 2) 4
2947* EVENING FALLS 8-9 G Hind (4) *dsptd ld, hrd drvn 2 fs out, wknd fnl furlong...................*(9 to 4 op 2 to 1) 5
3236[4] TOP SHOW (Ire) 8-12 A Culhane (5) *pckd badly and almost uns rdr leaving stalls, not reco'r...*(16 to 1 op 14 to 1) 6
Dist: ¾l, hd, 2l, ½l, 5l. 1m 0.20s. a 2.20s (6 Ran).
SR: 42/44/42/39/32/15/ (Pat FitzGerald), P C Haslam

3358 Rothmans Royals North South Challenge Series Handicap Class D (0-80 3-y-o and up) £4,077 1m........ (4:15)

3182[4] PRIDE OF PENDLE [62] 4-9-0 J Carroll (5) *patiently rdn, weaved through frm midfield last 2 fs, str run to ld cl hme..................* (10 to 1 op 9 to 1 tchd 11 to 1) 1
2930[6] HIGH LOW (USA) [75] 5-9-6 (7*) S Giles (2) *wtd wth, smooth hdwy to ld o'r one furlong out, ct cl hme.....* (16 to 1) 2
2926 PRENONAMOSS [75] 5-9-10 (3*) S D Williams (4) *trkd ldg bunch, took clr order last 2 fs, rng on finish...* (14 to 1) 3
3219[5] NORTHERN CHIEF [56] 3-7-12 (3*) S Maloney (10) *al hndy, led 2 fs out till o'r one out, kpt on same pace.* .... (25 to 1 op 20 to 1) 4
2954[2] LAWNSWOOD JUNIOR [67] 6-9-5 G Hind (9) *chsd alng to go pace hfwy, steady hdwy last 2 fs, nrst finish.* .... (16 to 1 op 14 to 1) 5
2931* NORTHERN RAINBOW [50] 5-8-2 Dale Gibson (12) *chsd ldg bunch, swtchd ins to improve o'r one furlong out, kpt on same pace.........* (15 to 2 op 16 to 1 tchd 7 to 1) 6
2816 HABETA (USA) [59] (bl) 7-8-11 B Raymond (1) *al pressing ldrs, drvn alng o'r 2 fs out, kpt on same pace.* (14 to 1) 7
3017[3] BALLERINA BAY [70] (v) 5-9-8 R Cochrane (14) *settled midfield, effrt on ins whn baulked o'r one furlong out, not rcvr.................................*(8 to 1 op 7 to 1) 8
3182[2] SOOTY TERN [62] 6-8-7 (7*) Mark Denaro (6) *nvr far away, drvn alng o'r 2 fs out, one pace.* .... (8 to 1 tchd 9 to 1 and 7 to 1) 9
3054[6] UMBUBUZI (USA) [66] 3-8-8 (3*) N Kennedy (16) *wth ldrs for o'r 5 fs, no extr.................* (20 to 1 op 14 to 1) 10
3012[9] PROTON [75] (v) 3-9-1 (5*) J Tate (17) *led, hdd and drvn alng o'r 2 fs out, fdd.............* (14 to 1 op 12 to 1) 11
2882 SALDA [60] 4-8-12 K Fallon (11) *chsd alng hfwy, nvr able to rch ldrs...........* (11 to 1 op 14 to 1 tchd 10 to 1) 12
3012 BROUGHTONS TURMOIL [56] 4-8-3 (5*) D McCabe (7) *sluggish strt, nvr able to reco'r........* (16 to 1 op 14 to 1) 13
2596* PIXTON (Ire) [77] 3-9-8 G Duffield (8) *tucked away, led briefly o'r 2 fs out, sn btn.......*(5 to 1 fav op 11 to 2) 14
3058[2] SPANISH VERDICT [71] 6-9-2 (7*) C Teague (3) *settled off the pace, nvr a factor..........* (12 to 1 op 10 to 1) 15
2624[8] RISE UP SINGING [64] 5-9-2 M Wigham (15) *in tch to strt, sn btn...............................*(9 to 1 op 10 to 1) 16
3058* SELF EXPRESSION [61] 5-8-6 (7*) D Thomas (13) *settled off the pace, nvr a factor.* (9 to 1 op 8 to 1 tchd 10 to 1) 17
2220[5] MYSILV [62] 3-8-7 N Carlisle (18) *trkd ldrs, squeezed out appr strt, sddl slpd, eased last 3 fs.* (25 to 1 op 20 to 1) 18
Dist: Nk, ¾l, ½l, 3l, nk, 2l, hd, 1½l, ½l, ¾l. 1m 41.10s. a 2.80s (18 Ran).
SR: 40/52/50/22/31/13/16/26/13/ (W B Imison), P Calver

3359 Wensleydale Maiden Stakes Class D (3-y-o and up) £3,552 5f.........(4:50)

3178[2] BALLET SHOES (Ire) 3-8-9 R Cochrane (2) *on toes in paddock, made all, kpt on strly fnl furlong.* ....(6 to 4 on op Evens) 1
3094[5] MAGIC PEARL 3-8-9 K Fallon (11) *al hndy, ev ch and rdn appr fnl furlong, kpt on same pace.* (8 to 1 tchd 9 to 1) 2
3132[4] CALAMANCO 3-8-9 S Webster (12) *nvr far away, ev ch o'r one furlong out, kpt on..........................*(20 to 1) 3
3059[5] DISCO BOY (bl) 3-8-7 (7*) S Sanders (8) *gd speed in frnt rnk, rdn and wknd appr fnl furlong.* .... (33 to 1 op 25 to 1) 4
3178[4] JAWAAL 3-9-0 B Raymond (6) *unruly in stalls, wth ldrs for o'r 3 fs, wknd quickly..........*(5 to 1 op 3 to 1) 5
2202[9] NO CONTRACT (USA) 3-9-0 G Hind (13) *chsd alng to go pace, styd on last 2 fs, nvr dngrs....*(10 to 1 op 8 to 1) 6
2580 FASHION QUEEN 3-8-9 N Connorton (4) *chsd alng in midfield, some hdwy o'r one furlong out, no imprsn.* ....(25 to 1 tchd 33 to 1) 7
2872[7] VICTORIAS PASSION 3-8-6 (3*) S D Williams (1) *sluggish strt, nvr a threat.................*(12 to 1 op 25 to 1) 8
3132[8] MISS RITZ 3-8-9 Dale Gibson (10) *chsd ldrs to hfwy, sn btn...............................* (33 to 1 op 25 to 1) 9
TARNSIDE BANKER 3-9-0 J Lowe (7) *sluggish strt, nvr dngrs.......................................* (33 to 1) 10
SAJA (USA) 3-8-9 N Carlisle (5) *drvn alng to keep up, nvr a factor.................*(10 to 1 op 9 to 1 tchd 12 to 1) 11
1562 STORM VIXEN 4-8-10 (3*) S Maloney (3) *sluggish strt, not reco'r.......................................* (50 to 1) 12
Dist: 2½l, hd, 5l, ¾l, ½l, 3l, 3½l, hd, ¾l, nk. 1m 0.40s. a 2.40s (12 Ran).
SR: 42/32/31/16/13/11/ (Lord Weinstock), R Charlton

SOUTHWELL (A.W) (std)
Saturday August 14th
Going Correction: NIL (race 1), PLUS 0.05 (2,3,4,5,6)

3360 Kirby-in-Ashfield Handicap Class E (0-70 3-y-o and up) £3,002 5f.... (2:20)

3253[3] ARC LAMP [49] 7-9-0 M Birch (1) *cl up centre, rdn to ld entering fnl furlong, ran on....*(7 to 2 fav tchd 4 to 1) 1
3136[4] MEESON TIMES [50] 5-8-8 (7*) H Bastiman (2) *in tch centre, rdn and hdwy o'r one furlong out, styd on ins last.* .... (4 to 1 tchd 9 to 2 and 5 to 1) 2
2777 SO SUPERB [59] (bl) 4-9-10 S Webster (7) *led stands side, rdn wl o'r one furlong out, hdd entering last, not quicken..........................*(12 to 1 op 10 to 1) 3
3085[4] DAL MISS [31] (bl) 6-7-10 N Adams (4) *cl up, rdn 2 fs out, kpt on one pace......*(10 to 1 op 14 to 1 tchd 16 to 1) 4
3220 GUSSIE FINK-NOTTLE (Ire) [57] (bl) 3-8-11 (7*) V Halliday (9) *cl up stands side, rdn 2 fs out, sn one pace....* (10 to 1) 5
3188[3] STRIP CARTOON (Ire) [58] 5-9-2 (7*) G Strange (8) *outpcd and rdn alng hfwy, styd on fnl furlong, nvr dngrs.* ....(4 to 1 op 3 to 1 tchd 9 to 2) 6
2919[4] COMET WHIRLPOOL (Ire) [59] (bl) 3-9-6 P Robinson (5) *chsd ldrs, rdn 2 fs out, sn btn............* (6 to 1 op 5 to 1) 7
3032 CONVENIENT MOMENT [54] 3-9-1 J Fortune (6) *chsd ldrs, rdn 2 fs out, sn wknd.................*(8 to 1 op 7 to 1) 8
2765[7] CRACKER JACK [42] (bl) 3-8-3 J Fanning (3) *chsd ldrs, rdn o'r 2 fs out, sn wknd.............* (16 to 1 op 12 to 1) 9
Dist: ½l, 1l, 2l, nk, hd, 2l, ½l, 7l. 1m 0.80s. a 2.90s (9 Ran).
SR: 42/41/46/10/31/35/24/17/-/ (B Bruce), J A Glover

3361 Blidworth Claiming Stakes Class F (3 & 4-y-o) £2,243 1m 3f........... (2:50)

3246* CLIBURNEL NEWS (Ire) 3-8-5 P Robinson (5) *trkd ldr, hdwy to ld on bit o'r 2 fs out, easily.* ....(5 to 4 on op Evens) 1
3170* EARLY TO RISE 3-8-7 (7*) J D Smith (6) *led, rdn 3 fs out, hdd o'r 2 out, kpt on und pres, no ch wth wnr.* .... (11 to 4 op 3 to 1 tchd 5 to 2) 2
3046 ABJAR 3-8-13 Gay Kelleway (3) *chsd ldrs, effrt and rdn 3 fs out, sn one pace...........* (9 to 2 op 5 to 2) 3
1416[5] MUNNASIB (Fr) 3-7-11 (7*) P McCabe (1) *chsd ldrs, rdn 4 fs out, sn wknd..........................*(12 to 1 op 7 to 1) 4
3092[5] LARKSPUR LEGEND 3-8-2 (5*) D Wright (2) *in tch, rdn hfwy, sn wknd............*(28 to 1 op 20 to 1) 5
3138[4] LADY MAGADI 3-7-9 N Adams (4) *al rear, wl beh hfwy.* .... (50 to 1 op 33 to 1) 6
Dist: 1½l, 8l, 20l, 20l, 12l. 2m 28.90s. a 7.10s (6 Ran).
SR: 26/32/15/ (East Lancs Newspapers Readers Club), M H Tompkins

3362 Garbos Night Club Maiden Auction Stakes Class F (2-y-o) £2,803 7f (3:20)

2785[2] INDEFENCE (Ire) 9-0 C Rutter (1) *cl up, led aftr 2 fs, quickened clr o'r two out, unchal.* ....(2 to 1 fav op 9 to 4 tchd 3 to 1) 1
2718[4] ROBBY (Ire) 9-0 P Robinson (12) *mid-div, hdwy hfwy, chsd wnr fnl 2 fs, kpt on und pres.* (20 to 1 op 14 to 1) 2
3091[4] WINNING LINE 9-0 M Birch (7) *in tch, hdwy 3 fs out, sn rdn, kpt on one pace....* (5 to 2 op 3 to 1 tchd 9 to 4) 3
2528[5] NOORAN 9-0 J Fortune (6) *mid-div, hdwy 3 fs out, sn rdn, one pace frm 2 out...................* (20 to 1 op 16 to 1) 4
2875[3] WINN'S PRIDE (Ire) 9-0 S Perks (11) *in tch, rdn 3 fs out, sn one pace...............................* (7 to 2 tchd 4 to 1) 5
3137[4] STRADISHALL (bl) 9-0 N Day (2) *outpcd and beh, styd on fnl 2 fs, nvr dngrs.................*(14 to 1 op 12 to 1) 6
LADY GREY (Swe) 8-9 R Price (9) *slwly into strd, al beh.* ....(20 to 1 op 14 to 1) 7
2652[4] HE SHALL REIGN 9-0 T Williams (5) *chsd ldrs, rdn 3 fs out, sn btn...............................*(6 to 1 op 9 to 2) 8
2687[6] WINGS OF HORAGE (Ire) 9-0 W Hood (10) *slwly into strd, al rear..* (33 to 1) 9
2836[9] RINUS MASTER (Ire) 9-0 J Weaver (3) *led 2 fs, cl up till rdn and wknd quickly 3 out..........* (50 to 1 op 33 to 1) 10
586[7] FIRE MUSIC (bl) 9-0 T Sprake (4) *chsd ldrs 3 fs, sn lost pl.* (14 to 1 op 20 to 1 tchd 50 to 1) 11
2586[9] OZZIE JONES 9-0 S Wood (8) *chsd ldrs, rdn 3 fs out, sn wknd..........................*(50 to 1 op 25 to 1) 12
Dist: 6l, 4l, 2l, 2½l, 2½l, 4l, 1½l, 2l, 4l, 5l. 1m 31.40s. a 5.30s (12 Ran).
SR: 26/8/-/-/-/-/ (Les Hamilton), M R Channon

3363 Derry Building Services And Bowmer & Kirkland Claiming Stakes Class F (2-y-o) £2,243 6f. . . . . (3:50)

2377^{2} PALACEGATE JO (Ire) 8-12 J Fortune (1) *dwlt, sn chasing ldrs, shaken up and quickened to ld wl o'r one furlong out, soon clr*. . . . .(7 to 4 fav op 5 to 2) 1
3082^{7} LEAP OF FAITH (Ire) 8-6 M Birch (3) *chsd ldrs, rdn alng and outpcd hfwy, styd on und pres fnl 2 fs*. . . . .(9 to 4 op 7 to 4) 2
3122^{4} BOLD ARISTOCRAT (Ire) 9-3 S Perks (7) *cl up, led hfwy, rdn and hdd wl o'r one furlong out, one pace*. . . . .(5 to 1 tchd 13 to 2) 3
2588^{4} TRENDY DANCER (Ire) (v) 9-0 (3*) O Pears (4) *chsd ldg pair, rdn 3 fs out, sn one pace*. . . . .(12 to 1 op 6 to 1) 4
SARAH'S OPERA (Ire) 8-12 T Sprake (5) *lost many ls strt, beh till styd on fnl 2 fs, nvr dngrs*. (40 to 1 op 20 to 1) 5
2933^{3} HENRY THE HAWK 8-1 (7*) V Halliday (8) *chsd ldrs, rdn hfwy, sn one pace*. . . . .(16 to 1 op 6 to 1) 6
3189^{2} THATCHED ROOF (Ire) 8-12 T Lucas (6) *dwlt, al rear*. . . . . (12 to 1 op 6 to 1) 7
2952* MOKAITE 8-3 S Wood (9) *led to hfwy, sn rdn, wknd quickly 2 fs out*. . . . .(7 to 1 op 4 to 1) 8
Dist: 2l, 1½l, 7l, 2½l, ½l, 3½l, 7l. 1m 17.90s. a 4.50s (8 Ran).
SR: 14/-/5/-/-/ (Palacegate Corporation Ltd), J Berry

3364 Rainworth Handicap Class D (0-80 3-y-o and up) £3,289 1m. . . . . (4:20)

3019^{9} GOLDEN CHIP (Ire) [60] 5-9-5 J Fortune (2) *made all, quickened clr 3 fs out, styd on strly ins last*. . . . .(3 to 1) 1
2930 HADEER'S DANCE [70] 3-9-8 R Price (1) *chsd ldg pair, effrt and hdwy 3 fs out, sn rdn, kpt on one pace frm 2 out*. . . . . (12 to 1 op 8 to 1) 2
3192* MOHICAN BRAVE (Ire) [72] 3-9-10 M Birch (3) *chsd ldrs, effrt and hdwy 3 fs out, rdn wl o'r one out, kpt on one pace*. . . . .(5 to 1 tchd 6 to 1) 3
3234* SET THE FASHION [59] (v) 4-9-4 C Rutter (6) *stumbled strt, steadied and beh, effrt and hdwy o'r 3 fs out, sn rdn, no imprsn*. . . . .(6 to 5 on op 5 to 4) 4
3140^{7} MISTER BLAKE [60] (bl) 3-8-9 (3*) Emma O'Gorman (5) *al beh*. . . . . (16 to 1 op 14 to 1) 5
2697^{6} DON'T JUMP (Ire) [72] 3-9-10 P Robinson (4) *chsd ldr, rdn and wknd 3 fs out*. . . . . .(8 to 1 op 7 to 1 tchd 10 to 1) 6
Dist: 5l, ¾l, 2l, 10l, 7l. 1m 43.30s. a 4.30s (6 Ran).
SR: 47/35/35/23/-/-/ (A H Jackson), A P Stringer

3365 Hucknall Handicap Class D (0-75 3-y-o and up) £3,494 7f. . . . . (4:55)

3180^{9} COLFAX CLASSIC [41] 3-7-7 S Wood (11) *prmnt, led aftr 3 fs to three out, cl up, rdn to ld appr last, ran on gmely und pres*. . . . .(33 to 1 op 20 to 1) 1
3190^{2} PENNY BANGER (Ire) [64] 3-9-2 T Williams (9) *beh, pushed alng hfwy, hdwy on outsd 2 and a half fs out, styd on to chal ins last, no extr nr finish*. . . . . (100 to 30 fav op 5 to 2 tchd 7 to 2) 2
2707^{4} INVIGILATE [56] 4-9-0 J Weaver (1) *cl up, led 3 fs out, rdn and hdd o'r one out, one pace ins last*. . . . .(7 to 1 op 6 to 1 tchd 15 to 2) 3
3190^{5} MUSIC DANCER [52] 4-8-10 J McLaughlin (7) *reared strt, beh, hdwy on ins o'r 2 fs out, kpt on und presssure inside last*. . . . .(6 to 1 op 7 to 2) 4
2469^{3} HERSHEBAR [66] (bl) 3-8-11 (7*) G Strange (2) *chsd ldrs, rdn o'r 2 fs out, styd on one pace*. . . (12 to 1 op 9 to 1) 5
3180* OBSIDIAN GREY [56] 6-8-11 (3*) O Pears (8) *led 2 fs, chsd ldrs, rdn two out, wknd appr last*. . . . . (11 to 2 op 5 to 1 tchd 6 to 1) 6
3190^{3} GLENFIELD GRETA [58] 5-8-11 (5*) D Wright (6) *chsd ldrs, rdn 3 fs out, wknd 2 out*. . . . . (5 to 1 op 4 to 1) 7
3190^{7} DREAM CARRIER (Ire) [66] 5-9-3 (7*) V Halliday (3) *hld up beh, some hdwy fnl 2 fs, nvr plcd to chal*. . . . . (14 to 1 op 9 to 1) 8
2639^{7} LORD NASKRA (USA) [50] (bl) 4-8-5 (3*) Emma O'Gorman (4) *wide strt, al beh*. . . . .(8 to 1 op 7 to 1) 9
521 HAWAII STORM (Fr) [60] 5-9-4 R Price (5) *cl up, led aftr 2 fs to 4 out, prmnt till rdn two and a half out, sn wknd*. . . . . (20 to 1 op 16 to 1 tchd 25 to 1) 10
Dist: 1½l, 1½l, hd, ½l, nk, 3l, nk, 2½l, nk. 1m 32.50s. a 6.40s (10 Ran).
SR: -/6/-/-/-/-/ (Colfax Window Systems Ltd), B S Rothwell

TRAMORE (IRE) (good to firm) Saturday August 14th

3366 Guillamene Maiden (4-y-o and up) £2,243 1¾m. . . . . (2:30)

2143 SIMPLY SWIFT 6-8-3 (8*) G M Moylan (6) . . . . (9 to 4 jt-fav) 1
3077^{4} LEAD ME LEAD MENOT (USA) (bl) 4-8-5 (6*) B J Walsh (5) . . . . (9 to 4 jt-fav) 2
HARRISTOWN LADY (bl) 6-8-1 (10*) D J Casey (1) . .(3 to 1) 3
3077 GLAD'S NIGHT (Ire) 4-8-11 B Coogan (2) . . . .(10 to 1) 4
3293^{3} WINTER DREAMS (Ire) 4-8-1 (10*) T Hagger (4) . . . . .(6 to 1) 5
3295 AFAWI (Ire) 5-9-0 N Byrne (3) . . . . (10 to 1) 6
Dist: 1l, nk, 4l, 5½l. 3m 11.30s. (6 Ran).
(J M Cusack), P Mullins

3367 Landrover Handicap (0-60 3-y-o and up) £2,588 1½m. . . . . (4:00)

3277* LAKE OF LOUGHREA (Ire) [-] 3-9-0 (6*,5ex) B J Walsh (2) . . . . (6 to 4 fav) 1
2842 REGAL PRETENDER (Ire) [-] 3-8-4 D V Smith (6) . . .(16 to 1) 2
3277^{9} GREEK CHIME (Ire) [-] 4-9-6 (6*) C Everard (8) . . . . . .(7 to 1) 3
3277^{4} RYE HILL QUEEN (Ire) [-] 3-8-10 N Byrne (4) . . . .(5 to 1) 4
2094^{8} WOODFIELD ROSE [-] 4-7-10^{2} (8*) B Fenton (3) . . . (12 to 1) 5
2677^{5} TAJARIB (Ire) [-] (bl) 3-9-2 B Coogan (5) . . . . (8 to 1) 6
3278^{4} KOI CORP [-] 9-8-0^{5} (8*) P J Smullen (1) . . . .(16 to 1) 7
3277^{6} AQUINAS [-] 7-7-13 (10*) R A Hennessy (7) . . . . (9 to 4) 8
SMOKE SCREEN (Fr) [-] 5-8-7 (8*) G M Moylan (9) (10 to 1) 9
Dist: 3l, 1½l, ¾l, hd. 2m 42.30s. (9 Ran).
(Bezwell Fixings Ltd), Kevin Prendergast

3368 Brownstown Head Maiden (3-y-o and up) £2,243 1½m. . . . . (5:00)

3164^{4} WICKLOW WAY (Ire) 3-8-2^{1} (6*) B J Walsh (2) . .(10 to 9 on) 1
2902^{6} DANCING VISION (Ire) 3-8-10 N Byrne (1) . . . . (12 to 1) 2
JAZZY REFRAIN (Ire) 3-7-13 (8*) B Fenton (5) . . . . . . (4 to 1) 3
2984^{6} MILLERS MILL (Ire) (bl) 3-8-2 (8*) G M Moylan (3) . . . (4 to 1) 4
3074^{8} LADYS BID (Ire) 3-8-7 D V Smith (4) . . . .(6 to 1) 5
Dist: ½l, 13l, ¾l, 2l. 2m 41.90s. (5 Ran).
(P Conlan), Kevin Prendergast

DEAUVILLE (FR) (good) Sunday August 15th

3369 Prix du Haras de Fresnay-le-Buffard Jacques le Marois-Group 1 (3-y-o and up) £119,474 1m. . . . . (3:00)

2905^{2} SAYYEDATI 3-8-8 W R Swinburn, *in rear early, effrt and quickened 2 fs out, led jst und one and a half furlongs out, ran on wl*. 1
2981* SKI PARADISE (USA) 3-8-8 Pat Eddery, *broke slwly, in rear, rdn and quickened one furlong out, fnshd fst, jst fld*. 2
1749* KINGMAMBO (USA) 3-8-11 C Asmussen, *prmnt, quickened to ld 2 fs out till hdd und one and a half furlongs out, no extr fnl furlong*. 3
2981^{3} ELIZABETH BAY (USA) 3-8-8 L Piggott, *mid-div, effrt and quickened 2 fs out to chal ldrs, one pace fnl furlong*. . . 4
1767* GOLD SPLASH (USA) 3-8-8 G Mosse, *mid-div, quickened 2 and a half fs out, chlgd for ld two out, one pace fnl furlong*. 5
2531^{3} SIAM (USA) 3-8-11 E Saint-Martin, *trkd ldrs, rdn and outpcd 2 fs out, made some late prog*. 6
2981^{7} ROUQUETTE 3-8-8 A Badel, *ran in last pl, effrt and quickened 2 fs out, sn wknd*. 7
1546^{7} HUDO (USA) 3-8-11 C Piccioni, *led till hdd 2 fs out, wknd quickly*. 8
Dist: Hd, nk, 2½l, ¾l, 1½l, 1½l, 6l. 1m 39.80s. a 4.80s (8 Ran).
SR: 22/21/23/12/10/8/-/-/ (Mohamed Obaida), C E Brittain

GELSENKIRCHEN (GER) (soft) Sunday August 15th

3370 Aral Pokal (Group 1) (3-y-o and up) £85,714 1½m. . . . . (3:45)

3022^{4} GEORGE AUGUSTUS (USA) 5-9-6 M Roberts, *hdwy 4 fs out, led ins fnl furlong, hng lft cl hme, kpt on, fnshd 1st, plcd second*. 1D
2259^{2} MONSUN (Ger) 3-8-7 M Kinane, *3rd strt, lost pl 2 fs out, rallied fnl furlong, hmpd cl hme, came second, awarded race*. 1
2839* SHREWD IDEA 3-8-7 L Dettori, *hdwy 2 fs out, ev ch ins fnl furlong, ran on*. 3
2771^{2} PETIT LOUP (USA) 4-9-6 B Raymond, *led or dsptd ld till ins fnl furlong, ran on one pace*. 4
2079^{2} SUGUNAS (Ger) 5-9-6 D Ilic, *hdwy fnl 2 fs, nvr plcd to chal*. 5
2259^{3} STERNKONIG (Ire) 3-8-7 M Hofer, *hdwy and 6th strt, one paced fnl 2 fs*. 6
2261^{2} APPLE TREE (Fr) 4-9-6 T Jarnet, *nvr plcd to chal*. 7
2837^{3} PROTEKTOR (Ger) 4-8-11 (9*) T Hellier, *prmnt till wknd fnl 3 fs*. 8
2979^{2} OUMNAZ (Fr) 4-9-6 M Boutin, *al beh*. 9
2644^{2} SPORTIVO (USA) 4-9-6 A Helfenbein. 10
2979^{3} VINCENZO (Ger) 4-9-6 O Schick. 11
Dist: Nk, hd, ½l, 2½l, ½l, 3½l, 4½l, 3l, 1½l, 1 ¾l. 2m 36.10s. (11 Ran).
(Baron G Von Ullmann), H Jentzsch

HOPPEGARTEN (GER) (good)
Sunday August 15th

3371 **BMW Europachampionat (Group 3) (3-y-o) £163,265 1½m............. (3:15)**

2837* KORNADO 9-2 M Rimmer, *rcd in 4th to strt, hdwy 2 fs out, led ins fnl furlong, drvn out*.................... 1
2259* LANDO (Ger) 9-2 A Tylicki, *wnt second 5 fs out, led 2 furlongs out till ins fnl furlong, no extr clsg stages*.... 2
2654* RIVER NORTH (Ire) 9-2 K Darley, *hld up in rear, cld up and 5th strt, ran on one pace fnl furlong*................ 3
2883³ BENEFICIAL 9-2 M Hills, *trkd ldrs, led 5 fs out to 2 out, lost 3rd pl cl hme*.................................... 4
2081* FORT WOOD (USA) 9-2 S Guillot, *set slow pace, hdd 5 fs out, 3rd strt, sn btn*.................................. 5
2837⁴ ALTER ADEL 9-2 L Pyritz, *hld up, rdn alng 5 fs out, last and btn in strt*.. 6
Dist: 1l, 3l, ½l, 5l, 5l. 2m 29.30s. (6 Ran).
(Stall Granum), Bruno Schuetz

OSTEND (BEL) (good to soft)
Sunday August 15th

3372 **Criterium de Vitesse (2-y-o and up) £5,964 5f...................... (2:30)**

EARTH AND FIRE (Bel) 5-9-6 1
MYASHA (USA) 4-9-9 2
GUSTAV LAKE (Fr) 4-9-11 3
3080* PLAY HEVER GOLF 3-9-13 D Holland, *dsptd ld 2 fs, one pace fnl quarter-m*.................................. 6
Dist: 1½l, 2½l, 1½l, 2l, ½l. 57.70s. (13 Ran).

HAMILTON (good)
Monday August 16th
Going Correction: MINUS 0.15 sec. per fur. (races 1,2,3), MINUS 0.20 (4,5,6)

3373 **Team Management Apprentice Handicap Class G (0-70 3-y-o and up) £2,574 1½m 17yds.................... (2:15)**

2871* BATABANOO [70] 4-10-0 S Maloney (10) *patiently rdn, smooth hdwy on bit 2 fs out, ridden to ld last 50 yards, ran on*............. (2 to 1 fav op 5 to 2 tchd 3 to 1) 1
2774⁷ IRON BARON (Ire) [40] 4-7-9 (3*) Claire Balding (4) *tried to make all, quickened 2 fs out, hdd and drifted lft last 50 yards, rallied, fnshd second, relegated to 4th.* ....(7 to 1 op 6 to 1) 2D
3146³ DOCTOR ROY [42] 5-8-0 F Norton (9) *wtd wth, dashed through on ins to chal entering fnl furlong, kpt on same pace, fnshd 3rd, plcd second*... (7 to 1 op 6 to 1) 2
2950⁵ HOT PUNCH [37] 4-7-9 A Garth (6) *nvr far away, ev ch entering fnl furlong, crowded last 50 yards, one pace, fnshd 4th, plcd 3rd*.......................... (16 to 1) 3
1894⁷ ASTURIAS [35] 10-7-7 N Kennedy (3) *trkd ldr, drvn alng last 2 fs, no extr*..................(33 to 1 op 20 to 1) 5
3240⁴ CARROLLS MARC (Ire) [53] 5-8-4 (7*) J Gracey (2) *trkd ldg bunch, drvn up to fltter aftr a m, no imprsn.* .... (10 to 1 op 7 to 1) 6
2740⁴ GREAT ORATION (Ire) [40] 4-7-12⁶ (3*) V Halliday (8) *missed break, reco'red to race in tch for over a m, fdd.* ....(5 to 1 tchd 6 to 1) 7
3116⁴ SHAMSHOM AL ARAB (Ire) [49] 5-8-7 Darren Moffatt (7) *settled midfield, effrt and drvn alng hfwy, fdd o'r 2 fs out*........(9 to 2 op 4 to 1 tchd 5 to 1 and 11 to 2) 8
2565³ MUFID (USA) [51] 4-8-6 (3*) J Marshall (5) *settled on ins, drvn alng whn pace lifted 2 fs out, sn btn.* ....(14 to 1 op 12 to 1 tchd 16 to 1) 9
3147⁷ GROUSE-N-HEATHER [58] 4-8-13 (3*) G Forster (1) *settled aftr fst break, effrt hfwy, btn o'r 2 fs out.* .... (50 to 1 op 16 to 1) 10
Dist: Hd, ¾l, ½l, 3l, hd, 3l, hd, 10l, 2½l. 2m 37.20s. a 4.20s (10 Ran).
SR: 54/23/23/17/9/26/7/15/-/ (P D Savill), Mrs M Reveley

3374 **Hazelbank Selling Handicap Class G (0-60 3-y-o and up) £2,721 1m 1f 36yds .... (2:45)**

2726³ SLOE BRANDY [38] 3-8-2 G Duffield (8) *al hndy, led 2 fs out, rdn and styd on wl.* ....(3 to 1 fav op 7 to 2 tchd 4 to 1) 1
2931⁴ DRUMDONNA (Ire) [45] 3-8-9 J Carroll (12) *settled midfield, drvn through appr fnl furlong, kpt on same pace.* ....(10 to 1 op 8 to 1 tchd 11 to 1) 2
3055⁴ MAJOR IVOR [57] 8-10-0 M Birch (2) *patiently rdn, improved to fltter 2 fs out, edgd rght, kpt on same pace.* .... (11 to 1 op 8 to 1) 3
3216* SLUMBER THYME (Ire) [36] (bl) 4-8-7¹ (5ex) K Fallon (13) *sluggish strt, improved into midfield hfwy, rdn and not quicken last 2 fs*.................. (9 to 2 tchd 5 to 1) 4
3144⁹ HOD-MOD (Ire) [40] 3-8-4 A Mackay (10) *wtd wth, pushed alng to improve last 3 fs, styd on.* ....(14 to 1 op 12 to 1 tchd 16 to 1) 5
2737⁴ PERSIAN LION [32] 4-8-3² Alex Greaves (9) *nvr far away, hrd at work 3 fs out, no imprsn*... (8 to 1 tchd 10 to 1) 6
3090⁹ WEAVER GEORGE (Ire) [36] 3-7-12¹ (3*) S Maloney (1) *settled off the pace, steady hdwy last 2 fs, nvr plcd to chal*.......................... (25 to 1 op 20 to 1) 7
3088 BOLD MELODY [46] 4-9-0 (3*) C Hodgson (5) *trkd ldrs, led o'r 4 fs out till 2 out, eased whn btn ins last.* ....(8 to 1 op 7 to 1) 8
3002 MISS EL ARAB (Ire) [38] 5-8-9 J Lowe (4) *in tch, drvn alng hfwy, nvr able to chal*..............(33 to 1 op 20 to 1) 9
2763² MY BALLYBOY [44] (bl) 3-8-1 (7*) W Hawksley (3) *pressed ldg quartet till fdd o'r 2 fs out*..... (25 to 1 op 10 to 1) 10
3216⁵ DANCES WITH GOLD [38] (bl) 3-8-2 R P Elliott (7) *led till hdd and wknd quickly o'r 4 fs out.* .... (10 to 1 op 8 to 1 tchd 11 to 1) 11
TREASURE BEACH [38] 4-8-2 (7*) G Forster (6) *trkd ldg trio, wknd quickly o'r 3 fs out, eased.* ....(50 to 1 tchd 100 to 1) 12
Dist: 2½l, 2l, 4l, hd, 4l, ¾l, hd, 2½l, 2l. 1m 58.20s. a 4.20s (12 Ran).
SR: 4/3/16/-/-/-/ (Lady Fairhaven), Sir Mark Prescott

3375 **Royal Scots Dragoon Guards Handicap Class D (0-80 3-y-o and up) £3,720 1m 65yds....................... (3:15)**

3089* TALENTED TING (Ire) [65] (v) 4-9-3 K Darley (4) *set str pace to hfwy, rgned ld o'r 2 fs out, kpt on gmely fnl furlong.* .... (5 to 4 fav tchd 6 to 4) 1
2799⁷ MENTALASANYTHIN [69] 4-9-7 A Mackay (3) *patiently rdn, drvn up to chal ins fnl furlong, not quicken cl hme*..................(5 to 1 op 4 to 1 tchd 11 to 2) 2
3169* LAUREL QUEEN (Ire) [73] 5-9-11 J Carroll (2) *wth wnr, nosed ahead hfwy till o'r 2 fs out, no extr ins last.* ....(9 to 2 op 4 to 1) 3
2680⁴ MEDIA MESSENGER [54] 4-8-6² K Fallon (5) *chsd ldrs, struggling to keep up hfwy, styd on fnl furlong.* .... (14 to 1 op 12 to 1) 4
3117 COUREUR [47] 4-7-13 J Fanning (6) *in tch, outpcd and drvn alng hfwy, styd on finish.* (20 to 1 tchd 25 to 1) 5
3146⁵ PUBLIC WAY (Ire) [54] 3-8-0 J Lowe (7) *chsd ldg bunch, rdn to improve hfwy, btn o'r 2 fs out*..(20 to 1 op 16 to 1) 6
3146 STRAW THATCH [56] 4-8-3 (5*) Stephen Davies (1) *trkd ldg pair, feeling pace hfwy, sn struggling.* ....(4 to 1 tchd 9 to 2) 7
Dist: ¾l, 3l, 1½l, 1½l, 5l, 5l. 1m 46.80s. a 2.80s (7 Ran).
SR: 42/44/39/15/3/-/-/ (Martin Wickens), P C Haslam

3376 **Rosebank Claiming Stakes Class F (3-y-o) £2,579 6f 5yds............ (3:45)**

3123* PALACEGATE TOUCH (v) 9-7 J Carroll (2) *broke smartly, made all, shaken up to go clr appr fnl furlong, easily.* ....(9 to 4 on op 2 to 1 on tchd 7 to 4 on) 1
3051⁸ RAIN SPLASH 8-7 (7*) Claire Balding (1) *sluggish strt, swtchd outsd to improve hfwy, effrt o'r one furlong out, sn rdn and btn*................ (7 to 4 op 6 to 4) 2
2651⁶ BALLY ROBERT 8-12 (5*) Stephen Davies (3) *bolted gng to post, missed break, sn tld off.* .... (25 to 1 op 20 to 1 tchd 33 to 1) 3
Dist: 5l, dist. 1m 13.60s. a 2.90s (3 Ran).
SR: 25/-/-/ (Palacegate Corporation Ltd), J Berry

3377 **EBF Silverwell House Maiden Stakes Class D (2-y-o) £4,163 6f 5yds... (4:15)**

3223⁴ KNAVE'S ASH (USA) 9-0 Paul Eddery (2) *settled gng wl, nosed ahead o'r one furlong out, quickened away towards finish*.......... (7 to 4 op 6 to 4 tchd 2 to 1) 1
2706³ JETHOU (Ire) 9-0 N Connorton (4) *al hndy, led briefly o'r one furlong out, not quicken towards finish.* ....(5 to 1 op 4 to 1 tchd 6 to 1) 2
3131² MARBLE 8-4 (5*) Darren Moffatt (5) *unruly in paddock, rcd wide, effrt and drvn alng 2 fs out, hng lft, one pace.* .... (50 to 1 op 33 to 1) 3
3001⁵ HILL REEF (Fr) 9-0 K Fallon (1) *broke wl to show gd speed for o'r 4 fs, grad wknd.* (9 to 1 op 6 to 1 tchd 10 to 1) 4
KRISTAL DIVA 8-9 Dean McKeown (8) *lost many ls strt, ran green through out, ran on finish, nvr nrr.* ....(11 to 10 fav op 5 to 4 tchd 6 to 4 and Evens) 5
2021 THUNDERBIRD TWO (Ire) 9-0 M Birch (9) *broke wl to ld for o'r 4 fs, wknd quickly*............ (100 to 1 op 33 to 1) 6
HESFINMENTALTOO 9-0 A Mackay (7) *missed break, nvr able to reco'r*.........(20 to 1 op 16 to 1 tchd 33 to 1) 7
1889⁹ PEASAN 9-0 J Fortune (6) *chsd ldr to hfwy, sn tld off.* .... (50 to 1 op 20 to 1) 8
Dist: 3½l, 2½l, 1½l, 2½l, 8l, 2l, dist. 1m 13.50s. a 2.80s (8 Ran).
SR: 20/6/-/-/-/ (Sheikh Mohammed), M R Stoute

3378 **Shulman Carpets Handicap Class E (0-70 3-y-o and up) £3,157 6f 5yds**

. . . . (4:45)

3253[6] CRAIGIE BOY [44] 3-7-12 (3*) S Maloney (10) *nvr far away, led wl o'r one furlong out, hld on grimly ins last.* . . . . (16 to 1 op 25 to 1) 1
2760[5] LAMSONETTI [48] 3-8-5 Alex Greaves (9) *chsd alng to improve on outsd hfwy, drw level fnl furlong, jst hld.* . . . . (25 to 1 op 20 to 1) 2
3354[4] KILLY'S FILLY [54] 3-8-11 J Carroll (4) *led for o'r 3 fs, rdn and kpt on same pace ins last.* . . . . (6 to 1 tchd 13 to 2) 3
3168[6] ABIGAILS BOY (Hol) [49] 4-8-10 G Hind (2) *nvr far away, drvn alng last 2 fs, not quicken.* . . . . (6 to 1 op 5 to 1 tchd 13 to 2) 4
3191[3] ISLAND KNIGHT (Ire) [63] 4-9-7 (3*) C Hodgson (5) *patiently rdn, effrt and shaken up 2 fs out, no imprsn.* . . . . (11 to 1 op 8 to 1) 5
3094[4] SECOND COLOURS (USA) [60] 3-9-3 K Darley (7) *wth ldrs, led o'r 2 fs out till wl over one out, fdd.* . . . . (7 to 4 fav op 2 to 1 tchd 5 to 2) 6
3085[8] PAGEBOY [62] 4-9-9 Dean McKeown (6) *squeezed out strt, rdn alng hfwy, nvr dngrs.* . . . . (7 to 1 op 6 to 1 tchd 8 to 1) 7
3148[5] BEST EFFORT [50] (v) 7-8-11 K Fallon (8) *chsd ldrs for o'r 4 fs, fdd.* . . . . (14 to 1 op 10 to 1 tchd 16 to 1) 8
3180[5] SYLVAN STARLIGHT [56] (v) 3-8-13 G Duffield (1) *chsd alng and wndrd hfwy, nvr nr to chal.* . . . (14 to 1 op 12 to 1) 9
1494 FRANCIS ANN [53] 5-9-0 J Fanning (3) *wl plcd stand side, drvn alng whn squeezed out ins fnl furlong, eased when btn.* . . . . (25 to 1 op 16 to 1) 10

Dist: Nk, 1½l, 1½l, ½l, 1½l, sht-hd, 1½l, 1½l, 5l. 1m 12.50s. a 1.80s (10 Ran).
SR: 27/30/30/23/35/22/27/9/5/ (C Tomkins), N Bycroft

ROSCOMMON (IRE) (good)
Monday August 16th

3379 Glebe Nursery (2-y-o) £2,245 7f (6:15)

3200[9] LUDDEN LADY (Ire) [-] 8-5 (4*) J J Behan (6) . . . . . . (12 to 1) 1
3026[3] ORANEDIN [-] 9-1 (4*) P Carberry (1) . . . . (6 to 1) 2
2704[6] MY RAGAMUFFIN (Ire) [-] 8-13 J P Murtagh (3) . . . . (14 to 1) 3
2745[6] MONICA'S CHOICE (Ire) [-] (bl) 7-11 (2*) R M Burke (8) . . . . (8 to 1) 4
3064[2] BACK FROM HEAVEN (Ire) [-] 9-0 C Roche (2) . . (7 to 4 fav) 5
2983[3] SHIOWEN (Ire) [-] 8-6 M J Kinane (9) . . . . (9 to 4) 6
2450[4] SUAVE REDSKIN (Ire) [-] 8-4 W J Supple (5) . . . . (10 to 1) 7
3073[6] TRIMBLEMILL (Ire) [-] 9-1 B Coogan (4) . . . . (8 to 1) 8
2037 DANCING BRIEF (Ire) [-] 7-10 (2*) D G O'Shea (7) . . (25 to 1) 9

Dist: ½l, nk, sht-hd, ¾l. 1m 35.60s. (9 Ran).
(B J Caffrey), Edward P Mitchell

3380 European Forestry Growers Race (3-y-o and up) £2,762 7f. . . . . (6:45)

2741[5] MISS MISTLETOES (Ire) 3-9-0 S Craine (1) . . . . (9 to 2) 1
2703* BRATA (USA) 3-9-0 M J Kinane (4) . . . . (5 to 4 fav) 2
2779[7] GLOWING VALUE (Ire) (bl) 3-8-10 J P Murtagh (2) . . (7 to 1) 3
3278[2] MISS CARMELLA (Ire) 3-8-2[1] (6*) B J Walsh (6) . . . . . (5 to 1) 4
2957[5] GOODIES TWO STEP (Ire) 3-8-9 (8*) D M McCullagh (7) . . . . (14 to 1) 5
2674* PEARL DAWN (Ire) 3-8-10 (4*) J J Behan (9) . . . . . . (10 to 1) 6
3297[2] MARY'S CASE (Ire) 3-8-10 C Roche (5) . . . . (10 to 1) 7
ANVIL SPARK (Ire) 3-8-7 J F Egan (8) . . . . (33 to 1) 8
788[7] KERMIS (Fr) 3-8-8 (2*) D G O'Shea (3) . . . . (50 to 1) 9

Dist: Nk, nk, 1½l, 2½l. 1m 34.80s. (9 Ran).
(R E Sangster), T Stack

3381 John J. Fogarty Memorial Handicap (0-70 3-y-o) £3,652 1¼m. . . . . (7:15)

2249 PENNY A DAY (Ire) [-] 8-11 C Roche (4) . . . . (8 to 1) 1
2881[3] ISLAND VISION (Ire) [-] 8-13 W J Supple (13) (7 to 2 jt-fav) 2
2984[5] SAINT HILDA (Ire) [-] 8-10 (6*) J A Heffernan (8) . . . (13 to 2) 3
3062[4] ANIMATE (Ire) [-] 7-12 (4*) J J Behan (12) . . . . (7 to 1) 4
2516[8] SHARP AT SIX (Ire) [-] (bl) 7-13 (4*) W J Smith (3) . . (20 to 1) 5
2449[5] RED MICKS WIFE (Ire) [-] 8-13 J P Murtagh (9) . . . . . (20 to 1) 6
3062[9] FESTIVAL GIRL (Ire) [-] 9-2 M J Kinane (2) . . . . (7 to 2 jt-fav) 7
2843[7] FAX ME NOW (Ire) [-] 8-8 J F Egan (7) . . . . (14 to 1) 8
3112[6] WARREN STREET (Ire) [-] 9-2 S Craine (1) . . . . (10 to 1) 9
3112 TERN DANCER (Ire) [-] (bl) 8-5 (6*) B J Walsh (6) . . . (10 to 1) 10
1856[7] MUSWELL BROOK (Ire) [-] 9-3 K J Manning (10) . . (10 to 1) 11
3274* OCEAN BLUE (Ire) [-] (bl) 9-2 (4*,5ex) P Carberry (11) (7 to 1) 12
2514 GIRARDELLI (Ire) [-] 7-13 (2*) D G O'Shea (5) . . . . . . (33 to 1) 13

Dist: 1l, 4½l, 2l, 3½l. 2m 17.00s. (13 Ran).
(Savio To), P Burke

3382 Abbey Maiden (3-y-o and up) £2,245 1 ¼m. . . . . (7:45)

3300[3] BOTHSIDESNOW (Ire) (bl) 3-8-10 (4*) P Carberry (2) (9 to 4) 1
KILADANTE (Ire) 4-9-5 S Craine (10) . . . . (20 to 1) 2
NANNAKA (USA) 3-8-11 K J Manning (6) . . . . (10 to 1) 3
2691[3] NORDIC THORN (Ire) 3-9-0 C Roche (5) . . . . (9 to 2) 4
WORLD'S VIEW 3-8-11 M J Kinane (9) . . . . (6 to 4 fav) 5
3274[4] SYDNEY SUSSEX (Ire) 3-9-0 W J Supple (7) . . . . (7 to 1) 6
CAPTAIN TANDY (Ire) 4-9-2 (6*) R V Skelly (1) . . . . . (25 to 1) 7
3198[6] TODDY MARK (Ire) 4-9-8 N Byrne (3) . . . . (50 to 1) 8
2703[9] BETTER GOODS (Ire) 3-8-11 J P Murtagh (8) . . . . . (16 to 1) 9

Dist: 3l, hd, 3½l, ½l. 2m 17.40s. (9 Ran).
(T J Duffy), Noel Meade

WINDSOR (good to firm)
Monday August 16th

Going Correction: MINUS 0.30 sec. per fur. (races 1,4,5), MINUS 0.05 (2,3,6)

3383 Additional Apprentices' Handicap Class G (0-70 3-y-o and up) £2,301 5f 10yds. . . . . (2:30)

3229[5] JUCEA [57] 4-9-8 R Painter (6) *wl beh till hdwy 2 fs out, str run ins last to ld post.* (9 to 1 op 6 to 1 tchd 10 to 1) 1
3108[3] SOPHISTICATED AIR [55] (bl) 3-9-0 (3*) D Griffiths (4) *chsd ldrs, ev ch o'r one furlong out, rallied ins last, jst fld.* . . . . (9 to 2 fav op 4 to 1 tchd 5 to 1) 2
3270[3] BATCHWORTH BOUND [54] 4-9-0 (5*) A Daly (7) *al prmnt, led gng wl o'r one furlong out, rdn ins last, ct fnl strds.* . . . . (11 to 2 op 4 to 1) 3
3180[6] CHOIR PRACTICE [56] 6-9-4 (3*) Sally Radford-Howes (2) *slwly into strd, wl beh till str run fnl furlong, fnshd well.* . . . . (16 to 1 op 12 to 1) 4
2967[2] AVRIL ETOILE [51] 3-8-5 (8*) Iona Wands (8) *al prmnt, rdn 2 fs out, styd on wl ins last.* . . . . (5 to 1 op 6 to 1) 5
2967* PERFECT PASSION [46] 3-8-7[2] (3*) Rachel Bridger (5) *led till hdd o'r one furlong out, wknd ins last.* . . . . (9 to 1 op 7 to 1 tchd 10 to 1) 6
3032[3] TOMMY TEMPEST [47] (bl) 4-8-4 (8*) L Suthern (3) *wth ldrs, ev ch o'r one furlong out, no extr.* . . . . (7 to 1 op 5 to 1 tchd 15 to 2) 7
2788[6] TREASURE TIME (Ire) [63] 4-9-6 (8*) T Fuggle (1) *prmnt on outsd, ev ch o'r one furlong out, wknd ins last.* . . . . (5 to 1 tchd 6 to 1 and 9 to 2) 8
3340[8] BARASSIE [36] 3-7-9 (3*) Sharon Millard (10) *speed to hfwy.* . . . . (16 to 1 op 25 to 1 tchd 33 to 1) 9
3229 THE ORDINARY GIRL (Ire) [55] (v) 3-9-3 D O'Neill (9) *speed to hfwy, sn btn.* . . . . (7 to 1 op 10 to 1) 10

Dist: Nk, sht-hd, sht-hd, nk, 2½l, 2l, ¾l, 2½l, 1½l. 1m 1.40s. a 2.40s (10 Ran).
SR: 30/24/25/26/17/2/-/11/-/ (A A Campbell), J L Spearing

3384 Belmead Selling Stakes Class G (3-y-o) £2,406 1¼m 7yds. . . . . (3:00)

2858[4] PATONG BEACH 8-9 R Hills (1) *chsd ldrs gng wl, led well o'r 2 fs out, hld on gmely ins last.* . . . . (4 to 1 op 7 to 2 tchd 9 to 2) 1
3007 MALZETA (Ire) 8-4 (5*) D Wright (13) *hld up, gd hdwy on outsd o'r 2 fs out, str chal last, jst fld.* . . . . (13 to 2 op 7 to 2) 2
3106[5] MISS MICHELLE 8-9 T Sprake (10) *beh till hdwy wl o'r 2 fs out, styd on, nvr nrr.* . . . . (8 to 1 op 6 to 1 tchd 10 to 1 and 12 to 1) 3
876 RITZY 8-9 W Newnes (6) *al hndy, ev ch wl o'r 2 fs out, kpt on same pace.* . . . . (14 to 1 op 10 to 1) 4
2712 MARAT (USA) 9-0 T Quinn (8) *midfield, rdn 3 fs out, kpt on ins last.* . . . . (12 to 1 op 7 to 1) 5
FREDDY SYLVESTER 9-0 W Ryan (7) *beh till hdwy wl o'r 3 fs out, no extr appr last.* (16 to 1 op 7 to 1 tchd 20 to 1) 6
3249[3] FILOU FILANT (Fr) 9-0 Pat Eddery (12) *led till hdd wl o'r 2 fs out, sn wknd.* . . . . (5 to 2 fav op 11 to 4 tchd 3 to 1 and 7 to 2) 7
2898 DOUBLE DEALING (Ire) (v) 8-7 (7*) G Rothwell (9) *beh and sn rdn alng, some hdwy 2 fs out, no dngr.* . . . . (25 to 1 op 20 to 1 tchd 33 to 1) 8
3301 ARRAS ROYALE 9-0 R Price (3) *midfield, rdn and no hdwy whn hmpd 2 fs out, not reco'r.* . . . . (33 to 1 op 16 to 1) 9
2684[8] OMIDJOY (Ire) (bl) 8-9 W Woods (4) *chsd ldg bunch, effrt 4 fs out, sn rdn and btn.* . . . . (8 to 1 op 6 to 1) 10
3221[6] PETITE JUNE (Ire) 8-9 T Williams (5) *chsd ldr, rdn o'r 3 fs out, sn wknd.* . . . . (20 to 1 op 14 to 1) 11
2833[2] TREBLE LASS 8-9 L Dettori (11) *chsd ldrs till rdn and wknd o'r 3 fs out.* . . . . . . (13 to 2 op 4 to 1 tchd 7 to 1) 12
3083[6] WHATONE BELL (bl) 9-0 S Raymont (14) *slwly into strd, reco'red to midfield till wknd wl over 4 fs out.* . . . . (33 to 1 op 25 to 1) 13

Dist: Sht-hd, 3l, ¾l, 4l, 2½l, 3l, 1l, 1l, nk, 12l. 2m 8.30s. a 5.80s (13 Ran).
SR: 32/31/25/23/20/15/9/7/5/ (Tim Newsome), J W Hills

3385 Theale Conditions Stakes Class D (3-y-o and up) £3,377 1¼m 7yds. . . (3:30)

2654 ICY SOUTH (USA) 3-8-8 L Dettori (6) *made all, jnd o'r one furlong out, pushed out, cmftbly.* . . . . (16 to 1 op 10 to 1 tchd 20 to 1) 1
2654[3] BLUE LION 3-9-0 M Roberts (9) *settled hndy, chlgd wnr o'r one furlong out, eased whn no imprsn fnl 100 yards.* . . . . (11 to 10 fav op Evens tchd 5 to 4 and 11 to 8) 2
VRATISLAV (USA) 4-9-0 Pat Eddery (8) *hld up, hdwy o'r 3 fs out, styd on same pace.* . . . . (10 to 1 op 8 to 1 tchd 12 to 1) 3

1974[5] BADIE (USA) 4-9-6 W Carson (1) *hld up, rdn 3 fs out, kpt on fnl furlong, nvr nrr*............(33 to 1 op 20 to 1) 4
2752* PETER QUINCE 3-8-10 W Ryan (3) *trkd ldr, rdn o'r 2 fs out, sn no extr*....................(5 to 4 op 11 to 8) 5
2617 MILZIG (USA) 4-9-0 J Williams (7) *trkd ldrs, rdn 3 fs out, sn btn*..................(20 to 1 op 25 to 1 tchd 33 to 1) 6
1719[5] SHIRO 3-8-10 A Munro (5) *took keen hold, hld up, shrtlvd effrt o'r 3 fs out, no dngr*..........(33 to 1 op 20 to 1) 7
JURA 5-9-5 P Robinson (4) *hld up, rdn 3 fs out, sn no imprsn*..............(16 to 1 op 12 to 1 tchd 20 to 1) 8
2992 STARLIGHT FLYER (bl) 6-9-3 R Price (2) *trkd ldrs, rdn o'r 4 fs out, wknd quickly, tld off*..............(100 to 1) 9

Dist: 2l, 2½l, ½l, nk, 1l, 1l, 1l, 25l. 2m 6.80s. a 4.30s (9 Ran).
SR: 46/48/43/48/37/39/33/40/-/ (Saeed Manana), J H M Gosden

3386 Coopers & Lybrand Nursery Class D (2-y-o) £4,776 5f 217yds.........(4:00)

3222* MAJOR SUCCESS (Ire) [79] 9-4 (7ex) D Holland (1) *rcd alone far side, made virtually all, swrvd rght and lft und pres frm o'r one furlong out, ran on strly.*
..................................(4 to 1 fav tchd 9 to 2) 1
2616[5] DARREN BOY (Ire) [80] 8-12 (7*) T G McLaughlin (13) *hld up, gd hdwy o'r 2 fs out and led stands side frm over one out, str run and veered lft fnl furlong, jst fld.*
..........................(7 to 1 op 6 to 1 tchd 8 to 1) 2
3222[6] DANCING LAWYER [70] 8-9 A Munro (4) *prmnt stands side, ev ch o'r one furlong out, no extr ins last.*
..........................(9 to 1 op 7 to 1 tchd 10 to 1) 3
2687* BLURRED IMAGE (Ire) [75] 9-0 Pat Eddery (7) *chsd ldrs till rdn and no hdwy fnl one and a half fs.*
..................................(11 to 2 op 4 to 1) 4
2528* HIGHLY FASHIONABLE (Ire) [73] 8-12 T Quinn (8) *led aftr 2 fs stands side till hdd o'r one out, wknd.*
..................................(8 to 1 op 6 to 1) 5
2825[4] ZORAHAYDA (Fr) [54] 7-0 (7*) Kim McDonnell (9) *beh till styd on fnl 2 fs, nvr able to chal.* (25 to 1 tchd 33 to 1) 6
3129 CONNECT (Ire) [68] (bl) 8-4 (3*) B Doyle (11) *midfield, moderate hdwy 2 fs out, no dngr.*
..........................(14 to 1 op 12 to 1 tchd 16 to 1) 7
3082[3] SHFNAK (Ire) [64] (v) 8-3 M Roberts (15) *chsd ldrs, rdn hfwy, sn one pace*......(8 to 1 op 7 to 1 tchd 10 to 1) 8
2929[2] MILLICENT NORTH [80] 9-5 J Williams (10) *prmnt stands side till no hdwy fnl 2 fs.*
..........................(9 to 1 op 8 to 1 tchd 10 to 1) 9
1602 STARISK [58] 7-6 (5*) D Wright (3) *al rear div*.....(20 to 1) 10
3303[2] LITTLE HOOLIGAN [57] 7-10 C Rutter (2) *chsd ldg bunch, rdn alng hfwy, stdly lost pl.*
..........................(8 to 1 op 7 to 1 tchd 9 to 1) 11
1920[4] MOUNT LEINSTER [82] 9-7 W Ryan (14) *led stands side 2 fs, sn wknd*..........................(20 to 1 op 16 to 1) 12
1988[3] SWAGGER LADY [77] 9-2 W Carson (12) *al beh.*
..................................(14 to 1 op 12 to 1) 13
2946* ADMIRING [67] 8-3 (3*) M Fenton (6) *al beh.*
..................................(10 to 1 op 7 to 1) 14

Dist: Sht-hd, 4l, 5l, 3l, nk, 1l, 2½l, ¾l, ¾l, 4l. 1m 11.50s. a 1.20s (14 Ran).
SR: 44/44/18/3/-/-/ (W J Gredley), B W Hills

3387 EBF Bracknell Maiden Stakes Class D (2-y-o) £4,342 5f 10yds..........(4:30)

3052[3] CRYSTAL MAGIC 8-9 Pat Eddery (8) *made all, clr o'r one furlong out, drvn out*............(9 to 4 fav op 3 to 1) 1
PHONEAHOLIC (Ire) 9-0 B Rouse (14) *al prmnt, chsd wnr frm hfwy, kpt on wl.*
.............(5 to 1 op 4 to 1 tchd 6 to 1 and 7 to 1) 2
3041[2] BIRD OF TIME (Ire) 8-9 W Carson (2) *rcd alone far side, ev ch till wknd ins last*.....(6 to 1 op 5 to 1 tchd 8 to 1) 3
2990[7] ROBSERA (Ire) 9-0 B Raymond (4) *chsd ldrs, rdn o'r 2 fs out, kpt on same pace*...(7 to 2 op 5 to 1 tchd 3 to 1) 4
2519[4] SPORTING START 9-0 N Adams (9) *al chasing ldrs, rdn o'r 2 fs out, unbl to quicken*..........(33 to 1 op 14 to 1) 5
3041[7] IRADAH (USA) 8-9 R Hills (6) *chsd ldrs till rdn and one pace fnl 2 fs*...................(7 to 2 tchd 11 to 2) 6
MAY LIGHT 8-9 W Ryan (12) *slwly away, beh till hdwy 2 fs out, kpt on, nvr nrr*..............(20 to 1 op 12 to 1) 7
SPRINGTIME AFFAIR 8-9 L Dettori (3) *slwly into strd, nvr able to chal*..................(33 to 1 op 14 to 1) 8
2571 AIRSPEED FLYER (USA) 9-0 T Quinn (5) *nvr better than midfield*..........................(12 to 1 op 14 to 1) 9
LADY HAWK 8-9 W Newnes (11) *outpcd.*
..................................(33 to 1 op 20 to 1) 10
3009[7] ARAFARAZ 9-0 A Munro (10) *chsd ldrs to hfwy.*
..................................(33 to 1 op 20 to 1) 11
1063 COMMENDATION DAY (Ire) 9-0 D Holland (1) *slwly away, al rear div*..........(25 to 1 op 12 to 1 tchd 33 to 1) 12
AVANTI XIQUET 9-0 C Avery (13) *al beh.*
..................................(33 to 1 op 20 to 1) 13
SHAYNES DOMAIN 9-0 P Robinson (7) *slwly away, al beh, tld off*..........................(33 to 1 op 14 to 1) 14

Dist: 1l, 3½l, nk, ¾l, 1l, 1l, 3½l, hd, sht-hd, hd. 1m 0.50s. a 1.50s (14 Ran).
SR: 35/36/17/21/18/9/5/-/-/ (D Sieff), R Hannon

3388 Quortina Challenge Cup Handicap Class D (0-80 3-y-o and up) £3,850 1m 3f 135yds......................(5:00)

2899[2] SHIRLEY ROSE [66] 3-8-12 M Roberts (2) *led till hdd 4 fs out, led and veered rght one out, drvn clr.*
..........................(6 to 4 fav op 7 to 4 tchd 2 to 1) 1
2942[4] FULL QUIVER [46] (v) 8-7-11 (5*) D Wright (8) *hld up, hdwy 3 fs out, hmpd one out, kpt on.*
..........................(6 to 1 op 7 to 1 tchd 11 to 2) 2
2913[5] INCHCAILLOCH (Ire) [66] 4-9-8 B Raymond (7) *al hndy, led 4 fs out till hdd one out, not quicken.*
..................................(3 to 1 tchd 7 to 2) 3
3010[4] MAHRAJAN [61] 9-9-3 T Quinn (4) *hld up in tch, rdn and hdwy o'r 3 fs out, sn ev ch, one pace fnl 2 furlongs.*
..........................(7 to 2 op 5 to 2 tchd 4 to 1) 4
2757[9] ROSE ELEGANCE [69] (bl) 4-9-6 (5*) V Slattery (5) *slwly into strd, pld hrd, effrt 3 fs out, sn btn.* (14 to 1 op 12 to 1) 5
3010[6] BO KNOWS BEST (Ire) [60] 4-9-2 B Rouse (1) *trkd ldr till wknd o'r 3 fs out*........(8 to 1 op 6 to 1 tchd 9 to 1) 6
AFTER THE FIRE [45] 4-8-1[1]4 (7*) T Fuggle (3) *in tch till lost pl o'r 4 fs out, sn in rear*..........(66 to 1 op 50 to 1) 7

Dist: 2l, 2l, 3l, 1½l, 2l, 10l. 2m 29.50s. a 6.50s (7 Ran).
SR: 27/13/29/18/23/10/-/ (Greenland Park Ltd), M Johnston

FOLKESTONE (firm (races 1,2,4,6), good to firm (3,5))
Tuesday August 17th
Going Correction: NIL (races 1,2,4,6), MINUS 0.20 (3,5)

3389 BBC Radio Kent Median Auction Maiden Fillies' Stakes Class F (2-y-o) £2,243 6f 189yds............... (1:45)

2718[3] PAT'S SPLENDOUR 8-8 (3*) C Hodgson (3) *cl up, led one and a half fs out, drvn out.*
..........................(7 to 1 op 8 to 1 tchd 10 to 1) 1
3218[4] TASHLA (v) 8-11 M Tebbutt (4) *trkd ldrs, ev ch ins fnl furlong, ran on*.....(2 to 1 fav tchd 9 to 4 and 7 to 4) 2
2234[3] PHYLIAN 8-11 W Woods (6) *chsd ldrs, rdn and ran on ins fnl furlong*..........................(6 to 1 op 5 to 1) 3
CARA CARLTON (USA) 8-11 W Newnes (10) *outpcd, hdwy one furlong out, ran on wl nr finish.*
..................................(40 to 1 op 20 to 1) 4
POSENZEE (Ire) 8-11 S Raymont (11) *strted slwly, hdwy o'r one furlong out, ran on ins last.* (14 to 1 op 7 to 1) 5
2895[6] ZUNO NOELYN 8-11 Paul Eddery (7) *chsd ldg 5, kpt on wl fnl furlong*..........................(20 to 1 op 14 to 1) 6
GOLDEN FERN 8-11 W Ryan (1) *outpcd, nvr on terms.*
..........................(12 to 1 op 7 to 1 tchd 14 to 1) 7
2844 HELLO MAMA 8-11 B Rouse (8) *outpcd and sn rdn alng, cld on ldg grp hfwy, soon btn*.....(20 to 1 op 10 to 1) 8
2325 SWITCH BLADE (Ire) (bl) 8-11 S O'Gorman (9) *cl up til rdn and wknd o'r one furlong out.*
..........................(3 to 1 op 5 to 2 tchd 4 to 1) 9
2826 BOLDANDPRETTY (bl) 8-8 (3*) D Harrison (5) *rcd freely, led til hdd one and a half fs out, wknd.*
..................................(40 to 1 op 20 to 1) 10
GHALIA (Ire) 8-4 (7*) R Painter (2) *outpcd, sn tld off.*
..................................(16 to 1 op 8 to 1) 11

Dist: ½l, ½l, sht-hd, sht-hd, ½l, 6l, 1l, 1½l, sht-hd, 20l. 1m 26.70s. a 5.80s (11 Ran).
SR: 10/8/6/5/4/2/ (Mrs Patricia Lunn), D Morris

3390 Dave Austin Breakfast Show Selling Stakes Class G (2-y-o) £2,070 6f 189yds........................(2:15)

2271 FOREVER BLUSHING 8-0[1] (7*) S Drowne (2) *beh, hdwy o'r one furlong out, led wl ins last, jst hld on.*
..................................(14 to 1 op 10 to 1) 1
2844[7] COMEONUP 8-11 S Raymont (4) *trkd ldrs, lost pl o'r 3 fs out, hdwy over one out, fnshd wl, jst fld.*
..........................(7 to 2 op 3 to 1 tchd 4 to 1) 2
3264[8] HIGH SWINGER (bl) 8-11 B Rouse (8) *sn led, hdd wl ins fnl furlong, no extr cl hme*.............(7 to 1 op 4 to 1) 3
3126[9] SALT STONE (Ire) (v) 7-13 (7*) S Mulvey (6) *hld up, hdwy 2 fs out, ev ch ins last, no extr nr finish.*
..................................(14 to 1 op 10 to 1) 4
3098[6] JOBISDUN 8-4 (7*) Mark Denaro (12) *trkd ldrs, pushed alng o'r 2 fs out, kpt on.*
..........................(16 to 1 op 10 to 1 tchd 20 to 1) 5
3166[8] SPORTING STORY (Ire) 8-6 A Clark (10) *beh, styd on wl fnl furlong*..........................(7 to 1 tchd 10 to 1) 6
GREEN'S IMPRESSION (Ire) 8-3 (3*) M Fenton (7) *trkd ldrs, pushed alng and ev ch o'r one furlong out, sn wknd.*
..............(100 to 30 jt-fav op 4 to 1 tchd 13 to 2) 7
3235[3] CELESTIAL DANCE 8-6 J Fortune (5) *cl up, rdn 2 fs out, wknd ins last.* (100 to 30 jt-fav op 2 to 1 tchd 7 to 2) 8
2271[7] CARNEGIE BLUE 8-6 W Ryan (1) *al beh.*
..........................(12 to 1 op 8 to 1 tchd 14 to 1) 9
2637[9] ROSE OF GLENN (v) 8-1 (5*) Stephen Davies (3) *trkd ldrs till rdn and wknd wl o'r one furlong out.*
..................................(8 to 1 op 6 to 1) 10
2819[6] SEMAH'S DREAM 8-6 W Woods (9) *trkd ldrs til wknd o'r 2 fs out*..........................(20 to 1 op 10 to 1) 11

1863^{5} ZIGGYS BOY 8-11 N Adams (11) *strted slwly, hdwy 3 fs out, sn btn*..........(14 to 1 op 10 to 1 tchd 16 to 1) 12
Dist: Sht-hd, nk, hd, 1l, ½l, ¾l, nk, 2l, sht-hd, 2½l. 1m 28.00s. a 7.10s (12 Ran).
(Miss M Bryant), P Butler

3391 Kentish Express Rating Related Maiden Stakes Class F (0-60 3-y-o) £2,243 6f.................... (2:45)

3168^{4} DOUBLE BOUNCE 9-0 W Newnes (7) *chsd ldrs, wnt second 2 fs out, rdn o'r one out, led nr finish.* ....(13 to 2 op 5 to 1 tchd 7 to 1) 1
2719^{2} RED ADMIRAL 8-11 (3*) C Hodgson (1) *led, clr o'r 2 fs out, ct nr finish*..........(7 to 4 fav op 9 to 4 tchd 5 to 2) 2
3168^{3} LORINS GOLD (bl) 9-0 S Dawson (3) *trkd ldrs till outpcd fnl 2 fs*..........(13 to 2 op 6 to 1 tchd 7 to 1) 3
719 BALLET 8-6 (3*) D Harrison (8) *cl up till outpcd o'r 2 fs out, kpt on ins last*......... (13 to 2 op 5 to 1 tchd 7 to 1) 4
3047^{3} ALMONTY (Ire) (bl) 9-0 Paul Eddery (12) *prmnt, hrd rdn o'r 2 fs out, sn wknd*......(13 to 2 op 5 to 1 tchd 9 to 1) 5
2918^{4} EXPORT MONDIAL (bl) 9-0 M Tebbutt (2) *outpcd hfwy, styd on ins fnl furlong.* ....(14 to 1 op 10 to 1 tchd 16 to 1) 6
3188^{7} LAID BACK BEN (bl) 9-0 A Clark (6) *nvr on terms.* ....(20 to 1 op 14 to 1) 7
3292^{6} SLIVOVITZ (bl) 8-9 (5*) Stephen Davies (11) *chsd ldrs till wknd o'r 2 fs out*.....(16 to 1 op 12 to 1 tchd 20 to 1) 8
3100^{7} KINTWYN (v) 9-0 T Williams (9) *outpcd frm hfwy.* ....(20 to 1 op 12 to 1) 9
3068^{4} DANNY BLUE (Ire) 8-9 (5*) D McCabe (5) *outpcd and beh whn stumbled o'r 4 fs out*............(8 to 1 op 5 to 1) 10
3305 GALLOP TO GLORY (v) 9-0 W Ryan (10) *outpcd.* ....(20 to 1 op 12 to 1) 11
2893^{3} ROYAL MUSIC 9-0 J Fortune (4) *outpcd.* ....(16 to 1 op 12 to 1 tchd 20 to 1) 12
Dist: Nk, 7l, ½l, 2½l, 2l, 2l, nk, 5l, ¾l, 2l. 1m 12.70s. a 1.70s (12 Ran).
SR: 42/41/13/6/1/-/ (Mrs P Scott-Dunn), K T Ivory

3392 Shepway Festival Apprentice Handicap Class F (0-70 3-y-o) £2,511 2m 93yds......................... (3:20)

2547^{3} TILTY (USA) [67] 9-2 (3*) D O'Neill (6) *nvr far away, led wl o'r one furlong out, styd on well.* ....(11 to 8 fav op 6 to 4 tchd 7 to 4) 1
3044^{3} MR COPYFORCE [62] (bl) 9-0 A Martinez (7) *led til hdd one and a half fs out, kpt on*.......... (11 to 4 op 2 to 1) 2
2937^{8} MENHAAD (Ire) [55] 7-13 (8*) C Dykes (5) *in tch, hmpd and lost pl ten fs out, hdwy 7 out, ev ch o'r 2 out, one pace.* ....(12 to 1 op 7 to 1 tchd 14 to 1) 3
3252^{5} FOREVER SHINEING [69] 9-4 (3*) Sarah Thompson (4) *chsd ldrs till outpcd frm o'r 3 fs out*....(14 to 1 op 10 to 1) 4
3232^{5} SANTA STELLAR [42] 7-8 Ruth Coulter (8) *chsd ldrs till outpcd fnl 5 fs*....... (25 to 1 op 20 to 1 tchd 33 to 1) 5
3078 CANDARELA [41] 7-7 Sally Radford-Howes (1) *cl up til wknd 3 fs out*.......................(33 to 1 op 20 to 1) 6
3097^{4} ROWLANDSONS GOLD (Ire) [41] 7-7 Wendy Jones (3) *al beh*....................(12 to 1 op 8 to 1 tchd 14 to 1) 7
2640^{2} IBTIKAR (USA) [45] (v) 7-11 M Baird (2) *al beh, tld off frm hfwy*.......................(4 to 1 op 3 to 1 tchd 9 to 2) 8
Dist: 4l, ¾l, 15l, ½l, 8l, 1½l, 20l. 3m 38.60s. a 7.60s (8 Ran).
SR: 29/20/11/10/-/ (Mrs P R Cock), R Hannon

3393 Kent Today Limited Stakes Class E (0-70 3-y-o and up) £2,976 6f.... (3:55)

3168* MY RUBY RING 6-8-8 (5*) Stephen Davies (1) *al prmnt, led appr 2 fs out, ran on wl.* ....(9 to 4 fav op 2 to 1 tchd 5 to 2) 1
3323^{2} MISS WHITTINGHAM (Ire) 3-8-9 J Fortune (3) *cl up, ev ch 2 fs out, sn hrd rdn and no extr.* ....(4 to 1 op 7 to 2 tchd 9 to 2) 2
3305^{4} ZEBOIM (bl) 7-8-11 (7*) Kim McDonnell (4) *in tch, hdwy o'r one furlong out, ran on*.............. (8 to 1 op 5 to 1) 3
3070^{2} MR NEVERMIND (Ire) 3-9-0 B Rouse (7) *cl up, hrd rdn one furlong out, one pace*... (3 to 1 op 7 to 2 tchd 4 to 1) 4
3060^{6} ASHGORE 3-9-0 T Williams (6) *led til hdd appr 2 fs out, no extr*..........(11 to 1 op 6 to 1 tchd 12 to 1) 5
3168 SPECTACLE JIM 4-9-4 N Adams (2) *strted slwly, cld hfwy, no imprsn frm o'r 2 fs out*.........(33 to 1 op 16 to 1) 6
3229* MARTINA 5-8-13 Paul Eddery (5) *hld up, effrt 2 fs out, no imprsn*...............................(4 to 1 op 3 to 1) 7
Dist: 2l, 1l, ½l, 1½l, 2l, 1½l. 1m 13.10s. a 2.10s (7 Ran).
SR: 33/21/26/20/14/10/-/ (Mrs Marion Wickham), D R Laing

3394 BBC Radio Kent/Kent Messenger Group Headline Handicap Class E (3-y-o and up) £3,131 1½m........ (4:30)

3125 BIG PAT [58] 4-9-5 (5*) J Tate (1) *chsd ldrs, hdwy o'r one furlong out, sstnd run to ld fnl strd.* ....(15 to 8 fav op 2 to 1 tchd 5 to 2 and 7 to 4) 1
3342^{8} THEMEDA [43] 4-8-6 (3*) D Harrison (5) *cl up, led 2 fs out till ct fnl strd.* ....(12 to 1 op 10 to 1 tchd 14 to 1 and 16 to 1) 2
2970^{8} LEXUS (Ire) [41] 5-8-0 (7*) Sarah Thompson (8) *trkd ldrs, reminder o'r 2 fs out, ran on ins last.* ....(7 to 1 op 8 to 1 tchd 10 to 1 and 6 to 1) 3
2942^{9} INCOLA [49] 7-9-1 S Dawson (7) *led til hdd 2 fs out, rallied und pres, no extr wl ins last.* ....(4 to 1 op 3 to 1 tchd 9 to 2) 4
2948^{2} BRONZE MAQUETTE (Ire) [59] (bl) 3-9-1 E Johnson (4) *hld up, effrt o'r 2 fs out, no imprsn.* ....(11 to 4 op 7 to 4 tchd 3 to 1) 5
SEVERINE (USA) [60] 4-9-12 W Ryan (6) *trkd ldrs till wknd o'r one furlong out, eased.* ....(12 to 1 op 10 to 1 tchd 14 to 1 and 16 to 1) 6
2032^{7} PHARLING [46] 3-8-2 G Hind (2) *hld up, outpcd o'r 6 fs out, tld off*..........................(14 to 1 op 8 to 1) 7
Dist: Nk, ¾l, ½l, 8l, 3l, 25l. 2m 38.80s. a 8.30s (7 Ran).
SR: 27/11/7/14/-/3/-/ (Burton Park Country Club), J Pearce

LAYTOWN (IRE) (hard) Tuesday August 17th

3395 Neptune Race (3-y-o and up) £1,727 5f ....(5:00)

3380^{6} PEARL DAWN (Ire) 3-8-13 (4*) P Carberry (3).......(6 to 1) 1
2879^{4} PAKOL (Ire) 4-8-5 (4*) W J Smith (7)...............(8 to 1) 2
3074 I'M NO LADY (Ire) 3-8-11 N Byrne (5)..............(50 to 1) 3
3328* YONOKA (Fr) (bl) 4-9-9 P V Gilson (6)............. (10 to 1) 4
2741^{4} PETITE EPAULETTE 3-8-11 J P Murtagh (12)...(7 to 4 fav) 5
2514^{8} NABEEL (USA) 7-9-3 D V Smith (8)................ (14 to 1) 6
3161^{8} SOUTHERN REVIEW (Ire) (bl) 3-9-0 W J Supple (13) (10 to 1) 7
3074^{2} LOWLACK (bl) 3-8-7 (4*) J J Behan (4)........... (10 to 1) 8
2780^{4} RECOLLECTION (Ire) (bl) 4-8-6 (8*) B J Halligan (2) (6 to 1) 9
3296^{9} WHY ME LINDA (Ire) 4-8-9 D Manning (11)........ (10 to 1) 10
2511^{9} FIVE LITTLE GIRLS (Ire) 3-8-11 K J Manning (16)..(20 to 1) 11
2877^{6} CELTICCARO (Ire) 5-8-12 J F Egan (10)...........(20 to 1) 12
TIR NA NOLLAIG (Ire) 5-8-1 (8*) G Coogan (1).....(66 to 1) 13
3296^{8} ICANSEEFORMILES (Ire) (bl) 5-9-3 S Craine (15)..(20 to 1) 14
2141 SPECIAL SECRET (Ire) 5-8-9 (8*) P O Casey (17)..(33 to 1) 15
2879 DONMIR LOVEBIRD (Ire) (bl) 3-8-5 (6*) R V Skelly (14) ....(25 to 1) 16
TOP DIVER (Ire) 3-8-8 (6*) B J Walsh (9)..........(20 to 1) 17
267 TANDRAGEE STARLET (Ire) 3-8-11 R Gordon (18) (100 to 1) 18
Dist: ¾l, ¾l, 2l, hd. (Time not taken) (18 Ran).
(Mrs M Chance), Noel T Chance

3396 Coca Cola Maiden (3-y-o and up) £2,072 1½m.................. (5:30)

870 ARAN EXILE 3-8-7 (4*) P Carberry (4)............ (10 to 1) 1
3197^{6} NURSES RUN (Ire) 3-8-7 (4*) J J Behan (6).........(7 to 2) 2
3366^{2} LEAD ME LEAD MENOT (USA) (bl) 4-9-5 (2*) R M Burke (9) ....(5 to 2) 3
2902 L'EQUIPE (Ire) 3-9-0 J F Egan (1)..................(7 to 2) 4
2484^{3} RICH LIFE (Ire) (bl) 3-8-10 (4*) W J Smith (8).... (9 to 4 fav) 5
3329^{4} GARDENVALE VIC (Ire) 3-9-0 S Craine (7)......... (10 to 1) 6
753^{5} BLENHEIM PALACE (USA) 6-9-10 H Rogers (5)... (14 to 1) pu
Dist: 3l, 4l, 1½l, 8l. (Time not taken) (7 Ran).
(Kerr Technology Ltd), Noel Meade

3397 Golden Lane Handicap (0-65 3-y-o and up) £2,072 1½m................(6:30)

3326^{6} CORAL SOUND (Ire) [-] 3-8-9 (4*) P Carberry (6)....(8 to 1) 1
2665^{6} MR GERAN (Ire) [-] 4-8-0 (4*) J J Behan (3)......... (14 to 1) 2
3367^{3} GREEK CHIME (Ire) [-] 4-9-6 J F Egan (15)...........(8 to 1) 3
3277^{8} SOUND PERFORMANCE (Ire) [-] 4-9-8 J P Murtagh (14) ....(14 to 1) 4
3277^{2} SPRING RITE [-] 6-7-6^{5} (8*) R T Fitzpatrick (10).....(5 to 1) 5
3112^{7} BENGALI (Ire) [-] 3-8-0 W J Supple (11).........(3 to 1 fav) 6
3367^{2} REGAL PRETENDER (Ire) [-] 3-7-13 D V Smith (5)...(8 to 1) 7
2556 TOMBARA (Ire) [-] 5-9-11 B Coogan (4).............(8 to 1) 8
1141 COLLECTED (Ire) [-] (bl) 4-7-13 Joanna Morgan (18) (20 to 1) 9
GRANDEUR (Ire) [-] 3-7-10 (2*) R M Burke (1)..... (16 to 1) 10
3326 MANGANS HILL (Ire) [-] (bl) 3-9-3 N Byrne (9)......(12 to 1) 11
2221^{3} DUCHESS AFFAIR (Ire) [-] 3-7-13 (8*) P J Smullen (7) ....(14 to 1) 12
2512^{8} BELLE O' THE BAY (Ire) [-] 4-7-11 (6*) R V Skelly (2) (33 to 1) 13
2498^{5} HUGH DANIELS [-] 5-6-12 (10*) J D Moore (17)....(12 to 1) 14
3061* TOAST AND HONEY (Ire) [-] 4-10-2 (6*,12ex) C Everard (16) ....(7 to 1) 15
851^{7} JUST FOUR (Ire) [-] (bl) 4-8-13 K J Manning (13)...(20 to 1) 16
Dist: 2l, 1l, 4l, 1½l. (Time not taken) (16 Ran).
(Mrs M Cahill), Noel Meade

3398 Kerins & Morrissey Q.R. Handicap (0-80 4-y-o and up) £2,417 1¾m (7:00)

3276* NANARCH (USA) [-] 9-11-4 (7*,2ex) Mr J Connolly (3) ....(100 to 30) 1
2841 HACKETTS CROSS (Ire) [-] 5-11-7 (7*) Miss J Lewis (2) ....(5 to 1) 2
2408^{6} UPPINGHAM [-] 7-10-8 Mr S R Murphy (7)..........(8 to 1) 3
2842 STEEL CHIMES (Ire) [-] (bl) 4-10-10 (5*) Mr J A Nash (8) ....(5 to 1) 4
1025^{8} TOOLITTLE TOOLATE (Ire) [-] 4-11-4 (3*) Mr A R Coonan (6) ....(33 to 1) 5

HEAD OF CHAMBERS (Ire) [-] 5-11-7 (3*) Mr D Marnane (4) ....(7 to 4 fav) 6

852 FROMTHEGETGO (Ire) [-] 4-10-10 (3*) Mr R Neylon (1) ....(14 to 1) 7

3245[2] SACULORE (Ire) [-] 5-10-11 (7*) Mr A Daly (5) ...... (9 to 1) 8

996[9] DARCARI ROSE (Ire) [-] 4-10-9 (7*) Mr M O'Connor (9) ....(25 to 1) 9

Dist: ½l, 1l, 1l. (Time not taken) (9 Ran).

(Mrs Kevin Prendergast), Kevin Prendergast

3399 Bettystown Handicap (0-70 3-y-o and up) £1,727 1m..................(7:30)

3296[2] BOLERO DANCER (Ire) [-] 5-8-0 (6*) R V Skelly (10) (10 to 1) 1

2922[7] KENTUCKY BABY (Ire) [-] 3-8-13 J P Murtagh (7)..(20 to 1) 2

3076[5] DAHAR'S LOVE (USA) [-] (bl) 4-8-3 W J Supple (9)..(9 to 1) 3

3112[3] LUCKY PRINCE (Ire) [-] 3-8-13 (4*) W J Smith (4)... (8 to 1) 4

3160[5] BARNAGEERA BOY (Ire) [-] 4-8-9 (2*) P Carberry (12) (4 to 1) 5

3076 SUTTON CENTENARY (Ire) [-] 5-7-11 Joanna Morgan (5) ....(16 to 1) 6

3160[4] TINCO PALENO [-] 9-9-3 (2*) R M Burke (2)........(4 to 1) 7

3244[5] CAROLINA RUA (USA) [-] 3-7-8[1] (4*) J J Behan (15) (16 to 1) 8

3160 LOVE OF ERIN (Ire) [-] 4-7-5 (2*) D G O'Shea (1)...(16 to 1) 9

3328[5] INISHMOT (Ire) [-] (bl) 3-9-0 P V Gilson (14).......(14 to 1) 10

3296 SHERAVISION (Ire) [-] (bl) 4-8-1[1] (8*) P O Casey (3) (20 to 1) 11

2323 REASON TO BELIEVE (Ire) [-] 4-7-10 (8*) R T Fitzpatrick (6) ....(16 to 1) 12

3327[3] MEJEVE [-] 5-10-1 S Craine (11)..............(9 to 4 fav) 13

649[6] TREBLE BOB (Ire) [-] 3-8-2[3] (10*) J J Byrne (8).... (20 to 1) 14

Dist: 3l, 2½l, 2l, 1l. (Time not taken) (14 Ran).

(Mrs B R Quigley), Thomas O'Neill

YORK (good to soft)
Tuesday August 17th

Going Correction: PLUS 0.20 sec. per fur. (races 1,2,3,4,6,7), PLUS 0.25 (5)

3400 Deploy Acomb Conditions Stakes Class B (2-y-o) £12,676 6f 214yds ....(2:05)

2968* CONCORDIAL (USA) 8-12 Pat Eddery (1) *trkd ldrs, rdn to ld entering fnl furlong, ran on wl*....(5 to 1 op 7 to 2) 1

3122* JUST HAPPY (USA) 8-12 W R Swinburn (2) *in tch, hdwy o'r 2 fs out, chlgd fnl furlong, no extr nr finish.* .... (11 to 2 op 9 to 2 tchd 6 to 1) 2

2792* GRAND LODGE (USA) 8-12 L Dettori (5) *dwlt, sn tracking ldrs, pushed alng o'r 2 fs out, ev ch entering last, one pace*......... (7 to 4 on op 6 to 4 on tchd 11 to 8 on) 3

2616[2] CULT HERO (Can) 8-10 J Reid (8) *prmnt, led o'r 2 fs out till entering last, sn btn*..................(8 to 1 op 6 to 1) 4

2429* MAZENTRE FORWARD (Ire) 8-10 M J Kinane (3) *cl up, ev ch o'r one furlong out, kpt on same pace.* .... (16 to 1 op 12 to 1 tchd 20 to 1) 5

LOMOND MIST (Ire) 8-10 A Culhane (7) *al beh, lost tch 2 fs out*......................... (66 to 1 op 33 to 1) 6

MERLINSRISK (Ire) 8-10 J Fanning (4) *al beh, lost tch 2 fs out*......................... (100 to 1 op 50 to 1) 7

3016[6] BLAZING HONDA (Ire) 8-10 M Roberts (6) *led till o'r 2 fs out, wknd quickly*................ (33 to 1 op 25 to 1) 8

Dist: Nk, 5l, nk, nk, 10l, 3l, 2l. 1m 25.91s. a 4.21s (8 Ran).

SR: 56/55/40/37/36/6/-/-/ (K Abdulla), R Charlton

3401 Melrose Rated Class B Handicap (0-100 3-y-o) £13,140 1m 5f 194yds ....(2:35)

2907[6] EDBAYSAAN (Ire) [91] 8-13 Pat Eddery (12) *trkd ldrs, led o'r 2 fs out, rdn and styd on wl*......... (6 to 1 op 5 to 1) 1

2907[5] LEAGUE LEADER (Ire) [85] 8-7 L Dettori (4) *in tch, effrt 3 fs out, chlgd ins last, no extr nr finish.* ....(4 to 1 tchd 9 to 2) 2

2623[4] MOONSHINE LAKE [85] 8-7 M Roberts (5) *led till o'r 2 fs out, kpt on same pace.* (10 to 1 op 8 to 1 tchd 11 to 1) 3

2561[2] MUJAWAB [85] 8-2 (5*) A Garth (2) *in tch, hdwy 3 fs out, kpt on same pace fnl 2 furlongs*................(20 to 1) 4

2907 DARMSTADT (USA) [85] 8-7 W Carson (3) *chsd ldrs, effrt 3 fs out, no hdwy*..................(12 to 1 op 10 to 1) 5

2963* LILLE HAMMER [87] 8-9 R Cochrane (10) *hld up, effrt 3 fs out, styd on, not rch ldrs*........ (3 to 1 fav op 4 to 1) 6

1637[3] THE SEER [85] 8-7 M J Kinane (1) *prmnt, rdn 3 fs out, fdd.* ....(16 to 1 op 20 to 1) 7

2259 DARECLIFF (USA) [93] 9-1 J Reid (6) *hld up, some hdwy 4 fs out, sn rdn and btn*...................... (12 to 1) 8

2963[2] SOLARTICA (USA) [85] 8-7 P Robinson (11) *al beh.* ....(14 to 1 op 10 to 1) 9

2907 DUSTY POINT (Ire) [85] 8-7 W R Swinburn (7) *al beh.* .... (12 to 1 op 10 to 1 tchd 14 to 1) 10

3217* TOMOS [102] 9-10 (3ex) L Piggott (9) *rcd wide, cl up till wknd o'r 2 fs out*...................................(20 to 1) 11

2360[4] ALJAZZAF [96] 9-4 B Raymond (8) *chsd ldrs, pushed alng one m out, wknd 4 fs out, sn lost tch, tld off.* .... (11 to 1 op 8 to 1) 12

Dist: Nk, 4l, nk, 2½l, 1l, 2l, 10l, 1½l, nk, 6l. 3m 1.50s. a 6.50s (12 Ran).

SR: 62/55/47/46/41/41/35/23/12/ (Sheikh Essa Bin Mubarak), H R A Cecil

3402 Juddmonte International Stakes Class A (Group 1) (3-y-o and up) £156,935 1¼m 85yds.................... (3:10)

1748[8] EZZOUD (Ire) (v) 4-9-6 W R Swinburn (3) *mid-div, effrt 3 fs out, styd on strly und pres to ld wl ins last.* .... (28 to 1 op 33 to 1 tchd 25 to 1) 1

2621 SABREHILL (USA) 3-8-12 M Roberts (4) *trkd ldrs, led o'r 2 fs out, quickened clr over one out, hdd and no extr wl ins last*............(7 to 4 fav op 6 to 4 tchd 15 to 8) 2

2650* SPARTAN SHAREEF (Ire) 4-9-6 R Cochrane (8) *chsd ldrs, effrt 3 fs out, kpt on wl und pres frm 2 out*....(50 to 1) 3

2531* REVELATION (Ire) 3-8-12 A Da Cruz (10) *trkd ldrs, ev ch o'r 2 fs out, kpt on same pace*.......... (9 to 1 op 8 to 1) 4

2791[2] WHITE MUZZLE 3-8-12 J Reid (5) *trkd ldrs, quickened to ld o'r 5 fs out, hdd over 2 out, fdd.* ....(2 to 1 op 7 to 4 tchd 9 to 4) 5

2261[4] BLUES TRAVELLER (Ire) 3-8-12 M J Kinane (7) *led till o'r 5 fs out, wknd over 2 out.* .... (15 to 1 op 14 to 1 tchd 16 to 1) 6

2791[8] TENBY 3-8-12 Pat Eddery (2) *beh, pushed alng o'r 4 fs out, no real hdwy*.....(15 to 2 op 8 to 1 tchd 10 to 1) 7

1888[3] GUADO D'ANNIBALE (Ire) 4-9-6 D Holland (1) *nvr dngrs.* .... (66 to 1 op 50 to 1) 8

2791[6] ENVIRONMENT FRIEND (v) 5-9-6 G Duffield (9) *hld up, hmpd 6 fs out, nvr nr ldrs.* .... (28 to 1 op 25 to 1 tchd 33 to 1) 9

2905[5] ALHIJAZ 4-9-6 W Carson (6) *beh, effrt o'r 3 fs out, no imprsn*.....................................(20 to 1) 10

2302[3] RED BISHOP (USA) 5-9-6 L Dettori (11) *beh, rdn 3 fs out, no imprsn*.....................(14 to 1 tchd 12 to 1) 11

Dist: 1½l, 5l, 1½l, 2l, 1½l, nk, 2l, 5l, 15l, 8l. 2m 12.16s. a 4.16s (11 Ran).

SR: 85/74/72/61/57/54/53/57/47/ (Maktoum Al Maktoum), M R Stoute

3403 Great Voltigeur Stakes Class A (Group 2) (3-y-o) £46,715 1m 3f 195yds ....(3:45)

1448[6] BOB'S RETURN (Ire) 8-9 P Robinson (4) *cl up, led o'r 2 fs out, rdn clr over one out, styd on wl.* ....(16 to 1 op 14 to 1) 1

2076[3] FORESEE 8-9 M Roberts (1) *chsd ldrs, pushed alng o'r 4 fs out, rdn over 2 out, kpt on, no ch wth wnr.* ....(4 to 1 op 7 to 2) 2

2174[2] DECLASSIFIED (USA) 8-9 R Cochrane (2) *hld up, swtchd ins 3 fs out, hdwy whn not clr run and hmpd wl o'r one out, switched outsd, styd on well.* .... (25 to 1 op 20 to 1 tchd 33 to 1) 3

2883[2] SHAREEK (USA) 8-9 W R Swinburn (8) *chsd ldrs, effrt o'r 3 fs out, one pace*..............................(12 to 1) 4

2883[6] MAJORITY (Ire) 8-9 D Holland (9) *led till o'r 2 fs out, sn rdn, wknd over one out*..............................(33 to 1) 5

2883* RIGHT WIN (Ire) 8-9 J Reid (3) *in tch, pushed alng o'r 3 fs out, no hdwy*......................(9 to 2 tchd 5 to 1) 6

1087[2] ARMIGER 8-9 Pat Eddery (5) *hld up in tch, pushed alng o'r 4 fs out, sn btn.* ...(11 to 10 on op Evens tchd 5 to 4 on and 11 to 10) 7

2883[8] TIOMAN ISLAND 8-9 T Quinn (6) *cl up till wknd o'r 3 fs out*................ (25 to 1 tchd 33 to 1 and 22 to 1) 8

1448 GEISWAY (Can) 8-9 A Da Cruz (7) *beh frm 5 fs out.* ....(20 to 1 op 16 to 1) 9

Dist: 6l, 1½l, 3½l, nk, 8l, 5l, sht-hd, 2l. 2m 31.49s. a 3.49s (9 Ran).

SR: 84/72/69/62/61/45/35/34/30/ (Mrs G A E Smith), M H Tompkins

3404 Eagle Lane Handicap Class C (0-100 3-y-o and up) £12,622 6f........ (4:15)

2987[3] HOW'S YER FATHER [79] 7-8-11 A Munro (6) *al prmnt, led ins fnl furlong, ran on wl*................ (8 to 1 jt-fav) 1

3148* DIET [69] (v) 7-7-10 (5*) J Marshall (8) *led till ins fnl furlong, no extr*.................................. (25 to 1) 2

2885[7] MARGARET'S GIFT [86] 3-9-0 J Carroll (14) *prmnt, rdn 2 fs out, kpt on wl fnl furlong*....................(25 to 1) 3

3270[5] PEERAGE PRINCE [67] (bl) 4-7-10 (3*) N Kennedy (21) *in tch, styd on wl fnl furlong, nrst finish*....... (25 to 1) 4

1485[5] DUPLICITY (Ire) [96] 5-10-0 J Reid (10) *in tch, hdwy 2 fs out, styd on fnl furlong, nrst finish.* ....(20 to 1 tchd 25 to 1) 5

3118* NORDAN RAIDER [67] 5-7-13 J Fanning (3) *in tch, effrt and ch 2 fs out, one pace fnl furlong.* ....(8 to 1 jt-fav tchd 9 to 1) 6

3153[6] DOMINUET [95] 8-9-13 K Darley (1) *chsd ldrs, no hdwy fnl furlong*........................ (14 to 1 tchd 12 to 1) 7

3034[5] SAGEBRUSH ROLLER [82] 5-9-0 G Duffield (9) *in tch, kpt on fnl 2 fs, not rch ldrs*........................ (20 to 1) 8

3051[6] MACS MAHARANEE [83] 6-8-10 (5*) D Wright (12) *beh, hdwy o'r 2 fs out, one pace fnl furlong*.......(20 to 1) 9

3127[3] MASTER PLANNER [90] 4-9-1 (7*) J D Smith (23) *cl up, hmpd o'r 2 fs out, sn btn*......... (16 to 1 op 14 to 1) 10

3034[8] CUMBRIAN WALTZER [88] 8-9-6 M Birch (22) *nvr dngrs.* ....(14 to 1 op 16 to 1) 11

2628[6] GILT THRONE [77] 6-8-9 P Robinson (5) *chsd ldrs till wknd entering fnl furlong.* (12 to 1 op 16 to 1 tchd 11 to 1) 12

3080[8] SOUTHERN MEMORIES (Ire) [81] (bl) 3-8-9 A Da Cruz (7) *prmnt till wknd o'r one furlong out*..........(16 to 1) 13

3034[9] DENSBEN [81] 9-8-13 K Fallon (2) *in tch till wknd 2 fs out.* ....(16 to 1) 14
3153[3] MACFARLANE [74] 5-8-6 W Carson (16) *sn chasing ldrs, wknd o'r one furlong out*........(10 to 1 tchd 12 to 1) 15
3261 BERTIE WOOSTER [76] 10-8-8 L Dettori (13) *in tch till wknd o'r one furlong out*......................(20 to 1) 16
3034 THE AUCTION BIDDER [77] 6-8-9 S Perks (4) *nvr dngrs.* ....(40 to 1 op 50 to 1) 17
2580* SO INTREPID (Ire) [84] 3-8-12 W R Swinburn (19) *nvr dngrs.* ....(12 to 1) 18
3153 SIR JOEY (USA) [75] 4-8-7 J Williams (17) *sn beh.* (20 to 1) 19
915[7] WHITE SHADOW (Ire) [90] 3-9-4 Pat Eddery (18) *chsd ldrs, hmpd o'r 2 fs out, sn no ch*.....................(12 to 1) 20
3034[2] PETITE-D-ARGENT [86] 4-9-4 T Quinn (20) *cl up, hng lft o'r 2 fs out, sn wknd*..............................(12 to 1) 21
3280[5] ANOTHER LANE [70] 6-8-2 J Quinn (11) *chsd ldrs, wkng whn hmpd o'r 2 fs out*............................(33 to 1) 22
17[6] PANIKIN [87] 5-9-2 (3*) S D Williams (15) *sn beh*... (50 to 1) 23
Dist: 2l, sht-hd, hd, ½l, nk, nk, hd, ¾l, 2½l, 2½l. 1m 13.09s. a 3.09s (23 Ran).
SR: 65/47/59/43/70/40/67/53/51/ (Unity Farm Holiday Centre Ltd), R J Hodges

3405 Lonsdale Stakes Class A (Listed Race) (3-y-o and up) £12,676 1m 7f 195yds........................(4:45)

1787[8] FURTHER FLIGHT 7-9-5 M Hills (8) *in tch, hdwy to ld o'r 2 fs out, styd on wl fnl furlong*..........(6 to 1 op 5 to 1) 1
2360[5] SILVERDALE (USA) 3-8-0 W Carson (1) *hld up, effrt o'r 2 fs out, drifted rght over one out, drvn out, not rch wnr.* ....(9 to 2 op 4 to 1 tchd 5 to 1) 2
2835[2] ALLEGAN (USA) 4-9-0 Pat Eddery (2) *cl up, led 5 fs out till o'r 2 out, one pace.* (7 to 2 jt-fav op 5 to 2 tchd 4 to 1) 3
WITNESS BOX (USA) 6-9-0 M Roberts (6) *trkd ldrs, pushed alng 4 fs out, wknd 2 out.* ....(7 to 2 jt-fav op 3 to 1 tchd 4 to 1) 4
2925[5] NOT IN DOUBT (USA) 4-9-0 J Reid (3) *in tch, pushed alng 5 fs out, no hdwy*..............................(10 to 1) 5
3283* POST IMPRESSIONIST (Ire) 4-8-9 K Darley (5) *al beh.* ....(66 to 1 op 100 to 1) 6
2925[3] ARCADIAN HEIGHTS 5-9-3 L Dettori (4) *in tch, effrt o'r 4 fs out, sn wknd*.....................(5 to 1 tchd 11 to 2) 7
2515[2] STRONG CASE (Ire) 5-9-0 W R Swinburn (9) *chsd ldrs till wknd o'r 6 fs out*................................(33 to 1) 8
1787[9] SILVERNESIAN (USA) 4-9-10 L Piggott (7) *led to 5 fs out, sn wknd*..........................(20 to 1 tchd 25 to 1) 9
Dist: 1½l, 6l, 12l, 7l, 5l, 8l, 3l, ¾l. 3m 26.54s. a 5.54s (9 Ran).
SR: 81/60/68/56/49/39/39/33/41/ (S Wingfield Digby), B W Hills

3406 Eglinton Nursery Class C (2-y-o) £12,622 6f 214yds..............(5:15)

3281[3] CALL TO MIND (Ire) [76] 8-5 M Birch (1) *cl up, led hfwy, ran on wl fnl furlong*..................(8 to 1 tchd 9 to 1) 1
2826* BARBAROJA [78] 8-7 W Carson (10) *in tch, effrt o'r 2 fs out, styd on wl fnl furlong, no extr nr finish.* ....(4 to 1 fav op 9 to 2 tchd 5 to 1) 2
2998[2] DIESAN (USA) [89] 9-4 M Roberts (14) *hld up, hdwy 3 fs out, ev ch one out, hng rght, one pace.* ....(9 to 1 op 8 to 1) 3
2973* OOH AH CANTONA [81] 8-10 A Culhane (9) *chsd ldrs, effrt o'r 2 fs out, ev ch over one out, one pace fnl furlong.* ....(14 to 1 op 12 to 1) 4
2866[3] OBVIOUS RISK [80] 8-9 Pat Eddery (3) *beh, styd on fnl 2 fs, not rch ldrs*.............(7 to 1 op 6 to 1 tchd 8 to 1) 5
3082* LADY PHYL [72] 7-12 (3*) B Doyle (2) *in tch, effrt 3 fs out, no hdwy*..........................(7 to 1 op 11 to 2) 6
3235[6] BRAMCOTE CENTURY [64] 7-4[2] (5*) D Wright (4) *led to hfwy, fdd*........(66 to 1 op 50 to 1 tchd 100 to 1) 7
2844* GINGERBIRD (Ire) [73] 8-2 A McGlone (6) *chsd ldrs till wknd 2 fs out*.......... (8 to 1 op 7 to 1 tchd 9 to 1) 8
3079* BUMAAN (Ire) [85] 9-0 R Hills (8) *prmnt till wknd wl o'r one furlong out*.........(11 to 1 op 10 to 1 tchd 12 to 1) 9
2796[6] BLASTER BATES (USA) [65] 7-8[1] J Fanning (7) *nvr dngrs.* ....(20 to 1 tchd 25 to 1) 10
2890[5] MOSAIC GOLD [79] 8-8 N Connorton (12) *nvr dngrs.* ....(14 to 1 op 16 to 1) 11
2890* SAIHAT (Ire) [92] 9-7 L Piggott (5) *chsd ldrs till wknd 3 fs out*...............................(16 to 1 op 14 to 1) 12
2546* CHICKAWICKA (Ire) [86] 9-1 S Whitworth (15) *in tch, effrt hfwy, sn btn*..........................(20 to 1 op 16 to 1) 13
2974* CLOSE TO REALITY [82] 8-11 K Fallon (11) *hmpd and stumbled aftr 2 fs, nvr dngrs*..................(10 to 1) 14
2988* ALPINE SKIER (Ire) [82] 8-11 K Darley (13) *in tch till wknd 3 fs out*.................(15 to 2 op 6 to 1 tchd 8 to 1) 15
Dist: ¾l, 2½l, 1½l, 5l, 2½l, 3½l, nk, ½l, ¾l, 2½l. 1m 27.00s. a 5.30s (15 Ran).
SR: 33/33/36/23/7/-/ (G Graham), M H Easterby

CARLISLE (good to firm) Wednesday August 18th

Going Correction: MINUS 0.35 sec. per fur. (races 1,2,3,6), MINUS 0.45 (4,5)

3407 Greylag Selling Stakes Class G (3-y-o and up) £2,364 1½m...........(2:10)

3283[4] FAMOUS BEAUTY 6-8-12 (7*) L Aspell (7) *sluggish strt, hld up, took clr order hfwy, brght wide strt, led o'r one furlong out, edgd rght, pushed out ins last.* ....(11 to 1 op 8 to 1) 1
3055* LE TEMERAIRE 7-9-10 Kim Tinkler (4) *led, shaken up entering strt, hdd o'r one furlong out, kpt on same pace*.................. (2 to 1 op 7 to 4 tchd 9 to 4) 2
3320[4] YEVEED (Ire) 3-8-6 (3*) S Maloney (8) *trkd ldrs, feeling pace and drvn alng 4 fs out, rallied, hrd rdn entering strt, not quicken fnl furlong.* ....(15 to 8 fav op 6 to 4 tchd 9 to 4) 3
3096[7] SHARP SENSATION 3-8-4 (5*) J Marshall (3) *pressed ldg bunch, effrt and rdn o'r 2 fs out, not much room over one out, no extr ins last*.............(25 to 1 op 16 to 1) 4
2888[4] ANAR (Ire) (v) 4-9-7 (3*) O Pears (5) *nvr far away, pushed alng entering strt, sn ev ch, one pace o'r one furlong out*...............................(14 to 1 op 12 to 1) 5
3121[5] LARA'S BABY (Ire) 5-9-5 A Clark (6) *cl up, ev ch entering strt, sn rdn alng, btn one furlong out.* ....(11 to 2 op 5 to 1 tchd 6 to 1) 6
2566[4] LORLANNE 3-8-4 A Mackay (1) *beh on outer, struggling o'r 4 fs out, tld off entering strt*.....(8 to 1 op 12 to 1) 7
3055[9] WITHOUT LEAVE 4-9-5 S Webster (2) *keen hold, pressed ldrs, rdn and lost tch o'r 4 fs out, tld off entering strt.* ....(200 to 1 op 100 to 1) 8
Dist: 2½l, 1½l, 1l, 3½l, 3½l, 25l, hd. 2m 34.50s. a 4.50s (8 Ran).
SR: 18/18/-/-/6/ (J E Bigg), R Hollinshead

3408 Conway Rental Handicap Class E (0-70 3-y-o and up) £3,183 7f 214yds ....(2:45)

2989[8] JAHANGIR (Ire) [66] 4-9-10 (3*) O Pears (6) *nvr far away, chlgd o'r 2 furlong sout, edgd rght and led ins last, hld on gmely*...........................(7 to 1 op 6 to 1) 1
3237[2] COOL ENOUGH [35] 12-7-10 A Mackay (10) *patiently rdn, gd hdwy to ld wl o'r one furlong out, hdd ins last, no extr towards finish*..............(9 to 2 fav op 5 to 1) 2
3124[3] MAROWINS [45] 4-8-1 (5*) D Wright (4) *slwly into strd, beh, effrt on outer entering strt, ran on ins fnl furlong.* ....(6 to 1 op 5 to 1) 3
3139[2] TOUCH ABOVE [53] 7-8-7 (7*) V Halliday (11) *settled rear, pushed alng hfwy, ran on entering strt, kpt on fnl furlong*......................(8 to 1 op 6 to 1) 4
3258[4] HAND ON HEART (Ire) [44] (v) 4-8-5 A Clark (13) *mid-div, rdn alng to improve entering strt, not clr run and swtchd a furlong out, kpt on same pace.* ....(6 to 1 op 5 to 1) 5
3142[3] PINKERTON'S SILVER [44] 3-7-11[1] (3*) S Maloney (7) *led, drvn alng o'r 3 fs out, hdd wl over one furlong out and not quicken ins last*...............(14 to 1 op 12 to 1) 6
2774 EXPRESS GIFT [67] 4-9-9 (5*) Darren Moffatt (14) *tucked away on ins, effrt and not clr run frm o'r one furlong out, no imprsn inside last*............(9 to 1 op 7 to 1) 7
3134[3] MASTER OFTHE HOUSE [48] 7-8-4 (5*) J Marshall (3) *keen hold, pressed ldg grp, effrt 2 fs out, not clr run ins last, no extr*..............................(9 to 1 op 12 to 1) 8
2480[8] HOT OFF THE PRESS [48] 3-8-3 A Culhane (1) *chsd ldrs, rdn ahflway, no extr o'r one furlong out*......(16 to 1) 9
2972 SILVER STANDARD [53] 3-8-8 L Charnock (8) *nvr far way, rdn alng entering strt, wknd o'r one furlong out.* ....(8 to 1 op 12 to 1) 10
3216 SKOLERN [36] 9-7-11 S Wood (2) *in tch on outer, rdn alng o'r 2 fs out, fdd*..............................(20 to 1) 11
JIM'S WISH (Ire) [44] 5-7-12 (7*) Claire Balding (9) *sluggish strt, al in rear*...................(100 to 1 op 50 to 1) 12
2831[6] EVER SO SHARP [33] 10-7-8[6] (5*) A Garth (12) *chsd ldrs till rdn and wknd 3 fs out, tld off*.... (100 to 1 op 66 to 1) 13
Dist: Nk, ½l, ¾l, sht-hd, sht-hd, 1½l, sht-hd, ½l, 2½l, 6l. 1m 39.90s. a 2.00s (13 Ran).
SR: 41/9/17/23/13/6/30/10/2/ (S W Macfarlane), B Hanbury

3409 Conway Vauxhall Handicap Class E (0-70 3-y-o and up) £3,158 6f 206yds ....(3:20)

3057[6] AFFORDABLE [53] 5-9-1 (3*) O Pears (11) *hld up, swtchd outsd gng wl entering strt, sstnd run to ld ins fnl furlong, ran on*.........................(5 to 1 op 4 to 1) 1
3057 ROCK OPERA (Ire) [51] 5-9-2 A Clark (7) *hld up, pushed alng o'r 3 fs out, improved over one furlong out, ev ch last 75 yards, held towards finish.* (14 to 1 op 12 to 1) 2
3094 NORLING (Ire) [50] 3-8-10 L Charnock (6) *led til hdd and no extr ins fnl furlong*..................(12 to 1 op 14 to 1) 3
3101[4] DIWALI DANCER [52] (v) 3-8-12 A Tucker (9) *slwly into strd, beh, effrt and squeezed through o'r one furlong out, kpt on towards finish*..............(10 to 1 op 9 to 1) 4
3140* CORONA GOLD [60] 3-9-6 S Perks (2) *nvr far away, chlgd entering strt, rdn and no extr ins fnl furlong.* ....(4 to 1 op 3 to 1) 5
3216[3] VANART [43] 4-8-8 S Webster (1) *chsd ldrs, effrt and rdn o'r 2 fs out, no extr over one furlong out.* ....(3 to 1 fav op 7 to 2 tchd 4 to 1) 6

4743a² KILTROUM (Fr) [40] 4-8-2 (3*) S Maloney (5) *keen hold, trkd ldr, rdn and ev ch entering strt, no extr o'r one furlong out*..........(14 to 1) 7
SWANK GILBERT [28] 7-7-3³ (7*) Claire Balding (10) *chsd ldrs, rdn entering strt, hng lft and btn o'r one furlong out*..........(100 to 1) 8
3004⁸ GANT BLEU (Fr) [53] 6-9-4 A Culhane (8) *mid-div, rdn alng entering strt, nvr able to chal*......(11 to 2 op 6 to 1) 9
3148³ ARABAT [63] 6-9-7 (7*) V Halliday (3) *settled on outer, drvn alng to improve hfwy, wknd 2 fs out.*..........(9 to 1 op 10 to 1) 10
1875⁹ JOTRA [44] 3-8-4 A Mackay (4) *beh, rdn alng hfwy, nvr on terms*.......... (25 to 1 op 33 to 1 tchd 40 to 1) 11
Dist: Nk, 1l, ¾l, ¾l, sht-hd, 2½l, 3l, 2½l, 3½l, 4l. 1m 27.30s. a 1.90s (11 Ran).
SR: 39/36/27/27/33/20/9/-/5/ (Q Irshid), S G Norton

3410 Matthew Brown Handicap Class D (0-80 3-y-o and up) £4,175 5f.... (3:55)

3280⁸ PALLIUM (Ire) [65] 5-8-13 A Culhane (11) *beh, effrt and rdn 2 fs out, ran on to ld ins fnl furlong, kpt on wl.*..........(12 to 1 op 10 to 1) 1
3118² FOLLOWMEGIRLS [58] 4-8-6¹ S Perks (13) *sluggish strt, beh til gd hdwy o'r one furlong out, fnshd wl.* (8 to 1) 2
3085² SINGING STAR [70] 7-8-11 (7*) Claire Balding (8) *beh on outer, gd hdwy 2 fs out, ran on ins last.*..........(8 to 1 op 7 to 1) 3
3220⁶ JADE CITY [75] 3-9-3 (3*) S D Williams (3) *in tch on outer, effrt and improved o'r one furlong out, ran on ins last.*..........(12 to 1 op 10 to 1) 4
3280² HERE COMES A STAR [66] 5-9-0 A Clark (6) *nvr far away, chlgd appr fnl furlong, no extr ins last*......(4 to 1 jt-fav op 9 to 2 tchd 11 to 2) 5
3280* ADMIRALS REALM [59] 4-8-7 (7ex) A Mackay (9) *al frnt rnk, led o'r one furlong out, hdd ins last, no extr.* (4 to 1 jt-fav op 5 to 1 tchd 11 to 2) 6
3094⁸ MILBANK CHALLENGER [60] 3-8-2 (3*) S Maloney (12) *tucked away beh ldrs, effrt and rdn o'r one furlong out, one pace ins last*..........(10 to 1 op 8 to 1) 7
FANGIO [80] 4-10-0 T Sprake (15) *led til hdd and no extr o'r one furlong out*..........(20 to 1 op 16 to 1) 8
2731⁵ TWO MOVES IN FRONT (Ire) [75] 3-8-13 (7*) P Roberts (4) *chsd ldrs, pushed alng hfwy, not quicken o'r one furlong out*..........(14 to 1 op 12 to 1) 9
3153 GONDO [74] 6-9-1 (7*) S Knott (10) *beh, shaken up o'r one furlong out, kpt on ins last, nvr dngrs.*..........(14 to 1 op 12 to 1) 10
3220⁴ WILLSHE GAN [74] 3-9-5 L Charnock (14) *trkd ldrs, rdn alng entering strt, btn o'r one furlong out.*..........(13 to 2 op 6 to 1 tchd 8 to 1) 11
3354 MISS ARAGON [48] 5-7-10 S Wood (1) *beh, rdn hfwy, shrtlvd effrt on outer 2 fs out, sn btn.*..........(25 to 1 op 20 to 1) 12
3378⁷ PAGEBOY [62] (bl) 4-8-7 (3*) N Kennedy (16) *chsd ldrs ins, rdn alng o'r 2 fs out, fdd*.......... (14 to 1 op 12 to 1) 13
1560 ABSOLUTELY NUTS [65] 4-8-13 A Tucker (5) *nvr far away, bustled alng appr strt, wknd o'r 2 fs out*......(20 to 1) 14
3051 JUST BOB [70] 4-8-11 (7*) M Proctor (7) *slwly into strd, al struggling in rear*..........(25 to 1 op 20 to 1) 15
3220 RED FAN (Ire) [70] (bl) 3-8-12 (3*) O Pears (2) *beh on outer, drvn alng appr strt, sn btn*..... (25 to 1 tchd 33 to 1) 16
Dist: 1½l, nk, nk, hd, sht-hd, 2½l, nk, hd, sht-hd, 1½l. 1m 0.10s. a 0.10s (16 Ran).
SR: 52/39/50/51/44/36/24/46/37/ (W J Kelly), M P Naughton

3411 EBF Conway After Sales Median Auction Maiden Stakes Class F (2-y-o) £2,924 5f.......... (4:25)

3001³ PALACEGATE JACK (Ire) 8-11 (3*) O Pears (5) *made all, clr o'r one furlong out, kpt on ins last.*..........(11 to 10 on op 5 to 4 on tchd Evens) 1
3001² GENERAL GUBBINS 8-11 (3*) S Maloney (4) *nvr far away, effrt and rdn o'r 2 fs out, outpcd and hng fire over one out, styd on towards finish.*..........(3 to 1 op 11 to 4 tchd 7 to 2) 2
PASTURES NEW (Ire) 8-9 S Wood (3) *pressed ldg bunch, not clr run 2 fs out, rdn and no imprsn fnl furlong.*..........(14 to 1 op 12 to 1) 3
2949⁴ SECONDS AWAY 9-0 A Mackay (2) *dwlt, beh on outer, rdn alng entering strt, not pace to chal.* (8 to 1 op 10 to 1) 4
2541⁶ BLAIN 9-0 A Clark (1) *chsd ldrs, pushed alng 2 fs out, not quicken o'r one furlong out.*..........(12 to 1 op 10 to 1 tchd 14 to 1) 5
2706 LOCHON 9-0 S Webster (6) *cl up, rdn alng 2 fs out, sn btn.*..........(50 to 1) 6
1529 CELTIC GOVERNESS 8-2 (7*) Claire Balding (9) *chsd ldrs, rdn alng 2 fs out, btn whn short of room ins last.*..........(33 to 1) 7
MARJAN (Ire) 8-4 (5*) A Garth (8) *slwly into strd, beh, shaken up entering strt, ran on fnl furlong, nvr able to chal*.......... (20 to 1 op 14 to 1) 8
1889⁵ IBERIAN MAGIC (Ire) 9-0 L Charnock (7) *pressed ldg grp, pushed alng hfwy, grad wknd*.... (25 to 1 op 20 to 1) 9
Dist: 1l, 3½l, sht-hd, 1½l, sht-hd, 3½l, nk, 10l. 1m 1.90s. a 1.90s (9 Ran).
SR: 17/13/-/-/-/-/ (Palacegate Corporation Ltd), J Berry

3412 White Front Maiden Handicap Class F (0-60 3-y-o and up) £2,668 1¾m 32yds.......... (4:55)

3239² SCALP 'EM (Ire) [31] 5-8-4 L Charnock (7) *pressed ldg grp, rdn to improve entering strt, ran on to chal ins fnl furlong, edgd rght, led post*.......(7 to 1 tchd 8 to 1) 1
2547⁶ ARC BRIGHT (Ire) [51] 3-8-12 S Perks (3) *nvr far away, improved to ld o'r 2 fs out, shaken up over one out, jnd ins last, ct post*..........(16 to 1 op 14 to 1) 2
3056⁴ FAIRWAYS ON TARGET [55] 7-9-11 (3*) S Maloney (12) *settled rear, improved into midfield aftr 4 fs, rdn alng o'r 3 furlongs out, kpt on fnl furlong, nvr dngrs.*..........(7 to 1 op 5 to 1) 3
3078⁶ SPANISH REFUGE [55] 3-9-2 R P Elliott (1) *mid-div, drvn alng 4 fs out, sn outpcd, styd on fnl 2 furlongs, no imprsn*..........(7 to 1 op 5 to 1) 4
3239³ DON'T CRY [23] 5-7-10 Kim Tinkler (6) *hld up and beh, took clr order 4 fs out, kpt on entering strt, nvr nrr.*..........(16 to 1 op 14 to 1) 5
3239⁶ INVISIBLE ARMOUR [32] (bl) 4-8-5 Dale Gibson (5) *led til hdd o'r 2 fs out, rdn and sn btn.* (16 to 1 tchd 20 to 1) 6
2573² INTREPID LASS [46] 6-9-5 C Rutter (13) *chsd ldrs, rdn and lost pl o'r 4 fs out, no imprsn entering strt.*..........(2 to 1 fav op 5 to 2 tchd 3 to 1) 7
3106⁴ BORROWED AND BLUE [55] 3-8-13 (3*) O Pears (8) *mid-div, drvn alng hfwy, btn o'r 3 fs out.*..........(8 to 1 op 7 to 1 tchd 9 to 1) 8
3033⁶ KINTAVI [50] 3-8-8 (3*) S D Williams (4) *cl up, drvn alng 5 fs out, wknd o'r 3 furlongs out*.......(10 to 1 op 8 to 1) 9
3146⁷ CORNFLAKE [44] 3-8-5 A Clark (2) *chsd ldrs, rdn to improve o'r 4 fs out, btn 3 furlongs out.*..........(6 to 1 op 5 to 1 tchd 7 to 1) 10
3239⁹ HAUT-BRION (Ire) [35] 4-8-8 S Webster (11) *mid-div, feeling pace hfwy, grad wknd*..........(100 to 1) 11
3219⁹ MAJOR JACK [49] 3-8-10 A Mackay (10) *hld up and beh, shaken up fnl 3 fs, eased a furlong out, nvr nr to chal.*..........(25 to 1) 12
2932⁸ BLAKENEY BOY [32] 3-7-4 (3*) N Kennedy (9) *slwly into strd, beh and sn niggled alng, lost tch hfwy, tld off.*..........(66 to 1 op 50 to 1) 13
Dist: Hd, 4l, 2l, ½l, 7l, 5l, 12l, nk, 1½l, 5l. 3m 4.70s. a 6.90s (13 Ran).
(Mrs L A Windsor), P D Evans

DEAUVILLE (FR) (good)
Wednesday August 18th
Going Correction: PLUS 0.15 sec. per fur.

3413 Prix de la Vallee d'Auge (Listed) (2-y-o) £14,337 5f.......... (2:30)

SHOALHAVEN (USA) 8-11 G Mosse,.......... 1
2980² KEY OF LUCK (USA) 8-11 F Head,.......... 2
WEZZO (USA) 8-8 C Asmussen,.......... 3
1692⁴ PETARD EXPRESS (Ire),.......... 4
CASLON (Fr),.......... 5
2144⁶ MY SIN (Ire),.......... 6
2647⁸ ROI D'O (Fr),.......... 7
Dist: ¾l, 2l, 1½l, 2½l, nk, hd. 59.00s. a 3.00s (7 Ran).
SR: 52/49/38/-/ (Sheikh Mohammed), J E Hammond

3414 Prix de Meautry (Group 2) (3-y-o and up) £23,895 6f.......... (3:30)

1786 MONDE BLEU 5-9-0 D Boeuf, *made all, set slow pace till rdn and quickened 2 fs out, ran on wl*.......... 1
3015⁶ CRACK REGIMENT (USA) 5-9-0 E Saint-Martin, *mid-div ins, rdn 2 fs out, hdwy one furlong out, ran on wl, got second nr line*.......... 2
2488* THREE FOR FANTASY (Ire) 3-8-10 O Peslier, *trkd ldr, rdn 2 fs out, kpt on, lost second cl hme*.......... 3
3015⁵ ZIETEN (USA) 3-9-0 T Jarnet, *hld up in rear, not clr run one and a half fs out, nvr able to chal*.......... 4
2488⁷ NIDD (USA) 3-8-10 , *mid-div on outsd, rdn 2 fs out, no hdwy*.......... 5
2981⁸ KENBU (Fr) 4-8-10 C Asmussen, *al in rear*.......... 6
Dist: 1½l, ½l, 1l, hd, ½l. 1m 12.50s. a 4.10s (6 Ran).
SR: 36/30/24/24/19/17/ (Daniel Wildenstein), A Fabre

GOWRAN PARK (IRE) (good)
Wednesday August 18th

3415 Cloghala E.B.F. Race (2-y-o) £3,797 1m.......... (5:45)

BALLYKETT NANCY (Ire) 8-11 K J Manning (1)..... (7 to 2) 1
2284* CORLEONIE (Ire) (bl) 9-7 W J Supple (5).......... (10 to 1) 2
2742* TIMINIYA (Ire) 9-4 J P Murtagh (3).......... (9 to 4) 3
NORTHERN BARS (Ire) 8-8 (6*) J A Heffernan (2).. (20 to 1) 4
2982² ACROSS THE TRACKS (Ire) 8-9 (2*) D G O'Shea (6) (8 to 1) 5
Dist: 2l, 5½l, 4½l, hd. 1m 39.10s. (5 Ran).
(Exors Of The Late N Keating), J S Bolger

3416 Goresbridge E.B.F. (C & G) Maiden (2-y-o) £3,797 1m................ (6:15)

1650^{4} SWIFT RIPOSTE (Ire) 9-0 K J Manning (12)........ (8 to 1) 1
ARKUB 9-0 W J Supple (10)........................ (6 to 1) 2
3159^{4} SHANKAR (Ire) 8-12 (2*) P Carberry (5)............ (7 to 2) 3
3159^{3} DANCING SUCCESS (USA) 9-0 S Craine (1)... (7 to 4 fav) 4
3243 WHEREWILITALL END (Ire) 9-0 P Shanahan (13).. (20 to 1) 5
3030^{6} ROSE BUNCH 9-0 P V Gilson (6)................ (5 to 1) 6
FRENCH VICTOR (Ire) 8-10 (4*) J J Behan (8)...... (8 to 1) 7
3159^{6} BUBBLY PROSPECT (USA) 8-6 (8*) A P McCoy (7) (14 to 1) 8
2778^{5} RUDI'S PRIDE (Ire) 9-0 J F Egan (4)............(12 to 1) 9
KAKASHDA (Ire) 9-0 J P Murtagh (11)............... (5 to 1) 10
1332 MONEYBROKER (Ire) 9-0 D Hogan (2)........... (20 to 1) 11
WUDITBEFAIRTOSAY (Ire) 8-12 (2*) R M Burke (3) (14 to 1) 12
2982^{6} BOB BARNES (Ire) 8-4 (10*) S Kelly (9)........... (14 to 1) 13

Dist: 1½l, 1½l, hd, 4½l. 1m 40.30s. (13 Ran).

(Mount Juliet), J S Bolger

3417 Thomastown Fillies Maiden (3-y-o and up) £2,762 1m..................(6:45)

1164 ALASKAN GIRL (Ire) 3-8-12 S Craine (15).........(11 to 4) 1
3242^{3} SKERRIES BELL 3-8-12 P V Gilson (8)............ (5 to 1) 2
3025^{4} CREATIVE CRAFT (USA) 3-8-12 P Shanahan (12) .... (9 to 4 fav) 3
2691^{8} ROLANDS GIRL (Ire) 3-8-6 (6*) J A Heffernan (6)...(16 to 1) 4
2781 DO-TELL-ME (Ire) 3-8-6 (6*) R V Skelly (13)......... (20 to 1) 5
LOVE HURTS (Ire) 3-8-12 W J Supple (14)........ (16 to 1) 6
3074^{7} LOOK NONCHALANT (Ire) 4-9-0 (4*) J J Behan (10) (12 to 1) 7
3062^{5} NORDIC ABU (Ire) 3-8-4 (8*) T E Durcan (1)....... (7 to 1) 8
SHANGANOIR (Ire) 3-8-10 (2*) P Carberry (2)...... (8 to 1) 9
3062^{3} SHPEEL (Ire) 3-8-6 (6*) B J Walsh (3)................ (7 to 1) 10
3161^{7} AURLIANO (Ire) 3-8-10 (2*) R M Burke (4)..........(25 to 1) 11
2843^{5} SHY TEACHER (Ire) 3-8-12 N Byrne (11)............ (16 to 1) 12
3074 ELEGANT NORA (Ire) 3-8-12 J F Egan (5).........(16 to 1) 13
3294 SILVER JAR (Ire) 3-8-4 (8*) G M Moylan (7).........(16 to 1) 14

Dist: 1½l, 1l, sht-hd, 1½l. 1m 41.50s. (14 Ran).

(Patrick H Burns), Declan Gillespie

3418 Derrinstown Apprentice Series Handicap (0-75 4-y-o and up) £3,797 1m 1f 130yds.......................... (7:15)

3076^{8} BRACKLOON BOY (Ire) [-] 4-8-12 (4*) C Everard (6) (12 to 1) 1
3296^{2} BLUES COMPOSER (Ire) [-] 4-8-1 (4*) B J Walsh (7) (7 to 2) 2
3296* THE BOWER (Ire) [-] (bl) 4-8-0 (6*,4ex) P M Donohue (3) .... (5 to 2) 3
2901 TOUCHDOWN [-] 6-8-7 (6*) G M Moylan (8).........(8 to 1) 4
3294^{3} SCOTSMAN'S BAY (Ire) [-] 4-8-2 (2*) J J Behan (9) .... (9 to 4 fav) 5
3296^{5} ACCELL (Ire) [-] (bl) 4-8-7 D G O'Shea (4).......... (8 to 1) 6
1515^{6} DONNASOO (Ire) [-] 4-10-0 P Carberry (2)......... (14 to 1) 7
3278^{5} SUTTONIAN (Ire) [-] (bl) 4-9-0 (2*) W J Smith (1)... (12 to 1) 8

Dist: Hd, nk, 1½l, ¾l. 2m 5.50s. (8 Ran).

(Seaview Stud Ltd), Ms E Cassidy

3419 Kilkenny Handicap (0-80 3-y-o) £2,762 7f............................. (7:45)

3294^{4} WHAT A PLEASURE (Ire) [-] 8-3 (6*) B J Walsh (10)..(5 to 1) 1
3327^{8} SLIGHTLY SCRUFFY (Ire) [-] 9-0 P V Gilson (6).... (11 to 2) 2
3242 SAMOT (Ire) [-] 8-12 J F Egan (7)................ (12 to 1) 3
3380^{2} BRATA (USA) [-] 9-1 (4*) W J Smith (9).......... (5 to 4 fav) 4
2556^{7} FAIRY BRIDE (Ire) [-] 7-10 Joanna Morgan (8)..... (14 to 1) 5
3328^{4} SARA MAURETTE (Ire) [-] 8-4 W J Supple (3)....... (10 to 1) 6
1611 EDENS LANDING (Ire) [-] 8-7 (4*) J J Behan (2).... (14 to 1) 7
3075^{8} VERITABLE GALLERY (Ire) [-] 7-13 (2*) R M Burke (1) ....(12 to 1) 8
3074^{6} BOSSY PATRICIA (Ire) [-] 7-6^{7} (8*) R T Fitzpatrick (4) (20 to 1) 9
2806^{5} ABEREDW (Ire) [-] 7-11 (2*) D G O'Shea (5)......... (9 to 1) 10

Dist: 1½l, ½l, 4l. 1m 27.50s. (10 Ran).

(Mrs Kevin Prendergast), Kevin Prendergast

KEMPTON (good to firm)
Wednesday August 18th

Going Correction: MINUS 0.30 sec. per fur. (races 1,2,3,4), MINUS 0.40 (5,6)

3420 Douglas Cameron Apprentice Handicap Class E (0-70 3-y-o and up) £3,366 1¼m.......................... (5:40)

2348^{6} WHO'S THE BEST (Ire) [45] 3-7-12 D McCabe (14) *al hndy, pushed alng frm 3 fs out, led jst o'r one out, cmftbly.* ....(12 to 1 op 8 to 1) 1
442^{6} VA UTU [47] 5-8-3 (5*) R Painter (10) *hld up and beh, hdwy o'r 3 fs out, kpt on fnl furlong, nrst finish.* .... (16 to 1 op 12 to 1) 2
3211^{6} RUTLAND WATER (USA) [63] 6-9-5 (5*) T Ashley (3) *in tch, smooth hdwy to ld wl o'r 2 fs out, hdd jst over one out, wknd ins last*......... (11 to 2 op 4 to 1 tchd 6 to 1) 3
1827 BIT ON THE SIDE (Ire) [63] 4-9-3 (7*) G Faulkner (5) *handily plcd, shaken up o'r 2 fs out, kpt on same pace.* .... (10 to 1 op 8 to 1) 4
3042^{7} ROSIETOES (USA) [38] 5-7-13 P McCabe (4) *al chasing ldrs, effrt 3 fs out, sn one pace*.. (20 to 1 tchd 33 to 1) 5
723 STRIKING IMAGE (Ire) [45] 4-8-3 (3*) D Gibbs (1) *chsd ldrs, rdn o'r 3 fs out, kpt on same pace fnl 2.* .... (33 to 1 op 25 to 1) 6
2894^{7} ALBERT [45] 6-8-1 (5*) Sharon Millard (6) *beh, pushed alng o'r 3 fs out, nvr able to chal.* ....(10 to 1 op 8 to 1 tchd 12 to 1) 7
3065^{5} SULA MOON [46] 3-7-13 B Russell (7) *midfield, rdn o'r 3 fs out, sn btn*.......................(33 to 1 op 20 to 1) 8
3228^{3} TAKE THE MICK [51] (bl) 3-8-4 T G McLaughlin (9) *wl beh till some hdwy o'r 2 fs out, sn rdn and btn.* ....(16 to 1 op 12 to 1 tchd 20 to 1) 9
3043* OVERPOWER [59] 9-9-6 S Mulvey (8) *hld up in midfield, rdn o'r 3 fs out, no imprsn*........... (4 to 1 op 3 to 1) 10
169 CRETOES DANCER (USA) [48] 4-8-9 Kim McDonnell (2) *midfield till lost pl frm hfwy, sn in rear.* .... (33 to 1 op 20 to 1) 11
3224* SANTANA LADY (Ire) [63] 4-9-5 (5*,5ex) Ruth Coulter (12) *led till hdd wl o'r 2 fs out, wknd quickly.* .... (5 to 2 fav tchd 3 to 1 and 100 to 30) 12
3229 SHADES OF JADE [37] 5-7-7 (5*) M Baird (13) *wth ldr till wknd quickly o'r 3 fs out, sn beh, tld off.* .... (33 to 1 op 20 to 1) 13
2847^{8} HEAVY ROCK (Ire) [34] 4-7-9^{2} L Newton (11) *prmnt 5 fs, wknd quickly, tld off.* ....(25 to 1 op 16 to 1 tchd 33 to 1) 14

Dist: 3l, ¾l, 2l, ½l, 2l, 6l, nk, ½l, 2½l, hd. 2m 5.16s. a 3.36s (14 Ran).

SR: 20/24/38/34/8/11/ (Mrs Ann Jarvis), A P Jarvis

3421 Mike Dickin Median Auction Maiden Stakes Class F (2-y-o) £3,522 6f (6:10)

2626^{3} FRIENDLY CHAMP (Ire) 9-0 R Price (15) *al prmnt far side, led jst o'r one furlong out, rdn out.* ....(9 to 2 op 5 to 2 tchd 5 to 1) 1
ARNDILLY 8-8^{4} (5*) A Procter (16) *chsd ldrs far side, gd hdwy to chal o'r one furlong out, kpt on wl.* .... (50 to 1 op 25 to 1) 2
3009^{3} ROYALE FIGURINE (Ire) 8-6 (3*) D Harrison (10) *in tch stands side, led grp frm wl o'r one furlong out, ran on strly*.................................(14 to 1 op 8 to 1) 3
WYCHWOOD SANDY 9-0 N Day (20) *prmnt far side, led hfwy till jst o'r one furlong out, no extr.* .... (50 to 1 op 25 to 1) 4
2994^{5} STORM SHIP (Ire) 9-0 L Dettori (7) *nvr far away stands side, rdn alng o'r 2 fs out, one pace.* ....(9 to 2 op 5 to 1 tchd 4 to 1) 5
2862 HARDING 9-0 J Williams (12) *hld up beh, hdwy fnl 2 fs, nvr plcd to chal*.....................(14 to 1 op 10 to 1) 6
2325 CHILIGRAY (bl) 8-9 (5*) Stephen Davies (8) *sn rdn alng stands side, some hdwy fnl 2 fs, nvr nrr.* .... (50 to 1 op 25 to 1) 7
3143^{2} TOM MORGAN 9-0 G Duffield (9) *chsd ldrs stands side, rdn o'r 2 fs out, unbl to quicken.* ....(4 to 1 fav op 3 to 1 tchd 9 to 2) 8
LETS GO BO (Ire) 9-0 B Rouse (5) *hld up and beh, steady hdwy fnl one and a half fs, nvr plcd to chal.* .... (25 to 1 op 12 to 1) 9
3222^{5} RAPIER POINT (Ire) 9-0 W Ryan (13) *sn chsd alng in midfield stands side, nvr able to chal.* ....(20 to 1 op 16 to 1 tchd 25 to 1) 10
COUCHANT (Ire) 9-0 S Whitworth (22) *slwly into strd, beh till ran on 2 fs out on far side, kpt on, nvr nrr.* ....(10 to 1 op 6 to 1 tchd 11 to 1) 11
3120^{5} MR BERGERAC (Ire) 8-11 (3*) C Hodgson (6) *led stands side grp till wl o'r one furlong out, sn wknd.* ....(16 to 1 tchd 50 to 1) 12
BELLO GALLICO (Ire) 9-0 S Raymont (17) *outpcd far side till ran on fnl 2 fs, no dngr.* ....(12 to 1 op 7 to 1 tchd 14 to 1) 13
3267^{4} SARMATIAN (USA) 9-0 Jaki Houston (3) *wth ldrs stands side till wknd 2 fs out*.............. (33 to 1 op 25 to 1) 14
2610^{7} MUSIC PRINCESS 8-4 (5*) B Russell (2) *chsd ldrs stands side 4 fs*...............................(50 to 1 op 33 to 1) 15
2147^{5} BANDITA 8-2 (7*) R Painter (21) *led far side grp to hfwy, sn wknd*.................................(50 to 1 op 25 to 1) 16
MAGIC MAGGIE 8-9 T Quinn (4) *nvr rch ldrs.* ....(25 to 1 op 12 to 1 tchd 33 to 1) 17
SAAFI (Ire) 9-0 M Wigham (11) *slwly away, al beh.* .... (20 to 1 op 10 to 1) 18
MUSICAL SQUIRREL 8-9 E Johnson (19) *al rear.* .... (50 to 1 op 25 to 1) 19
TOTALLY TICKLED (USA) 8-9 M Hills (1) *prmnt stands side till wknd quickly fnl 2 fs*............ (5 to 1 op 6 to 1) 20
3130 MISTER O'GRADY (Ire) 8-7 (7*) G Forster (14) *chsd ldrs far side till wknd wl o'r 2 fs out*....... (50 to 1 op 33 to 1) 21
DANDINI 9-0 N Adams (23) *al beh*.... (50 to 1 op 25 to 1) 22

Dist: ¾l, 2½l, 1l, 3½l, ¾l, nk, nk, ½l, 1½l, 1½l. 1m 13.45s. a 2.65s (22 Ran).

SR: 11/3/-/-/-/-/ (Dr Meou Tsen Geoffrey Yeh), R W Armstrong

3422 Pete Murray Maiden Stakes Class D (2-y-o) £3,786 7f................(6:40)

2968^{3} NICOLOTTE 9-0 M Hills (13) *al hndy gng wl, quickened to ld well o'r 2 fs out, sn clr, imprsv.* ....(6 to 4 on op 7 to 4 on tchd Evens) 1

2990[4] VARSAVIA (USA) 8-6 (3*) D Harrison (14) *trkd ldrs, rdn alng o'r 2 fs out, kpt on, no ch wth wnr.* ....(9 to 2 op 4 to 1 tchd 7 to 2 and 5 to 1) 2
687[4] SMART FAMILY (USA) 9-0 T Quinn (12) *chsd ldrs, rdn o'r 2 fs out, not quicken*...(10 to 1 op 12 to 1 tchd 14 to 1) 3
3130[5] WAYFARERS WAY (USA) 9-0 L Dettori (3) *pld hrd, prmnt, rdn wl o'r 2 fs out, sn one pace.* ....(5 to 1 op 6 to 1 tchd 9 to 2) 4
1706[7] FORGOTTEN DANCER (Ire) 9-0 S Raymont (6) *led till wl o'r 2 fs out, sn wknd*.................(33 to 1 op 25 to 1) 5
3079[4] DUELLO 9-0 N Adams (16) *chsd ldrs, rdn o'r 2 fs out, sn no extr*...........................(12 to 1 op 14 to 1) 6
TUDOR FLIGHT 8-9 M Wigham (4) *mid-div, outpcd and lost pl 3 fs out, ran on clsg stages.* (25 to 1 op 20 to 1) 7
2968 AL JINN 8-11 (3*) C Hodgson (11) *mid-div, niggled alng hfwy, nvr able to chal*.......................(50 to 1) 8
1489[5] REED MY LIPS (Ire) 9-0 G Duffield (10) *wth ldrs, rdn and wknd wl o'r 2 fs out.* (20 to 1 op 25 to 1 tchd 33 to 1) 9
POSSIBILITY 8-9 J Williams (5) *nvr a dngr.* ....(33 to 1 op 25 to 1) 10
JADY'S DREAM (Ire) 8-9 W Ryan (7) *slwly into strd, al beh.* ....(50 to 1 op 33 to 1) 11
WILD TRUFFES (Ire) 8-9 S Whitworth (8) *hld up beh, some hdwy o'r 3 fs out, eased whn btn.* ....(25 to 1 op 20 to 1 tchd 33 to 1) 12
CHOPENDOZ (USA) 9-0 M Tebbutt (1) *sn niggled alng, nvr a threat*..........................(33 to 1 op 14 to 1) 13
3166 A SUITABLE GIRL 8-9 S Dawson (9) *mid-div on outsd till wknd o'r 3 fs out, sn beh*......... (50 to 1 op 33 to 1) 14
SAHAH 9-0 B Rouse (15) *slwly away, al beh.* ....(50 to 1 op 33 to 1) 15
Dist: 4l, 2½l, 2l, ¾l, 2l, 3½l, nk, 1½l, ½l, 2l. 1m 25.29s. a 1.19s (15 Ran).
SR: 51/34/31/25/23/17/1/5/-/ (Mollers Racing), G Wragg

3423 Robbie Vincent Conditions Stakes Class D (2-y-o) £3,420 7f........(7:10)

2990[2] ALAFLAK (Ire) 8-11 T Quinn (3) *trkd ldr, sstnd chal frm 3 fs out, led last 100 yards, cleverly.* ......(11 to 8 on op 6 to 4 on tchd 2 to 1 on and 5 to 4 on) 1
2998[3] PETER ROWLEY 8-13 L Dettori (2) *sn led, jnd fnl 3 fs, no extr and hdd last 100 yards.* ....(11 to 4 op 7 to 2 tchd 5 to 2) 2
1983* COTTEIR CHIEF (Ire) 8-11 W Ryan (1) *swrvd lft strt, hld up last, hng left o'r 2 fs out, not rcvr, tld off.* ....(4 to 1 op 3 to 1 tchd 9 to 2) 3
Dist: Nk, dist. 1m 27.42s. a 3.32s (3 Ran).
SR: 16/17/-/ (Hamdan Al-Maktoum), J L Dunlop

3424 London Talkback Radio 1152 AM Handicap Class C (0-90 3-y-o and up) £4,962 1½m.................. (7:40)

3271* SUN OF SPRING [85] 3-9-5 (4ex) W Ryan (3) *hld up in tch, cld 5 fs out, led wl o'r 2 out, drvn clr.* ....(11 to 8 fav op 6 to 4 tchd 13 to 8 and 5 to 4) 1
3010[3] BARFORD LAD [70] 6-9-0 L Dettori (2) *hld up in tch, hdwy 5 fs out, chsd wnr frm 2 out, no imprsn.* ....(6 to 1 tchd 13 to 2) 2
3139* RIVAL BID (USA) [72] 5-9-2 N Day (1) *patiently rdn, hdwy 3 fs out, not much room o'r 2 out, kpt on same pace und pres*...............................(5 to 1 op 4 to 1) 3
3212[4] ROMALITO [60] (bl) 3-7-8 N Adams (5) *al hndy, led briefly 3 fs out, sn rdn and wknd.* ....(8 to 1 op 7 to 1 tchd 10 to 1) 4
2395[6] JUSTICE (Fr) [66] 5-8-10 G Duffield (4) *led 2 fs, hndy till squeezed out and lost pl 5 out, kpt on one pace und pres frm two out*.........(25 to 1 tchd 33 to 1 and 20 to 1) 5
3067[2] BLACKPATCH HILL [84] 4-10-0 W Carson (6) *pld hrd, led aftr 2 fs to 3 out, sn wknd, eased whn btn, fnshd lme.* ....(3 to 1 tchd 7 to 2 and 11 to 4) 6
Dist: 4l, 3l, 6l, sht-hd, 20l. 2m 31.72s. a 0.72s (6 Ran).
SR: 50/37/33/-/14/-/ (Sheikh Mohammed), M R Stoute

3425 Steve Allen Handicap Class E (0-70 3-y-o and up) £3,236 7f......... (8:10)

2940[3] TEANARCO (Ire) [61] 5-9-8 L Dettori (4) *chsd ldrs, pushed alng o'r 3 fs out, sstnd effrt frm one and a half out to ld on line*..........................(7 to 1 tchd 15 to 2) 1
3269[2] DANCING SENSATION (USA) [55] 6-9-2 T Quinn (14) *al hndy, ev ch frm o'r 2 fs out, hrd rdn to ld ins last, ct on line*...............................(7 to 4 fav op 9 to 4) 2
3302* PANCHELLITA (USA) [60] 4-9-7 (5ex) B Rouse (11) *led till ins fnl furlong, no extr*.................(11 to 2 op 9 to 2) 3
3169[6] JOLTO [38] 4-7-13 N Adams (7) *beh, rdn and styd on wl fnl 2 fs, nrst finish*...............(9 to 1 tchd 11 to 1) 4
2882 DIGPAST (Ire) [68] (bl) 3-9-7 (3*) D Harrison (12) *nvr far away, rdn and not much room o'r 2 fs out, ran on same pace*...................(10 to 1 op 8 to 1 tchd 12 to 1) 5
2712[6] THATCHED (Ire) [41] (bl) 3-7-11 N Carlisle (9) *hld up beh, rdn o'r 2 fs out, styd on, nvr nrr*...(33 to 1 op 25 to 1) 6
3302[2] ZINBAQ [35] 7-7-10 T Williams (3) *hld up mid-div, rdn o'r 2 fs out, kpt on ins last*.................(11 to 1 op 9 to 1) 7
3057* PUSEY STREET BOY [48] 6-8-9 M Hills (5) *prmnt, rdn and ev ch wl o'r one furlong out, wknd ins last.* ....(10 to 1 op 9 to 1) 8
2669 THRESHFIELD (USA) [44] 7-8-5 G Hind (2) *hld up, wide and some hdwy entering strt, nvr nr to chal.* ....(11 to 1 op 12 to 1 tchd 16 to 1 and 10 to 1) 9
3292[9] GALLANT HOPE [41] (bl) 11-7-11 (5*) D McCabe (10) *chsd ldg bunch, rdn and wknd 2 fs out.* ....(40 to 1 op 33 to 1 tchd 50 to 1) 10
2989[9] DANCING MISS (Ire) [34] 4-7-9 C Avery (6) *slwly into strd, al beh*.............. (40 to 1 op 25 to 1 tchd 50 to 1) 11
1563[6] FIRST GOLD [62] 4-9-9 J Williams (1) *hld up mid-div, rdn o'r 2 fs out, sn btn*...(20 to 1 op 16 to 1 tchd 25 to 1) 12
2944[6] TAJDID (Ire) [59] 3-9-1 W Carson (8) *prmnt till wknd o'r 3 fs out*.............................(12 to 1 tchd 14 to 1) 13
3175 RAPINSKI [36] (bl) 4-7-11[4] K Williamson (13) *prmnt to hfwy, sn wknd*........................(100 to 1 op 66 to 1) 14
Dist: Hd, 1½l, sht-hd, 1l, ¾l, ½l, ½l, ½l, 1½l, 5l. 1m 25.55s. a 1.25s (14 Ran).
SR: 47/40/40/17/39/10/7/18/12/ (B K Symonds), P G Murphy

YARMOUTH (good)
Wednesday August 18th

Going Correction: PLUS 0.10 sec. per fur. (races 1,2,3,4), MINUS 0.15 (5,6)

3426 Pleasure Beach Claiming Stakes Class F (2-y-o) £2,489 5f 43yds.. (2:20)

2370[4] RESONANT 9-0 M Hills (5) *made all, quickened to go clr last 2 fs, easily*............ (13 to 8 on op 11 to 8 on) 1
1999[3] MITSIS 8-11 (3*) B Doyle (4) *pushed alng to keep up hfwy, styd on grimly to chase wnr fnl furlong, no imprsn.* ....(15 to 2 op 4 to 1 tchd 8 to 1) 2
3210[6] LUCY'S GOLD (bl) 7-13 D Biggs (3) *nvr far away, feeling pace whn wnr quickened 2 fs out, no extr.* ....(12 to 1 tchd 14 to 1) 3
2933[4] NOSMO KING (Ire) 8-10 J Fortune (6) *broke wl, sn rdn and outpcd, some hdwy hfwy, no imprsn.* ....(12 to 1 op 8 to 1) 4
3167[5] SWIFT NICK NEVISON 8-7 (5*) K Rutter (1) *broke wl to dispute ld to hfwy, wknd quickly o'r one furlong out.* ....(25 to 1 op 16 to 1 tchd 33 to 1) 5
3103[2] CANDI DAS (Ire) (bl) 7-10 (7*) Antoinette Armes (2) *co'red up on ins, hrd at work hfwy, sn lost tch.* (6 to 1 op 4 to 1) 6
Dist: 4l, ¾l, 5l, 7l, 3½l. 1m 4.00s. a 3.30s (6 Ran).
SR: 45/29/11/2/-/-/ (Cheveley Park Stud), Sir Mark Prescott

3427 Britannia Pier Conditions Stakes Class C (3-y-o and up) £4,927 6f 3yds ....(2:50)

3178* STORM CANYON (Ire) 3-8-12 B Raymond (2) *tucked away on ins, quickened ahead o'r one furlong out, kpt on strly*..........(5 to 4 on tchd 11 to 10 on and Evens) 1
2362[6] FYLDE FLYER 4-10-0 J Fortune (4) *trkd ldg pair, outpcd and lost grnd o'r 2 fs out, rallied gmely fnl furlong.* ....(5 to 1 op 9 to 2) 2
2242[6] NIGHT MELODY (Ire) 3-9-0 M Hills (5) *steadied strt, rcd freely on outsd, kpt on wl ins fnl furlong.* ....(5 to 1 op 4 to 1) 3
3153 ROCK SYMPHONY 3-8-7 (5*) J Tate (3) *nvr far away, led briefly wl o'r one furlong out, not quicken ins last.* ....(16 to 1 op 12 to 1) 4
2746* PRESS GALLERY 3-9-0 P Robinson (1) *broke wl to dispute ld for o'r 4 fs, fdd*................(16 to 1 op 12 to 1) 5
2987 LORD OLIVIER (Ire) 3-8-12 M Tebbutt (6) *slight ld for o'r 4 fs, fdd*................(13 to 2 op 6 to 1 tchd 7 to 1) 6
Dist: 2l, ¾l, sht-hd, 3½l, 1½l. 1m 14.30s. a 3.30s (6 Ran).
SR: 44/52/35/32/20/12/ (Sheikh Mohammed), J H M Gosden

3428 Peddars Cross Nursery Class D (2-y-o) £3,406 6f 3yds............. (3:25)

3052* ONE ON ONE [80] 9-0 M Hills (5) *al gng wl, led aftr one and a half fs, quickened away ins last, imprsv.* ....(6 to 4 on op 5 to 4 on tchd Evens) 1
2417* NAKITA [80] 8-7 (7*) G Forster (4) *steadied strt, shaken up to improve last 2 fs, ran on, no ch wth wnr.* ....(12 to 1 op 8 to 1) 2
2473[5] PRIMA SILK [76] 8-10 D Biggs (7) *al hndy, chsd wnr o'r one furlong out, no imprsn whn eased and lost second pl last 50 yards*........(10 to 1 op 6 to 1 tchd 11 to 1) 3
3129[3] PERSIAN HERITAGE [78] 8-12 M Tebbutt (8) *steadied strt, improved on outsd hfwy, kpt on und pres fnl furlong.* ....(13 to 2 op 5 to 1 tchd 7 to 1) 4
2058[9] GOLDEN GRAND [68] 7-9 (7*) N Varley (3) *bumped leaving stalls, sn chasing ldrs, rdn o'r 2 fs out, one pace.* ....(33 to 1 op 10 to 1) 5
3133[3] MONKEY MUSIC [79] (bl) 8-13 J Fortune (2) *slight ld for one and a half fs, styd upsides til wknd o'r one furlong out.* ....(7 to 1 op 5 to 1) 6
2629[3] NERA [87] 9-7 B Raymond (1) *co'red up on ins, feeling pace over 2 fs out, sn btn*........... (8 to 1 op 9 to 2) 7
2209[4] WOODS VENTURE (Ire) [65] 7-13 A McGlone (6) *trkd ldrs, struggling to keep up o'r 2 fs out, sn btn.* ....(33 to 1 op 8 to 1) 8
Dist: 6l, nk, sht-hd, hd, 3l, 3l, 5l. 1m 15.50s. a 4.50s (8 Ran).
SR: 22/-/-/-/-/ (Cheveley Park Stud), W J Haggas

3429 Canon Fillies' Stakes Handicap Class E (0-70 3-y-o and up) £3,210 7f 3yds ....(4:00)

2944² ADAMPARIS [50] (bl) 3-8-3 P Robinson (8) *patiently rdn, brst through entering fnl furlong, ran on to ld last strd.* .... (13 to 2 op 7 to 1 tchd 6 to 1) 1
3219² RED COTTON [62] 3-9-1 P D'Arcy (5) *made most, hrd pressed last 2 fs, ran on, jst ct.* ....(7 to 2 fav tchd 4 to 1 and 3 to 1) 2
3184* KINNEGAD KID [45] (v) 4-7-12 (5*) N Gwilliams (6) *nvr far away, ev ch and rdn o'r one furlong out, one pace cl hme*............................(8 to 1 op 6 to 1) 3
3099⁸ SPRING HIGH [49] 6-8-7 G Bardwell (7) *rcd wide, rdn to dispute ld o'r 2 fs out, kpt on same pace.* .... (11 to 1 op 16 to 1 tchd 20 to 1) 4
3191* OCARA (USA) [62] 3-9-1 M Tebbutt (4) *tucked away, shaken up to improve last 2 fs, kpt on towards finish.* .... (11 to 2 op 9 to 2 tchd 6 to 1) 5
3237* ROYAL COMEDIAN [45] 4-7-10 (7*,6ex) N Varley (9) *swrvd rght leaving stalls, rcd wide, ev ch o'r 2 fs out, one pace*............................(8 to 1 op 7 to 1) 6
3358⁸ BALLERINA BAY [70] (v) 5-10-0 B Raymond (3) *tucked away on ins, feeling pace o'r 2 fs out, nvr able to chal.* ....(6 to 1 op 5 to 1 tchd 13 to 2) 7
2898⁸ LITTLE OSBORNE (Ire) [43] (bl) 3-7-10 F Norton (2) *in tch, feeling pace and rdn hfwy, no imprsn.* ....(33 to 1 op 16 to 1) 8
2874³ ASTERN (USA) [68] 3-9-7 G Hind (1) *wth ldrs for o'r 4 fs, eased whn btn last 2 furlongs*.......(7 to 1 op 4 to 1) 9

Dist: Sht-hd, 1l, sht-hd, ¾l, ½l, 1½l, 1l, dist. 1m 28.70s. a 5.50s (9 Ran).
SR: 17/28/13/16/22/8/28/-/-/ (Invoshire Ltd), G A Pritchard-Gordon

3430 21st Running Of The Botton Brothers Handicap Ladies' Class G (0-70 3-y-o and up) £2,385 1¾m 17yds......(4:30)

2729 MYSTERIOUS MAID (USA) [39] 6-10-0 Mrs L Pearce (5) *nvr far away, led o'r 3 fs out, drvn clr, readily.* ....(7 to 1 op 10 to 1) 1
2992³ SCENIC DANCER [48] 5-10-9 Miss L Hide (1) *tucked away on ins, swtchd outsd to improve last 3 fs, ran on, not rch wnr*......................(5 to 1 tchd 11 to 2) 2
3288³ ALLMOSA [60] 4-11-7 Mrs J Naughton (3) *al hndy, drvn alng whn pace quickened last 2 fs, kpt on same pace.* ....(6 to 1 op 5 to 1) 3
2992² THE KARAOKE KING [47] (bl) 4-10-8 Mrs J Boggis (10) *trkd ldrs, effrt and drvn alng o'r 3 fs out, outpcd last 2 furlongs*.......................(6 to 1 op 5 to 1) 4
3067³ LOOKINGFORARAINBOW (Ire) [59] 5-11-6 Miss D J Jones (7) *al hndy, wide strt, ev ch till hng lft and wknd o'r one furlong out*................(4 to 1 fav op 11 to 4) 5
3078 CATHOS (Fr) [33] 8-9-8 Miss Diana Jones (4) *co'red up beh ldrs, effrt entering strt, btn over 2 fs out.* ....(9 to 2 op 6 to 1) 6
2578⁷ MISS RIBBONS [37] 3-8-11 (3*) Miss S Chittenden (9) *trkd ldg bunch, struggling to keep up o'r 3 fs out, sn btn.* ....(33 to 1) 7
2948⁶ PRECUSSION [52] 3-10-1 Mrs M Haggas (2) *led till hdd o'r 3 fs out, wknd quickly last 2 furlongs.* ....(14 to 1 op 12 to 1) 8
3212⁶ TURFMANS VISION [50] 3-9-10 (3*) Miss S Boston (6) *chsd ldg bunch till wknd quickly entering strt.* ....(12 to 1 tchd 14 to 1) 9
3240³ HYDROPIC [25] 6-8-12¹ (3*) Miss R Clark (8) *sddl slpd sn aftr strt, pld up 7 fs out*.............(25 to 1 op 20 to 1) pu

Dist: 4l, 1½l, 6l, nk, 1l, 8l, 5l, 12l. 3m 7.90s. a 10.90s (10 Ran).
(D J Maden), J Pearce

3431 Cobholm Fillies' Handicap Class D (0-80 3-y-o) £3,611 1¼m 21yds.. (5:00)

2776⁵ PEARLY MIST (Ire) [76] 9-4 (3*) B Doyle (1) *patiently rdn, not much room appr strt, rallied to ld approaching last, forged clr*..................... (12 to 1 op 8 to 1) 1
3088* MISTY SILKS [66] 8-11 D Biggs (8) *settled gng wl, led on bit o'r 2 fs out till appr fnl furlong, one pace.* ....(6 to 1 op 5 to 1 tchd 8 to 1) 2
3083* SEAMA (USA) [63] 8-8 C Nutter (2) *led for 2 fs, led ag'n and came wide appr strt, hdd o'r two furlongs out, no extr.* ....(6 to 1 op 5 to 1 tchd 7 to 1) 3
2563⁵ FUNNY HILARIOUS (USA) [69] 9-0 P Robinson (4) *wtd wth, improved und pres o'r 2 fs out, styd on, no imprsn.* .... (11 to 2 op 6 to 1 tchd 7 to 1) 4
2940⁷ PETONELLAJILL [74] 9-5 G Bardwell (9) *trkd ldg bunch, effrt and rdn o'r 3 fs out, sn outpcd.* (10 to 1 op 6 to 1) 5
3282* BAY QUEEN [79] 9-7 (3*,4ex) M Fenton (3) *tucked away in midfield, not much room appr strt, fdd wl o'r one furlong out*..........................(5 to 2 fav op 7 to 4) 6
2749⁹ MISS KINABALU [52] 7-11 F Norton (6) *led aftr 2 fs till hdd appr strt, wknd quickly o'r two furlongs out.* .... (14 to 1 op 8 to 1 tchd 16 to 1) 7
2444⁴ DREAMS ARE FREE (Ire) [70] 9-1 A McGlone (7) *trkd ldrs, drvn alng o'r 3 fs out, tld off last 2 furlongs.* ....(8 to 1 op 5 to 1) 8
1625⁹ FAIR TO THE WIND (USA) [63] (bl) 8-8 B Raymond (5) *co'red up, drvn alng on ins whn squeezed for room over 3 fs out, tld off*.......................(10 to 1 op 6 to 1) 9

Dist: 5l, ½l, nk, 10l, 1½l, 12l, nk, 15l. 2m 7.80s. a 3.80s (9 Ran).
SR: 54/34/30/35/20/22/ (Sheikh Marwan Al Maktoum), C E Brittain

YORK (good)
Wednesday August 18th
Going Correction: PLUS 0.15 sec. per fur. (races 1,4,5,7), PLUS 0.10 (2,3,6)

3432 Rous Selling Stakes Class E (2-y-o) £8,610 6f.................... (2:05)

1742⁴ CIRCLE OF FRIENDS (Ire) 8-6 J Reid (10) *prmnt far side, led 2 fs out, ran on wl fnl furlong*............(9 to 2 jt-fav op 4 to 1) 1
3230⁸ MILLION LIGHTS (Ire) 8-6 L Dettori (15) *in tch stands side, ran on wl fnl 2 fs, not rch wnr*.......(6 to 1 op 5 to 1) 2
3236* JIMMY THE SKUNK (Ire) 8-11 J Carroll (4) *cl up far side, ev ch 2 fs out, kpt on und pres*...............(9 to 2 jt-fav op 4 to 1 tchd 5 to 1) 3
3215⁴ MONKEY'S WEDDING (bl) 8-11 G Duffield (1) *led far side to 2 fs out, kpt on und pres*.......... (16 to 1 op 14 to 1) 4
2866⁴ ELEVATOR SHAFT (Ire) (bl) 8-11 T Quinn (8) *prmnt far side, one pace fnl 2 fs*..............(14 to 1 tchd 16 to 1) 5
2569² TURTLE ROCK 8-11 K Darley (16) *chsd stands side ldrs, effrt and edgd lft 2 fs out, kpt on same pace.* .... (10 to 1 op 12 to 1) 6
3133⁶ CLARET BUMBLE 8-6 W Ryan (12) *chsd stands side ldrs, no hdwy fnl 2 fs*........(15 to 2 op 7 to 1 tchd 8 to 1) 7
2482⁵ BRITANNIA MILLS 8-6 K Fallon (21) *in tch stands side, no hdwy fnl 2 fs*..............................(33 to 1) 8
SLMAAT 8-6 M Roberts (3) *in tch far side till wknd 2 fs out*.......................... (10 to 1 op 8 to 1) 9
GLENUGIE 8-11 A Munro (18) *stands side, slwly into strd, beh till ran on fnl 2 fs, nrst finish.* (33 to 1 op 25 to 1) 10
3215⁹ FUSSY SIOUX 8-6 R Cochrane (23) *nvr dngrs*.... (33 to 1) 11
2772 BESCABY GIRL 8-6 J Fanning (11) *swtchd stands side strt, chsd ldrs, sn pushed alng, wknd o'r 2 fs out.* ....(33 to 1 op 25 to 1) 12
2129⁷ BEX BOY (Ire) 8-11 C Dwyer (9) *nvr dngrs*........(33 to 1) 13
3031⁸ FEATHERSTONE LANE 8-11 Dean McKeown (19) *in tch stands side to hfwy*..............................(33 to 1) 14
3186⁷ BOJOLLY 8-6 W Newnes (2) *slwly into strd, nvr dngrs.* .... (20 to 1 op 16 to 1 tchd 25 to 1) 15
3309⁴ ALLLEGSNOBRAIN (v) 8-11 D Holland (14) *led stands side grp for o'r 4 fs, sn wknd*......... (10 to 1 tchd 11 to 1) 16
2929⁸ RISKIE THINGS 7-13 (7*) Mark Denaro (20) *nvr dngrs.* ....(20 to 1) 17
CRAGLOUGH 8-11 Dale Gibson (22) *nvr dngrs*... (33 to 1) 18
2994 STEADY RISK 8-11 W R Swinburn (17) *in tch stands side to hfwy*.............................(16 to 1 tchd 20 to 1) 19
2973 PRINCE SKYBURD 8-11 J Lowe (6) *sn beh*....... (33 to 1) 20
3279 MATABUNGKAY 8-11 N Connorton (13) *swtchd to far side strt, sn beh*...(33 to 1) 21
3079 PATRICE 8-11 Pat Eddery (5) *sn beh.* ....(12 to 1 tchd 14 to 1) 22
2826 SONIC (Ire) 8-11 T Lucas (7) *sn beh*... (33 to 1 op 25 to 1) 23

Dist: 1½l, hd, hd, 3l, nk, 2l, 1½l, hd, ½l, sht-hd. 1m 14.82s. a 4.82s (23 Ran).
SR: 14/8/12/11/-/-/ (Mrs S H Spencer-Phillips), R Hannon

3433 Aston Upthorpe Yorkshire Oaks Class A (Group 1) (3-y-o and up) £78,598 1m 3f 195yds...................... (2:35)

2986² ONLY ROYALE (Ire) 4-9-7 R Cochrane (7) *hld up, hdwy to ld wl o'r one furlong out, sn clr, easily.* ....(10 to 1 tchd 11 to 1) 1
2986⁶ DANCING BLOOM (Ire) 3-8-11 W R Swinburn (4) *in tch, effrt 3 fs out, sn pushed alng, styd on wl fnl furlong, no ch wth wnr*.......................(14 to 1 tchd 16 to 1) 2
2791⁴ USER FRIENDLY 4-9-7 G Duffield (5) *trkd ldrs, pushed alng 3 fs out, kpt on fnl furlong*....(7 to 4 tchd 2 to 1) 3
3194² SPRING 4-9-7 T Quinn (8) *in tch, rdn to ld 2 fs out, sn hdd, one pace*.. (16 to 1) 4
3194³ OAKMEAD (Ire) 3-8-11 J Reid (2) *cl up, pushed alng 3 fs out, btn whn swtchd outsd o'r one out.* .... (15 to 2 op 7 to 1 tchd 8 to 1) 5
2986⁹ THAWAKIB (Ire) 3-8-11 W Carson (3) *led to 2 fs out, fdd.* ....(14 to 1 tchd 16 to 1) 6
2238* RAINBOW LAKE 3-8-11 Pat Eddery (9) *chsd ldrs, pushed alng o'r 3 fs out, wknd 2 out.* ....(13 to 8 fav op 11 to 8 tchd 7 to 4) 7
529 PREMIATA (Ire) 3-8-11 L Dettori (6) *in tch till wknd 4 fs out, tld off*..........................(50 to 1 op 33 to 1) 8

Dist: 3½l, ¾l, ½l, 3½l, 8l, hd, 30l. 2m 31.76s. a 3.76s (8 Ran).
SR: 81/64/72/71/54/38/37/-/ (G Sainaghi), L M Cumani

3434 150th Year Of The Tote Ebor Handicap Class B (3-y-o and up) £66,185 1m 5f 194yds....................... (3:10)

2655[7] SARAWAT [76] 5-8-2 T Quinn (9) *cl up, trkd ldr o'r 6 fs out till led gng wl over 3 out, styd on well frm 2 out.* ....(14 to 1 tchd 16 to 1) 1
2625* OH SO RISKY [97] 6-9-9 Pat Eddery (6) *dwlt, beh, hdwy 5 fs out, ran on strly frm 2 out, nrst finish.* ....(12 to 1 op 11 to 1 tchd 14 to 1) 2
3179[3] DREAMS END [82] 5-8-8 L Piggott (1) *in tch, hdwy 5 fs out, styd on und pres frm 2 out, nrst finish.* ....(16 to 1 tchd 14 to 1) 3
2393* KEY TO MY HEART (Ire) [95] 3-8-9 K Fallon (20) *nvr far away, chsd wnr o'r 2 fs out till wknd ins last.* ....(14 to 1 tchd 16 to 1) 4
2962 CASTORET [85] 7-8-8 (3*) D Harrison (19) *hld up, effrt 4 fs out, styd on, not trble ldrs*.......(16 to 1 tchd 20 to 1) 5
2617[5] MILLION IN MIND (Ire) [83] 4-8-9 W Newnes (18) *cl up, led o'r 6 fs out till over 3 out, fdd.* ....(18 to 1 op 16 to 1 tchd 20 to 1) 6
1682[5] CASTLE COURAGEOUS [94] 6-9-6 K Darley (13) *prmnt till wknd o'r 2 fs out*....(33 to 1 op 25 to 1) 7
2655* BRANDON PRINCE (Ire) [92] (bl) 5-9-4 (4ex) L Dettori (10) *mid-div, effrt o'r 3 fs out, no hdwy.* ....(7 to 1 op 10 to 1 tchd 11 to 1) 8
2907[2] SPIN DOCTOR (Ire) [89] 3-8-3[1] R Cochrane (4) *hld up, hdwy 5 fs out, rdn 3 out, sn btn*.......(5 to 1 fav tchd 6 to 1) 9
2907[8] PISTOL RIVER (Ire) [94] 3-8-8 J Reid (14) *nvr dngrs.* ....(12 to 1 op 11 to 1 tchd 14 to 1) 10
2061 QUICK RANSOM [90] 5-9-2 Dean McKeown (3) *prmnt till wknd frm 4 fs out*....(12 to 1 op 11 to 1) 11
3152 OPERA GHOST [83] 7-8-9 W R Swinburn (16) *nvr nr ldrs.* ....(25 to 1 tchd 28 to 1) 12
3067[4] DURSHAN (USA) [78] 4-8-4 J Lowe (7) *in tch, losing pl whn hmpd o'r 5 fs out, no dngr aftr*....(50 to 1) 13
2841 RISZARD (USA) [98] 4-9-10 C Roche (11) *nvr nr ldrs.* ....(40 to 1) 14
2393[4] LINDON LIME (USA) [94] 3-8-8 A Munro (15) *mid-div till wknd 3 fs out*....(20 to 1 tchd 16 to 1) 15
3067* GLIDE PATH (USA) [85] 4-8-11 (4ex) R Hills (17) *in tch till wknd o'r 3 fs out.* ....(11 to 1 op 12 to 1 tchd 14 to 1 and 10 to 1) 16
1380[5] ENCORE UNE FOIS (Ire) [82] 4-8-8 T Williams (12) *led till o'r 6 fs out, wknd quickly*....(40 to 1) 17
2962[8] NIGHT CLUBBING (Ire) [88] 4-9-0 D Holland (22) *nvr nr ldrs.* ....(33 to 1) 18
2360[7] SAINT KEYNE [99] 3-8-13 W Ryan (2) *in tch, hmpd o'r 5 fs out, effrt 4 out, sn btn*....(16 to 1) 19
2962[7] TURGENEV (Ire) [98] (v) 4-9-10 M Roberts (8) *in tch, some hdwy 6 fs out, wknd o'r 3 out*....(12 to 1) 20
2432[3] BOLOARDO [94] (v) 4-9-6 M Birch (21) *in tch till wknd 5 fs out, tld off*....(50 to 1) 21

Dist: 2½l, ¾l, hd, 7l, 1½l, 5l, 1½l, 5l, ½l, 1l. 2m 59.20s. a 4.20s (21 Ran).
SR: 60/76/59/59/47/42/43/38/13/ (S Aitken), R Akehurst

3435 Scottish Equitable Gimcrack Stakes Class A (Group 2) (2-y-o) £56,619 6f ....(3:45)

3200* TURTLE ISLAND (Ire) 9-5 J Reid (3) *cl up, chlgd o'r 2 fs out, ran on wl und pres to ld close hme*...(5 to 2 op 2 to 1) 1
2730* UNBLEST 9-0 G Duffield (2) *cl up, slight ld o'r 2 fs out, ran on wl und pres, ct close hme*........(4 to 1 op 7 to 2) 2
3223[2] TORCH ROUGE 9-0 D Holland (6) *swrvd lft strt, slwly into strd, sn in tch, effrt o'r 2 fs out, kpt on fnl furlong.* ....(10 to 1 op 8 to 1) 3
2335[6] ALANEES 9-0 W R Swinburn (5) *in tch, kpt on fnl 2 fs, not trble ldrs*....(50 to 1) 4
3200[3] FAST EDDY 9-0 L Dettori (7) *trkd ldrs, effrt o'r 2 fs out, kpt on same pace*..........(11 to 2 op 5 to 1 tchd 6 to 1) 5
2924* MISTER BAILEYS 9-3 Dean McKeown (4) *slight ld till o'r 2 fs out, wkng whn rdr lost whip wl over one out.* ....(15 to 8 fav op 7 to 4 tchd 2 to 1) 6
3222[2] PRINCE AZZAAN (Ire) 9-0 Pat Eddery (1) *hld up, effrt o'r 2 fs out, wknd over one out*........(28 to 1 op 50 to 1) 7
3200[6] TAKADOU (Ire) 9-0 D Harrison (8) *hld up, effrt o'r 2 fs out, sn wknd*............(40 to 1 op 33 to 1 tchd 50 to 1) 8

Dist: Hd, 2½l, 3l, nk, ½l, ¾l, 12l. 1m 13.49s. a 3.49s (8 Ran).
SR: 53/47/37/25/24/25/19/-/ (R E Sangster), P W Chapple-Hyam

3436 Roses Stakes Class A (Listed Race) (2-y-o) £10,672 5f..............(4:15)

2618[8] BID FOR BLUE 8-11 W R Swinburn (1) *cl up, led o'r 2 fs out, hrd pressed fnl furlong, kpt on wl und pres.* ....(11 to 1 op 10 to 1) 1
3200[5] GOLD LAND (USA) 9-0 A Munro (2) *trkd ldrs, effrt 2 fs out, hrd rdn to chal ins last, no extr cl hme.* ....(7 to 4 tchd 2 to 1) 2
2960[4] MOSCOW ROAD 8-11 K Darley (3) *led till o'r 2 fs out, wknd entering last*......(7 to 1 op 8 to 1 tchd 9 to 1) 3
2909* ELECTRIFY (USA) 8-11 Pat Eddery (6) *sn pushed alng and beh, nvr dngrs*......(6 to 4 fav op Evens tchd 13 to 8) 4
2745* IL CARAVAGGIO (Ire) (bl) 9-0 M J Kinane (5) *hld up, effrt and some hdwy hfwy, wknd entering fnl furlong.* ....(10 to 1) 5
3236[6] STORM REGENT 8-11 W Woods (4) *sn beh.* ....(66 to 1 op 100 to 1) 6

Dist: Hd, 4l, 3½l, ¾l, 8l. 1m 0.15s. a 2.85s (6 Ran).
SR: 55/57/38/24/24/-/ (Cheveley Park Stud), R Hannon

3437 Fulford Rated Class B Handicap (0-105 3-y-o and up) £10,377 1¼m 85yds........................(4:45)

2926 STONEY VALLEY [93] 3-8-6[1] J Reid (13) *led aftr 2 fs, ran on wl fnl furlong*.........(9 to 1 op 8 to 1 tchd 10 to 1) 1
2581[6] ALDERBROOK [91] 4-8-12 Paul Eddery (7) *chsd ldrs, effrt 3 fs out, ev ch one out, kpt on.* ....(7 to 1 op 8 to 1 tchd 10 to 1) 2
3158 CUMBRIAN CHALLENGE (Ire) [90] (bl) 4-8-11 M Birch (3) *led 2 fs, cl up, effrt two out, ev ch one out, kpt on.* ....(12 to 1 op 10 to 1 tchd 14 to 1) 3
2654[4] SALATIN (USA) [105] 3-9-4 W Carson (2) *hld up, hdwy 3 fs out, not clr run and swtchd entering last, styd on und pres*....(9 to 1 op 12 to 1) 4
MR CONFUSION (Ire) [92] 5-8-13 N Connorton (1) *in tch, hdwy hfwy, ch o'r one furlong out, kpt on same pace fnl furlong*....(16 to 1 op 14 to 1) 5
2413[3] MIZAAYA [100] 4-9-7 W R Swinburn (4) *hld up, hdwy o'r 3 fs out, rdn 2 out, sn btn and eased.* (10 to 1 op 8 to 1) 6
2774[2] SILVER SAMURAI [86] 4-8-7 J Lowe (8) *cl up till wknd 2 fs out*....(12 to 1 op 14 to 1) 7
2884[5] EFHARISTO [86] (v) 4-8-7 R Hills (12) *beh, some hdwy fnl 4 fs, nvr dngrs*....(12 to 1 op 10 to 1) 8
2962[9] CASPIAN TERN (USA) [86] 4-8-7 A Munro (6) *mid-div, reminder hfwy, sn btn*....(16 to 1) 9
2376[4] BOLD PURSUIT (Ire) [94] 4-9-1 K Fallon (10) *mid-div, pushed alng hfwy, sn beh*...... (25 to 1 tchd 33 to 1) 10
2907[3] GONE FOR A BURTON (Ire) [90] 3-8-3 K Darley (11) *loose bef strt, in tch, effrt o'r 3 fs out, sn btn.* ....(9 to 2 fav op 3 to 1 tchd 5 to 1) 11
2815* MECKLENBURG (Ire) [92] 3-8-5 M Roberts (5) *al beh.* ....(6 to 1 op 5 to 1 tchd 7 to 1) 12
2961[2] MIDNIGHT HEIGHTS [88] 3-8-1 T Williams (9) *mid-div till wknd 4 fs out*......... (6 to 1 op 5 to 1 tchd 13 to 2) 13

Dist: ¾l, nk, sht-hd, 2½l, 7l, sht-hd, 12l, 5l, 1½l, 2½l. 2m 12.38s. a 4.38s (13 Ran).
SR: 59/63/61/67/57/51/36/12/2/ (R E Sangster), P W Chapple-Hyam

3438 Falmouth Handicap Class C (0-100 3-y-o) £11,257 5f..............(5:15)

1213[7] IN CASE (USA) [90] 8-12 Pat Eddery (10) *in tch, hdwy 2 fs out, ran on wl to ld ins last.* ....(8 to 1 op 6 to 1 tchd 9 to 1) 1
2908* CALL ME I'M BLUE (Ire) [92] 9-0 L Piggott (13) *in tch, hdwy und pres 2 fs out, ev ch ins last, no extr nr finish.* ....(7 to 1 op 8 to 1) 2
2987 GARNOCK VALLEY [90] 8-12 A Munro (12) *beh, hdwy 2 fs out, ran on wl fnl furlong, nrst finish.* ....(12 to 1 tchd 14 to 1) 3
3153[5] MISTERTOPOGIGO (Ire) [86] 8-8 K Darley (9) *cl up, led gng wl o'r one furlong out, hdd ins last, no extr.* ....(10 to 1 op 8 to 1) 4
3108* TRAPEZIUM [83] 8-5 R Cochrane (7) *cl up, slight ld hfwy till o'r one furlong out, kpt on fnl furlong.* ....(8 to 1 op 6 to 1) 5
3051 MANOR ADVENTURE [71] 7-3[3] (7*) J Bramhill (2) *chsd ldrs, ev ch one furlong out, kpt on und pres.* ....(20 to 1 op 33 to 1) 6
2908[2] LOCH PATRICK [87] 8-9 J Reid (14) *chsd ldrs, ev ch one furlong out, no extr*...............(7 to 1 tchd 8 to 1) 7
2399[7] ELLE SHAPED (Ire) [95] 9-3 W R Swinburn (4) *in tch, no hdwy fnl 2 fs*....(25 to 1 op 20 to 1) 8
3081[6] JOBIE [75] 7-11 J Quinn (11) *nvr dngrs.* ....(14 to 1 op 12 to 1 tchd 16 to 1) 9
3153[2] STEPANOV (USA) [91] 8-13 M Roberts (15) *cl up, dsptd ld hfwy, wknd o'r one furlong out.* ....(5 to 2 fav op 7 to 2 tchd 4 to 1) 10
3348[5] ANOTHER JADE [78] 8-0 J Lowe (8) *slwly into strd, nvr dngrs*...............(11 to 1 op 12 to 1 tchd 14 to 1) 11
2855[3] SAINT EXPRESS [92] 9-0 Dean McKeown (5) *chsd ldrs till wknd 2 fs out*....(16 to 1 op 14 to 1) 12
2797[3] PLUM FIRST [71] (bl) 7-7 J Fanning (3) *cl up, led aftr 2 fs, sn hdd and wknd*.................. (25 to 1 tchd 20 to 1) 13
2746[4] HOTARIA [71] 7-2 (5*) D Wright (1) *led 2 fs, sn wknd.* ....(33 to 1) 14
2753[3] SABRE RATTLER [99] 9-7 J Carroll (6) *chsd ldrs to hfwy, sn wknd*.......................... (14 to 1 tchd 12 to 1) 15

Dist: Nk, nk, nk, nk, sht-hd, ½l, 2l, nk, nk, 4l. 1m 0.24s. a 2.94s (15 Ran).
SR: 54/55/52/47/43/30/44/44/23/ (K Abdulla), R Charlton

AYR (good)
Thursday August 19th

Going Correction: PLUS 0.30 sec. per fur. (races 1,2,4,6), PLUS 0.05 (3,5)

3439 Burns Median Auction Maiden Stakes Class E (3-y-o) £2,739 7f........(2:10)

3378[2] LAMSONETTI 8-9 Alex Greaves (7) *steadied strt, confidently rdn, improved 2 fs out, quickened to ld ins last, sn clr*........................... (20 to 1 op 12 to 1) 1

3178^{3} AQUILETTA 8-9 K Fallon (5) *hld up in tch, shaken up 3 fs out, improved to ld appr fnl furlong, hdd ins last, no extr*..........(5 to 4 fav op Evens tchd 11 to 8) 2

1869^{2} PERSIAN CHARMER (Ire) 9-0 J Fanning (2) *nvr far away, rdn and ev ch o'r 2 fs out, one pace ins fnl furlong.* ....(2 to 1 tchd 9 to 4) 3

MISS CHARLIE 8-9 A Mackay (3) *sluggish strt, sn reco'red to chase ldrs, effrt and rdn 3 fs out, not quicken ins last*..........(12 to 1 op 33 to 1) 4

3070^{7} PISTON (Ire) 8-11 (3*) O Pears (6) *keen hold, led aftr a furlong, shaken up o'r 2 fs out, hdd appr last, sn btn.* ....(6 to 1 op 5 to 1) 5

SABERAGE 8-9 S Perks (1) *tucked away on ins, shaken up o'r one furlong out, nvr plcd to chal.* ....(25 to 1 op 20 to 1 tchd 33 to 1) 6

3132^{5} SOBA UP 8-9 J Lowe (4) *led a furlong, styd hndy, rdn alng entering strt, wknd wl o'r one furlong out.* ....(8 to 1 op 7 to 1 tchd 9 to 1) 7

Dist: 3l, nk, nk, 1½l, ½l, 1½l. 1m 31.95s. a 7.95s (7 Ran).

SR: 7/-/2/-/ (Mrs Kate Hall), R M Whitaker

3440 Goukscroft Apprentice Handicap Class F (0-70 3-y-o and up) £2,595 7f ....(2:45)

2733 SUPER BENZ [61] 7-9-9 (5*) L Aspell (4) *set gd pace, clr o'r 3 fs out, shaken up over one out, hld on wl ins last.* ....(11 to 2 op 5 to 1 tchd 6 to 1) 1

2954^{4} CRESELLY [58] 6-9-4 (7*) I Jardine (6) *nvr far away, effrt and rdn o'r 2 fs out, kpt on und pres ins last.* ....(7 to 2 op 5 to 2) 2

3354^{3} LANGUEDOC [59] 6-9-7 (5*) D Thomas (3) *settled off the pace, improved o'r 2 fs out, shaken up over one out, no extr ins last*..........(3 to 1 fav tchd 11 to 4) 3

2764^{5} GOLD DESIRE [43] 3-8-0 (5*) M Baird (2) *chsd ldg pair, rdn alng o'r 2 fs out, kpt on same pace ins fnl furlong.* ....(9 to 1 op 6 to 1 tchd 10 to 1) 4

3378* CRAIGIE BOY [49] 3-8-6 (5*,5ex) C Teague (7) *beh, pushed alng hfwy, effrt 2 fs out, no imprsn fnl furlong.* ....(9 to 2 op 7 to 2) 5

3310^{4} THISONESFORALICE [35] 5-7-9 (7*) I Grantham (1) *slwly into strd, beh and sn detached, shaken up and styd on wl fnl 2 fs, nvr nrr*..........(6 to 1 op 8 to 1) 6

2737^{7} QUESSONG [33] 3-7-9^{6} (5*) J Dennis (5) *in tch, drvn alng appr strt, wknd 2 fs out*..........(25 to 1) 7

Dist: 2l, nk, 1l, nk, 5l, 10l. 1m 32.44s. a 8.44s (7 Ran).

SR: 19/10/10/-/ (Whitestonecliffe Racing Partnership), B Beasley

3441 Williams De Broe Nursery Class E (2-y-o) £2,845 5f.......... (3:15)

3133^{8} GREY TOPPA [51] 7-4^{1} (7*) C Teague (3) *in tch on outer, shaken up to improve hfwy, led appr fnl furlong, pushed out ins last*...(14 to 1 op 12 to 1 tchd 16 to 1) 1

2400^{9} MISTER PISTE (Ire) [76] 9-7 J Fanning (5) *led til hdd appr fnl furlong, rdn and rallied ins last.* ....(6 to 1 op 5 to 1 tchd 7 to 1) 2

2063^{7} ARTA [62] 8-7 A Culhane (4) *handily plcd, effrt and rdn o'r one furlong out, no extr ins last.* ....(14 to 1 op 12 to 1 tchd 16 to 1) 3

3133^{9} CHEEKY CHAPPY [61] 8-6 Alex Greaves (8) *co'red up on ins, effrt whn not clr run over one furlong out, swtchd and styd on inside last, nvr dngrs.* ....(14 to 1 op 12 to 1 tchd 16 to 1) 4

3279^{2} LUCIUS LOCKET (Ire) [56] 8-1 L Charnock (6) *in tch gng wl, effrt and rdn 2 fs out, one pace appr last.* ....(7 to 4 fav op Evens tchd 2 to 1) 5

3183^{2} SPRING STAR [66] 8-8 (3*) O Pears (2) *nvr far away, rdn alng o'r 2 fs out, btn appr last.* ....(14 to 1 op 12 to 1 tchd 16 to 1) 6

2652^{2} NO MEAN CITY (Ire) [70] 8-10 (5*) D Wright (1) *sn beh, pushed alng 3 out, nvr on terms*..... (4 to 1 op 3 to 1) 7

841^{5} SADDAM THE LOG [74] 9-5 A Mackay (7) *chsd ldrs on ins, rdn alng hfwy, wknd quickly wl o'r one furlong out.* *wnr*..........(3 to 1 op 6 to 1) 8

Dist: ½l, 1½l, 1½l, ½l, 5l, 2½l, 2½l. 1m 1.86s. a 3.76s (8 Ran).

SR: 12/35/15/8/1/ (D Ford), Denys Smith

3442 Dumfries Selling Stakes Class F (3-y-o and up) £2,377 1m 7f.......... (3:50)

3283^{3} REACH FOR GLORY 4-9-10 A Culhane (4) *trkd ldr, improved to ld o'r 2 fs out, sn clr, easily.* ....(10 to 1 op 8 to 1) 1

BEEKMAN STREET 7-9-10 J Fanning (6) *chsd ldg pair, outpcd and rdn o'r 2 fs out, styd on ins last, no ch wth wnr*..........(5 to 2 op 2 to 1) 2

2599^{3} SAOIRSE (Ire) (v) 5-9-0 K Fallon (5) *hld up in tch, rdn appr strt, kpt on und pres o'r one furlong out, nvr dngrs.* ....(3 to 1 tchd 100 to 30 and 7 to 2) 3

2888^{5} MYNYOSS 3-8-6 L Charnock (3) *set sedate pace, quickened hfwy, hdd o'r 2 fs out, btn wl over one furlong out*..........(100 to 1) 4

3283^{2} RAVENSPUR (Ire) 3-8-1 (5*) D Wright (1) *hld up in last pl, effrt and shaken up entering strt, nvr on terms.* ....(6 to 1 tchd 7 to 1) 5

2950^{4} REEL OF TULLOCH (Ire) 4-9-5 (5*) J Marshall (2) *keen hold, in tch, rdn alng 4 fs out, btn wl o'r 2 furlongs out.* ....(9 to 4 fav tchd 2 to 1) 6

Dist: 7l, 2½l, 1½l, 1½l, 7l. 3m 39.74s. (6 Ran).

(R M Whitaker), R M Whitaker

3443 EBF Kirkoswald Maiden Fillies Stakes Class D (2-y-o) £3,913 6f..........(4:20)

2909^{4} EN CACHETTE (Ire) 8-11 K Fallon (1) *nvr far away, chlgd o'r one furlong out, led ins last, rdn out.* ....(5 to 2 on tchd 9 to 4 on and 3 to 1 on) 1

1529^{8} PETITE MAXINE 8-11 S Perks (3) *dsptd ld, led o'r 2 fs out, jnd over one out, hdd ins last, no extr.* ....(20 to 1 tchd 25 to 1) 2

2203^{5} VANESSA ROSE 8-11 A Mackay (7) *tucked away beh ldrs, effrt and swtchd outsd o'r one furlong out, kpt on same pace ins fnl furlong.* (12 to 1 op 10 to 1 tchd 14 to 1) 3

1393^{5} ALACRITY 8-8 (3*) M Fenton (8) *trkd ldrs, pushed alng hfwy, not clr run and swtchd o'r one furlong out, one pace ins fnl furlong*..........(11 to 2 op 4 to 1) 4

STRANGERSARDANGERS (Ire) 8-6 (5*) D Wright (5) *hld up, shaken up and steady hdwy o'r one furlong out, can improve*..........(25 to 1 op 12 to 1) 5

2090^{4} LEADING PRINCESS (Ire) 8-11 J Fanning (6) *led til hdd o'r 2 fs out, rdn and sn btn.* (12 to 1 op 8 to 1 tchd 14 to 1) 6

2370^{6} GRANGE DANCER (Ire) 8-11 L Charnock (4) *nvr far away, pushed alng o'r 2 fs out, wknd wl over one furlong out.* ....(50 to 1 op 25 to 1) 7

3183^{3} CAPONATA (Ire) 8-11 J Lowe (2) *keen hold, co'red up beh ldrs, rdn alng over 2 fs out, btn over one out.* ....(8 to 1 op 6 to 1 tchd 9 to 1) 8

Dist: 1l, 3½l, nk, 3½l, 5l, 1½l, 1l. 1m 14.80s. a 3.90s (8 Ran).

SR: 25/21/7/6/-/ (R E Sangster), P W Chapple-Hyam

3444 Belmont Handicap Class D (0-80 3-y-o and up) £3,290 1¼m..........(4:50)

3373^{2} DOCTOR ROY [42] 5-7-7 (5*) D Wright (2) *nvr far away, shaken up to ld o'r one furlong out, pushed clr ins last.* ....(6 to 1 tchd 13 to 2) 1

2767^{3} TANODA [40] 7-7-10 J Lowe (5) *chsd ldrs on outer, effrt and rdn 3 fs out, kpt on ins last, no ch wth wnr.* ....(8 to 1 op 7 to 1 tchd 9 to 1) 2

3146^{2} PRINCIPAL PLAYER (USA) [57] 3-8-0 (5*) J Marshall (3) *tucked away on ins, improved to ld 3 fs out, hdd o'r one out, not quicken*..........(10 to 1 op 8 to 1) 3

3256^{2} BRACKENTHWAITE [51] 3-7-13 A Mackay (6) *hld up in rear, rdn entering strt, styd on fnl furlong, nvr dngrs.* ....(7 to 2 op 3 to 1) 4

3035* IMPERIAL BID (Fr) [70] 5-9-12 K Fallon (7) *hld up, shaken up to improve o'r 2 fs out, rdn over one out, sn btn.* ....(15 to 2 op 5 to 1 tchd 8 to 1) 5

3179^{8} MANILA BAY (USA) [75] 3-9-6 (3*) M Fenton (4) *hld up, pushed alng appr strt, shrtlvd effrt o'r 2 fs out, sn wknd*..........(5 to 2 fav op 7 to 2) 6

3050^{8} FLASHMAN [52] 3-8-0 L Charnock (1) *chsd ldrs, rdn entering strt, sn lost pl*..........(10 to 1 tchd 14 to 1) 7

1967^{3} AMERICAN HERO [53] 5-8-9 J Fanning (8) *led til hdd 3 fs out, rdn and sn btn*..... (7 to 1 op 6 to 1 tchd 8 to 1) 8

Dist: 3½l, 3½l, 2½l, 2½l, 7l, ½l, ¾l. 2m 13.13s. a 8.13s (8 Ran).

SR: 33/24/26/15/37/20/-/3/ (M C Newberry), N Bycroft

SALISBURY (good to firm)
Thursday August 19th
Going Correction: MINUS 0.40 sec. per fur.

3445 Woodford Apprentice Handicap Class F (0-80 3-y-o and up) £2,489 6f.. (5:40)

2993^{5} PRINCELY FAVOUR (Ire) [78] 3-9-6 (8*) Wendy Jones (7) *nvr far away, led o'r 2 fs out, hdd over one out, rallied to ld on line*..........(9 to 1 op 6 to 1) 1

3257^{7} COURTING NEWMARKET [40] 5-7-5^{2} (5*) D Toole (5) *beh early, gd hdwy 3 fs out, led o'r one out, ct on line.* ....(16 to 1 op 10 to 1 tchd 20 to 1) 2

3226^{7} WALNUT BURL (Ire) [55] (v) 3-7-9 (10*) Iona Wands (1) *slwly into strd, reco'red to chase ldrs, rdn and styd on wl ins last, nrst finish*..... (14 to 1 op 10 to 1 tchd 16 to 1) 3

3229^{2} DOUBLE SHIFT [55] 4-8-9 P Roberts (2) *wth ldrs, ev ch o'r one furlong out, no extr ins last.* ....(9 to 4 fav tchd 11 to 4) 4

3292^{4} UNVEILED [51] 5-8-5 D Gibbs (6) *prmnt till rdn and wknd wl o'r one furlong out*..........(3 to 1 op 7 to 2) 5

3088 DASHING MARCH [62] 4-9-2 R Painter (3) *wth ldrs till rdn and wknd o'r 2 fs out*..........(8 to 1 op 6 to 1) 6

3169^{4} SURE LORD (Ire) [68] 4-9-3 (5*) S McCarthy (4) *led till hdd o'r 2 fs out, wknd*..... (4 to 1 op 7 to 2 tchd 9 to 2) 7

Dist: Sht-hd, nk, 2½l, 3l, 8l, 2l. 1m 14.32s. a 1.82s (7 Ran).

SR: 30/-/5/-/ (C M Hamer), R Hannon

3446 Odstock Maiden Stakes Class D (2-y-o) £4,020 6f.......... (6:10)

1750[6] CANASKA DANCER (Ire) 9-0 D Holland (7) *al prmnt, led o'r 2 fs out, hrd rdn and found extr ins last.* ....(11 to 4 op 2 to 1 tchd 7 to 2 and 4 to 1) 1

2994[4] CALYPSO MONARCH (Ire) 8-7 (7*) Mark Denaro (8) *led till hdd o'r 2 fs out, rallied over one out till no extr ins last.* ....(5 to 2 fav op 5 to 2 tchd 3 to 1) 2

2316 TAILCOAT (USA) 9-0 C Rutter (9) *al hndy, rdn and ev ch frm o'r 2 fs out, one pace ins last.* (16 to 1 op 10 to 1) 3

COUNTRY LOVER 9-0 J Williams (4) *midfield till ran on wl fnl one and a half fs, nrst finish.* (16 to 1 tchd 25 to 1) 4

3209 LADY SILK 8-9 S Whitworth (10) *midfield, pushed alng frm o'r 3 fs out, ran on wl fnl furlong, nvr nrr.* .... (33 to 1 op 16 to 1) 5

1857[4] ROCKETEER (Ire) 8-7 (7*) Kim McDonnell (6) *prmnt on outsd, ev ch frm o'r 2 fs out till wknd appr last.* ....(16 to 1 op 14 to 1 tchd 20 to 1) 6

MONTICINO (Ire) 9-0 S Raymont (13) *midfield, hdwy o'r 2 fs out, no further imprsn appr last.* ....(7 to 1 op 7 to 2 tchd 8 to 1) 7

CONIC HILL (Ire) 9-0 F Norton (2) *chsd alng in midfield till no hdwy fnl 2 fs...*..................(10 to 1 op 6 to 1) 8

2626[8] DESERT PRESIDENT 8-9 (5*) J Tate (16) *trkd ldrs till wknd o'r 2 fs out*........................(25 to 1 op 14 to 1) 9

RAZINAH (Ire) 8-9 N Carlisle (11) *slwly away, ran green and nvr nr to chal....* (16 to 1 op 8 to 1 tchd 20 to 1) 10

LIVELY (Ire) 8-4 (5*) B Russell (12) *chsd ldrs and sn rdn alng, stdly lost pl fnl 2 and a half fs.* .... (66 to 1 op 33 to 1) 11

BODANTREE 8-9 (5*) V Slattery (15) *nvr trbld ldrs.* .... (66 to 1 op 33 to 1) 12

AWFULLY RISKY 8-9 B Rouse (1) *slwly away, al beh.* ....(25 to 1 op 16 to 1 tchd 33 to 1) 13

HOMEOFTHECLASSICS 8-9 S Dawson (5) *slwly away, al beh*..............................(66 to 1 op 33 to 1) 14

SALTCORN (Ire) 9-0 W Newnes (14) *midfield till lost pl frm hfwy*...............................(33 to 1 op 25 to 1) 15

Dist: ¾l, 1l, nk, ½l, 2l, nk, 2l, 2½l, 2l, ½l. 1m 14.50s. a 2.00s (15 Ran).

SR: 12/9/5/4/-/-/ (Mrs June M Sifton), P W Chapple-Hyam

3447 BBC Wiltshire Sound Claiming Handicap Class G (0-60 3-y-o and up) £3,015 6f 212yds......................(6:40)

3302[5] JOKIST [46] 10-9-0 J Williams (7) *wl beh till rapid hdwy frm 2 fs out, led ins last, sn clr*.....(11 to 1 op 10 to 1) 1

3305[7] MOGWAI (Ire) [54] (v) 4-9-8 S Whitworth (5) *beh, hdwy 2 fs out, ev ch ins last, not pace of wnr.* ....(14 to 1 op 12 to 1 tchd 16 to 1) 2

3042[8] NAVARESQUE [41] 8-8-2 (7*) S Drowne (9) *hld up beh, hdwy to ld 2 fs out, hdd and no extr ins last.* ....(14 to 1 op 12 to 1 tchd 16 to 1) 3

3042[4] OLD COMRADES [50] 6-8-11 (7*) Mark Denaro (11) *prmnt, ev ch wl o'r one furlong out, not quicken ins last.* ....(13 to 2 op 5 to 1 tchd 7 to 1) 4

3020 CONISTON LAKE (Ire) [54] (bl) 4-9-8 B Rouse (12) *mid-div, rdn wl o'r 2 fs out, kpt on fnl furlong.* ....(33 to 1 op 20 to 1) 5

3020[4] KISSAVOS [46] 7-9-0 F Norton (14) *mid-div, rdn wl o'r 2 fs out, kpt on ins last, not rch ldrs...* (11 to 1 op 10 to 1) 6

3047* MEDLAND (Ire) [47] 3-8-10 W Newnes (20) *slwly into strd, beh till ran on o'r one furlong out, not quicken ins last.* ....(8 to 1 op 6 to 1) 7

2868 CHICARD [44] 4-8-12 D Holland (10) *beh, some hdwy o'r one furlong out, nvr trble ldrs.....* (14 to 1 op 10 to 1) 8

3068[5] FIVEOFIVE (Ire) [57] 3-9-1 (5*) A Procter (8) *slwly into strd, sn reco'red to midfield, hdwy wl over one furlong out, no dngr*...............(17 to 2 op 8 to 1 tchd 9 to 1) 9

2863[8] SEASON'S STAR [51] (v) 3-9-0 S Dawson (3) *led aftr 2 fs to two out, sn wknd*..................(12 to 1 op 10 to 1) 10

2388[9] TWO LUMPS [59] 3-9-8 L Dettori (19) *trkd ldrs, rdn and wknd wl o'r one furlong out....* (6 to 1 fav op 12 to 1) 11

TEXAN CLAMOUR (Fr) [44] 5-8-12 S Raymont (13) *slwly away, wl beh till moderate late hdwy*........ (33 to 1) 12

3340[7] FAIR ENCHANTRESS [43] 5-8-4 (7*) Kim McDonnell (18) *wth ldrs, wknd wl o'r one furlong out.* (33 to 1 op 25 to 1) 13

3168[8] CEE-EN-CEE [55] (v) 9-9-9 A Tucker (6) *chsd alng in mid-div, effrt and not much room wl o'r one furlong out, sn btn*.............................. (20 to 1 op 16 to 1) 14

3180[3] SUSANNA'S SECRET [52] 6-9-1 (5*) J Tate (16) *wth ldrs, wknd o'r 2 fs out....*(14 to 1 op 12 to 1 tchd 16 to 1) 15

455[7] JORDYWRATH [53] 3-8-9 (7*) P McCabe (17) *nvr better than mid-div*...........................(33 to 1 op 25 to 1) 16

3302 KIRRIEMUIR [44] 5-8-12 N Carlisle (2) *in tch on outsd till wknd 3 fs out*.......................... (14 to 1 op 20 to 1) 17

2724[8] CALISAR [57] 3-9-1 (5*) Stephen Davies (4) *in tch till wknd 3 fs out*...........................(20 to 1 tchd 25 to 1) 18

NONANNO [42] 4-8-10 G Bardwell (15) *led 2 fs, stdly lost pl*.. (33 to 1) 19

Dist: 2½l, 2l, 1½l, sht-hd, hd, hd, ¾l, 3l, 1l, 2l. 1m 27.10s. a 1.50s (19 Ran).

SR: 35/35/16/20/23/14/9/9/8/ (William Jarvis), W Jarvis

3448 Nightfall Conditions Stakes Class D (2-y-o) £3,655 5f.................(7:10)

3114* BLUE SIREN 8-9 L Dettori (1) *trkd ldr till led wl o'r one furlong out, all out.* ....(15 to 8 on op 5 to 4 on tchd 2 to 1 on) 1

3267* DOLLAR GAMBLE (Ire) 8-3 (7*) Mark Denaro (2) *al hndy, rdn o'r 2 fs out, ran on strly ins last, jst fld.* ....(9 to 1 op 6 to 1) 2

2137* BASKERVILLE 9-0 J Williams (5) *beh early, rdn o'r 2 fs out, styd on wl fnl furlong, nvr nrr.* .... (11 to 1 op 8 to 1 tchd 12 to 1) 3

2618 HIGH DOMAIN (Ire) 9-6 W Carson (4) *led till wl o'r one furlong out, sn one pace*............(6 to 1 op 8 to 1) 4

3254 CYARNA QUINN (Ire) 8-9 C Rutter (6) *beh, rdn o'r 2 fs out, nvr able to chal*..... (25 to 1 op 33 to 1 tchd 40 to 1) 5

3167[2] ROXANIAN (Ire) 9-4 D Holland (3) *trkd ldrs, came wide o'r 3 fs out, sn racing alone, wknd appr last.* .... (7 to 1 op 6 to 1 tchd 15 to 2) 6

Dist: Hd, 2l, 1½l, 3l, 3l. 1m 0.26s. a 0.46s (6 Ran).

SR: 46/46/42/42/19/16/ (J C Smith), I A Balding

3449 Netheravon Maiden Stakes Class D (3-y-o and up) £3,494 1¾m......(7:40)

3173[6] COLLIER BAY 3-8-9 L Dettori (7) *in tch, hdwy o'r 3 fs out, led over 2 out, sn clr, readily.* .... (8 to 1 tchd 7 to 1 and 9 to 1) 1

1960[2] PAT OR ELSE 3-8-4 W Carson (5) *hld up in midfield, effrt o'r 4 fs out, not much room and swtchd lft over 2 out, styd on, no ch wth wnr*..............(4 to 1 op 6 to 1) 2

2158[2] BOHEMIAN CROWN (USA) 3-8-9 D Holland (8) *led one furlong, rgned ld 6 out, hdd o'r 2 out, one pace.* .... (11 to 4 op 2 to 1 tchd 3 to 1) 3

3173[3] QUILLON 3-8-9 A McGlone (3) *trkd ldrs, effrt o'r 5 fs out, sn rdn and no hdwy.* .... (15 to 8 fav op 7 to 4 tchd 13 to 8 and 2 to 1) 4

3225 ROYAL MANOEVRE 3-8-9 W Newnes (4) *trkd ldrs, rdn o'r 5 fs out, one pace*......(14 to 1 op 12 to 1 tchd 16 to 1) 5

2464[3] CYRUS THE BOLD (Ire) 3-8-9 S Raymont (2) *in tch, rdn o'r 4 fs out, sn btn*......... (9 to 1 op 8 to 1 tchd 10 to 1) 6

3012 AWAY GIRL 3-8-4 B Rouse (9) *nvr able to chal.* .... (14 to 1 op 50 to 1) 7

3173 SIANISKI 4-9-2 J Williams (1) *al beh.* ....(50 to 1 tchd 66 to 1) 8

3012 DAJAM 3-8-0[1] (5*) Stephen Davies (6) *led aftr one furlong to 6 out, sn wknd, tld off*.......... (66 to 1 op 50 to 1) 9

3292[8] BAYFAN (Ire) (bl) 3-8-2 (7*) Mark Denaro (10) *al beh, tld off.* ....(66 to 1 tchd 100 to 1) 10

Dist: 3l, 5l, 10l, 8l, 1½l, 8l, 5l, 20l, 1½l. 2m 59.20s. a 1.50s (10 Ran).

SR: 24/13/8/-/-/-/ (Lord Derby), J H M Gosden

3450 Netton Handicap Class D (0-80 3-y-o and up) £4,175 6f 212yds........(8:10)

3261[2] LORD ALFIE [48] 4-7-10 N Carlisle (1) *hld up beh, hdwy frm 2 fs out to ld ins last, ran on....* (10 to 1 op 8 to 1) 1

3257[2] TROOPING (Ire) [71] (bl) 4-9-5 W Carson (10) *al hndy, led jst ins fnl furlong, sn hdd, ran on...* (3 to 1 fav op 5 to 1) 2

2989* GRAND VITESSE (Ire) [70] 4-8-11 (7*) D Gibbs (8) *prmnt, led o'r one furlong out till jst ins last, not quicken.* ....(7 to 1 op 6 to 1) 3

3261 SIR OLIVER (Ire) [54] 4-8-2 A McGlone (9) *chsd ldrs, rdn and hmpd 2 fs out, kpt on ins last.* .... (20 to 1 op 16 to 1 tchd 25 to 1) 4

2869[8] SINGERS IMAGE [56] 4-8-4 J Williams (2) *last early, rdn and hdwy on outsd o'r 2 fs out, kpt on.* ....(14 to 1 tchd 12 to 1) 5

2410[3] FRIENDLY BRAVE (USA) [73] 3-9-2 L Dettori (11) *beh, swtchd and hdwy 2 fs out, kpt on ins last.* .... (14 to 1 op 12 to 1) 6

3261* COURT MINSTREL [61] 4-8-9 (6ex) J Reid (12) *hld up midfield, hdwy frm 2 fs out, swtchd rght ins last, nvr nrr.* .... (7 to 1 op 6 to 1 tchd 15 to 2) 7

3177 YOURS BY RIGHT [80] (v) 3-9-4 (5*) Stephen Davies (16) *wth ldr, wknd o'r one furlong out, eased whn btn.* .... (20 to 1 op 16 to 1) 8

3017[4] MY BEST VALENTINE [80] 3-9-9 F Norton (5) *beh, came wide and effrt wl o'r one furlong out, nvr trble ldrs.* .... (14 to 1 op 16 to 1) 9

3169[2] CHARMED KNAVE [70] 8-9-4 T Williams (17) *led till o'r one furlong out, sn wknd, eased whn btn.* ....(14 to 1 op 10 to 1 tchd 16 to 1) 10

3099[4] BLUE TOPAZE [76] 5-9-10 M Wigham (4) *nvr nr to chal.* .... (14 to 1 op 12 to 1 tchd 16 to 1) 11

2928[7] HALLORINA [63] 3-8-6 G Bardwell (13) *chsd ldrs, rdn and wknd wl o'r one furlong out*.......(25 to 1 op 20 to 1) 12

2715 TOP PET (Ire) [73] 3-8-9 (7*) L Carter (15) *chsd ldrs, lost pl fnl 2 fs*...........................(14 to 1 op 12 to 1) 13

3168 RAINBOW FLEET [53] 5-8-1 S Dawson (14) *mid-div, not clr run o'r 2 fs out, sn btn.* ....(40 to 1 op 33 to 1 tchd 50 to 1) 14

3261[4] SURREY RACING [62] 5-8-10 B Rouse (7) *prmnt, rdn alng and wkng whn hmpd 2 fs out*......(10 to 1 op 8 to 1) 15

2976* CITY ROCKET [75] 3-9-4 D Holland (6) *in tch, wknd o'r 2 fs out*.................................. (14 to 1 op 10 to 1) 16

3080[5] FEATHER FACE [78] 3-9-7 W Newnes (3) *chsd alng in midfield, lost pl hfwy*...........(20 to 1 tchd 25 to 1) 17

Dist: Nk, 2l, ¾l, sht-hd, sht-hd, sht-hd, 3½l, 4l, 1l, nk. 1m 26.98s. a 1.38s (17 Ran).

SR: 19/41/34/16/17/28/20/23/11/ (K C Gomm), B J Meehan

TIPPERARY (IRE) (good)
Thursday August 19th

3451 Stonepark E.B.F. Fillies Maiden (Div I) (2-y-o) £3,797 7f................(5:15)

3039² MISS KRISTIN (Ire) 9-0 K J Manning (4)........(5 to 4 on) 1
ZING PING (Ire) 9-0 S Craine (5)..................(10 to 1) 2
2742³ SARANGA (Ire) 9-0 J P Murtagh (9)...............(7 to 1) 3
3203³ DANCING AT LUNASA (Ire) 9-0 W J Supple (10)....(5 to 1) 4
3071² ALJAWZA (USA) (bl) 9-0 M J Kinane (6)............(7 to 2) 5
3071 DREAMS OF SUMMER (Ire) 9-0 J F Egan (2)......(16 to 1) 6
1442⁸ CAPATINA (Ire) 9-0 B Coogan (7)..................(12 to 1) 7
EVICTRESS (Ire) 8-10 (4*) J J Behan (11)..........(10 to 1) 8
3071 FAYR DILLY (Ire) 8-8 (6*) R V Skelly (12).........(20 to 1) 9
HELLS BELLS (Ire) 8-8 (6*) B J Walsh (1)..........(20 to 1) 10
3071 MONTEGO BAY (Ire) 9-0 P Shanahan (3)...........(14 to 1) 11
Dist: Hd, 5½l, 1l, 1l. 1m 37.50s. (11 Ran).
(Mrs Kristin Cherry Renfroe), J S Bolger

3452 Moanmore Race (3-y-o and up) £2,762 7f..............................(5:45)

3072² MILLIE'S CHOICE (Ire) 4-9-7 W J Supple (4)....(5 to 4 on) 1
2779* DOREG (Ire) 3-9-5 J P Murtagh (1)..................(2 to 1) 2
2779⁵ COMMON BOND (Ire) 3-8-12 S Craine (7).........(16 to 1) 3
3334⁶ RONDELLI (Ire) 3-9-1 K J Manning (3)...............(11 to 2) 4
BALLYTIGUE LORD 7-8-12 (8*) B Fenton (5).......(33 to 1) 5
3075 SOUNDPROOF (Ire) 3-8-10 (4*) J J Behan (6).....(11 to 1) 6
Dist: ¾l, 8l, 2l, ½l. 1m 39.80s. (6 Ran).
(Colm McEvoy), Kevin Prendergast

3453 Stonepark E.B.F. Fillies Maiden (Div II) (2-y-o) £3,797 7f............. (6:15)

3071³ RAZIDA (Ire) 9-0 K J Manning (6)....................(9 to 2) 1
3243⁹ GO MILLIE (Ire) 9-0 W J Supple (2)...................(8 to 1) 2
MARKET SLIDE (USA) 9-0 M J Kinane (8)...... (7 to 4 on) 3
3071⁹ SENDER VICTORIOUS (Ire) 8-10 (4*) J J Behan (1) (10 to 1) 4
BETTER STYLE (Ire) 9-0 J P Murtagh (7)...........(14 to 1) 5
FAIRY MUSIC (Ire) 8-12 (2*) P Carberry (9).........(12 to 1) 6
SAVE THE WEST (Ire) 9-0 J F Egan (4)............(20 to 1) 7
2745⁷ DACANI STAR (Ire) 9-0 P Shanahan (10)...........(20 to 1) 8
2742 LADY SAPIEN (Ire) 8-10 (4*) W J Smith (11).......(33 to 1) 9
PORT QUEEN (Ire) 9-0 S Craine (5)..................(20 to 1) 10
GREAC 8-12 (2*) D G O'Shea (3)...................(10 to 1) 11
Dist: ¾l, sht-hd, 5l, ¾l. 1m 38.80s. (11 Ran).
(D H W Dobson), J S Bolger

3454 Sportsmans Handicap (0-75 3-y-o and up) £2,762 1m 1f................ (6:45)

2041³ TINERANA (Ire) [-] 3-9-5 M J Kinane (2)........ (10 to 9 on) 1
3327² AULD STOCK (Ire) [-] 3-9-2 (6*) J R Barry (4).......(7 to 1) 2
3202³ LOVELY ALI (Ire) [-] (bl) 4-9-5 K J Manning (8)......(4 to 1) 3
2782² RAIN RITE (Ire) [-] 4-10-0 S Craine (6)..............(9 to 1) 4
3294 ALDENA (Ire) [-] 3-7-5 (2*) D G O'Shea (7)........(25 to 1) 5
3298⁴ VOUVRAY (Ire) [-] 3-8-1 Joanna Morgan (1)........(20 to 1) 6
3294⁵ VISTAGE (Ire) [-] 5-9-5 J P Murtagh (5).............(7 to 1) 7
3294 VLADIMIR'S WAY (Ire) [-] (bl) 4-9-5 W J Supple (9) (12 to 1) 8
2923⁷ MISS MAYTHORN (Ire) [-] 3-9-1 J F Egan (10).....(20 to 1) 9
Dist: 1½l, nk, 2l, 1l. 2m 0.30s. (9 Ran).
(Dr Paschal Carmody), E J O'Grady

3455 Slievenamon Maiden (3-y-o and up) £2,762 5f...................... (7:15)

2843⁸ MOONLIGHT PARTNER (Ire) 3-8-11 W J Supple (7) (7 to 2) 1
3300² NORDIC QUEEN (Ire) 3-8-11 K J Manning (5)........(4 to 1) 2
3330³ BENE MERENTI (Ire) (bl) 3-8-8 (6*) R V Skelly (1)....(6 to 1) 3
3161⁵ OROVILLE 3-8-11 S Craine (3)............. (11 to 10 fav) 4
3112⁹ CARRIG STAR (Ire) 4-9-1 (2*) P Carberry (4).........(8 to 1) 5
3330⁸ BLACKTRENCH LADY (Ire) (bl) 5-9-0 J P Murtagh (6) (8 to 1) 6
2556 SHESOMETHINGELSE (Ire) (bl) 3-8-1 (10*) P P O'Grady (2) ....(33 to 1) 7
Dist: 4l, hd, 1½l, 2l. 57.10s. (7 Ran).
(Patrick H Burns), Declan Gillespie

YARMOUTH (good)
Thursday August 19th
Going Correction: MINUS 0.30 sec. per fur. (races 1,6), PLUS 0.20 (2,3,4,5)

3456 John Beckett Maiden Stakes Class D (3-y-o and up) £4,077 1¼m 21yds (2:20)

3012³ DANISH FORT 3-8-12 W Ryan (6) *al hndy, led and quickend o'r 2 fs out, ran on strly*........ (9 to 4 op 6 to 4) 1
PERFECT VINTAGE 3-8-12 Paul Eddery (11) *patiently rdn, improved to chal o'r 2 fs out, not quicken fnl furlong.* ....(6 to 4 on op 5 to 4) 2
MELODY MOUNTAIN (Ire) 4-8-12 (3*) B Doyle (15) *al hndy, ev ch and drvn alng 2 fs out, outpcd ins fnl furlong.* .... (50 to 1 op 20 to 1) 3
3012⁶ CITTERN 3-8-12 A Clark (13) *nvr far away, effrt and drvn alng 2 fs out, styd on*...............(20 to 1 op 10 to 1) 4
2596² MO-ADDAB (Ire) 3-8-12 A McGlone (7) *settled to track ldrs, effrt and drvn alng ove 2 fs out, no extr.* ....(9 to 1 op 6 to 1 tchd 10 to 1) 5
1068⁶ MOULTAZIM (USA) 3-8-12 B Raymond (5) *nvr far away, drvn alng whn pace quickened 2 fs out, no extr.* ....(33 to 1 op 20 to 1) 6
2332 DANCING TRALTHEE (Ire) 3-8-0 (7*) Jo Hunnam (8) *al tracking ldrs, drvn alng whn pace lifted 2 fs out, fdd.* ....(50 to 1 op 20 to 1) 7
1068 SCORPIUS 3-8-12 P D'Arcy (12) *trkd ldrs, effrt on ins and not much room o'r 2 fs out, nvr able to chal.* ....(50 to 1 op 33 to 1) 8
3225 ON THE LEDGE (USA) 3-8-12 S Whitworth (3) *steadied strt, swtchd outsd and steady hdwy o'r 2 fs out, can improve*............................(50 to 1 op 16 to 1) 9
3272 COLIN MUSET 3-8-12 G Hind (10) *al hndy, led o'r 3 fs till over 2 furlongs out, fdd*.......... (50 to 1 op 20 to 1) 10
3225 REMEMBER THIS (Ire) 3-8-12 D Biggs (1) *sluggish strt, chsd alng to keep in tch, nvr dngrs.* ....(50 to 1 op 20 to 1) 11
1617⁸ MUSTAKIM (Ire) 3-8-12 R Price (14) *taken to post early, in tch for o'r 6 fs, fdd*............ (50 to 1 op 16 to 1) 12
3117 ROLLING WATERS 3-8-12 G Duffield (4) *dictated pace till hdd o'r 3 fs out, sn lost tch*........ (50 to 1 op 33 to 1) 13
DINNER AT EIGHT 3-8-12 M Wigham (2) *outpcd and drvn alng, nvr a threat*................(50 to 1 op 20 to 1) 14
LADY CONFESS 3-8-7 N Adams (9) *sluggish strt, al trailing*............................ (50 to 1 op 20 to 1) 15
Dist: 3l, 5l, nk, 1l, 3l, 1l, ¾l, 2l, 3½l, nk. 2m 7.10s. a 3.10s (15 Ran).
SR: 37/31/24/20/18/12/5/8/4/ (Sheikh Mohammed), H R A Cecil

3457 Wellington Pier Median Auction Maiden Stakes Class D (2-y-o) £4,080 6f 3yds........................ (2:50)

3137³ AMIDST 8-9 Paul Eddery (3) *trkd ldr, pld out to chal appr fnl furlong, led last 100 yards, ran on.* ....(3 to 1 op 9 to 4 tchd 100 to 30) 1
3215³ PAONIC (Ire) 8-11 (3*) C Hodgson (1) *edgy at strt, set out to make all, rdn and cauht last 100 yards.* ....(9 to 4 on op 2 to 1 on tchd 7 to 4 on) 2
MAGNETIC REEL 9-0 G Duffield (2) *sluggish strt, ran green thrght, nvr a factor*.......... (7 to 1 op 5 to 1) 3
Dist: 1l, 20l. 1m 15.10s. a 4.10s (3 Ran).
SR: 37/38/-/ (Sir Evelyn de Rothschild), M R Stoute

3458 Holden International Challenge Handicap Class D (0-80 3-y-o and up) £4,235 7f 3yds........................ (3:25)

2882 HOPEFUL BID (Ire) [64] (bl) 4-9-4 G Duffield (4) *chsd alng on ins, improved und pres to ld last 100 yards, hld on wl.* ....(4 to 1 fav) 1
3017 BRAVEBOY [59] 5-8-10 (3*) B Doyle (8) *settled off the pace, steady hdwy on outsd last 2 fs, ran on, jst fld.* (12 to 1) 2
3175³ BILL MOON [52] 7-8-1 (5*) D McCabe (5) *nvr far away, drvn alng o'r 2 fs out, kpt on same pace ins last.* (9 to 2) 3
3261⁸ AMADEUS AES [65] (bl) 4-9-2 (3*) C Hodgson (2) *tried to make all, 4 ls clr hfwy, wknd and ct last 100 yards.* ....(9 to 1 op 8 to 1) 4
2624⁷ LA BAMBA [74] 7-10-0 W Hood (6) *sluggish strt, bustled alng to improve frm off the pace last 2 fs, nvr able to chal*............................(10 to 1) 5
3211 ANNABELLE ROYALE [61] 7-9-1 N Adams (9) *uns rdr gng to post, broke wl to show speed for o'r 4 fs, sn btn.* (10 to 1) 6
1950⁸ PONDICHERRY (USA) [68] 3-9-3 W Woods (11) *sluggish strt, chsd alng to go pace thrght, nvr dngrs.* .... (6 to 1 op 11 to 2) 7
3132³ DESERT CHAMP (USA) [72] 4-9-12 B Raymond (7) *patiently rdn, pushed into midfield hfwy, nvr rch ldrs...* (5 to 1) 8
3070⁴ MISS GORGEOUS (Ire) [74] 3-9-6 (3*) Emma O'Gorman (10) *unruly in stalls, broke wl to chase ldr to hfwy, sn btn.* ....(11 to 2) 9
Dist: Sht-hd, 3l, 1l, ¾l, 6l, 2l, 3½l, 10l. 1m 29.90s. a 6.70s (9 Ran).
SR: 25/19/3/13/20/-/ (N Capon), R Hannon

3459 Bungay Fillies' Handicap Class E (0-70 3-y-o and up) £3,210 6f 3yds ....(4:00)

3099⁵ BEATLE SONG [49] 5-8-13 G Duffield (4) *nvr far away, drvn ahead ins fnl furlong, sn clr.* ....(4 to 1 op 7 to 2 tchd 9 to 2) 1
3229 BELMONT PRINCESS (Ire) [53] 3-8-13 A Clark (1) *al hndy, led o'r 2 fs out til ins fnl furlong, no extr.* .... (20 to 1 op 14 to 1) 2
2788⁵ BREAKFAST BOOGIE [60] 3-9-6 Paul Eddery (11) *al frnt rnk, bustled alng last 2 fs, kpt on same pace.* .... (11 to 2 op 5 to 1) 3
2945² JOIN THE CLAN [60] 4-9-3 (7*) E Husband (2) *jmpd path and lost grnd sn aftr strt, rallied hfwy, rdn and no extr or o'r one furlong out*....... (7 to 2 jt-fav tchd 4 to 1) 4
3270 CUDDLY DATE [50] (v) 3-8-3 (7*) S Eiffert (3) *settled beh ldrs, drvn through on ins last 2 fs, not rch lders.* .... (20 to 1 op 14 to 1) 5

2868^{5} MOVING IMAGE (Ire) [54] 3-9-0 C Dwyer (5) *trkd ldg bunch, drvn alng whn pace lifted 2 fs out, no extr*...(7 to 2 jt-fav op 9 to 2) 6

3305^{9} RUBY COOPER [52] 3-8-12 D Biggs (8) *pressed ldrs, rdn o'r 2 fs out, fdd*.............................(20 to 1) 7

2993^{4} TEE GEE JAY [52] (v) 3-8-12 B Raymond (13) *sluggish strt, steady hdwy whn hng lft o'r 2 fs out, nvr dngrs.* ....(8 to 1 op 5 to 1) 8

2401^{6} WHERE'S THE DANCE [65] (v) 3-9-8 (3*) B Doyle (12) *chsd ldrs for o'r 3 fs, fdd.* (11 to 1 op 10 to 1 tchd 12 to 1) 9

3343^{8} KENNEDYS PRIMA [63] (bl) 3-9-6 (3*) D Harrison (12) *chsd alng to keep up aftr 3 fs, sn btn*.....(10 to 1 op 6 to 1) 10

2940 GUANHUMARA [42] (v) 3-8-2 J Quinn (10) *early speed, drvn alng hfwy, sn btn*.................(20 to 1 op 14 to 1) 11

3247^{8} CAMINO A RONDA [29] 4-7-0 (7*) Antoinette Armes (7) *set gd clip for o'r 3 fs, fdd*...............................(33 to 1) 12

Dist: 4l, ½l, 1l, 2½l, 2½l, 1l, sht-hd, 5l, 1l, 2½l. 1m 15.50s. a 4.50s (12 Ran).

SR: 33/17/22/22/-/-/ (C John Hill), C J Hill

3460 Cromer Limited Stakes Class E (0-60 3-y-o and up) £3,132 1m 3yds... (4:30)

2953* AZOLA (Ire) (v) 3-8-8 M Tebbutt (7) *co'red up on ins, improved und presure to join ldr 2 fs out, styd on grimly to ld inside last*..............(6 to 1 op 9 to 2) 1

3364^{4} SET THE FASHION (v) 4-9-4 (3*) D Harrison (11) *nvr far away, nosed ahead o'r 2 fs out till ins last, kpt on same pace*...............(3 to 1 fav op 4 to 1 tchd 9 to 2) 2

2898* FORMAL AFFAIR 3-8-1 (7*) J D Smith (9) *in tch, pushed up to take clr order o'r 2 fs out, no imprsn appr last.* ....(9 to 2 op 7 to 2 tchd 5 to 1) 3

3269 CAPTAIN MARMALADE 4-9-2 (5*) K Rutter (13) *sluggish strt, improved into midfield hfwy, effrt 2 fs out, one pace*...............................(16 to 1 op 12 to 1) 4

2882 DIVINE BOY 3-8-13 D Biggs (3) *gd speed on outsd for 5 fs, no extr*....................................(6 to 1) 5

3191^{2} SAKURA QUEEN (Ire) 3-8-8 W Woods (8) *al pressing ldrs, effrt and drvn alng 2 fs out, fdd*.... (10 to 1 op 5 to 1) 6

3045^{4} NAHLATI (Ire) 3-8-5 (3*) B Doyle (14) *led aftr one and a half fs till o'r 3 furlongs out, fdd over one out.* ....(10 to 1 op 8 to 1) 7

2938^{7} DON TOCINO 3-8-13 G Hind (5) *wth ldrs, rdn o'r 2 fs out, fdd*..............................(12 to 1 op 7 to 1) 8

2757 LITTLE ROUSILLON 5-9-7 A Clark (4) *pressed ldrs, led o'r 3 fs out till over 2 furlongs out, sn btn.* ....(14 to 1 op 10 to 1) 9

2165^{5} TRIBAT 3-8-5 (3*) C Hodgson (2) *settled midfield, chsd alng o'r 2 fs out, sn btn*...........(25 to 1 op 16 to 1) 10

1588 TOP ONE 8-9-7 G Duffield (10) *led for one and a half fs, styd hndy till fdd o'r 2 furlongs out.* (12 to 1 op 7 to 1) 11

2864^{4} TRUNDLEY WOOD (bl) 3-8-8 Paul Eddery (12) *sluggish strt, nvr able to rch chalg pos*...........(7 to 1 op 6 to 1) 12

1618^{7} GENERAL JOHN (Ire) 4-9-7 Dale Gibson (6) *sluggish strt, niggled alng hfwy, nvr a factor*... (20 to 1 op 14 to 1) 13

Dist: ¾l, 5l, 1½l, ¾l, 3½l, nk, ¾l, hd, hd, 12l. 1m 41.90s. a 6.10s (13 Ran).

SR: 27/38/10/18/8/-/-/-/1/ (E J Loder), D R Loder

3461 Mundesley Maiden Handicap Class F (0-65 3-y-o and up) £2,892 1m 3f 101yds........................ (5:00)

2127 UTRILLO (USA) [40] (v) 4-8-10 B Raymond (5) *tucked away gng wl, quickened ahead appr fnl furlong, sn well clr.* ....(8 to 1 op 12 to 1) 1

3301^{3} RISPOTO [57] 3-9-4 G Duffield (12) *tried to make all, hdd appr fnl furlong, not pace of wnr*...(11 to 1 op 7 to 1) 2

2767^{6} MISTROY [52] 3-8-13 A Clark (2) *nvr far away, ev ch and drvn alng 2 fs out, one pace*....... (20 to 1 op 16 to 1) 3

2948^{3} PLATINUM VENTURE [59] 3-9-6 W Woods (17) *al hndy, drw level und pres 3 fs out, no extr appr fnl furlong.* ....(10 to 1 op 5 to 1) 4

2859^{5} ROSE NOBLE (USA) [54] 3-9-1 M Tebbutt (1) *settled off the pace, steady hdwy last 2 fs, ran on wl.* ....(25 to 1 op 20 to 1) 5

2737^{3} MAGNETIC POINT (USA) [47] 4-9-3 G Hind (13) *trkd ldg pair, drvn alng o'r 2 fs out, sn btn.* ....(10 to 1 op 9 to 1 tchd 12 to 1) 6

3185^{2} EDIREPUS [49] 5-9-5 Dale Gibson (10) *trkd ldg bunch, effrt on outsd o'r 2 fs out, no imprsn.* ....(7 to 1 op 6 to 1 tchd 15 to 2) 7

2576^{4} MATARIS [59] 3-9-6 J Quinn (15) *chsd ldg half dozen, rdn o'r 2 fs out, fdd*.....................(10 to 1 op 6 to 1) 8

3246^{3} BALL GOWN [49] 3-8-10 P D'Arcy (3) *patiently rdn, improved o'r 3 fs out, not pace to chal.* ....(16 to 1 op 12 to 1) 9

FAIRY FREE [58] 4-9-11 (3*) B Doyle (7) *pressed ldg trio, feeling pace o'r 2 fs out, sn btn.* ....(12 to 1 op 20 to 1 tchd 10 to 1) 10

2995^{4} SWEET DISORDER (Ire) [57] 3-9-4 Paul Eddery (8) *settled beh ldg bunch, pushed alng o'r 3 fs out, sn btn.* ....(12 to 1 op 9 to 1) 11

3212^{3} LA MENORQUINA (USA) [61] 3-9-5 (3*) C Hodgson (11) *chsd ldrs to strt, sn btn*... (7 to 2 fav op 5 to 2 tchd 4 to 1) 12

3192^{2} PACIFIC POWER [52] 3-8-10 (3*) Emma O'Gorman (6) *chsd ldrs, rdn o'r 3 fs out, sn btn*........(20 to 1 op 16 to 1) 13

3301^{2} FATHER DAN (Ire) [47] 4-9-3 Gay Kelleway (14) *trkd ldg bunch to strt, fdd o'r 2 fs out.* ....(7 to 1 op 5 to 1 tchd 8 to 1) 14

3106^{6} PRETTY BABY [53] 3-9-0 D Biggs (4) *in tch for o'r 6 fs, sn btn*.............................. (20 to 1 op 14 to 1) 15

3102^{5} STEPPE CLOSER [46] 3-8-4 (3*) D Harrison (18) *trkd ldrs till wknd quickly o'r 2 fs out, tld off*....(12 to 1 op 7 to 1) 16

Dist: 6l, nk, 3l, 1½l, nk, 1l, 1½l, 1l, ½l, nk. 2m 25.80s. a 2.30s (16 Ran).

SR: 40/36/30/31/23/24/24/22/10/ (S J Hammond), B J Curley

YORK (good)
Thursday August 19th
Going Correction: NIL

3462 Moorestyle Convivial Maiden Stakes Class D (2-y-o) £7,505 6f........(2:05)

2994^{3} OWINGTON 9-0 M Hills (7) *prmnt, led appr hfwy, quickened clr entering fnl 2 fs, eased nr finish, unchlgd.* ....(5 to 4 fav op 6 to 4 tchd 13 to 8) 1

PINKERTON'S PAL 9-0 M Birch (10) *dwlt, hdwy hfwy, ran green, swtchd wide wl o'r one furlong out, ran on strly ins last, improve*................(20 to 1 tchd 25 to 1) 2

2909^{2} JAZEEL (USA) 9-0 W Carson (3) *chsd ldrs, rdn alng hfwy, kpt on fnl 2 fs*.......... (4 to 1 op 3 to 1 tchd 9 to 2) 3

NIZAAL (USA) 9-0 R Hills (5) *cl up, rdn o'r 2 fs out, kpt on one pace.* (11 to 1 op 10 to 1 tchd 9 to 1 and 12 to 1) 4

FAWRAN (USA) 9-0 M Roberts (2) *chsd ldrs, rdn o'r 2 fs out, sn one pace*.....................(8 to 1 op 5 to 1) 5

WESTERN GENERAL 9-0 P Robinson (11) *beh, hdwy hfwy, sn rdn, not rch ldrs.* ....(12 to 1 op 16 to 1 tchd 20 to 1) 6

3079^{2} STASH THE CASH (Ire) 9-0 Pat Eddery (4) *led till appr hfwy, sn rdn, wknd 2 fs out.* ....(6 to 1 op 5 to 1 tchd 7 to 1) 7

2990^{6} RISKY TU 8-9 J Carroll (9) *al rear*...............(20 to 1) 8

MIDNIGHT LEGEND 9-0 R Cochrane (8) *al rear.* ....(14 to 1 op 12 to 1) 9

PERTEMPS FLYER 9-0 L Dettori (6) *chsd ldrs, rdn hfwy, wknd*...................................... (25 to 1) 10

COLWAY RAKE 9-0 W R Swinburn (1) *al rear.* ....(20 to 1 op 14 to 1) 11

Dist: 3½l, sht-hd, 2l, 3½l, 5l, 2½l, nk, 1½l, 1½l, 2l. 1m 12.24s. a 2.24s (11 Ran).

SR: 55/41/40/32/18/-/ (Baron G Von Ullmann), G Wragg

3463 Lowther Stakes Class A (Group 2) (2-y-o) £38,518 6f................. (2:35)

2473* VELVET MOON (Ire) 8-11 A Munro (4) *made all, rdn and edgd lft o'r one furlong out, put head in air, kpt on ins last*...............................(10 to 1 op 8 to 1) 1

2960* RISKY 9-0 W R Swinburn (1) *al prmnt, effrt and hdwy 2 fs out, sn rdn and ev ch, hng rght and no extr ins last.* ....(11 to 8 fav op Evens tchd 13 to 8) 2

3156* MEHTHAAF (USA) 8-11 W Carson (5) *chsd ldrs, effrt and rdn o'r 2 fs out, ev ch till not quicken appr last.* ....(9 to 4 op 5 to 2) 3

2790^{4} GREAT DEEDS 8-11 T Quinn (2) *chsd wnr, ev ch and rdn 2 fs out, wknd appr last*...........(10 to 1 tchd 11 to 1) 4

2790^{5} PROPHECY (Ire) 8-11 Pat Eddery (7) *chsd ldrs, effrt and rdn 2 fs out, kpt on one pace*.........(7 to 1 op 6 to 1) 5

3230^{2} SO SEDULOUS (USA) 8-11 M Hills (6) *hld up, hdwy hfwy, sn rdn, no imprsn*.............. (16 to 1 tchd 20 to 1) 6

3104^{3} NICE WELCOME 8-11 L Dettori (3) *in tch, rdn hfwy, sn btn*...(50 to 1) 7

1683^{3} TAMAR'S BRIGADE 8-11 J Reid (8) *speed stands side to hfwy, sn lost pl and beh*........................(33 to 1) 8

2575^{2} I'M YOUR LADY 8-11 J Fortune (9) *sn outpcd, beh and rdn hfwy*.......................................(50 to 1) 9

Dist: 2½l, ½l, 1½l, ½l, ¾l, 5l, 4l, ¾l. 1m 11.82s. a 1.82s (9 Ran).

SR: 61/54/49/43/41/38/18/2/-/ (Fahd Salman), P F I Cole

3464 Keeneland Nunthorpe Stakes Class A (Group 1) (2-y-o and up) £87,583 5f ....(3:10)

2927* LOCHSONG 5-9-3 L Dettori (5) *made all, quickened wl o'r one furlong out, kpt on strly ins last.* ....(10 to 1 op 8 to 1 tchd 12 to 1) 1

2927^{2} PARIS HOUSE 4-9-6 J Carroll (1) *chsd ldrs, effrt and hdwy one and a half fs out, sn rdn, kpt on wl.* ....(4 to 1 op 9 to 2 tchd 5 to 1) 2

3015* COLLEGE CHAPEL 3-9-3 L Piggott (10) *slwly into strd and beh, hdwy hfwy, effrt and rdn o'r one furlong out, hng lft and not quicken ins last.* ....(9 to 4 fav op 2 to 1 tchd 5 to 2) 3

2362^{7} ELBIO (v) 6-9-6 W R Swinburn (3) *dwlt, beh till hdwy 2 fs out, sn rdn, styd on ins last.* .... (6 to 1 op 11 to 2 tchd 13 to 2) 4

2927^{6} BLYTON LAD 7-9-6 S Webster (2) *chsd ldrs, rdn 2 fs out, kpt on ins last*...........................(33 to 1) 5

2927^{3} KEEN HUNTER (USA) 6-9-6 M Roberts (4) *chsd ldrs, rdn alng o'r 2 fs out, sn one pace.* ....(9 to 2 op 7 to 2 tchd 5 to 1) 6

2927 FREDDIE LLOYD (USA) 4-9-6 J Reid (8) *dwlt, sn chasing ldrs, rdn o'r 2 fs out, soon btn.* ....(80 to 1 op 66 to 1 tchd 100 to 1) 7
BOLD N' FLASHY (Can) 4-9-6 A Munro (9) *cl up, rdn hfwy, wknd*........(50 to 1 tchd 33 to 1) 8
1551* SEA GAZER (Ire) 3-9-3 K Darley (6) *cl up to hfwy, sn lost pl.* ....(50 to 1) 9
1406 MILLYANT 3-9-0 W Carson (7) *in tch to hfwy, sn outpcd and beh*........(100 to 1) 10
1807⁷ LYRIC FANTASY (Ire) 3-9-0 Pat Eddery (11) *rear, sn drvn alng, beh hfwy*........(8 to 1 op 7 to 1) 11
Dist: 1½l, ¾l, 1l, nk, 1l, 3½l, ½l, 2½l, 1½l, 1½l. 58.12s. a 0.82s (11 Ran).
SR: 87/84/78/77/76/72/58/56/43/ (J C Smith), I A Balding

3465 Bradford & Bingley Rated Class B Handicap (0-105 3-y-o and up) £21,241 7f 202yds........(3:45)

2794* DAWNING STREET (Ire) [97] 5-8-13 Pat Eddery (2) *trkd ldrs, hdwy o'r 2 fs out, led appr last, rdn clr, kpt on.* ....(6 to 1 op 5 to 1) 1
2926* PHILIDOR [91] 4-8-4 (3*) N Kennedy (5) *mid-div, hdwy on ins 2 fs out, swtchd appr last, ran on strly.* ....(8 to 1 tchd 9 to 1) 2
3158* TESHAMI (USA) [96] 3-8-6 M Roberts (3) *cl up, hdwy to ld o'r 2 fs out, sn rdn, hdd and not quicken appr last.* ....(3 to 1 fav op 11 to 4 tchd 100 to 30) 3
2926 PAY HOMAGE [103] 5-9-5 L Dettori (6) *beh, hdwy on outsd o'r 2 fs out, sn rdn, kpt on ins last*........(20 to 1) 4
2794⁴ RIBHI (USA) [96] 3-8-6 W Carson (7) *hdwy 3 fs out, effrt and rdn 2 out, one pace appr last.* ....(8 to 1 op 7 to 1 tchd 9 to 1) 5
2376³ ST NINIAN [101] 7-9-3 M Birch (1) *led, rdn 3 fs out, sn hdd, wknd appr last*........(16 to 1) 6
2926² LOST SOLDIER (USA) [102] 3-8-12 R Cochrane (11) *chsd ldrs, rdn 2 fs out, kpt on one pace.* (6 to 1 tchd 13 to 2) 7
2211⁵ ROYAL SEATON [91] 4-8-7 J Carroll (15) *beh, hdwy on ins o'r 2 fs out, sn rdn, styd on inside last, nvr dngrs.* ....(16 to 1) 8
2060⁸ TAUFAN BLU (Ire) [97] (bl) 4-8-13 J Fortune (14) *cl up, rdn and ev ch o'r 2 fs out, sn wknd*........(33 to 1) 9
3199* APPROACH THE BENCH (Ire) [110] 5-9-12 (3ex) J Reid (10) *nvr rch ldrs*........(25 to 1 op 16 to 1) 10
2794 BAND ON THE RUN [91] 6-8-7 T Quinn (4) *chsd ldrs, rdn 3 fs out, wknd*........(25 to 1) 11
2885⁵ MYSTIC GODDESS (USA) [94] 3-8-4 A Munro (9) *hld up beh, some hdwy 3 fs out, sn wknd*........(20 to 1) 12
2853⁶ TIK FA (USA) [104] (bl) 4-9-6 W R Swinburn (8) *in tch, rdn 3 fs out, sn wknd*........(20 to 1) 13
2793⁶ LITTLE BEAN [100] (v) 4-9-2 M Hills (12) *in tch, rdn o'r 3 fs out, sn wknd*........(12 to 1 tchd 14 to 1) 14
2254³ GYMCRAK PREMIERE [100] 5-9-2 K Darley (13) *beh, some hdwy on outsd 3 fs out, sn rdn and btn.* ....(10 to 1 tchd 12 to 1) 15
Dist: 3½l, ½l, hd, ¾l, nk, 1½l, 1½l, ¾l, 1½l, 6l. 1m 38.09s. a 1.79s (15 Ran).
SR: 72/55/52/64/49/59/49/39/43/ (Windflower Overseas Holdings Inc), J L Dunlop

3466 Ladbroke Knavesmire Handicap Class C (0-95 3-y-o and up) £12,817 1m 3f 195yds........(4:15)

2884⁶ YILDIZ [70] 4-9-0 W Carson (4) *led 2 fs, cl up, chlgd o'r two out, rdn to ld appr last, ran on*........(12 to 1) 1
3121* ROBERTY LEA [69] 5-8-13 T Quinn (17) *cl up, led aftr 2 fs, rdn o'r two, hdd appr last, kpt on wl und pres.* ....(14 to 1 op 10 to 1 tchd 16 to 1) 2
2433⁹ HIGHBROOK (USA) [84] 5-10-0 P Robinson (7) *mid-div, hdwy 3 fs out, effrt 2 out, sn rdn, kpt on ins last.* ....(14 to 1 op 10 to 1 tchd 16 to 1) 3
2696² LATVIAN [72] 6-9-2 N Connorton (21) *chsd ldrs, effrt 3 fs out, rdn 2 out, kpt on one pace.* (20 to 1 tchd 25 to 1) 4
3152* CUMBRIAN RHAPSODY [76] 3-8-7 (3*) S Maloney (12) *mid-div, hdwy 3 fs out, rdn 2 out, styd on, not rch ldrs.* ....(12 to 1 op 10 to 1) 5
2795* WHITECHAPEL (USA) [79] 5-9-9 A Munro (11) *hld up, not clr run o'r 5 fs out, hdwy on outsd 3 out, sn rdn, kpt on, not rch ldrs*........(7 to 1 fav op 8 to 1) 6
2395² AMBIGUOUSLY REGAL (USA) [78] 4-9-8 L Piggott (5) *slwly into strd and beh, hdwy 3 fs out, sn rdn, kpt on one pace*........(16 to 1 op 14 to 1) 7
2936² AEGAEN LADY [60] 4-8-4 J Carroll (1) *beh, hdwy on ins 4 fs out, not much room 2 out, kpt on und pres.* ....(50 to 1 op 33 to 1) 8
2433⁵ REDSTELLA (USA) [83] 4-9-13 J Reid (10) *beh, some hdwy o'r 3 fs out, nvr dngrs*........(25 to 1) 9
3067⁵ CRYSTAL CROSS (USA) [83] 4-9-13 L Dettori (15) *chsd ldrs, rdn 3 fs out, grad wknd*........(20 to 1) 10
3121³ MUCH SOUGHT AFTER [82] 4-9-12 R Hills (9) *chsd ldrs, rdn o'r 3 fs out, sn wknd*........(20 to 1 op 16 to 1) 11
3307 BIGWHEEL BILL (Ire) [62] 4-8-6 M Birch (18) *chsd ldrs on outsd, rdn 3 fs out, wknd 2 out*.... (25 to 1 op 20 to 1) 12
3179* ARKAAN (USA) [83] 3-9-3 W R Swinburn (2) *mid-div, hdwy on outsd 3 fs out, sn rdn, edgd lft and wknd 2 out.* ....(11 to 1 op 12 to 1 tchd 10 to 1) 13
3353² CHATHAM ISLAND [70] 5-9-0 J Fortune (16) *prmnt till rdn and wknd o'r 3 fs out*........(20 to 1 op 14 to 1) 14
2758* MOSCOW SEA (USA) [87] 3-9-7 M Roberts (19) *cl up, chsd ldr hfwy till rdn 3 fs out, sn wknd*... (9 to 1 op 8 to 1) 15
3018* MOSHAAJIR (USA) [73] 3-8-4 (3*) N Kennedy (8) *al rear.* ....(25 to 1 op 16 to 1) 16
2997⁶ DRUMMER HICKS [80] 4-9-10 Pat Eddery (3) *in tch on ins, rdn o'r 3 fs out, sn wknd*........(14 to 1 op 10 to 1) 17
3128* AZUREUS (Ire) [78] 5-9-3 (5*) Darren Moffatt (6) *al beh and rdn alng*........(33 to 1 op 20 to 1) 18
2963⁷ BLUE BLAZER [81] 3-9-1 M Hills (22) *slwly into strd, al rear*........(25 to 1 op 16 to 1) 19
2632⁵ BLUE LAWS (Ire) [70] 3-8-4 S Wood (14) *al rear.* ....(14 to 1 tchd 16 to 1) 20
3045* DRAGON'S TEETH (Ire) [82] 3-9-2 R Cochrane (20) *nvr a factor*........(10 to 1 op 8 to 1) 21
2204⁴ WHITE WILLOW [73] 4-9-3 K Darley (13) *al beh*... (12 to 1) 22
Dist: 2l, 1l, 3½l, ¾l, 1½l, 2½l, 2l, 4l, sht-hd, hd. 2m 32.05s. a 4.05s (22 Ran).
SR: 59/54/67/48/40/50/44/22/37/ (S Mino), B W Hills

3467 Galtres Stakes Class A (Listed Race) (3-y-o and up) £14,750 1m 3f 195yds........(4:45)

3173* KITHANGA (Ire) 3-8-8 R Cochrane (2) *hld up, hdwy o'r 3 fs out, led 2 out, sn rdn, ran on wl und pres ins last.* ....(13 to 8 fav op 7 to 4 tchd 15 to 8) 1
3163* ALOUETTE 3-8-8 C Roche (3) *trkd ldrs, rdn and outpcd 3 fs out, styd on und pres ins last.* ....(5 to 1 op 9 to 2 tchd 11 to 2) 2
2925⁴ ANNE BONNY 4-9-4 W R Swinburn (1) *trkd ldr, chlgd 3 fs out, ev ch till rdn and one pace o'r one out.* ....(7 to 1 op 6 to 1) 3
2962⁴ ANNA OF SAXONY 4-9-4 W Carson (7) *hld up, hdwy 3 fs out, sn rdn, kpt on one pace fnl 2 furlongs.* ....(4 to 1 op 3 to 1 tchd 9 to 2) 4
2238⁸ IVIZA (Ire) 3-8-8 M Roberts (6) *hld up, hdwy on outsd 3 fs out, ev ch 2 out, sn rdn and btn*...(11 to 2 tchd 6 to 1) 5
3096* MEAVY 3-8-8 T Quinn (4) *led, rdn o'r 3 fs out, hdd and wknd 2 out*........(25 to 1 op 20 to 1) 6
2963⁵ ALINOVA (USA) 3-8-8 W Ryan (5) *prmnt, rdn o'r 3 fs out, sn btn*........(8 to 1 op 6 to 1) 7
Dist: 3l, 2½l, ½l, 4l, 2l, sht-hd. 2m 33.14s. a 5.14s (7 Ran).
SR: 43/37/42/41/23/19/18/ (Fittocks Stud Limited), L M Cumani

3468 City Of York Stakes Class A (Listed Race) (3-y-o and up) £11,745 6f 214yds........(5:15)

2905⁸ TINNERS WAY (USA) 3-8-9 Pat Eddery (9) *slwly away, hdwy hfwy, squeezed through o'r 2 fs out, styd on wl to ld ins last, ran on*... (7 to 2 fav op 5 to 2 tchd 4 to 1) 1
3315⁵ ARDKINGLASS 3-9-3 W Ryan (5) *chsd ldrs, swtchd outsd and effrt 2 fs out, rdn to chal ins last, kpt on.* ....(6 to 1 op 5 to 1 tchd 13 to 2) 2
3177* EN ATTENDANT (Fr) 5-9-0 L Piggott (3) *hld up, hdwy on ins hfwy, led o'r 2 fs out, rdn appr one out, hdd and no extr inside last*........(9 to 2 tchd 5 to 1) 3
2789 THOUSLA ROCK (Ire) 4-9-0 J Reid (8) *prmnt, ev ch 2 fs out, sn rdn, wknd appr last*........(11 to 2 tchd 6 to 1) 4
2572³ HUMAM (Ire) 3-9-0 R Hills (6) *cl up, led aftr 2 fs, rdn and hdd o'r two out, wknd appr last*...(11 to 1 op 10 to 1) 5
2987⁵ VENTURE CAPITALIST (bl) 4-9-0 K Darley (11) *slwly into strd, beh till hdwy 3 fs out, styd on frm 2 out, nvr dngrs.* ....(16 to 1 op 25 to 1) 6
2985⁴ FITZCARRALDO (USA) 3-8-9 M Roberts (10) *chsd ldrs, rdn o'r 2 fs out, sn wknd.* (11 to 1 op 10 to 1 tchd 12 to 1) 7
2861⁷ ROSE FLYER (Ire) 3-8-4 P Robinson (1) *led 2 fs, wkng whn hmpd o'r two out, beh when hng lft over one out.* ....(100 to 1) 8
FRAAM 4-9-0 W R Swinburn (7) *cl up, effrt and riden o'r 2 fs out, sn wknd*........(25 to 1 tchd 33 to 1) 9
2853³ YOUNG SENOR (USA) (bl) 4-9-0 M Hills (2) *slwly away, hdwy on ins and rdn whn not clr run o'r 2 fs out, btn when hmpd over one out*........(5 to 1 tchd 11 to 2) 10
3023* BRANSTON ABBY (Ire) 4-9-0 T Quinn (4) *chsd ldrs, rdn aftr 2 fs, wknd hfwy, sn beh*........(10 to 1 op 8 to 1) 11
Dist: ¾l, 1l, 4l, nk, 3l, 4l, 2l, 2l, 6l, 25l. 1m 24.89s. a 3.19s (11 Ran).
SR: 47/53/47/35/34/25/8/-/1/ (K Abdulla), J H M Gosden

CHESTER (good to soft)
Friday August 20th
Going Correction: MINUS 0.10 sec. per fur.

3469 Wirral Apprentice Handicap Class E (0-70 3-y-o and up) £2,974 1¼m 75yds........(2:30)

3232² HEART OF SPAIN [58] 3-9-1 D Griffiths (4) *nvr far away, drvn ahead o'r one furlong out, styd on wl.* ....(15 to 2 op 7 to 1 tchd 8 to 1) 1
3308⁴ NO COMEBACKS [53] 5-9-1 (3*) S Knott (7) *steadied strt, weaved through frm last pl 2 fs out, put head in air, not run on*........(8 to 1 tchd 9 to 1) 2
3157⁴ WITHOUT A FLAG (USA) [56] 3-8-10 (3*) S James (8) *trkd ldg bunch, drvn through on ins 2 fs out, unbalanced inside last, one pace*........(8 to 1 op 7 to 1 tchd 9 to 1) 3

3043³ TAUNTING (Ire) [47] 5-8-12 S McCarthy (5) *al hndy, ev ch and drvn alng o'r 2 fs out, not quicken.* ....(6 to 1 op 5 to 1) 4
2641⁷ BEND SABLE (Ire) [62] 3-8-11 (8*) J Gracey (10) *nvr far away, ev ch and rdn 2 fs out, sn outpcd.* ....(14 to 1 op 10 to 1) 5
3307* GREEN'S CASSATT (USA) [52] 5-9-3 (7ex) J Dennis (9) *patiently rdn, weaved through frm midfield last 2 fs, nvr nrr*........(5 to 1 fav op 9 to 2) 6
3408⁸ MASTER OF THE HOUSE [48] 7-8-13 C Adamson (3) *trkd ldr gng wl, led on bit o'r 2 fs out, hdd over one furlong out, not run on*........(10 to 1) 7
2970⁵ AFFA [46] (v) 4-8-11 J O'Dwyer (1) *tucked away on ins, not much room bend aftr 2 and a half fs, rdn and btn o'r 3 furlongs out*........(11 to 2 op 5 to 1) 8
2920³ DIAMOND IN THE DARK (USA) [49] (v) 5-8-9 (5*) F Savage (6) *struggling to keep up hfwy, nvr rch chalg pos.* ....(20 to 1 op 16 to 1) 9
885 STOPROVERITATE [59] 4-9-10 L Aspell (12) *in tch, rdn o'r 5 fs out, sn btn*........(17 to 2 op 8 to 1 tchd 9 to 1) 10
2384 MUMMYS ROCKET [36] 4-7-7 (8*) W Hawksley (11) *struggling to keep up hfwy, nvr a factor.* ....(16 to 1 op 20 to 1 tchd 14 to 1) 11
3307⁸ DON'T FORGET MARIE (Ire) [56] (bl) 3-8-5 (8*) Angela Gallimore (2) *dictated pace, clr hfwy, hdd and wknd quickly o'r 2 fs out*........(14 to 1) 12

Dist: 1l, 1½l, 5l, hd, 1½l, 4l, 3l, 1½l, hd, 2½l. 2m 16.38s. a 7.28s (12 Ran).
SR: 18/19/11/-/6/1/ (F A Jackson), P J Bevan

3470 EBF Grey Friars Maiden Stakes Class D (2-y-o) £4,792 7f 2yds........(3:00)

2968 KING CURAN (USA) 9-0 G Duffield (7) *chsd ldg pair, drvn alng to go pace, improved hfwy, styd on grimly to ld wl ins fnl furlong.* (100 to 30 jt-fav op 5 to 1 tchd 3 to 1) 1
2968 RAGSAT AL OMOR (Ire) 9-0 P Robinson (6) *nvr far away, drvn alng last 2 fs, kpt on wl towards finish.* ....(10 to 1 op 8 to 1 tchd 12 to 1) 2
2571² JAREEF'S WAY (Ire) 9-0 K Darley (12) *set str pace, tried to make all, wknd and hdd wl ins fnl furlong.* ....(100 to 30 jt-fav op 2 to 1 tchd 7 to 2) 3
3031⁵ BEECHFIELD FLYER 9-0 J Carroll (10) *chsd ldg quartet, feeling pace and drvn alng 3 fs out, no imprsn.* ....(33 to 1 tchd 25 to 1) 4
1790⁶ ALJATHAAB (USA) 9-0 G Hind (11) *sluggish strt, improved into midfield hfwy, styd on, nvr able to chal.* ....(7 to 1 op 4 to 1) 5
SUPREME STAR (USA) 9-0 A McGlone (2) *settled midfield, pushed alng to keep up hfwy, no imprsn last 2 fs.* ....(15 to 2 op 5 to 1 tchd 8 to 1) 6
2571 PERSONAL PRIDE (Ire) 9-0 A Munro (5) *chsd alng in midfield, not pace to rch ldg bunch*... (16 to 1 op 14 to 1) 7
1497 ALTOBY 9-0 J Weaver (4) *sluggish strt, improved on outsd hfwy, kpt on, nvr able to chal*.....(50 to 1 op 33 to 1) 8
3362⁵ WINN'S PRIDE (Ire) 9-0 S Perks (1) *chsd ldg bunch, drvn alng hfwy, not pace to chal*........(20 to 1) 9
2299⁷ COURT JESTER 9-0 D Holland (3) *trkd ldg bunch, rdn hfwy, sn outpcd*........(20 to 1 op 16 to 1) 10
3377⁷ HESFINMENTALTOO 9-0 A Mackay (14) *swrvd rght and lost many ls strt, nvr able to reco'r.* (50 to 1 op 33 to 1) 11
2875² WAZIN (USA) 9-0 R Hills (9) *chsd ldr, rdn hfwy, btn o'r 2 fs out*........(6 to 1 op 4 to 1) 12
3218³ SANDMOOR CHAMBRAY 9-0 M Birch (8) *in tch for o'r 4 fs, grad wknd*........(25 to 1 op 16 to 1) 13
1949 MIAMI HURRICANE (Ire) 9-0 B Raymond (13) *sluggish strt, nvr a factor*........(20 to 1) 14

Dist: ½l, 2l, 3½l, 7l, ¾l, 2l, 2l, hd, 5l, nk. 1m 29.85s. a 4.45s (14 Ran).
SR: 23/21/15/4/-/-/ (Billy Maguire), M Bell

3471 Kidsons Impey Bonus Series Final Handicap Class C (0-100 3-y-o and up) £8,805 7f 2yds................ (3:30)

3177⁹ CORALS DREAM (Ire) [80] 4-9-9 W Woods (5) *al hndy, brght wide strt, ran on grimly to ld last 50 yards.* ....(10 to 1 op 9 to 1 tchd 12 to 1) 1
3004⁵ THORNTON GATE [72] 4-8-12 (3*) S Maloney (10) *al hndy, led aftr 2 fs till o'r two furlongs out, rallied ins last.* ....(6 to 1 op 11 to 2) 2
3155⁴ MARINE DIVER [70] 7-8-13 S Whitworth (8) *al wl plcd, led o'r 2 fs out, kpt to the inner entering strt, wknd and hdd last 50 yards*........(9 to 1 op 7 to 1) 3
2966² NOBBY BARNES [63] 4-8-6 D Holland (7) *nvr far away, drvn alng last 2 fs, kpt on same pace*........(5 to 1 jt-fav op 9 to 2) 4
3148⁴ DOKKHA OYSTON (Ire) [77] 5-9-6 J Carroll (4) *chsd alng in midfield, styd on last 2 fs, nvr nrr*....(8 to 1 op 7 to 1) 5
3155⁶ HIGHLAND MAGIC (Ire) [81] 5-9-10 C Rutter (1) *patiently rdn, improved o'r 2 fs, kpt on, nvr able to chal.* ....(11 to 2 op 5 to 1 tchd 6 to 1) 6
3177 VELOCE (Ire) [79] 5-9-8 A Mackay (3) *drvn alng in midfield, nvr able to rch chalg pos*........(6 to 1 op 7 to 1) 7
3177 TAJDIF (USA) [82] 3-9-6 R Hills (9) *bustled alng in midfield, effrt on outsd hfwy, edgd rght, no imprsn.* ....(7 to 1 op 6 to 1 tchd 8 to 1) 8
3190* TYRIAN PURPLE (Ire) [61] (bl) 5-8-1 (3*) D Harrison (6) *led for 2 fs, wknd rpdly hfwy, tld off.* (5 to 1 jt-fav op 4 to 1) 9

Dist: 1l, 1l, 2½l, 1½l, 1½l, hd, 3l. 1m 27.85s. a 2.45s (9 Ran).
SR: 61/50/45/30/39/38/35/24/-/ (Mrs C Hamson), C F Wall

3472 Combermere Fillies' Conditions Stakes Class C (2-y-o) £4,476 6f 18yds ....(4:00)

2996⁵ BELLA PARKES 8-10 J Carroll (1) *made all, quickened up to go clr entering fnl furlong, cmftbly.* ....(4 to 1 tchd 5 to 1) 1
3309* INDIAHRA 8-8 S Perks (3) *trkd wnr, rdn o'r one furlong out, no extr*........(3 to 1 tchd 7 to 2 and 11 to 4) 2
2996⁴ STAR SPEEDER (Ire) 8-5 (5*) D Wright (2) *nvr far away, effrt and drvn alng 2 fs out, kpt on same pace.* ....(7 to 4 fav op 13 to 8 tchd 2 to 1) 3
2618⁴ WELSH MIST 8-8 W Woods (4) *nvr far away, ev ch o'r 2 fs out, fdd appr fnl furlong.* ....(5 to 2 op 2 to 1 tchd 11 to 4) 4

Dist: 3l, sht-hd, 8l. 1m 16.82s. a 3.32s (4 Ran).
SR: 18/4/5/-/ (Joseph Heler), J Berry

3473 Black Friars Handicap Class D (0-80 3-y-o and up) £5,504 1m 7f 195yds ....(4:30)

2662³ WELSHMAN [57] 7-8-5 J Quinn (10) *al hndy, led 5 fs out, hrd pressed fnl furlong, hld on wl*... (9 to 1 op 7 to 1) 1
2467² AUDE LA BELLE (Fr) [61] 5-8-9 A McGlone (11) *wtd wth, dashed up to join issue appr strt, styd on wl fnl furlong*........(14 to 1 tchd 16 to 1) 2
2904* AAHSAYLAD [80] (bl) 7-10-0 G Duffield (2) *sluggish strt, chsd alng to improve frm off the pace last 3 fs, fnshd wl.* ....(15 to 2 op 6 to 1 tchd 8 to 1) 3
3125 OUR AISLING [70] 5-9-1 (3*) O Pears (3) *patiently rdn, improved gng wl entering strt, steadied ins fnl furlong, fnshd well*........(6 to 1 op 5 to 1) 4
3152⁷ PHILGUN [60] 4-8-5 (3*) S Maloney (6) *nvr far away, ev ch and drvn alng o'r 2 fs out, kpt on same pace.* ....(14 to 1 op 16 to 1) 5
3255⁶ CONTINUITY [61] 4-8-9 J Weaver (12) *chsd alng in midfield, effrt o'r 3 fs out, not pace to chal.* ....(12 to 1 tchd 14 to 1) 6
3231⁵ HUNTING GROUND [54] (bl) 5-8-2 A Mackay (7) *trkd ldg bunch, effrt and bustled alng o'r 3 fs out, fdd.* ....(10 to 1 op 8 to 1) 7
2166² KAYARTIS [48] 4-7-10 J Lowe (14) *settled midfield, effrt and drvn alng o'r 4 fs out, wknd entering strt.* ....(11 to 2 fav op 5 to 1 tchd 6 to 1) 8
3231⁶ FRENCH IVY (USA) [72] 6-9-6 D Holland (9) *wth ldrs till fdd appr strt*........(14 to 1) 9
3092* CIVIL LAW (Ire) [68] 3-7-11 (5*) A Garth (15) *settled off the pace, effrt hfwy, nvr able to chal.* (11 to 1 op 10 to 1) 10
3106* IMPECCABLE TASTE [62] 3-7-10 D Biggs (1) *tucked away on ins, struggling to hold pl whn badly baulked and snatched up o'r 2 fs out*........(11 to 1 op 10 to 1) 11
924 TEL E THON [45] (bl) 6-7-0 (7*) Antoinette Armes (8) *led till hdd and wknd quickly 5 fs out*........(50 to 1) 12
3125² ROSINA MAE [77] 4-9-11 A Munro (13) *trkd ldg half dozen, feeling pace and lost grnd o'r 4 fs out, sn btn.* ....(13 to 2 op 6 to 1 tchd 7 to 1) 13
3193³ ABALENE [49] 4-7-6 (5*) D Wright (5) *chsd ldrs for o'r a m, sn lost tch*........(14 to 1 op 12 to 1) 14
1155⁵ MY CHIARA [63] 7-8-11 B Crossley (4) *trkd ldrs for a m, sn lost tch*........(16 to 1 tchd 14 to 1) 15

Dist: Hd, 1l, nk, ½l, 10l, 1l, ½l, 1½l, 1l, 5l. 3m 34.21s. a 9.21s (15 Ran).
(Brian Oxton), M Blanshard

3474 Eastgate Rated Class B Handicap (0-95 3-y-o) £6,434 7f 2yds..... (5:00)

3376* PALACEGATE TOUCH [85] (bl) 8-11 (6ex) J Carroll (7) *made all, clr hfwy, shaken up o'r one furlong out, kpt on strly*........(5 to 1 co-fav op 4 to 1 tchd 11 to 2) 1
2987 TRUE PRECISION [85] 8-11 A Munro (9) *chsd alng to improve hfwy, effrt and rdn o'r one furlong out, nopt rch wnr*........(7 to 1 op 6 to 1) 2
3123³ THE SHARP BIDDER (Ire) [81] 8-7 K Darley (4) *beh, drvn alng to improve last 2 fs, nrst finish.* ....(10 to 1 tchd 12 to 1) 3
3312⁴ WINGED VICTORY (Ire) [95] 9-7 G Duffield (5) *missed break, drvn alng to take clr order hfwy, not pace to chal.* ....(13 to 2 op 5 to 1 tchd 7 to 1) 4
2657⁹ SPARK (Ire) [81] 8-4 (3*) S Maloney (6) *struggling to go pace hfwy, nvr a threat*........(14 to 1 op 12 to 1) 5
2572 CARBON STEEL (Ire) [88] 9-0 P Robinson (3) *chsd ldg trio for o'r 4 fs, sn btn*........(12 to 1 op 10 to 1) 6
2928⁹ ARID [81] 8-7 G Hind (10) *drvn alng to go pace, nvr a factor*........(6 to 1) 7
2479⁴ YAQTHAN (Ire) [83] 8-9 R Hills (2) *chsd ldg pair till fdd til pres 2 fs out*........(5 to 1 co-fav op 9 to 2) 8
2746³ HUFFA (USA) [82] 8-5 (3*) D Harrison (8) *chsd wnr for o'r 4 fs, sn btn*.......(5 to 1 co-fav op 9 to 2 tchd 11 to 2) 9

Dist: 3½l, 5l, ¾l, nk, 2½l, ¾l, 2½l, 6l. 1m 29.29s. a 3.89s (9 Ran).
SR: 28/17/-/10/-/-/ (Palacegate Corporation Ltd), J Berry

SANDOWN (good to firm)

Friday August 20th
Going Correction: NIL (races 1,7), MINUS 0.05 (2,3,4,5,6)

3475 Really Useful & Polydor Records Nursery Class D (2-y-o) £4,240 5f 6yds ....(2:00)

3250^{3} BRAVE EDGE [69] 8-9 Pat Eddery (4) *pressed ldrs, quickened to ld o'r one furlong out, pushed clr.* .... (4 to 1 op 11 to 4) 1
2278* TWICE IN BUNDORAN (Ire) [76] 8-11 (5*) L Newton (8) *trkd ldr, led o'r 2 fs out, rdn and hdd over one out, ran on same pace*..............(5 to 1 op 4 to 1 tchd 11 to 2) 2
3210^{2} HARPO'S SPECIAL [56] 7-10 W Carson (9) *bumped strt, hdwy frm rear hfwy, styd on ins fnl furlong.* ....(7 to 2 fav op 9 to 2 tchd 5 to 1) 3
2825^{2} WINDOW DISPLAY [62] 8-2 M Roberts (1) *in tch, swtchd rght and effrt und pres o'r one furlong out, kpt on one pace*..................... (12 to 1 op 8 to 1) 4
3086* ROCKY TWO [66] 8-6 T Quinn (2) *effrt o'r 2 fs out, rdn and no imprsn ins last*.......................... (9 to 1 op 7 to 1) 5
3167^{4} NAME THE TUNE [62] 8-2 Paul Eddery (6) *slwly into strd, rear till effrt and not clr run one furlong out, eased whn btn*............(16 to 1 op 20 to 1 tchd 25 to 1) 6
2826^{3} ROMAN REEL (USA) [77] 9-3 B Rouse (11) *chsd ldrs, no hdwy last 2 fs*.......(11 to 1 op 10 to 1 tchd 12 to 1) 7
3345^{2} CHARISMA GIRL [53] 7-7 N Adams (10) *outpcd.* .... (12 to 1 op 10 to 1) 8
2500^{8} INDIAN DREAMER [62] (bl) 8-2 M Hills (3) *led for o'r 2 fs, wknd quickly*........(10 to 1 op 8 to 1 tchd 12 to 1) 9
3082^{5} ADMIRALELLA [81] 9-7 J Reid (7) *outpcd aftr 2 fs.* .... (12 to 1 op 10 to 1) 10
3303^{7} CURBRIDGE (Ire) [59] (bl) 7-13 S O'Gorman (5) *mid-div till clipped heels of rival and brght dwn o'r one furlong out*....................(25 to 1 op 20 to 1 tchd 33 to 1) bd

Dist: 2½l, nk, 2½l, 4l, 1l, 2½l, ¾l, nk, nk. 1m 2.50s. a 3.00s (11 Ran).
SR: 35/32/11/7/-/-/ (C J Petyt), R Hannon

3476 Cats 12th Year Handicap Class C (0-90 3-y-o) £5,667 1m 14yds......... (2:35)

3177^{7} KASSBAAN (USA) [81] 8-13 W R Swinburn (10) *hld up, ran on frm 2 fs out, shaken up to ld last 100 yards.* .... (9 to 1 op 8 to 1 tchd 10 to 1) 1
1016^{2} AMERICAN SWINGER (USA) [70] 8-2 Paul Eddery (9) *ldg grp, ran on frm 3 fs out, slight ld entering last, hdd and one pace last 100 yards.* (15 to 2 op 8 to 1 tchd 9 to 1) 2
3005* EL GAHAR [78] 8-10 W Ryan (4) *hdwy ins last 2 fs, styd on nr finish*..............(10 to 1 op 8 to 1 tchd 11 to 1) 3
2361^{7} MARASTANI (USA) [89] 9-7 J Reid (8) *led aftr one furlong till entering last, not quicken*....(14 to 1 tchd 16 to 1) 4
3158^{2} CONEYBURY (Ire) [87] 9-5 R Cochrane (6) *hdwy frm rear o'r 2 fs out, styd on one pace fnl furlong.* ....(8 to 1 op 6 to 1 tchd 9 to 1) 5
3174^{2} KING PARIS (Ire) [77] 8-6 (3*) M Fenton (14) *wl plcd, rdn o'r one furlong out, wknd ins last*................(20 to 1) 6
3348^{2} CATHERINEOFARAGON [73] 8-5 J Williams (12) *in tch, no prog frm 2 fs out*.................. (12 to 1 op 16 to 1) 7
2697* EAST LIBERTY (USA) [85] 9-3 L Dettori (11) *hld up in tch, effrt o'r one furlong out, sn btn.* ....(6 to 1 fav tchd 8 to 1) 8
3117* MUJAAZAFAH (USA) [86] 9-4 M Roberts (2) *nvr nrr.* ....(8 to 1 tchd 9 to 1) 9
3017^{9} SALBUS [74] (v) 8-6 T Quinn (15) *mid-div, effrt o'r 2 fs out, rdn and wknd over one out.* ....(66 to 1 op 33 to 1 tchd 100 to 1) 10
1408^{5} TWICE THE GROOM (Ire) [72] 8-4^{3} W Newnes (5) *nvr trble ldrs*..................(25 to 1 op 20 to 1 tchd 33 to 1) 11
3158^{8} NAFUTH (USA) [77] 8-9 W Carson (13) *drpd rear aftr 2 fs.* .... (16 to 1 op 14 to 1) 12
3068* THE LITTLE FERRET [77] 8-9 B Rouse (7) *in tch till wknd 3 fs out*..............(16 to 1 op 20 to 1 tchd 25 to 1) 13
3101^{3} SILVER GROOM (Ire) [61] 7-7 N Adams (16) *squeezed out strt, al beh*.......................(40 to 1 op 33 to 1) 14
3177^{8} NORFOLK HERO [83] 9-1 L Piggott (1) *wl plcd on outsd till lost pos 3 fs out, eased whn btn*............... (16 to 1) 15
3119^{5} BEAUMAN [68] (bl) 8-0 T Williams (17) *led one furlong, chsd ldr till wknd wl o'r 2 out.* ....(20 to 1 op 16 to 1 tchd 25 to 1) 16
3225^{2} VILLAGE GREEN (Fr) [80] 8-12 Pat Eddery (3) *pressed ldrs till wknd quickly 3 fs out*..........(10 to 1 op 12 to 1) 17

Dist: ¾l, 1½l, ¾l, 1½l, 1½l, 2½l, sht-hd, 2l, ½l, 3½l. 1m 41.15s. a 2.05s (17 Ran).
SR: 62/49/52/61/54/39/27/38/33/ (Maktoum Al Maktoum), A A Scott

3477 Amazing Joseph Dream Mile Class A (formerly the Atlanta) Stakes (Listed Race) (3-y-o and up) £10,698 1m 14yds ....(3:10)

3093* LAP OF LUXURY 4-9-1 M Tebbutt (9) *hdwy frm rear on ins 3 fs out, ran on und pres to ld nr finish.* ....(20 to 1 tchd 25 to 1) 1
3225* REINE DE NEIGE 3-8-9 W R Swinburn (11) *led till hdd und pres nr finish*.........(8 to 1 op 10 to 1 tchd 12 to 1) 2
2885^{4} QUEEN'S VIEW (Fr) 3-8-9 M Roberts (12) *in tch, pressed ldrs 3 fs out, ev ch o'r one out, not quicken nr finish.* .... (7 to 4 fav op 2 to 1 tchd 9 to 4 and 13 to 8) 3
3017* TAHDID 3-8-9 W Carson (6) *wl plcd, rdn and ev ch o'r one furlong out, not quicken.* ....(9 to 1 op 8 to 1 tchd 10 to 1) 4
3286* GHOST TREE (Ire) 3-8-9 L Dettori (13) *mid-div, rdn alng and effrt o'r 2 fs out, one pace appr last.* ....(9 to 2 op 4 to 1 tchd 5 to 1) 5
703^{2} SOIREE (Ire) 4-9-1 Pat Eddery (8) *beh till moderate prog ins last 2 fs*..........(14 to 1 op 10 to 1) 6
3262^{5} INSTANT AFFAIR (USA) 3-8-12 T Quinn (4) *in tch, effrt o'r 3 fs out, wknd over 2 out*.............(12 to 1 op 8 to 1) 7
2885* MOON OVER MIAMI 3-9-2 J Reid (7) *wl plcd, ev ch 2 fs out, rdn and btn o'r one out.* ....(14 to 1 op 12 to 1 tchd 16 to 1) 8
3036^{3} GOLDEN GUEST 3-8-12 L Piggott (5) *ldg grp till lost pl 2 fs out*..............................(33 to 1 op 25 to 1) 9
1524^{8} GUSTAVIA (Ire) 3-8-9 R Price (14) *slwly into strd, al beh.* ....(33 to 1 tchd 40 to 1) 10
2853^{4} SOOTY SWIFT (Ire) 3-8-9 B Doyle (10) *mid-div, rdn and wknd wl o'r 2 fs out*..............(25 to 1 op 16 to 1) 11
3227^{2} ETOSHA 3-8-9 M Hills (3) *steadied strt, effrt o'r 2 fs out, sn rdn alng and lost pl.* (9 to 1 op 8 to 1 tchd 10 to 1) 12

Dist: 1l, ¾l, 1½l, 4l, 2l, 1½l, hd, ¾l, sht-hd, nk. 1m 41.02s. a 1.92s (12 Ran).
SR: 66/57/55/50/38/38/30/33/27/ (I C Hill-Wood), W Jarvis

3478 Sunset Boulevard Solario Stakes Class A (Group 3) (2-y-o) £21,816 7f 16yds........................ (3:40)

3122^{2} ISLAND MAGIC 8-11 K Fallon (2) *made all, rdn and quickened entering fnl furlong, eased cl hme.* ....(2 to 1 op 7 to 4) 1
2562* NEWS AND ECHO (USA) 8-6 W R Swinburn (1) *trkd wnr, rdn alng o'r 2 fs out, hng rght over one out, kpt on same pace*..................(85 to 40 op 9 to 4 tchd 5 to 2) 2
2906^{4} GOVERNOR GEORGE (USA) 8-11 L Dettori (3) *hld up, not clr run o'r one furlong out, sn rdn and no extr.* ....(6 to 4 fav op 11 to 10) 3

Dist: 2l, nk. 1m 31.08s. a 4.58s (3 Ran).
SR: 23/12/16/ (M R Charlton), Mrs J R Ramsden

3479 Phantom Stayers Handicap Class D (0-70 3-y-o and up) £3,777 2m 78yds ....(4:10)

3255* SUN GREBE (Ire) [70] 3-9-2 (4ex) Pat Eddery (15) *mid-div, ran on to ld 2 fs out, pushed out, cmftbly.* ....(9 to 2 fav op 4 to 1) 1
3087^{3} MOIDART [70] 3-9-2 W R Swinburn (8) *ldg grp, led 3 fs out to 2 out, kpt on same pace ins last.* ....(5 to 1 op 4 to 1 tchd 11 to 2) 2
3319^{4} DOYCE [62] (bl) 4-9-8 W Carson (3) *mid-div, rdn and ran on o'r 2 fs out, one pace appr last.* (7 to 1 tchd 8 to 1) 3
2386^{3} ELEGANT KING (Ire) [57] 4-9-3 L Dettori (6) *handily plcd, rdn and one pace 2 fs out*.........(25 to 1 op 20 to 1) 4
3087^{2} PEACH BRANDY [42] 4-8-2 N Adams (18) *led aftr 2 fs to 3 out, sn btn*..........(11 to 1 op 8 to 1 tchd 12 to 1) 5
2904^{6} TOUCHING TIMES [44] 5-8-4 A Clark (10) *ldg grp, ev ch o'r 3 fs out, wknd over 2 out.* ....(12 to 1 op 14 to 1 tchd 16 to 1) 6
3142* FAIRY WISHER (Ire) [40] 4-7-7 (7*) N Varley (1) *pressed ldrs, ev ch 3 fs out, sn rdn and btn*......(25 to 1 op 16 to 1) 7
3078^{3} HALLOW FAIR [35] (v) 8-7-9^{2} T Williams (13) *effrt frm rear o'r 3 fs out, nvr nrr.* (25 to 1 op 16 to 1 tchd 33 to 1) 8
3288^{6} FANATICAL (USA) [46] 7-8-6 W Newnes (5) *beh, effrt o'r 3 fs out, not rch frnt rnk*............... (25 to 1 op 16 to 1) 9
2850^{3} CONCINNITY (USA) [46] 4-8-6 C Avery (16) *rear most of way*.............................. (25 to 1 op 16 to 1) 10
3231^{4} CHUCKLESTONE [64] 10-9-10 T Quinn (2) *in tch in mid-div, pushed alng hfwy, wknd o'r 3 fs out.* ....(11 to 1 op 10 to 1 tchd 12 to 1) 11
3078^{5} CHILD STAR (Fr) [43] 4-8-3 S Dawson (4) *mid-div, no hdwy appr last 3 fs*.........(16 to 1 op 14 to 1 tchd 20 to 1) 12
3193 BARCHAM [41] 6-8-1 M Roberts (11) *lost pl aftr 4 fs, effrt o'r 5 out, wknd over 2 out*.........(6 to 1 tchd 7 to 1) 13
3173^{8} PRINCESS DAVID (USA) [62] 3-8-8 Paul Eddery (14) *nvr able to rch frnt rnk, tld off*.......... (14 to 1 tchd 16 to 1) 14
2471 WHERE ARE WE [36] 7-7-10^{6} (3*) B Doyle (17) *al beh, tld off*.....................................(66 to 1 op 50 to 1) 15
FAIRGROUNDPRINCESS [33] 5-7-0 (7*) Kim McDonnell (12) *wl plcd till wknd o'r 4 fs out, tld off.* .... (66 to 1 op 50 to 1) 16
3021 GHOSTLY GLOW [49] (v) 4-8-9 J Reid (9) *led 2 fs, lost tch 7 out, tld off*..........(33 to 1 op 25 to 1 tchd 40 to 1) 17
PANDY [58] 7-8-13 (5*) A Procter (7) *prmnt early, rdn alng and wknd bef hfwy, tld off last 6 fs.* .... (33 to 1 op 25 to 1) 18

Dist: 4l, 3½l, 3l, 2l, 4l, nk, nk, 1l, 5l, 3l. 3m 35.45s. a 6.45s (18 Ran).
SR: 29/25/27/19/2/-/ (Sir Thomas Pilkington), J L Dunlop

3480 Starlight Express Claiming Stakes Class F (3-y-o) £2,749 1m 1f.....(4:45)

3083^{2} REGALSETT 8-10 J Reid (3) *hdwy hfwy, ran on und pres to ld last 50 yards*...... (5 to 1 op 9 to 2 tchd 11 to 2) 1

2989[6] PREROGATIVE (v) 8-6 L Dettori (5) *led till rdn and hdd last 50 yards*..........................(7 to 1 tchd 8 to 1) 2
3269 ERLKING (Ire) 8-4 M Roberts (8) *ldg grp, ev ch und pres o'r one furlong out, not quicken*. ....(15 to 2 op 6 to 1 tchd 9 to 1) 3
3096[3] TOMSK 8-8 Pat Eddery (2) *pressed ldrs till lost pl o'r 3 fs out, styd on one pace appr last*...... (5 to 1 op 4 to 1) 4
2898[2] FANFOLD (Ire) 7-8 (5*) B Russell (1) *cl up, rdn and not much room o'r 2 fs out, btn over one out*. ....(9 to 2 op 4 to 1 tchd 5 to 1) 5
1342[4] FLASHFEET 8-8 N Adams (7) *hdwy 3 fs out, no extr ins last 2*............................ (12 to 1 op 14 to 1) 6
3083[3] DEE RAFT (USA) 8-11 W R Swinburn (4) *rear, rdn and no imprsn on ldrs fnl 3 fs*.......... (4 to 1 fav tchd 5 to 1) 7
3214[4] URRY URRY URRY 8-0 W Carson (6) *chsd ldrs to hfwy, sn rdn and drpd rear*................. (8 to 1 tchd 9 to 1) 8
3225 IVORY HUTCH 8-3[3] A Clark (10) *al beh*. .... (20 to 1 op 33 to 1) 9
3068[6] SEATTLE AFFAIR (Ire) 8-1 Dale Gibson (9) *beh, rdn hfwy, tld off*.............. (40 to 1 op 33 to 1 tchd 50 to 1) 10

Dist: 1½l, 1l, 3½l, ¾l, 5l, 4l, 3½l, 6l, 20l. 1m 54.83s. a 3.63s (10 Ran).
SR: 35/26/21/14/3/-/ (David S Lewis), M C Pipe

3481 Norma Desmond Handicap Class D (0-80 3-y-o and up) £3,761 5f 6yds ....(5:15)

2987 EDUCATED PET [66] 4-8-11 (3*) B Doyle (3) *beh, swtchd rght and str brst o'r one furlong out, led last 50 yards*. .... (10 to 1 op 12 to 1) 1
3383* JUCEA [57] 4-8-5 Paul Eddery (2) *ran on 2 fs out, led ins last, hdd and outpcd last 50 yards*... (5 to 1 op 6 to 1) 2
3266[3] BODARI [76] 4-9-10 M Roberts (1) *chsd ldrs, ran on und pres to ld o'r one furlong out, hdd ins last, ran on same pace*..........................(9 to 2 jt-fav op 7 to 2) 3
3266[2] NO EXTRAS (Ire) [79] 3-9-10 B Rouse (8) *mid-div, cld on ldrs o'r one furlong out, sn ev ch, no extr nr line*. ....(9 to 2 jt-fav op 7 to 2 tchd 5 to 1) 4
3099[2] ARAGROVE [77] 3-9-8 J Reid (9) *chsd ldrs, styd on one pace fnl furlong*........(11 to 2 op 5 to 1 tchd 6 to 1) 5
3229 VISIMOTION (USA) [60] 3-8-5 T Quinn (6) *in tch for o'r 3 fs*. .... (16 to 1 op 14 to 1) 6
3229 PURBECK CENTENARY [58] 3-8-3 W Ryan (11) *led centre one furlong, cl up till rdn and outpcd ins last*. .... (33 to 1 op 25 to 1) 7
3229 RAYS MEAD [47] 5-7-9 C Avery (12) *in tch, cld on ldrs 2 fs out, no extr ins last*................ (33 to 1 op 25 to 1) 8
3229[7] FARMER JOCK [60] 11-8-8 W Newnes (10) *outpcd*. .... (33 to 1 op 20 to 1 tchd 40 to 1) 9
3220 NEWBURY COAT [74] (bl) 3-9-5 A Clark (4) *led aftr one furlong till hdd and wknd quickly o'r one out*. ....(16 to 1 op 14 to 1 tchd 20 to 1) 10
3095[4] COCONUT JOHNNY [55] (v) 3-8-0 F Norton (5) *in tch, rdn alng and wknd appr fnl furlong*............. (20 to 1) 11
2965[5] BALIGAY [76] 8-9-10 L Dettori (7) *outpcd*. ....(8 to 1 op 7 to 1 tchd 10 to 1) 12
BREEZY DAY [78] 7-9-5 (7*) J Bramhill (13) *mid-div, rdn and wknd hfwy*...................(33 to 1 op 20 to 1) 13

Dist: ½l, ¾l, nk, 2½l, sht-hd, sht-hd, ½l, 2l, 2l, nk. 1m 2.22s. a 2.72s (13 Ran).
SR: 46/35/51/50/38/20/17/7/12/ (Billy Morgan), M Johnston

WEXFORD (IRE) (good)
Friday August 20th

3482 Genenelil Assiuraziani Maiden (3-y-o and up) £2,762 1m 5f........... (6:45)

3326[2] ALIBAR'S PET (Ire) 3-8-6 J F Egan (1)......... (5 to 4 fav) 1
3396[5] RICH LIFE (Ire) (bl) 3-8-9 P Shanahan (2).......... (5 to 1) 2
3274[2] TEBRE (USA) (bl) 3-8-6 W J Supple (6)............ (5 to 1) 3
3396[2] NURSES RUN (Ire) 3-8-2 (4*) J J Behan (5).........(4 to 1) 4
3164[5] NORDIC UNION (Ire) 3-8-0 (6*) J A Heffernan (3)....(4 to 1) 5

Dist: 11l, 5½l, ¾l, 1l. 2m 43.90s. (5 Ran).
(J F Grogan), A P O'Brien

3483 Guardian Royal Exchange Handicap (0-60 4-y-o and up) £2,762 2m... (7:15)

1013 SENSITIVE KING (Ire) [-] 5-8-5 (2*) R M Burke (7)... (7 to 1) 1
1962[3] ZUHAL [-] 5-9-7 (6*) C Everard (8)................. (3 to 1) 2
3276[2] RANDOM PRINCE [-] 9-8-2 W J Supple (4)..... (Evens fav) 3
3276[9] MARIAN YEAR [-] 7-7-13[3] (8*) B Fenton (1)........ (10 to 1) 4
2324[5] PRINCE YAZA [-] 6-9-4 (10*) D J Casey (3).........(4 to 1) 5
3276 ASTRA (Ire) [-] (bl) 4-9-7 (6*) J R Barry (2)..........(12 to 1) 6

Dist: 3l, ½l, 7l, 3½l. 3m 39.70s. (6 Ran).
(J C Harley), J C Harley

3484 Insurance Corporation Of Ireland Handicap (0-80 3-y-o) £2,762 1m 5f ....(7:45)

3163[8] SAFFRON CROCUS [-] 9-6 J P Murtagh (5).... (5 to 4 fav) 1
3367* LAKE OF LOUGHREA (Ire) [-] 8-2 (6*,12ex) B J Walsh (6) ....(9 to 2) 2
2881[8] BLUE DIANA (Ire) [-] 8-11 (6*) J R Barry (4).........(8 to 1) 3
2956* ALYREINA (USA) [-] (bl) 9-9 K J Manning (7)........(3 to 1) 4
3329* NORDICOLINI (Ire) [-] 8-4 (4*,3ex) W J Smith (3).... (8 to 1) 5
3294[8] DARK SWAN (Ire) [-] (bl) 8-3 W J Supple (8).......(14 to 1) 6
1757 POUNDWORLD (Ire) [-] 7-11 (8*) P J Smullen (2)...(33 to 1) 7

Dist: ¾l, hd, 10l, ½l. 2m 46.50s. (7 Ran).
(Sheikh Mohammed), John M Oxx

CHESTER (good to soft)
Saturday August 21st
Going Correction: MINUS 0.10 sec. per fur.

3485 Linenhall Conditions Stakes Class C (2-y-o) £4,914 6f 18yds..........(2:00)

2414[2] BALANDRA BAY (Ire) 8-12 Pat Eddery (1) *tucked away on ins, drvn alng last 2 fs, ran on to ld cl hme*. ....(100 to 30 op 5 to 2) 1
3069* SELHURSTPARK FLYER (Ire) 9-4 J Carroll (3) *trkd ldr, led o'r one furlong out, rdn and jst ct*. ....(7 to 4 fav op 6 to 4 tchd 15 to 8) 2
1998* BALLAH SHACK (USA) 8-5 (5*) D Wright (4) *al hndy, hrd drvn last 2 fs, kpt on same pace*......(9 to 2 op 3 to 1) 3
2030[3] GONE TO POT (bl) 8-5 (5*) Stephen Davies (2) *dictated pace for o'r 4 fs, rdn and no extr*....... (10 to 1 tchd 9 to 1) 4
3031[4] THREE IN ONE 8-10 W Carson (5) *chsd alng to keep up, nvr able to chal*.................... (4 to 1 op 3 to 1) 5

Dist: Nk, 1½l, 2l, 3l. 1m 16.31s. a 2.81s (5 Ran).
SR: 30/35/21/13/1/ (J A Lazzari), R Hannon

3486 Rowton Moor Handicap Class D (0-85 3-y-o and up) £7,304 5f 16yds... (2:30)

3404 MACFARLANE [74] 5-9-6 F Norton (4) *drvn alng to go pace, relentless prog to ld ins fnl furlong, kpt on strly*. ....(6 to 1 op 5 to 1) 1
3220* TUSCAN DAWN [85] 3-9-7 (7*) P Roberts (8) *tried to make all, brght wide bend o'r one furlong out, hdd and no extr ins last*........ (5 to 1 fav op 9 to 2 tchd 11 to 2) 2
3280[6] CRYSTAL JACK (Fr) [71] 5-9-3 S Perks (6) *nvr far away, bustled alng last 2 fs, kpt on same pace*. ....(6 to 1 op 9 to 2) 3
3251* JESS REBEC [57] 5-7-12 (5*) Stephen Davies (5) *outpcd and drvn alng, styd on grimly fnl furlong, nrst finish*. ....(10 to 1) 4
3354[8] PENNY HASSET [67] 5-8-13 W Carson (3) *outpcd and drvn alng, ran on wl ins fnl furlong, nvr nrr*. ....(6 to 1 op 5 to 1) 5
3280[9] SIR TASKER [54] 5-7-9 (5*) D Wright (12) *chsd ldrs, effrt and rdn 2 fs out, one pace*........(20 to 1 op 16 to 1) 6
3280 LOVE LEGEND [68] 8-9-0 Paul Eddery (10) *bustled alng to keep up, not pace of ldrs*.......... (14 to 1 op 10 to 1) 7
2896[2] LITTLE SABOTEUR [68] 4-9-0 Pat Eddery (2) *settled off the pace, drvn alng to improve hfwy, not much room o'r one furlong out, one pace*.........................(6 to 1) 8
2777* MY ABBEY [63] 4-8-6 (3*) S Maloney (7) *pressed ldg trio till fdd und pres last 2 fs*............. (8 to 1 tchd 9 to 1) 9
3136[6] SIMMIE'S SPECIAL [57] (bl) 5-8-3 W Ryan (9) *wth ldg pair for o'r 3 fs, fdd*.................... (20 to 1 op 12 to 1) 10
3280[4] KABCAST [53] (bl) 8-7-13 S Wood (11) *gd speed to dispute ld for 3 fs, wknd quickly*. ....(12 to 1 op 14 to 1 tchd 11 to 1) 11

Dist: 1½l, 1½l, sht-hd, ½l, ½l, 2l, 2½l, sht-hd, 3l, 1½l. 1m 2.36s. a 2.06s (11 Ran).
SR: 55/57/40/25/33/18/24/14/8/ (P Fetherston-Godley), M J Fetherston-Godley

3487 Rothmans Royals North South Challenge Series Handicap Class C (0-90 3-y-o and up) £8,155 7f 122yds.. (3:00)

2928[3] HUNTERS OF BRORA (Ire) [73] 3-8-10 W Carson (5) *outpcd and rdn alng, brght wide to improve entering strt, got up cl hme*........................ (6 to 1 tchd 13 to 2) 1
3158[7] TISSISAT (USA) [84] (v) 4-9-13 Pat Eddery (1) *al hndy, drvn ahead entering fnl furlong, ct cl hme*. ....(6 to 1 op 9 to 2 tchd 7 to 1) 2
3155[3] BOLD ANGEL [76] 6-9-2 (3*) S Maloney (10) *nvr far away, led o'r one furlong out till entering last, kpt on same pace*.......................(5 to 1 jt-fav tchd 6 to 1) 3
3290[8] LORD OBERON (Ire) [67] (v) 5-8-10 F Norton (8) *last and drvn alng, styd on wl last 2 fs, nrst finish*. ....(7 to 1 tchd 8 to 1) 4
3325[4] THEMAAM [50] 4-7-7 S Wood (9) *drvn up frm midfield to join ldrs o'r one furlong out, rdn and no extr*. .... (14 to 1 op 10 to 1) 5
2622 SUIVEZ [72] 3-8-9 J Carroll (4) *pressed ldg 5, hrd drvn whn not much room o'r one furlong out, no extr*. .... (25 to 1 op 16 to 1) 6
3375[2] MENTALASANYTHIN [69] 4-8-9 (3*) O Pears (3) *pressed ldrs, fdg whn not much room appr fnl furlong*. ...(5 to 1 jt-fav op 9 to 2) 7
3155[2] KUMMEL KING [54] 5-7-6 (5*) D Wright (7) *wth ldr, led aftr 2 fs till o'r one out, fdd*................ (7 to 1 op 6 to 1) 8
3302[3] WATERLORD (Ire) [64] 3-7-10 (5*) Stephen Davies (6) *pressed ldrs, drvn alng o'r 2 fs out, fdd*.... (14 to 1 op 12 to 1) 9

2211 GREEK GOLD (Ire) [66] 4-8-6 (3*) S D Williams (2) *led for 2 fs, struggling and lost pl o'r two out, eased.* .... (16 to 1 op 14 to 1) 10

Dist: ½l, 3½l, 1l, 1l, sht-hd, nk, 1l, ½l, 30l. 1m 35.27s. a 3.27s (10 Ran).
SR: 36/51/32/20/-/15/17/-/1/ (Robert Gibbons), J D Bethell

3488 Chester Rated Class A Handicap formerly the Tricity Bendix Series Six Chester Stakes (Listed Race) (0-105 3-y-o and up) £12,511 1m 5f 89yds ....(3:30)

2795² NASSMA (Ire) [89] 3-8-3 W Ryan (5) *patiently rdn, improved to nose ahead appr fnl furlong, hld on gmely.* ....(6 to 4 fav op 11 to 8 tchd 13 to 8) 1
2393³ AZHAR [103] 3-9-3 Paul Eddery (8) *tried to make all, hdd appr fnl furlong, rallied gmely*...... (2 to 1 op 7 to 4) 2
3152⁴ STAR PLAYER [82] 7-8-7 F Norton (3) *last and hld up, imprvg und pres whn hng rght o'r one furlong out, no imprsn*.......................... (7 to 1 tchd 8 to 1) 3
1579⁷ HEATHYARDS BOY [82] 3-7-10 M Humphries (4) *trkd ldg quartet, feeling pace and lost grnd 3 fs out, sn btn.* .... (25 to 1 op 20 to 1) 4
2962 ANCHORITE [90] 4-9-1 J Carroll (6) *trkd ldr, hrd drvn 3 fs out, sn lost tch*.. (8 to 1) 5
2625³ MICHELOZZO (USA) [96] 7-9-7 S Raymont (2) *tucked away on ins, struggling to hold pl o'r 3 fs out, tld off.* .... (11 to 1 op 12 to 1) 6

Dist: Sht-hd, 10l, ¾l, 25l, ½l. 2m 56.77s. a 6.77s (6 Ran).
SR: 8/21/-/ (Sheikh Ahmed Bin Saeed Al Maktoum), J R Fanshawe

3489 Paradise Maiden Stakes Class D (3-y-o and up) £4,305 7f 2yds...... (4:00)

2752² LACOTTE (Ire) 3-8-13 Pat Eddery (3) *al gng best, led on bit entering fnl furlong, smoothly.* ....(13 to 8 fav op 6 to 4 tchd 7 to 4) 1
2732⁵ DESERT GREEN (Fr) 4-9-4 P D'Arcy (7) *trkd ldg pair, drvn up on outsd to ld hfwy, hdd entering last, no ch wth wnr*............................. (3 to 1 tchd 7 to 2) 2
3132⁶ WILLOW RIVER (Can) 3-8-8 J Carroll (2) *wtd wth, took clr order o'r 2 fs out, rdn and styd on same pace.* .... (16 to 1 op 12 to 1) 3
BOLD STAR 3-8-13 S Perks (8) *last and niggled alng, styd on last 2 fs, nvr nrr*...............(50 to 1 op 33 to 1) 4
3286² JASARAH (Ire) 3-8-8 W Carson (4) *trkd ldrs, led 4 fs, fdd last 2 furlongs*.................... (9 to 4 tchd 2 to 1) 5
2773⁷ TRANQUIL LADY (Ire) 3-8-3 (5*) Stephen Davies (1) *dictated pace to hfwy, sn drvn alng, no extr.* .... (50 to 1 op 33 to 1) 6
3272 NAWAAYA (USA) 3-8-3 (5*) J Tate (5) *trkd ldg trio till wknd und pres 3 fs out, tld off*........... (50 to 1 op 33 to 1) 7
VIRILIS 3-8-13 W Ryan (9) *chsd ldg quartet to hfwy, sn tld off*.................................. (16 to 1 op 12 to 1) 8

Dist: 1l, 3l, 1½l, 1½l, 3l, 25l, 30l. 1m 28.85s. a 3.45s (8 Ran).
SR: 37/39/20/20/10/1/-/-/ (Sheikh Mohammed), J H M Gosden

3490 Levy Board Nursery Class C (2-y-o) £5,526 7f 2yds................. (4:30)

2844² LINK MILES [77] 9-7 W Ryan (6) *sluggish strt, rapid hdwy on outsd entering strt, crrd rght entering last, sn led, ran on wl*............... (13 to 2 op 5 to 1 tchd 7 to 1) 1
3041³ NORTHERN CELADON (Ire) [75] 9-0 (5*) K Rutter (5) *al hndy, led o'r 2 fs out, drifted rght and hdd entering fnl furlong, kpt on, fnshd second, plcd 3rd.* (7 to 1 op 6 to 1) 2D
3362* INDEFENCE (Ire) [72] 9-2 Pat Eddery (8) *co'red up gng wl, rdn and ev ch whn squeezed out entering fnl furlong, not rcvr, fnshd 3rd, plcd second.* ....(15 to 8 fav op 6 to 4 tchd 2 to 1) 2
2586* HEATHYARDS CRUSADE (Ire) [57] 7-8 (7*) M Humphries (9) *patiently rdn, steady hdwy 2 fs out, wndrd fnl furlong, ran on*.................. (7 to 1 op 6 to 1 tchd 8 to 1) 4
2102⁷ MICHELLISA [69] 8-13 W Carson (1) *beh and drvn alng, improved entering strt, styd on.* .... (10 to 1 op 8 to 1 tchd 12 to 1) 5
3351⁹ NOT FOR JOE [65] 8-9 A Tucker (4) *outpcd and beh, improved und pres 2 fs out, nvr dngrs.* .... (20 to 1 op 14 to 1) 6
908 MONKEY MAGIC (Ire) [68] 8-12 J Carroll (10) *wth ldrs till fdd und pres o'r one furlong out*...(16 to 1 op 10 to 1) 7
1810³ TIMES ZANDO [61] 8-0 (5*) D Wright (2) *tried to make all, hdd o'r 2 fs out, sn btn.* .... (11 to 1 op 7 to 1 tchd 12 to 1) 8
2974⁸ HALI (Ire) [63] 8-7 F Norton (7) *trkd ldrs for o'r 4 fs, fdd.* .... (14 to 1 op 8 to 1) 9
886* HILL FARM KATIE [65] 8-9 Paul Eddery (3) *trkd ldrs, feeling pace and rdn 3 fs out, sn btn*...... (10 to 1 op 8 to 1) 10

Dist: Nk, 3l, nk, 3l, 1l, 2½l, 1½l, 2l, hd. 1m 30.67s. a 5.27s (10 Ran).
SR: 17/14/2/-/-/-/ (The Winning Team), R Hannon

3491 Rouge Rose Maiden Fillies' Stakes Class D (3-y-o) £4,402 1½m 66yds ....(5:00)

3173² KERKURA (USA) 8-11 W Ryan (9) *wth ldr, led and quickened pace 7 fs out, styd on strly fnl furlong.* .... (5 to 4 fav op 5 to 4 on tchd 11 to 8) 1
1311⁵ KARDELLE 8-11 T Sprake (3) *patiently rdn, improved und pres entering strt, styd on*............(14 to 1 op 10 to 1) 2
ELATIS (USA) 8-11 J Carroll (2) *settled off the pace, effrt and drvn alng last 3 fs, no imprsn.* ....(11 to 1 op 10 to 1 tchd 8 to 1 and 12 to 1) 3
2310² BAWAETH (USA) 8-11 W Carson (7) *slight ld till hdd 7 fs out, struggling to hold pl appr strt, sn btn.* ....(7 to 2 op 5 to 2) 4
3012 TOKYO 8-6 (5*) J Tate (4) *trkd ldg bunch, feeling pace and rdn o'r 3 fs out, no imprsn*.................... (33 to 1) 5
3012 FIDA (Ire) 8-11 P D'Arcy (5) *nvr far away, rdn o'r 3 fs out, sn btn*............................(16 to 1 tchd 25 to 1) 6
3272 NAVAJO LOVE SONG (Ire) 8-11 Paul Eddery (10) *in tch, took clr order o'r 3 fs out, sn btn*...(20 to 1 op 14 to 1) 7
2579⁶ RANI (Ire) 8-11 Pat Eddery (8) *wth ldrs till wknd appr strt, tld off*..............(5 to 1 tchd 6 to 1 and 9 to 2) 8
2716⁸ SING A RAINBOW (Ire) 8-11 F Norton (1) *trkd ldg pair for almost a m, sn lost tch, tld off*.................(20 to 1) 9
3320⁷ ANNYBAN 8-11 S Perks (6) *last and niggled alng, tld off last 4 fs*..(50 to 1) 10

Dist: 2l, 5l, 7l, nk, nk, 3l, 20l, 1l, nk. 2m 44.33s. a 7.53s (10 Ran).
SR: 9/5/-/-/-/-/ (Lord Howard de Walden), H R A Cecil

CURRAGH (IRE) (good to yielding)
Saturday August 21st
Going Correction: PLUS 0.10 sec. per fur.

3492 Merrion (E.B.F.) (C & G) Maiden (2-y-o) £5,244 7f................... (2:00)

2840³ CASHEL MARKET (Ire) 9-0 K J Manning (13) ... (9 to 4 fav) 1
2982³ DAYESS (USA) 9-0 M J Kinane (8)................ (9 to 2) 2
2402⁹ REGAL ACCESS (USA) 8-12 (2*) P Carberry (6) ....(10 to 1) 3
3243⁴ CAIRNBRAE (Ire) 9-0 J F Egan (12).............. (16 to 1) 4
ALFRED THE BOLD (Ire) 9-0 W J Supple (11)..... (10 to 1) 5
3416⁷ FRENCH VICTOR (Ire) 8-10 (4*) J J Behan (4)..... (10 to 1) 6
2037 CROSS SWORDS (USA) 9-0 P Shanahan (5)......(10 to 1) 7
3203⁷ NORDIC AIR (Ire) 8-8 (6*) J A Heffernan (9)........(10 to 1) 8
2701 INCHINTAGGART 9-0 P V Gilson (10)............(10 to 1) 9
3243 ALL SHOW (Ire) 9-0 R Hughes (7)................(20 to 1) 10
TORDO (Ire) 9-0 S Craine (14).................... (8 to 1) 11
3030⁷ JACQUIMO (Ire) 9-0 J P Murtagh (15)............ (8 to 1) 12
2701⁹ LEO'S FRIEND (Ire) 9-0 M G Cleary (3)........... (16 to 1) 13
OLD SUNSHINE (Ire) 9-0 N Byrne (2)...............(14 to 1) 14
ADJALARI (Ire) 9-0 D Hogan (1).................. (7 to 2) 15

Dist: 2½l, nk, 2l, ½l. 1m 29.40s. a 6.20s (15 Ran).
SR: 18/10/9/3/1/-/ (Des Vere Hunt), J S Bolger

3493 E.B.F. Laidlaw Debutante Stakes (Listed) (2-y-o) £8,625 6f...........(2:30)

2804* LOW KEY AFFAIR (USA) 8-12 M J Kinane (8) *sn led, rdn one furlong out, kpt on strly*......................(6 to 4 on) 1
ANNA RALPH (USA) 8-9 S Craine (6) *mid-div, swtchd rght to chal one furlong out, styd on strly, nrst finish.* ....(14 to 1) 2
1332* JEDWA (Ire) 8-9 K J Manning (7) *trkd ldr, strly rdn frm 2 fs out, no extr cl hme*....................................(4 to 1) 3
3030³ BETTER FOLLY (Ire) 8-9 W J Supple (5) *rear, some prog 2 fs out, rdn and kpt on one pace, not rch ldrs*.... (14 to 1) 4
3039⁵ SOLAR ATTRACTION (Ire) 8-9 P Shanahan (1) *al rear, rdn and wknd one furlong out*...................(14 to 1) 5
2605² COMMON RUMPUS (Ire) 8-12 L Piggott (3) *hld up, rdn one furlong out, eased whn btn ins last*........... (5 to 2) 6

Dist: ½l, nk, 6l, 4l. 1m 16.50s. a 6.00s (6 Ran).
(Moyglare Stud Farm), D K Weld

3494 Herbert Lodge Handicap (0-90 3-y-o and up) £3,450 1¼m............(3:00)

2460* KHALYANI (Ire) [-] 3-9-0 J P Murtagh (4)..........(11 to 2) 1
3327* TRYARRA (Ire) [-] 3-8-8 (6*,5ex) B J Walsh (10)..... (7 to 1) 2
3197* UP SHE FLEW (USA) [-] 3-7-8 (4*) W J Smith (11)...(8 to 1) 3
1468⁷ LACKEL (Ger) [-] 5-9-5 K J Manning (6)........... (14 to 1) 4
1822⁴ SOLAS ABU (Ire) [-] 3-8-5 (6*) J A Heffernan (2)....(13 to 2) 5
2878⁴ LOKI (Ire) [-] 5-10-0 M J Kinane (5)...........(13 to 8 fav) 6
3075⁹ KAR OR [-] 3-8-13 R Hughes (1)..................(16 to 1) 7
2741⁸ OVERCAST (Ire) [-] (bl) 3-8-0 (4*) J J Behan (3).... (12 to 1) 8
3038⁷ CENTER MORICHES (Ire) [-] 3-8-7 (2*) P Carberry (7) ....(10 to 1) 9
2957⁷ GALLARDINI (Ire) [-] 4-9-3 (8*) M W Martin (9)..... (14 to 1) 10
1440 MAGNUM STAR (Ire) [-] 4-8-0 J F Egan (8)........ (13 to 2) 11

Dist: 3l, nk, 1½l, ¾l. 2m 7.20s. a 4.40s (11 Ran).
SR: 66/60/43/61/51/-/ (H H Aga Khan), John M Oxx

3495 Meld Stakes (Group 3) (3-y-o and up) £11,500 1¼m.................. (3:30)

1269⁵ LORD OF THE FIELD 6-9-1 W Newnes (2) *trkd ldr, prog to dispute ld hfwy, led 4 fs out, quickened clr 3 out, kpt on*..(5 to 1) 1
2077* VINTAGE CROP 6-9-1 P Shanahan (3) *rear, prog to track ldrs aftr 4 fs, ev ch 2 out, styd on strly cl hme.* (12 to 1) 2

3149* DANSE ROYALE (Ire) 3-8-7 L Piggott (8) *mid-div, prog 2 fs out, ev ch one out, no extr*.................... (13 to 8) 3
2405[8] TAKAROUNA (USA) 3-8-10 M J Kinane (7) *hld up, prog 2 fs out, swtchd to chal on far rail one out, not much room ins last, kpt on*.............................(6 to 4 fav) 4
2607[3] SEMPLE STADIUM (Ire) 3-8-7 P V Gilson (6) *wl plcd, prog to track ldr 3 fs out, ev ch 2 out, no extr and wknd ins last.* ....(12 to 1) 5
3333[5] MALVERNICO (Ire) (bl) 5-9-1 K J Manning (1) *mid-div, prog 3 fs out, sn rdn, wknd quickly aftr 2 out*........ (10 to 1) 6
MAGIC SPIRIT (Ire) 4-9-1 J F Egan (5) *led, jnd hfwy, hdd 4 fs out, rdn and wknd quickly 2 out*........... (50 to 1) 7
Dist: ½l, ½l, nk, ¾l. 2m 8.30s. a 5.50s (7 Ran).
SR: 56/55/46/48/43/-/-/ (Duke Of Devonshire), J A R Toller

3496 Rockingham Handicap (0-110 3-y-o and up) £6,900 5f...............(4:00)

3333[7] BRADAWN BREEVER (Ire) [-] (bl) 4-9-10 W J Supple (4) ....(12 to 1) 1
3027[3] DIAMONDS GALORE (Can) [-] 8-9-9 M J Kinane (3) (5 to 1) 2
3201[2] CLASSICAL AFFAIR (Ire) [-] 4-8-13 (4*,5ex) J J Behan (7) ....(5 to 1) 3
1201[6] LAVINIA FONTANA (Ire) [-] 4-9-2 P V Gilson (1) (6 to 4 fav) 4
3201* MY-O-MY (Ire) [-] 3-8-8 (7ex) S Craine (5).......... (4 to 1) 5
1825[6] GOLD BRAISIM (Ire) [-] 3-6-13 (8*) G M Moylan (2) (16 to 1) 6
3395[9] RECOLLECTION (Ire) [-] (bl) 4-7-7 Joanna Morgan (8) ....(16 to 1) 7
2187[7] CLANDOLLY (Ire) [-] 5-7-13 (2*) D G O'Shea (6)....(14 to 1) 8
Dist: ½l, 1l, sht-hd, sht-hd. 1m 0.80s. a 2.50s (8 Ran).
SR: 70/67/57/55/46/ (M A Murray), Kevin Prendergast

3497 McLoughlin Ashlee House Equi-Tred Race (3 & 4-y-o) £4,140 1m..... (4:30)

3074* STRATEGIC TIMING (Ire) (bl) 3-9-3 M J Kinane (4) .. (9 to 2) 1
3161[3] COUTURE DIAMANT (Ire) 3-8-8 (2*) R M Burke (12) (11 to 1) 2
3161* KILTIMONY 3-9-3 P V Gilson (9).................(10 to 1) 3
3025* CRYSTAL SHIP (Ire) 3-9-3 L Piggott (3)........ (6 to 4 fav) 4
3382[5] WORLD'S VIEW 3-8-10 J P Murtagh (10)..........(10 to 1) 5
3417[4] ROLANDS GIRL (Ire) 3-8-4 (6*) J A Heffernan (11) (50 to 1) 6
2902 GOLDEN SPHINX (Ire) 3-8-8 (2*) D G O'Shea (1)...(50 to 1) 7
1507[5] MYSTICAL CITY (Ire) 3-8-10 J F Egan (5).........(20 to 1) 8
3417* ALASKAN GIRL (Ire) 3-9-3 S Craine (8)............(9 to 2) 9
911[7] BACK TO BLACK (Ire) 4-9-0 M G Cleary (6).........(40 to 1) 10
3242* MARKIEVICZ (Ire) 3-8-9 (8*) G M Moylan (7).......(10 to 1) 11
282 COPSEWOOD (Ire) 3-8-10 D Manning (2).........(25 to 1) 12
Dist: 1l, sht-hd, ¾l, 1l. 1m 42.80s. a 6.20s (12 Ran).
SR: 22/12/18/16/6/-/ (Moyglare Stud Farm), D K Weld

3498 Flat Rath Handicap (0-75 3-y-o and up) £3,105 1m..................... (5:00)

3278* STATE PRINCESS (Ire) [-] 3-9-1 (6ex) R Hughes (10) (13 to 2) 1
3399[5] BARNAGEERA BOY (Ire) [-] 4-8-6 P V Gilson (8)...(10 to 1) 2
3327[5] FLORA WOOD (Ire) [-] 3-9-1 (6*) B J Walsh (7)......(6 to 1) 3
3381 MUSWELL BROOK (Ire) [-] (bl) 3-8-13 K J Manning (9) ....(16 to 1) 4
3294 TINA'S CHARM (Ire) [-] 4-8-13 (6*) C Everard (6)... (20 to 1) 5
3334[3] SKELLIG [-] (bl) 7-9-6 M J Kinane (2)................(3 to 1) 6
3242[4] NORDIC GLARE (Ire) [-] 3-8-7 (8*) T E Durcan (5).. (10 to 1) 7
2922* LA CENERENTOLA (Ire) [-] 3-9-8 (2*) P Carberry (3) ....(11 to 4 fav) 8
2901[5] LORD GLENVARA (Ire) [-] 5-8-7 (2*) R M Burke (1)... (5 to 1) 9
3294[6] MYRO BALANNE (Ire) [-] 3-8-0 (4*) W J Smith (4).. (16 to 1) 10
Dist: 1l, sht-hd, ¾l, 1l. 1m 42.50s. a 5.90s (10 Ran).
SR: 24/12/26/16/19/-/ (Sportsmans Inn Syndicate), D T Hughes

DEAUVILLE (FR) (good)
Saturday August 21st

Going Correction: PLUS 0.10 sec. per fur. (race 1), PLUS 0.20 (2,3)

3499 Challenge d'Or Piaget (Restricted Listed) (2-y-o) £179,211 7f......... (2:35)

2924[2] PRINCE BABAR 9-0 L Dettori,.......................... 1
SE SOUVENIR (Fr) 8-10 G Guignard,..................... 2
VOLOCHINE (Ire) 9-0 C Asmussen,...................... 3
DIRIGEANTE (Fr) 8-10 F Head,.......................... 4
2473[4] BEARALL (Ire),.. 6
3259[8] THE CHAIRMAN (Ire),.................................. 0
SOLID ILLUSION (USA) 9-0 E Legrix,.................... 0
Dist: ¾l, sht-nk, sht-hd, nk, ½l, ½l, nk, hd, hd. 1m 25.50s. a 3.50s (18 Ran).
SR: 58/52/55/50/ (Giles W Pritchard-Gordon), G A Pritchard-Gordon

3500 Prix Gontaut-Biron (Group 3) (4-y-o and up) £23,895 1¼m..........(3:05)

2437* URBAN SEA (USA) 4-8-11 C Asmussen, *mid-div, 4th strt, effrt and quickened 2 fs out, led jst und one furlong out, ran on wl*.. 1
2981[6] VERVEINE (USA) 4-8-7[1] D Boeuf, *in rear early, rdn 2 fs out on outsd, chlgd ldrs one and a half furlongs out, ran on*.. 2
3022[7] LUCKY LINDY (Ire) 4-8-9 L Dettori, *trkd ldrs, 3rd strt, led briefly jst und 2 fs out, one paced fnl furlong*.......... 3
1908[2] ARCHANGE (USA) 4-8-9 F Head, *last strt, rdn 2 fs out, ran on fnl furlong, nrst finish*................................. 4
2979* MARILDO (Fr) 6-9-4 G Guignard, *mid-div, second strt, led 2 fs out, hdd jst und two out, no extr fnl furlong*.......... 5
3154[3] HALF A TICK (USA) 5-8-11 G Mosse, *mid-div, rdn and outpcd frm 2 fs out*.. 6
392[4] IN QUARTO 4-8-9 P Bruneau, *led, hdd 2 fs out, sn wknd.* 7
Dist: ½l, ½l, ¾l, 2l, 3l, 10l. 2m 6.30s. a 4.60s (7 Ran).
SR: 71/66/67/65/70/57/35/ (David Tsui), J Lesbordes

3501 Piaget d'Or (Restricted Listed) (3-y-o) £179,211 1¼m.................. (4:10)

3262* DANA SPRINGS (Ire) 8-10 L Dettori,..................... 1
1722[3] DANCIENNE (Fr) 8-10 D Boeuf,.......................... 2
2409[4] DIS MOI TOUT (Fr) 8-10 J Reid,........................ 3
2531[2] TALLOIRES (USA) 9-0 T Jarnet,......................... 4
2485* KIROV PREMIERE,.. 5
2803[5] RANGER (Fr) 9-0 W Mongil,............................. 8
Dist: 1½l, 2l, hd, ¾l, nk, hd, 1½l, nk, 2l. 2m 7.20s. a 5.50s (11 Ran).
SR: 61/58/54/57/-/-/ (G Howard-Spink), R Hannon

RIPON (good to firm)
Saturday August 21st

Going Correction: MINUS 0.10 sec. per fur. (races 1,3,4), MINUS 0.40 (2,5,6)

3502 Knaresborough Conditions Stakes Class D (2-y-o) £3,552 6f........(2:15)

3254[5] RANDONNEUR (Ire) 8-10 G Hind (6) *nvr far away, improved to ld o'r one furlong out, rdn out ins last.* ....(14 to 1 op 12 to 1 tchd 16 to 1) 1
3000[3] KNAYTON LASS 8-12 T Lucas (7) *in tch on outer, pushed alng to improve o'r one furlong out, sn ev ch, no extr towards finish*............... (6 to 1 op 9 to 2) 2
1683[2] SINNERS REPRIEVE 8-12 M Birch (5) *co'red up beh ldrs, effrt and rdn over one furlong out, not quicken ins last.* ....(7 to 4 fav tchd 2 to 1) 3
2500[3] MISTER BLOY 9-3 L Charnock (3) *led til rdn and hdd o'r one furlong out, sn one pace*...... (14 to 1 op 12 to 1) 4
2895* LITTLE BEAUT 8-12 W Woods (2) *co'red up beh ldrs, edgd lft over 2 fs out, shaken up over one out, swtchd rght entering last, nvr nr to chal*........ (4 to 1 op 5 to 1) 5
3236[3] MISTER BEAT 8-13 R Cochrane (8) *dwlt, beh but in tch, pushed alng aftr 2 fs, not quicken fnl two furlongs.* ....(12 to 1) 6
2453* PRIZEFIGHTER 9-1 K Darley (4) *nvr far away, pushed alng to keep up hfwy, btn 2 fs out*... (5 to 1 op 3 to 1) 7
3254[7] BANDON CASTLE (Ire) 9-3 J Quinn (1) *keen hold, beh on inner, badly hmpd o'r 2 fs out, not rcvr and eased.* ....(16 to 1 op 14 to 1) 8
Dist: 1½l, 1½l, 1½l, 2l, 2l, 3l, 5l. 1m 13.70s. a 3.10s (8 Ran).
SR: 22/18/12/11/-/ (T A Scothern), E Weymes

3503 Billy Nevett Memorial Challenge Cup Handicap Stakes Class D (0-80 3-y-o and up) £4,207 1½m 60yds......(2:45)

3240[2] FIRST BID [60] 6-9-2 A Culhane (2) *pressed ldg grp, rdn to chal 2 fs out, led appr last, hld on gmely whn hrd pressed cl hme*......... (9 to 1 op 8 to 1 tchd 10 to 1) 1
2972[2] NAWAHIL [71] 3-9-3 R Hills (7) *tried to make all, jnd frm 3 fs out, edgd lft o'r 2 out, hdd appr last, rallied gmely.* ....(8 to 1 op 7 to 1 tchd 9 to 1) 2
3211[2] BARRATRY [68] (bl) 3-9-0 A McGlone (1) *settled mid-div, took clr order appr strt, chlgd 3 fs out, drvn and kpt on und pres ins last*................ (6 to 1 op 9 to 2) 3
3373* BATABANOO [70] 4-9-12 K Darley (12) *patiently rdn, improved hfwy, drvn alng o'r 2 fs out swtchd ins over one out, one pace and eased towards finish.* ....(9 to 4 fav op 4 to 1) 4
2997[5] MISBELIEF [71] 3-9-3 M Hills (3) *keen hold, nvr far away, improved to chal o'r 3 fs out, drvn last 2 furlongs, one pace ins last*........... (5 to 1 op 4 to 1 tchd 11 to 2) 5
2683[6] MINGUS (USA) [38] 6-7-8 J Lowe (6) *drpd out strt, hld up in rear, drvn to improve o'r 2 fs out, kpt on, nvr dngrs.* ....(20 to 1 op 16 to 1) 6
3119[3] ARGYLE CAVALIER (Ire) [62] 3-8-8 R Cochrane (8) *mid-div, rdn alng to improve hfwy, kpt on same pace fnl 2 fs.* ....(14 to 1 op 12 to 1 tchd 16 to 1) 7
3353[3] ALDERNEY PRINCE (USA) [75] 3-9-7 S Whitworth (10) *hld up and beh, effrt and rdn on outer 4 fs out, not rch ldrs.* ....(7 to 1) 8
1394 FREE TRANSFER (Ire) [38] 4-7-8[1] J Fanning (11) *co'red up on ins, rdn alng 4 fs out, no imprsn fnl 2 furlongs.* ....(50 to 1 op 25 to 1) 9
2641[3] SUGEMAR [54] 7-8-5 (5*) D McCabe (5) *settled towards rear, pushed alng o'r 3 fs out, not pace to chal.* ....(20 to 1 op 16 to 1) 10
3356 HARPOON LOUIE (USA) [71] 3-9-3 M Birch (4) *wl plcd, rdn to chal o'r 3 fs out, wknd over 2 out, eased.* ....(16 to 1 op 12 to 1) 11

366 DEMOKOS (Fr) [39] 8-7-9² J Quinn (9) *unruly bef strt, cl up, lost placing entering strt, sn btn*.......... (50 to 1) 12
Dist: Hd, 1l, sht-hd, sht-hd, 2l, nk, 2½l, ½l, 5l, 3l. 2m 37.30s. a 2.30s (12 Ran).
SR: 30/30/25/36/26/-/12/20/-/ (Thomlinson's), R M Whitaker

3504 Tote Great St Wilfrid Handicap Class B (0-105 3-y-o and up) £16,165 6f (3:15)

2987² HARD TO FIGURE [96] 7-9-3 (7*) S Drowne (23) *settled far side grp, headweay 2 fs out, str run to ld last 75 yards, styd on wl*......................(10 to 1 tchd 11 to 1) 1
3127* SAMSOLOM [79] 5-8-7 J Quinn (15) *pressed main bunch far side, effrt and rdn 2 fs out, led entering fnl furlong, hdd last 75 yards, no extr*........(10 to 1 tchd 11 to 1) 2
3404 MASTER PLANNER [90] 4-8-11 (7*) J D Smith (16) *nvr far away far side, improved to ld o'r one fs out, veered rght, hdd entering fnl furlong, no extr*..........(16 to 1) 3
3034* EVERGLADES (Ire) [98] 5-9-12 R Cochrane (12) *settled far side grp, drvn to improve o'r 2 fs out, not quicken ins last*................ (9 to 2 fav op 5 to 1 tchd 6 to 1) 4
2600² FOR THE PRESENT [82] 3-8-6 K Darley (6) *nvr far away stands side, led that grp hfwy, one pace o'r one furlong out, no ch wth far side.* ....(17 to 2 op 10 to 1 tchd 11 to 1) 5
2813⁸ CATHERINES WELL [81] 10-8-9 T Lucas (19) *handily plcd far side grp, rdn and ev ch 2 fs out, one pace ins last.* ....(25 to 1 op 20 to 1) 6
3034³ EURO FESTIVAL [79] 4-8-7 A McGlone (20) *in tch far side, drvn last 2 fs, kpt on same pace ins last.* ....(16 to 1 op 20 to 1) 7
3253* SENSE OF PRIORITY [67] 4-7-9 L Charnock (14) *pressed ldg trio far side, drvn alng hfwy, no extr o'r one furlong out*..................................(20 to 1) 8
2987⁴ MASTER OF PASSION [92] 4-9-6 M Tebbutt (18) *dwlt, beh, pushed alng bef hfwy, ran on fnl furlong, nvr danmgerous*......................(20 to 1 op 16 to 1) 9
2813 EWALD (Ire) [70] 5-7-7 (5*) A Garth (9) *cl up, led far side grp hfwy, hdd o'r one furlong out, no extr*........(33 to 1) 10
3196⁷ POKER CHIP [97] 3-9-7 M Hills (21) *in tch gng wl far side, effrt and rdn 2 fs out, nvr able to chal*..........(14 to 1) 11
2987 NAGIDA [89] 4-9-3 J Weaver (11) *beh far side, sn pushed alng, effrt 2 fs out, nvr dngrs*.................. (14 to 1) 12
2987 AMRON [87] 6-9-1 N Carlisle (17) *beh far side grp, pushed alng and kpt on o'r one furlong out, not rch ldrs.* ....(20 to 1) 13
3177⁵ FACE NORTH (Ire) [71] 5-7-8 (5*) B Russell (1) *tucked away on ins stands side, rdn and no imprsn fnl 2 fs.* ....(7 to 1 op 8 to 1) 14
3177 REALITIES (USA) [93] 3-9-3 R Hills (7) *chsd ldrs stands side til rdn and wknd fnl 2 fs*..........................(16 to 1) 15
3034⁴ FINJAN [80] 6-8-1 (7*) V Halliday (3) *prmnt stands side, drvn alng hfwy, btn 2 fs out*.................. (20 to 1) 16
3280 SHE'S SMART [77] (v) 5-8-5² M Birch (10) *led far side grp to hfwy, grad lost pl*..................(25 to 1 op 20 to 1) 17
2987 KIMBERLEY PARK [66] (bl) 5-7-8¹ J Lowe (2) *beh stands side, drvn alng frm hfwy, nvr on terms*........(33 to 1) 18
2919² FORMIDABLE LIZ [69] 3-7-3³ (7*) N Varley (13) *chsd alng beh ldg grp hfwy, sn lost tch*......................(50 to 1) 19
3051⁹ TARNSIDE ROSAL [71] 3-7-9 Dale Gibson (5) *stands side, swtchd centre 2 fs out, sn struggling*.......... (33 to 1) 20
3184⁵ BALLAD DANCER [70] 8-7-12 J Fanning (8) *in tch stands side, rdn alng 3 fs out, wknd frm 2 furlongs out.* ....(33 to 1 op 25 to 1) 21
2600⁹ RED ROSEIN [81] 7-8-9 A Culhane (22) *sluggish strt, nvr able to reco'r*.................................. (20 to 1) 22
3280 DRUM SERGEANT [76] (bl) 6-8-4 S Whitworth (4) *led stands side grp to hfwy, fdd*.................... (33 to 1) 23
Dist: 1l, ½l, 2½l, 1l, nk, hd, nk, sht-hd, ¾l, nk. 1m 11.60s. a 1.00s (23 Ran).
SR: 78/57/66/64/40/42/39/26/50/ (J W Mursell), R J Hodges

3505 Tattersalls Maiden Auction Series Stakes Qualifier Class D (2-y-o) £3,435 5f............................ (3:50)

MR B REASONABLE (Ire) 8-6 A McGlone (3) *trkd ldrs gng wl, effrt 2 fs out, rdn to ld ins last, kpt on well.* ....(16 to 1 op 20 to 1) 1
2370⁵ ELUNED MAY 8-3 A Culhane (2) *made most, rdn and edgd rght o'r one furlong out, hdd ins last, not quicken.* ....(13 to 2 op 6 to 1 tchd 7 to 1) 2
2502⁷ MON ROUGE (Ire) 8-6 W Woods (6) *sn pushed alng beh ldrs, effrt 2 fs out, not quicken ins last.* ....(8 to 1 op 7 to 1) 3
LINCOLN TREASURE (Ire) 8-2 (5*) D McCabe (5) *beh, outpcd and rdn aftr 2 fs, improved o'r one furlong out, kpt on wl towards finish*......................(33 to 1) 4
3120³ THREE OF HEARTS 8-1 L Charnock (4) *wth ldr, ev ch hfwy, not quicken o'r one furlong out.* ....(13 to 2 op 6 to 1) 5
3086⁴ NAPOLEON STAR (Ire) 8-6 G Hind (8) *dwlt, pressed ldg grp on outer, pushed alng hfwy, not clr run fnl furlong, one pace*.......... (9 to 4 fav op 7 to 4 tchd 5 to 2) 6
DIAMOND PANTHER 8-13 K Darley (9) *dwlt, sn in tch on outer, shaken up 2 fs out, soon btn.* ....(4 to 1 op 5 to 2 tchd 5 to 1) 7
POWER SHARE 8-9 Dale Gibson (1) *slwly into strd, sn outpcd and struggling, nvr on terms.* (9 to 1 op 7 to 1) 8

1672⁴ SHARP SUMMIT (Ire) 8-1 J Quinn (7) *chsd ldrs, feeling pace and lost grnd hfwy, sn btn*........(16 to 1 op 20 to 1) 9
Dist: 1l, 3l, ½l, 1½l, nk, 3l, 6l, 3½l. 1m 1.30s. a 3.30s (9 Ran).
SR: 15/8/-/-/-/-/ (Broughton Thermal Insulation), W J Musson

3506 Boroughbridge Maiden Stakes Class D (3-y-o and up) £3,757 1m..... (4:25)

3225³ CAMBARA 3-8-7 M Hills (10) *nvr far away, led appr strt, shaken up and quickened approaching fnl furlong, easily*..............................(4 to 1 op 3 to 1) 1
3117³ MAKIN (USA) 3-8-12 R Hills (13) *trkd ldrs, improved to chase wnr o'r 2 fs out, sn shaken up, eased whn hld towards finish*...................... (3 to 1 op 7 to 2) 2
TAJHIZ (USA) 3-8-12 G Hind (8) *keen hold early, wl plcd, shaken up o'r 3 fs out, outpcd well over one out.* ....(11 to 8 fav op 7 to 4 tchd 2 to 1 and 9 to 4) 3
3225⁹ SILK ISLAND 3-8-12 J Quinn (5) *chsd ldrs, pushed alng o'r 2 fs out, sn one pace*..............(14 to 1 op 12 to 1) 4
3012 ELTARA 3-8-7 M Tebbutt (9) *beh, shaken up o'r 2 fs out, styd on fnl furlong, nrst finish*.... (20 to 1 op 16 to 1) 5
FLINTLOCK (Ire) 3-8-12 J Weaver (15) *slwly into strd, beh, shaken up to improve fnl 2 fs, nvr dngrs.* ....(12 to 1 op 7 to 1) 6
3225⁵ WORDS OF WISDOM (Ire) 3-8-12 M Wigham (12) *settled towards rear, shaken up o'r 2 fs out, kpt on, nvr plcd to chal*..........................(10 to 1 op 7 to 1) 7
CHIPALA 3-8-7 (5*) D McCabe (11) *slwly into strd, beh, came wide strt, sn pushed alng, nvr rchd ldrs.* (50 to 1) 8
3092⁴ JASPER ONE 3-8-12 N Connorton (3) *led til hdd appr strt, rdn alng 4 fs out, stdly lost pl*.... (50 to 1 op 100 to 1) 9
3359 STORM VIXEN 4-8-13 M Wood (4) *chsd ldg bunch, pushed alng o'r 3 fs out, sn btn*...................... (50 to 1) 10
2596⁵ WARM TOES 3-8-0 (7*) K Sked (7) *rcd very keenly, prmnt, came wide strt, rdn and wknd o'r 3 fs out*..... (33 to 1) 11
GAYADD 3-8-7 (5*) A Garth (2) *slwly into strd, pushed alng 4 fs out, nvr on terms*......................... (33 to 1) 12
16 PINK CITY 3-8-5 (7*) J Edmunds (14) *beh, lost tch hfwy, tld off*... (100 to 1) 13
Dist: 3l, 4l, 6l, 1½l, ½l, 2l, 1l, 5l, 6l, 1½l. 1m 39.80s. a 1.50s (13 Ran).
SR: 23/19/7/-/-/-/ (Sheikh Mohammed), M R Stoute

3507 Harrogate Handicap Class D (0-80 3-y-o and up) £4,305 1¼m.......... (4:55)

3356² JUBRAN (USA) [69] 7-9-2 (5*) A Garth (18) *nvr far away, chlgd o'r 2 fs out, led wl over one out, rdn out ins last.* ....(9 to 1 op 10 to 1) 1
3211³ SOVEREIGN PAGE (USA) [74] 4-9-12 M Tebbutt (8) *hld up, steady hdwy o'r 3 fs out, not clr run appr last, swtchd and sn ev ch, one pace cl hme*.......(9 to 1 op 7 to 1) 2
3019⁵ SUPERTOP [62] 5-9-0 G Hind (12) *reared leaving stalls, improve into midfield aftr 3 fs, effrt on outer 4 furlongs out, kpt on same pace fnl furlong.* (12 to 1 op 10 to 1) 3
2961 DUVEEN (Ire) [70] 3-8-11 (3*) M Fenton (5) *pressed ldrs, rdn to chal 2 fs out, one pace ins fnl furlong*.....(6 to 1 jt-fav op 8 to 1 tchd 11 to 2) 4
3181* MAY HILLS LEGACY (Ire) [57] 4-8-9 M Hills (6) *nvr far away, improved to ld o'r 2 fs out, hdd wl over one out, no extr.* .... (6 to 1 jt-fav tchd 13 to 2) 5
3035³ ARAK (USA) [69] 5-9-7 T Williams (16) *led, rdn and hdd o'r 2 fs out, kpt on same pace*..................(14 to 1) 6
TAPATCH (Ire) [62] 5-9-0 J Fanning (9) *hld up, shaken up to improve fnl 2 fs, can improve*..... (50 to 1 op 33 to 1) 7
3175⁵ DARING PAST [61] (bl) 3-8-5 W Woods (11) *keen hold, chsd ldrs, hrd at work frm 3 fs out, btn o'r one furlong out.* ....(16 to 1) 8
3356⁸ FLOATING LINE [58] 5-8-10 M Wigham (14) *settled towards rear, pushed alng o'r 2 fs out, swtchd over one out, nvr nr to chal*...................................... (25 to 1) 9
3119⁷ WESTHOLME (USA) [62] 5-9-0 M Birch (7) *hld up, rdn to improve o'r 3 fs out, one pace fnl 2 furlongs.* ....(10 to 1 op 14 to 1) 10
2961 STORM VENTURE (Ire) [72] 3-9-2 R Cochrane (15) *tucked away on ins, pushed alng to hold pl 3 fs out, sn btn.* ....(9 to 1 op 10 to 1) 11
2066 TRIPPIANO [68] 3-8-12 A McGlone (1) *hld up, rdn alng 4 fs out, not pace to chal*.............. (10 to 1 op 8 to 1) 12
2633⁸ MHEMEANLES [69] 3-8-13 T Lucas (17) *cl up til lost pl o'r 3 fs out, sn eased*................(16 to 1 op 14 to 1) 13
2995² AJMAAN (USA) [71] 3-9-1 S Whitworth (3) *in rear, rdn alng o'r 3 fs out, nvr on terms*..........(8 to 1 tchd 9 to 1) 14
137³ MASTER'S CROWN (USA) [43] 5-7-9² J Quinn (2) *hld up and beh, nvr plcd to chal*........................ (33 to 1) 15
2064² BAMBURGH (USA) [75] (v) 3-9-5 R Hills (13) *nvr far away, drvn alng 4 fs out, sn wknd, tld off.* (8 to 1 op 7 to 1) 16
3219 BOLDVILLE BASH (Ire) [64] 3-8-8 K Darley (10) *hld up and beh, lost tch fnl 3 fs, tld off*........(12 to 1 op 10 to 1) 17
Dist: ½l, 3l, nk, 5l, 1½l, nk, 1½l, ¾l, hd, nk. 2m 5.20s. a 1.20s (17 Ran).
SR: 55/59/41/40/25/34/26/14/17/ (Mrs Elke Scullion), M Johnston

SANDOWN (good to firm)
Saturday August 21st
Going Correction: MINUS 0.05 sec. per fur. (races 1,2,3,5,6,7), NIL (4)

3508 Butlin's Holidays Selling Nursery Stakes Handicap Class E (2-y-o) £2,900 7f 16yds................ (2:05)

2705[4] SHERIFF [63] 9-4 J Williams (10) *hdwy frm rear on outsd 2 fs out, str run to get up last strds.* ....(16 to 1 op 14 to 1 tchd 20 to 1) 1
3210* GREENSON (Ire) [58] 8-13 T Quinn (16) *led for one furlong, led wl o'r 2 fs out, rdn clr one out, hdd last strds.* ....(3 to 1 fav op 5 to 1) 2
3126[2] PRINCESS CARMEN (Ire) [66] 9-7 B Raymond (13) *led aftr one furlong, hdd o'r 2 fs out, one pace appr fnl furlong.* ....(12 to 1 op 10 to 1) 3
3264[7] NORTHERN BAILIWICK (Ire) [53] (bl) 8-8 N Adams (8) *slwly into strd, ran on frm rear 2 fs out, nrst finish.* ....(12 to 1 op 8 to 1 tchd 14 to 1) 4
2988[5] STRAPPED [53] 8-8 C Rutter (6) *towards rear whn hmpd 4 fs out, cld on ldrs 3 out, one pace appr fnl furlong.* ....(16 to 1 tchd 20 to 1) 5
3236[5] MIGHTY KINGDOM (Ire) [53] (bl) 8-8 A Mackay (12) *hdwy 3 fs out, rdn and no extr o'r one out*..............(14 to 1) 6
3303[3] BET A PLAN (Ire) [57] 8-9 (3*) D Harrison (11) *mid-div, effrt 2 fs out, not rch ldrs*... (16 to 1 op 14 to 1 tchd 20 to 1) 7
3345[5] THORNY BISHOP [62] (bl) 9-3 S O'Gorman (15) *chsd ldrs till hmpd 4 fs out, rallied 3 out, no extr ins last 2 furlongs.* ....(33 to 1 op 25 to 1) 8
3129[5] ERRIS BOY [59] 9-0 A Clark (4) *in tch, rdn and no prog 2 fs out, wknd o'r one out*.........(11 to 1 op 8 to 1) 9
3084[4] WADDLE (Ire) [54] 8-9 P Robinson (5) *wl plcd, effrt o'r 2 fs out, wknd well over one out*..... (10 to 1 tchd 11 to 1) 10
3222[9] BROUGHTONS PARTNER [56] (bl) 8-11 D Biggs (9) *wl plcd for 5 fs*..........(25 to 1 op 20 to 1) 11
3126[3] MR ROUGH [57] 8-12 G Bardwell (3) *effrt frm mid-div o'r 2 furlong sout, wknd over one out.* ....(6 to 1 op 5 to 1 tchd 13 to 2) 12
3129[7] DOUBLE DANCER [61] 9-2 G Duffield (1) *pressed ldrs for o'r 4 fs, sn btn*.........(10 to 1 op 7 to 1 tchd 11 to 1) 13
2844 SOUTHDOWN GIRL [55] 8-5 (5*) L Newton (7) *chsd ldrs for 4 fs*..........(33 to 1 op 20 to 1 tchd 40 to 1) 14
3267[8] MARCH OF TIME [58] 8-13 D Holland (2) *al beh.* ....(33 to 1 op 20 to 1) 15
2988 KOONOONA LADY [58] (bl) 8-10 (3*) B Doyle (14) *mid-div till beh last 3 fs, tld off*................(33 to 1 op 20 to 1) 16

Dist: Nk, 2½l, 1½l, hd, 3½l, 5l, 3l, nk, 1l, 1½l. 1m 32.68s. a 6.18s (16 Ran).
SR: 6/-/-/-/-/ (Christopher P J Brown), J W Hills

3509 Vymura International Amateur Riders Conditions Stakes Class E (3-y-o and up) £3,225 1¼m 7yds........... (2:35)

2941[2] RIVER BOYNE (USA) 3-11-0 Miss A Harwood (16) *led for one furlong, wl plcd, led ag'n well o'r one furlong out, rdn clr and styd on*......... (6 to 4 on tchd 5 to 4 on) 1
3224[2] GILDERDALE 11-11-8 Mr C Vigors (3) *hld up, hdwy o'r 3 fs out, chsd wnr fnl furlong, no imprsn.* ....(9 to 2 tchd 5 to 1) 2
3090[2] CREDIT SQUEEZE 3-11-0 Miss E Johnson Houghton (11) *wth ldrs, led o'r 3 fs out, hdd wl over one out, ran on same pace*..........(8 to 1 tchd 10 to 1) 3
3385[6] MILZIG (USA) 4-11-8 Mrs P Nash (5) *hdwy o'r 2 fs out, styd on one pace appr fnl furlong, not rch wnr.* ....(12 to 1 op 10 to 1) 4
3096[2] HOME PARK (Ire) 3-11-0 Mrs M Cowdrey (7) *wl in tch, cld on ldrs o'r 3 fs out, no extr fnl furlong.* ....(7 to 1 op 6 to 1) 5
3385[9] STARLIGHT FLYER (bl) 6-11-10 (4*) Mr T Waters (17) *handily plcd til wknd o'r 2 fs out*................(150 to 1) 6
3240* SIR THOMAS BEECHAM 3-11-0 Mr T Cuff (4) *nvr nrr.* ....(20 to 1 op 14 to 1) 7
3221[4] FORTUNE STAR (Ire) 4-11-4 (4*) Miss M Bridger (12) *led aftr one furlong, hdd o'r 6 fs out, wknd over 3 out.* (150 to 1) 8
3225 DIXIE DIAMOND 3-10-9 Miss Harriet Glen (2) *nvr better than mid-div*..........(150 to 1) 9
3247[6] DUNMAGLASS 6-11-4 (4*) Mr M Mannish (6) *lost many ls leaving stalls, rapid hdwy to ld o'r 6 fs out, hdd and wknd over 3 out*.......... (150 to 1) 10
EASTERN EVENING 8-11-4 (4*) Mr J Poulton (8) *settled in mid-div, nvr trble frnt rnk frm 3 fs out*...... (150 to 1) 11
SOROPTIMIST (Fr) 4-11-3 Miss J Winter (15) *in tch for o'r 6 fs*.......... (150 to 1) 12
2992 LAMBOURN RAJA 7-11-5[1] (4*) Mr K Tork (9) *slwly into strd, nvr rch ldrs*.......... (150 to 1) 13
TIME OF GRACE (Ire) 3-10-10 (4*) Mr E Tolhurst (14) *al beh.* ....(150 to 1) 14
2658 MELLERIO 3-11-0 Mr K Santana (13) *sn in rear.* ....(100 to 1 op 6 to 1) 15
3286 MYJINKA 3-10-5 (4*) Miss K Martindale (1) *slwly into strd, al outpcd, tld off*.......... (150 to 1) 16
3225 BUY BY NIGHT 3-10-9 Mrs S Bosley (10) *mid-div till drpd rear 4 fs out, virtually pld up last 2 furlongs.* (150 to 1) 17

Dist: 2½l, 2½l, 3l, 5l, 10l, sht-hd, 4l, hd, 3l, nk. 2m 11.91s. a 8.01s (17 Ran).
SR: 43/46/33/35/17/11/ (K Abdulla), G Harwood

3510 Unifilla Conditions Stakes Class C (2-y-o) £4,025 1m 14yds........... (3:10)

3137* BLAZE AWAY (USA) 8-13 S O'Gorman (5) *hld up, ran on o'r 2 fs out, led over one out, rdn clr*.. (6 to 1 tchd 7 to 1) 1
3248[4] THREATENING 8-8 G Bardwell (6) *settled in 3rd pl, led o'r 3 fs out, hdd over one out, ran on same pace.* ....(8 to 1 op 7 to 1 tchd 9 to 1) 2
3130[4] LEAR DANCER (USA) 8-11 M Roberts (4) *hld up towards rear, ran on one pace last 2 fs*....... (7 to 1 op 8 to 1) 3
2924[4] CLASSIC SKY (Ire) 9-3 B Raymond (1) *hld up, rdn alng o'r 2 fs out, one pace appr fnl furlong.* ....(5 to 2 fav op 3 to 1 tchd 100 to 30) 4
3289[3] REPREHEND 8-13 T Quinn (2) *chsd ldr till lft in ld o'r 4 fs out, hdd over 3 out, hng left and btn 2 out.* ....(11 to 4 op 2 to 1) 5
2250* SILVER WEDGE (USA) 8-13 G Duffield (3) *led til veered lft and slpd up o'r 4 fs out*..........(11 to 2 op 7 to 1) su

Dist: 4l, 3½l, 3l, 3½l. 1m 43.92s. a 4.82s (6 Ran).
SR: 21/4/-/ (Paul Mellon), I A Balding

3511 Coloroll Rated Stakes Class B Handicap (0-100 3-y-o and up) £5,750 5f 6yds........................ (3:40)

3153* GORINSKY (Ire) [93] 5-9-7 T Quinn (11) *led for one furlong, cl up, shaken up to ld wl ins fnl furlong, hld on.* ....(9 to 2 fav op 4 to 1 tchd 5 to 1) 1
3410[8] FANGIO [80] 4-8-1 (7*) P McCabe (4) *led aftr one furlong, rdn and hdd wl ins fnl furlong, rallied last strd.* ....(14 to 1 op 12 to 1 tchd 16 to 1) 2
2872[4] METAL BOYS [79] 6-8-4 (3*) D Harrison (3) *mid-div, str run o'r one furlong out, fnshd wl*.... (10 to 1 tchd 12 to 1) 3
3105[4] HEAVENLY RISK [87] 3-8-5 (7*) Mark Denaro (5) *slwly into strd, ran on frm rear wl o'r one furlong out, fnshd well.* ....(11 to 1 op 10 to 1) 4
3105[3] FARFELU [89] (v) 6-9-3 D Holland (2) *chsd ldrs, rdn and kpt on ins fnl furlong*..........(7 to 1 tchd 8 to 1) 5
3105[2] SHIKARI'S SON [84] 6-8-12 G Duffield (9) *styd on frm rear o'r one furlong out, fnshd wl.* ....(9 to 1 op 8 to 1 tchd 10 to 1) 6
3291[8] INHERENT MAGIC (Ire) [80] 4-8-8 A Clark (7) *chsd frnt rnk, rdn and not quicken fnl furlong.* (12 to 1 tchd 14 to 1) 7
2969[7] MAGIC ORB [79] 3-8-4 A Mackay (12) *hdwy frm rear 2 fs out, styd on nr finish*....(7 to 1 op 8 to 1 tchd 9 to 1) 8
2987 BALLASECRET [88] 5-8-11 (5*) A Procter (6) *pressed ldrs til wknd o'r one furlong out.* ....(11 to 1 op 7 to 1 tchd 12 to 1) 9
3348[4] TERRHARS (Ire) [82] 5-8-10 M Roberts (13) *mid-div, effrt o'r one furlong out, no imprsn*......(11 to 2 op 6 to 1) 10
658[7] RESIST THE FORCE (USA) [81] 3-8-6 D Biggs (8) *chsd ldrs for o'r 3 fs, sn wknd*..........(20 to 1 op 16 to 1) 11
3034[6] BEAU VENTURE (USA) [82] 5-8-7 (3*) N Kennedy (1) *wl plcd til wknd o'r one furlong out*..... (14 to 1 tchd 16 to 1) 12
2255 OLIFANTSFONTEIN [79] (bl) 5-8-7 B Raymond (10) *slwly into strd, al beh*.......... (25 to 1 tchd 20 to 1) 13

Dist: Sht-hd, nk, hd, ½l, ½l, nk, ½l, nk, hd, 3l. 1m 1.26s. a 1.76s (13 Ran).
SR: 72/58/56/60/63/56/51/45/56/ (William Robertson), J Berry

3512 William Hill Stakes Handicap Class C (0-90 3-y-o and up) £4,515 1¼m 7yds ....(4:15)

2433[3] JAZILAH (Fr) [73] 5-9-1 T Quinn (7) *wl plcd, ran on 3 fs out, led jst o'r one out, pushed clr*........(5 to 1 op 7 to 2) 1
3012[8] KARSHI [80] 3-9-0 G Duffield (9) *chsd ldr, ev ch one furlong out, rdn and not quicken*.............. (20 to 1) 2
3179[2] EDEN'S CLOSE [71] 4-8-13 P Robinson (8) *mid-div, ran on 3 fs out, styd on one pace fnl furlong.* ....(17 to 2 op 8 to 1 tchd 9 to 1) 3
3018[5] LOBILIO (USA) [67] (v) 4-8-6 (3*) B Doyle (4) *prmnt till rdn and wknd o'r one furlong out, fnshd 4th, disqualified.* ....(16 to 1 tchd 20 to 1) 4D
3204* KNOCK KNOCK [75] 8-9-3 S O'Gorman (3) *hdwy frm rear last 2 fs, nvr nrr, fnshd 5th, plcd 4th.* ....(4 to 1 fav op 5 to 1 tchd 6 to 1) 4
3342* RAPPORTEUR (USA) [61] 7-8-3 D Holland (11) *led till o'r one furlong out, eased whn btn, fnshd 6th, plcd 5th.* ....(16 to 1 tchd 20 to 1) 5
3211[4] LET'S GET LOST [71] 4-8-13 N Day (10) *rear till moderate hdwy last 2 fs*......(10 to 1 op 8 to 1 tchd 12 to 1) 7
2854[4] PIQUANT [83] 6-9-8 (3*) D Harrison (2) *settled rear, effrt 3 fs out, sn btn*..........(12 to 1 op 10 to 1 tchd 14 to 1) 8
3301[4] WHATEVER'S RIGHT (Ire) [53] 4-7-9 N Adams (13) *al rear.* ....(20 to 1 op 16 to 1 tchd 25 to 1) 9
603* BELMOREDEAN [66] 8-8-8 D Biggs (12) *wth ldrs till wknd 2 fs out*..........(20 to 1) 10
3093[4] NASHVILLE BLUES (Ire) [82] 4-9-10 J Williams (14) *nvr on terms*..........(12 to 1 op 10 to 1 tchd 14 to 1) 11
3019[4] ABERDEEN HEATHER [70] 3-8-4 A Mackay (6) *chsd frnt rnk, ran wide and wknd o'r 3 fs out.* ....(25 to 1 op 20 to 1) 12
3282[6] VALLANCE [78] 5-9-6 A Clark (1) *in tch till wknd o'r 2 fs out*..........(14 to 1 op 16 to 1) 13
3036[4] MAP OF STARS (USA) [81] (v) 3-9-1 M Roberts (5) *mid-div till lost pos 4 fs out*.......... (10 to 1 tchd 12 to 1) 14

Dist: 3l, 2½l, 2l, sht-hd, ¾l, 2l, hd, 4l, 6l, 1l. 2m 7.50s. a 3.60s (14 Ran).
SR: 60/53/47/39/46/30/36/47/9/ (S Aitken), R Akehurst

3513 Texas Homecare Stakes Handicap Class D (0-80 3-y-o and up) £3,870 1 ¾m. . . . . (4:45)

3224[4] WINGS COVE [69] 3-8-6 J Williams (4) *pressed ldrs, led o'r 2 fs out, rdn clr appr fnl furlong.* . . . . (12 to 1 op 10 to 1 tchd 14 to 1) 1
2152[2] LAKE POOPO (Ire) [72] 3-8-9 D Holland (9) *wl plcd, rdn and outpcd 2 fs out, styd on ag'n ins fnl furlong.* . . . . (17 to 2 op 8 to 1 tchd 9 to 1) 2
3434* SARAWAT [75] 5-9-10 (4ex) T Quinn (3) *cl up, led o'r 8 fs out, hdd over 2 out, kpt on same pace fnl furlong.* . . . . (Evens fav op 5 to 4 tchd 11 to 8) 3
994 ABSENT RELATIVE [54] 5-8-3 A Clark (7) *hdwy frm rear o'r 3 fs out, not much room over one out, no imprsn.* . . . . (33 to 1 op 25 to 1 tchd 40 to 1) 4
3252[2] HOOSIE [72] 3-8-9 M Roberts (6) *led til hdd o'r 8 fs out, one pace frm 2 out*. . . . . (13 to 2 op 5 to 1 tchd 7 to 1) 5
2963[8] HILL OF DREAMS [74] 3-8-11 S O'Gorman (1) *beh til moderate prog last 2 fs*. . . . (11 to 1 op 10 to 1 tchd 12 to 1) 6
2913[3] MOONLIGHT QUEST [79] 5-9-11 (3*) D Harrison (11) *hld up in mid-div aftr 3 fs, effrt o'r three out, btn over 2 out.* . . . . (10 to 1 op 8 to 1 tchd 11 to 1) 7
2942[3] ACROBATE (USA) [61] 4-8-10 A Mackay (2) *stumbled leaving stalls, nvr better than mid-div.* . (12 to 1 op 8 to 1) 8
3066[5] WEDNESDAYS AUCTION (Ire) [44] 5-7-7 N Adams (10) *al beh*. . . . . (66 to 1 op 33 to 1) 9
3306[3] MAD CASANOVA [62] (bl) 8-8-11 D Biggs (5) *in tch til wknd 4 fs out*. . . . . (20 to 1 op 12 to 1) 10

Dist: 5l, 3l, ¾l, ½l, 4l, 1l, 7l, 3l, 6l. 3m 1.66s. a 7.36s (10 Ran).
SR: 11/4/13/-/-/-/4/-/-/ (Edwin N Cohen), Lady Herries

3514 Variety Club Childrens' Charity Maiden Fillies' Stakes Class D (3-y-o) £3,545 1m 14yds. . . . . (5:20)

423[9] JAVA QUEEN (USA) 8-11 S O'Gorman (13) *made all, pushed clr frm 2 fs out, unchlgd.* . . . . (12 to 1 op 7 to 1 tchd 16 to 1) 1
3117[5] LA SPEZIA 8-11 G Duffield (10) *chsd wnr thrght, rdn and not quicken 2 fs out*. . . (14 to 1 op 8 to 1 tchd 16 to 1) 2
BADRAH (USA) 8-11 A Clark (12) *wl plcd, styd on one pace last 2 fs*. . . . . (11 to 1 op 12 to 1 tchd 14 to 1) 3
POCKET PIECE (USA) 8-11 K Fallon (9) *mid-div, effrt o'r 3 fs out, no extr ins last 2 furlongs*. . . (12 to 1 op 7 to 1) 4
3272[2] TAP ON AIR 8-11 M Roberts (8) *handily plcd, shaken up hfwy, no prog last 2 fs*. . . . . (6 to 4 on tchd Evens) 5
1452[4] KEYLOCK (USA) 8-11 J Williams (4) *hld up, effrt o'r 3 fs out, no imprsn on ldrs last 2 furlongs.* . . . . (25 to 1 op 20 to 1 tchd 33 to 1) 6
821[9] ZANZE (USA) 8-11 B Crossley (5) *nvr nr to chal.* . . . . (33 to 1 op 20 to 1) 7
2401[4] KOSATA (Ire) 8-11 D Holland (2) *strted slwly, hdwy frm rear 3 fs out, wknd o'r one out*. . . . . (6 to 1 op 10 to 1) 8
3286[5] BOBBIE DEE 8-11 T Quinn (7) *nvr able to chal.* . . . . (8 to 1 op 6 to 1) 9
2937[9] EMMA WOODFORD 8-11 N Adams (11) *reared leaving stalls, al beh*. . . . . . . (25 to 1 op 16 to 1 tchd 33 to 1) 10
3286 TOUCHEE BOUCHEE 8-11 C Rutter (6) *sn racing towards rear, nvr on terms*. . . . . (66 to 1 op 33 to 1) 11
1454[7] RISK THE WITCH 8-6 (5*) L Newton (1) *al outpcd.* . . . . (50 to 1 op 33 to 1 tchd 66 to 1) 12

Dist: 3½l, 1½l, 2l, 2½l, 3l, 1l, nk, 4l, 8l, 2l. 1m 42.69s. a 3.59s (12 Ran).
SR: 37/26/21/15/7/-/ (Paul Mellon), I A Balding

DEAUVILLE (FR) (good)
Sunday August 22nd
Going Correction: PLUS 0.20 sec. per fur. (race 1), NIL (2,3)

3515 Prix Morny Agence Francaise 2yo Colts & Fillies £119,474 6f. . . . . . (2:30)

3014* COUP DE GENIE (USA) 8-8 C Asmussen, *al cl up, jnd ldr 2 fs out, led 150 yards out, ran on wl*. 1
2647* PSYCHOBABBLE (Ire) 8-11 F Head, *pld hrd, trkd ldrs, not clr run 2 fs out, found gap one out, fnshd wl*. 2
SPAIN LANE (USA) 8-8 W R Swinburn, *mid-div, slight ld wl o'r one furlong out till hdd 150 yards out, unbl to quicken*. 3
2980[3] CELTIC ARMS (Fr) 8-11 D Boeuf, *in rear till hdwy 2 fs out, kpt on fnl furlong, nvr rchd ldrs*. 4
3014[2] FOXHOUND (USA) 8-11 T Jarnet, *slwly into strd, sn in tch, rdn 2 fs out, one pace fnl furlong*. 5
3031* SOLAR WAGON (USA) 8-11 Pat Eddery, *led till wl o'r one furlong out*. 6
3014[4] FRED BONGUSTO (Ire) 8-11 E Legrix, *mid-div, not clr run 2 fs out, nvr able to chal*. 7
2647[3] FAR MIST (Fr) 8-8 O Peslier, *in tch on outsd till rdn and wknd 2 fs out*. 8

Dist: 1½l, sht-nk, 1l, ¾l, 1½l, ¾l, nk. 1m 13.10s. a 4.70s (8 Ran).
SR: 24/21/17/16/13/7/4/-/ (S S Niarchos), F Boutin

3516 Prix Kergorlay (Group 2) (3-y-o and up) £35,842 1m 7f. . . . . (4:35)

2646* RAINTRAP 3-8-7 Pat Eddery, *hld up, last strt, hdwy 2 fs out, ran on wl to ld 50 yards out*. 1
3241[2] SAMOURZAKAN (Ire) 4-9-4 G Mosse, *led to 5 fs out, 3rd strt, led 2 out till ct 50 yards out*. 2
3349[4] ZINAAD 4-9-8 W R Swinburn, *hld up, 4th strt, outpcd 2 fs out, some late prog*. 3
1787[3] TURGEON (USA) 7-9-4 C Asmussen, *trkd ldr, led 5 fs out to 2 out, one pace*. 4
EMBARCADERO (Ger) 5-9-4 J Reid, *second strt, rdn and wknd one and a half fs out*. 5

Dist: ½l, ¾l, ½l, 2½l. 3m 25.70s. a 16.30s (5 Ran).
(K Abdulla), A Fabre

OVREVOLL (NOR) (heavy)
Sunday August 22nd

3517 Fina Norsk Derby 1993 (Listed) (3-y-o) £47,755 1½m. . . . . (2:50)

LOROFINO (Nor) 9-2 G Nordling. 1
LAST ATTEMPT (Nor) 9-2 F Diaz. 2
ESTARELLA (Den) 9-2 J Fortune. 3
MCCUE (Nor) 9-2 M Santos. 4

Dist: 25l, 14l, 1l, ½l, 4½l, 1l, 13l, hd, 14l, 3½l. 2m 48.10s. (14 Ran).
Wido Neuroth

NOTTINGHAM (good)
Monday August 23rd
Going Correction: PLUS 0.10 sec. per fur.

3518 'Encourage Young' Selling Handicap Class G (0-60 3-y-o and up) £2,889 1m 1f 213yds. . . . . (2:15)

3107[5] TIGER CLAW (USA) [43] (bl) 7-8-11 A McGlone (12) *mid-div, hdwy 3 fs out, effrt 2 out, rdn to ld ins last, ran on.* . . . . (10 to 1 op 8 to 1) 1
4758a KATHY FAIR (Ire) [41] 4-8-4 (5*) B Russell (4) *beh, hdwy on ins 3 fs out, rdn 2 out, styd on strly inside last.* . . . . (9 to 1 op 7 to 1 tchd 12 to 1) 2
2384 GOTT'S DESIRE [39] (bl) 7-8-7 T Quinn (5) *hld up beh, hdwy on ins 4 fs out, effrt 2 out, sn led, rdn o'r one out, hdd and no extr inside last*. . . . . . . (25 to 1 op 12 to 1) 3
3240[7] NOT YET [29] 9-7-11 J Quinn (15) *beh, hdwy 3 fs out, rdn and ran on frm 2 out, nrst finish.* . . . . (10 to 1 op 7 to 1 tchd 11 to 1) 4
2197 PIMSBOY [44] 6-8-12 S Wood (13) *in tch, hdwy on outsd 4 fs out, ev ch 2 out, sn rdn, one pace appr last.* . . . . (33 to 1 op 20 to 1) 5
3310[8] YOUNG JASON [44] 10-8-12 S Perks (2) *hld up mid-div, effrt and swtchd wide 3 fs out, rdn 2 out, kpt on one pace*. . . . . (12 to 1 op 8 to 1) 6
3232* GALEJADE [53] 3-8-13 J Williams (16) *in tch, effrt o'r 2 fs out, sn rdn, one pace*. . . (8 to 1 op 7 to 1 tchd 9 to 1) 7
3322[8] RED SOMBRERO [31] 4-7-13 A Mackay (8) *cl up, led aftr 4 fs, rdn 3 out, hdd and wknd wl o'r one out*. . . . (25 to 1) 8
3246[6] BILLYBACK [54] 3-9-0 D Biggs (6) *nvr rch ldrs.* . . . . (14 to 1 op 10 to 1) 9
1961[3] GESNERA [30] 5-7-12 N Adams (1) *beh and rdn alng, some hdwy fnl 2 fs*. . . . . (14 to 1 op 12 to 1) 10
3055[7] ROLY WALLACE [52] (bl) 4-9-6 G Bardwell (9) *nvr rch ldrs.* . . . . (16 to 1 op 14 to 1) 11
3224[7] BRONZE RUNNER [35] (bl) 9-8-3 T Sprake (17) *prmnt, effrt 3 fs out, sn ev ch, rdn 2 out, soon wknd.* . . . . (14 to 1 op 8 to 1 tchd 16 to 1) 12
3374[4] SLUMBER THYME (Ire) [37] (bl) 4-8-5 W Ryan (22) *dwlt, beh and pld hrd, hdwy 4 fs out, sn rdn and no imprsn.* . . . . (11 to 1 op 8 to 1) 13
3042[6] PIPERS REEL [45] (v) 3-8-5 A Munro (14) *chsd ldrs, rdn 4 fs out, wknd*. . . . . (10 to 1 op 8 to 1) 14
1143 MARZOCCO [42] 5-8-10 T Williams (18) *in tch, lost pl and beh fnl 3 fs*. . . . . (16 to 1 op 12 to 1) 15
1035[6] DANCING BOAT [35] 4-8-3 D Holland (11) *cl up, rdn o'r 3 fs out, sn wknd*. . . . . (20 to 1 tchd 25 to 1) 16
3228 MEXICAN DANCER [42] 4-8-10 K Darley (20) *al rdn alng in rear*. . . . . (14 to 1 op 10 to 1) 17
3010[8] EVERY ONE A GEM [35] (bl) 6-8-3[2] A Clark (7) *hld up, effrt 4 fs out, sn rdn, no hdwy*. . . . . . . (4 to 1 fav op 14 to 1) 18
CANNONALE (Ire) [33] 4-8-1 P Robinson (10) *in tch, rdn 4 fs out, sn wknd*. . . . . (33 to 1) 19
3192 WRETS [60] 4-9-7 (7*) R Painter (21) *nvr a factor.* . . . . (50 to 1 op 33 to 1) 20
3088[8] DANSEUSE FRANCAISE (Ire) [40] 3-7-13[2] (3*) M Fenton (3) *led 4 fs, cl up till rdn and wknd four out, sn beh.* . . . . (20 to 1 op 14 to 1 tchd 25 to 1) 21
THRILL [40] 5-8-8 K Williamson (19) *in tch, rdn o'r 4 fs out, sn lost pl*. . . . . (66 to 1 op 33 to 1) 22

Dist: 1l, 1l, ½l, 2l, 4l, ½l, sht-hd, 2½l, hd, 1l. 2m 10.00s. a 7.00s (22 Ran).
SR: 37/33/29/18/29/21/21/6/16/ (Unity Farm Holiday Centre Ltd), R J Hodges

3519 W. J. Furse Conditions Stakes Class D (3-y-o) £3,318 1m 54yds........ (2:45)

2941[4] AJFAN (USA) 8-5 R Hills (4) *made all, rdn 2 fs out, ran on wl*..........................(13 to 8 fav op 5 to 2) 1
3268[6] EL DUCO (USA) 9-0 Pat Eddery (3) *in tch, effrt o'r 3 fs out, sn chasing wnr, rdn and hng lft 2 out, no imprsn.* ....(100 to 30 op 5 to 2) 2
3268[5] PLANETARY ASPECT (USA) 9-0 J Reid (2) *trkd wnr, effrt and rdn 3 fs out, not run on.* ....(4 to 1 op 7 to 2 tchd 5 to 1) 3
CROPTON 8-7 Paul Eddery (1) *chsd ldrs, rdn o'r 3 fs out, sn one pace*....................(14 to 1 tchd 16 to 1) 4
3268[3] DARBONNE (USA) 8-11 K Darley (5) *chsd ldrs, rdn o'r 3 fs out, hng lft, sn btn*..................(5 to 1 op 7 to 2) 5
3268[8] GREEN'S BID 9-0 T Quinn (6) *slwly into strd, al rear.* ....(33 to 1 op 25 to 1) 6

Dist: 3½l, 5l, 6l, 7l, 12l. 1m 43.20s. a 3.20s (6 Ran).
SR: 55/53/38/13/-/-/ (Hamdan Al-Maktoum), H Thomson Jones

3520 Tattersalls Maiden Auction Series Stakes Qualifier Class D (2-y-o) £3,845 6f 15yds...................... (3:15)

3166[4] YO-CANDO (Ire) 7-10 (5*) L Newton (12) *cl up gng wl, led on bit entering fnl furlong, shaken up ins last, ran on.* ....(6 to 1 tchd 8 to 1 and 5 to 1) 1
3260[6] LIME STREET BLUES (Ire) 8-11 Pat Eddery (16) *in tch, rdn 2 fs out, hdwy to chal ins last, not quicken nr finish.* ....(11 to 2 op 6 to 1 tchd 8 to 1) 2
2826[4] A MILLION WATTS 8-6 G Duffield (18) *led till appr hfwy, cl up and ev ch till rdn and one pace entering last.* ....(14 to 1 op 10 to 1) 3
3230[5] VENUS VICTORIOUS (Ire) 8-7 M Hills (17) *cl up gng wl, led appr hfwy, rdn and hdd entering last, no extr.* ....(5 to 2 fav op 7 to 4 tchd 11 to 4) 4
LA RESIDENCE 8-7 N Adams (14) *dwlt, sn in tch, rdn 2 fs out, kpt on*...................(33 to 1 op 50 to 1) 5
KID ORY 8-6 Dale Gibson (13) *dwlt, chsd ldrs hfwy, sn rdn, kpt on*................................(50 to 1) 6
3104[2] SEDIMENTARY 8-6 L Dettori (9) *prmnt, effrot and ev ch one and a half fs out, sn rdn, wknd entering last.* ....(8 to 1 op 5 to 1) 7
3250[5] VLAMINCK (Ire) 8-13 A McGlone (7) *not rch ldrs.* ....(20 to 1 op 16 to 1) 8
2706 UNCLE DOUG 8-12 J Fanning (15) *nvr rch ldrs*...(33 to 1) 9
3215[2] RAFFERTY'S RULES (Ire) 8-9 K Fallon (2) *steadied strt, mid-div till swtchd wide and hdwy 2 fs out, sn rdn, kpt on*.................................(6 to 1 op 7 to 2) 10
2179[6] SOMMERSBY (Ire) 8-10 R Hills (5) *nvr a factor.* ....(8 to 1 op 5 to 1) 11
2866[9] VICEROY RULER 8-11 S Whitworth (19) *chsd ldrs, rdn and wknd 2 fs out*..........................(25 to 1 op 3 to 1) 12
2224[4] PETITJEAN (Ire) 8-11 T Quinn (8) *nvr a factor.* ....(14 to 1 op 12 to 1) 13
CADEAUX PREMIERE 8-8 Alex Greaves (6) *nvr rch ldrs.* ....(50 to 1) 14
2695[7] RED DANCER 8-3 (3*) M Fenton (1) *outpcd, sn rdn alng, al beh*..............................(16 to 1 op 12 to 1) 15
3421 MISTER O'GRADY (Ire) 8-7 R Cochrane (4) *chsd ldrs, rdn hfwy, sn wknd*.....................(50 to 1 op 33 to 1) 16
KENILWORTH FORD 8-1 N Carlisle (3) *sn outpcd and beh.* ....(50 to 1) 17
2123 WILL GLOW 8-8 J Reid (11) *outpcd and wl beh hfwy.* ....(25 to 1 op 16 to 1) 18
VAX IT 8-1 K Darley (20) *slwly away, al beh.* ....(25 to 1 op 16 to 1) 19

Dist: Nk, 2l, sht-hd, ¾l, 1½l, hd, nk, hd, sht-hd, ½l. 1m 15.10s. a 3.60s (19 Ran).
SR: 27/36/23/23/20/13/12/18/16/ (Miss L Elliott), D J S Cosgrove

3521 Harcros Timber & Building Supplies Stayers Championship Series Handicap Qualifier Class D (0-80 3-y-o and up) £3,640 1¾m 15yds.......... (3:45)

3307[5] KADASTROF (Fr) [68] 3-8-5 T Quinn (8) *made all, rdn o'r 2 fs out, ran on strly*................(16 to 1 op 10 to 1) 1
3288[2] HIGH SUMMER [68] 3-8-5 L Dettori (18) *trkd wnr, chlgd 3 fs out, sn rdn, kpt on one pace.* (11 to 4 fav op 7 to 2) 2
3255[7] ELA BILLANTE [68] 3-8-5 P Robinson (11) *mid-div, hdwy 5 fs out, effrt 3 out, sn rdn, kpt on one pace.* ....(12 to 1 op 14 to 1) 3
BRODESSA [66] 7-9-1 M Birch (9) *hld up beh, hdwy on outsd 4 fs out, rdn o'r 2 out, kpt on.* ....(16 to 1 op 12 to 1 tchd 20 to 1) 4
3288[8] WHITE RIVER [45] 7-7-8[1] A Mackay (15) *hld up beh, hdwy 5 fs out, effrt on outsd 2 out, sn rdn, kpt on.* ....(20 to 1 op 14 to 1) 5
3356[7] SALU [53] 4-8-2[2] G Duffield (4) *beh, hdwy on ins 3 fs out, swtchd outsd wl o'r one out, kpt on, nvr dngrs.* ....(12 to 1 op 8 to 1) 6
2655[5] TAROUDANT [75] 6-9-10 K Darley (14) *chsd ldrs, effrt 4 fs out, rdn 3 out, wknd 2 out*..........(9 to 1 op 7 to 1) 7
3271[3] CALL THE GUV'NOR [68] 4-9-3 W Ryan (2) *in tch, effrt 3 fs out, sn rdn, one pace*.............(5 to 1 tchd 6 to 1) 8
3271[2] ALQAIRAWAAN [58] 4-8-7 B Rouse (7) *pld hrd, in tch, effrt 3 fs out, sn rdn and btn.* (7 to 1 op 5 to 1 tchd 8 to 1) 9
3307[2] WESTFIELD MOVES (Ire) [56] 5-7-12 (7*) C Hawksley (17) *nvr rch ldrs*..........................(10 to 1 op 8 to 1) 10
3116[5] SAMAIN (USA) [49] 6-7-12 N Carlisle (5) *slwly away, al rear*...(20 to 1) 11
420[8] KARAMOJA [53] 4-8-2 A Munro (10) *chsd ldrs, rdn 4 fs out, sn wknd*..........................(14 to 1 op 12 to 1) 12
3231[2] SWORD MASTER [75] 4-9-10 N Day (12) *al rear.* ....(11 to 1 op 8 to 1) 13
478[8] IOTA [73] 4-9-8 B Raymond (6) *prmnt, rdn o'r 3 fs out, sn wknd*..........................(10 to 1 tchd 12 to 1) 14
2776 SOLOMAN SPRINGS (USA) [72] 3-8-6 (3*) O Pears (1) *prmnt, rdn 5 fs out, sn wknd*..... (25 to 1 op 16 to 1) 15
3089[3] VICTOR ROMEO [44] (v) 4-7-3[1] (5*) D Wright (13) *mid-div, some hdwy hfwy, sn lost pl and beh*..........(66 to 1) 16
SADLER'S WAY [71] 4-9-6 Ann Stokell (16) *al beh, tld off fnl 4 fs*..(50 to 1) 17

Dist: 3½l, 1l, 1½l, ¾l, 1½l, 3½l, nk, ¾l, 3½l, sht-hd. 3m 4.00s. a 6.10s (17 Ran).
SR: 44/37/35/42/19/24/39/31/19/ (A P Paton), R Dickin

3522 'Children Admitted Free' Limited Stakes Class F (0-60 3-y-o and up) £2,892 1¾m 15yds............. (4:15)

2937[7] MAMARA REEF 3-8-7 R Cochrane (1) *made all, quickened 3 fs out, rdn 2 out, ran on wl*........(7 to 2 op 2 to 1) 1
3212[2] ARAADH (USA) 3-8-7 R Hills (6) *trkd wnr, chlgd o'r 2 fs out, sn rdn, one pace appr last.* ....(2 to 1 fav op 5 to 2 tchd 3 to 1) 2
3394* BIG PAT 4-9-5 (5*) J Tate (8) *hld up beh, hdwy hfwy, effrt 3 fs out, sn rdn, kpt on one pace*......(4 to 1 op 3 to 1) 3
3272 ASLAN (Ire) 5-9-10 K Fallon (4) *trkd ldrs, effrt 4 fs out, rdn 3 out, sn one pace*...... (6 to 1 op 5 to 1 tchd 7 to 1) 4
2148[4] HOPEFUL PROSPECT 3-8-7 J Williams (2) *chsd ldrs pulling hrd, rdn o'r 3 fs out, sn wknd.* (33 to 1 op 20 to 1) 5
3307[7] ROUSITTO 5-9-10 W Ryan (7) *al rear.* ....(8 to 1 op 10 to 1 tchd 12 to 1) 6
2992 MADAGANS GREY 5-9-10 Pat Eddery (3) *al rear.* ....(11 to 1 op 7 to 1 tchd 12 to 1) 7
2097[7] MONAZITE 3-8-12 P Robinson (5) *chsd ldrs, rdn 5 fs out, sn wknd*..........(16 to 1 op 14 to 1 tchd 20 to 1) 8

Dist: 2l, 7l, 6l, 6l, 10l, ¾l, nk. 3m 6.80s. a 8.90s (8 Ran).
SR: 18/14/17/5/-/ (Lord Halifax), L M Cumani

3523 'Playground' Handicap Class E (0-70 3-y-o and up) £3,572 1m 54yds.. (4:45)

3310[6] QUANTITY SURVEYOR [54] (v) 4-9-0 G Duffield (2) *chsd ldrs, effrt o'r 2 fs out, sn rdn, styd on ins last to ld nr finish*........................(10 to 1 op 8 to 1) 1
3124* EXCLUSION [68] 4-10-0 W Newnes (12) *chsd ldrs, effrt 3 fs out, sn rdn, styd on and ev ch ins last, not quicken nr finish*..........................(12 to 1 op 10 to 1) 2
2954* LEAVE IT TO LIB [62] 6-9-3 (5*) J Tate (18) *prmnt, hdwy 3 fs out, led 2 out, sn rdn, edgd lft ins last, hdd nr finish.* ....(12 to 1 op 10 to 1) 3
3310[2] PREMIER STAR [55] (bl) 3-8-9 L Dettori (16) *beh, hdwy on ins and not clr run 2 and a half fs out, swtchd one and a half out, styd on strly und pres inside last.* (4 to 1 jt-fav op 7 to 1) 4
3228[6] LEGAL RISK [41] (v) 3-7-9[1] A Mackay (9) *int ouch, hdwy 4 fs out, ev ch 2 out, sn rdn, kpt on.* ....(20 to 1 op 14 to 1 tchd 25 to 1) 5
2663[8] MUSTAHIL (Ire) [63] 4-9-9 A Munro (17) *chsd ldrs, rdn 2 fs out, kpt on*.....................(14 to 1 op 10 to 1) 6
3058[6] AVISHAYES (USA) [55] 6-9-1 K Darley (7) *hld up, hdwy on ins 2 fs out, not clr run, rdn and styd on inside last.* ....(8 to 1 op 7 to 1) 7
3216 SIR ARTHUR HOBBS [49] 6-8-6 (3*) N Kennedy (19) *in tch, effrt and rdn 3 fs out, kpt on one pace frm 2 out.* ....(14 to 1 op 10 to 1 tchd 16 to 1) 8
3234[4] NOEL (Ire) [46] 4-8-1 (5*) D Wright (1) *nvr dngrs.* ....(33 to 1 op 25 to 1) 9
1436 WILD PROSPECT [54] 5-9-0 M Birch (14) *cl up, rdn 3 fs out, wknd 2 out*..................(20 to 1 tchd 25 to 1) 10
MADAM CAPRICE [57] 3-8-8 (3*) D Harrison (8) *nvr dngrs.* ....(33 to 1) 11
3354 ETERNAL FLAME [63] 5-9-4 (5*) B Russell (15) *nvr rch ldrs.* ....(20 to 1 op 16 to 1) 12
3282[4] MBULWA [47] 7-8-7 Pat Eddery (11) *prmnt, effrt o'r 2 fs out, sn rdn and ev ch, wknd and eased appr last.* ....(4 to 1 jt-fav op 5 to 1 tchd 11 to 2) 13
3355[3] SABO'S EXPRESS [44] 3-7-12 D Biggs (20) *chsd ldrs, rdn 3 fs out, sn wknd*..................(12 to 1 tchd 14 to 1) 14
3365* COLFAX CLASSIC [41] 3-7-9 S Wood (5) *led, rdn 3 fs out, hdd and wknd 2 out*..................(14 to 1 op 10 to 1) 15
3233* MISS CRUSTY [40] 5-8-0 N Adams (6) *nvr rch ldrs.* ....(12 to 1 op 10 to 1) 16
3324[3] AVIATOR'S DREAM [55] 3-8-9 K Fallon (4) *mid-div, rdn and lost pl 3 fs out*.....................................(25 to 1) 17
ELEGANT FRIEND [60] 5-9-6 P Robinson (10) *slwly into strd, al beh*..........................(20 to 1 op 14 to 1) 18
3365 HAWAII STORM (Fr) [47] 5-8-2[2] (7*) R Painter (3) *al beh.* ....(33 to 1) 19

Dist: Nk, hd, sht-hd, 1½l, sht-hd, hd, ¾l, nk, hd, 1½l. 1m 46.00s. a 6.00s (19

Ran).
SR: 22/35/28/14/-/22/13/5/1/ (Lady Fairhaven), Sir Mark Prescott

TRALEE (IRE) (firm)
Monday August 23rd

3524 Ocathain Iasc Maiden (3-y-o and up) £3,452 1¾m.................. (6:00)

2185[4] CALIANDAK (Ire) 3-9-0 L Piggott (9)........... (5 to 4 on) 1
ALYREY (USA) 3-9-0 C Roche (6)................ (7 to 1) 2
552[4] UNCERTAIN AFFAIR (Ire) 3-8-11 M J Kinane (1).... (9 to 2) 3
KARAR (Ire) 3-9-0 D Hogan (7).................. (14 to 1) 4
WILD FANTASY (Ire) 5-9-9 J P Murtagh (3)........ (10 to 1) 5
3368[2] DANCING VISION (Ire) 3-9-0 W J Supple (2)...... (12 to 1) 6
MISS BUSYBODY (Ire) 3-8-11 D V Smith (10)..... (20 to 1) 7
DONE DEAL (Ire) 5-9-4 (8*) B Fenton (8).......... (50 to 1) 8
GLOWING LINES (Ire) 3-8-11 S Craine (5)........ (12 to 1) 9
SCENT JAR (Ire) 3-8-11 J F Egan (4)............. (16 to 1) 10
Dist: ½l, 5l, sht-hd, 9l. 3m 12.80s. (10 Ran).
(H H Aga Khan), John M Oxx

3525 Kerry Petroleum Shell Handicap (0-100 3-y-o and up) £6,902 1½m (6:30)

3037* ERZADJAN (Ire) [-] 3-8-9 J P Murtagh (7).......... (4 to 1) 1
3038[3] LYPHARD ABU (Ire) [-] (bl) 5-8-0 (6*) J A Heffernan (9) (8 to 1) 2
2955[4] MORNING SARGE [-] 5-7-8 (4*) J J Behan (2)...... (16 to 1) 3
2841[5] NATIVE PORTRAIT [-] 6-7-0 (8*) G M Moylan (6).... (6 to 1) 4
2513* FLAME OF PERSIA (Ire) [-] 3-9-2 R Hughes (3)..... (8 to 1) 5
3028[2] FERRYCARRIG HOTEL (Ire) [-] 4-7-10 (2*) D G O'Shea (1) .... (7 to 1) 6
3037[4] IMAD (USA) [-] 3-8-6 W J Supple (4).............. (11 to 1) 7
1573* POLITICAL SURGE (USA) [-] 3-8-7 M J Kinane (12) .... (7 to 4 fav) 8
487 NORDIC SIGN (Ire) [-] 4-7-7 Joanna Morgan (8)... (25 to 1) 9
Dist: 1l, sht-hd, 2l, 3½l. 2m 33.20s. (9 Ran).
(H H Aga Khan), John M Oxx

3526 Tend-R-Leen Sweet Feed Maiden (3-y-o) £3,452 1½m.............. (7:00)

2781[5] PUSH THE BUTTON (Ire) 8-11 M J Kinane (8).. (5 to 4 fav) 1
3455[2] NORDIC QUEEN (Ire) 8-11 K J Manning (2)........ (6 to 1) 2
3382[4] NORDIC THORN (Ire) 9-0 C Roche (3)............. (7 to 1) 3
HAWTHORN ROSE (Ire) 8-11 P Shanahan (7)..... (25 to 1) 4
3061[5] SPLENDID KING (Ire) 9-0 L Piggott (4)........... (15 to 2) 5
2743[7] DANCEALOT (Ire) 8-10 (4*) J J Behan (1)......... (20 to 1) 6
2956[5] GLENSTAL FLAGSHIP (Ire) 9-0 R Hughes (6)... (100 to 30) 7
EITLEAN ALAINN (Ire) 8-3 (8*) P J Smullen (5)..... (25 to 1) 8
Dist: 2l, ½l, 2½l, 12l. 2m 36.50s. (8 Ran).
(Moyglare Stud Farm), D K Weld

3527 O'Brien E.B.F. Cup (2-y-o) £3,797 1m ....(7:30)

DANCING ACTION (USA) 9-0 M J Kinane (11) (5 to 2 jt-fav) 1
3071[4] ICY TUNDRA 9-0 J P Murtagh (3)........... (5 to 2 jt-fav) 2
2742[6] DANITA (Ire) 9-0 C Roche (2)..................... (9 to 2) 3
3453[4] SENDER VICTORIOUS (Ire) 8-10 (4*) J J Behan (13) (10 to 1) 4
3453[9] LADY SAPIEN (Ire) 8-10 (4*) W J Smith (4)........ (50 to 1) 5
3453[7] SAVE THE WEST (Ire) 9-0 K J Manning (12)........ (33 to 1) 6
2880[6] FOOLISH FLIGHT (Ire) 9-0 P V Gilson (6)......... (10 to 1) 7
ACHTUNG LADY (Ire) 9-0 P Shanahan (1).......... (25 to 1) 8
2804[9] BETTER YET (Ire) 9-0 W J Supple (10)........... (50 to 1) 9
SUBARASHII (USA) 9-0 L Piggott (5)............... (4 to 1) 10
GRENNAN CLASSIC (Ire) 9-0 R Hughes (8)........ (25 to 1) 11
3451[6] DREAMS OF SUMMER (Ire) 9-0 J F Egan (9)...... (16 to 1) 12
Dist: 5l, 3l, 5l, sht-hd. 1m 41.90s. (12 Ran).
(Moyglare Stud Farm), D K Weld

BRIGHTON (good to firm)
Tuesday August 24th
Going Correction: MINUS 0.45 sec. per fur.

3528 EBF Rottingdean Maiden Stakes Class D (2-y-o) £3,949 5f 59yds..(2:00)

2766[5] MONIS (Ire) 9-0 W Carson (3) *led til hdd entering fnl furlong, rallied und pres to ld ag'n nr finish.* .... (5 to 1 tchd 6 to 1) 1
2374[7] BASHFUL BRAVE 9-0 M Hills (2) *hld up in tch, swtchd lft and str run to ld entering fnl furlong, rdn and hdd nr finish.*.................. (4 to 1 op 3 to 1 tchd 6 to 1) 2
3265[5] PRINCE OF GAELS 9-0 J Reid (1) *al prmnt, ev ch whn rdn 2 fs out, one pace aftr.* (13 to 2 op 5 to 1 tchd 7 to 1) 3
3387[2] PHONEAHOLIC (Ire) 9-0 B Rouse (6) *hld up in tch, rdn 2 fs out, one pace.*.....(5 to 4 on op 6 to 4 on tchd Evens) 4
3387[5] SPORTING START 9-0 N Adams (9) *al mid-div, eased whn btn one furlong out.* (20 to 1 op 12 to 1 tchd 25 to 1) 5
SECRATORIUS (Ire) 9-0 W Newnes (5) *nvr on terms.* .... (50 to 1 op 25 to 1) 6
3103 CRAFTY CRICKETER (bl) 9-0 A McGlone (8) *al beh.* .... (66 to 1 op 33 to 1) 7
3264 CLANCY'S EXPRESS (bl) 9-0 S Raymont (4) *speed to hfwy.* .... (66 to 1 op 33 to 1) 8
Dist: Hd, 5l, sht-hd, 6l, 4l, nk, 8l. 1m 0.90s. a 0.80s (8 Ran).
SR: 37/36/16/15/-/ (Hamdan Al-Maktoum), T Thomson Jones

3529 Queen's Park Spa Median Auction Maiden Stakes Class F (2-y-o) £2,243 5f 59yds......................(2:30)

POST MISTRESS (Ire) 8-11 G Duffield (2) *made virtually all, kpt up to work fnl 2 fs, all out.* (Evens fav op 5 to 4) 1
2278[4] LOVESCAPE 8-11 J Reid (3) *dsptd ld early, styd in tch, rdn and ran on ins fnl furlong.* .... (15 to 2 op 5 to 1 tchd 8 to 1) 2
3230[7] RAISA POINT 8-11 W R Swinburn (6) *chsd ldrs, lost tch o'r one furlong out.*.................. (2 to 1 op 13 to 8) 3
3421 MAGIC MAGGIE 8-11 W Woods (1) *al struggling to go pace, rdn and wknd wl o'r one furlong out.* .... (33 to 1 op 12 to 1) 4
3103 BURMA STAR 8-11 N Adams (4) *outpcd thrght.* .... (33 to 1 op 20 to 1 tchd 50 to 1) 5
AMAZING NEWS 8-11 W Carson (5) *slwly away, sn tld off.* .... (8 to 1 op 4 to 1 tchd 10 to 1) 6
Dist: ½l, 5l, 5l, 2l, 30l. 1m 1.40s. a 1.30s (6 Ran).
SR: 24/22/2/ (W E Sturt), Sir Mark Prescott

3530 Whitehawk Apprentice Selling Stakes Handicap Class G (0-60 3-y-o) £2,070 1m 3f 196yds................. (3:00)

2833[3] QUEENS CONTRACTOR [41] (bl) 9-1 P McCabe (5) *made all, quickened o'r 3 fs out, sn clr, cmftbly.* .... (5 to 2 tchd 9 to 4) 1
3306* BADAWI (Fr) [41] (bl) 9-1 G Forster (2) *trkd ldrs, hdwy to chase wnr 3 fs out, sn rdn, no imprsn.* .... (2 to 1 fav op 11 to 8 tchd 9 to 4) 2
3301 NIGHTMARE LADY [26] 8-0 C Hawksley (1) *in rear till hdwy 4 fs out, no imprsn on 1st 2 fnl two furlongs.* .... (7 to 1 tchd 6 to 1) 3
3392[5] SANTA STELLAR [37] (v) 8-6 (5*) A Whelan (4) *chsd wnr till wknd 3 fs out.*.................. (20 to 1 op 12 to 1) 4
3170[4] CHILTERN HUNDREDS (USA) [38] 8-5 (7*) G Faulkner (6) *al towards rear.*.................. (4 to 1 op 6 to 1) 5
699[8] EVE'S TREASURE [47] 9-7 B Russell (7) *slwly away, steadied in rear, nvr on terms.*..........(20 to 1 op 12 to 1) 6
3320 SUPPER WITH SUSIE [30] 8-4 N Varley (3) *mid-div, lost tch o'r 3 fs out.*.................. (10 to 1 tchd 14 to 1) 7
Dist: 5l, 2l, 6l, 1½l, 2l, 6l. 2m 34.60s. a 7.10s (7 Ran).
(P G Lowe), M J Heaton-Ellis

3531 Queen's Park Centenary Challenge Cup Handicap Class D (0-80 4-y-o and up) £3,817 6f 209yds............(3:30)

3105[7] CALEMAN [72] 4-9-6 W Carson (6) *made all, rdn clr fnl furlong.*............. (10 to 1 op 8 to 1 tchd 12 to 1) 1
2966[3] SILKY SIREN [70] 4-9-4 Pat Eddery (4) *hld up in rear, rdn and hdwy o'r 2 fs out, sn chsd wnr, no imprsn ins last.* .... (5 to 2 fav tchd 7 to 2) 2
3269 WAVE HILL [69] 4-9-3 J Reid (8) *hld up, hdwy o'r 2 fs out, not pace to chal.*.......(13 to 2 op 8 to 1 tchd 6 to 1) 3
3471[4] NOBBY BARNES [63] 4-8-11 J Williams (10) *nvr far off pace, rdn wl o'r one furlong out, no hdwy.* .... (15 to 2 op 5 to 1 tchd 8 to 1) 4
3228[2] CAPE PIGEON (USA) [68] (bl) 8-9-2 A Munro (3) *chsd ldrs, rdn 2 fs out, one pace aftr.* .... (15 to 2 op 8 to 1 tchd 7 to 1) 5
2733[6] PRINCE RODNEY [66] 4-8-7 (7*) D O'Neill (1) *in tch, no hdwy ins fnl 2 fs.*.................. (12 to 1 op 8 to 1) 6
3302[7] NIGEL'S LUCKY GIRL [50] 5-7-5 (7*) C Hawksley (11) *prmnt on outsd till wknd appr fnl furlong.* .... (14 to 1 op 8 to 1 tchd 16 to 1) 7
2854[6] HERORA (Ire) [80] (bl) 4-10-0 B Raymond (5) *rcd keenly, hld up in tch, short of room 2 fs out, sn btn.* ....(5 to 1 op 4 to 1) 8
3261[6] SUPEROO [66] (bl) 7-9-0 W R Swinburn (9) *al beh, rdn hfwy, nvr on terms.*.................. (6 to 1 op 4 to 1) 9
2327 ABSO [63] 5-8-11 G Duffield (7) *trkd wnr till wknd quickly 2 fs out, virtually pld up ins last*...(33 to 1 op 16 to 1) 10
Dist: 3½l, 4l, hd, 1½l, hd, 1½l, ½l, 5l, 5l. 1m 20.20s. a 0.20s (10 Ran).
SR: 56/43/30/23/23/20/-/27/-/ (M Berger), R Boss

3532 Arthur King Memorial Nursery Class E (2-y-o) £3,002 6f 209yds......(4:00)

2974[5] NONIOS (Ire) [76] 9-4 (3*) B Doyle (6) *trkd ldrs, led o'r 2 fs out, pushed out, cmftbly.* ....(13 to 2 op 7 to 1 tchd 8 to 1 and 6 to 1) 1
3351[7] PRINCE DANZIG (Ire) [63] 8-8 J Reid (8) *hld up in rear, hdwy on outsd 2 fs out, ran on and crrd lft ins last.* .... (16 to 1 op 12 to 1 tchd 20 to 1) 2
3287 HENRY'S LUCK [60] 8-5 W Woods (9) *hld up on outsd, wl beh hfwy, ran on and edgd lft fnl furlong.* .... (12 to 1 op 10 to 1 tchd 14 to 1) 3
3264[2] DULFORD LAD [69] 9-0 S Whitworth (3) *mid-div, ran on one pace fnl 2 fs.*.......(6 to 1 op 5 to 1 tchd 13 to 2) 4

3264[3] MADAME GREGOIRE [54] (bl) 7-10 (3*) N Kennedy (4) *al mid-div, hdwy 2 fs out, wknd entering last.* ....(9 to 2 tchd 5 to 1) 5
2539[7] IMPOSING GROOM (Ire) [71] 9-2 B Raymond (7) *in tch, wkng whn squeezed out entering fnl furlong.* ....(5 to 1 tchd 11 to 2) 6
1523 MAKE THE BREAK [72] 9-3 Pat Eddery (5) *hld up, nvr got into race*............ (4 to 1 fav op 5 to 1 tchd 7 to 2) 7
3235* KOMPLICITY [66] 8-11 W R Swinburn (1) *led til hdd o'r 2 fs out, sn btn and eased*... (9 to 2 op 4 to 1 tchd 5 to 1) 8
2588[3] BIEN CUIT [51] 7-10[1] T Williams (2) *trkd ldr till wknd o'r 2 fs out, sn btn*..........................(14 to 1 op 8 to 1) 9
Dist: 2l, sht-hd, 2½l, 1½l, ½l, 2½l, 5l, 5l. 1m 21.70s. a 1.70s (9 Ran).
SR: 34/15/11/12/-/7/ (J P Fleming), B J Meehan

3533 Lancing Rating Related Maiden Stakes Class F (3-y-o) £2,243 1m 1f 209yds........................ (4:30)

3306[4] ICE REBEL (bl) 9-0 W Newnes (7) *made all, kpt on gmely und pres ins last*...... (9 to 1 op 10 to 1 tchd 11 to 1) 1
3469[3] WITHOUT A FLAG (USA) 9-0 Pat Eddery (8) *hld up, hdwy on ins 3 fs out, ev ch whn edgd rght and slightly hmpd 3rd entering last, hrd rdn, no extr.* ....(3 to 1 fav op 7 to 1) 2
3225 DUBAI SUMMER (bl) 9-0 B Raymond (5) *al prmnt, wnt second o'r 3 fs out, rdn whn hng lft and bumped entering last, wknd ins*.....(11 to 2 op 7 to 1 tchd 10 to 1) 3
2087[4] LANDRAIL (USA) 8-9 D Holland (4) *al in tch, rdn o'r 2 fs out, one pace*........ (100 to 30 op 5 to 2 tchd 7 to 2) 4
2613[3] MARATHIA (v) 8-9 W Woods (6) *trkd wnr till wnt wide o'r 3 fs out, wknd stdly*..................(20 to 1 op 12 to 1) 5
3247[7] HAZY KAY (Ire) (bl) 8-9 Gay Kelleway (3) *mid-div, lost tch o'r 2 fs out*........................(12 to 1 op 10 to 1) 6
3341[6] VILLAVINA 8-9 G Duffield (2) *hld up, lost tch o'r 3 fs out.* ....(16 to 1 op 8 to 1) 7
3106[2] GOLD TASSEL 8-9 J Reid (1) *al struggling in rear.* ....(100 to 30 op 2 to 1 tchd 7 to 2) 8
Dist: Nk, 3½l, ¾l, 7l, 2½l, 2½l, 2½l. 2m 1.30s. a 3.10s (8 Ran).
SR: 24/23/16/9/-/ (J F Hansberry), Miss B Sanders

DEAUVILLE (FR) (good)
Tuesday August 24th
Going Correction: PLUS 0.60 sec. per fur.

3534 Prix de Lieurey (Listed) (3-y-o) £14,337 1m.......................... (2:55)

3195[2] LOST PRAIRIE (USA) 9-2 T Jarnet, ... 1
SEATTLE VICTORY (USA) 9-2 G Guignard, ... 2
1753[3] AISLA (USA) 9-2 C Asmussen, ... 3
2981[2] FRESHER 9-2 F Head, ... 4
Dist: ¾l, 1l, hd, ½l, nose, sht-hd, nk, 2½l, 1½l. 1m 43.00s. a 8.00s (10 Ran).
SR: 54/52/49/48/ (D Wildenstein), A Fabre

PONTEFRACT (good)
Tuesday August 24th
Going Correction: MINUS 0.35 sec. per fur.

3535 York & Westminster Apprentice Series Round Four Handicap Class G (0-70 3-y-o and up) £2,511 6f.... (2:45)

2480[7] KARINSKA [57] 3-8-13 D McCabe (13) *pushed alng, sn outpcd, hdwy last 2 fs, ran on to ld last strds.* (25 to 1) 1
3057[2] MU-ARRIK [53] 5-8-13 J Tate (14) *led one and a half fs, chsd alng to ld entering last, ct last strds.* ....(6 to 1 fav op 7 to 1 tchd 11 to 2) 2
3354[2] SOBERING THOUGHTS [68] 7-9-9 (5*) L Aspell (17) *led aftr one and a half fs, clr hfwy, hdd entering last, no extr.* ....(7 to 1) 3
3257[8] LIDA'S DELIGHT (Ire) [59] 3-8-12 (3*) P Johnson (12) *chsd ldg 5, feeling pace hfwy, rallied o'r one furlong out, kpt on*..(16 to 1) 4
2811[6] BLUE GRIT [64] 7-9-10 V Halliday (9) *pushed alng to improve frm midfield last 2 fs, kpt on, nvr able to chal.* ....(8 to 1 op 9 to 1) 5
3360[6] STRIP CARTOON (Ire) [56] 5-8-13 (3*) G Strange (10) *speed 3 fs, sn drvn alng, no imprsn appr last.* ....(11 to 1 op 10 to 1) 6
3258[7] HENBURY HALL (Ire) [37] 5-7-6 (5*) M Baird (3) *drvn alng to keep up, styd on last 2 fs, nvr nrr.* (100 to 1 op 50 to 1) 7
2368 ALL THE GIRLS (Ire) [35] 4-7-2 (7*) F Savage (4) *chsd alng to go pace, styd on last 2 fs, nvr nrr*............. (33 to 1) 8
3180[2] FORTIS PAVIOR (Ire) [60] 3-9-2 G Parkin (18) *outpcd and beh, kpt on appr fnl furlong, no imprsn*.......(12 to 1) 9
3365[3] INVIGILATE [56] 4-8-11 (5*) D Thomas (5) *chsd ldrs for o'r 3 fs, fdd*........................ (15 to 2 op 6 to 1) 10
3409[7] KILTROUM (Fr) [40] 4-8-0 Mark Denaro (8) *sluggish strt, outpcd and beh till ran on fnl furlong*........ (10 to 1) 11
2309[8] STATE FLYER [58] (v) 5-9-4 D Wright (11) *sluggish strt, late hdwy, nvr nrr*....................................(16 to 1) 12
3310 SHANNON EXPRESS [45] 6-7-12 (7*) W Hawksley (15) *chsd alng in midfield, not rch ldrs*...... (25 to 1 op 20 to 1) 13
3301[7] COUNTERCHECK (Ire) [41] 4-8-1 S Mulvey (1) *chsd ldg trio for o'r 4 fs, sn btn*................. (11 to 1 op 10 to 1) 14
2602[5] MAGICATION [53] 3-8-9 Claire Balding (6) *outpcd and beh, nvr a factor*......................(12 to 1 op 10 to 1) 15
3085[7] NILU (Ire) [44] 5-7-13 (5*) J Bramhill (7) *struggling to go pace, nvr dngrs*................. (16 to 1 op 14 to 1) 16
Dist: Nk, 4l, ½l, ½l, hd, ½l, ½l, hd, 1½l, 1½l. 1m 15.70s. a 1.00s (16 Ran).
SR: 37/36/35/20/27/18/-/-/13/ (Geoff Whiting), M C Chapman

3536 Timeform Card Selling Stakes Class G (3-y-o and up) £2,364 1¼m 6yds (3:15)

2670[2] VANROY (v) 9-9-7 L Dettori (9) *nvr far away, led o'r one furlong out, rdn out*............(2 to 1 fav op 9 to 4) 1
2763* ESSAYEFFSEE 4-9-0 K Darley (1) *led early, sn settled, ev ch and drvn alng last 2 fs, ran on wl.* (6 to 1 op 5 to 1) 2
3049[2] ANN HILL (Ire) 3-8-8 W Ryan (7) *settled midfield, drvn up on outsd last 2 fs, styd on finish.* ....(9 to 2 op 5 to 1 tchd 4 to 1) 3
3420 OVERPOWER 9-9-7 P Robinson (5) *co'red up on ins, effrt and drvn alng over 2 fs out, kpt on same pace.* ....(11 to 4 op 9 to 4) 4
2631[6] MY LINDIANNE 6-8-4 J Fanning (8) *slwly away, str hold, sn reco'red, effrt and rdn hfwy, no imprsn.* .... (66 to 1 op 50 to 1) 5
3239[8] INOVAR 3-8-1 G Hind (11) *nvr far away, led o'r 2 fs out till over one out, no extr*...................................(33 to 1) 6
ROMANTIC MOOD 4-8-9 J Quinn (4) *al wl plcd, feeling pace and rdn 2 fs out, sn btn*..................(25 to 1) 7
2931[5] OLICANA (Ire) 3-8-8 (5*) J Marshall (2) *patiently rdn, swtchd ins and hmpd o'r 4 fs out, not rcvr.* ....(8 to 1 op 10 to 1) 8
3135[6] WAWEEWAWOO (Ire) 5-7-13 (5*) Darren Moffatt (12) *sn led, drvn alng and hdd o'r 2 fs out, fdd.* .... (66 to 1 op 50 to 1) 9
1900 JOSEPH'S WINE (Ire) 4-8-8[1] (7*) H Bastiman (6) *struggling to go pace hfwy, tld off*.........................(14 to 1) 10
3216[8] GOLDEN ANCONA 10-9-7 M Wigham (10) *trkd ldg 4, effrt o'r 3 fs out, sn btn, tld off*..........................(66 to 1) 11
1928 METTERNICH 8-9-0 (7*) S Mulvey (3) *chsd ldrs, wknd quickly o'r 3 fs out, sn tld off*..................... (20 to 1) 12
Dist: Hd, ½l, 2l, 4l, ¾l, 5l, 2l, 5l, 20l, ½l. 2m 14.80s. a 6.60s (12 Ran).
SR: 6/-/-/-/-/-/ (J M Long), J R Jenkins

3537 Timeform Futurity Conditions Stakes Class D (2-y-o) £4,230 6f........(3:45)

3421* FRIENDLY CHAMP (Ire) 8-11 R Price (7) *sluggish strt, outpcd and struggling hfwy, styd on to ld o'r one furlong out, rdn out*.............................(10 to 1 op 7 to 1) 1
2968[4] OVERBURY (Ire) 8-11 L Dettori (5) *nvr far away, drw level o'r one furlong out, rdn and no extr cl hme.* ....(6 to 4 on op 11 to 10) 2
2996 OCHOS RIOS (Ire) 9-1 J Quinn (8) *sn last and outpcd, improved last 2 fs, ran on, not pace to chal.* ....(14 to 1 op 10 to 1 tchd 16 to 1) 3
3166* BRIERLEY 8-6 T Quinn (6) *speed wth ldg pair till rdn and no extr o'r one furlong out*.......... (10 to 1 op 8 to 1) 4
3289[2] BAROSSA VALLEY (Ire) 9-1 R Cochrane (3) *trkd ldrs gng wl, drvn alng 2 fs out, sn btn*....... (11 to 4 op 9 to 4) 5
3133 NORDICO PRINCESS 8-10 S Perks (4) *led for o'r 4 fs, wknd quickly*.......................(33 to 1 op 25 to 1) 6
2021[5] PLEASURE TRICK (USA) 8-11 K Darley (2) *wth ldr, drvn alng o'r 2 fs out, fdd*................(33 to 1 op 20 to 1) 7
Dist: ½l, 3l, 8l, 2l, 1½l. 1m 15.60s. a 0.90s (7 Ran).
SR: 37/35/27/-/ (Dr Meou Tsen Geoffrey Yeh), R W Armstrong

3538 Phil Bull Trophy Class C Conditions Stakes (3-y-o and up) £4,355 2m 1f 216yds........................ (4:15)

3319[3] KAISER WILHELM 4-9-5 W Ryan (6) *patiently rdn, improved to ld o'r 3 fs out, quickened, styd on strly fnl furlong*...................(2 to 1 fav tchd 9 to 4) 1
3319[6] JACK BUTTON (Ire) 4-9-11 N Day (4) *trkd ldr, drvn to chal last 3 fs, kpt on same pace ins last*... (9 to 4 op 2 to 1) 2
2904[4] MISS PLUM 4-9-0 L Dettori (2) *chsd ldg trio, effrt and drvn alng last 3 fs, styd on finish, nvr nrr.* ....(7 to 2 op 3 to 1) 3
3434 ENCORE UNE FOIS (Ire) 4-9-2 T Quinn (1) *sn clr, jnd hfwy, hdd and rdn o'r 3 fs out, rallied, one pace.* ....(7 to 1 op 6 to 1 tchd 8 to 1) 4
3116* GREY POWER 6-9-0 K Darley (3) *in tch, drvn alng to improve 3 fs out, no imprsn fnl furlong.* ....(13 to 2 op 8 to 1 tchd 9 to 1 and 6 to 1) 5
CHAPELSTREET BLUES 6-8-9 (3*) O Pears (5) *last and niggled alng hfwy, tld off last 5 fs.* .... (100 to 1 tchd 500 to 1) 6
Dist: 1l, 1½l, 4l, 7l, dist. 4m 3.00s. a 11.50s (6 Ran).
(Charles H Wacker III), H R A Cecil

3539 Timeform Nursery Class D (2-y-o) £4,425 6f........................ (4:45)

3386[2] DARREN BOY (Ire) [80] 9-7 T Quinn (5) *al frnt rnk, led hfwy, quickened fnl furlong, readily.* ....(5 to 4 on op 11 to 10 on) 1

2988 CULSYTH FLYER [71] 8-12 W Ryan (2) *nvr far away, effrt and drvn alng o'r one furlong out, ran on same pace.* ....(11 to 1 op 10 to 1) 2
2876[8] DANTE'S RUBICON (Ire) [53] 7-3 (5*) D Wright (6) *pressed ldrs, effrt and drvn alng last 2 fs, kpt on same pace.* ....(12 to 1 tchd 11 to 1) 3
3131* BENEFICIARY [69] 8-10 M Birch (1) *dsptd ld to hfwy, drvn and no extr o'r one furlong out*.....(13 to 2 op 6 to 1) 4
3236[7] DOUBLE SIXTEEN [58] 7-10 (3*) S Maloney (3) *steadied aftr fst strt, outpcd hfwy, hdwy last 2 fs, not rch ldrs.* ....(10 to 1 op 7 to 1) 5
3363* PALACEGATE JO (Ire) [73] 9-0 J Carroll (7) *slight ld on outsd to hfwy, wknd und pres o'r one furlong out.* ....(11 to 2 op 7 to 1) 6
2845[9] SIGANCA [74] 8-12 (3*) M Fenton (4) *chsd alng to keep up, nvr able to chal*....(25 to 1 op 16 to 1) 7
Dist: 3l, nk, 6l, ¾l, 1½l, hd. 1m 16.10s. a 1.40s (7 Ran).
SR: 37/16/-/-/ (D F Allport), P F I Cole

3540 Timeform Perspective And Ratings Handicap Class D (0-80 3-y-o and up) £3,289 1m 4yds.......... (5:15)

3358* PRIDE OF PENDLE [66] 4-9-4 K Darley (7) *niggled alng to go pace hfwy, improved o'r one furlong out, led last strd*....(11 to 2 op 6 to 1) 1
2233[5] MUTAKALLAM (USA) [68] 3-9-0 R Hills (9) *al hndy, drvn to ld entering fnl furlong, ct last strd.* ....(14 to 1 tchd 16 to 1) 2
3117[4] NORTHERN BRED (Ire) [74] 3-9-6 R Cochrane (3) *trkd ldg 4, ev ch and drvn alng fnl furlong, ran on.* ....(11 to 8 fav op 5 to 4 tchd 7 to 4) 3
3257[4] CAUSLEY [72] 8-9-10 T Quinn (2) *led till entering fnl furlong, no extr last 50 yards*.... (10 to 1 tchd 11 to 1) 4
3358[7] HABETA (USA) [58] 7-8-10 W Ryan (6) *co'red up beh ldrs, not clr run appr fnl furlong, ran on finish.* ....(14 to 1 op 12 to 1) 5
3375[4] MEDIA MESSENGER [52] 4-8-4 K Fallon (4) *pressed ldrs, drvn alng last 2 fs, kpt on same pace.* ....(33 to 1 op 20 to 1) 6
3017 POLEDEN (USA) [62] 3-8-8 A Mackay (1) *co'red up beh ldrs, effrt and drvn alng last 2 fs, styd on.* ....(25 to 1 op 20 to 1) 7
3358[3] PRENONAMOSS [76] (v) 5-9-11 (3*) S D Williams (5) *wtd wth, effrt on ins o'r 2 fs out, no imprsn.* ....(9 to 1 op 8 to 1 tchd 10 to 1) 8
3358 MYSILV [62] 3-8-8 P Robinson (11) *chsd alng to keep up hfwy, no imprsn last 2 fs.* ....(10 to 1 op 20 to 1 tchd 8 to 1) 9
3050[3] KRYPTOS (USA) [60] 3-8-6 L Dettori (8) *nvr far away, feeling pace and rdn 2 fs out, sn btn.* ....(10 to 1 op 8 to 1 tchd 11 to 1) 10
1375[5] GROUND NUT (Ire) [69] 3-9-1 S Dawson (10) *chsd alng to go pace, nvr able to rch ldrs*.....(20 to 1 op 16 to 1) 11
3101[6] REGAL AURA (Ire) [66] (v) 3-8-12 A Clark (12) *wth ldrs for o'r 5 fs*....(14 to 1 op 10 to 1) 12
Dist: Hd, ½l, 1½l, 1l, hd, sht-hd, ½l, 1l, 3½l, 5l. 1m 43.00s. a 0.90s (12 Ran).
SR: 49/44/48/47/30/23/26/44/21/ (W B Imison), P Calver

TRALEE (IRE) (good)
Tuesday August 24th

3541 Paddy Norris E.B.F. Maiden (2-y-o) £3,797 7f.......... (5:00)

3203[2] PEACE ROLE (USA) (bl) 9-0 M J Kinane (11).....(13 to 8) 1
2403[5] BASSMAAT (USA) 8-11 C Roche (3).....(5 to 4 fav) 2
CRYSTAL LAKE (Ire) 8-11 P V Gilson (6).....(12 to 1) 3
OUT IN THE SUN (USA) 8-11 K J Manning (4).....(20 to 1) 4
3243[5] SALMON RIVER (USA) 9-0 W J Supple (13).....(7 to 1) 5
SUN MARK (Ire) 9-0 N Byrne (2).....(25 to 1) 6
THREE LEAVES (Ire) 8-6 (8*) B Fenton (5).....(33 to 1) 7
TINERANA ROSE (Ire) 8-3 (8*) P J Smullen (1).....(33 to 1) 8
3332[8] APPEARANCE MONEY (Ire) 8-11 J F Egan (10).... (20 to 1) 9
3243 SEANEE SQUAW 8-11 B Coogan (7).....(20 to 1) 10
3243[3] STELFOX (Ire) 8-10 (4*) J J Behan (15).....(16 to 1) 11
1643[4] RUSTIC LEAGUE (Ire) 8-12 (2*) P Carberry (8).....(33 to 1) 12
3039[8] COOLOWEN FLASH (Ire) 8-11 D V Smith (12).....(33 to 1) 13
2284[9] SALTONIC (Ire) 9-0 S Craine (14).....(14 to 1) 14
3064[4] STRANGFORD LOUGH (Ire) 9-0 P Shanahan (9)...(33 to 1) 15
Dist: ½l, 4½l, 4½l, ½l. 1m 28.90s. (15 Ran).
(Moyglare Stud Farms Ltd), D K Weld

3542 Irish National Bookmakers Association Handicap (0-100 3-y-o and up) £5,177 7f.......... (7:00)

3202[6] WANDERING THOUGHTS (Ire) [-] 4-8-4 W J Supple (7) ....(7 to 1) 1
3027[4] EL ZORRO DORADO (Ire) [-] 3-8-13 S Craine (2)....(4 to 1) 2
3452[4] RONDELLI (Ire) [-] 3-8-10 (8*) T E Durcan (3)..... (16 to 1) 3
ROBERTOLOMY (USA) [-] 4-8-1 (2*) R M Burke (9) (14 to 1) 4
2039[8] SEEK THE FAITH (USA) [-] (bl) 4-8-6 M J Kinane (10) (6 to 1) 5
3027[6] PERSIAN CREEK (Ire) [-] 4-9-13 C Roche (4).......(7 to 1) 6
665[9] TAKE NO CHANCES (Ire) [-] 3-8-9 (4*) J J Behan (1) (14 to 1) 7
3201[4] NORDIC OAK (Ire) [-] (bl) 5-9-3 K J Manning (5).....(8 to 1) 8
3300* LOCK'S HEATH (Can) [-] 3-8-13 J P Murtagh (12) ....(7 to 2 fav) 9
2878[8] LEGAL FLAIR (Ire) [-] 3-9-6 P V Gilson (6).........(14 to 1) 10
3334[5] CLASSIC MATCH (Ire) [-] 5-9-4 (2*) P Carberry (11) (14 to 1) 11
Dist: 1l, 1½l, ½l, ¾l. 1m 29.10s. (11 Ran).
(W Mythen), A P O'Brien

3543 Carrolls Festival Handicap (0-70 3-y-o and up) £3,452 1m 3f.......... (7:30)

3381[2] ISLAND VISION (Ire) [-] 3-8-12 W J Supple (5)......(8 to 1) 1
3418[3] THE BOWER (Ire) [-] (bl) 4-8-6 (8*,6ex) P M Donohue (1) ....(7 to 1) 2
3277[3] PREMIER LEAP (Ire) [-] 4-8-3 (8*) B Fenton (4).....(14 to 1) 3
3298* PHASE IN [-] 3-9-11 (7ex) M J Kinane (3)..... (13 to 8 fav) 4
3028[6] SIR ALWAH (Ire) [-] 4-8-6 P Shanahan (6).......(12 to 1) 5
3296[7] JUST ONE CANALETTO [-] 5-8-10 J P Murtagh (13) (16 to 1) 6
3418[5] SCOTSMAN'S BAY (Ire) [-] 4-8-6 (4*) J J Behan (15) (9 to 1) 7
2842 HIND VISION (Ire) [-] 3-9-1 J F Egan (8)..........(16 to 1) 8
3294[9] CARAVELLE LAD (Ire) [-] 3-8-9 P V Gilson (2)..... (20 to 1) 9
2692 DIAMOND CLUSTER [-] 3-7-6 (8*) R T Fitzpatrick (10) ....(20 to 1) 10
3482* ALIBAR'S PET (Ire) [-] 3-9-3 (6*,5ex) J R Barry (14)..(6 to 1) 11
3076 VICOSA (Ire) [-] 4-7-11 (2*) D G O'Shea (11).......(14 to 1) 12
2461[8] ALL YOURS (Ire) [-] 4-8-13 (6*) C Everard (7).......(25 to 1) 13
3275[5] SOLAR FLASH (Ire) [-] 4-7-8[2] (4*) W J Smith (12).. (16 to 1) 14
2842 PULMICORT [-] (bl) 3-9-3 S Craine (9)...........(10 to 1) 15
Dist: 1l, 3½l, 2½l, 2½l. 2m 21.90s. (15 Ran).
(Mrs M O'Connell), Kevin Prendergast

3544 Smirnoff Handicap (0-75 3-y-o and up) £3,452 7f.......... (8:00)

3327[6] HANG A RIGHT [-] 6-9-3 (6*) T P Treacy (2)....... (12 to 1) 1
3395[4] YONOKA (Fr) [-] (bl) 4-9-3 P Shanahan (6)........ (14 to 1) 2
3399[2] KENTUCKY BABY (Ire) [-] 3-8-9 J P Murtagh (14)..(12 to 1) 3
3076 TORCH SINGER [-] 3-8-0 (2*) R M Burke (8)...... (20 to 1) 4
3330 NORDIC SAINT (Ire) [-] 4-9-2 (6*) J A Heffernan (4) (16 to 1) 5
3330[6] MASTER WORK [-] 5-7-6 (4*) J J Behan (1)........(16 to 1) 6
3399[3] DAHAR'S LOVE (USA) [-] (bl) 4-7-6[5] (8*) R T Fitzpatrick (12) ....(14 to 1) 7
3497[3] KILTIMONY [-] 3-9-6 P V Gilson (11).............. (7 to 2) 8
3419[5] FAIRY BRIDE (Ire) [-] 3-8-3 Joanna Morgan (10)... (25 to 1) 9
3294[2] FLORAL STREET [-] 4-9-0 (6*) C Everard (3)...... (10 to 1) 10
3498[7] NORDIC GLARE (Ire) [-] 3-8-5 (8*) T E Durcan (7).. (14 to 1) 11
3294[7] ALBERTA ROSE (Ire) [-] 4-8-13 (6*) J R Barry (13)..(13 to 2) 12
3161[2] GREAT CABARET (Ire) [-] (bl) 3-9-7 M J Kinane (9) ....(13 to 8 fav) 13
3498[6] SKELLIG [-] 7-9-6 J F Egan (15).................(10 to 1) 14
3455[4] OROVILLE [-] 3-9-6 S Craine (5).................(10 to 1) 15
Dist: Hd, 1½l, ½l, ½l. 1m 29.60s. (15 Ran).
(Thomas Mullins), P Mullins

BRIGHTON (good to firm)
Wednesday August 25th
Going Correction: MINUS 0.35 sec. per fur.

3545 Newhaven Nursery Class E (2-y-o) £2,950 5f 59yds.......... (2:10)

3386* MAJOR SUCCESS (Ire) [80] 9-12 (6ex) D Holland (4) *broke wl, made virtually all, clr appr fnl furlong, hld on, cmftbly*.....(11 to 8 fav op Evens tchd 13 to 8) 1
3475[8] CHARISMA GIRL [53] 7-13 N Adams (7) *sn rdn alng towards rear, crrd rght wl o'r one furlong out, str run ins last, gng on finish*.............(16 to 1 op 10 to 1) 2
2996 TUTU SIXTYSIX [71] (bl) 9-3 G Duffield (8) *midfield, edgd rght wl o'r one furlong out, styd on well ins last.* ....(8 to 1 tchd 10 to 1) 3
3041* LAUNE (Aus) [75] 9-7 B Raymond (2) *rdn alng early, gd hdwy o'r 2 fs out and sn ev ch, not quicken appr last.* ....(7 to 2 op 5 to 1 tchd 3 to 1) 4
3267[2] VEDO NUDO [69] 9-1 M Hills (5) *prmnt, ev ch 2 fs out, unbl to quicken*............(10 to 1 op 8 to 1 tchd 12 to 1) 5
2947[5] ANTONIA'S FOLLY [73] 9-5 T Quinn (1) *dwlt, sn reco'red to midfield, ran on one pace fnl 2 fs.* (16 to 1 op 14 to 1) 6
2886[8] COLNE VALLEY [63] (bl) 8-9 J Reid (9) *wth ldrs till rdn and wknd wl o'r one furlong out*.....(10 to 1 tchd 11 to 1) 7
3103[7] PETRATHENE [47] (bl) 7-7 T Wilson (6) *outpcd.* ....(25 to 1 op 16 to 1) 8
3222 SUN CHIEF (Ire) [64] 8-10 N Day (10) *al beh.* ....(16 to 1 op 10 to 1 tchd 20 to 1) 9
3321[5] READY-FREDDIE [55] (bl) 7-10 (5*) D Wright (3) *dsptd ld, ev ch wl o'r one furlong out, sn wknd.* ....(12 to 1 tchd 14 to 1) 10
Dist: Nk, 1½l, 1l, 2l, 2½l, nk, nk, nk, 2½l. 1m 1.80s. a 1.70s (10 Ran).
SR: 41/13/25/25/11/5/ (W J Gredley), B W Hills

3546 Seagulls Selling Stakes Class G (2-y-o) £2,070 6f 209yds.......... (2:40)

3532[3] HENRY'S LUCK 8-4 (7*) R Painter (1) *tucked away, smooth hdwy frm 3 fs out to ld entering fnl furlong, pushed out, cmftbly*..........(11 to 2 tchd 9 to 2 and 6 to 1) 1

3137[6] STARSPORT (Ire) (bl) 8-11 T Quinn (10) *led one furlong, rgned ld 2 fs out, hdd entering last, not pace of wnr.* .... (9 to 1 op 7 to 1 tchd 10 to 1) 2
2385[3] TSWANA (Ire) 8-11 B Raymond (16) *ran in snatches chasing ldrs, rdn alng wl o'r 2 fs out, kpt on ins last.* .... (9 to 2 op 3 to 1 tchd 5 to 1) 3
2911[6] FLAIR LADY 8-11 T Sprake (8) *al prmnt, hrd rdn and ev ch o'r 2 fs out, wknd appr last*........ (14 to 1 op 8 to 1) 4
3390* FOREVER BLUSHING 8-4 (7*) S Drowne (7) *beh till styd on fnl 2 fs, nvr a dngr*........ (10 to 1 op 7 to 1) 5
3390[7] GREEN'S IMPRESSION (Ire) 8-6 M Hills (6) *led aftr one furlong till hdd 2 fs out, sn rdn and btn*......(7 to 2 jt-fav op 9 to 2 tchd 5 to 1) 6
2331 INDIAN CASTLE (Ire) (bl) 8-11 S Whitworth (3) *chsd ldg bunch, rdn wl o'r 2 furlogs out and sn one pace.* .... (33 to 1 op 20 to 1) 7
2331[5] FOREST LOCH 7-13 (7*) Antoinette Armes (11) *wl beh till some hdwy and edgd lft o'r 2 fs out, nvr able to chal.* ....(7 to 2 jt-fav op 3 to 1 tchd 4 to 1) 8
3264 LUCKY HELEN (v) 8-6 F Norton (9) *nvr better than mid-div*........(33 to 1 op 20 to 1) 9
3166 ESOTERIC (Ire) 8-6 S O'Gorman (5) *al towards rear.* .... (33 to 1 op 20 to 1) 10
3303[5] KINGSCOURT JOHN-A (Ire) 8-11 N Adams (15) *chsd ldrs to hfwy, sn wknd*........(12 to 1 op 8 to 1 tchd 14 to 1) 11
3345[6] HUMMINBIRDPRINCESS 8-6 B Rouse (13) *al beh.* .... (33 to 1 op 16 to 1) 12
3126 HOODLUM (v) 8-11 G Duffield (14) *midfield till came wide wl o'r 3 fs out, sn in rear.* .... (25 to 1 op 14 to 1 tchd 33 to 1) 13
3303[8] MAJOR ROWAN 8-11 C Avery (12) *sn rdn alng in midfield, lost pl frm hfwy*........(20 to 1 op 16 to 1) 14
Dist: 2½l, 3l, 4l, 1½l, 3l, nk, 2l, 2l, 2½l, 4l. 1m 22.10s. a 2.10s (14 Ran).
SR: 29/21/12/-/-/-/ (T W Langley), M R Channon

3547 Saddlescombe Claiming Stakes Class G (Div I) (3-y-o and up) £2,070 7f 214yds........ (3:10)

3046* SHARP GAZELLE 3-7-12 (5*) Stephen Davies (6) *trkd ldrs on ins, swtchd rght wl o'r 2 fs out and sn ev ch, rdn and sstnd effrt to ld well inside last.* .... (5 to 1 op 7 to 2 tchd 11 to 2) 1
3175[9] DODGY (v) 6-8-12 J Quinn (3) *al hndy, led 3 fs out till hdd and not quicken wl ins last*........(6 to 1 op 5 to 1) 2
3228[7] TOUT DE VAL 4-8-6 T Sprake (5) *slwly into strd, mid-div, hrd rdn o'r 3 fs out, put head in air and kpt on clsg stages*........(50 to 1 op 20 to 1) 3
3480[5] FANFOLD (Ire) 3-8-7 T Quinn (4) *trkd ldrs, hdwy to join issue 3 fs out, no extr fnl furlong.* ....(11 to 8 fav tchd 5 to 4 and 6 to 4) 4
3480[9] IVORY HUTCH 3-8-3 D Biggs (2) *chsd ldrs, rdn o'r 3 fs out, kpt on same pace*........(50 to 1 op 20 to 1) 5
ARAMON 3-8-8 (7*) M Payne (1) *outpcd and wl beh till styd on fnl 2 fs, nvr nrr.* .... (16 to 1 op 8 to 1 tchd 20 to 1) 6
3340[4] CANADIAN CAPERS 4-8-7 C Rutter (8) *wth ldr till wknd wl o'r 2 fs out*........ (7 to 2 op 3 to 1 tchd 4 to 1) 7
3047 DELAY NO MORE (v) 3-7-13 S O'Gorman (7) *led till hdd 3 fs out, sn wknd*........(50 to 1 op 14 to 1) 8
3007[8] SUNLEY SPARKLE 5-8-5 M Hills (10) *chsd ldrs till rdn and wknd o'r 3 fs out*......(8 to 1 op 7 to 1 tchd 10 to 1) 9
261[8] DIVINE GLORY 4-8-6 S Dawson (9) *beh and rdn alng hfwy, tld off*........(50 to 1 op 20 to 1) 10
Dist: 3l, sht-hd, ½l, nk, 2l, 4l, 7l, 3l, 30l. 1m 35.00s. a 2.60s (10 Ran).
SR: 8/8/1/-/-/1/ (M Pattimore), B Smart

3548 A. R. Dennis Bookmakers Handicap Class E (0-70 3-y-o and up) £4,620 1m 3f 196yds........ (3:40)

3021[7] DR ZEVA [31] 7-7-4 (7*) Kim McDonnell (1) *tucked in hndy, pushed alng and hdwy o'r 3 fs out, sstnd effrt to ld ins last*........(20 to 1 op 16 to 1) 1
3430[5] LOOKINGFORARAINBOW (Ire) [59] 5-9-11 N Day (6) *al hndy, led 6 fs out, clr o'r 2 out, wknd and hdd ins last.* .... (15 to 2 op 7 to 1 tchd 9 to 1) 2
HEAD TURNER [27] 5-7-7 N Adams (11) *hld up, gd hedway on outsd o'r 3 fs out, kpt on ins last, nrst finish.* ....(50 to 1) 3
3461* UTRILLO (USA) [45] 4-8-11 (5ex) B Raymond (8) *al prmnt, rdn o'r 4 fs out, unbl to quicken, eased whn btn ins last.* ....(2 to 1 fav op 5 to 4 tchd 9 to 4) 4
3420[2] VA UTU [47] 5-8-6 (7*) R Painter (2) *patiently rdn, hdwy o'r 3 fs out, kpt on same pace fnl 2 furlongs.* ....(5 to 1 op 6 to 1 tchd 7 to 1) 5
2942[2] ROCQUAINE BAY [44] 6-8-10 C Rutter (12) *beh and rdn alng o'r 5 fs out, came wide entering strt, kpt on und pres fnl 2 furlongs, no dngr.* .... (12 to 1 op 10 to 1 tchd 14 to 1) 6
3152 BALADIYA [62] 6-9-11 (3*) C Hodgson (7) *led till hdd 6 fs out, rdn o'r 4 out and sn btn.* .... (25 to 1 op 16 to 1 tchd 33 to 1) 7
SPARKLER GEBE [45] (bl) 7-8-11 J Quinn (9) *hld up in midfield, rdn o'r 4 fs out, sn no imprsn.* .... (14 to 1 op 16 to 1 tchd 20 to 1) 8
3430[3] ALLMOSA [60] 4-9-12 D Holland (10) *nvr far away, chsd ldr frm 5 fs out till wknd wl o'r 2 out, eased whn btn.* .... (5 to 1 op 8 to 1 tchd 10 to 1) 9
3044[5] BRANSBY ROAD (Ire) [44] 3-8-0 F Norton (13) *prmnt till hrd rdn o'r 4 fs out, stdly wknd, eased whn btn fnl 2 furlongs*........ (14 to 1 op 8 to 1 tchd 16 to 1) 10
3394[2] THEMEDA [36] 4-8-2 M Hills (3) *chsd ldrs till wknd o'r 5 fs out*........ (5 to 1 tchd 11 to 2 and 9 to 2) 11
3018[4] CORINTHIAN GOD (Ire) [32] 4-7-12[1] A McGlone (5) *chsd ldrs to hfwy, sn struggling*........(25 to 1 op 16 to 1) 12
3430[6] CATHOS (Fr) [36] (bl) 8-8-2[3] G Duffield (4) *slwly away and reluctant to race, al tld off.* .... (16 to 1 op 14 to 1 tchd 20 to 1) 13
Dist: 1½l, 1l, 2½l, 2l, ½l, 2l, 4l, 4l, 12l, ½l. 2m 29.80s. a 2.30s (13 Ran).
SR: 18/43/9/22/20/16/30/5/12/ (G R Butterfield), M Dixon

3549 George Robey Challenge Trophy Limited Stakes Class E (3-y-o) £3,028 6f 209yds........ (4:10)

3060* QUINSIGIMOND 8-9 G Duffield (2) *made all, rdn o'r 2 fs out, styd on gmely.* .... (11 to 10 fav op Evens tchd 11 to 8) 1
2736[4] DEVIOUS DANCER 8-9 (5*) D McCabe (7) *beh and outpcd appr hfwy, gd hdwy o'r one furlong out, hng lft ins last, ran on, nvr nrr*...(12 to 1 op 7 to 1 tchd 14 to 1) 2
3302[6] DESERT NOMAD 8-4 (5*) D Wright (3) *al prmnt, chlgd wnr frm o'r 2 fs out till no extr appr fnl furlong.* .... (11 to 2 op 9 to 2 tchd 6 to 1) 3
3450 HALLORINA 8-9 G Bardwell (5) *prmnt till rdn and lost pl wl o'r 2 fs out, kpt on ag'n ins last.* ....(16 to 1 op 14 to 1 tchd 12 to 1 and 20 to 1) 4
1312 PATSY GRIMES 8-9 S Raymont (1) *slwly into strd, reco'red to track ldrs till wknd appr fnl furlong.* .... (16 to 1 op 20 to 1 tchd 14 to 1) 5
2897[8] GREEN'S FAIR (Ire) (v) 9-0 M Hills (8) *trkd ldrs on outsd, effrt o'r 2 fs out, sn one pace.* ....(7 to 1 op 9 to 2 tchd 8 to 1) 6
2009[3] MARK'S CLUB (Ire) (bl) 9-0 A Clark (6) *prmnt till rdn and wknd wl o'r 2 fs out*...(12 to 1 op 8 to 1 tchd 14 to 1) 7
3070[3] COALISLAND (v) 9-0 A McGlone (4) *chsd ldg bunch, rdn o'r 3 fs out, wknd*...... (5 to 1 op 9 to 2 tchd 4 to 1) 8
Dist: 1½l, ½l, ¾l, 2l, ½l, 4l, 5l. 1m 22.20s. a 2.20s (8 Ran).
SR: 25/25/18/16/10/13/1/-/ (A E T Mines), Sir Mark Prescott

3550 Saddlescombe Claiming Stakes Class G (Div II) (3-y-o and up) £2,070 7f 214yds........ (4:40)

3233[9] SUPERENSIS (v) 3-7-12 (7*) Kim McDonnell (4) *made virtually all, kicked clr o'r 2 fs out, styd on strly.* ....(5 to 1 op 7 to 2) 1
3190[6] BASSIO (Bel) (h) 4-8-8 W Hood (1) *wth ldr till rdn and outpcd o'r 2 fs out, kpt on*........ (7 to 1 op 4 to 1) 2
3228 GATHERING 4-8-13 T Quinn (6) *beh, hdwy o'r 3 fs out, kpt on und pres ins last, nvr nrr.* .... (33 to 1 op 16 to 1 tchd 50 to 1) 3
2869[4] GREAT HAND 7-9-6 J Reid (3) *al chasing ldrs, rdn o'r 3 fs out, no real imprsn*.....(11 to 4 op 3 to 1 tchd 4 to 1) 4
2684[7] LER CRU (Ire) (bl) 4-8-10 A McGlone (7) *chsd ldrs early, rdn bef hfwy, sn wknd.* (9 to 4 fav op 5 to 2 tchd 11 to 4) 5
2724 BIRD TROUBLE (Ire) 3-8-3 C Avery (9) *chsd ldrs 3 fs, sn wknd*........(50 to 1 op 25 to 1) 6
3213[6] THE WEND 3-7-3 (5*) D Wright (5) *wth ldrs till rdn and wknd wl o'r 3 fs out*.... (5 to 1 op 4 to 1 tchd 6 to 1) 7
3174[7] EASTERN CHARLY (Bel) (bl) 3-8-1 G Hind (2) *chsd ldrs to hfwy, sn rdn and wknd.* .... (10 to 1 op 16 to 1 tchd 25 to 1) 8
3221[7] ABSOLUTELY HUMMING (v) 7-8-8 R Price (8) *in tch 2 fs, pushed alng and struggling hfwy, wl beh whn broke shoulder o'r two out, destroyed*... (50 to 1 op 33 to 1) pu
Dist: 2½l, hd, 3l, 7l, 2½l, 2½l, 1½l. 1m 34.90s. a 2.50s (9 Ran).
SR: 12/7/11/9/-/-/ (A J de V Patrick), W R Muir

3551 Brighton Amateur Riders' Handicap Class G (0-70 3-y-o and up) £2,637 1m 1f 209yds........ (5:10)

3308[6] KELIMUTU [36] 4-9-6 Mrs L Pearce (3) *took keen hold, tucked away in midfield, hdwy o'r 2 fs out, str run fnl furlong to ld cl hme*..... (5 to 1 op 4 to 1 tchd 6 to 1) 1
3107[4] DON'T DROP BOMBS (USA) [35] 4-9-5 Miss J Feilden (9) *led, quickened clr wl o'r 2 fs out, ct cl hme.* ....(8 to 1 tchd 10 to 1) 2
3447[7] MEDLAND (Ire) [47] 3-9-9 Miss D J Jones (10) *chsd ldr, outpcd wl o'r 2 fs out, unbl to quicken.* .... (10 to 1 op 6 to 1) 3
3342[4] TORGHIA [51] 6-10-2 (5*) Miss M Sandercock (5) *chsd ldg bunch, rdn and some hdwy o'r 2 fs out, kpt on one pace*........(20 to 1 op 12 to 1 tchd 25 to 1) 4
3340* MULCIBER [65] 5-11-7 Miss A Harwood (18) *midfield, rdn alng and hng rght o'r 2 fs out, kpt on ins last.* .... (13 to 2 op 4 to 1 tchd 7 to 1) 5
2422[7] BACK TO FORM [30] 8-8-13[4] (5*) Mrs C Price (4) *hld up, hdwy on ins whn not clr run o'r 2 fs out, kpt on fnl furlong, nvr nr to chal*........ (50 to 1 op 20 to 1) 6

3340[5] GAMEFULL GOLD [35] 4-9-5 Mr T Cuff (8) *chsd ldrs till rdn and lost pl o'r 2 fs out*............(50 to 1 op 12 to 1) 7
402 STRAT'S LEGACY [45] 6-10-1 Mrs D Arbuthnot (13) *hld up and beh, pld wide and steady hdwy o'r 3 fs out, kpt on, nvr able to chal*......(5 to 2 fav op 7 to 2 tchd 4 to 1) 8
3090[6] BREEZED WELL [40] 7-9-10 Mrs H Noonan (11) *midfield, hdwy to chase ldrs o'r 3 fs out, sn rdn and no extr.* ......(25 to 1 op 10 to 1) 9
3430[7] MISS RIBBONS [38] 3-8-9 (5*) Miss S Chittenden (7) *beh hfwy till moderate late hdwy*......(50 to 1 op 33 to 1) 10
2948[8] TAYLORS PRINCE [47] (v) 6-10-3 Mr P Close (12) *hld up and beh, pld wide and not clr run o'r 3 fs out, nvr a dngr.* ......(12 to 1 op 8 to 1) 11
2195[5] HERETICAL MISS [50] 3-9-12 Mrs J Boggis (17) *prmnt till rdn and wknd o'r 3 fs out.* ......(16 to 1 op 8 to 1 tchd 20 to 1) 12
2532[7] AEDEAN [35] 4-9-5 Mrs D McHale (15) *beh till shrtlvd effrt o'r 4 fs out, sn btn*..............(20 to 1 op 12 to 1) 13
CANDLE KING (Ire) [40] (bl) 5-9-10 Mrs S Bosley (14) *midfield, shrtlvd effrt o'r 4 fs out, sn wknd.* ......(50 to 1 op 20 to 1) 14
3420[3] RUTLAND WATER (USA) [61] 6-11-3 Mr T McCarthy (16) *chsd ldrs till rdn and wknd o'r 2 fs out.* ......(4 to 1 tchd 5 to 1) 15
2847 EMERALD EARS [30] 4-8-13[4] (5*) Miss E Mills (2) *pld hrd in midfield on ins, beh frm 4 fs out*... (50 to 1 op 20 to 1) 16
3509 LAMBOURN RAJA [61] 7-11-3[7] (5*) Mr K Tork (6) *prmnt till wknd wl o'r 3 fs out, tld off*.......(50 to 1 op 33 to 1) 17
Dist: 1l, 6l, nk, 1½l, nk, hd, 1l, 3½l, hd, 2l. 2m 2.20s. a 4.00s (17 Ran).
SR: 31/28/20/31/42/6/10/18/6/ (James Furlong), J Pearce

REDCAR (good to firm)
Wednesday August 25th
Going Correction: NIL (races 1,4,5), PLUS 0.10 (2,3,6,7)

3552 Runswick Bay Selling Handicap Stakes Class G (0-60 3-y-o and up) £2,070 1¾m 19yds............ (1:50)

3373[6] CARROLLS MARC (Ire) [50] 5-10-0 R Cochrane (3) *patiently rdn, improved entering strt, led o'r one furlong out, drvn out*.......................(13 to 2 op 7 to 1) 1
3503[9] FREE TRANSFER (Ire) [30] 4-8-8 J Fanning (10) *settled gng wl, improved frm midfield to chal o'r one furlong out, ran on und pres.* (11 to 2 jt-fav op 9 to 2 tchd 6 to 1) 2
3442* REACH FOR GLORY [45] 4-9-9 (5ex) A Culhane (16) *nvr far away, chlgd und pres last 2 fs, not quicken nr finish.* ......(11 to 2 jt-fav op 6 to 1) 3
3049[4] BAJAN AFFAIR [32] 3-7-12[3] (3*) D Harrison (14) *settled gng wl, led on bit o'r 3 fs out, hdd over one out, edgd lft, no extr*......(12 to 1 op 10 to 1) 4
3430 HYDROPIC [23] 6-8-1 S Wood (2) *wth ldr, led o'r 4 fs out till over 3 out, wkng whn squeezed for room and snatched up ins last*..............(12 to 1 op 10 to 1) 5
2343[4] GREY COMMANDER [25] 5-8-3 A Mackay (8) *settled beh ldrs, drvn alng to improve last 3 fs, not pace to chal.* ......(10 to 1) 6
3407* FAMOUS BEAUTY [45] 6-9-2 (7*,5ex) L Aspell (11) *steadied strt, wl beh hfwy, styd on last 2 fs, nvr nrr*..... (6 to 1) 7
3355[2] MR ABBOT [37] 3-8-3 J Lowe (15) *settled beh ldrs, drvn alng entering strt, no response*...... (6 to 1 op 5 to 1) 8
FILM LIGHTING GIRL [22] 7-7-9 (5*) Darren Moffatt (13) *chsd alng appr strt, nvr a factor*.......(33 to 1 op 25 to 1) 9
3056[7] MEDIA STAR [26] 8-8-4[1] Alex Greaves (7) *settled beh ldrs, drvn alng entering strt, nvr nr to chal.* ......(14 to 1 op 10 to 1) 10
290 QUEENS TOUR [30] 8-8-8 S Webster (4) *pressed ldg pair, wknd quickly entering strt*......(33 to 1) 11
3239[5] NANCY (Ire) [33] (bl) 3-7-13 T Williams (1) *led till o'r 4 fs out, wknd rpdly*..........(14 to 1 op 12 to 1 tchd 16 to 1) 12
3283[5] ALIZARI (USA) [37] 4-9-1 R P Elliott (5) *pressed ldrs, und pres appr strt, sn lost tch*......(33 to 1) 13
3142[4] EVERSO IRISH [34] 4-8-12 L Dettori (6) *pressed ldg trio, hrd drvn appr strt, sn lost tch*......(12 to 1) 14
Dist: Hd, 2l, 2½l, 1l, 5l, ½l, 1½l, 1l, 2½l, ¾l. 3m 6.90s. a 10.40s (14 Ran).
SR: 10/-/-/-/-/ (P I P Electrics Limited), P C Haslam

3553 Furniture Factors Racing Schools Limited Stakes For Apprentice Riders Class E (0-70 3-y-o and up) £2,898 1m ....(2:20)

2915[2] DANCING DOMINO 3-8-8 S Maloney (1) *settled gng wl, swtchd outsd to ld o'r one furlong out, drvn clr.* ......(9 to 4 op 7 to 4) 1
3365[5] HERSHEBAR (bl) 3-8-5[1] (4*) G Strange (4) *nvr far away, effrt and drvn alng last 2 fs, styd on one pace.* ......(16 to 1 op 12 to 1) 2
3375* TALENTED TING (Ire) (v) 4-9-0 J Weaver (5) *slight ld, edgd lft and rdn o'r 2 fs out, hdd over one out, sn btn.* ......(7 to 4 fav op 11 to 8) 3
3358 SPANISH VERDICT 6-8-10 (4*) C Teague (2) *nvr far away, effrt and niggled alng hfwy, outpcd o'r one furlong out, kpt on*......(3 to 1) 4
3440[2] CRESELLY 6-8-1 (8*) I Jardine (6) *wth ldr, drvn alng o'r 2 fs out, sn outpcd*....... (8 to 1 op 7 to 1 tchd 9 to 1) 5
3185[5] THROW AWAY LINE 4-8-5 (4*) S Copp (3) *last and bustled alng hfwy, sn lost tch*...........(100 to 1 op 50 to 1) 6
Dist: 3l, 3l, hd, 3½l, 20l. 1m 40.00s. a 5.10s (6 Ran).
SR: 30/21/18/17/1/-/ (P D Savill), M H Easterby

3554 Andersons Conditions Stakes Class D (2-y-o) £3,289 7f...............(2:50)

ASKERN 8-10 E Johnson (5) *patiently rdn, shaken up and ran green o'r 2 fs out, swtchd and ran on to ld last 50 yards*......(20 to 1 op 16 to 1) 1
3250* SURIS (Ire) 9-0 R Cochrane (1) *al hndy, drvn alng to ld appr fnl furlong, hdd last 50 yards, no extr.* ......(5 to 4 fav tchd 11 to 8) 2
2836* PAVAKA (v) 8-10 L Dettori (7) *wth ldr, led hfwy till appr fnl furlong, kpt on same pace*..........(5 to 1 op 9 to 2) 3
GOLDEN HELLO 8-10 M Birch (8) *patiently rdn, shaken up o'r 2 fs out, ran on, better for race.* ......(25 to 1 op 20 to 1) 4
2812[4] OUBECK BLUE 8-11 W Ryan (4) *sluggish strt, last and outpcd hfwy, ran on appr fnl furlong, nvr nrr.* ......(11 to 2 op 4 to 1) 5
3000[2] PLAINSONG 8-5 K Fallon (3) *pressed ldrs, feeling pace and pushed alng o'r 2 fs out, wknd.* (7 to 1 op 6 to 1) 6
2528[2] NIGHT SNOW 8-2 (3*) M Fenton (2) *slight ld to hfwy, fdd und pres o'r one furlong out*.......(10 to 1 op 8 to 1) 7
3502[8] BANDON CASTLE (Ire) 8-13 (3*) D Harrison (9) *rcd freely on outsd, ev ch hfwy, eased whn btn o'r one furlong out.* ......(11 to 1 op 10 to 1 tchd 12 to 1) 8
LADY GWEN (Ire) 8-5 Dale Gibson (6) *chsd ldrs for o'r 4 fs, fdd*.............................. (25 to 1 op 20 to 1) 9
Dist: 1½l, 3l, 1½l, 5l, 3l, sht-hd, 4l, 3½l. 1m 26.00s. a 4.20s (9 Ran).
SR: 44/43/30/25/11/-/ (J Hanson), J Hanson

3555 Mulgrave Limited Stakes Class E (0-70 3-y-o and up) £3,080 1¼m (3:20)

3388* SHIRLEY ROSE 3-8-8 L Dettori (5) *made all, quickened o'r 3 fs out, jnd and rdn appr last, hld on gmely.* ......(9 to 4 fav op 7 to 4 tchd 5 to 2) 1
3255[9] BLUE GROTTO (Ire) (bl) 3-8-13 N Connorton (6) *al hndy, drw level und pres o'r one furlong out, kpt on wl.* ......(10 to 1 op 14 to 1) 2
2930[8] SCORCHED AIR 3-8-5 (3*) B Doyle (2) *nvr far away, ev ch and drvn alng o'r 2 fs out, kpt on same pace*....(6 to 1) 3
3507[4] DUVEEN (Ire) 3-8-10 (3*) M Fenton (1) *pressed ldg pair, ev ch and rdn o'r 2 fs out, styd on same pace.* ......(7 to 2 op 3 to 1) 4
MARADONNA (USA) 4-9-7 R Cochrane (4) *trkd ldrs, feeling pace o'r 3 fs out, styd on wl nr finish.* ......(10 to 1 op 8 to 1) 5
3101[7] SUNTARA (Ire) 3-8-8 W Ryan (7) *settled gng wl, effrt and drvn alng o'r 2 fs out, not pace to chal.* ......(5 to 1 op 4 to 1) 6
3256[3] I'M A DREAMER (Ire) 3-8-13 Dale Gibson (3) *chsd ldrs, drvn alng entering strt, kpt on, nvr able to chal.* ......(12 to 1 op 10 to 1) 7
3142[5] DONIA (USA) 4-9-2 A Munro (8) *settled midfield, effrt and pushed alng o'r 2 fs out, nvr able to chal.* ......(14 to 1 op 16 to 1) 8
Dist: Sht-hd, 2l, ¾l, 1l, 1½l, ¾l, 10l. 2m 6.80s. a 5.60s (8 Ran).
SR: 38/42/33/36/42/26/29/12/ (Greenland Park Ltd), M Johnston

3556 Yorkshire Television Handicap Class E (0-70 3-y-o) £3,080 1m 5f 135yds ....(3:50)

3056[2] MONDRAGON [68] 9-7 J Lowe (8) *patiently rdn, last strt, styd on to ld o'r one furlong out, drifted lft, ran on.* ......(9 to 1 op 8 to 1) 1
3147[2] MILNGAVIE (Ire) [48] 8-1 T Williams (3) *settled midfield, swrvd rght o'r 4 fs out, chalg whn hmpd appr last, kpt on*......(10 to 1) 2
3049* SIDE BAR [44] (bl) 7-11 A Tucker (11) *al hndy, led 3 fs out till o'r one out, kpt on*.............(12 to 1 op 10 to 1) 3
3308[3] GIORDANO (Ire) [62] 9-1 L Dettori (9) *trkd ldrs, drvn to chal o'r 2 fs out, kpt on same pace*.... (10 to 1 tchd 11 to 1) 4
3356[3] DUPLICATE [62] 9-1 M Birch (9) *nvr far away, not much room and swtchd ins 2 fs out, kpt on same pace.* ......(6 to 1 fav op 11 to 2) 5
3322* POETIC FORM (Ire) [41] (bl) 7-8[1] Dale Gibson (10) *al hndy, led briefly o'r 3 fs out, one pace whn hmpd ins last.* ......(10 to 1 op 8 to 1) 6
3320[3] POINT THE WAY (Ire) [66] 9-0 (5*) J Tate (2) *co'red up, effrt and drvn alng over 2 fs out, not pace to chal.* (12 to 1) 7
3412[2] ARC BRIGHT (Ire) [53] (bl) 8-6[2] S Perks (13) *chsd ldrs, effrt on outsd entering strt, no imprsn last 2 fs.* ......(9 to 1 op 10 to 1 tchd 8 to 1) 8
1831 RUN TO AU BON (Ire) [60] 8-13 R Cochrane (12) *wtd wth, effrt and drvn alng entering strt, not rch ldrs.* ......(20 to 1 op 16 to 1) 9
2888* HO-JOE (Ire) [57] 8-10 K Fallon (1) *settled midfield, nvr trble ldrs*......(14 to 1) 10

3097² MONSIEUR DUPONT (Ire) [65] 9-1 (3*) D Harrison (7) *in tch, effrt on outsd whn bumped o'r 4 fs out, nvr able to chal.* ....(8 to 1) 11
3320⁹ PUGET DANCER (USA) [54] (v) 8-4 (3*) M Fenton (5) *hld up in tch, effrt entering staight, nvr able to chal.* ....(20 to 1 op 14 to 1) 12
3097* SO SAUCY [60] 8-10 (3*) B Doyle (4) *led till hdd and wknd o'r 3 fs out*........(7 to 1) 13
3256⁷ KAHLO [52] 8-5 J Carroll (14) *chsd ldrs to strt, sn btn.* ....(14 to 1 tchd 20 to 1 and 12 to 1) 14
Dist: 2l, 1l, 2l, ½l, ¾l, 1½l, 3l, 2½l, 1½l, 4l. 2m 59.60s. a 9.70s (14 Ran).
SR: 10/-/-/-/-/- (Skeltools Ltd), Mrs M Reveley

3557 Westerdale Maiden Auction Stakes Class E (2-y-o) £2,872 5f........(4:20)

1229³ ELEUTHERA 8-9 L Dettori (8) *al gng wl, led o'r one furlong out, pushed out, readily*......(5 to 4 on op 7 to 4 on) 1
MARY HINGE 8-9 Paul Eddery (6) *al wl plcd, drw level o'r one furlong out, kpt on well*........(5 to 1 op 9 to 2) 2
2203² CHASTIZE (Ire) 9-0 W Ryan (7) *co'red up, swtchd outsd to improve last 2 fs, ran on same pace.* ....(7 to 2 op 4 to 1 tchd 9 to 2) 3
NEVER SO TRUE 8-9 J Weaver (1) *in tch, pushed alng to go pace hfwy, ran on fnl furlong, nvr nrr.* ....(14 to 1 tchd 20 to 1) 4
IT MUST BE MILLIE 8-9 Dale Gibson (4) *pressed ldrs for o'r 3 fs, rdn and no extr*........(25 to 1 op 20 to 1) 5
2586⁷ BOLD TIME MONKEY 8-9 J Carroll (5) *slight ld for o'r 3 fs, fdd*........(25 to 1 op 20 to 1) 6
3505⁹ SHARP SUMMIT (Ire) 8-6 (3*) D Harrison (3) *speed on ins for 3 fs, sn rdn and no extr*........(50 to 1 op 33 to 1) 7
3411³ PASTURES NEW (Ire) 8-9 S Wood (2) *speed on ins, hng lft o'r 2 fs out, wknd quickly over one out.* ....(14 to 1 op 10 to 1) 8
Dist: 1l, 2½l, 3½l, ½l, ¾l, 8l, nk. 1m 0.50s. a 3.80s (8 Ran).
SR: 29/25/20/1/-/ (Lucayan Stud), D R Loder

3558 Whitley Handicap Class C (0-90 3-y-o and up) £5,300 7f...............(4:50)

3158⁶ AMAZING FEAT (Ire) [83] 4-9-9 R Cochrane (4) *settled gng wl, quickened ahead o'r one furlong out, drvn clr.* ....(6 to 1 op 5 to 1) 1
3237⁴ NORTH ARDAR [62] 3-7-11 T Williams (3) *nvr far away, led briefly o'r one furlong out, kpt on same pace.* ....(11 to 1 op 9 to 1 tchd 12 to 1) 2
3219⁴ OK BERTIE [74] 3-8-9 M Birch (2) *tucked away on ins, not much room o'r 2 fs out, kpt on wl fnl furlong.* ....(11 to 1 op 8 to 1 tchd 12 to 1) 3
3404 DENSBEN [81] 9-9-7 K Fallon (12) *pushed alng to improve last 2 fs, fnshd wl*........(14 to 1 op 12 to 1) 4
3504⁷ EURO FESTIVAL [79] 4-9-2 (3*) D Harrison (13) *wtd wth, improved to go hndy 2 fs out, styd on same pace.* ....(6 to 1 op 5 to 1) 5
3375³ LAUREL QUEEN (Ire) [73] 5-8-13 J Carroll (9) *wth ldr, drvn alng o'r one furlong out, sn btn.* ......(100 to 30 fav op 8 to 1 tchd 9 to 1 and 3 to 1) 6
3350 BEWARE OF AGENTS [87] 4-9-13 R P Elliott (11) *beh, hmpd and swtchd ins hfwy, drvn alng and switched outsd one furlong out, ran on.* (8 to 1 op 7 to 1 tchd 9 to 1) 7
3280³ SAVAHRA SOUND [68] 8-8-8 S Webster (8) *led till o'r 3 fs out, fdd*........(14 to 1) 8
2854 PARLIAMENT PIECE [84] 7-9-10 W Ryan (1) *wth ldrs, led o'r 3 fs out till over one out, fdd.* ....(11 to 1 op 7 to 1 tchd 12 to 1) 9
2830⁵ NOYAN [83] (v) 3-9-1 (3*) M Fenton (5) *chsd alng in midfield, struggling last 2 fs*........(9 to 1 tchd 10 to 1) 10
3182⁵ CELESTINE [54] (v) 4-7-8 J Fanning (7) *in tch, bustled alng in midfield hfwy, sn btn*........(20 to 1 op 14 to 1) 11
1269⁹ BANDMASTER (USA) [88] 4-10-0 Paul Eddery (6) *steadied strt, effrt and pushed alng hfwy, sn lost tch.* ....(20 to 1 op 14 to 1) 12
3409⁹ GANT BLEU (Fr) [54] 6-7-8¹ Dale Gibson (10) *chsd ldrs on outsd, wknd and eased last 2 fs*....(20 to 1 op 14 to 1) 13
Dist: 2½l, nk, 1l, 1½l, 3½l, 1½l, 5l, 1½l, 15l, ¾l. 1m 26.30s. a 4.50s (13 Ran).
SR: 52/18/29/38/31/14/23/-/-/ (P D Savill), Mrs M Reveley

TRALEE (IRE) (good)
Wednesday August 25th

3559 Beamish Stout Ruby Stakes (Listed) (3-y-o and up) £8,625 1m....... (3:30)

3452² DOREG (Ire) 3-8-10 P V Gilson (11) *wl plcd, cld on ldrs 3 fs out, led one out, ran on well*........(12 to 1) 1
3465 APPROACH THE BENCH (Ire) 5-9-7 W J Supple (1) *hld up, prog on outsd entering strt, styd on strly fnl furlong.* ....(9 to 2) 2
3199⁴ ARABIC TREASURE (USA) 3-8-10 P Shanahan (9) *wl plcd, rdn in 4th 2 fs out, ran on well fnl furlong*..... (7 to 1) 3
2957⁸ THATCHING CRAFT (Ire) 4-8-13 J J Behan (3) *led till hdd one furlong out, sn wknd*........(14 to 1) 4
3162⁴ DASHING COLOURS (Ire) 4-9-4 P Carberry (6) *hld up, brght wide to chal entering strt, kpt on one pace*..... (5 to 1) 5
3029⁴ CHANZI (USA) (bl) 3-8-12 J P Murtagh (10) *trkd ldr till rdn and wknd 2 fs out*........(4 to 1) 6
2809* PRE-EMINENT (bl) 6-9-7 M J Kinane (2) *trkd ldrs till rdn and lost pl 2 fs out, eased fnl furlong*.......(7 to 4 fav) 7
3333⁴ SALMON EILE (Ire) 5-9-7 S Craine (4) *rear, slightly hmpd hfwy, nvr rchd ldrs*........(7 to 1) 8
3454⁴ RAIN RITE (Ire) 4-8-13 R Hughes (5) *al rear*.......(25 to 1) 9
Dist: Hd, sht-hd, 2l, nk. 1m 38.40s. (9 Ran).
(Patrick F Headon), Declan Gillespie

3560 Carling Gold Cup Handicap (0-110 3-y-o and up) £13,150 1¾m.........(4:00)

3328² COMMAND 'N CONTROL [-] 4-6-13 (8*) G M Moylan (7) ....(20 to 1) 1
3336* SHIRLEY'S DELIGHT (Ire) [-] 3-8-8 (2*,7ex) P Carberry (11) ....(6 to 1) 2
3336³ PARNALA (USA) [-] 3-8-5 (2*) D G O'Shea (1).......(6 to 1) 3
3275² FONTANAYS (Ire) [-] 5-7-9 Joanna Morgan (4).....(20 to 1) 4
2038 RIYOOM (USA) [-] 3-9-2 K J Manning (9)........(14 to 1) 5
2841² PADASHPAN (USA) [-] 4-8-3 (4*) J J Behan (2)..(100 to 30) 6
2841* SHANKORAK [-] 6-8-8 W J Supple (6)........(7 to 1) 7
2841⁸ NEMURO (USA) [-] (bl) 5-9-0 (6*) C Everard (10)...(20 to 1) 8
3336² TBAAREEH (USA) [-] 3-9-2 C Roche (5)........(6 to 1) 9
2881⁷ MARILYN (Ire) [-] 4-8-3 J F Egan (8)........(20 to 1) 10
2955* GARBONI (USA) [-] 4-9-7 M J Kinane (3).......(3 to 1 fav) 11
Dist: Nk, 2l, 8l, 3½l. 3m 9.70s. (11 Ran).
(J E Mulhern), J E Mulhern

3561 Denis Moriarty Plant Hire Handicap Sprint (0-90 3-y-o and up) £4,140 5f ....(4:30)

2879⁶ MACGILLYCUDDY (Ire) [-] (bl) 4-8-9 (8*) R T Fitzpatrick (8) ....(9 to 2) 1
3496⁵ MY-O-MY (Ire) [-] 3-10-3 S Craine (9)........(4 to 1) 2
3330⁴ ASTA MADERA (Ire) [-] 3-8-3 J F Egan (3)........(6 to 1) 3
3395² PAKOL (Ire) [-] 4-8-0 (4*) W J Smith,........(14 to 1) 4
3452³ COMMON BOND (Ire) [-] 3-9-1 C Roche (7)...(11 to 4 fav) 5
3395⁵ PETITE EPAULETTE [-] (bl) 3-9-3 J P Murtagh (2)..(14 to 1) 6
3330 OICHE MHAITH [-] (bl) 3-8-8 R Hughes (1)........(10 to 1) 7
3201⁹ SHOOT THE DEALER (Ire) [-] 3-8-5 (8*) G Coogan (5) ....(14 to 1) 8
3244⁸ KILLEEN STAR (Ire) [-] 3-8-8 M J Kinane (4)........(9 to 1) 9
Dist: Nk, 1l, ¾l. 1m 2.50s. (9 Ran).
(Mrs Rita Hale), Patrick Prendergast

3562 Bernard Dillon E.B.F. (C & G) Maiden (2-y-o) £3,795 1m...............(5:00)

3030⁹ RAHAL (Ire) 9-0 M J Kinane (5)........(13 to 8 on) 1
NUN'S ISLAND (Ire) 9-0 B Coogan (10)........(12 to 1) 2
3415⁴ NORTHERN BARS (Ire) 9-0 C Roche (6)........(100 to 30) 3
3416 KAKASHDA (Ire) 9-0 J P Murtagh (8)........(9 to 1) 4
FAIRY TRYST (Ire) 9-0 J F Egan (4)........(9 to 1) 5
3332⁹ BRIEF RESPITE (Ire) 9-0 P Shanahan (3)........(12 to 1) 6
ALEXANDER KAHYASI 9-0 N Byrne (7)........(20 to 1) 7
2982 DUGORT STRAND (Ire) 8-8 (6*) B Bowens (1).....(20 to 1) 8
Dist: 1l, hd, 5l, 2½l. 1m 40.10s. (8 Ran).
(Andrea Schiavi), D K Weld

EDINBURGH (firm)
Thursday August 26th
Going Correction: MINUS 0.30 sec. per fur. (races 1,2,3,5), MINUS 0.50 (4,6)

3563 Royal Scots Club Nursery Class E (2-y-o) £2,815 7f 15yds............ (2:10)

3236² MISS MAH-JONG [77] 9-7 G Duffield (8) *dsptd ld thrght, led o'r one furlong out, ran on strly.* ....(9 to 2 op 5 to 1 tchd 11 to 2) 1
2996 DISTINCTIVE AIR [70] 9-0 L Dettori (7) *trkd ldrs, crrd wide strt, effrt and drvn alng last 2 fs, fnshd wl.* ....(15 to 2 op 7 to 1 tchd 8 to 1) 2
3235² PASSION SUNDAY [62] 8-6 M Birch (11) *tried to make all, rdn and hdd 2 fs out, kpt on same pace.* ....(4 to 1 fav op 7 to 2) 3
3210⁵ CAPITAL LADY (Ire) [49] 7-7 S Wood (6) *beh and drvn alng hfwy, rapid hdwy entering fnl furlong, fnshd fst.* ....(33 to 1 op 20 to 1) 4
3215⁷ THE HAPPY LOON (Ire) [60] 8-4 K Fallon (5) *took keen hold in midfield, effrt and drvn alng o'r 2 fs out, ran on wl.* ....(10 to 1 op 8 to 1) 5
3279⁵ HELLABY [63] 8-7 T Williams (10) *pressed ldg trio, drvn ahead o'r 2 fs out, hdd over one furlong out, one pace.* ....(14 to 1 op 12 to 1 tchd 16 to 1) 6
3235⁷ MONSIEUR BLEU [55] 7-13 J Fanning (9) *pushed alng in midfield, effrt o'r 2 fs out, kpt on same pace*... (16 to 1) 7
3259 KARSEAM (Ire) [71] 9-1 N Connorton (12) *wth ldrs, came wide and rdn strt, fdd und pres last 2 fs.* ....(17 to 2 op 8 to 1 tchd 10 to 1) 8
2679⁴ OLYMPIC BID [59] 8-3¹ J Carroll (4) *outpcd and drvn alng hfwy, nvr nr to chal*........(12 to 1) 9
3235⁵ MISS FREEBIE (Ire) [50] 7-8¹ Dale Gibson (1) *chsd alng to go pace, nvr a factor*........(10 to 1 op 8 to 1) 10

2825^{5} STORM HEIGHTS [50] 7-8^{1} J Lowe (2) *beh and drvn alng hfwy, nvr a threat*.......(33 to 1 op 25 to 1) 11
2946^{4} HONEST WOMAN [55] 7-10^{2} (5*) D McCabe (3) *steadied strt, effrt and drvn alng hfwy, nvr dngrs.* ....(10 to 1 op 8 to 1) 12
Dist: 1½l, 1½l, nk, sht-hd, hd, ¾l, 7l, 7l, 1l, ½l. 1m 28.00s. a 2.80s (12 Ran).
SR: 34/22/9/-/5/7/ (R Robinson (Wigan)), M Johnston

3564 Edmonds Handicap Class E (0-70 3-y-o) £2,944 7f 15yds..............(2:40)

3358^{4} NORTHERN CHIEF [56] 8-11 (3*) S Maloney (9) *al travelling wl, led o'r 2 fs out, shaken up and sprinted clr fnl furlong*..........(11 to 2 jt-fav op 5 to 1 tchd 6 to 1) 1
3409^{3} NORLING (Ire) [50] 8-8 S Morris (14) *slight ld to hfwy, rallied und pres last 2 fs, no ch wth wnr.* ....(12 to 1 op 10 to 1) 2
3247* NICHODOULA [60] 9-4 G Duffield (13) *nvr far away, drvn alng whn pace quickened last 2 fs, one pace.* ....(6 to 1 op 5 to 1 tchd 13 to 2) 3
3378^{3} KILLY'S FILLY [53] 8-11 J Carroll (8) *chsd alng in midfield, styd on last 2 fs, nvr able to chal*.....(8 to 1 op 6 to 1) 4
3365^{2} PENNY BANGER (Ire) [57] 9-1 T Williams (15) *wth ldr, led hfwy till o'r 2 fs out, rdn and no extr.* ....(15 to 2 op 7 to 1 tchd 8 to 1) 5
3094^{7} MY GODSON [61] 9-5 L Dettori (7) *in tch, drvn into midfield o'r 2 fs out, not pace of ldrs.* (12 to 1 tchd 14 to 1) 6
3439* LAMSONETTI [53] 8-11 (5ex) Alex Greaves (11) *settled midfield, effrt and drvn alng o'r 2 fs out, kpt on, nvr able to chal*.............(11 to 2 jt-fav op 9 to 2 tchd 6 to 1) 7
3310 NELLIE'S GAMBLE [40] 7-9 (3*) N Kennedy (6) *patiently rdn, steady hdwy whn not much room last 2 fs, nvr nrr.* ....(12 to 1 tchd 14 to 1) 8
2764^{7} GRINNELL [49] 8-7 J Fanning (5) *beh, chsd alng to improve on outsd o'r 2 fs out, nrst finish*..............(16 to 1) 9
2953^{6} KEEP BATTLING [51] (v) 8-9 S Webster (2) *nvr far away, hrd at work o'r 2 fs out, no extr*..............(20 to 1) 10
3219^{8} BIRCHWOOD SUN [62] (bl) 9-6 J Weaver (4) *settled off the pace, swtchd ins and ran on last 2 fs, nvr nrr.* ....(14 to 1 op 12 to 1) 11
3219^{6} CICERONE [57] 9-1 Dale Gibson (1) *chsd alng beh ldg bunch, no imprsn last 2 fs*..................(16 to 1) 12
3302 DAYTONA BEACH (Ire) [60] 9-4 S Perks (10) *pressed ldg trio, hrd at work o'r 2 fs out, sn btn.* ....(16 to 1 op 14 to 1) 13
3325 SPORTING SPIRIT [45] 8-3 S Wood (12) *chsd ldg bunch, effrt and drvn alng o'r 2 fs out, sn btn*.......(50 to 1) 14
2057 CARLTON EXPRESS (Ire) [45] 8-3^{1} N Connorton (16) *outpcd and drvn alng hfwy, nvr a factor*............(50 to 1) 15
Dist: 6l, ½l, nk, 2l, nk, hd, 2½l, ½l, 1½l, 2l. 1m 27.10s. a 1.90s (15 Ran).
SR: 40/16/24/16/14/17/8/-/-/ (T C Chiang), M H Easterby

3565 Royal Scots Handicap Class E (0-70 3-y-o and up) £2,927 1½m 31yds (3:10)

3373 IRON BARON (Ire) [40] 4-7-7 (5*) D Wright (6) *dictated pace to hfwy, rallied und pres to rgn ld o'r one furlong out, styd on wl*..........(9 to 2 op 4 to 1 tchd 5 to 1) 1
3342^{5} PIE HATCH (Ire) [44] (bl) 4-8-2 G Duffield (1) *trkd ldr, led and quickened pace hfwy, sn clr, hdd o'r one furlong out, kpt on*..........................(5 to 1 op 9 to 2) 2
3373^{3} HOT PUNCH [37] 4-7-9 Dale Gibson (4) *trkd ldg pair, hrd at work whn pace quickened entering strt, styd on, no imprsn*..................(8 to 1 tchd 9 to 1) 3
3282^{2} FAIR FLYER (Ire) [61] 4-9-5 R P Elliott (2) *last and hld up, effrt on ins appr strt, drvn alng last 2 fs, one pace.* ....(9 to 2 op 5 to 1 tchd 4 to 1) 4
3503^{4} BATABANOO [70] 4-9-11 (3*) S Maloney (5) *patiently rdn, improved appr strt, sn hrd drvn, nvr able to chal.* ....(7 to 4 fav tchd 2 to 1) 5
3373^{5} ASTURIAS [35] 10-7-7^{3} (3*) N Kennedy (7) *settled to track ldg bunch, feeling pace entering strt, no imprsn.* ....(14 to 1 op 12 to 1) 6
3240^{9} BORING (USA) [43] 4-8-1 J Fanning (3) *chsd ldrs to strt, sn lost tch, tld off*..................(25 to 1 op 16 to 1) 7
Dist: 3½l, 2½l, 3½l, 3l, 2l, dist. 2m 35.10s. a 2.30s (7 Ran).
SR: 24/21/9/26/29/-/-/ (Raymond Gomersall), Mrs V A Aconley

3566 Salamanca Selling Stakes Class G (2-y-o) £2,368 5f..................(3:40)

3432 ALLLEGSNOBRAIN 9-2 L Dettori (10) *al travelling wl, quickened up to ld stands side hfwy, sprinted clr fnl furlong*.............(13 to 8 fav op 2 to 1 tchd 6 to 4) 1
3321* FLOATING TRIAL (v) 8-11 J Carroll (4) *dictated pace stands side to hfwy, kpt on, not pace of wnr.* ....(9 to 2 op 7 to 2 tchd 5 to 1) 2
3411^{6} LOCHON 8-11 S Webster (9) *pushed alng to improve frm midfield last 2 fs, ran on finish.* ....(20 to 1 op 16 to 1 tchd 25 to 1) 3
UPEX LE GOLD (Ire) 8-11 J Fanning (1) *gd speed stands side thrght, kpt on same pace fnl furlong.* ....(50 to 1 op 33 to 1) 4
3411^{7} CELTIC GOVERNESS 7-13 (7*) Claire Balding (3) *chsd alng beh ldrs, effrt 2 fs out, kpt on, nvr able to chal.* ....(66 to 1 op 25 to 1) 5
3254 INDIAN CRYSTAL 8-11 T Williams (6) *sluggish strt, sn outpcd and drvn alng, styd on last 2 fs, nvr nrr.* ....(8 to 1 op 6 to 1) 6
2949^{7} RED GRIT (Ire) (bl) 8-6 J Weaver (13) *led centre, drvn alng hfwy, kpt on same pace last 2 fs*... (20 to 1 op 12 to 1) 7
3001 HONG KONG FUTURE (Ire) (bl) 8-11 J Fortune (14) *sluggish strt, chsd alng to improve hfwy, kpt on, nvr able to chal*..........................(16 to 1 tchd 50 to 1) 8
2103^{8} SALTPETRE (Ire) 8-11 A Mackay (2) *drvn alng beh ldg bunch, no imprsn last 2 fs*.......(100 to 1 op 33 to 1) 9
3254^{8} MAD ABOUT MEN 8-11 N Connorton (8) *sluggish strt, drvn into midfield hfwy, nvr rchd chalg pos.* ....(11 to 1 op 7 to 1 tchd 12 to 1) 10
3183^{6} KAYDARAJ 8-6 M Birch (7) *trkd ldrs, shaken up hfwy, grad wknd last 2 fs*................(7 to 1 op 9 to 2) 11
3215^{8} REGINA ALICIA 8-6 G Duffield (5) *chsd alng in midfield, nvr able to chal*..................(10 to 1 op 8 to 1) 12
3345^{7} GRECIAN GARDEN 8-11 J O'Reilly (11) *sluggish strt, bustled alng thrght, nvr dngrs*.......(25 to 1 op 14 to 1) 13
3235^{8} MAZINA 8-6 A Culhane (16) *chsd alng to go pace hfwy, sn btn*..........................(33 to 1 op 20 to 1) 14
3321^{9} ARKINDALE SPIRIT (Ire) (v) 8-4 (7*) C Munday (15) *struggling to keep up aftr 2 fs, nvr a factor.* ....(33 to 1 op 20 to 1) 15
3377^{8} PEASAN 8-8 (3*) S Maloney (17) *broke wl to show speed far side to hfwy, wknd quickly*..... (100 to 1 op 33 to 1) 16
3321 SUZY LLOYD 8-6 S Wood (12) *sn drvn alng to keep up, nvr a factor*...........(100 to 1 op 25 to 1) 17
Dist: 2l, 2½l, 1½l, 2½l, 2½l, nk, 1½l, 1½l, 10l, ¾l. 58.70s. a 0.90s (17 Ran).
SR: 34/21/11/5/-/-/ (M Woodall), P D Evans

3567 Gaymers Olde English Cyder Claiming Stakes Class F (3-y-o and up) £2,595 1m 7f 16yds.............(4:10)

3092^{3} FOLLINGWORTH GIRL (Ire) 3-8-3 (3*) S Maloney (5) *made all, quickened up entering strt, styd on strly last 2 fs.* ....(4 to 1 tchd 9 to 2 and 5 to 1) 1
3322^{2} ANNABEL'S BABY (Ire) 4-8-12 (7*) N Varley (7) *nvr far away, stumbled entering strt, rallied and ev ch last 2 fs, kpt on same pace*..........(12 to 1 tchd 16 to 1) 2
3442^{2} BEEKMAN STREET 7-9-12 J Fanning (4) *trkd ldg quartet, ev ch and drvn alng o'r 2 fs out, not quicken.* ....(2 to 1 op 3 to 1 tchd 4 to 1) 3
2950^{7} ALPHA HELIX (v) 10-9-0 G Duffield (1) *last but in tch, effrt and bustled alng o'r 3 fs out, not pace to chal.* ....(33 to 1 tchd 50 to 1) 4
3128^{3} RASAYEL (USA) 3-7-11 (3*) D Harrison (6) *trkd wnr, hrd at work o'r 2 fs out, found little.* ....(5 to 4 fav op 11 to 8 on tchd 11 to 8 and 6 to 4) 5
2775^{7} ASTRAC TRIO (USA) 3-8-11 A Mackay (3) *settled aftr fst break, drvn alng whn pace quickened entering strt, sn btn*..........................(33 to 1 op 25 to 1) 6
3552 EVERSO IRISH 4-9-4 L Dettori (2) *chsd ldrs to strt, sn lost tch*.................. (40 to 1 op 33 to 1 tchd 50 to 1) 7
Dist: 1½l, 4l, 4l, 3½l, 12l, 2½l. 3m 19.50s. a 7.50s (7 Ran).
(John L Holdroyd), S G Norton

3568 Pergoda Apprentice Handicap Class G (0-70 3-y-o and up) £2,316 5f.. (4:40)

3229^{4} TREVORSNINEPOINTS [60] 3-8-10 (5*) S Copp (1) *made all stands side, quickened to go clr entering fnl furlong, readily*...................(7 to 1 op 6 to 1) 1
2682^{5} LANGTONIAN [49] (bl) 4-8-2 (5*) Ruth Coulter (2) *pressed wnr stands side thrght, kpt on same pace ins fnl furlong*............................ (20 to 1 op 16 to 1) 2
3486 KABCAST [53] (bl) 8-8-11 D Harrison (14) *dominated far side thrght, kpt on wl ins fnl furlong.* ....(7 to 1 op 6 to 1) 3
3481^{2} JUCEA [63] 4-9-2 (5*,7ex) R Painter (3) *drvn alng to improve frm off the pace last 2 fs, fnshd wl.* ....(5 to 1 op 11 to 2 tchd 13 to 2) 4
3486 SIMMIE'S SPECIAL [57] (bl) 5-8-10 (5*) J Dennis (7) *chsd ldr centre, drvn alng last 2 fs, kpt on same pace.* ....(14 to 1 op 12 to 1) 5
3032^{9} BARBEZIEUX [46] 6-8-1 (3*) D McCabe (9) *sn drvn alng to go pace, kpt on appr fnl furlong, nvr nrr.* ....(14 to 1 op 12 to 1) 6
3032^{5} MISS SIHAM (Ire) [45] 4-8-0 (3*) Claire Balding (11) *chsd alng to join far grp hfwy, rdn and not quicken o'r one furlong out*........................ (8 to 1 op 6 to 1) 7
3391^{2} RED ADMIRAL [55] 3-8-10 C Hodgson (6) *gd speed centre for 3 fs, no extr*... (9 to 2 jt-fav op 5 to 1 tchd 11 to 2) 8
3136^{7} NIFTY FIFTY (Ire) [66] 4-9-5 (5*) P Roberts (10) *broke wl to show gd speed far side 3 fs, fdd*.... (16 to 1 op 14 to 1) 9
MINIZEN MUSIC (Ire) [35] 5-7-7^{3} (3*) J Marshall (12) *wth ldrs far side till fdd und pres to fs out.* (50 to 1 op 33 to 1) 10
3504 EWALD (Ire) [70] 5-10-0 A Garth (13) *gd speed far side, drvn alng 2 fs out, wknd*................(10 to 1 op 8 to 1) 11
3216 ROBIX (Ire) [41] 3-7-10 D Wright (8) *sluggish strt, al struggling to go pace*.................(50 to 1 op 33 to 1) 12
3238^{3} GEMINI FIRE [55] 9-8-13 J Weaver (5) *sluggish strt, drvn alng and some hdwy hfwy, eased whn btn 2 fs out.* ....(9 to 2 jt-fav op 6 to 1 tchd 7 to 1) 13
Dist: 3½l, nk, 1½l, nk, 1½l, 1½l, ½l, ½l, 3½l, 10l. 58.30s. a 0.50s (13 Ran).
SR: 41/19/22/26/19/2/-/-/12/ (T S Child), Mrs M Reveley

LINGFIELD (good)
Thursday August 26th
Going Correction: MINUS 0.25 sec. per fur. (races 1,2,3,5), MINUS 0.45 (4)

3569 Britvic Soft Drinks Claiming Stakes Class F (Div I) (2-y-o) £2,623 6f. . (2:20)

3084* SISTER SUSAN 8-6 W Ryan (4) *sn chsd alng in rear, swtchd rght and hdwy wl o'r one furlong out, ran on to ld cl hme*..........................(4 to 1 op 3 to 1) 1
3432⁴ MONKEY'S WEDDING (bl) 8-9 T Quinn (3) *unruly stalls, cl up, led one and a half fs out to till hdd close hme.* ....(11 to 10 fav op 7 to 4) 2
3267⁵ ANSELLADY 8-7¹ J Reid (1) *in tch, hrd rdn 2 fs out, ev ch ins last, no extr*.......(16 to 1 op 6 to 1 tchd 20 to 1) 3
1955⁶ NATURAL PATH 8-4 A Munro (9) *led til hdd one and a half fs out, one pace*........(8 to 1 op 6 to 1 tchd 10 to 1) 4
3222⁷ KNIGHTRIDER 8-10 J Williams (8) *trkd ldrs till wknd ins fnl furlong*...........(12 to 1 op 6 to 1 tchd 14 to 1) 5
2493³ CURTIS THE FIRST 8-9 A Clark (7) *chsd ldrs till outpcd aftr 2 fs, styd on ins last*..........(33 to 1 op 14 to 1) 6
3446⁶ ROCKETEER (Ire) 9-0 (7*) Kim McDonnell (6) *outpcd.* ....(6 to 1 op 7 to 2) 7
3167⁶ CHARLIE CHARLIE 9-0 A McGlone (2) *outpcd frm hfwy.* .... (33 to 1 op 14 to 1) 8

Dist: Hd, nk, 4l, 2l, sht-hd, 1½l, 3½l. 1m 12.21s. a 3.21s (8 Ran).
(T A Johnsey), R Hannon

3570 Murphys Irish Stout Conditions Stakes Class D (2-y-o) £3,377 7f 140yds (2:50)

2964³ SAWLAJAN (USA) 8-10 W Carson (4) *cl up, led o'r 4 fs out, pushed clr ins last, not extended.* .... (15 to 8 op 7 to 4 tchd 9 to 4) 1
2844⁵ YOUNG AT HEART (Ire) 8-10 R Cochrane (3) *beh, hdwy o'r 2 fs out, kpt on one pace.* .... (40 to 1 op 33 to 1 tchd 50 to 1) 2
3176⁵ IZZA 8-5 Pat Eddery (5) *hld up beh ldrs, cld o'r 3 fs out, rdn alng 2 out, one pace appr last.* .... (5 to 4 fav op 11 to 10 tchd 11 to 8) 3
2592² ORANGE PLACE (Ire) 9-0 M Hills (7) *trkd ldrs till lost pl wl o'r 2 fs out, styd on ins fnl furlong.* ....(10 to 1 op 8 to 1 tchd 12 to 1 and 14 to 1) 4
3423² PETER ROWLEY 8-12 J Reid (1) *trkd ldrs till wknd wl o'r one furlong out.* ....(5 to 1 op 9 to 2 tchd 11 to 2 and 6 to 1) 5
1857⁹ SWEET CAROLINE 8-5 J Quinn (2) *al beh.* ....(50 to 1 op 33 to 1 tchd 100 to 1) 6
2911* KATHANNA 8-5 D Holland (6) *led til hdd o'r 4 fs out, wknd over 3 out*..........(20 to 1 op 14 to 1) 7

Dist: 4l, 1½l, 4l, 2½l, ½l, 5l. 1m 31.86s. a 3.56s (7 Ran).
SR: 14/2/-/-/ (Hamdan Al-Maktoum), J L Dunlop

3571 Whitbread Conditions Stakes Class C (3-y-o and up) £4,308 5f.........(3:50)

2927⁸ ARTISTIC REEF 4-9-0 W Carson (9) *hng lft thrght, al prmnt, shaken up and ran on to ld fnl strds.* .... (11 to 4 op 9 to 4 tchd 3 to 1) 1
2399² PALACEGATE EPISODE (Ire) 3-9-4 Pat Eddery (3) *led til hdd fnl strds*...........(15 to 8 fav op 9 to 4 tchd 7 to 4) 2
2252⁵ BOLD LEZ 6-9-9 R Cochrane (6) *chsd ldrs, rdn and hdwy wl o'r one furlong out, ran on*....... (5 to 1 op 6 to 1) 3
3427³ NIGHT MELODY (Ire) 3-9-1 M Hills (7) *sn drvn alng, kpt on wl fnl furlong*..........(7 to 1 op 5 to 1) 4
3348⁹ FOOD OF LOVE 5-8-9 J Williams (5) *prmnt till lost pl 2 fs out, ran on ins last*..........(14 to 1 op 10 to 1) 5
3266⁴ BELLSABANGING (v) 3-8-11 S Whitworth (2) *in tch, hrd rdn o'r one furlong out, ran on*....(25 to 1 op 16 to 1) 6
3438⁸ ELLE SHAPED (Ire) 3-9-0 (5*) Stephen Davies (1) *chsd ldrs, pushed alng o'r 2 fs out, hrd rdn over one out, wknd ins last*..........(12 to 1 op 8 to 1 tchd 14 to 1) 7
3348 LOVE RETURNED 6-9-1 M Tebbutt (4) *hld up, effrt 2 fs out, not pace to chal*..........(14 to 1 op 10 to 1) 8
3420 SHADES OF JADE 5-8-9 G Bardwell (8) *speed to hfwy.* ....(100 to 1 op 50 to 1) 9

Dist: Nk, 1½l, 1l, nk, hd, 2l, ½l, 8l. 57.48s. a 0.58s (9 Ran).
SR: 63/66/65/53/46/47/47/41/3/ (R A Mohammed), G H Eden

3572 Boddingtons Bitter Handicap Class D (0-80 3-y-o and up) £3,494 1m 3f 106yds...................... (4:20)

2972* SUMMER PAGEANT [74] 3-9-7 W Ryan (3) *led til hdd 2 fs out, led ag'n ins last, rdn out*......(11 to 4 op 2 to 1) 1
4714a⁶ SURE HAVEN (Ire) [72] 4-10-0 C Nutter (4) *trkd ldr, sn pushed alng, led appr 2 fs out till hdd and no extr ins last*..........(25 to 1 op 14 to 1) 2
3263* BOBBYSOXER [75] 3-9-8 Pat Eddery (7) *beh, hdwy 4 fs out, cld appr fnl furlong, swshd tail and one pace ins last*..........(11 to 10 fav tchd 5 to 4) 3
2921² HAROLDON (Ire) [62] 4-9-4 D Holland (2) *dwlt, sn chasing ldrs, chsd ldg pair into strt, rdn and one pace frm 2 out.* .... (16 to 1 op 14 to 1 tchd 20 to 1) 4
3479 FAIRGROUNDPRINCESS [37] 5-7-7 N Adams (1) *trkd ldrs, outpcd hfwy, styd on fnl 2 fs*.....(100 to 1 op 50 to 1) 5
1951 BARBARY REEF (Ire) [37] 5-7-7 G Bardwell (9) *beh till styd on fnl 2 fs, nvr nr to chal*..........(50 to 1 op 33 to 1) 6
SPRING TO GLORY [37] 6-7-3³ (7*) A Whelan (6) *nvr on terms*..........(100 to 1 op 50 to 1) 7
3271⁷ HOLIDAY ISLAND [63] 4-9-5 T Quinn (5) *trkd ldrs to hfwy.* ....(13 to 2 op 7 to 1 tchd 10 to 1) 8
1345 DOM WAC [63] 5-9-5 J Reid (10) *hld up, al beh.* ....(9 to 1 op 8 to 1 tchd 10 to 1) 9
3384³ MISS MICHELLE [48] 3-7-9² A Tucker (8) *al beh, tld off.* ....(16 to 1 op 20 to 1) 10

Dist: 1l, 1l, ½l, 2½l, 1½l, ½l, 8l, 2½l, 15l. 2m 24.98s. a 0.78s (10 Ran).
SR: 47/52/44/39/9/6/5/15/10/ (Cheveley Park Stud), J R Fanshawe

3573 Britvic Soft Drinks Claiming Stakes Class F (Div II) (2-y-o) £2,623 6f (4:50)

3265⁷ FERRYMAN (USA) 8-13 Pat Eddery (7) *al prmnt, led 2 fs out, drvn out*........(100 to 30 op 7 to 2 tchd 4 to 1) 1
3281⁷ UP THE MARINERS (Ire) 8-0 (5*) K Rutter (1) *al prmnt, led briefly appr 2 fs out, ev ch ins last, no extr nr finish.* ....(7 to 1 op 6 to 1 tchd 8 to 1) 2
3267⁶ TOTON LAD 8-11 W Newnes (3) *took keen hold, trkd ldrs, rdn o'r one furlong out, swshd tail and no extr ins last.* ....(12 to 1 op 10 to 1 tchd 14 to 1 and 16 to 1) 3
2419⁶ INZAR 9-2 J Reid (4) *in tch, sn pushed alng and outpcd hfwy, ran on fnl furlong.* ....(2 to 1 fav op 5 to 4 tchd 9 to 4) 4
3103⁶ MACE EL REEM 8-4 W Ryan (2) *took keen hold, trkd ldrs, rdn 2 fs out, wknd ins last*......(14 to 1 tchd 16 to 1) 5
2819⁷ LEGAL CONQUEST 7-13 J Quinn (8) *led til hdd 2 fs out, sn wknd*..........(33 to 1 op 16 to 1) 6
3390⁶ SPORTING STORY (Ire) 8-4 N Adams (5) *reared strt and beh, swtchd lft and hdwy o'r 3 fs out, wknd 2 out.* .... (10 to 1 op 8 to 1) 7
REMINISCENCE (Ire) 8-9 (7*) Mark Denaro (9) *in tch till ran green and outpcd frm hfwy*..........(9 to 1 op 6 to 1) 8
RISK OF FIRE 9-7 Paul Eddery (6) *outpcd.* ....(9 to 1 op 8 to 1 tchd 11 to 1) 9

Dist: 1½l, 1l, nk, 2l, 3l, 1l, hd, nk. 1m 13.47s. a 4.47s (9 Ran).
(K Abdulla), G Harwood

LINGFIELD (A.W) (std)
Thursday August 26th
Going Correction: MINUS 0.20 sec. per fur.

3574 Bulmers Cider Handicap Class E (0-70 3-y-o) £2,821 2m............... (3:20)

3509⁷ SIR THOMAS BEECHAM [60] (e/s) 8-12 T Quinn (1) *wtd wth, cld o'r 7 fs out, led over 2 out, clr over one out, eased close hme*..........(100 to 30 op 9 to 4) 1
3344* USK THE WAY [69] 9-7 W Ryan (6) *trkd ldr, led o'r 6 fs out, hrd rdn 3 out, hdd over 2 out, one pace.* ....(6 to 4 fav op 7 to 4 tchd 9 to 4) 2
3193⁴ CRIMINAL RECORD (USA) [59] (v) 8-11 J Reid (7) *al prmnt, ev ch o'r 2 fs out, one pace.* ....(8 to 1 op 6 to 1 tchd 9 to 1) 3
3346³ JULIASDARKINVADER [50] 8-0⁵ (7*) L Carter (4) *hld up, took keen hold, rdn and cld o'r 4 fs out, sn outpcd.* ....(12 to 1) 4
3232³ BILJAN (USA) [57] 8-9 A Munro (3) *beh, rcd wide, effrt o'r 5 fs out, no response*.....(10 to 1 op 9 to 2 tchd 13 to 2) 5
3361² EARLY TO RISE [51] 7-10 (7*) J D Smith (2) *prmnt til wknd quickly o'r 6 fs out, tld off.* .... (10 to 1 op 8 to 1 tchd 12 to 1) 6
3053⁸ MOUJEEB (USA) [42] (v) 7-8 J Quinn (5) *led til hdd o'r 6 fs out, sn wknd, tld off.* (16 to 1 op 14 to 1 tchd 20 to 1) 7

Dist: 4l, sht-hd, 6l, sht-hd, 12l, 30l. 3m 25.14s. a 3.14s (7 Ran).
SR: 35/40/29/14/20/2/-/ (Mrs Heather Chakko), S Dow

3575 Taunton Cider Handicap Class D (0-80 3-y-o and up) £3,406 7f......... (5:20)

3364² HADEER'S DANCE [70] 3-8-13 R Price (3) *al prmnt, led o'r 2 fs out, rdn and ran on wl*.......... (7 to 1 op 5 to 1) 1
3020⁶ PERSIAN GUSHER (Ire) [67] (e/s) 3-8-10 T Quinn (8) *in tch, hdwy o'r 2 fs out, chsd wnr frm over one out, ran on.* ....(8 to 1 op 7 to 1 tchd 10 to 1 and 11 to 1) 2
1309⁸ SLEEPTITE (Fr) [53] 3-7-10 J Quinn (6) *slwly into strd, sn tld off in rear, hdwy o'r 2 fs out, styd on ins last.* ....(20 to 1) 3
3305⁶ STARDUST EXPRESS [68] 3-8-11 J Reid (2) *led til hdd o'r 2 fs out, one pace*.......... (13 to 2 op 6 to 1) 4
3325² BRAVE HERO (USA) [50] 3-7-7 G Bardwell (7) *outpcd, hdwy o'r 2 fs out, nvr nrr*..........(12 to 1 tchd 14 to 1) 5
3302⁹ INVOCATION [78] 6-9-12 N Adams (10) *in tch, rdn and no hdwy fnl 2 fs*..........(9 to 1 op 7 to 1 tchd 10 to 1) 6
3471³ MARINE DIVER [70] 7-9-4 S Whitworth (4) *in tch, lost pl o'r 4 fs out, sn pushed alng, no hdwy.* .... (7 to 1 op 6 to 1 tchd 15 to 2) 7
3445⁷ SURE LORD (Ire) [68] (bl) 4-9-2 A Munro (1) *cl up, rdn alng o'r 2 fs out, sn btn*...(12 to 1 op 10 to 1 tchd 14 to 1) 8
3100⁵ TRUTHFUL IMAGE [71] (bl) 4-9-5 D Biggs (9) *in tch til wknd o'r 2 fs out*..........(9 to 2 fav op 7 to 2 tchd 5 to 1) 9

3340[2] DAILY SPORT DON [63] 3-8-6 A McGlone (5) *trkd ldrs till wknd 3 fs out*......... (11 to 2 op 4 to 1 tchd 6 to 1) 10
Dist: 1½l, 2½l, 1l, nk, sht-hd, 2½l, 1½l, nk, 2l. 1m 25.31s. a 1.91s (10 Ran).
SR: 49/41/19/31/12/44/28/21/23/ (Khalifa Dasmal), R W Armstrong

TRALEE (IRE) (good)
Thursday August 26th

3576 BRC Australian Jockey Club Handicap (0-75 3-y-o) £3,450 1m.......... (3:00)

3381* PENNY A DAY (Ire) [-] 8-11 (5ex) C Roche (2)..(10 to 3 fav) 1
3544[4] TORCH SINGER [-] 7-12 (2*) R M Burke (11)....... (7 to 1) 2
3498[4] MUSWELL BROOK (Ire) [-] (bl) 8-12 K J Manning (7) (12 to 1) 3
3544[3] KENTUCKY BABY (Ire) [-] 8-7 J P Murtagh (1).......(7 to 2) 4
639 SHOWBOAT MELODY (Ire) [-] 7-12 (8*) B Fenton (3) (14 to 1) 5
3419[3] SAMOT (Ire) [-] 9-3 J F Egan (6)................... (8 to 1) 6
3419[2] SLIGHTLY SCRUFFY (Ire) [-] 9-5 P V Gilson (10).... (5 to 1) 7
3278[3] ICEFLOW (Fr) [-] 8-4 (6*) R V Skelly (12)..........(10 to 1) 8
3484[6] DARK SWAN (Ire) [-] (bl) 8-6 (2*) D G O'Shea (5)... (14 to 1) 9
1123[8] LAUNCH INTO SONG (Ire) [-] 8-10 S Craine (9).....(14 to 1) 10
3399[4] LUCKY PRINCE (Ire) [-] (bl) 8-10 M J Kinane (8).... (7 to 1) 11
Dist: 1l, ¾l, hd, 4l. 1m 41.50s. (11 Ran).
(Savio To), P Burke

3577 Denny Havasnack QR Race (4-y-o and up) £6,900 2m 1f............... (4:00)

3165[2] MUBADIR (USA) 5-11-7 Mr S R Murphy (2)...(5 to 2 jt-fav) 1
2881* CLIVEDEN GAIL (Ire) 4-10-13 (5*) Mr J A Nash (1) (5 to 2 jt-fav) 2
2515* BIG MATT (Ire) 5-11-0 (7*) Mr J Connolly (3)........(8 to 1) 3
2035 NORDIC SUN (Ire) 5-11-0 Mr P Fenton (9)........ (10 to 1) 4
1024[2] EYELID 7-10-7 (7*) Mr D J Kavanagh (6)............(3 to 1) 5
2841[3] EBONY AND IVORY (Ire) 4-10-11 (7*) Mr A K Wyse (5) ....(6 to 1) 6
3452[5] BALLYTIGUE LORD 7-10-12 (7*) Mr G P FitzGerald (4) ....(33 to 1) 7
WOLF WINTER 8-11-0 (7*) Mr P A Roche (10).....(14 to 1) 8
3524[5] WILD FANTASY (Ire) 5-10-9 (7*) Mr G F Ryan (7)...(33 to 1) 9
3077[8] LEAP INTO SPRING (Ire) 4-11-7 Mr A P O'Brien (8) (14 to 1) 10
Dist: 3l, 1l, 2l, 2l. 3m 46.90s. (10 Ran).
(Liam Keating), Noel Meade

3578 Dunnes Stores Rose Of Tralee Ladies Race (3-y-o and up) £3,450 1½m (4:30)

3197[4] SHARKASHKA (Ire) 3-9-9 (3ex) Miss L Robinson (2) ....(9 to 4 fav) 1
3197[2] SHAWGATNY (USA) 3-10-0 (8ex) Miss C Hutchinson (9) ....(5 to 2) 2
3367[5] WOODFIELD ROSE 4-9-6 (2*) Miss S J Leahy (3)..(20 to 1) 3
3449[2] PAT OR ELSE 3-9-9 (8ex) Mrs M Cowdrey (7)....... (4 to 1) 4
3326[5] PRINTOUT (Ire) 3-9-1 Miss A Gilsenan (12)....... (12 to 1) 5
NORA ANN (Ire) 4-9-6 (2*) Miss H Finlay (10).......(12 to 1) 6
2902[3] KEPPOLS HARRIER (Ire) 3-9-4 Miss O Glennon (4) (10 to 1) 7
3326* SIMPLY MARILYN (Ire) 4-11-0 (8ex) Mrs J M Mullins (11) ....(7 to 1) 8
3245[8] CAT FIGHT 6-9-6 (2*) Miss G Morgan (8).......... (66 to 1) 9
1987 TANAISTE (USA) (bl) 4-9-10[1] (2*) Miss R Hickey (5) (66 to 1) 10
3197[4] VELMA (USA) 3-9-13 (3ex) Miss U Smyth (1).......(7 to 1) 11
TAN PRINCESS 6-9-6 (2*) Miss F Loughran (6).... (50 to 1) 12
Dist: Nk, ½l, sht-hd, 6l. 2m 36.20s. (12 Ran).
(Lady Clague), John M Oxx

3579 Spectra Photo Labs Maiden (3-y-o and up) £3,450 1m..................(5:00)

3297[4] BELLISSI (Ire) 3-8-1 (8*) P J Smullen (6)..........(10 to 1) 1
CERTAIN PROSPECT 3-8-9 J P Murtagh (3)....... (9 to 2) 2
1106 MAYASTA (Ire) 3-8-9 P V Gilson (4)............ (7 to 4 on) 3
1078 LOS ANGELES (Ire) 4-9-1 C Roche (1)........... (12 to 1) 4
3297[5] MY KERRY DANCER (USA) 3-8-12 S Craine (5).... (6 to 1) 5
3297[3] KUDDAM (Ire) 3-8-9 M J Kinane (2)................(7 to 1) 6
3417[8] NORDIC ABU (Ire) 3-8-1 (8*) B A Hunter (7)....... (12 to 1) 7
3380[8] ANVIL SPARK (Ire) 3-8-9 J F Egan (9)............ (20 to 1) 8
3382[7] CAPTAIN TANDY (Ire) 4-9-2 (2*) P Carberry (8).... (16 to 1) 9
SCALPEL (Ire) 3-8-9 K M O'Callaghan (11).........(33 to 1) 10
NATIVE WOODFIRE (Ire) 4-9-1 K J Manning (10).. (16 to 1) 11
Dist: ½l, ½l, 3½l, 2½l. 1m 41.80s. (11 Ran).
(T F Lacy), T F Lacy

3580 Joe Donnelly Handicap (0-70 3-y-o and up) £3,450 2m..................(5:30)

3063 SYLVIA FOX [-] 6-9-10 M J Kinane (16)........ (2 to 1 fav) 1
3483* SENSITIVE KING (Ire) [-] 5-8-1 (2*,4ex) R M Burke (17) ....(9 to 1) 2
2842[3] SENSE OF VALUE [-] 4-9-10 J P Murtagh (3)......(12 to 1) 3
3560* COMMAND 'N CONTROL [-] 4-8-13 (6*) J R Barry (2) (8 to 1) 4
3494 MAGNUM STAR (Ire) [-] 4-9-8 C F Swan (8)....... (33 to 1) 5
3381[4] ANIMATE (Ire) [-] 3-7-12 (8*) J J Stack (14)........(16 to 1) 6
2664[3] ONOMATOPOEIA (Ire) [-] 3-8-10 P V Gilson (11)....(16 to 1) 7
2692[2] RASSETTE (Ire) [-] 3-7-13 (6*) J A Heffernan (19).. (12 to 1) 8
2881[2] ASSERT STAR [-] 3-8-12 (4*) J J Behan (13)........(4 to 1) 9
3482[5] NORDIC UNION (Ire) [-] 3-8-10 C Roche (7).......(16 to 1) 10
2557* LET IT RIDE (Ire) [-] 4-9-4 (6*) C Everard (12)...... (10 to 1) 11
2094[4] SOPHISM (USA) [-] 4-9-1 P Shanahan (9).........(20 to 1) 12
3483[4] MARIAN YEAR [-] 7-7-8 (2*) D G O'Shea (5).......(20 to 1) 13
2143 ACTION DANCER [-] 7-7-11 (6*) R V Skelly (1).... (33 to 1) 14
3277[5] RIYADH DANCER (Ire) [-] 3-7-13[1] J F Egan (20).... (12 to 1) 15
CANDID LAD [-] 6-9-8 (6*) T P Treacy (15)........ (12 to 1) 16
3397* CORAL SOUND (Ire) [-] 3-8-8 (2*,4ex) P Carberry (6) ....(12 to 1) 17
3197[3] BONNIFER (Ire) [-] 4-10-0 R Hughes (4)..........(20 to 1) 18
3077 SIR ALFRED (USA) [-] 8-7-7[8] (8*) R T Fitzpatrick (18) ....(50 to 1) pu
Dist: 1l, ½l, hd, 3l. 3m 33.09s. (19 Ran).
(Mrs C L Weld), D K Weld

BADEN-BADEN (GER) (good)
Friday August 27th

3581 Kronimus-Rennen (Listed) (2-y-o) £10,205 7f.................... (2:45)

GERMANY (USA) 8-12 M Rimmer,.................. 1
CATTANO (Ger) 8-9 A Helfenbein,................. 2
3475[7] ROMAN REEL (USA) 8-7 B Rouse,..................... 3
PROGRESSOR 9-0 A Riding,........................ 4
Dist: 8l, sht-hd, 3l, 5l, 5l. 1m 23.63s. (6 Ran).
(Jaber Abdullah), B Schutz

3582 Spreti-Rennen (Group 3) (4-y-o and up) £30,612 1¼m...............(3:25)

2253[4] KARINGA BAY 6-8-12 B Rouse, *mid-div, 4th hfwy, second four fs out, led 2 and a half out, hld on wl.* (5 to 4 on) 1
3370[5] SUGUNAS (Ger) 5-8-12 A Boschert, *al tracking wnr, str chal fnl furlong*.......................... (47 to 10) 2
1882[2] LE JARDIN (Ger) 5-8-9 M Rimmer, *al prmnt, one pace fnl furlong*.............................. (67 to 10) 3
2644* IRON FIGHTER (Ger) 4-8-12 R Hillis, *wtd wth, ran on wl fnl furlong*............................... (64 to 10) 4
3022[5] APIS (Ger) 4-8-9 O Schick, *led for 7 and a half fs.* (13 to 1) 5
FABRIANO 4-8-9 T Hellier, *mid-div, rdn and unbl to quicken 3 fs out*........................... (20 to 1) 6
3206[2] CHESA PLANA 4-8-5 A Best, *nvr a factor*...... (76 to 10) 7
AKTIONAR (Fr) 6-8-9 E Schindler, *prmnt early, sn btn.* ....(37 to 1) 8
Dist: ½l, 2l, 1 ¼l, 2l, ½l, 1 ¼l. 2m 4.45s. (8 Ran).
(K Higson), G L Moore

CLAIREFONTAINE (FR) (good)
Friday August 27th

3583 Grand Prix de Clairefontaine (Listed) (3-y-o and up) £19,116 1m 3f.... (2:35)

BEDAVA (Fr) 3-8-6 N Jeanpierre,.................. 1
2644 EXTRA POINT 3-8-9 W Mongil,.................... 2
DAJRAAN (Ire) 4-9-0 T Jarnet,..................... 3
LITTLE WASSL (Fr) 4-9-4 O Doleuze,............... 4
Dist: 1l, 2l, ½l, ½l, 1l, nose, 3l. 2m 22.60s. (8 Ran).
(Mme R Reeves), F Doumen

GOODWOOD (good)
Friday August 27th
Going Correction: MINUS 0.30 sec. per fur.

3584 Furniture Village Apprentice Handicap Class E (0-70 3-y-o and up) £3,947 5f.......................... (2:10)

3383[4] CHOIR PRACTICE [56] 6-8-12 (5*) Sally Radford-Howes (4) *slwly into strd, outpcd till hdwy wl o'r one furlong out, drifted rght, led ins last.* (8 to 1 op 6 to 1 tchd 9 to 1) 1
3229[3] ABERLADY [59] 3-9-3 K Rutter (7) *hld up in tch, hdwy to ld wl o'r one furlong out, rdn and hdd ins last.* ....(5 to 1 fav op 4 to 1) 2
3383[3] BATCHWORTH BOUND [53] 4-8-7 (7*) A Daly (9) *hld up, hdwy 2 fs out, ev ch entering last, no extr fnl 100 yards.* ....(11 to 2 op 9 to 2) 3
3220 GO FLIGHTLINE (Ire) [55] 3-8-10 (3*) D McCabe (8) *outpcd early, styd on ins fnl 2 fs, nvr nrr*...(10 to 1 op 8 to 1) 4
2728[5] TEE-EMM [52] 3-8-5 (5*) Debbie Biggs (14) *nvr far away, led hfwy till wl o'r one furlong out, one pace aftr.* ....(25 to 1 op 16 to 1) 5
3340[9] DISTANT DYNASTY [35] 3-7-2 (5*) Wendy Jones (11) *beh, hdwy frm hfwy, nvr nr to chal.* ....(50 to 1 op 33 to 1 tchd 66 to 1) 6
3383[8] TREASURE TIME (Ire) [63] 4-9-7 (3*) G Forster (5) *prmnt, wkng whn short of room o'r one furlong out.* ....(9 to 1 op 8 to 1) 7
3459[2] BELMONT PRINCESS (Ire) [51] 3-8-4 (5*) D Gibbs (3) *led aftr one furlong till o'r 3 out, wknd over one out.* ....(9 to 1 op 8 to 1 tchd 10 to 1) 8

3011^9 PAT POINDESTRES [45] 3-8-3 N Gwilliams (13) *prmnt, led o'r 3 fs out to hfwy, sn btn.* .... (12 to 1 op 14 to 1 tchd 20 to 1) 9
3481 COCONUT JOHNNY [55] 3-8-8 (5*) R Painter (15) *mid-div on outsd, wknd o'r one furlong out.* .... (16 to 1 op 12 to 1) 10
2305^7 SERIOUS HURRY [55] 5-9-2 A Procter (2) *led one furlong, wknd hfwy*...................... (16 to 1 op 14 to 1) 11
3270^9 CASTLE MAID [39] 6-8-0^6 (3*) S Drowne (12) *al struggling.* .... (12 to 1 op 10 to 1) 12
3360^4 DAL MISS [32] (bl) 6-7-7 D Wright (1) *speed stands side to hfwy*............... (20 to 1 op 14 to 1 tchd 25 to 1) 13
249 BANBURY FLYER [52] 5-8-13 A Garth (10) *al rear.* .... (16 to 1 op 20 to 1) 14
3251^7 SKI CAPTAIN [43] 9-7-13 (5*) L Carter (6) *outpcd.* .... (16 to 1 op 14 to 1) 15
Dist: 1½l, 1l, 3½l, sht-hd, nk, hd, nk, hd, 1½l, 1l. 58.36s. a 1.56s (15 Ran).
SR: 42/36/29/14/10/-/22/6/-/ (Stephen Chapman), W J Haggas

3585 Schroder Investment Management Handicap Class C (0-90 3-y-o) £9,942 1m.......................... (2:40)

3158^4 FOURFORFUN [85] 9-4 B Raymond (11) *al tracking ldrs, strly rdn entering fnl furlong, ran on to ld ins last.* .... (15 to 2 op 6 to 1 tchd 8 to 1) 1
3261^3 AWESTRIKE (USA) [77] 8-10 Paul Eddery (14) *nvr far away, rdn o'r 2 fs out, ran on strly to go second wl ins last.* ....(4 to 1 fav tchd 9 to 2 and 7 to 2) 2
3219* NAIF (USA) [85] 9-4 R Cochrane (5) *led early, styd prmnt, led o'r 2 fs out, rdn and hdd ins last.* .... (9 to 1 op 7 to 1 tchd 10 to 1) 3
3290^2 CARELAMAN [88] 9-7 M Hills (10) *mid-div, styd on ins fnl 2 fs, nvr nrr*....................... (14 to 1 op 12 to 1) 4
3080^3 BELFRY GREEN (Ire) [73] 8-6^2 C Asmussen (6) *hld up, ran on ins fnl 2 fs, nvr nrr*... (7 to 1 op 6 to 1 tchd 8 to 1) 5
3350 WISHAM (USA) [81] 9-0 A McGlone (12) *mid-div, hdwy 2 fs out, one pace fnl furlong*.......... (20 to 1 op 16 to 1) 6
3290* POLAR STORM (Ire) [79] 8-12 J Williams (4) *wl beh till styd on ins fnl 2 fs, nvr nrr*............. (8 to 1 tchd 9 to 1) 7
989^4 CLOUDED ELEGANCE [85] 9-4 L Dettori (13) *beh, effrt 3 fs out, no imprsn frm 2 out*..........(10 to 1 op 12 to 1) 8
3476 NORFOLK HERO [83] 9-2 C Rutter (9) *pld hrd, chsd ldrs till rdn and wknd appr fnl furlong.* .... (20 to 1 op 14 to 1 tchd 25 to 1) 9
3272^9 SEASONAL SPLENDOUR (Ire) [76] (bl) 8-9 W Newnes (8) *beh, rdn 2 fs out, no imprsn*...... (20 to 1 op 14 to 1) 10
3146* SHARAAR (USA) [80] 8-13 J Reid (15) *sn led, hdd o'r 2 fs out, wknd*.......... (16 to 1 op 12 to 1 tchd 20 to 1) 11
3181^2 DUTOSKY [74] 8-7 A Munro (1) *beh, effrt o'r 2 fs out, sn btn*................ (14 to 1 op 12 to 1 tchd 16 to 1) 12
3269^8 WAHEM (Ire) [65] 7-7 (5*) D Wright (3) *al beh.* ....(12 to 1 tchd 14 to 1) 13
3012 PISTOL (Ire) [72] 8-5 D Holland (2) *al beh.* .... (33 to 1 op 20 to 1) 14
3226* KNOBBLEENEEZE [67] (v) 8-0 J Quinn (7) *mid-div till wknd quickly o'r 2 fs out*... (14 to 1 op 12 to 1 tchd 16 to 1) 15
Dist: ¾l, 1l, 1½l, sht-hd, 2l, sht-hd, ½l, 1l, 1l, ½l. 1m 38.41s. a 1.21s (15 Ran).
SR: 50/40/45/43/27/29/26/30/25/ (Mrs R F Knipe), R Hannon

3586 Butlin's Southcoast World Prestige Stakes Class A (Group 3) (2-y-o) £17,300 7f.................... (3:10)

2754* GLATISANT 8-9 M Hills (4) *hld up, hdwy o'r 2 fs out, shaken up entering last, ran green and edgd rght, led nr finish*................... (2 to 1 on tchd 6 to 4 on) 1
3265* WILD PLANET (USA) 8-9 C Asmussen (3) *led, rdn appr fnl furlong, faltered and hdd nr finish.* (4 to 1 op 3 to 1) 2
3176^6 SPOT PRIZE (USA) 8-9 R Cochrane (5) *hld up rear, hdwy 2 fs out, ran on wl fnl furlong, nvr nrr.* .... (33 to 1 op 16 to 1) 3
3347^4 MILD REBUKE 8-9 L Dettori (6) *chsd ldrs, rdn 2 fs out, kpt on one pace*.................... (10 to 1 tchd 12 to 1) 4
3176^3 SONG OF YEARS (Ire) 8-9 B Raymond (2) *trkd ldr to 2 fs out, wknd quickly appr last.* .... (20 to 1 op 12 to 1 tchd 25 to 1) 5
3176^7 GREAT TRIVIALITY 8-9 Paul Eddery (1) *in tch 4 fs.* .... (25 to 1 op 20 to 1 tchd 33 to 1) 6
Dist: Hd, 1½l, 1l, 5l, 12l. 1m 26.14s. a 1.54s (6 Ran).
SR: 40/39/34/31/16/-/ (Sir Philip Oppenheimer), G Wragg

3587 Furniture Village Trophy Handicap Class C (0-95 3-y-o and up) £7,895 1½m.......................... (3:40)

3353* GENERAL MOUKTAR [72] 3-8-7 C Asmussen (10) *hld up in tch, al gng wl, cruised into ld appr fnl furlong, cmftbly.* ....(5 to 1 co-fav tchd 11 to 2) 1
2961^3 AL SENAFI (Ire) [87] 3-9-8 R Cochrane (6) *hld up rear, rdn and hdwy o'r 2 fs out, ran on to go second cl hme.* ....(5 to 1 co-fav tchd 6 to 1) 2
2152* PRINCE HANNIBAL [83] 6-10-0 J Reid (7) *mid-div, hdwy to dispute ld 2 fs out, outpcd fnl furlong.* ....(10 to 1 tchd 14 to 1) 3
2632^3 ALMAMZAR (USA) [86] 3-9-7 B Raymond (11) *led till appr fnl furlong, kpt on one pace*.......(14 to 1 op 10 to 1) 4
2991* DAY OF HISTORY (Ire) [60] 4-8-5^2 W Newnes (4) *rear till styd on ins fnl 2 fs*... (16 to 1 op 12 to 1 tchd 20 to 1) 5
3152^5 CROMARTY [76] 3-8-11 A McGlone (2) *al abt same pl, one pace fnl 2 fs*......................(12 to 1 op 10 to 1) 6
3263^3 EL VOLADOR [64] 6-8-9 J Quinn (9) *rear, hdwy o'r 3 fs out, wknd 2 out*............................(7 to 1 tchd 8 to 1) 7
3356* HARD TASK [79] 3-9-0 Paul Eddery (3) *chsd ldrs till wknd o'r 2 fs out*................(5 to 1 co-fav tchd 6 to 1) 8
2991^2 MARROS MILL [77] (v) 3-8-12 M Hills (5) *frnt rnk till wknd quickly 2 fs out*...................... (16 to 1 op 14 to 1) 9
2758^5 KIMBERLEY BOY [74] 3-8-9 D Holland (8) *al beh.* .... (11 to 2 op 5 to 1 tchd 6 to 1) 10
3179^6 ROBENKO (USA) [66] 4-8-11 L Dettori (1) *al beh.* .... (16 to 1 op 12 to 1) 11
Dist: 2l, nk, 2l, 2½l, nk, 6l, ¾l, 1l, 10l, 12l. 2m 35.36s. a 2.36s (11 Ran).
SR: 33/44/49/38/17/22/8/11/7/ (A S Helaissi), M C Pipe

3588 Horse Racing Abroad Claiming Handicap Class F (0-70 3-y-o) £3,366 1¼m ....(4:10)

3078 BROUGHTONS FORMULA [52] 7-12 (5*) D McCabe (7) *hld up mid-div, rdn and hdwy on ins 3 fs out, short of room till entering last, ran on strly, sn led, cmftbly.* ....(14 to 1 op 10 to 1) 1
3346^2 TROPICAL JUNGLE (USA) [59] 8-3 (7*) J D Smith (6) *led, rdn o'r one furlong out, hdd ins last, outpcd*...... (10 to 1) 2
3512 ABERDEEN HEATHER [70] 9-7 C Asmussen (1) *sn tracking ldr, ev ch 2 fs out, rdn and kpt on one pace.* .... (12 to 1 op 6 to 1) 3
3007^4 DARING KING [48] 7-13 A McGlone (11) *mid-div, effrt o'r 2 fs out, kpt on ins last.* ....(12 to 1 op 10 to 1 tchd 14 to 1) 4
2834* LEGAL ARTIST (Ire) [55] 8-6 B Raymond (5) *pld hrd, prmnt, rdn o'r 2 fs out, one pace aftr.* ....(6 to 1 op 5 to 1 tchd 13 to 2) 5
3384^2 MALZETA (Ire) [45] 7-5 (5*) D Wright (8) *beh, hdwy o'r 2 fs out, kpt on one pace*.... (8 to 1 op 6 to 1 tchd 9 to 1) 6
3374* SLOE BRANDY [42] 7-7 (4ex) J Quinn (9) *trkd ldrs till rdn and wknd wl o'r one furlong out.* .... (11 to 4 fav op 3 to 1 tchd 100 to 30) 7
3551^3 MEDLAND (Ire) [49] 8-0^2 A Munro (3) *reared strt, nvr on terms*................ (11 to 1 op 8 to 1 tchd 12 to 1) 8
3053^6 MORSTOCK [61] 8-5 (7*) S Drowne (4) *hld up rear, nvr on terms*............... (14 to 1 op 12 to 1 tchd 16 to 1) 9
2907 COMPLETE MADNESS [70] 9-7 D Holland (10) *prmnt till wknd o'r 2 fs out, eased*............. (8 to 1 op 6 to 1) 10
3226^3 LOCHORE [59] 8-10 A Tucker (2) *slwly away, nvr got into race*................. (10 to 1 op 8 to 1 tchd 11 to 1) 11
Dist: 2l, 2½l, hd, ½l, ¾l, nk, 3l, 1½l, 1½l, 7l. 2m 9.69s. a 4.19s (11 Ran).
SR: 17/20/26/3/9/-/-/-/3/ (Broughton Thermal Insulation), W J Musson

3589 Southernprint Median Auction Maiden Stakes Class E (2-y-o) £3,392 6f (4:45)

3421^2 ARNDILLY 8-9 C Asmussen (12) *trkd ldrs, hdwy 2 fs out, hng lft appr last, strly rdn to ld on line.* ....(5 to 2 fav tchd 3 to 1 and 9 to 4) 1
3421^5 STORM SHIP (Ire) 9-0 B Raymond (13) *made most, rdn ins fnl furlong, hdd on line.* ....(12 to 1 op 6 to 1 tchd 14 to 1) 2
3082^8 MERLIN'S FIELD (Ire) 9-0 L Dettori (7) *al prmnt stands side, ev ch appr fnl furlong, kpt on.* .... (10 to 1 op 8 to 1 tchd 12 to 1) 3
CO PILOT (Ire) 8-9 A Munro (15) *mid-div, hdwy hfwy, ran on ins fnl furlong*.... (25 to 1 op 20 to 1 tchd 33 to 1) 4
KEFAHI (Ire) 9-0 J Quinn (10) *hld up, hdwy 2 fs out, ran on wl ins last*.......... (20 to 1 op 14 to 1 tchd 25 to 1) 5
2626^5 BILLIE GREY 8-9 G Hind (18) *prmnt far side, ev ch entering fnl furlong, kpt on one pace*... (25 to 1 op 20 to 1) 6
2137^7 SOUTHERN RIDGE 9-0 J Williams (2) *prmnt on stands side till outpcd 2 fs out, ran on ins last.* .... (12 to 1 op 8 to 1 tchd 14 to 1) 7
3143^7 CURIE CRUSADER (Ire) 9-0 B Crossley (8) *dsptd ld, hrd rdn 2 fs out, wkng whn hmpd appr last.* ....(25 to 1 tchd 50 to 1) 8
2429^5 JUDGE DREAD 9-0 R Cochrane (4) *wtd wth, hdwy 2 fs out, wknd entering last.* (7 to 2 op 4 to 1 tchd 9 to 2) 9
2659 ROCKSTINE (Ire) 8-9 S O'Gorman (1) *al mid-div.* .... (50 to 1 op 33 to 1) 10
3130 BALLYMORRIS (Ire) 9-0 Paul Eddery (16) *mid-div, rdn 2 fs out, sn btn*.................................. (33 to 1) 11
MAZIRAH 9-0 T Sprake (5) *slwly away, nvr on terms.* .... (50 to 1 op 20 to 1) 12
3287^4 PLATINI (Ire) 9-0 J Reid (6) *al rear*..... (8 to 1 op 6 to 1) 13
GREATEST HOPES 9-0 C Rutter (3) *outpcd.* .... (50 to 1 op 33 to 1) 14
GOLD'N SHROUD (Ire) 9-0 W Newnes (20) *rcd far side, beh fnl 2 fs*..........................(50 to 1 op 33 to 1) 15
3267^3 SMOOTH HOUND 9-0 D Holland (19) *prmnt far side till wknd 2 fs out, eased.* (10 to 1 op 7 to 1 tchd 12 to 1) 16
2990^5 NORDANCE PRINCE (Ire) 8-9 (5*) D McCabe (11) *al rear.* ....(14 to 1 tchd 16 to 1) 17
2964^9 NOTHING TO WEAR 9-3^3 Lorna Vincent (14) *al beh.* .... (50 to 1 op 33 to 1) 18
2096^9 PAPPA'S PET 9-0 M Hills (17) *in tch far side to hfwy, sn beh*................. (20 to 1 op 14 to 1 tchd 25 to 1) 19

Dist: Hd, 1½l, sht-hd, ½l, ½l, hd, 3l, 1½l, 1l, 1½l. 1m 12.50s. a 2.10s (19 Ran).
SR: 17/21/15/9/12/5/9/-/-/ (Olympic Racing), C R Egerton

3590 West Dean Maiden Stakes Class D (3-y-o) £4,020 1¼m. . . . . (5:20)

3272³ WINTER FOREST (USA) 9-0 A McGlone (17) *al prmnt, led o'r 2 fs out, strly rdn entering last, kpt on.* . . . . (5 to 2 fav tchd 3 to 1) 1
DARRERY 8-9 R Cochrane (16) *in tch, hdwy to chase wnr fnl 2 fs, swshd tail ins last, no imprsn.* . . . . (8 to 1 tchd 10 to 1) 2
3225⁶ CUFF LINK (Ire) 9-0 J Reid (4) *chsd ldrs, rdn 3 fs out, styd on one pace frm 2 out.* (10 to 1 op 8 to 1 tchd 12 to 1) 3
TOUJOURS RIVIERA 9-0 M Hills (5) *chsd ldr till one pace ins fnl 3 fs.* . . . . (5 to 1 op 4 to 1) 4
2883⁷ PEACHES POLLY 8-9 Paul Eddery (13) *rear, hdwy 4 fs out, nvr nr to chal.* . . . . (5 to 1 op 7 to 1 tchd 8 to 1 and 9 to 2) 5
3272⁸ DARK DEN (USA) 9-0 C Asmussen (9) *led till o'r 2 fs out, sn btn.* . . . . (16 to 1 op 12 to 1 tchd 20 to 1) 6
3117⁶ WEFY (USA) 9-0 W Newnes (2) *pld hrd, prmnt on outsd till wknd 3 fs out.* . . . . (25 to 1 op 16 to 1 tchd 33 to 1) 7
3272⁵ BOMBLET 8-9 L Dettori (3) *mid-div, pushed alng hfwy, nvr nr to chal.* . . . . (12 to 1 op 8 to 1 tchd 14 to 1) 8
3272⁴ LIKE THE SUN (USA) 8-9 B Raymond (6) *in tch, pld hrd, no ch fnl 3 fs.* . . . . (10 to 1 op 7 to 1) 9
2598² ADMIRAL'S WELL (Ire) 9-0 B Crossley (8) *rear early, nvr nr to chal.* . . . . (20 to 1 op 14 to 1) 10
1004³ OLD RED (Ire) 9-0 A Munro (14) *mid-div, no hdwy fnl 4 fs.* . . . . (20 to 1 op 12 to 1) 11
3225⁴ ARVOLA 8-9 G Hind (15) *nvr on terms.* (14 to 1 op 8 to 1) 12
751 MAASHAI LAWM (Ire) 8-9 (5*) K Rutter (1) *al beh.* . . . . (50 to 1 op 33 to 1) 13
523 SWORD SAIL 8-9 D Holland (12) *al beh.* . . . . (20 to 1 op 16 to 1 tchd 25 to 1) 14
3480 SEATTLE AFFAIR (Ire) 8-9 J Quinn (10) *swshd tail strt, al beh, tld off.* . . . . (50 to 1) 15
3456 DINNER AT EIGHT 9-0 J Williams (11) *al beh, tld off hfwy.* . . . . (50 to 1 op 33 to 1) 16
Dist: 1½l, 6l, 7l, ½l, 1½l, 3½l, nk, sht-hd, 2½l, 2l. 2m 6.69s. a 1.19s (16 Ran).
SR: 58/50/43/29/23/25/18/12/11/ (Sheikh Mohammed), H R A Cecil

NEWMARKET (JULY) (good)
Friday August 27th
Going Correction: MINUS 0.20 sec. per fur.

3591 Beaufort Selling Handicap Class E (0-60 3 & 4-y-o) £4,016 7f. . . . . (2:00)

2520⁹ BLOWING (USA) [45] 3-8-4 (7*) Gaye Harwood (17) *made most of rng centre of course, clr appr last 2 fs, styd on strly.* . . . . (33 to 1 op 25 to 1) 1
3175⁶ DEAD CALM [50] (v) 3-9-2 M Tebbutt (9) *slwly into strd, prog far side 2 fs out, ran on ins fnl furlong.* . . . . (20 to 1 op 14 to 1) 2
3270⁷ OUR SHADEE (USA) [55] (v) 3-9-7 M Wigham (29) *hdwy whn hmpd o'r 2 fs out, rdn and kpt on ins fnl furlong.* . . . . (16 to 1) 3
3047⁹ CLEAR LOOK [50] (bl) 3-9-2 T Quinn (28) *trkd ldrs stands side, one pace ins fnl furlong.* . . . . (16 to 1 tchd 20 to 1) 4
3447² MOGWAI (Ire) [54] (v) 4-9-11 S Whitworth (6) *ran on frm 2 fs out, nrst at finish.* . . . . (11 to 1 op 10 to 1) 5
3068³ BAN RI (Ire) [44] 3-8-10 F Norton (25) *str hdwy frm 2 furlogs out, fnshd fst.* . . . . (20 to 1 op 14 to 1) 6
3425⁶ THATCHED (Ire) [41] (bl) 3-8-7 N Day (3) *styd on far side last 2 fs.* . . . . (12 to 1 tchd 14 to 1) 7
3440⁵ CRAIGIE BOY [49] 3-9-1 (5ex) G Duffield (5) *pressed ldrs far side for o'r 5 fs.* . . . . (16 to 1) 8
3247² GUESSTIMATION (USA) [47] (bl) 4-9-4 G Bardwell (2) *cld on ldrs 2 out, not quicken fnl furlong.* (12 to 1 op 8 to 1) 9
1414 ARAGONA [31] 4-7-9 (7*) Martin Dwyer (12) *in tch centre of course, one pace fnl 2 fs.* . . . . (33 to 1) 10
3311⁹ VILAMAR (Ire) [55] 3-9-7 K Fallon (4) *cl up far side, led that grp o'r 2 fs out, no imprsn on wnr appr fnl furlong.* . . . . (20 to 1) 11
3459⁸ TEE GEE JAY [52] 3-9-1 (3*) D Harrison (1) *chsd far side ldrs, no extr o'r one out.* . . . . (20 to 1 tchd 16 to 1) 12
3391⁵ ALMONTY (Ire) [44] (bl) 3-8-10 M Roberts (18) *nvr nrr.* . . . . (10 to 1 jt-fav tchd 11 to 1) 13
3144² VIKING WATERS [40] (bl) 3-8-3 (3*) N Kennedy (10) *wl plcd to hfwy.* . . . . (20 to 1) 14
3447⁹ FIVEOFIVE (Ire) [57] 3-9-9 Pat Eddery (13) *nvr plcd to chal.* . . . . (10 to 1 jt-fav tchd 9 to 1) 15
3249 LITTLE PARK [38] 4-8-9 P Robinson (14) *no hdwy fnl 2 fs.* . . . . (20 to 1 op 16 to 1) 16
3228⁵ MAN OF THE SEASON (USA) [40] 4-8-11 W Carson (19) *wth ldrs stands side til wknd o'r 2 fs out.* . . . . (12 to 1 op 10 to 1) 17
3523 SABO'S EXPRESS [44] 3-8-10 D Biggs (11) *led far side grp for o'r 4 fs.* . . . . (25 to 1 tchd 33 to 1) 18
2719⁶ FRIENDLY SMILE [43] (v) 3-8-6 (3*) C Hodgson (22) *no imprsn on ldrs frm 2 fs out.* . . . . (33 to 1 op 25 to 1) 19
3088⁶ RIVER FIRE (Ire) [39] (bl) 3-8-5 N Adams (20) *nvr dngrs.* . . . . (33 to 1 op 25 to 1) 20
ALTO PRINCESS [34] 4-8-5 R Price (27) *wth stands side ldrs till rdn and veered lft o'r 2 out, sn btn.* . . . . (40 to 1 op 33 to 1) 21
2775⁸ RIVA ROCK [47] 3-8-6 (7*) G Faulkner (21) *nvr on terms.* . . . . (20 to 1) 22
3249 FESTIN [46] (bl) 3-8-12 W Ryan (7) *wl plcd far side for 5 fs.* . . . . (20 to 1 op 16 to 1) 23
3459⁵ CUDDLY DATE [49] 3-9-1 L Piggott (15) *nvr trbld frnt rnk.* . . . . (16 to 1) 24
10⁶ ANOTHER VINTAGE [52] 4-9-2 (7*) D Griffiths (26) *wl plcd stands side til wknd o'r 2 fs out.* . . . (40 to 1 op 33 to 1) 25
2590⁸ DANDY DESIRE [36] (v) 4-8-4 (3*) S D Williams (16) *speed for 4 fs.* . . . . (33 to 1 op 25 to 1) 26
3174⁵ POP TO STANS [57] (bl) 4-9-9 (5*) J Tate (24) *speed for o'r 4 fs.* . . . . (33 to 1 op 25 to 1) 27
3550² BASSIO (Bel) [37] (h) 4-8-8 W Hood (8) *dwlt, sn wth ldrs, wknd o'r 2 fs out, far side.* . . . . (16 to 1 tchd 20 to 1) 28
3216⁶ BOLD LINE [37] (bl) 3-8-3 N Carlisle (23) *reluctant to race, virtually took no part.* . . . . (16 to 1) 29
Dist: 2½l, ½l, ¾l, nk, nk, 1l, nk, ¾l, 5l, 1½l. 1m 26.83s. a 2.63s (29 Ran).
SR: 37/34/37/30/38/22/16/23/24/ (G Harwood), G Harwood

3592 Port Of Tilbury Maiden Stakes Class D (2-y-o) £4,662 7f. . . . . (2:35)

3130² INNISHOWEN (USA) 9-0 Pat Eddery (27) *led stands side grp, hng lft to join far side ldr 2 fs out, edgd left und pres ins fnl furlong, all out.* . . . . (100 to 30 fav op 9 to 4 tchd 7 to 2) 1
FLORID (USA) 9-0 W Ryan (12) *wl plcd, led far side grp o'r 2 fs out, hdd and hmpd ins fnl furlong, jst fld.* . . . . (7 to 2 op 9 to 4 tchd 4 to 1) 2
TREE OF HEAVEN 8-9 M Tebbutt (6) *wl plcd far side, styd on appr fnl furlong.* . . . . (33 to 1 op 20 to 1) 3
2964⁷ BRAVE PATRIARCH (Ire) 9-0 G Duffield (10) *missed break, prog hfwy, rdn and no extr appr fnl furlong.* . . . . (33 to 1 op 20 to 1) 4
VIRTUAL REALITY 8-11 (3*) D Harrison (18) *handily plcd, rdn and not quicken frm 2 fs out.* . . . . (50 to 1) 5
ROMAN CAMP (Fr) 8-11 (3*) B Doyle (28) *ldg grp, kpt on one pace last 2 fs.* . . . . (20 to 1) 6
3352 CONVOY POINT (Ire) 9-0 K Fallon (22) *styd on frm 2 out, not trble frnt rnk.* . . . . . . (8 to 1 op 14 to 1 tchd 6 to 1) 7
SADLER'S IMAGE (Ire) 9-0 M Roberts (5) *wl in tch far side for 5 fs.* . . . . (8 to 1 op 5 to 1 tchd 10 to 1) 8
913⁶ JUST FLAMENCO 9-0 D Biggs (9) *ldg grp far side, no hdwy frm 2 fs out.* . . . . (40 to 1 op 33 to 1) 9
IRISH SENOR (Ire) 8-9 (5*) L Newton (23) *chsd ldrs for 5 fs.* . . . . (40 to 1 op 33 to 1) 10
RINGMASTER (Ire) 9-0 P Robinson (24) *nvr nrr.* . . (33 to 1) 11
3130⁶ SHOOFK 9-0 L Piggott (17) *rcd in mid-div, no imprsn frm 2 fs out.* . . . . (12 to 1 op 6 to 1) 12
3259 UNPREJUDICE 9-0 V Smith (3) *led far side grp for o'r 4 fs.* . . . . (33 to 1 op 20 to 1) 13
3259² RUPAN 9-0 W R Swinburn (14) *dsptd ld centre of course for o'r 4 fs, eased whn btn.* . . . . (6 to 1 op 4 to 1 tchd 13 to 2) 14
STOLLER (USA) 9-0 T Quinn (21) *cl up stands side til outpcd frm 2 fs out.* . . . (14 to 1 op 10 to 1 tchd 20 to 1) 15
AHSANT MTOTO 9-0 R Price (2) *speed far side for 4 fs.* . . . . (33 to 1 op 20 to 1) 16
CHILLY LAD 8-7 (7*) P McCabe (4) *beh hfwy.* . . . . (40 to 1 op 33 to 1) 17
2720⁸ MENTMORE LAD 9-0 M Wigham (7) *rcd far side in tch for o'r 5 fs, eased whn btn.* . . . . (50 to 1) 18
CLOUDY GEM 8-9 N Day (16) *nvr trbld frnt rnk.* . . . . (40 to 1 op 25 to 1) 19
RISING SPRAY 9-0 F Norton (25) *strted slwly, nvr wth ldrs.* . . . . (50 to 1) 20
MUCH TOO CLEVER 9-0 S Whitworth (19) *speed to hfwy.* . . . . (50 to 1) 21
HAVE IT READY (Ire) 9-0 S Dawson (1) *al towards rear.* . . . . (25 to 1 op 20 to 1 tchd 33 to 1) 22
KINDERGARTEN BOY (Ire) 9-0 W Carson (20) *strted slwly, chsd ldrs aftr 2 fs, wknd two out.* (20 to 1 op 14 to 1) 23
3218⁹ PLUM DENNIS 9-0 T Rogers (8) *beh hfwy.* . . . . (50 to 1) 24
2642 SAPORE DI SALE 9-0 N Adams (26) *nvr on terms.* . . . . (25 to 1 tchd 33 to 1) 25
PILIB (Ire) 9-0 G Bardwell (15) *rear most of way.* (50 to 1) 26
TRANS SIBERIA 9-0 W Woods (11) *beh frm hfwy.* (50 to 1) 27
RIVER JUNCTION (Ire) 9-0 N Carlisle (13) *nvr on terms.* . . . . (50 to 1) 28
Dist: Sht-hd, 2½l, 2½l, 2½l, 1½l, hd, hd, 1l, 1½l, nk. 1m 27.16s. a 2.96s (28 Ran).
SR: 35/34/21/18/10/5/4/3/-/ (Conal Kavanagh), R Hannon

3593 Baxi Solo Apprentice Handicap Class E (0-80 3-y-o and up) £4,893 6f. . (3:05)

3460 GENERAL JOHN (Ire) [58] 4-8-3 (5*) C Adamson (10) *rcd centre of course, cl up, led o'r 2 fs out, styd on wl* . . . . (33 to 1 tchd 50 to 1) 1
3313* GREAT HALL [72] (bl) 4-9-3 (5*) D Griffiths (11) *hld up, ran on frm 2 fs out, styd on wl ins fnl furlong.* . . . . (10 to 1) 2
3404⁴ PEERAGE PRINCE [65] (bl) 4-9-1 N Kennedy (9) *trkd far side ldrs, styd on ins fnl furlong.* . . . . (7 to 1 op 6 to 1) 3

3051[7] PETRACO (Ire) [73] 5-9-9 S D Williams (17) *led stands side grp, kpt on one pace frm 2 fs out*...(14 to 1 op 12 to 1) 4
3229 ELTON LEDGER (Ire) [56] (bl) 4-8-6 J Tate (15) *hld up, hdwy appr fnl furlong, ran on und pres nr line.* ....(14 to 1 op 12 to 1) 5
3459* BEATLE SONG [54] 5-8-4 (5ex) D Harrison (8) *wl in tch far side, rdn and not quicken appr fnl furlong.* ....(6 to 1 op 5 to 1) 6
3168[9] BALLYHAYS (Ire) [52] 4-7-13 (3*) B Russell (2) *styd on frm 2 out, not rch wnr*....(20 to 1 op 16 to 1) 7
3140[5] MARTINOSKY [62] 7-8-12 C Hodgson (4) *nvr better than mid-div*....(20 to 1) 8
3535[2] MU-ARRIK [53] 5-8-3 F Norton (13) *hld up in tch, effrt 2 out, not quicken fnl furlong*....(8 to 1 op 7 to 1) 9
2788[2] BRIGHT PARAGON (Ire) [48] 4-7-9 (3*) C Hawksley (5) *wl plcd far side til wknd 2 out*....(11 to 1 op 10 to 1) 10+
3438 ANOTHER JADE [78] 3-9-5 (5*) G McGrath (1) *led far side grp for 4 fs, fdd*....(20 to 1 op 16 to 1) 10+
3168 LEIGH CROFTER [50] (bl) 4-7-9 (5*) Martin Dwyer (3) *nvr nr to chal*....(25 to 1) 12
2686[8] SCENT OF POWER [63] 3-8-6 (3*) Michael Denaro (16) *chsd stands side ldrs for 4 fs*....(25 to 1) 13
3354* ASTERIX [56] 5-8-3 (3*) Mark Denaro (12) *nvr rchd frnt rnk.* ....(12 to 1 tchd 14 to 1) 14
2723[9] RESTORE [47] (bl) 10-7-11[4] B Doyle (14) *nvr able to chal frm 2 out*....(33 to 1) 15
3020[8] LADY SABO [59] 4-8-9 M Fenton (7) *early pace, no hdwy frm hfwy*....(16 to 1 tchd 20 to 1) 16
3094[9] FARNDALE [43] 6-7-4 (3*) N Varley (6) *in tch far side for 4 fs*....(20 to 1 op 10 to 1) 17
3127[2] ROCA MURADA (Ire) [69] 4-9-2 (3*) P McCabe (18) *cld on ldrs hfwy, btn and eased appr fnl furlong.* ....(11 to 2 fav op 6 to 1) 18

Dist: 1½l, hd, sht-hd, nk, nk, 1l, 1½l, 1½l, nk, dd-ht. 1m 13.11s. a 1.41s (18 Ran).
SR: 42/50/42/49/31/28/22/26/11/ (Lord Scarsdale), P C Haslam

3594 Hopeful Stakes Class A (Listed Race) (3-y-o and up) £9,855 6f.........(3:35)

2855[2] STACK ROCK 6-9-1 K Fallon (5) *made all, drvn out and hld on wl fnl furlong*....(9 to 1 op 8 to 1) 1
2927 GARAH 4-8-12 W Ryan (6) *hld up towards rear, cld on ldrs 2 furlong out, rdn and kpt on same pace ins fnl furlong*....(7 to 1 op 6 to 1) 2
2987* KING'S SIGNET (USA) 4-9-0 M Roberts (7) *ldg grp, rdn and ev ch 2 fs out, no extr ins fnl furlong.* ....(13 to 8 fav op 5 to 4 tchd 7 to 4) 3
2574[5] SPLICE 4-9-1 Pat Eddery (4) *hld up towards rear, gd hdwy 2 out, rdn and not quicken wl ins fnl furlong.* ....(6 to 1 op 9 to 2) 4
3162[2] MONTENDRE 6-9-6 P Gilson (1) *sn pushed alng, cld on ldrs hfwy, ev ch 2 out, btn o'r one out.* ....(15 to 2 op 5 to 1 tchd 8 to 1) 5
3153[7] STAR FAMILY FRIEND (Ire) 3-8-11 P Robinson (3) *speed for o'r 3 fs*....(33 to 1 op 25 to 1) 6
3291[5] WAFFLE ON 3-8-5 G Duffield (8) *cl up til wknd 2 out.* ....(16 to 1 op 25 to 1) 7
3313[4] ARABELLAJILL 4-8-9 T Quinn (2) *pressed ldrs, ev ch 2 out, wknd o'r one out*....(25 to 1 op 20 to 1) 8
3315[7] SIWAAYIB 3-8-6[1] W R Swinburn (9) *steadied leaving stalls, settled in rear, rdn alng 2 out, no imprsn, eased clsg stages*....(7 to 1 op 8 to 1 tchd 9 to 1) 9

Dist: Nk, 1l, hd, 4l, 2l, nk, sht-hd, 6l. 1m 11.87s. a 0.17s (9 Ran).
SR: 74/70/68/68/57/40/33/36/9/ (Castle Racing), E J Alston

3595 Breheny Handicap Class C (0-95 3-y-o and up) £6,004 1¾m 175yds.....(4:05)

2963[3] MY PATRIARCH [90] 3-9-5 W Carson (8) *pld hrd to hfwy, chsd ldr, led o'r 3 fs out, rdn and styd on ins fnl furlong*....(11 to 2 op 4 to 1) 1
3319* BOLD RESOLUTION (Ire) [72] 5-9-0 Pat Eddery (9) *hld up, improved o'r 3 fs out, rdn and not quicken frm over one out*....(11 to 2 op 9 to 2) 2
3449* COLLIER BAY [72] 3-7-12 (3*,4ex) D Harrison (1) *in tch, hdwy 4 out, rdn alng o'r 2 out, one pace fnl furlong.* ....(6 to 4 fav op 11 to 8 tchd 7 to 4) 3
3434[3] DREAMS END [82] 5-9-10 L Piggott (4) *hld up towards rear, cld on ldrs ins last 2 fs, btn whn eased inside fnl furlong*....(13 to 2 op 8 to 1) 4
2755[2] REQUESTED [80] 6-9-8 T Quinn (5) *strted slwly, hld up in rear, pld to outsd 4 out, rdn and one pace appr fnl furlong*....(14 to 1 op 12 to 1 tchd 16 to 1) 5
3125[8] MULL HOUSE [77] 6-9-5 W R Swinburn (2) *handily plcd til rdn and wknd frm 2 fs out, tld off*....(20 to 1) 6
3217[3] VISHNU (USA) [89] 3-9-4 W Ryan (6) *chsd ldrs til lost pl 3 fs out, tld off*....(20 to 1 op 16 to 1 tchd 25 to 1) 7
3263[2] NORTHERN BOUND (Ire) [83] 3-8-12 M Roberts (3) *led til hdd and wknd o'r 3 fs out, tld off*...(10 to 1 op 8 to 1) 8
3193[5] MODEST HOPE (USA) [57] 6-7-13 D Biggs (7) *in tch in mid-div, lost pos frm hfwy, tld off*....(25 to 1 op 50 to 1) 9

Dist: 1½l, 1l, 3l, nk, 20l, sht-hd, ½l, 30l. 3m 15.60s. a 9.60s (9 Ran).
(Peter S Winfield), J L Dunlop

3596 Blue Peter Conditions Stakes Class D (2-y-o) £3,427 6f................(4:35)

2994* FOREST GAZELLE (USA) 9-1 Pat Eddery (3) *rcd keenly, led aftr 2 fs, shaken up appr fnl furlong, pushed out.* ....(5 to 2 on op 9 to 4 on tchd 2 to 1 on) 1
3537* FRIENDLY CHAMP (Ire) 9-1 (4ex) R Price (2) *hld up, cld on wnr 2 out, rdn and not quicken one furlong out, styd on same pace*....(3 to 1 op 5 to 2 tchd 100 to 30) 2
3223[3] BATTLING BLUE 9-1 W R Swinburn (1) *led for 2 fs, rdn and outpcd frm two furlongs out*....(11 to 1 op 8 to 1) 3
3130 FOURTH OF JUNE (USA) 8-11 M Roberts (4) *speed to hfwy, sn btn*....(20 to 1 op 25 to 1 tchd 33 to 1) 4

Dist: 1½l, 5l, 2l. 1m 13.53s. a 1.83s (4 Ran).
SR: 40/34/14/2/ (K Abdulla), R Charlton

3597 Saxham Nursery Class C (2-y-o) £5,174 1m.....................(5:05)

3406[2] BARBAROJA [78] 9-3 W R Swinburn (14) *hld up, ran on 3 fs out, led wl o'r one out, wndrd ins fnl furlong, held on.* ....(100 to 30 fav op 3 to 1 tchd 7 to 2 and 4 to 1) 1
2988[4] SHARP TYCOON (Ire) [71] 8-7 (3*) B Doyle (12) *hdwy frm rear 2 out, ran on ins fnl furlong, edgd lft nr finish.* ....(12 to 1 op 14 to 1 tchd 16 to 1) 2
3009[2] ARZ (USA) [69] 8-8 N Carlisle (7) *hld up towards rear, ran on o'r one out, fnshd wl*....(6 to 1 op 10 to 1) 3
3363[2] LEAP OF FAITH (Ire) [66] (v) 8-5 T Quinn (11) *pressed ldrs, ev ch frm 2 out, no extr whn bumped nr finish.* ....(20 to 1 tchd 25 to 1) 4
3259[3] BONAIGUA (Ire) [81] 9-6 Pat Eddery (8) *in tch, rdn and ev ch 2 out, one pace appr fnl furlong.* ....(12 to 1 op 8 to 1 tchd 14 to 1) 5
2718[2] MOMENT OF GLORY (Ire) [66] 8-5 D Biggs (4) *made most of rng for o'r 6 fs, kpt on same pace.* ....(16 to 1 op 14 to 1 tchd 20 to 1) 6
3351[8] HEATHCLIFF (Ire) [70] (v) 8-9 M Wigham (3) *wl in tch, rdn and no prog appr fnl furlong*....(20 to 1 op 16 to 1) 7
2988[3] JASARI (Ire) [75] 8-7 (7*) Mark Denaro (13) *rear grp most of way*....(8 to 1 op 9 to 1 tchd 10 to 1) 8
3351* DUTY TIME [82] 9-7 W Carson (6) *beh aftr 2 fs.* ....(9 to 2 op 4 to 1 tchd 7 to 2) 9
3362[6] STRADISHALL [60] (bl) 7-11[1] (3*) D Harrison (10) *cl up til wknd o'r 2 out*....(33 to 1 tchd 50 to 1) 10
2929[4] CHIEF EXECUTIVE [58] 7-11 N Adams (2) *mid-div, effrt o'r 2 out, sn rdn and btn.* ....(14 to 1 tchd 12 to 1 and 16 to 1) 11
3166[6] YAWARA [76] 9-1 M Roberts (1) *chsd ldrs to hfwy.* ....(16 to 1 op 14 to 1) 12
2996 SAWTID [72] 8-8 (3*) C Hodgson (9) *wl plcd for 5 fs.* ....(16 to 1 op 14 to 1 tchd 25 to 1) 13
3281 BERNIE'S SISTER (Ire) [54] 7-7 G Bardwell (5) *ldg grp til wknd frm hfwy*....(50 to 1 op 33 to 1) 14

Dist: Nk, nk, nk, 1½l, nk, 12l, 3½l, 4l, 2l, 2½l. 1m 41.10s. a 3.20s (14 Ran).
SR: 31/23/20/16/26/10/ (Marquesa de Moratalla), J G FitzGerald

THIRSK (good to firm (races 1,2,3,5,6), firm (4))

Friday August 27th

Going Correction: NIL

3598 James Lambie Selling Stakes Class G (2-y-o) £3,036 7f................(2:20)

3362[3] WINNING LINE 8-11 M Birch (7) *cl up gng wl, hdwy to ld 2 and a half fs out, pushed out*....(5 to 2 fav op 2 to 1) 1
2933[2] HICKLETON LADY (Ire) 8-6 K Darley (4) *beh, hdwy on outsd o'r 2 fs out, styd on strly ins last.* ....(3 to 1 tchd 100 to 30) 2
3186[5] MONKEY WENCH (Ire) 8-6 J Fortune (2) *chsd ldrs, rdn 2 fs out, styd on ins last*....(14 to 1) 3
3279[4] GAELIC STAR (Ire) 8-11 S Perks (11) *al prmnt, effrt and ev ch 2 fs out, sn rdn and one pace appr last.* ....(8 to 1 op 6 to 1) 4
3377[3] MARBLE 8-1 (5*) Darren Moffatt (6) *in tch, rdn o'r 2 fs out, sn one pace*....(10 to 1 tchd 12 to 1) 5
2554 GLENLYON DUCHESS 8-6 J Weaver (10) *mid-div, some hdwy fnl 2 fs, nvr dngrs*....(50 to 1 op 33 to 1) 6
2852[2] LAUREL ROMEO (Ire) 9-3 J Carroll (9) *in tch, rdn wl o'r 2 fs out, sn one pace*....(13 to 2 op 6 to 1 tchd 7 to 1) 7
2679[3] WINGS AHEAD 8-11 N Connorton (14) *mid-div, hdwy o'r 2 fs out, sn rdn, kpt on one pace*....(16 to 1) 8
3235 MINIBAR 8-6 A Mackay (13) *chsd ldrs, effrt on outer o'r 2 fs out, sn rdn, edgd lft and one pace.* ....(50 to 1 op 33 to 1) 9
2472[8] POLHYMNIA 8-6 R Hills (15) *slwly into strd, hdwy 3 fs out, sn rdn and wknd 2 furlongs out*....(9 to 1 op 8 to 1) 10
3432 SONIC (Ire) (bl) 8-11 T Lucas (3) *led, rdn and hdd 2 and a half fs out, grad wknd*....(33 to 1 tchd 25 to 1) 11
GYPSOPHILA 8-6 J Fanning (12) *nvr rchd ldrs*...(33 to 1) 12
607[7] FREE TYSON 8-8 (3*) S Maloney (5) *chsd ldr, rdn 3 fs out, sn wknd*....(50 to 1 op 33 to 1) 13
2826 CRANFIELD CHARGER 8-6 L Charnock (1) *slwly into strd, al beh*....(50 to 1 op 33 to 1) 14
NOWT SPOILING 8-11 S Morris (8) *slwly away, al beh.* ....(50 to 1) 15
3309[8] DUNDEELIN 8-12 Dale Gibson (16) *pld hrd on outer, in tch till ran very wide strt, sn beh*....(20 to 1) 16

Dist: 3½l, ¾l, hd, 2½l, 2l, nk, 3l, nk, ½l, 2l. 1m 28.60s. a 5.80s (16 Ran).
SR: 10/-/-/-/-/-/ (The Winning Line), M H Easterby

3599 Doug Moscrop Handicap Class D (0-75 3-y-o and up) £3,552 2m........ (2:50)

3521[6] SALU [51] 4-8-6 J Carroll (2) *hld up, gd hdwy 5 fs out, led 3 furlongs out, ran on wl*............ (7 to 1 tchd 8 to 1) 1
3125[3] PROVENCE [71] 6-9-12 M Birch (6) *al cl up, effrt 3 fs out, sn rdn and ev ch, one pace fnl 2 furlongs.* ....(9 to 4 fav op 2 to 1) 2
3473[8] KAYARTIS [48] 4-8-3 J Lowe (1) *trkd ldrs, rdn and outpcd o'r 3 fs out, kpt on fnl 2 furlongs*.....(4 to 1 op 3 to 1) 3
3473[5] PHILGUN [60] (v) 4-8-12 (3*) S Maloney (4) *chsd ldrs, effrt 3 fs out, sn rdn and one pace fnl 2 furlongs.* .... (5 to 1 op 9 to 2 tchd 11 to 2) 4
3193[6] HASTA LA VISTA [54] (bl) 3-7-9 L Charnock (7) *led, rdn 4 fs out, hdd 3 furlongs out and sn btn*............ (8 to 1) 5
2683[7] SEXY MOVER [39] 6-7-8[1] J Fanning (9) *chsd ldrs, rdn o'r 3 fs out, sn one pace*.................. (33 to 1 op 25 to 1) 6
3405[6] POST IMPRESSIONIST (Ire) [49] 4-8-4 K Darley (5) *cl up, rdn 4 fs out, sn wknd*...................................(7 to 1) 7
BALLAD RULER [46] 7-8-1[4] T Williams (10) *hld up and beh, effrt o'r 3 fs out, sn rdn and btn*.......................(50 to 1) 8
2640[5] DESERT LAUGHTER (Ire) [52] 3-7-7 A Mackay (3) *al rear.* ....(20 to 1) 9
3356 ROLLING THE BONES (USA) [57] 4-8-12 J Weaver (8) *al rear*..............................(25 to 1 op 20 to 1) 10
1305[7] MASTER OF THE ROCK [40] 4-7-9 S Wood (11) *cl up, rdn alng hfwy, sn lost pl and beh*.....(33 to 1 op 25 to 1) 11

Dist: 2½l, 5l, 2l, ¾l, 4l, 10l, 5l, 1l, 1½l, 12l. 3m 30.00s. a 6.00s (11 Ran).
SR: 32/49/21/31/9/4/4/-/-/ (W N Lumley), J Etherington

3600 Ray Gilpin Nursery Class E (2-y-o) £3,158 6f...................... (3:20)

3281 JOHNNIE THE JOKER [56] (v) 8-5 J Weaver (9) *cl up, led appr hfwy, rdn 2 fs out, kpt on ins last.* .... (12 to 1 op 10 to 1) 1
3115[6] WIXI (Ire) [72] 9-0 (7*) S Mulvey (8) *beh, hdwy hfwy, effrt to chal entering last, sn rdn, edgd rght, kpt on.* .... (10 to 1 op 8 to 1) 2
3309[5] MERISSA [53] 8-2 L Charnock (6) *trkd ldrs, effrt and not much room 2 fs out, rdn and styd on ins last.* ....(8 to 1 op 6 to 1) 3
3281[4] HASTY BANK [58] 8-7 J Lowe (7) *led till appr hfwy, cl up, rdn 2 fs out, wknd approaching last.* ....(13 to 8 fav op 2 to 1 tchd 9 to 4) 4
2890[6] POTSCLOSE [70] 9-5 T Williams (3) *chsd ldrs, rdn alng hfwy, kpt on one pace.* (13 to 2 op 6 to 1 tchd 7 to 1) 5
2586[2] FOUR OF SPADES [60] 8-9 J Fortune (2) *cl up, ev ch 2 fs out, sn rdn, wndrd and wknd entering last.* ....(6 to 1 op 9 to 2) 6
767[3] BATIEN'S RIVER [57] 8-6 Dale Gibson (5) *in tch, rdn o'r 2 fs out, sn wknd*.......................(12 to 1 op 10 to 1) 7
3236[9] SPRING LOADED [66] 9-1 K Darley (1) *chsd ldrs, rdn o'r 2 fs out, sn btn*............. (8 to 1 op 7 to 1 tchd 9 to 1) 8
3281[9] FORREST MASTER (Ire) [48] 7-11 J Fanning (4) *cl up, rdn alng hfwy and sn lost pl*............ (25 to 1 op 20 to 1) 9

Dist: 1½l, ½l, 1½l, 2l, 1l, 1l, 7l, 1l. 1m 15.20s. a 5.20s (9 Ran).
(Miss M Carrington-Smith), J P Leigh

3601 Matt Seymour Apprentice Rating Related Maiden Stakes Class F (0-70 3-y-o) £2,534 7f................ (3:50)

2834[3] CLEVER MINSTREL (USA) 8-9 (5*) P Houghton (5) *trkd ldrs, hdwy to ld 2 fs out, pushed out.* .... (6 to 5 fav op 11 to 10 on tchd 5 to 4) 1
3312[3] CITY TIMES (Ire) (bl) 8-9 S Sanders (3) *cl up, led hfwy, rdn and hdd 2 fs out, kpt on*............(7 to 4 op 6 to 4) 2
3006[4] NOBLE MEASURE (Ire) (bl) 8-9 (5*) G Strange (1) *dwlt and sn pushed alng, effrt 3 fs out, no ch whn bumped 2 furlongs out*.........................(8 to 1 op 7 to 1) 3
3047[7] WOODLANDS ELECTRIC (v) 8-9 (5*) M Baird (4) *pld hrd, led till led wide strt, rdn and wkng whn hng rght 2 fs out, sn beh*......................... (50 to 1 op 25 to 1) 4
1656[6] SARAH HEIGHTS 8-9 V Halliday (2) *beh frm hfwy.* .... (9 to 1 op 12 to 1) 5

Dist: 3l, 6l, 12l, 1l. 1m 28.10s. a 5.30s (5 Ran).
SR: 21/7/ (Seymour Cohn), G Harwood

3602 EBF Victor Green Maiden Stakes Class D (2-y-o) £4,628 6f........ (4:20)

3317[6] FAWAAKEH (USA) 8-9 R Hills (5) *cl up, led hfwy, quickened clr 2 fs out, unchlgd.* ....(6 to 4 on op 13 to 8 on tchd 5 to 4 on) 1
3114[6] SURPRISE GUEST (Ire) 9-0 T Williams (8) *al prmnt, rdn 2 fs out, kpt on one pace*... (13 to 2 op 8 to 1 tchd 6 to 1) 2
3031[6] SUSHI BAR (Ire) 9-0 K Darley (7) *hld up on heels of ldrs, tenderly rdn and some prog appr fnl furlong, nvr plcd to chal*.......................(12 to 1 op 10 to 1) 3
RINUS MAJOR (Ire) 9-0 J Weaver (10) *pushed alng hfwy, styd on fnl 2 fs, nvr dngrs*........................(33 to 1) 4
3091[7] DINOT (Ire) 9-0 S Perks (9) *led to hfwy, cl up till rdn 2 fs out and sn wknd*....(14 to 1 tchd 16 to 1 and 12 to 1) 5
HARPHAM HERO 9-0 J Lowe (4) *outpcd and beh frm hfwy*.......................... (50 to 1 op 33 to 1) 6
3411[5] BLAIN 9-0 J Carroll (3) *cl up, rdn hfwy and sn lost pl.* ....(25 to 1 op 16 to 1 tchd 33 to 1) 7

Dist: 6l, nk, 3l, 3½l, 7l, 2l. 1m 14.90s. a 4.90s (7 Ran).
(Hamdan Al-Maktoum), R W Armstrong

3603 John Morgan Handicap Class E (0-70 3-y-o and up) £3,786 5f......... (4:50)

3032[7] KALAR [45] (bl) 4-8-3 S Wood (3) *led far side, o'rall ldr hfwy, rdn and ran on wl fnl furlong.* ....(20 to 1 op 16 to 1) 1
2456[8] LE CHIC [45] 7-8-3 R Hills (2) *chsd wnr far side, effrt to chal appr fnl furlong, sn rdn and not quicken.* ....(33 to 1 op 25 to 1) 2
3410[5] HERE COMES A STAR [69] 5-9-13 K Darley (1) *chsd ldrs far side, rdn one and a half fs out, kpt on ins last.* ....(12 to 1 op 10 to 1) 3
3280[7] SLADES HILL [60] 6-8-11 (7*) V Halliday (5) *cl up far side, ev ch o'r one fs out, sn rdn and not quicken ins last.* ....(12 to 1 op 10 to 1) 4
2494[5] SADDLEHOME (USA) [56] 4-8-11 (3*) O Pears (6) *rcd centre, gd hdwy 2 fs out and sn ev ch, rdn and one pace entering last*................................. (25 to 1) 5
3251[4] BRISAS [35] (v) 6-7-7 J Fanning (12) *in tch, rdn 2 fs out and kpt on*.......................... (10 to 1 op 7 to 1) 6
3438 PLUM FIRST [69] (v) 3-9-7 (3*) S Maloney (7) *rcd centre, rdn 2 fs out, styd on ins last, nrst finish*..........(14 to 1) 7
3360* ARC LAMP [57] 7-9-1 J Fortune (13) *prmnt stands side, rdn 2 fs out, sn one pace*...............(8 to 1 op 7 to 1) 8
3504 BALLAD DANCER [70] 8-10-0 M Birch (14) *chsd ldr stands side, rdn and outpcd 2 fs out, styd on ins last.* (12 to 1) 9
3410[3] SINGING STAR [70] 7-9-7 (7*) Claire Balding (15) *dwlt and beh, swtchd lft and hdwy 2 fs out, kpt on, nvr dngrs.* ....(13 to 2 op 5 to 1 tchd 7 to 1) 10
3251[5] SUPER ROCKY [67] 4-9-4 (7*) H Bastiman (10) *cl up stands side till rdn and one pace fnl 2 fs*.............(10 to 1) 11
2951[3] ABSOLUTION [64] 9-9-8 J Weaver (8) *gd speed centre o'r 3 fs*.................................(14 to 1 op 12 to 1) 12
3032 LUCKY MILL [43] (bl) 3-7-12 L Charnock (11) *cl up stands side till rdn and wknd 2 fs out*............... (25 to 1) 13
3059[4] DAYJUZ (Ire) [58] (bl) 3-8-13 S Perks (17) *led stands side and o'rall ldr to hfwy, sn rdn adnd wknd 2 fs out.* ....(3 to 1 fav op 8 to 1) 14
3032 NORTH OF WATFORD [43] 8-8-1 J Lowe (16) *cl up stands side till rdn and wknd fnl 2 fs*...... (8 to 1 op 12 to 1) 15
2132[6] FIRST PLAY [66] 3-9-7 J Carroll (9) *prmnt stands side till rdn and wknd o'r 2 fs out*....................(20 to 1) 16
2231[8] HUMBER'S SUPREME (Ire) [46] (bl) 3-8-1 A Mackay (4) *al rear*..............................(33 to 1 op 25 to 1) 17

Dist: 1½l, ¾l, ¾l, 1½l, 2l, nk, nk, sht-hd, ½l, sht-hd. 59.80s. a 2.60s (17 Ran).
SR: 37/31/52/40/30/1/31/21/33/ (E Stockdale), D W Chapman

TRALEE (IRE) (good) Friday August 27th

3604 Derrinstown Apprentice Series Handicap (0-75 3-y-o and up) £3,797 1m 5f ....(5:00)

2516* TROPICAL LAKE (Ire) [-] 3-8-10 R M Burke (12)... (10 to 1) 1
3397[5] SPRING RITE [-] (bl) 6-7-1 (6*) G M Moylan (1).... (10 to 1) 2
2900[5] OPEN MARKET (USA) [-] 4-9-5 (6*) D J O'Donoghue (3) ....(4 to 1 co-fav) 3
3543[3] PREMIER LEAP (Ire) [-] 4-8-1 (6*) B Fenton (2).......(9 to 2) 4
3484[2] LAKE OF LOUGHREA (Ire) [-] 3-8-7 (4*,12ex) B J Walsh (11) ....(4 to 1 co-fav) 5
3525[2] LYPHARD ABU (Ire) [-] (bl) 5-9-12 (2*) J A Heffernan (8) ....(4 to 1 co-fav) 6
3397 TOAST AND HONEY (Ire) [-] 4-9-10 (4*) C Everard (5) ....(12 to 1) 7
3367[7] KOI CORP [-] 9-7-7 D G O'Shea (10)..................(25 to 1) 8
3484[7] POUNDWORLD (Ire) [-] (bl) 3-8-2 (6*) P J Smullen (4) ....(25 to 1) 9
3396* ARAN EXILE [-] 3-9-0 (5ex) P Carberry (13)....... (10 to 1) 10
OLD MAN RIVER [-] 8-8-3 (2*) W J Smith (6)...... (16 to 1) 11

Dist: 1½l, ½l, hd, ½l. 2m 52.70s. (11 Ran).
(G Redford), Michael Hourigan

3605 B.R.C. Waterford Crystal Maiden (3-y-o and up) £4,052 7f........... (5:30)

2877[2] MONOPOLY MONEY (Ire) 3-8-10 P Shanahan (4)...(6 to 4) 1
INTIMACY (USA) 3-8-7 J F Egan (2)...............(8 to 1) 2
3576[3] MUSWELL BROOK (Ire) (bl) 3-8-10 K J Manning (3) (10 to 1) 3
3029[5] GOODNIGHT KISS (bl) 3-8-7 M J Kinane (6)....(6 to 4 on) 4
3327 WHAT MAGIC (Ire) 3-7-13 (8*) P J Smullen (5).....(25 to 1) 5
BOLD CAT (Ire) 4-8-11 (4*) J J Behan (7)......... (100 to 1) 6
3417 ELEGANT NORA (Ire) 3-8-5 (2*) R M Burke (1).....(33 to 1) 7

Dist: 2l, 5l, 1l, 2l. 1m 27.30s. (7 Ran).
(A McLean), C Collins

3606 Tom McGiff Liberator Handicap (0-75 3-y-o and up) £3,452 5f......... (6:00)

3244³ DAIRINE'S DELIGHT (Ire) [-] 3-7-7 Joanna Morgan (6) ....(12 to 1) 1
3244⁶ LADY PRESIDENT (Ire) [-] (bl) 4-8-9 (8*) R T Fitzpatrick (3) ....(3 to 1) 2
3561⁴ PAKOL (Ire) [-] 4-8-12 (4*) W J Smith (2) ....(8 to 1) 3
3561³ ASTA MADERA (Ire) [-] 3-8-13 (2*) P Carberry (1) ....(13 to 8 fav) 4
2320⁷ JOHNS DANCER (Ire) [-] 4-6-13 (8*) G M Moylan (10) ....(33 to 1) 5
3395 FIVE LITTLE GIRLS (Ire) [-] 3-8-7 K J Manning (8) ..(16 to 1) 6
3244² BUSINESS CENTRE (Ire) [-] 3-8-5 J F Egan (5) ....(10 to 1) 7
3455⁵ CARRIG STAR (Ire) [-] 4-8-11 (4*) J J Behan (12) ...(10 to 1) 8
3395⁷ SOUTHERN REVIEW (Ire) [-] (bl) 3-9-4 W J Supple (9) ....(14 to 1) 9
310 SOME FUN [-] 6-9-1 (10*) D W O'Sullivan (11) .....(16 to 1) 10
3561⁸ SHOOT THE DEALER (Ire) [-] (bl) 3-9-3 (8*) G Coogan (4) ....(14 to 1) 11
Dist: Nk, 5½l, ½l, hd. 1m 1.60s. (11 Ran).
(Seamus MacCrosain), Michael Cunningham

3607 Oyster Tavern Nursery (2-y-o) £4,142 1m.....(6:30)

1332 JOMACOON (Ire) [-] 7-11 (6*) J A Heffernan (1) ....(14 to 1) 1
2983⁷ ZOE BAIRD [-] 7-8² (4*) J J Behan (6) ....(12 to 1) 2
3415² CORLEONIE (Ire) [-] (bl) 9-2 W J Supple (5) (100 to 30 fav) 3
3379² ORANEDIN [-] 8-12 (6*) B J Walsh (7) ....(7 to 2) 4
1432* SHARE A DREAM (Ire) [-] 8-5 (2*) R M Burke (2) ...(10 to 1) 5
3379⁵ BACK FROM HEAVEN (Ire) [-] (bl) 9-3 K J Manning (8) ....(13 to 2) 6
3026⁵ PAUGIM (Ire) [-] (bl) 9-2 M J Kinane (3) ....(9 to 2) 7
2982⁷ EAS GEIPTINE [-] 7-10 (6*) R V Skelly (4) ....(16 to 1) 8
3379⁴ MONICA'S CHOICE (Ire) [-] (bl) 7-12 Joanna Morgan (9) ....(5 to 1) 9
Dist: 1½l, 2l, 3l, 1½l. 1m 39.70s. (9 Ran).
(T F Brennan), J S Bolger

3608 Slieve Mish Auction Race (2-y-o) £3,452 1m.....(7:00)

3073⁴ MASCOT 8-2 J F Egan (4) ....(8 to 1) 1
3416⁴ DANCING SUCCESS (USA) 8-8 M J Kinane (16) (7 to 4 fav) 2
3332² TONGABEZI (Ire) 8-0 (2*) R M Burke (1) ....(11 to 2) 3
3203⁵ SINGING DANCER (Ire) 8-1 (4*) J J Behan (3) ....(6 to 1) 4
3073⁵ QUASIMODO (Ire) (bl) 8-1 (4*) W J Smith (11) ....(12 to 1) 5
3416 MONEYBROKER (Ire) 8-8 K J Manning (2) ....(33 to 1) 6
3073² WAQAR (Ire) 8-5 P Shanahan (12) ....(11 to 1) 7
3073⁸ AVALIN (Ire) 7-8 (8*) R T Fitzpatrick (6) ....(14 to 1) 8
3273² CLANCY NOSSEL (Ire) 8-5 W J Supple (8) ....(12 to 1) 9
MELODIC SOUND (Ire) 9-0 S Craine (9) ....(8 to 1) 10
3273³ JENZSOPH (Ire) 8-2 A J Nolan (10) ....(20 to 1) 11
3416⁹ RUDI'S PRIDE (Ire) 8-6 (2*) D G O'Shea (15) ....(16 to 1) 12
3073 DR LEUNT (Ire) 7-13 (6*) J A Heffernan (13) ....(33 to 1) 13
3073 JINGLING SILVER (Ire) (bl) 7-11 (8*) J J Mullins (7) (16 to 1) 14
3273⁷ SEAPARK LADY (Ire) 7-10 (6*) R V Skelly (5) ....(40 to 1) 15
Dist: 3l, ½l, 1l, ½l. 1m 39.90s. (15 Ran).
(Rudy Weiss), M J Grassick

ARLINGTON (USA) (good)
Saturday August 28th

3609 Beverly D Stakes (Grade 1) (3-y-o and up) £198,675 1m 1f 110yds.....

3150* FLAWLESSLY (USA) 5-8-11 C McCarron (2) ....(2 to 1 on) 1
VIA BORGHESE (USA) 4-8-11 J Velasquez (4) ....(7 to 1) 2
3150³ LET'S ELOPE (NZ) 6-8-11 P Valenzuela (6) ....(7 to 2) 3
HERO'S LOVE (USA) 5-8-11 E Fires (5) ....(15 to 1) 4
AQUILEGIA (USA) 4-8-11 Julie Krone (1) ....(12 to 1) 5
2793⁴ LUPESCU 5-8-11 L Dettori (7) ....(27 to 1) 6
SKIMBLE (USA) 4-8-11 P Day (3) ....(16 to 1) 7
Dist: Nose, nk, nose, 2 ¼l, 1 ¼l, ¾l. 1m 55.60s. (7 Ran).
(Harbor View Farm), C Whittingham

CURRAGH (IRE) (good to firm)
Saturday August 28th
Going Correction: MINUS 0.10 sec. per fur. (races 1,2,3,4,5), MINUS 0.40 (6,7)

3610 Stewards Handicap (0-90 3-y-o) £3,450 7f.....(2:00)

2877* GLACIAL ARCTIC (USA) [-] 9-2 M J Kinane (5) ..(6 to 4 fav) 1
1511⁵ RAJAURA (Ire) [-] 8-12 J P Murtagh (8) ....(5 to 1) 2
1199 KURDISTAN (Ire) [-] 9-2 R Hughes (7) ....(12 to 1) 3
3334² UKUD (USA) [-] 9-0 W J Supple (9) ....(6 to 1) 4
3576* PENNY A DAY (Ire) [-] 7-8¹ (8*,10ex) B A Hunter (4) (9 to 1) 5
3496⁶ GOLD BRAISIM (Ire) [-] 8-8 C Roche (6) ....(16 to 1) 6
2779³ ABEL TASMAN (USA) [-] 9-4 P V Gilson (10) ....(6 to 1) 7
3380³ GLOWING VALUE (Ire) [-] (bl) 9-1 (6*) J A Heffernan (3) ....(12 to 1) 8
3395* PEARL DAWN (Ire) [-] 8-2 (4*) J J Behan (1) ....(14 to 1) 9
3029⁶ ELIZABETH'S PET (Ire) [-] 9-2 L Piggott (2) ....(6 to 1) 10
Dist: Hd, ¾l, 1l, ½l. 1m 25.10s. a 1.90s (10 Ran).
SR: 63/58/60/55/40/-/ (Andrea Schiavi), D K Weld

3611 E.B.F. Anglesey Stakes (Group 3) (2-y-o) £14,375 6f 63yds.....(2:30)

3200⁴ KERAKA (USA) 8-7 M J Kinane (5) *wl plcd, quickened to ld ins fnl furlong, styd on*....(9 to 4) 1
LUZARCHES (Ire) 8-7 S Craine (3) *hld up, prog 2 fs out, rdn one out, kpt on*....(11 to 2) 2
3223* AVERTI (Ire) 8-10 W Newnes (6) *sn led, rdn appr fnl furlong, hdd ins last, wknd cl hme*....(7 to 4 fav) 3
3451* MISS KRISTIN (Ire) 8-7 C Roche (7) *trkd ldr, rdn 2 fs out, kpt on one pace ins last*....(100 to 30) 4
3335⁹ DILIGENT DODGER (Ire) 8-10 W J Supple (4) *hld up, prog 2 fs out, ev ch one out, no extr ins last*....(14 to 1) 5
3453* RAZIDA (Ire) 8-7 K J Manning (2) *rear, kpt on one pace fnl 2 fs, not rch ldrs*....(14 to 1) 6
3026⁴ KING SANCHO (Ire) 8-10 R Hughes (1) *mid-div, rdn 2 fs out, wknd one out*....(20 to 1) 7
Dist: 1l, nk, hd, hd. 1m 18.60s. a 4.10s (7 Ran).
(H H Aga Khan), John M Oxx

3612 E.B.F. Futurity Stakes (Group 3) (2-y-o) £14,375 1m.....(3:00)

2605* COIS NA TINE (Ire) 8-10 C Roche (3) *dsptd ld, led 3 fs out, rdn and quickened one and a half out, kpt on strly*....(9 to 4 fav) 1
3415* BALLYKETT NANCY (Ire) 8-7 K J Manning (5) *wl plcd, rdn 2 fs out, styd on strly ins last, nrst finish*....(8 to 1) 2
2807² CITY NIGHTS (Ire) 8-10 M J Kinane (4) *dsptd ld to 3 fs out, rdn 2 out, wknd one out*....(7 to 1) 3
2807* BARTOK (Ire) 8-10 P V Gilson (7) *trkd ldrs, rdn and wknd one furlong out*....(5 to 2) 4
2840* MUSICAL INSIGHT (Ire) 8-10 J P Murtagh (8) *al rear, rdn 2 fs out, wknd one out*....(3 to 1) 5
3541⁵ SALMON RIVER (USA) 8-10 W J Supple (1) *mid-div, rdn and wknd 2 fs out*....(25 to 1) 6
3335⁴ DANISH (Ire) 8-7 R Hughes (6) *al rear, rdn and wknd aftr 2 fs out*....(10 to 1) 7
Dist: ¾l, 2l, 2½l, sht-hd. 1m 41.50s. a 4.90s (7 Ran).
SR: 11/6/3/-/ (Niall Quinn), J S Bolger

3613 Tattersalls Breeders Stakes (Listed) (2-y-o) £73,750 6f.....(3:30)

3411* PALACEGATE JACK (Ire) 8-10 S Craine (12) *sn led, quickened 2 fs out, styd on strly, eased cl hme*....(7 to 1) 1
3493⁴ BETTER FOLLY (Ire) 8-7 B J Walsh (18) *wl plcd, strly rdn 2 fs out, kpt on one pace, not rch wnr*....(8 to 1) 2
3492⁸ NORDIC AIR (Ire) (bl) 8-10 C Roche (5) *rear, kpt on strly frm 2 fs out, nrst finish*....(10 to 1) 3
2804⁵ QUINTILIANI (Ire) 8-10 J P Murtagh (10) *rear, hmpd 2 fs out, kpt on ins last, nrst finish*....(12 to 1) 4
2603⁵ STRATHTORE DREAM (Ire) 8-7 R M Burke (13) *wl plcd, rdn 2 fs out, no extr ins last*....(25 to 1) 5
3400⁸ BLAZING HONDA (Ire) 8-10 J Weaver (16) *rear, kpt on wl fnl 2 fs, nrst finish*....(16 to 1) 6
3332⁷ CATWALKER (Ire) (bl) 8-10 R Hughes (15) *mid-div, prog 2 fs out, rdn and wknd ins last*....(12 to 1) 7
2037⁸ MOMENTS TO CARE (Ire) 8-7 P V Gilson (17) *prmnt far side, rdn 2 fs out, wknd ins last*....(12 to 1) 8
1044⁴ SOMETHING SUPER 8-10 W J Supple (14) *wl plcd, rdn 2 fs out, wknd one out*....(9 to 1) 9
3389⁵ POSENZEE (Ire) 8-7 W Newnes (4) *rear, kpt on fnl 2 fs, nrst finish*....(9 to 1) 10
3071 SMART ROSIE (Ire) 8-7 P Shanahan (9) *mid-div, rdn and kpt on one pace frm 2 fs out*....(50 to 1) 11
2618 PAPAGAYOS (Ire) 8-10 B Doyle (11) *mid-div, rdn and wknd 2 fs out*....(9 to 1) 12
COLLECTOR GENERAL (Ire) 8-10 D G O'Shea (19) *al rear*....(25 to 1) 13
2909⁸ DIAMOND FRONTIER (Ire) 8-10 K J Manning (3) *mid-div, rdn and wknd 2 fs out*....(20 to 1) 14
3273⁶ MEGLIO CHE POSSO (Ire) 8-7 J J Behan (1) *al rear*....(33 to 1) 15
3287² STAR JAZZ (Ire) 8-8¹ L Piggott (6) *trkd ldr, rdn and wknd quickly 2 fs out*....(9 to 2 fav) 16
3166³ MUSIC OF DANCE (Ire) 8-7 M Tebbutt (8) *trkd ldr, rdn 2 fs out, wknd one out*....(7 to 1) 17
2666* SOPHIE'S PET (Ire) 8-7 J F Egan (7) *wl plcd, rdn and lost pl 2 fs out*....(7 to 1) 18
3379⁶ SHIOWEN (Ire) (bl) 8-10 M J Kinane (2) *prmnt early, rdn 3 fs out, hmpd 2 out, wknd quickly*....(11 to 1) 19
Dist: 2l, 1l, ½l, 1½l, sht-hd, sht-hd, nk, 1l, hd, ½l. 1m 13.00s. a 2.50s (19 Ran).
SR: 34/23/22/20/11/13/12/8/7/ (Palacegate Corporation Ltd), J Berry

3614 DataPac Handicap (0-80 3-y-o and up) £3,805 6f.....(4:00)

3330* CISEAUX (USA) [-] 4-9-12 (8*,5ex) D J O'Donohoe (10) ....(2 to 1 fav) 1
3561⁷ OICHE MHAITH [-] (bl) 3-9-0 R Hughes (12) ....(9 to 1) 2
3027⁸ PILGRIM BAY (Ire) [-] 3-9-7 M J Kinane (1) ....(4 to 1) 3
3455³ BENE MERENTI (Ire) [-] (bl) 3-8-12 (6*) R V Skelly (8) (9 to 1) 4
3544⁵ NORDIC SAINT (Ire) [-] 4-8-11 (6*) J A Heffernan (4) (12 to 1) 5
1444⁷ COMMODITY MARKET (Ire) [-] 3-8-9 J P Murtagh (3) ....(12 to 1) 6

3075⁵ IBDA [-] 3-8-6 (6*) B J Walsh (9) ......(8 to 1) 7
1822⁸ KESS (Ire) [-] 4-7-10³ (2*) R M Burke (13) ......(25 to 1) 8
3330⁹ SOUTHERN RULE [-] (bl) 6-7-6¹ (2*) D G O'Shea (14) ......(12 to 1) 9
3330⁷ CLONALEENAN [-] 4-7-7 Joanna Morgan (2) ......(10 to 1) 10
3296 SHEBA'S PAL [-] 6-6-13 (8*) G M Moylan (7) ......(25 to 1) 11
3027⁹ SAND OR STONE (Ire) [-] 5-9-9 A J Nolan (11) ......(25 to 1) 12
3544 OROVILLE [-] (bl) 3-9-2 S Craine (5) ......(10 to 1) 13

Dist: 1l, sht-hd, hd, 1l. 1m 13.10s. a 2.60s (13 Ran).
SR: 56/32/38/34/29/-/ (G Olivero), D K Weld

3615 Dee Handicap (0-105 3-y-o and up) £6,900 1¼m...... (4:30)

3494² TRYARRA (Ire) [-] 3-8-5 (4*,5ex) J J Behan (9) ......(6 to 1) 1
3038* MAMOURA (Ire) [-] (bl) 3-9-2 J P Murtagh (3) ......(7 to 2) 2
3202⁴ OENOTHERA (Ire) [-] 3-8-7 S Craine (8) ......(7 to 1) 3
2958⁵ ROYAL VISION (Ire) [-] 4-9-5 K J Manning (4) ......(7 to 1) 4
3075² GENERAL CHAOS (Ire) [-] 3-8-6 P V Gilson (6) ......(7 to 1) 5
3494 GALLARDINI (Ire) [-] 4-9-6 C Roche (5) ......(14 to 1) 6
2922⁵ HOLIWAY STAR (Ire) [-] 3-7-7 Joanna Morgan (1) ..(14 to 1) 7
2808* SKIPO (USA) [-] (bl) 3-9-3 M J Kinane (2) ......(2 to 1 fav) 8
3494⁹ CENTER MORICHES (Ire) [-] 3-8-2 P Braiden (7) ..(14 to 1) 9

Dist: Nk, 1½l, 2½l, 2l. 2m 2.00s. b 0.80s (9 Ran).
SR: 63/69/57/64/47/-/ (Mrs K Doyle), A P O'Brien

3616 Martinstown (E.B.F.) Maiden (3-y-o and up) £3,450 1¼m...... (5:00)

BALAWHAR (Ire) 3-9-0 M J Kinane (9) ......(13 to 8 on) 1
3025² ALBERTAZZI (Ire) 3-9-0 C Roche (7) ......(6 to 1) 2
3198² ENDSONG (USA) 3-8-11 L Piggott (1) ......(6 to 1) 3
2877⁴ TALES OF HEARSAY (Ger) 3-9-0 W J Supple (4) ...(15 to 2) 4
3299² RETURN AGAIN (Ire) 3-8-11 R Hughes (2) ......(8 to 1) 5
3497⁸ MYSTICAL CITY (Ire) 3-8-11 J F Egan (5) ......(25 to 1) 6
3198⁵ RED GLITTER (USA) 3-8-10 (4*) J J Behan (3) ......(20 to 1) 7
3382⁸ TODDY MARK (Ire) 4-9-2 (6*) C Everard (8) ......(33 to 1) 8

Dist: ½l, hd, sht-hd, ½l. 2m 4.40s. a 1.60s (8 Ran).
SR: 44/43/39/41/37/ (H H Aga Khan), John M Oxx

DEAUVILLE (FR) (good)
Saturday August 28th
Going Correction: PLUS 0.40 sec. per fur. (races 1,2), PLUS 0.25 (3)

3617 Prix Michel Houyvet (Listed) (3-y-o) £14,337 1½m 110yds...... (2:35)

TRIARIUS (USA) 9-2 T Jarnet, ... 1
RANGE RIDER (Ire) 9-2 F Sanchez, ... 2
2208⁴ HURTEVENT (Fr) 9-2 D Boeuf, ... 3
DIACO (USA) 9-2 C Asmussen, ... 4

Dist: ¾l, 1l, 2½l, 2l, ¾l, ½l, 1½l, 5l. 2m 46.70s. a 10.20s (9 Ran).
SR: 50/48/46/41/

3618 Prix Quincey (Group 3) (3-y-o and up) £23,895 1m...... (3:05)

3285* BON POINT 3-8-8 T Jarnet (5) *trkd ldr, led und 2 fs out to one out, rallied fnl 100 yards to ld on line.* (11 to 10 fav) 1
2081⁷ SHARMAN (USA) 3-8-12 S Guillot (4) *mid-div, rdn 2 fs out, led 110 yards out till fnl strds* ......(178 to 10) 2
3468³ EN ATTENDANT (Fr) 5-8-13 E Saint-Martin (7) *hld up in rear, rdn 2 fs out, fnshd wl* ......(201 to 10) 3
3337² FASTNESS (Ire) 3-8-8 F Head (10) *pld hrd in rear, swtchd outsd 2 fs out, led one out till fnl 110 yards, one pace.* ......(47 to 10) 4
2981⁵ BALLINAMALLARD (USA) 4-8-10 O Peslier (3) *prmnt, rdn and kpt on one pace 2 fs out* ......(68 to 10) 5
2803* ASTAIR (Fr) 3-8-12 G Mosse (9) *hld up in last, rdn 2 fs out, nrst finish* ......(93 to 10) 6
1364 KHORAZ (USA) 3-8-8 Jacqueline Freda (8) *pld hrd rear, swtchd to outsd 2 fs out, kpt on one pace* ......(44 to 1) 7
2055⁶ TRESOR DU MESNIL (Fr) 3-8-8 F Sanchez (2) *prmnt till rdn and wknd 2 fs out* ......(43 to 1) 8
2803⁸ CAESOUR (USA) 3-8-8 C Asmussen (1) *prmnt till rdn and wknd 2 fs out* ......(94 to 10) 9
2650³ PROSPECTIVE RULER (USA) (bl) 5-9-4 G Guignard (11) *led till rdn and hdd jst und 2 fs out* ......(36 to 1) 0
HYLANDRA (USA) 4-8-10 O Doleuze (12) *mid-div till wknd 2 fs out* ......(54 to 1) 0
3285² SANDCREEK (Ire) 3-8-8 D Boeuf (6) *prmnt till rdn and wknd 2 fs out* ......(8 to 1) 0

Dist: Nk, sht-nk, nose, ½l, sht-nk, 1l, 1½l, ½l, ¾l. 1m 40.20s. a 5.20s (12 Ran).
SR: 64/67/67/61/61/62/55/50/48/ (K Abdulla), A Fabre

3619 Prix du Cercle (Listed) (3-y-o and up) £14,337 5f...... (4:05)

431³ KASHANI (USA) 3-8-9 T Jarnet, ... 1
1086⁶ TENGA (USA) 3-8-6 C Asmussen, ... 2
MYZA (USA) 3-8-6 S Guillot, ... 3
MOT DE FRANCE (Fr) 5-8-11 A Badel, ... 4
2488⁶ DREAM TALK (bl) 6-8-11 D Boeuf, ... 5

Dist: Hd, ½l, sht-nk, 1l, ½l, dd-ht, 1½l, 2l, hd. 58.60s. a 2.60s (13 Ran).
SR: 68/64/62/66/-/- (K Abdulla), A Fabre

GOODWOOD (good to firm (races 1,4), good (2,3,5,6,7))
Saturday August 28th
Going Correction: MINUS 0.25 sec. per fur.

3620 Sport On 5 March Stakes Class A (Listed Race) (3-y-o) £9,894 1¾m... (2:00)

3318⁴ SHAIBA (USA) 8-11 M Roberts (3) *pld hrd, trkd ldr, led 2 fs out, rdn out* ......(11 to 2 op 4 to 1 tchd 6 to 1) 1
3217² AZILIAN (Ire) (v) 8-11 Pat Eddery (4) *hld up in 3rd pl, outpcd 4 fs out, styd on frm 2 out to go second ins last.* ......(15 to 8 fav op 6 to 4 tchd 2 to 1) 2
2314* URGENT REQUEST (Ire) 8-11 D Holland (2) *led, quickened 4 fs out, hdd 2 out, rdn and one pace ins last.* ......(2 to 1 op 6 to 4 tchd 9 to 4) 3
3012* TOCHAR BAN (USA) 8-6 W Carson (1) *al last, outpcd 4 fs out, nvr on terms aftr* ......(7 to 2 op 5 to 1) 4

Dist: ¾l, 2½l, 7l. 3m 1.86s. a 4.56s (4 Ran).
SR: 16/14/9/-/ (Sheikh Ahmed Al Maktoum), M R Stoute

3621 Ladbroke Racing Sprint Handicap Class C (0-95 3-y-o and up) £14,655 6f ...... (2:30)

3404³ MARGARET'S GIFT [87] 3-9-6 D Holland (8) *in tch, hrd rdn o'r one furlong out, ran on wl to ld nr finish.* ......(12 to 1 op 10 to 1 tchd 14 to 1) 1
3504³ MASTER PLANNER [90] 4-9-6 (7*) J D Smith (13) *al prmnt, led o'r one furlong out, ran on, ct nr finish.* ......(10 to 1 tchd 11 to 1) 2
3504² SAMSOLOM [81] 5-9-4 J Quinn (2) *hld up stands side, rdn o'r one furlong out, ran on wl fnl stages.* ......(7 to 1 op 6 to 1) 3
3313⁷ FASCINATION WALTZ [76] 6-8-8 (5*) A Procter (12) *mid-div, hdwy wl o'r one furlong out, ran on strly cl hme.* ......(20 to 1 op 14 to 1 tchd 25 to 1) 4
3468⁶ VENTURE CAPITALIST [91] 4-10-0 Pat Eddery (11) *slwly into strd, hdwy 2 fs out, ran on ins last, no imprsn cl hme* ......(8 to 1 tchd 9 to 1) 5
2987 MASNUN (USA) [72] 8-8-9 D Biggs (17) *chsd ldrs, ev ch entering fnl furlong, one pace* ...(14 to 1 tchd 16 to 1) 6
3410² FOLLOWMEGIRLS [58] 4-7-9 S Dawson (16) *rcd far side, hdwy o'r one furlong out, kpt on one pace ins last.* ......(20 to 1 op 16 to 1 tchd 25 to 1) 7
3404* HOW'S YER FATHER [85] 7-9-1 (7*) S Drowne (6) *nvr far away, rdn o'r one furlong out, no extr ins last.* ......(5 to 1 fav op 6 to 1 tchd 13 to 2) 8
3313⁹ DARK EYED LADY (Ire) [79] 3-8-12 T Quinn (4) *led till rdn and hdd o'r one furlong out, wknd ins last.* ......(16 to 1 op 14 to 1 tchd 20 to 1) 9
3348 PADDY CHALK [86] 7-9-9 J Reid (7) *mid-div, kpt on ins fnl furlong, nvr dngrs* ......(12 to 1 op 14 to 1) 10
3291⁴ YAKIN (USA) [84] 3-9-3 W Carson (3) *speed to hfwy.* ......(20 to 1 op 16 to 1) 11
3313⁸ CAROMISH (USA) [59] 6-7-10 N Adams (14) *speed far side, fdd o'r one furlong out* ......(33 to 1) 12
3438⁹ JOBIE [73] 3-8-6 W Woods (10) *mid-div, effrt wl o'r one furlong out, wknd ins last* ......(20 to 1 op 16 to 1) 13
3481³ BODARI [77] 4-9-0 M Roberts (9) *speed 4 fs.* ......(14 to 1 op 12 to 1 tchd 16 to 1) 14
3393* MY RUBY RING [70] 6-8-4 (3*) Stephen Davies (5) *speed 4 fs.* ......(12 to 1 op 10 to 1) 15
3105⁵ ASSIGNMENT [71] 7-8-8 A McGlone (1) *al beh.* ......(20 to 1 op 16 to 1) 16
3348⁸ AUGHFAD [80] (v) 7-9-3 W Ryan (15) *in tch early, drpd out quickly 2 fs out, tld off* ......(12 to 1 op 14 to 1) 17

Dist: Nk, nk, sht-hd, ½l, ½l, hd, 1½l, hd, nk, 1l. 1m 11.11s. a 0.71s (17 Ran).
SR: 62/68/58/52/65/44/29/50/39/ (Mrs T G Holdcroft), J Berry

3622 Tripleprint Celebration Mile Class A (Group 2) (3-y-o and up) £36,223 1m ...... (3:10)

3315³ SWING LOW 4-9-3 J Reid (5) *hld up in last pl, rdn 2 fs out, str run on outsd to ld nr finish.* ......(10 to 1 op 12 to 1 tchd 14 to 1) 1
2803⁴ MISTLE CAT (USA) 3-8-8 W Woods (2) *set steady pace, jnd 2 fs out, rdn and kpt on, hdd nr finish.* ......(11 to 2 op 8 to 1 tchd 5 to 1) 2
2803² EMPEROR JONES (USA) 3-8-8 Pat Eddery (1) *trkd ldr, dsptd ld frm 2 fs out till cl hme* ....(4 to 1 tchd 9 to 2) 3
3315* INCHINOR 3-8-8 T Quinn (3) *trkd ldrs, rdn and ev ch appr fnl furlong, one pace ins.* ......(13 to 8 fav op 6 to 4 tchd 7 to 4) 4
3315⁴ GABR 3-8-8 W Carson (4) *hld up, hdwy o'r 2 fs out, ev ch entering last, not much room and wknd wl ins.* ......(11 to 1 op 10 to 1 tchd 12 to 1) 5
2853² HALF TERM (USA) 3-8-8 M Roberts (6) *pld hrd, rdn 2 fs out, short of room appr last, no extr.* (9 to 2 op 3 to 1) 6

Dist: ½l, shrt-hd, nk, 1½l, nk. 1m 38.94s. a 1.74s (6 Ran).
SR: 47/36/35/34/29/28/ (Roldvale Limited), R Hannon

3623 Richmond-Brissac Trophy Handicap Class E Gentleman Amateur Riders (0-90 3-y-o and up) £3,687 1m 1f (3:40)

2884[9] TALENT (USA) [84] (v) 5-11-9 Mr L A Urbano (9) *sn led, rdn clr o'r 2 fs out, easily*............ (6 to 1 tchd 15 to 2) 1
3257* DANCING BEAU (Ire) [54] 4-9-7 Mr T Cuff (7) *slwly away, hdwy 3 fs out, short of room on ins 2 out, kpt on, no ch wth wnr*.......................... (10 to 1 op 7 to 1) 2
3509[3] CREDIT SQUEEZE [74] 3-10-6 Mr G Johnson Houghton (4) *beh, hdwy o'r 2 fs out, ran on, nvr nrr.* ....(8 to 1 op 6 to 1 tchd 9 to 1) 3
3509[2] GILDERDALE [75] 11-11-0 Mr C Vigors (8) *mid-div, hdwy o'r 3 fs out, sn rdn, kpt on one pace.* .... (100 to 30 fav op 3 to 1 tchd 7 to 2) 4
1785 GLEN ECHO (Ire) [81] 3-10-13 Mr J Durkan (6) *rear, some hdwy ins fnl 2 fs*.................. (8 to 1 tchd 9 to 1) 5
3269[9] AKKAZAO (Ire) [70] 5-10-9 Mr K Santana (3) *in tch, rdn 3 fs out, sn btn*............. (6 to 1 op 5 to 1 tchd 7 to 1) 6
3258* BATTLE COLOURS (Ire) [85] 4-11-10 Mr S Swiers (5) *chsd ldrs, no ch fnl 3 fs*..... (9 to 1 op 7 to 1 tchd 10 to 1) 7
3408* JAHANGIR (Ire) [69] 4-10-8 Mr F Grasso Caprioli (1) *broke wl, chsd wnr to 3 fs out, wknd quickly.* ....(6 to 1 op 4 to 1 tchd 13 to 2) 8
2873[8] WALKING THE PLANK [72] (v) 4-10-11 Mr P Macewan (2) *al beh*.............. (14 to 1 op 12 to 1) 9

Dist: 5l, 1l, sht-hd, 3l, 6l, ¾l, 1l, 1½l. 1m 55.85s. a 3.85s (9 Ran).
SR: 46/6/17/24/17/1/14/-/-/ (The Queen), Lord Huntingdon

3624 Chichester Observer Rated Class B Handicap (0-100 3-y-o and up) £6,419 7f............................. (4:15)

3350[9] YOUNG ERN [91] 3-8-11 T Quinn (8) *trkd ldr, led o'r 2 fs out, kpt up to work, ran on wl.* .... (15 to 2 op 10 to 1 tchd 11 to 1) 1
2757[8] NOBLE PET [82] 4-8-7 W Ryan (7) *trkd ldrs, hrd rdn appr fnl furlong, ran on ins last*....... (16 to 1 op 14 to 1) 2
3315 SON PARDO [100] 3-9-6 M Roberts (9) *led till o'r 2 fs out, rdn and kpt on one pace.* .... (16 to 1 op 14 to 1 tchd 20 to 1) 3
3471* CORALS DREAM (Ire) [84] 4-8-9 W Woods (6) *rear, hdwy o'r 2 fs out, ran on*..... (15 to 2 op 7 to 1 tchd 8 to 1) 4
2361[3] TYCHONIC [84] 3-8-4 Pat Eddery (3) *hld up, effrt on ins 2 fs out, hrd rdn and wknd inside last.* ....(15 to 8 fav op 9 to 4 tchd 5 to 2) 5
3350[2] KAYVEE [96] 4-9-7 W Carson (1) *al rear, rdn 2 fs out, nvr nr to chal*.............. (9 to 2 op 4 to 1 tchd 5 to 1) 6
2926 FAIRY STORY (Ire) [82] 3-8-2 D Holland (5) *chsd ldrs, rdn and wknd 2 fs out*................(10 to 1 op 14 to 1) 7
3350[3] NO RESERVATIONS (Ire) [87] 3-8-7 J Reid (4) *in tch till wknd 2 fs out, eased*....(9 to 1 op 7 to 1 tchd 10 to 1) 8
3350[4] SUNDAY'S HILL [91] (bl) 4-9-2 J Quinn (2) *al beh, tld off fnl 2 fs*.................................(9 to 1 op 8 to 1) 9

Dist: 2l, 1l, ½l, 1l, 3½l, 4l, 10l, 1½l. 1m 24.72s. a 0.12s (9 Ran).
SR: 69/59/69/56/48/54/23/-/2/ (M F Kentish), S Dow

3625 EBF Solent Maiden Fillies' Stakes Class D (2-y-o) £5,127 7f........ (4:45)

ZAMA (USA) 8-11 Pat Eddery (11) *made all, rdn entering fnl furlong, jst hld on.* .... (7 to 4 fav op 6 to 4 tchd 5 to 4 and 15 to 8) 1
WIND IN HER HAIR (Ire) 8-11 D Holland (10) *in tch, swtchd lft o'r 2 fs out, hrd rdn and ran on ins last, jst fld.* ....(8 to 1 op 6 to 1 tchd 9 to 1) 2
LUANA 8-11 M Roberts (1) *slwly into strd, sn prmnt on outsd, ev ch appr fnl furlong, eased whn hld, prmsg.* .... (10 to 1 op 8 to 1 tchd 12 to 1) 3
2542[3] SOOLAIMON (Ire) 8-11 J Reid (7) *in tch till one pace fnl 2 fs*..................... (9 to 1 op 8 to 1 tchd 10 to 1) 4
3209[7] BE EXCITING (Ire) 8-11 W Carson (6) *mid-div, rdn 2 fs out, kpt on one pace*......(10 to 1 op 12 to 1 tchd 20 to 1) 5
STATE CRYSTAL (Ire) 8-11 W Ryan (8) *trkd wnr till wknd wl o'r one furlong out*............ (3 to 1 tchd 7 to 2) 6
2250[8] LIMOSA 8-11 J Quinn (2) *slwly away, effrt o'r 2 fs out, nvr dngrs*................(33 to 1 op 20 to 1 tchd 50 to 1) 7
BEWAILS (Ire) 8-11 A McGlone (3) *mid-div, rdn 2 fs out, no hdwy*................(20 to 1 op 14 to 1 tchd 25 to 1) 8
REGAL PURSUIT (Ire) 8-11 W Woods (4) *prmnt till wknd sn aftr hfwy*......................... (50 to 1 op 20 to 1) 9
1660[4] GIFT BOX (Ire) 8-7[1] (5*) A Procter (5) *mid-div, lost tch o'r 2 fs out*................(10 to 1 op 8 to 1 tchd 11 to 1) 10
3317 BELLA RAGAZZA 8-4 (7*) Mark Denaro (9) *al beh, tld off.* .... (20 to 1 op 14 to 1 tchd 25 to 1) 11

Dist: Sht-hd, 3½l, 1½l, ½l, 3½l, 4l, 4l, 4l, sht-hd, 12l. 1m 27.62s. a 3.02s (11 Ran).
SR: 25/24/13/8/6/-/ (Sheikh Mohammed), J H M Gosden

3626 Pilley Green Nursery Handicap Class D (2-y-o) £3,525 6f.............. (5:15)

3345* NORISKI'MARINGER [61] 8-8 Pat Eddery (2) *made all, hrd rdn entering fnl furlong, hld on gmely.* ....(7 to 4 fav op 5 to 4) 1
3508[5] STRAPPED [53] 8-0 N Adams (4) *in rear, hdwy hfwy, swtchd lft o'r one furlong out, ran on und pres, jst fld.* .... (11 to 2 op 6 to 1 tchd 5 to 1) 2
841[3] THATCHERELLA [74] 9-7 D Biggs (5) *chsd ldrs, rdn to press wnr entering fnl furlong, wknd ins.* ....(7 to 2 op 3 to 1 tchd 4 to 1) 3
3166[2] RAJMAPATA [72] 8-12 (7*) Mark Denaro (3) *chsd ldr till wl o'r one furlong out, short of room and outpcd ins last.* ....(3 to 1 op 5 to 2) 4
3082[6] SON OF HADEER [49] 7-10 J Quinn (1) *slwly away, outpcd ins fnl 2 fs*........................(6 to 1 tchd 5 to 1) 5

Dist: Sht-hd, 3l, nk, 8l. 1m 13.38s. a 2.98s (5 Ran).
SR: 4/-/4/1/-/ (Roldvale Limited), G Lewis

NEWCASTLE (good to firm)
Saturday August 28th

Going Correction: MINUS 0.10 sec. per fur. (races 1,2,3), MINUS 0.35 (4,5,6)

3627 Newgate Maiden Fillies' Stakes Class D (2-y-o) £3,816 7f.............. (2:15)

3352[2] HAWAJISS 8-11 B Raymond (6) *nvr far away, improved to ld o'r 2 fs out, shaken up whn chlgd ins last, ran on wl.* .... (6 to 4 on op 2 to 1 on tchd 11 to 10 on) 1
3186[3] MUMTAZ FLYPAST 8-11 K Darley (2) *tucked away beh ldrs, not clr run hfwy, improved on inner o'r one furlong out, chlgd ins last, no extr towards finish.* .... (10 to 1 op 7 to 1) 2
3091[2] SALSKA 8-11 G Duffield (1) *nvr far away, ev ch o'r 2 fs out, outpcd over one out.* .... (12 to 1 op 10 to 1 tchd 14 to 1) 3
2785[3] I FEAR NOTHING 8-11 F Norton (11) *tucked away on ins, rdn alng o'r 2 fs out, sn outpcd, improved over one furlong out, no imprsn*............ (12 to 1 op 8 to 1) 4
CURLEW CALLING (Ire) 8-8 (3*) M Fenton (9) *trkd ldrs, pushed alng whn pace quickened 2 fs out, one pace.* .... (5 to 1 op 10 to 1 tchd 4 to 1) 5
OPUS ONE 8-11 S Webster (3) *fractious at stalls, lost prmnt pitch aftr a furlong, sn pushed alng, kpt on o'r one out, no imprsn*................ (33 to 1 op 20 to 1) 6
2603[2] DURHAM DRAPES 8-11 M Birch (10) *wth ldr, rdn alng o'r 2 fs out, sn btn*................ (25 to 1 op 20 to 1) 7
3001[8] AJNAS (Ire) 8-11 N Carlisle (5) *hld up, weaved through hfwy, ev ch o'r 2 fs out, fdd*....... (33 to 1 op 20 to 1) 8
FIVE AND UP FIVE 8-11 J Fanning (7) *co'red up beh ldrs, drvn alng hfwy, btn 2 fs out*......(33 to 1 op 16 to 1) 9
3377[5] KRISTAL DIVA 8-11 R P Elliott (4) *chsd ldrs on outer, edgd rght thrght, drvn alng 3 fs out, fdd.* .... (11 to 1 op 6 to 1 tchd 12 to 1) 10
2875[6] SHARONE 8-11 N Connorton (8) *led til hdd and wknd o'r 2 fs out*..................................... (33 to 1) 11

Dist: 1l, 5l, 2l, 2½l, hd, ½l, 2l, 1½l, ¾l, 1½l. 1m 27.77s. a 3.77s (11 Ran).
SR: 30/27/12/6/-/-/ (Maktoum Al Maktoum), M R Stoute

3628 Gallowgate Apprentice Claiming Stakes Class G (3-y-o and up) £2,406 6f........................... (2:50)

3365[6] OBSIDIAN GREY 6-8-13 D McCabe (2) *al wl plcd, drw level o'r one furlong out, led ins last, rdn and ran on well.* ....(6 to 1 tchd 11 to 2) 1
2711[5] MARCHMAIN 3-8-2 (3*) P Roberts (10) *nvr far away, improved to ld o'r 2 fs out, hng lft and jnd over one out, hdd ins last, no extr*...........(7 to 2 fav tchd 4 to 1) 2
3213[5] RUPERT COURT 3-7-10 (7*) Kimberley Hart (11) *in tch, shaken up fnl 2 fs, not quicken final furlong.* .... (25 to 1 op 20 to 1) 3
3237[6] MISSED THE BOAT (Ire) 3-8-3 V Halliday (5) *chsd ldrs, sn pushed alng, outpcd and drvn o'r 2 fs out kpt on ins last, no dngr*......................(12 to 1 op 10 to 1) 4
3184[8] LARN FORT (v) 3-8-9 P McCabe (6) *in tch, drvn alng hfwy, not quicken o'r one furlong out*... (12 to 1 op 10 to 1) 5
3216[9] SYKE LANE 4-8-1[4] (3*) G Parkin (3) *chsd ldrs, effrt and pushed alng 2 fs out, kpt on same pace*.......(25 to 1) 6
3504 DRUM SERGEANT (bl) 6-9-4 (5*) S Copp (13) *hld up, effrt on inner o'r 2 fs out, one pace over one out.* ....(4 to 1 op 7 to 2 tchd 9 to 2) 7
3376[2] RAIN SPLASH 3-8-8 Claire Balding (7) *dwlt, beh, shaken up to improve hfwy, no imprsn o'r one furlong out.* ....(4 to 1) 8
91 PREMIER ENVELOPE (Ire) 4-8-9 J Marshall (4) *led til hdd o'r 2 fs out, rdn and sn btn*........... (50 to 1 op 33 to 1) 9
3409 ARABAT (v) 6-9-9 N Varley (8) *baulked leaving stalls, beh and sn outpcd, drvn frm hfwy, nvr able to chal.* ....(10 to 1 op 8 to 1) 10
3311 FREDDIE JACK 3-8-7 M Humphries (9) *sn pushed alng beh ldrs, drvn along hfwy, soon btn*... (40 to 1 op 33 to 1) 11
3506 PINK CITY (v) 3-8-0 (7*) J Edmunds (1) *beh on outer, pushed alng, struggling frm hfwy*............(50 to 1) 12
3005[7] RICHER SPIRIT 4-8-1 (5*) D Thomas (12) *in tch stands side, rdn alng appr hfwy, grad wknd*...(33 to 1 op 25 to 1) 13

Dist: 1l, 3½l, 3l, hd, nk, 1l, ¾l, 1½l, 2l, 2l. 1m 14.50s. a 2.50s (13 Ran).
SR: 37/25/9/-/2/-/11/-/-/ (Miss L C Siddall), Miss L C Siddall

3629 Armada Nursery Class C (2-y-o) £7,245 5f. .... (3:25)

3254² SMART PET [71] 8-12 N Connorton (6) *trkd ldrs, not clr run hfwy, swtchd ins and ran on to ld a furlong out, sn clear*..........(3 to 1 fav op 11 to 4 tchd 100 to 30) 1
3279* LADY SHERIFF [75] 9-2 T Lucas (8) *nvr far away, rdn and hng lft hfwy, kpt on same pace ins fnl furlong.* .... (13 to 2 op 5 to 1) 2
3441⁷ NO MEAN CITY (Ire) [67] 8-8 L Charnock (7) *chsd ldrs, rdn hfwy, hng lft frm 2 fs out, hdd one out, no extr ins last.* .... (12 to 1 op 10 to 1) 3
3520 RAFFERTY'S RULES (Ire) [80] 9-0 (7*) D Thomas (1) *settled on outer, improved on bit o'r one furlong out, shaken up and no imprsn whn slightly hmpd ins last.* ....(4 to 1 op 9 to 2 tchd 7 to 2) 4
3441⁴ CHEEKY CHAPPY [61] (bl) 8-2 G Duffield (5) *hmpd strt, sn outpcd and beh, improved o'r one furlong out, nrst finish*...........................(10 to 1 op 8 to 1) 5
3284* IVA'S FLYER (Ire) [72] 8-13 K Darley (4) *cl up, chlgd 2 fs out, sn pushed alng, one pace appr last.* (7 to 2 op 3 to 1) 6
3441³ ARTA [65] 8-6 N Carlisle (2) *led til hdd 2 fs out, sn btn.* .... (12 to 1 op 10 to 1) 7
2199⁶ WARTHILL WHISPERS [54] 7-9 J Lowe (3) *chsd ldrs, pushed alng hfwy, btn wl o'r one furlong out.* .... (11 to 1 op 10 to 1 tchd 12 to 1) 8

Dist: 3½l, nk, 1l, 4l, 1½l, 3½l, 2l. 1m 0.97s. a 2.07s (8 Ran).
SR: 47/37/28/37/2/7/-/-/ (Mrs George Ward), Miss S E Hall

3630 Thomas Lonsdale Gallagher Handicap Class D (0-75 3-y-o and up) £3,915 1¼m 32yds. .... (4:00)

3113³ ATHERTON GREEN (Ire) [64] 3-9-3 M Birch (9) *hld up, took clr order hfwy, rdn to chal o'r one furlong out, led and edgd lft ins last, ran on gmely.* .... (6 to 1 op 11 to 2 tchd 13 to 2) 1
3444⁷ FLASHMAN [50] (bl) 3-8-3 N Carlisle (2) *led one furlong, styd hndy, rgned ld and jnd o'r 2 out, hdd ins last, kpt on same pace*..................... (20 to 1 op 16 to 1) 2
2591⁶ SHARQUIN [37] 6-7-12 J Lowe (4) *pressed ldrs, chlgd o'r 2 fs out, rdn and no extr ins fnl furlong.* .... (10 to 1 op 12 to 1) 3
3256* EFIZIA [71] 3-9-10 K Darley (1) *settled on ins, effrt and rdn 2 fs out, one pace inside fnl furlong.* ....(4 to 1 tchd 9 to 2) 4
3444* DOCTOR ROY [47] 5-8-3 (5*) D Wright (8) *mid-div, lost pl appr strt, rdn o'r 2 fs out, kpt on ins last, no imprsn.* .... (5 to 2 fav op 3 to 1 tchd 100 to 30) 5
3408⁵ HAND ON HEART (Ire) [44] (v) 4-8-2 (3*) S Maloney (5) *dwlt, hld up, rdn to improve entering strt, not quicken fnl 2 fs*...................................(10 to 1 op 8 to 1) 6
3308⁸ GOLDEN TORQUE [60] 6-9-0 (7*) H Bastiman (10) *drpd out strt, hld up, shaken up to improve fnl 2 fs, nvr nr to chal*.........(11 to 1 op 8 to 1 tchd 12 to 1) 7
3439³ PERSIAN CHARMER (Ire) [70] 3-9-9 B Raymond (3) *settled rear, niggled alng appr strt, rdn 3 fs out, no imprsn.* ....(8 to 1) 8
3408 SILVER STANDARD [51] (v) 3-8-4 G Duffield (7) *wth ldr, led aftr one furlong, hdd o'r 2 out, wknd over one out.* .... (11 to 1 op 10 to 1) 9
OUR JOEY [32] 4-7-7 J Fanning (6) *chsd ldg pair till rdn and wknd entering strt, tld off*.... (50 to 1 op 33 to 1) 10

Dist: 1½l, nk, 2½l, 1½l, nk, 2l, 2½l, 3½l, 20l. 2m 8.70s. a 2.20s (10 Ran).
SR: 45/28/22/43/24/20/32/29/3/ (Atherton And Green), J A Glover

3631 Westgate Maiden Handicap Class E (0-70 3-y-o and up) £3,262 1m... (4:30)

3375⁵ COUREUR [44] 4-9-1 G Duffield (7) *beh, plenty to do o'r 2 fs out, not clr run and swtchd wl over one out, not much room, str run ins last to ld post.* ....(14 to 1 tchd 16 to 1) 1
3523⁴ PREMIER STAR [55] (bl) 3-9-3 (3*) M Fenton (2) *dwlt, beh, rdn to improve entering strt, ran on wl to ld ins fnl furlong, ct post*.......................(5 to 1 op 4 to 1) 2
2099⁸ SHAMGAAN (USA) [58] 3-9-9 B Raymond (6) *settled beh ldrs, shaken up o'r 2 fs out, chlgd ins last, one pace.* .... (12 to 1 op 10 to 1) 3
3374 DANCES WITH GOLD [33] 3-7-12 F Norton (5) *nvr far away, improved to ld briefly ins fnl furlong, one pace.* .... (16 to 1 op 14 to 1) 4
2388⁴ CLAIRIFICATION (Ire) [46] 3-8-11 J Fanning (17) *mid-div, effrt and rdn 3 fs out, one pace fnl furlong.* ....(9 to 2 fav op 7 to 1 tchd 4 to 1) 5
2978⁸ FORT VALLY [54] 3-8-12 (7*) G Parkin (15) *hld up, improved on outer 2 fs out, styd on finish*... (20 to 1 op 16 to 1) 6
3249² LETTERMORE [37] 3-8-2 J Lowe (14) *hld up, improved fnl 2 fs, edgd lft, kpt on same pace towards finish.* ....(9 to 1 op 8 to 1) 7
3408⁶ PINKERTON'S SILVER [44] (bl) 3-8-9 M Birch (4) *nvr far away, effrt and ev ch appr last, sn one pace.* .... (10 to 1 op 8 to 1) 8
2953⁴ FLASHELLA (Ire) [54] (v) 3-9-2 (3*) O Pears (12) *beh, pushed alng 3 fs out, swtchd outsd o'r one out, no imprsn.* .... (20 to 1 op 14 to 1) 9
3469⁵ BEND SABLE (Ire) [59] 3-9-7 (3*) S Maloney (3) *tucked away on ins, effrt and rdn o'r 2 fs out, not quicken over one out*.............................. (16 to 1 op 14 to 1) 10
3308 DOUBLE THE STAKES (USA) [25] (bl) 4-7-10 L Charnock (8) *al prmnt, led o'r 2 fs out, edgd lft, hdd ins last, sn wknd*..................................(25 to 1 op 20 to 1) 11
3461 SWEET DISORDER (Ire) [55] (bl) 3-9-6 N Carlisle (18) *mid-div, pushed alng 3 fs, one pace whn hmpd wl o'r one out*.................................. (16 to 1 op 10 to 1) 12
3461⁶ MAGNETIC POINT (USA) [46] 4-8-12 (5*) J Tate (11) *in tch, improve to fltter o'r one furlong out, sn btn.* .... (12 to 1 op 10 to 1) 13
3311⁵ BREAKING HEARTS (Ire) [44] 3-8-4 (5*) J Marshall (10) *beh, nvr on terms*.......................(33 to 1 op 25 to 1) 14
3374⁵ HOD-MOD (Ire) [39] 3-8-4¹ N Connorton (16) *hld up, shaken up on ins entering strt, nvr able to chal.* .... (20 to 1 op 16 to 1) 15
3139⁷ CANNY LAD [45] (bl) 3-8-5 (5*) D McCabe (1) *led til rdn and hdd o'r 2 fs out, sn btn.* ....(16 to 1 op 14 to 1 tchd 20 to 1) 16
3447 TWO LUMPS [56] (v) 3-9-7 K Darley (9) *nvr far away, drvn alng entering strt, wknd 2 fs out*....(10 to 1 op 8 to 1) 17
3320 NISHARA [22] (v) 5-7-3¹ (5*) D Wright (13) *beh, rdn appr strt, sn struggling, tld off*.............................(50 to 1) 18

Dist: Sht-hd, 2½l, ½l, 1l, ½l, sht-hd, 1½l, 1½l, ¾l, sht-hd. 1m 41.59s. a 2.59s (18 Ran).
SR: 20/24/19/-/2/8/ (Robert Gibbons), J D Bethell

3632 Wide Open Handicap Class D (0-80 3-y-o) £4,012 1m............... (5:00)

3503 HARPOON LOUIE (USA) [69] 9-7 K Darley (2) *nvr far away, jnd issue 2 fs out, led one out, ran on wl, cmftbly.* ....(11 to 10 fav op 6 to 4) 1
3054³ SCOFFERA [61] 8-13 Kim Tinkler (3) *led, jnd 2 fs out, hdd one out, no extr ins last.* (4 to 1 op 3 to 1 tchd 9 to 2) 2
3408⁹ HOT OFF THE PRESS [46] 7-7 (5*) D Wright (6) *hld up in tch, took clr order aftr 3 fs, rdn 2 out, kpt on same pace ins last*..(7 to 2 op 11 to 4) 3
2365⁴ MELODYS DAUGHTER [48] 8-0 F Norton (4) *took keen hold, chsd ldrs, rdn alng o'r 2 fs out, sn btn.* .... (10 to 1 op 8 to 1) 4
3440⁴ GOLD DESIRE [42] 7-8 J Lowe (1) *rcd freely, trkd ldrs, rdn 3 fs out, fdd*............................(6 to 1 op 5 to 1) 5

Dist: 1½l, hd, 5l, 3½l. 1m 43.87s. a 4.87s (5 Ran).
(P D Savill), M H Easterby

NEWMARKET (JULY) (good)
Saturday August 28th
Going Correction: MINUS 0.25 sec. per fur.

3633 Park Lodge Maiden Stakes Class D (2-y-o) £4,077 6f. .... (2:10)

WATANI (USA) 9-0 R Hills (8) *ldg grp, led wl o'r one out, quickened clr ins fnl furlong.* ....(100 to 30 op 5 to 2 tchd 9 to 4 and 7 to 2) 1
3120⁴ HIGH HOLME (v) 9-0 N Day (10) *led, sn clr, hdd wl o'r one furlong out, kpt on same pace*.....(33 to 1 op 20 to 1) 2
2472² IN LIKE FLYNN 9-0 M Hills (16) *wl plcd, ev ch 2 out, rdn and not quicken appr fnl furlong.* .... (13 to 2 op 4 to 1 tchd 7 to 1) 3
TORTUGA (USA) 9-0 J Carroll (5) *hdwy o'r 2 fs out, styd on ins fnl furlong, not rch wnr*........ (14 to 1 op 6 to 1) 4
TATAMI (USA) 9-0 R Cochrane (9) *slwly into strd, rdn and towards rear til ran on frm 2 fs out.* .... (8 to 1 op 4 to 1 tchd 10 to 1) 5
STORM NYMPH (USA) 8-9 W R Swinburn (3) *trkd ldrs, hng badly lft entering last 2 fs, eased whn btn fnl furlong.* ....(7 to 4 fav op 2 to 1 tchd 5 to 2) 6
SALT LAKE 9-0 P Robinson (2) *speed for 4 fs*..... (12 to 1) 7
SPARKLING LYRIC 8-4 (5*) K Rutter (1) *in tch, rdn and no prog frm 2 fs out*.... (33 to 1 op 25 to 1 tchd 50 to 1) 8
2571⁸ TANBIH 9-0 J Williams (12) *al towards rear.* .... (25 to 1 op 14 to 1 tchd 33 to 1) 9
TRUTH MOUNTAIN (Ire) 8-9 W Hood (13) *rcd in mid-div, rdn and no hdwy frm 2 fs out*.....(50 to 1 op 25 to 1) 10
BRUZ 9-0 S Perks (4) *nvr nr to chal.* .... (50 to 1 op 25 to 1 tchd 66 to 1) 11
LITTLE IBNR 9-0 M Wigham (17) *slwly into strd, al outpcd.* .... (50 to 1 op 20 to 1) 12
CHIEFTAIN'S CROWN (USA) 9-0 Paul Eddery (11) *mid-div, outpcd appr last 2 fs*.............. (14 to 1 op 8 to 1) 13
DOUBLE DIP 9-0 S Whitworth (7) *settled in mid-div, rdn hfwy, sn btn*...............................(33 to 1 op 25 to 1) 14
TRINITY HOUSE 9-0 A Munro (6) *al outpcd.* .... (20 to 1 op 12 to 1) 15
SHAMARDAL (Ire) 9-0 K Fallon (15) *dwlt, al rear grp.* .... (33 to 1 op 20 to 1 tchd 40 to 1) 16
BIX 8-11 (3*) S D Williams (14) *chsd ldr to hfwy, lost pl quickly*..........(50 to 1 op 25 to 1 tchd 66 to 1) 17

Dist: 4l, hd, 1l, 2l, hd, 2½l, ½l, 2l, 1l, 5l. 1m 12.73s. a 1.03s (17 Ran).
SR: 49/33/32/28/20/14/9/2/-/ (Hamdan Al-Maktoum), R W Armstrong

3634 Lonsdale Claiming Stakes Class E (3-y-o) £4,142 7f.................. (2:45)

2912[5] FUCHU 8-10 A Munro (10) *wl in tch, cld on ldr frm 2 out, led ins fnl furlong, rdn out*.........(7 to 1 op 11 to 2) 1
3476[6] KING PARIS (Ire) 9-4 M Hills (6) *handily plcd, led 3 fs out, hdd und pres ins last, kpt on same pace.* ....(5 to 2 fav op 3 to 1 tchd 9 to 4) 2
2864[3] PERDITION (Ire) 8-7 R Hills (9) *hld up, prog 3 fs out, not much room 2 out, swtchd lft, styd on ins fnl furlong.* .... (13 to 2 op 6 to 1 tchd 7 to 1) 3
2712[4] TRIANGLEPOINT (Ire) (bl) 8-1 P Robinson (14) *steadied leaving stalls and hld up, cld on ldrs gng easily 2 out, no extr ins fnl furlong*..............(8 to 1 op 6 to 1) 4
418[7] ARAWA 8-7 K Fallon (12) *ran on frm rear 2 fs out, styd on nr finish*.........................(66 to 1 op 50 to 1) 5
3439[5] PISTON (Ire) 8-12 W R Swinburn (13) *trkd ldrs, rdn and not quicken 2 fs out, one pace fnl furlong.* ....(8 to 1 op 6 to 1) 6
3425[5] DIGPAST (Ire) (bl) 9-1 (3*) D Harrison (7) *ldg grp, rdn and wknd frm 2 fs out*...................(5 to 1 op 9 to 2) 7
2832 DANCING DIAMOND (Ire) 7-9 Dale Gibson (2) *mid-div, rdn alng and outpcd frm hfwy.* .... (14 to 1 op 12 to 1 tchd 16 to 1) 8
1488[9] LADY RELKO 7-9 G Bardwell (4) *in tch to hfwy.* ....(33 to 1 tchd 50 to 1) 9
725[9] EXPRESS MARIECURIE (Ire) 7-11 (7*) Kim McDonnell (5) *led for 4 fs, wknd 2 out*...............(33 to 1 op 16 to 1) 10
3550[8] EASTERN CHARLY (Bel) 7-7 (7*) C Hawksley (1) *al outpcd.* ....(33 to 1 op 20 to 1) 11
3123[4] PEA FORTY FIVE 8-4 A Proud (3) *nvr nr to chal.* (33 to 1) 12
3359[8] VICTORIAS PASSION 7-12 A Mackay (8) *speed for 2 fs, sn drpd rear*............ (14 to 1 op 8 to 1 tchd 16 to 1) 13
2765[5] CIZARD (Ire) 7-7[1] (3*) N Kennedy (11) *al beh.* ....(66 to 1 op 50 to 1) 14

Dist: 1l, hd, ¾l, 1½l, 2½l, 1½l, ¾l, 2½l, 1l, ¾l. 1m 26.86s. a 2.66s (14 Ran).
SR: 30/35/23/15/16/13/14/-/-/ (C E Brittain), C E Brittain

3635 Boadicea Nursery Class C (2-y-o) £15,010 6f..................... (3:20)

3129[6] ROYAL INSIGNIA [83] 9-3 A Munro (6) *made virtually all, drvn out fnl furlong, styd on wl*.... (10 to 1 op 8 to 1) 1
3502[2] KNAYTON LASS [85] 9-0 (5*) L Newton (4) *wth wnr thrght, ev ch ins fnl furlong, not quicken nr finish.* ....(8 to 1 op 7 to 1 tchd 9 to 1) 2
3309[9] BEATS WORKING [79] 8-13 K Fallon (5) *mid-div, hdwy 2 fs out, edgd lft o'r one out, rdn and styd on cl hme.* ....(7 to 4 fav op 2 to 1 tchd 5 to 2) 3
3406[5] OBVIOUS RISK [80] 9-0 R Cochrane (3) *hld up, not clr run and snatched up wl o'r one furlong out, squeezed through ins fnl furlong, fnshd well.* .... (5 to 1 op 4 to 1 tchd 11 to 2) 4
3432[3] JIMMY THE SKUNK (Ire) [75] 8-9 J Carroll (7) *pressed ldrs, hmpd one furlong out, no extr last 100 yards.* ....(5 to 1 tchd 11 to 2) 5
3248[5] KISSININTHEBACKROW (USA) [86] 9-6 R Hills (10) *improved frm hfwy, rdn and not quicken appr fnl furlong*.............(14 to 1 tchd 16 to 1) 6
3448[3] BASKERVILLE [87] 9-7 Paul Eddery (9) *slwly into strd, nvr able to rch frnt rnk*................(8 to 1 tchd 9 to 1) 7
3406[6] LADY PHYL [72] 8-6 S Whitworth (2) *cld on ldrs hfwy, not clr run and wknd wl o'r one furlong out.* .... (6 to 1 op 5 to 1 tchd 13 to 2) 8

Dist: ½l, sht-hd, 1½l, ½l, 1½l, 3l, 3l. 1m 13.40s. a 1.70s (8 Ran).
SR: 39/39/32/27/20/25/14/-/ (Fahd Salman), M Bell

3636 Danepak Bacon Rated Class B Handicap (0-100 3-y-o and up) £9,472 1¼m ....(3:50)

3314[3] SHARJAH (USA) [88] 3-8-1 P Robinson (10) *hld up, lost pos and shaken up 3 out, ran on und pres to ld ins fnl furlong, styd on*........... (4 to 1 co-fav tchd 5 to 1) 1
3437[6] MIZAAYA [99] 4-9-6 W R Swinburn (7) *handily pl, rdn to ld wl o'r one out, hdd and not quicken ins fnl furlong.* ....(10 to 1 op 8 to 1) 2
1785[7] BLACK DRAGON (Ire) [86] 3-7-10 (3*) D Harrison (6) *pressed ldrs, led o'r 3 fs out, hdd wl over one out, kpt on.* .... (15 to 2 op 8 to 1 tchd 9 to 1) 3
2830[2] LUCKY GUEST [97] 6-9-4 M Hills (1) *hld up, prog 4 fs out, one pace ins last 2 furlongs.* ....(9 to 2 op 7 to 1 tchd 8 to 1) 4
2941[5] JACKPOT STAR [86] 3-7-13 G Bardwell (4) *towards rear, rdn alng to improve 3 fs out, styd on one pace appr fnl furlong*............(11 to 1 op 10 to 1 tchd 12 to 1) 5
1845[2] RAMBO'S HALL [100] 8-9-4 (3*) S D Williams (2) *hld up in rear, moderate prog last 2 fs, nrst finish.* ....(14 to 1 tchd 12 to 1) 6
3509* RIVER BOYNE (USA) [96] 3-8-9 Paul Eddery (5) *cld on ldrs o'r 3 out, rdn alng over 2 out, eased whn btn fnl furlong*.............(4 to 1 co-fav op 5 to 2 tchd 9 to 2) 7
2962[5] DUKE OF EUROLINK [98] 4-9-5 R Cochrane (8) *hld up towards rear, rdn and no prog fnl 2 fs*......(4 to 1 co-fav op 5 to 1 tchd 11 to 2) 8
PREVENE (Ire) [90] 3-8-3 A Munro (3) *al beh, tld off.* ....(25 to 1 op 20 to 1) 9
2254[4] HOST (Ire) [86] 4-8-7 J Carroll (9) *led til hdd o'r 3 fs out, wknd quickly, tld off*.....................(16 to 1) 10

Dist: 1l, 2l, ¾l, nk, nk, hd, 2½l, 25l, ½l. 2m 4.41s. a 2.21s (10 Ran).
SR: 40/57/32/49/29/50/37/42/-/ (Sheikh Ahmed Al Maktoum), M A Jarvis

3637 Multiyork Handicap Class C (0-95 3-y-o) £6,165 7f.................... (4:20)

3313[5] CHILI HEIGHTS [77] (v) 8-10 J Williams (4) *hld up, str brst appr fnl furlong, led last 25 yards.* ....(14 to 1 tchd 12 to 1) 1
2758 DIXIELAND MELODY (USA) [82] 9-1 R Hills (12) *hld up, hdwy o'r 2 fs out, rdn and not quicken over one out, ran on nr line*....................(20 to 1 op 16 to 1) 2
3269[7] PRAIRIE GROVE [68] 8-1 G Bardwell (7) *pressed ldrs, rdn to ld o'r one furlong out, hdd and no extr last 25 yards.* ....(10 to 1 op 8 to 1) 3
3476* KASSBAAN (USA) [87] 9-6 W R Swinburn (5) *cld on ldrs hfwy, rdn and edgd rght o'r one furlong out, styd on same pace*..........(7 to 2 fav tchd 3 to 1 and 4 to 1) 4
3017[2] FIELD OF VISION (Ire) [81] 9-0 T Williams (6) *hld up, improved o'r 2 fs out, rdn and not much room appr fnl furlong, kpt on nr finish*........... (8 to 1 op 6 to 1) 5
3101[5] ROYAL ROLLER (Ire) [76] 8-2 (7*) G Forster (8) *led, wndrd rght o'r 2 fs out, hdd over one out, no extr.* ....(10 to 1 op 14 to 1) 6
2928 SIMPLY FINESSE [78] 8-11 A Munro (11) *cl up til rdn and lost pl o'r one furlong out.* .... (15 to 2 op 6 to 1 tchd 8 to 1) 7
3385[7] SHIRO [88] 9-7 Paul Eddery (13) *slwly into strd, beh til styd on appr fnl furlong, nvr nrr.* (20 to 1 op 16 to 1) 8
3214[2] CROIRE (Ire) [76] 8-9 M Hills (1) *rcd in mid-div, effrt o'r 2 fs out, no imprsn on frnt rnk*......(10 to 1 tchd 11 to 1) 9
3474[3] THE SHARP BIDDER (Ire) [79] 8-12 S Perks (10) *handily plcd, rdn and not much room o'r one furlong out, no extr*.......................(20 to 1 op 16 to 1) 10
3474[5] SPARK (Ire) [79] 8-12 J Carroll (9) *chsd ldrs to hfwy.* .... (12 to 1 op 16 to 1 tchd 20 to 1) 11
3080[2] AL MOULOUKI [83] 9-2 R Cochrane (2) *steadied leaving stalls, hld up in rear, nvr on terms.* ....(6 to 1 tchd 13 to 2) 12
2491[8] BALLON [65] 7-12 Dale Gibson (3) *chsd ldrs to hfwy, wknd quickly*.....................................(33 to 1) 13

Dist: ½l, hd, 1½l, ¾l, hd, 3½l, 4l, 2l, ½l, nk. 1m 25.90s. a 1.70s (13 Ran).
SR: 44/47/32/46/38/32/23/21/3/ (B T Attenborough), G B Balding

3638 La Grange Handicap Class C (0-95 3-y-o and up) £5,427 5f......... (4:50)

3348 PRINCESS OBERON (Ire) [69] 3-8-6 M Hills (8) *led till hdd ins fnl furlong, rallied to get up ag'n last strd.* ....(20 to 1 op 16 to 1) 1
3438[4] MISTERTOPOGIGO (Ire) [86] 3-9-9 A Munro (4) *pressed ldr, rdn to ld ins fnl furlong, hdd last strd.* .... (9 to 1 op 8 to 1 tchd 10 to 1) 2
3404[9] MACS MAHARANEE [81] 6-9-7 G Hind (18) *hld up, ran on frm 2 fs out, kpt on und pres nr finish.* ....(16 to 1 tchd 20 to 1) 3
3238* GIPSY FIDDLER [87] (v) 5-9-10 (3*) S D Williams (16) *ran on frm 2 fs out, styd on und pres wl ins last*...... (16 to 1) 4
3348[3] CALL TO THE BAR (Ire) [69] 4-8-9 K Fallon (10) *hdwy frm 2 out, ran on ins fnl furlong*..........(9 to 1 op 7 to 1) 5
3593[3] PEERAGE PRINCE [67] (bl) 4-8-4 (3*) N Kennedy (6) *trkd ldrs, rdn and not quicken o'r one furlong out, no extr clsg stages*..........................(14 to 1 tchd 16 to 1) 6
3486[4] JESS REBEC [57] 5-7-11 G Bardwell (1) *prmsg effrt hfwy, rdn and one pace fnl furlong*.................. (20 to 1) 7
3571[5] FOOD OF LOVE [80] 5-9-6 J Williams (2) *speed for o'r 3 fs.* ....(20 to 1 op 16 to 1) 8
3350 TROON [87] 3-9-3 (7*) G Milligan (12) *sn outpcd, some late prog, nvr nrr*........ (16 to 1 op 14 to 1 tchd 20 to 1) 9
3511[3] METAL BOYS [79] 6-9-0 (5*) K Rutter (17) *hdwy frm rear 2 fs out, not rch ldrs*...... (9 to 1 op 10 to 1 tchd 12 to 1) 10
3410* PALLIUM (Ire) [71] 5-8-11 A Culhane (5) *slwly into strd, nvr on terms*......................(16 to 1 tchd 20 to 1) 11
3410 PAGEBOY [60] 4-8-0 Dale Gibson (9) *chsd ldrs, rdn and no hdwy frm 2 fs out*................ (20 to 1 op 16 to 1) 12
3348* HEAVEN-LIEGH-GREY [73] 5-8-13 J Carroll (14) *speed for 3 fs*.................................. (6 to 1 fav op 7 to 1) 13
3177 FIGHTER SQUADRON [65] 4-8-5 P Robinson (13) *nvr on terms*................(16 to 1 op 14 to 1 tchd 20 to 1) 14
3481* EDUCATED PET [71] 4-8-11 R Hills (11) *al beh.* .... (11 to 1 op 12 to 1 tchd 10 to 1) 15
2813[6] EAGER DEVA [86] 6-9-5 (7*) L Aspell (7) *reared leaving stalls, nvr dngrs*..... (16 to 1 op 14 to 1 tchd 20 to 1) 16
2813[4] NED'S BONANZA [73] 4-8-13 R Cochrane (15) *shwd speed for 3 fs*..............................(10 to 1 op 12 to 1) 17
3251[3] STORMY HEIGHTS [62] (bl) 3-7-13 T Wilson (3) *in tch til rdn and btn wl o'r one furlong out*.... (20 to 1 op 16 to 1) 18

Dist: Sht-hd, 1l, nk, hd, sht-hd, 1½l, ½l, hd, nk, nk. 1m 1.36s. a 2.66s (18 Ran).
SR: 14/30/24/29/10/7/-/12/15/ (R P B Michaelson), M Bell

3639 Stanley House Maiden Stakes Class D (3-y-o and up) £3,915 1m....... (5:25)

CAMPANA (Ire) 3-8-6 J Carroll (7) *mid-div, gd hdwy 2 out, bumped and crrd rght entering fnl furlong, led last 100 yards, sn clr.*......(7 to 1 op 12 to 1 tchd 14 to 1) 1

3514[4] POCKET PIECE (USA) 3-8-6 K Fallon (12) *hld up, ran on 3 fs out, led wl o'r one out, veered badly rght entering fnl furlong, sn hdd and outpcd.* ....(7 to 4 fav op 3 to 1 tchd 7 to 2) 2

2410[4] CHUMMY'S SAGA 3-8-11 R Cochrane (3) *pressed ldrs, ev ch entering fnl furlong, outpcd last 100 yards.* ....(13 to 2 op 5 to 1 tchd 7 to 1) 3

3506[7] WORDS OF WISDOM (Ire) 3-8-11 M Wigham (1) *wl in tch til lost pl 3 fs out, ran on ag'n und pres appraoching fnl furlong, fnshd well.* (14 to 1 op 10 to 1 tchd 16 to 1) 4

3261 ERTLON 3-8-11 G Bardwell (2) *cl up, led o'r 3 fs out, hdd wl over one out, ran on one pace.* ....(13 to 2 op 5 to 1 tchd 7 to 1) 5

LABUDD (USA) 3-8-11 R Hills (11) *hld up, hdwy und pres o'r 2 fs out, not quicken fnl furlong.* ....(4 to 1 op 2 to 1 tchd 9 to 2) 6

917[6] SEA BARON 3-8-11 A Munro (8) *chsd ldrs til wknd ins fnl 2 fs.*..........(10 to 1 op 20 to 1) 7

3456 REMEMBER THIS (Ire) 3-8-11 Dale Gibson (10) *in tch, rdn alng and effrt 3 fs out, wknd last 2 furlongs.* ....(50 to 1 op 33 to 1) 8

3514[6] KEYLOCK (USA) 3-8-1 (5*) K Rutter (9) *slwly into strd, al in rear.*..........(33 to 1 op 25 to 1) 9

3506[6] FLINTLOCK (Ire) 3-8-11 G Hind (4) *in tch in mid-div for 5 fs, sn wknd.*..........(16 to 1 op 14 to 1 tchd 20 to 1) 10

2275 QUEST FOR THE BEST 4-8-12 P Robinson (5) *led for o'r 4 fs, wknd over 2 out.*..........(33 to 1 tchd 50 to 1) 11

BIDDER (Ire) 3-8-8 (3*) S D Williams (13) *towards rear and rdn alng hfwy, sn lost tch, tld off.* ....(25 to 1 op 10 to 1 tchd 33 to 1) 12

DARINGLY 4-9-3 A Culhane (6) *beh most of way, tld off.* ....(66 to 1 op 50 to 1) 13

Dist: 3l, 1l, hd, 1l, 3l, 4l, 5l, hd, 1l, 4l. 1m 40.96s. a 3.06s (13 Ran).
SR: 16/7/9/8/5/-/ (Sheikh Mohammed), J H M Gosden

SARATOGA (USA) (firm)
Saturday August 28th

3640 Whitney Handicap (Grade 1) (3-y-o and up) £99,338 1m 1f..............

BRUNSWICK (USA) 4-7-12 M Smith,..........(13 to 2) 1

2262[3] WEST BY WEST (USA) 4-8-3 J-L Samyn,..........(2 to 1) 2

2838[2] DEVIL HIS DUE (USA) 4-8-10 H McCauley,......(5 to 3 on) 3

MICHELLE CAN PASS (USA) 5-7-13 R Migliore,...(13 to 1) 4

2262[5] JACKSONPORT (USA) 4-7-9 R Rojas,..........(32 to 1) 5

1541[8] SAND LIZARD (USA) 4-8-1 J Santos,..........(8 to 1) 6

DIGNITAS (USA) 4-8-2 J D Bailey,..........(2 to 1) 7

Dist: 3½l, ¾l, 7½l, 3½l, 2l, 2 ¾l. 1m 47.10s. (7 Ran).
(J Denker), A Margotta

WINDSOR (good to firm)
Saturday August 28th
Going Correction: NIL (races 1,2), MINUS 0.15 (3,4,5,6)

3641 Bradfield Selling Stakes Class G (2-y-o) £1,968 5f 217yds..........(5:20)

2119[5] GIPSY KID 7-13 (7*) C Hawksley (2) *al prmnt rdn to ld wl ins fnl furlong, drvn out.* ....(15 to 2 op 6 to 1 tchd 8 to 1) 1

RAFTER-J 8-6 (5*) B Russell (21) *dwlt, gd prog hfwy, led o'r one furlong out till hdd wl ins last, ran on* ....(14 to 1 op 20 to 1 tchd 10 to 1) 2

3279[9] MONSIEUR PETONG 8-4 (7*) R Painter (7) *mid-div 2 fs out, ev ch ins last, ran on.* ....(5 to 1 fav op 10 to 1 tchd 12 to 1) 3

3508[8] THORNY BISHOP (bl) 8-11 S O'Gorman (4) *prmnt, hng badly lft o'r 2 fs out, ev ch ins last, not quicken nr finish.*..........(20 to 1 op 14 to 1) 4

CLASSICAL (Ire) 8-11 S Whitworth (12) *chsd ldrs, styd on one pace fnl 2 fs, nvr nrr.*..........(10 to 1 op 5 to 1) 5

3223[6] ROYAL INTERPRETER (bl) 8-11 S Raymont (5) *mid-div, styd on fnl 2 fs, nvr nrr.*..........(10 to 1 op 6 to 1) 6

3303 PINATUBO 8-11 S Dawson (13) *rear till styd on stdly frm o'r one furlong out, nvr nr to chal.* (33 to 1 op 20 to 1) 7

3091[8] SNOWDON SLIGHTS 7-13 (7*) S Mulvey (15) *mid-div hrd rdn 2 fs, kpt on one pace.* ....(14 to 1 op 8 to 1 tchd 16 to 1) 8

2786[9] CLASSICAL DON (Ire) 8-11 N Day (8) *al mid-div.* ....(14 to 1 op 12 to 1 tchd 20 to 1) 9

3189[5] BESSIE'S WILL (v) 8-6 A Mackay (6) *cl up till wknd wl o'r one furlong out.*...... (10 to 1 op 8 to 1 tchd 12 to 1) 10

3303[4] SPORT RACING CLUB (bl) 8-3 (3*) Stephen Davies (11) *prmnt till hrd rdn and wknd o'r one furlong out.* ....(14 to 1 op 10 to 1) 11

3546 KINGSCOURT JOHN-A (Ire) (bl) 8-4 (7*) D Gibbs (1) *chsd ldrs, hrd rdn and veered rght wl o'r one furlong out, wknd.*..........(20 to 1 op 10 to 1) 12

1583 WHITCHURCH SILK (Ire) 8-6 R Price (19) *led till o'r one furlong out, wknd rpdly.*..........(16 to 1 op 10 to 1) 13

3264 DREAM MISSY 8-1 (5*) N Gwilliams (20) *prmnt till wknd 2 fs out.*..........(25 to 1 op 20 to 1) 14

2946[6] DAVIDS DIAMOND 8-1[2] (7*) Sally Wall (22) *no show.* ....(25 to 1 op 20 to 1 tchd 33 to 1) 15

3345[4] ROCKABYE BAILEYS 7-13 (7*) Antoinette Armes (16) *al beh.* ....(16 to 1 op 12 to 1) 16

3508 SOUTHDOWN GIRL (v) 8-1 (5*) L Newton (9) *prmnt till wknd o'r 2 fs out.*..........(14 to 1 op 12 to 1) 17

3209 DISH OF THE DAY (Ire) 8-6 C Rutter (14) *chsd ldrs to hfwy, sn wknd.*..........(12 to 1 tchd 16 to 1) 18

2377[8] LOUGH KEY LADY (Ire) 8-6 T Sprake (18) *nvr nr ldrs.* ....(16 to 1 op 12 to 1 tchd 20 to 1) 19

DUTCH MISS 8-0[1] (7*) S Drowne (10) *missed break, al wl beh.*..........(14 to 1 op 8 to 1) 20

MASTER HAMELETTE 8-11 A Tucker (3) *strted slwly, sn rdn alng al wl beh.*..........(33 to 1 op 20 to 1) 21

Dist: Hd, ¾l, ½l, 4l, ¾l, nk, 2l, 1l, 1l, 1½l. 1m 13.40s. a 3.10s (21 Ran).
SR: 30/34/31/29/13/10/9/-/-/ (Mrs Lesley Mills), R Guest

3642 Lords Taverners Maiden Auction Stakes Class F (2-y-o) £2,721 5f 217yds ....(5:45)

STRUMPET CITY 8-9 S Raymont (9) *al prmnt, rdn to ld o'r one furlong out, ran on wl.* ....(11 to 1 op 8 to 1 tchd 12 to 1) 1

3009[5] LADY WILLIAMS (Ire) 8-6 (3*) D Harrison (14) *prog frm mid-div 2 fs out, ran on wl ins fnl furlong, not rch wnr.* ....(4 to 1 op 11 to 4 tchd 9 to 2) 2

MATHANDAN 8-6 (3*) Stephen Davies (8) *al prmnt, rdn and unbl to quicken 2 fs out, ran on ag'n ins last.* ....(33 to 1 op 20 to 1) 3

CIZARGA 8-4 (5*) L Newton (11) *chsd ldr, hrd rdn o'r 2 fs out, kpt on one pace ins last.* (7 to 2 co-fav op 6 to 1) 4

2179[2] CAPTAIN SCARLET (Ire) 9-0 S Whitworth (4) *mid-div, rdn and prog 2 fs out, styd on one pace.*........(7 to 2 co-fav op 3 to 1 tchd 4 to 1) 5

3287[9] MIDSEAS 9-0 T Sprake (16) *al chasing ldrs, rdn and one pace fnl 2 fs.* ....(20 to 1 op 14 to 1 tchd 33 to 1 and 40 to 1) 6

2836[2] WESTERN FLEET (USA) 9-0 T Quinn (15) *mid-div, hrd rdn o'r 2 fs out, no prog.* ....(7 to 2 co-fav op 3 to 1 tchd 4 to 1) 7

3079[8] SUPERLATIVECASTING 9-0 A Tucker (6) *rear, hrd rdn and styd on fnl 2 fs, nvr dngrs.*........(25 to 1 op 16 to 1) 8

GADGE 9-0 C Rutter (7) *beh, rdn hfwy, nvr nrr.* ....(20 to 1 op 14 to 1 tchd 25 to 1) 9

3215[6] LIGHTNING BELLE (bl) 8-2 (7*) J D Smith (13) *clr ldr till rdn and hdd o'r one furlong out.* ....(16 to 1 op 14 to 1 tchd 20 to 1) 10

2021[8] NORTHGATE SYMPHONY 9-0 A Mackay (2) *rdn hfwy, al mid-div.*..........(50 to 1 op 25 to 1) 11

2687[5] SCREWBALL ANACONDA 8-7 (7*) C Hawksley (5) *nvr dngrs.*..........(33 to 1) 12

1870[5] LIFE'S TOO SHORT (Ire) 8-2 (7*) A Martinez (1) *al beh.* ....(25 to 1 tchd 33 to 1) 13

POLY SCREEN 9-0 Lorna Vincent (18) *wl beh till moderate late prog.*..........(20 to 1 op 14 to 1 tchd 25 to 1) 14

AT THE SAVOY (Ire) 9-0 N Day (17) *chsd ldrs till wknd o'r one furlong out, eased whn btn.* ....(16 to 1 op 12 to 1 tchd 20 to 1) 15

ROODMAS (Ire) 8-2 (7*) Antoinette Armes (3) *strted slwly, al beh.*..........(25 to 1 op 16 to 1) 16

2866 ONLY FOOLS 9-0 R Price (12) *mid-div, wknd hfwy.* ....(50 to 1 op 33 to 1) 17

3546 ESOTERIC (Ire) 8-9 S O'Gorman (10) *al beh.* ....(50 to 1 op 33 to 1) 18

Dist: 1½l, 4l, 3l, ½l, nk, 1½l, sht-hd, sht-hd, nk, 1l. 1m 12.80s. a 2.50s (18 Ran).
SR: 45/39/23/11/14/13/7/6/5/ (Mrs M Bryce-Smith), R Charlton

3643 Frillies Fillies' Handicap Class D (0-80 3-y-o and up) £4,050 1m 67yds. . (6:10)

3290[4] MOON SPIN [79] 4-10-0 Paul Eddery (9) *trkd ldrs, led appr fnl furlong, shaken up and ran on wl.* ....(3 to 1 fav op 5 to 2) 1

3042[4] PRECIOUS AIR (Ire) [54] 5-7-12 (5*) B Russell (10) *in tch, prog and rdn o'r 2 fs out, ev ch ins last, ran on one pace.*..........(5 to 1 op 7 to 1) 2

3261[5] OARE SPARROW [67] 3-8-10 T Quinn (2) *led, rdn 3 fs out, hdd appr last, one pace.*..........(5 to 1 tchd 11 to 2) 3

2882[8] VAYAVAIG [78] 3-9-7 W R Swinburn (1) *in tch, rdn o'r 2 fs out, styd on, nvr able to chal.* ....(9 to 2 op 4 to 1 tchd 5 to 1) 4

3341[2] PRINCESS HAYLEY [67] 3-8-10 D Holland (3) *chsd ldr, rdn 3 fs out, ev ch o'r one furlong out, wknd ins last.* ....(6 to 1 op 5 to 1) 5

2832[8] SINGER ON THE ROOF [69] (v) 3-8-12 S O'Gorman (8) *wtd wth, prog and rdn o'r 2 fs out, ch appr last, no extr.* ....(9 to 1 op 8 to 1 tchd 10 to 1) 6

3057[7] KELLY'S KITE [44] 5-7-4[4] (7*) C Hawksley (4) *dwlt, prog to join ldrs 5 fs out, wknd and rdn 3 furlongs out.* ....(33 to 1 op 20 to 1) 7

OVERNIGHT SUCCESS (Ire) [64] 3-8-7 C Avery (5) *chsd ldrs, rdn and wknd 3 fs out*.......................(33 to 1) 8
2534* STARLIGHT ROSE (Ire) [56] 3-7-13 E Johnson (7) *hld up, hrd rdn o'r 3 fs out, sn wknd.* ....(17 to 2 op 7 to 1 tchd 9 to 1) 9
Dist: ¾l, 2l, ¾l, nk, nk, 5l, 8l, sht-hd. 1m 46.10s. a 5.10s (9 Ran).
SR: 19/-/-/2/-/-/ (Mrs W R Hern), Major W R Hern

3644 Winter Hill Stakes Class A (Listed Race) (3-y-o and up) £10,845 1¼m 7yds.......................... (6:40)

2962* USAIDIT 4-9-7 J Reid (4) *hld up, prog 3 fs out, hrd rdn to chal o'r one out, led ins last, ran on wl.* ....(7 to 1 op 6 to 1 tchd 8 to 1) 1
2962³ SOURCE OF LIGHT 4-9-0 Pat Eddery (1) *hld up, smooth prog 3 fs out, led wl o'r one out, hrd rdn and hdd ins last, ran on well*....(11 to 8 fav op 7 to 4 tchd 2 to 1) 2
2962² MUHAYAA (USA) 4-9-4 W R Swinburn (2) *led for 2 fs, prmnt aftr, rdn and unbl to quicken o'r two out.* ....(15 to 2 op 6 to 1 tchd 8 to 1) 3
3282³ SEEK THE PEARL 3-8-1 M Roberts (6) *rear, pushed alng o'r 4 fs out, styd on und pres appr last, nvr rch ldrs.* ....(25 to 1 op 20 to 1) 4
3337⁴ PORT LUCAYA (bl) 3-8-13 W Carson (3) *chsd ldrs, rdn and not quicken 4 fs out, btn whn hmpd o'r one out, kpt on.* ....(5 to 1 op 4 to 1 tchd 11 to 2) 5
2621³ YOUNG BUSTER (Ire) 5-9-10 M Hills (5) *prmnt, led o'r 4 fs out, rdn 3 out, hdd and wknd wl over one out.* ....(6 to 1 op 5 to 1 tchd 13 to 2) 6
2835* MACK THE KNIFE (bl) 4-9-4 Paul Eddery (7) *led aftr 2 fs till hdd o'r 4 out, wkng whn not much room over one out.* ....(6 to 1 op 5 to 1) 7
Dist: Hd, 5l, nk, 2½l, 3½l, 3l. 2m 3.90s. a 1.40s (7 Ran).
SR: 78/70/64/46/53/57/45/ (Mrs Pauline Merrick), T G Mills

3645 Stepping Stones Conditions Stakes Class D (3-y-o and up) £3,260 1m 3f 135yds....................... (7:10)

3456* DANISH FORT 3-8-7 W Ryan (1) *settled 3rd, prog to ld wl o'r 2 fs out, hrd rdn appr last, ran on strly, imprsv.* ....(100 to 30 op 9 to 2 tchd 3 to 1) 1
2793² TREMOLANDO (USA) 3-8-7 Pat Eddery (2) *hld up last, cld 3 fs out, hrd rdn to chal o'r one furlongs out, sn one pace*..........................(5 to 4 fav tchd 6 to 4) 2
3385³ VRATISLAV (USA) 4-9-1 M Roberts (3) *pushed alng to chase ldr, led briefly 3 fs out, sn rdn and btn.* ....(9 to 2 op 3 to 1 tchd 5 to 1) 3
3262⁶ BASHAYER (USA) 3-8-2 W Carson (4) *clr ldr till hdd 3 fs out, hrd rdn and wknd.* ....(3 to 1 op 5 to 2 tchd 100 to 30) 4
Dist: 7l, 3l, 8l. 2m 24.70s. a 1.70s (4 Ran).
SR: 59/45/47/18/ (Sheikh Mohammed), H R A Cecil

3646 Harpoon Louie's Limited Stakes Class F (3-y-o and up) £2,285 1m 3f 135yds ....(7:40)

3555* SHIRLEY ROSE 3-8-6 M Roberts (2) *led for 5 fs, rdn to ld ag'n 2 out, pushed out ins last.* ...(6 to 5 on op 11 to 10 tchd 5 to 4 and 11 to 8 on) 1
3513* WINGS COVE 3-8-11 J Williams (4) *led aftr 5 fs till rdn and hdd 2 out, ev ch ins last, no extr.* ....(6 to 4 op Evens tchd 13 to 8) 2
3307 KHALIDI (Ire) 4-9-7 A McGlone (1) *prmnt till rdn and btn o'r 2 fs out, kpt on und pres ins last.* ....(25 to 1 op 20 to 1 tchd 33 to 1 and 50 to 1) 3
3388³ INCHCAILLOCH (Ire) 4-9-7 T Quinn (3) *keen hold and hld up, prog gng wl 3 fs out, rdn 2 out and found nothing.* ....(7 to 1 op 8 to 1 tchd 9 to 1) 4
1146 CIRCUIT COURT (Ire) 5-9-7 S Whitworth (5) *hld up last, rdn and lost tch 3 fs out, eased ins last.* ....(33 to 1 op 25 to 1 tchd 50 to 1) 5
Dist: Nk, 10l, sht-hd, 12l. 2m 27.40s. a 4.40s (5 Ran).
SR: 31/35/25/24/-/ (Greenland Park Ltd), M Johnston

BADEN-BADEN (GER) (good)
Sunday August 29th

3647 Furstenberg-Rennen (Group 3) (3-y-o) £30,612 1m 3f...................(3:20)

3370⁶ STERNKONIG (Ire) 8-9 N Grant, *wtd wth, swtchd to outsd one and a half fs out, led one out, sn clr, very easily*... 1
2433* BARON FERDINAND 8-9 R Cochrane, *rcd in 4th, cld up 3 fs out, led briefly one and a half out, ran on one pace.* 2
DREAM FOR FUTURE (Ire) 8-9 J Reid, *rcd in 3rd, kpt on wl fnl 2 fs, no extr cl hme*.. 3
105³ SHARPELA 8-11 O Poirier, *wtd wth, wnt for gap one and a half fs out, no room, swtchd fnl furlong, ran on wl, fnshd 5th, plcd 4th*.. 4
PENOL (Ger) 8-9 A Tylicki, *led, quickened hfwy till one and a half fs out, one pace, fnshd 4th, plcd 5th*....... 5
3151* ZIMZALABIM 9-4 D Holland, *wtd wth, chlgd on outsd 2 fs out, one pace*.. 6
2259 LAMBADA (Ger) 8-9 K Woodburn, *trkd ldr, rdn and wknd 2 fs out*.. 7
Dist: 2½l, sht-hd, sht-hd, 4l. 2m 13.53s. (7 Ran).
(Gestut Rottgen), T Grieper

3648 Preis des Casino Baden-Baden (Listed) (3-y-o) £16,327 1m......... (4:30)

3285⁴ BERINSFIELD 8-12 S Guillot, *hld up in tch, jnd ldrs o'r one furlong out, led last strds*........................ 1
2572⁴ LITTLE MUNCHKIN (Ire) 9-2 D Holland, *al in tch, led 2 fs out till ct last strds*........................ 2
TRANSFORMATOR (Fr) 8-7 M Hofer, *led to 2 fs out, ev ch one furlong out, ran on*........................ 3
Dist: Sht-hd, 1l, nk, 1l, 1½l, 1l. 1m 37.75s. (10 Ran).
(Sheikh Mohammed), A Fabre

DEAUVILLE (FR) (good to firm)
Sunday August 29th

Going Correction: PLUS 0.25 sec. per fur. (races 1,2), PLUS 0.10 (3)

3649 Grand Prix de Deauville Lancel (Group 2) (3-y-o and up) £59,737 1½m 110yds........................ (2:30)

2302⁷ SNURGE 6-9-8 T Quinn (2) *pld hrd early, second strt, rdn 2 fs out, hng lft, led 100 yards out, all out*...(165 to 10) 1
3370⁴ PETIT LOUP (USA) 4-9-2 W R Swinburn (4) *trkd ldr, 4th strt, led briefly und 2 fs out till 110 yards out, kpt on gmely*..................................(48 to 10) 2
3241* HUSBAND (USA) 3-8-7 C Asmussen (9) *in rear, 8th strt, rdn and swtchd 2 fs out, kpt on, not rch ldrs.* (37 to 10) 3
2261³ MODHISH (Ire) 4-9-5 T Jarnet (1) *mid-div, 6th strt, effrt 2 fs out, ran on, not rch ldrs*..................(Evens fav) 4
3194⁵ HALESIA (USA) (bl) 4-8-13 D Boeuf (6) *mid-div, rdn 2 fs out, one pace fnl furlong*..................(29 to 1) 5
3500⁵ MARILDO (Fr) (bl) 6-9-5 G Guignard (8) *led till jst und 2 fs out, wknd*..................................(10 to 1) 6
GLANVILLE (USA) 4-9-2 E Legrix (5) *trkd ldr, 3rd strt, rdn and wknd 2 fs out*..................................(30 to 1) 7
3109* DABARA (Ire) 3-8-7 E Saint-Martin (7) *al rear*.... (64 to 10) 8
2302⁵ SAPIENCE 7-9-5 W Carson (3) *prominenet early, 5th strt, rdn and wknd 2 fs out*..................................(21 to 1) 9
Dist: Sht-hd, 2l, nose, nose, 2l, 3l, 2l, ½l. 2m 42.60s. a 7.10s (9 Ran).
SR: 68/61/48/59/52/54/45/32/43/ (M Arbib), P F I Cole

3650 Prix de la Nonette (Group 3) (3-y-o) £23,895 1¼m.................. (3:05)

1722* SHEMAKA (Ire) 9-2 G Mosse (4) *rcd in 3rd to strt, led jst o'r 2 fs out, ran on wl*..................... (11 to 10 jt-fav) 1
2409⁷ BAYA (USA) 9-2 T Jarnet (2) *last strt, rdn and outpcd 2 fs out, ran on wl fnl furlong*...........................(5 to 2) 2
2238² TALENTED 9-2 W Carson (6) *trkd ldr, second strt, rdn and ev ch 2 fs out, lost second on line*.............(77 to 10) 3
3149² VIVIANA (USA) 9-2 Pat Eddery (5) *4th strt, kpt on one pace fnl 2 fs*..................................(33 to 10) 4
2690² ADORED SLEW (USA) 9-2 D Boeuf (3) *5th strt, no hdwy fnl 2 fs*..................................(49 to 10) 5
MOULOUDYA (Ire) 9-2 D Bonilla (1) *led till jst o'r 2 fs out.* ....(11 to 10 jt-fav) 6
Dist: ½l, nose, 2½l, ½l, 8l. 2m 6.80s. a 5.10s (6 Ran).
SR: 76/75/74/69/68/52/ (H H Aga Khan), A de Royer-Dupre

3651 Prix du Calvados (Group 3) (2-y-o) £23,895 7f..................... (3:35)

3515⁸ FAR MIST (Fr) 8-9 G Mosse (6) *last early, swtchd outsd and hdwy o'r 2 fs out, led wl ins last, all out.* (177 to 10) 1
CHEROKEE ROSE (Ire) 8-9 Pat Eddery (3) *al prmnt, led briefly ins fnl furlong, hrd rdn, ran on*.........(5 to 1) 2
2647⁶ BLUE BURGEE (USA) 8-9 D Boeuf (5) *mid-div, not clr run 2 fs out, kpt on wl fnl furlong*..................(5 to 1) 3
2980* ETERNAL REVE (USA) 8-9 C Asmussen (2) *trkd ldr, led o'r one furlong out till ins last, one pace*..........(2 to 1) 4
ENSORCELLES MOI (USA) 8-9 T Jarnet (8) *mid-div, effrt 2 fs out, one pace ins last*..................(13 to 10 fav) 5
SENSAZIONE 8-9 M Esposito (7) *rear till some hdwy fnl 2 fs, nvr able to chal*..........................(19 to 2) 6
YTALSA ROYALE (Fr) 8-9 G Guignard (4) *al beh*... (29 to 1) 7
2648* MICHELLE HICKS 8-9 M Hills (1) *led till o'r one furlong out*..................................(13 to 1) 8
3413³ WEZZO (USA) 8-9 W R Swinburn (8) *mid-div till rdn and wknd 2 fs out*..................................(23 to 2) 9
Dist: Sht-hd, 1½l, ¾l, 1l, 1½l, 2l, nose, 6l. 1m 25.30s. a 3.30s (9 Ran).
SR: 56/55/50/48/45/40/34/33/15/ (J Lore), F Flachi

OSTEND (BEL) (good)
Sunday August 29th

3652 Prix Gutt Tattersalls (2-y-o) £5,964 7f ....(1:00)

3176[4] OVERACT (Ire) 8-11 K Darley, *wnt second aftr 2f, led wl o'r 2f out, ran on well*... 1
CALVA'S GLOW (Ire) 8-9 P Massage,... 2
SALT PEANUTS (Ire) 8-11 P Smith,... 3
Dist: 2l, 1l, ½l. 1m 36.40s. (9 Ran).
(Lady Hayward), D R Loder

ARLINGTON (USA) (soft)
Sunday August 29th

3653 Secretariat Stakes (Grade 1) 3yo (Turf) £158,940 1¼m ....

AWAD (USA) 8-10 J Velasquez,... 1
2442[5] EXPLOSIVE RED (Can) 8-11 S Sellers,... 2
1548[4] BRAZANY (USA) 8-2 K Desormeaux,... 3
Dist: 1 ¼l, hd, 1 ¼l, 2½l, ¾l, 1l, 9l, 11l, 8l, 1 ¼l. 2m 8.60s. (14 Ran).

3654 Arlington Million (Grade 1) (3-y-o and up) £397,350 1¼m..................

2084* STAR OF COZZENE (USA) 5-9-0 J Santos,... 1
EVANESCENT (USA) 6-9-0 A Gryder,... 2
JOHANN QUATZ (Fr) 4-9-0 K Desormeaux,... 3
2261[5] DEAR DOCTOR (Fr) 6-9-0 C Black,... 4
2926 PETER DAVIES (USA) 5-9-0 L Dettori, *rcd in 3rd to wl o'r one furlong out, 4th strt, sn wknd*... 5
COAXING MATT (USA) 4-9-0 E Fires,... 6
LITTLE BRO LANTIS (USA) 5-9-0 ,... 7
3205[2] LEGER CAT (Arg) 7-9-0 C Nakatani,... 8
Dist: ¾l, 2½l, 2½l, 3½l, 2½l, 2½l, 1l. 2m 7.40s. (8 Ran).
(J Siegel), F Boutin

CHEPSTOW (good to firm)
Monday August 30th
Going Correction: MINUS 0.25 sec. per fur.

3655 Severn Bridge Handicap Class E (0-70 3-y-o and up) £3,668 1¼m 36yds (1:50)

3043[4] EIRAS MOOD [38] 4-7-10 C Avery (10) *prog on outsd o'r 4 fs out, led over 2 out, hld on wl fnl furlong*. ...(25 to 1 op 20 to 1) 1
3263[6] MUTAMANNI [70] 3-9-6 W Carson (6) *al cl up, led briefly 3 fs out, hrd rdn appr fnl furlong, styd on*. ...(10 to 1 op 8 to 1) 2
3340[3] CELIA BRADY [46] 5-8-4 C Rutter (1) *hdwy 3 fs out, ev ch ins last, ran on*...(8 to 1 op 6 to 1) 3
2633[7] TELEPHUS [50] 4-8-3 (5*) D Wright (5) *slwly into strd, gd prog on ins 3 fs out, hrd drvn and not quicken last 150 yards*...(9 to 1 op 8 to 1) 4
3288[4] SWIFT ROMANCE (Ire) [49] 5-8-7 J Williams (12) *beh till gd hdwy appr fnl furlong, fnshd fst*. (14 to 1 op 10 to 1) 5
3310[3] MAI PEN RAI [43] 5-8-1 N Adams (16) *styd on last 2 fs, not rch ldrs*...(10 to 1 op 6 to 1) 6
3107[2] COURAGEOUS KNIGHT [70] 4-10-0 L Dettori (4) *effrt o'r 4 fs out, rdn 3 out, not real prog last 2 furlongs*. ...(7 to 2 fav op 9 to 2 tchd 5 to 1) 7
3420 CRETOES DANCER (USA) [40] 4-7-5 (7*) Kim McDonnell (13) *pressed ldrs till wknd 3 fs out*...(25 to 1 op 20 to 1) 8
3420[6] STRIKING IMAGE (Ire) [41] 4-7-13[1] S O'Gorman (15) *nvr rch ldrs*...(16 to 1 op 14 to 1) 9
3358[9] SOOTY TERN [61] 6-8-12 (7*) Michael Bradley (2) *led till hdd 3 fs out, btn appr fnl furlong*...(10 to 1 op 8 to 1) 10
2834[8] HOMEMAKER [47] 3-7-11 T Wilson (7) *chsd ldrs till rdn and wknd o'r 3 fs out*...(14 to 1 tchd 16 to 1) 11
3518* TIGER CLAW (USA) [48] (bl) 7-8-6 (5ex) R Price (9) *wl plcd till wknd o'r 3 fs out*...(10 to 1 op 8 to 1) 12
3512[5] RAPPORTEUR (USA) [60] 7-9-4 A Munro (14) *pressed ldg grp till wknd o'r 3 fs out*...(9 to 1 op 8 to 1) 13
2939[9] SENOR L'AMOUR [50] 3-8-0[7] (7*) Mark Denaro (8) *rcd keenly, prmnt till wknd 4 fs out, tld off*. ...(25 to 1 op 20 to 1) 14
Dist: 1l, hd, ¾l, sht-hd, hd, hd, 3l, ¾l, ½l, ½l. 2m 7.70s. a 4.10s (14 Ran).
SR: 15/37/20/22/20/13/39/3/2/ (S E Salimeni), B Palling

3656 John Hylton Watts Memorial Claiming Stakes Class F (3-y-o and up) £2,770 1 ½m 23yds.................... (2:20)

3193[2] PREMIER DANCE 6-8-11 (5*) D Wright (1) *chsd ldg pair, led o'r 2 fs out till over one out, led ins last, ran on wl*. ...(10 to 1 op 7 to 1) 1+
3078[4] PICKLES 5-9-10 A Munro (10) *dwlt, improved aftr 5 fs, led o'r one out till ins last, ran on wl*. ...(14 to 1 tchd 20 to 1) 1+
3522[6] ROUSITTO 5-9-6 L Dettori (3) *al chasing ldrs, rdn o'r 2 fs out, kpt on same pace*... (7 to 1 op 5 to 1 tchd 8 to 1) 3
3128[2] TEMPLE KNIGHT 4-9-10 W Carson (2) *beh, rdn 5 fs out, styd on last 2 furlongs, not rch ldrs*. ...(3 to 1 op 7 to 2 tchd 4 to 1) 4
3518 GESNERA 5-8-4 (5*) A Procter (9) *chsd ldr till rdn and wknd ins last 3 fs*... (33 to 1 op 20 to 1) 5
2162[9] ELIZA WOODING (v) 5-8-5 N Adams (5) *missed break, effrt 5 fs out, wknd o'r 2 out*...(33 to 1 op 20 to 1) 6
2381[4] CRACKLING 4-9-2 (3*) D Harrison (6) *in tch till wknd 3 fs out*...(14 to 1 op 16 to 1) 7
3304[3] FLAMING MIRACLE (Ire) (bl) 3-9-0 C Rutter (7) *led till hdd o'r 2 fs out, sn wknd*... (10 to 1 op 8 to 1) 8
2820[3] GENERAL CHASE 3-8-5 R Price (4) *rdn and effrt o'r 4 fs out, wknd 3 furlongs out*... (7 to 4 fav op 5 to 4) 9
3050[7] IRISH GROOM (bl) 6-9-2 A Clark (11) *al in rear*. ...(40 to 1 op 33 to 1) 10
PALACE MAN (USA) 5-9-10 J Williams (8) *al in rear, tld off fnl 5 fs*...(40 to 1 op 33 to 1) 11
Dist: Dd-ht, 5l, 3l, ¾l, sht-hd, nk, 3l, 7l, 8l, 30l. 2m 36.10s. a 4.60s (11 Ran).
SR: 26/34/20/18/1/-/9/-/-/ (Mrs Carol Sheppard & David Currie), D Haydn Jones & R Lee

3657 Tattersalls Auction Series Nursery Qualifier Class D (2-y-o) £3,231 5f 16yds........................ (2:50)

3387* CRYSTAL MAGIC [72] 9-2 L Dettori (4) *made virtually all, pushed clr fnl furlong, readily*. ...(11 to 10 fav op 6 to 4) 1
3103[4] DANCES WITH RISK [63] 8-4 (3*) D Harrison (5) *al chasing ldrs, rdn 2 fs out, swtchd lft appr fnl furlong, not quicken ins last*...(11 to 2 op 5 to 1) 2
3529[5] BURMA STAR [49] 7-7 N Adams (7) *gd prog on stands rls o'r one furlong out, kpt on ins last*. ...(25 to 1 op 20 to 1) 3
2996[8] MIRIAM [70] 9-0 A Munro (6) *al wl plcd, one pace fnl 2 fs*. ...(7 to 1 op 4 to 1) 4
3432[5] ELEVATOR SHAFT (Ire) [68] 8-12 R Price (3) *wth ldrs till wknd ins last 2 fs*...(8 to 1 op 5 to 1) 5
3448[5] CYARNA QUINN (Ire) [77] 9-7 W Carson (1) *pressed ldrs 4 fs*. ...(7 to 1 op 6 to 1) 6
3363[3] BOLD ARISTOCRAT (Ire) [71] 9-1 S Perks (2) *hmpd aftr one furlong, rdn 2 fs out, sn struggling*. (8 to 1 tchd 9 to 1) 7
3386 STARISK [55] 7-8 (5*) D Wright (8) *outpcd*...(20 to 1) 8
Dist: 3l, nk, 3l, ½l, 5l, 1l, 1½l. 59.30s. a 2.30s (8 Ran).
SR: 31/10/-/4/-/ (D Sieff), R Hannon

3658 EBF Romeo Maiden Stakes Class D (2-y-o) £4,435 1m 14yds........ (3:20)

3352[8] UNCLE OSWALD 9-0 L Dettori (2) *al cl up, led o'r 2 fs out, ran on wl*...(3 to 1 op 5 to 2) 1
3259[4] ZUBOON (USA) 9-0 W Carson (8) *al wl plcd, ev ch 2 fs out, kpt on und pres towards finish*. ...(9 to 4 fav op 5 to 2 tchd 3 to 1 and 2 to 1) 2
3259 TOWER GREEN 9-0 J Williams (5) *hld up, hdwy o'r 2 fs out, not quicken fnl furlong*...(12 to 1 op 10 to 1) 3
3079[6] ARABOYBILL 9-0 A Clark (4) *improved hfwy, no imprsn last 2 fs*...(12 to 1 op 16 to 1 tchd 20 to 1) 4
STAR MASTER 9-0 A Munro (12) *steady prog appr fnl furlong, better for race*...(7 to 1 op 6 to 1) 5
TOTAL JOY (Ire) 9-0 C Rutter (13) *al in tch, no prog last 2 fs*...(20 to 1 op 14 to 1) 6
3287 FOOT TAPPER (Ire) 9-0 R Price (9) *dsptd ld till led o'r 3 fs out, hdd over 2 out, sn btn*... (33 to 1 op 25 to 1) 7
ALASKAN HEIR 8-9 (5*) A Procter (10) *nvr rch ldrs*. ...(33 to 1 op 20 to 1) 8
SHREWD ALIBI 9-0 S O'Gorman (3) *mid-div till no ch last 2 fs*...(12 to 1 op 6 to 1) 9
3084[2] PACIOLI 8-9 (5*) D Wright (14) *led o'r 4 fs, wknd over 2 furlongs out*...(14 to 1 tchd 20 to 1) 10
2502 SEA SPOUSE 9-0 N Adams (6) *hld up, al beh*... (33 to 1) 11
3079[9] EXPLORE MONDIAL (Ire) 8-11 (3*) D Harrison (11) *chsd ldrs 5 fs*... (12 to 1 op 10 to 1) 12
3009 SPEEDY SNAPS IMAGE 8-7 (7*) Mark Denaro (7) *pressed ldrs 5 fs*... (33 to 1 tchd 50 to 1) 13
Dist: Nk, 3½l, 3l, sht-hd, 2l, 4l, 1l, 1½l, 3l, 1½l. 1m 35.40s. a 3.00s (13 Ran).
SR: 25/24/13/4/3/-/ (Nimrod Company), R Hannon

3659 EBF Juliet Maiden Fillies' Stakes Class D (2-y-o) £4,435 1m 14yds (3:50)

3186[2] BONNY BRIDE (Ire) 8-11 L Dettori (13) *al wl plcd, drvn alng 3 fs out, led appr fnl furlong, hld on well*. ...(9 to 2 op 3 to 1) 1
3317[5] LYPHARD STREET (USA) 8-11 A Munro (9) *al frnt rnk, led 2 fs out till jst o'r one out, ran on*. (6 to 4 fav op 5 to 2) 2
2887 AZHAAR (USA) 8-11 W Carson (5) *al handily plcd, rdn 2 and a half fs out, styd on ins last*. (12 to 1 op 10 to 1) 3
3352[5] LA RIVERAINE (USA) 8-8 (3*) D Harrison (2) *prog 3 fs out, rdn 2 out, kpt on same pace*... (9 to 2 op 3 to 1) 4
2583[6] RARE BIRD (USA) 8-11 S Perks (7) *pressed ldrs till wknd wl o'r one furlong out*...(14 to 1 op 8 to 1) 5
3351[3] ROSE CIEL (Ire) 8-4 (7*) Mark Denaro (10) *chsd ldrs, no imprsn last 2 fs*...(10 to 1 op 6 to 1) 6
3389[7] GOLDEN FERN 8-6 (5*) D Wright (8) *trkd ldrs, wknd o'r 2 fs out*... (50 to 1 op 25 to 1) 7
3260[5] TANDIA 8-4 (7*) L Carter (16) *led 6 fs, sn lost pl*. ...(16 to 1 op 14 to 1 tchd 20 to 1) 8
3422[7] TUDOR FLIGHT 8-11 R Price (3) *nvr a factor*. ...(25 to 1 op 16 to 1) 9
MISTY WISE 8-11 S O'Gorman (11) *al beh*. ...(25 to 1 op 20 to 1) 10

2695 MISS TEMERITY 8-11 N Adams (12) *al in rear.* .... (50 to 1 op 33 to 1) 11
3422 JADY'S DREAM (Ire) 8-11 A Clark (15) *al struggling.* .... (33 to 1 op 25 to 1 tchd 50 to 1) 12
CRAZY FOR YOU 8-11 C Rutter (14) *sn badly outpcd.* .... (50 to 1 op 20 to 1) 13
3264 POETIC FANCY 8-4 (7*) D O'Neill (6) *rdn bef hfwy, sn toiling, tld off*.................... (50 to 1 op 33 to 1) 14
3389 GHALIA (Ire) 8-11 A Culhane (1) *sn wl beh, tld off.* .... (50 to 1 op 33 to 1) 15
3137² RUBY ESTATE (Ire) 8-11 J Williams (4) *virtually pld up o'r 2 fs out, sddl slpd*.....(11 to 1 op 14 to 1 tchd 20 to 1) 16
Dist: Hd, ¾l, 1½l, 1½l, 2l, 2l, ½l, 4l, 1½l, 2½l. 1m 34.90s. a 2.50s (16 Ran).
SR: 30/29/27/22/17/11/5/3/-/ (E J Loder), D R Loder

3660 Frankie Dettori Ton-up Fillies Conditions Stakes Class D (3-y-o and up) £3,231 7f 16yds............... (4:25)

3477³ QUEEN'S VIEW (Fr) 3-9-3 A Munro (2) *hld up gng wl, rdn to ld o'r one furlong out, wndrd ins last, ridden out.* .... (11 to 10 on op Evens tchd 5 to 4 on) 1
3312* KATIBA (USA) 3-9-1 W Carson (4) *hld up, sn outpcd, prog 2 fs out, hrd rdn last 200 yards, styd on*.........(3 to 1) 2
3474⁴ WINGED VICTORY (Ire) 3-9-3 L Dettori (1) *led till hrd drvn and hdd o'r one furlong out, kpt on same pace.* .... (100 to 30 op 5 to 2 tchd 7 to 2) 3
2971⁸ CARRANITA (Ire) 3-9-3 R Price (5) *chsd ldr to hfwy, wknd ins last 2 fs*..........................(10 to 1 op 7 to 1) 4
LADY MAVIS 3-8-9 J Williams (3) *slwly away, al tld off.* .... (40 to 1 op 100 to 1) 5
Dist: ½l, 2l, 5l, 30l. 1m 20.70s. a 0.70s (5 Ran).
SR: 66/62/58/43/-/ (Sheikh Mohammed), L M Cumani

3661 Caerwent Apprentice Maiden Handicap Class F (0-65 3-y-o and up) £2,812 6f 16yds...................... (4:55)

3229 BEVELED EDGE [49] 4-9-0 (5*) Wendy Jones (1) *made all, swtchd to race towards stands side, edgd lft ins last 2 fs, hld on wl*....................(16 to 1 tchd 20 to 1) 1
3305³ POYLE AMBER [53] 4-9-4 (5*) S McCarthy (3) *al frnt rnk, ev ch fnl furlong, kpt on*... (9 to 2 op 4 to 1 tchd 5 to 1) 2
3535⁸ ALL THE GIRLS (Ire) [35] 4-7-12 (7*) F Savage (8) *gd late hdwy, fnshd wl*............................ (20 to 1) 3
3100³ NO GAIN [52] 3-8-11 (7*) W Hawksley (7) *outpcd, gd hdwy wl o'r one furlong out, rdn entering fnl furlong, fnshd fst*.............................(8 to 1 tchd 13 to 2) 4
3481⁶ VISIMOTION (USA) [58] 3-9-5 (5*) Ruth Coulter (2) *al cl up, ev ch appr fnl furlong, not quicken ins last.* .... (10 to 1 op 12 to 1 tchd 14 to 1) 5
771 TAKE IT IN CASH [44] 4-8-4 (10*) Michelle Thomas (4) *hdwy appr fnl furlong, kpt on*..........(14 to 1 op 10 to 1) 6
3383² SOPHISTICATED AIR [56] (bl) 3-9-0 (8*) D Griffiths (6) *pressed ldrs, ev ch o'r one furlong out, no extr last 200 yards.* ....(3 to 1 fav op 4 to 1) 7
3383⁵ AVRIL ETOILE [51] 3-8-7 (10*) Iona Wands (10) *pressed ldrs till not quicken appr fnl furlong.* .... (7 to 1 op 9 to 2 tchd 15 to 2) 8
2350⁹ HULLO MARY DOLL [27] 4-7-4 (7*) A Daly (5) *strted slwly, nvr nrr*.......................................(50 to 1) 9
3313 CHRISTIAN WARRIOR [33] (v) 4-7-12 (5*) A Whelan (13) *chsd ldrs, rdn o'r 2 fs out, sn btn*..................(16 to 1) 10
3100⁹ SUI GENERIS (Ire) [35] 3-7-11¹ (5*) J Dennis (12) *beh fnl 2 fs.* ....(33 to 1) 11
4747a⁶ M A EL-SAHN [56] 3-8-12 (10*) E Greehy (11) *chsd ldrs to hfwy*............... (14 to 1 op 12 to 1 tchd 16 to 1) 12
LAWNSWOOD PRINCE (Ire) [36] 4-7-13 (7*) L Suthern (15) *no ch last 2 fs*..................... (20 to 1 tchd 25 to 1) 13
3305⁸ NANQUIDNO [33] 3-7-8 (5*) Sharon Millard (9) *al beh.* .... (50 to 1 op 33 to 1) 14
3007 MY BOY BUSTER [32] 4-7-11 (5*) M Baird (14) *speed to hfwy*..(20 to 1) 15
Dist: Nk, nk, sht-hd, hd, ¾l, ½l, 1l, 1½l, 1l, 4l. 1m 11.70s. a 2.20s (15 Ran).
SR: 31/34/15/27/32/19/25/16/-/ (Christopher J Mason), B Palling

DOWNPATRICK (IRE) (good to firm)
Monday August 30th

3662 B.J. Eastwood Irelands Leading Bookmaker Organisation Race (3-y-o and up) £1,380 1m 3f 208yds........ (4:00)

3482³ TEBRE (USA) (bl) 3-8-3 (6*) B J Walsh (8).......... (4 to 1) 1
3299⁵ CLASSY KAHYASI (Ire) 3-8-9 P Shanahan (2)..(11 to 4 fav) 2
3293² SUNSET CAFE (Ire) (bl) 3-8-7 (2*) R M Burke (1).... (6 to 1) 3
3482⁴ NURSES RUN (Ire) (bl) 3-8-3 (6*) R V Skelly (10).... (4 to 1) 4
3397 MANGANS HILL (Ire) 3-9-0 Joanna Morgan (9)....(16 to 1) 5
3245⁴ BASSETJA (Ire) 4-9-5 R Hughes (3)..............(5 to 1) 6
3074⁹ PAKED (Ire) 3-8-9 D V Smith (6)................ (25 to 1) 7
3396³ LEAD ME LEAD MENOT (USA) (bl) 4-8-9 (10*) D J Finnegan (4)...(7 to 1) 8
BLUSHING BUNNY 7-9-6 (4*) W J Smith (5)...... (20 to 1) pu
Dist: 3l, hd, 2½l, 4½l. (Time not taken) (9 Ran).
(Mrs H de Burgh), Kevin Prendergast

3663 Cork Dry Gin Ulster Cesarewitch (0-65 3-y-o and up) £1,725 2m 1f 172yds ....(4:30)

3398* NANARCH (USA) [-] 9-9-13 (6*,3ex) B J Walsh (7) .... (6 to 4 fav) 1
3398⁵ TOOLITTLE TOOLATE (Ire) [-] 4-9-12 J Collins (4)..(13 to 2) 2
3398⁴ STEEL CHIMES (Ire) [-] (bl) 4-9-6 P Shanahan (6) (100 to 30) 3
3245⁶ LUCK OF A LADY (Ire) [-] 4-8-2 (6*) R V Skelly (1)..(33 to 1) 4
2484 LEAVING CERT [-] 6-8-0 Joanna Morgan (5)...... (16 to 1) 5
3397 BELLE O' THE BAY (Ire) [-] 4-8-1 (2*) R M Burke (2) (33 to 1) 6
3397 HUGH DANIELS [-] 5-6-12 (10*) J D Moore (8)......(3 to 1) 7
1508 SINGHANA (Ire) [-] (bl) 5-8-9 (8*) R T Fitzpatrick (3) (10 to 1) 8
Dist: 3½l, 11l, 2½l, hd. (Time not taken) (8 Ran).
(Mrs Kevin Prendergast), Kevin Prendergast

EPSOM (good)
Monday August 30th

Going Correction: MINUS 0.40 sec. per fur. (races 1,2,4,6,7), MINUS 0.45 (3), MINUS 0.30 (5)

3664 Ladas Rating Related Maiden Stakes Class E (0-70 2-y-o) £2,820 6f... (2:05)

3167³ KERRIE-JO 8-9 B Raymond (2) *hdwy hfwy, rdn and styd on to ld last 50 yards*.... (5 to 1 op 6 to 1 tchd 7 to 1) 1
2412⁴ ASKING FOR ACES 8-9 Pat Eddery (4) *sn led, rdn alng 2 fs out, hdd und pres last 50 yards.* ....(9 to 4 fav op 2 to 1 tchd 5 to 2) 2
3387³ BIRD OF TIME (Ire) 8-9 Paul Eddery (3) *ldg grp, rdn and one pace ins last 2 fs*.........................(7 to 2 op 3 to 1) 3
776⁹ LORD SKY 9-0 T Quinn (7) *in tch, rdn alng o'r 3 fs out, no extr 2 out*............. (9 to 2 op 7 to 2 tchd 5 to 1) 4
3210⁴ NORTHERN STORM (Ire) 9-0 W Woods (6) *sn pushed alng in rear, rdn o'r 2 fs out, nvr on terms.* .... (16 to 1 op 12 to 1) 5
3345³ GIGUE 8-9 G Hind (8) *settled rear, rdn alng hfwy, nvr nr to chal*............................(12 to 1 op 8 to 1) 6
3508⁹ ERRIS BOY (bl) 9-0 G Bardwell (5) *pld hrd, wl plcd till rdn and outpcd 3 fs out*................(10 to 1 op 8 to 1) 7
Dist: 1l, 2l, 3½l, nk, ½l, 6l. 1m 10.85s. a 2.95s (7 Ran).
(Mrs Maureen Day), M J Haynes

3665 Sherwood Maiden Stakes Class D (3-y-o and up) £3,590 7f.......... (2:35)

1842³ CANASKA STAR 3-9-0 T Quinn (2) *led aftr 100 yards, sn wl clr, shaken up o'r one furlong out, styd on well.* ....(5 to 4 fav op 6 to 4 on) 1
3511 RESIST THE FORCE (USA) 3-9-0 Pat Eddery (4) *hdwy aftr 3 fs, chsd wnr o'r 2 out, sn hrd rdn, not quicken ins last.* ....(9 to 2 op 4 to 1 tchd 7 to 2) 2
3450⁶ FRIENDLY BRAVE (USA) 3-9-0 Paul Eddery (3) *ran on 3 fs out, hrd rdn and styd on appr last, not rch wnr.* ....(7 to 1 op 8 to 1 tchd 9 to 1) 3
3286³ DESERT VENUS 3-8-9 B Raymond (5) *sn chasing wnr, lost pl o'r 2 fs out, wknd one out*.........(6 to 1 op 5 to 1) 4
THUNDER STRIKE (USA) 3-9-0 G Hind (6) *outpcd, tld off.* .... (11 to 2 op 4 to 1 tchd 6 to 1) 5
3509 MYJINKA (bl) 3-8-6 (3*) M Fenton (1) *led 100 yards, wknd 4 fs out, tld off*....... (66 to 1 op 50 to 1 tchd 100 to 1) 6
Dist: 2l, ½l, 3l, 15l, 4l. 1m 22.29s. a 1.89s (6 Ran).
SR: 30/24/22/8/-/-/ (Mrs June M Sifton), P W Chapple-Hyam

3666 Moet & Chandon Silver Magnum Class E Limited Handicap For Gentleman Amateur Riders (0-90 3-y-o and up) £8,237 1½m 10yds.......... (3:10)

3388⁶ BO KNOWS BEST (Ire) [61] 4-10-0 Mr L A Urbano (7) *hld up in tch, rdn alng o'r 2 fs out, str run to ld wl ins last.* .... (13 to 2 op 5 to 1 tchd 7 to 1) 1
3353⁶ SHADOWS OF SILVER [73] 5-10-12¹ Mr E McMahon (3) *led aftr one furlong, pushed alng 2 out, hdd wl ins last, no extr*..................(10 to 1 op 8 to 1 tchd 11 to 1) 2
3353⁷ SATIN DANCER [77] 3-10-6 Mr J Durkan (8) *led one furlong, pressed ldrs, rdn 3 out, no extr appr last.* ....(7 to 1 op 6 to 1 tchd 8 to 1) 3
3263⁷ BLAZON OF TROY [61] 4-10-0 Mr F Grasso Caprioli (10) *mid-div, cld on ldrs 4 fs out, one pace 3 out.* .... (33 to 1 op 16 to 1) 4
3466⁹ REDSTELLA (USA) [83] (v) 4-11-8² Mr S Whitaker (1) *dwlt, beh till moderate hdwy last 2 fs, nrst finish.* .... (9 to 1 op 8 to 1 tchd 10 to 1) 5
3434⁵ CASTORET [84] 7-11-9 Mr C Vigors (6) *nvr better than mid-div, shaken up and no response frm 3 fs out.* ....(7 to 2 fav op 3 to 1 tchd 4 to 1) 6
3252* FARMER'S PET [85] 4-11-10 Mr P Pritchard-Gordon (2) *wl plcd till wknd hfwy*.... (7 to 1 op 6 to 1 tchd 8 to 1) 7
3574* SIR THOMAS BEECHAM [71] 3-10-0 (2ex) Mr T Cuff (4) *al rear*..........................(12 to 1 tchd 14 to 1) 8
3152⁶ SHUJAN (USA) [78] 4-11-3 Mr M Armytage (5) *pressed ldrs till wknd quickly o'r 2 fs out.* .... (11 to 2 op 5 to 1 tchd 6 to 1) 9

3509[4] MILZIG (USA) [85] 4-11-10 Mr S Swiers (9) *al beh.* ....(8 to 1 op 6 to 1 tchd 9 to 1) 10
Dist: 1½l, 2½l, 2½l, 3l, hd, 2l, 1l, 1l, sht-hd. 2m 36.48s. a 0.98s (10 Ran).
SR: 50/59/48/37/53/53/50/24/39/ (Nigel Goldman), J Sutcliffe

3667 Tadworth Nursery Class D (2-y-o) £4,542 7f...................... (3:40)

3209[4] HELLO IRELAND [67] 8-6 Pat Eddery (9) *pressed ldr, hrd rdn entering fnl furlong, led last strds.* ....(7 to 4 fav op 5 to 2) 1
3532* NONIOS (Ire) [81] 9-6 (5ex) W Woods (2) *handily plcd, rdn alng and edgd lft ins fnl furlong, str brst, jst fld.* ....(4 to 1 op 5 to 2 tchd 9 to 2) 2
3485[3] BALLAH SHACK (USA) [80] 9-5 Paul Eddery (8) *led till hrd rdn and hdd last strds*...(9 to 2 op 7 to 2 tchd 5 to 1) 3
3428[5] GOLDEN GRAND [65] 8-4 G Bardwell (1) *mid-div, pushed alng 4 fs out, ran on o'r 2 out, not rch ldrs.* .... (20 to 1 op 12 to 1) 4
3508[4] NORTHERN BAILIWICK (Ire) [54] (bl) 7-0 (7*) Antoinette Armes (7) *slwly away, cld on ldrs aftr 2 fs, wknd 3 out.* ....(12 to 1 op 10 to 1 tchd 14 to 1) 5
2862* PERSIAN AFFAIR (Ire) [74] 8-10 (3*) M Fenton (6) *ldg grp till rdn and wknd o'r 2 fs out*..........(8 to 1 op 6 to 1) 6
2845[8] MR DEVIOUS [82] 9-7 B Raymond (4) *in tch, pushed alng 4 fs out, no hdwy appr 3 out.* ....(12 to 1 op 10 to 1 tchd 14 to 1) 7
3386 LITTLE HOOLIGAN [57] 7-10 N Carlisle (3) *outpcd.* ....(8 to 1 op 7 to 1 tchd 9 to 1) 8
Dist: Sht-hd, nk, 6l, 1l, 2½l, 2l, nk. 1m 22.54s. a 2.14s (8 Ran).
SR: 18/31/29/-/-/ (Cliveden Stud), R Charlton

3668 Tote Bookmakers Sprint Rated Class B Handicap (0-100 3-y-o and up) £9,420 5f...................... (4:10)

3438 SABRE RATTLER [97] 3-9-7 G Hind (2) *cl up, led hfwy, rdn and styd on strly ins fnl furlong.* ....(12 to 1 op 10 to 1 tchd 14 to 1) 1
3266* PRESS THE BELL [82] 3-7-13 (7*) P Roberts (5) *led to hfwy, kpt on und pres ins fnl furlong*.... (7 to 2 tchd 4 to 1) 2
3266[6] ALLTHRUTHENIGHT (Ire) [80] 4-8-7 T Quinn (8) *hld up, cld on ldrs o'r one furlong out, not quicken fnl 100 yards.* .... (11 to 2 op 7 to 1 tchd 8 to 1) 3
3438* IN CASE (USA) [94] 3-9-4 Pat Eddery (1) *pressed ldrs, rdn hfwy, one pace ins fnl furlong*... (3 to 1 fav op 2 to 1) 4
3291[6] MISS VAXETTE [91] 4-8-11 (7*) M Humphries (7) *slwly into strd, rear till swtchd lft hfwy, no imprsn on ldrs fnl furlong*..............(12 to 1 op 8 to 1 tchd 14 to 1) 5
3571[8] LOVE RETURNED [85] 6-8-12 W Woods (3) *effrt und pres on outsd 2 fs out, sn btn*..........(12 to 1 op 10 to 1) 6
3348[7] ASHTINA [87] 8-9-0 Paul Eddery (6) *wth ldrs to hfwy, sn btn*....................(11 to 2 op 5 to 1 tchd 6 to 1) 7
3511 TERRHARS (Ire) [82] 5-8-9 B Raymond (4) *mid-div, not pace to chal frm 2 fs out*..............(11 to 2 op 8 to 1) 8
Dist: 1½l, ¾l, ¾l, nk, 3l, ¾l, ½l. 55.01s. a 0.31s (8 Ran).
SR: 71/50/48/56/55/37/36/29/ (H B Hughes), J Berry

3669 Cicero Claiming Stakes Class E (3-y-o) £3,054 1¼m 18yds......... (4:40)

3173[7] BAG OF TRICKS (Ire) 9-7 Pat Eddery (1) *wl plcd, not much room on ins o'r 2 fs out, hrd rdn to ld well inside last, all out*....................(4 to 1 op 9 to 4 tchd 9 to 2) 1
3431[3] SEAMA (USA) 9-0 C Nutter (8) *led till hdd und pres wl ins fnl furlong*....................(9 to 2 op 7 to 2) 2
3185[3] GYPSY CRYSTAL (USA) 8-0 N Carlisle (2) *pressed ldr, rdn and not quicken appr fnl furlong.* ....(20 to 1 op 14 to 1 tchd 33 to 1) 3
3507[8] DARING PAST (bl) 8-13 B Raymond (6) *mid-div, effrt und pres o'r 2 fs out, kpt on one pace.* (16 to 1 op 10 to 1) 4
3246[5] SPARKY'S SONG 8-8 T Quinn (4) *mid-div, reminders hfwy, rdn alng 3 fs out, no imprsn 2 out.* ....(10 to 1 op 7 to 1 tchd 11 to 1) 5
3460[3] FORMAL AFFAIR 8-1 (7*) J D Smith (3) *ldg grp till rdn and wknd 2 fs out*..........(4 to 1 op 7 to 2 tchd 9 to 2) 6
2087[3] MIND THE ROOF (Ire) 8-0 G Bardwell (9) *nvr on terms.* ....(7 to 2 fav tchd 3 to 1 and 4 to 1) 7
3461[4] PLATINUM VENTURE 8-7 W Woods (5) *in tch, rdn and wknd o'r 3 fs out*......(13 to 2 op 6 to 1 tchd 7 to 1) 8
3341[7] MISS COPYFORCE 7-9 (5*) B Russell (10) *al beh.* ....(20 to 1 op 16 to 1) 9
1793[6] BAYYINAT (USA) 8-4 (3*) M Fenton (7) *slwly into strd, lost tch o'r 4 fs out*...... (33 to 1 op 25 to 1 tchd 40 to 1) 10
Dist: Hd, 3l, 2l, 3½l, nk, 3½l, 4l, 1l, 5l. 2m 6.81s. a 2.51s (10 Ran).
SR: 42/34/14/23/11/10/ (K Abdulla), G Harwood

3670 Ranmore Fillies' Handicap Class D (0-80 3-y-o and up) £4,737 1m 114yds ....(5:10)

3088[2] MISS FASCINATION [61] 3-8-6 W Woods (1) *mid-div, led o'r 3 fs out, drvn out, styd on cl hme*...(6 to 1 tchd 7 to 1) 1
3507[5] MAY HILLS LEGACY (Ire) [56] 4-8-8 T Quinn (9) *wth ldrs, led 4 fs out till edgd rght and hdd o'r 3 out, sstnd chal frm 2 out, jst fld*............. (8 to 1 op 7 to 1 tchd 10 to 1) 2
2926 QUEEN WARRIOR [69] 4-9-7 Pat Eddery (8) *rear till ran on und pres o'r 2 fs out, fnshd wl.* (3 to 1 fav tchd 4 to 1) 3
3269* SAAFEND [73] 5-9-11 B Raymond (11) *hld up in mid-div, rdn and not quicken und pres o'r 2 fs out, rallied nr line*..................(11 to 2 op 5 to 1 tchd 13 to 2) 4
3290 EXHIBIT AIR (Ire) [70] 3-8-8 (7*) D Gibbs (6) *handily plcd in mid-div, hrd rdn o'r one furlong out, styd on.* ....(10 to 1 tchd 12 to 1) 5
3549[3] DESERT NOMAD [56] 3-8-1 G Hind (5) *ldg grp, cl up 3 fs out, rdn and no extr wl o'r one out, eased whn btn.* ....(10 to 1 op 7 to 1) 6
3447[8] CHICARD [42] 4-7-8 G Bardwell (2) *prog frm rear o'r 3 fs out, sn und pres, wknd aftr 2 out.* .... (14 to 1 op 10 to 1 tchd 16 to 1) 7
3121[6] PLAY WITH ME (Ire) [71] 3-9-2 Paul Eddery (10) *in tch till lost pl o'r 2 fs out*..................(9 to 1 op 10 to 1) 8
3429* ADAMPARIS [53] (bl) 3-7-12 N Carlisle (4) *al beh.* ....(8 to 1 op 7 to 1) 9
992[7] KENESHA (Ire) [74] 3-8-12 (7*) A Martinez (7) *led to 4 fs out, wknd 3 out*.................... (50 to 1 op 33 to 1) 10
3088[3] FRANCIA [57] 3-7-9 (7*) Antoinette Armes (3) *al rear.* ....(20 to 1 op 10 to 1) 11
3206[6] DOUBLE FLUTTER [76] 4-9-11 (3*) M Fenton (12) *prmnt till wknd o'r 3 fs out*..................(12 to 1 op 10 to 1) 12
Dist: Nk, hd, ¾l, 1½l, 2½l, ¾l, 3½l, 1½l, 3l, ½l. 1m 43.52s. a 1.52s (12 Ran).
SR: 18/19/31/33/18/-/ (N S Yong), M A Jarvis

NEWCASTLE (good to firm) Monday August 30th

Going Correction: MINUS 0.35 sec. per fur. (races 1,2,3,6), MINUS 0.20 (4,5)

3671 Rafa Wings Appeal Nursery Stakes Class D (2-y-o) £3,200 7f........(2:15)

3490[2] INDEFENCE (Ire) [72] 9-1 L Piggott (1) *made virtually all, rdn entering fnl furlong, hld on wl.* ....(9 to 4 fav tchd 11 to 4) 1
3176[9] CUT THE RED TAPE (Ire) [78] 9-7 T Williams (3) *trkd ldrs, chlgd o'r one furlong out, ev ch ins fnl furlong, no extr cl hme*....................(5 to 1 op 7 to 2) 2
3563[8] KARSEAM (Ire) [71] 9-0 N Connorton (6) *trkd ldrs, effrt o'r 2 fs out, kpt on ins last*..............(20 to 1 op 12 to 1) 3
3115[3] LUCKY MESSAGE (USA) [67] 8-10 W Newnes (4) *hld up, hdwy 2 fs out, one pace fnl furlong.* ....(7 to 2 op 4 to 1 tchd 9 to 2) 4
3598[8] WINGS AHEAD [58] 7-10 (5*) Darren Moffatt (2) *prmnt, effrt o'r 2 fs out, sn btn*....(16 to 1 op 14 to 1 tchd 20 to 1) 5
3475[3] HARPO'S SPECIAL [63] 8-6 K Fallon (5) *in tch, sn pushed alng, nvr dngrs*..................(7 to 2 op 5 to 2) 6
3411[4] SECONDS AWAY [62] 8-5 A McGlone (7) *in tch till wknd 2 fs out*..........(11 to 1 op 12 to 1 tchd 10 to 1) 7
Dist: Nk, 2l, sht-hd, 2½l, 2½l, 5l. 1m 26.65s. a 2.65s (7 Ran).
SR: 25/30/17/12/ (Les Hamilton), M R Channon

3672 EBF Hedgehope Maiden Stakes Class D (2-y-o) £4,235 7f..............(2:50)

3352 ERHAAB (USA) 9-0 W Newnes (5) *trkd ldrs, effrt o'r 2 fs out, hdwy to ld ins fnl furlong, pushed clr.* .... (11 to 2 op 9 to 2 tchd 6 to 1) 1
2364[2] ALLEZ CYRANO (Ire) 9-0 M Hills (3) *led till hdd wl o'r one furlong out, kpt on ins last.* .... (Evens fav tchd 11 to 10 and 6 to 5) 2
3352[3] PICCOLO 9-0 L Piggott (1) *dwlt, sn tracking ldrs, led wl o'r one furlong out, hdd ins last, no extr.* ....(2 to 1 op 6 to 4 tchd 9 to 4) 3
2502[2] MILL FORCE 9-0 J Fanning (2) *prmnt, chlgd 2 fs out, sn rdn and btn*.................... (8 to 1) 4
3143[5] SINBAD 9-0 N Connorton (4) *in tch till wknd o'r 2 fs out.* .... (40 to 1 op 33 to 1) 5
ESPLEY NIPPER 8-11 (3*) S D Williams (6) *al beh.* .... (25 to 1 op 14 to 1) 6
3218[6] MANOLETE 9-0 K Fallon (7) *chsd ldr to hfwy, sn wknd.* .... (50 to 1 op 33 to 1) 7
Dist: 2½l, sht-hd, 4l, 12l, 2½l, 6l. 1m 25.29s. a 1.29s (7 Ran).
SR: 44/36/35/23/ (Hamdan Al-Maktoum), J L Dunlop

3673 Leaf Claiming Stakes Class G (2-y-o) £2,490 5f...................... (3:20)

3432 FEATHERSTONE LANE 8-5 W Newnes (3) *beh, hdwy on outsd hfwy, led o'r one furlong out, ran on wl.* .... (25 to 1 op 16 to 1) 1
2412[7] KING RAT (Ire) 8-9 T Williams (8) *al prmnt, chlgd o'r one furlong out, kpt on ins fnl furlong*..(9 to 2 op 4 to 1) 2
3279 DANGEROUS SHADOW 8-2 (5*) Darren Moffatt (2) *beh, sn pushed alng, hdwy 2 fs out, wnt lft jst ins fnl furlong, nrst finish*..................(5 to 2 fav tchd 11 to 4) 3
3279[6] PAGODA 7-12 (3*) S Maloney (7) *wth ldrs, led briefly o'r one furlong out, wknd fnl furlong.* ....(8 to 1 op 7 to 1 tchd 9 to 1) 4
3426[4] NOSMO KING (Ire) (bl) 8-6[1] L Piggott (10) *beh till styd on und pres fnl 2 fs, not trble ldrs*......(11 to 1 op 8 to 1) 5
2814[3] DOCKYARD DORA 8-2 M Hills (6) *wth ldrs, wkng whn hmpd jst ins fnl furlong*........... (10 to 1 op 8 to 1) 6

3321^{4} PELAMIS 8-5^{2} (3*) S D Williams (4) *chsd ldrs till wknd o'r one furlong out*.................... (14 to 1 op 8 to 1) 7
CHADWELL HALL 8-7 K Fallon (9) *nvr dngrs*. .... (33 to 1 op 16 to 1) 8
3566 KAYDARAJ (v) 8-0 A McGlone (5) *prmnt till wknd 2 fs out*. .... (14 to 1 op 10 to 1) 9
3441^{5} LUCIUS LOCKET (Ire) 8-4 J Fanning (1) *slight ld till hdd o'r one furlong out, wknd quickly*...... (9 to 2 op 7 to 2) 10
Dist: 1½l, 2l, 2½l, 1l, 1½l, nk, 1½l, 3½l, 2½l. 1m 0.83s. a 1.93s (10 Ran).
SR: 17/15/5/-/-/-/ (Mrs Barbara Holroyd), Miss L C Siddall

3674 Virginia Rated Class A Handicap (Listed Race) (0-105 3-y-o and up) £9,437 1 ¼m 32yds..................... (3:55)

2207* LICORNE [80] 3-7-13 A McGlone (5) *trkd ldrs, led o'r one furlong out, drvn clr*...........................(6 to 1) 1
2997* FORTHWITH [88] 3-8-7 M Hills (7) *cl up, led 7 fs out, hdd o'r one out, kpt on, no ch wth wnr*. ....(9 to 2 op 5 to 1 tchd 6 to 1) 2
2884* ROSE ALTO [93] 5-9-6 K Fallon (2) *unruly stalls, trkd ldrs, kpt on same pace frm 3 fs out*....... (6 to 1 op 5 to 1) 3
3036* SILVERLOCKS [84] 3-8-3 N Connorton (4) *trkd ldrs, outpcd 3 fs out, no dngr aftr*................ (9 to 1 op 8 to 1) 4
2334 SUMOTO [93] 3-8-12 W Newnes (3) *hld up, effrt 3 out, no hdwy*................(10 to 1 op 8 to 1 tchd 11 to 1) 5
3262^{2} ANDROMAQUE (USA) [98] 3-9-3 T Sprake (1) *dwlt, hld up, rdn 3 fs out, no hdwy*... (9 to 2 op 3 to 1 tchd 5 to 1) 6
3262^{4} GISARNE (USA) [102] 3-9-7 L Piggott (6) *led 3 fs, chsd ldr till wknd 2 out*. (11 to 4 fav op 3 to 1 tchd 100 to 30) 7
Dist: 5l, 3½l, ½l, 1½l, 1½l, 1½l. 2m 6.60s. a 0.10s (7 Ran).
SR: 64/62/68/50/56/58/59/ (Lord Howard de Walden), H R A Cecil

3675 Perkins Memorial Cup Handicap Class C (0-90 3-y-o and up) £4,751 2m 19yds......................... (4:30)

3473* WELSHMAN [64] 7-8-5^{2} K Fallon (5) *prmnt, led o'r 2 fs out, hrd pressed fnl two furlongs, styd on gmely*. ....(13 to 2 op 6 to 1 tchd 7 to 1) 1
2239^{2} HIGHFLYING [87] 7-10-0 W Newnes (3) *trkd ldrs gng wl, chlgd 2 fs out, rdn entering fnl furlong, no extr towards finish*...................(5 to 2 op 2 to 1 tchd 11 to 4) 2
3125^{7} GOOD HAND (USA) [83] 7-9-10 N Connorton (2) *sn pushed alng and beh, styd on fnl 3 fs, nrst finish*. .... (13 to 2 op 6 to 1) 3
3401^{3} MOONSHINE LAKE [85] 3-8-12 A McGlone (1) *led till hdd o'r 2 fs out, sn btn*. (2 to 1 fav op 11 to 4 tchd 3 to 1) 4
2755^{9} FREE MOVER (Ire) [77] 4-9-4 L Piggott (4) *hld up, effrt 5 fs out, btn 3 out*............................ (9 to 1 op 7 to 1) 5
2801* MERRY NUTKIN [80] 7-9-7 J Fanning (6) *chsd ldr till wknd o'r 3 fs out*.......................... (8 to 1 op 7 to 1) 6
Dist: ½l, 6l, 8l, 8l, 4l. 3m 27.70s. a 1.70s (6 Ran).
SR: 42/64/54/34/32/31/ (Brian Oxton), M Blanshard

3676 Cheviot Handicap Class D (0-80 3-y-o and up) £3,817 7f...............(5:05)

3060^{4} ROYAL GIRL [61] 6-9-3 N Connorton (4) *trkd ldrs, effrt 2 fs out, led ins last, ran on wl*......... (6 to 1 tchd 7 to 1) 1
3558^{2} NORTH ARDAR [62] 3-8-13 T Williams (7) *trkd ldrs, drvn to ld 2 fs out, hdd ins last*................ (9 to 2 op 4 to 1) 2
3450* LORD ALFIE [53] 4-8-9 M Hills (8) *hld up in tch, hdwy o'r 2 fs out, one pace fnl furlong*...... (3 to 1 fav op 7 to 2) 3
2572 CAVATINA [77] 3-9-11 (3*) S D Williams (9) *slight ld till hdd 2 fs out, one pace*.................................(25 to 1) 4
3504 TARNSIDE ROSAL [70] 3-9-7 W Newnes (2) *in tch, chsd alng hfwy, kpt on same pace*...... (12 to 1 op 10 to 1) 5
3535^{5} BLUE GRIT [64] (bl) 7-9-6 L Piggott (3) *beh, hrd rdn 2 fs out, not rch ldrs*......................... (8 to 1 op 7 to 1) 6
3504^{8} SENSE OF PRIORITY [66] 4-9-5 (3*) S Maloney (6) *reared strt, hld up in tch, effrt o'r 2 fs out, no hdwy*. ....(7 to 1 op 8 to 1 tchd 9 to 1) 7
3088^{5} WORKINGFORPEANUTS (Ire) [43] (v) 3-7-8 J Fanning (5) *cl up till wknd o'r 2 fs out*............(8 to 1 tchd 9 to 1) 8
3440^{3} LANGUEDOC [59] 6-9-1 K Fallon (1) *in tch till wknd o'r 2 fs out*.................................(7 to 1 op 6 to 1) 9
Dist: ½l, 2½l, 1½l, hd, hd, hd, 5l, ¾l. 1m 26.08s. a 2.08s (9 Ran).
SR: 35/29/17/31/23/21/22/-/-/ (Miss S E Hall), Miss S E Hall

RIPON (good to firm) Monday August 30th

Going Correction: NIL (races 1,3), MINUS 0.25 (2,4,5,6)

3677 Stainley Selling Stakes Class G (2-y-o) £2,868 6f.................. (2:00)

2973^{4} AMORET (Ire) 8-7^{1} R Cochrane (1) *made most stands side, quickened clr o'r one furlong out, readily*. ....(7 to 1 op 12 to 1 tchd 13 to 2) 1
3052^{5} DAILY STAR 8-6 J Carroll (2) *wth ldrs, drvn alng o'r 2 fs out, not quicken over one out*...... (8 to 1 op 10 to 1) 2
3133^{5} CERTIFICATE-X 8-11 R Hills (11) *pressed ldg grp on outsd, effrt and rdn o'r 2 fs out, edgd lft over one out, not quicken*............ (2 to 1 fav op 6 to 4 tchd 9 to 4) 3
3098^{2} RANDOM 8-6 J Lowe (8) *settled midfield, shaken up and swtchd to improve 2 fs out, kpt on ins last*. .... (17 to 2 op 8 to 1 tchd 9 to 1) 4
3114^{5} DEMON DANCER (Ire) 8-11 M Roberts (3) *nvr far away, rdn hfwy, not quicken wl o'r one furlong out*. (16 to 1) 5
2637^{7} REAL POPCORN (Ire) 8-6 P Robinson (6) *rcd beh ldrs, pushed alng to improve o'r 2 fs out, no imprsn over one out*............................. (50 to 1 op 33 to 1) 6
3432^{7} CLARET BUMBLE 8-11 K Darley (12) *dsptd ld centre to hfwy, sn drvn alng, btn wl o'r one out*. ....(7 to 1 op 5 to 1) 7
3539^{4} BENEFICIARY 8-11 M Birch (7) *chsd ldrs, shaken up hfwy, wknd 2 fs out*.... (4 to 1 op 7 to 2 tchd 11 to 2) 8
CULRAIN 8-11 S Webster (13) *beh and sn wl outpcd, hdwy o'r one furlong out, not rch ldrs*. .... (20 to 1 op 16 to 1) 9
3363^{8} MOKAITE 8-6 (5*) J Marshall (10) *cl up centre, rdn and wknd wl o'r 2 fs out*........... (20 to 1 op 16 to 1) 10
3281 TILQUHILLIE ROSE (bl) 8-6 T Lucas (9) *beh, drvn and veered rght hfwy, nvr on terms*................ (33 to 1) 11
EILIEHUSH 8-6 Alex Greaves (5) *beh, pushed alng aftr 2 fs, nvr a factor*..................(50 to 1 op 33 to 1) 12
3303 PITIARA 8-6 S Wood (4) *dsptd ld to hfwy, drvn alng and sn lost pl, tld off*..............................(50 to 1) 13
Dist: 5l, 1l, 3l, 2l, 1l, ¾l, hd, 2½l, 2l, nk. 1m 13.50s. a 2.90s (13 Ran).
SR: 35/14/15/-/-/-/ (W J Whitaker), Sir Mark Prescott

3678 BonusPrint Rating Related Maiden Stakes Class D (2-y-o) £3,590 1m (2:30)

3259^{5} BLAIR CASTLE (Ire) 9-0 R Cochrane (4) *sn led, shaken up 2 fs out, edgd lft appr last, drw clr*.....(9 to 4 op 2 to 1) 1
3421^{6} HARDING 9-0 W R Swinburn (2) *trkd ldr, effrt and rdn o'r 2 fs out, not quicken ins last, eased nr finish*. .... (5 to 2 op 9 to 4 tchd 11 to 4) 2
3351^{2} MIDUSHI (USA) 8-9 K Darley (1) *nvr far away, outpcd and rdn o'r 3 fs out, effrt und pres 2 out, one pace ins last*. ....(11 to 8 fav op 5 to 4 tchd 6 to 4) 3
3259^{9} RIVA'S BOOK (USA) (bl) 9-0 J Carroll (5) *hld up in last, rdn 4 fs out, no extr fnl 2 furlongs*.......(11 to 1 op 10 to 1) 4
Dist: 2l, 1½l, 7l. 1m 42.90s. a 4.60s (4 Ran).
SR: 1/ (Highflyers), I A Balding

3679 BonusPrint Champion Two Years Old Trophy, 1993 Class A (Listed Race) £9,056 6f..................... (3:00)

3230* EHTFAAL (Ire) 8-6 R Hills (4) *trkd ldrs gng wl, led o'r one furlong out, rdn and ran on well whn hrd pressed ins last*............ (4 to 1 op 7 to 2 tchd 9 to 2) 1
3435^{4} ALANEES 8-11 W R Swinburn (2) *settled beh ldrs, improved and pld wide o'r 2 fs out, ran on chal ins last, no extr nr finish*.......... (13 to 2 op 7 to 1) 2
3436* BID FOR BLUE 9-2 K Darley (5) *nvr far away, led aftr 2 fs, drvn alng and hdd o'r one out, kpt on same pace ins last*.................................. (9 to 2 op 7 to 2) 3
3357* HANNAH'S MUSIC 8-9 R Cochrane (1) *tucked away on ins, sn pushed alng, swtchd and improved o'r one furlong out, kpt on inside last, nvr dngrs*. ....(7 to 1 tchd 15 to 2) 4
2301^{4} SNIPE HALL 8-11 P Robinson (7) *co'red up beh ldrs, rdn 2 fs out, sn one pace*...............(7 to 2 op 3 to 1) 5
3357^{4} MR M-E-N (Ire) 8-11 J Carroll (6) *veered rght leaving stalls, chsd ldrs on outsd, rdn o'r 2 fs out, no extr*. .... (8 to 1 op 14 to 1) 6
3545* MAJOR SUCCESS (Ire) 8-11 M Roberts (3) *veered to stands rail leaving stalls, led 2 fs, drvn hfwy, btn and eased fnl two furlongs*.......(9 to 2 tchd 5 to 1 and 4 to 1) 7
Dist: ½l, 2½l, ¾l, 2½l, 3½l, hd. 1m 12.60s. a 2.00s (7 Ran).
SR: 52/55/50/40/32/18/17/ (Hamdan Al-Maktoum), H Thomson Jones

3680 Ripon Rowels Handicap Class C (0-100 3-y-o and up) £7,505 1m.. (3:30)

3506* CAMBARA [82] 3-8-9 M Roberts (1) *trkd ldr gng wl, led 3 fs out, quickened fnl furlong, readily*. ....(3 to 1 fav op 5 to 2) 1
3179^{5} JURA FOREST [84] 3-8-11 W R Swinburn (7) *hld up, not clr run 2 fs out, swtchd lft, improved and switched ins appr last, kpt on same pace towards finish*. ....(8 to 1 op 7 to 1) 2
3314^{4} BRIGANTE DI CIELO [92] 3-9-5 R Cochrane (2) *nvr far away, chlgd 3 fs out, rdn and not quicken appr last*. ....(5 to 1 tchd 11 to 2) 3
3540* PRIDE OF PENDLE [72] 4-8-5 (6ex) K Darley (4) *hld up, effrt whn not clr run wl o'r one furlong out, swtchd and sn hmpd, ran on ins fnl furlong, nvr dngrs*. ....(7 to 1 op 6 to 1) 4
3465^{9} TAUFAN BLU (Ire) [95] 4-9-7 (7*) D Thomas (3) *chsd ldrs on ins, pushed alng 3 fs out, one pace o'r one out*. .... (20 to 1 op 16 to 1) 5
3135^{3} NO SUBMISSION (USA) [65] 7-7-12 S Wood (8) *led till 3 fs out, sn drvn alng, no extr 2 out*. (20 to 1 tchd 25 to 1) 6

2926 FOREVER DIAMONDS [84] 6-9-3 M Birch (5) *hld up, effrt on outsd o'r 2 fs out, btn over one out*.........(6 to 1) 7
2926[5] NORTHERN BIRD [85] 3-8-12 R Hills (6) *keen hold early, mid-div, effrt and rdn o'r 2 fs out, sn btn*. ....(7 to 1 op 6 to 1) 8
3512[8] PIQUANT [82] 6-9-1 J Carroll (9) *tucked away on ins, swtchd outsd 4 fs out, effrt and rdn 3 out, btn whn not much room and eased fnl furlong*....(8 to 1 op 7 to 1) 9
Dist: 3l, ½l, 1½l, 2l, sht-hd, 1½l, 1l, 5l. 1m 39.30s. a 1.00s (9 Ran).
SR: 50/43/49/30/47/16/30/22/10/ (Sheikh Mohammed), M R Stoute

3681 Pateley Handicap Class E (0-70 3-y-o) £4,305 1¼m.................... (4:00)

3301* TINSASHE (Ire) [54] 8-6 R Hills (12) *tucked away on ins, effrt and rdn o'r 2 fs out, led over one out, pushed clr inside last*........................(6 to 1 tchd 13 to 2) 1
3394[5] BRONZE MAQUETTE (Ire) [57] 8-9[8] (7*) J Gracey (10) *hld up, hdwy 3 fs out, ev ch o'r one out, no extr ins last*. ....(14 to 1 op 10 to 1) 2
1661[2] JONSALAN [66] 9-4 J Carroll (2) *settled mid-div, rdn to improve o'r 3 fs out, styd on und pres ins last, nvr dngrs*.......................(10 to 1 op 8 to 1) 3
3306[2] LEAR KING (USA) [69] (bl) 9-7 W R Swinburn (11) *nvr far away, rdn o'r 2 fs out, wknd one out*. ....(5 to 1 op 6 to 1 tchd 13 to 2) 4
3113[2] DODGY DANCER [66] 9-4 S Whitworth (7) *hld up, drvn 3 fs out, edgd rght, kpt on same pace ins last*. ....(9 to 2 fav op 11 to 2 tchd 6 to 1) 5
3355 MERRY MERMAID [47] 7-13 L Charnock (4) *hld up, pushed alng and not clr run 3 fs out, kpt on fnl furlong, nvr able to chal*.......................(10 to 1 tchd 11 to 1) 6
3507 MHEMEANLES [63] (bl) 9-1 M Birch (1) *tacked o'r to ins rail leaving stalls, led, clr into strt, rdn over 2 fs out, hdd over one out, sn btn*....(9 to 1 op 7 to 1 tchd 10 to 1) 7
3256[6] ROYAL DIVA [54] 8-6 M Roberts (3) *in tch, sn niggled alng, drvn 3 fs out, soon one pace*.........(9 to 1 op 8 to 1) 8
2859 MONASTIC FLIGHT (Ire) [45] 7-11 S Wood (5) *hld up, drvn alng to take clr order o'r 3 fs out, wknd 2 furlongs out*. ....(16 to 1 op 12 to 1) 9
1812[3] GREYSTYLE [42] 7-8[1] J Lowe (14) *co'red up on ins, rdn entering strt, btn over 2 fs out*..................(33 to 1) 10
2448[2] ARMENIAN COFFEE (Ire) [69] (bl) 9-7 R Cochrane (6) *settled midfield, pushed alng 3 fs out, sn btn*. ....(9 to 1 op 7 to 1) 11
2631 HABEEBITTI NADIA [41] 7-7[7] (7*) K Sked (9) *beh and sn struggling, nvr a factor*.......(50 to 1 op 33 to 1) 12
2822[3] TRY N' FLY (Ire) [60] 8-12 K Darley (13) *chsd ldrs, rdn entering strt, btn o'r 3 fs out, tld off*. (10 to 1 op 8 to 1) 13
2914[3] BLOWEDIFIKNOW [63] 9-1 P Robinson (8) *trkd ldg pair, pushed alng 4 fs out, sn btn, tld off*. ....(16 to 1 op 14 to 1) 14
Dist: 3l, 7l, 1½l, sht-hd, 1½l, ¾l, ½l, nk, ½l, nk. 2m 6.90s. a 2.90s (14 Ran).
SR: 38/35/30/30/26/4/18/8/-/ (A Foustok), W Jarvis

3682 Grassington Maiden Fillies' Stakes Class D (3-y-o) £3,348 1½m 60yds ....(4:30)

2752[3] TREE OF LIFE 8-11 R Cochrane (2) *hld up in tch, took clr order entering strt, improved to ld o'r one furlong out, hng rght and swshd tail, ran on ins last*. ....(11 to 8 fav op 6 to 4 tchd 7 to 4) 1
3491[3] ELATIS (USA) 8-11 M Roberts (3) *nvr far away, rdn o'r 3 fs out, chlgd 2 out, not quicken ins last*..........(7 to 2) 2
3491[2] KARDELLE 8-11 W R Swinburn (4) *trkd ldrs, drpd rear 6 out, not much room and swtchd 4 four fs out, rdn 3 out, one pace and eased ins last*. ....(11 to 4 op 5 to 2 tchd 3 to 1) 3
3272 EDITHMEAD (Ire) 8-11 S Whitworth (6) *led, slightly wide strt, rdn o'r 3 fs out, hdd over one out, no extr*. ....(16 to 1 op 20 to 1) 4
3491[5] TOKYO 8-11 K Darley (1) *hld up in last, lost tch o'r 3 fs out, tld off*...........(11 to 1 op 8 to 1 tchd 12 to 1) 5
RYNAVEY 8-11 J Lowe (5) *slwly into strd, sn reco'red to track ldrs, chlgd entering strt, rdn and lost tch over 3 out, tld off*............(6 to 1 op 7 to 2 tchd 13 to 2) 6
Dist: 2½l, 3l, 3l, 30l, 3l. 2m 37.40s. a 2.40s (6 Ran).
SR: 42/37/31/25/-/-/ (Lord Halifax), L M Cumani

ROSCOMMON (IRE) (good to firm) Monday August 30th

3683 Cloonbrackna E.B.F. Maiden (2-y-o) £3,452 7f...................... (5:45)

3039[4] MANAAFIS (Ire) 9-0 W J Supple (8)..........(9 to 4 jt-fav) 1
2701[3] UNBUCKLE (Ire) 9-0 M J Kinane (11)..............(5 to 2) 2
SHELWA (USA) 8-11 C Roche (1)............(9 to 4 jt-fav) 3
3071[7] MAKE THAT CALL (Ire) 8-11 P V Gilson (7)........(14 to 1) 4
3453[5] BETTER STYLE (Ire) 8-11 J P Murtagh (4).........(16 to 1) 5
2804 EUPHORIC (Ire) 8-12 (2*) D G O'Shea (9)..........(14 to 1) 6
TRAGIC POINT (Ire) 8-3 (8*) T E Durcan (5).........(20 to 1) 7
3541[8] TINERANA ROSE (Ire) 8-3 (8*) P J Smullen (3)......(16 to 1) 8
3332 THE MARDYKE (Ire) 9-0 K J Manning (2).........(12 to 1) 9
2294[6] PASTELLE 8-11 R Dolan (10)...................(16 to 1) 10
3030 EMELIA'S PET (Ire) 9-0 J F Egan (6).............(20 to 1) 11
Dist: 2l, 2l, 3l, 4½l. 1m 32.00s. (11 Ran).
(Hamdan Al-Maktoum), Kevin Prendergast

3684 Fuerty Handicap (0-70 3-y-o and up) £2,762 1½m.................. (6:45)

3580[3] SENSE OF VALUE [-] 4-9-8 J P Murtagh (1)........(3 to 1) 1
3604[3] OPEN MARKET (USA) [-] (bl) 4-10-0 M J Kinane (5) ....(5 to 2 fav) 2
FORTUNE'S GIRL [-] 5-8-6 P V Gilson (10).......(12 to 1) 3
3604[2] SPRING RITE [-] (bl) 6-6-13 (8*) G M Moylan (12)...(5 to 1) 4
3368* WICKLOW WAY (Ire) [-] 3-8-12 W J Supple (7)......(8 to 1) 5
3580 NORDIC UNION (Ire) [-] 3-8-12 C Roche (3).......(12 to 1) 6
2806[6] INAUGURATION (Ire) [-] 4-8-12 (4*) J J Behan (4)...(6 to 1) 7
3397 GRANDEUR (Ire) [-] 3-7-6[1] (2*) D G O'Shea (2)....(16 to 1) 8
3543[9] CARAVELLE LAD (Ire) [-] 3-7-11 (8*) J J Mullins (6) (16 to 1) 9
2035 SPECIAL OFFER (Ire) [-] 3-8-10 (6*) J A Heffernan (9) ....(12 to 1) 10
944[8] THE SALTY FROG (Ire) [-] 3-8-4 J F Egan (8)......(16 to 1) 11
Dist: 1l, 2l, 1½l, 2l. 2m 37.80s. (11 Ran).
(F Dunne), F Dunne

3685 Dunnes Stores Ladies Fashion Series (3-y-o and up) £3,452 1½m......(7:45)

2451[5] PRINCIPLE MUSIC (USA) (bl) 5-9-13 (3ex) Miss U Smyth (2) ....(7 to 4 on) 1
2881 TOP GENERATION 4-9-2 (2*) Miss T Cunningham (1) (7 to 1) 2
3578[9] CAT FIGHT 6-9-2 (2*) Miss G Morgan (5).........(25 to 1) 3
3382[9] BETTER GOODS (Ire) 3-8-11 Miss A Gilsenan (3)..(14 to 1) 4
MIZRAHI (USA) 4-9-12 (8ex) Miss C Hutchinson (4) (9 to 4) pu
Dist: 1½l, 10l, 2l. 2m 42.40s. (5 Ran).
(Michael W J Smurfit), D K Weld

WARWICK (good to firm) Monday August 30th

Going Correction: MINUS 0.35 sec. per fur. (races 1,3,4,5,6,8), MINUS 0.40 (2,7)

3686 Rugby Maiden Auction Stakes Class F (2-y-o) £2,070 7f...............(2:00)

3490[8] TIMES ZANDO 8-9 J Fortune (4) *led aftr a furlong, pushed clr entering strt, unchlgd*............(8 to 1 op 6 to 1) 1
3287[8] POLAR QUEST 9-0 S Raymont (3) *in tch, hdwy to chase wnr fnl 2 fs, kpt on ins last*........(11 to 2 op 7 to 2) 2
1583[5] QUEENS STROLLER (Ire) 8-9 D Holland (8) *al wl plcd, rdn o'r a furlong out, one pace*. ....(7 to 4 fav op 5 to 2 tchd 7 to 2) 3
3390[2] COMEONUP 9-0 J Reid (10) *hld up, effrt o'r 2 fs out, kpt on one pace*............(3 to 1 op 7 to 2 tchd 2 to 1) 4
2687[4] HARLEQUIN WALK (Ire) 8-2 (7*) N Varley (11) *pressed ldrs, rdn 2 fs out, sn outpcd*............(16 to 1 op 10 to 1) 5
3528[6] SECRATORIUS (Ire) 8-11 (3*) Stephen Davies (2) *chsd ldrs for 5 fs, sn rdn and one pace*......(33 to 1 op 25 to 1) 6
SAN DIEGO CHARGER (Ire) 8-11 (3*) O Pears (5) *hld up, effrt 2 fs out, nvr nr to chal*........(20 to 1 op 14 to 1) 7
3422 CHOPENDOZ (USA) 9-0 F Norton (6) *pressed ldrs, rdn and outpcd blw dist*..................(14 to 1 op 8 to 1) 8
3218[5] MILAIRIOUS (Ire) 9-0 A Mackay (12) *speed o'r 4 fs*. ....(10 to 1 op 7 to 1) 9
3126 ARIAN SPIRIT (Ire) 8-4 (5*) D McCabe (9) *sn rdn alng, nvr nr ldrs*..............................(33 to 1 op 25 to 1) 10
2274 POLAR CAP 8-11 (3*) N Kennedy (1) *al in rear*. ....(25 to 1 op 14 to 1) 11
2705 DUCHESS DAISY (bl) 8-9 Kim Tinkler (7) *led for a furlong, prmnt till rdn and wknd entering strt*. ....(50 to 1 op 25 to 1) 12
Dist: 3l, 1½l, 1½l, 2½l, ¾l. 1m 26.30s. a 2.50s (12 Ran).
SR: 21/17/7/7/-/-/ (Times Of Wigan), Capt J Wilson

3687 North Warwickshire Pony Club Claiming Stakes Class E (Div I) (3-y-o and up) £2,954 5f...................(2:30)

3343[3] FIRST OPTION 3-9-3 D Holland (10) *hdwy hfwy, rdn o'r one furlong out, ran on to ld wl ins last*. ....(9 to 2 op 7 to 2 tchd 11 to 2) 1
3100* SAMSON-AGONISTES 7-8-9 (7*) S Sanders (9) *wth ldr, slight ld hfwy, hdd and no extr wl ins fnl furlong*. ....(3 to 1 op 9 to 4 tchd 100 to 30) 2
3229[8] SEAMERE (bl) 10-8-3 (7*) C Hawksley (2) *hdwy 2 fs out, hmpd and swtchd rght fnl furlong, ran on strly*. ....(25 to 1 op 14 to 1) 3
3486[6] SIR TASKER 5-9-0 A Mackay (6) *hdwy entering fnl furlong, hrd rdn, fnshd wl*...........(14 to 1 op 12 to 1) 4
3425 FIRST GOLD 4-9-4 J Reid (11) *took clr order hfwy, kpt on ins fnl furlong, nvr able to chal*... (16 to 1 op 10 to 1) 5
3253[2] VERY DICEY 5-9-0 J Fortune (5) *slight ld to hfwy, hrd rdn and wknd o'r a furlong out*. ....(11 to 4 fav op 7 to 2 tchd 5 to 2) 6
3220[5] HICKORY BLUE 3-8-11 (3*) O Pears (3) *gd speed for 3 fs*. ....(4 to 1 op 11 to 2) 7
2352[8] IRON KING 7-7-13 (5*) A Garth (4) *chsd ldrs o'r 3 fs, sn rdn and outpcd*......................(10 to 1 tchd 16 to 1) 8

3127 WADERS DREAM (Ire) 4-8-11 (5*) L Newton (7) *nvr gng pace of ldrs*............................ (16 to 1 op 6 to 1) 9

PINEAPPLE PRINCE 3-8-3 (7*) S Drowne (8) *outpcd, tld off.* .... (33 to 1 op 20 to 1) 10

CEE DEE 4-8-3 K Williamson (1) *strted slwly, al tld off.* .... (66 to 1 op 33 to 1) 11

Dist: 1½l, ½l, hd, ¾l, 2l, nk, ½l, 1½l, 15l, 15l. 58.80s. a 0.60s (11 Ran).
SR: 51/44/36/39/40/28/27/15/21/ (P D Savill), M H Easterby

3688 Avonvale Volvo Nursery Class E (2-y-o) £3,027 6f.................. (3:00)

3428[3] PRIMA SILK [75] 8-7 (7*) P McCabe (4) *outpcd, hdwy 2 fs out, sn rdn, ran on to ld ins fnl furlong.* ....(4 to 1 op 3 to 1) 1

3475* BRAVE EDGE [82] 9-7 J Reid (1) *led till ins fnl furlong, hrd rdn, unbl to quicken*...........(13 to 8 fav op 9 to 4) 2

877[7] KENNET BOY [60] 7-13 F Norton (2) *slwly into strd, beh and outpcd, hdwy blw dist, ran on.* (9 to 2 op 3 to 1) 3

3626[2] STRAPPED [54] 7-2[2] (7*) N Varley (6) *outpcd, hdwy o'r one furlong out, strly rdn and ran on fnl furlong.* ....(4 to 1 op 5 to 2) 4

3475[4] WINDOW DISPLAY [64] 8-3 A Mackay (5) *chsd ldr, ran very wide entering strt, sn lost tch tld off.* .... (13 to 2 op 6 to 1 tchd 7 to 1) 5

Dist: 1½l, 1½l, nk, 15l. 1m 13.50s. a 1.80s (5 Ran).
SR: 21/22/ (Three Ply Racing), M J Ryan

3689 St Nicholas Selling Stakes Class G (3-y-o and up) £2,070 1¼m 169yds (3:30)

3536[3] ANN HILL (Ire) 3-8-5 (5*) A Garth (8) *patiently rdn, steady hdwy 4 fs out, quickened to ld entering fnl furlong, ran on strly*......(4 to 1 op 5 to 1 tchd 6 to 1 and 7 to 2) 1

3221* KIAWAH 3-8-3 (7*) N Varley (7) *slwly into strd, hld up, hdwy entering strt, pld wide, str run fnl furlong, jst fld*.................. (3 to 1 fav op 2 to 1 tchd 7 to 2) 2

2358[5] TEJANO GOLD (USA) 3-8-12 J Reid (11) *al cl up, led o'r 2 fs out, hdd entering fnl furlong, one pace.* ....(6 to 1 op 4 to 1) 3

3407[2] LE TEMERAIRE 7-9-10 Kim Tinkler (15) *led aftr 2 fs, hdd o'r two furlongs out, kpt on same pace.* (5 to 1 op 3 to 1) 4

3518[3] GOTT'S DESIRE (bl) 7-9-5 (5*) V Slattery (16) *settled midfield, effrt 3 fs out, sn rdn and not pace to chal.* .... (14 to 1 op 12 to 1 tchd 16 to 1) 5

WE'RE IN THE MONEY 9-9-2 F Norton (14) *hld up, hdwy o'r 2 fs out, nvr nrr*................(33 to 1 op 20 to 1) 6

2833[7] NIGELS PROSPECT 3-8-12 A Mackay (1) *hld up in rear, hdwy 3 fs out, styd on*.................(20 to 1 op 14 to 1) 7

3506[9] JASPER ONE 3-8-9 (3*) O Pears (6) *led 2 fs, wknd o'r two furlongs out*......... (14 to 1 op 20 to 1 tchd 25 to 1) 8

MONTAGNE 4-8-9 (7*) S Drowne (12) *pressed ldrs for o'r 6 fs, sn lost tch*.................... (20 to 1 op 12 to 1) 9

3536[7] ROMANTIC MOOD 4-9-4 (3*) N Kennedy (5) *tucked away in midfield, hdwy o'r 2 fs out, sn rdn and wknd.* .... (33 to 1 op 16 to 1) 10

2162 CLEAR LIGHT 6-9-10 Dale Gibson (13) *chsd ldrs, rdn o'r 3 fs out, grad fdd.* ....(16 to 1 op 20 to 1 tchd 25 to 1 and 14 to 1) 11

3514 TOUCHEE BOUCHEE 3-8-7 A Tucker (10) *wtd wth, took clr order 4 fs out, rdn and wknd fnl 2 furlongs.* .... (33 to 1 op 20 to 1) 12

3384[6] FREDDY SYLVESTER 3-8-12 D Holland (3) *nvr a factor.* ....(7 to 1 op 4 to 1) 13

3509[8] FORTUNE STAR (Ire) 4-9-3 (7*) Rachel Bridger (2) *al beh, tld off*....................................(40 to 1 op 20 to 1) 14

3425 RAPINSKI 4-9-7 K Williamson (9) *al beh, tld off.* .... (50 to 1 op 20 to 1) 15

Dist: ½l, 3½l, 3½l, hd, 1½l, hd, 3½l, 2½l, ½l, 4l. 2m 16.70s. a 3.90s (15 Ran).
SR: 19/18/13/18/17/6/1/-/-/ (A S Hill), R Hollinshead

3690 Listers Audi Volkswagen Warwick Cesarewitch Handicap Class D (0-80 3-y-o and up) £3,582 2m 20yds.. (4:00)

3473[2] AUDE LA BELLE (Fr) [64] 5-9-1 A Mackay (7) *hld up, took clr order 6 fs out, styd on to ld jst ins fnl furlong, sn clr.* .... (4 to 1 jt-fav tchd 9 to 2) 1

3319[7] WESTERN DYNASTY [70] 7-9-0 (7*) P McCabe (6) *sn chasing ldr, led o'r 2 fs out till ins fnl furlong, no extr.* ....(6 to 1 op 5 to 1) 2

3231[3] MONARDA [67] 6-8-11 (7*) D Goggin (10) *wtd wth, hdwy 6 fs out, effrt appr fnl furlong, not pace to chal.* ....(6 to 1 op 9 to 2) 3

3231* SPECTACULAR DAWN [76] 4-9-13 J Reid (8) *led till hdd o'r 2 fs out, hmpd entering strt, sn wknd.* ....(9 to 2 op 7 to 2) 4

3473[9] FRENCH IVY (USA) [65] 6-8-11 (5*) A Garth (5) *trkd ldrs, styd on same pace fnl 2 fs.* .... (8 to 1 op 10 to 1 tchd 14 to 1) 5

3121[4] LEGION OF HONOUR [61] 5-8-5 (7*) V Halliday (1) *al in tch, hrd rdn o'r 2 fs out, sn btn*........ (14 to 1 op 10 to 1) 6

2904[9] PATROCLUS [44] 8-7-9[2] S Dawson (4) *al in rear, tld off fnl 4 fs*.................................. (33 to 1 op 25 to 1) 7

3152[8] MY ROSSINI [64] 4-8-8 (7*) C Hawksley (2) *lost pl bef hfwy, tld off*................ (10 to 1 op 8 to 1 tchd 12 to 1) 8

2204[3] DIME BAG [69] 4-9-6 D Holland (11) *hld up, effrt 5 fs out, sn rdn and wknd, eased whn btn, tld off*.....(4 to 1 jt-fav op 9 to 2 tchd 7 to 2) 9

SUEZ CANAL (Ire) [69] 4-9-3 (3*) Stephen Davies (9) *cl up till lost pl hfwy, tld off*............... (20 to 1 op 16 to 1) 10

Dist: 4l, 4l, 10l, ¾l, 2l, 8l, 2l, 8l, 6l. 3m 27.80s. a 2.30s (10 Ran).
SR: 22/24/17/16/3/-/ (Mrs Val Rapkins), Mrs L Piggott

3691 Listers Vauxhall Conditions Stakes Class D (2-y-o) £3,915 7f........(4:30)

2964* ESCARPMENT (USA) 8-12 J Reid (1) *made all, drw clr o'r 3 fs out, canter*...............(25 to 1 on op 20 to 1 on) 1

BRENSHAM FOLLY 8-8 A Mackay (2) *dsptd ld to hfwy, sn rdn and wknd, eased whn btn, tld off.* .... (14 to 1 op 10 to 1 tchd 16 to 1) 2

Won by Dist. 1m 28.20s. a 4.40s (2 Ran).
SR: -/-/ (R E Sangster), P W Chapple-Hyam

3692 North Warwickshire Pony Club Claiming Stakes Class E (Div II) (3-y-o and up) £2,929 5f.................... (5:00)

3638 EAGER DEVA 6-9-1 (5*) S Wynne (10) *chsd ldr, shaken up to ld wl ins fnl furlong.* .... (2 to 1 fav op 7 to 4 tchd 6 to 4 and 9 to 4) 1

3404 ANOTHER LANE 6-8-11 D Holland (2) *al prmnt, swtchd rght blw dist, fnshd wl.* (5 to 1 op 4 to 1 tchd 6 to 1) 2

3011* THE NOBLE OAK (Ire) (bl) 5-8-10 J Reid (3) *led, quickened clr o'r a furlong out, hdd and no extr wl ins last.* .... (11 to 4 op 4 to 1 tchd 5 to 1) 3

3459[6] MOVING IMAGE (Ire) 3-8-8[2] C Dwyer (5) *hdwy o'r a furlong out, fnshd wl*..................... (14 to 1 op 12 to 1) 4

3360[8] CONVENIENT MOMENT 3-7-7 (7*) P Fessey (9) *chsd ldrs, effrt und pres 2 fs out, unbl to quicken.* .... (12 to 1 op 10 to 1) 5

3378[8] BEST EFFORT 7-8-3 (7*) V Halliday (7) *outpcd till hdwy appr fnl furlong, nvr nrr*......... (20 to 1 op 12 to 1) 6

2352[4] LUCEDEO 9-9-6 A Mackay (1) *mid-div, effrt o'r a furlong out, not pace to chal*.............. (12 to 1 op 8 to 1) 7

3100[4] JEWEL THIEF (v) 3-7-13 (7*) N Varley (6) *chsd ldrs o'r 3 fs.* .... (12 to 1 op 10 to 1 tchd 14 to 1) 8

3220[8] THE FED 3-8-9 Dale Gibson (8) *gd speed 3 fs.* .... (14 to 1 op 8 to 1) 9

2226[9] MARSH WARBLER (bl) 5-7-12 (7*) P McCabe (4) *outpcd, tld off*................................ (50 to 1 op 25 to 1) 10

Dist: 1l, sht-hd, 1l, ¾l, nk, nk, 1½l, 3½l, 8l. 59.50s. a 1.30s (10 Ran).
SR: 40/27/25/19/8/17/26/6/-/ (Mrs E G Faulkner), R Hollinshead

3693 Barford Maiden Fillies' Stakes Class D (3-y-o and up) £3,845 1m..... (5:30)

3012[5] WANNABE 3-8-11 J Reid (15) *rcd mid-div, rdn 3 fs out, kpt on to ld wl ins last.* .... (7 to 4 fav op 2 to 1 tchd 7 to 2) 1

3286[4] COMMON LAW (Ire) 3-8-11 S Raymont (5) *led, drvn clr wl o'r a furlong out, wknd and hdd towards finish.* .... (11 to 4 op 3 to 1 tchd 7 to 4) 2

MAJHOLA (Ire) 3-8-11 D Holland (6) *dwlt, hdwy o'r 2 fs out, kpt on wl ins fnl furlong*........(5 to 1 op 4 to 1) 3

3433[8] PREMIATA (Ire) 3-8-8 (3*) Stephen Davies (7) *took clr order hfwy, rdn entering strt, styd on*.... (10 to 1 op 5 to 1) 4

4720a[6] WESSHAUN 3-8-4 (7*) P McCabe (8) *ran on fnl 2 fs, nvr rch ldrs*..................... (50 to 1 op 33 to 1) 5

3431[7] MISS KINABALU 3-8-11 F Norton (1) *pressed ldrs, rdn o'r 2 fs out, sn btn*......................(25 to 1 op 12 to 1) 6

3491[9] SING A RAINBOW (Ire) 3-8-11 A Tucker (9) *cl up, chsd ldr frm hfwy, wknd blw dist*.......... (14 to 1 op 10 to 1) 7

3005[4] PROMITTO 3-8-11 J Fortune (2) *al chasing ldrs, rdn and wknd wl o'r a furlong out*......... (14 to 1 op 16 to 1) 8

2032[3] LADY SABINA 3-8-6 (5*) V Slattery (17) *prmnt till wknd 2 fs out*................. (10 to 1 op 12 to 1 tchd 14 to 1) 9

3233 EASY TOUCH 3-8-11 A Mackay (10) *trkd ldrs till wknd o'r 2 fs out*....................................(66 to 1) 10

SHARP GEM 3-8-4 (7*) N Varley (4) *nvr plcd to chal.* .... (20 to 1 op 33 to 1) 11

LADY BUCHAN 4-9-3 Kim Tinkler (16) *al in rear.* .... (20 to 1 op 14 to 1) 12

LA VILLA ROSE (Fr) 3-8-11 C Dwyer (3) *al beh.* .... (20 to 1 op 33 to 1) 13

POLLY LEACH 3-8-4 (7*) S Drowne (12) *prmnt, sn drvn alng, lost pl hfwy*............. (66 to 1 op 25 to 1) 14

MAID OF CADIZ 3-8-11 S Dawson (14) *nvr a factor.* .... (20 to 1 op 10 to 1) 15

RHAZYA 5-9-0 (3*) N Kennedy (13) *tld off.* .... (66 to 1 op 50 to 1) 16

3518 THRILL 5-9-3 K Williamson (11) *al in rear, tld off.* .... (66 to 1 op 33 to 1) 17

Dist: 1½l, 3½l, 1½l, 8l, nk, sht-hd, 1½l, ½l, nk, nk. 1m 37.60s. a 0.80s (17 Ran).
SR: 43/38/27/22/-/-/ (Michael Davey), L M Cumani

YARMOUTH (good)
Monday August 30th

Going Correction: MINUS 0.30 sec. per fur.

3694 Coppice Claiming Stakes Class G (3-y-o and up) £2,070 2m.......... (2:10)

3288[7] EDGE OF DARKNESS 4-8-13 G Duffield (6) *in tch, led hfwy, clr wl o'r 2 fs out, eased dwn ins last.* ....(15 to 8 fav op 2 to 1) 1
2784[2] NOMADIC FIRE 3-8-4 J Weaver (3) *hld up, hdwy 6 out, styd on same pace fnl 3 fs.* ....(9 to 4 op 5 to 2 tchd 2 to 1) 2
3522[8] MONAZITE (bl) 3-8-2 D Biggs (2) *effrt hfwy, sn chasing wnr, rdn o'r 4 fs out, not quicken*...(10 to 1 op 8 to 1) 3
3574[6] EARLY TO RISE 3-8-6 P D'Arcy (4) *tucked in hndy, rdn and outpcd o'r 4 fs out, no real imprsn.* ....(5 to 1 op 9 to 2 tchd 11 to 2) 4
3246[9] FRAGMENT (Ire) 3-8-6 M Tebbutt (1) *beh, rdn o'r 4 fs out, no dngr*..............(20 to 1 op 25 to 1) 5
626 CHASMARELLA 8-8-12 E Johnson (5) *led to hfwy, wknd.* ....(33 to 1 op 25 to 1) 6
3479 GHOSTLY GLOW 4-9-1 J Quinn (7) *trkd ldr till niggled alng frm hfwy, wknd 4 fs out.* ....(8 to 1 op 7 to 1 tchd 9 to 1) 7

Dist: 3½l, sht-hd, 1½l, 15l, 25l, 15l. 3m 31.80s. (7 Ran).
(Mrs Marie Tinkler), J W Hills

3695 Merevale Maiden Auction Fillies Stakes Class E (2-y-o) £1,830 6f 3yds ....(2:40)

3052[7] PURSUIT OF GLORY 8-11 G Duffield (5) *al hndy, sstnd chal frm o'r one furlong out, led last 100 yards, drvn out*.............. (2 to 1 op 7 to 4 tchd 9 to 4) 1
1071[2] DUBALL REMY 8-11 Gay Kelleway (4) *prmnt, rdn 2 fs out, flashed tail, kpt on nr finish.* ....(9 to 2 op 4 to 1 tchd 5 to 1) 2
MOORLAND DANCER (Ire) 8-11 N Day (1) *led till hdd last 100 yards, no extr*..............(15 to 8 fav op 6 to 4) 3
1456[7] CAZANOVE'S PET 8-8 (3*) C Hodgson (3) *chsd ldrs to hfwy, sn rdn and wknd*.............. (7 to 1 op 5 to 1) 4
LOOKIN' ROSIE 8-11 M Tebbutt (2) *speed one and a half fs, sn struggling*..... (12 to 1 op 10 to 1 tchd 16 to 1) 5

Dist: 2½l, hd, 6l, 20l. 1m 13.90s. a 2.90s (5 Ran).
SR: 3/-/ (Gerald Leigh), C A Cyzer

3696 Spinney Selling Nursery Stakes Class G (2-y-o) £1,725 1m 3yds....... (3:15)

3546* HENRY'S LUCK [67] 9-1 (7*,7ex) R Painter (1) *rcd keenly, led o'r 4 fs out, clr wl over one out, edgd lft ins last, rdn out*.............. (3 to 1 op 11 to 4 tchd 5 to 2) 1
3508 MR ROUGH [57] 8-9 (3*) C Hodgson (5) *dwlt, reco'red to track ldrs, swtchd lft and effrt over 2 fs out, kpt on same pace*..............(7 to 2 tchd 9 to 2) 2
3508[3] PRINCESS CARMEN (Ire) [66] 9-7 G Duffield (6) *in tch on outsd, niggled alng frm hfwy, kpt on ins last.* ....(2 to 1 fav tchd 9 to 4) 3
3189[3] SHUTTLECOCK [61] 9-2 J Weaver (2) *al prmnt, rdn o'r 2 fs out, sn btn*.............. (8 to 1 op 6 to 1 tchd 9 to 1) 4
3386[8] SHFNAK (Ire) [64] 8-12 (7*) Sally Radford-Howes (4) *led o'r 3 fs, rdn and wknd over 2 out*.............. (7 to 1 op 6 to 1) 5
3390[4] SALT STONE (Ire) [56] (v) 8-4 (7*) S Mulvey (3) *al beh, tld off.* .... (12 to 1 op 7 to 1) 6

Dist: 2½l, sht-hd, ¾l, 4l, 25l. 1m 39.30s. a 3.50s (6 Ran).
SR: 20/2/10/3/-/-/ (T W Langley), M R Channon

3697 Rothmans Royals North South Challenge Series Handicap Class D (0-80 3-y-o and up) £3,980 1m 3yds... (3:45)

2300* SAIFAN [75] (bl) 4-9-6 (3*) C Hodgson (3) *patiently rdn tracking ldrs, smooth hdwy o'r one furlong out, sn chlgd, ran on und pres to led nr finish.* ....(8 to 1 op 6 to 1) 1
1976[3] VELASCO (Ire) [67] 3-8-9 G Duffield (2) *al hndy, rdn to ld ins last, ct nr finish*.... (13 to 2 op 5 to 1 tchd 7 to 1) 2
3269 SHINING JEWEL [71] 6-8-12 (7*) G Milligan (10) *led till ins last, kpt on*.............. (11 to 1 op 7 to 1 tchd 12 to 1) 3
3460[4] CAPTAIN MARMALADE [51] 4-7-13 D Biggs (1) *track ldrs far side, ev ch wl o'r one furlong out, not quicken ins last*.............. (7 to 1 op 10 to 1) 4
3429[2] RED COTTON [64] 3-8-6 P D'Arcy (9) *trkd ldrs, rdn o'r 2 fs out, styd on same pace*..............(6 to 1 fav op 5 to 1) 5
3177 BLOCKADE (USA) [74] 4-9-3 (5*) J Tate (11) *in tch, rdn wl o'r 2 fs out, sn btn*..............(7 to 1 op 5 to 1) 6
3314 WYNONA (Ire) [76] 3-9-4 M Tebbutt (5) *beh till rdn and shrtlvd effrt o'r 3 fs out, not trble ldrs.* .... (16 to 1 op 14 to 1) 7
3458[2] BRAVEBOY [62] 5-8-7 (3*) B Doyle (4) *rdn alng early, some hdwy o'r 3 fs out, nvr a dngr.* ....(7 to 1 op 6 to 1 tchd 8 to 1) 8
756[3] SAND TABLE [80] 4-10-0 M Wigham (6) *beh and niggled alng hfwy, no hdwy*..............(10 to 1 op 6 to 1) 9
2882 BUZZARDS BELLBUOY [73] (v) 4-9-7 J Quinn (12) *prmnt on stands side, hrd rdn o'r 2 fs out, sn wknd.* ....(7 to 1 op 5 to 1) 10
3269 BRAVURA [76] 4-9-10 N Day (7) *midfield, rdn and not much room o'r 2 fs out, wknd*.......(8 to 1 op 7 to 1) 11
3132* AWESOME VENTURE [80] 3-9-8 J Weaver (8) *hld up and beh, rdn o'r 3 fs out, eased whn wl btn ins last.* .... (10 to 1 op 7 to 1) 12

Dist: Hd, 1l, sht-hd, 2½l, 5l, 2l, hd, 2l, ½l, ½l. 1m 36.60s. a 0.80s (12 Ran).
SR: 61/46/53/32/31/32/22/13/25/ (Mrs Rosalie Hawes), D Morris

3698 EBF Aston Maiden Stakes Class D (2-y-o) £4,664 7f 3yds............. (4:20)

CRACKLING SIKE 8-9 M Tebbutt (5) *al hndy, led 2 fs out, rdn clr, eased nr finish.* (3 to 1 op 6 to 1 tchd 5 to 2) 1
NEPTUNALIA 8-9 P D'Arcy (9) *al prmnt, led aftr 2 fs till hdd two out, sn outpcd by wnr till rallied nr finish.* ....(12 to 1 op 7 to 1 tchd 14 to 1) 2
3421 COUCHANT (Ire) 9-0 G Duffield (12) *nvr far away, outpcd 2 fs out, ran on wl ins last.* ....(7 to 4 fav op 6 to 4 tchd 9 to 4) 3
2796[2] ONE WILD OAT 8-4 (5*) J Tate (4) *led 2 fs, styd hndy, rdn o'r two out, no extr wl ins last.* ....(5 to 1 op 4 to 1 tchd 6 to 1 and 7 to 1) 4
SPANISH STRIPPER (USA) 9-0 J Weaver (10) *midfield, some hdwy and ran green o'r 2 fs out, nvr nr to chal.* .... (6 to 1 op 10 to 1) 5
3422 POSSIBILITY 8-2 (7*) G Milligan (3) *midfield till hng rght and some hdwy o'r 2 fs out, sn one pace.* .... (16 to 1 op 14 to 1) 6
OBELOS (USA) 9-0 D Biggs (2) *slwly away, beh till some hdwy hfwy, sn rdn and btn*......... (8 to 1 op 4 to 1) 7
3421 MUSICAL SQUIRREL 8-9 E Johnson (1) *chsd ldrs till rdn hfwy and sn wknd*.............. (33 to 1) 8
CHAPTER TWO 9-0 N Day (13) *chsd ldrs till wknd 3 fs out.* .... (14 to 1 op 10 to 1) 9
2818[8] SUNDAY RISK 9-0 W Hood (11) *chsd ldrs till rdn and wknd o'r 3 fs out, tld off*.............. (33 to 1) 10
HOLLY ST GERMAINE (Ire) 8-6 (3*) C Hodgson (6) *in tch till lost pl quickly hfwy, tld off, sddl slpd*........(33 to 1) 11
VAYELLO 9-0 J Quinn (7) *slwly into strd, al outpcd, tld off*..............(16 to 1 op 12 to 1) 12
METALWORK (Ire) 8-11 (3*) B Doyle (8) *wth ldrs till lost pl quickly aftr 3 fs, broke pastern, destroyed.* .... (10 to 1 op 6 to 1) pu

Dist: 2½l, sht-hd, hd, 4l, 2l, 7l, 1½l, ¾l, 20l, 10l. 1m 25.20s. a 2.00s (13 Ran).
SR: 34/26/30/24/17/6/ (Lord Hartington), D Morley

3699 Stewards Limited Stakes Class F (3-y-o and up) £1,725 1m 3f 101yds (4:50)

3522[3] BIG PAT 4-9-2 (5*) J Tate (8) *hld up, pld wide and hdwy o'r 3 fs out, sstnd effrt to ld jst ins last, ran on strly.* ....(7 to 2 op 5 to 2) 1
3461[5] ROSE NOBLE (USA) 3-8-6 M Tebbutt (3) *tucked in hndy, ev ch frm 3 fs out, wndrd und pres till kpt on ins last.* ....(11 to 4 jt-fav op 6 to 1 tchd 9 to 4) 2
3461[2] RISPOTO 3-8-6 G Duffield (9) *nvr far away, rdn o'r 3 fs out, kpt on one pace appr last*..............(11 to 4 jt-fav op 2 to 1 tchd 3 to 1) 3
2873[7] ROMOLA NIJINSKY 5-9-2 N Day (7) *led, rdn frm wl o'r 2 fs out, hdd jst ins last and no extr*...(7 to 1 tchd 8 to 1) 4
3460[7] NAHLATI (Ire) 3-8-3 (3*) B Doyle (4) *trkd ldr, rdn 3 fs out, not clr run wl o'r one out and ag'n ins last, unbl to quicken*..............(8 to 1 op 6 to 1) 5
1457[7] DEBACLE (USA) 4-9-7 E Johnson (5) *settled midfield till rdn and wknd o'r 3 fs out*...........(9 to 1 op 7 to 1) 6
COUNT BARACHOIS (USA) 5-9-4 (3*) C Hodgson (2) *hld up and beh, rdn o'r 4 fs out, sn wknd*........... (33 to 1) 7
3306[5] MUTAWALI (Ire) 3-8-11 J Weaver (6) *handily plcd on outsd till rdn and wknd wl o'r 3 fs out.* ....(7 to 1 op 6 to 1 tchd 8 to 1) 8

Dist: 1l, 1½l, hd, 1½l, 15l, 15l, 1½l. 2m 27.90s. a 4.40s (8 Ran).
SR: 29/12/9/18/5/ (Burton Park Country Club), J Pearce

SARATOGA (USA) (firm)
Monday August 30th

3700 Spinaway Stakes (Grade 1) (2-y-o) £79,470 6f..........................

STRATEGIC MANEUVER (USA) 8-7 J Santos,......(6 to 1) 1
ASTAS FOXY LADY (USA) 8-7 C Perret,.........(37 to 10) 2
DELTA LADY (USA) 8-7 P Day,...............(147 to 10) 3
FOOTING (USA) 8-7 M Smith,................ (66 to 10) 4
CAT ATTACK (USA) 8-7 R Davis,............(13 to 10 fav) 5
CONSIDER THE LILY (USA) 8-7 J R Velasquez,.. (62 to 10) 6
SAM'S IN CONTROL (USA) 8-7 J Chavez,........(48 to 1) 7
SHOO BABY (USA) 8-7 E Maple,...............(20 to 1) 8
PRINCESS TRU (USA) 8-7 J Bailey,..............(33 to 1) 9

Dist: 1½l, 2 ¾l, 1½l, hd, 2l, 2l, 1 ¼l, 1½l. 1m 10.20s. (9 Ran).
(P Teinowitz), F S Shulhofer

BADEN-BADEN (GER) (good)
Tuesday August 31st

3701 Preis von Gaggenau (2-y-o) £4,898 6f ....(1:00)

DYHIM (USA) 9-2 A Boschert, ... 1
FLY ON TIME (USA) 9-0 M Rimmer, ... 2
ADRASTOS (Fr) 8-12 N Grant, ... 3
3265[6] SWINGING SIXTIES (Ire) 9-0 B Rouse, *nvr rch chalg pos.* 6
Dist: 3l, hd, 2½l, hd, 2½l, 1 ¼l. 1m 11.55s. (9 Ran).
(Jaber Abdullah), A Wohler

3702 Hatzfeldt-Rennen (Claimer) (3-y-o) £6,939 1¼m.................. (2:10)

LEPENAC (Ger) 9-2 O Schick, ... 1
MEXICANOS (Ger) 8-9 R Hillis, ... 2
SWINGING DANCER 9-6 T Mundry, ... 3
3346[5] SMART DAISY 9-0 B Rouse, *hdwy 3 out, one pace fnl 2 fs.* 6
Dist: 1 ¼l, nk, nk, hd, 7l, ½l. 2m 5.16s. (10 Ran).
(B Gisler), H Blume

3703 Oettingen-Rennen (Group 3) (3-y-o and up) £30,612 1m............ (4:25)

2298[3] ZABAR 5-9-0 T Hellier, *rcd in 3rd, second 2 fs out, led one out, ran on wl*.. 1
2985[2] VISTO SI STAMPI (Ire) 3-8-0 A Munro, *led till one furlong out, kpt on*.. 2
3465[4] PAY HOMAGE 5-9-0 L Dettori, *mid-div, 6th strt, kpt on fnl 2 fs*.. 3
3013[2] TROPICAL KING (Ger) 3-8-5 M Rimmer, *nrst finish*........ 4
3022[2] KOMTUR (USA) 3-8-5 K Woodburn, *5th strt, one pace*.... 5
3196[3] QUEBRADA (Ire) 3-8-5 P Schiergen, *4th strt, no extr fnl 2 fs*.. 6
3582* KARINGA BAY 6-9-2 B Rouse, *prmnt till 3 fs out, sn rdn and btn*.. 7
3013* TIMELY THREAT (USA) 3-8-7 N Grant, *al rear*............ 8
3013[8] YOUNG MOON 7-9-2 J McLaughlin, *second till wknd 2 fs out*.. 9
GALLERY OF ZURICH (Ire) 4-8-9 J Chevrolet, *al beh*....... 0
1289[6] INFORMANT 3-8-0 C Asmussen, *nvr plcd to chal*......... 0
3013[4] IROKESE (Ger) 3-8-5 A Helfenbein, *nvr a factor*.......... 0
Dist: 1l, 4l, ½l, 1½l, 1 ¼l, ½l. 1m 35.88s. (12 Ran).
(Gerald Leigh), J E Pease

EPSOM (good to firm)
Tuesday August 31st
Going Correction: MINUS 0.40 sec. per fur. (races 1,2,3,4,5,7), MINUS 0.45 (6)

3704 Heathcote Maiden Stakes Class D (2-y-o) £3,377 1m 114yds.......... (2:15)

3352 PAMPERED GUEST (Ire) 9-0 M Hills (7) *led to 3 fs out, rdn and edgd lft entering last, led last strd, all out.* ....(9 to 2 op 6 to 1 tchd 8 to 1) 1
3130[9] WEST BUOYANT (USA) 9-0 T Quinn (1) *trkd ldr, led 3 fs out, wnt clr wth wnr o'r 2 out, hdd last strd.* ....(5 to 1 op 6 to 1 tchd 7 to 1) 2
3091[3] DYNAMIC DELUXE (USA) 9-0 R Cochrane (8) *chsd ldrs, outpcd 3 fs out, hrd rdn, kpt on one pace.* ....(5 to 1 op 3 to 1) 3
3129[8] WICKLOW BOY (Ire) 9-0 A McGlone (4) *chsd ldrs, outpcd 3 fs out, rdn and kpt on one pace.* ....(25 to 1 op 14 to 1 tchd 33 to 1) 4
3510[3] LEAR DANCER (USA) 9-0 J Reid (3) *mid-div, rdn o'r 2 fs out, no imprsn*.......(7 to 2 fav op 9 to 4 tchd 4 to 1) 5
3079 ART TATUM (Ire) 9-0 R Hills (2) *hld up, shaken up 3 fs out, not pace to chal*..................(14 to 1 op 8 to 1) 6
SUNDAY NEWS'N'ECHO (USA) 8-9 Pat Eddery (5) *mid-div, no hdwy fnl 3 fs*....................(9 to 2 op 3 to 1) 7
1949 STOMPIN 8-11 (3*) B Doyle (9) *mid-div, lost tch fnl 3 fs.* ....(33 to 1 op 25 to 1) 8
3520 PETITJEAN (Ire) 9-0 J Williams (10) *slwly away, nvr on terms*..........................(25 to 1 op 14 to 1) 9
2964[5] PLUNDER BAY (USA) 9-0 B Raymond (11) *chsd ldrs, rdn 3 fs out, wknd quickly*..............(14 to 1 op 8 to 1) 10
3166[7] RICH MISS 8-9 A Clark (12) *al beh*... (33 to 1 op 25 to 1) 11
3259 FATALIST 9-0 M Roberts (6) *sn beh.* ....(20 to 1 op 14 to 1 tchd 25 to 1) 12
Dist: Sht-hd, 5l, sht-hd, 2½l, 3l, 3½l, 2½l, 1l, ½l, ½l. 1m 44.18s. a 2.18s (12 Ran).
SR: 16/15/-/-/-/-/ (J L C Pearce), M Bell

3705 Leatherhead Median Auction Maiden Stakes Class E (2-y-o) £3,184 7f (2:45)

3352 MIGHTY FORUM 9-0 J Williams (8) *hld up, rdn and styd on frm 2 fs out, swtchd rght entering last, sn led, drw clr*.............................. (14 to 1 tchd 20 to 1) 1
3470[3] JAREEF'S WAY (Ire) 9-0 Pat Eddery (11) *chsd ldrs, outpcd o'r 2 fs out, styd on to go second ins last.* ....(6 to 4 fav op 11 to 8 tchd 5 to 4 and 2 to 1) 2
3387[4] ROBSERA (Ire) 9-0 B Raymond (9) *chsd ldrs, outpcd o'r 2 fs out, rdn and hdwy whn short of room entering last, ran on wl*.................(4 to 1 op 5 to 1 tchd 7 to 2) 3
1949[5] DONTFORGET INSIGHT (Ire) 9-0 T Quinn (3) *led to 3 fs out, edgd lft and led briefly one out, sn outpcd.* .... (11 to 2 op 3 to 1 tchd 6 to 1) 4
3352[9] SECUNDUS (Ire) 9-0 M Roberts (1) *slwly into strd, rdn and sn trkd ldr, led 3 fs out, wkng whn hmpd and hdd one out, eased*..............(8 to 1 op 6 to 1 tchd 9 to 1) 5
2129[5] CAPTAIN STARLIGHT (Ire) 9-0 M Hills (2) *beh, nvr got into race*..................(12 to 1 op 8 to 1 tchd 14 to 1) 6
2968 LITTLE GENT (Ire) 8-7 (7*) L Carter (4) *chsd ldrs till outpcd hfwy, sn beh*.................................... (33 to 1) 7
3421[9] LETS GO BO (Ire) 9-0 A McGlone (7) *al beh.* ....(10 to 1 op 12 to 1 tchd 14 to 1) 8
3589 NORDANCE PRINCE (Ire) 9-0 M Wigham (10) *al beh.* ....(20 to 1 op 14 to 1) 9
3387 ARAFARAZ 9-0 J Reid (5) *chsd ldrs early, beh hfwy.* ....(50 to 1 op 33 to 1) 10
Dist: 3l, 1½l, 1½l, 4l, 3½l, 1½l, 3½l, nk, 1½l. 1m 22.55s. a 2.15s (10 Ran).
SR: 26/17/12/7/-/-/ (R J Tory), D R C Elsworth

3706 Steve Donoghue Apprentice Limited Stakes Class E (0-70 3-y-o and up) £3,557 1½m 10yds............. (3:20)

3512 LOBILIO (USA) (v) 4-9-2 (3*) B Doyle (8) *led one and a half fs, trkd ldr, led 2 out, shaken up and styd on ins last.* ....(9 to 2 op 7 to 2 tchd 5 to 1) 1
3344[2] FOOLS ERRAND (Ire) 3-8-1 (8*) D O'Neill (3) *chsd ldrs, rdn and styd on to go second ins fnl furlong.* ....(9 to 2 op 7 to 2 tchd 5 to 1) 2
3392[2] MR COPYFORCE (v) 3-8-4 (5*) A Martinez (9) *led aftr one and a half fs to 2 out, rdn and one pace fnl furlong.* ....(9 to 2 op 7 to 2) 3
3224[6] SONG OF SIXPENCE (USA) 9-8-11 (8*) D Griffiths (5) *rear, styd on ins fnl 2 fs, nvr nrr.* ....(9 to 1 op 7 to 1 tchd 10 to 1) 4
3394[4] INCOLA 7-8-13 (6*) Antoinette Armes (2) *hld up mid-div, ran on one pace fnl 2 fs.* ....(10 to 1 op 8 to 1 tchd 12 to 1) 5
3272 MODI (USA) 3-8-1 (3*) D Harrison (1) *mid-div, effrt on ins o'r 2 fs out, rdn and wknd over one out.* ......(100 to 30 fav op 7 to 2 tchd 4 to 1 and 3 to 1) 6
3473 IMPECCABLE TASTE 3-7-12 (6*) J D Smith (4) *chsd ldrs, wknd 2 fs out*..................(10 to 1 op 7 to 1) 7
NORTHERN VILLAGE 6-9-5 F Norton (6) *al beh, no ch fnl 5 fs, tld off*..........................(50 to 1 op 33 to 1) 8
42[5] CLIFTON CHASE 4-9-5 D Wright (7) *al beh, tld off.* ....(50 to 1 op 25 to 1) 9
Dist: 3l, 1½l, hd, 1½l, 2l, 1l, 12l, 10l. 2m 36.69s. a 1.19s (9 Ran).
SR: 45/29/26/35/32/13/11/2/-/ (The Dowager Lady Beaverbrook), C E Brittain

3707 Ladbroke Group Sprint Handicap Class E (0-70 3-y-o and up) £3,850 6f ....(3:50)

3292* AGWA [42] 4-8-0 F Norton (16) *al gng wl, trkd ldrs, shaken up to ld one and a half fs out, ran on well.* ....(9 to 2 fav op 7 to 2) 1
3391[3] LORINS GOLD [54] (bl) 3-8-8 S Dawson (4) *led till rdn and hdd one and a half fs out, kpt on one pace.* ....(20 to 1 op 16 to 1) 2
3261 BAYSHAM (USA) [66] (bl) 7-9-10 S Whitworth (7) *frnt rnk, kpt on one pace ins fnl 2 fs*...... (12 to 1 tchd 14 to 1) 3
2363 CONFRONTER [70] 4-9-11 (3*) D Harrison (17) *mid-div, ran on fnl 2 fs, nvr nr to chal*.........(16 to 1 op 14 to 1) 4
3481[9] FARMER JOCK [58] 11-9-2 J Reid (12) *chsd ldrs, rdn 2 fs out, one pace*..................... (16 to 1 op 14 to 1) 5
3425 GALLANT HOPE [37] (bl) 11-7-9 G Bardwell (6) *beh till ran on fnl 2 fs, nvr dngrs*........... (25 to 1 tchd 33 to 1) 6
3486[7] LOVE LEGEND [65] 8-9-9 T Quinn (13) *mid-div, kpt on one pace fnl 2 fs*..................... (12 to 1 tchd 14 to 1) 7
3584[4] GO FLIGHTLINE (Ire) [55] 3-8-9 J Williams (5) *mid-div, nvr nr to chal*.............(8 to 1 op 7 to 1 tchd 10 to 1) 8
3445[2] COURTING NEWMARKET [44] 5-7-9 (7*) D Toole (9) *beh till some late hdwy*.................(10 to 1 tchd 11 to 1) 9
3445[3] WALNUT BURL (Ire) [49] (v) 3-8-3 A McGlone (11) *slwly away, nvr on terms*..................(8 to 1 op 7 to 1) 10
3270[8] BELLE SOIREE [43] 3-7-7[1] (5*) B Russell (14) *rcd on outsd, nvr on terms*.................. (14 to 1 op 12 to 1) 11
2309[9] PRECENTOR [47] (v) 7-8-5 R Hills (3) *slwly into strd, nvr got into race*..................(10 to 1 op 12 to 1) 12
STERLING PRINCESS [45] 3-7-8 (5*) D Wright (15) *chsd ldrs till rdn and wknd o'r 2 fs out*..................... (33 to 1) 13
3225 GARRY'S CHOICE [47] 4-8-5 Dale Gibson (18) *outpcd.* ....(50 to 1) 14
1492[8] GAYNOR GOODMAN (Ire) [44] 3-7-12 C Avery (8) *mid-div, wknd o'r 2 fs out*.................................... (20 to 1) 15
3638 STORMY HEIGHTS [62] (bl) 3-9-2 M Roberts (1) *al beh.* ....(10 to 1 tchd 12 to 1) 16
Dist: 2l, 2l, ½l, 2½l, hd, 1½l, hd, 3½l, 1½l, hd. 1m 8.92s. a 1.02s (16 Ran).
SR: 18/18/26/28/6/-/6/-/-/ (I A Baker), R J O'Sullivan

3708 CPM Field Marketing Fillies' Maiden Stakes Class D (3-y-o and up) £3,260 1 ¼m 18yds..................... (4:20)

3514[2] LA SPEZIA 3-8-9 M Roberts (1) *set steady pace, quickened 3 fs out, cmftbly*..................(Evens fav op 5 to 4 on) 1
2937[3] LAMBAST 3-8-9 Pat Eddery (4) *rcd in 3rd, rdn 2 fs out, ran on to go second ins last*............(5 to 2 tchd 3 to 1) 2

2716[2] DIPLOMATIST 3-8-9 J Reid (3) *trkd wnr, rdn o'r 2 fs out, one pace and lost second pl ins last.* .... (3 to 1 op 5 to 2 tchd 100 to 30) 3
1713[9] LA POSADA 3-8-9 A McGlone (2) *al last, no ch fnl 3 fs.* .... (20 to 1 op 14 to 1 tchd 33 to 1) 4
Dist: 2½l, 1l, 10l. 2m 10.46s. a 6.16s (4 Ran).
(Sheikh Mohammed), J H M Gosden

3709 Redhill Selling Stakes Class F (3-y-o and up) £3,080 5f. ....(4:50)

29654 NEVER IN THE RED (bl) 5-9-0 L Piggott (6) *trkd ldr, smooth hdwy fnl furlong to ld nr finish, cleverly.* .... (11 to 10 on op 5 to 4 on tchd Evens) 1
3238[5] SIGAMA (USA) 7-9-0 R Lappin (2) *broke wl, led and set str pace, wknd fnl half furlong, hdd nr finish.* ....(5 to 1 op 7 to 2 tchd 6 to 1) 2
3584[7] TREASURE TIME (Ire) 4-8-9 C Avery (3) *sn rdn, kpt on fnl furlong, no ch wth 1st 2*............(12 to 1 op 6 to 1) 3
3253[4] KILDEE LAD 3-8-11 J Williams (5) *slwly away, ran on one pace fnl 2 fs*....................(20 to 1 tchd 33 to 1) 4
3383[6] PERFECT PASSION 3-7-13 (7*) Antoinette Armes (1) *chsd ldrs on outsd, one pace fnl 2 fs*.... (33 to 1 op 25 to 1) 5
2728[4] MAID WELCOME (v) 6-8-2 (7*) S Drowne (8) *btn hfwy.* .... (20 to 1 op 14 to 1 tchd 25 to 1) 6
3393[7] MARTINA 5-9-0 Pat Eddery (7) *al beh, outpcd.* ....(4 to 1 op 5 to 1 tchd 7 to 2) 7
Dist: ½l, 3½l, 4l, 2½l, 1l, 1½l. 54.79s. a 0.09s (7 Ran).
SR: 53/51/32/18/3/2/1/ (Robert Aird), J Berry

3710 Chalk Lane Handicap Class D (0-80 3-y-o and up) £3,817 1¼m 18yds (5:20)

3551* KELIMUTU [40] 4-7-8 (4ex) G Bardwell (9) *hld up, rdn and hdwy 2 fs out, str run to ld last strd.* .... (6 to 1 op 5 to 1 tchd 13 to 2) 1
2884 KNOWTH (Ire) [73] 4-9-13 T Quinn (12) *hld up, hdwy to ld wl o'r one furlong out, ran on, ct last strd.* ....(9 to 2 op 4 to 1 tchd 5 to 1) 2
2976[2] GREEN KILT [70] 3-9-2 W R Swinburn (6) *mid-div, styd on ins fnl 2 fs, nvr nrr*...................(8 to 1 op 10 to 1) 3
3512[4] KNOCK KNOCK [74] 8-10-0 R Cochrane (5) *mid-div, rdn o'r 2 fs out, kpt on, nvr nrr.* ....(7 to 2 fav op 9 to 2 tchd 5 to 1) 4
3221[2] VANBOROUGH LAD [51] 4-8-5 B Raymond (8) *al abt same pl, one pace fnl 2 fs*............ (16 to 1 op 12 to 1) 5
3044[2] CAST THE LINE [67] 3-8-13 A McGlone (10) *prmnt till no hdwy fnl 2 fs*..........(8 to 1 op 7 to 1 tchd 10 to 1) 6
3533[2] WITHOUT A FLAG (USA) [56] 3-7-10[1] (7*) J D Smith (2) *led, rdn and hdd one and a half fs out, wknd quickly.* ....(8 to 1 tchd 10 to 1) 7
3487[4] LORD OBERON (Ire) [66] 5-9-6 D Biggs (4) *trkd ldr, rdn and wknd 2 fs out*.......(12 to 1 op 10 to 1 tchd 14 to 1) 8
3044[6] ERICOLIN (Ire) [70] (v) 3-9-2 M Roberts (1) *slwly away, al rear*...(20 to 1) 9
3054[4] DANNY BOY [70] 3-9-2 J Reid (7) *in tch on ins, rdn and wknd o'r 2 fs out*.................(20 to 1 tchd 25 to 1) 10
3420[7] ALBERT [44] 6-7-5 (7*) Sharon Millard (3) *al beh.* ....(20 to 1 tchd 33 to 1) 11
1912[9] BAYDON BELLE (USA) [53] 3-7-10 (3*) D Harrison (11) *in tch, rdn 3 fs out, sn beh*...............(33 to 1 op 20 to 1) 12
3101 DALALAH [66] 3-8-12 R Hills (13) *chsd ldrs on outsd, wknd wl o'r 2 fs out, eased*............(20 to 1 tchd 33 to 1) 13
Dist: Sht-hd, 3l, hd, 2½l, ¾l, 2l, ½l, 2l, 2l, hd. 2m 6.07s. a 1.77s (13 Ran).
SR: 22/54/37/48/20/26/11/28/20/ (James Furlong), J Pearce

RIPON (good to firm)
Tuesday August 31st

Going Correction: MINUS 0.25 sec. per fur. (races 1,3,5), MINUS 0.45 (2,4,6)

3711 Claro Maiden Auction Stakes Class E (2-y-o) £3,080 5f. ....(2:30)

3287 GOOD FETCH 8-9 W Carson (3) *nvr far away, drvn ahead ins fnl furlong, ran on wl.* ....(4 to 1 op 2 to 1 tchd 9 to 2) 1
3421 MR BERGERAC (Ire) 9-0 D Holland (8) *chsd alng in midfield, imprvg whn continually hng lft fnl furlong, kpt on finish*.............(7 to 1 op 10 to 1 tchd 6 to 1) 2
1401[3] ANTANANARIVO (Ire) 9-0 K Darley (7) *wl plcd on outsd, bustled alng frm hfwy, styd on ins fnl furlong.* ....(5 to 4 fav op 15 to 8) 3
3183[8] PETRINA BAY 8-9 A Culhane (5) *led, hdd and rdn ins fnl furlong, no extr*........................(12 to 1 op 8 to 1) 4
1082[4] FAIR SWOP (Ire) 8-9 M Birch (2) *sluggish strt, hld up and beh, hdwy last 2 fs, nvr plcd to chal.* ....(11 to 1 op 7 to 1 tchd 12 to 1) 5
3505[4] LINCOLN TREASURE (Ire) 8-9 (5*) D McCabe (4) *pushed alng in midfield, effrt whn crowded ins fnl furlong, snatched up last 50 yards*.....................(12 to 1) 6
3443[8] CAPONATA (Ire) 8-9 J Carroll (6) *sluggish strt, reco'red to press ldr for over 3 fs, fdd*.........(12 to 1 op 10 to 1) 7
3120[6] COLONEL SINCLAIR (Ire) 9-0 S Perks (1) *sn outpcd and drvn alng, nvr a factor*...........(50 to 1 op 33 to 1) 8
Dist: 1½l, nk, 2l, 2½l, ½l, 1l, sht-hd. 1m 0.20s. a 2.20s (8 Ran).
SR: 26/25/24/11/1/4/-/-/ (Elite Racing Club), P F I Cole

3712 Deverell Claiming Stakes Class F (3-y-o and up) £3,340 1m..........(3:00)

3540[4] CAUSLEY 8-8-10 W Carson (8) *led aftr a furlong, made rst, quickened 2 fs out, hld on wl.* ....(100 to 30 op 4 to 1 tchd 3 to 1) 1
3409* AFFORDABLE 5-8-5 (3*) O Pears (18) *patiently rdn, improved on outsd o'r 2 fs out, hng rght fnl furlong, not go past*..........................(14 to 1 tchd 16 to 1) 2
3258[2] LOMBARD SHIPS (bl) 6-8-0 A Mackay (15) *al hndy, ev ch and rdn last 2 fs, styd on.* ....(13 to 2 op 6 to 1 tchd 7 to 1) 3
3311[2] KELLY MAC 3-8-4 Paul Eddery (16) *unruly and strt, led one furlong, styd hndy till not quicken fnl furlong.* ....(10 to 1 tchd 9 to 1) 4
3623[7] BATTLE COLOURS (Ire) 4-8-12 G Duffield (11) *nvr far away, hrd drvn o'r 2 fs out, one pace.* ....(11 to 4 fav op 5 to 2 tchd 3 to 1) 5
3603[9] BALLAD DANCER 8-8-6 M Birch (19) *wtd wth, improved on ins hfwy, reminder o'r one furlong out, eased whn btn*.............................. (14 to 1 op 12 to 1) 6
3536[8] OLICANA (Ire) 3-7-8[1] (5*) J Marshall (1) *in tch, drvn up frm midfield o'r 2 fs out, styd on same pace*........(16 to 1) 7
2175 COASTAL EXPRESS 4-8-4 G Hind (12) *al chasing ldrs, drvn alng last 2 fs, no extr*........................(25 to 1) 8
3558[9] PARLIAMENT PIECE 7-9-6 K Darley (6) *chsd ldg bunch, effrt o'r 2 fs out, no imprsn*.........(13 to 2 op 7 to 2) 9
3518[5] PIMSBOY 6-8-6 S Wood (5) *struggling to keep in tch hfwy, styd on, nvr able to chal*....(33 to 1 op 25 to 1) 10
3506[8] CHIPALA 3-8-4[3] (3*) S D Williams (17) *bustled alng in midfield, not pace of ldrs*....................(50 to 1) 11
1833[5] CHICKCHARNIE 3-8-1 (5*) J Tate (14) *settled midfield, effrt and rdn o'r 2 fs out, sn btn*........(16 to 1 op 14 to 1) 12
1657[5] ROYAL VACATION 4-9-6 J Fanning (7) *beh thrght, nvr a factor*..(25 to 1) 13
2307[4] SEA-AYR (Ire) 3-7-8 J Lowe (2) *struggling to keep up hfwy, nvr a factor*................ (50 to 1 op 33 to 1) 14
CELTIC RISING 3-8-4[4] Alex Greaves (9) *beh thrght.* ....(50 to 1) 15
2827[6] MELTONBY 4-7-13 Kim Tinkler (4) *al struggling.* (50 to 1) 16
MEESONS (Ire) 3-7-8 L Charnock (3) *sluggish strt, not reco'r*.. (33 to 1) 17
SILVER WILL 3-8-6 S Webster (13) *sluggish strt, al beh.* .... (50 to 1 op 33 to 1) 18
Dist: ½l, ¾l, 2½l, 1l, 4l, 1½l, 1½l, hd, 3½l, 1½l. 1m 40.00s. a 1.70s (18 Ran).
SR: 16/12/2/-/3/-/-/-/13/ (Henry Pearce), B A McMahon

3713 EBF Sapper Maiden Stakes Class D (2-y-o) £4,306 6f................(3:30)

DELTA ONE (Ire) 8-11 (3*) Stephen Davies (7) *made virtually all, ran very green o'r one furlong out, shaken up, kpt on wl*.........(9 to 4 on op 2 to 1 on tchd 5 to 2 on) 1
3114[7] KILLY'S RAYNJA (Ire) 9-0 J Carroll (6) *sn outpcd and drvn alng, gd hdwy to join issue o'r one furlong out, styd on.* ....(20 to 1) 2
3317[7] EDWINA (Ire) 8-6 (3*) M Fenton (9) *al hndy, ev ch and rdn o'r one furlong out, kpt on same pace.* ....(5 to 1 tchd 13 to 2) 3
1778[3] SKY DIVER 9-0 K Darley (8) *broke wl to race in frnt rnk for o'r 4 fs, eased whn btn, can improve.* .... (12 to 1 op 10 to 1) 4
BLUE DOMAIN 9-0 S Perks (4) *struggling to go pace thrght, nvr dngrs*...........................(20 to 1) 5
2370[7] WOODTONG 9-0 J Fanning (1) *broke wl, struggling to go pace and lost grnd hfwy, sn btn*............. (33 to 1) 6
CALDER KING 9-0 N Adams (5) *sluggish strt, al outpcd.* .... (50 to 1 op 25 to 1) 7
EZEKIEL 9-0 Paul Eddery (2) *steadied strt, feeling pace hfwy, nvr a threat*.................. (7 to 1 op 5 to 1) 8
Dist: 1½l, sht-hd, 2½l, 6l, sht-hd, 8l, 1½l. 1m 13.90s. a 3.30s (8 Ran).
SR: 4/-/-/-/-/ (R E Sangster), P W Chapple-Hyam

3714 Steve Nesbitt Challenge Trophy Handicap Class D (0-80 4-y-o and up) £5,572 1¼m...........................(4:00)

3346* DASHING FELLOW (Ire) [54] 5-8-5 J Quinn (10) *patiently rdn, improved to ld o'r 2 fs out, hld on wl fnl furlong.* .... (7 to 1 op 5 to 1 tchd 15 to 2) 1
3507[7] TAPATCH (Ire) [59] 5-8-10 J Fanning (1) *wtd wth, improved into midfield o'r 3 fs out, squeezed for room appr fnl furlong, fnshd wl*..................(15 to 2 op 6 to 1) 2
3507* JUBRAN (USA) [73] 7-9-5 (5*) A Garth (3) *al hndy, ev ch and drvn alng last 2 fs, kpt on gmely*............(7 to 2 jt-fav op 3 to 1 tchd 4 to 1) 3

3507[9] FLOATING LINE [52] 5-8-3 A Culhane (2) *unruly in paddock, nvr far away, drvn alng last 3 fs, one pace.* ....(6 to 1 op 5 to 1) 4
3523[7] AVISHAYES (USA) [55] 6-8-6 K Darley (7) *nvr striding out, last hfwy, not pace of ldrs*..................(7 to 2 jt-fav op 4 to 1 tchd 100 to 30) 5
3469[9] DIAMOND INTHE DARK (USA) [44] (v) 5-7-4 (5*) Darren Moffatt (6) *chsd alng to keep in tch, effrt o'r 3 fs out, no imprsn*..................................(25 to 1) 6
2954[5] ROUTING [53] 5-7-13 (5*) J Marshall (8) *rcd freely on ins, quickened up to ld entering strt, hdd jst o'r 2 fs out, sn btn*..............................(12 to 1 op 10 to 1) 7
3630[3] SHARQUIN [42] 6-7-7 J Lowe (5) *chsd alng to keep up, nvr a factor*..................................(12 to 1) 8
3290[5] WELLINGTON ROCK (USA) [74] 4-9-11 P Robinson (4) *led till hdd entering strt, fdd und pres o'r 2 fs out.* ....(7 to 1 op 6 to 1) 9
Dist: Nk, 1l, 3l, 4l, 1½l, 1½l, ¾l, 4l. 2m 4.70s. a 0.70s (9 Ran).
SR: 40/44/56/29/24/10/16/2/26/ (Mrs Val Rapkins), Mrs L Piggott

3715 Curfew Nursery Class E (2-y-o) £3,132 5f............................(4:30)

3441* GREY TOPPA [59] 7-3 (7*) C Teague (2) *nvr far away, drvn through to ld o'r one furlong out, ran on strly.* (12 to 1) 1
3537[6] NORDICO PRINCESS [76] 8-13 S Perks (1) *gd speed stand side, ev ch fnl furlong, kpt on same pace.* ....(16 to 1 op 14 to 1 tchd 20 to 1) 2
3566[2] FLOATING TRIAL [57] (v) 7-8 L Charnock (7) *al hndy, drvn alng and ev ch o'r one furlong out, not quicken.* ....(2 to 1 fav op 11 to 4) 3
2947[6] ALZIANAH [76] 8-13 G Duffield (4) *chsd alng to improve frm midfield hfwy, kpt on und pres fnl furlong.* ....(10 to 1 op 8 to 1) 4
3309[7] KANGRA VALLEY [66] 8-3 J Quinn (10) *tried to make all, hdd and rdn o'r one furlong out, no extr.* ....(20 to 1 op 14 to 1) 5
2886 DANCE OF THE SWANS (Ire) [75] 8-12 K Darley (11) *sluggish strt, drvn into midfield hfwy, kpt on, nvr able to chal.* ....(9 to 1 op 8 to 1 tchd 10 to 1) 6
3505[2] ELUNED MAY [66] 8-3 A Culhane (9) *chsd alng beh ldrs, kpt on, nvr able to chal*............(10 to 1 op 8 to 1) 7+
3421 RAPIER POINT (Ire) [76] (v) 8-6 (7*) C Adamson (6) *sluggish strt, styd on last 2 fs, nrst finish.* ....(10 to 1 op 14 to 1 tchd 16 to 1) 7+
3475[2] TWICE IN BUNDORAN (Ire) [84] 9-2 (5*) L Newton (5) *gd speed for o'r 3 fs, fdd*................(6 to 1 op 9 to 2) 9
3629[5] CHEEKY CHAPPY [61] (bl) 7-12 W Carson (3) *bustled alng beh ldrs, nvr able to rch chalg poss.* (10 to 1 op 8 to 1) 10
3001[4] BOLLIN MARY [66] 8-0 (3*) S Maloney (8) *broke wl to show speed to hfwy, eased whn btn o'r one furlong out.* ....(7 to 1 op 9 to 2) 11
Dist: 1½l, sht-hd, 1½l, 1l, hd, 1½l, dd-ht, 1½l, ¾l, 2½l. 59.60s. a 1.60s (11 Ran).
SR: 25/36/16/29/15/23/8/18/20/ (D Ford), Denys Smith

3716 Wakeman Stayers Handicap Class E (0-70 3-y-o and up) £4,175 2m... (5:00)

3521 SAMAIN (USA) [49] 6-9-0 N Carlisle (13) *patiently rdn, improved on ins whn not much room o'r 2 fs out, led inside last, ran on wl*..............(10 to 1 op 8 to 1) 1
3021[3] JAWANI (Ire) [53] (v) 5-9-4 J Quinn (3) *nvr far away, ev ch and drvn alng 2 fs out, kpt on*...... (9 to 1 op 15 to 2) 2
901[2] CHANTRY BARTLE [41] 7-8-6 J Fanning (15) *al hndy, led o'r 2 fs out till ins last, one pace*... (14 to 1 op 12 to 1) 3
3056[6] BILBERRY [38] 4-8-0 (3*) N Kennedy (8) *ran in snatches, improved on outsd 2 fs out, kpt on same pace.* ....(12 to 1 op 8 to 1) 4
3252[4] BRIGGSMAID [49] 5-9-0 M Tebbutt (12) *patiently rdn, improved on outsd to chal 2 fs out, kpt on.* ....(9 to 1 op 10 to 1 tchd 8 to 1) 5
3503[6] MINGUS (USA) [38] 6-8-3 J Lowe (4) *co'red up on ins, improved last 2 fs, nrst finish*.................(14 to 1) 6
3473[7] HUNTING GROUND [52] (bl) 5-9-3 A Mackay (6) *trkd ldg 6, effrt and drvn alng o'r 2 fs out, one pace.* ....(7 to 1 tchd 13 to 2) 7
3356 PEANUTS PET [38] 8-8-3 P Robinson (2) *trkd ldrs, feeling pace o'r 2 fs out, no extr.* ....(25 to 1 op 20 to 1 tchd 33 to 1) 8
3599[6] SEXY MOVER [28] 6-7-8[1] L Charnock (17) *settled midfield, effrt and not much room o'r 2 fs out, no imprsn.* ....(14 to 1) 9
3567* FOLLINGWORTH GIRL (Ire) [53] 3-8-1 (3*,5ex) S Maloney (16) *made most till o'r 3 fs out, wknd 2 out.* ....(12 to 1 op 10 to 1) 10
3087[6] WAKT [48] 3-7-13 W Carson (14) *dsptd ld, led o'r 3 fs out till over 2 out, fdd*..........................(8 to 1) 11
3239* MR WOODCOCK [59] 8-9-10 K Darley (5) *wth ldrs, lost grnd entering strt, fdd o'r 2 fs out.* ....(11 to 2 fav op 5 to 1 tchd 6 to 1) 12
3503 DEMOKOS (Fr) [29] 8-7-7 S Wood (7) *beh and drvn alng hfwy, nvr a factor*................ (50 to 1 op 33 to 1) 13
3134[5] STATIA (Ire) [28] 5-7-7 Kim Tinkler (10) *struggling hfwy, nvr a factor*..........................(50 to 1 op 33 to 1) 14
2709[4] A GENTLEMAN TWO [34] 7-7-13 N Adams (1) *settled off the pace, nvr able to chal*.........................(20 to 1) 15
HAMANAKA (USA) [50] 4-9-1 G Duffield (11) *settled midfield, feeling pace o'r 3 fs out, fdd.* (20 to 1 op 14 to 1) 16
3473[6] CONTINUITY [59] 4-9-10 J Weaver (9) *last aftr 3 fs, broke dwn hfwy, tld off*................ (14 to 1 op 10 to 1) 17
Dist: 1l, sht-hd, nk, nk, ¾l, ¾l, hd, 6l, 7l, 1½l. 3m 27.70s. a 2.70s (17 Ran).
SR: 1/4/-/-/-/-/ (Countrywide Classics Limited), J A Glover

BADEN-BADEN (GER) (good) Wednesday September 1st

3717 Jacobs Goldene Peitsche (Group 2) (3-y-o and up) £51,020 6f........(3:25)

3015[7] ROBIN DES PINS (USA) 5-9-3 C Asmussen, *hld up, hdwy o'r one furlong out, str run ins fnl furlong to ld last strds*.. 1
1807[8] SURPRISE OFFER 3-8-11 B Raymond, *led aftr 2 fs till wknd and ct last strds*.................................. 2
3196[2] NASR ALLAH (USA) 3-8-11 A Starke, *hdwy o'r 2 fs out, second one out, one pace*................................ 3
1365[9] ARRANVANNA 5-8-12 Jacqueline Freda, *mid-div, ran on fnl furlong*.. 4
3015[9] RUSTIC CRAFT (Ire) 3-8-11 B Rouse, *hdwy fnl 2 fs, nrst finish*.. 5
3015[8] BORODISLEW (USA) 3-8-7 O Doleuze, *hdwy fnl 2 fs, nrst finish*.. 6
1465[6] MAMMA'S TOO 4-8-12 M Hofer, *al prmnt, chsd ldr aftr 2 fs to one out, kpt on one pace*......................... 7
3015[2] DANAKAL (USA) 3-8-11 G Mosse, *nvr rch chalg pos*...... 8
2242[4] MONTEPULCIANO (USA) 4-9-3 G Bocskai, *prmnt for o'r 4 fs*... 9
3196[8] NEW EUROPE 3-8-7 L Mader, *al beh*........................ 0
2242[3] MORE WIND (Ger) 7-9-3 D Ilic, *led for 2 fs, wknd o'r one out*... 0
3023[2] FANTOMAS (Ger) 5-9-3 K Woodburn, *prmnt for 4 fs*....... 0
REKORD (Ger) 3-8-11 T Mundry, *al beh*.................. 0
Dist: Nk, 2l, ¾l, nk, nose, sht-hd. 1m 8.55s. (13 Ran).
(S S Niarchos), F Boutin

3718 Milka Steher Cup (Listed) (3-y-o and up) £20,408 2m................(4:35)

MATAHIF (Ire) 5-9-2 N Grant,.............................. 1
3516[4] TURGEON (USA) 7-9-6 C Asmussen,...................... 2
2744* SHAIYBARA (Ire) 3-8-1 A McGlone,...................... 3
1042[7] IBIANO (Ire) 4-9-6 O Schick,......................... 4
3405[9] SILVERNESIAN (USA) 4-9-0 B Raymond, *led 4 fs till 2 out.* 5
Dist: Nose, nk, 4l, 4½l, 1 ¾l, dist. 3m 20.58s. (10 Ran).
(S Ekman), L Reuterskjold

BALLINROBE (IRE) (good to firm) Wednesday September 1st

3719 Cong (C&G) E.B.F. Maiden (2-y-o) £3,107 6f..................... (5:30)

3335[7] MULMUS (Ire) 9-0 R Hughes (6)..................(5 to 1) 1
3039[3] STAGE LEFT EVEN (Ire) 8-12 (2*) P Carberry (3) (11 to 8 fav) 2
3039 PETERS BIRD (Ire) 9-0 P V Gilson (5)............ (20 to 1) 3
3379[8] TRIMBLEMILL (Ire) 9-0 P Shanahan (7)............(9 to 1) 4
3332[5] YAHTHAB (Ire) 9-0 W J Supple (8)................(5 to 1) 5
3243[2] THE BREADMAN (Ire) 9-0 M J Kinane (2)..........(4 to 1) 6
PENZAAD (Ire) 8-8 (6*) B J Walsh (1).............(33 to 1) 7
3541 SALTONIC (Ire) 9-0 S Craine (4)................(12 to 1) 8
Dist: Nk, 4l, 2l, 2l. 1m 15.70s. (8 Ran).
(Thomas G Cahill), G T Hourigan

3720 Corrib Orange Maiden (3-y-o and up) £2,762 6f..................... (6:00)

3242[2] RETICENT BRIDE (Ire) 3-8-11 M J Kinane (3)... (5 to 4 fav) 1
3160[9] VLADIVOSTOK 3-9-0 P V Gilson (8)...............(8 to 1) 2
ANOTHER SKY-LARK (Ire) 5-9-2 (2*) P Carberry (2) (33 to 1) 3
3161[4] TORC MOUNTAIN (Ire) (bl) 3-8-10 (4*) J J Behan (6) (9 to 4) 4
3455[6] BLACKTRENCH LADY (Ire) 5-8-13 (2*) R M Burke (5) (5 to 1) 5
3419[7] EDENS LANDING (Ire) 3-8-11 J F Egan (1).........(8 to 1) 6
3395 TOP DIVER (Ire) (bl) 3-9-0 R Hughes (4).......... (20 to 1) 7
Dist: 1l, 3l, 1l, 4l. 1m 14.50s. (7 Ran).
(Michael Watt), D K Weld

3721 Lough Mask Handicap (0-65 3-y-o and up) £2,245 1¼m................(6:30)

3543[6] JUST ONE CANALETTO [-] 5-9-0 W J Supple (7)..(10 to 1) 1
3418[2] BLUES COMPOSER (Ire) [-] 4-8-10 (6*) B J Walsh (10) ....(9 to 4 fav) 2
3294* MORNING NURSE (Ire) [-] 4-9-8 (2*) P Carberry (5) (5 to 2) 3
3112[5] NORDIC MINE (Ire) [-] 3-8-1 (6*) J A Heffernan (1) (10 to 1) 4
3296[6] SON OF TEMPO (Ire) [-] 4-8-0 J F Egan (11)...... (16 to 1) 5
3399[6] SUTTON CENTENARY (Ire) [-] 5-7-7 (10*) D A O'Sullivan (12) ....(14 to 1) 6
3484[5] NORDICOLINI (Ire) [-] (bl) 3-9-10 M J Kinane (9)....(8 to 1) 7
3399* BOLERO DANCER (Ire) [-] 5-8-11 (6*,5ex) R V Skelly (3) ....(8 to 1) 8

2484 COUNTESS PAHLEN (Ire) [-] 4-7-11 (4*) J J Behan (4) ....(25 to 1) 9
3397[7] REGAL PRETENDER (Ire) [-] (bl) 3-7-10 (8*) G M Moylan (6) ....(12 to 1) 10
PERSIAN HILL (Ire) [-] 4-7-13 (6*) B Bowens (8)...(16 to 1) 11
3294 MISS MARESE (Ire) [-] (bl) 3-9-3 R Hughes (2).....(20 to 1) 12
Dist: ¾l, 6l, ½l, 2½l. 2m 16.50s. (12 Ran).
(Jacques Van T Hart), Adrian Taylor

YORK (good to firm)
Wednesday September 1st
Going Correction: MINUS 0.25 sec. per fur. (races 1,3,5,6,7), NIL (2,4)

3722 Levy Board McIvor Scotch Whisky Claiming Stakes Class D (3-y-o and up) £5,526 1m 205yds.......... (2:00)

3234[2] JADE VALE 4-8-11 (3*) D Harrison (2) *trkd ldr, led 3 fs out, sn quickened clr, eased nr finish.* ....(2 to 1 fav tchd 9 to 4 and 7 to 4) 1
3450[3] GRAND VITESSE (Ire) 4-9-1 (7*) D Gibbs (9) *led to 3 fs out, kpt on, no ch wth wnr*...(7 to 1 op 8 to 1 tchd 6 to 1) 2
3342[3] SURREY DANCER 5-9-5 W Ryan (1) *in tch, effrt and ch 3 fs out, kpt on same pace und pres.* ....(17 to 2 op 8 to 1 tchd 9 to 1) 3
3469 STOPROVERITATE 4-8-9 A Munro (6) *beh, effrt o'r 3 fs out, styd on frm 2 out, not trble ldrs.* ....(20 to 1 op 16 to 1 tchd 25 to 1) 4
3437 BOLD PURSUIT (Ire) (bl) 4-9-7 W R Swinburn (3) *trkd ldrs, effrt and ch 3 fs out, sn rdn and btn.* (5 to 1 op 3 to 1) 5
3480[7] DEE RAFT (USA) 3-8-13 D Holland (4) *in tch, effrt 3 fs out, no hdwy*......................(10 to 1 tchd 12 to 1) 6
2794 LEIF THE LUCKY (USA) 4-9-8 N Connorton (8) *dwlt, hld up, hdwy 4 fs out, rdn 3 out, sn btn.* ....(10 to 1 op 12 to 1 tchd 14 to 1) 7
1901[3] GREENBANK (USA) 3-8-13 L Dettori (7) *chsd ldrs, pushed alng 4 fs out, wknd 3 out.* ....(13 to 2 op 7 to 1 tchd 6 to 1) 8
3355* INFANTRY GLEN (v) 3-8-10 M Birch (5) *al beh, lost tch fnl furlong*......................(25 to 1 tchd 33 to 1) 9
Dist: 8l, sht-hd, 1l, 3½l, 1½l, ½l, 4l, 10l. 1m 50.16s. a 0.96s (9 Ran).
SR: 52/36/32/19/20/7/14/-/-/ (Mrs S Bosher), J W Hills

3723 Best Buy Products Conditions Stakes Class C (2-y-o) £4,639 5f........ (2:30)

3472[4] WELSH MIST 8-5 M Roberts (3) *cl up, led 2 fs out, kpt on wl fnl furlong*.............................(7 to 2) 1
312* CAPE MERINO 8-7 S Webster (2) *slwly into strd, hld up in tch, hdwy to dispute ld one furlong out, no extr ins last*..................(11 to 1 op 10 to 1 tchd 14 to 1) 2
3529* POST MISTRESS (Ire) 8-5 G Duffield (1) *sn cl up, ev ch 2 fs out, kpt on same pace*..................(4 to 1 op 3 to 1) 3
3436[3] MOSCOW ROAD 9-0 W R Swinburn (6) *led to 2 fs out, sn btn*..............(7 to 4 fav op 5 to 4 tchd 15 to 8) 4
3448[4] HIGH DOMAIN (Ire) 9-2 W Carson (4) *in tch, sn pushed alng, wknd 2 fs out*..................(9 to 2 op 4 to 1) 5
Dist: 1½l, 2½l, 2½l, sht-hd. 59.41s. a 2.11s (5 Ran).
SR: 49/45/33/32/33/ (P Asquith), R Boss

3724 Batleys Cash & Carry Handicap Class C (0-90 3-y-o and up) £6,056 1m 5f 194yds....................... (3:00)

1717[2] HASTEN TO ADD (USA) [80] 3-9-0 G Duffield (4) *prmnt, led o'r one furlong out, styd on wl.* ....(11 to 4 fav op 5 to 2 tchd 3 to 1) 1
3503* FIRST BID [66] 6-8-11 A Culhane (3) *chsd ldrs, pushed alng o'r 3 fs out, hdwy und prerssure over one out, kpt on.* ....(12 to 1 tchd 14 to 1) 2
3353[5] FLIGHT LIEUTENANT (USA) [78] 4-9-9 J Reid (6) *hld up, effrt o'r 3 fs out, styd on wl fnl furlong, nrst finish.* ....(7 to 1 op 6 to 1) 3
3521* KADASTROF (Fr) [75] 3-8-9 (3ex) T Quinn (2) *led till o'r one furlong out, kpt on same pace*.....(11 to 1 op 12 to 1) 4
3466* YILDIZ [77] 4-9-8 W Carson (5) *trkd ldr, ev ch 2 fs out, kpt on same pace*..................(9 to 2 tchd 5 to 1) 5
3466 WHITE WILLOW [71] 4-9-2 K Darley (1) *hld up in tch, some hdwy o'r 2 fs out, staying on whn not clr run fnl furlong*..........................(10 to 1 tchd 9 to 1) 6
2871[6] BOLD ELECT [52] 5-7-11 L Charnock (9) *in tch, effrt o'r 3 fs out, no hdwy*..................(25 to 1 op 20 to 1) 7
SUBSONIC (Ire) [79] 5-9-10 W Ryan (8) *hld up, nvr nr ldrs.* ....(20 to 1 op 16 to 1 tchd 25 to 1) 8
3595[2] BOLD RESOLUTION (Ire) [72] 5-9-3 M Roberts (10) *in tch, effrt o'r 3 fs out, sn btn*..............(7 to 2 op 11 to 4) 9
3401 DUSTY POINT (Ire) [84] 3-9-4 W R Swinburn (7) *trkd ldrs, wknd quickly 5 fs out, tld off*......(16 to 1 op 12 to 1) 10
Dist: 2½l, 1l, hd, 2l, 1½l, 8l, 5l, 12l. 2m 59.25s. a 4.25s (10 Ran).
SR: 23/15/25/10/19/10/ (Pin Oak Stable), Sir Mark Prescott

3725 Lawrence Batley Rated Class B Handicap (0-105 3-y-o and up) £13,627 6f ....(3:30)

3621[2] MASTER PLANNER [91] 4-8-0 (7*) J D Smith (7) *cl up, led hfwy, ran on wl fnl furlong.* ....(6 to 1 fav tchd 13 to 2 and 11 to 2) 1
3468 BRANSTON ABBY (Ire) [100] 4-9-2 M Roberts (4) *in tch, hdwy to chase wnr o'r one furlong out, kpt on wl.* ....(14 to 1 op 12 to 1) 2
2698[4] BRIGG FAIR [98] 3-8-11 K Darley (1) *in tch, hdwy o'r 2 fs out, kpt on fnl furlong*..............(14 to 1 op 12 to 1) 3
3404[5] DUPLICITY (Ire) [96] 5-8-12 J Reid (2) *in tch, styd on fnl 2 fs, nrst finish*....................(8 to 1 tchd 10 to 1) 4
3504 POKER CHIP [94] 3-8-7 L Dettori (15) *trkd ldrs, effrt 2 fs out, kpt on same pace.* ....(11 to 1 op 10 to 1 tchd 12 to 1) 5
3504* HARD TO FIGURE [101] 7-8-10 (7*) S Drowne (5) *beh, effrt o'r 2 fs out, not clr run till styd on wl fnl furlong, not rch ldrs*......................(7 to 1 op 6 to 1) 6
3427[4] ROCK SYMPHONY [93] 3-8-1 (5*) J Tate (10) *pld hrd early, effrt o'r 2 fs out, kpt on same pace.* (16 to 1 op 14 to 1) 7
3638[9] TROON [91] 3-7-11 (7*) G Milligan (9) *chsd ldrs, one pace fnl 2 fs*......................(20 to 1 op 16 to 1) 8
3153[4] SIR HARRY HARDMAN [94] 5-8-10 S Perks (12) *prmnt till wknd o'r one furlong out*.........(11 to 1 op 10 to 1) 9
2252[4] MEDAILLE D'OR [100] (v) 5-9-2 A Munro (3) *chsd ldrs till wknd 2 fs out*....................(16 to 1 op 14 to 1) 10
3438[3] GARNOCK VALLEY [91] 3-8-4 J Carroll (13) *in tch, effrt whn not clr run o'r one furlong out, nvr dngrs.* ....(13 to 2 op 6 to 1 tchd 7 to 1) 11
3474[2] TRUE PRECISION [91] 3-8-1 (3*) D Harrison (14) *chsd ldrs till wknd 2 fs out*..........................(20 to 1) 12
4712a[4] ISAIAH [91] 4-8-7 Paul Eddery (8) *prmnt till wknd hfwy.* ....(33 to 1 op 25 to 1) 13
2753* REGAL CHIMES [105] 4-9-7 T Quinn (6) *led to hfwy, wknd 2 fs out*..........................(14 to 1 op 12 to 1) 14
3404[7] DOMINUET [94] 8-8-10 G Hind (11) *reared, slwly into strd, beh whn hmpd o'r one furlong out, nvr dngrs.* ....(10 to 1 op 8 to 1 tchd 12 to 1) 15
Dist: 1½l, 2l, ½l, ¾l, 1½l, ½l, nk, nk, 2l, ½l. 1m 11.36s. a 1.36s (15 Ran).
SR: 66/69/56/55/47/51/38/35/40/ (R M Cyzer), C A Cyzer

3726 Flintlock Cider Handicap Class D (0-80 3-y-o and up) £5,253 7f 202yds.. (4:00)

3639[5] ERTLON [75] 3-9-6 L Dettori (1) *made all, rdn o'r one furlong out, jst hld on*...........(16 to 1 op 14 to 1) 1
2794 WAINWRIGHT (USA) [75] 4-9-11 M Roberts (6) *prmnt, chsd wnr o'r 2 fs out, kpt on wl nr finish, jst fld.* ....(6 to 1 op 5 to 1 tchd 13 to 2) 2
1720[5] SWEET MIGNONETTE [72] 5-9-3 (5*) Darren Moffatt (2) *beh, hdwy 3 fs out, styd on wl fnl furlong, nrst finish.* ....(9 to 1 op 8 to 1) 3
3456 MUSTAKIM (Ire) [58] 3-8-3 W Carson (9) *chsd wnr, kpt on same pace fnl 2 fs*..........................(14 to 1) 4
3269[3] KINGCHIP BOY [55] (v) 4-8-5 D Biggs (10) *hld up, hdwy to chase ldrs hfwy, kpt on same pace fnl 2 fs.* ....(7 to 1 op 6 to 1) 5
3558[5] EURO FESTIVAL [77] 4-9-13 W R Swinburn (8) *beh, sn pushed alng, kpt on fnl 3 fs, not rch ldrs.* ....(10 to 1 op 8 to 1) 6
3450 FEATHER FACE [74] 3-9-5 J Reid (4) *chsd ldrs till wknd 2 fs out*....................(20 to 1 op 16 to 1) 7
3358 SELF EXPRESSION [60] 5-8-3 (7*) D Thomas (5) *slwly into strd, nvr trble ldrs*..................(9 to 1 op 8 to 1) 8
2522 TAAHHUB (Ire) [71] 3-9-2 R Hills (12) *chsd ldrs till wknd 3 fs out*....................(12 to 1 op 10 to 1) 9
2884 DOUBLE ECHO (Ire) [69] 5-9-5 A Munro (7) *al beh.* ....(11 to 1 op 10 to 1 tchd 12 to 1) 10
3553* DANCING DOMINO [70] 3-9-1 K Darley (11) *in tch till wknd 3 fs out*..................(5 to 2 fav op 11 to 4) 11
SEAGULL HOLLOW (Ire) [69] 4-9-5 M Birch (3) *beh hfwy.* ....(33 to 1) 12
Dist: Hd, 1l, ½l, 3l, nk, 1l, sht-hd, 12l, 2½l, 1l. 1m 37.81s. a 1.51s (12 Ran).
SR: 53/57/51/30/23/44/33/23/-/ (C E Brittain), C E Brittain

3727 Mayfield Bitter & Lager Maiden Stakes Class D (3-y-o) £4,503 1¼m 85yds........................ (4:30)

3117[2] ICE POOL (USA) 8-9 M Roberts (8) *prmnt, led o'r 3 fs out, styd on wl*..........................(9 to 2 op 7 to 2) 1
3456[2] PERFECT VINTAGE 9-0 W R Swinburn (5) *in tch, hdwy hfwy, ev ch 3 fs out, sn rdn, kpt on same pace.* ....(6 to 4 op 5 to 4 on tchd 11 to 10 on) 2
3506[2] MAKIN (USA) 9-0 W Carson (7) *in tch, pushed alng 3 fs out, swtchd wl o'r one out, styd on fnl furlong.* ....(13 to 2 op 6 to 1) 3
515 RIBBOLD 9-0 A Munro (4) *led till o'r 3 fs out, kpt on same pace*..........................(25 to 1) 4
2937[6] CHUMMY'S PAL (USA) 9-0 J Reid (9) *trkd ldr, effrt o'r 3 fs out, sn btn*..........(16 to 1 op 14 to 1 tchd 20 to 1) 5
3272 MAJBOOR YAFOOZ (USA) 9-0 G Hind (1) *slwly into strd, nvr nr to chal*..................(25 to 1 op 20 to 1) 6
1145[2] MT TEMPLEMAN (USA) 9-0 L Dettori (3) *chsd ldrs till wknd 3 fs out*..........................(8 to 1 op 7 to 1) 7
3318[7] GENTLEMAN SID 9-0 J Lowe (2) *in tch till wknd o'r 3 fs out*..........................(100 to 1 op 50 to 1) 8

3489^{4} BOLD STAR 9-0 S Perks (10) *al beh.* (20 to 1 tchd 25 to 1) 9
TROY BOY 9-0 K Darley (6) *al beh, tld off.* ....(33 to 1 op 25 to 1) 10
Dist: 2l, ¾l, 2½l, 5l, 1½l, ¾l, 1½l, 1½l, 30l. 2m 12.19s. a 4.19s (10 Ran).
SR: 27/28/26/21/11/8/6/3/-/ (Sheikh Mohammed), H R A Cecil

3728 Wachenfeld German Wines Maiden Stakes Class D (2-y-o) £4,308 7f 202yds........................ (5:00)

PEARL KITE (USA) 8-9 M Roberts (3) *in tch, pushed alng to ld entering fnl furlong, styd on wl*..........(11 to 8 jt-fav op 5 to 4 tchd 6 to 4) 1
2756^{5} MUWAFIK 9-0 R Hills (4) *led till entering fnl furlong, no extr*..........................(11 to 8 jt-fav op Evens) 2
2990 EL BAILADOR (Ire) 9-0 L Dettori (2) *chsd ldr, hng lft o'r 2 fs out, sn wknd*..........................(9 to 2 op 8 to 1) 3
517 CLUBS ARE TRUMPS (Ire) 9-0 J Lowe (5) *in tch till outpcd o'r 4 fs out, sn tld off*............ (20 to 1 tchd 25 to 1) 4
Dist: 3l, 10l, 12l. 1m 39.52s. a 3.22s (4 Ran).
SR: 17/13/-/-/ (Saeed Manana), M Johnston

GOWRAN PARK (IRE) (good)
Thursday September 2nd

3729 Posen 2-Y-0 EBF Fillies Maiden (Div 1) £4,485 7f...................... (4:00)

3541^{3} CRYSTAL LAKE (Ire) 9-0 P V Gilson (1) ....(5 to 2 jt-fav) 1
GOSPEL SINGER (USA) 9-0 P Shanahan (6) .... (6 to 1) 2
3527^{3} DANITA (Ire) 9-0 C Roche (9) .... (3 to 1) 3D
3451^{8} EVICTRESS (Ire) 9-0 R Hughes (3) .... (12 to 1) 3
ZARA'S BIRTHDAY (Ire) 8-12 (2*) P Carberry (8) ... (10 to 1) 5
3453^{6} FAIRY MUSIC (Ire) 9-0 J P Murtagh (11) .... (12 to 1) 6
FRIARY TOWN (Ire) 8-10 (4*) J J Behan (4) ....(33 to 1) 7
3613^{2} BETTER FOLLY (Ire) 9-0 W J Supple (12) ......(5 to 2 jt-fav) 8
IMPLICIT VIEW 9-0 N G McCullagh (7) .... (14 to 1) 9
3451^{9} FAYR DILLY (Ire) 8-8 (6*) R V Skelly (5).............(33 to 1) 10
3332 PERFECT CADENCE (Ire) (bl) 8-12 (2*) D G O'Shea (2) ....(25 to 1) 11
3527^{8} ACHTUNG LADY (Ire) 9-0 D Manning (10)........ (12 to 1) 12
Dist: 1½l, 1l, sht-hd, 6l. 1m 33.20s. (12 Ran).
(Mrs D V O'Brien), Charles O'Brien

3730 Posen 2-Y-0 EBF Fillies Maiden (Div 2) £4,485 7f...................... (4:30)

3527^{2} ICY TUNDRA 9-0 M J Kinane (2).............. (Evens fav) 1
3527 SUBARASHII (USA) 9-0 P V Gilson (10)...............(6 to 1) 2
3451^{4} DANCING AT LUNASA (Ire) (bl) 9-0 J P Murtagh (11) (6 to 1) 3
3453^{2} GO MILLIE (Ire) 9-0 W J Supple (7)..................(4 to 1) 4
1442^{5} POSTPONE (Ire) 9-0 C Roche (8)...................(6 to 1) 5
3451^{7} CAPATINA (Ire) (bl) 8-12 (2*) P Carberry (3)........(16 to 1) 6
3613 MEGLIO CHE POSSO (Ire) 9-0 B Coogan (6).......(25 to 1) 7
SECRET WAR (Ire) 9-0 R Hughes (4).............. (12 to 1) 8
SALIENCE (Ire) 9-0 P Shanahan (9)................ (10 to 1) 9
GLAD YOU ASKED ME (Ire) 8-10 (4*) J J Behan (5) (33 to 1) 10
3243^{8} NOREASTER (Ire) 9-0 K J Manning (1)........... (16 to 1) 11
Dist: 1l, ¾l, 5l, 2l. 1m 32.10s. (11 Ran).
(Sheikh Mohammed), John M Oxx

3731 Bob Back (C&G) E.B.F. Maiden (2-y-o) £4,485 7f...................... (5:00)

2982^{5} CLIFDON FOG (Ire) (bl) 9-0 C Roche (2)......(7 to 4 jt-fav) 1
3608 MELODIC SOUND (Ire) 9-0 S Craine (1)........... (10 to 1) 2
2982^{9} MAJESTIC MAN (Ire) 9-0 J F Egan (5)............(66 to 1) 3
ARTEMA (Ire) 9-0 M J Kinane (14)............(7 to 4 jt-fav) 4
3492^{7} CROSS SWORDS (USA) 9-0 P V Gilson (13)....... (7 to 1) 5
3562^{4} KAKASHDA (Ire) 9-0 J P Murtagh (11)...............(8 to 1) 6
SCHNAPPS 8-12 (2*) P Carberry (7)...................(8 to 1) 7
CONTRASTING (Ire) 9-0 Joanna Morgan (6)....... (20 to 1) 8
3608^{4} SINGING DANCER (Ire) 9-0 W J Supple (12)....... (8 to 1) 9
3335 SEAFORTH (Ire) (bl) 9-0 R Hughes (9)............. (20 to 1) 10
2778^{8} FINAL REMINDER (Ire) 9-0 P Shanahan (4).......... (14 to 1) 11
2840^{9} BERGERACONHOLIDAY (Ire) 9-0 N G McCullagh (3) ....(16 to 1) 12
RAINBOW IDOL (Ire) 9-0 K J Manning (10).........(33 to 1) 13
Dist: Sht-hd, 7l, nk, 2l. 1m 30.90s. (13 Ran).
(J P Hill), J S Bolger

3732 Bagenalstown Handicap (0-75 3-y-o) £2,760 1m 1f.................... (5:30)

3498* STATE PRINCESS (Ire) [-] 9-6 (6ex) R Hughes (8)... (5 to 1) 1
1652^{3} DEVIL'S HOLIDAY (USA) [-] 9-2 P V Gilson (9)......(10 to 1) 2
3454* TINERANA (Ire) [-] 9-11 (7ex) M J Kinane (4).... (2 to 1 fav) 3
3298^{2} MY GOSSIP (Ire) [-] 8-4 N G McCullagh (6)..........(9 to 2) 4
3494^{3} UP SHE FLEW (USA) [-] 8-10 (4*) W J Smith (2).....(7 to 1) 5
3329^{2} HAANEM [-] 8-11 W J Supple (1)................... (20 to 1) 6
3061^{7} TOUCHING MOMENT (Ire) [-] 8-11 (10*) J D Moore (3) ....(20 to 1) 7
3454^{2} AULD STOCK (Ire) [-] 9-2 (6*) J R Barry (7).......... (6 to 1) 8
3278^{6} VALAMIR (Ire) [-] 8-9 (6*) B Bowens (5)........... (50 to 1) 9
3293* NO DUNCE (Ire) [-] 9-4 S Craine (10)................ (8 to 1) 10
Dist: Sht-hd, 3l, 1½l, 1l. 2m 0.80s. (10 Ran).
(Sportsmans Inn Syndicate), D T Hughes

3733 Ballylinch Stud Maiden (3-y-o) £3,450 1m 1f 130yds.................. (6:00)

3616^{2} ALBERTAZZI (Ire) 9-0 C Roche (7)...............(2 to 1 on) 1
3579^{5} MY KERRY DANCER (USA) 9-0 S Craine (3)....... (6 to 1) 2
3497^{6} ROLANDS GIRL (Ire) 8-7 (4*) J J Behan (6)........(12 to 1) 3
3417^{5} DO-TELL-ME (Ire) 8-5 (6*) R V Skelly (1)..........(16 to 1) 4
3382^{3} NANNAKA (USA) 8-11 K J Manning (4).............(6 to 1) 5
1333 TERESIAN GIRL (Ire) 8-9 (2*) P Carberry (5).......(20 to 1) 6
3395^{3} I'M NO LADY (Ire) 8-11 N Byrne (2)............... (12 to 1) 7
Dist: ¾l, 2l, 3l, 2½l. 2m 18.80s. (7 Ran).
(Mrs J S Bolger), J S Bolger

SALISBURY (good to firm)
Thursday September 2nd

Going Correction: MINUS 0.25 sec. per fur. (races 1,2,3,4,5), MINUS 0.40 (6)

3734 Winterbourne Limited Stakes Class F (0-65 3-y-o and up) £3,049 1m 1f 209yds........................ (2:20)

3344^{3} NEMEA (USA) 3-8-4 T Quinn (15) *trkd ldr, led o'r 2 fs out, sn hdd, rallied gmely to ld ag'n wl ins last.* ....(6 to 1 op 7 to 2) 1
3551^{5} MULCIBER 5-9-2 M Hills (1) *al in tch on outsd, hdwy to ld 2 fs out, rdn and hdd wl ins last.* ....(7 to 1 op 6 to 1 tchd 8 to 1) 2
2118^{2} QUICK SILVER BOY 3-8-2 (7*) S Drowne (10) *led till hdd o'r 2 fs out, kpt on one pace*..........(12 to 1 op 10 to 1) 3
3232^{6} SHALHOLME 3-8-5[1] J Williams (12) *al prmnt, kpt on one pace fnl 2 fs*..........................(33 to 1 op 25 to 1) 4
2273* MISTY VIEW 4-8-6 (5*) K Rutter (13) *hld up in tch, rdn 3 fs out, one pace aftr*..................(8 to 1 op 7 to 1) 5
3681^{2} BRONZE MAQUETTE (Ire) 3-7-13 (5*) D Wright (14) *hld up in rear, styd on fnl 2 fs, nvr dngrs*.....(5 to 1 op 14 to 1) 6
3119^{6} JADE GREEN 4-8-11 J Reid (5) *in tch, rdn 3 fs out, no hdwy fnl 2*..................................(12 to 1 op 10 to 1) 7
1699^{3} STORM FREE (USA) 7-9-2 A Munro (2) *mid-div, no hdwy fnl 3 fs*...........................(10 to 1 tchd 12 to 1) 8
3461 FAIRY FREE 4-8-8 (3*) B Doyle (3) *al mid-div, no hdwy fnl 3 fs*..................................... (20 to 1 op 16 to 1) 9
3088 JADIRAH (USA) 3-8-4 R Hills (9) *mid-div, rdn 3 fs out, sn btn*..................................... (12 to 1 op 10 to 1) 10
3506^{4} SILK ISLAND 3-8-9 Pat Eddery (4) *hld up in tch, rdn o'r 3 fs out, sn btn*......(3 to 1 fav tchd 7 to 2 and 11 to 4) 11
3549^{8} COALISLAND 3-8-9 J Weaver (11) *al towards rear.* ....(33 to 1 op 20 to 1) 12
3549^{5} PATSY GRIMES 3-8-4 S Raymont (6) *slwly away, effrt hfwy, beh fnl 3 fs*.....................(33 to 1 op 20 to 1) 13
3391^{7} LAID BACK BEN 3-8-9 A Clark (7) *slwly away, ran wide hfwy, al beh*.......................................(66 to 1) 14
3447 NONANNO 4-9-2 M Perrett (8) *al beh, tld off.* ....(66 to 1 op 50 to 1) 15
Dist: 1½l, ½l, 2l, ¾l, ½l, ¾l, 3l, 2l, 3l, 2½l. 2m 7.74s. a 3.74s (15 Ran).
SR: 28/37/29/21/25/17/22/21/12/ (B E Nielsen), J R Fanshawe

3735 Konig-Pilsener Conditions Stakes Class C (3-y-o) £4,680 1¾m..... (2:50)

3403^{8} TIOMAN ISLAND 9-3 T Quinn (4) *trkd ldr, led aftr 5 fs, shaken up o'r 2 furlongs out, styd on grimly.* ....(9 to 4 op 2 to 1 tchd 11 to 4) 1
3401* EDBAYSAAN (Ire) 9-2 Pat Eddery (5) *set steady pace 1st 5 fs, steadied in mid-div, rdn to chal o'r 3 furlongs out, one pace fnl 2.* ....(Evens fav op 11 to 10 on tchd 5 to 4 on) 2
1638^{9} BRIGHT SPELLS 8-5 J Williams (1) *hld up, rdn and hdwy o'r 2 fs out, one pace fnl furlong*.....(8 to 1 op 7 to 1) 3
2432^{4} ACANTHUS (Ire) 9-4 R Hills (2) *al abt same pl, lost tch fnl 3 fs*...(8 to 1 op 7 to 1) 4
3578^{4} PAT OR ELSE 8-5 A Munro (3) *hld up in tch, trkd wnr aftr 5 fs, wknd quickly 3 out.* ....(16 to 1 op 12 to 1 tchd 20 to 1) 5
Dist: 3l, nk, 15l, 12l. 3m 3.19s. a 5.49s (5 Ran).
SR: 13/6/ (H R H Sultan Ahmad Shah), P F I Cole

3736 EBF 'Wessex Stallions' Fillies Handicap Class C (0-90 3-y-o and up) £9,195 6f 212yds...................... (3:20)

1829* SILENT EXPRESSION [70] 3-8-4 (3*) C Hodgson (13) *al lying hndy, rdn to ld appr fnl furlong, ran on strly.* ....(16 to 1 op 14 to 1) 1
3425* TEANARCO (Ire) [64] 5-8-5 J Williams (8) *hld up in rear, gd hdwy 2 fs out, ran on wl ins last.* ....(7 to 1 op 6 to 1 tchd 8 to 1) 2
3511^{9} BALLASECRET [87] 5-9-9 (5*) D Meredith (2) *trkd ldr, led 3 fs out, hdd appr last, ran on one pace.* ....(25 to 1 op 16 to 1) 3
3312^{2} LACERTA (Ire) [89] 3-9-9 (3*) Stephen Davies (6) *rdn frm hfwy, styd on ins fnl one and a half fs.* ....(12 to 1 op 10 to 1) 4

3269[5] NITOUCHE [64] 3-7-12 (3*) D Harrison (5) *chsd ldrs, sn rdn alng, one pace ins fnl 2 fs.........* (10 to 1 op 16 to 1) 5
3051* PLUCK [81] 3-9-4 Pat Eddery (4) *hld up, effrt 2 fs out, rdn and no extr ins last.* ....(9 to 4 fav op 11 to 4 tchd 3 to 1) 6
2193[2] QUAVER (USA) [74] 3-8-11 G Hind (7) *chsd ldrs, wknd wl o'r one furlong out, eased..........* (10 to 1 op 7 to 1) 7
3343[2] TRINITY HALL [65] 3-8-2 T Williams (12) *hld up, hdwy hfwy, rdn 2 fs out, sn btn........*(16 to 1 tchd 14 to 1) 8
3450[8] YOURS BY RIGHT [77] (bl) 3-9-0 T Sprake (9) *in tch till rdn 3 fs out, wknd 2 out.* (14 to 1 op 12 to 1 tchd 16 to 1) 9
3476[8] EAST LIBERTY (USA) [84] 3-9-7 M Hills (1) *rcd wide, wknd o'r 2 fs out.............* (8 to 1 op 6 to 1 tchd 9 to 1) 10
3341* LAKAB (USA) [75] 3-8-12 R Hills (3) *al in rear.* ....(10 to 1 tchd 12 to 1) 11
3643[3] OARE SPARROW [67] (v) 3-8-4 T Quinn (11) *led till hdd 3 fs out, wknd stdly......*(10 to 1 tchd 8 to 1 and 11 to 1) 12
3481 BALIGAY [75] 8-9-2 A Munro (10) *outpcd and al in rear.* .... (20 to 1 op 16 to 1) 13
Dist: 2l, nk, ¾l, ¾l, ½l, 1l, hd, 5l, 6l, 3l. 1m 26.84s. a 1.24s (13 Ran).
SR: 48/40/62/58/31/46/36/26/23/ (Mrs Rosalie Hawes), D Morris

3737 Dick Poole Fillies Conditions Stakes Class B (2-y-o) £6,116 6f........(3:50)

3463[5] PROPHECY (Ire) 8-11 Pat Eddery (2) *outpcd in rear, rdn o'r 2 fs out, picked up wl to ld ins last, cmftbly.* ....(7 to 2 op 3 to 1 tchd 4 to 1) 1
3448* BLUE SIREN 8-13 M Hills (1) *trkd ldrs, hdwy to ld one furlong out, kpt on, hdd ins.* ....(11 to 2 op 5 to 1 tchd 13 to 2) 2
3657* CRYSTAL MAGIC 8-13 (2ex) B Raymond (5) *trkd ldr, rdn and outpcd fnl furlong............* (7 to 1 tchd 8 to 1) 3
3317* ARECIBA (USA) 8-11 J Reid (4) *hld up, rdn 2 fs, no response.......................*(7 to 4 fav op 2 to 1) 4
3347[3] TRICORNE 8-11 T Quinn (6) *led, shaken up 2 fs out, hdd one out, sn btn.........*(11 to 4 op 9 to 4 tchd 3 to 1) 5
Dist: ¾l, 4l, 1½l, ½l. 1m 13.73s. a 1.23s (5 Ran).
SR: 42/41/25/17/15/ (K Abdulla), J H M Gosden

3738 EBF Quidhampton Maiden Fillies' Stakes Class D (2-y-o) £5,020 6f 212yds........................(4:20)

BALANCHINE (USA) 8-11 J Reid (14) *trkd ldr, al gng wl, shaken up to ld appr fnl furlong, pushed out, cmftbly.* ....(2 to 1 on op 6 to 4 on) 1
3230[3] DEVOTEE 8-11 M Hills (2) *led till hdd appr fnl furlong, ran on one pace.......*(9 to 1 op 7 to 1 tchd 10 to 1) 2
OH SUSANNAH 8-11 A Munro (16) *broke wl, trkd ldrs, rdn well o'r one furlong out, one pace.* ....(11 to 1 op 8 to 1 tchd 12 to 1) 3
2571 IOLANI 8-11 S Raymont (7) *prmnt till outpcd ins fnl 2 fs.* .... (33 to 1 op 20 to 1) 4
3443[4] ALACRITY 8-11 J Williams (9) *hld up in mid-div, hdwy 2 fs out, rdn appr last, one pace.* ....(25 to 1 op 16 to 1 tchd 33 to 1) 5
REALIZE 8-11 Pat Eddery (1) *beh, ran on wl ins fnl 2 fs, nvr nrr, prmsg....................* (10 to 1 op 5 to 1) 6
3265[4] PERYLLYS 8-8 (3*) Stephen Davies (3) *mid-div, hdwy on outsd o'r 2 fs out, rdn and wknd over one out.* ....(25 to 1 op 16 to 1 tchd 33 to 1) 7
ARYAAH 8-11 R Hills (11) *slwly away, no imprsn fnl 2 fs.* .... (14 to 1 op 10 to 1) 8
2754[8] PIZZAZZ 8-11 T Quinn (17) *chsd ldrs, rdn and wknd o'r one furlong out..................* (50 to 1 op 25 to 1) 9
HIGH TYPHA 8-11 A McGlone (8) *al towards rear.* .... (20 to 1 op 14 to 1) 10
PERICARDIA 8-11 B Raymond (5) *speed till wknd o'r 2 fs out..........*(10 to 1 tchd 12 to 1 and 14 to 1) 11
2546 LEGENDARY LADY 8-11 J Weaver (6) *speed to hfwy.* .... (100 to 1 op 50 to 1) 12
PRINCESS TALLULAH 8-11 N Adams (4) *outpcd frm hfwy.* .... (66 to 1 op 20 to 1) 13
3230 JANE HERRING 8-4 (7*) S Drowne (10) *in tch to hfwy, sn beh, tld off.......................*(100 to 1 op 50 to 1) 14
3287 SEE MY GUEST (Fr) 8-11 A Clark (12) *al beh, tld off.* .... (100 to 1 op 33 to 1) 15
Dist: 3l, 1l, 4l, 1½l, 1l, 1½l, sht-hd, 1l, 6l, 1l. 1m 27.42s. a 1.82s (15 Ran).
SR: 43/34/31/19/14/11/6/5/2/ (R E Sangster), P W Chapple-Hyam

3739 Blandford Handicap Class D (0-80 3-y-o and up) £3,552 5f.............(4:50)

3621 BODARI [77] 4-9-8 (3*) D Harrison (12) *made all, edgd lft appr fnl furlong, ran on wl..........*(10 to 1 op 9 to 1) 1
3584[3] BATCHWORTH BOUND [54] 4-8-2 C Rutter (4) *hld up, ran on wl to go second ins fnl furlong.* ....(9 to 1 op 8 to 1 tchd 10 to 1) 2
3270[2] SUPREME BOY [56] 4-8-4 G Hind (8) *trkd wnr, rdn entering fnl furlong, one pace........*(7 to 1 tchd 8 to 1) 3
3099[8] RHYTHMIC DANCER [73] 5-9-7 A Mackay (7) *chsd ldrs, ev ch one and a half fs out, one pace.* (16 to 1 op 14 to 1) 4
3571[6] BELLSABANGING [74] 3-9-3 (3*) Stephen Davies (11) *hld up, hdwy 2 fs out, kpt on one pace..*(5 to 1 op 6 to 1) 5
3584* CHOIR PRACTICE [56] 6-7-11 (7*) Sally Radford-Howes (5) *towards rear, hdwy and not much room o'r 2 fs out, kpt on one pace.........* (3 to 1 fav op 7 to 2 tchd 4 to 1) 6
3270* LYNDON'S LINNET [70] 5-9-4 J Weaver (1) *rcd on outsd, nvr nr to chal..........................*(9 to 2 op 4 to 1) 7
3226[5] MURPHY'S HOPE (Ire) [50] (bl) 3-7-10 N Adams (3) *gd speed till wknd appr fnl furlong.........*(33 to 1 op 25 to 1) 8
3348 BELLS OF LONGWICK [72] 4-9-6 T Williams (6) *speed to hfwy, sn beh...................*(10 to 1 tchd 12 to 1) 9
3584 SERIOUS HURRY [55] 5-8-3 T Quinn (9) *speed to hfwy, wknd 2 fs out, eased..............* (20 to 1 op 16 to 1) 10
3229[6] JEREMIAHS BOY [50] 3-7-10[1] F Norton (10) *al beh.* .... (10 to 1 op 9 to 1 tchd 12 to 1) 11
3305 HOME SAFE [47] (v) 3-7-3[1] (5*) D Wright (2) *al beh.* .... (40 to 1 op 33 to 1) 12
Dist: 2½l, 1l, ½l, hd, ¾l, 3l, 1½l, 1l, ¾l, ¾l. 1m 0.39s. a 0.59s (12 Ran).
SR: 59/26/24/39/37/18/20/-/12/ (R J Thomas), D A Wilson

YARMOUTH (good)
Thursday September 2nd

Going Correction: MINUS 0.20 sec. per fur. (races 1,2,3,4,5), MINUS 0.45 (6)

3740 Smestow Brook Maiden Stakes Class D (3-y-o and up) £3,465 1m 3f 101yds ....(2:10)

3456[8] SCORPIUS 3-8-11 K Darley (6) *outpcd and pushed alng in rear hfwy, hdwy on outer 3 fs out, effrt and edgd lft 2 out, rdn to ld bef last, kpt on.....* (7 to 4 tchd 11 to 4) 1
3272[6] RUMPUS (Ire) 3-8-6 R Cochrane (3) *trkd ldrs gng wl, smooth hdwy to ld o'r 3 fs out, rdn 2 out, hdd and not quicken appr last.* .... (11 to 10 fav op Evens tchd 5 to 4 and 5 to 4 on) 2
3487[6] SUIVEZ 3-8-11 J Quinn (1) *hld up and beh, gd hdwy 3 fs out, effrt and ev ch 2 out, rdn and not quicken appr last..*............................(16 to 1 op 6 to 1) 3
3173[5] CLASSIC CABOOSE (USA) 3-8-4 (7*) Michael Denaro (2) *outpcd and beh, hdwy 3 fs out, styd on fnl 2, nvr dngrs.* ....(16 to 1 op 10 to 1 tchd 20 to 1) 4
3509[5] HOME PARK (Ire) 3-8-11 P D'Arcy (7) *effrt and rdn 3 fs out, sn one pace...........* (7 to 1 op 3 to 1 tchd 15 to 2) 5
DEVILS DEN (Ire) 3-8-11 D Biggs (9) *chsd ldrs, hdwy to chal o'r 4 fs out, sn rdn and wknd 3 out.* .... (20 to 1 op 12 to 1) 6
PLAIN SAILING (Fr) 3-8-11 M Tebbutt (8) *chsd ldr, led o'r 4 fs out, rdn and hdd over 3 out, sn btn.* .... (20 to 1 op 10 to 1) 7
3590 MAASHAI LAWM (Ire) (bl) 3-8-11 P Robinson (5) *chsd ldrs, rdn 3 fs out, sn wknd..............*(25 to 1 op 16 to 1) 8
DARSING 3-8-11 G Duffield (4) *pld hrd, led, rdn and hdd o'r 4 fs out, wknd quickly.........* (33 to 1 op 16 to 1) 9
Dist: 1½l, 3l, 5l, 2½l, 8l, hd, 12l, 15l. 2m 26.00s. a 2.50s (9 Ran).
SR: 49/41/40/30/25/9/8/-/-/ (Sheikh Mohammed), M R Stoute

3741 Waterbridge Selling Stakes Class G (3-y-o and up) £2,070 1¼m 21yds (2:40)

3192[6] COSMIC STAR 3-8-10 W Ryan (8) *trkd ldrs, hdwy 4 fs out, shaken up to ld 2 out, sn rdn and ran on wl ins last.* .... (10 to 1 op 8 to 1) 1
3258[5] ELEGANT HUSSAR 3-8-10 J Quinn (3) *trkd ldr, hdwy to ld 4 fs out, rdn 3 out, hdd 2 out, kpt on und pres.* ....(9 to 2 tchd 5 to 1) 2
3518 ROLY WALLACE (v) 4-9-10 M Wigham (5) *trkd ldrs, pushed alng hfwy, hdwy o'r 2 fs out, effrt and swtchd appr last, sn rdn and kpt on one pace...*(14 to 1 op 10 to 1) 3
83 STREPHON (Ire) 3-8-10 P Robinson (4) *led, rdn and hdd 4 fs out, kpt on one pace und pres...*(16 to 1 op 14 to 1) 4
3536* VANROY (v) 9-9-10 R Cochrane (7) *hld up, hdwy o'r 3 fs out, effrt on outer and ev ch over one out, sn rdn and hng badly rght, wknd entering last.* ....(6 to 4 fav op 11 to 10 tchd 7 to 4) 5
3461 PRETTY BABY 3-8-5 D Biggs (2) *cl up, rdn 3 fs out, grad wknd..*............................(20 to 1 op 16 to 1) 6
3374[3] MAJOR IVOR 8-9-10 K Darley (6) *hld up, hdwy on outer o'r 3 fs out, sn rdn, wknd 2 furlongs out and virtually pld up..*..............(3 to 1 tchd 7 to 2 and 11 to 4) 7
Dist: 1½l, nk, sht-hd, ¾l, 1½l, dist. 2m 11.50s. a 7.50s (7 Ran).
SR: 1/-/11/-/8/-/-/ (Arashan Ali), S P C Woods

3742 EBF Canal Barge Maiden Stakes Class D (2-y-o) £4,056 1m 3yds. .(3:10)

2968[5] KING'S THEATRE (Ire) 9-0 W Ryan (5) *al prmnt, led o'r 2 fs out, clr appr last..*.........(3 to 1 on op 2 to 1 on) 1
3130 SHERMAN (Ire) 9-0 G Duffield (4) *al prmnt, effrt 2 fs out, sn rdn and kpt on, no ch wth wnr.....* (25 to 1 op 8 to 1) 2
3079 PRISCIAN'S HEAD 9-0 P Robinson (3) *prmnt, rdn and outpcd 2 and a half fs out, styd on und pres ins last.* .... (25 to 1 op 8 to 1) 3
3592 SHOOFK 9-0 L Piggott (8) *prmnt, rdn o'r 2 fs out and sn one pace..*..........................(10 to 1 op 3 to 1) 4
3137[5] OCEAN PARK 9-0 R Cochrane (6) *in tch, rdn alng hfwy, sn one pace..........* (11 to 1 op 8 to 1 tchd 12 to 1) 5

3230 NAWAFELL 8-4 (5*) J Tate (1) *led, rdn 2 and a half fs out, sn hdd and wknd*.................(25 to 1 op 14 to 1) 6
KHATIR (Can) 9-0 K Darley (7) *steadied strt, pushed alng hfwy, nvr a factor*.............(20 to 1 op 10 to 1) 7
466 CHINESE TREASURE (Ire) 9-0 M Tebbutt (2) *al rear*. ....(14 to 1 op 33 to 1 tchd 50 to 1) 8
3546 HOODLUM 8-7 (7*) S Eiffert (9) *hld up, some hdwy on outer hfwy, sn rdn and wknd*.... (100 to 1 op 50 to 1) 9
Dist: 5l, 1l, 1l, 3l, 1½l, 7l, 2½l, 1l. 1m 39.20s. a 3.40s (9 Ran).
SR: 25/10/7/4/-/-/ (Michael Poland), H R A Cecil

3743 September Nursery Class E (2-y-o) £3,106 7f 3yds.................(3:40)

3189[4] BENFLEET [55] 8-4 R Price (2) *hld up and beh, swtchd rght and hdwy 2 fs out, effrt and rdn o'r one out, styd on ins last to ld nr finish*. ....(11 to 1 op 7 to 1 tchd 12 to 1) 1
3386 ADMIRING [64] 8-10 (3*) M Fenton (6) *chsd ldrs, hdwy to ld 2 fs out, rdn appr last, hdd and no extr nr finish*. ....(12 to 1 op 8 to 1) 2
3091[6] LUNAR MISSION (Ire) [72] 9-7 K Darley (4) *chsd ldrs, hdwy 2 fs out, effrt to chal appr last, sn rdn and not quicken*. .....(100 to 30 fav op 3 to 1 tchd 11 to 4 and 7 to 2) 3
3600* JOHNNIE THE JOKER [63] (v) 8-12 (7ex) R Cochrane (5) *led, rdn 3 fs out, hdd 2 out and one pace*. ....(5 to 1 op 3 to 1 tchd 11 to 2) 4
3695[2] DUBALL REMY [54] 8-3 S O'Gorman (7) *cl up, ev ch 2 fs out, sn rdn and btn*..........(6 to 1 op 8 to 1) 5
2414[4] EWAR EMPRESS (Ire) [66] 9-1 W Ryan (8) *prmnt, rdn o'r 2 fs out, sn one pace*................(16 to 1 op 10 to 1) 6
3432 BOJOLLY [55] 8-4 G Duffield (3) *chsd ldrs, rdn 2 fs out and sn btn*................(8 to 1 op 7 to 1 tchd 10 to 1) 7
3390[3] HIGH SWINGER [62] (v) 8-11 J Quinn (10) *in tch, riden alng 3 fs out, sn btn*........(10 to 1 op 6 to 1 tchd 12 to 1) 8
3009 HERR TRIGGER [56] 8-5 G Bardwell (1) *al rear*. ....(8 to 1 tchd 10 to 1) 9
3426[2] MITSIS [62] 8-11 N Carlisle (9) *slwly into strd, al rear*. ....(7 to 1 op 5 to 1) 10
Dist: 2l, hd, 3l, hd, ½l, 2½l, 3l, 8l, 7l. 1m 26.60s. a 3.40s (10 Ran).
SR: 18/21/28/10/-/10/ (C G Donovan), R W Armstrong

3744 Valley Park Claiming Stakes Class F (3-y-o and up) £2,243 7f 3yds....(4:10)

3697[3] SHINING JEWEL 6-9-7 L Piggott (3) *cl up, led 2 fs out, shaken up ins last and ran on*. ....(11 to 10 on op 5 to 4 tchd 5 to 4 on) 1
3447* JOKIST 10-8-13 M Tebbutt (4) *hld up, gd hdwy o'r 2 fs out, effrt to chal entering last, sn rdn and not quicken*. ....(6 to 1 op 4 to 1) 2
3591[3] OUR SHADEE (USA) (v) 3-8-7 R Cochrane (1) *hld up and beh, hdwy 2 fs out, rdn and kpt on one pace appr last*. ....(9 to 2 op 7 to 2 tchd 5 to 1) 3
2670[5] CHAFF 6-8-8 B Crossley (2) *al chasing ldrs, rdn 2 fs out, sn one pace*........................(50 to 1 op 20 to 1) 4
3213[3] EASTERN GLOW (bl) 3-7-7[7] (7*) A Liggins (6) *hdwy hfwy, rdn 2 fs out, plugged on one pace*. ....(8 to 1 op 6 to 1 tchd 11 to 1) 5
3591 LITTLE PARK 4-7-4 (7*) Antoinette Armes (11) *beh, hdwy on outer 3 fs out, sn rdn and no imprsn*. ....(20 to 1 op 10 to 1 tchd 25 to 1) 6
3384[7] FILOU FILANT (Fr) 3-8-4 K Darley (7) *nvr rchd ldrs*. .... (14 to 1 op 6 to 1) 7
3550* SUPERENSIS (v) 3-8-6 (7*) Kim McDonnell (8) *led, rdn and hdd 2 fs out, sn wknd*.......(25 to 1 op 10 to 1) 8
1177 COURTENAY BEE 4-9-5 N Day (10) *chsd ldrs, rdn 3 fs out, sn wknd*...........................(50 to 1 op 16 to 1) 9
3174[8] BALLYGRIFFIN BELLE 4-8-2 (7*) S Mulvey (12) *chsd ldrs, rdn 3 fs out, sn wknd*. ....(33 to 1 op 20 to 1 tchd 50 to 1) 10
3535[7] HENBURY HALL (Ire) 5-8-9 J Quinn (5) *chsd ldrs to hfwy, sn lost pl*...........................(50 to 1 op 20 to 1) 11
3180 FOR GOLD 3-7-11 Dale Gibson (9) *al rear*. ....(50 to 1 op 20 to 1) 12
Dist: 1½l, 3l, 1½l, 5l, ¾l, 2l, 2½l, 1½l, 5l, hd. 1m 26.00s. a 2.80s (12 Ran).
SR: 44/31/16/12/-/-/ (D W Rolt), Mrs L Piggott

3745 Autumn Handicap Class E (0-70 3-y-o and up) £3,261 6f 3yds..........(4:40)

3378[9] SYLVAN STARLIGHT [53] (bl) 3-8-12 G Duffield (16) *outpcd and beh stands side, gd hdwy o'r 2 fs out, rdn and styd on wl to ld ins last, ran on*.......(14 to 1 tchd 16 to 1) 1
3593 RESTORE [43] (bl) 10-8-5 R Price (15) *al cl up stands side, led o'r 2 fs out, sn rdn, hdd and not quicken entering last*.........................(50 to 1 op 16 to 1) 2
3638[7] JESS REBEC [57] 5-9-0 (5*) L Newton (13) *in tch stands side, gd hdwy to chal 2 fs out, sn rdn and not quicken entering last*.........(11 to 1 op 10 to 1 tchd 12 to 1) 3
3429[4] SPRING HIGH [49] 6-8-11 G Bardwell (17) *chsd ldrs stand side, effrt and swtchd 2 fs out, sn rdn and kpt on*. ....(15 to 2 op 7 to 1 tchd 8 to 1) 4
2758 PAIR OF JACKS (Ire) [60] 3-9-5 R Cochrane (14) *o'rall ldr stands side, rdn and hdd over 2 fs out, kpt on one pace*. ....(9 to 1 op 12 to 1 tchd 8 to 1) 5
3458[3] BILL MOON [50] 7-8-5 (7*) Michael Denaro (3) *chsd ldrs far side, effrt and hdwy 2 fs out, kpt on one pace ins last*. ....(8 to 1 op 7 to 1 tchd 9 to 1) 6
3564[2] NORLING (Ire) [50] 3-8-9 L Piggott (11) *prmnt stands side, rdn o'r 2 fs out, grad wknd*. ....(7 to 1 op 6 to 1 tchd 8 to 1) 7
3591 FRIENDLY SMILE [43] (bl) 3-8-2 Dale Gibson (12) *slwly into strd and beh till some hdwy fnl 2 fs, nvr dngrs*. ....(33 to 1 op 16 to 1) 8
3292[3] AROOM [65] (bl) 3-9-10 P Robinson (4) *chsd ldr far side, rdn 2 fs out, one pace*. (11 to 1 op 8 to 1 tchd 12 to 1) 9
2831[2] QUICK STEEL [58] (bl) 5-8-13 (7*) S Mulvey (7) *nvr rchd ldrs*. ....(12 to 1 op 5 to 1) 10
3593 BRIGHT PARAGON (Ire) [48] 4-8-10 J Quinn (1) *nvr rchd ldrs*...........................(16 to 1 op 12 to 1) 11
3568* TREVORSNINEPOINTS [60] 3-9-5 K Darley (8) *led far side, rdn 2 fs out, sn wknd*............(9 to 4 fav op 7 to 2) 12
3270[6] PRINCE SONGLINE [52] (v) 3-8-11 W Ryan (9) *in tch stands side, effrt and rdn o'r 2 fs out, sn btn*. ....(14 to 1 op 12 to 1) 13
3591 CUDDLY DATE [48] (v) 3-8-7 D Biggs (10) *cl up stands side o'r 3 fs*...........................(33 to 1 op 14 to 1) 14
3593[5] ELTON LEDGER (Ire) [56] (bl) 4-8-13 (5*) J Tate (2) *rcd far side, effrt and hdwy o'r 2 fs out, sn rdn and btn*. ....(7 to 1 tchd 8 to 1) 15
3593[8] MARTINOSKY [62] (bl) 7-9-10 N Day (5) *chsd ldrs far side o'r 3 fs*...........................(25 to 1 op 14 to 1) 16
3270[4] GEMINI BAY [35] (bl) 4-7-11[1] S Dawson (6) *chsd ldrs far side till rdn and wknd quickly 2 fs out*. ....(25 to 1 op 16 to 1) 17
Dist: 1½l, 1½l, 1½l, 1½l, hd, ¾l, ½l, sht-hd, ½l, 1½l. 1m 11.30s. a 0.30s (17 Ran).
SR: 38/25/33/19/21/13/7/-/19/ (Mrs R A Johnson), Sir Mark Prescott

YORK (good to firm)
Thursday September 2nd

Going Correction: MINUS 0.05 sec. per fur. (races 1,2,6), NIL (3,4,5)

3746 Haxby Maiden Stakes Class D (2-y-o) £5,390 6f.....................(2:00)

3462[2] PINKERTON'S PAL 9-0 M Birch (4) *prmnt, slight ld wl o'r one furlong out, hld on well und pres*. ....(7 to 2 op 3 to 1) 1
GNEISS (USA) 9-0 Paul Eddery (2) *dwlt, hld up, hdwy hfwy, ev ch ins fnl furlong, no extr und pres*. ....(6 to 1 op 5 to 1 tchd 13 to 2) 2
MUR TAASHA (USA) 8-9 W Carson (3) *unruly in stalls, dwlt, sn in tch, chlgd wl o'r one furlong out, ev ch till no extr nr finish*. (11 to 10 on op Evens tchd 11 to 10) 3
2909[6] GALLANT SPIRIT (Ire) 9-0 L Dettori (6) *led till wl o'r one furlong out, kpt on same pace*......(10 to 1 op 8 to 1) 4
ZILZAL ZAMAAN (USA) 9-0 W R Swinburn (8) *trkd ldrs, effrt 2 fs out, sn btn*.... (7 to 1 op 4 to 1 tchd 15 to 2) 5
3432 GLENUGIE 9-0 A Culhane (9) *prmnt till wknd 2 fs out*. ....(25 to 1 tchd 33 to 1) 6
MILL CITY 9-0 W Newnes (7) *sn beh*. (50 to 1 op 33 to 1) 7
KING BRUCE 9-0 D Holland (1) *beh hfwy*. ....(16 to 1 op 12 to 1) 8
3259 RICH GLOW 9-0 Alex Greaves (5) *chsd ldrs till wknd o'r 2 fs out*.........................(50 to 1 op 33 to 1) 9
Dist: Hd, sht-hd, 3l, 2½l, 3½l, 4l, ½l, nk. 1m 13.76s. a 3.76s (9 Ran).
SR: 19/18/12/5/-/-/ (Miss E G Macgregor), C E Brittain

3747 Quintin Gilbey Silver Trophy Handicap Class E (0-75 3-y-o and up) £5,244 6f 214yds......................(2:30)

3535* KARINSKA [57] 3-8-6 (5*) D McCabe (1) *beh, not clr run 3 fs out, hdwy 2 out, str run to ld ins last, ran on wl*. ....(9 to 1 op 10 to 1) 1
3425[7] ZINBAQ [36] 7-7-8[1] J Lowe (2) *chsd ldrs, led wl o'r one furlong out till ins last, no extr*....(16 to 1 op 20 to 1) 2
3535 STATE FLYER [58] (v) 5-8-9 (7*) G Forster (21) *hld up, headway 3 fs out, rdn o'r one out, styd on wl*.....(33 to 1) 3
1902 BAYIN (USA) [36] 4-7-8[1] R Street (15) *hld up in tch, styd on fnl 2 fs, nrst finish*............................(100 to 1) 4
3504 KIMBERLEY PARK [60] (bl) 5-9-4 W R Swinburn (7) *chsd ldrs, effrt o'r 2 fs out, kpt on same pace*. ....(12 to 1 tchd 14 to 1) 5
3237[3] MCA BELOW THE LINE [62] (v) 5-9-6 S Webster (23) *chsd ldrs, kpt on same pace fnl 2 fs*.......................(16 to 1) 6
3553[4] SPANISH VERDICT [70] 6-9-7 (7*) C Teague (22) *chsd ldrs, ev ch 2 fs out, one pace*........................ (20 to 1) 7
3261[9] TAKENHALL [56] 8-9-0 M Roberts (20) *beh, pushed alng, some hdwy fnl 3 fs, not trble ldrs*. ....(11 to 2 op 9 to 2 tchd 6 to 1) 8
3182[6] MAJAL (Ire) [57] 4-9-1 L Charnock (9) *in tch, not clr run o'r 2 fs out, styd on fnl furlong*....... (25 to 1 op 33 to 1) 9
3628* OBSIDIAN GREY [60] 6-9-1 (3*) O Pears (3) *prmnt till wknd wl o'r one furlong out*.................. (14 to 1) 10
2966[4] CLAYBANK (USA) [66] 4-9-10 D Holland (12) *chsd ldrs, effrt 3 fs out, wknd o'r one out*......... (16 to 1 op 14 to 1) 11

3564* NORTHERN CHIEF [62] 3-8-13 (3*,6ex) S Maloney (18) *chsd ldrs, ev ch 2 fs out, sn rdn and wknd, eased whn btn fnl furlong*............(5 to 1 fav op 9 to 2) 12
3504 FORMIDABLE LIZ [61] 3-9-1 K Fallon (4) *chsd ldrs till wknd 2 fs out*..............(20 to 1 tchd 25 to 1) 13
3564[7] LAMSONETTI [72] 3-9-12 Alex Greaves (17) *nvr dngrs.* ....(25 to 1) 14
3174[6] GRANVILLE CORNER [58] (bl) 3-8-12 W Newnes (11) *nvr dngrs*..............(16 to 1 op 14 to 1) 15
3410[7] MILBANK CHALLENGER [59] 3-8-13 M Birch (13) *cl up till wknd 2 furlong out*..............(20 to 1) 16
SPANISH PERFORMER [43] 4-8-1 N Connorton (16) *nvr better than mid-div*..............(50 to 1) 17
3124[6] TUMBLING (USA) [44] 5-8-2 W Carson (10) *beh most of way*..............(10 to 1 op 14 to 1) 18
3603[7] PLUM FIRST [68] 3-9-8 Paul Eddery (6) *led till wl o'r one furlong out, sn wknd*..............(25 to 1) 19
2707[7] FILICAIA [39] 7-7-11 Kim Tinkler (14) *al beh*......(100 to 1) 20
3409[2] ROCK OPERA (Ire) [53] 5-8-11 A Culhane (8) *dwlt, al beh.* ....(16 to 1) 21
3676[3] LORD ALFIE [53] 4-8-11 S Whitworth (5) *in tch, effrt o'r 2 fs out, staying on whn hmpd and brght dwn over one out.* ....(10 to 1) bd
Dist: 3l, nk, hd, 2l, ½l, hd, nk, nk, 1l, ½l. 1m 24.81s. a 3.11s (22 Ran).
SR: 45/19/40/17/35/35/42/27/27/ (Geoff Whiting), M C Chapman

3748 Strensall Stakes Class A (Listed Race) (3-y-o and up) £11,257 1m 205yds ....(3:00)

3268* MUHTARRAM (USA) 4-9-1 W Carson (3) *in tch, hdwy on bit 3 fs out, shaken up to ld entering last, ran on wl.* ....(13 to 8 on op 2 to 1 on tchd 6 to 4 on) 1
3644[5] PORT LUCAYA (bl) 3-8-12 L Dettori (2) *led, rdn 2 fs out, hdd entering last, ran on wl*..............(3 to 1 op 4 to 1) 2
3154[2] COLWAY ROCK (USA) 3-8-9 W R Swinburn (4) *trkd ldr, effrt 3 fs out, wknd 2 out*..............(5 to 1 op 9 to 2) 3
3268[4] SPANISH STORM (Ire) (bl) 4-9-1 W Woods (1) *beh, effrt o'r 3 fs out, sn btn and lost tch*..............(16 to 1 op 14 to 1) 4
Dist: Nk, 10l, 8l. 1m 51.19s. a 1.99s (4 Ran).
SR: 71/67/34/16/ (Hamdan Al-Maktoum), J H M Gosden

3749 Sun Life Of Canada Centenary Rated Class B Handicap (0-105 3-y-o) £12,509 1m 3f 195yds..............(3:30)

3401[2] LEAGUE LEADER (Ire) [90] 8-9 W R Swinburn (5) *trkd ldr, led o'r 2 fs out, rdn and styd on wl.* ....(15 to 8 op 7 to 4 tchd 2 to 1) 1
3401[8] DARECLIFF (USA) [91] 8-10 W Newnes (4) *hld up, shaken up and hdwy o'r 2 fs out, chsd wnr fnl furlong, styd on, no imprsn*..............(6 to 1 op 7 to 1) 2
3467[6] MEAVY [88] 8-7 W Carson (3) *led till o'r 2 fs out, sn rdn and no extr*..............(10 to 1 op 8 to 1) 3
3403[5] MAJORITY (Ire) [102] 9-7 M Roberts (1) *trkd ldrs, effrt o'r 2 fs out, kpt on same pace.* ....(11 to 2 op 5 to 1 tchd 6 to 1) 4
2360* SPRING TO ACTION [102] 9-7 L Dettori (2) *hld up, effrt o'r 2 fs out, sn rdn and one pace.* ....(13 to 8 fav op 6 to 4 tchd 7 to 4) 5
Dist: 1l, 1½l, hd, hd. 2m 32.28s. a 4.28s (5 Ran).
SR: 52/51/45/58/57/ (Lord Weinstock), M R Stoute

3750 'Go Racing In Yorkshire' Nursery Class C (2-y-o) £5,952 7f 202yds (4:00)

3281[2] BALLARD RING (Ire) [66] 9-3 J Fanning (3) *chsd ldrs, led o'r one furlong out, rdn fnl furlong, jst hld on.* ....(13 to 2 op 6 to 1 tchd 7 to 1) 1
3667[5] NORTHERN BAILIWICK (Ire) [53] (bl) 8-4 Paul Eddery (5) *hld up, effrt and swtchd 2 fs out, styd on wl und pres fnl furlong, jst fld*..............(12 to 1 op 10 to 1) 2
3281[6] OVIDEO [61] (bl) 8-12 J Lowe (1) *led to fnl furlonog, kpt on*..............(8 to 1 tchd 9 to 1) 3
3377[4] HILL REEF (Fr) [68] 9-5 K Fallon (8) *hld up, styd on fnl 2 fs, nrst finish*..............(13 to 2 op 5 to 1 tchd 7 to 1) 4
3386[5] HIGHLY FASHIONABLE (Ire) [70] 9-7 L Dettori (6) *mid-div, effrt whn not clr run o'r 2 fs out, swtchd and one pace.* ....(7 to 1 tchd 8 to 1) 5
3696* HENRY'S LUCK [66] 9-3 (6ex) S Whitworth (9) *hld up, hdwy to track ldrs 3 fs out, rdn 2 out, sn btn.* ....(7 to 2 op 3 to 1) 6
3126* SILVER SLIPPER [65] 9-2 M Roberts (7) *mid-div, wkng whn hmpd 2 fs out*..............(11 to 4 fav op 3 to 1) 7
2862[8] CHANTRY BEATH [62] 8-13 W Carson (2) *chsd ldr, wkng whn bumped o'r 2 fs out*..............(16 to 1) 8
2714[8] JEAN DE FLORETTE (USA) [66] 9-3 D Holland (4) *chsd ldrs till wknd quickly 3 fs out, tld off*..............(16 to 1) 9
Dist: Sht-hd, 2½l, 3l, 1½l, 1½l, 3½l, 8l. 1m 40.73s. a 4.43s (9 Ran).
SR: 37/23/23/21/18/9/ (J H Pickard), J S Wainwright

3751 Huntington Fillies Conditions Stakes Class D (2-y-o) £4,464 6f........(4:30)

2301[6] BRAARI (USA) 9-0 W Carson (4) *trkd ldrs, led o'r 2 fs out, shaken up and drw clr fnl furlong*..............(9 to 4 jt-fav tchd 11 to 4) 1
3000* PROMISE FULFILLED (USA) 9-3 (3*) O Pears (3) *cl up, led briefly o'r 2 fs out, kpt on und pres, no ch wth wnr.* ....(7 to 2 op 3 to 1) 2
3347[6] DOUBLE DOWN 9-0 L Dettori (5) *led till wl o'r 2 fs out, sn rdn and btn*..............(9 to 4 jt-fav op 7 to 4) 3
3463[8] TAMAR'S BRIGADE 9-0 M Birch (1) *cl up, rdn o'r 2 fs out, sn btn*..............(12 to 1 op 10 to 1) 4
3679[4] HANNAH'S MUSIC 9-4 W R Swinburn (2) *beh frm hfwy.* ....(4 to 1 op 7 to 2) 5
Dist: 3½l, 1½l, 2l, 7l. 1m 13.16s. a 3.16s (5 Ran).
SR: 31/23/11/3/-/ (Hamdan Al-Maktoum), B W Hills

BADEN-BADEN (GER) (good)
Friday September 3rd

3752 Preis der Stadt Baden-Baden (Listed) (3-y-o and up) £16,327 1¼m.....(2:10)

3636[4] LUCKY GUEST 6-9-6 L Piggott, *rcd in 4th, led one furlong out, very easily*.............. 1
3494[6] LOKI (Ire) 5-9-0 M Hills, *wtd wth, ran on wl fnl furlong, took second on line*.............. 2
3582[6] FABRIANO 4-9-2 N Grant,.............. 3
FAVOURED NATIONS (Ire) 5-9-2 -,.............. 4
3019[6] ONE OFF THE RAIL (USA) 3-8-5 B Rouse, *led for 7 fs, sn wknd*.............. 0
Dist: 1 ¼l, nk, 2½l, hd, 1 ¾l, nk. 2m 4.98s. (13 Ran).
(Windflower Overseas Holdings Inc), J L Dunlop

3753 Moet & Channon-Rennen (Group 2) (2-y-o) £40,816 6f................(3:25)

3462* OWINGTON 9-2 M Hills, *al prmnt, chlgd one and a half fs out, led ins last, jst hld on*.............. 1
2906[3] FUMO DI LONDRA (Ire) 9-2 L Piggott, *led till ins fnl furlong, kpt on gmely, jst fld*.............. 2
OASIS HAWK (USA) 9-2 M Rimmer, *al prmnt on ins, kpt on wl 2 fs out, no extr fnl furlong*.............. 3
2845[2] POLISH ADMIRAL 9-2 N Day, *no ch frm hfwy*.............. 4
3581[3] ROMAN REEL (USA) 9-2 B Rouse, *no ch frm 3 fs out*...... 5
DRINSKI 9-2 A Helfenbein, *prmnt early, outpcd frm hfwy.* 6
Dist: Sht-hd, 1½l, 7l, 9l, 9l. 1m 10.94s. (6 Ran).
(Baron G Von Ullmann), G Wragg

HAYDOCK (good to firm)
Friday September 3rd

Going Correction: MINUS 0.10 sec. per fur. (races 1,2,3,5), NIL (4,6,7)

3754 EBF Birkenhead Maiden Stakes Class D (2-y-o) £4,479 5f..............(2:15)

1091[7] BLUE BOMBER 9-0 K Darley (12) *wl plcd centre, quickened ahead 2 fs out, sprinted clr fnl furlong.* ....(10 to 1 op 7 to 1) 1
1955[2] ROBIN LAKE (Ire) 8-9 L Dettori (3) *sn handily plcd, led aftr 3 fs till 2 furlongs out not pace of wnr.* ....(5 to 2 op 2 to 1 tchd 11 to 4) 2
3528[2] BASHFUL BRAVE 9-0 G Duffield (16) *chsd alng to improve on outsd hfwy, styd on ins fnl furlong.* ....(7 to 4 fav op 2 to 1) 3
RECAPTURED DAYS (Ire) 9-0 B Raymond (4) *squeezed out strt, improved into midfield hfwy, styd on wl fnl furlong*..............(8 to 1 op 6 to 1 tchd 9 to 1) 4
3284[6] MY GALLERY (Ire) (bl) 8-9 A Mackay (15) *squeezed out strt, chsd alng to improve centre last 2 fs, ran on finish.* ....(20 to 1 op 14 to 1) 5
3569[4] NATURAL PATH 8-9 W Carson (11) *broke wl to ld centre for 3 fs, fdd o'r one furlong out.* ....(14 to 1 op 12 to 1 tchd 16 to 1) 6
3284[8] MISS PIGALLE 8-9 J Fanning (10) *bustled alng in midfield, styd on und pres fnl furlong, nvr nrr.* ....(20 to 1 op 14 to 1) 7
2342[7] MONKEY BOY (Ire) 9-0 J Carroll (8) *broke wl, shwd gd speed for o'r 3 fs, fdd*..............(33 to 1 op 20 to 1) 8
THE WITCHBOY 9-0 W Hood (2) *nvr far away, feeling pace and rdn 2 fs out, sn btn*......(20 to 1 op 16 to 1) 9
DEAR SILVERS 8-9 K Fallon (7) *chsd alng to keep up, kpt on last 2 fs, no imprsn*..............(33 to 1) 10
3957 MUZZ (Ire) 9-0 T Williams (14) *drvn alng to improve frm midfield hfwy, kpt on, nvr plcd to chal.* ....(10 to 1 op 8 to 1 tchd 12 to 1) 11
2706[9] PRIMUM TEMPUS 8-9 M Birch (6) *sluggish strt, steady hdwy hfwy, nvr plcd to chal*......(20 to 1 op 14 to 1) 12
COURSE FISHING 8-7 (7*) S Sanders (17) *chsd alng to go pace, nvr a threat*..............(33 to 1 op 25 to 1) 13
3387 COMMENDATION DAY (Ire) 9-0 D Holland (5) *drvn alng to keep in tch, nvr trble ldrs*.........(20 to 1 op 16 to 1) 14
3520 KENILWORTH FORD 8-9 J Fortune (13) *squeezed out strt, nvr able to reco'r*..............(50 to 1 op 33 to 1) 15
1203[5] ROYAL CAPE 9-0 T Quinn (9) *sn struggling to keep up, nvr a factor*..............(10 to 1 op 8 to 1 tchd 11 to 1) 16

GRANGE VENTURE 8-9 (5*) Darren Moffatt (1) *coltly in paddock, very slow away, tld off*............ (33 to 1) 17

Dist: 5l, 3½l, sht-hd, sht-hd, nk, 1½l, ½l, hd, ½l, ¾l. 1m 0.63s. a 1.83s (17 Ran).

SR: 53/28/19/18/12/11/5/8/7/ (Cheveley Park Stud), R Hannon

3755 Bold Heath Claiming Stakes Class F (2-y-o) £3,032 6f................(2:50)

3357[6] TOP SHOW (Ire) 8-10 J Weaver (3) *made all far side, hrd pressed fnl furlong, hld on grimly*... (8 to 1 op 6 to 1) 1

3545[3] TUTU SIXTYSIX (v) 8-4 G Duffield (7) *wl plcd far side, drw level und pres fnl furlong, kpt on*....(6 to 1 op 9 to 2) 2

3423[3] COTTEIR CHIEF (Ire) 9-3 M Perrett (15) *steadied strt, beh whn swtchd to race far side hfwy, str run fnl furlong, unlucky*. .... (5 to 2 fav op 9 to 2 tchd 5 to 1 and 9 to 4) 3

3673[3] DANGEROUS SHADOW 8-11[1] K Darley (16) *wl plcd sides side, kpt on to ld that grp entering last, veered lft, one pace*....................(11 to 2 op 5 to 1 tchd 6 to 1) 4

3539[2] CULSYTH FLYER 8-11 W Carson (13) *wl plcd stands side, effrt and drvn alng 2 fs out, not quicken*. ....(7 to 1 op 6 to 1) 5

2103* ROCHE ABBEY (Ire) 8-2 T Williams (11) *dictated pace stands side, hdd entering fnl furlong, no extr*. .... (12 to 1 op 10 to 1) 6

3528[3] PRINCE OF GAELS 8-1 A Tucker (1) *chsd alng to improve frm off the pace last 2 fs, fnshd wl*. (12 to 1 op 10 to 1) 7

3598[7] LAUREL ROMEO (Ire) 8-4 J Carroll (14) *gd speed wth ldrs stands side for 4 fs, no extr*. .... (11 to 1 op 10 to 1 tchd 12 to 1) 8

3259 HADI (Ire) 8-12 S Whitworth (12) *chsd alng towards stands side, styd on und pres fnl furlong, nvr nrr*. .... (20 to 1 op 14 to 1) 9

3713[6] WOODTONG (v) 8-2 J Fanning (2) *gd speed far side to hfwy, fdd*.......................................(33 to 1) 10

1964 SUPER TIMES 7-7 G Bardwell (4) *chsd alng in midfield hfwy, styd on last 2 fs, nvr nrr*................(33 to 1) 11

2973[8] BROWLEA LYNDENE 7-8[1] L Charnock (6) *drvn alng in midfield hfwy, kpt on, nvr able to chal*........(33 to 1) 12

3443[7] GRANGE DANCER (Ire) 7-2 (5*) Darren Moffatt (5) *outpcd and drvn alng, nvr able to chal*....................(33 to 1) 13

3432 FUSSY SIOUX 7-11 N Carlisle (9) *steadied strt, pld hrd to hfwy, nvr a factor*................ (16 to 1 op 14 to 1) 14

3443[5] STRANGERSARDANGERS (Ire) 7-4 (5*) D Wright (10) *bustled alng to keep up hfwy, nvr a factor*. ....(8 to 1 op 7 to 1) 15

2176[7] GOVERNOR'S BAY 8-0 A Mackay (8) *early speed, struggling frm hfwy*...............................(33 to 1) 16

Dist: Hd, nk, 3½l, 4l, 1½l, nk, 2½l, 1l, 1l, nk. 1m 14.45s. a 2.85s (16 Ran).

SR: 27/20/32/2/-/-/ (P J White), K W Hogg

3756 Melling Limited Stakes Class D (0-80 3-y-o) £3,551 6f................ (3:25)

3051[3] ALASIB 8-6 L Dettori (6) *made most, quickened up 2 fs out, kpt on strly fnl furlong*. ....(13 to 8 fav op 7 to 4 tchd 2 to 1) 1

3291[9] SIMPLY SOOTY 8-6 J Lowe (5) *tucked away on ins, pushed alng 2 fs out, ran on strly towards finish*. .... (20 to 1 op 16 to 1) 2

3511[8] MAGIC ORB 8-6 A Mackay (9) *sluggish strt, chsd alng to improve hfwy, kpt on same pace fnl furlong*. ....(6 to 1 op 5 to 1) 3

3445* PRINCELY FAVOUR (Ire) 8-11 T Quinn (8) *broke wl to dispute ld for o'r 3 fs, fdd appr fnl furlong*. .... (6 to 1 op 5 to 1 tchd 13 to 2) 4

3343* JAAZIM 8-11 W Carson (2) *co'red up on ins, feeling pace 2 fs out, styd on fnl furlong*. .... (5 to 1 tchd 9 to 2 and 11 to 2) 5

3220[9] BENZOE (Ire) 8-11 T Lucas (7) *broke wl to dispute ld, lost action and hng rght o'r one furlong out, sn btn*. .... (8 to 1 op 12 to 1) 6

3637 THE SHARP BIDDER (Ire) 8-11 K Darley (4) *sluggish strt, chsd alng to improve hfwy, staying on whn baulked o'r one furlong out*.................. (10 to 1 op 7 to 1) 7

3410[9] TWO MOVES IN FRONT (Ire) 8-4 (7*) P Roberts (3) *badly outpcd and drvn alng hfwy, swtchd outsd 2 fs out, nvr nrr*..........................(10 to 1 op 8 to 1) 8

3213[7] BOLD SEVEN (Ire) 8-6 S Perks (1) *lost many ls leaving stalls, nvr able to reco'r*.....................(20 to 1) 9

Dist: ¾l, 2l, 3l, hd, 1½l, nk, 1½l, 4l. 1m 13.58s. a 1.98s (9 Ran).

SR: 40/37/29/22/21/15/14/8/-/ (A Foustok), W Jarvis

3757 Kirkby Handicap Class D (0-80 3-y-o) £3,824 1¼m 120yds............ (4:00)

3308 DORAZINE [63] 7-13 (7*) P McCabe (1) *enterprisingly rdn, led aftr a furlong, quickened clr entering strt, hld on gmely cl hme*......................(14 to 1 op 12 to 1) 1

3466 BLUE BLAZER [78] 9-7 D Holland (9) *hld up and beh, hmpd and snatched up aftr 3 fs, rapid hdwy fnl 2 furlongs, jst fld*..................(14 to 1 op 12 to 1 tchd 16 to 1) 2

1831[6] BEDEVIL (USA) [73] 9-2 J Carroll (3) *nvr far away, rdn whn pace quickened entering strt, styd on finish*. ....(5 to 1 op 6 to 1) 3

3053* LT WELSH (USA) [72] (v) 9-1 L Dettori (12) *nvr far away, drvn alng entering strt, kpt on ins fnl furlong*. ....(4 to 1 fav op 9 to 2 tchd 7 to 2) 4

3588* BROUGHTONS FORMULA [56] 7-13 (4ex) A Mackay (14) *trkd ldg bunch, improved on outsd last 2 fs, not pace to chal*......................................(6 to 1 op 9 to 2) 5

3710[9] ERICOLIN (Ire) [70] 8-10 (3*) B Doyle (6) *sluggish strt, improved into midfield hfwy, sn drvn alng, styd on same pace fnl furlong*............. (20 to 1 op 16 to 1) 6

3503[8] ALDERNEY PRINCE (USA) [74] 8-10 (7*) S Drowne (8) *trkd ldrs, outpcd and drvn alng entering strt, no imprsn last 2 fs*...(12 to 1) 7

2991[5] MISS SHAGRA (USA) [72] 9-1 B Raymond (10) *led one furlong, styd hndy but drvn alng entering strt, no imprsn last 2 fs*........(6 to 1 op 11 to 2 tchd 13 to 2) 8

1836 RICH ASSET (Ire) [51] 7-8[1] L Charnock (4) *struggling and beh hfwy, no imprsn last 3 fs*................. (33 to 1) 9

2776[6] TREAD CAREFULLY [73] 9-2 G Duffield (5) *chsd ldg bunch, effrt on outsd o'r 3 fs out, not pace to chal*. ....(10 to 1 tchd 11 to 1) 10

3585 SEASONAL SPLENDOUR (Ire) [76] 9-5 T Quinn (13) *wth ldrs, feeling pace and drvn alng entering strt, btn o'r 2 fs out*............................ (16 to 1 op 14 to 1) 11

3488[4] HEATHYARDS BOY [75] 9-4 S Perks (2) *tucked away on ins, struggling to hold pl entering strt, btn o'r 2 fs out*. .... (25 to 1 op 20 to 1) 12

1306[2] DOC COTTRILL [73] 9-2 K Fallon (7) *patiently rdn, drvn alng whn not much room o'r 3 fs out, nvr dngrs*. ....(9 to 1 op 7 to 1 tchd 10 to 1) 13

3139[8] PRESTON GUILD (Ire) [63] 8-6 W Carson (11) *chsd ldg bunch, effrt and not much room on ins o'r 3 fs out, nvr a threat*....................................... (10 to 1) 14

Dist: Hd, 1½l, 1l, 5l, ½l, sht-hd, 7l, 1l, nk, ¾l. 2m 17.03s. a 6.03s (14 Ran).

SR: 31/45/37/34/8/21/24/-/-/ (C John Hill), C J Hill

3758 Outland Selling Handicap Class G (0-60 3-y-o and up) £2,878 6f.... (4:30)

3410 MISS ARAGON [45] 5-8-9 (5*) D McCabe (18) *settled gng wl, quickened ahead well o'r one furlong out, ran on strly*................(16 to 1 op 20 to 1 tchd 25 to 1) 1

3429[8] LITTLE OSBORNE (Ire) [39] (bl) 3-8-2 (3*) M Fenton (20) *nvr far away, determined chal ins fnl furlong, kpt on wl*. .... (25 to 1 op 20 to 1) 2

3253[5] SWINGING TICH [46] 4-9-1 L Dettori (23) *pressed ldrs stands side, effrt und pres o'r one furlong out, kpt on same pace*.............. (11 to 1 op 10 to 1 tchd 12 to 1) 3

3568[6] BARBEZIEUX [46] 6-8-8 (7*) V Halliday (24) *sluggish strt, drvn up frm off the pace o'r 2 fs out, kpt on same pace*. .... (25 to 1 op 20 to 1) 4

3584 COCONUT JOHNNY [52] 3-8-11 (7*) R Painter (14) *drvn alng in midfield, styd on und pres appr fnl furlong, nvr nrr*................................ (25 to 1 op 20 to 1) 5

3535 MAGICATION [53] 3-8-12 (7*) Claire Balding (1) *rcd alone far side frm hfwy, effrt o'r one furlong out, kpt on same pace*..................................... (25 to 1 op 20 to 1) 6

3460 TOP ONE [54] 8-9-2 (7*) P McCabe (21) *chsd alng wth stands side bunch, not quicken last 2 fs*. .... (16 to 1 op 12 to 1) 7

3535 KILTROUM (Fr) [38] (v) 4-8-7 M Birch (3) *pushed alng in midfield, styd on appr fnl furlong, nrst finish*. .... (25 to 1 op 33 to 1) 8

3123[2] SING AS WE GO [39] 3-8-5 N Carlisle (12) *bustled alng in midfield, effrt o'r 2 fs out, kpt on, nvr nrr*. .... (16 to 1 op 14 to 1) 9

3568[2] LANGTONIAN [49] (bl) 4-8-11 (7*) Ruth Coulter (15) *pushed alng to improve centre hfwy, ev ch o'r one furlong out, not quicken*......................(12 to 1 op 20 to 1) 10

3575[4] STARDUST EXPRESS [44] (bl) 3-8-10 T Williams (16) *chsd alng to show speed in centre for o'r 4 fs, no extr*. .... (12 to 1 op 10 to 1) 11

3593* GENERAL JOHN (Ire) [50] 4-9-5 K Darley (4) *chsd alng centre, effrt 2 fs out, not pace to chal*. ....(2 to 1 fav tchd 7 to 4 and 9 to 4) 12

3591[8] CRAIGIE BOY [49] 3-9-1 G Duffield (6) *bustled alng centre, nvr able to trble ldrs*...........(10 to 1 tchd 11 to 1) 13

3140[8] GREENWICH CHALENGE [48] (v) 3-9-0 M Wigham (22) *slow away, swtchd to race far side aftr one furlong, switched centre o'r one furlong out, nrst finish*. ....(33 to 1) 14

3354[6] SUMMER EXPRESS [50] 4-9-5 A Mackay (10) *bustled alng to go pace hfwy, nvr able to rch ldrs*.......... (12 to 1) 15

3687[3] SEAMERE [55] (bl) 10-9-10 J Lowe (9) *chsd ldg bunch centre, nvr nr to chal*.................(10 to 1 op 7 to 1) 16

2914[4] BLUE RADIANCE [50] 3-9-2 J Fanning (7) *drvn alng to go pace hfwy, nvr a threat*..................... (33 to 1) 17

3095[6] SAY SUNPAK [40] 3-8-6 J Carroll (19) *unruly at strt, speed to chase ldrs stands side till wknd and eased o'r one furlong out*................................(50 to 1) 18

3354 COAT OF DREAMS [35] 4-8-4 S Dawson (5) *sn outpcd and drvn alng, nvr a factor*.......................... (50 to 1) 19

2544[8] FAIRFORD [37] (bl) 4-8-6 L Charnock (13) *broke wl to chase ldrs centre for o'r 4 fs, sn btn*...................(50 to 1) 20

3661 LAWNSWOOD PRINCE (Ire) [36] (bl) 4-8-5 T Quinn (17) *dictated pace stands side till hdd and wknd wl o'r one furlong out*....................................(25 to 1) 21

3568 ROBIX (Ire) [41] 3-8-7 S Wood (11) *sn struggling to go pace, nvr a factor*..........(25 to 1 op 33 to 1) 22
4773a[3] JOCKS JOKER [60] 3-9-12 J Fortune (2) *broke wl to show speed on outsd to hfwy, sn btn*..........(33 to 1) 23
3506 STORM VIXEN [39] (v) 4-8-8 K Fallon (8) *beh and drvn alng, nvr nr to chal*..........(33 to 1) 24
Dist: ½l, 2½l, 1l, 2l, ½l, ¾l, sht-hd, 2l, sht-hd, ¾l. 1m 14.35s. a 2.75s (24 Ran).
SR: 33/22/22/18/13/12/13/-/-/ (T Charlesworth), Miss L C Siddall

3759 Birkdale Handicap Class E (0-70 3-y-o) £3,257 1m 3f 200yds..........(5:05)

3255[5] HAZARD A GUESS (Ire) [62] 9-1 K Fallon (17) *settled gng wl, led well o'r one furlong out, hld on well ins last 100 yards*..........(7 to 1 op 5 to 1) 1
3424[4] ROMALITO [59] 8-12 K Darley (1) *wtd wth, drvn through frm midfield last 2 fs, fnshd wl*.... (20 to 1 op 14 to 1) 2
3431[4] FUNNY HILARIOUS (USA) [68] 9-7 T Quinn (2) *trkd ldrs, pushed through on ins and ev ch 2 fs out, kpt on same pace*..........(8 to 1 op 6 to 1 tchd 9 to 1) 3
3256[4] PRINCESS TATEUM (Ire) [65] 8-11 (7*) R Painter (7) *nvr far away, led aftr 4 fs till appr strt, kpt on same pace fnl furlong*..........(16 to 1 op 12 to 1) 4
3314 KARACHI [66] 9-2 (3*) B Doyle (15) *pld hrd, trkd ldg bunch, improved on outsd last 2 fs, kpt on.*
..........(9 to 1 op 12 to 1 tchd 8 to 1) 5
3392[4] FOREVER SHINEING [63] 9-2 W Carson (4) *al hndy, led appr strt till hdd 2 fs out, no extr.* (20 to 1 op 16 to 1) 6
3556[4] GIORDANO (Ire) [62] (v) 9-1 L Dettori (18) *al hndy, led briefly 2 fs out, sn drvn alng, no extr fnl furlong.*
..........(9 to 2 fav op 6 to 1 tchd 4 to 1) 7
2773[9] AMIARGE [45] 7-12 A Mackay (12) *trkd ldg bunch, effrt and drvn alng o'r 2 fs out, not pace to chal.*
..........(33 to 1 op 25 to 1) 8
3556[2] MILNGAVIE (Ire) [48] 8-1 T Williams (13) *settled gng wl, ev ch and pushed alng o'r 2 fs out, one pace.*
..........(15 to 2 op 8 to 1 tchd 9 to 1 and 7 to 1) 9
2388[3] SKY BURST [44] 7-11 N Carlisle (19) *wth ldrs, drvn alng o'r 2 fs out, one pace whn baulked over one furlong out, no extr*..........(16 to 1 op 14 to 1 tchd 20 to 1) 10
3225 RIZ BIZ (USA) [50] 8-0 (3*) M Fenton (9) *chsd ldg bunch, effrt and drvn alng o'r 2 fs out, no imprsn.*
..........(16 to 1 tchd 20 to 1) 11
2685[2] JOLIS ABSENT [43] 7-10 G Bardwell (3) *settled midfield, rdn whn pace quickened o'r 3 fs out, nvr dngrs.*
..........(8 to 1 op 5 to 1) 12
3087 KEDGE [56] 8-9 J Carroll (14) *trkd ldrs, rdn o'r 2 fs out, fdd*..........(10 to 1 op 16 to 1) 13
1495[4] DOC SPOT [61] 9-0 J Fortune (5) *settled midfield, struggling to keep up o'r 3 fs out, no imprsn*..........(20 to 1) 14
3469 DON'T FORGET MARIE (Ire) [51] 7-13 (5*) D Wright (8) *in tch, effrt on outsd entering strt, nvr able to chal*...(20 to 1) 15
AMILLIONMEMORIES [68] 9-7 S Webster (16) *chsd ldg bunch for a m, fdd*..........(50 to 1) 16
880[8] OLIVADI (Ire) [62] 9-1 J Weaver (20) *trkd ldrs to strt, fdd o'r 2 fs out*..........(14 to 1 op 12 to 1) 17
3473 CIVIL LAW (Ire) [67] 9-6 S Perks (10) *in tch, rdn o'r 3 fs out, nvr dngrs*..........(16 to 1 op 14 to 1) 18
2737 RAQS ASSAYF [41] 7-8 J Fanning (6) *chsd ldrs to strt, sn btn*..........(25 to 1) 19
3556 KAHLO [52] (bl) 8-5 M Birch (11) *led for 4 fs, wknd quickly entering strt, eased whn btn*..........(20 to 1) 20
Dist: Nk, 1½l, ½l, nk, 1½l, 1½l, 1½l, ¾l, 1½l, 2l. 2m 35.60s. a 5.80s (20 Ran).
SR: 43/39/45/41/41/35/31/11/12/ (Mrs D Ridley), Mrs J R Ramsden

3760 Clock Face Median Auction Maiden Stakes Class E (2-y-o) £3,176 1m 30yds..........(5:35)

3222[3] ALCOVE 9-0 L Dettori (1) *al hndy, led hfwy, drvn alng o'r one furlong out, kpt on wl*..... (13 to 8 fav op 7 to 4) 1
SWEDISH INVADER 9-0 B Raymond (14) *patiently rdn, swtchd outsd to improve o'r one furlong out, put head in air, kpt on*..........(12 to 1 op 8 to 1) 2
LADY FAIRFAX 8-9 G Duffield (6) *al hndy, rdn to draw level o'r 2 fs out, one pace fnl furlong.*
..........(14 to 1 op 8 to 1) 3
3457[3] MAGNETIC REEL 9-0 J Carroll (5) *nvr far away, drvn alng whn pace quickened o'r 2 fs out, one pace.*
..........(25 to 1 op 14 to 1) 4
FAWLTY TOWERS (Ire) 9-0 T Quinn (7) *sluggish strt, bustled alng thrght, styd on last 2 fs.*
..........(5 to 2 tchd 9 to 2 and 9 to 4) 5
WILCUMA 9-0 K Darley (2) *patiently rdn, shaken up o'r 2 fs out, steady late hdwy, nrst finish.*
..........(10 to 1 tchd 14 to 1) 6
3352 SCUD MISSILE (Ire) 9-0 D Holland (9) *beh and pushed alng hfwy, styd on last 2 fs, nrst finish*... (7 to 1 op 6 to 1) 7
3079 TOMMY COOPER 9-0 S Webster (13) *al chasing ldrs, feeling pace and rdn o'r 2 fs out, not pace to chal.*
..........(50 to 1 op 33 to 1) 8
3641[2] RAFTER-J 9-0 M Perrett (10) *beh, drvn alng and some hdwy last 2 fs, nvr dngrs*..........(16 to 1) 9
1998[6] MISS MILLIPEDE 8-9 A Culhane (8) *chsd ldg bunch for o'r 4 fs, fdd*..........(25 to 1 op 20 to 1) 10
3143[6] JOE JAGGER (Ire) 9-0 M Birch (3) *slight ld to hfwy, wknd quickly o'r 2 fs out*..........(25 to 1 op 20 to 1) 11
2836[3] CRISTAL SPRINGS 8-9 J Fortune (15) *wth ldrs for o'r 4 fs, fdd*..........(14 to 1 op 10 to 1 tchd 16 to 1) 12
OLIVER-J 8-11 (3*) O Pears (12) *chsd alng to go pace hfwy, nvr a factor*..........(33 to 1 op 25 to 1) 13
3554[9] LADY GWEN (Ire) 8-9 K Fallon (11) *in tch to strt, wknd quickly*..........(33 to 1) 14
3264[9] TROPICAL VISTA 8-9 J Lowe (4) *uns rdr gng to strt, led all the way to start, tld off frm hfwy.* (50 to 1 op 33 to 1) 15
Dist: ¾l, 2½l, 3½l, 2½l, 3½l, 1l, 2l, 3l, 3l, 2½l. 1m 45.85s. a 5.25s (15 Ran).
SR: 21/19/6/-/-/-/ (Highclere Thoroughbred Racing Ltd), R Hannon

KEMPTON (good)
Friday September 3rd
Going Correction: MINUS 0.25 sec. per fur. (races 1,2,6), MINUS 0.20 (3,4,5)

3761 Watford Handicap Class E (0-70 3-y-o and up) £3,933 1¾m 92yds..........(2:05)

2729 POPSI'S LEGACY [57] 6-8-8 (7*) D Toole (11) *hld up, hdwy on outsd 2 fs out, sstnd run to ld nr line.*
..........(25 to 1 op 16 to 1) 1
1495[2] SAFETY IN NUMBERS [60] 3-8-7 J Quinn (7) *ldg grp, led o'r 3 fs out, sn clr, rdn and hdd nr line.*
..........(12 to 1 tchd 14 to 1) 2
3320[2] FIRST FLING (Ire) [47] 4-8-2 (3*) D Harrison (5) *pushed alng in mid-div o'r 4 fs out, ran on und pres 2 out, styd on cl hme*..........(14 to 1 op 12 to 1 tchd 16 to 1) 3
3152[2] HARLESTONE BROOK [68] 3-9-1 R Cochrane (3) *handily plcd, outpcd 3 fs out, ran on o'r 2 out, not quicken ins last*..........(5 to 1 jt-fav tchd 11 to 2) 4
LAND AFAR [68] 6-9-12 R Lappin (13) *improved hfwy, styd on one pace last 2 fs*..........(33 to 1 op 25 to 1) 5
3078* PRINCESS ERMYN [48] 4-8-6 A Clark (8) *chsd ldrs, outpcd 3 fs out, no imprsn ins last 2*..........(9 to 1 op 8 to 1) 6
3521[9] ALQAIRAWAAN [58] 4-9-2 Pat Eddery (10) *in tch, pushed alng o'r 3 fs out, effrt over 2 out, sn btn and eased.*
..........(5 to 1 jt-fav op 7 to 2) 7
3521[3] ELA BILLANTE [68] 3-9-1 P Robinson (9) *hmpd aftr 2 fs, settled mid-div, effrt o'r two out, no extr appr last.*
..........(7 to 1 op 6 to 1 tchd 8 to 1) 8
3430[2] SCENIC DANCER [49] 5-8-0 (7*) N Varley (4) *al rear.*
..........(9 to 1 op 7 to 1) 9
3288 WITH GUSTO [44] 6-8-2[1] A Munro (2) *al rear.*
..........(20 to 1 op 14 to 1 tchd 25 to 1) 10
3706[7] IMPECCABLE TASTE [60] 3-8-7 J Williams (1) *pressed ldrs, ev ch o'r 3 fs out, wknd over 2 out.*
..........(14 to 1 op 12 to 1 tchd 16 to 1) 11
3424[5] JUSTICE (Fr) [58] 5-9-2 M Roberts (12) *nvr nr ldrs.*
..........(20 to 1 tchd 16 to 1 and 25 to 1) 12
3479[9] FANATICAL (USA) [43] (bl) 7-8-1 A McGlone (14) *in tch in mid-div, rdn and wknd o'r 2 fs out.* (14 to 1 op 10 to 1) 13
3556 SO SAUCY [60] (bl) 3-8-7 W R Swinburn (6) *led till o'r 3 fs out, wknd over 2 out.* (14 to 1 op 10 to 1 tchd 16 to 1) 14
Dist: ½l, nk, 2½l, nk, 8l, 1l, hd, 1½l, nk, sht-hd. 3m 9.26s. (14 Ran).
(M J Haynes), M J Haynes

3762 Stanmore Nursery Class D (2-y-o) £4,012 6f..........(2:35)

3457* AMIDST [76] 9-3 Paul Eddery (9) *wl plcd, pushed alng frm hfwy, led one furlong out, hld on nr line.*
..........(9 to 2 fav tchd 5 to 1) 1
3001[6] DOMINO QUEEN (Ire) [62] 8-3 A Munro (10) *trkd frnt rnk, pushed alng o'r 2 fs out, ran on fnl furlong, fnshd wl, jst fld*..........(7 to 1 op 8 to 1) 2
3259[7] WAAFED (USA) [76] (bl) 9-3 W R Swinburn (11) *pressed ldr, slight ld o'r one furlong out, sn hdd, kpt on same pace.*
..........(6 to 1 op 5 to 1) 3
3406 CHICKAWICKA (Ire) [80] 9-7 R Cochrane (3) *hdwy o'r 2 fs out, edgd rght over one out, styd on wl nr finish.*
..........(16 to 1 op 12 to 1 tchd 20 to 1) 4
3657[6] CYARNA QUINN (Ire) [77] 9-4 J Reid (7) *slwly into strd, hdwy frm rear o'r one furlong out, nrst finish.*
..........(16 to 1 op 14 to 1) 5
3626* NORISKI'MARINGER [67] 8-8 (6ex) Pat Eddery (5) *chsd ldrs, rdn and not much room o'r one furlong out, not rcvr.*
..........(13 to 2 op 5 to 1 tchd 7 to 1) 6
3545[2] CHARISMA GIRL [53] 7-8 N Adams (4) *nvr rch frnt rnk.*
..........(6 to 1 op 9 to 2) 7
3041[4] HELLO MISTER [70] 8-11 M Roberts (12) *led till o'r one furlong out, sn wknd*..........(12 to 1) 8
3421[7] CHILIGRAY [66] 8-7 R Hills (2) *nvr on terms.*
..........(14 to 1 op 12 to 1) 9
3303[6] SWEET WHISPER [58] 7-13 A McGlone (1) *outpcd.*
..........(12 to 1 op 10 to 1 tchd 14 to 1) 10
3641 WHITCHURCH SILK (Ire) [52] 7-3[3] (7*) N Varley (8) *rdn alng in rear whn hmpd 2 fs out, no dngr aftr.*
..........(50 to 1 op 33 to 1 tchd 66 to 1) 11
2909[9] RUNIC SYMBOL [64] 8-5 J Quinn (13) *in tch to hfwy.*
..........(14 to 1 op 16 to 1) 12
Dist: Hd, ¾l, ½l, 2½l, 3½l, 3½l, ¾l, ½l, nk, 1l. 1m 12.33s. a 1.53s (12 Ran).
SR: 42/27/38/40/27/3/ (Sir Evelyn de Rothschild), M R Stoute

3763 Milcars Chertsey Lock Conditions Stakes Class C (2-y-o) £4,082 7f (3:10)

3596^2 FRIENDLY CHAMP (Ire) 8-13 R Price (4) *settled in 3rd pl, chsd ldr 3 fs out, led o'r 2 out, rdn clr last 100 yards.* ....(3 to 1 op 11 to 4 tchd 100 to 30) 1
3289* STAR TALENT (USA) 9-3 R Cochrane (7) *hld up, cld on wnr appr fnl furlong, rdn and not quicken final 100 yards.* ....(6 to 4 fav op 5 to 4 tchd 7 to 4) 2
3400^5 MAZENTRE FORWARD (Ire) 8-11 Pat Eddery (3) *beh till styd on last 2 fs, no ch wth ldrs.* ....(9 to 2 op 5 to 1 tchd 6 to 1 and 4 to 1) 3
RAINBOW HEIGHTS 8-11 R Hills (5) *slwly into strd, al outpcd*............................(20 to 1 op 12 to 1) 4
2430^7 THE FLYING PHANTOM 8-13 P Robinson (1) *clr till rdn and hdd o'r 2 fs out, wknd over one out.* ....(20 to 1 op 12 to 1) 5
TAJANNAB 8-11 W R Swinburn (2) *al rear, lost tch hfwy.* ....(8 to 1 op 9 to 2) 6
2845^7 ARECIBO (Ire) 8-11 M Roberts (6) *trkd ldr 4 fs, sn wknd.* ....(50 to 1 op 25 to 1) 7
Dist: 2½l, 4l, nk, 5l, 1l, 5l. 1m 26.16s. a 2.06s (7 Ran).
SR: 47/43/25/24/11/6/-/ (Dr Meou Tsen Geoffrey Yeh), R W Armstrong

3764 Milcars Temple Fortune Stakes Class A (Listed Race) (3-y-o and up) £11,550 1m..........................(3:40)

3468* TINNERS WAY (USA) 3-9-1 Pat Eddery (6) *chsd ldr aftr 3 fs, shaken up to ld last 100 yards, pushed out.* ....(11 to 4 fav op 3 to 1 tchd 7 to 2) 1
1118^5 CLOUD OF DUST 4-9-4 J Reid (4) *rcd keenly in rear, ran on o'r 2 fs out, styd on und pres ins last.* ....(9 to 1 op 7 to 1 tchd 10 to 1) 2
3468^2 ARDKINGLASS 3-9-4 W Ryan (2) *mid-div, pushed alng to improve o'r 3 fs out, rdn and not quicken ins last.* ....(4 to 1 op 3 to 1) 3
3636^2 MIZAAYA 4-9-0 W R Swinburn (3) *clr, rdn alng and hng rght o'r 2 fs out, hdd and no extr last 100 yards.* ....(4 to 1 op 7 to 2) 4
3434 LINDON LIME (USA) 3-8-9 A Munro (5) *mid-div, outpcd 3 fs out, kpt on clsg stages.* ....(25 to 1 op 33 to 1 tchd 40 to 1) 5
3350* IHTIRAZ 3-8-9 R Hills (1) *hld up, rdn alng and effrt 3 fs out, no hdwy ins last 2.* ....(100 to 30 op 5 to 2 tchd 7 to 2) 6
REPORTED (Ire) 4-9-6 R Cochrane (7) *chsd ldr 3 fs, sn wknd, tld off*....................(50 to 1 op 33 to 1) 7
Dist: 1½l, ¾l, 2½l, 1½l, 1½l, 30l. 1m 36.96s. a 0.16s (7 Ran).
SR: 75/73/71/59/49/44/-/ (K Abdulla), J H M Gosden

3765 Milcars Fillies Conditions Stakes Class C (2-y-o) £4,345 7f........(4:10)

3248* DANCE TO THE TOP 8-10 W R Swinburn (6) *hld up, not much room entering last 2 fs, pushed alng to ld one out, ran on, cleverly.* ....(13 to 8 on op 7 to 4 on tchd 15 to 8 on) 1
3317^8 DIAMOND PARK (Ire) 8-8 Pat Eddery (1) *beh till ran on und pres 2 fs out, styd on ins last*...... (25 to 1 op 20 to 1) 2
1393^3 OMNIA (USA) 8-8 A Munro (2) *in tch, rdn alng o'r 2 fs out, not quicken over one out, styd on nr finish.* ....(12 to 1 tchd 14 to 1) 3
3472^3 STAR SPEEDER (Ire) 8-5 (5*) B Russell (5) *led till hdd and rdn one furlong out, sn btn*.......(8 to 1 tchd 10 to 1) 4
3186* MISS RINJANI 8-10 Paul Eddery (3) *trkd ldr, ev ch whn edgd rght entering last 2 fs, sn rdn and one pace.* ....(5 to 1 op 9 to 2) 5
GILBERTINA (USA) 8-8 R Street (4) *strted slwly, effrt frm rear hfwy, no prog appr last 2 fs*...(25 to 1 op 20 to 1) 6
2562^4 PALANA (USA) 8-12 R Cochrane (7) *hld up rear, rdn alng o'r 2 fs out, no imprsn*............(20 to 1 op 12 to 1) 7
Dist: ¾l, ½l, 1½l, 2l, hd, nk. 1m 26.24s. a 2.14s (7 Ran).
SR: 43/39/37/34/28/25/28/ (Cheveley Park Stud), M R Stoute

3766 Radlett Maiden Handicap Class F (0-65 3-y-o and up) £3,786 7f.... (4:40)

3233^2 CASTING SHADOWS [50] 4-9-3 Pat Eddery (14) *hld up, pushed alng o'r 2 fs out, ran on und pres to ld nr line.* ....(11 to 2 jt-fav op 5 to 1) 1
3358 BROUGHTONS TURMOIL [50] 4-9-3 D Biggs (6) *cl up, led wl o'r 2 fs out, sn hrd rdn, hdd nr line.* ....(16 to 1 op 14 to 1) 2
3712^4 KELLY MAC [56] 3-9-5 J Reid (2) *ldg grp, rdn and not quicken frm 2 fs out, kpt on cl hme*........(11 to 2 jt-fav op 6 to 1 tchd 13 to 2) 3
3692^8 JEWEL THIEF [48] (v) 3-8-11 J Williams (15) *ran on frm rear last 2 fs, fnshd wl*.... (12 to 1 op 10 to 1 tchd 14 to 1) 4
3634^5 ARAWA [45] 3-8-8 R Cochrane (17) *beh, hdwy and swtchd rght 2 fs out, styd on one pace wl ins last.* ....(13 to 2 op 5 to 1 tchd 7 to 1) 5
3575^3 SLEEPTITE (Fr) [53] 3-9-2 W Ryan (7) *hdwy frm rear 2 fs out, nrst finish*.................... (8 to 1 tchd 9 to 1) 6
3247^3 FROSTY MORNING [64] 3-9-13 M Roberts (13) *mid-div, rdn and effrt o'r one furlong out, styd on cl hme.* ....(9 to 1 op 7 to 1) 7
3168 FINDON ACADEMY (Ire) [50] (bl) 3-8-13 A Morris (12) *cld on ldrs 4 fs out, rdn and not quicken 2 out, no extr ins last.* ....(33 to 1 op 25 to 1 tchd 50 to 1) 8
SOUTHAMPTON [45] 3-8-1 (7*) N Varley (4) *rear till some hdwy o'r 2 fs out, not rch frnt rnk.* (50 to 1 op 33 to 1) 9
3661^3 ALL THE GIRLS (Ire) [35] 4-8-2 C Rutter (18) *slwly into strd, al rear*..............(10 to 1 op 6 to 1 tchd 12 to 1) 10
1275 ANNIVERSAIRE [60] 3-9-9 P Robinson (1) *ldg grp, rdn and lost pl one furlong out*............ (20 to 1 op 16 to 1) 11
2577 STEPPIN HIGH [57] 3-9-3 (3*) D Harrison (3) *trkd ldrs till wknd last 2 fs*.......(14 to 1 op 12 to 1 tchd 16 to 1) 12
3340^6 ASCOM PAGER TOO [43] 3-8-6 J Quinn (16) *mid-div, effrt o'r 2 fs out, btn over one out*......(16 to 1 op 12 to 1) 13
3487^9 WATERLORD (Ire) [63] 3-9-12 Paul Eddery (8) *led till wl o'r 2 fs out, sn lost pl*............... (10 to 1 tchd 12 to 1) 14
SPRING SAINT [52] 4-9-5 A Munro (11) *handily plcd till wknd o'r 2 fs out*................(50 to 1 op 25 to 1) 15
3634^9 LADY RELKO [42] 3-8-5 N Adams (10) *strted slwly, sn chasing ldrs, not much room and wknd wl o'r one furlong out*......................(50 to 1 op 33 to 1) 16
3518 CANNONALE (Ire) [33] 4-8-0 Dale Gibson (9) *mid-div, rdn alng o'r 2 fs out, wknd wl over one out, tld off.* ....(50 to 1 op 20 to 1) 17
Dist: Sht-hd, 1l, sht-hd, sht-hd, ¾l, nk, 2l, 5l, 2l, 1l. 1m 26.50s. a 2.20s (17 Ran).
SR: 44/43/42/33/29/35/45/25/5/ (S Skelding), B W Hills

BELMONT PARK (USA) (firm)
Saturday September 4th

3767 Gazelle Handicap (Grade 1) (3-y-o) £59,603 1m 1f......................

2440^4 DISPUTE (USA) 8-8 J D Bailey,................ (2 to 1 fav) 1
2440^3 SILKY FEATHER (USA) 8-5 R Migliore,............ (10 to 1) 2
935^3 IN HER GLORY (USA) 8-0 E Maple,..............(33 to 1) 3
2440^2 FUTURE PRETENSE (USA) 8-6 C Perret,........(26 to 10) 4
2999^4 TRUE AFFAIR (USA) 8-5 J Chavez,.............. (13 to 1) 5
762^7 AZTEC HILL (USA) 8-5 R Davis,.................(99 to 10) 6
2802^4 FORTUNATE FAITH (USA) 8-3 M Smith,.........(28 to 10) 7
MORNING MEADOW (USA) 8-2 J Santos,........(13 to 1) 8
Dist: 7½l, hd, nose, 1l, 5l, 1½l, 14l. 1m 47.20s. (8 Ran).
(O M Phipps), C R McGaughey

FAIRYHOUSE (IRE) (good to firm)
Saturday September 4th

3768 Great Commotion E.B.F. Maiden (3-y-o) £4,140 7f................. (2:00)

3614^4 BENE MERENTI (Ire) (bl) 8-8 (6*) R V Skelly (3)......(9 to 2) 1
3380^7 MARY'S CASE (Ire) (bl) 9-0 C Roche (5)........... (8 to 1) 2
3497^5 WORLD'S VIEW 8-11 J P Murtagh (4)..............(5 to 2) 3
2320^3 LIBRAN ROCK (Ire) 9-0 P Shanahan (6)............ (9 to 2) 4
2810^2 RENEWED DYNASTY (USA) 9-0 M J Kinane (1) (6 to 4 fav) 5
3605^7 ELEGANT NORA (Ire) 8-9 (2*) R M Burke (2)...... (33 to 1) 6
Dist: ¾l, ¾l, 1½l, 1l. 1m 29.10s. (6 Ran).
(J F Bailey Jun), J F Bailey Jun

3769 Newmarket Claiming Race (3-y-o and up) £2,760 1m 1f............... (2:30)

3328^6 GILT DIMENSION 6-9-0 M J Kinane (14)...........(9 to 2) 1
3497^7 GOLDEN SPHINX (Ire) 3-7-12 (2*) D G O'Shea (7) (20 to 1) 2
3328^3 LENANTO (Ire) 5-8-12 R Hughes (9)........... (5 to 2 fav) 3
3605^3 MUSWELL BROOK (Ire) (bl) 3-8-5 P V Gilson (4)....(5 to 1) 4
3061^3 HERMES GOLD (Ire) 3-8-0 W J Supple (5).........(4 to 1) 5
3399 INISHMOT (Ire) 3-7-10 Joanna Morgan (11).......(16 to 1) 6
KARAMID (USA) 6-8-10 P Shanahan (2)..........(16 to 1) 7
3417 SHPEEL (Ire) 3-7-12 (4*) W J Smith (13)........... (8 to 1) 8
2516^5 FAIRY FANTASY (Ire) 3-7-6 (8*) G M Moylan (12)...(14 to 1) 9
3061^8 DIGNIFIED (Ire) 3-7-10^2 (2*) R M Burke (1)........(14 to 1) 10
2923^8 HAVIN' A BALL (Ire) 4-8-9 N Byrne (8)............(50 to 1) 11
3330 NOBLE SAM (Ire) (bl) 4-8-0 (6*) J A Heffernan (6).. (20 to 1) 12
1251 CLANROSIE (Ire) (bl) 4-7-13 (4*) J J Behan (10)....(16 to 1) 13
Dist: 1l, 1½l, hd, sht-hd. 1m 54.90s. (13 Ran).
(Mrs J M Mullins), W P Mullins

3770 Tolka Handicap (0-105 3-y-o and up) £6,900 1m 1f.................. (3:00)

3542 CLASSIC MATCH (Ire) [-] 5-9-3 (2*) P Carberry (6) (14 to 1) 1
3202* SWEET NASHA (Ire) [-] 4-9-9 P V Gilson (9)........ (7 to 2) 2
3164* MADANIYYA (USA) [-] 3-8-12 M J Kinane (7)... (9 to 4 fav) 3
3399^7 TINCO PALENO [-] 9-7-7 Joanna Morgan (2)......(14 to 1) 4
2406^8 SIR SLAVES [-] (bl) 3-8-0 (6*) D J O'Donohoe (4)...(12 to 1) 5
3542^4 ROBERTOLOMY (USA) [-] 4-8-4 N G McCullagh (3) (11 to 2) 6
3615^6 GALLARDINI (Ire) [-] 4-9-2 C Roche (8)...........(12 to 1) 7
3615* TRYARRA (Ire) [-] 3-8-8 (4*,5ex) J J Behan (10)..... (5 to 1) 8
3559^4 THATCHING CRAFT (Ire) [-] 4-9-4 J P Murtagh (1).. (8 to 1) 9
3615^9 CENTER MORICHES (Ire) [-] 3-7-12 W J Supple (5) (25 to 1) 10
Dist: Nk, hd, 2½l, nk. 1m 54.20s. (10 Ran).

(Ms P Haselden), Noel Meade

3771 Woodpark Stud (EBF) (C&G) Maiden (2-y-o) £5,865 7f. . . . . (3:30)

BAWARDI (Ire) 9-0 J P Murtagh (4) . . . .(9 to 4) 1
3613[3] NORDIC AIR (Ire) (bl) 9-0 C Roche (10) . . . . (8 to 1) 2
2982[4] CONCEPT HOUSE (Ire) 9-0 N Byrne (8) . . . . (8 to 1) 3
MOOBAKKR (USA) 9-0 M J Kinane (2) . . . . (Evens fav) 4
3492[6] FRENCH VICTOR (Ire) 9-0 R Hughes (11) . . . .(10 to 1) 5
2701[4] BEAUCHAMP IMPERIAL 9-0 P Shanahan (1) . . . . . . (10 to 1) 6
3273[8] NORTHERN FANCY (Ire) 9-0 W J Supple (7) . . . . . . (50 to 1) 7
WOODY 8-12 (2*) P Carberry (9) . . . .(10 to 1) 8
2701 INNOVATIVE (Ire) 9-0 D Hogan (12) . . . .(25 to 1) 9
3608 JINGLING SILVER (Ire) (bl) 9-0 P V Gilson (5) . . . .(50 to 1) 10
TWILIGHT HOUR (Ire) 8-12 (2*) D G O'Shea (6) . . . .(25 to 1) 11
3159[7] IAN MY BOY (Ire) 9-0 Joanna Morgan (3) . . . . (50 to 1) 12
Dist: 2½l, 1l, 1l, 2l. 1m 28.50s. (12 Ran).

(H H Aga Khan), John M Oxx

3772 Jareer Handicap (0-80 3-y-o) £3,450 1 ½m. . . . . (4:00)

2496* GLENBRACK [-] 9-0 (6*) J R Barry (2) . . . . (5 to 1) 1
2743* BRAVE RAIDER (Ire) [-] 9-5 M J Kinane (7) . . . .(5 to 2 jt-fav) 2
3076 GLAS AGUS OR (Ire) [-] (bl) 7-13 (6*) J A Heffernan (4)
. . . .(10 to 1) 3
3484* SAFFRON CROCUS [-] (bl) 9-4 (6*,4ex) C Everard (8)
. . . . (5 to 2 jt-fav) 4
2781[4] UNCONDITIONAL (Fr) [-] 9-4 P Shanahan (9) . . . .(6 to 1) 5
3498[3] FLORA WOOD (Ire) [-] 9-1 W J Supple (6) . . . .(5 to 1) 6
3381 OCEAN BLUE (Ire) [-] (bl) 8-5 P V Gilson (5) . . . .(14 to 1) 7
3578[7] KEPPOLS HARRIER (Ire) [-] 8-3 N G McCullagh (1) (14 to 1) 8
Dist: 1½l, nk, 1l, 6l. 2m 37.80s. (8 Ran).

(John Bernard O'Connor), Patrick Joseph Flynn

3773 Dunnes Stores Ladies Fashion Series (3-y-o and up) £3,450 1½m. . . . . (4:30)

3616[5] RETURN AGAIN (Ire) 3-8-11 Miss C E Hyde (9) . . . . . (3 to 1) 1
2186[7] SHARASTAMINA (USA) 4-9-1 (2*) Miss C Bowden (3)
. . . .(10 to 1) 2
3111* PETOFI 3-9-8[3] Miss U Smyth (1) . . . . (6 to 1) 3
3578[2] SHAWGATNY (USA) 3-9-10[8] Miss C Hutchinson (2)
. . . .(2 to 1 fav) 4
3524[4] KARAR (Ire) 3-9-5[5] Ms L Robinson (8) . . . .(5 to 1) 5
3276[8] INDIANA GOLD (Ire) 5-9-3[2] (2*) Ms W Fox (10) . . . . (20 to 1) 6
SECOND SCHEDUAL 8-9-11[2] Miss A M McMahon (5)
. . . .(10 to 1) 7
1576[8] MOUNTAIN BLOOM (Ire) (bl) 5-9-4 (2*) (4) . . . . (14 to 1) 8
3685[2] TOP GENERATION 4-9-1 (2*) Miss T Cunningham (6)
. . . .(10 to 1) 9
3685[4] BETTER GOODS (Ire) 3-9-0[3] Miss A H Marshall (7) (25 to 1) 10
Dist: 3l, 3½l, ½l, 1l. 2m 39.40s. (10 Ran).

(Mrs J R Mullion), D T Hughes

HAYDOCK (good to firm)
Saturday September 4th
Going Correction: NIL (races 1,2,3,6,7), MINUS 0.20 (4,5)

3774 Stanley Leisure Group Handicap Class C (0-90 3-y-o and up) £9,339 7f 30yds. . . . . (2:00)

3531* CALEMAN [80] 4-9-4 W Carson (9) *made all, quickened o'r 2 fs out, kpt on strly fnl furlong.*
. . . . (11 to 2 op 5 to 1 tchd 6 to 1) 1
3450[9] MY BEST VALENTINE [79] 3-8-13 F Norton (2) *tucked away on ins, edgd away frm rls o'r one furlong out, kpt on same pace.* . . . .(11 to 1 op 10 to 1) 2
3465 BAND ON THE RUN [87] 6-9-4 (7*) S Sanders (3) *trkd ldrs, drvn through on ins last 2 fs, styd on.*
. . . . (14 to 1 op 12 to 1 tchd 16 to 1) 3
3471[2] THORNTON GATE [74] 4-8-9 (3*) S Maloney (7) *al hndy, ev ch and rdn last 2 fs, one pace.*
. . . . (13 to 2 op 5 to 1 tchd 7 to 1) 4
3637[8] SHIRO [86] 3-9-6 M Roberts (1) *steadied strt, hmpd entering strt, not clr run o'r 2 fs out, ran on finish.*
. . . .(8 to 1 op 6 to 1) 5
3177[4] PRINCESS KRIS [82] 3-9-2 K Darley (11) *stumbled strt, chsd alng to improve hfwy, kpt on, nvr nr to chal.*
. . . .(9 to 2 fav op 5 to 1 tchd 6 to 1) 6
3471[7] VELOCE (Ire) [77] 5-9-1 L Piggott (6) *nvr far away, drvn alng whn hmpd o'r one furlong out, no extr.*
. . . . (17 to 2 op 9 to 1 tchd 8 to 1) 7
3488[5] ANCHORITE [81] 4-9-5 L Dettori (10) *bustled alng in midfield, styd on last 2 fs, nrst finish.*
. . . . (11 to 1 op 12 to 1 tchd 14 to 1) 8
2715 DOMICKSKY [64] 5-8-2[1] J Carroll (13) *pressed ldg quartet, feeling pace o'r 2 fs out, no extr.* (14 to 1 tchd 16 to 1) 9
1835 BOURSIN (Ire) [62] 4-8-0 Dale Gibson (5) *settled midfield, effrt hfwy, eased whn btn o'r one furlong out.*
. . . . (20 to 1 op 14 to 1) 10
3404 PANIKIN [83] 5-9-4 (3*) S D Williams (8) *in tch, hrd at work on ins o'r 2 fs out, no imprsn.* . . . .(16 to 1 tchd 20 to 1) 11
3575[7] MARINE DIVER [70] 7-8-8 A Mackay (12) *wth ldrs, feeling pace and rdn o'r 2 fs out, sn btn.* . . . (11 to 1 op 8 to 1) 12
HOME COUNTIES (Ire) [90] 4-10-0 S Dawson (4) *last and hld up, nvr nr to chal.* . . . . (33 to 1 op 20 to 1) 13
3365[7] GLENFIELD GRETA [55] (bl) 5-7-2 (5*) D Wright (16) *chsd ldrs on outsd for o'r 4 fs, fdd.* . . . .(20 to 1 op 14 to 1) 14
1629 HOTEL CALIFORNIA (Ire) [59] 3-7-7 S Wood (15) *chsd ldg bunch for o'r 3 fs, fdd.* . . . . (50 to 1 op 33 to 1) 15
Dist: 1½l, 1½l, 2l, 1½l, ¾l, 1½l, 1½l, 4l, nk, 2l. 1m 30.49s. a 3.29s (15 Ran).
SR: 55/45/52/33/36/30/24/23/-/ (M Berger), R Boss

3775 Preserving Nature's Goodness Rated Class B Handicap (0-100 3-y-o and up) £9,296 1m 3f 200yds. . . . . (2:30)

3401 ALJAZZAF [91] 3-8-3 M Roberts (2) *trkd ldr, led o'r 2 fs out, hdd briefly over one out, rallied and ran on.*
. . . .(9 to 2 op 4 to 1) 1
3434 GLIDE PATH (USA) [86] 4-8-7 L Dettori (5) *patiently rdn, drvn up to nose ahead briefly o'r one furlong out, edgd lft, one pace.* . . . .(2 to 1 fav op 9 to 4) 2
3314[2] JOHNS ACT (USA) [86] 3-7-12 A Mackay (4) *last and hld up, effrt and drvn alng o'r 2 fs out, styd on same pace.*
. . . . (11 to 4 op 9 to 4 tchd 3 to 1) 3
3434[6] MILLION IN MIND (Ire) [86] 4-8-7 W Newnes (6) *set modest pace, quickened o'r 3 fs out, hdd over 2 out, no extr.*
. . . . (11 to 2 op 5 to 1 tchd 6 to 1) 4
3385[4] BADIE (USA) [94] 4-9-1 W Carson (3) *trkd ldg pair, effrt and rdn o'r 2 fs out, no real imprsn.* (7 to 1 op 6 to 1) 5
3465[6] ST NINIAN [100] 7-9-4 (3*) S Maloney (1) *wl plcd on ins, hrd at work o'r 3 fs out, btn 2 out.*
. . . . (15 to 2 op 5 to 1 tchd 8 to 1) 6
Dist: 1l, 1½l, 1½l, 1l, 5l. 2m 36.29s. a 6.49s (6 Ran).
SR: 24/26/14/20/26/22/ (Mohamed Obaida), C E Brittain

3776 Campsie Spring Conditions Stakes Class C (2-y-o) £6,553 1m 30yds (3:00)

3259* CHARITY CRUSADER 8-9 (3*) Stephen Davies (4) *led aftr one and a half fs till hdd o'r 2 out, rallied, styd on wl ins last.* . . . .(9 to 4 op 7 to 4) 1
3423* ALAFLAK (Ire) 8-12 W Carson (2) *patiently rdn, improved to ld briefly o'r 2 fs out, wndrd, ridden and no extr.*
. . . . (5 to 4 on tchd Evens) 2
PORTESHAM (USA) 8-10 M Roberts (1) *last and outpcd most of way, styd on fnl furlong, nvr nrr.*
. . . .(6 to 1 op 5 to 1 tchd 7 to 1) 3
2887[5] SLIP A COIN 8-5 L Dettori (3) *led for one and a half fs, styd hndy till fdd o'r one furlong out.*
. . . . (10 to 1 op 8 to 1 tchd 12 to 1) 4
Dist: 3l, 8l, ½l. 1m 44.06s. a 3.46s (4 Ran).
SR: 46/37/11/4/ (Express Marie Curie Racing Club), P W Chapple-Hyam

3777 Hazlewood Foods Sprint Cup Class A (Group 1) (2-y-o and up) £81,701 6f . . . .(3:30)

3315[2] WOLFHOUND (USA) 4-9-9 M Roberts (3) *settled midfield, quickened up to ld entering fnl furlong, ran on strly.*
. . . .(7 to 2 op 5 to 1) 1
2574* CATRAIL (USA) 3-9-6 J Carroll (1) *in tch, drvn up on outsd to chal appr fnl furlong, edgd lft, kpt on same pace.*
. . . . (10 to 1 op 14 to 1 tchd 16 to 1) 2
3464* LOCHSONG 5-9-6 L Dettori (6) *set str pace, hdd and rdn entering fnl furlong, no extr.*
. . . . (11 to 4 op 3 to 1 tchd 7 to 2) 3
3464[3] COLLEGE CHAPEL 3-9-6 L Piggott (2) *sn struggling to go pace, improved und pres o'r one furlong out, nvr able to chal.* . . . . (5 to 2 fav op 7 to 4) 4
3196* PIPS PRIDE 3-9-6 S Raymont (5) *pressed ldg pair, feeling pace and rdn o'r one furlong out, no extr.*
. . . . (16 to 1 op 14 to 1) 5
3196[4] SHARP PROD (USA) 3-9-6 K Darley (4) *outpcd and drvn alng aftr 2 fs, nvr a factor.* . . . .(66 to 1 op 50 to 1) 6
2362* HAMAS (Ire) 4-9-9 W Carson (7) *chsd ldr, rdn wl o'r one furlong out, fdd.* . . . .(7 to 2 op 5 to 2) 7
Dist: 1l, 1½l, 3l, nk, 4l, hd. 1m 10.98s. b 0.62s (7 Ran).
SR: 97/90/84/72/71/55/57/ (Sheikh Mohammed), J H M Gosden

3778 Be Friendly Handicap Class D (0-80 3-y-o and up) £5,901 6f. . . . . (4:00)

3558[3] OK BERTIE [75] 3-9-3 (3*) S Maloney (16) *wth ldr, led hfwy, clr o'r one furlong out, kpt on wl.* . . . . (12 to 1) 1
3292[2] FACE THE FUTURE [62] 4-8-10 W Newnes (5) *chsd alng to keep up, gd hdwy frm off the pace fnl furlong, fnshd wl.* . . . .(10 to 1) 2
3504 RED ROSEIN [79] 7-9-13 M Roberts (19) *chsd ldg bunch, brst through entering fnl furlong, ran on wl.*
. . . . (16 to 1 op 14 to 1) 3
2987 LETSBEONESTABOUTIT [64] (v) 7-8-12 L Dettori (1) *nvr far away, rdn 2 fs out, kpt on same pace.* . . . .(20 to 1) 4
3558[4] DENSBEN [80] 9-10-0 W Carson (10) *chsd alng in midfield, improved entering fnl furlong, fnshd wl.*
. . . . (10 to 1 op 8 to 1) 5
3404 THE AUCTION BIDDER [75] 6-9-4 (5*) S Wynne (13) *bustled alng to improve frm midfield last 2 fs, styd on.* (20 to 1) 6

3148[2] EGG [61] (bl) 3-7-13 (7*) V Halliday (14) *sluggish strt, weaved through last 2 fs, ran on finish.* .... (12 to 1 op 9 to 1) 7
2915[7] BERNSTEIN BETTE [56] 7-7-13 (5*) D Wright (11) *outpcd and drvn alng, improved on outsd o'r one furlong out, nvr nrr*.......................... (14 to 1 op 16 to 1) 8
1877[7] BOLD STREET (Ire) [62] 3-8-7 F Norton (9) *chsd ldg bunch, feeling pace o'r 2 fs out, kpt on, no imprsn*.... (25 to 1) 9
3410[6] ADMIRALS REALM [60] 4-8-8 A Mackay (18) *pressed ldrs, drvn alng to hold pl 2 fs out, fdd.* (14 to 1 op 12 to 1) 10
3712[6] BALLAD DANCER [69] 8-9-3 K Darley (8) *pushed alng in midfield, not pace to trble ldrs*................ (16 to 1) 11
3558[8] SAVAHRA SOUND [66] 8-9-0 S Webster (12) *settled midfield, effrt whn baulked and snatched up o'r 2 fs out, sn btn*.. (20 to 1) 12
3621[7] FOLLOWMEGIRLS [58] 4-8-6 S Dawson (17) *speed to chase ldrs centre for o'r 4 fs, fdd*........ (12 to 1 op 14 to 1) 13
3593[2] GREAT HALL [74] (bl) 4-9-1 (7*) D Griffiths (6) *chsd ldg bunch, swtchd outsd o'r 2 fs out, nvr dngrs*... (12 to 1) 14
3410 GONDO [72] (v) 6-8-13 (7*) S Knott (4) *sluggish strt, swtchd outsd to improve hfwy, fdd o'r one furlong out.* ....(14 to 1 tchd 16 to 1) 15
3471[5] DOKKHA OYSTON (Ire) [75] 5-9-9 J Carroll (3) *pushed alng to go pace, nvr rch chalg pos.* .... (10 to 1 op 12 to 1 tchd 14 to 1) 16
3486[3] CRYSTAL JACK (Fr) [70] 5-9-4 S Perks (2) *broke wl to show speed in frnt rnk for o'r 4 fs, fdd.* .... (12 to 1 op 10 to 1 tchd 14 to 1) 17
3638 EDUCATED PET [70] 4-9-1 (3*) B Doyle (15) *chsd alng beh ldg bunch, nvr able to chal*...... (12 to 1 tchd 14 to 1) 18
3404[2] DIET [70] (v) 7-9-4 L Piggott (20) *slight ld stands side to hfwy, wknd quickly o'r one furlong out.* ....(9 to 2 fav op 8 to 1 tchd 10 to 1) 19
3002 SULLY'S CHOICE (USA) [45] (bl) 12-7-7 S Wood (7) *gd speed in frnt rnk till wknd quickly o'r one furlong out.* ....(25 to 1) 20

Dist: ½l, sht-hd, 1½l, sht-hd, 1l, 1½l, hd, hd, nk, 1l. 1m 13.65s. a 2.05s (20 Ran).
SR: 41/29/45/24/39/30/7/4/6/ (R A Fahey), R A Fahey

3779 Fri d'Or Maiden Stakes Class D (2-y-o) £6,149 7f 30yds................ (4:30)

3537[2] OVERBURY (Ire) 9-0 M Roberts (11) *nvr far away, quickened ahead o'r one furlong out, readily.* .... (7 to 4 fav op Evens tchd 9 to 4) 1
MUTAKDDIM (USA) 9-0 W Carson (3) *sluggish strt, improved into midfield hfwy, styd on, not rch wnr.* .... (11 to 4 op 4 to 1 tchd 5 to 2) 2
2964[2] WISHING (USA) 9-0 L Dettori (4) *trkd ldg 6, effrt and drvn alng last 2 fs, kpt on same pace.* .... (5 to 2 op 2 to 1 tchd 11 to 4) 3
1778[5] TO CROWN IT ALL (USA) 9-0 S Wood (2) *tried to make all, hdd and rdn o'r one furlong out, no extr.* .... (25 to 1 op 20 to 1) 4
MOVING ARROW 8-11 (3*) S Maloney (9) *patiently rdn, steady hdwy on fence last 2 fs, ran on, one to note.* ....(25 to 1) 5
3352 MAKE A STAND 9-0 W Newnes (13) *nvr far away, effrt and drvn alng o'r 2 fs out, not quicken fnl furlong.* .... (25 to 1 op 20 to 1) 6
1715[6] ALPINE JOHNNY 9-0 S Perks (6) *pressed ldr, rdn 2 fs out, fdd*................................ (20 to 1 op 16 to 1) 7
SHARP FALCON (Ire) 8-9 A Mackay (10) *settled off the pace, steady hdwy on outsd last 2 fs, nvr plcd to chal.* ....(33 to 1) 8
FRUSTRATED POET (USA) 9-0 K Darley (7) *outpcd and drvn alng hfwy, nvr nr to chal*.... (25 to 1 op 20 to 1) 9
INDIAN SERENADE 9-0 F Norton (12) *patiently rdn, swtchd ins and not much room o'r one furlong out, can improve*..........................(25 to 1 op 20 to 1) 10
MUSIC BLITZ 9-0 J Carroll (5) *chsd alng to keep up aftr 2 fs, nvr dngrs*............................ (33 to 1) 11
3485[4] GONE TO POT (v) 9-0 L Piggott (1) *wl plcd on ins for 5 fs, sn btn*................................(9 to 1 op 14 to 1) 12
3602[4] RINUS MAJOR (Ire) 9-0 G Bardwell (8) *wth ldrs for o'r 4 fs, wknd quickly*................................ (33 to 1) 13

Dist: 2½l, ½l, 4l, 2½l, ¾l, ½l, 1½l, ½l, 3½l, 3½l. 1m 31.22s. a 4.02s (13 Ran).
SR: 40/32/30/18/10/8/6/-/-/ (Sheikh Mohammed), D R Loder

3780 Speke Limited Stakes Class F (0-65 3-y-o and up) £3,961 1m 30yds.. (5:00)

3460[2] SET THE FASHION (v) 4-8-11 (3*) D Harrison (12) *confidently rdn, quickened ahead 2 fs out, easily.* .... (11 to 2 op 5 to 1 tchd 6 to 1) 1
2940[5] QUEEN OF SHANNON (Ire) (v) 5-8-6 (3*) B Doyle (9) *trkd ldg bunch, improved o'r one furlong out, edgd lft, styd on.* ....(10 to 1) 2
3460* AZOLA (Ire) (v) 3-8-5[1] L Dettori (5) *tucked away in midfield, improved o'r one furlong out, styd on.* ....(9 to 4 fav op 5 to 2 tchd 3 to 1) 3
3226[4] MR CUBE (Ire) 3-8-9 W Carson (6) *settled midfield, drvn alng o'r 2 fs out, styd on same pace*........... (8 to 1) 4
2534[4] CRYSTAL REAY 3-8-4 M Roberts (4) *trkd ldg bunch, effrt and drvn alng o'r 2 fs out, one pace.* (7 to 1 op 6 to 1) 5
3553[2] HERSHEBAR (bl) 3-8-4[2] (7*) G Strange (8) *al hndy, led o'r 3 fs out out till hdd 2 out, no extr.* (16 to 1 tchd 20 to 1) 6
3439[7] SOBA UP 3-8-5[1] S Webster (18) *co'red up in midfield, ran green and wndrd hfwy, ran on wl towards finish.* ....(33 to 1) 7
3036[5] SPRING FLYER (Ire) 3-7-13 (5*) D Wright (11) *shwd up wl for o'r 6 fs, fdd*................................(20 to 1) 8
2757 GARTH (bl) 5-9-0 S Perks (13) *chsd ldg bunch, feeling pace and rdn o'r 2 fs out, nvr able to chal*..... (33 to 1) 9
3680[6] NO SUBMISSION (USA) 7-9-0 S Wood (10) *wth ldr, chsd alng o'r 2 fs out, grad wknd*....... (14 to 1 op 12 to 1) 10
3712[3] LOMBARD SHIPS (bl) 6-8-9 L Piggott (16) *beh and drvn alng hfwy, nvr nr to chal*............(6 to 1 op 5 to 1) 11
3409[4] DIWALI DANCER 3-8-2 (7*) Angela Gallimore (3) *sluggish strt, improved on ins o'r 2 fs out, nvr able to chal.* ....(33 to 1) 12
3632[2] SCOFFERA 3-8-4 Kim Tinkler (2) *led till hdd o'r 3 fs out, fdd last 2 furlongs*............................(16 to 1) 13
2954[6] WHITE CREEK (Ire) (v) 3-8-9 J Carroll (1) *settled midfield, drvn alng whn pace quickened o'r 2 fs out, sn btn.* .... (14 to 1 op 12 to 1) 14
3060[3] PEACEFULL REPLY (USA) 3-8-9 K Darley (14) *trkd ldg quartet for o'r 5 fs, fdd*............ (14 to 1 op 12 to 1) 15
3523[3] LEAVE IT TO LIB 6-8-4 (5*) J Tate (15) *trkd ldg bunch, effrt whn struck into o'r 2 fs out, eased*... (6 to 1 op 5 to 1) 16
3032 SICILY OAK 3-8-4 G Bardwell (7) *outpcd and drvn alng thrght, nvr a factor*.............. (50 to 1 op 33 to 1) 17
LOUDEST WHISPER 5-8-11 (3*) S D Williams (17) *chsd ldg bunch for o'r 5 fs, fdd*..................... (100 to 1) 18

Dist: 3l, 2½l, 2½l, 2l, hd, 2l, nk, 1½l, sht-hd, 1l. 1m 43.98s. a 3.38s (18 Ran).
SR: 49/35/23/19/8/12/2/-/5/ (The Queen), Lord Huntingdon

KEMPTON (good (races 1,2,4,5,6), good to firm (3,7))

Saturday September 4th

Going Correction: MINUS 0.10 sec. per fur. (races 1,2,5), MINUS 0.30 (3,4,6,7)

3781 EBF Arion Maiden Fillies' Stakes Class D (2-y-o) £4,485 6f........(2:10)

3317[4] RELATIVELY SPECIAL 8-11 R Cochrane (9) *cl up, rdn to ld appr fnl furlong, ran on wl.* ....(13 to 8 fav op 7 to 4 tchd 6 to 4) 1
3156[3] REDRESS (USA) 8-11 A Munro (12) *led til hdd appr fnl furlong, ran on one pace.* ....(4 to 1 op 3 to 1 tchd 5 to 1) 2
ZIFTA (USA) 8-11 W R Swinburn (11) *trkd ldrs, shaken up 2 fs out, one pace, improve*........... (10 to 1 op 4 to 1) 3
3260[2] BAHRAIN STAR (USA) 8-11 J Reid (10) *al prmnt, one pace appr fnl 2 fs*..........(12 to 1 op 8 to 1 tchd 14 to 1) 4
SULITELMA (USA) 8-11 S O'Gorman (4) *beh, rdn and hdwy o'r 2 fs out, styd on*.............. (33 to 1 op 20 to 1) 5
BINTALSHAATI 8-11 R Hills (3) *wth ldrs till wknd 2 fs out.* .... (10 to 1 op 5 to 1) 6
ZIPPY ZOE 8-11 M Tebbutt (7) *chsd ldrs till wknd o'r 2 fs out*.................. (9 to 1 op 20 to 1 tchd 25 to 1) 7
ECHARDE 8-11 D Holland (5) *outpcd, nvr on terms.* .... (33 to 1 op 20 to 1) 8
3317 KHAYA 8-11 C Rutter (2) *chsd ldrs to hfwy.* .... (66 to 1 op 50 to 1) 9
3387[8] SPRINGTIME AFFAIR 8-11 M Hills (8) *trkd ldrs till wknd o'r 2 fs out*....................... (33 to 1 op 16 to 1) 10
MNAAFA (Ire) 8-11 Pat Eddery (14) *outpcd.* .... (16 to 1 op 10 to 1 tchd 20 to 1) 11
3317 BROOKS MASQUERADE 8-11 W Ryan (1) *strted slwly, al beh*.......................... (20 to 1 tchd 33 to 1) 12
3446 LIVELY (Ire) 8-11 J Williams (6) *chsd ldrs to hfwy.* .... (66 to 1 op 33 to 1) 13
EFFICACY 8-11 J Quinn (13) *al beh.* (66 to 1 op 33 to 1) 14

Dist: 2l, 4l, 3½l, nk, 4l, nk, 1l, 3l, 2½l, 2½l. 1m 12.35s. a 1.55s (14 Ran).
SR: 54/46/30/16/15/-/ (Helena Springfield Ltd), L M Cumani

3782 Teddington Fillies' Conditions Stakes Class D (3-y-o and up) £3,055 6f (2:40)

2334 ZARANI SIDI ANNA (USA) (v) 3-9-1 W R Swinburn (4) *co'red up in cl tch, pushed alng over one furlong out, shaken up to ld wl ins fnl furlong, cmftbly.* .... (5 to 2 op 13 to 8 tchd 11 to 4) 1
3438[5] TRAPEZIUM 3-9-1 R Cochrane (2) *pld hrd, led, quickened hfwy, hdd and no extr wl ins fnl furlong.* ....(5 to 1 tchd 6 to 1) 2
3594[2] GARAH 4-9-5 W Ryan (3) *hld up in last pl, hrd rdn o'r one furlong out, no imprsn*....(11 to 8 on tchd 13 to 8 on) 3
3709[5] PERFECT PASSION 3-8-4 (7*) Antoinette Armes (1) *wth ldr till wknd wl o'r 2 fs out.* ....(100 to 1 op 50 to 1 tchd 200 to 1) 4

Dist: ¾l, 4l, 10l. 1m 11.88s. a 1.08s (4 Ran).
SR: 67/64/52/4/ (Maktoum Al Maktoum), M R Stoute

3783 Geoffrey Hamlyn Handicap Class D (0-80 3-y-o) £3,845 1m.......... (3:10)

3214[3] PERSIANSKY (Ire) [73] 9-0 M Hills (11) *mid-div, rdn and hdwy 2 fs out, squeezed through to ld wl ins last.* ....(12 to 1) 1
3290 RAKIS (Ire) [78] (bl) 9-5 J Williams (5) *led til hdd wl ins fnl furlong, ran on*.................. (40 to 1 op 33 to 1) 2
3234[3] GRAN SENORUM (USA) [71] 8-12 A Munro (3) *trkd ldrs, ev ch o'r one furlong out, edgd rght and one pace cl hme.* .... (10 to 1 op 12 to 1) 3
417* TABKIR (USA) [80] 9-7 W Ryan (12) *strted slwly, beh, plenty to do strt, hdwy o'r 2 fs out, ran on wl.* .... (20 to 1 op 16 to 1) 4
3080[4] DISKETTE [71] 8-12 W R Swinburn (16) *mid-div, hdwy 2 fs out, slightly hmpd and one pace cl hme.* ....(7 to 1 tchd 15 to 2 and 13 to 2) 5
3070* AHJAY [52] 7-7 J Quinn (2) *mid-div, prog whn hmpd 2 fs out, ran on ins last*................(10 to 1 op 7 to 1) 6
3480[6] FLASHFEET [67] 8-8 N Adams (9) *chsd ldrs, rdn o'r 2 fs out, one pace frm over one out*.... (40 to 1 op 33 to 1) 7
3476 TWICE THE GROOM (Ire) [66] 8-7 J Reid (15) *mid-div, no hdwy fnl 2 fs*......................(14 to 1 op 12 to 1) 8
2182[8] SOVIET EXPRESS [58] 7-6 (7*) A Daly (4) *chsd ldrs, swshd tail and wknd o'r one furlong out.* (33 to 1 op 25 to 1) 9
1313[7] KNYAZ [62] 8-3 D Holland (10) *mid-div, lost pl o'r 3 fs out, some modest late prog*............ (40 to 1 op 33 to 1) 10
3053[4] GREEN CHILI [58] 7-13 D Biggs (8) *reluctant to race, al beh*................................(16 to 1 op 14 to 1) 11
3476 THE LITTLE FERRET [74] 8-8 (7*) Mark Denaro (14) *trkd ldrs till rdn and wknd quickly appr fnl furlong.* .... (20 to 1 op 14 to 1) 12
2578[3] ANORAK (USA) [74] 9-1 Pat Eddery (6) *hld up towards rear, effrt on ins o'r 2 fs out, sn no imprsn.* ....(14 to 1 tchd 16 to 1) 13
3054* SUSQUEHANNA DAYS (USA) [66] 8-7 S O'Gorman (1) *trkd ldrs till rdn 2 fs out, btn quickly*... (12 to 1 op 10 to 1) 14
3476 SILVER GROOM (Ire) [54] 7-2 (7*) N Varley (18) *al beh.* ....(16 to 1 tchd 14 to 1) 15
2563 AMOREM [59] (v) 8-0 C Rutter (7) *cl up, pushed alng 3 fs out, sn wknd*........................(33 to 1 op 25 to 1) 16
3540[2] MUTAKALLAM (USA) [72] 8-13 R Hills (13) *cl up, wkng whn hmpd 2 fs out*.....................(6 to 1 fav op 5 to 1) 17
3314 FORTENSKY (USA) [78] 9-5 R Cochrane (17) *mid-div, rdn to cl o'r 4 fs out, wknd quickly over 2 out.* .... (9 to 1 op 8 to 1 tchd 10 to 1) 18
Dist: Nk, 1l, sht-hd, 1l, 1½l, nk, 1½l, nk, sht-hd, 1l. 1m 39.20s. a 2.40s (18 Ran).
SR: 28/32/22/30/18/-/8/2/-/ (Mrs J M Beeby), B Hanbury

3784 BonusPrint September Stakes Class A (Group 3) (3-y-o and up) £25,830 1m 3f 30yds........................ (3:40)

3402[3] SPARTAN SHAREEF (Ire) 4-9-3 A Munro (3) *trkd ldg pair, led 3 fs out, rdn alng and ran on strly.* .... (5 to 1 op 9 to 2 tchd 11 to 2) 1
2621* BOBZAO (Ire) 4-9-0 J Reid (9) *dwlt, hld up, cld 3 fs out, hrd rdn o'r one out, ran on wl.* ....(4 to 1 op 7 to 2 tchd 9 to 2) 2
2079[5] CAPTAIN HORATIUS (Ire) 4-9-5 W Ryan (7) *hld up, pushed alng 3 fs out, hdwy o'r one out, kpt on.* .... (14 to 1 op 16 to 1) 3
3403[9] GEISWAY (Can) 3-8-6 M Hills (5) *chsd ldrs, hrd rdn o'r 2 fs out, one pace over one out.* .... (20 to 1 op 25 to 1 tchd 33 to 1) 4
3403[3] DECLASSIFIED (USA) 3-8-6 R Cochrane (2) *trkd ldr, rdn alng o'r 2 fs out, one pace frm over one out.* ....(8 to 1 tchd 10 to 1) 5
3644[2] SOURCE OF LIGHT 4-9-0 Pat Eddery (4) *hld up, nvr gng wl, hrd 3 fs out, never nrr.* ......(100 to 30 fav op 9 to 2 tchd 5 to 1 and 3 to 1) 6
3500[3] LUCKY LINDY (Ire) 4-9-5 R Hills (6) *trkd ldrs, pushed alng 3 fs out, sn btn*..........(10 to 1 op 8 to 1 tchd 11 to 1) 7
2174* WINGED VICTORY (USA) 3-8-6 D Holland (1) *hld up, effrt 3 fs out, sn btn*..........(10 to 1 op 8 to 1 tchd 11 to 1) 8
2211 HIGHLAND DRESS 4-9-0 W R Swinburn (8) *led til hdd 3 fs out, wknd*............ (13 to 2 op 5 to 1 tchd 7 to 1) 9
Dist: Nk, 3l, 2½l, sht-hd, 6l, 1l, 2½l, ½l. 2m 20.23s. a 2.93s (9 Ran).
SR: 40/36/35/17/16/12/15/-/4/ (C T Olley), C E Brittain

3785 BonusPrint Sirenia Stakes Class A (Listed Race) (2-y-o) £8,975 6f...(4:10)

3633* WATANI (USA) 8-11 R Hills (2) *trkd ldr, led o'r 3 fs out, ran on wl*........................ (Evens fav tchd 11 to 10) 1
3260* MAJESTIC EAGLE (Ire) 8-11 M Hills (3) *rcd in 3rd pl, pushed alng and cld on wnr o'r 2 fs out, hng rght and one pace over one out*.............. (2 to 1 op 6 to 4) 2
3478[3] GOVERNOR GEORGE (USA) 8-11 J Reid (1) *pld hrd, sn led, hdd o'r 3 fs out, wknd*............... (7 to 2 op 4 to 1) 3
Dist: 3½l, 10l. 1m 12.22s. a 1.42s (3 Ran).
SR: 57/43/3/ (Hamdan Al-Maktoum), R W Armstrong

3786 Spelthorne Handicap Class C (0-90 3-y-o and up) £7,765 1½m..... (4:40)

3078[2] SUPREME MASTER [69] 3-8-5 J Williams (6) *beh, hdwy 3 fs out, led appr last, ran on wl.* .... (11 to 1 op 8 to 1 tchd 12 to 1) 1
3587* GENERAL MOUKTAR [79] 3-9-1 M Perrett (2) *hld up, hdwy on bit o'r 2 fs out, squeezed through on far rail over one out, sn ev ch, no extr nr finish.* ....(2 to 1 fav op 5 to 2 tchd 3 to 1) 2
3434 OPERA GHOST [79] 7-9-10 J Reid (1) *hld up beh, hdwy 4 fs out, ev ch ins last, no extr cl hme*............. (12 to 1) 3
3466 ARKAAN (USA) [82] 3-9-4 W R Swinburn (8) *chsd ldg pair, led o'r 3 fs out till hdd appr last, one pace.* .... (9 to 1 op 8 to 1 tchd 10 to 1) 4
3314[6] NESSUN DORMA [81] 3-9-3 M Hills (10) *chsd ldrs till rdn and wknd o'r 2 fs out*..............(7 to 1 tchd 8 to 1) 5
4750a[3] CASPIAN BELUGA [60] 5-8-5 J Quinn (7) *wth ldr, led o'r 5 fs out till hdd over 3 out, sn wknd.* ....(33 to 1 tchd 66 to 1) 6
3572[3] BOBBYSOXER [76] 3-8-12 Pat Eddery (4) *trkd ldrs, ev ch 2 fs out, sn btn*.........................(7 to 1 op 6 to 1) 7
875 YAJEED (USA) [87] 3-9-9 R Hills (3) *beh, hrd rdn 5 fs out, no imprsn*.............................(50 to 1 tchd 66 to 1) 8
3424[2] BARFORD LAD [72] 6-9-3 W Ryan (11) *mid-div, beh frm hfwy*..(12 to 1 op 10 to 1) 9
3513[7] MOONLIGHT QUEST [78] 5-9-9 D Holland (5) *chsd ldrs till wknd o'r 4 fs out*.....(16 to 1 op 14 to 1 tchd 20 to 1) 10
3572[2] SURE HAVEN (Ire) [76] 4-9-7 G Duffield (9) *led til hdd o'r 5 fs out, wknd over 3 out*... (13 to 2 op 5 to 1 tchd 7 to 1) 11
Dist: 1l, nk, 2½l, 15l, ½l, 2½l, 8l, 6l, 2½l, nk. 2m 31.69s. a 0.69s (11 Ran).
SR: 48/56/64/53/22/9/11/6/-/ (Harry W Hopgood), R Hannon

3787 Grebe Apprentices Handicap Class F (0-70 3-y-o and up) £3,496 1¼m (5:10)

3290[6] LADY LACEY [56] 6-8-11 (7*) Iona Wands (1) *hld up in mid-div, hdwy 2 fs out, led o'r one out, ran on strly.* .... (12 to 1 op 7 to 1 tchd 14 to 1) 1
3420[4] BIT ON THE SIDE (Ire) [62] 4-9-10 D McCabe (9) *dwlt, hld up beh, hdwy 2 fs out, ran on wl.* ....(7 to 1 op 6 to 1 tchd 9 to 1) 2
3518[2] KATHY FAIR (Ire) [43] 4-8-5 B Russell (7) *took keen hold in mid-div, hdwy o'r 3 fs out, led briefly over one out, one pace*.......................... (6 to 1 op 5 to 1 tchd 7 to 1) 3
3420* WHO'S THE BEST (Ire) [52] 3-8-4 (3*) D Gibbs (5) *cl up till lost pl 4 fs out, hrd rdn 2 out, kpt on ins last.* ....(5 to 1 fav tchd 11 to 2 and 4 to 1) 4
3551[2] DON'T DROP BOMBS (USA) [39] 4-8-1 Kim McDonnell (10) *led, clr 3 fs out till hdd and wknd o'r one out.* .... (11 to 2 op 5 to 1 tchd 15 to 2) 5
3263[8] WELL SUITED [66] 3-9-2 (5*) D O'Neill (4) *trkd ldrs till wknd o'r one furlong out*........................(7 to 1 op 6 to 1) 6
2989[5] MON PETITNAMOUR (Ire) [40] 4-8-2 N Varley (8) *chsd ldrs, outpcd fnl 2 fs*..........................(12 to 1 op 8 to 1) 7
3518[9] BILLYBACK [52] 3-8-1[1] (7*) T Beaver (6) *beh, effrt 3 fs out, sn no imprsn*............................(20 to 1 op 12 to 1) 8
NOCATCHIM [52] 4-9-0 J D Smith (12) *chsd ldrs till wknd wl o'r one furlong out*..................(10 to 1 op 20 to 1) 9
2712[8] JUST JAMIE [50] 3-8-2 (3*) L Carter (11) *chsd ldrs, hrd rdn 3 fs out, sn btn*........ (20 to 1 op 16 to 1 tchd 25 to 1) 10
3420[8] SULA MOON [39] 3-7-3 (5*) Wendy Jones (15) *beh whn ran wide into strt, no imprsn*.......... (50 to 1 op 33 to 1) 11
YOUNG FACT [58] 8-9-6 Michael Denaro (2) *al beh.* .... (50 to 1 op 33 to 1) 12
3341[5] SEA SIREN [62] 3-9-3 Antoinette Armes (14) *cl up till wknd o'r 2 fs out*.......... (12 to 1 op 10 to 1 tchd 14 to 1) 13
Dist: 3½l, 2½l, 6l, 1½l, nk, ¾l, 1½l, 2½l, 12l, 1½l. 2m 5.48s. a 3.68s (13 Ran).
SR: 37/36/12/2/-/12/ (Mrs K L Perrin), G B Balding

THIRSK (firm (races 1,3,4,5,6), good to firm (2,7))

Saturday September 4th

Going Correction: MINUS 0.10 sec. per fur. (races 1,3,4,5,6), NIL (2,7)

3788 Falcon Selling Stakes Class G (3-y-o and up) £2,532 1m.............(2:15)

3088[4] PARFAIT AMOUR 4-8-13 A Culhane (3) *nvr far away, led 2 fs out, hng rght and ran on wl whn hrd pressed fnl furlong*.......... (6 to 5 on op 5 to 4 on tchd Evens) 1
3631 DOUBLE THE STAKES (USA) (bl) 4-9-0 R Lappin (12) *led til hdd 2 fs out, sn rdn alng and rallied, rnwd chal fnl furlong, no extr towards finish*.... (50 to 1 op 33 to 1) 2
3593 LADY SABO 4-8-8 (5*) A Garth (2) *dwlt, sn reco'red into midfield, imprvg whn not clr run and swtchd over one out, chlgd ins last, kpt on towards finish.* ....(9 to 1 op 8 to 1) 3
2365[8] HAWAYMYSON (Ire) 3-8-9 T Quinn (5) *tucked away beh ldrs, rdn alng o'r 2 fs out, kpt on ins fnl furlong.* ....(16 to 1 tchd 20 to 1) 4
3374[2] DRUMDONNA (Ire) 3-8-8 J Fortune (9) *al prmnt, wide strt, ev ch 2 fs out, edgd lft, no extr ins last*........ (5 to 1) 5
3324[4] FORMAESTRE (Ire) 3-8-5 (3*) O Pears (11) *pressed ldg grp on outer, wide strt, improved 2 fs out, rdn and no extr appr last*......... (16 to 1 op 14 to 1 tchd 20 to 1) 6
3376[3] BALLY ROBERT 3-8-9 J Weaver (6) *hld up, shaken up 2 fs out, nvr nr to chal*............... (33 to 1 op 25 to 1) 7

4810a INTREPID FORT (bl) 4-8-7 (7*) G Parkin (8) *sn beh, pushed alng aftr 3 fs, rdn to improve o'r 2 furlongs out, wknd appr last*..........................(50 to 1 op 33 to 1) 8
3246[4] BARLEY CAKE (v) 3-8-8 J Fanning (10) *hld up, pushed alng appr strt, not pace to chal.* ....(15 to 2 op 6 to 1 tchd 8 to 1) 9
3631[4] DANCES WITH GOLD 3-8-4 T Williams (1) *nvr far away, came wide strt, sn pushed alng, wknd 2 fs out.* ....(14 to 1 op 12 to 1) 10
2736[8] DESIRABLE MISS (v) 3-8-3 (5*) J Marshall (4) *tucked away on ins, rdn alng 3 fs out, nvr on terms.* ....(33 to 1 op 25 to 1) 11
2797[6] ANGELS ANSWER (Ire) 4-8-8 (5*) Darren Moffatt (7) *sddl slpd sn aftr strt, keen hold in tch, pushed alng entering strt, soon btn*..................................(33 to 1) 12

Dist: ½l, hd, 2½l, hd, 3l, ½l, 1½l, 4l, 2½l, 2l. 1m 41.30s. a 5.40s (12 Ran).

SR: 6/5/3/-/-/-/ (R M Whitaker), R M Whitaker

3789 Yorkshire Racing Club Maiden Stakes Class D (3-y-o and up) £3,523 6f (2:45)

3489[2] DESERT GREEN (Fr) 4-9-0 P D'Arcy (14) *taken early to post, wth ldrs, led o'r 2 fs out, shaken up and ran on wl ins last*......... (6 to 4 on op 11 to 10 on tchd Evens) 1
3458[8] DESERT CHAMP (USA) 4-9-0 B Raymond (12) *al frnt rnk, rdn and hng lft 2 fs out, sn ev ch, edgd rght and kpt on same pace ins last*.................(10 to 1 op 8 to 1) 2
3359[3] CALAMANCO 3-8-6 P Robinson (6) *led til hdd o'r 2 fs out, sn rdn and rallied, no extr ins fnl furlong*.....(10 to 1) 3
3359[6] NO CONTRACT (USA) 3-8-11 G Hind (10) *nvr far away, pushed alng o'r 2 fs out, outpcd wl over one out.* ....(10 to 1 tchd 12 to 1) 4
3006[9] HALL BANK COTTAGE 3-8-6 J Weaver (5) *beh, shaken up hfwy, kpt on o'r one furlong out, nvr nr to chal.* ....(33 to 1) 5
3359 TARNSIDE BANKER 3-8-11 J Lowe (13) *chsd ldg bunch on inner, pushed alng hfwy, kpt on same pace*... (50 to 1) 6
WESTERN FRIEND (USA) 3-8-6 T Quinn (11) *trkd ldrs, pushed alng o'r 2 fs out, sn outpcd.* (8 to 1 op 6 to 1) 7
3631[9] FLASHELLA (Ire) 3-8-6 Paul Eddery (9) *beh, shaken up o'r 2 fs out, not clr run over one out, sn eased, nvr nr to chal.* ....(25 to 1) 8
3178[6] FILL 3-8-6 A McGlone (1) *pressed ldg bunch on outer, pushed alng hfwy, btn 2 fs out*..... (10 to 1 op 7 to 1) 9
3634 CIZARD (Ire) (bl) 3-8-3 (3*) N Kennedy (7) *dwlt, sn reco'red to press ldg bunch, rdn alng hfwy, btn 2 fs out.* (66 to 1) 10
UNFINISHEDBUSINESS 3-8-11 L Charnock (4) *beh on outer, struggling hfwy, nvr on terms.* ....(33 to 1 op 25 to 1) 11
2366[7] MOLLY BRAZEN 3-8-6 M Birch (3) *beh, pushed alng frm hfwy, nvr wnt pace*..........................(33 to 1) 12
2634[6] OSCAR THE SECOND (Ire) 3-8-11 J Fanning (2) *pressed ldg bunch, rdn alng 2 fs out, sn btn*..............(50 to 1) 13
3514 RISK THE WITCH 3-8-1 (5*) L Newton (8) *chsd ldrs, sn pushed alng, lost tch frm hfwy*.... (50 to 1 op 25 to 1) 14

Dist: 1½l, 1½l, 6l, 2½l, 1½l, sht-hd, sht-hd, nk, 2l, 2½l. 1m 13.30s. a 3.30s (14 Ran).

SR: 34/28/14/-/-/-/ (Mana Al Maktoum), M R Stoute

3790 Hambleton Cup Handicap Class D (0-80 3-y-o and up) £4,542 1½m (3:15)

3503[5] MISBELIEF [73] 3-9-2 T Quinn (12) *nvr far away, improved to ld 4 fs out, hdd o'r one furlong out, rallied to rgn lead ins last, kpt on wl.* ....(11 to 2 fav op 5 to 1 tchd 6 to 1) 1
3548[2] LOOKINGFORARAINBOW (Ire) [62] 5-9-0 N Day (9) *settled midfield, improved on bit to ld o'r one furlong out, shaken up and hdd ins last, not run on*...... (7 to 1) 2
1967[8] IN THE MONEY (Ire) [58] 4-8-3 (7*) M Humphries (3) *chsd ldg pair, feeling pace appr strt, sn rdn, ran on o'r one furlong out, nrst finish*..........................(25 to 1) 3
3466[4] LATVIAN [72] 6-9-10 J Weaver (5) *hld up, effrt and came wide strt, sn drvn alng, kpt on ins fnl furlong, nrst finish*..............................(6 to 1 op 5 to 1) 4
3469[6] GREEN'S CASSATT (USA) [50] 5-7-11 (5*) A Garth (11) *in tch on ins, pushed alng entering strt, kpt on und pres inside fnl furlong*..............................(10 to 1) 5
2977* SUPER BLUES [49] 6-8-1 T Williams (1) *mid-div, improved on bit and ev ch 2 fs out, wknd appr last.* .... (13 to 2 op 8 to 1 tchd 9 to 1) 6
3356[6] DUNNELLON [74] 3-9-3 K Fallon (2) *hld up towards rear, pushed alng aftr 4 fs, drvn along entering strt, one pace fnl 2 furlongs*...............(25 to 1 op 20 to 1) 7
2233[6] QUEENS CONSUL (Ire) [68] 3-8-11 J Fortune (10) *dwlt, hld up, pushed alng appr strt, nvr rchd ldrs.* ....(20 to 1 op 16 to 1) 8
3630* ATHERTON GREEN (Ire) [70] 3-8-13 M Birch (6) *hld up and beh, steady hdwy fnl 2 fs, nvr plcd to chal.* ....(9 to 1 op 8 to 1) 9
2506[8] EIRE LEATH-SCEAL [44] 6-7-10 J Lowe (7) *led 2 and a half fs, styd hndy, rdn alng o'r 5 out, wknd entering strt.* ....(12 to 1) 10
3356 PERSIAN SOLDIER [47] 6-7-13 J Fanning (8) *prmnt, led aftr 2 and a half fs, hdd 4 furlongs out, sn pushed alng, wknd o'r two out*...................(6 to 1 op 5 to 1) 11
3139[3] SAFIR (USA) [77] 3-9-6 B Raymond (4) *pressed ldrs, drpd rear o'r 4 fs out, no imprsn and eased entering strt.* ....(9 to 1 op 8 to 1) 12

Dist: 1½l, 1½l, 1½l, nk, sht-hd, 4l, ½l, ½l, 1½l, 4l. 2m 34.00s. a 3.80s (12 Ran).

SR: 52/47/40/51/28/26/34/27/28/ (T & J Vestey), J R Fanshawe

3791 Phoenix Rated Class B Handicap (0-95 3-y-o and up) £6,709 1m........ (3:45)

3637[2] DIXIELAND MELODY (USA) [84] 3-9-1 B Raymond (6) *set modest pace, made all, jnd 2 fs out, ran on strly ins last.* ....(3 to 1 fav op 9 to 4) 1
3177 WATHIK (USA) [87] (bl) 3-9-4 N Carlisle (4) *trkd ldr, effrt and drifted rght 2 fs out, sn drvn alng, kpt on und pres ins last*..............................(25 to 1 op 20 to 1) 2
3350[8] EMBANKMENT (Ire) [85] 3-9-2 T Quinn (1) *nvr far away, improved to chal 2 fs out, rdn and no extr ins fnl furlong*..........................(11 to 2 op 7 to 1) 3
2657[3] TAWAFIJ (USA) [77] 4-8-13 J Fanning (2) *hld up in tch, pushed alng o'r 2 fs out, swtchd over one out, no imprsn*..............................(5 to 1 op 4 to 1) 4
3643* MOON SPIN [84] 4-9-6 Paul Eddery (7) *nvr far away, effrt and drvn alng 2 fs out, swtchd lft o'r one out, sn one pace*..............................(7 to 2 tchd 4 to 1) 5
3487[3] BOLD ANGEL [76] 6-8-12 M Birch (3) *steadied strt, hld up, shaken up and hdwy 2 fs out, nvr nr to chal.* ....(4 to 1 tchd 9 to 2) 6
3558[7] BEWARE OF AGENTS [85] 4-9-7 R P Elliott (5) *chsd ldrs on outer, drpd rear hfwy, lost tch fnl 2 fs.* ....(10 to 1 tchd 11 to 1) 7

Dist: 1½l, nk, 3l, ½l, 1½l, 10l. 1m 40.80s. a 4.90s (7 Ran).

SR: 16/14/11/-/4/-/-/ (Saeed Suhail), B Hanbury

3792 Highflyer Maiden Auction Stakes Class F (2-y-o) £3,297 7f........ (4:15)

2875[5] MHEANMETOO 9-0 M Birch (6) *trkd ldr gng wl, improved to ld o'r 2 fs out, rdn out ins last.* ....(3 to 1 fav tchd 7 to 2) 1
3520[3] A MILLION WATTS 9-0 P Robinson (9) *nvr far away, drvn alng entering strt, kpt on ins fnl furlong.* ....(4 to 1 op 5 to 1 tchd 7 to 2) 2
3642[7] WESTERN FLEET (USA) 9-0 T Quinn (15) *settled towards rear, took clr order hfwy, effrt and rdn 2 out, edgd lft, ran on strly ins last*..........................(6 to 1) 3
2772[4] BOLD ALEX 8-11 (3*) O Pears (5) *set gd pace, rdn entering strt, hdd o'r 2 fs out, btn appr last.* ....(5 to 1 op 7 to 1 tchd 8 to 1) 4
3642[5] CAPTAIN SCARLET (Ire) 9-0 S Whitworth (2) *chsd ldg 3, effrt and drvn alng three fs out, one pace appr last.* .... (11 to 2 op 9 to 2) 5
3362[7] LADY GREY (Swe) 8-9 R Price (11) *in tch, drvn alng appr strt, not quicken o'r one furlong out*......... (50 to 1) 6
2876 LEGAL TRAIN 9-0 J Lowe (13) *keen hold, mid-div, shaken up entering strt, one pace fnl 2 fs*............ (33 to 1) 7
3218[2] MAURANGI 9-0 Paul Eddery (16) *sn pushed alng beh ldrs, rdn o'r 3 fs out, one pace fnl 2 furlongs*.......(10 to 1) 8
3598[3] MONKEY WENCH (Ire) 8-9 J Fortune (10) *beh and sn pushed alng, drvn along entering strt, kpt on fnl furlong, nvr dngrs*..............................(14 to 1) 9
ICANSPELL 9-0 A McGlone (12) *beh, shaken up 2 fs out, nvr able to chal*..............................(20 to 1) 10
1998 BARNPARK 9-0 Alex Greaves (8) *beh, pushed alng o'r 2 fs out, not rch ldrs*..............................(50 to 1) 11
2772 GALLIC GENT 9-0 T Lucas (1) *sn beh, shaken up entering strt, nvr on terms*..............................(50 to 1) 12
1897 AUNTIE FAY (Ire) 8-9 K Fallon (3) *chsd ldrs, rdn appr strt, sn btn*.......................... (50 to 1 op 33 to 1) 13
2766[9] DROP THE DONKEY 8-9 L Charnock (7) *sluggish strt, beh and pushed alng 3 fs out, nvr on terms*.......(100 to 1) 14
900 YOUNG MEDIC 9-0 J Fanning (4) *dwlt, beh, struggling fnl 3 fs, tld off*................................ (50 to 1) 15
BIRCHWOOD STAR 8-2 (7*) M Humphries (14) *lost many ls strt, nvr able to reco'r*.......... (16 to 1 tchd 20 to 1) 16

Dist: 2½l, 1½l, ½l, 1½l, 2l, 3l, 4l, 2l, ¾l, ¾l. 1m 28.20s. a 5.40s (16 Ran).

SR: 8/-/-/-/-/-/ (Ken Dyke), M H Easterby

3793 Underwood Maiden Stakes Class D (2-y-o) £3,494 1m................. (4:45)

3470[2] RAGSAT AL OMOR (Ire) 9-0 P Robinson (4) *chsd ldg 3, ld wl o'r 2 fs out, hdd over one out, rallied and rgned lead ins last, rdn out.* (5 to 2 on op 11 to 4 on tchd 9 to 4 on) 1
3259 CLIFTON BEAT (USA) 9-0 K Fallon (2) *nvr far away, rdn to ld o'r one furlong out, hdd ins last, no extr.* ....(4 to 1 tchd 9 to 2) 2
3470 SANDMOOR CHAMBRAY 9-0 M Birch (5) *led, hdd entering strt, sn pushed alng, wknd o'r one furlong out.* ....(12 to 1) 3
3137[8] HARLESTONE FIRS 9-0 S Whitworth (1) *in tch, pushed alng hfwy, drvn entering strt, no imprsn fnl 2 fs.* .... (16 to 1 op 12 to 1) 4
FRIENDLY MONET 9-0 J Fanning (7) *hld up, took clr order hfwy, rdn and swtchd 2 fs out, sn btn, tld off.* .... (16 to 1 op 12 to 1) 5

3411[9] IBERIAN MAGIC (Ire) (v) 9-0 L Charnock (6) *rcd keenly, trkd ldr, led entering strt, hdd wl o'r 2 fs out, sn wknd, tld off*.................................... (33 to 1) 6
Dist: 2½l, 8l, 3l, 15l, 2l. 1m 41.90s. a 6.00s (6 Ran).
(Sheikh Ahmed Al Maktoum), M A Jarvis

3794 Crathorne Maiden Handicap Class F (0-60 3-y-o and up) £3,027 5f.... (5:15)

3747[4] BAYIN (USA) [33] 4-8-2 R Street (15) *dwlt, hld up gng wl, improved to ld ins fnl furlong, styd on strly*. ....(5 to 1 tchd 11 to 2) 1
3758[8] KILTROUM (Fr) [35] (v) 4-8-4 K Fallon (10) *swtchd to stand rail sn aftr strt, prmnt and soon drvn alng, kpt on ins fnl furlong, no ch wth wnr*..........(7 to 1 op 6 to 1) 2
3603 LUCKY MILL [41] (bl) 3-8-5 (3*) N Kennedy (5) *in tch gng wl far side, improved and ev ch appr last, no extr*. ....(10 to 1 tchd 12 to 1) 3
3354[5] MISS BRIGHTSIDE [38] (bl) 5-8-7 M Birch (3) *made most far side, hng lft appr last, hdd and no extr ins fnl furlong*. ....(10 to 1 tchd 12 to 1) 4
3006[8] PRETTY CHIC [27] (bl) 4-7-10 J Fanning (7) *nvr far away, chlgd centre 2 fs out, rdn and not quicken ins last*. ....(33 to 1 op 25 to 1) 5
3591[4] CLEAR LOOK [50] (bl) 3-9-3 T Quinn (12) *cl up stand side, pushed alng aftr 2 fs, kpt on same pace appr last*. ....(11 to 4 fav op 7 to 2) 6
3354 PAULINUS [31] 5-8-0 L Charnock (1) *chsd ldrs on wide outsd, rdn alng frm hfwy, no imprsn o'r one furlong out*..(14 to 1) 7+
3100[6] RICKY'S TORNADO (Ire) [59] 4-10-0 J Weaver (11) *settled beh ldrs stand side, improved o'r one furlong out, no extr ins last*..........(11 to 1 op 10 to 1 tchd 12 to 1) 7+
2481[8] GATE OF HEAVEN [26] 3-7-2 (5*) Darren Moffatt (2) *sn pushed alng beh ldrs far side, one pace fnl 2 fs*. (33 to 1) 9
1516[4] RUSSIA WITH LOVE [56] 3-9-9 B Raymond (4) *chsd ldrs far side, pushed alng hfwy, btn o'r one furlong out*. ....(10 to 1 tchd 11 to 1 and 12 to 1) 10
3553[6] THROW AWAY LINE [36] 4-7-12 (7*) G Forster (8) *in tch centre, effrt and drvn alng last 2 fs, one pace*. (33 to 1) 11
3140[9] SENSABO [32] 3-7-13 J Lowe (14) *chsd ldrs stand side, rdn alng hfwy, sn btn*. ....(11 to 1 op 14 to 1 tchd 16 to 1) 12
3391 ROYAL MUSIC [42] 3-8-2 (7*) P Roberts (6) *cl up far side, drvn alng hfwy, fdd wl o'r one furlong out*....(16 to 1) 13
3603 HUMBER'S SUPREME (Ire) [43] (bl) 3-8-10 J Fortune (13) *sn drvn alng beh ldrs stand side, btn 2 fs out*.....(16 to 1) 14
3619 BRIGADORE GOLD [47] 3-9-0 R Lappin (9) *prmnt stand side, rdn alng hfwy, grad wknd*... (12 to 1 op 20 to 1) 15
Dist: 3½l, nk, 1l, 1l, sht-hd, 2½l, dd-ht, nk, nk, 2½l. 59.80s. a 2.60s (15 Ran).
SR: 36/24/27/22/7/27/-/28/-/ (Trevor Barker), M D I Usher

BADEN-BADEN (GER) (good)
Sunday September 5th

3795 Grosser Preis von Baden (Group 1) (3-y-o and up) £122,449 1½m...... (3:00)

3371[2] LANDO (Ger) 3-8-9 A Tylicki (1) *rcd in 6th, prog 4 fs out, 3rd strt, str chal to ld one out, ran on wl*................ 1
2791 PLATINI (Ger) 4-9-6 M Rimmer (4) *rcd in 3rd, took clr order 4 fs out, led 2 out till one out, rallied wl*............ 2
3370 GEORGE AUGUSTUS (USA) 5-9-6 M Roberts (5) *rcd in 4th, ran on one pace strt, nvr able to chal*.................. 3
3022[3] HONDO MONDO (Ire) (bl) 5-9-6 Manfred Hofer (7) *last till kpt on fnl 3 fs*.. 4
3370 SPORTIVO (USA) 4-9-6 A Helfenbein (6) *led, clr hfwy till hdd and one pace 2 and a half fs out*.................. 5
1727* RUBY TIGER 6-9-2 B Raymond (2) *rcd in 5th, rdn and btn 3 fs out*... 6
3649[9] SAPIENCE 7-9-6 B Rouse (3) *rcd in second, led briefly 2 and a half fs out, wknd quickly*........................ 7
Dist: Nk, 6l, 3l, 2l, 1 ¼l, 1½l. 2m 28.20s. (7 Ran).
(Gestut Haus Ittlingen), H Jentzsch

CAPANNELLE (ITY) (good to firm)
Sunday September 5th

3796 Premio Villa Borghese (Listed) (3-y-o) £20,173 1m 3f.................. (2:00)

1888[6] MR RICHARD (Ire) 8-8 M Pasquale,.............................. 1
2925[9] DI GIACOMO 8-8 F Jovine, *rcd in second, led 4 fs out till one and a half out, one pace*..................................... 2
1322[3] DARK STREET (Ire) 8-8 B Jovine,.............................. 3
1364[7] MAD MARTIGAN 8-8 G Bietolini,.............................. 4
1364 LIFE EXTENSION 5
Dist: 2l, 1l, 6l, 10l. 2m 18.00s. (5 Ran).
(Scuderia Ri Ma), L Camici

3797 Premio Mexico Maiden (2-y-o) £5,603 1m.......................................(3:00)

SIR DANCER (Ity) 8-11 D Zarroli,.............................. 1
MR EUGENE (Ire) 8-11 A Corniani,.............................. 2
LETROIS MAILLETZ (Ire) 8-11 S Morales,.............................. 3
3218[7] BARACCA (Ire) 8-11 F Jovine, *nvr dngrs*.............................. 6
Dist: 1l, 4l, nk, 2 ¼l, ¾l, 1½l, 1l, hd, 2l, hd. 1m 39.80s. (17 Ran).
(R Del Gizzi), A Bellogi

FLORENCE (ITY) (good)
Sunday September 5th

3798 Premio Toscana (Listed) (2-y-o) £20,173 7f 110yds.............. (3:50)

2257* SPAGHETTI WESTERN (Ire) 8-11 J Reid, *made all, ran on wl fnl furlong*.. 1
PETER COYOTE (Ire) 8-8 L Dettori,.............................. 2
2145* ASHOKA 8-8 E Tasende,.............................. 3
2649[8] STONY BEST (Ire) 8-8 G Scardino,.............................. 4
SKY MELODY (Ire) 8-8 S Landi,.............................. 5
SOLDATI (Ity) 8-8 C Colombi,.............................. 6
1647[5] ANOTHER BOLD (Ity) 8-8 A Luongo,.............................. 7
2649[6] CASTEL RUNDEGG (Ity) 8-11 A Sauli,.............................. 8
Dist: 1½l, 1l, ½l. (Time not taken) (8 Ran).
(Gerecon Italia), J L Dunlop

LONGCHAMP (FR) (good)
Sunday September 5th

3799 Prix d'Arenberg (Group 3) (2-y-o) £23,895 5f...................... (1:25)

3413[2] KEY OF LUCK (USA) 8-11 W R Swinburn (2) *led, rdn and quickened one furlong out, ran on wl fnl furlong*. ....(29 to 10) 1
EAGLE EYED (USA) 8-11 Pat Eddery (1) *rcd in 3rd, rdn 2 fs out, ran on, no ch wth wnr*..................(18 to 10) 2
3413[5] CASLON (Fr) 8-8 D Boeuf (4) *rcd in 4th, effrt 2 fs out, one pace*.......................................(89 to 10) 3
3413* SHOALHAVEN (USA) 8-11 G Mosse (3) *rcd in second, rdn 2 fs out, wknd one out*.......................(10 to 7 on) 4
Dist: 3l, 1l, 1½l. 57.90s. a 2.40s (4 Ran).
SR: 29/17/10/7/ (Mme F Boutin), F Boutin

3800 Emirates Prix du Moulin de Longchamp (Group 1) (3-y-o and up) £107,527 1m.................. (3:10)

3369[3] KINGMAMBO (USA) 3-8-11 C Asmussen (9) *prmnt, 3rd strt, led o'r one and a half fs out till one out, led 110 yards out, ran on wl*..........................(27 to 10) 1
3369[2] SKI PARADISE (USA) 3-8-8 T Jarnet (6) *prmnt, 4th strt, rdn to join ldr one and a half fs out, led one out till fnl 110 yards*..(27 to 10) 2
2905* BIGSTONE (Ire) 3-8-11 D Boeuf (3) *mid-div, 7th strt, rdn on outsd 2 fs out, ran on wl fnl furlong*.....(6 to 4 fav) 3
2253[5] BARATHEA (Ire) 3-8-11 Pat Eddery (11) *mid-div, 8th strt, swtchd to outsd 2 fs out, fnshd wl, no ch wth wnr*. ....(81 to 10) 4
3618[6] ASTAIR (Fr) 3-8-11 W Mongil (2) *rear early, 6th strt, effrt and quickened 2 fs out, no extr fnl furlong*....(29 to 1) 5
3369[5] GOLD SPLASH (USA) 3-8-8 G Mosse (4) *rear, 9th strt, rdn 2 fs out, nrst finish*..........................(17 to 1) 6
1749[3] VENTIQUATTROFOGLI (Ire) 3-8-11 W Carson (1) *al prmnt, 5th strt, rdn 2 fs out, no extr fnl furlong*.......(36 to 1) 7
3468[7] FITZCARRALDO (USA) 3-8-11 W R Swinburn (10) *trkd ldr, ev ch 2 fs out, sn wknd*..................... (81 to 10) 8
2905[4] CULTURE VULTURE (USA) 4-8-13 T Quinn (7) *rear till some late hdwy*.......................................(92 to 10) 9
2298[4] TAKE RISKS (Fr) 4-9-2 F Head (5) *al beh*..............(35 to 1) 0
3369[8] HUDO (USA) 3-8-11 E Saint-Martin (8) *led till jst und 2 fs out*...(27 to 10) 0
Dist: Hd, nose, 1½l, ½l, 1l, nk, 3l, 2l, 2½l. 1m 37.60s. a 0.10s (11 Ran).
SR: 72/68/70/65/63/57/59/50/46/ (S S Niarchos), F Boutin

3801 Prix des Tourelles (Listed) (3-y-o and up) £14,337 1½m...............(4:45)

1033[8] ENCOREMOI (USA) 3-8-7 E Saint-Martin,.............................. 1
EGYPTOWN (Fr) 4-9-5 O Doleuze,.............................. 2
ERDIYA (USA) 3-8-7 G Mosse,.............................. 3
3149[4] AUBE INDIENNE (Fr) 3-8-11 C Asmussen,.............................. 4
DELLAGRAZIA (USA) 3-8-7 O Peslier,.............................. 5
LA FRANCESA (Arg) 5-9-1 F Head,.............................. 6
Dist: ½l, hd, 3l, ½l, 1l, 1½l, 2½l. 2m 30.40s. a 1.30s (8 Ran).
SR: 56/67/54/52/-/-/ (Mrs Lucy Young Boutin), F Boutin

SAN SIRO (ITY) (good to soft)
Sunday September 5th

3802 Premio Nova (2-y-o) £5,603 7f 110yds ....(2:20)

BEAT OF DRUMS 8-11 E Botti,.............................. 1
MR ARTISTIC (USA) 8-11 L Sorrentino, *rcd in 3rd, led 2 and a half fs out till one and a half out, one pace*.......... 2

EL RASHID (Ire) 8-11 S Soto, ... 3
Dist: 3½l, 1l, ½l, 3½l, 5½l, ½l, 14l. 1m 34.60s. (8 Ran).
(Dr Carlo Vittadini), G Botti

3803 Premio Eupili (Listed) (2-y-o) £20,173 6f............................ (3:20)

3339* STRAIGHT ARROW 8-11 A Munro, *made all, very easily.* 1
1221* ULTIMO IMPERATORE 8-8 L Piggott, *rcd in 3rd, second 2 fs out, no imprsn..*.................................... 2
SPRINT BEST (Ire) 8-8 L Sorrentino, ... 3
BOLDROUS 8-8 M Esposito, ... 4
GOFFREDO GORI (Ire) 8-8 S Dettori, ... 5
WINNER RUSH (Ire) 8-8 M Tellini, ... 6
BAONERO (Ire) 8-8 M Botti, ... 7
Dist: 2½l, 5l, nk, 1l, nose, ¾l. 1m 12.20s. (7 Ran).
(J R Bailey), Lord Huntingdon

BELMONT PARK (USA) (firm)
Sunday September 5th

3804 Go For Wand Stakes (Group 1) (3-y-o and up) £79,470 1m.................

1691* TURNBACK THE ALARM (USA) 4-8-11 C Antley, ... (6 to 5) 1
3207[4] NANNERL (USA) 6-8-4 J D Bailey, ...(43 to 10) 2
3207[2] NOVEMBER SNOW (USA) 4-8-4 M Smith, ...(Evens fav) 3
TEDDY'S TOP TEN (USA) 4-8-2 J Santos, ... (10 to 1) 4
Dist: 1 ¼l, hd, 1l. 1m 36.02s. (4 Ran).
(Moyglare Stud Farm), W Terrill

GALWAY (IRE) (good to firm)
Monday September 6th

3805 Waterford Crystal Handicap (0-90 3-y-o and up) £7,022 1½m.......... (5:30)

3772* GLENBRACK [-] 3-8-10 (6*,5ex) J A Heffernan (7) ...(4 to 1) 1
3382* BOTHSIDESNOW (Ire) [-] (bl) 3-8-9 (2*) P Carberry (10) ....(7 to 1) 2
3560[3] PARNALA (USA) [-] 3-9-3 J P Murtagh (1)...... (7 to 2 fav) 3
3732 NO DUNCE (Ire) [-] 3-7-10 (8*) R T Fitzpatrick (9).. (12 to 1) 4
3604[6] LYPHARD ABU (Ire) [-] (bl) 5-9-0 C Roche (8).......(8 to 1) 5
3525[4] NATIVE PORTRAIT [-] 6-7-10 (6*) R V Skelly (2) .....(6 to 1) 6+
2842 WESBEST (Ire) [-] 4-8-5 N G McCullagh (6) .... (14 to 1) 6+
3336[6] AIYBAK (Ire) [-] 5-9-11 M J Kinane (3) .... (6 to 1) 8
3484[3] BLUE DIANA (Ire) [-] 3-8-8 J F Egan (5) ....(14 to 1) 9
3578[8] SIMPLY MARILYN (Ire) [-] 4-8-10 (4*) J J Behan (12) (10 to 1) 10
3525[7] IMAD (USA) [-] 3-9-1 W J Supple (4) .... (10 to 1) 11
3336[9] SUPER FLAME (Can) [-] (bl) 6-9-7 P V Gilson (11)....(8 to 1) 12
Dist: 2l, 2l, 2½l, 3l. 2m 39.70s. (12 Ran).
(John Bernard O'Connor), Patrick Joseph Flynn

3806 O'Leary Off Licence & Lounge Bar Nursery (2-y-o) £3,452 7f........(6:00)

3683* MANAAFIS (Ire) [-] 9-3 (2ex) W J Supple (7).... (2 to 1 fav) 1
3611[6] RAZIDA (Ire) [-] 9-2 C Roche (4)................. (9 to 4) 2
3243* NEVER TOLD (Ire) [-] 8-11 P V Gilson (5) ....(6 to 1) 3
3379[3] MY RAGAMUFFIN (Ire) [-] 8-13 J P Murtagh (8) .....(7 to 1) 4
3379[9] DANCING BRIEF (Ire) [-] 7-7 (2*) D G O'Shea (2)...(20 to 1) 5
3416[5] WHEREWILITALL END (Ire) [-] 7-13 (4*) J J Behan (3) ....(12 to 1) 6
3613 SHIOWEN (Ire) [-] 8-0 (6*) D J O'Donohoe (6) ......(10 to 1) 7
3243[7] MALT LEAF (Ire) [-] 7-7 Joanna Morgan (1) ....(12 to 1) 8
Dist: Nk, 2l, 1l, 2l. 1m 31.30s. (8 Ran).
(Hamdan Al-Maktoum), Kevin Prendergast

3807 Castlegar E.B.F. (Fillies) Maiden (2-y-o) £3,797 7f.................. (6:30)

PROFIT RELEASE (Ire) 9-0 M J Kinane (2)...... (7 to 4 on) 1
3683[7] TRAGIC POINT (Ire) 9-0 C Roche (8) .... (10 to 1) 2
3451[3] SARANGA (Ire) 9-0 J P Murtagh (10) .... (9 to 2) 3
3110[3] ASTRADANE (Ire) 9-0 W J Supple (1) .... (12 to 1) 4
2666[3] INSUPERABLE (Ire) 9-0 N G McCullagh (12) ...... (10 to 1) 5
QUEEN OF ALL BIRDS (Ire) 9-0 P V Gilson (11)... (14 to 1) 6
2344[3] ONE DAY LATE 9-0 P Shanahan (5) .... (16 to 1) 7
CLODAGHS FANCY (Ire) 8-8 (6*) J A Heffernan (6) (25 to 1) 8
3071[6] SHEER STYLE (Ire) 8-12 (2*) P Carberry (9) .... (10 to 1) 9
3527[6] SAVE THE WEST (Ire) 9-0 J F Egan (7).............(20 to 1) 10
2959[5] LADY COUNSEL (Ire) 9-0 R Hughes (4) ....(20 to 1) 11
MARROWFAT LADY (Ire) 9-0 B Coogan (3) .... (16 to 1) 12
Dist: 6l, 1½l, nk, 4l. 1m 31.30s. (12 Ran).
(Moyglare Stud Farm), D K Weld

3808 Lydon House Maiden (3-y-o and up) £3,452 1m 100yds.............. (7:00)

RADICAL TACTIC (USA) 3-9-0 M J Kinane (14) (9 to 4 fav) 1
3616[4] TALES OF HEARSAY (Ger) 3-9-0 S Craine (4) ..... (11 to 4) 2
BAJAN QUEEN (Ire) 3-8-11 P V Gilson (9) .... (10 to 1) 3
2703[2] ADOLESCENCE (Ire) 3-8-11 P Shanahan (10) ...... (6 to 1) 4
3417[9] SHANGANOIR (Ire) 3-8-9 (2*) P Carberry (7) ...... (20 to 1) 5
3242[6] SCALP (Ire) 3-9-0 K J Manning (11) .... (12 to 1) 6
3720[3] ANOTHER SKY-LARK (Ire) 5-9-5 N Byrne (6) ......(20 to 1) 7
MERSADA (Ire) 3-8-11 C Roche (12) .... (10 to 1) 8
3497[2] COUTURE DIAMANT (Ire) 3-8-9 (2*) R M Burke (13) (10 to 1) 9
3579[8] ANVIL SPARK (Ire) 3-8-11 J F Egan (2) .... (33 to 1) 10
3579[2] CERTAIN PROSPECT 3-8-11 J P Murtagh (15) ..... (6 to 1) 11
2675[6] SLEET (Ire) 3-8-3 (8*) J J Mullins (3) ....(20 to 1) 12
577[8] RUNNING GUEST (Ire) 3-8-11 D Hogan (5) .... (20 to 1) 13
Dist: Nk, 1½l, sht-hd, 3l. 1m 49.20s. (13 Ran).
(Moyglare Stud Farm), D K Weld

HAMILTON (firm)
Monday September 6th

Going Correction: MINUS 0.35 sec. per fur. (races 1,2), MINUS 0.50 (3,4,5,6)

3809 EBF Lord Hamilton Of Dalzell Median Auction Maiden Stakes Class E (2-y-o) £4,142 6f 5yds................... (2:15)

3597[8] JASARI (Ire) 9-0 L Dettori (3) *made most, drw clr frm 2 fs out, easily*............ (5 to 1 op 4 to 1 tchd 11 to 2) 1
3589[5] KEFAHI (Ire) 9-0 B Raymond (6) *dsptd ld, rdn o'r 2 fs out, kpt on, no ch wth wnr*........ (2 to 1 on op 7 to 4 on) 2
3143[9] GOOD SPIRITS 8-9 M Birch (1) *in tch, outpcd hfwy, kpt on fnl 2 fs*.........................(50 to 1 op 25 to 1) 3
3443[3] VANESSA ROSE 8-9 A Mackay (5) *slwly into strd, sn in tch, one pace fnl 2 fs*................ (6 to 1 op 5 to 1) 4
BEE DEE BEST (Ire) 9-0 J Fanning (4) *dsptd ld till wknd o'r 2 fs out*.......................... (50 to 1 op 25 to 1) 5
RED MARCH HARE 8-9 J Fortune (2) *chsd ldrs till rdn and wknd o'r 2 fs out*.................(50 to 1 op 25 to 1) 6
MARGOT'S BOY 9-0 G Duffield (8) *strted slwly, al beh.* ....(50 to 1 op 25 to 1) 7
3613 DIAMOND FRONTIER (Ire) (bl) 9-0 J Carroll (7) *cl up to hfwy, sn wknd*.......................... (12 to 1 op 8 to 1) 8
Dist: 5l, 2l, 1l, 4l, 6l, sht-hd, 3½l. 1m 11.60s. a 0.90s (8 Ran).
SR: 40/20/7/3/-/ (The Winning Team), R Hannon

3810 EBF 'Myson Compact' Maiden Stakes Class D (2-y-o) £4,142 6f 5yds...(2:45)

3589[2] STORM SHIP (Ire) 9-0 B Raymond (9) *made all, styd on wl und pres fnl furlong.* ....(7 to 4 on op 6 to 4 on tchd 11 to 8 on) 1
2804[7] FRISKY MISS (Ire) 8-9 J Carroll (4) *wth wnr, ev ch one furlong out, no extr und pres.* .... (12 to 1 op 10 to 1 tchd 14 to 1) 2
3713[4] SKY DIVER 9-0 K Darley (6) *trkd ldrs, ev ch 2 fs out, kpt on same pace*............................(3 to 1 op 9 to 4) 3
3183 MONKEY FACE 8-2 (7*) P Roberts (7) *in tch, sn pushed alng, kpt on fnl 2 fs, not trble ldrs.* (50 to 1 op 25 to 1) 4
3602[2] SURPRISE GUEST (Ire) 9-0 G Duffield (5) *slwly into strd, sn in tch, rdn and wknd o'r 2 fs out*.... (6 to 1 op 5 to 1) 5
3470 HESFINMENTALTOO 9-0 A Mackay (2) *slwly into strd, wl beh till some late hdwy, nvr dngrs.* ....(20 to 1 tchd 25 to 1) 6
3377[6] THUNDERBIRD TWO (Ire) (v) 9-0 M Birch (1) *pld hrd early, swrvd aftr one furlong, prmnt till wknd quickly hfwy, tld off*...........................(66 to 1 op 50 to 1) 7
3566 PEASAN 8-11 (3*) S D Williams (3) *trkd ldrs till rdn and wknd quickly o'r 2 fs out, tld off*...................(100 to 1) 8
Dist: 2l, 4l, 5l, 3l, nk, 20l, 6l. 1m 11.60s. a 0.90s (8 Ran).
SR: 40/27/16/-/-/ (Jimmy Strauss), A A Scott

3811 Hamilton Palace Claiming Stakes Class F (3-y-o) £3,184 1m 65yds (3:15)

3634[2] KING PARIS (Ire) (bl) 9-4 M Hills (11) *trkd ldr, led 3 fs out, sn clr, eased fnl furlong, very easily.* ....(5 to 4 fav op 11 to 8 tchd 6 to 4) 1
1892* NUTTY BROWN (v) 9-0 (3*) O Pears (13) *led till hdd 3 fs out, kpt on, no ch wth wnr*..............(8 to 1 op 7 to 1) 2
3311[7] AMERIGUE 8-8 N Connorton (10) *mid-div, hdwy 4 fs out, kpt on same pace fnl 2 furlongs.* ....(17 to 2 op 7 to 1 tchd 10 to 1) 3
3628[4] MISSED THE BOAT (Ire) 8-9 L Dettori (15) *mid-div, outpcd 3 fs out, kpt on wl fnl furlong*.......(12 to 1 op 10 to 1) 4
3564 DAYTONA BEACH (Ire) (bl) 9-7 K Darley (1) *in tch, hdwy o'r 3 fs out, one pace 2 out*...........(20 to 1 op 14 to 1) 5
3788[5] DRUMDONNA (Ire) 8-8 J Carroll (5) *in tch, no hdwy fnl 3 fs.* .... (10 to 1 op 8 to 1) 6
3631 HOD-MOD (Ire) 8-11 A Mackay (6) *prmnt, ev ch 3 fs out, one pace*..........(16 to 1 tchd 20 to 1 and 25 to 1) 7
3355 VELVET HEART (Ire) (v) 7-7 (7*) C Adamson (9) *mid-div, hdwy o'r 3 fs out, wknd 2 out*....(10 to 1 tchd 12 to 1) 8
2005[3] EURYTHMIC 9-2 J Fanning (7) *in tch, effrt o'r 3 fs out, sn btn*................................(7 to 1 op 6 to 1) 9
2454[7] SAINTED SUE 7-13 (3*) S Maloney (3) *prmnt till wknd quickly o'r 2 fs out, tld off.* ....(66 to 1 op 50 to 1 tchd 100 to 1) 10
3355[8] MAGIC FAN (Ire) (bl) 8-9 B Raymond (14) *al beh, tld off.* ....(33 to 1) 11
3301[5] SAXON MAGIC 8-10 J Weaver (12) *prmnt till wknd o'r 2 fs out, eased whn btn, tld off.* .... (20 to 1 op 16 to 1 tchd 33 to 1) 12

136[5] BALLACASCADE 8-6 (7*) J Gracey (8) *al beh, tld off.* ....(25 to 1) 13
3407[7] LORLANNE 8-6 T Williams (4) *dwlt, al beh, tld off.* ....(66 to 1 op 25 to 1 tchd 100 to 1) 14
CINDERS GIRL 9-2 J Fortune (2) *in tch till wknd quickly o'r 3 fs out, wl tld off*..........(50 to 1 op 33 to 1) 15
Dist: 3l, 1l, nk, 1l, 2l, nk, 1l, ¾l, 15l, nk. 1m 45.50s. a 1.50s (15 Ran).
SR: 20/10/-/-/7/-/ (Mrs Pauline Karpidas), M Bell

3812 William Hill Scottish Trophy Handicap Class E (0-70 3-y-o and up) £7,750 1m 65yds........................ (3:45)

2944[4] BALLYRANTER [48] (v) 4-8-6 M Hills (9) *in tch, steady hdwy 3 fs out, slight ld jst ins fnl furlong, just hld on.* ....(12 to 1 tchd 14 to 1 and 10 to 1) 1
3507[6] ARAK (USA) [66] 5-9-10 G Duffield (12) *cl up, chlgd jst ins fnl furlong, kpt on, just hld*..... (10 to 1 tchd 12 to 1) 2
3553[3] TALENTED TING (Ire) [69] (v) 4-9-13 J Weaver (8) *cl up, led o'r 3 fs out, hdd jst ins fnl furlong, no extr.* ....(12 to 1 op 10 to 1) 3
3042[3] DIACO [58] 8-9-2 A Munro (14) *mid-div, effrt 3 fs out, kpt on same pace fnl 2 furlongs*..........(8 to 1 op 7 to 1) 4
3444[5] IMPERIAL BID (Fr) [68] 5-9-12 N Connorton (16) *chsd ldrs, kpt on same pace fnl 3 fs*.......... (14 to 1 op 12 to 1) 5
3374[8] BOLD MELODY [46] 4-7-11 (7*) C Adamson (7) *in tch, kpt on fnl 3 fs, not rch ldrs*............(25 to 1 op 20 to 1) 6
3429[5] OCARA (USA) [61] 3-9-0 L Dettori (17) *chsd ldrs, rdn o'r 2 fs out, grad wknd.* ....(11 to 2 fav op 7 to 1 tchd 8 to 1 and 5 to 1) 7
3712[2] AFFORDABLE [56] 5-8-11 (3*) O Pears (11) *hld up in tch, effrt o'r 2 fs out, sn btn*..............(7 to 1 op 6 to 1) 8
3714[5] AVISHAYES (USA) [55] 6-8-13 J Fanning (4) *dwlt, nvr nr ldrs*.................(9 to 1 op 8 to 1 tchd 10 to 1) 9
3444[4] BRACKENTHWAITE [51] 3-8-4 T Williams (15) *nvr dngrs.* ....(16 to 1 tchd 20 to 1) 10
3310 MATTS BOY [44] 5-7-13 (3*) S Maloney (13) *nvr dngrs.* ....(20 to 1 op 16 to 1) 11
3375[6] PUBLIC WAY (Ire) [52] 3-8-5 S Webster (5) *al beh.* (33 to 1) 12
3676[6] BLUE GRIT [62] 7-9-6 J Lowe (18) *nvr dngrs.* ....(16 to 1 tchd 20 to 1) 13+
3408[7] EXPRESS GIFT [65] 4-9-4 (5*) Darren Moffatt (3) *al beh.* ....(12 to 1 op 10 to 1 tchd 14 to 1) 13+
3692[6] BEST EFFORT [47] 7-8-5 A Culhane (6) *nvr dngrs.* (33 to 1) 15
3487[7] MENTALASANYTHIN [70] 4-10-0 A Mackay (2) *chsd ldrs till wknd o'r 2 fs out*............................ (16 to 1) 16
3632* HARPOON LOUIE (USA) [75] 3-10-0 K Darley (1) *mid-div till wknd o'r 2 fs out*................ (7 to 1 tchd 8 to 1) 17
3535 SHANNON EXPRESS [45] (v) 6-7-12 (5*) D Wright (10) *led till hdd o'r 3 fs out, wknd 2 out*....................(25 to 1) 18
Dist: Sht-hd, 1½l, 3½l, ¾l, 1½l, sht-hd, nk, 1½l, 1½l, 2l. 1m 44.20s. a 0.20s (18 Ran).
SR: 27/44/42/20/28/1/10/9/3/ (P J Byrnes), H J Collingridge

3813 MacAllan Highland Malt Scotch Whisky Conditions Stakes Class D (2-y-o) £3,785 1m 65yds........... (4:15)

3470* KING CURAN (USA) 9-2 M Hills (5) *wth ldr, led o'r 2 fs out, sn clr, cmftbly*..................(Evens fav tchd 5 to 4) 1
2796* MAKE A NOTE (USA) 9-2 K Darley (2) *trkd ldrs, pushed alng o'r 3 fs out, rdn 2 out, kpt on, no ch wth wnr.* ....(13 to 8 op Evens) 2
3546[2] STARSPORT (Ire) (bl) 8-10 J Carroll (4) *slight ld till hdd o'r 2 fs out, sn btn*..........(11 to 1 op 8 to 1 tchd 12 to 1) 3
2102[9] DEER IN THE GLEN 8-5 J Weaver (3) *hld up and beh, effrt 3 fs out, no real hdwy*.............. (25 to 1 op 14 to 1) 4
PRISCILLA ROSE 8-5 G Duffield (1) *trkd ldrs, effrt 3 fs out, wknd 2 out*...........................(5 to 1 op 6 to 1) 5
Dist: 2½l, 4l, 1l, 4l. 1m 46.10s. a 2.10s (5 Ran).
SR: 9/1/ (Billy Maguire), M Bell

3814 W. H. Robertson-Aikman Memorial Handicap Class E (0-70 3-y-o and up) £4,077 1½m 17yds............. (4:45)

3444[8] AMERICAN HERO [53] 5-9-6 J Weaver (13) *made all, clr o'r one furlong out, eased towards finish, unchlgd.* ....(14 to 1 op 10 to 1) 1
3356 SEA PADDY [48] 5-8-8 (7*) H Bastiman (12) *mid-div, effrt 3 fs out, kpt on wl fnl furlong, no ch wth wnr.* ....(12 to 1 op 10 to 1) 2
3565* IRON BARON (Ire) [46] 4-8-8 (5*) D Wright (1) *chsd wnr, ev ch 3 fs out, wndrd und pres one out, no extr.* ....(11 to 2 op 9 to 2) 3
3003[5] KINOKO [50] 5-9-3 K Darley (2) *hld up, hdwy o'r 3 fs out, one pace fnl 2 furlongs*.............. (7 to 1 op 6 to 1) 4
3759[9] MILNGAVIE (Ire) [49] 3-8-7 T Williams (5) *mid-div, effrt o'r 3 fs out, kpt on same pace*..............(8 to 1 op 7 to 1) 5
3552[4] BAJAN AFFAIR [35] 3-7-2 (5*) Darren Moffatt (6) *sn beh, slightly hmpd 7 fs out and 6 out, not trble ldrs.* ....(12 to 1 op 10 to 1) 6
3655[9] STRIKING IMAGE (Ire) [40] 4-8-7 G Duffield (3) *chsd ldrs till wknd o'r 2 fs out*.......(5 to 1 tchd 6 to 1 and 9 to 2) 7
3790[6] SUPER BLUES [49] 6-9-2 L Dettori (9) *mid-div, rdn alng hfwy, some hdwy und pres 5 fs out, wknd o'r 2 out.* ....(9 to 2 fav op 5 to 1 tchd 6 to 1) 8
3530[2] BADAWI (Fr) [39] (bl) 3-7-11 A Mackay (8) *in tch, slightly hmpd 7 fs out, rdn alng 4 out, sn btn.* ....(17 to 2 op 8 to 1 tchd 9 to 1) 9
3466[8] AEGAEN LADY [57] 4-9-10 J Carroll (4) *hld up, some hdwy 4 fs out, wknd o'r 2 out*..........(8 to 1 op 10 to 1) 10
3552[7] FAMOUS BEAUTY [45] 6-8-5 (7*) L Aspell (7) *al beh.* ....(14 to 1 op 10 to 1) 11
3681 HABEEBITTI NADIA [37] 3-7-9 J Lowe (11) *chsd ldrs, sn pushed alng, wknd 4 fs out, tld off*............(50 to 1) 12
Dist: 5l, 1½l, sht-hd, 2½l, 2½l, nk, 2½l, 2l, nk, 1½l. 2m 32.90s. b 0.10s (12 Ran).
SR: 47/32/27/30/15/-/9/13/-/ (David S Leggate), R Allan

NOTTINGHAM (firm)
Monday September 6th
Going Correction: MINUS 0.30 sec. per fur. (races 1,2), MINUS 0.20 (3,4,5,6,7)

3815 Newport Selling Nursery Stakes Class G (2-y-o) £2,070 6f 15yds....... (2:30)

3677[2] DAILY STAR [62] 9-7 W R Swinburn (12) *nvr far away, improved to ld o'r one furlong out, pushed clr ins last.* ....(11 to 2 op 5 to 1 tchd 13 to 2) 1
3641[3] MONSIEUR PETONG [58] 8-10 (7*) R Painter (17) *tucked away on ins, effrt and pushed alng 2 fs out, kpt on inside last, no ch wth wnr*...........(8 to 1 op 5 to 1) 2
3126[4] WARWICK WARRIOR (Ire) [53] 8-12 T Quinn (14) *pressed ldrs, effrt and swtchd ins 2 fs out, kpt on same pace inside last*..........................(7 to 1 op 10 to 1) 3
3597 CHIEF EXECUTIVE [55] 9-0 Pat Eddery (10) *led till hdd o'r 2 fs out, sn drvn alng, one pace over one out.* ....(7 to 1 op 5 to 1) 4
3490[9] HALI (Ire) [59] 9-4 F Norton (1) *wth ldrs, led o'r 2 fs out, hdd over one out, edgd lft and sn one pace.* ....(14 to 1 op 8 to 1) 5
3715 CHEEKY CHAPPY [57] (bl) 9-2 A McGlone (6) *nvr far away, drvn alng last 2 fs, not quicken*....(14 to 1 op 10 to 1) 6
3657[3] BURMA STAR [49] 8-8 N Adams (4) *chsd ldrs, sn pushed alng, unbl to quicken fnl 2 fs.* ....(10 to 1 op 8 to 1 tchd 14 to 1) 7
3600[7] BATIEN'S RIVER [53] (v) 8-12 Dale Gibson (8) *mid-div, drvn hfwy, no imprsn o'r one furlong out.* ....(20 to 1 op 16 to 1) 8+
3598 SONIC (Ire) [45] (bl) 8-4 L Charnock (16) *in tch, rdn alng hfwy, not quicken fnl 2 fs*....................(33 to 1) 8+
3189[9] SNUGFIT ANNIE [50] 8-9 A Tucker (9) *dwlt, beh and sn pushed alng, kpt on ins last, nvr able to chal.* (25 to 1) 10
3546[4] FLAIR LADY [54] 8-13 T Sprake (3) *pressed ldrs on outer, effrt and drvn alng hfwy, btn wl o'r one furlong out.* ....(16 to 1 op 12 to 1) 11
2695[8] TAUFELIANE [56] 9-1 Paul Eddery (15) *sn pushed alng beh ldg grp, struggling frm hfwy.* (100 to 30 fav op 5 to 1) 12
3563 HONEST WOMAN [52] (bl) 8-11 W Carson (13) *pressed ldg bunch, drvn alng hfwy, fdd*..... (14 to 1 tchd 16 to 1) 13
3236[8] CREEK VALLEY [52] 8-11 K Fallon (2) *beh, shaken up hfwy, swtchd ins wl o'r one furlong out, nvr nr to chal.* ....(9 to 1 op 8 to 1 tchd 10 to 1) 14
3566 GRECIAN GARDEN [52] (bl) 8-11 J O'Reilly (7) *sluggish strt, al beh*..........................(16 to 1 op 8 to 1) 15
3686 DUCHESS DAISY [45] (bl) 8-4 Kim Tinkler (11) *strted slwly, sn outpcd and al wl beh*...........(50 to 1 op 25 to 1) 16
Dist: 3l, ½l, 2l, ¾l, ¾l, 3l, ½l, dd-ht, 1l, 1½l. 1m 13.40s. a 1.90s (16 Ran).
SR: 33/17/10/4/5/-/ (Express Newspapers Plc), J Berry

3816 Tattersalls Maiden Auction Series Stakes Qualifier Class D (2-y-o) £3,816 6f 15yds...................... (3:00)

3557[2] MARY HINGE 8-2 Paul Eddery (14) *nvr far away, improved to ld o'r 2 fs out, rdn and kpt on ins fnl furlong*..............(7 to 4 fav tchd 2 to 1) 1
3520[5] LA RESIDENCE 8-7 N Adams (13) *dsptd ld, hdd o'r 2 fs out, sn drvn alng, kpt on ins last.* ....(7 to 1 op 8 to 1 tchd 10 to 1) 2
2179[9] STOREY'S GATE (Ire) 8-8 W R Swinburn (11) *pressed ldrs, effrt and rdn last 2 fs, kpt on und pres ins last.* ....(16 to 1 op 12 to 1) 3
3432[2] MILLION LIGHTS (Ire) 8-4 W Ryan (9) *dsptd ld for wl o'r 3 fs, drvn alng and one pace appr last.* ....(6 to 1 op 5 to 1 tchd 13 to 2) 4
3287[7] NOBLE SPIRIT (Ire) 8-11 A McGlone (15) *beh stands side, not clr run o'r 2 fs out, swtchd and styd on strly fnl furlong, nrst finish*.............. (20 to 1 op 16 to 1) 5
3642 AT THE SAVOY (Ire) 8-6 K Fallon (17) *beh on ins, pushed alng aftr 2 fs, improved o'r one out, nvr nrr.* ....(33 to 1 op 20 to 1) 6
3520[2] LIME STREET BLUES (Ire) 8-11 Pat Eddery (7) *prmnt, drvn alng o'r 2 fs out, no extr over one out.* ....(11 to 4 op 2 to 1 tchd 3 to 1) 7
3711[3] ANTANANARIVO (Ire) 8-7 W Carson (2) *in tch on outer, bustled alng whn pace quickened 2 fs out, no extr.* ....(17 to 2 op 6 to 1 tchd 9 to 1) 8

LEVIATHAN MYSTERY 8-7 J Williams (1) *chsd ldg grp, shaken up o'r 2 fs out, no imprsn over one out.* ....(20 to 1 op 16 to 1) 9

3520[9] UNCLE DOUG 8-12 J Quinn (10) *chsd ldrs gng wl, shaken up 2 fs out, one pace, not knocked abt.* ....(20 to 1 op 12 to 1) 10

SPANISH DAWN 8-4 T Quinn (12) *chsd ldrs till rdn and wknd fnl 2 fs*......................(10 to 1 op 4 to 1) 11

2453[4] BEDAZZLE 8-8 M Wigham (4) *dwlt, pushed alng in rear hfwy, not rch ldrs*..........(33 to 1 op 20 to 1) 12

1814[3] WHARFEDALE MUSIC 8-1 Dale Gibson (3) *pressed ldrs on outer, feeling pace o'r 2 fs out, fdd.* (20 to 1 op 16 to 1) 13

3573[9] RISK OF FIRE 8-6 D Harrison (8) *dwlt, pushed alng in rear hfwy, nvr on terms*..........(20 to 1 op 14 to 1) 14

1863[8] LUNAR RHAPSODY 8-1 G Hind (6) *co'red up beh ldrs, rdn alng hfwy, sn btn*..........(33 to 1 op 25 to 1) 15

3520 RED DANCER 8-3 (3*) M Fenton (5) *beh, struggling aftr 2 fs, nvr wnt pace*..... (25 to 1 op 20 to 1 tchd 33 to 1) 16

3052[9] SKELTON PRINCESS (Ire) 7-8 (7*) M Humphries (16) *slwly into strd, sn reco'red to press ldg grp, wknd frm hfwy.* ....(33 to 1 op 25 to 1) 17

Dist: ¾l, sht-hd, 1l, 2½l, nk, 2l, 2l, ½l, hd, 3½l. 1m 12.70s. a 1.20s (17 Ran).
SR: 28/30/30/22/19/13/10/-/-/ (Mrs J Cecil), Mrs J Cecil

3817 British Gas Autumn Campaign Maiden Stakes Class D (3-y-o and up) £3,523 1m 54yds............... (3:30)

MEADOW PIPIT (Can) 4-9-1 G Hind (5) *pressed ldrs, improved on ins to ld o'r 2 fs out, shaken up and styd on fnl furlong*.....................(10 to 1 op 9 to 2) 1

3272[7] KESTON POND (Ire) 3-9-0 W R Swinburn (8) *trkd ldr, rdn and ev ch 3 fs out, styd on ins last, not rch wnr.* .... (4 to 1 tchd 9 to 2 and 7 to 2) 2

3456[4] CITTERN 3-9-0 W Carson (9) *trkd ldg 3, pushed alng o'r three fs out, sn outpcd, kpt on ins last.* ....(4 to 1 op 2 to 1) 3

3456 ROLLING WATERS 3-9-0 W Ryan (4) *chsd main bunch on inner, shaken up o'r 3 fs out, no imprsn over one out.* .... (40 to 1 op 25 to 1 tchd 50 to 1) 4

3132[2] AUTUMNIS (USA) 3-9-0 Pat Eddery (6) *trkd ldg pair, shaken up o'r 3 fs out, hng rght, sn one pace, eased last*.........................(13 to 8 on op 5 to 4 on) 5

3384 PETITE JUNE (Ire) 3-8-4 (5*) N Gwilliams (1) *led till hdd o'r 3 fs out, rdn and grad wknd*........ (66 to 1 op 33 to 1) 6

3356 HAYDON BRIDGE (Ire) 3-9-0 Paul Eddery (10) *hld up, drvn alng o'r 3 fs out, btn 2 out*........ (25 to 1 op 16 to 1) 7

1762[6] TUSCANIA 3-8-9 Kim Tinkler (3) *beh, detached appr strt, nvr on terms*..................... (66 to 1 op 50 to 1) 8

686[9] FARANDOLE 3-9-0 S Whitworth (2) *sluggish strt, sn pushed alng, detached and struggling aftr 3 fs.* ....(66 to 1 op 50 to 1) 9

Dist: 1½l, 2l, 3½l, 3l, sht-hd, ½l, 7l, 1½l. 1m 42.90s. a 2.90s (9 Ran).
SR: 33/27/21/10/1/-/ (Sheikh Mohammed), J H M Gosden

3818 Levy Board Limited Stakes Class E (0-70 3-y-o) £3,183 1m 54yds.... (4:00)

3670[5] EXHIBIT AIR (Ire) 8-9 Pat Eddery (3) *chsd ldg pair, pushed alng appr strt, pld wide and drvn 3 fs out, ran on to ld ins last, sn clr*.... (11 to 10 fav op Evens tchd 11 to 8) 1

3585 KNOBBLEENEEZE (v) 9-0 S Whitworth (4) *led one furlong, styd upsides, rgned ld o'r 3 out, drvn 2 out, hdd ins last, no extr*............................(8 to 1 op 6 to 1) 2

3219 BALIANA 8-9 K Fallon (1) *sluggish strt, beh and sn outpcd, drvn appr strt, styd on fnl furlong, nvr dngrs.* ....(14 to 1 op 10 to 1) 3

3489[3] WILLOW RIVER (Can) 8-9 W Carson (2) *led aftr one furlong, hdd o'r 3 out, sn rdn and grad wknd.* .... (5 to 4 tchd Evens) 4

Dist: 2½l, 4l, 7l. 1m 43.10s. a 3.10s (4 Ran).
SR: 24/21/4/-/ (Archie Hornall), R Hannon

3819 EBF Hagley Maiden Stakes Class D (2-y-o) £4,092 1m 54yds........... (4:30)

3462[9] MIDNIGHT LEGEND 9-0 W R Swinburn (8) *nvr far away, jnd issue 2 fs out, shaken up and led ins last, ran on wl.* ....(8 to 1 op 5 to 1) 1

3592 IRISH SENOR (Ire) 8-9 (5*) L Newton (5) *chsd ldrs, rdn frm 3 fs out, kpt on wl ins last*.......... (7 to 1 tchd 8 to 1) 2

3009 GAY DEVIL 9-0 Pat Eddery (2) *led, jnd 2 fs out, hdd ins last, no extr, eased towards finish.* (10 to 1 op 5 to 1) 3

3470[6] SUPREME STAR (USA) 9-0 W Ryan (7) *nvr far away, shaken up o'r 3 fs out, one pace over one out.* ....(9 to 4 op 7 to 4 tchd 7 to 2) 4

3592[3] TREE OF HEAVEN 8-9 M Tebbutt (4) *fractious at strt, hld up, effrt and rdn 3 fs out, edgd rght, kpt on ins last, nvr able to chal*.........(6 to 4 fav op 5 to 4 tchd 7 to 4) 5

3592 AHSANT MTOTO 9-0 W Carson (1) *keen hold early, tucked away on ins, effrt and shaken up 3 fs out, wknd wl o'r one out*....................(11 to 1 op 8 to 1) 6

3633 LITTLE IBNR 9-0 M Wigham (3) *sluggish strt, beh, pushed alng entering strt, not pace to chal.* ....(33 to 1 op 16 to 1) 7

PERSIAN LINNET 9-0 K Fallon (6) *hld up in tch, shaken up o'r 2 fs out, sn btn*................(16 to 1 op 10 to 1) 8

Dist: Nk, 1½l, 1½l, 1l, 5l, 1½l, 7l. 1m 45.80s. a 5.80s (8 Ran).
(Umm Qarn Racing), L M Cumani

3820 Bloxwich Limited Stakes Class E (0-70 3-y-o and up) £3,054 1m 1f 213yds ....(5:00)

3572[4] HAROLDON (Ire) 4-9-0 (7*) P McCabe (3) *missed break, keen hold, dsptd ld hfwy, led 2 fs out, edgd lft and ran on gmely ins last*....... (5 to 1 op 6 to 1 tchd 13 to 2) 1

3655[2] MUTAMANNI 3-9-0 W Carson (7) *led, jnd hfwy, hdd 2 fs out, rallied, no extr towards finish.* ....(7 to 4 jt-fav tchd 9 to 4) 2

3456[5] MO-ADDAB (Ire) 3-9-0 A McGlone (4) *hld up in tch, shaken up 4 fs out, drvn 2 out, ran on strly ins last.* ....(4 to 1 op 7 to 2) 3

3710[3] GREEN KILT 3-9-0 W R Swinburn (2) *nvr far away, drvn alng o'r 2 fs out, one pace appr last*..........(7 to 4 jt-fav op 6 to 4) 4

3693 LADY BUCHAN 4-9-2 Kim Tinkler (5) *pressed ldg 4, outpcd appr strt, no dngr fnl 2 fs*.........(25 to 1 op 16 to 1) 5

3324[2] BY QUEEN (Ire) 3-8-9 J Williams (1) *in tch, outpcd o'r 3 fs out, sn btn*.......................(25 to 1 op 16 to 1) 6

MISS KINGFISHER (USA) 4-9-2 Paul Eddery (6) *dwlt, hld up in rear, shaken up 3 fs out, sn btn and eased.* ....(50 to 1 op 33 to 1) 7

Dist: Nk, hd, 3l, 10l, 2l, 1½l. 2m 7.60s. a 4.60s (7 Ran).
SR: 41/33/32/26/8/-/1/ (Lamb Brook Associates), B Palling

3821 Brewood Handicap Class E (0-70 3-y-o and up) £3,494 2m 9yds.........(5:30)

3716[5] BRIGGSMAID [49] 5-8-10 M Tebbutt (6) *confidently rdn in rear, not clr run and weaved through frm 3 fs out, led appr last, pushed clear.* ....(10 to 1 op 8 to 1 tchd 11 to 1) 1

3125[9] IRISH STAMP (Ire) [67] 4-10-0 W Carson (5) *tucked away on ins, effrt and drvn alng 3 fs out, kpt on inside last, no ch wth wnr*........... (8 to 1 op 12 to 1 tchd 14 to 1) 2

3306[7] SPORTS VIEW [41] 4-8-2 Paul Eddery (3) *hld up, took clr order appr strt, ran on to ld 2 fs out, hdd approaching last, one pace*........(14 to 1 op 12 to 1 tchd 16 to 1) 3

3288[9] SINGING REPLY (USA) [36] 5-7-11 J Quinn (14) *hld up, cld entering strt, styd on fnl 2 fs, nrst finish.* ....(16 to 1 op 12 to 1) 4

3716* SAMAIN (USA) [52] 6-8-13 (7ex) N Carlisle (13) *patiently rdn, smooth hdwy 6 fs out, chlgd o'r 2 out, no extr appr last*................ (9 to 4 fav op 2 to 1 tchd 5 to 2) 5

3690[5] FRENCH IVY (USA) [65] (v) 6-9-12 W R Swinburn (18) *nvr far away, improved to ld o'r 3 fs out, hdd 2 out, kpt on same pace*.........................(14 to 1 op 10 to 1) 6

3479[7] FAIRY WISHER (Ire) [40] 4-7-8 (7*) N Varley (2) *chsd ldrs on ins, pushed alng o'r 3 fs out, one pace fnl 2 furlongs.* .... (14 to 1 tchd 16 to 1 and 12 to 1) 7

3456[3] MELODY MOUNTAIN (Ire) [64] 4-9-8 (3*) B Doyle (20) *hld up, beh till styd on o'r 2 fs out, nvr dngrs.* .... (10 to 1 op 7 to 1 tchd 11 to 1) 8

SERAPHIM (Fr) [38] 4-7-13 D Harrison (16) *settled midfield, drvn alng o'r 6 fs out, styd on fnl 2, nvr nrr.* ....(33 to 1 op 25 to 1) 9

3567[2] ANNABEL'S BABY (Ire) [36] 4-7-5[1] (7*) C Hawksley (8) *nvr far away, pushed alng entering strt, no extr fnl 2 fs.* ....(14 to 1 op 12 to 1) 10

3599[8] BALLAD RULER [40] 7-8-1 R Street (15) *drpd out strt, wl beh till styd on fnl 2 fs, nvr nr to chal*.........(50 to 1) 11

3572[5] FAIRGROUNDPRINCESS [32] 5-7-7 N Adams (7) *hld up in tch, pushed alng entering strt, btn o'r 2 fs out.* ....(16 to 1 op 12 to 1) 12

3392[8] IBTIKAR (USA) [45] (v) 3-7-7 L Charnock (9) *co'red up in midfield, took clr order hfwy, rdn appr strt, wknd over 3 fs out*.......................(16 to 1 op 14 to 1) 13

3392[3] MENHAAD (Ire) [54] 3-8-2 A McGlone (11) *midfield, took clr order 7 fs out, rdn and wknd 3 out.* ....(5 to 1 op 6 to 1 tchd 8 to 1) 14

3552[5] HYDROPIC [32] 6-7-7 S Wood (12) *cl up till rdn and wknd entering strt*........ (50 to 1 op 33 to 1 tchd 66 to 1) 15

3556[8] ARC BRIGHT (Ire) [53] (bl) 3-7-10 (5*) A Garth (10) *set gd pace, led till hdd o'r 3 fs out, sn wknd, tld off.* (14 to 1) 16

3572[6] BARBARY REEF (Ire) [33] 5-7-8[1] Dale Gibson (4) *beh, hmpd bend aftr 4 fs, wide strt, sn btn, tld off.* ....(25 to 1 op 20 to 1) 17

3147[6] FATAL SHOCK [45] (bl) 3-7-7 G Bardwell (1) *chsd ldrs, drvn alng 6 fs out, wknd entering strt, tld off.* .... (20 to 1 op 33 to 1 tchd 50 to 1) 18

35[6] STATION EXPRESS (Ire) [33] 5-7-8[4] (3*) N Kennedy (17) *beh, sn struggling, tld off frm hfwy*.... (50 to 1 op 33 to 1) 19

3572[9] DOM WAC [56] 5-9-0 (3*) M Fenton (19) *settled on outer, drvn alng o'r 6 fs out, btn whn broke dwn and pld up over 3 out, destroyed*................ (11 to 1 op 8 to 1) pu

Dist: 3l, nk, 3½l, 1l, ½l, 1l, 3½l, 1½l, ½l, ½l. 3m 27.40s. a 3.20s (20 Ran).
SR: 32/47/20/11/26/38/12/32/4/ (F W Briggs/Park Lane Racing), J M P Eustace

BELMONT PARK (USA) (firm)
Monday September 6th

3822 Jerome Handicap (Grade 1) (3-y-o) £79,470 1m.

SCHOSSBERG (Can) 8-1 J D Bailey,............(24 to 10) 1
WILLIAMSTOWN (USA) 8-6 C Perret,............(6 to 4) 2
779 MI CIELO (USA) 8-4 M Smith,............(6 to 4) 3
1542[5] VIRGINIA RAPIDS (USA) 8-7 E Maple,........(11 to 10 fav) 4
APPRENTICE (USA) 8-0 R Davis,................(13 to 1) 5
Dist: Hd, ½l, ½l, 2½l. 1m 35.53s. (5 Ran).
(S Stavro), P England

DEL MAR (USA) (firm)
Monday September 6th

3823 Del Mar Derby (Grade 1) (3-y-o) £109,271 1m 1f.

1546[3] GUIDE (Fr) 8-10 K Desormeaux,................(11 to 2) 1
4704a[8] FUTURE STORM (USA) 8-10 P Valenzuela,........(86 to 10) 2
THE REAL VASLAV (USA) 8-10 C Nakatani,.....(105 to 10) 3
NONPRODUCTIVEASSET (USA) 8-10 P Atkinson, (29 to 1) 4D
2531[4] FATHERLAND (Ire) 8-10 E Delahoussaye,....(48 to 10 fav) 4
3402[6] BLUES TRAVELLER (Ire) 8-10 A Gryder,.........(73 to 10) 5
1546[5] HAWK SPELL (USA) 8-10 P Day,..................(79 to 10) 6
ZIGNEW (USA) 8-10 D Flores,.................(103 to 10) 7
ART OF LIVING (USA) 8-10 C Black,.............(27 to 1) 8
MANNY'S PROSPECT (USA) 8-10 C McCarron,...(14 to 1) 9
DEVOTED BRASS (USA) 8-10 L Pincay Jr,........(15 to 2) 0
DARE TO DUEL (USA) 8-10 G Stevens,..........(97 to 10) 0
Dist: 1½l, hd, nose, ½l, hd, nose, 1½l, nk, ½l, hd. 1m 49.60s. (12 Ran).
(Exors Of Sir Robin McAlpine), E Bartholomew

GALWAY (IRE) (good to firm)
Tuesday September 7th

3824 Ardilaun House Hotel Oyster Stakes (Listed) (3-y-o and up) £8,627 1½m ....(5:00)

3467[2] ALOUETTE 3-8-7 C Roche (5) *mid-div, rdn 6 fs out, prog to ld 3 out, kpt on strly strt*..............(6 to 4 fav) 1
3199[6] TARAKANA (USA) 3-8-7 R Hughes (7) *hld up, prog 3 out, trkd ldr and ev ch one out, rdn and no extr ins last.* ....(9 to 2) 2
2744[3] JUDICIAL FIELD (Ire) (bl) 4-9-5 M J Kinane (2) *trkd ldr, rdn 3 out, kpt on one pace*...............(7 to 1) 3
3615[3] OENOTHERA (Ire) 3-8-7 S Craine (6) *rear, prog 3 out, rdn, no extr and wknd appr fnl furlong*............(14 to 1) 4
3199[2] KRISDALINE (USA) 3-8-9[2] J P Murtagh (1) *mid-div, prog to track ldrs 3 fs out, rdn and no extr one and a half out, eased whn btn ins last*...............(2 to 1) 5
3542[3] RONDELLI (Ire) 3-8-10 K J Manning (3) *led, quickened 5 out, cld aftr 4 fs*.............(12 to 1) 6
Dist: 1½l, 6l, 1l, 4l. 2m 41.30s. (6 Ran).
(Miss K Rausing), J S Bolger

3825 Long Walk (C&G) E.B.F. Maiden (2-y-o) £3,797 1m 100yds..........(5:30)

3608[2] DANCING SUCCESS (USA) 8-10 (4*) J J Behan (12) (7 to 2) 1
NORDIC VALLEY (Ire) 9-0 C Roche (5)............(6 to 1) 2
3562[2] NUN'S ISLAND (Ire) 9-0 B Coogan (3)............(4 to 1) 3
3683[2] UNBUCKLE (Ire) 9-0 M J Kinane (9)...........(9 to 4 fav) 4
3541[6] SUN MARK (Ire) 9-0 R Hughes (15)..............(14 to 1) 5
3731 RAINBOW IDOL (Ire) 9-0 K J Manning (4).........(25 to 1) 6
WOLFIES RASCAL (Ire) 9-0 P V Gilson (7).........(12 to 1) 7
3492 TORDO (Ire) 9-0 S Craine (14)...................(14 to 1) 8
3608 DR LEUNT (Ire) 9-0 J F Egan (6).................(33 to 1) 9
3731[7] SCHNAPPS 8-12 (2*) P Carberry (13)............(10 to 1) 10
3562[7] ALEXANDER KAHYASI 9-0 N Byrne (11)...........(33 to 1) 11
2666[9] ASTRO REEF (Ire) 9-0 P Shanahan (2)...........(25 to 1) 12
2982 ACTION LAD (Ire) 9-0 N G McCullagh (8).........(33 to 1) 13
3541 RUSTIC LEAGUE (Ire) 9-0 J P Murtagh (1).........(20 to 1) 14
Dist: 1l, ½l, 4l, 2½l. 1m 51.00s. (14 Ran).
(Frederick J Ellis), Liam Browne

3826 Derrinstown Apprentice Handicap (0-75 3-y-o and up) £3,797 1m 100yds ....(6:00)

3544* HANG A RIGHT [-] 6-9-10 (4*,3ex) T P Treacy (1)...(4 to 1) 1
3418[6] ACCELL (Ire) [-] 4-7-13 (6*) G M Moylan (9).......(7 to 1) 2
3770[4] TINCO PALENO [-] 9-9-5 R M Burke (2)........(7 to 2 fav) 3
3418* BRACKLOON BOY (Ire) [-] 4-9-4 (4*) C Everard (4)..(6 to 1) 4
2517[8] TRANQUIL BEAUTY (Ire) [-] 4-9-3 P Carberry (5)....(7 to 1) 5
2692[6] LAST EMPEROR (USA) [-] 6-8-6 (8*) A P Colgan (10) ....(14 to 1) 6
3732[7] TOUCHING MOMENT (Ire) [-] 3-9-3 (8*) J D Moore (6) ....(14 to 1) 7
3543[4] PHASE IN [-] 3-9-3 (8*) W J Walsh (3)..............(4 to 1) 8
2957[9] BOBROSS (Ire) [-] 3-9-1 (8*) W Ryan (7)...........(12 to 1) 9
1645[9] DENZILLE LANE (Ire) [-] 3-7-10 (6*) G Coogan (8)..(40 to 1) 10
Dist: Sht-hd, 1l, ¾l, 2l. 1m 49.90s. (10 Ran).
(Thomas Mullins), P Mullins

3827 Irish Shell Unleaded Handicap (0-65 3-y-o and up) £3,452 7f.........(6:30)

3721[6] SUTTON CENTENARY (Ire) [-] 5-7-8[1] (10*) D A O'Sullivan (9) ....(16 to 1) 1
3576 LUCKY PRINCE (Ire) [-] (bl) 3-9-10 M J Kinane (12) (6 to 1) 2
3544[2] YONOKA (Fr) [-] (bl) 4-10-0 P V Gilson (5)......(2 to 1 fav) 3
3544[6] MASTER WORK [-] (bl) 5-8-0 (4*) J J Behan (2).....(7 to 1) 4
3544[7] DAHAR'S LOVE (USA) [-] (bl) 4-8-6 W J Supple (16) (8 to 1) 5
3076 ARDLEA HOUSE (Ire) [-] 4-7-6 (8*) G M Moylan (1) (12 to 1) 6
3112 BRAZEN ANGEL (Ire) [-] 3-9-4 (6*) J R Barry (14)... (7 to 1) 7
3244* SHESLOOKINATME (Ire) [-] 4-8-13 J P Murtagh (10) (6 to 1) 8
3296[4] OUT OF STEP (Ire) [-] 4-8-1 J F Egan (13)..........(8 to 1) 9
3040[6] RIFLEBIRD (Ire) [-] 3-9-2 P Shanahan (11)........(10 to 1) 10
3578 TAN PRINCESS [-] 6-7-7 Joanna Morgan (3)........(50 to 1) 11
2248 SANDCHORUS (Ire) [-] 3-9-0 (8*) G Coogan (8)....(33 to 1) 12
3160[7] BOLD MOLLY (Ire) [-] (bl) 4-8-4 (2*) R M Burke (15)..(7 to 1) 13
Dist: 1l, 2½l, hd, hd. 1m 13.80s. (13 Ran).
(D G McArdle), D G McArdle

LEICESTER (good to firm)
Tuesday September 7th

Going Correction: MINUS 0.25 sec. per fur. (races 1,2,3,6,7), MINUS 0.35 (4,5)

3828 EBF Filbert Maiden Fillies' Stakes Class D (2-y-o) £4,270 1m 8yds..(2:15)

3659[8] TANDIA 8-11 J Weaver (11) *made all, rdn and ran on wl fnl 2 fs, readily*..... (25 to 1 op 14 to 1 tchd 33 to 1) 1
CUT ADRIFT 8-11 K Darley (6) *trkd ldrs, shaken up frm 2 fs out, kpt on*..................... (10 to 1 op 6 to 1) 2
COIGACH 8-11 W Ryan (7) *outpcd and beh, gd hdwy frm 2 fs out, fnshd wl*......(11 to 2 op 4 to 1 tchd 6 to 1) 3
3209[2] SHORTFALL 8-11 L Dettori (3) *drvn alng frm 3 fs out, styd on und pres fnl furlong.* ....(6 to 4 on tchd 5 to 4 on and 13 to 8 on) 4
3317 VIRGINIA WATER (USA) 8-11 A Munro (9) *chsd ldrs, effrt ins fnl 2 fs, wknd final furlong*.... (33 to 1 op 14 to 1) 5
3659 CRAZY FOR YOU 8-11 G Duffield (8) *pressed wnr early, wknd o'r 2 fs out*.................(33 to 1 op 20 to 1) 6
3625[7] LIMOSA 8-11 P Robinson (4) *mid-div, shaken up and some prog fnl 2 fs*............... (33 to 1 op 20 to 1) 7
GALYPH (USA) 8-11 M Roberts (2) *in tch 5 fs, fdd.* ....(9 to 1 op 5 to 1) 8
WILLOW 8-11 J Quinn (15) *mid-div, nvr rchd ldrs.* ....(25 to 1 op 20 to 1 tchd 33 to 1) 9
DANIELLE HABIBI (Ire) 8-11 Paul Eddery (12) *nvr rchd ldrs.* ....(33 to 1 op 20 to 1) 10
SUGAR TOWN (Ire) 8-11 W Carson (14) *mid-div till wknd fnl 2 fs*........................(16 to 1 op 7 to 1) 11
OUR STELLA 8-11 K Fallon (1) *dwlt, al beh.* ....(50 to 1 op 20 to 1) 12
3592 CLOUDY GEM 8-11 N Connorton (16) *prmnt till wknd o'r 2 fs out*........................(50 to 1 op 20 to 1) 13
2917[6] MISS TUT (Ire) 8-11 N Carlisle (5) *in tch early, sn beh.* ....(100 to 1 op 33 to 1) 14
2862 AVONDALE ROSE 8-11 D Harrison (10) *prmnt to hfwy.* ....(50 to 1 op 20 to 1) 15
ST KITTS 8-11 T Sprake (13) *al outpcd.* ....(50 to 1 op 20 to 1) 16
Dist: 1½l, ¾l, ½l, ¾l, 2½l, 4l, 1½l, 5l, 2l, 5l. 1m 38.00s. a 2.90s (16 Ran).
SR: 24/19/17/15/13/5/ (Trevor Painting), M C Pipe

3829 Rancliffe Nursery Selling Handicap Class G (2-y-o) £2,721 1m 8yds (2:45)

3696[2] MR ROUGH [54] 8-8 (3*) C Hodgson (6) *hdwy 3 fs out, led one and a half out, rdn, edgd lft and kpt on ins last.* ....(7 to 1 op 7 to 2) 1
3563[7] MONSIEUR BLEU [53] 8-10 J Fanning (19) *in tch, led 2 and a half fs out, hdwy one and a half out, kpt on.* ....(12 to 1 op 10 to 1) 2
2973[6] DRAGON MAN [60] 9-3 J Weaver (11) *al in tch, shaken up and kpt on fnl 2 fs*.............. (16 to 1 op 12 to 1) 3
3390[8] CELESTIAL DANCE [52] 8-9 J Carroll (9) *hdwy frm 2 fs out, ran on ins last*........ (9 to 1 op 6 to 1 tchd 10 to 1) 4
3569[5] KNIGHTRIDER [57] 9-0 L Dettori (15) *pressed ldrs, chlgd o'r 2 fs out, wknd ins last*.............(12 to 1 op 7 to 1) 5
3264[4] NORTHERN STARLIGHT [52] (v) 8-9 N Adams (14) *wth ldrs, ev ch 2 fs out, wknd fnl furlong.* ....(12 to 1 op 8 to 1 tchd 14 to 1) 6
2216[3] RITA'S JOY [59] 8-9 (7*) P McCabe (12) *pressed ldrs till wknd 2 fs out*....... (14 to 1 op 10 to 1 tchd 16 to 1) 7
3563[4] CAPITAL LADY (Ire) [48] 8-5 D Harrison (7) *nvr rchd ldrs.* ....(14 to 1 op 8 to 1) 8
3598[9] MINIBAR [47] 8-4 A Mackay (18) *chsd ldrs till wknd o'r 2 fs out*........................ (25 to 1 op 16 to 1) 9
3235[4] GREEK NIGHT OUT (Ire) [50] 8-7 M Roberts (2) *wth ldrs till wknd ins fnl 3 fs*.... (10 to 1 op 7 to 1 tchd 11 to 1) 10
3508 DOUBLE DANCER [57] 9-0 L Charnock (13) *in tch till wknd frm 3 fs out*................ (14 to 1 op 12 to 1) 11
3508 BROUGHTONS PARTNER [52] 8-9 W Carson (17) *nvr rchd ldrs*...............(14 to 1 op 8 to 1) 12

3563 MISS FREEBIE (Ire) [49] 8-6 A Culhane (5) *nvr dngrs.* .... (33 to 1 op 16 to 1) 13
3098^{7} MILLY'S PET [50] 8-7 J Quinn (16) *beh, rdn hfwy, no response*.......... (7 to 2 fav op 12 to 1 tchd 14 to 1) 14
3563^{3} PASSION SUNDAY [62] 9-5 K Darley (10) *al beh.* ....(7 to 1 op 6 to 1 tchd 8 to 1) 15
2705^{7} STEANARD BOY [48] 8-5 F Norton (8) *nvr dngrs.* .... (33 to 1 op 20 to 1) 16
3189^{6} SUPER SYMPHONIC [64] 9-7 P Robinson (1) *made most till hdd 2 and a half fs out, wknd quickly.* .... (14 to 1 op 8 to 1) 17
3390^{9} CARNEGIE BLUE [49] 8-6 G Duffield (3) *in tch to hfwy.* .... (20 to 1 op 10 to 1) 18
3303^{9} FINISHING KIND [42] 7-13 G Bardwell (20) *sn beh.* .... (33 to 1 op 20 to 1) 19
3390 SEMAH'S DREAM [47] 8-4 J O'Reilly (4) *strted slwly, sn wl beh*.............................. (33 to 1 op 20 to 1) 20
Dist: 1½l, ½l, 3½l, hd, 1½l, 1½l, 3l, 1½l, 2l, 4l. 1m 39.10s. a 4.00s (20 Ran).
SR: 7/1/6/-/-/-/ (Robin Akehurst), D Morris

3830 Swan Handicap Class E (0-70 3-y-o and up) £3,600 7f 9yds.......... (3:15)

3047 UNIFICATION (Ire) [41] 4-8-0 A Munro (13) *trkd ldrs, led o'r 2 fs out, drvn out*................ (25 to 1 tchd 33 to 1) 1
3564^{3} NICHODOULA [60] 3-9-1 G Duffield (10) *sn frnt rnk, chlgd frm o'r 2 fs out till no extr wl ins last*........... (8 to 1) 2
3302^{8} YUNUS EMRE (Ire) [45] (v) 3-8-0 D Biggs (9) *hdwy 2 fs out, ran on fnl furlong*............... (16 to 1 op 12 to 1) 3
2371* WILL SOON [63] 4-9-1 (7*) Antoinette Armes (2) *led till hdd o'r 2 fs out, kpt on one pace*....... (14 to 1 op 12 to 1) 4
3458* HOPEFUL BID (Ire) [68] (bl) 4-9-13 Pat Eddery (14) *in tch, kpt on fnl furlong*................ (7 to 1 tchd 8 to 1) 5
3447^{6} KISSAVOS [44] 7-8-3 W Carson (6) *trkd ldrs, drvn and kpt on fnl furlong*................(12 to 1 op 16 to 1) 6
3591^{2} DEAD CALM [52] (v) 3-8-7 M Tebbutt (4) *chsd ldrs, one pace fnl 2 fs*............................(14 to 1 op 12 to 1) 7
3783^{6} AHJAY [52] 3-8-7 J Quinn (5) *in tch, rdn o'r 2 fs out, not pace to chal*.................. (11 to 2 fav op 5 to 1) 8
3564 CICERONE [52] 3-8-7 Dale Gibson (3) *nvr gng pace of ldrs.* .... (25 to 1 op 20 to 1) 9
3593^{6} BEATLE SONG [57] 5-9-2 N Adams (11) *trkd ldrs till wknd 2 fs out*.............. (15 to 2 op 6 to 1 tchd 8 to 1) 10
3747^{9} MAJAL (Ire) [57] 4-9-2 L Charnock (20) *pressed ldrs 5 fs.* .... (16 to 1 op 14 to 1) 11
3661^{2} POYLE AMBER [53] 4-8-12 K Darley (15) *chsd ldrs for o'r 4 fs*.................................(11 to 1 op 10 to 1) 12
3523 ETERNAL FLAME [61] 5-9-1 (5*) B Russell (16) *effrt hfwy, sn wknd*.......................... (10 to 1 op 8 to 1) 13
3468^{8} ROSE FLYER (Ire) [57] 3-8-7 (5*) D McCabe (17) *wth ldrs to hfwy*..(14 to 1) 14
3780 DIWALI DANCER [50] (bl) 3-8-5 F Norton (12) *nvr rchd ldrs.* ....(14 to 1) 15
3447 KIRRIEMUIR [40] 5-7-10^{2} (5*) A Garth (7) *speed 4 fs.* .... (50 to 1 op 33 to 1) 16
3531 ABSO [57] 5-9-2 M Roberts (1) *nvr gng pace of ldrs.* ....(20 to 1) 17
3060 HELLO HOBSON'S (Ire) [65] 3-8-13 (7*) H Bastiman (18) *slwly away, al beh*................ (16 to 1 tchd 25 to 1) 18
NUCLEAR EXPRESS [58] 6-8-10 (7*) S Drowne (8) *chsd ldrs 4 fs*...(25 to 1) 19
1991 KOA [54] (v) 3-8-9 Paul Eddery (19) *nvr dngrs.* .... (33 to 1 op 25 to 1) 20
Dist: Nk, 1½l, 1½l, ¾l, nk, nk, 1¾l, 1½l, 2l, 1½l. 1m 24.40s. a 2.50s (20 Ran).
SR: 22/36/16/33/36/11/14/9/4/ (New House Farm Livery Stables), R Akehurst

3831 Stag Handicap Class E (0-70 3-y-o and up) £4,137 1m 1f 218yds........ (3:45)

1712^{6} GOLD BLADE [48] 4-8-10 W Ryan (18) *gd hdwy o'r 2 fs out, quickened to ld ins last, kpt on wl.* (33 to 1 op 20 to 1) 1
3710* KELIMUTU [47] 4-8-9 (5ex) G Bardwell (13) *drvn and hdwy ins fnl 2 fs, str run final furlong, kpt on.* ....(8 to 1 op 5 to 1 tchd 9 to 1) 2
3656^{3} ROUSITTO [50] 5-8-12 L Dettori (8) *chsd ldrs till led 2 and a half fs out, hdd and outpcd ins last.* (9 to 1 op 14 to 1) 3
3655^{4} TELEPHUS [50] 4-8-12 Pat Eddery (17) *hdwy 4 fs out, ev ch 2 out, kpt on same pace.* .... (7 to 1 tchd 9 to 1 and 6 to 1) 4
3361* CLIBURNEL NEWS (Ire) [55] 3-8-10 P Robinson (7) *hdwy o'r 2 fs out, drvn and styd on same pace frm over one out.* .... (10 to 1 op 6 to 1) 5
3587 ROBENKO (USA) [61] 4-9-9 J Weaver (5) *beh till ran on fnl 2 fs, not a dngr*...................(20 to 1 op 16 to 1) 6
3507^{3} SUPERTOP [60] 5-9-8 Paul Eddery (2) *hdwy o'r 4 fs out, drvn and no imprsn frm over 2 out.* .... (9 to 1 op 10 to 1 tchd 8 to 1) 7
3595^{9} MODEST HOPE (USA) [49] 6-8-6 (5*) A Garth (6) *nvr rchd ldrs*..............................(14 to 1 op 16 to 1) 8
3681* TINSASHE (Ire) [59] 3-9-0 (5ex) M Tebbutt (16) *chsd ldrs, rdn 3 fs out, sn wknd*................. (7 to 2 fav op 5 to 2) 9
3089^{7} ZAAHEYAH (USA) [53] 3-8-8 G Duffield (15) *led till hdd 2 and a half fs out, sn wknd*........ (33 to 1 op 20 to 1) 10
3551^{4} TORGHIA [51] 6-8-13 Dale Gibson (9) *in tch, pressed ldrs o'r 2 fs out, wknd last quarter m*...(33 to 1 op 20 to 1) 11
3630^{7} GOLDEN TORQUE [58] 6-8-13 (7*) H Bastiman (12) *slwly into strd, al beh*.................. (20 to 1 op 16 to 1) 12
$4661a^{2}$ COMTEC'S LEGEND [57] 3-8-12 K Fallon (19) *sn chasing ldrs, wknd o'r 2 fs out*............. (33 to 1 op 25 to 1) 13
2497^{5} TAUTEN (Ire) [56] 3-8-11 S Dawson (11) *al beh*.... (33 to 1) 14
2019^{4} JALCANTO [67] 3-9-8 K Darley (1) *beh frm hfwy.* .... (12 to 1 op 10 to 1) 15
3224^{8} QAMOOS (Ire) [69] 3-9-3 (7*) Lisa Jacobs (4) *in tch till wknd o'r 3 fs out*..................... (25 to 1 tchd 33 to 1) 16
3173 WORTHY MEMORIES [48] 4-8-10 N Carlisle (14) *chsd ldrs till wknd 3 fs out*.................(33 to 1 op 25 to 1) 17
3308* LOWAWATHA [54] 5-8-13 (3*) C Hodgson (3) *pressed ldrs, ev ch 2 and a half fs out, wknd rpdly.* .... (10 to 1 op 7 to 1) 18
3012 WADIA (USA) [67] 3-9-8 W Carson (10) *sn wl beh.* .... (25 to 1 op 20 to 1) 19
Dist: 1l, 1l, 1½l, ¾l, 3l, 1½l, 1½l, nk, 1½l, sht-hd. 2m 4.70s. a 1.80s (19 Ran).
SR: 43/40/41/38/34/41/37/23/25/ (Richard Berenson), N A Graham

3832 Leicestershire Maiden Stakes Class D (3-y-o and up) £3,669 1m 1f 218yds ....(4:15)

COUNT OF FLANDERS (Ire) 3-9-0 M Roberts (8) *in tch, led o'r 2 fs out, quickened clr over one out, easily.* ....(2 to 1 tchd 13 to 8) 1
3512^{2} KARSHI 3-9-0 G Duffield (10) *sn chasing ldrs, outpcd 2 fs out, rdn and ran on ag'n ins last.* ....(11 to 8 fav op 7 to 4) 2
3590^{8} BOMBLET 3-8-9 J Carroll (7) *in tch, led gng wl ins fnl 3 fs, hdd o'r 2 out, styd on same pace*...(16 to 1 op 10 to 1) 3
3590 ADMIRAL'S WELL (Ire) 3-9-0 L Dettori (11) *slwly into strd and beh, hdwy o'r 2 fs out, kpt on same pace.* .... (10 to 1 op 8 to 1) 4
WELLWOTDOUTHINK 7-9-2 K Darley (6) *hdwy 4 fs out, wknd o'r 2 out*........................ (14 to 1 op 16 to 1) 5
3101^{8} RAGAZZO (Ire) 3-9-0 L Charnock (9) *chsd ldrs to hfwy.* ....(66 to 1) 6
EVER SO LYRICAL 3-9-0 W Ryan (12) *beh till some prog last 2 fs*.......................... (50 to 1 op 33 to 1) 7
3491^{7} NAVAJO LOVE SONG (Ire) 3-8-9 W Carson (5) *al beh.* ....(25 to 1) 8
3456 LADY CONFESS 3-8-9 N Adams (1) *al beh*....... (66 to 1) 9
KAMIKAZE 3-9-0 J Weaver (3) *slwly into strd, al beh.* .... (12 to 1 op 6 to 1) 10
2275^{9} SHIP'S TWINE (Ire) 3-8-9 Paul Eddery (2) *chsd ldrs, chlgd 3 fs out, wknd o'r 2 out*............. (20 to 1 op 14 to 1) 11
2776 SILVER SEA (Ire) 3-8-9 P Robinson (4) *led till hdd ins fnl 3 fs, wknd quickly*................ (25 to 1 op 20 to 1) 12
3489^{8} VIRILIS 3-9-0 A Munro (13) *al beh*.... (25 to 1 op 20 to 1) 13
Dist: 1½l, 5l, 3½l, 2½l, ¾l, hd, 7l, 3l, 3l, 2l. 2m 4.60s. a 1.70s (13 Ran).
SR: 48/45/30/28/25/21/20/1/-/ (Sheikh Mohammed), M R Stoute

3833 Rempstone Maiden Stakes Class D (2-y-o) £4,050 7f 9yds............. (4:45)

MYTILENE (Ire) 8-9 L Dettori (5) *al gng wl intch, led one and a half fs out, cmftbly.* ....(9 to 2 op 4 to 1 tchd 5 to 1) 1
3130^{8} RORY 9-0 Paul Eddery (9) *chsd ldrs, shaken up and outpcd fnl furlong, rallied to take second cl hme.* .... (20 to 1 op 16 to 1 tchd 25 to 1) 2
COOL JAZZ 9-0 M Roberts (6) *led till hdd one and a half fs out, eased and ct for second cl hme.* ....(9 to 4 fav op 4 to 1) 3
3265^{2} ASTRAL WEEKS (Ire) 9-0 K Darley (15) *in tch, outpcd 2 fs out, rallied and ran on ag'n ins last.* .... (9 to 1 op 5 to 1 tchd 10 to 1) 4
AUGUSTAN 9-0 J Weaver (17) *drvn to chase ldrs hfwy, no imprsn fnl 2 fs*...................... (33 to 1 op 16 to 1) 5
3592^{9} JUST FLAMENCO 9-0 D Biggs (18) *chsd ldrs, ev ch one and a half fs out, sn fdd*.......................(33 to 1) 6
WALDO 9-0 D Harrison (4) *trkd ldrs, no imprsn frm 2 fs out*.............................. (33 to 1 op 20 to 1) 7
SWALLOWS DREAM (Ire) 9-0 A Munro (11) *beh, effrt 3 fs out, no imprsn frm o'r 2 out*....... (33 to 1 op 14 to 1) 8
DAWN DEFENDER (Ire) 9-0 N Adams (8) *beh till kpt on fnl 2 fs, not a dngr*..................(33 to 1 op 20 to 1) 9
MAKHRAJ (USA) 9-0 W Carson (12) *al in rear.* .... (12 to 1 op 8 to 1 tchd 14 to 1) 10
NIGHT BOAT 9-0 S Raymont (3) *al beh.* .... (50 to 1 op 20 to 1) 11
1456^{3} ICY HOT (Ire) 9-0 W Ryan (2) *chsd ldrs 5 fs.* ....(6 to 1 op 4 to 1) 12
GOLDEN BALL (Ire) 9-0 Pat Eddery (1) *prmnt, pressed ldrs hfwy, wknd o'r 2 fs out.* (9 to 2 op 7 to 4 tchd 5 to 1) 13
3446 SALTCORN (Ire) 9-0 N Connorton (16) *chsd ldrs o'r 4 fs.* .... (50 to 1 op 33 to 1) 14
3589 PAPPA'S PET 9-0 P Robinson (13) *al beh.* .... (33 to 1 op 25 to 1) 15
DOUBLING DICE 9-0 K Fallon (20) *nvr rchd ldrs.* .... (33 to 1 op 20 to 1) 16
ENVIRONMENTALIST (Ire) 9-0 G Duffield (10) *al in rear.* .... (33 to 1 op 25 to 1) 17
2147^{6} COVENTRY KID 9-0 J Carroll (19) *mid-div to hfwy.* .... (33 to 1 op 20 to 1) 18

SHAWN CUDDY 9-0 W Hood (7) *al beh.* .... (50 to 1 op 25 to 1) 19
THE DEACONESS 8-9 S Dawson (14) *al beh.* .... (50 to 1 op 20 to 1) 20
Dist: 2½l, sht-hd, sht-hd, 2½l, ¾l, 1l, 1½l, 3l, ½l, 2l. 1m 25.20s. a 3.30s (20 Ran).
SR: 19/16/15/14/6/4/1/-/-/ (P G Goulandris), J H M Gosden

3834 Prestwold Conditions Stakes Class D (3-y-o and up) £3,720 5f 2yds....(5:15)

3571* ARTISTIC REEF 4-9-4 W Carson (1) *made all, drvn out fnl furlong*.......... (6 to 5 on op 7 to 4 on tchd Evens) 1
3571^{4} NIGHT MELODY (Ire) 3-9-1 K Darley (7) *pushed alng hfwy, rdn and ran on fnl furlong, fnshd wl.* ....(9 to 2 op 7 to 2 tchd 5 to 1) 2
3438 SAINT EXPRESS 3-9-2 A Culhane (8) *in tch, ev ch one furlong out, kpt on*.......(12 to 1 op 8 to 1) 3
3709* NEVER IN THE RED (bl) 5-8-10 J Carroll (5) *hdwy o'r one furlong out, ran on ins last.* ....(5 to 1 op 8 to 1 tchd 9 to 2) 4
3692* EAGER DEVA 6-9-3 (5*) S Wynne (2) *chsd ldrs, ev ch one and a half fs out, wknd.* ....(14 to 1 op 10 to 1 tchd 16 to 1) 5
3474^{9} HUFFA (USA) 3-8-8 L Dettori (3) *pressed ldrs, ev ch appr fnl furlong, sn outpcd.* ....(16 to 1 op 20 to 1 tchd 25 to 1) 6
3638 PALLIUM (Ire) 5-9-4 M Roberts (6) *outpcd.* ....(16 to 1 op 12 to 1 tchd 20 to 1) 7
SCOTT'S RISK 3-8-8 A Mackay (4) *slwly away, al wl beh.* ....(100 to 1 op 50 to 1) 8
Dist: Nk, sht-hd, ¾l, 2½l, ¾l, 2½l, 10l. 59.30s. a 0.60s (8 Ran).
SR: 67/63/63/54/56/39/39/-/ (R A Mohammed), G H Eden

LINGFIELD (good to firm)
Tuesday September 7th
Going Correction: MINUS 0.45 sec. per fur.

3835 Crockham Hill Rating Related Maiden Stakes Class E (0-70 2-y-o) £2,821 6f ....(2:00)

3664^{2} ASKING FOR ACES 8-9 T Quinn (5) *pressed ldrs, led and hng lft o'r 2 fs out, veered badly left over one out, rdn out*........(13 to 8 fav op 9 to 4 tchd 5 to 2) 1
3705^{5} SECUNDUS (Ire) 8-7 (7*) A Lakeman (1) *wl-plcd on outsd, ev ch whn hmpd and crrd badly lft one furlong out, not reco'r*........(5 to 1 op 4 to 1 tchd 6 to 1) 2
3762^{8} HELLO MISTER 8-11 (3*) M Fenton (4) *hld up in tch, pushed alng 3 out, kpt on one pace fnl furlong.* ....(14 to 1 op 10 to 1 tchd 16 to 1) 3
3569^{3} ANSELLADY 8-9 R Cochrane (3) *hld up, pushed alng to improve frm hfwy, not quicken fnl furlong.* ....(5 to 2 op 2 to 1 tchd 7 to 4) 4
3532^{7} MAKE THE BREAK 9-0 J Reid (2) *in tch, pushed alng frm hfwy, rdn and no extr fnl furlong.* ....(7 to 1 op 4 to 1 tchd 8 to 1) 5
3573^{3} TOTON LAD 9-0 W Newnes (6) *led for o'r 3 fs, wknd fnl furlong*........(16 to 1 op 8 to 1) 6
Dist: 1½l, 1l, sht-hd, 1l, 3½l. 1m 11.24s. a 2.24s (6 Ran).
(Mrs G R Smith), N A Callaghan

3836 EBF Nutfield Maiden Stakes Class D (2-y-o) £4,950 7f................(3:00)

998^{9} GREATEST 9-0 R Price (2) *chsd ldrs, ran on o'r 2 fs out, led over one out, hng lft ins fnl furlong, styd on.* ....(8 to 1 op 7 to 1 tchd 9 to 1) 1
2419^{4} JAFEICA (Ire) 9-0 J Reid (1) *hdwy hfwy, not much room o'r 2 fs out, rdn and hmpd ins fnl furlong, not quicken.* ....(5 to 2 fav op 3 to 1 tchd 9 to 4) 2
793^{8} KELLYSI 9-0 M Hills (12) *al wl plcd, styd on one pace appr fnl furlong*........(25 to 1 op 20 to 1 tchd 33 to 1) 3
1602 RED VALERIAN 9-0 S O'Gorman (15) *ldg grp, rdn alng o'r 2 out, one pace appr fnl furlong*........(10 to 1 op 8 to 1) 4
3265^{9} ROUSAY 8-11 (3*) B Doyle (11) *wth ldr, led o'r 2 fs out, hdd over one out, no extr.* ....(12 to 1 tchd 14 to 1 and 10 to 1) 5
3698^{6} POSSIBILITY 8-9 L Piggott (6) *led for o'r 4 fs, btn over one out*........(12 to 1) 6
3698^{7} OBELOS (USA) 9-0 R Hills (14) *slwly into strd, some hdwy last 2 fs, not rch ldrs*... (11 to 2 op 8 to 1 tchd 5 to 1) 7
3352 BIRD ISLAND 9-0 W Newnes (4) *ldg grp til wknd und pres o'r 2 fs out*........(20 to 1 op 16 to 1) 8
FAIR COURT 9-0 R Cochrane (3) *dwlt, nvr nr to chal.* ....(8 to 1 op 4 to 1) 9
2419^{8} TANAH MERAH (Ire) 9-0 T Quinn (13) *mid-div, no prog last 2 fs*........(8 to 1 op 6 to 1 tchd 9 to 1) 10
3446 HOMEOFTHECLASSICS 8-9 W Woods (16) *mid-div, rdn and wknd o'r 2 fs out*........(33 to 1) 11
3016^{9} CRETAN GIFT 9-0 A McGlone (8) *in tch in mid-div, no prog appr last 2 fs*........(25 to 1 op 14 to 1) 12
2968 SOUTH EASTERN FRED 9-0 V Smith (9) *outpcd*...(33 to 1) 13
3422 WILD TRUFFES (Ire) 8-9 D Holland (1) *cl up til lost pl wl o'r 2 fs out*........(33 to 1 op 20 to 1) 14
KISSAIR (Ire) 9-0 B Rouse (5) *slwly into strd, al beh.* ....(33 to 1 op 20 to 1) 15
Dist: 1l, 4l, nk, sht-hd, nk, 1½l, ¾l, 1l, ¾l, nk. 1m 22.72s. a 2.02s (15 Ran).
SR: 22/19/7/6/5/-/ (Miss Therese Sevremont), R W Armstrong

3837 Swiss Life Handicap Class D (0-80 3-y-o and up) £3,786 7f............(3:30)

3531^{5} CAPE PIGEON (USA) [65] (bl) 8-9-3 D Holland (8) *pressed ldrs, led o'r 2 fs out, hdd over one out, rgned advantage ins fnl furlong, all out*.........(16 to 1 op 14 to 1) 1
3745^{9} AROOM [65] (bl) 3-8-13 M Hills (10) *steadied leaving stalls, hdwy o'r 2 fs out, ev ch and not quicken wl ins fnl furlong*........(14 to 1 tchd 16 to 1) 2
3425^{3} PANCHELLITA (USA) [60] 4-8-12 B Rouse (5) *cl up, rdn hfwy, led o'r one furlong out, hdd and not quicken ins last*........(7 to 1 tchd 8 to 1) 3
3450^{7} COURT MINSTREL [60] 4-8-12 J Reid (11) *hld up in rear, swtchd lft and ran on frm 2 fs out, one pace last 100 yards*........(5 to 1 fav tchd 6 to 1) 4
2413^{7} HELIOS [73] (bl) 5-9-11 W Woods (15) *handily plcd, rdn hfwy, not quicken ins last 2 fs*......(9 to 1 op 7 to 1) 5
3531^{6} PRINCE RODNEY [64] 4-8-9 (7*) Mark Denaro (13) *mid-div till drpd rear hfwy, styd on ag'n clsg stages*..(12 to 1) 6
3017^{5} SECOND CHANCE (Ire) [73] 3-9-7 W Newnes (4) *in tch, rdn and no imprsn on ldrs last 2 fs*.....(14 to 1 op 12 to 1) 7
2864^{2} TONY'S MIST [67] 3-8-8 (7*) D Gibbs (14) *nvr nrr.* ....(10 to 1 op 6 to 1 tchd 11 to 1) 8
3450 CHARMED KNAVE [68] 8-9-6 T Williams (1) *in tch on outsd to hfwy*........(14 to 1 op 12 to 1) 9
3707^{4} CONFRONTER [70] 4-9-8 R Cochrane (3) *rcd alone on outsd and in tch to hfwy, wknd o'r 2 fs out.* ....(9 to 1 op 8 to 1 tchd 10 to 1) 10
3450^{4} SIR OLIVER (Ire) [53] 4-8-5 A McGlone (9) *nvr nr to chal.* ....(9 to 1 op 6 to 1) 11
3450 TOP PET (Ire) [70] 3-9-4 T Quinn (16) *nvr rchd frnt rnk.* ....(10 to 1 tchd 9 to 1) 12
3474^{8} YAQTHAN (Ire) [80] 3-10-0 R Hills (7) *chsd ldrs to hfwy, beh fnl 2 fs*........(16 to 1 op 10 to 1) 13
3588^{3} ABERDEEN HEATHER [68] 3-9-2 L Piggott (6) *squeezed for room leaving stalls, al in rear.* ....(9 to 1 tchd 12 to 1 and 8 to 1) 14
1412^{6} FULL FEATHER (USA) [80] 3-10-0 G Hind (12) *led for o'r 4 fs, sn wknd*........(9 to 1 op 7 to 1) 15
Dist: 1½l, sht-hd, hd, 1½l, 2½l, sht-hd, 1l, sht-hd, hd, hd. 1m 21.52s. a 0.82s (15 Ran).
SR: 43/34/32/31/39/22/26/17/21/ (E J S Gadsden), L G Cottrell

3838 Marsh Green Maiden Stakes Class D (3-y-o) £3,357 1m 3f 106yds..... (4:30)

3491^{8} RANI (Ire) 8-6 (3*) B Doyle (1) *led for one furlong, trkd ldr, pushed alng to rgn advantage o'r one furlong out, not extended*........(3 to 1 op 2 to 1) 1
3587^{2} AL SENAFI (Ire) 9-0 R Cochrane (2) *led aftr one furlong, rdn and hdd o'r one out, no extr.* .... (10 to 3 on op 11 to 4 on tchd 5 to 2 on) 2
4676a EL GRANDO 9-0 S Whitworth (3) *al beh, ran wide and lost tch entering last 3 fs, tld off.* ....(33 to 1 tchd 25 to 1 and 40 to 1) 3
Dist: 3l, 30l. 2m 27.08s. a 2.88s (3 Ran).
SR: 14/13/-/ (Mohammed Obaid Al Maktoum), C E Brittain

3839 Hartfield Maiden Stakes Class D (3-y-o and up) £3,406 7f........... (5:00)

3585^{5} BELFRY GREEN (Ire) 3-9-0 D Holland (11) *hld up wl in tch, squeezed through and bumped 2 fs out, led ins fnl furlong, hrd held*.......(4 to 1 op 9 to 2 tchd 5 to 1) 1
3489^{5} JASARAH (Ire) 3-8-9 R Hills (1) *ldg grp, led 2 fs out, hdd and not quicken ins fnl furlong.* (100 to 30 op 2 to 1) 2
3476 VILLAGE GREEN (Fr) 3-9-0 S Whitworth (5) *handily plcd, rdn and ev ch 2 out, outpcd ins fnl furlong.* ....(10 to 1 op 6 to 1 tchd 11 to 1) 3
DOMOVOY 3-8-9 W Newnes (9) *dwlt, styd on frm rear last 2 fs, nrst finish*........(33 to 1 op 20 to 1) 4
3214^{5} NOBLE RISK (bl) 3-9-0 J Reid (7) *led for 5 fs, wknd o'r one out*........(8 to 1 op 6 to 1 tchd 10 to 1) 5
3639^{2} POCKET PIECE (USA) 3-8-9 R Cochrane (8) *hld up in mid-div, hng rght and bumped 2 fs out, not reco'r.* .... (13 to 8 fav op 5 to 4 tchd 7 to 4 and 2 to 1) 6
4709a^{6} JOY OF FREEDOM 3-8-6 (3*) B Doyle (4) *rdn alng hfwy, nvr rch frnt rnk*.....(50 to 1 op 3 to 1 tchd 100 to 1) 7
3666^{5} THUNDER STRIKE (USA) 3-9-0 G Hind (3) *in tch til rdn and wknd last 2 fs*........(20 to 1 op 14 to 1) 8
3425 DANCING MISS (Ire) 4-8-13 M Perrett (10) *outpcd most of way*........(100 to 1 op 50 to 1) 9
3707 STERLING PRINCESS 3-8-9 B Crossley (6) *prmnt til lost pl aftr 2 fs, tld off*........(100 to 1 op 33 to 1) 10
1746 ROADRUNNER 3-8-9 (5*) A Procter (2) *in tch til lost pos and stumbled 4 fs out, tld off*.....(100 to 1 op 50 to 1) 11
Dist: 1½l, 4l, 1l, nk, nk, 2½l, 5l, 5l, 15l, 7l. 1m 22.38s. a 1.68s (11 Ran).
SR: 28/18/11/3/7/1/ (John Kelsey-Fry), C A Horgan

LINGFIELD (A.W) (std)
Tuesday September 7th

Going Correction: MINUS 0.40 sec. per fur.

3840 Harrier Selling Handicap Class G (0-60 3-y-o and up) £2,553 1¼m (2:30)

3655[8] CRETOES DANCER (USA) [40] (bl) 4-8-9 (7*) Kim McDonnell (13) *ldg grp, led o'r 5 fs out, wl clr over 3 out, unchlgd.* ....(8 to 1 op 6 to 1) 1
3469[4] TAUNTING (Ire) [47] 5-9-9 R Cochrane (3) *chsd ldrs, rdn alng o'r 4 fs out, wnt second appr fnl furlong, not rch wnr*....(9 to 2 op 4 to 1) 2
3384[4] RITZY [42] 3-8-11 W Newnes (14) *wth ldrs, led 7 fs out, hdd o'r 5 out, sn hrd rdn, one pace last 3 furlongs.* ....(16 to 1 op 14 to 1 tchd 20 to 1) 3
3523[5] LEGAL RISK [56] (v) 3-9-11 J Reid (1) *handily plcd, rdn and outpcd last 4 fs*....(9 to 1 op 6 to 1 tchd 10 to 1) 4
3766[6] SLEEPTITE (Fr) [53] 3-9-8 T Quinn (9) *moderate hdwy clsg stages, nvr rch frnt rnk.* ....(7 to 2 fav op 4 to 1 tchd 3 to 1) 5
3518 PIPERS REEL [53] (v) 3-9-8 M Hills (10) *hdwy o'r 5 fs out, no prog over 3 out*....(8 to 1 tchd 10 to 1) 6
3461[9] BALL GOWN [47] 3-9-2 J Lowe (6) *mid-div, rdn to improve hfwy, wknd o'r 3 out*....(12 to 1 op 10 to 1) 7
3240 SHARE A MOMENT (Can) [46] 3-9-1 S Perks (12) *shrtlvd effrt frm rear o'r 4 fs out, sn btn*....(12 to 1) 8
3346[6] FIABA [47] 5-9-2 (7*) S Mulvey (7) *chsd ldrs to hfwy, sn lost pl*....(25 to 1 op 6 to 1 tchd 33 to 1) 9
3741[3] ROLY WALLACE [50] (v) 4-9-12 M Wigham (11) *slwly into strd, al towards rear*....(10 to 1 op 8 to 1) 10
3325 SIE AMATO (Ire) [48] 4-9-10 J Fortune (4) *led for 2 fs, wknd frm hfwy*....(12 to 1 op 10 to 1) 11
3634 EASTERN CHARLY (Bel) [39] 3-8-1 (7*) S Eiffert (2) *al outpcd in rear*....(25 to 1 op 20 to 1 tchd 33 to 1) 12
3246[7] FASHIONABLE DANCER [56] 3-9-8 (3*) B Doyle (5) *led aftr 2 fs, hdd 7 out, wknd 4 out.* ....(25 to 1 op 16 to 1 tchd 33 to 1) 13
3449[7] AWAY GIRL [45] 3-9-0 D Holland (8) *nvr on terms.* ....(10 to 1 op 8 to 1) 14

Dist: 10l, 2l, sht-hd, 6l, 1½l, 3l, sht-hd, nk, 5l, ¾l. 2m 6.18s. a 2.98s (14 Ran).
SR: 32/19/3/16/1/-/ (Mrs W K Ong), W R Muir

3841 Levy Board Nursery Class E (2-y-o) £2,950 1m.... (4:00)

3686* TIMES ZANDO [62] 8-8 (5ex) J Fortune (6) *wth ldr, rdn to gain slight advantage wl o'r one out, jst hld on.* ....(4 to 1 fav op 3 to 1 tchd 9 to 2) 1
3532[2] PRINCE DANZIG (Ire) [71] 9-3 J Reid (1) *wl plcd, rdn and outpcd 2 out, str run und pres ins fnl furlong, jst fld.* ....(11 to 2 op 5 to 1) 2
3671* INDEFENCE (Ire) [77] 9-9 (5ex) L Piggott (5) *led til hdd wl o'r one furlong out, kpt on same pace*...(9 to 2 op 7 to 2) 3
3386[6] ZORAHAYDA (Fr) [50] 7-3 (7*) Kim McDonnell (7) *ldg grp, rdn alng one pace fnl 2 fs*....(7 to 1 op 6 to 1) 4
3750[2] NORTHERN BAILIWICK (Ire) [65] (bl) 8-11 M Wigham (4) *sn pushed alng towards rear, not rchd ldrs und pres last 2 fs*....(11 to 2 op 5 to 1) 5
2973 DEMI-PLIE [75] (v) 9-7 R Cochrane (8) *sn rdn alng and outpcd, lost tch aftr 2 fs, moderate effrt o'r 3 out, nvr dngrs*....(12 to 1 op 10 to 1 tchd 14 to 1) 6
3688[3] KENNET BOY [60] 8-6 T Quinn (3) *sn pushed alng in tch, wknd frm 3 out*....(6 to 1 op 5 to 1) 7
3532[9] BIEN CUIT [50] (e/s) 7-5 (5*) D Wright (2) *rdn alng and beh frm hfwy*....(12 to 1 op 10 to 1 tchd 14 to 1) 8

Dist: Sht-hd, 1l, 3½l, 1½l, 1½l, 5l, 5l. 1m 39.72s. a 3.52s (8 Ran).
SR: -/1/4/-/-/ (Times Of Wigan), Capt J Wilson

LONGCHAMP (FR) (good to firm)
Tuesday September 7th

3842 Prix Ridgway (Listed) (3-y-o) £14,337 1¼m.... (2:10)

3337[3] JEUNE HOMME (USA) 8-9 G Mosse,.... 1
3644[3] MUHAYAA (USA) 9-1 W R Swinburn, *rcd in 3rd, led 5 fs out, rdn 2 and a half out till one out, kpt on*.... 2
3500[4] ARCHANGE (USA) 9-1 F Head,.... 3
3241[7] DONDOOK (USA) 8-9 D Boeuf,.... 4

Dist: 4l, ½l, ½l, 1½l, ½l, nose, hd. 2m 6.30s. a 4.20s (8 Ran).
SR: 53/51/50/43/ (Yoshio Asakawa), F Boutin

3843 Prix Gladiateur (Group 3) (3-y-o and up) £26,284 1m 7f 110yds.... (3:45)

3434[2] OH SO RISKY 6-9-0 J Williams (1) *mid-div, 6th strt, rdn 2 fs out, led jst und one out, ran on wl*....(68 to 10) 1
3241[3] NON PARTISAN (USA) 4-9-6 T Jarnet (2) *4th strt, rdn 2 fs out, led one and a half out, hdd jst und one out, one pace*....(46 to 10) 2
3194[4] SOUGHT OUT (Ire) 5-9-5 M Boutin (3) *led till one and a half fs out, one pace*....(23 to 10) 3
NAVIRE (Fr) 4-9-0 N Jeanpierre (6) *rear and 7th strt, rdn 2 fs out, hmpd ins fnl furlong, not reco'r*.... (102 to 10) 4
3370[9] OUMNAZ (Fr) 4-9-4 R Laplanche (8) *rcd in last, rdn 2 fs out, one pace*....(21 to 1) 5
2771[4] DJAIS (Fr) 4-9-0 G Mosse (5) *prmnt, second strt, rdn and wknd 2 fs out*....(18 to 10 fav) 6
CUTTING REEF (Ire) (bl) 4-8-10 A Badel (4) *prmnt early, 5th strt, one pace 2 fs out*....(16 to 1) 7
VACATION (Fr) 5-8-10 D Boeuf (7) *pld hrd early, mid-div till rdn and wknd o'r 2 fs out*....(83 to 10) 8

Dist: 2l, sht-nk, ½l, sht-nk, ½l, 1½l, 3l. 3m 22.90s. a 6.40s (8 Ran).
SR: 36/40/38/32/35/30/24/21/ (The Oh So Risky Syndicate), D R C Elsworth

3844 Prix de Liancourt (Listed) (3-y-o) £14,337 1m.... (4:40)

3534[3] AISLA (USA) 8-11 G Mosse,.... 1
3195* BINT LARIAAF (USA) 9-2 W R Swinburn,.... 2
COX ORANGE (USA) 8-11 S Guillot,.... 3
3195[3] SHOWGUM (Fr) 9-2 G Dubroeucq,.... 4
1693[4] ALLEGED SARON (USA) 8-12 D Boeuf,.... 5
3477[2] REINE DE NEIGE 8-12 B Raymond, *trkd ldr, second strt, effrt and one pace 2 fs out*.... 6
1086[8] KIRUNA (USA) 8-12 T Jarnet,.... 7
3149[6] LOCHNAU LADY (Fr) 8-12 F Sanchez,.... 8

Dist: 1l, ½l, 1l, 1½l, ¾l, nk, sht-nk. 1m 38.80s. a 2.80s (8 Ran).
SR: 55/57/50/52/43/41/40/39/ (Nicolo Incisa Della Rocchetta), F Boutin

DONCASTER (good to soft (races 1,2), soft (3,4,5,6))
Wednesday September 8th

Going Correction: MINUS 0.10 sec. per fur. (races 1,3,5), PLUS 0.20 (2,4,6)

3845 EBF Carrie Red Fillies' Nursery Handicap Class C (2-y-o) £17,730 6f 110yds.... (2:00)

3626[4] RAJMAPATA [70] 8-2 K Darley (9) *trkd ldr far side, led wl o'r one out, ran on well*....(16 to 1) 1
3597 YAWARA [72] 8-1 (3*) B Doyle (8) *rcd far side, led till hdd wl o'r one out, kpt on well*....(25 to 1) 2
3091* MONAASSABAAT (USA) [85] 9-3 W R Swinburn (20) *cl up, led stands side grp for o'r 2 out, ran on wl, not rch 1st two*....(11 to 4 fav op 5 to 2 tchd 3 to 1) 3
3600[2] WIXI (Ire) [74] 8-6 P Robinson (1) *in tch far side, kpt on wl fnl furlong*....(20 to 1) 4
3421[3] ROYALE FIGURINE (Ire) [72] 8-4 M Roberts (11) *swtchd stands side sn aftr strt, prmnt, no extr fnl furlong.* ....(8 to 1) 5
3389[6] ZUNO NOELYN [66] 7-12 D Harrison (18) *chsd ldrs stands side, kpt on same pace fnl 2 fs*....(14 to 1) 6
3688* PRIMA SILK [80] 8-5 (7*,5ex) P McCabe (21) *in tch stands side, effrt whn swrvd lft o'r one out, kpt on same pace.* ....(14 to 1) 7
3309[3] LEGATEE [80] 8-12 M Birch (10) *rcd far side, in tch, kpt on same pace fnl 2 fs*....(25 to 1 op 20 to 1) 8
3472* BELLA PARKES [86] 9-4 J Carroll (22) *led stands side grp till hdd o'r 2 out, wknd over one out.* (8 to 1 op 7 to 1) 9
3743[2] ADMIRING [64] 7-10 A Mackay (17) *rcd stands side, nvr nr ldrs*....(14 to 1 tchd 16 to 1) 10
2988[8] RAMBOLD [76] 8-8 J Williams (13) *rcd stands side, nvr dngrus*....(20 to 1 op 25 to 1) 11
3499[6] BEARALL (Ire) [89] 9-7 B Rouse (15) *rcd stands side, nvr dngrs*....(16 to 1) 12
3287* LADY-BO-K [73] 8-5 R Hills (7) *rcd far side, nvr dngrs.* ....(10 to 1 op 9 to 1) 13
3115[5] MY LIFETIME LADY (Ire) [74] 8-6[1] S Perks (16) *rcd stands side, nvr dangrous*....(25 to 1) 14
3762[5] CYARNA QUINN (Ire) [77] 8-9 Pat Eddery (4) *rcd far side, nvr dngrs*....(14 to 1) 15
3629* SMART PET [84] 9-2 N Connorton (14) *rcd stands side, nvr dngrs*....(14 to 1) 16
3626[3] THATCHERELLA [73] 8-5 T Quinn (5) *rcd far side, chsd ldrs till wknd 2 out*....(16 to 1) 17
3629[2] LADY SHERIFF [77] 8-9 T Lucas (2) *rcd far side, beh frm hfwy*....(25 to 1) 18
3432* CIRCLE OF FRIENDS (Ire) [74] 8-6 J Reid (19) *rcd stands side, in tch to hfwy*....(10 to 1 op 9 to 1) 19
3625 GIFT BOX (Ire) [67] 7-13 G Bardwell (3) *rcd far side, cl up to hfwy*....(20 to 1) 20

Dist: 1½l, ½l, 1½l, 2l, ¾l, 1½l, hd, 1½l, 3l, 1½l. 1m 20.78s. a 3.38s (20 Ran).
SR: 7/3/14/-/-/-/ (Peter Green), R Hannon

3846 Worthington Best Bitter Park Hill Stakes Class A (Group 3) (3-y-o and up) £22,013 1¾m 132yds.... (2:35)

3467[4] ANNA OF SAXONY 4-9-3 L Dettori (5) *trkd ldr gng wl, led o'r one out, sn clr, easily*....(8 to 1 op 6 to 1) 1
3401[6] LILLE HAMMER 3-8-5 R Cochrane (4) *hld up, hdwy 4 out, chsd wnr o'r one out, kpt on, no imprsn.* ....(9 to 1 op 7 to 1 tchd 10 to 1) 2
3433[4] SPRING 4-9-3 W Carson (9) *trkd ldrs, led wl o'r 2 out, hdd over one out, kpt on same pace.* ....(100 to 30 op 3 to 1 tchd 7 to 2) 3
3262[3] MAGICAL RETREAT (USA) 3-8-5 K Darley (1) *beh, pushed alng hfwy, kpt on fnl 3 fs, not rch ldrs.* ....(10 to 1 op 8 to 1) 4

3467^{3} ANNE BONNY 4-9-3 W R Swinburn (8) *trkd ldr, led o'r 3 out, sn hdd, wknd 2 out*...........(10 to 1 op 8 to 1) 5
3467^{5} IVIZA (Ire) (bl) 3-8-5 M Roberts (2) *led till hdd o'r 3 out, sn btn*.................. (12 to 1 op 8 to 1 tchd 14 to 1) 6
3433^{7} RAINBOW LAKE 3-8-5 Pat Eddery (3) *in tch, effrt o'r 3 out, wknd over 2 out*.................(9 to 4 fav tchd 5 to 2) 7
1789^{5} ABURY (Ire) 3-8-6^{1} J Reid (6) *hld up, effrt o'r 3 out, no hdwy*..................(9 to 1 op 7 to 1 tchd 10 to 1) 8
3401^{9} SOLARTICA (USA) 3-8-5 T Quinn (7) *in tch till wknd 4 out, tld off*.............................(33 to 1 op 20 to 1) 9
Dist: 5l, 4l, 4l, 5l, 7l, 2½l, nk, 25l. 3m 11.63s. a 7.13s (9 Ran).
SR: 61/39/43/23/25/-/ (Sheikh Mohammed), J H M Gosden

3847 Doncaster Bloodstock Sales Scarbrough Stakes Class A (Listed Race) (3-y-o and up) £9,855 5f.........(3:10)

3594^{3} KING'S SIGNET (USA) 4-9-2 M Roberts (3) *chsd ldrs, quickened to ld o'r one out, ran on wl*.............(2 to 1 jt-fav op 7 to 4) 1+
3162^{6} MARINA PARK 3-8-11 L Dettori (9) *trkd ldrs, effrt o'r one out, ran on wl towards finish*. (2 to 1 jt-fav op 7 to 4) 1+
2574^{6} RAIN BROTHER (USA) 3-8-13 J Reid (10) *led till hdd o'r one out, no extr*....................(10 to 1 op 8 to 1) 3
1258^{6} ANONYMOUS 3-8-5 B Doyle (1) *cl up, ev ch o'r one out, kpt on same pace*...............(50 to 1 op 33 to 1) 4
3725 DOMINUET 8-8-11 G Hind (2) *slwly into strd, nvr rch ldrs*. ....(14 to 1 tchd 16 to 1) 5
3464^{7} FREDDIE LLOYD (USA) 4-9-4 Pat Eddery (4) *prmnt till wknd entering fnl furlong*. .... (5 to 1 op 7 to 2 tchd 11 to 2) 6
TITLE ROLL (Ire) 5-8-13 M Hills (5) *al beh*. .... (12 to 1 op 8 to 1) 7
Dist: Dd-ht, 3l, 2½l, 2½l, 3½l, 1½l. 1m 0.35s. a 1.55s (7 Ran).
SR: 61/57/47/29/25/18/7/ (Sheikh Mohammed & Greenland Park Ltd), J H M Gosden & M Johnston

3848 Harcros Timber & Building Supplies Stayers Championship Final Handicap Class B (3-y-o and up) £21,500 1 ¾m 132yds.....................(3:40)

3724^{3} FLIGHT LIEUTENANT (USA) [78] 4-8-10 J Reid (11) *hld up, hdwy o'r 3 out, rdn over one out, styd on wl to ld cl hme*...........................(8 to 1 op 7 to 1) 1
3466^{2} ROBERTY LEA [73] 5-8-5 K Darley (17) *cl up, led 8 out, rdn o'r 2 out, hdd and no extr close hme*. .... (9 to 1 op 7 to 1 tchd 10 to 1) 2
3434 QUICK RANSOM [88] 5-9-6 L Dettori (12) *in tch, hdwy to chase ldrs o'r 4 out, rdn over 2 out, ev ch ins fnl furlong, no extr towards finish*. .... (9 to 1 op 8 to 1 tchd 10 to 1) 3
3434^{7} CASTLE COURAGEOUS [93] 6-9-11 W Ryan (20) *trkd ldrs, outpcd o'r 3 out, styd on wl fnl 2 fs*. (20 to 1 op 16 to 1) 4
3152^{3} CHIEF MINISTER (Ire) [71] 4-8-3 W Carson (15) *chsd ldrs, outpcd 3 out, styd on wl und pres fnl furlong*. ....(14 to 1 tchd 16 to 1) 5
3488^{3} STAR PLAYER [78] 7-8-10 J Williams (9) *in tch, hdwy 5 out, kpt on same pace fnl 2 fs*.........(20 to 1 tchd 25 to 1) 6
3690^{2} WESTERN DYNASTY [70] 7-7-9 (7*) P McCabe (18) *in tch, hdwy to track ldrs 7 out, ev ch o'r 2 out, wknd fnl furlong*..........................(14 to 1 op 12 to 1) 7
3271^{6} HIERARCH (USA) [70] 4-8-2 A Munro (13) *in tch, kpt on fnl 2 fs, nvr dngrs*.......................(16 to 1 op 14 to 1) 8
3599* SALU [61] 4-7-7 J Lowe (4) *hld up, some hdwy fnl 3 fs, not rch ldrs*.......................(20 to 1 tchd 25 to 1) 9
3252^{3} EIGHTANDAHALF (Ire) [64] 4-7-7 (3*) N Kennedy (5) *hld up, effrt 4 out, no real hdwy*.......... (16 to 1 op 14 to 1) 10
2857^{3} MYSTIC MEMORY [61] 4-7-3^{1} (5*) Darren Moffatt (3) *nvr dngrs*... (20 to 1) 11
3513^{3} SARAWAT [84] 5-9-2 T Quinn (16) *hld up, gd hdwy to track ldr 6 out, rdn 3 out, wknd 2 out*. .... (9 to 1 op 8 to 1 tchd 10 to 1) 12
3255^{8} KING WILLIAM [61] 8-7-0 (7*) Kim McDonnell (10) *nvr nr ldrs*..............................(100 to 1 op 66 to 1) 13
3749* LEAGUE LEADER (Ire) [94] 3-9-0 (4ex) W R Swinburn (8) *middiv, lost pl 4 out*........................(8 to 1 op 6 to 1) 14
3724^{6} WHITE WILLOW [71] 4-8-3 J Carroll (7) *trkd ldrs, pushed alng 6 out, sn wknd*. ....(11 to 2 fav op 5 to 1 tchd 6 to 1) 15
3521^{8} CALL THE GUV'NOR [66] (bl) 4-7-12 A McGlone (14) *chsd ldrs, pushed alng 6 out, wknd 4 out*. .... (12 to 1 op 10 to 1) 16
3288* SUMMER WIND (Ire) [74] 3-7-8 G Bardwell (2) *slight ld till hdd 8 out, sn wknd, tld off*......... (10 to 1 op 8 to 1) 17
3116^{2} CONTRACT ELITE (Ire) [75] 3-7-9^{2} A Mackay (6) *al beh. tld off*............................(100 to 1 op 66 to 1) 18
Dist: Nk, 1½l, ¾l, ½l, nk, 1½l, 3½l, 8l, 10l, 2l. 3m 12.98s. a 8.48s (18 Ran).
SR: 40/34/46/49/26/32/21/14/-/ (P & S Lever Partners), R Hannon

3849 Tote-Portland Handicap Class B (0-110 3-y-o and up) £17,432 5f 140yds ....(4:10)

3504 AMRON [86] 6-9-0 N Carlisle (9) *in tch, hdwy 2 out, styd on wl to ld cl hme*................(12 to 1 op 14 to 1) 1
3468^{4} THOUSLA ROCK (Ire) [98] 4-9-12 J Reid (15) *trkd ldrs, led jst ins fnl furlong, hdd and no extr cl hme*.....(12 to 1) 2
3438^{2} CALL ME I'M BLUE (Ire) [94] 3-9-5 L Piggott (19) *chsd ldrs, rdn 2 out, kpt on fnl furlong*...................(10 to 1) 3
3638^{2} MISTERTOPOGIGO (Ire) [90] 3-9-1 A Munro (16) *trkd ldrs, effrt o'r one out, kpt on same pace*........... (12 to 1) 4
3834^{2} NIGHT MELODY (Ire) [94] 3-9-5 K Darley (3) *al prmnt, no extr fnl furlong*..............(16 to 1 tchd 20 to 1) 5
2018 RISTON LADY (Ire) [83] 3-8-8 J Fortune (1) *led till hdd and wknd jst ins fnl furlong*..................... (33 to 1) 6
3177 HOB GREEN [81] 4-8-9 K Fallon (4) *chsd ldrs, chlgd jst ins fnl furlong, sn rdn and wknd*. (6 to 1 fav tchd 13 to 2) 7
3668^{5} MISS VAXETTE [91] 4-8-12 (7*) M Humphries (2) *prmnt till wknd o'r one out*.............................. (16 to 1) 8
3739* BODARI [83] 4-8-6 (5*,7ex) D McCabe (12) *chsd ldrs till wknd o'r one out*..............(12 to 1 tchd 14 to 1) 9
3571^{3} BOLD LEZ [96] 6-9-10 R Cochrane (17) *dwlt, not trble ldrs*. ....(12 to 1) 10
2987 CASTLEREA LAD [91] 4-9-5 W Ryan (13) *not trble ldrs*. ....(12 to 1 tchd 14 to 1) 11
3725^{5} POKER CHIP [94] 3-9-5 L Dettori (5) *in tch, effrt hfwy, no hdwy*..........................(8 to 1 op 7 to 1) 12
3065^{3} DOUBLE BLUE [90] 4-9-4 M Roberts (14) *prmnt till wknd hfwy*..(10 to 1) 13
3621^{3} SAMSOLOM [83] 5-8-11 J Quinn (7) *in tch, effrt hfwy, sn btn*...................................(9 to 1 op 8 to 1) 14
3504^{6} CATHERINES WELL [80] 10-8-8 T Lucas (8) *in tch till wknd hfwy*..........................(16 to 1 tchd 20 to 1) 15
2927^{7} EL YASAF (Ire) [100] 5-10-0 Pat Eddery (21) *chsd ldrs till wknd 2 out*.......................................(16 to 1) 16
3511^{2} FANGIO [82] 4-8-3 (7*) P McCabe (20) *rcd stands side, beh frm hfwy*.........................(9 to 1 op 10 to 1) 17
3668^{6} LOVE RETURNED [85] 6-8-13 M Tebbutt (22) *rcd stands side, beh frm hfwy*..........................(20 to 1) 18
Dist: ½l, 3l, sht-hd, ¾l, ¾l, nk, 1½l, 1½l, 1½l, nk. 1m 8.12s. a 1.02s (18 Ran).
SR: 68/78/59/54/55/41/41/45/31/ (Roy Peebles), J Berry

3850 Cowies Plc Limited Stakes Class D (0-80 3-y-o) £4,542 1¼m 60yds..(4:40)

2930^{5} TICKERTY'S GIFT 8-11 B Rouse (7) *prmnt, rdn to chase ldr 2 out, styd on wl to ld ins fnl furlong, sn clr*. .... (20 to 1 op 16 to 1) 1
3101^{2} STAY WITH ME BABY 8-6 T Quinn (9) *led, rdn o'r 2 out, hdd ins fnl furlong, no extr*............... (8 to 1 op 7 to 1) 2
2708* SOLOMON'S DANCER (USA) 8-11 P Robinson (8) *hld up in tch, pushed alng 4 out, styd on fnl 2 fs, not rch ldrs*. ....(9 to 2 op 7 to 2) 3
2907^{9} LANKRIDGE 8-11 W Carson (4) *chsd ldrs, kpt on same pace frm 3 out*......................(11 to 2 op 4 to 1) 4
1488^{3} SPECIAL DAWN (Ire) 8-11 W Ryan (6) *beh, styd on fnl 2 fs, not trble ldrs*...........(7 to 1 op 6 to 1 tchd 8 to 1) 5
3401^{7} THE SEER 8-11 Pat Eddery (1) *in tch till rdn and wknd o'r 3 out*.........................(11 to 4 fav op 5 to 2) 6
3585 WAHEM (Ire) 8-11 M Roberts (3) *chsd ldr, grad wknd frm 4 out*.................. (12 to 1 op 10 to 1 tchd 14 to 1) 7
3585 DUTOSKY 8-6 A Munro (2) *chsd ldrs till wknd quickly 3 out*...................................(6 to 1 tchd 13 to 2) 8
3639^{4} WORDS OF WISDOM (Ire) 8-11 K Darley (10) *al beh, lost tch fnl 3 fs*...............(11 to 1 op 10 to 1 tchd 12 to 1) 9
Dist: 3l, 1½l, 2l, 8l, 8l, ¾l, 4l, 8l. 2m 13.50s. a 6.80s (9 Ran).
SR: 50/39/41/37/21/5/3/-/-/ (K Higson), R Hannon

EVRY (FR) (good to soft)
Wednesday September 8th
Going Correction: PLUS 0.20 sec. per fur.

3851 Prix Saint-Roman (Group 3) (2-y-o) £23,895 1m 1f..................(2:55)

ZINDARI (USA) 8-9 G Mosse (5) *led, rdn and quickened 2 fs out, sn clr, easily*.................................(8 to 5) 1
FAIR FABULOUS (Fr) 8-9 D Boeuf (2) *last strt, hdwy 2 fs out, one pace ins last*...........................(7 to 2) 2
BAHAMIAN SUNSHINE (USA) 8-9 T Jarnet (3) *3rd strt, effrt o'r 2 fs out, unbl to quicken fnl one and a half furlongs*. ....(5 to 4 on) 3
ROBUR (Fr) 8-9 O Peslier (1) *second strt, effrt o'r 2 fs out, one pace and wknd over one out*...............(7 to 1) 4
Dist: 8l, 3l, 5l. 1m 57.58s. a 6.28s (4 Ran).
SR: 28/12/6/-/ (K Abdulla), F Boutin

GALWAY (IRE) (good to firm)
Wednesday September 8th

3852 Northern Telecom Meridian-1 Race (3-y-o and up) £3,450 7f........... (3:00)

3610^{8} GLOWING VALUE (Ire) (bl) 3-9-0 J P Murtagh (5)... (7 to 1) 1
3297* CORTIJA PARK (Ire) 3-9-4 R Hughes (1)............(6 to 1) 2
3497^{4} CRYSTAL SHIP (Ire) (bl) 3-9-4 W J Supple (3)....... (7 to 2) 3
3610^{3} KURDISTAN (Ire) 3-9-7 P V Gilson (6)..........(7 to 4 fav) 4
308 FOR REG (Ire) 4-8-12 (6*) J R Barry (7)............(10 to 1) 5
3497 MARKIEVICZ (Ire) 3-8-10 (8*) G M Moylan (4)..... (10 to 1) 6

3419⁴ BRATA (USA) (bl) 3-9-4 M J Kinane (2) ....(5 to 1) 7
Dist: Nk, 1½l, ¾l, 5l. 1m 27.90s. (7 Ran).
(F Dunne), F Dunne

3853 Galway City Vitners Handicap (0-70 3-y-o and up) £3,795 1¾m...... (4:00)

3580² SENSITIVE KING (Ire) [-] 5-8-2 (2*) R M Burke (12) ....(2 to 1 fav) 1
3295* THIS IS MY LIFE (Ire) [-] 4-9-0 R Hughes (6) ....(10 to 1) 2
3604⁴ PREMIER LEAP (Ire) [-] 4-8-12 W J Supple (11) .....(9 to 2) 3
2842 SPOUT HOUSE (Ire) [-] 4-9-0 S Craine (10) .... (7 to 1) 4
3543 ALIBAR'S PET (Ire) [-] 3-9-3 (6*) J R Barry (3) ....(8 to 1) 5
3277 CONCERT ORCHESTRA (Ire) [-] 4-7-8 (2*) D G O'Shea (8) ....(12 to 1) 6
3580 RIYADH DANCER (Ire) [-] 3-8-2 J F Egan (5) ....(10 to 1) 7
3397² MR GERAN (Ire) [-] (bl) 4-7-12 (4*) J J Behan (1) .... (9 to 1) 8
819⁵ INNOCENT MAN (Ire) [-] (bl) 3-7-9 (8*) R T Fitzpatrick (15) ....(25 to 1) 9
1508⁷ VIVERE (Ire) [-] 4-8-3 N G McCullagh (4) ....(8 to 1) 10
2900⁸ BEAU BEAUCHAMP [-] 6-9-6 (2*) P Carberry (9) ....(8 to 1) bd
2958⁹ RIYASHA (Ire) [-] 5-7-7 Joanna Morgan (16) ....(40 to 1) bd
1295 DAMHSA (Den) [-] (bl) 4-9-0 (8*) M W Martin (7) .... (20 to 1) su
Dist: 1½l, 6l, nk, 1½l. 3m 10.00s. (13 Ran).
(J C Harley), J C Harley

3854 Carrolls Festival Handicap (0-70 3-y-o and up) £3,450 1½m............(4:30)

3684³ FORTUNE'S GIRL [-] 5-8-6 P V Gilson (11) ....(7 to 1) 1
3721⁴ NORDIC MINE (Ire) [-] 3-7-11 (2*) R M Burke (14) .. (16 to 1) 2
3560⁴ FONTANAYS (Ire) [-] 5-8-13 (6*) C Everard (2) ...... (9 to 1) 3
2901 ZORIA (Ire) [-] 5-8-13 N G McCullagh (8) ....(20 to 1) 4
3772³ GLAS AGUS OR (Ire) [-] (bl) 3-8-7 (6*) J A Heffernan (16) ....(11 to 2) 5
3684² OPEN MARKET (USA) [-] (bl) 4-10-0 M J Kinane (9) (5 to 1) 6
3543 DIAMOND CLUSTER [-] 3-7-5 (8*) R T Fitzpatrick (15) ....(25 to 1) 7
3662* TEBRE (USA) [-] (bl) 3-8-11 (6*,4ex) B J Walsh (3) ..(10 to 1) 8
3326⁴ GRECIAN LADY (Ire) [-] 4-8-11 W J Supple (10) .... (14 to 1) 9
3245⁷ ALVATUR (Ire) [-] 4-6-13 (8*) G M Moylan (12) ...... (20 to 1) 10
3684⁷ INAUGURATION (Ire) [-] 4-8-12 (4*) J J Behan (1) .. (14 to 1) 11
3580⁷ ONOMATOPOEIA (Ire) [-] 3-8-13 J F Egan (7) ..(11 to 4 fav) 12
3381⁶ RED MICKS WIFE (Ire) [-] 3-8-5 (4*) W J Smith (4) ..(25 to 1) 13
3580⁶ ANIMATE (Ire) [-] 3-8-9 S Craine (6) .... (14 to 1) 14
3381⁷ FESTIVAL GIRL (Ire) [-] (bl) 3-9-0 R Hughes (17) ... (14 to 1) 15
3295⁸ KILCSEM EILE (Ire) [-] (bl) 4-8-1 (2*) D G O'Shea (13) ....(66 to 1) 16
Dist: Nk, 2l, 1½l, ½l. 2m 39.20s. (16 Ran).
(Talk Of The Town Syndicate), M Halford

3855 Galway Bay Seafood Handicap (0-80 3-y-o and up) £3,450 1m 100yds (5:00)

3732² DEVIL'S HOLIDAY (USA) [-] 3-8-13 P V Gilson (5) ... (7 to 2) 1
3497* STRATEGIC TIMING (Ire) [-] (bl) 3-9-6 M J Kinane (1) ....(11 to 10 fav) 2
3164² COOLRAIN LADY (Ire) [-] 3-9-1 S Craine (7) ....(4 to 1) 3
3576⁶ SAMOT (Ire) [-] 3-9-1 J F Egan (2) ....(7 to 1) 4
3380⁵ GOODIES TWO STEP (Ire) [-] 3-9-6 N G McCullagh (6) ....(12 to 1) 5
3616⁷ RED GLITTER (USA) [-] 3-8-9 (4*) J J Behan (4) ....(16 to 1) 6
Dist: 1l, 2l, 1½l, 2l. 1m 49.10s. (6 Ran).
(Sheikh Mohammed), Michael Kauntze

CLONMEL (IRE) (good)
Thursday September 9th

3856 Kilcash Claiming Race (3-y-o) £2,243 1 ¼m............................ (4:00)

3368⁴ MILLERS MILL (Ire) 7-13 (2*) R M Burke (4) .... (6 to 1) 1
3769⁵ HERMES GOLD (Ire) 8-0 W J Supple (1) ...... (11 to 8 fav) 2
CAPTURE THE MAGIC (Ire) 8-0 J F Egan (3) .... (8 to 1) 3
3454⁵ ALDENA (Ire) 7-10 (2*) D G O'Shea (12) .... (10 to 1) 4
3769⁹ FAIRY FANTASY (Ire) 7-6 (8*) G M Moylan (9) ......(12 to 1) 5
SARAMY (Ire) 7-10 (4*) W J Smith (6) ....(16 to 1) 6
2285⁹ BUTTERNUT (Ire) 8-2 N G McCullagh (2) ....(14 to 1) 7
3298³ CHAMPAGNE NIGHT (Fr) (bl) 7-11 (6*) R V Skelly (7) (4 to 1) 8
3524⁹ GLOWING LINES (Ire) 8-10 S Craine (11) ....(12 to 1) 9
2806⁹ DRESS DANCE (Ire) 8-5 A J Nolan (8) ....(20 to 1) 10
3721 REGAL PRETENDER (Ire) 7-13 (4*) J J Behan (10) .. (8 to 1) 11D
Dist: Hd, 2½l, 1l, 1l. 2m 3.00s. (11 Ran).
(L M K Racing Club), E McNamara

3857 Suir Maiden (4-y-o and up) £2,243 2m ....(4:30)

3405⁸ STRONG CASE (Ire) 5-8-10 (4*) J J Behan (1) ..(10 to 9 on) 1
3577⁹ WILD FANTASY (Ire) 5-8-11 W J Supple (7) .... (6 to 1) 2
3580 SOPHISM (USA) 4-9-0 M J Kinane (9) ....(8 to 1) 3
MAY GALE (Ire) 5-8-11 N Byrne (5) .... (16 to 1) 4
ENNEREILLY RIVER 10-8-4 (10*) S P Kelly (6) .....(12 to 1) 5
3077² EASTER SIXTEEN 7-9-0 K J Manning (10) .... (4 to 1) 6
3299⁶ PHARACH (Ire) 4-9-0 N G McCullagh (8) .... (10 to 1) 7
3524⁸ DONE DEAL (Ire) 5-8-6 (8*) B Fenton (2) ....(33 to 1) 8
RED BARONS LADY (Ire) 4-8-11 R Hughes (3) .... (25 to 1) 9
3077⁶ CARES OF TOMORROW 6-8-6 (8*) A P McCoy (4) ..(9 to 1) pu
Dist: 3½l, 3l, 7l, 8l. 3m 38.40s. (10 Ran).
(J A Stewart), Liam Browne

3858 September Handicap (0-75 3-y-o and up) £2,243 1¼m................(5:00)

3544 GREAT CABARET (Ire) [-] 3-9-8 M J Kinane (2) ..... (4 to 1) 1
3397⁴ SOUND PERFORMANCE (Ire) [-] (bl) 4-8-13 J P Murtagh (4) ....(12 to 1) 2
3419* WHAT A PLEASURE (Ire) [-] 3-9-2 (6*) B J Walsh (7) (5 to 1) 3
3721³ MORNING NURSE (Ire) [-] 4-9-2 W J Supple (9) ..... (4 to 1) 4
3381³ SAINT HILDA (Ire) [-] 3-8-8 (6*) R V Skelly (1) .. (11 to 4 fav) 5
2346⁴ KEDWICK (Ire) [-] 4-10-0 N G McCullagh (8) ...... (10 to 1) 6
2460⁵ ARCH-T-GLEN (Ire) [-] 3-8-4 (8*) D M McCullagh (6) (40 to 1) 7
3721⁵ SON OF TEMPO (Ire) [-] 4-7-5 (2*) D G O'Shea (5) .. (9 to 1) 8
2743⁶ JU JU'S GIRL (Ire) [-] 3-8-13 K J Manning (3) ..... (12 to 1) 9
Dist: ½l, 2l, 1½l, 3l. 2m 3.60s. (9 Ran).
(R E Sangster), D K Weld

DONCASTER (soft)
Thursday September 9th
Going Correction: PLUS 0.25 sec. per fur.

3859 Queen's Own Yorkshire Dragoons Conditions Stakes Class D (2-y-o) £5,316 7f..................... (1:35)

3422* NICOLOTTE 9-1 M Hills (2) *trkd ldrs, quickened to ld o'r one out, pushed clr, cmftbly.* ....(11 to 10 on op Evens tchd 5 to 4) 1
3352* PENCADER (Ire) 9-1 J Reid (1) *led, shaken up hfwy, hdd o'r one out, no extr*........(11 to 10 on op 11 to 8 on) 2
Won by 2½l. 1m 29.44s. a 6.04s (2 Ran).
SR: 37/29/ (Mollers Racing), G Wragg

3860 May Hill Stakes Class A (Group 3) (2-y-o) £17,767 1m................(2:05)

3627* HAWAJISS 8-8 W R Swinburn (3) *sn tracking ldr, shaken up o'r 2 out, rdn wl over one out, styd on well to ld ins fnl furlong*....... (5 to 2 jt-fav op 7 to 4 tchd 11 to 4) 1
2592* KISSING COUSIN (Ire) 8-8 M Roberts (2) *led, shaken up o'r 2 out, rdn over one out, hdd and no extr fnl furlong.* ....(5 to 2 jt-fav op 7 to 4) 2
3478² NEWS AND ECHO (USA) 8-8 R Cochrane (6) *in tch, rdn and outpcd 3 out, kpt on fnl furlong, no ch wth 1st 2.* ....(11 to 2 op 9 to 2 tchd 6 to 1) 3
3652* OVERACT (Ire) 8-8 L Dettori (5) *trkd ldrs, rdn o'r 3 out, grad wknd*..........................(4 to 1 op 3 to 1) 4
3625³ LUANA 8-8 Pat Eddery (1) *dwlt, in tch till wknd quickly 3 out, tld off.* ....(13 to 2 op 7 to 1 tchd 10 to 1 and 6 to 1) 5
Dist: 2l, 10l, ½l, 15l. 1m 40.61s. a 3.91s (5 Ran).
SR: 65/59/29/27/-/ (Maktoum Al Maktoum), M R Stoute

3861 Doncaster Cup Class A (Group 3) (3-y-o and up) £20,082 2¼m....... (2:35)

3349² ASSESSOR (Ire) 4-9-7 T Quinn (2) *hld up, smooth hdwy 3 out, led entering fnl furlong, styd on strly.* ....(5 to 4 fav tchd 11 to 8 and 11 to 10) 1
3405* FURTHER FLIGHT 7-9-3 M Hills (6) *hld up, effrt 3 out, led 2 out, sn rdn, hdd entering fnl furlong, no extr.* ....(15 to 8 op 6 to 4 tchd 2 to 1) 2
3538² JACK BUTTON (Ire) 4-9-0 N Connorton (3) *chsd ldr, sn pushed alng, drvn to ld o'r 4 out, hdd 2 out, one pace.* ....(8 to 1 op 10 to 1 tchd 12 to 1) 3
3405⁴ WITNESS BOX (USA) 6-9-0 M Roberts (1) *led till hdd o'r 4 out, grad wknd*..................... (5 to 1 op 7 to 2) 4
3599⁷ POST IMPRESSIONIST (Ire) 4-8-11 K Darley (5) *hld up, pushed alng 6 out, lost tch 5 out, tld off.* ....(100 to 1 op 50 to 1) 5
Dist: 4l, 5l, 7l, dist. 4m 3.84s. a 11.84s (5 Ran).
SR: 34/26/18/11/-/ (B E Nielsen), R Hannon

3862 Kiveton Park Stakes Class A (Group 3) (3-y-o and up) £22,196 1m...... (3:10)

3622* SWING LOW 4-9-7 J Reid (9) *in tch, effrt 3 out, styd on wl fnl furlong, led last strd*..........(7 to 2 co-fav op 3 to 1 tchd 4 to 1) 1
3622³ EMPEROR JONES (USA) 3-8-13 M Roberts (1) *pld hrd early, led, rdn o'r one out, wknd ins fnl furlong, ct last strd*............ (7 to 2 co-fav op 3 to 1 tchd 4 to 1) 2
3622² MISTLE CAT (USA) 3-8-9 W Woods (4) *chsd ldr, rdn o'r 2 out, hng rght over one out, kpt on fnl furlong, no extr nr finish*.................... (7 to 2 co-fav op 5 to 2) 3
2905 INNER CITY (Ire) 4-9-4 R Cochrane (3) *in tch, effrt 3 out, one pace*......... (7 to 2 co-fav op 3 to 1 tchd 4 to 1) 4
3748³ COLWAY ROCK (USA) 3-8-9 W R Swinburn (10) *chsd ldrs, rdn o'r 3 out, sn btn.* (12 to 1 op 14 to 1 tchd 16 to 1) 5
3468 YOUNG SENOR (USA) 4-9-0 M Hills (2) *strted slwly, tld off whn pld up aftr 3 fs, lme*......................(8 to 1) pu
Dist: Sht-hd, hd, 7l, 3½l. 1m 42.79s. a 6.09s (6 Ran).

SR: 46/37/32/20/-/-/ (Roldvale Limited), R Hannon

3863 Doncaster Free Press Ladies Day Handicap Class C (0-90 3-y-o and up) £5,617 7f...................... (3:40)

3070[5] FINAL FRONTIER (Ire) [70] 3-8-7 T Quinn (11) *wth ldrs till lost pl hfwy, rdn to ld entering fnl furlong, hld on wl.* ....(8 to 1 op 10 to 1) 1
3540[8] PRENONAMOSS [75] (v) 5-9-2 J Reid (16) *trkd ldrs, effrt 2 out, kpt on wl und pres fnl furlong.* ....(11 to 1 op 10 to 1) 2
3269[4] ALBEMINE (USA) [66] 4-8-7 Paul Eddery (14) *al prmnt, ev ch o'r one out, kpt on same pace.* ....(4 to 1 fav tchd 9 to 2) 3
3575 DAILY SPORT DON [68] 3-8-5 K Darley (5) *trkd ldrs, effrt o'r 2 out, ev ch over one out, no extr fnl furlong.* (8 to 1) 4
3458[5] LA BAMBA [71] 7-8-12 W Hood (15) *beh, effrt 3 out, styd on wl fnl furlong, not rch ldrs.* ....(9 to 2 op 3 to 1 tchd 5 to 1) 5
3670 KENESHA (Ire) [74] 3-8-11 R Cochrane (17) *beh, swtchd outsd o'r 2 out, hdwy and ev ch over one out, one pace fnl furlong*..........................(33 to 1 op 25 to 1) 6
1939* DEBSY DO (USA) [75] 4-8-13 (3*) O Pears (1) *cl up, slight ld 2 out, hdd and wknd entering fnl furlong.* ....(10 to 1 tchd 11 to 1) 7
3523[2] EXCLUSION [70] 4-8-11 W Newnes (7) *cl up, led 4 out til hdd 2 out, wknd entering fnl furlong.* ....(9 to 2 op 4 to 1 tchd 5 to 1) 8
3778 BALLAD DANCER [69] 8-8-10 M Birch (10) *slight ld till hdd 4 out, wknd o'r 2 out*..............(14 to 1 op 16 to 1) 9
3404 BERTIE WOOSTER [74] 10-9-1 M Hills (6) *al beh.* ....(20 to 1 op 16 to 1) 10
3593 ROCA MURADA (Ire) [69] 4-8-3 (7*) P McCabe (2) *dwlt, sn chasing ldrs, ev ch 2 out, wknd quickly o'r one out.* ....(13 to 2 op 6 to 1 tchd 7 to 1) 11

Dist: Nk, 3l, ¾l, 1½l, sht-hd, ¾l, 3½l, 3l, ½l, 3½l. 1m 28.08s. a 4.68s (11 Ran).
SR: 49/57/39/35/37/35/38/22/12/ (A D Spence), R Akehurst

3864 Kyoto Sceptre Stakes Class A formerly the Reference Point Sceptre Stakes (Listed Race) (3-y-o and up) £10,965 7f..................... (4:10)

2885[2] ARJUZAH (Ire) 3-8-6 W Carson (8) *trkd ldrs gng wl, bumped o'r one out, quickened to ld entering fnl furlong, sn clr, very easily.* ....(9 to 4 fav op 2 to 1 tchd 5 to 2) 1
3477[8] MOON OVER MIAMI 3-8-10 Pat Eddery (5) *beh, effrt whn not much room 2 out, hmpd o'r one out, styd on wl to take second ins fnl furlong, no ch wth wnr.* ....(7 to 1 op 6 to 1 tchd 8 to 1) 2
3680[5] TAUFAN BLU (Ire) 4-8-10 K Darley (7) *beh, hdwy 3 out, ch whn hmpd entering fnl furlong, kpt on.* ....(15 to 2 op 12 to 1 tchd 7 to 1) 3
3227* STELLA MYSTIKA (USA) 3-8-6 M Roberts (6) *cl up, slight ld hfwy, drifted rght o'r one out, wknd entering fnl furlong*..........................(4 to 1 op 5 to 2) 4
1030[3] RIBBONWOOD (USA) 3-8-6 L Dettori (4) *trkd ldrs, effrt 3 out, one pace*..........................(5 to 1 op 3 to 1) 5
3315 MOUNTAIN ASH 4-9-4 J Reid (9) *slight ld till hdd hfwy, wkng whn bumped o'r one out*.......(7 to 1 op 6 to 1) 6
3477[4] TAHDID 3-8-6 R Hills (3) *wth ldrs till wknd 3 out.* ....(9 to 1 op 10 to 1 tchd 12 to 1) 7

Dist: 5l, 1½l, ¾l, 1l, 8l, 10l. 1m 27.46s. a 4.06s (7 Ran).
SR: 57/46/41/35/32/20/-/ (Hamdan Al-Maktoum), J H M Gosden

3865 Levy Board Nursery Class C (2-y-o) £5,663 1m..................... (4:40)

3597[9] DUTY TIME [82] 9-3 W Carson (15) *beh, effrt 3 out, styd on wl und pres to ld towards finish*...(14 to 1 op 12 to 1) 1
3351[4] BALI WARRIOR (Ire) [69] 8-4 M Hills (5) *cl up, slight ld o'r 3 out till hdd and no extr towards finish.* ....(10 to 1 tchd 12 to 1) 2
3750* BALLARD RING (Ire) [73] 8-8 (7ex) J Fanning (1) *beh, hdwy whn hmpd 2 out, kpt on wl fnl furlong.* ....(16 to 1 op 14 to 1 tchd 20 to 1) 3
3635[3] BEATS WORKING [83] 9-4 K Fallon (4) *in tch, hdwy 3 out, slightly hmpd 2 out, ev ch one out, no extr.* ....(6 to 1 fav tchd 7 to 1) 4
2465* CARAPELLE [63] 7-12[4] (3*) S Maloney (14) *chsd ldrs, outpcd o'r 3 out, styd on wl fnl furlong.* ....(15 to 2 op 6 to 1 tchd 8 to 1) 5
3510 SILVER WEDGE (USA) [82] 9-3 Pat Eddery (16) *cl up, ev ch o'r one out, no extr*....(9 to 1 op 8 to 1 tchd 10 to 1) 6
3597[3] ARZ (USA) [75] 8-10 R Hills (12) *chsd ldrs, kpt on same pace fnl 2 fs*..........................(10 to 1 op 8 to 1) 7
2890[3] SECRET SERENADE [83] (v) 9-4 M Birch (9) *beh, hdwy on outsd o'r 3 out, ch over one out, wknd fnl furlong.* ....(14 to 1 op 12 to 1 tchd 16 to 1) 8
3597[2] SHARP TYCOON (Ire) [78] 8-13 W R Swinburn (7) *led or dsptd ld till wknd o'r one out*.....(11 to 1 op 10 to 1) 9
2492[3] BANDAR PERAK [69] (v) 8-4[1] T Quinn (3) *prmnt, rdn 3 out, wknd o'r one out*..........................(20 to 1) 10
3592 PLUM DENNIS [58] 7-3[1] (5*) D Wright (2) *chsd ldrs till wknd 2 out*..........................(66 to 1 op 50 to 1) 11
2759[2] MANHATTAN SUNSET (USA) [75] 8-10 J Reid (6) *beh till some late hdwy, nvr dngrs*.......(11 to 1 op 10 to 1) 12
3490[4] HEATHYARDS CRUSADE (Ire) [59] 7-8[8] (7*) M Humphries (11) *in tch till wknd 3 out*..........................(20 to 1) 13
2988[9] SECOND SIGHT (Ire) [77] 8-12 M Roberts (8) *chsd ldrs till wknd 2 out*.........(11 to 1 op 12 to 1 tchd 10 to 1) 14
3281* HAM N'EGGS [86] 9-7 L Dettori (10) *cl up till wknd o'r 3 out*..........................(13 to 2 op 5 to 1 tchd 7 to 1) 15
3389[3] PHYLIAN [67] 8-2 W Woods (13) *beh most of way.* ....(12 to 1 tchd 14 to 1) 16
2465[6] TWO D'S [60] 7-9 J Lowe (17) *chsd ldrs till wknd o'r 3 out.* ....(20 to 1 tchd 25 to 1) 17

Dist: Nk, 1½l, hd, 2½l, 3½l, 1½l, 1l, 2l, nk, sht-hd. 1m 42.35s. a 5.55s (17 Ran).
SR: 50/36/35/44/16/24/12/17/6/ (Aubrey Ison), J L Dunlop

FOLKESTONE (good)
Thursday September 9th
Going Correction: NIL (races 1,3,7,8), MINUS 0.15 (2,4,5,6)

3866 New Inn Sandwich Maiden Fillies' Stakes Class D (3-y-o and up) £3,494 1m 1f 149yds.................. (1:45)

3693[3] MAJHOLA (Ire) 3-8-7 A Munro (10) *wtd wth in tch, shaken up to ld jst ins fnl furlong, pushed out.* ....(5 to 4 fav op 7 to 4) 1
3708[3] DIPLOMATIST 3-8-7 W Ryan (4) *nvr far away, hdwy o'r 3 fs out, led briefly entering last, kpt on one pace.* ....(5 to 1 op 7 to 2 tchd 11 to 2) 2
1911[4] LAILATI (USA) 3-8-7 B Raymond (1) *led aftr one fs, rdn 2 out, hdd entering fnl furlong*........(7 to 1 op 3 to 1) 3
3514[7] ZANZE (USA) 3-8-7 G Hind (9) *hld up in tch, rdn 3 fs out, one pace aftr*...........(7 to 2 op 5 to 2 tchd 4 to 1) 4
3693 LA VILLA ROSE (Fr) 3-8-7 J Quinn (6) *mid-div, no hdwy ins fnl 3 fs*..........................(50 to 1 op 25 to 1) 5
992 ALYVAIR 3-8-7 P Robinson (12) *al mid-div, no ch fnl 3 fs.* ....(50 to 1 op 25 to 1) 6
SWALLOW RIDGE (Ire) 4-9-0 D Biggs (8) *beh, rdn and hdwy o'r 2 fs out, nvr nr to chal*...(50 to 1 op 33 to 1) 7
CLELIA 3-8-7 D Harrison (11) *al towards rear.* ....(50 to 1 op 25 to 1) 8
3693[7] SING A RAINBOW (Ire) 3-8-7 S Whitworth (5) *nvr on terms.* ....(33 to 1 op 16 to 1) 9
3693[5] WESSHAUN 3-8-7 T Sprake (13) *led 1st furlong, lost tch 3 fs out*..........................(50 to 1 op 33 to 1) 10
GECKO ROUGE 3-8-7 S Dawson (2) *slwly away, al wl beh*..........................(50 to 1 op 25 to 1) 11
3514[8] KOSATA (Ire) 3-8-7 J Williams (7) *pld hrd, sn trkd ldr, sddl slpd, wknd rpdly o'r 2 fs, virtually pulled up.* ....(10 to 1 op 7 to 1 tchd 12 to 1) 12
DOUNHURST 6-9-0 A Clark (3) *al beh, tld off fnl 4 fs.* ....(40 to 1 op 25 to 1) 13

Dist: 2l, 1½l, 8l, sht-hd, 8l, hd, 1l, 2½l, hd, 10l. 2m 5.70s. a 8.10s (13 Ran).
SR: 12/8/5/-/-/-/ (Sultan Mohammed), Lord Huntingdon

3867 South East London Mercury Claiming Stakes Class G (Div I) (2-y-o) £2,070 6f ....(2:15)

3657[5] ELEVATOR SHAFT (Ire) (bl) 8-6 A Munro (4) *made all, drw clr o'r 2 fs out, pushed out, easily.* ....(7 to 2 op 5 to 2 tchd 4 to 1) 1
3264 MANDEVILLE GEORGE 9-0 W Ryan (2) *sn rdn alng, styd on to go second ins fnl furlong.* ....(10 to 1 op 7 to 1 tchd 12 to 1) 2
3658 SPEEDY SNAPS IMAGE 8-6 J Williams (8) *mid-div, rdn o'r 2 fs out, kpt on one pace ins last*...(25 to 1 op 20 to 1) 3
3641[8] SNOWDON SLIGHTS 8-1 P Robinson (11) *wl beh and outpcd, styd on ins fnl 2 fs, nvr nrr.* (16 to 1 tchd 25 to 1) 4
3573[2] UP THE MARINERS (Ire) 8-7 (5*) K Rutter (1) *slwly away, nvr rch ldrs*..........................(9 to 1 op 5 to 1) 5
3363[5] SARAH'S OPERA (Ire) 8-9 T Sprake (7) *speed till outpcd ins fnl 2 fs*..........................(33 to 1 op 20 to 1) 6
FOXTOWNS GIRL 8-0 (5*) N Gwilliams (6) *al outpcd.* ....(33 to 1 op 25 to 1) 7
3755[7] PRINCE OF GAELS (bl) 8-8 A Clark (3) *prmnt, chsd wnr hfwy till wknd wl o'r one furlong out.* ....(13 to 2 op 5 to 1 tchd 7 to 1) 8
3321[7] SPORTING HEIR (Ire) (bl) 9-1 N Adams (5) *speed, beh frm hfwy*..........................(10 to 1 op 7 to 1) 9
3633 TRUTH MOUNTAIN (Ire) 8-4 (5*) L Newton (9) *shwd early speed, sn beh*.......(2 to 1 fav op 9 to 4 tchd 5 to 2) 10
3546[6] GREEN'S IMPRESSION (Ire) 7-13 (3*) M Fenton (10) *prmnt on outsd to hfwy, rdn and sn btn.* ....(13 to 2 op 5 to 1 tchd 4 to 1 and 7 to 1) 11

Dist: 5l, 1½l, 3½l, 2½l, 2l, nk, hd, 2½l, 4l, nk. 1m 14.50s. a 3.50s (11 Ran).
SR: 4/-/-/-/-/-/ (Christopher Wright), D W P Arbuthnot

3868 St Margaret's Bay Median Auction Maiden Stakes Class F (3-y-o) £2,243 1m 7f 92yds....................(2:45)

3344[4] GUESTWICK 9-0 B Raymond (6) *pld hrd, trkd ldrs, wnt second 6 fs out, rdn to ld o'r 2 out, pushed clr.* (2 to 1 jt-fav op 7 to 4) 1
2507[5] CHARLOTTE DUNDAS 8-9 G Hind (5) *trkd ldrs till 6 fs out, styd in tch, rdn and kpt on one pace fnl 2 furlongs.* ....(4 to 1 op 5 to 2) 2
538 MR LUCIANO (Ire) 8-11 (3*) B Doyle (4) *in rear till took clr order frm hfwy, one pace fnl 3 fs*.....(9 to 1 op 8 to 1) 3
3740[5] HOME PARK (Ire) 9-0 W Ryan (3) *made most till hdd o'r 2 fs out, rdn and sn btn*............(2 to 1 jt-fav op 6 to 4) 4
3392[6] CANDARELA (bl) 8-9 J Quinn (1) *slwly away, al beh, tld off frm hfwy*.......................(25 to 1 op 14 to 1) 5
3344[5] COMBELLINO 9-0 G Duffield (2) *in tch till ran wide on bend aftr 6 fs, sn tld off*...........(10 to 1 op 14 to 1) 6
Dist: 5l, 12l, ½l, 30l, 25l. 3m 31.00s. a 12.50s (6 Ran).
(Sir Gordon Reece), J L Dunlop

3869 South East London Mercury Claiming Stakes Class G (Div II) (2-y-o) £2,070 6f ....(3:15)

3641* GIPSY KID 7-11 (7*) C Hawksley (3) *made all, pushed clr ins fnl furlong*......(9 to 4 fav op 5 to 2 tchd 2 to 1) 1
3641 BESSIE'S WILL 7-11 A Mackay (8) *pressed wnr till outpcd fnl furlong*............(9 to 1 op 8 to 1 tchd 10 to 1) 2
1964[4] BADGER'S BEND 8-3 P Robinson (7) *chsd ldrs, rdn 2 fs out, styd on ins last*................(9 to 2 op 7 to 2) 3
3762[7] CHARISMA GIRL 8-6 G Duffield (9) *chsd ldrs, rdn and styd on one pace ins fnl 2 fs*........................(3 to 1) 4
3529[4] MAGIC MAGGIE 7-11 T Williams (2) *speed till wknd o'r one furlong out*..........(11 to 1 op 8 to 1 tchd 12 to 1) 5
3641 DISH OF THE DAY (Ire) 7-12[1] D Harrison (10) *prmnt on outsd, rdn and wknd wl o'r one furlong out.* ....(33 to 1 op 20 to 1) 6
3633 DOUBLE DIP 9-0 M Tebbutt (1) *beh frm hfwy, collapsed aftr line, dead*.....................(10 to 1 op 8 to 1) 7
3698 SUNDAY RISK 8-4 A McGlone (11) *in tch to hfwy.* ....(33 to 1 op 20 to 1) 8
3387 AVANTI XIQUET 9-0 C Avery (6) *al towards rear.* ....(20 to 1 tchd 25 to 1) 9
GUTO NYTH BRAN 8-10 S Whitworth (5) *slwly away, outpcd, al beh*...........(11 to 1 op 8 to 1 tchd 12 to 1) 10
CLASSIC MELODY 8-2 D Biggs (4) *slwly away, tld off frm hfwy*.....................(33 to 1 op 20 to 1) 11
Dist: 3l, nk, 2l, ¾l, 3l, 2½l, 2l, sht-hd, 12l, 7l. 1m 15.30s. a 4.30s (11 Ran).
(Mrs Lesley Mills), R Guest

3870 EBF Margate Rating Related Maiden Stakes Class F (2-y-o) £2,950 5f (3:45)

3642 LIGHTNING BELLE (bl) 8-9 A Clark (1) *made all, rdn hfwy, kpt on ins fnl furlong*.............(12 to 1 op 8 to 1) 1
3545[7] COLNE VALLEY 8-9 A McGlone (6) *sn chsd wnr, rdn o'r one furlong out, no imprsn ins.* ....(9 to 2 op 4 to 1 tchd 5 to 1) 2
3421 BANDITA 8-9 Dale Gibson (2) *mid-div, ran on one pace ins fnl 2 fs*..........(12 to 1 op 14 to 1 tchd 20 to 1) 3
1229[7] PRIMO STAMPARI 8-9 W Ryan (9) *in tch on outsd, no hdwy appr fnl furlong*.............(7 to 2 tchd 4 to 1) 4
3426[6] CANDI DAS (Ire) 8-9 D Harrison (7) *mid-div, effrt hfwy, one pace appr fnl furlong*............(10 to 1 op 8 to 1) 5
3641 SPORT RACING CLUB (v) 8-9 M Tebbutt (4) *broke wl, no hdwy fnl 2 fs*.....................(33 to 1 op 25 to 1) 6
3743[8] HIGH SWINGER (v) 9-0 J Quinn (3) *outpcd, nvr nr to chal.* ....(12 to 1) 7
3664[7] ERRIS BOY (bl) 9-0 D Biggs (10) *chsd ldrs till wknd wl o'r one furlong out*......(11 to 1 op 10 to 1 tchd 12 to 1) 8
3573[5] MACE EL REEM 8-9 G Duffield (8) *speed till wknd hfwy.* ....(20 to 1 op 12 to 1) 9
3711[2] MR BERGERAC (Ire) 8-11 (3*) Stephen Davies (5) *prmnt, sddl sn slpd, wkng whn uns rdr ins fnl furlong.* ....(3 to 1 fav op 2 to 1) ur
Dist: 1l, 2½l, 2½l, ¾l, ½l, sht-hd, sht-hd, 4l. 1m 1.50s. a 2.90s (10 Ran).
SR: 22/18/8/-/-/-/ (Mrs Satu Marks), M McCormack

3871 Kent Enterprise Office Nursery Class E (2-y-o) £3,183 5f..............(4:15)

3657[2] DANCES WITH RISK [63] 8-4 D Harrison (2) *sn trkd ldr, led jst ins fnl furlong, rdn out*..........(7 to 2 op 5 to 2) 1
3715[4] ALZIANAH [76] 9-3 P Robinson (4) *wtd wth in tch, short of room hfwy, outpcd appr last, ran on wl to go second ins*...................(6 to 1 op 5 to 1 tchd 13 to 2) 2
3426* RESONANT [80] 9-7 G Duffield (1) *led, hng lft 1st 2 fs, rdn and hdd jst ins last, no extr.* ....(7 to 4 fav op 5 to 2 tchd 11 to 4) 3
3566* ALLLEGSNOBRAIN [75] 9-2 A Munro (8) *al prmnt on outsd, rdn and ev ch appr last, no extr ins.* (4 to 1 op 3 to 1) 4
3528[7] CRAFTY CRICKETER [52] (bl) 7-3[3] (7*) N Varley (7) *speed on outsd for 3 fs*........................(33 to 1 op 20 to 1) 5
3475[9] INDIAN DREAMER [57] 7-12[3] (3*) M Fenton (6) *speed till rdn and wknd wl o'r one furlong out.* (14 to 1 op 10 to 1) 6
3529[2] LOVESCAPE [76] 9-3 A Clark (5) *in tch 3 fs.* ....(9 to 1 op 8 to 1 tchd 10 to 1) 7
3641 SOUTHDOWN GIRL [52] 7-7 G Bardwell (3) *al beh, lost tch hfwy*.....................................(33 to 1) 8
Dist: 1l, 1½l, 1½l, 7l, 2½l, ¾l, 3l. 1m 0.90s. a 2.30s (8 Ran).
SR: 29/38/36/25/-/ (Roldvale Limited), G Lewis

3872 Eight Bells Canterbury Handicap Class E (0-70 3-y-o and up) £3,106 1m 7f 92yds......................(4:45)

3716[7] HUNTING GROUND [52] (bl) 5-9-6 G Duffield (8) *nvr out of 1st 3, chsd wnr 6 fs out, hrd rdn o'r 2 out, ran on gmely to ld on line*...................(3 to 1 fav op 11 to 4) 1
3479[5] PEACH BRANDY [41] 4-8-9 N Adams (2) *led, strly rdn 2 fs out, ran on, hdd on line.* ....(5 to 1 op 9 to 2 tchd 11 to 2) 2
3759 JOLIS ABSENT [43] (bl) 3-7-13 G Bardwell (5) *chsd ldrs, hrd rdn 3 fs out, no imprsn on 1st 2 ins last two furlongs.* ....(9 to 2 op 11 to 4) 3
3394[3] LEXUS (Ire) [38] 5-8-6 D Biggs (7) *mid-div, styd on und pres ins fnl 2 fs*.....................(5 to 1 op 6 to 1) 4
3521[5] WHITE RIVER [44] 7-8-12 J Williams (3) *mid-div till lost pl hfwy, styd on fnl 2 fs*............................(7 to 1) 5
1607 BITTER ALOE [56] 4-9-10 B Raymond (6) *beh, effrt hfwy, sn rdn, not pace to chal*...........(16 to 1 op 14 to 1) 6
3548[6] ROCQUAINE BAY [44] 6-8-12 C Rutter (1) *beh till hdwy 4 fs out, wknd 2 out*...................(10 to 1 op 8 to 1) 7
2471[4] ROMANIAN (Ire) [42] 5-8-10 J Quinn (9) *in tch till wknd o'r 2 fs out*...........................(10 to 1 op 8 to 1) 8
3590 SEATTLE AFFAIR (Ire) [48] (bl) 3-8-4 A Clark (4) *mid-div, rdn to go second briefly sn aftr hfwy, wknd rpdly o'r 2 fs out*...............................(33 to 1 op 20 to 1) 9
Dist: Sht-hd, 2l, 1½l, 2l, nk, 4l, 8l, 7l. 3m 33.70s. a 15.20s (9 Ran).
(Esprit de Corps Racing), A Bailey

3873 Sun Inn St Nicholas At Wade Limited Stakes Class E (0-70 3-y-o and up) £3,054 1½m................... (5:15)

3456[7] DANCING TRALTHEE (Ire) 3-8-7 J Weaver (7) *wtd wth in tch, hdwy o'r 3 fs out, led one and a half out, drvn out.* ....(7 to 2 fav tchd 5 to 1) 1
3587[7] EL VOLADOR 6-9-7 W Ryan (6) *hld up, gd hdwy 5 fs out, rdn to chal wl o'r one furlong out, swtchd rght ins, ran on*..................................(7 to 1 op 5 to 1) 2
3314 MITRAAS (USA) (bl) 3-8-12 N Carlisle (4) *led till hdd one and a half fs out, one pace aftr*...............(7 to 1) 3
3288 ADDICTED TO LOVE (bl) 4-9-2 A Munro (9) *chsd ldrs, rdn 3 fs out, no hdwy fnl 2*..............(11 to 2 op 5 to 1) 4
3212[5] INDIAN FLASH (Ire) 3-8-7 D Harrison (10) *chsd ldrs till wknd wl o'r one furlong out*.........(6 to 1 op 7 to 2) 5
3681[4] LEAR KING (USA) 3-8-12 M Perrett (3) *trkd ldrs, rdn 3 fs out, sn btn*.................................(8 to 1) 6
3518[7] GALEJADE 3-8-7 J Williams (1) *al in rear.* ....(10 to 1 op 7 to 1 tchd 12 to 1) 7
1936[3] QAFFAL (USA) 3-8-12 B Raymond (5) *mid-div sn aftr hfwy.* ....(8 to 1 op 7 to 1) 8
3507 STORM VENTURE (Ire) 3-8-12 G Duffield (8) *chsd ldr till wknd rpdly o'r 3 fs out, tld off*.......(5 to 1 op 4 to 1) 9
3388[7] AFTER THE FIRE 4-9-2 (5*) K Rutter (2) *al beh, lost tch by hfwy, tld off*...............(50 to 1 op 20 to 1) 10
Dist: 1½l, 6l, 3l, 4l, 10l, ¾l, 2l, 1l, dist. 2m 41.40s. a 10.90s (10 Ran).
(Sheikh Ahmed Al Maktoum), L M Cumani

CAPANNELLE (ITY) (good)
Friday September 10th

3874 Premio Aringo (Listed) (3-y-o and up) £20,173 6f.................... (3:00)

1365[2] IMPREVEDIBILE (Ire) 3-8-10 A Parravani,................. 1
REFERENCE LIGHT (USA) 6-8-9 M Tellini,................. 2
1362[6] VINTAGE ONLY 5-8-9 B Jovine,........................ 3+
COMPUTER KID 4-8-9 A Luongo,........................ 3+
3348 VERDE ALITALIA (Ire) 4-8-9 F Jovine, *pressed ldr till wknd wl o'r one furlong out*.............................. 7
Dist: 1 ¼l, 2 ¼l, dd-ht, 2 ¼l, ½l, sht-hd, 4l. 1m 9.00s. (8 Ran).
(Scuderia Gianni Daniele), P Ceriotti

3875 Premio Angri (Maiden) (2-y-o) £5,603 5f............................ (3:30)

KATHY FAIRUZ (Ire) 8-8 A Corniani,...................... 1
GOLDEN COMPLIANCE (USA) 8-11 S Morales,........... 2
BIG PIER (Ire) 8-11 O Fancera,.......................... 3
3545[5] VEDO NUDO 8-11 F Jovine, *trkd ldrs till wknd o'r one furlong out*.. 5
Dist: ¾l, 1½l, 1½l, 3l, 1½l, 2½l. 59.00s. (10 Ran).
(Allevamento Pian Di Neve), A Peraino

DONCASTER (soft)
Friday September 10th
Going Correction: PLUS 0.20 sec. per fur.

3876 Laurent-Perrier Rose Champagne Maiden Stakes For Injured Jockeys' Fund Class D (2-y-o) £3,840 1m (1:35)

2359² SHEPTON MALLET (Ire) 9-0 J Reid (12) *cl up, chlgd 2 out, rdn fnl furlong, kpt on wl to ld close hme.* ....(11 to 10 fav op 6 to 4 tchd 11 to 10 on) 1
DOVER STRAITS (USA) 9-0 W R Swinburn (1) *in tch, gd hdwy o'r 2 out, led jst ins fnl furlong, kpt on, ct cl hme.* ....(9 to 1 op 5 to 1 tchd 10 to 1) 2
3316² THABIT (USA) 9-0 R Hills (14) *led aftr 2 fs, hdd jst ins last, no extr*............(11 to 2 op 7 to 2 tchd 6 to 1) 3
2559² SHERIDAN (Ire) 9-0 Pat Eddery (8) *led 2 fs, cl up, kpt on same pace fnl two furlongs.* ....(6 to 1 op 5 to 1 tchd 13 to 2) 4
3352⁴ SOUTHERN POWER (Ire) 9-0 L Dettori (11) *trkd ldrs, hdwy and ev ch 2 out, sn wknd*............(10 to 1 op 6 to 1) 5
3760⁴ MAGNETIC REEL 9-0 J Carroll (3) *sn beh, kpt on frm 3 out, not trble ldrs*............(33 to 1) 6
3589 BALLYMORRIS (Ire) 8-11 (3*) B Doyle (13) *prmnt till wknd 3 out*............(100 to 1 op 50 to 1) 7
3658 EXPLORE MONDIAL (Ire) 9-0 M Tebbutt (9) *beh till some late hdwy, nvr nr ldrs*............(50 to 1 op 33 to 1) 8
SILENCE IN COURT (Ire) 9-0 A Mackay (10) *chsd ldrs till wknd o'r 3 out*............(50 to 1 op 33 to 1) 9
ASTRAL INVASION (USA) 9-0 K Fallon (6) *sn beh and pushed alng, nvr nr ldrs*............(20 to 1 op 12 to 1) 10
3505⁶ NAPOLEON STAR (Ire) 9-0 J Williams (4) *al beh.* ....(50 to 1 op 20 to 1 tchd 66 to 1) 11
NORTHERN HIGHLIGHT 9-0 J Fortune (7) *chsd ldrs till wknd o'r 3 out*............(50 to 1 op 33 to 1) 12
3400⁷ MERLINSRISK (Ire) 9-0 G Duffield (2) *in tch till wknd o'r 3 out*............(100 to 1 op 50 to 1) 13
2299 ZOES PET 8-9 Dale Gibson (5) *al beh.* ....(100 to 1 op 50 to 1) 14
Dist: Sht-hd, 1½l, nk, 8l, 5l, ½l, nk, 1½l, nk, 6l. 1m 43.01s. a 6.21s (14 Ran).
SR: 31/30/25/24/-/-/ (R E Sangster), P W Chapple-Hyam

3877 British Coal Handicap Stakes Class D (0-80 3-y-o and up) £3,840 5f.... (2:05)

3220² PRIMULA BAIRN [66] (v) 3-8-12 K Fallon (9) *al prmnt, effrt 2 out, ran on wl to ld cl hme.* ....(5 to 1 op 4 to 1 tchd 11 to 2) 1
3486* MACFARLANE [79] 5-9-13 F Norton (1) *trkd ldrs, led o'r one out, rdn fnl furlong, hdd and no extr cl hme.* ....(4 to 1 fav op 3 to 1) 2
3603⁵ SADDLEHOME (USA) [56] 4-8-4 G Duffield (7) *cl up, led 2 out, hdd o'r one out, kpt on wl fnl furlong.* ....(11 to 1 op 8 to 1 tchd 12 to 1) 3
3603* KALAR [52] (bl) 4-8-0 S Wood (11) *slight ld till hdd 2 out, kpt on fnl furlong*............(8 to 1 op 6 to 1) 4
3668³ ALLTHRUTHENIGHT (Ire) [79] 4-9-13 J Reid (13) *al chasing ldrs, no extr fnl furlong*............(9 to 1 op 7 to 1) 5
3603⁸ ARC LAMP [56] 7-8-4 J Fortune (2) *prmnt, rdn 2 out, kpt on same pace*............(12 to 1) 6
3638⁸ FOOD OF LOVE [80] 5-10-0 J Williams (12) *chsd ldrs, one pace fnl 2 fs*............(16 to 1 op 12 to 1) 7
3136⁵ LOCAL HEROINE [69] 3-9-1 J Carroll (5) *chsd ldrs, one pace fnl 2 fs*............(14 to 1 op 10 to 1) 8
2935⁴ PRINCE BELFORT [60] 5-8-8 N Adams (6) *nvr dngrs.* ....(12 to 1) 9
3504 SHE'S SMART [74] 5-9-5 (3*) S Maloney (3) *dsptd ld to hfwy, grad wknd*.... (16 to 1 op 14 to 1 tchd 20 to 1) 10
3486⁸ LITTLE SABOTEUR [68] 4-9-2 W R Swinburn (10) *nvr dngrs.* ....(9 to 1 op 6 to 1) 11
3603 ABSOLUTION [61] 9-8-9 Pat Eddery (8) *in tch, rdn hfwy, sn btn*............(9 to 1 op 8 to 1) 12
Dist: ½l, hd, sht-hd, 2l, 2l, 1½l, 2½l, nk, nk, sht-hd. 1m 2.23s. a 3.43s (12 Ran).
SR: 49/62/38/33/52/21/39/16/8/ (Kavli), Mrs J R Ramsden

3878 Coal Trade Benevolent Association Conditions Stakes Class B (3-y-o and up) £7,680 1¼m 60yds..........(2:35)

3644⁶ YOUNG BUSTER (Ire) 5-9-6 Pat Eddery (6) *hld up, hdwy on bit o'r 2 out, quickened to ld wl ins fnl furlong, cleverly*............(11 to 2 op 5 to 1 tchd 6 to 1) 1
3437⁴ SALATIN (USA) 3-8-11 R Hills (1) *trkd ldrs, led o'r one out, hdd wl ins fnl furlong, no extr*... (2 to 1 fav op 7 to 4) 2
3385* ICY SOUTH (USA) 3-8-12 L Dettori (2) *led till hdd o'r one out, kpt on same pace*... (3 to 1 op 7 to 2 tchd 9 to 4) 3
FRENCHPARK 3-8-13 J Carroll (3) *trkd ldr, rdn and wknd o'r one out*............(14 to 1 op 10 to 1 tchd 16 to 1) 4
3784⁴ GEISWAY (Can) 3-9-1 W R Swinburn (4) *in tch, rdn 2 out, sn btn*............(9 to 2 op 3 to 1 tchd 5 to 1) 5
3437* STONEY VALLEY 3-9-1 J Reid (5) *hld up, hdwy 3 out, rdn and wknd 2 out*............(8 to 1 op 7 to 1) 6
Dist: ½l, 3l, 2½l, 3½l, ¾l. 2m 13.45s. a 6.75s (6 Ran).
SR: 59/49/44/40/35/33/ (Mollers Racing), G Wragg

3879 O & K Troy Stakes Class A formerly the Troy Stakes (Listed Race) (3-y-o) £9,942 1½m.................. (3:05)

3318* PRINCE OF ANDROS (USA) 8-11 L Dettori (8) *hld up gng wl, steady hdwy to ld 2 out, hrd pressed fnl furlong, styd on well*............(5 to 1 op 9 to 4) 1
3434⁴ KEY TO MY HEART (Ire) 8-11 K Fallon (7) *trkd ldrs gng wl, shaken up to chal one out, ev ch till no extr towards finish*............(8 to 1 tchd 9 to 1) 2
1364⁹ PERSIAN BRAVE (Ire) 8-11 G Duffield (3) *trkd ldrs, slight ld o'r 2 out, sn hdd, kpt on same pace.* ....(100 to 30 fav op 3 to 1 tchd 4 to 1) 3
3318² KUSAMBA (USA) 8-11 J Reid (4) *sn tracking ldr, ev ch o'r 2 out, one paced*............(7 to 1 op 5 to 1 tchd 15 to 2) 4
3620³ URGENT REQUEST (Ire) 8-11 Pat Eddery (6) *sn led, hdd o'r 2 out, grad wknd*............(9 to 1 op 8 to 1 tchd 10 to 1) 5
3272* DEL DEYA (Ire) 8-6 L Piggott (5) *hld up, hdwy 4 out, rdn o'r 2 out, sn wknd*............(9 to 2 op 5 to 1) 6
890⁶ DESERT SECRET (Ire) 9-0 W R Swinburn (2) *hld up, effrt 3 out, no hdwy*............(12 to 1 op 10 to 1 tchd 14 to 1) 7
1638² MASHAIR (USA) 8-6 R Hills (1) *in tch, effrt 3 out, sn btn.* ....(11 to 2 op 5 to 1 tchd 6 to 1) 8
Dist: ½l, 2½l, 3½l, 2½l, 3l, 3½l, 3l. 2m 35.70s. a 5.20s (8 Ran).
SR: 69/68/63/56/51/40/41/27/ (Lucayan Stud), D R Loder

3880 Laurent-Perrier Champagne Stakes Class A (Group 2) (2-y-o) £38,274 7f ....(3:35)

3435² UNBLEST 8-11 G Duffield (2) *hld up in tch, shaken up and quickened entering fnl furlong, sn rdn, ran on wl to ld towards finish*..... (3 to 1 op 5 to 2 tchd 7 to 2) 1
2619* STATE PERFORMER (USA) 8-11 J Reid (4) *trkd ldrs, led wl o'r one out, rdn and quickened entering fnl furlong, hdd and no extr towards finish.* ....(Evens fav op 11 to 10 tchd 5 to 4 on) 2
2430* BLUEGRASS PRINCE (Ire) 8-11 L Dettori (3) *made most till hdd wl o'r one out, sn btn*............(10 to 1 op 7 to 1) 3
2359* BAL HARBOUR 8-11 Pat Eddery (1) *wth ldr, ev ch o'r one out, wknd fnl furlong*... (3 to 1 op 5 to 2 tchd 7 to 2) 4
Dist: ¾l, 6l, 2½l. 1m 28.36s. a 4.96s (4 Ran).
SR: 44/42/24/16/ (Lord Vestey), J R Fanshawe

3881 H. Leverton Handicap Stakes Class C (0-100 3-y-o and up) £4,480 1½m (4:05)

3724² FIRST BID [66] 6-8-7 A Culhane (7) *chsd ldrs, pushed alng hfwy, led o'r one out, drvn clr.* (4 to 1 fav tchd 5 to 1) 1
3434 PISTOL RIVER (Ire) [92] 3-9-10 J Reid (6) *sn pushed alng and beh, kpt on frm 3 out to take second ins fnl furlong, nrst finish*............(9 to 2 op 7 to 2) 2
3479³ DOYCE [65] 4-8-6 R Hills (3) *led till hdd o'r one out, no extr*............(9 to 1 op 8 to 1) 3
3033² BROCTUNE BAY [69] 4-8-10 M Birch (9) *in tch, hdwy to track ldr 8 out, outpcd 3 out, no dngr aftr.* ....(6 to 1 op 5 to 1) 4
3466 DRUMMER HICKS [78] 4-9-5 Pat Eddery (1) *prmnt till wknd o'r 2 out*............(6 to 1 op 5 to 1) 5
3252⁷ MISS PIN UP [72] 4-8-13 G Duffield (2) *dwlt, beh, some hdwy 3 out, wknd o'r one out*....(14 to 1 tchd 16 to 1) 6
2783⁶ LUNAR RISK [61] 3-7-7 J Lowe (8) *beh, effrt o'r 3 out, no hdwy*............(16 to 1 op 14 to 1) 7
3790⁸ QUEENS CONSUL (Ire) [68] 3-7-9 (5*) D Wright (4) *in tch, rdn 5 out, sn btn*..... (20 to 1 op 16 to 1 tchd 25 to 1) 8
3401⁵ DARMSTADT (USA) [82] (v) 3-9-0 L Dettori (5) *trkd ldrs, effrt 3 out, sn btn and eased*............(11 to 2 op 4 to 1) 9
Dist: 3l, 2l, 6l, 3½l, ¾l, 2½l, 6l, 6l. 2m 36.80s. a 6.30s (9 Ran).
SR: 54/65/43/35/37/29/4/-/1/ (Thomlinson's), R M Whitaker

3882 Sun Princess Conditions Stakes Class C (3-y-o) £4,480 1m.............(4:35)

3519* AJFAN (USA) 8-8 R Hills (3) *made all, styd on wl fnl 2 fs.* ....(Evens fav op 5 to 4 on) 1
3660² KATIBA (USA) 8-9 Pat Eddery (4) *in tch, pushed alng hfwy, outpcd o'r 2 out, styd on und pres to take second one out, not rch wnr*............(9 to 2 op 4 to 1) 2
1001⁵ TAOS (Ire) 9-7 L Dettori (1) *in tch, steady hdwy 3 out, one paced frm 2 out*............(4 to 1 op 7 to 2) 3
1950 JETBEEAH (Ire) 8-8 W R Swinburn (2) *chsd ldr, effrt o'r 2 out, one paced*.... (9 to 2 op 4 to 1 tchd 5 to 1) 4
Dist: 2½l, 1½l, sht-hd. 1m 41.69s. a 4.99s (4 Ran).
SR: 43/36/43/29/ (Hamdan Al-Maktoum), H Thomson Jones

GOODWOOD (good to soft)
Friday September 10th
Going Correction: PLUS 0.25 sec. per fur.

3883 Country Lady Rose Handicap Class C (0-90 3-y-o and up) £5,385 1m 1f (2:10)

3710² KNOWTH (Ire) [73] 4-9-4 T Quinn (17) *trkd ldrs al gng wl, led appr fnl furlong, drvn out.* ....(4 to 1 fav op 5 to 1 tchd 11 to 2 and 7 to 2) 1
2475² WAKIL (Ire) [66] 4-8-11 A Munro (10) *al cl up, ev ch appr fnl furlong, kpt on one pace*............ (14 to 1 tchd 16 to 1) 2
3353⁴ GOOGLY [73] 4-9-4 G Bardwell (16) *mid-div and sn pushed alng, not much room frm 3 fs out, swtchd lft o'r one out, ran on*............(8 to 1 op 7 to 1) 3
2581³ BOLD STROKE [77] 4-9-8 W Carson (18) *beh, pushed alng and hdwy on ins 3 fs out, styd on one pace.* ....(7 to 1 op 5 to 1) 4

3670[2] MAY HILLS LEGACY (Ire) [56] 4-8-1 R Price (5) *chsd ldrs, led o'r 2 fs out till hdd appr last, no extr.* ....(10 to 1 op 8 to 1 tchd 11 to 1) 5
3531[3] WAVE HILL [68] 4-8-13 J Weaver (14) *beh, effrt o'r 2 fs out, staying on ins last.*...............(12 to 1 op 14 to 1) 6
3179[7] SWIFT SILVER [58] 6-8-3 A McGlone (15) *hld up beh, styd on frm o'r one furlong out, nrst finish.* ....(20 to 1 op 14 to 1 tchd 25 to 1) 7
3269[6] DEEVEE [65] 4-8-10 P Robinson (2) *hld up in mid-div, hdwy 2 fs out, wknd ins last.*......(14 to 1 op 10 to 1) 8
3477 GUSTAVIA (Ire) [80] 3-9-5 M Roberts (6) *mid-div, rdn alng o'r 3 fs out, no hdwy.* (14 to 1 op 10 to 1 tchd 16 to 1) 9
3585[3] NAIF (USA) [85] 3-9-10 R Cochrane (4) *trkd ldrs, ev ch o'r 2 fs out, sn btn and eased.*..........(14 to 1 op 10 to 1) 10
3639[7] SEA BARON [66] 3-8-5 D Harrison (11) *trkd ldrs till wknd o'r one furlong out.*..............(33 to 1 op 25 to 1) 11
3271[4] MIROSWAKI (USA) [73] 3-8-12 Paul Eddery (13) *nvr plcd to chal.*..........................(33 to 1 op 20 to 1) 12
3585[8] CLOUDED ELEGANCE [83] 3-9-8 W Ryan (12) *al beh.* ....(12 to 1 op 10 to 1) 13
3697 BUZZARDS BELLBUOY [73] (v) 4-9-4 J Quinn (7) *nvr dngrs.* ....(33 to 1 op 25 to 1) 14
1374[5] YOUNG FREEMAN (USA) [73] 4-9-4 M Perrett (9) *hdd o'r 2 fs out, wknd quickly.*..........................(33 to 1) 15
3314 BRANDONHURST [82] 3-9-7 M Hills (20) *nvr better than mid-div.*............(12 to 1 op 10 to 1 tchd 14 to 1) 16
3623[6] AKKAZAO (Ire) [69] 5-9-0 B Raymond (3) *wth ldrs till wknd o'r 3 fs out.*.........(20 to 1 op 16 to 1 tchd 25 to 1) 17
3290 NORTH ESK (USA) [63] 4-8-3 (5*) D McCabe (19) *al beh.* ....(33 to 1 op 25 to 1) 18
Dist: 1½l, 2l, 1½l, ¾l, 1l, hd, 1l, 2l, 1l, 1½l. 1m 59.35s. a 7.35s (18 Ran).
SR: 28/16/17/16/-/2/ (Ruelles Partners), R Akehurst

3884 Stardom Stakes Class A (Listed Race) (2-y-o) £10,867 1m............. (2:40)

3592* INNISHOWEN (USA) 8-11 T Quinn (6) *sn led, quickened o'r one furlong out, ran on strly.*........(6 to 1 op 5 to 1) 1
3691* ESCARPMENT (USA) 8-11 M Roberts (5) *cl up, drvn alng 3 fs out, outpcd o'r one out, ran on ins last.* ....(2 to 1 fav op 7 to 4 tchd 9 to 4) 2
2419* HARVEST MOUSE 8-11 R Cochrane (4) *dwlt, hld up in cl tch, closed 3 fs out, hrd rdn o'r one out, one pace.* ....(9 to 4 op 3 to 1) 3
3659* BONNY BRIDE (Ire) 8-6 K Darley (3) *hld up, outpcd o'r 2 fs out, styd on ins last.* (12 to 1 op 10 to 1 tchd 14 to 1) 4
3510* BLAZE AWAY (USA) 8-11 M Hills (2) *trkd ldrs till wknd o'r one furlong out.*..................(4 to 1 op 5 to 2) 5
3667[2] NONIOS (Ire) 8-11 W Ryan (1) *hld up, hdwy o'r 2 fs out, wknd over one out.*...............(20 to 1 op 14 to 1) 6
Dist: 2½l, nk, nk, 3l, hd. 1m 43.62s. a 6.42s (6 Ran).
SR: 31/23/22/16/12/11/ (Conal Kavanagh), R Hannon

3885 Country Gentlemen's Association Rated Class B Handicap (0-100 3-y-o and up) £6,465 7f................(3:10)

3624[4] CORALS DREAM (Ire) [84] 4-8-9 W Woods (10) *trkd ldrs, pushed alng o'r 2 fs out, led ins last, ran on wl.* ....(7 to 1 op 5 to 1 tchd 15 to 2) 1
3477[5] GHOST TREE (Ire) [84] 3-8-5 M Roberts (2) *hld up towards rear, pushed alng and not clr run 2 out, hdwy o'r one out, ran on and ev ch ins last, no extr cl hme.* ....(6 to 1 op 9 to 2 tchd 13 to 2) 2
3624[3] SON PARDO [100] 3-9-7 K Darley (3) *hld up beh, hdwy o'r one furlong out, ev ch and one pace ins last.* ....(16 to 1 op 12 to 1) 3
3637[5] FIELD OF VISION (Ire) [82] 3-8-3 T Williams (4) *mid-div, hdwy 2 fs out, kpt on one pace.*..(10 to 1 tchd 12 to 1) 4
3736[3] BALLASECRET [87] 5-8-12 R Cochrane (8) *led til hdd ins fnl furlong, no extr.*.............(16 to 1 op 12 to 1) 5
3624* YOUNG ERN [97] 3-9-4 T Quinn (1) *hld up, hdwy o'r 2 fs out, ev ch over one out, sn btn.*......(7 to 1 op 6 to 1) 6
3637[4] KASSBAAN (USA) [87] 3-8-8 B Raymond (5) *hld up in mid-div, drvn alng 2 fs out, btn o'r one out.* ....(8 to 1 op 7 to 1 tchd 9 to 1) 7
3774* CALEMAN [83] 4-8-8 (3ex) W Carson (9) *prmnt, pushed alng and ev ch o'r 2 fs out, btn over one out, eased.* ....(11 to 4 fav op 3 to 1 tchd 100 to 30) 8
3350[5] ROCKY WATERS (USA) [89] 4-9-0 B Rouse (7) *cl up till wknd quickly wl o'r 2 fs out.*.... (12 to 1 tchd 14 to 1) 9
3624[2] NOBLE PET [84] 4-8-9 W Ryan (6) *prmnt till wknd quickly wl o'r 2 fs out.*........ (15 to 2 op 7 to 1 tchd 8 to 1) 10
Dist: Nk, nk, 2l, ¾l, 1½l, 4l, 3½l, 4l, 3½l. 1m 30.25s. a 5.65s (10 Ran).
SR: 36/31/46/22/29/30/8/-/-/ (Mrs C Hamson), C F Wall

3886 Abtrust Select Stakes Class A (Group 3) (3-y-o and up) £21,120 1¼m.. (3:40)

3154* KNIFEBOX (USA) 5-9-3 M Roberts (6) *made all, rdn alng o'r 2 fs out, ran on strly.*......(6 to 4 fav tchd 2 to 1) 1
3371[3] RIVER NORTH (Ire) 3-8-10 K Darley (1) *hld up, rdn and hdwy o'r 2 fs out, not quicken ins last.* ....(4 to 1 tchd 9 to 2 and 7 to 2) 2
3622[5] GABR 3-8-7 W Carson (3) *hld up, hdwy o'r 2 fs out, kpt on und pres ins last, no extr nr finish.* ....(7 to 1 op 6 to 1) 3
2986* LYPHARD'S DELTA (USA) 3-8-9 W Ryan (2) *trkd ldrs, rdn and not much room o'r one furlong out, sn wknd.* ....(9 to 2 op 9 to 4) 4
3748[2] PORT LUCAYA (bl) 3-8-7 B Raymond (5) *cl up, rdn o'r 2 fs out, wknd ins last.*......(8 to 1 op 7 to 1 tchd 9 to 1) 5
3402[9] ENVIRONMENT FRIEND 5-9-0 Paul Eddery (4) *in tch till wknd o'r 2 fs out.*..............(10 to 1 tchd 12 to 1) 6
Dist: ¾l, 1½l, 3l, sht-hd, 2½l. 2m 11.88s. a 6.38s (6 Ran).
SR: 64/55/49/45/42/44/ (Sheikh Mohammed), J H M Gosden

3887 High Wood Claiming Handicap Class G (0-60 3-y-o and up) £4,094 1m (4:15)

3269 DASWAKI (Can) [60] 5-10-0 B Rouse (25) *trkd ldrs, led appr fnl furlong, quickened clr, easily.* ....(7 to 1 op 6 to 1 tchd 8 to 1) 1
3523 HAWAII STORM (Fr) [40] 5-8-4[3] (7*) R Painter (11) *beh, hdwy frm 3 fs out, styd on wl, no ch wth wnr.* ....(33 to 1 op 20 to 1) 2
3734 PATSY GRIMES [59] (bl) 3-9-1 (7*) Mark Denaro (8) *al cl up, led o'r 2 fs out till hdd appr last, one pace.* ....(33 to 1 op 25 to 1 tchd 40 to 1) 3
2727[7] LYN'S RETURN (Ire) [47] 4-8-8 (7*) G Rothwell (21) *hdwy on ins whn not clr run o'r one furlong out, ran on inside last.*..........................(20 to 1 op 12 to 1) 4
3634[8] DANCING DIAMOND (Ire) [42] 3-8-5 W Woods (13) *5th, mid-div, rdn and styd on ins fnl furlong.* ....(20 to 1 op 14 to 1 tchd 25 to 1) 5
3591[7] THATCHED (Ire) [39] 3-8-2 A McGlone (12) *chsd ldrs, hrd rdn o'r one furlong out, one pace.* (16 to 1 op 14 to 1) 6
3261 SCOTS LAW [45] (bl) 6-8-8 (5*) D McCabe (2) *styd on fnl 2 fs, nvr nrr.*.......... (16 to 1 op 10 to 1 tchd 20 to 1) 7
3550[3] GATHERING [42] 4-8-10 C Rutter (5) *beh, hdwy und pres fnl 2 fs, nvr nrr.* (16 to 1 op 10 to 1 tchd 20 to 1) 8
2684[4] NORTHERN CONQUEROR (Ire) [45] 5-8-13 Paul Eddery (7) *nvr nr to chal.*......(14 to 1 op 12 to 1 tchd 16 to 1) 9
3550[4] GREAT HAND [45] 7-8-13 M Perrett (22) *beh, hrd rdn o'r 2 fs out, no imprsn.*...............(12 to 1 tchd 14 to 1) 10
3224 PIGALLE WONDER [43] (bl) 5-8-11 D Biggs (24) *led til hdd o'r 2 fs out, wknd.*................(8 to 1 tchd 9 to 1) 11
3447[4] OLD COMRADES [48] (bl) 6-9-2 A Munro (3) *chsd ldrs till wknd 2 fs out.*........ (10 to 1 op 8 to 1 tchd 11 to 1) 12
3139[9] KYRENIA GAME [55] 3-9-4 S O'Gorman (9) *al beh.* ....(16 to 1 op 12 to 1 tchd 20 to 1) 13
3588[8] MEDLAND (Ire) [46] 3-8-9 D Harrison (19) *cl up til wknd 2 fs out.*.............................(12 to 1 op 10 to 1) 14
3312[5] LADY BROKER [53] 3-9-2 A Tucker (10) *al beh.* ....(14 to 1 op 12 to 1) 15
3512[9] WHATEVER'S RIGHT (Ire) [50] 4-9-4 T Quinn (1) *cl up till wknd 3 fs out.*...... (12 to 1 op 10 to 1 tchd 14 to 1) 16
3588[7] SLOE BRANDY [42] 3-8-5 M Roberts (16) *pushed alng to chase ldrs, wknd o'r 2 fs out, eased whn btn over two furlongs out.*....(6 to 1 fav op 4 to 1 tchd 13 to 2) 17
3325[5] WOODMANS STAR [40] 3-8-3 R Price (17) *trkd ldrs till wknd 3 fs out.*...... (25 to 1 op 20 to 1 tchd 33 to 1) 18
2725[7] WEST END GIRL [40] 3-8-3 T Sprake (4) *nvr dngrs.* ....(33 to 1 op 20 to 1) 19
3286[8] JOAN'S GIFT [40] 3-8-3 T Williams (23) *strted slwly, al beh.* ....(33 to 1 op 20 to 1 tchd 50 to 1) 20
3643[8] OVERNIGHT SUCCESS (Ire) [58] 3-9-7 C Avery (18) *beh frm hfwy.*............ (33 to 1 op 25 to 1 tchd 40 to 1) 21
DE LA BILLIERE (Ire) [40] 5-8-8 S Whitworth (20) *al beh.* ....(33 to 1 op 25 to 1 tchd 50 to 1) 22
3783 GREEN CHILI [58] 3-9-7 M Hills (6) *swshd tail and refused to race, took no part.*............ (16 to 1 op 12 to 1) 0
Dist: 5l, ½l, nk, 2½l, 1l, ¾l, 2l, 1½l, 2l, nk. 1m 43.31s. a 6.11s (23 Ran).
SR: 52/17/29/21/3/-/6/-/-/ (David Allen), G L Moore

3888 Goodwood Motor Circuit Maiden Stakes Class D (2-y-o) £3,757 6f (4:45)

SIXPEES 9-0 W Woods (8) *chsd alng beh ldrs, led o'r one furlong out, sn clr, easily.*......(20 to 1 tchd 33 to 1) 1
3462[5] FAWRAN (USA) 9-0 M Roberts (2) *chsd ldrs, pushed alng o'r 2 fs out, kpt on ins last.*..........(3 to 1 op 2 to 1) 2
2909[7] ROOFTOP FLYER (Ire) 9-0 K Darley (12) *led til hdd o'r one furlong out, one pace und pres.* ....(8 to 1 op 10 to 1 tchd 12 to 1) 3
3400[4] CULT HERO (Can) 9-0 W Carson (4) *wth ldr, ev ch 2 fs out, one pace und pres o'r one out.* ....(13 to 8 fav op 6 to 4 tchd 7 to 4) 4
3446[7] MONTICINO (Ire) 9-0 R Cochrane (7) *in tch, ev ch 2 fs out, btn o'r one out, eased.*..............(8 to 1 tchd 10 to 1) 5
3421[4] WYCHWOOD SANDY 9-0 A Munro (5) *chsd ldrs o'r 4 fs.* ....(10 to 1 op 12 to 1 tchd 14 to 1) 6
2990 THE LONE DANCER 9-0 S O'Gorman (6) *wth ldr til wknd und pres o'r 2 fs out.* (25 to 1 op 14 to 1 tchd 33 to 1) 7
3209 BERMUDA LADY (USA) 8-9 D Harrison (1) *nvr on terms.* ....(50 to 1 op 33 to 1) 8
FARNHAM (Ire) 9-0 M Hills (9) *slwly into strd, effrt and cld hfwy, btn wl o'r one out.*...........(10 to 1 op 6 to 1) 9
3589 MAZIRAH 9-0 W Ryan (3) *slwly into strd, nvr on terms wth ldrs.*..................... (50 to 1 op 33 to 1) 10
2866 DANCING ROSINA (Ire) 8-9 W Newnes (11) *outpcd.* ....(50 to 1 op 33 to 1) 11
3260[7] LAKE PARVA 9-0 C Rutter (10) *outpcd.* .... (33 to 1 op 25 to 1 tchd 50 to 1) 12

Dist: 4l, nk, 3l, ½l, 3l, nk, 3l, sht-hd, ¾l, 8l. 1m 14.79s. a 4.39s (12 Ran).
SR: 42/26/25/13/11/-/ (Mrs N K Crook), M R Channon

3889 Carnes Seat Conditions Stakes Class D (3-y-o) £3,348 7f..............(5:20)

3519^{2} EL DUCO (USA) 8-12 Paul Eddery (1) *made all, ran on strly ins fnl furlong*.....(9 to 4 jt-fav op 2 to 1 tchd 5 to 2) 1
2885^{6} MATILA (Ire) 8-7 W Carson (4) *hld up in last pl, hdwy o'r 2 fs out, chsd wnr frm over one out, ran on.* ....(11 to 4 op 3 to 1 tchd 5 to 2) 2
3725^{3} BRIGG FAIR 9-0 K Darley (5) *pld hrd, cl up, pushed alng 2 fs out, one pace*.....(7 to 2 op 5 to 2) 3
3514* JAVA QUEEN (USA) 8-7 M Hills (2) *pld hrd, cl up, outpcd fnl 2 fs, tld off*.....(9 to 4 jt-fav tchd 11 to 4) 4
Dist: 2½l, 2l, 12l. 1m 29.64s. a 5.04s (4 Ran).
SR: 49/36/37/-/ (K Abdulla), R Charlton

BELMONT PARK (USA) (soft)
Saturday September 11th

3890 Flower Bowl Handicap (Grade 1) (3-y-o and up) £59,603 1¼m...........

FAR OUT BEAST (USA) 6-7-13 J-L Samyn,.....(175 to 10) 1
DAHLIA'S DREAMER (USA) 4-7-12^{1} J R Velasquez, (14 to 1) 2
LADY BLESSINGTON (Fr) 5-8-6 P Day,.......(24 to 10 fav) 3
3501^{3} DIS MOI TOUT (Fr) 3-8-2^{2} C Antley,..............(10 to 1) 4
FAIRY GARDEN (USA) 5-8-8 M Smith,..........(36 to 10) 5
3187^{6} ROYAL PAGEANT (USA) 4-7-13^{1} J Bailey,.......(39 to 10) 6
SARATOGA SOURCE (USA) 4-8-1 J Santos,.......(5 to 1) 7
GARENDARE 4-8-0 R Davis,..................(102 to 10) 8
FRENCH STEEL (USA) 4-7-12 J Cruguet,......(392 to 10) 9
COZZENE'S FLITE (USA) 4-7-12 J Bravo,......(755 to 10) 10
Dist: ½l, ½l, 3 ¾l, 2½l, ¾l, 1 ¾l, 4½l, nose, 1½l. 2m 3.88s. (10 Ran).
(Sullimar Stable), P Johnson

CHEPSTOW (good to firm)
Saturday September 11th
Going Correction: PLUS 0.10 sec. per fur. (races 1,2), MINUS 0.05 (3,4,5,6)

3891 Clearwell Handicap Class D (0-80 3-y-o and up) £3,991 1¼m 36yds....(1:50)

3282^{8} WASSL THIS THEN (Ire) [58] 4-8-10 R Price (12) *mid-div, prog 2 and a half fs out, kpt on to ld nr line.* .....(20 to 1 op 14 to 1) 1
3710^{5} VANBOROUGH LAD [50] 4-8-2^{1} G Duffield (4) *led o'r one furlong, remained cl up, led 2 fs out, hdd nr line.* .....(8 to 1 op 6 to 1) 2
HIGHLAND SPIRIT [54] 5-8-6 D Harrison (3) *settled in rear, hdwy 2 fs out, kpt on wl last 150 yards.* .....(8 to 1 op 6 to 1 tchd 9 to 1) 3
3655^{6} MAI PEN RAI [43] 5-7-2 (7*) Kim McDonnell (13) *hld up in rear, hdwy 3 fs out, kpt on same pace fnl furlong.* .....(10 to 1 op 7 to 1 tchd 12 to 1) 4
3157^{3} CHANDIGARH [50] 5-7-12^{1} (5*) J Tate (9) *slwly away, pld hrd, led o'r 8 fs out, hdd 2 furlongs out, no extr.* .....(14 to 1 op 10 to 1) 5
2353^{8} IBSEN [42] 5-7-8^{5} (5*) B Russell (7) *chsd ldrs, drvn alng o'r 2 fs out, styd on same pace.* .....(9 to 2 fav op 8 to 1 tchd 4 to 1) 6
3469^{8} AFFA [43] (v) 4-7-9 A Tucker (8) *improved 3 fs out, btn one and a half furlongs out*.....(14 to 1 op 10 to 1) 7
3211* SCOTTISH BAMBI [75] 5-9-6 (7*) Mark Denaro (2) *nvr able to chal*.....(6 to 1 tchd 13 to 2) 8
MAHONG [57] 5-8-9 T Sprake (10) *pressed ldrs, rdn o'r 2 fs out, wknd appr fnl furlong*.....(25 to 1) 9
3655* EIRAS MOOD [41] 4-7-7 C Avery (6) *chsd ldrs, hrd rdn 3 and a half fs out, sn lost pl*.....(10 to 1 op 7 to 1) 10
3734^{8} STORM FREE (USA) [58] 7-8-10 N Carlisle (11) *cl up, lost pl ins last 3 fs*.....(14 to 1 op 12 to 1) 11
3655 SOOTY TERN [60] 6-8-5 (7*) Michael Bradley (14) *prmnt on outsd early, sn beh*.....(16 to 1 op 12 to 1) 12
3089^{2} MARCHMAN [58] 8-8-10 R Hills (1) *lost pos bef hfwy, rallied ins last half m, wknd o'r 2 fs out.* .....(10 to 1 tchd 11 to 1) 13
3656^{9} GENERAL CHASE [63] 3-8-1 (7*) S Drowne (5) *mid-div till beh last 3 fs, pld up and dismounted ins last.* .....(10 to 1 op 8 to 1) pu
Dist: Hd, ¾l, nk, 1½l, hd, 3l, nk, 1l, hd, 7l. 2m 11.20s. a 7.60s (14 Ran).
SR: 30/21/23/11/15/6/1/32/12/ (Mrs Josephine Carter), D W P Arbuthnot

3892 Brecon Conditions Stakes Class D (3-y-o and up) £3,260 1¼m 36yds..(2:20)

357* UM ALGOWAIN (USA) 3-8-11 P D'Arcy (2) *made virtually all, pushed alng o'r one out, kpt on wl.* .....(100 to 30 op 4 to 1) 1
1204^{7} FRESCADE (USA) 3-8-7 C Rutter (1) *pressed wnr till rdn and outpcd 2 and a half fs out, styd on ag'n ins last.* .....(11 to 2 op 4 to 1 tchd 6 to 1) 2
3385^{8} JURA 5-9-5 G Duffield (3) *hld up in rear, effrt 2 fs out, hrd drvn appr fnl furlong, unbl to quicken.* .....(7 to 2 op 3 to 1 tchd 11 to 4) 3
3645^{4} BASHAYER (USA) 3-8-6 R Hills (4) *steadied strt, jnd wnr 2 fs out, no extr fnl furlong.* .....(11 to 8 fav op 11 to 10 tchd 6 to 4) 4
Dist: 1½l, nk, ½l. 2m 9.20s. a 5.60s (4 Ran).
SR: 51/44/55/41/ (Sheikh Ahmed Al Maktoum), M R Stoute

3893 Straight Mile Maiden Stakes Class D (3-y-o and up) £3,582 1m 14yds (2:50)

3639^{6} LABUDD (USA) 3-9-0 R Hills (1) *al frnt rnk, led 2 and a half fs out, pushed alng o'r one out, ran on wl.* .....(11 to 10 on op Evens) 1
MISLEMANI (Ire) 3-9-0 C Dwyer (3) *led 5 and a half fs, kpt on same pace*.....(12 to 1 op 10 to 1) 2
3783 ANORAK (USA) 3-8-7 (7*) Kim McDonnell (6) *al cl up, styd on same pace last 2 fs.* (15 to 2 op 5 to 1 tchd 8 to 1) 3
752^{8} FADAKI HAWAKI (USA) 3-8-9 W Woods (12) *al handily plcd, no extr last 2 fs*... (8 to 1 op 6 to 1 tchd 10 to 1) 4
3693^{9} LADY SABINA 3-8-9 C Rutter (13) *styd on fnl 2 fs, nvr able to chal*.....(10 to 1 op 8 to 1) 5
3693 EASY TOUCH 3-8-9 R Price (7) *no prog last 2 fs.* .....(50 to 1 op 33 to 1 tchd 66 to 1) 6
3012 AMY COME HOME 3-8-9 D Harrison (5) *no imprsn last 2 fs.* .....(25 to 1 op 20 to 1 tchd 33 to 1) 7
3547^{6} ARAMON 3-8-7 (7*) M Payne (11) *nvr trble ldrs.* .....(12 to 1 op 14 to 1) 8
2937 GREAT PLOVER 3-9-0 T Sprake (10) *pressed ldrs 5 fs.* .....(66 to 1 op 33 to 1) 9
MR PERKY 3-9-0 N Carlisle (2) *strted slwly, al struggling, tld off*.....(50 to 1 op 33 to 1) 10
2596^{8} JIMMY HIMSELF (bl) 3-9-0 G Duffield (4) *al in rear, tld off.* .....(20 to 1 tchd 25 to 1) 11
3509 SOROPTIMIST (Fr) 4-9-0 A Tucker (8) *cl up o'r 4 fs, tld off.* .....(66 to 1 op 33 to 1) 12
3687 PINEAPPLE PRINCE 3-8-7 (7*) S Drowne (9) *dwlt, al in rear, tld off*.....(50 to 1 op 20 to 1) 13
SIGNORE DE ANGLES 4-8-12 (7*) Mark Denaro (14) *cl up stands side o'r 4 fs, wknd quickly, tld off.* .....(66 to 1 op 33 to 1) 14
Dist: 2l, ½l, 1½l, ½l, 4l, 1½l, 6l, hd, 8l, ¾l. 1m 35.60s. a 3.20s (14 Ran).
SR: 46/40/38/28/26/14/9/-/-/ (Hamdan Al-Maktoum), J H M Gosden

3894 Ryeford Conditions Stakes Class D (2-y-o) £3,318 5f 16yds............(3:30)

3448^{2} DOLLAR GAMBLE (Ire) 8-3 (7*) Mark Denaro (2) *al wl plcd, led ins last 2 fs, ran on well*.....(3 to 1 jt-fav op 11 to 4 tchd 100 to 30) 1
3436^{2} GOLD LAND (USA) 9-12 C Rutter (1) *al cl up, ev ch one and a half fs out, unbl to quicken ins last.* .....(7 to 2 tchd 4 to 1) 2
3183* ANN'S PEARL (Ire) 8-5 T Sprake (8) *cl up stands side, ev ch appr fnl furlong, edgd lft ins last, not quicken.* .....(7 to 2 op 3 to 1) 3
3723^{3} POST MISTRESS (Ire) 8-5 G Duffield (3) *led till hdd wl o'r one furlong out, hld whn not much room ins last.* .....(3 to 1 jt-fav tchd 100 to 30) 4
3016^{4} BILLY CRUNCHEON 8-10 W Woods (7) *outpcd to hfwy, no real prog last 2 fs*.....(50 to 1 op 33 to 1) 5
3472^{2} INDIAHRA 8-9 S Perks (4) *frnt rnk till wknd one and a half fs out*.....(8 to 1 tchd 7 to 1) 6
2886 WINSOME WOOSTER 8-9 D Harrison (5) *dwlt, al beh.* .....(20 to 1 op 12 to 1) 7
Dist: 1½l, nk, 3½l, 2l, ¾l, 1l. 59.10s. a 2.10s (7 Ran).
SR: 49/59/37/23/20/16/12/ (J A Leek), R Hannon

3895 Mansion Median Auction Maiden Fillies' Stakes Class E (2-y-o) £3,129 6f 16yds.........................(4:05)

3166^{5} FROMAGE 8-11 R Price (7) *wtd wth, effrt one and a half fs out, weaved through to ld ins fnl furlong, ran on.* .....(12 to 1 op 8 to 1) 1
AMNESIA (Ire) 8-11 G Duffield (8) *led o'r 3 fs, ev ch fnl furlong, kpt on*.....(7 to 2 op 9 to 4 tchd 4 to 1) 2
3633^{8} SPARKLING LYRIC 8-6 (5*) K Rutter (9) *slwly into strd, hdwy one and a half fs out, kpt on ins last.* .....(4 to 1 op 3 to 1 tchd 9 to 2) 3
ARAGON HOLLY 8-11 W Woods (4) *sn cl up, led ins last 2 fs, hdd and no extr last 150 yards.* .....(7 to 1 op 12 to 1 tchd 20 to 1) 4
2887 NORFOLK LAVENDER (Can) 8-11 C Rutter (6) *al frnt rnk, led 2 and a half fs out, hdd o'r one out, no extr ins last.* .....(9 to 4 fav op 7 to 4) 5
3387^{7} MAY LIGHT 8-11 S O'Gorman (2) *hld up, effrt 2 fs out, btn one out*.....(15 to 2 op 5 to 1 tchd 8 to 1) 6
NUIN-TARA 8-11 T Sprake (1) *missed break, sn chasing ldrs, wknd o'r one furlong out*.....(66 to 1 op 33 to 1) 7
3287 NO WHAT I MEAN (Ire) 8-4 (7*) Mark Denaro (3) *outpcd frm hfwy, sn tld off.* ....(20 to 1 op 25 to 1 tchd 33 to 1 and 16 to 1) 8
LORELEI ROCK 8-11 N Carlisle (5) *sn struggling, tld off frm hfwy*.....(40 to 1 op 33 to 1) 9
Dist: ½l, nk, 2½l, sht-hd, 4l, 5l, 15l, dist. 1m 12.90s. a 3.40s (9 Ran).

SR: 23/21/20/10/9/-/ (Mrs P G Goulandris), D R Laing

3896 Redbrook Apprentice Handicap Class G (0-70 3-y-o and up) £2,679 6f 16yds ....(4:35)

3707^{9} COURTING NEWMARKET [44] 5-7-11^{2} (7*) Marie Plowright (14) *al gng easily, led 3 and a half fs out, readily.* ....(20 to 1 tchd 25 to 1) 1
3155^{7} DARUSSALAM [52] 6-8-5 (5*) L Aspell (4) *cl up far side, kpt on same pace ins last 2 fs*........(10 to 1 tchd 11 to 1) 2
3593 ASTERIX [56] 5-9-0 Mark Denaro (3) *styd on last one and a half fs, kpt on wl towards finish*....(11 to 1 op 7 to 1) 3
3447^{3} NAVARESQUE [42] 8-8-0^{1} S Drowne (12) *hdwy wl o'r one furlong out, ran on*..............(12 to 1 tchd 14 to 1) 4
3305* FAY'S SONG (Ire) [58] 5-8-13 (3*) L Carter (7) *prog 2 fs out, kpt on ins last*......(6 to 1 fav op 5 to 1 tchd 13 to 2) 5
3305^{5} TURTLE BEACH [35] 4-7-7 Antoinette Armes (9) *led 2 and a half fs, not quicken appr fnl furlong.* ....(14 to 1 tchd 16 to 1) 6
3118^{5} SPLASH OF SALT (Ire) [64] 3-9-0 (5*) T Ashley (1) *took clr order 2 and a half fs out, hrd drvn o'r one out, no real imprsn*..............(11 to 1 op 10 to 1 tchd 14 to 1) 7
3213^{4} KARUKERA [48] 3-8-3 Kim McDonnell (16) *styd on appr fnl furlong, nvr able to chal*.............(14 to 1 op 10 to 1) 8
3621 MY RUBY RING [70] 6-9-9 (5*) S Eiffert (13) *effrt 2 fs out, not rch ldrs*.....................(10 to 1 tchd 11 to 1) 9
3707^{3} BAYSHAM (USA) [65] (bl) 7-9-9 C Hawksley (18) *missed break, nvr rch ldrs*.................. (7 to 1 op 6 to 1) 10
3445^{5} UNVEILED [49] 5-8-7 M Humphries (2) *nrst finish.* .... (12 to 1 op 10 to 1 tchd 14 to 1) 11
3233 OLIVIA VAL [39] 3-7-8^{1} B Russell (8) *missed break, al beh.* ....(33 to 1 tchd 25 to 1) 12
3661* BEVELED EDGE [51] 4-8-4 (5*) Wendy Jones (6) *fly-jmpd leaving stalls, chsd ldrs 4 fs out, wknd wl o'r one out.* .... (9 to 1 op 10 to 1) 13
3758^{7} TOP ONE [52] 8-8-7 (3*) R Painter (19) *nvr a factor.* ....(8 to 1 op 6 to 1 tchd 9 to 1) 14
3002 JACK GRAY [46] 5-8-4^{6} (5*) J Dennis (11) *nvr wnt pace.* .... (33 to 1 op 25 to 1) 15
3523 MISS CRUSTY [38] 5-7-10 Claire Balding (10) *speed o'r 3 fs.* ....(20 to 1 tchd 25 to 1) 16
1416 MR JAZZ DANCER (Ire) [45] 3-8-0^{7} (5*) Michael Bradley (5) *al struggling, tld off*............................(50 to 1) 17
3408 EVER SO SHARP [35] 10-7-0 (7*) F Savage (17) *al toiling, tld off*..(50 to 1) 18
3053^{9} SUPER SCENARIO [38] 3-7-2 (5*) M Baird (15) *gd speed to hfwy, tld off*.............................(50 to 1 op 33 to 1) 19
Dist: 1½l, ½l, hd, sht-hd, ½l, 1l, sht-hd, hd, ¾l, ½l. 1m 11.70s. a 2.20s (19 Ran).
SR: 38/40/42/27/42/17/39/22/46/ (Geo Taylor), Mrs A Knight

DONCASTER (good to soft (races 1,2,6,7), soft (3,4,5))
Saturday September 11th
Going Correction: NIL (races 1,2,6,7), PLUS 0.10 (3,4,5)

3897 Coalite Rated Class B Handicap (0-105 3-y-o and up) £20,137 1m (2:00)

3468^{9} FRAAM [91] 4-8-7 W R Swinburn (13) *in tch, hdwy 2 out, led jst ins fnl furlong, ran on wl*...(33 to 1 op 25 to 1) 1
3285^{8} BEAUCHAMP HERO [94] 3-8-5 Pat Eddery (7) *beh, steady hdwy 3 out, led entering fnl furlong, sn hdd, kpt on same pace*.............(13 to 2 op 6 to 1 tchd 7 to 1) 2
3558* AMAZING FEAT (Ire) [91] 4-8-7 K Darley (10) *hld up, hdwy o'r 2 fs out, kpt on wl fnl furlong.* (9 to 2 fav op 4 to 1) 3
3489* LACOTTE (Ire) [91] 3-8-2 J Carroll (1) *trkd ldrs, effrt 2 out, kpt on fnl furlong*..................(13 to 2 op 5 to 1) 4
2926^{3} SHOW FAITH (Ire) [96] 3-8-7 W Ryan (9) *hld up, effrt 2 out, styd on, not rch ldrs*.............(6 to 1 tchd 13 to 2) 5
2654^{9} MELLOTTIE [105] 8-9-7 J Lowe (11) *beh, pushed alng hfwy, styd on fnl furlong, not rch ldrs.* .... (16 to 1 op 14 to 1) 6
2789^{7} NEW CAPRICORN (USA) [96] 3-8-7 J Reid (5) *led till hdd o'r 2 out, grad wknd*...............(12 to 1 tchd 14 to 1) 7
3437^{8} EFHARISTO [91] 4-8-7 J Weaver (2) *cl up, led o'r 2 fs out, sn rdn, hdd entering fnl furlong, soon wknd.* ....(20 to 1 op 25 to 1 tchd 33 to 1) 8
3703^{3} PAY HOMAGE [103] 5-9-5 L Dettori (8) *hld up, effrt o'r 2 fs out, no hdwy*..................(16 to 1 tchd 20 to 1) 9
3585* FOURFORFUN [91] 3-8-2 M Hills (3) *trkd ldrs, effrt and ev ch 2 out, wknd entering fnl furlong.* (9 to 1 op 10 to 1) 10
3465 GYMCRAK PREMIERE [97] 5-8-13 J Williams (4) *in tch till wknd o'r 2 out*.................. (20 to 1 op 16 to 1) 11
3465^{8} ROYAL SEATON [91] 4-8-7 A Mackay (6) *chsd ldrs, pushed alng hfwy, wknd o'r 2 fs out*.....(12 to 1 tchd 14 to 1) 12
3350^{6} CROFT VALLEY [97] 6-8-13 T Quinn (14) *rcd alone stands side, beh fnl 2 fs*.................(12 to 1 tchd 14 to 1) 13
3437^{3} CUMBRIAN CHALLENGE (Ire) [92] (bl) 4-8-8 M Birch (12) *prmnt till wknd o'r 2 fs out*.......(14 to 1 op 12 to 1) 14
Dist: 1l, 1½l, ½l, 1½l, 2½l, ½l, ¾l, nk, 2l, 3½l. 1m 39.18s. a 2.38s (14 Ran).
SR: 57/52/49/42/42/48/32/30/41/ (Maktoum Al Maktoum), A A Scott

3898 Tripleprint Flying Childers Stakes Class A (Group 2) (2-y-o) £25,473 5f ....(2:30)

2960^{2} IMPERIAL BAILIWICK (Ire) 8-6 J Williams (5) *hld up in tch, not much room wl o'r one furlong out, str run fnl furlong to ld cl hme*............... (12 to 1 op 10 to 1) 1
3463^{4} GREAT DEEDS 8-6 T Quinn (2) *chsd ldrs, led hfwy, clr whn rdn one furlong out, hdd cl hme*.........(7 to 2) 2
3485^{2} SELHURSTPARK FLYER (Ire) 8-11 J Carroll (4) *prmnt, pushed alng hfwy, rallied and ran on wl fnl furlong.* .... (11 to 2 op 7 to 1) 3
2210^{2} YA MALAK 8-11 R Cochrane (6) *trkd ldrs, effrt whn not clr run wl o'r one furlong out, swtchd rght and kpt on well fnl furlong*.............(7 to 2 op 3 to 1 tchd 4 to 1) 4
3357^{3} ISABELLA SHARP 8-6 L Dettori (8) *sn disputing ld, kpt on same pace fnl 2 fs*.... (12 to 1 op 10 to 1 tchd 14 to 1) 5
3435^{7} PRINCE AZZAAN (Ire) 8-11 Pat Eddery (1) *hld up, effrt 2 out, kpt on same pace.* (17 to 2 op 10 to 1 tchd 8 to 1) 6
3347^{2} STIMULANT 8-6 W R Swinburn (3) *led or dsptd ld till hdd hfwy, sn pushed alng, fdd*.......(3 to 1 fav op 2 to 1) 7
3357^{2} CRAGGANMORE 8-11 M Hills (7) *beh frm hfwy.* ....(16 to 1 tchd 20 to 1) 8
Dist: Nk, 1l, 1½l, 1½l, 1½l, 3l, 1l. 1m 0.44s. a 1.64s (8 Ran).
SR: 59/58/59/53/42/41/24/25/ (Dr Ian R Shenkin), M D I Usher

3899 Coalite St Leger Stakes Class A (Group 1) (3-y-o) £194,720 1¾m 132yds........................ (3:05)

3403* BOB'S RETURN (Ire) 9-0 P Robinson (9) *pld hrd early, trkd ldr frm hfwy, led wl o'r 2 fs out, rdn over one out, styd on well*.............................(3 to 1 fav op 4 to 1) 1
3403^{7} ARMIGER 9-0 Pat Eddery (8) *led aftr 2 fs, hdd wl o'r two out, sn rdn, kpt on, no imprsn on wnr.* ....(4 to 1 op 3 to 1 tchd 9 to 2) 2
3735^{2} EDBAYSAAN (Ire) 9-0 W Ryan (7) *prmnt till pushed alng and outpacd o'r over 5 fs out, styd on wl und pres fnl 2 furlongs, not rch 1st two*.........(25 to 1 tchd 33 to 1) 3
3403^{4} SHAREEK (USA) 9-0 W R Swinburn (5) *in tch, effrt o'r 3 fs out, kpt on same pace.* .... (13 to 1 op 14 to 1 tchd 12 to 1) 4
3645* DANISH FORT 9-0 C Asmussen (4) *hld up, hdwy o'r 4 fs out, effrt over 3 out, sn btn.* .... (13 to 2 op 6 to 1 tchd 7 to 1) 5
3349* AZZILFI 9-0 T Quinn (6) *trkd ldrs, rdn wl o'r 3 out, sn wknd, eased whn btn*... (7 to 2 op 9 to 4 tchd 4 to 1) 6
3405^{2} SILVERDALE (USA) 9-0 L Dettori (1) *hld up, effrt o'r 4 fs out, sn rdn and wknd*.............. (7 to 1 op 8 to 1) 7
3784^{8} WINGED VICTORY (USA) 9-0 R Cochrane (2) *hld up, hdwy to track ldrs hfwy, wknd o'r 3 fs out.* .... (16 to 1 op 12 to 1 tchd 20 to 1) 8
3620^{2} AZILIAN (Ire) (v) 9-0 M Hills (3) *led 2 fs, cl up till wknd quickly 6 out, tld off*............(33 to 1 tchd 50 to 1) 9
Dist: 3½l, 1½l, ½l, 8l, 12l, 2½l, 7l, 30l. 3m 7.85s. a 3.35s (9 Ran).
SR: 81/74/71/70/54/30/25/11/-/ (Mrs G A E Smith), M H Tompkins

3900 Ladbroke Handicap Class C (0-95 3-y-o and up) £14,532 1¼m 60yds... (3:40)

3465^{5} RIBHI (USA) [95] 3-10-0 M Hills (9) *trkd ldrs gng wl, quickened to ld ins fnl furlong, ran on well.* .... (10 to 1 op 8 to 1) 1
3512* JAZILAH (Fr) [81] 5-9-7 T Quinn (12) *cl up, led 2 fs out, hdd ins fnl furlong, no extr.* ....(11 to 2 fav op 5 to 1 tchd 6 to 1) 2
3308^{5} MAD MILITANT (Ire) [70] 4-8-10 K Darley (7) *trkd ldrs, ev ch o'r one furlong out, kpt on same pace*.........(12 to 1) 3
3476 BEAUMAN [65] 3-7-12 A Mackay (6) *in tch, kpt on wl fnl 3 fs, nrst finish*..................(10 to 1 tchd 11 to 1) 4
3437^{7} SILVER SAMURAI [83] 4-9-9 L Dettori (4) *hld up, effrt and swtchd 2 fs out, styd on, not trble ldrs.* .... (10 to 1 op 14 to 1) 5
1064^{9} CEZANNE [76] 4-9-2 W R Swinburn (3) *in tch, hdwy 3 fs out, one pace fnl 2 furlongs.* .... (7 to 1 op 6 to 1 tchd 15 to 2) 6
3630^{8} PERSIAN CHARMER (Ire) [63] (bl) 3-7-10 J Fanning (2) *cl up till outpcd and lost pl o'r 4 fs out, no dngr aftr.* ....(20 to 1 tchd 16 to 1) 7
3466 MOSCOW SEA (USA) [84] 3-9-3 W Ryan (5) *in tch, effrt 3 fs out, sn btn*........................ (7 to 1 tchd 8 to 1) 8
3740^{3} SUIVEZ [70] 3-8-3 J Carroll (11) *cl up, led o'r 4 fs out, hdd 2 out, sn wknd*......... (14 to 1 op 12 to 1 tchd 16 to 1) 9
3179^{4} BENTICO [70] 4-8-10 Pat Eddery (8) *trkd ldrs, effrt 3 fs out, wknd 2 out*...................................(7 to 1) 10
3757 DOC COTTRILL [70] (bl) 3-8-3 J Weaver (10) *in tch till wknd o'r 2 fs out*...................................(7 to 1) 11
3714^{3} JUBRAN (USA) [74] 7-9-0 J Reid (1) *led till hdd o'r 4 fs out, sn btn*............................(8 to 1 tchd 9 to 1) 12
Dist: 1½l, 2½l, 1l, 4l, 8l, 6l, sht-hd, 1l, 4l, ½l. 2m 11.83s. a 5.13s (12 Ran).
SR: 73/63/47/33/50/27/-/15/-/ (Hamdan Al-Maktoum), D Morley

3901 Rothmans Royals North South Challenge Series Semi-final Handicap Class C (0-100 3-y-o and up) £12,908

1m. . . . . (4:15)

3726[8] SELF EXPRESSION [58] 5-8-4 J Weaver (6) *beh, hdwy o'r 2 fs out, styd on und pres to ld ins fnl furlong, all out.* . . . .(12 to 1) 1

1017* HI NOD [80] 3-9-7 N Connorton (3) *cl up, slight ld wl o'r one out, hdd ins fnl furlong, kpt on.* (10 to 1 op 8 to 1) 2

3487* HUNTERS OF BRORA (Ire) [77] 3-9-4 W R Swinburn (11) *beh, effrt and swtchd o'r 2 fs out, styd on und pres, not rch ldrs.* . . . . (9 to 2 fav op 4 to 1) 3

3680[7] FOREVER DIAMONDS [82] 6-10-0 M Birch (8) *hld up, hdwy 2 fs out, kpt on und pres ins fnl furlong.* . . . .(8 to 1 tchd 9 to 1) 4

3726[3] SWEET MIGNONETTE [74] 5-9-6 R Cochrane (5) *beh, gd hdwy to chal 2 fs out, sn rdn and no extr.* . . . .(7 to 1 op 8 to 1) 5

3812 MENTALASANYTHIN [70] 4-9-2 A Mackay (4) *cl up, ev ch 3 fs out, sn rdn, wknd 2 out.* . . . . (14 to 1) 6

2733[2] LEGEND DULAC (Ire) [55] 4-8-1 P Robinson (10) *rcd wide, led till hdd wl o'r one furlong out, sn wknd.* . . . .(12 to 1 tchd 14 to 1) 7

3791[6] BOLD ANGEL [74] 6-9-6 Pat Eddery (7) *prmnt till wknd wl o'r 2 fs out.* . . . . (15 to 2 op 7 to 1 tchd 8 to 1) 8

3680[4] PRIDE OF PENDLE [71] 4-9-3 K Darley (2) *in tch, hdwy to chal 2 fs out, sn rdn and wknd.* . . . . (11 to 2 op 5 to 1) 9

3747 NORTHERN CHIEF [65] 3-8-3 (3*) S Maloney (1) *chsd ldrs till wknd o'r 2 fs out.* . . . .(9 to 1 op 8 to 1 tchd 10 to 1) 10

3540[5] HABETA (USA) [58] 7-8-4 M Hills (9) *al beh.* . . . .(10 to 1 tchd 12 to 1) 11

Dist: ¾l, 1½l, ½l, nk, 7l, ½l, hd, 1½l, ½l, 2½l. 1m 41.61s. a 4.91s (11 Ran).

SR: 28/43/35/43/34/9/-/10/2/ (Jonathan Ramsden), Mrs J R Ramsden

3902 Rous Conditions Stakes Class D (2-y-o) £4,191 6f. . . . . (4:45)

3672[3] PICCOLO 8-11 T Quinn (4) *dwlt, trkd ldrs, led entering fnl furlong, ran on wl.* . . . .(4 to 1 op 5 to 2) 1

3754* BLUE BOMBER 9-1 K Darley (5) *hld up, swtchd and hdwy hfwy, chlgd 2 fs out, ev ch one out, no extr.* . . . . (13 to 8 fav op 7 to 4 tchd 6 to 4 and 15 to 8) 2

3528* MONIS (Ire) 9-1 L Dettori (2) *dwlt, trkd ldrs, effrt whn bumped and stumbled wl o'r one furlong out, ev ch one out, no extr.* . . . .(15 to 2 op 8 to 1 tchd 10 to 1 and 7 to 1) 3

3602* FAWAAKEH (USA) 8-10 R Hills (3) *led till hdd wl o'r one furlong out, kpt on same pace.* . . . . (7 to 4 op 6 to 4 tchd 15 to 8) 4

3629[3] NO MEAN CITY (Ire) (bl) 8-11 A Mackay (1) *pld hrd early, cl up till rdn and wknd wl o'r one furlong out.* . . . . (25 to 1 op 16 to 1) 5

Dist: 2l, sht-hd, 3½l, 6l. 1m 14.70s. a 3.30s (5 Ran).

SR: 31/27/26/7/-/ (T Leigh), M R Channon

3903 Battle Of Britain Nursery Class D (2-y-o) £4,932 6f. . . . . (5:15)

3629[4] RAFFERTY'S RULES (Ire) [79] 9-0 J Weaver (8) *wnt rght strt, beh, hdwy hfwy, led o'r one furlong out, pushed out, cmftbly.* . . . .(9 to 2 op 5 to 1 tchd 6 to 1) 1

3715[7] RAPIER POINT (Ire) [76] 8-11 R Cochrane (10) *prmnt, led o'r 2 fs out, hdd over one out, kpt on wl.* . . . .(14 to 1 op 12 to 1 tchd 16 to 1) 2

2430[6] BROCTUNE GOLD [86] 9-7 K Darley (13) *al prmnt, kpt on fnl furlong, no ch wth 1st 2.* . . . . (8 to 1 tchd 9 to 1) 3

3755[5] CULSYTH FLYER [73] 8-8 W Ryan (9) *bumped strt, beh, effrt whn bumped hfwy, styd on fnl 2 fs, not rch ldrs.* . . . . (11 to 1 op 10 to 1) 4

3563[6] HELLABY [62] 7-8 (3*) N Kennedy (3) *rcd centre, chsd ldrs, no hdwy fnl 2 fs.* . . . .(20 to 1 op 14 to 1) 5

3673[6] DOCKYARD DORA [59] (bl) 7-2[1] (7*) N Varley (2) *rcd centre, led till hdd o'r 2 fs out, grad wknd.* . . . .(20 to 1 op 16 to 1 tchd 25 to 1) 6

3635[4] OBVIOUS RISK [81] 9-2 Pat Eddery (12) *in tch, effrt o'r 2 fs out, no real hdwy.* (6 to 4 fav op 9 to 4 tchd 11 to 8) 7

3254[3] CHILIOLA [73] 8-5 (3*) S Maloney (7) *nvr nr to chal.* . . . . (10 to 1 op 7 to 1) 8

3490[5] MICHELLISA [66] 8-1 J Lowe (1) *rcd centre, nvr dngrs.* . . . .(10 to 1 tchd 12 to 1) 9

3441[8] SADDAM THE LOG [67] 8-2 A Mackay (11) *chsd ldr to hfwy.* . . . . (14 to 1 op 12 to 1 tchd 16 to 1) 10

3755[6] ROCHE ABBEY (Ire) [58] 7-7 J Fanning (5) *chsd ldrs till wknd o'r 2 fs out.* . . . . .(10 to 1 op 8 to 1 tchd 11 to 1) 11

3084[3] CHEERFUL GROOM (Ire) [58] 7-7 S Wood (6) *prmnt till wknd o'r 2 fs out.* . . . .(16 to 1) 12

3321[2] KENTUCKY FLYER [59] 7-8 L Charnock (4) *prmnt till wknd o'r 2 fs out.* . . . .(16 to 1) 13

Dist: 2l, 7l, 1½l, 3l, nk, ¾l, ¾l, 1l, 1l, ¾l. 1m 14.78s. a 3.38s (13 Ran).
SR: 32/21/3/-/-/-/ (O Soberg-Olsen), Mrs J R Ramsden

GOODWOOD (good to soft)
Saturday September 11th

Going Correction: PLUS 0.30 sec. per fur. (races 1,2,4,5,6,7), PLUS 0.25 (3)

3904 Barkers Trident Conditions Stakes Class C (3-y-o and up) £6,906 1½m . . . . (2:15)

3488[2] AZHAR 3-8-11 Paul Eddery (1) *made all, quickened o'r 3 fs out, pushed wl clr last 2, eased.* . . . . (11 to 10 on op 5 to 4 on tchd Evens) 1

3262[9] IVORY PALM (USA) 3-8-0 G Hind (3) *trkd wnr most of way, rdn and not quicken 3 fs out, outpcd 2 out.* . . . .(7 to 1 op 6 to 1 tchd 8 to 1) 2

2937* ALKHAFJI 4-9-2 A McGlone (2) *in tch till rdn and outpcd o'r 3 fs out, styd on ag'n appr fnl furlong.* . . . . (11 to 4 op 9 to 4 tchd 3 to 1) 3

3431* PEARLY MIST (Ire) 3-8-2 B Doyle (4) *al in rear, rdn and wl outpcd o'r 3 fs out, tld off.* . . . . (9 to 2 op 5 to 1 tchd 11 to 2) 4

Dist: 4l, sht-hd, 15l. 2m 41.88s. a 8.88s (4 Ran).

SR: 44/25/40/-/ (Sheikh Ahmed Al Maktoum), M R Stoute

3905 Highland Spring/ROA Nursery Handicap Class D (2-y-o) £4,045 7f. . . (2:45)

3406[3] DIESAN (USA) [93] 9-7 G Hind (7) *in tch, squeezed through to ld o'r one furlong out, styd on cleverly.* . . . . (13 to 2 op 6 to 1) 1

3625[5] BE EXCITING (Ire) [68] 7-10 T Williams (11) *cl up, led o'r 3 fs out, hdd over one out, not quicken.* (11 to 2 op 4 to 1) 2

3597[4] LEAP OF FAITH (Ire) [71] (v) 7-8 (5*) A Garth (2) *rear til rdn and ran on o'r 2 fs out, one pace ins fnl furlong.* . . . . (11 to 1 op 10 to 1) 3

3589* ARNDILLY [77] 8-2 (3*) M Fenton (4) *wl plcd, rdn and one pace last 2 fs.* . . . . . . (4 to 1 fav op 7 to 2 tchd 5 to 1) 4

3264* DOWN D ISLANDS [76] (bl) 8-4 A Munro (9) *pressed ldrs, rdn and bumped wl o'r one furlong out, not rcvr.* . . . . (6 to 1 op 9 to 2 tchd 13 to 2) 5

3347[7] SWEET DECISION (Ire) [84] 8-12 M Wigham (13) *chsd ldrs till rdn and wknd o'r 2 fs out.* . . . . (20 to 1 op 16 to 1 tchd 25 to 1) 6

3352[6] JEYPORE JO [76] 7-11 (7*) D Gibbs (1) *led aftr one furlong, hdd o'r 3 out, wknd fnl furlong.* . . . .(7 to 1 op 6 to 1 tchd 8 to 1) 7

3658[4] ARABOYBILL [70] 7-12 D Biggs (10) *effrt frm rear 3 fs out, no extr ins last 2 furlongs.* . . . . (12 to 1 op 10 to 1) 8

3589 ROCKSTINE (Ire) [65] 7-2 (5*) D Wright (3) *al beh.* . . . . (50 to 1 op 20 to 1) 9

3613 PAPAGAYOS (Ire) [85] 8-10 (3*) B Doyle (6) *pressed ldrs till wknd o'r 2 fs out.* . . . .(20 to 1 op 16 to 1 tchd 25 to 1) 10

3573* FERRYMAN (USA) [73] 8-1[2] Paul Eddery (5) *led for one furlong, wknd 4 out.* . . .(13 to 2 op 6 to 1 tchd 7 to 1) 11

3760 TROPICAL VISTA [65] 7-7 N Adams (8) *lost pos aftr 2 fs, beh rst of way.* . . . . (66 to 1 op 33 to 1 tchd 100 to 1) 12

Dist: 1l, 3½l, 1l, 2½l, 1l, 3½l, 2½l, 3l, 7l, 3½l. 1m 30.53s. a 5.93s (12 Ran).

SR: 50/22/14/17/8/13/ (Sheikh Ahmed Al Maktoum), J H M Gosden

3906 William Hill Sprint Cup Handicap Class C (0-95 3-y-o and up) £16,262 6f . . . . (3:20)

3885[5] BALLASECRET [88] 5-9-4[1] (5*) D Meredith (11) *made virtually all stand side grp, styd on wl cl hme.* . . . . (20 to 1 op 14 to 1) 1

3266[7] BORN TO BE [76] 4-8-10 G Hind (20) *ldg grp, rdn and brief advantage ins fnl furlong, jst fld.* . . . . (33 to 1) 2

3404 PETITE-D-ARGENT [85] 4-9-5 A Munro (19) *pressed ldrs, ev ch ins fnl furlong, no extr last strds.* . . . .(16 to 1) 3

3476[7] CATHERINEOFARAGON [76] 3-8-7 G Bardwell (17) *sn rdn alng, str run o'r one furlong out, fnshd wl.* . . .(8 to 1 jt-fav op 10 to 1) 4

2940* NEITHER NOR [79] 4-8-8 (5*) D McCabe (6) *beh til gd hdwy appr fnl furlong, ran on cl hme.* . . . .(8 to 1 jt-fav tchd 7 to 1) 5

3593[4] PETRACO (Ire) [74] 5-8-5 (3*) S D Williams (23) *rcd alone far side, dsptd ld til rdn and no extr ins fnl furlong.* . . . .(14 to 1 op 16 to 1 tchd 20 to 1) 6

3184[2] HONEY SEEKER [63] 4-7-11 J Quinn (8) *mid-div, rdn alng and styd on one pace o'r one furlong out.* . . . .(12 to 1 tchd 14 to 1) 7

3621[6] MASNUN (USA) [72] 8-8-6 D Biggs (22) *hld up, ran on last 2 fs, styd on cl hme.* . . . . (16 to 1) 8

3404 WHITE SHADOW (Ire) [88] 3-9-5 S Raymont (21) *nvr nrr.* . . . . (20 to 1 op 16 to 1) 9

3504[5] FOR THE PRESENT [82] 3-8-13 Paul Eddery (10) *trkd ldrs, rdn and ev ch wl o'r one furlong out, no extr.* . . . .(12 to 1 op 10 to 1) 10

3778* OK BERTIE [80] 3-8-4 (7*) P McCabe (15) *in tch til wknd o'r one furlong out.* . . . . (10 to 1 op 12 to 1) 11

3393[5] ASHGORE [68] 3-7-13 N Adams (2) *pressed ldrs for o'r 3 fs, fdd.* . . . .(25 to 1) 12

3778[9] BOLD STREET (Ire) [62] 3-7-2 (5*) D Wright (9) *ldg grp til rdn and wknd o'r one furlong out.* . . . .(20 to 1) 13

2136* ECHO-LOGICAL [88] 4-9-8 A McGlone (13) *styd on one pace last 2 fs, not rch frnt rnk.* . . . .(16 to 1 op 14 to 1) 14

3474* PALACEGATE TOUCH [93] 3-9-3 (7*) P Roberts (3) *cl up til wknd und pres 2 fs out.* . . . . (12 to 1 op 14 to 1 tchd 16 to 1) 15

3486[5] PENNY HASSET [66] 5-7-9 (5*) L Newton (14) *ldg grp for o'r 3 fs*..............................(10 to 1 tchd 11 to 1) 16
3665[2] RESIST THE FORCE (USA) [78] 3-8-2 (7*) J D Smith (5) *outpcd frm hfwy*.............................(20 to 1) 17
3621[4] FASCINATION WALTZ [77] 6-8-6 (5*) A Procter (18) *chsd ldrs, rdn alng o'r 2 fs out, wknd over one out.* ....(12 to 1 tchd 14 to 1) 18
3621 ASSIGNMENT [69] 7-8-3 T Williams (4) *al beh*.....(20 to 1) 19
3725[7] ROCK SYMPHONY [91] 3-9-8 B Raymond (12) *hld up intch, rdn and wknd wl o'r one furlong out*... (12 to 1) 20
1485 GREEN DOLLAR [83] 10-9-3 F Norton (1) *al in rear.* ....(25 to 1 op 20 to 1) 21
3778 EDUCATED PET [70] 4-8-1 (3*) B Doyle (16) *rear grp most of way*...(25 to 1) 22

Dist: Nk, sht-hd, ¾l, nk, nk, 2l, ½l, nk, ½l, hd. 1m 13.82s. a 3.42s (22 Ran).
SR: 70/57/65/50/55/49/30/37/49/ (R J Adams), R Dickin

3907 Alexandra Trophy Handicap Class C (0-90 3-y-o and up) £5,131 2m... (3:55)

3479[2] MOIDART [73] 3-8-10 A Munro (3) *wl plcd, shaken up to ld 3 fs out, sn clr, eased nr finish.* ....(9 to 2 fav op 7 to 2 tchd 5 to 1) 1
2397[4] BARDOLPH (USA) [68] 6-9-4 A Clark (4) *hdwy 7 fs out, chsd wnr 2 out, ran on one pace*........(15 to 2 op 10 to 1) 2
3538[4] ENCORE UNE FOIS (Ire) [78] 4-9-11 (3*) B Doyle (5) *ldg grp, rdn and one pace wl o'r 2 fs out.* (10 to 1 tchd 11 to 1) 3
3587[4] ALMAMZAR (USA) [84] 3-9-7 Paul Eddery (2) *beh til styd on appr last 2 fs, not rch wnr.* .... (15 to 2 op 6 to 1 tchd 8 to 1) 4
3304* ELBURG (Ire) [72] 3-8-9 G Hind (6) *made most of rng til hdd 3 fs out, sn btn*.......(16 to 1 op 14 to 1 tchd 20 to 1) 5
3125[4] STAR QUEST [73] 6-9-9 A McGlone (7) *rcd in mid-div, pushed alng and no prog fnl 3 fs.* (12 to 1 op 10 to 1) 6
3675* WELSHMAN [68] 7-9-4 J Quinn (1) *dsptd ld til 3 fs out, sn wknd*..............................(11 to 2 op 7 to 1) 7
3521 SWORD MASTER [72] 4-9-8 M Wigham (10) *beh most of way*.................(11 to 1 op 10 to 1 tchd 12 to 1) 8
3521 IOTA [71] 4-9-7 B Raymond (12) *settled towards rear, rdn alng o'r 3 fs out, no hdwy.* .... (7 to 1 op 6 to 1 tchd 15 to 2) 9
3761* POPSI'S LEGACY [60] 6-8-3 (7*) D Toole (8) *hld up in rear, rdn alng o'r 2 fs out, no imprsn.* .... (6 to 1 op 5 to 1 tchd 13 to 2) 10
3171* RAGTIME SONG [43] 4-7-7 N Adams (11) *chsd ldrs til lost pl o'r 3 fs out, tld off*............(20 to 1 tchd 25 to 1) 11

Dist: 2l, 2½l, 4l, 4l, ½l, 1l, 1l, ½l, nk, 15l. 3m 35.14s. a 11.14s (11 Ran).
SR: 33/39/46/35/19/32/26/29/27/ (Sir David Wills), J R Fanshawe

3908 EBF Goldings Maiden Stakes Class D (2-y-o) £4,503 1m.............. (4:30)

CICERAO (Ire) 9-0 A McGlone (10) *led til hdd 3 fs out, led ag'n one out, kpt on nr finish.* ....(9 to 4 op 3 to 1 tchd 9 to 2) 1
TWIN FALLS (Ire) 9-0 A Munro (7) *rcd keenly wth ldrs, led 3 fs out, reminder and hdd one out, ran on.* ....(15 to 8 fav op 6 to 4) 2
EHTEFAAL (USA) 9-0 Paul Eddery (6) *chsd ldrs aftr 2 fs, rdn and outpcd o'r 3 out.* ....(8 to 1 op 7 to 1 tchd 9 to 1) 3
CLARION CALL (Ire) 9-0 M Tebbutt (9) *mid-div, outpcd last 3 fs*..................................(9 to 1 op 7 to 1) 4
VINTAGE TIMES 9-0 D Biggs (8) *effrt frm rear o'r 3 fs out, sn rdn and no hdwy.* (20 to 1 op 16 to 1 tchd 25 to 1) 5
STONECROP 9-0 Dale Gibson (1) *pressed ldrs til outpcd frm 3 fs out*......................(33 to 1 op 20 to 1) 6
MAJOR CLINTON 9-0 A Clark (4) *slwly into strd, beh most of way*...................(8 to 1 op 5 to 1 tchd 9 to 1) 7
STETTIN 9-0 B Raymond (3) *chsd ldrs for 3 fs, sn wknd.* ....(8 to 1 op 6 to 1) 8
IN BEHIND (Ire) 8-9 B Rouse (5) *al beh.* ....(20 to 1 tchd 25 to 1) 9
MILOS 9-0 J Quinn (2) *in tch til drpd rear o'r 3 fs out.* ....(16 to 1 tchd 25 to 1) 10

Dist: ¾l, 12l, 2½l, 2l, sht-hd, 2l, 3l, 1½l, 3l. 1m 46.85s. a 9.65s (10 Ran).
(Ivan Allan), H R A Cecil

3909 Foxhall Maiden Stakes Class D (3-y-o) £4,077 1¼m.................. (5:00)

3590[2] DARRERY 8-9 Paul Eddery (10) *made virtually all, quickened o'r one furlong out, pushed clr, eased nr finish.* ....(11 to 10 fav tchd 5 to 4 and Evens) 1
3590[4] TOUJOURS RIVIERA 9-0 F Norton (8) *hld up in rear, swtchd lft and ran on 3 fs out, one pace appr fnl furlong*.................. (8 to 1 op 6 to 1 tchd 10 to 1) 2
WAJIH (USA) 9-0 A Clark (7) *chsd frnt rnk, rdn and swtchd rght o'r 2 fs out, no extr appr fnl furlong.* ....(20 to 1 op 12 to 1 tchd 25 to 1) 3
2485[5] ECU DE FRANCE (Ire) 9-0 T Williams (1) *ldg grp, rdn and one pace fnl 2 fs*........(5 to 1 op 4 to 1 tchd 11 to 2) 4
482[8] PURPLE SPLASH 9-0 A Munro (4) *jnd wnr aftr 4 fs, no extr und pres 2 out*........ (25 to 1 op 20 to 1 tchd 33 to 1) 5
3225 VALBRA 8-9 A McGlone (2) *cl up til wknd 2 fs out.* ....(20 to 1 op 8 to 1) 6
583[2] NUMBER ONE SPOT 8-9 B Raymond (3) *mid-div, wknd o'r 2 fs out*..................(3 to 1 op 7 to 2 tchd 9 to 2) 7
3509[9] DIXIE DIAMOND 8-9 N Adams (5) *lost several ls leaving stalls, al beh, tld off.* ....(66 to 1 op 50 to 1 tchd 100 to 1) 8
COMMANCHE STAR 8-11 (3*) S D Williams (9) *chsd ldrs for 7 fs, tld off*..........(66 to 1 op 33 to 1 tchd 100 to 1) 9

Dist: 3l, 1l, 1½l, ¾l, 4l, 10l, 20l, ¾l. 2m 15.15s. a 9.65s (9 Ran).
SR: 29/28/26/23/21/8/ (Sheikh Mohammed), M R Stoute

3910 Battle Of Britain Westhampnett Limited Stakes Class G Amateur Riders (3-y-o and up) £3,370 7f.........(5:30)

3780* SET THE FASHION (v) 4-10-9 Mrs M Cowdrey (17) *in tch, ran on 3 fs out, reminder to ld o'r one out, eased cl hme.* .... (15 to 8 fav op 2 to 1 tchd 9 to 4 and 7 to 4) 1
3440* SUPER BENZ 7-10-9 Mr R Hale (13) *led aftr one furlong, hdd o'r one out, ran on same pace*... (6 to 1 op 4 to 1) 2
3425[8] PUSEY STREET BOY 6-10-4 (5*) Mrs S Bosley (3) *dsptd second pl, rdn and one pace appr fnl furlong.* .... (16 to 1 op 14 to 1 tchd 20 to 1) 3
3780[2] QUEEN OF SHANNON (Ire) 5-10-4 Mr J Rees (19) *hdwy o'r 2 fs out, ev ch over one out, not quicken.* ....(9 to 2 op 5 to 1 tchd 6 to 1) 4
3551 HERETICAL MISS (bl) 3-9-9 (5*) Mrs J Boggis (14) *hdwy on ins last 2 fs, not rch wnr.* ....(20 to 1 op 16 to 1 tchd 33 to 1) 5
3549* QUINSIGIMOND 3-10-0 Miss Diana Jones (5) *rcd in 3rd pl, rdn and ev ch o'r one furlong out, wknd fnl 100 yards.* ....(9 to 2 op 7 to 2 tchd 5 to 1) 6
2868[7] GREY CHARMER (Ire) 4-10-4 (5*) Mr E James (4) *rdn to improve appr last 2 fs, styd on one pace approaching last*.............................. (12 to 1 tchd 14 to 1) 7
3709[6] MAID WELCOME (v) 6-9-13 (5*) Miss A Sanders (2) *led for one furlong, dsptd second pl til wknd o'r one out.* ....(25 to 1 op 16 to 1 tchd 50 to 1) 8
3447[5] CONISTON LAKE (Ire) 4-10-4 (5*) Mr J Keller (16) *mid-div, rdn and not rch ldrs o'r 2 fs out.* ....(50 to 1 op 20 to 1 tchd 66 to 1) 9
3509[6] STARLIGHT FLYER (bl) 6-10-4 (5*) Mr T Waters (10) *some late hdwy, nvr nrr*..................(66 to 1 op 50 to 1) 10
3228[4] DON'T GIVE UP 5-10-4 (5*) Miss V Haigh (1) *nvr nr to chal.* ....(50 to 1 op 20 to 1) 11
DOMINANT FORCE 4-10-4 (5*) Mrs D McHale (7) *in tch in mid-div, rdn and wknd last 2 fs*... (50 to 1 op 33 to 1) 12
3020 EXCESS BAGGAGE (Ire) 3-10-0 (5*) Miss F Burke (9) *nvr rchd ldrs*..............(50 to 1 op 20 to 1 tchd 66 to 1) 13
3019[8] SYLVAN SABRE (Ire) 4-10-9 Mr R Teal (8) *hrd rdn and effrt 3 out, wknd ins last 2 fs.* ....(13 to 2 op 8 to 1 tchd 10 to 1) 14
3661[6] TAKE IT IN CASH 4-9-13 (5*) Miss S Duckett (20) *not clr run on ins o'r 5 fs out, nvr on terms aftrwards.* ....(50 to 1 op 20 to 1 tchd 66 to 1) 15
3551 LAMBOURN RAJA 7-11-4[14] (5*) Mr K Tork (11) *strted slwly, hrd rdn hfwy, al beh.* ....(66 to 1 op 50 to 1 tchd 100 to 1) 16
3665[6] MYJINKA (bl) 3-9-9 (5*) Miss K Martindale (6) *dwlt, al outpcd*..............................(66 to 1 op 50 to 1) 17
3460 TRIBAT 3-9-9 (5*) Mrs L Morris (12) *in tch to hfwy.* ....(50 to 1 op 20 to 1 tchd 66 to 1) 18
3257[9] SUPREME OPTIMIST (bl) 9-10-4 (5*) Mrs C Peacock (18) *badly hmpd 5 fs out, not reco'r*.... (66 to 1 op 50 to 1) 19
3007 PRINCESS JESSICA 6-9-13 (5*) Mr M Mannish (15) *chsd ldrs til wknd o'r 3 fs out*..........(66 to 1 op 50 to 1) 20

Dist: 2½l, 1l, 1½l, hd, 2l, 2l, hd, 1½l, sht-hd, 1l. 1m 32.87s. a 8.27s (20 Ran).
SR: 30/22/19/9/4/-/1/-/-/ (The Queen), Lord Huntingdon

LEOPARDSTOWN (IRE) (good) Saturday September 11th

3911 Guinness Extra Stout E.B.F. Maiden (2-y-o) £5,520 6f............... (2:15)

PERUGINO (USA) 9-0 L Piggott (15)..........(10 to 9 on) 1
3453[3] MARKET SLIDE (USA) 8-11 M J Kinane (7)........ (3 to 1) 2
2880 AINE'S PET (Ire) 8-9 (2*) P Carberry (10)..........(12 to 1) 3
2742[9] KRAYYALEI (Ire) 8-11 S Craine (17)..............(20 to 1) 4
ANSARIYA (USA) 8-11 J P Murtagh (3)...............(8 to 1) 5
2804[6] CELESTIAL PLAIN (Ire) 8-11 N G McCullagh (5).... (14 to 1) 6
3683[6] EUPHORIC (Ire) 8-12 (2*) D G O'Shea (9).......... (12 to 1) 7
1824[8] FIONN DE COOL (Ire) 9-0 C Roche (4)..............(12 to 1) 8
2742[4] AL NAAYY 8-11 W J Supple (11).....................(7 to 1) 9
3332[4] ABSOLUTE RULER (Ire) 9-0 R Hughes (16)........ (16 to 1) 10
2804 IMPOSING TIME 9-0 P Shanahan (1)............ (33 to 1) 11
3719[3] PETERS BIRD (Ire) 9-0 P V Gilson (12).............(20 to 1) 12
3039 INDIAN EXPRESS 8-11 B Coogan (13)...............(20 to 1) 13
3731 BERGERACONHOLIDAY (Ire) 9-0 A J Nolan (2)....(50 to 1) 14
3719[7] PENZAAD (Ire) 9-0 K Fallon (6).....................(66 to 1) 15
3683 EMELIA'S PET (Ire) 9-0 J F Egan (14)...............(66 to 1) 16

Dist: Hd, 6l, 2½l, 1l. 1m 14.20s. a 2.70s (16 Ran).
SR: 28/24/-/-/-/-/ (R E Sangster), M V O'Brien

3912 Arthur Guinness E.B.F. Flying Five (Group 3) (2-y-o and up) £14,375 5f

.................................(2:45)

3162* TROPICAL (bl) 3-9-9 M J Kinane (7) *trkd ldrs, smooth prog one and a half fs out to ld o'r 100 yards out, cmftbly.* ....(6 to 4 fav) 1
3594* STACK ROCK 6-9-7 K Fallon (9) *broke smartly, pressed ldr frm hfwy, kpt on fnl furlong*.....................(5 to 1) 2
3571² PALACEGATE EPISODE (Ire) 3-9-5 M Roberts (6) *led 4 fs out till hdd ins fnl furlong, kpt on*.....................(8 to 1) 3
3162⁸ UP AND AT 'EM (bl) 3-9-8 W Carson (8) *trkd ldrs, rdn and not quicken one and a half fs out, styd on*.... (10 to 1) 4
3291² LUCKY PARKES 3-9-5 L Piggott (3) *wl plcd till rdn and wknd 2 fs out*...................................(7 to 1) 5
3496* BRADAWN BREEVER (Ire) 4-9-10 W J Supple (4) *slwly away and sn rdn, styd on fnl furlong*.........(10 to 1) 6
3455* MOONLIGHT PARTNER (Ire) 3-9-5 R Hughes (10) *rear, outpcd frm hfwy*.....................................(33 to 1) 7
3542² EL ZORRO DORADO (Ire) 3-9-8 S Craine (2) *al rear.* ....(14 to 1) 8
2927⁹ SOVEREIGN GRACE (Ire) 4-9-7 J P Murtagh (5) *led till hdd 4 fs out, rdn and wknd 2 out*.................. (20 to 1) 9
3464⁹ SEA GAZER (Ire) 3-9-12 P V Gilson (1) *wl plcd till rdn and wknd o'r 2 fs out*..........................(10 to 1) 10
Dist: 2½l, nk, 1l, 3l. 59.40s. a 0.70s (10 Ran).
SR: 80/68/65/64/49/-/ (The Sussex Stud Limited), D K Weld

3913 Guinness Champion Stakes (Group 1) (3-y-o and up) £84,300 1¼m.....(3:30)

3748* MUHTARRAM (USA) 4-9-4 W Carson (3) *al wl plcd, rdn to chal one and a half fs out, led 150 yards out, ran on well*...............................(7 to 1) 1
2791* OPERA HOUSE 5-9-4 M Roberts (6) *trkd ldrs till prog on fnl turn to ld o'r one furlong out, no extr cl hme.* ....(Evens fav) 2
3495* LORD OF THE FIELD 6-9-4 W Newnes (9) *rear till styd on wl fnl 2 fs*...............................(25 to 1) 3
3022* MARKET BOOSTER (USA) 4-9-1 M J Kinane (4) *led 8 fs out till hdd and wknd o'r one out*............. (100 to 30) 4
3559² APPROACH THE BENCH (Ire) 5-9-4 J F Egan (10) *rear till prog into mid-div 4 fs out, rcd wide on fnl turn, styd on.* ....(50 to 1) 5
3495⁴ TAKAROUNA (USA) 3-8-8 J P Murtagh (8) *mid-div, rdn entering strt, nvr rch ldrs*.....................(14 to 1) 6
3495³ DANSE ROYALE (Ire) 3-8-8 W J Supple (7) *led till hdd 8 fs out, second in strt, sn wknd*................. (20 to 1) 7
3402⁴ REVELATION (Ire) 3-8-11 S Craine (1) *wl plcd till rdn and wknd 3 fs out*...............................(14 to 1) 8
2074* IVORY FRONTIER (Ire) 3-8-11 K J Manning (2) *al rear.* ....(25 to 1) 9
941* PERFECT IMPOSTER (Ire) 3-8-11 C Roche (5) *mid-div till rdn and lost pl 4 fs out*........................(20 to 1) 10
Dist: ½l, 2½l, 2½l, 1l, sht-hd, hd, 1l, 1½l, ¾l. 2m 6.10s. a 1.40s (10 Ran).
SR: 75/74/69/61/62/51/50/51/48/ (Hamdan Al-Maktoum), J H M Gosden

3914 St. James's Gate Handicap (3-y-o and up) £4,140 1¼m.................(4:00)

3202² SAIBOT (USA) [-] (bl) 4-9-9 M J Kinane (3)......... (3 to 1) 1
3494* KHALYANI (Ire) [-] 3-9-7 (6*) C Everard (8)...... (6 to 4 fav) 2
3855³ COOLRAIN LADY (Ire) [-] 3-8-6 (2*) P Carberry (5) .. (8 to 1) 3
3494⁷ KAR OR [-] 3-8-10 (6*) B J Walsh (2)............. (20 to 1) 4
3525⁶ FERRYCARRIG HOTEL (Ire) [-] 4-8-2 (6*) J A Heffernan (9) ....(8 to 1) 5
3543⁷ SCOTSMAN'S BAY (Ire) [-] 4-7-7² (4*) J J Behan (11) ....(12 to 1) 6
3327⁴ THE BURSER [-] 7-9-3 J F Egan (10).............(10 to 1) 7
2808⁴ SECOND REVOLUTION (Ire) [-] 4-9-2 C Roche (7) .. (8 to 1) 8
3772⁶ FLORA WOOD (Ire) [-] (bl) 3-8-10 W J Supple (12) (12 to 1) 9
3163⁵ COCKNEY LAD (Ire) [-] 4-8-10 P Shanahan (1) .... (14 to 1) 10
2677⁹ CLANFLUTHER (Ire) [-] 3-7-5 (2*) D G O'Shea (6) .. (50 to 1) 11
3662⁷ PAKED (Ire) [-] 3-7-6³ (4*) W J Smith (4)......... (200 to 1) 12
Dist: Hd, 4l, hd, 4l. 2m 7.40s. a 2.70s (12 Ran).
SR: 67/70/43/50/34/-/ (Michael W J Smurfit), D K Weld

3915 Guinness Toucan Handicap (3-y-o and up) £6,900 1¾m.................(4:30)

3494⁴ LACKEL (Ger) [-] 5-7-11 (6*) J A Heffernan (8)..... (14 to 1) 1
3577² CLIVEDEN GAIL (Ire) [-] 4-8-7 M J Kinane (4) ... (5 to 4 fav) 2
3336⁵ MASAI WARRIOR [-] 6-7-8 (2*) R M Burke (9)...... (16 to 1) 3
3560² SHIRLEY'S DELIGHT (Ire) [-] 3-8-0 W Carson (13) .. (4 to 1) 4
ROSE APPEAL [-] 7-7-11 (4*) J J Behan (1)....... (10 to 1) 5
3398² HACKETTS CROSS (Ire) [-] 5-7-5⁵ (8*) R T Fitzpatrick (5) ....(20 to 1) 6
3577⁶ EBONY AND IVORY (Ire) [-] 4-9-0 W J Supple (6) .. (12 to 1) 7
665⁵ LADAKIYA (USA) [-] 3-8-4 M Roberts (12)...........(8 to 1) 8
3163² CURRENCY BASKET (Ire) [-] 4-8-8 C Roche (7).... (9 to 1) 9
3578* SHARKASHKA (Ire) [-] 3-7-10 (2*) D G O'Shea (3) ..(10 to 1) 10
3063* OFTEN AHEAD (Ire) [-] 5-7-11 N G McCullagh (2) ... (8 to 1) 11
3577⁵ EYELID [-] 7-9-7 S Craine (11)...................(14 to 1) 12
GORGEOUS DANCER (Ire) [-] 4-9-0 J F Egan (10) (25 to 1) 13
Dist: 1l, 3½l, 2l, hd. 2m 57.30s. a 1.30s (13 Ran).
SR: 55/57/39/39/39/-/ (Mrs E Kube), J S Bolger

3916 Perfect Pint E.B.F. Race (3-y-o and up) £4,140 1m 1f...................(5:00)

788² IDRIS (Ire) 3-9-5 J P Murtagh (4)..............(Evens fav) 1
3452* MILLIE'S CHOICE (Ire) 4-9-9 W J Supple (5).......(8 to 1) 2
3559³ ARABIC TREASURE (USA) 3-9-5 M J Kinane (7)....(6 to 1) 3
3770² SWEET NASHA (Ire) 4-9-12 P V Gilson (6)........ (13 to 2) 4
3165⁴ FAIRY LORE (Ire) 3-8-8 (4*) J J Behan (8).........(10 to 1) 5
3495⁵ SEMPLE STADIUM (Ire) 3-9-3 L Piggott (3).........(8 to 1) 6
2903* LOUGHMOGUE (Ire) 3-9-0 N G McCullagh (1).... (10 to 1) 7
3733* ALBERTAZZI (Ire) 3-9-1 C Roche (2)..............(10 to 1) 8
3164⁷ RAFFERTY'S INNER (Ire) 3-9-1 S Craine (9).......(50 to 1) 9
997⁵ ELA-MANA-SUE (Ire) 4-8-6 (8*) D McCullagh (10) (100 to 1) 10
Dist: 2l, sht-hd, 2l, 2l. 1m 53.40s. a 2.90s (10 Ran).
SR: 41/41/36/39/21/-/ (H H Aga Khan), John M Oxx

3917 Guinness Hopstore Nursery Handicap (2-y-o) £4,140 1m..............(5:30)

3541* PEACE ROLE (USA) [-] (bl) 9-10 (6ex) M J Kinane (5) (7 to 4) 1
3335⁶ ZAVALETA (Ire) [-] 9-1 C Roche (1)............ (5 to 4 fav) 2
3332⁶ INISHMANN (Ire) [-] 8-4 J F Egan (8)..............(9 to 1) 3
3030 METROELLA (Ire) [-] 8-5 W J Supple (4)........... (6 to 1) 4
1994⁶ YOUR VILLAGE (Ire) [-] 8-0 (4*) J A Heffernan (6) .. (14 to 1) 5
3806⁵ DANCING BRIEF (Ire) [-] 7-5 (2*) D G O'Shea (7) ...(16 to 1) 6
2319 FANCY BOOTS (Ire) [-] 8-2 N G McCullagh (3).....(14 to 1) 7
Dist: 2l, 2l, sht-hd, sht-hd. 1m 46.10s. a 8.10s (7 Ran).
(Moyglare Stud Farms Ltd), D K Weld

SAN SIRO (ITY) (heavy)
Saturday September 11th

3918 Premio Valcamonica (Maiden) (2-y-o) £5,603 1m..................... (2:55)

TABLET (Ire) 8-11 A Carboni,................................ 1
GISELLE PENN (USA) 8-8 E Botti,............................ 2
RAPIDDIMA (Ire) 8-11 V Panici,.............................. 3
MARINA GRIMALDI (Ire) 8-8 S Whitworth, *mid-div till rdn and wknd 3 fs out*.................................. 0
Dist: 1l, ¾l, 6l, 1l, 1½l, ½l, 4l, sht-hd, 3½l, 6l. 1m 43.90s. (11 Ran).
G Miliani

3919 Premio Cortina (2-y-o) £5,603 6f (4:10)

SEA DREAMS (Ire) 8-11 S Whitworth, *al frnt rnk, led one and a half fs out, hld on wl*.......................... 1
DOWN BOUND TRAIN (Ity) 8-8 A Carboni,................ 2
MR LOVE (Ire) 8-11 C Bertolini,.......................... 3
Dist: Nk, nk, 1l, 3l, 3½l, 5l, 2l, 7l. 1m 16.10s. (9 Ran).
(P E Wragg), P W Chapple-Hyam

CAPANNELLE (ITY) (good)
Sunday September 12th

3920 Premio Archidamia (Listed) (3-y-o and up) £20,173 1¼m...............(3:30)

3437 MIDNIGHT HEIGHTS 3-8-4 W Ryan, *rcd in 4th, led 2 fs out, sn clr, easily*.. 1
1222² ROSE VIOLET (USA) 3-8-4 F Jovine,....................... 2
2650⁵ DAMA GRANDE 4-8-9 G Bietolini,.......................... 3
1727⁴ OLLI STAR (Ire) 3-8-4 M Jerome,.......................... 4
694⁸ LIFTING (Ire) 3-8-4 M Pasquale,........................... 5
FIRM FRIEND (Ire) 3-8-4 A Luongo,......................... 6
VERNON STREET (USA) 4-8-9 L Ficuciello,................ 7
ANA SYROS (USA) 3-8-4 G Ligas,.......................... 8
694⁶ JEU DE CARTES (USA) 3-8-4 B Jovine,.................... 9
Dist: 4l, 2 ¼l, 1 ¼l, ¾l, 1l, nk, 1 ¼l, 3½l. 2m 2.30s. (9 Ran).
(Ettore Landi), J L Dunlop

3921 Premio Ezio Vanoni (Listed) (4-y-o and up) £20,173 1½m...............(4:30)

3784³ CAPTAIN HORATIUS (Ire) 4-8-10 W Ryan, *rcd in 3rd, chlgd 2 and a half fs out, led appr fnl furlong, ran on wl*.... 1
1323⁵ JACK LANG 5-8-8 M Pasquale,............................ 2
3402⁸ GUADO D'ANNIBALE (Ire) 4-8-8 F Jovine,................. 3
957⁴ ALMANOR 4-8-8 V Mezzatesta,............................ 4
1085⁷ LABUAN CROOM (Ire) 4-8-8 A Luango,.................... 5
BANDOL (Ire) 5-9-1 E Tasende,............................. 6
Dist: ¾l, sht-nk, ½l, hd, 8l. 2m 31.70s. (6 Ran).
(D R Hunnisett), J L Dunlop

CURRAGH (IRE) (good to yielding)
Sunday September 12th
Going Correction: PLUS 0.35 sec. per fur.

3922 Athgarvan (EBF) Maiden (2-y-o) £5,244 1m..................... (2:15)

3492³ REGAL ACCESS (USA) 8-12 (2*) P Carberry (13) ....(6 to 1) 1
DEVASTATING STORM (Ire) 9-0 M J Kinane (12) (2 to 1 fav) 2
3731² MELODIC SOUND (Ire) 9-0 S Craine (1)........... (9 to 2) 3
IVORY REEF (Ire) 9-0 C Roche (7)..................(3 to 1) 4
3416³ SHANKAR (Ire) 9-0 M Roberts (9)................(10 to 1) 5

3492[9] INCHINTAGGART 9-0 P Shanahan (14)...........(12 to 1) 6
CLOUD INSPECTOR (Ire) 9-0 P V Gilson (11).....(12 to 1) 7
3159[5] SHOREWOOD (Ire) 9-0 R Hughes (5).............(12 to 1) 8
MUZRAK (Can) 9-0 W J Supple (8)................(8 to 1) 9
NIYAZI (Ire) 9-0 D Hogan (2)......................(10 to 1) 10
PIPER ZERO (Ire) 9-0 J P Murtagh (3)............(10 to 1) 11
CLEAR CRACK (Ire) 8-10 (4*) J J Behan (10)......(20 to 1) 12
Dist: ¾l, 1½l, ¾l, 1½l. 1m 45.20s. a 8.60s (12 Ran).
SR: 13/11/6/4/-/-/ (Mrs Rita Holly), Noel Meade

3923 Trusted Partner Matron Stakes (Group 3) (3-y-o and up) £14,375 1m.... (2:45)

3559[6] CHANZI (USA) (bl) 3-8-9 M Roberts (2) *mid-div, prog 3 fs out, styd on strly ins last to ld on line*.........(14 to 1) 1
3333* ASEMA (USA) 3-8-13 M J Kinane (4) *hld up, prog 3 fs out, led one out, rdn, hdd on line*.............(11 to 8 on) 2
3764[2] CLOUD OF DUST 4-9-0 W Carson (6) *rear, dsptd ld 3 fs out, led bef 2 out, hdd one out, kpt on one pace*. (9 to 4) 3
3072* KAYFA (Ire) 4-9-0 P Carberry (1) *trkd ldr, rdn 2 fs out, wknd one out*.............................(12 to 1) 4
3029* EUROSTORM (USA) 3-8-9 P V Gilson (3) *mid-div, prog 3 fs out, rdn 2 out, slightly hmpd whn btn one furlong out*..(6 to 1) 5
3770[9] THATCHING CRAFT (Ire) 4-9-0 J J Behan (5) *led, jnd 3 fs out, hdd bef 2 out, wknd*.........................(33 to 1) 6
Dist: Sht-hd, ¾l, 1l, 2l. 1m 42.00s. a 5.40s (6 Ran).
SR: 56/59/58/55/44/-/ (Sheikh Mohammed), John M Oxx

3924 Diners Club Autumn Handicap (0-95 3-y-o and up) £4,140 1m 3f...... (3:15)

3824[4] OENOTHERA (Ire) [-] 3-8-13 S Craine (7)..........(7 to 1) 1
3525[8] POLITICAL SURGE (USA) [-] (bl) 3-9-1 M J Kinane (3) (6 to 1) 2
3770[3] MADANIYYA (USA) [-] 3-9-0 (6*) C Everard (5)..(2 to 1 fav) 3
2449* PLATINUM EMPIRE (USA) [-] 3-8-13 L Piggott (2)...(5 to 2) 4
3770[7] GALLARDINI (Ire) [-] 4-9-10 C Roche (4)..........(12 to 1) 5
3062* LIMBO LADY (USA) [-] 3-8-9 (4*) J J Behan (1)....(10 to 1) 6
3525[5] FLAME OF PERSIA (Ire) [-] 3-9-10 R Hughes (8)....(10 to 1) 7
1072 THRILL SEEKER (Ire) [-] (bl) 4-7-6[14] (8*) R T Fitzpatrick (9)..(66 to 1) 8
Dist: Sht-hd, 3l, 1½l, 4½l. 2m 26.30s. (8 Ran).
(R E Sangster), T Stack

3925 Moyglare Stud Stakes (Group 1) (2-y-o) £56,100 7f................ (3:50)

2301* LEMON SOUFFLE 8-11 L Piggott (12) *mid-div, prog 2 fs out, led o'r one out, quickened clr ins last*..(100 to 30) 1
3515[3] SPAIN LANE (USA) 8-11 W R Swinburn (8) *wl plcd, prog 2 fs out, ev ch one out, rdn and no extr ins last*...(11 to 10 fav) 2
3493* LOW KEY AFFAIR (USA) 8-11 M J Kinane (10) *mid-div, kpt on wl 2 fs out, nrst finish*.....................(8 to 1) 3
3335[2] GOTHIC DREAM (Ire) 8-11 R Hughes (13) *wl plcd, rdn 2 fs out, kpt on one pace ins last*..................(12 to 1) 4
3611* KERAKA (USA) 8-11 J P Murtagh (11) *hld up, prog 2 fs out, kpt on ins last*...................................(10 to 1) 5
3586[2] WILD PLANET (USA) 8-11 K Darley (1) *led, rdn 2 fs out, hdd o'r one out, wknd*...................................(9 to 1) 6
3159* ZORINA 8-11 M Roberts (5) *mid-div, prog 3 fs out, rdn 2 out, sn wknd*...(14 to 1) 7
3612[2] BALLYKETT NANCY (Ire) 8-11 K J Manning (7) *trkd ldrs, rdn 3 fs out, wknd 2 out*..............................(14 to 1) 8
3806[2] RAZIDA (Ire) 8-11 C Roche (3) *prmnt early, rdn 3 fs out, wknd*...(16 to 1) 9
3729[8] BETTER FOLLY (Ire) 8-11 W J Supple (9) *al rear*...(50 to 1) 10
3379* LUDDEN LADY (Ire) 8-11 J J Behan (4) *mid-div, rdn and wknd 2 fs out*.................................(66 to 1) 11
Dist: 4l, ½l, hd, nk. 1m 27.50s. a 4.30s (11 Ran).
SR: 69/57/55/54/53/-/ (Lord Carnarvon), R Hannon

3926 Irish Cambridgeshire Handicap (0-110 3-y-o and up) £9,750 1m........ (4:25)

3542* WANDERING THOUGHTS (Ire) [-] 4-8-2 (5ex) N G McCullagh (13)...(6 to 1) 1
3770* CLASSIC MATCH (Ire) [-] 5-9-0 (2*,5ex) P Carberry (14)..(12 to 1) 2
3824[6] RONDELLI (Ire) [-] 3-8-7 C Roche (19)............(12 to 1) 3
3732* STATE PRINCESS (Ire) [-] 3-7-1 (8*,5ex) G M Moylan (10)..(7 to 1) 4
3610* GLACIAL ARCTIC (USA) [-] 3-8-6 (5ex) M J Kinane (4)..(4 to 1 fav) 5
3336[7] TONY'S FEN [-] 4-9-1 W J Supple (17)...........(20 to 1) 6
3610 ELIZABETH'S PET (Ire) [-] 3-8-2[1] K Darley (6).....(20 to 1) 7
3498[8] LA CENERENTOLA (Ire) [-] 3-7-7 N Carlisle (7)....(14 to 1) 8
3615[5] GENERAL CHAOS (Ire) [-] 3-7-9 (2*) R M Burke (12) (16 to 1) 9
3559[8] SALMON EILE (Ire) [-] 5-9-10 J P Murtagh (18)....(16 to 1) 10
3452[6] SOUNDPROOF (Ire) [-] 3-7-7 (4*) J J Behan (2)....(16 to 1) 11
2245[4] ALALJA (Ire) [-] 3-8-9 J F Egan (15)...............(16 to 1) 12
2878[7] NEVER BACK DOWN (Ire) [-] 3-7-9 (4*) W J Smith (3)..(20 to 1) 13
3165[3] ANLACE [-] 4-8-3 M Roberts (11)..................(5 to 1) 14
3334[7] COLOUR PARTY (USA) [-] 3-9-0 P V Gilson (16)...(20 to 1) 15
2843* LADIES GALLERY (Ire) [-] 3-7-5 (2*) D G O'Shea (9) (16 to 1) 16
3615[4] ROYAL VISION (Ire) [-] 4-8-3 (4*) J A Heffernan (8) (16 to 1) 17

3826[5] TRANQUIL BEAUTY (Ire) [-] 4-7-5[6] (8*) R T Fitzpatrick (1)..(25 to 1) 18
Dist: 1½l, ½l, ¾l, sht-hd. 1m 42.10s. a 5.50s (18 Ran).
SR: 48/57/46/32/42/-/ (W Mythen), A P O'Brien

3927 Go And Go EBF Round Tower Stakes (Listed) (2-y-o) £8,625 6f........ (4:55)

MORCOTE (Ire) 8-8 M J Kinane (6) *wl plcd, quickened to ld one furlong out, styd on strly*..............(5 to 4 fav) 1
3611[5] DILIGENT DODGER (Ire) 8-11 W J Supple (4) *hld up, prog 2 fs out, ev ch one out, no extr ins last*..........(9 to 1) 2
3611[4] MISS KRISTIN (Ire) 8-8 C Roche (8) *trkd ldrs, rdn 2 fs out, lost pl one out, kpt on ag'n clsg stages*.........(7 to 2) 3
3110* PEACE TOKEN (Ire) 8-8 B Coogan (9) *wl plcd, dsptd ld 3 fs out, led 2 out till one out, wknd*...............(14 to 1) 4
3026[2] THE PUZZLER (Ire) 9-2 P V Gilson (1) *mid-div, ev ch 2 fs out, sn rdn, wknd ins last*.........................(6 to 1) 5
1854* MEMORIES (Ire) 8-8 N G McCullagh (3) *al rear*....(12 to 1) 6
3451[2] ZING PING (Ire) 8-8 S Craine (7) *led, jnd 3 fs out, hdd 2 out, rdn and wknd one out, eased*.................(7 to 2) 7
Dist: 1l, ¾l, 2l, 2l. 1m 16.00s. a 5.50s (7 Ran).
SR: 26/25/19/11/11/-/-/ (Dieter H Hofemeier), John M Oxx

3928 Mooneys Of Monasterevin Handicap (0-90 3-y-o and up) £4,140 6f.... (5:25)

3768* BENE MERENTI (Ire) [-] (bl) 3-8-6 (6*) R V Skelly (12) (14 to 1) 1
3544[8] KILTIMONY [-] 3-8-3 (8*) J J Mullins (5)...........(14 to 1) 2
2604[4] KINDNESS ITSELF (Ire) [-] 3-9-8 M J Kinane (11)...(7 to 1) 3
3614[3] PILGRIM BAY (Ire) [-] 3-8-11 (2*) R M Burke (17)...(10 to 1) 4
3330[2] MACQUARIE RIDGE (USA) [-] 5-7-5 (2*) D G O'Shea (6)..(5 to 1) 5
3561[9] KILLEEN STAR (Ire) [-] (bl) 3-7-10 (8*) G M Moylan (8)..(25 to 1) 6
3561[6] PETITE EPAULETTE [-] 3-8-6 (8*) D A O'Sullivan (19)..(20 to 1) 7
2604[9] SHRAGRADDY LASS (Ire) [-] 3-7-5[1] (8*) R T Fitzpatrick (10)..(16 to 1) 8
3334[8] BOURREE [-] 5-8-9 J F Egan (18)...............(25 to 1) 9
3610[4] UKUD (USA) [-] 3-9-5 W J Supple (2)..............(7 to 1) 10
3614* CISEAUX (USA) [-] 4-9-11 (6*,6ex) D J O'Donohoe (3)..(7 to 2 fav) 11
3614 SAND OR STONE (Ire) [-] 5-9-0 A J Nolan (4).....(20 to 1) 12
3614[2] OICHE MHAITH [-] (bl) 3-7-12 (6*) J A Heffernan (13) (9 to 1) 13
3614[6] COMMODITY MARKET (Ire) [-] 3-8-1 N G McCullagh (1)..(12 to 1) 14
3542[8] NORDIC OAK (Ire) [-] (bl) 5-10-0 C Roche (9)......(12 to 1) 15
3542[7] TAKE NO CHANCES (Ire) [-] 3-9-8 (4*) J J Behan (7) (12 to 1) 16
3606[3] PAKOL (Ire) [-] 4-7-12 (4*) W J Smith (14).........(20 to 1) 17
3720[2] VLADIVOSTOK [-] 3-7-11[7] (8*) P J Smullen (16)...(25 to 1) 18
3202[5] HAPPY ROVER [-] 8-9-11 J P Murtagh (15).......(16 to 1) 19
Dist: 3l, sht-hd, ½l, 1l. 1m 14.70s. a 4.20s (19 Ran).
SR: 56/43/53/42/18/-/ (J F Bailey Jun), J F Bailey Jun

HANOVER (GER) (good)
Sunday September 12th

3929 Preis der Hannovereschen Sparkassen und der VH (3 & 4-y-o) £24,490 1½m......................... (3:45)

PIRANGA (Ire) 3-8-9 W Newnes, *rcd in 3rd, chlgd fnl furlong to ld 100 yards out*............................... 1
3846[4] MAGICAL RETREAT (USA) 3-8-9 D Biggs, *dsptd ld till hdd 2 fs out, rallied to lead one out, ct cl hme*............ 2
3206[3] SHINE SHARE (Ire) 3-8-9 N Grant, *hld up, ran on fnl 2 fs, not rch wnr*.. 3
ELISHA (Ger) 4-9-6 R Ludtke, *hld up, ran on fnl 2 fs*...... 4
3206[5] ELACATA (Ger) 3-8-9 A Best, *prmnt 3 fs out, no extr fnl 2 furlongs*.. 5
RACING BLUE 3-8-9 L Mader, *one pace fnl 3 fs*.......... 6
2690[4] RIVE (USA) 3-8-9 N Jeanpierre, *4th strt, no extr*......... 7
1395[7] VAL D'ISERE (Ger) 3-8-9 R Hillis, *nvr a factor*............ 8
3582[7] CHESA PLANA 4-9-6 P Schiergen, *dsptd ld, led 2 fs out, wknd quickly*.. 9
3206[4] ARKONA (Ger) 3-8-9 O Schick, *prmnt early, sn btn*....... 0
TRIADE (Ger) 3-8-9 P Bloomfield,........................ 0
Dist: Nk, 1 ¾l, 1l, 1l, 1l. 2m 37.70s. (11 Ran).
(Gestut Wiedingen), A Wohler

LONGCHAMP (FR) (soft)
Sunday September 12th

Going Correction: PLUS 0.50 sec. per fur. (races 1,2,4), PLUS 0.30 (3)

3930 Prix Foy Escada (Group 3) (4-y-o and up) £23,895 1½m.............. (1:25)

3433* ONLY ROYALE (Ire) 4-8-12 R Cochrane (1) *rcd in 3rd, hdwy one and a half fs out, led jst ins last, ran on wl*..(2 to 1 on) 1
3649[4] MODHISH (Ire) 4-9-2 T Jarnet (4) *led, quickened 2 fs out, hdd jst ins last, ran on*...................... (23 to 10) 2

2261[6] VERT AMANDE (Fr) 5-9-2 D Boeuf (3) *trkd ldr, chlgd 2 fs out, one pace fnl furlong*.................. (28 to 10) 3
DARIYOUN (USA) 5-9-2 F Head (2) *al last, kpt on one pace fnl 2 fs*.................................... (13 to 1) 4
Dist: 1l, 1l, 1l. 2m 51.60s. a 22.50s (4 Ran).
(G Sainaghi), L M Cumani

3931 Prix Vermeille Escada (Group 1) (3-y-o) £119,474 1½m............. (2:55)

2405[4] INTREPIDITY 9-2 T Jarnet (4) *rear till rdn 2 fs out, jnd ldr one and a half out, led o'r one out, ran on wl.* (5 to 2) 1
2405* WEMYSS BIGHT 9-2 Pat Eddery (1) *mid-div, 5th strt, rdn and not clr run 2 fs out, fnshd fst, unlucky.* ....(11 to 10 fav) 2
3194* BRIGHT MOON (USA) (bl) 9-2 S Guillot (8) *3rd strt, rdn and quickened 2 fs out, chlgd one and a half out, kpt on.* ....(39 to 10) 3
3331[2] ROYAL BALLERINA (Ire) 9-2 R Cochrane (7) *prmnt, second strt, chlgd 2 fs out, one pace one and a half out.* ....(84 to 10) 4
3501* DANA SPRINGS (Ire) 9-2 J Reid (2) *led till o'r one furlong out, no extr*..(8 to 1) 5
1789[4] BRIGHT GENERATION (Ire) 9-2 A Munro (3) *4th strt, rdn 2 fs out, nvr plcd to chal*..........................(35 to 1) 6
2054[4] CORRAZONA (USA) 9-2 O Doleuze (6) *slwly away, last strt, rdn 2 fs out, nvr plcd to chal*.............(18 to 1) 7
3149[9] ACCOMMODATING (USA) 9-2 E Saint-Martin (5) *al rear.* ....(36 to 1) 8
Dist: Hd, 1½l, 3l, ¾l, sht-hd, ½l, 20l. 2m 36.80s. a 7.70s (8 Ran).
SR: 85/84/81/75/73/72/71/31/ (Sheikh Mohammed), A Fabre

3932 Prix de la Salamandre (Group 1) (2-y-o) £59,737 7f................. (3:30)

3515* COUP DE GENIE (USA) 8-8 C Asmussen (4) *rcd in 3rd, led one and a half fs out, imprsv*.............. (5 to 2 on) 1
3335* MAJESTIC ROLE (Fr) 8-8 J Reid (2) *trkd ldr, led 2 and a half fs out to one and a half out, one pace*... (79 to 10) 2
3499[3] VOLOCHINE (Ire) 8-11 W Mongil (6) *last till hdwy 2 and a half fs out, took 3rd one and a half out, one pace fnl furlong*..(14 to 1) 3
3515[4] CELTIC ARMS (Fr) 8-11 G Mosse (5) *rear till effrt 2 fs out, kpt on one pace fnl furlong*..................(98 to 10) 4
BECCARI (USA) 8-11 T Jarnet (3) *some late prog, nvr dngrs*..(9 to 2) 5
3338 SIMPLY TRICKY (USA) (bl) 8-11 O Doleuze (1) *led till 2 and a half fs out, sn rdn and wknd*.............. (106 to 10) 6
Dist: 3l, 2l, sht-hd, sht-hd, 1½l. 1m 23.10s. a 3.60s (6 Ran).
SR: 72/63/60/59/58/53/ (S S Niarchos), F Boutin

3933 Prix Niel Escada (Group 2) (3-y-o) £47,790 1½m.................. (4:05)

2076[2] HERNANDO (Fr) 9-2 C Asmussen (6) *second strt, rdn and quickened 2 fs out, led jst und one and a half out, ran on wl*.. (5 to 2 on) 1
3337* DERNIER EMPEREUR (USA) 9-2 S Guillot (2) *3rd strt, rdn and quickened 2 fs out, jnd ldrs one and a half out, no ch wth wnr*..(34 to 10) 2
3501[2] DANCIENNE (Fr) 8-13 D Boeuf (5) *4th strt, outpcd o'r 2 fs out, some hdwy fnl furlong, took 3rd cl hme.* (33 to 10) 3
2771[3] TURNERS HILL 9-2 Pat Eddery (3) *trkd ldr, led 5 fs out till jst und one and a half out, sn wknd*.............. (8 to 1) 4
3800 HUDO (USA) 9-2 E Saint-Martin (4) *led till 5 fs out, wknd 4 out, sn tld off*.. (5 to 2 on) 5
Dist: 1½l, 1½l, ½l, dist. 2m 36.70s. a 7.60s (5 Ran).
SR: 86/83/77/79/-/ (S S Niarchos), F Boutin

SAN SIRO (ITY) (soft)
Sunday September 12th

3934 Premio Pietro Bessero (Listed) (3-y-o and up) £20,173 1m........... (3:20)

JULY GIRL 4-8-8 M Esposito,.. 1
CIVIDALE (Ire) 4-8-8 M Planard,.. 2
VAGHEZZA (Ire) 4-8-8 S Soto,.. 3
2981[9] ANCESTRAL DANCER 3-8-10 M Hills, *rcd in 5th, some hdwy 2 fs out, nvr dngrs*.. 4
CU NA MARA 4-8-8 M Tellini,.. 5
FOOLISH HEART (Ire) 3-8-8 L Sorrentino,.. 6
SIDDHARTA (USA) 5-8-8 G Vericelli,.. 7
Dist: 1½l, ½l, ¾l, sht-hd, 2½l, dist. 1m 40.80s. (7 Ran).
(North Ridge Farm), V Caruso

3935 Premio Federico Tesio (Group 3) (4-y-o and up) £28,161 1m 3f.......(3:40)

2253[2] MISIL (USA) 5-8-12 L Dettori, *rcd in 3rd, led 2 and a half fs out, sn clr, easily*.. 1
1888[5] GREEN SENOR (USA) 5-8-12 L Sorrentino, *led till 2 and a half fs out, kpt on, no ch wth wnr*.. 2
1323* BIG TOBIN (Ity) 4-9-1 O Fancera, *rcd in second, unbl to quicken fnl 2 fs*.. 3
PATRIK OF IRELAND (Ire) 5-8-12 M Tellini, *nvr able to chal.* 4
4727a[8] GIROLAMO 4-8-12 P Bugattella, *refused to race early stages, al beh*.. 5
Dist: 8l, 3l, 3½l, dist. 2m 19.50s. (5 Ran).
(Scuderia Laghi), V Caruso

TABY (SWE) (good)
Sunday September 12th

3936 Stockholm Plaza Open Sprint Championship (Group 3) (3-y-o and up) £28,011 6f...................... (1:50)

3291* BUNTY BOO 4-9-0 A Mackay,.. 1
GREEN TURBAN 5-9-4 G Nordling,.. 2
GLENLIVET (Swe) 5-9-4 O Larsen,.. 3
NEVER SO SURE 5-9-4 Yvonne Durant,.. 4
3427[2] FYLDE FLYER 4-9-4 J Carroll,.. 5
KILLIGO (Swe) 5-9-4 Kim Andersen,.. 6
SIMMERING 3-8-9 M Santos,.. 7
SIDE WINGER (USA) 5-9-4 J Tandari,.. 8
MARACAIBO (Den) 4-9-4 S Meacock,.. 9
HATTA FORT 6-9-4 A Boschert,.. 0
3174[3] SIZZLING SAGA (Ire) 5-9-4 C Cordrey,.. 0
DESERT SPORT (Fr) 5-9-4 F Diaz,.. 0
PARIOS (Fr) 5-9-4 F Johansson,.. 0
3725[2] BRANSTON ABBY (Ire) 4-9-0 M Birch,.. 0
HOT RUN (Den) 5-9-4 John Fortune,.. 0
Dist: 1l, 1l, nk, 1½l, ½l, ½l, 1l, 2l, ½l, 1½l. 1m 10.90s. (15 Ran).
(Mrs R C Mayall), B A McMahon

BATH (good)
Monday September 13th
Going Correction: MINUS 0.10 sec. per fur.

3937 Faulkland Maiden Stakes Class D (3-y-o) £3,752 1m 3f 144yds........(2:00)

BALLET PRINCE (Ire) 9-0 L Dettori (7) *al prmnt, led entering fnl 2 fs, pushed clr, cmftbly.* .... (5 to 1 op 5 to 2 tchd 11 to 2) 1
489 SPRING MARATHON (USA) 9-0 A Mackay (10) *wl beh til gd prog fnl 2 fs, not rch wnr*.......... (20 to 1 op 14 to 1) 2
3590[6] DARK DEN (USA) 9-0 W Newnes (1) *led til hdd and no extr entering fnl quarter m*........... (3 to 1 fav op 6 to 1) 3
3102[3] CUTLASS (Ire) 8-9 J Reid (9) *in tch, no prog fnl 3 fs.* ....(4 to 1 op 7 to 2) 4
3740[4] CLASSIC CABOOSE (USA) 9-0 R Cochrane (6) *nvr trbld ldrs*.......................... (4 to 1 op 7 to 2) 5
1068 SPANISH SAHARA (Ire) 9-0 S Whitworth (2) *nvr rchd ldrs.* .... (20 to 1 op 12 to 1) 6
3590 OLD RED (Ire) 9-0 A Munro (8) *chsd ldr til wknd 3 fs out.* .... (14 to 1 op 10 to 1 tchd 16 to 1) 7
DESTINY CALLS 9-0 A McGlone (4) *slwly away, nvr dngrs*..............................(50 to 1 op 20 to 1) 8
3693 POLLY LEACH 8-2 (7*) S Drowne (3) *prmnt til hfwy.* .... (50 to 1 op 33 to 1) 9
2315[3] THALEROS 9-0 M Perrett (5) *wl plcd til wknd 4 fs out.* ....(4 to 1 op 5 to 2) 10
3660[5] LADY MAVIS 8-9 N Adams (11) *tld off fnl 5 fs.* .... (50 to 1 op 33 to 1) 11
Dist: 2½l, 1½l, 2l, 2½l, sht-hd, 1l, 1½l, 5l, 7l, 30l. 2m 33.00s. a 6.00s (11 Ran).
SR: 28/23/20/11/11/10/8/5/-/ (Lord Weinstock), M R Stoute

3938 Autumn Selling Handicap Class G (0-60 3 & 4-y-o) £2,742 1m 5yds (2:30)

3591[5] MOGWAI (Ire) [55] (bl) 4-10-0 S Whitworth (18) *mid-div, gd hdwy o'r 2 fs out, led appr fnl furlong, hld on wl.* .... (12 to 1 op 10 to 1 tchd 14 to 1) 1
3766 ALL THE GIRLS (Ire) [35] 4-8-1 (7*) P McCabe (12) *prog o'r 2 fs out, styd on wl fnl furlong*...... (14 to 1 op 10 to 1) 2
3655 HOMEMAKER [42] 3-8-10 L Dettori (16) *hdwy 3 fs out, led one and a half out, sn hdd, kpt on.* .... (11 to 2 op 7 to 2 tchd 6 to 1) 3
3670[7] CHICARD [38] 4-8-11 R Cochrane (11) *mid-div til styd on fnl quarter m*......... (12 to 1 op 8 to 1 tchd 14 to 1) 4
3910[5] HERETICAL MISS [46] (bl) 3-8-7 (7*) Mark Denaro (7) *chsd ldr til wknd 2 fs out*..... (7 to 1 op 6 to 1 tchd 8 to 1) 5
3766[8] FINDON ACADEMY (Ire) [47] (bl) 3-9-1 B Rouse (15) *in tch, no prog fnl 3 fs*..................(20 to 1 op 10 to 1) 6
3591* BLOWING (USA) [53] 3-9-7 J Reid (6) *led til hdd one and a half fs out, sn btn*..... (6 to 1 tchd 7 to 1 and 5 to 1) 7
3766[3] KELLY MAC [57] 3-9-11 Paul Eddery (14) *chsd ldrs til wknd appr fnl 2 fs*.. (4 to 1 fav op 3 to 1 tchd 9 to 2) 8
3095[7] RIVER REFUGE [44] 3-8-12 W Newnes (9) *al abt same pl.* .... (16 to 1 op 14 to 1) 9
3591 ALMONTY (Ire) [40] (bl) 3-8-3 (5*) N Gwilliams (5) *prmnt til wknd o'r 2 fs out*..............(14 to 1 op 10 to 1) 10
3228 SHALOU [40] (bl) 4-8-13 A Munro (8) *cl up til lost pl appr fnl 2 fs*..............(14 to 1 op 10 to 1) 11
3547[5] IVORY HUTCH [42] 3-8-10 D Biggs (13) *nvr rchd ldrs.* .... (6 to 1 op 10 to 1 tchd 14 to 1) 12
3310[7] MALCESINE (Ire) [40] (v) 4-8-13 J Fortune (10) *slwly into strd, nvr dngrs*..................(12 to 1 op 8 to 1) 13

3689[7] NIGELS PROSPECT [42] 3-8-10 A Mackay (2) nvr trbld ldrs..............................(16 to 1 op 12 to 1) 14
1377[5] CHUMMY'S FRIEND (Ire) [43] 3-8-11 R Hills (4) nvr dngrs. ....(14 to 1 op 8 to 1 tchd 16 to 1) 15
1375[7] MUSICAL PHONE [41] 3-8-9 A Tucker (3) nvr nr ldrs. ....(33 to 1 op 20 to 1) 16
3689[9] MONTAGNE [40] 4-8-6 (7*) S Drowne (17) nvr in the hunt. ....(33 to 1 op 20 to 1) 17
3887 WEST END GIRL [40] (bl) 3-8-8 T Sprake (1) prmnt to hfwy. ....(33 to 1 op 20 to 1) 18

Dist: Nk, nk, 3l, hd, 1½l, 2½l, sht-hd, 3l, 2½l, 1½l. 1m 43.40s. a 4.40s (18 Ran).
SR: 36/15/16/8/10/6/4/7/-/ (Anthony Pye-Jeary), R F Johnson Houghton

3939 Sherston Fillies' Conditions Stakes Class D (2-y-o) £4,020 1m 5yds..(3:00)

2447* HIGHLAND LEGEND (USA) 8-12 W Ryan (1) chsd ldrs, hrd rdn to ld ins fnl furlong, styd on wl. (7 to 4 op 5 to 4) 1
3828[6] CRAZY FOR YOU 8-8 Paul Eddery (5) led til hdd and outpcd ins fnl furlong............(33 to 1 op 20 to 1) 2
2583[4] JANGADA 8-8 J Reid (4) chsd ldr til edgd rght 2 fs out, one pace..............................(4 to 1 op 3 to 1) 3
2887[4] LOCHBELLE 8-8 L Dettori (6) chsd ldrs, drvn alng 3 fs out, no imprsn.......... (6 to 4 fav op 7 to 4 tchd 2 to 1) 4
VOLTERRA 8-8 A McGlone (3) nvr dngrs. ....(12 to 1 op 8 to 1) 5
3389[4] CARA CARLTON (USA) 8-8 W Newnes (2) rdn hfwy, sn outpcd.............................(12 to 1 op 8 to 1) 6

Dist: 2l, 4l, 2½l, 2l, 4l. 1m 43.90s. a 4.90s (6 Ran).
SR: 13/3/-/ (Angus Dundee Ltd), H R A Cecil

3940 Bathford Nursery Class C (2-y-o) £5,047 1m 5yds................ (3:30)

3792[5] CAPTAIN SCARLET (Ire) [69] 8-7 (3*) B Doyle (12) cl up, led one furlong out, rdn out............ (10 to 1 op 8 to 1) 1
3760* ALCOVE [80] 9-7 L Dettori (14) wth ldrs, ev ch fnl 2 fs, kpt on..............................(7 to 2 fav op 4 to 1) 2
3705[3] ROBSERA (Ire) [70] 8-11 B Raymond (11) al prmnt, rdn o'r 3 fs out, styd on wl nr finish. ....(7 to 1 op 6 to 1 tchd 8 to 1) 3
3554[7] NIGHT SNOW [65] 8-6 M Hills (1) led til hdd one furlong out, 3rd and btn whn snatched up nr finish. .... (11 to 1 op 10 to 1 tchd 12 to 1) 4
3762 RUNIC SYMBOL [60] 8-1 A Munro (13) mid-div, styd on fnl quarter m............................(16 to 1 op 10 to 1) 5
3260[4] SCARLET DIVA [73] 9-0 R Cochrane (3) in tch, effrt 2 fs out, no extr ins last..................... (9 to 1 op 8 to 1) 6
3686[3] QUEENS STROLLER (Ire) [58] 7-13 D Harrison (9) wl plcd til wknd ins fnl 2 fs....................... (4 to 1 op 5 to 1) 7
3841[5] NORTHERN BAILIWICK (Ire) [59] 8-0 R Street (5) strted slwly, nvr rchd ldrs... (11 to 1 op 8 to 1 tchd 12 to 1) 8
3829[6] NORTHERN STARLIGHT [52] (v) 7-7 N Adams (10) effrt hfwy, rdr lost irons, wknd o'r 2 fs out. ....(16 to 1 op 12 to 1) 9
3704[9] PETITJEAN (Ire) [62] 8-3 A McGlone (7) nvr dngrs. ....(14 to 1 op 12 to 1) 10
3667[8] LITTLE HOOLIGAN [56] 7-11[2] F Norton (2) no ch frm hfwy. ....(10 to 1 op 8 to 1) 11
2176[6] SILVERISTE (Ire) [52] 7-7 E Johnson (4) chsd ldrs to hfwy. ....(33 to 1 op 20 to 1) 12
3362[2] ROBBY (Ire) [60] 8-1 Paul Eddery (6) al rear grp. ....(12 to 1 op 10 to 1) 13
2216[7] SWORDSMANSHIP [62] 8-3 G Hind (8) no ch fnl 4 fs. ....(10 to 1 op 7 to 1) 14

Dist: Hd, 1l, 1½l, 1l, ½l, 1½l, 2½l, 12l, 1½l, 10l. 1m 43.00s. a 4.00s (14 Ran).
SR: 24/34/21/11/3/14/ (Patrick G O'Sullivan), B J Meehan

3941 EBF Tormarton Maiden Stakes Class D (2-y-o) £4,521 5f 161yds.......(4:00)

3230[6] REASON TO DANCE 8-9 R Cochrane (1) chsd ldrs, quickened to ld ins fnl furlong, readily....(6 to 1 op 4 to 1) 1
3446[3] TAILCOAT (USA) 9-0 M Perrett (7) pressed ldr, ev ch entering fnl furlong, sn outpcd. .... (9 to 1 op 6 to 1 tchd 10 to 1) 2
3528[4] PHONEAHOLIC (Ire) 9-0 B Rouse (8) led til hdd and no extr ins fnl furlong.................... (10 to 1 op 7 to 1) 3
3781[2] REDRESS (USA) 8-9 A Munro (4) cl up, not quicken fnl quarter m. .... (6 to 4 fav op 13 to 8 tchd 7 to 4 and 11 to 8) 4
3284[3] RANKAIDADE 8-9 W Ryan (10) al prmnt, ev ch 2 fs out, no extr..............................(16 to 1 op 10 to 1) 5
EBONY BLAZE 9-0 B Raymond (6) mid-div, rdn alng hfwy, no prog.....................(25 to 1 op 14 to 1) 6
ARZINA (USA) 8-9 J Reid (5) slwly away, outpcd towards rear til styd on fnl 2 fs............(12 to 1 op 10 to 1) 7
LOUISIANA SPORT 8-2 (7*) Wendy Jones (3) missed break, nvr rchd ldrs.....................(25 to 1 op 14 to 1) 8
3446[2] CALYPSO MONARCH (Ire) 9-0 L Dettori (2) wth ldrs til wknd quickly 2 fs out... (3 to 1 op 5 to 2 tchd 4 to 1) 9
3705[8] LETS GO BO (Ire) 9-0 A McGlone (11) no ch fnl 3 fs. ....(25 to 1 op 12 to 1) 10
CATAWAMPUS 9-0 W Newnes (12) nvr wnt pace. ....(50 to 1 op 33 to 1) 11
DOWSONG 9-0 Paul Eddery (9) mid-div til wknd hfwy. ....(8 to 1 op 6 to 1 tchd 10 to 1) 12

Dist: 2½l, 1½l, hd, 3½l, 1½l, 1½l, ¾l, 5l, 2l, sht-hd. 1m 11.50s. a 2.10s (12 Ran).
SR: 41/36/30/24/10/9/ (Mrs D Joly), D R C Elsworth

3942 September Handicap Class D (0-80 3-y-o and up) £4,175 5f 161yds. . (4:30)

3709[4] KILDEE LAD [54] 3-8-1 Dale Gibson (10) prog 2 fs out, ran on to ld nr finish......(14 to 1 op 8 to 1 tchd 16 to 1) 1
3778[4] LETSBEONESTABOUTIT [64] (v) 7-9-0 L Dettori (15) wth ldrs, ev ch fnl 2 fs, kpt on wl...... (6 to 1 tchd 8 to 1) 2
2896[7] UMBRIA [50] 4-8-0 N Adams (9) prmnt, led hfwy til hdd cl hme..............................(9 to 2 fav op 3 to 1) 3
3391* DOUBLE BOUNCE [62] 3-8-9 W Newnes (12) hdwy hfwy, styd on fnl furlong..................(8 to 1 op 7 to 1) 4
3568[4] JUCEA [61] 4-8-11 Paul Eddery (14) styd on und pres fnl 2 fs, not rch ldrs............................ (5 to 1 op 4 to 1) 5
3758 SEAMERE [55] (bl) 10-7-12 (7*) C Hawksley (7) chsd ldrs, no prog fnl 2 fs.............................(12 to 1 op 8 to 1) 6
3549[7] MARK'S CLUB (Ire) [57] (bl) 3-8-4 D Biggs (3) trkd ldrs til wknd 2 fs out.......................... (14 to 1 op 10 to 1) 7
3178[5] PENNY FAN [63] 3-8-10 A Munro (4) chsd ldrs to hfwy. .... (7 to 1 op 10 to 1) 8
2671 FIVESEVENFIVEO [72] 5-9-8 R Cochrane (13) nvr nr to chal.................................(7 to 1 op 5 to 1) 9
3313[2] DOMULLA [77] 3-9-10 J Reid (8) prmnt til wknd 2 fs out. ....(6 to 1 op 4 to 1) 10
3726[7] FEATHER FACE [71] (bl) 3-9-4 A McGlone (11) led to hfwy, btn 2 fs out..........................(20 to 1 op 12 to 1) 11
2967[6] FOLLY VISION (Ire) [54] 3-7-12 (3*) B Doyle (6) slwly away, al rear.............................(16 to 1 op 12 to 1) 12

Dist: Nk, ¾l, 1l, 1½l, ¾l, ½l, ½l, sht-hd, 2½l, 3l. 1m 11.40s. a 2.00s (12 Ran).
SR: 36/48/31/36/32/23/20/24/35/ (J F O'Donovan), A P Jones

3943 Kennet Maiden Handicap Class E (0-70 3-y-o and up) £3,325 1m 5f 22yds ....(5:00)

3548[3] HEAD TURNER [30] 5-7-10 (3*) B Doyle (8) hdwy frm rear 3 fs out, led appr fnl furlong, hld on wl. ....(10 to 1 op 8 to 1) 1
3461 LA MENORQUINA (USA) [58] 3-9-3 R Cochrane (10) mid-div, hdwy entering strt, ev ch fnl furlong, kpt on. ....(8 to 1 op 7 to 1 tchd 12 to 1) 2
3759 RIZ BIZ (USA) [45] 3-8-4 M Hills (5) wnt prmnt aftr 5 fs, not quicken last quarter m............ (33 to 1 op 16 to 1) 3
3759[2] ROMALITO [62] 3-9-7 A Munro (12) hld up, effrt 4 fs out, one pace fnl 2 furlongs.............. (6 to 1 op 5 to 1) 4
3759 KEDGE [52] 3-8-11 B Raymond (11) cl up, led 3 fs out till hdd appr fnl furlong, sn btn..... (16 to 1 op 12 to 1) 5
3787[3] KATHY FAIR (Ire) [43] 4-8-7 (5*) B Russell (6) effrt und pres 3 fs out, no further prog............ (10 to 1 op 6 to 1) 6
2992 TIME FOR A FLUTTER [52] (bl) 4-9-7 W Newnes (14) chsd ldrs till wknd o'r 2 fs out.......... (33 to 1 op 20 to 1) 7
3513 MAD CASANOVA [57] (bl) 8-9-12 D Biggs (4) rear div til rdn and styd on fnl 3 fs............... (20 to 1 op 10 to 1) 8
3821[3] SPORTS VIEW [41] 4-8-10 Paul Eddery (2) mid-div, short lived effrt 3 fs out...(5 to 2 fav op 2 to 1 tchd 11 to 4) 9
3694[3] MONAZITE [45] (bl) 3-8-4 L Dettori (13) led til wknd 3 fs out, eased whn btn............................ (10 to 1 op 8 to 1) 10
3821 ARC BRIGHT (Ire) [53] (bl) 3-8-12 W Ryan (3) in tch til lost pl 4 fs out..............................(20 to 1 op 12 to 1) 11
2051[2] ASSEMBLY DANCER [58] 6-9-13 N Adams (15) al rear. ....(33 to 1 op 20 to 1) 12
3522[2] ARAADH (USA) [62] 3-9-7 R Hills (7) prmnt til wknd o'r 5 fs out......... (9 to 2 op 6 to 1 tchd 13 to 2 and 4 to 1) 13
3420[9] TAKE THE MICK [46] (bl) 3-8-5 T Sprake (1) chsd ldrs til wknd entering strt................(16 to 1 op 10 to 1) 14

Dist: ¾l, 4l, ¾l, 2½l, 3l, 8l, ½l, 1½l, 20l, ½l. 2m 53.50s. a 5.20s (14 Ran).
SR: 20/36/15/30/15/10/3/7/-/ (I Jerrard), C P Wildman

EVRY (FR) (soft)
Monday September 13th
Going Correction: PLUS 0.75 sec. per fur.

3944 Prix de la Cochere (Listed) (3-y-o) £14,337 1¼m.................. (3:20)

1033[4] INSIJAAM (USA) 9-2 W R Swinburn, ... 1
GLOIRE DE ROSE 9-2 T Jarnet, ... 2
3534[2] SEATTLE VICTORY (USA) 9-2 G Guignard, ... 3
2080[4] SARLIYA (Ire) 9-2 G Mosse, ... 4
1506[3] ELITE GUEST (Ire) , ... 0
2080[3] PELAGIC 9-2 E Saint-Martin, ... 6

Dist: 1l, hd, 1½l, hd, 1l, sht-nk, sht-hd, sht-hd, 3l. 2m 17.52s. a 13.52s (11 Ran).
SR: 42/40/39/36/-/-/ (Maktoum Al Maktoum), Mrs C Head

LEICESTER (good to soft)
Monday September 13th
Going Correction: PLUS 0.30 sec. per fur.

3945 Golden Hand Selling Stakes Class G (3-y-o) £2,721 1m 1f 218yds..... (2:20)

3249[6] MULLED ALE (Ire) 8-6 G Duffield (8) *chsd ldrs, improved and hng rght o'r 2 fs out, led appr last, drvn out.* ....(8 to 1 op 6 to 1) 1
3741[6] PRETTY BABY (bl) 8-6 W Carson (3) *patiently rdn, imprvg whn badly baulked o'r 2 fs out, swtchd, fnshd wl.* ....(10 to 1) 2
3689[8] JASPER ONE 8-11 N Connorton (6) *nvr far away, ev ch whn squeezed out appr fnl furlong, swtchd, kpt on.* ....(20 to 1 op 14 to 1) 3
3355[4] JENDORCET 8-6 J Fanning (5) *al hndy, led o'r 3 fs out till appr fnl furlong, one pace*........(20 to 1 op 16 to 1) 4
2023[4] SOLO CHARTER 8-4 (7*) S Mulvey (15) *settled midfield, drvn alng to improve o'r 2 fs out, kpt on, nvr able to chal*...........(4 to 1 jt-fav op 3 to 1 tchd 9 to 2) 5
3741[2] ELEGANT HUSSAR (v) 8-11 M Birch (10) *trkd ldrs, effrt on ins o'r 2 fs out, kpt on same pace*.... (7 to 1 op 6 to 1) 6
3588[6] MALZETA (Ire) 8-1 (5*) D Wright (7) *trkd ldrs, hrd at work o'r 2 fs out, not quicken.* ....(15 to 2 op 6 to 1 tchd 8 to 1) 7
3689[3] TEJANO GOLD (USA) 8-11 T Quinn (11) *settled midfield, effrt on ins o'r 2 fs out, rdn and no extr*......(4 to 1 jt-fav op 5 to 1 tchd 6 to 1) 8
3533[5] MARATHIA (v) 8-6 W Woods (17) *led till hdd o'r 3 fs out, fdd und pres 2 out*..............(10 to 1 op 9 to 1) 9
2221[9] CATCH ME STARSKY (Ire) 8-11 S Dawson (14) *rdn to keep in tch hfwy, outpcd o'r 2 fs out, sn btn.* ....(16 to 1 op 12 to 1) 10
3572 MISS MICHELLE 8-6 C Rutter (4) *in tch to strt, fdd und pres o'r 2 fs out*...... (16 to 1 op 12 to 1 tchd 20 to 1) 11
2750[6] BLACK BEAN 8-11 J Quinn (2) *pressed ldrs for o'r 5 fs, sn struggling*...............(33 to 1) 12
3759 RAQS ASSAYF (v) 8-11 A Culhane (12) *shwd up wl for o'r 5 fs, wknd quickly*...............(25 to 1 op 16 to 1) 13
3817[9] FARANDOLE (bl) 8-11 J Carroll (9) *struggling to keep up hfwy, tld off*...............(33 to 1 op 20 to 1) 14
4661a SOUNDS RISKY 8-6 J Lowe (13) *chsd ldrs to strt, tld off last 3 fs*...............(33 to 1) 15
3689 FREDDY SYLVESTER 8-11 K Darley (1) *pressed ldrs for o'r 5 fs, sn tld off*...............(12 to 1 op 8 to 1) 16

Dist: 1½l, ¾l, hd, ¾l, ½l, 3l, 4l, 3½l, 10l, 2½l. 2m 14.40s. a 11.50s (16 Ran).
SR: 7/4/7/1/4/3/ (W J Bridge), C F Wall

3946 Leicester Sound FM Limited Stakes Class F (3-y-o and up) £3,395 5f 218yds ....(2:50)

3535[9] FORTIS PAVIOR (Ire) 3-8-11 A Culhane (14) *chsd alng to improve frm midfield 2 fs out, kpt on to ld cl hme.* ....(16 to 1 op 12 to 1) 1
3739[2] BATCHWORTH BOUND 4-8-9 C Rutter (11) *patiently rdn, steady hdwy o'r 2 fs out, ev ch fnl furlong, kpt on.* ....(8 to 1 op 7 to 1 tchd 9 to 1) 2
3896[2] DARUSSALAM 6-8-9 Pat Eddery (16) *wtd wth, steady hdwy to join issue last 2 fs, kpt on cl hme.* ....(100 to 30 fav op 5 to 1 tchd 11 to 2) 3
3359[4] DISCO BOY 3-8-4 (7*) S Sanders (12) *wl plcd centre, led o'r 2 fs out, hrd drvn fnl furlong, ct cl hme.* ....(33 to 1 op 20 to 1) 4
3778[8] BERNSTEIN BETTE 7-8-9 J Williams (17) *patiently rdn, prmsg effrt whn squeezed out ins fnl furlong, unlucky.* ....(7 to 1 op 11 to 2) 5
3564 BIRCHWOOD SUN (bl) 3-8-11 W Woods (20) *trkd ldrs, effrt and drvn alng last 2 fs, kpt on, nvr nrr*........(12 to 1) 6
3637 BALLON (v) 3-8-6 J Quinn (15) *settled midfield, improved frm off the pace last 2 fs, ran on*... (16 to 1 op 12 to 1) 7
3687[5] FIRST GOLD 4-9-0 M Birch (18) *improved into midfield hfwy, effrt o'r one furlong out, styd on.* ....(9 to 1 op 12 to 1) 8
3745* SYLVAN STARLIGHT (bl) 3-8-6 G Duffield (10) *chsd ldrs, rdn to improve last 2 fs, nvr nrr*...............(6 to 1 op 5 to 1) 9
3811[5] DAYTONA BEACH (Ire) (bl) 3-8-11 K Darley (4) *co'red up stand side, effrt and rdn 2 fs out, no responce.* ....(16 to 1 op 12 to 1) 10
3744[3] OUR SHADEE (USA) (v) 3-8-11 M Wigham (19) *chsd alng to improve into midfield hfwy, styd on, nvr able to chal.* ....(20 to 1 op 16 to 1) 11
3535[6] STRIP CARTOON (Ire) 5-8-7 (7*) G Strange (6) *gd speed centre for o'r 4 fs, fdd*............ (16 to 1 op 12 to 1) 12
3535 NILU (Ire) (bl) 5-8-9 A Clark (21) *gd speed centre till fdd und pres o'r one furlong out*...............(33 to 1) 13
3758[6] MAGICATION 3-7-13 (7*) Claire Balding (7) *chsd alng stand side, nvr trble ldrs*...............(20 to 1) 14
3766 ANNIVERSAIRE 3-8-11 M Tebbutt (8) *drvn alng to go pace hfwy, no imprsn*...............(25 to 1 op 33 to 1) 15
3745[5] PAIR OF JACKS (Ire) (bl) 3-8-11 T Quinn (3) *broke wl to ld stand side grp for o'r 3 fs, fdd*..... (12 to 1 op 10 to 1) 16
3549[4] HALLORINA 3-8-6 G Bardwell (5) *sluggish strt, nvr a factor*...............(16 to 1 op 14 to 1) 17
3190 MANADEL (v) 3-8-6 N Connorton (9) *early speed, struggling frm hfwy*...............(50 to 1) 18
3535[4] LIDA'S DELIGHT (Ire) 3-8-6[2] (7*) P Johnson (1) *settled wth stand side bunch, struggling hfwy, sn btn.* ....(14 to 1 op 12 to 1) 19

Dist: Nk, sht-hd, nk, ½l, 2l, ¾l, ¾l, nk, hd, 1l. 1m 16.00s. a 5.60s (19 Ran).
SR: 21/18/17/18/14/8/-/5/-/ (D Gill), R M Whitaker

3947 Wren Handicap Class D (0-80 3-y-o and up) £4,305 5f 2yds.........(3:20)

3739[6] CHOIR PRACTICE [63] 6-8-12 C Rutter (17) *missed break, last hfwy, weaved through fnl furlong, led last 50 yards*...............(10 to 1 op 7 to 1) 1
3628[7] DRUM SERGEANT [68] 6-9-3 N Connorton (14) *nvr far away, ev ch fnl furlong, kpt on.* ....(12 to 1 op 8 to 1 tchd 14 to 1) 2
3603[3] HERE COMES A STAR [69] 5-9-4 L Piggott (4) *patiently rdn, steady hdwy to chal ins fnl furlong, ran on same pace*...............(8 to 1 co-fav op 6 to 1) 3
3220 SHADOW JURY [74] 3-9-7 K Darley (11) *wl plcd centre, ev ch o'r 2 fs out, not quicken last 100 yards.* ....(14 to 1 op 12 to 1) 4
3584[2] ABERLADY [62] 3-8-4 (5*) K Rutter (19) *nvr far away, led o'r one furlong out till ct last 50 yards.* ....(9 to 1 op 8 to 1 tchd 10 to 1) 5
3360[7] COMET WHIRLPOOL (Ire) [47] (bl) 3-7-8 J Quinn (13) *al chasing ldrs, feeling pace 2 fs out, kpt on same pace.* ....(20 to 1 tchd 25 to 1) 6
3621 AUGHFAD [79] (v) 7-10-0 K Fallon (5) *pressed ldrs thrght, rdn and no imprsn appr fnl furlong.* ....(14 to 1 op 16 to 1) 7
3758[4] BARBEZIEUX [45] 6-7-3 (5*) D Wright (1) *patiently rdn, steady hdwy last 2 fs, kpt on*...... (12 to 1 op 10 to 1) 8
2829 NORDOORA (Ire) [48] 4-7-6 (5*) Darren Moffatt (18) *rcd centre, led aftr 2 fs till o'r one furlong out, no extr.* ....(20 to 1 op 16 to 1) 9
3739[9] BELLS OF LONGWICK [70] 4-9-5 T Williams (9) *chsd alng to go pace, effrt hfwy, kpt on, nvr able to chal.* (8 to 1 co-fav op 7 to 1) 10
3188[5] NO QUARTER GIVEN [67] 8-9-2 J Lowe (15) *bustled alng to chase ldrs for 3 fs, fdd*............(20 to 1 op 16 to 1) 11
3621[9] DARK EYED LADY (Ire) [78] 3-9-11 T Quinn (2) *chsd alng in midfield, not pace of ldrs*...(8 to 1 co-fav tchd 10 to 1) 12
3568[3] KABCAST [54] (bl) 8-8-3 S Wood (8) *led for 2 fs, wknd quickly two out*...............(16 to 1 op 12 to 1) 13
1076[3] SOBA GUEST (Ire) [68] 4-9-3 J Carroll (10) *chsd alng in midfield to hfwy, sn btn*........ (12 to 1 tchd 14 to 1) 14
2738[3] JOELLISE [46] (v) 3-7-3[3] (7*) Claire Balding (3) *sluggish strt, nvr able to reco'r*...............(25 to 1) 15
3481 BREEZY DAY [76] 7-9-4 (7*) S Sanders (16) *chsd ldrs for 3 fs, fdd*...............(20 to 1 op 16 to 1) 16
3343[7] CHARITY EXPRESS (Ire) [68] 3-9-1 M Wigham (7) *sluggish strt, nvr able to reco'r*............(20 to 1 op 14 to 1) 17
3360[3] SO SUPERB [59] (bl) 4-8-8 W Woods (6) *struggling to keep up aftr 2 fs, nvr a factor*..........(14 to 1 op 12 to 1) 18

Dist: 1½l, nk, 1l, 1l, hd, 2½l, hd, nk, nk, ¾l. 1m 2.60s. a 3.90s (18 Ran).

SR: 50/49/49/48/32/16/40/5/7/ (Stephen Chapman), W J Haggas

3948 Charnwood Claiming Stakes Class F (3 & 4-y-o) £3,370 5f 218yds..... (3:50)

3794[7] RICKY'S TORNADO (Ire) 4-8-6 J Weaver (17) *al hndy, led in centre aftr one and a half fs, kpt on strly ins last.* ....(10 to 1 op 8 to 1) 1
3758[3] SWINGING TICH 4-7-11 T Williams (21) *nvr far away, effrt and drvn alng fnl furlong, kpt on same pace.* ....(5 to 1 op 4 to 1 tchd 6 to 1) 2
3324 MELODIC DRIVE 3-8-11 J Lowe (8) *sluggish strt, steady hdwy frm off the pace last 2 fs, fnshd wl.* ....(25 to 1 op 20 to 1) 3
3020[7] RED LEADER (Ire) 3-7-13 W Carson (14) *drvn into midfield hfwy, effrt o'r one furlong out, kpt on same pace.* ....(7 to 2 fav op 3 to 1) 4
3593 LEIGH CROFTER (bl) 4-8-6 J Williams (20) *patiently rdn, improved to join issue last 2 fs, ran on same pace.* ....(9 to 1 op 10 to 1) 5
3780[6] HERSHEBAR (bl) 3-8-4 (7*) G Strange (11) *al hndy, drvn alng last 2 fs, one pace*...............(12 to 1) 6
3391[9] KINTWYN 3-8-7 R Price (12) *bustled alng to improve into midfield hfwy, rdn and not quicken o'r one furlong out*...............(33 to 1 op 25 to 1) 7
3325[9] DONTBETALKING (Ire) 3-7-8 J Quinn (9) *chsd ldrs, effrt and rdn last 2 fs, styd on*.........(33 to 1 op 25 to 1) 8
3758 BLUE RADIANCE (v) 3-7-8 J Fanning (1) *chsd alng beh ldrs, styd on appr fnl furlong, nvr nrr.* (16 to 1 op 12 to 1) 9
54[8] GYMCRAK TYCOON 4-8-2 Julie Bowker (5) *sluggish strt, improved hfwy, kpt on, no imprsn*........... (14 to 1) 10
3228* HARVEST ROSE 4-9-2 (5*) V Slattery (10) *chsd alng beh ldrs, no imprsn last 2 fs*...........(12 to 1 op 10 to 1) 11
RAVE-ON-HADLEY (Ire) 3-8-8 (7*) W Hollick (13) *broke wl to show early speed, fdd frm hfwy*... (33 to 1 op 25 to 1) 12
3766[4] JEWEL THIEF 3-8-3 A Clark (4) *beh and drvn alng aftr 2 fs, nvr rch ldrs*...............(10 to 1 op 7 to 1) 13
3591 ARAGONA 4-7-11 L Charnock (15) *settled on outsd, effrt and drvn alng hfwy, eased whn btn o'r one furlong out*...............(33 to 1 op 25 to 1) 14
3628[9] PREMIER ENVELOPE (Ire) 4-8-1 (5*) Darren Moffatt (22) *gd speed on outsd till fdd und pres o'r one furlong out.* ....(50 to 1) 15+

3311 GLIMPSE OF HEAVEN (v) 3-7-3 (5*) D Wright (16) *drvn alng to keep up, nvr a threat.* .... (14 to 1 op 12 to 1 tchd 16 to 1) 15+
2719^9 TASSAGH BRIDGE (Ire) 3-7-8 N Carlisle (18) *bustled alng to keep up, nvr rch chalg pos*.................. (33 to 1) 17
3144^8 CANAZEI (v) 3-7-8 Kim Tinkler (19) *drvn alng beh ldrs, struggling frm hfwy*.............. (33 to 1 op 50 to 1) 18
3046^4 FIVE ISLANDS 3-8-6 T Quinn (6) *sluggish strt, nvr able to rch ldrs*.................... (10 to 1 op 6 to 1) 19
1480 BELL LAD (Ire) 3-7-9^1 (5*) D McCabe (3) *settled midfield, feeling pace hfwy, fdd*...................... (33 to 1) 20
3766 CANNONALE (Ire) (bl) 4-8-6 G Bardwell (2) *broke wl to ld for one and a half fs, wknd quickly hfwy, tld off.* .... (33 to 1 op 50 to 1) 21

Dist: 1l, hd, nk, 1½l, nk, 1½l, nk, 1l, ¾l, ½l. 1m 15.70s. a 5.30s (21 Ran).
SR: 22/9/22/9/10/14/4/-/-/ (J Parkes), J Parkes

3949 Kegworth Conditions Stakes Class D (2-y-o) £3,260 7f 9yds.......... (4:20)

3672* ERHAAB (USA) 9-1 W Carson (4) *tucked away, reminders 3 fs out, responded and sn led, drw clr fnl furlong.* .... (6 to 5 fav op 6 to 4 tchd Evens) 1
2845^3 KUTBEYA (USA) 8-10 G Duffield (1) *patiently rdn, checked o'r one furlong out, kpt on, no ch wth wnr.* .... (7 to 1 op 5 to 1) 2
3436^4 ELECTRIFY (USA) 9-1 Pat Eddery (5) *wth ldr, drvn alng whn pace quickened last 2 fs, no extr.* .... (7 to 4 op 6 to 4 tchd 9 to 4) 3
3537^3 OCHOS RIOS (Ire) 9-1 J Quinn (2) *outpcd and drvn alng hfwy, kpt on, nvr able to chal.* .... (11 to 1 op 8 to 1 tchd 12 to 1) 4
3596^3 BATTLING BLUE 9-1 K Darley (3) *slight ld for o'r 4 fs, fdd und pres*......................... (13 to 2 op 5 to 1) 5

Dist: 7l, 3½l, ¾l, 1½l. 1m 29.50s. a 7.60s (5 Ran).
SR: 19/-/ (Hamdan Al-Maktoum), J L Dunlop

3950 River Nursery Class D (2-y-o) £3,980 5f 218yds......................... (4:50)

2090^3 TEETOTALLER (Ire) [60] 8-5 J Carroll (5) *al gng wl, led o'r 2 fs out, ran on strly*................. (3 to 1 op 7 to 2) 1
2911^3 ANTIGUAN SKY [55] 8-0 J Fanning (3) *patiently rdn, improved to chal o'r 2 fs out, ridden and one pace ins last*........................... (5 to 2 fav op 2 to 1) 2
3520 VICEROY RULER [60] (v) 8-5 W Carson (4) *al hndy, feeling pace and rdn 2 fs out, kpt on same pace.* .... (5 to 1 tchd 6 to 1) 3
3688^5 WINDOW DISPLAY [61] 8-6 J Lowe (1) *led till hdd o'r 2 fs out, rdn and no extr*........... (16 to 1 op 10 to 1) 4
2554* ONCE MORE FOR LUCK (Ire) [75] 9-6 K Darley (8) *settled on ins, swrvd and hit rail o'r 3 fs out, btn 2 out.* .... (4 to 1 op 3 to 1 tchd 5 to 1) 5
3815^7 BURMA STAR [49] 7-8^1 J Quinn (6) *nvr far away, drvn alng whn pace quickened 2 fs out, sn btn.* .... (16 to 1 op 12 to 1) 6
3779^7 ALPINE JOHNNY [76] 9-7 S Perks (7) *speed to press ldrs for 5 fs, sn btn*.......................... (8 to 1 op 6 to 1) 7

Dist: 2½l, 1½l, 1½l, 5l, ¾l, 1½l. 1m 17.80s. a 7.40s (7 Ran).
(Highflyers), J Berry

ROSCOMMON (IRE) (good to firm)
Monday September 13th

3951 Creggs Apprentice Handicap (0-65 3-y-o and up) £2,243 1½m...... (3:30)

3483^2 ZUHAL [-] 5-9-11 B Fenton (1).................... (6 to 1) 1
3854 ONOMATOPOEIA (Ire) [-] 3-9-7 J J Stack (6).... (9 to 2 fav) 2
3858^2 SOUND PERFORMANCE (Ire) [-] (bl) 4-9-7 (2*) W J Walsh (13) .... (8 to 1) 3
3721^2 BLUES COMPOSER (Ire) [-] 4-9-4 (2*) I Browne (17) (11 to 2) 4
3853^2 THIS IS MY LIFE (Ire) [-] 4-9-5 B Halligan (3)....... (5 to 1) 5
3826^6 LAST EMPEROR (USA) [-] 6-9-9 (2*) K Hopkins (2) (12 to 1) 6
3482^2 RICH LIFE (Ire) [-] (bl) 3-9-6 D J Donohoe (12)..... (10 to 1) 7
3543^8 HIND VISION (Ire) [-] 3-9-6 (2*) S P Cooke (9)..... (12 to 1) 8
3062^8 HAIL TO HOME (Ire) [-] 3-9-3 D McCullagh (4).... (33 to 1) 9
3854^5 GLAS AGUS OR (Ire) [-] (bl) 3-9-7 T E Durcan (18).. (8 to 1) 10
2958^7 AT YOUR SERVICE (Ire) [-] 4-9-7 T J Daly (15)..... (20 to 1) 11
3604^9 POUNDWORLD (Ire) [-] 3-9-3 P J Smullen,....... (20 to 1) 12
3772^7 OCEAN BLUE (Ire) [-] (bl) 3-9-7 G M Moylan (11).. (16 to 1) 13
MOOREFIELD GIRL (Ire) [-] 4-9-0 (2*) S P Kelly,.... (8 to 1) 14
2956 OMESMACJOY (Ire) [-] 3-7-11^4 R T Fitzpatrick (16) (33 to 1) 15
3616^8 TODDY MARK (Ire) [-] 4-10-0 A P McCoy (14)..... (33 to 1) 16

Dist: ¾l, 1½l, 2l, ½l. 2m 41.01s. (16 Ran).
(Jacques Van T Hart), Adrian Taylor

3952 Tully Maiden (3-y-o) £2,243 1½m (4:00)

2691^5 PARTICULAR (Ire) 9-0 J P Murtagh (4)............ (4 to 1) 1
3526^3 NORDIC THORN (Ire) 9-0 K J Manning (6)......... (7 to 2) 2
2692 LIMAHEIGHTS (Ire) 8-3 (8*) P J Smullen (2)....... (20 to 1) 3
3616^3 ENDSONG (USA) 8-11 P V Gilson (3).......... (5 to 4 on) 4
3858^7 ARCH-T-GLEN (Ire) 8-6 (8*) D M McCullagh (7).... (20 to 1) 5
2249 SELUNE (Fr) (bl) 8-11 N McCullagh (1)........... (7 to 1) 6

Dist: 3l, 1l, 15l, sht-hd. 2m 40.00s. (6 Ran).
(N Stassen), Joseph M Canty

3953 Glenamaddy Fillies E.B.F. Maiden (Div I) (2-y-o) £3,105 7f.......... (5:00)

3683^3 SHELWA (USA) 9-0 C Roche (3)............ (11 to 10 fav) 1
3730^8 SECRET WAR (Ire) 9-0 J F Egan (15)............ (14 to 1) 2
3613^8 MOMENTS TO CARE (Ire) 9-0 N G McCullagh (8).. (10 to 1) 3
3527 GRENNAN CLASSIC (Ire) 8-12 (2*) R M Burke (4).. (33 to 1) 4+
STAGEWALK (Ire) 9-0 S Craine (9)................ (7 to 1) 4+
3683^5 BETTER STYLE (Ire) 9-0 J P Murtagh (5).......... (10 to 1) 6
LIFE DANCING (Ire) 9-0 K J Manning (11)......... (10 to 1) 7
3608^8 AVALIN (Ire) 8-6 (8*) R T Fitzpatrick (10)........... (10 to 1) 8
3729^3 EVICTRESS (Ire) 8-10 (4*) J J Behan (1)........... (4 to 1) 9
3729^7 FRIARY TOWN (Ire) 9-0 W J Supple (14).......... (12 to 1) 10
3807 LADY COUNSEL (Ire) 8-12 (2*) P Carberry (13).... (33 to 1) 11
3729 ACHTUNG LADY (Ire) 9-0 P V Gilson (7).......... (25 to 1) 12
3453 GREAC 8-4 (10*) S P Kelly (2)................. (33 to 1) 13
BELLE VIVE (Ire) 9-0 M G Cleary (6).............. (33 to 1) 14

Dist: 3½l, sht-hd, 1l, dd-ht. 1m 33.00s. (14 Ran).
(Hilal Salem), J S Bolger

3954 Glenamaddy Fillies E.B.F. Maiden (Div II) (2-y-o) £3,105 7f......... (5:30)

LADY'S VISION (Ire) 9-0 J F Egan (7).............. (5 to 1) 1
SORALENA (Ire) 9-0 W J Supple (14)............. (12 to 1) 2
3039^7 JOYFUL MUSIC (Ire) 8-6 (8*) J J Stack (13)........ (6 to 1) 3
3683^8 TINERANA ROSE (Ire) 8-6 (8*) P J Smullen (10).... (16 to 1) 4
ALMOST A LADY (Ire) 9-0 P V Gilson (8).......... (10 to 1) 5
CNOCMA (Ire) 9-0 K J Manning (9).............. (16 to 1) 6
1792^6 NOBLE CHOICE (Ire) 9-0 Ann O'Rourke (3)....... (14 to 1) 7
3541^4 OUT IN THE SUN (USA) 9-0 S Craine (1)....... (4 to 1 fav) 8
FUTURE PLAN (Ire) 9-0 J P Murtagh (5)........... (8 to 1) 9
3527^4 SENDER VICTORIOUS (Ire) 8-10 (4*) J J Behan (2).. (5 to 1) 10
3730 GLAD YOU ASKED ME (Ire) (bl) 8-12 (2*) P Carberry (6) .... (20 to 1) 11
3243^6 FINAL EXHIBIT (Ire) 9-0 C Roche (15)............. (6 to 1) 12
NOBODYS CHILD (Ire) 8-8 (6*) R V Skelly (12)..... (16 to 1) 13
POSCIMUR (Ire) 9-0 N G McCullagh (11)......... (14 to 1) 14

Dist: 3½l, nk, nk, 2l. 1m 33.60s. (14 Ran).
(Michael W J Smurfit), Patrick Joseph Flynn

SANDOWN (soft)
Tuesday September 14th

Going Correction: PLUS 0.05 sec. per fur. (races 1,4), PLUS 0.55 (2,3,5,6,7)

3955 Willow Claiming Stakes Class F (3-y-o and up) £2,983 5f 6yds......... (2:20)

3638 METAL BOYS 6-8-0 (7*) P McCabe (12) *al prmnt, led appr 2 fs out, rdn clr ins last.* (11 to 2 op 5 to 1 tchd 6 to 1) 1
1806 GONE SAVAGE 5-9-2 Pat Eddery (15) *cl up, led briefly hfwy, ev ch 2 fs out, one pace ins last.* .... (7 to 2 fav op 3 to 1) 2
3692^2 ANOTHER LANE 6-8-2 J Quinn (10) *al prmnt, rdn and one pace fnl 2 fs*................. (12 to 1 op 8 to 1) 3
3059^3 SOBER LAD (Ire) (bl) 3-8-6 J Reid (1) *led to hfwy, sn hrd rdn, one pace*....... (20 to 1 op 14 to 1 tchd 25 to 1) 4
3849^9 BODARI 4-8-9 (5*) D McCabe (9) *wth ldrs, rdn o'r 2 fs out, one pace*............ (6 to 1 op 5 to 1 tchd 13 to 2) 5
3081* SEA-DEER 4-8-9 J Williams (7) *outpcd, ran on ins fnl furlong, nrst finish*.............. (20 to 1 op 12 to 1) 6
3849 DOUBLE BLUE 4-9-5 M Roberts (13) *wth ldrs till pushed alng and wknd o'r 2 fs out*.......... (5 to 1 op 6 to 1) 7
3692^5 CONVENIENT MOMENT 3-7-3 (7*) P Fessey (14) *cl up, rdn 2 fs out, wknd ins last*............. (25 to 1 op 16 to 1) 8
3687* FIRST OPTION 3-8-10 K Darley (5) *slwly into strd, rdn and hdwy 2 fs out, no imprsn o'r one out.* (8 to 1 op 7 to 1) 9
3709^7 MARTINA 5-8-1 Paul Eddery (6) *nvr rchd chalg pos.* .... (20 to 1 op 16 to 1) 10
2024^6 WALK THE BEAT 3-9-1 W Woods (11) *took keen hold in rear, short lived effrt hfwy*...... (14 to 1 tchd 16 to 1) 11
3220^7 MY BONUS 3-8-1 (5*) L Newton (4) *prmnt, pushed alng hfwy, sn wknd*.................... (14 to 1 op 10 to 1) 12
3766 LADY RELKO 3-7-10 N Adams (2) *sn chsd alng, nvr on terms*......................... (66 to 1 op 50 to 1) 13
3519^6 GREEN'S BID 3-9-3 T Quinn (8) *prmnt 2 fs, sn lost pl.* .... (20 to 1 op 14 to 1) 14
3707 BELLE SOIREE 3-7-8^3 (5*) B Russell (3) *reluctant to race, al tld off*............................. (33 to 1) 15

Dist: 4l, 1½l, ¾l, ¾l, hd, nk, hd, 2½l, 3l, ½l. 1m 1.42s. a 1.92s (15 Ran).
SR: 60/53/33/34/39/33/42/18/22/ (R J Wilkinson), Miss L C Siddall

3956 Godfrey Merritt Amiss Group Fillies' Handicap Class C (0-95 3-y-o) £4,879 1m 14yds....................... (2:50)

3757* DORAZINE [67] 7-11 (5*) D Wright (6) *made all, rdn alng 2 fs out, clr ins last, ran on strly.* .... (11 to 2 op 4 to 1 tchd 6 to 1) 1
3693* WANNABE [79] 9-0 R Cochrane (4) *beh, tacked across to stands side strt, sn rdn, ran on und pres ins last.* .... (9 to 2 op 11 to 4 tchd 5 to 1) 2

3883[9] GUSTAVIA (Ire) [80] (bl) 9-1 M Roberts (2) *strted slwly, beh, tacked across to stands side strt, hdwy 3 fs out, sn hrd rdn, one pace ins last.* (11 to 2 op 5 to 1 tchd 6 to 1) 3
2882* COMANCHE COMPANION [70] 8-0 (5*) A Garth (3) *sn trkd wnr, one pace fnl 2 fs*............(5 to 2 fav op 3 to 1) 4
1231 GUV'S JOY (Ire) [76] 8-11 Pat Eddery (1) *trkd ldrs, tacked across to stands side strt, rdn o'r 2 out, wknd one out.* ....(10 to 1 op 7 to 1) 5
3519[4] CROPTON [86] 9-7 Paul Eddery (8) *trkd ldrs, hrd rdn o'r one furlong out, sn btn*..........(12 to 1 tchd 14 to 1) 6
3585[7] POLAR STORM (Ire) [77] 8-12 J Williams (5) *hld up, effrt 2 fs out, nvr on terms*...................(9 to 2 op 5 to 1) 7
3459[9] WHERE'S THE DANCE [63] 7-12 J Quinn (7) *hld up, al beh.* ....(25 to 1 op 16 to 1) 8

Dist: 2½l, ¾l, 3½l, nk, 1½l, 1½l, 3l. 1m 47.52s. a 8.42s (8 Ran).
SR: 28/32/31/10/15/20/6/-/ (C John Hill), C J Hill

3957 Woodchester L.M.S. Handicap Class D (0-80 3-y-o and up) £4,591 7f 16yds ....(3:25)

3887* DASWAKI (Can) [64] 5-8-12 (4ex) B Rouse (15) *sn pushed alng to track ldrs, led wl o'r one furlong out, soon clr, eased nr finish*...... (7 to 2 fav op 4 to 1 tchd 9 to 2) 1
3637[7] SIMPLY FINESSE [75] 3-9-5 T Quinn (3) *chsd ldrs, kpt on wl und pres ins last*....... (15 to 2 op 8 to 1 tchd 9 to 1) 2
3726[6] EURO FESTIVAL [75] 4-9-4 (5*) D McCabe (14) *beh, remained far side entering strt, hdwy 3 fs out, led o'r 2 out till hdd wl over one out, one pace.* ....(9 to 1 op 8 to 1 tchd 10 to 1) 3
3747[5] KIMBERLEY PARK [59] 5-8-7 R Cochrane (10) *beh, pushed alng o'r 2 fs out, ran on ins last.* ....(8 to 1 op 7 to 1 tchd 9 to 1) 4
3623[8] JAHANGIR (Ire) [68] 4-9-2 A Munro (5) *chsd ldrs, pushed alng 3 fs out, styd on one pace*......(12 to 1 op 8 to 1) 5
2522 BOLD THATCHER [68] 3-8-12 Paul Eddery (1) *beh, effrt o'r 2 fs out, some modest prog, nvr nrr.* (12 to 1 op 10 to 1) 6
2601[3] BOLD ACRE [67] 3-8-11 R Price (8) *led til hdd o'r 3 fs out, sn wknd*..............(14 to 1 op 10 to 1 tchd 16 to 1) 7
3531[2] SILKY SIREN [73] 4-9-7 Pat Eddery (2) *hld up in mid-div, no prog fnl 3 fs*...................(8 to 1 tchd 10 to 1) 8
3789[2] DESERT CHAMP (USA) [72] 4-9-6 W R Swinburn (7) *trkd ldrs gng wl, wknd quickly 2 fs out.* ....(10 to 1 op 8 to 1 tchd 12 to 1) 9
3637[3] PRAIRIE GROVE [70] 3-9-0 J Reid (11) *al beh.* ....(13 to 2 op 5 to 1 tchd 7 to 1) 10
3226[8] SECRET ASSIGNMENT (USA) [60] 3-8-4 D Biggs (6) *rear, effrt 3 fs out, nvr on terms*.........(20 to 1 op 16 to 1) 11
3863[6] KENESHA (Ire) [65] 3-8-9 J Williams (4) *strted slwly, al beh, tld off*..........................(12 to 1 tchd 14 to 1) 12
3774 PANIKIN [80] 5-9-11 (3*) S D Williams (13) *trkd ldr, remained far side, led o'r 3 fs out till hdd over 2 out, wknd quickly, tld off*..............(33 to 1 op 25 to 1) 13

Dist: 5l, sht-hd, ¾l, 4l, ½l, ¾l, 1l, sht-hd, hd, ¾l. 1m 33.44s. a 6.94s (13 Ran).
SR: 52/44/47/29/26/20/17/24/22/ (David Allen), G L Moore

3958 Tattersalls Maiden Auction Series Stakes Qualifier Class D (2-y-o) £3,285 5f 6yds.......................(3:55)

3762[2] DOMINO QUEEN (Ire) 8-9 A Munro (2) *made virtually all, shaken up o'r one furlong out, ran on wl.* ....(7 to 2 op 4 to 1) 1
3287[3] JAYANNPEE 9-0 R Cochrane (6) *trkd wnr, led briefly one and a half fs out, no extr ins last.* (9 to 4 fav op 5 to 4) 2
3642[9] GADGE 9-0 B Rouse (4) *trkd ldg pair, one pace und pres appr fnl furlong*..... (16 to 1 op 12 to 1 tchd 20 to 1) 3
FORT KNOX (Ire) 9-0 R Price (9) *strted slwly, hdwy 2 fs out, one pace frm o'r one out.* ....(7 to 2 op 6 to 1 tchd 7 to 1) 4
3642[2] LADY WILLIAMS (Ire) 8-9 D Harrison (5) *slwly into strd, sn reco'red to track ldrs, pushed alng hfwy, outpcd frm over one furlong out*.................(3 to 1 op 5 to 2) 5
3746[8] KING BRUCE 9-0 J Reid (8) *trkd ldrs till wknd wl o'r one furlong out*......................(10 to 1 tchd 12 to 1) 6
3816 RISK OF FIRE 9-0 Paul Eddery (7) *nvr on terms.* ....(33 to 1 op 14 to 1) 7
3642 ONLY FOOLS 9-0 J Williams (10) *outpcd.* ....(33 to 1 op 16 to 1) 8

Dist: 1l, 4l, nk, 3l, 1½l, 4l, sht-hd. 1m 2.37s. a 2.87s (8 Ran).
SR: 43/44/28/27/10/9/-/-/ (J G K Borrett), J W Payne

3959 Woodchester Credit Lyonnais Futurity Conditions Stakes Class C (2-y-o) £4,478 1m 14yds................ (4:30)

3779* OVERBURY (Ire) 8-13 M Roberts (1) *hld up, led 2 fs out, edgd rght, rdn and ran on wl.* ....(11 to 4 on op 5 to 2 on tchd 3 to 1 on) 1
2990[8] PARTY SEASON 8-11 K Darley (3) *cl up, led o'r 3 fs out, hdd 2 out, ran on wl.* (16 to 1 op 14 to 1 tchd 20 to 1) 2
3763[3] MAZENTRE FORWARD (Ire) 8-11 Pat Eddery (4) *led til hdd o'r 3 fs out, sn rdn and outpcd, eased whn hld.* ....(3 to 1 op 7 to 4 tchd 100 to 30) 3
1949[9] DEBLYN 8-11 A Munro (2) *in cl tch till wknd 3 fs out.* ....(66 to 1 op 33 to 1 tchd 100 to 1) 4

Dist: Nk, 6l, 15l. 1m 48.96s. a 9.86s (4 Ran).
SR: 17/14/-/-/ (Sheikh Mohammed), D R Loder

3960 EBF Wey Maiden Fillies Stakes Class D (2-y-o) £4,279 1m 14yds...... (5:00)

3352 FRAGRANT BELLE (USA) 8-11 J Williams (6) *hld up beh, hdwy o'r one furlong out, sstnd run to ld wl ins last.* ....(7 to 2 op 3 to 1 tchd 4 to 1) 1
3627[4] I FEAR NOTHING 8-11 K Darley (8) *led one furlong, led ag'n o'r 3 fs out, quickened clr over one out, hdd wl ins last*..............................(6 to 1 tchd 7 to 1) 2
3659[2] LYPHARD STREET (USA) 8-11 A Munro (4) *hld up, cld 3 fs out, pushed alng and stumbled 2 out, one pace.* ....(2 to 1 fav op 5 to 4 tchd 9 to 4) 3
3209 JEMIMA PUDDLEDUCK 8-11 R Price (3) *trkd ldrs, rdn alng and outpcd fnl 2 fs*...............(50 to 1 op 25 to 1) 4
3698[2] NEPTUNALIA 8-11 Paul Eddery (9) *hld up beh ldrs, cld 3 fs out, sn pushed alng, wknd o'r one out, eased.* ....(7 to 2 op 9 to 4) 5
THIRD DAM 8-11 J Reid (1) *took keen hold, led aftr one furlong till hdd o'r 3 out, sn wknd.* ....(12 to 1 op 7 to 1 tchd 14 to 1) 6
RED POINT 8-11 R Cochrane (7) *outpcd, tld off.* ....(11 to 1 op 8 to 1 tchd 12 to 1) 7
TADELLAL (Ire) 8-11 W R Swinburn (2) *wth ldrs till wknd quickly 3 fs out, tld off.* (9 to 1 op 8 to 1 tchd 10 to 1) 8

Dist: ½l, 8l, 2½l, 5l, 10l, 7l, 15l. 1m 48.68s. a 9.58s (8 Ran).
SR: 19/17/-/-/-/ (W H O'Gorman), D R C Elsworth

3961 'Sandown 20th Anniversary' Handicap Class E (0-70 3-y-o) £3,087 1¼m 7yds ....(5:35)

3710[7] WITHOUT A FLAG (USA) [54] 8-5 M Roberts (6) *hld up, hdwy 3 fs out, edgd rght and led one out, ran on wl.* ....(7 to 1 op 10 to 1) 1
3341[3] SHERGRESS [57] 8-8 K Darley (5) *hld up, hdwy 4 fs out, led briefly o'r one out, ran on one pace.* ....(20 to 1 op 16 to 1 tchd 25 to 1) 2
3540[9] MYSILV [60] 8-11 W Woods (13) *cl up, led o'r 3 fs out till hdd 2 and a half out, kpt on one pace.* ....(14 to 1 op 12 to 1 tchd 16 to 1) 3
3540 GROUND NUT (Ire) [62] 8-13 J Williams (7) *hld up in rear, hdwy o'r one furlong out, ran on wl.* ....(14 to 1 tchd 20 to 1) 4
3314[8] MARIUS (Ire) [64] 9-1 Pat Eddery (1) *trkd ldrs, led 2 and a half fs out till hdd o'r one out, no extr.* ....(9 to 2 fav op 7 to 2 tchd 11 to 2) 5
2151[3] ANUSHA [62] 8-13 A Clark (11) *beh, hdwy fnl 2 fs, styd on.* ....(20 to 1) 6
3883 SEA BARON [66] 9-3 J Quinn (8) *mid-div, cld 4 fs out, effrt 2 out, one pace*..........(33 to 1 op 25 to 1) 7
1690[7] KISMETIM [60] 8-11 T Quinn (10) *beh, hdwy 3 fs out, nrst finish*...............(20 to 1 op 14 to 1 tchd 25 to 1) 8
3639[9] KEYLOCK (USA) [52] 8-3 R Hills (16) *beh, slightly hmpd o'r 2 fs out, sn hrd rdn, ran on cl hme.* (25 to 1 op 20 to 1) 9
3469* HEART OF SPAIN [65] 8-9 (7*) C Hawksley (2) *mid-div, hdwy 4 fs out, wknd 2 out*....... (10 to 1 tchd 12 to 1) 10
3850* TICKERTY'S GIFT [73] 9-10 (4ex) B Rouse (17) *pushed alng to chase ldrs, wknd quickly 2 fs out.* ....(11 to 2 op 5 to 1 tchd 6 to 1) 11
2963 PHROSE [65] 9-2 M Perrett (19) *trkd ldrs till wknd o'r one furlong out*.......... (25 to 1 op 20 to 1 tchd 33 to 1) 12
3460[8] DON TOCINO [59] 8-10 J Reid (15) *mid-div, swtchd rght 2 fs out, sn btn*......................(20 to 1 op 16 to 1) 13
3734[6] BRONZE MAQUETTE (Ire) [63] 9-0 E Johnson (12) *al beh.* ....(12 to 1 tchd 14 to 1) 14
3757[5] BROUGHTONS FORMULA [56] 8-2 (5*) D McCabe (4) *beh, hdwy und pres o'r one furlong out, wknd entering last, eased*................ (12 to 1 op 10 to 1 tchd 14 to 1) 15
3757 HEATHYARDS BOY [66] 9-3 S Perks (14) *beh fnl 3 fs.* ....(12 to 1 op 10 to 1 tchd 14 to 1) 16
2713[5] BERING ISLAND (USA) [54] 8-5 Paul Eddery (3) *chsd ldrs till wknd o'r 2 fs out*.....(9 to 1 op 10 to 1 tchd 12 to 1) 17
3540 KRYPTOS (USA) [56] 8-7 A Munro (9) *chsd ldrs till wknd quickly o'r 2 fs out*................(16 to 1 op 12 to 1) 18
3358 PROTON [70] 9-7 W R Swinburn (20) *mid-div, drpd rear o'r 3 fs out*............. (25 to 1 op 20 to 1 tchd 33 to 1) 19
3783 AMOREM [53] (bl) 8-4 C Rutter (18) *led til hdd o'r 3 fs out, wknd quickly*..................(50 to 1 op 33 to 1) 20

Dist: 1½l, ½l, 1½l, 1l, 1½l, 3l, nk, ½l, 2l, 2l. 2m 14.60s. a 10.70s (20 Ran).
SR: 39/39/41/40/40/35/33/26/17/ (R M Cyzer), C A Cyzer

YARMOUTH (soft)
Tuesday September 14th
Going Correction: PLUS 0.70 sec. per fur. (races 1,2), PLUS 0.15 (3,4,5,6)

3962 Brooke Claiming Stakes Class F (3-y-o) £3,002 1m 3f 101yds........(2:30)

3304[2] GWEEK (Ire) 8-2 P Robinson (2) *tucked away on ins, steady hdwy entering strt, led o'r one furlong out, forged clr*........................(6 to 1 tchd 13 to 2) 1

3669^{2} SEAMA (USA) 9-5 G Duffield (3) *led early, styd hndy and gng wl, led o'r 3 fs out till over 2 out, kpt on same pace.* ....(11 to 4 fav op 5 to 2) 2
3588^{2} TROPICAL JUNGLE (USA) 9-3 L Dettori (4) *settled gng wl, led on bit o'r 2 fs out, hdd over one out, rdn and no response*..............(9 to 2 op 5 to 1 tchd 11 to 2) 3
3556^{9} RUN TO AU BON (Ire) 8-7 J Weaver (5) *patiently rdn, improved o'r 3 fs out, sn drvn alng, one pace.* ....(8 to 1 op 6 to 1) 4
3246 ROSE OF MEDINA 7-12 F Norton (1) *last and hld up, hmpd appr strt, effrt o'r 2 fs out, no extr.* ....(33 to 1 tchd 40 to 1) 5
3412^{8} BORROWED AND BLUE 8-8 B Raymond (7) *trkd ldg quartet, hrd at work entering strt, sn lost tch.* ....(14 to 1 op 12 to 1) 6
3759^{6} FOREVER SHINEING 9-1 G Bardwell (8) *sn led, hdd and rdn o'r 3 fs out, lost tch quickly last 2 furlongs.* ....(100 to 30 op 3 to 1 tchd 7 to 2) 7
2640^{4} WALSHAM WITCH 8-2^{2} (5*) K Rutter (6) *niggled alng to keep up, struggling entering strt, tld off.* ....(14 to 1 op 20 to 1) 8
BIG GEM 8-3 J Carroll (9) *co'red up, struggling whn pace lifted entering strt, tld off.* ....(66 to 1 op 50 to 1 tchd 100 to 1) 9
Dist: 6l, 1½l, sht-hd, 3l, 15l, nk, 2l, 20l. 2m 36.40s. a 12.90s (9 Ran).
SR: 39/44/39/28/13/-/ (Henry B H Chan), M H Tompkins

3963 John Musker Fillies Stakes Class A (Listed Race) (3-y-o and up) £11,550 1 ¼m 21yds...................... (3:00)

3674^{2} FORTHWITH 3-8-5 M Hills (1) *made all, quickened up to go clr o'r 2 fs out, styd on wl.* ....(4 to 1 op 7 to 2 tchd 9 to 2) 1
3644^{4} SEEK THE PEARL 3-8-5 B Raymond (2) *tucked away on ins, drvn alng to chase wnr last 3 fs, no imprsn.* ....(12 to 1 op 8 to 1) 2
3674^{3} ROSE ALTO 5-8-12 G Duffield (9) *in tch, struggling to keep up entering strt, styd on und pres last 2 fs, nvr nrr.* ....(7 to 2 jt-fav op 3 to 1) 3
3708* LA SPEZIA 3-8-5 J Carroll (8) *trkd ldg trio, effrt and drvn alng o'r 3 fs out, struggling last 2 furlongs.* ....(20 to 1 op 12 to 1) 4
3838* RANI (Ire) 3-8-5 B Doyle (6) *patiently rdn, effrt entering strt, sn ridden, btn 3 fs out*........(12 to 1 op 10 to 1) 5
2433^{8} GROVE DAFFODIL (Ire) (v) 3-8-5 P Robinson (5) *sluggish strt, flt out entering strt, sn lost tch.* ....(16 to 1 op 20 to 1 tchd 25 to 1) 6
3639* CAMPANA (Ire) 3-8-5 L Dettori (4) *settled midfield, came wide and flounded o'r 3 fs out, sn lost tch*....(7 to 2 jt-fav op 3 to 1 tchd 4 to 1) 7
3674* LICORNE 3-8-13 W Ryan (3) *trkd wnr, ev ch entering strt, wknd rpdly last 2 fs, tld off*.........(9 to 2 op 3 to 1) 8
Dist: 5l, 7l, 4l, 4l, 1l, 4l, 15l. 2m 14.00s. a 10.00s (8 Ran).
SR: 61/51/44/29/21/19/11/-/ (L H J Ward), J W Hills

3964 Brian Taylor Memorial Handicap Class C (0-90 3-y-o and up) £5,253 6f 3yds.......................... (3:30)

3603^{4} SLADES HILL [59] 6-7-12 A Mackay (9) *patiently rdn, weaved through to chal appr fnl furlong, ran on to ld last 50 yards*..........................(7 to 1 op 14 to 1) 1
3393^{2} MISS WHITTINGHAM (Ire) [66] 3-8-2 J Carroll (10) *al hndy, led o'r one furlong out, hdd last 50 yards, kpt on.* ....(9 to 1 op 8 to 1) 2
2987 MERRYHILL MAID (Ire) [65] 5-8-1 (3*) B Doyle (5) *wl plcd centre, definite advantage hfwy, hdd o'r one furlong out, kpt on same pace*.............(14 to 1 op 10 to 1) 3
3830 ROSE FLYER (Ire) [57] 3-7-7 G Bardwell (11) *reared leaving stalls, sn led, hdd hfwy, rdn and no extr fnl furlong.* ....(25 to 1 op 20 to 1) 4
3511^{6} SHIKARI'S SON [84] 6-9-9 W Ryan (7) *beh and pushed alng hfwy, kpt on wl appr fnl furlong, nrst finish.* ....(9 to 1 op 8 to 1 tchd 10 to 1) 5
3906 FASCINATION WALTZ [77] 6-8-11 (5*) K Rutter (4) *al tracking ldrs, effrt and drvn alng last 2 fs, kpt on same pace.* ....(8 to 1 op 7 to 1) 6
3638^{3} MACS MAHARANEE [82] 6-9-7 G Hind (8) *trkd ldg quartet, gng wl hfwy, rdn alng o'r one furlong out, no extr.* ....(13 to 2 op 5 to 1) 7
3594^{7} WAFFLE ON [86] 3-9-8 G Duffield (3) *last and bustled alng hfwy, nvr able to rch chalg pos*......(6 to 1 op 5 to 1) 8
3427^{5} PRESS GALLERY [88] 3-9-10 P Robinson (6) *co'red up beh ldrs, effrt hfwy, sn rdn and no imprsn.* ....(12 to 1 op 8 to 1) 9
3747 CLAYBANK (USA) [63] 4-8-2 M Hills (2) *chsd alng in midfield, struggling o'r 2 fs out, sn btn.* ....(12 to 1 op 8 to 1 tchd 14 to 1) 10
3638* PRINCESS OBERON (Ire) [73] 3-8-9 L Dettori (1) *shwd up on outsd to hfwy, eased whn btn 2 fs out.* ....(5 to 1 fav op 7 to 2 tchd 11 to 2) 11
Dist: ¾l, 2½l, ¾l, nk, 4l, nk, 4l, 7l, ½l, 5l. 1m 14.00s. a 3.00s (11 Ran).
SR: 42/43/35/21/50/27/31/16/-/ (James E Greaves), T D Barron

3965 Caister Selling Stakes Class G (3-y-o and up) £2,532 6f 3yds..........(4:05)

3095^{5} TRENTESIMO (Ire) 3-9-2 J Carroll (9) *made all, shaken up to go clr o'r one furlong out, readily*..........(5 to 1 jt-fav op 7 to 2 tchd 11 to 2) 1
1454^{5} WESTERING 3-8-6 P Robinson (11) *sluggish strt, gd hdwy frm off the pace last 2 fs, ran on, nvr nrr.* ....(8 to 1 op 14 to 1) 2
3180^{8} ACROSS THE BAY (v) 6-9-5 W Ryan (6) *bustled alng to go pace hfwy, styd on appr fnl furlong, ran on wl.* ....(11 to 1 op 7 to 1) 3
3591 TEE GEE JAY (v) 3-8-11 B Raymond (7) *sluggish strt, drvn alng to keep up hfwy, effrt o'r one furlong out, one pace*.................................(12 to 1 op 8 to 1) 4
3249 WALK THAT WALK 4-9-0 G Duffield (5) *bustled alng in midfield, effrt 2 fs out, not pace to chal.* ....(7 to 1 op 8 to 1 tchd 10 to 1) 5
3747 OBSIDIAN GREY 6-9-2 (3*) O Pears (3) *gd speed centre, drvn alng o'r 2 fs out, sn btn*... (5 to 1 jt-fav op 7 to 2) 6
3460 TRUNDLEY WOOD 3-8-11 L Dettori (4) *trkd wnr, hrd at work o'r 2 fs out, fdd*.... (6 to 1 op 5 to 1 tchd 7 to 1) 7
3709^{3} TREASURE TIME (Ire) 4-8-9 (5*) K Rutter (1) *broke wl to show speed on outsd for o'r 3 fs, fdd.* (7 to 1 op 7 to 2) 8
3744^{2} JOKIST 10-9-5 M Tebbutt (2) *co'red up beh ldrs, struggling to hold pl hfwy, sn lost tch*...............(6 to 1) 9
Dist: 2l, 2½l, 3½l, 4l, 5l, ¾l, 4l, 8l. 1m 15.10s. a 4.10s (9 Ran).
SR: 38/20/23/1/-/-/ (B R Allen), J Berry

3966 Jack Leader Memorial Challenge Trophy Fillies Nursery Handicap Class C (2-y-o) £4,980 7f 3yds...........(4:35)

3677* AMORET (Ire) [68] 8-9 J Weaver (9) *made all, shaken up to quicken o'r one furlong out, forged clr.* ....(9 to 4 fav op 6 to 4 tchd 5 to 2) 1
3389^{2} TASHLA [68] (v) 8-9 L Dettori (4) *al hndy, drvn alng whn wnr quickened o'r one furlong out, no imprsn.* ....(5 to 1 op 7 to 1 tchd 8 to 1) 2
3563* MISS MAH-JONG [80] 9-7 G Duffield (6) *nvr far away, effrt and drvn alng 2 fs out, not quicken.* ....(7 to 1 tchd 8 to 1) 3
3845^{4} WIXI (Ire) [74] 9-1 P Robinson (1) *al chasing ldrs, outpcd and drvn alng o'r one furlong out, no impresion.* ....(11 to 2 op 5 to 1 tchd 6 to 1) 4
3321^{6} JUST GREENWICH [57] 7-7 (5*) N Gwilliams (5) *trkd ldrs, feeling pace and rdn last 2 fs, nvr able to chal.* ....(25 to 1 op 12 to 1 tchd 33 to 1) 5
3738^{5} ALACRITY [79] 9-6 W Ryan (8) *al wl plcd, feeling pace and rdn 2 fs out, sn struggling*..........(13 to 2 op 9 to 2) 6
3351^{6} FOOTSTEPS (Ire) [79] 9-1 (5*) J Tate (3) *sn hndy, hrd at work 2 fs out, fdd*...... (7 to 1 op 6 to 1 tchd 8 to 1) 7
3686^{5} HARLEQUIN WALK (Ire) [55] 7-10 G Bardwell (2) *sluggish strt, sn outpcd, tld off*............(33 to 1 op 16 to 1) 8
3713^{3} EDWINA (Ire) [76] 9-0 (3*) M Fenton (7) *sluggish strt, tld off aftr 2 fs*..............(10 to 1 op 8 to 1 tchd 11 to 1) 9
Dist: 5l, hd, 6l, 3l, sht-hd, 1l, dist, 20l. 1m 28.80s. a 5.60s (9 Ran).
SR: 27/12/23/-/-/-/ (W J Whitaker), P C Haslam

3967 Regent Rating Related Maiden Stakes Class F (3-y-o and up) £2,794 5f 43yds ....(5:05)

3459^{3} BREAKFAST BOOGIE 3-8-7 G Duffield (5) *made all, edgd lft thrght, sprinted clr fnl furlong.* ....(11 to 10 fav op 5 to 4) 1
3568^{8} RED ADMIRAL 3-8-9 (3*) C Hodgson (3) *wth wnr, drvn alng whn pace lifted o'r one furlong out, kpt on same pace*...........................(5 to 2 tchd 11 to 4) 2
3593 SCENT OF POWER 3-8-12 J Carroll (2) *nvr far away, hrd at work o'r one furlong out, sn outpcd.* ....(6 to 1 tchd 13 to 2 and 11 to 2) 3
3188^{4} LAURA 4-8-9 B Crossley (1) *broke wl, chsd alng on outsd hfwy, outpcd o'r one furlong out.* (6 to 1 tchd 8 to 1) 4
2365^{5} KIMMY'S PRINCESS 3-8-7 P Robinson (4) *steadied strt, effrt hfwy, rdn o'r one furlong out, no response.* ....(20 to 1 tchd 25 to 1) 5
Dist: 8l, 6l, 4l, 8l. 1m 3.80s. a 3.10s (5 Ran).
SR: 46/19/ (Mrs Mary Watt), J R Fanshawe

BEVERLEY (good to soft)
Wednesday September 15th

Going Correction: PLUS 0.10 sec. per fur. (races 1,2,3,4,6,7), NIL (5)

3968 Humber Estuary Nursery Selling Handicap Class G (2-y-o) £3,049 7f 100yds...................... (2:10)

3126^{8} GLORIETTE [-] 9-3 K Fallon (14) *al cl up, improved to ld 2 fs out, drvn and edgd rght ins last, kpt on gmely.* ....(10 to 1 op 8 to 1) 1
3563 STORM HEIGHTS [-] 8-1 J Lowe (16) *led till hdd 2 fs out, styd upsides, not much room and swtchd ins last, kpt on*...(20 to 1) 2

3671[5] WINGS AHEAD [-] 8-7 (3*) S Maloney (4) *co'red up beh ldg grp, improved entering strt, swtchd rght over one furlong out, not much room and switched lft ins last, kpt on*.......... (16 to 1 op 14 to 1) 3

3563[9] OLYMPIC BID [-] 9-0 A Munro (12) *settled on ins, pushed alng to improve whn not clr run entering strt, kpt on fnl furlong, nvr dngrs*.......... (16 to 1 op 14 to 1) 4

3829[7] RITA'S JOY [-] 8-9 (7*) S Drowne (10) *nvr far away, effrt and rdn entering strt, one pace whn baulked ins fnl furlong*.......... (9 to 1 op 8 to 1) 5

3281[5] SURPRISE BREEZE [-] 8-8 A Culhane (11) *stall slow to open, beh, rdn whn not much room entering strt, improved wl o'r one furlong out, no extr ins last.* .... (5 to 1 fav op 9 to 2) 6

3627 SHARONE [-] 8-9 S Morris (2) *wnt lft strt, beh, effrt and rdn 2 fs out, swtchd ins and kpt on inside last, nrst finish*.......... (11 to 1 op 10 to 1 tchd 12 to 1) 7

3597 STRADISHALL [-] 8-12 A McGlone (5) *stall slow to open, tucked away on ins, swtchd and drvn entering strt, kpt on fnl furlong, no imprsn*.......... (12 to 1 op 10 to 1) 8

3600[8] SPRING LOADED [-] 9-7 K Darley (1) *patiently rdn, tacked o'r to stands rail entering strt, shaken up, nvr plcd to chal*.......... (8 to 1 tchd 9 to 1) 9

3677[5] DEMON DANCER (Ire) [-] 9-0 N Connorton (3) *in tch on outer, drvn alng last 2 fs, kpt on same pace.* .... (8 to 1 tchd 10 to 1) 10

3696[4] SHUTTLECOCK [-] 9-0 R Cochrane (7) *chsd ldrs, came to stands rail entering strt, rdn and sn one pace.* .... (11 to 2 op 6 to 1 tchd 9 to 2) 11

3829[9] MINIBAR [-] 8-4 J Fanning (8) *beh, drvn alng fnl 3 fs, nvr able to chal*.......... (33 to 1) 12

1759[3] TENPIN PROPHET (Ire) [-] (bl) 8-9 J Fortune (13) *settled mid-div, pushed alng entering strt, sn btn.* .... (16 to 1 tchd 20 to 1) 13

3865 TWO D'S [-] 9-3 M Birch (6) *nvr far away, pushed alng entering strt, sn lost pl*.......... (12 to 1) 14

3815[8] SONIC (Ire) [-] (bl) 8-2 L Charnock (15) *pressed ldg grp, pushed alng to keep in tch entering strt, fdd, tld off.* .... (16 to 1 op 14 to 1) 15

2949[5] CAPTAIN TAFFY [-] (v) 8-11 Paul Eddery (17) *trkd ldrs, reminders hfwy, rdn and wknd entering strt, tld off.* .... (10 to 1 op 8 to 1) 16

Dist: 1½l, 2l, ½l, sht-hd, ½l, ½l, sht-hd, ¾l, nk, sht-hd. 1m 35.70s. a 5.40s (16 Ran).

SR: 33/12/15/17/18/8/7/9/16/ (J W Biswell), R Guest

3969 Tattersalls Maiden Auction Series Stakes Qualifier Class D (2-y-o) £4,110 7f 100yds.......... (2:40)

3613 STAR JAZZ (Ire) 8-9 Paul Eddery (3) *nvr far away, improved to ld o'r one furlong out, sn jnd, kpt on gmely ins fnl furlong*.......... (5 to 1 op 9 to 2) 1

3130[7] IRON GENT (USA) 9-0 R Cochrane (1) *hld up, rdn to chal o'r one furlong out, hng rght and kpt on ins last, jst fld*.......... (4 to 1 op 3 to 1) 2

1877[9] BURES (Ire) (v) 9-0 P Robinson (12) *led till hdd o'r one furlong out, drvn alng and one pace whn not much room towards finish*.......... (25 to 1 tchd 33 to 1) 3

3627[2] MUMTAZ FLYPAST 8-9 K Darley (4) *in tch, rdn to improve entering strt, ch o'r one furlong out, not quicken ins last*.......... (Evens fav op 11 to 10) 4

YENGEMA 8-9 N Connorton (13) *slwly into strd, beh and ran green, shaken up to improve fnl 2 fs, kpt on, nrst finish*.......... (25 to 1 op 14 to 1) 5

3792 BARNPARK 9-0 L Charnock (8) *beh, rdn alng o'r 2 fs out, kpt on ins last, nvr dngrs*.......... (50 to 1) 6

3671[3] KARSEAM (Ire) 9-0 J Fanning (10) *nvr far away, pushed alng entering strt, ch o'r one furlong out, grad wknd.* .... (16 to 1 op 14 to 1) 7

TU OPES 9-0 Dale Gibson (2) *hld up, shaken up o'r 2 fs out, nvr nr to chal*.......... (33 to 1 op 16 to 1) 8

3711[5] FAIR SWOP (Ire) 8-9 M Birch (7) *trkd ldrs on ins, drvn last 2 fs, grad wknd*.......... (12 to 1 op 8 to 1) 9

3792 AUNTIE FAY (Ire) 8-9 J Fortune (6) *settled midfield, drvn alng 3 fs out, edgd rght 2 furlongs out, sn btn*. (50 to 1) 10

3779 MUSIC BLITZ 9-0 K Fallon (9) *hld up towards rear, drvn alng entering strt, no imprsn o'r one furlong out.* .... (33 to 1) 11

STROLLING MINSTREL (Ire) 9-0 D Harrison (5) *dwlt, beh, chsd alng entering strt, nvr on terms.* .... (16 to 1 op 33 to 1) 12

3742[8] CHINESE TREASURE (Ire) 9-0 A McGlone (11) *trkd ldg pair, drvn alng o'r 2 fs out, sn btn, tld off.* .... (25 to 1 op 20 to 1) 13

Dist: Sht-hd, 1l, 2l, 2½l, 4l, 2l, 1½l, nk, 2½l, nk. 1m 34.80s. a 4.50s (13 Ran).

SR: 39/43/40/29/21/14/8/3/-/ (Southgate Racing), Mrs J Cecil

3970 Rambo Dancer Handicap Class D (0-80 3-y-o and up) £4,045 1m 3f 216yds.......... (3:10)

3555[5] MARADONNA (USA) [66] 4-9-4 R Cochrane (10) *nvr far away, not clr run o'r 2 fs out, styd on to ld ins last, kpt on wl*.......... (3 to 1 fav op 11 to 4 tchd 7 to 2) 1

3521 WESTFIELD MOVES (Ire) [52] 5-8-4 J Quinn (9) *led one furlong, styd hndy, rdn to rgn ld one out, hdd ins last, one pace*.......... (6 to 1 op 5 to 1) 2

3831[3] ROUSITTO [49] 5-7-10 (5*) A Garth (7) *mid-div, improved and ev ch o'r one furlong out, no extr ins last.* .... (10 to 1 op 6 to 1) 3

3356[5] CANNY CHRONICLE [65] 5-9-3 P Robinson (2) *keen hold, hld up and beh, gd hdwy o'r one furlong out, styd on, nrst finish*.......... (6 to 1 op 5 to 1 tchd 13 to 2) 4

3466 BLUE LAWS (Ire) [65] 3-8-8 K Fallon (5) *nvr far away, drvn alng fnl 3 fs, one pace ins last*.......... (12 to 1 op 10 to 1) 5

3353[8] AJALAN (Ire) [77] 3-9-6 Paul Eddery (13) *led aftr a furlong, shaken up 2 out, hdd one out, no extr.* .... (13 to 2 op 6 to 1 tchd 7 to 1) 6

3538[5] GREY POWER [72] 6-9-10 K Darley (8) *steadied strt, hld up and beh, took clr order o'r 4 fs out, drvn last 3, one pace appr last*.......... (6 to 1 op 5 to 1 tchd 13 to 2) 7

3033[7] BOLD AMBITION [42] 6-7-8[1] J Lowe (1) *pressed ldr, ev ch entering strt, sn drvn alng, wknd o'r one furlong out.* .... (20 to 1 op 16 to 1) 8

2131[2] MADAM GYMCRAK [59] 3-8-2 Julie Bowker (6) *hld up in rear, cld o'r 4 fs out, pushed alng entering strt, no imprsn*.......... (16 to 1 op 12 to 1) 9

3759 DOC SPOT [60] 3-8-3[1] J Fortune (3) *trkd ldrs, ev ch o'r 2 fs out, hng lft and sn btn*.......... (16 to 1 op 14 to 1) 10

1900[9] PERSIAN FOUNTAIN (Ire) [63] (v) 3-8-6 D Harrison (11) *hld up, hdwy o'r 3 fs out, btn over one out*.......... (12 to 1) 11

SATIN LAKE (USA) [44] 6-7-10[3] A Mackay (12) *beh, drvn appr strt, sn btn*.......... (33 to 1 tchd 50 to 1) 12

DESERT PEACE (Ire) [70] 4-9-8 Dale Gibson (14) *hld up, rdn entering strt, sn lost tch*.......... (16 to 1 op 14 to 1) 13

Dist: 1l, 1½l, nk, ¾l, 1½l, 2l, 1l, 2½l, ½l, 1l. 2m 41.60s. a 10.60s (13 Ran).

SR: 10/-/-/3/-/1/1/-/-/ (Gerald Leigh), L M Cumani

3971 Snowy Gray Memorial Maiden Stakes Class D (3-y-o and up) £3,525 2m 35yds.......... (3:40)

3271[9] RIVIERE ACTOR (USA) 3-8-8 Paul Eddery (1) *nvr far away, led o'r 3 fs out, came wide strt, rdn last 2 furlongs, edgd rght, styd on strly*.......... (6 to 1 op 9 to 2) 1

3449[4] QUILLON 3-8-8 A McGlone (5) *nvr far away, rdn and ev ch 2 fs out, one pace appr last.* .... (9 to 4 op 2 to 1 tchd 5 to 2) 2

3727[5] CHUMMY'S PAL (USA) 3-8-8 M Birch (8) *keen hold, pressed ldrs, pushed alng appr strt, styd on fnl furlong, nvr dngrs*.......... (8 to 1 op 7 to 1) 3

3740[2] RUMPUS (Ire) 3-8-6[3] R Cochrane (3) *settled beh ldrs, improved gng wl appr strt, rdn 2 fs out, sn one pace.* .... (2 to 1 fav op 7 to 4) 4

COEUR BATTANT (Fr) 3-8-8 Kim Tinkler (6) *slwly into strd, sn beh, detached hfwy, pushed alng o'r 3 fs out, styd on fnl furlong, nvr nrr*.......... (25 to 1 op 20 to 1) 5

3832[5] WELLWOTDOUTHINK 7-9-2 K Darley (7) *hld up, improved 5 fs out, rdn entering strt, sn outpcd.* .... (4 to 1 op 7 to 2 tchd 9 to 2) 6

3727 TROY BOY 3-8-8 N Connorton (4) *led, rdn o'r 5 fs out, hdd over 3 out, fdd, tld off*.......... (33 to 1 op 25 to 1) 7

LIGHT THE BAY 3-8-3 D Harrison (2) *keen hold, in tch, rdn o'r 6 fs out, lost touch appr strt, tld off.* .... (50 to 1 op 33 to 1) 8

Dist: 3l, ½l, 3l, 12l, 1½l, 6l, 15l. 3m 42.70s. a 13.70s (8 Ran).

(S Khaled), J L Dunlop

3972 Burton Agnes Maiden Stakes Class D (2-y-o) £4,337 5f.......... (4:10)

MULTI NATIONAL 9-0 K Fallon (20) *hld up in tch far side, improved to ld o'r one furlong out, edgd lft and forged clr ins last, readily*.......... (9 to 2 op 10 to 1) 1

3589[6] BILLIE GREY 8-9 A Munro (15) *trkd ldrs, improved to ld briefly o'r one furlong out, outpcd by wnr ins last.* .... (4 to 1 fav op 11 to 4) 2

3816[8] ANTANANARIVO (Ire) 9-0 K Darley (14) *nvr far away, rdn and ev ch o'r one furlong out, not quicken ins last.* .... (9 to 2 op 6 to 1) 3

3520[6] KID ORY 9-0 Dale Gibson (10) *mid-div, drvn alng aftr 2 fs, kpt on last, nvr dngrs*.......... (12 to 1 op 33 to 1) 4

3284[2] SKIPTAMALOO 8-9 R Cochrane (6) *chsd ldrs stands side, ev ch 2 fs out, eased whn btn fnl furlong.* .... (10 to 1 op 8 to 1) 5

PURPLE FLING 9-0 M Birch (12) *hmpd strt, beh, shaken up hfwy, kpt on fnl furlong, nrst finish.* .... (8 to 1 op 4 to 1) 6

3673[8] CHADWELL HALL 9-0 A McGlone (21) *wth ldrs, led hfwy, hng lft and hdd o'r one furlong out, no extr*.......... (33 to 1) 7

3810[4] MONKEY FACE 8-2 (7*) P Roberts (13) *veered lft strt, beh, swtchd rght hfwy, styd on fnl furlong, nvr nrr.* .... (16 to 1) 8

3557[5] IT MUST BE MILLIE 8-9 G Bardwell (5) *nvr far away stands side, pushed alng fnl 2 fs, one pace*.......... (14 to 1) 9

2042[5] MYSTICAL MICKEY (Ire) 8-11 (3*) S D Williams (11) *mid-div, sn pushed alng, no imprsn fnl 2 fs*.......... (33 to 1) 10

3633 BRUZ 9-0 S Perks (9) *beh, drvn alng aftr 2 fs, styd on o'r one out, not rch ldrs*.......... (33 to 1 op 25 to 1) 11

3755 SUPER TIMES 8-9 J Fortune (3) *pressed ldg bunch stands side, rdn alng hfwy, not pace to chal.* .... (33 to 1 op 25 to 1) 12
3754 KENILWORTH FORD 8-6 (3*) O Pears (19) *cl up, ev ch hfwy, rdn and btn wl o'r one furlong out*..... (50 to 1) 13
3754 COURSE FISHING 9-0 A Mackay (22) *pressed ldg grp on outer, effrt and drvn alng 2 fs out, sn btn.* .... (33 to 1 op 25 to 1) 14
1837[8] HOTCROFT (v) 8-9 A Culhane (16) *led till hdd hfwy, rdn and grad wknd*.................. (20 to 1 op 16 to 1) 15
THE TESTER 8-7 (7*) S Drowne (7) *beh and sn pushed alng, stumbled aftr one furlong, nvr on terms.* .... (33 to 1 op 25 to 1) 16
3557[8] PASTURES NEW (Ire) 8-9 D Harrison (1) *beh stands side, sn drvn alng, nvr wnt pace*..........(20 to 1 op 16 to 1) 17
3746[9] RICH GLOW 9-0 L Charnock (8) *beh, shaken up o'r 2 fs out, nvr a factor*................. (33 to 1 op 25 to 1) 18
2754[7] ROSY LYDGATE 8-9 Paul Eddery (2) *prmnt stands side till rdn and wknd frm hfwy*...........(10 to 1 op 7 to 1) 19
RISKY PRINCESS 8-6 (3*) S Maloney (4) *beh stands side, chsd alng thrght, nvr a factor*............... (33 to 1) 20
3793[5] FRIENDLY MONET 9-0 J Fanning (23) *prmnt on outer, pushed alng hfwy, sn struggling*.............(33 to 1) 21
Dist: 3½l, 3½l, 1l, 1½l, 1½l, sht-hd, hd, 1l, 2l, 1½l. 1m 4.30s. a 2.60s (21 Ran).
SR: 48/29/20/16/5/4/3/-/-/ (L Mann), Mrs J R Ramsden

3973 Battle Of Britain Wings Appeal Handicap Stakes Class D (0-80 3-y-o and up) £2,880 1m 100yds.......... (4:40)

3358 SALDA [55] 4-8-9 A Culhane (8) *nvr far away, led o'r 3 fs out, hrd pressed over one out, styd on gmely ins last, jst hld on*......................................(6 to 1) 1
3623[2] DANCING BEAU (Ire) [55] 4-8-9 K Darley (10) *chsd ldrs, lost grnd hfwy, imprvg und pres whn not clr run o'r one out, swtchd and styd on strly, jst fld.* (5 to 1 op 9 to 2) 2
2820[6] CAN CAN CHARLIE [48] 3-7-11 J Fanning (11) *handily plcd, rdn to chal o'r one furlong out, no extr ins last.* .... (12 to 1 op 10 to 1) 3
3783* PERSIANSKY (Ire) [76] 3-9-11 R Cochrane (6) *nvr far away, pushed alng o'r 2 fs out, one pace ins last.* ....(9 to 2 fav op 5 to 1) 4
3308[2] RED INDIAN [42] 7-7-10 Dale Gibson (9) *hld up in rear, drvn alng to improve o'r 2 fs out, no imprsn ins last.* .... (11 to 2 op 6 to 1 tchd 5 to 1) 5
RETENDER (USA) [62] 4-9-2 K Fallon (5) *hld up, pushed alng 2 fs out, not quicken o'r one out.* .... (12 to 1 op 10 to 1) 6
3358[6] NORTHERN RAINBOW [49] 5-8-3 J Quinn (4) *beh on outer, drvn alng hfwy, swtchd ins o'r one furlong out, reminders and kpt on, nvr dngrs.* (12 to 1 op 10 to 1) 7
3712* CAUSLEY [72] 8-9-12 M Birch (2) *slight ld till hdd o'r 3 fs out, btn over one out, eased*......... (7 to 1 op 5 to 1) 8
3676[4] CAVATINA [75] 3-9-7 (3*) S D Williams (7) *slwly into strd, beh, rdn alng entering strt, fdd, tld off.* .... (16 to 1 op 14 to 1) 9
3364[3] MOHICAN BRAVE (Ire) [58] 3-8-7 Paul Eddery (3) *pressed ldrs, rdn alng o'r 3 fs out, grad wknd, tld off.* ....(6 to 1 op 5 to 1) 10
3487 GREEK GOLD (Ire) [59] 4-8-10 (3*) S Maloney (1) *keen hold, in tch on outer, drvn alng aftr entering strt, sn btn, tld off*..............................(14 to 1 op 12 to 1) 11
Dist: Hd, 1½l, 2½l, 1½l, nk, 1½l, 3½l, 20l, 1½l, 2½l. 1m 48.60s. a 5.80s (11 Ran).
SR: 21/20/3/23/-/8/-/2/-/ (E R Thomas), R M Whitaker

3974 EBF Garrowby Maiden Stakes Class D (2-y-o) £4,127 7f 100yds.........(5:10)

3633[5] TATAMI (USA) 9-0 R Cochrane (8) *trkd ldrs, lft and rdn 2 fs out, led ins last, drifted left, styd on wl.* .... (6 to 4 fav tchd 2 to 1) 1
3597[5] BONAIGUA (Ire) 9-0 K Darley (5) *tucked away beh ldrs, outpcd and drvn entering strt, ran on fnl furlong, not rch wnr*...........................(6 to 1 op 5 to 1) 2
3592[4] BRAVE PATRIARCH (Ire) 9-0 J Lowe (4) *nvr far away, improved to ld wl o'r 2 fs out, hdd ins last, no extr.* ....(4 to 1 op 3 to 1) 3
3592 RUPAN 9-0 J Fortune (3) *chsd ldrs, effrt entering strt, hng rght and not quicken o'r one furlong out.* .... (13 to 2 op 5 to 1) 4
1020 DIVERTIMIENTO 9-0 K Fallon (10) *wth ldr, ev ch o'r 2 fs out, rdn and sn one pace*.........(10 to 1 op 14 to 1) 5
3592 RISING SPRAY 9-0 M Birch (2) *keen hold, hld up, bustled alng entering strt, kpt on ins last, nvr nrr.* .... (25 to 1 op 20 to 1) 6
3760[5] FAWLTY TOWERS (Ire) 9-0 A Munro (1) *settled on outer, pushed alng entering strt, btn wl o'r one furlong out.* ....(6 to 1 op 9 to 2) 7
3833 SHAWN CUDDY 9-0 W Hood (12) *led till hdd wl o'r 2 fs out, btn well over one out*........ (50 to 1 op 33 to 1) 8
KILERNAN 9-0 J Fanning (7) *slwly into strd, beh, shaken up entering strt, nvr a factor*......(33 to 1 op 25 to 1) 9
3633 CHIEFTAIN'S CROWN (USA) 9-0 Paul Eddery (9) *tucked away on ins, effrt and pushed alng o'r 2 fs out, fdd.* .... (14 to 1 op 12 to 1) 10

3746[7] MILL CITY 9-0 A McGlone (6) *pressed ldg grp, rdn alng entering strt, sn btn*..............(20 to 1 op 16 to 1) 11
Dist: 3½l, ½l, 4l, hd, ¾l, 4l, 2l, nk, ½l, ¾l. 1m 35.90s. a 5.60s (11 Ran).
SR: 27/16/14/2/1/-/ (Sheikh Mohammed), L M Cumani

DOWNPATRICK (IRE) (good)
Wednesday September 15th

3975 S.P. Graham Maiden (3-y-o and up) £1,380 1m 3f 208yds............(5:00)

3662[3] SUNSET CAFE (Ire) (bl) 3-8-7 (4*) W J Smith (3) .... (5 to 1) 1
3856 REGAL PRETENDER (Ire) 3-8-10 (4*) J J Behan (9) (16 to 1) 2
3662[2] CLASSY KAHYASI (Ire) 3-8-11 P Shanahan (4) ..... (7 to 2) 3
3381[9] WARREN STREET (Ire) 3-9-0 S Craine (1) ....(7 to 1) 4
3732[6] HAANEM 3-8-5 (6*) B J Walsh (5) .... (13 to 8 fav) 5
3274[3] DARK HYACINTH (Ire) (bl) 3-8-11 W J Supple (6) .. (13 to 2) 6
3914 CLANFLUTHER (Ire) 3-8-12 (2*) D G O'Shea (10) .. (20 to 1) 7
3579[9] CAPTAIN TANDY (Ire) 4-9-2 (6*) C Everard (8) ..... (20 to 1) 8
3381 TERN DANCER (Ire) (bl) 3-8-11 N G McCullagh (12) (16 to 1) 9
SERANERA (Ire) 3-8-11 R Hughes (7) .... (7 to 1) 10
3856[6] SARAMY (Ire) 3-8-3 (8*) D A O'Sullivan (2) .... (12 to 1) 11
Dist: 5l, nk, 2½l, 1½l. (Time not taken) (11 Ran).
(Seamus Burns), M Halford

3976 Sean Graham Bookmaker Maiden (4-y-o and up) £1,380 1m 5f........(5:30)

3578[6] NORA ANN (Ire) 4-9-5 (6*) C Everard (7) .... (9 to 2) 1
1576 ALOHA (Ire) 4-9-11 M Duffy (1) .... (10 to 1) 2
3854 ALVATUR (Ire) 4-10-0 W J Supple (5) .... (20 to 1) 3
3578[3] WOODFIELD ROSE 4-9-11 S Craine (3) .... (Evens fav) 4
3662[6] BASSETJA (Ire) 4-9-5 (6*) T P Treacy (2) .... (7 to 2) 5
3662[8] LEAD ME LEAD MENOT (USA) 4-9-9 (2*) R M Burke (6) ....(6 to 1) 6
3663[4] LUCK OF A LADY (Ire) 4-9-1 (10*) C McCormack (4) (12 to 1) 7
Dist: 4½l, 8l, ½l, 3l. (Time not taken) (7 Ran).
(Mrs Ann Ennis), Francis Ennis

LONGCHAMP (FR) (soft)
Wednesday September 15th
Going Correction: PLUS 1.10 sec. per fur.

3977 Prix d'Aumale (Group 3) (2-y-o) £23,895 1m.................... (1:55)

BONASH 8-9 Pat Eddery (4) *made all, quickened 2 fs out, hld on wl und pres fnl furlong*.............(10 to 9 on) 1
FLAGBIRD (USA) 8-9 T Jarnet (1) *mid-div, second strt, rdn 2 fs out, ran on wl fnl furlong*............ (29 to 10) 2
SIERRA MADRE (Fr) 8-9 G Mosse (5) *trkd ldrs, 3rd strt, rdn 2 fs out, kpt on*................................(19 to 1) 3
MURADIAMA (Fr) 8-9 C Asmussen (3) *hld up, last strt, hdwy 2 fs out, no extr ins last*...............(52 to 10) 4
3651[3] BLUE BURGEE (USA) 8-9 O Peslier (2) *4th strt, rdn 2 fs out, wknd one out*................................ (26 to 10) 5
Dist: Hd, ½l, ¾l, 2l. 1m 49.20s. a 13.20s (5 Ran).
SR: 29/28/26/24/18/ (K Abdulla), A Fabre

SANDOWN (soft)
Wednesday September 15th
Going Correction: NIL (races 1,5), PLUS 0.55 (2,3,4,6,7)

3978 'Battle Of Britain' Nursery Class D (2-y-o) £4,240 5f 6yds............ (2:20)

3835[3] HELLO MISTER [66] 8-4 (7*) P McCabe (6) *hld up, rdn and gd hdwy o'r one furlong out, str run to ld ins last, drvn out*..................................(8 to 1 tchd 10 to 1) 1
3815* DAILY STAR [66] 8-11 (6ex) J Carroll (7) *made most till rdn and hdd ins last, unbl to quicken.* ....(2 to 1 fav op 6 to 4) 2
3871[2] ALZIANAH [76] 9-7 G Duffield (5) *trkd ldrs, rdn o'r one furlong out, stumbled ins last, ran on cl hme.* .... (100 to 30 op 3 to 1 tchd 9 to 2) 3
3421 SARMATIAN (USA) [68] 8-13 J Reid (4) *al prmnt, ev ch wl o'r one furlong out, wknd ins last.* (5 to 1 tchd 4 to 1) 4
3815[2] MONSIEUR PETONG [58] 8-3 T Quinn (3) *al prmnt, rdn and ev ch o'r one furlong out, wknd.* .... (13 to 2 op 5 to 1 tchd 7 to 1) 5
3677[4] RANDOM [56] 8-1 T Williams (1) *in tch, rdn and effrt o'r 2 fs out, wknd appr last.* .... (11 to 1 op 10 to 1 tchd 12 to 1) 6
3867[9] SPORTING HEIR (Ire) [57] (bl) 8-2 M Roberts (2) *rdn alng hfwy, nvr able to chal.* .... (16 to 1 op 12 to 1 tchd 20 to 1) 7
Dist: 1½l, 1½l, 1l, nk, 2l, ¾l. 1m 2.30s. a 2.80s (7 Ran).
SR: 41/35/39/27/16/6/4/ (Brian Mitten), J O'Donoghue

3979 EBF 'Hawker Hurricane' Maiden Stakes Class D (2-y-o) £4,110 7f 16yds

.................................(2:50)

LUHUK (USA) 9-0 T Quinn (11) *beh, hdwy frm o'r 2 fs out, wndrd over one out, ran on to ld ins last.* ....(6 to 1 op 7 to 2 tchd 7 to 1) 1
WILLIAM TELL 9-0 J Reid (1) *al prmnt, led o'r 2 fs out till hdd ins last, not quicken.* ....(10 to 1 op 20 to 1 tchd 33 to 1) 2
1489⁴ RORY CREEK (USA) 9-0 L Dettori (14) *led 2 fs, styd prmnt, ev ch o'r one out, one pace.* ....(11 to 2 op 5 to 1 tchd 7 to 1) 3
3463⁶ SO SEDULOUS (USA) 8-9 M Hills (10) *chsd ldg bunch, rdn o'r 2 fs out, flashed tail and kpt on same pace ins last.* ....(9 to 4 fav op 6 to 4 tchd 5 to 2) 4
SAKIC (USA) 9-0 S O'Gorman (6) *beh, pushed alng and hdwy o'r 2 fs out, wnt rght over one out, kpt on, nvr nrr*.............................. (33 to 1 op 20 to 1) 5
3130 FARAS ELNAAS 9-0 M Roberts (4) *led aftr 2 fs till hdd o'r two out, not much room over one out, wknd.* ....(7 to 1 op 6 to 1 tchd 8 to 1) 6
FAIR AND FANCY (Fr) 9-0 B Rouse (2) *al prmnt, ev ch o'r 2 fs out, sn rdn and wknd*...........(20 to 1 op 12 to 1) 7
DANISH HEIGHTS (Ire) 9-0 R Price (12) *trkd ldrs, ev ch o'r 2 fs out, stdly lost pl*....(13 to 2 op 7 to 1 tchd 11 to 2) 8
3642 POLY SCREEN 8-7 (7*) R Painter (3) *nvr nr to chal.* ....(50 to 1 op 33 to 1 tchd 66 to 1) 9
3819³ GAY DEVIL 8-7 (7*) Mark Denaro (13) *beh, rdn 3 fs out, no imprsn*...........................(10 to 1 op 8 to 1) 10
3421 BELLO GALLICO (Ire) 9-0 A Clark (5) *midfield till rdn o'r 3 fs out, wknd*.......................... (50 to 1 op 20 to 1) 11
3738 PRINCESS TALLULAH 8-9 N Adams (8) *slwly away, beh, rdn and swshd tail wl o'r 2 fs out, no dngr.* ....(50 to 1 tchd 66 to 1) 12
HILLSWICK 9-0 G Duffield (15) *slwly away, hdwy on ins o'r 3 fs out, sn rdn and wknd*......(50 to 1 op 33 to 1) 13

Dist: ¾l, 1½l, hd, 3l, 3l, 1½l, hd, 3½l, ½l, 1½l. 1m 34.59s. a 8.09s (13 Ran).
SR: 36/34/29/23/19/10/5/4/-/ (Hamdan Al-Maktoum), J L Dunlop

3980 'Supermarine Spitfire' Fillies' Maiden Stakes Class D (3-y-o) £4,084 1¼m 7yds.......................... (3:20)

1200⁴ FELAWNAH (USA) 8-11 M Roberts (1) *al hndy, came wide strt and led 3 fs out, clr o'r one out, easily.* ....(2 to 1 on op 4 to 1 on tchd 15 to 8 on) 1
GEORDIE SONG 8-11 J Carroll (4) *set muddling pace till hdd 3 fs out, sn rdn alng, kpt on same pace.* ....(7 to 1 op 6 to 1) 2
SHADY BANK (USA) 8-11 R Price (6) *took keen hold, hld up, hdwy on ins 3 fs out, ran on one pace.* .... (6 to 1 op 10 to 1) 3
3708² LAMBAST 8-11 J Williams (3) *hld up in tch, some hdwy o'r 3 fs out, no further imprsn*..........(6 to 1 op 9 to 2) 4
3866⁸ CLELIA 8-11 G Duffield (5) *trkd ldr, rdn o'r 3 fs out, sn wknd*.......................... (66 to 1 op 50 to 1) 5
3689 TOUCHEE BOUCHEE 8-4 (7*) R Painter (2) *hld up in tch, rdn 3 fs out, wknd*..........................(100 to 1) 6

Dist: 3½l, 4l, 1½l, 12l, 5l. 2m 15.11s. a 11.21s (6 Ran).
SR: 40/33/25/22/-/-/ (Sheikh Ahmed Al Maktoum), J H M Gosden

3981 Harry Brind Testimonial Handicap Class E (0-70 3-y-o) £3,160 1m 14yds ....(3:55)

3783 SILVER GROOM (Ire) [53] 8-5 T Quinn (10) *midfield till hdwy o'r 3 fs out, led wl over one out, sn clr, easily.* .... (12 to 1 op 10 to 1) 1
3710 DANNY BOY [66] 9-4 J Reid (9) *midfield, came wide strt, hdwy o'r 2 fs out and sn ev ch, ran on one pace.* ....(9 to 1 op 10 to 1 tchd 11 to 1 and 8 to 1) 2
3722⁸ GREENBANK (USA) [64] 9-2 L Dettori (7) *midfield, came wide strt, sn rdn alng, ran on in snatches.* ....(8 to 1 tchd 10 to 1) 3
3670* MISS FASCINATION [64] 9-2 J Carroll (13) *trkd ldg bunch, rdn alng o'r 3 fs out, ran on over one out till not quicken ins last*.............................(3 to 1 jt-fav tchd 11 to 4 and 100 to 30) 4
3226² SMART TEACHER (USA) [50] 8-2 M Hills (12) *led till hdd wl o'r one furlong out, wknd.* ....(8 to 1 op 5 to 1 tchd 9 to 1) 5
3697² VELASCO (Ire) [69] (v) 9-7 G Duffield (5) *chsd ldr, chlgd o'r 2 fs out, sn no extr*...........................(3 to 1 jt-fav op 2 to 1 tchd 100 to 30) 6
3226⁹ JALIB (Ire) [47] 7-13 T Williams (1) *midfield early, rdn and lost pl o'r 3 fs out, no further dngr.* ....(25 to 1 op 20 to 1 tchd 33 to 1) 7
3459⁷ RUBY COOPER [48] 8-0 B Crossley (2) *chsd ldrs, rdn o'r 3 fs out, sn lost pl*..................(25 to 1 op 16 to 1) 8
3384⁹ ARRAS ROYALE [49] 8-1⁸ R Price (4) *al beh*.... (100 to 1) 9
3214⁶ THE SNOUT [54] 8-6 J Williams (3) *slwly into strd, al beh.* ....(10 to 1 op 7 to 1 tchd 11 to 1) 10
3226 AKHLAK (Ire) [51] (v) 8-3 A Clark (11) *chsd ldg pair, sddld slpd forward frm bef hfwy, lost pl o'r 3 fs out.* (12 to 1) 11

Dist: 5l, 1l, 1½l, 5l, 1½l, 4l, 1l, sht-hd, ½l, 4l. 1m 47.79s. a 8.69s (11 Ran).
SR: 27/25/20/15/-/-/ (Mrs Anne-Marie Hamilton), A P Jarvis

3982 'Squadron Scramble' Claiming Stakes Class E (2-y-o) £2,931 5f 6yds...(4:25)

3867* ELEVATOR SHAFT (Ire) (bl) 8-4 T Quinn (12) *al prmnt, led hfwy, hld on wl ins last*..........(9 to 2 fav op 4 to 1) 1
3422⁵ FORGOTTEN DANCER (Ire) 8-12 G Duffield (5) *chsd ldrs, rdn wl o'r one furlong out, ran on strly ins last, nrst finish*.............................(6 to 1 tchd 7 to 1) 2
3677³ CERTIFICATE-X 7-13 T Williams (3) *chsd ldrs, rdn alng frm hfwy, styd on wl ins last.* ....(6 to 1 op 4 to 1 tchd 13 to 2) 3
2845⁶ CHAMPAGNE GIRL 8-0 T Sprake (4) *chsd ldrs, ran on o'r one furlong out, no extr ins last 100 yards.* ....(6 to 1 op 5 to 1 tchd 7 to 1) 4
3641⁴ THORNY BISHOP 8-2 S O'Gorman (8) *midfield, hdwy wl o'r one furlong out, kpt on ins last.* ....(16 to 1 tchd 20 to 1) 5
3309 LEFT STRANDED 8-13 J Reid (10) *broke wl, led to hfwy, styd prmnt till wknd ins fnl furlong.* (5 to 1 op 7 to 2) 6
3505* MR B REASONABLE (Ire) 9-1 W Newnes (9) *beh till hdwy o'r 2 fs out, kpt on, nvr nr to chal.* ....(9 to 1 op 7 to 1 tchd 10 to 1) 7
3629⁶ IVA'S FLYER (Ire) 8-0 N Adams (1) *gd early speed to dispute ld till wknd fnl furlong.* ....(10 to 1 op 8 to 1 tchd 11 to 1) 8
3386 MOUNT LEINSTER 8-5 J Williams (7) *chsd ldg bunch to hfwy, sn btn*...................(6 to 1 tchd 7 to 1) 9
3641⁵ CLASSICAL (Ire) 8-0 (7*) A Lakeman (2) *al beh.* ....(25 to 1 op 20 to 1 tchd 33 to 1) 10
BATON BLEU 8-13 L Dettori (6) *slwly away, reco'red to midfield till wknd over 2 fs out, tld off.* ....(12 to 1 op 10 to 1) 11
BETAWAYDECKERWAY 8-2 S Dawson (11) *missed break, al outpcd, tld off*..............................(33 to 1) 12

Dist: ¾l, nk, ¾l, ¾l, nk, 2½l, sht-hd, ¾l, 5l, 15l. 1m 2.76s. a 3.26s (12 Ran).
SR: 25/30/16/14/13/23/15/-/1/ (Christopher Wright), D W P Arbuthnot

3983 'Chocs Away' Limited Stakes Class D (3-y-o) £4,318 7f 16yds..........(5:00)

3756⁴ PRINCELY FAVOUR (Ire) 9-2 L Dettori (6) *made all, clr fnl furlong, easily*......(100 to 30 op 5 to 2 tchd 7 to 2) 1
2612⁷ ABLE CHOICE (Ire) 9-2 M Hills (2) *hld up in tch, hdwy o'r 2 fs out, kpt on und pres ins last.* ....(9 to 1 op 8 to 1 tchd 10 to 1) 2
3080 HILARY GERRARD (USA) 9-2 G Duffield (4) *hld up in tch, hdwy o'r 2 fs out, kpt on one pace fnl furlong.* ....(13 to 2 op 5 to 1 tchd 7 to 1) 3
3756² SIMPLY SOOTY 8-11 J Reid (3) *wth ldr, rdn o'r 2 fs out, no extr fnl furlong*.....(11 to 4 fav op 9 to 4 tchd 3 to 1) 4
2293⁴ CHAPKA (Ire) 8-11 J Williams (1) *slwly into strd, rdn o'r 3 fs out, nvr a dngr*.................. (10 to 1 op 8 to 1) 5
3736* SILENT EXPRESSION 8-8 (3*) C Hodgson (5) *trkd ldg pair, rcd alone on ins frm 3 fs out, sn rdn and wknd.* ....(3 to 1 op 5 to 2 tchd 100 to 30) 6

Dist: 3l, ½l, ¾l, 4l, 10l. 1m 33.89s. a 7.39s (6 Ran).
SR: 49/40/38/31/19/-/ (C M Hamer), R Hannon

3984 'Angels One Five' Apprentice Handicap Class F (0-80 3-y-o and up) £2,853 1m 3f 91yds....................(5:35)

3761⁶ PRINCESS ERMYN [46] 4-8-13 D Gibbs (1) *made all, rdn wl o'r 2 fs out, well clr fnl furlong, eased nr finish.* ....(7 to 4 fav op 9 to 4 tchd 5 to 2) 1
3572⁸ HOLIDAY ISLAND [57] 4-9-7 (3*) L Carter (4) *beh til effrt 4 fs out, hrd rdn wl o'r 2 out, not quicken, no ch wth wnr.* ....(9 to 2 op 11 to 8 tchd 5 to 1) 2
3787⁷ MON PETITNAMOUR (Ire) [37] 4-7-13 (5*) A Whelan (3) *al hndy, came wide strt, sn rdn and one pace.* ....(7 to 2 tchd 3 to 1 and 4 to 1) 3
MY SENOR [34] 4-7-10 (5*) Iona Wands (2) *al beh.* ....(8 to 1 op 6 to 1 tchd 10 to 1) 4
3572⁷ SPRING TO GLORY [28] 6-7-4 (5*) Wendy Jones (5) *trkd ldrs till rdn and wknd wl o'r 2 fs out.* ....(9 to 2 op 6 to 1 tchd 7 to 1) 5

Dist: 12l, ½l, 15l, nk. 2m 35.56s. a 15.56s (5 Ran).
SR: 7/-/ (J Daniels), M Dixon

YARMOUTH (good to soft)
Wednesday September 15th

Going Correction: PLUS 0.40 sec. per fur. (races 1,2), PLUS 0.20 (3,4,5,6,7)

3985 Courage Newtown Selling Stakes Class G (3-y-o and up) £2,490 1¼m 21yds......................... (2:30)

3840⁷ BALL GOWN 3-8-0 (5*) L Newton (12) *confidently rdn, cruised ahead o'r 2 fs out, shaken up fnl furlong, readily*............................(10 to 1 op 6 to 1) 1
3734⁷ JADE GREEN 4-9-3 W Ryan (4) *last and hld up, effrt and not clr run o'r 3 fs out, got through fnl furlong, not rch wnr*.................(6 to 5 on op 5 to 4 tchd 6 to 4) 2

3887[4] LYN'S RETURN (Ire) 4-9-1 (7*) G Rothwell (8) *nvr far away, led jst o'r 3 fs till over 2 out, sn rdn and not quicken.* ....(4 to 1 tchd 9 to 2) 3
3536[6] INOVAR 3-8-10 G Hind (6) *al hndy, hrd at work whn pace lifted o'r 2 fs out, no extr.*....... (20 to 1 tchd 25 to 1) 4
2564[7] JUNCTION TWENTYTWO 3-8-10 (5*) V Slattery (7) *trkd ldg 5, drvn alng whn pace quickened o'r 2 fs no extr.* .... (12 to 1 op 7 to 1) 5
3866[6] ALYVAIR 3-8-5 D Biggs (5) *co'red up, effrt entering strt, drvn alng over 2 fs out, sn btn.*....(20 to 1 op 16 to 1) 6
3689 ROMANTIC MOOD 4-9-3 B Raymond (9) *dictated pace till jst o'r 3 fs out, rdn and btn 2 out.* .... (40 to 1 op 20 to 1 tchd 50 to 1) 7
709[4] APPLIANCEOFSCIENCE (bl) 6-9-3 (5*) K Rutter (3) *tucked away on ins, effrt and drvn alng o'r 3 fs out, sn btn.* .... (25 to 1 op 16 to 1) 8
3693 THRILL 5-8-12 K Williamson (10) *wth ldr, hrd at work o'r 2 fs out, sn btn.*.....................(66 to 1 op 33 to 1) 9
Dist: 2½l, 10l, 2l, hd, 10l, 5l, ¾l, ½l. 2m 14.20s. a 10.20s (9 Ran).
SR: 29/36/21/5/9/-/ (C V Lines), C V Lines

3986 Golden Jubilee Challenge Trophy Handicap Class C (0-90 3-y-o and up) £5,628 1¼m 21yds............. (3:00)

3476[2] AMERICAN SWINGER (USA) [75] 3-9-2 W R Swinburn (3) *set modest pace, quickened up jst o'r 2 fs out, styd on strly.* ....(4 to 1 op 9 to 4) 1
3224[3] PORT SUNLIGHT (Ire) [69] 5-9-3 W Carson (6) *nvr far away, chlgd und pres last 2 fs, kpt on same pace.* ....(13 to 8 fav op 9 to 4) 2
2581 TOP SHIEL [76] 5-9-10 J Weaver (7) *settled gng wl, swtchd outsd to chal last 2 fs, ran on one pace.* ....(6 to 1 tchd 8 to 1) 3
2670[3] WELL APPOINTED (Ire) [68] 4-9-2 J O'Reilly (1) *took keen hold, effrt and bustled alng o'r 2 fs out, kpt on, not pace to chal*......................(16 to 1 op 12 to 1) 4
3549[6] GREEN'S FAIR (Ire) [61] 3-8-2 R Hills (2) *last and gng wl, effrt and shaken up o'r 2 fs out, one pace.* ....(14 to 1 op 12 to 1 tchd 16 to 1) 5
3458[7] PONDICHERRY (USA) [64] 3-8-5 W Woods (4) *tucked away on ins, effrt o'r 2 fs out, sn rdn and outpcd.* ....(14 to 1 op 12 to 1 tchd 16 to 1) 6
3786[9] BARFORD LAD [69] 6-8-10 (7*) N Varley (11) *took str hold, sddl slpd aftr 2 fs, eased o'r two furlongs out.* ....(5 to 1 op 7 to 2) 7
Dist: 1½l, 2½l, ¾l, ½l, 10l, ½l. 2m 18.30s. a 14.30s (7 Ran).
(Triple (Crowners I), P W Harris

3987 Fosters Norfolk Farmers Conditions Stakes Class D (3-y-o and up) £4,230 6f 3yds.......................... (3:30)

3427* STORM CANYON (Ire) 3-9-7 B Raymond (4) *patiently rdn, swtchd outsd and shaken up o'r one furlong out, ran on strly to ld last 100 yards.* ....(11 to 8 fav op 5 to 4 tchd 6 to 4) 1
2885[9] MITHL AL HAWA 3-8-6 W R Swinburn (2) *led for 2 fs, styd hndy and drvn alng two furlongs out, stayed on, not rch wnr*..........................(5 to 2 op 2 to 1) 2
3906 ROCK SYMPHONY 3-8-9 (5*) J Tate (3) *al hndy, led aftr 2 fs, quickened appr last, hdd and no extr last 100 yards.* .... (11 to 1 op 8 to 1) 3
3621 YAKIN (USA) 3-8-6 R Hills (5) *wtd wth, shaken up to improve o'r one furlong out, styd on same pace.* ....(10 to 1 op 14 to 1 tchd 16 to 1) 4
3427[6] LORD OLIVIER (Ire) 3-9-1 M Tebbutt (6) *nvr far away, feeling pace and drvn alng 2 fs out, no imprsn.* ....(20 to 1 op 14 to 1 tchd 25 to 1) 5
3889[3] BRIGG FAIR (bl) 3-9-3 W Carson (1) *broke wl to show speed on outsd for 4 fs, fdd*............... (5 to 1 op 9 to 2) 6
Dist: 1½l, nk, 1½l, nk, 12l. 1m 13.80s. a 2.80s (6 Ran).
SR: 75/54/61/47/55/9/ (Sheikh Mohammed), J H M Gosden

3988 Shadwell Stud Apprentice Series Handicap Class F (0-70 3-y-o and up) £3,611 7f 3yds................. (4:00)

3290[9] DUCKEY FUZZ [54] 5-9-2 Michael Denaro (13) *tucked away gng wl, led o'r one furlong out, sprinted clr.* ....(8 to 1 op 6 to 1) 1
3747* KARINSKA [66] 3-9-10 D McCabe (7) *beh, drvn up frm off the pace last 2 fs, styd on, no ch wth wnr.* ....(5 to 2 fav tchd 3 to 1) 2
3774 GLENFIELD GRETA [51] (bl) 5-8-13 Claire Balding (6) *al hndy, hrd at work whn pace quickened one furlong out, one pace*................... (20 to 1 op 14 to 1) 3
3555[8] DONIA (USA) [57] (bl) 4-9-5 Stephen Davies (12) *led and sn clr, began to tire and hdd o'r one furlong out, no extr.* ....(16 to 1 op 12 to 1 tchd 20 to 1) 4
3634* FUCHU [69] 3-9-13 B Doyle (2) *beh and plenty to do hfwy, swtchd outsd to improve 2 fs out, kpt on, nvr able to chal*...................................(7 to 1 op 6 to 1) 5
3506[5] ELTARA [58] 3-9-2 K Rutter (8) *settled midfield, effrt and drvn alng o'r 2 fs out, one pace.* ....(12 to 1 op 8 to 1 tchd 14 to 1) 6
3670[9] ADAMPARIS [51] (bl) 3-8-9 M Fenton (14) *broke wl, feeling pace and lost grnd hfwy, kpt on ag'n fnl furlong.* ....(17 to 2 op 7 to 1 tchd 10 to 1) 7
3325[3] MAY SQUARE (Ire) [40] 5-8-2 D Wright (4) *wtd wth, effrt and bustled alng o'r 2 fs out, not pace to chal.* ....(15 to 2 op 6 to 1 tchd 9 to 1) 8
3639[8] REMEMBER THIS (Ire) [57] 3-9-1 J D Smith (5) *chsd alng to go pace hfwy, no imprsn last 2 fs.* (25 to 1 op 20 to 1) 9
2015[4] ERIK ODIN [40] 6-7-11 (5*) G Milligan (9) *settled centre, drvn alng to go pace o'r 2 fs out, sn struggling.* ....(20 to 1 op 16 to 1) 10
3593[7] BALLYHAYS (Ire) [50] 4-8-7 (5*) T Ashley (15) *co'red up on ins, not much room hfwy, btn 2 fs out.* ....(11 to 2 op 5 to 1 tchd 6 to 1) 11
3531[7] NIGEL'S LUCKY GIRL [48] 5-8-10 C Hawksley (1) *sluggish strt, chsd alng hfwy, nvr a factor.* (16 to 1 op 12 to 1) 12
3687[9] WADERS DREAM (Ire) [66] (v) 4-10-0 L Newton (11) *squeezed strt, improved into midfield hfwy, btn o'r 2 fs out.* ....(33 to 1 op 12 to 1) 13
Dist: 5l, 1l, nk, ½l, hd, 3½l, 1½l, 3½l, 2½l, ¾l. 1m 30.00s. a 6.80s (13 Ran).
SR: 21/14/-/5/11/-/ (Mrs W M Faletti), R M Flower

3989 John Smiths Halvergate Rating Related Maiden Stakes Class F (2-y-o) £2,377 6f 3yds................. (4:35)

3432[6] TURTLE ROCK 9-0 W Ryan (4) *nvr far away, quickened up to ld appr fnl furlong, forged clr.* (7 to 2 op 3 to 1) 1
3743[6] EWAR EMPRESS (Ire) (v) 8-6 (3*) B Doyle (3) *sluggish strt, swtchd to race stands side, led aftr one and a half fs to hfwy, no ch wth wnr ins last*....... (9 to 1 op 7 to 1) 2
2419[7] KILLING TIME 9-0 B Raymond (5) *led for one and a half fs, hng lft and drvn alng hfwy, rallied fnl furlong.* ....(9 to 2 op 7 to 2 tchd 5 to 1) 3
3754[3] BASHFUL BRAVE 8-11 (3*) M Fenton (1) *al hndy, led hfwy till appr fnl furlong, eased whn btn.* ....(5 to 4 fav op 11 to 8 tchd 13 to 8) 4
3762[9] CHILIGRAY (bl) 9-0 W Carson (2) *wth ldrs, struggling aftr 2 fs, sn lost tch*...................... (8 to 1 op 7 to 1) 5
Dist: 5l, 2½l, sht-hd, 7l. 1m 17.00s. a 6.00s (5 Ran).
SR: 4/-/ (P D Savill), S G Norton

3990 Miller Pilsner Lifeboat Maiden Stakes Class D (2-y-o) £4,175 7f 3yds...(5:05)

INDHAR 8-9 (5*) L Newton (14) *al gng wl, drvn up to ld stands side appr fnl furlong, ran on strly.* .... (10 to 1 op 5 to 1) 1
3592 STOLLER (USA) 9-0 W Woods (18) *clr o'rall ldr stands side for over 5 fs, rallied towards finish.* .... (25 to 1 op 14 to 1) 2
3809[2] KEFAHI (Ire) 9-0 B Raymond (15) *wl plcd stands side, ev ch and hrd drvn o'r one furlong out, kpt on same pace.* .... (10 to 1 op 8 to 1) 3
3633[4] TORTUGA (USA) 9-0 G Hind (5) *wth ldrs far side, crossed o'r to centre and led that grp last 2 fs, nvr able to chal.* ....(13 to 8 fav op 2 to 1 tchd 6 to 4) 4
3592 RIVER JUNCTION (Ire) 9-0 N Carlisle (19) *wl plcd stands side, drvn alng o'r one furlong out, grad wknd.* .... (50 to 1 op 33 to 1) 5
3592 PILIB (Ire) 9-0 M Wigham (13) *pressed ldrs stands side for o'r 5 fs, no extr*......................(50 to 1 op 33 to 1) 6
HESELL STREET (Ire) 9-0 J Weaver (4) *pressed ldrs far side, feeling pace hfwy, nvr able to chal.* .... (20 to 1 op 10 to 1) 7
LUCKY TUCKY 9-0 F Norton (11) *trkd ldrs stands side for 5 fs, fdd*.......................... (40 to 1 op 25 to 1) 8
ENCORE SENOR (USA) 8-9 (5*) J Tate (16) *patiently rdn, shaken up and steady hdwy stands side last 2 fs, nrst finish*...........................(40 to 1 op 20 to 1) 9
ZAMHAREER (USA) 8-11 (3*) B Doyle (12) *missed break, chsd alng thrght, nvr nr to chal*.. (33 to 1 op 20 to 1) 10
2502 LORD WELLINGTON (Ire) 8-11 (3*) M Fenton (17) *chsd ldrs stands side, struggling frm hfwy.* (50 to 1 op 25 to 1) 11
SAMBA SHARPLY 8-9 (5*) K Rutter (2) *wth ldrs far side, feeling pace hfwy, fdd last 2 fs*.... (50 to 1 op 33 to 1) 12
ZAHRAN (Ire) 9-0 W Ryan (1) *wth ldrs far side, struggling frm hfwy, eased whn no ch last 2 fs.* ....(7 to 2 op 5 to 1 tchd 7 to 1) 13
3833[6] JUST FLAMENCO 9-0 D Biggs (8) *gd speed far side, eased whn btn 2 fs out*................. (25 to 1 op 20 to 1) 14
3592 MUCH TOO CLEVER 9-0 S Whitworth (10) *sluggish strt, chsd alng far side, nvr dngrs*..... (50 to 1 op 33 to 1) 15
ETHBAAT (USA) 9-0 R Hills (7) *steadied strt, led far side aftr a furlong, grad wknd last 2 fs.* ....(5 to 1 tchd 6 to 1 and 4 to 1) 16
MANFATH (Ire) 8-9 W Carson (3) *struggling to go pace far side aftr 3 fs, sn lost tch*.......(14 to 1 op 12 to 1) 17
JUNDI (Ire) 9-0 W R Swinburn (6) *struggling aftr 2 fs, lost tch far side frm hfwy*..............(10 to 1 op 8 to 1) 18
BOLD GREEK 9-0 M Tebbutt (9) *struggling far side aftr 2 fs, tld off*..........................(40 to 1 op 20 to 1) 19
Dist: 1l, nk, 7l, 2½l, 1l, 2½l, ¾l, ¾l, ½l, 4l. 1m 28.70s. a 5.50s (19 Ran).
SR: 39/36/35/14/6/3/ (Miss P Rovera), J E Banks

3991 Kronenbourg 1664 North Sea Handicap Class D (0-80 3-y-o and up) £4,556

1m 3yds. . . . . (5:40)

3655[3] CELIA BRADY [47] 5-8-0 C Rutter (7) *tucked away gng wl, not clr run o'r one furlong out, brst through to ld ins last, drvn out*. (9 to 2 op 11 to 2) 1
731 MAHOOL (USA) [71] 4-9-10 W R Swinburn (10) *made most till hdd and rdn ins fnl furlong, kpt on same pace.* . . . . (16 to 1 op 10 to 1) 2
3512[7] LET'S GET LOST [68] 4-9-7 W Ryan (2) *al hndy, drw level und pres o'r one furlong out, not quicken.* . . . . (9 to 2 op 7 to 2) 3
3766* CASTING SHADOWS [53] 4-8-6 R Hills (5) *settled gng wl, continually denied clr run last 2 fs, unlucky.* . . . . (7 to 2 fav tchd 4 to 1) 4
3811* KING PARIS (Ire) [77] (bl) 3-9-8 (3*,4ex) M Fenton (11) *wl plcd thrght, drvn alng o'r one furlong out, no extr.* . . . . (6 to 1 op 5 to 1) 5
3670[4] SAAFEND [73] 5-9-7 (5*) K Rutter (3) *rcd very freely on outsd till wknd 2 fs out.* (6 to 1 op 9 to 2 tchd 13 to 2) 6
2182[5] TIME HONORED (USA) [66] 3-9-0 C Nutter (9) *trkd ldrs, drvn alng whn pace quickened last 2 fs, sn btn.* . . . . (12 to 1 op 7 to 1) 7
3631[3] SHAMGAAN (USA) [58] 3-8-6 B Raymond (1) *wth ldrs for o'r 5 fs, fdd*. (8 to 1 op 5 to 1) 8
Dist: 2½l, ½l, ½l, 4l, 1l, sht-hd, 20l. 1m 42.70s. a 6.90s (8 Ran).
SR: 6/22/17/-/7/5/-/-/ (Mrs David Blackburn), H Candy

AYR (good to firm)
Thursday September 16th

Going Correction: MINUS 0.30 sec. per fur. (races 1,5,6,7), MINUS 0.70 (2,3,4)

3992 EBF Hall Farm Stud Maiden Stakes Class D (2-y-o) £4,396 7f. . . . . (2:00)

3462[3] JAZEEL (USA) 9-0 W Carson (5) *trkd ldrs, rdn o'r one furlong out, ran on wl to ld well ins fnl furlong.* . . . .(6 to 5 fav op 11 to 8 tchd 6 to 4) 1
3779[5] MOVING ARROW 9-0 N Connorton (7) *trkd ldrs, led o'r one furlong out, rdn, hdd and no extr wl ins fnl furlong.* . . . . (100 to 30 op 7 to 2 tchd 4 to 1) 2
2250[3] DANGER POINT 9-0 K Darley (8) *hld up, hdwy 3 out, ev ch entering fnl furlong, kpt on same pace*. . . . . (8 to 1) 3
2389[2] AMBER VALLEY (USA) 9-0 E Johnson (1) *led till hdd o'r one furlong out, kpt on same pace*. . . . . . . (3 to 1 op 5 to 2) 4
WILD ROSE OF YORK 8-9 G Duffield (4) *prmnt, effrt o'r 2 fs out, wkng whn not clr run and swtchd over one out.* . . . . (33 to 1 op 14 to 1) 5
3809[7] MARGOT'S BOY 9-0 J Fanning (2) *chsd ldr till wknd o'r one furlong out*. . . . . (500 to 1 op 200 to 1) 6
3810[6] HESFINMENTALTOO (bl) 9-0 A Mackay (3) *dwlt, al wl beh.* . . . . (50 to 1 op 33 to 1) 7
3672[6] ESPLEY NIPPER 9-0 J Carroll (9) *al beh, lost tch o'r 2 fs out*. (50 to 1) 8
Dist: Nk, 2l, hd, 5l, 3½l, 6l, nk. 1m 25.71s. a 1.71s (8 Ran).
SR: 43/42/36/35/15/9/-/-/ (Hamdan Al-Maktoum), J L Dunlop

3993 Tattersalls Maiden Auction Series Fillies' Stakes Qualifier Class D (2-y-o) £3,501 6f. . . . . (2:35)

1418 ZANZARA (Ire) 8-6 J Fortune (1) *chsd ldrs, ran on wl to ld jst ins fnl furlong, pushed out.* . . . . (20 to 1 tchd 25 to 1 and 16 to 1) 1
3810[2] FRISKY MISS (Ire) 8-3 J Carroll (8) *led till hdd jst ins fnl furlong, rdn and no extr*. . . . . . . (13 to 8 fav op 7 to 4) 2
ENCHANTEUR 8-5 M Birch (4) *dwlt, beh, hdwy 2 fs out, ran on wl fnl furlong, nrst finish.* (14 to 1 op 12 to 1) 3
3776[4] SLIP A COIN 8-6 K Darley (2) *cl up till wknd entering fnl furlong*. (4 to 1 op 5 to 2) 4
3695[3] MOORLAND DANCER (Ire) 8-4 R Hills (3) *trkd ldrs gng wl, effrt 2 fs out, sn ev ch, wknd fnl furlong.* . . . .(9 to 4 op 5 to 2 tchd 3 to 1) 5
2766[7] PORTITE SOPHIE 8-3 J Lowe (5) *prmnt early, outpcd and lost tch frm hfwy*. . . . . (25 to 1 op 20 to 1) 6
3755 STRANGERSARDANGERS (Ire) 8-4 A Mackay (7) *dwlt, al wl beh*. (20 to 1 op 14 to 1) 7
Dist: 1l, 1l, 1½l, 2½l, 6l, 3l. 1m 11.56s. a 0.66s (7 Ran).
(Skyline Racing Ltd), J Berry

3994 Timeform Harry Rosebery Trophy Class A (Listed Race) (2-y-o) £7,904 5f . . . . (3:10)

3613* PALACEGATE JACK (Ire) 9-3 J Carroll (1) *cl up, led o'r 3 fs out, hld on wl fnl furlong*. . . . . (7 to 1 op 6 to 1) 1
3746* PINKERTON'S PAL 8-11 M Birch (4) *dwlt, in tch, swtchd outsd and effrt 2 fs out, edgd lft and rdr drpd reins one out, ran on wl towards finish*. . . (3 to 1 tchd 100 to 30) 2
3679[3] BID FOR BLUE 9-3 K Darley (5) *trkd ldrs, effrt 2 fs out, ev ch one out, kpt on wl*. . . . . (4 to 1 op 3 to 1) 3
3679* EHTFAAL (Ire) 8-12 R Hills (2) *trkd ldrs, chlgd 2 fs out, no extr fnl furlong*. . . . . (5 to 4 fav tchd 11 to 8) 4
3715[2] NORDICO PRINCESS 8-6 S Perks (6) *beh frm hfwy.* . . . . (33 to 1 op 25 to 1) 5
3441[2] MISTER PISTE (Ire) 8-11 J Fanning (3) *led till hdd o'r 3 out, wknd 2 out*. (33 to 1 op 25 to 1) 6
Dist: Nk, hd, ¾l, 5l, 1l. 57.84s. b 0.26s (6 Ran).
SR: 38/31/36/28/2/3/ (Palacegate Corporation Ltd), J Berry

3995 Champagne Pannier Handicap Class D (0-75 3-y-o and up) £4,572 5f. . (3:40)

3404 SIR JOEY (USA) [72] 4-9-5 (7*) S Drowne (2) *in tch gng wl, hdwy 2 fs out, led ins fnl furlong, all out.* . . . . (25 to 1 op 16 to 1) 1
3638[5] CALL TO THE BAR (Ire) [69] 4-9-9 A Clark (9) *in tch, hdwy to ld o'r one furlong out, hdd ins fnl furlong, kpt on.* . . . .(7 to 1 fav op 8 to 1 tchd 13 to 2) 2
3778 GONDO [71] (v) 6-9-4 (7*) S Knott (11) *al chasing ldrs, kpt on fnl furlong*. . . . .(14 to 1 op 16 to 1) 3
3877 ABSOLUTION [61] 9-9-1 K Fallon (5) *in tch, kpt on wl fnl furlong*. . . . .(20 to 1) 4
3410 JUST BOB [69] 4-9-9 J Fortune (10) *al chasing ldrs, kpt on same pace fnl 2 fs*. . . . . (25 to 1 op 20 to 1) 5
3947[4] SHADOW JURY [74] 3-9-12 K Darley (7) *prmnt, one pace fnl 2 fs*. . . . .(10 to 1 tchd 12 to 1) 6
3568[5] SIMMIE'S SPECIAL [55] (bl) 5-8-4 (5*) A Garth (6) *sn cl up, chlgd 2 fs out, hng lft, wknd entering fnl furlong.* . . . . (20 to 1 op 16 to 1) 7
3261[7] JIGSAW BOY [74] 4-10-0 M Birch (13) *beh till ran on fnl 2 fs, nrst finish*. . . . .(10 to 1 tchd 11 to 1) 8
3603 SINGING STAR [68] 7-9-1 (7*) Claire Balding (1) *beh, some hdwy hfwy, nvr dngrs*. . . . .(12 to 1) 9
3709[2] SIGAMA (USA) [70] 7-9-10 R Lappin (8) *led till hdd o'r one furlong out, sn btn*. . . . .(10 to 1 op 12 to 1) 10
2935[5] LOFT BOY [53] (bl) 10-8-7 R Hills (4) *dwlt, nvr dngrs.* . . . .(14 to 1) 11
3603[6] BRISAS [40] (v) 6-7-8[1] J Fanning (20) *nvr dngrs.* . . . . (25 to 1 op 20 to 1) 12
3947 KABCAST [54] (bl) 8-8-8 N Connorton (18) *chsd ldrs till wknd 2 out*. . . . .(16 to 1) 13
2951[4] OUR MICA [53] (bl) 3-7-12 (7*) P Roberts (16) *chsd ldrs till wknd 2 out*. . . . .(16 to 1) 14
3834[7] PALLIUM (Ire) [70] 5-9-5 (5*) D McCabe (14) *sn beh.* (14 to 1) 15
2935[8] MURRAY'S MAZDA (Ire) [72] 4-9-12 J Carroll (15) *chsd ldrs to hfwy*. . . . . (14 to 1 tchd 16 to 1) 16
3758 LANGTONIAN [49] (bl) 4-7-10 (7*) P Fessey (12) *nvr better than mid-div*. . . . .(25 to 1 op 20 to 1) 17
3410 WILLSHE GAN [74] 3-9-12 W Carson (19) *sn beh.* . . . .(12 to 1 tchd 14 to 1) 18
3568 MINIZEN MUSIC (Ire) [40] 5-7-8[1] J Lowe (17) *sn beh.* . . . .(50 to 1) 19
3059[6] BOLD COUNTY [61] (bl) 3-8-13 G Duffield (3) *sn beh.* . . . .(14 to 1 op 12 to 1 tchd 16 to 1) 20
Dist: Sht-hd, 2½l, 2l, 2½l, nk, 1l, hd, hd, ¾l, hd. 57.20s. b 0.90s (20 Ran).
SR: 60/56/48/30/28/30/9/27/20/ (Mrs A G Sims), P G Murphy

3996 Sam Hall Rated Class B Handicap (0-95 3-y-o and up) £6,187 7f. . . . (4:10)

3901[2] HI NOD [80] 3-8-5 N Connorton (3) *chsd ldrs, led o'r one furlong out, ran on wl.* . . . .(13 to 8 fav op 2 to 1 tchd 9 to 4) 1
3897[3] AMAZING FEAT (Ire) [91] 4-9-6 K Darley (5) *hld up, effrt 2 fs out, ran on wl fnl furlong.* . . . . (5 to 1 op 4 to 1 tchd 11 to 2) 2
3885[4] FIELD OF VISION (Ire) [80] 3-8-5 T Williams (1) *in tch, gd hdwy o'r one furlong out, edgd lft and kpt on wl fnl furlong*. (7 to 1 op 8 to 1) 3
2732[3] ABSOLUTE MAGIC [90] 3-9-1 R Hills (7) *cl up, slight ld wl o'r one furlong out, sn hdd and one pace.* . . . .(9 to 1 op 7 to 1) 4
3864[3] TAUFAN BLU (Ire) [92] 4-9-7 J Fortune (4) *hld up, effrt 2 fs out, kpt on, not rch ldrs*. . . . . (7 to 1 op 6 to 1) 5
3774[5] SHIRO [84] 3-8-9 W Carson (6) *trkd ldrs, pushed alng o'r 2 fs out, btn whn not much room fnl furlong.* . . . .(6 to 1 op 5 to 1) 6
3477[6] SOIREE (Ire) [90] 4-9-5 G Duffield (2) *led till hdd wl o'r one furlong out, wkng whn hmpd entering fnl furlong.* . . . .(20 to 1 op 14 to 1) 7
Dist: 1l, ½l, 3l, hd, 2l, 3l. 1m 25.05s. a 1.05s (7 Ran).
SR: 44/56/39/40/45/27/28/ (Brian Nordan), M J Camacho

3997 Dick Peacock Nursery Class D (2-y-o) £3,696 1m. (4:40)

3865[4] BEATS WORKING [83] 9-7 K Fallon (4) *hld up in tch, hdwy o'r 2 fs out, styd on wl to ld cl hme*. . . . .(3 to 1 jt-fav tchd 7 to 2) 1
3658[2] ZUBOON (USA) [82] 9-6 W Carson (6) *slwly into strd, sn chasing ldrs, led hfwy, kpt on wl fnl furlong, ct cl hme.* . . . .(100 to 30 op 7 to 2 tchd 4 to 1 and 3 to 1) 2
3129[2] HIT THE CANVAS (USA) [73] 8-11 K Darley (7) *chsd ldrs, chlgd 2 fs out, ev ch till no extr ins fnl furlong.* . . . .(3 to 1 jt-fav tchd 7 to 2) 3
3750[8] CHANTRY BEATH [56] 7-8 J Fanning (2) *beh, styd on wl fnl 2 fs, not rch ldrs*. . . . .(33 to 1 op 25 to 1) 4
3406 MOSAIC GOLD [79] 9-3 N Connorton (3) *in tch, hmpd hfwy, styd on wl fnl 2 fs, not rch ldrs.* . . . .(16 to 1 op 14 to 1) 5

3677^{8} BENEFICIARY [64] 7-11 (5*) Darren Moffatt (10) *trkd ldrs, ev ch 2 fs out, wknd entering fnl furlong.* ....(14 to 1 op 12 to 1) 6
3678^{4} RIVA'S BOOK (USA) [64] 8-2 R Hills (1) *beh, not much room and swtchd o'r 2 fs out, styd on fnl furlong, not trble ldrs*..(12 to 1) 7
3563^{2} DISTINCTIVE AIR [69] 8-7 M Birch (8) *trkd ldrs, ev ch 2 fs out, sn wknd*..........(15 to 2 op 7 to 1 tchd 8 to 1) 8
3816 BEDAZZLE [56] 7-8^{1} A Mackay (5) *led 2 fs, chsd ldrs, fdd frm 3 out*....................................(33 to 1) 9
3672^{5} SINBAD [67] 8-5 J Lowe (9) *led aftr 2 fs till hdd hfwy, fdd.* ....(16 to 1 op 14 to 1) 10
Dist: Hd, 1½l, sht-hd, sht-hd, 2l, nk, 2l, 1l, 4l. 1m 39.84s. a 2.14s (10 Ran).
SR: 39/37/23/5/27/6/5/4/-/ (M R Charlton), Mrs J R Ramsden

3998 Bogside Cup Handicap Class C (0-95 3-y-o) £4,901 1m 7f.............(5:10)

3513^{2} LAKE POOPO (Ire) [74] 8-11 K Darley (1) *made all, styd on wl fnl furlong.* ....(5 to 2 op 11 to 4 tchd 3 to 1 and 9 to 4) 1
3556* MONDRAGON [73] 8-10 J Lowe (4) *dwlt, beh, pushed alng hfwy, hdwy 4 fs out, ch o'r one out, kpt on, no imprsn.* ....(3 to 1 op 9 to 4) 2
3759^{4} PRINCESS TATEUM (Ire) [65] 8-2 W Carson (3) *trkd ldrs, pushed alng 5 fs out, wknd 2 out*...(6 to 1 tchd 7 to 1) 3
1605* THE WHERE WITHAL [78] 9-1 G Duffield (5) *hld up, pushed alng 5 fs out, hng lft and wknd 3 out.* (8 to 1 op 5 to 1) 4
3401^{4} MUJAWAB [84] 9-7 R Hills (2) *trkd ldr, pushed alng 5 fs out, wknd o'r 2 out*............ (9 to 4 fav tchd 5 to 2) 5
Dist: ½l, 5l, 5l, ½l. 1m 13.65s. (5 Ran).
(R E Sangster), B W Hills

DUNDALK (IRE) (good)
Thursday September 16th

3999 Riverstown Maiden (3-y-o and up) £2,243 1½m................... (3:30)

3773^{5} KARAR (Ire) 3-9-0 M J Kinane (1)............. (6 to 4 fav) 1
3526^{2} NORDIC QUEEN (Ire) 3-8-11 K J Manning (8)...... (7 to 2) 2
3808^{5} SHANGANOIR (Ire) 3-8-10^{1} (2*) P Carberry (9)......(7 to 4) 3
3733^{6} TERESIAN GIRL (Ire) 3-8-11 N Byrne (7)..........(25 to 1) 4
3684^{9} CARAVELLE LAD (Ire) (bl) 3-9-0 P V Gilson (4).....(14 to 1) 5
3497 BACK TO BLACK (Ire) 4-9-1 (4*) C Everard (6).....(14 to 1) 6
DESERT WALTZ (Ire) 4-9-8 J F Egan (5)..........(20 to 1) 7
3857^{7} PHARACH (Ire) 4-9-8 J P Murtagh (3)............(14 to 1) 8
ANNADOT (Ire) 3-8-11 N G McCullagh (2)........(12 to 1) 9
Dist: Nk, 4½l, 9l, ½l. 2m 34.60s. (9 Ran).
(H H Aga Khan), John M Oxx

4000 Mullacrew Claiming Race (2-y-o) £2,243 7f 166yds............... (4:00)

3562^{6} BRIEF RESPITE (Ire) 8-9 P Shanahan (10)........ (10 to 1) 1
2666^{4} BRUGATTI (Ire) 8-2 W J Supple (4).................(7 to 2) 2
3608 JENZSOPH (Ire) 7-2 (8*) G M Moylan (2)..........(10 to 1) 3
3071 GENEVIEVE FLEUR (Ire) 7-12 (2*) D G O'Shea (13) (20 to 1) 4
3416^{6} ROSE BUNCH 8-9 P V Gilson (8).................(3 to 1 jt-fav) 5
NORDIC COLOURS (Ire) 7-10^{2} (2*) R M Burke (11)..(6 to 1) 6
MISSUS MURHILL (Ire) 8-8 M J Kinane (6)... (3 to 1 jt-fav) 7
2959^{6} ARTFULNESS (Ire) (bl) 7-5 (8*) R T Fitzpatrick (12) (14 to 1) 8
2880 LOVELY DEISE (Ire) 8-0 J F Egan (1).............(14 to 1) 9
YOUNGER DAYS (Ire) 8-5 (4*) J A Heffernan (9)... (25 to 1) 10
3273^{5} REMAIN ANONYMOUS (Ire) 7-8 (4*) J J Behan (5) (10 to 1) 11
3807^{9} SHEER STYLE (Ire) 8-2 N G McCullagh (7).........(6 to 1) 12
Dist: 1½l, hd, nk, hd. 1m 39.00s. (12 Ran).
(Mrs B Keogh), Declan Gillespie

4001 Heinz Custom Foods Handicap (0-70 3-y-o and up) £2,768 1m 1f...... (4:30)

3543^{2} THE BOWER (Ire) [-] (bl) 4-8-7 (8*) P M Donohue (10) (4 to 1) 1
2691^{6} MAJESTIC PADDY (Ire) [-] 3-9-4 J P Murtagh (8)...(16 to 1) 2
3721* JUST ONE CANALETTO [-] 5-8-11 (4*,8ex) J J Behan (3) ....(8 to 1) 3
3827^{6} ARDLEA HOUSE (Ire) [-] 4-7-6 (2*) D G O'Shea (2) (10 to 1) 4
3827^{5} DAHAR'S LOVE (USA) [-] (bl) 4-8-0 W J Supple (4) (10 to 1) 5
640 ALBONA [-] 5-9-10 H Rogers (15)...............(33 to 1) 6
3732^{4} MY GOSSIP (Ire) [-] 3-8-11 N G McCullagh (11) (3 to 1 fav) 7
3244^{7} CAMEY'S CHOICE (Ire) [-] 3-7-0 (8*) G M Moylan (14) ....(25 to 1) 8
3544 FLORAL STREET [-] 4-9-11 (2*) P Carberry (9).... (10 to 1) 9
3418^{4} TOUCHDOWN [-] 6-9-4 R Hughes (5)..............(7 to 1) 10
3721^{8} BOLERO DANCER (Ire) [-] 5-8-5 (6*) R V Skelly (6) (14 to 1) 11
1163 SWEET REALM [-] (bl) 4-7-5^{3} (8*) R T Fitzpatrick (7) (25 to 1) 12
3454^{6} VOUVRAY (Ire) [-] (bl) 3-8-3 (2*) R M Burke (16)....(16 to 1) 13
3543 VICOSA (Ire) [-] 4-7-8 (4*) W J Smith (1)..........(12 to 1) 14
3826^{4} BRACKLOON BOY (Ire) [-] 4-9-7 (4*) C Everard (13) (7 to 1) 15
Dist: Nk, nk, nk, nk. 1m 58.00s. (15 Ran).
(Mrs C Collins), C Collins

LINGFIELD (soft)
Thursday September 16th

Going Correction: PLUS 0.40 sec. per fur. (races 1,2,4,5,6), PLUS 0.20 (3,7)

4002 Levy Board Maiden Stakes Class D (Div I) (2-y-o) £3,582 7f 140yds.. (2:20)

3763^{4} RAINBOW HEIGHTS 9-0 M Hills (11) *nvr far away, led appr 3 fs out, rdn out.* ....(11 to 8 on op 6 to 4 on tchd Evens) 1
SILVER HUT (USA) 8-9 S Raymont (4) *al prmnt, took keen hold early, ev ch ins fnl furlong, ran on.* ....(5 to 1 op 7 to 2) 2
3421 SAAFI (Ire) 9-0 M Wigham (2) *dwlt, rcd far side, rdn 3 fs out, ran on wl frm o'r one out*..... (25 to 1 op 20 to 1) 3
2836^{6} SPARKLING ROBERTA 8-9 M Roberts (10) *led till hdd 4 fs out, one pace*........ (14 to 1 op 10 to 1 tchd 16 to 1) 4
1909^{8} LITTLE LUKE (Ire) 9-0 R Cochrane (3) *led far side trio till wknd o'r one furlong out*.................... (33 to 1) 5
LICENTIOUS 8-9 Paul Eddery (1) *dwlt, wth ldr on far side, outpcd wl o'r one furlong out.* ....(12 to 1 op 7 to 1 tchd 14 to 1) 6
GINGER JIM 9-0 M Perrett (5) *took keen hold beh ldrs, outpcd fnl 3 fs*............ (25 to 1 op 20 to 1) 7
STAR JESTER (Ire) 8-9 J Williams (9) *chsd ldrs till outpcd hfwy*..................(8 to 1 op 4 to 1 tchd 10 to 1) 8
RAMSHAW (Ire) 9-0 B Raymond (6) *missed break, al beh.* .... (8 to 1 op 7 to 1 tchd 10 to 1) 9
3705^{7} LITTLE GENT (Ire) 8-7 (7*) L Carter (8) *wth ldr, led 4 fs out till appr 3 out, wknd*............. (20 to 1 op 14 to 1) 10
GOLDEN BULLION 8-9 G Hind (7) *missed break and beh, reminders 3 fs out, no imprsn*................ (33 to 1) 11
Dist: Nk, 6l, 1l, 3½l, 1½l, 1½l, 2l, hd, 5l, 1l. 1m 37.46s. a 9.16s (11 Ran).
SR: 9/3/-/-/-/-/ (Broughton Homes Ltd), B W Hills

4003 Levy Board Maiden Stakes Class D (Div II) (2-y-o) £3,552 7f 140yds.. (3:20)

3658^{8} ALASKAN HEIR 9-0 C Rutter (4) *trkd ldrs, al gng wl, led one and a half fs out, rdn out*..... (50 to 1 op 20 to 1) 1
AEROKING (USA) 9-0 Paul Eddery (5) *dwlt, sn trkd ldrs, rdn 2 fs out, ev ch ins last, no extr nr finish.* ....(6 to 4 op 6 to 4) 2
AFFIRM 9-0 T Quinn (6) *cl up, rdn o'r 2 fs out, one pace.* .... (12 to 1 op 4 to 1 tchd 14 to 1) 3
3569^{8} CHARLIE CHARLIE 9-0 A Tucker (2) *took keen hold, led till hdd one and a half fs out, one pace.* ....(25 to 1 op 16 to 1 tchd 33 to 1 and 50 to 1) 4
2364^{3} LAFTAH (USA) 9-0 M Roberts (1) *strted slwly, beh, hdwy to track ldrs o'r 4 fs out, shaken up over 2 out, eased whn hld ins last.* .... (11 to 8 fav op 5 to 4 on tchd 6 to 4) 5
FRUSTRATION 8-9 J Williams (7) *nvr on terms.* .... (16 to 1 op 8 to 1 tchd 20 to 1) 6
2866 HEALTHY RISK 9-0 J Quinn (8) *chsd ldrs, rdn alng o'r one furlong out, sn wknd*............ (50 to 1 op 20 to 1) 7
3792^{6} LADY GREY (Swe) 8-9 M Hills (10) *pld hrd, cl up 2 fs, sn drpd rear*.......................(50 to 1 op 20 to 1) 8
CORCOVADO 9-0 R Cochrane (3) *dwlt, al beh.* .... (16 to 1 op 5 to 1 tchd 20 to 1) 9
STEAM ON 9-0 M Wigham (9) *sn beh, tld off.* ....(33 to 1 op 14 to 1) 10
Dist: Nk, 2l, 1½l, nk, 3l, 4l, 3½l, 2½l, 15l. 1m 38.86s. a 10.56s (10 Ran).
(N D Bowyer), D J G Murray Smith

4004 AHJ 20th Anniversary Fillies' Conditions Stakes Class D (2-y-o) £3,377 6f ....(3:50)

984^{2} FRENCH GIFT 8-8 R Cochrane (6) *chsd ldg pair far side, hrd rdn and ran on to ld wl ins fnl furlong.* (11 to 4 co-fav op 2 to 1 tchd 3 to 1) 1
2748* SUAAD (Ire) 8-12 M Hills (1) *tacked across to far side, led aftr one furlong, hrd rdn o'r one out, hdd wl ins last.* ....(3 to 1 op 5 to 2) 2
3816* MARY HINGE 8-12 Paul Eddery (4) *rcd far side, sn rdn alng to chase ldr, ev ch und pres ins fnl furlong, not quicken*........ (11 to 4 co-fav op 5 to 2 tchd 2 to 1) 3
3765^{4} STAR SPEEDER (Ire) 8-7 (5*) B Russell (5) *rcd alone stands side, led one furlong, in tch till outpcd o'r 2 out.* ....(11 to 4 co-fav op 7 to 2) 4
AILEENS GIRL 8-8 J Williams (2) *outpcd, tld off.* .... (50 to 1 op 33 to 1) 5
Dist: ¾l, ¾l, 5l, 30l. 1m 13.61s. a 4.61s (5 Ran).
SR: 26/27/24/4/-/ (Raymond Tooth), D R C Elsworth

4005 Nicholson Graham & Jones Conditions Stakes Class D (3-y-o and up) £3,406 7f..................... (4:20)

3674^{5} SUMOTO 3-8-8 M Hills (5) *trkd ldr far side grp, quickened to ld one and a hlf fs out, ran on gmely und pres, jst hld on*................... (9 to 1 op 7 to 1 tchd 10 to 1) 1
3660* QUEEN'S VIEW (Fr) 3-9-3 M Roberts (2) *in tch far side, rdn alng o'r 2 fs out, ran on und pres ins last, jst fld.* ....(5 to 2 fav op 9 to 4 tchd 11 to 4) 2
3624^{9} SUNDAY'S HILL (v) 4-9-1 J Quinn (6) *led far side grp, ev ch o'r 2 fs out, kpt on one pace.* ....(16 to 1 op 14 to 1 tchd 20 to 1) 3

3885[6] YOUNG ERN 3-9-4 T Quinn (9) *rcd stands side, led o'r 2 fs out till hdd one and a half out, one pace.* ....(9 to 2 op 7 to 2 tchd 5 to 1) 4
3717[5] RUSTIC CRAFT (Ire) 3-9-4 R Cochrane (8) *rcd far side, hld up, effrt o'r 2 fs out, nvr on terms.* .... (5 to 1 op 4 to 1 tchd 11 to 2) 5
DESERT SHOT 3-9-0 B Raymond (3) *in tch far side, no hdwy frm o'r 2 fs out*.............. (7 to 1 op 5 to 1) 6
2698[3] KNOCK TO ENTER (USA) 5-8-12 J Williams (1) *al beh.* ....(6 to 1 tchd 13 to 2) 7
3885[9] ROCKY WATERS (USA) 4-9-2 B Rouse (7) *rcd stands side, led till hdd o'r 2 fs out, sn wknd*... (12 to 1 op 10 to 1) 8
AVENUE FOCH (Ire) 4-8-11 M Wigham (4) *outpcd and tld off*.................................(50 to 1 op 33 to 1) 9
Dist: Sht-hd, 3½l, ½l, ¾l, ½l, 5l, 7l, 20l. 1m 25.82s. a 5.12s (9 Ran).
SR: 59/67/54/55/53/47/30/13/-/ (Sir Philip Oppenheimer), G Wragg

4006 Courvoisier Napoleon Handicap Class D (0-80 3-y-o and up) £3,728 1 ¾m.......................... (4:50)

3761[2] SAFETY IN NUMBERS [62] 3-8-8 J Quinn (8) *trkd ldrs al gng wl, led well o'r one furlong out, quickened clr, imprsv*.............................(4 to 1 fav op 9 to 2) 1
3761[4] HARLESTONE BROOK [66] 3-8-12 Paul Eddery (1) *al prmnt, styd on wl und pres fnl 2 fs*...(7 to 1 op 6 to 1) 2
3706[2] FOOLS ERRAND (Ire) [67] 3-8-13 M Hills (12) *cl up, led hfwy, quickened o'r 2 fs out till hdd over one out, one pace*..................... (8 to 1 op 6 to 1 tchd 9 to 1) 3
3513[4] ABSENT RELATIVE [54] 5-8-10 B Rouse (7) *trkd ldrs, pushed alng and ev ch o'r 2 fs out, one pace.* ....(12 to 1 op 14 to 1) 4
3666[8] SIR THOMAS BEECHAM [65] 3-8-11 J Williams (10) *hld up, hdwy o'r 5 fs out, sn btn*...........(10 to 1 op 8 to 1) 5
3821[4] SINGING REPLY (USA) [37] 5-7-3[3] (7*) N Varley (4) *nvr nrr.* ....(20 to 1 op 16 to 1) 6
3044* RUNAWAY PETE (USA) [78] 3-9-10 T Quinn (3) *trkd ldrs till wknd und pres o'r 2 fs out.* ....(10 to 1 op 6 to 1 tchd 11 to 1) 7
3522* MAMARA REEF [68] 3-9-0 R Cochrane (9) *led to hfwy, cl up, ev ch 3 fs out, sn btn*.............(9 to 2 op 5 to 2) 8
3466 MOSHAAJIR (USA) [75] 3-9-2 (5*) K Rutter (11) *slwly into strd and beh, hdwy hfwy, btn 5 fs out.* ....(14 to 1 tchd 16 to 1) 9
3656[4] TEMPLE KNIGHT [56] 4-8-12 M Roberts (2) *hld up, shrtlvd effrt o'r 5 fs out*..................... (9 to 2 op 7 to 2) 10
3787 YOUNG FACT [50] 8-8-1 (5*) B Russell (6) *al beh, tld off.* ....(25 to 1 op 20 to 1) 11
Dist: 8l, 2½l, 4l, 2l, 1½l, sht-hd, 4l, 8l, 8l, 25l. 3m 14.43s. a 19.43s (11 Ran).
(Edwin N Cohen), Lady Herries

4007 Renown Stakes Limited Stakes Class E (0-70 3-y-o and up) £3,598 7f 140yds ....(5:20)

3558[6] LAUREL QUEEN (Ire) 5-8-9 T Quinn (9) *cl up, led 5 fs out, clr o'r one out, easily.* (11 to 4 fav op 2 to 1 tchd 3 to 1) 1
1730[7] ROCALITY 4-8-9 Paul Eddery (12) *chsd ldrs, hrd rdn o'r 2 fs out, styd on wl*........(8 to 1 op 6 to 1 tchd 9 to 1) 2
3393[4] MR NEVERMIND (Ire) 3-8-10 B Rouse (1) *trkd ldg pair, rdn and one pace fnl 2 fs*................ (6 to 1 op 5 to 1) 3
3837 CONFRONTER (v) 4-9-0 J Williams (5) *beh till ran on ins fnl furlong, nrst finish*............ (10 to 1 tchd 12 to 1) 4
3676[5] TARNSIDE ROSAL (v) 3-8-6[1] R Cochrane (3) *chsd ldrs, rdn and not imprsn fnl 2 fs*............(7 to 1 tchd 8 to 1) 5
3766 SPRING SAINT 4-9-0 S Raymont (7) *chsd ldrs, rdn 3 fs out, no imprsn*...........................(50 to 1 op 33 to 1) 6
3883[6] WAVE HILL 4-9-0 M Perrett (8) *hld up beh, nvr plcd to chal*.................... (7 to 1 op 6 to 1 tchd 8 to 1) 7
3292[7] WILD AND LOOSE 5-9-0 B Raymond (11) *sn pushed alng in rear, al beh*...... (16 to 1 op 12 to 1 tchd 20 to 1) 8
3219[3] CHAMPAGNE 'N ROSES 3-8-5 M Roberts (2) *led till hdd 5 fs out, cl up till wknd 3 out.* ....(11 to 2 op 5 to 1 tchd 6 to 1 and 13 to 2) 9
2113 DUTY SERGEANT (Ire) 4-8-7 (7*) Mark Denaro (4) *al beh.* ....(50 to 1 op 33 to 1) 10
3643[5] PRINCESS HAYLEY 3-8-5 M Hills (10) *trkd ldrs till wknd o'r 2 fs out*............ (10 to 1 op 7 to 1 tchd 12 to 1) 11
Dist: 5l, hd, 2½l, 2½l, ¾l, ½l, 1l, hd, 8l, 7l. 1m 34.14s. a 5.84s (11 Ran).
SR: 54/39/39/35/19/25/23/20/10/ (Laurel (Leisure) Limited), J Berry

4008 McCall Group Maiden Handicap Class E (0-70 3-y-o and up) £2,976 5f.. (5:50)

3734 COALISLAND [54] 3-9-5 (5*) B Russell (2) *rdn thrght, chsd ldrs, led one furlong out, drvn out.* (9 to 2 op 10 to 1) 1
3758[2] LITTLE OSBORNE (Ire) [44] (bl) 3-9-0 M Hills (1) *led till hdd one furlong out, kpt on.* ....(4 to 1 co-fav op 7 to 2 tchd 9 to 2) 2
3047 HARD ROCK MINER [33] 3-8-0[4] (7*) S Mulvey (6) *outpcd, rdn and hdwy o'r one furlong out, ran on ins last.* ....(50 to 1 op 33 to 1) 3
3661[7] SOPHISTICATED AIR [56] (bl) 3-9-12 R Cochrane (9) *tacked across to far side grp, hrd rdn o'r 2 fs out, ev ch one out, one pace*................(9 to 2 op 5 to 2 tchd 5 to 1) 4
2939[5] CHILI LADY [53] 3-9-9 T Quinn (3) *trkd ldrs, ev ch one furlong out, one pace.* ....(4 to 1 co-fav op 7 to 2 tchd 9 to 2) 5
3661[8] AVRIL ETOILE [50] 3-9-6 J Williams (8) *rcd stands side, effrt o'r 2 fs out, nvr on terms*......(4 to 1 co-fav op 7 to 2) 6
2939[8] AMBIVALENTATTITUDE [27] (bl) 3-7-11 J Quinn (5) *outpcd.* ....(33 to 1) 7
3099[7] BELTHORN [42] 4-9-0 S O'Gorman (4) *cl up till wknd wl o'r one furlong out*.................. (12 to 1 op 14 to 1) 8
3707 GAYNOR GOODMAN (Ire) [42] 3-8-12 M Perrett (7) *rcd stands side, sn outpcd, tld off*...... (14 to 1 op 6 to 1) 9
3584[6] DISTANT DYNASTY [30] 3-7-7 (7*) Wendy Jones (10) *rcd stands side, sn beh, tld off.* ....(25 to 1 op 20 to 1 tchd 33 to 1) 10
Dist: Nk, hd, 1½l, 1l, 4l, 3½l, nk, 10l, 20l. 1m 1.45s. a 4.55s (10 Ran).
SR: 39/28/16/33/26/7/ (P McKernan), R Ingram

LINGFIELD (A.W) (std)
Thursday September 16th
Going Correction: MINUS 0.20 sec. per fur.

4009 Hammersmith Selling Stakes Class G (2-y-o) £2,532 1m.............. (2:50)

3743[9] HERR TRIGGER (bl) 8-6 (5*) K Rutter (6) *slwly into strd and beh, pushed alng hfwy, hdwy 3 fs out, led entering last, sn clr*...................... (25 to 1 op 12 to 1) 1
3696[3] PRINCESS CARMEN (Ire) (bl) 8-6 R Cochrane (8) *prmnt, ev ch whn put head in air one furlong out, ran on nr finish*...(2 to 1 fav op 7 to 4 tchd 5 to 2 and 11 to 4) 2
3546[3] TSWANA (Ire) 8-11 B Raymond (5) *prmnt, led one and a half fs out till entering last, one pace.* ....(5 to 1 op 3 to 1) 3
3362[4] NOORAN 8-11 T Quinn (11) *rdn alng thrght, in rear till hdwy o'r 3 fs out, styd on one pace.* ....(15 to 2 op 6 to 1 tchd 8 to 1) 4
3841[4] ZORAHAYDA (Fr) 8-6 B Rouse (9) *outpcd in rear till ran on appr fnl furlong, nrst finish*........(15 to 2 op 8 to 1) 5
3870[8] ERRIS BOY (bl) 8-11 M Roberts (3) *led till hdd one and a half fs out, wknd quickly.* .... (10 to 1 op 12 to 1 tchd 8 to 1) 6
3829[5] KNIGHTRIDER 8-11 J Quinn (10) *chsd ldrs till wknd o'r 3 fs out*...................................... (10 to 1) 7
3664[6] GIGUE 8-6 Paul Eddery (2) *cl up, rdn alng o'r 4 fs out, wknd und pres over 2 out*...........(10 to 1 op 7 to 1) 8
3546[9] LUCKY HELEN 8-6 G Hind (12) *rcd wide, prmnt till rdn alng o'r 4 fs out, sn wknd*......... (50 to 1 op 16 to 1) 9
3641 ROCKABYE BAILEYS 8-6 M Wigham (4) *sn pushed alng, al beh*.............................(25 to 1 op 16 to 1) 10
3658 PACIOLI 8-11 J Williams (7) *al beh.* ....(14 to 1 op 12 to 1 tchd 16 to 1) 11
3264[5] MR MYSTICAL (Ire) (bl) 8-4 (7*) Mark Denaro (1) *wtd wth, beh ldrs till lost pl quickly appr hfwy, tld off.* ....(10 to 1 op 6 to 1) 12
Dist: 4l, 5l, 2l, 4l, 2½l, 2l, hd, 2½l, hd, 2l. 1m 39.95s. a 3.75s (12 Ran).
SR: 17/-/-/-/-/-/ (Mrs Corinne Fleming), Dr J D Scargill

MAISONS-LAFFITTE (FR) (heavy)
Thursday September 16th
Going Correction: PLUS 0.40 sec. per fur.

4010 Prix de Seine-et-Oise (Group 3) (4-y-o and up) £23,895 6f............. (3:10)

3196[5] DOLPHIN STREET (Fr) 3-8-11 C Asmussen (8) *hld up, pld out o'r 2 fs out, led jst ins fnl furlong, ran on wl.* ....(114 to 10) 1
1289* VOLERIS (Fr) 4-9-2 F Sanchez (9) *trkd ldr, led one and a half furlong out till ins last*..................(16 to 1) 2
3162[3] MIDHISH 3-8-11 W R Swinburn (7) *mid-div, hdwy 2 fs out, ev ch o'r one out, kpt on one pace*............(10 to 1) 3
3015[3] MATELOT (USA) 3-8-11 T Jarnet (5) *mid-div, swtchd outsd 2 and a half fs out, hdwy to chal two out, wknd fnl furlong*.................................(21 to 10 fav) 4
3619* KASHANI (USA) 3-8-11 Pat Eddery (2) *prmnt, rdn 2 fs out, sn one pace*..................................(5 to 2) 5
3717[8] DANAKAL (USA) 3-8-11 G Mosse (10) *mid-div and not clr run 3 fs out, some late hdwy*................(58 to 10) 6
3414[2] CRACK REGIMENT (USA) 5-9-0 E Saint-Martin (6) *in tch till wknd wl o'r one furlong out*..................(14 to 1) 7
3619[5] DREAM TALK (bl) 6-9-4 D Boeuf (3) *led for o'r 4 fs.* ....(89 to 10) 8
3717[4] ARRANVANNA 5-8-13 Jacqueline Freda (1) *in tch whn hng lft 2 fs out, sn btn*..........................(19 to 1) 9
KENTUCKY COFFEE (Fr) (bl) 5-9-0 O Peslier (4) *trkd ldrs till wknd 2 fs out*...............................(89 to 10) 0
3619[2] TENGA (USA) 3-8-8 W Mongil (11) *al beh*.........(16 to 1) 0
Dist: 2l, 2½l, 1l, 2½l, nk, ½l, sht-nk, ½l, 1½l. 1m 13.10s. a 3.60s (11 Ran).
SR: 73/70/55/51/41/40/41/44/37/ (S S Niarchos), J E Hammond

YARMOUTH (good to soft)
Thursday September 16th

Going Correction: PLUS 0.25 sec. per fur.

4011 EBF Courage Gorleston Maiden Fillies' Stakes Class D (2-y-o) £4,464 6f 3yds.......................... (2:30)

GLIMPSE 8-11 J Weaver (6) *steadied strt, gng wl but not clr run 2 fs out, squeezed through fnl furlong, led post.* .... (12 to 1 op 7 to 1) 1
RAKNAH (Ire) 8-11 M Tebbutt (4) *al wl plcd, led on bit 2 fs out, ran on, jst ct*........(9 to 2 op 3 to 1 tchd 5 to 2) 2
3156[7] BRADWELL (Ire) 8-11 P Robinson (7) *al hndy, effrt and bustled alng o'r one furlong out, crowded ins last, kpt on*.............................. (33 to 1 op 20 to 1) 3
3586[6] GREAT TRIVIALITY 8-8 (3*) B Doyle (3) *nvr far away, hrd at work o'r one furlong out, kpt on towards finish.* ....(11 to 4 fav op 7 to 2 tchd 5 to 2) 4
TANSY 8-11 F Norton (5) *missed break, drvn into midfield hfwy, styd on und pres, nvr nrr.* .... (11 to 2 op 7 to 2 tchd 6 to 1) 5
3765[6] GILBERTINA (USA) 8-11 W Ryan (8) *tried to make all, hdd 2 fs out, wndrd and hmpd ins last, eased whn btn.* ....(9 to 2 op 6 to 1 tchd 4 to 1) 6
BEAMING 8-11 L Dettori (2) *settled midfield, effrt und pres o'r 2 fs out, not quicken.* ....(8 to 1 op 6 to 1 tchd 9 to 1) 7
3813[5] PRISCILLA ROSE 8-11 N Carlisle (1) *speed on outsd for o'r 3 fs, wknd quickly*... (10 to 1 tchd 12 to 1 and 8 to 1) 8
Dist: Sht-hd, ½l, 1l, ½l, 1½l, sht-hd, 12l. 1m 16.70s. a 5.70s (8 Ran).
SR: 13/12/10/6/4/ (G Keller), L M Cumani

4012 Fosters Breydon Water Handicap Class E (0-70 3-y-o and up) £3,366 6f 3yds.......................... (3:00)

3778[2] FACE THE FUTURE [65] 4-10-0 P Robinson (5) *settled travelling wl, brst through to ld ins fnl furlong, ran on well*...............................(4 to 1 op 11 to 4) 1
3692[4] MOVING IMAGE (Ire) [54] 3-9-0 C Dwyer (7) *nvr far away, ev ch and rdn ins fnl furlong, kpt on same pace.* ....(9 to 2 op 7 to 2) 2
3481[7] PURBECK CENTENARY [55] 3-9-1 W Ryan (6) *tried to make all, clr 2 fs out, wknd and hdd ins fnl furlong, no extr.* .... (12 to 1 op 7 to 1) 3
3310[9] VERRO (USA) [30] (bl) 6-7-7 G Bardwell (8) *scrubbed alng thrght, styd on grimly ins fnl furlong, nvr nrr.* .... (33 to 1 op 25 to 1) 4
3839[5] NOBLE RISK [66] 3-9-12 L Dettori (2) *co'red up, flttered und pres over one furlong out, found little.* ....(3 to 1 fav op 5 to 1) 5
3745[2] RESTORE [46] (bl) 10-8-9 R Price (3) *nvr far away, hrd at work last 2 fs, one pace*............. (7 to 1 tchd 8 to 1) 6
A LITTLE PRECIOUS [47] 7-8-10 S Whitworth (4) *last and outpcd most of way, styd on grimly fnl furlong, nvr nrr*................... (20 to 1 op 16 to 1 tchd 25 to 1) 7
3942[2] LETSBEONESTABOUTIT [64] (v) 7-9-6 (7*) E Husband (1) *drvn alng the whole way, nvr a factor.* ....(9 to 2 op 3 to 1) 8
Dist: 1½l, 1½l, nk, hd, ½l, 1½l, 10l. 1m 15.60s. a 4.60s (8 Ran).
SR: 52/32/27/4/36/17/12/-/ (Mrs P W Harris), P W Harris

4013 Great Yarmouth Stayers Handicap Class C (0-95 3-y-o and up) £5,628 2¼m 51yds..................... (3:30)

3599[2] PROVENCE [72] 6-8-7 W Ryan (2) *track ldr, styd centre in strt, led o'r 2 fs out, kpt on strly.* .... (9 to 1 op 6 to 1 tchd 10 to 1) 1
3861[3] JACK BUTTON (Ire) [93] 4-10-0 M Tebbutt (3) *nvr far away, drvn up to fltter o'r one furlong out, not quicken towards finish*....................(5 to 1 tchd 11 to 2) 2
3538[3] MISS PLUM [80] 4-9-1 L Dettori (1) *trkd ldg quartet, bustled alng o'r 2 fs out, styd on.* ....(9 to 2 op 5 to 1 tchd 11 to 2 and 4 to 1) 3
3479* SUN GREBE (Ire) [77] 3-7-12 D Biggs (6) *patiently rdn, last strt, feeling pace o'r 2 fs out, rallied.* ....(6 to 4 fav op 7 to 4 tchd 9 to 4) 4
3125 RUSTY REEL [72] 3-7-7 G Bardwell (4) *led, styd alone far side in strt, hdd o'r 2 fs out, fdd*... (40 to 1 op 20 to 1) 5
3319[5] GREEN LANE (USA) [74] 5-8-9 S Whitworth (7) *trkd ldrs, crossed o'r to race alone stands side in strt, no imprsn last 2 fs*.......................... (6 to 1 op 9 to 2) 6
3690* AUDE LA BELLE (Fr) [72] 5-8-7 L Piggott (5) *wtd wth, improved into midfield hfwy, fdd last 2 fs.* .... (11 to 2 op 9 to 2) 7
Dist: 3l, 1½l, ½l, 7l, hd, 4l. 4m 10.60s. a 9.60s (7 Ran).
SR: 43/61/46/28/16/31/25/ (Mrs P W Harris), P W Harris

4014 EBF John Smiths Hastings Maiden Stakes Class D (2-y-o) £4,464 1m 3yds ....(4:00)

3592[2] FLORID (USA) 9-0 W Ryan (2) *rcd keenly on outsd, led o'r 3 fs out, sprinted clr, imprsv.* (4 to 1 on op 7 to 2 on tchd 3 to 1 on and 5 to 1 on) 1
DARONNE 9-0 J Weaver (4) *settled aftr fst break, drvn alng last 3 fs, kpt on, no ch wth wnr.* (9 to 1 op 7 to 1) 2
3836[5] ROUSAY 8-11 (3*) B Doyle (7) *al hndy, struggling whn pace quickened o'r 2 fs out, no imprsn.* ....(9 to 1 op 6 to 1) 3
3742[7] KHATIR (Can) 9-0 M Tebbutt (6) *patiently rdn, not much room and lost grnd o'r 2 fs out, rallied fnl furlong.* ....(25 to 1 op 16 to 1) 4
3592 TRANS SIBERIA 9-0 W Woods (5) *narrow ld on stands rls till o'r 3 fs out, btn 2 furlongs out.* (66 to 1 op 33 to 1) 5
3833 DOUBLING DICE 9-0 P D'Arcy (1) *settled midfield, rdn whn pace lifted o'r 2 fs out, sn btn.* (25 to 1 op 14 to 1) 6
BOLD FLAME 9-0 G Bardwell (3) *missed break, outpcd and drvn alng hfwy, nvr a factor*..... (66 to 1 op 33 to 1) 7
Dist: 5l, 4l, 3l, nk, 1½l, 2l. 1m 42.60s. a 6.80s (7 Ran).
SR: 28/13/1/-/ (Lord Howard de Walden), H R A Cecil

4015 Lottie And Albert Botton Memorial Nursery Class D (2-y-o) £4,012 1m 3yds......................... (4:30)

3743* BENFLEET [62] 7-10 D Biggs (2) *trkd ldrs centre, rdn and edgd rght 2 fs out, styd on to ld entering fnl furlong, drvn out*........................ (14 to 1 op 8 to 1) 1
3554[3] PAVAKA [74] (v) 8-8 L Dettori (6) *trkd ldrs stands side, effrt and edgd lft o'r 2 fs out, rallied fnl furlong, ran on.* ....(5 to 1 op 7 to 1) 2
3829* MR ROUGH [59] 7-6[6] (7*,5ex) C Hawksley (8) *sluggish strt, reco'red to ld over 2 fs out, hdd entering last, one pace.* ....(7 to 1 op 8 to 1) 3
3865[2] BALI WARRIOR (Ire) [69] 8-0 (3*) M Fenton (4) *co'red up centre, squeezed out and baulked over 2 fs out, rallied fnl furlong, nvr nrr.* ....(6 to 5 fav op 7 to 4 tchd 11 to 10) 4
3763[5] THE FLYING PHANTOM [84] 9-4 P Robinson (1) *chsd alng centre, slightly hmpd and swtchd o'r 2 fs out, rng on finish*.................(14 to 1 op 8 to 1 tchd 16 to 1) 5
3406[8] GINGERBIRD (Ire) [73] 8-7 W Ryan (9) *led stands side, hrd at work and hdd o'r 2 fs out, sn btn* .... (12 to 1 op 8 to 1 tchd 14 to 1) 6
3698[4] ONE WILD OAT [74] 8-8 L Piggott (5) *made most centre till o'r 2 fs out, sn btn*..................(10 to 1 op 8 to 1) 7
3406[9] BUMAAN (Ire) [87] 9-7 N Carlisle (3) *broke wl centre, struggling whn slightly hmpd o'r 2 fs out, sn btn.* .... (25 to 1 op 12 to 1) 8
3659[6] ROSE CIEL (Ire) [79] 8-13 W Woods (7) *wth ldr stands side for o'r 5 fs, wknd quickly*..........(10 to 1 op 7 to 1) 9
Dist: ½l, 1l, nk, 2½l, 10l, 3l, ½l, 8l. 1m 42.70s. a 6.90s (9 Ran).
SR: 9/19/1/10/17/-/ (C G Donovan), R W Armstrong

4016 Miller Pilsner Yarmouth Roads Maiden Handicap Class F (0-60 3-y-o and up) £3,652 1m 3yds.........(5:00)

3631[5] CLAIRIFICATION (Ire) [44] 3-8-13 P Robinson (9) *chsd alng to improve on wide outsd o'r 2 fs out, led entering fnl furlong, drvn out*..............(3 to 1 fav op 5 to 1) 1
3102[9] KALOKAGATHOS [25] 4-7-12 D Biggs (11) *drvn alng to improve frm off the pace o'r 2 fs out, fnshd strly.* .... (20 to 1 op 25 to 1) 2
2859[6] MARY MACBLAIN [34] 4-8-7 M Tebbutt (5) *squeezed out strt, weaved through last 2 fs, fnshd wl.* ....(8 to 1 tchd 7 to 1) 3
3766 ASCOM PAGER TOO [40] 3-8-9 B Crossley (7) *al hndy, nosed ahead 2 fs out, hdd entering fnl furlong, one pace*.......................... (25 to 1 tchd 33 to 1) 4
3588[4] DARING KING [46] 3-9-1 L Dettori (14) *trkd ldr stands side, ev ch and rdn o'r 2 fs out, kpt on same pace.* .... (6 to 1 tchd 11 to 2 and 7 to 1) 5
3745[8] FRIENDLY SMILE [38] (bl) 3-8-7 J Weaver (15) *steadied strt, weaved through frm off the pace to flttr o'r one furlong out, not quicken*............. (12 to 1 op 8 to 1) 6
3533[3] DUBAI SUMMER [56] (bl) 3-9-11 W Woods (13) *led stands side, drvn alng o'r one furlong out, no extr.* ....(8 to 1 op 6 to 1) 7
3744[6] LITTLE PARK [33] 4-8-1 (5*) L Newton (4) *bustled alng in midfield, no imprsn last 2 fs.* ....(16 to 1 op 14 to 1 tchd 20 to 1) 8
1875[7] PYTCHLEY DAWN [48] 3-9-3 N Carlisle (16) *unruly in stalls, drvn alng in midfield, kpt on, not pace to chal.* ....(16 to 1) 9
3574[7] MOUJEEB (USA) [42] (v) 3-8-4 (7*) P McCabe (3) *made most centre for 6 fs, fdd*.................(11 to 1 op 8 to 1) 10
3726[4] MUSTAKIM (Ire) [59] 3-10-0 R Price (1) *chsd alng to go pace hfwy, nvr a threat*............. (7 to 1 op 5 to 1) 11
3789 RISK THE WITCH [30] 3-7-12[2] (3*) M Fenton (10) *bustled alng to chase ldrs for o'r 5 fs, fdd.* (33 to 1 op 20 to 1) 12
3591 RIVER FIRE (Ire) [34] (v) 3-8-3 F Norton (8) *drvn alng in midfield hfwy, sn outpcd*..........(33 to 1 op 20 to 1) 13
3699[7] COUNT BARACHOIS (USA) [36] 5-8-6 (3*) C Hodgson (2) *wth ldr centre till wknd last 2 fs.* ....(20 to 1 tchd 25 to 1 and 16 to 1) 14
3794[9] GATE OF HEAVEN [26] 3-7-9[5] (3*) B Doyle (12) *drvn alng to go pace, nvr a factor*..........................(33 to 1) 15
3896 OLIVIA VAL [35] 3-8-4 G Bardwell (6) *beh and rdn hfwy, nvr a threat*...........(8 to 1 op 10 to 1 tchd 6 to 1) 16
Dist: Nk, 2½l, ½l, nk, ½l, 3½l, nk, 3½l, ½l, 4l. 1m 44.00s. a 8.20s (16 Ran).
SR: 6/-/-/-/-/-/ (Mrs S Hallam), J Wharton

AYR (good to firm)
Friday September 17th
Going Correction: MINUS 0.30 sec. per fur. (races 1,2,3,6,7), MINUS 0.45 (4,5)

4017 Kilkerran Amateur Riders' Conditions Stakes Class G (4-y-o and up) £2,814 1 ¼m 192yds.................... (2:00)

3645^{3} VRATISLAV (USA) 4-10-12 Mrs L Pearce (8) *trkd ldrs, prog to ld 2 fs out, quickened clr, ran on strly, easily.* ....(10 to 3 on op 4 to 1 on tchd 3 to 1 on) 1
2801^{7} TRUBEN (USA) 4-10-9 Mr M Buckley (7) *pressed ldr 3 fs, effrt and ev ch 2 furlongs out, no chance wth wnr.* ....(12 to 1 op 10 to 1 tchd 14 to 1) 2
3814* AMERICAN HERO 5-11-1 Mr S Swiers (3) *led 3 fs, led ag'n entering strt, hdd and wknd 2 out.* (5 to 1 tchd 6 to 1) 3
1531^{8} PERSUASIVE 6-10-10 (5*) Miss L Robertson (2) *beh, prog o'r 2 fs out, ran on wl ins last.*.... (16 to 1 op 14 to 1) 4
1056^{8} ONE FOR THE POT 8-10-12 Mrs A Farrell (5) *al mid-div, kpt on one pace in strt.*............ (66 to 1 op 50 to 1) 5
2761^{2} FLING IN SPRING 7-10-12 Mr J Bradburne (10) *trkd ldrs till wknd entering strt*...........................(50 to 1) 6
470^{5} NEGD (USA) 3-10-0 (5*) Mrs D Kettlewell (4) *al rear.* ....(16 to 1 tchd 20 to 1) 7
3551 MISS RIBBONS 3-9-9 (5*) Miss S Chittenden (1) *al rear.* ....(200 to 1) 8
2347 MEESON CODE 6-10-7 (5*) Mr V Lukaniuk (9) *led aftr 3 fs till hdd entering strt, rdn and wknd 2 out*....(500 to 1) 9
VERBAL WARNING 5-10-7 (5*) Miss S Storey (6) *in tch till wknd appr strt, tld off*........(500 to 1 op 1000 to 1) 10

Dist: 5l, 10l, nk, 5l, 8l, hd, 3l, 2l, 20l. 2m 18.76s. a 4.76s (10 Ran).
SR: 46/33/19/18/5/-/ (Sheikh Mohammed), J H M Gosden

4018 EBF Inheritress Fillies' Handicap Class C (0-90 3-y-o and up) £10,796 1 ¼m.......................... (2:35)

3514^{5} TAP ON AIR [77] 3-9-8 K Darley (5) *hld up mid-div, prog o'r 2 fs out, rdn to ld ins last, readily.* ....(4 to 1 fav op 5 to 1) 1
3469^{2} NO COMEBACKS [55] 5-8-6 K Fallon (1) *dwlt, rear till prog entering strt, effrt 2 fs out, led briefly ins last, sn hdd and no extr*.....................................(12 to 1) 2
3670^{3} QUEEN WARRIOR [71] 4-9-3 (5*) D Wright (6) *in tch in rear, cld up 2 fs out, kpt on ins last*...... (11 to 2 op 5 to 1) 3
3674^{4} SILVERLOCKS [82] 3-9-13 N Connorton (10) *al prmnt, effrt 2 fs out, ev ch ins last, no extr*.....(6 to 1 tchd 7 to 1) 4
3757 SEASONAL SPLENDOUR (Ire) [70] 3-9-1 D Biggs (4) *al prmnt, effrt 2 fs out, ch ins last, styd on*.......(20 to 1) 5
3185* SEROTINA (Ire) [72] (bl) 3-8-10 (7*) D Gibbs (9) *rear, prog o'r 2 fs out, no imprsn fnl furlong*.......(9 to 1 op 7 to 1) 6
3431^{6} BAY QUEEN [83] 3-9-11 (3*) M Fenton (2) *trkd ldrs, led o'r 2 fs out, hdd and not quicken ins last.* ....(10 to 1 op 8 to 1) 7
3883^{3} GOOGLY [73] 4-9-10 M Hills (7) *in tch, effrt o'r 2 fs out, sn rdn and btn*.........................(11 to 2 op 5 to 1) 8
3444^{2} TANODA [43] 7-7-8^{1} J Lowe (8) *chsd up into ld, hdd and wknd o'r 2 fs out*............... (14 to 1 tchd 12 to 1) 9
3637 SPARK (Ire) [75] 3-9-3 (3*) S Maloney (3) *trkd ldrs, effrt o'r 2 fs out, sn wknd*......................... (20 to 1 op 16 to 1) 10
3818^{3} BALIANA [68] 3-8-13 A Culhane (11) *trkd ldr, effrt and ev ch 2 fs out, sn rdn and wknd quickly.* .... (33 to 1 op 25 to 1) 11

Dist: 1½l, ½l, ¾l, hd, 1l, sht-hd, 1½l, 3½l, 3½l, 12l. 2m 7.49s. a 2.49s (11 Ran).
SR: 53/34/49/52/39/39/49/42/-/ (Sheikh Mohammed), M R Stoute

4019 Ladbroke Ayrshire Handicap Class C (0-90 3-y-o and up) £14,720 1m. . (3:05)

3726^{2} WAINWRIGHT (USA) [79] 4-9-7 W R Swinburn (4) *mid-div, 7th strt, cld up 2 fs out, led briefly o'r one out, sn rdn, styd on to ld ag'n last strd*..........(11 to 2 op 6 to 1) 1
3812^{2} ARAK (USA) [66] 5-8-8 J Weaver (6) *led, rdn and hdd briefly o'r one furlong out, led ag'n till headed fnl strd.* ....(5 to 1 op 7 to 1) 2
3973^{2} DANCING BEAU (Ire) [55] 4-7-8 (3*) N Kennedy (7) *in tch, prog 2 fs out, styd on ins last*................ (10 to 1) 3
3812 HARPOON LOUIE (USA) [75] 3-8-13 K Darley (9) *trkd ldr, second strt, ev ch o'r one furlong out, wknd ins last.* ....(16 to 1 op 14 to 1) 4
3791^{5} MOON SPIN [84] 4-9-12 Paul Eddery (3) *trkd ldrs, 5th strt, effrt 2 fs out, wknd o'r one out*.... (14 to 1 op 12 to 1) 5
3747^{7} SPANISH VERDICT [69] 6-8-11 K Fallon (12) *trkd ldrs, 3rd strt, kpt on one pace fnl 2 fs*.....(20 to 1 op 16 to 1) 6
3780 NO SUBMISSION (USA) [62] 7-8-4 J Fanning (11) *rear, prog o'r 2 fs out, not get on terms*......(25 to 1 op 20 to 1) 7
3812^{5} IMPERIAL BID (Fr) [68] 5-8-10 M Birch (15) *rear, prog 2 fs out, not rch ldrs*..............................(33 to 1) 8
3901 HABETA (USA) [58] 7-8-0 J Lowe (8) *in tch, no imprsn in strt*............................ (16 to 1 tchd 20 to 1) 9
3726 DOUBLE ECHO (Ire) [67] (v) 5-8-9 J Carroll (13) *trkd ldrs, 4th strt, wknd 2 fs out*...................(25 to 1 op 20 to 1) 10
3783^{4} TABKIR (USA) [80] 3-9-4 W Carson (10) *trkd ldrs, 6th strt, wknd o'r 2 fs out*... (11 to 4 fav op 5 to 2 tchd 3 to 1) 11
3774 HOME COUNTIES (Ire) [86] 4-9-9 (5*) Darren Moffatt (1) *al rear*..(100 to 1) 12
3747^{8} TAKENHALL [54] 8-7-10 L Charnock (2) *in tch, till wknd 3 fs out*............................(14 to 1 op 10 to 1) 13
3850^{9} WORDS OF WISDOM (Ire) [76] 3-9-0 M Hills (14) *rear, effrt o'r 2 fs out, sn btn*............................ (25 to 1) 14
3631^{2} PREMIER STAR [58] (bl) 3-7-10 D Biggs (5) *pld hrd, hld up mid-div, wknd o'r 2 fs out*........................(12 to 1) 15

Dist: Hd, 2l, 2½l, ¾l, ½l, nk, sht-hd, 1l, 1½l, sht-hd. 1m 38.12s. a 0.42s (15 Ran).
SR: 65/51/34/42/53/36/28/33/20/ (Sheikh Mohammed), J H M Gosden

4020 Shadwell Stud Firth Of Clyde Stakes Class A (Listed Race) (2-y-o) £18,269 6f............................ (3:35)

3751* BRAARI (USA) 8-8 W Carson (1) *trkd ldr, led one and a half fs out, hng rght ins last, rdn out.* ....(7 to 4 fav op 2 to 1) 1
3635^{2} KNAYTON LASS 8-8 T Lucas (3) *hld up, cld up o'r one furlong out, ev ch ins last, kpt on.* (20 to 1 op 16 to 1) 2
3502* RANDONNEUR (Ire) 8-8 G Hind (5) *cld up 2 fs out, consistantly denied clr run and checked ins last.* ....(25 to 1 op 16 to 1) 3
3428* ONE ON ONE 8-8 M Hills (2) *led till one and a half fs out, hng rght ins last, checked and no ch aftr.* ....(9 to 4 op 2 to 1) 4
3845^{3} MONAASSABAAT (USA) 8-8 W R Swinburn (4) *wth ldr, rdn o'r one furlong out, no imprsn whn badly hmpd ins last*............................. (2 to 1 tchd 9 to 4) 5

Dist: Nk, 1½l, 3½l, 4l. 1m 10.62s. b 0.28s (5 Ran).
SR: 46/45/39/25/9/ (Hamdan Al-Maktoum), B W Hills

4021 Ladbroke Racing Nursery Class D (2-y-o) £3,745 6f.................. (4:05)

3902^{5} NO MEAN CITY (Ire) [68] (bl) 8-6 A Mackay (6) *made all, rdn out fnl furlong*.................................. (8 to 1) 1
3406 CLOSE TO REALITY [80] 9-4 K Fallon (7) *chsd ldr through out, ev ch ins last, no extr*...... (9 to 4 fav op 7 to 2) 2
3715* GREY TOPPA [66] 7-13 (5*) Darren Moffatt (4) *trkd ldrs, effrt o'r one furlong out, sn rdn and wknd.* ....(9 to 2 op 7 to 2 tchd 5 to 1) 3
3792^{2} A MILLION WATTS [72] 8-10 W Carson (8) *sn pushed alng, nvr on terms*........... (9 to 2 op 7 to 2 tchd 5 to 1) 4
2630^{7} LANCASHIRE LIFE (Ire) [57] 7-4 (5*) D Wright (3) *beh, some prog o'r 2 fs out, sn btn*..........(20 to 1 tchd 25 to 1) 5+
3386^{9} MILLICENT NORTH [78] 9-2 Paul Eddery (1) *rear, some prog o'r 2 fs out, sn btn*...............(10 to 1 op 8 to 1) 5+
3115^{4} BEST KEPT SECRET [83] 9-7 J Carroll (5) *chsd ldrs, rdn and wknd o'r 2 fs out*............(5 to 1 tchd 11 to 2) 7
2974^{9} LUCKY FOURTEEN [68] (bl) 8-6 J Fanning (2) *rdn and btn hfwy*.......................................(25 to 1) 8

Dist: 1½l, 3½l, 1½l, 3½l, dd-ht, 3l, 10l. 1m 10.71s. b 0.19s (8 Ran).
SR: 42/48/20/20/-/12/5/-/ (Mrs M O'Donnell), A Bailey

4022 Brodick Claiming Stakes Class G (3-y-o and up) £3,048 1m.......... (4:35)

3712^{5} BATTLE COLOURS (Ire) 4-8-12 K Darley (6) *made all, wnt clr entering strt, kpt on wl*...........(3 to 1 op 5 to 2) 1
3811^{6} DRUMDONNA (Ire) 3-7-9 N Carlisle (10) *chsd ldr through out, 3rd strt, no imprsn fnl 2 fs*..................(14 to 1) 2
3780 LOMBARD SHIPS (bl) 6-7-11 A Mackay (13) *rear, prog 3 fs out, styd on ins last, nrst finish.* ....(9 to 4 fav op 5 to 2 tchd 11 to 4) 3
3747 ROCK OPERA (Ire) (v) 5-7-12^{1} (5*) D McCabe (15) *rear, last strt, prog 2 fs out, styd on wl ins last.* ....(10 to 1 op 8 to 1) 4
2681^{2} RUNRIG (Ire) 3-7-13 J Fanning (7) *prmnt, 7th strt, chsd ldrs frm 2 fs out, no imprsn*........... (14 to 1 op 12 to 1) 5+
2371^{9} PANTHER (Ire) 3-8-1 (3*) N Kennedy (9) *prmnt, 6th strt, kpt on one pace fnl 2 fs*...........................(33 to 1) 5+
3812 MATTS BOY 5-7-13 (3*) S Maloney (3) *nvr on terms, nrst finish*.............................(20 to 1 tchd 25 to 1) 7
3794^{7} PAULINUS 5-8-2 L Charnock (12) *al mid-div*..... (66 to 1) 8
3812^{8} AFFORDABLE 5-9-0 Paul Eddery (1) *rear, some prog o'r 2 fs out, sn btn*.........................(8 to 1 op 7 to 1) 9
3727^{9} BOLD STAR 3-8-10 W Carson (5) *prmnt, 8th strt, wknd o'r 2 fs out*.............. (10 to 1 op 8 to 1 tchd 12 to 1) 10
3632^{5} GOLD DESIRE 3-7-11 (5*) J Marshall (11) *prmnt, 5th strt, wknd o'r 2 fs out*................................. (50 to 1) 11
3656 PALACE MAN (USA) 5-8-3 (7*) S Drowne (8) *rear, rdn o'r 2 fs out, nvr dngrs*.................... (100 to 1 op 50 to 1) 12
ANNE'S BAY (Ire) 3-7-5^{1} (5*) Darren Moffatt (4) *trkd ldrs, 4th strt, wknd o'r 2 fs out*...........................(100 to 1) 13
2993^{9} MONTONE (Ire) 3-8-6 A Culhane (14) *al beh.* ....(20 to 1 op 16 to 1) 14
3788 DESIRABLE MISS (v) 3-7-8^{1} J Lowe (2) *prmnt to hfwy, sn wknd*.. (33 to 1) 15

Dist: 2½l, 1½l, ¾l, ¾l, dd-ht, 3½l, 5l, 1½l, ½l, 4l. 1m 38.71s. a 1.01s (15 Ran).
SR: 47/22/19/22/17/22/9/-/1/ (Garth Insoll), Sir Mark Prescott

4023 Eglinton & Winton Handicap Class D (0-75 3-y-o and up) £4,299 2m 1f 105yds. . . . . (5:05)

3872* HUNTING GROUND [54] (bl) 5-9-4 (3ex) W Carson (5) *al prmnt, led hfwy, drw clr frm 3 fs out, eased ins last.* ....(5 to 1 op 9 to 2) 1
3821⁹ SERAPHIM (Fr) [38] 4-8-2 K Darley (4) *prmnt, prog to track ldr 5 fs out, kpt on one pace frm 3 out.* ....(14 to 1 op 12 to 1) 2
3716³ CHANTRY BARTLE [43] 7-8-7 J Fanning (2) *prmnt, prog and 3rd into strt, kpt on one pace.* (8 to 1 tchd 9 to 1) 3
3716⁶ MINGUS (USA) [38] 6-8-2 J Lowe (6) *rear to hfwy, prog and 4th into strt, kpt on one pace.* (14 to 1 op 10 to 1) 4
3821* BRIGGSMAID [52] 5-9-2 (3ex) M Tebbutt (1) *settled beh, prog 5 fs out, 6th strt, sn rdn, no imprsn last 2 furlongs.* ....(9 to 4 fav op 5 to 2 tchd 11 to 4) 5
3716⁴ BILBERRY [39] 4-8-0 (3*) N Kennedy (10) *in tch, prog and 5th strt, sn rdn and kpt on one pace.* ....(8 to 1 tchd 9 to 1) 6
3716² JAWANI (Ire) [55] (v) 5-9-0 (5*) K Rutter (3) *trkd ldr, pushed alng whn lost pl quickly 7 fs out, no dngr aftr.* ....(5 to 1 op 4 to 1) 7
3716⁹ SEXY MOVER [30] 6-7-8¹ L Charnock (11) *trkd ldr till wknd 6 fs out*....................(33 to 1) 8
3599 ROLLING THE BONES (USA) [50] 4-8-9 (5*) D McCabe (8) *led to hfwy, wknd 5 fs out*.......... (25 to 1 op 16 to 1) 9
3821⁸ MELODY MOUNTAIN (Ire) [64] 4-10-0 M Birch (7) *in tch till wknd 4 fs out*....... (12 to 1 op 14 to 1 tchd 16 to 1) 10

Dist: 3½l, 2l, 1½l, sht-hd, 2½l, 12l, 10l, 12l, 8l. 3m 47.65s. a 3.65s (10 Ran).
SR: 15/-/-/-/4/-/ (Esprit de Corps Racing), A Bailey

NEWBURY (good to soft) Friday September 17th

Going Correction: PLUS 0.30 sec. per fur.

4024 Winchester Asset Management Handicap Class C (0-90 3-y-o and up) £5,816 7f 64yds. . . . . (2:05)

3957⁴ KIMBERLEY PARK [59] 5-7-11 (3*) B Doyle (12) *hld up, hdwy o'r 2 fs out, led appr last, pushed out.* ....(10 to 1 tchd 12 to 1) 1
3837⁸ TONY'S MIST [67] 3-7-11 (7*) A Whelan (5) *wl beh, hdwy o'r one furlong out, weaved through to take second nr finish*....................(25 to 1 op 12 to 1) 2
3665³ FRIENDLY BRAVE (USA) [72] 3-8-9 J Reid (4) *hld up, slightly hmpd o'r 2 fs out, styd on ins last.* ....(12 to 1 op 25 to 1) 3
3885² GHOST TREE (Ire) [84] 3-9-7 M Roberts (7) *hld up, ran on ins fnl 2 fs, one pace nr finish.* ....(9 to 2 op 5 to 1 tchd 11 to 2) 4
2237⁶ SHARP PROSPECT [77] 3-9-0 W Ryan (11) *al prmnt, led briefly one and a half fs out, rdn and no extr ins last.* ....(14 to 1 op 10 to 1 tchd 16 to 1) 5
3783² RAKIS (Ire) [80] (bl) 3-9-3 R Hills (3) *led aftr one furlong till one and a half out, one pace*...... (14 to 1 tchd 8 to 1) 6
3637* CHILI HEIGHTS [81] 3-9-4 J Williams (9) *wl in rear, styd on one pace fnl 2 fs*....................(9 to 1 op 7 to 1) 7
3957* DASWAKI (Can) [67] 5-8-8 (7ex) B Rouse (14) *mid-div, rdn hfwy, sn btn*........ (2 to 1 fav op 9 to 4 tchd 5 to 2) 8
2194⁵ LEE ARTISTE [87] 5-10-0 T Quinn (2) *hld up, making hdwy whn badly hmpd o'r 2 fs out, eased when held ins last.* ....(16 to 1 op 12 to 1 tchd 20 to 1) 9
3830⁴ WILL SOON [63] 4-8-4 W Newnes (6) *pressed ldrs, rdn 3 fs out, hmpd sn aftr, wknd*........(14 to 1 tchd 16 to 1) 10
1808⁸ MOORISH [88] 3-9-4 (7*) T G McLaughlin (1) *slwly away, al beh*.................... (12 to 1 tchd 14 to 1) 11
3830 ABSO [57] (bl) 5-7-12 G Bardwell (8) *chsd ldrs, rdn 3 fs out, hmpd and wknd o'r 2 out*......... (50 to 1 op 33 to 1) 12
3261 POETS COVE [66] 5-8-7 A Clark (10) *slwly away, al beh.* ....(50 to 1 op 33 to 1) 13
3736² TEANARCO (Ire) [66] 5-8-7 Pat Eddery (13) *led for one furlong, wknd and eased 2 out.* ....(8 to 1 op 6 to 1 tchd 9 to 1) 14

Dist: 1l, ¾l, ¾l, 1½l, hd, 3½l, 2½l, ¾l, ½l, ¾l. 1m 32.33s. a 5.03s (14 Ran).
SR: 43/44/47/57/45/47/37/19/37/ (G W Mills), D W P Arbuthnot

4025 Tony Stratton Smith Memorial Conditions Stakes Class B (3-y-o and up) £6,508 5f 34yds. . . . . (2:40)

3717² SURPRISE OFFER (bl) 3-9-2 B Raymond (8) *in tch stands side, led fnl furlong, ran on.* ....(6 to 4 fav op 5 to 4 tchd 13 to 8) 1
3511* GORINSKY (Ire) 5-9-10 T Quinn (5) *al prmnt, ev ch entering fnl furlong, outpcd nr finish.* (8 to 1 tchd 10 to 1) 2
3486² TUSCAN DAWN 3-9-2 Pat Eddery (3) *led centre till ins last, rdn and rallied nr finish.* ....(6 to 1 op 7 to 1 tchd 8 to 1) 3
3127⁵ PETERSFORD GIRL (Ire) 3-8-9 J Reid (7) *outpcd till kpt on wl ins fnl furlong*.... (25 to 1 op 20 to 1 tchd 33 to 1) 4
3725 MEDAILLE D'OR (v) 5-9-2 J Williams (4) *in tch till outpcd fnl 2 fs*................(5 to 1 tchd 9 to 2 and 11 to 2) 5
3847⁴ ANONYMOUS 3-8-8 B Doyle (6) *outpcd.* ....(20 to 1 op 16 to 1 tchd 25 to 1) 6
1551⁵ SPANIARDS CLOSE 5-9-5 L Piggott (1) *chsd ldr on outsd, wknd sn aftr hfwy*................(7 to 2 tchd 4 to 1) 7

Dist: 1l, ¾l, hd, 4l, 7l, 1½l. 1m 3.39s. a 3.09s (7 Ran).
SR: 72/76/65/57/48/12/17/ (Lord Carnarvon), R Hannon

4026 Starflight Aviation Fillies' Conditions Stakes Class B (2-y-o) £6,679 7f (3:10)

3738* BALANCHINE (USA) 8-10 J Reid (1) *made all, imprsv.* .... (11 to 2 op 7 to 2 on tchd 10 to 3 on) 1
LALA MUSA 8-8 M Roberts (2) *rcd 3rd, rdn o'r 2 fs out, ran on to take second entering last, no ch wth wnr.* ....(9 to 1 op 5 to 1 tchd 10 to 1) 2
NOBLISSIMA (Ire) 8-8 T Quinn (4) *hld up, took second hfwy, rdn and wknd appr fnl furlong.* ....(9 to 1 op 5 to 1) 3
2866 CHITA RIVERA 8-8 B Raymond (3) *trkd wnr to hfwy, lost tch wl o'r one furlong out*........ (33 to 1 op 12 to 1) 4

Dist: 7l, ¾l, 6l. 1m 30.64s. a 6.54s (4 Ran).
SR: 29/6/4/-/ (R E Sangster), P W Chapple-Hyam

4027 Haynes, Hanson And Clark Conditions Stakes Class B (2-y-o) £6,369 1m (3:40)

3742* KING'S THEATRE (Ire) 8-13 W Ryan (4) *made all, ran on wl ins fnl 2 fs*.......... (13 to 8 fav op Evens tchd 7 to 4) 1
1020² STAR SELECTION 8-11 T Quinn (2) *in tch, hdwy to take second sn aftr hfwy, rdn o'r one out, no imprsn.* ....(3 to 1 op 4 to 1 tchd 9 to 2 and 11 to 4) 2
2250⁶ KHAMASEEN 8-11 L Piggott (7) *hld up rear, hdwy wl o'r one furlong out, styd on, nvr nrr.* ....(10 to 1 op 8 to 1 tchd 12 to 1) 3
3260⁸ PERSIAN SAINT (Ire) 8-11 J Williams (3) *rear, ran past btn horses fnl furlong*.... (25 to 1 op 20 to 1 tchd 33 to 1) 4
3316⁴ BRANDON COURT (Ire) 8-11 B Raymond (8) *prmnt till 2 fs out, one pace aftr*.............. (20 to 1 tchd 25 to 1) 5
RUBHAHUNISH (Ire) 8-11 J Reid (6) *hld up, effrt o'r 2 fs out, one pace aftr*..... (12 to 1 op 8 to 1 tchd 14 to 1) 6
3833⁴ ASTRAL WEEKS (Ire) 8-11 M Roberts (5) *chsd wnr till wknd 3 fs out*.......... (10 to 1 op 8 to 1 tchd 7 to 1) 7
NEW ALBION (USA) 8-11 Pat Eddery (1) *in tch on outsd to hfwy, sn beh, eased*.... (5 to 1 op 9 to 2 tchd 11 to 2) 8

Dist: 4l, nk, ¾l, 3l, nk, 6l, 15l. 1m 43.94s. a 6.84s (8 Ran).
SR: 32/18/17/15/6/5/-/-/ (Michael Poland), H R A Cecil

4028 Trinifold Silver Clef Handicap Ladies Class E (0-70 3-y-o and up) £6,255 1½m 5yds. . . . . (4:10)

3656⁷ CRACKLING [36] 4-9-7 Miss K Marks (21) *wtd wth, steady hdwy 3 fs out, styd on to ld ins last.* ....(11 to 2 fav op 7 to 1 tchd 8 to 1) 1
3655 RAPPORTEUR (USA) [59] 7-10-11 (5*) Miss A Elsey (8) *mid-div, hdwy 5 fs out, led o'r 3 out, edgd rght and hdd ins last*................(25 to 1 op 16 to 1 tchd 33 to 1) 2
1775² MATCHING GREEN [54] 4-10-6 (5*) Miss K Greaney (3) *hld up, hdwy 5 fs out, ev ch 2 out, no extr ins last.* ....(16 to 1 op 12 to 1) 3
3821⁷ FAIRY WISHER (Ire) [40] 4-9-11 Miss A Harwood (6) *chsd ldrs, rdn o'r 2 fs out, one pace aftr.* (20 to 1 op 14 to 1) 4
3872⁴ LEXUS (Ire) [38] 5-9-9 Mrs M Cowdrey (20) *wtd wth, hdwy o'r 2 fs out, sn rdn, one pace.* ....(13 to 2 op 8 to 1 tchd 6 to 1) 5
3706⁴ SONG OF SIXPENCE (USA) [60] 9-11-3 Miss C Balding (18) *mid-div, effrt o'r 2 fs out, nvr dngrs.* ....(8 to 1 op 12 to 1 tchd 14 to 1) 6
3761⁹ SCENIC DANCER [47] 5-10-4 Miss L Hide (11) *mid-div, effrt o'r 2 fs out, no imprsn on ldrs.* ....(14 to 1 op 12 to 1 tchd 16 to 1) 7
3425⁹ THRESHFIELD (USA) [42] 7-9-8 (5*) Mrs K Walsh (17) *chsd ldrs, hdwy on ins o'r 3 fs out, sn rdn, one pace inside fnl 2 furlongs*....... (16 to 1 op 10 to 1 tchd 20 to 1) 8
DISTANT MEMORY [52] 4-10-9 Mrs S Hobbs (7) *chsd ldrs till wknd 2 fs out*.....(20 to 1 op 12 to 1 tchd 25 to 1) 9
3943* HEAD TURNER [35] 5-9-6 (5ex) Mrs S Bosley, *al mid-div.* ....(8 to 1 op 7 to 1 tchd 10 to 1) 10
3119² SAINT CIEL (USA) [64] 5-11-7 Miss Diana Jones (19) *rear till effrt 3 fs out, nvr nr to chal.* ....(10 to 1 op 7 to 1 tchd 11 to 1) 11
3669⁵ SPARKY'S SONG [52] 3-9-10 (5*) Miss S Francome (13) *mid-div, no hdwy fnl 3 fs*.............. (20 to 1 op 16 to 1) 12
644⁶ LATIN LEADER [66] 3-10-10 (5*) Miss V Snowdon (5) *mid-div, no hdwy fnl 3 fs.* (20 to 1 op 16 to 1 tchd 25 to 1) 13
3710 ALBERT [43] 6-10-0 Mrs P Nash (1) *al towards rear.* ....(8 to 1 tchd 10 to 1) 14
3548⁷ BALADIYA [61] 6-10-13 (5*) Mrs L Morris (10) *prmnt, led o'r 5 fs out till over 3 out, wknd stdly.* (20 to 1 op 16 to 1) 15
MERRY MARIGOLD [44] 7-9-10 (5*) Miss A Sanders (4) *mid-div, wknd o'r 3 fs out.* ....(25 to 1 op 20 to 1 tchd 33 to 1) 16
KALAMOSS [42] 4-9-13 Miss S Mitchell (14) *al beh.* ....(66 to 1 op 50 to 1) 17
3727⁸ GENTLEMAN SID [50] 3-9-8 (5*) Miss S Duckett (2) *slwly away, sn in tch, wknd o'r 3 fs out.* (33 to 1 op 20 to 1) 18

3689 FORTUNE STAR (Ire) [38] 4-9-4 (5*) Miss M Bridger (22) *chsd ldrs till wknd o'r 3 fs out*.........(66 to 1 op 50 to 1) 19
3551[8] STRAT'S LEGACY [45] 6-10-2 Mrs D Arbuthnot (15) *al beh.* ....(10 to 1 op 8 to 1) 20
3786[6] CASPIAN BELUGA [57] 5-11-0 Miss S A Billot (12) *led till o'r 5 fs out, sn btn, tld off.* ....(12 to 1 op 10 to 1 tchd 14 to 1) 21
VERSATILE [60] 9-11-3 Miss L Eaton (9) *in tch to hfwy, sn beh, tld off*.....................(66 to 1 op 50 to 1) 22
Dist: ½l, ½l, 4l, 4l, nk, 1l, hd, 5l, nk, nk. 2m 42.98s. a 13.38s (22 Ran).
SR: 9/31/25/3/-/14/ (Denis Marchant), D Marks

4029 Victor Chandler Nursery Class C (2-y-o) £5,309 7f 64yds............ (4:40)

3704 PLUNDER BAY (USA) [65] 8-10 B Raymond (4) *made all, rdn appr fnl furlong, styd on*......(12 to 1 op 10 to 1) 1
3625[4] SOOLAIMON (Ire) [69] 9-0 J Reid (7) *nvr far away, ev ch appr fnl furlong, kpt on one pace.* ....(11 to 2 op 9 to 2 tchd 6 to 1) 2
3633[9] TANBIH [65] 8-10 R Hills (1) *slwly into strd, hdwy on ins hfwy, kpt on one pace fnl 2 fs out.* (20 to 1 op 16 to 1) 3
3845[2] YAWARA [72] 9-0 (3*) B Doyle (2) *trkd ldrs, no hdwy entering fnl furlong*.................(7 to 2 tchd 4 to 1) 4
3422[9] REED MY LIPS (Ire) [75] 9-6 P Robinson (5) *trkd wnr, rdn 3 fs out, wknd entering last*...........(25 to 1 op 20 to 1) 5
3386[4] BLURRED IMAGE (Ire) [72] 9-3 Pat Eddery (11) *hld up, effrt hfwy, hng lft o'r one furlong out, eased whn btn.* ....(7 to 1 tchd 8 to 1) 6
2542[9] WIZARD KING [55] 8-0 G Bardwell (3) *towards rear, some hdwy 2 fs out, nvr dngrs.* ....(14 to 1 op 16 to 1 tchd 20 to 1) 7
3230 FOLLY FINNESSE [66] 8-11 S Whitworth (10) *pld hrd, rdn 2 fs out, sn btn*......................(25 to 1 op 16 to 1) 8
3287 SANGARE (Ire) [65] 8-10 T Quinn (6) *in tch till wknd o'r 2 fs out*...................(8 to 1 op 6 to 1 tchd 9 to 1) 9
3537[4] BRIERLEY [76] 9-7 R Perham (8) *in tch, rdn o'r 2 fs out, sn wknd*..........................(10 to 1 tchd 12 to 1) 10
3589 PLATINI (Ire) [67] 8-12 M Roberts (9) *slwly away, al struggling*...........................(5 to 2 fav tchd 9 to 4) 11
Dist: ¾l, nk, 2l, ½l, 1½l, 1½l, 7l, 1½l, 2l, 1l. 1m 34.67s. a 7.37s (11 Ran).
SR: 18/20/15/16/17/9/ (Mrs Shirley Robins), G Lewis

4030 Kintbury Maiden Stakes Class D (3-y-o) £3,720 1m................. (5:10)

1713[4] WINDRUSH LADY 8-9 J Reid (9) *hld up, hdwy 2 fs out, led ins last, cmftbly*.........(9 to 2 op 8 to 1 tchd 4 to 1) 1
3839[3] VILLAGE GREEN (Fr) (v) 9-0 T Quinn (1) *in tch, led o'r 2 fs out, rdn and hdd ins last*.........(7 to 1 tchd 8 to 1) 2
3506[3] TAJHIZ (USA) 9-0 R Hills (2) *led till o'r 2 fs out, kpt on one pace*................(2 to 1 fav op 6 to 4 tchd 9 to 4) 3
FIRE CARPET (USA) 9-0 M Roberts (6) *beh, struggling hfwy, past btn horses ins fnl 2 fs.* ....(6 to 1 op 4 to 1 tchd 7 to 1) 4
3727[7] MT TEMPLEMAN (USA) 9-0 Pat Eddery (3) *prmnt till rdn and wknd 2 fs out*......(3 to 1 op 7 to 2 tchd 4 to 1) 5
KATIE'S KID 9-0 T Rogers (7) *al rear*. (50 to 1 op 33 to 1) 6
3783[7] FLASHFEET 9-0 N Adams (4) *chsd ldrs till wknd wl o'r 2 fs out*..................(16 to 1 op 14 to 1 tchd 20 to 1) 7
ROYAL EXECUTIVE (Ire) 8-11 (3*) B Doyle (5) *al struggling in rear*..........................(25 to 1 op 20 to 1) 8
LUNAR PRINCE 9-0 G Bardwell (8) *beh aftr 2 fs, tld off hfwy*..............................(50 to 1 op 33 to 1) 9
Dist: 4l, 4l, 4l, 1½l, 5l, 5l, 7l, dist. 1m 43.84s. a 6.74s (9 Ran).
SR: 30/23/11/-/-/-/ (M A Wilkins), M McCormack

SOUTHWELL (A.W) (std)
Friday September 17th

Going Correction: PLUS 0.10 sec. per fur. (races 1,2,3,5,6), NIL (4)

4031 Newark Maiden Handicap Stakes Class F (0-70 3-y-o and up) £2,243 7f ....(2:30)

3020[3] FAMILY ROSE [44] 4-8-8 (3*) Stephen Davies (2) *chsd ldrs, gd hdwy 2 fs out, styd on to ld ins last, rdn and hld on wl*..(8 to 1) 1
818[7] WEE SARAH [59] 5-9-5 (7*) V Halliday (1) *mid-div, hdwy on outer 2 fs out, sn rdn and ran on strly ins last, jst fld.* ....(9 to 1 op 10 to 1 tchd 8 to 1) 2
3693[6] MISS KINABALU [47] 3-8-10 F Norton (5) *chsd ldrs, effrt 2 fs out, rdn to chal ins last, no extr nr finish.* ....(8 to 1 op 7 to 1) 3
3601[3] NOBLE MEASURE (Ire) [37] (bl) 3-8-0 J Quinn (7) *chsd ldrs, effrt 2 fs out, rdn and one pace appr last*....(6 to 1 jt-fav op 5 to 1) 4
3628 FREDDIE JACK [40] (bl) 3-8-3 J Fortune (13) *chsd ldg pair, hdwy to ld o'r one and a half fs out, sn rdn, hdd and wknd ins last*...................(20 to 1 op 16 to 1) 5
3794[2] KILTROUM (Fr) [40] (v) 4-8-7 L Dettori (6) *al prmnt, effrt o'r 2 fs out, sn rdn and one pace*...(6 to 1 jt-fav op 4 to 1) 6
3788[2] DOUBLE THE STAKES (USA) [36] (bl) 4-8-3 R Lappin (15) *led to hfwy, sn rdn, wknd fnl 2 fs*....... (7 to 1 op 5 to 1) 7
3469 MUMMYS ROCKET [32] (bl) 4-7-13 A Tucker (9) *sn outpcd and rdn alng, styd on fnl 2 fs, nvr dngrs*......(16 to 1) 8
2634[5] COVEN MOON [53] (v) 3-9-2 D Holland (11) *nvr plcd to chal*..........................(11 to 1 op 8 to 1) 9
3631[7] LETTERMORE [35] 3-7-12 D Harrison (4) *slwly into strd, effrt and some hdwy 2 fs out, sn rdn and no imprsn.* ....(10 to 1 op 7 to 1) 10
3661 CHRISTIAN WARRIOR [31] (v) 4-7-12[1] A McGlone (14) *cl up, led hfwy, rdn 2 fs out, sn hdd and wknd.* ....(16 to 1 op 14 to 1) 11
2499 BLUE TRUMPET [52] 3-9-1 R Price (10) *al rear*....(10 to 1) 12
3789 MOLLY BRAZEN [53] 3-9-2 G Duffield (3) *slwly into strd, sn chasing ldrs, wknd 3 fs out*........(11 to 1 op 10 to 1) 13
1463[9] BECKYHANNAH [33] 3-7-10 Dale Gibson (8) *in tch, rdn hfwy, sn wknd*..................................(33 to 1) 14
3794[5] PRETTY CHIC [40] (bl) 4-8-7 S Wood (12) *al rear.* ....(16 to 1 op 14 to 1) 15
2365[6] SAMANTHAS JOY [47] 3-8-7 (3*) C Hodgson (16) *beh frm hfwy*..........................(25 to 1 op 16 to 1) 16
Dist: Sht-hd, nk, 3l, nk, 2l, 1½l, hd, 2½l, 1l, 3l. 1m 31.50s. a 5.40s (16 Ran).
SR: 27/41/24/5/7/5/ (J Naughton), Miss Gay Kelleway

4032 Asfordby Well Done Selling Stakes Class G (2-y-o) £2,070 7f........(3:00)

3667[4] GOLDEN GRAND 9-2 R Cochrane (1) *trkd ldrs, smooth hdwy to ld o'r 2 fs out, rdn and ran on fnl furlong.* ....(9 to 2 op 3 to 1) 1
3082 CHARLIES DREAM (Ire) 8-6 J Quinn (3) *chsd ldrs, hdwy o'r 2 fs out, rdn to chal and ev ch one furlong out, no extr ins last*..............(7 to 1 op 5 to 1 tchd 8 to 1) 2
3819[7] LITTLE IBNR 8-11 M Wigham (4) *slwly into strd and beh, hdwy hfwy, styd on fnl 2 fs*......(9 to 4 fav op 4 to 1) 3
3813[3] STARSPORT (Ire) (bl) 8-11 J Fortune (14) *chsd ldrs, rdn o'r 2 fs out, kpt on one pace*............(6 to 1 op 4 to 1) 4
3131[5] SUPERHOO 8-11 T Williams (10) *outpcd and beh, styd on fnl 2 fs, nvr rch ldrs*..............(16 to 1 op 14 to 1) 5
3508 WADDLE (Ire) 8-4 (7*) S Mulvey (12) *beh till some hdwy fnl 2 fs, nvr dngrs*...................(14 to 1 op 10 to 1) 6
3363[7] THATCHED ROOF (Ire) 8-7[1] C Dwyer (15) *in tch, rdn 3 fs out and sn wknd*..................(12 to 1 op 8 to 1) 7
3641[7] PINATUBO 8-4 (7*) Sarah Holland (7) *nvr rch ldrs.* ....(20 to 1 op 12 to 1) 8
3321[8] TOOGOODFORYOU 8-11 W Woods (9) *al mid-div.* ....(33 to 1 op 16 to 1) 9
SHARADA 8-6 A McGlone (11) *nvr rch ldrs.* ....(20 to 1 op 10 to 1) 10
3695[5] LOOKIN' ROSIE 8-6 S Webster (6) *chsd ldr, rdn o'r 2 fs out, not much room and sn wknd.* (20 to 1 op 16 to 1) 11
3557[7] SHARP SUMMIT (Ire) 8-6 D Harrison (5) *nvr a factor.* ....(20 to 1 op 16 to 1) 12
3490[6] NOT FOR JOE (bl) 8-11 L Dettori (2) *led, rdn and hdd o'r 2 fs out, sn wknd*..................(6 to 1 op 5 to 1) 13
3573[7] SPORTING STORY (Ire) (bl) 8-6 D Holland (13) *al rear.* ....(20 to 1 op 10 to 1) 14
3131[7] RISKY GIFT 8-11 G Duffield (8) *chsd ldrs, rdn 3 fs out, sn wknd*..............................(8 to 1 op 5 to 1) 15
Dist: 3l, 7l, 2½l, 10l, ½l, ¾l, 2l, hd, 1½l, nk. 1m 31.20s. a 5.10s (15 Ran).
SR: 36/17/1/-/-/-/ (D A Johnson), R J R Williams

4033 EBF Reed Farmers Publishing Group Maiden Stakes Class D (2-y-o) £4,270 1m..........................(3:30)

3592[7] CONVOY POINT (Ire) 9-0 R Cochrane (3) *trkd ldrs, hdwy on inner to ld one and a half fs out, rdn and ran on fnl furlong*..........(3 to 1 fav op 5 to 2 tchd 100 to 30) 1
3490 NORTHERN CELADON (Ire) 9-0 W Woods (1) *cl up, led hfwy, rdn and hdd one and a half fs out, kpt on.* ....(100 to 30 op 7 to 2 tchd 3 to 1) 2
2357[6] WAVELET 8-9 D Holland (2) *led to hfwy, cl up till rdn o'r 2 fs out and grad wknd*................(8 to 1 op 5 to 1) 3
3841[2] PRINCE DANZIG (Ire) 9-0 G Duffield (7) *beh still styd on fnl 3 fs, nvr dngrs*........................(5 to 1 op 4 to 1) 4
3659 RUBY ESTATE (Ire) 8-9 J Quinn (6) *chsd ldrs, rdn o'r 2 fs out, sn one pace*....................(9 to 1 op 10 to 1) 5
3833[7] WALDO 9-0 D Harrison (8) *nvr rch ldrs.* ....(15 to 2 op 5 to 1 tchd 8 to 1) 6
3836[3] KELLYSI 9-0 C Rutter (5) *nvr a factor*. (13 to 2 op 4 to 1) 7
3470[8] ALTOBY 8-11 (3*) Stephen Davies (4) *prmnt, rdn 3 fs out and sn wknd*...................(25 to 1 op 20 to 1) 8
3658[7] FOOT TAPPER (Ire) 9-0 R Price (9) *al rear.* ....(16 to 1 op 14 to 1) 9
3659 MISTY WISE 8-9 L Dettori (10) *in tch to hfwy, sn lost pl and beh*..(12 to 1) 10
Dist: 3l, 7l, 2l, 3l, 5l, 1½l, 7l, 7l, 7l. 1m 44.30s. a 5.30s (10 Ran).
SR: 33/24/-/-/-/-/ (Sultan Mohammed), M R Stoute

4034 British Gas Conditions Stakes Class D (2-y-o) £3,348 5f................(4:00)

2825[7] THE FERNHILL FLYER (Ire) (v) 8-7 J Fortune (3) *cl up, rdn to ld one and a half fs out, kpt on wl und pres.* ....(12 to 1 op 10 to 1) 1
3557* ELEUTHERA 8-7 L Dettori (5) *al prmnt, ev ch 2 fs out, sn rdn and not quicken entering last.* ....(6 to 4 on op 5 to 4 on tchd 6 to 5 on) 2

3657[7] BOLD ARISTOCRAT (Ire) 8-10 S Perks (1) *cl up on outer, effrt and ev ch one and a half fs out, sn rdn and kpt on one pace ins last*.......... (12 to 1 op 8 to 1) 3
3715[5] KANGRA VALLEY 8-9 J Quinn (7) *led one and a half fs, cl up till rdn and wknd appr fnl furlong*. .... (20 to 1 op 14 to 1) 4
3711[6] LINCOLN TREASURE (Ire) 8-10 A McGlone (6) *in tch, rdn and outpcd 2 fs out, kpt on ins last*. .... (33 to 1 op 20 to 1) 5
3363[4] TRENDY DANCER (Ire) 8-7 (3*) O Pears (8) *cl up, rdn hfwy and sn wknd*.......... (12 to 1 op 6 to 1) 6
2400[6] HILTONS TRAVEL (Ire) (bl) 8-10 S Webster (2) *prmnt on outer, led aftr one and a half fs till one and a half furlongs out, sn hng lft and wknd*. .... (14 to 1 tchd 20 to 1) 7
3950[4] WINDOW DISPLAY 8-10 Dale Gibson (9) *slwly into strd, sn cl up, rdn hfwy and soon wknd*... (25 to 1 op 14 to 1) 8
3679[7] MAJOR SUCCESS (Ire) 9-4 D Holland (4) *sddld slpd strt, beh fnl 3 fs*.......... (9 to 2 op 5 to 2) 9
Dist: 2½l, ½l, 2½l, 2½l, 2l, 1½l, 6l, 3½l. 1m 0.60s. a 2.70s (9 Ran).
SR: 39/29/30/19/10/2/ (P J Evans), J Berry

4035 Foy & Co. Limited Stakes Class F (0-60 3-y-o and up) £2,243 1¾m...... (4:30)

3087[8] MUST BE MAGICAL (USA) 5-9-7 L Dettori (8) *al prmnt, hdwy 5 fs out, rdn 3 furlongs out, styd on wl to ld ins last, ran on strly*.......... (12 to 1) 1
2977[2] ARCTIC GUEST (Ire) 3-8-6 T Williams (6) *al prmnt, effrt to chal 3 fs out, sn rdn, led one and a half furlongs out, edgd rght and hdd ins last*.......... (7 to 2 op 9 to 4) 2
3706[9] CLIFTON CHASE (bl) 4-9-7 D Holland (10) *led, rdn 2 and a half fs out, hdd one and a half furlongs out and sn one pace*.......... (12 to 1 op 10 to 1) 3
3848[9] SALU 4-9-2 G Duffield (11) *trkd ldrs, hdwy 4 fs out, rdn 3 furlongs out and sn one pace*.... (7 to 4 fav op 5 to 2) 4
3761[3] FIRST FLING (Ire) 4-9-2 S Webster (1) *al abt same pl*. .... (7 to 1 op 6 to 1) 5
3322[6] NORTHERN JUDY (Ire) 3-8-6 S Perks (4) *sn beh, some hdwy fnl 3 fs, nvr a factor*.......... (20 to 1) 6
3521 KARAMOJA 4-9-7 A McGlone (7) *chsd ldrs, rdn 4 fs out and sn wknd*.......... (8 to 1 op 6 to 1) 7
3552* CARROLLS MARC (Ire) 5-9-7 R Cochrane (2) *al rear*. .... (8 to 1 op 6 to 1) 8
182 SAILOR BOY (bl) 7-9-4 (3*) Stephen Davies (5) *cl up till wknd quickly hfwy, sn tld off*.......... (25 to 1) 9
3306[6] UP ALL NIGHT 4-9-2 Dale Gibson (9) *sn beh, tld off frm hfwy*.......... (16 to 1 op 14 to 1) 10
1161[7] MRS NORMAN 4-8-13 (3*) C Hodgson (3) *sn struggling, tld off frm hfwy*.......... (33 to 1) 11
Dist: 4l, 3l, 3l, 2½l, 8l, 1½l, ¾l, dist, 7l, nk. 3m 9.60s. a 9.60s (11 Ran).
SR: 25/2/11/-/-/-/ (The County Group), J Mackie

4036 KPMG Peat Marwick Handicap Class E (0-70 3-y-o and up) £3,805 1½m .... (5:00)

3521[2] HIGH SUMMER [62] 3-8-13 D Harrison (7) *made all, clr 2 and a half fs out, easily*........ (9 to 2 fav tchd 5 to 1) 1
3656* PREMIER DANCE [42] 6-8-1 R Price (4) *hld up, hdwy to join ldrs hfwy, effrt to chase wnr 2 fs out, sn rdn and no imprsn*.......... (10 to 1 op 7 to 1) 2
2827[5] PHARLY DANCER [65] 4-9-10 S Webster (13) *al prmnt, effrt 3 fs out, sn rdn and one pace*...... (14 to 1 op 10 to 1) 3
3786 SURE HAVEN (Ire) [69] 4-10-0 G Duffield (14) *al prmnt, effrt and rdn 3 fs out, sn one pace*...... (8 to 1 op 10 to 1) 4
2529* GOODBYE MILLIE [62] 3-8-10 (3*) O Pears (1) *mid-div, effrt 3 fs out, sn rdn, sayed on appr fnl furlong, nvr dngrs*. .... (10 to 1 op 7 to 1) 5
3840[2] TAUNTING (Ire) [47] 5-8-6 R Cochrane (5) *chsd ldrs, rdn and one pace fnl 3 fs*.......... (14 to 1 op 12 to 1) 6
3831[8] MODEST HOPE (USA) [66] 6-9-6 (5*) A Garth (12) *hld up, gd hdwy 4 fs out, rdn 3 furlongs out and sn wknd*. .... (12 to 1) 7
3790[2] LOOKINGFORARAINBOW (Ire) [64] 5-9-9 L Dettori (10) *hld up, gd hdwy 4 fs out, rdn 3 furlongs out, sn wknd*. .... (13 to 2 op 9 to 2) 8
3221[3] NOTED STRAIN (Ire) [49] 5-8-8 D Holland (3) *nvr rch ldrs*. .... (14 to 1 op 12 to 1) 9
3556[6] POETIC FORM (Ire) [48] (bl) 3-7-13 F Norton (15) *prmnt, hdwy to chase wnr hfwy, rdn o'r 4 fs out and sn wknd*. .... (14 to 1 op 10 to 1) 10
2196[5] VAIGLY SUNTHYME [58] 3-8-9 S Morris (6) *nvr dngrs*. .... (16 to 1 op 20 to 1) 11
3873[7] GALEJADE [49] 3-8-0 A McGlone (2) *nvr a factor*. .... (14 to 1 op 10 to 1) 12
2631[9] SUNTAN (Fr) [49] (bl) 4-8-8 S Perks (11) *al beh*.... (25 to 1) 13
3630[5] DOCTOR ROY [46] 5-8-5 W Woods (16) *beh frm hfwy*. .... (14 to 1 op 12 to 1) 14
3780 LOUDEST WHISPER [53] (v) 5-8-12 J Fortune (8) *prmnt till rdn and lost pl hfwy, sn beh*...... (25 to 1 op 20 to 1) 15
3714* DASHING FELLOW (Ire) [58] 5-9-3 J Quinn (9) *chsd ldrs, rdn and lost pl 5 fs out, sn wl beh*..... (5 to 1 tchd 11 to 2) 16
Dist: 2½l, 2l, 8l, 8l, nk, ¾l, hd, 2l, 12l, 4l. 2m 39.90s. a 6.00s (16 Ran).
SR: 51/34/53/41/10/2/19/16/-/ (The Queen), Lord Huntingdon

AYR (good to firm)
Saturday September 18th
Going Correction: MINUS 0.50 sec. per fur. (races 1,3,5,7), MINUS 0.65 (2,4,6)

4037 Johnnie Walker Whisky Handicap Class C (0-90 3-y-o and up) £5,015 1m 5f 13yds.......... (1:25)

3512[3] EDEN'S CLOSE [71] 4-9-7 P Robinson (5) *cl up, led o'r 3 fs out, sn clr, wknd towards finish, jst hld on*. .... (13 to 2 op 6 to 1 tchd 7 to 1) 1
3848 WHITE WILLOW [70] 4-9-6 K Darley (9) *hld up, gd hdwy 3 fs out, ran on wl fnl furlong, not rch wnr*. .... (7 to 1 tchd 8 to 1) 2
3690[6] LEGION OF HONOUR [59] 5-8-9 K Fallon (4) *in tch, chsd wnr fnl 2 fs till no extr wl ins last*. .... (20 to 1 tchd 16 to 1) 3
3881* FIRST BID [72] 6-9-8 J Fanning (2) *beh, gd hdwy o'r 2 fs out, styd on same pace fnl furlong*. (11 to 2 op 9 to 2) 4
3466 AZUREUS (Ire) [74] 5-9-10 M Perrett (8) *hld up, steady hdwy 3 fs out, kpt on wl fnl furlong, nrst finish*. .... (16 to 1 op 12 to 1) 5
3790 EIRE LEATH-SCEAL [44] 6-7-8[1] J Lowe (6) *cl up till wknd o'r 2 fs out*.......... (25 to 1) 6
3740* SCORPIUS [79] 3-9-6 W Carson (7) *in tch, pushed alng 4 out, hdwy o'r 2 out, hng lft and wknd over one out*. .... (2 to 1 fav tchd 7 to 4 and 9 to 4) 7
3706[3] MR COPYFORCE [61] (v) 3-7-11 (5*) D Wright (10) *prmnt till wknd o'r 2 fs out*.......... (14 to 1 op 10 to 1) 8
3790[4] LATVIAN [70] 6-9-6 J Weaver (3) *beh, hdwy hfwy, rdn 3 fs out, sn wknd*.......... (13 to 2 op 6 to 1 tchd 7 to 1) 9
3599[4] PHILGUN [57] (v) 4-8-4 (3*) N Kennedy (1) *led till stumbled badly and hdd o'r 3 fs out, sn beh, tld off*. .... (14 to 1 op 12 to 1) 10
Dist: Nk, hd, 1½l, 1½l, 10l, 1l, 1l, nk, 20l. 2m 45.81s. b 0.19s (10 Ran).
SR: 44/42/30/40/39/-/13/-/10/ (Mrs M Barwell), M H Tompkins

4038 Ladbroke Ayr Silver Cup Handicap Class B (3-y-o and up) £12,427 6f (1:55)

3535[3] SOBERING THOUGHTS [68] 7-8-8 W Ryan (10) *cl up far side, slight ld o'r 2 fs out, hld on wl fnl furlong*. .... (25 to 1 op 20 to 1) 1
3756[6] BENZOE (Ire) [73] (bl) 3-8-10 T Lucas (12) *trkd ldrs far side, chalr 2 fs out, ev ch till no extr towards finish*. (33 to 1) 2
3995* SIR JOEY (USA) [75] 4-8-8 (7*,3ex) S Drowne (3) *in tch far side, hdwy hfwy, rdn entering fnl furlong, kpt on wl*. .... (14 to 1 op 12 to 1) 3
3849[7] HOB GREEN [81] 4-9-7 K Fallon (6) *rcd far side, beh, hdwy o'r 2 fs out, ran on wl fnl furlong, nrst finish*. .... (11 to 2 fav op 10 to 1 tchd 5 to 1) 4
3105[8] RUNNING GLIMPSE (Ire) [80] 5-9-1 (5*) D Wright (5) *al prmnt far side, no extr fnl furlong*.......... (33 to 1) 5
3791[4] TAWAFIJ (USA) [77] 4-9-3 J Fanning (9) *al chasing ldrs far side, no extr fnl furlong*.......... (25 to 1) 6
3756[8] TWO MOVES IN FRONT (Ire) [73] 3-8-10 D Holland (1) *chsd ldrs far side, no hdwy fnl 2 fs*.......... (33 to 1) 7
3812 BLUE GRIT [64] (bl) 7-8-4 J Weaver (7) *rcd far side, beh, rdn 2 fs out, styd on, not trble ldrs*.......... (40 to 1) 8
3995[8] JIGSAW BOY [74] 4-9-0 J Williams (14) *in tch stand side, ran on wl to ld stand side grp ins fnl furlong*. .... (14 to 1 op 12 to 1) 9
3774[7] VELOCE (Ire) [77] 5-9-3 A Mackay (8) *rcd far side, sn pushed alng, nvr dngrs*.......... (28 to 1 op 33 to 1) 10
3410[4] JADE CITY [75] (bl) 3-8-12 M Birch (29) *prmnt stand side, effrt o'r 2 fs out, kpt on fnl furlong*.......... (25 to 1) 11
3849 SAMSOLOM [81] 5-9-7 J Quinn (23) *in tch stand side, kpt on fnl 2 fs, nvr dngrs*.......... (16 to 1) 12
3778[5] DENSBEN [80] 9-9-6 W Carson (17) *rcd stand side, nvr dngrs*.......... (16 to 1) 13
3778 DOKKHA OYSTON (Ire) [75] 5-9-1 J Carroll (13) *in tch, hdwy to ld stand side grp o'r 2 out, wknd emtering fnl furlong*.......... (25 to 1) 14
3906[5] NEITHER NOR [79] 4-9-5 G Duffield (2) *in tch far side till wknd o'r 2 fs out*.....(11 to 1 op 14 to 1 tchd 16 to 1) 15
3906 FOR THE PRESENT [82] 3-9-5 K Darley (19) *rcd stand side, hdwy to dispute ld 2 out, wknd entering fnl furlong*. .... (20 to 1 op 16 to 1) 16
3877[9] PRINCE BELFORT [60] 5-8-0 L Charnock (24) *dsptd ld stand side till wknd 2 fs out*.......... (50 to 1) 17
3778[3] RED ROSEIN [79] 7-9-5 J Fortune (26) *chsd ldrs stand side till wknd 2 fs out*.......... (12 to 1 op 14 to 1) 18
3906[4] CATHERINEOFARAGON [76] 3-8-13 M Perrett (21) *rcd stand side, nvr dngrs*.......... (16 to 1 op 14 to 1) 19
3778 DIET [70] (v) 7-8-5 (5*) J Marshall (4) *rcd far side, led till hdd o'r 2 fs out, sn wknd*. (20 to 1 op 25 to 1 tchd 33 to 1) 20
3778 GREAT HALL [72] 4-8-12 R Cochrane (18) *rcd stand side. nvr dngrs*.......... (25 to 1) 21
3946 HALLORINA [60] 3-7-11 Dale Gibson (15) *rcd stand side, in tch till wknd o'r 2 fs out*.......... (50 to 1) 22
3057 RESOLUTE BAY [63] (v) 7-8-3 N Carlisle (25) *rcd stand side, al beh*.......... (50 to 1) 23

3778[7] EGG [61] (bl) 3-7-12 J Lowe (22) *rcd stand side, al beh.* ...(33 to 1) 24
3964* SLADES HILL [63] 6-8-3 (3ex) A McGlone (20) *rcd stand side, beh frm hfwy*...(16 to 1 op 14 to 1) 25
3877* PRIMULA BAIRN [66] (v) 3-8-3 P Robinson (11) *in tch far side, rdn o'r 2 fs out, sn btn*...(14 to 1) 26
3638 FIGHTER SQUADRON [65] (bl) 4-8-2 (3*) S D Williams (28) *dsptd ld stand side till wknd o'r 2 fs out.* ...(25 to 1 op 20 to 1) 27
3354[9] GENTLE HERO (USA) [56] 7-7-10[9] (7*) P McCabe (27) *rcd stand side, al beh*...(50 to 1) 28
Dist: Nk, ¾l, nk, 1½l, ½l, 2½l, nk, ¾l, sht-hd, hd. 1m 8.98s. b 1.92s (28 Ran).
SR: 54/55/57/62/55/50/33/26/33/ (W E Solomon), J L Eyre

4039 Semi Chem Doonside Cup Class A (Listed Race) (3-y-o and up) £9,354 1 ¼m 192yds.................... (2:25)

JOHN BALLIOL (USA) 5-9-1 K Darley (1) *trkd ldr, led entering fnl furlong, sn rdn, hld on wl.* ...(5 to 1 op 6 to 1 tchd 9 to 2) 1
3644[7] MACK THE KNIFE (bl) 4-9-1 M Birch (2) *led, hdd entering fnl furlong, kpt on wl und pres*...(9 to 2 op 7 to 2) 2
3879[2] KEY TO MY HEART (Ire) 3-8-4 K Fallon (3) *hld up, effrt o'r 2 fs out, sn rdn, styd on wl ins last.* ...(15 to 8 fav op 2 to 1 tchd 7 to 4) 3
3775* ALJAZZAF 3-8-4 W Ryan (6) *trkd ldrs, rdn o'r one furlong out, kpt on, no imprsn*...(9 to 2 op 4 to 1) 4
3466[3] HIGHBROOK (USA) 5-8-6 P Robinson (4) *hld up, effrt 3 fs out, sn btn*...(13 to 2 op 6 to 1 tchd 7 to 1) 5
3879[7] DESERT SECRET (Ire) 3-9-0 W Carson (5) *hld up, effrt 3 fs out, sn btn*...(16 to 1 op 12 to 1) 6
Dist: Nk, 1l, nk, 10l, 8l. 2m 17.29s. a 3.29s (6 Ran).
SR: 14/13/-/ (Sheikh Mohammed), D R Loder

4040 Ladbrokes Ayr Gold Cup Handicap Class B (3-y-o and up) £50,427 6f (3:05)

3725[6] HARD TO FIGURE [101] 7-9-6 R Cochrane (8) *in tch far side, gd hdwy 2 out, quickened to ld jst ins fnl furlong, rdn and ran on wl*...(12 to 1 op 14 to 1) 1
3575[9] TRUTHFUL IMAGE [82] (bl) 4-7-10[2] (7*) P McCabe (17) *al chasing ldrs far side, kpt on wl fnl furlong*...(50 to 1) 2
3621[5] VENTURE CAPITALIST [91] (bl) 4-8-10 J Williams (9) *rcd far side, beh till styd on wl und pres fnl furlong, nrst finish*...(12 to 1 op 14 to 1 tchd 16 to 1) 3
3725[9] SIR HARRY HARDMAN [94] 5-8-13 S Perks (2) *rcd far side, chsd ldrs, rdn entering fnl furlong, kpt on wl.* (40 to 1) 4
3849* AMRON [93] 6-8-12 (7ex) N Carlisle (12) *rcd far side, beh, hrd rdn o'r one furlong out, ran on wl fnl furlong, nrst finish*...(18 to 1 op 20 to 1) 5
3621[8] HOW'S YER FATHER [85] 7-8-4 A McGlone (14) *in tch far side, rdn o'r 2 fs out, kpt on wl fnl furlong, nrst finish.* ...(16 to 1 op 14 to 1) 6
3504[4] EVERGLADES (Ire) [97] 5-9-2 W Carson (4) *chsd ldrs far side, rdn and ch o'r one fs out, no extr fnl furlong.* ...(7 to 1 fav op 8 to 1) 7+
3594[8] ARABELLAJILL [90] 4-8-9 W Newnes (10) *rcd far side, beh till styd on fnl 2 fs, not rch ldrs*...(25 to 1 op 20 to 1) 7+
3725[4] DUPLICITY (Ire) [96] 5-9-1 M Perrett (3) *rcd far side, beh till styd on und pres fnl furlong. not rch ldrs.* ...(14 to 1 op 16 to 1) 9
3849 CASTLEREA LAD [91] 4-8-10 W Ryan (22) *rcd stand side, in tch, ran on wl fnl 2 fs, nvr dngrs*...(20 to 1) 10
3725 REGAL CHIMES [105] 4-9-10 A Mackay (24) *led stand side grp, no extr fnl furlong*...(50 to 1) 11
3906 PALACEGATE TOUCH [93] (bl) 3-8-2 (7*) P Roberts (26) *al chasing stand side ldr, no extr fnl furlong.* ...(50 to 1 op 33 to 1) 12
2854[9] ABERGELE [86] (bl) 3-8-2 K Fallon (11) *chsd ldrs far side till wknd o'r one furlong out*...(25 to 1 op 33 to 1) 13
3511[4] HEAVENLY RISK [88] 3-7-12[1] (7*) Mark Denaro (29) *rcd stand side, beh till styd on wl fnl 2 fs, nvr dngrs.* ...(33 to 1) 14
3906[3] PETITE-D-ARGENT [85] 4-8-4 J Fortune (5) *cl up far side, rdn to ld o'r one fs out, hdd jst ins last, sn wknd.* ...(14 to 1 op 16 to 1) 15
3847[5] DOMINUET [94] 8-8-13 J Lowe (7) *rcd far side, not trble ldrs*...(20 to 1) 16
3725* MASTER PLANNER [97] 4-8-9 (7*,7ex) J D Smith (1) *chsd ldrs far side till wknd 2 fs out.* ...(12 to 1 op 14 to 1 tchd 16 to 1 and 11 to 1) 17
3504[9] MASTER OF PASSION [92] 4-8-11 M Tebbutt (18) *prmnt stand side, rdn 2 fs out, sn wknd.* (40 to 1 op 33 to 1) 18
3849[8] MISS VAXETTE [91] 4-8-3 (7*) M Humphries (25) *rcd stand side, in tch till wknd o'r 2 fs out*...(50 to 1) 19
3725 GARNOCK VALLEY [91] 3-8-7 J Carroll (28) *in tch stand side till wknd o'r 2 fs out.* ...(18 to 1 op 20 to 1 tchd 16 to 1) 20
3936[5] FYLDE FLYER [105] 4-9-7 (3*) Emma O'Gorman (23) *chsd ldrs stand side till wknd 2 fs out*...(50 to 1 op 40 to 1) 21
3906 ECHO-LOGICAL [88] 4-8-7 K Darley (21) *in tch stand side till wknd o'r 2 fs out*...(25 to 1 op 22 to 1) 22
3227[3] FIRST VEIL [90] 3-8-6 G Duffield (15) *rcd far side, nvr dngrs*...(33 to 1) 23
3404 CUMBRIAN WALTZER [86] 8-8-5 M Birch (27) *rcd stand side, in tch till wknd 2 fs out*...(20 to 1 tchd 25 to 1) 24
3511[5] FARFELU [89] (v) 6-8-8 P Robinson (20) *chsd ldrs stand side till wknd 2 fs out*...(33 to 1) 25
3849 EL YASAF (Ire) [101] (bl) 5-9-1 (5*) D Wright (16) *rcd far side, slight ld till hdd o'r one furlong out, wknd quickly.* ...(50 to 1 op 33 to 1) 26
3906 GREEN DOLLAR [83] 10-7-11 (5*) D McCabe (6) *rcd far side, sn beh*...(33 to 1) 27
3621* MARGARET'S GIFT [94] 3-8-10 (7ex) D Holland (13) *in tch far side till wknd 2 fs out*...(14 to 1) 28
3350 BRIGADE [88] (v) 4-8-2 (5*) K Rutter (19) *rcd stand side, beh frm hfwy*...(40 to 1 op 33 to 1) 29
Dist: ½l, 1½l, hd, sht-hd, sht-hd, ½l, dd-ht, sht-hd, 1l, nk. 1m 9.05s. b 1.85s (29 Ran).
SR: 65/44/47/49/47/38/48/41/46/ (J W Mursell), R J Hodges

4041 EBF Top Flight Leisure Median Auction Maiden Stakes Class E (2-y-o) £3,718 1m...................... (3:35)

3672[4] MILL FORCE 9-0 K Darley (3) *trkd ldr, led 3 fs out, pushed out, cmftbly*...(3 to 1 on op 5 to 2 on tchd 2 to 1 on) 1
CLIMB THE HEIGHTS (Ire) 9-0 J Carroll (1) *led till hdd 3 fs out, kpt on, no ch wth wnr*...(11 to 4 op 9 to 4) 2
3792 BIRCHWOOD STAR 8-9 S Perks (2) *in tch till outpcd 3 out.* ...(16 to 1 op 12 to 1) 3
Dist: 3½l, 7l. 1m 41.65s. a 3.95s (3 Ran).
(R Meredith), Mrs M Reveley

4042 Western Meeting Selling Stakes Class E (2-y-o) £4,494 5f.............. (4:10)

3871[3] RESONANT 9-2 G Duffield (4) *made all, ran on wl fnl furlong*...(6 to 5 fav op 11 to 8 tchd 6 to 4) 1
3673[2] KING RAT (Ire) 9-2 J Weaver (8) *al cl up, rdn o'r one furlong out, kpt on, no imprsn on wnr.* ...(7 to 1 tchd 6 to 1 and 15 to 2) 2
3809[5] BEE DEE BEST (Ire) 8-11 J Fanning (3) *in tch, styd on wl fnl furlong, nrst finish*...(33 to 1 op 20 to 1) 3
3715[6] DANCE OF THE SWANS (Ire) 8-11 K Darley (6) *chsd ldrs, rdn 2 fs out, kpt on same pace*...(7 to 2 op 5 to 2) 4
3475[5] ROCKY TWO 9-2 J Fortune (10) *wth wnr, rdn 2 fs out, grad wknd*...(12 to 1 op 8 to 1) 5
3569[2] MONKEY'S WEDDING (bl) 8-11 J Carroll (2) *chsd ldrs, rdn 2 fs out, sn btn*...(5 to 1 tchd 6 to 1) 6
3600[9] FORREST MASTER (Ire) 8-4 (7*) R Havlin (9) *nvr dngrs.* ...(100 to 1) 7
3754[7] MISS PIGALLE 8-6 Dale Gibson (1) *sn pushed alng and beh*...(33 to 1 op 20 to 1) 8
3673[5] NOSMO KING (Ire) (bl) 8-11 W Carson (7) *sn beh.* (20 to 1) 9
Dist: 1½l, 2½l, nk, 1½l, 1½l, 1½l, nk, 8l. 57.81s. b 0.29s (9 Ran).
SR: 43/37/22/21/20/9/3/-/-/ (Cheveley Park Stud), Sir Mark Prescott

4043 Sinclair Lang Handicap Class D (0-75 3-y-o and up) £5,356 1¼m..... (4:40)

3710[4] KNOCK KNOCK [74] 8-10-0 R Cochrane (11) *hld up, smooth hdwy 3 out, led o'r one furlong out, quickened clr, easily*...(9 to 4 fav tchd 5 to 2) 1
3555[2] BLUE GROTTO (Ire) [72] (v) 3-9-6 D Holland (1) *prmnt, slight ld 2 fs out, sn hdd, kpt on, no ch wth wnr.* ...(15 to 2 op 7 to 1 tchd 8 to 1) 2
3714[2] TAPATCH (Ire) [62] 5-9-2 W Newnes (13) *beh, hdwy 3 fs out, not clr run and swtchd fnl furlong, ran on, nrst finish.* ...(7 to 1) 3
3631* COUREUR [49] 4-8-3 G Duffield (2) *prmnt, chlgd 2 fs out, sn rdn and one pace*...(6 to 1 op 5 to 1) 4
3820[2] MUTAMANNI [69] (v) 3-9-3 W Carson (12) *trkd ldrs, ev ch 2 fs out, one pace*...(4 to 1 op 6 to 1) 5
3564[9] GRINNELL [46] (v) 3-7-8[1] J Fanning (9) *in tch, effrt o'r 2 fs out, kpt on same pace*...(20 to 1) 6
3146[4] SUSPECT [46] 3-7-8 J Quinn (10) *mid-div, effrt 3 fs out, hrd rdn 2 out, sn btn*...(20 to 1) 7
3375[7] STRAW THATCH [54] 4-8-8 J Weaver (4) *nvr trble ldrs.* ...(14 to 1 tchd 16 to 1) 8
3714[8] SHARQUIN [40] 6-7-8[1] J Lowe (7) *led till hdd 2 fs out, sn wknd*...(16 to 1 tchd 20 to 1) 9
3412 CORNFLAKE [47] 3-7-9[2] L Charnock (6) *chsd ldrs till wknd 2 fs out*...(33 to 1 op 25 to 1) 10
3812 BRACKENTHWAITE [49] 3-7-11 A Mackay (5) *al beh.* ...(20 to 1 op 16 to 1) 11
3840 SIE AMATO (Ire) [39] 4-7-2 (5*) D Wright (3) *prmnt till outpcd and lost pl hfwy, sn beh, tld off*...(33 to 1) 12
Dist: 3l, sht-hd, 2l, 1l, 2l, nk, 5l, hd, 1½l, ½l. 2m 5.20s. a 0.20s (12 Ran).
SR: 62/48/43/26/38/11/10/14/-/ (G M Smart), I A Balding

CATTERICK (good to soft)
Saturday September 18th
Going Correction: PLUS 0.30 sec. per fur.

4044 EBF Sandhurst Maiden Stakes Class D (Div I) (2-y-o) £4,020 5f 212yds (1:45)

3792[4] BOLD ALEX 9-0 N Connorton (2) *al hndy, bustled alng to nose ahead entering fnl furlong, shaken up, ran on wl.* ...(11 to 10 fav op 6 to 4) 1

3566[3] LOCHON 9-0 S Webster (7) *led aftr one furlong, kicked clr o'r 2 fs out, hdd entering last, rallied.* ......(11 to 2 op 4 to 1) 2
3742[6] NAWAFELL 8-4 (5*) J Tate (3) *nvr far away, effrt and ran green 2 fs out, rallied, fnshd fst*......(4 to 1 op 9 to 4) 3
3490[7] MONKEY MAGIC (Ire) 9-0 B Crossley (5) *slight ld for one furlong, styd hndy and pushed alng hfwy, outpcd o'r one out*......(9 to 2) 4
3754 PRIMUM TEMPUS 8-6 (3*) S Maloney (6) *trkd ldrs, drvn alng whn pace lifted o'r 2 fs out, no extr.* ......(14 to 1 op 8 to 1) 5
KATHYS RAINBOW 8-9 F Norton (1) *sn outpcd and drvn alng, ran green and came wide strt, nvr dngrs.* ......(14 to 1 op 20 to 1) 6
WHISPERS HILL 8-6 (3*) O Pears (4) *missed break, al last and struggling*......(33 to 1 op 25 to 1) 7
Dist: ½l, sht-hd, 4l, hd, 10l, 5l. 1m 16.00s. a 5.00s (7 Ran).
SR: 36/34/28/17/11/-/-/ (G Charlesworth), S G Norton

4045 Great Catterick Racing Game Gamble Fillies' Handicap Class E (0-70 3-y-o and up) £3,444 7f......(2:15)

3558 CELESTINE [50] (v) 4-8-9 (3*) O Pears (1) *made most, styd centre in strt, hld on wl fnl furlong.* (6 to 1 op 7 to 1) 1
3788* PARFAIT AMOUR [62] 4-9-10 A Culhane (7) *al hndy, determined chal entering fnl furlong, ran on.* ......(5 to 1 fav tchd 11 to 2) 2
3564[8] NELLIE'S GAMBLE [38] 3-7-10[6] (5*) L Newton (4) *sluggish strt, steady hdwy gng wl hfwy, swtchd wide strt, fnshd strly*......(10 to 1 op 14 to 1 tchd 16 to 1) 3
3632[4] MELODYS DAUGHTER [46] 3-8-4 F Norton (2) *al hndy, rdn fnl 2 fs, one pace*......(9 to 1 op 8 to 1) 4
2151[5] MISS OFFIE [40] 3-7-7 (5*) A Garth (3) *al frnt rnk, drvn alng last 2 fs, not quicken*......(14 to 1 op 12 to 1) 5
2697[9] SPICE AND SUGAR [61] (bl) 3-9-5 A Clark (6) *nvr far away, bustled alng last 2 fs, styd on*......(7 to 1) 6
3794 THROW AWAY LINE [36] 4-7-12[9] (5*) J Tate (10) *chsd ldg bunch, effrt and drvn alng hfwy, not pace of ldrs.* ......(25 to 1 op 20 to 1) 7
3831 COMTEC'S LEGEND [50] 3-8-3 (5*) Darren Moffatt (9) *chsd ldg bunch, swtchd wide to improve strt, nrst finish.* ......(14 to 1 op 12 to 1 tchd 16 to 1) 8
3747 SPANISH PERFORMER [40] 4-8-2 N Connorton (12) *chsd alng in midfield, no imprsn last 2 fs.* ......(16 to 1 op 14 to 1) 9
3057 PATIENCE PLEASE [54] 4-8-13 (3*) S Maloney (13) *wth ldrs, brght wide strt, rdn and btn 2 fs out.* ......(11 to 2 op 9 to 2) 10
3523 COLFAX CLASSIC [37] 3-7-2 (7*) C Adamson (14) *wth ldrs for o'r 5 fs, btn 2 out*......(9 to 1 op 8 to 1) 11
3794 BRIGADORE GOLD [42] 3-8-0 R Lappin (5) *pressed ldrs, rdn o'r 2 fs out, sn btn*......(16 to 1) 12
2425 DON'T BE SAKI (Ire) [38] 3-7-10 A Tucker (8) *missed break, nvr able to reco'r*......(20 to 1 op 16 to 1) 13
3774 HOTEL CALIFORNIA (Ire) [53] 3-8-11 S Wood (11) *pressed ldrs for 4 fs, sn btn*......(20 to 1) 14
Dist: Hd, ¾l, 3l, 1½l, 2l, ½l, ½l, hd, 1l, hd. 1m 29.50s. a 6.50s (14 Ran).
SR: 32/43/13/12/1/16/-/1/-/ (M J Grace), T Fairhurst

4046 Skyram Limited Stakes Class G (0-60 3-y-o) £2,758 1m 7f 177yds......(2:50)

3239[7] MOUNTAIN WILLOW 7-12 (7*) S Mulvey (1) *sn led, hdd and drvn appr strt, led ag'n o'r one furlong out, edgd rght, styd on.* (14 to 1 op 12 to 1 tchd 16 to 1 and 20 to 1) 1
3193 SCOTTISH WEDDING 8-3[1] (3*) O Pears (3) *patiently rdn, improved to chal o'r 2 fs out, edgd lft, not quicken fnl furlong*......(9 to 4 fav op 2 to 1) 2
3716 FOLLINGWORTH GIRL (Ire) 8-2 (3*) S Maloney (5) *took keen hold, led appr strt till o'r one furlong out, rdn and one pace*......(7 to 2 op 3 to 1) 3
3682[5] TOKYO 8-0 (5*) J Tate (2) *led early, styd hndy till rdn o'r 2 fs out, sn outpcd*......(5 to 2 tchd 3 to 1) 4
2633[6] THE PREMIER EXPRES 8-10 R Lappin (4) *trkd ldrs, drvn alng whn pace quickened o'r 2 fs out, no imprsn.* ......(4 to 1 op 5 to 1) 5
Dist: 1½l, 2½l, 6l, 1½l. 3m 41.50s. a 20.00s (5 Ran).
(P Aconley), Mrs V A Aconley

4047 Constant Security Services Ltd. Maiden Stakes Class D (3-y-o) £3,435 7f......(3:20)

3866 KOSATA (Ire) 8-6 (3*) S Maloney (2) *missed break, improved hfwy, brght stand side strt, ran on to ld fnl furlong.* ......(5 to 1 tchd 6 to 1) 1
3789 UNFINISHEDBUSINESS 9-0 N Connorton (1) *led aftr a furlong, made most after, rdn and hdd fnl furlong, one pace*......(33 to 1) 2
3341[4] NEWINGTON BUTTS (Ire) 8-9 A Clark (5) *al hndy, ev ch and rdn last 2 fs, not on same pace*......(4 to 1 op 7 to 2) 3
3268[7] MISWAKI DANCER (USA) 8-9 (5*) J Tate (9) *patiently rdn, pushed alng to improve last 2 fs, ran on finish.* ......(2 to 1 fav op 5 to 2) 4

2476[8] SALVATORE GIULIANO 8-11 (3*) O Pears (4) *wth ldrs, drvn alng 2 fs out, one pace.* ......(16 to 1 op 33 to 1 tchd 50 to 1) 5
3839[4] DOMOVOY 8-4 (5*) A Garth (6) *pressed ldrs through out, not quicken appr fnl furlong*......(3 to 1 op 9 to 4) 6
3132[7] DUELETTA 8-9 A Culhane (8) *steadied strt, shaken up o'r 2 fs out, nvr plcd to chal*......(14 to 1 op 12 to 1) 7
3839[8] THUNDER STRIKE (USA) 9-0 B Crossley (7) *wl plcd for o'r 4 fs, sn rdn and btn*......(12 to 1) 8
3712 SILVER WILL 9-0 S Webster (3) *led for a furlong, styd hndy till wknd 2 out*......(50 to 1 op 25 to 1) 9
3506 WARM TOES 8-9 R P Elliott (10) *rcd freely to hfwy, fdd o'r 2 fs out*......(25 to 1 op 20 to 1) 10
Dist: 3½l, 3½l, hd, ¾l, 1½l, 4l, 3½l, 1l, ½l. 1m 30.30s. a 7.30s (10 Ran).
SR: 17/11/-/-/-/-/ (R E Sangster), B W Hills

4048 'Go Racing In Yorkshire' Ladies Rating Related Maiden Stakes Class F (3-y-o and up) £2,444 1½m 44yds.. (3:50)

3699[3] RISPOTO 3-9-8 Miss Diana Jones (1) *led aftr 2 fs, quickened appr strt, styd on strly last two furlongs.* ......(11 to 8 fav op 5 to 4 on) 1
3552 NANCY (Ire) (bl) 3-9-1 (7*) Miss A Elsey (4) *nvr far away, jnd wnr appr strt, rdn and styd on same pace last 2 fs.* ......(20 to 1 op 16 to 1) 2
3307[9] BAHER (USA) 4-10-7 Mrs L Pearce (7) *patiently rdn, steady hdwy appr strt, ridden and one pace last 2 fs.* ......(17 to 2 op 9 to 1 tchd 8 to 1) 3
3840[8] SHARE A MOMENT (Can) 3-9-8 (5*) Miss J Southall (3) *chsd ldg bunch, drvn alng hfwy, nvr nr to chal.* ......(7 to 1 op 6 to 1) 4
3355[7] BONNY PRINCESS 3-9-1 (7*) Miss S Storey (2) *led for 2 fs, bustled alng to hold pl hfwy, sn lost tch.* ......(66 to 1 op 50 to 1) 5
3868[4] HOME PARK (Ire) (v) 3-9-13 Mrs M Cowdrey (6) *in tch, struggling to go pace hfwy, nvr a factor.* ......(7 to 4 op 2 to 1 tchd 9 to 4) 6
3171[5] LAST APPEARANCE 4-9-9 (7*) Miss C Lake (5) *wth ldr to hfwy, sn lost tch*......(50 to 1) 7
3811 BALLACASCADE 3-9-6 (7*) Miss A Armitage (8) *struggling to go pace aftr 4 fs, tld off frm hfwy.* ......(33 to 1 op 20 to 1) 8
Dist: 8l, 6l, 15l, 6l, 4l, 5l, 20l. 2m 46.00s. a 11.00s (8 Ran).
SR: 35/19/20/-/-/ (P G Goulandris), Sir Mark Prescott

4049 Dartmouth Selling Stakes Class G (3-y-o) £2,448 1m 5f 175yds......(4:25)

3741[4] STREPHON (Ire) 8-3 (7*) S Mulvey (7) *slight ld for 5 fs, rallied to rgn lead o'r one out, rdn out.* ......(13 to 2 op 6 to 1 tchd 7 to 1) 1
3669[3] GYPSY CRYSTAL (USA) 8-5 A Culhane (2) *in tch, drvn up to take clr order entering strt, kpt on und pres fnl furlong*......(6 to 1 op 9 to 2 tchd 13 to 2) 2
3556 HO-JOE (Ire) 9-0 Julie Bowker (5) *settled gng wl, led aftr 5 fs till rdn and hdd o'r one out, wknd rpdly last 100 yards*......(6 to 1 op 5 to 1) 3
3945[3] JASPER ONE 8-10 F Norton (4) *pressed ldrs, niggled alng thrght, one pace last 2 fs*......(8 to 1 tchd 9 to 1) 4
3945[4] JENDORCET 8-5 S Wood (9) *in tch, drvn up to join issue hfwy, rdn entering strt, no extr*......(10 to 1 op 8 to 1) 5
3407[3] YEVEED (Ire) 8-6 (3*) S Maloney (8) *trkd ldg bunch, effrt appr strt, btn o'r 2 fs out*......(13 to 8 fav op 7 to 2) 6
3681[8] ROYAL DIVA 8-9 N Connorton (6) *settled midfield, drvn alng appr strt, sn lost tch*......(5 to 1 op 4 to 1) 7
3049[9] HIGH CHAIR 7-12 (7*) C Adamson (3) *chsd ldrs, struggling appr strt, no imprsn*......(20 to 1) 8
3694[5] FRAGMENT (Ire) 8-10 A Clark (1) *struggling and beh hfwy, tld off last 3 fs*......(16 to 1 op 12 to 1) 9
Dist: ¾l, 10l, 2½l, 5l, 10l, 2l, 2l, dist. 3m 10.30s. a 14.80s (9 Ran).
(Mark Tompkins Elite), M H Tompkins

4050 EBF Sandhurst Maiden Stakes Class D (Div II) (2-y-o) £3,984 5f 212yds (4:55)

2866[7] QUEENS COTTAGE (Ire) 8-9 A Clark (7) *al hndy, led entering strt, drifted lft fnl furlong, ran on.* ......(6 to 1 op 20 to 1) 1
3746[6] GLENUGIE 9-0 A Culhane (5) *pushed alng beh ldrs, hng lft 2 fs out, rallied fnl furlong, nvr nrr.* ......(11 to 10 fav op 5 to 4 on) 2
3131[8] WESTCOAST 9-0 F Norton (6) *led till hdd and rdn entering strt, kpt on same pace fnl furlong.* ......(25 to 1 op 20 to 1) 3
LITTLE SENOR (Ire) 8-7 (7*) J Gracey (3) *trkd ldrs, lost grnd whn pace lifted o'r 2 fs out, styd on.* (7 to 1 op 6 to 1) 4
3215[5] K-REG 9-0 M Wigham (1) *bolted gng to post, unruly in stalls, wl plcd and drvn alng, no extr o'r one furlong out*......(3 to 1 op 9 to 4 tchd 7 to 2) 5
SHERGAL 8-9 C Dwyer (2) *missed break, tld off frm hfwy.* ......(100 to 1 op 33 to 1) 6
Dist: 2½l, ½l, 2l, nk, 30l. 1m 17.50s. a 6.50s (6 Ran).
SR: 1/-/-/ (Dozen Dreamers Partnership), R T Phillips

4051 Cranwell Nursery Class E (2-y-o) £3,158 7f......(5:25)

3563[5] THE HAPPY LOON (Ire) [55] 7-3 (5*) Darren Moffatt (1) *made all, quickened up entering strt, edgd lft fnl furlong, ran on wl*.............. (5 to 1 op 7 to 1 tchd 9 to 2) 1
3903[9] MICHELLISA [64] 8-3[2] A Clark (5) *improved to go hndy hfwy, ev ch o'r one furlong out, kpt on same pace*. .... (16 to 1 op 14 to 1) 2
3793[2] CLIFTON BEAT (USA) [72] 8-11 M Wigham (9) *nvr far away, ev ch and drvn alng last 2 fs, kpt on same pace*. .... (100 to 30 op 9 to 2 tchd 6 to 1) 3
3406[4] OOH AH CANTONA [82] 9-7 A Culhane (10) *al hndy, rdn 2 fs out, not quicken*..............................(8 to 1) 4
3750[3] OVIDEO [64] (bl) 7-12 (5*) J Tate (2) *gd speed in frnt rnk for o'r 5 fs, no extr*.......(12 to 1 op 10 to 1 tchd 14 to 1) 5
2274[3] NON VINTAGE (Ire) [71] 8-10 S Wood (12) *sluggish strt, improved into midfield hfwy, kpt on, nvr nrr*. .... (12 to 1 op 10 to 1) 6
3841* TIMES ZANDO [65] 8-3[2] (3*) O Pears (4) *sluggish strt, steady hdwy last 2 fs, nvr nrr*...... (10 to 1 op 8 to 1) 7
3600[4] HASTY BANK [57] (bl) 7-10 F Norton (11) *gd speed in frnt rnk till wknd und pres last 2 fs*..... (10 to 1 op 8 to 1) 8
3792* MHEANMETOO [77] 8-13 (3*) S Maloney (3) *trkd ldrs, effrt stands side o'r 2 fs out, sn rdn, no imprsn fnl furlong*. ....(5 to 2 fav op 3 to 1) 9
3755[8] LAUREL ROMEO (Ire) [60] 7-13 B Crossley (8) *chsd ldg bunch for 5 fs, fdd*............... (14 to 1 op 12 to 1) 10
2505[4] WOODLAND WHISPER [59] 7-5 (7*) C Adamson (7) *sluggish strt, nvr a threat*..................(25 to 1 op 20 to 1) 11
3532[8] KOMPLICITY [64] 8-3 N Connorton (13) *broke wl to show speed for o'r 4 fs, fdd*.............(14 to 1 op 12 to 1) 12
2772[8] TANFIRION CHIEF [62] 8-1 A Tucker (6) *sluggish strt, nvr able to reco'r*..................(20 to 1 op 16 to 1) 13
Dist: 2l, 2l, 3l, hd, 1½l, hd, hd, 1l, 3l, nk. 1m 29.60s. a 6.60s (13 Ran).
SR: 13/16/18/19/-/2/-/-/3/ (Jim Blair), Denys Smith

CURRAGH (IRE) (good to yielding)
Saturday September 18th
Going Correction: PLUS 0.65 sec. per fur.

4052 Kildare Hotel & Country Club Nursery Handicap (2-y-o) £5,520 6f...... (2:10)

2778[4] DON'T KNOW (Ire) [-] 8-5 (4*) J A Heffernan (7).....(9 to 1) 1
3927[4] PEACE TOKEN (Ire) [-] 8-12 (8*) G Coogan (8)......(5 to 1) 2
3719[4] TRIMBLEMILL (Ire) [-] 7-13 (8*) R T Fitzpatrick (3)..(14 to 1) 3
3807[4] ASTRADANE (Ire) [-] 8-2 M Roberts (4)............(8 to 1) 4
3613[7] CATWALKER (Ire) [-] (bl) 8-10 M J Kinane (2)........(9 to 2) 5
3613[9] SOMETHING SUPER [-] 8-7 W J Supple (9)........(6 to 1) 6
3806[3] NEVER TOLD (Ire) [-] 8-5 P V Gilson (10).......(4 to 1 fav) 7
3203[8] BUTLER BRENNAN (Ire) [-] 7-1 (8*) G M Moylan (5) (20 to 1) 8
1608[7] JOIN FORCES (Ire) [-] (bl) 8-0 N G McCullagh (6)..(20 to 1) 9
3607[9] MONICA'S CHOICE (Ire) [-] 7-7 A J Nolan (11).....(10 to 1) 10
2745[5] WAVE THE WAND (Ire) [-] 8-10 J F Egan (1).......(10 to 1) 11
Dist: 1l, ½l, 1½l, 2l. 1m 17.60s. a 7.10s (11 Ran).
SR: 31/38/23/12/12/-/ (Mrs Una Manning), J S Bolger

4053 Macdonagh Boland Stakes (Listed Race) (3-y-o and up) £8,625 7f...(2:40)

3916[2] MILLIE'S CHOICE (Ire) 4-8-9 W J Supple (1) *wl plcd, prog 2 fs out, dsptd ld one out, led ins last, styd on strly*. .... (10 to 3 fav) 1
3559[7] PRE-EMINENT (bl) 6-9-2 M J Kinane (2) *led, rdn 2 fs out, jnd one out, hdd ins last, kpt on*.............. (5 to 1) 2
3559[5] DASHING COLOURS (Ire) 4-8-9 J Reid (7) *hld up, rdn 2 fs out, styd on ins last wthout threatening ldrs*...(7 to 2) 3
3559* DOREG (Ire) 3-8-12 P V Gilson (4) *trkd ldr, rdn 2 fs out, no extr and wknd one out*........................(6 to 1) 4
2805[4] PERNILLA (Ire) 3-8-12 C Roche (8) *rear, rdn and kpt on one pace fnl 2 fs wthout threatening ldrs*.......(5 to 1) 5
NECTARINE (Ire) 3-8-5 J F Egan (6) *trkd ldr, rdn 2 fs out, wknd one out*............................ (16 to 1) 6
3605[2] INTIMACY (USA) 3-8-5 N G McCullagh (5) *al rear, rdn 2 fs out, sn wknd*.................................(12 to 1) 7
3912[8] EL ZORRO DORADO (Ire) 3-8-8 S Craine (3) *al rear, rdn 2 fs out, no extr and wknd o'r one out, eased*......(10 to 1) 8
Dist: 1l, 2l, 2l, hd. 1m 36.40s. a 13.20s (8 Ran).
(Colm McEvoy), Kevin Prendergast

4054 Smurfit National Stakes (Group 1) (2-y-o) £60,100 7f................ (3:10)

3203* MANNTARI (Ire) 9-0 J P Murtagh (6) *dsptd ld, advantage 4 fs out, rdn 2 out, quickened four ls clr one out, drw clear ins last, imprsv*...........................(6 to 1) 1
3612[3] CITY NIGHTS (Ire) 9-0 T Quinn (5) *hld up, rdn 2 fs out, styd on one pace ins last*.............................(14 to 1) 2
3880[2] STATE PERFORMER (USA) 9-0 J Reid (2) *wl plcd, trkd ldr 3 fs out, rdn 2 out, no extr appr last, wknd*... (9 to 4 on) 3
3731* CLIFDON FOG (Ire) (bl) 9-0 C Roche (4) *dsptd ld early on, rdn 3 fs out, wknd 2 out*....................... (14 to 1) 4
3917* PEACE ROLE (USA) (bl) 9-0 M J Kinane (3) *dsptd ld, hdd 4 fs out, rdn 2 out, sn wknd*........................(6 to 1) 5
3612[5] MUSICAL INSIGHT (Ire) 9-0 L Dettori (1) *wl plcd, rdn 2 fs out, wknd quickly*...............................(12 to 1) 6
Dist: 10l, sht-hd, 4½l, 4½l, 4l. 1m 29.70s. a 6.50s (6 Ran).
SR: 70/40/39/25/11/-/ (H H Aga Khan), John M Oxx

4055 Jefferson Smurfit Memorial Irish St.Leger (Group 1) (3-y-o and up) £87,600 1¾m................... (3:45)

3495[2] VINTAGE CROP 6-9-8 M J Kinane (4) *wl plcd, prog to dispute ld 3 fs out, quickened to lead 2 out, styd on strly*...(9 to 2) 1
3861* ASSESSOR (Ire) 4-9-8 J Reid (5) *rear, prog 3 fs out, kpt on wl ins fnl 2 wthout threatening wnr*............(9 to 2) 2
3403[2] FORESEE (bl) 3-8-12 M Roberts (8) *mid-div, rdn 4 fs out, ev ch 2 out, kpt on one pace*......................(9 to 2) 3
3349[3] SONUS (Ire) (bl) 4-9-8 L Piggott (6) *hld up, prog 3 fs out, ev ch 2 out, no extr one out, wknd*.................. (9 to 1) 4
2791[5] DRUM TAPS (USA) 7-9-8 L Dettori (3) *led, hdd aftr 6 fs, dsptd ld 3 furlongs out, rdn and headed 2 out, wknd one out*...(5 to 1) 5
3649* SNURGE 6-9-8 T R Quinn (2) *mid-div, prog 4 fs out, rdn 2 out, no extr and wknd appr fnl furlong*... (11 to 4 fav) 6
3370[3] SHREWD IDEA 3-8-12 J P Murtagh (1) *trkd ldr, quickened to ld aftr 6 fs, jnd 3 out, sn hdd, wknd 2 out*... (20 to 1) 7
3241[4] LINPAC WEST 7-9-8 G Hind (7) *al rear, rdn 4 fs out, wknd 3 out*.. (25 to 1) 8
Dist: 2½l, nk, 3l, 4l, ½l, 5l, 15l. 3m 6.70s. a 11.20s (8 Ran).
SR: 87/82/71/75/67/66/46/26/ (Michael W J Smurfit), D K Weld

4056 Smurfit Paribas Bank Handicap (0-110 3-y-o and up) £9,750 6f......... (4:20)

3912[6] BRADAWN BREEVER (Ire) [-] (bl) 4-9-10 W J Supple (10) ....(14 to 1) 1
3610[9] PEARL DAWN (Ire) [-] 3-7-5[6] (8*) R T Fitzpatrick (18) (25 to 1) 2
3928[3] KINDNESS ITSELF (Ire) [-] 3-7-10 (2*) D G O'Shea (5) (8 to 1) 3
3334* MYSTERIOUS WAYS (Ire) [-] 3-9-3 L Piggott (11) (3 to 1 fav) 4
3928[2] KILTIMONY [-] 3-6-13 (8*) J J Mullins (4)..........(10 to 1) 5
2805[6] ROSIE'S MAC (Ire) [-] (bl) 4-9-1 N G McCullagh (13) (10 to 1) 6
3928 CISEAUX (USA) [-] 4-8-1 (6*) D J O'Donohoe (6)... (12 to 1) 7
3496[4] LAVINIA FONTANA (Ire) [-] 4-8-13 P V Gilson (16)...(8 to 1) 8
3542[6] PERSIAN CREEK (Ire) [-] 4-9-0 C Roche (15)......(10 to 1) 9
3928 NORDIC OAK (Ire) [-] (bl) 5-8-0 (4*) J A Heffernan (14) ....(20 to 1) 10
3928 SAND OR STONE (Ire) [-] (bl) 5-7-1 A J Nolan (8).. (25 to 1) 11
3544 SKELLIG [-] 7-7-7 L O'Shea (9)..................(20 to 1) 12
665[8] NAIVITY (Ire) [-] 4-7-13[6] J F Egan (17)............(14 to 1) 13
3496[3] CLASSICAL AFFAIR (Ire) [-] 4-8-8 (6*) R V Skelly (7) (10 to 1) 14
3496[2] DIAMONDS GALORE (Can) [-] 8-9-8 M J Kinane (12) ....(10 to 1) 15
3912[7] MOONLIGHT PARTNER (Ire) [-] 3-6-13 (8*) G M Moylan (1) ....(8 to 1) 16
Dist: 1l, nk, hd, sht-hd. 1m 17.20s. a 6.70s (16 Ran).
SR: 54/19/23/41/16/-/ (M A Murray), Kevin Prendergast

4057 Corporate Sport & Leisure Handicap (0-80 3-y-o and up) £3,805 1m... (4:50)

3827[7] BRAZEN ANGEL (Ire) [-] 3-8-8 J F Egan (10)...... (25 to 1) 1
2345[6] NUNIVAK (USA) [-] 5-8-13 (6*) R V Skelly (1)...... (12 to 1) 2
1856[8] BASIE NOBLE [-] 4-9-4 N G McCullagh (9)...... (12 to 1) 3
3580[4] COMMAND 'N CONTROL [-] 4-8-3 (8*) G Coogan (12) ....(14 to 1) 4
3855[4] SAMOT (Ire) [-] 3-8-10 (6*) D O'Donohoe (2).......(12 to 1) 5
3852[2] CORTIJA PARK (Ire) [-] 3-9-1 R Hughes (4)..... (3 to 1 fav) 6
3769 NOBLE SAM (Ire) [-] 4-7-13[2] W J Supple (3)...... (50 to 1) 7
1106[6] PENNINE'S DAUGHTER [-] 3-9-3 B Coogan (5)... (12 to 1) 8
1649* MANZALA (USA) [-] 3-9-3 J P Murtagh (14)......... (9 to 2) 9
3855[2] STRATEGIC TIMING (Ire) [-] (bl) 3-9-7 M J Kinane (11) ....(5 to 1) 10
3916[9] RAFFERTY'S INNER (Ire) [-] 3-8-10 S Craine (6)... (20 to 1) 11
1570[2] ISLAND HEATHER (Ire) [-] (bl) 5-9-5 (4*) C Everard (18) ....(14 to 1) 12
753[3] TIME IT RIGHT (Ire) [-] 4-9-1 (10*) (13)...........(20 to 1) 13
1513 WASSL'S NANNY (Ire) [-] 4-8-11 (6*) T P Treacy (21) (20 to 1) 14
3498[5] TINA'S CHARM (Ire) [-] 4-8-9 (2*) P Carberry (7)... (20 to 1) 15
3160 BERESFORD LADY (Ire) [-] 3-8-4 P V Gilson (15)... (14 to 1) 16
3769[2] GOLDEN SPHINX (Ire) [-] 3-7-11 (2*) D G O'Shea (19) ....(14 to 1) 17
3858[3] WHAT A PLEASURE (Ire) [-] 3-8-11 (6*) B J Walsh (20) ....(12 to 1) 18
3928[6] KILLEEN STAR (Ire) [-] (bl) 3-8-4 (8*) G M Moylan (17) ....(20 to 1) 19
1443[7] THREE MUSKETEERS (Ire) [-] 4-8-4 (4*) J A Heffernan (8) ....(25 to 1) 20
3924[8] THRILL SEEKER (Ire) [-] 4-7-6 (8*) R T Fitzpatrick (22) .... (33 to 1) 21
Dist: 2½l, 2l, nk, sht-hd. 1m 45.90s. a 9.30s (21 Ran).
SR: 32/35/28/20/24/-/ (Albany Syndicate), Patrick Joseph Flynn

4058 Charles Caldwell (E.B.F) Maiden (2-y-o) £5,244 7f.................. (5:20)

3719[5] YAHTHAB (Ire) 9-0 W J Supple (1)............... (14 to 1) 1
3030[2] FLAG FEN (USA) 9-0 J P Murtagh (3)...........(5 to 2 fav) 2
MISS SACHA (Ire) 8-11 P V Gilson (5).............(11 to 4) 3
FLY THE CREST (USA) 9-0 N Byrne (14)..........(16 to 1) 4
3807[2] TRAGIC POINT (Ire) 8-11 C Roche (2)................(8 to 1) 5
FLYING EAGLE 9-0 D Hogan (6).......................(6 to 1) 6
2037[4] UNDER SIEGE (Ire) 9-0 S Craine (13)...............(5 to 1) 7

3030[8] LESLEY'S ANGEL (Ire) 9-0 P Lowry (8) .... (20 to 1) 8
3771[4] MOOBAKKR (USA) 9-0 M J Kinane (12) .... (9 to 2) 9
3771[7] NORTHERN FANCY (Ire) 8-12 (2*) D G O'Shea (15) (20 to 1) 10
BURKEAN MELODY (Ire) 9-0 N G McCullagh (11) (12 to 1) 11
DONT BUG ME (Ire) 8-8 (6*) B J Walsh (4) .... (20 to 1) 12
3825 SCHNAPPS 9-0 R Hughes (10) .... (16 to 1) 13
3771 TWILIGHT HOUR (Ire) (bl) 9-0 (9) .... (25 to 1) 14
Dist: Sht-hd, 2l, 3l, 1l. 1m 32.50s. a 9.30s (14 Ran).
SR: 29/28/19/13/7/-/ (Hamdan Al Maktoum), Kevin Prendergast

DOWN ROYAL (IRE) (good)
Saturday September 18th

4059 Down Royal E.B.F. Maiden (2-y-o) £2,415 5f..................... (3:00)

3613 SMART ROSIE (Ire) 8-11 P Shanahan (10) .... (9 to 2) 1
3492 ALL SHOW (Ire) 9-0 D V Smith (12) .... (10 to 1) 2
BUI-DOI (Ire) 8-3 (8*) B Fenton (1) ....(8 to 1) 3
2450[8] CAN BUT DREAM (Ire) 8-9 (2*) R M Burke (9) ...... (8 to 1) 4
3527[7] FOOLISH FLIGHT (Ire) 8-3 (8*) P M Donohue (6) ..(3 to 1 jt-fav) 5
1824[7] ZURYAF STAR (Ire) 9-0 K J Manning (5) ......(3 to 1 jt-fav) 6
3073 MEGAN'S DREAM (Ire) 8-7 (4*) W J Smith (8) ..... (12 to 1) 7
3729 FAYR DILLY (Ire) 8-3 (8*) P J Smullen (2) .... (4 to 1) 8
3911 PENZAAD (Ire) (bl) 8-6 (8*) D McCullagh (3) .... (14 to 1) 9
3731[8] CONTRASTING (Ire) 9-0 D J Smith (11) ....(10 to 1) 10
SHAHNAAD (Ire) 9-1[1] F Woods (7) .... (6 to 1) 11
3073 GREENRIDGE COURT (Ire) 8-5 (6*) B Bowens (4) ..(14 to 1) 12
Dist: 2l, ¾l, ½l, hd. (Time not taken) (12 Ran).
(Anthony Broughan), Owen Weldon

4060 Ulster Bank Fillies Maiden (3-y-o and up) £1,380 7f.................. (4:00)

3395[8] LOWLACK (bl) 3-9-1[1] F Woods (6) ....(7 to 1) 1
3579[6] KUDDAM (Ire) (bl) 3-9-0 P Shanahan (8) .... (4 to 1) 2
2667[3] ARROGANT LADY 3-8-6 (8*) P M Donohue (1) ..... (5 to 1) 3
3579[4] LOS ANGELES (Ire) 4-9-4 K J Manning (5) ..... (6 to 4 fav) 4
3576[8] ICEFLOW (Fr) (bl) 3-8-6 (8*) P J Smullen (3) .... (8 to 1) 5
3399[8] CAROLINA RUA (USA) 3-8-6 (8*) B Fenton (7) .....(20 to 1) 6
3074 ELLE A TED (Ire) 3-8-10 (4*) W J Smith (4) .... (12 to 1) 7
3074[5] TEGEMEZA (Ire) 3-8-12 (2*) R M Burke (2) .... (12 to 1) 8
Dist: 4l, 1l, hd, ¾l. (Time not taken) (8 Ran).
(O Brady), Miss I T Oakes

NEWBURY (good to soft)
Saturday September 18th
Going Correction: PLUS 0.10 sec. per fur.

4061 Highclere Nursery Class C (2-y-o) £7,252 5f 34yds................ (1:30)

3845[5] ROYALE FIGURINE (Ire) [70] 8-9 W R Swinburn (7) *trkd ldr, led 2 fs out, sn clr, cmftbly.* .... (11 to 2 op 7 to 2 tchd 6 to 1) 1
3688[2] BRAVE EDGE [82] 9-7 Pat Eddery (1) *chsd ldrs, ran on ins fnl furlong, no ch wth wnr.* .... (5 to 1 op 4 to 1 tchd 11 to 2) 2
3978* HELLO MISTER [75] 8-11 (3*,7ex) M Fenton (6) *hld up, ran on wl ins fnl furlong, nvr nrr*..... (7 to 1 tchd 15 to 2) 3
3673* FEATHERSTONE LANE [69] 8-8 B Rouse (10) *slwly away, ran on ins fnl 2 fs*..... (10 to 1 op 8 to 1 tchd 12 to 1) 4
3894[5] BILLY CRUNCHEON [70] 8-9 W Woods (8) *trkd ldrs, outpcd ins fnl 2 fs*....................... (25 to 1 op 20 to 1) 5
3715[3] FLOATING TRIAL [60] (v) 7-13 N Adams (5) *led till hdd 2 fs out, sn btn*............(11 to 2 op 3 to 1 tchd 6 to 1) 6
3871* DANCES WITH RISK [68] 8-7 D Harrison (4) *in tch till wknd wl o'r one furlong out.* .... (9 to 2 fav op 5 to 1 tchd 11 to 2 and 6 to 1) 7
3664[4] LORD SKY [64] 8-3 C Rutter (9) *rcd alone stands side, speed for 3 fs*.......................(10 to 1 op 8 to 1) 8
3978[5] MONSIEUR PETONG [61] 7-11 (3*) Stephen Davies (2) *outpcd thrght*.......................(12 to 1 op 10 to 1) 9
3436[8] STORM REGENT [58] 7-11 D Biggs (3) *slwly away, sn in tch, wknd quickly 2 fs out*.........(25 to 1 op 16 to 1) 10
Dist: 3l, sht-hd, 2½l, sht-hd, 3½l, nk, nk, 7l, 1l. 1m 3.24s. a 2.94s (10 Ran).
SR: 47/47/39/23/23/-/6/1/-/ (Ms Christine Walker), M J Fetherston-Godley

4062 Rokeby Farms Mill Reef Stakes Class A (Group 2) (2-y-o) £29,030 6f 8yds .... (2:00)

2075* POLISH LAUGHTER (USA) 8-11 W R Swinburn (4) *made virtually all, rdn and edgd lft ins fnl furlong, ran on.* ....(4 to 1 op 9 to 2 tchd 5 to 1) 1
3679[2] ALANEES 8-11 B Raymond (6) *hld up, hdwy to press wnr ins fnl furlong*.................. (14 to 1 op 12 to 1) 2
2906* FIRST TRUMP 9-1 M Hills (5) *slwly into strd, sn in tch, rdn 2 fs out, outpcd entering last.* ....(6 to 4 jt-fav op 5 to 4 tchd 13 to 8) 3
2845* BIG SQUEEZE (USA) 8-11 D Biggs (2) *dsptd ld till wknd o'r one furlong out*.................. (33 to 1 op 25 to 1) 4
3596* FOREST GAZELLE (USA) 8-11 Pat Eddery (3) *pld hrd, in tch till wknd wl o'r one furlong out, eased*. . .(6 to 4 jt-fav op 5 to 4 tchd 13 to 8) 5
Dist: Sht-hd, 2½l, nk, 5l. 1m 15.59s. a 3.89s (5 Ran).
SR: 31/30/24/19/-/ (Juma Humaid), B Hanbury

4063 Courage Rated Class B Handicap (0-110 3-y-o and up) £15,593 1¼m 6yds ....(2:30)

3764[5] LINDON LIME (USA) [91] 3-8-5 C Rutter (12) *hld up in tch, steady hdwy to ld appr fnl furlong, edgd rght, drvn out*.............................(25 to 1 tchd 33 to 1) 1
3636[5] JACKPOT STAR [87] 3-8-1 D Biggs (5) *hld up, hdwy on outsd o'r 2 fs out, edgd and jinked lft ins last, kpt on.* .... (16 to 1 op 14 to 1) 2
3437 GONE FOR A BURTON (Ire) [90] 3-8-4 T Sprake (4) *hld up in tch, hdwy whn hmpd o'r 2 fs out, several poss till ran on ins last*........... (11 to 1 op 8 to 1 tchd 12 to 1) 3
3434 BOLOARDO [87] 4-8-4 (3*) B Doyle (7) *trkd ldr, led o'r 2 fs out, rdn and hdd appr last, kpt on one pace.* (25 to 1) 4
3476[5] CONEYBURY (Ire) [87] 3-8-1 D Harrison (1) *chsd ldrs, kpt on one pace fnl 2 fs.* (11 to 1 op 12 to 1 tchd 10 to 1) 5
1329[3] SOVIET LINE (Ire) [103] 3-9-3 W R Swinburn (8) *wtd wth, ran on ins fnl 2 fs, nvr nrr.* ....(11 to 1 op 10 to 1 tchd 12 to 1) 6
3437[5] MR CONFUSION (Ire) [92] 5-8-12 B Raymond (9) *prmnt on outsd, squeezed for room and hmpd wl o'r one furlong out, swtchd rght, styd on ins last.* ....(9 to 2 fav op 4 to 1 tchd 11 to 2) 7
3314[7] WESTERN CAPE (USA) [96] 3-8-10 Pat Eddery (2) *hld up in mid-div, hdwy o'r 3 fs out, not clr run frm 2 out, eased ins last*............................(10 to 1 op 8 to 1) 8
3282 LYFORD CAY (Ire) [87] (bl) 3-7-12 (3*) Stephen Davies (11) *hld up, no hdwy fnl 3 fs*............. (20 to 1 tchd 22 to 1) 9
3879[3] PERSIAN BRAVE (Ire) [107] 3-9-7 M Hills (6) *led till hdd o'r 2 fs out, wknd quickly, eased.* ....(8 to 1 op 7 to 1 tchd 9 to 1) 10
3158[5] RISK MASTER [91] 4-8-11 W Woods (3) *slwly away, al in rear*..............................(16 to 1 op 20 to 1) 11
3900* RIBHI (USA) [99] 3-8-13 R Hills (10) *hld up in rear, nvr on terms*............................. (6 to 1 op 11 to 2) 12
3437[2] ALDERBROOK [94] 4-9-0 Paul Eddery (14) *mid-div, rdn o'r 3 fs out, sn btn*..................... (9 to 1 op 10 to 1) 13
3752* LUCKY GUEST [96] 6-9-2 B Rouse (13) *hld up in rear, effrt o'r 3 fs out, sn btn*................ (10 to 1 tchd 9 to 1) 14
Dist: ½l, ½l, 1l, ½l, ½l, nk, 6l, 1½l, sht-hd, ½l. 2m 8.92s. a 5.92s (14 Ran).
SR: 42/37/39/40/33/48/42/28/16/ (Fahd Salman), P F I Cole

4064 Tote Autumn Cup Handicap Class C (0-95 3-y-o and up) £15,962 1m 5f 61yds......................... (3:00)

3666[6] CASTORET [82] 7-9-12 D Harrison (3) *hld up, rdn and hdwy o'r 2 fs out, led ins last, jst held on.* .... (10 to 1 op 8 to 1 tchd 12 to 1) 1
3010* BAGALINO (USA) [82] 3-9-3 Pat Eddery (16) *al prmnt, led o'r 2 fs out, rdn and hdd ins last, rallied gmely, jst fld.* .... (10 to 1 op 11 to 1) 2
3761 JUSTICE (Fr) [51] 5-7-9[3] (3*) B Doyle (11) *mid-div, hdwy o'r 3 fs out, outpcd ins fnl 2.* .... (40 to 1 op 50 to 1 tchd 66 to 1) 3
3892* UM ALGOWAIN (USA) [93] 3-9-11 Paul Eddery (13) *mid-div, pushed alng o'r 4 fs out, kpt on one pace fnl 3.* .... (10 to 1 op 8 to 1 tchd 11 to 1) 4
3892[2] FRESCADE (USA) [84] 3-8-12 (7*) T G McLaughlin (4) *chsd ldrs, rdn o'r 2 fs out, one pace*..... (20 to 1 op 16 to 1) 5
3848[2] ROBERTY LEA [77] 5-9-2 (5*) A Procter (7) *chsd ldrs, rdn 3 fs out, one pace*................ (10 to 1 tchd 12 to 1) 6
3749[3] MEAVY [87] 3-9-8 R Hills (19) *chsd ldr till wknd o'r 2 fs out*................. (25 to 1 op 20 to 1 tchd 33 to 1) 7
3318[5] SCOTTISH PEAK (Ire) [88] 3-9-9 W R Swinburn (6) *in rear, styd on one pace fnl 3 fs*.......................... (20 to 1) 8
3735[3] BRIGHT SPELLS [89] 3-9-10 R Price (1) *towards rear, nvr nr to chal*........................(20 to 1 op 16 to 1) 9
3271[5] TIGER SHOOT [54] 6-7-12 T Williams (10) *al mid-div.* .... (25 to 1 op 20 to 1 tchd 33 to 1) 10
3466 CRYSTAL CROSS (USA) [82] 4-9-5 (7*) D Griffiths (17) *in rear, effrt on outsd 3 fs out, nvr dngrs.* .... (25 to 1 op 20 to 1 tchd 33 to 1) 11
3466[5] CUMBRIAN RHAPSODY [76] 3-8-11 D Biggs (12) *mid-div, nvr dngrs*.......................(10 to 1 op 8 to 1) 12
3724[4] KADASTROF (Fr) [75] 3-8-10 C Rutter (20) *led till hdd o'r 2 fs out, wknd quickly*........... (12 to 1 tchd 14 to 1) 13
2963[6] COMME D'HABITUDE (USA) [75] 3-8-10 M Hills (2) *mid-div, beh fnl 3 fs*............................. (33 to 1) 14
3850[6] THE SEER [76] 3-8-11 S Raymont (8) *al towards rear.* .... (25 to 1 op 20 to 1 tchd 33 to 1) 15
3666* BO KNOWS BEST (Ire) [66] 4-8-10 B Rouse (14) *beh frm hfwy*.............................. (10 to 1 op 12 to 1) 16
3587[8] HARD TASK [77] 3-8-12 S Whitworth (18) *mid-div, lost tch o'r 3 fs out*..................... (20 to 1 op 25 to 1) 17
1976[6] GRAND APPLAUSE (Ire) [68] 3-7-12[2] (7*) G Rothwell (9) *slwly away, came wide into strt, btn o'r 3 fs out.* .... (66 to 1 op 50 to 1) 18
3786* SUPREME MASTER [74] 3-8-9 B Raymond (15) *al in rear.* ....(10 to 1) 19

3786² GENERAL MOUKTAR [82] 3-9-0 (3*) Stephen Davies (5) *in rear, came wide into strt, btn o'r 3 fs out.* ....(5 to 1 fav op 7 to 1) 20
Dist: Sht-hd, 5l, 2l, hd, 6l, 3l, 1l, 5l, 3l, ¾l. 2m 56.77s. a 10.57s (20 Ran).
SR: 20/10/-/4/-/-/ (Lady d'Avigdor-Goldsmid), J W Hills

4065 Rothmans Royals North South Challenge Series Semi-final Handicap Class C (0-100 3-y-o and up) £15,660 1m 7yds.......................(3:30)

2794² PENNY DROPS [79] 4-9-6 D Harrison (18) *hld up, gd hdwy o'r 2 fs out, ran on to ld ins last, pushed out.* ....(5 to 1 fav op 7 to 1) 1
3623⁹ WALKING THE PLANK [70] (v) 4-8-11 W R Swinburn (4) *nvr far away, led one and a half fs out, rdn and hdd ins last, no extr*......................(16 to 1 op 14 to 1) 2
3697* SAIFAN [78] (bl) 4-9-2 (3*) C Hodgson (8) *hld up, hdwy o'r 2 fs out, rdn appr last, one pace*... (10 to 1 tchd 11 to 1) 3
3774 MARINE DIVER [67] 7-8-8 S Whitworth (9) *mid-div, gd hdwy o'r one furlong out, nvr nrr.* .... (14 to 1 op 12 to 1 tchd 16 to 1) 4
3487² TISSISAT (USA) [87] (v) 4-10-0 Pat Eddery (15) *hld up in mid-div, rdn and gd hdwy o'r 2 fs out, outpcd ins last.* .... (15 to 2 op 8 to 1 tchd 7 to 1) 5
3624⁸ NO RESERVATIONS (Ire) [85] 3-9-5 (3*) Stephen Davies (5) *led till hdd one and a half fs out, wknd ins last.* .... (16 to 1 op 20 to 1) 6
3697⁹ SAND TABLE [78] 4-9-5 B Rouse (12) *towards rear till ran on ins fnl 2 fs, nvr nrr*.......... (14 to 1 tchd 16 to 1) 7
2757⁵ PROUD BRIGADIER (Ire) [57] 5-7-12 C Rutter (13) *mid-div, rdn 2 fs out, one pace*.......................(20 to 1) 8
3697⁷ WYNONA (Ire) [70] 3-8-4 (3*) M Fenton (3) *mid-div, no hdwy fnl 2 fs*.. (20 to 1) 9
3655⁷ COURAGEOUS KNIGHT [69] 4-8-10 B Raymond (1) *hld up in tch, rdn and wknd o'r one furlong out.* ....(14 to 1 tchd 16 to 1) 10
3710⁸ LORD OBERON (Ire) [66] (v) 5-8-7 N Adams (6) *al mid-div.* .... (11 to 1 op 10 to 1 tchd 12 to 1) 11
3623³ CREDIT SQUEEZE [74] 3-8-11 R Hills (2) *chsd ldrs, rdn 3 fs out, wknd quickly appr last*................ (14 to 1) 12
3358⁵ LAWNSWOOD JUNIOR [66] 6-8-7 Paul Eddery (16) *al towards rear*.........(16 to 1 op 12 to 1 tchd 25 to 1) 13
3531⁴ NOBBY BARNES [62] 4-7-10 (7*) Sharon Millard (20) *nvr on terms*..........................(20 to 1 tchd 25 to 1) 14
3429⁷ BALLERINA BAY [68] 5-8-2 (7*) S Eiffert (17) *very slwly away, al in rear*................(20 to 1 tchd 25 to 1) 15
3358² HIGH LOW (USA) [78] 5-8-12 (7*) S Giles (10) *al beh, lost tch 3 fs out*...........................(10 to 1 op 8 to 1) 16
3697⁶ BLOCKADE (USA) [72] 4-8-13 M Hills (7) *chsd ldr till wknd quickly 2 fs out*...... (11 to 1 op 10 to 1 tchd 12 to 1) 17
3766² BROUGHTONS TURMOIL [55] 4-7-10³ D Biggs (11) *in tch till wknd quickly o'r 2 fs out*.....(14 to 1 tchd 16 to 1) 18
3177² INDIAN SLAVE (Ire) [71] 5-8-5 (7*) C Hawksley (19) *al in rear.* .... (12 to 1 op 10 to 1) 19
3697 AWESOME VENTURE [76] 3-8-13 W Woods (14) *chsd ldrs, wknd rpdly o'r 2 fs out*...........(33 to 1 op 25 to 1) 20
Dist: 2l, 2l, 2l, 2½l, ¾l, ¾l, 1l, nk, 1½l, ¾l. 1m 39.13s. a 3.33s (20 Ran).
SR: 68/53/55/38/50/42/37/13/21/ (Stanley J Sharp), Lord Huntingdon

4066 Arlington Conditions Stakes Class C (3-y-o and up) £5,057 1m 7yds.. (4:00)

MAROOF (USA) 3-9-0 R Hills (5) *trkd ldr, led aftr 2 fs, shaken up entering last, ran on wl.* ....(7 to 4 fav tchd 11 to 8 and 15 to 8) 1
3268² REDENHAM (USA) 3-8-11 B Raymond (2) *hld up, hdwy o'r 2 fs out, ran on to go second wl ins last.* ....(2 to 1 op 6 to 4 tchd 9 to 4) 2
3882³ TAOS (Ire) 3-9-6 Pat Eddery (4) *pld hrd, led for 2 fs, chsd wnr, rdn and outpcd ins last.* .... (11 to 4 op 5 to 2 tchd 7 to 2) 3
3748⁴ SPANISH STORM (Ire) (v) 4-9-0 W Woods (1) *hld up, rdn o'r 2 fs out, sn wknd*......(8 to 1 op 10 to 1 tchd 12 to 1) 4
WUFUD (USA) 3-8-10 Paul Eddery (3) *hld up in rear, lost tch 2 fs out*.......................(20 to 1 op 14 to 1) 5
Dist: 1½l, nk, 10l, 1½l. 1m 39.95s. a 4.15s (5 Ran).
SR: 50/42/50/14/5/ (Hamdan Al-Maktoum), R W Armstrong

4067 EBF Harwell Maiden Stakes Class D (2-y-o) £4,500 6f 8yds..........(4:30)

3589⁷ SOUTHERN RIDGE 9-0 D Harrison (5) *trkd ldrs, led 2 fs out, pushed out ins last.* .... (7 to 1 op 12 to 1 tchd 14 to 1) 1
LATTAM (USA) 9-0 R Hills (11) *nvr far away, hdwy 2 fs out, chsd wnr fnl furlong.* (10 to 1 op 8 to 1 tchd 12 to 1) 2
WAFAYT (Ire) 9-0 W R Swinburn (15) *slwly away, hdwy o'r 2 fs out, short of room and swtchd lft appr last, ran on wl ins*.........................(7 to 4 fav op 5 to 2) 3
JANGLE (Ire) 9-0 Pat Eddery (16) *mid-div, hdwy o'r 2 fs out, ran on one pace*... (5 to 1 op 4 to 1 tchd 11 to 2) 4
3781⁵ SULITELMA (USA) 8-9 S O'Gorman (6) *led aftr 2 fs, hdd two out, one pace after*...........(10 to 1 op 7 to 1) 5
3230⁹ SALANKA (Ire) 8-9 S Whitworth (13) *chsd ldrs till outpcd ins fnl furlong*.................. (33 to 1 op 16 to 1) 6
1689⁷ RED SLANEY (Ire) 8-9 (5*) B Russell (1) *mid-div, no hdwy fnl 2 fs*.................................(33 to 1 op 20 to 1) 7
FORENSIC EVIDENCE (Ire) 8-11 (3*) C Hodgson (7) *in tch till wknd wl o'r one furlong out*................(33 to 1) 8
ROSSINI BLUE 9-0 M Hills (4) *settled in rear, made some late hdwy*.......... (14 to 1 op 16 to 1 tchd 20 to 1) 9
EVANRO (Ire) 9-0 B Rouse (2) *intch till wknd 2 fs out.* ....(33 to 1) 10
3781⁸ ECHARDE 8-9 Paul Eddery (18) *al beh.* .... (33 to 1 op 20 to 1) 11
3260³ KENTAVRUS WAY (Ire) 9-0 S Raymont (17) *speed for 4 fs.* .... (14 to 1 op 10 to 1) 12
PEVERIL PRINCESS 8-9 N Adams (9) *al in rear.* .... (33 to 1 op 20 to 1) 13
MISTER MAYBE 9-0 R Perham (8) *slwly away, al beh.* .... (33 to 1 op 20 to 1) 14
POLISH CONSUL 9-0 B Procter (3) *mid-div, beh fnl 2 fs.* ....(16 to 1 tchd 20 to 1) 15
BOLD MICK 9-0 C Rutter (12) *mid-div, hrd rdn o'r 2 fs out, sn btn*......................................(33 to 1) 16
FRED'S DELIGHT (Ire) 9-0 W Woods (14) *in tch, wknd sn aftr hfwy*.....................................(33 to 1) 17
3746⁴ GALLANT SPIRIT (Ire) 9-0 B Raymond (19) *chsd ldrs till wknd quickly sn aftr hfwy.* ....(11 to 2 op 3 to 1 tchd 6 to 1) 18
3589 GREATEST HOPES 9-0 T Williams (10) *led 1st 2 fs, wknd hfwy*...(33 to 1) 19
Dist: 2½l, 2½l, 1l, 3l, 2½l, ½l, nk, 1½l, nk, sht-hd. 1m 15.47s. a 3.77s (19 Ran).
SR: 37/27/17/13/-/-/ (Bill Brown), D R C Elsworth

BELMONT PARK (USA) (soft)
Saturday September 18th

4068 Woodward Stakes (Grade 1) (3-y-o and up) £198,675 1m 1f..............

2838³ BERTRANDO (USA) 4-9-0 G Stevens,........ (10 to 9 on) 1
3640³ DEVIL HIS DUE (USA) 4-9-0 H McCauley,....... (29 to 10) 2
2838* VALLEY CROSSING (USA) 5-9-0 C Antley,..... (152 to 10) 3
2243⁵ MISSIONARY RIDGE 6-9-0 E Delahoussaye,.. (10 to 9 on) 4
MINER'S MARK (USA) 3-8-9 C McCarron,.......(42 to 10) 5
3640² WEST BY WEST (USA) 4-9-0 J-L Samyn,..........(9 to 2) 6
Dist: 14l, 3l, hd, 12l, 6l. 1m 47.00s. (6 Ran).
(Nahem, 505 Stable & Headley), B Headley

4069 Futurity Stakes (Grade 1) (2-y-o) £45,934 7f..........................

HOLY BULL (USA) 8-10 M Smith,............... (31 to 10) 1
DEHERE (USA) 8-10 C McCarron,.............(5 to 2 on) 2
PRENUP (USA) 8-10 C Antley,..................(344 to 10) 3
SACRED HONOUR (USA) 8-10 E Delahoussaye, (129 to 10) 4
SIR JOE (USA) 8-10 J Chavez,...................(55 to 1) 5
SLEW GIN FIZZ (USA) 8-10 J Bailey,............(53 to 10) 6
Dist: ½l, 5l, 8l, 21l, 16l. 1m 23.31s. (6 Ran).
(W J Croll Jr), W J Croll Jr

4070 Matron Stakes (Grade 1) (2-y-o) £46,808 7f..........................

3700* STRATEGIC MANEUVER (USA) 8-7 J Santos, ...(5 to 4 on) 1
3700² ASTAS FOXY LADY (USA) 8-7 C Perret, ...(56 to 10) 2
SOVEREIGN KITTY (USA) 8-7 J R Velasquez,.....(10 to 1) 3
THE BINK (USA) 8-7 E Maple,................. (64 to 10) 4
OFFICER FALLON (USA) 8-7 R Baez,...........(39 to 10) 5
LADY HUNTER (USA) 8-7 R Migliore,............ (23 to 1) 6
3700⁹ PRINCESS TRU (USA) 8-7 J Chavez,............ (45 to 1) 7
WONDERLAN (USA) 8-7 J Bailey,................ (38 to 1) 8
Dist: 13l, 6½l, 5l, 2l, 11l, 1l. 1m 23.84s. (8 Ran).
(P Teinowitz), F S Shulhofer

4071 Man O' War Stakes (Grade 1) (3-y-o and up) £158,940 1m 3f..............

3654* STAR OF COZZENE (USA) 5-9-0 J Santos, ... (5 to 4 on) 1
2771* SERRANT (USA) 5-9-0 M Smith,................(9 to 2) 2
3187³ DR KIERNAN (USA) 4-9-0 C Antley,........... (147 to 10) 3
3654⁴ DEAR DOCTOR (Fr) 6-9-0 G Stevens,...........(69 to 10) 4
FURIOUSLY (USA) 4-9-0 K Desormeaux,........(88 to 10) 5
597² BIEN BIEN (USA) 4-9-0 C McCarron,........... (61 to 10) 6
3187* SPECTACULAR TIDE (USA) 4-9-0 J Bailey,.....(194 to 10) 7
ANTARTIC WINGS (USA) 5-9-0 R Davis,.......... (75 to 1) 8
Dist: 5½l, nk, nk, 3½l, 12l, 9l, dist. 2m 23.14s. (8 Ran).
(J Siegel), F Boutin

EVRY (FR) (soft)
Saturday September 18th
Going Correction: PLUS 0.15 sec. per fur.

4072 Prix du Point du Jour (Listed) (4-y-o and up) £14,337 1m............ (3:05)

ROI DES CHAMPS 4-8-11 O Doleuze,.................... 1
KITWOOD (USA) 4-8-11 T Jarnet,....................... 2

WHAT KAY DID (USA) 4-8-8 C Asmussen, ... 3
4726a[8] SEBA LE ROUGE (Fr) 6-8-11 W Mongil, ... 4
Dist: ½l, ¾l, nose, 1½l, hd, hd, 10l. 1m 41.83s. a 4.43s (8 Ran).
SR: 49/47/42/44/ (Mlle M Head), Dom Boulard

FRANKFURT (GER) (good)
Sunday September 19th

4073 Team Trophy der Volksbanken Raiffeisenbanken (Group 2) (3-y-o and up) £48,980 1¼m.................. (3:45)

3703[5] KOMTUR (USA) 3-8-5 K Woodburn, *made all, clr one furlong out, ran on strly*................................. 1
2259 THAGUS (Ger) 3-8-5 N Grant, *al in tch, 3rd strt, second one and a half fs out, no imprsn*..................... 2
3913[8] REVELATION (Ire) 3-8-9 T Quinn, *hld up, 6th strt, hdwy wl o'r one furlong out, one pace fnl furlong*.............. 3
3582[3] LE JARDIN (Ger) 5-9-1 Manfred Hofer, *last till 4 fs out, 7th strt, ran on fnl 2 furlongs, nrst finish*................ 4
3582[2] SUGUNAS (Ger) 5-9-3 A Boschert, *hdwy hfwy, 5th strt, 4th 2 fs out, sn one pace*................................ 5
3784* SPARTAN SHAREEF (Ire) 4-9-3 M Roberts, *prmnt, 4th strt, wknd o'r one furlong out*............................ 6
3370 VINCENZO (Ger) 4-9-1 W Newnes, *trkd ldr till wknd o'r one furlong out*...................................... 7
3582[4] IRON FIGHTER (Ger) 4-9-3 R Hillis, *prmnt till rdn and wknd o'r 3 fs out*...................................... 8
2644[5] SAN FRANZISCO (Ger) 6-9-1 A Riding, *al rear*............ 9
Dist: 3l, ¾l, 1 ¼l, 1½l, nk, 1l, 10l, 4l. 2m 6.22s. (9 Ran).
(H Hasler & A Pereira), H Remmert

LONGCHAMP (FR) (soft)
Sunday September 19th
Going Correction: PLUS 0.55 sec. per fur.

4074 Prix la Rochette (Group 3) (2-y-o) £23,895 1m.................... (3:10)

CHIMES BAND (USA) 9-2 D Boeuf (2) *made all, kpt on wl.* ....(11 to 1) 1
SUNSHACK 9-2 Pat Eddery (1) *trkd ldr, chlgd 2 fs out, kpt on strly*.................................. (10 to 7 on) 2
LOST WORLD (Ire) 9-2 O Peslier (3) *pld hrd mid-div, 5th strt, effrt and one pace 2 fs out, ran on fnl furlong.* ....(37 to 10) 3
3048* BARODET (USA) 9-2 T Jarnet (5) *slwly away, pld hrd mid-div, 4th strt, rdn 2 fs out, one pace ins last*... (37 to 10) 4
ARDANA (Ire) 9-2 E Saint-Martin (7) *hld up rear, rdn and swtchd outsd 2 fs out, some late prog*.........(19 to 1) 5
3499 SOLID ILLUSION (USA) 9-2 W Mongil (4) *prmnt early, 3rd strt, rdn 2 fs out, sn wknd*.................. (24 to 1) 6
OCEAN INDIEN (Fr) 9-2 C Asmussen (6) *pld hrd rear, 6th strt, nvr plcd to chal*.........................(89 to 10) 7
Dist: Hd, 1½l, ¾l, 2l, hd, sht-hd. 1m 48.90s. a 12.90s (7 Ran).
(Ecurie I M Fares), P Bary

4075 Prix du Prince d'Orange (Group 3) (3-y-o and up) £23,895 1¼m....... (3:40)

3370[7] APPLE TREE (Fr) (bl) 4-9-4 T Jarnet (3) *trkd ldr, rdn 2 fs out, led one and a half out, drw clr ins fnl furlong.* ....(2 to 1 on) 1
3649[6] MARILDO (Fr) (bl) 6-9-4 G Guignard (1) *led till one and a half fs out, kpt on one pace*.................(31 to 10) 2
2803[6] JACKDIDI (Fr) 3-8-9 D Boeuf (2) *rcd in 3rd, effrt 2 fs out, kpt on fnl furlong*.............................(13 to 2) 3
PENCOMBE (USA) 3-8-9 C Asmussen (4) *al last.* (28 to 10) 4
Dist: 2½l, ½l, 3l. 2m 14.82s. a 12.72s (4 Ran).
SR: 32/27/17/11/ (Paul de Moussac), A Fabre

4076 Prix du Pin (Listed) (3-y-o and up) £14,337 7f..................... (4:10)

3777[6] SHARP PROD (USA) 3-8-9 L Piggott, *made all, rdn o'r one out, all out fnl furlong*................................ 1
3015 ACTEUR FRANCAIS (USA) 5-8-11 T Jarnet,.............. 2
NEVERNEYEV (USA) 3-8-9 O Doleuze,.................... 3
3015 GOTHLAND (Fr) 4-9-1 F Sanchez,........................ 4
3285[3] TRUE BEARING (USA) 3-8-9 F Head,..................... 5
3501[8] RANGER (Fr) 3-9-2 W Mongil,.......................... 6
3208 INTERVALLO (USA) 3-8-9 C Asmussen,................... 7
3618 SANDCREEK (Ire) 3-8-9 O Peslier,...................... 8
QUARTANNIER (Fr) 4-8-11 G Mosse,...................... 9
WAJIHOR (Fr) 3-8-9 G Toupel,.......................... 10
Dist: 1l, 1l, ½l, 1½l, nose, nose, 1½l, nose, 2l. 1m 24.70s. a 5.20s (10 Ran).
SR: 75/74/69/73/62/68/60/55/56/ (The Queen), Lord Huntingdon

SAN SIRO (ITY) (soft)
Sunday September 19th

4077 Premio Novella (Listed) (2-y-o) £20,173 7f 110yds.............. (2:00)

3651[6] SENSAZIONE 8-10 M Esposito,.......................... 1
GOLDEN TAJNIAK (Ire) 8-10 O Fancera,.................. 2
JARRE BOVE (Ire) 8-8 S Dettori,....................... 3
TYCOON LADY (Ire) 8-8 J Carroll,...................... 4
3651[8] MICHELLE HICKS 8-10 J Reid, *dsptd ld 4 fs out, wknd 3 out*... 5
IMEME (Ity) 8-8 M Planard,............................ 6
Dist: 4l, 3½l, nk, hd, nk. 1m 33.30s. (6 Ran).
(Scuderia Blueberry), V Caruso

4078 Gran Premio d'Italia (Group 1) (3-y-o) £97,165 1½m.................. (4:00)

3403[6] RIGHT WIN (Ire) 9-2 J Reid, *rcd in 5th, hdwy 2 fs out, led appr fnl furlong, ran on wl*......................... 1
3899[6] AZZILFI 9-2 W Carson, *rcd in 4th, dsptd ld strt, led briefly o'r one furlong out, ran on*......................... 2
3501[4] TALLOIRES (USA) 9-2 S Guillot, *dsptd ld strt, led 2 fs out, swrvd and hdd one and a half out, not reco'r*......... 3
3878[4] FRENCHPARK 9-2 J Carroll, *trkd ldr, dsptd ld strt, ran on one pace 2 fs out*.................................. 4
3796* MR RICHARD (Ire) 9-2 M Pasquale, *rear early, rcd alone and 4th strt, sn wknd*................................ 5
3796[5] LIFE EXTENSION 9-2 O Fancera, *led till wknd quickly appr strt*.. 6
Dist: ¾l, 1½l, 1 ¾l, dist, dist. 2m 28.70s. (6 Ran).
(Conal Kavanagh), R Hannon

BELMONT PARK (USA) (heavy)
Sunday September 19th

4079 Ruffian Handicap (Grade 1) (3-y-o and up) £79,470 1m 110yds...............

2802[3] SHARED INTEREST (USA) 5-8-2 R Davis, ...(134 to 10) 1
3767* DISPUTE (USA) 3-8-3 K Desormeaux, ... (32 to 10) 2
3804* TURNBACK THE ALARM (USA) 4-8-11 C Antley, ... (5 to 2) 3
2802* YOU'D BE SURPRISED (USA) 4-8-6 M Smith, ... (9 to 2) 4
2645[2] PASEANA (Arg) 6-8-13 C McCarron, ...(2 to 1 on) 5
Dist: 2½l, 3l, 2 ¼l, 13l. 1m 41.92s. (5 Ran).
(R S Evans), F S Schulhofer

WOODBINE (CAN) (firm)
Sunday September 19th

4080 Molson Export Million (Grade 2) (3-y-o) £310,880 1m 1f..................

2442* PETESKI (Can) 8-9 C Perret,.......................... 1
2442[2] CHEERY KNIGHT (Can) 8-5 D Seymour,................. 2
1542[7] SEA HERO (USA) 9-0 J D Bailey,....................... 3
1542[2] KISSIN KRIS (USA) 9-0 P Day,......................... 4
779 TRUTH OF IT ALL (USA) 8-7 M Walls,.................... 5
1542* COLONIAL AFFAIR (USA) 9-0 J Santos,.................. 6
Dist: 4½l, 1l, 3l, ¾l, 3l. 1m 49.20s. (6 Ran).
(Earle I Mack), R Attfield

EDINBURGH (good to soft)
Monday September 20th
Going Correction: PLUS 0.10 sec. per fur.

4081 Tote Placepot Claiming Stakes Class F (2-y-o) £1,605 7f 15yds........ (2:15)

3968 SHUTTLECOCK 8-3 J Weaver (1) *cl up, led 4 fs out, clr one out, cmftbly*.........................(5 to 1 op 7 to 2) 1
3829[4] CELESTIAL DANCE 8-2 J Carroll (10) *beh, styd on wl fnl 2 fs, nrst finish*.................... (11 to 2 op 4 to 1) 2
3792[7] LEGAL TRAIN 8-13 J Lowe (6) *led for one furlong, prmnt, outpcd o'r 2 out, swtchd and styd on fnl furlong.* .... (10 to 1 op 16 to 1) 3
3968[3] WINGS AHEAD 8-11 B Rouse (4) *chsd ldrs, kpt on same pace frm 2 out*...................(8 to 1 tchd 10 to 1) 4
3809[6] RED MARCH HARE 8-1 (5*) J Tate (2) *prmnt, chsd wnr frm 3 out, no imprsn, wknd fnl furlong.* ....(10 to 1 op 25 to 1 tchd 33 to 1) 5
3903 ROCHE ABBEY (Ire) 8-1 E Johnson (3) *led aftr one furlong, stumbled 4 out, sn hdd, wknd o'r one out.* .... (10 to 1 op 8 to 1) 6
3968 TWO D'S 8-13 G Bardwell (12) *sn beh, nvr dngrs.* .... (20 to 1 op 14 to 1) 7
3566 MAZINA 7-7 (5*) D Wright (7) *nvr dngrs*........... (33 to 1) 8
3841[8] BIEN CUIT 7-13 (3*) N Kennedy (8) *beh, effrt 3 fs out, sn btn*............................. (20 to 1 op 16 to 1) 9
JERSEY MONKEY (Ire) 7-9 (7*) P Roberts (11) *beh frm hfwy.* .... (33 to 1 op 25 to 1) 10
3869[3] BADGER'S BEND (v) 8-8 Dale Gibson (5) *mid-div till wknd o'r 2 out*....................... (4 to 1 fav tchd 5 to 1) 11
3903[5] HELLABY 8-11 T Williams (9) *mid-div, hdwy 3 fs out, wknd o'r one out, eased whn btn*.... (5 to 1 op 7 to 2) 12
Dist: 4l, hd, hd, 2½l, 8l, 1½l, 1½l, 1½l, 3½l, 2½l. 1m 30.80s. a 5.60s (12 Ran).
SR: 16/3/13/10/-/-/ (Lord Scarsdale), P C Haslam

4082 Gaymers Olde English Cyder Nursery Class E (2-y-o) £1,966 7f 15yds. . (2:45)

3966³ MISS MAH-JONG [80] 9-7 J Weaver (8) *trkd ldr, led 2 fs out, rdn fnl furlong, jst hld on.* ....(5 to 4 on op Evens tchd 11 to 10 and 11 to 8 on) 1
3598⁶ GLENLYON DUCHESS [54] 7-4 (5*) D Wright (1) *mid-div, effrt on outsd 3 fs out, sn rdn, styd on wl fnl furlong, jst fld*.......................(25 to 1 tchd 33 to 1) 2
3966⁴ WIXI (Ire) [75] 9-2 Dale Gibson (7) *hld up, hdwy 3 fs out, ev ch entering fnl furlong, no extr.* ....(4 to 1 op 3 to 1 tchd 9 to 2) 3
3760 CRISTAL SPRINGS [61] 8-2 T Williams (6) *al prmnt, pushed alng o'r 2 fs out, kpt on same pace.* ....(10 to 1 tchd 12 to 1) 4
3968² STORM HEIGHTS [52] 7-7 J Lowe (3) *led till hdd 2 fs out, wknd fnl furlong*.....................(10 to 1 op 8 to 1) 5
3792⁹ MONKEY WENCH (Ire) [55] 7-3 (7*) P Fessey (4) *beh, effrt 3 fs out, no real hdwy*...............(16 to 1 op 10 to 1) 6
3218 UN PARFUM DE FEMME (Ire) [68] 8-9 G Bardwell (5) *in tch, pushed alng 3 fs out, wknd 2 out.* (20 to 1 op 12 to 1) 7
3743⁷ BOJOLLY [53] 7-8⁴ (3*) N Kennedy (2) *al beh.* ....(16 to 1 op 10 to 1) 8

Dist: Sht-hd, 2½l, 1l, nk, 2½l, hd, ½l. 1m 31.90s. a 6.70s (8 Ran).
SR: 17/-/3/-/-/ (R Robinson (Wigan)), M Johnston

4083 Tote Credit Maiden Handicap Class F (Div I) (0-60 3-y-o and up) £2,242 7f 15yds. . . . . (3:15)

3591⁹ GUESSTIMATION (USA) [45] 4-9-3 G Bardwell (3) *in tch, effrt o'r 2 out, rdn to ld ins fnl furlong, ran on wl.* ....(6 to 1 tchd 7 to 1) 1
4047⁵ SALVATORE GIULIANO [42] 3-8-10 J Carroll (4) *al prmnt, led one furlong out, sn hdd, no extr.* ....(7 to 1 op 6 to 1 tchd 8 to 1) 2
4022⁵ PANTHER (Ire) [60] 3-9-9 (5*) J Tate (6) *beh, hdwy hfwy, kpt on same pace fnl 2 fs*............ (20 to 1 op 12 to 1) 3
2978⁶ JOMOVE [37] 4-8-4 (5*) D Wright (8) *beh, hdwy 3 fs out, styd on, not rch ldrs*...................(7 to 1 op 5 to 1) 4
3789⁵ HALL BANK COTTAGE [44] 3-8-12 J Weaver (7) *beh till styd on und pres fnl 2 fs, not rch ldrs*.... (10 to 1 op 7 to 1) 5
3887⁶ THATCHED (Ire) [36] (bl) 3-8-4 T Williams (1) *led till hdd one furlong out, sn btn*............. (4 to 1 fav op 7 to 2) 6
3628⁶ SYKE LANE [27] 4-7-13 Dale Gibson (5) *trkd ldrs, effrt 3 fs out, wknd o'r one out.* ....(16 to 1 op 14 to 1 tchd 20 to 1) 7
3631⁸ PINKERTON'S SILVER [41] 3-8-9 J Lowe (10) *prmnt till lost pl 4 fs out, no dngr aftr*..............(9 to 2 op 4 to 1) 8
3533⁷ VILLAVINA [51] 3-9-2 (3*) N Kennedy (2) *trkd ldrs, effrt on outsd 3 fs out, wknd 2 out.* ....(17 to 2 op 7 to 1 tchd 12 to 1) 9
3811 SAINTED SUE [28] 3-7-3 (7*) C Adamson (9) *prmnt till grad wknd frm 3 fs out*..................... (25 to 1 op 16 to 1) 10

Dist: 1l, 1½l, 1½l, 1l, 3½l, 5l, ½l, ¾l, nk. 1m 30.50s. a 5.30s (10 Ran).
SR: 34/24/37/13/13/-/ (Quintet Partnership), J Pearce

4084 EBF Tote Dual Forecast Fillies' Rating Related Maiden Stakes Class F (2-y-o) £2,179 5f. . . . . (3:45)

3903⁶ DOCKYARD DORA (bl) 8-11 G Bardwell (4) *chsd ldrs, kpt on wl und pres to ld ins fnl furlong, all out.* ....(8 to 1 op 7 to 1 tchd 10 to 1) 1
3557⁶ BOLD TIME MONKEY 8-11 Dale Gibson (6) *dwlt, in tch, rdn 2 fs out, kpt on wl und pres ins fnl furlong.* ....(14 to 1 op 10 to 1 tchd 16 to 1) 2
3870² COLNE VALLEY (v) 8-11 T Williams (1) *led, rdn o'r one furlong out, hdd ins fnl furlong, no extr.* ....(6 to 4 fav op 5 to 4 tchd 2 to 1) 3
3711⁷ CAPONATA (Ire) 8-11 J Carroll (3) *chsd ldr, chlgd 2 fs out, ev ch till wknd fnl furlong*.........(4 to 1 tchd 5 to 1) 4
3673⁴ PAGODA 8-11 J Weaver (5) *trkd ldrs, effrt 2 fs out, sn rdn and no hdwy*...........(3 to 1 op 4 to 1 tchd 9 to 2) 5
3972 HOTCROFT 8-11 J Lowe (2) *prmnt till wknd hfwy.* ....(14 to 1 op 10 to 1) 6

Dist: Nk, nk, 1½l, 2l, 6l. 1m 2.20s. a 4.40s (6 Ran).
SR: 19/18/17/11/3/-/ (G G Ashton), M Brittain

4085 Tote Credit Maiden Handicap Class F (Div II) (0-60 3-y-o and up) £2,242 7f 15yds. . . . . (4:15)

3440⁶ THISONESFORALICE [33] 5-9-5 J Lowe (7) *sn beh and pushed alng, hdwy 3 fs out, styd on wl to ld ins fnl furlong*.............. (8 to 1 op 7 to 1 tchd 9 to 1) 1
3216⁴ ALBEIT [31] 3-8-13 T Williams (5) *trkd ldrs, effrt o'r 2 fs out, rdn to ld one out, sn hdd, no extr.* ....(9 to 2 op 4 to 1 tchd 5 to 1) 2
4031⁶ KILTROUM (Fr) [35] (v) 4-9-7 Dale Gibson (10) *led till hdd one furlong out, kpt on*...........(6 to 1 op 5 to 1) 3
3788 DANCES WITH GOLD [32] 3-9-0 E Johnson (9) *cl up, ev ch o'r one furlong out, kpt on same pace.* ....(10 to 1 op 8 to 1) 4
4022⁵ RUNRIG (Ire) [46] (v) 3-9-7 (7*) R Havlin (8) *al chasing ldrs, kpt on same pace fnl 2 fs*.........(8 to 1 tchd 10 to 1) 5
3256⁸ PANIC BUTTON (Ire) [43] 3-9-11 J Carroll (2) *in tch, sn pushed alng, kpt on fnl 2 fs, nvr dngrs.* ....(25 to 1 op 12 to 1) 6
3591 VIKING WATERS [37] (bl) 3-9-0 (5*) J Tate (6) *beh, styd on fnl 2 fs, not rch ldrs*...............(10 to 1 op 8 to 1) 7
3948 GLIMPSE OF HEAVEN [42] 3-9-3 (7*) G Parkin (4) *in tch, rdn 3 fs out, sn btn*..................(20 to 1 op 16 to 1) 8
3591 FESTIN [41] (bl) 3-9-9 J Weaver (3) *prmnt till wknd o'r 2 fs out*...............(15 to 2 op 6 to 1 tchd 8 to 1) 9
3107⁶ FLYING WIND [40] (bl) 4-9-12 B Rouse (1) *dwlt, sn in tch, wknd o'r 2 fs out*..............(7 to 2 fav tchd 4 to 1) 10

Dist: 1½l, ½l, 1l, hd, sht-hd, ½l, 8l, 4l, ½l. 1m 32.10s. a 6.90s (10 Ran).
SR: 12/1/7/-/10/6/ (Willie Smith), A Harrison

4086 Bet With The Tote Handicap Class E (0-70 3-y-o and up) £2,008 1½m 31yds . . . . (4:45)

3831² KELIMUTU [50] 4-8-12 G Bardwell (7) *hld up gng wl, hdwy 5 fs out, led o'r one out, pushed clr, easily.* ....(9 to 4 fav tchd 5 to 2) 1
3831⁵ CLIBURNEL NEWS (Ire) [53] 3-8-7 Dale Gibson (5) *beh, hdwy 4 fs out, ch 2 out, kpt on, no chance wth wnr.* ....(5 to 1 op 4 to 1) 2
2870⁷ MOONSHINE DANCER [40] 3-7-3 (5*) D Wright (6) *prmnt till lost pl and beh 5 fs out, rdn 3 out, styd on wl fnl 2 furlongs*...................(16 to 1 op 10 to 1) 3
3814⁵ MILNGAVIE (Ire) [47] 3-8-1 E Johnson (11) *in tch, hdwy to track ldrs 8 fs out, ev ch 2 out, kpt on same pace.* ....(9 to 1 op 8 to 1 tchd 12 to 1) 4
3301⁶ CUTTHROAT KID (Ire) [50] (v) 3-8-4 J Carroll (8) *led or dsptd ld till hdd o'r one furlong out, sn btn.* ....(14 to 1 op 8 to 1) 5
4017³ AMERICAN HERO [61] 5-9-9 J Weaver (3) *chsd ldr, chlgd 4 fs out, ev ch till wknd wl o'r one out.* ....(4 to 1 tchd 9 to 2) 6
4043⁹ SHARQUIN [37] 6-7-13 J Lowe (10) *nvr nr ldrs.* ....(14 to 1 op 12 to 1) 7
3567⁶ ASTRAC TRIO (USA) [44] 3-7-9 (3*) N Kennedy (9) *mid-div till wknd o'r 4 fs out*..............(66 to 1 op 50 to 1) 8
3752 ONE OFF THE RAIL (USA) [55] 3-8-9 B Rouse (4) *beh most of way*...................................(6 to 1 tchd 7 to 1) 9
J P MORGAN [46] (v) 5-8-3 (5*) J Tate (2) *in tch, pushed alng hfwy, wknd o'r 3 fs out*...... (33 to 1 op 20 to 1) 10
JUPITER MOON [62] 4-9-10 T Williams (1) *chsd ldrs till wknd o'r 4 fs out*...................(40 to 1 op 33 to 1) 11

Dist: 3½l, 1½l, 2l, 2½l, 6l, 8l, 4l, 2½l, 3½l, ½l. 2m 41.20s. a 8.40s (11 Ran).
SR: 26/14/-/1/-/6/ (James Furlong), J Pearce

FOLKESTONE (good to soft (races 1,2,3,4), good (5,6))

Monday September 20th

Going Correction: PLUS 0.20 sec. per fur. (races 1,2,3,5,6), PLUS 0.05 (4)

4087 Deal Handicap Class E (0-70 3-y-o) £2,118 1m 1f 149yds. . . . . (1:50)

3681 ARMENIAN COFFEE (Ire) [65] (bl) 9-2 Pat Eddery (15) *made all, rdn 2 fs out, styd on gmely.* ....(5 to 1 tchd 6 to 1 and 9 to 2) 1
3820³ MO-ADDAB (Ire) [70] 9-7 S Whitworth (6) *settled midfield, gd hdwy wl o'r 2 fs out, chlgd appr last, ran on.* ....(6 to 1 op 4 to 1) 2
2942⁸ WOLLBOLL [47] 7-12 N Adams (14) *al hndy, chlgd 2 fs out, kpt on one pace und pres ins last.* (25 to 1 op 16 to 1) 3
3533⁴ LANDRAIL (USA) [60] 8-11 D Holland (2) *trkd ldrs, ev ch o'r 2 fs out, not quicken ins last*...... (10 to 1 tchd 8 to 1) 4
2972 MENA [49] 8-0 D Biggs (13) *beh till styd on fnl 2 fs, nrst finish*..........................(12 to 1 tchd 14 to 1) 5
3745 PRINCE SONGLINE [50] 8-1 T Sprake (4) *beh till gd hdwy frm o'r 3 fs out, styd on, nvr nrr*... (20 to 1 op 14 to 1) 6
3533* ICE REBEL [58] (bl) 8-9 W Newnes (11) *bustled alng to track ldr till rdn and wknd appr fnl furlong.* ....(3 to 1 fav op 4 to 1 tchd 5 to 2) 7
3832⁶ RAGAZZO (Ire) [45] 7-10 L Charnock (5) *trkd ldrs, rdn o'r 2 fs out, wndrd over one out, no extr.* ....(12 to 1 tchd 16 to 1) 8
1976⁷ NIGHT EDITION [48] 7-13 A Tucker (3) *wl beh till some hdwy o'r 3 fs out, nvr able to chal.* (33 to 1 op 20 to 1) 9
3783⁸ TWICE THE GROOM (Ire) [63] 9-0 A Clark (1) *nvr better than mid-div*..................... (12 to 1 tchd 20 to 1) 10
3783 KNYAZ [60] 8-11 N Carlisle (8) *al towards rear.* ....(20 to 1 op 14 to 1) 11
3178⁸ LADY HONDA (Ire) [45] 7-10³ (3*) B Doyle (7) *al beh.* ....(33 to 1 op 25 to 1) 12
3817⁴ ROLLING WATERS [57] 8-8 W Woods (12) *chsd ldrs till rdn and wknd o'r 4 fs out.* ....(11 to 1 op 10 to 1 tchd 12 to 1) 13
3574⁴ JULIASDARKINVADER [45] 7-9⁴ (5*) B Russell (9) *al beh.* ....(33 to 1 op 20 to 1) 14
3549² DEVIOUS DANCER [65] 8-11 (5*) D McCabe (10) *hld up and beh, shrtlvd effrt o'r 3 fs out, sn wknd.* ....(10 to 1 tchd 11 to 1) 15

Dist: ¾l, ¾l, 1l, ½l, sht-hd, 2l, 2½l, 3l, 8l, ½l. 2m 7.10s. a 9.50s (15 Ran).

SR: 27/30/5/16/4/4/8/-/-/ (Az Agr Associate Srl), J L Dunlop

4088 Hastings Claiming Stakes Class F (3-y-o) £1,941 1m 1f 149yds........(2:20)

3887[5] DANCING DIAMOND (Ire) 8-3 W Woods (4) led aftr 3 fs, drvn clr 2 furlongs out, unchlgd. .... (11 to 2 op 6 to 1 tchd 8 to 1) 1

3759 SKY BURST 8-8 N Carlisle (1) chsd ldrs, rdn o'r 2 fs out, styd on same pace appr last, no ch wth wnr. .... (11 to 1 op 8 to 1 tchd 12 to 1) 2

3311[4] GUV'NORS GIFT 8-10 P Robinson (10) al hndy, rdn o'r 2 fs out, kpt on one pace............. (7 to 4 fav op 3 to 1) 3

THE COUNTRY DANCER 8-5[1] M Wigham (7) led 3 fs, styd hndy till rdn and not quicken fnl 2. .... (33 to 1 op 25 to 1) 4

3945[2] PRETTY BABY (bl) 8-8 D Biggs (11) handily plcd, rdn o'r 2 fs out, no extr.................. (5 to 1 tchd 11 to 2) 5

3811 SAXON MAGIC (bl) 8-8 D Holland (12) chsd ldrs, rdn o'r 2 fs out, sn btn..................... (14 to 1 op 10 to 1) 6

3634 EXPRESS MARIECURIE (Ire) 8-1 (5*) D McCabe (3) beh, came wide and some hdwy und pres wl o'r one furlong out, not a dngr............................. (14 to 1) 7

3591[6] BAN RI (Ire) 7-11 (5*) B Russell (2) prmnt till rdn and wknd 2 fs out........................... (7 to 1 op 5 to 1) 8

3887 KYRENIA GAME 8-8 W Newnes (9) nvr nr to chal. .... (12 to 1 op 10 to 1) 9

1627[9] SOOJAMA (Ire) 9-1 Pat Eddery (8) beh, rdn and hdwy o'r 2 fs out, eased whn btn fnl furlong. (12 to 1 op 10 to 1) 10

3981[9] ARRAS ROYALE 8-7 A Tucker (5) ldg grp till wknd 3 fs out. .... (33 to 1 op 25 to 1 tchd 50 to 1) 11

3955 LADY RELKO 8-0 N Adams (14) al beh......... (33 to 1) 12

2669 CALIBRATE 8-8 (3*) B Doyle (13) midfield, shrtlvd effrt o'r 3 fs out, sn wknd............... (20 to 1 op 14 to 1) 13

3170[5] ESERIE DE CORES (USA) 8-7 A Clark (6) al beh. .... (20 to 1 op 10 to 1 tchd 25 to 1) 14

GENERAL BUNCHING 9-7 B Raymond (15) missed break, al tld off............................ (25 to 1) 15

Dist: 10l, nk, 2l, hd, 2l, 2½l, nk, hd, 1l, nk. 2m 7.50s. a 9.90s (15 Ran).

SR: 10/-/-/-/-/-/ (The Equema Partnership), C F Wall

4089 EBF Lysander Insurance Maiden Fillies' Stakes Class D (2-y-o) £4,556 6f 189yds........................ (2:50)

2069[5] DARING DESTINY 8-11 T Sprake (6) settled midfield gng wl, pld wide and smooth hdwy 2 fs out, led ins last, cmftbly............. (6 to 1 op 10 to 1 tchd 12 to 1) 1

3209[8] DELIVER (Ire) 8-11 Pat Eddery (5) al hndy, led o'r one furlong out, hdd ins last, swshd tail and eased whn btn................ (7 to 2 op 3 to 1 tchd 5 to 1) 2

3248[6] SARIYAA 8-11 B Raymond (9) beh, pushed alng o'r 2 fs out, styd on wl fnl furlong, nvr nrr. .... (9 to 1 op 7 to 1 tchd 10 to 1) 3

3828 SUGAR TOWN (Ire) 8-11 A Clark (8) beh, rdn o'r 2 fs out, kpt on fnl one and a half furlong, nrst finish. .... (20 to 1 op 16 to 1 tchd 25 to 1) 4

2316[4] HADDIAH 8-11 W Newnes (12) led aftr one furlong till hdd o'r one furlong out, sn rdn and no extr. .... (9 to 1 op 7 to 1) 5

2394[3] EARTH CHARTER 8-8 (3*) B Doyle (2) beh till styd on und pres fnl one and a half fs, nvr nrr. (16 to 1 op 12 to 1) 6

KIROV ROYALE 8-11 M Wigham (4) slwly away, last and outpcd till kpt on fnl one and a half fs, no dngr. .... (50 to 1 op 33 to 1) 7

3738[2] DEVOTEE 8-11 L Charnock (11) led one furlong, styd hndy till rdn wl o'r one furlong out, sn wknd. .... (6 to 4 fav tchd 7 to 4) 8

DONA BIANCA 8-11 A Geran (10) dwlt, sn reco'red to chase ldg bunch till wknd wl over 2 fs out. .... (33 to 1 tchd 50 to 1) 9

2417[5] RADIANT DANCER 8-11 P Robinson (1) trkd ldrs till wknd o'r 2 fs out.......... (40 to 1 op 33 to 1 tchd 50 to 1) 10

3659[5] RARE BIRD (USA) 8-11 D Holland (3) prmnt till hrd rdn 2 fs out, wknd quickly..... (11 to 2 op 7 to 1 tchd 5 to 1) 11

2909 LOOSE CHANGE 8-11 A Morris (7) slwly into strd, al beh. .... (50 to 1 op 33 to 1) 12

Dist: 3½l, 2½l, ¾l, ½l, ½l, 3½l, nk, sht-hd, 1½l, 2l. 1m 27.10s. a 6.20s (12 Ran).

SR: 25/14/6/4/2/-/ (Mrs Ann E M Wright), K R Burke

4090 Scottish Equitable Handicap Class D (0-80 3-y-o and up) £3,933 6f.... (3:20)

3774[9] DOMICKSKY [61] 5-8-6 (3*) B Doyle (3) made all, hld on wl und pres ins last............................ (10 to 1) 1

3445[4] DOUBLE SHIFT [58] 4-8-6 S Whitworth (2) hld up, hdwy o'r 2 fs out, chlgd fnl furlong, jst fld. (12 to 1 op 10 to 1) 2

3942* KILDEE LAD [61] 3-8-6 (7ex) B Raymond (8) beh early, hdwy wl o'r one furlong out, kpt on.......... (10 to 1) 3

3942[7] MARK'S CLUB (Ire) [57] (bl) 3-8-2 D Biggs (7) slwly into strd, rdn alng hfwy, styd on fnl furlong, nrst finish. .... (8 to 1) 4

3393[6] SPECTACLE JIM [50] (bl) 4-7-12[6] (5*) D McCabe (13) midfield, hdwy o'r one furlong out, not trble ldrs. (20 to 1) 5

3378[5] ISLAND KNIGHT (Ire) [62] 4-8-5 (5*) K Rutter (1) midfield, gd hdwy o'r one furlong out, no extr ins last..... (14 to 1) 6

3621 JOBIE [72] 3-9-3 W Woods (6) beh till styd on fnl one and a half fs, nvr nrr.......................... (8 to 1) 7

3404 GILT THRONE [74] 6-9-8 P Robinson (17) rcd alone far side to hfwy, styd on same pace fnl one and a half fs. .... (6 to 1 op 7 to 1) 8

3778[6] THE AUCTION BIDDER [74] 6-9-3 (5*) S Wynne (16) beh till some hdwy fnl furlong, no dngr................ (10 to 1) 9

3942[4] DOUBLE BOUNCE [62] 3-8-7 W Newnes (15) nvr far away, ev ch o'r 2 fs out, sn rdn and btn............... (6 to 1) 10

3707[2] LORINS GOLD [56] (bl) 3-8-1 N Adams (11) prmnt till wknd o'r 2 fs out.............................. (7 to 1) 11

3947[7] AUGHFAD [79] (v) 7-9-6 (7*) R Painter (10) speed 4 fs, sn rdn and wknd.................................. (10 to 1) 12

3837[7] SECOND CHANCE (Ire) [71] 3-9-2 A Clark (5) rdn alng early and in tch to hfwy, sn wknd................. (12 to 1) 13

3942[3] UMBRIA [50] 4-7-8[1] (5*) B Russell (12) prmnt, rdn frm hfwy, btn whn snatched up o'r one furlong out. .... (9 to 2 fav) 14

3668[8] TERRHARS (Ire) [80] 5-10-0 D Holland (9) chsd ldg bunch till wknd o'r 2 fs out.............. (12 to 1 op 10 to 1) 15

3745 GEMINI BAY [45] 4-7-7 N Carlisle (4) al beh...... (33 to 1) 16

Dist: Nk, 3l, 1½l, 1l, ¾l, 1l, sht-hd, ½l, sht-hd, 1l. 1m 13.80s. a 2.80s (16 Ran).

SR: 45/41/29/19/11/20/23/27/25/ (M J Watson), M R Channon

4091 Broadstairs Claiming Stakes Class G (3-y-o and up) £1,957 1½m...... (3:50)

3655[5] SWIFT ROMANCE (Ire) 5-8-12 S Whitworth (1) hld up and wl beh, rapid hdwy o'r 3 fs out, led over one out, sn clr, unchlgd........................ (8 to 1 tchd 9 to 1) 1

3962[2] SEAMA (USA) 3-8-9 C Nutter (3) led till hdd o'r one furlong out, sn rdn and not pace of wnr. .... (3 to 1 tchd 100 to 30) 2

3666 MILZIG (USA) (bl) 4-9-10 Pat Eddery (6) nvr far away, not much room wl o'r one furlong out, sn rdn and no extr. .... (5 to 4 fav op Evens) 3

1318[6] MYFONTAINE 6-9-4 M Wigham (9) rdn and headweay appr hfwy, sn in tch, ev ch wl o'r one furlong out, one pace............ (12 to 1 op 10 to 1 tchd 14 to 1) 4

3887 WOODMANS STAR 3-8-3 (5*) K Rutter (4) chsd ldg bunch till rdn and not quicken fnl 2 fs... (50 to 1 op 33 to 1) 5

3962[7] FOREVER SHINEING 3-8-3 D Biggs (2) chsd ldrs till rdn and wknd 3 fs out...... (9 to 1 op 10 to 1 tchd 8 to 1) 6

ABU DANCER (Ire) 3-8-12 L Charnock (11) slwly into strd, wl beh till some hdwy o'r 3 fs out, nvr able to chal. .... (33 to 1 op 25 to 1 tchd 50 to 1) 7

1143 QUADRANT 4-9-0 N Adams (8) al rear div. .... (16 to 1 op 10 to 1 tchd 20 to 1) 8

2670 CASTLE-VIEW 3-7-11 A Tucker (7) in tch to hfwy, wknd quickly......................... (50 to 1 op 25 to 1) 9

3551[6] BACK TO FORM 8-8-6 T Sprake (5) chsd ldrs till rdn hfwy, wknd............... (16 to 1 op 20 to 1 tchd 33 to 1) 10

3909[9] COMMANCHE STAR 3-8-4 N Carlisle (12) in tch to hfwy, sn in rear........... (33 to 1 op 25 to 1 tchd 50 to 1) 11

3669 BAYYINAT (USA) (v) 3-8-4[2] A Clark (10) tld off frm hfwy. .... (50 to 1 op 25 to 1) 12

Dist: 10l, hd, 4l, 3l, 3l, ¾l, 10l, 1l, 5l, 5l. 2m 41.40s. a 10.90s (12 Ran).

SR: 13/-/4/-/-/-/ (Mrs Nerys Dutfield), B R Millman

4092 Pedlinge Amateur Riders' Limited Stakes Class F (0-70 3-y-o and up) £1,730 6f 189yds................ (4:20)

425 CHIEF OF STAFF 4-10-12 Mrs L Pearce (8) settled midfield, hdwy 3 fs out, led one out, ran on wl. .... (7 to 1 tchd 6 to 1 and 8 to 1) 1

3910[8] MAID WELCOME (v) 6-10-2 (5*) Miss A Sanders (9) trkd ldr, rdn and ev ch 2 fs out, kpt on ins last. .... (25 to 1 op 16 to 1) 2

3736 OARE SPARROW 3-10-3 Mrs M Cowdrey (16) made most till hdd one furlong out, not quicken. .... (3 to 1 fav op 4 to 1 tchd 9 to 2) 3

3837 TOP PET (Ire) 3-10-3 (5*) Mr T McCarthy (10) trkd ldrs, ev ch 2 fs out, kpt on same pace ins last.... (8 to 1 op 7 to 1) 4

3313[3] RELENTLESS PURSUIT (Ire) 5-10-7 (5*) Mrs J Chapple-Hyam (7) chsd ldrs till not hdwy fnl one and a half fs out............................ (5 to 1 op 7 to 2) 5

3302 KRAYYAN DAWN 3-10-8 Mr J Rees (2) beh till some hdwy und pres 2 fs out, styd on, nvr nrr. (25 to 1 op 20 to 1) 6

LILLAH DARAK (USA) 5-10-7 (5*) Miss A Whitfield Jones (15) slwly into strd, beh till kpt on fnl one and a half fs, not a dngr.................... (20 to 1 op 16 to 1) 7

3745[6] BILL MOON 7-10-12 Miss J Feilden (13) pld hrd, chsd ldg bunch, ev ch 2 fs out, sn rdn and wknd. .... (8 to 1 op 7 to 1) 8

3634[4] TRIANGLEPOINT (Ire) 3-9-13[1] (5*) Mr P Pritchard-Gordon (6) midfield, hdwy on outsd o'r 2 fs out and sn ev ch, wknd quickly appr last.................... (14 to 1) 9

3910 SYLVAN SABRE (Ire) (v) 4-10-12 Mr R Teal (5) trkd ldg bunch till rdn o'r 2 fs out, wknd. .... (20 to 1 op 16 to 1 tchd 25 to 1) 10

3007[6] GEORGE ROPER 3-10-3 (5*) Mrs J Moore (4) al rear div. .... (33 to 1 op 25 to 1 tchd 40 to 1) 11

4016 MOUJEEB (USA) 3-10-3 (5*) Miss S Chittenden (14) beh whn hmpd 3 fs out, nvr a dngr. .... (25 to 1 op 20 to 1 tchd 33 to 1) 12

3910 STARLIGHT FLYER (bl) 6-10-7 (5*) Mr T Waters (3) *slwly away and reluctant to race, al beh.* ....(25 to 1 op 20 to 1) 13

3509 MELLERIO (bl) 3-10-3 (5*) Mr K Santana (1) *missed break, al wl beh.* ....(33 to 1) 14

1700^{6} THREEOFUS 3-10-3 (5*) Mr D Marshall (11) *al beh.* ....(25 to 1 tchd 33 to 1) 15

4007^{4} CONFRONTER (v) 4-10-7 (5*) Mr T Cuff (12) *chsd ldrs till badly hmpd and uns rdr 3 fs out*... (7 to 2 tchd 4 to 1) ur

Dist: 2l, ½l, ¾l, 5l, 1½l, ½l, hd, 1½l, hd, hd. 1m 27.60s. a 6.70s (16 Ran).
SR: 46/35/29/32/21/12/14/13/-/ (The Exclusive Partnership), J Pearce

LISTOWEL (IRE) (good to yielding)
Monday September 20th

4093 Pierse Contracting Nursery (2-y-o) £5,520 1m.................... (2:15)

3416* SWIFT RIPOSTE (Ire) [-] 9-0 K J Manning (3) ..(9 to 2 jt-fav) 1
2982* MISS NUTWOOD (Ire) [-] 8-11 P Shanahan (9) ......(7 to 1) 2
3730^{3} DANCING AT LUNASA (Ire) [-] 8-6 P V Gilson (5) (9 to 2 jt-fav) 3
3541 STELFOX (Ire) [-] 7-11 (2*) R M Burke (6) ....(8 to 1) 4
3825^{4} UNBUCKLE (Ire) [-] (bl) 8-5 M J Kinane (4) ....(5 to 1) 5
3953^{3} MOMENTS TO CARE (Ire) [-] 8-3 N G McCullagh (10) (7 to 1) 6
3806^{4} MY RAGAMUFFIN (Ire) [-] 8-0 (8*) R T Fitzpatrick (2) (9 to 1) 7
3917^{5} YOUR VILLAGE (Ire) [-] $8\text{-}0^{3}$ (4*) J A Heffernan (8) ..(16 to 1) 8
2244^{7} SUSIE SUNSHINE (Ire) [-] 7-13 (4*) W J Smith (1) .. (16 to 1) 9
3608^{9} CLANCY NOSSEL (Ire) [-] 8-0 W J Supple (14) .... (12 to 1) 10
4052^{8} BUTLER BRENNAN (Ire) [-] (bl) 7-2 (8*) G M Moylan (13) ....(33 to 1) 11
3731^{3} MAJESTIC MAN (Ire) [-] $7\text{-}10^{1}$ (6*) R V Skelly (15) .. (16 to 1) 12
3607^{8} EAS GEIPTINE [-] (bl) $7\text{-}12^{2}$ G Coogan (11) .... (20 to 1) 13
3917^{3} INISHMANN (Ire) [-] 8-1 J F Egan (12) .... (12 to 1) 14
3416 BOB BARNES (Ire) [-] 8-0 (2*) D G O'Shea (7) ...... (16 to 1) 15

Dist: 4l, ¾l, hd, 1l. 1m 45.10s. (15 Ran).
(Mount Juliet), J S Bolger

4094 Golf Hotel Claiming Race (3-y-o and up) £3,795 1m.................(2:45)

3923^{6} THATCHING CRAFT (Ire) 4-9-1 (6*) R V Skelly (7) ....(11 to 8 fav) 1
3328^{7} DARCY'S THATCHER 9-8-8 M J Kinane (3) .... (6 to 1) 2
3769* GILT DIMENSION 6-9-0 P V Gilson (14) .... (6 to 1) 3
3826* HANG A RIGHT 6-8-12 (2*) P Carberry (11) .... (4 to 1) 4
2518^{6} BLACK PIPER (Ire) 3-8-7 J F Egan (1) ....(25 to 1) 5
3454^{7} VISTAGE (Ire) 5-9-2 J P Murtagh (2) ....(14 to 1) 6
4001 TOUCHDOWN 6-8-1 (8*) G M Moylan (9) ....(10 to 1) 7
3382^{6} SYDNEY SUSSEX (Ire) 3-9-2 W J Supple (8) .... (14 to 1) 8
3769^{4} MUSWELL BROOK (Ire) (bl) $3\text{-}7\text{-}13^{1}$ (4*) J A Heffernan (10) ....(8 to 1) 9
2404^{9} LEADING TIME (Fr) 4-9-6 R Hughes (5) ....(10 to 1) 10
2452^{7} SKEAF (Ire) 3-7-12 (8*) G Coogan (12) ....(25 to 1) 11
1574 EFFICIENT FUNDING (Ire) 3-7-11 (2*) D G O'Shea (6) ....(50 to 1) 12

Dist: 4l, 3½l, 1l, ¾l. 1m 43.20s. (12 Ran).
(Hugh McMahon), Hugh McMahon

4095 Listowel Racecourse Bookmakers QR Handicap (0-105 4-y-o and up) £8,380 2m.......................... (3:20)

3560^{6} PADASHPAN (USA) [-] 4-10-5 (5*) Mrs J M Mullins (12) ....(6 to 1 jt-fav) 1
3685* PRINCIPLE MUSIC (USA) [-] (bl) 5-10-7 (5*) Mr J A Nash (4) ....(7 to 1) 2
575^{5} BITOFABANTER [-] 6-10-4 (7*) Mr H Murphy (8).... (8 to 1) 3
3915^{6} HACKETTS CROSS (Ire) [-] 5-10-5 (3*) Mr A R Coonan (7) ....(10 to 1) 4
3560^{7} SHANKORAK [-] 6-10-4 (7*) Mr D J Kavanagh (2) ..(13 to 2) 5
4057^{4} COMMAND 'N CONTROL [-] 4-9-11 (3*) Miss C Hutchinson (10) ....(6 to 1 jt-fav) 6
3577^{7} BALLYTIGUE LORD [-] 7-10-13 (7*) Mr G P FitzGerald (5) ....(25 to 1) 7
3915^{5} ROSE APPEAL [-] 7-11-1 Mr T Mullins (9) ....(7 to 1) 8
2461^{2} DOMINO'S RING (Ire) [-] (bl) 4-10-12 (7*) Miss S Kauntze (6) ....(14 to 1) 9
2296^{7} THATCH AND GOLD (Ire) [-] 5-10-7 (7*) Mr E Norris (13) ....(14 to 1) 10
3915* LACKEL (Ger) [-] 5-11-10 (7ex) Mr A P O'Brien (11) (7 to 1) 11
3857^{5} ENNEREILLY RIVER [-] 10-9-13 (3*) Mrs M Mullins (1) ....(16 to 1) 12

Dist: 6l, 1l, nk, 2l. 3m 54.90s. (12 Ran).
(William Brennan), W P Mullins

NOTTINGHAM (good to soft (races 1,2,3), soft (4,5,6,7))
Monday September 20th

Going Correction: PLUS 0.40 sec. per fur. (races 1,2,3), PLUS 0.50 (4,5,6,7)

4096 Arnold Limited Stakes Class E (0-70 3-y-o and up) £3,261 6f 15yds... (2:00)

3404^{6} NORDAN RAIDER 5-8-9 N Connorton (5) *al travelling wl, not clr run hfwy, led on bit well o'r one furlong out, sprinted clear.* ....(9 to 4 fav op 3 to 1 tchd 7 to 2 and 2 to 1) 1

3863 ROCA MURADA (Ire) 4-8-7 (7*) P McCabe (4) *chsd alng to improve frm off the pace last 2 fs, ran on, no ch wth wnr*....(10 to 1 op 8 to 1 tchd 11 to 1) 2

1954 OUR RITA 4-8-9 L Piggott (2) *patiently rdn, shaken up to improve on outsd o'r one furlong out, kpt on same pace*.... (8 to 1 op 6 to 1) 3

3343^{4} CHILLY BREEZE 3-8-6 G Duffield (7) *sluggish strt, drvn into midfield hfwy, styd on same pace fnl furlong.* ....(13 to 2 op 5 to 1) 4

3638^{6} PEERAGE PRINCE (bl) 4-9-0 R Cochrane (6) *co'red up on ins, led briefly 2 fs out, rdn and no extr entering fnl furlong*.... (9 to 1 op 6 to 1) 5

3955^{3} ANOTHER LANE 6-8-9 J Quinn (1) *tucked away in midfield, effrt and rdn 2 fs out, not quicken.* ....(9 to 1 op 8 to 1) 6

3050^{6} HAWAYAH (Ire) 3-8-1 (5*) S Drowne (8) *chsd alng to go pace, nvr able to trble ldrs*........(20 to 1 op 12 to 1) 7

3896^{9} MY RUBY RING 6-8-6 (3*) Stephen Davies (3) *shwd up wl on outsd for o'r 4 fs, fdd.* ....(10 to 1 op 7 to 1 tchd 11 to 1) 8

3747 PLUM FIRST 3-8-11 Paul Eddery (11) *made most for 4 fs, fdd o'r one furlong out*............(12 to 1 op 10 to 1) 9

3946^{4} DISCO BOY 3-8-4 (7*) S Sanders (10) *broke wl to show gd speed in frnt rnk 4 fs, sn btn*......(20 to 1 op 14 to 1) 10

3948* RICKY'S TORNADO (Ire) 4-9-0 M Roberts (9) *wth ldr 4 fs, wknd quickly, virtually pld up, broke blood vessel.* ....(10 to 1 op 7 to 1) 11

Dist: 1½l, hd, 1l, 5l, 1½l, 3l, 3½l, sht-hd, 1½l, dist. 1m 16.10s. a 4.60s (11 Ran).
SR: 51/50/44/37/25/14/ (Miss J A Camacho), M J Camacho

4097 Colwick Fillies' Nursery Class E (2-y-o) £3,598 6f 15yds........... (2:30)

3309^{2} STEADFAST ELITE (Ire) [54] 8-10 W Carson (5) *made virtually all, pushed alng last 2 fs, kpt on strly.* ....(7 to 2 op 3 to 1 tchd 4 to 1) 1

3755^{4} DANGEROUS SHADOW [64] 9-1 (5*) Darren Moffatt (6) *al hndy, drw level o'r 2 fs out, edgd lft fnl furlong, no extr*........(6 to 1 op 5 to 1) 2

3569* SISTER SUSAN [64] 9-6 M Roberts (7) *nvr far away, drvn alng whn pace quickened 2 fs out, styd on same pace.* ....(7 to 2 op 2 to 1 tchd 4 to 1) 3

3265^{8} CHINA ROBIN [60] 9-2 Paul Eddery (11) *tucked away on ins, hmpd and checked aftr one and a half fs, rallied, no extr fnl furlong*............. (20 to 1 op 14 to 1) 4

2595^{3} DOUCE MAISON (Ire) [62] 9-4 T Quinn (4) *co'red up, improved centre over 2 fs out, no imprsn appr fnl furlong*............(5 to 2 fav op 3 to 1) 5

3836^{6} POSSIBILITY [65] 9-7 L Piggott (1) *chsd alng on wide outsd, feeling pace o'r 2 fs out, fdd.* (9 to 1 op 6 to 1) 6

3284^{5} TRYSAIL [58] 9-0 J Quinn (8) *chsd alng in midfield, rdn and no imprsn last 2 fs.* ....(16 to 1 op 12 to 1 tchd 20 to 1) 7

3816 LUNAR RHAPSODY [57] 8-13 R Price (10) *tucked away in midfield, drvn alng whn pace lifted 2 fs out, sn btn.* ....(20 to 1 op 16 to 1 tchd 25 to 1) 8

1774 SOTTISES (Ire) [45] 7-8 (7*) N Varley (3) *chsd alng to go pace hfwy, no imprsn last 2 fs*.............(33 to 1) 9

3235^{9} MACAROON LADY [60] 9-2 G Duffield (2) *broke wl to show speed to hfwy, btn 2 fs out*....... (16 to 1 op 14 to 1) 10

2949^{8} WILLWIN [57] 8-13 J Williams (9) *lost many ls strt, nvr able to reco'r*....... (14 to 1 op 10 to 1 tchd 16 to 1) 11

Dist: 1½l, 2l, 4l, 3l, 2½l, sht-hd, 2½l, ¾l, 8l, 12l. 1m 18.20s. a 6.70s (11 Ran).
SR: 10/14/6/-/-/-/ (Steadfast Engineering Company Ltd), J J O'Neill

4098 Levy Board Maiden Stakes Class D (2-y-o) £4,225 6f 15yds........... (3:00)

3746^{2} GNEISS (USA) 9-0 Paul Eddery (3) *al cantering far side, led hfwy, clr last 2 fs, imprsv.* ....(15 to 8 on op 2 to 1 on tchd 6 to 4 on) 1

3352 SHIKAREE (Ire) 9-0 A McGlone (8) *chsd ldrs far side, styd on grimly fnl furlong, no ch wth wnr*........ (12 to 1) 2

3009^{9} AWS (Ire) 9-0 W Carson (4) *trkd ldrs far side, rdn alng o'r 2 fs out, styd on same pace fnl furlong.* ....(20 to 1 op 10 to 1) 3

3462 PERTEMPS FLYER 9-0 T Quinn (12) *unruly at strt, chsd ldrs far side, kpt on same pace last 2 fs.* ....(20 to 1 op 50 to 1) 4

TRYPANIS (Ire) 8-9 R Cochrane (10) *trkd ldrs far side, effrt on outsd 2 fs out, kpt on one pace.* (12 to 1 op 10 to 1) 5

WARHURST (Ire) 8-7 (7*) S Mulvey (21) *drvn alng wth stands side bunch, styd on und pres fnl furlong, nvr able to chal*............(33 to 1) 6

3779^{8} SHARP FALCON (Ire) 8-9 J Quinn (15) *wth stands side bunch, led that side o'r 2 fs out, no imprsn fnl furlong.* ....(9 to 1 op 14 to 1) 7

3317 PAB'S CHOICE 8-9 M Birch (2) *pressed ldrs far side, feeling pace o'r 2 fs out, no extr*............... (66 to 1) 8

CHANTELYS 8-2 (7*) P McCabe (14) *chsd alng to go pace hfwy, nvr able to rch chalg pos*.......(33 to 1) 9
3754 DEAR SILVERS 8-9 R Perham (7) *chsd ldrs far side, rdn and no imprsn last 2 fs*.......(50 to 1) 10
3754[9] THE WITCHBOY 9-0 W Hood (5) *broke wl to ld far side to hfwy, fdd last 2 fs*.......(33 to 1) 11
WADADA 8-11 (3*) O Pears (11) *drvn alng far side, no imprsn last 2 fs*.......(100 to 1) 12
3833 THE DEACONESS 8-6[2] (5*) V Slattery (22) *bustled alng wth stands side bunch, nvr a threat*.......(100 to 1) 13
NORMA'S LADY 8-9 M Hills (20) *rcd stands side, outpcd and drvn alng hfwy, nvr a threat*.
.......(11 to 2 op 9 to 2 tchd 7 to 1) 14
JUST DUGGIE 9-0 R Price (18) *chsd alng stands side, nvr able to chal*.......(100 to 1) 15
3084 WENLOCH LAD 9-0 T Wall (17) *drvn alng to keep up thrght, nvr a threat*.......(100 to 1) 16
3781 EFFICACY 8-9 W R Swinburn (6) *wl plcd far side for o'r 3 fs, fdd*.......(33 to 1) 17
L'AVENTURE (Ire) 9-0 T Rogers (1) *sn outpcd and struggling, tld off far side frm hfwy*.......(100 to 1) 18
MISS NANUSHKA 8-6 (3*) S D Williams (16) *missed break, nvr a factor*.......(100 to 1) 19
3633 BIX 9-0 S Raymont (13) *wth ldrs far side till wknd o'r 2 fs out*.......(100 to 1) 20
EVENING BRIGADIER 9-0 G Duffield (19) *led stands side bunch till o'r 2 fs out, sn lost tch*.......(50 to 1) 21

Dist: 10l, ¾l, 1l, nk, 3l, nk, ½l, 1½l, 3½l, ½l. 1m 16.60s. a 5.10s (21 Ran).

SR: 46/6/3/-/-/-/ (Matthew Oram), Mrs J Cecil

4099 EBF Nottingham Maiden Stakes Class D (2-y-o) £4,807 1m 54yds...... (3:30)

3836[2] JAFEICA (Ire) 8-11 L Dettori (14) *led for 2 fs, rgned ld hfwy, styd on strly last two furlongs*.
.......(11 to 4 fav op 4 to 1 tchd 5 to 1) 1
WAITING 8-11 T Quinn (16) *al hndy, ev ch and drvn alng last 2 fs, styd on same pace*.
.......(11 to 2 op 3 to 1 tchd 6 to 1) 2
1456[9] BSHEER (USA) 8-11 W R Swinburn (18) *sluggish strt, weaved through into midfield 3 fs out, styd on wl towards finish*.......(14 to 1 op 7 to 1) 3
3592[8] SADLER'S IMAGE (Ire) 8-11 M Roberts (17) *led aftr 2 fs till hdd hfwy, styd hndy till not quicken fnl furlong*.
.......(9 to 2 op 3 to 1) 4
3742[2] SHERMAN (Ire) 8-11 L Piggott (9) *settled off the pace, swtchd outsd and 2 reminders o'r one furlong out, fnshd wl*.......(6 to 1 op 4 to 1) 5
3422[6] DUELLO 8-11 J Quinn (10) *tucked away on ins, not clr run and checked appr strt, ev ch o'r 2 fs out, no extr fnl furlong*.......(14 to 1 op 8 to 1) 6
3130 ELSDON (Ire) 8-4 (7*) S Mulvey (13) *chsd ldg bunch, drvn alng whn pace quickened o'r 2 fs out, one pace*.
.......(33 to 1 op 25 to 1) 7
3836[9] FAIR COURT 8-11 R Cochrane (8) *trkd ldg bunch, ev ch on ins o'r 2 fs out, grad wknd*.......(20 to 1 op 12 to 1) 8
2862 ANZUM 8-4 (7*) P McCabe (2) *chsd ldg bunch for o'r 5 fs, rdn and no extr*.......(100 to 1 op 33 to 1) 9
MARSH ARAB 8-11 J Williams (12) *trkd ldg trio, drvn alng entering strt, fdd o'r 2 fs out*.......(100 to 1 op 66 to 1) 10
3592[5] VIRTUAL REALITY 8-11 A McGlone (1) *in tch, bustled alng entering strt, not pace of ldrs*.......(10 to 1 op 6 to 1) 11
3446[8] CONIC HILL (Ire) 8-11 M Hills (4) *settled midfield, effrt and chsd alng entering strt, nvr able to chal*.
.......(12 to 1 op 6 to 1) 12
3592 HAVE IT READY (Ire) 8-11 W Carson (3) *in tch to strt, fdd last 3 fs*.......(16 to 1 op 8 to 1) 13
UNBELIEVABLE 8-11 G Duffield (5) *trkd ldrs, drvn alng entering strt, fdd o'r 2 fs out*.......(14 to 1 op 7 to 1) 14
3400[6] LOMOND MIST (Ire) 8-11 Paul Eddery (11) *settled midfield, pushed alng o'r 3 fs out, sn btn*.
.......(16 to 1 op 20 to 1 tchd 25 to 1) 15
1666 FIGHTING SPIRIT 8-11 M Birch (7) *trkd ldg half dozen, bustled alng last 3 fs, fdd*.......(100 to 1 op 50 to 1) 16
BRIDIE'S PRIDE 8-6 (5*) S Drowne (15) *very slow away, al tld off*.......(33 to 1 tchd 50 to 1) 17

Dist: 3l, 1l, ½l, nk, 3l, hd, 4l, nk, 1½l, hd. 1m 50.00s. a 10.00s (17 Ran).

SR: 9/-/-/-/-/-/ (N T C (Racing) Limited), R Hannon

4100 Trent Conditions Stakes Class D (3-y-o and up) £3,143 1m 1f 213yds (4:00)

3878[3] ICY SOUTH (USA) 3-9-0 L Dettori (4) *made all, rcd wide to strt, quickened clr last 2 fs, readily*. (6 to 1 op 9 to 2) 1
3385[2] BLUE LION 3-9-2 M Roberts (1) *took keen hold, effrt and drvn alng o'r 2 fs out, styd on same pace fnl furlong*.
.......(6 to 1 op 9 to 2) 2
3878[2] SALATIN (USA) 3-8-12 W Carson (6) *nvr far away, feeling pace and drvn alng o'r 2 fs out, styd on grimly ins fnl furlong*.......(7 to 4 jt-fav tchd 9 to 4) 3
3832* COUNT OF FLANDERS (Ire) 3-8-12 W R Swinburn (3) *trkd wnr, hrd at work whn pace lifted o'r 2 fs out, sn outpcd*.......(7 to 4 jt-fav op 5 to 2 tchd 6 to 4) 4
2885[8] MAGIQUE ROND POINT (USA) 3-8-6 A McGlone (2) *trkd ldrs, feeling pace and drvn alng o'r 2 fs out, sn rdn and btn*.......(9 to 1 op 9 to 2 tchd 10 to 1) 5
SPEAKER'S HOUSE (USA) 4-9-4 T Quinn (5) *chsd ldrs, rdn and lost grnd quickly 3 fs out, tld off*. (9 to 1 op 5 to 1) 6

Dist: 2l, ½l, 5l, ¾l, dist. 2m 13.90s. a 10.90s (6 Ran).

SR: 41/39/34/24/16/-/ (Saeed Manana), J H M Gosden

4101 Gelding Handicap Class D (0-80 3-y-o and up) £4,371 1m 1f 213yds.... (4:30)

3961[3] MYSILV [60] 3-8-7 W Carson (11) *al wl plcd, led o'r 3 fs out, pushed out wth hands and heels fnl furlong*.
.......(10 to 1 op 9 to 1 tchd 12 to 1) 1
3722[3] SURREY DANCER [67] 5-9-1 (5*) Darren Moffatt (10) *patiently rdn, gd hdwy last 2 fs, chalg whn hng lft fnl furlong, no extr*.
.......(7 to 2 fav op 7 to 1 tchd 8 to 1 and 9 to 1) 2
3883[7] SWIFT SILVER [57] 6-8-10 W R Swinburn (6) *al tracking ldrs, effrt and drvn alng o'r 2 fs out, styd on same pace*.
.......(12 to 1 op 10 to 1) 3
3831* GOLD BLADE [53] 4-8-6 M Roberts (7) *patiently rdn, improved frm off the pace o'r 2 fs out, styd on one pace ins last*.......(8 to 1 op 9 to 1 tchd 10 to 1) 4
3157[2] LIGHT HAND [63] 7-8-9 (7*) S Mulvey (5) *sluggish strt, improved into midfield 3 fs out, kpt on, nvr able to chal*.
.......(9 to 1 op 6 to 1) 5
3722[4] STOPROVERITATE [56] 4-8-9 Paul Eddery (3) *shwd up wl on outsd, effrt and rdn alng o'r 2 fs out, no extr*.
.......(14 to 1 op 10 to 1) 6
3507 WESTHOLME (USA) [58] 5-8-11 M Birch (16) *wth ldrs, led entering strt till o'r 3 fs out, fdd last 2 furlongs*.
.......(16 to 1 op 14 to 1) 7
2598* DESERT POWER [72] 4-9-6 (5*) V Slattery (2) *trkd ldg bunch, effrt ant rdn alng o'r 2 fs out, no imprsn*.
.......(25 to 1 op 20 to 1) 8
3523* QUANTITY SURVEYOR [57] (v) 4-8-10 G Duffield (22) *in tch, improved frm midfield o'r 2 fs out, nvr able to chal*.
.......(20 to 1) 9
3891[2] VANBOROUGH LAD [52] 4-8-5 M Hills (8) *trkd ldg bunch for o'r 6 fs, no extr*.......(20 to 1) 10
3699[4] ROMOLA NIJINSKY [55] 5-8-5 (3*) C Hodgson (23) *pressed ldr, ev ch and rdn entering strt, fdd o'r 2 fs out*.
.......(12 to 1 op 10 to 1 tchd 8 to 1) 11
3540[3] NORTHERN BRED (Ire) [77] 3-9-10 R Cochrane (18) *settled midfield, drvn alng whn pace quickened o'r 2 fs out, nvr able to chal*.
.......(13 to 2 op 5 to 1 tchd 4 to 1 and 7 to 1) 12
3314[9] FRONTIER FLIGHT (USA) [78] 3-9-11 S Raymont (15) *chsd ldg bunch, hrd at work o'r 2 fs out, sn btn*.
.......(33 to 1 op 20 to 1) 13
3957[7] BOLD ACRE [67] 3-9-0 R Price (21) *beh and pushed alng hfwy, nvr nr to chal*.......(25 to 1) 14
3790[9] ATHERTON GREEN (Ire) [67] 3-9-0 J Williams (14) *settled off the pace, effrt and rdn alng o'r 3 fs out, nvr able to chal*.......(14 to 1 op 10 to 1) 15
3263[5] ELAINE TULLY (Ire) [75] 5-10-0 L Dettori (19) *pressed ldg bunch till wknd and eased o'r 2 fs out*.......(20 to 1) 16
3035[8] RAGGERTY (Ire) [55] 3-8-2 F Norton (4) *beh and pushed alng, nvr nr to chal*.......(33 to 1) 17
3192[4] AWESTRUCK [72] 3-9-5 T Wall (17) *settled midfield, feeling pace entering strt, sn btn*.......(33 to 1) 18
3820* HAROLDON (Ire) [70] 4-9-2 (7*) P McCabe (9) *in tch for o'r 6 fs, fdd*.......(16 to 1 op 12 to 1) 19
3555[7] I'M A DREAMER (Ire) [63] 3-8-7 (3*) S D Williams (13) *tucked away in midfield, feeling pace o'r 3 fs out, sn struggling*.......(25 to 1 tchd 33 to 1) 20
3431[8] DREAMS ARE FREE (Ire) [67] 3-9-0 A McGlone (20) *wth ldrs till fdd o'r 3 fs out*.......(20 to 1 op 16 to 1) 21
3669* BAG OF TRICKS (Ire) [72] 3-9-5 T Quinn (1) *struggling frm hfwy, tld off*.......(20 to 1 op 16 to 1) 22
3734[9] FAIRY FREE [55] 4-8-8[3] L Piggott (12) *led till hdd entering strt, lost tch o'r 2 fs out*.......(33 to 1) 23

Dist: 2l, 3½l, hd, 8l, 1½l, 2l, ¾l, sht-hd, hd, nk. 2m 12.90s. a 9.90s (23 Ran).

SR: 44/53/36/31/25/15/13/25/9/ (Jack Fisher), C F Wall

4102 Carlton Handicap Class E (0-70 3-y-o and up) £3,727 2m 9yds.........(5:00)

2235[6] FIVE TO SEVEN (USA) [63] 4-9-11 (3*) O Pears (2) *made all, clr entering strt, jnd 2 fs out, kpt on grimly fnl furlong*.
.......(9 to 1 op 7 to 1 tchd 10 to 1) 1
3125 BALLY KNIGHT [59] 7-9-7 (3*) C Hodgson (16) *patiently rdn, improved to draw level last 2 fs, ridden and not go past*.......(14 to 1 op 12 to 1) 2
3479 CHILD STAR (Fr) [41] 4-8-6 R Cochrane (17) *wtd wth, drvn up frm midfield entering strt, styd on, no imprsn fnl furlong*.......(4 to 1 op 5 to 1 tchd 7 to 2) 3
AUTHORSHIP (USA) [45] 7-8-10 W R Swinburn (20) *patiently rdn, effrt and snatched up in midfield appr strt, styd on ag'n fnl 2 fs, nvr nrr*. (25 to 1 op 16 to 1) 4
559 GO SOUTH [55] 9-9-6 T Quinn (7) *in tch, drvn alng to keep up appr strt, styd on last 2 fs, nvr nrr*.......(33 to 1) 5
3552[6] GREY COMMANDER [28] (v) 5-7-2 (5*) Darren Moffatt (13) *beh and pushed alng, relentless prog last 3 fs, nvr nrr*.
.......(25 to 1 op 33 to 1) 6
3288 CHARMED LIFE [42] 4-8-6[4] (5*) V Slattery (4) *chsd ldg bunch, effrt and drvn alng entering strt, kpt on, nvr able to chal*.......(33 to 1 op 20 to 1) 7

2921[3] BEAU QUEST [42] (bl) 6-8-7 G Duffield (11) *trkd ldg 6, effrt and rdn o'r 3 fs out, kpt on same pace.* ....(33 to 1 op 20 to 1) 8
MISS MARIGOLD [36] 4-8-0[4] (5*) S Drowne (6) *reluctant to enter stalls, nvr far away, drvn alng 3 fs out, one pace.* ....(33 to 1) 9
KAUSAR (USA) [50] 6-9-1 Paul Eddery (10) *trkd ldg grp, bustled alng entering strt, outpcd last 3 fs.* ....(8 to 1 op 14 to 1) 10
NORTHERN KINGDOM (USA) [63] 4-9-11 (3*) Stephen Davies (14) *struggling to keep up hfwy, nvr nr to chal.* ....(33 to 1) 11
3868* GUESTWICK [64] 3-9-3 L Dettori (3) *wl plcd for 5 fs, struggling appr strt, sn lost tch*......(3 to 1 fav tchd 7 to 2) 12
3556[5] DUPLICATE [61] 3-9-0 M Birch (5) *wth ldrs, rdn alng hfwy, lost tch o'r 3 fs out*................(10 to 1 op 6 to 1) 13
3873[8] QAFFAL (USA) [64] 3-9-3 W Carson (15) *chsd ldrs, drvn up to go second o'r 6 fs out, fdd over 3 out.* ....(14 to 1 op 8 to 1) 14
3556[3] SIDE BAR [45] (bl) 3-7-12[1] F Norton (18) *trkd ldg quartet, rdn alng o'r 3 fs out, sn btn*.........(14 to 1 op 8 to 1) 15
3574[2] USK THE WAY [69] 3-9-8 A McGlone (8) *pressed ldrs to hfwy, fdd entering strt.* (4 to 1 op 9 to 2 tchd 7 to 1) 16
CLASSIC STATEMENT [47] 7-8-12 M Roberts (12) *al struggling and beh, tld off*..............(16 to 1 op 14 to 1) 17
MYSTICAL GUEST [50] 7-9-1 R Price (1) *al last, tld off.* ....(33 to 1) 18
Dist: ½l, 7l, 1½l, 1½l, 2l, 4l, 4l, 4l, 2l, 4l. 3m 43.50s. a 19.30s (18 Ran).
(The Five To Seven Partnership), S G Norton

PONTEFRACT (good)
Monday September 20th

Going Correction: PLUS 0.10 sec. per fur. (races 1,2,3,4,7), PLUS 0.20 (5,6)

4103 EBF Poppin Lane Maiden Stakes Class D (2-y-o) £4,270 6f.........(2:10)

3462[4] NIZAAL (USA) 9-0 R Hills (5) *made all, shaken up entering strt, pushed clr ins last.* ....(5 to 4 fav op 6 to 4 tchd 11 to 10) 1
3781[3] ZIFTA (USA) 8-9 J Reid (6) *keen hold, nvr far away, rdn and ev ch ins fnl furlong, one pace.* ....(3 to 1 op 9 to 4 tchd 7 to 2) 2
3941[2] TAILCOAT (USA) 9-0 M Perrett (9) *settled on outsd, improved appr strt, shaken up and kpt on ins fnl furlong*.................. (6 to 1 op 5 to 1 tchd 13 to 2) 3
SONNET (USA) 8-9 D Harrison (11) *al hndy, pushed alng entering strt, kpt on same pace*...... (8 to 1 op 7 to 1) 4
TOPNOTCH 8-9 A Culhane (8) *trkd ldrs, pushed alng 2 fs out, not quicken o'r one out*.......(20 to 1 op 14 to 1) 5
EQUERRY 9-0 W Ryan (2) *reluctant to enter stalls, strted slwly, beh, steady hdwy on bit o'r one furlong out, prmsg*...........................(14 to 1 op 10 to 1) 6
2429 STAR PERFORMER (Ire) 9-0 K Darley (3) *tucked away beh ldrs, not clr run appr strt, shaken up and not much room entering fnl furlong, improve.* ....(14 to 1 op 10 to 1) 7
CHAMPAGNE ATEASTER 8-9 K Fallon (10) *in tch, pushed alng hfwy, fdd entering strt.* ....(16 to 1 op 25 to 1 tchd 14 to 1) 8
CITY OF MY DREAMS (Ire) 8-9 J Fanning (4) *trkd ldrs on ins, rdn alng appr strt, wknd*...................(33 to 1) 9
STEEL SOVEREIGN 9-0 F Norton (1) *missed break, beh, pushed alng o'r 2 fs out, nvr on terms*........ (20 to 1) 10
MUSICAL STAR 8-9 R P Elliott (7) *nvr far away, rdn alng o'r 2 fs out, sn btn*...................(16 to 1 op 14 to 1) 11
Dist: 2l, 5l, ¾l, nk, 1l, 2l, 2½l, 3½l, 3l, 3l. 1m 18.40s. a 3.70s (11 Ran).
SR: 38/25/10/2/1/2/ (Hamdan Al-Maktoum), H Thomson Jones

4104 Neat Market Selling Handicap Class G (0-60 3-y-o and up) £2,889 1m 4yds ....(2:40)

3887[9] NORTHERN CONQUEROR (Ire) [42] 5-8-10 D Harrison (5) *hld up, plenty to do appr strt, str run o'r one furlong out, led nr finish*.................(12 to 1 op 10 to 1) 1
3938 MALCESINE (Ire) [40] 4-8-8 S Wood (18) *slwly into strd, beh, prog on outsd frm 3 fs out, led ins last, ct nr finish.* ....(20 to 1 op 16 to 1) 2
3536[2] ESSAYEFFSEE [51] 4-9-5 K Darley (17) *nvr far away, led entering strt till ins fnl furlong, kpt on same pace.* ....(8 to 1) 3
3812[4] DIACO [56] 8-9-10 W Ryan (9) *hld up, imprvg whn short of room entering strt, styd on strly ins fnl furlong.* ....(11 to 2 fav op 5 to 1) 4
3409[6] VANART [42] 4-8-10 S Webster (20) *beh, improved to midfield hfwy, styd on fnl furlong, nrst finish*.... (12 to 1) 5
3408[2] COOL ENOUGH [37] 12-8-5 K Fallon (15) *patiently rdn, improved appr strt, kpt on ins last.* ....(7 to 1 op 6 to 1 tchd 8 to 1) 6
3523[8] SIR ARTHUR HOBBS [47] 6-9-1 R Lappin (2) *prmnt, drvn alng o'r 2 fs out, no extr fnl furlong.* ....(11 to 1 op 10 to 1 tchd 12 to 1) 7
3811[4] MISSED THE BOAT (Ire) [47] 3-8-4 (7*) V Halliday (7) *hld up beh, hdwy on outsd fnl 2 fs, nrst finish.* ....(16 to 1 tchd 20 to 1) 8
3518[6] YOUNG JASON [42] 10-8-10 S Perks (10) *patiently rdn, improved on bit 2 fs out, swtchd and styd on ins last, nvr plcd to chal*..................(15 to 2 op 7 to 1) 9
3714[6] DIAMOND INTHE DARK (USA) [39] (v) 5-8-2 (5*) A Garth (19) *in tch, drvn alng hfwy, no extr fnl 2 fs*........(16 to 1) 10
3788[6] FORMAESTRE (Ire) [42] 3-8-3 (3*) S Maloney (22) *mid-div, drvn alng o'r 3 fs out, kpt on same pace entering strt.* ....(16 to 1) 11
STYLISH GENT [45] 6-8-13 J O'Reilly (3) *in tch, drvn alng hfwy, not quicken fnl 2 fs.* ....(14 to 1 op 20 to 1 tchd 12 to 1) 12
3140[3] YOUNG VALENTINE [50] 4-9-4 A Culhane (16) *chsd ldrs, pushed alng appr strt, sn btn*.....(14 to 1 op 12 to 1) 13
3812[6] BOLD MELODY [44] 4-8-7 (5*) J Marshall (8) *mid-div, drvn alng last 3 fs, no imprsn*........................(12 to 1) 14
2017[2] KHALLOOF (Ire) [48] 4-9-2 R Hills (6) *tucked away beh ldrs, imprvg whn no room appr strt, no imprsn.* ....(12 to 1 op 14 to 1) 15
2768[5] GOLD SURPRISE (Ire) [48] 4-9-2 J Fortune (1) *chsd ldrs, drvn alng hfwy, fdd appr strt*................(12 to 1) 16
3090[8] LAZY RHYTHM (USA) [37] 7-8-5 F Norton (13) *beh, drvn alng 3 fs out, nvr a factor*........ (14 to 1 op 16 to 1) 17
3812 SHANNON EXPRESS [44] (v) 6-8-12 Julie Bowker (14) *led aftr 2 fs till entering strt, wknd quickly.* ....(16 to 1 op 14 to 1) 18
2338[8] STATE TACOMA [40] (v) 3-8-4 A Mackay (21) *sluggish strt, al beh*................................(33 to 1) 19
4799a LORD VIVIENNE (Ire) [60] 4-10-0 M Perrett (12) *trkd ldr, drvn alng 3 fs out, fdd*........................(25 to 1) 20
3948[9] BLUE RADIANCE [50] (v) 3-9-0 J Fanning (4) *led 2 fs, hndy till rdn and wknd o'r 3 out*........ (25 to 1 op 20 to 1) 21
Dist: Nk, ½l, nk, sht-hd, 1½l, 2l, nk, ¾l, nk, 3½l. 1m 47.60s. a 5.50s (21 Ran).
SR: 26/23/32/36/21/11/15/10/7/ (Mrs J T Naughton), T J Naughton

4105 New Hall Rating Related Maiden Stakes Class E (0-70 2-y-o) £2,898 5f ....(3:10)

3671[4] LUCKY MESSAGE (USA) 8-9 J Reid (3) *nvr far away, rdn entering strt, led ins fnl furlong, kpt on wl.* ....(6 to 4 fav op 2 to 1) 1
3870 MR BERGERAC (Ire) 9-0 D Harrison (6) *nvr far away, rdn to ld entering strt, edgd lft, hdd ins fnl furlong, no extr.* ....(7 to 2 op 3 to 1 tchd 4 to 1) 2
2128[2] FADE AWAY (Ire) 8-9 K Darley (1) *dwlt, beh, rdn alng hfwy, improved o'r one furlong out, no ch wth 1st 2*...(8 to 1) 3
3598[4] GAELIC STAR (Ire) 9-0 W Ryan (7) *presed ldrs, drvn alng hfwy, outpcd entering strt*...........(8 to 1 op 6 to 1) 4
3715[7] ELUNED MAY 8-9 A Culhane (2) *trkd ldrs, drvn alng o'r 2 fs out, sn outpcd*................ (8 to 1 op 6 to 1) 5
3592 MENTMORE LAD 9-0 A Mackay (5) *made most till entering strt, fdd*..........................(10 to 1 op 8 to 1) 6
3677[6] REAL POPCORN (Ire) 8-9 J Fortune (4) *trkd ldrs, drvn alng hfwy, outpcd entering strt*........ (12 to 1 op 10 to 1) 7
Dist: 1½l, 10l, hd, 2l, hd, nk. 1m 4.80s. a 3.60s (7 Ran).
SR: 33/32/-/-/ (W L Armitage), J Etherington

4106 Graham Kitchen & Bathroom Nursery Class D (2-y-o) £4,815 1m 4yds. .(3:40)

3865[7] ARZ (USA) [75] 8-13 R Hills (7) *settled gng wl, imprvg whn not clr run o'r one furlong out, squeezed through to ld ins last, ran on strly*... (9 to 2 tchd 5 to 1 and 4 to 1) 1
3865[8] SECRET SERENADE [83] 9-7 J Fortune (9) *tucked away beh ldrs, drvn alng hfwy, chalg whn edgd lft ins last, kpt on same pace*..........................(12 to 1) 2
3865 PHYLIAN [67] 8-5 D Harrison (6) *settled midfield, imprvg and hng rght o'r one furlong out, chalg whn baulked ins last, one pace*................. (20 to 1 op 16 to 1) 3
3539[5] DOUBLE SIXTEEN [57] 7-9 J Fanning (10) *hld up, stumbled and lost grnd aftr 2 fs, imprvg whn not clr run o'r one furlong out, swtchd lft ins last, ran on strly.* ....(5 to 1 op 7 to 2) 4
3406 ALPINE SKIER (Ire) [80] 9-4 K Darley (1) *led half a furlong, trkd ldr, led o'r 2 out, hng rght and hdd ins last, no extr*................................(7 to 1 op 5 to 1) 5
3143[3] ALL IN THE MIND [74] 8-12 K Fallon (5) *co'red up on ins, improved and swtchd rght entering strt, kpt on fnl furlong, nvr dngrs*..........................(14 to 1) 6
3052[8] SUSELJA (Ire) [56] 7-8[1] A Mackay (8) *beh, drvn alng 3 fs out, no imprsn entering strt*....... (25 to 1 op 20 to 1) 7
3836 TANAH MERAH (Ire) [65] 8-3 C Rutter (2) *tucked away on ins, drvn alng to improve o'r 2 fs out, sn btn.* ....(10 to 1 op 8 to 1) 8
3218* SYABAS (Ire) [80] 9-4 J Reid (3) *led aftr half a furlong, hdd o'r 2 out, fdd*...................... (7 to 2 fav op 3 to 1) 9
3627[7] DURHAM DRAPES [64] 7-13 (3*) S Maloney (4) *nvr far away, drvn alng hfwy, wknd entering strt, tld off.* ....(7 to 1 op 12 to 1 tchd 14 to 1) 10
3903[4] CULSYTH FLYER [73] 8-11 W Ryan (12) *beh, rdn alng hfwy, sn struggling, tld off*...... (10 to 1 tchd 11 to 1) 11
3750[9] JEAN DE FLORETTE (USA) [60] (bl) 7-7 (5*) A Garth (13) *in tch on outsd, drvn alng o'r 3 fs out, wknd, tld off.* ....(25 to 1 op 20 to 1) 12

3554[5] OUBECK BLUE [79] 9-3 M Tebbutt (11) *in tch on outsd, drvn alng hfwy, wknd o'r 2 fs out, eased, tld off.* .... (20 to 1 op 16 to 1) 13
Dist: 1½l, 1l, hd, 1l, sht-hd, 10l, 1½l, 4l, 10l, 5l. 1m 48.70s. a 6.60s (13 Ran).
SR: 12/15/-/-/5/-/ (Hamdan Al-Maktoum), H Thomson Jones

4107 Dalby Screw-driver Rated Class B Handicap (0-90 4-y-o and up) £7,509 1¼m 6yds..................... (4:10)

3900[6] CEZANNE [75] 4-8-7 W Ryan (3) *trkd ldrs, pushed alng 4 fs out, ran on to ld appr last, styd on wl.* .... (7 to 2 op 4 to 1 tchd 11 to 4) 1
3883[4] BOLD STROKE [77] 4-8-9 J Reid (2) *led, shaken up entering strt, hdd appr last, no extr fnl 100 yards.* ....(11 to 4 fav op 5 to 2 tchd 3 to 1) 2
3158[9] AMAZE [89] 4-9-7 K Darley (7) *tucked away beh ldrs, improved 3 fs out, rdn and outpcd entering strt, kpt on ins last*.................. (9 to 1 op 7 to 1 tchd 10 to 1) 3
3722[7] LEIF THE LUCKY (USA) [75] 4-8-7 N Connorton (6) *keen hold, in tch, cld o'r 2 fs out, not quicken over one out.* .... (14 to 1 op 12 to 1) 4
2433 LAST EMBRACE (Ire) [80] 4-8-12 D Harrison (4) *beh, sn niggled alng, drvn to improve o'r 3 fs out, nvr able to chal*.................... (13 to 2 op 5 to 1 tchd 7 to 1) 5
4043* KNOCK KNOCK [77] 8-8-9 (3ex) S O'Gorman (9) *settled on outsd, pushed alng 4 fs out, nvr able to chal, eased fnl furlong*........................... (11 to 2 op 4 to 1) 6
3424[3] RIVAL BID (USA) [75] 5-8-7 M Tebbutt (1) *settled rear, improved and ev ch o'r 2 fs out, wknd over one out.* .... (12 to 1) 7
3714[4] FLOATING LINE [75] 5-8-7 A Culhane (8) *trkd ldrs, feeling pace o'r 3 fs out, wknd wl over 2 out, tld off.* .... (50 to 1 op 33 to 1) 8
2198 ROYAL CITIZEN (Ire) [75] 4-8-7 K Fallon (5) *beh, struggling last half-m, tld off*.............................(33 to 1) 9
3900[5] SILVER SAMURAI [80] 4-8-9 (3*) S Maloney (10) *cl up, pushed alng 4 fs out, wknd, tld off.* ....(13 to 2 tchd 7 to 1) 10
Dist: 1½l, 2l, 2l, 7l, 1l, ½l, 12l, 5l, 6l. 2m 13.60s. a 5.40s (10 Ran).
SR: 59/58/66/48/39/34/31/7/-/ (Sheikh Mohammed), M R Stoute

4108 Frier Wood Conditions Stakes Class C (3-y-o and up) £4,408 1½m 8yds (4:40)

3909* DARRERY 3-8-3 K Darley (4) *trkd ldr, rdn to ld entering fnl furlong, styd on strly.* ....(7 to 4 fav op 2 to 1 tchd 13 to 8) 1
3318[6] TRAMMEL 3-8-8 K Fallon (1) *trkd ldg pair, outpcd and drvn alng o'r 3 fs out, styd on wl fnl furlong, wnt second cl hme*.......... (9 to 1 op 6 to 1 tchd 10 to 1) 2
3590* WINTER FOREST (USA) 3-8-8 W Ryan (2) *led, rdn o'r 2 fs out, hdd entering last, no extr.* .... (15 to 8 op 6 to 4 tchd 2 to 1) 3
2654[8] BREAK BREAD (USA) 4-9-3 J Reid (3) *hld up last, lost tch o'r 2 fs out, eased, tld off.* .... (11 to 4 op 5 to 2 tchd 3 to 1) 4
Dist: 3½l, ½l, 20l. 2m 41.90s. a 6.90s (4 Ran).
SR: 44/42/41/10/ (Sheikh Mohammed), M R Stoute

4109 Nevison Handicap Class E (0-70 3-y-o and up) £3,340 5f............... (5:10)

3747 MILBANK CHALLENGER [58] 3-8-12 (3*) S Maloney (10) *wth ldr, rdn to ld ins fnl furlong, hld on wl*........(14 to 1) 1
3995[5] JUST BOB [69] 4-10-0 J Fortune (16) *in tch on outsd, pushed alng and wide strt, kpt on wl fnl furlong.* .... (11 to 1 op 10 to 1 tchd 12 to 1) 2
3877[3] SADDLEHOME (USA) [57] 4-9-2 J Reid (4) *nvr far away, effrt whn not much room one furlong out, squeezed through and ran on nr finish*.... (5 to 1 fav op 6 to 1) 3
3948[5] LEIGH CROFTER [47] (bl) 4-8-6 G Hind (14) *pressed ldrs, effrt and rdn 2 fs out, ev ch ins last, one pace.* ....(12 to 1 tchd 14 to 1) 4
3947[9] NORDOORA (Ire) [48] 4-8-5[5] (7*) G Strange (9) *led, rdn 2 fs out, hdd ins last, no extr*.........................(20 to 1) 5
3745 BRIGHT PARAGON (Ire) [47] 4-8-6 J Quinn (5) *beh, drvn appr strt, styd on strly ins fnl furlong, nrst finish.* .... (10 to 1 op 9 to 1) 6
3995[7] SIMMIE'S SPECIAL [55] (bl) 5-8-9 (5*) A Garth (11) *nvr far away, pushed alng hfwy, not quicken ins fnl furlong.* .... (16 to 1 op 14 to 1) 7
3745[3] JESS REBEC [57] 5-8-11 (5*) L Newton (7) *chsd ldrs, drvn alng hfwy, kpt on ins fnl furlong*.... (8 to 1 op 7 to 1) 8
3947 SO SUPERB [59] (bl) 4-9-4 S Webster (1) *beh on ins, effrt 2 fs out, kpt on inside last*.....................(20 to 1) 9
3323[3] COVENT GARDEN GIRL [62] 3-9-5 T Lucas (3) *chsd ldrs, ch entering strt, wknd appr last*.... (10 to 1 tchd 9 to 1) 10
3877[6] ARC LAMP [54] 7-8-13 W Ryan (17) *beh on outsd, pushed alng to improve last 2 fs, nvr dngrs.* .... (14 to 1 op 12 to 1) 11
3955[8] CONVENIENT MOMENT [51] 3-8-8 K Darley (12) *pressed ldrs, rdn alng hfwy, no imprsn*.............. (14 to 1) 12
3778 ADMIRALS REALM [59] 4-9-4 A Mackay (15) *beh, drvn alng last 2 fs, not pace to chal*.........(12 to 1 op 10 to 1) 13
3877[4] KALAR [53] (bl) 4-8-12 S Wood (13) *reared strt, sn in tch, pushed alng appr strt, btn o'r one furlong out.* .... (11 to 1 op 10 to 1) 14
3758 JOCKS JOKER [57] 3-9-0 J Fanning (2) *beh, drvn alng hfwy, not pace to chal*........................(25 to 1) 15
ORIENT AIR [57] 5-9-2 N Connorton (18) *beh on outsd, rdn and no ch entering strt*...................... (25 to 1) 16
3486[9] MY ABBEY [62] 4-9-7 K Fallon (6) *chsd ldrs, drvn alng appr strt, wknd wl o'r one furlong out.* .... (10 to 1 op 12 to 1) 17
2934[6] KIMBOLTON KORKER [52] 3-8-2 (7*) Claire Balding (8) *sn beh, struggling hfwy*........... (20 to 1 tchd 16 to 1) 18
Dist: ½l, hd, hd, hd, ¾l, nk, ¾l, nk, ¾l, ½l. 1m 6.70s. a 5.50s (18 Ran).
SR: 1/12/-/-/-/-/ (C H Stevens), M H Easterby

KEMPTON (soft)
Tuesday September 21st
Going Correction: PLUS 0.50 sec. per fur. (races 1,3,5,6,7), PLUS 0.35 (2,4)

4110 Tangmere Maiden Stakes Class D (3-y-o) £3,728 1½m.............. (1:45)

3682[2] ELATIS (USA) 8-9 J Carroll (15) *al prmnt, led 2 fs out, kpt on wl*............................ (6 to 1 op 9 to 2) 1
3909[5] PURPLE SPLASH 9-0 A Munro (3) *sn in tch, led 3 fs out to 2 out, styd on und pres.* .... (14 to 1 op 12 to 1 tchd 16 to 1) 2
3590[3] CUFF LINK (Ire) 9-0 J Reid (12) *in tch, drvn alng 3 fs out, hrd driven and styd on fnl furlong.* (6 to 1 op 5 to 1) 3
3937[2] SPRING MARATHON (USA) 9-0 J Williams (19) *wl beh, reminders aftr 4 fs, shaken up 5 out, ran on o'r 2 out, fnshd well*.....................(4 to 1 fav op 6 to 1) 4
2117[4] PRINCESS SIOUX 8-9 B Raymond (7) *str hold in rear, sn chasing ldrs, shaken up 2 fs out, outpcd appr last.* .... (12 to 1 op 10 to 1 tchd 14 to 1) 5
3909[4] ECU DE FRANCE (Ire) 9-0 T Quinn (6) *sn chasing ldrs, rdn 2 fs out, wknd o'r one out.* (9 to 2 op 4 to 1 tchd 5 to 1) 6
3832 KAMIKAZE 9-0 J Weaver (8) *hdwy o'r 2 fs out, sn wknd.* .... (25 to 1 op 16 to 1 tchd 33 to 1) 7
2907 ERCKULE 8-11 (3*) B Doyle (18) *in tch till wknd 2 fs out.* .... (20 to 1 op 14 to 1) 8
557[8] PRIDWELL 9-0 S Raymont (17) *prmnt till wknd o'r 3 fs out*.............. (20 to 1 op 16 to 1 tchd 25 to 1) 9
3173[4] ALASAD 9-0 W Carson (9) *chsd ldrs, led 7 fs out to 3 out, eased whn btn fnl furlong*.......... (6 to 1 op 5 to 1) 10
3173 AMAZING AIR (USA) 9-0 R Price (1) *hdwy 5 fs out, wknd 2 and a half out*...... (25 to 1 op 33 to 1 tchd 20 to 1) 11
3831 TAUTEN (Ire) 8-9 B Rouse (14) *hdwy 6 fs out, wknd o'r 3 out*............................ (66 to 1 op 50 to 1) 12
3866 GECKO ROUGE 8-9 R Perham (16) *al beh.* .... (50 to 1 op 33 to 1) 13
3740[7] PLAIN SAILING (Fr) 9-0 R Hills (10) *pressed ldrs till wknd 4 fs out*............... (25 to 1 op 20 to 1 tchd 33 to 1) 14
3173 BALMORAL BELLE 8-9 M Simonaggio (5) *al beh.* .... (25 to 1 op 16 to 1 tchd 33 to 1) 15
3225 CUCKMERE VENTURE 8-9 N Adams (4) *sn prmnt, rdn 4 fs out, wknd 3 out*.................. (66 to 1 op 50 to 1) 16
3682[3] KARDELLE 8-9 Pat Eddery (13) *led 5 fs, wknd quickly.* .... (13 to 2 op 9 to 2 tchd 7 to 1) 17
BARNIEMEBOY 9-0 M Perrett (2) *al beh, tld off.* .... (66 to 1 op 50 to 1) 18
ALLEZ PABLO (bl) 9-0 A Clark (11) *al beh, tld off.* .... (50 to 1 op 33 to 1) 19
Dist: 1½l, sht-hd, 6l, 1½l, hd, 3l, 10l, sht-hd, 4l, 8l. 2m 41.76s. a 10.76s (19 Ran).
SR: 48/50/49/37/29/33/26/6/5/ (Sheikh Mohammed), J H M Gosden

4111 Kenley Fillies' Conditions Stakes Class C (2-y-o) £4,111 1m.......(2:15)

3845 BEARALL (Ire) 8-10 B Rouse (3) *chsd ldr, led 5 fs out, hdd briefly 3 out, drvn out fnl furlong.* (10 to 1 op 8 to 1) 1
3939[2] CRAZY FOR YOU 8-8 T Quinn (2) *led 3 fs, styd chasing wnr, rdn 2 out, rallied cl hme.* .... (16 to 1 op 12 to 1 tchd 20 to 1) 2
3765[3] OMNIA (USA) 8-8 A Munro (1) *al in tch, drvn o'r 3 fs out, one pace appr last*..... (3 to 1 op 11 to 4 tchd 7 to 2) 3
2968[2] LOVING LEGACY 8-8 R Hills (5) *steadied sn aftr strt, hld up, effrt 3 fs out, rdn and no imprsn frm 2 out.* .... (11 to 10 fav op 5 to 4 on tchd 6 to 5) 4
3698* CRACKLING SIKE 8-10 M Tebbutt (4) *chsd ldrs, styd alone far side, led briefly 3 fs out, outpcd frm 2 out.* ....(4 to 1 op 7 to 2) 5
Dist: ¾l, 2½l, 1½l, hd. 1m 46.50s. a 9.70s (5 Ran).
(Mr And Mrs M Winterford), R Hannon

4112 West Malling Hurricane Conditions Stakes Class D (3-y-o and up) £3,172 5f ....(2:45)

3912[5] LUCKY PARKES 3-9-7 J Carroll (3) *made all, rdn and kpt on wl fnl furlong.* .... (11 to 8 fav op 11 to 10 on tchd 6 to 4) 1

3511[7] INHERENT MAGIC (Ire) 4-9-0 A Clark (1) *outpcd and beh, ran on o'r one furlong out, fnshd wl.* ......(14 to 1 op 12 to 1) 2
3782[2] TRAPEZIUM 3-8-13 J Weaver (2) *hdwy o'r 2 fs out, pressed wnr one out, sn rdn, no extr*...... (5 to 2 tchd 11 to 4) 3
3987[3] ROCK SYMPHONY 3-8-12 (5*) J Tate (4) *chsd ldrs till wknd ins fnl 2 fs*.......... (100 to 30 op 4 to 1 tchd 9 to 2) 4
3849 FANGIO 4-9-2 T Sprake (6) *chsd ldrs till wknd hfwy*. ......(10 to 1 tchd 14 to 1) 5
Dist: ½l, sht-hd, 5l, 2½l. 1m 3.16s. a 4.96s (5 Ran).
SR: 58/49/47/31/20/ (Joseph Heler), J Berry

4113 Heathrow Maiden Stakes Class D (2-y-o) £4,807 1m................. (3:15)

3704[3] DYNAMIC DELUXE (USA) 9-0 S O'Gorman (18) *al frnt rnk, led ins fnl 2 fs, all out.* (8 to 1 op 7 to 1 tchd 10 to 1) 1
3462[7] STASH THE CASH (Ire) 9-0 Pat Eddery (12) *made most till ins fnl 2 fs, rallied und pres, jst fld.* ....(11 to 2 fav op 5 to 2 tchd 6 to 1) 2
REHLAT FARAH (USA) 9-0 J Weaver (22) *in tch, rdn and kpt on frm o'r one furlong out.* ......(6 to 1 op 4 to 1 tchd 13 to 2) 3
VILLAGE EAGLE (Fr) 8-11 (3*) B Doyle (19) *pressed ldrs, ev ch 2 fs out, styd on same pace*......(6 to 1 tchd 7 to 1) 4
PEMBRIDGE PLACE 9-0 W Carson (21) *in tch, hdwy to chase ldrs 3 fs out, ev ch 2 out, styd on same pace.* ......(8 to 1 op 6 to 1 tchd 10 to 1) 5
3819[6] AHSANT MTOTO 9-0 R Price (8) *hdwy o'r 3 fs out, rdn and wknd one and a half out.* ......(14 to 1 op 10 to 1 tchd 16 to 1) 6
DURABLE 9-0 B Raymond (20) *beh, hdwy hfwy, no prog frm o'r 2 fs out*......(7 to 1 op 3 to 1) 7
LYPHARD'S FABLE (USA) 9-0 R Hills (16) *effrt into mid-div 3 fs out, styd on same pace.* ......(8 to 1 op 6 to 1 tchd 9 to 1) 8
MELNIK 9-0 T Quinn (1) *in tch hfwy, shaken up and no imprsn fnl 2 fs*......(7 to 1 op 4 to 1) 9
3642[6] MIDSEAS 9-0 R Perham (2) *pressed ldrs till wknd o'r 2 fs out*......(33 to 1 op 20 to 1) 10
ECHO WOOD 9-0 N Adams (7) *sn beh, reminder, nvr rch ldrs*......(50 to 1 op 25 to 1) 11
NORTHERN UNION (Can) 9-0 P Robinson (13) *sn beh, nvr dngrs*......(10 to 1 op 8 to 1 tchd 12 to 1) 12
3760[7] SCUD MISSILE (Ire) 9-0 J Carroll (10) *nvr better than mid-div*......(14 to 1 op 12 to 1 tchd 16 to 1) 13
3939[6] CARA CARLTON (USA) 8-4 (5*) D Wright (6) *al beh.* ......(16 to 1 op 12 to 1 tchd 20 to 1) 14
QUICK DECISION (Ire) 9-0 W Hood (24) *in tch 4 fs.* ......(14 to 1 op 10 to 1) 15
LINDON LAD 9-0 A Clark (9) *al beh*...(50 to 1 op 33 to 1) 16
BRAVE TORNADO 9-0 J Williams (23) *dwlt, al beh.* ......(25 to 1 op 20 to 1) 17
3908[6] STONECROP 9-0 J Reid (11) *chsd ldrs 5 fs.* ......(25 to 1 op 16 to 1 tchd 33 to 1) 18
3686[8] CHOPENDOZ (USA) 9-0 M Tebbutt (14) *nvr better than mid-div*......(33 to 1 op 16 to 1) 19
3836 KISSAIR (Ire) 9-0 B Rouse (17) *prmnt 5 fs.* ......(50 to 1 op 33 to 1) 20
2546 ABACUSAM 9-0 S Whitworth (5) *al beh.* ......(50 to 1 op 33 to 1) 21
HE'S BIZZI (Ire) 9-0 A Morris (4) *sn beh.* ......(50 to 1 op 33 to 1) 22
Dist: Nk, ¾l, 1½l, 1l, 2½l, nk, 2l, 3l, 2½l, ½l. 1m 43.41s. a 6.61s (22 Ran).
SR: 43/42/40/35/32/24/23/17/8/ (Urs E Schwarzenbach), I A Balding

4114 Duxford Nursery Class D (2-y-o) £3,494 5f....................... (3:45)

3754[5] MY GALLERY (Ire) [64] (bl) 7-8 (5*) D Wright (6) *steadied strt, hdwy frm 2 fs out, led ins last, wnt clr.* ......(10 to 1 op 8 to 1 tchd 12 to 1) 1
4061[5] BILLY CRUNCHEON [70] 8-5 W Woods (4) *chsd ldrs, led o'r one furlong out till ins last, styd on same pace.* ......(8 to 1 op 6 to 1 tchd 9 to 1) 2
3871[5] CRAFTY CRICKETER [58] (bl) 7-7 N Adams (8) *beh and outpcd, drvn and hdwy o'r one furlong out, fnshd wl.* ......(50 to 1 op 33 to 1 tchd 66 to 1) 3
3815[4] CHIEF EXECUTIVE [58] 7-3[3] (7*) N Varley (3) *pressed ldrs, led 2 and a half fs out till o'r one out, styd on one pace.* ......(14 to 1 op 10 to 1 tchd 16 to 1) 4
3657[4] MIRIAM [68] 8-3 A Munro (10) *led one furlong, frnt rnk till wknd one and a half out.* ......(12 to 1 op 10 to 1 tchd 14 to 1) 5
3529[3] RAISA POINT [71] 8-6 T Quinn (1) *led aftr one furlong till 2 and a half out, btn two out.* ......(12 to 1 op 10 to 1 tchd 14 to 1) 6
4061[2] BRAVE EDGE [82] 9-3 Pat Eddery (5) *chsd ldrs till fdd appr fnl furlong*......(15 to 8 fav op 9 to 4 tchd 5 to 2) 7
3982[9] MOUNT LEINSTER [75] 8-5 (5*) S Drowne (9) *outpcd.* ......(12 to 1 op 10 to 1 tchd 14 to 1) 8
3845 LADY-BO-K [70] 8-5 W Carson (13) *wnt rght strt, sn reco'red to press ldrs, wknd 2 fs out.* (6 to 1 op 5 to 1) 9
3569[7] ROCKETEER (Ire) [74] 8-9 W Newnes (7) *sn outpcd.* ......(14 to 1 op 12 to 1 tchd 16 to 1) 10
3845 THATCHERELLA [71] 8-6 J Reid (12) *mid-div, lost tch frm 2 fs out*......(8 to 1 op 7 to 1 tchd 9 to 1) 11
Dist: 5l, 2½l, nk, sht-hd, 1l, 1l, 1l, ½l, sht-hd, ¾l. 1m 3.43s. a 5.23s (11 Ran).
SR: 30/16/-/-/2/1/8/ / / (Gordon Mytton), A Bailey

4115 Hendon Selling Stakes Class G (3-y-o and up) £2,763 1m 1f........... (4:15)

402[3] COLTRANE (v) 5-9-3 A Munro (6) *led aftr one furlong, drvn clr appr last*......(6 to 1 tchd 8 to 1) 1
3985[3] LYN'S RETURN (Ire) 4-8-10 (7*) G Rothwell (2) *hdwy 4 fs out, shaken up and ran on fnl furlong, no imprsn on wnr*......(14 to 1 tchd 16 to 1) 2
3910 DON'T GIVE UP (bl) 5-9-8[10] (5*) D Meredith (16) *beh, hdwy o'r 3 fs out, styd on wl fnl furlong.* (50 to 1 op 33 to 1) 3
3891[5] CHANDIGARH 5-9-3 J Williams (9) *hdwy 3 fs out, no imprsn o'r one out*......(8 to 1 op 10 to 1) 4
3631 SWEET DISORDER (Ire) 3-8-4 (3*) B Doyle (19) *prmnt till outpcd fnl 2 fs*......(8 to 1 tchd 7 to 1) 5
3518 MEXICAN DANCER 4-8-12 B Crossley (11) *sn prmnt, rdn o'r 2 fs out, soon wknd*......(50 to 1 op 25 to 1) 6
3840 ROLY WALLACE (bl) 4-9-3 M Wigham (10) *slwly into strd, nvr rch ldrs*......(25 to 1 op 16 to 1 tchd 33 to 1) 7
229[8] LOCK KEEPER (USA) 7-8-10 (7*) P McCabe (15) *mid-div, hdwy 3 fs out, rdn and sddl slpd 2 out, not reco'r.* ......(12 to 1 op 10 to 1 tchd 14 to 1) 8
3741[5] VANROY (v) 9-9-3 T Quinn (8) *hdwy 4 fs out, pressed ldrs 3 out, wknd ins fnl 2*...... (6 to 1 op 5 to 1 tchd 7 to 1) 9
3887 OVERNIGHT SUCCESS (Ire) 3-8-4 (3*) M Fenton (5) *pressed ldrs till wknd 2 fs out*......(50 to 1 op 33 to 1) 10
3460[9] LITTLE ROUSILLON (bl) 5-9-3 J Reid (20) *steadied in rear, effrt 3 fs out, nvr dngrs*......(7 to 1 op 6 to 1) 11
WAVE MASTER 6-8-12 (5*) S Drowne (7) *beh most of way.* ......(50 to 1 op 25 to 1) 12
990 PRIMO FIGLIO 3-8-12 Pat Eddery (13) *led one furlong, styd frnt rnk, rdn o'r 3 out, sn wknd.* ......(3 to 1 fav op 9 to 4 tchd 100 to 30) 13
3547[3] TOUT DE VAL 4-8-12 R Perham (3) *prmnt till wknd 4 fs out*......(25 to 1 op 20 to 1 tchd 33 to 1) 14
3945[7] MALZETA (Ire) 3-8-2 (5*) D Wright (1) *beh hfwy.* ......(25 to 1 op 16 to 1 tchd 33 to 1) 15
3744 HENBURY HALL (Ire) (v) 5-9-3 Ann Stokell (14) *prmnt, edgd rght o'r 4 fs out, sn wknd*......(50 to 1 op 33 to 1) 16
1771[8] SHEFFORD 3-8-7 A Clark (17) *slwly into strd, al beh.* ......(20 to 1 tchd 25 to 1) 17
ALTON BELLE 4-8-5 (7*) Debbie Biggs (18) *al beh.* ......(50 to 1 op 33 to 1) 18
3945 CATCH ME STARSKY (Ire) (bl) 3-8-12 B Rouse (12) *chsd ldrs, wkng whn hmpd and lost pl o'r 4 fs out.* ......(25 to 1 op 50 to 1) 19
2163[9] KAWASIR (Can) 3-8-5 (7*) Nicola Howarth (4) *al beh.* ......(25 to 1 op 20 to 1 tchd 33 to 1) 20
Dist: 4l, 1½l, ¾l, 4l, hd, 3l, ½l, nk, 8l, 3l. 1m 59.91s. a 9.91s (20 Ran).
SR: 22/10/10/3/-/-/ (M L Oberstein), Lord Huntingdon

4116 Biggin Hill Handicap Class C (0-90 3-y-o and up) £5,638 1m........... (4:45)

3791[3] EMBANKMENT (Ire) [85] 3-9-6 Pat Eddery (11) *in tch till lost pl o'r 3 fs out, rallied and str run und pres appr last, led nr finish*......(12 to 1 tchd 14 to 1) 1
3885* CORALS DREAM (Ire) [87] 4-9-12 W Woods (10) *sn frnt rnk, led 2 fs out, kpt on und pres fnl furlong, ct cl hme.* ......(14 to 1 op 12 to 1) 2
3786[8] YAJEED (USA) [77] 3-8-12 J Reid (2) *hdwy o'r 4 fs out, chlgd frm 2 out, no extr wl ins last*......(33 to 1) 3
1027 FOX SPARROW [73] 3-8-8 S Raymont (3) *hdwy frm 2 fs out, kpt on fnl furlong, not pace to rch ldrs.* ......(14 to 1 tchd 12 to 1 and 16 to 1) 4
3787* LADY LACEY [61] (v) 6-7-7 (7*) N Varley (9) *broke wl, steadied, hdwy o'r 2 fs out, styd on fnl furlong.* ......(9 to 1 op 10 to 1 tchd 8 to 1) 5
3863[8] EXCLUSION [69] 4-8-8 W Newnes (8) *mid-div, hdwy and rdn ins fnl 2 fs, kpt on.* ......(14 to 1 tchd 12 to 1 and 16 to 1) 6
3988* DUCKEY FUZZ [54] 5-7-2 (5*) D Wright (16) *beh, plenty to do 4 fs out, hdwy o'r 2 out, hrd rdn and one pace fnl furlong*......(11 to 4 fav tchd 7 to 2) 7
3783 MUTAKALLAM (USA) [70] 3-8-5 R Hills (5) *prmnt, pressed ldrs o'r 2 fs out, wknd two out*......(20 to 1 op 16 to 1) 8
3637 AL MOULOUKI [82] 3-9-3 W Hood (15) *beh, some prog appr fnl furlong, no dngr*......(12 to 1 op 10 to 1) 9
4024[8] DASWAKI (Can) [74] 5-8-13 (5ex) B Rouse (4) *led to 2 fs out, sn btn*...... (12 to 1 op 10 to 1 tchd 14 to 1) 10
3670 DOUBLE FLUTTER [72] 4-8-11 T Quinn (1) *hdwy 4 fs out, chsd ldrs 3 out, wknd o'r 2 out*... (12 to 1 tchd 14 to 1) 11
945 MULLITOVER [83] 3-9-4 A Munro (18) *beh, nvr plcd to chal*......(33 to 1 op 25 to 1) 12
3956* DORAZINE [72] 3-8-0 (7*,5ex) P McCabe (6) *in tch, rdn and effrt o'r 2 fs out, sn wknd.* ......(13 to 2 op 8 to 1 tchd 6 to 1) 13
3585[2] AWESTRIKE (USA) [79] 3-9-0 J Carroll (14) *in tch 5 fs.* ......(8 to 1 tchd 10 to 1) 14
3837 SIR OLIVER (Ire) [55] 4-7-8[1] G Bardwell (12) *chsd ldrs for o'r 5 fs*......(33 to 1 tchd 20 to 1) 15
3558 BANDMASTER (USA) [80] 4-9-5 B Raymond (13) *prmnt till wknd 3 fs out*......(33 to 1) 16
1839[6] ZAJIRA (Ire) [76] 3-8-11 W Carson (7) *beh fnl 3 fs.* ......(14 to 1 tchd 16 to 1) 17

3558 NOYAN [80] 3-8-12 (3*) M Fenton (17) *in tch, rdn 4 fs out, sn wknd*.......................... (20 to 1 tchd 25 to 1) 18
Dist: Nk, nk, 1l, 1l, 1½l, 1l, sht-hd, 1½l, 1l, 1l. 1m 43.83s. a 6.83s (18 Ran).
SR: 64/69/54/47/36/39/21/32/39/ (Lady Tennant), R Hannon

LISTOWEL (IRE) (soft)
Tuesday September 21st

4117 Three Mermaids EBF Maiden (2-y-o) £5,670 6f...................... (2:00)

3451^{5} ALJAWZA (USA) 9-0 M J Kinane (6)........... (7 to 4 fav) 1
3807^{6} QUEEN OF ALL BIRDS (Ire) 9-0 P V Gilson (1).....(20 to 1) 2
3953^{2} SECRET WAR (Ire) 9-0 J F Egan (3)............... (11 to 2) 3
3953^{9} EVICTRESS (Ire) 9-0 R Hughes (2)................ (8 to 1) 4
3729 PERFECT CADENCE (Ire) (bl) 8-12 (2*) D G O'Shea (4) ....(66 to 1) 5
1571^{8} GREENCASTLE ROSE (Ire) 8-12 (2*) P Carberry (5) (14 to 1) 6
3953^{4} STAGEWALK (Ire) 9-0 S Craine (9)................. (4 to 1) 7
3911 INDIAN EXPRESS (bl) 9-0 B Coogan (8)........... (14 to 1) 8
4000^{6} NORDIC COLOURS (Ire) 8-6 (8*) A P McCoy (7)... (12 to 1) 9
PETIT NOM (Ire) 9-0 C Roche (11).................. (12 to 1) 10
3954 GLAD YOU ASKED ME (Ire) (bl) 9-0 W J Supple (13) (33 to 1) 11
3453^{8} DACANI STAR (Ire) 9-0 P Shanahan (12)...........(20 to 1) 12
3953^{4} GRENNAN CLASSIC (Ire) 8-12 (2*) R M Burke (10) (10 to 1) 13
Dist: 8l, 1½l, 1½l, ¾l. 1m 26.20s. (13 Ran).
(Hamdan Al Maktoum), D K Weld

4118 Brandon Hotel Maiden (3-y-o) £4,685 7f.............................. (2:35)

CORPORATE SPORT (Ire) 9-0 N G McCullagh (14)..(6 to 1) 1
3605^{4} GOODNIGHT KISS 8-11 M J Kinane (1)........(7 to 4 fav) 2
3768^{3} WORLD'S VIEW 8-11 J P Murtagh (2).............. (3 to 1) 3
3526^{7} GLENSTAL FLAGSHIP (Ire) 9-0 C Roche (15)..... (10 to 1) 4
577 ANOTHER FIDDLE (Ire) 9-0 R Hughes (13)......... (10 to 1) 5
3808 RUNNING GUEST (Ire) 8-11 P Shanahan (12)..... (12 to 1) 6
3856^{9} GLOWING LINES (Ire) (bl) 8-11 S Craine (10)...... (25 to 1) 7
3808^{8} MERSADA (Ire) 8-3 (8*) T E Durcan (4)............(14 to 1) 8
ESTAFETTE (Ire) 8-11 P V Gilson (3)............. (14 to 1) 9
3417^{6} LOVE HURTS (Ire) 8-11 W J Supple,.............. (14 to 1) 10
3768^{6} ELEGANT NORA (Ire) 8-9 (2*) R M Burke (7)...... (50 to 1) 11
MATCHLESS PRINCE (Ire) 9-0 J F Egan (11)...... (14 to 1) 12
ITSGOTTOBE (Ire) 8-9 (2*) D G O'Shea (9)........ (20 to 1) 13
3579 SCALPEL (Ire) 8-11 M G Quigley (5)...............(66 to 1) 14
Dist: Hd, nk, 1l, 2½l. 1m 34.30s. (14 Ran).
(D S Dunne), D Hanley

4119 Gerard Lynch Handicap (0-75 3-y-o and up) £3,795 2m..............(3:10)

3399 TREBLE BOB (Ire) [-] 3-8-6 M J Kinane (17).......(10 to 1) 1
3976^{4} WOODFIELD ROSE [-] 4-7-6 (2*) D G O'Shea (3)... (12 to 1) 2
3952* PARTICULAR (Ire) [-] 3-9-8 (5ex) J P Murtagh (5)....(5 to 1) 3
3275^{3} L-WAY FIRST (Ire) [-] 3-8-5 W J Supple (19)........(16 to 1) 4
3853^{7} RIYADH DANCER (Ire) [-] 3-7-11 (4*) J J Behan (11) (16 to 1) 5
852 PLUMBOB (Ire) [-] 4-7-11^{4} (8*) P J Smullen (13).... (20 to 1) 6
3580 MARIAN YEAR [-] 7-7-6^{6} (8*) R T Fitzpatrick (15)... (14 to 1) 7
3951 MOOREFIELD GIRL (Ire) [-] 4-8-11 R Hughes (8).. (14 to 1) 8
1797* KARABAKH (Ire) [-] 4-10-0 P V Gilson (4)........... (8 to 1) 9
3856* MILLERS MILL (Ire) [-] 3-9-1 (2*,5ex) P Carberry (7) (10 to 1) 10
3663^{2} TOOLITTLE TOOLATE (Ire) [-] 4-9-12 J Collins (6)..(12 to 1) 11
3684 THE SALTY FROG (Ire) [-] 3-7-6 (8*) G M Moylan (14) ....(33 to 1) 12
3951^{2} ONOMATOPOEIA (Ire) [-] 3-8-13 J F Egan (12)..(5 to 2 fav) 13
3975* SUNSET CAFE (Ire) [-] (bl) 3-8-6 (4*) W J Smith (10) (10 to 1) 14
2517^{9} CARBON FIVE (Ire) [-] 4-7-13 (4*) J A Heffernan (18) (33 to 1) 15
SKEOUGH (Ire) [-] 5-9-1 C Roche (2)............... (8 to 1) 16
3298^{5} BOLD NOT BEAT (Ire) [-] 3-7-11 (2*) R M Burke (16) (33 to 1) ur
2094^{6} QUIET CITY [-] 6-7-11 N G McCullagh (1).........(33 to 1) su
Dist: 2l, 10l, ¾l, ½l. 4m 1.00s. (18 Ran).
(Mrs S Khan), D K Weld

NOTTINGHAM (soft (races 1,2,3), heavy (4,5,6,7))
Tuesday September 21st
Going Correction: PLUS 1.10 sec. per fur.

4120 Mapperley Limited Stakes Class F (0-65 3-y-o and up) £3,273 1m 54yds ....(2:00)

4024^{2} TONY'S MIST 3-8-10 K Darley (16) *nvr far away, styd on und pres to ld o'r one furlong out, ran on wl*. ....(100 to 30 fav op 5 to 2) 1
1818^{5} AUSTRAL JANE 3-8-5 K Fallon (10) *trkd ldrs, improved und pres on outsd last 2 fs, styd on finish*. ....(8 to 1 tchd 10 to 1) 2
3747^{6} MCA BELOW THE LINE (bl) 5-9-0 S Webster (1) *al hndy, drvn alng whn pace quickened o'r 2 fs out, styd on same pace*.. (10 to 1) 3
3961^{7} SEA BARON 3-8-10 J Quinn (6) *settled midfield, effrt and drvn alng o'r 2 fs out, styd on same pace*. .... (12 to 1 op 8 to 1) 4
3757 TREAD CAREFULLY 3-8-5 W Ryan (13) *tried to make all, quickened clr entering strt, wknd and hdd o'r one furlong out, sn btn*.................(7 to 1 op 4 to 1) 5
3973* SALDA 4-9-0 A Culhane (7) *wth ldrs, ev ch o'r 3 fs out, hrd drvn 2 out, fdd*..................(5 to 1 tchd 6 to 1) 6
3881^{8} QUEENS CONSUL (Ire) 3-8-5 D Harrison (4) *settled midfield, struggling to keep up o'r 2 fs out, sn outpcd*. ....(12 to 1 tchd 14 to 1) 7
3656 IRISH GROOM 6-9-0 R Cochrane (8) *beh and drvn alng hfwy, nvr nr to chal*............. (25 to 1 op 20 to 1) 8
3910^{4} QUEEN OF SHANNON (Ire) 5-8-9 M Hills (11) *settled gng wl, smooth hdwy o'r 3 fs out, rdn 2 out, found nothing*. ....(7 to 1 op 5 to 1) 9
3460^{6} SAKURA QUEEN (Ire) 3-8-5 C Rutter (5) *slow away, nvr able to reco'r*.................................... (20 to 1) 10
3310* NORMAN WARRIOR (bl) 4-8-11 (3*) C Hodgson (3) *trkd ldrs to strt, fdd o'r 3 fs out*. ....(10 to 1 op 12 to 1 tchd 14 to 1) 11
3523^{6} MUSTAHIL (Ire) 4-9-0 A McGlone (2) *trkd ldrs for o'r 5 fs, wknd quickly*........................(7 to 1 op 6 to 1) 12
3780^{9} GARTH (bl) 5-9-0 S Perks (15) *sluggish strt, nvr able to reco'r*................................(25 to 1 op 20 to 1) 13
Dist: 2½l, 2½l, 3l, ¾l, 2l, nk, 4l, 2½l, ¾l, 2l. 1m 52.70s. a 12.70s (13 Ran).
SR: 42/29/30/17/10/13/3/-/-/ (Mrs Chris Harrington), R Hannon

4121 EBF Colwick Maiden Fillies' Stakes Class D (2-y-o) £4,485 1m 54yds (2:30)

VIOLET CROWN (Ire) 8-11 R Cochrane (3) *al gng wl, smooth hdwy to ld well o'r one furlong out, sn drw clr*. ....(7 to 2 op 5 to 2) 1
3828^{3} COIGACH 8-11 W Ryan (6) *trkd ldg pair, led o'r 2 fs out till wl over one out, no ch wth wnr*. .... (Evens fav op 6 to 4 tchd 13 to 8) 2
CLYDE GODDESS (Ire) 8-11 K Darley (2) *trkd ldrs, ran green and shaken up o'r 2 fs out, styd on, improve*. ....(14 to 1 op 8 to 1) 3
3781 SPRINGTIME AFFAIR 8-11 L Dettori (1) *pressed ldg trio, drvn alng whn pace quickened o'r 2 fs out, sn struggling*..................................(25 to 1 op 14 to 1) 4
3738^{3} OH SUSANNAH 8-11 W R Swinburn (4) *led one and a half fs, led ag'n entering strt, hdd o'r 2 out, sn btn*. .... (11 to 4 op 5 to 4) 5
3828 DANIELLE HABIBI (Ire) 8-11 M Hills (8) *led aftr one and a half fs till entering strt, fdd und pres frm 2 out*. .... (33 to 1 op 25 to 1) 6
MY FIORE 8-4 (7*) C Hawksley (7) *drvn to keep up aftr 3 fs, sn struggling*...................(50 to 1 tchd 100 to 1) 7
3828 MISS TUT (Ire) 8-11 N Carlisle (5) *missed break, al beh*. ....(100 to 1 op 50 to 1) 8
3389^{8} HELLO MAMA 8-11 G Duffield (9) *trkd ldg 4, struggling entering strt, sn lost tch*............(25 to 1 op 16 to 1) 9
Dist: 6l, 2l, 6l, 3½l, ½l, 8l, hd, 1½l. 1m 56.70s. a 16.70s (9 Ran).
(Sheikh Mohammed), L M Cumani

4122 Nottingham Goose Fair Nursery Class D (2-y-o) £3,757 1m 1f 213yds... (3:00)

3968^{8} STRADISHALL [55] 8-1 F Norton (14) *patiently rdn, improved to ld o'r 2 fs out, ran on strly*. ....(25 to 1 op 20 to 1) 1
3705^{6} CAPTAIN STARLIGHT (Ire) [60] 8-6 M Hills (16) *trkd ldrs, drvn alng to improve o'r 2 fs out, styd on towards finish*..............(9 to 1 op 10 to 1 tchd 12 to 1) 2
2216^{4} MEMORABLE [64] 8-10 K Darley (4) *wtd wth, improved frm off the pace o'r 2 fs out, styd on, not rch wnr*. ....(12 to 1 op 11 to 1) 3
3598* WINNING LINE [68] 9-0 M Birch (21) *trkd ldrs, chal o'r 2 fs out, rdn and one pace fnl furlong*. (10 to 1 op 6 to 1) 4
3940^{3} ROBSERA (Ire) [70] 9-2 Paul Eddery (3) *tucked away, improved to chal 3 fs out, styd on same pace ins last*. .... (6 to 1 fav op 7 to 1 tchd 8 to 1 and 5 to 1) 5
3968^{7} SHARONE [52] 7-12 L Charnock (1) *missed break, chsd alng entering strt, styd on, nvr nrr*. ....(12 to 1 op 10 to 1) 6
3742^{4} SHOOFK [68] 9-0 L Piggott (7) *nvr far away, led o'r 3 fs out till over 2 out, fdd*. ....(11 to 1 op 10 to 1 tchd 12 to 1) 7
3686^{4} COMEONUP [60] 8-6 W Ryan (2) *wth ldrs, drvn alng o'r 2 fs out, fdd*......................... (10 to 1 op 8 to 1) 8
4009 MR MYSTICAL (Ire) [49] (v) 7-9 J Quinn (12) *trkd ldrs, feeling pace o'r 2 fs out, fdd*............................ (25 to 1) 9
4033^{4} PRINCE DANZIG (Ire) [73] 9-5 W R Swinburn (20) *rcd wide, effrt appr strt, nvr dngrs*..........................(12 to 1) 10
3642 LIFE'S TOO SHORT (Ire) [51] 7-11^{1} D Harrison (15) *chsd alng beh ldrs, nvr able to chal*. ....(11 to 1 op 10 to 1 tchd 12 to 1) 11
3841^{6} DEMI-PLIE [70] (v) 9-2 L Dettori (10) *chsd ldrs, struggling 3 fs out, sn btn*.................................(12 to 1) 12
2705^{6} SHARPISH WORDS [54] (bl) 8-0 Dale Gibson (18) *rcd wide, in tch to strt, sn btn*...............(33 to 1 op 20 to 1) 13
3829 SEMAH'S DREAM [47] 7-7 J O'Reilly (8) *led aftr 3 fs till o'r three out, sn btn*..................................(50 to 1) 14
3422^{8} AL JINN [72] 9-4 R Cochrane (13) *struggling to keep up hfwy, sn lost tch*..................................(20 to 1) 15
3829^{3} DRAGON MAN [64] 8-5 (5*) J Marshall (9) *trkd ldrs till wknd o'r 2 fs out*.......................... (10 to 1) 16

3828* TANDIA [75] 9-7 A McGlone (5) *chsd ldrs, struggling hfwy, sn btn*..............................(10 to 1 op 7 to 1) 17
3886[9] MILAIRIOUS (Ire) [60] 8-6 G Duffield (17) *in tch for o'r 4 fs, wknd quickly*....................................... (16 to 1) 18
3570[6] SWEET CAROLINE [60] 8-3 (3*) N Kennedy (19) *struggling frm hfwy, tld off*.....................(25 to 1 op 20 to 1) 19
2844[4] EMMA GRIMES (Ire) [64] 8-10 D Holland (6) *led 3 fs, wknd rpdly o'r three out, tld off*........(20 to 1 op 16 to 1) 20
Dist: 1½l, nk, 3l, 1½l, 1½l, 10l, 6l, 6l, hd, ¾l. 2m 19.50s. a 16.50s (20 Ran).
SR: 32/34/37/35/34/13/9/-/-/ (Davie Wong), G C Bravery

4123 Burton Joyce Fillies' Handicap Class E (0-70 3-y-o and up) £3,598 6f 15yds ....(3:30)

3887[3] PATSY GRIMES [58] (bl) 3-8-12 (7*) Mark Denaro (1) *made all far side, kpt on strly fnl furlong*...(14 to 1 op 12 to 1) 1
3887 LADY BROKER [50] 3-8-11 A Tucker (16) *outpcd and beh, gd hdwy frm off the pace last 2 fs, fnshd wl*... (20 to 1) 2
1416[4] APACHE MYTH [54] 3-9-1 L Dettori (7) *sluggish strt, improved far side hfwy, styd on wl fnl furlong.* ....(14 to 1 op 12 to 1) 3
3138[5] PETAL'S JARRED [32] 3-7-2 (5*) Darren Moffatt (12) *chsd alng centre, styd on strly appr fnl furlong.* ....(7 to 1 op 8 to 1 tchd 10 to 1) 4
3830 POYLE AMBER [52] 4-9-2 R Cochrane (14) *speed centre, feeling pace hfwy, styd on fnl furlong.* ....(12 to 1 op 11 to 1) 5
3190[8] HEATHYARDS GEM [54] 3-9-1 S Perks (8) *wl plcd far side thrght, kpt on same pace fnl furlong*..........(16 to 1) 6
3906 PENNY HASSET [64] 5-10-0 T Lucas (5) *patiently rdn, steady hdwy far side last 2 fs, ran on.* ....(12 to 1 op 11 to 1 tchd 14 to 1) 7
3946[5] BERNSTEIN BETTE [56] 7-9-6 W Ryan (9) *chsd alng in mid-div, kpt fnl furlong, nvr nrr.* ....(6 to 1 fav op 11 to 2 tchd 7 to 1) 8
3910 TAKE IT IN CASH [43] 4-8-7 C Rutter (3) *bustled alng far side, styd on same pace last 2 fs*... (14 to 1 op 10 to 1) 9
3429[3] KINNEGAD KID [45] 4-8-4 (5*) N Gwilliams (2) *chsd alng to go pace, kpt on, nvr able to chal*....(10 to 1 op 8 to 1) 10
3634 VICTORIAS PASSION [46] 3-8-4 (3*) S D Williams (10) *chsd far side ldrs, rdn and no imprsn last 2 fs*...... (20 to 1) 11
2089[2] COLMAR [34] 3-7-9 A Mackay (22) *wth ldr stand side for o'r 4 fs, fdd*..........................(14 to 1 op 20 to 1) 12
3946[3] DARUSSALAM [53] 6-9-0 (3*) O Pears (11) *broke wl to show speed centre for 4 fs, fdd.* (7 to 1 op 6 to 1 tchd 8 to 1) 13
3447 SEASON'S STAR [48] 3-8-2 (7*) Antoinette Armes (21) *led stand side bunch, drvn alng o'r 2 fs out, sn btn.* ....(16 to 1 tchd 20 to 1) 14
2723[4] SCARLET PRINCESS [37] 5-8-1 F Norton (20) *bustled alng towards centre, outpcd frm hfwy*.... (8 to 1 op 6 to 1) 15
3634 PEA FORTY FIVE [43] 3-8-4 A Proud (15) *outpcd and drvn alng, nvr dngrs*..................(33 to 1 op 25 to 1) 16
1171[8] I'M YOURS [61] 3-9-8 K Darley (18) *beh and drvn alng, nvr a factor*.. (20 to 1) 17
3965[5] WALK THAT WALK [55] (bl) 4-9-5 R Lappin (17) *struggling to go pace in centre, nvr dngrs*.................. (25 to 1) 18
3830 HELLO HOBSON'S (Ire) [60] 3-9-0 (7*) H Bastiman (13) *sluggish strt, tld off*....................(20 to 1 op 16 to 1) 19
2699[7] FORDALLIA [35] 3-7-7 (3*) N Kennedy (6) *chsd ldrs far side to hfwy, sn tld off*.................(33 to 1 op 25 to 1) 20
Dist: 1½l, nk, 1½l, nk, sht-hd, ½l, 4l, 2½l, 1½l, 4l. 1m 21.30s. a 9.80s (20 Ran).
SR: 41/27/30/2/24/22/33/9/-/ (J K Grimes), M P Muggeridge

4124 Bunny Rating Related Maiden Stakes Class D (0-80 2-y-o) £3,260 6f 15yds ....(4:00)

3816[7] LIME STREET BLUES (Ire) 9-0 A McGlone (3) *outpcd and beh, rapid hdwy to ld ins fnl furlong, forged clr.* ....(10 to 1 op 7 to 1) 1
3421[8] TOM MORGAN 9-0 D Holland (2) *trkd ldrs, drvn through to ld briefly ins fnl furlong, not quicken.* ....(5 to 1 op 4 to 1) 2
3903[2] RAPIER POINT (Ire) 9-0 K Darley (6) *made most till hdd o'r 2 fs out, rallied, no extr last 50 yards.* ....(4 to 1 op 7 to 2 tchd 5 to 1) 3
3457[2] PAONIC (Ire) 9-0 R Cochrane (7) *wth ldrs, led o'r 2 fs out till ins last, no extr*............. (7 to 4 fav op 2 to 1) 4
3589[3] MERLIN'S FIELD (Ire) 9-0 L Dettori (4) *al hndy, ev ch ins fnl furlong, no extr*......................(6 to 1 op 4 to 1) 5
3762[3] WAAFED (USA) (bl) 9-0 W R Swinburn (5) *sluggish strt, drvn alng to improve o'r one furlong out, nvr nrr.* ....(11 to 2 op 3 to 1) 6
3641[6] ROYAL INTERPRETER (v) 9-0 M Hills (8) *al chasing ldrs, drvn alng frm hfwy, nvr able to chal.* ....(25 to 1 op 20 to 1) 7
3389 BOLDANDPRETTY (bl) 8-9 D Harrison (1) *speed on outsd for 3 fs, wknd quickly*............(25 to 1 op 20 to 1) 8
Dist: 2½l, ½l, ½l, hd, nk, 4l, 10l. 1m 21.20s. a 9.70s (8 Ran).
SR: 38/28/26/24/23/22/6/-/ (D B Gallop), R Hannon

4125 Fiskerton Maiden Stakes Class D (Div I) (3-y-o and up) £3,494 1m 54yds (4:30)

3590 ARVOLA 3-8-9 L Dettori (3) *wtd wth in rear, smooth hdwy 3 fs out, led on bit blw dist, very easily.* ....(7 to 2 op 5 to 2 tchd 9 to 2) 1
3817[2] KESTON POND (Ire) 3-9-0 W R Swinburn (10) *led 2 fs, led 3 out to blw dist, sn outpcd*........(6 to 4 fav op 5 to 4) 2
3893[5] LADY SABINA 3-8-9 C Rutter (7) *wtd wth, hdwy 3 fs out, kpt on appr last, not pace to chal.* ....(12 to 1 tchd 14 to 1) 3
PRIMA SINFONIA 3-8-9 D Holland (12) *al cl up, rdn and ev ch 2 fs out, no extr appr last.* ....(7 to 1 op 4 to 1 tchd 15 to 2) 4
3817[7] HAYDON BRIDGE (Ire) 3-9-0 Paul Eddery (5) *trkd ldrs, shaken up 3 fs out, wknd blw dist.* (33 to 1 op 20 to 1) 5
3439[4] MISS CHARLIE 3-8-9 A Mackay (8) *missed break, pld hrd and ld aftr 2 fs, hdd 3 out, grad wknd.* ....(10 to 1 op 12 to 1) 6
YA MAI 3-8-9 A McGlone (11) *slwly into strd, sn reco'red to chase ldrs, wknd over 2 fs out.* ....(10 to 1 op 6 to 1 tchd 12 to 1) 7
3893[8] ARAMON 3-8-9 (5*) B Russell (2) *strted slwly, al in rear.* ....(16 to 1 op 14 to 1) 8
FARAGINGO 3-9-0 S Webster (9) *sn bustled alng, nvr gng pace of ldrs*....................................(33 to 1) 9
3893 MR PERKY 3-9-0 T Wall (6) *nvr a factor*......... (50 to 1) 10
FETES GALANTES (Ire) 3-8-9 R Cochrane (1) *strted slwly, sn in tch, wknd o'r 3 fs out, tld off.* ....(7 to 1 op 5 to 1 tchd 8 to 1) 11
3893 PINEAPPLE PRINCE 3-9-0 J Quinn (13) *chsd ldrs 6 fs, sn rdn and wknd, tld off*.................... (50 to 1) 12
Dist: 4l, 1½l, 1½l, 6l, 3½l, ¾l, hd, 3½l, ½l, 20l. 1m 54.60s. a 14.60s (12 Ran).
SR: 12/5/-/-/-/-/ (Sheikh Mohammed), J H M Gosden

4126 Fiskerton Maiden Stakes Class D (Div II) (3-y-o and up) £3,465 1m 54yds ....(5:00)

3740[6] DEVILS DEN (Ire) 3-9-0 D Harrison (9) *al chasing ldrs, shaken up 2 fs out, led jst ins last, ran on wl.* ....(20 to 1 op 16 to 1) 1
3282[5] RAFTERS 4-9-4 M Hills (5) *led, rdn o'r a furlong out, hdd and no extr fnl furlong.* ....(7 to 1 op 10 to 1 tchd 6 to 1) 2
SILVER MAPLE (USA) 3-8-9 G Hind (8) *sluggish strt, wtd wth in rear, steady hdwy fnl 2 fs, nvr nrr.* ....(6 to 1 op 7 to 2) 3
2752 PRIME OF LIFE (Ire) 3-9-0 K Darley (1) *al wl plcd, rdn blw dist, sn btn*..................(2 to 1 fav op 5 to 4) 4
3948 RAVE-ON-HADLEY (Ire) 3-8-7 (7*) W Hollick (11) *chsd ldr, ev ch 2 fs out, ran on one pace*.................... (25 to 1) 5
1884 MISSED FLIGHT 3-9-0 G Duffield (2) *strted slwly, hdwy o'r 3 fs out, not rch ldrs*.............. (3 to 1 tchd 4 to 1) 6
3590[7] WEFY (USA) 3-9-0 W R Swinburn (7) *patiently rdn, effrt 3 fs out, sn wknd, eased whn btn*.....(10 to 1 op 8 to 1) 7
COOL ETOILE 3-8-2 (7*) A Eddery (6) *al in rear.* ....(25 to 1 op 20 to 1) 8
3286[6] POLAR MOON 3-8-9 J Fortune (10) *al in rear.* ....(10 to 1 op 5 to 1) 9
FAVLIENT 3-8-9 J Lowe (12) *in tch till wknd o'r 2 fs out, tld off*..........................(25 to 1 op 20 to 1) 10
WEB OF STEEL 3-9-0 T Rogers (3) *trkd ldrs, rdn and wknd o'r 3 fs out, tld off*..........(33 to 1 op 25 to 1) 11
Dist: 3l, 4l, 2½l, nk, ½l, 12l, 5l, 3l, 5l, 2l. 1m 52.60s. a 12.60s (11 Ran).
SR: 46/41/20/17/16/14/ (P A Kelleway), P A Kelleway

BRIGHTON (good to firm)
Wednesday September 22nd
Going Correction: MINUS 0.25 sec. per fur.

4127 EBF Kemp Town Maiden Stakes Class D (2-y-o) £4,306 5f 213yds.......(2:00)

3129[9] SHEPHERD MARKET (Ire) 9-0 R Price (4) *made all, quickened clr o'r 2 fs out, easily.* ....(4 to 1 tchd 5 to 1 and 7 to 2) 1
2619[2] BAGSHOT 9-0 A Munro (10) *mid-div, rdn alng 2 fs out, swtchd rght o'r one out, kpt on, no ch wth wnr.* ....(15 to 8 fav op 7 to 4 tchd 5 to 2) 2
2325[8] SAGASAN 9-0 W Newnes (3) *dwlt, mid-div, hdwy o'r one furlong out, ran on wl*............(33 to 1 op 16 to 1) 3
3958[3] GADGE 9-0 B Rouse (13) *prmnt till rdn and one pace fnl 2 fs*..................................(14 to 1 op 7 to 1) 4
2720[7] TONE CONTROL 9-0 W Woods (1) *cl up, rdn alng o'r 2 fs out, one pace*...................(50 to 1 op 25 to 1) 5
COOL EDGE (Ire) 9-0 P Robinson (7) *slwly away, hdwy o'r one furlong out, nvr nrr*..........(50 to 1 op 16 to 1) 6
3870[3] BANDITA 8-5[3] (7*) R Painter (11) *mid-div, not much room and swtchd lft o'r one furlong out, kpt on.* ....(50 to 1 op 25 to 1) 7
3867[3] SPEEDY SNAPS IMAGE 9-0 L Dettori (14) *nvr dngrs.* ....(33 to 1 op 20 to 1) 8
2817[5] WIDE OUTSIDE (Ire) 8-9 A Morris (9) *chsd ldrs, wknd o'r one furlong out*.................(50 to 1 op 25 to 1) 9
SEGALA (Ire) 9-0 G Duffield (5) *strted slwly, nvr dngrs.* ....(16 to 1 op 12 to 1) 10
GINZA LIGHTS (Ire) 9-0 Paul Eddery (12) *cl up, pushed alng o'r 2 fs out, sn wknd*....(3 to 1 op 9 to 2 tchd 5 to 2) 11

LADY VALENSINA (Ire) 8-9 J Williams (8) *slwly into strd, nvr on terms*....................... (12 to 1 op 6 to 1) 12
HALLIARD 9-0 R Perham (15) *outpcd*............ (33 to 1) 13
STERRETJIE (Ire) 8-9 J Reid (6) *cl up till wknd wl o'r 2 fs out*.................................. (50 to 1 op 20 to 1) 14
Dist: 5l, 1½l, ½l, sht-hd, 1l, 1½l, sht-hd, 3½l, ¾l, ½l. 1m 10.00s. a 1.60s (14 Ran).
SR: 38/18/12/10/9/5/ (Hugh Hart), R W Armstrong

4128 Steine Claiming Stakes Class E (2-y-o) £3,261 6f 209yds........... (2:30)

3870[5] CANDI DAS (Ire) 8-2 D Harrison (8) *mid-div, hdwy to ld appr fnl furlong, ran on wl*.................. (16 to 1) 1
3835[5] MAKE THE BREAK 8-10 (7*) D O'Neill (9) *beh, hdwy whn not much room aftr 2 fs out, weaved through ins last, ran on*.. (12 to 1) 2
4032[6] WADDLE (Ire) 7-13[1] (7*) S Mulvey (16) *sn pushed alng to track ldrs, lost pl 3 fs out, hdwy 2 out, one pace.* .... (66 to 1) 3
3390 ROSE OF GLENN 7-10 N Adams (18) *beh, hdwy o'r one furlong out, ran on*.................................. (16 to 1) 4
3940 LITTLE HOOLIGAN (v) 8-3 C Rutter (2) *chsd ldrs, hrd rdn 3 fs out, kpt on one pace*........................ (14 to 1) 5
3546[5] FOREVER BLUSHING 7-10 (5*) L Newton (5) *chsd ldrs, wide strt, sn rdn, wknd 2 fs out*......... (16 to 1 op 20 to 1) 6
3867[2] MANDEVILLE GEORGE 8-11 J Reid (14) *trkd ldrs, lost pl hfwy, kpt on frm 2 fs out*......................... (7 to 1) 7
3755[2] TUTU SIXTYSIX (v) 8-6 T Quinn (6) *cl up, led aftr 2 fs till appr last, wknd quickly*.... (11 to 8 on tchd 5 to 4 on) 8
1933 MY SONG OF SONGS 7-12 J Quinn (3) *nvr nrr*... (50 to 1) 9
3905 FERRYMAN (USA) 9-7 Paul Eddery (1) *cl up, ev ch o'r 2 fs out, wknd und pres over one out*... (10 to 1 op 9 to 1) 10
3978[7] SPORTING HEIR (Ire) 8-7[1] M Wigham (15) *led 2 fs, cl up till wknd o'r two out*............................. (20 to 1) 11
3126[7] EASY D'OR 8-6 (3*) M Fenton (10) *sn pushed alng in rear, al beh*.. (50 to 1) 12
969[4] LEESON STREET LADY (Ire) (bl) 8-0 D Biggs (17) *cl up, ev ch 3 fs out, sn wknd, eased*.......................... (66 to 1) 13
3869[5] MAGIC MAGGIE 7-12 T Williams (7) *trkd ldrs, wknd wl o'r 2 fs out*... (50 to 1) 14
3869 CLASSIC MELODY 8-1 A McGlone (4) *outpcd, sn tld off.* .... (66 to 1) 15
Dist: ¾l, 2l, 1½l, ¾l, 4l, hd, nk, sht-hd, 2l, ¾l. 1m 23.40s. a 3.40s (15 Ran).
SR: 11/24/6/-/-/-/ (Giles W Pritchard-Gordon), G A Pritchard-Gordon

4129 Friend-James Memorial Limited Stakes Class E (0-70 3-y-o and up) £3,339 1m 3f 196yds........... (3:00)

3555[3] SCORCHED AIR 3-8-6 M Hills (12) *trkd ldrs, ran on to ld wl ins fnl furlong*...... (8 to 1 op 7 to 1 tchd 10 to 1) 1
3820[4] GREEN KILT 3-8-11 A Munro (3) *wtd wth in mid-div, hdwy and not much room o'r 2 fs out, ran on wl nr finish.* .... (9 to 1 op 8 to 1 tchd 10 to 1) 2
3759[3] FUNNY HILARIOUS (USA) 3-8-6 T Quinn (1) *trkd ldr, led 2 and a half fs out till wl ins last*...... (5 to 1 op 4 to 1) 3
3866[2] DIPLOMATIST 3-8-6 J Reid (8) *hld up beh, hdwy 5 fs out gng wl, not much room 3 out, kpt on.* .... (11 to 1 op 7 to 1 tchd 12 to 1) 4
3850[5] SPECIAL DAWN (Ire) 3-8-11 W Carson (9) *chsd ldrs, pushed alng o'r 3 fs out, not much room over one out, kpt on.* .... (11 to 2 op 5 to 1 tchd 7 to 1) 5
3018[2] WARM SPELL 3-8-11 B Rouse (13) *trkd ldrs, rdn 2 fs out, one pace*.............. (12 to 1 op 6 to 1 tchd 14 to 1) 6
1028[9] BUSMAN (Ire) 4-9-5 W Newnes (11) *nvr nr to chal.* .... (50 to 1 op 25 to 1) 7
3873* DANCING TRALTHEE (Ire) 3-8-6 R Cochrane (7) *keen, led to 2 and a half fs out, wknd quickly.* .... (2 to 1 fav op 7 to 4 tchd 9 to 4) 8
3787[6] WELL SUITED (bl) 3-8-11 L Dettori (5) *hld up, effrt and hdwy 3 fs out, btn o'r one out*...... (12 to 1 op 7 to 1) 9
874[9] HONEY DANCER 9-8-12 (7*) R Painter (4) *al beh, tld off.* .... (200 to 1 op 66 to 1) 10
3310[5] BROADWAY RUCKUS (Can) 4-8-11 (3*) Stephen Davies (2) *trkd ldrs till wknd 4 fs out, tld off.* .... (100 to 1 op 33 to 1) 11
441 SUNBEAM CHARLIE 3-8-6 (5*) B Russell (6) *trkd ldrs, rdn alng o'r 4 fs out, sn btn, tld off*... (200 to 1 op 50 to 1) 12
Dist: Nk, nk, 2½l, nk, 3l, ¾l, hd, 2l, 20l, 10l. 2m 30.50s. a 3.00s (12 Ran).
SR: 32/36/30/25/29/23/29/15/16/ (Michael Wauchope), J W Hills

4130 Hill Conditions Stakes Class D (2-y-o) £3,348 5f 213yds............... (3:30)

3667[3] BALLAH SHACK (USA) 8-12 Paul Eddery (5) *cl up, pushed alng o'r 2 fs out, led ins last, ran on wl.* .... (12 to 1 op 6 to 1) 1
3751[3] DOUBLE DOWN 8-9 L Dettori (2) *sn led, hdd ins fnl furlong, no extr*........ (5 to 2 fav op 4 to 1 tchd 9 to 2) 2
3902[3] MONIS (Ire) 9-0 W Carson (4) *broke wl, steadied to track ldg pair, drvn 2 fs out, not quicken.* .... (3 to 1 op 9 to 4 tchd 100 to 30) 3
3902[2] BLUE BOMBER 9-0 J Reid (3) *hld up in rear, cld 2 fs out, one pace*........................ (11 to 4 op 2 to 1) 4
3104* AL BATTAR (USA) 9-0 R Cochrane (6) *hld up in tch, effrt 2 fs out, no imprsn*...... (11 to 2 op 3 to 1 tchd 6 to 1) 5
1665[2] GO WITH BO (Ire) 8-10 B Rouse (1) *hld up in tch, outpcd wl o'r one furlong out*............ (33 to 1 op 16 to 1) 6
Dist: 2½l, ¾l, sht-hd, 4l, 3½l. 1m 10.10s. a 1.70s (6 Ran).
SR: 34/21/23/22/6/-/ (Abdulla Al Khalifa), G Lewis

4131 Win With The Tote Handicap Class E (0-70 3-y-o and up) £3,261 6f 209yds ....(4:00)

3896 UNVEILED [49] 5-8-6 (5*) S Drowne (18) *beh, pushed alng o'r 3 fs out, hdwy over one out, str run to ld wl ins last.* .... (20 to 1 op 14 to 1 tchd 25 to 1) 1
3707 WALNUT BURL (Ire) [49] (v) 3-8-7 J Reid (12) *hld up rear, hdwy o'r one furlong out, ran on wl.* .... (11 to 1 op 10 to 1 tchd 12 to 1) 2
3634[7] DIGPAST (Ire) [66] 3-9-10 T Quinn (13) *mid-div, hdwy 2 fs out, ev ch ins last, no extr cl hme*... (9 to 1 op 10 to 1) 3
3896[8] KARUKERA [48] 3-8-6 J Williams (15) *hld up rear, hdwy o'r one furlong out, ran on.* .... (20 to 1 op 16 to 1 tchd 25 to 1) 4
3522[7] MADAGANS GREY [50] 5-8-12 G Duffield (17) *beh, hdwy appr fnl furlong, ran on.* .... (25 to 1 op 20 to 1 tchd 33 to 1) 5
3830 BEATLE SONG [56] 5-8-11 (7*) P McCabe (3) *chsd ldrs, rdn and one pace fnl 2 fs*.............. (14 to 1 op 10 to 1) 6
3670[6] DESERT NOMAD [57] 3-8-10 (5*) D Wright (8) *trkd ldrs, led 2 fs out till wl ins last, no extr*....... (15 to 2 op 12 to 1) 7
3591 FIVEOFIVE (Ire) [52] (bl) 3-8-10 L Dettori (9) *chsd ldrs, rdn alng o'r 2 fs out, no hdwy.* .... (12 to 1 op 7 to 1 tchd 14 to 1) 8
3818[2] KNOBBLEENEEZE [67] (v) 3-9-11 S Whitworth (14) *cl up, led briefly 2 and a half fs out, sn btn.* .... (11 to 1 op 8 to 1 tchd 12 to 1) 9
3837[3] PANCHELLITA (USA) [61] 4-9-9 B Rouse (6) *trkd ldrs, wknd o'r one furlong out*............ (7 to 1 jt-fav op 6 to 1) 10
1992[3] NYMPH ERRANT [59] 3-9-3 A Munro (5) *beh, effrt o'r 2 fs out, no imprsn*........ (10 to 1 op 8 to 1 tchd 12 to 1) 11
3783 THE LITTLE FERRET [70] (bl) 3-9-7 (7*) D Gibbs (11) *wide, trkd ldrs till wknd 2 fs out.* .... (14 to 1 op 10 to 1 tchd 16 to 1) 12
3837[9] CHARMED KNAVE [65] 8-9-13 T Williams (10) *nvr dngrs.* .... (16 to 1 op 12 to 1 tchd 20 to 1) 13
3896[4] NAVARESQUE [43] 8-8-5 A McGlone (1) *nvr gng wl, al beh.* .... (7 to 1 jt-fav op 6 to 1 tchd 8 to 1) 14
3178[7] KAPUCHKA (Ire) [57] 3-9-1 Paul Eddery (2) *al beh.* .... (20 to 1 tchd 33 to 1) 15
3946 PAIR OF JACKS (Ire) [58] 3-9-2 W Woods (7) *cl up till wknd o'r 2 fs out, eased*................ (20 to 1 op 12 to 1) 16
3887[7] SCOTS LAW [43] (bl) 6-8-5 J Quinn (4) *chsd ldrs till wknd o'r 2 fs out, eased, tld off*.......... (10 to 1 op 8 to 1) 17
3575[8] SURE LORD (Ire) [66] (v) 4-10-0 W Carson (16) *led to 2 and a half fs out, drpd out tamely, tld off.* .... (25 to 1 op 16 to 1) 18
Dist: Nk, 1l, ¾l, ¾l, 1½l, sht-hd, 1½l, 1l, 2l, 1½l. 1m 22.50s. a 2.50s (18 Ran).
SR: 33/28/42/22/26/27/23/13/25/ (Mrs K M Burge), R J Hodges

4132 Waterhall Conditions Stakes Class D (3-y-o and up) £3,260 7f 214yds. .(4:30)

3585[4] CARELAMAN 3-8-10 J Reid (2) *chsd ldrs, cld 2 fs out, led one out, sn clr*.................. (5 to 1 tchd 11 to 2) 1
3800[8] FITZCARRALDO (USA) (bl) 3-8-10 R Cochrane (5) *cl up, hrd rdn to ld 2 fs out, sn edgd lft, hdd one out, no extr.* .... (2 to 1 fav op 6 to 4 tchd 9 to 4) 2
1801[7] BARIK (Ire) 3-9-0 R Hills (3) *pld hrd, hld up, hdwy 3 fs out, sn rdn and one pace*..... (8 to 1 op 7 to 2 tchd 9 to 1) 3
4066[4] SPANISH STORM (Ire) (v) 4-9-0 W Woods (9) *led, clr hfwy, hdd and btn 2 fs out*..... (6 to 1 op 5 to 1 tchd 7 to 1) 4
2926 SHAMAM (USA) 3-9-4 W Carson (8) *outpcd till styd on ins fnl furlong, nvr dngrs*............ (6 to 1 tchd 7 to 1) 5
3964[5] SHIKARI'S SON 6-9-8 G Duffield (6) *beh, cld hfwy, wknd wl o'r one furlong out*.............. (10 to 1 op 8 to 1) 6
3744* SHINING JEWEL 6-9-2 L Piggott (1) *keen hold, trkd ldr till wknd 2 fs out*........................ (12 to 1 op 16 to 1) 7
4005[9] AVENUE FOCH (Ire) 4-9-1 M Wigham (7) *outpcd.* .... (20 to 1 op 33 to 1 tchd 66 to 1) 8
3474[6] CARBON STEEL (Ire) (bl) 3-8-11 L Dettori (4) *chsd ldrs, pushed alng o'r th fs out, sn btn and eased.* .... (16 to 1 op 14 to 1 tchd 20 to 1) 9
Dist: 3l, 6l, nk, 3l, 2½l, 1½l, nk, 6l. 1m 34.50s. a 2.10s (9 Ran).
SR: 35/26/12/11/6/2/ (P G Goulandris), J L Dunlop

4133 Eric Simms Memorial Handicap Class D (0-80 3-y-o and up) £4,079 7f 214yds ....(5:00)

3726[5] KINGCHIP BOY [53] (v) 4-7-10 (7*) P McCabe (14) *rcd freely, made all, sn clr, tired ins fnl furlong, jst hld on.* .... (5 to 1 op 9 to 2) 1
3257[5] AITCH N'BEE [72] 10-9-8 L Dettori (13) *beh, rdn alng o'r 3 fs out, hdwy 2 out, ran on wl.* .... (9 to 1 op 8 to 1 tchd 10 to 1) 2
3736 LAKAB (USA) [72] 3-9-4 R Hills (6) *trkd ldrs, rdn and one pace fnl 2 fs*........(20 to 1 op 14 to 1 tchd 25 to 1) 3
3837[4] COURT MINSTREL [61] 4-8-11 J Reid (4) *mid-div, hdwy o'r one furlong out, ran on*........ (4 to 1 fav tchd 5 to 1) 4

3450[5] SINGERS IMAGE [55] (v) 4-8-5 J Williams (8) *beh, styd on ins fnl furlong, nvr nrr.* (8 to 1 op 6 to 1 tchd 9 to 1) 5
3450[2] TROOPING (Ire) [75] (bl) 4-9-11 R Cochrane (10) *chsd wnr, hrd rdn 2 fs out, wknd ins last.*......(7 to 1 op 4 to 1) 6
3883 NORTH ESK (USA) [62] 4-8-12 M Wigham (11) *mid-div, effrt o'r one furlong out, nvr on terms.* ....(14 to 1 op 16 to 1 tchd 25 to 1) 7
3476 NAFUTH (USA) [75] 3-9-7 W Carson (12) *chsd ldrs, rdn 2 fs out, btn o'r one out.* (11 to 1 op 10 to 1 tchd 14 to 1) 8
3643[2] PRECIOUS AIR (Ire) [57] 5-8-7 B Rouse (1) *beh, effrt 2 fs out, eased whn no imprsn one out.* ....(7 to 1 op 8 to 1 tchd 10 to 1) 9
3837[6] PRINCE RODNEY [62] 4-8-5 (7*) Mark Denaro (2) *trkd ldrs, wknd appr 2 fs out.*...............(14 to 1 op 10 to 1) 10
3906 ASSIGNMENT [67] 7-9-3 T Williams (3) *beh, hrd drvn o'r 3 fs out, no imprsn.*..................(25 to 1 op 16 to 1) 11
3942 FOLLY VISION (Ire) [54] (bl) 3-7-11 (3*) B Doyle (15) *outpcd, tld off.*..........................(33 to 1 op 20 to 1) 12
1425* MOUGINS (Ire) [78] (bl) 4-10-0 T Quinn (5) *veered lft leaving stalls and crashed through rls.* ....(16 to 1 op 14 to 1 tchd 20 to 1) ro
Dist: Nk, 1½l, 2l, 2½l, ½l, hd, 5l, 2½l, 3½l, 5l. 1m 33.80s. a 1.40s (13 Ran).
SR: 38/56/47/34/20/38/24/18/-/ (Four Jays Racing Partnership), M J Ryan

LISTOWEL (IRE) (soft)
Wednesday September 22nd

4134 Ballinruddery (Fillies) E.B.F. Maiden (Div 1) (2-y-o) £5,865 1m........(3:50)

3911[5] ANSARIYA (USA) 9-0 J P Murtagh (5).........(11 to 8 on) 1
3954[8] OUT IN THE SUN (USA) 9-0 K J Manning (8)......(12 to 1) 2
3729 DANITA (Ire) 9-0 C Roche (4).....................(3 to 1) 3
3683[4] MAKE THAT CALL (Ire) 9-0 P V Gilson (12).........(8 to 1) 4
1994[7] BOARDWALKER (Ire) 9-0 W J Supple (9).........(33 to 1) 5
CARANNA 9-0 J F Egan (7).....................(14 to 1) 6
3953 FRIARY TOWN (Ire) 9-0 P Shanahan (2)...........(50 to 1) 7
BELLA SIGURA (USA) 9-0 S Craine (13).........(10 to 1) 8
3807 SAVE THE WEST (Ire) 8-12 (2*) P Carberry (10)......(33 to 1) 9
CLASSIC QUEEN (Ire) 9-0 N G McCullagh (6).....(14 to 1) 10
LEMOIRE (Ire) 8-7 (7*) S N Donohoe (3)..........(50 to 1) 11
ACUMEN (Ire) 9-0 R Hughes (1).................(12 to 1) 12
Dist: 2l, 2l, 1½l, 2l. 1m 49.10s. (12 Ran).
(H H Aga Khan), John M Oxx

4135 Ballinruddery (Fillies) E.B.F. Maiden (Div 2) (2-y-o) £5,865 1m........(4:25)

CREATIVE BLOOM (USA) 9-0 M J Kinane (8)... (7 to 4 on) 1
3954[5] ALMOST A LADY (Ire) 9-0 P V Gilson (12).........(12 to 1) 2
3954[2] SORALENA (Ire) 9-0 W J Supple (13)..............(6 to 1) 3
3954 SENDER VICTORIOUS (Ire) 9-0 R Hughes (5).....(16 to 1) 4
3953[7] LIFE DANCING (Ire) 9-0 K J Manning (2)..........(14 to 1) 5
GRACEFUL RESIGN 9-0 N G McCullagh (3)........(14 to 1) 6
GLIMMERING GIRL (USA) 9-0 S Craine (6).........(10 to 1) 7
3954[3] JOYFUL MUSIC (Ire) 8-6 (8*) J J Stack (7)........(12 to 1) 8
3807 MARROWFAT LADY (Ire) 9-0 B Coogan (1).......(33 to 1) 9
3729[6] FAIRY MUSIC (Ire) 9-0 J F Egan (4)..............(16 to 1) 10
3954 POSCIMUR (Ire) 8-10 (4*) J J Behan (9)..........(50 to 1) 11
3953 BELLE VIVE (Ire) 9-0 M G Cleary (10)..........(100 to 1) 12
CANGERAC (Ire) 8-6 (8*) A P McCoy (11)........(100 to 1) 13
Dist: 7l, nk, 4l, 4l. 1m 48.50s. (13 Ran).
(Moyglare Stud Farm), D K Weld

4136 Tom Browne Memorial Handicap (0-85 3-y-o and up) £3,795 1m...(5:00)

3327[7] ALSHOU (Ire) [-] 4-7-10 (6*) R V Skelly (6).........(12 to 1) 1
3926[4] STATE PRINCESS (Ire) [-] 3-9-8 R Hughes (11) (11 to 4 fav) 2
3542[5] SEEK THE FAITH (USA) [-] (bl) 4-9-11 M J Kinane (13) ....(100 to 30) 3
3808[6] SCALP (Ire) [-] 3-8-11 K J Manning (2)............(14 to 1) 4
3928 UKUD (USA) [-] 3-9-6 (6*) B J Walsh (5)..........(10 to 1) 5
3380* MISS MISTLETOES (Ire) [-] 3-9-8 S Craine (14).....(6 to 1) 6
3576[4] KENTUCKY BABY (Ire) [-] 3-7-10 (8*) G M Moylan (10) ....(12 to 1) 7
4001[6] ALBONA [-] 5-8-13 N Byrne (4)..................(14 to 1) 8
3826[9] BOBROSS (Ire) [-] 3-8-12 (4*) J A Heffernan (9)....(25 to 1) 9
3399 MEJEVE [-] 5-9-2 (4*) C Everard (1)..............(10 to 1) 10
4057[9] MANZALA (USA) [-] 3-9-2 J P Murtagh (7)..........(10 to 1) 11
3160 FAIRYDEL (Ire) [-] 3-8-5 (8*) P J Smullen (3)....... (33 to 1) 12
4057* BRAZEN ANGEL (Ire) [-] 3-8-12 (5ex) J F Egan (8)...(5 to 1) 13
3926 SOUNDPROOF (Ire) [-] (bl) 3-9-6 (4*) J J Behan (12) (14 to 1) 14
Dist: 1½l, 1l, ½l, 3½l. 1m 45.10s. (14 Ran).
(J Morrison), J Morrison

4137 Sean O'Sullivan Memorial Maiden (3-y-o and up) £3,795 1¾m........ (5:30)

3524[3] UNCERTAIN AFFAIR (Ire) 3-8-6 M J Kinane (11) (7 to 4 fav) 1
3857[2] WILD FANTASY (Ire) 5-9-2 W J Supple (2).......... (3 to 1) 2
3198[3] CARRICK PIKE (USA) (bl) 3-8-9 C Roche (10)......(6 to 1) 3
FURIETTO (Ire) 3-8-2[3] (10*) A J Dempsey (4)......(33 to 1) 4
3524[6] DANCING VISION (Ire) 3-8-1 (8*) B Fenton (9).....(10 to 1) 5
3526[4] HAWTHORN ROSE (Ire) 3-8-6 P Shanahan (3)..... (8 to 1) 6
3772[8] KEPPOLS HARRIER (Ire) 3-8-9 A J Nolan (1)......(16 to 1) 7
MILFORD MATCH (Ire) 5-9-2 P V Gilson (16).......(8 to 1) 8
3999[9] ANNADOT (Ire) 3-8-6 N G McCullagh (17)........(33 to 1) 9
3295[7] MARYJO (Ire) 4-9-0 (2*) P Carberry (5)..........(100 to 1) 10
3524[7] MISS BUSYBODY (Ire) 3-8-6 D V Smith (13)......(33 to 1) 11
3952[3] LIMAHEIGHTS (Ire) 3-7-12 (8*) P J Smullen (14).... (7 to 1) 12
3198[4] ROYAL ANTELOPE (Fr) 3-8-6 R Hughes (7)........(5 to 1) 13
YELLOW FORD ROSE (Ire) 3-8-6 D Manning (12)..(50 to 1) 14
Dist: 4l, 4l, 4l, hd. 3m 18.60s. (14 Ran).
(Moyglare Stud Farm), D K Weld

SAN SIRO (ITY) (good)
Wednesday September 22nd

4138 Premio Colorno Maiden (2-y-o) £5,603 7f 110yds......................(4:00)

SUPLIZI (Ire) 8-8 J Weaver, *trkd ldrs, led 2 fs out, sn clr, very easily*.. 1
CAROMARCO (Ity) 8-11 S Dettori,...................... 2
TRAGIC HERO (USA) 8-11 B Jovine,...................... 3
Dist: 8l, 3½l, 2 ¼l, 2l, 2l, 4l, ½l, 10l. 1m 31.80s. (10 Ran).
(Scuderia Rencati Srl), L M Cumani

ASCOT (good to soft)
Thursday September 23rd

Going Correction: PLUS 0.20 sec. per fur. (races 1,2,4,6,7), PLUS 0.45 (3,5)

4139 Clarence House Conditions Stakes Class B (3-y-o and up) £8,019 7f (2:00)

1786 PETARDIA 3-8-12 M Hills (4) *hld up, hdwy one and a half fs out, bumped jst ins last, quickened to ld nr finish.* ....(3 to 1 fav op 5 to 2 tchd 7 to 2) 1
2237 CELESTIAL KEY (USA) 3-9-2 K Darley (1) *pressed ldr, led 3 fs out, edgd lft ins last, hdd and no extr cl hme.* ....(6 to 1 op 8 to 1 tchd 9 to 1) 2
3468[5] HUMAM (Ire) 3-8-9 R Hills (5) *chsd ldrs, rdn and one pace fnl 2 fs*..................(7 to 2 op 5 to 2 tchd 4 to 1) 3
658[6] SERIOUS 3-8-6 W R Swinburn (3) *hld up, effrt o'r 2 fs out, sn rdn and one pace*................(4 to 1 op 7 to 2) 4
4005[5] RUSTIC CRAFT (Ire) (bl) 3-8-10 R Cochrane (2) *led 4 fs, wknd 2 out*............(7 to 2 op 11 to 4 tchd 4 to 1) 5
Dist: 1l, 2l, 2½l, 4l. 1m 31.78s. a 5.48s (5 Ran).
SR: 37/38/25/14/6/ (Mollers Racing), G Wragg

4140 Hoover Rated Class B Handicap (0-100 3-y-o and up) £9,507 1m..(2:30)

3636[6] RAMBO'S HALL [99] 8-9-7 P Robinson (6) *beh, pld out and hdwy 2 and a half fs out, led jst ins fnl two, drvn out.* ....(11 to 2 op 3 to 1 tchd 6 to 1) 1
3214* HE'S A KING (USA) [85] 3-8-3 L Dettori (7) *led till ins fnl 2 fs, hrd drvn, kpt on wl, not pace of wnr.* ....(10 to 1 op 8 to 1) 2
4063 RISK MASTER [91] 4-8-13 D Holland (4) *beh, hdwy one and a half fs out, rdn and kpt on wl fnl furlong.* ....(7 to 1 op 8 to 1 tchd 9 to 1) 3
497[4] LORD CHICKNEY (USA) [96] 4-9-4 M Roberts (2) *trkd ldrs, str chal 2 fs out, outpcd fnl furlong.* ....(11 to 2 op 5 to 1 tchd 13 to 2) 4
3897 FOURFORFUN [89] 3-8-7 B Raymond (3) *beh, hdwy 3 fs out, ev ch ins fnl 2, not quicken.* ....(11 to 1 op 8 to 1 tchd 12 to 1) 5
2009[2] JUST YOU DARE (Ire) [86] 3-8-4 G Duffield (1) *str hold, prmnt till wknd appr 2 fs out.* ....(7 to 1 op 6 to 1 tchd 15 to 2) 6
3897* FRAAM [96] 4-9-4 W R Swinburn (5) *beh, hdwy to press ldrs o'r 2 fs out, sn wknd, eased whn btn fnl furlong.* ....(2 to 1 fav op 9 to 4 tchd 5 to 2) 7
3636 HOST (Ire) [85] 4-8-4 (3*) B Doyle (8) *pressed ldrs till wknd 2 fs out.*.......................... (20 to 1 tchd 25 to 1) 8
Dist: 1l, hd, nk, hd, 10l, 1½l, ¾l. 1m 44.30s. a 5.30s (8 Ran).
SR: 52/31/40/44/32/-/8/-/ (B Dixon), J A Glover

4141 Hoover Cumberland Lodge Stakes Class A (Group 3) (3-y-o and up) £28,080 1½m................. (3:05)

3879* PRINCE OF ANDROS (USA) 3-8-6 L Dettori (6) *3rd till chsd ldr 3 fs out, led one and a half out, rdn and edgd rght ins last, drvn out.*.. (2 to 1 fav op 13 to 8 tchd 5 to 2) 1
3784[2] BOBZAO (Ire) 4-9-0 J Reid (1) *beh, hdwy to track ldrs aftr 5 fs, rdn o'r 2 out, ran on wl fnl furlong, edgd rght and not rch wnr.*..........(5 to 2 tchd 9 to 4 and 11 to 4) 2
3842[2] MUHAYAA (USA) 4-9-0 W R Swinburn (5) *led to one and a half fs out, hld whn hmpd ins last.* ....(6 to 1 op 5 to 1 tchd 13 to 2) 3
3784[7] LUCKY LINDY (Ire) 4-9-5 Pat Eddery (4) *rear, rdn 3 fs out, styd on one pace frm 2 out.*....... (6 to 1 tchd 13 to 2) 4
1805[5] GARDEN OF HEAVEN (USA) 4-9-5 M Roberts (3) *beh, rdn 3 fs out, not pace to rch ldrs frm o'r 2 out.* ....(8 to 1 op 7 to 1 tchd 9 to 1) 5
1484[4] ROLL A DOLLAR 7-9-3 B Rouse (2) *chsd ldr 9 fs, wknd o'r 2 out.*.................(16 to 1 op 8 to 1 tchd 20 to 1) 6

Dist: Hd, 2l, 3½l, 1l, 8l. 2m 40.55s. a 12.35s (6 Ran).
SR: 23/30/26/24/22/4/ (Lucayan Stud), D R Loder

4142 Blue Seal Conditions Stakes Class B (2-y-o) £10,233 6f. . . . . (3:40)

TABLAH (USA) 8-8 W Carson (7) *mid-div, pushed alng 3 fs out, led ins fnl 2, pushed out*...... (14 to 1 op 10 to 1) 1
TZU'MU 8-8 M Hills (6) *in tch, effrt whn not much room ins fnl 2 fs, rdn and no imprsn inside last.* ....(5 to 1 op 7 to 2) 2
ISLAND OF SILVER (USA) 8-8 M Roberts (4) *str hold, steadied rear, hdwy appr fnl furlong, ran on.* ....(5 to 1 tchd 9 to 2) 3
VERDIGRIS (Ire) 8-8 R Cochrane (9) *prmnt, led 3 fs out till ins fnl 2, kpt on one pace*..........(7 to 2 jt-fav op 9 to 2 tchd 4 to 1) 4
BALAABEL (USA) 8-8 R Hills (1) *chsd ldrs, rdn and kpt on same pace o'r one furlong out*. ....(7 to 2 jt-fav op 3 to 1 tchd 4 to 1) 5
4011² RAKNAH (Ire) 8-8 B Raymond (2) *in tch hfwy, wknd 2 fs out*.................... (4 to 1 op 5 to 1 tchd 11 to 2) 6
ZILZILAH (USA) 8-8 W R Swinburn (3) *outpcd.* ....(12 to 1 tchd 14 to 1) 7
MUTINIQUE 8-8 R Price (5) *led 3 fs, sn wknd.* ....(100 to 1 op 50 to 1) 8

Dist: 2½l, ¾l, ½l, 1½l, 4l, 5l, 15l. 1m 18.22s. a 4.82s (8 Ran).
SR: 22/12/9/7/1/ (Hamdan Al-Maktoum), P T Walwyn

4143 Gordon Carter Handicap Class C (0-95 3-y-o and up) £12,135 2m 45yds (4:10)

4006* SAFETY IN NUMBERS [66] 3-8-0 (4ex) J Quinn (7) *settled mid-div, hdwy 3 fs out, quickened to ld ins fnl 2, sn clr.* ....(7 to 2 fav op 11 to 4 tchd 4 to 1) 1
2655³ RITTO [76] 3-8-10 D Holland (12) *slwly into strd, hld up beh, hdwy 4 fs out, led o'r 2 out till ins fnl two, styd on one pace*....................... (12 to 1 tchd 14 to 1) 2
3392* TILTY (USA) [70] 3-8-4 K Darley (8) *beh, hdwy o'r 2 fs out, kpt on wl fnl furlong*...........(14 to 1 tchd 16 to 1) 3
3724⁹ BOLD RESOLUTION (Ire) [72] 5-9-4 Pat Eddery (13) *beh, hdwy to track ldrs 7 fs out, rdn and no imprsn 2 out.* ....(7 to 1 op 6 to 1 tchd 15 to 2) 4
3881³ DOYCE [65] 4-8-11 W Carson (10) *chsd ldrs, rdn alng 3 fs out, one pace*.................... (10 to 1 op 12 to 1) 5
3848⁶ STAR PLAYER [78] 7-9-10 J Williams (4) *beh, ran on o'r 2 fs out, nrst finish*................(20 to 1 tchd 25 to 1) 6
3907⁹ IOTA [69] 4-9-1 M Roberts (14) *beh, nvr rch ldrs.* ....(16 to 1 op 14 to 1 tchd 20 to 1) 7
3706* LOBILIO (USA) [68] (v) 4-8-11 (3*) B Doyle (15) *beh, nvr better than mid-div.* (20 to 1 op 14 to 1 tchd 25 to 1) 8
3907* MOIDART [81] 3-9-1 A Munro (5) *chsd ldrs, rdn 4 fs out, wknd 3 out*............(4 to 1 tchd 7 to 2 and 9 to 2) 9
3255³ CHAKALAK [72] 5-9-4 T Quinn (11) *chsd ldrs ten fs.* ....(20 to 1 tchd 25 to 1) 10
3848⁸ HIERARCH (USA) [69] (v) 4-9-1 W R Swinburn (6) *pressed ldrs, led 4 fs out till o'r 2 out, sn wknd.* ....(20 to 1 op 16 to 1 tchd 22 to 1) 11
3434 DURSHAN (USA) [74] 4-9-6 J Reid (1) *chsd ldrs till wknd quickly 4 fs out*.... (25 to 1 op 20 to 1 tchd 33 to 1) 12
3848⁷ WESTERN DYNASTY [72] 7-8-11 (7*) P McCabe (2) *hdwy to chase ldrs aftr 4 fs, chlgd 6 out, wknd 3 out.* ....(20 to 1 op 16 to 1 tchd 25 to 1) 13
3907³ ENCORE UNE FOIS (Ire) [78] 4-9-10 L Dettori (9) *led to 4 fs out, pressed ldrs till wknd quickly o'r 2 out.* ....(11 to 1 op 16 to 1 tchd 20 to 1) 14
3943 ASSEMBLY DANCER [58] 6-8-4 N Adams (3) *nvr better than mid-div*..............................(100 to 1) 15

Dist: 4l, 2½l, 1l, 4l, ¾l, sht-hd, 2l, 3l, 6l, ½l. 3m 36.85s. a 11.85s (15 Ran).
SR: 41/47/38/51/40/51/41/38/36/ (Edwin N Cohen), Lady Herries

4144 Golden Gates Nursery Handicap Class C (2-y-o) £9,162 6f. . . . . (4:40)

3978³ ALZIANAH [79] 8-13 L Dettori (10) *al prmnt, quickened to ld ins last, ran on wl*... (13 to 2 op 8 to 1 tchd 6 to 1) 1
3810* STORM SHIP (Ire) [81] 9-1 B Raymond (8) *led till ins last, styd on, not pace of wnr.* ....(14 to 1 op 10 to 1 tchd 16 to 1) 2
3762* AMIDST [79] 8-13 Paul Eddery (5) *hdwy hfwy, rdn and outpcd frm one and a half fs out.* ....(7 to 1 op 11 to 2 tchd 8 to 1) 3
3762⁴ CHICKAWICKA (Ire) [80] 9-0 R Cochrane (7) *chsd ldrs, styd on same pace fnl 2 fs*.............. (10 to 1 op 8 to 1) 4
3966* AMORET (Ire) [75] 8-9 (7ex) J Weaver (9) *rdn and outpcd 3 fs out, no imprsn frm 2 out.* ....(5 to 2 fav op 2 to 1 tchd 11 to 4) 5
3386³ DANCING LAWYER [74] 8-5 (3*) B Doyle (3) *outpcd stands side, some prog fnl furlong.* ....(25 to 1 op 16 to 1 tchd 33 to 1) 6
4061* ROYALE FIGURINE (Ire) [77] 8-11 (7ex) W R Swinburn (2) *stands side, pressed ldrs 3 fs out till wknd ins fnl 2.* ....(11 to 2 op 9 to 2 tchd 6 to 1) 7
3835* ASKING FOR ACES [68] 8-2 W Carson (4) *led stands side grp 3 fs*................(11 to 1 op 10 to 1 tchd 12 to 1) 8
3816⁵ NOBLE SPIRIT (Ire) [73] 8-7 A McGlone (1) *prmnt stands side for o'r 3 fs*.......... (8 to 1 op 7 to 1 tchd 9 to 1) 9
4061³ HELLO MISTER [75] 8-2 (7*,7ex) P McCabe (6) *outpcd.* ....(12 to 1 op 10 to 1 tchd 14 to 1) 10

Dist: 1½l, 6l, hd, 3l, 3½l, 2½l, sht-hd, nk. 1m 17.02s. a 3.62s (10 Ran).
SR: 51/47/21/21/4/-/ (Sheikh Amin Dahlawi), G A Pritchard-Gordon

4145 Bishopsgate Fillies' Apprentice Stakes Class E (3-y-o and up) £4,230 7f . . . . (5:10)

3817* MEADOW PIPIT (Can) 4-8-10 (3*) P McCabe (4) *led 3 and a half fs out, drvn and hld on gmely fnl furlong.* ....(9 to 4 tchd 5 to 2 and 2 to 1) 1
3660³ WINGED VICTORY (Ire) 3-8-6 (5*) D Griffiths (3) *4th till hdwy 2 fs out, jnd wnr fnl furlong and str chal till no extr last strds*.............................. (5 to 2) 2
4040⁷ ARABELLAJILL 4-8-9 (3*) Mark Denaro (2) *trkd ldrs, rdn ins fnl 2 fs, one pace final furlong.* ....(2 to 1 fav op 7 to 4 tchd 9 to 4) 3
3906* BALLASECRET 5-9-6 D Meredith (1) *led to 3 and a half fs out, wknd 2 out*....... (5 to 1 op 4 to 1 tchd 11 to 2) 4

Dist: Hd, 3½l, 6l. 1m 31.65s. a 5.35s (4 Ran).
SR: 40/37/27/17/ (Sheikh Mohammed), J H M Gosden

LISTOWEL (IRE) (good to yielding) Thursday September 23rd

4146 Pitman-Moore I.S.C.O.M Vaccine E.B.F (C&G) Maiden (2-y-o) £5,865 1m . . . . (2:00)

3731⁴ ARTEMA (Ire) 9-0 M J Kinane (2)..............(13 to 8 fav) 1
3492⁵ ALFRED THE BOLD (Ire) 9-0 P V Gilson (9)....... (14 to 1) 2
3416² ARKUB 9-0 W J Supple (8)...................... (3 to 1) 3
3608⁶ MONEYBROKER (Ire) 9-0 K J Manning (5)........(33 to 1) 4
3922 NIYAZI (Ire) 9-0 J P Murtagh (12)............. (14 to 1) 5
3825³ NUN'S ISLAND (Ire) 9-0 B Coogan (17)............(6 to 1) 6
ARCTIC PARK (Ire) 9-0 C Roche (6)...............(5 to 2) 7
GUIDED TOUR (Ire) 9-0 J F Egan (3)..............(20 to 1) 8
SEA FISHER (Ire) 8-6 (8*) B Fenton (4)..........(50 to 1) 9
3541⁷ THREE LEAVES (Ire) 9-0 N G McCullagh (1).......(20 to 1) 10
3562⁸ DUGORT STRAND (Ire) 8-8 (6*) B Bowens (14).... (50 to 1) 11
2701 MAIN REFRAIN (Ire) 8-10 (4*) J A Heffernan (15)... (33 to 1) 12
1104⁸ BOY IN BLACK (Ire) 8-8 (6*) R V Skelly (13).......(33 to 1) 13
3825 ALEXANDER KAHYASI 9-0 N Byrne (7)..............(25 to 1) 14
2701 ZARA ZAREEN (Ire) 9-0 P Shanahan (10).......... (50 to 1) 15
GOVERNMENT GRANT (Ire) 9-0 S Craine (16).....(20 to 1) 16
3825 RUSTIC LEAGUE (Ire) 8-12 (2*) P Carberry (11)....(50 to 1) 17

Dist: 3l, 3½l, 1½l, sht-hd. 1m 45.50s. (17 Ran).
(Saleh Y Al-Homaisi), D K Weld

4147 Helena Sheahan Memorial Handicap (0-85 3-y-o and up) £3,795 1½m (4:50)

3914⁵ FERRYCARRIG HOTEL (Ire) [-] 4-8-0 (8*) P J Smullen (12) ....(14 to 1) 1
3038² SOVIET CHOICE (Ire) [-] 3-9-4 M J Kinane (13).. (Evens fav) 2
3494⁵ SOLAS ABU (Ire) [-] 3-9-1 K J Manning (4)........(12 to 1) 3
3805⁴ NO DUNCE (Ire) [-] 3-8-1 (6*) R V Skelly (14)....... (12 to 1) 4
3924* OENOTHERA (Ire) [-] 3-9-7 (4ex) S Craine (7).......(7 to 1) 5
3525³ MORNING SARGE [-] 5-8-5 (4*) J J Behan (10).... (12 to 1) 6
3805 SUPER FLAME (Can) [-] 6-9-9 P V Gilson (8)...... (14 to 1) 7
3805 IMAD (USA) [-] 3-9-4 W J Supple (1)............. (14 to 1) 8
3914⁴ KAR OR [-] 3-8-9 (6*) B J Walsh (2)............. (14 to 1) 9
3773² SHARASTAMINA (USA) [-] 4-8-12 N G McCullagh (15) ....(12 to 1) 10
3063² SAFE CONDUCT (Ire) [-] 3-9-2 J P Murtagh (3).... (14 to 1) 11
3914⁸ SECOND REVOLUTION (Ire) [-] 4-9-2 C Roche (6) (16 to 1) 12
4057³ BASIE NOBLE [-] 4-8-13 R Hughes (16).......... (14 to 1) 13
MRS KEPPEL [-] 5-8-4 J F Egan (11).............(33 to 1) 14
2041 MAYFIELD PRINCE (Ire) [-] 4-9-2 (6*) B Bowens (17) (14 to 1) 15
1046⁷ DOYROY (Ire) [-] 3-8-1 (2*) D G O'Shea (9)........ (25 to 1) 16
3805* GLENBRACK [-] 3-9-6 (6*,6ex) J R Barry (5)........(5 to 1) 17

Dist: 8l, ½l, 4½l, 1½l. 3m 4.50s. (17 Ran).
(J C Lacy), T F Lacy

ASCOT (good to soft) Friday September 24th

Going Correction: PLUS 0.35 sec. per fur. (race 1), PLUS 0.05 (2,4,6,7), PLUS 0.50 (3,5)

4148 Shadwell Estates Handicap Private Stakes (3-y-o and up) £0 1¼m. . .(1:30)

3139⁴ RAHIL (Ire) [76] 3-11-10 Bill Smith (5) *made all, kpt on wl fnl 2 fs*.............(100 to 30 op 5 to 2 tchd 7 to 2) 1
3831 QAMOOS (Ire) [64] (bl) 3-10-12 Wally Swinburn, *beh, pushed alng frm 5 fs out, ran on to chase wnr ins last, no imprsn*.................(8 to 1 op 6 to 1 tchd 10 to 1) 2
3790 SAFIR (USA) [73] 3-11-7 Greville Starkey (6) *hdwy on rls 3 fs out, chsd wnr 2 out till one pace ins last.* ....(5 to 2 fav op 11 to 4 tchd 7 to 2) 3
3832⁴ ADMIRAL'S WELL (Ire) [70] 3-11-4 Robin Gray (1) *hdwy to chase ldrs 6 fs out, styd on same pace frm 2 out.* ....(7 to 1 op 5 to 1 tchd 8 to 1) 4

4043[5] MUTAMANNI [69] 3-11-3 Brough Scott (4) *in tch, hdwy to track ldrs 4 fs out, rdn and wknd ins fnl 2.* ....(6 to 1 op 5 to 1 tchd 7 to 1) 5
4024[6] RAKIS (Ire) [80] (bl) 3-12-0 Peter Scudamore (3) *chsd wnr to 2 fs out, sn wknd*.........................(7 to 2 tchd 4 to 1) 6
Dist: 1½l, 3l, ½l, 3½l, 3½l. 2m 15.79s. a 12.09s (6 Ran).
SR: 52/37/40/36/28/32/ (Hamdan Al-Maktoum), H Thomson Jones

4149 Forces Help Society Conditions Stakes Class B (2-y-o) £10,464 7f (2:00)

3779[2] MUTAKDDIM (USA) 8-11 W Carson (6) *in tch, quickened to ld jst ins fnl 2 fs, cmftbly.* ....(7 to 4 on tchd 13 to 8 on and 15 to 8 on) 1
RUN SOFTLY (USA) 8-11 Pat Eddery (5) *beh, hdwy o'r 2 fs out, quickened to chase wnr one out, eased whn hld cl hme*....................................(4 to 1 op 3 to 1) 2
MAPENGO 8-11 M Hills (2) *mid-div, pushed alng hfwy, drvn and ran on fnl furlong*.......(25 to 1 op 12 to 1) 3
TRANSOM (USA) 8-11 M Perrett (7) *beh, shaken up 3 fs out, rdn and ran on fnl furlong.* ....(10 to 1 op 6 to 1 tchd 12 to 1) 4
3704[7] SUNDAY NEWS'N'ECHO (USA) 8-6 R Cochrane (3) *led till jst ins fnl 2 fs, sn outpcd.* ....(20 to 1 op 10 to 1 tchd 25 to 1) 5
3833[5] AUGUSTAN 8-11 M Roberts (1) *prmnt, rdn o'r 2 fs out, sn wknd*................(11 to 1 op 6 to 1 tchd 12 to 1) 6
3990[9] ENCORE SENOR (USA) 8-11 B Raymond (4) *chsd ldrs, wknd appr fnl 2 fs*............... (25 to 1 op 10 to 1) 7
STATELY HOME (Ire) 8-11 J Williams (8) *wnt rght strt, al beh, lost tch hfwy.* (66 to 1 op 33 to 1 tchd 100 to 1) 8
Dist: 2½l, 3l, ½l, 1½l, 3l, 8l, 25l. 1m 31.61s. a 5.31s (8 Ran).
SR: 23/15/6/4/-/ (Hamdan Al-Maktoum), J H M Gosden

4150 Lord Roberts Workshop Rated Class B Handicap (0-100 3-y-o) £7,689 1¼m ....(2:30)

4018* TAP ON AIR [85] 8-7 (3ex) M Roberts (5) *mid-div, rdn alng 3 fs out, quickened to ld one furlong out, ran on wl.* ....(5 to 1 op 4 to 1 tchd 11 to 2) 1
3838[2] AL SENAFI (Ire) [88] 8-10 R Cochrane (2) *beh, hdwy o'r 2 fs out, ran on fnl furlong, not pace of wnr.* ....(10 to 1 op 8 to 1 tchd 12 to 1) 2
4063[3] GONE FOR A BURTON (Ire) [90] 8-12 Pat Eddery (8) *beh, pushed alng 3 fs out, hdwy o'r one out, no imprsn fnl furlong*.......... (5 to 2 fav tchd 11 to 4 and 9 to 4) 3
3401 TOMOS [99] 9-7 M Hills (3) *led to one furlong out, sn outpcd*..................................(25 to 1 op 20 to 1) 4
3749[2] DARECLIFF (USA) [93] 9-1 J Reid (4) *beh, shaken up and styd on appr fnl furlong, nrst finish.* .... (9 to 1 op 8 to 1 tchd 10 to 1) 5
3757[2] BLUE BLAZER [85] 8-7 W Carson (1) *beh, lost tch hfwy, pushed alng and ran on appr fnl furlong.* ....(7 to 1 tchd 8 to 1) 6
3963[2] SEEK THE PEARL [85] 8-7 B Raymond (7) *chsd ldr 7 fs, wknd ins fnl 2*.........(11 to 2 op 5 to 1 tchd 6 to 1) 7
3636[3] BLACK DRAGON (Ire) [86] 8-8 D Holland (6) *prmnt, chsd ldr 3 fs out till wknd appr last, eased whn btn.* .... (13 to 2 op 11 to 2 tchd 7 to 1) 8
Dist: 1½l, ¾l, 2½l, nk, 1½l, ½l, 1½l. 2m 11.83s. a 8.13s (8 Ran).
SR: 62/62/62/66/59/48/47/45/ (Sheikh Mohammed), M R Stoute

4151 Army Benevolent Fund Rated Class B Handicap (0-105 3-y-o and up) £13,372 5f............................ (3:05)

3849[3] CALL ME I'M BLUE (Ire) [93] 3-8-8 L Piggott (6) *trkd ldrs, led ins fnl 2 fs, clr final furlong, readily.* .... (5 to 1 op 9 to 2 tchd 11 to 2) 1
3849[4] MISTERTOPOGIGO (Ire) [90] 3-8-5 W Carson (9) *chsd ldrs, kpt on to chase wnr fnl furlong, no imprsn.* .... (9 to 1 op 7 to 1 tchd 10 to 1) 2
3849 BOLD LEZ [94] 6-8-11 R Cochrane (8) *mid-div and pushed alng, hdwy o'r one furlong out, ran on ins last.* ....(8 to 1 tchd 10 to 1) 3
4025[2] GORINSKY (Ire) [96] 5-8-13 Pat Eddery (5) *led till ins fnl 2 fs, sn outpcd*....................(3 to 1 fav tchd 4 to 1) 4
4025[4] PETERSFORD GIRL (Ire) [91] 3-8-6[1] J Reid (4) *beh, sn lost tch, rapid hdwy one furlong out, fnshd wl.* ....(14 to 1 tchd 20 to 1) 5
3438[7] LOCH PATRICK [90] 3-8-5 A McGlone (7) *steadied strt, beh, hdwy o'r one furlong out, sn one pace.* ....(9 to 1 op 8 to 1) 6
4025[7] SPANIARDS CLOSE [104] 5-9-7 B Raymond (3) *outpcd, nvr rch ldrs*...........(12 to 1 op 10 to 1 tchd 14 to 1) 7
3594[6] STAR FAMILY FRIEND (Ire) [92] 3-8-7 P Robinson (1) *mid-div, sn rdn alng, outpcd hfwy*....... (8 to 1 op 7 to 1) 8
3906[2] BORN TO BE [90] 4-8-7 M Roberts (11) *pressed ldrs to hfwy*................(16 to 1 op 14 to 1 tchd 20 to 1) 9
4112[4] ROCK SYMPHONY [90] (bl) 3-8-0 (5*) J Tate (2) *pressed ldrs to hfwy*......................... (12 to 1 tchd 10 to 1) 10
3668[7] ASHTINA [90] 8-8-7 J Quinn (10) *pressed ldrs till wknd quickly 2 fs out*........ (11 to 1 op 10 to 1 tchd 12 to 1) 11
Dist: 3½l, 2l, ¾l, nk, 1½l, 2l, nk, ½l, 4l, nk. 1m 2.01s. a 1.71s (11 Ran).
SR: 65/48/46/45/37/30/38/23/21/ (Harsh (Tipping Gears)), N Tinkler

4152 Ewar Stud Farms For Apprentices Handicap Class E (0-80 3-y-o and up) £4,854 1½m.................. (3:35)

3307[3] HILLZAH (USA) [56] 5-9-0 H Bastiman (5) *mid-div, hdwy o'r 2 fs out, ran on wl to ld appr last, drvn out.* ....(10 to 1 tchd 12 to 1) 1
3970[4] CANNY CHRONICLE [65] 5-9-9 S Mulvey (9) *hld up rear, plenty to do o'r 2 fs out, rapid hdwy appr last, fnshd wl, too much to do*............ (3 to 1 fav tchd 7 to 2) 2
3961[8] KISMETIM [60] 3-8-5 (5*) D O'Neill (8) *in tch till outpcd 5 fs out, ran on frm 2 out, no imprsn ins last.* ....(10 to 1 tchd 12 to 1) 3
3681[3] JONSALAN [66] 3-9-2 C Hawksley (4) *hdwy 5 fs out, pressed ldrs 3 out, one pace appr last.* .... (9 to 1 op 8 to 1 tchd 10 to 1) 4
3548* DR ZEVA [37] 7-7-4 (5*) Wendy Jones (3) *beh, hdwy 5 fs out, wknd 2 out*.....................(14 to 1 tchd 16 to 1) 5
1372[3] SON OF SHARP SHOT (Ire) [74] 3-9-10 T G McLaughlin (11) *pld hrd, led o'r 4 fs out till hdd and wknd appr last.* .... (10 to 1 op 8 to 1) 6
3961* WITHOUT A FLAG (USA) [58] 3-8-8 (4ex) J D Smith (2) *beh, some prog 3 fs out, not rch ldrs*...... (9 to 2 op 4 to 1) 7
3689[2] KIAWAH [55] 3-8-5 N Varley (12) *sn in tch, chsd ldrs 3 fs out, wknd ins fnl 2*....................(10 to 1 op 8 to 1) 8
2685[7] LAMU LADY (Ire) [70] 3-8-13 (7*) Kate Dovey (6) *chsd ldrs, wknd appr last 2 fs*........................(33 to 1 op 16 to 1) 9
3873[2] EL VOLADOR [64] 6-9-8 B Russell (1) *beh, effrt on outsd 4 fs out, sn wknd*......... (7 to 1 op 5 to 1 tchd 8 to 1) 10
3984[3] MON PETITNAMOUR (Ire) [37] 4-7-5[1] (5*) A Whelan (7) *hdwy 5 fs out, pressed ldrs 3 out, sn wknd.* .... (14 to 1 op 10 to 1 tchd 16 to 1) 11
IVORS GUEST [48] (v) 7-8-1 (5*) D Griffiths (10) *led till o'r 4 fs out, wknd ins fnl 3*.................................. (33 to 1) 12
Dist: ¾l, ¾l, 1½l, 3l, 1½l, ¾l, nk, 3l, sht-hd, 5l. 2m 40.29s. a 12.09s (12 Ran).
SR: 39/46/31/34/7/33/15/11/20/ (Mrs P Churm), R Bastiman

4153 Rosemary Rated Class A Handicap (Listed Race) (0-105 3-y-o) £12,838 1m ....(4:05)

3674[6] ANDROMAQUE (USA) [97] 9-4 S Raymont (6) *hld up rear, hdwy frm 2 fs out, led ins last, cmftbly.* .... (7 to 1 tchd 8 to 1 and 6 to 1) 1
3882[4] JETBEEAH (Ire) [90] 8-11 W R Swinburn (8) *beh, hrd rdn 3 fs out, kpt on und pres fnl furlong.* ....(8 to 1 op 6 to 1 tchd 9 to 1) 2
3680* CAMBARA [90] 8-11 M Roberts (9) *prmnt, led 2 fs out till ins last, not quicken.* ....(15 to 8 fav op 2 to 1 tchd 5 to 2 and 7 to 4) 3
3882[2] KATIBA (USA) [93] 9-0 W Carson (2) *beh, pushed alng hfwy, ran on appr fnl furlong, styd on.* ....(8 to 1 op 7 to 1 tchd 9 to 1) 4
3736[4] LACERTA (Ire) [89] 8-10 J Reid (3) *al frnt rnk, rdn appr fnl furlong, styd on same pace*......... (12 to 1 op 8 to 1) 5
3680[8] NORTHERN BIRD [86] 8-7 D Holland (10) *in tch, rdn 2 fs out, no imprsn fnl furlong*..........(12 to 1 op 8 to 1) 6
3620[4] TOCHAR BAN (USA) [88] 8-9 T Quinn (4) *chsd ldrs till wknd 2 fs out*..........................(12 to 1 tchd 14 to 1) 7
3844[6] REINE DE NEIGE [95] 9-2 B Raymond (11) *made most to 2 fs out, sn wknd*..........................(12 to 1 op 8 to 1) 8
3864[2] MOON OVER MIAMI [100] 9-7 L Piggott (5) *sn mid-div, shaken up appr 2 fs out, wknd approaching last.* .... (12 to 1 op 10 to 1 tchd 14 to 1) 9
3864[4] STELLA MYSTIKA (USA) [95] 9-2 R Cochrane (7) *slwly into strd, beh, effrt o'r 2 fs out, sn wknd.* .... (12 to 1 op 8 to 1 tchd 14 to 1) 10
3864[7] TAHDID [90] 8-11 M Hills (12) *prmnt till wknd ins fnl 2 fs.* .... (16 to 1 op 14 to 1 tchd 20 to 1) 11
856[4] WOODWARDIA (USA) [94] 9-1 Pat Eddery (1) *dsptd ld early, wknd 3 fs out*...............(16 to 1 op 12 to 1) 12
Dist: 2½l, sht-hd, hd, nk, 3½l, 2½l, nk, 1½l, 5l, 4l. 1m 43.97s. a 4.97s (12 Ran).
SR: 35/20/19/21/16/2/-/2/2/ (Dr Carlos E Stelling), R Charlton

4154 Kensington Palace Conditions Stakes Class B (2-y-o) £9,855 5f........(4:40)

3898[3] SELHURSTPARK FLYER (Ire) 9-3 W Carson (1) *led 2 fs, styd prmnt, led one and a half out, pushed out.* ....(11 to 4 op 3 to 1 tchd 100 to 30) 1
3972* MULTI NATIONAL 8-13 K Fallon (4) *outpcd, shaken up o'r 2 fs out, ran on appr last, not pace of wnr.* .... (5 to 2 op 9 to 4 tchd 11 to 4) 2
3860[5] LUANA 8-6 M Roberts (5) *chsd ldrs till outpcd and rdn hfwy, kpt on fnl furlong*.......... (20 to 1 op 12 to 1) 3
3166 ALL THE JOYS 8-6 J Williams (2) *outpcd, moderate prog fnl furlong*.......................(100 to 1 op 50 to 1) 4
3515[6] SOLAR WAGON (USA) 8-13 Pat Eddery (7) *led aftr 2 fs to one and a half out, wknd rpdly.* .....(13 to 8 fav op 5 to 4 tchd 11 to 10 and 7 to 4) 5
3737[3] CRYSTAL MAGIC 8-10 J Reid (6) *chsd ldrs till wknd quickly ins fnl 2 fs*.......(8 to 1 op 6 to 1 tchd 9 to 1) 6
3982[5] THORNY BISHOP (v) 8-11 S O'Gorman (3) *outpcd.* .... (100 to 1 op 50 to 1) 7
Dist: 2l, 5l, 3l, hd, 2½l, 7l. 1m 2.57s. a 2.27s (7 Ran).

SR: 63/51/24/12/18/5/-/ (Chris Deuters), J Berry

HAYDOCK (good to soft)
Friday September 24th

Going Correction: PLUS 0.45 sec. per fur. (races 1,3,4,6), PLUS 0.25 (2,5)

4155 Stanley Sportsline Maiden Stakes Class D (3-y-o) £3,844 1¼m 120yds ....(2:15)

3909[3] WAJIH (USA) 9-0 W Ryan (9) *nvr far away, squeezed through to chal o'r one furlong out, edgd lft, led ins last, pushed out.* ...(11 to 10 on op 11 to 8 tchd 6 to 4 and 6 to 5 on) 1
DILI (USA) 8-9 L Dettori (12) *patiently rdn, improved to ld o'r one furlong out, hdd ins last, one pace towards finish*...............................(7 to 1 op 7 to 2) 2
3780[7] SOBA UP 8-9 A Culhane (5) *pressed ldg grp, drpd rear aftr 2 fs, rdn o'r 3 out, kpt on fnl furlong, no ch wth 1st two.* ....(25 to 1 op 20 to 1) 3
3832[7] EVER SO LYRICAL 9-0 G Hind (3) *keen hold, trkd ldrs, not much room and rdn alng o'r 2 fs out, sn outpcd.* ....(20 to 1 tchd 25 to 1) 4
1027 BEVERLY KNIGHT 9-0 D Biggs (8) *led til hdd wl o'r 2 fs out, sn drvn alng, wknd over one out.* ....(16 to 1 op 10 to 1) 5
3639[3] CHUMMY'S SAGA 8-11 (3*) S Maloney (4) *pressed ldr, led wl o'r 2 fs out, sn pushed alng, hdd over one out, fdd.* ....(5 to 1 op 7 to 2) 6
SHILLELAGH BAY (Ire) 9-0 N Adams (10) *hld up, rdn entering strt, nvr able to chal*........(25 to 1 tchd 33 to 1) 7
GLOWING JADE 8-2 (7*) R Painter (2) *steadied strt, drvn alng wl o'r 2 fs out, sn btn*.........(10 to 1 op 7 to 1) 8
3439[6] SABERAGE 8-9 S Perks (6) *nvr far away, effrt and drvn alng 3 fs out, grad wknd*.......... (25 to 1 op 16 to 1) 9
REGAL JEST 8-3[1] (7*) G Parkin (11) *missed break, beh, rdn entering strt, sn btn, tld off*...................(50 to 1) 10
VINTAGE RED 9-0 W Newnes (7) *settled on outer, pushed alng 4 fs out, sn wknd, tld off*..... (33 to 1 op 25 to 1) 11
COUSIN WENDY 8-4 (5*) A Garth (1) *missed break, sn tld off and virtually pld up aftr one furlong*......(50 to 1) 12
Dist: Nk, 10l, 2l, ½l, 2l, 7l, ½l, 2l, 15l, 7l. 2m 20.27s. a 9.27s (12 Ran).
SR: 55/49/29/30/29/25/11/5/1/ (Hamdan Al-Maktoum), Major W R Hern

4156 Stanley Credit Claiming Handicap Class E (0-70 3-y-o and up) £3,485 6f ....(2:45)

4109[4] LEIGH CROFTER [47] (bl) 4-8-10 W Newnes (23) *made all stand side, rdn and jnd ins fnl furlong, ran on gmely towards finish*...................(13 to 2 op 5 to 1) 1
3758[5] COCONUT JOHNNY [49] 3-8-2 (7*) R Painter (18) *settled on ins stand side, weaved through o'r one furlong out, hng lft, chlgd inside last, no extr cl hme.* ....(12 to 1 tchd 14 to 1) 2
3946 OUR SHADEE (USA) [54] (v) 3-9-0 M Wigham (22) *pressed ldrs stand side, drvn alng last 2 fs, kpt on towards finish*...................................(14 to 1) 3
3168 WESTERN VALLEY [55] 3-9-1 W Ryan (16) *chsd ldrs stand side, effrt and rdn 2 fs out, kpt on same pace ins last.* .... (12 to 1 op 10 to 1 tchd 14 to 1) 4
3946[6] BIRCHWOOD SUN [59] (bl) 3-9-5 L Dettori (20) *beh and sn pushed alng stand side, swtchd hfwy, kpt on fnl furlong, no imprsn*..........................(12 to 1 op 10 to 1) 5
3354[7] SARTIGILA [61] 4-9-5 (5*) J Marshall (6) *in tch far side, ev ch that grp o'r one furlong out, one pace.* .... (12 to 1 op 14 to 1 tchd 16 to 1) 6
2851[4] SUDDEN SPIN [62] (v) 3-9-1 (7*) P Roberts (10) *dsptd ld far side, drvn alng o'r 2 fs out, not quicken over one out.* ....(14 to 1) 7
4038 GENTLE HERO (USA) [54] 7-9-3 J Fortune (14) *pressed ldg grp stand side, effrt and improved 2 fs out, no extr appr last*...................................(16 to 1) 8
4008[2] LITTLE OSBORNE (Ire) [44] (bl) 3-8-1 (3*) M Fenton (13) *frnt rnk stand side, rdn 2 fs out, grad wknd.* ....(6 to 1 fav op 7 to 1) 9
4012[4] VERRO (USA) [31] (bl) 6-7-8[1] N Carlisle (4) *sn beh far side, improved o'r 2 fs out, kpt on ins last.* ....(25 to 1 op 20 to 1) 10
4012[7] A LITTLE PRECIOUS [47] 7-8-10 S Whitworth (2) *settled beh ldrs stand side, pushed alng 2 fs out, no imprsn.* ....(33 to 1 op 25 to 1) 11
3946* FORTIS PAVIOR (Ire) [64] 3-9-10 (5ex) A Culhane (19) *hld up stand side, effrt and rdn o'r 2 fs out, eased whn btn ins last*............................ (8 to 1 tchd 9 to 1) 12
4123 COLMAR [35] (bl) 3-7-9[1] A Tucker (15) *chsd alng in mid-div stand side, one pace fnl 2 fs*.....................(25 to 1) 13
3292 DONTDRESSFORDINNER [48] 3-8-8 R Perham (5) *chsd ldrs far side, drvn alng o'r 2 fs out, sn btn.* ....(33 to 1 op 25 to 1) 14
3863[9] BALLAD DANCER [65] 8-10-0 G Hind (12) *settled on outer stand side, drvn alng o'r 2 fs out, sn btn.* ....(16 to 1 op 14 to 1) 15
3758 SUMMER EXPRESS [48] 4-8-4 (7*) L Suthern (7) *prmnt far side, drvn alng hfwy, fdd*........ (25 to 1 op 20 to 1) 16
3896* COURTING NEWMARKET [49] 5-8-5 (7*) Marie Plowright (1) *dsptd ld far side til shaken up and wknd wl o'r one furlong out*.........(11 to 1 op 10 to 1 tchd 12 to 1) 17
3758 COAT OF DREAMS [31] 4-7-8[1] A Mackay (21) *trkd ldrs stand side, rdn hfwy, grad wknd*............ (25 to 1) 18
2602[2] NICKNAME [46] 3-8-6 D Biggs (17) *speed 4 fs, rdn and grad wknd*...........(9 to 1 op 7 to 1 tchd 10 to 1) 19
4090[6] ISLAND KNIGHT (Ire) [62] 4-9-6 (5*) A Procter (9) *pressed ldrs far side, rdn alng o'r 2 fs out, nvr a factor.* ....(14 to 1 op 10 to 1) 20
2481[7] SUPREME DESIRE [40] 5-8-3 M Wood (11) *chsd ldrs stand side til rdn and wknd 2 fs out*................(25 to 1) 21
3409 JOTRA [39] 3-7-13 N Adams (3) *prmnt far side til wknd o'r 2 fs out*........................(25 to 1 tchd 33 to 1) 22
Dist: Hd, 2l, nk, ¾l, 5l, ½l, hd, nk, 4l, ½l. 1m 15.95s. a 4.35s (22 Ran).
SR: 39/37/34/34/35/20/16/10/-/ (P D Cundell), P D Cundell

4157 Stanley Racing Handicap Class C (0-90 3-y-o and up) £5,485 1m 3f 200yds....................... (3:15)

3466 MUCH SOUGHT AFTER [80] 4-9-10 L Dettori (3) *made all, quickened 3 fs out, ran on gmely ins last.* ....(9 to 2 tchd 5 to 1) 1
3761[5] LAND AFAR [67] 6-8-11 R Lappin (8) *hld up beh, outpcd and drvn o'r 2 fs out, ran on wl fnl furlong.* ....(11 to 2 op 9 to 2) 2
3587[9] MARROS MILL [74] (v) 3-8-7 (3*) M Fenton (5) *trkd ldg 3, ev ch frm three fs out, edgd lft o'r one out, no extr last 75 yards*..........................(7 to 1 op 6 to 1) 3
2961 MIDYAN BLUE (Ire) [71] 3-8-4 (3*) N Kennedy (6) *keen hold, hld up in tch, outpcd and rdn o'r 3 fs out, styd on ins last*..........................(4 to 1 jt-fav) 4
3036[7] SAVOY TRUFFLE (Fr) [80] 3-9-2 W Ryan (2) *nvr far away, pushed alng 3 fs out, not quicken fnl furlong.* .... (11 to 2 op 5 to 1 tchd 6 to 1) 5
LIABILITY ORDER [62] 4-8-6 W Newnes (4) *mid-div, drpd rear hfwy, pushed alng to improve o'r 2 fs out, no extr ins last*...................................(20 to 1) 6
4037[3] LEGION OF HONOUR [59] 5-8-3 J Fortune (7) *nvr far away, chlgd 3 fs out, sn rdn, no extr o'r one out*. ...(4 to 1 jt-fav tchd 9 to 2) 7
ADMIRALS SEAT [57] 5-7-12 (3*) S Maloney (1) *patiently rdn, shaken up 3 fs out, not pace to chal.* .... (12 to 1 op 10 to 1 tchd 14 to 1) 8
BIRD WATCHER [56] 4-7-9 (5*) J Marshall (9) *hld up, lost tch entering strt, tld off*.........................(25 to 1) 9
Dist: ½l, ½l, 1l, ½l, 1½l, 2½l, 1½l, 30l. 2m 42.00s. a 12.20s (9 Ran).
SR: 42/28/26/21/29/16/8/3/-/ (The MSA Partnership), D Morley

4158 Stanley Leisure Organisation Dream Mile Handicap Class D (0-85 3-y-o and up) £6,157 1m 30yds............(3:50)

3900[4] BEAUMAN [64] 3-8-8 A Mackay (4) *mid-div, rdn to improve 3 fs out, edgd rght, ran on to ld ins last, styd on wl.* .... (15 to 2 op 7 to 1 tchd 8 to 1) 1
3487[8] KUMMEL KING [53] 5-7-10 (5*) A Garth (1) *led or dsptd ld thrght, styd alone far side entering strt, ran on wl frm 2 fs out, no extr towards finish*......(16 to 1 op 14 to 1) 2
3681[7] MHEMEANLES [61] (bl) 3-8-2 (3*) S Maloney (2) *wth ldr, led stand side grp entering strt, wndrd and hdd o'r one furlong out, no extr ins last.* .... (14 to 1 op 12 to 1 tchd 16 to 1) 3
3408[3] MAROWINS [46] 4-7-8 N Adams (8) *hld up, improved hfwy, led o'r one furlong out, hdd ins last, one pace.* ....(10 to 1 op 12 to 1) 4
3983[3] HILARY GERRARD (USA) [77] 3-9-7 D Biggs (12) *chsd ldrs, drvn alng o'r 3 fs out, outpcd 2 out.* ....(14 to 1 op 10 to 1) 5
3957[5] JAHANGIR (Ire) [68] 4-9-2 W Ryan (7) *chsd ldrs, effrt and rdn 3 fs out, btn o'r one out*....... (10 to 1 op 8 to 1) 6
3900 DOC COTTRILL [69] 3-8-6 (7*) D Thomas (9) *patiently rdn, shaken up 3 fs out, nvr able to chal.* ....(16 to 1 op 14 to 1) 7
3893* LABUDD (USA) [75] 3-9-5 L Dettori (3) *slwly into strd, sn reco'red into midfield, pushed alng 3 fs out, unbl to quicken*........... (6 to 4 fav op 5 to 4 tchd 13 to 8) 8
2799[6] PRINCESS OF ORANGE [48] 4-7-10 N Carlisle (6) *reared strt stalls, keen hold, sn midfield, effrt and rdn wl o'r 2 fs out, wknd over one out*........ (40 to 1 op 33 to 1) 9
1940[5] COOL LUKE (Ire) [79] 4-9-13 W Newnes (10) *hld up, rdn 3 fs out, sn btn, tld off*.... (8 to 1 op 10 to 1 tchd 12 to 1) 10
3863[7] DEBSY DO (USA) [73] 4-9-4 (3*) O Pears (11) *settled on outsd, drvn alng o'r 3 fs out, wknd, tld off.* ....(9 to 1 op 8 to 1) 11
1153[5] GREAT STEPS [79] 3-9-9 G Hind (5) *beh, pushed alng appr strt, drvn 3 fs out, fdd, tld off*.................(25 to 1) 12
Dist: ½l, 1l, ½l, 12l, sht-hd, sht-hd, hd, 1½l, 8l, 4l. 1m 48.65s. a 8.05s (12 Ran).
SR: 29/20/21/8/-/-/ (Mrs B Facchino), B A McMahon

4159 Stanley Snooker Nursery Class D (2-y-o) £3,629 6f.................. (4:20)

3635^{5} JIMMY THE SKUNK (Ire) [75] 9-2 L Dettori (6) *al prmnt, hng lft frm 2 fs out, led o'r one out, rdn out ins last.* ....(4 to 1 op 7 to 2) 1

4044^{4} MONKEY MAGIC (Ire) [62] 8-3 J Fortune (2) *nvr far away, rdn and ev ch o'r one furlong out, no extr wl ins last.* ....(11 to 1 op 8 to 1 tchd 12 to 1) 2

3845^{8} LEGATEE [80] 9-7 W Ryan (1) *hld up, effrt and swtchd lft o'r 2 fs out, ev ch appr last, no extr last 50 yards.* ....(10 to 1 tchd 11 to 1) 3

3443^{6} LEADING PRINCESS (Ire) [55] 7-7 (3*) N Kennedy (7) *pressed ldrs, not clr run o'r 2 fs out, swtchd and improved over one out, no extr ins last.* ....(14 to 1 op 12 to 1 tchd 16 to 1) 4

4021* NO MEAN CITY (Ire) [75] (bl) 9-2 (7ex) A Mackay (5) *sn led, rdn hfwy, hdd o'r one furlong out, one pace.* ....(4 to 1 tchd 9 to 2) 5

3950^{2} ANTIGUAN SKY [55] 7-10 D Biggs (8) *pressed ldg 3, pushed alng aftr 2 fs, not quicken o'r one out.* ....(3 to 1 fav op 9 to 4) 6

3602^{5} DINOT (Ire) [62] 7-12 (5*) A Garth (9) *beh on ins, rdn hfwy, one pace o'r one furlong out.* ....(12 to 1 tchd 10 to 1 and 14 to 1) 7

4034^{7} HILTONS TRAVEL (Ire) [73] 8-7 (7*) S Knott (3) *chsd ldrs, shaken up hfwy, hng badly lft and sn btn.* ....(20 to 1 op 12 to 1) 8

3600^{3} MERISSA [54] 7-9 N Adams (4) *walked to post, missed break, reco'red aftr 2 fs, rdn and wknd quickly after two out*....................................(7 to 1 op 6 to 1) 9

Dist: 1l, sht-hd, 2l, ½l, 1½l, ¾l, 1½l, 12l. 1m 17.76s. a 6.16s (9 Ran).
SR: 9/-/9/-/-/-/ (J David Abell), J Berry

4160 Stanley Clubs Conditions Stakes Class D (3-y-o and up) £3,454 1¾m ....(4:50)

3319^{2} DOVER PATROL (Ire) 3-8-7 W Ryan (2) *nvr far away, led entering strt, shaken up, ran on gmely fnl 2 fs.* ....(11 to 8 on op 11 to 10 on) 1

4017* VRATISLAV (USA) 4-9-1 L Dettori (1) *hld up beh, steady hdwy to chal o'r 2 fs out, sn rdn, one pace appr last, eased last 100 yards*....................(2 to 1 op 13 to 8) 2

3775^{5} BADIE (USA) 4-9-3 G Hind (3) *pressed ldrs, rdn alng 3 fs out, hng badly lft, sn btn*...............(6 to 1 op 5 to 1) 3

KING UBAD (USA) 4-8-12 (3*) S Maloney (5) *rcd wide, led, hdd entering strt, rdn and sn btn, tld off.* ....(20 to 1 op 16 to 1) 4

HONDEGHEM 7-9-1 W Newnes (4) *trkd ldrs on outsd, outpcd hfwy, tld off fnl 5 fs*....................(50 to 1) 5

Dist: 3l, 8l, 20l, 25l. 3m 12.76s. a 15.26s (5 Ran).
SR: 3/5/ (L B Holliday), H R A Cecil

LISTOWEL (IRE) (good to yielding)
Friday September 24th

4161 Murphy Auctioneers Handicap (0-65 4-y-o and up) £3,795 1¾m..... (4:20)

4119^{2} WOODFIELD ROSE [-] 4-7-8 (2*) D G O'Shea (9) ... (6 to 1) 1
2900^{4} TIME IS UP (Ire) [-] 4-9-2 J P Murtagh,............ (8 to 1) 2
4094^{7} TOUCHDOWN [-] 6-9-9 R Hughes (15)...........(12 to 1) 3
2693 SWIFT PAL [-] 8-7-7 L O'Shea (12)...................(8 to 1) 4
3951^{5} THIS IS MY LIFE (Ire) [-] 4-8-12 (4*) C Everard,..... (8 to 1) 5
3663^{3} STEEL CHIMES (Ire) [-] (bl) 4-9-4 M J Kinane (4).... (6 to 1) 6
3853^{3} PREMIER LEAP (Ire) [-] 4-8-6 (8*) B Fenton (3).....(10 to 1) 7
3976^{3} ALVATUR (Ire) [-] (bl) 4-7-13[1] W J Supple (2)...... (25 to 1) 8
2881^{5} ANGAREB (Ire) [-] 4-9-5 (6*) J R Barry (13)........(10 to 1) 9
4119^{6} PLUMBOB (Ire) [-] 4-7-11[2] (8*) P J Smullen (1)..... (33 to 1) 10
3277 NORDIC RACE [-] 6-9-1 (4*) J A Heffernan (7).....(10 to 1) 11
3397^{3} GREEK CHIME (Ire) [-] 4-9-6 P McWilliams (8).....(12 to 1) 12
3663^{5} LEAVING CERT [-] 6-7-9[1] (4*) W J Smith (11)......(20 to 1) 13
3395 ICANSEEFORMILES (Ire) [-] 5-7-8 (8*) R T Fitzpatrick (16) ....(33 to 1) 14
3853^{4} SPOUT HOUSE (Ire) [-] (bl) 4-9-2 S Craine (5)...(5 to 1 fav) 15
3580^{5} MAGNUM STAR (Ire) [-] 4-9-8 C F Swan (14)......(12 to 1) 16
3366* SIMPLY SWIFT [-] 6-8-11 (8*) G M Moylan (6)....... (8 to 1) ur

Dist: 2½l, 1l, 5l, hd. 3m 14.00s. (17 Ran).
(T F Roe), Augustine Leahy

4162 Harp Lager Maiden (3-y-o and up) £4,140 1¼m.................. (5:30)

3579^{3} MAYASTA (Ire) 3-8-11 P V Gilson (3)...............(6 to 1) 1
3808^{2} TALES OF HEARSAY (Ger) 3-9-0 N G McCullagh (9) ....(2 to 1 fav) 2
2956^{4} MAGIC FEELING (Ire) 3-8-9 (2*) D G O'Shea (10).. (12 to 1) 3
4118^{4} GLENSTAL FLAGSHIP (Ire) 3-8-8 (6*) R V Skelly (13) ....(12 to 1) 4
4001^{2} MAJESTIC PADDY (Ire) 3-9-0 P Shanahan (1)..... (12 to 1) 5
3808 CERTAIN PROSPECT 3-8-11 J P Murtagh (17).... (10 to 1) 6
1963^{5} SCHMEICHEL (Ire) 3-9-0 S Craine (8)............ (14 to 1) 7
2903^{3} SHEER OPULANCE (Ire) 3-9-0 M J Kinane (14)..... (9 to 4) 8
3999^{2} NORDIC QUEEN (Ire) 3-8-7 (4*) J A Heffernan (15) (10 to 1) 9
CATCHMENOT (Ire) 3-8-3 (8*) B Fenton (11)....... (33 to 1) 10
4057^{8} PENNINE'S DAUGHTER 3-8-11 R Hughes (6).....(10 to 1) 11
CHARTY (Ire) 3-9-0 W J Supple (5)................(20 to 1) 12
3951 POUNDWORLD (Ire) 3-8-3 (8*) P J Smullen (4).... (50 to 1) 13
2902 RISKY GALORE 3-8-6 (8*) R T Fitzpatrick (7)......(33 to 1) 14
3951 AT YOUR SERVICE (Ire) 4-9-4 (2*) P Carberry (2).. (66 to 1) 15
309 LA MAJA (Ire) 4-8-7 (10*) A J Dempsey,.......... (66 to 1) 16
BOTANIC VERSES (Ire) 3-8-11 J F Egan,......... (16 to 1) 17

Dist: ¾l, 1½l, 2½l, hd. 2m 15.70s. (17 Ran).
(J H McLoughlin), C Collins

REDCAR (good)
Friday September 24th
Going Correction: MINUS 0.40 sec. per fur.

4163 Scarborough Selling Stakes Class G (2-y-o) £2,070 6f.................(2:20)

3082^{4} MOCKINGBIRD (v) 8-6 D Harrison (5) *nvr far away, quickened to ld o'r one furlong out, ran on wl.* ....(8 to 1 op 12 to 1) 1

4044^{2} LOCHON 8-11 S Webster (6) *led, gng wl hfwy, hdd and rdn o'r one furlong out, ran on same pace.* ....(7 to 1 tchd 6 to 1) 2

3950^{5} ONCE MORE FOR LUCK (Ire) 9-4 K Darley (15) *patiently rdn, hdwy centre o'r 2 fs out, drvn alng one out, ran on wl*..................................(5 to 1 op 9 to 2) 3

3539^{6} PALACEGATE JO (Ire) 8-13 J Carroll (9) *wtd wth, weaved through frm midfield last 2 fs, kpt on same pace.* ....(7 to 2 fav op 9 to 2 tchd 5 to 1) 4

3598^{5} MARBLE 8-1 (5*) Darren Moffatt (3) *shwd up wl on outsd, ev ch o'r 2 fs out, one pace*... (33 to 1 op 25 to 1) 5

3120^{7} MISS KATIE LOUISE 8-1 (5*) D Wright (8) *chsd far side grp, effrt o'r one furlong out, ran on same pace.* ....(33 to 1 op 25 to 1) 6

4081^{5} RED MARCH HARE 8-6 Dale Gibson (7) *pressed ldrs centre, ev ch and drvn alng last 2 fs, kpt on one pace.* (25 to 1) 7

3566^{8} HONG KONG FUTURE (Ire) 8-11 A Munro (23) *drvn alng stands side, speed for o'r 4 fs, no extr*......... (14 to 1) 8

3557^{4} NEVER SO TRUE 8-6 J Weaver (4) *chsd ldrs, effrt far side 2 fs out, not quicken*................(7 to 1 op 6 to 1) 9

3432 BESCABY GIRL 8-6 J Fanning (20) *chsd alng stands side, kpt on, not pace to chal*......... (12 to 1 tchd 14 to 1) 10

3363^{6} HENRY THE HAWK 8-4 (7*) V Halliday (17) *drvn alng in midfield, styd on last 2 fs, nvr nrr*..................(33 to 1) 11

3969^{9} FAIR SWOP (Ire) 8-6 M Birch (13) *speed centre for o'r 4 fs, fdd*................ (12 to 1 op 10 to 1 tchd 14 to 1) 12

DENTON QUEEN 8-6 F Norton (22) *sluggish strt, last hfwy, str run fnl furlong, fnshd wl*.......... (50 to 1) 13

3972 RICH GLOW 8-11 L Charnock (11) *trkd ldrs centre, drvn alng o'r 2 fs out, fdd*........................(100 to 1) 14

3421 MUSIC PRINCESS 8-6 C Rutter (21) *pressed ldrs stands side for o'r 4 fs, sn btn*........................ (50 to 1) 15

3867^{5} UP THE MARINERS (Ire) 8-8 (5*) K Rutter (18) *chsd ldrs, rdn alng o'r 2 fs out, fdd*..............(16 to 1 op 12 to 1) 16

3972 MYSTICAL MICKEY (Ire) 8-8 (3*) S D Williams (12) *sn drvn alng, nvr a factor*..............................(50 to 1) 17

3664^{5} NORTHERN STORM (Ire) 8-4 (7*) P McCabe (1) *chsd alng far side, struggling hfwy*...................... (33 to 1) 18

4044^{5} PRIMUM TEMPUS 8-6 T Lucas (14) *settled off the pace, nvr plcd to chal*.............................. (25 to 1) 19

830^{6} CAPTAIN KEYSTONE 8-11 N Connorton (10) *outpcd and drvn alng, nvr a factor*...........(33 to 1 op 25 to 1) 20

3566^{9} SALTPETRE (Ire) 8-11 G Bardwell (19) *early speed stands side, wknd quickly last 2 fs*.................. (50 to 1) 21

BUOING 8-6 J Lowe (16) *sluggish strt, tld off hfwy.* ....(100 to 1) 22

Dist: 2l, 2½l, 1l, ¾l, ¾l, ¾l, 2l, hd, ½l, 3l. 1m 11.50s. a 1.80s (22 Ran).

SR: 8/5/2/-/-/-/ (Lord Carnarvon), Lord Huntingdon

4164 Mississippi Amateur Riders' Handicap Class E (0-70 3-y-o and up) £4,090 1m...........................(2:50)

3910^{3} PUSEY STREET BOY [50] 6-9-11 (5*) Mrs S Bosley (9) *patiently rdn, steady hdwy hfwy, ran on to ld ins fnl furlong, jst lasted*................(10 to 1 op 9 to 1) 1

TARDA [52] 6-9-13 (5*) Mr L Donnelly (22) *trkd ldrs centre, brst through appr fnl furlong, ran on, jst hld.* ....(33 to 1 op 25 to 1) 2

4092^{8} BILL MOON [50] 7-10-2 Miss J Feilden (26) *wl plcd stands side, o'rall ldr over 2 fs out, hdd fnl furlong, kpt on same pace*........................(12 to 1 op 10 to 1) 3

3134^{9} ROAR ON TOUR [34] 4-8-9 (5*) Miss A Yardley (5) *settled to track ldg bunch, drvn through centre last 2 fs, styd on same pace*..................................(50 to 1) 4

3540^{6} MEDIA MESSENGER [51] 4-9-12 (5*) Miss M Carson (28) *pressed ldrs thrght, ev ch stands side o'r 2 fs out, kpt on one pace*.........................(20 to 1 op 14 to 1) 5

2849^{6} OUR EDDIE [40] (v) 4-9-1 (5*) Mrs M Busby (30) *wl plcd stands side thrght, drvn alng o'r 2 fs out, one pace.* ....(16 to 1 op 14 to 1) 6

3938^{5} HERETICAL MISS [46] (bl) 3-9-3 (5*) Mrs J Boggis (18) *chsd ldrs stands side, improved und pres o'r 2 fs out, kpt on one pace*.....................(25 to 1 op 20 to 1) 7

3831 JALCANTO [62] 3-10-10 Mr M Buckley (7) *trkd ldrs centre, effrt o'r 2 fs out, kpt on one pace.* (14 to 1 op 12 to 1) 8

3628 ARABAT [59] 6-10-6 (5*) Mr R D Green (25) *patiently rdn, improved centre last 2 fs, kpt on, nvr nrr.* .... (33 to 1 op 25 to 1) 9
3184[6] DUKE OF DREAMS [60] 3-10-8 Mrs M Cowdrey (15) *bustled alng to improve centre hfwy, kpt on, not pace to chal.* .... (14 to 1) 10
3257[6] MAINLY ME [55] 4-10-7 Mrs L Pearce (13) *settled stands side, gng wl hfwy, kpt on appr fnl furlong, nvr able to chal.* .... (7 to 1 jt-fav op 8 to 1 tchd 6 to 1) 11
3643[7] KELLY'S KITE [34] 5-8-9 (5*) Mr P Close (14) *trkd centre grp, effrt and drvn alng o'r 2 fs out, not pace of ldrs.* .... (20 to 1 op 16 to 1) 12
3863[5] LA BAMBA [69] 7-11-2 (5*) Mr P Pritchard-Gordon (11) *patiently rdn, improved far side to ld o'r 2 fs out, drvn alng appr fnl furlong, fdd.* .... (8 to 1 tchd 10 to 1) 13
4104 LAZY RHYTHM (USA) [37] 7-9-1[3] (5*) Mrs C Hirst (8) *chsd alng to keep in tch hfwy, styd on, nvr able to chal.* .... (50 to 1) 14
3812 PUBLIC WAY (Ire) [48] 3-9-7[2] (5*) Miss C Metcalfe (17) *sluggish strt, drvn alng hfwy, nvr rch ldrs.* .... (25 to 1 op 20 to 1) 15
3090[4] THUNDERING [39] 8-9-5[3] Miss Diana Jones (20) *chsd alng stands side, struggling o'r 2 fs out, sn btn.* .... (10 to 1 op 8 to 1) 16
3910 TRIBAT [43] 3-9-2[2] (5*) Mrs L Morris (10) *chsd alng to keep up hfwy, nvr rch ldrs.* .... (100 to 1) 17
3323[6] APPEALING TIMES (USA) [52] 4-9-13 (5*) Miss R Clark (16) *pushed alng to go pace hfwy, nvr a serious threat.* .... (50 to 1 op 33 to 1) 18
3788 ANGELS ANSWER (Ire) [48] 4-9-9 (5*) Mr R Barrett (27) *drvn alng and struggling hfwy, sn btn.* .... (100 to 1) 19
3634[3] PERDITION (Ire) [61] 3-10-4 (5*) Mrs S Wray (2) *bustled alng hfwy, nvr a threat.* .... (16 to 1) 20
3631 BREAKING HEARTS (Ire) [42] 3-9-4[9] (5*) Mr D Parker (24) *shwd up wl stands side for o'r 4 fs, fdd.* .... (33 to 1) 21
3991[3] LET'S GET LOST [68] 4-11-1 (5*) Mrs M Haggas (4) *chsd ldrs far side to hfwy, sn btn.* .... (10 to 1 op 8 to 1) 22
3896 JACK GRAY [43] 5-9-4 (5*) Miss C Spearing (21) *outpcd and drvn alng hfwy, sn lost tch.* .... (50 to 1) 23
3002 BRAVE MELODY [34] 7-8-9 (5*) Miss J Bond (6) *drvn alng to go pace hfwy, nvr a factor.* .... (100 to 1) 24
3124[8] BIDWEAYA (USA) [34] 6-9-0 Mrs A Farrell (1) *dictated pace far side till rdn and hdd 3 fs out, sn btn.* .... (33 to 1) 25
4019[3] DANCING BEAU (Ire) [55] 4-10-2 (5*) Mr T Cuff (3) *chsd alng far side, struggling frm hfwy.* .. (7 to 1 jt-fav op 6 to 1) 26
NOBBY [45] 7-9-11[9] Mr R Hale (23) *tld off frm hfwy.* .... (33 to 1 op 25 to 1) 27

Dist: Hd, 1l, 3l, 1½l, sht-hd, 1½l, sht-hd, 1½l, sht-hd, hd. 1m 38.10s. a 3.20s (27 Ran).

SR: 20/21/16/-/3/-/-/3/-/ (M A Wilkins), J R Bosley

4165 Tattersalls Auction Series Nursery Qualifier Class E (2-y-o) £3,416 6f .... (3:20)

3448[6] ROXANIAN (Ire) [88] 9-8 A Munro (1) *made all, tacked o'r to centre last 2 fs, kpt on strly fnl furlong.* .... (8 to 1 op 9 to 1 tchd 10 to 1) 1
3845[7] PRIMA SILK [81] 8-8 (7*) P McCabe (6) *chsd alng beh ldrs, improved appr fnl furlong, kpt on und pres.* ... (7 to 1) 2
3539[3] DANTE'S RUBICON (Ire) [59] 7-3[1] (5*) D Wright (5) *nvr far away, effrt and drvn alng last 2 fs, kpt on same pace.* .... (12 to 1 op 10 to 1) 3
3816[4] MILLION LIGHTS (Ire) [71] 8-5 G Duffield (10) *sn pressing ldrs, effrt and drvn alng last 2 fs, kpt on one pace.* .... (7 to 2 fav op 3 to 1) 4
3903[3] BROCTUNE GOLD [86] 9-6 K Darley (4) *broke wl to show gd speed centre for o'r 4 fs, no extr.* .... (11 to 2 op 5 to 1 tchd 6 to 1) 5
3816 UNCLE DOUG [62] 7-10 J Fanning (11) *settled midfield, chsd alng hfwy, no imprsn appr fnl furlong.* ... (6 to 1) 6
3502[3] SINNERS REPRIEVE [86] 9-6 M Birch (12) *settled gng wl stands side, effrt and shaken up 2 fs out, not quicken.* .... (6 to 1) 7
3903 CHEERFUL GROOM (Ire) [59] 7-3[1] (5*) Darren Moffatt (8) *impeded sn aftr leaving stalls, chsd alng hfwy, kpt on, nvr nrr.* .... (33 to 1) 8
3993[6] PORTITE SOPHIE [60] 7-8[1] J Lowe (9) *chsd alng to go pace hfwy, nvr a factor.* .... (50 to 1 op 33 to 1) 9
3428[6] MONKEY MUSIC [75] (bl) 8-9 J Carroll (2) *broke wl to show speed on outsd for o'r 4 fs, wknd.* (14 to 1 op 12 to 1) 10
3816 WHARFEDALE MUSIC [63] 7-11 Dale Gibson (3) *drvn alng to go pace hfwy, nvr a threat.* .... (20 to 1) 11
3502[6] MISTER BEAT [73] (bl) 8-7 Paul Eddery (7) *crossed o'r sharply to show speed stands side for over 3 fs, sn btn.* .... (14 to 1 op 12 to 1) 12

Dist: 1l, 3½l, hd, 3½l, ½l, ½l, 2½l, ½l, 8l, 2½l. 1m 10.40s. a 0.70s (12 Ran).

SR: 46/35/-/10/11/-/7/-/-/ (Mrs Elaine Mitchell), M J Heaton-Ellis

4166 British Gas Northern Handicap Class C (0-90 3-y-o and up) £5,554 7f.. (3:55)

3774[2] MY BEST VALENTINE [82] 3-9-5 F Norton (9) *trkd ldrs centre, drvn ahead o'r one furlong out, hld on grimly cl hme.* .... (9 to 1 co-fav op 8 to 1 tchd 10 to 1) 1
3638[4] GIPSY FIDDLER [87] (v) 5-9-11 (3*) S D Williams (11) *settled midfield, bustled alng to improve last 2 fs, ran on, jst fld.* .... (10 to 1 op 9 to 1) 2
3957[3] EURO FESTIVAL [75] 4-8-9 (7*) P McCabe (7) *co'red up in midfield, improved over one furlong out, ran on towards finish.* .... (10 to 1 op 8 to 1) 3
2431[8] SEA DEVIL [77] 7-9-4 N Connorton (15) *patiently rdn, weaved through frm midfield last 2 fs, kpt on wl.* .... (12 to 1) 4
3182[3] PRINCESS MAXINE (Ire) [56] 4-7-11 J Fanning (12) *nvr far away, effrt and pushed alng last 2 fs, styd on.* .... (12 to 1 op 10 to 1) 5
3791[2] WATHIK (USA) [88] (bl) 3-9-11 R Hills (21) *settled gng wl, dsptd ld hfwy, rdn and not quicken ins fnl furlong.* .... (9 to 1 co-fav op 8 to 1) 6
3774 BOURSIN (Ire) [59] 4-8-0 Dale Gibson (8) *broke wl to ld centre for o'r 5 fs, rdn and no extr.* (25 to 1 op 16 to 1) 7
4019[6] SPANISH VERDICT [69] 6-8-3 (7*) C Teague (14) *pressed ldrs, feeling pace and drvn alng 2 fs out, grad wknd.* .... (16 to 1) 8
3637[9] CROIRE (Ire) [73] 3-8-10 Paul Eddery (6) *patiently rdn, improved into midfield hfwy, styd on, nvr able to chal.* .... (12 to 1) 9
3747[3] STATE FLYER [60] (v) 5-8-1[1] R Price (4) *pressed ldrs on outsd, bustled alng o'r 2 fs out, fdd.* .... (14 to 1 op 12 to 1) 10
3747 TUMBLING (USA) [52] 5-7-3[1] (5*) D Wright (19) *chsd alng beh ldg bunch, no imprsn last 2 fs.* .... (20 to 1 op 100 to 1) 11
3995 PALLIUM (Ire) [70] 5-8-4 (7*) V Halliday (16) *sluggish strt, improved into midfield hfwy, not pace to chal.* (33 to 1) 12
3676[2] NORTH ARDAR [65] 3-8-2 J Weaver (3) *chsd ldrs on outsd for o'r 5 fs, fdd.* .... (12 to 1 tchd 14 to 1) 13
3458[4] AMADEUS AES [62] (v) 4-8-3 G Duffield (2) *gd speed on wide outsd till wknd 2 fs out.* .... (12 to 1 tchd 14 to 1) 14
3680[9] PIQUANT [80] (v) 6-9-7 D Harrison (17) *in tch, struggling in midfield aftr 3 fs, sn btn.* .... (9 to 1 co-fav op 8 to 1 tchd 10 to 1) 15
3756[7] THE SHARP BIDDER (Ire) [75] 3-8-12 K Darley (1) *chsd alng on wide outsd, nvr able to rch ldrs.* (25 to 1 op 20 to 1) 16
3995 WILLSHE GAN [74] (bl) 3-8-11 L Charnock (13) *wth ldrs, drifted rght und pres o'r 2 fs out, sn btn.* ...... (33 to 1) 17
3780 SCOFFERA [60] 3-7-11 Kim Tinkler (10) *bustled alng in midfield hfwy, nvr a threat.* .... (33 to 1) 18
3910[2] SUPER BENZ [65] 7-8-6 A Munro (18) *chsd ldrs, feeling pace and drvn alng o'r 2 fs out, sn btn.* .... (10 to 1) 19
3901[8] BOLD ANGEL [72] 6-8-13 M Birch (20) *drpd back to rear hfwy, eased whn no ch last 2 fs.* .... (12 to 1) 20
3410 RED FAN (Ire) [66] (bl) 3-8-3 J Lowe (5) *chsd alng on outsd, wknd quickly frm hfwy.* .... (50 to 1) 21

Dist: Nk, 1l, hd, hd, ½l, 1½l, 4l, 1l, ¾l, 3½l. 1m 22.60s. a 0.80s (21 Ran).

SR: 51/59/44/45/23/49/19/17/14/ (The Valentines), P W Harris

4167 Newby Median Auction Maiden Stakes Class E (2-y-o) £3,779 7f (4:25)

3633[3] IN LIKE FLYNN 9-0 A Munro (10) *nvr far away, chalg whn hng fire o'r one furlong out, rdn to last strds.* .... (4 to 1 op 3 to 1) 1
3658[3] TOWER GREEN 9-0 D Harrison (4) *al hndy, led 2 fs out, ran on, jst ct.* .... (7 to 1 tchd 8 to 1 and 9 to 1) 2
3816[3] STOREY'S GATE (Ire) 9-0 J Carroll (8) *al pressing ldrs, effrt and drvn alng last 2 fs, kpt on same pace.* .... (10 to 1 tchd 12 to 1) 3
KINGS CAY (Ire) 9-0 M Tebbutt (2) *nvr far away, drvn alng o'r one furlong out, not quicken.* .... (4 to 1 op 5 to 2) 4
3833[2] RORY 9-0 Paul Eddery (1) *tried to make all, hdd and rdn 2 fs out, grad wknd.* .. (3 to 1 fav op 4 to 1 tchd 5 to 1) 5
KAITAK (Ire) 9-0 S Morris (7) *patiently rdn, steady hdwy last 2 fs, can improve.* .... (50 to 1) 6
3969[4] MUMTAZ FLYPAST 8-9 K Darley (6) *co'red up in midfield, swtchd ins to improve over one furlong out, nrst finish.* .... (12 to 1 op 8 to 1) 7
3686[2] POLAR QUEST 9-0 A Clark (9) *al chasing ldrs, drvn alng 2 fs out, no imprsn.* .... (16 to 1 op 14 to 1) 8
JASDAN 9-0 C Rutter (14) *pushed alng in midfield hfwy, no imprsn last 2 fs.* .... (10 to 1 op 7 to 1) 9
CASUAL WATER (Ire) 9-0 M Birch (12) *jinked, lft strt, drvn into midfield hfwy, sn rdn and btn.* .... (50 to 1 op 33 to 1) 10
DALERIVER 9-0 E Johnson (3) *broke wl to show gd speed for 5 fs, better for race.* .... (33 to 1 op 25 to 1) 11
3990[3] KEFAHI (Ire) 9-0 R Hills (16) *broke wl to show speed for o'r 5 fs, wknd.* .... (10 to 1 op 8 to 1) 12
3091[5] IN A MOMENT (USA) 9-0 N Connorton (5) *pressed ldrs, feeling pace o'r 2 fs out, fdd.* .... (25 to 1) 13
3131[3] WALWORTH LADY 8-9 S Webster (15) *drvn alng aftr 3 fs, wknd o'r 2 furlongs out.* .... (66 to 1) 14
3218[6] SIMPLY A SEQUEL (Ire) 9-0 G Duffield (13) *chsd alng hfwy, outpcd last 2 fs.* .... (20 to 1) 15
3972 RISKY PRINCESS 8-9 L Charnock (11) *bumped strt, sn tld off.* .... (100 to 1) 16

Dist: Nk, 3½l, hd, 1½l, 1l, 1l, 2½l, 3½l, 1½l, 1½l. 1m 23.80s. a 2.00s (16 Ran).

SR: 28/27/16/15/10/7/ (M M Matalon), R Hannon

4168 Hornsea Handicap Class D (0-80 3-y-o and up) £3,845 6f............... (5:00)

3794* BAYIN (USA) [45] 4-7-7 R Street (15) *settled gng wl, quickened up frm midfield 2 fs out, led ins fnl furlong, easily.* ....(7 to 1 fav tchd 8 to 1 and 6 to 1) 1
3739³ SUPREME BOY [57] 4-8-5² M Birch (22) *al hndy, ev ch and drvn alng fnl furlong, not pace of wnr.* ....(10 to 1 op 8 to 1) 2
3758* MISS ARAGON [53] 5-7-10² (7*) P McCabe (21) *nvr far away, ev ch and bustled alng last 2 fs, kpt on same pace.*....(12 to 1 op 10 to 1) 3
3535 INVIGILATE [55] 4-8-3 K Darley (14) *pressed ldrs, rdn to draw level entering fnl furlong, kpt on same pace.* ....(25 to 1) 4
3906⁶ PETRACO (Ire) [74] 5-9-5 (3*) S D Williams (9) *made most in centre till hdd and not quicken ins fnl furlong.* ....(10 to 1 op 9 to 1) 5
3758 CRAIGIE BOY [48] (bl) 3-7-7 L Charnock (2) *rcd far side, al frnt rnk, rdn and no extr fnl furlong*....(33 to 1) 6
2110⁸ PHARAOH'S DANCER [66] 6-9-0 A Clark (4) *nvr far away, effrt and drvn alng o'r one furlong out, kpt on same pace*....(9 to 1 op 8 to 1 tchd 10 to 1) 7
4012⁸ LETSBEONESTABOUTIT [64] (bl) 7-8-12 C Rutter (19) *al chasing ldrs, rdn last 2 fs, no imprsn*....(16 to 1) 8
4038⁸ BLUE GRIT [59] (bl) 7-8-7 J Lowe (20) *sluggish strt, improved into midfield hfwy, styd on, nvr nrr.* ....(12 to 1 op 10 to 1) 9
3504 FINJAN [79] 6-9-13 J Weaver (1) *broke wl to show speed far side, drvn alng last 2 fs, no extr.* ....(25 to 1 tchd 33 to 1) 10
3947³ HERE COMES A STAR [69] 5-9-3 W Woods (3) *al chasing ldrs, rdn o'r 2 fs out, no imprsn*....(12 to 1 op 11 to 1) 11
4090⁹ THE AUCTION BIDDER [74] 6-9-3 (5*) S Wynne (13) *bustled alng beh ldg bunch, no imprsn last 2 fs.* ....(20 to 1 tchd 25 to 1) 12
4109 KALAR [53] (bl) 4-7-8 (7*) Claire Balding (8) *chsd alng in midfield, nvr trble ldrs*....(33 to 1) 13
2969⁹ EASY LINE [80] 10-10-0 G Duffield (10) *sluggish strt, improved hfwy, nvr able to chal.* (20 to 1 tchd 25 to 1) 14
3004 BLOW DRY (Ire) [72] 3-9-3 Dale Gibson (11) *chsd ldrs, drvn alng o'r 2 fs out, not pace to chal.* ....(16 to 1 tchd 20 to 1) 15
3354 PINE RIDGE LAD (Ire) [64] 3-8-9 A Munro (16) *chsd ldrs, drvn alng hfwy, no imprsn*....(14 to 1) 16
3995 MINIZEN MUSIC (Ire) [45] 5-7-3¹ (5*) D Wright (7) *drvn alng to go pace hfwy, nvr a threat*....(100 to 1) 17
4038 DENSBEN [80] 9-10-0 N Connorton (17) *struggling frm hfwy, nvr dngrs*....(10 to 1 op 9 to 1) 18
CLASSIC STORM [75] 3-9-6 J Carroll (5) *broke wl to show early speed, fdd last 3 fs*....(14 to 1 op 12 to 1) 19
3745⁴ SPRING HIGH [48] (bl) 6-7-10 G Bardwell (12) *struggling to keep up hfwy, sn lost tch*....(14 to 1 op 12 to 1) 20
GLENCROFT [48] (bl) 9-7-10 J Fanning (6) *chsd alng far side for o'r 3 fs, sn lost tch*....(66 to 1) 21
Dist: 2l, hd, hd, 1½l, ½l, ½l, 2l, 1l, nk, ½l. 1m 10.10s. a 0.40s (21 Ran).
SR: 23/27/22/23/36/5/24/14/5/ (Trevor Barker), M D I Usher

ST-CLOUD (FR) (soft)
Friday September 24th
Going Correction: PLUS 0.40 sec. per fur.

4169 Prix Coronation (Listed) (3-y-o) £14,337 1m....(2:20)

4738a⁴ ZIGREEN (Fr) 8-11 W Mongil, 1
1545⁵ LA GROUPIE (Fr) 8-11 O Doleuze, 2
3195⁴ SHAMSIYA (USA) 8-11 G Mosse, 3
WEST COAST 8-11 T Jarnet, 4
Dist: 2½l, ½l, nk, ½l, nk, nk, 2l, 5l. 1m 44.10s. a 5.60s (9 Ran).
SR: 61/53/51/50/ (Mme B Houillion), A Spanu

ASCOT (good to soft)
Saturday September 25th
Going Correction: PLUS 0.30 sec. per fur. (races 1,3), PLUS 0.35 (2,4,5,6)

4170 Diadem Stakes Class A (Group 3) (3-y-o and up) £41,580 6f....(1:30)

3777² CATRAIL (USA) 3-8-11 M Roberts (1) *trkd ldrs, al gng wl, led well o'r one furlong out, sn clr, easily.* ....(11 to 10 on op 5 to 4 on tchd Evens) 1
3847* MARINA PARK 3-8-8 L Dettori (2) *trkd ldrs, not much room appr 2 fs out, kpt on und pres ins last.* ....(8 to 1 op 10 to 1 tchd 11 to 1) 2
3782* ZARANI SIDI ANNA (USA) (v) 3-8-8 W R Swinburn (8) *cl up, ev ch 2 fs out, shaken up o'r one out, one pace.* ....(8 to 1 op 5 to 1) 3
4040* HARD TO FIGURE 7-9-0 R Cochrane (6) *outpcd, hdwy entering fnl furlong, ran on wl*....(20 to 1) 4
3315⁶ LOOK WHO'S HERE (Ire) 3-8-11 C Asmussen (5) *trkd ldrs, effrt 2 fs out, no imprsn*....(50 to 1 tchd 66 to 1) 5
3594⁵ MONTENDRE 6-9-0 J Reid (9) *in tch, hdwy o'r 2 fs out, wknd one out*....(12 to 1) 6
3594⁴ SPLICE 4-8-11 M Hills (3) *al beh*.... (20 to 1 op 14 to 1) 7
3333² EUROLINK THUNDER 3-8-11 Pat Eddery (4) *hld up, hrd rdn 2 fs out, no imprsn*....(10 to 1 tchd 11 to 1) 8
3777⁷ HAMAS (Ire) (v) 4-9-6 W Carson (7) *led til hdd wl o'r one furlong out, drpd out quickly.* ....(11 to 1 op 8 to 1 tchd 12 to 1) 9
Dist: 4l, ½l, 2½l, 1l, 1½l, 2l, hd, 3l. 1m 15.63s. a 2.23s (9 Ran).
SR: 88/69/67/63/56/53/42/41/38/ (Sheikh Mohammed), J H M Gosden

4171 Fillies' Mile Class A (Group 1) (2-y-o) £93,420 1m....(2:05)

3176* FAIRY HEIGHTS (Ire) 8-10 C Asmussen (2) *hld up in rear, al gng wl, hdwy o'r one furlong out, quickened to ld well ins last*....(11 to 1 op 10 to 1) 1
3765* DANCE TO THE TOP 8-10 W Carson (8) *took keen hold early, cl up, led briefly ins fnl furlong, ran on one pace.* ....(8 to 1 op 7 to 1 tchd 9 to 1) 2
3860² KISSING COUSIN (Ire) 8-10 M Roberts (5) *led til hdd ins fnl furlong, not quicken*.... (7 to 1 op 6 to 1 tchd 8 to 1) 3
3781* RELATIVELY SPECIAL 8-10 R Cochrane (11) *beh, hdwy whn not clr run 2 fs out, checked one out, ran on ins fnl furlong*....(16 to 1 op 14 to 1 tchd 20 to 1) 4
3586³ SPOT PRIZE (USA) 8-10 D Harrison (3) *beh, rdn alng 2 fs out, hdwy und pres appr last, sn one pace.* ....(16 to 1 op 14 to 1 tchd 20 to 1) 5
3860* HAWAJISS 8-10 W R Swinburn (1) *trkd ldrs, rdn alng 3 fs out, btn o'r one out.* ....(2 to 1 fav op 9 to 4 tchd 11 to 4) 6
3833* MYTILENE (Ire) 8-10 L Dettori (7) *mid-div, hdwy 3 fs out, rdn o'r 2 out, wknd wl ins last.* ....(7 to 1 op 5 to 1 tchd 15 to 2) 7
3925⁸ BALLYKETT NANCY (Ire) 8-10 C Roche (6) *mid-div, pushed alng o'r 4 fs out, sn outpcd*.... (20 to 1 tchd 25 to 1) 8
3248² AVERTI (USA) 8-10 Pat Eddery (10) *hld up beh, hrd rdn and hdwy o'r 2 fs out, sn btn.* ....(11 to 2 op 5 to 1 tchd 6 to 1) 9
3860³ NEWS AND ECHO (USA) 8-10 S Whitworth (4) *cl up till rdn and wknd o'r 2 fs out*....(50 to 1 tchd 66 to 1) 10
2790* A SMOOTH ONE (Ire) 8-10 J Reid (9) *chsd ldrs, pushed alng 4 fs out, drvn and btn o'r 2 out.* ....(20 to 1 op 16 to 1) 11
Dist: 1½l, ¾l, nk, nk, nk, hd, 6l, 2½l, ½l, nk. 1m 44.44s. a 4.94s (11 Ran).
SR: 64/59/57/56/55/54/53/35/27/ (Frank W Golding), N A Callaghan

4172 Tote Festival Handicap Class B (3-y-o and up) £51,061 7f....(2:40)

4005⁴ YOUNG ERN [96] 3-8-12 (5ex) W Ryan (17) *wtd wth in mid-div gng wl, cld o'r 2 fs out, led well over one out, quickened clr*....(25 to 1 op 20 to 1) 1
4065* PENNY DROPS [84] 4-8-4 (5ex) D Harrison (4) *hld up, hdwy 2 fs out, kpt on ins last, not rch wnr.* ....(6 to 1 op 7 to 1 tchd 8 to 1) 2
3624⁶ KAYVEE [96] 4-9-2 W R Swinburn (13) *mid-div, hdwy appr 2 fs out, kpt on*....(33 to 1 tchd 40 to 1) 3
3504 FACE NORTH (Ire) [73] 5-7-2 (5*) D Wright (20) *cl up gng wl, ev ch 2 fs out, hrd rdn and not quicken.* ....(25 to 1 tchd 33 to 1) 4
3774³ BAND ON THE RUN [90] 6-8-10 C Asmussen (21) *al prmnt, rdn 2 fs out, one pace*.... (14 to 1 op 25 to 1) 5
3987* STORM CANYON (Ire) [95] 3-8-11 (5ex) M Roberts (6) *hld up in mid-div, hdwy o'r 2 fs out, eased whn no imprsn wl ins last*....(11 to 2 fav op 6 to 1 tchd 7 to 1) 6
3504 REALITIES (USA) [93] 3-8-9 R Cochrane (16) *chsd ldrs, hdwy 2 fs out, btn one out*....(50 to 1 op 33 to 1) 7
3764⁶ IHTIRAZ [105] 3-9-7 R Hills (19) *beh, hdwy 2 fs out, sn no extr*....(33 to 1 op 25 to 1) 8
3863² PRENONAMOSS [76] (v) 5-7-10 J Quinn (12) *mid-div, not much room 2 fs out, ran on ins last*....(25 to 1) 9
3404⁸ SAGEBRUSH ROLLER [82] 5-8-2 P Robinson (25) *beh, hdwy 2 fs out, not clr run and btn entering fnl furlong.* ....(25 to 1 op 20 to 1) 10
3618³ EN ATTENDANT (Fr) [104] 5-9-10 L Piggott (26) *hld up in mid-div gng wl, rdn and hdwy 2 fs out, btn one out, eased*....(11 to 1 op 20 to 1 tchd 10 to 1) 11
3936 BRANSTON ABBY (Ire) [100] 4-9-6 L Dettori (7) *hld up in mid-div, effrt and no hdwy fnl 2 fs*....(20 to 1) 12
3897⁷ NEW CAPRICORN (USA) [96] 3-8-12 J Reid (8) *trkd ldrs till wknd 2 fs out*....(33 to 1 op 25 to 1) 13
2413⁴ UNDERWATER (USA) [98] 4-9-4 Pat Eddery (14) *hld up in rear, rdn and no response frm o'r 2 fs out.* ....(12 to 1 op 14 to 1) 14
4065⁶ NO RESERVATIONS (Ire) [87] (v) 3-7-12 (5*) B Russell (18) *led til hdd wl o'r one furlong out, sn wknd.* ....(33 to 1 op 25 to 1) 15
3726* ERTLON [80] 3-7-10³ (3*,5ex) B Doyle (24) *cl up til wknd wl o'r one furlong out*...(20 to 1 op 16 to 1 tchd 25 to 1) 16
3996⁴ ABSOLUTE MAGIC [90] 3-8-6 M Hills (22) *prmnt till wknd quickly 2 fs out*.... (50 to 1 op 33 to 1) 17
4038⁴ HOB GREEN [81] 4-8-1 K Fallon (11) *hld up, rdn and no imprsn 3 fs out*....(8 to 1 op 7 to 1 tchd 10 to 1) 18
3885³ SON PARDO [100] 3-9-2 W Newnes (5) *al beh.* ....(20 to 1 tchd 25 to 1) 19
3471⁶ HIGHLAND MAGIC (Ire) [81] 5-8-1 T Williams (23) *beh, hdwy und pres o'r 2 fs out, wknd one out.* ....(25 to 1 tchd 33 to 1) 20

1635* TIME AGAIN [79] 3-7-9^{7} (5*) N Gwilliams (15) *chsd ldrs till rdn and wknd o'r 2 fs out*.........(25 to 1 op 20 to 1) 21
3896 BAYSHAM (USA) [73] 7-7-4^{4} (7*) N Varley (9) *al beh*. ....(100 to 1 op 50 to 1) 22
3926^{3} RONDELLI (Ire) [91] 3-8-7 C Roche (10) *al beh*. ....(28 to 1 op 25 to 1 tchd 33 to 1) 23
3712^{9} PARLIAMENT PIECE [84] (v) 7-7-13 (5*) Darren Moffatt (1) *al beh*..................(40 to 1 op 33 to 1 tchd 50 to 1) 24
3889^{2} MATILA (Ire) [90] 3-8-6 W Carson (2) *chsd ldrs, hrd rdn and wknd o'r 2 fs out*................(16 to 1 tchd 20 to 1) 25
FIRST CENTURY (Ire) [73] 4-7-7 G Bardwell (3) *cl up 3 fs, sn btn*.............................(100 to 1 op 66 to 1) 26
Dist: 3l, ¾l, hd, 1½l, nk, 1½l, 1½l, 1l, nk, hd. 1m 30.03s. a 3.73s (26 Ran).
SR: 74/57/67/43/55/55/48/55/27/ (M F Kentish), S Dow

4173 Queen Elizabeth II Stakes Class A (Group 1) (3-y-o and up) £194,280 1m ....(3:25)

3800^{3} BIGSTONE (Ire) 3-9-0 Pat Eddery (6) *hld up, pushed alng o'r 4 fs out, hdwy 2 out, sstnd run und pres to ld ins last, ran on*..........(100 to 30 op 7 to 2 tchd 3 to 1) 1
3800^{4} BARATHEA (Ire) 3-9-0 M Roberts (9) *took keen hold, trkd ldrs, squeezed through on ins rail to ld wl o'r one furlong out, hdd inside last, ran on*. ....(9 to 1 op 8 to 1 tchd 10 to 1) 2
3800* KINGMAMBO (USA) 3-9-0 C Asmussen (1) *hld up beh, hdwy o'r one furlong out, no imprsn ins last*. ....(5 to 2 fav op 9 to 4 tchd 2 to 1) 3
3369* SAYYEDATI 3-8-11 W R Swinburn (3) *hld up in rear, hdwy o'r one furlong out, sn no extr*. ....(3 to 1 op 9 to 4 tchd 100 to 30) 4
3862* SWING LOW 4-9-4 J Reid (8) *hld up, hdwy o'r one furlong out, one pace*. ....(15 to 2 op 10 to 1 tchd 12 to 1 and 7 to 1) 5
3402 ALHIJAZ 4-9-4 W Carson (5) *sn led, hdd wl o'r one furlong out, wknd und pres*.............(33 to 1 tchd 40 to 1) 6
3622^{6} HALF TERM (USA) 3-9-0 L Dettori (2) *took keen hold, trkd ldrs, rdn alng 3 fs out, sn wknd*. ....(25 to 1 op 20 to 1 tchd 33 to 1) 7
3862^{3} MISTLE CAT (USA) 3-9-0 W Woods (4) *prmnt till wknd 2 fs out*..................(25 to 1 op 20 to 1 tchd 33 to 1) 8
3862^{4} INNER CITY (Ire) 4-9-4 R Cochrane (7) *trkd ldr, ev ch 2 fs out, wknd*..........(40 to 1 op 33 to 1 tchd 50 to 1) 9
Dist: 1½l, 2½l, 1½l, nk, 1½l, 2½l, 5l, 4l. 1m 42.89s. a 3.39s (9 Ran).
SR: 91/86/78/70/76/71/59/44/36/ (Daniel Wildenstein), E Lellouche

4174 Royal Lodge Stakes Class A (Group 2) (2-y-o) £59,940 1m............. (4:00)

3435^{6} MISTER BAILEYS 8-10 L Dettori (7) *chsd ldrs, pushed alng o'r 2 fs out, led one and a half out, rdn out*. ....(100 to 30 jt-fav op 3 to 1 tchd 7 to 2) 1
3400* CONCORDIAL (USA) 8-10 Pat Eddery (6) *took keen hold early, hld up in rear, hdwy 2 fs out gng wl, sn rdn and not quicken, kpt on cl hme*. ....(7 to 2 op 9 to 4 tchd 4 to 1) 2
3959* OVERBURY (Ire) 8-10 M Roberts (9) *hld up in cl tch, quickened to hold ev ch o'r one furlong out, no extr close hme*........(15 to 2 op 8 to 1 tchd 9 to 1 and 7 to 1) 3
3959^{2} PARTY SEASON 8-10 C Asmussen (3) *hld up beh, hdwy fnl furlong, nrst finish*. ....(20 to 1 op 16 to 1 tchd 33 to 1) 4+
3130* HAWKER HUNTER (USA) 8-10 J Reid (4) *trkd ldr, ev ch 2 fs out, one pace*....................(8 to 1 tchd 10 to 1) 4+
3779^{3} WISHING (USA) 8-10 W R Swinburn (1) *led til hdd one and a half fs out, wknd*. (33 to 1 op 20 to 1 tchd 40 to 1) 6
4014* FLORID (USA) 8-10 W Ryan (2) *in tch, effrt 3 fs out, sn btn*. ....(100 to 30 jt-fav op 4 to 1 tchd 9 to 2) 7
3833^{3} COOL JAZZ 8-10 R Cochrane (8) *slwly into strd, beh, cld o'r 2 fs out, outpcd over one out*. (14 to 1 tchd 16 to 1) 8
3570* SAWLAJAN (USA) 8-10 W Carson (5) *cl up, wkng whn hmpd appr 2 fs out*....(10 to 1 op 8 to 1 tchd 11 to 1) 9
Dist: ½l, sht-hd, 2½l, dd-ht, ½l, 8l, 5l, 4l. 1m 45.14s. a 5.64s (9 Ran).
SR: 53/51/50/42/42/40/16/1/-/ (G R Bailey Ltd (Baileys Horse Feeds)), M Johnston

4175 Ascot Handicap Class B (3-y-o and up) £47,437 1½m.................. (4:35)

3848 LEAGUE LEADER (Ire) [88] 3-8-10 (4ex) W Carson (1) *rcd alone on far rail, al prmnt, jnd main grp o'r 7 fs out, led 2 out, rdn and hld on wl*.........(10 to 1 tchd 11 to 1) 1
3466^{6} WHITECHAPEL (USA) [79] 5-8-9 W R Swinburn (9) *trkd ldrs, pushed alng 3 fs out, ran on wl nr finish*.....(5 to 1 jt-fav tchd 11 to 2 and 9 to 2) 2
3848^{3} QUICK RANSOM [88] 5-9-4 L Dettori (3) *keen hold early, trkd ldrs, rdn alng 3 fs out, kpt on one pace*. ....(13 to 2 op 7 to 1 tchd 8 to 1) 3
1346^{9} DEER HUNT [82] 4-8-12 C Asmussen (5) *cl up, led o'r 7 fs out, hdd 2 out, ev ch one out, no extr*. ....(14 to 1 tchd 16 to 1) 4
4039^{5} HIGHBROOK (USA) [84] 5-9-0 P Robinson (7) *hld up beh, steady hdwy frm 5 fs out, ch o'r 2 out, outpcd over one out*....................(8 to 1 op 7 to 1 tchd 9 to 1) 5
3595^{4} DREAMS END [82] 5-8-12 R Cochrane (4) *beh, hdwy o'r one furlong out, styd on*.........(12 to 1 tchd 14 to 1) 6
3900^{3} MAD MILITANT (Ire) [70] 4-8-0 J Quinn (2) *beh, rdn and hdwy o'r 3 fs out, nvr nr to chal*..............(33 to 1) 7
3775^{4} MILLION IN MIND (Ire) [83] 4-8-13 W Newnes (11) *chsd ldrs, pushed alng o'r 5 fs out, btn 3 out*. (25 to 1 op 20 to 1) 8
3848* FLIGHT LIEUTENANT (USA) [82] 4-8-12 (4ex) J Reid (8) *chsd ldrs till outpcd fnl 2 fs*. ....(15 to 2 op 10 to 1 tchd 11 to 1) 9
3931^{5} DANA SPRINGS (Ire) [101] 3-9-9 (4ex) Pat Eddery (12) *hld up in rear, nvr gng wl, al beh*..................(5 to 1 jt-fav op 4 to 1 tchd 11 to 2) 10
4063^{7} MR CONFUSION (Ire) [92] 5-9-8 L Piggott (13) *al beh*. ....(15 to 2 op 8 to 1 tchd 9 to 1) 11
4064* CASTORET [89] 7-9-5 (4ex) D Harrison (6) *chsd ldrs till lost pl o'r 4 fs out*.......(12 to 1 op 10 to 1 tchd 14 to 1) 12
4063^{4} BOLOARDO [94] 4-9-10 M Roberts (10) *led, til hdd o'r 7 fs out, pushed alng over 5 out, sn lost pl*. ....(33 to 1 op 20 to 1) 13
Dist: Hd, 1½l, nk, 7l, 1l, 8l, 2½l, 1½l, ¾l, 10l. 2m 37.32s. a 9.12s (13 Ran).
SR: 47/45/51/44/32/28/-/8/4/ (Lord Weinstock), M R Stoute

HAYDOCK (soft)
Saturday September 25th
Going Correction: PLUS 0.45 sec. per fur.

4176 September Maiden Handicap Class E (0-70 3-y-o and up) £3,597 1¾m (2:15)

3961^{9} KEYLOCK (USA) [47] 3-7-12 (3*) N Kennedy (13) *keen hold, settled beh ldg grp, effrt and rdn 3 fs out, led o'r one out, forged clr*......................(10 to 1 op 7 to 1) 1
3821 MENHAAD (Ire) [50] 3-8-4 J Carroll (8) *settled midfield, improved and ev ch o'r 2 fs out, kpt on same pace appr last*................................(11 to 1 op 8 to 1) 2
3883 MIROSWAKI (USA) [70] 3-9-10 A Munro (17) *mid-div, took clr order entering strt, rdn o'r 2 fs out, one pace over one out*.............(11 to 1 op 10 to 1 tchd 12 to 1) 3
3552^{2} FREE TRANSFER (Ire) [35] 4-7-13 J Lowe (7) *hld up, drvn to improve entering strt, tracking ldrs 2 fs out, one pace*. ....(13 to 2 co-fav op 5 to 1) 4
3971^{3} CHUMMY'S PAL (USA) [68] 3-9-8 T Quinn (18) *nvr far away, improved to ld hfwy, drvn o'r 2 fs out, hdd over one out, no extr*............. (13 to 2 co-fav op 6 to 1) 5
3970^{5} BLUE LAWS (Ire) [65] (bl) 3-9-5 T Lucas (14) *keen hold, trkd ldrs, drvn entering strt, ev ch o'r 3 fs out, sn btn, eased fnl furlong*..........................(8 to 1 op 6 to 1) 6
NEEDWOOD POPPY [29] 5-7-0 (7*) C Teague (11) *wl beh, shaken up and steady hdwy fnl 3 fs, nvr nr to chal*. ....(33 to 1) 7
3943^{3} RIZ BIZ (USA) [45] 3-7-10 (3*) M Fenton (5) *trkd ldrs, effrt and rdn 3 fs out, wknd wl o'r one out*......(13 to 2 co-fav op 7 to 1 tchd 8 to 1) 8
3872^{6} BITTER ALOE [55] 4-9-5 B Raymond (16) *pressed ldrs, took clr order hfwy, pushed alng entering strt, wknd 2 fs out*................................(11 to 1 op 8 to 1) 9
BAND SARGEANT (Ire) [46] 4-8-10 D Biggs (20) *pressed ldg grp on outer, improved to track ldrs 6 fs out, rdn 4 out, weaked 3 out*..................................(25 to 1) 10
3943 ARC BRIGHT (Ire) [50] 3-7-11 (7*) D Denby (2) *hld up, pushed alng entering strt, nvr able to chal*. ....(16 to 1 op 12 to 1) 11
3759 AMILLIONMEMORIES [60] 3-9-0 S Webster (9) *mid-div, shaken up entering strt, nvr on terms*.........(25 to 1) 12
3757^{9} RICH ASSET (Ire) [42] 3-7-10 L Charnock (4) *settled on outer, rdn alng 5 fs out, no imprsn*. (25 to 1 op 20 to 1) 13
4035 MRS NORMAN [30] 4-7-8 N Adams (12) *beh, shaken up appr strt, sn btn, tld off*......................(33 to 1) 14
3970 DOC SPOT [57] 3-8-11 J Fortune (6) *frnt rnk, feeling pace and rdn o'r 3 fs out, fdd and tld off*. ....(16 to 1 op 14 to 1) 15
3384 TREBLE LASS [41] 3-7-9 N Carlisle (10) *towards rear, pushed alng appr strt, grad lost tch, tld off*. ....(14 to 1 op 12 to 1) 16
3442^{3} SAOIRSE (Ire) [43] 5-8-7^{1} J Williams (15) *beh, struggling 6 fs out, nvr a factor, tld off*.........(10 to 1 tchd 12 to 1) 17
3442^{5} RAVENSPUR (Ire) [46] 3-7-7 (7*) F Savage (19) *settled beh ldrs, drvn alng 5 fs out, sn lost tch, tld off*. ....(20 to 1 op 16 to 1) 18
3308 CIVIL ACTION (Ire) [45] 3-7-13 F Norton (1) *keen hold, tucked away on ins, rdn alng appr strt, sn wknd, tld off*..(33 to 1) 19
3089^{6} MAJOR RISK [39] 4-8-3^{17} (7*) R Painter (3) *led til hdd hfwy, grad lost pl, eased whn no ch entering strt, tld off*. ....(25 to 1 op 20 to 1 tchd 33 to 1) 20
Dist: 5l, hd, 2½l, 2½l, 12l, 2l, ½l, 1½l, 2½l, 8l. 3m 12.10s. a 14.60s (20 Ran).
SR: 4/-/16/-/4/-/ (Lord Howard de Walden), W Jarvis

4177 Sale Fillies' Conditions Stakes Class B (2-y-o) £6,040 7f 30yds........(2:45)

3510^{2} THREATENING 8-13 D Biggs (2) *pressed ldg trio, improved to ld o'r one furlong out, rdn out ins last*. ....(9 to 2 op 7 to 2 tchd 5 to 1) 1
3865^{3} BALLARD RING (Ire) 8-13 T Quinn (6) *trkd ldg pair, pushed alng 3 fs out, swtchd lft and effrt o'r one out, no extr ins last*..........................(7 to 2 tchd 4 to 1) 2

2648[4] WHATCOMBE (USA) 9-5 A Munro (5) *led half a furlong, trkd ldr, drvn and ev ch o'r 2 out, one pace ins last.* ....(2 to 1 fav tchd 13 to 8 and 9 to 4) 3
2102[4] HEATHYARDS LADY (USA) 8-11 S Perks (3) *hld up on ins, not clr run o'r one furlong out, swtchd lft, one pace inside last*........................ (20 to 1 op 16 to 1) 4
3317 AWTAAR (USA) 8-11 B Raymond (7) *led aftr half a furlong, shaken up o'r 2 out, hdd over one out, sn btn.* ....(10 to 1 op 8 to 1) 5
3723[2] CAPE MERINO 8-13 S Webster (1) *rcd very keenly, hld up, rdn alng 2 fs out, no response*......(7 to 2 tchd 4 to 1) 6
Dist: 1l, 1l, 1½l, 4l, 3½l. 1m 37.46s. a 10.26s (6 Ran).
(Lord Matthews), R J R Williams

4178 Akzo Group Handicap Class C (0-90 3-y-o and up) £5,962 1¼m 120yds ....(3:15)

3812 EXPRESS GIFT [64] 4-8-11 J Williams (11) *patiently rdn, improved on ins rail o'r 2 fs out, led over one out, drw clr inside last*....................(12 to 1 tchd 14 to 1) 1
4107* CEZANNE [74] 4-9-7 (4ex) B Raymond (6) *trkd ldrs gng wl, improved and ev ch 2 fs out, outpcd by wnr ins last.* ....(2 to 1 fav op 6 to 4) 2
3724[5] YILDIZ [77] 4-9-10 J Fortune (10) *nvr far away, rdn to ld wl o'r 2 fs out, hdd over one out, edgd lft and not quicken*......................(8 to 1 tchd 7 to 1) 3
3759* HAZARD A GUESS (Ire) [66] 3-8-6 A Munro (8) *keen hold, in tch, improved and ev ch 2 fs out, rdn and outpcd appr last*................................ (6 to 1 op 5 to 1) 4
4018[6] SEROTINA (Ire) [71] (bl) 3-8-4 (7*) D Gibbs (4) *sluggish strt, sn reco'red to press ldg grp, ev ch over 3 fs out, rdn and one pace fnl 2 furlongs*.......................(12 to 1) 5
4064 TIGER SHOOT [50] 6-7-11 J Lowe (3) *led til rdn and hdd wl o'r 2 fs out, unbl to quicken*................(20 to 1) 6
3503[7] ARGYLE CAVALIER (Ire) [62] 3-8-2 L Charnock (1) *trkd ldrs, drvn alng entering strt, btn o'r 2 fs out.* ....(16 to 1 op 12 to 1) 7
4018[2] NO COMEBACKS [57] 5-8-4 N Adams (12) *slwly into strd, hld up, smooth hdwy to chase ldrs 3 fs out, sn rdn alng, wknd wl o'r one out*..................(13 to 2 op 10 to 1) 8
3814 AEGAEN LADY [55] 4-8-2 J Carroll (7) *pressed ldrs, effrt and drvn alng o'r 2 fs out, nvr able to chal and eased fnl furlong*......................(14 to 1 op 20 to 1) 9
4019[7] NO SUBMISSION (USA) [60] 7-8-7 T Lucas (9) *beh, feeling pace entering strt, nvr a factor*................(25 to 1) 10
3883[5] MAY HILLS LEGACY (Ire) [56] 4-8-3 T Quinn (5) *trkd ldg pair, rdn o'r 3 fs out, grad wknd, tld off*........(8 to 1) 11
3970 PERSIAN FOUNTAIN (Ire) [60] 3-8-0 N Carlisle (2) *tucked away on ins, drvn 5 fs out, sn outpcd, tld off.* ....(14 to 1 op 12 to 1) 12
Dist: 4l, 3½l, hd, 5l, 5l, 6l, ½l, 1½l, 2½l, 12l. 2m 19.86s. a 8.86s (12 Ran).
SR: 56/58/54/35/30/6/ (M W Horner, H Young, And D S Arnold), Mrs M Reveley

4179 Countrywide Freight Maiden Stakes Class D (Div I) (2-y-o) £3,551 7f 30yds ....(3:50)

3763[6] TAJANNAB 9-0 B Raymond (2) *al wl plcd, effrt and rdn 2 fs out, led o'r one out, edgd lft ins last, drvn out.* ....(5 to 4 fav op 11 to 10 tchd 6 to 4) 1
3833 MAKHRAJ (USA) 9-0 J Williams (5) *nvr far away, shaken up o'r one furlong out, kpt on wl ins last, jst hld.* ....(6 to 1 op 9 to 2) 2
3779[9] FRUSTRATED POET (USA) 9-0 L Charnock (6) *dwlt, hld up in rear, steady hdwy on ins 2 fs out, not much room and swtchd inside last, can improve.* .... (9 to 1 op 8 to 1 tchd 10 to 1) 3
WHISPERING LOCH (Ire) 9-0 F Norton (9) *chsd ldrs, outpcd and drvn o'r 3 fs out, improved over one out, no extr ins last*.......................(16 to 1 op 12 to 1) 4
3974[5] DIVERTIMIENTO 9-0 T Lucas (7) *sluggish strt, hld up, improved gng wl o'r 2 fs out, reminder and edgd lft one out, kpt on same pace*.............. (5 to 1 op 4 to 1) 5
3876 NORTHERN HIGHLIGHT 9-0 T Quinn (4) *trkd ldrs, not clr run o'r one furlong out, shaken up whn hmpd entering last, not rcvr, can improve*........ (20 to 1 op 16 to 1) 6
MAZ (Ire) 8-9 A Munro (1) *led, hdd 3 fs out, styd upsides, rgned ld briefly o'r one furlong out, sn btn.* ....(8 to 1 op 12 to 1 tchd 14 to 1) 7
NEEDWOOD JOKER 8-11 (3*) C Hodgson (8) *missed break, shrtlvd effrt on outsd 3 fs out, wnt lft, sn btn.* ....(50 to 1 op 33 to 1) 8
SHERBLU 9-0 J Lowe (3) *chsd ldrs on outsd, improved to ld 3 fs out, hdd o'r one out, sn wknd, eased ins last.* ....(50 to 1 op 33 to 1) 9
Dist: Nk, 2l, 2l, ¾l, 4l, 1½l, 2½l, 5l. 1m 40.36s. a 13.16s (9 Ran).
(Maktoum Al Maktoum), M R Stoute

4180 Leigh Handicap Class C (0-90 3-y-o and up) £5,797 5f..............(4:20)

4090* DOMICKSKY [66] 5-8-2 (7*,5ex) R Painter (11) *in tch stands side grp, improved o'r one furlong out, led ins last, ran on gmely*..........................(11 to 1 op 10 to 1) 1
3947* CHOIR PRACTICE [68] 6-8-11 J Williams (8) *beh centre, rdn hfwy, improved o'r one furlong out, ev ch ins last, jst hld*....................................(7 to 1 op 6 to 1) 2
3995[3] GONDO [71] (v) 6-8-7 (7*) S Knott (12) *nvr far away stands side, rdn to ld o'r one furlong out, hdd ins last, no extr.* ....(9 to 1 op 7 to 1) 3
4123[7] PENNY HASSET [64] (bl) 5-8-7 T Lucas (15) *bumped badly leaving stalls, beh stands side, pushed alng to improve 2 fs out, one pace ins last.* ....(11 to 1 op 10 to 1 tchd 12 to 1) 4
4109 COVENT GARDEN GIRL [62] 3-7-12 (5*) L Newton (7) *prmnt centre, drvn alng o'r 2 fs out, no extr entering last.* ....(16 to 1 op 14 to 1) 5
3438[6] MANOR ADVENTURE [70] 3-8-11 J Fortune (3) *dwlt, sn chasing ldrs far side, pushed alng 2 fs out, no extr ins last*.................(12 to 1 op 10 to 1 tchd 14 to 1) 6
3707[7] LOVE LEGEND [62] (bl) 8-8-5 A Munro (1) *in tch far side, effrt and rdn 2 fs out, one pace ins last.* ....(20 to 1 op 16 to 1) 7
3849[6] RISTON LADY (Ire) [81] 3-9-3 (5*) A Procter (21) *pressed ldrs stands side, rdn alng 2 fs out, no imprsn one out.* ....(10 to 1 tchd 11 to 1) 8
3877[2] MACFARLANE [81] 5-9-10 F Norton (19) *pressed ldg grp stands side, rdn alng o'r 2 fs out, btn over one out.* ....(15 to 2 op 6 to 1) 9
4109[9] SO SUPERB [57] (bl) 4-8-0 L Charnock (6) *gd speed far side, pushed alng o'r 2 fs out, eased whn btn fnl furlong.* ....(25 to 1 op 20 to 1) 10
3955[4] SOBER LAD (Ire) [65] (bl) 3-8-6 J Carroll (13) *wth ldr stands side, rdn alng hfwy, wknd o'r one furlong out.* ....(10 to 1 tchd 12 to 1) 11
3603[2] LE CHIC [50] 7-7-7 N Adams (16) *pressed ldrs stands side, rdn hfwy, sn btn*..................(16 to 1 op 14 to 1) 12
3359* BALLET SHOES (Ire) [76] 3-9-3 T Quinn (4) *in tch far side, pushed alng appr hfwy, sn no imprsn.* ....(5 to 1 fav op 8 to 1) 13
3359[2] MAGIC PEARL [67] 3-8-8 B Raymond (17) *slight ld stands side, hdd o'r one furlong out, wknd quickly.* ....(10 to 1 op 8 to 1) 14
3511 BEAU VENTURE (USA) [79] 5-9-5 (3*) N Kennedy (2) *pressed ldg 3 far side, rdn hfwy, fdd*......(16 to 1 op 14 to 1) 15
1494 SONDERISE [68] 4-8-11 N Carlisle (18) *chsd ldg grp stands side, drvn hfwy, sn btn*.........(14 to 1 tchd 16 to 1) 16
3568 GEMINI FIRE [55] 9-7-12 J Lowe (20) *baulked leaving stalls, beh stands side, rdn hfwy, nvr on terms.* ....(14 to 1 tchd 16 to 1 and 12 to 1) 17
Dist: Hd, 2½l, nk, 2½l, 1½l, nk, 1l, 1l, ½l, sht-hd. 1m 3.75s. a 4.95s (17 Ran).
SR: 41/42/35/27/13/15/8/21/19/ (M J Watson), M R Channon

4181 Castle Irwell Handicap Class D (0-80 3-y-o) £4,900 7f 30yds.......... (4:50)

3837 YAQTHAN (Ire) [77] 9-7 N Carlisle (12) *made all, jnd o'r one furlong out, ran on gmely ins last.* (14 to 1 op 12 to 1) 1
3343[5] CHAMPAGNE GRANDY [64] 8-1 (7*) R Painter (6) *mid-div, improved and ev ch o'r one furlong out, not quicken ins last*..............................(10 to 1 op 12 to 1) 2
4038 EGG [58] (bl) 8-2 J Lowe (1) *hld up, rdn alng o'r 2 fs out, styd on fnl furlong, nrst finish*................(8 to 1) 3
3830[7] DEAD CALM [50] (v) 7-5[4] (7*) C Hawksley (11) *in tch on outsd, cld o'r 3 fs out, not quicken appr last*...(20 to 1) 4
3830[9] CICERONE [49] 7-2[2] (7*) F Savage (4) *al prmnt, pushed alng 4 fs out, chlgd o'r one out, wknd ins last.* ....(20 to 1 op 16 to 1) 5
3973[4] PERSIANSKY (Ire) [76] 9-6 B Raymond (9) *tucked away beh ldrs, effrt and rdn o'r 2 fs out, not quicken over one out.* ....(6 to 1 op 5 to 1) 6
1109[5] CELESTIAL CHOIR [62] 8-6 N Adams (2) *missed break, beh, rdn alng 3 fs out, improved o'r one out, no imprsn ins last*..............................(25 to 1) 7
3726 DANCING DOMINO [71] 9-1 L Charnock (5) *hld up in rear, not clr run and swtchd o'r 2 fs out, shaken up and hng lft, nvr able to chal*...................(7 to 1 op 5 to 1) 8
3783[3] GRAN SENORUM (USA) [71] 9-1 A Munro (10) *trkd ldrs on outsd, pushed alng 3 fs out, grad wknd.* ....(5 to 1 tchd 11 to 2) 9
3358 PIXTON (Ire) [72] (bl) 9-2 F Norton (8) *nvr far away, rdn alng o'r 3 fs out, btn over 2 out*... (12 to 1 op 10 to 1) 10
3893[4] FADAKI HAWAKI (USA) [53] 7-8 (3*) N Kennedy (3) *settled beh ldrs, pushed alng o'r 2 fs out, sn btn.* ....(4 to 1 fav op 9 to 4 tchd 9 to 2) 11
2635* LIVONIAN [69] 8-13 J Carroll (7) *hld up, shrtlvd effrt 3 fs out, fdd*..............................(9 to 2 op 6 to 1) 12
Dist: 2½l, 1½l, ¾l, 1l, 2½l, 2l, 1½l, 5l, 2l, 2½l. 1m 35.76s. a 8.56s (12 Ran).
SR: 28/7/-/-/-/1/ (Hamdan Al-Maktoum), H Thomson Jones

4182 Countrywide Freight Maiden Stakes Class D (Div II) (2-y-o) £3,532 7f 30yds ....(5:20)

XYLEM (USA) 9-0 J Carroll (6) *hld up, smooth hdwy 3 fs out, led 2 out, pushed alng and drw clr ins last.* ....(4 to 1 op 5 to 2) 1
3704[2] WEST BUOYANT (USA) 9-0 T Quinn (7) *cl up, led aftr a furlong, hdd 2 out, rdn and one pace.* ....(6 to 4 on op 5 to 4 tchd 13 to 8 on) 2

3470[9] WINN'S PRIDE (Ire) 9-0 S Perks (8) *pressed ldg grp, rdn o'r 2 fs out, not pace to chal.* ....(12 to 1 op 14 to 1 tchd 20 to 1) 3

2554 MR TOWSER 8-11 (3*) C Hodgson (5) *led one furlong, styd upsides, rdn o'r 2 out, one pace whn hng badly rght over one out*........ (50 to 1 op 33 to 1) 4

3713[7] CALDER KING 9-0 N Adams (1) *pressed ldrs on ins, pushed alng o'r 2 fs out, sn btn*....(50 to 1 op 33 to 1) 5

AGADIR (Ire) 9-0 A Munro (2) *beh, outpcd and drvn alng entering strt, nvr a threat*.......... (5 to 1 op 7 to 2) 6

3602[6] HARPHAM HERO 9-0 J Lowe (3) *nvr far away, rdn alng 3 fs out, grad wknd, tld off*.........(40 to 1 op 33 to 1) 7

ELLASTYLE (Ire) 8-9 J Fortune (4) *lost many ls strt, nvr able to reco'r, tld off*.............. (25 to 1 op 20 to 1) 8

Dist: 6l, 1½l, 1½l, 12l, 2½l, 12l, 15l. 1m 36.91s. a 9.71s (8 Ran).
SR: 3/-/-/-/-/ (Sheikh Mohammed), J H M Gosden

LISTOWEL (IRE) (yielding to soft)
Saturday September 25th

4183 Listowel Arms Auction Race (2-y-o) £4,140 7f..................... (1:30)

4000[7] MISSUS MURHILL (Ire) 8-5 M J Kinane (12).... (6 to 4 fav) 1
3608[3] TONGABEZI (Ire) 7-11 (2*) R M Burke (1).......... (7 to 2) 2
3607[2] ZOE BAIRD 7-13 J F Egan (7).................... (6 to 1) 3
NORTHREEL 8-5 P V Gilson (16)................. (9 to 1) 4
2959[4] SEE YOU (Ire) 8-5 W J Supple (9)................ (8 to 1) 5
3613 COLLECTOR GENERAL (Ire) 8-6[1] S Craine (6)..... (8 to 1) 6
3953[8] AVALIN (Ire) 7-5 (8*) R T Fitzpatrick (8)..........(14 to 1) 7
4000[3] JENZSOPH (Ire) 7-13 A J Nolan (15).............(10 to 1) 8
PERSIAN BLOOM (Ire) 7-7 (6*) R V Skelly (3)......(14 to 1) 9
CAPITAL GAIN 8-7 (4*) J A Heffernan (4)..........(10 to 1) 10
CIARA CANE (Ire) 7-12 (4*) W J Smith (5).........(33 to 1) 11
2188[7] LAXEY LEAP (Ire) 8-8 N G McCullagh (14)........ (25 to 1) 12
THE DREAM FACTORY (Ire) 7-11 (2*) D G O'Shea (11) ....(14 to 1) 13

Dist: ½l, 4l, 2l, 1l. 1m 32.20s. (13 Ran).
(Miss K McGann), D K Weld

4184 Kaliber Handicap (0-80 3-y-o and up) £4,140 6f..................... (2:00)

3928 COMMODITY MARKET (Ire) [-] (bl) 3-8-8 P V Gilson (4) ....(14 to 1) 1
3928[4] PILGRIM BAY (Ire) [-] 3-9-6 (4*) C Everard (14)......(7 to 1) 2
3928[8] SHRAGRADDY LASS (Ire) [-] 3-8-7 N G McCullagh (5) ....(7 to 1) 3
3561* MACGILLYCUDDY (Ire) [-] (bl) 4-9-6 (8*) R T Fitzpatrick (8) ....(7 to 1) 4
3606* DAIRINE'S DELIGHT (Ire) [-] 3-7-6 (2*) D G O'Shea (6) ....(8 to 1) 5
3928[5] MACQUARIE RIDGE (USA) [-] 5-8-1 W J Supple (7) ....(3 to 1 fav) 6
3928 PAKOL (Ire) [-] 4-8-7 (4*) W J Smith (12).......... (16 to 1) 7
3614[9] SOUTHERN RULE [-] (bl) 6-6-13 (8*) G M Moylan (9) ....(16 to 1) 8
1646[7] HAWAIAN TASCA (Ire) [-] 4-7-7 L O'Shea (2)...... (25 to 1) 9
4057 ISLAND HEATHER (Ire) [-] (bl) 5-9-7 (2*) P Carberry (11) ....(7 to 1) 10
3827[8] SHESLOOKINATME (Ire) [-] 4-7-9 (2*) R M Burke (3) (10 to 1) 11
3606[7] BUSINESS CENTRE (Ire) [-] 3-8-1 J F Egan (1).... (14 to 1) 12
3720[6] EDENS LANDING (Ire) [-] (bl) 3-8-6 (4*) J J Behan (13) ....(25 to 1) 13
3334[4] DOBIE (USA) [-] 5-9-12 M J Kinane (10)........... (9 to 2) 14

Dist: 1½l, sht-hd, 2l, 1½l. 1m 23.50s. (14 Ran).
(Mrs Sarah Hughes), Edward Lynam

4185 Carrolls Handicap (Series Final) (3-y-o and up) £8,280 1¼m........ (3:00)

3826[8] PHASE IN [-] 3-9-10 M J Kinane (12)..............(6 to 1) 1
3854[2] NORDIC MINE (Ire) [-] 3-7-11 (2*) R M Burke (4).... (12 to 1) 2
3543* ISLAND VISION (Ire) [-] 3-9-2 W J Supple (10)...... (9 to 2) 3
3854[3] FONTANAYS (Ire) [-] 5-9-2 S Craine (6)..........(3 to 1 fav) 4
4136 MEJEVE [-] 5-9-10 (4*) C Everard (9)............. (12 to 1) 5
3914[6] SCOTSMAN'S BAY (Ire) [-] 4-8-7 N G McCullagh (13) (7 to 1) 6
3951 GLAS AGUS OR (Ire) [-] (bl) 3-8-9 (4*) J A Heffernan (5) ....(14 to 1) 7
3858[4] MORNING NURSE (Ire) [-] 4-9-1 R Hughes (8)......(9 to 1) 8
3543 PULMICORT [-] (bl) 3-9-2 P V Gilson (3).......... (10 to 1) 9
3854[4] ZORIA (Ire) [-] 5-8-8 (2*) P Carberry (14).......... (12 to 1) 10
3854 INAUGURATION (Ire) [-] 4-8-7 (4*) J J Behan (11)... (14 to 1) 11
4001[3] JUST ONE CANALETTO [-] 5-8-12 J F Egan (1)... (12 to 1) 12
4001 VICOSA (Ire) [-] 4-7-7 (2*) D G O'Shea (2)......... (16 to 1) 13
3576[9] DARK SWAN (Ire) [-] 3-8-3 (6*) R V Skelly (7)...... (20 to 1) su

Dist: 2l, sht-hd, 2l, 1l. 2m 16.40s. (14 Ran).
(Michael Hilary Burke), D K Weld

4186 Listowel Supporters Club Slan Abhaile QR Race (4-y-o and up) £6,900 2m........................... (4:30)

3336[4] DUHARRA (Ire) (bl) 5-11-5 (5*) Mr J A Nash (8)..(7 to 4 fav) 1
3915 EYELID 7-11-7 (7*) Mr D J Kavanagh (7)............(5 to 2) 2
2515[4] BACK DOOR JOHNNY 7-11-0 Mr J P Dempsey (4) (12 to 1) 3
TEMPLERAINEY (Ire) 5-11-3 Mr A P O'Brien (6)... (10 to 1) 4
3915[7] EBONY AND IVORY (Ire) 4-11-4 (7*) Mr J Connolly (2) ....(5 to 2) 5
4119[9] KARABAKH (Ire) 4-10-12 (5*) Mrs J M Mullins (3)... (8 to 1) 6
3773[6] INDIANA GOLD (Ire) 5-10-4 (7*) Ms W Fox (1)..... (50 to 1) 7

Dist: 1½l, nk, 3l, hd. 4m 0.80s. (7 Ran).
(Mrs M Togher), D K Weld

REDCAR (good)
Saturday September 25th
Going Correction: PLUS 0.05 sec. per fur.

4187 Reynard Selling Handicap Class G (0-60 3-y-o and up) £2,805 1¼m (2:00)

4104[3] ESSAYEFFSEE [51] 4-9-10 K Darley (17) *settled midfield, drvn alng to improve 2 fs out, kpt on to ld last strds.* ....(11 to 2 fav op 6 to 1 tchd 7 to 1) 1

3681[6] MERRY MERMAID [43] 3-8-7 (3*) S Maloney (9) *tucked away in midfield, improved to ld entering fnl furlong, ran on, jst ct*........ (7 to 1 op 5 to 1) 2

4104 DIAMOND INTHE DARK (USA) [39] (v) 5-8-12 J Weaver (8) *al hndy, drvn ahead wl o'r 2 fs out, hdd entering fnl furlong, one pace*.............. (16 to 1 tchd 20 to 1) 3

3868[3] MR LUCIANO (Ire) [49] (v) 3-9-2 A McGlone (1) *nvr far away, ev ch and rdn last 2 fs, kpt on same pace.* .... (10 to 1 op 7 to 1) 4

4104[9] YOUNG JASON [42] 10-9-1 R Lappin (11) *patiently rdn, chsd alng to improve last 2 fs, nrst finish.* .... (15 to 2 op 8 to 1) 5

3565[3] HOT PUNCH [37] 4-8-10 Dale Gibson (5) *trkd ldrs, effrt and rdn 2 fs out, kpt on same pace.* (10 to 1 op 7 to 1) 6

4049[6] YEVEED (Ire) [48] (bl) 3-9-1 M Birch (14) *wth ldr, led briefly 3 fs out, wknd und pres appr fnl furlong*......(10 to 1) 7

2972 ZONK [45] 3-8-7 (5*) J Tate (15) *chsd ldg bunch, effrt und pres o'r 2 fs out, not pace of ldrs.* .... (10 to 1 op 12 to 1 tchd 8 to 1) 8

1307 SPRAY OF ORCHIDS [40] 4-8-13 C Rutter (16) *nvr far away, rdn o'r 2 fs out, fdd*........(11 to 1 op 10 to 1) 9

4115[7] ROLY WALLACE [50] (bl) 4-9-9 M Wigham (2) *missed break, nvr able to reco'r*.................(20 to 1 op 16 to 1) 10

4104 STYLISH GENT [45] 6-9-4 J O'Reilly (6) *in tch, hrd drvn o'r 3 fs out, nvr dngrs*..............(20 to 1 op 16 to 1) 11

3489[6] TRANQUIL LADY (Ire) [51] 3-9-1 (3*) Stephen Davies (13) *slight ld till hdd 3 fs out, fdd 2 furlongs out*... (25 to 1) 12

3249[8] STRIKE-A-POSE [50] 3-9-3 G Duffield (3) *al tracking ldrs, rdn o'r 2 fs out, sn btn*..............(7 to 1 op 6 to 1) 13

4045[9] SPANISH PERFORMER [36] 4-8-9 N Connorton (7) *patiently rdn, steady hdwy on ins whn not clr run 3 fs out, eased when btn*...(8 to 1 op 12 to 1 tchd 14 to 1) 14

3788[4] HAWAYMYSON (Ire) [48] 3-9-1 Paul Eddery (4) *chsd ldrs till fdd o'r 3 fs out*.................. (14 to 1 op 16 to 1) 15

3689[5] GOTT'S DESIRE [39] (bl) 7-8-12 A Tucker (10) *took fierce hold, stopped pulling o'r 3 fs out, sn btn.* ....(8 to 1 op 7 to 1) 16

2631[7] UCKERBY MOOR [43] 4-8-9 (7*) V Halliday (12) *beh, whn slpd up appr strt*.......................... (20 to 1) su

Dist: Hd, 1½l, 1½l, 1½l, nk, 2l, ¾l, 1l, 3½l, 1½l. 2m 8.90s. a 7.70s (17 Ran).
SR: 38/23/22/23/19/13/14/9/8/ (Mrs S D Murray), Mrs M Reveley

4188 Cleveland Limited Stakes Class D (0-75 3-y-o and up) £3,728 1m 3f (2:30)

4107[6] KNOCK KNOCK 8-9-7 S O'Gorman (6) *patiently rdn, improved to join issue 3 fs out, led ins fnl furlong, ran on wl*........................ (9 to 2 op 4 to 1) 1

3623[4] GILDERDALE 11-9-0 (7*) M Henry (5) *patiently rdn, improved on outsd to ld o'r 2 fs out, hdd ins last, rallied*.......................... (14 to 1 op 12 to 1) 2

3646* SHIRLEY ROSE 3-8-9 J Weaver (4) *made most till hdd and rdn o'r 2 fs out, rallied gmely fnl furlong.* ....(4 to 1 op 3 to 1) 3

4036[4] SURE HAVEN (Ire) 4-9-7 G Duffield (7) *nvr far away, ev ch and rdn 2 fs out, kpt on same pace.* .... (12 to 1 op 14 to 1 tchd 10 to 1) 4

LARRIKIN (USA) 4-9-2 M Birch (3) *al pressing ldrs, effrt and drvn alng o'r 2 fs out, one pace.* ....(100 to 30 fav op 5 to 1) 5

3246[8] MONSIGNOR PAT (USA) 3-9-0 A McGlone (8) *tucked away on ins, ev ch 3 fs out, fdd wl o'r one furlong out.* ....(14 to 1) 6

4017[2] TRUBEN (USA) 4-8-9 (7*) R Havlin (9) *drvn alng to keep up hfwy, styd on und pres last 2 fs, nvr nrr.* .... (12 to 1 op 10 to 1) 7

4043[2] BLUE GROTTO (Ire) (v) 3-9-0 N Connorton (12) *wtd wth, improved on outsd to fltter entering strt, btn o'r 2 fs out*................................(8 to 1 op 7 to 1) 8

3630[4] EFIZIA 3-8-9 K Darley (10) *patiently rdn, effrt and drvn alng o'r 3 fs out, no imprsn*.......... (5 to 1 op 8 to 1) 9

3866[3] LAILATI (USA) 3-8-9 Paul Eddery (1) *dsptd ld for o'r 7 fs, fdd und pres 2 furlongs out*.......(16 to 1 op 12 to 1) 10

3821 BARBARY REEF (Ire) (bl) 5-9-7 A Mackay (2) *in tch, bustled alng to keep up hfwy, nvr a factor*..........(500 to 1) 11

3821 FAIRGROUNDPRINCESS 5-9-2 C Rutter (11) *sn struggling to keep up, lost tch entering strt*............ (200 to 1) 12

Dist: Hd, ½l, 1½l, 8l, nk, sht-hd, 2l, 6l, 7l, 4l. 2m 20.50s. a 5.10s (12 Ran).

SR: 62/61/48/57/36/33/34/28/11/ (G M Smart), I A Balding

4189 Northern Lights Rated Class B Handicap (0-95 3-y-o and up) £6,500 1¾m 19yds......................... (3:00)

3848[4] CASTLE COURAGEOUS [94] 6-9-7 K Darley (6) *patiently rdn, improved to ld 2 fs out, forged clr last 100 yards.* ....(7 to 2 op 3 to 1) 1
3675[3] GOOD HAND (USA) [82] 7-8-9 N Connorton (1) *last and outpcd hfwy, styd on grimly last 2 fs, not rch wnr.* .... (14 to 1 op 10 to 1) 2
3907[4] ALMAMZAR (USA) [84] 3-8-1 Paul Eddery (4) *nvr far away, nosed ahead briefly o'r 2 fs out, rdn and outpcd fnl furlong*................ (13 to 2 op 6 to 1 tchd 7 to 1) 3
3405[5] NOT IN DOUBT (USA) [93] 4-9-6 G Duffield (3) *led for 3 fs, led ag'n entering strt till o'r 2 furlongs out, fdd.* (9 to 2) 4
4064 CRYSTAL CROSS (USA) [80] 4-8-0 (7*) D Griffiths (7) *al in tch, effrt and rdn entering strt, outpcd last 2 fs.* .... (10 to 1 op 7 to 1) 5
3538* KAISER WILHELM [89] 4-9-2 A McGlone (5) *nvr far away, ev ch entering strt, fdd o'r 2 fs out.* .... (3 to 1 fav tchd 7 to 2) 6
4064[5] FRESCADE (USA) [80] 3-7-11 C Rutter (2) *led aftr 3 fs till entering strt, fdd und pres o'r 2 furlongs out*... (7 to 1) 7
MANAARAH (USA) [80] 3-7-11 J Fanning (8) *trkd ldrs, ev ch and rdn o'r 3 fs out, tld off last 2 furlongs.* .... (14 to 1 op 12 to 1) 8

Dist: 6l, 4l, 1½l, ½l, ¾l, 1½l, 12l. 3m 1.60s. a 5.10s (8 Ran).
SR: 63/39/23/39/25/32/10/-/ (Lady Mary Mumford), Lady Herries

4190 Tetley Tea Maiden Fillies' Stakes Class D (2-y-o) £3,991 7f........ (3:35)

TUFA 8-11 K Darley (7) *nvr far away, shaken up to ld wl ins fnl furlong, ran on well*.................... (5 to 1) 1
BABY LOVES 8-11 Paul Eddery (3) *wtd wth, drvn up to ld o'r one furlong out, hdd wl ins fnl furlong, kpt on.* ....(9 to 2 op 3 to 1) 2
3738[6] REALIZE 8-11 G Hind (12) *wl plcd stands side, effrt and drvn alng o'r 2 fs out, kpt on same pace*......(9 to 4 jt-fav op 2 to 1) 3
BLUSHINGBIRD (Ire) 8-11 A McGlone (2) *dictated pace for o'r 5 fs, no extr ins last*......................(9 to 4 jt-fav op 7 to 4 tchd 5 to 2) 4
MEGDALE (Ire) 8-11 N Connorton (13) *sluggish strt, pushed alng to improve hfwy, styd on, nrst finish.* .... (16 to 1 op 12 to 1 tchd 20 to 1) 5
DREAM LANE 8-8 (3*) S Maloney (4) *pushed alng to chase ldrs, rdn and no imprsn last 2 fs*... (50 to 1 op 20 to 1) 6
BECKENHAM LADY (Ire) 8-11 G Duffield (5) *wth ldr, hrd at work 2 fs out, fdd*................ (40 to 1 op 50 to 1) 7
2342[6] DUNSLOW ROAD 8-11 M Birch (10) *steadied strt, rcd freely centre for o'r 4 fs, fdd*.................. (33 to 1) 8
3792 DROP THE DONKEY 8-11 A Culhane (11) *in tch, feeling pace and drvn alng hfwy, nvr dngrs*........(100 to 1) 9
3422 A SUITABLE GIRL 8-11 A Mackay (9) *gd speed stands side for 5 fs, fdd*...................... (40 to 1 op 33 to 1) 10
CHAMPERS GALORE 8-6 (5*) J Tate (1) *gd speed in frnt rnk till wknd 2 fs out*............(100 to 1 op 50 to 1) 11
NILEGUNNER 8-6 (5*) A Garth (8) *wth ldrs stands side, wknd and hng badly lft o'r one furlong out, tld off.* ....(50 to 1) 12

Dist: Hd, 3l, 1½l, 3½l, 8l, 5l, 3l, hd, 2½l, 1l. 1m 26.80s. a 5.00s (12 Ran).
SR: 27/26/17/12/1/-/ (K Abdulla), R Charlton

4191 Transmore Van Hire Maiden Stakes Class D (3-y-o and up) £3,582 7f (4:15)

3909[7] NUMBER ONE SPOT 3-8-9 Paul Eddery (12) *trkd ldrs, shaken up to improve o'r one furlong out, ran on strly to ld last 50 yards*....... (4 to 1 op 7 to 2 tchd 9 to 2) 1
3957[9] DESERT CHAMP (USA) 4-8-13 (5*) J Tate (4) *tried to make all, veered lft entering fnl furlong, hdd and no extr last 50 yards*..................................(5 to 1 op 4 to 1) 2
3981[3] GREENBANK (USA) (v) 3-9-0 S O'Gorman (7) *nvr far away, effrt and drvn alng last 2 fs, not pace of ldg pair.* ....(9 to 1 op 8 to 1) 3
3839[2] JASARAH (Ire) 3-8-9 M Birch (13) *chsd ldrs, rdn 2 fs out, not quicken*.............. (2 to 1 fav op 3 to 1) 4
1212 NAFIHA (USA) 3-8-9 R Price (8) *al chasing ldrs, effrt and rdn o'r 2 fs out, one pace*.......... (11 to 2 op 5 to 1) 5
REMEESON 3-8-9[2] (7*) H Bastiman (15) *sn beh and drvn alng, kpt on wl last 2 fs, nvr dngrs.* .... (100 to 1 op 50 to 1) 6
872 CORN CIRCLE (Ire) 3-8-9 K Darley (14) *chsd alng in midfield, effrt o'r 2 fs out, nvr able to chal.* .... (16 to 1 op 12 to 1) 7
WOT NO PERKS 3-9-0 M Tebbutt (9) *settled midfield, drvn alng hfwy, nvr nr to chal*........ (25 to 1 op 10 to 1) 8
3789[4] NO CONTRACT (USA) 3-9-0 G Hind (1) *speed on outsd till fdd und pres 2 fs out*............. (11 to 1 op 10 to 1) 9
GYMCRAK DIAMOND (Ire) 3-9-0 Julie Bowker (11) *sluggish strt, nvr able to reco'r*........ (66 to 1 op 50 to 1) 10
3789[6] TARNSIDE BANKER 3-9-0 G Duffield (10) *outpcd and drvn alng, nvr a threat*........................... (16 to 1) 11
2464 JARIN ROSE (Ire) 3-8-4 (5*) A Garth (3) *drvn alng on outsd, swshd tail und pres hfwy, sn lost tch*........ (200 to 1) 12
GOLD FORT (bl) 3-8-7 (7*) G Parkin (5) *chsd ldrs, drvn alng in midfield hfwy, sn lost tch*................. (50 to 1) 13
1850[4] MILLEMAY 3-8-9 J Weaver (6) *early speed, struggling to hold pl hfwy, sn lost tch*............................(50 to 1) 14
4047[9] SILVER WILL 3-8-11 (3*) S Maloney (2) *broke wl to show speed to hfwy, sn lost tch*............................(50 to 1) 15

Dist: 1½l, 7l, ½l, 8l, 1l, 2l, 1l, 2½l, 7l, 2l. 1m 25.40s. a 3.60s (15 Ran).
SR: 46/50/25/18/-/-/ (Helena Springfield Ltd), R Charlton

4192 EBF Reg Boyle Bookmakers Maiden Stakes Class D (2-y-o) £4,127 1m 1f .... (4:45)

DOUBLE TRIGGER (Ire) 9-0 J Weaver (3) *patiently rdn, swtchd frm midfield to improve hfwy, led 2 fs out, forged clr fnl furlong*...........(14 to 1 op 7 to 1) 1
3554[4] GOLDEN HELLO 9-0 M Birch (1) *trkd ldg trio, drvn alng o'r 2 fs out, styd on, no ch wth wnr.* .... (11 to 10 fav op 5 to 4 on tchd 6 to 5) 2
3627[6] OPUS ONE 8-9 N Connorton (4) *al hndy, led briefly o'r 2 fs out, kpt on same pace fnl furlong.* ....(6 to 1 op 4 to 1 tchd 7 to 1) 3
3819[8] PERSIAN LINNET 9-0 K Darley (6) *dictated pace till hdd o'r 2 fs out, grad wknd*............... (12 to 1 op 14 to 1) 4
FROM THE LEFT (Ire) 9-0 Paul Eddery (7) *stumbled leaving stalls, drvn up frm last pl entering strt, no imprsn last 2 fs*.................................(14 to 1 op 7 to 1) 5
NORAGAN 9-0 G Duffield (9) *trkd ldrs, feeling pace and rdn o'r 2 fs out, sn btn*..............(16 to 1 op 12 to 1) 6
3908[4] CLARION CALL (Ire) 9-0 C Rutter (8) *trkd ldg pair, rdn o'r 2 fs out, sn btn*............(7 to 2 op 4 to 1 tchd 9 to 2) 7
CORSAGE 8-11 (3*) S Maloney (2) *chsd ldrs, drvn alng o'r 2 fs out, sn lost tch*............... (33 to 1 op 20 to 1) 8
GIMLICK 8-9 A Culhane (5) *pressed ldrs, struggling to hold pl o'r 2 fs out, sn btn*........ (66 to 1 op 50 to 1) 9

Dist: 10l, 3l, 4l, nk, ½l, 3l, 12l, 1½l. 1m 53.90s. a 5.40s (9 Ran).
SR: 26/6/-/-/-/-/ (R W Huggins), M Johnston

4193 Bridlington Nursery Class E (2-y-o) £3,442 5f...................... (5:15)

2886[5] ALLWIGHT THEN (Ire) [78] 9-5 Paul Eddery (7) *al hndy, led hfwy, ran on strly fnl furlong*... (4 to 1 fav op 8 to 1) 1
4042[2] KING RAT (Ire) [70] 8-11 J Weaver (6) *nvr far away, determined effrt entering fnl furlong, kpt on wl.* .... (11 to 2 op 5 to 1) 2
4105* LUCKY MESSAGE (USA) [72] 8-13 (5ex) M Birch (18) *settled midfield, improved o'r one furlong out, kpt on und pres fnl furlong*........................(8 to 1 op 7 to 1) 3
4042* RESONANT [80] 9-7 G Duffield (4) *nvr far away, led briefly appr hfwy, kpt on same pace fnl furlong.* ....(6 to 1 op 5 to 1) 4
2102[6] ORIENTAL AIR (Ire) [62] 8-3 Dale Gibson (10) *chsd alng to go pace, styd on appr fnl furlong, nrst finish.* .... (12 to 1 op 10 to 1) 5
3990 JUST FLAMENCO [60] 8-1 D Biggs (17) *drvn alng to keep up, improved last 2 fs, ran on, nvr nrr.* .... (8 to 1 op 10 to 1) 6
3845 LADY SHERIFF [77] (bl) 9-4 K Darley (2) *gd speed in frnt rnk for o'r 3 fs, no extr*.............. (14 to 1 op 12 to 1) 7
3532[5] MADAME GREGOIRE [52] 7-0 (7*) C Adamson (16) *bustled alng in midfield, kpt on same pace last 2 fs.* .... (14 to 1 op 12 to 1) 8
4021[5] LANCASHIRE LIFE (Ire) [56] 7-11[3] S O'Gorman (9) *chsd alng in midfield, not pace of ldrs last 2 fs.* .... (25 to 1 op 20 to 1) 9
3715 BOLLIN MARY [63] 8-1 (3*) S Maloney (13) *chsd alng, effrt whn not clr run hfwy, nvr able to chal.* .... (14 to 1 op 10 to 1) 10
3978[4] SARMATIAN (USA) [68] 8-9 A McGlone (15) *chsd alng in midfield, nvr a serious threat*........(8 to 1 op 7 to 1) 11
3566 MAD ABOUT MEN [53] 7-1 (7*) P Fessey (5) *missed break, nvr able to reco'r*..............(25 to 1 op 16 to 1) 12
3086[7] OLD HOOK (Ire) [60] 8-1 A Mackay (11) *chsd ldrs to hfwy, sn btn*.......................... (16 to 1 op 10 to 1) 13
3566[7] RED GRIT (Ire) [52] (v) 7-7 J O'Reilly (14) *sluggish strt, nvr able to reco'r*................................ (33 to 1) 14
3183[4] DAUNTLESS FORT [57] 7-12 A Tucker (8) *drvn alng in midfield, outpcd frm hfwy*........(25 to 1 op 20 to 1) 15
3673[9] KAYDARAJ [54] 7-7[3] (5*) A Garth (3) *broke wl to ld hfwy, wknd o'r one furlong out*.........(33 to 1 op 25 to 1) 16
3815[6] CHEEKY CHAPPY [54] (bl) 7-9 J Fanning (1) *gd speed on outsd to hfwy, sn btn*............................(20 to 1) 17

Dist: 1l, 1l, 2½l, ¾l, hd, ¾l, nk, 2l, 1l, 1½l. 59.80s. a 3.10s (17 Ran).
SR: 48/36/34/32/11/8/22/-/-/ (P J Cosgrove), F H Lee

COLOGNE (GER) (heavy) Saturday September 25th

4194 Grosser Kaufhof Preis (Group 2) (3-y-o and up) £29,592 1m......... (3:40)

3717[3] NASR ALLAH (USA) 3-8-9 A Starke, *3rd strt, led 2 fs out, ran on wl*.. 1

3703[4] TROPICAL KING (Ger) 3-8-9 M Rimmer, ... 2
1882[7] LASKO (Ger) 3-8-9 M Hofer, *rear early, ran on wl fnl 2 fs, nvr nrr*......... 3
JOHN ROSE 4-9-2 T Hellier, *mid-div, nrst finish*......... 4
3703[8] TIMELY THREAT (USA) 3-8-12 N Grant, *prmnt, second hfwy, no extr 2 fs out*......... 5
ANDINO (Ger) 3-8-9 S Eccles, *led till wknd 2 fs out*....... 6
WILL OF STEEL (Fr) 4-9-2 M Trinker, *nvr dngrs*........... 7
MARS (Su) 4-9-2 A Tylicki, *second till wknd quickly hfwy*. 8
1882[6] MEERWIND (Ger) 4-9-2 G Bocskai, *al beh*.............. 9
3208* ENHARMONIC (USA) 6-9-4 K Woodburn, *al beh*........... 10
Dist: 1½l, 3½l, 1½l, 2l, 4l, 6l, 10l, 1½l. 1m 43.88s. (10 Ran).
(Stall Mabrouk), F Scheffer

EVRY (FR) (soft)
Saturday September 25th
Going Correction: PLUS 0.05 sec. per fur. (race 1), PLUS 0.70 (2)

4195 Criterium d'Evry (Listed) (2-y-o) £14,337 6f..................... (2:45)

3799* KEY OF LUCK (USA) 9-2 F Head, ... 1
3651[4] ETERNAL REVE (USA) 8-10 G Mosse, ... 2
3014[6] FILHA DO AR (USA) 8-6 O Peslier, ... 3
3338[3] WEST MAN (USA) 8-9 M Boutin, ... 4
3799[2] EAGLE EYED (USA) 8-9 T Jarnet, ... 5
3803[2] ULTIMO IMPERATORE 8-9 D Holland, *rcd in 4th, rdn 2 and a half fs out, eased whn btn fnl furlong*............... 6
Dist: Nose, 2l, 1l, 3l, 3l. 1m 12.79s. a 2.49s (6 Ran).
SR: 58/51/39/38/26/14/ (Mme F Boutin), F Boutin

4196 Prix du Lion d'Angers (Listed) (3-y-o) £14,337 1¼m.................. (3:55)

TOT OU TARD (Ire) 8-12 O Peslier, ... 1
SOVETSKY 8-12 T Jarnet, ... 2
2208[3] EMBROS (USA) 8-12 G Mosse, ... 3
3583* BEDAVA (Fr) 9-2 N Jeanpierre, ... 4
958[5] WOOTTON RIVERS (USA) 8-12 D Holland, *rear till ran on fnl one and a half fs*............ 5
3337[6] IRISH PROSPECTOR (Fr) 8-12 D Boeuf, ... 6
3583[2] EXTRA POINT 8-12 W Mongril, ... 7
1149[7] OKEEDOKEE (Fr) 8-12 O Doleuze, ... 8
VERSAINVILLE (Fr) 8-12 F Head, ... 9
201* PRINCE DIANON (Fr) 8-12 A Bredillet, ... 0
1410[7] PALAIROS (Fr) 8-12 G Guignard, ... 0
JUST IN TIME (Fr) 8-12 G Dubroeucq, ... 0
Dist: ¾l, ¾l, 1½l, ½l, nk, sht-hd, 4l, ¾l, sht-nk. 2m 14.03s. a 10.03s (12 Ran).
SR: 68/66/64/65/60/59/58/50/48/ (M Kura), Y Porzier

CAPANNELLE (ITY) (soft)
Sunday September 26th

4197 Premio Divino Amore (Listed) (2-y-o) £20,173 5f...................... (2:25)

2260[4] LATE PARADE (Ire) 8-8 Jacqueline Freda, ... 1
3515[7] FRED BONGUSTO (Ire) 9-2 B Jovine, ... 2
3014[8] ANGEL OF THE NIGHT (USA) 8-8 F Jovine, ... 3
3898[5] ISABELLA SHARP 8-5 M Hills, *al mid-div*............... 4
2649 BISCUITER (Ire) 8-8 A Luongo, ... 5
LUCIFIC (Ire) 8-5 M Pasquale, ... 6
3875* KATHY FAIRUZ (Ire) 8-5 A Corniani, ... 7
Dist: 5l, 2l, ¾l, 1l, ¾l, 1l. 58.20s. (7 Ran).
(A J B Stable), A Renzoni

4198 Premio Rumon (Listed) (2-y-o) £20,173 1m............................ (3:15)

2649[2] LEAR WHITE (USA) 8-8 V Mezzatesta, ... 1
2649[5] SUGARLAND EXPRESS (Ire) 8-8 W Ryan, ... 2
1647[6] GOLDEN BENGAL (USA) 8-8 A Luongo, ... 3
3798[4] STONY BEST (Ire) 8-8 B Jovine, ... 4
SIR DANCER (Ire) 8-8 D Zarroli, ... 5
3478* ISLAND MAGIC 9-1 Jacqueline Freda, *led o'r 3 fs out, wknd quickly 2 out*.......... 6
2649[4] SECRELLY (USA) 8-8 L Ficuciello, ... 7
Dist: 1l, sht-hd, 3l, 6l, 2l, 4l. 1m 41.20s. (7 Ran).
(Scuderia General Horse), F Brogi

4199 Premio Lydia Tesio (Group 2) (3-y-o and up) £43,553 1¼m...........(3:40)

3206[7] PRACER (USA) 3-8-8 O Poirier, *made all, quickened one and a half fs out, ran on wl*.............. 1
3920* MIDNIGHT HEIGHTS 3-8-8 W Ryan, *5th strt, ev ch one and a half fs out, kpt on one pace fnl furlong*............. 2
3963* FORTHWITH 3-8-8 M Hills, *trkd ldr, second strt, chlgd 3 fs out, ev ch one and a half out, kpt on*............... 3
3920[2] ROSE VIOLET (USA) 3-8-8 F Jovine, *3rd strt, outpcd wl o'r one furlong out, rallied fnl furlong, fnshd well*........ 4
3920[3] DAMA GRANDE 4-9-0 G Bietolini, *hdwy into 4th strt, wknd 2 fs out*.......................... 5
3920[6] FIRM FRIEND (Ire) 3-8-8 Jacqueline Freda, *al rear*......... 6
SEEING (USA) 3-8-8 M Vargiu, *nvr able to chal*.......... 7
Dist: 1 ¼l, hd, nk, 7l, nk, 20l. 2m 4.20s. (7 Ran).
(G Borghi), A de Royer Dupre

COLOGNE (GER) (heavy)
Sunday September 26th

4200 Iduna Nova Flieger Preis (Listed) (2-y-o and up) £8,163 5f........... (2:40)

3912[3] PALACEGATE EPISODE (Ire) 3-9-5 J Carroll, *made all, pushed out fnl furlong*.............. 1
2242[7] FLEET FOR EUROPE 4-9-12 A Bond, ... 2
3717[9] MONTEPULCIANO (USA) 4-9-12 G Bocskai, ... 3
VICEROY 6-9-12 T Hellier, ... 4
3936 HATTA FORT 6-9-12 A Boschert, ... 5
3936 PARIOS (Fr) 5-9-12 K Woodburn, ... 6
PARK DANCE 3-9-5 M Hofer, ... 7
Dist: 1 ¼l, 3½l, sht-hd, nk, 2l, 7l. 1m 0.41s. (7 Ran).
(Palacegate Corporation Ltd), J Berry

4201 EMS Kurierpost Europa Preis (Group 1) (3-y-o and up) £122,449 1½m (3:55)

3370* MONSUN (Ger) 3-8-10 A Tylicki, *trkd ldr, led 3 fs out, ran on wl fnl furlong*............ 1
3371* KORNADO 3-8-10 M Rimmer, *rcd in 4th, 5th strt, chlgd 2 fs out, one pace fnl furlong*.......... 2
3647* STERNKONIG (Ire) 3-8-10 N Grant, *hld up, 6th strt, ran on fnl 2 fs*.............. 3
4055[6] SNURGE 6-9-6 T Quinn, *rcd in 3rd, second strt, one pace appr fnl furlong*.............. 4
3370[8] PROTEKTOR (Ger) 4-9-6 T Hellier, *led till 3 fs out*......... 5
3516[5] EMBARCADERO (Ger) 5-9-6 P Schiergen, *4th strt, sn wknd*.............. 6
GIMN (Su) 3-8-10 D Ilic, *al beh*........................ 7
3929[9] CHESA PLANA 4-9-2 A Best, *al rear*..................... 8
Dist: 3½l, 4l, 1 ¼l, ¾l, 1½l, 4l, 4½l. 2m 42.23s. (8 Ran).
(Baron G Von Ullmann), H Jentzsch

DUINDIGT (HOL) (heavy)
Sunday September 26th

4202 Central Beheer Grote Prijs der Nederlanden (3-y-o and up) £10,870 1 ¼m 110yds.........................

3424[6] BLACKPATCH HILL 4-9-4 Paul Eddery, *mid-div, rdn one and a half fs out, led o'r one out, cmftbly*............ 1
VIBRACOX 3-8-7 C Phelippeau, ... 2
DOLLAR'S PERSIA (Ire) 3-8-3 M Watlow, ... 3
Dist: 1½l, 2½l, 11l, 20l, 11l, nose. 2m 22.10s. (10 Ran).
(J L Dunlop), J L Dunlop

MERANO (ITY) (heavy)
Sunday September 26th

4203 Premio Racines (3-y-o and up) £8,966 1½m...............................

1178[3] FORMATO UNI (Ire) 3-8-6 C Colombi, *rcd in second, led jst o'r 2 fs out, ran on wl*.............. 1
3921[4] ALMANOR 4-9-2 P Yanez, ... 2
DIAMOND (Pol) 3-8-6 E Mezzo, ... 3
Dist: 1 ¾l, dist, 6l, dist. (Time not taken) (5 Ran).
(Gerecon Italia), J L Dunlop

4204 Premio Europa (2-y-o) £8,966 1m.....

ALASTOR (Fr) 8-10 E Mezzo, ... 1
JESSI-JANE (Pol) 8-9 W Lord, ... 2
2836[7] TECHNICOLORED 8-5 C Colombi, ... 3
Dist: 10l, sht-hd, 1l, ½l, 10l, 2l, 6l, 15l, 10l. (Time not taken) (11 Ran).
(Scuderia San Bartolomeo), G Verricelli

OVREVOLL (NOR) (soft)
Sunday September 26th

4205 Oslo Cup (Group 3) (3-y-o and up) £19,102 1½m.......................

KATEB (Ire) 4-9-4 K Andersen, ... 1
3848[5] CHIEF MINISTER (Ire) 4-9-4 P Harley, *al prmnt, led 2 fs out till 100 yards out, ran on wl*............ 2
REGAL PARADE 9-9-4 J Tandari, ... 3
Dist: Hd, 7l, 4½l, 6½l, 1½l, 2l, 1½l, 5l, 20l. 2m 41.50s. (13 Ran).
(Hamdan Al-Maktoum), R W Armstrong

BATH (good)
Monday September 27th
Going Correction: MINUS 0.15 sec. per fur.

4206 Aldie Apprentice Maiden Handicap Class E (0-75 3-y-o and up) £2,847 1m 5yds. . . . . (1:35)

3233^{3} MY MINNIE [51] 3-8-2 S Drowne (9) *sn tracking ldrs, led 2 and a half fs out, cmftbly*. . . . . (5 to 1 op 11 to 4) 1
4126^{2} RAFTERS [73] 4-10-0 S Giles (2) *sn prmnt, chsd wnr fnl 2 fs, no imprsn*. . . . . (4 to 1 jt-fav op 11 to 4) 2
4115 TOUT DE VAL [38] 4-7-5^{3} (5*) A Whelan (10) *slwly into strd, sn in tch, hdwy 2 fs out, one pace appr last.* . . . . (16 to 1 op 10 to 1 tchd 20 to 1) 3
4007^{6} SPRING SAINT [47] (bl) 4-8-2 P McCabe (6) *beh, hrd drvn frm o'r 3 fs out, nrst finish*. . . . . (4 to 1 jt-fav op 5 to 1 tchd 100 to 30) 4
3938^{2} ALL THE GIRLS (Ire) [38] 4-7-0 (7*) F Savage (5) *mid-div and rdn hfwy, nvr dngrs*. . . . . (5 to 1 op 4 to 1 tchd 6 to 1) 5
3988^{6} ELTARA [56] 3-8-7 M Humphries (7) *al mid-div.* . . . . (6 to 1 op 5 to 1) 6
2576^{9} MIM [42] 3-7-7 N Varley (1) *beh most of way.* . . . . (20 to 1 op 10 to 1) 7
4022 BOLD STAR [56] 3-8-2 (5*) J Dennis (8) *al beh.* . . . . (16 to 1 op 10 to 1 tchd 20 to 1) 8
3887 WHATEVER'S RIGHT (Ire) [47] (bl) 4-7-11 (5*) A Lakeman (3) *led till hdd and wknd rpdly 2 and a half fs out.* . . . . (16 to 1 op 8 to 1) 9
2350^{8} WESSEX MILORD [40] (bl) 8-7-9^{9} (7*) W Hawksley (4) *chsd ldrs for o'r 4 fs, wknd quickly*. . . . . (50 to 1 op 20 to 1) 10

Dist: 6l, 3l, 2½l, 2½l, 2½l, sht-hd, 2l, 2½l, 10l. 1m 41.10s. a 2.10s (10 Ran).
SR: 39/47/3/4/-/-/ (Mrs W Protheroe-Beynon), R J Hodges

4207 Morris Dancer Conditions Stakes Class C (3-y-o and up) £4,501 1m 5yds . . . . (2:05)

4005^{6} DESERT SHOT 3-8-12 R Cochrane (4) *in tch, chsd ldr 4 fs out, led 2 out, drvn out.* . . . . (9 to 4 fav op 2 to 1 tchd 11 to 4) 1
3878^{5} GEISWAY (Can) 3-9-5 J Reid (2) *led to 2 fs out, rdn and styd on und pres frm o'r one out.* . . . . (11 to 4 op 2 to 1 tchd 3 to 1) 2
3892^{4} BASHAYER (USA) (bl) 3-8-7 W Carson (3) *chsd ldr 4 fs, rdn 3 out, kpt on fnl furlong*. . . . . (4 to 1 tchd 9 to 2) 3
4005^{7} KNOCK TO ENTER (USA) 5-9-2 J Williams (1) *al 4th, rdn and one pace fnl 2 fs.* (16 to 1 op 12 to 1 tchd 20 to 1) 4
3897^{9} PAY HOMAGE 5-9-12 L Dettori (5) *hld up, effrt 2 fs out, btn fnl furlong*. . . . . (11 to 4 op 5 to 2) 5

Dist: 3l, 1l, hd, sht-hd. 1m 42.70s. a 3.70s (5 Ran).
SR: 25/23/8/16/25/ (Maktoum Al Maktoum), M R Stoute

4208 EBF Dodington Maiden Stakes Class D (2-y-o) £4,175 1¼m 46yds. . . . . (2:35)

2502 BLAAZIING JOE (Ire) 9-0 T Quinn (3) *trkd ldrs, slight ld 2 and a half fs out, hdd two out, rallied to lead ins last, drvn out*. . . . . (8 to 1 op 5 to 1 tchd 10 to 1) 1
3997^{2} ZUBOON (USA) 9-0 W Carson (13) *str hold, prmnt, led gng wl 2 fs out, hdd ins last, rdn and no extr.* . . . . (Evens fav tchd 5 to 4) 2
3876 ASTRAL INVASION (USA) 9-0 J Reid (6) *beh, hdwy 4 fs out, styd on same pace frm 2 out*. . . . . (5 to 1 op 4 to 1) 3
3940^{9} NORTHERN STARLIGHT (v) 9-0 J Williams (14) *str hold, prmnt, kpt on same pace fnl 3 fs*. . . (33 to 1 op 20 to 1) 4
3908^{5} VINTAGE TIMES 9-0 D Biggs (10) *hdwy o'r 2 fs out, styd on one pace*. . . . . (10 to 1 op 7 to 1) 5
3760^{8} TOMMY COOPER 9-0 W Newnes (11) *chsd ldrs, wknd o'r 2 fs out*. . . . . (50 to 1 op 33 to 1) 6
3959^{4} DEBLYN 9-0 G Duffield (12) *led to 2 and a half fs out, wknd rpdly*. . . . . (33 to 1 op 20 to 1 tchd 50 to 1) 7
4067 MISTER MAYBE 9-0 A McGlone (1) *chsd ldrs 6 fs.* . . . . (16 to 1 op 10 to 1) 8
3446 BODANTREE 8-9 (5*) V Slattery (5) *al beh.* . . . . (66 to 1 op 33 to 1) 9
3968^{5} RITA'S JOY 8-4 (5*) P McCabe (15) *prmnt 6 fs*. . . . . (33 to 1) 10
3828 ST KITTS 8-9 T Sprake (2) *prmnt to hfwy.* . . . . (66 to 1 op 20 to 1) 11
LITTLE BROOK 9-0 R Perham (9) *chsd ldrs, faltered 5 fs out, wknd quickly*. . . . . (66 to 1 op 33 to 1) 12
3908^{7} MAJOR CLINTON 9-0 L Dettori (7) *in tch 5 fs.* . . . . (10 to 1 op 9 to 2 tchd 12 to 1) 13
4099 BRIDIE'S PRIDE 9-0 N Adams (4) *al beh.* . . . . (66 to 1 op 33 to 1) 14
4098 L'AVENTURE (Ire) (bl) 9-0 T Rogers (8) *dwlt, sn drvn to chase ldrs, wknd quickly 5 fs out.* (66 to 1 op 25 to 1) 15

Dist: Nk, 8l, 12l, 2l, ½l, 1l, nk, ½l, ¾l, 4l. 2m 12.50s. a 6.10s (15 Ran).
SR: 24/23/7/-/-/-/ (Mrs Linda Gardiner), P F I Cole

4209 Mere Maiden Stakes Class D (3-y-o and up) £4,045 1¼m 46yds. . . . . . (3:05)

1911^{3} DUKRAME 3-8-7 W Newnes (3) *hld up mid-div, str run 2 fs out to ld ins last, cmftbly*. . . . . (5 to 1 co-fav op 4 to 1) 1
FAWARAN (USA) 3-8-12 W Carson (6) *in tch, led 2 fs out, shaken up appr one out, hdd and outpcd ins last.* . . . . (5 to 1 co-fav op 5 to 2 tchd 11 to 2) 2
ULTIMATE WARRIOR 3-8-12 D Biggs (13) *chsd ldrs, styd on same pace fnl 2 fs*. . . . . (25 to 1 op 14 to 1) 3
3491^{4} BAWAETH (USA) 3-8-7 M Hills (15) *led to 3 and a half fs out, sn one pace*. . . . . (6 to 1) 4
3850^{4} LANKRIDGE 3-8-12 J Reid (14) *sn prmnt, led 3 and a half fs out to 2 out, wknd fnl furlong*. . . . . (5 to 1 co-fav) 5
MASTER MURPHY 4-9-4 J Williams (10) *slwly into strd, moderate prog fnl 2 fs*. . . . . (33 to 1 op 25 to 1) 6
4110^{5} PRINCESS SIOUX 3-8-7 G Duffield (8) *pressed ldrs till wknd 3 fs out*. . . . . (5 to 1 co-fav op 4 to 1) 7
4788a HASTY SPARK 5-9-1 (3*) Stephen Davies (7) *prmnt till wknd o'r 2 fs out*. . . . . (50 to 1 op 20 to 1) 8
3893^{6} EASY TOUCH 3-8-7 S Whitworth (1) *chsd ldrs 6 fs.* . . . . (33 to 1 op 25 to 1) 9
BUNDERBURG (USA) 3-8-12 D Holland (11) *pressed ldrs, rdn whn hmpd and snatched up o'r 4 fs out.* . . . . (6 to 1 op 4 to 1) 10
825 HARD EIGHT 3-8-12 A McGlone (12) *al beh.* . . . . (25 to 1 op 14 to 1) 11
SPIKE 3-8-12 T Rogers (5) *al beh*. . . . (50 to 1 op 33 to 1) 12
2937 EUSTATIA 3-8-7 C Rutter (4) *hdwy 6 fs out, wknd o'r 3 out.* . . . . (50 to 1 op 33 to 1) 13
2596^{6} SYLVIA MACUSHLA 3-8-7 T Quinn (2) *al beh.* . . . . (33 to 1 op 25 to 1) 14
DISTANT MILL (Ire) 5-9-5^{6} (5*) D Meredith (9) *slwly into strd, al beh*. . . . . (50 to 1 op 33 to 1) 15

Dist: 2l, 4l, hd, 2l, 8l, 5l, 4l, ¾l, ½l, 8l. 2m 12.50s. a 6.10s (15 Ran).
SR: 17/18/10/4/5/-/ (P G Goulandris), H Candy

4210 Tattersalls Maiden Auction Series Stakes Qualifier Class D (2-y-o) £3,379 5f 11yds. . . . . (3:35)

DOMINION KING 8-6 T Quinn (3) *chsd ldrs, led jst ins fnl furlong, drvn out*. . . . . (33 to 1 op 25 to 1) 1
SALVEZZA (Ire) 7-12 (3*) Stephen Davies (7) *mid-div, drvn alng hfwy, rapid hdwy ins last, jst fld.* . . . . (11 to 8 fav op 2 to 1) 2
4105^{2} MR BERGERAC (Ire) 8-6 D Holland (5) *chsd ldrs, rdn and styd on fnl furlong*. . . . . (14 to 1 op 12 to 1) 3
3633^{2} HIGH HOLME (v) 8-6 G Duffield (10) *led till jst ins fnl furlong, sn outpcd*. . . . . (5 to 1 op 7 to 2) 4
3520^{4} VENUS VICTORIOUS (Ire) 8-7 M Hills (2) *chsd ldrs till outpcd appr fnl furlong.* (10 to 1 op 6 to 1 tchd 11 to 1) 5
4067 EVANRO (Ire) 8-6 J Reid (14) *pressed ldrs, one pace fnl 2 fs.* . . . . (33 to 1 op 25 to 1) 6
BONNY MELODY 7-8 (7*) N Varley (9) *nvr rch ldrs.* . . . . (33 to 1 op 20 to 1) 7
3816^{9} LEVIATHAN MYSTERY 8-7 J Williams (13) *outpcd, nrst finish*. . . . . (25 to 1 op 12 to 1 tchd 33 to 1) 8
3982 CLASSICAL (Ire) 8-5 (3*) B Doyle (4) *outpcd most of way.* . . . . (33 to 1 op 25 to 1) 9
3941^{3} PHONEAHOLIC (Ire) 8-7 B Rouse (11) *pressed ldrs, rdn o'r 2 fs out, wknd quickly one and a half out.* . . . . (10 to 1 op 7 to 1) 10
MINNIE NORTH 8-1 T Sprake (12) *outpcd most of way.* . . . . (33 to 1) 11
3958^{2} JAYANNPEE 8-9 L Dettori (8) *in tch, rdn hfwy, wknd 2 fs out*. . . . . (7 to 2 tchd 3 to 1) 12
3816^{2} LA RESIDENCE 8-7 N Adams (1) *sn outpcd.* . . . . (11 to 1 op 7 to 1 tchd 12 to 1) 13
3728^{4} CLUBS ARE TRUMPS (Ire) 8-7 R Cochrane (15) *outpcd.* . . . . (33 to 1) 14
3816 SPANISH DAWN 8-4 C Rutter (6) *sn outpcd.* . . . . (33 to 1 op 12 to 1) 15

Dist: ½l, hd, 2½l, ½l, 1l, ½l, 3l, ½l, 1½l, ¾l. 1m 2.60s. a 2.10s (15 Ran).
SR: 35/28/32/22/21/16/9/3/2/ (Mrs D E Kaine), B A McMahon

4211 Farleaze Fillies' Conditions Stakes Class D (2-y-o) £3,557 5f 11yds. . (4:05)

3941* REASON TO DANCE 8-12 R Cochrane (4) *in tch, shaken up and swtchd rght one furlong out, quickened to ld nr finish.* . . (6 to 5 on op 11 to 10 on tchd 5 to 4 on and Evens) 1
3357^{5} EVENING FALLS 9-2 J Reid (6) *chsd ldr, led 2 fs out, edgd lft one out, ct cl hme*. . . . . (4 to 1 op 100 to 30) 2
CROESO-I-CYMRU 8-8 T Quinn (3) *pressed ldrs, ev ch 2 fs out till outpcd ins last*. . . . . (25 to 1 op 20 to 1) 3
3905^{6} SWEET DECISION (Ire) 8-8 J Williams (5) *reared strt, some prog appr fnl furlong, nrst finish.* . . . . (8 to 1 op 5 to 1 tchd 9 to 1) 4
PUELLA BONA 8-8 D Holland (1) *nvr trble ldrs.* . . . . (7 to 1 op 9 to 2 tchd 8 to 1) 5
3894^{6} INDIAHRA 8-12 S Perks (2) *led to 2 fs out, sn outpcd.* . . . . (5 to 1 op 4 to 1) 6

Dist: 1l, nk, 3l, 1½l, ½l. 1m 3.00s. a 2.50s (6 Ran).
SR: 33/33/24/12/6/8/ (Mrs D Joly), D R C Elsworth

4212 Westmoreland Handicap Class D (0-80 3-y-o and up) £4,305 2m 1f 34yds (4:35)

4013^{6} GREEN LANE (USA) [72] 5-9-11 J Reid (7) *mid-div, hdwy o'r 3 fs out, led 2 out, pushed out*. . . (13 to 2 op 8 to 1) 1
3907^{5} ELBURG (Ire) [71] 3-8-12 L Dettori (16) *beh, hdwy 3 fs out, ran on fnl furlong, no ch wth wnr.* (14 to 1 op 16 to 1) 2
3907^{2} BARDOLPH (USA) [70] 6-9-9 T Quinn (4) *prmnt, led o'r 3 fs out to 2 out, sn one pace*. . . . . . (6 to 1 jt-fav op 7 to 1) 3

3998[4] THE WHERE WITHAL [76] (bl) 3-9-3 G Duffield (10) *hld lup, hdwy o'r 3 fs out, no imprsn frm 2 out.* .... (15 to 2 op 5 to 1 tchd 8 to 1) 4
420[5] SCOTONI [45] 7-7-12 D Biggs (12) *chsd ldrs, pushed alng hfwy, no imprsn fnl 3 fs*.......... (25 to 1 op 20 to 1) 5
3868[6] COMBELLINO [58] 3-7-13 C Rutter (11) *prmnt, chsd ldrs 3 fs out, sn wknd*.................. (33 to 1 op 20 to 1) 6
3690[7] PATROCLUS [40] 8-7-7 N Adams (2) *beh, pushed alng hfwy, nrst finish*.................. (50 to 1 op 33 to 1) 7
3971* RIVIERE ACTOR (USA) [72] 3-8-13 W Carson (1) *mid-div most of way*.................. (6 to 1 jt-fav op 9 to 2) 8
3937[6] SPANISH SAHARA (Ire) [70] 3-8-11 D Holland (3) *hdwy hfwy, wknd 4 fs out*............... (14 to 1 op 12 to 1) 9
4064 KADASTROF (Fr) [74] 3-9-1 R Cochrane (14) *prmnt till wknd 4 fs out*......... (10 to 1 op 8 to 1 tchd 11 to 1) 10
3479 CHUCKLESTONE [62] 10-9-1 S Whitworth (13) *chsd ldrs, sn pushed alng, wkng whn hmpd 5 fs out.* .... (11 to 1 op 8 to 1) 11
3761 SO SAUCY [55] 3-7-10[3] (3*) B Doyle (6) *led till o'r 4 fs out, sn wknd*.......................... (20 to 1 op 16 to 1) 12
2865[4] DAZZLING FIRE (Ire) [40] 4-7-7 Kim McDonnell (17) *beh most of way*.................................... (33 to 1) 13
3690[4] SPECTACULAR DAWN [75] 4-10-0 M Hills (8) *prmnt, wth ldrs hfwy, led o'r 4 fs out till over 3 out, wknd quickly.* .... (11 to 1 op 8 to 1 tchd 12 to 1) 14
3690[8] MY ROSSINI [60] 4-8-6 (7*) C Hawksley (9) *al beh.* .... (16 to 1 op 33 to 1) 15
4013[7] AUDE LA BELLE (Fr) [70] 5-9-2 (7*) G Milligan (18) *prmnt till wknd hfwy*......................... (10 to 1 op 7 to 1) 16
Dist: 4l, nk, 1½l, 6l, nk, 2l, 3½l, ½l, 10l, 8l. 3m 47.10s. a 3.10s (16 Ran).
SR: 54/37/47/39/14/14/6/22/19/ (R N C Lynch), R Akehurst

HAMILTON (good)
Monday September 27th

Going Correction: MINUS 0.20 sec. per fur. (races 1,2,3,6), NIL (4,5)

4213 Daily Record Claiming Stakes Class F (3-y-o and up) £3,184 1m 3f 16yds ....(2:00)

4019[8] IMPERIAL BID (Fr) 5-9-6 K Fallon (1) *beh and sn pushed alng, hdwy 4 out, rdn to ld one furlong out, ran on wl.* .... (3 to 1 op 7 to 2 tchd 4 to 1) 1
3962* GWEEK (Ire) 3-8-4 P Robinson (11) *trkd ldrs, led o'r one furlong out, sn hdd, kpt on.* .... (9 to 4 fav op 2 to 1 tchd 5 to 2) 2
3811[9] EURYTHMIC 3-8-5 Dale Gibson (7) *in tch, hdwy o'r 3 fs out, styd on fnl furlong, nrst finish.* .... (20 to 1 op 14 to 1) 3
4104 GOLD SURPRISE (Ire) 4-9-3 J Fortune (13) *nvr far away, rdn o'r 2 fs out, kpt on same pace.* .... (14 to 1 op 12 to 1 tchd 16 to 1) 4
3811[2] NUTTY BROWN (v) 3-8-10 (3*) O Pears (3) *led till hdd o'r one furlong out, wknd fnl furlong*............. (8 to 1) 5
4101 RAGGERTY (Ire) 3-8-11 J Lowe (5) *sn beh, styd on fnl 3 fs, not trble ldrs*....................... (33 to 1 op 20 to 1) 6
4049[5] JENDORCET 3-7-7[1] (3*) N Kennedy (6) *mid-div, effrt 3 fs out, no hdwy*...................... (20 to 1 op 16 to 1) 7
4091[2] SEAMA (USA) 3-8-12 M Birch (12) *cl up till wknd o'r 2 fs out*.................................... (9 to 2 op 7 to 2) 8
3117 QUARTZ HILL (USA) (v) 4-9-7 J Weaver (14) *prmnt till wknd 3 fs out*.......................... (66 to 1 op 50 to 1) 9
3216 TOLL BOOTH 4-8-2 J Quinn (8) *prmnt, rdn o'r 2 fs out, wknd quickly, tld off*.......................(200 to 1) 10
3681 TRY N' FLY (Ire) 3-8-13 K Darley (4) *sn beh, tld off.* .... (20 to 1 op 14 to 1) 11
3985[4] INOVAR 3-8-6 A Culhane (9) *nvr better than mid-div, wknd 3 fs out, tld off*............. (40 to 1 op 33 to 1) 12
1077[9] HIGHLAND PRINCESS 3-7-9 L Charnock (2) *al beh, tld off.* .... (100 to 1) 13
4022 ANNE'S BAY (Ire) 3-7-8 (5*) Darren Moffatt (10) *al beh, lost tch hfwy, wl tld off*.......................... (100 to 1) 14
Dist: 1l, 1l, 2½l, 4l, 3½l, nk, 6l, 1½l, 15l, hd. 2m 24.90s. a 4.90s (14 Ran).
SR: 35/17/16/23/11/2/ (Lord Durham), Denys Smith

4214 EBF Bothwell Bridge Median Auction Maiden Stakes Class E (2-y-o) £3,348 1m 65yds.....................(2:30)

3895[2] AMNESIA (Ire) 8-9 M Birch (2) *trkd ldr, shaken up to ld wl o'r one fs out, sn clr*.......................... (Evens jt-fav op 11 to 10 tchd 5 to 4) 1
3969[3] BURES (Ire) (v) 9-0 P Robinson (3) *led, drvn alng o'r 2 fs out, hdd wl over one out, sn btn*............. (Evens jt-fav op 5 to 4 on tchd 11 to 10) 2
3813[4] DEER IN THE GLEN 8-9 J Weaver (1) *in tch, rdn o'r 2 fs out, sn btn*............. (7 to 1 op 6 to 1 tchd 8 to 1) 3
Dist: 8l, 1½l. 1m 48.00s. a 4.00s (3 Ran).
SR: 10/-/-/ (G D Waters), Sir Mark Prescott

4215 Letheby & Christopher Premier Cuvee Nursery Class E (2-y-o) £3,523 1m 65yds......................... (3:00)

3813[2] MAKE A NOTE (USA) [76] 9-7 K Darley (4) *prmnt, rdn o'r 2 fs out, led ins fnl furlong, pushed out.* .... (9 to 2 tchd 6 to 1 and 4 to 1) 1
4082[2] GLENLYON DUCHESS [54] 7-8 (5*) D Wright (14) *chsd ldr, led o'r 2 fs out, hdd ins fnl furlong, no extr.* .... (10 to 1 op 7 to 1) 2
3968[4] OLYMPIC BID [57] 8-2 R Hills (11) *chsd ldrs, effrt 3 fs out, kpt on fnl furlong*................ (14 to 1 op 12 to 1) 3
3829[2] MONSIEUR BLEU [58] 7-12 (5*) J Marshall (7) *chsd ldrs, effrt 3 fs out, kpt on same pace.* .... (9 to 1 op 10 to 1 tchd 12 to 1) 4
3189[7] BANG IN TROUBLE (Ire) [55] 8-0 Dale Gibson (1) *beh, some hdwy 3 fs out, kpt on fnl furlong, nrst finish.* (33 to 1) 5
4082[8] BOJOLLY [52] (bl) 7-11 L Charnock (16) *mid-div, effrt 3 fs out, styd on fnl furlong*....................... (33 to 1) 6
3865 PLUM DENNIS [50] 7-9 J Quinn (10) *slwly into strd, beh till some late hdwy, not rch ldrs*..... (20 to 1 tchd 25 to 1) 7
4081[4] WINGS AHEAD [53] 7-9 (3*) N Kennedy (5) *mid-div, effrt 3 fs out, no hdwy*.................. (14 to 1 tchd 16 to 1) 8
3940[4] NIGHT SNOW [65] (bl) 8-7 (3*) M Fenton (12) *led till hdd o'r 2 fs out, sn wknd*.................. (7 to 1 tchd 8 to 1) 9
3865 SECOND SIGHT (Ire) [74] 9-5 M Birch (6) *nvr better than mid-div*.......................... (25 to 1 op 14 to 1) 10
4082[4] CRISTAL SPRINGS [61] 8-6 J Lowe (13) *nvr dngrs.* .... (20 to 1 op 16 to 1) 11
1926[5] BELLROI (Ire) [58] (v) 8-3 P Robinson (3) *prmnt till wknd 3 out*................ (16 to 1 op 12 to 1 tchd 20 to 1) 12
4051 WOODLAND WHISPER [57] (bl) 8-2[1] J Weaver (15) *strted slwly, al beh*.......................... (33 to 1 op 25 to 1) 13
4032[4] STARSPORT (Ire) [64] 8-9 J Fortune (9) *chsd ldrs till wknd 3 out*.......................... (25 to 1 op 14 to 1) 14
4106[4] DOUBLE SIXTEEN [57] 8-2 K Fallon (8) *beh, effrt hfwy, no hdwy*.............. (2 to 1 fav op 5 to 2 tchd 3 to 1) 15
2705* HIGHFIELD LAD [71] 8-13 (3*) O Pears (2) *chsd ldrs till wknd o'r 3 fs out*.......... (20 to 1 op 16 to 1) 16
Dist: 1½l, 3l, hd, sht-hd, 1½l, sht-hd, 1½l, nk, 6l, hd. 1m 49.10s. a 5.10s (16 Ran).
SR: 6/-/-/-/-/-/ (P D Savill), R Hannon

4216 Tennent's Lager Conditions Stakes Class D (3-y-o and up) £3,984 6f 5yds ....(3:30)

3849[5] NIGHT MELODY (Ire) 3-9-4 K Darley (7) *trkd ldrs, smooth hdwy to ld o'r one furlong out, drvn out.* .... (15 to 8 fav op 7 to 4 tchd 2 to 1) 1
3996[5] TAUFAN BLU (Ire) (bl) 4-9-4 (3*) O Pears (1) *slwly into strd, beh, hdwy o'r 2 fs out, rdn over one out, styd on fnl furlong, not rch wnr*............................ (8 to 1) 2
3987[5] LORD OLIVIER (Ire) 3-9-1 M Tebbutt (4) *slightly ld till hdd o'r one furlong out, kpt on same pace*......... (6 to 1) 3
3955[7] DOUBLE BLUE (bl) 4-9-2 J Weaver (3) *wth ldrs till wknd o'r one furlong out*...... (7 to 1 op 6 to 1 tchd 8 to 1) 4
3834[3] SAINT EXPRESS 3-9-5 A Culhane (5) *in tch, rdn 2 fs out, no hdwy*........................... (7 to 1 op 6 to 1) 5
3725 ISAIAH 4-9-6 J Quinn (2) *chsd ldrs till wknd 2 fs out.* .... (20 to 1 tchd 16 to 1) 6
3987[4] YAKIN (USA) 3-8-6 R Hills (6) *dwlt, in tch, effrt o'r 2 fs out, sn btn*................ (13 to 2 op 7 to 1 tchd 8 to 1) 7
4040 PETITE-D-ARGENT 4-9-0 J Fortune (8) *dsptd ld till wknd 2 fs out*.............................. (6 to 1 tchd 7 to 1) 8
Dist: 1½l, 1½l, 1½l, 3l, ½l, 1l, 1½l. 1m 13.00s. a 2.30s (8 Ran).
SR: 58/55/43/38/29/28/10/12/ (P D Savill), R Hannon

4217 Tennents 80/- Apprentice Handicap Class F (0-70 3-y-o and up) £3,054 6f 5yds.......................... (4:00)

4168[6] CRAIGIE BOY [48] (bl) 3-8-4 S Copp (1) *chsd ldrs, effrt 2 fs out, ran on wl to ld cl hme*.................... (6 to 1) 1
3593[9] MU-ARRIK [57] 5-8-11 (5*) J Gracey (9) *cl up, led o'r one furlong out, hdd and no extr close hme.* .... (5 to 1 op 11 to 2 tchd 6 to 1) 2
3676[9] LANGUEDOC [57] 6-9-2 D Thomas (3) *cl up gng wl, chlgd 2 fs out, rdn and wknd entering fnl furlong*...... (7 to 1) 3
3638 PAGEBOY [56] 4-8-12 (3*) C Adamson (4) *led till hdd o'r one furlong out, sn btn*............. (9 to 2 op 4 to 1) 4
3964[2] MISS WHITTINGHAM (Ire) [68] 3-9-7 (3*) Ruth Coulter (5) *chsd ldrs, ev ch 2 fs out, one pace.* .... (3 to 1 fav op 11 to 4 tchd 7 to 2) 5
4104 KHALLOOF (Ire) [48] 4-8-4 (3*) C Teague (6) *nvr dngrs.* .... (14 to 1 tchd 16 to 1) 6
3564 KEEP BATTLING [46] 3-7-8 (8*) I Grantham (7) *nvr dngrs.* .... (20 to 1 op 16 to 1) 7
4038 DIET [69] (v) 7-9-9 (5*) A Eddery (2) *prmnt till wknd 2 fs out.* .... (11 to 2 op 5 to 1 tchd 6 to 1) 8
3536[9] WAWEEWAWOO (Ire) [34] 5-7-2 (5*) D Denby (8) *al beh.* .... (100 to 1) 9
Dist: Sht-hd, 2½l, sht-hd, 1l, 3l, 1½l, 6l, 1½l. 1m 13.70s. a 3.00s (9 Ran).
SR: 30/41/31/29/34/5/ (C Tomkins), N Bycroft

4218 Captain J. C. Stewart Memorial Handicap Class E (0-70 3-y-o and up) £5,127 1½m 17yds................... (4:30)

4037[6] EIRE LEATH-SCEAL [41] 6-7-13 J Lowe (10) *led to hfwy, cl up, styd on wl fnl furlong to ld post*.......... (16 to 1) 1

3970² WESTFIELD MOVES (Ire) [55] 5-8-13 J Quinn (5) *prmnt, rdn to ld jst ins fnl furlong, ct post*.....(6 to 1 tchd 7 to 1) 2
4046⁵ THE PREMIER EXPRES [56] 3-8-6 R Lappin (1) *cl up, led hfwy, hdd jst ins fnl furlong, kpt on wl*.......(33 to 1) 3
4036³ PHARLY DANCER [58] 4-9-2 S Webster (11) *al prmnt, ev ch whn not much room entering fnl furlong, kpt on*. ....(12 to 1) 4
4086³ MOONSHINE DANCER [43] 3-7-2 (5*) Darren Moffatt (14) *beh, hdwy 4 fs out, ch o'r one out, not extr fnl furlong*. ....(14 to 1 op 12 to 1 tchd 16 to 1) 5
3307⁴ DEB'S BALL [50] 7-8-8 M Birch (12) *beh till styd on wl fnl 3 fs, nrst finish*........(11 to 1 op 10 to 1 tchd 12 to 1) 6
4037 PHILGUN [56] (v) 4-8-11 (3*) N Kennedy (7) *trkd ldrs, rdn o'r 2 fs out, one pace*..............(10 to 1 op 8 to 1) 7
4086² CLIBURNEL NEWS (Ire) [53] 3-8-3 P Robinson (3) *in tch, hdwy to track ldrs 3 fs out, wknd 2 out*. ....(5 to 1 tchd 6 to 1) 8
3373⁹ MUFID (USA) [47] 4-8-5 J Weaver (9) *in tch, effrt 3 fs out, no hdwy*..............(33 to 1) 9
3521⁴ BRODESSA [66] 7-9-10 K Darley (8) *beh, hdwy 4 fs out, wknd 2 out*..............(5 to 1 op 4 to 1) 10
2823⁶ APACHE SQUAW [52] 3-7-11 (5*) D Wright (13) *hld up, steady hdwy to track ldrs 4 fs out, not clr run o'r 2 out, rdn over one out, sn btn*. ....(20 to 1 op 16 to 1 tchd 25 to 1) 11
4086⁴ MILNGAVIE (Ire) [47] 3-7-11 Dale Gibson (6) *in tch till wknd o'r 2 fs out*. ....(11 to 1 op 10 to 1 tchd 12 to 1 and 14 to 1) 12
910⁴ CORNET [49] (v) 7-8-7 K Fallon (4) *al beh*.........(33 to 1) 13
3373⁷ GREAT ORATION (Ire) [37] (v) 4-7-9² L Charnock (16) *beh, hdwy to track ldrs hfwy, wknd o'r 2 fs out*....(33 to 1) 14
3552³ REACH FOR GLORY [48] 4-8-6 A Culhane (15) *prmnt, rdn o'r 2 fs out, wknd quickly*.........(16 to 1 op 14 to 1) 15
3430* MYSTERIOUS MAID (USA) [45] 6-8-3 G Bardwell (2) *chsd ldrs till stumbled and lost pl hfwy, sn beh*. ....(9 to 2 fav op 4 to 1 tchd 5 to 1) 16

Dist: Sht-hd, hd, 1l, hd, 3½l, 1l, 1l, nk, ¾l, 1½l. 2m 36.70s. a 3.70s (16 Ran).
SR: 24/37/29/37/13/21/25/12/13/ (Mel Brittain), M Brittain

MAISONS -LAFFITTE (FR) (heavy)
Monday September 27th
Going Correction: PLUS 0.50 sec. per fur.

4219 La Coupe de Maisons-Laffitte (Group 3) (3-y-o and up) £23,895 1¼m.. (3:55)

1971⁴ HATOOF (USA) 4-9-3 W R Swinburn (1) *mid-div, not much room 3 fs out, led on bit 2 out, drw clr fnl furlong, easily*..............(5 to 2) 1
3650² BAYA (USA) 3-8-13 T Jarnet (2) *hld up on outsd, hdwy 2 and a half fs out, rdn one and a half out, styd on*. ....(23 to 10 fav) 2
2979⁴ SAWASDEE (Fr) 3-8-11 W Mongil (9) *mid-div, trkd wnr till one furlong out, one pace ins last*..............(8 to 1) 3
2979⁸ FUNNY BABY (Fr) 5-9-2 A Badel (5) *mid-div, rdn and one pace 2 fs out*..............(19 to 1) 4
CHEF SUPREME (USA) 4-9-0 O Doleuze (8) *sn led, hdd and wknd 2 fs out*..............(5 to 2) 5
3647⁴ SHARPELA 3-9-2 O Poirer (4) *prmnt till rdn and wknd 2 fs out*..............(14 to 1) 6
3618⁹ CAESOUR (USA) 3-8-11 C Asmussen (3) *hld up on outsd, rdn 2 fs out, wknd ins last*..............(7 to 1) 7
HOMME DE LOI (Ire) 4-8-13 O Peslier (7) *trkd ldr till 2 fs out, wknd quickly*..............(4 to 1) 8
1546⁶ FANTASTIC DREAM (Ire) 3-8-9 D Boeuf (6) *prmnt till 2 fs out, wknd quickly*..............(20 to 1) 9

Dist: 4l, sht-nk, 4l, sht-hd, 4l, 2½l, nk, 8l. 2m 8.00s. a 6.60s (9 Ran).
SR: 87/75/72/69/66/60/50/51/31/ (Maktoum Al Maktoum), Miss C Head

SOUTHWELL (good (races 1,2), soft (3,4,5,6,7,8))
Monday September 27th
Going Correction: MINUS 0.05 sec. per fur.

4220 Tettenhall Median Auction Maiden Stakes Class F (Div I) (2-y-o) £2,243 7f ....(2:15)

3895³ SPARKLING LYRIC 8-9 W Woods (6) *chsd ldrs, gd hdwy on inner to ld wl o'r 2 fs out, quickened clr, easily*. ....(7 to 4 fav op 11 to 4) 1
3760² SWEDISH INVADER 9-0 B Raymond (14) *chsd ldrs, hdwy on outer 2 fs out, sn chasing wnr, rdn o'r one out, soon one pace*..............(85 to 40 op Evens tchd 9 to 4) 2
MCGILLYCUDDY REEKS (Ire) 8-9 W Ryan (4) *slwly into strd, beh till hdwy on outer 2 fs out, styd on strly ins last*..............(33 to 1) 3
SUCCESS STORY 8-9 D Harrison (7) *chsd ldrs, hdwy o'r 2 fs out, sn rdn and kpt on one pace*. (12 to 1 op 7 to 1) 4
3659⁷ GOLDEN FERN 8-9 Paul Eddery (13) *chsd ldrs, effrt and hdwy on outer 2 fs out, sn rdn, wknd ins last*. ....(14 to 1 op 10 to 1) 5
3695⁴ CAZANOVE'S PET 8-9 A Munro (15) *cl up, rdn o'r 2 fs out, sn one pace*..............(20 to 1) 6
GINKA 8-9 B Procter (1) *beh, some hdwy fnl 2 fs, nvr dngrs*..............(14 to 1 op 7 to 1) 7
3828 OUR STELLA 8-9 G Hind (2) *in tch, effrt and hdwy o'r 2 fs out, sn rdn and wknd over one out*. ....(33 to 1 op 20 to 1) 8
3816⁶ AT THE SAVOY (Ire) 9-0 N Connorton (9) *led, rdn 4 fs out, sn hdd and grad wknd*..............(12 to 1 op 8 to 1) 9
2968 PEARL DAISY 8-9 N Carlisle (5) *nvr a factor*......(33 to 1) 10
4003⁷ HEALTHY RISK 9-0 J Carroll (8) *chsd ldrs, rdn o'r 2 fs out, wknd over one out*..............(50 to 1 op 33 to 1) 11
2933⁶ CHELSEA LADY (Ire) 8-9 M Wood (12) *nvr rchd ldrs*. ....(50 to 1) 12
4103 STEEL SOVEREIGN 9-0 J Fanning (10) *chsd ldrs to hfwy, sn wknd*..............(16 to 1 op 14 to 1) 13
3091⁹ THE ARDINGLY FAIR (Ire) 8-11 (3*) C Hodgson (11) *cl up, rdn 3 fs out, sn wknd*..............(50 to 1) 14
3209 HALL OF PEARLS 8-9 A Clark (3) *al beh*. ....(50 to 1 op 33 to 1) 15

Dist: 5l, ¾l, ¾l, 2l, 4l, 2l, hd, 1½l, 6l, 1½l. 1m 30.90s. a 3.90s (15 Ran).
SR: 31/21/14/12/6/-/ (N S Yong), M A Jarvis

4221 Sedgeley Selling Stakes Class G (3-y-o) £2,070 6f..............(2:45)

3965* TRENTESIMO (Ire) 9-4 J Carroll (1) *made all, rdn appr fnl furlong, ran on wl ins last*. ....(11 to 8 fav op 5 to 2 tchd 11 to 4) 1
3837 FULL FEATHER (USA) 9-4 Pat Eddery (12) *hld up, gd hdwy on inner 3 fs out, swtchd wide and effrt 2 out, sn rdn, one pace ins last*..............(7 to 2 op 2 to 1) 2
3378⁶ SECOND COLOURS (USA) 9-4 W Ryan (7) *cl up, chsd wnr hfwy, rdn and ev ch one and a half fs out, one pace ins last*..............(7 to 1 op 5 to 1) 3
3896⁷ SPLASH OF SALT (Ire) 8-13 Paul Eddery (4) *chsd ldrs, rdn and ch 2 fs out, sn one pace*. ....(6 to 1 op 5 to 1 tchd 7 to 1) 4
3946 MAGICATION 7-13 (7*) Claire Balding (5) *slwly into strd, hdwy o'r 2 fs out, styd on ins last*. (14 to 1 op 10 to 1) 5
4012² MOVING IMAGE (Ire) 8-13 C Dwyer (10) *chsd ldrs, rdn o'r 2 fs out, sn one pace*.....(9 to 1 op 7 to 1 tchd 10 to 1) 6
3948⁴ RED LEADER (Ire) 8-11 (7*) T G McLaughlin (6) *al mid-div*. ....(10 to 1 op 6 to 1) 7
4031 SAMANTHAS JOY 8-4¹ (3*) C Hodgson (11) *very slwly away, some hdwy fnl 2 fs, nvr a factor*........(50 to 1) 8
4109 JOCKS JOKER 8-11 A Mackay (3) *slwly into strd, al rear*. ....(25 to 1 op 20 to 1) 9
2769⁶ BRIGHT GEM 8-13 J Fanning (8) *chsd ldrs, rdn hfwy, sn wknd*..............(25 to 1) 10
3692⁹ THE FED (v) 9-4 B Raymond (2) *cl up, rdn 3 fs out, wknd quickly, eased 2 out*..............(14 to 1 op 12 to 1) 11
1273 MATTHEW DAVID 8-11 (7*) G Strange (9) *al beh*...(33 to 1) 12

Dist: 1½l, ½l, 3l, 3½l, nk, 2½l, 1½l, 1½l, 1½l, 2½l. 1m 16.70s. a 2.70s (12 Ran).
SR: 44/38/36/19/-/4/ (B R Allen), J Berry

4222 Coca Cola Schweppes Apprentice Maiden Stakes Class G (3-y-o) £2,070 6f..............(3:15)

3948³ MELODIC DRIVE 8-7 (7*) J Edmunds (6) *very slwly away, outpcd and wl beh, hdwy on wide outsd o'r one furlong out, fnshd strly to ld nr line*..............(4 to 1) 1
4180 MAGIC PEARL 8-1 (8*) S Knott (8) *al prmnt, chsd ldr 2 and a half fs out and sn rdn, led wl ins last, ct nr line*. ....(7 to 2 fav tchd 4 to 1) 2
3628² MARCHMAIN 8-11 (3*) P Roberts (5) *led, rdn 2 fs out, wknd and hdd wl ins last*. ....(4 to 1 op 3 to 1 tchd 9 to 2) 3
4031⁴ NOBLE MEASURE (Ire) (bl) 8-8 (6*) G Strange (1) *rdn and outpcd 2 and a half fs out, styd on wl appr last*. ....(10 to 1) 4
3459 KENNEDYS PRIMA 8-9 D Gibbs (7) *beh till styd on fnl 2 fs*. ....(9 to 2 op 7 to 2) 5
3948⁸ DONTBETALKING (Ire) 8-9 R Painter (9) *beh till styd on fnl 2 fs*..........(14 to 1 op 20 to 1 tchd 12 to 1) 6
3794³ LUCKY MILL (bl) 8-4 (5*) D Griffiths (2) *cl up till rdn and wknd 2 and a half fs out*...........(9 to 1 op 8 to 1) 7
4126⁸ COOL ETOILE 8-6⁵ (8*) L Aspell (4) *mid-div, effrt and some hdwy o'r 2 fs out, sn wknd*..............(33 to 1) 8
3693⁸ PROMITTO 8-1 (8*) J Bramhill (3) *chsd ldrs till wknd 2 and a half fs out*..............(11 to 1 op 10 to 1) 9
3794 RUSSIA WITH LOVE 7-13 (10*) K Sked (11) *al rear*. (16 to 1) 10
GREAT INDY 8-7⁴ (6*) M Harris (10) *slwly away, al rear*. ....(50 to 1) 11

Dist: Hd, ¾l, 1½l, ¾l, ½l, 5l, hd, 6l, 10l, nk. 1m 17.60s. a 3.60s (11 Ran).
SR: 22/16/18/12/4/2/ (Mrs C M Stevens), P S Felgate

4223 Levy Board Conditions Stakes Class D (2-y-o) £3,523 7f..............(3:45)

3755³ COTTEIR CHIEF (Ire) 8-10 D Harrison (5) *mid-div and pushed alng, hdwy 3 fs out, rdn and styd on to ld ins last, ran on*..........(9 to 2 op 5 to 1 tchd 6 to 1) 1
3905* DIESAN (USA) 9-8 M Roberts (9) *chsd ldrs, hdwy o'r 2 fs out, led one and a half out, sn rdn, hdd and no extr ins last*..............(5 to 4 fav tchd 11 to 8) 2

3865 HAM N'EGGS 8-9 (7*) Mark Denaro (1) *chsd ldr, led 2 and a half fs out, rdn and hdd one and a half out, sn one pace*............(7 to 1 op 4 to 1) 3
3753^{4} POLISH ADMIRAL 9-0 W Woods (4) *mid-div, hdwy to chase ldrs hfwy, rdn 2 fs out and one pace.* ....(6 to 1 op 5 to 1) 4
3554* ASKERN 9-2 E Johnson (6) *chsd ldrs, rdn o'r 2 fs out, sn one pace*..........................(11 to 2 op 3 to 1) 5
3974^{8} SHAWN CUDDY 8-10 Paul Eddery (3) *outpcd and wl beh till some hdwy fnl 2 fs, nvr a factor*.......... (66 to 1) 6
4159^{8} HILTONS TRAVEL (Ire) (v) 8-3 (7*) S Knott (7) *led till hdd and wknd quickly 2 and a half fs out.* (20 to 1 op 50 to 1) 7
CAZZUTO (Ire) 9-2 A Munro (8) *chsd ldrs, rdn o'r 2 fs out, sn wknd*.......................... (8 to 1 op 6 to 1) 8
2819* LOVE OF THE NORTH (Ire) 8-13³ T Wall (2) *beh frm hfwy.* ....(50 to 1) 9
3940 SILVERISTE (Ire) 8-10 M Wigham (10) *beh frm hfwy.* ....(66 to 1) 10

Dist: 2l, 4l, 5l, 10l, 1l, 1½l, sht-hd, 8l, 10l. 1m 30.80s. a 3.80s (10 Ran).
SR: 34/40/22/5/-/-/ (M & N Plant Ltd), M C Pipe

4224 Black Country Limited Stakes Class F (0-60 3-y-o and up) £3,004 7f.... (4:15)

3830 ETERNAL FLAME 5-8-9 B Raymond (2) *chsd ldrs on inner and not much room 3 fs out, swtchd wide and rdn 2 out, styd on ins last to ld nr finish*..... (14 to 1 op 12 to 1) 1
4045* CELESTINE (v) 4-8-9 J Fanning (11) *chsd ldrs, effrt to ld one and a half fs out, sn rdn, hdd and no extr nr finish.* ....(11 to 2 fav op 9 to 2) 2
4045^{3} NELLIE'S GAMBLE 3-8-0 (5*) L Newton (7) *hld up and beh, gd hdwy on outer 2 fs out, rdn and ev ch entering last, no extr*...........................(8 to 1 op 12 to 1) 3
3788^{3} LADY SABO 4-8-4 (5*) A Garth (6) *chsd ldrs, rdn 2 fs out, kpt on one pace*.......................... (14 to 1) 4
3745 QUICK STEEL (bl) 5-9-0 R Price (13) *chsd ldrs, effrt and ev ch 2 fs out, sn rdn and wknd appr last*....... (10 to 1) 5
403 SIRTELIMAR (Ire) 4-9-0 A Mackay (10) *outpcd and beh till styd on fnl 2 fs*.................(14 to 1 op 16 to 1) 6
3901^{7} LEGEND DULAC (Ire) 4-9-0 J Carroll (5) *cl up, led aftr 2 fs, jnd and rdn two out, sn hdd and wknd.* ....(7 to 1 tchd 8 to 1) 7
3946 STRIP CARTOON (Ire) 5-8-7 (7*) G Strange (8) *pushed alng in mid-div, nvr dngrs*............ (16 to 1 op 14 to 1) 8
4038 PRINCE BELFORT 5-9-0 A Clark (12) *cl up, effrt and ev ch 2 fs out, sn rdn and wknd appr last.* (8 to 1 op 6 to 1) 9
3988^{3} GLENFIELD GRETA (bl) 5-8-2 (7*) Claire Balding (14) *al rear.* .... (10 to 1 op 8 to 1) 10
3896^{3} ASTERIX 5-8-7 (7*) Mark Denaro (9) *al rear.* ....(7 to 1 op 5 to 1) 11
4104 LORD VIVIENNE (Ire) 4-9-0 F Norton (4) *prmnt till rdn and wknd o'r 2 fs out*.......................... (33 to 1) 12
3707^{5} FARMER JOCK 11-9-0 M Roberts (1) *led 2 fs, cl up till rdn 3 out, sn wknd*.....................(12 to 1 op 8 to 1) 13
3964^{4} ROSE FLYER (Ire) 3-8-0 (5*) N Carlisle (3) *unruly strt, reared and uns rdr leaving stalls.* ....(12 to 1 tchd 14 to 1) ur

Dist: ½l, 1½l, 1l, 1½l, ¾l, 1½l, nk, 2½l, 1½l, ½l. 1m 32.30s. a 5.30s (14 Ran).
SR: 10/8/-/-/-/-/ (Cliffe Rowlands), J Hetherton

4225 Codsall Nursery Handicap Class E (2-y-o) £3,416 6f.................. (4:45)

3968^{9} SPRING LOADED [60] 7-12 J Fanning (11) *hld up and beh, gd hdwy 2 fs out, str run to ld ins last, sn clr.* (14 to 1) 1
4044* BOLD ALEX [64] 7-13 (3*) S Maloney (5) *chsd ldr, effrt to ld one and a half fs out, rdn and hdd ins last, wknd nr finish*.................(11 to 2 op 5 to 1 tchd 6 to 1) 2
3779 GONE TO POT [74] (v) 8-12 A Clark (2) *al prmnt, ev ch 2 fs out, sn rdn, kpt on ins last*...................(14 to 1) 3
3705^{2} JAREEF'S WAY (Ire) [75] (v) 8-13 Paul Eddery (4) *chsd ldrs, effrt and hdwy 2 fs out, sn rdn and kpt on one pace fnl furlong*............................ (9 to 2 op 7 to 2) 4
4124^{6} WAAFED (USA) [79] (bl) 9-3 B Raymond (10) *led, rdn 2 fs out, sn hdd and wknd*.............(10 to 1 op 8 to 1) 5
3120^{2} QUEEN'S TRUST [68] 8-6 A Munro (3) *chsd ldrs, rdn 2 fs out, sn wknd*...........................(9 to 1 op 6 to 1) 6
4034^{5} LINCOLN TREASURE (Ire) [60] 7-12 N Carlisle (9) *nvr rchd ldrs*...............................(33 to 1 op 50 to 1) 7
3978^{2} DAILY STAR [71] 8-9 J Carroll (8) *chsd ldrs, rdn 2 fs out, sn wknd*.............................. (6 to 1 op 9 to 2) 8
3845^{6} ZUNO NOELYN [64] 8-2 D Harrison (12) *al beh*.... (10 to 1) 9
3809* JASARI (Ire) [75] 8-13 M Roberts (1) *hld up and beh, effrt and rdn 2 fs out, no hdwy*......(7 to 2 fav tchd 9 to 2) 10
3069^{2} MARJORIE'S MEMORY (Ire) [83] 9-7 W Ryan (6) *prmnt, rdn o'r 2 fs out, ridden and wknd quickly.* ....(9 to 1 op 5 to 1) 11

Dist: 2½l, hd, hd, 2l, 4l, ½l, 2½l, 1½l, 1½l, 12l. 1m 17.40s. a 3.40s (11 Ran).
SR: 10/4/13/13/9/-/ (P D Savill), Mrs M Reveley

4226 West Midland Fillies' Handicap Class D (0-80 3-y-o and up) £3,816 1½m ....(5:15)

4116 ZAJIRA (Ire) [76] 3-9-7 R Price (14) *hld up, gd hdwy o'r 4 fs out, cl up 2 out, shaken up to ld wl ins last, ran on.* ....(11 to 1 op 10 to 1 tchd 12 to 1) 1
3891^{3} HIGHLAND SPIRIT [55] 5-8-8 D Harrison (5) *hld up, hdwy 5 fs out, led 2 out, rdn appr fnl furlong, hdd and no extr wl ins last*..........(3 to 1 fav op 7 to 4 tchd 7 to 2) 2
3461^{8} MATARIS [57] (v) 3-8-2 Paul Eddery (6) *al prmnt, effrt and ev ch 2 fs out, sn rdn and one pace appr fnl furlong.* ....(12 to 1) 3
4018^{9} TANODA [42] 7-7-9¹ A Mackay (9) *hld up, hdwy 4 fs out, effrt and rdn 2 out, kpt on*................. (14 to 1) 4
3814 FAMOUS BEAUTY [41] 6-7-7⁴ (5*) A Garth (1) *in tch, effrt and hdwy 5 fs out, rdn 3 out, kpt on one pace.* (20 to 1) 5
3970^{9} MADAM GYMCRAK [57] 3-8-2 Julie Bowker (3) *hld up, hdwy o'r 2 fs out, kpt on, not rch ldrs.* .... (10 to 1 op 14 to 1) 6
4028 BALADIYA [58] 6-8-8 (3*) C Hodgson (2) *chsd ldrs, rdn alng 5 fs out, sn wknd*................(8 to 1 tchd 10 to 1) 7
3786^{7} BOBBYSOXER [73] 3-9-4 B Raymond (13) *led, rdn and hdd 2 fs out, sn wknd*..................(6 to 1 op 4 to 1) 8
3866^{4} ZANZE (USA) [59] 3-8-4 M Roberts (15) *trkd ldrs, hdwy 4 fs out, rdn o'r 2 out, sn wknd.* ....(11 to 2 op 4 to 1 tchd 6 to 1) 9
4101 ROMOLA NIJINSKY [55] 5-8-5 (3*) S Maloney (7) *cl up, rdn 4 fs out, sn lost pl*.............................. (14 to 1) 10
4101 ELAINE TULLY (Ire) [75] 5-10-0 J Carroll (4) *chsd ldrs, rdn hfwy, sn beh*.....................(12 to 1 op 8 to 1) 11
3820^{5} LADY BUCHAN [55] 4-8-8 Kim Tinkler (12) *al beh.* (20 to 1) 12

Dist: 1½l, 2l, 1½l, 2½l, nk, 15l, 7l, 3½l, nk, 2½l. 2m 44.60s. a 10.60s (12 Ran).
(Hamdan Al-Maktoum), R W Armstrong

4227 Tettenhall Median Auction Maiden Stakes Class F (Div II) (2-y-o) £2,243 7f ....(5:45)

3974^{7} FAWLTY TOWERS (Ire) 9-0 A Munro (5) *al cl up, led 2 and a half fs out, rdn appr last, ran on wl*........(7 to 2 co-fav op 4 to 1 tchd 9 to 2 and 3 to 1) 1
2862^{7} SALOME'S DANCE 8-9 M Roberts (3) *chsd ldrs, rdn o'r 2 fs out, styd on appr last*......(7 to 2 co-fav tchd 5 to 1) 2
RESPONSE 9-0 G Hind (7) *beh, hdwy on ins 2 fs out, rdn appr last, styd on*.......................... (33 to 1) 3
WACKY (Ire) 8-9 J Carroll (8) *beh and ran green, hdwy on outsd 2 fs out, hng lft one and a half out, kpt on ins last*............................. (10 to 1 op 7 to 1) 4
4103^{7} STAR PERFORMER (Ire) 9-0 J Fanning (13) *chsd ldrs, effrt and ev ch 2 fs out, sn rdn, wknd appr last.* ....(7 to 1 op 6 to 1) 5
4026^{4} CHITA RIVERA 8-9 Paul Eddery (9) *in tch and rdn, outpcd hfwy, styd on one pace fnl 2 fs.* ....(7 to 2 co-fav op 2 to 1) 6
FAMILIAR ART 8-9 W Ryan (14) *in tch, effrt and hdwy 2 fs out, sn rdn and one pace.* .... (9 to 1 op 6 to 1 tchd 10 to 1) 7
3137^{7} WORLD TRAVELLER 9-0 B Raymond (12) *in tch, effrt 2 and a half fs out, sn rdn and btn.* (20 to 1 tchd 33 to 1) 8
3760 OLIVER-J 9-0 D Harrison (2) *chsd ldrs 3 fs, sn wknd.* .... (50 to 1 op 25 to 1) 9
3997^{9} BEDAZZLE 9-0 M Wigham (10) *chsd ldrs, sn rdn, lost pl hfwy*.......................... (33 to 1 op 25 to 1) 10
2862^{9} GWERNYMYNYDD 8-6 (3*) S Maloney (11) *slwly into strd, hdwy on outsd to join ldrs hfwy, rdn 2 fs out, wkng whn hmpd one and a half out.* .... (7 to 1 op 8 to 1 tchd 10 to 1) 11
3166 MY MOONA 8-9 A Clark (1) *slwly into strd, al rear.* .... (50 to 1 op 25 to 1) 12
1263^{8} CHARLYMOON 8-9 C Dwyer (4) *led, rdn and hdd 2 and a half fs out, sn wknd*........................(50 to 1) 13
2278^{7} ANGELIC DANCER (v) 8-9 N Connorton (6) *in tch, effrt 2 and a half fs out, sn rdn and wknd.* .... (20 to 1 op 50 to 1) 14

Dist: 1½l, ¾l, 1l, ¾l, 3l, sht-hd, 1l, ¾l, 1½l, ¾l. 1m 33.90s. a 6.90s (14 Ran).
(Fahd Salman), P F I Cole

BRIGHTON (good to soft)
Tuesday September 28th
Going Correction: MINUS 0.10 sec. per fur.

4228 Final Selling Stakes Class G (2-y-o) £2,070 5f 59yds................ (2:10)

4193^{2} KING RAT (Ire) 8-11 M Roberts (12) *pushed alng stands side frm hfwy, led wl o'r one furlong out, quickened clr*..................(Evens fav op 5 to 4 tchd 6 to 4) 1
4114^{4} CHIEF EXECUTIVE 8-11 W Carson (5) *chsd ldrs, ran on 2 fs out, one pace fnl furlong*..........(14 to 1 op 10 to 1) 2
3815 FLAIR LADY (bl) 8-1 (5*) P McCabe (4) *handily plcd, kpt on one pace appr fnl furlong*....... (20 to 1 tchd 33 to 1) 3
3098* LITTLE EMMELINE 8-6 N Carlisle (14) *led on far side till hdd by wnr wl o'r one furlong out, no extr.* .... (10 to 1 op 7 to 1) 4
4084^{3} COLNE VALLEY (bl) 8-6 J Reid (8) *ldg grp, rdn and outpcd appr fnl furlong*...................(8 to 1 op 6 to 1) 5
3903 SADDAM THE LOG 8-6 A Mackay (11) *styd on one pace last 2 fs*........................(12 to 1 op 10 to 1) 6
3870^{6} SPORT RACING CLUB (bl) 8-3 (3*) Stephen Davies (16) *nvr rchd ldrs*..........................(50 to 1 op 33 to 1) 7
3978^{6} RANDOM 8-6 W Newnes (7) *mid-div most of way.* .... (16 to 1 op 14 to 1) 8

4128 SPORTING HEIR (Ire) 8-11 M Wigham (9) *outpcd.* ....(33 to 1 tchd 50 to 1) 9

2689[7] EUROCHEM LAD (Ire) (bl) 8-11 B Rouse (6) *chsd ldr to hfwy, wknd 2 fs out.* (16 to 1 op 20 to 1 tchd 33 to 1) 10

3835[6] TOTON LAD 8-11 L Dettori (10) *speed for 3 fs.* ....(9 to 1 op 5 to 1) 11

3869[2] BESSIE'S WILL 8-6 S Whitworth (2) *mid-div, rdn and outpcd frm hfwy.*.................(20 to 1 op 14 to 1) 12

4009[8] GIGUE 8-6 T Quinn (3) *chsd ldrs for o'r 2 fs, wknd.* ....(33 to 1 op 20 to 1) 13

4193 OLD HOOK (Ire) 8-8 (3*) B Doyle (13) *nvr able to chal.* ....(20 to 1 op 12 to 1) 14

3432 RISKIE THINGS 8-0[1] (7*) Mark Denaro (1) *mid-div, outpcd last 2 fs.*....................(12 to 1 tchd 14 to 1) 15

Dist: 4l, 2l, 2½l, hd, 2l, 1l, 1l, nk, 2l, 2l. 1m 2.30s. a 2.20s (15 Ran).

SR: 43/27/14/4/3/-/ (The 2nd Kingsley House Partnership), M Johnston

4229 EBF Sompting Maiden Stakes Class D (2-y-o) £4,378 6f 209yds.........(2:40)

3888[2] FAWRAN (USA) 9-0 M Roberts (11) *in tch, ran on to ld o'r 2 fs out, quickened clr fnl furlong.....* (7 to 2 op 2 to 1) 1

3990[7] HESELL STREET (Ire) 9-0 R Cochrane (3) *cld on ldrs aftr 3 fs, ev ch 2 out, not quicken fnl furlong.* ....(6 to 1 op 8 to 1 tchd 9 to 1) 2

3979[7] FAIR AND FANCY (Fr) 9-0 W Carson (5) *ldg grp, rdn and not quicken appr fnl furlong.* ....(16 to 1 op 12 to 1 tchd 20 to 1) 3

4033[6] WALDO 9-0 D Harrison (6) *chsd frnt rnk, rdn and kpt on one pace last 2 fs.*....................(33 to 1 op 20 to 1) 4

3958[4] FORT KNOX (Ire) 9-0 R Price (1) *made most til hdd o'r 2 fs out, no extr fnl furlong.*............(7 to 2 op 5 to 1) 5

1905 NO SPEECHES (Ire) 9-0 D Biggs (7) *outpcd towards rear til moderate prog last 2 fs.*....................(33 to 1) 6

4127[2] BAGSHOT 9-0 A Munro (9) *in tch, rdn and no hdwy frm 2 fs out.*.......(6 to 1 op 7 to 1 tchd 9 to 1 and 5 to 1) 7

3979[3] RORY CREEK (USA) 9-0 L Dettori (2) *towards rear most of way.*...............(5 to 2 fav op 9 to 4 tchd 11 to 4) 8

4002 GOLDEN BULLION 8-9 G Hind (8) *slwly into strd, nvr on terms.*....................(50 to 1 op 20 to 1) 9

2257[6] EL TEL (Fr) 9-0 T Quinn (10) *cl up for o'r 4 fs, wknd.* ....(20 to 1 op 12 to 1 tchd 25 to 1) 10

GREEN CRUSADER 9-0 W Ryan (12) *speed to hfwy.* ....(14 to 1 op 10 to 1 tchd 16 to 1) 11

3833[9] DAWN DEFENDER (Ire) 9-0 R Hills (4) *al beh.* ....(20 to 1 op 12 to 1) 12

ABLE FUN 9-0 M Hills (13) *mid-div til wknd 2 fs out.* ....(50 to 1 op 20 to 1) 13

Dist: 3½l, 2½l, 3l, hd, ½l, sht-hd, ½l, 3½l, 2l, ½l. 1m 23.20s. a 3.20s (13 Ran).

SR: 41/30/22/13/12/10/9/7/-/ (Sheikh Ahmed Al Maktoum), J H M Gosden

4230 Brighthelmstone Nursery Class E (2-y-o) £3,340 6f 209yds...........(3:10)

4029[7] WIZARD KING [55] 7-7 G Bardwell (4) *cl up, led o'r 2 fs out, rdn out.*....................(14 to 1 op 10 to 1) 1

3974[4] RUPAN [78] 9-2 R Cochrane (8) *hrd rdn and ran on frm rear last 2 fs, fnshd wl.*...................(12 to 1 op 8 to 1) 2

3664[3] BIRD OF TIME (Ire) [64] 8-2 W Carson (5) *hdwy und pres o'r 2 fs out, not quicken fnl furlong....* (10 to 1 op 8 to 1) 3

3865[9] SHARP TYCOON (Ire) [78] 9-2 L Dettori (13) *trkd ldrs, kpt on one pace last 2 fs.*................(11 to 2 op 6 to 1) 4

4082[3] WIXI (Ire) [75] 8-13 P Robinson (7) *improved und pres o'r 2 fs out, no extr ins fnl furlong.*.........(14 to 1 op 8 to 1) 5

3905[5] DOWN D ISLANDS [74] (bl) 8-12 J Reid (14) *led for 2 fs, wknd two out.*.........(11 to 2 op 8 to 1 tchd 9 to 1) 6

4106[8] TANAH MERAH (Ire) [66] (bl) 8-4[1] T Quinn (11) *nvr nr to chal.*...................(25 to 1 op 20 to 1 tchd 33 to 1) 7

3836[4] RED VALERIAN [70] (v) 8-8 S O'Gorman (12) *wl in tch for 4 fs, wknd.*.........................(14 to 1 op 8 to 1) 8

3753[5] ROMAN REEL (USA) [72] 8-10 B Rouse (10) *wl plcd for 4 fs, sn lost pl.*...................(33 to 1 op 16 to 1) 9

3223[5] BEAUTETE [80] 9-4 W Ryan (6) *nvr trbld frnt rnk.* ....(20 to 1 op 14 to 1 tchd 25 to 1) 10

4127* SHEPHERD MARKET (Ire) [83] 9-7 (5ex) R Price (2) *led aftr 2 fs, hdd o'r two out, wknd rpdly.* ....(7 to 2 fav op 5 to 2 tchd 4 to 1) 11

3974[2] BONAIGUA (Ire) [83] (bl) 9-7 M Hills (3) *al towards rear.* ....(7 to 1 op 6 to 1 tchd 15 to 2) 12

3657[8] STARISK [55] 7-2 (5*) D Wright (9) *outpcd.* ....(14 to 1 op 33 to 1 tchd 12 to 1) 13

3166 BUNNY RUN [57] 7-9[2] J Quinn (1) *outpcd.* ....(33 to 1 op 25 to 1) 14

Dist: ¾l, 2½l, nk, nk, 1l, 6l, nk, hd, nk, 5l. 1m 23.60s. a 3.60s (14 Ran).

SR: 15/36/14/27/23/19/ (Sheikh Ahmed Bin Saeed Al Maktoum), Sir Mark Prescott

4231 Eastbourne Limited Stakes Class F (0-65 3-y-o) £2,243 7f 214yds.... (3:40)

3830[2] NICHODOULA 8-9 M Roberts (4) *pressed ldrs, led o'r 3 fs out, rdn clr fnl furlong*..............(2 to 1 fav tchd 5 to 2) 1

3710 DALALAH 8-9 R Hills (10) *in tch, ran on 3 fs out, rdn and not quicken o'r one out.* (7 to 1 op 5 to 1 tchd 8 to 1) 2

3588 LOCHORE 9-0 A Tucker (8) *ran on und pres frm rear 2 fs out, one pace fnl furlong.* ....(14 to 1 op 12 to 1 tchd 16 to 1) 3

3780[4] MR CUBE (Ire) 9-0 T Quinn (6) *handily plcd, ev ch o'r 2 fs out, no extr appr fnl furlong.* ....(11 to 2 op 5 to 1 tchd 6 to 1) 4

3780[5] CRYSTAL REAY 8-9 R Cochrane (7) *nvr nrr.* ....(8 to 1 op 7 to 1) 5

4012[5] NOBLE RISK 9-0 J Reid (11) *in tch in mid-div, rdn and no prog frm hfwy.*...................(5 to 1 tchd 11 to 2) 6

3325[8] STEVIE'S WONDER (Ire) 9-0 N Carlisle (5) *speed for 3 fs, sn lost tch.*............. (16 to 1 op 14 to 1 tchd 20 to 1) 7

3981[5] SMART TEACHER (USA) 9-0 G Hind (3) *wth ldrs til wknd frm 3 fs out.*............(9 to 1 op 8 to 1 tchd 10 to 1) 8

1861 M'BEBE 8-9 (5*) B Russell (9) *dwlt, al beh, tld off.* (50 to 1) 9

3547* SHARP GAZELLE 8-6 (3*) Stephen Davies (1) *made most of rng til o'r 3 fs out, eased clsg stages, tld off.* ....(8 to 1 op 5 to 1) 10

Dist: 2½l, hd, 3l, 5l, 2l, ½l, ½l, 20l, 1½l. 1m 35.60s. a 3.20s (10 Ran).

SR: 35/27/31/22/2/1/ (Hesmonds Stud), Sir Mark Prescott

4232 Steyning Fillies' Conditions Stakes Class D (2-y-o) £3,143 6f 209yds (4:10)

3176[8] QUEENBIRD 9-4 W Ryan (4) *pressed ldrs, led o'r one furlong out, drvn alng, hld on last strds.* ....(7 to 4 jt-fav op 2 to 1 tchd 11 to 4) 1

1726[5] MICROLITE (USA) 8-8 T Quinn (2) *hld up beh, ran on und pres o'r 2 fs out, ev ch ins fnl furlong, jst fld.* ....(25 to 1 op 10 to 1) 2

3949[2] KUTBEYA (USA) 8-12 W Carson (1) *in tch, led o'r 2 fs out, hdd over one out, rallied last 100 yards, jst fld.* ....(5 to 2 op 2 to 1 tchd 11 to 4) 3

4011* GLIMPSE 8-12 R Cochrane (5) *wth ldrs til rdn and outpcd o'r 2 fs out.*...................(7 to 4 jt-fav op 5 to 4) 4

2754[6] CADENABBIA (USA) 8-8 J Reid (3) *led til hdd o'r 2 fs out, sn btn.*............... (25 to 1 op 10 to 1 tchd 33 to 1) 5

Dist: Hd, sht-hd, 3l, 5l. 1m 25.30s. a 5.30s (5 Ran).

SR: 14/3/6/-/-/ (A S Reid), H R A Cecil

4233 Saltdean Maiden Stakes Class D (3-y-o and up) £3,289 7f 214yds.... (4:40)

3456 COLIN MUSET 3-9-3 M Roberts (1) *rcd keenly, led o'r 3 fs out, pushed clr fnl furlong.*........(7 to 2 tchd 4 to 1) 1

3893[2] MISLEMANI (Ire) 3-9-3 C Dwyer (6) *led til rdn and hdd o'r 3 fs out, swtchd lft over one out, not quicken.* ....(11 to 10 on op Evens tchd 5 to 4) 2

3937 THALEROS 3-9-3 W Carson (5) *dwlt, sn wth ldr, rdn and one pace appr last 2 fs.* ....(15 to 8 op 11 to 8 tchd 2 to 1) 3

3980[5] CLELIA 3-8-12 D Harrison (4) *chsd ldrs til lost tch frm 3 fs out.*................(50 to 1 op 20 to 1 tchd 66 to 1) 4

3866[7] SWALLOW RIDGE (Ire) 4-9-2 D Biggs (2) *al outpcd, lost tch 3 fs out.*............ (50 to 1 op 20 to 1 tchd 66 to 1) 5

4088[4] THE COUNTRY DANCER 3-8-12 M Wigham (3) *in tch til wknd o'r 3 fs out, eased and lost pos.* ....(40 to 1 op 25 to 1 tchd 50 to 1) 6

Dist: 3½l, 2½l, 15l, 15l, 5l. 1m 36.30s. a 3.90s (6 Ran).

SR: 33/22/14/ (Sheikh Mohammed), J H M Gosden

4234 Levy Board Maiden Handicap Class E (0-70 3-y-o and up) £3,287 1m 3f 196yds........................ (5:10)

3716 WAKT [46] 3-8-4 W Carson (2) *improved frm hfwy, led and edgd rght o'r 2 fs out, rdn clr fnl furlong.* ....(8 to 1 tchd 9 to 1) 1

4129[2] GREEN KILT [68] 3-9-12 A Munro (10) *hld up, hdwy und pres o'r 3 fs out, styd on one pace ins last.* ....(6 to 4 fav op 5 to 2 tchd 3 to 1) 2

MAHAASIN [33] 5-7-13 A Mackay (13) *hdwy frm rear o'r 3 fs out, rdn and no imprsn on wnr fnl furlong.* ....(5 to 1 op 12 to 1 tchd 9 to 2) 3

1685 QUELQUE CHOSE [50] 3-8-5 (3*) B Doyle (9) *made most til hdd and bumped o'r 2 fs out, no extr.* ....(16 to 1 op 12 to 1 tchd 20 to 1) 4

3551[7] GAMEFULL GOLD [34] 4-8-0 N Adams (4) *hdwy 4 fs out, rdn and hng lft ins last 2, not rch wnr.* ....(33 to 1 op 16 to 1) 5

4087[9] NIGHT EDITION [48] 3-8-6 T Quinn (5) *in tch, took clr order 5 fs out, wknd ins last 2.*.......... (33 to 1 op 16 to 1) 6

4091[5] WOODMANS STAR [36] 3-7-8 N Carlisle (8) *beh til styd on o'r 2 fs out, nrst finish.*........... (20 to 1 op 14 to 1) 7

3971[4] RUMPUS (Ire) [67] 3-9-11 R Cochrane (12) *hld up towards rear, short lived effrt 3 fs out, sn btn.* ....(8 to 1 op 5 to 1 tchd 10 to 1) 8

4115 ALTON BELLE [29] 4-7-9[2] J Quinn (7) *beh most of way.* ....(33 to 1 tchd 40 to 1) 9

3523 MADAM CAPRICE [56] 3-9-0 D Harrison (6) *wl plcd til rdn alng 5 fs out, sn wknd.* ....(10 to 1 op 8 to 1 tchd 11 to 1) 10

4087[5] MENA [49] 3-8-7 M Roberts (1) *chsd frnt rnk til lost pos o'r 3 fs out.*..................(7 to 1 op 4 to 1 tchd 8 to 1) 11

3096[4] SPICE BOX (USA) [60] 3-9-4 L Dettori (3) *cl up, dsptd ld 4 fs out, wknd 3 out.*.................... (7 to 1 op 6 to 1) 12

4187[4] MR LUCIANO (Ire) [49] 3-8-7 W Ryan (11) *wth ldrs, rdn alng hfwy, wknd o'r 3 fs out.*.......(10 to 1 op 5 to 1) 13

Dist: 3½l, 3½l, 2½l, ½l, 3½l, 2½l, 1l, 15l, 1l, 1½l. 2m 35.80s. a 8.30s (13 Ran).

SR: -/10/-/-/-/-/ (Hamdan Al-Maktoum), D Morley

NEWCASTLE (good)
Tuesday September 28th

Going Correction: MINUS 0.20 sec. per fur. (races 1,2,3,4), MINUS 0.10 (5,6,7)

4235 Newcastle Members Subscription Handicap Class E (0-70 3-y-o and up) £3,496 7f..................... (2:00)

3973^{3} CAN CAN CHARLIE [48] 3-8-4 J Weaver (8) *rcd far side, made all, rdn and ran on wl fnl furlong.* ....(7 to 1 op 6 to 1) 1

3965^{9} JOKIST [55] 10-9-1 M Tebbutt (6) *trkd ldrs far side, chsd wnr appr fnl furlong, kpt on und pres.* .... (14 to 1 op 12 to 1) 2

4166^{5} PRINCESS MAXINE (Ire) [56] 4-9-2 J Fanning (18) *rcd stands side, hld up, hdwy 2 fs out, sn rdn, styd on appr last.* ....(6 to 1 fav op 5 to 1) 3

4156 A LITTLE PRECIOUS [45] 7-8-5 G Duffield (19) *rcd stands side, slwly into strd and beh till styd on wl fnl furlong, nrst finish*........... (14 to 1 op 16 to 1 tchd 20 to 1) 4

4120^{3} MCA BELOW THE LINE [61] (bl) 5-9-7 S Webster (7) *prmnt far side, rdn o'r 2 fs out, kpt on one pace*...... (12 to 1) 5

3965^{3} ACROSS THE BAY [62] (v) 6-9-8 K Darley (1) *chsd ldrs far side, rdn 2 fs out, kpt on one pace.* (14 to 1 op 12 to 1) 6

3523 MBULWA [45] 7-8-5 J Fortune (3) *cl up far side, rdn 2 fs out, wknd*........................... (12 to 1 op 10 to 1) 7

AYIA NAPA [53] 6-8-6 (7*) N Kinnon (20) *beh till styd on fnl 2 fs, nvr dngrs*.................... (100 to 1 op 66 to 1) 8

4181^{5} CICERONE [49] 3-8-5 Dale Gibson (14) *cl up stands side, effrt 2 fs out, sn rdn, wknd appr last*........... (16 to 1) 9

4168^{9} BLUE GRIT [59] 7-9-5 K Fallon (15) *mid-div, effrt and rdn o'r 2 fs out, no imprsn*............. (12 to 1 op 10 to 1) 10

4166 TUMBLING (USA) [46] 5-8-6^{3} Pat Eddery (11) *prmnt stands side, rdn wl o'r 2 fs out, sn btn*.... (12 to 1 op 10 to 1) 11

3429^{6} ROYAL COMEDIAN [45] 4-8-5 J Carroll (16) *led stands side grp, rdn 2 fs out, sn hdd and one pace*........ (16 to 1) 12

3789^{8} FLASHELLA (Ire) [50] 3-8-6 B Raymond (5) *nvr a factor.* .... (20 to 1 op 16 to 1) 13

4038 RESOLUTE BAY [61] (v) 7-9-7 S Perks (9) *rcd far side, slwly into strd, al rear*..................(25 to 1 tchd 20 to 1) 14

4104 YOUNG VALENTINE [50] 4-8-10 A Culhane (17) *nvr rch ldrs*.. (20 to 1) 15

3523 WILD PROSPECT [52] 5-8-12 M Birch (13) *prmnt stands side 4 fs, sn lost pl*..................(14 to 1 op 12 to 1) 16

4022 MONTONE (Ire) [53] 3-8-9 W R Swinburn (2) *nvr a factor.* ....(25 to 1) 17

3948 GYMCRAK TYCOON [68] 4-9-11 (3*) S Maloney (10) *trkd ldrs far side, effrt and rdn 2 fs out, sn btn and eased.* .... (25 to 1 op 20 to 1) 18

3758 GREENWICH CHALENGE [48] (v) 3-8-4 E Johnson (12) *chsd ldrs stands side, rdn and wknd wl o'r 2 fs out.* .... (7 to 1 op 12 to 1) 19

Dist: ¾l, 1l, 1½l, 1l, 2l, ¾l, sht-hd, nk, sht-hd, hd. 1m 26.83s. a 2.83s (19 Ran).

SR: 27/36/34/18/31/26/7/14/5/ (A W Robinson), M Johnston

4236 Brunton Lane Rating Related Maiden Stakes Class F (0-70 2-y-o) £2,623 7f ....(2:30)

4044^{3} NAWAFELL 8-9 W R Swinburn (5) *in tch, pushed alng 2 fs out, hdwy and swtchd entering last, rdn and squeezed through to ld nr line*.............. (7 to 1 op 10 to 1) 1

3972^{3} ANTANANARIVO (Ire) 9-0 J Carroll (2) *led centre, rdn one furlong out, hng rght ins last, hdd nr finish.* .... (10 to 1 op 8 to 1) 2

3750^{4} HILL REEF (Fr) 9-0 K Fallon (7) *cl up gng wl, chlgd 2 fs out, rdn and ev ch ins last, edgd lft and wkng whn hmpd nr finish*.............................. (8 to 1 op 6 to 1) 3

4021^{4} A MILLION WATTS 9-0 G Duffield (3) *chsd ldrs, rdn 2 fs out, sn one pace*............ (5 to 1 op 4 to 1 tchd 6 to 1) 4

3969^{7} KARSEAM (Ire) 9-0 J Fanning (6) *pld hrd, chsd ldrs, effrt and rdn 2 fs out, wknd and eased ins last*..... (12 to 1) 5

3876^{8} EXPLORE MONDIAL (Ire) 9-0 M Tebbutt (4) *outpcd and beh, styd on fnl 2 fs, nvr dngrs*......... (11 to 1 op 10 to 1) 6

3810^{3} SKY DIVER 9-0 K Darley (1) *chsd ldrs, rdn o'r 2 fs out, sn wknd*...(7 to 1) 7

4027^{7} ASTRAL WEEKS (Ire) 9-0 Pat Eddery (9) *slwly into strd, sn cl up, ev ch o'r 2 fs out, soon rdn, wknd wl over one out.* ....(13 to 8 fav op 6 to 4 tchd 2 to 1) 8

3281^{8} GLENVALLY 8-2 (7*) G Parkin (8) *in tch, rdn hfwy and sn beh*................. (16 to 1 op 12 to 1 tchd 20 to 1) 9

3642 NORTHGATE SYMPHONY 9-0 J Lowe (11) *speed 3 fs, sn beh*..(50 to 1) 10

3809^{3} GOOD SPIRITS 8-9 M Birch (10) *cl up, rdn and wknd quickly hfwy, sn beh*...............(25 to 1 op 16 to 1) 11

Dist: Nk, sht-hd, 6l, 1½l, 4l, sht-hd, 1½l, 2½l, 15l, 15l. 1m 28.48s. a 4.48s (11 Ran).

SR: 7/11/10/-/-/-/ (Maktoum Al Maktoum), A A Scott

4237 EBF Polwarth Maiden Stakes Class D (2-y-o) £4,378 6f................(3:00)

3754^{4} RECAPTURED DAYS (Ire) 9-0 W R Swinburn (10) *trkd ldrs gng wl, hdwy on bit o'r one furlong out, quickened to ld ins last, sn clr*.....(2 to 1 fav op 9 to 4 tchd 3 to 1) 1

3979^{6} FARAS ELNAAS 9-0 W Woods (12) *chsd ldrs, hdwy 2 fs out, rdn and ran on strly ins last*.... (4 to 1 op 5 to 2) 2

3993^{2} FRISKY MISS (Ire) 8-9 J Carroll (3) *led, rdn o'r one furlong out, hdd and wknd ins last*.........(7 to 1 op 6 to 1) 3

NORTH REEF (Ire) 9-0 G Duffield (7) *slwly into strd, beh till styd on wl fnl 2 fs*................... (7 to 1 op 6 to 1) 4

3613^{5} STRATHTORE DREAM (Ire) 8-9 K Darley (5) *cl up, rdn and ev ch wl o'r one furlong out, sn wknd.* ....(7 to 1 tchd 8 to 1) 5

3411^{2} GENERAL GUBBINS 9-0 B Raymond (2) *prmnt, rdn 2 fs out, sn btn*.......................... (6 to 1 op 5 to 1) 6

4042^{3} BEE DEE BEST (Ire) 9-0 J Fanning (1) *mid-div, hdwy o'r 2 fs out, sn rdn and wknd*............(12 to 1 op 10 to 1) 7

4044^{7} WHISPERS HILL 8-6 (3*) O Pears (9) *cl up 3 fs.* .... (33 to 1 op 20 to 1) 8

3972^{7} CHADWELL HALL 9-0 A McGlone (8) *in tch to hfwy.* ....(20 to 1) 9

TARNSIDE TURBO 9-0 M Birch (4) *prmnt, rdn 2 fs out, sn wknd*........................ (25 to 1 op 16 to 1) 10

CAFE SOLO 8-9 L Charnock (11) *slwly away, some hdwy hfwy, sn wknd*...................(40 to 1 op 16 to 1) 11

PAPARAZZO 9-0 Pat Eddery (6) *slwly into strd, al beh.* ....(7 to 1 tchd 5 to 1) 12

Dist: 1l, 3l, 3½l, nk, 1½l, 2l, 3½l, 3½l, 1l, 1½l. 1m 14.10s. a 2.10s (12 Ran).

SR: 34/30/13/4/-/-/ (K Khurbash), A A Scott

4238 Newcastle University Turf Club Conditions Stakes Class C (3-y-o and up) £4,195 5f...................... (3:30)

4112* LUCKY PARKES 3-9-3 J Carroll (6) *made all, rdn one and a half fs out, ran on strly*........ (2 to 1 fav tchd 9 to 4) 1

4216* NIGHT MELODY (Ire) 3-9-0 K Darley (7) *chsd ldrs, effrt 2 fs out, sn rdn, ran on ins last.* ....(7 to 2 op 3 to 1 tchd 4 to 1) 2

4025^{5} MEDAILLE D'OR (bl) 5-9-1 B Raymond (5) *cl up, effrt and ev ch one and a half fs out, sn rdn, wknd ins last.* ....(7 to 1) 3

4040^{4} SIR HARRY HARDMAN 5-9-2 S Perks (2) *chsd ldrs, effrt and rdn 2 fs out, kpt on one pace*.... (8 to 1 op 7 to 1) 4

3571^{7} ELLE SHAPED (Ire) 3-9-2 W R Swinburn (3) *nvr rch ldrs.* .... (16 to 1 op 14 to 1) 5

3995^{4} ABSOLUTION 9-8-12 K Fallon (4) *sn drvn alng, al rear.* .... (50 to 1 op 33 to 1) 6

3834* ARTISTIC REEF 4-9-2 Pat Eddery (1) *prmnt, rdn hfwy, sn lost pl*............. (3 to 1 op 11 to 4 tchd 100 to 30) 7

Dist: 2l, ½l, 1½l, 4l, 1½l, ½l. 59.30s. a 0.40s (7 Ran).

SR: 75/64/63/58/42/32/34/ (Joseph Heler), J Berry

4239 Newcastle Future Stayers And Cesarewitch Trial Rated Class B Handicap (0-95 3-y-o) £6,975 2m 19yds ....(4:00)

3595* MY PATRIARCH [95] 9-7 Pat Eddery (1) *set slow pace, quickened 4 fs out, rdn o'r one out, hng rght ins last, hld on gmely*.............(5 to 4 on tchd 11 to 10 on) 1

3724* HASTEN TO ADD (USA) [89] 9-1 G Duffield (2) *hld up, hdwy 3 fs out, rdn to chal o'r one out, staying on and ev ch whn bumped nr line, jst fld.* ....(5 to 4 tchd 11 to 10 and 11 to 8) 2

3595^{7} VISHNU (USA) [83] 8-9 A McGlone (3) *trkd ldr, effrt and rdn 2 fs out, sn one pace*.............. (8 to 1 tchd 9 to 1) 3

Dist: Sht-hd, 6l. 3m 31.64s. a 5.64s (3 Ran).

SR: 35/28/16/ (Peter S Winfield), J L Dunlop

4240 EBF Princes Maiden Stakes Class D (2-y-o) £4,592 1m...............(4:30)

3876^{4} SHERIDAN (Ire) 9-0 Pat Eddery (6) *trkd ldr, led o'r 2 fs out, rdn and ran on fnl furlong.* ....(6 to 5 on tchd 11 to 10 on) 1

4099^{3} BSHEER (USA) 9-0 W R Swinburn (8) *trkd ldrs, hdwy o'r 2 fs out, sn chasing wnr, rdn and ran on ins last.* .... (11 to 2 op 9 to 2 tchd 6 to 1) 2

3992^{3} DANGER POINT 9-0 K Darley (3) *in tch, hdwy 2 fs out, sn rdn, styd on ins last*................(7 to 1 op 6 to 1) 3

3779^{4} TO CROWN IT ALL (USA) 9-0 S Perks (4) *chsd ldrs, rdn 2 fs out, kpt on one pace*............(16 to 1 tchd 20 to 1) 4

3992^{4} AMBER VALLEY (USA) 9-0 E Johnson (2) *pld hrd, hld up beh, hdwy 2 fs out, styd on ins last, not rch ldrs.* (7 to 1) 5

3742^{3} PRISCIAN'S HEAD 9-0 Paul Eddery (5) *in tch, rdn 3 fs out, sn wknd*............ (9 to 1 op 7 to 1 tchd 10 to 1) 6

3819^{4} SUPREME STAR (USA) 9-0 A McGlone (9) *led, rdn and hdd o'r 2 fs out, sn wknd*.............. (9 to 1 op 10 to 1) 7

3969^{6} BARNPARK 9-0 L Charnock (7) *in tch, rdn 3 fs out, sn wknd*.. (50 to 1) 8

DOCKMASTER 9-0 G Duffield (1) *slwly into strd, al rear.* .... (33 to 1 op 20 to 1) 9

Dist: 1l, 4l, 1l, nk, 5l, 2½l, 2½l, 8l. 1m 43.31s. a 4.31s (9 Ran).

SR: 23/20/8/5/4/-/ (Cyril Humphris), J L Dunlop

4241 Newlands Claiming Stakes Class F (3-y-o) £3,210 1m. . . . . (5:00)

3981[2] DANNY BOY 8-13 Pat Eddery (12) *al prmnt, led 2 fs out, rdn and styd on fnl furlong, eased nr finish.* . . . . (3 to 1 fav op 4 to 1) 1
4126* DEVILS DEN (Ire) 8-12 K Darley (11) *trkd ldrs, hdwy to chase wnr fnl 2 fs, sn rdn, ran on ins last.* . . . . (4 to 1 op 7 to 2) 2
2995[5] KEYWAY (USA) 8-13 G Duffield (3) *hmpd aftr one and a half fs and beh, rdn and swtchd wide 2 furlongs out, styd on ins last.* . . . . (5 to 1 op 4 to 1) 3
4047[4] MISWAKI DANCER (USA) 8-3 Paul Eddery (14) *in tch, hdwy o'r 2 fs out, sn rdn, kpt on one pace.* (6 to 1 op 5 to 1) 4
4083[3] PANTHER (Ire) 7-13 (3*) N Kennedy (2) *beh till styd on fnl 2 fs, nvr dngrs.* . . . . (9 to 1 op 8 to 1) 5
2769[3] QUEEN OF THE QUORN 8-4 J Fanning (9) *led, rdn and hdd 2 fs out, sn wknd.* . . . . (14 to 1 tchd 12 to 1) 6
4031 LETTERMORE 7-8 J Lowe (8) *beh, hdwy 2 and a half fs out, kpt on one pace.* . . . . (20 to 1) 7
4022[2] DRUMDONNA (Ire) 7-12 L Charnock (5) *prmnt, rdn wl o'r 2 fs out, sn wknd.* . . . . (9 to 1 op 10 to 1) 8
4017[7] NEGD (USA) 8-4 J Fortune (10) *in tch, rdn o'r 2 fs out, sn btn.* . . . . (33 to 1 op 25 to 1) 9
3681 GREYSTYLE 7-13 (3*) S Maloney (7) *beh, effrt hfwy, sn drvn alng, no imprsn.* . . . . (33 to 1) 10
4022 GOLD DESIRE 7-11 (5*) J Marshall (6) *al mid-div.* (33 to 1) 11
4045[4] MELODYS DAUGHTER 7-13 F Norton (15) *chsd ldr till rdn and wknd quickly o'r 2 fs out.* . . . . (20 to 1 op 16 to 1) 12
4045[6] SPICE AND SUGAR (bl) 8-4 J Carroll (4) *nvr rch ldrs.* . . . . (12 to 1) 13
MIDNIGHT MISCHIEF (bl) 7-4 (5*) Darren Moffatt (13) *mid-div, hdwy hfwy, rdn o'r 2 fs out, sn wknd.* . . . . (20 to 1) 14
2566[7] FRIENDLY KNIGHT 8-0 Dale Gibson (1) *slwly away, al beh.* . . . . (33 to 1 op 25 to 1) 15

Dist: Nk, 5l, nk, 2l, ¾l, 2½l, hd, 1½l, 3l, nk. 1m 41.39s. a 2.39s (15 Ran).
SR: 51/49/35/24/17/17/-/2/3/ (Ivan Twigden), R Hannon

EVRY (FR) (soft)
Wednesday September 29th
Going Correction: PLUS 0.35 sec. per fur.

4242 Prix Herod (Listed) (2-y-o) £14,337 1m . . . . (4:20)

DARE AND GO (USA) 8-11 O Doleuze, ... 1
3014[5] TELLURIUM (USA) 8-11 F Head, ... 2
PRESS BARON (USA) 8-11 T Jarnet, ... 3
BEFUTO (Fr) 8-11 A Badel, ... 4

Dist: ¾l, 1l, 1½l, ½l, 1l. 1m 48.37s. a 10.97s (6 Ran).
(J Wertheimer), Mrs C Head

4243 Prix Joubert (Listed) (3-y-o) £14,337 1½m. . . . . (4:50)

RING PINK (USA) 8-11 O Doleuze, ... 1
3650[5] ADORED SLEW (USA) 8-11 D Boeuf, ... 2
3194[7] VALLEY QUEST 8-11 C Asmussen, ... 3
LA BARBERINA (USA) 8-11 T Jarnet, ... 4

Dist: 2½l, sht-nk, 1½l, 4l. 2m 39.29s. a 8.49s (5 Ran).
SR: 54/49/48/45/ (J Wertheimer), Miss C Head

FAIRYHOUSE (IRE) (good to yielding)
Wednesday September 29th

4244 Kilcloon E.B.F. Race (2-y-o) £4,140 7f . . . . (2:30)

3335[3] VIA CONDOTTI (Ire) 9-2 K J Manning (16) . . . . (5 to 2) 1
4058[6] FLYING EAGLE 8-10 J P Murtagh (8) . . . . (7 to 1) 2
3927[2] DILIGENT DODGER (Ire) 9-6 W J Supple (5) . . . . (6 to 1) 3
3335[5] ASTRONAVE (Ire) 8-13 M J Kinane (19) . . . . (7 to 4 fav) 4
SHARP TRY (Ire) 8-10 R Hughes (12) . . . . (14 to 1) 5
4058[4] FLY THE CREST (USA) 8-10 N Byrne (3) . . . . (12 to 1) 6
4058 NORTHERN FANCY (Ire) 8-4 (6*) B J Walsh (1) . . . . (40 to 1) 7
3807[8] CLODAGHS FANCY (Ire) 8-3 (4*) J A Heffernan (17) (25 to 1) 8
ONE FALSE MOVE (Ire) 8-7 P V Gilson (20) . . . . (10 to 1) 9
4183[4] NORTHREEL 8-10 S Craine (14) . . . . (12 to 1) 10
3039 BILLY BUZZ (Ire) 8-7 N G McCullagh (18) . . . . (20 to 1) 11
CARABAWN (Ire) 8-6 (4*) J J Behan (4) . . . . (16 to 1) 12
BOLD ENCOUNTER (Ire) 8-5 (2*) R M Burke (9) . . . . (10 to 1) 13
PHARDY (Ire) 8-0 (10*) P P O'Grady (11) . . . . (40 to 1) 14
3073 NANCYS WOOD (Ire) 7-13 (8*) R T Fitzpatrick (6) . . (25 to 1) 15
AARDWOLF 8-8 (2*) P Carberry (15) . . . . (12 to 1) 16
4058 DONT BUG ME (Ire) 8-2 (8*) B Fenton (7) . . . . (50 to 1) 17
4059 GREENRIDGE COURT (Ire) 7-13 (8*) G M Moylan (13) . . . . (50 to 1) 18
3825[5] SUN MARK (Ire) 8-10 P Shanahan (2) . . . . (16 to 1) 19

Dist: 5l, 2l, 1l, ½l. 1m 30.00s. (19 Ran).
(D H W Dobson), J S Bolger

4245 Clonalvey Race (3-y-o and up) £3,450 1m 1f. . . . . (4:00)

3924[7] FLAME OF PERSIA (Ire) 3-9-2 R Hughes (11) . . . . (10 to 1) 1
1199[3] SHARP REVIEW (Ire) 5-9-11 M J Kinane (14) . . . . (2 to 1) 2
3616* BALAWHAR (Ire) 3-9-1 J P Murtagh (13) . . . . (5 to 4 fav) 3
LADY OLEIN (Ire) 5-9-4 J F Egan (2) . . . . (14 to 1) 4
7874 FOREST CONCERT (Ire) 4-9-8 S Craine (15) . . . . (10 to 1) 5
4118* CORPORATE SPORT (Ire) 3-9-3 N G McCullagh (9) (7 to 1) 6
3579* BELLISSI (Ire) 3-8-4 (8*) P J Smullen (18) . . . . (10 to 1) 7
4057 GOLDEN SPHINX (Ire) 3-8-5 (2*) D G O'Shea (19) (12 to 1) 8
PROUD MOMENT (Ire) 3-8-6 (4*) J J Behan (6) . . . . (20 to 1) 9
3926 TRANQUIL BEAUTY (Ire) 4-9-2 (2*) P Carberry (22) (20 to 1) 10
3999[4] TERESIAN GIRL (Ire) 3-8-7 D Manning (8) . . . . (33 to 1) 11
ALPENCROCUS (Ire) 3-8-7 P Shanahan (3) . . . . (20 to 1) 12
3852[3] CRYSTAL SHIP (Ire) (bl) 3-8-12 P V Gilson (1) . . . . (10 to 1) 13
JOSH'S BEN (Ire) 4-9-2 D Hogan (7) . . . . (20 to 1) 14
3808[7] ANOTHER SKY-LARK (Ire) 5-9-2 N Byrne (17) . . . . (20 to 1) 15
LADY HOSTESS (Ire) 4-8-11 (2*) R M Burke (5) . . . . (50 to 1) 16
3916[8] ALBERTAZZI (Ire) (bl) 3-9-1 K J Manning (4) . . . . (10 to 1) 17
3111[2] DAHLIA'S BEST (USA) 3-8-10 W J Supple (21) . . . . (14 to 1) su
BAVARIAN BALLAD (Ire) 3-8-3 (4*) W J Smith (10) (25 to 1) 18

Dist: 1½l, ¾l, 2½l, sht-hd. 2m 8.00s. (19 Ran).
(E Flynn), Michael Kauntze

4246 Palmerstown Handicap (0-80 3-y-o) £2,760 1½m. . . . . (4:30)

2955[2] MICKS DELIGHT (Ire) [-] 9-3 (2*) P Carberry (8) . . . . (7 to 1) 1
4147[4] NO DUNCE (Ire) [-] 8-13 P V Gilson (13) . . . . (14 to 1) 2
3028[5] HOPESVILLE (Ire) [-] 8-12 (4*) J J Behan (4) . . . . (12 to 1) 3
3684[5] WICKLOW WAY (Ire) [-] 8-5 W J Supple (23) . . . . (12 to 1) 4
4147[9] KAR OR [-] 9-3 (4*) C Everard (14) . . . . (16 to 1) 5
3773* RETURN AGAIN (Ire) [-] 9-7 R Hughes (7) . . . . (4 to 1 jt-fav) 6
3733[2] MY KERRY DANCER (USA) [-] 9-2 S Craine (22) . . . (12 to 1) 7
1980[4] MRS SNUGGS (Ire) [-] 7-7 (8*) R T Fitzpatrick (2) . . (12 to 1) 8
3772[2] BRAVE RAIDER (Ire) [-] 9-5 M J Kinane (5) . . . . (4 to 1 jt-fav) 9
4147[3] SOLAS ABU (Ire) [-] 9-7 K J Manning (15) . . . . (12 to 1) 10
2842 BOBADIL (Ire) [-] 7-12[3] (8*) P J Smullen (20) . . . . (20 to 1) 11
2781[7] NEW LOVE (Ire) [-] 7-12 (2*) R M Burke (1) . . . . (6 to 1) 12
3616[6] MYSTICAL CITY (Ire) [-] 8-8 J F Egan (21) . . . . (10 to 1) 13
3299* TROUBLE SHOOT (USA) [-] 9-5 N G McCullagh (10) . . . . (14 to 1) 14
4185[7] GLAS AGUS OR (Ire) [-] (bl) 8-1 (4*) J A Heffernan (19) . . . . (12 to 1) 15
4119[3] PARTICULAR (Ire) [-] 9-0 (5ex) J P Murtagh (11) . . . . (7 to 1) 16
819* SPORTSTYLE (Ire) [-] 8-12 N Byrne (3) . . . . (16 to 1) 17
3497 COPSEWOOD (Ire) [-] 7-10 (8*) G M Moylan (17) . . (25 to 1) 18
3914 PAKED (Ire) [-] 7-3 (4*) W J Smith (18) . . . . (50 to 1) 19
3951[8] HIND VISION (Ire) [-] (bl) 8-4 (2*) D G O'Shea (12) . . (14 to 1) 20
3604[5] LAKE OF LOUGHREA (Ire) [-] 8-4[1] (6*) B J Walsh (6) . . . . (120 to 1) 21
3380[9] KERMIS (Fr) [-] 7-12 (8*) B J Halligan (9) . . . . (50 to 1) 22

Dist: ¾l, ¾l, 3l, sht-hd. 2m 50.50s. (22 Ran).
(M J McCarthy), Noel Meade

NEWMARKET (good to soft)
Wednesday September 29th
Going Correction: PLUS 0.15 sec. per fur. (races 1,2), PLUS 0.30 (3,4,5,6)

4247 Shadwell Stud Apprentice Series Final Handicap Class E (0-85 3-y-o and up) £8,415 1¼m. . . . . (2:00)

4028[6] SONG OF SIXPENCE (USA) [58] 9-7-13 (7*) C Scudder (13) *patiently rdn, shaken up to improve o'r one furlong out, ran on wl to ld cl hme.* . . . . (14 to 1 tchd 16 to 1) 1
3787[2] BIT ON THE SIDE (Ire) [64] 4-8-12 L Newton (2) *wtd wth, improved o'r 2 fs out, led last 100 yards, ct cl hme.* . . . . (12 to 1 op 10 to 1) 2
3555[6] SUNTARA (Ire) [69] 3-8-11 Michael Denaro (14) *tucked away in midfield, improved to ld o'r one furlong out, hdd last 100 yards, one pace.* . . . . (20 to 1 op 16 to 1 tchd 25 to 1) 3
4036 DASHING FELLOW (Ire) [58] 5-8-1 (5*) G Milligan (1) *settled gng wl, improved on bit o'r 2 fs out, styd on same pace fnl furlong.* . . . . (16 to 1 op 14 to 1) 4
3507[2] SOVEREIGN PAGE (USA) [76] 4-9-10 J Tate (3) *settled mid-field, chlgd 2 fs out, not quicken fnl furlong.* . . . . (20 to 1 op 12 to 1) 5
3420 SANTANA LADY (Ire) [63] 4-8-6 (5*) Ruth Coulter (7) *nvr far away, led o'r 2 fs out till over one out, no extr.* . . . . (25 to 1 op 20 to 1) 6
3973[6] RETENDER (USA) [60] 4-8-8 B Russell (19) *beh, drvn alng hfwy, styd on und pres fnl furlong, nvr nrr.* . . . . (11 to 1 op 8 to 1 tchd 12 to 1) 7
3831 LOWAWATHA [54] 5-8-2[3] C Hodgson (4) *wtd wth, improved on outsd o'r 2 fs out, wknd ins last.* . . . . (20 to 1 op 16 to 1) 8
3985* BALL GOWN [54] 3-7-10[1] Stephen Davies (17) *settled off the pace, improved hfwy, effrt o'r 2 fs out, no imprsn.* . . . . (10 to 1 op 8 to 1) 9
2794[9] PERFAY (USA) [80] 5-10-0 B Doyle (20) *beh, chsd alng hfwy, styd on und pres last 2 fs, nvr nrr.* . . . . (33 to 1 tchd 50 to 1) 10

3555[4] DUVEEN (Ire) [68] 3-8-10 M Fenton (12) *wtd wth, pushed alng o'r 2 fs out, no extr.* ....(14 to 1 op 12 to 1 tchd 16 to 1) 11
MAJED (Ire) [78] 5-9-12 Darren Moffatt (11) *settled off the pace, swtchd ins to improve o'r 2 fs out, nvr able to chal.*..............................(14 to 1 op 12 to 1) 12
3986[2] PORT SUNLIGHT (Ire) [71] 5-9-0 (5*) D O'Neill (16) *pressed ldrs, hrd drvn o'r 2 fs out, fdd.* (8 to 1 fav tchd 9 to 1) 13
2059[7] LYPHANTASTIC (USA) [71] 4-9-5 K Rutter (5) *nevr far away, feeeling pace o'r 2 fs out, fdd.* ....(25 to 1 op 20 to 1 tchd 33 to 1) 14
4088* DANCING DIAMOND (Ire) [51] 3-7-7 (5ex) C Hawksley (15) *shwd up wl on ins till fdd last 2 fs.* ....(10 to 1 op 12 to 1 tchd 8 to 1) 15
4107[2] BOLD STROKE [77] 4-9-11 J D Smith (10) *trkd ldrs, bustled alng o'r 2 fs out, fdd*....(9 to 1 op 7 to 1 tchd 10 to 1) 16
4018[3] QUEEN WARRIOR [72] 4-9-6 D Wright (8) *shwd up wl for o'r 6 fs, fdd 2 out*......(11 to 1 op 8 to 1 tchd 12 to 1) 17
4043[3] TAPATCH (Ire) [64] 5-8-12 O Pears (18) *trkd ldrs, effrt gng wl hfwy, fdd o'r 2 fs out*...........(12 to 1 op 10 to 1) 18
2894* MR TATE (Ire) [70] 4-8-13 (5*) T Ashley (9) *co'red up in midfield, drvn alng whn pace quickened over 2 fs out, fdd*..............................(14 to 1 op 12 to 1) 19
4035[3] CLIFTON CHASE [45] (bl) 4-7-7 A Garth (6) *led till o'r 2 fs out, fdd*..............................(33 to 1 op 20 to 1) 20

Dist: Hd, 2l, ¾l, nk, 1½l, nk, 2½l, hd, ¾l, sht-hd. 2m 8.93s. a 6.23s (20 Ran).
SR: 45/50/45/38/55/39/35/24/17/ (Paul Mellon), I A Balding

4248 Hunter Price Partnership Rated Class B Handicap (0-100 3-y-o and up) £7,884 1½m.................... (2:35)

3434 NIGHT CLUBBING (Ire) [84] 4-9-1 T Quinn (6) *trkd ldg pair, led o'r 2 fs out, hrd pressed fnl furlong, kpt on wl.* ....(100 to 30 fav op 7 to 2) 1
3881[2] PISTOL RIVER (Ire) [94] (v) 3-9-3 J Reid (8) *tucked away on ins, chalg whn squeezed for room o'r 2 fs out, bumped appr last, kpt on, unlucky.* ....(9 to 2 op 7 to 2 tchd 5 to 1) 2
3786[3] OPERA GHOST [81] 7-8-12 W R Swinburn (2) *patiently rdn, improved frm off the pace whn edgd lft o'r 2 fs out and over one out, kpt on*..........(5 to 1 tchd 11 to 2) 3
1314[2] CAPTAIN'S GUEST (Ire) [96] 3-9-5 R Hills (7) *settled midfield, improved on outsd whn edgd rght o'r 2 fs out, one pace ins last*........... (8 to 1 op 7 to 1 tchd 10 to 1) 4
4064[7] MEAVY [83] 3-8-6 M Tebbutt (9) *al hndy, led o'r 7 fs out till over 2 out, wknd appr last*..........(10 to 1 op 7 to 1) 5
3963[6] GROVE DAFFODIL (Ire) [84] (v) 3-8-7 P Robinson (1) *patiently rdn, drvn alng to improve 3 fs out, ridden and outpcd 2 out*.....(14 to 1 op 12 to 1 tchd 16 to 1) 6
3587[3] PRINCE HANNIBAL [84] 6-9-1 Pat Eddery (4) *last and hld up, drvn alng whn pace quickened o'r 2 fs out, sn lost tch*.................... (10 to 1 op 7 to 1 tchd 12 to 1) 7
4064[3] JUSTICE (Fr) [76] 5-8-4 (3*) B Doyle (3) *led till o'r 7 fs out, drvn alng over 2 out, sn lost tch.* (33 to 1 tchd 50 to 1) 8
3904[3] ALKHAFJI [90] 4-9-7 W Ryan (5) *trkd ldg trio, struggling o'r 2 fs out, sn lost tch.* (13 to 2 op 5 to 1 tchd 7 to 1) 9

Dist: 1l, sht-hd, 1l, 10l, nk, 15l, 2½l, 6l. 2m 36.48s. a 6.88s (9 Ran).
SR: 50/50/44/49/16/16/ (Sheikh Essa Bin Mubarak), R Akehurst

4249 Tattersalls Houghton Sales Conditions Stakes Class B (2-y-o) £26,796 7f .... (3:05)

3753[2] FUMO DI LONDRA (Ire) 9-0 L Piggott (28) *led centre grp, o'rall ldr ins fnl furlong, hld on gmely.* ....(16 to 1 tchd 20 to 1) 1
3859* NICOLOTTE 9-0 M Hills (14) *wl plcd centre, led o'r one furlong out till ins last, rallied.* ....(7 to 4 fav op 2 to 1 tchd 9 to 4) 2
3902* PICCOLO 9-0 W Woods (12) *wl plcd centre, drvn alng ins fnl furlong, kpt on same pace*....(33 to 1 tchd 50 to 1) 3
4004* FRENCH GIFT 8-9 R Cochrane (9) *chsd stands side ldrs, styd on ins fnl furlong, nrst finish.* ....(25 to 1 tchd 33 to 1) 4+
3463* VELVET MOON (Ire) 8-9 A Munro (5) *led stands side till o'r one furlong out, kpt on same pace.* (11 to 2 op 6 to 1) 4+
3435[3] TORCH ROUGE 9-0 D Holland (10) *wl plcd stands side, bustled alng ins fnl furlong, kpt on well.* .... (8 to 1 op 7 to 1 tchd 10 to 1) 6
3446* CANASKA DANCER (Ire) 9-0 J Reid (6) *wth ldrs stands side, drvn alng entering fnl furlong, kpt on.* ....(50 to 1 op 33 to 1) 7
3597* BARBAROJA 9-0 W R Swinburn (19) *wl plcd centre, feeling pace o'r one furlong out, rallied.* (20 to 1 tchd 33 to 1) 8
3729* CRYSTAL LAKE (Ire) 8-9 M Roberts (16) *chsd alng to improve frm midfield last 2 fs, styd on finish.* ....(25 to 1 op 20 to 1 tchd 33 to 1) 9
4027[2] STAR SELECTION 9-0 T Quinn (7) *pressed ldrs stands side, drvn alng o'r one furlong out, kpt on same pace.* ....(25 to 1 op 20 to 1 tchd 33 to 1) 10
3625[2] WIND IN HER HAIR (Ire) 8-9 R Hills (25) *chsd alng centre, improved o'r one furlong out, ran on finish.* ....(20 to 1 tchd 25 to 1) 11
3462[6] WESTERN GENERAL 9-0 P Robinson (2) *sluggish strt, improved frm off the pace last 2 fs, fnshd wl.* ....(100 to 1 op 66 to 1) 12
3659[4] LA RIVERAINE (USA) 8-9 J Carroll (21) *bustled alng hfwy, improved centre fnl furlong, fnshd wl.* ....(100 to 1 op 66 to 1) 13
3635[6] KISSININTHEBACKROW (USA) 8-9 J Williams (11) *sluggish strt, improved to press stands side ldrs hfwy, one pace last 2 fs*..............................(100 to 1 op 66 to 1) 14
3908* CICERAO (Ire) 9-0 W Ryan (15) *chsd alng centre, styd on last 2 fs, nvr able to chal*........... (10 to 1 op 8 to 1) 15
4062[4] BIG SQUEEZE (USA) 9-0 D Biggs (8) *pressed ldrs stands side for o'r 5 fs, no extr*............(33 to 1 op 20 to 1) 16
3828[4] SHORTFALL 8-9 L Dettori (23) *chsd ldrs centre, effrt hfwy, no imprsn last 2 fs*... (40 to 1 op 33 to 1 tchd 50 to 1) 17
3596[4] FOURTH OF JUNE (USA) 9-0 B Doyle (3) *bustled alng to keep up, styd on last 2 fs, nvr nrr.* (100 to 1 op 66 to 1) 18
4113[2] STASH THE CASH (Ire) 9-0 G Bardwell (4) *tucked away stands side, not much room and swtchd o'r one furlong out, nvr able to chal.* ....(66 to 1 op 50 to 1 tchd 100 to 1) 19
3159[2] IRRESTIBLE LADY (Ire) 8-9 C Roche (1) *sluggish strt, bustled alng stands side, nvr able to chal.* ....(40 to 1 op 33 to 1 tchd 50 to 1) 20
3570[3] IZZA 8-9 S Whitworth (20) *outpcd and drvn alng, nvr rch chalg pos*............(40 to 1 op 33 to 1 tchd 50 to 1) 21
3422[2] VARSAVIA (USA) 8-9 D Harrison (27) *drvn alng centre, nvr nr to chal*..............................(33 to 1) 22
3960[2] I FEAR NOTHING 8-9 K Darley (18) *bustled alng midfield, nvr rch ldrs*......................(50 to 1 op 33 to 1) 23
2704[2] GIULIO ROMANO (Ire) 9-0 M Tebbutt (26) *chsd alng to keep up, nvr dngrs*..............................(66 to 1) 24
3940[2] ALCOVE 9-0 A McGlone (22) *outpcd and drvn alng, nvr nr to chal*...........(50 to 1 op 33 to 1 tchd 66 to 1) 25
3888[9] FARNHAM (Ire) 9-0 Stephen Davies (13) *speed centre for o'r 4 fs, sn lost tch*..................(100 to 1 op 66 to 1) 26
3592[6] ROMAN CAMP (Fr) 9-0 M Birch (17) *outpcd and drvn alng most of way, nvr dngrs*..........(100 to 1 op 33 to 1) 27
3658* UNCLE OSWALD 9-0 R Perham (30) *wth ldrs centre for o'r 4 fs, fdd*............(50 to 1 op 33 to 1 tchd 66 to 1) 28
3765[2] DIAMOND PARK (Ire) 8-9 Pat Eddery (24) *struggling to go pace hfwy, nvr dngrs.* ....(25 to 1 op 20 to 1 tchd 33 to 1) 29
4058[7] UNDER SIEGE (Ire) (bl) 9-0 G Duffield (29) *speed centre to hfwy, wknd rpdly*.............. (100 to 1 op 66 to 1) 30

Dist: Hd, 1½l, hd, dd-ht, ½l, nk, nk, ½l, sht-hd, sht-hd. 1m 28.39s. a 4.89s (30 Ran).
SR: 58/57/52/46/46/49/48/47/40/ (Gerecon Italia), J L Dunlop

4250 Shadwell Stud Cheveley Park Stakes Class A (Group 1) (2-y-o) £73,122 6f ....(3:40)

3737* PROPHECY (Ire) 8-11 Pat Eddery (1) *patiently rdn, last hfwy, brst through fnl furlong, ran on to ld cl hme.* ....(12 to 1 op 10 to 1 tchd 14 to 1) 1
3463[2] RISKY 8-11 W R Swinburn (3) *led, quickened and clr 2 fs out, wknd last 100 yards, ct cl hme.* ....(7 to 2 op 3 to 1 tchd 4 to 1) 2
3925* LEMON SOUFFLE 8-11 L Piggott (4) *al hndy, struck into o'r 2 fs out, ev ch whn lost action fnl furlong, rallied.* ....(6 to 4 on op 2 to 1 on tchd 11 to 8 on) 3
2301[3] ROHITA (Ire) 8-11 T Quinn (6) *nvr far away, drvn alng whn pace quickened o'r 2 fs out, one pace.* ....(16 to 1 op 12 to 1 tchd 20 to 1) 4
3898* IMPERIAL BAILIWICK (Ire) 8-11 J Williams (5) *pressed ldrs, drvn alng whn pace quickened o'r 2 fs out, sn outpcd.* ....(12 to 1 op 16 to 1 tchd 20 to 1) 5
1844* MARAGON 8-11 R Cochrane (2) *wtd wth, effrt and drvn alng o'r 2 fs out, no extr.* ....(16 to 1 op 14 to 1 tchd 20 to 1) 6

Dist: ½l, 2l, 3½l, hd, 3½l. 1m 14.68s. a 3.28s (6 Ran).
SR: 67/65/57/43/42/28/ (K Abdulla), J H M Gosden

4251 EBF Jersey Lily Fillies' Nursery Handicap Class C (2-y-o) £20,225 7f.. (4:10)

3865 MANHATTAN SUNSET (USA) [72] 8-7 J Reid (9) *patiently rdn, weaved through appr fnl furlong, ran on wl to ld on line*..............(14 to 1 op 16 to 1 tchd 20 to 1) 1
3902[4] FAWAAKEH (USA) [80] 9-1 R Hills (10) *tucked away midfield, led entering fnl furlong, ran on, ct on line.* ....(16 to 1 tchd 20 to 1) 2
3463[7] NICE WELCOME [86] 9-0 (7*) C Hawksley (8) *beh, improved frm off the pace to ld o'r one furlong out, hdd entering last, kpt on*..............................(33 to 1) 3
3809[4] VANESSA ROSE [62] 7-6 (5*) D Wright (13) *outpcd and pushed alng hfwy, str run entering fnl furlong, rng on whn hmpd last 50 yards, unlucky*............(25 to 1) 4
3765[7] PALANA (USA) [83] 9-4 M Hills (12) *patiently rdn, weaved through frm midfield appr fnl furlong, styd on, nvr nrr*..............................(25 to 1) 5
3966[2] TASHLA [69] (v) 8-4 W Ryan (6) *made most till entering fnl furlong, kpt on same pace*........(14 to 1 op 12 to 1) 6
4004[4] STAR SPEEDER (Ire) [78] 8-8 (5*) B Russell (5) *chsd ldg bunch, effrt and swtchd lft entering fnl furlong, kpt on, nvr nrr*.................... (8 to 1 fav op 12 to 1) 7
3905[4] ARNDILLY [77] 8-12 W R Swinburn (4) *nvr far away, hrd drvn last 2 fs, no extr*...........(14 to 1 tchd 16 to 1) 8

3905[2] BE EXCITING (Ire) [73] 8-8 R Cochrane (2) *speed frnt rnk till rdn and no extr ins fnl furlong*.... (12 to 1 op 10 to 1) 9
3972[2] BILLIE GREY [70] 8-5 D Holland (15) *wl plcd on outsd, kpt on same pace ins fnl furlong*...... (14 to 1 op 16 to 1) 10
3667* HELLO IRELAND [74] 8-9 Pat Eddery (3) *tucked away on ins, effrt 2 fs out, not pace to chal*............(12 to 1) 11
4097[2] DANGEROUS SHADOW [64] 7-8 (5*) Darren Moffatt (1) *wl plcd stands side, ev ch 2 fs out, wkng whn hmpd and snatched up ins last*.............(12 to 1 tchd 14 to 1) 12
3958[5] LADY WILLIAMS (Ire) [66] 8-1 D Harrison (16) *speed frnt rnk 5 fs*.......................................(10 to 1 op 7 to 1) 13
3284[4] EXOTIC FOREST [62] 7-10[2] (3*) B Doyle (20) *chsd ldrs, effrt and swtchd outsd whn clipped rival's heels and almost brght dwn 2 fs out, not reco'r*.................(50 to 1) 14
3941[4] REDRESS (USA) [73] 8-8 A Munro (14) *wtd wth, effrt whn squeezed for room o'r one furlong out, nvr able to chal*. ....(10 to 1 op 14 to 1) 15
3671[2] CUT THE RED TAPE (Ire) [82] 9-3 L Dettori (7) *settled midfield, ev ch and rdn 2 fs out, wknd fnl furlong*. ....(14 to 1 op 16 to 1) 16
4002[4] SPARKLING ROBERTA [60] 7-9 R Street (21) *struggling to go pace hfwy, sn btn*.......................(33 to 1) 17
3966[6] ALACRITY [76] 8-11 J Williams (18) *trkd ldrs, feeling pace o'r 2 fs out, fdd*...................(33 to 1 op 25 to 1) 18
4029[4] YAWARA [74] 8-9 M Roberts (11) *in tch, struggling to go pace hfwy, sn btn*.................(14 to 1 op 12 to 1) 19
3845* RAJMAPATA [78] 8-13 K Darley (17) *frnt rnk, hmpd 2 fs out, sn btn*....................................(12 to 1) 20
3865[5] CARAPELLE [66] 8-1[3] (3*) S Maloney (22) *settled gng wl, swtchd outsd and ev ch whn hmpd 2 fs out, eased when no chance*.. (12 to 1 op 10 to 1 tchd 14 to 1) 21
3750[5] HIGHLY FASHIONABLE (Ire) [69] 8-4 T Quinn (19) *pressed ldrs, effrt whn baulked 2 fs out, eased when btn*. ....(20 to 1) 22

Dist: Sht-hd, nk, 1l, hd, hd, 1½l, 2½l, hd, sht-hd, ½l. 1m 29.34s. a 5.84s (22 Ran).
SR: 37/44/49/22/42/27/31/22/17/ (R E Sangster), P W Chapple-Hyam

4252 EBF Myson Compact Maiden Stakes Class D (2-y-o) £5,127 1m.......(4:40)

THE DEEP (Ire) 9-0 D Holland (10) *sluggish strt, improved hfwy, ran on strly to ld last 50 yards*. (7 to 1 op 6 to 1) 1
3876[2] DOVER STRAITS (USA) 9-0 L Dettori (18) *trkd ldrs gng wl, led o'r 2 fs out, wknd and ct last 50 yards*. ....(2 to 1 on op 6 to 4 on tchd 5 to 4 on) 2
4099[2] WAITING 9-0 A Munro (7) *pressed ldrs stands side, drvn alng appr fnl furlong, kpt on same pace*. ....(14 to 1 op 10 to 1) 3
PTOTO 9-0 R Cochrane (6) *settled midfield, effrt and drvn alng last 2 fs, kpt on same pace*. ....(20 to 1 op 12 to 1) 4
EUROLINK CHIEFTAIN 9-0 W Ryan (5) *patiently rdn, shaken up to improve on bit o'r one furlong out, ran on, prmsg*...........(33 to 1 op 16 to 1 tchd 50 to 1) 5
APACHE PLUME (USA) 9-0 M Roberts (9) *wtd wth, swtchd outsd to improve frm midfield last 2 fs, improve*. ....(14 to 1 op 12 to 1 tchd 20 to 1) 6
SILVER HUNTER (USA) 9-0 T Quinn (14) *al hndy, drvn alng whn pace quickened o'r one furlong out, one pace*. ....(16 to 1 op 10 to 1) 7
3287 TRADE WIND 9-0 J Williams (1) *beh and pushed alng hfwy, styd on last 2 fs, nrst finish*. ....(25 to 1 op 16 to 1 tchd 33 to 1) 8
4027[6] RUBHAHUNISH (Ire) 9-0 J Reid (12) *tucked away in midfield, gng wl hfwy, fdd appr fnl furlong*. ....(20 to 1 op 7 to 1) 9
ALWAYS ALOOF (USA) 9-0 W R Swinburn (15) *beh and chsd alng hfwy, styd on last 2 fs, nvr nrr*. ....(14 to 1 op 12 to 1 tchd 20 to 1) 10
3802[2] MR ARTISTIC (USA) 9-0 D Harrison (11) *wl plcd stands side, led o'r 3 fs out till over 2 out, fdd*. ....(25 to 1 op 12 to 1 tchd 33 to 1) 11
MUNTAFI 9-0 R Hills (3) *trkd ldrs, shaken up hfwy, wknd o'r one furlong out*...(33 to 1 op 14 to 1 tchd 50 to 1) 12
TAAJ (USA) 9-0 J Carroll (8) *settled midfield, effrt and ran green hfwy, wknd 2 fs out*.........(25 to 1 op 16 to 1) 13
POLO KIT (Ire) 9-0 G Duffield (2) *beh and chsd alng hfwy, nvr nr to chal*.........(20 to 1 op 10 to 1 tchd 25 to 1) 14
CUANGO (Ire) 9-0 K Darley (4) *beh and drvn alng hfwy, nvr dngrs*..............................(50 to 1 op 33 to 1) 15
THUNDERHEART 8-11 (3*) C Hodgson (13) *chsd ldrs centre for o'r 5 fs, fdd*.....................(50 to 1 op 33 to 1) 16
ACERBUS DULCIS 8-11 (3*) B Doyle (19) *shwd up wl on outsd till wknd last 2 fs*........... (50 to 1 op 20 to 1) 17
MATO 9-0 M Hills (16) *chsd alng midfield, struggling last 2 fs*...............................(50 to 1 op 20 to 1) 18
1828 PERHAPS 9-0 P Robinson (17) *led till o'r 3 fs out, fdd 2 out*...(50 to 1 op 25 to 1) 19

Dist: 1½l, ½l, nk, 2½l, ½l, ½l, 2½l, nk, 1½l, 1½l. 1m 43.39s. a 6.19s (19 Ran).
SR: 43/38/36/35/27/25/23/15/14/ (K Al-Said), B W Hills

SALISBURY (soft)
Wednesday September 29th

Going Correction: PLUS 0.05 sec. per fur. (races 1,3,5,6,7), PLUS 0.15 (2,4)

4253 EBF London Trust Securities Maiden Stakes Class D (Div I) (2-y-o) £4,306 1m..............................(2:25)

3908[2] TWIN FALLS (Ire) 9-0 B Raymond (6) *al prmnt, led o'r 3 fs out, ran on wl ins last*........ (2 to 1 on op 6 to 4 on) 1
MYSTIC HILL 9-0 S Raymont (11) *pld hrd, al in tch on outsd, ev ch 2 fs out till swrvd badly rght ins last*. .... (6 to 1 op 9 to 4 tchd 13 to 2) 2
4002[3] SAAFI (Ire) 9-0 W Carson (4) *slwly into strd, sn prmnt, led hfwy, hdd o'r 3 fs out, outpcd ins fnl 2*. ....(7 to 1 op 5 to 1 tchd 8 to 1) 3
3260[9] INDIAN TEMPLE 9-0 M Wigham (8) *al prmnt, led aftr 2 fs, hdd bef hfwy, lost tch ins fnl two*. (50 to 1 op 33 to 1) 4+
4067 PEVERIL PRINCESS 8-9 N Adams (12) *wtd wth, styd on fnl 2 fs, nvr dngrs*................(50 to 1 op 20 to 1) 4+
4002[6] LICENTIOUS 8-9 A Clark (3) *nvr on terms*. .... (20 to 1 op 12 to 1 tchd 25 to 1) 6
3979[9] POLY SCREEN 9-0 K Fallon (7) *beh, rdn o'r 3 fs out, nvr on terms*............... (33 to 1 op 25 to 1 tchd 50 to 1) 7
RUN WITH JOY (Ire) 9-0 W Newnes (5) *led for 2 fs, wknd sn aftr hfwy*..........................(16 to 1 op 10 to 1) 8
STRATH KITTEN 8-9 R Price (2) *al beh*.......... (50 to 1) 9
3869 GUTO NYTH BRAN 9-0 J Lowe (1) *al towards rear, outpcd frm hfwy*...(50 to 1) 10
2331[9] READY MONEY RILEY 9-0 E Johnson (10) *outpcd thrght, tld off*............................(50 to 1 op 33 to 1) 11

Dist: 2½l, 12l, 4l, dd-ht, 3l, nk, 3l, 3l, 2½l, 20l. 1m 46.77s. a 7.27s (11 Ran).
(Fahd Salman), R Hannon

4254 Hertz No.1 Club Gold Handicap Class E (0-70 3-y-o and up) £3,652 1m 1f 209yds.......................(2:55)

4028 CASPIAN BELUGA [55] 5-9-2 J Quinn (2) *led aftr one furlong, styd alone on far side frm hfwy, sn clr, pushed out, cmftbly*.......... (20 to 1 op 16 to 1 tchd 25 to 1) 1
3891[9] MAHONG [55] 5-9-2 T Sprake (13) *mid-div, hdwy to chase wnr fnl 2 fs, ran on ins last*...... (14 to 1 tchd 16 to 1) 2
4101* MYSILV [66] 3-9-7 (5ex) W Carson (5) *led 1st furlong, came o'r to centre hfwy, chsd wnr till wknd 2 fs out*. ....(4 to 1 fav op 6 to 1) 3
3961[6] ANUSHA [61] 3-9-2 A Clark (11) *in rear, making hdwy whn edgd lft o'r 2 fs out, kpt on one pace*. .... (13 to 2 op 8 to 1) 4
3646[4] INCHCAILLOCH (Ire) [66] 4-9-8 (5*) A Procter (15) *in rear, styd on fnl 2 fs, nvr nrr*. ....(20 to 1 op 16 to 1 tchd 25 to 1) 5
4116[5] LADY LACEY [61] 6-9-1 (7*) N Varley (9) *hld up, effrt 3 fs out, nvr dngrs*...........(8 to 1 op 7 to 1 tchd 9 to 1) 6
4091* SWIFT ROMANCE (Ire) [54] 5-9-1 (5ex) J Lowe (6) *beh, some hdwy ins fnl 3 fs, nvr dngrs*....... (7 to 1 op 11 to 2) 7
3986[5] GREEN'S FAIR (Ire) [59] 3-9-0 J Weaver (14) *hld up in tch, rdn o'r 2 fs out, one pace*.......... (20 to 1 op 16 to 1) 8
3985[2] JADE GREEN [56] 4-9-3 C Rutter (4) *al abt same pl, no hdwy fnl 3 fs*........(16 to 1 op 14 to 1 tchd 20 to 1) 9
3225[8] WELSH HERITAGE (Ire) [61] 3-9-2 B Raymond (3) *pld hrd, prmnt till wknd o'r 2 fs out*.........(10 to 1 op 8 to 1) 10
3832[3] BOMBLET [70] 3-9-11 Paul Eddery (10) *al beh*. .... (20 to 1 op 12 to 1) 11
3088[7] TIFFANY'S CASE (Ire) [54] 4-9-1 E Johnson (17) *al beh*. .... (20 to 1 op 12 to 1) 12
4091[4] MYFONTAINE [57] 6-9-4 M Wigham (16) *mid-div, wknd o'r 3 fs out*.................. (20 to 1 op 16 to 1) 13
2898[9] WATER GYPSY [66] 3-9-7 S Raymont (18) *chsd ldrs till wknd o'r 3 fs out*.................(20 to 1 op 14 to 1) 14
3643[6] SINGER ON THE ROOF [67] (v) 3-9-8 S O'Gorman (12) *prmnt, wkng whn bumped o'r 2 fs out, eased*. .... (16 to 1 op 14 to 1) 15
3670[8] PLAY WITH ME (Ire) [68] 3-9-9 W Newnes (7) *chsd ldrs till wknd o'r 3 fs out*...............(14 to 1 op 10 to 1) 16
4102 MYSTICAL GUEST [50] 7-8-11 R Price (1) *al beh, tld off*. .... (66 to 1 op 33 to 1) 17

Dist: 2½l, 3½l, ¾l, ¾l, 7l, 7l, nk, ½l, 2½l, 1½l. 2m 11.19s. a 7.19s (17 Ran).
SR: 45/40/38/31/40/21/ (L J Hawkings), Mrs A Knight

4255 Westbury Motor Auctions Sia Trophy Conditions Stakes Class C (2-y-o) £5,578 6f 212yds...............(3:25)

3974* TATAMI (USA) 8-12 J Weaver (1) *hld up, hdwy o'r 2 fs out, led appr last, ran green, jst held on*. ....(11 to 4 op 5 to 2 tchd 3 to 1) 1
3949* ERHAAB (USA) 9-0 W Carson (3) *trkd ldr, shaken up to ld o'r 2 fs out, hdd appr last, rallied und pres, jst fld*. .... (13 to 8 on op 11 to 8 on tchd 5 to 4 on) 2
3880[3] BLUEGRASS PRINCE (Ire) 9-0 W Newnes (2) *led, rdn and hdd o'r 2 fs out, one pace aftr*.......(9 to 2 op 5 to 2) 3

Dist: Sht-hd, 3½l. 1m 28.64s. a 3.04s (3 Ran).
SR: 58/59/48/ (Sheikh Mohammed), L M Cumani

4256 Caribbean Connection Claiming Handicap Class G (0-60 3-y-o and up) £3,517 1¾m.................. (3:55)

3872[3] JOLIS ABSENT [42] (bl) 3-7-10 (5*) P McCabe (10) *al frnt rnk, led 2 fs out, edgd rght jst ins last, all out, fnshd 1st, plcd second*.........(9 to 1 op 8 to 1 tchd 10 to 1) 1D

4028 HEAD TURNER [34] 5-8-3 Paul Eddery (15) *hld up in rear, gd hdwy on far rail 3 fs out, chlgd entering last, short of room, jst fld, fnshd second, plcd 1st.* ....(7 to 1 op 12 to 1 tchd 14 to 1) 1

4049* STREPHON (Ire) [49] 3-8-1 (7*) S Mulvey (11) *led till hdd 2 fs out, rdn and rallied wl entering last, no extr fnl 50 yards*..............................(7 to 1 tchd 8 to 1) 3

2530[4] SMILES AHEAD [57] 5-9-5 (7*) R Painter (13) *nvr far away, ev ch one and a half fs out, kpt on one pace*..(16 to 1) 4

4152[3] KISMETIM [56] 3-9-1 K Fallon (1) *mid-div, hdwy 5 fs out, not pace to chal ins fnl 2*.........(5 to 1 fav op 9 to 2) 5

4028[5] LEXUS (Ire) [36] 5-8-5 J Quinn (5) *hld up, hdwy o'r 4 fs out, one pace fnl 2*.....................(10 to 1 op 8 to 1) 6

3962[4] RUN TO AU BON (Ire) [51] 3-8-10 J Weaver (8) *prmnt till rdn and wknd 2 fs out*....(12 to 1 op 10 to 1 tchd 14 to 1) 7

3761 IMPECCABLE TASTE [56] 3-9-1 A Clark (2) *mid-div, hdwy hfwy, wknd o'r 2 fs out*..........(20 to 1 op 14 to 1) 8

3943[5] KEDGE [50] 3-8-9 B Raymond (17) *mid-div, one pace fnl 3 fs*..............................(16 to 1 tchd 20 to 1) 9

2124 GALACTIC FURY [56] 3-9-1 Dale Gibson (19) *beh, nvr nr to chal*..............................(25 to 1 op 20 to 1) 10

3170[2] BOXBOY [36] 3-7-9 N Carlisle (6) *beh, nvr nr to chal.* ....(12 to 1 op 8 to 1) 11

3761 FANATICAL (USA) [40] (bl) 7-8-9 W Newnes (16) *pld hrd, chsd ldr hfwy till wknd o'r 3 fs out.* ....(16 to 1 tchd 20 to 1) 12

4028 MERRY MARIGOLD [42] 7-8-6 (5*) S Drowne (12) *hld up, hdwy o'r 3 fs out, wknd over 2 out.* ....(16 to 1 op 10 to 1 tchd 20 to 1) 13

3872[5] WHITE RIVER [43] 7-8-12 A Mackay (7) *mid-div, hdwy 6 fs out, wknd 3 out*.....(14 to 1 op 10 to 1 tchd 16 to 1) 14+

KILLSHANDRA (Ire) [33] 4-8-2 R Price (3) *al beh*...(33 to 1) 14+

960[5] PALACE PARADE (USA) [56] 3-9-1 J Lowe (14) *al beh, tld off*..(25 to 1) 16

FEELING FOOLISH (Ire) [41] 4-8-10 N Adams (4) *al beh, tld off*..............................(25 to 1 op 20 to 1) 17

966 FITZROY LAD [45] 3-8-4 C Rutter (9) *al beh, tld off fnl 4 fs.* ....(33 to 1) 18

4110 AMAZING AIR (USA) [51] 3-8-10 W Carson (18) *prmnt to hfwy, sn beh, tld off*.............(12 to 1 op 10 to 1) 19

Dist: Sht-hd, 1½l, 1½l, 1½l, 2½l, 3l, 7l, 2l, 4l, ¾l. 3m 10.05s. a 12.35s (19 Ran).

(I Jerrard), C P Wildman

4257 Swettenham Stud Conditions Stakes Class D (2-y-o) £3,678 6f........(4:25)

3959[3] MAZENTRE FORWARD (Ire) 9-0 W Newnes (5) *made all, stretched out wl fnl furlong*.........(3 to 1 op 5 to 2) 1

3642* STRUMPET CITY 8-7 S Raymont (4) *trkd ldrs, rdn and ran green 2 fs out, wnt second appr last, one pace.* ....(11 to 4 op 3 to 1) 2

2998[4] ABSOLUTELY FAYRE 9-2 Paul Eddery (1) *chsd wnr till wknd o'r 2 fs out*.......(9 to 1 op 6 to 1 tchd 10 to 1) 3

3785[2] MAJESTIC EAGLE (Ire) 9-2 B Raymond (2) *hld up, hdwy to go second o'r 2 fs out, wknd quickly appr last.* ....(11 to 10 fav op 5 to 4 tchd 11 to 8) 4

MARYKIRK 8-7 J Quinn (3) *swrvd violently lft leaving stalls, virtually took no part, tld off.* ....(33 to 1 op 20 to 1 tchd 50 to 1) 5

Dist: 4l, 5l, 2l, dist. 1m 15.21s. a 2.71s (5 Ran).

SR: 52/29/18/10/-/ (The Winning Team), R Hannon

4258 Valletta Surfacing 'Ultrimac' Handicap Class E (0-70 3-y-o and up) £3,574 1m ....(4:55)

4065 LAWNSWOOD JUNIOR [65] 6-9-12 G Hind (9) *trkd ldrs, led jst ins last, ran on gmely*.......(14 to 1 tchd 16 to 1) 1

3981* SILVER GROOM (Ire) [59] 3-9-2 J Quinn (17) *hld up in tch, rdn to ld briefly entering fnl furlong, ran on.* .... (3 to 1 fav op 7 to 2 tchd 4 to 1 and 9 to 2) 2

4120[4] SEA BARON [62] 3-9-5 K Fallon (15) *nvr far away, hdwy to ld 2 fs out, hdd entering last, kpt on.* ....(16 to 1 op 12 to 1 tchd 20 to 1) 3

4133[4] COURT MINSTREL [61] 4-9-8 W Newnes (16) *hld up in rear, gd hdwy one and a half fs out, ran on strly ins last*.............(12 to 1 op 8 to 1 tchd 14 to 1) 4

4104* NORTHERN CONQUEROR (Ire) [49] 5-8-5 (5*,7ex) P McCabe (10) *beh, hdwy whn short of room 2 fs out, found gap and ran on strly ins last.* ....(14 to 1 op 10 to 1 tchd 16 to 1) 5

3643[9] STARLIGHT ROSE (Ire) [51] 3-8-8 E Johnson (7) *mid-div, not pace to chal fnl 2 fs.* (20 to 1 op 16 to 1 tchd 25 to 1) 6

3518 WRETS [52] 4-8-13 A Mackay (1) *in rear, hdwy o'r 2 fs out, nvr dngrs*..............................(50 to 1) 7

3991[4] CASTING SHADOWS [53] 4-9-0 B Raymond (4) *in tch till rdn and wknd 2 fs out*.............(8 to 1 op 6 to 1) 8

3850[2] STAY WITH ME BABY [70] 3-9-13 Paul Eddery (6) *led till hdd 2 fs out, wknd, eased ins last*....(9 to 1 op 7 to 1) 9

3747 LORD ALFIE [53] 4-9-0 N Carlisle (5) *in tch till rdn and wknd 2 fs out*..........(8 to 1 op 7 to 1 tchd 9 to 1) 10

4019 PREMIER STAR [55] (bl) 3-8-12 J Weaver (13) *in tch till rdn 3 fs out, sn btn*.......(10 to 1 op 9 to 1 tchd 11 to 1) 11

4133[5] SINGERS IMAGE [55] (v) 4-8-9 (7*) N Varley (18) *beh, effrt on ins 3 fs out, nvr dngrs.* (9 to 1 op 8 to 1 tchd 10 to 1) 12

4024 ABSO [51] (bl) 5-8-12 J Lowe (11) *prmnt till wknd quickly 2 fs out*..............................(33 to 1) 13

3981 AKHLAK (Ire) [51] (v) 3-8-8 W Carson (8) *prmnt to hfwy, tld off*..................(14 to 1 tchd 12 to 1 and 16 to 1) 14

3957 SECRET ASSIGNMENT (USA) [57] (bl) 3-9-0 A Clark (2) *trkd o'r to centre, prmnt till wknd 3 fs out, tld off.* ....(16 to 1 op 12 to 1) 15

4088[3] GUV'NORS GIFT [59] 3-8-9 (7*) S Mulvey (3) *chsd ldrs till wknd sn aftr hfwy, tld off.* ....(14 to 1 op 8 to 1 tchd 16 to 1) 16

2120* MAASTRICHT [59] 3-9-2 R Price (12) *prmnt to hfwy, sn beh, tld off*..........(14 to 1 op 12 to 1 tchd 16 to 1) 17

Dist: Nk, nk, nk, nk, 7l, nk, ½l, ¾l, ½l, 1½l. 1m 45.37s. a 5.87s (17 Ran).

SR: 30/19/21/23/10/-/-/-/1/ (Graham Treglown), J L Spearing

4259 EBF London Trust Securities Maiden Stakes Class D (Div II) (2-y-o) £4,306 1m..........................(5:25)

4014[2] DARONNE 9-0 J Weaver (8) *led aftr 2 fs, rdn o'r one out, ran on, all out.* ....(9 to 2 op 4 to 1 tchd 5 to 1 and 7 to 2) 1

4027[3] KHAMASEEN 9-0 B Raymond (5) *hld up in tch, outpcd o'r 2 fs out, rallied and ran on strly ins last.* ....(9 to 4 op 5 to 2 tchd 3 to 1) 2

WEIGH ANCHOR 9-0 S O'Gorman (2) *in tch, outpcd o'r 2 fs out, rdn and styd on ag'n fnl furlong.* ....(12 to 1 op 14 to 1 tchd 20 to 1) 3

3876[3] THABIT (USA) 9-0 W Carson (9) *pld hrd in tch, hdwy to chal 2 fs out, sn hard rdn, one pace fnl furlong.* ....(11 to 8 on op Evens tchd 5 to 4) 4

3836[7] OBELOS (USA) 9-0 Paul Eddery (3) *mid-div, rdn 3 fs out, wknd 2 out*.................(16 to 1 op 14 to 1) 5

3625[9] REGAL PURSUIT (Ire) 8-9 Dale Gibson (4) *rdn hfwy, no hdwy fnl 3 fs*.....................(50 to 1 op 33 to 1) 6

3979 HILLSWICK 8-11[2] (5*) A Procter (7) *led 2 fs, rdn o'r two out, sn btn*..........................(50 to 1 op 33 to 1) 7

4113 BRAVE TORNADO 9-0 N Adams (6) *al beh.* ....(50 to 1 op 33 to 1) 8

CLIFTON SET 8-9 (5*) S Drowne (10) *outpcd thrght.* ....(50 to 1 op 25 to 1) 9

CHRIS'S LAD 9-0 A Clark (11) *slwly away, al beh.* ....(50 to 1 op 25 to 1) 10

3589 NOTHING TO WEAR 9-0 C Rutter (1) *al beh.* ....(33 to 1 op 20 to 1) 11

Dist: Hd, ¾l, 1½l, 15l, nk, 1l, 2½l, 6l, ¾l, nk. 1m 45.16s. a 5.66s (11 Ran).

SR: 21/20/18/13/-/-/ (Sheikh Mohammed), L M Cumani

GOWRAN PARK (IRE) (heavy) Thursday September 30th

4260 Thomastown Race (3-y-o and up) £2,760 1¾m.................. (2:30)

1198[8] PORTRAIT GALLERY (Ire) 3-9-5 P V Gilson (6)..... (3 to 1) 1
3852[5] FOR REG (Ire) 4-9-0 (6*) J R Barry (7)............ (7 to 1) 2
3163[7] SLEET SKIER 6-10-1 M J Kinane (10)......... (6 to 4 fav) 3
HAUNTING ANGLE (Ire) 4-8-13 (4*) C Everard (9)..(16 to 1) 4
2692[5] NORTHMAID (Ire) (bl) 4-9-2 (6*) T P Treacy (2).....(12 to 1) 5
4162 RISKY GALORE 3-8-10 J P Murtagh (4)..........(25 to 1) 6
3999[7] DESERT WALTZ (Ire) 4-9-6 J F Egan (5)..........(20 to 1) 7
2213[2] TRIPLE 3-8-8 (2*) D G O'Shea (1)................(4 to 1) 8

Dist: 15l, 7l, 14l, 4l. 3m 31.40s. (8 Ran).

(Mrs M V O'Brien), Charles O'Brien

4261 Kilkenny EBF Fillies Maiden (2-y-o) £3,795 1m.................... (3:00)

BROADMARA (Ire) 9-0 R Hughes (2).............. (7 to 2) 1
3911[9] AL NAAYY 9-0 W J Supple (10)....................(8 to 1) 2
3729[5] ZARA'S BIRTHDAY (Ire) 8-12 (2*) P Carberry (7).... (8 to 1) 3
KOTAMA (USA) 9-0 M J Kinane (12)...........(7 to 4 fav) 4
3730[2] SUBARASHII (USA) 9-0 N G McCullagh (5)........ (7 to 1) 5
INCHARDER (Ire) 9-0 P V Gilson (3)...............(10 to 1) 6
4093[9] SUSIE SUNSHINE (Ire) 8-10 (4*) J J Behan (14)....(14 to 1) 7
MERCY BIEN (Ire) 9-0 P Shanahan (6)............(20 to 1) 8
4134 CLASSIC QUEEN (Ire) 9-0 Ann O'Rourke (11)..... (20 to 1) 9
DEEP IN SEPTEMBER (Ire) 8-12 (2*) R M Burke (1) (14 to 1) 10
4134[6] CARANNA 9-0 J F Egan (4)......................(14 to 1) 11
CHAMPAGNE HURLEY (Ire) 9-0 S Craine (13).....(14 to 1) 12
4134 ACUMEN (Ire) 8-4 (10*) R McAuliffe (9)............(33 to 1) 13
1044[5] BIG STORY 9-0 C Roche (16).......................(7 to 1) 14
3954 NOBODYS CHILD (Ire) 8-12 (2*) D G O'Shea (15)..(33 to 1) 15
3953 GREAC 9-0 J P Murtagh (8)........................(33 to 1) 16

Dist: ½l, ¾l, 5½l, 2l. 1m 50.10s. (16 Ran).

(Mrs Clodagh Kean), A J Maxwell

4262 Waterford Crystal Nursery (2-y-o) £5,040 1m.................... (3:30)

3917[4] METROELLA (Ire) [-] 7-8[3] (4*) J J Behan (8)........ (8 to 1) 1
3562* RAHAL (Ire) [-] (bl) 8-2 M J Kinane (4)..........(6 to 4 fav) 2
3608* MASCOT [-] 8-2 J F Egan (5)......................(6 to 1) 3
4093[7] MY RAGAMUFFIN (Ire) [-] 8-3 N G McCullagh (2)..(12 to 1) 4

3379[7] SUAVE REDSKIN (Ire) [-] 7-7[4] (4*) W J Smith (3) . . . (14 to 1) 5
4058* YAHTHAB (Ire) [-] 8-11 W J Supple (1) . . . . (11 to 2) 6
3607* JOMACOON (Ire) [-] (bl) 7-13[2] (4*) J A Heffernan (6) (8 to 1) 7
3807[3] SARANGA (Ire) [-] 7-12 (2*) D G O'Shea (7) . . . . (6 to 1) 8
Dist: Nk, 2½l, 1l, 1½l. 1m 50.60s. (8 Ran).

(M Hanrahan), A P O'Brien

LINGFIELD (soft)
Thursday September 30th
Going Correction: PLUS 0.40 sec. per fur. (races 1,2,3,4,7,8), PLUS 0.85 (5,6)

4263 EBF Sleeping Partner Maiden Stakes Class D (Div I) (2-y-o) £4,413 6f. .(1:50)

4067[3] WAFAYT (Ire) 9-0 D Holland (12) *made virtually all, quickened clr 2 out, hrd hld.* . . . .(9 to 4 on op 5 to 2 on tchd 7 to 4 on) 1
CAJUN CADET 9-0 T Sprake (11) *ran on frm rear 2 fs out, took second pl nr line.* (10 to 1 op 6 to 1 tchd 11 to 1) 2
4067 BOLD MICK 9-0 C Rutter (1) *al wl plcd, rdn and outpcd last 2 fs* . . . . (25 to 1 op 16 to 1) 3
INSPIRATION POINT 8-9 W Newnes (5) *mid-div, styd on one pace last 2 fs* . . . . (14 to 1 op 10 to 1) 4
POSITIVO 9-0 K Fallon (7) *hdwy frm rear o'r one furlong out, no ch wth wnr* . . . . (14 to 1 op 10 to 1) 5
SUGAR RISK 8-9 J Weaver (2) *ldg grp til wknd o'r one furlong out* . . . . (16 to 1 tchd 25 to 1) 6
BOLD-MAX 9-0 T Quinn (10) *chsd wnr for 4 fs, no extr.* . . . . (16 to 1 op 10 to 1) 7
TELEPHONE TAP 9-0 R Perham (8) *slwly into strd, al outpcd* . . . . (11 to 1 op 6 to 1 tchd 12 to 1) 8
3895[4] ARAGON HOLLY 8-9 W Woods (9) *in tch to hfwy.* . . . . (10 to 1 op 8 to 1 tchd 12 to 1) 9
3287 INFRA BLUE (Ire) 8-4 (5*) B Russell (6) *outpcd.* . . . . (33 to 1 op 20 to 1) 10
877[4] HOLLINGTON SONG 8-9 A McGlone (3) *speed for o'r 2 fs, sn drpd rear* . . . . (25 to 1 op 16 to 1) 11
Dist: 2½l, nk, 3l, 2½l, 5l, 3½l, 4l, ¾l, 10l, 4l. 1m 16.17s. a 7.17s (11 Ran).

SR: 5/-/-/-/-/-/ (Sheikh Ahmed Al Maktoum), J H M Gosden

4264 Bletchingly Claiming Stakes Class F (2-y-o) £2,243 6f. . . . .(2:20)

SHARPENING 8-8 G Duffield (6) *wl in tch far side, ran on to ld well ins fnl furlong.* (8 to 1 op 4 to 1 tchd 9 to 1) 1
3982* ELEVATOR SHAFT (Ire) (bl) 9-3 T Quinn (1) *clr ldr far side til hdd und pres wl ins fnl furlong.* . . . .(4 to 1 op 7 to 2 tchd 5 to 1) 2
3573[8] REMINISCENCE (Ire) 8-2 S Raymont (12) *chsd stands side ldrs, ran on to ld that grp ins fnl furlong, fnshd wl.* . . . . (16 to 1 tchd 20 to 1) 3
4089[5] HADDIAH (bl) 8-8 W Newnes (3) *rcd far side, styd on one pace last 2 fs* . . . . (7 to 1 op 7 to 2) 4
3982[4] CHAMPAGNE GIRL 8-6 T Sprake (14) *led stands side grp til hdd and no extr ins fnl furlong.* . . . . (3 to 1 fav tchd 4 to 1) 5
3264[6] PRIMOST 8-7 N Adams (8) *outpcd on far side til styd on und pres frm 2 fs out* . . . . (25 to 1 op 16 to 1) 6
4105[4] GAELIC STAR (Ire) 8-7 S Perks (5) *chsd far side ldr, no extr appr fnl furlong* . . . . (20 to 1 op 16 to 1) 7
2825[6] LADY WESTBURY (Ire) 8-6 J Quinn (11) *nvr better than mid-div stands side.* (16 to 1 op 25 to 1 tchd 33 to 1) 8
4128[8] TUTU SIXTYSIX (v) 8-4 P Robinson (9) *trkd stands side grp, no hdwy frm 2 fs out* . . . (7 to 1 op 7 to 2 tchd 15 to 2) 9
BALATA BAY 9-3 R Hills (13) *outpcd stands side most of way* . . . . (12 to 1 op 10 to 1 tchd 14 to 1) 10
4009 PACIOLI (bl) 8-7 M Wigham (16) *rcd stands side, nvr nr to chal.* . . . . (33 to 1 op 20 to 1) 11
FRESH EDGE 8-12 A McGlone (15) *rcd stands side, nvr on terms* . . . . (25 to 1 op 20 to 1) 12
3867[7] FOXTOWNS GIRL 7-13 (5*) N Gwilliams (7) *rcd far side, sn outpcd* . . . . (33 to 1) 13
4061 STORM REGENT (bl) 8-11 W Woods (10) *wl plcd stands side for 4 fs, wknd* . . . (14 to 1 op 12 to 1 tchd 16 to 1) 14
4097 WILLWIN (bl) 8-2[2] J Weaver (4) *speed far side for 4 fs.* . . . . (33 to 1 op 25 to 1) 15
3686[6] SECRATORIUS (Ire) 8-6 (3*) Stephen Davies (2) *outpcd far side* . . . . (33 to 1 op 25 to 1) 16
Dist: 2l, sht-hd, 1l, ½l, nk, 2l, 2½l, 2l, nk, 1½l. 1m 15.72s. a 6.72s (16 Ran).

SR: 8/9/-/-/-/-/ (Cheveley Park Stud), Sir Mark Prescott

4265 Lynn Spaulding Maiden Stakes Class D (2-y-o) £3,845 5f. . . . .(2:50)

3941[7] ARZINA (USA) 8-9 D Holland (2) *rcd far side, led aftr one furlong, styd on wl ins fnl furlong.* (12 to 1 op 8 to 1) 1
3941[5] RANKAIDADE 8-9 S Perks (10) *ldg grp, rdn and ran on ins fnl furlong* . . . . (14 to 1 op 8 to 1) 2
4127[6] COOL EDGE (Ire) 9-0 P Robinson (12) *rcd centre of course, ran on frm 2 out, fnshd wl.* . . . . (12 to 1 op 8 to 1 tchd 14 to 1) 3
INDIAN LAMENT 8-4 (5*) S Drowne (9) *strted slwly, hdwy frm rear o'r one out, fnshd wl* . . . . (50 to 1 op 33 to 1) 4
4067[5] SULITELMA (USA) 8-9 S O'Gorman (6) *wl in tch far side, not quicken appr fnl furlong.* . . . . (6 to 1 op 7 to 2 tchd 13 to 2) 5
2817[6] INSIDER TRADER 9-0 D Biggs (11) *rcd centre of course, wl in tch, not quicken o'r one furlong out.* . . . . (16 to 1 op 12 to 1 tchd 20 to 1) 6
3993[5] MOORLAND DANCER (Ire) 8-9 R Hills (3) *rcd far side, led for one furlong, wth wnr til wknd o'r one out.* . . . . (16 to 1 op 8 to 1) 7
3941 DOWSONG 9-0 R Perham (15) *chsd stands side ldrs for o'r 3 fs* . . . . (10 to 1 op 33 to 1) 8
3339[4] CALLABONNA 8-9 G Duffield (14) *wl plcd stands side to hfwy* . . . . (5 to 2 fav tchd 7 to 2) 9
3908 MILOS 9-0 A McGlone (5) *outpcd.* . . . . (15 to 2 op 10 to 1 tchd 7 to 1) 10
UPPER GROSVENOR (Ire) 9-0 T Quinn (8) *slwly into strd, al beh* . . . .(8 to 1 tchd 7 to 1 and 10 to 1) 11
4114[2] BILLY CRUNCHEON 9-0 W Woods (16) *led stands side grp for o'r 3 fs* . . . .(11 to 2 op 8 to 1 tchd 5 to 1) 12
4067 GREATEST HOPES 9-0 T Williams (1) *outpcd.* . . . . (50 to 1 op 25 to 1) 13
SOUND OF THE BLUES (Ire) 8-9 S Raymont (4) *chsd ldrs far side, rdn and wknd frm 2 out* . . . . . .(14 to 1 op 10 to 1) 14
4032 LOOKIN' ROSIE 8-9 K Fallon (7) *speed to hfwy.* . . . . (50 to 1 op 33 to 1) 15
3982 BETAWAYDECKERWAY 9-0 N Adams (13) *slwly into strd, al beh, tld off* . . . . (50 to 1 op 33 to 1) 16
Dist: 1½l, ¾l, 5l, ¾l, sht-hd, 5l, nk, ¾l, sht-hd, nk. 1m 1.84s. a 4.94s (16 Ran).

SR: 36/30/32/7/4/8/ (Sheikh Mohammed), B W Hills

4266 Upham Nursery Handicap Class E (2-y-o) £3,675 7f. . . . . (3:20)

4033[2] NORTHERN CELADON (Ire) [80] 9-2 (5*) K Rutter (13) *pressed ldr, led 2 out, rdn and edgd rght wl ins fnl furlong, kpt on.* . . . .(14 to 1) 1
4015[9] ROSE CIEL (Ire) [79] (bl) 9-6 R Hills (12) *cld on ldrs o'r 2 out, ev ch ins fnl furlong, no extr whn hmpd nr line.* . . . . (25 to 1 op 20 to 1 tchd 33 to 1) 2
3743[3] LUNAR MISSION (Ire) [75] 9-2 P Robinson (8) *hld up, hdwy o'r 2 out, ev ch one out, not quicken last 100 yards.* . . . .(9 to 2 fav op 8 to 1) 3
4032* GOLDEN GRAND [62] 8-3 D Biggs (14) *in tch, cld on ldrs o'r 2 out, wknd ins fnl furlong.* . . . . (10 to 1 op 7 to 1 tchd 12 to 1) 4
4082[7] UN PARFUM DE FEMME (Ire) [68] 8-9 S Raymont (3) *beh til ran on o'r 2 out, nrst at finish* . . . . (25 to 1) 5
3865 BANDAR PERAK [68] (v) 8-9 G Hind (4) *styd on one pace last 2 fs, nvr nrr* . . . .(16 to 1 tchd 20 to 1) 6
1602* SLASHER JACK (Ire) [78] 9-5 G Duffield (7) *beh til moderate prog ins last 2 fs* . . . .(7 to 1 op 6 to 1) 7
3895* FROMAGE [74] 9-1 B Rouse (5) *mid-div, no imprsn on ldrs appr fnl furlong* . . . .(7 to 1 tchd 9 to 1) 8
4032[2] CHARLIES DREAM (Ire) [60] 8-1 N Adams (11) *led til hdd 2 out, wknd o'r one out.* . . . . (16 to 1 op 14 to 1 tchd 20 to 1) 9
4003[4] CHARLIE CHARLIE [65] 8-6 A Tucker (6) *wl plcd for o'r 4 fs.* . . . .(6 to 1 op 7 to 1 tchd 8 to 1) 10
3876[7] BALLYMORRIS (Ire) [65] 8-6 R Perham (16) *in tch for 4 fs.* . . . . (16 to 1 op 10 to 1) 11
3845 ADMIRING [67] 8-5 (3*) M Fenton (2) *ldg grp til wknd o'r 2 fs out* . . . .(11 to 1 op 8 to 1 tchd 12 to 1) 12
4122 EMMA GRIMES (Ire) [64] 8-5 T Quinn (9) *al beh.* . . . . (33 to 1 op 25 to 1) 13
3982[7] MR B REASONABLE (Ire) [73] 9-0 A McGlone (15) *beh appr last 2 fs* . . . . (8 to 1 op 5 to 1 tchd 9 to 1) 14
3428[4] PERSIAN HERITAGE [74] 9-1 K Fallon (10) *beh fnl 3 fs.* . . . .(7 to 1 op 8 to 1) 15
Dist: ¾l, 2l, 5l, ¾l, 1½l, 1l, sht-hd, ¾l, nk, 5l. 1m 29.11s. a 8.41s (15 Ran).

SR: 23/20/10/-/-/-/ (R P Marchant), M A Jarvis

4267 Autumn Maiden Stakes Class D (3-y-o) £3,435 1¾m. . . . . (3:50)

4110[7] KAMIKAZE 9-0 J Weaver (13) *hdwy 6 fs out, led appr fnl furlong, pushed clr* . . . (10 to 1 op 7 to 1 tchd 12 to 1) 1
4006[3] FOOLS ERRAND (Ire) 9-0 G Duffield (2) *ldg grp, led 3 fs out, hdd o'r one out, one pace.* . . . .(9 to 2 op 6 to 1 tchd 7 to 1) 2
3682[4] EDITHMEAD (Ire) 8-9 S Whitworth (12) *hdwy frm rear 5 fs out, rdn and not quicken appr fnl furlong.* . . . . (11 to 2 op 4 to 1 tchd 6 to 1) 3
3971[2] QUILLON 9-0 A McGlone (7) *led aftr 3 fs, hdd three furlongs out, sn wknd.* (11 to 4 fav op 7 to 4 tchd 3 to 1) 4
2937 PISH KESH 8-9 D Holland (11) *wl plcd til rdn and wknd 2 fs out* . . . . (16 to 1 tchd 25 to 1) 5
3937[8] DESTINY CALLS 9-0 B Rouse (3) *moderate prog last 3 fs, not rch ldrs* . . . . (25 to 1 tchd 33 to 1) 6
3937[7] OLD RED (Ire) 9-0 T Quinn (15) *hdwy hfwy, rdn and wknd o'r 2 fs out* . . . . (20 to 1 op 16 to 1) 7
4110[9] PRIDWELL 9-0 S Raymont (8) *pressed ldr aftr 3 fs, wknd three furlongs out* . . . .(9 to 1 op 16 to 1) 8
1746[8] SCHOOLGIRL CRUSH 8-9 K Fallon (9) *nvr nr to chal.* . . . .(33 to 1) 9
4091[7] ABU DANCER (Ire) 9-0 R Perham (6) *led for 3 fs, wknd o'r 4 furlongs out* . . . . (66 to 1 op 50 to 1) 10

4110[6] ECU DE FRANCE (Ire) 9-0 W Newnes (14) *chsd ldrs til rdn and lost pl hfwy*.....................(5 to 1 op 7 to 2) 11
3590 DINNER AT EIGHT 9-0 D Biggs (4) *in tch til beh last 6 fs*. ....(33 to 1 op 25 to 1) 12
1935[5] MOHAYA (USA) 9-0 C Rutter (1) *al racing towards rear*. ....(50 to 1) 13
4110 ALLEZ PABLO 8-11 (3*) S D Williams (10) *al beh, tld off aftr 4 fs*.................................(66 to 1 op 50 to 1) 14
3787 SULA MOON 8-9 J Quinn (5) *al in rear, tld off frm hfwy*. ....(66 to 1 op 50 to 1) 15
Dist: 3½l, 3l, 7l, 3l, 12l, 2½l, 3l, 8l, 1½l, 4l. 3m 19.60s. a 24.60s (15 Ran).
(Sheikh Mohammed), L M Cumani

4268 Lewes Amateur Riders' Limited Stakes Class G (0-65 3-y-o and up) £2,805 1m 3f 106yds...........(4:20)

4028[2] RAPPORTEUR (USA) 7-10-5 (7*) Miss A Elsey (1) *led for 2 fs, lost pl, led o'r 5 furlongs out, forged clr last 3 furlongs*. ....(100 to 30 op 11 to 4 tchd 7 to 2) 1
4048* RISPOTO 3-10-0 Miss Diana Jones (8) *ldg grp, led o'r 6 fs out, hdd over 5 furlongs out, one pace last 3 furlongs*. ....(3 to 1 fav op 2 to 1 tchd 100 to 30) 2
4218 MYSTERIOUS MAID (USA) 6-10-7 Mrs L Pearce (6) *mid-div, ran on 4 fs out, one pace last 2 furlongs*. ....(13 to 2 op 6 to 1 tchd 7 to 1) 3
3831[9] TINSASHE (Ire) 3-9-7 (7*) Miss I Foustok (15) *mid-div and pushed alng hfwy, styd on one pace frm 3 fs out*. ....(6 to 1 op 5 to 1) 4
3873[5] INDIAN FLASH (Ire) 3-10-0 Mrs M Cowdrey (9) *chsd ldrs til rdn and wknd o'r 2 out*. ....(100 to 30 op 5 to 1 tchd 3 to 1) 5
2127 NATIVE CHIEFTAN 4-10-5 (7*) Mr T Cuff (2) *wl plcd til wknd 6 fs out*...........................(7 to 1 op 6 to 1) 6
4028 FORTUNE STAR (Ire) 4-10-5 (7*) Miss M Bridger (12) *nvr rchd ldrs*..........................(50 to 1 op 33 to 1) 7
3887 GREAT HAND 7-10-7 (5*) Mr G Lewis (14) *rcd in mid-div, no hdwy fnl 4 fs*...........................(20 to 1 op 16 to 1) 8
1321 ICE MAGIC 6-10-5 (7*) Miss S Yardley (7) *nvr on terms, tld off*...(50 to 1) 9
4092 MELLERIO 3-9-12 (7*) Mr K Santana (4) *beh most of way, tld off*.................................(50 to 1 op 33 to 1) 10
2536[3] QUIET RIOT 11-10-5 (7*) Miss Susan Davies (11) *slwly into strd, improved aftr 4 fs, wknd last four furlongs, tld off*...............................(16 to 1 op 14 to 1) 11
4088 ARRAS ROYALE 3-9-12 (7*) Mrs D McHale (13) *mid-div til lost tch 4 fs out, tld off*.............................(50 to 1) 12
3910 EXCESS BAGGAGE (Ire) 3-9-12 (7*) Miss F Burke (3) *wl plcd, led o'r 9 fs out, hdd over 6 furlongs out, wknd 3 out, tld off*...............................(50 to 1 op 33 to 1) 13
3689 RAPINSKI 4-10-5 (7*) Mrs H Noonan (10) *beh aftr 3 fs, tld off*...............................(50 to 1 op 33 to 1) 14
4092 STARLIGHT FLYER (bl) 6-10-5 (7*) Mr T Waters (5) *beh most of way, tld off fnl 5 fs*. ....(33 to 1 op 25 to 1 tchd 50 to 1) 15
Dist: 7l, 3l, 6l, 4l, 8l, 2l, hd, 15l, 2l, 2l. 2m 41.32s. a 17.12s (15 Ran).
SR: 53/27/28/9/1/-/ (Richard Berenson), C C Elsey

4269 EBF Sleeping Partner Maiden Stakes Class D (Div II) (2-y-o) £4,378 6f (4:50)

3888[3] ROOFTOP FLYER (Ire) 9-0 R Hills (11) *pressed ldrs, led und pres one furlong out, styd on cl hme*. ....(6 to 4 fav op Evens tchd 7 to 4 and 15 to 8) 1
4098[2] SHIKAREE (Ire) 9-0 A McGlone (1) *al chasing ldrs, rdn alng hfwy, ran on und pres fnl furlong, fnshd wl*. ....(5 to 2 op 4 to 1 tchd 5 to 1) 2
3888[5] MONTICINO (Ire) 9-0 S Raymont (4) *led til hdd one furlong out, no extr nr line*.....(5 to 2 op 6 to 4 tchd 11 to 4) 3
3972[5] SKIPTAMALOO 8-9 D Holland (6) *handily plcd, rdn and outpcd appr fnl furlong*............(14 to 1 op 7 to 1) 4
4113 KISSAIR (Ire) 8-9 (5*) B Russell (8) *mid-div, rdn and no imprsn on ldrs frm 2 fs out*........(25 to 1 op 12 to 1) 5
3781[9] KHAYA 8-9 A Clark (12) *in tch, no hdwy ins last 2 fs*. ....(20 to 1 op 12 to 1) 6
DEEPLY VALE (Ire) 9-0 B Rouse (5) *slwly into strd, nvr on terms*........................(25 to 1 op 20 to 1) 7
THEE AND ME 8-9 S Perks (10) *mid-div, rdn and outpcd frm hfwy*.........................(25 to 1 op 14 to 1) 8
MANATEE 8-9 P Robinson (9) *outpcd*. ....(20 to 1 op 10 to 1 tchd 25 to 1) 9
AUNT TATE 8-9 T Williams (3) *strted slwly, al outpcd*. ....(20 to 1 op 12 to 1) 10
3833 PAPPA'S PET 9-0 G Duffield (2) *sn outpcd*. ....(20 to 1 op 16 to 1 tchd 25 to 1) 11
3833 SALTCORN (Ire) 9-0 W Newnes (7) *chsd ldrs for o'r 2 fs, lost pl quickly*.........................(25 to 1 op 14 to 1) 12
Dist: 1½l, sht-hd, 2½l, 1½l, 2l, 2l, 1l, 1½l, 2½l, 1½l. 1m 16.58s. a 7.58s (12 Ran).
(Miss L J Vickers), R Hannon

4270 Levy Board Handicap Class E (0-70 3-y-o) £3,675 7f................ (5:20)

3564[5] PENNY BANGER (Ire) [55] (bl) 8-6 J Weaver (12) *made virtually all, drw clr last 2 fs, eased nr line*. ....(6 to 1 tchd 10 to 1) 1
3830[8] AHJAY [50] 8-1 J Quinn (9) *beh til styd on und pres ins last 2 fs, not rch wnr*...................(11 to 1 op 8 to 1) 2
3343[9] TARTIB (Ire) [60] 8-11 R Hills (1) *pressed wnr til outpcd frm 2 fs out*..................(25 to 1 op 20 to 1 tchd 33 to 1) 3
3766[5] ARAWA [46] 7-8 (3*) A Tucker (11) *ran on und pres frm rear o'r 2 fs out, one pace fnl furlong*....(10 to 1 op 8 to 1) 4
3794[6] CLEAR LOOK [53] 8-4[3] T Quinn (7) *chsd ldrs for 5 fs, no extr*...................................(16 to 1 op 10 to 1) 5
4090[4] MARK'S CLUB (Ire) [55] (bl) 8-6 D Biggs (4) *slwly into strd, nvr able to chal*..........(7 to 1 op 6 to 1 tchd 8 to 1) 6
4131[4] KARUKERA [48] 7-13 A Mackay (13) *moderate effrt frm rear o'r 2 out, no imprsn on frnt rnk*............(6 to 1) 7
4123 SEASON'S STAR [48] (v) 7-13 C Rutter (5) *cl up til lost pl o'r 2 fs out*...........................(20 to 1 op 14 to 1) 8
4206* MY MINNIE [51] 8-0[3] (5*) S Drowne (10) *nvr better than mid-div*............(11 to 2 fav op 7 to 2 tchd 6 to 1) 9
3736[8] TRINITY HALL [64] 9-1 D Holland (16) *rcd in mid-div, no hdwy appr last 2 fs, eased*.......(14 to 1 tchd 16 to 1) 10
3575[2] PERSIAN GUSHER (Ire) [60] 8-11 G Duffield (15) *wl plcd to hfwy, sn lost pos*..................(12 to 1 op 10 to 1) 11
3965[2] WESTERING [61] 8-12 P Robinson (6) *beh fnl 3 fs*. ....(14 to 1 op 10 to 1) 12
1697[5] SOAKING [70] 9-7 B Rouse (2) *ldg grp til lost pl hfwy*. ....(6 to 1 tchd 7 to 1) 13
3988[9] REMEMBER THIS (Ire) [52] 8-3 K Fallon (3) *beh frm hfwy*. ....(25 to 1 op 20 to 1) 14
4131[2] WALNUT BURL (Ire) [49] (v) 8-0 A McGlone (14) *al outpcd in rear*.................................(10 to 1 op 8 to 1) 15
Dist: 10l, ½l, 4l, ½l, 1½l, 2½l, 2l, ½l, 2l, 8l. 1m 29.34s. a 8.64s (15 Ran).
SR: 4/-/-/-/-/-/ (R W Huggins), M Johnston

NEWMARKET (good)
Thursday September 30th
Going Correction: PLUS 0.15 sec. per fur.

4271 Godolphin Stakes Class A (Listed Race) (3-y-o and up) £9,594 1½m (1:35)

4141[3] MUHAYAA (USA) 4-8-13 W R Swinburn (5) *trkd ldr, led o'r 3 fs out till over one out, rallied to rgn ld last 70 yards, hld on wl*..........(11 to 4 fav op 9 to 4 tchd 3 to 1) 1
3385[5] PETER QUINCE 3-8-8 W Ryan (2) *patiently rdn, improved to ld o'r one furlong out, ridden and hdd last 70 yards, rallied*.....................(5 to 1 op 6 to 1 tchd 7 to 1) 2
4063 PERSIAN BRAVE (Ire) 3-8-5 M Hills (1) *wtd wth, improved o'r 3 fs out, hrd at work last 2 furlongs, kpt on same pace*...................(9 to 2 op 7 to 2 tchd 5 to 1) 3
4039* JOHN BALLIOL (USA) 5-9-5 M Roberts (4) *trkd ldg quartet, effrt and drvn alng o'r 3 fs out, one pace entering fnl furlong*...(3 to 1 op 9 to 4) 4
3572* SUMMER PAGEANT 3-8-0 W Carson (6) *dictated pace till hdd o'r 3 fs out, fdd last 2 furlongs*. ....(10 to 1 op 8 to 1 tchd 12 to 1) 5
4086* KELIMUTU 4-8-8 G Bardwell (8) *unruly bef race, sluggish strt, effrt and chsd alng o'r 5 fs out, sn struggling*. ....(33 to 1 tchd 40 to 1) 6
3590[5] PEACHES POLLY 3-8-0 B Doyle (7) *tucked away on ins, hrd at work o'r 5 fs out, sn rdn and btn*. ....(25 to 1 tchd 33 to 1) 7
3879[5] URGENT REQUEST (Ire) 3-8-5 Pat Eddery (3) *trkd ldg trio, drvn alng whn pace quickened o'r 2 fs out, sn btn*. ....(14 to 1 op 10 to 1) 8
Dist: Sht-hd, 3½l, 2l, 12l, 1l, 7l, 1l. 2m 34.79s. a 5.19s (8 Ran).
SR: 65/59/49/59/16/22/-/3/ (Maktoum Al Maktoum), A A Scott

4272 Bailey's Horse Feeds Nursery Class C (2-y-o) £7,635 5f................(2:05)

4159[5] NO MEAN CITY (Ire) [74] (bl) 8-8 A Mackay (7) *broke smartly, made all, ran on strly to remain clr ins fnl furlong*. (14 to 1 op 12 to 1 tchd 10 to 1 and 16 to 1) 1
3435[8] TAKADOU (Ire) [85] 9-5 W R Swinburn (9) *sluggish strt, improved centre hfwy, str run fnl furlong, no extr cl hme*...............................(12 to 1 tchd 14 to 1) 2
3869* GIPSY KID [59] (bl) 7-7 J Lowe (11) *nvr far away, hrd at work ins fnl furlong, kpt on same pace*. ....(8 to 1 op 7 to 1 tchd 9 to 1) 3
3894* DOLLAR GAMBLE (Ire) [87] 9-0 (7*) Mark Denaro (1) *al chasing ldrs, improved centre hfwy, ev ch o'r one furlong out, kpt on same pace*.............(8 to 1 tchd 9 to 1) 4
4114* MY GALLERY (Ire) [71] (bl) 8-0 (5*,7ex) D Wright (3) *sluggish strt, chsd alng to keep up, gd hdwy last 2 fs, fnshd wl*. ....(11 to 2 jt-fav op 4 to 1 tchd 6 to 1) 5
2996 TINKER OSMASTON [78] 8-12 Pat Eddery (5) *nvr far away, feeling pace 2 fs out, rdn and kpt on same pace ins fnl furlong*...............................(7 to 1 tchd 8 to 1) 6
3635[7] BASKERVILLE [80] 9-0 J Reid (8) *sluggish strt, drvn alng to improve frm off the pace last 2 fs, nvr nrr*. ....(14 to 1 op 10 to 1) 7
3982[3] CERTIFICATE-X [71] 8-5 M Roberts (13) *broke wl to show gd speed in frnt rnk for o'r 3 fs, fdd*. ....(12 to 1 op 8 to 1 tchd 14 to 1) 8
3222[8] CABCHARGE PRINCESS (Ire) [73] 8-0 (7*) S Mulvey (10) *chsd alng on ins, nvr able to rch chalg pos*. ....(25 to 1 op 16 to 1 tchd 33 to 1) 9

3993* ZANZARA (Ire) [80] 9-0 J Carroll (2) *struggling to go pace aftr a furlong, styd on appr fnl furlong, nvr dngrs.* ......(12 to 1 tchd 14 to 1) 10
3958* DOMINO QUEEN (Ire) [69] 8-3 A Munro (12) *shwd up wl beh ldg pair, drvn alng 2 fs out, fdd*.............(11 to 2 jt-fav op 6 to 1 tchd 5 to 1) 11
3994[5] NORDICO PRINCESS [79] 8-13 W Ryan (6) *settled midfield, hrd at work to hold pl hfwy, eased whn btn o'r one furlong out*.........(33 to 1 op 25 to 1 tchd 50 to 1) 12
4114[5] MIRIAM [68] 8-2 W Carson (4) *speed to chase ldrs to hfwy, sn lost tch*..........(33 to 1 op 20 to 1 tchd 40 to 1) 13
Dist: 1½l, ¾l, hd, 1½l, 1½l, nk, 3l, 2½l, ¾l, 3l. 1m 2.37s. a 3.77s (13 Ran).
SR: 34/39/10/37/15/16/17/-/-/ (Mrs M O'Donnell), A Bailey

4273 Newgate Stud Middle Park Stakes Class A (Group 1) (2-y-o) £91,233 6f ....(2:35)

4062[3] FIRST TRUMP 9-0 M Hills (5) *settled midfield, pushed alng and boxed in hfwy, got through fnl furlong, ran on strly to ld last 50 yards.* ......(6 to 1 op 5 to 1 tchd 13 to 2) 1
3753* OWINGTON 9-0 Pat Eddery (1) *al hndy, led o'r 2 fs out, drvn alng ins fnl furlong, ran on, jst ct*........ (5 to 1) 2
1788[3] REDOUBTABLE (USA) 9-0 L Dettori (3) *wtd wth, drvn up on outsd to join issue entering fnl furlong, kpt on same pace*.......................... (10 to 1 tchd 12 to 1) 3
3435* TURTLE ISLAND (Ire) 9-0 J Reid (7) *wth ldrs, led o'r 3 fs out till over 2 out, hrd drvn ins last, not quicken last 100 yards*............ (85 to 40 fav op 7 to 4 tchd 9 to 4) 4
3763[2] STAR TALENT (USA) 9-0 R Cochrane (4) *steadied leaving stalls, shaken up to improve o'r 2 fs out, not quicken fnl furlong*........................ (12 to 1 tchd 14 to 1) 5
4098* GNEISS (USA) 9-0 Paul Eddery (8) *wth ldrs, hrd at work whn pace lifted o'r one furlong out, no extr.* ......(15 to 2 op 7 to 1 tchd 8 to 1) 6
3994[2] PINKERTON'S PAL 9-0 M Roberts (2) *chsd alng to keep up, nvr a serious threat*............... (20 to 1 op 16 to 1) 7
3785* WATANI (USA) 9-0 W Carson (6) *wnt freely to pace, slight ld for o'r 2 fs, wknd rpdly two furlongs out, lme.* ......(5 to 1 tchd 11 to 2) 8
Dist: Hd, ¾l, 1l, 2½l, 2½l, 3½l, 7l. 1m 13.74s. a 2.34s (8 Ran).
SR: 71/70/67/63/53/43/29/1/ (Mollers Racing), G Wragg

4274 Ladbroke Handicap Class C (0-100 3-y-o) £8,090 1¼m............ (3:10)

3314* CHATOYANT [93] 9-5 W R Swinburn (9) *al travelling wl, swtchd ins to ld fnl furlong, ran on strly.* ......(5 to 1 fav tchd 6 to 1) 1
3986* AMERICAN SWINGER (USA) [80] 8-6 Pat Eddery (11) *al wl plcd, led o'r 3 fs out till ins fnl furlong, styd on same pace*.................. (11 to 2 op 9 to 2 tchd 6 to 1) 2
989[8] BUROOJ [80] 8-6 W Carson (1) *co'red up in midfield, drvn alng whn pace quickened over 2 fs out, rallied, styd on finish*...............(10 to 1 op 14 to 1 tchd 16 to 1) 3
3963[4] LA SPEZIA [77] 8-3 J Carroll (5) *nvr far away, rdn to draw level o'r one furlong out, ridden and kpt on same pace.* ......(12 to 1 op 10 to 1) 4
4018[4] SILVERLOCKS [82] 8-8 N Connorton (6) *settled gng wl, bustled alng and lost grnd o'r 2 fs out, styd on ag'n last 100 yards*.......................... (10 to 1 op 7 to 1) 5
3783[5] DISKETTE [70] 7-10 D Harrison (2) *patiently rdn, shaken up to improve on outsd o'r 2 fs out, ran on finish.* ......(13 to 2 op 5 to 1 tchd 7 to 1) 6
3681[5] DODGY DANCER [67] 7-2 (5*) D Wright (4) *rcd freely thrght, drvn alng o'r 3 fs out, not pace to chal.* ......(25 to 1 op 16 to 1) 7
929[5] MARCO MAGNIFICO (USA) [80] 8-6 M Hills (10) *tucked away on ins, effrt and not much room o'r 2 fs out, nvr able to chal*...................(25 to 1 op 16 to 1) 8
3262[8] SURPRISE SURPRISE [90] 8-9 (7*) Antoinette Armes (13) *dictated pace till hdd o'r 3 fs out, fdd 2 out.* ......(12 to 1 op 14 to 1) 9
4063* LINDON LIME (USA) [95] 9-7 A Munro (12) *trkd ldrs, drvn alng on ins whn pace quickened o'r 2 fs out, no extr.* ......(7 to 1 op 8 to 1) 10
405[6] HOTSOCKS [67] 7-7 Kim McDonnell (7) *in tch, drvn alng in midfield o'r 3 fs out, sn btn.* ......(100 to 1 op 66 to 1 tchd 150 to 1) 11
3883 BRANDONHURST [80] 8-6 L Dettori (8) *in tch, effrt and drvn alng o'r 3 fs out, sn outpcd.* ......(12 to 1 op 10 to 1 tchd 14 to 1) 12
3996[6] SHIRO [81] 8-7 M Roberts (3) *chsd ldg bunch, hrd at work o'r 3 fs out, sn lost tch.* (15 to 2 op 6 to 1 tchd 8 to 1) 13
Dist: 1½l, 1½l, 1l, 1l, sht-hd, 2½l, 1½l, 5l, nk, ½l. 2m 8.90s. a 6.20s (13 Ran).
SR: 58/42/39/34/37/24/16/26/26/ (Lord Derby), J W Watts

4275 Rous Stakes Class A (Listed Race) (3-y-o and up) £9,681 5f.......... (3:40)

3561[2] MY-O-MY (Ire) 3-8-4 M Roberts (10) *bustled alng in midfield, str run entering fnl furlong, quickened ahead last 50 yards*.......(11 to 1 op 10 to 1 tchd 12 to 1) 1
4170[7] SPLICE 4-8-9 W R Swinburn (9) *patiently rdn, steady hdwy o'r 2 fs out, ran on strly fnl furlong, fnshd fst.* ......(11 to 2 op 6 to 1 tchd 7 to 1) 2
3464[5] BLYTON LAD 7-9-0 S Webster (4) *led early, styd hndy till led ag'n o'r one furlong out, rdn and hdd cl hme, no extr*..(100 to 30 jt-fav op 2 to 1 tchd 7 to 2) 3
4151* CALL ME I'M BLUE (Ire) 3-8-9 L Piggott (8) *nvr far away, bustled alng to draw level ins fnl furlong, not quicken cl hme*.........(100 to 30 jt-fav op 7 to 2 tchd 3 to 1) 4
4025* SURPRISE OFFER (bl) 3-9-2 B Raymond (1) *steadied leaving stalls, improved to go hndy hfwy, rdn and no extr last 100 yards*.......... (11 to 2 op 4 to 1 tchd 6 to 1) 5
4216[5] SAINT EXPRESS 3-8-9 W Carson (3) *settled aftr fst break, effrt and pushed alng last 2 fs, kpt on same pace.* ......(33 to 1 op 20 to 1) 6
3291[3] SHEILA'S SECRET (Ire) 3-8-5[1] Pat Eddery (6) *al chasing ldrs, hrd at work 2 fs out, no imprsn.* ......(8 to 1 op 12 to 1) 7
3668* SABRE RATTLER 3-8-9 J Carroll (2) *sn led, hdd and drvn alng o'r one furlong out, fdd*....... (10 to 1 op 8 to 1) 8
4040 REGAL CHIMES 4-9-0 A Munro (5) *chsd ldg quartet, hrd at work hfwy, lost tch o'r one furlong out.* ......(10 to 1 op 12 to 1 tchd 14 to 1) 9
4025[6] ANONYMOUS 3-8-4 B Doyle (7) *outpcd and drvn alng thrght, nvr a factor*............... (50 to 1 op 33 to 1) 10
Dist: ½l, nk, hd, 1l, 2½l, 1l, 1½l, 1½l, hd. 1m 0.81s. a 2.21s (10 Ran).
SR: 61/64/68/62/65/48/40/38/37/ (R E Sangster), T Stack

4276 EBF Westley Maiden Stakes Class D (2-y-o) £5,595 7f.................(4:10)

DARNAY 9-0 L Dettori (5) *patienty rdn, steady hdwy o'r one furlong out, drvn ahead last 50 yards, ran on wl.* ......(7 to 1 op 5 to 1 tchd 8 to 1) 1
1975[3] RIVER DEEP (USA) 9-0 A Munro (11) *al hndy, led towards stands side o'r 3 fs out, rdn and hdd last 50 yards, no extr*............................ (7 to 1 tchd 10 to 1) 2
PORPHYRIOS 9-0 M Hills (1) *steadied strt, steady hdwy o'r 2 fs out, effrt ins fnl furlong, ran on same pace.* ......(33 to 1 op 20 to 1) 3
CHOCOLAT DE MEGURO (USA) 9-0 M Perrett (16) *settled in midfield, effrt and chsd alng o'r one furlong out, ran on same pace*..........(9 to 1 op 8 to 1 tchd 12 to 1) 4
TRIPLE TIE (USA) 8-9 J Reid (4) *wl plcd stands side, feeling pace and rdn o'r one furlong out, not quicken.* ......(16 to 1 op 8 to 1 tchd 20 to 1) 5
3979[2] WILLIAM TELL 9-0 K Darley (6) *patiently rdn, pushed alng to improve frm midfield last 2 fs, ran on.* ......(10 to 1 op 7 to 1) 6
4067[2] LATTAM (USA) 9-0 W Carson (7) *wl plcd stands side, hrd at work 2 fs out, no extr*....(7 to 1 op 6 to 1 tchd 8 to 1) 7
4113[3] REHLAT FARAH (USA) 9-0 M Roberts (21) *trkd far side bunch, drvn alng last 2 fs, one pace.* ......(6 to 1 fav op 5 to 1 tchd 7 to 1) 8
DANCE TURN 9-0 R Price (27) *wl plcd far side, drvn alng o'r 2 fs out, no extr*..................(50 to 1 op 20 to 1) 9
WINTER COAT (USA) 9-0 B Crossley (14) *wth ldrs far side, feeling pace o'r 2 fs out, no extr*... (33 to 1 op 20 to 1) 10
DESERT CONQUEROR (USA) 9-0 W R Swinburn (24) *settled off the pace, slightly hmpd o'r 3 fs out, staying on fnl furlong*.......................... (10 to 1 op 9 to 2) 11
CZARNA (Ire) 8-11 (3*) B Doyle (2) *led stands side till o'r 3 fs out, grad wknd*.................(50 to 1 op 33 to 1) 12
2571[4] GLITTERAZZI 9-0 J Williams (12) *chsd alng in midfield, no imprsn last 2 fs*...... (33 to 1 op 20 to 1 tchd 50 to 1) 13
IRKUTSK (USA) 9-0 W Ryan (8) *bustled alng to improve centre o'r 2 fs out, not pace of ldrs.* ......(12 to 1 op 8 to 1 tchd 14 to 1) 14
SAMSONESQUE 8-9 G Bardwell (3) *settled midfield, drvn alng o'r 2 fs out, nvr nr to chal*.... (50 to 1 op 33 to 1) 15
3990[8] LUCKY TUCKY 9-0 F Norton (18) *settled midfield, hrd at work o'r 2 fs out, no imprsn*.... (50 to 1 tchd 100 to 1) 16
4026[3] NOBLISSIMA (Ire) 8-9 L Piggott (20) *chsd alng far side, wknd o'r 2 fs out*.....(25 to 1 op 14 to 1 tchd 33 to 1) 17
BOLAS 8-9 Pat Eddery (23) *patiently rdn, steady hdwy far side hfwy, nvr plcd to chal.* ......(9 to 1 op 8 to 1 tchd 10 to 1) 18
DECENT COVE 9-0 M Tebbutt (17) *drvn alng far side, no imprsn last 2 fs*...................(50 to 1 op 33 to 1) 19
BLUSHING FLAME (USA) 9-0 R Cochrane (19) *outpcd and drvn alng aftr 2 fs, nvr dngrs*......(20 to 1 op 10 to 1) 20
LUCAYAN CAY (Ire) 8-7 (7*) Mark Denaro (25) *chsd alng wth far side bunch, fdd o'r 2 fs out.* ......(50 to 1 op 20 to 1 tchd 66 to 1) 21
2250[4] SANS ECOCIDE 9-0 V Smith (28) *led far side bunch till o'r 3 fs out, fdd*.........................(50 to 1 op 33 to 1) 22
4003[9] CORCOVADO 9-0 D Harrison (13) *drvn alng to chase far side ldrs for o'r 4 fs, fdd.* ......(50 to 1 op 33 to 1 tchd 66 to 1) 23
3969[8] TU OPES 9-0 Dale Gibson (15) *patiently rdn, steady hdwy far side hfwy, nvr plcd to chal.* ......(50 to 1 tchd 100 to 1) 24
NIGHT IN A MILLION 9-0 Paul Eddery (26) *drvn alng hfwy, sn outpcd*....(50 to 1 op 20 to 1 tchd 66 to 1) 25
ACCESS ADVENTURER (Ire) 9-0 A Culhane (10) *sluggish strt, nvr able to reco'r*.......... (50 to 1 tchd 66 to 1) 26
TWISP 9-0 J Lowe (22) *struggling frm hfwy.* ......(20 to 1 op 12 to 1) 27
FLEUR DE TAL 8-9 J Carroll (9) *chsd alng to go pace hfwy, sn btn*........................ (50 to 1 op 33 to 1) 28

Dist: Hd, 1½l, 1½l, 3l, 1½l, 2l, ¾l, nk, hd, 1½l. 1m 30.34s. a 6.84s (28 Ran).
SR: 13/12/7/2/-/-/ (Sheikh Mohammed), J H M Gosden

4277 Fitzwilliam Handicap Class D (0-80 3-y-o) £3,882 5f. . . . . (4:40)

66^{3} SASEEDO (USA) [77] 9-7 J Williams (13) *al wl plcd, gd run through on ins fnl furlong, ran on to ld last 50 yards.* . . . . (14 to 1 tchd 16 to 1) 1
3947 DARK EYED LADY (Ire) [76] 9-6 L Dettori (10) *al hndy, ev ch fnl furlong, swshd tail and swrvd last 50 yards, no extr.* . . . . (9 to 1 op 8 to 1 tchd 10 to 1) 2
3438 HOTARIA [67] 8-11 A Culhane (16) *tried to make all, clr hfwy, wknd and hdd last 50 yards, hmpd, no extr.* . . . . (16 to 1 op 14 to 1 tchd 20 to 1) 3
3947 CHARITY EXPRESS (Ire) [66] (e/c) 8-10 M Wigham, *bustled alng to go pace hfwy, swtchd through to improve o'r one furlong out, ran on finish.* . . . . (12 to 1 op 20 to 1) 4
4092 MOUJEEB (USA) [49] (v) 7-7 Kim McDonnell (4) *wl plcd stands side, hrd at work last 2 fs, kpt on same pace.* . . . . (50 to 1 op 66 to 1) 5
3955^{9} FIRST OPTION [70] 9-0 K Darley (6) *trkd ldg pair far side, bustled alng o'r one furlong out, not quicken.* . . . . (9 to 2 fav op 6 to 1 tchd 7 to 1) 6
3481^{5} ARAGROVE [77] 9-7 J Reid (7) *trkd far side bunch, effrt and rdn 2 fs out, one pace.* . . . . (12 to 1 op 10 to 1 tchd 14 to 1) 7
3942 DOMULLA [76] 9-6 D Harrison (3) *drvn alng to chase stands side bunch, kpt on, not pace to chal.* . . . . (10 to 1 op 8 to 1 tchd 12 to 1) 8
3906 BOLD STREET (Ire) [60] 8-4 F Norton (5) *chsd ldrs far side, drvn alng 2 fs out, no extr.* . . . . (8 to 1 tchd 9 to 1 and 7 to 1) 9
4090^{3} KILDEE LAD [58] 8-2 Dale Gibson (9) *sluggish strt, chsd alng far side, nvr able to chal.* . . . . (15 to 2 op 6 to 1 tchd 8 to 1) 10
2582^{3} RACING TELEGRAPH [58] 8-2 G Bardwell (8) *drvn alng to keep up, nvr able to trble ldrs.* . . . (10 to 1 tchd 12 to 1) 11
3947 JOELLISE [49] (v) 7-2^{2} (7*) Claire Balding (12) *sn outpcd and drvn alng, nvr nr to chal.* . . . . (50 to 1 op 33 to 1) 12
4090^{7} JOBIE [72] 9-2 Pat Eddery (11) *chsd alng far side, struggling hfwy, sn btn.* . . . . . . (8 to 1 op 7 to 1 tchd 9 to 1) 13
3964 PRINCESS OBERON (Ire) [72] 9-2 M Hills (1) *broke wl to show speed stands side for o'r 3 fs, fdd.* . . . . (15 to 2 op 7 to 1 tchd 8 to 1) 14
3593 ANOTHER JADE [76] 9-6 W R Swinburn (2) *broke wl to show speed wth stands side bunch till wknd o'r one furlong out.* . . . . (12 to 1 tchd 14 to 1) 15
4123 FORDALLIA [49] 7-7 J Lowe (14) *drvn alng wth far side bunch, nvr able to trble ldrs.* . . . . . . (50 to 1 op 66 to 1) 16
Dist: 1½l, 2l, nk, hd, nk, sht-hd, sht-hd, 1½l, nk, 1½l. 1m 1.52s. a 2.92s (16 Ran).
SR: 64/57/40/38/20/40/46/44/22/ (S Fustok), W A O'Gorman

NEWMARKET (good) Friday October 1st

Going Correction: PLUS 0.30 sec. per fur. (races 1,3,4,5), PLUS 0.20 (2,6)

4278 Snowdens Marquees Fillies' Rated Class B Handicap (0-105 3-y-o and up) £8,204 6f. . . . . (1:50)

4172 BRANSTON ABBY (Ire) [102] 4-9-7 M Roberts (5) *hld up rear, hdwy o'r one furlong out, hrd rdn ins last, led last strds.* . . . . (6 to 1 jt-fav op 5 to 1 tchd 13 to 2) 1
3756* ALASIB [88] 3-8-5 L Dettori (2) *cl up, rdn to ld appr fnl furlong, hdd last strds.* . . . . (12 to 1 tchd 14 to 1) 2
3504 NAGIDA [88] 4-8-7 J Weaver (6) *hdwy frm rear and swtchd rght o'r one furlong out, dsptd ld last 100 yards, jst fld.* . . . . (6 to 1 jt-fav tchd 13 to 2) 3
3964^{8} WAFFLE ON [89] 3-8-6^{1} J Reid (3) *in tch, rdn and not quicken o'r one furlong out, kpt on wl nr finish.* . . . . (20 to 1 op 16 to 1 tchd 25 to 1) 4
4024^{9} LEE ARTISTE [88] (bl) 5-8-7 Pat Eddery (11) *hdwy frm rear o'r one furlong out, sn ev ch, one pace last 100 yards.* . . . . (10 to 1 tchd 12 to 1) 5
4145^{3} ARABELLAJILL [89] 4-8-8 K Darley (7) *trkd ldrs, pushed alng 2 fs out, one pace fnl furlong.* (7 to 1 tchd 8 to 1) 6
4151^{8} STAR FAMILY FRIEND (Ire) [92] 3-8-9 P Robinson (12) *hld up, hdwy 2 fs out, rdn and crrd rght o'r one out, no extr.* . . . . (12 to 1 op 10 to 1) 7
2304^{9} AMIRATI (USA) [88] 3-8-0 (5*) J Tate (9) *trkd ldrs till wknd ins last 2 fs.* . . . . (16 to 1 op 14 to 1 tchd 20 to 1) 8
1806 MASSIBA (Ire) [94] 4-8-13 B Raymond (10) *led till hdd und pres appr fnl furlong, wknd.* . . . . . . (20 to 1 op 16 to 1) 9
4040^{2} TRUTHFUL IMAGE [88] (bl) 4-8-2 (5*) P McCabe (1) *ldg grp, rdn alng o'r one furlong out, outpcd clsg stages.* . . . . (15 to 2 op 6 to 1 tchd 8 to 1) 10
3849 POKER CHIP [90] 3-8-7 M Hills (4) *hld up, effrt 2 fs out, sn btn.* . . . . (12 to 1 op 10 to 1 tchd 14 to 1) 11
3983^{4} SIMPLY SOOTY [88] 3-8-5 A Mackay (13) *chsd ldrs 4 fs, sn wknd.* . . . . (50 to 1 op 25 to 1 tchd 66 to 1) 12
4040 DOMINUET [92] 8-8-11 J Lowe (8) *hld up, shrtlvd effrt 2 fs out, no hdwy o'r one out.* . . . . (12 to 1 op 10 to 1 tchd 14 to 1) 13
4040 MARGARET'S GIFT [91] 3-8-8 J Carroll (14) *in tch till wknd 2 fs out, eased fnl furlong.* . . . . (11 to 1 op 10 to 1 tchd 12 to 1) 14
Dist: Hd, hd, 1l, 1l, hd, ½l, 1½l, hd, sht-hd, 1½l. 1m 15.17s. a 3.77s (14 Ran).
SR: 68/51/52/47/44/44/43/33/40/ (J David Abell), M Johnston

4279 Racing Post Claiming Stakes Class E (3-y-o and up) £4,815 1½m. . . . . . (2:25)

1827 FAUGERON 4-9-4 R Cochrane (3) *trkd ldrs, led o'r 3 fs out, clr 2 out, styd on wl.* . . (16 to 1 op 8 to 1 tchd 20 to 1) 1
3980^{4} LAMBAST 3-8-7 Pat Eddery (12) *hld up, hdwy and not clr run o'r 2 fs out, ran on appr last, styd on cl hme.* . . . . (11 to 4 fav op 7 to 2 tchd 4 to 1 and 5 to 2) 2
SAFFAAH (USA) 6-9-4 J Carroll (11) *ldg grp, effrt and rdn o'r 2 fs out, kpt on same pace.* . . . . (9 to 1 op 8 to 1 tchd 10 to 1) 3
4234^{3} MAHAASIN 5-8-8 A Mackay (4) *mid-div, effrt 3 fs out, rdn and one pace frm 2 out.* . . . . (11 to 1 op 8 to 1 tchd 12 to 1) 4
4152^{8} KIAWAH 3-7-8 (7*) N Varley (15) *hld up, rdn alng and styd on one pace fnl 2 fs.* . . . (10 to 1 op 8 to 1 tchd 11 to 1) 5
2023^{3} RUFFLE 3-8-7 J Reid (1) *hld up, prog o'r 2 fs out, not quicken appr last, sn btn.* . . . . (11 to 1 op 7 to 1 tchd 12 to 1) 6
3669^{8} PLATINUM VENTURE 3-8-7 W Woods (10) *led aftr 2 fs till o'r 3 out, wknd over one out.* . . . . (25 to 1 op 14 to 1 tchd 33 to 1) 7
4028 SPARKY'S SONG 3-8-3 R Hills (6) *chsd ldrs till wknd o'r 2 fs out.* . . . . (20 to 1 op 14 to 1 tchd 33 to 1) 8
SHINGLE PATH 3-8-5 M Roberts (13) *al rear.* . . . . (33 to 1 op 14 to 1) 9
4006^{7} RUNAWAY PETE (USA) 3-9-6 M Hills (9) *led 2 fs, wknd o'r 3 out.* . . . . (6 to 1 op 9 to 2) 10
REJECTS REPLY 3-8-6 G Hind (5) *al beh, tld off.* . . . . (40 to 1 op 20 to 1 tchd 50 to 1) 11
FIREBIRD LAD 5-8-13 J Lowe (8) *al rear, tld off.* . . . . (40 to 1 op 33 to 1 tchd 50 to 1) 12
3945^{5} SOLO CHARTER 3-8-6 P Robinson (7) *prmnt till lost pl quickly 5 fs out, tld off.* . . . . (20 to 1 op 12 to 1 tchd 25 to 1) 13
4037^{5} AZUREUS (Ire) 5-9-9 K Darley (2) *refused to race.* . . . . (6 to 1 op 4 to 1 tchd 13 to 2) I
Dist: 1½l, 2½l, 2½l, nk, 1½l, 4l, ¾l, hd, 1½l, 20l. 2m 38.84s. a 9.24s (14 Ran).
SR: 36/22/28/13/5/8/ (Normandy Developments (London)), R Akehurst

4280 Charles Wells Eagle Bitter Rated Class B Handicap (0-100 3-y-o and up) £8,566 7f. . . . . (2:55)

4140^{7} FRAAM [96] 4-9-6 W R Swinburn (4) *al gng wl on heels of ldrs, led o'r one furlong out, pushed clr.* . . . . (10 to 1 tchd 12 to 1) 1
4172^{7} REALITIES (USA) [91] 3-8-12 R Cochrane (10) *slwly into strd, rdn alng 3 fs out, ran on o'r one out, styd on nr finish.* . . . . (20 to 1 op 12 to 1) 2
4172^{3} KAYVEE [94] 4-9-4 M Perrett (12) *hld up, hdwy 2 fs out, str run appr last, fnshd wl.* . . . . (12 to 1 op 10 to 1) 3
4040 ECHO-LOGICAL [86] 4-8-10 K Darley (6) *hld up rear, hdwy und pres o'r one furlong out, styd on clsg stages.* . . . . (25 to 1 op 16 to 1) 4
4153^{3} CAMBARA [90] 3-8-11 M Roberts (15) *wl plcd, rdn and not quicken appr fnl furlong.* . . . . (7 to 1 op 6 to 1 tchd 8 to 1) 5
4040^{9} DUPLICITY (Ire) [95] 5-9-5 J Reid (9) *hld up, improved o'r 2 fs out, styd on ins last.* . . . . (12 to 1 op 14 to 1) 6
3897 CROFT VALLEY [96] 6-9-6 D Harrison (5) *led till hdd and wknd o'r one furlong out.* . . . . (16 to 1 tchd 14 to 1 and 20 to 1) 7
3624^{5} TYCHONIC [83] (bl) 3-8-4 Pat Eddery (11) *missed break, cld on ldrs 3 fs out, no extr appr last.* . . . . (6 to 1 fav op 8 to 1 tchd 10 to 1) 8
4040 HEAVENLY RISK [87] 3-8-8 M Hills (7) *hld up, hdwy on outsd 2 fs out, no imprsn appr last.* (25 to 1 op 20 to 1) 9
4040 MASTER PLANNER [97] 4-9-0 (7*) J D Smith (2) *hld up, effrt 2 fs out, hng lft and not trble frnt rnk appr last.* . . . . (20 to 1 tchd 25 to 1) 10
3791* DIXIELAND MELODY (USA) [88] 3-8-9 B Raymond (3) *effrt hfwy, no prog last 2 fs.* . . . . (8 to 1 tchd 10 to 1) 11
4040 GREEN DOLLAR [83] 10-8-7 T Sprake (8) *wl plcd for o'r 4 fs.* . . . . (50 to 1) 12
4066^{5} WUFUD (USA) [89] 3-8-10 W Carson (1) *nvr trble ldrs.* . . . . (25 to 1 tchd 33 to 1) 13
3885 NOBLE PET [83] 4-8-7 J Carroll (13) *pressed ldrs till lost pl ins last 2 fs.* . . . . (16 to 1 op 14 to 1 tchd 20 to 1) 14
4038 NEITHER NOR [83] 4-8-7 P Robinson (18) *in tch, no hdwy o'r 2 fs out.* . . . . (16 to 1 op 20 to 1 tchd 25 to 1) 15
4145^{2} WINGED VICTORY (Ire) [91] 3-8-12 L Dettori (16) *in tch, effrt o'r 2 fs out, sn btn.* . . . . (10 to 1 tchd 11 to 1) 16
4166^{2} GIPSY FIDDLER [87] (v) 5-8-8 (3*) S D Williams (14) *pressed ldrs till wknd quickly 2 fs out.* . . . . (10 to 1 op 12 to 1) 17
4116^{2} CORALS DREAM (Ire) [87] 4-8-11 W Woods (17) *cl up on outsd, wknd quickly 2 fs out.* . . . . (15 to 2 op 10 to 1 tchd 6 to 1) 18

Dist: 3l, ¾l, nk, ½l, nk, sht-hd, 2l, 2l, sht-hd, nk. 1m 28.35s. a 4.85s (18 Ran).
SR: 65/48/52/43/42/49/49/27/25/ (Maktoum Al Maktoum), A A Scott

4281 Somerville Tattersall Stakes Class A (Listed Race) (2-y-o) £10,116 7f (3:25)

3400^3 GRAND LODGE (USA) 8-11 Pat Eddery (7) *al gng wl, led o'r one furlong out, pushed clr, easily.* .... (7 to 2 op 11 to 4 tchd 4 to 1) 1
3316* COLONEL COLLINS (USA) 9-1 J Reid (2) *wl plcd, chlgd and veered rght o'r one furlong out, outpcd ins last.* .... (11 to 10 fav tchd 6 to 4 and Evens) 2
3435^5 FAST EDDY 8-11 L Dettori (1) *mid-div, rdn alng 3 fs out, styd on one pace fnl furlong.* .... (11 to 1 op 10 to 1 tchd 12 to 1) 3
3884* INNISHOWEN (USA) 9-1 K Darley (8) *led for o'r 3 fs, led 2 out, hdd and hmpd over one out, not rcvr.* .... (7 to 1 op 6 to 1 tchd 8 to 1) 4
2924^5 MR EUBANKS (USA) 8-11 R Cochrane (9) *slwly into strd, rdn and effrt 3 fs out, not rch ldrs.* (66 to 1 op 33 to 1) 5
STAR CARNIVAL (USA) 8-11 W R Swinburn (6) *pushed alng 3 fs out, nvr able to chal.* .... (25 to 1 op 20 to 1 tchd 16 to 1 and 33 to 1) 6
YOUNG CLIFFORD (USA) 8-11 M Hills (5) *outpcd most of way.* .... (20 to 1 tchd 25 to 1) 7
3763* FRIENDLY CHAMP (Ire) 8-11 R Price (3) *pressed ldr, led o'r 3 fs out to 2 out, not clr run and wknd over one out.* .... (8 to 1 op 7 to 1 tchd 9 to 1) 8
4067* SOUTHERN RIDGE 8-11 D Harrison (4) *chsd frnt rnk, effrt 3 fs out, wknd 2 out.* .... (20 to 1 tchd 25 to 1) 9
Dist: 3½l, 2½l, 2½l, ½l, ½l, 1l, hd, 2½l. 1m 27.52s. a 4.02s (9 Ran).
SR: 68/61/49/45/39/37/34/33/25/ (Lord Howard de Walden), W Jarvis

4282 Main Reef Stakes Class A (Listed Race) (3-y-o and up) £10,377 1m (3:55)

3886^3 GABR 3-8-10 W Carson (2) *trkd ldr, rdn to ld o'r 2 fs out, pushed clr fnl furlong.* .... (7 to 2 co-fav tchd 5 to 2 and 4 to 1) 1
1749^4 WHARF (USA) 3-8-10 Pat Eddery (6) *hld up, hdwy on ins and not much room o'r one furlong out, styd on last 100 yards.* .... (7 to 2 co-fav op 5 to 2 tchd 4 to 1) 2
4172 EN ATTENDANT (Fr) 5-9-0 B Raymond (4) *wl plcd, rdn and not quicken ins last 2 fs, kpt on gmely.* .... (8 to 1 op 7 to 1 tchd 9 to 1) 3
4063^6 SOVIET LINE (Ire) 3-8-10 W R Swinburn (5) *led till o'r 2 fs out, edgd lft over one out, ran on same pace.* (7 to 2 co-fav op 5 to 1) 4
3465^7 LOST SOLDIER (USA) 3-8-10 M Roberts (3) *rcd keenly in mid-div, effrt o'r 2 fs out, not quicken.* .... (15 to 2 op 7 to 1 tchd 10 to 1) 5
1921* WAGON MASTER (Fr) 3-8-10 R Hills (7) *hld up, improved on outsd 3 fs out, no prog ins last 2 furlongs.* .... (7 to 1 tchd 8 to 1) 6
4005* SUMOTO 3-8-5 M Hills (1) *ldg grp till rdn and wknd wl o'r one furlong out.* .... (8 to 1 op 7 to 1 tchd 9 to 1) 7
Dist: 2½l, 1l, nk, 3½l, 3½l, 5l. 1m 42.41s. a 5.21s (7 Ran).
SR: 54/46/47/42/31/20/-/ (Hamdan Al-Maktoum), R W Armstrong

4283 Stayers' Handicap Class C (0-90 3-y-o and up) £5,754 1¾m........ (4:30)

3873^4 ADDICTED TO LOVE [60] (bl) 4-8-7 T Sprake (2) *hdwy frm rear 4 fs out, led o'r 2 out, pushed out.* .... (33 to 1 tchd 50 to 1) 1
4036^8 LOOKINGFORARAINBOW (Ire) [64] 5-8-11 M Wigham (1) *hld up, cld on ldrs o'r 3 fs out, chsd wnr appr last, not quicken.* .... (33 to 1) 2
4143^3 TILTY (USA) [70] 3-8-8 K Darley (8) *improved frm rear 4 fs out, styd on one pace from 2 out.* .... (10 to 1 op 8 to 1 tchd 12 to 1) 3
3970* MARADONNA (USA) [72] 4-9-5 R Cochrane (4) *mid-div, pushed alng hfwy, ran on o'r 3 fs out, one pace frm 2 out.* .... (7 to 2 fav op 3 to 1 tchd 4 to 1) 4
3881^6 MISS PIN UP [71] 4-9-4 W R Swinburn (13) *slwly into strd, hld up, ran on and not much room o'r 2 fs out, nrst finish.* .... (11 to 1 op 16 to 1) 5
4037^4 FIRST BID [72] 6-9-5 A Culhane (15) *hld up, hdwy o'r 3 fs out, rdn and one pace 2 out.* .... (8 to 1 op 14 to 1 tchd 16 to 1) 6
3646^2 WINGS COVE [78] 3-9-2 J Reid (14) *hdwy hfwy, chsd ldr o'r 3 fs out, no extr frm 2 out.* .... (4 to 1 op 6 to 1) 7
3724^8 SUBSONIC (Ire) [77] 5-9-10 W Carson (10) *beh till effrt o'r 2 fs out, no imprsn on ldrs.* .... (16 to 1 op 20 to 1) 8
3734* NEMEA (USA) [63] 3-8-1 P Robinson (11) *ldg grp till rdn and wknd ins last 2 fs.* (11 to 1 op 8 to 1 tchd 12 to 1) 9
2751^5 DEDUCE [73] 4-9-6 M Hills (9) *ldg grp till lost pl o'r 3 fs out.* .... (20 to 1 tchd 16 to 1) 10
3998* LAKE POOPO (Ire) [77] 3-9-1 D Holland (12) *chsd ldr, led o'r 4 fs out till over 2 out, eased whn btn.* (9 to 1 op 7 to 1) 11
4064 HARD TASK [75] 3-8-13 J Carroll (7) *al rear.* .... (33 to 1 op 25 to 1) 12
3666^9 SHUJAN (USA) [75] 4-9-8 R Price (17) *led till o'r 4 fs out, sn btn.* .... (25 to 1 tchd 33 to 1) 13
4150^6 BLUE BLAZER [81] 3-9-5 B Raymond (18) *nvr able to chal.* .... (20 to 1 op 12 to 1) 14
462^2 CRYSTAL SPIRIT [75] 6-9-8 L Dettori (3) *in tch till outpcd 3 fs out.* .... (10 to 1 op 20 to 1) 15
2003^4 REFUGIO [85] 3-9-9 M Roberts (16) *trkd ldrs till rdn and wknd o'r 3 fs out.* .... (12 to 1 tchd 14 to 1) 16
3998^5 MUJAWAB [83] 3-9-7 R Hills (5) *pressed ldrs ten fs.* .... (20 to 1 tchd 25 to 1) 17
3271^8 PHARAMINEUX [75] 7-9-8 Pat Eddery (6) *al beh, lost tch 6 fs out, tld off.* .... (25 to 1 op 16 to 1 tchd 33 to 1) 18
Dist: 2½l, 3l, 3l, nk, nk, 2½l, 10l, 1½l, ½l, 3½l. 3m 4.09s. a 8.09s (18 Ran).
SR: 40/39/30/35/33/33/25/13/-/ (Mascalls Stud), P J Makin

CURRAGH (IRE) (yielding to soft)
Saturday October 2nd

Going Correction: PLUS 0.50 sec. per fur. (races 1,5,6), PLUS 0.80 (2,3,4,7)

4284 Derrinstown Apprentice Series Handicap Final (0-85 3-y-o and up) £8,280 1 ¼m........ (2:00)

4001* THE BOWER (Ire) [-] (bl) 4-7-11 (6*,3ex) P M Donohue (16) .... (10 to 1) 1
3914* SAIBOT (USA) [-] 4-9-10 (4*) D J O'Donohoe (11) ... (7 to 1) 2
3926* WANDERING THOUGHTS (Ire) [-] 4-10-0 (4*) J R Barry (18) .... (4 to 1 fav) 3
4147* FERRYCARRIG HOTEL (Ire) [-] 4-8-10 (6*,8ex) P J Smullen (8) .... (11 to 2) 4
3826^2 ACCELL (Ire) [-] 4-7-3 (6*) G M Moylan (7) .... (14 to 1) 5
4161^3 TOUCHDOWN [-] (bl) 6-7-13 (4*) P P Murphy (9) ... (12 to 1) 6
3914^9 FLORA WOOD (Ire) [-] (bl) 3-8-7 (4*) B J Walsh (15) (14 to 1) 7
3327^9 SAFAYN (USA) [-] (bl) 3-9-4 (2*) W J Smith (17) .... (12 to 1) 8
3924^5 GALLARDINI (Ire) [-] 4-9-3 (6*) T E Durcan (10) .... (14 to 1) 9
2984^3 VALONA (Ire) [-] 3-9-2 (2*) J A Heffernan (1) .... (10 to 1) 10
4147 MRS KEPPEL [-] 5-7-12 (6*) G Coogan (2) .... (20 to 1) 11
3951^4 BLUES COMPOSER (Ire) [-] 4-7-5 (8*) J P Cornally (13) .... (14 to 1) 12
3926^7 ELIZABETH'S PET (Ire) [-] 3-9-6 (2*) C Everard (6) (10 to 1) 13
4057 WHAT A PLEASURE (Ire) [-] 3-8-2 (8*) I Browne (14) (16 to 1) 14
3924^6 LIMBO LADY (USA) [-] 3-8-13 (2*) J J Behan (19) .. (12 to 1) 15
4094^4 HANG A RIGHT [-] 6-9-1 (4*) T P Treacy (5) .... (11 to 1) 16
3826^3 TINCO PALENO [-] 9-8-7 R M Burke (12) .... (14 to 1) 17
4185^8 MORNING NURSE (Ire) [-] 4-8-3 D G O'Shea (3) ... (14 to 1) 18
3330^5 WALLY WALLENSKY (Ire) [-] 3-9-7 P Carberry (4) .. (10 to 1) 19
Dist: Sht-hd, 2l, 2½l, ¾l. 2m 13.10s. a 10.30s (19 Ran).
SR: 36/60/60/39/16/-/ (Mrs C Collins), C Collins

4285 GRE Nursery (2-y-o) £3,795 6f...(2:30)

4052^9 JOIN FORCES (Ire) [-] 7-12 (4*) W J Smith (9) ..... (25 to 1) 1
4052^3 TRIMBLEMILL (Ire) [-] 7-13 (8*) R T Fitzpatrick (7) ... (5 to 1) 2
3611^7 KING SANCHO (Ire) [-] 9-2 M J Kinane (5) .... (13 to 2) 3
4052^4 ASTRADANE (Ire) [-] 8-4 J F Egan (2) .... (8 to 1) 4
3730^4 GO MILLIE (Ire) [-] 8-8 S Craine (10) .... (10 to 1) 5
3719^2 STAGE LEFT EVEN (Ire) [-] 8-12 (2*) P Carberry (4) .... (3 to 1 fav) 6
4117^5 PERFECT CADENCE (Ire) [-] (bl) 7-7 (2*) D G O'Shea (3) .... (16 to 1) 7
3731^5 CROSS SWORDS (USA) [-] (bl) 7-10 (4*) J J Behan (11) .... (10 to 1) 8
3110^4 EASTROP DANCER (Ire) [-] 6-13 (8*) G M Moylan (12) .... (16 to 1) 9
3110^2 MAHASEAL (USA) [-] 8-6 W J Supple (6) .... (7 to 1) 10
3911^8 FIONN DE COOL (Ire) [-] 8-3 (4*) J A Heffernan (8) (12 to 1) 11
2983^8 BONNIE CRATHIE (Ire) [-] 8-9 P V Gilson (1) .... (8 to 1) 12
Dist: Nk, hd, sht-hd, 2½l. 1m 18.70s. a 8.20s (12 Ran).
SR: 20/24/32/19/13/-/ (Mrs M A O'Toole), M A O'Toole

4286 C L Weld EBF Park Stakes (Group 3) (2-y-o) £14,375 7f........ (3:00)

3927* MORCOTE (Ire) 8-10 D Hogan (6) *mid-div, shaken up appr fnl furlong, led 150 yards out, ran on strly.* .... (5 to 2) 1
3925^9 RAZIDA (Ire) 8-10 K J Manning (8) *wl plcd, led 2 fs out, hdd and wknd 150 yards out.* .... (10 to 1) 2
FAIRY WATER 8-10 W J Supple (9) *prog frm rear 3 fs out, kpt on fnl furlong, nvr dngrs.* .... (14 to 1) 3
INSTAMATIC 8-10 S Craine (4) *rear till styd on fnl 2 fs.* .... (7 to 1) 4
3415^3 TIMINIYA (Ire) (bl) 8-10 R Hughes (5) *prmnt, led briefly 2 and a half fs out, wknd appr last.* .... (7 to 1) 5
3807* PROFIT RELEASE (Ire) 8-10 M J Kinane (2) *led to 2 and a half fs out, wknd quickly.* .... (7 to 4 fav) 6
HONEYSPIKE (Ire) 8-10 P V Gilson (1) *slwly away, rdn and no imprsn hfwy.* .... (10 to 1) 7
4117^3 SECRET WAR (Ire) 8-10 J F Egan (3) *trkd ldrs, niggled alng hfwy, wknd appr 2 fs out.* .... (25 to 1) 8
3925^7 ZORINA 8-10 P Shanahan (10) *al rear, eased fnl furlong.* .... (12 to 1) 9
Dist: 2½l, sht-hd, 2½l, 2l. 1m 31.00s. a 7.80s (9 Ran).
SR: 63/55/54/46/40/-/ (Dieter H Hofemeier), John M Oxx

4287 Waterford Testimonial Stakes (Listed) (3-y-o and up) £8,625 6f........ (3:30)

4056* BRADAWN BREEVER (Ire) (bl) 4-8-11 W J Supple (3) *settled mid-div, prog appr fnl furlong, chlgd ins last, ran on wl to ld nr line*......(3 to 1 fav) 1
4056[8] LAVINIA FONTANA (Ire) 4-8-8 P V Gilson (9) *mid-div, hdwy hfwy, led one furlong out till cl hme*......(4 to 1) 2
1050 HIGH TYCOON (Ire) 3-8-8 M J Kinane (8) *wl plcd, chlgd 2 fs out, wknd ins last*......(8 to 1) 3
3912[4] UP AND AT 'EM (bl) 3-8-8 P Shanahan (12) *hld up, chlgd one and a half fs out, fdd*......(4 to 1) 4
4057[6] CORTIJA PARK (Ire) 3-8-5 P Carberry (7) *kpt on frm mid-div, nvr dngrs*......(16 to 1) 5
4056 NAIVITY (Ire) 4-8-8 J F Egan (6) *rear, kpt on und pres fnl 2 fs*......(20 to 1) 6
4056 CLASSICAL AFFAIR (Ire) (bl) 4-8-11 K J Manning (10) *led aftr one furlong till appr last, wknd quickly*......(12 to 1) 7
ADRIEN DE VRIES (Ire) 3-8-8 S Craine (11) *nvr trble ldrs.*......(33 to 1) 8
4056[3] KINDNESS ITSELF (Ire) 3-8-5 R Hughes (5) *led for one furlong, wl plcd till rdn and wknd 2 out*......(12 to 1) 9
4056 SAND OR STONE (Ire) 5-8-11 A J Nolan (2) *wl plcd till hfwy, sn btn*......(50 to 1) 10
4056[6] ROSIE'S MAC (Ire) (bl) 4-9-1 N G McCullagh (1) *mid-div till rdn and wknd 2 fs out*......(8 to 1) 11
4056 MOONLIGHT PARTNER (Ire) (bl) 3-8-5 W J Smith (4) *mid-div till rdn and btn 3 fs out*......(14 to 1) 12
Dist: Hd, 3l, 1½l, 2½l. 1m 17.00s. a 6.50s (12 Ran).
SR: 63/59/47/41/28/-/ (M A Murray), Kevin Prendergast

4288 Irish Cesarewitch Handicap (0-110 3-y-o and up) £6,900 2m........ (4:00)

3915[2] CLIVEDEN GAIL (Ire) [-] 4-9-3 M J Kinane (20)......(9 to 1) 1
3915[4] SHIRLEY'S DELIGHT (Ire) [-] 3-8-7 (2*) P Carberry (16)......(7 to 1) 2
3604* TROPICAL LAKE (Ire) [-] 3-6-13 (8*) G M Moylan (15)......(12 to 1) 3
4147[6] MORNING SARGE [-] 5-7-4 (6*) P P Murphy (7)......(20 to 1) 4
4095[3] BITOFABANTER [-] 6-8-2 (2*) R M Burke (10)......(8 to 1) 5
3926[8] TONY'S FEN [-] 4-9-4 (6*) B J Walsh (18)......(20 to 1) 6
2676[2] CAMDEN BUZZ (Ire) [-] 5-8-1 (4*) J J Behan (8) (5 to 1 fav) 7
4095 LACKEL (Ger) [-] 5-8-13 (4*) J A Heffernan (22)......(16 to 1) 8
2841[4] RISING WATERS (Ire) [-] 5-8-9 S Craine (6)......(20 to 1) 9
4147[8] IMAD (USA) [-] 3-8-0 W J Supple (1)......(20 to 1) 10
3915[8] LADAKIYA (USA) [-] 3-8-9 R Hughes (9)......(12 to 1) 11
3951* ZUHAL [-] 5-7-6[7] (8*,4ex) R T Fitzpatrick (5)......(20 to 1) 12
3924[4] PLATINUM EMPIRE (USA) [-] 3-8-11 A J Nolan (19) (14 to 1) 13
3853[5] ALIBAR'S PET (Ire) [-] 3-6-13 (8*) B J Halligan (21) (20 to 1) 14
4147 SHARASTAMINA (USA) [-] 4-7-7 (6*) D J O'Donohoe (12)......(16 to 1) 15
CHIRKPAR [-] 6-8-12 K J Manning (14)......(12 to 1) 16
3772[4] SAFFRON CROCUS [-] (bl) 3-8-0 (2*) D G O'Shea (13)......(14 to 1) 17
4147[7] SUPER FLAME (Can) [-] 6-8-5 P V Gilson (3)......(16 to 1) 18
3063[5] LOSHIAN (Ire) [-] 4-8-7 J F Egan (17)......(8 to 1) 19
3580* SYLVIA FOX [-] 6-7-7 (4*) W J Smith (25)......(10 to 1) 20
3684* SENSE OF VALUE [-] 4-7-13 N G McCullagh (2)...(16 to 1) 21
2808[7] KHAZARI (USA) [-] (bl) 5-8-0 L O'Shea (11)......(25 to 1) 22
CHANUSKA [-] 10-7-9[2] P Braiden (24)......(66 to 1) 23
Dist: Nk, 6l, 1l, 6l. 3m 38.40s. a 16.90s (23 Ran).
SR: 14/5/-/-/-/-/ (Int Thoroughbred Breeders Inc), D K Weld

4289 Solonaway Race (Listed) (3-y-o and up) £8,625 1m 1f................ (4:30)

3916* IDRIS (Ire) 3-8-10 M J Kinane (4) *trkd ldrs, led appr 2 fs out, quickened clr ins last, easily*......(13 to 8 on) 1
3913[5] APPROACH THE BENCH (Ire) 5-9-6 J F Egan (6) *hld up, effrt 2 fs out, kpt on one pace ins last*......(7 to 2) 2
3926 NEVER BACK DOWN (Ire) 3-8-7 W J Supple (7) *hdwy frm rear 2 fs out, hmpd one out, ran on*......(25 to 1) 3
3333[8] BE MY HOPE (Ire) 4-8-13 N G McCullagh (5) *5th strt, rdn to chal 2 fs out, sn wknd*......(8 to 1) 4
4162[2] TALES OF HEARSAY (Ger) (bl) 3-8-10 P V Gilson (3) *wl plcd till wknd appr fnl furlong*......(14 to 1) 5
3824[5] KRISDALINE (USA) 3-8-7 R Hughes (2) *led till rdn and hdd appr 2 fs out, wknd quickly*......(7 to 1) 6
4053[6] NECTARINE (Ire) 3-8-7 S Craine (1) *mid-div till rdn and lost pl 4 fs out*......(25 to 1) 7
Dist: 4½l, 1l, 3l, nk. 2m 2.60s. a 13.10s (7 Ran).
(H H Aga Khan), John M Oxx

4290 Cut Bush EBF Maiden (2-y-o) £5,244 6f ....(5:00)

3071[5] CLARADANE (Ire) 8-11 W J Supple (6)......(9 to 2) 1
LIMANDA (Ire) 8-11 M J Kinane (8)......(11 to 10 fav) 2
4146[8] GUIDED TOUR (Ire) 9-0 J F Egan (5)......(20 to 1) 3
RINJANI 9-0 R Hughes (13)......(9 to 2) 4
2244[4] SAFKANA (Ire) 8-11 D Hogan (14)......(10 to 1) 5
BE GIVING (Ire) 8-11 N G McCullagh (1)......(14 to 1) 6
4117 GLAD YOU ASKED ME (Ire) (bl) 8-11 N Byrne (4)...(50 to 1) 7
REGAL DOMAIN (Ire) 8-8 (6*) B J Walsh (11)......(10 to 1) 8
BLAKE'S HOTEL 9-0 K J Manning (12)......(16 to 1) 9
TRIGGER HAPPY JOHN (Ire) 9-0 P Shanahan (10) (16 to 1) 10
4059[9] PENZAAD (Ire) 8-12 (2*) P Carberry (9)......(33 to 1) 11
2778[7] PEARL OF ORIENT (Ire) 8-12 (2*) R M Burke (2)...(25 to 1) 12
4059[3] BUI-DOI (Ire) 8-9 (2*) D G O'Shea (7)......(14 to 1) 13
4117[6] GREENCASTLE ROSE (Ire) 8-11 S Craine (3)......(14 to 1) 14
Dist: 1½l, 1l, 3l, ½l. 1m 19.20s. a 8.70s (14 Ran).
SR: 19/13/12/-/-/-/ (Mrs A E Butler), A Butler

LOUISIANA DOWNS (USA) (firm)
Saturday October 2nd

4291 Super Derby (Grade 1) (3-y-o) £298,013 1¼m......................

779 WALLENDA (USA) 9-0 H McCauley,......(202 to 10) 1
SAINTLY PROSPECTOR (USA) 9-0 R Lester,......(34 to 10) 2
4080* PETESKI (Can) 9-0 C Perret,......(10 to 7 on) 3
4080[4] KISSIN KRIS (USA) 9-0 P Day,......(34 to 10) 4
3823 DEVOTED BRASS (USA) 9-0 L Pincay Jr,......(88 to 10) 5
3823[2] FUTURE STORM (USA) 9-0 P Valenzuela,......(12 to 1) 6
585[3] FOXTRAIL (USA) 9-0 B Walker Jr,......(81 to 10) 7
1070[9] HEGAR (USA) 9-0 C Bourque,......(56 to 1) 8
3823[6] HAWK SPELL (USA) 9-0 K Desormeaux,......(29 to 1) 9
EL BAKAN (USA) 9-0 L Snyder,......(56 to 1) 0
ZARBYCAT (USA) 9-0 B Thomas,......(47 to 1) 0
PREMIER CHEER (USA) 9-0 R Ardoin,......(34 to 10) 0
Dist: Hd, hd, hd, ¾l, 2½l, 10l, 1 ¼l, 1 ¼l, 2l, 3½l. 2m 2.30s. (12 Ran).

LONGCHAMP (FR) (heavy)
Saturday October 2nd
Going Correction: PLUS 0.80 sec. per fur.

4292 CIGA Prix de Royallieu (Group 2) (3-y-o and up) £35,842 1½m 110yds (2:20)

3649[5] HALESIA (USA) 4-9-0 D Boeuf (4) *hld up gng wl, chlgd 2 fs out, led one out, drvn out*......(7 to 1) 1
3331* RAYSEKA (Ire) 3-8-8 J Murtagh (5) *drpd out in last pl, rdn and effrt 3 fs out, led 2 out, edgd lft und pres and hdd one out, not quicken*......(6 to 4) 2
3846[2] LILLE HAMMER 3-8-8 R Cochrane (3) *hld up beh, hdwy und pres fnl 2 fs, styd on ins last*......(14 to 1) 3
3801* ENCOREMOI (USA) 3-8-8 E Saint-Martin (7) *hld up, prog in 3rd pl wl o'r 2 fs out, styd on one pace over one out.*......(82 to 10) 4
3801[2] EGYPTOWN (Fr) 4-9-0 O Doleuze (8) *set moderate pace, hdd 2 fs out, wknd and btn one out*......(5 to 1) 5
3488* NASSMA (Ire) 3-8-8 M Roberts (2) *pld hrd, prmnt, rdn wl o'r 2 fs out, sn lost pl, tld off*......(24 to 1) 6
3824* ALOUETTE 3-8-8 C Roche (6) *rdn hfwy, last and floundering strt, sn tld off*......(29 to 1) 7
1506* APOGEE 3-8-8 Pat Eddery (1) *sn chasing ldrs, wknd o'r 2 fs out, eased whn btn, tld off*......(19 to 10) 8
Dist: 1½l, ¾l, 3l, hd, 8l, 4l, ¾l. 2m 49.00s. a 13.70s (8 Ran).
SR: 63/54/52/46/51/29/21/19/ (E Sarasola), E Lellouche

4293 CIGA Grand Criterium (Group 1) (2-y-o) £143,369 1m...............(2:50)

4074[3] LOST WORLD (Ire) 8-11 O Peslier (3) *midfield, rdn and effrt 3 fs out, led 2 out, hld on gmely und pres.* (91 to 10) 1
3338* SIGNE DIVIN (USA) 8-11 T Jarnet (7) *hld up in last pl, sstnd prog fnl 2 fs, ran on strly ins last*......(12 to 1) 2
3515[2] PSYCHOBABBLE (Ire) 8-11 C Asmussen (5) *hld up, rdn o'r 2 fs out, edgd lft, und pres fnl furlong, no imprsn.*......(10 to 7 on) 3
3851* ZINDARI (USA) 8-11 Pat Eddery (2) *led aftr one furlong, rdn and hdd 2 out, ran on one pace*......(23 to 10) 4
4074* CHIMES BAND (USA) 8-11 D Boeuf (4) *led one furlong, chsd ldr, rdn and ev ch 2 out, wknd fnl furlong.*......(94 to 10) 5
3014[3] GREEN TUNE (USA) 8-11 O Doleuze (1) *prmnt, lost pl o'r 2 fs out*......(93 to 10) 6
4074[6] SOLID ILLUSION (USA) 8-11 G Mosse (6) *hld up, rdn wl o'r 2 fs out, sn btn*......(42 to 1) 7
Dist: ¾l, 1½l, 1½l, hd, 3l, 3l. 1m 45.90s. a 8.40s (7 Ran).
SR: 67/65/60/55/54/45/36/ (D Wildenstein), E Lellouche

4294 CIGA Prix du Cadran (Group 1) (4-y-o and up) £59,737 2½m...........(4:00)

4055[2] ASSESSOR (Ire) 4-9-2 J Reid (1) *hld up rear, hdwy 3 fs out, led 2 out, sn clr, ran on strly*......(6 to 5 fav) 1
3843[3] SOUGHT OUT (Ire) 5-8-13 G Mosse (4) *chsd ldr, led aftr 9 fs to 2 out, ran on one pace, swshd tail fnl furlong.*......(47 to 10) 2
4055[4] SONUS (Ire) 4-9-2 Pat Eddery (3) *drpd out in last pl, hdwy 4 fs out, 3rd and drvn strt, no imprsn fnl furlong.*......(29 to 10) 3
DOUBLE BLASH 4-9-2 D Boeuf (5) *mid-div, chsd ldrs into strt, ran on one pace*......(15 to 1) 4
3843[7] CUTTING REEF (Ire) 4-8-13 A Badel (7) *set fst pace, hdd aftr 9 fs, chsd ldr till wl o'r 2 out, wknd quickly.*......(40 to 1) 5
3718[2] TURGEON (USA) 7-9-2 M Roberts (10) *hld up, rdn 6 fs out, wnt 4th und pres strt, sn btn, fnshd tired*.... (29 to 10) 6
3843[6] DJAIS (Fr) 4-9-2 C Asmussen (9) *chsd ldrs, lost tch 5 fs out, tld off 3 out*......(17 to 1) 7

3583³ DAJRAAN (Ire) 4-9-2 T Jarnet (8) *hld up mid-div, lost tch 5 fs out, tld off 3 out*..........................(29 to 10) 8
3843* OH SO RISKY 6-9-2 J Williams (2) *hld up beh, struggling 6 fs out, tld off 4 out*..........................(43 to 10) 9
KUANG LIEN (Fr) 4-9-2 B Marchand (6) *mid-div, struggling hfwy, tld off fnl 6 fs*.......................... (33 to 1) 10
RIVER TEST (USA) 7-9-2 F Head (11) *prmnt, rdn 9 fs out, btn 6 out, tld off 4 out*.......................... (30 to 1) 11
Dist: 6l, sht-nk, 4l, 6l, 10l, 20l, 6l, 2½l, 5l. 4m 38.20s. a 24.20s (11 Ran).
SR: 20/11/13/9/-/-/ (B E Nielsen), R Hannon

4295 CIGA Prix Dollar (Group 2) (3-y-o and up) £35,842 1m 1f 165yds....... (4:35)

3886* KNIFEBOX (USA) 5-9-0 M Roberts (4) *made all, clr most of way, rdn alng and ran on strly fnl 3 fs, unchlgd.*..........................(14 to 10 fav) 1
2298* FANMORE (USA) 5-9-0 Pat Eddery (1) *drpd out last, effrt on bit to go second strt, sn rdn, drvn and no imprsn o'r 2 fs out*..........................(53 to 10) 2
4075² MARILDO (Fr) 6-9-4 G Guignard (5) *chsd wnr to 4 fs out, sn btn*..........................(78 to 10) 3
2253⁶ ARCANGUES (USA) 5-9-6 T Jarnet (2) *hld up, effrt appr strt, sn rdn and btn*..........................(2 to 1) 4
3842* JEUNE HOMME (USA) 3-8-9 C Asmussen (3) *chsd ldrs to 5 fs out, sn beh, tld off*.......................... (29 to 10) 5
Dist: 8l, 1½l, nk, 8l. 2m 7.70s. a 8.70s (5 Ran).
SR: 87/63/62/63/28/ (Sheikh Mohammed), J H M Gosden

4296 CIGA Prix de Lutece (Group 3) (3-y-o) £26,284 1m 7f.................. (5:10)

3718³ SHAIYBARA (Ire) 8-6 G Mosse (6) *hld up, chlgd 2 fs out, quickened one out, led und pres fnl 50 yards.* (23 to 10) 1
3516* RAINTRAP 9-2 Pat Eddery (4) *chsd ldr to hfwy, shaken up to ld 2 fs out, hrd drvn and hdd cl hme*.....(10 to 6 on) 2
JO KNOWS (USA) 8-6 D Bonilla (2) *hng lft early, led till drvn and hdd 2 fs out, ran on one pace*....... (26 to 1) 3
3842⁴ DONDOOK (USA) 8-10 O Peslier (5) *hld up, cl up, wnt second hfwy, ev ch one and a half fs out, not quicken ins last*..........................(12 to 1) 4
3617³ HURTEVENT (Fr) 8-9 D Boeuf (1) *hld up, rdn and effrt 3 fs out, no imprsn*.......................... (67 to 10) 5
SABINO (Ire) 8-10 T Jarnet (3) *chsd ldrs, rdn hfwy, lost tch o'r 3 fs out, tld off*..........................(76 to 10) 6
Dist: Sht-nk, 2l, nk, 4l, 8l. 3m 38.20s. a 28.20s (6 Ran).
(H H Aga Khan), John M Oxx

NEWMARKET (good to soft)
Saturday October 2nd
Going Correction: PLUS 0.30 sec. per fur.

4297 NGK Spark Plugs Quality Handicap Class C (0-90 3-y-o and up) £7,564 7f ....(1:55)

3697⁸ BRAVEBOY [60] 5-7-12 (3*) B Doyle (1) *wl plcd stands side, led o'r one furlong out, hld on*.....(25 to 1 op 20 to 1) 1
4096³ OUR RITA [67] 4-8-8 D Holland (20) *hdwy and not clr run o'r 2 fs out, swtchd rght and lft over one out, fnshd fst.*..........................(20 to 1 tchd 25 to 1) 2
4172 TIME AGAIN [77] 3-9-1 J Weaver (3) *ran on frm 2 fs out, fnshd wl*............(16 to 1 op 14 to 1 tchd 20 to 1) 3
4172 PARLIAMENT PIECE [76] 7-9-3 W Ryan (4) *hld up, hdwy 2 fs out, rdn and styd on ins last*.... (33 to 1 op 25 to 1) 4
1830 RURAL LAD [58] 4-7-8 (5*) A Garth (2) *in tch stands side, kpt on und pres ins fnl furlong.* (20 to 1 tchd 25 to 1) 5
3830⁵ HOPEFUL BID (Ire) [66] 4-8-7 K Darley (6) *ldg grp stands side, ev ch o'r one furlong out, not quicken.*..........................(14 to 1 tchd 12 to 1) 6
3885⁸ CALEMAN [87] 4-10-0 G Duffield (17) *led far side grp, one pace ins fnl furlong.* (20 to 1 op 16 to 1 tchd 25 to 1) 7
3531⁸ HERORA (Ire) [76] (bl) 4-9-3 W Carson (15) *wl plcd far side, not quicken o'r one furlong out.*..........................(14 to 1 op 12 to 1 tchd 16 to 1) 8
4172⁹ PRENONAMOSS [75] (v) 5-9-2 W R Swinburn (16) *trkd ldrs towards far side, no extr fnl furlong.*..........................(14 to 1 op 12 to 1 tchd 16 to 1) 9
4007² ROCALITY [67] 4-8-8 Paul Eddery (8) *led stands side grp for o'r 5 fs*..........................(11 to 1 jt-fav op 10 to 1) 10
3450 BLUE TOPAZE [75] 5-9-2 M Wigham (10) *slwly into strd, nvr nrr*..........................(25 to 1 tchd 20 to 1) 11
4005³ SUNDAY'S HILL [85] (v) 4-9-12 J Quinn (18) *in tch far side, effrt o'r 2 fs out, btn fnl furlong*... (16 to 1 op 14 to 1) 12
4024³ FRIENDLY BRAVE (USA) [72] 3-8-10 J Carroll (5) *pressed ldrs stands side, wknd and eased appr fnl furlong.*..........................(14 to 1 op 16 to 1) 13
4022* BATTLE COLOURS (Ire) [75] 4-9-2 K Fallon (11) *wl plcd stands side till lost pl 2 fs out*......(16 to 1 op 12 to 1) 14
4133⁶ TROOPING (Ire) [72] 4-8-13 M Hills (21) *chsd ldrs far side 5 fs*..........................(16 to 1 tchd 20 to 1) 15
4166 PIQUANT [76] 6-9-3 D Harrison (7) *mid-div stands side till wknd 3 fs out*........ (14 to 1 op 12 to 1 tchd 16 to 1) 16
4166³ EURO FESTIVAL [76] 4-9-3 L Dettori (22) *effrt hfwy, no imprsn on ldrs last 2 fs*............ (14 to 1 op 12 to 1) 17
4065 NOBBY BARNES [59] 4-7-7 (7*) Sharon Millard (9) *slwly into strd, outpcd most of way*........(25 to 1 op 20 to 1) 18
3956⁷ POLAR STORM (Ire) [75] 3-8-13 T Quinn (14) *trkd far side ldrs till wknd o'r 2 fs out*.......... (14 to 1 op 12 to 1) 19
4116³ YAJEED (USA) [78] 3-9-2 B Raymond (23) *no prog frm hfwy*..........(11 to 1 jt-fav op 10 to 1 tchd 12 to 1) 20
1458⁷ TURRET GATES [57] 4-7-12 N Carlisle (12) *in tch till outpcd o'r 2 fs out*.......................... (33 to 1 tchd 40 to 1) 21
3955* METAL BOYS [82] 6-9-9 D Biggs (19) *nvr nr to chal.*..........................(25 to 1 tchd 33 to 1) 22
3983⁶ SILENT EXPRESSION [76] 3-8-11 (3*) C Hodgson (13) *nvr on terms*..........................(20 to 1) 23
Dist: ¾l, nk, nk, 1½l, 1½l, hd, 1½l, sht-hd, ¾l, ½l. 1m 29.04s. a 5.54s (23 Ran).
SR: 35/40/46/47/24/27/47/31/29/ (The Dowager Lady Beaverbrook), C E Brittain

4298 Sun Chariot Stakes Class A (Group 2) (3-y-o and up) £35,380 1¼m.....(2:25)

3650³ TALENTED 3-8-8 W Carson (8) *led 2 fs, led 4 out, pushed out, hld on gmely*...... (4 to 1 op 7 to 2 tchd 9 to 2) 1
4153* ANDROMAQUE (USA) 3-8-8 M Hills (1) *hld up, prog 3 fs out, rdn and kpt on ins last.*..........................(11 to 2 op 5 to 1 tchd 6 to 1) 2
3980* FELAWNAH (USA) 3-8-8 L Dettori (5) *jnd wnr 4 fs out, ev ch ins last, not quicken.*..........................(11 to 4 fav op 5 to 2 tchd 3 to 1) 3
3886⁴ LYPHARD'S DELTA (USA) 3-8-11 W Ryan (4) *hld up, cld on ldrs 3 fs out, rdn and no extr ins last.*..........................(5 to 1 op 9 to 2 tchd 11 to 2) 4
3795⁶ RUBY TIGER 6-9-3 T Quinn (3) *led aftr 2 fs, hdd 4 out, wknd o'r two out*... (7 to 2 tchd 4 to 1 and 100 to 30) 5
3879⁶ DEL DEYA (Ire) 3-8-8 L Piggott (6) *hld up in tch, rdn and wknd o'r 2 fs out*.......... (16 to 1 tchd 20 to 1) 6
2907⁴ SEREN QUEST 3-8-8 D Harrison (7) *strted slwly, al beh, lost tch o'r 3 fs out, tld off*....... (20 to 1 tchd 25 to 1) 7
Dist: Nk, sht-hd, 1½l, 5l, ½l, 30l. 2m 9.61s. a 6.91s (7 Ran).

SR: 55/54/53/53/49/39/-/ (P G Goulandris), J L Dunlop

4299 NGK Spark Plugs Performance Nursery Class C (2-y-o) £7,895 6f.... (3:00)

3903* RAFFERTY'S RULES (Ire) [87] 9-7 K Fallon (10) *pushed alng hfwy, hdwy 2 fs out, edgd lft and led ins fnl furlong, sn clr*..........................(2 to 1 fav tchd 9 to 4) 1
4029⁶ BLURRED IMAGE (Ire) [70] 8-4 D Biggs (3) *ran on and not clr run 2 fs out, styd on to take second pl nr finish.*..........................(14 to 1 op 12 to 1 tchd 16 to 1) 2
4004³ MARY HINGE [83] 9-3 Paul Eddery (1) *led hfwy, hdd and hng rght ins fnl furlong, no extr*.....(6 to 1 op 9 to 2) 3
4034² ELEUTHERA [83] 9-3 L Dettori (2) *chsd frnt rnk, rdn and not quicken o'r one furlong out, kpt on nr finish.*..........................(6 to 1 op 7 to 1 tchd 15 to 2) 4
3678³ MIDUSHI (USA) [77] 8-11 K Darley (5) *styd on frm rear fnl furlong, nrst finish*.......... (12 to 1 op 14 to 1) 5
3845 RAMBOLD [74] 8-8 R Perham (9) *led to hfwy, wth ldr til wknd o'r one furlong out*..........(25 to 1 op 20 to 1) 6
4163* MOCKINGBIRD [62] (v) 7-10 D Harrison (4) *wl plcd, not much room 2 fs out, wknd o'r one out.*............(11 to 2 op 5 to 1 tchd 9 to 2 and 6 to 1) 7
3845 MY LIFETIME LADY (Ire) [70] 8-4 W Ryan (6) *trkd ldrs for 4 fs, sn btn*.......................... (25 to 1 op 20 to 1) 8
4225⁵ WAAFED (USA) [79] (bl) 8-13 W R Swinburn (7) *cl up til lost pl frm 2 fs out*..........................(14 to 1 tchd 16 to 1) 9
4061⁴ FEATHERSTONE LANE [71] 8-5² W Newnes (12) *hmpd leaving stalls, pushed alng and outpcd most of way.*..........................(14 to 1 op 12 to 1) 10
4106 JEAN DE FLORETTE (USA) [61] (v) 7-9² A Mackay (11) *veered rght leaving stalls, nvr on terms*.......................... (50 to 1) 11
Dist: 2½l, nk, ¾l, 1½l, 1½l, nk, 6l, 6l, 1½l, 7l. 1m 15.48s. a 4.08s (11 Ran).

SR: 61/34/46/43/31/22/9/-/-/ (J E Swiers), Mrs J R Ramsden

4300 William Hill Cambridgeshire Handicap Class B (3-y-o and up) £54,788 1m 1f.............................. (3:40)

4172² PENNY DROPS [84] 4-7-13 (5ex) D Harrison (18) *al gng wl stands side, quickened to ld o'r 2 fs out, clr appr last.*..........................(7 to 1 fav tchd 9 to 1) 1
3623* TALENT (USA) [84] (v) 5-7-13 A Munro (28) *led far side grp frm hfwy, styd on wl ins fnl furlong.*..........................(33 to 1 op 25 to 1 tchd 40 to 1) 2
4140* RAMBO'S HALL [105] 8-9-6 (5ex) P Robinson (2) *mid-div, ran on o'r 2 fs out, styd on ins last.*..........................(8 to 1 op 6 to 1 tchd 9 to 1) 3

3752^{2} LOKI (Ire) [85] (v) 5-8-0 K Darley (21) *hdwy o'r 2 fs out, ran on ins last*..........(16 to 1 op 14 to 1 tchd 20 to 1) 4
3897^{8} EFHARISTO [85] (v) 4-7-11 (3*) B Doyle (12) *hdwy 3 fs out, rdn and one pace appr last*......(33 to 1 tchd 50 to 1) 5
3465* DAWNING STREET (Ire) [106] 5-9-7 L Piggott (6) *in tch stands side, cld 3 fs out, no extr o'r one out.* ....(9 to 1 tchd 10 to 1) 6
3897^{6} MELLOTTIE [105] 8-9-6 J Lowe (16) *styd on last 2 fs, no ch wth wnr*..(25 to 1) 7
3963^{3} ROSE ALTO [93] 5-8-8 G Duffield (22) *slwly into strd, improved appr last 2 fs, nrst finish.* ....(33 to 1 tchd 40 to 1) 8
3897^{2} BEAUCHAMP HERO [94] 3-8-4 T Quinn (1) *chsd stands side grp, effrt o'r 2 fs out, no extr over one out.* ....(12 to 1 tchd 14 to 1) 9
3897^{5} SHOW FAITH (Ire) [96] 3-8-6 L Dettori (13) *rcd centre, hdwy o'r 3 fs out, one pace frm 2 out*..............(16 to 1) 10
3883* KNOWTH (Ire) [78] 4-7-2 (5*) D Wright (17) *wl plcd stands side aftr 3 fs, rdn and one pace frm 2 out*.....(12 to 1) 11
4063^{2} JACKPOT STAR [86] 3-7-10^{2} D Biggs (19) *nvr nrr.* ....(20 to 1 tchd 25 to 1) 12
3182* CROSSILLION [85] 5-8-0 F Norton (3) *rcd stands side, one pace last 2 fs*..............................(33 to 1) 13
3986^{3} TOP SHIEL [78] 5-7-7 J Quinn (24) *styd on one pace frm 2 fs out*..................................(33 to 1 tchd 40 to 1) 14
4018^{8} GOOGLY [78] 4-7-7 G Bardwell (32) *swtchd to stands side 4 fs out, no imprsn on ldrs frm 2 out*..........(50 to 1) 15
3913^{3} LORD OF THE FIELD [109] 6-9-10 W Newnes (8) *hld up stands side, shrtlvd effrt o'r 3 fs out, sn btn.* ....(16 to 1 op 20 to 1) 16
4116* EMBANKMENT (Ire) [85] 3-7-9 N Adams (36) *slwly into strd, rcd far side, nvr on terms*...(33 to 1 tchd 25 to 1) 17
3643^{4} VAYAVAIG [83] 3-7-4^{4} (7*) N Varley (31) *nvr on terms.* ....(100 to 1 op 66 to 1) 18
3897^{4} LACOTTE (Ire) [86] 3-7-10 B Crossley (35) *chsd far side ldrs 6 fs*..(20 to 1) 19
3636* SHARJAH (USA) [93] 3-8-3 (5ex) J Carroll (33) *speed far side for o'r 5 fs*....................(25 to 1 tchd 28 to 1) 20
2926^{4} FROGMARCH (USA) [91] 3-8-1^{1} Paul Eddery (30) *rear most of way*..................................(50 to 1 tchd 66 to 1) 21
4065 BALLERINA BAY [78] (v) 5-7-7 Kim McDonnell (25) *nvr trble ldrs*..................................(100 to 1 op 66 to 1) 22
3680^{3} BRIGANTE DI CIELO [93] 3-8-3^{1} B Raymond (26) *nvr dngrs.* ....(25 to 1 tchd 33 to 1) 23
4140^{2} HE'S A KING (USA) [85] 3-7-9 N Carlisle (14) *outpcd.* ....(25 to 1 tchd 33 to 1) 24
3901^{6} MENTALASANYTHIN [78] 4-7-0 (7*) F Savage (34) *led far side grp to hfwy, sn wknd*..................(100 to 1) 25
3897 ROYAL SEATON [88] 4-8-3 A Mackay (23) *outpcd.* ....(33 to 1 tchd 40 to 1) 26
4065 HIGH LOW (USA) [79] 5-7-8^{1} J Fanning (5) *cl up, led stands side grp hfwy, hdd and wknd o'r 2 fs out.* ....(50 to 1 tchd 100 to 1) 27
4140^{6} JUST YOU DARE (Ire) [86] 3-7-10 Dale Gibson (15) *beh last 3 fs*..................................(33 to 1 tchd 40 to 1) 28
4116 DOUBLE FLUTTER [78] 4-7-0 (7*) Antoinette Armes (27) *beh hfwy*..................................(100 to 1 op 66 to 1) 29
3956^{4} COMANCHE COMPANION [83] 3-7-6^{4} (5*) A Garth (20) *pressed stands side ldrs 6 fs, sn lost pl.* ....(50 to 1 tchd 66 to 1) 30
3764^{7} REPORTED (Ire) [106] 4-9-2 (5*) D McCabe (37) *beh most of way*..................................(100 to 1 op 66 to 1) 31
3465^{2} PHILIDOR [92] 4-8-4 (3*) N Kennedy (38) *nvr nr ldrs.* ....(20 to 1 tchd 25 to 1) 32
4063^{5} CONEYBURY (Ire) [91] (bl) 3-8-1^{5} J Weaver (7) *led stands side grp to hfwy, wknd 3 fs out, sddl slpd*.....(25 to 1) 33
Dist: 6l, nk, 1½l, ½l, 1l, 3l, ½l, ½l, nk, 4l. 1m 53.39s. a 3.69s (33 Ran).

SR: 70/52/72/47/45/63/53/39/33/ (Stanley J Sharp), Lord Huntingdon

4301 Jockey Club Cup Class A (Group 3) (3-y-o and up) £19,014 2m........(4:15)

3861^{2} FURTHER FLIGHT 7-9-3 M Hills (3) *hld up in rear, ran on 4 fs out, shaken up to ld o'r one out, sn clr.* ....(2 to 1 op 7 to 4 tchd 9 to 4) 1
3899^{3} EDBAYSAAN (Ire) 3-8-3 W Ryan (6) *in tch, jnd ldr 4 fs out, ev ch o'r 2 out till appr last, one pace.* ....(6 to 4 fav op 11 to 8 tchd 5 to 4 and 13 to 8) 2
3516^{3} ZINAAD 4-9-5 W R Swinburn (1) *hld up, led 4 fs out till o'r one out, rdn and no extr.* ....(11 to 2 op 5 to 1 tchd 6 to 1) 3
3349^{5} SHAMBO 6-9-5 W Carson (2) *hld up rear, rdn and wknd 5 fs out, tld off*..........(9 to 1 op 8 to 1 tchd 10 to 1) 4
3405^{7} ARCADIAN HEIGHTS 5-9-0 L Dettori (4) *chsd ldr, led briefly o'r 4 fs out, lost tch over 3 out, tld off.* ....(11 to 1 op 10 to 1 tchd 12 to 1) 5
1681^{4} MELLABY (USA) 5-9-0 B Raymond (5) *led till o'r 4 fs out, wknd quickly, tld off.* ....(66 to 1 op 50 to 1 tchd 100 to 1) 6
Dist: 2l, sht-hd, dist, 15l, dist. 3m 31.97s. a 7.97s (6 Ran).

SR: 71/55/70/ (S Wingfield Digby), B W Hills

4302 Oh So Sharp Stakes Class A (Listed Race) (2-y-o) £7,995 7f..........(4:45)

3130^{3} BULAXIE 8-8 W Carson (5) *made all, pushed clr ins fnl furlong, eased nr line.* ....(7 to 4 fav op 9 to 4 tchd 5 to 2) 1
3760^{3} LADY FAIRFAX 8-8 G Duffield (4) *rcd keenly, dsptd second till lost pl o'r one furlong out, styd on clsg stages.* ....(8 to 1 op 12 to 1) 2
3586^{4} MILD REBUKE 8-11 K Darley (3) *dsptd second pl, ev ch o'r one furlong out, not quicken.* ....(11 to 2 op 2 to 1 tchd 6 to 1) 3
LEONOVA 8-8 J Weaver (1) *hld up, outpcd 2 fs out, styd on wl last 100 yards*.....(7 to 1 op 5 to 1 tchd 8 to 1) 4
3737^{2} BLUE SIREN 8-8 M Hills (6) *hld up, cld on ldrs o'r 2 fs out, sn rdn alng, wknd ins last.* ....(9 to 4 op 7 to 4 tchd 5 to 2) 5
3828^{8} GALYPH (USA) 8-8 L Dettori (2) *rcd keenly, in tch till wknd last 2 fs*.............(20 to 1 op 12 to 1 tchd 25 to 1) 6
Dist: 2l, ¾l, 1½l, 1l, 10l. 1m 31.98s. a 8.48s (6 Ran).
(P G Goulandris), J L Dunlop

4303 Alington Maiden Fillies' Stakes Class D (2-y-o) £4,737 6f..............(5:20)

FINGER OF LIGHT 8-11 W R Swinburn (5) *trkd ldrs, shaken up to ld o'r one furlong out, hld on cl hme.* ....(100 to 30 op 5 to 2 tchd 7 to 2) 1
NOBLE ROSE (Ire) 8-11 J Weaver (1) *dwlt, cld on ldrs hfwy, not quicken o'r one furlong out, rallied close hme*..................................(8 to 1 op 10 to 1) 2
3870^{4} PRIMO STAMPARI 8-11 L Dettori (3) *wth ldr, led hfwy till o'r one furlong out, kpt on wl.* ....(14 to 1 op 16 to 1 tchd 20 to 1) 3
ISTIBSHAR (USA) 8-11 W Carson (4) *improved hfwy, ev ch o'r one furlong out, styd on same pace.* ....(7 to 4 fav op 6 to 4 tchd 15 to 8) 4
2785^{6} WALSHAM WHISPER (Ire) 8-11 P Robinson (13) *dwlt, settled mid-div, outpcd last 2 fs.* ....(20 to 1 op 33 to 1 tchd 50 to 1) 5
TRUMPS HIGH (USA) 8-11 W Ryan (9) *steadied strt, shrtlvd effrt frm rear o'r 2 fs out, wknd over one out.* ....(4 to 1 op 5 to 1 tchd 6 to 1) 6
MUTIARA 8-11 K Darley (7) *outpcd most of way.* ....(50 to 1 op 33 to 1) 7
CHOWPOR 8-8 (3*) B Doyle (6) *mid-div, pushed alng hfwy, outpcd last 2 fs*.............(33 to 1 op 20 to 1) 8
DESERT MAIDEN 8-11 Paul Eddery (8) *settled mid-div, wknd 2 fs out*........(16 to 1 op 10 to 1 tchd 20 to 1) 9
4179^{7} MAZ (Ire) 8-11 A Mackay (11) *led to hfwy, wknd frm 2 fs out*..................................(20 to 1 tchd 33 to 1) 10
4142^{8} MUTINIQUE 8-11 N Adams (10) *cl up on outsd, wknd und pres o'r 2 fs out*..............(50 to 1 tchd 66 to 1) 11
Dist: Nk, ¾l, hd, 5l, 2½l, 1½l, hd, 5l, 2½l, 3½l. 1m 17.39s. a 5.99s (11 Ran).
SR: 13/12/9/8/-/-/ (The Snailwell Stud Company Limited), M R Stoute

DORTMUND (GER) (heavy)
Sunday October 3rd

4304 Dortmunder Fliegerpreis (Listed) (3-y-o and up) £24,408 5f..........(3:00)

4200* PALACEGATE EPISODE (Ire) 3-8-7 J Carroll, *made all, cmftbly*... 1
4200^{3} MONTEPULCIANO (USA) 4-9-1 G Bocskai,...................... 2
3936^{4} NEVER SO SURE 5-9-1 J McLaughlin,...................... 3
4200^{5} HATTA FORT 6-8-13 A Boschert,...................... 4
2242^{5} TI ZINO (Fr) 3-,...................... 5
3717^{7} MAMMA'S TOO 4-,...................... 6
3936^{3} GLENLIVET (Swe) 5-,...................... 7
4200^{2} FLEET FOR EUROPE 4-,...................... 8
4200^{6} PARIOS (Fr) 5-,...................... 9
3717 FANTOMAS (Ger) 5-,...................... 10
3013^{6} INDIAN LAKE 4-,...................... 11
MORE WIND (Ire) 7-,...................... 12
Dist: 2½l, nk, ½l, 3l, ¾l, nk, 2½l. 59.90s. (12 Ran).
(Palacegate Corporation Ltd), J Berry

4305 Grosser Preis der Continentale (Deutsches St Leger) Group 2 (3-y-o) £48,890 1¾m.................(3:45)

PINOT (Ger) 9-2 A Best, *rear strt, str run to ld ins fnl furlong, ran on wl*...................................... 1
4078^{2} AZZILFI 9-2 L Piggott, *led till hdd ins fnl furlong*........ 2
3929^{6} RACING BLUE 8-12^{1} W J Supple, *rcd in 4th, styd on one pace fnl furlong*...................................... 3
PALMETTO EXPRESS 9-2 G Bocskai, *rcd in second, wknd o'r one furlong out*...................................... 4
2259 LAW'S ANSWER (Ire) 9-2^{1} L Mader, *nvr able to chal*...... 5
4078^{4} FRENCHPARK 9-2 J Carroll, *3rd strt, wknd o'r 2 fs out*... 6
3929* PIRANGA (Ire) 8-12 A Boschert, *nvr plcd to chal*.......... 7
1369^{6} WIRGILIAN (Ger) 9-2 M Hofer, *al beh*.................... 8
3702^{3} SWINGING DANCER 9-2 T Mundry, *al outpcd*............ 9
Dist: 1 ¾l, 2½l, 3l, dist, 2½l, 8l, dist. 3m 12.90s. (9 Ran).
B Schutz

HOPPEGARTEN (GER) (good)

Sunday October 3rd

4306 Prix Zino Davidoff (Group 3) (3-y-o and up) £114,286 1¼m.............(3:20)

4073* KOMTUR (USA) 3-8-13 K Woodburn, *made all, nvr threatened*.. 1
3752[3] FABRIANO 4-9-6 T Hellier, *mid-div, ran on strly fnl 2 fs.* 2
4073[5] SUGUNAS (Ger) 5-9-6 L Pyritz, *second strt, no extr fnl furlong, kpt on one pace*.. 3
4073[2] THAGUS (Ger) 3-8-13 N Grant, *wtd wth, effrt o'r 2 fs out, one pace fnl furlong*.. 4
3647[3] DREAM FOR FUTURE (Ire) 3-8-13 W Newnes, *rcd in 6th, nvr nrr to chal*.. 5
3921* CAPTAIN HORATIUS (Ire) 4-9-6 W Ryan, *mid-div, chlgd 2 fs out, one pace fnl furlong*.. 6
3795[4] HONDO MONDO (Ire) 5-9-6 B Raymond, *cl up till 2 fs out, no extr*.. 7
3582[5] APIS (Ger) 4-9-6 P Schiergen, *nvr dngrs*................ 8
3795[5] SPORTIVO (USA) 4-9-6 T J Manning, *nvr a factor*........ 9

Dist: 1½l, 2½l, sht-hd, nk, hd, 3½l. 2m 3.60s. (9 Ran).
(H Hasler & A Pereira), H Remmert

LONGCHAMP (FR) (heavy) Sunday October 3rd

Going Correction: PLUS 0.60 sec. per fur. (races 1,2,3,4,5), PLUS 0.80 (6)

4307 Prix Charles Laffitte (Listed) (3-y-o) £14,337 1¼m.................. (2:00)

3944* INSIJAAM (USA) 9-0 W R Swinburn (3) *made all, drvn one furlong out, hld on gmely*................ (10 to 9 on) 1
3944[3] SEATTLE VICTORY (USA) 8-9 G Guignard (7) *chsd wnr, hrd rdn one furlong out, no imprsn fnl 100 yards*... (5 to 1) 2
ROYAL CHANTOU 9-0 M J Kinane (2) *hld up, chalg whn not much room ins fnl furlong, unlucky*..... (44 to 10) 3
SAHARA SUN (USA) 8-9 G Mosse (1) *hld up, effrt o'r 2 fs out, drvn and not quicken*.................. (20 to 1) 4
3801[4] AUBE INDIENNE (Fr) 9-0 C Asmussen (6) *chsd ldrs, drvn entering strt, one pace*.....................(71 to 10) 5
3944[2] GLOIRE DE ROSE 8-9 T Jarnet (5) *last early, nvr able to chal*..(11 to 1) 6
DAHAR'S BEST (USA) 8-9 E Saint-Martin (8) *midfield, wknd o'r 2 fs out*.......................... (28 to 1) 7
296[2] APPLIANCE 8-9 Pat Eddery (4) *al beh*..........(78 to 10) 8

Dist: ½l, ½l, 1½l, 1½l, 2½l, ½l, 5l. 2m 13.90s. a 11.60s (8 Ran).
SR: 44/38/42/34/36/26/25/15/ (Maktoum Al Maktoum), Mrs C Head

4308 CIGA Prix du Rond-Point (Group 2) (3-y-o and up) £47,790 1m......... (2:35)

4010[2] VOLERIS (Fr) 4-9-0 C Asmussen (2) *chsd ldrs, 5th strt, quickened und pres one furlong out, brst through to ld fnl 100 yards*.............................. (92 to 10) 1
2905[6] ALFLORA (Ire) 4-9-2 M J Kinane (9) *chsd ldrs, 6th and gng wl strt, led 2 fs out till hdd and not quicken und pres fnl 100 yards*..............................(44 to 10) 2
4066* MAROOF (USA) 3-8-12 W Carson (5) *chsd ldr, led entering strt, hdd 2 fs out, one pace und pres*......... (56 to 10) 3
3618[4] FASTNESS (Ire) 3-8-12 F Head (11) *9th and rdn strt, effrt on outsd o'r 2 fs out, drvn and no imprsn fnl furlong.* ....(26 to 1) 4
3618* BON POINT 3-8-12 Pat Eddery (8) *hld up, effrt and 4th strt, ev ch 2 fs out, sn outpcd*.................. (28 to 10) 5
3862[2] EMPEROR JONES (USA) 3-8-12 M Roberts (10) *hld up and beh, nvr plcd to chal*..........................(11 to 2) 6
4072[2] KITWOOD (USA) (bl) 4-9-0 T Jarnet (1) *last to strt, nvr on terms*......................................(11 to 2) 7
3800[6] GOLD SPLASH (USA) 3-8-13 G Mosse (3) *prmnt, 3rd strt, sn lost pl*............................. (21 to 10 fav) 8
4076[4] GOTHLAND (Fr) 4-9-0 J Reid (4) *7th strt, nvr able to chal.* ....(36 to 1) 9
2853[5] THOURIOS 4-9-0 T Quinn (6) *led till entering strt, lost pl quickly, eased o'r one furlong out*.............. (36 to 1) 10

Dist: 1½l, 2l, 1l, 2½l, ½l, 1½l, ½l, 4l, 8l. 1m 42.10s. a 6.10s (10 Ran).
SR: 81/78/68/65/57/55/52/49/38/ (D B Thompson), J E Hammond

4309 CIGA Prix de l'Opera (Group 2) (3-y-o and up) £47,790 1m 1f 55yds.... (3:10)

3500[2] VERVEINE (USA) 4-8-13 O Peslier (3) *settled mid-div, pushed into ld 2 fs out, sn clr, cmftbly*....(19 to 10 fav) 1
LA FRANCESA (Arg) 5-8-13 F Head (6) *chsd ldg pair, rdn strt, styd on to go second wl ins fnl furlong, no ch wth wnr*..(216 to 10) 2
3369[4] ELIZABETH BAY (USA) 3-8-9 T Jarnet (1) *chsd ldr, ev ch 2 fs out, btn whn edgd rght ins last*............. (22 to 10) 3
3882* AJFAN (USA) 3-8-9 R Hills (7) *led to 2 fs out, btn whn not much room cl hme*..............................(137 to 10) 4
2986[5] MARILLETTE (USA) 3-8-9 Pat Eddery (8) *steadied strt, 6th and drvn alng strt, nvr able to chal*.......... (22 to 10) 5
3931[7] CORRAZONA (USA) 3-8-9 O Doleuze (2) *chsd ldrs, 4th and rdn strt, sn outpcd*......................... (64 to 10) 6
3923[2] ASEMA (USA) 3-8-9 M J Kinane (10) *7th strt, nvr trble ldrs.* ....(48 to 10) 7
4169* ZIGREEN (Fr) 4-8-9 W Mongil (4) *al last pair, no ch fnl 3 fs.* ....(71 to 10) 8
3923[3] CLOUD OF DUST 4-8-13 M Roberts (9) *al last pair, rdn and no ch 3 fs out*............................ (163 to 10) 9

Dist: 4l, ¾l, ½l, 1½l, ½l, 2l, 2½l, sht-nk. 1m 58.90s. a 6.90s (9 Ran).
SR: 79/67/61/59/54/52/46/38/41/ (D Wildenstein), E Lellouche

4310 Prix Marcel Boussac (Group 1) (2-y-o) £95,579 1m.................. (3:45)

3977[3] SIERRA MADRE (Fr) 8-11 G Mosse (7) *steadied strt, last to strt, str chal and edgd rght one furlong out, drvn to ld nr finish*.............................. (349 to 10) 1
3977[2] FLAGBIRD (USA) 8-11 T Jarnet (5) *prmnt, 4th strt, led 2 fs out, drvn and hdd cl hme*..................(64 to 10) 2
3463[3] MEHTHAAF (USA) 8-11 W Carson (4) *keen hold, chsd ldr to 2 fs out, not quicken und pres ins last*.......(114 to 10) 3
3925[4] GOTHIC DREAM (Ire) 8-11 M J Kinane (6) *hld up, 6th strt, staying on at one pace whn hmpd one furlong out.* ....(225 to 10) 4
3932* COUP DE GENIE (USA) 8-11 C Asmussen (8) *hld up, 7th strt, rdn and little response 2 fs out, btn whn slightly hmpd one out*........................... (10 to 3 on) 5
SAIL STORM (USA) 8-11 O Doleuze (1) *prmnt, 3rd strt, no extr o'r one furlong out*......................(79 to 10) 6
DANSEUSE DU NORD (Ire) 8-11 D Boeuf (2) *chsd ldrs, 5th strt, sn btn*.............................. (162 to 10) 7
3932[2] MAJESTIC ROLE (Fr) 8-11 L Dettori (3) *led to 2 fs out, wknd und pres*............................. (102 to 10) 8

Dist: Hd, ¾l, ¾l, nk, sht-hd, 2½l, 3l. 1m 45.40s. a 7.90s (8 Ran).
SR: 50/49/47/45/44/43/35/26/ (J L Bouchard), P Bary

4311 CIGA Prix de l'Arc de Triomphe (Group 1) (3-y-o and up) £597,372 1½m ....(4:30)

3500* URBAN SEA (USA) 4-9-1 E Saint-Martin (9) *al cl up, sstnd chal frm 2 fs out, led one out, ran on gmely*... (37 to 1) 1
3402[5] WHITE MUZZLE 3-8-11 J Reid (23) *beh till gd hdwy appr strt, chlgd 2 fs out, ev ch thrght fnl furlong, ran on wl, al jst hld*.............................. (54 to 1) 2
3913[2] OPERA HOUSE 5-9-4 M Roberts (15) *rcd freely, chsd ldrs, effrt 3 fs out, led 2 out to one out, ev ch till not quicken wl ins last*..............................(39 to 10) 3
3931* INTREPIDITY 3-8-8 T Jarnet (14) *hdwy outsd o'r 2 fs out, fnshd strly*.............................. (39 to 10) 4
3930* ONLY ROYALE (Ire) 4-9-1 R Cochrane (16) *hld up and beh, hdwy 4 fs out, chasing ldrs whn hmpd in strt, not quicken o'r one out*..........................(19 to 1) 5
3899* BOB'S RETURN (Ire) 3-8-11 P Robinson (12) *prmnt, led o'r 2 fs out, sn hdd, styd on same pace*......... (126 to 10) 6
3935* MISIL (USA) 5-9-4 L Dettori (11) *hld up, effrt 3 fs out, kpt on, unbl to chal, lost plate*..........................(9 to 1) 7
4078[3] TALLOIRES (USA) 3-8-11 O Peslier (19) *gd hdwy to chal and ev ch o'r 2 fs out, hng violently rght and lft aftr.* ....(51 to 1) 8
3930[3] VERT AMANDE (Fr) 5-9-4 F Head (10) *strted slwly, sn scrubbed alng, nvr nr to chal*................ (20 to 1) 9
3913[4] MARKET BOOSTER (USA) 4-9-1 M J Kinane (20) *prog hfwy, chsd ldrs 3 fs out, sn lost pl*................. (77 to 1) 10
3930[4] DARIYOUN (USA) 5-9-4 O Doleuze (8) *led till o'r 2 fs out, sn lost pl*.............................. (138 to 1) 11
3933[3] DANCIENNE (Fr) 3-8-8 D Boeuf (5) *nvr nr ldrs*.... (25 to 1) 12
3795[2] PLATINI (Ger) 4-9-4 M Rimmer (17) *struggling in rear most of way*.............................. (46 to 1) 13
1544[6] BADOLATO (USA) 3-8-11 J-M Breux (7) *mid-div, drvn appr strt, not quicken*.......................... (114 to 1) 14
3899[2] ARMIGER 3-8-11 W Carson (2) *prmnt till wknd wl o'r 2 fs out*..............................(4 to 1) 15
3933* HERNANDO (Fr) 3-8-11 C Asmussen (13) *midfield, no dngr aftr hfwy*............................(37 to 10 fav) 16
3402* EZZOUD (Ire) (v) 4-9-4 W R Swinburn (18) *wl beh most of way, no ch whn eased one furlong out*........(55 to 1) 17
3931[3] BRIGHT MOON (USA) 3-8-8 S Guillot (6) *chsd ldrs to hfwy.* ....(47 to 1) 18
4141[5] GARDEN OF HEAVEN (USA) 4-9-4 T Quinn (22) *strted slwly, last hfwy, rapid hdwy to press ldrs on outsd and hanging entering strt, drpd back rpdly*...........(137 to 1) 19
3194[6] ALWAYS FRIENDLY 5-9-1 A Munro (21) *strted slwly, rapid prog to second aftr 3 fs, lost pl appr strt*......(140 to 1) 20
3931[2] WEMYSS BIGHT 3-8-8 Pat Eddery (4) *hld up chasing ldrs, brief effrt 4 fs out, sn btn, eased clsg stages*.....(4 to 1) 21
3433[3] USER FRIENDLY 4-9-1 G Duffield (1) *rcd freely, wth ldrs but hmpd twice bef hfwy, not reco'r, sn drpd out.* ....(118 to 10) 22
3650* SHEMAKA (Ire) 3-8-8 G Mosse (3) *prmnt 7 fs, tld off.* ....(78 to 10) 23

Dist: Nk, ½l, ¾l, 1l, 1½l, ¾l, ½l, 1½l, 1½l, 1½l. 2m 37.90s. a 8.80s (23 Ran).
SR: 91/86/92/80/85/78/83/75/79/ (David Tsui), J Lesbordes

4312 CIGA Prix de l'Abbaye de Longchamp (Group 1) (2-y-o and up) £83,632 5f ....(5:20)

3777[3] LOCHSONG 5-9-8 L Dettori (9) *broke fst, clr ld thrght, pushed alng o'r one furlong out, unchlgd*...... (2 to 1) 1
3912[2] STACK ROCK 6-9-8 K Fallon (6) *rcd in 3rd, no ch wth wnr, drvn and ran on gmely to snatch second on line.* .... (28 to 1) 2
3414* MONDE BLEU (bl) 5-9-11 S Guillot (4) *sn chasing wnr, unbl to chal frm hfwy*........................... (81 to 10) 3
3414[4] ZIETEN (USA) 3-9-11 T Jarnet (8) *midfield, kpt on ins fnl furlong, nvr nrr*.........................(6 to 4 co-fav) 4
3912* TROPICAL (bl) 3-9-8 M J Kinane (2) *sn rdn alng, nvr better than mid-div, kpt on ins fnl furlong*......... (31 to 10) 5
4170[3] ZARANI SIDI ANNA (USA) (bl) 3-9-8 W R Swinburn (7) *slwly into strd, improved to 4th at hfwy, sn btn*..... (21 to 1) 6
3777* WOLFHOUND (USA) 4-9-11 M Roberts (11) *nvr able to get on terms*.............................. (6 to 4 co-fav) 7
4010[8] DREAM TALK (bl) 6-9-11 D Boeuf (10) *nvr better than midfield*.......................................(32 to 1) 8
4010[7] CRACK REGIMENT (USA) (bl) 5-9-11 E Saint-Martin (1) *outpcd*...(34 to 1) 9
3847* KING'S SIGNET (USA) 4-9-11 Pat Eddery (5) *no ch frm hfwy, tld off*..........................(6 to 4 co-fav) 10
3414[3] THREE FOR FANTASY (Ire) 3-9-8 F Head (3) *sn outpcd, tld off aftr hfwy*................................. (21 to 1) 11

Dist: 6l, sht-hd, ½l, ¾l, sht-nk, 4l, sht-hd, 4l, 5l. 59.70s. a 4.20s (11 Ran).
SR: 104/80/82/80/74/73/60/59/43/ (J C Smith), I A Balding

SAN SIRO (ITY) (heavy)
Sunday October 3rd

4313 Premio Morengo (2-y-o) £11,207 7f ....(2:55)

3554[2] SURIS (Ire) 8-7 J Weaver, *made all, fnshd very tired*...... 1
GOFFREDO GORI 8-10 S Dettori, ... 2
MILD DANCER 8-7 M Latorre, ... 3
BEST OF DRUMS, ... 4
SULFORICH (USA), ... 5
PALACIOS (Ity), ... 6

Dist: 1l, sht-hd, 4l, 9l, 16l. 1m 35.50s. (6 Ran).
(Scuderia Rencati Srl), L M Cumani

4314 Premio Del Dado (Listed) (2-y-o) £20,173 1m.................... (3:20)

2257[2] CHOCOLUNE (Ity) 8-9 S Dettori, ... 1
3803[3] SPRINT BEST (Ire) 8-9 L Sorrentino, ... 2
MORIGI 8-9 M Tellini, ... 3
3798* SPAGHETTI WESTERN (Ire) 9-0 A Parravani, *trkd ldr, chlgd 3 fs out, sn wknd*.................................... 4

Dist: 6l, 4l, 7l. 1m 48.40s. (4 Ran).
(Scuderia Viorel), A Pandolfi

FLORENCE (ITY) (heavy)
Sunday October 3rd

4315 Premio Cascine (Listed) (3-y-o and up) £20,173 7f 110yds.............. (1:00)

1548[5] NIGHT MANOEUVRES 4-8-8 F Jovine, ... 1
3648[2] LITTLE MUNCHKIN (Ire) 3-8-5 Paul Eddery, ... 2
FLAGPOLE (Ire) 4-8-4 E Baldacci, ... 3
POWER OF POLLY (USA) 3-8-5 A Herrera, ... 4
3934[5] CU NA MARA 4-8-4 S Landi, ... 5
MESSALA (Ire) 3-8-5 V Foglia, ... 6
DIAMOND MINE (Ire) 4-8-7 E Tasende, ... 7

Dist: 1 ¼l, nk, 1l, 6l, 6l, sht-hd. (Time not taken) (7 Ran).
(P G Goulandris), H Candy

PONTEFRACT (soft)
Monday October 4th
Going Correction: PLUS 0.55 sec. per fur.

4316 EBF Claxton Bay Maiden Stakes Class D (2-y-o) £4,698 1¼m 6yds......(2:10)

3728[2] MUWAFIK 9-0 R Hills (13) *al hndy, led jst o'r 2 fs out, pushed clr, kpt on strly*.............(7 to 2 op 9 to 2) 1
4192[2] GOLDEN HELLO 9-0 M Birch (1) *nvr far away, feeling pace o'r 2 fs out, styd on grimly last, nrst finish.* .... (10 to 1 op 7 to 1) 2
4027[5] BRANDON COURT (Ire) 9-0 L Dettori (5) *trkd ldg bunch, improved to chase wnr 2 fs out, no extr fnl furlong.* .... (4 to 1 op 3 to 1) 3
4192[5] FROM THE LEFT (Ire) 9-0 J Weaver (10) *drvn up frm off the pace hfwy, styd on fnl furlong, nvr able to chal.* .... (14 to 1 op 12 to 1) 4
4014[4] KHATIR (Can) 9-0 K Darley (8) *dsptd ld, definite advantage o'r 3 fs out, hdd jst over 2 out, sn outpcd.* .... (16 to 1 op 12 to 1) 5
4111[2] CRAZY FOR YOU 8-9 Paul Eddery (7) *slight ld to wl o'r 3 fs out, not much room entering strt, sn btn.* ....(11 to 4 fav op 5 to 2 tchd 3 to 1) 6
4225[7] LINCOLN TREASURE (Ire) 8-9 (5*) D McCabe (9) *outpcd and drvn alng, styd on und pres last 2 fs, nrst finish.* .... (33 to 1) 7
LIGHTNING QUEST (Ire) 9-0 W Newnes (12) *missed break, drvn alng to keep up, late hdwy, nvr nrr.* .... (14 to 1 op 12 to 1) 8
4113[6] AHSANT MTOTO 9-0 R Price (3) *chsd ldg bunch, rdn 3 fs out, fdd last 2*.......... (7 to 1 tchd 8 to 1 and 6 to 1) 9
4182[3] WINN'S PRIDE (Ire) 9-0 S Perks (4) *pressed ldrs for o'r 6 fs, sn rdn and btn*.................. (20 to 1 op 16 to 1) 10
REBECCAS SECRET (Ire) 9-0 K Fallon (14) *steadied strt, al beh, tld off last 3 fs*................(50 to 1 op 33 to 1) 11
933[9] BURRINGHAM BOY 9-0 J Quinn (6) *trkd ldg 5 to hfwy, tld off last 3 fs*..................(100 to 1 op 33 to 1) 12
4208[9] BODANTREE (bl) 9-0 V Slattery (11) *chsd alng in midfield, effrt und pres hfwy, tld off last 3 fs.* .... (100 to 1 op 33 to 1) 13

Dist: 2l, 1½l, 3l, 1½l, 1l, 6l, ¾l, 2l, 1l, dist. 2m 20.80s. a 12.60s (13 Ran).
SR: 29/25/22/16/13/6/ (Hamdan Al-Maktoum), J L Dunlop

4317 Buccoo Reef Claiming Stakes Class F (3-y-o) £3,003 6f................(2:40)

4031 BECKYHANNAH (bl) 7-11 L Charnock (10) *broke wl, led aftr 2 fs, clr whn drifted rght ins fnl furlong, kpt on.* ....(66 to 1 op 50 to 1 tchd 100 to 1) 1
4156[2] COCONUT JOHNNY 8-3[1] (7*) R Painter (16) *al chasing ldrs, improved 2 fs out, shied frm whip o'r one out, kpt on und pres*.......................... (6 to 1 fav op 7 to 1) 2
4166 THE SHARP BIDDER (Ire) 8-13 S Perks (14) *al hndy, ev ch and drvn alng 2 fs out, crowded entering last, kpt on same pace*.......................... (8 to 1 op 7 to 1) 3
4222[6] DONTBETALKING (Ire) (bl) 7-12 J Quinn (9) *al pressing ldrs, effrt and bustled alng last 2 fs, kpt on same pace.* .... (40 to 1 op 33 to 1) 4
4156[4] WESTERN VALLEY 8-5 (3*) B Doyle (8) *pushed alng to improve frm midfield hfwy, crowded and wndrd ins fnl furlong, one pace.* ....(15 to 2 op 8 to 1 tchd 10 to 1 and 7 to 1) 5
4156[5] BIRCHWOOD SUN (bl) 8-12 L Dettori (15) *sluggish strt, weaved through into midfield hfwy, rng on whn squeezed out ins fnl furlong, nvr nrr.* .... (10 to 1 op 9 to 1) 6
3687[7] HICKORY BLUE (bl) 8-6 (3*) O Pears (1) *sluggish strt, pulling hrd whn badly baulked on ins aftr one and a half fs, rallied 2 out, kpt on same pace*.............(7 to 1) 7
3995[6] SHADOW JURY 9-0 K Darley (13) *led on outsd for 2 fs, styd hndy till fdd appr last*..............(8 to 1 op 7 to 1) 8
3756[9] BOLD SEVEN (Ire) 8-6 Paul Eddery (11) *chsd alng in midfield, effrt 2 fs out, no imprsn*................(12 to 1) 9
3564[6] MY GODSON (bl) 8-6 (5*) J Tate (4) *settled on ins, stumbled badly aftr one and a half fs, rdn o'r 2 out, no imprsn.* .... (10 to 1) 10
MIGHTY WRATH 8-9 N Adams (12) *sluggish strt, steady hdwy hfwy, kpt on fnl furlong*.... (12 to 1 op 10 to 1) 11
4156[3] OUR SHADEE (USA) (v) 8-12 M Wigham (7) *drvn alng to chase ldg bunch, no imprsn last 2 fs*...........(12 to 1) 12
4156[7] SUDDEN SPIN (v) 8-13 J Carroll (2) *bustled alng to go pace, hmpd aftr a furlong, nvr a serious threat.* .... (8 to 1 tchd 9 to 1) 13
1852 HIGH ROMANCE 7-13 (5*) Darren Moffatt (5) *sluggish strt, effrt and rdn alng hfwy, nvr nr to chal*....... (25 to 1) 14
3533[6] HAZY KAY (Ire) 8-4 A McGlone (17) *chsd alng beh ldg bunch, no imprsn frm hfwy*.................(20 to 1) 15
3955 MY BONUS 8-10 D Biggs (6) *drvn alng in midfield, outpcd last 2 fs*..........(10 to 1 op 8 to 1 tchd 12 to 1) 16D
4031[5] FREDDIE JACK (bl) 8-7 R Lappin (3) *chsd alng to go pace, nvr a dngr*.................................(50 to 1) 17

Dist: ¾l, ½l, 1l, hd, nk, 2l, 2½l, hd, 1½l, 3l. 1m 21.90s. a 7.20s (17 Ran).
SR: 5/14/16/-/6/9/ (Terry Pitts), R Bastiman

4318 Levy Board Nursery Class E (2-y-o) £3,262 6f......................(3:10)

4193[6] JUST FLAMENCO [58] 8-2 D Biggs (2) *chsd alng to improve midfield hfwy, styd on to ld ins fnl furlong, forged clr.* ....(7 to 1 op 6 to 1) 1
4228[2] CHIEF EXECUTIVE [53] 7-11 G Bardwell (5) *nvr far away, effrt and drvn alng last 2 fs, kpt on same pace.* ....(8 to 1 op 7 to 1) 2
4225[2] BOLD ALEX [64] 8-1 (7*) N Varley (8) *al wl plcd, led well o'r 2 fs out, clr till wknd and ct ins fnl furlong.* .... (12 to 1 op 8 to 1) 3
4097* STEADFAST ELITE (Ire) [61] 8-5 L Dettori (9) *rcd wide, al hndy, hng badly rght o'r one furlong out, no imprsn.* ....(13 to 2 op 7 to 1 tchd 8 to 1 and 6 to 1) 4
4159[4] LEADING PRINCESS (Ire) [52] 7-7 (3*) N Kennedy (3) *chsd alng in midfield, effrt hfwy, not pace to chal.* (14 to 1) 5
3829 BROUGHTONS PARTNER [49] 7-7 N Adams (13) *sn outpcd and drvn alng, some hdwy last 2 fs, nvr dngrs.* .... (40 to 1 op 20 to 1) 6
1846[5] FEARLESS WONDER [60] 8-1 (3*) S Maloney (14) *missed break, steady hdwy frm hfwy, nvr plcd to chal.* .... (25 to 1 op 16 to 1) 7
4097[8] LUNAR RHAPSODY [52] 7-10 J Lowe (11) *bustled alng in midfield, not pace of ldrs*..........(50 to 1 op 33 to 1) 8

698⁹ GRANDMAN (Ire) [55] 7-8 (5*) Darren Moffatt (12) *chsd ldrs, rdn o'r 2 fs out, sn btn.*..........(33 to 1) 9
4051* THE HAPPY LOON (Ire) [60] 8-4 K Fallon (7) *broke wl to ld till well o'r 2 fs out, fdd*..........(6 to 1 tchd 11 to 2) 10
3627⁸ AJNAS (Ire) [57] 8-1 N Carlisle (4) *bustled alng in midfield, wknd und pres 2 fs out*..........(14 to 1 tchd 16 to 1) 11
4163 RICH GLOW [51] 7-9¹ L Charnock (10) *in tch, rdn alng to go pace hfwy, sn btn*..........(50 to 1 op 33 to 1) 12
4225* SPRING LOADED [66] 8-10 (6ex) K Darley (15) *chsd alng in midfield, eased whn btn last 2 fs.* ....(4 to 1 fav op 9 to 2 tchd 5 to 1) 13
2356⁴ ROSIE VALENTINE [54] 7-12 J Quinn (1) *chsd alng to go pace hfwy, sn lost tch*..........(14 to 1 op 16 to 1) 14
4159* JIMMY THE SKUNK (Ire) [77] 9-7 J Carroll (6) *pressed ldrs, drvn alng o'r 2 fs out, eased whn btn over one out.* ....(6 to 1 tchd 13 to 2) 15

Dist: 4l, hd, 5l, 7l, ¾l, nk, ½l, 1½l, nk, ¾l. 1m 20.90s. a 6.20s (15 Ran).
SR: 30/9/19/-/-/-/ (Mrs S M Martin), M J Ryan

4319 York & Westminster Apprentice Series Final Round Handicap Class E (0-70 3-y-o and up) £3,132 1½m 8yds ....(3:40)

3970⁷ GREY POWER [70] 6-9-11 (3*) S Copp (7) *al travelling wl, led o'r 2 fs out, pushed clr ins last, readily*...(4 to 1 jt-fav tchd 9 to 2) 1
4218 REACH FOR GLORY [48] 4-8-6 G Parkin (5) *nvr far away, ev ch whn slightly hmpd 2 fs out, hrd rdn fnl furlong, one pace*..........(12 to 1 op 10 to 1) 2
4157⁸ ADMIRALS SEAT [54] 5-8-7 (5*) D Thomas (10) *patiently rdn, steady hdwy frm midfield 2 fs out, shaken up ins last, ran on wl*..........(5 to 1 tchd 9 to 2 and 11 to 2) 3
4218³ THE PREMIER EXPRES [56] 3-8-6 J Tate (4) *al hndy, led o'r 4 fs out till over 2 out, no extr.* (4 to 1 jt-fav tchd 7 to 2) 4
4226⁵ FAMOUS BEAUTY [41] 6-7-13 A Garth (9) *wtd wth, took clr order hfwy, rdn and outpcd last 2 fs.* ....(14 to 1 op 10 to 1) 5
826 PONDERED BID [35] 9-7-7 N Varley (2) *last and drvn alng hfwy, styd on fnl 2 fs, nrst finish.* (66 to 1 op 50 to 1) 6
3971⁷ TROY BOY [43] (bl) 3-7-4 (3*) C Teague (6) *settled midfield, feeling pace o'r 3 fs out, no imprsn.* ....(25 to 1 op 20 to 1 tchd 33 to 1) 7
3440⁷ QUESSONG [43] 3-7-2 (5*) A Whelan (3) *co'red up in midfield, drvn alng whn pace quickened last 3 fs, fdd.* ....(66 to 1 op 50 to 1) 8
3523 ELEGANT FRIEND [57] 5-9-1 S Mulvey (14) *pushed alng in midfield, outpcd last 3 fs.* ....(12 to 1 op 10 to 1 tchd 14 to 1) 9
4086⁷ SHARQUIN [36] 6-7-3 (5*) C Adamson (12) *made most till hdd o'r 4 fs out, fdd appr strt*.....(20 to 1 op 12 to 1) 10
4176 CIVIL ACTION (Ire) [43] 3-7-0 (7*) F Savage (1) *in tch, drvn alng in midfield hfwy, sn btn*.....(66 to 1 op 50 to 1) 11
4048³ BAHER (USA) [37] 4-7-2 (7*) Carol Davison (13) *wth ldrs to hfwy, lost tch o'r 3 fs out*..........(20 to 1) 12
4036⁷ MODEST HOPE (USA) [48] 6-8-6 Claire Balding (11) *chsd alng to keep in tch hfwy, sn beh.* ....(8 to 1 op 7 to 1 tchd 10 to 1) 13
3134⁸ SIR EDWARD HENRY (Ire) [44] (bl) 3-7-3 (5*) G Milligan (8) *pressed ldrs, struggling to hold pl o'r 3 fs out, sn lost tch*..........(14 to 1 op 12 to 1) 14

Dist: 3½l, 2½l, 4l, ½l, 5l, sht-hd, 8l, 1½l, 4l, 12l. 2m 47.80s. a 12.80s (14 Ran).
SR: 52/23/24/10/2/-/ (A Frame), Mrs M Reveley

4320 Maraval Handicap Class D (0-80 3-y-o) £5,845 1m 4yds..........(4:10)

3431² MISTY SILKS [67] 8-8 D Biggs (15) *in tch, improved frm midfield hfwy, str run to ld cl hme*..........(14 to 1) 1
4019⁴ HARPOON LOUIE (USA) [74] 9-1 K Darley (8) *al hndy, styd on to ld ins fnl furlong, jst ct*.......(9 to 1 op 8 to 1) 2
2290⁵ WEAVER BIRD [77] 9-4 W Newnes (2) *tucked away on ins, swtchd to improve o'r one furlong out, kpt on wl towards finish*......(14 to 1 op 12 to 1 tchd 16 to 1) 3
4233* COLIN MUSET [66] 8-7 (6ex) L Dettori (14) *al hndy, led o'r 2 fs out till hdd ins last, found little.* ....(7 to 4 fav op 5 to 2) 4
4016* CLAIRIFICATION (Ire) [52] (bl) 7-7 J Quinn (10) *nvr far away, rdn o'r 2 fs out, styd on same pace.* ....(12 to 1 tchd 14 to 1) 5
4007⁵ TARNSIDE ROSAL [64] 8-5 J Carroll (4) *struggling in midfield hfwy, styd on grimly fnl furlong, nvr nrr.* ....(20 to 1 op 16 to 1) 6
3988² KARINSKA [66] 8-2 (5*) D McCabe (11) *beh, swtchd wide to improve o'r 2 fs out, ran on finish*...(9 to 1 op 8 to 1) 7
4158⁷ DOC COTTRILL [67] 8-8 K Fallon (5) *beh and drvn alng, styd on last 2 fs, nvr able to chal*... (7 to 1 op 16 to 1) 8
3699⁸ MUTAWALI (Ire) [52] 7-7 J Lowe (3) *trkd ldrs, feeling pace and rdn o'r 3 fs out, no imprsn*..........(14 to 1) 9
4133⁸ NAFUTH (USA) [70] 8-11 J Weaver (7) *wth ldr, led aftr 2 fs till o'r two out, rdn and no extr*.....(14 to 1 op 8 to 1) 10
4132³ BARIK (Ire) [80] 9-7 A McGlone (13) *chsd ldg bunch, effrt o'r 3 fs out, not pace to chal*......(12 to 1 op 10 to 1) 11
4016 MUSTAKIM (Ire) [59] 8-0² R Price (9) *al chasing ldrs, edgd lft und pres fnl furlong, nvr dngrs*..........(16 to 1) 12
4116⁸ MUTAKALLAM (USA) [68] 8-9 R Hills (16) *pressed ldrs, feeling pace o'r 3 fs out, fdd*..........(12 to 1) 13
3956⁵ GUV'S JOY (Ire) [75] 9-2 D Holland (6) *drvn alng in midfield, some hdwy whn hmpd ins fnl furlong, eased when btn*..........(12 to 1 op 10 to 1) 14
542⁹ MR BUTCH [75] 8-9 (7*) R Painter (12) *trkd ldg bunch, feeling pace o'r 3 fs out, sn lost tch.* (33 to 1 op 25 to 1) 15
3334⁷ PURE MADNESS (USA) [54] 7-9 N Carlisle (1) *led for 2 fs, tld off last 3*..........(50 to 1) 16

Dist: Nk, ½l, ½l, nk, 2½l, sht-hd, hd, 4l, 1½l, 1½l. 1m 50.40s. a 8.30s (16 Ran).
SR: 35/41/42/29/14/18/19/19/-/ (P E Axon), M J Ryan

4321 Trinidad & Tobago Handicap Class E (0-70 3-y-o and up) £3,366 2m 1f 22yds ....(4:40)

2310⁹ WORLD WITHOUT END (USA) [30] 4-7-8 J Quinn (4) *wth ldr, led aftr 3 fs, hrd pressed 2 out, hld on gmely.* ....(14 to 1 tchd 16 to 1 and 12 to 1) 1
4102² BALLY KNIGHT [64] 7-9-11 (3*) C Hodgson (13) *patiently rdn, pushed up frm midfield to chal 2 fs out, ridden and no extr towards finish*..........(12 to 1 op 10 to 1) 2
3412⁵ DON'T CRY [29] 5-7-7 Kim Tinkler (5) *settled midfield, improved to flter 2 fs out, styd on same pace fnl furlong*..........(33 to 1) 3
4102⁴ AUTHORSHIP (USA) [45] 7-8-4 (5*) D McCabe (1) *nvr far away, feeling pace and drvn alng o'r 5 fs out, rallied, wndrd over one out, no imprsn.* ....(11 to 1 op 8 to 1 tchd 12 to 1) 4
4023⁴ MINGUS (USA) [39] 6-8-3² K Fallon (8) *chsd ldg bunch, drvn alng whn pace lifted o'r 3 fs out, nvr able to chal.* ....(14 to 1 op 10 to 1) 5
3716 A GENTLEMAN TWO [30] 7-7-8 J Lowe (3) *led for 3 fs, styd hndy till wknd und pres o'r three furlongs out.* ....(33 to 1 op 25 to 1) 6
4212⁷ PATROCLUS [34] 8-7-12 N Adams (15) *slow into strd, drvn into midfield last 6 fs, kpt on, no imprsn.* ....(14 to 1 op 12 to 1 tchd 16 to 1) 7
3147⁵ BRIDGE PLAYER [29] 6-7-3¹ (5*) Darren Moffatt (2) *in tch, drvn alng to improve o'r 4 fs out, not pace of ldrs.* ....(16 to 1) 8
4023⁵ BRIGGSMAID [54] 5-9-4 M Tebbutt (7) *beh, chsd alng, some hdwy o'r 3 fs out, nvr dngrs*.......(10 to 1 op 8 to 1) 9
4102 SIDE BAR [44] (bl) 3-7-11 D Biggs (19) *settled midfield, drvn alng whn pace quickened last 4 fs, nvr rch ldrs.* ....(20 to 1) 10
857 ADMINISTER [52] (bl) 5-8-13 (3*) S Maloney (9) *in tch for o'r a m, drvn alng over 4 fs out, sn struggling.* ....(33 to 1 op 25 to 1) 11
4035⁴ SALU [56] 4-9-6 J Carroll (18) *settled midfield, drvn up on outsd o'r 4 fs out, wknd quickly over 2 out.* ....(7 to 1 op 10 to 1 tchd 11 to 1) 12
4006² HARLESTONE BROOK [66] 3-9-5 Paul Eddery (10) *chsd ldg 5, struggling to hold pl o'r 4 fs out, sn btn.* ....(5 to 2 fav op 7 to 2) 13
4023² SERAPHIM (Fr) [40] 4-8-4 K Darley (11) *pressed ldrs till wknd quickly o'r 4 fs out.* ....(15 to 2 op 7 to 1 tchd 8 to 1) 14
4176 MRS NORMAN [32] 4-7-10⁶ (3*) B Doyle (12) *chsd ldg bunch for o'r a m, struggling last 4 fs*.......(100 to 1) 15
3821⁵ SAMAIN (USA) [52] 6-9-2 N Carlisle (16) *beh and drvn alng hfwy, nvr a factor*..........(12 to 1 op 10 to 1) 16
ATTADALE [55] 5-9-5 M Birch (6) *al beh, tld off last 4 fs.* ....(25 to 1 op 20 to 1) 17

Dist: ½l, 5l, 6l, 1l, 3½l, 3l, 1l, ½l, 1½l, 4l. 4m 1.00s. a 21.50s (17 Ran).
(Mrs Angela Norton), S G Norton

4322 Caroni Maiden Stakes Class D (3-y-o) £4,971 1m 4yds..........(5:10)

4126⁶ MISSED FLIGHT 9-0 P Robinson (3) *al travelling wl, led entering fnl furlong, sprinted clr*.... (9 to 2 op 7 to 2) 1
4120⁷ QUEENS CONSUL (Ire) 8-9 J Quinn (6) *made most till hdd appr fnl furlong, kpt on, no ch wth wnr*..... (25 to 1) 2
3909² TOUJOURS RIVIERA 9-0 Paul Eddery (11) *al hndy, rdn to nose ahead briefly appr fnl furlong, sn ridden and one pace*..........(6 to 5 fav op 11 to 10 on tchd 5 to 4) 3
4030² VILLAGE GREEN (Fr) (v) 9-0 K Darley (7) *al hndy, feeling pace and drvn alng o'r 2 fs out, kpt on same pace.* ....(14 to 1 op 10 to 1) 4
WATER SKIER 9-0 D Holland (15) *in tch, imprvg whn came very wide into strt, nvr able to chal.* (9 to 1 op 10 to 1) 5
4047⁶ DOMOVOY 8-9 W Newnes (4) *patiently rdn, shaken up to improve o'r 3 fs out, not rch ldrs*..........(25 to 1) 6
FLOWING OCEAN 9-0 L Dettori (16) *beh, chsd alng to improve last 3 fs, nrst finish*.......(10 to 1 op 5 to 1) 7
4125⁷ YA MAI 8-9 A McGlone (12) *settled midfield, effrt and drvn alng o'r 3 fs out, styd on same pace.* ....(20 to 1 op 16 to 1) 8
4155⁸ GLOWING JADE 8-9 K Fallon (8) *chsd ldg bunch, feeling pace o'r 3 fs out, sn struggling*.....(12 to 1 op 10 to 1) 9
GEMIKOSIX (Fr) 8-9 (5*) J Tate (14) *beh and drvn alng hfwy, nvr a threat*..........(50 to 1) 10
4181⁷ CELESTIAL CHOIR 8-9 N Adams (1) *tucked away on ins, feeling pace hfwy, fdd*..........(25 to 1 op 50 to 1) 11
3983² ABLE CHOICE (Ire) 9-0 R Hills (2) *co'red up on ins, drvn alng hfwy, sn btn*..... (9 to 1 op 8 to 1 tchd 10 to 1) 12

4221[8] SAMANTHAS JOY 8-6 (3*) C Hodgson (5) *beh and drvn alng hfwy, nvr a factor*......(50 to 1) 13
2892[4] DO TELL 8-11 (3*) S D Williams (10) *led for 2 fs, styd hndy till wknd frm hfwy*......(50 to 1 op 33 to 1) 14
4191 GYMCRAK DIAMOND (Ire) 8-11 (3*) S Maloney (13) *rcd freely, pressed ldrs for o'r 4 fs, sn btn*......(50 to 1) 15
BURROUGH HILL LASS 8-2 (7*) S Sanders (9) *drvn alng to keep in tch hfwy, sn beh*......(50 to 1) 16
Dist: 6l, ½l, nk, 2½l, 4l, 1l, 2½l, 1l, 8l, nk. 1m 49.80s. a 7.70s (16 Ran).
SR: 51/28/31/30/22/5/7/-/-/ (Walter Grubmuller), C F Wall

ROSCOMMON (IRE) (yielding)
Monday October 4th

4323 Fairymount Auction Race (2-y-o) £2,243 7f...... (4:00)

4183[2] TONGABEZI (Ire) 8-0 (2*) R M Burke (10)......(7 to 2) 1
4261[3] ZARA'S BIRTHDAY (Ire) 8-2 J F Egan (6)......(5 to 2 fav) 2
4093[6] MOMENTS TO CARE (Ire) 8-2 N G McCullagh (13)..(7 to 1) 3
1121[8] EASY STEP (Ire) 7-12 (10*) I Browne (2)......(25 to 1) 4
4183[5] SEE YOU (Ire) (bl) 8-8 W J Supple (12)......(12 to 1) 5
4183[6] COLLECTOR GENERAL (Ire) 8-4 (4*) J J Behan (7) (10 to 1) 6
4183[9] PERSIAN BLOOM (Ire) 7-8 (8*) G M Moylan (9)....(16 to 1) 7
DAMERS DUKE (Ire) 8-5 D V Smith (4)......(8 to 1) 8
2742 ALBERTA DIAMOND 8-8 P Shanahan (3)......(14 to 1) 9
2037 ALKEN (Ire) 8-8 M J Kinane (5)......(7 to 2) 10
4117 GRENNAN CLASSIC (Ire) 7-12 (4*) W J Smith (14) (14 to 1) 11
4093 BUTLER BRENNAN (Ire) 8-2[1] (4*) J A Heffernan (1) (33 to 1) 12
4183 THE DREAM FACTORY (Ire) 8-0 (2*) D G O'Shea (8) (33 to 1) 13
4183 CIARA CANE (Ire) 7-11 (8*) R T Fitzpatrick (11)....(33 to 1) 14
Dist: 2l, 4l, 1l, 1½l. 1m 37.00s. (14 Ran).
(J C Harley), J C Harley

4324 Crosswell Handicap (0-75 3-y-o) £2,243 7f...... (4:30)

3827[2] LUCKY PRINCE (Ire) [-] (bl) 8-6 (6*) D J O'Donohoe (1)......(8 to 1) 1
4057 RAFFERTY'S INNER (Ire) [-] 8-11 W J Supple (7)..(13 to 2) 2
4184* COMMODITY MARKET (Ire) [-] (bl) 9-0 (5ex) P V Gilson (8)......(9 to 2) 3
3062[7] LADY NOBLE (Ire) [-] 9-1 J F Egan (6)......(12 to 1) 4
4060[7] ELLE A TED (Ire) [-] 8-2 (4*) W J Smith (9)......(14 to 1) 5
4136 MANZALA (USA) [-] 9-5 J P Murtagh (3)......(7 to 1) 6
3827 SANDCHORUS (Ire) [-] (bl) 8-3 A J Nolan (5)......(33 to 1) 7
1923[3] SOMERTON BOY (Ire) [-] 9-6 M J Kinane (4)....(2 to 1 fav) 8
3614[7] IBDA [-] 8-4 (8*) R T Fitzpatrick (2)......(6 to 1) 9
Dist: 5l, ¾l, hd, 2l. 1m 37.70s. (9 Ran).
(Bezwell Fixings Ltd), D K Weld

ST-CLOUD (FR) (heavy)
Monday October 4th
Going Correction: PLUS 0.65 sec. per fur.

4325 Prix Eugene de Savoie (Listed) (3-y-o and up) £14,337 1m...... (3:20)

1723[4] NORTHERN CRYSTAL 5-9-4 T Jarnet,...... 1
4196[3] EMBROS (USA) 3-8-11 C Asmussen,...... 2
SIGNORETTO (Fr) 6-9-0 G Guignard,...... 3
3842[3] ARCHANGE (USA) 4-9-0 F Head,...... 4
Dist: 1½l, hd, 1l, 2½l, ¾l. 1m 49.10s. a 10.60s (6 Ran).
SR: 23/11/13/10/ (Sheikh Mohammed), A Fabre

WARWICK (soft)
Monday October 4th
Going Correction: PLUS 0.45 sec. per fur. (races 1,3,4,5,6,8), NIL (2,7)

4326 Tattersalls Maiden Auction Series Stakes Qualifier Class D (Div I) (2-y-o) £3,465 6f...... (1:30)

WHITE SHOOT (Ire) 8-1 A Tucker (5) *slwly away, gd hdwy on outsd o'r 2 fs out, led entering fnl furlong, ran on wl*......(33 to 1) 1
4159[2] MONKEY MAGIC (Ire) (bl) 8-10 L Piggott (4) *sn led, rdn and hdd entering fnl furlong, one pace*......(4 to 1 co-fav op 7 to 2) 2
2179[4] SCHNOZZLE (Ire) 8-11 W R Swinburn (7) *chsd ldrs, rdn appr fnl furlong, one paced*......(9 to 2 op 4 to 1) 3
1857[2] RED CLOUD (Ire) 8-8 P Robinson (8) *hld up, hdwy hfwy, rdn o'r one out, one pace ins*......(9 to 2 op 7 to 2 tchd 5 to 1) 4
3972 COURSE FISHING 8-6 A Mackay (3) *chsd ldr till wknd appr fnl furlong*......(33 to 1) 5
4089 RADIANT DANCER 8-3[2] G Duffield (1) *al mid-div*......(25 to 1 op 20 to 1) 6
4098[5] TRYPANIS (Ire) 8-3 M Hills (6) *al beh*......(4 to 1 co-fav op 5 to 2) 7
FLORA BELLE 8-5 D Harrison (11) *slwly away, al beh*......(12 to 1 op 6 to 1) 8
PAVACINI 8-6 A Munro (2) *chsd ldrs till rdn and wknd sn aftr hfwy*......(33 to 1) 9
3557[3] CHASTIZE (Ire) 8-11 W Ryan (9) *sn beh, nvr on terms*......(4 to 1 co-fav op 3 to 1) 10
3520 VAX IT 8-3[2] G Hind (10) *outpcd thrght*......(50 to 1 op 33 to 1) 11
Dist: 1½l, 1½l, ¾l, 1½l, 1½l, ½l, 5l, sht-hd, 3l, 6l. 1m 18.20s. a 6.50s (11 Ran).
SR: 11/14/9/3/-/-/ (Major D N Chappell), Major D N Chappell

4327 Prince Rupert Maiden Handicap Class D (0-70 3-y-o and up) £3,523 5f.. (2:00)

4222[2] MAGIC PEARL [65] 3-9-7 (7*) S Knott (12) *al prmnt, led wl o'r one furlong out, sn clr, easily*....(8 to 1 op 7 to 1) 1
4123[9] TAKE IT IN CASH [41] 4-8-5 C Rutter (1) *slwly away, in rear till hdwy on ins o'r 2 fs out, ran on to go second inside last*......(20 to 1 op 14 to 1) 2
4156[9] LITTLE OSBORNE (Ire) [45] (bl) 3-8-8 M Hills (14) *al frnt rnk, came wide into strt, ev ch 2 fs out, kpt on one pace*......(7 to 1 op 5 to 1) 3
4096 DISCO BOY [55] 3-9-4 T Quinn (10) *chsd ldrs, kpt on one pace ins fnl 2 fs*......(7 to 1 op 8 to 1) 4
4008[5] CHILI LADY [51] 3-9-0 A Munro (13) *prmnt till outpcd ins fnl 2 fs*......(10 to 1 op 6 to 1) 5
4008[4] SOPHISTICATED AIR [55] (bl) 3-9-4 R Cochrane (7) *led to hfwy, rdn and no extr appr fnl furlong*......(13 to 2 op 6 to 1 tchd 7 to 1) 6
3948[2] SWINGING TICH [46] 4-8-10 A Mackay (4) *slwly away, hdwy hfwy, nvr dngrs*......(7 to 1 op 6 to 1) 7
4090 LORINS GOLD [56] (bl) 3-9-5 L Piggott (6) *chsd ldrs, rdn wl o'r one furlong out, sn btn, eased*......(11 to 1 op 8 to 1 tchd 12 to 1) 8
4222[3] MARCHMAIN [60] 3-9-9 W Carson (11) *led hfwy, rdn o'r 2 fs out, hdd and wknd wl over one out*......(7 to 1 op 6 to 1) 9
4090[2] DOUBLE SHIFT [63] (v) 4-9-13 S Whitworth (9) *outpcd thrght*......(6 to 1 fav op 5 to 1 tchd 13 to 2) 10
3707 GARRY'S CHOICE [42] 4-8-6 Dale Gibson (2) *outpcd thrght*......(33 to 1 op 20 to 1) 11
3946 MANADEL [31] (v) 3-7-8[1] E Johnson (16) *al towards rear*......(50 to 1 op 33 to 1) 12
4031 CHRISTIAN WARRIOR [32] (bl) 4-7-10[2] J Fanning (5) *speed to hfwy*......(33 to 1 op 25 to 1) 13
4221[9] JOCKS JOKER [51] 3-9-0 J Fortune (3) *al beh*......(33 to 1 op 25 to 1) 14
4156 JOTRA [36] (v) 3-7-13 T Williams (15) *outpcd thrght*......(33 to 1 op 25 to 1) 15
4123 VICTORIAS PASSION [43] 3-8-6 W Ryan (8) *al in rear, tld off*......(33 to 1) 16
Dist: 6l, ¾l, 1½l, 1½l, sht-hd, ½l, 1l, nk, 1½l, 2l. 1m 1.40s. a 3.20s (16 Ran).
SR: 50/3/3/7/-/-/ (G G Sanderson), E J Alston

4328 Arden Conditions Stakes Class C (3-y-o and up) £4,690 1¼m 169yds (2:30)

4100[3] SALATIN (USA) 3-8-10 W Carson (4) *trkd ldr, led o'r 3 fs out, pushed clr fnl furlong*......(11 to 10 op Evens tchd 11 to 10 on) 1
1269[3] MESLEH 6-9-2 Pat Eddery (1) *hld up, hdwy to go second 3 fs out, hrd rdn o'r one out, eased whn held ins last*......(6 to 5 on op 11 to 8 on tchd 11 to 10 on) 2
FORGE BAY 6-8-7 (7*) C Hawksley (2) *pld hrd, al same pl, lost tch 2 fs out*......(100 to 1 op 50 to 1) 3
4022 PALACE MAN (USA) 5-8-9 (5*) S Drowne (3) *led till hdd o'r 3 fs out, sn beh, tld off*......(100 to 1 op 50 to 1) 4
Dist: 8l, 15l, 30l. 2m 24.50s. a 11.70s (4 Ran).
SR: 27/17/-/-/ (Hamdan Al-Maktoum), P T Walwyn

4329 Vauxhall Master Hire Nursery Handicap Class E (0-75 2-y-o) £3,753 1m ......(3:00)

4122[7] SHOOFK [66] 9-1 L Piggott (21) *sn in tch, short of room and swtchd lft o'r one furlong out, led jst ins last, all out*......(20 to 1 op 16 to 1) 1
4236* NAWAFELL [65] 9-0 (7ex) W R Swinburn (16) *hld up, hdwy o'r 2 fs out, hrd rdn and edgd lft entering last, rallied and pressed wnr to line*. (9 to 2 op 5 to 1 tchd 6 to 1) 2
3704[6] ART TATUM (Ire) [70] 9-5 M Hills (8) *mid-div, drvn to make hdwy ins fnl 2 fs, nvr nrr*......(14 to 1 op 12 to 1 tchd 16 to 1) 3
3940 SWORDSMANSHIP [57] (bl) 8-6 G Duffield (17) *led 1st 3 fs, led wl o'r 2 out, hrd rdn and hdd jst ins last, no extr*......(20 to 1 op 12 to 1) 4
4208[4] NORTHERN STARLIGHT [50] (v) 7-13[3] D Harrison (19) *prmnt, rdn and wkng whn slightly hmpd entering fnl furlong, no extr*......(20 to 1 op 14 to 1) 5
3940[5] RUNIC SYMBOL [58] 8-7 A Munro (14) *chsd ldrs, rdn o'r 2 fs out, one paced*......(25 to 1 op 20 to 1) 6
3792[3] WESTERN FLEET (USA) [65] 9-0 T Quinn (15) *trkd ldrs, ev ch till wknd entering fnl furlong*....(9 to 1 op 6 to 1) 7
4122 AL JINN [65] 8-7 (7*) Sarah Thompson (1) *beh, nvr on terms*......(50 to 1 op 25 to 1) 8
4009[4] NOORAN [54] 8-3 W Carson (18) *prmnt till hmpd sn aftr hfwy, nvr dngrs after*......(16 to 1 op 14 to 1) 9

4122 LIFE'S TOO SHORT (Ire) [47] 7-10 J Fanning (4) *led aftr 3 fs, hdd wl o'r 2 furlongs out, wknd appr last.* ....(25 to 1 op 20 to 1) 10
4081³ LEGAL TRAIN [62] 8-11 J Williams (13) *prmnt to hfwy.* ....(20 to 1 op 16 to 1) 11
3428⁸ WOODS VENTURE (Ire) [60] 8-9 W Woods (6) *prmnt till wknd o'r 2 fs out*........................(33 to 1 op 25 to 1) 12
4128⁵ LITTLE HOOLIGAN [49] (v) 7-12⁴ C Rutter (3) *nvr on terms.* ....(25 to 1 op 16 to 1) 13
3126⁵ EXPRESS LINE [45] 7-1 (7*) M Baird (12) *bolted bef strt, al beh*........................(50 to 1 op 33 to 1) 14
4113* DYNAMIC DELUXE (USA) [72] 9-7 S O'Gorman (5) *prmnt till rdn and wknd 2 fs out.* ....(3 to 1 fav op 9 to 4 tchd 7 to 2) 15
3532⁴ DULFORD LAD [69] 9-4 S Whitworth (2) *al beh.* ....(14 to 1 tchd 16 to 1) 16
3972 KENILWORTH FORD [55] 8-4 J Fortune (9) *al beh.* ....(50 to 1 op 33 to 1) 17
3815 CREEK VALLEY [49] 7-12 Dale Gibson (10) *al beh.* ....(33 to 1 op 20 to 1) 18
4113 CARA CARLTON (USA) [64] 8-13 W Ryan (11) *al beh.* ....(50 to 1 op 25 to 1) 19
3867⁴ SNOWDON SLIGHTS [46] 7-9 E Johnson (7) *al beh.* ....(25 to 1 op 20 to 1) 20
3835² SECUNDUS (Ire) [70] 9-5 B Rouse (20) *hld up in rear, al beh*........................(20 to 1 op 14 to 1) 21

Dist: Hd, 3½l, nk, 1½l, hd, nk, 8l, nk, hd, 1½l. 1m 46.30s. a 9.50s (21 Ran).
SR: 13/11/5/-/-/-/ (Ali K Al Jafleh), Mrs L Piggott

4330 Tattersalls Maiden Auction Series Stakes Qualifier Class D (Div II) (2-y-o) £3,435 6f...................... (3:30)

4210² SALVEZZA (Ire) 8-1 W Carson (6) *steadied strt, sn pushed alng and prmnt, rdn to ld 2 fs out, drw clr.* ....(2 to 1 on op 7 to 4 on tchd 13 to 8 on) 1
4210 PHONEAHOLIC (Ire) 8-7 B Rouse (2) *slwly away, hld up, hdwy hfwy, styd on to chase wnr fnl furlong.* ....(12 to 1 op 7 to 1) 2
4097⁶ POSSIBILITY 8-3 G Duffield (3) *broke wl, trkd ldr, rdn o'r 2 fs out, rallied and kpt on one pace.* (12 to 1 op 8 to 1) 3
4220 HEALTHY RISK 8-6 T Quinn (1) *in rear, styd on fnl 2 fs, nvr nrr*..(50 to 1) 4
3387 SHAYNES DOMAIN (bl) 8-11 J Williams (4) *hld up, rdn and ran on one pace ins fnl 2 fs*........................ (50 to 1) 5
3642⁴ CIZARGA 7-13³ (5*) L Newton (10) *led till rdn and hdd 2 fs out, wknd*........................(8 to 1 op 4 to 1) 6
4127⁵ TONE CONTROL 8-11 W Woods (5) *chsd ldr till rdn and wknd o'r 2 fs out*........................(14 to 1 op 12 to 1) 7
SOUPERFICIAL 8-6 J Fortune (7) *in tch till wknd sn aftr hfwy*..(33 to 1) 8
WHITE TOP (Ire) 8-8 D Harrison (9) *slwly away, al beh, tld off*..(10 to 1 op 5 to 1) 9
BADGE OF COURAGE 8-2¹ A Munro (8) *outpcd thrght, tld off*..(14 to 1 op 10 to 1) 10

Dist: 8l, hd, ¾l, 2½l, nk, 1½l, 3½l, 7l, 12l. 1m 18.40s. a 6.70s (10 Ran).
SR: 7/-/-/-/-/-/ (Skyline Racing Ltd), P W Chapple-Hyam

4331 Queen Bess Claiming Apprentice Stakes Class F (3-y-o and up) £2,870 6f ....(4:00)

4168 FINJAN 6-8-4 (5*) J Dennis (13) *hld up, gd hdwy o'r one furlong out, led ins last, ran on.* ....(100 to 30 fav op 3 to 1 tchd 4 to 1) 1
4008⁶ AVRIL ETOILE 3-7-5 (5*) Iona Wands (17) *mid-div, hdwy on outsd o'r 2 fs out, led entering last, sn hdd, one paced.* ....(10 to 1 op 6 to 1) 2
4123³ APACHE MYTH 3-8-6 (5*) Wendy Jones (5) *outpcd in rear, hdwy 2 fs out, ran on, nvr nrr*..... (6 to 1 tchd 7 to 1) 3
4221⁷ RED LEADER (Ire) 3-7-8 (7*) A Daly (14) *hld up, gd hdwy o'r one furlong out, kpt on ins*.........(10 to 1 op 8 to 1) 4
4180 SOBER LAD (Ire) 3-9-2 P Roberts (15) *chsd ldrs, rdn and one pace entering fnl furlong*........(6 to 1 op 5 to 1) 5
3661⁴ NO GAIN 3-7-9 (7*) W Hawksley (3) *slwly away, hdwy on ins wl o'r one furlong out, ran on, nvr nrr*.... (16 to 1) 6
2787⁶ OLYMPIA 3-7-12 (7*) L Suthern (11) *chsd ldrs till wknd wl o'r one furlong out, disqualified*........(16 to 1) 7D
THE OLD CHAPEL 4-8-13 (5*) J Bramhill (2) *prmnt, led hfwy till rdn and hdd entering last, wknd.* ....(10 to 1 op 4 to 1) 8
4224⁸ STRIP CARTOON (Ire) (bl) 5-8-6 (3*) G Strange (6) *led to hfwy, prmnt till wknd ins fnl furlong.* ....(12 to 1 op 8 to 1) 9
3628⁵ LARN FORT (v) 3-8-3³ (7*) J Gracey (9) *mid-div, slightly hmpd 2 fs out, nvr dngrs*........................(10 to 1) 10
4156 COLMAR 3-7-0 (7*) D Denby (1) *speed to hfwy*... (33 to 1) 11
3550⁷ THE WEND 3-7-2 (5*) M Baird (8) *prmnt till wknd 2 fs out.* ....(50 to 1) 12
4206⁵ ALL THE GIRLS (Ire) 4-7-6⁴ (7*) S Jones (16) *slwly away, al beh*........................(12 to 1 op 8 to 1) 13
3249 ANOTHER KINGDOM 3-8-7 L Carter (7) *slwly away, al beh*........................(33 to 1 op 20 to 1) 14
3981⁸ RUBY COOPER 3-8-9 (5*) Debbie Biggs (12) *prmnt early, beh frm hfwy*..(50 to 1) 15
3655 SENOR L'AMOUR (bl) 3-8-2 (5*) D O'Neill (10) *chsd ldrs till wknd quickly o'r 2 fs out, tld off*............ (20 to 1) 16

Dist: ¾l, ½l, sht-hd, ½l, 1½l, ½l, 1½l, nk, ½l, ¾l. 1m 18.70s. a 7.00s (16 Ran).
SR: 9/-/6/-/8/-/ (Mrs R Olivier), Martyn Wane

4332 Wroxhall Conditions Stakes Class C (2-y-o) £4,232 5f................(4:30)

3898⁴ YA MALAK 8-13 R Cochrane (2) *made all, rdn appr fnl furlong, drvn out.* ....(7 to 4 on op 13 to 8 on tchd 2 to 1 on) 1
3723⁴ MOSCOW ROAD 9-1 W R Swinburn (6) *trkd wnr, rdn and swtchd lft appr fnl furlong, no imprsn, eased cl hme.* ....(7 to 2 op 5 to 2 tchd 4 to 1) 2
3715⁹ TWICE IN BUNDORAN (Ire) 8-6 T Quinn (3) *chsd ldrs, no imprsn fnl 2 fs*........................(7 to 1 op 4 to 1) 3
3982⁸ IVA'S FLYER (Ire) 8-1 (7*) P Roberts (1) *rcd on ins, effrt hfwy, btn wl o'r one furlong out.* (16 to 1 op 14 to 1) 4
3537⁷ PLEASURE TRICK (USA) 8-11 A Clark (5) *outpcd thrght.* ....(33 to 1 op 16 to 1) 5
ANOTHER SOLOMON 8-6 (5*) K Rutter (4) *slwly away, al beh*........................(50 to 1 op 33 to 1) 6

Dist: 1½l, 3½l, 3½l, 5l, 2l. 1m 1.10s. a 2.90s (6 Ran).
SR: 41/37/14/2/-/-/ (G Jabre), J W Payne

4333 Kingsbury Limited Stakes Class F (0-60 3-y-o and up) £3,295 7f.... (5:00)

4065⁸ PROUD BRIGADIER (Ire) 5-9-0 T Quinn (2) *al prmnt, led one and a half fs out, sn clr, cmftbly.* ....(14 to 1 op 12 to 1 tchd 16 to 1) 1
4270* PENNY BANGER (Ire) (bl) 3-8-6 T Williams (3) *led aftr 2 and a half fs, rdn one and a half out, one pace.* ....(7 to 4 fav op 5 to 2) 2
3325⁶ ON Y VA (USA) 6-8-2 (7*) Sarah Thompson (18) *al prmnt on outsd, ev ch 2 fs out, one pace aftr.* (16 to 1 op 8 to 1) 3
4277 RACING TELEGRAPH 3-8-11 M Wigham (16) *hld up, gd hdwy 2 fs out, hrd rdn appr last, no extr ins.* ....(14 to 1 op 10 to 1 tchd 16 to 1) 4
4164* PUSEY STREET BOY 6-9-0 C Rutter (19) *hld up, ran on ins fnl 2 fs, nvr nrr*........(7 to 1 op 6 to 1 tchd 10 to 1) 5
3409⁵ CORONA GOLD 3-8-11 W R Swinburn (11) *al abt same pl, no imprsn ins fnl 2 fs*........................(12 to 1 op 7 to 1) 6
PERSIAN BUD (Ire) 5-9-0 S Raymont (6) *mid-div, some hdwy fnl 2 fs*........................(50 to 1 op 33 to 1) 7
4224² CELESTINE (v) 4-8-9 J Fanning (4) *mid-div, no hdwy fnl 2 fs*..(12 to 1 op 7 to 1) 8
3910⁷ GREY CHARMER (Ire) 4-9-0 S Whitworth (1) *slwly away, hdwy on ins fnl 2 fs, nvr dngrs*..... (14 to 1 op 8 to 1) 9
3591 VILAMAR (Ire) 3-8-1² (7*) S Knott (14) *chsd ldrs till wknd 2 fs out*........................(20 to 1 op 25 to 1) 10
2639³ GALLERY ARTIST (Ire) 5-8-7 (7*) S Eiffert (15) *chsd ldrs till wknd 2 fs out*........................(25 to 1 op 10 to 1) 11
3311 FINAL OAK 3-8-6 J Fortune (9) *speed till wknd 3 fs out.* ....(50 to 1 op 20 to 1) 12
3766 WATERLORD (Ire) 3-8-11 A Clark (8) *trkd ldrs till wknd hfwy*........................(20 to 1 op 11 to 1) 13
4224⁶ SIRTELIMAR (Ire) 4-9-0 A Mackay (5) *al beh.* ....(25 to 1 op 20 to 1) 14
3991⁷ TIME HONORED (USA) 3-8-11 G Duffield (17) *in tch till wknd quickly 2 fs out*............ (14 to 1 op 9 to 1) 15
4131* UNVEILED 5-8-4 (5*) S Drowne (7) *al towards rear.* ....(14 to 1 op 8 to 1) 16
3447 CEE-EN-CEE (v) 9-9-0 A Tucker (13) *outpcd frm strt.* ....(33 to 1 op 20 to 1) 17
4235 YOUNG VALENTINE 4-9-0 W Woods (10) *al beh.* ....(33 to 1 op 14 to 1) 18
2396⁷ DESERT SPLENDOUR (bl) 5-8-9 (5*) P McCabe (20) *speed to hfwy, tld off*........................(33 to 1 op 20 to 1) 19
881⁵ AMETHYSTINE (USA) 7-8-9 A Munro (12) *led 2 and a half fs, wknd quickly, tld off.* ....(8 to 1 op 7 to 1 tchd 11 to 1 and 12 to 1) 20

Dist: 3½l, nk, 1½l, ¾l, nk, 4l, sht-hd, 2l, sht-hd, ½l. 1m 30.70s. a 6.90s (20 Ran).
SR: 44/25/27/24/25/21/12/6/5/ (M T Lawrance), M R Channon

FOLKESTONE (soft)
Tuesday October 5th

Going Correction: PLUS 0.85 sec. per fur. (races 1,2,3,4,5,8), PLUS 0.65 (6,7)

4334 Levy Board Apprentice Maiden Stakes Class F (3-y-o and up) £1,548 1 ½m........................... (1:40)

4129⁴ DIPLOMATIST 3-8-1 (5*) M Baird (8) *trkd ldrs, led o'r 2 fs out, rdn and styd on wl fnl furlong*.........(15 to 8 jt-fav op 9 to 4 tchd 5 to 2 and 7 to 4) 1
4036 VAIGLY SUNTHYME 3-8-11 B Russell (1) *prog 3 fs out, chsd wnr fnl furlong, not quicken.* ....(9 to 1 op 10 to 1 tchd 14 to 1) 2
3937⁵ CLASSIC CABOOSE (USA) 3-8-11 Michael Denaro (7) *wl plcd, rdn and one paced ins last 2 fs*........(15 to 8 jt-fav op 2 to 1 tchd 9 to 4) 3
3503² NAWAHIL 3-7-13 (7*) C Dykes (4) *slwly into strd, led aftr 4 fs, hdd and ran wide o'r 2 furlongs out, sn btn.* ....(3 to 1 op 6 to 4) 4

ROYAL GLINT 4-8-7 (7*) A Daly (6) *towards rear til styd on last 2 fs, not rch ldrs*............. (50 to 1 op 20 to 1) 5

3868[5] CANDARELA 3-8-1 (5*) Debbie Biggs (3) *led til ran wide on bend aftr 2 fs, prmnt until lost pl two furlongs out.* .... (66 to 1 op 33 to 1) 6

CASTLE ORCHARD 9-9-2 (3*) D Gibbs (5) *lft in ld aftr 2 fs, hdd 8 furlongs out, wknd 5 out*...(100 to 1 op 33 to 1) 7

4110 BALMORAL BELLE 3-7-13 (7*) Jo Hunnam (2) *nvr on terms frm hfwy*........... (20 to 1 op 12 to 1 tchd 25 to 1) 8

TINAS LASS 4-8-9 (5*) D Toole (9) *chsd ldrs til lost pl quickly aftr 4 fs, tld off*.......... (100 to 1 op 33 to 1) 9

Dist: 3½l, 3l, 7l, sht-hd, 4l, 10l, 5l, 25l. 2m 52.30s. a 21.80s (9 Ran).

(Mrs S Page), W Jarvis

4335 Sedlescombe Claiming Stakes Class F (3-y-o and up) £1,800 1m 1f 149yds ....(2:10)

2291 SARAH-CLARE 5-8-12 D Holland (7) *wl plcd, chsd ldr frm 4 out, led well o'r one out, rdn clr.* ....(5 to 2 fav tchd 3 to 1 and 9 to 4) 1

4115 PRIMO FIGLIO (bl) 3-8-5 P Robinson (9) *chsd frnt rnk, kpt on one pace frm 2 out*.............. (10 to 1 op 7 to 1) 2

4241[3] KEYWAY (USA) 3-8-13 G Duffield (5) *wl in tch, rdn and not quicken frm 2 fs out*...............(7 to 2 tchd 9 to 2) 3

4101 FRONTIER FLIGHT (USA) 3-8-13 S Raymont (14) *led til hdd and wknd wl o'r one furlong out.* ....(5 to 1 op 4 to 1 tchd 6 to 1) 4

4115[2] LYN'S RETURN (Ire) 4-8-12 (7*) G Rothwell (3) *effrt o'r 3 fs out, not rch ldrs last 2 furlongs.* .... (9 to 1 op 5 to 1 tchd 10 to 1) 5

4088 SOOJAMA (Ire) 3-8-5 N Adams (4) *slwly into strd, effrt 3 out, no imprsn last 2*............ (33 to 1 op 20 to 1) 6

2499 ONE-O-EIGHT 3-8-0 T Williams (13) *beh til styd on one pace frm 2 out*...................(66 to 1 op 50 to 1) 7

4115[9] VANROY (v) 9-9-1 S Whitworth (8) *mid-div 4 furlong out, rdn and no extr last 3 fs*........... (8 to 1 op 10 to 1) 8

CORDILLERO 7-8-7 B Rouse (11) *outpcd in mid-div, no hdwy frm 3 out*...................(14 to 1 op 20 to 1) 9

3938 NIGELS PROSPECT 3-7-13 (5*) D Wright (1) *beh most of way*.............................. (66 to 1 op 25 to 1) 10

3945[9] MARATHIA 3-8-3[1] W Woods (15) *chsd ldrs to hfwy, sn btn.* .... (33 to 1 op 14 to 1) 11

4129 SUNBEAM CHARLIE 3-7-8 (5*) B Russell (12) *wl plcd to hfwy, sn wknd*...................(66 to 1 op 33 to 1) 12

4031[9] COVEN MOON (v) 3-7-8 G Bardwell (2) *effrt 6 fs out, wknd o'r 3 furlongs out*................ (25 to 1 op 14 to 1) 13

3839[9] DANCING MISS (Ire) 4-8-0 T Sprake (6) *chsd ldr for o'r 5 fs, wknd 3 out*.......................... (33 to 1 op 25 to 1) 14

3866[5] LA VILLA ROSE (Fr) 3-7-8 E Johnson (10) *strted slwly, al beh, tld off*.........................(33 to 1 op 20 to 1) 15

Dist: 2l, 5l, 1½l, 10l, 1½l, 7l, hd, 2½l, 1l, 5l. 2m 13.80s. a 16.20s (15 Ran).

SR: 21/10/8/-/-/-/ (Miss Clare Coyne), R Akehurst

4336 Brede Limited Stakes Class F (0-60 3-y-o and up) £2,337 1m 1f 149yds ....(2:40)

4115* COLTRANE (v) 5-9-3 D Holland (9) *led aftr one furlong, made rst, rdn wl clr o'r one out.* (9 to 4 fav op 3 to 1) 1

3961[2] SHERGRESS 3-8-1 (5*) J Tate (12) *chsd wnr aftr 3 fs, ev ch 2 out, outpcd fnl furlong.* ....(3 to 1 op 5 to 2 tchd 7 to 2) 2

4101[9] QUANTITY SURVEYOR (v) 4-9-3 G Duffield (1) *in tch, styd on one pace last 2 fs*.....(7 to 1 op 8 to 1 tchd 6 to 1) 3

3669[4] DARING PAST (bl) 3-8-11 S Raymont (4) *hdwy 4 fs out, found no extr ins last 2.* .... (16 to 1 op 12 to 1 tchd 20 to 1) 4

3910 DOMINANT FORCE 4-9-3 P Robinson (7) *improved hfwy, no imprsn on ldrs frm 2 out*.......(33 to 1 op 20 to 1) 5

4152 MON PETITNAMOUR (Ire) 4-8-9 (3*) B Doyle (5) *rcd in mid-div, no hdwy last 3 fs*............... (33 to 1 op 14 to 1) 6

3102[7] NOVA SPIRIT 5-8-12 R Price (3) *nvr better than fnl placing*.............. (16 to 1 op 14 to 1 tchd 20 to 1) 7

4091[8] QUADRANT 4-8-12 (5*) D McCabe (10) *wl plcd for 6 fs.* .... (33 to 1 op 20 to 1) 8

3986[6] PONDICHERRY (USA) 3-8-6 W Woods (8) *in tch til wknd o'r 2 fs out*..........(16 to 1 op 12 to 1 tchd 20 to 1) 9

4271[6] KELIMUTU 4-8-12 G Bardwell (14) *strted slwly, sn pushed alng, effrt o'r 3 fs out, no ch wth ldrs.* ....(4 to 1 op 5 to 2 tchd 9 to 2) 10

WIDE SUPPORT 8-9-3 B Rouse (11) *beh most of way.* .... (33 to 1 op 20 to 1) 11

4131 NYMPH ERRANT 3-8-6 T Sprake (13) *nvr nr to chal frm hfwy*........................ (20 to 1 op 12 to 1) 12

4035 UP ALL NIGHT (bl) 4-8-7 (5*) D Wright (2) *beh fnl 4 fs.* .... (50 to 1 op 33 to 1 tchd 66 to 1) 13

1714[9] INONDER 3-8-6 T Williams (6) *led for one furlong, wknd aftr 3 fs*..............................(50 to 1 op 33 to 1) 14

Dist: 7l, 10l, 4l, 8l, 12l, nk, 1½l, nk, sht-hd, 5l. 2m 11.90s. a 14.30s (14 Ran).

SR: 45/20/11/-/-/-/ (M L Oberstein), Lord Huntingdon

4337 Hurst Green Maiden Auction Stakes Class E (Div I) (2-y-o) £2,005 6f 189yds ....(3:10)

4127 SEGALA (Ire) 8-13 G Duffield (2) *chsd ldrs, rdn to ld jst o'r one out, forged clr*..............(11 to 4 fav op 3 to 1) 1

3940[7] QUEENS STROLLER (Ire) 8-6 D Holland (6) *led aftr 2 fs, hng lft and hdd jst o'r one out, no extr*... (6 to 1 op 7 to 2) 2

ARTIC COURIER 8-9 (5*) L Newton (7) *improved frm rear 3 out, rdn and kpt on one pace last 2.* .... (14 to 1 op 12 to 1 tchd 20 to 1) 3

3960[4] JEMIMA PUDDLEDUCK 8-8 R Price (3) *took clr order frm hfwy, outpcd last 2 fs*... (7 to 1 op 5 to 1 tchd 8 to 1) 4

4236[2] ANTANANARIVO (Ire) 8-11 B Rouse (5) *led for 2 fs, prmnt til wknd ins last two furlongs*....... (100 to 30 op 2 to 1) 5

4098[6] WARHURST (Ire) 8-11 P Robinson (8) *chsd ldrs, shaken up and not quicken o'r 2 out, wknd wl over one out.* ....(5 to 1 op 9 to 2 tchd 6 to 1) 6

4229[9] GOLDEN BULLION 7-11 (5*) B Russell (9) *early speed, lost pl hfwy*.............(25 to 1 op 12 to 1 tchd 33 to 1) 7

UP IN FLAMES (Ire) 8-10 R Perham (1) *dwlt, outpcd last 3 fs*..................(11 to 2 op 4 to 1 tchd 10 to 1) 8

4014[7] BOLD FLAME 8-9 G Bardwell (4) *al towards rear, tld off.* .... (40 to 1 op 20 to 1 tchd 50 to 1) 9

Dist: 4l, 6l, 2½l, 1l, nk, 12l, nk, 20l. 1m 30.60s. a 9.70s (9 Ran).

SR: 42/23/13/-/-/-/ (Mrs Michael Ennever), Sir Mark Prescott

4338 Hurst Green Maiden Auction Stakes Class E (Div II) (2-y-o) £2,005 6f 189yds ....(3:40)

4167[6] KAITAK (Ire) 8-12 S Morris (1) *chsd ldr, rdn alng to ld one furlong out, styd on last 100 yards.* ....(5 to 2 op 4 to 1 tchd 2 to 1) 1

4165[4] MILLION LIGHTS (Ire) (v) 8-8 W Woods (6) *led til hdd one furlong out, one pace fnl 100 yards.* ....(2 to 1 fav op 5 to 4 tchd 5 to 2) 2

PHIL'S TIME 8-11 B Rouse (5) *dwlt, chsd ldrs aftr 2 fs, ev ch o'r one out, no extr.* .... (12 to 1 op 6 to 1 tchd 14 to 1) 3

3446[5] LADY SILK 8-7 S Whitworth (2) *ldg grp, rdn and one pace appr fnl furlong*....................(3 to 1 op 2 to 1) 4

4113 QUICK DECISION (Ire) 8-6 (5*) D Wright (8) *beh til effrt 2 out, no imprsn o'r one out.* .... (20 to 1 op 12 to 1 tchd 25 to 1) 5

4032 SPORTING STORY (Ire) 8-3 R Price (3) *chsd ldr for 5 fs, no extr*...............................(33 to 1 op 12 to 1) 6

3421 DANDINI 8-8 N Adams (4) *nvr rchd chalg pos.* ....(40 to 1 op 20 to 1 tchd 50 to 1) 7

3426[3] LUCY'S GOLD 7-9 (7*) M Baird (7) *ldg grp til rdn and wknd 2 out*................(12 to 1 op 6 to 1 tchd 14 to 1) 8

4002[5] LITTLE LUKE (Ire) 8-3 (5*) L Newton (9) *outpcd til hrd rdn o'r 2 out, not rch ldrs.* (12 to 1 op 5 to 1 tchd 14 to 1) 9

Dist: 2l, 3½l, 4l, 1½l, sht-hd, 6l, 2l, 6l. 1m 32.20s. a 11.30s (9 Ran).

SR: 18/8/-/-/-/-/ (F Carr), J M Carr

4339 EBF Ashford Median Auction Maiden Stakes Class E (2-y-o) £2,495 6f (4:10)

3982[2] FORGOTTEN DANCER (Ire) 9-0 R Perham (6) *made virtually all, shaken up and styd on ins fnl furlong.* ....(13 to 8 fav op 5 to 4 tchd 7 to 4) 1

4210[8] LEVIATHAN MYSTERY 9-0 P Robinson (1) *hmpd leaving stalls, improved frm hfwy, chsd wnr last 2 fs, not quicken*.......................... (7 to 1 tchd 14 to 1) 2

4124[2] TOM MORGAN 9-0 G Duffield (8) *al handily plcd, styd on one pace frm 2 fs out*.............. (2 to 1 op 5 to 2) 3

3589 SMOOTH HOUND 9-0 D Holland (11) *pressed ldrs, rdn and outpcd appr fnl furlong.* ....(11 to 1 op 7 to 1 tchd 12 to 1) 4

4004[5] AILEENS GIRL 8-9 N Adams (5) *ran on frm rear last 2 fs, not rch ldrs*.......(66 to 1 op 33 to 1 tchd 100 to 1) 5

3958[6] KING BRUCE 9-0 C Rutter (7) *chsd ldrs til lost pl 2 out.* .... (25 to 1 op 20 to 1 tchd 33 to 1) 6

4127[9] WIDE OUTSIDE (Ire) 8-9 A Morris (10) *cl up for 4 fs, no extr.* .... (66 to 1 op 33 to 1) 7

FOOD BROKER FELLA (Ire) 8-9 (5*) B Russell (13) *al beh.* .... (33 to 1 op 14 to 1) 8

BO KNOWS NIGEL (Ire) 9-0 B Rouse (14) *outpcd.* .... (20 to 1 op 12 to 1 tchd 25 to 1) 9

SPORTING SCRIPT (Ire) 9-0 R Price (4) *mid-div, rdn and outpcd o'r 2 fs out*... (50 to 1 op 20 to 1 tchd 66 to 1) 10

3950[3] VICEROY RULER (v) 9-0 S Whitworth (15) *wl plcd for 4 fs.* .... (20 to 1 op 12 to 1 tchd 25 to 1) 11

4098 EFFICACY 8-4 (5*) D Wright (9) *speed for o'r 3 fs.* .... (50 to 1 op 33 to 1) 12

ARCTIC SHREWD 8-4 (5*) L Newton (16) *outpcd.* .... (50 to 1 op 20 to 1) 13

4003 STEAM ON 9-0 T Williams (3) *swrvd lft leaving stalls, beh hfwy, tld off*........(50 to 1 op 20 to 1 tchd 66 to 1) 14

3895[9] LORELEI ROCK 8-9 G Bardwell (12) *beh hfwy, tld off whn virtually pld up fnl furlong*....... (66 to 1 op 33 to 1) 15

Dist: 1l, 3½l, 5l, hd, nk, 1½l, ½l, hd, sht-hd, 1½l. 1m 19.40s. a 8.40s (15 Ran).

SR: 10/6/-/-/-/-/ (G A Bosley), R Hannon

4340 Northiam Handicap Class E (0-70 3-y-o and up) £2,267 6f............. (4:40)

1209[7] EFRA [65] 4-9-12 S Raymont (3) *hdwy frm rear and swtchd rght 2 out, led o'r one out, quickened clr.* .... (15 to 2 op 8 to 1 tchd 7 to 1) 1

3747[2] ZINBAQ [38] 7-7-13 T Williams (2) *hdwy 3 out, led wl o'r one out, sn hdd and one pace.* ....(4 to 1 fav op 5 to 1 tchd 6 to 1) 2
3896[6] TURTLE BEACH [35] 4-7-10 Kim McDonnell (10) *led til hdd wl o'r one out, sn outpcd*........ (12 to 1 tchd 10 to 1) 3
3910[6] QUINSIGIMOND [65] 3-9-10 G Duffield (13) *pressed ldrs, ev ch 2 out, not quicken appr fnl furlong.* .... (15 to 2 op 6 to 1 tchd 8 to 1) 4
4156* LEIGH CROFTER [52] (bl) 4-8-13 S Whitworth (16) *cl up, ev ch wl o'r one out, no extr*............ (6 to 1 op 7 to 2) 5
3226[6] BICHETTE [55] 3-9-0 B Rouse (12) *chsd ldr for 4 fs.* .... (12 to 1 op 16 to 1 tchd 20 to 1) 6
4008[3] HARD ROCK MINER [37] 3-7-3 (7*) M Baird (7) *towards rear til rdn and kpt on frm 2 out*.........(8 to 1 op 6 to 1) 7
4156 VERRO (USA) [32] (bl) 6-7-7 G Bardwell (11) *wl plcd for o'r 4 fs*.. (33 to 1) 8
4123[5] POYLE AMBER [52] (bl) 4-8-13 W Woods (15) *trkd ldrs to hfwy*..................(9 to 1 op 7 to 1 tchd 10 to 1) 9
3047 PEGGOTTY [38] 5-7-6 (7*) Wendy Jones (9) *outpcd in mid-div most of way*.................. (25 to 1 op 20 to 1) 10
4131[7] DESERT NOMAD [55] 3-8-9 (5*) D Wright (8) *rcd in mid-div, no hdwy last 2 fs*................. (12 to 1 op 10 to 1) 11
3938 CHUMMY'S FRIEND (Ire) [38] 3-7-11 C Rutter (6) *mid-div whn bumped 2 fs out, not reco'r.* .... (16 to 1 op 14 to 1 tchd 20 to 1) 12
2671[8] COPPERMILL LAD [42] 10-7-10 (7*) Iona Wands (14) *al outpcd, lost tch hfwy*.................(12 to 1 op 8 to 1) 13
4164[3] BILL MOON [50] 7-8-6 (5*) D McCabe (4) *nvr on terms.* .... (13 to 2 op 6 to 1 tchd 7 to 1) 14
4090 GEMINI BAY [33] (bl) 4-7-8 N Adams (5) *slwly into strd, cld on ldrs on outsd appr hfwy, wknd 2 fs out.* ....(20 to 1 tchd 25 to 1) 15

Dist: 4l, 4l, 1½l, 1½l, 1½l, nk, nk, ¾l, sht-hd, ½l. 1m 18.00s. a 7.00s (15 Ran).
SR: 50/7/-/10/-/-/ (Mrs P Jubert), R Hannon

4341 Robertsbridge Handicap Class E (0-70 3-y-o) £2,267 1½m............ (5:10)

4129[6] WARM SPELL [69] 9-7 B Rouse (3) *prog 5 out, rdn to ld ins last 2 fs, edgd lft one out, drvn out.* .... (11 to 2 op 6 to 1 tchd 7 to 1) 1
4256 JOLIS ABSENT [42] (bl) 7-8 G Bardwell (2) *rdn alng to cl on ldrs 4 out, swtchd rght o'r one out, ev ch ins fnl furlong, jst fld*..........(2 to 1 fav op 9 to 4 tchd 5 to 2) 2
4234[4] QUELQUE CHOSE [50] 7-13 (3*) B Doyle (6) *ldg grp, rdn alng one pace appr fnl furlong*..... (10 to 1 op 8 to 1) 3
3998[3] PRINCESS TATEUM (Ire) [65] 9-3 G Duffield (4) *trkd ldr, led o'r 3 fs out, hdd ins last 2 furlongs, sn btn.* .... (11 to 1 op 8 to 1 tchd 12 to 1) 4
3787[4] WHO'S THE BEST (Ire) [51] 7-12 (5*) D McCabe (11) *beh til styd on appr last 2 fs, nrst at finish.* .... (14 to 1 op 10 to 1) 5
4087[3] WOLLBOLL [48] 8-0 T Sprake (1) *in tch til wknd o'r 2 out.* ....(8 to 1 op 7 to 1 tchd 9 to 1) 6
3821 IBTIKAR (USA) [41] (v) 7-7 Kim McDonnell (10) *hld up, effrt o'r 3 out, not rch frnt rnk.* .... (14 to 1 op 12 to 1 tchd 16 to 1) 7
4087* ARMENIAN COFFEE (Ire) [69] (bl) 9-7 D Holland (12) *led til hdd o'r 3 fs out, eased aftr wkng over one out.* .... (13 to 2 op 4 to 1) 8
3840[4] LEGAL RISK [41] 7-4[2] (5*) D Wright (8) *chsd ldrs for 9 fs, sn wknd*................(12 to 1 op 8 to 1 tchd 14 to 1) 9
4092[4] TOP PET (Ire) [64] 9-2 R Perham (13) *hld up in tch, wknd quickly 4 fs out*.....................(10 to 1 op 8 to 1) 10
4256 BOXBOY [41] 7-7 N Adams (9) *al beh.* (25 to 1 op 14 to 1) 11
3881[7] LUNAR RISK [59] 8-11 W Woods (5) *al rear grp.* .... (14 to 1 op 12 to 1) 12
4741a CONBRIO STAR [45] 7-11[4] T Williams (7) *hdwy frm rear and hmpd aftr 5 fs, wknd five furlongs out, tld off.* .... (50 to 1 op 25 to 1) 13

Dist: Hd, 7l, 3l, 2l, 6l, 3l, 1l, 4l, 3½l, 2l. 2m 52.90s. a 22.40s (13 Ran).
(K Higson), R Simpson

REDCAR (good to soft) Tuesday October 5th

Going Correction: PLUS 0.25 sec. per fur. (races 1,4,5,6,7), PLUS 0.45 (2,3)

4342 Malton Claiming Stakes Class F (2-y-o) £3,139 7f................. (2:15)

3997[6] BENEFICIARY 7-12 (3*) S Maloney (18) *al prmnt, led 2 fs out, rdn appr last, ran on wl*.......(7 to 1 tchd 9 to 1) 1
3432[9] SLMAAT 7-8 (7*) Sally Radford-Howes (16) *chsd ldrs, hdwy o'r 2 fs out, ev ch entering last, kpt on.* .... (16 to 1 op 10 to 1) 2
4163[9] NEVER SO TRUE 7-2 (7*) C Adamson (28) *led stands side grp, rdn and hdd 2 fs out, hng lft entering last, kpt on.* ....(16 to 1 op 14 to 1 tchd 20 to 1) 3
GINGERLY (USA) 8-9 Pat Eddery (3) *in tch, hdwy to join ldrs o'r 2 fs out, sn ev ch, rdn appr last, one pace.* ....(5 to 1 op 5 to 2) 4
4051 LAUREL ROMEO (Ire) (bl) 8-10 J Carroll (14) *led centre grp, ev ch 2 fs out, sn rdn, wkng whn hmpd entering last.* .... (25 to 1 op 20 to 1) 5
2973[2] CELESTIAL RUMOUR (Ire) 9-0 K Darley (2) *chsd ldrs far side, hdwy and ch o'r 2 fs out, sn rdn, one pace appr last*..................(9 to 1 op 8 to 1 tchd 10 to 1) 6
4033 MISTY WISE 7-6 (7*) N Varley (1) *cl up far side, rdn wl o'r 2 fs out, sn one pace*............... (20 to 1 op 16 to 1) 7
4081[2] CELESTIAL DANCE 7-11 L Charnock (6) *o'rall ldr far side to hfwy, sn one pace*................. (16 to 1 op 14 to 1) 8
4122 DRAGON MAN 8-4 J Weaver (30) *styd on fnl 2 fs, nvr dngrs*................................(12 to 1 op 10 to 1) 9
4167 WALWORTH LADY 8-7 S Webster (27) *slwly into strd, beh till styd on fnl 2 fs*.................................. (50 to 1) 10
4122 SEMAH'S DREAM 8-1 J O'Reilly (22) *nvr rch ldrs.* ....(100 to 1) 11
3236 RAVEN'S RETURN (Ire) 8-12 S Perks (19) *prmnt centre, rdn o'r 2 fs out, sn btn*.................(14 to 1 op 10 to 1) 12
4163 DENTON QUEEN 8-3 F Norton (20) *nvr rch ldrs.* .... (40 to 1 op 33 to 1) 13
4041[3] BIRCHWOOD STAR 7-7[1] (7*) M Humphries (5) *in tch far side 4 fs*......................(50 to 1 op 33 to 1) 14
CROFT POOL 8-7 (3*) S D Williams (15) *al mid-div.* .... (50 to 1 op 20 to 1) 15
3968* GLORIETTE 8-3 K Fallon (21) *nvr rch ldrs.* ....(4 to 1 fav op 3 to 1) 16
4084[6] HOTCROFT 7-10 (5*) P McCabe (25) *in tch stands side, rdn and beh hfwy*.............................. (50 to 1) 17
3627[9] FIVE AND UP FIVE 7-13 J Fanning (9) *nvr rch ldrs.* ....(16 to 1 tchd 20 to 1) 18
3235 ASTROLOGY 8-1 Kim Tinkler (26) *al rear.* .... (66 to 1 op 50 to 1) 19
4128 MAGIC MAGGIE 7-11 S Wood (12) *nvr a factor.* .... (33 to 1 op 25 to 1) 20
3760 LADY GWEN (Ire) 8-9 Dale Gibson (10) *beh hfwy.* (50 to 1) 21
3972[8] MONKEY FACE 7-11 J Lowe (24) *nvr a factor*.... (20 to 1) 22
4081 JERSEY MONKEY (Ire) 7-4 (7*) P Fessey (13) *al rear.* .... (66 to 1 op 50 to 1) 23
3598 NOWT SPOILING 8-2[5] (7*) G Parkin (11) *al rear.* (100 to 1) 24
4050[4] LITTLE SENOR (Ire) 8-3[2] (7*) J Gracey (7) *nvr a factor.* ....(25 to 1) 25
4192[8] CORSAGE (bl) 8-5[1] M Birch (23) *sn pushed alng, al rear.* .... (40 to 1 op 33 to 1) 26
3406[7] BRAMCOTE CENTURY 7-6 (5*) Darren Moffatt (8) *chsd ldrs far side to hfwy, sn wknd*......................(33 to 1) 27
4032[9] TOOGOODFORYOU 8-6 J Quinn (29) *slwly into strd, al rear*..(100 to 1) 28
ONE FOR THE LADIES 8-7 (7*) J Edmunds (17) *slwly into strd, al beh*..(50 to 1) 29

Dist: 1½l, 1½l, hd, 1½l, ½l, 1½l, 1½l, 1l, 1½l, 1½l. 1m 27.90s. a 6.10s (29 Ran).
SR: 22/17/6/19/15/17/ (Reg Griffin), M H Easterby

4343 Scarborough Handicap Class E (0-70 3-y-o and up) £3,572 1m 1f..... (2:45)

4188[9] EFIZIA [67] 3-9-6 K Darley (16) *in tch, hdwy on outsd 3 fs out, rdn o'r one out, styd on to ld ins last.* .... (9 to 1 op 8 to 1 tchd 10 to 1) 1
4164[5] MEDIA MESSENGER [50] 4-8-8 N Connorton (11) *prmnt, chlgd one and a half fs out, sn rdn, ev ch ins last, not quicken nr finish*................(14 to 1 tchd 16 to 1) 2
4178[8] NO COMEBACKS [55] 5-8-13 K Fallon (13) *hld up, hdwy 3 fs out, effrt and not much room entering last, kpt on.* ....(7 to 1 op 8 to 1) 3
4178 NO SUBMISSION (USA) [55] 7-8-13 S Wood (10) *chsd ldr, led 3 and a half fs out, rdn wl o'r one out, hdd and no extr ins last*.................................... (14 to 1) 4
4241[5] PANTHER (Ire) [59] 3-8-12 J Carroll (14) *chsd ldrs, rdn 2 fs out, edgd lft and one pace entering last.* .... (11 to 1 op 10 to 1 tchd 12 to 1) 5
2874[5] BILOELA [59] 3-8-12 Pat Eddery (1) *hld up, hdwy 3 fs out, rdn o'r one out, kpt on one pace*.... (9 to 1 op 10 to 1) 6
4022[4] ROCK OPERA (Ire) [52] 5-8-10 L Dettori (7) *in tch, rdn 3 fs out, kpt on same pace frm 2 out*............... (12 to 1) 7
3901* SELF EXPRESSION [63] 5-9-0 (7*) D Thomas (9) *mid-div, hdwy on outsd 3 fs out, rdn 2 out, sn one pace.* ....(5 to 1 fav op 4 to 1) 8
SHAKE TOWN (USA) [69] (v) 5-9-13 T Wall (8) *slwly into strd, al rear*.................................... (33 to 1) 9
4235[8] AYIA NAPA [53] 6-8-11 J Quinn (12) *chsd ldrs, rdn o'r 3 fs out, wknd*...................................(25 to 1) 10
3356[9] BRILLIANT [61] 5-9-5 M Wigham (2) *al rear.* .... (15 to 2 op 6 to 1 tchd 8 to 1) 11
4019[9] HABETA (USA) [55] 7-8-13 B Raymond (15) *nvr rch ldrs.* .... (9 to 1 op 8 to 1 tchd 10 to 1) 12
3247[4] MAWAYED (USA) [55] 3-8-8 R Hills (3) *chsd ldrs, rdn 3 fs out, wknd 2 out*................(14 to 1 op 12 to 1) 13
1520[4] INVERTIEL [57] 9-9-1 J Weaver (5) *led, rdn and hdd 3 and a half fs out, sn wknd.* .... (40 to 1 op 33 to 1 tchd 50 to 1) 14
4092* CHIEF OF STAFF [70] 4-10-0 S Webster (6) *slwly into strd, al rear*.............................(10 to 1 op 8 to 1) 15

Dist: ¾l, 1½l, nk, 1l, 2½l, 2½l, nk, 1½l, nk, 3l. 1m 57.60s. a 9.10s (15 Ran).
SR: 30/16/16/14/9/-/ (Mrs H I S Calzini), Mrs M Reveley

4344 Brotton Seafoods Handicap Class D (0-80 3-y-o and up) £5,343 1¾m 19yds ....(3:15)

4143* SAFETY IN NUMBERS [75] 3-9-3 J Quinn (7) *in tch, hdwy 4 fs out, led 2 and a half out, sn clr, unchlgd.* ....(7 to 4 fav op 2 to 1 tchd 9 to 4) 1
3595[3] COLLIER BAY [75] 3-9-3 L Dettori (4) *mid-div, hdwy 5 fs out, effrt on outsd 3 out, sn ev ch, chsd wnr frm 2 out, no imprsn*.......... (100 to 30 op 11 to 4 tchd 7 to 2) 2
3998[2] MONDRAGON [75] 3-9-3 J Lowe (3) *hld up beh, hdwy 3 fs out, rdn and styd on frm 2 out, nrst finish.* ....(9 to 1 op 8 to 1) 3
4143 WESTERN DYNASTY [69] 7-9-1 (5*) P McCabe (12) *prmnt, chlgd 3 fs out, sn rdn, one pace*............... (14 to 1) 4
3724[7] BOLD ELECT [51] 5-8-2[3] A Culhane (1) *hld up beh, hdwy 3 fs out, styd on und pres frm 2 out, not rch ldrs.* .... (33 to 1 op 25 to 1) 5
3881[4] BROCTUNE BAY [67] 4-9-4 K Darley (5) *in tch, hdwy to chase ldrs 4 fs out, sn rdn, one pace.* .... (12 to 1 op 10 to 1) 6
4064 CUMBRIAN RHAPSODY [73] 3-9-1 M Birch (6) *chsd ldrs, led o'r 3 fs out, sn rdn, hdd 2 and a half out, wknd.* ....(7 to 1 op 6 to 1) 7
3513[6] HILL OF DREAMS [73] 3-9-1 Pat Eddery (9) *chsd ldr, rdn 4 fs out, sn wknd*........................ (14 to 1 op 12 to 1) 8
4064 COMME D'HABITUDE (USA) [71] 3-8-13 J Carroll (8) *led, rdn o'r 3 fs out, sn hdd and wknd*..... (14 to 1 op 12 to 1) 9
1276[5] VAIN PRINCE [49] 6-8-0 L Charnock (2) *al rear.* .... (20 to 1 op 25 to 1 tchd 16 to 1) 10
4226 LADY BUCHAN [55] 4-8-6 Kim Tinkler (11) *al rear*. (33 to 1) 11
TRIENNIUM (USA) [77] 4-10-0 J Weaver (10) *al rear, tld off hfwy, virtually pld up 5 fs out*..............(100 to 1) 12
Dist: 4l, 1½l, 3½l, nk, 4l, 7l, 8l, 2½l, 15l, 12l. 3m 7.20s. a 10.70s (12 Ran).
SR: 59/51/48/44/25/33/16/-/-/ (Edwin N Cohen), Lady Herries

4345 EBF Pickering Maiden Fillies' Stakes Class D (2-y-o) £4,270 6f........(3:45)

4011[5] TANSY 8-11 F Norton (1) *chsd ldrs, hdwy o'r 2 fs out, led one and a half out, rdn and ran on wl.* ....(7 to 1 op 4 to 1) 1
4011[7] BEAMING 8-11 B Raymond (3) *chsd ldrs, led o'r 2 fs out to one and a half out, kpt on und pres.* (7 to 1 op 5 to 1) 2
3781[6] BINTALSHAATI 8-11 R Hills (7) *chsd ldrs, effrt and ev ch one and a half fs out, sn rdn, kpt on.* .... (12 to 1 op 10 to 1) 3
680[5] BUSTLE'EM (Ire) 8-11 K Darley (12) *in tch stands side, rdn and styd on one pace fnl 2 fs*...... (33 to 1 op 50 to 1) 4
4103[8] CHAMPAGNE ATEASTER 8-11 K Fallon (5) *rcd centre, o'rall ldr till rdn and hdd over 2 fs out, sn one pace.* .... (33 to 1 op 50 to 1) 5
4103[5] TOPNOTCH 8-11 A Culhane (9) *chsd ldrs, rdn o'r 2 fs out, sn one pace*............................ (20 to 1 op 16 to 1) 6
4098[9] CHANTELYS 8-6 (5*) P McCabe (6) *in tch, rdn alng hfwy, no hdwy*.. (33 to 1) 7
4237 CAFE SOLO 8-11 L Charnock (2) *cl up centre, rdn hfwy, sn wknd*.. (100 to 1) 8
4142[3] ISLAND OF SILVER (USA) 8-11 L Dettori (10) *cl up stands side, rdn and ev ch o'r 2 fs out, sn btn.* ....(15 to 8 on op 13 to 8 on) 9
4103[9] CITY OF MY DREAMS (Ire) 8-6 (5*) Darren Moffatt (4) *al rear.* ....(100 to 1) 10
4190[6] DREAM LANE 8-11 M Birch (11) *beh hfwy.* .... (33 to 1 op 20 to 1) 11
4182[8] ELLASTYLE (Ire) 8-11 S Wood (8) *rear, rdn and hng lft hfwy*..(100 to 1) 12
1632[6] SATLEY LASS 8-4 (7*) J Gracey (13) *cl up stands side to hfwy, sn beh*.................................. (100 to 1) 13
Dist: 1½l, hd, 3l, 1l, 2½l, 1½l, ½l, sht-hd, 2½l, 10l. 1m 13.90s. a 4.20s (13 Ran).
SR: 43/37/36/24/20/10/4/2/1/ (Sheikh Mohammed), G Wragg

4346 Guisborough Maiden Stakes Class D (3-y-o) £3,377 6f...............(4:15)

3693[2] COMMON LAW (Ire) 8-9 Pat Eddery (7) *made all, rdn 2 fs out, styd on wl*...............(11 to 10 fav op Evens) 1
4030[3] TAJHIZ (USA) 9-0 R Hills (8) *cl up, effrt and ev ch 2 fs out, sn rdn, not quicken appr last.* ....(7 to 4 op 6 to 4 tchd 2 to 1) 2
4222[5] KENNEDYS PRIMA 8-9 B Raymond (4) *prmnt, rdn hfwy, sn one pace*......................... (7 to 1 op 8 to 1) 3
PRIDE'S DESIRE 8-2 (7*) V Halliday (6) *beh, rdn hfwy, kpt on fnl 2 fs, not rch ldrs*........... (50 to 1 op 33 to 1) 4
4222 RUSSIA WITH LOVE 8-9 L Dettori (3) *chsd ldrs, rdn hfwy, sn wknd*.................................. (20 to 1 op 16 to 1) 5
4191 TARNSIDE BANKER 9-0 J Lowe (2) *rdn alng aftr 2 fs, sn outpcd and beh*...... (33 to 1 op 20 to 1 tchd 50 to 1) 6
4191 MILLEMAY 8-9 J Weaver (5) *in tch and rdn alng, beh hfwy*........................... (66 to 1 op 50 to 1) 7
Dist: 2½l, 8l, 2½l, 20l, 2l, 6l. 1m 13.40s. a 3.70s (7 Ran).
SR: 51/46/9/-/ (Mrs Nicole Myers), R Charlton

4347 Castleton Conditions Stakes Class D (3-y-o and up) £3,260 7f........(4:45)

1208[4] PATER NOSTER (USA) 4-9-2 R Hills (3) *made all, rdn and quickened 2 fs out, clr appr last, ran on wl.* ....(2 to 1 op 7 to 4) 1
4040[3] VENTURE CAPITALIST (bl) 4-9-2 Pat Eddery (1) *dwlt, sn in tch, pushed alng and hdwy 2 and a half fs out, chsd wnr und pres appr last, no imprsn.* ....(11 to 8 fav tchd 6 to 4) 2
4040 MASTER OF PASSION 4-9-0 M Tebbutt (4) *cl up, rdn 2 fs out, sn one pace*....................(6 to 1 op 5 to 1) 3
4040 BRIGADE 4-9-4 L Dettori (2) *cl up, rdn alng o'r 2 fs out, sn one pace*..(5 to 1) 4
Dist: 3½l, 2½l, nk. 1m 25.80s. a 4.00s (4 Ran).
SR: 68/57/47/50/ (Martin Myers), Mrs J Cecil

4348 Settrington Handicap Class E (0-70 3-y-o) £3,779 7f................ (5:15)

3736[5] NITOUCHE [62] 9-2 K Darley (9) *chsd ldrs centre, rdn 2 fs out, styd on to ld appr last, kpt on wl.* ....(14 to 1 tchd 16 to 1) 1
4158[3] MHEMEANLES [61] (bl) 8-12 (3*) S Maloney (20) *cl up stands side, led one and a half fs out, rdn, edgd lft and hdd appr last, rallied and edged rght ins last.* .... (10 to 1 op 8 to 1 tchd 11 to 1) 2
3213* GLEN MILLER [60] 9-0 L Dettori (13) *o'rall ldr centre, rdn and hdd one and a half fs out, kpt on und pres.* .... (16 to 1 op 14 to 1) 3
2953[3] MUSTN'T GRUMBLE (Ire) [58] 8-12 J Carroll (6) *in tch centre, effrt 2 fs out, sn rdn, kpt on one pace.* .... (12 to 1 op 10 to 1) 4
4043[7] SUSPECT [42] 7-5 (5*) Darren Moffatt (8) *rcd centre, beh till styd on fnl 2 fs*.................................. (33 to 1) 5
4031[3] MISS KINABALU [47] 8-1 F Norton (14) *cl up centre, rdn 2 fs out, kpt on one pace*.............. (20 to 1 op 14 to 1) 6
3630[9] SILVER STANDARD [45] (bl) 7-13 J Quinn (4) *led far side grp, rdn and one pace fnl 2 fs*..... (16 to 1 op 14 to 1) 7
3863[4] DAILY SPORT DON [67] 9-7 Pat Eddery (16) *dispuuted ld stands side, rdn and hng lft o'r one and a half fs out, sn wknd*............................ (12 to 1 op 10 to 1) 8
4181[3] EGG [56] (bl) 8-10 J Lowe (18) *chsd ldrs, rdn o'r 2 fs out, no imprsn*........................(6 to 1 fav tchd 7 to 1) 9
4235* CAN CAN CHARLIE [54] 8-8 (6ex) J Weaver (23) *chsd ldrs stands side, rdn o'r 2 fs out, sn btn*.. (7 to 1 op 5 to 1) 10
3745[7] NORLING (Ire) [50] 8-4 L Charnock (21) *chsd ldrs stands side, rdn and wknd o'r 2 fs out*.... (20 to 1 op 16 to 1) 11
3564 SPORTING SPIRIT [39] 7-7 S Wood (27) *nvr rch ldrs.* ....(50 to 1) 12+
4181 FADAKI HAWAKI (USA) [50] 8-4[1] B Raymond (11) *cl up centre, rdn and wknd o'r 2 fs out.* (20 to 1 op 16 to 1) 12+
3460[5] DIVINE BOY [56] (v) 8-5 (5*) P McCabe (22) *chsd ldrs stands side 4 fs*......................... (20 to 1 tchd 25 to 1) 14
3280 OUBECK [65] 9-5 M Tebbutt (1) *prmnt 4 fs far side.* ....(33 to 1) 15
4317[2] COCONUT JOHNNY [53] 8-2[2] (7*) R Painter (7) *nvr rch ldrs.* .... (9 to 1 op 10 to 1 tchd 12 to 1) 16
4045 BRIGADORE GOLD [39] 7-4[4] (7*) A Whelan (24) *nvr a factor*.. (50 to 1) 17
4235 MONTONE (Ire) [53] 8-7 K Fallon (3) *rcd far side, beh hfwy.* ....(33 to 1) 18
3794 HUMBER'S SUPREME (Ire) [41] (v) 7-4[2] (7*) N Varley (26) *al rear*..............................(50 to 1 op 33 to 1) 19
4224[3] NELLIE'S GAMBLE [42] 7-3 (7*) C Adamson (5) *outpcd.* .... (8 to 1 op 10 to 1) 20
3758 ROBIX (Ire) [39] 7-2[2] (7*) C Teague (10) *slwly into strd, al rear*...(50 to 1) 21
4166 NORTH ARDAR [63] 9-3 R P Elliott (15) *nvr rch ldrs.* ....(20 to 1) 22
4217[7] KEEP BATTLING [47] (v) 8-1[1] R Lappin (17) *beh hfwy.* ....(50 to 1 op 33 to 1) 23
4018 BALIANA [60] (bl) 9-0 A Culhane (25) *al beh.* .... (25 to 1 op 20 to 1) 24
3358 UMBUBUZI (USA) [63] 9-3 S Perks (12) *cl up centre, rdn and wknd o'r 2 fs out*...........................(33 to 1) 25
3789 OSCAR THE SECOND (Ire) [41] 7-9 J Fanning (19) *chsd ldrs stands side, rdn and wknd 3 fs out*...........(50 to 1) 26
Dist: ½l, 2½l, 3l, 1l, nk, 1½l, sht-hd, 1l, 1½l, 3½l. 1m 27.20s. a 5.40s (26 Ran).
SR: 47/44/35/24/5/9/2/23/9/ (D A Shekells), A Hide

WARWICK (soft (races 1,2,3), heavy (4,5,6,7,8))

Tuesday October 5th

Going Correction: PLUS 0.70 sec. per fur.

4349 EBF Maiden Fillies' Stakes Class D (Div I) (2-y-o) £4,378 7f..........(1:30)

715[7] FORGOTTEN LADY (Ire) 8-11 T Quinn (7) *made all, clr hfwy, tacked across to stands side strt, tired ins fnl furlong*.............. (10 to 1 op 8 to 1 tchd 11 to 1) 1
4098[7] SHARP FALCON (Ire) 8-11 J Williams (4) *mid-div, rdn and ran on frm o'r one furlong out, kpt on wl.* ....(6 to 1 op 6 to 1) 2
LITTLE BEDWYN (USA) 8-11 J Reid (1) *dwlt, beh, cld on ldrs hfwy, ran on fnl furlong.* ....(2 to 1 fav op 6 to 4 tchd 9 to 4) 3
LESLEY'S FASHION 8-11 L Piggott (8) *beh, rdn alng o'r 2 fs out, styd on ins last, nvr dngrs*..... (10 to 1 op 6 to 1) 4

3960^{6} THIRD DAM 8-11 R Street (6) *strted slwly, hdwy o'r 2 fs out, nvr nr to chal*..... (10 to 1 op 8 to 1 tchd 7 to 1) 5
SHUTTLINGSLOW 8-11 M Hills (10) *outpcd till ran on ins fnl furlong*..................... (10 to 1 op 7 to 1) 6
3186^{6} SHIFTING MIST 8-11 C Nutter (9) *chsd ldrs till outpcd fnl 2 fs*............................ (12 to 1 tchd 10 to 1) 7
4121^{6} DANIELLE HABIBI (Ire) 8-11 W Newnes (11) *outpcd*. ....(33 to 1) 8
2668^{9} BIRD OF THE WIND 8-11 D Harrison (3) *cl up till wknd wl o'r one furlong out*......................... (50 to 1) 9
625^{8} MISS RISKY 8-11 A McGlone (5) *cl up till lost pl quickly 4 fs out*.. (10 to 1) 10
3979 PRINCESS TALLULAH 8-6 (5*) S Drowne (2) *cl up, rdn alng o'r 3 fs out, btn wl over one out*.............. (50 to 1) 11
Dist: ½l, hd, 10l, 4l, ¾l, ½l, nk, 5l, 5l, 2½l. 1m 34.80s. a 11.00s (11 Ran).
SR: 5/3/2/-/-/-/ (Mrs Linda Gardiner), P F I Cole

4350 EBF Maiden Fillies' Stakes Class D (Div II) (2-y-o) £4,342 7f......... (2:00)

4089^{4} SUGAR TOWN (Ire) 8-11 T Quinn (5) *trkd ldrs, led o'r 3 fs out, edgd lft and hdd briefly over one out, ran on wl*. .... (11 to 2 op 6 to 1 tchd 7 to 1) 1
3828^{5} VIRGINIA WATER (USA) 8-11 A Munro (2) *cl up, led 4 fs out till o'r 3 out, led ag'n briefly over one out, ev ch ins last, no extr nr finish*.............. (3 to 1 fav tchd 4 to 1) 2
3389^{9} SWITCH BLADE (Ire) 8-11 M Hills (9) *beh, hdwy 3 fs out, kpt on one pace*.................... (7 to 1 op 6 to 1) 3
4089^{8} DEVOTEE 8-11 Paul Eddery (4) *trkd ldrs, pushed alng and one pace frm o'r 2 fs out*............ (4 to 1 op 3 to 1) 4
3939^{5} VOLTERRA 8-11 A McGlone (1) *trkd ldrs, rdn and outpcd appr 2 fs out*...................... (6 to 1 op 5 to 1) 5
1955^{9} IT'S SO EASY 8-11 J Fortune (3) *chsd ldrs till outpcd o'r 2 fs out*.................................. (8 to 1 op 6 to 1) 6
3895^{7} NUIN-TARA 8-8 (3*) Stephen Davies (10) *al beh*... (50 to 1) 7
HI KIKI 8-11 A Tucker (6) *strted very slwly, cld on ldrs hfwy, rdn o'r 2 fs out, wknd over one out*..... (33 to 1) 8
RED BOUQUET 8-11 C Nutter (7) *rdn alng thrght, al beh*. ....(7 to 1 op 6 to 1) 9
TEN-TO-SIX GIRL (bl) 8-11 L Piggott (8) *rcd freely, led, sn clr, hdd and wknd quickly 4 fs out*...(7 to 1 op 5 to 2) 10
Dist: 1l, 5l, 5l, 4l, hd, ¾l, nk, 6l, 10l. 1m 34.50s. a 10.70s (10 Ran).
SR: 10/7/-/-/-/-/ (Lord Portman), P F I Cole

4351 Toplis And Harding Nursery Class E (2-y-o) £3,418 7f................ (2:30)

3490* LINK MILES [83] 9-7 J Reid (14) *made all, clr appr 2 fs out, drvn out ins last*...(5 to 1 jt-fav op 3 to 1 tchd 6 to 1) 1
4230* WIZARD KING [59] 7-11 (8ex) D Biggs (9) *chsd ldrs, chased wnr fnl 2 fs, kpt on*........... (5 to 1 jt-fav op 5 to 2) 2
3905^{8} ARABOYBILL [67] 8-5 A Clark (13) *trkd ldrs, rdn o'r 2 fs out, sn outpcd*.................. (16 to 1 op 14 to 1) 3
3958^{7} RISK OF FIRE [60] 7-12 D Harrison (12) *cl up, rdn alng o'r 2 fs out, sn outpcd*.................. (6 to 1 op 10 to 1) 4
4251 EXOTIC FOREST [62] 8-0 N Carlisle (8) *outpcd, hdwy o'r 2 fs out, nvr nrr*.................. (16 to 1 tchd 12 to 1) 5
3009 RED TAR [63] 8-1^{1} A Munro (11) *trkd ldrs till wknd wl o'r 2 fs out*..................... (20 to 1 op 16 to 1) 6
4165 MONKEY MUSIC [70] (bl) 8-8 T Quinn (15) *chsd ldrs, cld hfwy, drvn o'r 2 fs out, sn btn*..... (14 to 1 op 10 to 1) 7
3287 JOYRIDER [61] 7-13^{1} A Mackay (3) *sn beh*. .... (14 to 1 op 12 to 1) 8
4114 ROCKETEER (Ire) [69] 8-7 W Newnes (2) *mid-div, cld on ldrs 4 fs out, wknd appr 3 out*................ (16 to 1) 9
4021^{5} MILLICENT NORTH [77] 9-1 J Williams (6) *al beh*. .... (8 to 1 op 16 to 1) 10
3989^{3} KILLING TIME [65] 8-3 A McGlone (5) *al beh*. ....(11 to 1 op 10 to 1 tchd 14 to 1) 11
4105^{6} MENTMORE LAD [58] 7-10^{6} (3*) N Kennedy (10) *beh, hdwy o'r 3 fs out, btn over 2 out*......... (20 to 1 op 16 to 1) 12
4051^{7} TIMES ZANDO [65] 8-3 J Fortune (1) *broke wl, cl up till lost pl aftr 3 fs*..............(9 to 1 op 8 to 1 tchd 10 to 1) 13
3743 MITSIS [60] 7-12 W Carson (7) *strted slwly, al beh, tld off*. ....(16 to 1) 14
Dist: 1½l, 12l, sht-hd, 3l, 1½l, 4l, 4l, 1l, 10l, 1½l. 1m 32.70s. a 8.90s (14 Ran).
SR: 47/18/-/-/-/-/ (The Winning Team), R Hannon

4352 Autumn Conditions Stakes Class D (3-y-o and up) £3,143 1½m 115yds (3:00)

3904^{2} IVORY PALM (USA) 3-8-3 Paul Eddery (1) *led, rdn alng o'r 6 fs out, hdd over 5 out, rallied und pres to ld ag'n wl ins last*.. (7 to 2 op 3 to 1) 1
4150^{4} TOMOS 3-8-12 M Hills (2) *trkd ldr, led o'r 5 fs out, hdd and no extr wl ins last*.............. (7 to 4 jt-fav op 6 to 4) 2
4160^{3} BADIE (USA) (bl) 4-9-6 W Carson (5) *hld up in tch, rdn alng 5 fs out, outpcd 3 out, styd on frm o'r one out*. .... (6 to 1 tchd 11 to 2 and 13 to 2) 3
3727* ICE POOL (USA) 3-8-7 M Roberts (3) *hld up in tch, rdn alng o'r 4 fs out, btn wl over 2 out, eased*......(7 to 4 jt-fav op 6 to 4 tchd 2 to 1) 4
924 CITY LINE 4-9-2 A Tucker (4) *al beh, tld off fnl 4 fs*. .... (33 to 1 op 25 to 1) 5
Dist: 1l, 20l, 15l, 1½l. 2m 57.80s. a 19.90s (Flag start) (5 Ran).
(K Abdulla), J H M Gosden

4353 Racing Schools Tote Apprentices' Handicap Class F (0-70 3-y-o and up) £2,892 2m 20yds............... (3:30)

4046^{3} FOLLINGWORTH GIRL (Ire) [52] 3-8-8 D Harrison (12) *rcd wide thrght, al hndy, led 9 fs out, clr o'r 3 out, styd on wl*.................... (9 to 1 op 7 to 1 tchd 10 to 1) 1
4176* KEYLOCK (USA) [56] 3-8-12 N Kennedy (7) *nvr far away, chsd wnr frm o'r 3 fs out, ev ch one out, sn no extr*. ....(2 to 1 fav op 3 to 1) 2
4102^{3} CHILD STAR (Fr) [41] 4-8-8 Claire Balding (9) *beh, hdwy 6 fs out, styd on frm 2 out*... (5 to 1 op 9 to 2 tchd 7 to 1) 3
3943^{9} SPORTS VIEW [41] 4-8-8 S Drowne (14) *hld up in rear, hdwy hfwy, kpt on und pres fnl 2 fs*. (9 to 1 op 5 to 1) 4
3412^{7} INTREPID LASS [44] 6-8-8 (3*) S Drake (6) *led aftr 4 fs till hdd 9 furlongs out, lost pl o'r 6 out, styd on fnl 2 furlongs*....(15 to 2 op 6 to 1 tchd 8 to 1 and 9 to 1) 5
4102^{8} BEAU QUEST [40] (bl) 6-8-7 A Garth (10) *beh, hdwy o'r 6 fs out, rdn and btn 2 out*............(20 to 1 op 16 to 1) 6
4086 JUPITER MOON [57] 4-9-3 (7*) Carol Davison (4) *dsptd ld 4 fs, trkd ldrs till drpd out hfwy*............... (33 to 1) 7
4234^{5} GAMEFULL GOLD [34] 4-7-12 (3*) A Martinez (5) *mid-div, cld hfwy, outpcd frm o'r 3 fs out*. .... (16 to 1 op 14 to 1 tchd 20 to 1) 8
4046^{2} SCOTTISH WEDDING [54] (v) 3-8-10 S Sanders (3) *took keen hold in mid-div, effrt hfwy, wknd o'r 3 fs out*. .... (9 to 1 op 7 to 1 tchd 10 to 1) 9
ACCESS SUN [48] 6-9-1 Mark Denaro (13) *trkd ldrs till rdn and wknd o'r 2 fs out*............ (25 to 1 op 16 to 1) 10
4046* MOUNTAIN WILLOW [55] 3-8-11 S Mulvey (1) *dsptd ld 4 fs, cl up till rdn and wknd 6 furlongs out*. .... (9 to 1 op 8 to 1 tchd 10 to 1) 11
4267 MOHAYA (USA) [45] 3-8-1^{4} (3*) D Griffiths (11) *dsptd ld 4 fs, lost pl hfwy*.. (33 to 1) 12
2943^{3} NAAWY [56] 3-8-12 K Rutter (8) *al beh, tld off*. .... (20 to 1 op 16 to 1) 13
Dist: 2½l, 12l, 4l, 1l, 5l, 1l, ¾l, 10l, 1½l, 1½l. 3m 54.70s. a 29.20s (13 Ran).
(John L Holdroyd), S G Norton

4354 Vauxhall Master Hire Claming Handicap Class F (0-60 3-y-o and up) £3,015 1¼m 169yds................... (4:00)

4088^{2} SKY BURST [42] 3-8-5 N Carlisle (8) *made all, rdn alng o'r one furlong out, ran on wl*........ (14 to 1 op 12 to 1) 1
3891^{4} MAI PEN RAI [43] 5-8-13 A Munro (5) *al prmnt, chsd wnr into strt, one pace und pres*........(7 to 1 tchd 8 to 1) 2
4110 TAUTEN (Ire) [47] 3-8-10 J Reid (14) *hdwy to chase ldrs hfwy, 3rd strt, one pace und pres*.... (6 to 1 op 4 to 1) 3
4256* HEAD TURNER [40] 5-8-10 (6ex) Paul Eddery (6) *rdn and hdwy 3 fs out, hrd drvn to hold ev ch one out, sn one pace*.................................. (11 to 2 fav op 7 to 1) 4
4213^{4} GOLD SURPRISE (Ire) [46] 4-9-2 J Fortune (10) *chsd ldrs, rdn alng 3 fs out, one pace*..........(6 to 1 op 5 to 1) 5
4036^{2} PREMIER DANCE [44] 6-9-0 A Mackay (19) *trkd ldrs, rdn 2 fs out, eased whn hld ins last*................. (8 to 1) 6
3669^{6} FORMAL AFFAIR [52] 3-8-8 (7*) J D Smith (13) *chsd ldrs till wknd 4 fs out*......... (7 to 1 op 6 to 1 tchd 15 to 2) 7
2673 ROCK THE BARNEY (Ire) [48] 4-9-1 (3*) C Hodgson (15) *beh, some modest late hdwy, nvr nr to chal*........ (20 to 1) 8
4187^{7} YEVEED (Ire) [45] (bl) 3-8-8 M Roberts (2) *beh, hdwy hfwy, wknd 3 fs out*.......................................(10 to 1) 9
4115^{4} CHANDIGARH [50] 5-8-13 (7*) P Bowe (16) *chsd ldrs till wknd o'r 5 fs out*.................(14 to 1 op 12 to 1) 10
4087^{6} PRINCE SONGLINE [50] 3-8-13 W Ryan (9) *nvr dngrs*. ....(11 to 1 op 10 to 1 tchd 12 to 1) 11
3759 DON'T FORGET MARIE (Ire) [45] 3-8-8 W Carson (1) *cl up till lost pl hfwy*..................... (14 to 1 tchd 12 to 1) 12
ROXY RIVER [48] 4-9-4 A Tucker (20) *al beh*...... (33 to 1) 13
3981 THE SNOUT [49] 3-8-12 T Rogers (17) *beh, shortlived effrt 5 fs out, sn btn*...(33 to 1) 14
3655 TIGER CLAW (USA) [46] (bl) 7-9-2 A McGlone (12) *wth wnr till wknd o'r 4 fs out*.............. (16 to 1 op 14 to 1) 15
3734^{4} SHALHOLME [45] 3-8-8 J Williams (3) *al beh*. ....(8 to 1 op 7 to 1) 16
4035^{6} NORTHERN JUDY (Ire) [44] (v) 3-8-2 (5*) A Garth (4) *al beh*. ....(20 to 1 tchd 33 to 1) 17
SULTAN'S SON [54] 7-9-10 V Slattery (18) *nvr gng wl, sn beh, tld off*...........................(33 to 1 op 20 to 1) 18
Dist: 2l, sht-hd, hd, 4l, 7l, 12l, ¾l, 10l, 2l, hd. 2m 30.90s. a 18.10s (Flag start) (18 Ran).
(Mrs D Jenks), L G Cottrell

4355 Ann Hathaway Limited Stakes Class D (0-70 3-y-o and up) £3,786 1m... (4:30)

4090 SECOND CHANCE (Ire) 3-9-0 W Newnes (11) *made all, rdn out*...................... (14 to 1 op 12 to 1) 1
4258* LAWNSWOOD JUNIOR 6-9-4 G Hind (8) *mid-div, cld hfwy, chsd wnr into strt, ev ch one furlong out, no extr*. .... (11 to 2 op 4 to 1) 2
4131^{9} KNOBBLEENEEZE (v) 3-9-0 T Quinn (3) *trkd ldrs, pushed alng o'r 2 fs out, one pace*......... (12 to 1 op 10 to 1) 3
4241* DANNY BOY 3-9-0 J Reid (9) *chsd ldrs, outpcd fnl 2 fs*. ....(9 to 4 fav op 7 to 2 tchd 4 to 1) 4

4087 KNYAZ 3-9-0 N Carlisle (4) *sn tld off in rear, styd on frm o'r one furlong out*..............(33 to 1 op 20 to 1) 5
3983^{5} CHAPKA (Ire) 3-8-9 L Piggott (10) *trkd ldrs till rdn and wknd o'r 2 fs out*.....(11 to 1 op 10 to 1 tchd 12 to 1) 6
3883 YOUNG FREEMAN (USA) 4-9-4 M Perrett (6) *cl up till wknd 2 fs out*..........................(16 to 1 op 12 to 1) 7
4092 CONFRONTER (v) 4-9-4 W Ryan (7) *chsd ldrs, cld o'r 3 fs out, btn wl over 2 out.* (11 to 1 op 6 to 1 tchd 12 to 1) 8
3986^{7} BARFORD LAD 6-9-4 W Carson (1) *prmnt til drpd out hfwy, eased whn btn*............(8 to 1 tchd 10 to 1) 9
2227^{4} ALASKAN PRINCESS (Ire) 3-8-9 A Munro (2) *beh, effrt and cld hfwy, sn btn*....................(12 to 1 op 8 to 1) 10
747^{3} TIMOTHY CASEY 3-9-0 A Tucker (12) *stumbled strt, sn tld off*...................(16 to 1 op 14 to 1 tchd 20 to 1) 11
4024 WILL SOON 4-8-11 (7*) S Drake (5) *prmnt, pushed alng hfwy, sn lost pl*..................(14 to 1 op 12 to 1) 12

Dist: 2l, 10l, 6l, 3l, ¾l, ¾l, 6l, 6l, 8l, 1½l. 1m 47.00s. a 10.20s (12 Ran).

SR: 31/29/-/-/-/-/ (Down And Outs Racing), P Mitchell

4356 EBF Brinklow Maiden Stakes Class D (2-y-o) £4,807 7f.................(5:00)

3990^{2} STOLLER (USA) 9-0 Paul Eddery (18) *made all, shaken up 2 fs out, easily*......................(7 to 2 op 5 to 2) 1
3352 CASTLE COMBE (Ire) 9-0 J Reid (19) *chsd ldrs, pushed alng hfwy, chased wnr frm o'r one furlong out, one pace*..............................(10 to 1 op 3 to 1) 2
4192^{7} CLARION CALL (Ire) 9-0 A Munro (15) *al cl up, rdn and one pace fnl 2 fs*......................(16 to 1 op 12 to 1) 3
698^{6} PASSING PLAYER (USA) 9-0 M Hills (17) *trkd ldrs, one pace fnl 2 fs*............................(16 to 1 op 8 to 1) 4
4127^{3} SAGASAN 9-0 W Newnes (10) *chsd ldrs, rdn and cld 2 fs out, sn one pace*.................. (16 to 1 op 10 to 1) 5
COLONEL COLT 8-12^{3} (5*) A Procter (16) *mid-div styd on frm o'r one furlong out, nrst finish.* ....(50 to 1 op 20 to 1) 6
4099^{8} FAIR COURT 9-0 R Cochrane (12) *nvr nr to chal.* ....(20 to 1 op 12 to 1) 7
3979 GAY DEVIL 9-0 A Clark (2) *chsd ldrs till wknd o'r 2 fs out.* .... (20 to 1 op 14 to 1) 8
REAL MADRID 9-0 M Perrett (14) *nvr better than mid-div.* .... (50 to 1 op 20 to 1) 9
3264 GRANBY BELL (bl) 9-0 A Mackay (20) *wth wnr till wknd 2 fs out*............................(33 to 1 op 16 to 1) 10
DIA GEORGY 8-7 (7*) S Eiffert (11) *al beh.* ....(33 to 1 op 20 to 1) 11
4149^{3} MAPENGO 9-0 W Carson (1) *missed break, slwly into strd, al beh*.........(5 to 2 fav op 5 to 4 tchd 11 to 4) 12
4210 CLUBS ARE TRUMPS (Ire) 9-0 D Biggs (9) *chsd ldrs till wknd hfwy*......................(50 to 1 op 25 to 1) 13
3352 RAVEN'S ROOST (Ire) 9-0 A Tucker (6) *nvr dngrs.* .... (15 to 2 op 33 to 1 tchd 6 to 1) 14
4033^{7} KELLYSI 9-0 T Quinn (4) *chsd ldrs, beh frm hfwy.* .... (25 to 1 op 10 to 1) 15
3713^{5} BLUE DOMAIN 9-0 W Ryan (3) *strted slwly, reco'red quickly to track ldrs, wknd over 2 fs out*...... (33 to 1) 16
4029^{5} REED MY LIPS (Ire) 9-0 J Williams (7) *al beh.* .... (9 to 1 op 10 to 1) 17
3793^{4} HARLESTONE FIRS 9-0 A McGlone (8) *strted slwly, al beh.* .... (25 to 1 op 16 to 1) 18
RONALDSWAY 9-0 D Harrison (5) *al beh.* .... (16 to 1 op 8 to 1) 19

Dist: 3½l, 3½l, ½l, 2l, 8l, 2l, ½l, ¾l, ½l, 1½l. 1m 35.10s. a 11.30s (19 Ran).
SR: 4/-/-/-/-/-/ (Dr Howard J Baker), Mrs J Cecil

HAYDOCK (soft)
Wednesday October 6th
Going Correction: PLUS 0.50 sec. per fur.

4357 Racing Schools' Apprentices' Handicap Class E (0-70 3-y-o and up) £3,095 1¾m..........................(2:10)

4218^{7} PHILGUN [56] (v) 4-9-5 N Kennedy (3) *al hndy, led and kicked for hme o'r 3 fs out, styd on wl fnl furlong.* ....(12 to 1 tchd 14 to 1) 1
4218^{5} MOONSHINE DANCER [40] 3-7-2 (6*) D Denby (11) *nvr far away, chsd alng last 3 fs, ev ch ins last, kpt on same pace*................(12 to 1 tchd 16 to 1 and 10 to 1) 2
3239^{4} DOMINANT SERENADE [41] 4-8-4 J Marshall (13) *trkd ldg quartet, and drvn alng last 3 fs, styd on ins fnl furlong.* ....(16 to 1) 3
4143 HIERARCH (USA) [65] 4-10-0 D Harrison (1) *settled off the pace, swtchd o'r to race stands side strt, styd on last 2 fs, nvr nrr*............................(10 to 1 op 8 to 1) 4
3943^{2} LA MENORQUINA (USA) [61] 3-9-1 J Weaver (20) *patiently rdn, improved entering strt, kpt on wl last 2 fs, nvr nrr.* ....(8 to 1) 5
4036^{5} GOODBYE MILLIE [66] 3-9-3 (3*) T Marsden (9) *tucked away on ins, effrt and pushed alng entering strt, styd on, not pace to chal*.............................. (12 to 1) 6
3961 HEATHYARDS BOY [60] 3-9-0 A Garth (2) *trkd ldg bunch, swtchd to race stands side strt, rdn and no imprsn last 2 fs*............................(20 to 1 tchd 16 to 1) 7
4035^{5} FIRST FLING (Ire) [48] 4-8-11 K Rutter (16) *settled midfield, feeling pace and drvn alng entering strt, sn struggling.* ....(12 to 1 op 10 to 1) 8
702^{5} SILLARS STALKER (Ire) [54] 5-9-3 Stephen Davies (18) *patiently rdn, steady hdwy entering strt, styd on last 3 fs, nvr nrr*.............(9 to 1 op 7 to 1 tchd 10 to 1) 9
3412* SCALP 'EM (Ire) [37] 5-8-0 R Havlin (19) *settled midfield, bustled alng o'r 3 fs out, sn outpcd*............(14 to 1) 10
4256^{3} STREPHON (Ire) [49] 3-8-3 S Mulvey (6) *dictated pace, jnd hfwy, hdd o'r 3 fs out, fdd*.........(8 to 1 tchd 9 to 1) 11
MY TURN NEXT [30] 5-7-6^{5} (6*) A Eddery (14) *sluggish strt, drvn alng hfwy, nvr a factor*................. (50 to 1) 12
4102 KAUSAR (USA) [48] 6-8-11 J Tate (8) *trkd ldg trio, rdn whn pace quickened o'r 3 fs out, one pace.* ....(11 to 1 op 12 to 1 tchd 10 to 1) 13
4129 HONEY DANCER [41] 9-8-4^{3} R Painter (12) *trkd ldrs, drw level hfwy, rdn alng 3 fs out, fdd.* (50 to 1 op 33 to 1) 14
1929^{4} ENFANT DU PARADIS (Ire) [36] 5-7-13 Claire Balding (10) *trkd ldg pair, rdn o'r 3 fs out, sn btn*.........(16 to 1) 15
4102 QAFFAL (USA) [61] (bl) 3-9-1 S Maloney (15) *trkd ldg half dozen, effrt appr strt, btn 3 fs out*.............(20 to 1) 16
CENTENARY STAR [40] 8-8-3^{8} (3*) D Griffiths (17) *chsd ldg bunch to strt, sn struggling*....................(20 to 1) 17+
4017^{4} PERSUASIVE [60] 6-9-6 (3*) S Copp (5) *drvn alng in rear thrght, nvr a factor*.............(6 to 1 fav op 5 to 1) 17+
626^{2} ISLAND BLADE (Ire) [60] 4-9-9 L Carter (7) *co'red up in midfield, swtchd to race stands side strt, nvr a factor.* ....(10 to 1) 19
4176 RAVENSPUR (Ire) [42] 3-7-7 (3*) M Baird (4) *beh and drvn alng hfwy, nvr a factor*......................(33 to 1) 20

Dist: 2l, 1½l, 4l, 5l, 1½l, 5l, 3l, 2l, 3½l, 12l. 3m 17.18s. a 19.68s (20 Ran).

(C D Barber-Lomax), C W C Elsey

4358 Maple Selling Nursery Class G (2-y-o) £2,589 6f...................... (2:40)

4042^{6} MONKEY'S WEDDING [66] (bl) 9-3 J Carroll (2) *made all far side, quickened up last 2 fs, kpt on wl fnl furlong.* ....(14 to 1) 1
4165^{8} CHEERFUL GROOM (Ire) [52] 8-0 (3*) N Kennedy (3) *chsd alng far side, gd hdwy last 2 fs, fnshd strly*... (33 to 1) 2
4032^{3} LITTLE IBNR [50] 8-1 D Harrison (19) *dictated stands side thrght, ev ch and rdn 2 fs out, styd on same pace.* ....(6 to 1 fav op 10 to 1) 3
4081^{6} ROCHE ABBEY (Ire) [57] 8-8 J Weaver (14) *wl plcd stands side, bustled alng 2 fs out, kpt on same pace.* .... (14 to 1 op 12 to 1) 4
4106^{7} SUSELJA (Ire) [53] 8-4 S Whitworth (1) *chsd far side ldrs, effrt and rdn hfwy, not quicken last 2 fs*...... (33 to 1) 5
3762 SWEET WHISPER [54] 8-5 K Darley (8) *chsd far side ldrs, effrt hfwy, rdn and one pace fnl furlong.* .... (11 to 1 op 10 to 1) 6
4163^{3} ONCE MORE FOR LUCK (Ire) [66] 9-3 R Cochrane (11) *bustled alng and sn outpcd, improved towards centre last 2 fs, nvr nrr*..................... (7 to 1 tchd 15 to 2) 7
4269^{4} SKIPTAMALOO [61] 8-12 A Munro (22) *pressed stands side ldrs, drvn alng o'r 2 fs out, kpt on one pace.* .... (7 to 1 op 11 to 2) 8
3386^{7} CONNECT (Ire) [65] 8-9 (7*) A Lakeman (20) *shwd up wl stands side, rdn 2 fs out, not quicken*......... (14 to 1) 9
4228^{6} SADDAM THE LOG [62] 8-13 A Mackay (7) *pressed wnr far side, rdn o'r 2 fs out, btn appr fnl furlong.* ....(11 to 1 op 10 to 1 tchd 12 to 1) 10
4163^{5} MARBLE [52] 7-12 (5*) Darren Moffatt (9) *drvn alng far side, effrt hfwy, no imprsn last 2 fs*................(16 to 1) 11
4163^{6} MISS KATIE LOUISE [52] 8-3 G Hind (4) *chsd far side ldrs, effrt and drvn alng o'r 2 fs out, not pace to chal.* ....(25 to 1) 12
2502^{9} ELLARUTH (Ire) [57] 8-8 P Robinson (6) *bustled alng beh far side ldrs, no imprsn last 2 fs*....(16 to 1 op 14 to 1) 13
3390^{5} JOBISDUN [59] 8-3 (7*) Mark Denaro (17) *chsd alng to keep up, no imprsn last 2 fs*............(16 to 1 op 14 to 1) 14
3688^{4} STRAPPED [56] 8-7 N Adams (24) *drvn alng stands side, no imprsn frm hfwy*..............(11 to 1 op 10 to 1) 15
4114^{8} MOUNT LEINSTER [69] 9-1 (5*) S Drowne (12) *rdn to go pace hfwy, nvr on terms*..........(16 to 1 op 12 to 1) 16
3903 KENTUCKY FLYER [52] 8-3 L Charnock (5) *drvn alng far side, nvr able to rch ldrs*..........(20 to 1 op 16 to 1) 17
3993^{7} STRANGERSARDANGERS (Ire) [50] 7-8 (7*) Angela Gallimore (15) *missed break, nvr a factor*..... (33 to 1 op 25 to 1) 18
4318 ROSIE VALENTINE [54] 8-2 (3*) Stephen Davies (21) *drvn alng stands side, nvr trble ldrs*..... (10 to 1 op 8 to 1) 19
4193 CHEEKY CHAPPY [50] (bl) 8-1 A McGlone (13) *struggling to go pace aftr 2 fs, nvr a threat*.................. (33 to 1) 20
3539^{7} SIGANCA [70] 9-4 (3*) M Fenton (23) *chsd stands side ldrs to hfwy, sn btn*....................(10 to 1 op 8 to 1) 21
3052 CA IRA (Ire) [50] 7-10 (5*) A Garth (18) *drvn alng to go pace hfwy, nvr on terms*...............(33 to 1 op 25 to 1) 22
4163^{7} RED MARCH HARE [51] 8-2 T Williams (10) *drvn alng centre, struggling frm hfwy*..................(20 to 1) 23
4021^{8} LUCKY FOURTEEN [60] (bl) 8-11 K Fallon (16) *rdn aftr 3 fs, nvr on terms*..................................(20 to 1) 24

Dist: ½l, 4l, sht-hd, hd, 1l, nk, ¾l, 1½l, nk, ¾l. 1m 18.31s. a 6.71s (24 Ran).
SR: 29/13/-/1/-/-/4/-/-/ (The Monkey Racing Club Limited), J Berry

MALLOW (IRE) (good to yielding)

Wednesday October 6th

4359 Southern E.B.F. Maiden (2-y-o) £3,105 1m 1f..........................(4:30)

4134³ DANITA (Ire) 8-11 C Roche (1)................(3 to 1 fav) 1
3771³ CONCEPT HOUSE (Ire) 9-0 N Byrne (7)...........(4 to 1) 2
4093⁵ UNBUCKLE (Ire) (bl) 9-0 M J Kinane (9)...........(5 to 1) 3
3771⁵ FRENCH VICTOR (Ire) 9-0 J F Egan (2)...........(6 to 1) 4
3492⁴ CAIRNBRAE (Ire) 9-0 R Hughes (4)...............(50 to 1) 5
4146 MAIN REFRAIN (Ire) 8-10 (4*) J J Behan (8).......(20 to 1) 6
4146⁶ NUN'S ISLAND (Ire) 9-0 B Coogan (10)...........(5 to 1) 7
3771 JINGLING SILVER (Ire) (bl) 8-6 (8*) J J Mullins (11) (25 to 1) 8
4323 BUTLER BRENNAN (Ire) 9-0 W J Supple (5).......(50 to 1) 9
4261 GREAC 8-1 (10*) M J Cullen (3).................(33 to 1) 10
Dist: Hd, 6l, 3l, 5l. 1m 58.70s. (10 Ran).
(John Hayes), J S Bolger

4360 Kinsale Nursery Handicap (2-y-o) £2,243 1m 1f....................(5:00)

4261⁷ SUSIE SUNSHINE (Ire) [-] 8-13 C Roche (11)......(12 to 1) 1
3806⁸ MALT LEAF (Ire) [-] 7-1 (6*) P P Murphy (4)........(14 to 1) 2
4000* BRIEF RESPITE (Ire) [-] 8-13 (6*) B J Walsh (13)...(10 to 1) 3
3608 RUDI'S PRIDE (Ire) [-] 8-10 P V Gilson (15).........(6 to 1) 4
4183³ ZOE BAIRD [-] 7-12 (8*) B Fenton (2)..............(11 to 2) 5
4262* METROELLA (Ire) [-] 8-13 (4*,7ex) J J Behan (17)...(6 to 1) 6
4262² RAHAL (Ire) [-] (bl) 9-3 M J Kinane (5)..........(9 to 4 fav) 7
3527⁵ LADY SAPIEN (Ire) [-] 8-0 (4*) W J Smith (16)......(14 to 1) 8
3273* WINTER'S OVER [-] 7-12 (8*) G M Moylan (7)......(8 to 1) 9
4093 BOB BARNES (Ire) [-] 8-8 (4*) J A Heffernan (9).....(25 to 1) 10
2983⁹ SALLY'S TRUST (Ire) [-] 8-0 (2*) R M Burke (14)...(20 to 1) 11
4093 EAS GEIPTINE [-] 8-6 A J Nolan (10)..............(20 to 1) 12
3954⁷ NOBLE CHOICE (Ire) [-] 8-10 N G McCullagh (8)...(10 to 1) 13
4262⁵ SUAVE REDSKIN (Ire) [-] 8-8 W J Supple (12).....(12 to 1) 14
3527 DREAMS OF SUMMER (Ire) [-] 8-7 J F Egan (3)...(14 to 1) 15
3917⁶ DANCING BRIEF (Ire) [-] 7-8 (2*) D G O'Shea (6)...(14 to 1) pu
Dist: ½l, ¾l, hd, sht-hd. 1m 58.70s. (16 Ran).
(Woodgrove Syndicate), A P O'Brien

YORK (heavy)
Wednesday October 6th

Going Correction: PLUS 0.90 sec. per fur. (races 1,2,4,5,6), PLUS 0.65 (3,7)

4361 Monkgate Median Auction Maiden Fillies' Stakes Class D (2-y-o) £4,542 7f 202yds........................(2:00)

4121³ CLYDE GODDESS (Ire) 8-11 W Carson (3) *led aftr one fs, styd far rls strt, rdn o'r one out, stayed on wl ins last.* ....(9 to 2 op 5 to 1 tchd 4 to 1) 1
3819⁵ TREE OF HEAVEN 8-11 M Tebbutt (1) *in tch, wide strt, hdwy 3 fs out, rdn 2 out, ev ch ins last, kpt on.* ....(7 to 1 op 7 to 6 to 1) 2
4190⁵ MEGDALE (Ire) 8-11 M Birch (2) *al prmnt, chsd wnr far side 4 fs out, effrt and ev ch ins last, kpt on.* ....(16 to 1 op 12 to 1) 3
4220³ MCGILLYCUDDY REEKS (Ire) 8-11 W Ryan (6) *hld up, wide strt, hdwy o'r 3 fs out, styd on one pace fnl 2 furlongs, nvr dngrs.*...........(11 to 1 op 10 to 1 tchd 12 to 1) 4
3828² CUT ADRIFT 8-11 W R Swinburn (8) *chsd ldrs, wide strt, effrt 3 fuyrlongs out, rdn 2 out, sn wknd.* ....(3 to 1 op 9 to 4) 5
3895⁵ NORFOLK LAVENDER (Can) 8-11 J Reid (9) *mid-div, wide strt, effrt and hdwy o'r 3 fs out, sn rdn and btn.* ....(12 to 1 op 10 to 1) 6
3960⁷ RED POINT 8-11 L Dettori (4) *led one furlong, chsd wnr till wide strt, rdn 3 out, sn wknd.* (16 to 1 op 14 to 1) 7
3969 AUNTIE FAY (Ire) 8-11 S Wood (5) *cl up, wide strt, rdn 4 fuirlongs out, sn wknd.*..........(100 to 1 op 33 to 1) 8
2123⁷ COME GO 8-11 M Roberts (7) *rcd wide, in tch, rdn alng aftr 3 fs, sn wknd, tld off and virtually pld up three out.*...............................(14 to 1 op 12 to 1) 9
AVIRA 8-11 Pat Eddery (10) *in tch on outer, pushed alng aftr 3 fs and sn beh, tld off and virtually pld up o'r three out.*..........(9 to 4 fav op 6 to 4 tchd 11 to 4) 10
Dist: 1½l, sht-hd, 12l, 3l, 20l, 3½l, nk, dist, 3l. 1m 46.80s. a 12.50s (10 Ran).
SR: 18/13/12/-/-/-/ (Cyril Humphris), J L Dunlop

4362 Micklegate Conditions Stakes Class C (3-y-o and up) £5,346 7f 202yds..(2:30)

4207³ BASHAYER (USA) (v) 3-8-7 W Carson (1) *made all, sn clr, styd on wl fnl 2 fs*.....................(4 to 1 op 7 to 2) 1
4066² REDENHAM (USA) 3-8-11 Pat Eddery (5) *in tch, pushed alng hfwy, hrd drvn to chase wnr fnl 2 fs, no imprsn.* ....(2 to 1 op 7 to 4) 2
4100² BLUE LION 3-9-0 M Roberts (4) *chsd ldr, effrt 3 fs out, rdn 2 out, sn wknd*..................(13 to 8 fav op 6 to 4) 3
1116⁶ MR MARTINI (Ire) 3-8-11 (3*) B Doyle (3) *chsd ldr, rdn 3 fs out, sn one pace*..........(10 to 1 tchd 12 to 1) 4
4132⁸ AVENUE FOCH (Ire) 4-9-1 M Wigham (2) *al rear, wl beh fnl 3 fs*...........................(33 to 1 op 25 to 1) 5
Dist: 4l, 3l, ½l, 10l. 1m 44.80s. a 8.50s (5 Ran).
SR: 74/66/60/58/29/ (Hamdan Al-Maktoum), Major W R Hern

4363 Newington Hotel York Racegoers Handicap Class D (0-80 3-y-o and up) £6,254 5f......................(3:00)

4109⁷ SIMMIE'S SPECIAL [55] (bl) 5-8-5² W Ryan (2) *rcd far rls, made virtually all, rdn appr last, ran on gmely.* ....(16 to 1 tchd 20 to 1) 1
4109³ SADDLEHOME (USA) [58] 4-8-8 J Reid (3) *prmnt far side, hdwy to chal 2 fs out, hrd rdn and ev ch ins last, no extr nr finish*..........(7 to 1 jt-fav op 8 to 1 tchd 9 to 1) 2
3946² BATCHWORTH BOUND [54] 4-8-4 C Rutter (15) *rcd centre, beh till styd on strly appr fnl furlong, drifted lft ins last, nrst finish*......(14 to 1 op 10 to 1 tchd 16 to 1) 3
4180⁸ RISTON LADY (Ire) [79] 3-9-9 (5*) A Procter (7) *led centre grp, rdn 2 fs out, kpt on one pace.* ....(16 to 1 tchd 20 to 1) 4
4096⁵ PEERAGE PRINCE [66] (bl) 4-9-2 J Quinn (4) *chsd ldrs far side, rdn 2 fs out, kpt on one pace*............(16 to 1) 5
3687⁴ SIR TASKER [54] 5-8-4 Paul Eddery (6) *cl up far side, rdn 2 fs out, grad wknd*.........................(16 to 1) 6
4180³ GONDO [70] (v) 6-8-13 (7*) S Knott (13) *chsd ldrs centre, rdn 2 fs out, kpt on one pace*..... (12 to 1 op 10 to 1) 7
4168 KALAR [52] (bl) 4-8-2 S Wood (16) *speed centre, rdn 2 fs out, one pace*..................(33 to 1 op 25 to 1) 8
3687² SAMSON-AGONISTES [70] 7-8-13 (7*) S Sanders (12) *in tch centre, rdn 2 fs out, no hdwy.* ....(16 to 1 op 12 to 1 tchd 20 to 1) 9
3947 BREEZY DAY [72] 7-9-8 T Quinn (5) *chsd ldrs far side, rdn and wknd o'r 2 fs out.* ....(25 to 1 op 20 to 1 tchd 33 to 1) 10
4238⁶ ABSOLUTION [58] 9-8-8 J Lowe (14) *al prmnt centre, rdn 2 fs out, one pace*..................(20 to 1 op 16 to 1) 11
4180⁷ LOVE LEGEND [60] (v) 8-8-10 L Dettori (8) *chsd ldrs centre, rdn o'r 2 fs out, sn btn*..............(14 to 1 op 12 to 1) 12
1925⁷ FLORAC (Ire) [55] 3-8-4 M Hills (17) *al beh stand side.* ....(25 to 1 op 20 to 1) 13
4277 ANOTHER JADE [76] 3-9-11 W R Swinburn (20) *al beh stand side*..............(25 to 1 op 20 to 1) 14
4180* DOMICKSKY [71] 5-9-7 Pat Eddery (21) *al beh stand side.* ....(7 to 1 jt-fav tchd 8 to 1) 15
4109* MILBANK CHALLENGER [62] 3-8-11 M Birch (22) *speed stand side, rdn alng hfwy, sn beh.* (14 to 1 op 10 to 1) 16
4180 SONDERISE [66] 4-9-2 W Newnes (10) *chsd ldrs centre, rdn alng hfwy, sn btn*.............(20 to 1 op 16 to 1) 17
4180 SO SUPERB [55] (bl) 4-8-5 S Webster (18) *beh stand side frm hfwy*....................(20 to 1 op 25 to 1) 18
2524 LORD HIGH ADMIRAL (Can) [76] 5-9-12 M Roberts (9) *prmnt centre, rdn hfwy, sn wknd and eased.* ....(14 to 1 op 12 to 1) 19
4109 MY ABBEY [60] 4-8-10 D Holland (1) *prmnt far side 3 fs.* ....(25 to 1 op 20 to 1 tchd 33 to 1) 20
4180 GEMINI FIRE [52] 9-8-2 F Norton (11) *in tch centre to hfwy, sn beh*..........................(33 to 1 op 25 to 1) 21
4168 HERE COMES A STAR [69] 5-9-5 L Piggott (23) *al rear.* ....(16 to 1 op 12 to 1) 22
4090 AUGHFAD [77] 7-9-10 (3*) S D Williams (19) *speed stand side 2 fs, sn wl beh*..............(33 to 1 op 20 to 1) 23
Dist: Hd, 2½l, 1½l, 1½l, 2l, nk, ¾l, ¾l, ¾l, sht-hd. 1m 2.90s. a 5.60s (23 Ran).
SR: 44/46/32/50/32/12/27/6/21/ (D Coppenhall), R Hollinshead

4364 Goodramgate Handicap Class D (0-80 3-y-o and up) £6,072 1¼m 85yds (3:30)

4247² BIT ON THE SIDE (Ire) [64] 4-9-3 Pat Eddery (13) *hld up, hdwy 4 fs out, effrt to ld 2 out, rdn appr last, styd on gmely*........... (5 to 1 jt-fav op 9 to 2 tchd 11 to 2) 1
4178* EXPRESS GIFT [71] 4-9-10 J Williams (4) *hld up, gd hdwy on outer 3 fs out, styd on to chal and ev ch ins last, kpt on*..........................(5 to 1 jt-fav tchd 11 to 2) 2
4101³ SWIFT SILVER [56] 6-8-9 J Quinn (16) *hld up and beh, gd hdwy o'r 2 fs out, ev ch ins last, kpt on.* ....(12 to 1 tchd 14 to 1) 3
4043⁴ COUREUR [48] 4-8-1 W Carson (3) *trkd ldrs gng wl, quickened to ld 3 fs out, rdn and hdd 2 out, wknd appr last.* ....(12 to 1 tchd 14 to 1) 4
4247* SONG OF SIXPENCE (USA) [58] 9-8-4 (7*) C Scudder (8) *hld up, gd hdwy on outer 3 fs out, ch 2 out, sn rdn and wknd*...........................(7 to 1 tchd 8 to 1) 5
3790³ IN THE MONEY (Ire) [58] 4-8-11 W Ryan (15) *hld up, hdwy 4 fs out, ev ch o'r 2 out, sn rdn and wknd*.......(14 to 1) 6
4143⁸ LOBILIO (USA) [66] (v) 4-9-5 M Roberts (12) *rcd wide, pushed alng hfwy, nvr dngrs.* ....(11 to 1 op 10 to 1 tchd 12 to 1) 7
3891* WASSL THIS THEN (Ire) [61] 4-9-0 T Quinn (14) *hdwy on outer 3 fs out, rdn o'r 2 out, sn one pace.* ....(12 to 1 tchd 14 to 1) 8
1738⁷ DOCTOR'S REMEDY [40] 7-7-7 J Lowe (1) *led, rdn and hdd 3 fs out, sn wknd*.........................(100 to 1) 9
4188⁵ LARRIKIN (USA) [70] 4-9-9 W R Swinburn (11) *hld up, hdwy and in tch whn rdn 2 fs out, sn btn.* ....(13 to 2 op 6 to 1 tchd 7 to 1) 10
4178 PERSIAN FOUNTAIN (Ire) [55] (bl) 3-8-2 S Wood (9) *nvr a factor*...........................(33 to 1 op 25 to 1) 11
2622⁷ EXPO MONDIAL (Ire) [74] 3-9-7 M Tebbutt (7) *al rear.* ....(33 to 1) 12

4064 THE SEER [70] 3-9-3 D Holland (10) *chsd ldr till rdn and wknd quickly o'r 3 fs out*.........(14 to 1 op 12 to 1) 13
3630^2 FLASHMAN [51] (bl) 3-7-12 N Carlisle (2) *chsd ldrs, rdn and wknd 4 fs out*....................(16 to 1 op 14 to 1) 14
3211^9 CIRCUS COLOURS [74] (bl) 3-9-7 L Dettori (5) *wide strt, sn rdn and wknd 4 fs out, tld off*.....(14 to 1 op 12 to 1) 15
Dist: ½l, 1l, 5l, 12l, 8l, 10l, ½l, nk, nk, ¾l. 2m 22.10s. a 14.10s (15 Ran).
SR: 57/63/46/28/14/-/ (Mike Hawkett), W J Musson

4365 Walmgate Nursery Class C (2-y-o) £6,888 7f 202yds............... (4:00)

4167* IN LIKE FLYNN [80] 9-4 Pat Eddery (1) *made virtually all, rdn clr 2 fs out, styd on strly*.........(8 to 1 op 7 to 1) 1
4215^2 GLENLYON DUCHESS [59] 7-4 (7*) N Varley (3) *al prmnt, chsd wnr fnl 2 fs, no imprsn*.................... (16 to 1) 2
4051^6 NON VINTAGE (Ire) [71] 8-9 L Dettori (16) *beh, hdwy on outer 2 fs out, styd on und pres ins last*. .... (14 to 1 op 12 to 1) 3
4122^4 WINNING LINE [68] 8-6 M Birch (10) *beh, hdwy 2 fs out, rdn and styd on ins last*...........(12 to 1 op 10 to 1) 4
3969* STAR JAZZ (Ire) [70] 8-8 Paul Eddery (14) *cl up, ev ch o'r 2 fs out, sn rdn and grad wknd*..........(8 to 1 op 6 to 1) 5
3997^7 RIVA'S BOOK (USA) [61] 7-13 J Fanning (17) *mid-div, styd on fnl 2 fs, nvr dngrs*........................ (20 to 1) 6
4215^7 PLUM DENNIS [56] 7-8^1 N Carlisle (12) *beh till some some hdwy fnl 2 fs, not rch ldrs*.........(50 to 1 op 33 to 1) 7
4015^3 MR ROUGH [62] 8-0 J Quinn (9) *in tch, rdn 3 fs out, sn wknd*.................................... (12 to 1) 8
3997^5 MOSAIC GOLD [79] 9-3 N Connorton (18) *in tch, rdn alng hfwy, sn one pace*................(16 to 1 op 14 to 1) 9
3281 NEW INN [79] 9-3 W R Swinburn (7) *chsd ldrs, rdn 3 fs out, sn btn and eased*................(25 to 1 op 20 to 1) 10
4106^6 ALL IN THE MIND [72] 8-10 L Piggott (8) *wl beh till styd on fnl 2 fs*................................ (12 to 1) 11
3940* CAPTAIN SCARLET (Ire) [74] 8-9 (3*) B Doyle (15) *cl up till rdn and wknd 3 fs out*......................(14 to 1) 12
3974^3 BRAVE PATRIARCH (Ire) [82] 9-6 W Carson (4) *in tch, rdn alng o'r 3 fs out, hng lft and sn btn*. (9 to 1 op 8 to 1) 13
4051^5 OVIDEO [64] (bl) 8-2 J Lowe (6) *chsd ldrs till rdn and wknd 3 fs out*......................................(16 to 1) 14
4014^3 ROUSAY [70] 8-8 M Roberts (13) *prmnt, rdn 4 fs out, sn wknd*.........................(16 to 1 op 12 to 1) 15
3813* KING CURAN (USA) [83] 9-7 M Hills (5) *in tch whn badly hmpd 3 fs out, no ch aftr*. ....(4 to 1 fav op 6 to 1 tchd 7 to 1) 16
4214^2 BURES (Ire) [75] (v) 8-13 T Quinn (11) *al rear*......(16 to 1) 17
4251^4 VANESSA ROSE [62] 7-9 (5*) D Wright (2) *beh, some hdwy whn badly hmpd and uns rdr o'r 3 fs out*. .... (11 to 2 op 9 to 2 tchd 6 to 1) ur
Dist: 3½l, 3l, hd, 1l, 5l, 6l, 2½l, 2½l, 8l, nk. 1m 47.80s. a 11.50s (18 Ran).
SR: 40/8/11/7/6/-/ (M M Matalon), R Hannon

4366 Gillygate Conditions Stakes Class C (3-y-o and up) £5,078 1m 5f 194yds ....(4:30)

3861^4 WITNESS BOX (USA) 6-9-5 M Roberts (3) *chsd ldr, ld aftr 5 fs, quickened clr o'r 3 out, eased ins last*. ....(11 to 8 tchd 6 to 4) 1
4160* DOVER PATROL (Ire) 3-8-11 W Ryan (2) *hld up, took clr order hfwy, rdn o'r 3 fs out, plugged on one pace und pres*..................... (11 to 8 on tchd 6 to 5 on) 2
3524* CALIANDAK (Ire) 3-8-9 L Piggott (4) *bolted bef strt, rcd wide, led 5 fs, rdn 3 out, wknd 2 out*. ....(16 to 1 op 14 to 1 tchd 20 to 1) 3
3759^5 KARACHI 3-8-8 (3*) B Doyle (1) *in tch till rdn and wknd 4 fs out, sn tld off*..................(20 to 1 op 16 to 1) 4
Dist: 20l, 5l, dist. 3m 15.10s. a 20.10s (4 Ran).
SR: 30/ (Sheikh Mohammed), J H M Gosden

4367 EBF Spurriergate Maiden Stakes Class D (2-y-o) £5,580 6f........(5:00)

4174^8 COOL JAZZ 9-0 M Roberts (3) *hld up, hdwy and hng lft to far rail o'r 2 fs out, rdn to ld appr last, ran on*. .... (15 to 8 op 3 to 1 tchd 7 to 4) 1
4240^5 AMBER VALLEY (USA) 9-0 W Carson (4) *led, rdn 2 fs out, hdd appr last, kpt on*....(9 to 2 op 4 to 1 tchd 5 to 1) 2
SATIN VELVET (USA) 8-9 L Dettori (1) *trkd ldrs gng wl, effrt and ev ch 2 fs out, sn rdn and not quicken appr last, eased*.......................... (6 to 4 fav op 5 to 4 on) 3
ROYAL HILL 9-0 L Piggott (5) *sn pushed alng, styd on fnl 2 fs, nvr dngrs*.....................(10 to 1 tchd 12 to 1) 4
4067^9 ROSSINI BLUE 9-0 J Reid (7) *chsd ldr, rdn hfwy, wknd 2 fs out*.. (10 to 1) 5
CHURCHWORTH 9-0 T Quinn (6) *prmnt till rdn and wknd wl o'r 2 fs out, eased*................................(16 to 1) 6
4220 THE ARDINGLY FAIR (Ire) 8-11 (3*) C Hodgson (2) *chsd ldrs, rdn and wknd hfwy, sn beh*...... (33 to 1 op 20 to 1) 7
Dist: 2l, 4l, 2l, 2l, 7l, 5l. 1m 19.40s. a 9.40s (7 Ran).
(Saeed Manana), C E Brittain

PUNCHESTOWN (IRE) (heavy)
Thursday October 7th

4368 Beggars End Race (3-y-o and up) £2,760 1m 3f.................. (2:30)

4246^7 MY KERRY DANCER (USA) 3-8-11 P Shanahan (8) (8 to 1) 1
4162* MAYASTA (Ire) 3-9-0 P V Gilson (9)................(9 to 2) 2
4137^4 FURIETTO (Ire) 3-8-4^3 (10*) A J Dempsey (2)......(10 to 1) 3
3976^2 ALOHA (Ire) 4-9-1 J P Murtagh (21)..............(20 to 1) 4
2449^2 KADASSA (Ire) 3-8-8 D Hogan (23)..................(8 to 1) 5
2781^6 ANDANTE (Ire) 3-8-8 C Roche (20)...................(4 to 1) 6
4245 DAHLIA'S BEST (USA) 3-8-11 W J Supple (1)......(9 to 2) 7
3975 SERANERA (Ire) 3-8-7^1 (2*) P Carberry (22)....... (20 to 1) 8
4162^7 SCHMEICHEL (Ire) 3-8-11 S Craine (10)..............(14 to 1) 9
3952^5 ARCH-T-GLEN (Ire) 3-8-3 (8*) D M McCullagh (15) (20 to 1) 10
4260^6 RISKY GALORE 3-8-1 (10*) R McCauliffe (24).....(25 to 1) 11
911^5 SARAKAYA 8-9-1 N G McCullagh (3).............(33 to 1) 12
4162 CATCHMENOT (Ire) 3-8-8 D V Smith (6)..........(25 to 1) 13
4137* UNCERTAIN AFFAIR (Ire) 3-9-0 M J Kinane (4)..(5 to 2 fav) 14
KERRYKEEL LADY (Ire) 3-8-2 (6*) P P Murphy (19) (20 to 1) 15
3062^6 QUIET CONFIDENCE (Ire) 3-8-6 (2*) D G O'Shea (13) ....(12 to 1) 16
GOLD VISION (Ire) 3-8-7 (4*) J J Behan (18).......(14 to 1) 17
1986 DYEGETME (Ire) 4-8-11 (4*) W J Smith (7)........ (50 to 1) 18
3952^4 ENDSONG (USA) 3-8-8 R Hughes (11)................(10 to 1) 19
SCHOOL LAB (Ire) 3-8-3 (8*) G M Moylan (25).....(25 to 1) 20
4162 CHARTY (Ire) 3-8-5 (6*) B J Walsh (17)........... (20 to 1) 21
4137^7 KEPPOLS HARRIER (Ire) (bl) 3-8-11 A J Nolan (12) (20 to 1) 22
847 CARHUE STAR (Ire) 3-8-6 (2*) R M Burke (5)....... (20 to 1) 23
VAGUELY DREAM (Ger) 3-8-8 J F Egan (14)...... (33 to 1) 24
4137^3 CARRICK PIKE (USA) (bl) 3-8-11 K J Manning (16) (10 to 1) I
Dist: 2l, 2½l, 1½l, sht-hd. 2m 36.20s. (25 Ran).
(Hudson Valley Equine Inc), P Mullins

4369 Elverstown EBF Maiden (2-y-o) £3,795 6f.............................(3:00)

CAJARIAN (USA) 9-0 J P Murtagh (1).......... (Evens fav) 1
4290^2 LIMANDA (Ire) 8-11 M J Kinane (3)...................(5 to 2) 2
4285 FIONN DE COOL (Ire) (bl) 9-0 K J Manning (15)....(14 to 1) 3+
3492 LEO'S FRIEND (Ire) 8-10 (4*) J A Heffernan, ...(16 to 1) 3+
3071 SCHONBEIN (Ire) 8-11 W J Supple (8)............ (10 to 1) 5
4135^8 JOYFUL MUSIC (Ire) 8-11 C Roche (17)............(10 to 1) 6
4117^9 NORDIC COLOURS (Ire) 8-1 (10*) D Quirke (2)..... (14 to 1) 7
4244 GREENRIDGE COURT (Ire) 8-3 (8*) G M Moylan (4) (50 to 1) 8
4117 PETIT NOM (Ire) 8-11 N G McCullagh (11)......... (20 to 1) 9
3073 RING-A-RUAN (Ire) 8-10 (4*) J J Behan (16).......(20 to 1) 10
2037 MY TRIVET (Ire) 9-0 S Craine (14)..................(33 to 1) 11
HI HANDSOME (Ire) 9-0 J F Egan (13)................(12 to 1) 12
1022^9 FORTY QUID (Ire) 8-5 (6*) B J Walsh (12).......... (20 to 1) 13
SECRET SENSATION (Ire) 8-11 P V Gilson (10).... (14 to 1) 14
4135 POSCIMUR (Ire) 8-3 (8*) R T Fitzpatrick (5)..........(33 to 1) 15
ANOTHER MUNCHKIN (Ire) 8-11 P Shanahan (9)..(12 to 1) 16
3243 BANZAI (Ire) 8-5^2 (8*) B P Gowran (6)............ (16 to 1) 17
NORSE VICTOR (Ire) 9-0 R Hughes (7)............ (10 to 1) 18
Dist: Hd, 3l, dd-ht, 1l. 1m 17.80s. (18 Ran).
(H H Aga Khan), John M Oxx

4370 Craddockstown Handicap (0-65 3-y-o and up) £2,760 7f 110yds........(3:30)

4136^7 KENTUCKY BABY (Ire) [-] 3-9-3 (4*) J A Heffernan (3) (8 to 1) 1
4161 ICANSEEFORMILES (Ire) [-] (bl) 5-7-8 (8*) R T Fitzpatrick (4) ....(16 to 1) 2
4184^6 MACQUARIE RIDGE (USA) [-] (bl) 5-9-2 M J Kinane (1) ....(9 to 2) 3
4001 BOLERO DANCER (Ire) [-] 5-9-2 J F Egan,........(12 to 1) 4
3827* SUTTON CENTENARY (Ire) [-] 5-7-12 (8*) D A O'Sullivan (2) ....(8 to 1) 5
3244 MUGNANO [-] 7-9-4 (8*) P J Smullen (18)..........(12 to 1) 6
3295 KAWA-KAWA [-] 6-8-1 (6*) P P Murphy (12)........ (20 to 1) 7
3951 TODDY MARK (Ire) [-] 4-9-3 (8*) T E Durcan (7).... (20 to 1) 8
4001^5 DAHAR'S LOVE (USA) [-] (bl) 4-8-4 W J Supple (14) (10 to 1) 9
3399^9 LOVE OF ERIN (Ire) [-] (bl) 4-6-13 (8*) G M Moylan (6) ....(20 to 1) 10
2511^7 NEWYORK CONNECTION (Ire) [-] 3-8-13 N Byrne (16) ....(16 to 1) 11
3398^9 DARCARI ROSE (Ire) [-] (bl) 4-8-8 (6*) B J Walsh (17) (14 to 1) 12
960^9 SUNBED SUE (Ire) [-] 3-8-8 (2*) P Carberry (13) (4 to 1 fav) 13
3916 ELA-MANA-SUE (Ire) [-] 4-8-5 (8*) D M McCullagh (15) ....(20 to 1) 14
4060^8 TEGEMEZA (Ire) [-] 3-9-4 (2*) R M Burke (5).......(12 to 1) 15
3827^4 MASTER WORK [-] 5-7-12 (4*) J J Behan (9).......(8 to 1) 16
3576^2 TORCH SINGER [-] 3-9-2 P V Gilson (10)..........(7 to 1) 17
3856^8 CHAMPAGNE NIGHT (Fr) [-] (bl) 3-9-5 N G McCullagh (8) ....(12 to 1) 18
Dist: 1½l, 3½l, 2l, ½l. 1m 45.40s. (18 Ran).
(P G Tierney), Edward Lynam

YORK (heavy)
Thursday October 7th
Going Correction: PLUS 1.10 sec. per fur.

4371 Badger Hill Fillies' Conditions Stakes Class C (2-y-o) £4,901 6f 214yds (2:00)

37514 TAMAR'S BRIGADE 8-10 A Clark (3) *made all, quickened 3 fs out, clr one out, ran on wl*........(7 to 2 op 9 to 4) 1
41115 CRACKLING SIKE 8-10 B Raymond (1) *cl up till outpcd 3 fs out, no dngr aftr*.......(2 to 1 op 7 to 4 tchd 5 to 2) 2
4089* DARING DESTINY 8-10 T Sprake (2) *in tch, effrt 3 fs out, ev ch 2 out, sn rdn, wknd fnl furlong.*
....(Evens fav op 5 to 4) 3
Dist: 7l, 1½l. 1m 32.77s. a 11.07s (3 Ran).
SR: 45/24/19/ (P R Cruden), M McCormack

4372 Ainsty Maiden Stakes Class D (3-y-o) £4,503 1¼m 85yds............. (2:30)

41263 SILVER MAPLE (USA) 8-9 B Crossley (2) *beh, hdwy 6 fs out, rdn 3 out, swtchd rght ins last, styd on wl to ld cl hme.*
....(7 to 1 op 9 to 2) 1
41102 PURPLE SPLASH 9-0 A Munro (1) *chsd ldrs, led wl o'r one furlong out, hdd and no extra cl hme.*
....(5 to 2 fav tchd 3 to 1) 2
7195 CHIEF'S SONG 9-0 K Darley (3) *in tch, pushed alng o'r 4 fs out, styd on frm 2 out*.........(10 to 1 op 8 to 1) 3
37273 MAKIN (USA) 9-0 W Carson (8) *led till wl o'r one furlong out, wknd fnl furlong*..............(7 to 2 op 3 to 1) 4
19315 PIPERS POOL (Ire) 8-9 M Roberts (6) *beh, pushed alng o'r 4 fs out, no hdwy, lost tch frm 2 out, tld off.*
....(5 to 1 op 7 to 2) 5
40304 FIRE CARPET (USA) 9-0 Pat Eddery (5) *beh, pushed alng hfwy, lost tch fnl 2 fs, tld off*.......(9 to 2 op 7 to 2) 6
FAIRLEAD 8-9 M Hills (7) *cl up till wknd quickly 4 fs out, tld off*............(16 to 1 tchd 14 to 1 and 20 to 1) 7
Dist: ¾l, 3l, 4l, 20l, sht-hd, 5l. 2m 24.83s. a 16.83s (7 Ran).
SR: 42/45/39/31/ (Sheikh Mohammed), J H M Gosden

4373 Allied Dunbar Rated Class B Handicap (0-105 3-y-o and up) £6,546 7f ....(3:00)

39962 AMAZING FEAT (Ire) [92] 4-8-10 K Darley (9) *hld up in tch, not clr run 3 fs out, ran on wl frm 2 out, led ins last.*
........................(7 to 4 fav op 2 to 1 tchd 9 to 4) 1
42162 TAUFAN BLU (Ire) [93] (bl) 4-8-8 (3*) O Pears (8) *beh, hdwy 4 fs out, led wl o'r one out, sn rdn, hdd ins last, no extr.*
....(7 to 1 op 6 to 1) 2
41404 LORD CHICKNEY (USA) [96] 4-9-0 M Roberts (6) *beh, sn pushed alng, styd on wl fnl 2 fs, not rch ldrs.*
..............................(9 to 2 op 3 to 1 tchd 5 to 1) 3
4172 NEW CAPRICORN (USA) [92] 3-8-7 W Carson (5) *cl up, led wl o'r 2 fs out till well over one out, one pace.*
.......................(10 to 1 op 8 to 1 tchd 12 to 1) 4
41725 BAND ON THE RUN [89] 6-8-7 A Mackay (4) *chsd ldrs, ev ch o'r 2 fs out, sn rdn and btn.*
.......................(11 to 2 op 5 to 1 tchd 6 to 1) 5
3725 TRUE PRECISION [89] 3-8-4 A Munro (1) *chsd ldrs, wknd 2 fs out*..........................(20 to 1 op 16 to 1) 6
4040 FYLDE FLYER [103] (bl) 4-9-7 J Carroll (7) *prmnt till wknd o'r 2 fs out*......................(16 to 1 op 14 to 1) 7
3897 GYMCRAK PREMIERE [93] (v) 5-8-11 R Cochrane (2) *led till wl o'r 2 fs out, sn rdn and wknd.* (16 to 1 tchd 20 to 1) 8
3897 CUMBRIAN CHALLENGE (Ire) [90] (bl) 4-8-8 M Birch (3) *in tch till wknd 3 fs out, tld off*......(12 to 1 op 10 to 1) 9
Dist: ¾l, 2½l, 1½l, 1½l, 7l, 5l, 1l, 15l. 1m 32.42s. a 10.72s (9 Ran).
SR: 51/50/45/33/28/4/6/-/-/ (P D Savill), Mrs M Reveley

4374 British Gas N. E. Apprentice Handicap Class E (0-70 3-y-o and up) £7,044 1m 3f 195yds...............(3:30)

41872 MERRY MERMAID [46] 3-7-11 M Humphries (2) *hld up, hdwy to ld o'r 3 fs out, styd on wl.* (14 to 1 op 12 to 1) 1
41015 LIGHT HAND [60] 7-9-5 S Mulvey (3) *hld up mid-div, hdwy o'r 4 fs out, ev ch 2 out, one pace*.....(6 to 1 op 9 to 2) 2
42262 HIGHLAND SPIRIT [55] 5-9-0 S Drowne (4) *trkd ldrs gng wl, effrt 2 fs out, sn rdn, kpt on same pace.*
..............................(9 to 2 fav tchd 5 to 1) 3
4152* HILLZAH (USA) [60] 5-9-5 H Bastiman (8) *hld up, hdwy to track ldrs o'r 3 fs out, rdn 2 out, kpt on same pace.*
....(7 to 1 op 8 to 1) 4
32565 BEAUMONT (Ire) [61] 3-8-12 T G McLaughlin (18) *beh, styd on fnl 3 fs, not trble ldrs*.........(14 to 1 tchd 16 to 1) 5
39703 ROUSITTO [50] 5-8-4 (5*) J Dennis (13) *beh, styd on fnl 3 fs, not trble ldrs*.................(10 to 1 tchd 12 to 1) 6
4218* EIRE LEATH-SCEAL [46] 6-8-5 (5ex) Michael Denaro (16) *in tch, hdwy to chase wnr 3 fs out, sn rdn and wknd.*
.......................(11 to 1 op 10 to 1 tchd 12 to 1) 7
4036 DOCTOR ROY [46] 5-8-5[5] (5*) S Copp (7) *in tch, rdn 4 fs out, no hdwy*........(16 to 1 op 14 to 1 tchd 20 to 1) 8
14953 ROSMARINO [52] 3-7-11[1] (7*) G Mills (19) *nvr trble ldrs.*
....(20 to 1) 9
39708 BOLD AMBITION [40] 6-7-8 (5*) M Baird (9) *nvr dngrs.*
....(25 to 1) 10
40175 ONE FOR THE POT [51] 8-8-10 V Halliday (20) *chsd ldrs, ev ch o'r 3 fs out, sn rdn and wknd*...(20 to 1 op 16 to 1) 11
40482 NANCY (Ire) [42] (bl) 3-7-7 Claire Balding (17) *in tch till wknd o'r 3 fs out*..................(25 to 1 op 20 to 1) 12
ALKABAR [49] 5-8-8 B Russell (5) *prmnt, led hfwy till o'r 3 fs out, sn wknd*..................(50 to 1 op 33 to 1) 13
35654 FAIR FLYER (Ire) [59] 4-9-4 N Varley (6) *prmnt, ev ch o'r 3 fs out, sn wknd*.......(11 to 1 op 10 to 1 tchd 12 to 1) 14
39625 ROSE OF MEDINA [42] 3-7-2 (5*) Sally Radford-Howes (15) *chsd ldrs till wknd o'r 4 fs out, tld off*........(33 to 1) 15
41887 TRUBEN (USA) [68] 4-9-10 (3*) R Havlin (1) *prmnt, chlgd o'r 3 fs out, wknd quickly, tld off*... (14 to 1 tchd 16 to 1) 16
42189 MUFID (USA) [48] 4-8-7[6] (5*) L Aspell (10) *beh most of way, tld off*..(33 to 1) 17
41576 LIABILITY ORDER [61] 4-9-6 J Marshall (14) *beh most of way, tld off*.........(12 to 1 op 10 to 1 tchd 14 to 1) 18
4086 J P MORGAN [43] (v) 5-8-2 C Munday (11) *sn beh, tld off.*
..............................(20 to 1 tchd 25 to 1) 19
37888 INTREPID FORT [34] (bl) 4-7-0 (7*) F Savage (21) *dwlt, led aftr one furlong, hdd hfwy, wknd o'r 4 out, tld off.*
..............................(50 to 1 op 33 to 1) 20
4115 KAWASIR (Can) [42] 3-7-5[3] (5*) Nicola Howarth (12) *led one furlong, cl up till wknd quickly 5 out, tld off.*
..............................(50 to 1 op 33 to 1) 21
Dist: 3½l, nk, 1l, 8l, 4l, ½l, 8l, nk, 2l, ½l. 2m 48.52s. a 20.52s (21 Ran).
SR: 10/25/19/22/-/-/ (Mrs O K Steele), J F Bottomley

4375 Malton Nursery Handicap Class C (2-y-o) £6,056 6f.................. (4:00)

4124* LIME STREET BLUES (Ire) [83] 9-5 Pat Eddery (3) *in tch, sn pushed alng, ran on wl und pres to ld nr finish.*
........(15 to 8 fav op 2 to 1 tchd 5 to 2 and 7 to 4) 1
39978 DISTINCTIVE AIR [69] 8-5 K Darley (10) *trkd ldrs, led entering fnl furlong, hdd and no extr nr finish*.....(12 to 1) 2
41653 DANTE'S RUBICON (Ire) [59] 7-9[1] W Carson (5) *made most till o'r 2 fs out, led over one out, sn hdd, kpt on.*
....(9 to 1 op 7 to 1) 3
40502 GLENUGIE [60] 7-10 N Carlisle (8) *trkd ldrs, effrt o'r 2 fs out, hng lft, kpt on fnl furlong.* (10 to 1 tchd 11 to 1) 4
41774 HEATHYARDS LADY (USA) [74] 8-10 S Perks (7) *dsptd ld, led o'r 2 fs out till over one out, wknd quickly.*
..............................(12 to 1 op 10 to 1) 5
41593 LEGATEE [80] 9-2 M Birch (2) *chsd ldrs till wknd quickly 2 fs out*..............(11 to 1 op 10 to 1 tchd 12 to 1) 6
4144* ALZIANAH [85] 9-7 D Harrison (1) *in tch till wknd quickly 2 fs out*...............(11 to 4 op 2 to 1 tchd 3 to 1) 7
4097 MACAROON LADY [57] 7-4[2] (5*) D Wright (9) *al beh.*
..............................(50 to 1 op 25 to 1) 8
41243 RAPIER POINT (Ire) [80] 9-2 R Cochrane (4) *cl up till wknd quickly 2 fs out, tld off whn pld up and dismounted fnl furlong*..........................(7 to 1 op 8 to 1) pu
Dist: ½l, ¾l, ¾l, 12l, 2½l, 3l, 4l. 1m 19.86s. a 9.86s (9 Ran).
SR: 40/24/11/9/-/-/ (D B Gallop), R Hannon

4376 Green Howards Cup Claiming Stakes Class D (3-y-o and up) £4,737 1¼m 85yds.......................... (4:30)

42412 DEVILS DEN (Ire) 3-8-4 D Harrison (6) *trkd ldrs gng wl, led o'r 2 fs out, sn clr, easily*........(2 to 1 fav op 9 to 4) 1
41527 WITHOUT A FLAG (USA) 3-8-5 M Roberts (7) *in tch, hdwy o'r 3 fs out, chsd wnr frm 2 out, no imprsn.*
........................(11 to 2 op 6 to 1 tchd 7 to 1) 2
41586 JAHANGIR (Ire) 4-9-4 B Raymond (2) *trkd ldrs, ev ch o'r 2 fs out, kpt on same pace*.........(10 to 1 tchd 11 to 1) 3
42135 NUTTY BROWN (v) 3-8-0 F Norton (4) *led one furlong, cl up, led o'r 3 out till over 2 out, sn wknd.*
........................(14 to 1 op 12 to 1 tchd 16 to 1) 4
39562 WANNABE 3-8-6[1] R Cochrane (9) *in tch, pushed alng and outpcd o'r 4 fs out, no dngr aftr*..... (3 to 1 op 2 to 1) 5
37222 GRAND VITESSE (Ire) 4-8-5 (7*) D Gibbs (10) *led aftr one furlong till o'r 3 out, sn btn*........(4 to 1 tchd 5 to 1) 6
36015 SARAH HEIGHTS 3-7-9 N Carlisle (3) *in tch, pushed alng o'r 4 fs out, sn beh*.................(50 to 1 op 33 to 1) 7
3523 AVIATOR'S DREAM 3-7-12[1] (3*) S Maloney (5) *al beh.*
....(33 to 1) 8
Dist: 12l, 6l, 6l, 2½l, 3½l, 6l, 2½l. 2m 25.26s. a 17.26s (8 Ran).
SR: 33/10/11/-/-/ (P A Kelleway), P A Kelleway

4377 EBF Sancton Maiden Stakes Class D (2-y-o) £5,253 7f 202yds.........(5:00)

41135 PEMBRIDGE PLACE 9-0 W Carson (6) *cl up, led o'r 4 fs out till over 3 out, led 2 out, styd on wl.*
..............................(11 to 8 fav op 6 to 4 tchd 5 to 4) 1
41137 DURABLE 9-0 B Raymond (4) *cl up, ev ch wl o'r one furlong out, kpt on same pace*.......(9 to 2 op 5 to 2) 2
40154 BALI WARRIOR (Ire) 9-0 M Hills (2) *cl up, led aftr 2 fs till o'r 4 out, led over 3 out to two out, sn btn.*
....(9 to 4 op 3 to 1) 3
38769 SILENCE IN COURT (Ire) 9-0 A Mackay (3) *in tch till wknd 3 fs out*..........................(10 to 1 op 20 to 1) 4
27147 GREENFINCH (Can) 9-0 M Roberts (1) *led 2 fs, sn pushed alng, wknd 3 out*.....................(10 to 1 op 8 to 1) 5
Dist: 4l, 3½l, 3l, 6l. 1m 51.33s. a 15.03s (5 Ran).
SR: 7/-/ (Lady Cohen), J L Dunlop

BELMONT PARK (USA) (firm)
Saturday October 9th

4378 Turf Classic (Grade 1) (3-y-o and up) £198,675 1½m......................

4075* APPLE TREE (Fr) 4-9-0 M Smith, ... (47 to 10) 1
SOLAR SPLENDOUR (USA) 6-9-0 H McCauley, .. (74 to 10) 2
3795³ GEORGE AUGUSTUS (USA) 5-9-0 J Bailey, ... (17 to 1) 3
4071* STAR OF COZZENE (USA) 5-9-0 J Santos, ... (2 to 1 on) 4
597³ FRAISE (USA) 5-9-0 P Valenzuela, ... (33 to 10) 5
Dist: 2 ¼l, ½l, 1l, 1 ¼l. 2m 28.31s. (5 Ran).
(Paul de Moussac), A Fabre

4379 Vosburgh Stakes (Grade 1) (3-y-o and up) £79,470 7f......................

BIRDONTHEWIRE (USA) 4-9-0 M Smith, ... (27 to 10) 1
TAKE ME OUT (USA) 5-9-0 P Valenzuela, ... (39 to 10) 2
LION CAVERN (USA) 4-9-0 J Bailey, ... (39 to 10) 3
IBERO (Arg) 6-9-0 J Santos, ... (24 to 10) 4
ALYDEED (Can) 4-9-0 C Perret, ... (7 to 5 fav) 5
LOACH (USA) 5-9-0 H McCauley, ... (25 to 1) 6
Dist: 2½l, 3 ¼l, hd, 10l, 5½l. 1m 22.28s. (6 Ran).
(R Kaufman), P Serpe

CURRAGH (IRE) (soft to heavy)
Saturday October 9th
Going Correction: PLUS 1.05 sec. per fur.

4380 Cill Dara EBF Maiden (2-y-o) £5,244 1m........................... (2:00)

AKHIYAR (Ire) 9-0 M J Kinane (4) .... (Evens fav) 1
4244 AARDWOLF 9-0 W Carson (27) .... (10 to 1) 2
TWO SHONAS (Ire) 8-11 J F Egan (23) .... (20 to 1) 3
4244 CARABAWN (Ire) 9-0 L Piggott (26) .... (12 to 1) 4
3415⁵ ACROSS THE TRACKS (Ire) 8-9 (2*) D G O'Shea (22) .... (10 to 1) 5
4146⁴ MONEYBROKER (Ire) 9-0 K J Manning (19) .... (14 to 1) 6
IXWORTH 9-0 R Hughes (25) .... (10 to 1) 7
THEATRE FLIGHT (USA) 8-11 D V Smith (10) ..... (33 to 1) 8
4135⁵ LIFE DANCING (Ire) 8-7 (4*) J J Behan (9) .... (12 to 1) 9
DEELISH (Ire) 8-11 P Shanahan (16) .... (20 to 1) 10
4244⁶ FLY THE CREST (USA) 9-0 R Lappin (5) .... (10 to 1) 11
2701⁷ PRINCESS SHERA (Ire) (bl) 8-5 (6*) D J O'Donohoe (12) .... (20 to 1) 12
4146 ZARA ZAREEN (Ire) 8-6 (8*) G M Moylan (29) ...... (33 to 1) 13
2402⁷ OPULENT 9-0 P V Gilson (2) .... (10 to 1) 14
3541 STRANGFORD LOUGH (Ire) 8-6 (8*) R T Fitzpatrick (8) .... (33 to 1) 15
4146 GOVERNMENT GRANT (Ire) 9-0 S Craine (3) ...... (20 to 1) 16
4146³ ARKUB 9-0 W J Supple (6) .... (11 to 2) 17
MYSTIC MOMENT (Ire) 8-11 D Manning (13) ...... (20 to 1) 18
4261⁹ CLASSIC QUEEN (Ire) 8-11 N G McCullagh (18) ... (20 to 1) 19
KNIGHT OF VISION (Ire) 9-0 J P Murtagh (15) ..... (14 to 1) 20
3562³ NORTHERN BARS (Ire) 9-0 C Roche (7) .... (8 to 1) 21
4261 DEEP IN SEPTEMBER (Ire) 8-1 (10*) S Kelly (24) ... (33 to 1) 22
3492 JACQUIMO (Ire) 9-0 D Hogan (28) .... (14 to 1) 23
4183 CAPITAL GAIN 8-6 (8*) A P McCoy (11) .... (20 to 1) 24
4058 BURKEAN MELODY (Ire) 9-0 L O'Shea (17) .... (20 to 1) 25
WONDERFUL VENTURE (Ire) 8-12 (2*) P Carberry (21) .... (16 to 1) 26
KILNOE (Ire) 8-5 (6*) P P Murphy (1) .... (33 to 1) 27
Dist: 3½l, 2½l, 4½l, nk. 1m 53.70s. a 17.10s (27 Ran).
(H H Aga Khan), John M Oxx

4381 Blandford Stakes (Group 2) (3-y-o and up) £23,000 1½m.............. (2:30)

4055³ FORESEE (bl) 3-8-8¹ J P Murtagh (2) *3rd, rdn appr 2 fs out, prog to ld one out, contact wth second, styd on.* .... (13 to 8 on) 1
4260* PORTRAIT GALLERY (Ire) (bl) 3-8-10 L Piggott (1) *sn led, rdn 2 fs out, hdd one out, contact wth wnr, rnwd effrt cl hme, jst fld.* .... (7 to 2) 2
4245³ BALAWHAR (Ire) 3-8-7 M J Kinane (4) *hld up, prog hfwy, rdn and no extr appr fnl furlong, wknd.* .... (8 to 1) 3
4055⁷ SHREWD IDEA 3-8-12 W Carson (3) *trkd ldr, rdn 2 fs out, sn wknd, eased wehn btn ins last.* .... (5 to 1) 4
Dist: Sht-hd, 6l, 5½l. 2m 45.70s. a 16.20s (4 Ran).
SR: 58/59/44/38/ (Sheikh Mohammed), John M Oxx

4382 Juddmonte EBF Beresford Stakes (Group 3) (2-y-o) £17,250 1m.... (3:00)

4240* SHERIDAN (Ire) 8-11 W Carson (3) *wl plcd, prog 3 fs out, quickened to ld one and a half out, styd on strly.* .... (100 to 30) 1
4054² CITY NIGHTS (Ire) 8-11 M J Kinane (1) *hld up, prog 3 fs out, ev ch 2 out, sn rdn, kpt on one pace.* ..... (3 to 1 jt-fav) 2
3771* BAWARDI (Ire) 8-11 J P Murtagh (6) *mid-div, rdn 2 fs out, kpt on ins last wthout threatening wnr.* .. (3 to 1 jt-fav) 3
4054⁴ CLIFDON FOG (Ire) (bl) 8-11 C Roche (5) *led early, rdn appr 2 fs out, no extr and wknd one out, kpt on ins last.* .... (8 to 1) 4
3806* MANAAFIS (Ire) 8-11 W J Supple (2) *mid-div, rdn 2 fs out, styd on one pace.* .... (8 to 1) 5
MR RESPECTFULL 8-11 N G McCullagh (9) *rear, rdn 2 fs out, kpt on.* .... (14 to 1) 6
4134² OUT IN THE SUN (USA) 8-8 K J Manning (7) *al rear, kpt on ins fnl 2 fs.* .... (16 to 1) 7
4244⁵ SHARP TRY (Ire) 8-11 R Hughes (8) *trkd ldr, led aftr 2 fs, rdn two out, sn hdd and wknd.* .... (14 to 1) 8
NEW TRIBE (Ire) 8-11 S Craine (4) *trkd ldrs, rdn 3 fs out, slightly hmpd 2 out, sn wknd.* .... (8 to 1) 9
Dist: 4l, 5l, ½l, 3l. 1m 47.30s. a 10.70s (9 Ran).
SR: 63/51/36/34/25/-/ (Cyril Humphris), J L Dunlop

4383 Diamond Stakes (Listed) (3-y-o and up) £8,625 1¼m................ (3:30)

3923⁵ EUROSTORM (USA) (bl) 3-8-12 P V Gilson (2) *trkd ldr, prog to ld bef 2 fs out, 4 ls clr appr one out, hld on whn chlgd cl hme.* .... (7 to 1) 1
3770⁸ TRYARRA (Ire) 3-8-8 L Piggott (5) *hld up, prog 4 fs out, styd on strly ins last, nrst finish.* .... (14 to 1) 2
4153⁴ KATIBA (USA) 3-8-8 W Carson (10) *mid-div, some prog 2 fs out, kpt on wl ins last wthout rching wnr.* ..... (4 to 1) 3
3824² TARAKANA (USA) 3-8-8 J P Murtagh (4) *hld up, gd prog appr fnl furlong, kpt on till wknd cl hme...* (7 to 2 fav) 4
4147⁵ OENOTHERA (Ire) 3-8-8 S Craine (12) *mid-div, rdn 2 fs out, no extr and wknd ins last.* .... (12 to 1) 5
4289⁴ BE MY HOPE (Ire) 4-9-0 N G McCullagh (13) *slwly away, kpt on ins fnl 2 fs wthout threatening ldrs....* (10 to 1) 6
4245* FLAME OF PERSIA (Ire) 3-8-8 P Carberry (6) *wl-plcd, rdn appr 2 fs out, kpt on one pace.* .... (9 to 1) 7
3923* CHANZI (USA) (bl) 3-9-1 R Hughes (11) *mid-div, rdn 2 fs out, no extr and wknd appr fnl furlong.* .... (7 to 1) 8
4147² SOVIET CHOICE (Ire) 3-8-8 M J Kinane (9) *trkd ldrs, rdn 2 fs out, no extr and wknd one out.* .... (10 to 1) 9
3916⁵ FAIRY LORE (Ire) 3-8-4 (4*) J J Behan (1) *al rear, rdn and wknd 2 fs out.* .... (14 to 1) 10
4368⁶ ANDANTE (Ire) 3-8-8 C Roche (14) *wl plcd, rdn 2 fs out, wknd.* .... (16 to 1) 11
4186⁵ EBONY AND IVORY (Ire) 4-9-0 W J Supple (3) *led till hdd o'r 2 fs out, sn wknd.* .... (16 to 1) 12
4289³ NEVER BACK DOWN (Ire) 3-8-8 J F Egan (8) *al rear, rdn and wknd 2 fs out.* .... (10 to 1) 13
4246 MYSTICAL CITY (Ire) 3-8-8 P Shanahan (7) *al rear.* (50 to 1) 14
Dist: ½l, sht-hd, hd, 3l. 2m 18.30s. a 15.50s (14 Ran).
SR: 48/43/42/41/35/-/ (Mrs G W Jennings), C Collins

4384 Glengarriff Handicap (0-105 3-y-o and up) £6,900 1m.................. (4:00)

4284³ WANDERING THOUGHTS (Ire) [-] 4-8-12 J P Murtagh (2) .... (3 to 1) 1
2878 CHEVIOT AMBLE (Ire) [-] 5-9-4 (6*) J R Barry (4) ... (12 to 1) 2
4245² SHARP REVIEW (Ire) [-] 5-9-2 M J Kinane (3) ... (5 to 2 fav) 3
3029⁷ SABAYA (USA) [-] 3-8-11 W J Supple (9) .... (12 to 1) 4
3610² RAJAURA (Ire) [-] 3-8-1 (2*) D G O'Shea (12) .... (7 to 1) 5
3202⁷ BIZANA (Ire) [-] 3-7-12 J F Egan (1) .... (12 to 1) 6
4284⁹ GALLARDINI (Ire) [-] 4-8-3 D Manning (11) .... (16 to 1) 7
4172 RONDELLI (Ire) [-] 3-8-12 C Roche (6) .... (8 to 1) 8
3926⁸ LA CENERENTOLA (Ire) [-] 3-7-4 (6*) P P Murphy (10) .... (12 to 1) 9
576⁹ TOPOGRAPHE (Fr) [-] 3-7-11 (6*) D J O'Donohoe (7) .... (14 to 1) 10
3916⁷ LOUGHMOGUE (Ire) [-] 3-8-2 N G McCullagh (8) .. (12 to 1) 11
4060⁴ LOS ANGELES (Ire) [-] 4-7-2 (8*) G M Moylan (13) (20 to 1) 12
850² DIFFERENT TIMES (Ire) [-] 3-7-11 (4*) J J Behan (5) (12 to 1) 13
Dist: 3l, 1l, 1l, 2l. 1m 51.10s. a 14.50s (13 Ran).
SR: 7/10/-/-/-/-/ (W Mythen), A P O'Brien

4385 Waterford Lodge Handicap (0-95 3-y-o and up) £3,105 6f.............. (4:30)

4184³ SHRAGRADDY LASS (Ire) [-] 3-7-2 (8*) B Halligan (2) (7 to 1) 1
3928⁷ PETITE EPAULETTE [-] 3-8-4 (8*) G M Moylan (13) (14 to 1) 2
4056⁷ CISEAUX (USA) [-] 4-10-0 M J Kinane (6) ...... (6 to 1 fav) 3
3417 AURLIANO (Ire) [-] 3-7-2 (6*) P P Murphy (7) ...... (50 to 1) 4
4370³ MACQUARIE RIDGE (USA) [-] (bl) 5-7-6¹ (2*) D G O'Shea (15) .... (8 to 1) 5
3606² LADY PRESIDENT (Ire) [-] (bl) 4-8-0 (4*) J J Behan (14) .... (9 to 1) 6
4287⁶ NAIVITY (Ire) [-] 4-8-11 R Hughes (4) .... (9 to 1) 7
4287⁸ ADRIEN DE VRIES (Ire) [-] 3-9-0 P V Gilson (10) ... (10 to 1) 8
4057⁵ SAMOT (Ire) [-] (bl) 3-8-6 P Shanahan (12) .... (12 to 1) 9
3928* BENE MERENTI (Ire) [-] (bl) 3-9-3 N G McCullagh (9) (8 to 1) 10
1513² DIXIE FAVOR (USA) [-] 4-8-7 (8*) P M O'Donohoe (5) .... (16 to 1) 11
3330 MAGIC DON (Ire) [-] (bl) 4-8-1 (8*) R T Fitzpatrick (18) .... (12 to 1) 12
1853⁴ ST MARTHA (Ire) [-] (bl) 3-9-1 C Roche (3) .... (8 to 1) 13
4184² PILGRIM BAY (Ire) [-] 3-8-7 (6*) D J O'Donohoe (16) (7 to 1) 14
3298⁷ ANOTHER FLYER (Ire) [-] 3-7-7 L O'Shea (8) ...... (50 to 1) 15
3768² MARY'S CASE (Ire) [-] 3-8-4 W J Supple (11) ...... (14 to 1) 16
3928⁹ BOURREE [-] 5-8-3 J F Egan (17) .... (14 to 1) 17
Dist: 3½l, hd, ½l, nk. 1m 21.00s. a 10.50s (17 Ran).
SR: -/-/15/-/-/-/ (Mrs J M Mullins), W P Mullins

4386 Swilly EBF Race (3-y-o and up) £3,795 7f.............................. (5:00)

2285* DINESEN 3-8-13 R Hughes (5) .... (4 to 1) 1

4056[4] MYSTERIOUS WAYS (Ire) 3-9-3 L Piggott (9) . . . (7 to 4 on) 2
3852[4] KURDISTAN (Ire) 3-8-13 P V Gilson (3) . . . . (7 to 1) 3
4136[6] MISS MISTLETOES (Ire) 3-9-0 S Craine (8) . . . . (7 to 1) 4
4057 WASSL'S NANNY (Ire) 4-8-8 N G McCullagh (7) . . . (20 to 1) 5
4118 MATCHLESS PRINCE (Ire) 3-8-8 J F Egan (4) . . . . . (25 to 1) 6
4094[8] SYDNEY SUSSEX (Ire) 3-8-8 W J Supple (2) . . . . (50 to 1) 7
4245 LADY HOSTESS (Ire) 4-8-8 K J Manning (6) . . . . (50 to 1) 8
Dist: Hd, 4l, 2l, 10l. 1m 36.40s. a 13.20s (8 Ran).
SR: 11/14/-/-/-/ (William J Betz), D Hanley

4387 Children's Medical & Research Foundation Charity Private Sweepstakes (3-y-o and up) £0 1¾m. . . . .(5:15)

4288 IMAD (USA) 3-11-3 Capt John Ledingham (5) . . . (7 to 4 on) 1
SLANEY FOOD 6-11-12 Nicholas Cousins (1) . . . . . . (6 to 1) 2
4368 SARAKAYA 8-11-9 Capt William Hayes (2) . . . . (10 to 1) 3
4368[4] ALOHA (Ire) 4-12-11[6] Tommy Murphy (8) . . . . (3 to 1) 4
753 MIDNIGHT COURT (USA) 10-12-7 Capt Ger O'Grady (3) . . . . (10 to 1) 5
2484[6] SHY GAL (Ire) 5-11-11[2] Pat Kane (9) . . . . (12 to 1) 6
2514 PERCY LANE (Ire) 3-11-11[1] Lt Col J H Murphy (7) (10 to 1) 7
3853[6] CONCERT ORCHESTRA (Ire) 4-11-13[4] Capt Niall O'Donohue (6) . . . . (7 to 1) 8
POST MASTER 7-11-12 Linus Fahy (4) . . . . (8 to 1) 9
Dist: 4l, 7l, 2½l, 2½l. (Time not taken) (9 Ran).
(Hamdan Al-Maktoum), Kevin Prendergast

DOWN ROYAL (IRE) (good to yielding) Saturday October 9th

4388 Isuzu EBF Fillies Maiden (2-y-o) £2,588 7f. (3:45)

KILMOOD LASS (Ire) 8-6 (8*) P J Smullen (11) . . . . . (16 to 1) 1
4286[8] SECRET WAR (Ire) 8-12 (2*) R M Burke (8) . . . . (10 to 1) 2
ANTIQUITY (Ire) 8-10 (4*) J A Heffernan (6) . . . .(7 to 1) 3
4261[2] AL NAAYY 8-8 (6*) B J Walsh (4) . . . . (5 to 1) 4
4135[9] MARROWFAT LADY (Ire) 9-0 B Coogan (3) . . . . (20 to 1) 5
3954[6] CNOCMA (Ire) 9-0 . . . . (20 to 1) 6
4134 LEMOIRE (Ire) 8-4 (10*) S N Donohue (13) . . . . (25 to 1) 7
BLACKDABRONZE (Ire) 8-4 (10*) I Browne (9) . . . . . (20 to 1) 8
CAN'T AFFORD IT (Ire) 9-0 N Byrne (2) . . . . (8 to 1) 9
CHANGED AROUND (Ire) 8-6 (8*) B P Gowran (10) (20 to 1) 10
GESHA (Ire) 8-6 (8*) T E Durcan (5) . . . . (20 to 1) 11
POOR PRINTER (Ire) 9-0 D J Smith (7) . . . . (20 to 1) 12
4059[7] MEGAN'S DREAM (Ire) 8-10 (4*) W J Smith (14) . . . (20 to 1) 13
FOUR DUSTY ROADS (Ire) 8-4 (10*) (16) . . . . (20 to 1) 14
2666 COOLAGOWN DOME (Ire) 9-0 A J Nolan (15) . . . . . . (20 to 1) 15
FALLING IN LOVE (Ire) 9-0 F Woods (12) . . . . (5 to 4 on) 16
Dist: ½l, 5½l, 1½l, ½l. (Time not taken) (16 Ran).
(Miss Marie McGrattan), Daniel J Murphy

4389 Pandoro Handicap (0-60 3-y-o and up) £1,380 5f. . . . . (4:15)

4184[5] DAIRINE'S DELIGHT (Ire) [-] 3-8-11 (6*) B J Walsh (2) . . . . (6 to 4 fav) 1
4184[9] HAWAIAN TASCA (Ire) [-] 4-8-3 (4*) J A Heffernan (9) . . . . (14 to 1) 2
4370[4] BOLERO DANCER (Ire) [-] 5-9-4 (4*) C Everard (8) . . (7 to 1) 3
4184[8] SOUTHERN RULE [-] (bl) 6-8-2 (8*) T J Daly (6) . . . . (11 to 2) 4
3606[6] FIVE LITTLE GIRLS (Ire) [-] 3-9-9 N Byrne (3) . . . . . . (10 to 1) 5
3330 FILL MY GLASS [-] 9-8-4 (4*) W J Smith (1) . . . . (14 to 1) 6
DUNSFORD [-] 7-7-13[4] (8*) P J Smullen (11) . . . . . . (14 to 1) 7
3294 TIGNES (Ire) [-] 5-8-9 (8*) B P Gowran (10) . . . . (7 to 1) 8
2667 SILVER SHARP (Ire) [-] 3-8-10 A J Nolan (4) . . . . (20 to 1) 9
3827 BOLD MOLLY (Ire) [-] 4-8-9 (2*) R M Burke (5) . . . . . . (8 to 1) 10
3244[9] SNATCH IT (Ire) [-] (bl) 3-8-2 (8*) G Coogan (7) . . . . (10 to 1) 11
Dist: 1½l, hd, sht-hd, nk. (Time not taken) (11 Ran).
(Seamus MacCrosain), Michael Cunningham

SANTA ANITA (USA) (firm) Saturday October 9th

4390 Oak Leaf Stakes (Grade 1) (2-y-o) £79,470 1m 110yds. . . . .

PHONE CHATTER (USA) 8-5[2] L Pincay Jr, ... (5 to 1) 1
SARDULA (USA) 8-4[1] E Delahoussaye, ... (5 to 1 on) 2
TRICKY CODE (USA) 8-3 G Stevens, ... (11 to 2) 3
RHAPSODIC (USA) 8-3 C McCarron, ... (5 to 1 on) 4
EMERALD COLONY (USA) 8-3 C Black, ... (17 to 1) 5
VIZ (USA) 8-3 A Solis, ... (25 to 1) 6
Dist: ½l, 7½l, 3l, ½l, 8l. 1m 41.78s. (6 Ran).
(H Sarkowsky), R Mandella

YORK (heavy) Saturday October 9th

Going Correction: PLUS 0.95 sec. per fur. (races 1,4,5,6,7), PLUS 1.00 (2,3)

4391 Crowther Homes Handicap Class D (0-80 3-y-o and up) £9,325 1m 205yds . . . .(2:15)

3881[5] DRUMMER HICKS [76] 4-9-13 L Dettori (8) *made most and wide strt till hdd o'r 2 fs out, sn hrd rdn, edgd rght and rallied to ld nr finish.* . . . . (12 to 1) 1
4116[4] FOX SPARROW [73] 3-9-5 Pat Eddery (20) *rcd wide, al cl up, effrt to ld o'r 2 fs out, sn rdn, edgd lft ins last, hdd nr finish.* . . . . (13 to 2 op 5 to 1 tchd 7 to 1) 2
4155[5] BEVERLY KNIGHT [66] 3-8-12 J Reid (18) *al prmnt, effrt in centre 3 fs out, rdn and kpt on one pace fnl 2 furlongs.* . . . . (16 to 1 op 14 to 1 tchd 20 to 1) 3
4101[6] STOPROVERITATE [55] 4-8-6 N Connorton (14) *mid-div, hdwy o'r 2 fs out, styd on und pres ins last.* . . . . (16 to 1 op 14 to 1) 4
4101[4] GOLD BLADE [52] 4-8-3 W Ryan (1) *in tch, effrt and hdwy o'r 2 fs out, sn rdn and one pace.* . .(12 to 1 op 14 to 1) 5
4336* COLTRANE [64] (v) 5-9-1 (4ex) A Munro (11) *prmnt, effrt in centre and ev ch 3 fs out, sn rdn, grad wknd fnl 2 furlongs.* . . . . (11 to 4 fav op 7 to 2 tchd 5 to 2) 6
4120[6] SALDA [58] 4-8-9 A Culhane (9) *chsd ldrs, rdn 3 fs out, grad wknd.* . . . .(12 to 1 op 10 to 1 tchd 14 to 1) 7
4235 RESOLUTE BAY [57] 7-8-8 S Perks (13) *mid-div, effrt and hdwy o'r 2 fs out, sn rdn, nvr dngrs.* . . . .(33 to 1) 8
2354[9] INFERRING [45] 5-7-5 (5*) D Wright (12) *nvr rch ldrs.* . . . .(25 to 1 tchd 33 to 1) 9
4258[5] NORTHERN CONQUEROR (Ire) [49] 5-8-0 D Harrison (7) *al mid-div.* . . . . (12 to 1 op 10 to 1) 10
4343[3] NO COMEBACKS [55] 5-8-6 K Fallon (2) *rear, rdn 3 fs out, no hdwy.* . . . .(12 to 1 op 10 to 1 tchd 14 to 1) 11
4115[8] LOCK KEEPER (USA) [47] 7-7-12 J Lowe (4) *al rear.* . . . . (14 to 1 op 12 to 1) 12
4258[2] SILVER GROOM (Ire) [61] 3-8-7 T Quinn (10) *in tch, effrt and hdwy 3 fs out, rdn and wknd 2 furlongs out.* . . . . (7 to 1 op 10 to 1) 13
55[3] EUROTWIST [65] 4-8-9 (7*) V Halliday (19) *al beh.* (33 to 1) 14
4158[4] MAROWINS [46] 4-7-11 N Adams (6) *al rear.* . . . . (16 to 1 op 14 to 1) 15
4016[3] MARY MACBLAIN [43] 4-7-8[1] J Quinn (16) *chsd ldrs, rdn hfwy, sn wknd.* . . . . (50 to 1) 16
CHIEFS BABU [60] 5-8-11 M Birch (5) *prmnt to hfwy, sn lost pl and beh.* . . . .(66 to 1 op 50 to 1) 17
4188 BARBARY REEF (Ire) [42] 5-7-7 G Bardwell (3) *al rear.* . . . .(100 to 1) 18
Dist: Sht-hd, 5l, 2½l, nk, 1½l, 3l, 5l, 1½l, hd, 2l. 2m 1.41s. a 12.21s (18 Ran).
SR: 59/50/28/14/10/17/2/-/-/ (Mrs N Napier), E Weymes

4392 ANC Rockingham Stakes Class A (Listed Race) (2-y-o) £10,173 6f. . . . . (2:45)

3994* PALACEGATE JACK (Ire) 9-2 J Carroll (2) *made all, quickened o'r 2 fs out, rdn ins last and ran on wl.* . . . . (11 to 4 op 2 to 1 tchd 3 to 1) 1
2947[4] NIGHTITUDE 8-6 W Ryan (4) *hld up, hdwy 2 fs out, effrt to chal and ev ch ins last, sn rdn and not quicken.* . . . . (12 to 1 op 8 to 1) 2
3994[4] EHTFAAL (Ire) 8-11 R Hills (3) *trkd ldg pair gng wl, smooth hdwy and ev ch 2 fs out, sn rdn, wknd quickly appr fnl furlong.* . . . .(100 to 30 op 9 to 4) 3
4257* MAZENTRE FORWARD (Ire) 8-11 Pat Eddery (1) *cl up, pushed alng hfwy, rdn wl o'r 2 fs out and sn btn.* . . . .(6 to 5 on op 11 to 8 tchd 5 to 4 on) 4
Dist: ½l, 5l, 10l. 1m 18.86s. a 8.86s (4 Ran).
SR: 45/33/18/-/ (Palacegate Corporation Ltd), J Berry

4393 Coral Sprint Trophy Handicap Class C (0-100 3-y-o and up) £13,500 6f. . (3:15)

4038[2] BENZOE (Ire) [77] (bl) 3-8-8 T Lucas (11) *led aftr one furlong and swtchd to far rail, sn clr, ran on wl fnl furlong.* . . . .(12 to 1 tchd 14 to 1) 1
4038[9] JIGSAW BOY [72] 4-8-0 (5*) S Drowne (1) *trkd ldrs far side, hdwy 2 fs out, rdn to chase wnr appr last, no imprsn.* . . . .(8 to 1 jt-fav op 7 to 1 tchd 10 to 1) 2
4096* NORDAN RAIDER [72] 5-8-5 L Charnock (22) *speed stands side, swtchd to centre, rdn 2 fs out, kpt on one pace.* . . . . (8 to 1 jt-fav op 10 to 1) 3
4151[9] BORN TO BE [78] 4-8-11 G Hind (2) *led one furlong, al prmnt far side, rdn 2 fs out, kpt on.* . . . .(25 to 1) 4
4168[5] PETRACO (Ire) [73] 5-8-6 G Duffield (6) *chsd ldrs, rdn and kpt on one pace fnl 2 fs.* . . . .(16 to 1 op 14 to 1) 5
4040 GARNOCK VALLEY [90] 3-9-7 K Darley (8) *prmnt, rdn 2 fs out, grad wknd.* . . . . (16 to 1 op 14 to 1) 6
4040 CUMBRIAN WALTZER [83] 8-9-2 M Birch (7) *mid-div, effrt and hdwy 2 fs out, sn rdn, kpt on one pace.* . . . . (10 to 1 op 12 to 1 tchd 14 to 1) 7
3404 SO INTREPID (Ire) [80] 3-8-11 Paul Eddery (18) *slwly into strd and beh, gd hdwy centre hfwy, rdn and one pace wl o'r one furlong out.* . . . . (20 to 1 tchd 25 to 1) 8
4297 SUNDAY'S HILL [81] (v) 4-9-0 T Quinn (3) *cl up far side, rdn o'r 2 fs out, grad wknd.* . . . . (16 to 1 op 14 to 1 tchd 20 to 1) 9
4040[6] HOW'S YER FATHER [85] 7-9-4 A Munro (20) *mid-div centre, effrt o'r 2 fs out, sn rdn and no hdwy.* . . . . (12 to 1 op 14 to 1) 10

4151[5] PETERSFORD GIRL (Ire) [80] 3-8-11 J Reid (12) *nvr rch ldrs.* ....(11 to 1 op 12 to 1 tchd 10 to 1) 11
4280 NEITHER NOR [79] 4-8-12 J Williams (19) *nvr rch ldrs.* ....(25 to 1) 12
3756[3] MAGIC ORB [77] 3-8-8 A Mackay (13) *nvr a factor.* ....(25 to 1 op 20 to 1) 13
4278 TRUTHFUL IMAGE [88] (bl) 4-9-7 D Biggs (4) *in tch far side to hfwy, sn wknd*.............................(20 to 1) 14
4280 GREEN DOLLAR [78] 10-8-11 M Tebbutt (14) *nvr rch ldrs.* ....(33 to 1) 15
4040 PALACEGATE TOUCH [91] (bl) 3-9-8 J Carroll (23) *speed stands side, swtchd to centre hfwy, sn rdn and btn.* ....(25 to 1) 16
4038* SOBERING THOUGHTS [73] 7-8-6 W Ryan (9) *nvr rch ldrs.* ....(18 to 1 op 14 to 1) 17
4278 DOMINUET [91] 8-9-10 J Lowe (15) *al rear*....... (25 to 1) 18
4278[7] STAR FAMILY FRIEND (Ire) [89] (bl) 3-9-6 P Robinson (16) *nvr rch ldrs*..(20 to 1) 19
4363 ANOTHER JADE [75] 3-7-13 (7*) M Baird (17) *chsd ldrs to hfwy, sn wknd*.......(33 to 1 op 20 to 1 tchd 40 to 1) 20
3127[7] SO RHYTHMICAL [80] 9-8-13 G Bardwell (5) *slwly into strd, al rear*...................................(20 to 1) 21
4278[3] NAGIDA [89] 4-9-8 J Weaver (10) *al beh*............(10 to 1) 22
4168 DENSBEN [78] 9-8-11 K Fallon (21) *al outpcd and beh.* ....(20 to 1 op 16 to 1) 23

Dist: 5l, 1½l, hd, 2l, 2l, 1l, sht-hd, 1l, sht-hd, hd. 1m 17.52s. a 7.52s (23 Ran).
SR: 64/41/35/40/27/34/25/19/18/ (Tony Fawcett), M W Easterby

4394 Carling Black Label Lager Handicap Class D (0-80 3-y-o and up) £6,664 6f 214yds........................ (3:45)

4297[2] OUR RITA [70] 4-9-5 D Holland (1) *in tch far side, hdwy o'r 2 fs out, effrt to ld appr fnl furlong, sn rdn and ran on wl*...................(9 to 2 fav op 7 to 1 tchd 4 to 1) 1
4333[5] PUSEY STREET BOY [53] 6-8-2 Paul Eddery (9) *chsd ldg pair, hdwy to ld 2 and a half fs out, rdn and hdd appr last, kpt on*......................................(16 to 1) 2
3901 NORTHERN CHIEF [63] 3-8-9 M Birch (2) *mid-div, hdwy far side 3 fs out, rdn 2 furlongs out, styd on ins last.* ....(16 to 1) 3
3168[7] PALACEGATE GOLD (Ire) [53] 4-8-2 A Munro (15) *in tch, hdwy centre 3 fs out, rdn 2 out, kpt on ins last.* (25 to 1) 4
3887[2] HAWAII STORM (Fr) [45] 5-7-8[1] R Street (4) *beh, gd hdwy far rls 2 fs out, sn rdn, styd on ins last*...........(20 to 1) 5
4156[6] SARTIGILA [60] 4-8-4 (5*) J Marshall (24) *mid-div centre, effrt and hdwy o'r 2 fs out, sn rdn and kpt on.* (25 to 1) 6
4172 SAGEBRUSH ROLLER [79] 5-10-0 G Duffield (5) *mid-div, hdwy far side 3 fs out, rdn and kpt on same pace appr fnl furlong*.............................(8 to 1 tchd 9 to 1) 7
3830[6] KISSAVOS [44] 7-7-0 (7*) Antoinette Armes (7) *in tch, hdwy centre 3 fs out, rdn 2 out, sn one pace*.........(33 to 1) 8
4156[8] GENTLE HERO (USA) [50] (v) 7-7-13 D Harrison (6) *chsd ldr, rdn 3 fs out, grad wknd*......................(33 to 1) 9
4320[7] KARINSKA [66] 3-8-7 (5*) D McCabe (12) *slwly into strd and beh, some hdwy fnl 2 fs*..................(20 to 1) 10
4297 BATTLE COLOURS (Ire) [73] 4-9-8 K Fallon (11) *mid-div, hdwy centre 2 fs out, kpt on one pace.* ....(20 to 1 op 16 to 1) 11
4107[4] LEIF THE LUCKY (USA) [73] 4-9-8 N Connorton (13) *mid-div, wide strt and hdwy 3 fs out, sn rdn, nvr rch ldrs.* ....(10 to 1 op 12 to 1) 12
4297[5] RURAL LAD [57] 4-8-6 Pat Eddery (20) *hld up, styd on fnl 2 fs, nvr dngrs*....................(10 to 1 tchd 9 to 1) 13
3774[4] THORNTON GATE [73] 4-9-5 (3*) S Maloney (23) *rcd wide, speed to hfwy*.....................(20 to 1 op 16 to 1) 14
3365[8] DREAM CARRIER (Ire) [48] 5-7-11 F Norton (16) *al mid-div.* ....(25 to 1 op 20 to 1) 15
3778 SAVAHRA SOUND [65] 8-9-0 S Webster (17) *prmnt in centre till rdn and wknd o'r 3 fs out*.............(33 to 1) 16
1286 TWILIGHT FALLS [46] 8-7-9 L Charnock (8) *al rear.* ....(20 to 1 op 16 to 1) 17
4333 YOUNG VALENTINE [47] 4-7-10 N Carlisle (14) *nvr a factor.* ....(33 to 1) 18
4181[4] DEAD CALM [50] (v) 3-7-10 J Lowe (25) *al rear*....(33 to 1) 19
3988[5] FUCHU [68] 3-8-11 (3*) B Doyle (22) *nvr a factor.* (20 to 1) 20
4166[4] SEA DEVIL [77] 7-9-12 L Dettori (19) *beh, swtchd far side hfwy, no hdwy*.........(8 to 1 op 9 to 1 tchd 7 to 1) 21
4235[4] A LITTLE PRECIOUS [44] 7-7-7 J Quinn (18) *al rear.* ....(16 to 1 tchd 20 to 1) 22
4166[7] BOURSIN (Ire) [57] (bl) 4-8-6 Dale Gibson (3) *led far rls, hdd and wknd 2 and a half fs out.* ....(20 to 1 op 16 to 1 tchd 25 to 1) 23
3439[2] AQUILETTA [67] 3-8-13 T Quinn (21) *slwly into strd, al beh.* ....(25 to 1) 24
4270[3] TARTIB (Ire) [60] 3-8-6 R Hills (10) *chsd ldrs, rdn and wknd 3 fs out*..(25 to 1) 25

Dist: 1l, hd, sht-hd, 2½l, ½l, sht-hd, 3½l, 8l, ½l, nk. 1m 32.03s. a 10.33s (25 Ran).
SR: 50/30/36/28/12/25/43/-/-/ (A C Edwards), Dr J D Scargill

4395 Bramham Moor Conditions Stakes Class B (3-y-o and up) £7,270 1m 3f 195yds........................ (4:15)

1018[8] MASHAALLAH (USA) 5-9-12 L Dettori (3) *hdwy to ld 4 fs out, quickened 2 out, ran on wl fnl furlong.* ....(5 to 4 tchd 6 to 5) 1
4271[2] PETER QUINCE 3-8-9 W Ryan (2) *hld up, hdwy to chase wnr 4 fs out, effrt and rdn 2 out, ev ch, kpt on.* ....(5 to 4 on op 6 to 4 on) 2
4341 LUNAR RISK (v) 3-8-9 A Munro (1) *led and sn clr, wknd and hdd 4 fs out, soon wl beh and eased.* ....(20 to 1 op 33 to 1 tchd 50 to 1) 3

Dist: 1l, dist. 2m 48.21s. a 20.21s (3 Ran).
SR: 24/5/-/ (Sheikh Ahmed Al Maktoum), J H M Gosden

4396 Coldstream Guards Association Cup Maiden Fillies' Stakes Class D (2-y-o) £5,253 7f 202yds................ (4:45)

4002[2] SILVER HUT (USA) 8-11 Pat Eddery (4) *led, wide strt, hdd briefly 2 fs out, sn rgned ld, quickened appr fnl furlong, rdn and ran on ins last.* ....(13 to 8 fav op 6 to 4 tchd 7 to 4) 1
4232[2] MICROLITE (USA) 8-11 T Quinn (6) *trkd ldg pair, effrt o'r 2 fs out, sn rdn, styd on wl ins last*.... (3 to 1 op 9 to 4) 2
3659[3] AZHAAR (USA) 8-11 R Hills (1) *cl up, slight ld 2 fs out, sn hdd, rdn appr fnl furlong, wknd wl ins last.* ....(5 to 2 op 9 to 4 tchd 11 to 4) 3
4149[5] SUNDAY NEWS'N'ECHO (USA) 8-11 D Harrison (5) *hld up in tch, hdwy 3 fs out and sn pushed alng, rdn approachiang fnl furlong, styd on wl nr finish.* ....(10 to 1 tchd 12 to 1) 4
TAHITI BEACH 8-11 C Rutter (3) *hld up in tch, effrt 2 and a half fs out, sn pushed alng, one pace.* ....(14 to 1 op 10 to 1) 5
2044[5] GILBOA 8-11 Paul Eddery (2) *wnt rght strt, chsd ldrs till rdn o'r 3 fs out, wknd quickly*..... (12 to 1 op 10 to 1) 6

Dist: ½l, 1l, hd, 5l, 20l. 1m 51.95s. a 15.65s (6 Ran).
(Dr Carlos E Stelling), R Charlton

4397 Stamford Bridge Conditions Stakes Class D (2-y-o) £5,162 6f 214yds (5:15)

4263* WAFAYT (Ire) 9-1 L Dettori (3) *made all, quickened clr on bit one and a half fs out, unchlgd.* ....(11 to 10 on tchd Evens) 1
4103* NIZAAL (USA) 9-1 R Hills (4) *trkd ldr, pushed alng o'r 2 fs out, sn rdn and wknd wl over one out.* ....(11 to 8 op Evens) 2
KINGSWOOD LEADER (USA) 8-11 K Darley (1) *chsd ldg pair, rdn alng hfwy, sn wl adrift*.... (9 to 1 op 6 to 1) 3
ALCIAN BLUE 8-11 W Ryan (2) *slwly away, al outpcd and beh*..................(16 to 1 op 12 to 1 tchd 20 to 1) 4

Dist: 6l, 1½l, 3l. 1m 34.55s. a 12.85s (4 Ran).
SR: 8/ (Sheikh Ahmed Al Maktoum), J H M Gosden

DUSSELDORF (GER) (heavy)
Sunday October 10th

4398 Grosser Preis von Dusseldorf (Group 2) (3-y-o and up) £32,653 1m 110yds ....(3:45)

3886[5] PORT LUCAYA 3-8-7 L Dettori, *rcd in 3rd, led o'r 2 fs out, ran on strly*.. 1
JOY OF GLORY (USA) 4-9-0 W R Swinburn, *rcd in 4th, ran on fnl 2 fs, unbl to rch wnr*.............................. 2
ART SEBAL (Ity) 5-9-0 J-M Breux, *rear early, ran on fnl 2 fs, nrst finish*.. 3
4073[4] LE JARDIN (Ger) 5-9-0 Manfred Hofer, *hld up, hdwy fnl 2 fs, nvr able to chal*.. 4
4194[3] LASKO (Ger) 3-8-7 A Best, *hld up, styd on one pace fnl 2 fs, nvr nrr*.. 5
ANDREA DORIA (Ger) 7-9-0 N Grant, *trkd ldr till 3 fs out.* 6
4194[7] WILL OF STEEL (Fr) 4-9-0 N Trinker, *nvr plcd to chal*...... 7
3013[7] AUTOCRACY (Ire) 4-9-0 K Woodburn, *prmnt for 5 fs*...... 8
3703[2] VISTO SI STAMPI (Ire) 3-8-7 B Raymond, *led till 2 and a half fs out, wknd quickly*.. 9

Dist: 2½l, 1 ¾l, 1 ¼l, nk, 1 ¾l, 7l, 1 ¼l. 1m 49.60s. (9 Ran).
(Lucayan Stud), R Hannon

LONGCHAMP (FR) (soft)
Sunday October 10th
Going Correction: PLUS 0.80 sec. per fur.

4399 Prix de Conde (Group 3) (2-y-o) £23,895 1m 1f.................. (2:55)

3932[4] CELTIC ARMS (Fr) 8-11 D Boeuf, *last strt, rdn and hdwy o'r one furlong out, ran on wl to ld nr line*............ 1
THREE ANGELS (USA) 8-8 C Asmussen, *trkd ldr, rdn one and a half fs out, led jst ins fnl furlong, ct on line*..... 2
4074[2] SUNSHACK 8-11 Pat Eddery, *led till jst ins fnl furlong, one pace*.. 3
MARTIEN (USA) 8-11 T Jarnet, *3rd strt, rdn and one pace 2 fs out*.. 4
SAMIRI (Fr) 8-11 G Mosse, *4th strt, sn btn*............... 5

Dist: Sht-hd, ¾l, 1½l, 4l. 2m 1.50s. a 12.50s (5 Ran).
SR: 17/13/11/6/-/ (J L Bouchard), P Bary

4400 Prix de la Foret (Group 1) (2-y-o and up) £59,737 7f..................(3:55)

4010* DOLPHIN STREET (Fr) 3-9-10 C Asmussen, *3rd strt, not much room 2 and a half fs out, swtchd one and a half out, fnshd fst, got up on line*..................(18 to 10) 1
3800² SKI PARADISE (USA) 3-9-7 T Jarnet, *4th strt, chlgd 2 and a half fs out, led jst und one and a half out, ct cl hme.*..(10 to 7 on) 2
3764* TINNERS WAY (USA) 3-9-10 Pat Eddery, *trkd ldr, rdn o'r 2 out, led briefly one and a half out, kpt on*....(56 to 10) 3
4076² ACTEUR FRANCAIS (USA) 5-9-12 S Guillot, *led till jst und one and a half fs out, wknd quickly*.......... (16 to 1) 4
4010⁶ DANAKAL (USA) 3-9-10 G Mosse, *al last*........(66 to 10) 5
Dist: Hd, ¾l, 4l, 3l. 1m 26.90s. a 7.40s (5 Ran).
SR: 83/79/80/70/59/ (S S Niarchos), J E Hammond

MUNICH (GER) (good)
Sunday October 10th

4401 Grosser Silicon Bavaria Sprint Preis (Listed) (3-y-o and up) £24,490 6f (4:00)

4076* SHARP PROD (USA) 3-9-1 L Piggott, *made all, ran on wl fnl furlong, all out*.. 1
4315² LITTLE MUNCHKIN (Ire) 3-8-12 K Darley, *str chal fnl one and a half fs, ev ch ins last, not quicken cl hme*....... 2
4304⁷ GLENLIVET (Swe) 5-9-1 L McGarrity, *wl beh till hdwy fnl one and a half fs, nrst finish*................................ 3
LEAD THE DANCE 4-9-1 A Boschert,.................... 4
1908⁶ WHAT KATY DID (USA) 4-8-10 M Roberts,................ 5
3315 ADJMAL (Ire) 4-8-10 A Bond,........................... 6
GREAT LAKES 7-9-1 G Huber,............................. 7
3023³ CATALAN (USA) 4-8-10 J-P Carvalho,.................. 8
SEIGNEUR D'ALLERAY (Fr) 6-8-10 P Heugi,................. 9
DAWSON PLACE (USA) 5-8-10 R Morse,...................... 0
3013⁵ BANNIER (Ger) 6-9-3 D Wildman,....................... 0
4304³ NEVER SO SURE 5-9-1 J D Hillis,...................... 0
1786⁷ STREET REBEL (Can) 5-8-13 P Choppin,................. 0
3717 NEW EUROPE 3-8-7 L Mader,............................. 0
Dist: Nk, 1½l, sht-hd, ½l, 1 ¼l, ¾l, 2l, hd, 1½l, nk. 1m 19.50s. (14 Ran).
(The Queen), Lord Huntingdon

SAN SIRO (ITY) (heavy)
Sunday October 10th

4402 Premio Dormello (Group 3) (2-y-o) £29,533 1m..................... (3:15)

2258³ ALPRIDE (Ire) 8-11 P Perlanti, *made all alone far side, jst hld on*...(86 to 10) 1
4077* SENSAZIONE 8-11 M Esposito, *rcd in second stands side, rdn 2 fs out, ran on wl fnl furlong*........(22 to 10 fav) 2
4077² GOLDEN TAJNIAK (Ire) 8-11 D Holland, *trkd ldrs, rdn o'r 2 fs out, no extr fnl furlong*.......................(42 to 1) 3
4177³ WHATCOMBE (USA) 8-11 A Munro, *al prmnt, rdn and one pace 2 fs out*......................................(5 to 1) 4
4074⁵ ARDANA (Ire) 8-11 Jacqueline Freda, *al mid-divsion.*...(5 to 1) 5
2980⁴ LA GRANDE CASCADE (USA) 8-11 W Mongil, *rear till some late hdwy*..(29 to 10) 6
CARMEN THE BEST (Ire) 8-11 A Corniani, *al mid-div.*...(36 to 1) 7
SECRING (USA) 8-11 V Mezzatesta, *rcd in 3rd, rdn 4 fs out, sn wknd*..(11 to 1) 8
SINSA MONTE 8-11 M Jerome, *prmnt till wknd fnl furlong*..(24 to 1) 9
QUEEN OF LEGHORN (Ire) 8-11 G Forte, *nvr dngrs.*...(14 to 1) 0
1726³ STREISAND 8-11 E Botti, *al beh*..................(34 to 1) 0
2258² KARPACKA (Ire) 8-11 S Dettori, *al beh*.............(23 to 1) 0
ZARA WHETEI (Ity) 8-11 M Vargiu, *outpcd*....... (80 to 1) 0
Dist: Nk, 10l, ¾l, ¾l, ½l, 5l, 22l, 3l, 2½l, 7l. 1m 50.80s. (13 Ran).
(Scuderia Briantea), M Ciciarelli

4403 Premio Vittorio di Capua (Group 1) (3-y-o and up) £135,858 1m.......(4:35)

4173⁶ ALHIJAZ 4-8-12 W Carson (3) *led till o'r 4 fs out, led wl over 3 out, ran on well*...............(16 to 10 jt-fav) 1
PELDER (Ire) 3-8-9 S Soto (1) *3rd strt, effrt rls and hmpd 3 fs out, ran on one pace*.........................(22 to 10) 2
2334⁹ NICER (Ire) 3-8-6 D Holland (5) *trkd ldr, led o'r 4 fs out, rcd wide strt, hdd wl over 3 out*...................(82 to 10) 3
3369⁷ ROUQUETTE 3-8-6 A Badel (2) *rear till some late hdwy fnl 2 fs*..(22 to 1) 4
4173⁵ SWING LOW 4-8-12 J Reid (4) *nvr able to chal.*.......................................(16 to 10 jt-fav) 5
1548⁸ GOLDEN BECHETT (Ire) 3-8-9 Jacqueline Freda (6) *al rear.*...(19 to 1) 6
1548⁶ GOLDEN MINTAGE (USA) 5-8-12 L Sorrentino, *al rear.*...(21 to 1) 7

Dist: 1 ¾l, 6l, 3l, 1½l, ¾l, ½l. 1m 47.90s. (7 Ran).
(Prince A A Faisal), J L Dunlop

SANTA ANITA (USA) (firm)
Sunday October 10th

4404 Oak Tree Invitational (Grade 1) (3-y-o and up) £119,205 1½m..............

3205* KOTASHAAN (Fr) 5-8-12 K Desormeaux,.......(2 to 1 on) 1
1124² LUAZUR (Fr) 4-8-12 P Day,.....................(29 to 10) 2
3609³ LET'S ELOPE (NZ) 6-8-9 P Valenzuela,.........(43 to 10) 3
3187⁷ D'ARROS (Ire) 4-8-12 G Stevens,................(12 to 1) 4
Dist: 4l, 5½l, 2l. 2m 25.06s. (4 Ran).
(La Presle Farm), R Mandella

NAVAN (IRE) (soft)
Tuesday October 12th

4405 Bohermeen E.B.F. Maiden (2-y-o) £3,795 5f...................... (2:30)

RIDGEWOOD BEN 9-0 D Hogan (10)..........(5 to 4 on) 1
3911³ AINE'S PET (Ire) 8-9 (2*) P Carberry (7)............(3 to 1) 2
YANKEE SINGER (Ire) 8-11 W J Supple (5).......(10 to 1) 3
4134⁸ BELLA SIGURA (USA) 8-3 (8*) J J Stack (4)........(33 to 1) 4
4369 MY TRIVET (Ire) 9-0 P Lowry (1)...................(33 to 1) 5
664⁵ MUSICAL SUNSET (Ire) 9-0 P V Gilson (15).......(12 to 1) 6
GLOWING ACCOUNT (Ire) 9-0 R Hughes (2)......(16 to 1) 7
4117⁷ STAGEWALK (Ire) 8-11 S Craine (9)..................(16 to 1) 8
4369⁷ NORDIC COLOURS (Ire) 8-1 (10*) D Quirke (14)...(16 to 1) 9
3039⁶ OVERSEAS TRANSFER (Ire) (bl) 9-0 P Shanahan (12)..(8 to 1) 10
4244 BILLY BUZZ (Ire) 8-11 N G McCullagh (8).........(20 to 1) 11
4059 CONTRASTING (Ire) 8-12 (2*) D G O'Shea (13).....(33 to 1) 12
3911 BERGERACONHOLIDAY (Ire) 9-0 A J Nolan (3)....(20 to 1) 13
ACRABOY LADY (Ire) 8-11 N Byrne (6)...........(25 to 1) 14
4059² ALL SHOW (Ire) (bl) 8-10 (4*) J A Heffernan (11)...(10 to 1) 15
Dist: 8l, sht-hd, 1l, ½l. 1m 5.20s. (15 Ran).
(Mrs Anne Coughlan), John M Oxx

4406 Royal Tara E.B.F. Maiden (3-y-o) £3,795 1m................... (3:00)

4058⁵ TRAGIC POINT (Ire) 8-11 K J Manning (9)............(8 to 1) 1
3922⁷ CLOUD INSPECTOR (Ire) 9-0 N Byrne (14)..........(9 to 1) 2
4146⁵ NIYAZI (Ire) 9-0 R Hughes (3).......................(7 to 1) 3
3922² DEVASTATING STORM (Ire) 9-0 P Shanahan (1) (5 to 4 on) 4
4244 NORTHREEL 8-10 (4*) J J Behan (2)..................(14 to 1) 5
4369⁵ SCHONBEIN (Ire) 8-11 W J Supple (4)...............(10 to 1) 6
4323⁷ PERSIAN BLOOM (Ire) 8-1 (10*) S P Cooke (13)....(16 to 1) 7
DAY LIGHT (Ire) 8-11 P V Gilson (6)..................(10 to 1) 8
4134⁵ BOARDWALKER (Ire) 8-7 (4*) J A Heffernan (18)....(20 to 1) 9
DARK POET (Ire) 9-0 S Craine (8).....................(10 to 1) 10
4000 SHEER STYLE (Ire) (bl) 8-9 (2*) P Carberry (16)....(12 to 1) 11
4290 PENZAAD (Ire) (bl) 8-8 (6*) B J Walsh (5)............(40 to 1) 12
4323 CIARA CANE (Ire) 9-0 P Lowry,.......................(33 to 1) 13
3825⁷ WOLFIES RASCAL (Ire) 9-0 N G McCullagh (17)....(14 to 1) 14
3825⁸ TORDO (Ire) 8-4 (10*) P P O'Grady (11)............(25 to 1) 15
4261 ACUMEN (Ire) 8-1 (10*) M J Cullen (15)............(33 to 1) 16
FULL OF SPARKLE (Ire) 8-9 (2*) R M Burke (10).....(10 to 1) 17
Dist: Nk, nk, 4l, sht-hd. 1m 49.20s. (17 Ran).
(Mrs Patricia O'Rourke), J S Bolger

4407 Batterstown Maiden (5-y-o) £2,760 1m ....(3:30)

4289⁵ TALES OF HEARSAY (Ger) (bl) 9-0 N G McCullagh (3)................................(9 to 4 fav) 1
1610² BRITANNIA BAY (Ire) 9-0 P V Gilson (13)............(4 to 1) 2
4118⁵ ANOTHER FIDDLE (Ire) 8-10 (4*) J A Heffernan (5)...(8 to 1) 3
4368⁷ DAHLIA'S BEST (USA) 9-0 W J Supple (10)............(8 to 1) 4
4118⁸ MERSADA (Ire) 8-3 (8*) T E Durcan (8)..............(14 to 1) 5
4118³ WORLD'S VIEW 8-11 R Hughes (9)...................(9 to 2) 6
4385⁸ ADRIEN DE VRIES (Ire) 9-0 S Craine (2).............(5 to 1) 7
3914³ COOLRAIN LADY (Ire) 8-9 (2*) P Carberry (12).......(6 to 1) 8
3417 SHY TEACHER (Ire) (bl) 8-11 N Byrne (7)...........(25 to 1) 9
DANCING SEER 8-11 R Dolan (11)....................(14 to 1) 10
4386⁶ MATCHLESS PRINCE (Ire) 9-0 K J Manning (6)....(25 to 1) 11
4368 CHARTY (Ire) 8-8 (6*) B J Walsh (1)................(14 to 1) 12
4609a TAUM GO LEOR (Ire) 8-6 (8*) R T Fitzpatrick (4)... (25 to 1) 13
Dist: 3½l, 3l, ¾l, 1l. 1m 48.80s. (13 Ran).
(Dr Peter Harms), D Hanley

4408 Commons Handicap (0-75 3-y-o and up) £2,760 1m..................(4:00)

4136 BRAZEN ANGEL (Ire) [-] 3-8-13 (6*) J R Barry (10) (12 to 1) 1
UNCLE BABY (Ire) [-] 5-7-5 (2*) D G O'Shea (18)...(33 to 1) 2
4057 THREE MUSKETEERS (Ire) [-] 4-8-6 (2*) R M Burke (1)..(33 to 1) 3
4284⁵ ACCELL (Ire) [-] 4-7-11 (8*) G M Moylan (7).........(8 to 1) 4
4284 BLUES COMPOSER (Ire) [-] 4-8-9 W J Supple (3)..(10 to 1) 5
3855* DEVIL'S HOLIDAY (USA) [-] 3-9-9 P V Gilson (5).... (8 to 1) 6

1444 HELLO EXCUSE ME (USA) [-] 3-7-12 (6*) P P Murphy (16) ....(33 to 1) 7
4370* KENTUCKY BABY (Ire) [-] 3-8-10 (4*,5ex) J A Heffernan (13) ....(7 to 1) 8
4370^{5} SUTTON CENTENARY (Ire) [-] 5-7-7^{1} (4*) W J Smith (14) ....(12 to 1) 9
3498^{2} BARNAGEERA BOY (Ire) [-] 4-8-6 N G McCullagh (6) (8 to 1) 10
3975^{5} HAANEM [-] 3-8-3 (6*) B J Walsh (15) ....(16 to 1) 11
4324* LUCKY PRINCE (Ire) [-] (bl) 3-9-2 (6*,7ex) D J O'Donohoe (11) ....(6 to 1 fav) 12
4094^{6} VISTAGE (Ire) [-] 5-9-3 (2*) P Carberry (8) ....(14 to 1) 13
4060^{5} ICEFLOW (Fr) [-] (bl) 3-8-1 (10*) D J Cassey (4) ....(25 to 1) 14
4370 TORCH SINGER [-] 3-7-9 (10*) Ann Corish (2) .....(16 to 1) 15
4118 ELEGANT NORA (Ire) [-] 3-7-7 (8*) R T Fitzpatrick (9) ....(33 to 1) 16
4162^{5} MAJESTIC PADDY (Ire) [-] 3-9-5 R Hughes (17) ......(8 to 1) 17
3614^{8} KESS (Ire) [-] 4-7-9^{1} (4*) J J Behan (12) ....(16 to 1) 18

Dist: Sht-hd, nk, hd, 1l. 1m 48.20s. (18 Ran).

(Albany Syndicate), Patrick Joseph Flynn

4409 Clonee Fillies Handicap (0-80 3-y-o and up) £2,760 1¼m............(4:30)

4246^{4} WICKLOW WAY (Ire) [-] 3-8-5 (6*) B J Walsh (7) .....(8 to 1) 1
4284 MRS KEPPEL [-] 5-8-10 (2*) P Carberry (6) ....(14 to 1) 2
4288 SHARASTAMINA (USA) [-] 4-9-0 (6*) T P Treacy (16) (10 to 1) 3
4094^{5} BLACK PIPER (Ire) [-] 3-9-0 N Byrne (11) ....(12 to 1) 4
3576^{5} SHOWBOAT MELODY (Ire) [-] 3-7-11 (8*) G Coogan (14) ....(12 to 1) 5
3854^{8} TEBRE (USA) [-] (bl) 3-9-1 W J Supple (2) ....(14 to 1) 6
4370^{7} KAWA-KAWA [-] 6-7-5 (6*) P P Murphy (15) ....(33 to 1) 7
3926 LADIES GALLERY (Ire) [-] 3-9-10 P V Gilson (19) ....(8 to 1) 8
4246 HIND VISION (Ire) [-] 3-8-10 K J Manning (8) ......(16 to 1) 9
4246^{3} HOPESVILLE (Ire) [-] 3-9-8 C Roche (17) ....(5 to 2 fav) 10
4136^{8} ALBONA [-] 5-8-13 (4*) W J Smith (3) ....(14 to 1) 11
4001^{8} CAMEY'S CHOICE (Ire) [-] 3-6-13 (8*) G M Moylan (12) ....(20 to 1) 12
4288 SENSE OF VALUE [-] 4-9-8 N G McCullagh (5) .....(8 to 1) 13
4185^{6} SCOTSMAN'S BAY (Ire) [-] 4-7-11 (8*) B J Halligan (13) ....(8 to 1) 14
4060^{2} KUDDAM (Ire) [-] (bl) 3-8-11 (6*) D J O'Donahoe (1) (8 to 1) 15
4368 QUIET CONFIDENCE (Ire) [-] 3-8-13 (2*) R M Burke (18) ....(16 to 1) 16
3854^{9} GRECIAN LADY (Ire) [-] 4-7-13 (4*) J J Behan (9) .. (12 to 1) 17
4245 TRANQUIL BEAUTY (Ire) [-] 4-8-13 R Hughes (4) .. (12 to 1) 18
4137 YELLOW FORD ROSE (Ire) [-] 3-8-1 (4*) J A Heffernan (10) ....(33 to 1) 19

Dist: 4l, 4½l, sht-hd, ¾l. 2m 16.30s. (19 Ran).

(P Conlan), Kevin Prendergast

4410 Mollies Maiden (3-y-o) £2,760 1¼m ....(5:00)

4162^{3} MAGIC FEELING (Ire) 8-9 (2*) P Carberry (6) .... (7 to 2) 1
4162^{4} GLENSTAL FLAGSHIP (Ire) 9-0 C Roache (5) ....(8 to 1) 2
2609^{6} NA-AMMAH (Ire) 8-11 W J Supple (10) ....(5 to 1) 3
3808^{3} BAJAN QUEEN (Ire) 8-11 P V Gilson (7) ....(3 to 1 fav) 4
BRIEF MERGER (Ire) 8-11 P Shanahan (4) .... (7 to 2) 5
GALLETINA (Ire) 8-11 N G McCullagh (11) .... (6 to 1) 6
4245 TERESIAN GIRL (Ire) 8-11 N Byrne (8) ....(20 to 1) 7
4368 GOLD VISION (Ire) 8-10 (4*) J J Behan (2) .... (16 to 1) 8
4137^{9} ANNADOT (Ire) 8-11 A J Nolan (3) .... (20 to 1) 9
4368 CARRICK PIKE (USA) (bl) 9-0 K J Manning (9) .....(10 to 1) 10
GILLAROO GIRL (Ire) 8-7 (4*) J A Heffernan (1) ....(20 to 1) 11

Dist: ½l, nk, nk, 2½l, 10l. 2m 16.20s. (11 Ran).

(Mrs J M Ryan), A P O'Brien

4411 Garlow Q.R. Maiden Race (4-y-o and up) £2,760 1¾m................(5:30)

NIGHTMAN 4-11-9 Mr A J Martin (9) ....(9 to 2) 1
COMMON POLICY (Ire) 4-11-2 (7*) Mr J Connolly (2) (4 to 1) 2
4186^{4} TEMPLERAINEY (Ire) 5-11-9 Mr A P O'Brien (10) (7 to 4 fav) 3
309 DUNFERNE CLASSIC (Ire) 4-11-9 Mr P Fenton (8) ....(100 to 30) 4
4260^{4} HAUNTING ANGLE (Ire) 4-11-3 (3*) Mr A R Coonan (6) ....(8 to 1) 5
4186^{7} INDIANA GOLD (Ire) 5-10-13 (7*) Ms W Fox (4) ....(14 to 1) 6
AMARI QUEEN 6-10-13 (7*) Miss J Lewis (3) ......(20 to 1) 7
4137^{8} MILFORD MATCH (Ire) 5-11-1 (5*) Mrs J M Mullins (1) ....(10 to 1) 8
MASALA (Ire) 4-11-3 (3*) Mr R Neylon (5) .... (25 to 1) 9
SHABRA CONNECTION 6-11-2 (7*) Mr D J Kavanagh (7) ....(66 to 1) 10

Dist: 1½l, 3½l, 3½l, 2l. 3m 23.90s. (10 Ran).

(Mrs A Manning), Charles O'Brien

ST-CLOUD (FR) (heavy)
Tuesday October 12th
Going Correction: PLUS 0.80 sec. per fur.

4412 Prix Eclipse (Group 3) (2-y-o) £23,895 6f 110yds......................(3:15)

WOOD OF BINN (USA) 8-13 F Sanchez (3) *rcd in 3rd, wndrd und pres 2 fs out, hrd rdn fnl furlong to ld cl hme*........(51 to 10) 1
3932^{3} VOLOCHINE (Ire) 9-2 W Mongil (2) *rcd in second, led 2 fs out, hrd rdn fnl furlong, hdd cl hme*....... (Evens fav) 2
4195^{2} ETERNAL REVE (USA) 8-13 C Asmussen (1) *led till 2 fs out, kpt on fnl furlong*........(16 to 10) 3
3932^{6} SIMPLY TRICKY (USA) (bl) 9-2 O Doleuze (4) *rcd in 4th, rdn 2 fs out, ev ch ins last, unbl to quicken*......(34 to 10) 4

Dist: ¾l, nk, sht-nk. 1m 27.50s. a 8.80s (4 Ran).
SR: 27/27/23/25/ (Henri Chalhoub), J E Hammond

LONGCHAMP (FR) (heavy)
Thursday October 14th
Going Correction: PLUS 1.35 sec. per fur.

4413 Prix Casimir Delamarre (Listed) (3-y-o) £14,337 7f................(4:15)

3844^{3} COX ORANGE (USA) 8-12 T Jarnet,........ 1
WILD JEWEL (Can) 8-12 F Sanchez,........ 2
4169^{3} SHAMSIYA (USA) 8-12 G Mosse,........ 3
3844* AISLA (USA) 9-2 E Saint-Martin,........ 4
ZELDA (Ire) 8-12 M Boutin,........ 5
LIA'S DANCE 8-12 G Guignard,........ 6
LADY EXPRESS (Ire) 8-12 F Head,........ 7

Dist: Hd, 1l, 1½l, 6l, 6l, 15l. 1m 31.10s. a 11.60s (7 Ran).
SR: 66/65/62/61/39/21/-/ (Sheikh Mohammed), A Fabre

NEWMARKET (good to soft)
Thursday October 14th
Going Correction: PLUS 0.35 sec. per fur.

4414 Greene King Rated Class B Handicap (0-95 3-y-o and up) £8,900 1½m (1:35)

1752 DERAB (USA) [76] 7-8-7 B Rouse (21) *al hndy, feeling pace o'r 2 fs out, swtchd appr last, styd on to ld cl hme.* ....(50 to 1) 1
4175^{2} WHITECHAPEL (USA) [83] 5-9-0 W R Swinburn (15) *led, quickened 3 fs out, rdn ins last, ct cl hme.* ....(7 to 1 fav op 8 to 1 tchd 9 to 1) 2
4018^{5} SEASONAL SPLENDOUR (Ire) [76] 3-7-13 G Bardwell (17) *wtd wth, pushed alng to improve last 2 fs, kpt on strly nr finish*......(50 to 1 op 33 to 1 tchd 66 to 1) 3
4175^{5} HIGHBROOK (USA) [82] 5-8-13 P Robinson (2) *patiently rdn, hdwy o'r 2 fs out, fnshd wl.* ....(9 to 1 op 8 to 1 tchd 10 to 1) 4
3682* TREE OF LIFE [82] 3-8-5 R Cochrane (12) *tucked away beh ldrs, pushed alng whn pace quickened 3 fs out, styd on fnl furlong*........(10 to 1 op 8 to 1) 5
3900^{2} JAZILAH (Fr) [83] 5-9-0 T Quinn (7) *nvr far away, effrt and drvn alng o'r 2 fs out, kpt on same pace.* ....(10 to 1 op 7 to 1) 6
4175^{4} DEER HUNT [84] 4-9-1 C Asmussen (1) *al hndy, drvn alng 3 fs out, styd on one pace.* ....(9 to 1 op 7 to 1 tchd 10 to 1) 7
3437^{9} CASPIAN TERN (USA) [81] (bl) 4-8-12 C Rutter (19) *sluggish strt, improved into midfield hfwy, rdn and not quicken last 2 fs*........ (20 to 1 op 25 to 1) 8
4175^{6} DREAMS END [80] 5-8-11 L Piggott (14) *patiently rdn, improved o'r 3 fs out, no imprsn appr last.* ....(14 to 1 tchd 16 to 1) 9
4248^{2} PISTOL RIVER (Ire) [95] (v) 3-9-4 Pat Eddery (9) *nvr far away, drvn alng 3 fs out, not quicken.* ....(9 to 1 op 8 to 1 tchd 10 to 1) 10
4218^{2} WESTFIELD MOVES (Ire) [76] 5-8-7 W Carson (5) *reared strt, improved into midfield hfwy, drvn alng o'r 2 fs out, fdd*........(50 to 1) 11
4300 JACKPOT STAR [87] 3-8-10 B Raymond (20) *tucked away on ins, feeling pace 3 fs out, btn 2 out.* ....(20 to 1 op 16 to 1) 12
3503^{3} BARRATRY [76] 3-7-13 F Norton (11) *in tch, effrt on outsd o'r 3 fs out, not pace to chal*...... (33 to 1 op 20 to 1) 13
4209* DUKRAME [81] 3-8-4^{1} W Newnes (6) *in tch, pushed alng o'r 3 fs out, no imprsn*........(14 to 1 op 16 to 1) 14
4160^{2} VRATISLAV (USA) [90] 4-9-7 L Dettori (10) *co'red up beh ldrs, effrt hfwy, fdd over 3 fs out.* (14 to 1 tchd 16 to 1) 15
4018^{7} BAY QUEEN [82] 3-8-2 (3*) M Fenton (16) *nvr far away, feeling pace 3 fs out, wknd.* ....(25 to 1 op 20 to 1 tchd 33 to 1) 16
727^{5} OUR SLIMBRIDGE [76] 5-8-7 J Curant (13) *beh and pushed alng hfwy, nvr a factor*........(200 to 1) 17
4150* TAP ON AIR [89] 3-8-12 M Roberts (4) *trkd ldrs, struggling to hold pl 3 fs out, sn btn.* ....(9 to 1 op 8 to 1 tchd 10 to 1) 18
3775^{2} GLIDE PATH (USA) [87] 4-9-4 R Perham (18) *settled midfield, bustled alng o'r 3 fs out, sn btn.* ....(25 to 1 op 20 to 1) 19
4175 CASTORET [85] 7-9-2 W Ryan (3) *settled gng wl, effrt hfwy, fdd last 3 fs*........(16 to 1 tchd 20 to 1) 20
4178^{3} YILDIZ [77] 4-8-8 D Holland (8) *settled midfield, struggling to hold pl o'r 3 fs out, sn btn*......(20 to 1 op 16 to 1) 21

Dist: Hd, 2l, nk, hd, 1½l, nk, nk, 6l, 1l, ½l. 2m 38.72s. a 9.12s (21 Ran).

SR: 44/50/31/44/35/41/41/37/24/ (Mrs E Brown), S E Sherwood

4415 Fordham Handicap Class C (0-95 3-y-o and up) £6,664 7f...............(2:05)

1016[6] SHINTILLO (Ire) [87] 3-9-3 R Cochrane (26) *nvr far away, led o'r 2 fs out, drifted lft wl ins last, kpt on, fnshd 1st, plcd 3rd*.................(14 to 1 co-fav) 1D

3585[9] NORFOLK HERO [80] (bl) 3-8-10 Pat Eddery (16) *nvr far away, rdn and ev ch fnl furlong, drifted rght last 50 yards, no extr, fnshd second, awarded race*. ....(16 to 1 tchd 20 to 1) 1

4038 JADE CITY [74] 3-8-4 N Carlisle (22) *sn wl plcd, ev ch and rdn appr fnl furlong, hmpd last 50 yards, fnshd 3rd, pld second*...................... (20 to 1 tchd 25 to 1) 2

801[5] ALLINSON'S MATE (Ire) [71] 5-8-4 J Fortune (29) *chsd ldrs far side, drvn to chal last 2 fs, styd on same pace*. ....(33 to 1) 4

4278[4] WAFFLE ON [87] 3-9-3 W Carson (3) *pushed alng stands side, styd on appr fnl furlong, nrst finish*..... (16 to 1) 5

4216[6] ISAIAH [83] 4-9-2 C Asmussen (4) *led stands side grp, feeling pace o'r 2 fs out, styd on fnl furlong*. ....(14 to 1 co-fav tchd 16 to 1) 6

4300[5] EFHARISTO [85] (v) 4-9-4 L Dettori (15) *chsd alng beh ldrs, improved centre last 2 fs, styd on*.......(14 to 1 co-fav) 7

4038 VELOCE (Ire) [74] 5-8-2 (5*) D Wright (21) *pressed ldrs far side, kpt on same pace fnl furlong*. ....(33 to 1 tchd 40 to 1) 8

4024[4] GHOST TREE (Ire) [85] 3-9-1 M Roberts (19) *chsd alng to improve frm midfield hfwy, effrt 2 fs out, one pace*. ....(14 to 1 co-fav tchd 16 to 1) 9

4096[2] ROCA MURADA (Ire) [71] 4-8-4 P Robinson (28) *chsd far side ldrs, feeling pace hfwy, kpt on, no imprsn*. .... (16 to 1 op 14 to 1) 10

4247 PERFAY (USA) [74] 5-8-7 M Wigham (25) *chsd far side ldrs, drvn alng o'r 2 fs out, not pace to chal*.......(33 to 1) 11

4297[4] PARLIAMENT PIECE [76] 7-8-9 W Ryan (1) *sluggish strt, drvn alng to improve stands side hfwy, styd on, nvr nrr*...............................(16 to 1 tchd 20 to 1) 12

3476[4] MARASTANI (USA) [89] 3-9-5 C Rutter (12) *chsd ldrs, effrt stands side o'r 2 fs out, no imprsn*. (33 to 1 op 25 to 1) 13

4280[4] ECHO-LOGICAL [86] 4-9-5 B Raymond (6) *chsd alng stands side, nvr rch chalg pos*... (16 to 1 tchd 20 to 1) 14

4116[9] AL MOULOUKI [81] 3-8-11 W Hood (27) *bustled alng to go pace far side, no imprsn last 2 fs*. ....(16 to 1 op 14 to 1 tchd 20 to 1) 15

3758 GENERAL JOHN (Ire) [62] 4-7-2 (7*) C Adamson (23) *led far side grp till o'r 2 fs out, wknd quickly*.........(33 to 1) 16

3531[9] SUPEROO [65] 7-7-12 N Adams (24) *chsd alng far side, nvr trble ldrs*........(33 to 1 op 25 to 1 tchd 40 to 1) 17

4278[5] LEE ARTISTE [84] (bl) 5-8-10 (7*) T G McLaughlin (7) *wth ldr stands side, drvn alng o'r 2 fs out, fdd*. ....(20 to 1 tchd 25 to 1) 18

4280[3] KAYVEE [95] 4-10-0 A Clark (2) *sluggish strt, drvn alng stands side hfwy, nvr on terms*.... (20 to 1 op 14 to 1) 19

3957[2] SIMPLY FINESSE [76] 3-8-6 D Holland (5) *wth ldg pair stands side for o'r 5 fs, fdd*. ....(14 to 1 co-fav tchd 12 to 1 and 16 to 1) 20

4172 ABSOLUTE MAGIC [85] 3-8-8 (7*) Sally Radford-Howes (11) *outpcd and drvn alng most of way*..............(50 to 1) 21

2011 CYPRIAN DANCER (USA) [75] 3-8-5 T Quinn (18) *drvn alng to keep up hfwy, nvr a factor*.................(33 to 1) 22

4024[5] SHARP PROSPECT [75] 3-8-5 W Newnes (17) *in tch, struggling to go pace hfwy, sn btn*.............(14 to 1 co-fav tchd 12 to 1) 23

4132[6] SHIKARI'S SON [83] 6-9-2 L Piggott (14) *drvn alng hfwy, sn outpcd*...................... (33 to 1 tchd 50 to 1) 24

4164 LA BAMBA [67] 7-8-0 T Williams (9) *missed break, improved into midfield hfwy, wknd 2 fs out*. .... (20 to 1 op 16 to 1) 25

4278[8] AMIRATI (USA) [85] 3-9-1 W R Swinburn (8) *pressed ldrs, feeling pace hfwy, sn btn*........................(25 to 1) 26

3358 RISE UP SINGING [63] 5-7-10 G Bardwell (20) *struggling hfwy, sn btn*..................(20 to 1 op 16 to 1) 27

3983* PRINCELY FAVOUR (Ire) [80] 3-8-10 W Woods (10) *pressed ldrs stands side 5 fs*.......(14 to 1 co-fav tchd 16 to 1) 28

Dist: ½l, hd, 1½l, sht-hd, nk, ½l, sht-hd, 2½l, 2l, nk. 1m 28.43s. a 4.93s (28 Ran).

SR: 66/57/50/45/57/55/55/43/43/ (Lady D M Watts), D J G Murray Smith

4416 Tattersalls Sales Nursery Final Class C (2-y-o) £11,647 6f.............(2:35)

4127[4] GADGE [64] 8-7 M Roberts (5) *al hndy, drvn ahead o'r one furlong out, ran on und pres*... (10 to 1 op 8 to 1) 1

4167[3] STOREY'S GATE (Ire) [74] 9-3 W R Swinburn (9) *al hndy, rdn to draw level o'r one furlong out, kpt on wl und pres*........(9 to 1 jt-fav op 10 to 1 tchd 8 to 1) 2

4225[6] QUEEN'S TRUST [59] 8-2 N Carlisle (12) *pressed ldg trio, ev ch and drvn alng last 2 fs, styd on same pace*. ....(12 to 1 tchd 14 to 1) 3

4220[9] AT THE SAVOY (Ire) [60] 8-3 C Rutter (11) *settled midfield, drvn alng to improve last 2 fs, styd on finish*. ....(25 to 1 tchd 33 to 1) 4

4210[4] HIGH HOLME [70] (v) 8-13 P Robinson (6) *nvr far away, ev ch and rdn 2 fs out, no extr*........(10 to 1 op 8 to 1) 5

4272 DOMINO QUEEN (Ire) [69] 8-12 R Cochrane (4) *pressed ldg 5, ev ch and rdn 2 fs out, no extr*.............(12 to 1) 6

4210 JAYANNPEE [68] 8-11 B Raymond (1) *drvn alng in midfield, effrt o'r 2 fs out, not pace to chal*. ....(11 to 1 op 10 to 1 tchd 12 to 1) 7

4210[3] MR BERGERAC (Ire) [75] 9-4 D Holland (10) *beh and chsd alng, styd on last 2 fs, nvr dngrs*..................(14 to 1) 8

4375[3] DANTE'S RUBICON (Ire) [58] 7-10 (5*) D Wright (2) *prmnt on outsd, drvn alng 2 fs out, no extr*............(9 to 1 jt-fav op 8 to 1 tchd 10 to 1) 9

4264[2] ELEVATOR SHAFT (Ire) [78] (bl) 9-7 T Quinn (16) *made most for o'r 4 fs, fdd*..................(10 to 1 tchd 11 to 1) 10

4061[7] DANCES WITH RISK [68] 8-11 Pat Eddery (8) *drvn alng in midfield hfwy, btn 2 fs out*. ....(11 to 1 op 10 to 1 tchd 12 to 1) 11

4330[2] PHONEAHOLIC (Ire) [72] 9-1 B Rouse (15) *chsd alng in midfield, no imprsn last 2 furlonsg*. ....(16 to 1 tchd 20 to 1) 12

4351[7] MONKEY MUSIC [70] (bl) 8-13 N Adams (3) *chsd alng to go pace hfwy, btn 2 fs out*.......... (25 to 1 tchd 33 to 1) 13

3520 MISTER O'GRADY (Ire) [60] (bl) 8-3 G Bardwell (17) *sluggish strt, not reco'r*...............................(50 to 1) 14

4266 MR B REASONABLE (Ire) [69] 8-12 W Newnes (13) *drvn alng to keep up hfwy, nvr a threat*. ....(10 to 1 tchd 11 to 1) 15

4332[3] TWICE IN BUNDORAN (Ire) [77] 9-6 L Dettori (14) *frnt rnk for o'r 4 fs, fdd*.................. (12 to 1 tchd 14 to 1) 16

4210 LA RESIDENCE [69] (bl) 8-12 W Carson (7) *struggling hfwy, sn lost tch*....................... (11 to 1 op 10 to 1) 17

Dist: ½l, 1l, 3½l, sht-hd, ¾l, sht-hd, ¾l, hd, 3l, 2½l. 1m 17.00s. a 5.60s (17 Ran).

SR: 23/31/12/-/8/4/2/6/-/ (J B R Leisure Ltd), J Sutcliffe

4417 Challenge Stakes Class A (Group 2) (3-y-o and up) £38,037 7f........(3:10)

4170* CATRAIL (USA) 3-8-11 M Roberts (4) *patiently rdn, hdwy 2 fs out, led ins last, jst lasted*. ....(5 to 4 on op 7 to 4 on tchd 6 to 5 on) 1

3717* ROBIN DES PINS (USA) 5-9-3 C Asmussen (6) *co'red up on ins, pushed alng to improve 2 fs out, str run fnl furlong, jst fld*..................(5 to 1 tchd 9 to 2 and 11 to 2) 2

3889* EL DUCO (USA) 3-8-11 Pat Eddery (7) *led, quickened hfwy, rdn and hdd ins fnl furlong, no extr*. .... (12 to 1 op 14 to 1) 3

4280* FRAAM 4-9-0 W R Swinburn (3) *pressed ldg pair, rdn to draw level o'r one furlong out, no extr last 100 yards*. ....(7 to 1 tchd 8 to 1) 4

4308 THOURIOS 4-9-0 T Quinn (1) *trkd ldr, bustled alng 2 fs out, no extr*.......... (14 to 1 op 8 to 1 tchd 16 to 1) 5

3315[8] HAZAAM (USA) 4-9-0 L Dettori (5) *last and pushed alng hfwy, nvr rch ldrs*.... (10 to 1 op 7 to 1 tchd 11 to 1) 6

1362[2] CASTEDDU 4-9-0 W Carson (2) *co'red up in midfield, feeling pace over 2 fs out, sn outpcd*. ....(20 to 1 tchd 25 to 1) 7

Dist: Hd, 2½l, 1½l, 3½l, hd, 3½l. 1m 27.92s. a 4.42s (7 Ran).

SR: 67/72/58/56/45/44/33/ (Sheikh Mohammed), J H M Gosden

4418 Buckenham Selling Stakes Class E (2-y-o) £4,955 7f..................(3:40)

4342[2] SLMAAT 8-6 M Roberts (29) *wth ldrs far side, led one furlong out, hld on wl cl hme*. ....(7 to 1 op 5 to 1 tchd 8 to 1) 1

4165 MISTER BEAT 9-2 D Holland (26) *o'rall ldr far side, clr hfwy, hdd one furlong out, rallied*. ....(14 to 1 op 12 to 1 tchd 16 to 1) 2

4338[2] MILLION LIGHTS (Ire) 8-6 Pat Eddery (14) *led stands side grp, outpcd o'r 2 fs out, ran on und pres, fnshd wl*. ....(5 to 1 fav op 4 to 1 tchd 11 to 2) 3

4342[6] CELESTIAL RUMOUR (Ire) 9-2 W Ryan (23) *in tch, pushed alng to improve far side o'r 2 fs out, one pace fnl furlong*.......................... (14 to 1 op 10 to 1) 4

4264[3] REMINISCENCE (Ire) 8-6 S Raymont (19) *pressed ldrs far side, drvn alng o'r 2 fs out, not quicken*. ....(9 to 1 op 7 to 1 tchd 10 to 1) 5

4228 GIGUE 8-2[3] (7*) R Painter (3) *wth ldrs stands side, drvn alng o'r 2 fs out, styd on finish*.... (33 to 1 op 20 to 1) 6

4215[9] NIGHT SNOW 8-3 (3*) M Fenton (10) *pushed alng to improve stands side o'r 2 fs out, kpt on same pace fnl furlong*.........(16 to 1 op 14 to 1 tchd 20 to 1) 7

4358[7] ONCE MORE FOR LUCK (Ire) 9-2 W Newnes (22) *bustled alng far side, hdwy last 2 fs, ran on*. ....(12 to 1 tchd 14 to 1) 8

3966[5] JUST GREENWICH 8-1 (5*) N Gwilliams (7) *wth ldrs stands side, feeling pace o'r 2 fs out, nvr nr to chal*. ....(20 to 1 tchd 25 to 1) 9

3508 KOONOONA LADY 8-1 (5*) D Wright (2) *chsd ldrs stands side, feeling pace o'r 2 fs out, not pace to chal*. (33 to 1) 10

3597[6] MOMENT OF GLORY (Ire) 8-11 R Cochrane (8) *bustled alng stands side, kpt on, not pace to chal*. .... (6 to 1 op 10 to 1 tchd 11 to 2) 11

4358[3] LITTLE IBNR 8-11 L Dettori (11) *chsd stands side ldrs, rdn alng hfwy, nvr on terms*. ....(11 to 1 op 8 to 1 tchd 12 to 1) 12

4342[8] CELESTIAL DANCE 8-6 G Bardwell (4) *bustled alng stands side, effrt hfwy, not pace to chal*. (25 to 1 op 20 to 1) 13

4228 TOTON LAD 8-11 M Wigham (18) *chsd alng on far side for o'r 4 fs, fdd*.......................... (33 to 1 op 25 to 1) 14
4351[4] RISK OF FIRE 8-11 B Raymond (25) *drvn alng to go pace far side, nvr rch chalg pos*.........(20 to 1 op 14 to 1) 15
3841[7] KENNET BOY (bl) 8-11 T Quinn (15) *drvn alng far side, not rch ldrs*........................ (16 to 1 tchd 20 to 1) 16
4338[6] SPORTING STORY (Ire) 8-6 R Price (9) *drvn alng stands side, nvr rch frnt rnk*........................ (33 to 1) 17
3126[6] MR MORIARTY (Ire) 8-6 (5*) K Rutter (20) *pressed far side ldrs 5 fs*.. (33 to 1) 18
4329 SNOWDON SLIGHTS 8-6 P Robinson (27) *outpcd far side, drvn alng hfwy, nvr on terms*..... (33 to 1 op 20 to 1) 19
4329 EXPRESS LINE 8-6 A Clark (13) *drvn alng to go pace, nvr on terms*...(33 to 1) 20
4081* SHUTTLECOCK 8-9 (7*) C Adamson (6) *bustled alng stands side, struggling o'r 2 fs out, sn btn*. ....(20 to 1 tchd 25 to 1) 21
4122[9] MR MYSTICAL (Ire) 8-11 B Rouse (24) *chsd ldrs far side, struggling o'r 2 fs out, sn btn*................ (33 to 1) 22
4032[8] PINATUBO 8-4 (7*) Sarah Holland (21) *prmnt far side 5 fs*. ....(33 to 1) 23
4128[3] WADDLE (Ire) 8-4 (7*) S Mulvey (12) *chsd ldrs stands side, struggling hfwy*.....................(33 to 1 op 20 to 1) 24
4210[9] CLASSICAL (Ire) 8-11 R Perham (5) *pressed stands side ldrs for o'r 4 fs, sn btn*................ (33 to 1 op 25 to 1) 25
3958[8] ONLY FOOLS 8-11 S Whitworth (30) *struggling hfwy*. ....(33 to 1) 26
4358[9] CONNECT (Ire) 9-2 L Piggott (17) *chsd alng, speed centre 5 fs, sn btn*........................ (25 to 1 op 16 to 1) 27
3641 KINGSCOURT JOHN-A (Ire) 8-4 (7*) Mark Denaro (16) *outpcd and drvn alng hfwy, nvr a factor*.........(33 to 1) 28
4339[5] AILEENS GIRL 8-6 N Adams (1) *chsd ldrs stands side to hfwy, sn btn*...................... (33 to 1 op 25 to 1) 29
4236[4] A MILLION WATTS (bl) 8-11 W R Swinburn (28) *chsd ldr far side for o'r 5 fs, wknd quickly*. .... (11 to 1 op 7 to 1 tchd 12 to 1) 30

Dist: Nk, sht-hd, 4l, hd, hd, ½l, 2l, hd, 1l, 2l. 1m 29.97s. a 6.47s (30 Ran).
SR: 32/41/30/28/17/16/14/18/7/ (Ali K Al Jafleh), W J Haggas

4419 EBF Chesterton Maiden Stakes Class D (Div I) (2-y-o) £5,936 1m......... (4:10)

4259[3] WEIGH ANCHOR 9-0 L Dettori (18) *nvr far away, led wl o'r one furlong out, quickened away ins last, kpt on strly*. ....(4 to 1 jt-fav op 7 to 1 tchd 8 to 1) 1
TOM WALLER (Ire) 9-0 Pat Eddery (19) *tucked away on ins, effrt and drvn alng last 2 fs, not pace of wnr*. .... (10 to 1 op 7 to 1) 2
4240[2] BSHEER (USA) 9-0 W R Swinburn (7) *frnt rnk, led o'r 4 fs out till wl over one out, kpt on same pace*....(4 to 1 jt-fav op 7 to 2 tchd 5 to 1) 3
COUNTY SET 9-0 A Clark (14) *trkd ldrs, effrt and bustled alng 2 fs out, one pace*............ (25 to 1 op 20 to 1) 4
DOUBLE DAGGER 9-0 W Ryan (20) *led till o'r 4 fs out, wknd quickly over one out*. .... (10 to 1 op 8 to 1 tchd 11 to 1) 5
3908[8] STETTIN 9-0 M Tebbutt (17) *settled midfield, effrt and shaken up o'r 2 fs out, not pace to chal*. .... (12 to 1 op 8 to 1 tchd 14 to 1) 6
TAKE A PEW 9-0 M Roberts (15) *co'red up on ins, feeling pace and drvn alng hfwy, no imprsn*. .... (16 to 1 op 14 to 1) 7
4276[8] REHLAT FARAH (USA) 9-0 R Cochrane (16) *settled to track ldrs, effrt hfwy, eased whn btn 2 fs out*. .... (10 to 1 op 6 to 1 tchd 11 to 1) 8
4252 ACERBUS DULCIS 9-0 C Asmussen (3) *steadied strt, hdwy into midfield last 2 fs, prmsg*. .... (33 to 1 op 25 to 1) 9
BONIFACCIO BANDIT (Ire) 9-0 B Rouse (2) *nvr far away, hrd drvn whn pace quickened o'r 2 fs out, no extr*. ....(33 to 1) 10
SIBELIAN SOUND 9-0 P Robinson (8) *chsd ldrs, drvn alng whn pace quickened o'r 2 fs out, no imprsn*. .... (14 to 1 op 12 to 1 tchd 16 to 1) 11
4208 LITTLE BROOK 9-0 R Perham (13) *in tch, bustled alng hfwy, sn outpcd*...(33 to 1) 12
4252 POLO KIT (Ire) 8-7 (7*) N Varley (9) *chsd ldrs for o'r 5 fs*. .... (14 to 1 op 10 to 1) 13
MESHED 9-0 B Raymond (1) *steadied strt, hdwy on outsd o'r 2 fs out, nvr plcd to chal*. .... (14 to 1 op 12 to 1 tchd 16 to 1) 14
ANIF (USA) 9-0 W Carson (11) *wth ldr, lost grnd whn pace quickened o'r 2 fs out, sn btn*....... (8 to 1 op 6 to 1) 15
FLAWED LOGIC (Ire) 9-0 D Holland (4) *midfield till wknd and eased o'r 2 fs out*..............(10 to 1 op 6 to 1) 16
4252 PERHAPS 9-0 V Smith (10) *chsd alng in midfield for o'r 5 fs, sn lost tch*..(33 to 1) 17
KEEN BID (Ire) 9-0 W Woods (5) *outpcd and drvn alng hfwy*.. (25 to 1 op 16 to 1) 18
4339 SPORTING SCRIPT (Ire) 9-0 R Price (6) *frnt rnk for o'r 5 fs*. ....(33 to 1) 19

Dist: 4l, 2½l, 1½l, 2½l, 3l, 2l, ¾l, sht-hd, 3l, 1½l. 1m 43.08s. a 5.88s (19 Ran).
SR: 54/42/34/29/21/12/6/4/3/ (Robert Hitchins), I A Balding

4420 Severals Conditions Stakes Class B (3-y-o and up) £6,918 1¼m......(4:45)

4145* MEADOW PIPIT (Can) 4-8-11 M Roberts (9) *nvr far away, effrt and edgd lft o'r one furlong out, drvn to ld ins last, kpt on*........... (7 to 1 op 5 to 1 tchd 15 to 2) 1
3892[3] JURA 5-9-1 W R Swinburn (10) *co'red up on ins, drvn to ld appr fnl furlong, hdd inside last, rallied*. .... (20 to 1 op 16 to 1) 2
3878* YOUNG BUSTER (Ire) 5-9-12 Pat Eddery (6) *patiently rdn, improved to chal whn crowded o'r one furlong out, sn ev ch, no extr last 50 yards*......... (9 to 2 op 3 to 1) 3
4141[4] LUCKY LINDY (Ire) (v) 4-9-6 T Quinn (8) *trkd ldg trio, led o'r 2 fs out till appr last, rdn and one pace*. .... (11 to 2 op 3 to 1) 4
4150[3] GONE FOR A BURTON (Ire) 3-8-8 L Piggott (5) *wtd wth, improved on outsd o'r 2 fs out, not pace of ldrs*. ....(8 to 1 tchd 10 to 1) 5
293[8] TOP REGISTER (USA) 4-9-3 C Asmussen (3) *settled midfield, drvn alng o'r 2 fs out, nvr able to chal*. .... (25 to 1 op 16 to 1 tchd 33 to 1) 6
4100* ICY SOUTH (USA) 3-8-13 L Dettori (7) *led till o'r 2 fs out, fdd appr last*....... (7 to 2 fav op 4 to 1 tchd 9 to 2) 7
PERPENDICULAR 5-9-6 W Ryan (2) *wl plcd on outsd, effrt and rdn o'r 2 fs out, fdd*............ (9 to 2 op 7 to 2) 8
4175 BOLOARDO 4-9-5 W Woods (1) *trkd ldr, struggling to hold pl o'r 2 fs out, sn btn*....... (33 to 1 tchd 40 to 1) 9
GRANACHE (Ire) 4-9-0 D Holland (4) *trkd ldg 4 till wknd und pres o'r 2 fs out*......................... (100 to 1) 10

Dist: Hd, 2l, 2½l, 5l, 6l, ½l, 8l, 2l, 20l. 2m 9.89s. a 7.19s (10 Ran).
SR: 60/63/70/59/37/34/29/20/15/ (Sheikh Mohammed), J H M Gosden

4421 EBF Chesterton Maiden Stakes Class D (Div II) (2-y-o) £5,936 1m......(5:15)

4174[6] WISHING (USA) 9-0 Pat Eddery (9) *alway hndy, led o'r one furlong out till ins last, rallied to ld last 50 yards*. ....(5 to 2 fav tchd 3 to 1 and 9 to 4) 1
TOP GUIDE (USA) 9-0 W R Swinburn (20) *unruly strt, nvr far away, drvn alng to ld ins fnl furlong, hdd and no extr last 50 yards*.......(13 to 2 op 5 to 1 tchd 7 to 1) 2
WIJDAN (USA) 8-9 W Carson (16) *al wl plcd, led o'r 3 fs out till over one out, kpt on same pace*...(7 to 1 op 4 to 1) 3
IKIS GIRL 8-6 (3*) M Fenton (19) *patiently rdn, hdwy on ins hfwy, swtchd appr fnl furlong, ran on, prmsg*. .... (50 to 1 op 25 to 1) 4
TRUCKHAVEN SECRET 9-0 W Ryan (15) *sluggish strt, hdwy into midfield hfwy, styd on fnl furlong, improve*. .... (10 to 1 op 5 to 1 tchd 12 to 1) 5
MOUNTAIN BALLET 8-9 B Raymond (14) *settled midfield, bustled alng to go pace hfwy, styd on, no imprsn*. .... (33 to 1 op 16 to 1) 6
HIGH ACCOUNT (USA) 9-0 D Holland (7) *tucked away in midfield, effrt and pushed alng 3 fs out, outpcd appr last*................... (7 to 1 op 6 to 1 tchd 15 to 2) 7
4316[8] LIGHTNING QUEST (Ire) 9-0 W Newnes (18) *led till o'r 3 fs out, fdd appr last*............... (33 to 1 op 16 to 1) 8
4252 THUNDERHEART 9-0 R Cochrane (5) *settled off the pace, shaken up to improve last 2 fs, nvr plcd to chal*. .... (33 to 1 op 16 to 1) 9
4259[6] REGAL PURSUIT (Ire) 8-9 T Williams (13) *chsd ldrs, feeling pace and rdn hfwy, not rch lders*. (50 to 1 op 33 to 1) 10
SEA RAVEN (Ire) 9-0 L Dettori (17) *trkd ldrs, ran green and pushed alng 3 fs out, nvr able to chal*. ....(8 to 1 op 6 to 1 tchd 9 to 1) 11
3833 ENVIRONMENTALIST (Ire) 9-0 V Smith (11) *pressed ldrs till o'r 2 fs out, sn btn*..............(50 to 1 op 33 to 1) 12
4249 ROMAN CAMP (Fr) 9-0 T Quinn (12) *bustled alng to keep up hfwy, nvr trble ldrs*............ (33 to 1 op 16 to 1) 13
ABDULLAH (USA) 9-0 W Woods (2) *beh and chsd alng hfwy, nvr a factor*..............(33 to 1 tchd 50 to 1) 14
3760[6] WILCUMA 9-0 C Asmussen (4) *settled off the pace, nvr plcd to chal*.........(10 to 1 op 20 to 1 tchd 25 to 1) 15
4252 TAAJ (USA) 9-0 M Roberts (8) *missed break, improved into midfield hfwy, fdd last 2 fs*. ....(20 to 1 op 14 to 1 tchd 25 to 1) 16
4276 DECENT COVE 9-0 M Tebbutt (10) *chsd ldrs, ev ch hfwy, fdd*.............................. (50 to 1 op 33 to 1) 17
SADLER'S WALK 9-0 P Robinson (1) *shaped wl on outsd for o'r 5 fs, better for race*. .... (14 to 1 op 10 to 1 tchd 16 to 1) 18
SANDY ARBUTHNOT 8-9 (5*) K Rutter (3) *struggling hfwy*. .... (33 to 1 op 20 to 1) 19
4099 UNBELIEVABLE 8-7 (7*) C Hawksley (6) *chsd alng to keep in tch hfwy, nvr dngrs*............ (50 to 1 op 33 to 1) 20

Dist: ½l, 3l, 1l, 1½l, 10l, nk, 1l, ¾l, sht-hd, 2½l. 1m 43.38s. a 6.18s (20 Ran).
SR: 49/47/33/30/30/-/ (M W Grant), R Hannon

REDCAR (soft)
Thursday October 14th
Going Correction: PLUS 1.00 sec. per fur.

4422 EBF Maiden Fillies' Stakes Class D (2-y-o) £11,326 7f................. (1:50)

4190[2] BABY LOVES 8-11 Paul Eddery (8) *in tch, pushed alng o'r 2 out, styd on wl fnl furlong to ld post*.... (5 to 2 jt-fav) 1
3589[4] CO PILOT (Ire) 8-11 A Munro (4) *led, rdn fnl furlong, wknd towards finish, ct post*............. (9 to 1 op 10 to 1) 2

4302[2] LADY FAIRFAX 8-11 G Duffield (9) *hld up, gd hdwy to track ldr hfwy, sn pushed alng, styd on fnl furlong.* ....(5 to 2 jt-fav op 2 to 1 tchd 11 to 4) 3
MWAARED 8-11 R Hills (3) *trkd ldrs, outpcd 3 fs out, styd on fnl furlong*..................(16 to 1 op 14 to 1) 4
MINSTREL'S GIFT 8-11 J Carroll (7) *chsd ldrs, edgd lft o'r 2 fs out, kpt on same pace*..........(4 to 1 op 7 to 2) 5
3992[5] WILD ROSE OF YORK 8-11 J Weaver (6) *in tch till wknd 3 out, sn beh*..............(8 to 1 op 7 to 1 tchd 9 to 1) 6
4190[4] BLUSHINGBIRD (Ire) 8-11 A McGlone (5) *chsd ldrs, rdn 3 fs out, sn btn*..................(5 to 1) 7
4350[9] RED BOUQUET 8-11 M Birch (2) *in tch till wknd 3 out, sn beh*..................(50 to 1 op 20 to 1) 8
Dist: Sht-hd, 1l, 1½l, ½l, 12l, 4l, hd. 1m 33.40s. a 11.60s (8 Ran).
SR: 28/27/24/19/17/ (S S Niarchos), Mrs J Cecil

4423 Tote Two-year-old Trophy Class B (2-y-o) £88,900 6f................ (2:20)

4177[6] CAPE MERINO 7-7 J Lowe (4) *made all, clr halway, hrd rdn 2 fs out, ran on wl*..................(33 to 1) 1
4250[2] RISKY 8-1 M Hills (11) *al chasing wnr, rdn 2 fs out, kpt on, no imprsn*..........(11 to 10 fav op 11 to 10 on) 2
3994[3] BID FOR BLUE 8-7 J Reid (14) *al prmnt, effrt o'r 2 fs out, kpt on same pace*..........(14 to 1 op 12 to 1) 3
4272[2] TAKADOU (Ire) 7-12 D Harrison (16) *in tch, kpt on und pres fnl 2 fs, nrst finish*..................(20 to 1) 4
4351[3] ARABOYBILL 8-1 S Maloney (5) *mid-div, rdn o'r 2 fs out, kpt on fnl furlong*..................(200 to 1) 5
3115[2] BRAILLE (Ire) 8-1 J Weaver (6) *al chasing ldrs, no extr fnl 2 fs*..................(16 to 1) 6
3351[5] PERUSAL 8-1 A McGlone (20) *mid-div, kpt on same pace fnl 2 fs*..................(50 to 1 op 33 to 1) 7
4193 SARMATIAN (USA) 7-12 Stephen Davies (2) *in tch, hdwy und pres hfwy, kpt on same pace fnl 2 fs*.....(200 to 1) 8
3949[4] OCHOS RIOS (Ire) 7-12 S Wood (10) *in tch, rdn hfwy, no hdwy*..................(66 to 1) 9
3679[5] SNIPE HALL 7-10 J Quinn (23) *rcd stands side, in tch, no extr fnl 2 fs*..................(12 to 1 op 10 to 1) 10
4276[6] WILLIAM TELL 8-1 Paul Eddery (26) *rcd stands side, in tch, no extr fnl 2 fs*..................(33 to 1) 11
3613[6] BLAZING HONDA (Ire) 8-1 B Doyle (21) *nvr dngrs*. (50 to 1) 12
2996[3] THE MULTIYORKER (Ire) 7-10 Dale Gibson (8) *nvr dngrs*. ....(50 to 1) 13
4210[6] EVANRO (Ire) 8-2[1] R Hills (13) *mid-div, bumped hfwy, no hdwy*..................(150 to 1 op 100 to 1) 14
4144 HELLO MISTER 8-1 P McCabe (12) *chsd ldrs till wknd o'r 2 fs out*..................(100 to 1) 15
4318 THE HAPPY LOON (Ire) 7-12 C Teague (17) *chsd ldrs till wknd o'r 2 fs out*..................(100 to 1) 16
4244[3] DILIGENT DODGER (Ire) 8-4 W Supple (22) *in tch till wknd o'r 2 fs out*..................(20 to 1) 17
4021[3] GREY TOPPA 7-7 A Mackay (19) *in tch till wknd o'r 2 fs out*..................(100 to 1 tchd 150 to 1) 18
3679[6] MR M-E-N (Ire) 8-1 J Carroll (15) *chsd ldrs till weakneed quickly 2 fs out*..................(40 to 1 op 33 to 1) 19
4345[6] TOPNOTCH 8-3[1] A Culhane (9) *sn beh*. ....(200 to 1 op 100 to 1) 20
3635* ROYAL INSIGNIA 8-4 A Munro (25) *rcd stands side, beh frm hfwy*..................(33 to 1) 21
4223[7] HILTONS TRAVEL (Ire) (v) 8-2[1] K Fallon (1) *sn beh*. ....(200 to 1 op 100 to 1) 22
4211[6] INDIAHRA 8-2 A Garth (3) *sn beh*.....(66 to 1 op 50 to 1) 23
1461* PETE AFRIQUE (Ire) 8-1 K Darley (24) *dwlt, sn in tch, wknd quickly o'r 2 fs out*..........(10 to 1 op 8 to 1) 24
4144[2] STORM SHIP (Ire) 8-1 G Hind (7) *sn beh*. ....(14 to 1 op 12 to 1) 25
4165* ROXANIAN (Ire) 8-2[1] G Duffield (18) *in tch till wknd quickly o'r 2 fs out*...(12 to 1 op 14 to 1 tchd 10 to 1) 26
Dist: 1½l, 1½l, 3l, 1½l, ¾l, sht-hd, 1½l, sht-hd, 1½l, 2½l. 1m 17.60s. a 7.90s (26 Ran).
SR: 41/43/43/22/19/16/15/6/5/ (Hugh Ellis), A Smith

4424 Redcar October Handicap Class C (0-90 3-y-o and up) £5,469 1m... (2:50)

4322* MISSED FLIGHT [81] 3-9-5 (6ex) G Duffield (8) *hld up, smooth hdwy to ld 2 fs out, quickened clr, easily*. ....(2 to 1 fav op 11 to 4 tchd 3 to 1 and 15 to 8) 1
4247 MAJED (Ire) [75] 5-8-10 (7*) S Copp (10) *beh, hdwy 3 out, styd on wl fnl furlong, not rch wnr*. (9 to 1 op 12 to 1) 2
4320[8] DOC COTTRILL [67] 3-8-5 K Fallon (1) *in tch, hdwy 3 fs out, ch 2 out, kpt on same pace*....(12 to 1 op 14 to 1) 3
3722[9] INFANTRY GLEN [56] (v) 3-7-8[1] A Mackay (12) *beh, hdwy 3 out, kpt on same pace fnl 2 fs*..................(33 to 1) 4
3938* MOGWAI (Ire) [58] (bl) 4-8-0 D Harrison (6) *mid-div, effrt 3 fs out, kpt on same pace*..........(20 to 1 op 16 to 1) 5
3996[3] FIELD OF VISION (Ire) [80] 3-9-4 J Weaver (9) *beh, styd on fnl 3 fs, not trble ldrs*..................(12 to 1) 6
4320[2] HARPOON LOUIE (USA) [74] 3-8-12 K Darley (19) *nvr nr to chal*..................(10 to 1 op 8 to 1) 7
4140[8] HOST (Ire) [80] 4-9-5 (3*) B Doyle (18) *in tch, kpt on fnl 2 fs, nvr dngrs*..................(20 to 1) 8
KIVETON TYCOON (Ire) [65] 4-8-7 M Birch (11) *nvr nr ldrs*. ....(50 to 1) 9
4206[2] RAFTERS [72] 4-9-0 M Hills (16) *prmnt, rdn 2 fs out, edgd lft and wknd quickly*..........(12 to 1 tchd 14 to 1) 10
4158 COOL LUKE (Ire) [77] (bl) 4-9-0 (5*) J Tate (13) *trkd ldrs, led 3 fs out, hdd 2 out, wknd quickly*..........(20 to 1) 11
4343[2] MEDIA MESSENGER [51] 4-7-3[1] (5*) Darren Moffatt (3) *chsd ldrs till weakneed o'r 2 fs out*..................(16 to 1) 12
4166[8] SPANISH VERDICT [67] 6-8-2 (7*) C Teague (4) *wth ldrs till wknd o'r 2 fs out*..................(33 to 1) 13
4376[3] JAHANGIR (Ire) [67] 4-8-9 R Hills (17) *mid-div, pushed alng hfwy, no hdwy*..................(25 to 1) 14
4348[2] MHEMEANLES [61] (bl) 3-7-12[2] (3*) S Maloney (5) *wth ldrs till wknd 3 fs out*..................(8 to 1 op 7 to 1) 15
4104 SHANNON EXPRESS [53] (v) 6-7-9[2] J Quinn (14) *chsd ldrs to hfwy*..................(100 to 1) 16
4019* WAINWRIGHT (USA) [86] 4-10-0 J Carroll (2) *prmnt till wknd 3 fs out*..................(10 to 1 op 8 to 1) 17
4355[4] DANNY BOY [77] 3-9-1 J Reid (15) *slight ld till hdd 3 out, wknd quickly*..........(20 to 1 op 16 to 1) 18
4024 MOORISH [85] 3-9-9 A Munro (7) *lost tch 3 fs out, tld off*. ....(12 to 1) 19
Dist: 2½l, 3½l, 2½l, 6l, ½l, hd, ¾l, nk, ½l, 2l. 1m 45.30s. a 10.40s (19 Ran).
SR: 69/59/36/17/5/21/14/22/6/ (Walter Grubmuller), C F Wall

4425 Leslie Petch Memorial Rated Class B Handicap (0-95 3-y-o and up) £6,465 1 ¾m 19yds.................... (3:20)

4344* SAFETY IN NUMBERS [78] 3-8-0 (3ex) J Quinn (4) *hld up, smooth hdwy 3 out, chsd ldr 2 out, led ins fnl furlong, styd on wl*..........(13 to 8 on op 11 to 8 on) 1
4175[3] QUICK RANSOM [90] 5-9-7 J Weaver (5) *in tch, smooth hdwy o'r 3 fs out, quickened to ld over 2 out, hdd ins fnl furlong, no extr*..........(6 to 1 op 5 to 1) 2
4143[6] STAR PLAYER [76] 7-8-7 J Williams (7) *hld up, effrt o'r 2 fs out, styd on same pace*..................(16 to 1) 3
4107[5] LAST EMBRACE (Ire) [76] 4-8-7 A Munro (6) *chsd ldr till wknd 2 fs out*..........(10 to 1 op 8 to 1) 4
4157* MUCH SOUGHT AFTER [83] 4-9-0 G Duffield (1) *chsd ldrs, pushed alng 4 out, not much room 3 out, wknd 2 out*. ....(10 to 1 op 8 to 1) 5
4064[6] ROBERTY LEA [76] 5-8-7 K Darley (3) *led till hdd o'r 2 fs out, sn wknd*..........(9 to 1 op 8 to 1 tchd 10 to 1) 6
4175[9] FLIGHT LIEUTENANT (USA) [82] 4-8-13 J Reid (2) *beh, pushed alng 6 out, no hdwy*..........(8 to 1 op 6 to 1) 7
Dist: 2l, 5l, 4l, 4l, nk, 5l. 3m 14.20s. a 17.70s (7 Ran).
SR: 49/66/42/34/33/25/21/ (Edwin N Cohen), Lady Herries

4426 Levy Board Handicap Class E (0-70 3-y-o and up) £3,235 1m 5f 135yds ....(3:50)

4344[5] BOLD ELECT [48] 5-8-12 L Charnock (9) *in tch, chlgd o'r 3 fs out, led entering fnl furlong, styd on wl*. ....(7 to 2 op 5 to 1) 1
4319[5] FAMOUS BEAUTY [40] 6-7-13 (5*) A Garth (10) *hld up, hdwy 4 fs out, ev ch frm 3 out till no extr ins fnl furlong*. ....(20 to 1 op 16 to 1) 2
4374* MERRY MERMAID [46] 3-7-8 (7*) M Humphries (7) *hld up, came wide strt, gd hdwy to ld 3 out, hdd entering fnl furlong, no extr*..........(11 to 4 fav op 9 to 4) 3
2467[4] SHAFFIC (Fr) [58] 6-9-8 J Fanning (3) *al chasing ldrs, ev ch 2 fs out, no extr fnl furlong*..........(14 to 1 op 12 to 1) 4
3937[4] CUTLASS (Ire) [69] 3-9-10 J Reid (5) *mid-div, pushed alng 5 fs out, styd on fnl 2 furlongs, not trble ldrs*. ....(15 to 2 op 7 to 1 tchd 8 to 1) 5
4357[7] HEATHYARDS BOY [60] 3-9-1 S Perks (12) *beh, styd on fnl 3 fs, not trble ldrs*....(12 to 1 op 10 to 1 tchd 14 to 1) 6
4353[9] SCOTTISH WEDDING [54] 3-8-6 (3*) O Pears (4) *hld up in tch, effrt 4 fs out, no hdwy*..................(20 to 1) 7
BANK VIEW [55] 8-9-5 Kim Tinkler (13) *nvr dngrs*. (50 to 1) 8
4319[2] REACH FOR GLORY [45] 4-8-9 A Culhane (8) *in tch, sn pushed alng, wknd o'r 2 fs out*..................(10 to 1) 9
1783[5] KING'S GUEST (Ire) [56] 4-9-1 (5*) J Tate (6) *led till hdd o'r 3 fs out, sn wknd*..........(25 to 1 op 20 to 1) 10
4218 APACHE SQUAW [51] 3-8-6 G Duffield (11) *chsd ldrs, ev ch 3 fs out, wknd 2 out*..........(12 to 1 op 10 to 1) 11
3831[6] ROBENKO (USA) [57] 4-9-4 (3*) B Doyle (2) *chsd ldr, rdn 5 fs out, wknd 4 out*..........(9 to 1 op 8 to 1) 12
1305[3] BEAUMOOD [39] (v) 7-8-3 K Fallon (15) *prmnt, led o'r 3 fs out, sn hdd and wknd*..................(20 to 1) 13
WSOM (Ire) [40] 5-8-4 S Morris (1) *al beh, tld off*. (50 to 1) 14
Dist: ½l, ¾l, 1½l, 12l, ¾l, 4l, hd, 3l, hd, nk. 3m 10.20s. a 20.30s (14 Ran).
SR: 30/21/16/34/12/1/ (Mrs J L Wigham), P Wigham

4427 Cub Hunters Rating Related Maiden Stakes Class E (0-70 2-y-o) £3,028 1m ....(4:20)

4329[3] ART TATUM (Ire) 9-0 J Reid (5) *chsd ldrs, led wl o'r one furlong out, pushed clr, easily*...(9 to 4 fav op 7 to 4) 1
3829 MISS FREEBIE (Ire) 8-9 A Culhane (11) *beh, hdwy hfwy, styd on wl fnl furlong, no ch wth wnr*..........(50 to 1) 2
4215 CRISTAL SPRINGS 8-9 K Darley (7) *beh, styd on fnl 3 fs, nrst finish*..................(25 to 1 op 16 to 1) 3
4251 ALACRITY 8-9 J Williams (10) *in tch, hdwy 3 fs out, kpt on same pace fnl 2 furlongs*. ....(9 to 1 op 8 to 1 tchd 10 to 1) 4
3793[3] SANDMOOR CHAMBRAY 9-0 M Birch (8) *led till hdd wl o'r one furlong out, wknd ins fnl furlong*..........(14 to 1) 5

4167 KEFAHI (Ire) (bl) 9-0 J Quinn (6) *trkd ldrs, chlgd o'r 2 fs out, wknd quickly over one out*........(3 to 1 tchd 7 to 2) 6

4240^{8} BARNPARK 9-0 L Charnock (12) *prmnt till wknd o'r 2 fs out, eased whn btn*..............................(33 to 1) 7

2785^{4} CALLING (USA) 9-0 M Hills (9) *trkd ldrs, effrt 3 fs out, sn btn*..............................(7 to 1 tchd 8 to 1) 8

4342 ASTROLOGY 8-9 Kim Tinkler (1) *sn beh*.........(100 to 1) 9

4179^{5} DIVERTIMIENTO 9-0 K Fallon (3) *prmnt till wknd o'r 2 fs out, eased whn btn*................(4 to 1 op 11 to 4) 10

4051 TANFIRION CHIEF 9-0 R P Elliott (4) *cl up till wknd quickly 3 fs out*..............................(33 to 1) 11

4159^{7} DINOT (Ire) 9-0 S Perks (2) *in tch till wknd 3 fs out*..............................(20 to 1) 12

Dist: 8l, 2½l, nk, sht-hd, 10l, 5l, 5l, ½l, nk, 3½l. 1m 47.80s. a 12.90s (12 Ran).

SR: 27/-/-/-/-/ (R Cohen & Mr A F Merritt), R Hannon

4428 Egton Conditions Stakes Class C (3-y-o) £4,232 7f.................. (4:50)

4238^{2} NIGHT MELODY (Ire) 9-4 K Darley (3) *cl up gng wl, led o'r 2 fs out, pushed clr, cmftbly*..... (7 to 4 fav tchd 6 to 4) 1

4158 GREAT STEPS 8-9 J Quinn (6) *slight ld till hdd o'r 2 fs out, kpt on und pres*..............................(16 to 1) 2

4139^{2} CELESTIAL KEY (USA) 9-9 (3*) O Pears (4) *cl up, chlgd 3 fs out, rdn 2 out, one pace*............. (5 to 2 op 6 to 4) 3

3900^{9} SUIVEZ 8-9 (3*) B Doyle (1) *cl up, rdn hfwy, sn btn*..............................(20 to 1 tchd 25 to 1) 4

TATIKA 8-12 M Hills (5) *in tch, effrt 3 fs out, no hdwy*..............................(8 to 1 op 6 to 1 tchd 9 to 1) 5

FAEZ 8-12 R Hills (2) *in tch, effrt 3 out, sn btn*..............................(3 to 1 op 7 to 2 tchd 4 to 1) 6

Dist: 7l, sht-hd, 6l, 4l, 4l. 1m 35.20s. a 13.40s (6 Ran).

SR: 8/-/-/ (P D Savill), R Hannon

THURLES (IRE) (good)
Thursday October 14th

4429 Glen Maiden (3-y-o and up) £2,243 1½m 110yds.................... (4:00)

3952^{2} NORDIC THORN (Ire) 3-8-6 (8*) T E Durcan (14).... (7 to 1) 1

4368^{5} KADASSA (Ire) 3-8-11 D Hogan (3)................(9 to 2) 2

URBAN DANCING (USA) 4-9-4 (4*) J J Behan (7)... (8 to 1) 3

3856^{2} HERMES GOLD (Ire) 3-8-5 (6*) B J Walsh (6)........(7 to 1) 4

DRUMS OF FREEDOM (USA) 3-8-11 R Hughes (5)..............................(4 to 1 fav) 5

4368^{8} SERANERA (Ire) 3-8-9 (2*) P Carberry (4).........(12 to 1) 6

3999^{6} BACK TO BLACK (Ire) 4-9-1 (4*) C Everard (15).....(5 to 1) 7

4368 ARCH-T-GLEN (Ire) 3-8-6 (8*) D M McCullagh (9).. (25 to 1) 8

3733^{5} NANNAKA (USA) 3-8-11 N G McCullagh,..............(6 to 1) 9

3975^{3} CLASSY KAHYASI (Ire) 3-8-11 P Shanahan (13).... (8 to 1) 10

3396^{6} GARDENVALE VIC (Ire) (bl) 3-9-0 K J Manning (2) (12 to 1) 11

3684^{8} GRANDEUR (Ire) 3-9-0 P V Gilson (11)...........(12 to 1) 12

BISSTAMI (Ire) 3-9-0 S Craine (12)...............(12 to 1) 13

959 STEEL GEM (Ire) (bl) 4-9-6 (2*) R M Burke (10).... (16 to 1) 14

4368 SCHOOL LAB (Ire) 3-9-0 C Roche (18)...........(12 to 1) 15

488 LEOS LITTLE BIT (Ire) 3-8-7 (4*) J A Heffernan (16) (33 to 1) 16

GENTLE REEF (Ire) 3-8-5 (6*) B Bowens (1).......(25 to 1) 17

2693 ONODI (Ire) 3-8-9 (2*) D G O'Shea (8)............(33 to 1) 18

Dist: 1l, nk, ¾l, 7l. 2m 47.20s. (18 Ran).

(D H W Dobson), J S Bolger

4430 Babs Babes Welter Race (4-y-o and up) £2,760 2m.................. (5:00)

4260^{2} FOR REG (Ire) 4-9-4 (6*) J R Barry (12)............ (6 to 1) 1

IF YOU SAY YES (Ire) 5-9-7 K J Manning (8)...... (12 to 1) 2

4383 EBONY AND IVORY (Ire) 4-9-8 (6*) B J Walsh (7)... (5 to 1) 3

3577^{3} BIG MATT (Ire) 5-10-1 C Roche (15)............(Evens fav) 4

2902^{4} CHANCERY QUEEN (Ire) 4-9-7 N Byrne (13)...... (10 to 1) 5

FRANTESA 7-9-5 (2*) P Carberry (2).............. (16 to 1) 6

4161 SIMPLY SWIFT 6-9-6 (6*) T P Treacy (16)......... (12 to 1) 7

4411^{4} DUNFERNE CLASSIC (Ire) 4-9-10 C F Swan (9)... (12 to 1) 8

4288^{9} RISING WATERS (Ire) 5-9-10 S Craine (4).........(10 to 1) 9

3580 CANDID LAD 6-10-1 N G McCullagh (3)..........(16 to 1) 10

3276^{3} CLASS ACT 7-9-0 (10*) A J Dempsey (1)......... (25 to 1) 11

4260^{5} NORTHMAID (Ire) (bl) 4-9-4 (8*) G M Moylan (5)... (16 to 1) 12

4095 THATCH AND GOLD (Ire) 5-9-7 (10*) S P Cooke (14) (14 to 1) 13

TOUREEN GIRL 6-9-7 M P Kelly (6)...............(14 to 1) 14

4095^{7} BALLYTIGUE LORD 7-9-7 (8*) B Fenton (10)...... (20 to 1) 15

Dist: 1½l, ½l, 3½l, 8l. 3m 40.60s. (15 Ran).

(D H O'Reilly), Patrick Joseph Flynn

CATTERICK (soft)
Friday October 15th
Going Correction: PLUS 0.75 sec. per fur.

4431 Craven Apprentice Maiden Stakes Class G (3-y-o) £2,511 1m 3f 214yds ....(2:20)

4176^{5} CHUMMY'S PAL (USA) 9-0 S McCarthy (8) *nvr far away, led o'r 2 fs out, shaken up and ran on wl fnl furlong*..............................(2 to 1 fav tchd 9 to 4) 1

4334^{2} VAIGLY SUNTHYME 9-0 G Parkin (4) *hld up, rdn to improve 4 fs out, ev ch 2 out, one pace ins last*..............................(7 to 2 op 3 to 1 tchd 4 to 1) 2

4176 ARC BRIGHT (Ire) 8-9 (5*) D Denby (6) *led till hdd o'r 2 fs out, rdn and no extr appr fnl furlong*......... (25 to 1) 3

1423^{7} MOONLIGHT ECLIPSE 9-0 S Knott (12) *settled mid-div, drvn alng to improve o'r 3 fs out, no imprsn entering strt*..............................(20 to 1) 4

4319^{7} TROY BOY (v) 9-0 C Teague (10) *tucked away in mid-div, outpcd and drvn alng hfwy, improved und pres fnl 2 fs, nrst finish*..............................(33 to 1) 5

3233 IJAB (Can) 9-0 M Baird (2) *trkd ldrs, drvn alng 4 fs out, wknd entering strt*..............................(25 to 1) 6

3311^{8} COBBS CROSS 8-9 (5*) W Hollick (14) *al hndy, jnd issue o'r 5 fs out, rdn over 3 out, wknd entering strt*..............................(66 to 1 op 50 to 1) 7

4110 GECKO ROUGE 8-4 (5*) M Henry (1) *settled midfield, took clr order hfwy, rdn and btn appr strt, tld off*..............................(20 to 1 op 14 to 1) 8

4110 PLAIN SAILING (Fr) 9-0 J Dennis (7) *keen hold early, trkd ldrs, drvn alng o'r 5 fs out, sn btn, tld off*..............................(14 to 1 tchd 16 to 1) 9

4322 GEMIKOSIX (Fr) 9-0 R Havlin (11) *slwly into strd, beh, pushed alng 5 fs out, grad lost tch, tld off*..............................(10 to 1 op 33 to 1) 10

4322 GYMCRAK DIAMOND (Ire) 9-0 L Aspell (9) *sluggish strt, beh, rdn alng whn pace lifted 4 fs out, sn btn, tld off*..............................(50 to 1) 11

4377a TINSTONE 8-9 R Painter (3) *trkd ldg bunch, pushed alng o'r 3 fs out, wknd quickly, tld off*.............. (33 to 1) 12

1297^{5} ROSSCOYNE 8-9 S Copp (13) *chsd ldrs on outer, drpd rear hfwy, sn btn, tld off*..............................(11 to 4 op 9 to 4 tchd 3 to 1) 13

CITY LIGHTER 8-9 D Griffiths (5) *trkd ldrs, lost pl bef hfwy, sn struggling, tld off*.....(66 to 1 op 100 to 1) 14

Dist: 1½l, 3½l, 10l, 1½l, 3l, 6l, 6l, ¾l, 3½l, 3l. 2m 46.50s. (14 Ran).

(B W Hills), B W Hills

4432 Hornby Castle Handicap Class D (0-75 3-y-o and up) £4,050 1m 3f 214yds ....(2:50)

2740^{8} ABSALOM'S PILLAR [50] 3-7-12 L Charnock (13) *patiently rdn, prog 4 fs out, led appr last, ridden and ran on wl*..............................(33 to 1) 1

4129^{3} FUNNY HILARIOUS (USA) [69] 3-9-3 K Fallon (2) *trkd ldrs, effrt and rdn entering strt, kpt on wl fnl furlong*..............................(8 to 1 tchd 9 to 1) 2

4037^{2} WHITE WILLOW [71] 4-9-13 J Fanning (18) *settled rear, improved appr strt, rdn and kpt on fnl furlong*..............................(7 to 1 op 6 to 1) 3

4035^{8} CARROLLS MARC (Ire) [57] 5-8-13 A Clark (16) *slwly into strd, beh, improved appr strt, ev ch one furlong out, no extr last 50 yards*..............................(20 to 1) 4

3814^{4} KINOKO [49] 5-8-0 (5*) A Garth (3) *nvr far away, rdn to ld wl o'r one furlong out, hdd appr last, no extr*..............................(11 to 1 op 10 to 1 tchd 12 to 1) 5

4107^{8} FLOATING LINE [50] 5-8-6 A Culhane (9) *al hndy, ev ch entering strt, rdn and not quicken fnl furlong*. (25 to 1) 6

4226^{4} TANODA [41] 7-7-11 J Lowe (6) *tucked away on ins, effrt and drvn alng 3 fs out, no imprsn o'r one out*. (16 to 1) 7

4037^{9} LATVIAN [67] (bl) 6-9-9 J Weaver (10) *hld up and beh, shaken up 3 fs out, kpt on fnl furlong, nvr nr to chal*..............................(20 to 1) 8

4148^{4} ADMIRAL'S WELL (Ire) [70] 3-9-4 G Hind (14) *beh, effrt and improved appr strt, eased whn btn o'r one furlong out*..............................(9 to 1 op 8 to 1) 9

4374^{6} ROUSITTO [50] 5-8-6 S Perks (4) *patiently rdn, improved o'r 3 fs out, ridden and no extr fnl 2 furlongs*..............................(16 to 1 op 14 to 1) 10

4374 J P MORGAN [43] 5-7-13 T Williams (20) *beh and sn pushed alng, drvn hfwy, styd on entering strt, nvr dngrs*..............................(40 to 1 op 33 to 1) 11

4374 ALKABAR [49] 5-8-0 (5*) P McCabe (1) *trkd ldrs, drvn alng appr strt, wknd wl o'r one furlong out*..............................(66 to 1 op 50 to 1) 12

4013^{5} RUSTY REEL [61] 3-8-9 M Birch (7) *led 3 fs, styd hndy, drvn alng entering strt, fdd*...... (16 to 1 op 14 to 1) 13

4283 HARD TASK [74] (bl) 3-9-8 J Carroll (8) *trkd ldg grp, improved hfwy, drvn alng o'r 3 fs out, wknd over 2 out*..............................(16 to 1) 14

1268^{3} BROUGHTON'S TANGO (Ire) [60] 4-8-11 (5*) D Wright (12) *settled rear, pushed alng 4 fs out, nvr able to chal*..............................(15 to 2 op 8 to 1 tchd 9 to 1) 15

4226^{3} MATARIS [57] (v) 3-8-5 G Duffield (5) *nvr far away, rdn alng 4 fs out, fdd*..........(12 to 1 op 8 to 1) 16

3373^{8} SHAMSHOM AL ARAB (Ire) [46] 5-7-11 (5*) Darren Moffatt (19) *settled on outer, effrt 5 fs out, sn btn*..... (14 to 1) 17

3356^{4} RUSSIAN EMPIRE [63] 3-8-11 D Holland (17) *cl up, led aftr 3 fs, rdn and hdd wl o'r one furlong out, wknd quickly*..............................(7 to 2 fav op 4 to 1) 18

4023^{9} ROLLING THE BONES (USA) [45] (v) 4-7-13^{1} (3*) S Maloney (15) *mid-div on outer, rdn hfwy, grad lost pl*..............................(40 to 1 op 33 to 1) 19

4047^{2} UNFINISHEDBUSINESS [69] 3-9-3 N Connorton (11) *keen hold, trkd ldrs till lost pl hfwy, tld off entering strt*..............................(14 to 1 tchd 12 to 1) 20

Dist: ¾l, nk, nk, 1½l, 7l, sht-hd, sht-hd, 7l, 3½l, sht-hd. 2m 46.60s. (20 Ran).
(N Hetherton), J Hetherton

4433 Brettanby Handicap Class D (0-80 3-y-o) £3,494 1m 7f 177yds......... (3:20)

4353* FOLLINGWORTH GIRL (Ire) [52] 7-8 (5*) Darren Moffatt (6) *pressed ldg pair, led 7 fs out, ran on wl whn pressed fnl 2 furlongs*......................(7 to 4 fav op 6 to 4) 1
4212² ELBURG (Ire) [74] 9-7 G Duffield (2) *hld up, niggled alng aftr 7 fs, took clr order 4 out, came to stand rail entering strt, not quicken o'r one out*.....(4 to 1 op 7 to 2) 2
4357² MOONSHINE DANCER [46] 7-2 (5*) D Wright (1) *steadied strt, hld up, improved to track ldrs hfwy, hdwy on bit appr strt, ev ch 2 fs out, one pace ins last*.......(7 to 2) 3
4212⁸ RIVIERE ACTOR (USA) [70] 9-3 J Carroll (5) *nvr far away, drvn alng 5 fs out, wknd entering strt, eased*. ....(7 to 2 tchd 4 to 1) 4
4374⁹ ROSMARINO [52] 7-13 T Williams (4) *made most till hdd 7 fs out, sn drvn alng and lost tch, tld off entering strt*. .... (10 to 1 op 12 to 1) 5
832⁵ MASTER FIDDLER [48] 7-9 J Fanning (3) *trkd ldg 3, drpd rear hfwy, tld off appr strt*........(20 to 1 op 16 to 1) 6
Dist: 2l, nk, 25l, dist, 10l. 3m 42.60s. a 21.10s (6 Ran).
SR: -/12/-/ (John L Holdroyd), S G Norton

4434 EBF Evening Gazette Maiden Stakes Class D (Div I) (2-y-o) £4,342 5f 212yds ....(3:55)

4345² BEAMING 8-9 K Fallon (10) *beh, drvn alng hfwy, imprvg and swtchd ins o'r one furlong out, quickened through gap to ld wl inside last*. ....(9 to 4 fav tchd 2 to 1 and 5 to 2) 1
4237³ FRISKY MISS (Ire) 8-9 J Carroll (4) *prmnt, led aftr 2 fs, rdn two out, hdd wl ins last, no extr*.... (6 to 1 op 11 to 2) 2
3156⁴ AS SHARP AS 8-9 D Holland (1) *trkd ldrs, improved and ev ch last 2 fs, no extr wl ins last*...... (7 to 2 op 11 to 4) 3
3156² ASDAF (USA) 8-9 G Duffield (6) *trkd ldrs, drvn alng appr strt, eased whn btn o'r one furlong out*. ....(7 to 2 op 5 to 1) 4
4103⁶ EQUERRY 9-0 W Woods (9) *beh, pushed alng hfwy, nvr able to chal*........................ (5 to 1 op 3 to 1) 5
BETABETCORBETT 9-0 N Connorton (3) *trkd ldrs, outpcd and drvn alng hfwy, btn 2 fs out*. (50 to 1 op 33 to 1) 6
4345⁸ CAFE SOLO 8-9 L Charnock (5) *beh, pushed alng 3 fs out, nvr on terms*............................(50 to 1 op 33 to 1) 7
4163⁸ HONG KONG FUTURE (Ire) 9-0 J Fortune (2) *led 2 fs, styd upsides, drvn entering strt, fdd*............... (33 to 1) 8
4220 STEEL SOVEREIGN 9-0 J Fanning (8) *sn beh and outpcd, struggling frm hfwy*...............(50 to 1 op 33 to 1) 9
Dist: 1½l, 1½l, 4l, 1½l, hd, 8l, 2½l, 3½l. 1m 18.30s. a 7.30s (9 Ran).
SR: 39/33/27/11/10/9/ (Mrs Dare Wigan), J R Fanshawe

4435 EBF Zetland Median Auction Maiden Fillies' Stakes Class E (2-y-o) £3,321 7f ....(4:25)

4266² ROSE CIEL (Ire) (bl) 8-11 D Holland (7) *al wl plcd, led o'r one furlong out, edgd lft and ran on strly ins last*. ....(6 to 4 fav op 5 to 4 on) 1
3209⁶ CINDY'S STAR (Ire) 8-11 W Woods (12) *nvr far away, ev ch o'r one furlong out, no extr ins last*. ....(14 to 1 op 12 to 1) 2
4227² SALOME'S DANCE 8-11 G Duffield (8) *sn led, hdd o'r one furlong out, not quicken ins fnl furlong*.......(5 to 1) 3
4227⁴ WACKY (Ire) 8-11 J Weaver (1) *pressed ldrs, effrt and shaken up 2 fs out, not quicken*.... (5 to 1 tchd 6 to 1) 4
3411⁸ MARJAN (Ire) 8-6 (5*) A Garth (3) *dwlt, sn reco'red to press ldg grp, drvn entering strt, no extr*............. (25 to 1) 5
TULU 8-11 K Fallon (10) *unruly strt, slwly into strd, beh and sn rdn alng, took clr order hfwy, no imprsn o'r one furlong out*............................ (6 to 1 op 7 to 1) 6
3235 GRETELS PET 8-11 L Charnock (2) *chsd ldrs on ins, rdn appr strt, btn 2 fs out*............ (100 to 1 op 66 to 1) 7
4227⁷ FAMILIAR ART 8-11 J Lowe (4) *mid-div, drvn alng hfwy, wknd entering strt*.... (12 to 1 op 8 to 1 tchd 14 to 1) 8
4358 STRANGERSARDANGERS (Ire) (bl) 8-11 A Mackay (5) *pressed ldg grp, effrt and drvn alng hfwy, btn entering strt*.................................(33 to 1 op 25 to 1) 9
4237⁸ WHISPERS HILL 8-8 (3*) O Pears (11) *beh, pushed alng aftr 2 fs, btn frm hfwy*........................ (50 to 1) 10
4345 CITY OF MY DREAMS (Ire) 8-6 (5*) Darren Moffatt (6) *beh and sn rdn alng, nvr a factor*......(50 to 1 op 33 to 1) 11
4190⁷ BECKENHAM LADY (Ire) 8-11 N Connorton (9) *trkd ldrs to hfwy, sn lost pl, struggling fnl 2 fs*........... (33 to 1) 12
4082⁶ MONKEY WENCH (Ire) 8-11 J Carroll (13) *sn beh, struggling frm hfwy, nvr a threat*. .... (25 to 1 op 20 to 1 tchd 33 to 1) 13
Dist: 1½l, hd, 4l, 2½l, 3½l, 4l, sht-hd, 6l, 3½l, hd. 1m 32.80s. a 9.80s (13 Ran).
SR: 29/24/23/11/3/-/ (Lady Tennant), R Hannon

4436 Ilkley Nursery Class E (2-y-o) £3,701 5f ....(4:55)

3871⁶ INDIAN DREAMER [54] 7-2 (5*) Darren Moffatt (18) *in tch, swept into ld wl o'r one furlong out, sn clr, easily*. ....(16 to 1 op 14 to 1) 1
3894⁴ POST MISTRESS (Ire) [78] 9-3 G Duffield (2) *wth ldr, drvn alng 2 fs out, not quicken ins last*.............. (7 to 1) 2
4163² LOCHON [63] 8-2 S Webster (6) *trkd ldg grp, drvn alng last 2 fs, kpt on same pace ins last*............ (10 to 1) 3
4193 MAD ABOUT MEN [55] 7-8¹ J Lowe (3) *al prmnt, pushed alng 2 fs out, no extr fnl furlong*...(25 to 1 op 20 to 1) 4
4042⁵ ROCKY TWO [60] 7-13 A Mackay (16) *bumped leaving stalls, beh, imprvg whn checked o'r one furlong out, styd on finish*.................. (12 to 1 tchd 14 to 1) 5
3629⁷ ARTA [64] 8-3 A Culhane (19) *pressed ldg grp on outer, effrt 2 fs out, kpt on ins fnl furlong*. ....(25 to 1 op 20 to 1) 6
4193⁷ LADY SHERIFF [77] (bl) 9-2 T Lucas (8) *slight ld till hdd wl o'r one furlong out, no extr ins fnl furlong*. ....(12 to 1 op 10 to 1) 7
4318³ BOLD ALEX [65] 8-4 N Connorton (4) *chsd alng in midfield, effrt 2 fs out, no imprsn ins last*. (9 to 4 fav op 5 to 1) 8
4318 RICH GLOW [54] (bl) 7-3³ (7*) N Varley (13) *nvr far away, rdn whn ducked rght o'r one furlong out, sn one pace*. ....(50 to 1) 9
2629⁵ DON'T BE KOI (Ire) [70] 8-9 T Williams (14) *pressed ldg grp, drvn alng 2 fs out, btn one out*. ....(8 to 1 op 7 to 1 tchd 9 to 1) 10
3845 CYARNA QUINN (Ire) [72] 8-11 K Fallon (12) *chsd ldrs, hrd at work hfwy, wknd wl o'r one furlong out*... (12 to 1) 11
4084* DOCKYARD DORA [59] (bl) 7-7 (5*) D Wright (20) *beh and sn pushed alng, kpt on fnl furlong, no imprsn*... (12 to 1) 12
4272 NORDICO PRINCESS [75] 9-0 S Perks (1) *prmnt far rail, pushed alng hfwy, wknd o'r one furlong out*. (20 to 1) 13
3755* TOP SHOW (Ire) [82] 9-7 J Weaver (17) *chsd ldrs till rdn and wknd frm hfwy*...............(14 to 1 op 10 to 1) 14
3972 PASTURES NEW (Ire) [55] 7-8 S Wood (15) *beh and sn pushed alng, nvr on terms*.................... (20 to 1) 15
4105³ FADE AWAY (Ire) [55] 7-8 Dale Gibson (10) *beh, pushed alng hfwy, sn struggling*............... (16 to 1 op 14 to 1) 16
4358 KENTUCKY FLYER [56] 7-9² L Charnock (7) *trkd ldrs, drvn alng hfwy, sn lost pl*..............................(33 to 1) 17
4097⁴ CHINA ROBIN [57] 7-10 A Tucker (5) *chsd ldg grp centre, rdn alng o'r 2 fs out, fdd*......... (20 to 1 op 16 to 1) 18
4061⁶ FLOATING TRIAL [60] (bl) 7-13 N Adams (9) *reared leaving stalls, al struggling in rear*......................(12 to 1) 19
Dist: 2½l, hd, hd, ¾l, sht-hd, nk, sht-hd, nk, 2½l, 1½l. 1m 4.00s. a 6.50s (19 Ran).
SR: 24/38/22/13/15/18/30/17/5/ (R B Holt), M Bell

4437 EBF Evening Gazette Maiden Stakes Class D (Div II) (2-y-o) £4,342 5f 212yds ....(5:25)

4237⁴ NORTH REEF (Ire) 9-0 G Duffield (5) *beh and sn pushed alng, improved to track ldrs hfwy, drvn to ld ins fnl furlong, kpt on wl*...............(2 to 1 fav op 5 to 4) 1
4265² RANKAIDADE 8-9 S Perks (2) *led, rdn 2 fs out, hdd ins last, no extr*.............(4 to 1 tchd 9 to 2 and 7 to 2) 2
4167 CASUAL WATER (Ire) 9-0 M Birch (8) *pressed ldrs, improved appr strt, sn rdn, not quicken 2 fs out*. ....(16 to 1) 3
4375⁴ GLENUGIE (v) 9-0 A Culhane (6) *nvr far away, ev ch and rdn entering strt, btn wl o'r one furlong out*. ....(10 to 1 tchd 12 to 1) 4
4177⁵ AWTAAR (USA) 8-9 D Holland (10) *rcd wide, beh, effrt and rdn o'r 2 fs out, eased whn btn over one out*. ....(4 to 1 tchd 5 to 1) 5
3589⁸ CURIE CRUSADER (Ire) 9-0 J Carroll (4) *trkd ldrs, drvn alng entering strt, grad wknd*...... (10 to 1 op 8 to 1) 6
BARRIER BOY 9-0 J Fortune (9) *pressed ldrs, rdn 3 fs out, btn 2 out*.......................................(33 to 1) 7
3686⁷ SAN DIEGO CHARGER (Ire) 9-0 Dale Gibson (7) *slwly into strd, al struggling in rear*......... (33 to 1 op 25 to 1) 8
3763⁷ ARECIBO (Ire) 9-0 J Weaver (1) *cl up, outpcd and drvn alng hfwy, fdd entering strt*. ....(5 to 1 op 7 to 1 tchd 9 to 2) 9
Dist: 1½l, 6l, ¾l, 5l, 3½l, hd, 4l, sht-hd. 1m 18.50s. a 7.50s (9 Ran).
SR: 40/29/10/7/-/-/ (W E Sturt), Sir Mark Prescott

MEADOWLANDS (USA) (firm)
Friday October 15th

4438 Meadowlands Cup (Grade 1) (3-y-o and up) £198,675 1m 1f..............

2243⁴ MARQUETRY (USA) 6-8-8 K Desormeaux,.....(5 to 2 fav) 1
3640⁴ MICHELLE CAN PASS (USA) 5-7-12¹ J R Velazquez, ...(43 to 1) 2
2262⁷ NORTHERN TREND (USA) 5-8-0 J Bravo,........(30 to 1) 3
4068³ VALLEY CROSSING (USA) 5-8-5 C Antley,.........(3 to 1) 4
2838⁶ SNAPPY LANDING (USA) 4-8-0² R Davis,........(26 to 1) 5
EXCELLENT TIPPER (USA) 5-8-3 C Perret,........(11 to 1) 6
146* SIBERIAN SUMMER (USA) 4-8-4 J Santos,........(17 to 2) 7
DUSTY SCREEN (USA) 5-8-3 E King,..............(48 to 10) 8
PRESS CARD (USA) 3-8-0¹ M Smith,..............(34 to 10) 9
Dist: 8l, ¾l, hd, nose, 1 ¾l, 5l, ¾l, 10l. 1m 47.20s. (9 Ran).
(K Abdulla), R Frankel

NEWMARKET (good to soft)
Friday October 15th
Going Correction: PLUS 0.25 sec. per fur.

4439 Newmarket Challenge Cup Class G (2-y-o) £0 7f. . . . . (1:30)

4339[3] TOM MORGAN (v) 9-0 Pat Eddery (2) *made all, quickened hfwy, pushed alng fnl furlong, styd on wl.* . . . . (11 to 8 tchd 5 to 4 and 6 to 4) 1
4220[2] SWEDISH INVADER 9-0 W R Swinburn (1) *trkd wnr gng wl, ev ch whn put head in air fnl furlong, not keen.* . . . . (Evens fav op 5 to 4 tchd 11 to 10 on) 2
4227[3] RESPONSE 9-0 R Cochrane (3) *trkd ldg pair, niggled alng to go pace frm hfwy, rdn and no response appr fnl furlong.* . . . . (7 to 1 op 7 to 2 tchd 8 to 1) 3
Dist: 1½l, 6l. 1m 29.63s. a 6.13s (3 Ran).
SR: 34/29/11/ (P T Walwyn), P T Walwyn

4440 EBF Snailwell Maiden Stakes Class D (Div I) (2-y-o) £5,708 6f. . . . .(2:00)

4142[2] TZU'MU 8-9 M Hills (1) *patiently rdn, improved on outsd last 2 fs, str run to ld cl hme.* . . . . (9 to 2 op 3 to 1) 1
1020[7] TABOOK (Ire) 9-0 W R Swinburn (13) *led, quickened o'r 2 fs out, hrd pressed fnl furlong, edgd rght und pres, jst ct.* . . . . (7 to 2 fav op 7 to 2) 2
NUMBERED ACCOUNT 9-0 R Hills (18) *nvr far away, drvn to chal entering fnl furlong, edgd lft, not quicken last 50 yards.* . . . . (33 to 1 op 20 to 1 tchd 50 to 1) 3
KALKABRINO (USA) 9-0 J Reid (11) *al hndy, chlgd and squeezed out entering fnl furlong, rallied and hmpd last 50 yards.* . . . . (4 to 1 op 6 to 4 tchd 9 to 2) 4
ST LOUIS LADY 8-9 M Tebbutt (2) *chsd alng to go pace hfwy, hdwy on outsd last 2 fs, nrst finish.* . . . . (66 to 1 op 33 to 1 tchd 100 to 1) 5
YET MORE ROSES 9-0 R Cochrane (15) *nvr far away, effrt and bustled alng 2 fs out, eased whn btn, better for race.* . . . . (6 to 1 op 4 to 1 tchd 13 to 2) 6
4003[5] LAFTAH (USA) 9-0 M Roberts (12) *sluggish strt, improved into midfield hfwy, styd on fnl furlong.* . . . . (16 to 1 op 10 to 1 tchd 20 to 1) 7
COUNTRY STAR (Ire) 9-0 A Munro (10) *pressed ldrs, feeling pace and drvn alng 2 fs out, no extr.* . . . . (25 to 1 op 14 to 1) 8
DONA DELLE ROSE (USA) 8-9 W Newnes (16) *co'red up in midfield, effrt over 2 fs out, not pace of ldrs.* . . . . (66 to 1 op 33 to 1 tchd 100 to 1) 9
DIABAIG 8-9 P Robinson (4) *sluggish strt, hdwy o'r 2 fs out, ran on, improve.* . . . . (33 to 1 op 20 to 1) 10
CLASSY 8-9 W Carson (3) *patiently rdn, shaken up and hdwy last 2 fs, prmsg.* . . . . (20 to 1 op 12 to 1 tchd 25 to 1) 11
RED EARTH (USA) 9-0 Pat Eddery (5) *sluggish strt, pushed alng hfwy, some late hdwy, nvr nrr.* . . . . (13 to 2 op 5 to 1 tchd 9 to 1) 12
4276 NIGHT IN A MILLION 9-0 Paul Eddery (17) *sluggish strt, hrd drvn aftr 2 fs, nvr a factor.* . . . . (50 to 1 op 20 to 1 tchd 66 to 1) 13
SHARP REBUFF 9-0 T Sprake (9) *sluggish strt, not reco'r.* . . . . (66 to 1 op 33 to 1 tchd 100 to 1) 14
4127 LADY VALENSINA (Ire) 8-9 C Asmussen (8) *outpcd and bustled alng, nvr trble ldrs.* . . . . (50 to 1 op 14 to 1 tchd 66 to 1) 15
4330[5] SHAYNES DOMAIN 9-0 J Williams (19) *outpcd and drvn alng hfwy, nvr a factor.* . . . . (66 to 1 op 33 to 1 tchd 100 to 1) 16
2990 PRESENTLY 8-9 W Ryan (7) *speed for o'r 4 fs.* . . . . (50 to 1 op 20 to 1 tchd 66 to 1) 17
4269[7] DEEPLY VALE (Ire) 9-0 B Rouse (6) *pressed ldrs for o'r 4 fs.* . . . . (66 to 1 op 33 to 1 tchd 100 to 1) 18
TOP TYCOON (Ire) 9-0 K Darley (14) *sluggish strt, not reco'r.* . . . . (25 to 1 op 12 to 1) 19
Dist: Nk, 2l, ½l, 2l, hd, 2l, ¾l, nk, 1l, nk. 1m 14.99s. a 3.59s (19 Ran).
SR: 53/57/49/47/34/38/30/27/21/ (Sir Philip Oppenheimer), G Wragg

4441 Baring International Darley Stakes Class A (Listed Race) (3-y-o and up) £10,116 1m 1f. . . . . (2:35)

4282[2] WHARF (USA) 3-8-10 Pat Eddery (4) *trkd ldg pair, drvn ahead o'r 2 fs out, kpt on gmely fnl furlong.* . . . . (11 to 4 fav op 7 to 2 tchd 4 to 1) 1
4373* AMAZING FEAT (Ire) 4-9-0 K Darley (8) *patiently rdn, hdwy hfwy, ev ch entering fnl furlong, kpt on wl.* . . . . (12 to 1 op 8 to 1) 2
4282[4] SOVIET LINE (Ire) 3-8-10 W R Swinburn (3) *al hndy, led o'r 5 fs out till over 2 out, kpt on same pace.* . . . . (15 to 2 op 6 to 1 tchd 8 to 1) 3
2907 REVERE (Ire) 3-8-10 A Munro (5) *led till o'r 5 fs out, hrd drvn whn pace quickened 2 out, rallied.* . . . . (20 to 1 op 33 to 1 tchd 50 to 1) 4
4309[9] CLOUD OF DUST 4-8-9 J Reid (6) *wtd wth, effrt and pushed alng hfwy, styd on same pace last 2 fs.* . . . . (11 to 2 op 4 to 1 tchd 6 to 1) 5
4153[2] JETBEEAH (Ire) (v) 3-8-5 B Raymond (1) *last and niggled alng hfwy, styd on last 2 fs, nvr able to chal.* . . . . (14 to 1 op 10 to 1 tchd 16 to 1) 6
4282* GABR 3-9-0 W Carson (11) *wl plcd centre, effrt and drvn alng 2 fs out, outpcd fnl furlong.* . . . . (100 to 30 op 9 to 4 tchd 7 to 2) 7
4066[3] TAOS (Ire) (v) 3-8-10 L Dettori (10) *settled midfield, effrt 3 fs out, sn rdn and outpcd.* . . . . (13 to 2 op 5 to 1 tchd 7 to 1) 8
4362[4] MR MARTINI (Ire) 3-8-10 R Cochrane (9) *trkd ldg 4, struggling o'r 2 fs out, sn btn.* . . . . (33 to 1 op 25 to 1 tchd 40 to 1) 9
672 FISIO SANDS 4-8-9 J Quinn (7) *prmnt 5 fs, lost tch o'r 2 out.* . . . . (100 to 1 tchd 200 to 1) 10
Dist: 1l, 3½l, hd, 2½l, 5l, ½l, ¾l, 3l, 8l. 1m 53.15s. a 3.45s (10 Ran).
SR: 77/78/63/62/53/34/41/35/26/ (K Abdulla), H R A Cecil

4442 Tattersalls Rockfel Stakes Class A (Group 3) (2-y-o) £16,425 7f. . . . . (3:05)

4171[4] RELATIVELY SPECIAL 8-8 R Cochrane (8) *al gng wl, led o'r 2 fs out, sprinted clr ins last.* . . . .(11 to 8 fav op 6 to 4 tchd 7 to 4) 1
4177[2] BALLARD RING (Ire) 8-8 K Darley (6) *nvr far away, lost grnd whn pace quickened o'r 2 fs out, rallied fnl furlong, ran on.* . . . . (50 to 1 op 33 to 1 tchd 66 to 1) 2
4211* REASON TO DANCE 8-8 C Asmussen (5) *patiently rdn, not much room in midfield o'r 2 fs out, swtchd, fnshd strly.* . . . . (9 to 1 op 8 to 1 tchd 10 to 1) 3
4177* THREATENING 8-8 G Bardwell (7) *pressed ldg trio, hrd drvn whn pace quickened o'r 2 fs out, one pace.* . . . . (25 to 1 op 20 to 1 tchd 33 to 1) 4
4142* TABLAH (USA) 8-8 R Hills (2) *al hndy, feeling pace and hrd drvn o'r 2 fs out, no extr.* . . . . (13 to 2 op 8 to 1 tchd 6 to 1) 5
4171[3] KISSING COUSIN (Ire) 8-8 M Roberts (9) *led till o'r 2 fs out, wknd quickly fnl furlong.* . . . . (7 to 2 op 11 to 4 tchd 4 to 1) 6
4020* BRAARI (USA) 8-8 W Carson (1) *co'red up on ins, drvn alng whn lost action and snatched up over 2 fs out, not rcvr.* . . . .(7 to 1 op 6 to 1) 7
4330* SALVEZZA (Ire) 8-8 J Reid (3) *sluggish strt, hmpd and checked aftr 2 fs, rdn and no imprsn frm hfwy.* . . . . (12 to 1 op 8 to 1 tchd 14 to 1) 8
4303[8] CHOWPOR 8-8 L Dettori (4) *sluggish strt, effrt and drvn alng hfwy, sn btn.* . .(50 to 1 op 33 to 1 tchd 100 to 1) 9
Dist: 5l, ¾l, ½l, sht-hd, 1l, 2½l, 1l, 2½l. 1m 27.82s. a 4.32s (9 Ran).
SR: 56/41/38/37/36/33/25/22/14/ (Helena Springfield Ltd), L M Cumani

4443 Dewhurst Stakes Class A (Group 1) (2-y-o) £117,724 7f. . . . . (3:40)

4281* GRAND LODGE (USA) 9-0 Pat Eddery (1) *keen hold, improved gng wl hfwy, chalg whn not much room appr fnl furlong, ran on well to ld cl hme.* . . . . (9 to 4 fav op 2 to 1 tchd 7 to 4 and 5 to 2) 1
2906[2] STONEHATCH (USA) 9-0 J Reid (7) *set modest pace, quickened o'r 2 fs out, rdn and hdd cl hme, no extr.* . . . .(7 to 1 op 6 to 1 tchd 8 to 1) 2
4249[2] NICOLOTTE 9-0 M Hills (2) *settled gng wl, quickened to chal appr fnl furlong, kpt on und pres.* . . . .(9 to 2 op 5 to 1 tchd 6 to 1) 3
4062* POLISH LAUGHTER (USA) 9-0 W R Swinburn (5) *al frnt rnk, led briefly appr fnl furlong, not quicken und pres cl hme.* . . . . (13 to 2 op 6 to 1 tchd 7 to 1) 4
4273[3] REDOUBTABLE (USA) 9-0 L Dettori (3) *co'red up in midfield, bustled up to chal appr fnl furlong, ran on same pace.* . . . . (7 to 1 op 6 to 1 tchd 8 to 1) 5
4293[3] PSYCHOBABBLE (Ire) 9-0 C Asmussen (4) *nvr far away, ev ch whn drifted lft o'r one furlong out, rdn and not quicken.* . . . .(15 to 2 op 6 to 1 tchd 8 to 1) 6
4276[2] RIVER DEEP (USA) 9-0 A Munro (10) *trkd ldrs towards outsd, drvn alng whn pace quickened o'r 2 fs out, no extr.* . . . .(33 to 1 tchd 25 to 1 and 40 to 1) 7
4149* MUTAKDDIM (USA) 9-0 W Carson (6) *trkd ldrs, struggling to hold pl whn pace quickened o'r 2 fs out, sn btn.* . . . .(12 to 1 tchd 14 to 1) 8
4113[4] VILLAGE EAGLE (Fr) 9-0 M Roberts (9) *trkd ldg pair, und pres o'r 2 fs out, fdd.* . . . .(150 to 1 op 100 to 1 tchd 200 to 1) 9
4062[2] ALANEES 9-0 B Raymond (8) *patiently rdn, improved on outsd hfwy, ridden and btn o'r 2 fs out.* . . . . (25 to 1 op 20 to 1 tchd 33 to 1) 10
Dist: ½l, nk, 1l, nk, ½l, 1½l, 1½l, nk, 1½l. 1m 28.27s. a 4.77s (10 Ran).
SR: 55/53/52/49/48/46/41/36/35/ (Lord Howard de Walden), W Jarvis

4444 Fen Ditton Nursery Class C (2-y-o) £9,325 1m. (4:15)

3779[6] MAKE A STAND [74] 8-5 W Newnes (19) *pushed alng in midfield, improved on outsd o'r one furlong out, ran on strly to ld cl hme.* . . . . (25 to 1 op 20 to 1 tchd 33 to 1) 1
3940[8] NORTHERN BAILIWICK (Ire) [62] (bl) 7-0 (7*) C Adamson (13) *al hndy, led o'r 3 fs out, hrd drvn fnl furlong, ct cl hme.* . . . . (50 to 1 op 33 to 1 tchd 66 to 1) 2

4227* FAWLTY TOWERS (Ire) [78] 8-9 A Munro (3) *co'red up in midfield, rdn to improve over one furlong out, kpt on strly nr finish*......................(20 to 1 op 14 to 1) 3
3793* RAGSAT AL OMOR (Ire) [77] 8-8 C Asmussen (9) *chsd alng to improve frm off the pace last 2 fs, fnshd wl.* ....(6 to 1 op 7 to 1) 4
4276 SANS ECOCIDE [70] (bl) 8-1 N Carlisle (23) *al hndy, dsptd ld o'r 3 fs out, rdn and not quicken fnl furlong.* ....(33 to 1) 5
3508* SHERIFF [69] 7-11 (3*) B Doyle (20) *nvr far away, hrd drvn last 2 fs, kpt on same pace.* ....(25 to 1 op 20 to 1 tchd 33 to 1) 6
4122[5] ROBSERA (Ire) [72] 8-3 D Harrison (2) *settled midfield, pushed alng to improve last 2 fs, styd on finish.* ....(20 to 1 op 16 to 1) 7
4128[2] MAKE THE BREAK [67] 7-12[1] A McGlone (12) *chsd alng hfwy, str run entering fnl furlong, fnshd wl.* ....(14 to 1 op 12 to 1 tchd 16 to 1) 8
4230[4] SHARP TYCOON (Ire) [78] 8-9 B Raymond (15) *pressed ldrs, drvn alng o'r 2 fs out, no imprsn*...(25 to 1 op 20 to 1) 9
4329[2] NAWAFELL [64] 7-9 J Quinn (16) *chsd alng in midfield, no imprsn last 2 fs*.......................... (7 to 1 tchd 8 to 1) 10
4015[2] PAVAKA [83] (v) 9-0 L Dettori (18) *pressed ldrs, feeling pace o'r 2 fs out, fdd*......................(14 to 1 tchd 16 to 1) 11
3865* DUTY TIME [90] 9-7 J Reid (7) *settled midfield, effrt and drvn alng o'r 2 fs out, no extr.* ....(16 to 1 op 14 to 1 tchd 20 to 1) 12+
4230 BONAIGUA (Ire) [80] 8-11 R Cochrane (1) *chsd alng on outsd, not pace of ldrs last 2 fs*.... (25 to 1 op 20 to 1) 12+
4229* FAWRAN (USA) [87] 9-4 M Roberts (4) *rcd keenly beh ldrs for o'r 4 fs*........... (5 to 1 fav op 6 to 1 tchd 9 to 2) 14
3667[7] MR DEVIOUS [78] 8-9 W R Swinburn (6) *drvn alng in midfield, nvr able to rch frnt rnk.* (33 to 1 op 25 to 1) 15
4167[5] RORY [72] 8-3 Paul Eddery (11) *chsd ldg bunch to hfwy, fdd o'r 2 fs out*....................(14 to 1 tchd 16 to 1) 16
2592[4] LUGANO [72] 8-3 K Darley (14) *settled midfield, bustled alng o'r 2 fs out, sn btn*..........(16 to 1 tchd 20 to 1) 17
3570[4] ORANGE PLACE (Ire) [86] 9-3 M Hills (10) *led till o'r 3 fs out, fdd appr last*........(25 to 1 op 20 to 1 tchd 33 to 1) 18
4122 SWEET CAROLINE [62] 7-7 Kim McDonnell (24) *sn struggling, nvr a factor*................ (50 to 1 op 66 to 1) 19
4253[3] SAAFI (Ire) [67] 7-12 W Carson (22) *rcd midfield, pushed alng hfwy, nvr dngrs*.........(16 to 1 tchd 20 to 1) 20
4124[5] MERLIN'S FIELD (Ire) [77] 8-8 Pat Eddery (5) *bustled alng to keep up, nvr a factor.* ....(16 to 1 op 14 to 1 tchd 20 to 1) 21
3678[2] HARDING [78] 8-9 J Williams (17) *speed for o'r 5 fs.* ....(16 to 1 tchd 20 to 1) 22
3597[7] HEATHCLIFF (Ire) [67] 7-12 F Norton (21) *frnt rnk for o'r 5 fs*.. (33 to 1) 23
Dist: Hd, 1½l, 1l, ½l, ¾l, sht-hd, 1l, 1½l, 1½l, 5l. 1m 42.03s. a 4.83s (23 Ran).
SR: 49/36/47/43/34/31/33/25/31/ (R Barnett), H Candy

4445 Greene King Handicap Class C (0-95 3-y-o) £5,481 1¾m.............. (4:50)

4274[8] MARCO MAGNIFICO (USA) [73] 8-10 M Hills (9) *tucked away, quickened to ld appr fnl furlong, hdd last 50 yards, rallied to lead last strds.* ....(11 to 2 op 5 to 1 tchd 4 to 1 and 6 to 1) 1
4110[3] CUFF LINK (Ire) [84] 9-7 W Ryan (4) *settled midfield, improved o'r 2 fs out, swtchd to chal appr last, led last 50 yards, hdd and no extr last strds.* ....(16 to 1 op 14 to 1 tchd 20 to 1) 2
4344[3] MONDRAGON [73] 8-10 K Darley (6) *wnt freely to post, patiently rdn, hdwy to chal last 2 fs, not quicken wl ins last*.................... (5 to 1 op 4 to 1 tchd 11 to 2) 3
4267[5] PISH KESH [56] 7-7 Kim McDonnell (5) *al hndy, led o'r 5 fs out till appr last, rdn and no extr.* ....(40 to 1 op 33 to 1 tchd 50 to 1) 4
4344[2] COLLIER BAY [75] 8-12 L Dettori (2) *nvr far away, ev ch and drvn alng o'r 3 fs out, outpcd appr last.* ....(7 to 4 fav op 2 to 1 tchd 9 to 4) 5
4344[8] HILL OF DREAMS [73] 8-10 R Cochrane (11) *tucked away, drvn up o'r 2 fs out, rdn and no imprsn appr last.* ....(33 to 1 op 25 to 1) 6
4267[2] FOOLS ERRAND (Ire) [66] 8-3 W Carson (10) *trkd ldrs, hrd drvn o'r 3 fs out, fdd 2 out.* ....(8 to 1 op 7 to 1 tchd 9 to 1) 7
4189[3] ALMAMZAR (USA) [82] 9-5 M Roberts (7) *settled gng wl, effrt and bustled alng o'r 3 fs out, fdd 2 out.* ....(11 to 1 op 8 to 1 tchd 12 to 1) 8
4283 BLUE BLAZER [80] 9-3 B Raymond (8) *trkd ldrs, effrt and drvn alng o'r 3 fs out, sn outpcd.* ....(20 to 1 op 12 to 1 tchd 25 to 1) 9
3757[6] ERICOLIN (Ire) [66] 8-0 (3*) B Doyle (12) *led till o'r 5 fs out, wknd und pres over 2 out.* ....(25 to 1 op 20 to 1 tchd 33 to 1) 10
4334* DIPLOMATIST [69] 8-6 J Reid (3) *co'red up on ins, effrt and not much room over 3 fs out, ch 2 out, fdd.* ....(12 to 1 op 10 to 1) 11
4176[3] MIROSWAKI (USA) [72] 8-9 Paul Eddery (1) *wl plcd, feeling pace and rdn alng o'r 3 fs out, sn btn.* ....(14 to 1 op 10 to 1) 12
Dist: Nk, 6l, 1l, 2½l, 4l, 6l, ¾l, ¾l, nk, ½l. 3m 5.45s. a 9.45s (12 Ran).
SR: 37/47/24/5/19/9/-/4/-/ (Mrs Leonard Simpson), B W Hills

4446 EBF Snailwell Maiden Stakes Class D (Div II) (2-y-o) £5,663 6f......... (5:15)

4154[3] LUANA 8-9 M Roberts (10) *al hndy, drvn ahead entering fnl furlong, kpt on strly to go clr last 100 yards.* .... (11 to 2 op 9 to 2 tchd 6 to 1) 1
1265[4] RAMANI (USA) 9-0 W R Swinburn (6) *wl plcd centre, led 2 fs out till entering last, rdn and kpt on same pace.* ....(9 to 1 op 6 to 1 tchd 10 to 1) 2
3941[9] CALYPSO MONARCH (Ire) 9-0 K Darley (1) *rcd alone stands side, led to 2 fs out, not quicken fnl furlong.* ....(10 to 1 tchd 12 to 1) 3
DIME TIME 9-0 L Dettori (4) *settled midfield, drvn to improve last 2 fs, styd on.* ....(12 to 1 op 5 to 1 tchd 14 to 1) 4
STAR OF THE DANCE (USA) 8-9 J Reid (12) *settled midfield, shaken up to improve 2 fs out, no imprsn fnl furlong*..........(7 to 4 fav op 6 to 4 tchd 2 to 1) 5
4276 GLITTERAZZI 9-0 Pat Eddery (17) *pressed ldrs, pushed alng o'r 2 fs out, one pace.* ....(14 to 1 op 6 to 1 tchd 16 to 1) 6
BY CANDLELIGHT (Ire) 8-9 M Tebbutt (16) *shaped wl for o'r 4 fs, better for race*................(25 to 1 tchd 33 to 1) 7
4269[2] SHIKAREE (Ire) (bl) 9-0 A McGlone (5) *nvr far away, drvn alng o'r 2 fs out, fdd.* (16 to 1 op 14 to 1 tchd 20 to 1) 8
GIGGLESWICK GIRL 8-9 C Rutter (15) *in tch, effrt and chsd alng o'r 2 fs out, not pace to chal.* ....(8 to 1 tchd 10 to 1) 9
HAWAIIAN DREAM 8-9 B Rouse (8) *sn outpcd and drvn alng, nvr trble ldrs*...(33 to 1 op 25 to 1 tchd 50 to 1) 10
3990 SAMBA SHARPLY 9-0 J Williams (14) *struggling hfwy, nvr a factor*...............................(50 to 1 op 33 to 1) 11
LE DOME (Ire) 9-0 R Cochrane (3) *sn outpcd and drvn alng, nvr on terms*.... (14 to 1 op 8 to 1 tchd 16 to 1) 12
BAJAN (Ire) 9-0 P Robinson (7) *bustled alng and outpcd aftr 3 fs, sn btn*..........................(33 to 1 op 20 to 1) 13
4303[6] TRUMPS HIGH (USA) 8-9 W Ryan (18) *trkd ldrs 4 fs.* ....(7 to 1 op 9 to 2 tchd 8 to 1) 14
IVANHOE 9-0 R Hills (11) *sluggish strt, not reco'r.* ....(25 to 1 op 20 to 1 tchd 33 to 1) 15
4179[9] SHERBLU 9-0 A Munro (13) *wl plcd for o'r 3 fs*... (50 to 1) 16
4269[9] MANATEE 8-9 B Raymond (9) *outpcd.* .... (33 to 1 op 20 to 1) 17
Dist: 3½l, 6l, 1l, ¾l, ¾l, hd, sht-hd, 1½l, 1½l, nk. 1m 14.92s. a 3.52s (17 Ran).
SR: 55/46/22/18/10/12/6/10/-/ (Saeed Manana), C E Brittain

BELMONT PARK (USA) (firm)
Saturday October 16th

4447 Jockey Club Gold Cup (Grade 1) (3-y-o and up) £337,748 1¼m...............

4068[5] MINER'S MARK (USA) 3-8-9 C McCarron, ...(84 to 10) 1
4080[6] COLONIAL AFFAIR (USA) 3-8-9 J Santos, ...(68 to 10) 2
3640* BRUNSWICK (USA) 4-9-0 M Smith, ...(19 to 10 fav) 3
4068[2] DEVIL HIS DUE (USA) 4-9-0 H McCauley, ...(22 to 10) 4
DIAZO (USA) 3-8-9 L Pincay Jr, ... (21 to 10) 5
Dist: Nose, 2 ¾l, 1 ¼l, nk. 2m 2.79s. (5 Ran).
(O Phipps), C R McGaughey

4448 Champagne Stakes (Grade 1) (2-y-o) £198,675 1m.........................

4069[2] DEHERE (USA) 8-10 C McCarron, ...(10 to 3 on) 1
CRARY (USA) 8-10 C Perret, ...(34 to 10) 2
AMATHOS (USA) 8-10 M Smith, ...(20 to 1) 3
4069[4] SACRED HONOUR (USA) 8-10 P Day, ...(89 to 10) 4
PERSONAL ESCORT (USA) 8-10 J D Bailey, ...(13 to 1) 5
MOVING VAN (USA) 8-10 R Davis, ...(28 to 1) 6
Dist: 4l, ¾l, ½l, 6½l, 18l. 1m 35.91s. (6 Ran).
(Due Process Stable), R Nobles

4449 Frizette Stakes (Grade 1) (2-y-o) £99,338 1m.........................

HEAVENLY PRIZE (USA) 8-7 M Smith, ...(24 to 10) 1
FACTS OF LOVE (USA) 8-7 C Perret, ...(46 to 1) 2
3700[4] FOOTING (USA) 8-7 P Day, ...(69 to 10) 3
4070[3] SOVEREIGN KITTY (USA) 8-7 J R Valazquez, ...(32 to 1) 4
SHE RIDES TONITE (USA) 8-7 F Alvarado, ... (33 to 1) 5
AVIE'S FANCY (USA) 8-7 C McCarron, ...(40 to 1) 6
4070* STRATEGIC MANEUVER (USA) 8-7 J Santos, (10 to 4 on) 7
Dist: 7l, 4 ¾l, 2½l, 2½l, 6l, 7l. 1m 35.46s. (7 Ran).
(O Phipps), C R McGaughey

4450 Beldame Stakes (Grade 1) (3-y-o and up) £99,338 1m 1f....................

4079[2] DISPUTE (USA) 3-8-7 J D Bailey, ... (14 to 10 fav) 1
4079* SHARED INTEREST (USA) 5-8-11 R Davis, ...(69 to 10) 2
1691[6] VIVANO (USA) 4-8-11 C McCarron, ...(18 to 1) 3
4079[3] TURNBACK THE ALARM (USA) 4-8-11 C Antley, ...(6 to 4) 4
AVIAN ASSEMBLY (USA) 4-8-11 E Maple, ...(40 to 1) 5
3804[3] NOVEMBER SNOW (USA) 4-8-11 M Smith, ... (41 to 10) 6
Dist: 1 ¾l, nk, 1 ¾l, ½l, 6l. 1m 47.22s. (6 Ran).

(O M Phipps), C R McGaughey

4451 Lawrence Realization (Grade 3) (Turf) (3-y-o) £49,987 1½m.

STROLLING ALONG (USA) 8-2^{1} C McCarron, ... (54 to 10) 1
SCATTERED STEPS (USA) 8-1 E Maple, ... (15 to 1) 2
NOBLE SHEBA (USA) 8-2^{1} J Santos, ... (42 to 1) 3
3784^{5} DECLASSIFIED (USA) 8-1 P Day, ... (56 to 10) 4
JODI'S THE BEST (USA) 8-1 J-L Samyn, ... (41 to 1) 5
GROOMED TO WIN (USA) 8-1 R Davis, ... (5 to 1) 6
3653^{3} BRAZANY (USA) 8-1 M Smith, ... (23 to 10 fav) 7
SENTIMENTAL MOI (USA) 8-1 J D Bailey, ... (41 to 10) 8
PROUD SHOT (USA) 8-1 H McCauley, ... (17 to 1) 9
4362^{2} REDENHAM (USA) 8-1 C Perret, ... (22 to 1) 0
COMPADRE (USA) 8-2^{1} C Antley, ... (17 to 1) 0
CAVEAT'S IMAGE (USA) 8-1 J Chavez, ... (32 to 1) 0
Dist: ¾l, 1l, ½l, 1 ¼l, ¾l, ¾l, 5l, nk, ¾l, 2l. 2m 32.70s. (12 Ran).
(O Phipps), C R McGaughey III

CATTERICK (good to soft)
Saturday October 16th

Going Correction: PLUS 0.75 sec. per fur. (races 1,4,5), PLUS 0.50 (2,3,6,7)

4452 EBF North Riding Maiden Stakes Class D (2-y-o) £4,985 5f. .... (2:05)

4269^{3} MONTICINO (Ire) 9-0 D Holland (17) *dsptd ld, advantage o'r one furlong out, rdn and ran on wl ins last.* ... (2 to 1 fav tchd 7 to 4 and 6 to 4) 1
3972^{6} PURPLE FLING 9-0 K Darley (15) *nvr far away, rdn alng 2 fs out, kpt on same pace ins fnl furlong.* ... (3 to 1 tchd 7 to 2) 2
4098^{4} PERTEMPS FLYER 9-0 Paul Eddery (5) *in tch, drvn up o'r one furlong out, no extr ins last....* (10 to 1 op 7 to 1) 3
2876^{4} KING RAMBO 9-0 S Perks (8) *handly paced, effrt and drvn alng last 2 fs, kpt on same pace.* ... (11 to 2 op 3 to 1) 4
3566^{5} CELTIC GOVERNESS 8-9 J Fortune (14) *in tch, rdn alng hfwy, not quicken o'r one furlong out.* ... (50 to 1 op 33 to 1) 5
4084^{2} BOLD TIME MONKEY 8-9 J Carroll (7) *chsd ldrs, pushed alng bef hfwy, not quicken o'r one furlong out.* ... (12 to 1 tchd 11 to 1) 6
4193 RED GRIT (Ire) (bl) 8-9 J Weaver (1) *slight ld far side till hdd o'r one furlong out, fdd......* (25 to 1 op 20 to 1) 7
4163 MYSTICAL MICKEY (Ire) 9-0 S D Williams (19) *beh, shaken up hfwy, styd on ins fnl furlong, nrst finish.* ... (50 to 1 op 33 to 1) 8
4303 MAZ (Ire) 8-9 L Charnock (4) *prmnt, rdn alng hfwy, wknd o'r one furlong out....* (8 to 1 op 14 to 1 tchd 20 to 1) 9
BAIRN GLEN 8-6 (3*) S Maloney (3) *pushed alng beh ldg grp hfwy, no imprsn o'r one furlong out.* ... (10 to 1 op 16 to 1 tchd 20 to 1) 10
4237^{9} CHADWELL HALL 9-0 K Fallon (18) *mid-div, pushed alng hfwy, unbl to quicken.* ... (25 to 1 op 20 to 1 tchd 33 to 1) 11
4237 TARNSIDE TURBO 9-0 A Culhane (10) *beh, shaken up hfwy, nvr able to chal.* ... (20 to 1) 12
4182^{5} CALDER KING 8-11 (3*) O Pears (13) *settled beh ldg grp, pushed alng to improve o'r 2 fs out, no imprsn.* ... (50 to 1 op 33 to 1) 13
4342 ONE FOR THE LADIES 9-0 Kim Tinkler (9) *beh, drvn alng hfwy, not rch ldrs.* ... (50 to 1 op 33 to 1) 14
4182^{7} HARPHAM HERO 9-0 A Tucker (12) *slwly into strd, beh and sn outpcd, nvr a factor.......* (50 to 1 op 33 to 1) 15
4330^{6} CIZARGA 8-9 M Wigham (16) *beh and sn struggling, nvr on terms.* ... (12 to 1 op 10 to 1) 16
1798 RENNYHOLME 9-0 S Morris (2) *chsd ldrs, rdn alng hfwy, sn btn.* ... (50 to 1 op 33 to 1) 17
MA FOLIE 8-9 J Fanning (11) *wnt lft strt, sn wl outpcd, nvr on terms.* ... (50 to 1 op 25 to 1) 18
EILEEN'S DARLING 8-6 (3*) N Kennedy (6) *al beh, struggling aftr 2 fs.* ... (50 to 1 op 33 to 1) 19
Dist: 1½l, 2½l, 4l, nk, 1½l, ½l, 1½l, nk, ¾l, nk. 1m 4.00s. a 6.50s (19 Ran).
SR: 45/39/29/13/7/1/ (Mrs Rupert Hambro), R Charlton

4453 Moulton Nursery Class E (2-y-o) £3,418 5f 212yds. .... (2:40)

4272^{8} CERTIFICATE-X [70] 8-10 J Weaver (3) *trkd ldrs, rdn to ld a furlong out, edgd lft and ran on gmely.* ... (14 to 1 op 12 to 1) 1
4375^{5} HEATHYARDS LADY (USA) [70] 8-10 S Perks (5) *hld up, improved on inner 2 fs out, ev ch fnl furlong, no extr last 50 yards.* ... (16 to 1) 2
4318 SPRING LOADED [66] 8-6 K Darley (4) *chsd ldg grp, effrt and pushed alng 2 fs out, sn ev ch, one pace ins last.* ... (9 to 1 op 8 to 1) 3
3254^{6} ARCTIC DIAMOND [60] 7-9 (5*) B Russell (2) *hld up, shaken up and improved 2 fs out, ran on ins fnl furlong.* ... (10 to 1 op 8 to 1 tchd 11 to 1) 4
4358* MONKEY'S WEDDING [72] (bl) 8-12 J Carroll (10) *prmnt, rdn to ld 2 fs out, hdd one out, no extr.........* (9 to 1) 5
4227^{5} STAR PERFORMER (Ire) [72] 8-12 L Charnock (1) *dwlt, beh, rdn to improve entering strt, no extr ins fnl furlong.* ... (14 to 1 op 10 to 1) 6
4318^{7} FEARLESS WONDER [60] 8-0 J Fanning (6) *steadied strt, hld up and beh, hdwy last 2 fs, nvr plcd to chal.* ... (14 to 1 op 20 to 1 tchd 25 to 1) 7
4265* ARZINA (USA) [69] 8-9 D Holland (13) *nvr far away, rdn alng entering strt, unbl to quicken.* ... (11 to 10 on op 5 to 4 tchd 11 to 8) 8
4029 BRIERLEY [70] 8-10 R Perham (8) *mid-div, drvn alng o'r 2 fs out, not quicken over one out...* (14 to 1 op 16 to 1) 9
3671^{7} SECONDS AWAY [61] 7-12 (3*) S Maloney (9) *beh, effrt and pushed alng entering strt, btn and eased fnl furlong.* ... (33 to 1) 10
4165^{5} BROCTUNE GOLD [81] 9-7 K Fallon (11) *nvr far away, rdn alng entering strt, wknd wl o'r one furlong out.* ... (14 to 1) 11
4050^{3} WESTCOAST [59] 7-13 T Williams (12) *led, hdd 2 fs out, rdn and grad wknd.* ... (20 to 1) 12
3502^{7} PRIZEFIGHTER [78] 9-4 Paul Eddery (7) *beh, wide strt, nvr able to chal.* ... (12 to 1) 13
Dist: ½l, 1½l, hd, 1½l, hd, ¾l, hd, 1l, 2½l, hd. 1m 17.90s. a 6.90s (13 Ran).
SR: 18/16/6/-/5/4/ (The 2nd Kingsley House Partnership), M Johnston

4454 Yorkshire Evening Post Limited Stakes Class F (0-60 3-y-o and up) £3,248 1m 5f 175yds. .... (3:15)

4321 SALU 4-8-13 J Carroll (15) *patiently rdn, shaken up to improve o'r 4 fs out, led over 2 out, forged clr.* ... (8 to 1 op 10 to 1 tchd 7 to 1) 1
3848 MYSTIC MEMORY 4-8-6 (7*) S Copp (8) *hld up, gd hdwy entering strt, kpt on fnl furlong, not rch wnr.* ... (8 to 1 op 7 to 1) 2
4353^{2} KEYLOCK (USA) 3-8-1 (3*) N Kennedy (11) *patiently rdn, took clr order appr strt, ridden and no extr o'r one furlong out.* ... (3 to 1 fav op 5 to 2) 3
4218^{6} DEB'S BALL 7-8-6 (7*) S Sanders (5) *beh, rdn hfwy, wide and hdwy entering strt, hrd ridden and ran on wl.* ... (10 to 1 op 8 to 1) 4
4087^{4} LANDRAIL (USA) 3-8-4 D Holland (1) *hld up, gd hdwy 4 fs out, rdn alng o'r 2 out, btn over one out.* ... (8 to 1 op 6 to 1) 5
4357* PHILGUN (v) 4-9-4 J Weaver (4) *trkd ldr, led o'r 4 fs out, hdd over 2 out, sn btn.* ... (6 to 1 op 9 to 2) 6
HELIOPSIS 5-8-13 (5*) J Marshall (6) *settled on ins, effrt 5 fs out, kpt on inside last, nvr able to chal.* ... (25 to 1 op 20 to 1) 7
4268^{2} RISPOTO 3-8-4 K Darley (12) *led til hdd o'r 4 fs out, drvn alng and wknd entering strt.* ... (5 to 1 op 4 to 1 tchd 11 to 2) 8
SILVERDALE FOX 6-9-4 S Perks (3) *settled on ins, rdn alng 6 fs out, btn 3 out.* ... (20 to 1 op 16 to 1) 9
4353^{7} JUPITER MOON 4-9-4 Paul Eddery (9) *trkd ldrs, hrd at work aftr 6 fs, grad wknd, tld off entering strt.* ... (25 to 1 op 20 to 1) 10
4157^{7} LEGION OF HONOUR 5-9-4 K Fallon (2) *prmnt, drvn alng 6 fs out, wknd o'r 4 out, tld off.......* (10 to 1 op 8 to 1) 11
1531^{6} DECIDED (Can) 10-9-1 (3*) O Pears (10) *trkd ldrs, drvn to hold pl aftr 6 fs, grad wknd, tld off entering strt.* ... (20 to 1 op 14 to 1) 12
4176 DOC SPOT 3-8-9 J Fortune (14) *trkd ldrs, outpcd hfwy, tld off entering strt.* ... (25 to 1 op 20 to 1) 13
3552 MEDIA STAR 8-8-6 (7*) M Baird (13) *slwly into strd, beh and sn niggled alng, stuggling frm hfwy, tld off.* ... (50 to 1 op 33 to 1) 14
SUREST DANCER (USA) (v) 7-9-1 (3*) S Maloney (7) *beh and sn pushed alng, lost tch hfwy, tld off.* ... (50 to 1 op 33 to 1) 15
Dist: 3½l, ¾l, 1½l, 3l, 5l, 2½l, 8l, 1½l, 10l, 2½l. 3m 12.30s. a 16.80s (15 Ran).
(W N Lumley), J Etherington

4455 Faverdale Handicap Class C (0-90 3-y-o and up) £5,166 5f. .... (3:50)

4327* MAGIC PEARL [75] 3-8-6 (7*) S Knott (6) *bumped sn aftr strt, pressed ldg grp, improved to ld wl o'r one furlong out, kpt on well ins last.* ... (10 to 1 op 8 to 1) 1
4038 PRIMULA BAIRN [69] 3-8-7 K Fallon (2) *pressed ldg bunch, improved to chal 2 fs out, kpt on fnl furlong, no extr towards finish.* ... (12 to 1 tchd 14 to 1) 2
4363 DOMICKSKY [71] 5-8-3 (7*) R Painter (19) *cl up stand side, drvn frm hfwy, hng lft fnl furlong, kpt on same pace.* ... (10 to 1 op 8 to 1) 3
4180^{2} CHOIR PRACTICE [72] 6-8-11 P Robinson (14) *beh and sn pushed alng, improved o'r one furlong out, styd on wl.* ... (15 to 2 op 8 to 1 tchd 9 to 1) 4
3834^{4} NEVER IN THE RED [81] (bl) 5-9-6 J Carroll (10) *trkd ldrs, effrt and rdn last 2 fs, kpt on same pace.* ... (14 to 1 op 10 to 1) 5
4038^{7} TWO MOVES IN FRONT (Ire) [71] (bl) 3-8-9 J Fortune (5) *made most till hdd wl o'r one furlong out, not quicken.* ... (16 to 1 op 12 to 1) 6
4277^{3} HOTARIA [68] 3-8-6 A Culhane (13) *pressed ldrs centre, effrt and rdn 2 fs out, one pace ins last.* ... (14 to 1 op 12 to 1) 7

4317[8] SHADOW JURY [72] 3-8-10 K Darley (17) *beh and sn outpcd, hdwy o'r one furlong out, styd on finish.* .... (14 to 1 op 12 to 1) 8
4363 BREEZY DAY [66] 7-7-12 (7*) S Sanders (12) *chsd alng in mid-div, kpt on o'r one furlong out, nvr dngrs.* .... (14 to 1 op 20 to 1) 9
4224[9] PRINCE BELFORT [56] 5-7-9[1] L Charnock (3) *wth ldrs far side, rdn hfwy, btn o'r one furlong out*........(20 to 1) 10
4217[4] PAGEBOY [55] 4-7-1 (7*) C Adamson (9) *chsd alng beh main grp far side, improved o'r one furlong out, kpt on towards finish*..................................(20 to 1) 11
1841 ANSELLMAN [86] 3-9-3 (7*) Mark Denaro (16) *chsd ldrs stand side, rdn o'r 2 fs out, no imprsn ins last.* (33 to 1) 12
4363* SIMMIE'S SPECIAL [59] (bl) 5-7-8[3] (7*) M Humphries (4) *nvr far away, pushed alng hfwy, btn o'r one furlong out.* ....(10 to 1 tchd 11 to 1) 13
4363 MILBANK CHALLENGER [62] 3-7-12[1] (3*) S Maloney (15) *mid-div, bustled alng o'r 2 fs out, not pace to chal.* .... (14 to 1 op 12 to 1) 14
4363 ABSOLUTION [58] 9-7-11[2] T Williams (20) *rcd stand side, in tch til rdn and btn 2 fs out.* ....(20 to 1 op 16 to 1 tchd 25 to 1) 15
3947[2] DRUM SERGEANT [70] 6-8-9 Paul Eddery (8) *bumped sn aftr strt, pushed alng after 2 fs, nvr a threat.* .... (14 to 1 op 12 to 1) 16
4297 METAL BOYS [82] 6-9-7 A Clark (11) *beh and sn outpcd, nvr a factor*....................(16 to 1 op 14 to 1) 17
1957[9] PALEY PRINCE (USA) [71] 7-8-10 R Street (18) *slwly into strd, sn beh, struggling frm hfwy*..................(20 to 1) 18
4363[4] RISTON LADY (Ire) [77] 3-8-11[1] (5*) A Procter (7) *bumped sn aftr strt, pressed main bunch till rdn and wknd frm hfwy*..................................(14 to 1 op 12 to 1) 19
4363[2] SADDLEHOME (USA) [61] 4-8-0 J Fanning (1) *taken early to post, cl up till rdn and wknd frm hfwy.* ....(6 to 1 fav op 9 to 1) 20

Dist: ½l, 1l, 1½l, hd, ½l, sht-hd, hd, 1½l, sht-hd, sht-hd. 1m 3.30s. a 5.80s (20 Ran).

SR: 58/50/49/44/52/39/35/38/27/ (G G Sanderson), E J Alston

4456 Otley Conditions Stakes Class D (2-y-o) £3,582 5f.................. (4:25)

4299[3] MARY HINGE 8-10 Paul Eddery (7) *nvr far away, improved to ld one furlong out, shaken up and ran on strly*..........................(3 to 1 op 11 to 4) 1
4237* RECAPTURED DAYS (Ire) 9-1 J Fortune (1) *trkd ldrs, led wl o'r one furlong out, hdd one out, no extr.* ....(9 to 4 fav op 11 to 4) 2
4004[2] SUAAD (Ire) 8-10 R Hills (4) *led till hdd and no extr wl o'r one furlong out*..................(7 to 2 op 3 to 1) 3
4020[4] ONE ON ONE 8-10 P Robinson (5) *wth ldr, drvn alng o'r 2 fs out, wknd over one out*.......... (3 to 1 op 11 to 4) 4
4098 JUST DUGGIE 8-11 K Fallon (2) *sn outpcd and wl beh, styd on fnl furlong, nvr dngrs*....(100 to 1 op 66 to 1) 5
4034* THE FERNHILL FLYER (Ire) (v) 8-12 J Carroll (3) *pressed ldrs, outpcd and drvn alng hfwy, fdd.* (16 to 1 op 14 to 1) 6

Dist: 2½l, 2½l, 5l, 2½l, 1½l. 1m 3.90s. a 6.40s (6 Ran).

SR: 43/38/23/3/-/-/ (Mrs J Cecil), Mrs J Cecil

4457 Batley Claiming Stakes Class F (3-y-o and up) £3,272 1m 3f 214yds.... (5:00)

4213[3] EURYTHMIC 3-8-2 K Darley (8) *keen hold early, co'red up in rear, gd hdwy appr strt, rdn to ld wl ins fnl furlong.* .... (10 to 1 op 6 to 1) 1
4213[2] GWEEK (Ire) 3-8-4 P Robinson (7) *nvr far away, led o'r 2 fs out, sn rdn, hdd wl ins last, no extr.* (6 to 1 op 7 to 1) 2
4335[2] PRIMO FIGLIO (bl) 3-8-8 R Perham (14) *keen hold in mid-div, took clr order hfwy, effrt and rdn 2 fs out, hng lft ins last, no extr*.................... (6 to 1 op 4 to 1) 3
1836[5] YOUNG TESS 3-8-2 Paul Eddery (2) *patiently rdn, steady hdwy frm 4 fs out, drvn alng 2 out, one pace appr last.* ....(7 to 1 tchd 8 to 1) 4
4187 TRANQUIL LADY (Ire) 3-8-0 (3*) S Maloney (4) *hld up, improved o'r 3 fs out, rdn entering strt, kpt on ins last, nrst finish*..................................(33 to 1) 5
4374 FAIR FLYER (Ire) 4-9-2 J Weaver (12) *hld up and beh, shaken up and hdwy last 2 fs, nvr nr to chal.* .... (12 to 1 op 10 to 1) 6
4247 DANCING DIAMOND (Ire) 3-8-0 (5*) B Russell (19) *hld up and beh, styd on fnl 2 fs, nvr nrr*.... (9 to 1 op 8 to 1) 7
4187[9] SPRAY OF ORCHIDS 4-8-8 A Culhane (11) *keen hold, co'red up beh ldrs, drvn alng appr strt, no extr last 2 fs.* ....(33 to 1) 8
4120[2] AUSTRAL JANE 3-8-7 K Fallon (17) *settled towards rear, effrt and rdn appr strt, nvr able to chal.* ....(4 to 1 fav op 9 to 2 tchd 11 to 2) 9
3407[5] ANAR (Ire) (v) 4-8-13 (3*) O Pears (3) *led, rdn 6 fs out, hdd o'r 2 out, fdd*....................(25 to 1 op 20 to 1) 10
4256[9] KEDGE (v) 3-8-3 A Clark (10) *keen hold, trkd ldrs, drvn appr strt, grad wknd*.............(14 to 1 tchd 16 to 1) 11
3565[7] BORING (USA) 4-9-4 J Fortune (1) *tucked away on ins, effrt and drvn alng appr strt, nvr able to chal.* (50 to 1) 12
4279[4] MAHAASIN 5-8-7 L Charnock (16) *chsd ldrs, improved hfwy, drvn 3 fs out, sn btn*.......... (9 to 1 op 8 to 1) 13
4374 INTREPID FORT 4-8-2 (7*) G Parkin (5) *pressed ldr, drvn alng hfwy, losing pl whn hmpd o'r 4 fs out, sn beh.* ....(50 to 1) 14
3716 STATIA (Ire) 5-8-9 Kim Tinkler (15) *beh, struggling fnl 4 fs, tld off*..................................(100 to 1) 15
4206[4] SPRING SAINT (bl) 4-8-12 J Carroll (13) *keen hold, mid-div on outer, took clr order hfwy, wknd 4 fs out, tld off.* .... (50 to 1 op 33 to 1) 16
4357 RAVENSPUR (Ire) 3-8-3 J Fanning (9) *nvr far away, drvn 3 fs out, sn btn, tld off entering strt.* (50 to 1 op 33 to 1) 17
652[6] SAVINGS BANK 3-8-1 (7*) V Halliday (20) *beh, lost tch fnl 5 fs, tld off entering strt*..................(50 to 1) 18
FLORA LADY 3-7-13[1] (3*) N Kennedy (18) *slwly into strd, beh, lost tch hfwy, tld off and virtually pld up entering strt*..................................(50 to 1) 19
3066[8] APRIL CITY 4-8-9 D Holland (6) *trkd ldrs, lost pl and rdn hfwy, tld off entering strt, virtually pld up*... (33 to 1) 20

Dist: Nk, 2l, 1½l, 5l, 1½l, 1l, 1½l, nk, 1½l, 1l. 2m 46.50s. (20 Ran).

(J Shack), Mrs M Reveley

4458 Ripley Handicap Class E (0-70 3-y-o and up) £3,522 7f.............. (5:30)

4181[2] CHAMPAGNE GRANDY [65] 3-9-2 (7*) R Painter (11) *nvr far away, led o'r one furlong out, quickened clr, easily.* ....(6 to 1 fav op 7 to 1 tchd 8 to 1) 1
4333[3] ON Y VA (USA) [54] 6-8-8 (7*) Sarah Thompson (13) *nvr far away, effrt and rdn 3 fs out, kpt on ins last, no ch wth wnr*..................................(9 to 1 op 8 to 1) 2
3354 MAM'ZELLE ANGOT [58] 3-9-2 J Fortune (1) *beh, rdn 3 fs out, styd on wl fnl 2, nrst finish*... (16 to 1 op 33 to 1) 3
4235[6] ACROSS THE BAY [59] (v) 6-9-6 K Darley (14) *beh, rdn to improve entering strt, kpt on ins fnl furlong.* .... (16 to 1 op 12 to 1) 4
3631[6] FORT VALLY [52] 3-8-3 (7*) G Parkin (2) *dwlt, beh till gd hdwy 2 fs out, kpt on wl*....................(20 to 1) 5
4235[5] MCA BELOW THE LINE [60] (v) 5-9-7 S Webster (5) *mid-div, rdn alng o'r 2 fs out, kpt on ins last, nvr dngrs.* .... (10 to 1 op 12 to 1) 6
4166 SUPER BENZ [64] 7-9-4 (7*) L Aspell (10) *led, clr entering strt, hdd o'r one furlong out, fdd.* (12 to 1 op 10 to 1) 7
4322[2] QUEENS CONSUL (Ire) [66] 3-9-5 (5*) A Procter (9) *hld up, steady hdwy fnl 2 fs, nrst finish*..................(12 to 1) 8
4217[3] LANGUEDOC [57] 6-8-11 (7*) D Thomas (8) *trkd ldr, effrt and rdn entering strt, grad wknd.* (16 to 1 op 14 to 1) 9
4235 BLUE GRIT [56] 7-9-3 L Charnock (19) *beh, drvn alng hfwy, no imprsn o'r one furlong out*............ (20 to 1) 10
4354 CHANDIGARH [49] (bl) 5-8-5 (5*) P McCabe (12) *dwlt, sn reco'red to track ldrs, rdn alng hfwy, one pace entering strt*.......................... (25 to 1 op 20 to 1) 11
4156 BALLAD DANCER [63] 8-9-10 J Carroll (4) *hld up, pushed alng entering strt, styd on fnl furlong, nvr dngrs.* ....(20 to 1) 12
4123[6] HEATHYARDS GEM [54] 3-8-12 S Perks (3) *in tch, bustled alng entering strt, btn 2 fs out*.................. (16 to 1) 13
4333[8] CELESTINE [53] (v) 4-9-0 J Fanning (15) *chsd ldrs, outpcd and rdn hfwy, no dngr entering strt.* .... (12 to 1 op 10 to 1) 14
3378 FRANCIS ANN [51] 5-8-5 (7*) R Havlin (17) *mid-div, pushed alng o'r 3 fs out, fdd entering strt*............ (20 to 1) 15
4031[2] WEE SARAH [55] 5-9-2 Paul Eddery (6) *beh, drvn aftr 3 fs, nvr on terms*.......... (13 to 2 op 6 to 1 tchd 7 to 1) 16
3965[6] OBSIDIAN GREY [65] 6-9-9 (3*) O Pears (18) *mid-div, drvn alng hfwy, wknd entering strt*.................. (20 to 1) 17
3747 LAMSONETTI [60] 3-9-4 Alex Greaves (7) *sluggish strt, beh, drvn hfwy, nvr a factor*...... (16 to 1 op 14 to 1) 18
4333[6] CORONA GOLD [56] 3-9-0 K Fallon (16) *beh and sn pushed alng, nvr wnt pace*..................(11 to 1 op 10 to 1) 19
4166 RED FAN (Ire) [62] (bl) 3-9-6 Dale Gibson (20) *al beh, lost tch hfwy, virtually pld up, tld off*.................. (33 to 1) 20

Dist: 5l, 2½l, 2l, ¾l, hd, 1½l, nk, hd, ¾l, nk. 1m 30.50s. a 7.50s (20 Ran).
SR: 49/26/19/17/5/15/14/12/5/ (Grandy Girls), M R Channon

NAAS (IRE) (good to yielding)
Saturday October 16th
Going Correction: PLUS 0.35 sec. per fur.

4459 Tifrums E.B.F. Fillies Maiden (2-y-o) £4,485 6f...................... (2:00)

3911[2] MARKET SLIDE (USA) 8-10 P Shanahan (11)..... (15 to 8) 1
CASTLE GARDENS (Ire) 8-10 D Hogan (6)........ (10 to 1) 2
2804[2] MASAWA (Ire) 8-10 R Hughes (21)............ (6 to 4 fav) 3
MISS POTTER (Ire) 8-6 (4*) J A Heffernan (13).....(25 to 1) 4
4117[2] QUEEN OF ALL BIRDS (Ire) 8-10 P V Gilson (17).. (12 to 1) 5
4388[4] AL NAAYY 8-10 W J Supple (16).................(12 to 1) 6
BLUE DOMINION (Ire) 8-8 (2*) P Carberry (8)......(12 to 1) 7
4261 CHAMPAGNE HURLEY (Ire) 8-10 D Manning (7)...(25 to 1) 8
4380 PRINCESS SHERA (Ire) (bl) 8-4 (6*) D J O'Donohoe (20) ....(16 to 1) 9
4369[9] PETIT NOM (Ire) 8-10 C Roche (22)..............(25 to 1) 10
MISS PROVIDER (Ire) 8-10 S Craine (2)............(6 to 1) 11
HOUSE MUSIC (Ire) 8-6 (4*) J J Behan (1)........ (12 to 1) 12
4388[2] SECRET WAR (Ire) 8-8 (2*) D G O'Shea (15).......(14 to 1) 13
TOP PERFORMER (Ire) 8-10 G Curran (19)....... (16 to 1) 14
ORINOCO BAY (USA) 8-10 J F Egan (5)...........(12 to 1) 15

ANGUILLITA (Ire) 8-10 K J Manning (9) .... (20 to 1) 16
THISTLE HILL (Ire) 8-0 (10*) I Browne (3) .... (25 to 1) 17
4290 GREENCASTLE ROSE (Ire) 8-10 N G McCullagh (10) .... (25 to 1) 18
4406[7] PERSIAN BLOOM (Ire) 8-0 (10*) S P Cooke (12) ... (20 to 1) 19
4369 SECRET SENSATION (Ire) 8-0 (10*) T M Finn (4) ... (33 to 1) 20
4135 CANGERAC (Ire) 8-2 (8*) P J Smullen (18) .... (50 to 1) 21
Dist: ½l, hd, hd, 3l. 1m 13.90s. a 4.40s (21 Ran).
SR: 50/48/47/46/34/-/ (Moyglare Stud Farm), D K Weld

4460 Castlemartin Stud E.B.F. (C&G) Maiden (2-y-o) £5,175 6f........ (2:30)

4290[3] GUIDED TOUR (Ire) 9-0 J F Egan (18) .... (7 to 1) 1
NIGHT CITY 9-0 R Hughes (11) .... (5 to 4 on) 2
IRISH ARMADA (USA) 9-0 P Shanahan (13) .... (7 to 1) 3
3719[8] SALTONIC (Ire) 8-6 (8*) J J Stack (15) .... (33 to 1) 4
3771[8] WOODY 8-12 (2*) P Carberry (3) .... (5 to 1) 5
JAKDUL (Ire) 8-10 (4*) J A Heffernan (16) .... (14 to 1) 6
ROYAL CRIMSON 9-0 K J Manning (6) .... (33 to 1) 7
3416 WUDITBEFAIRTOSAY (Ire) 8-8 (6*) D J O'Donohoe (7) .... (33 to 1) 8
3613[4] QUINTILIANI (Ire) 9-0 S Craine (9) .... (7 to 1) 9
BAYDUR (Ire) 9-0 D V Smith (14) .... (14 to 1) 10
4323[4] EASY STEP (Ire) 9-0 W J Supple (2) .... (8 to 1) 11
4146[9] SEA FISHER (Ire) 9-0 C Roche (5) .... (14 to 1) 12
MORE JUSTICE (Ire) 8-12 (2*) R M Burke (12) ..... (20 to 1) 13
CLASSIC PAL (USA) 9-0 P V Gilson (19) .... (14 to 1) 14
MURAAFQ (Ire) 8-8 (6*) B J Walsh (10) .... (14 to 1) 15
3492 ADJALARI (Ire) 9-0 D Hogan (4) .... (10 to 1) 16
HOW'S IT GOIN (Ire) 8-10 (4*) J J Behan (8) .... (20 to 1) 17
3608[7] WAQAR (Ire) 9-0 N G McCullagh (17) .... (10 to 1) 18
4369[3] LEO'S FRIEND (Ire) 8-10 (4*) C Everard (1) .... (10 to 1) 19
Dist: 4l, 2½l, sht-hd, 1l. 1m 13.70s. a 4.20s (19 Ran).
SR: 58/42/32/31/27/-/ (J A O'Gorman), Patrick Joseph Flynn

4461 Pitman Moore "Equip" Vaccine Handicap (0-105 3-y-o and up) £6,900 1m 3f .... (3:30)

4246[5] KAR OR [-] (bl) 3-7-11[3] (2*) R M Burke (16) .... (14 to 1) 1
4383 NEVER BACK DOWN (Ire) [-] 3-8-1 J F Egan (8) ... (10 to 1) 2
2143 ENQELAAB (USA) [-] 5-7-7 (4*) J J Behan (14) ..... (16 to 1) 3
4288[6] TONY'S FEN [-] 4-9-4 W J Supple (7) .... (8 to 1) 4
ELIADE (Ire) [-] 4-8-4 N G McCullagh (3) .... (14 to 1) 5
3245* SHIRWAN (Ire) [-] 4-7-7[3] (4*) W J Smith (13) .... (14 to 1) 6
3334[9] LIFEWATCH VISION [-] (bl) 6-9-7 P Shanahan (4) .. (12 to 1) 7
3615[2] MAMOURA (Ire) [-] (bl) 3-8-11 R Hughes (6) .... (6 to 1) 8
4409 HOPESVILLE (Ire) [-] 3-6-13 (8*) G M Moylan (9) ... (14 to 1) 9
4284[2] SAIBOT (USA) [-] (bl) 4-8-3 (6*) D J O'Donohoe (12) .... (3 to 1 fav) 10
3805[5] LYPHARD ABU (Ire) [-] (bl) 5-7-6 (6*) P P Murphy (11) .... (12 to 1) 11
4284 VALONA (Ire) [-] (bl) 3-7-13 D Manning (18) .... (14 to 1) 12
3915 SHARKASHKA (Ire) [-] 3-8-2 (2*) D G O'Shea (2) ... (14 to 1) 13
4147 MAYFIELD PRINCE (Ire) [-] 4-7-11 (6*) R V Skelly (5) (20 to 1) 14
4147 BASIE NOBLE [-] 4-7-8 Ann O'Rourke (10) .... (16 to 1) 15
4147 GLENBRACK [-] 3-8-0[1] (10*) S P Cooke (1) .... (10 to 1) 16
3198* TIGERSONG (USA) [-] 3-8-8 D V Smith (17) .... (10 to 1) 17
3915 OFTEN AHEAD (Ire) [-] 5-7-12 Joanna Morgan (15) (12 to 1) 18
Dist: ¾l, hd, ½l, 1l. 2m 27.40s. a 10.90s (18 Ran).
SR: 13/15/10/30/14/-/ (Edward Lynam), Edward Lynam

4462 Derrinstown Stud Birdcatcher Nursery (2-y-o) £16,250 6f.......... (4:00)

3917[2] ZAVALETA (Ire) [-] 8-2 (4*) J A Heffernan (12) .... (5 to 1) 1
4117* ALJAWZA (USA) [-] 8-1 (6*) D J O'Donohoe (10) (3 to 1 fav) 2
3719* MULMUS (Ire) [-] 8-7 R Hughes (15) .... (8 to 1) 3
4093[3] DANCING AT LUNASA (Ire) [-] 7-9 (4*) J J Behan (11) (7 to 1) 4
3613 SOPHIE'S PET (Ire) [-] 7-4 (8*) G M Moylan (9) ..... (16 to 1) 5
4285[5] GO MILLIE (Ire) [-] 8-0 W J Supple (8) .... (12 to 1) 6
4059* SMART ROSIE (Ire) [-] 7-9[2] Joanna Morgan (5) .... (20 to 1) 7
4052* DON'T KNOW (Ire) [-] 8-8 K J Manning (16) .... (10 to 1) 8
3608[5] QUASIMODO (Ire) [-] (bl) 7-7 (4*) W J Smith (4) ..... (20 to 1) 9
4323* TONGABEZI (Ire) [-] 7-13 (2*,6ex) R M Burke (13) .. (14 to 1) 10
3954* LADY'S VISION (Ire) [-] 8-6 J F Egan (6) .... (8 to 1) 11
4052[2] PEACE TOKEN (Ire) [-] 8-7 (8*) G Coogan (3) .... (12 to 1) 12
4285[2] TRIMBLEMILL (Ire) [-] 7-7 (8*) R T Fitzpatrick (2) ... (10 to 1) 13
3071* NEWPORT MADAM (Ire) [-] 8-10 S Craine (7) ...... (10 to 1) 14
4369[3] FIONN DE COOL (Ire) [-] (bl) 8-0[1] D Manning (1) ... (16 to 1) 15
1854[9] AVONDALE FOREST (Ire) [-] 8-4 N G McCullagh (14) .... (25 to 1) 16
4285[4] ASTRADANE (Ire) [-] 7-7 (2*) D G O'Shea (17) ..... (12 to 1) 17
Dist: ½l, nk, 3½l, 1½l. 1m 13.60s. a 4.10s (17 Ran).
SR: 52/51/50/28/21/-/ (Mrs Catherine Shubotham), J S Bolger

4463 Ali Retza & Mamadi Soudavar Garnet Race (Listed) (3-y-o and up) £8,625 7f .... (4:30)

4094* THATCHING CRAFT (Ire) 4-8-11 J J Behan (7) *trkd ldr, led 2 fs out, styd on strly* .... (12 to 1) 1
4386[4] MISS MISTLETOES (Ire) 3-8-8 S Craine (10) *rear, prog far side 2 fs out, styd on strly, not rch wnr* .... (14 to 1) 2
4053* MILLIE'S CHOICE (Ire) 4-9-2 W J Supple (11) *mid-div, rdn 2 fs out, styd on strly ins last* .... (7 to 2) 3
4053[3] DASHING COLOURS (Ire) 4-9-2 P V Gilson (14) *rear, prog 3 fs out, kpt on one pace* .... (6 to 1) 4
4172 NO RESERVATIONS (Ire) 3-8-8 R M Burke (1) *wl plcd, rdn 2 fs out, kpt on one pace* .... (12 to 1) 5
4384[2] CHEVIOT AMBLE (Ire) 5-8-11 J F Egan (5) *led, rdn 3 fs out, hdd 2 out, wknd* .... (5 to 2 fav) 6
4284[8] SAFAYN (USA) (bl) 3-8-8 C Roche (13) *trkd ldr, rdn 3 fs out, hmpd one and a half out, kpt on* .... (16 to 1) 7
2410* DAGNY JUEL (USA) 3-8-8 K J Manning (12) *mid-div, prog 3 fs out, drifted lft 2 out, sn rdn, wknd* .... (6 to 1) 8
4053[7] INTIMACY (USA) 3-8-8 N G McCullagh (16) *trkd ldr, rdn 3 fs out, wknd 2 out* .... (14 to 1) 9
4118[2] GOODNIGHT KISS (bl) 3-8-8 P Shanahan (3) *wl plcd, rdn 2 fs out, wknd one out* .... (8 to 1) 10
3733[3] ROLANDS GIRL (Ire) 3-8-8 J A Heffernan (4) *mid-div, rdn 3 fs out, wknd 2 out* .... (50 to 1) 11
4245[7] BELLISSI (Ire) 3-8-8 P J Smullen (6) *mid-div, rdn 3 fs out, wknd 2 out* .... (16 to 1) 12
4245[8] GOLDEN SPHINX (Ire) 3-8-8 D G O'Shea (8) *al rear.* .... (33 to 1) 13
4287[5] CORTIJA PARK (Ire) 3-8-8 P Carberry (15) *hld up, rdn 3 fs out, wknd 2 out* .... (14 to 1) 14
3852[6] MARKIEVICZ (Ire) (bl) 3-8-8 D Hogan (9) *al rear* ... (25 to 1) 15
3162 DAWNSIO (Ire) 3-8-13 R Hughes (2) *al rear* ...... (10 to 1) 16
Dist: 2l, ½l, hd, 1l. 1m 26.90s. a 4.30s (16 Ran).
SR: 69/60/66/65/54/-/ (Hugh McMahon), Hugh McMahon

NEWMARKET (good)
Saturday October 16th
Going Correction: PLUS 0.15 sec. per fur.

4464 Bedford Lodge Hotel Bentinck Stakes Class A (Listed Race) (3-y-o and up) £10,464 6f.......... (1:50)

4170[6] MONTENDRE 6-9-2 J Reid (13) *patiently rdn, improved far side o'r 2 fs out, drvn to ld ins last, hld on gmely.* .... (16 to 1 op 12 to 1 tchd 20 to 1) 1
4170[2] MARINA PARK 3-8-10 L Dettori (10) *tucked away, drvn to chal ins fnl furlong, fnshd wl.* .... (4 to 1 fav op 7 to 2 tchd 9 to 2) 2
4275[3] BLYTON LAD 7-9-2 S Webster (7) *made most, quickened 2 fs out, hdd and rdn ins last, no extr cl hme.* .... (6 to 1 op 9 to 2 tchd 13 to 2) 3
4312[6] ZARANI SIDI ANNA (USA) 3-8-6 W R Swinburn (1) *wtd wth, str run on outsd to chal entering fnl furlong, rdn and no extr last 50 yards* ... (11 to 2 op 4 to 1 tchd 6 to 1) 4
4282[3] EN ATTENDANT (Fr) 5-8-12 L Piggott (9) *co'red up in midfield, effrt gng wl over 2 fs out, sn rdn, one pace.* .... (12 to 1 op 10 to 1) 5
4170[4] HARD TO FIGURE 7-8-12 R Cochrane (11) *settled beh ldrs, outpcd and drvn alng hfwy, styd on fnl furlong, nrst finish* .... (8 to 1 tchd 12 to 1) 6
4275[2] SPLICE 4-8-11 Pat Eddery (6) *nvr far away, ev ch and rdn o'r 2 fs out, not quicken appr last.* (5 to 1 tchd 11 to 2) 7
4280[7] CROFT VALLEY 6-9-2 T Quinn (5) *dsptd ld, feeling pace and drvn alng o'r 2 fs out, fdd.* .... (40 to 1 op 33 to 1 tchd 50 to 1) 8
3936* BUNTY BOO 4-9-0 A Mackay (12) *pressed ldrs for o'r 3 fs, fdd appr last* .... (16 to 1 op 14 to 1 tchd 20 to 1) 9
4278* BRANSTON ABBY (Ire) 4-8-11 M Roberts (3) *settled midfield, drvn alng whn pace quickened o'r 2 fs out, no imprsn* .... (8 to 1 op 7 to 1) 10
4373[7] FYLDE FLYER 4-9-2 G Duffield (4) *trkd ldg pair, hrd drvn o'r 2 fs out, btn appr last.* .... (20 to 1 op 16 to 1 tchd 25 to 1) 11
4018 SPARK (Ire) 3-8-6 A Munro (2) *struggling aftr 2 fs, sn lost tch* .... (200 to 1 op 100 to 1) 12
Dist: Nk, 1l, ½l, 1½l, 1½l, 2l, 2l, hd, ½l, 2½l. 1m 13.32s. a 1.92s (12 Ran).
SR: 82/75/77/65/65/59/50/47/44/ (David Mort), M McCormack

4465 Olivier Douieb Memorial Rated Class B Handicap (0-100 3-y-o and up) £8,580 5f.......... (2:20)

3668[4] IN CASE (USA) [94] 3-9-0 Pat Eddery (18) *nvr far away, led appr fnl furlong, ran on strly* .... (9 to 1 op 8 to 1) 1
3127 CRADLE DAYS [86] 4-8-7 M Roberts (12) *tucked away in midfield, bustled through entering fnl furlong, ran on finish* .... (16 to 1 tchd 20 to 1) 2
4038[3] SIR JOEY (USA) [86] 4-8-2 (5*) S Drowne (22) *trkd ldrs far side, lost grnd whn pace quickened o'r 2 fs out, rallied nr finish* .... (14 to 1 op 12 to 1 tchd 16 to 1) 3
4278[2] ALASIB [89] 3-8-9 L Dettori (11) *wl plcd till rdn and lost grnd o'r 2 fs out, styd on fnl furlong, fnshd well.* .... (9 to 1 op 8 to 1) 4
4278[9] MASSIBA (Ire) [92] 4-8-8 (5*) D McCabe (1) *tucked away in midfield, effrt and drvn alng o'r one furlong out, kpt on same pace* .... (20 to 1 tchd 25 to 1) 5
3668[2] PRESS THE BELL [86] 3-7-13 (7*) P Roberts (17) *rcd centre, led for o'r 3 fs, rdn and no extr wl ins last.* .... (16 to 1 tchd 20 to 1) 6
4393* BENZOE (Ire) [90] (bl) 3-8-10 T Lucas (16) *sn chsd alng, improved frm midfield hfwy, effrt entering fnl furlong, not quicken* .... (6 to 1 fav op 8 to 1 tchd 9 to 1) 7

3955[2] GONE SAVAGE [86] 5-8-7 J Reid (8) *chsd ldrs, effrt and rdn 2 fs out, styd on same pace.* ....(14 to 1 op 12 to 1 tchd 16 to 1) 8
4151[2] MISTERTOPOGIGO (Ire) [90] 3-8-10 A Munro (13) *wth ldr centre, feeling pace o'r one furlong out, not quicken.* ....(10 to 1 op 12 to 1) 9
4151[3] BOLD LEZ [92] 6-8-13 R Cochrane (6) *outpcd and drvn alng aftr 2 fs, rapid hdwy appr last, fnshd wl.* ....(12 to 1 tchd 14 to 1) 10
4180[9] MACFARLANE [86] 5-8-7 F Norton (21) *chsd alng in midfield, effrt hfwy, not pace to chal.* (20 to 1 op 16 to 1) 11
3481[4] NO EXTRAS (Ire) [86] 3-8-6 B Rouse (4) *drvn alng to keep up hfwy, styd on appr fnl furlong, nvr nrr.* ....(25 to 1 op 20 to 1 tchd 33 to 1) 12
3955[5] BODARI [86] 4-8-7 D Harrison (9) *sn outpcd and drvn alng, kpt on last 2 fs, no imprsn*... (33 to 1 op 20 to 1) 13
4151 ASHTINA [86] 8-8-7 J Quinn (19) *trkd ldrs, feeling pace and rdn 2 fs out, no extr*.........(20 to 1 tchd 25 to 1) 14
4238[3] MEDAILLE D'OR [94] (bl) 5-9-1 B Raymond (10) *sluggish strt, styd on last 2 fs, nvr dngrs.* ....(20 to 1 op 16 to 1 tchd 25 to 1) 15
4277[2] DARK EYED LADY (Ire) [86] 3-8-6 T Quinn (15) *chsd ldrs, struggling hfwy, sn outpcd*......(20 to 1 tchd 25 to 1) 16
4238[4] SIR HARRY HARDMAN [93] (bl) 5-9-0 M Hills (20) *speed for o'r 3 fs*............................(16 to 1 op 14 to 1) 17
4151[7] SPANIARDS CLOSE [100] 5-9-7 W R Swinburn (2) *sn struggling to keep up, nvr a factor*......(25 to 1 op 20 to 1) 18
1945[6] HOPE HALL (Ire) [86] 5-8-7 W Ryan (5) *outpcd and drvn alng, nvr a factor*............................(66 to 1) 19
4373[6] TRUE PRECISION [86] 3-8-6 L Piggott (7) *struggling to go pace aftr 2 fs*....................(25 to 1 tchd 33 to 1) 20
4275[6] SAINT EXPRESS [91] 3-8-11 W Carson (3) *in tch to hfwy, sn btn*.............. (20 to 1 op 16 to 1 tchd 25 to 1) 21
4040 EL YASAF (Ire) [96] (bl) 5-9-0 (3*) Stephen Davies (14) *bolted gng to post, tld off most of way.* (25 to 1 tchd 33 to 1) 22

Dist: 1½l, ½l, ½l, ¾l, ¾l, sht-hd, 1l, sht-hd, sht-hd, ½l. 1m 0.71s. a 2.11s (22 Ran).

SR: 73/60/58/58/59/49/52/45/47/ (K Abdulla), R Charlton

4466 Tote Cesarewitch Handicap Class B (3-y-o and up) £50,915 2¼m.....(3:00)

3473[3] AAHSAYLAD [81] (bl) 7-8-12 J Williams (21) *settled off the pace, improved into midfield hfwy, styd on wl to ld cl hme*................................(12 to 1 op 10 to 1) 1
4143[2] RITTO [77] 3-7-10[1] D Harrison (30) *patiently rdn, last entering strt, hdwy to ld wl ins fnl furlong, jst ct.* ....(12 to 1 op 10 to 1) 2
3255[2] MY DESIRE [79] 5-8-5 (5*) Darren Moffatt (23) *sn beh, weaved through frm off the pace whn hmpd o'r 2 fs out, rallied, fnshd wl*................(33 to 1 tchd 40 to 1) 3
4239[2] HASTEN TO ADD (USA) [80] 3-7-13 G Duffield (9) *settled gng wl, led on bit o'r 3 fs out, hdd appr last, rallied, hng rght und pres ins last, no extr*....(3 to 1 fav op 4 to 1) 4
4143[5] DOYCE [65] 4-7-10 G Bardwell (25) *in tch, improved into midfield o'r 3 fs out, styd on ins last.* ....(50 to 1 tchd 66 to 1) 5
4239* MY PATRIARCH [95] 3-9-0 Pat Eddery (28) *settled gng wl, improved o'r 5 fs out, hmpd 2 out, rcvred to ld appr last, hdd and no extr last 50 yards*......(12 to 1 op 10 to 1) 6
3548[9] ALLMOSA [63] 4-7-8[1] A Mackay (20) *in tch, chsd alng whn pace quickened o'r 3 fs out, styd on ins last, fnshd wl.* ....(66 to 1) 7
4102[5] GO SOUTH [62] 9-7-7 S Wood (17) *sn beh, styd on und pres last 3 fs, rng on finish*....................(66 to 1) 8
4013* PROVENCE [72] 6-8-3 W Ryan (2) *nvr far away, ev ch o'r 3 fs out, hmpd 2 out, rdn, no extr.* (14 to 1 tchd 16 to 1) 9
4102* FIVE TO SEVEN (USA) [63] 4-7-8 J Quinn (13) *set gd pace, clr entering strt, hdd o'r 3 fs out, fdd appr last.* ....(25 to 1 tchd 33 to 1) 10
4283[5] MISS PIN UP [72] 4-8-3 B Rouse (8) *sluggish strt, beh till styd on wl last 3 fs, nvr nrr*.................. (50 to 1) 11
2422[2] MARDOOD [63] 8-7-3[2] (7*) N Varley (24) *chsd ldrs, effrt and drvn alng o'r 3 fs out, not pace to chal.* ....(25 to 1 tchd 33 to 1) 12
2061 RODEO STAR (USA) [73] 7-8-4 N Carlisle (27) *wth ldrs, ev ch hfwy, fdd last 3 fs*............(33 to 1 tchd 40 to 1) 13
4013[2] JACK BUTTON (Ire) [93] 4-9-10 N Connorton (22) *co'red up on ins, not clr run over 5 fs out, swtchd centre, kpt on, nvr nrr*.........................(33 to 1 tchd 40 to 1) 14
4319* GREY POWER [72] 6-8-3 A Munro (26) *sn beh, drvn alng to improve centre o'r 3 fs out, not rch ldrs.* ....(33 to 1 tchd 40 to 1) 15
3907 POPSI'S LEGACY [62] 6-7-5[5] (7*) D Toole (6) *in tch on outsd, drvn alng o'r 4 fs out, not pace of ldrs.* (50 to 1) 16
4013[4] SUN GREBE (Ire) [77] 3-7-10 W Carson (12) *in tch, improved into midfield o'r 4 fs out, rdn and nvr able to chal*..(14 to 1) 17
4212* GREEN LANE (USA) [74] 5-8-5 T Quinn (31) *chsd ldg bunch, drvn alng o'r 4 fs out, nvr dngrs*................ (20 to 1) 18
4283[3] TILTY (USA) [74] 3-7-7 N Adams (15) *beh and pushed alng hfwy, nvr rch chalg pos.* ....(25 to 1 op 33 to 1 tchd 20 to 1) 19
2061[2] BALASANI (Fr) [91] 7-9-8 M Perrett (5) *patiently rdn, effrt o'r 5 fs out, nvr able to chal*....... (12 to 1 op 10 to 1) 20
1688[5] TOP SPIN [71] (v) 4-7-13 (3*) B Doyle (7) *chsd ldrs, effrt hfwy, feeling pace o'r 4 fs out, fdd.* ....(33 to 1 op 50 to 1 tchd 66 to 1) 21
4143 ENCORE UNE FOIS (Ire) [78] 4-8-9 J Reid (14) *wth ldrs, feeling pace and rdn o'r 4 fs out, fdd.* ....(50 to 1 tchd 66 to 1) 22
3675[5] FREE MOVER (Ire) [77] 4-8-8 B Raymond (11) *pressed ldrs to hfwy, fdd und pres o'r 4 fs out*............ (50 to 1) 23
3473 ROSINA MAE [76] 4-8-7 L Dettori (10) *co'red up on ins, effrt in midfield over 4 fs out, nvr nr to chal*... (33 to 1) 24
4212[3] BARDOLPH (USA) [68] 6-7-13 C Rutter (4) *chsd ldrs, drvn into midfield o'r 4 fs out, sn struggling*........ (25 to 1) 25
3907[8] SWORD MASTER [72] 4-8-3 M Hills (3) *in tch, struggling to keep up hfwy, fdd o'r 4 fs out*..................(66 to 1) 26
3821[2] IRISH STAMP (Ire) [67] 4-7-12 J Lowe (29) *wl plcd to strt, lost tch last 4 fs*...... (12 to 1 op 10 to 1 tchd 14 to 1) 27
4143 CHAKALAK [72] 5-8-3 G Hind (16) *trkd ldrs, feeling pace o'r 4 fs out, sn lost tch*............(50 to 1 tchd 66 to 1) 28
4714a[3] MAAMUR (USA) [67] 5-7-12[2] A McGlone (18) *chsd ldrs, struggling to hold pl o'r 4 fs out, sn btn.* ....(33 to 1 tchd 40 to 1) 29
4143[4] BOLD RESOLUTION (Ire) [74] 5-8-5 M Roberts (1) *in tch, struggling entering strt, sn lost touch*......... (25 to 1) 30
4357 ISLAND BLADE (Ire) [62] 4-7-2 (5*) D Wright (19) *in tch, improved into midfield hfwy, wknd quickly o'r 4 fs out.* ....(33 to 1 tchd 40 to 1) 31

Dist: Hd, 2½l, nk, ¾l, nk, 1½l, sht-hd, 2½l, 3l, 2½l. 3m 59.52s. a 9.52s (31 Ran).

SR: 30/13/24/12/7/24/2/-/7/ (Ms M Horan), J White

4467 Dubai Champion Stakes Class A (Group 1) (3-y-o and up) £205,707 1¼m ....(3:40)

4219* HATOOF (USA) 4-9-0 W R Swinburn (1) *settled centre gng wl, led o'r 3 fs out, quickened clr last 2 furlongs, imprsv*..........................(5 to 2 fav tchd 11 to 4) 1
4311 EZZOUD (Ire) (v) 4-9-3 B Raymond (5) *nvr far away, led briefly o'r 3 fs out, rdn appr last, not pace of wnr.* ....(8 to 1 op 7 to 1 tchd 9 to 1) 2
3933[2] DERNIER EMPEREUR (USA) 3-8-12 T Jarnet (9) *chsd ldrs, struggling to go pace o'r 3 fs out, kpt on wl fnl furlong.* ....(7 to 1 tchd 13 to 2 and 8 to 1) 3
3402[7] TENBY 3-8-12 Pat Eddery (2) *led centre grp, rdn to join o'rall ldr over 3 fs out, not quicken fnl furlong.* ....(10 to 1 op 16 to 1) 4
3886[6] ENVIRONMENT FRIEND 5-9-3 M Hills (3) *trkd ldrs centre, drw level o'r 3 fs out, rdn and one pace ins last.* ....(66 to 1 tchd 100 to 1) 5
4141[2] BOBZAO (Ire) 4-9-3 J Reid (6) *tucked away beh ldrs, pushed alng whn pace quickened o'r 2 fs out, kpt on fnl furlong*.............. (20 to 1 op 33 to 1) 6
3913* MUHTARRAM (USA) 4-9-3 W Carson (8) *al hndy, hrd drvn whn pace quickened o'r 3 fs out, sn btn.* ....(9 to 2 op 5 to 2 tchd 5 to 1) 7
3433[2] DANCING BLOOM (Ire) 3-8-9 L Dettori (10) *trkd ldr, ev ch o'r 3 fs out, fdd frm 2 out*....... (16 to 1 tchd 20 to 1) 8
4295* KNIFEBOX (USA) 5-9-3 M Roberts (7) *led till o'r 3 fs out, fdd und pres frm 2 out.* (13 to 2 op 6 to 1 tchd 7 to 1) 9
4140[3] RISK MASTER 4-9-3 W Woods (11) *tucked away on ins, effrt o'r 3 fs out, rdn and outpcd frm 2 out.* ....(200 to 1 op 100 to 1) 10
4073[3] REVELATION (Ire) 3-8-12 T Quinn (4) *trkd ldrs centre, ev ch o'r 3 fs out, wknd 2 out*.......... (33 to 1 tchd 40 to 1) 11
4308[2] ALFLORA (Ire) 4-9-3 L Piggott (12) *co'red up on ins, effrt and rdn over 3 fs out, eased whn btn 2 out.* ....(16 to 1 tchd 20 to 1) 12

Dist: 3l, sht-hd, 2l, nk, nk, ¾l, ½l, 4l, 1½l, 2l. 2m 6.80s. a 4.10s (12 Ran).

SR: 74/71/65/61/65/64/62/53/53/ (Maktoum Al Maktoum), Mrs C Head

4468 Rothmans Royals North South Challenge Series Final Handicap Class B (3-y-o and up) £28,660 1m...... (4:15)

4065[3] SAIFAN [78] (bl) 4-9-5 (3*) C Hodgson (19) *patiently rdn, quickened to ld ins fnl furlong, hrd drvn, hld on wl.* ....(12 to 1 tchd 14 to 1) 1
4065[7] SAND TABLE [75] 4-9-5 J Reid (14) *tucked away, brst through to chal fnl furlong, edgd rght und pres, kpt on*................... (11 to 2 op 6 to 1 tchd 13 to 2) 2
4065[5] TISSISAT (USA) [84] (v) 4-10-0 L Dettori (12) *wtd wth, hdwy to chal entering fnl furlong, rdn and found little last 50 yards*................(14 to 1 op 12 to 1 tchd 16 to 1) 3
3996* HI NOD [84] 3-9-11 R Cochrane (11) *wl plcd, led well o'r 2 fs out till ins last, wknd cl hme.* ....(4 to 1 fav op 6 to 1 tchd 7 to 1) 4
4333* PROUD BRIGADIER (Ire) [66] 5-8-10 T Quinn (18) *tucked away far side, effrt whn squeezed for room entering fnl furlong, not quicken.* ....(16 to 1 op 14 to 1 tchd 20 to 1) 5
4065[4] MARINE DIVER [66] 7-8-10 S Whitworth (7) *chsd ldrs centre, effrt o'r 2 fs out, styd on same pace.* ....(16 to 1 op 14 to 1 tchd 20 to 1) 6
4343[8] SELF EXPRESSION [63] 5-8-2 (5*) S Drowne (10) *patiently rdn, improve o'r 2 fs out, no imprsn entering last.* ....(14 to 1 op 12 to 1) 7

4300 MENTALASANYTHIN [68] 4-8-12 A Mackay (6) *in tch, feeling pace and rdn alng hfwy, kpt on, no imprsn.* ....(33 to 1) 8

3901[5] SWEET MIGNONETTE [74] 5-9-4 A Munro (9) *settled midfield, effrt and rdn o'r 2 fs out, nvr able to chal.* ....(12 to 1 tchd 14 to 1) 9

4297 NOBBY BARNES [56] 4-8-0 B Crossley (5) *co'red up in midfield, drvn alng whn hmpd twice over 2 fs out, not rcvr*........(14 to 1 op 20 to 1) 10

4065[9] WYNONA (Ire) [66] 3-8-7 B Raymond (3) *beh and drvn alng hfwy, styd on last 2 fs, nvr dngrs.* (20 to 1 op 16 to 1) 11

4300 BALLERINA BAY [67] (v) 5-8-11 Pat Eddery (16) *beh and chsd alng hfwy, styd on, nvr nrr.* ....(25 to 1 tchd 33 to 1) 12

4224[7] LEGEND DULAC (Ire) [52] 4-7-10 J Quinn (8) *led or dsptd ld, led hfwy, hdd o'r 2 fs out, fdd...* (33 to 1 tchd 40 to 1) 13

4065 INDIAN SLAVE (Ire) [69] 5-8-13 D Harrison (4) *wth ldrs, ev ch hfwy, fdd o'r 2 fs out.* ....(14 to 1 op 12 to 1 tchd 16 to 1) 14

3901[9] PRIDE OF PENDLE [70] 4-9-0 W Ryan (13) *settled off the pace, drvn alng hfwy, nvr able to chal.* ....(20 to 1 tchd 25 to 1) 15

4065[2] WALKING THE PLANK [73] (v) 4-9-3 W R Swinburn (1) *trkd ldrs, effrt and rdn o'r 3 fs out, fdd 2 out.* ....(12 to 1 tchd 14 to 1) 16

4394[3] NORTHERN CHIEF [64] 3-8-5 M Birch (17) *wth ldrs, gng wl hfwy, wknd o'r 2 fs out, eased whn btn.* ....(14 to 1 op 12 to 1 tchd 16 to 1) 17

4065 CREDIT SQUEEZE [70] 3-8-11 L Piggott (21) *settled midfield, feeling pace 3 fs out, nvr dngrs.* ....(25 to 1 op 20 to 1) 18

4065 BLOCKADE (USA) [68] 4-8-12 M Hills (20) *led or dsptd ld to hfwy, fdd o'r 2 fs out.* ....(20 to 1 op 16 to 1 tchd 25 to 1) 19

4343 HABETA (USA) [54] (bl) 7-7-12 J Lowe (15) *beh and drvn alng thrght*........(33 to 1 op 25 to 1) 20

4065 LORD OBERON (Ire) [65] (v) 5-8-9 M Roberts (2) *rcd wide, rdn alng hfwy, nvr dngrs.* ....(20 to 1 op 16 to 1 tchd 25 to 1) 21

Dist: Hd, ½l, ¾l, 2l, 1l, ½l, sht-hd, nk, 2l, 1½l. 1m 41.06s. a 3.86s (21 Ran).

SR: 67/63/70/65/44/41/36/40/45/ (Mrs Rosalie Hawes), D Morris

4469 Houghton Conditions Stakes Class B (2-y-o) £9,084 7f.................(4:45)

3990* INDHAR 8-12 J Quinn (6) *settled gng wl, led o'r 2 fs out, quickened, drvn out fnl furlong.* (10 to 1 tchd 14 to 1) 1

4138* SUPLIZI (Ire) 9-0 (2ex) R Cochrane (1) *nvr far away, drvn alng whn pace quickened last 2 fs, kpt on wl.* ....(11 to 4 jt-fav op 9 to 4) 2

MASNAD (USA) 8-12 R Price (8) *nvr far away, ev ch and drvn alng o'r 2 fs out, ran on, prmsg.* ....(20 to 1 op 14 to 1 tchd 25 to 1) 3

4276 DESERT CONQUEROR (USA) 8-12 W R Swinburn (9) *nvr far away, feeling pace o'r 2 fs out, rallied, improve.* ....(13 to 2 op 5 to 1 tchd 7 to 1) 4

4397* WAFAYT (Ire) 8-12 L Dettori (10) *clr till hdd and rdn o'r 2 fs out, no extr*......(11 to 4 jt-fav op 5 to 2 tchd 3 to 1) 5

3979* LUHUK (USA) 8-12 W Carson (2) *sluggish strt, effrt and drvn alng o'r 2 fs out, one pace.* ....(100 to 30 op 5 to 2 tchd 7 to 2) 6

BROADWAY FLYER (USA) 8-12 M Hills (7) *sluggish strt, outpcd and drvn alng most of way, nvr dngrs.* ....(50 to 1 op 33 to 1 tchd 66 to 1) 7

DUMAANI (USA) 8-12 Pat Eddery (3) *pressed ldrs, hrd drvn whn pace quickened o'r 2 fs out, sn btn.* ....(12 to 1 op 10 to 1 tchd 14 to 1) 8

4276 CZARNA (Ire) 8-12 M Roberts (4) *in tch, chsd alng on ins hfwy, fdd o'r one furlong out.* ....(33 to 1 op 20 to 1 tchd 50 to 1) 9

Dist: 1l, ½l, 2l, 2½l, ½l, ¾l, hd, 1½l. 1m 28.48s. a 4.98s (9 Ran).

SR: 39/38/34/28/20/18/16/15/10/ (Miss P Rovera), J E Banks

4470 Westfield House Handicap Class D (0-85 3-y-o and up) £6,258 1m...(5:20)

4297[9] PRENONAMOSS [72] 5-9-4 J Williams (10) *co'red up in midfield, quickened to ld ins fnl furlong, drvn out.* ....(20 to 1 op 16 to 1 tchd 25 to 1) 1

4274[3] BUROOJ [82] 3-9-11 W Carson (13) *settled midfield, drvn to chal ins fnl furlong, kpt on wl.* (10 to 1 op 12 to 1) 2

4019[2] ARAK (USA) [72] 5-9-4 G Duffield (26) *led far side grp till ins fnl furlong, kpt on same pace.* (10 to 1 op 14 to 1) 3

4247[7] RETENDER (USA) [58] 4-8-4 G Hind (5) *clr of stands side grp thrght, rdn 2 fs out, styd on wl.* ....(11 to 1 op 10 to 1 tchd 12 to 1) 4

1530[6] ARANY [80] 6-9-5 (7*) S Mulvey (14) *wl plcd far side, drvn alng last 2 fs, kpt on same pace.* (25 to 1 tchd 33 to 1) 5

4297[6] HOPEFUL BID (Ire) [65] (bl) 4-8-11 J Reid (7) *tucked away in midfield, ran on last 2 fs, nrst finish.* ....(16 to 1 tchd 20 to 1) 6

4133[2] AITCH N'BEE [75] 10-9-7 L Dettori (12) *settled wth centre grp, effrt 2 fs out, kpt on same pace.* ....(8 to 1 fav op 12 to 1 tchd 7 to 1) 7

4348* NITOUCHE [66] 3-8-9 D Harrison (22) *wl plcd far side, rdn and not quicken appr fnl furlong.* (20 to 1 op 16 to 1) 8

4045[2] PARFAIT AMOUR [63] 4-8-9 A Mackay (29) *wth ldr far side, drvn alng 2 fs out, no extr*......(20 to 1 tchd 16 to 1) 9

4297* BRAVEBOY [64] 5-8-7 (3*) B Doyle (28) *chsd ldrs centre, drvn alng last 2 fs, no extr.* ....(9 to 1 op 14 to 1 tchd 8 to 1) 10

3388[5] ROSE ELEGANCE [67] 4-8-13 V Slattery (1) *chsd ldg pair stands side, rdn and no imprsn last 2 fs*......(33 to 1) 11

3512 NASHVILLE BLUES (Ire) [80] 4-9-12 M Hills (18) *chsd alng to go pace far side, styd on last 2 fs, nvr nrr.* ....(20 to 1 op 16 to 1) 12

4364[3] SWIFT SILVER [58] 6-8-4 A McGlone (3) *sluggish strt, bustled alng hfwy, late hdwy, nvr nrr.* ....(20 to 1 tchd 25 to 1) 13

4107[7] RIVAL BID (USA) [69] 5-9-1 M Tebbutt (11) *chsd alng in midfield, no imprsn last 2 fs.* ....(20 to 1 op 16 to 1 tchd 25 to 1) 14

4258[3] SEA BARON [63] 3-8-6 J Quinn (9) *pushed alng in centre grp, no imprsn last 2 fs*..........(33 to 1 op 25 to 1) 15

4209[5] LANKRIDGE [73] 3-9-2 W R Swinburn (4) *chsd ldr stands side, drvn alng o'r 2 fs out, fdd.* (20 to 1 tchd 25 to 1) 16

4297 ROCALITY [64] 4-8-10 W Woods (30) *pressed ldrs far side, ev ch o'r 2 fs out, fdd.* (20 to 1 op 16 to 1 tchd 25 to 1) 17

4116[7] DUCKEY FUZZ [61] 5-8-7 W Ryan (23) *trkd ldrs far side, feeling pace o'r 2 fs out, fdd*.....(16 to 1 tchd 20 to 1) 18

3308[9] MISTY GODDESS (Ire) [57] 5-8-0[2] (5*) K Rutter (24) *chsd ldrs far side till fdd o'r 2 fs out*......(25 to 1 tchd 33 to 1) 19

4343 BRILLIANT [60] 5-8-6 M Wigham (21) *sluggish strt, not reco'r*..........(33 to 1 op 25 to 1) 20

4164 LET'S GET LOST [67] 4-8-13 L Piggott (19) *settled midfield, effrt and rdn hfwy, nvr nr to chal.* ....(20 to 1 op 16 to 1 tchd 25 to 1) 21

3850[8] DUTOSKY [70] 3-8-13 R Cochrane (20) *speed to ld centre grp, rdn and wknd last 2 fs.* ....(25 to 1 op 20 to 1 tchd 33 to 1) 22

4116[6] EXCLUSION [68] 4-9-0 W Newnes (16) *wl plcd centre, rdn o'r 2 fs out, sn btn*...(20 to 1 op 16 to 1 tchd 25 to 1) 23

4116 DASWAKI (Can) [74] 5-9-6 B Rouse (8) *speed centre for o'r 5 fs, fdd*..........(14 to 1 op 16 to 1 tchd 20 to 1) 24

3991[5] KING PARIS (Ire) [73] 3-8-13 (3*) M Fenton (15) *chsd ldrs centre till wknd o'r 2 fs out.* ....(25 to 1 op 20 to 1 tchd 33 to 1) 25

4116 MULLITOVER [80] 3-9-9 A Munro (6) *in tch, struggling in centre grp o'r 2 fs out, sn btn*.....(33 to 1 op 20 to 1) 26

2198[8] FABRIANA [82] 3-9-11 T Quinn (25) *chsd alng far side, nvr a threat*..........(33 to 1 op 25 to 1) 27

2025[6] ELANMATINA (Ire) [70] 4-9-2 B Raymond (2) *chsd ldg trio stands side, nvr a factor*..........(33 to 1) 28

4297 YAJEED (USA) [77] 3-9-6 M Roberts (17) *trkd ldrs centre till wknd quickly o'r 2 fs out.* ....(20 to 1 op 16 to 1 tchd 25 to 1) 29

Dist: Nk, 1½l, nk, 1l, hd, hd, 1½l, ½l, sht-hd, 1l. 1m 41.65s. a 4.45s (29 Ran).

SR: 55/61/49/34/53/37/46/29/27/ (Mrs W A Oram), D W P Arbuthnot

BELMONT PARK (USA) (soft)
Sunday October 17th

4471 Long Island Handicap (Grade 2) (3-y-o and up) £45,536 1½m...............

3187 TRAMPOLI (USA) 4-8-7 M Smith,..........(11 to 10 fav) 1

3931[6] BRIGHT GENERATION (Ire) 3-8-2 H McCauley,..(13 to 10) 2

NORTHERN EMERALD (USA) 3-7-10 J Bravo,...(53 to 10) 3

PALACE REVOLT (USA) 5-7-13 J Chavez,........(15 to 1) 4

MY TOMBOLA (USA) 4-7-12 J Cruguet,..........(12 to 1) 5

Dist: Nk, 4 ¾l, 11l, 12l. 2m 31.57s. (5 Ran).

(P de Moussac), A Fabre

KEENELAND (USA) (heavy)
Sunday October 17th

4472 Spinster Stakes (Grade 1) (3-y-o and up) £138,823 1m 1f.................

4079[5] PASEANA (Arg) 6-8-11 C McCarron,..........(6 to 5 fav) 1

GRAY CASHMERE (USA) 4-8-11 P Day,.........(47 to 10) 2

JACODY (USA) 3-8-7 T Turner,.................(51 to 10) 3

2802[5] DEPUTATION (USA) 4-8-11 F Alvarado,..........(19 to 1) 4

3767[4] FUTURE PRETENSE (USA) 3-8-7 C Perret,......(86 to 10) 5

2441[6] ADDED ASSET (USA) 3-8-7 S Sellers,............(19 to 1) 6

560[5] ERICA'S DREAM (USA) 5-8-11 W Martinez,.......(30 to 1) 7

WILDERNESS SONG (Can) 5-8-11 D Clark,........(9 to 1) 8

FOWDA (USA) 5-8-11 P Migliore,...............(13 to 1) 9

Dist: 1l, 4l, 1l, 1½l, 8l, 1½l, 6l, 12l. 1m 48.40s. (9 Ran).

(S H Craig), R McAnally

LONGCHAMP (FR) (heavy)
Sunday October 17th
Going Correction: PLUS 0.80 sec. per fur.

4473 Prix de Saint-Cyr (Listed) (3-y-o) £14,337 1m 1f.................(2:50)

132[2] WAKRIA (Ire) 8-11 D Boeuf,.......................... 1

4307[2] SEATTLE VICTORY (USA) 8-11 G Guignard, ... 2
4307[4] SAHARA SUN (USA) 8-11 G Mosse, ... 3
4169[4] WEST COAST 8-11 T Jarnet, ... 4
Dist: Sht-nk, 1½l, 3l, 4l, 2l, 3l. 1m 58.40s. a 9.40s (7 Ran).
SR: 64/63/58/49/ (Sultan Al Kabeer), R Collet

4474 Prix du Conseil de Paris (Group 2) (3-y-o and up) £35,842 1½m. ...... (3:55)

4311 DANCIENNE (Fr) 3-8-6 D Boeuf (5) *trkd ldr, 4th strt, rdn 2 fs out, led one out, ran on wl*... (14 to 10 fav) 1
3933[4] TURNERS HILL 3-8-9 T Jarnet (6) *hld up in tch, hdwy 4 fs out, 3rd strt, led 2 out till one out, kpt on*.... (28 to 10) 2
4311[9] VERT AMANDE (Fr) 5-9-6 O Peslier (1) *hld up in tch, last strt, some prog fnl one and a half fs, nvr dngrs.* ... (52 to 10) 3
4201[4] SNURGE 6-9-4 T Quinn (7) *mid-div, hdwy hfwy, second strt, ev ch 2 fs out, one pace*... (5 to 2) 4
4311 GARDEN OF HEAVEN (USA) 4-9-0 M Roberts (4) *led till 2 fs out, wknd ins fnl furlong*... (86 to 10) 5
4292[4] ENCOREMOI (USA) 3-8-6 E Saint-Martin (3) *mid-div, 5th strt, rdn and wknd 2 fs out*... (138 to 10) 6
Dist: 3l, 1l, 4l, 2½l, 2½l. 2m 47.70s. a 18.60s (6 Ran).
SR: 2/-/8/ (H Yokoyama), E Lellouche

SAN SIRO (ITY) (heavy)
Sunday October 17th

4475 Premio Duca d'Aosta (Listed) (3-y-o and up) £20,173 1m 7f. .... (2:50)

2650[8] STEVE LUCKY (Ire) 3-8-7 M Esposito, ... 1
4727a[4] STRONG LIFE (Ire) 5-9-0 M Tellini, ... 2
4292[3] LILLE HAMMER 3-8-4 R Cochrane, *mid-div, 4th strt, nvr able to chal*... 3
SICUTERAT 6-9-0 L Sorrentino, ... 4
957[3] JUNGLE DANCER (Ire) 5-9-0 G Forte, ... 5
4294[5] CUTTING REEF (Ire) 4-9-0 A Badel, ... 6
4203* FORMATO UNI (Ire) 3-8-7 L Piggott, ... pu
Dist: 6l, ¾l, 2l, 1½l, dist. 3m 34.50s. (7 Ran).
(Flying Fox Farm), A Mattei

4476 Premio Omenoni (Group 3) (3-y-o and up) £33,733 5f. .... (3:45)

4010[9] ARRANVANNA 5-8-4 Jacqueline Freda, *made all, sn clr, easily*... 1
3847[3] RAIN BROTHER (USA) 3-8-7 D Holland, *rcd in second, rdn o'r 2 fs out, jst hld on to second pl cl hme*... 2
MARIBEN (Ity) 3-8-7 A Di Nardo, *mid-div, ran on wl fnl furlong, jst fld to take second*... 3
4312[9] CRACK REGIMENT (USA) 5-8-7 L Piggott, *mid-div till some prog fnl 2 fs*... 4
3936 SIZZLING SAGA (Ire) 5-8-7 S Soto, *nvr nrr*... 5
3874* IMPREVEDIBILE (Ire) 3-8-7 A Parravani, *al abt same pl*.... 6
JEWELLERY QUARTER (Ire) 4-8-7 R Cochrane, *nvr able to chal*... 7
1365[8] ETEREA KING (Ire) 3-8-4 G Di Chio, *al beh*... 8
1373 RUSHANES 6-8-7 A Scobie, *al rear*... 9
3874[7] VERDE ALITALIA (Ire) 4-8-7 L Dettori, *al beh, tld off*... 0
NORD'S LUCY (Ire) 3-8-4 M Esposito, *prmnt till fdd o'r 3 fs out*... 0
Dist: 6½l, hd, 1l, ½l, ¾l, 1l, hd, 7l, ¾l, dist. 1m 2.00s. (11 Ran).
(Antonio Balzarini), A Renzoni

4477 Gran Premio del Jockey Club e Coppa d'Oro (Group 1) (3-y-o and up) £208,204 1½m. .... (4:15)

4311[7] MISIL (USA) 5-9-3 L Dettori, *4th strt, chlgd 2 fs out, led o'r one and a half out, sn clr, ran on wl*... 1
3649[2] PETIT LOUP (USA) 4-9-3 W R Swinburn, *3rd strt, led 3 and a half fs out till one and a half out, one pace fnl furlong*... 2
4196[5] WOOTTON RIVERS (USA) 3-8-11 D Holland, *prmnt, second strt, rdn and wknd 2 fs out*... 3
4311[5] ONLY ROYALE (Ire) 4-9-0 R Cochrane, *mid-div, 5th strt, one pace 2 fs out*... 4
3935[4] PATRIK OF IRELAND (Ire) (bl) 5-9-3 S Dettori, *last till some late prog, nrst finish*... 5
3718[5] SILVERNESIAN (USA) (bl) 4-9-3 L Piggott, *led till strt, wknd quickly*... 6
4203[2] ALMANOR 4-9-3 V Mezzatesta, *nvr dngrs*... 7
3935[2] GREEN SENOR (USA) 5-9-3 B Jovine, *cl up till wknd 3 fs out*... 8
3935[3] BIG TOBIN (Ity) 4-9-3 O Fancera, *al rear*... 9
Dist: 2½l, 7l, 2½l, 2l, 8l, dist, 3l, hd. 2m 46.30s. (9 Ran).
(Scuderia Laghi), V Caruso

WOODBINE (CAN) (soft)
Sunday October 17th

4478 Rothmans Ltd International (Grade 1) (3-y-o and up) £322,850 1½m. ....

3649[3] HUSBAND (USA) 3-8-7 C Asmussen, ... (98 to 10) 1
596[8] COZZENE'S PRINCE (Can) 6-9-0 D Seymour, ... (12 to 1) 2
3337[5] REGENCY 3-8-7 Pat Eddery, ... (66 to 10) 3
3930[2] MODHISH (Ire) 4-9-0 G Stevens, ... (9 to 5 fav) 4
3654[2] EVANESCENT (USA) 6-9-0 A Gryder, ... (46 to 10) 5
4071[3] DR KIERNAN (USA) 4-9-0 C Antley, ... (97 to 10) 6
4071[4] DEAR DOCTOR (Fr) 6-9-0 J Santos, ... (8 to 1) 7
3653* AWAD (USA) 3-8-7 J Velasquez, ... (12 to 1) 8
3653[2] EXPLOSIVE RED (Can) 3-8-7 E Fires, ... (20 to 1) 9
3665* CANASKA STAR 3-8-7 M Walls, ... (54 to 1) 0
2442[4] FLASHY REGENT (Can) 3-8-7 J Lauzon, ... (45 to 1) 0
Dist: 5l, ½l, 3l, 2½l, ¾l, hd, 5½l, 19l, 12l. 2m 36.40s. (11 Ran).
(Mlle P Augustus), J Fellows

FOLKESTONE (soft)
Monday October 18th
Going Correction: PLUS 0.85 sec. per fur.

4479 Hardres Handicap Class E (0-70 3-y-o) £3,390 1m 1f 149yds. .... (1:50)

4341[8] ARMENIAN COFFEE (Ire) [66] (bl) 9-3 L Piggott (4) *made all, drvn appr fnl furlong, styd on gmely.* ... (13 to 2 op 5 to 1 tchd 7 to 1) 1
3757 PRESTON GUILD (Ire) [61] 8-12 J Reid (11) *hdwy o'r 3 fs out, styd on wl und pres to take second pl nr finish.* ... (9 to 1 op 7 to 1 tchd 10 to 1) 2
3670 FRANCIA [50] 7-10 (5*) P McCabe (1) *ldg grp, ev ch wl o'r one furlong out, ran on same pace.* ... (10 to 1 tchd 12 to 1) 3
4354[3] TAUTEN (Ire) [48] 7-13 T Williams (12) *cld on ldrs 6 fs out, rdn and one pace appr fnl furlong.* ... (16 to 1 op 10 to 1 tchd 20 to 1) 4
4320[9] MUTAWALI (Ire) [50] 8-1 A McGlone (14) *trkd ldr, hrd rdn o'r one furlong out, found no extr.* (16 to 1 op 14 to 1) 5
4254[4] ANUSHA [60] 8-11 A Clark (8) *rdn alng in rear hfwy, ran on o'r 3 fs out, not quicken appr fnl furlong.* ... (4 to 1 fav op 5 to 1) 6
3353[9] HOME FROM THE HILL (Ire) [70] 9-4 (3*) M Fenton (10) *sn racing in rear, styd on one pace last 2 fs, nrst at finish.* ... (20 to 1 op 12 to 1) 7
3226 SPRING SUNRISE [49] 8-0 F Norton (13) *nvr better than mid-div*... (25 to 1 op 16 to 1 tchd 33 to 1) 8
4256 PALACE PARADE (USA) [52] 8-3 N Carlisle (15) *pressed ldrs til rdn and wknd frm 2 fs out*..... (33 to 1 op 25 to 1) 9
3961 BERING ISLAND (USA) [51] 8-2 D Harrison (7) *nvr nr to chal*... (11 to 1 op 6 to 1) 10
4274[7] DODGY DANCER [64] 9-1 S Whitworth (2) *gd hdwy 4 fs out, rdn and wknd ins last 2 furlongs*.... (5 to 1 op 7 to 2) 11
1090[4] MIGAVON [65] 9-2 G Duffield (5) *nvr on terms.* ... (20 to 1 op 14 to 1) 12
3311* GLOWING PATH [66] (v) 8-12 (5*) S Drowne (3) *rcd in mid-div til drpd rear frm hfwy.* ... (6 to 1 tchd 13 to 2 and 7 to 1) 13
4376[2] WITHOUT A FLAG (USA) [60] 8-11 D Holland (6) *gd hdwy frm rear 4 fs out, wknd 2 out*........(5 to 1 op 5 to 2) 14
Dist: ½l, nk, 2½l, sht-hd, hd, 2½l, 2½l, nk, 10l, nk. 2m 13.60s. a 16.00s (14 Ran).
SR: 28/22/10/3/4/13/18/-/-/ (Az Agr Associate Srl), J L Dunlop

4480 EBF Burwash Maiden Stakes Class D (2-y-o) £4,985 6f 189yds. .... (2:20)

SUMMER HAIL (Ire) 8-7 (7*) T G McLaughlin (4) *chsd frnt rnk, shaken up and ran on to ld ins fnl furlong, sn clr.* ... (25 to 1 op 20 to 1 tchd 33 to 1) 1
4240[3] DANGER POINT 9-0 J Reid (13) *pressed ldrs, not much room o'r 2 fs out, styd on one pace fnl furlong.* ... (15 to 8 fav op 9 to 4 tchd 3 to 1 and 5 to 2) 2
4356[3] CLARION CALL (Ire) 9-0 T Quinn (10) *led for o'r one furlong, led ag'n over 2 out, hdd and no extr ins fnl furlong*... (5 to 1 op 4 to 1) 3
4337[8] UP IN FLAMES (Ire) 9-0 R Perham (14) *ran on 3 fs out, not much room and swtchd lft o'r one out, styd on one pace*... (25 to 1 op 14 to 1) 4
4067[8] FORENSIC EVIDENCE (Ire) 9-0 F Norton (9) *styd on last 2 fs, not trble frnt rnk*.... (12 to 1 op 10 to 1 tchd 14 to 1) 5
4338[3] PHIL'S TIME 9-0 B Rouse (8) *hdwy last 2 fs, nrst at finish.* ... (11 to 2 op 7 to 1) 6
3833[8] SWALLOWS DREAM (Ire) 9-0 L Piggott (1) *cl up, led o'r 5 fs out, hdd over 3 out, eased whn btn fnl furlong.* ... (7 to 2 op 7 to 4) 7
3573[4] INZAR 9-0 M Tebbutt (11) *nvr on terms.* ... (10 to 1 op 7 to 1 tchd 12 to 1) 8
NORTH TO GLORY 8-9 W Newnes (2) *pressed ldrs til lost pl 2 fs out*... (50 to 1 op 25 to 1) 9
4356[9] REAL MADRID 9-0 M Perrett (7) *moderate effrt 3 fs out, sn rdn and btn*... (50 to 1 op 33 to 1) 10
4276 FLEUR DE TAL 8-9 G Duffield (5) *nvr plcd to chal.* ... (33 to 1 op 20 to 1) 11
4220[8] OUR STELLA 8-9 D Holland (6) *outpcd aftr one furlong, effrt on outsd hfwy, wknd appr last 2 fs.* ... (50 to 1 op 25 to 1) 12
4263[8] TELEPHONE TAP 9-0 S Raymont (3) *cl up, led o'r 3 fs out till hdd and wknd over 2 out*...... (20 to 1 op 14 to 1) 13

1279[4] RICHARD'S ERROR 9-0 D Harrison (12) *in tch to hfwy, tld off*...............................(50 to 1 op 33 to 1) 14
Dist: 3½l, 3½l, ¾l, hd, ½l, nk, 3½l, 5l, 2½l, 2½l. 1m 32.20s. a 11.30s (14 Ran).
SR: 20/9/-/-/-/-/ (Fahd Salman), P F I Cole

4481 Biddenden Claiming Stakes Class F (3-y-o) £2,243 6f 189yds.........(2:50)

4340[6] BICHETTE 8-7 B Rouse (3) *made all, rdn alng o'r one furlong out, kpt on strly*.......... (10 to 1 op 7 to 1) 1
4376[4] NUTTY BROWN 8-13 (3*) O Pears (4) *pressed ldrs, rdn and not quicken 2 out, styd on ins fnl furlong.* ....(11 to 1 op 7 to 1 tchd 12 to 1) 2
4331[4] RED LEADER (Ire) 8-6 T Quinn (2) *ldg grp, hrd rdn and not quicken o'r one out, wknd ins fnl furlong.* ....(8 to 1 op 7 to 1) 3
4354[7] FORMAL AFFAIR 8-4 (7*) J D Smith (9) *improved o'r 3 fs out, rdn and one pace ins last 2 furlongs.* ....(8 to 1 op 6 to 1 tchd 9 to 1) 4
4335[3] KEYWAY (USA) (bl) 9-4 G Duffield (15) *handily plcd, rdn alng and wknd o'r one furlong out.* ....(3 to 1 op 4 to 1 tchd 9 to 2) 5
4164[7] HERETICAL MISS (bl) 8-3[1] R Perham (11) *in tch, no imprsn on ldrs frm 2 fs out*...............(14 to 1 op 10 to 1) 6
1674[6] TAKE YOUR PARTNER (Ire) 7-13 A McGlone (7) *wl plcd, wknd appr last 2 fs.* (12 to 1 op 10 to 1 tchd 14 to 1) 7
4355[5] KNYAZ 9-0 N Carlisle (6) *nvr nrr*..... (20 to 1 op 14 to 1) 8
4317[4] DONTBETALKING (Ire) (bl) 7-12 (5*) P McCabe (16) *chsd ldrs, rdn and wknd 2 fs out*.......(20 to 1 op 14 to 1) 9
3965[4] TEE GEE JAY 8-3 D Harrison (1) *al towards rear.* ....(16 to 1 op 8 to 1 tchd 20 to 1) 10
3811[7] HOD-MOD (Ire) 8-5 (5*) D Wright (13) *settled in mid-div, wknd last 3 fs*.......(20 to 1 op 14 to 1 tchd 25 to 1) 11
4331[3] APACHE MYTH 8-9 J Reid (8) *nvr rchd frnt rnk.* ....(2 to 1 fav op 3 to 1) 12
4088[6] SAXON MAGIC (bl) 8-5 D Holland (12) *mid-div, no hdwy appr fnl 2 fs*.....................(20 to 1 op 14 to 1) 13
4088[8] BAN RI (Ire) 8-1 T Williams (14) *prmsg run whn hmpd o'r 2 fs out, sn lost pl*...............(20 to 1 op 16 to 1) 14
2120[9] WHYALLA RAIN 8-7 R Price (5) *outpcd, tld off fnl 2 fs.* ....(20 to 1 op 14 to 1 tchd 25 to 1) 15
Dist: 2l, 3½l, ½l, 2½l, 1½l, hd, 4l, 3l, 1½l, sht-hd. 1m 30.60s. a 9.70s (15 Ran).
SR: 38/41/20/23/22/2/ (Peter L Higson), G L Moore

4482 Levy Board Rating Related Maiden Stakes Class F (Div I) (2-y-o) £2,579 6f ....(3:20)

4122[8] COMEONUP 9-0 J Reid (4) *hld up, hdwy frm rear o'r 2 fs out, led one out, quickened wl clr.* ....(7 to 2 fav op 2 to 1 tchd 4 to 1) 1
4418[9] JUST GREENWICH 8-4 (5*) N Gwilliams (3) *hld up in tch, rdn alng o'r one furlong out, sn outpcd.* ....(6 to 1 op 4 to 1) 2
4009[6] ERRIS BOY 9-0 A Clark (6) *pressed ldrs, led 2 fs out, hdd und pres and outpcd one out.* .... (8 to 1 op 6 to 1 tchd 10 to 1) 3
4167 SIMPLY A SEQUEL (Ire) 9-0 G Duffield (7) *wl in tch, effrt und pres 2 fs out, one pace fnl furlong.* .... (10 to 1 op 4 to 1) 4
4124[7] ROYAL INTERPRETER (v) 9-0 R Perham (2) *led for 4 fs, sn wknd*.............................(5 to 1 op 8 to 1) 5
4127[8] SPEEDY SNAPS IMAGE 9-0 M Perrett (10) *nvr rchd frnt rnk*..........................(14 to 1 op 10 to 1) 6
3941 LETS GO BO (Ire) (bl) 9-0 B Rouse (11) *chsd ldrs on outsd for o'r 3 fs*...........................(9 to 2 op 9 to 4) 7
3642 SCREWBALL ANACONDA 9-0 W Newnes (9) *squeezed for room leaving stalls, al towards rear.* ....(20 to 1 op 12 to 1 tchd 33 to 1) 8
4418 PINATUBO 8-7 (7*) Karron Fitchett (8) *no imprsn on frnt rnk frm hfwy*.............(33 to 1 op 14 to 1) 9
3816 RED DANCER 8-6 (3*) M Fenton (1) *outpcd.* ....(7 to 1 op 6 to 1 tchd 8 to 1) 10
4236 NORTHGATE SYMPHONY (bl) 9-0 T Quinn (5) *cl up til lost pl quickly o'r 2 fs out*.............(20 to 1 op 12 to 1) 11
Dist: 6l, ¾l, sht-hd, 7l, 6l, 1l, 1½l, hd, 2½l, 1½l. 1m 19.10s. a 8.10s (11 Ran).
SR: 40/11/13/12/-/-/ (David Roberts), R Hannon

4483 Levy Board Rating Related Maiden Stakes Class F (Div II) (2-y-o) £2,556 6f ....(3:50)

4029[8] FOLLY FINNESSE 8-9 S Whitworth (4) *hdwy hfwy, led o'r one furlong out, sn clr, ran on strly.* ....(5 to 1 op 9 to 2 tchd 6 to 1 and 7 to 1) 1
4418[6] GIGUE 8-2 (7*) R Painter (6) *cl up, slight advantage o'r 2 fs out, hdd over one out, ran on same pace*....(7 to 2 co-fav op 5 to 2 tchd 4 to 1) 2
4220[6] CAZANOVE'S PET 8-9 J Weaver (3) *ldg grp, rdn and not quicken appr fnl furlong.* ....(7 to 1 op 6 to 1 tchd 8 to 1) 3
4330[4] HEALTHY RISK 9-0 T Quinn (2) *led aftr one furlong, hdd o'r 2 out, outpcd over one out.* ....(7 to 2 co-fav tchd 4 to 1) 4
4339[7] WIDE OUTSIDE (Ire) 8-9 B Rouse (8) *hld up in mid-div, short lived effrt o'r 2 fs out, no imprsn on ldrs.* .... (16 to 1 op 14 to 1) 5
3546[8] FOREST LOCH (v) 8-9 D Harrison (9) *cl up for o'r 3 fs.* ....(7 to 2 co-fav op 9 to 4 tchd 4 to 1) 6
886 WILKS DREAM (Ire) 8-4 (5*) P McCabe (1) *led for one furlong, lost pl hfwy*................ (33 to 1 op 25 to 1) 7
4227 GWERNYMYNYDD 8-9 D Holland (7) *outpcd.* .... (11 to 1 op 5 to 1 tchd 12 to 1) 8
4358 MISS KATIE LOUISE 8-4 (5*) D Wright (10) *speed on outsd to hfwy, sn wknd*......(16 to 1 op 12 to 1 tchd 20 to 1) 9
4263 INFRA BLUE (Ire) 8-9 Dale Gibson (5) *al outpcd.* .... (33 to 1 op 14 to 1) 10
Dist: 5l, 12l, 2½l, 2½l, 1½l, 5l, 10l, 2½l, 10l. 1m 20.00s. a 9.00s (10 Ran).
SR: 17/-/-/-/-/-/ (Richard Withers), B R Millman

4484 Cliff Rating Related Maiden Stakes Class F (2-y-o) £2,691 5f........ (4:20)

4061[8] LORD SKY (bl) 9-0 T Quinn (8) *wl plcd stands side, led one furlong out, pushed out*...........(10 to 1 op 8 to 1) 1
4265[5] SULITELMA (USA) 8-9 J Reid (12) *rcd prmntly far side, swtchd stands side wl o'r one furlong out, not quicken ins fnl furlong*.................. (4 to 1 op 3 to 1) 2
4265[9] CALLABONNA 8-9 G Duffield (4) *led stands side til hdd one furlong out, ran on und pres.* ....(3 to 1 fav op 5 to 2) 3
4339[6] KING BRUCE 9-0 D Holland (6) *wl plcd stands side, rdn and outpcd appr fnl furlong*.......(10 to 1 op 8 to 1) 4
4326[6] RADIANT DANCER (bl) 8-9 A Clark (14) *in tch far side, one pace last 2 fs*.....................(33 to 1 op 20 to 1) 5
3629[8] WARTHILL WHISPERS 8-9 T Williams (2) *chsd stands side ldrs, no hdwy o'r one furlong out.* (50 to 1 op 20 to 1) 6
4127[7] BANDITA 8-9 Dale Gibson (7) *rcd stands side, outpcd frm 2 fs out*..........................(33 to 1 op 14 to 1) 7
4351 MITSIS 8-11 (3*) B Doyle (5) *rcd stands side, one pace frm 2 fs out*..............(12 to 1 op 8 to 1 tchd 14 to 1) 8
4265[7] MOORLAND DANCER (Ire) (bl) 8-9 D Harrison (3) *handily plcd stands side til wknd o'r one furlong out.* ....(14 to 1 op 10 to 1) 9
4416 MISTER O'GRADY (Ire) 9-0 R Perham (16) *rcd in mid-div far side, no hdwy last 2 fs*.........(50 to 1 op 33 to 1) 10
4269[5] KISSAIR (Ire) 9-0 B Rouse (10) *outpcd centre of course.* ....(16 to 1 op 10 to 1) 11
4265[6] INSIDER TRADER 9-0 J Weaver (13) *led far side grp for o'r 3 fs, wknd*........... (16 to 1 op 8 to 1 tchd 20 to 1) 12
4114[3] CRAFTY CRICKETER (bl) 9-0 W Newnes (9) *rcd centre of course, nvr able to chal frm hfwy.* ....(20 to 1 op 10 to 1 tchd 25 to 1) 13
4356 GRANBY BELL (bl) 8-9 (5*) D Wright (15) *al outpcd far side.* ....(50 to 1 op 20 to 1) 14
4330[3] POSSIBILITY 8-9 L Piggott (1) *al beh stands side, tld off last 2 fs*............... (5 to 1 op 7 to 2 tchd 11 to 2) 15
Dist: 1½l, ¾l, 6l, 1l, nk, hd, hd, 1½l, nk, sht-hd. 1m 6.10s. a 7.50s (15 Ran).
SR: 35/24/21/2/-/-/ (Stephen Crown), P F I Cole

4485 Herstmonceux Limited Stakes Class E (3-y-o and up) £2,950 6f.........(4:50)

4394* OUR RITA 4-8-9 D Holland (7) *handily plcd gng wl, led entering fnl furlong, sn clr, hrd hld.* (7 to 4 op 5 to 4) 1
4333[2] PENNY BANGER (Ire) (bl) 3-8-7 J Weaver (8) *led for one furlong, led ag'n o'r 2 out, hdd and outpcd ins fnl furlong*..............(11 to 2 op 6 to 1 tchd 10 to 1) 2
4096[8] MY RUBY RING 6-8-9 T Williams (2) *hmpd leaving stalls, led aftr one furlong, hdd o'r 2 out, one pace over one out*........................... (12 to 1 op 8 to 1) 3
4340* EFRA 4-9-0 S Raymont (4) *badly hmpd leaving stalls, improved appr hfwy, no extr ins last 2 fs.* ....(13 to 8 fav op 9 to 4 tchd 5 to 2) 4
4096[4] CHILLY BREEZE 3-8-7 G Duffield (5) *badly hmpd leaving stalls, sn chasing frnt rnk, one pace appr fnl furlong.* ....(7 to 1 op 5 to 1 tchd 9 to 1 and 10 to 1) 5
4363[5] PEERAGE PRINCE (bl) 4-9-0 J Reid (1) *in tch, shaken up and found nothing ins last 2 fs.* .... (12 to 1 op 8 to 1 tchd 14 to 1) 6
1876[4] PRINCE ROONEY (Ire) 5-8-9 (5*) S Drowne (3) *badly hmpd leaving stalls, not reco'r.* .... (25 to 1 op 20 to 1 tchd 33 to 1) 7
3343 ROYAL DEED (USA) 3-8-7 R Perham (6) *swrvd badly lft leaving stalls, not keen to race, al beh.* .... (33 to 1 op 25 to 1) 8
Dist: 4l, 4l, ½l, ¾l, 5l, 5l, 3½l. 1m 18.60s. a 7.60s (8 Ran).
SR: 45/27/13/16/6/ (A C Edwards), Dr J D Scargill

4486 Leeds Amateur Riders' Handicap Stakes Class G (0-75 3-y-o and up) £2,070 1½m.................. (5:20)

2721[3] PONDERING [74] (v) 3-11-5 Mr N Moore (10) *mid-div, ran on 4 fs out, led o'r one out, sn clr, easily.* ....(8 to 1 op 4 to 1) 1
4268[3] MYSTERIOUS MAID (USA) [45] 6-9-11 Mrs L Pearce (17) *ran on frm rear last 2 fs, nrst at finish.*..........(4 to 1 jt-fav op 5 to 1 tchd 11 to 2) 2
4355[7] YOUNG FREEMAN (USA) [69] 4-11-7 Miss A Harwood (6) *led, wl clr hfwy, hdd and wknd o'r one furlong out.* ....(20 to 1) 3
4333[7] PERSIAN BUD (Ire) [43] 5-9-9 Mrs S Bosley (14) *prog 3 fs out, one pace ins last 2 furlongs*... (20 to 1 op 14 to 1) 4

4028* CRACKLING [42] 4-9-8 Miss K Marks (9) *styd on frm rear last 2 fs*..........(4 to 1 jt-fav op 5 to 1 tchd 6 to 1) 5
3466 BIGWHEEL BILL (Ire) [55] 4-10-7 Mr P Pritchard-Gordon (8) *chsd ldr til o'r 3 fs out, wknd wl over one out.* .... (7 to 1 op 10 to 1) 6
3548 THEMEDA [40] 4-9-6 Mrs C Dunwoody (19) *wl plcd, no extr last 2 fs*.............................. (25 to 1 op 16 to 1) 7
4028[3] MATCHING GREEN [58] 4-10-10 Miss K Greaney (13) *stumbled and drpd rear aftr one furlong, nvr nrr.* ....(8 to 1 op 5 to 1 tchd 9 to 1) 8
3961 TICKERTY'S GIFT [73] 3-11-4 Miss K Hannon (3) *in tch for o'r 8 fs*..........(12 to 1 op 10 to 1 tchd 14 to 1) 9
4268* RAPPORTEUR (USA) [64] 7-11-2 Miss A Elsey (2) *mid-div, no imprsn on ldrs frm 3 fs out.* ....(15 to 2 op 5 to 1 tchd 8 to 1) 10
4129 BROADWAY RUCKUS (Can) [40] 4-9-6 Mr R Barrett (18) *nvr nr to chal*...........(33 to 1 op 20 to 1 tchd 50 to 1) 11
4129[5] SPECIAL DAWN (Ire) [70] 3-11-1 Miss E Johnson Houghton (11) *wl plcd til lost pos 2 fs out.* ....(13 to 2 op 7 to 1 tchd 8 to 1) 12
2755[7] AMAZON EXPRESS [65] 4-11-3 Mr P Taiano (12) *trkd frnt rnk for 8 fs, sn btn*................ (14 to 1 op 10 to 1) 13
4457 MAHAASIN [43] 5-9-9 Miss E Gatehouse (4) *handily plcd, rdn alng hfwy, wknd o'r 3 fs out.* (14 to 1 op 10 to 1) 14
DANCING YEARS (USA) [55] 4-10-7 Mr J Keller (1) *beh frm hfwy*................................ (50 to 1 op 25 to 1) 15
ARMASHOCKER [40] 5-9-6 Miss D J Jones (5) *al beh.* .... (50 to 1 op 25 to 1) 16
EVENING RAIN [40] 7-9-6 Miss S Mitchell (16) *nvr trbld ldrs*...................................(50 to 1 op 25 to 1) 17
393a BEYOND OUR REACH [62] 5-11-0 Miss A Sanders (15) *al beh*.................................. (50 to 1 op 25 to 1) 18
4268 STARLIGHT FLYER [46] (bl) 6-9-12 Mr T Waters (20) *in tch for 7 fs*..............................(50 to 1 op 25 to 1) 19
3011 BLUE TAIL [46] 5-9-12[6] Mr M Mannish (7) *in tch til drpd rear fnl 4 fs*........................ (33 to 1 op 20 to 1) 20
Dist: 8l, 1½l, nk, 2l, sht-hd, 5l, ¾l, 4l, 2½l, 4l. 2m 51.50s. a 21.00s (20 Ran).
SR: 25/-/8/-/-/-/ (M C Pipe), M C Pipe

NOTTINGHAM (soft)
Monday October 18th
Going Correction: PLUS 0.55 sec. per fur. (race 1), PLUS 0.75 (2,3,4,5,6,7,8)

4487 Kegworth Limited Stakes Class F (0-65 3-y-o and up) £3,094 5f 13yds ....(2:00)

3789[3] CALAMANCO 3-8-9 S Webster (21) *trkd ldrs stands side, shaken up to ld o'r one furlong out, kpt on wl nr finish.* ....(11 to 2 fav op 7 to 1 tchd 8 to 1 and 5 to 1) 1
4123* PATSY GRIMES (bl) 3-8-3[1] (7*) Mark Denaro (19) *chsd alng stands side, ran on strly appr fnl furlong, fnshd wl.* ....(7 to 1 op 7 to 2) 2
4331[5] SOBER LAD (Ire) (bl) 3-9-0 J Carroll (7) *wl plcd, rdn to ld far side grp one furlong out, kpt on und pres fnl furlong.* .... (14 to 1 op 12 to 1) 3
3955 MARTINA 5-8-5 (5*) B Russell (24) *pressed ldr stands side, led hfwy till o'r one furlong out, not quicken entering last*...............................(16 to 1 op 12 to 1) 4
4363[3] BATCHWORTH BOUND 4-8-10 C Rutter (18) *pressed ldrs stands side, rdn and kpt on same pace appr fnl furlong*.............................. (8 to 1 op 6 to 1) 5
4109[6] BRIGHT PARAGON (Ire) 4-9-1 J Quinn (17) *chsd ldrs stands side, drvn alng hfwy, no extr appr fnl furlong.* .... (25 to 1 op 20 to 1) 6
4394 SAVAHRA SOUND 8-8-8 (7*) G Strange (15) *wl plcd centre, drvn alng last 2 fs, styd on finish.* .... (20 to 1 op 16 to 1 tchd 25 to 1) 7
2719[5] CLANROCK 3-9-0 A Culhane (4) *promient, led far side grp 2 fs out till o'r one out, no extr*................ (25 to 1) 8
3251[6] JOE SUGDEN 9-9-1 R Cochrane (11) *trkd far side ldrs, effrt 2 fs out, styd on*............................ (50 to 1) 9
3676[7] SENSE OF PRIORITY (v) 4-9-1 M Birch (14) *wl plcd centre, rdn 2 fs out, not quicken*.......... (16 to 1 op 12 to 1) 10
4277[4] CHARITY EXPRESS (Ire) 3-8-9 M Wigham (9) *bustled alng far side, styd on und pres last 2 fs, nvr able to chal.* .... (10 to 1 op 6 to 1) 11
1136 VICTORIA HALL 3-8-9 Paul Eddery (2) *broke frm stalls bef race, speed far side for o'r 3 fs, fdd.* (12 to 1 op 10 to 1) 12
4092[7] LILLAH DARAK (USA) 5-9-1 J Williams (22) *chsd ldrs stands side, struggling 2 fs out, no imprsn.* .... (25 to 1 op 16 to 1) 13
2047[2] HARCLIFF (v) 4-9-1 J Lowe (8) *bustled alng to go pace far side, nvr rch ldrs*................................ (33 to 1) 14
4327[4] DISCO BOY 3-9-0 A Mackay (5) *chsd alng far side, not pace of ldrs last 2 fs*............................(33 to 1) 15
3603 SUPER ROCKY 4-8-8 (7*) H Bastiman (10) *drvn alng aftr 2 fs, nvr a factor*.........................(20 to 1 op 16 to 1) 16
3947 NO QUARTER GIVEN 8-9-1 K Fallon (16) *struggling stands side aftr 2 fs*......... (20 to 1 op 16 to 1 tchd 25 to 1) 17
4109[5] NORDOORA (Ire) 4-8-5 (5*) Darren Moffatt (23) *led stands side grp to hfwy, fdd o'r one furlong out.* .... (14 to 1 op 10 to 1) 18
4317 HIGH ROMANCE 3-8-6 (3*) S Maloney (3) *bustled alng far side, outpcd aftr 2 fs*..............................(50 to 1) 19
4191[7] CORN CIRCLE (Ire) 3-8-9 L Dettori (12) *drvn alng to keep up, nvr a threat*...................(16 to 1 op 10 to 1) 20
4008* COALISLAND 3-9-0 A Tucker (13) *struggling to go pace hfwy*..............................(20 to 1 tchd 25 to 1) 21
4012[3] PURBECK CENTENARY 3-9-0 W Ryan (1) *led far side grp 3 fs, wknd quickly*................................ (33 to 1) 22
Dist: ¾l, 1½l, ½l, ½l, 1½l, sht-hd, sht-hd, 1½l, hd, sht-hd. 1m 3.40s. a 5.20s (22 Ran).
SR: 46/43/42/36/34/33/32/30/25/ (Hugh Ellis), A Smith

4488 Rainworth Claiming Stakes Class F (3-y-o and up) £3,161 1m 54yds.... (2:30)

3364[6] DON'T JUMP (Ire) 3-8-10 P Robinson (6) *made all, quickened clr o'r 2 fs out, rdn and kpt on ins last.* (9 to 2 jt-fav op 3 to 1) 1
1849[7] ALWAYS RISKY 3-7-13 J Lowe (3) *patiently rdn, hdwy into midfield hfwy, wndrd 2 fs out, str run ins last, ran on*................................(20 to 1 op 16 to 1) 2
4104[4] DIACO 8-8-13 A Munro (8) *wtd wth, weaved through into midfield hfwy, chsd wnr appr fnl furlong, one pace last 50 yards*......................(10 to 1 tchd 8 to 1) 3
4343[9] SHAKE TOWN (USA) (v) 5-8-6 (3*) N Kennedy (9) *sluggish strt, hdwy gng wl entering strt, shaken up last 2 fs, no imprsn*..............................(16 to 1 op 14 to 1) 4
4354[9] YEVEED (Ire) (bl) 3-7-13[3] (3*) S Maloney (12) *trkd ldrs, effrt and not much room o'r 2 fs out, kpt on same pace fnl furlong*.............................(14 to 1 op 12 to 1) 5
3837 ABERDEEN HEATHER 3-9-7 J Williams (14) *in tch, pushed alng to improve entering strt, kpt on same pace last 2 fs.* ....(14 to 1 op 10 to 1) 6
4343[5] PANTHER (Ire) 3-8-8 K Fallon (11) *nvr far away, ev ch and rdn 3 fs out, no extr frm 2 out*................(10 to 1) 7
120[4] EAST BARNS (Ire) 5-8-6 (7*) Kimberley Hart (18) *patiently rdn, hdwy on outsd last 2 fs, nrst finish.* ....(33 to 1 op 20 to 1 tchd 50 to 1) 8
3891 EIRAS MOOD 4-8-8 (5*) A Garth (19) *chsd ldrs, feeling pace o'r 2 fs out, no imprsn*............................ (50 to 1) 9
3518 SLUMBER THYME (Ire) 4-8-13 A Mackay (5) *wtd wth, effrt on ins whn not much room o'r 2 fs out, nvr dngrs.* ....(50 to 1) 10
4115[6] MEXICAN DANCER 4-8-11 B Crossley (17) *prmnt till wknd o'r 2 fs out*.................... (25 to 1 tchd 33 to 1) 11
3181[4] ESSEX GIRL (v) 3-8-10 L Dettori (13) *wth ldrs, struggling o'r 2 fs out, sn btn*.............. (9 to 2 jt-fav op 7 to 2) 12
120[3] WATCH ME GO (Ire) 4-9-3 N Connorton (2) *pressed ldg pair, hrd drvn o'r 2 fs out, fdd*.......................(50 to 1) 13
2015[3] AMENABLE 8-9-3 J McLaughlin (20) *settled off the pace, nvr plcd to chal*............................. (6 to 1 op 5 to 1) 14
3323[7] SWEET ROMEO 3-8-9 J Carroll (10) *in tch till wknd entering strt*.................................. (14 to 1 op 12 to 1) 15
210 TYNRON DOON 4-9-3 M Wigham (7) *sluggish strt, beh and drvn alng, nvr a factor*........................ (33 to 1) 16
3447 SUSANNA'S SECRET (bl) 6-8-12 J Quinn (1) *wth ldrs for o'r 5 fs*.................................... (20 to 1 op 14 to 1) 17
4394 TWILIGHT FALLS 8-8-13 L Charnock (15) *pressed ldrs, struggling o'r 2 fs out, sn btn*......(16 to 1 op 14 to 1) 18
INVITE D'HONNEUR (NZ) 11-8-13 V Slattery (4) *beh and reminders aftr one furlong, nvr a factor.* ....(20 to 1 op 14 to 1 tchd 25 to 1) 19
4667a BRIDGE STREET BOY 4-8-11 T Sprake (16) *in tch, not much room on ins 3 fs out, sn lost touch*.......(50 to 1) 20
Dist: 1l, ½l, 7l, 3½l, 3½l, nk, 1l, 1½l, ¾l, 3l. 1m 49.10s. a 9.10s (20 Ran).
SR: 52/38/50/25/4/15/1/3/-/ (Mark Tompkins Racing), M H Tompkins

4489 EBF Whatton Manor Stud Maiden Stakes Class D (2-y-o) £5,673 1m 54yds........................ (3:00)

GOLDEN MEMORIES (Ire) 9-0 J Carroll (1) *made all, quickened clr o'r 2 fs out, drvn alng fnl furlong, kpt on wl.* ....(14 to 1 op 12 to 1 tchd 16 to 1) 1
4229[3] FAIR AND FANCY (Fr) 9-0 W Carson (16) *tucked away beh ldrs, chsd alng to improve last 2 fs, styd on, not rch wnr*...................(7 to 2 op 8 to 1 tchd 10 to 1) 2
4259[7] HILLSWICK 9-0 B Procter (2) *trkd ldg pair, drvn alng whn pace quickened o'r 2 fs out, styd on same pace.* ....(66 to 1 op 50 to 1) 3
4167[4] KINGS CAY (Ire) 9-0 L Dettori (14) *chsd ldg 6, rdn o'r 2 fs out, one pace*.......................(7 to 2 op 7 to 4) 4
4349[6] SHUTTLINGSLOW 8-9 R Hills (12) *pushed alng in midfield, effrt o'r 2 fs out, not pace to chal.* ....(20 to 1 op 16 to 1) 5
4179[6] NORTHERN HIGHLIGHT 9-0 A Mackay (3) *trkd ldrs, feeling pace and drvn alng o'r 2 fs out, sn outpcd.* ....(20 to 1 tchd 14 to 1) 6
RAINBOWS RHAPSODY 8-9 L Charnock (9) *patiently rdn, shaken up and hdwy on ins o'r 2 fs out, better for race.* .... (66 to 1 op 50 to 1) 7
2836[5] MELODY DANCER 9-0 S Perks (13) *settled midfield, effrt and drvn alng o'r 3 fs out, nvr nr to chal.* ....(40 to 1 op 25 to 1) 8
4316 BURRINGHAM BOY 9-0 J Quinn (7) *co'red up on ins, lost grnd whn pace quickened over 2 fs out, sn btn.* ....(66 to 1 op 50 to 1) 9

1640 SHARP THRILL 8-7 (7*) Mark Denaro (11) *in tch, chsd alng entering strt, nvr able to rch ldrs.* (66 to 1 op 50 to 1) 10
ERIN'S LAD 9-0 N Adams (15) *settled midfield, pushed alng o'r 2 fs out, fdd*............(66 to 1 op 50 to 1) 11
4264 WILLWIN (bl) 8-4 (5*) Darren Moffatt (5) *trkd ldrs, effrt and drvn alng entering strt, outpcd last 3 fs.* ....(66 to 1 op 33 to 1) 12
3974[9] KILERNAN 9-0 J Fanning (10) *settled off the pace, nvr nr to chal*............(66 to 1 op 50 to 1) 13
UNISON 9-0 J Williams (18) *beh and drvn alng hfwy, nvr a factor*............(66 to 1 op 50 to 1) 14
DAWN ROCK 9-0 R Cochrane (4) *sluggish strt, al beh.* ....(20 to 1 op 16 to 1) 15
DORIC 9-0 M Hills (17) *sn pushed alng to go pace, lost tch entering strt*............(14 to 1 op 7 to 1 tchd 16 to 1) 16
4377[5] GREENFINCH (Can) 9-0 W Ryan (6) *pressed ldg trio, effrt o'r 3 fs out, wknd quickly 2 out*....(25 to 1 op 20 to 1) 17
4149[8] STATELY HOME (Ire) 9-0 B Crossley (8) *tracking ldr whn ran out entering strt*............(66 to 1 op 50 to 1) ro

Dist: 1½l, 5l, 3l, nk, sht-hd, 4l, 6l, sht-hd, nk, nk. 1m 50.90s. a 10.90s (18 Ran).
SR: 29/24/9/-/-/-/ (F J Sainsbury), M J Heaton-Ellis

4490 Gamston Handicap Class D (0-80 3-y-o and up) £4,020 1m 54yds....... (3:30)

4120* TONY'S MIST [71] 3-9-5 L Dettori (15) *nvr far away, improved to ld o'r one furlong out, rdn and hld on gmely cl hme*............(6 to 1 op 9 to 2) 1
4336[3] QUANTITY SURVEYOR [55] (bl) 4-8-6 W Ryan (10) *patiently rdn, hdwy on outsd o'r 2 fs out, styd on wl, jst fld.* ....(12 to 1 op 10 to 1) 2
4343 CHIEF OF STAFF [64] 4-9-1 J McLaughlin (7) *sluggish strt, last entering strt, rapid hdwy appr fnl furlong, fnshd fst*............(20 to 1) 3
4320* MISTY SILKS [70] 3-9-4 W Carson (14) *settled midfield, improved o'r 2 fs out, styd on ins last.* ....(6 to 1 op 7 to 1 tchd 11 to 2) 4
4355[2] LAWNSWOOD JUNIOR [68] 6-9-5 G Hind (8) *patiently rdn, weaved through frm midfield last 2 fs, ran on finish.* ....(11 to 1 op 10 to 1) 5
4394 BATTLE COLOURS (Ire) [71] 4-9-8 K Fallon (18) *dashed into ld aftr 3 fs, drvn clr entering strt, hdd o'r one out, one pace*............(14 to 1 op 12 to 1) 6
2869[5] BRESIL (USA) [50] 4-8-1 J Lowe (12) *patiently rdn, hdwy on outsd o'r 2 fs out, ran on, nvr plcd to chal.* ....(20 to 1 tchd 33 to 1) 7
3258[3] SCOTTISH PARK [53] 4-8-4 J Quinn (16) *nvr far away, ev ch and rdn o'r 2 fs out, no extr fnl furlong*.... (20 to 1) 8
4277[9] BOLD STREET (Ire) [57] 3-8-5 N Connorton (2) *wtd wth, hdwy on ins 3 fs out, not pace of ldrs appr last.* ....(33 to 1 op 20 to 1) 9
3961[5] MARIUS (Ire) [63] 3-8-11 M Hills (6) *al hndy, rdn alng o'r 2 fs out, no extr*......(11 to 2 fav op 6 to 1 tchd 5 to 1) 10
4394 RURAL LAD [56] 4-8-2 (5*) A Garth (19) *co'red up in midfield, drvn alng whn pace quickened over 2 fs out, no imprsn*............(12 to 1 op 10 to 1) 11
4038 FIGHTER SQUADRON [63] (bl) 4-9-0 S D Williams (9) *beh and niggled alng hfwy, hdwy whn not clr run o'r 2 fs out, nvr able to chal*............(33 to 1) 12
4158[9] PRINCESS OF ORANGE [44] 4-7-9[1] J Fanning (4) *sluggish strt, beh and chsd alng hfwy, nvr dngrs*......(50 to 1) 13
4393[5] PETRACO (Ire) [72] 5-9-9 Paul Eddery (13) *led 3 fs, hndy till wknd and eased 2 out*............(25 to 1) 14
4125[5] HAYDON BRIDGE (Ire) [50] 3-7-12 N Adams (3) *trkd ldrs, drvn alng and lost grnd o'r 2 fs out, sn btn*....(50 to 1) 15
1861[9] WOLF POWER (Ire) [53] 3-7-13[1] (3*) S Maloney (5) *settled off the pace, no dngr last 3 fs*......... (20 to 1 op 25 to 1) 16
4231[3] LOCHORE [60] 3-8-8 A Tucker (11) *in tch, wide strt, btn o'r 2 fs out*............(14 to 1 tchd 16 to 1) 17
2134[4] EYE WITNESS (Ire) [64] (bl) 3-8-12 A Munro (17) *bustled alng to chase ldg 6, fdd thre fs out*......(16 to 1 op 14 to 1) 18
EARLY STAR [74] 4-9-11 Alex Greaves (1) *steadied strt, co'red up on ins, reminders over 3 fs out, sn btn.* ....(66 to 1 op 50 to 1) 19
651[2] JUNGLE KNIFE [70] 7-9-7 P Robinson (20) *sluggish strt, jnd ldrs aftr 2 fs, fdd und pres o'r two out.* ....(8 to 1 op 7 to 1) 20

Dist: Sht-hd, 1l, ½l, ¾l, hd, ½l, 3½l, 2½l, 2l, hd. 1m 49.50s. a 9.50s (20 Ran).
SR: 55/41/47/48/47/49/26/18/11/ (Mrs Chris Harrington), R Hannon

4491 Horserace Betting Levy Board Median Auction Maiden Stakes Class F (Div I) (2-y-o) £2,601 1m 1f 213yds..... (4:00)

4122[2] CAPTAIN STARLIGHT (Ire) 9-0 M Hills (2) *trkd ldr, niggled alng and edgd lft entering strt, drvn ahead o'r 2 fs out, hld on cl hme*............(6 to 4 fav op 11 to 10) 1
4329[4] SWORDSMANSHIP (bl) 9-0 W Ryan (9) *led, drvn alng and hdd o'r 2 fs out, rallied ins last, kpt on.* ....(9 to 2 op 3 to 1) 2
3462[8] RISKY TU 8-9 R Cochrane (6) *ran in snatches, hmpd twice appr strt, hrd drvn 3 fs out, styd on wl fnl furlong.* ....(7 to 1 op 6 to 1) 3
GREETLAND HALL 9-0 K Fallon (12) *sluggish strt, last and outpcd hfwy, styd on wl last 2 fs, nvr nrr.* ....(20 to 1 op 16 to 1) 4
4215[8] WINGS AHEAD 9-0 N Connorton (1) *nvr far away, hrd drvn o'r 2 fs out, no extr appr last.* (16 to 1 op 12 to 1) 5
4208[8] MISTER MAYBE 9-0 L Dettori (7) *trkd ldg trio, drvn alng o'r 3 fs out, outpcd frm 2 out*........(12 to 1 op 8 to 1) 6
ESTIMRAAR (Ire) 9-0 R Hills (5) *missed break, hdwy into midfield entering strt, effrt o'r 2 fs out, fdd.* ....(8 to 1 op 3 to 1) 7
ADMIRAL ROUS 9-0 M Wigham (8) *beh and drvn alng hfwy, nvr able to rch ldrs*......... (16 to 1 op 14 to 1) 8
4318[9] GRANDMAN (Ire) 8-9 (5*) Darren Moffatt (11) *wtd wth, hdwy on outsd o'r 3 fs out, fdd 2 out.* ....(16 to 1 op 50 to 1) 9
4097[9] SOTTISES (Ire) 8-2 (7*) N Varley (4) *sluggish strt, beh and chsd alng appr strt, nvr a factor*............(50 to 1) 10
2911[8] PETITE BIJOU 8-9 A Mackay (10) *chsd ldrs, feeling pace o'r 3 fs out, sn lost tch*............(66 to 1 op 50 to 1) 11
4326 VAX IT 8-9 G Hind (3) *sluggish strt, drvn up on ins aftr 3 fs, fdd entering strt, tld off*............(50 to 1) 12

Dist: ½l, nk, 5l, 7l, 8l, hd, 3l, nk, 7l, hd. 2m 18.00s. a 15.00s (12 Ran).
SR: 25/24/18/13/-/-/ (R P B Michaelson), M Bell

4492 Horserace Betting Levy Board Median Auction Maiden Stakes Class F (Div II) (2-y-o) £2,601 1m 1f 213yds..... (4:30)

4316[5] KHATIR (Can) 9-0 W Carson (9) *al hndy, swtchd ins to ld o'r 2 fs out, drvn alng fnl furlong, styd on.* ....(11 to 4 fav op 3 to 1 tchd 4 to 1) 1
4003[3] AFFIRM 9-0 C Rutter (1) *patiently riden, swtchd ins to improve o'r 2 fs out, styd on fnl furlong, not quicken cl hme*............(3 to 1 op 6 to 4) 2
4099[9] ANZUM 9-0 V Slattery (2) *trkd ldg 4, drvn alng to chal last 2 fs, styd on same pace ins last*..... (6 to 1 op 10 to 1) 3
4128[4] ROSE OF GLENN 8-6 (3*) S Maloney (3) *nvr far away, ev ch and drvn alng 2 fs out, kpt on same pace fnl furlong.* ....(25 to 1) 4
4215[3] OLYMPIC BID 8-9 J Carroll (8) *patiently rdn, hmpd aftr 3 fs, effrt and ridden o'r 2 out, one pace.* ....(7 to 1 op 6 to 1 tchd 8 to 1) 5
4350[7] NUIN-TARA 8-6 (3*) Stephen Davies (12) *rcd keenly, led till o'r 2 fs out, fdd*............(50 to 1) 6
4215[4] MONSIEUR BLEU 9-0 J Fanning (11) *al hndy, drvn alng whn pace quickened 2 fs out, fdd.* ....(12 to 1 tchd 14 to 1) 7
3990[5] RIVER JUNCTION (Ire) 9-0 R Cochrane (7) *tucked away in midfield, effrt and not much room 2 fs out, sn rdn and no imprsn*............(6 to 1 op 7 to 2) 8
LADY TJONGER 8-9 J Williams (5) *beh and pushed alng hfwy, nvr able to rch ldrs*......... (25 to 1 op 20 to 1) 9
3905 TROPICAL VISTA 8-9 N Adams (6) *beh and bustled alng hfwy, nvr on terms*............(50 to 1) 10
4128[9] MY SONG OF SONGS 8-9 J Quinn (10) *wtd wth, improved on outsd whn sddl slpd entering strt, rdr without irons last 2 fs, eased*............(50 to 1) 11
LADY DARING (bl) 8-9 A Munro (4) *sluggish strt, tld off last 3 fs*............(50 to 1) 12

Dist: 1½l, ¾l, ¾l, 5l, 12l, 8l, 2l, 2½l, 3l, 8l. 2m 18.80s. a 15.80s (12 Ran).
SR: 17/14/12/5/-/-/ (Hamdan Al-Maktoum), D Morley

4493 St Anns Maiden Stakes Class D (3-y-o and up) £3,816 1¾m 15yds...... (5:00)

1092[8] FLAKEY DOVE 7-9-0 T Sprake (9) *al gng best, led o'r 2 fs out, readily*............(8 to 1 op 4 to 1 tchd 9 to 1) 1
4110[4] SPRING MARATHON (USA) 3-8-10 J Williams (7) *in tch, drvn to improve entering strt, styd on ins fnl furlong, not rch wnr*.........(13 to 8 fav op Evens tchd 7 to 4) 2
4334[4] NAWAHIL 3-8-5 W Carson (12) *al hndy, drvn alng o'r 2 fs out, kpt on same pace.* (13 to 2 op 5 to 1 tchd 7 to 1) 3
791[4] FIRM BUT FAIR 3-8-10 R Cochrane (6) *patiently rdn, improved frm midfield o'r 2 fs out, styd on same pace.* ....(9 to 2 op 7 to 4 tchd 5 to 1) 4
4431[3] ARC BRIGHT (Ire) 3-8-10 S Perks (3) *led one furlong, styd hndy, led wl o'r 3 out till over 2 out, sn outpcd.* (25 to 1) 5
SNOW DREAM 3-8-5 P Robinson (16) *sluggish strt, drvn into midfield appr strt, outpcd last 2 fs.* ....(25 to 1 op 20 to 1 tchd 33 to 1) 6
3449[9] DAJAM 3-8-2 (3*) Stephen Davies (14) *led aftr one furlong till wl o'r 3 out, sn lost tch*............(100 to 1) 7
3832[9] LADY CONFESS 3-8-5 N Adams (15) *wtd wth, improved to track ldrs entering strt, wknd quickly o'r 2 fs out.* ....(50 to 1) 8
MUNIR (USA) 4-9-5 L Dettori (5) *chsd alng to press ldrs for o'r one m, wknd and eased last 3 fs.* ....(14 to 1 op 10 to 1) 9
4457 STATIA (Ire) (v) 5-9-0 Kim Tinkler (4) *reluctant to race, reminders aftr 2 fs, some hdwy entering strt, nvr a factor*............(100 to 1) 10
4209[8] HASTY SPARK 5-8-12 (7*) Mark Denaro (17) *chsd ldg 4, feeling pace entering strt, sn lost tch*.........(100 to 1) 11
80[9] MISS IN-A-BIT 3-8-5 Paul Eddery (1) *chsd alng hfwy, wl beh last 3 fs*............(100 to 1) 12
HARQUIN 3-8-10 A Munro (2) *chsd ldrs, struggling entering strt, sn lost tch, tld off.* ....(14 to 1 op 25 to 1 tchd 33 to 1) 13
RAINY STORM 4-9-5 S D Williams (13) *struggling aftr 4 fs, tld off*............(100 to 1) 14

Dist: 2l, 1½l, 4l, 7l, 12l, 1l, 6l, sht-hd, nk, 30l. 3m 16.90s. a 19.00s (14 Ran).
SR: 15/7/-/-/-/-/ (J T Price), R J Price

4494 Woodborough Handicap Class D (0-80 3-y-o and up) £3,611 2m 9yds... (5:30)

4357[9] SILLARS STALKER (Ire) [54] 5-9-4 K Fallon (8) *settled mid-field, pushed up hfwy, led wl o'r 2 fs out, wnt clr, styd on ins last*.......... (100 to 30 op 6 to 4 tchd 7 to 2) 1
559[4] VADO VIA [44] 5-8-8 A Munro (6) *beh and outpcd hfwy, rapid hdwy last 2 fs, kpt on same pace cl hme*. .... (10 to 1 op 11 to 2) 2
4256[4] SMILES AHEAD [56] 5-8-13 (7*) C Hawksley (2) *led aftr 2 fs till wl o'r two out, rallied, kpt on same pace fnl furlong*. ....(7 to 1 op 9 to 2) 3
3872[2] PEACH BRANDY [42] 4-8-6 N Adams (1) *led 2 fs, styd hndy, jnd ldr entering strt, feeling pace o'r two out, fdd*..............................(5 to 2 fav op 4 to 1) 4
BAYBEEJAY [40] 6-8-4 A Mackay (7) *chsd ldg 5, hrd drvn 3 fs out, no imprsn*.................(50 to 1 op 33 to 1) 5
4133a SUPER RITCHART [37] 5-8-1 J Lowe (4) *trkd ldg 4, hrd drvn entering strt, outpcd last 3 fs*. (25 to 1 op 33 to 1) 6
3479 PRINCESS DAVID (USA) [58] 3-8-12 G Bardwell (9) *trkd ldrs, struggling whn pace quickened o'r 2 fs out, fdd*. ....(16 to 1) 7
727[4] ZEALOUS KITTEN (USA) [58] 5-9-8 L Dettori (10) *settled gng wl, niggled alng appr strt, wknd quickly 3 fs out*. ....(6 to 1 tchd 7 to 1) 8
4102[7] CHARMED LIFE [40] 4-8-4 S Wood (3) *trkd ldg pair, struggling to hold pl appr strt, sn lost tch*. ....(14 to 1 op 10 to 1 tchd 16 to 1) 9
JUST MY BILL [60] (bl) 7-9-10 Kim Tinkler (5) *al last, struggling hfwy, tld off*..................(12 to 1 op 7 to 1) 10

Dist: ½l, 2l, 15l, 4l, sht-hd, 5l, 6l, 15l, 15l, dist. 3m 49.40s. a 25.20s (10 Ran).
(Sillars Civil Engineering), Mrs J R Ramsden

CHEPSTOW (soft)
Tuesday October 19th
Going Correction: PLUS 0.50 sec. per fur.

4495 Annual Flat v Jump Jockeys Challenge Handicap Class G (0-70 3-y-o and up) £2,286 7f 16yds.........(1:30)

4333 WATERLORD (Ire) [56] 3-10-10 W R Swinburn (3) *in tch, rdn o'r one furlong out, ran on und pres to ld nr finish*. ....(11 to 1 op 8 to 1) 1
4394[2] PUSEY STREET BOY [55] 6-10-7 (5*) P Niven (1) *prmnt, led appr fnl furlong, shaken up and ct last strds*. ....(9 to 4 fav op 7 to 4 tchd 5 to 2) 2
4355[3] KNOBBLEENEEZE [63] (v) 3-10-12 (5*) G McCourt (11) *pressed ldrs, led 2 fs out, hdd appr fnl furlong, outpcd ins last*.............................(10 to 1 op 8 to 1) 3
4120 GARTH [49] 5-10-1 (5*) L Harvey (12) *mid-div, rdn and styd on fnl 2 fs*.......................................(33 to 1) 4
3783[9] SOVIET EXPRESS [55] (bl) 3-10-5[1] (5*) J Frost (8) *led till hdd 2 fs out, sn fdd*.....................(12 to 1 op 7 to 1) 5
3943 TAKE THE MICK [51] (bl) 3-10-5 M Hills (7) *outpcd and drvn alng, some prog fnl furlong*........(33 to 1 op 25 to 1) 6
4224 ASTERIX [58] 5-11-1 J Reid (5) *al mid-div*. .... (12 to 1 op 10 to 1) 7
4258 LORD ALFIE [51] 4-10-8 G Duffield (9) *al beh and outpcd*. ....(7 to 1 op 5 to 1) 8
4340 BILL MOON [50] 7-10-2 (5*) B Powell (10) *chsd ldrs o'r 4 fs*. .... (11 to 2 op 5 to 1 tchd 13 to 2) 9
4258 ABSO [48] (bl) 5-10-5 W Carson (2) *speed 4 fs, eased whn no ch fnl furlong*.................(25 to 1 op 20 to 1) 10
2300 BLUE FLAG (USA) [67] 4-11-10 R Cochrane (6) *nvr gng pace of ldrs*..........................(12 to 1 op 10 to 1) 11
3320a PROFIT A PRENDRE [53] 9-10-5 (5*) M Dwyer (4) *speed to hfwy*........................ (20 to 1 op 16 to 1) 12

Dist: Hd, 2l, 7l, ¾l, ½l, 1½l, nk, 3½l, 2l, 3l. 1m 29.40s. a 9.40s (12 Ran).
SR: 36/37/36/4/5/-/4/-/-/ (Mrs Francoise Jansen), M J Heaton-Ellis

4496 EBF Meadow Maiden Fillies' Stakes Class D (Div I) (2-y-o) £4,232 7f 16yds ....(2:00)

GIRL FROM IPANEMA 8-11 T Quinn (8) *al frnt rnk, rdn and outpcd o'r one furlong out, rallied gmely und pres to ld nr finish*.............(9 to 1 op 5 to 1 tchd 11 to 1) 1
CAMBREL (Ire) 8-11 W Ryan (12) *prmnt, led wl o'r 2 fs out, shaken up and edgd lft ins last, ct nr finish*. ....(4 to 1 op 9 to 4) 2
4351 MILLICENT NORTH 8-6 (5*) S Drowne (15) *hdwy 2 fs out, styd on fnl furlong*................(20 to 1 op 12 to 1) 3
4349[3] LITTLE BEDWYN (USA) 8-11 J Reid (2) *led till hdd wl o'r 2 fs out, sn outpcd*.................... (7 to 2 op 3 to 1) 4
3941[8] LOUISIANA SPORT 8-11 W Woods (13) *sn chasing ldrs, no hdwy fnl 2 fs*.......................(20 to 1 op 16 to 1) 5
4253[4] PEVERIL PRINCESS 8-11 J Williams (1) *beh, moderate prog ins fnl 2 fs*...................... (25 to 1 op 20 to 1) 6
FAVILLA (Ire) 8-11 D Holland (3) *pressed ldrs o'r 4 fs*. .... (20 to 1 op 12 to 1) 7
ARAFEL 8-11 W Newnes (9) *al outpcd*. ....(100 to 1 op 50 to 1) 8
4227 MY MOONA 8-11 A Tucker (11) *chsd ldrs 4 fs*. ....(100 to 1 op 66 to 1) 9
LADY TETRUS 8-11 M Hills (7) *dwlt, nvr rchd ldrs*. ....(16 to 1 op 10 to 1) 10
3642 ROODMAS (Ire) 8-4 (7*) M Handley (5) *prmnt o'r 4 fs*. ....(50 to 1 op 33 to 1) 11
4002[8] STAR JESTER (Ire) 8-11 D Harrison (4) *beh frm hfwy*. ....(25 to 1 op 12 to 1) 12
CRYSTAL HEART (Ire) 8-11 M Wigham (10) *al beh*. ....(100 to 1 op 50 to 1) 13
3738 SEE MY GUEST (Fr) 8-11 S Raymont (6) *sn beh, tld off*. ....(100 to 1 op 66 to 1) 14
ATHENE (Ire) 8-11 W R Swinburn (14) *iron snapped and pld up aftr one furlong*.............(7 to 4 fav op 5 to 2) pu

Dist: ¾l, 12l, nk, 3½l, ¾l, sht-hd, 2½l, 3l, nk, 1l. 1m 27.70s. a 7.70s (15 Ran).
SR: 34/32/-/-/-/-/ (Christopher Wright), P F I Cole

4497 EBF Meadow Maiden Fillies' Stakes Class D (Div II) (2-y-o) £4,202 7f 16yds ....(2:30)

3625[6] STATE CRYSTAL (Ire) 8-11 W Ryan (5) *made virtually all, pushed out fnl furlong, hld on wl*. ....(6 to 1 op 7 to 2 tchd 13 to 2) 1
4276[5] TRIPLE TIE (USA) 8-11 J Reid (3) *trkd wnr, rdn o'r one furlong out, styd on und pres, not quite get up*. ....(5 to 4 fav op 6 to 4) 2
3446 RAZINAH (Ire) 8-11 W Carson (1) *in tch, rdn 2 fs out, styd on, not a dngr*...................(14 to 1 op 10 to 1) 3
4342[4] GINGERLY (USA) (v) 8-11 W R Swinburn (14) *pressed ldrs till outpcd ins fnl 2 fs*. ..(6 to 1 op 4 to 1 tchd 13 to 2) 4
CLASSIC LIGHT (Ire) 8-11 M Hills (12) *sn chasing ldrs, outpcd fnl 2 fs*......................(40 to 1 op 25 to 1) 5
4396[5] TAHITI BEACH 8-11 T Quinn (13) *pressed ldrs till outpcd fnl 2 fs*............................. (6 to 1 op 7 to 2) 6
BAYBELLINA (Ire) 8-11 M Wigham (6) *slwly away, styd on frm o'r one furlong out*...........(50 to 1 op 33 to 1) 7
3738 HIGH TYPHA 8-11 W Woods (10) *pressed ldrs till wknd fnl 2 fs*.................................. (20 to 1 op 10 to 1) 8
KARLINE KA (Fr) 8-11 C Rutter (11) *strted slwly, al in rear*. .... (50 to 1 op 40 to 1) 9
1583 COURT SERENADE 8-11 R Cochrane (9) *outpcd most of way*...................................(66 to 1 op 50 to 1) 10
4349[7] SHIFTING MIST 8-11 G Duffield (15) *al outpcd*. ....(20 to 1 op 14 to 1) 11
DAKOTA GIRL 8-11 J Williams (2) *dwlt, al outpcd*. ....(25 to 1 op 20 to 1) 12
SILKY MAGNA 8-11 R Price (4) *in tch o'r 4 fs*. ....(50 to 1 op 25 to 1) 13
VITE ETOILE 8-6 (5*) S Drowne (7) *al beh*. ....(66 to 1 op 33 to 1) 14
NORTHLAND STAR (Ire) 8-11 N Adams (8) *slwly away, al beh, tld off*...........................(66 to 1 op 40 to 1) 15

Dist: ½l, 10l, nk, hd, sht-hd., 8l, ¾l, 3l, 3l, nk. 1m 27.10s. a 7.10s (15 Ran).
SR: 43/41/11/10/9/8/ (Michael Poland), H R A Cecil

4498 Pat Eddery 200-in-a-season Maiden Stakes Class D (2-y-o) £4,055 1m 14yds........................ (3:00)

3422[4] WAYFARERS WAY (USA) 9-0 W Ryan (14) *mid-div, hdwy o'r one furlong out, str run fnl furlong to ld on line*. ....(10 to 1 op 6 to 1 tchd 14 to 1) 1
LON ISA 8-9 D Holland (16) *prmnt, str chal fnl 2 fs, jst fld*. ....(100 to 1 op 33 to 1) 2
4281[7] YOUNG CLIFFORD (USA) 9-0 T Quinn (11) *prmnt, led o'r 2 fs out, hrd drvn fnl furlong, ct on line*. ....(3 to 1 op 3 to 1) 3
4356[2] CASTLE COMBE (Ire) 9-0 J Reid (4) *al pressing ldrs, styd on one pace frm o'r 2 fs out*..........(7 to 1 op 4 to 1) 4
4027[4] PERSIAN SAINT (Ire) 9-0 D Harrison (13) *in tch, drvn and kpt on one pace fnl 2 fs*. (9 to 1 op 8 to 1 tchd 10 to 1) 5
4253[2] MYSTIC HILL 9-0 W R Swinburn (18) *prmnt, led o'r 4 fs out, hdd over 2 out, wknd appr fnl furlong*. ....(5 to 2 fav op 2 to 1) 6
4252[8] TRADE WIND 9-0 J Williams (17) *mid-div, some prog frm o'r one furlong out*. (16 to 1 tchd 20 to 1 and 14 to 1) 7
MR BROWNING (USA) 9-0 R Cochrane (9) *chsd ldrs o'r 5 fs*. ....(33 to 1 op 20 to 1) 8
DURHAM 9-0 C Rutter (1) *wnt lft strt, in tch 5 fs*. ....(16 to 1 op 12 to 1) 9
4113[8] LYPHARD'S FABLE (USA) 9-0 M Hills (15) *nvr gng pace to chal ldrs*..........................(16 to 1 op 20 to 1) 10
DIGGERS WELL (USA) 9-0 G Duffield (19) *prmnt till wknd o'r 2 fs out*..........................(16 to 1 op 10 to 1) 11
EPICA 9-0 W Newnes (10) *al outpcd*. (33 to 1 op 12 to 1) 12
TINGLE FACTOR 9-0 S O'Gorman (2) *al outpcd*. ....(20 to 1 op 12 to 1) 13
TARTHOOTH (Ire) 9-0 W Carson (3) *dwlt, al beh*. ....(20 to 1 op 10 to 1) 14
4259[9] CLIFTON SET 8-9 (5*) S Drowne (7) *al beh*. ....(66 to 1 op 33 to 1) 15
DRIMARD (Ire) 8-7 (7*) T G McLaughlin (12) *al in rear*. ....(40 to 1 op 20 to 1) 16

4113 ECHO WOOD 9-0 N Adams (5) *sn beh.* .... (66 to 1 op 33 to 1) 17
4253^{4} INDIAN TEMPLE 9-0 M Wigham (6) *pressed ldrs o'r 4 fs.* .... (33 to 1 op 25 to 1) 18
4098 EVENING BRIGADIER 9-0 A Clark (20) *al beh.* .... (50 to 1 op 33 to 1) 19
NANDURA 8-9 W Woods (8) *led till hdd o'r 4 fs out, wknd quickly*.......... (33 to 1 op 20 to 1) 20
Dist: Sht-hd, hd, 1½l, 1½l, nk, 1½l, 8l, nk, hd, 3½l. 1m 40.80s. a 8.40s (20 Ran).
SR: 34/28/32/27/22/21/16/-/-/ (Lady Tennant), R Hannon

4499 Spinney Conditions Stakes Class D (3-y-o and up) £3,405 1m 14yds.... (3:30)

4393^{9} SUNDAY'S HILL 4-9-2 J Williams (10) *in tch, rdn 2 fs out, led appr fnl furlong, drvn out*..... (14 to 1 op 12 to 1) 1
1030^{2} FAYFA (Ire) 3-8-10 W Ryan (5) *pressed ldr till led 4 fs out, hdd appr fnl furlong, kpt on same pace.* .... (15 to 8 fav op 13 to 8 tchd 9 to 4) 2
WOODCHAT (USA) 3-9-1 W Carson (7) *chsd ldrs, rdn and one pace fnl 2 fs*.......... (7 to 1 op 6 to 1) 3
3477 ETOSHA (bl) 3-8-10 M Hills (8) *dwlt, sn reco'red to chase ldrs, rdn over 2 fs out, soon outpcd.* (9 to 1 op 7 to 1) 4
4172 UNDERWATER (USA) 4-9-4 W R Swinburn (2) *chsd ldrs, rdn o'r 2 fs out, eased whn btn fnl furlong.* .... (7 to 2 op 3 to 1 tchd 9 to 4 and 4 to 1) 5
4030* WINDRUSH LADY 3-8-10 J Reid (6) *chsd ldrs, rdn 3 fs out, wknd 2 out*.......... (6 to 1 op 7 to 1) 6
MELISIO 3-8-6 C Rutter (4) *al beh*...(100 to 1 op 25 to 1) 7
4441 FISIO SANDS 4-8-9 B Rouse (11) *al beh.* .... (50 to 1 op 33 to 1) 8
SOOTHFAST (USA) 4-9-0 W Newnes (9) *al in rear.* .... (40 to 1 op 16 to 1 tchd 50 to 1) 9
GARRALLAN 3-8-11 D Holland (3) *led, rcd alone, hdd 4 fs out, wknd quickly*... (50 to 1 op 25 to 1 tchd 66 to 1) 10
4100^{6} SPEAKER'S HOUSE (USA) (bl) 4-9-4 T Quinn (1) *nvr gng wl, al beh*.......... (9 to 1 op 7 to 1) 11
SPARKY'S GIRL 3-8-7[1] M Wigham (12) *sn beh and tld off.* .... (40 to 1 op 12 to 1 tchd 50 to 1) 12
Dist: 1l, 2½l, 5l, 5l, hd, 2½l, ¾l, nk, 12l, 3½l. 1m 40.70s. a 8.30s (12 Ran).
SR: 37/28/25/5/-/-/ (Stanley Hinton), M Blanshard

4500 Copse Nursery Handicap Class E (2-y-o) £3,267 6f 16yds............ (4:00)

4251 DANGEROUS SHADOW [68] 8-10 (5*) Darren Moffatt (7) *made all, quickened clr ins last.* .... (3 to 1 fav tchd 5 to 2 and 100 to 30) 1
4229^{7} BAGSHOT [72] 9-5 W Carson (2) *beh, swtchd rght and hdwy one and a half fs out, kpt on fnl furlong, no imprsn on wnr*.......... (6 to 1 op 5 to 1) 2
4358^{2} CHEERFUL GROOM (Ire) [57] 8-1 (3*) N Kennedy (4) *mid-div, rdn and hdwy o'r one furlong out, styd on.* .... (7 to 1 op 11 to 2 tchd 8 to 1) 3
4356 KELLYSI [60] (bl) 8-7 T Quinn (8) *pressed ldrs till outpcd appr fnl furlong*.......... (10 to 1 op 8 to 1) 4
4356 REED MY LIPS (Ire) [70] (v) 9-3 D Holland (14) *drvn and hdwy to chase ldrs hfwy, wknd o'r one furlong out.* .... (14 to 1 op 10 to 1) 5
4264^{6} PRIMOST [65] (v) 8-12 N Adams (1) *pressed ldrs till wknd one and a half fs out*.......... (14 to 1 op 10 to 1) 6
3475 ADMIRALELLA [73] 9-1 (5*) D McCabe (5) *pressed ldrs 4 fs.* .... (12 to 1 op 10 to 1 tchd 14 to 1) 7
1583^{4} EUROPHARM LASSIE [73] 9-6 B Rouse (10) *swrvd strt, moderate prog frm o'r one furlong out*.......... (20 to 1) 8
4358 MOUNT LEINSTER [65] (bl) 8-7 (5*) S Drowne (9) *drvn out and hdwy hfwy, wknd 2 fs out*.... (20 to 1 op 16 to 1) 9
2610^{8} QUEEN'S ADMIRAL [50] 7-6 (5*) D Wright (3) *early speed.* .... (20 to 1) 10
4272^{9} CABCHARGE PRINCESS (Ire) [70] 9-3 P Robinson (12) *nvr rchd ldrs*.......... (20 to 1 op 10 to 1) 11
3009^{6} CHILLY TIME [58] 8-5 J Williams (11) *al in rear.* .... (8 to 1 tchd 9 to 1) 12
4265 GREATEST HOPES [55] 8-2 T Williams (6) *chsd ldrs o'r 3 fs.* .... (40 to 1 op 25 to 1) 13
4266^{8} FROMAGE [74] 9-0 (7*) N Varley (13) *effrt and wnt rght 2 fs out, sn btn*.......... (14 to 1 op 10 to 1) 14
Dist: 2l, 1½l, 1l, 2l, 1½l, nk, 2l, sht-hd, 3l, 1l. 1m 15.60s. a 6.10s (14 Ran).
SR: 39/35/14/13/15/4/11/3/-/ (Prime Maintenance), Mrs M Reveley

4501 Orchard Handicap Class D (0-80 3-y-o and up) £3,847 6f 16yds.........(4:30)

4340^{5} LEIGH CROFTER [52] (bl) 4-8-2 G Hind (6) *made virtually all, shaken up and quickened appr fnl furlong.* .... (14 to 1 op 12 to 1 tchd 16 to 1) 1
4394^{4} PALACEGATE GOLD (Ire) [54] 4-8-1 (3*) B Doyle (17) *al frnt rnk, kpt on fnl furlong, not pace of wnr.* .... (11 to 1 op 8 to 1) 2
4090^{8} GILT THRONE [72] 6-9-8 P Robinson (2) *gd hdwy o'r one furlong out, kpt on fnl furlong.* .... (14 to 1 op 10 to 1 tchd 16 to 1) 3
4038 CATHERINEOFARAGON [76] 3-9-10 W Ryan (18) *rcd stands side, kpt on fnl 2 fs, no imprsn*......(11 to 1 op 8 to 1) 4
3837* CAPE PIGEON (USA) [69] (bl) 8-9-5 D Holland (5) *led 2 fs, styd frnt rnk till wknd fnl furlong.* .... (12 to 1 tchd 11 to 1) 5
4393^{2} JIGSAW BOY [73] 4-9-9 J Williams (7) *outpcd, rdn fnl 2 fs, not pace to chal*.......... (2 to 1 fav op 7 to 2) 6
4168^{7} PHARAOH'S DANCER [64] 6-9-0 J Reid (19) *chsd ldr stands side, no prog frm o'r 2 fs out.* (13 to 2 op 8 to 1) 7
4168 THE AUCTION BIDDER [73] 6-9-4 (5*) S Wynne (3) *chsd ldrs 4 fs*.......... (25 to 1 op 20 to 1) 8
4333^{9} GREY CHARMER (Ire) [58] 4-8-8 W Newnes (16) *nvr gng pace of ldrs*.......... (20 to 1 op 14 to 1) 9
4327 DOUBLE SHIFT [62] 4-8-12 S Whitworth (13) *outpcd, nrst finish*.......... (16 to 1 op 14 to 1) 10
4331* FINJAN [78] 6-9-7 (7*) S McCarthy (9) *nvr dngrs.* .... (25 to 1 op 14 to 1) 11
4297 BLUE TOPAZE [72] 5-9-8 M Wigham (4) *slwly away, not reco'r*.......... (12 to 1 op 10 to 1) 12
4116 SIR OLIVER (Ire) [51] 4-8-1 Dale Gibson (8) *sn outpcd.* .... (25 to 1 op 20 to 1) 13
3947 BELLS OF LONGWICK [69] 4-9-5 T Williams (14) *drvn to chase ldrs hfwy, wknd ins fnl 2 fs.* (20 to 1 op 16 to 1) 14
3942^{9} FIVESEVENFIVEO [70] 5-9-1 (5*) S Drowne (1) *outpcd.* .... (33 to 1 op 16 to 1) 15
4348 COCONUT JOHNNY [55] 3-8-3 G Duffield (12) *sn outpcd.* .... (14 to 1 op 12 to 1) 16
4393 ANOTHER JADE [73] 3-9-7 W R Swinburn (20) *speed stands side o'r 3 fs*.......... (25 to 1 op 20 to 1) 17
2898^{6} NOEPROB (USA) [56] 3-8-4 R Perham (15) *al outpcd.* .... (50 to 1 op 33 to 1) 18
4038 HALLORINA [57] 3-8-5 G Bardwell (10) *sn beh.* .... (40 to 1 op 33 to 1) 19
BATTLING BELLA (USA) [52] 4-8-2 A Morris (11) *beh frm hfwy*.......... (66 to 1 op 50 to 1) 20
Dist: 1½l, 1l, 1l, 1l, 3l, 2½l, hd, ½l, sht-hd, ½l. 1m 14.70s. a 5.20s (20 Ran).
SR: 44/40/54/52/43/35/16/24/7/ (Peter Dimmock), P D Cundell

4502 Pasture Handicap Class D (0-80 3-y-o) £3,561 1½m 23yds............. (5:00)

4341* WARM SPELL [74] 9-2 B Rouse (1) *in tch, smooth hdwy to ld o'r 3 fs out, cmftbly.* (10 to 1 op 8 to 1 tchd 11 to 1) 1
4256^{5} KISMETIM [56] 7-9 (3*) B Doyle (4) *beh, hdwy frm 3 fs out, ran on und pres fnl 2 furlongs, not rch wnr.* .... (11 to 1 op 8 to 1) 2
4274^{6} DISKETTE [69] 8-11 W R Swinburn (5) *mid-div till lost pos 6 fs out, gd hdwy 3 out, rdn and styd on one pace fnl 2 furlongs*.......... (6 to 1 tchd 13 to 2) 3
2135^{3} TOP RANK [76] 9-4 D Harrison (13) *led till hdd o'r 3 fs out, sn outpcd*.......... (10 to 1 op 12 to 1) 4
4335^{6} SOOJAMA (Ire) [51] (bl) 7-7 G Bardwell (2) *slwly away, sn reco'red to chase ldrs, one pace fnl 3 fs*........ (50 to 1) 5
3759 CIVIL LAW (Ire) [64] 8-6 W Carson (12) *slwly away and beh, some prog frm o'r 2 fs out*.......... (16 to 1 op 14 to 1) 6
4267^{9} SCHOOLGIRL CRUSH [51] 7-4[2] (5*) Darren Moffatt (9) *nvr rchd ldrs*.......... (50 to 1) 7
4189^{7} FRESCADE (USA) [79] (bl) 9-7 T Quinn (11) *prmnt till wknd o'r 2 fs out*.......... (12 to 1 op 10 to 1) 8
4391^{3} BEVERLY KNIGHT [66] 8-8 J Reid (6) *chsd ldrs, wkng whn hmpd o'r 2 fs out*.......... (8 to 1 op 6 to 1) 9
2547^{5} ALLESCA [71] 8-13 N Adams (3) *strted slwly, drvn and hdwy 3 fs out, wknd o'r 2 out*...... (8 to 1 tchd 9 to 1) 10
4157^{5} SAVOY TRUFFLE (Fr) [79] 9-7 W Ryan (7) *in tch, rdn 4 fs out, sn wknd*.......... (8 to 1 op 7 to 1) 11
1244* ELECTROLYTE [51] 7-5[3] (5*) D Wright (10) *chsd ldrs till wknd frm 3 fs out*.... (11 to 1 op 12 to 1 tchd 14 to 1) 12
4274^{4} LA SPEZIA [77] 9-5 D Holland (8) *prmnt, reminders 5 fs out, hrd drvn 4 out, wknd ins fnl 3 furlongs.* .... (3 to 1 fav op 9 to 2) 13
Dist: 2½l, 6l, 1l, 2½l, 2l, hd, 3½l, 2l, 10l, 2½l. 2m 46.20s. a 14.70s (13 Ran).
SR: 15/-/-/-/-/-/ (K Higson), R Simpson

CHESTER (soft)
Tuesday October 19th
Going Correction: PLUS 0.60 sec. per fur.

4503 EBF Saltney Maiden Stakes Class D (Div I) (2-y-o) £4,175 7f 122yds.. (1:50)

3230^{4} SHALBOURNE (USA) 8-6 (3*) Stephen Davies (6) *settled off the pace, improved und pres 2 fs out, ran on to ld last strd*.......... (9 to 2 op 4 to 1 tchd 5 to 1) 1
3876^{5} SOUTHERN POWER (Ire) 9-0 L Dettori (5) *settled gng wl, led on bit o'r one furlong out, shaken up too late, ct last strd*.......... (9 to 4 on op 2 to 1 on) 2
1897^{8} ASTRAC (Ire) 8-11 (3*) O Pears (4) *wth ldr, led hfwy, quickened, hdd o'r one furlong out, sn outpcd.* .... (14 to 1 op 10 to 1) 3
3972 BRUZ 9-0 S Perks (2) *slight ld to hfwy, hrd drvn 2 fs out, sn btn*.......... (33 to 1 op 25 to 1 tchd 50 to 1) 4
EL SALVADOR 9-0 J Carroll (1) *trkd ldg pair, feeling pace o'r 2 fs out, fdd*........(15 to 2 op 5 to 1 tchd 8 to 1) 5
3992^{7} HESFINMENTALTOO (bl) 9-0 A Mackay (3) *sluggish strt, bustled alng thrght, tld off hfwy.* .... (33 to 1 op 25 to 1 tchd 50 to 1) 6
Dist: Sht-hd, 8l, 2l, 1½l, 20l. 1m 43.16s. a 11.16s (6 Ran).
(R E Sangster), P W Chapple-Hyam

4504 Queensferry Conditions Stakes Class D (2-y-o) £4,370 6f 18yds........(2:20)

4423 MR M-E-N (Ire) 9-6 J Carroll (3) *wtd wth, quickened to join ldr hfwy, led o'r one furlong out, sn clr.* ....(2 to 1 op 6 to 4) 1
4269* ROOFTOP FLYER (Ire) 9-2 L Dettori (1) *led, jnd and niggled alng hfwy, hdd o'r one furlong out, sn outpcd.* ....(9 to 4 on op 7 to 4 on) 2
4190 NILEGUNNER 8-2 (5*) A Garth (2) *trkd ldr, rdn and outpcd hfwy, sn lost tch.*........(33 to 1) 3
Dist: 12l, 12l. 1m 21.54s. a 8.04s (3 Ran).
SR: 17/-/-/ (Mrs M Taylor), J Berry

4505 Tattenhall Rated Class B Handicap (0-95 3-y-o and up) £7,231 1m 7f 195yds........(2:50)

3907⁷ WELSHMAN [68] 7-8-11 J Quinn (5) *al gng wl, quickened to ld o'r 4 fs out, wnt clr frm 2 out, styd on well.* ....(5 to 2 fav op 2 to 1 tchd 11 to 4) 1
4212 AUDE LA BELLE (Fr) [68] 5-8-11 A Mackay (4) *wtd wth, niggled alng whn pace quickened o'r 6 fs out, styd on appr last, nrst finish.*........(6 to 1 op 5 to 1) 2
4425³ STAR PLAYER [76] 7-9-5 L Dettori (6) *patiently rdn, last hfwy, improved to chase wnr fnl furlong, ridden and no extr last 50 yards.*........(7 to 2 op 9 to 2) 3
MALAMUTE SALOON (USA) [78] (v) 7-9-7 Paul Eddery (2) *sluggish strt, wnt hndy aftr one circuit, rdn o'r 2 fs out, wknd.*........(16 to 1 op 12 to 1) 4
4357⁶ GOODBYE MILLIE [64] 3-7-5¹ (7*) C Hawksley (3) *trkd ldg pair, struggling to hold pl o'r 4 fs out, sn btn.* ....(5 to 1 op 4 to 1) 5
4239³ VISHNU (USA) [80] 3-8-13 A McGlone (1) *led till hdd and rdn o'r 4 fs out, wknd quickly appr strt.* ....(4 to 1 op 3 to 1 tchd 9 to 2) 6
Dist: 4l, ½l, 8l, nk, 2l. 3m 49.39s. a 24.39s (6 Ran).
(Brian Oxton), M Blanshard

4506 Bunbury Fillies' Handicap Class D (0-80 3-y-o and up) £4,630 1¼m 75yds ....(3:20)

4155³ SOBA UP [55] 3-8-7 A Culhane (3) *co'red up in midfield, outpcd and looked btn over 3 fs out, styd on to ld last 70 yards.*........(12 to 1 op 10 to 1 tchd 14 to 1) 1
4022³ LOMBARD SHIPS [57] (bl) 6-9-0 A Mackay (7) *patiently rdn, improved on outsd to ld one furlong out, hdd and no extr last 70 yards.*........(6 to 1 tchd 13 to 2) 2
4283⁹ NEMEA (USA) [62] 3-9-0 J Carroll (4) *trkd ldg 4, led wl o'r 2 fs out to one out, rdn and one pace.* ....(11 to 2 op 4 to 1 tchd 6 to 1) 3
4336² SHERGRESS [59] 3-8-11 M Birch (8) *wtd wth, hdwy to join ldrs appr strt, rdn and found little fnl furlong.* ....(5 to 1 fav op 9 to 2) 4
4341⁴ PRINCESS TATEUM (Ire) [64] 3-8-9 (7*) R Painter (11) *nvr far away, feeling pace and drvn alng last 2 fs, kpt on same pace.*........(9 to 1 op 8 to 1) 5
3587⁶ CROMARTY [72] 3-9-10 A McGlone (5) *trkd ldrs, effrt and drvn alng 4 fs out, styd on, nvr nrr.* (8 to 1 op 7 to 1) 6
4391 NO COMEBACKS [55] 5-8-12 K Fallon (10) *settled off the pcae, drvn up on outsd o'r 3 fs out, not rch ldrs.* ....(8 to 1 op 7 to 1) 7
4258 AKHLAK (Ire) [45] 3-7-11 J Quinn (12) *in tch, effrt and drvn alng hfwy, outpcd last 3 fs.*........(33 to 1) 8
3988⁴ DONIA (USA) [55] (bl) 4-8-12 A Munro (9) *led till wl o'r 2 fs out, sn rdn and btn.*........(12 to 1) 9
4348⁶ MISS KINABALU [45] 3-7-11 F Norton (6) *chsd ldrs, hrd drvn o'r 4 fs out, sn lost tch.*........(14 to 1) 10
4178 MAY HILLS LEGACY (Ire) [53] 4-8-10 Paul Eddery (1) *trkd ldr, pushed alng hfwy, rdn and btn o'r 4 fs out.* ....(10 to 1) 11
4152⁹ LAMU LADY (Ire) [68] 3-9-3 (3*) Stephen Davies (2) *sn beh, struggling hfwy, tld off.*........(12 to 1 op 8 to 1) 12
Dist: 1½l, 2l, hd, 1l, nk, 7l, 6l, 2½l, 2l, 12l. 2m 20.89s. a 11.79s (12 Ran).
SR: 37/41/37/33/36/43/17/-/-/ (Mrs M Hills), J Etherington

4507 October Handicap Class C (0-95 3-y-o and up) £5,270 6f 18yds........(3:50)

4393³ NORDAN RAIDER [72] 5-8-8 L Charnock (9) *nvr far away, hmpd aftr 2 fs, drvn to ld ins last, kpt on wl.* ....(15 to 8 fav op 9 to 4) 1
3660⁴ CARRANITA (Ire) [86] 3-9-3 (3*) Stephen Davies (11) *nvr far away, led o'r 2 fs out till ins last, rdn and no extr.* ....(20 to 1 op 14 to 1) 2
4278⁶ ARABELLAJILL [88] (bl) 4-9-10 L Dettori (6) *pressed ldrs, drvn alng last 2 fs, styd on same pace.* ....(9 to 1 op 8 to 1 tchd 10 to 1) 3
4455³ DOMICKSKY [71] 5-8-2² (7*) R Painter (13) *sluggish strt, drvn alng to improve into midfield hfwy, styd on finish.*........(12 to 1 op 10 to 1 tchd 14 to 1) 4
4415⁸ VELOCE (Ire) [74] 5-8-10 A Mackay (3) *sn drvn alng to keep up, styd on last 2 fs, nvr nrr.*........(12 to 1 op 10 to 1) 5
4363⁷ GONDO [70] (v) 6-8-0¹ (7*) S Knott (14) *sluggish strt, chsd alng to improve last 2 fs, fnshd wl.* (12 to 1 op 10 to 1) 6
4317³ THE SHARP BIDDER (Ire) [70] 3-8-4 Paul Eddery (2) *sluggish strt, improved into midfield hfwy, effrt whn hmpd o'r 2 fs out, nvr nr to chal.*........(16 to 1) 7
4278 SIMPLY SOOTY [78] 3-8-12 J Lowe (7) *chsd alng in midfield, no imprsn last 2 fs.*........(20 to 1 op 16 to 1) 8
3947 SOBA GUEST (Ire) [64] 4-8-0 A Munro (10) *pressed ldrs, feeling pace and rdn o'r 2 fs out, sn btn.* ....(20 to 1 op 16 to 1) 9
4145⁴ BALLASECRET [91] 5-9-8 (5*) D Meredith (12) *al hndy, drvn alng o'r 2 fs out, fdd.*........(14 to 1 op 12 to 1) 10
4217⁸ DIET [69] (v) 7-8-0 (5*) J Marshall (5) *led one and a half fs, rdn and lost grnd o'r 2 out, sn btn.*........(20 to 1) 11
4216⁸ PETITE-D-ARGENT [85] 4-9-7 J Carroll (8) *led aftr one and a half fs till o'r 2 out, sn btn.*........(9 to 1 op 14 to 1) 12
4393 TRUTHFUL IMAGE [86] (bl) 4-9-8 D Biggs (1) *sn outpcd and drvn alng, nvr a factor.*........(16 to 1 op 12 to 1) 13
3725⁸ TROON [85] 3-9-5 L Piggott (4) *settled off the pace, pushed alng hfwy, nvr a factor.* ....(11 to 1 op 10 to 1 tchd 12 to 1) 14
Dist: 1l, 1½l, hd, ½l, nk, 4l, 2l, 5l, 3l, ½l. 1m 20.72s. a 7.22s (14 Ran).
SR: 22/30/28/10/11/6/ (Miss J A Camacho), M J Camacho

4508 EBF Saltney Maiden Stakes Class D (Div II) (2-y-o) £4,175 7f 122yds..(4:20)

4252³ WAITING 9-0 A Munro (1) *sluggish strt, reco'red quickly to join ldr hfwy, led over 2 fs out, ran on wl.* ....(9 to 4 on op 7 to 4 on tchd 6 to 4 on) 1
4316 WINN'S PRIDE (Ire) 9-0 S Perks (4) *al wll plcd, slight ld 4 fs out till o'r 2 out, styd on same pace.* ....(25 to 1 op 20 to 1) 2
4377³ BALI WARRIOR (Ire) 8-11 (3*) M Fenton (6) *led one furlong, outpcd and lost grnd hfwy, styd on fnl furlong.* ....(6 to 1 op 9 to 2) 3
MORGANA (USA) 8-6 (3*) Stephen Davies (2) *slwly away, tld off till ran on wl last 2 fs, nrst finish.* ....(8 to 1 op 5 to 1) 4
4435⁹ STRANGERSARDANGERS (Ire) (bl) 8-9 A Mackay (3) *led aftr one furlong till hdd and rdn 4 out, sn lost tch.* (50 to 1) 5
3779 RINUS MAJOR (Ire) 9-0 J Weaver (5) *chsd ldrs, struggling to hold pl hfwy, tld off.*........(50 to 1 op 33 to 1) 6
PRINCE DE BERRY 9-0 L Dettori (7) *chsd ldrs, struggling hfwy, virtually pld up last 3 fs.*..... (8 to 1 op 7 to 1) 7
Dist: 5l, 6l, 5l, 12l, 20l, dist. 1m 43.78s. a 11.78s (7 Ran).
(Fahd Salman), P F I Cole

DEAUVILLE (FR) (heavy)
Tuesday October 19th
Going Correction: PLUS 0.80 sec. per fur.

4509 La Coupe Piaget des Deux Ans (Restricted Listed) (2-y-o) £17,921 1m ....(1:55)

REBENAC (Fr) 8-11 F Sanchez,........ 1
SUPPERCUT (Fr) 8-11 T Jarnet,........ 2
LISE DU BERLAIS (Fr) 8-8 O Peslier,........ 3
3413⁴ PETARD EXPRESS (Ire) 8-8 O Doleuze,........ 4
Dist: ¾l, 5l, ½l. 1m 50.30s. a 15.30s (4 Ran).
(Mme S Desmarais), J-F Bernard

4510 La Coupe Piaget (Restricted Listed) (3-y-o) £17,921 1¼m........(4:20)

ZOUC MACHINE (Fr) 8-11 F Grenet,........ 1
JAWLENSKY (Fr) 8-11 C Asmussen,........ 2
2803 DIODEME (Fr) 8-11 M Boutin,........ 3
CHINESE GORDON (Ire) 8-11 T Jarnet,........ 4
POM POM GIRL (Fr) 8-8 T Gillet,........ 5
SECRET BABY (Fr) 8-8 L Huart,........ 6
Dist: 2l, sht-nk, 1½l, ¾l, 6l. 2m 17.90s. a 16.20s (6 Ran).
SR: 15/11/10/7/2/-/ (Mme D G Jacob), P Bary

CHESTER (soft)
Wednesday October 20th
Going Correction: PLUS 1.05 sec. per fur. (races 1,2), PLUS 1.25 (3,4), PLUS 1.40 (5,6)

4511 Carden Conditions Stakes Class D (2-y-o) £3,899 7f 2yds........(2:00)

4223* COTTEIR CHIEF (Ire) 9-1 Pat Eddery (3) *patiently rdn, rapid hdwy on outsd to ld appr fnl furlong, forged clr.* ....(11 to 8 fav op 6 to 4 tchd 13 to 8) 1
3865⁶ SILVER WEDGE (USA) (bl) 9-1 A Munro (2) *dashed up to ld sn aftr strt, drvn alng frm hfwy, hdd appr fnl furlong, one pace.*........(12 to 1 op 10 to 1) 2
4339* FORGOTTEN DANCER (Ire) 8-13 J Reid (4) *led early, styd upsides and ev ch 2 fs out, rdn and not quicken.* ....(13 to 2 op 5 to 1) 3
4423⁶ BRAILLE (Ire) 8-13 M Roberts (6) *wtd wth, drvn up on outsd to fltter o'r 2 fs out, no extr fnl furlong.* ....(9 to 4 tchd 5 to 2 and 2 to 1) 4

4326* WHITE SHOOT (Ire) 8-10 A Tucker (1) *steadied strt, effrt on ins o'r 2 fs out, rdn and not quicken.* ....(25 to 1 op 20 to 1) 5
4264* SHARPENING 8-6 D Harrison (5) *trkd ldrs, hrd at work o'r 2 fs out, sn lost tch*................(7 to 1 op 11 to 2) 6
Dist: 3½l, 2½l, hd, ½l, 15l. 1m 36.36s. a 10.96s (6 Ran).
SR: 47/36/26/25/20/-/ (M & N Plant Ltd), M C Pipe

4512 Marford Maiden Stakes Class D (2-y-o) £3,647 6f 18yds........... (2:30)

4367² AMBER VALLEY (USA) 9-0 W Carson (1) *al travelling wl, led o'r 2 fs out, quickened away, easily.* ....(5 to 4 fav op 11 to 8) 1
4367⁶ CHURCHWORTH 9-0 T Quinn (7) *chsd ldg quartet, outpcd and struggling hfwy, str run fnl furlong, prmsg.* ....(20 to 1 op 16 to 1) 2
4167 IN A MOMENT (USA) (v) 8-11 (3*) O Pears (4) *sn led, set gd pace for o'r 3 fs, no extr ins fnl furlong.* ....(25 to 1 op 20 to 1) 3
4225³ GONE TO POT (bl) 9-0 J Reid (9) *led early, styd hndy and ev ch hfwy, rdn and no extr fnl furlong.* ....(6 to 1 op 13 to 2 tchd 8 to 1) 4
4440 TOP TYCOON (Ire) 9-0 L Dettori (6) *sluggish strt, drvn into midfield aftr 2 fs, outpcd hfwy, no imprsn.* ....(12 to 1 op 10 to 1) 5
4326² MONKEY MAGIC (Ire) (bl) 9-0 J Carroll (8) *broke wl to show speed in frnt rnk for o'r 4 fs, sn btn.* ....(9 to 1 op 10 to 1 tchd 8 to 1) 6
4113 NORTHERN UNION (Can) 9-0 P Robinson (3) *outpcd and drvn alng most of way, styd on late, nvr dngrs.* ....(16 to 1) 7
4263³ BOLD MICK (bl) 9-0 C Rutter (5) *chsd ldg 5, hrd at work hfwy, sn lost tch*........(10 to 1) 8
4179³ FRUSTRATED POET (USA) 9-0 L Charnock (2) *sn drvn alng to keep in tch, nvr a factor.* ....(15 to 2 op 11 to 2 tchd 8 to 1) 9
3950⁷ ALPINE JOHNNY 9-0 S Perks (12) *outpcd and drvn alng thrght*........(16 to 1) 10
2493⁶ REGAL RAMBLER (Can) 9-0 N Adams (11) *chsd ldg half dozen, struggling hfwy, sn lost tch.* ....(50 to 1 op 33 to 1) 11
RINUS MANOR (Ire) 9-0 J Weaver (10) *sluggish strt, struggling thrght*........(50 to 1) 12
Dist: 8l, hd, 1l, 5l, 3½l, 1½l, 3½l, ½l, 7l, 3½l. 1m 22.47s. a 8.97s (12 Ran).
SR: 47/15/14/10/-/-/ (J Hanson), J Hanson

4513 Frodsham Rated Class B Handicap (0-95 3-y-o and up) £7,509 1¼m 75yds ....(3:00)

4424² MAJED (Ire) [75] 5-8-2 (5*) Darren Moffatt (2) *patiently rdn, effrt and plenty to do o'r 3 fs out, str brst to ld post.* ....(5 to 4 fav op 11 to 8 tchd 6 to 4) 1
4101⁸ DESERT POWER [75] 4-8-7 R Price (7) *nvr far away, drvn ahead ins fnl furlong, ran on, ct post.* ....(20 to 1 op 16 to 1) 2
4132* CARELAMAN [92] 3-9-5 W Carson (10) *patiently rdn, improved appr strt, ev ch fnl furlong, kpt on.* ....(9 to 1 op 8 to 1 tchd 10 to 1) 3
4107³ AMAZE [89] 4-9-7 T Quinn (8) *settled gng wl, led o'r 4 fs out till ins fnl furlong, no extr*....(5 to 1 tchd 11 to 2) 4
4300 SHOW FAITH (Ire) [94] 3-9-7 Pat Eddery (9) *wtd wth, drvn up frm off the pace appr strt, rdn and not quicken fnl furlong*........(6 to 1 op 5 to 1) 5
4158* BEAUMAN [75] 3-8-2 A Mackay (6) *tucked away beh ldrs, effrt appr strt, eased whn btn fnl furlong.* ....(14 to 1 op 12 to 1) 6
4414 BARRATRY [75] (bl) 3-8-2 W Ryan (3) *dictated pace till hdd o'r 4 fs out, fdd und pres.* ....(12 to 1 op 10 to 1 tchd 14 to 1) 7
4019 HOME COUNTIES (Ire) [80] 4-8-12 K Fallon (4) *nvr far away, hrd at work o'r 3 fs out, fdd entering strt.* ....(33 to 1) 8
4175⁷ MAD MILITANT (Ire) [75] 4-8-7 L Dettori (1) *last and outpcd hfwy, nvr a factor*........(8 to 1 tchd 10 to 1) 9
3956⁶ CROPTON [82] 3-8-9 Paul Eddery (5) *sluggish strt, improved into midfield hfwy, lost tch appr strt.* ....(14 to 1 op 12 to 1) 10
Dist: Sht-hd, ¾l, 2½l, 8l, ¾l, 2½l, 2l, 12l, 12l. 2m 25.77s. a 16.67s (10 Ran).
SR: 54/53/63/60/44/23/18/24/-/ (Laurel (Leisure) Limited), Mrs M Reveley

4514 Tarporley Handicap Class D (0-80 3-y-o and up) £5,348 7f 122yds...... (3:30)

4394⁷ SAGEBRUSH ROLLER [77] 5-9-11 G Duffield (13) *settled off the pace, weaved through last 2 fs, ran on to ld last 50 yards*........(13 to 2 jt-fav op 7 to 1 tchd 8 to 1 and 6 to 1) 1
4300 COMANCHE COMPANION [69] 3-8-9 (5*) A Garth (1) *patiently rdn, improved to ld appr fnl furlong, hdd and no extr last 50 yards*........(12 to 1 op 10 to 1) 2
4470⁵ ARANY [80] 6-10-0 P Robinson (10) *al hndy, drw level und pres 2 fs out, rdn and outpcd fnl furlong.* ....(12 to 1 op 10 to 1) 3
4394 THORNTON GATE [72] 4-9-3 (3*) S Maloney (14) *pushed up frm midfield to join issue hfwy, rdn and no extr fnl furlong*........(16 to 1 op 14 to 1) 4
4391⁶ COLTRANE [66] (v) 5-9-0 A Munro (8) *chsd alng in midfield hfwy, gd hdwy entering fnl furlong, fnshd wl.* (7 to 1) 5
4133* KINGCHIP BOY [57] (v) 4-8-0 (5*) P McCabe (9) *set str pace, clr hfwy, hdd and fdd appr fnl furlong.* ....(14 to 1 op 12 to 1) 6
4158² KUMMEL KING [55] 5-7-12 (5*) D Wright (4) *nvr far away, hrd at work o'r 2 fs out, sn btn*........(12 to 1) 7
4123² LADY BROKER [53] 3-7-12 A Mackay (3) *bustled alng in midfield, effrt o'r 2 fs out, nvr able to chal.* ....(15 to 2 op 6 to 1 tchd 8 to 1) 8
3863* FINAL FRONTIER (Ire) [74] 3-9-5 T Quinn (2) *chsd ldg half dozen till fdd und pres o'r 2 fs out*........(13 to 2 jt-fav op 5 to 1 tchd 7 to 1) 9
1674⁵ BACKSTABBER [53] 3-7-12 J Lowe (16) *chsd alng to go pace, nvr able to rch ldrs*........(20 to 1) 10
4172 HIGHLAND MAGIC (Ire) [77] 5-9-11 M Roberts (6) *sluggish strt, outpcd thrght*.....(15 to 2 op 7 to 1 tchd 8 to 1) 11
3957⁸ SILKY SIREN [72] 4-9-6 Pat Eddery (15) *struggling to keep in tch hfwy, nvr a factor*........(12 to 1 op 10 to 1) 12
4355* SECOND CHANCE (Ire) [70] 3-9-1 W Newnes (12) *chsd ldrs, feeling pace hfwy, fdd 2 fs out*.....(12 to 1 op 10 to 1) 13
2424* HEART BROKEN [67] 3-8-12 K Fallon (7) *settled midfield, drvn alng hfwy, sn outpcd*........(16 to 1 op 12 to 1) 14
4362⁵ AVENUE FOCH (Ire) [75] 4-9-9 M Wigham (11) *last and drvn alng, nvr a factor*........(25 to 1) 15
4155⁶ CHUMMY'S SAGA [70] 3-9-1 D Holland (5) *trkd ldg trio, struggling to hold pl hfwy, sn lost tch.* ....(14 to 1 op 12 to 1) 16
Dist: ½l, 8l, 2½l, hd, 2l, 2l, 1½l, ¾l, 8l, 7l. 1m 45.32s. a 13.32s (16 Ran).
SR: 52/39/29/13/6/-/ (A K Collins), J W Watts

4515 Heswall Conditions Stakes Class D (3-y-o and up) £4,175 1½m 66yds.. (4:05)

3937* BALLET PRINCE (Ire) 3-8-13 W R Swinburn (6) *confidently rdn, nosed ahead o'r 4 fs out, brght wide to go clr strt, easily*........(3 to 1 tchd 7 to 2) 1
3477⁷ INSTANT AFFAIR (USA) 3-8-8 T Quinn (5) *trkd ldg trio, drvn up to join wnr 3 fs out, outpcd fnl furlong.* ....(7 to 2 op 11 to 4) 2
4328² MESLEH 6-9-5 M Roberts (4) *nvr far away, drw level aftr a m, rdn and outpcd appr fnl furlong.* ....(11 to 10 fav op Evens tchd 6 to 5) 3
4420 GRANACHE (Ire) 4-8-9 (7*) R Painter (2) *last and niggled alng hfwy, styd on grimly last 2 fs, no imprsn.* ....(33 to 1 tchd 50 to 1) 4
1901* GRAEGOS (Ire) 3-8-13 W Ryan (1) *made most till hdd o'r 4 fs out, sn tld off*........(6 to 1 tchd 13 to 2) 5
4191 JARIN ROSE (Ire) 3-7-13 (5*) J Tate (3) *chsd ldg quartet, struggling last 5 fs, tld off.* ....(66 to 1 op 50 to 1 tchd 100 to 1) 6
Dist: 7l, 7l, 8l, dist, 15l. 3m 1.70s. a 24.90s (6 Ran).
SR: 22/3/-/ (Lord Weinstock), M R Stoute

4516 Beeston Castle Nursery Class D (2-y-o) £5,348 6f 18yds........... (4:35)

4163⁴ PALACEGATE JO (Ire) [60] 7-11 L Charnock (4) *al frnt rnk, drvn ahead o'r 2 fs out, kpt on wl fnl furlong.* (12 to 1) 1
4436 CYARNA QUINN (Ire) [72] (v) 8-2 (7*) R Painter (7) *trkd ldg 5, ev ch and drvn alng last 2 fs, kpt on same pace.* ....(25 to 1 op 20 to 1) 2
4437² RANKAIDADE [66] 7-12 (5*) A Garth (12) *al hndy, ev ch and rdn 2 fs out, one pace*........(10 to 1 op 8 to 1) 3
4349² SHARP FALCON (Ire) [65] 7-13 (3*) B Doyle (8) *patiently rdn, steady hdwy on ins o'r 2 fs out, fnshd strly.* ....(11 to 1 op 7 to 1) 4
4097³ SISTER SUSAN [64] 8-1 G Duffield (9) *pushed up frm off the pace o'r 2 fs out, kpt on, not pace of ldrs.* ....(11 to 1 op 8 to 1) 5
4193⁵ ORIENTAL AIR (Ire) [61] 7-12 Dale Gibson (3) *settled midfield, effrt and drvn alng long last 2 fs, kpt on same pace*........(8 to 1 op 14 to 1) 6
4144⁷ ROYALE FIGURINE (Ire) [75] 8-12 W R Swinburn (2) *tried to make all, hdd o'r 2 fs out, no extr*...(13 to 2 op 6 to 1) 7
4272⁵ MY GALLERY (Ire) [69] (bl) 8-1 (5*) D Wright (13) *al pressing ldrs, feeling pace o'r 2 fs out, fdd.* ....(6 to 1 fav tchd 13 to 2) 8
4375⁶ LEGATEE [80] 9-3 M Birch (6) *co'red up beh ldg bunch, improved hfwy, nvr able to chal*...(25 to 1 op 20 to 1) 9
4436 DOCKYARD DORA [59] (bl) 7-10 G Bardwell (14) *sluggish strt, chsd alng thrght, nvr nr to chal.* ....(25 to 1 op 20 to 1) 10
4165² PRIMA SILK [84] 9-2 (5*) P McCabe (11) *chsd ldg bunch, hrd at work hfwy, no imprsn*.....(14 to 1 op 12 to 1) 11
4051² MICHELLISA [66] 8-3 W Carson (15) *broke wl, struggling in midfield hfwy, sn btn*........(12 to 1) 12
3711* GOOD FETCH [68] 8-5 T Quinn (5) *chsd ldg 6, struggling to hold pl o'r 2 fs out, fdd.* (8 to 1 op 7 to 1 tchd 9 to 1) 13
4251 YAWARA [70] 8-7 M Roberts (1) *pressed ldg pair for o'r 4 fs, sn btn*........(11 to 1 op 10 to 1 tchd 12 to 1) 14
4225⁸ DAILY STAR [71] 8-8 J Carroll (10) *pressed ldg quartet till fdd o'r 2 fs out*........(16 to 1) 15
Dist: 2½l, 3½l, 1l, 1l, 1½l, ¾l, 2½l, ¾l, 12l, 2½l. 1m 24.50s. a 11.00s (15 Ran).

SR: 31/33/13/8/3/-/5/-/-/ (Palacegate Corporation Ltd), J Berry

MAISONS-LAFFITTE (FR) (heavy)
Thursday October 21st
Going Correction: PLUS 0.55 sec. per fur.

4517 Prix Phil Drake (Listed) (4-y-o and up) £14,337 1m.................. (2:50)

BORAGE (Fr) 5-8-11 D Boeuf,...................................... 1
4219[8] HOMME DE LOI (Ire) 4-8-11 T Jarnet,.................... 2
4325[3] SIGNORETTO (Fr) 6-8-11 G Guignard,...................... 3
3618[5] BALLINAMALLARD (USA) 4-8-8 C Asmussen,............ 4
4076[9] QUARTANNIER (Fr) 4-8-11 O Peslier,........................ 5
PREMONITORY DREAM (Can) 4-8-11 F Sanchez,........... 6
MOGILNY (USA) 4-8-11 M Boutin,..................................... 7
Dist: 1½l, 2½l, ¾l, sht-hd, 3l, 4l. 1m 41.60s. a 6.90s (7 Ran).
SR: 60/55/47/42/44/35/23/ (F Sabban), G Lellouche

NEWBURY (good to soft)
Thursday October 21st
Going Correction: PLUS 0.70 sec. per fur. (races 1,4,6), PLUS 0.60 (2,3,5,7,8)

4518 Vodafone British And Northern Racing Schools Apprentice Handicap Class F (0-80 3-y-o and up) £3,346 7f.... (2:05)

4470 DUCKEY FUZZ [61] 5-8-12 Michael Denaro (24) *hld up in tch, hdwy o'r 2 fs out, led appr last, ran on wl.* ....(7 to 1 op 8 to 1 tchd 6 to 1) 1
4024 TEANARCO (Ire) [66] 5-9-3 D Harrison (15) *wtd wth, hdwy o'r 2 fs out, ev ch entering last, ran on.* .... (10 to 1 op 8 to 1) 2
1876[6] BUDDY'S FRIEND (Ire) [55] 5-8-3[1] (4*) Sarah Thompson (10) *prmnt, outpcd appr last, rallied and ran on wl.* ....(20 to 1) 3
4131 CHARMED KNAVE [62] 8-8-13 P Bowe (25) *led aftr 2 fs till appr last, no extr fnl 100 yards*...............(20 to 1) 4
2940 SPANISH LOVE [42] 7-7-3 (4*) M Baird (5) *mid-div, hdwy 2 fs out, fnshd wl*.......................(33 to 1 op 25 to 1) 5
4038 GREAT HALL [70] 4-9-3 (4*) D Griffiths (13) *outpcd early, ran on ins fnl 2 fs*.................(12 to 1 op 10 to 1) 6
3492a YOUNG DUKE (Ire) [66] 5-8-13 (4*) A Martinez (7) *prmnt centre, one pace appr fnl furlong*.............(50 to 1) 7
3837[5] HELIOS [71] 5-9-4 (4*) S McCarthy (19) *rear, ran on ins fnl 2 fs*.............................. (20 to 1 op 16 to 1) 8
4458* CHAMPAGNE GRANDY [71] 3-9-5 (6ex) R Painter (2) *in tch on outsd, rdn 2 fs out, one pace aftr.* .... (100 to 30 fav op 7 to 2 tchd 9 to 2) 9
4019 TAKENHALL [52] 8-8-0[1] (4*) A Lakeman (6) *chsd ldrs, no hdwy fnl 2 fs*..................(16 to 1 tchd 20 to 1) 10
3739[5] BELLSABANGING [74] 3-9-8 Stephen Davies (21) *al rear.* .... (20 to 1 op 14 to 1) 11
4481[6] HERETICAL MISS [45] (bl) 3-7-0 (7*) Rhona Gent (4) *prmnt on outsd till wknd wl o'r one furlong out.* .... (33 to 1 op 25 to 1 tchd 40 to 1) 12
3948 HARVEST ROSE [60] 4-8-11 Claire Balding (22) *nvr nr to chal*.............................. (33 to 1 op 20 to 1) 13
3624[7] FAIRY STORY (Ire) [79] 3-9-13 J Marshall (18) *prmnt till wknd o'r 2 fs out*.................(20 to 1 op 16 to 1) 14
4393 GREEN DOLLAR [75] 10-9-12 S Drowne (3) *in tch on outsd 4 fs*.............................. (33 to 1 op 25 to 1) 15+
3957 PRAIRIE GROVE [69] 3-9-3 Mark Denaro (16) *al beh.* ....(14 to 1 tchd 16 to 1) 15+
2509[2] SYLVAN (Ire) [66] 4-8-13 (4*) Sally Radford-Howes (9) *mid-div, lost tch 2 fs out*..............................(12 to 1) 17
3988 BALLYHAYS (Ire) [48] 4-7-13 L Carter (17) *al beh.* .... (20 to 1 op 12 to 1) 18
4181[9] GRAN SENORUM (USA) [69] 3-9-3 D Meredith (8) *in tch till wknd hfwy*.........(16 to 1 op 14 to 1 tchd 20 to 1) 19
3450 CITY ROCKET [72] 3-9-6 S Mulvey (20) *outpcd*....(20 to 1) 20
4270 WALNUT BURL (Ire) [51] (v) 3-7-9 (4*) Iona Wands (12) *slwly away, al beh*..........................(25 to 1 op 20 to 1) 21
4007[9] CHAMPAGNE 'N ROSES [60] (bl) 3-8-8 A Garth (11) *led 2 fs, wknd o'r two out, eased*..........(20 to 1 op 16 to 1) 22
3830* UNIFICATION (Ire) [45] 4-7-6 (4*) D Toole (1) *slwly away, rcd alone far side, eased whn btn wl o'r one furlong out, tld off*...................(10 to 1 tchd 8 to 1 and 11 to 1) 23
Dist: ½l, nk, 2½l, ½l, 1½l, nk, hd, ¾l, hd, 2½l. 1m 32.41s. a 8.31s (23 Ran).
SR: 47/50/38/37/15/38/33/37/32/ (Mrs W M Faletti), R M Flower

4519 Vodafone Group Handicap Class C (0-90 3-y-o and up) £4,980 2m.. (2:40)

3690[3] MONARDA [66] 6-8-11 T Quinn (6) *hld up, hdwy o'r 3 fs out, short of room and swtchd rght one and a half out, styd on to ld wl ins last*............(5 to 1 tchd 6 to 1) 1
4466 ENCORE UNE FOIS (Ire) [76] 4-9-7 M Roberts (1) *wtd wth in tch, rdn 3 fs out, led one and a half out till wl ins last.* ....(4 to 1 op 7 to 2 tchd 9 to 2) 2
4466 SWORD MASTER [71] 4-9-2 M Wigham (4) *sn tracking ldr, rdn to ld 2 and a half fs out, hdd one and a half out, kpt on one pace*...................(8 to 1 tchd 9 to 1) 3
4064[2] BAGALINO (USA) [84] 3-9-5 Pat Eddery (5) *led to 2 and a half fs out, rdn entering last, sn btn, eased.* ....(5 to 4 fav tchd 6 to 4) 4
IVOR'S FLUTTER [79] 4-9-10 J Williams (2) *hld up, lost tch sn aftr hfwy, tld off*..............(8 to 1 tchd 10 to 1) 5
4267 ECU DE FRANCE (Ire) [80] 3-9-1 W Carson (3) *trkd ldrs till wknd 4 fs out, tld off.* (12 to 1 op 10 to 1 tchd 14 to 1) 6
Dist: 1l, 3l, 5l, 25l, 12l. 3m 46.86s. a 20.86s (6 Ran).
(Fahd Salman), P F I Cole

4520 Vodafone Horris Hill Stakes Class A (Group 3) (2-y-o) £25,376 7f 64yds ....(3:10)

4255* TATAMI (USA) 8-12 M Roberts (2) *wtd wth, rdn o'r 2 fs out, styd on to ld cl hme*..... (4 to 1 op 3 to 1 tchd 9 to 2) 1
4252* THE DEEP (Ire) 8-12 D Holland (4) *wtd wth, hdwy hfwy, led 2 fs out, clr entering last, strd shortened, hdd cl hme*..................................(4 to 1 op 5 to 2) 2
4255[2] ERHAAB (USA) 8-12 W Carson (8) *trkd ldr, led briefly o'r 2 fs out, styd on one pace.* (4 to 1 op 7 to 2 tchd 5 to 1) 3
3705* MIGHTY FORUM 8-12 J Williams (7) *steadied strt, rstrained in rear, ran on ins fnl furlong, nvr nrr.* .... (10 to 1 op 16 to 1) 4
4255[3] BLUEGRASS PRINCE (Ire) 8-12 J Reid (1) *led till rdn and hdd o'r 2 fs out, wknd ins last*...............(20 to 1) 5
4299* RAFFERTY'S RULES (Ire) 8-12 K Fallon (3) *al beh, rdn o'r 2 fs out, nvr dngrs*...............(3 to 1 fav tchd 4 to 1) 6
3803* STRAIGHT ARROW 9-1 Pat Eddery (6) *pld hrd in mid-div, wknd o'r 2 fs out*....................(10 to 1 tchd 12 to 1) 7
1565* SERIOUS OPTION (Ire) 8-12 T Quinn (5) *trkd ldrs, wknd quickly wl o'r one furlong out, tld off.* .... (12 to 1 op 14 to 1) 8
Dist: Sht-hd, 2½l, 1½l, ¾l, 1½l, 6l, 10l. 1m 35.63s. a 8.33s (8 Ran).
SR: 38/37/29/24/22/17/2/-/ (Sheikh Mohammed), L M Cumani

4521 Newbury Breeders Cup Gala Evening Rated Class B Handicap (0-110 3-y-o and up) £7,811 6f 8yds..........(3:40)

4464 BRANSTON ABBY (Ire) [104] 4-9-7 M Roberts (5) *trkd ldrs, short of room o'r one furlong out, squeezed through to ld wl ins last*..........(13 to 2 op 6 to 1 tchd 7 to 1) 1
4415 ECHO-LOGICAL [90] 4-8-7 W Ryan (6) *hld up rear, hdwy o'r 2 fs out, ev ch one out, no extr wl ins last.* .... (12 to 1 op 10 to 1 tchd 14 to 1) 2
4373[4] NEW CAPRICORN (USA) [90] 3-8-5 Pat Eddery (4) *prmnt, led 2 fs out till wl ins last, no extr*...........(6 to 1 jt-fav op 5 to 1 tchd 13 to 2) 3
4170[5] LOOK WHO'S HERE (Ire) [103] 3-9-4 T Quinn (13) *hld up, hdwy o'r 2 fs out, ran on ins last.* ....(6 to 1 jt-fav op 5 to 1) 4
4465 BOLD LEZ [92] 6-8-9 B Raymond (2) *hld up in tch, rdn o'r one furlong out, kpt on ins last*.....(8 to 1 op 7 to 1) 5
4393 PALACEGATE TOUCH [90] (bl) 3-7-12 (7*) P Roberts (8) *led to 2 fs out, wknd ins last*...........(10 to 1 tchd 11 to 1) 6
4216[3] LORD OLIVIER (Ire) [92] 3-8-7 M Tebbutt (12) *outpcd early, effrt hfwy, one pace ins fnl 2 fs*.............. (14 to 1) 7
4465[2] CRADLE DAYS [90] 4-8-7 J Reid (3) *prmnt till wknd appr fnl furlong*...........(7 to 1 op 6 to 1 tchd 15 to 2) 8
4455 ANSELLMAN [90] 3-7-13[1] (7*) Mark Denaro (1) *speed till wknd wl o'r one furlong out*................. (33 to 1) 9
4465[5] MASSIBA (Ire) [92] 4-8-9 J Williams (7) *chsd ldrs till wknd one and a half fs out*...............(8 to 1 op 7 to 1) 10
4347[3] MASTER OF PASSION [90] 4-8-7 W Newnes (9) *in tch till rdn o'r 2 fs out, sn beh*........... (16 to 1 op 14 to 1) 11
4393 HOW'S YER FATHER [90] 7-8-7 A McGlone (11) *outpcd early, effrt hfwy, eased whn btn.* (12 to 1 op 10 to 1) 12
4465 SPANIARDS CLOSE [100] (v) 5-9-3 L Dettori (10) *in tch to hfwy, sn btn, eased, tld off*.................... (14 to 1) 13
Dist: 1½l, ½l, ½l, hd, 3l, ½l, ¾l, hd, ¾l, 2l. 1m 18.25s. a 6.55s (13 Ran).
SR: 60/40/36/47/37/21/21/18/15/ (J David Abell), M Johnston

4522 PCL Handicap Class C (0-90 3-y-o and up) £6,027 1¼m 6yds..........(4:10)

4300 GOOGLY [72] 4-9-4 J Reid (1) *hld up, hdwy whn short of room and swtchd lft 2 fs out, led wl ins last, sn clr.* .... (9 to 1 op 10 to 1 tchd 11 to 1) 1
4300 EMBANKMENT (Ire) [87] 3-10-0 Pat Eddery (5) *mid-div, hdwy to ld 2 fs out, rdn and hdd ins last.* ....(10 to 1 tchd 12 to 1) 2
4364[8] WASSL THIS THEN (Ire) [60] 4-8-6 R Price (8) *hld up in tch, rdn and ev ch 2 fs out, kpt on one pace ins last.* .... (14 to 1 op 12 to 1) 3
3786[5] NESSUN DORMA [77] 3-9-4 M Hills (13) *hld up, hdwy 3 fs out, ev ch appr last, no extr*......(8 to 1 tchd 10 to 1) 4
3883[2] WAKIL (Ire) [70] 4-9-2 N Carlisle (6) *prmnt, ev ch till one pace ins fnl 2 fs*..... (11 to 1 op 10 to 1 tchd 12 to 1) 5
4431* CHUMMY'S PAL (USA) [66] 3-8-7 D Holland (4) *hld up, hdwy 3 fs out, one pace appr last*............. (10 to 1) 6
4028 SAINT CIEL (USA) [63] 5-8-9 A Clark (7) *mid-div, ran on one pace fnl 2 fs*....(12 to 1 op 14 to 1 tchd 16 to 1) 7
4274[2] AMERICAN SWINGER (USA) [84] 3-9-11 Paul Eddery (15) *hld up in mid-div, rdn o'r 2 fs out, wknd entering last.* ....(6 to 1 fav tchd 13 to 2) 8

TUDOR ISLAND [60] 4-8-6 M Roberts (10) *trkd ldr, led 4 fs out till o'r 2 out, wknd*.......................(20 to 1) 9
4152^{6} SON OF SHARP SHOT (Ire) [74] 3-9-1 W Ryan (9) *mid-div, lost tch o'r 2 fs out*..............(12 to 1 op 10 to 1) 10
4254^{6} LADY LACEY [59] 6-8-5 J Williams (3) *hld up rear, nvr nr to chal*.................(11 to 1 op 10 to 1 tchd 12 to 1) 11
4320^{3} WEAVER BIRD [78] 3-9-5 W Newnes (12) *al rear*. ....(7 to 1 op 6 to 1 tchd 15 to 2) 12
4247 MR TATE (Ire) [67] 4-8-13 T Quinn (14) *chsd ldrs, rdn to ld briefly o'r 2 fs out, wknd quickly*. (12 to 1 op 10 to 1) 13
1483^{5} DYAB (USA) [78] 3-9-5 W Carson (16) *led to 4 fs out, wknd quickly o'r 2 out, eased*.......................(16 to 1) 14
4019 DOUBLE ECHO (Ire) [65] 5-8-11 L Dettori (11) *chsd ldrs till wknd quickly o'r 2 fs out*. ....(12 to 1 op 16 to 1 tchd 20 to 1) 15

Dist: 3½l, 1l, 2l, nk, 1½l, 3½l, ½l, 4l, 2½l, 2l. 2m 13.79s. a 10.79s (15 Ran).
SR: 56/59/35/43/40/28/23/38/11/ (A G Lansley), W G R Wightman

4523 EBF Theale Maiden Stakes Class D (2-y-o) £5,439 6f 8yds............. (4:40)

4263^{2} CAJUN CADET 9-0 Pat Eddery (15) *mid-div, pushed alng hfwy, led wl o'r one furlong out, rdn, all out*. ....(15 to 2 op 5 to 1 tchd 8 to 1) 1
MOON MISTRESS 8-9 M Roberts (9) *hld up, hdwy 2 fs out, ran on strly ins last, jst fld*......... (14 to 1 op 7 to 1) 2
4276^{7} LATTAM (USA) 9-0 W Carson (4) *stumbled strt, settled mid-div, hdwy 2 fs out, ran on, nvr nrr*...(9 to 1 op 6 to 1) 3
CASHEW 8-9 R Perham (23) *hld up, hdwy o'r 2 fs out, ran on one pace ins last*.............. (66 to 1 op 33 to 1) 4
4440^{4} KALKABRINO (USA) 9-0 J Reid (5) *prmnt, led briefly 2 fs out, rdn and no extr*........... (6 to 4 on op 11 to 10) 5
3738 PERICARDIA 8-9 L Dettori (13) *mid-div, kpt on ins fnl 2 fs, nvr dngrs*............(10 to 1 op 12 to 1 tchd 14 to 1) 6
HUMBERT'S LANDING (Ire) 9-0 T Quinn (1) *frnt rnk, ev ch o'r 2 fs out, wknd appr last*.......(16 to 1 op 10 to 1) 7
4350^{8} HI KIKI 8-9 A Tucker (7) *chsd ldrs, one pace fnl 2 fs*. ....(33 to 1) 8
4446^{9} GIGGLESWICK GIRL 8-9 M Hills (19) *frnt rnk till wknd wl o'r one furlong out*....(12 to 1 op 8 to 1 tchd 14 to 1) 9
KEYS OF SILCA 9-0 Paul Eddery (2) *al mid-div*. ....(20 to 1 op 16 to 1) 10
4154^{4} ALL THE JOYS 8-9 S Whitworth (11) *prmnt 4 fs*. ....(66 to 1 op 33 to 1) 11
JULIA DOMNA 8-9 W Ryan (6) *nvr on terms*. ....(66 to 1 op 33 to 1) 12
4210 MINNIE NORTH 8-4 (5*) S Drowne (10) *nvr on terms*. ....(66 to 1 op 33 to 1) 13
3941^{6} EBONY BLAZE 9-0 B Raymond (14) *led to 2 fs out, wknd quickly*...................(33 to 1 op 16 to 1) 14
4339^{9} BO KNOWS NIGEL (Ire) 9-0 B Rouse (16) *al rear*. ....(40 to 1 op 33 to 1 tchd 66 to 1) 15
PERFECT BRAVE 9-0 J Williams (21) *al beh*. ....(20 to 1 op 16 to 1) 16
MAGIC JUNCTION (USA) 9-0 D Harrison (12) *al rear*. ....(20 to 1 op 16 to 1) 17
4419 SPORTING SCRIPT (Ire) 9-0 R Price (22) *al beh*. ....(66 to 1 op 33 to 1) 18
4263^{7} BOLD-MAX 8-7 (7*) Mark Denaro (8) *speed to hfwy*. ....(66 to 1 op 33 to 1) 19
OGGI 9-0 D Holland (20) *speed to hfwy*. ....(66 to 1 op 33 to 1) 20
DOZENS DIVINE 9-0 A Clark (17) *outpcd, tld off*. ....(66 to 1 op 33 to 1) 21

Dist: Sht-hd, 3l, 1l, ½l, 3l, 1½l, nk, 1½l, 2l, 2l. 1m 19.10s. a 7.40s (21 Ran).
SR: 36/30/23/14/17/-/ (Michael Pescod), R Charlton

4524 Enborne Maiden Stakes Class D (Div I) (3-y-o) £3,817 1¼m 6yds...... (5:10)

4391^{2} FOX SPARROW 9-0 S Raymont (12) *mid-div, hdwy frm 4 fs out, led one out, styd on*. ....(Evens fav op 5 to 4 tchd 11 to 8) 1
4209 BUNDERBURG (USA) 9-0 A Clark (5) *led till rdn and hdd one furlong out, one pace*......... (20 to 1 op 16 to 1) 2
4155^{2} DILI (USA) 8-9 S Whitworth (3) *mid-div, styd on one pace fnl 3 fs*.................(5 to 2 op 6 to 4 tchd 11 to 4) 3
4125^{3} LADY SABINA 8-9 M Wigham (6) *pld hrd, wnt second o'r 3 fs out, rdn and wknd ins last, eased and lost 3rd on line*...............................(20 to 1 op 16 to 1) 4
CASCASSI (USA) 8-9 C Nutter (4) *hld up rear, hdwy 3 fs out, rdn and wknd wl o'r one out*....(8 to 1 op 5 to 1) 5
1344 SIR KRISPIN 9-0 A Tucker (2) *nvr nr to chal*. ....(50 to 1 op 33 to 1) 6
515^{8} LATHERON (Ire) 9-0 R Perham (10) *al beh*. ....(16 to 1 op 10 to 1 tchd 20 to 1) 7
1997^{5} TIGHT FIST (Ire) 9-0 S Dawson (9) *prmnt till wknd wl o'r 3 fs out, tld off*........ (11 to 1 op 20 to 1 tchd 10 to 1) 8
4110 CUCKMERE VENTURE 8-9 T Rogers (7) *pld hrd, trkd ldr, rdn and wknd o'r 3 fs out, tld off*. (50 to 1 op 33 to 1) 9
4088 GENERAL BUNCHING 9-0 R Price (13) *al beh, tld off*. ....(50 to 1 op 33 to 1) 10
3693 SHARP GEM 8-9 B Crossley (11) *slwly away, al rear, tld off*..................................(50 to 1 op 33 to 1) 11

Dist: 3l, 2l, sht-hd, 5l, 8l, ¾l, 10l, 10l, 5l, 5l. 2m 17.38s. a 14.38s (11 Ran).
SR: 16/10/1/-/-/-/ (Miss M Sheriffe), R Charlton

4525 Enborne Maiden Stakes Class D (Div II) (3-y-o) £3,817 1¼m 6yds..... (5:40)

MINATINA (Ire) 8-9 B Crossley (3) *hld up, hdwy o'r 2 fs out, led one out, ran on*.....(6 to 1 op 4 to 1 tchd 13 to 2) 1
515^{9} PALACE OF GOLD 9-0 A Clark (8) *pld hrd, led, quickened 4 fs out, rdn and hdd one out, edgd lft, no extr*. ....(20 to 1 tchd 16 to 1) 2
FAIR SHIRLEY (Ire) 8-9 S Whitworth (7) *trkd ldr, outpcd o'r one furlong out, short of room and swtchd rght ins last, kpt on*.................... (7 to 1 op 5 to 1) 3
4322^{3} TOUJOURS RIVIERA 9-0 M Wigham (4) *wtd wth in tch, rdn and wnt lft one furlong out, no extr*.........(3 to 1 jt-fav op 5 to 2 tchd 7 to 2) 4
3682^{6} RYNAVEY 8-9 M Tebbutt (2) *prmnt, one pace fnl 2 fs*. ....(10 to 1 op 12 to 1 tchd 14 to 1) 5
4209^{7} PRINCESS SIOUX 8-9 R Price (1) *al mid-div, one pace fnl 3 fs*...............................(16 to 1 op 10 to 1) 6
HYPHENATE (USA) 9-0 C Dwyer (11) *mid-div, lost tch fnl 3 fs*...... (3 to 1 jt-fav tchd 5 to 2 and 100 to 30) 7
4322^{5} WATER SKIER 9-0 R Street (10) *pld hrd, al rear*. .... (9 to 2 tchd 5 to 1 and 4 to 1) 8
4030^{6} KATIE'S KID 9-0 T Rogers (6) *al beh*..............(33 to 1) 9
4209 EUSTATIA 8-9 S Raymont (5) *al beh*. (33 to 1 tchd 40 to 1) 10
4115 SHEFFORD 8-9 A Tucker (13) *chsd ldrs till wknd 3 fs out*. ....(33 to 1 tchd 40 to 1) 11
4355 TIMOTHY CASEY 9-0 V Smith (12) *in tch till wknd 4 fs out*. ....(20 to 1 op 16 to 1 tchd 33 to 1) 12
GREENHILL WONDER 8-9 R Perham (9) *slwly away, al beh, tld off*......................(33 to 1 tchd 50 to 1) 13

Dist: 1½l, 2½l, 1l, nk, 3½l, 12l, 5l, 1l, ¾l, ½l. 2m 18.44s. a 15.44s (13 Ran).
SR: 1/3/-/-/-/-/ (K Abdulla), J H M Gosden

PONTEFRACT (good to soft) Thursday October 21st

Going Correction: PLUS 0.40 sec. per fur.

4526 Brockadale Maiden Auction Stakes Class F (Div I) (2-y-o) £2,905 6f.. (1:55)

4434^{2} FRISKY MISS (Ire) 8-9 J Carroll (5) *broke smartly, made all, hrd pressed o'r one furlong out, kpt on strly*. .... (11 to 2 op 6 to 1 tchd 7 to 1) 1
4303^{5} WALSHAM WHISPER (Ire) 8-9 P Robinson (12) *missed break, chsd alng and a lot to do hfwy, ran on strly fnl furlong, jst fld*......................(6 to 1 tchd 5 to 1) 2
3972^{4} KID ORY 9-0 Dale Gibson (13) *nvr far away, ev ch and rdn last 2 fs, kpt on wl und pres*....... (14 to 1 op 12 to 1) 3
4316^{7} LINCOLN TREASURE (Ire) 8-9 (5*) D McCabe (6) *al pressing ldrs, hrd at work 2 fs out, rallied ins fnl furlong*. .... (33 to 1 op 25 to 1) 4
4276 TU OPES 9-0 N Adams (11) *sluggish strt, bustled alng to improve last 2 fs, ran on wl finish*.............(20 to 1) 5
4339^{2} LEVIATHAN MYSTERY 9-0 A Munro (3) *al hndy, ev ch whn hng lft o'r one furlong out, rdn and kpt on same pace*. ....(9 to 4 fav op 7 to 4) 6
4210^{7} BONNY MELODY 8-9 W R Swinburn (8) *trkd ldg 5, hrd at work 2 fs out, styd on finish*.......(6 to 1 op 11 to 2) 7
3362^{9} WINGS OF HORAGE (Ire) 9-0 R Cochrane (10) *chsd alng in midfield, no imprsn frm hfwy*.....(33 to 1 op 25 to 1) 8
4435^{6} TULU 8-6 (3*) S Maloney (15) *pushed alng in midfield, nvr able to rch chalg pos*............. (16 to 1 op 12 to 1) 9
4337^{5} ANTANANARIVO (Ire) 9-0 J Lowe (4) *gd speed in frnt rnk 4 fs, fdd*.................... (8 to 1 op 12 to 1) 10
4345^{4} BUSTLE'EM (Ire) 8-9 R Hills (14) *wl plcd on outsd for o'r 4 fs, sn btn*............................(10 to 1 op 8 to 1) 11
NEEDWOOD SWIFT 8-6 (3*) C Hodgson (1) *sluggish strt, al wl beh*...............................(33 to 1 op 25 to 1) 12
4361^{9} COME GO 8-9 G Duffield (2) *sluggish strt, drvn into midfield hfwy, sn lost tch*............(16 to 1 op 14 to 1) 13
4342 CORSAGE 9-0 M Birch (7) *sn outpcd and drvn alng, tld off*...............................(33 to 1 op 25 to 1) 14

Dist: ½l, ¾l, 1½l, nk, sht-hd, 3l, 8l, nk, hd, 2½l. 1m 20.20s. a 5.50s (14 Ran).
SR: 33/31/33/27/26/25/8/-/-/ (Mrs Margaret Sinanan), J Berry

4527 Brockadale Maiden Auction Stakes Class F (Div II) (2-y-o) £2,905 6f (2:25)

3760^{9} RAFTER-J 9-0 J Quinn (6) *chsd alng in midfield, gd hdwy o'r one furlong out, ran on to ld last strds*. ....(13 to 2 op 12 to 1 tchd 14 to 1 and 6 to 1) 1
4483^{2} GIGUE 8-9 C Rutter (15) *al wl plcd, led and quickened well o'r one furlong out, wnt clr, ct last strds*. ....(8 to 1 op 7 to 1) 2
4361^{4} MCGILLYCUDDY REEKS (Ire) 8-9 S Perks (13) *al hndy, feeling pace o'r one furlong out, kpt on und pres, no imprsn*......................... (9 to 2 jt-fav op 3 to 1) 3
3505^{5} THREE OF HEARTS 8-9 N Adams (2) *dashed up to join ldrs sn aftr strt, led after 2 fs till wl o'r one furlong out, fdd*. ....(10 to 1) 4
GROVE PRIMROSE (Ire) 8-9 P Robinson (12) *nvr far away, effrt and not much room entering fnl furlong, kpt on same pace*.........................(16 to 1 op 12 to 1) 5

3779 INDIAN SERENADE 9-0 G Duffield (8) *unruly in stalls, al chasing ldrs, hrd at work o'r 2 fs out, no imprsn.* ....(9 to 2 jt-fav op 7 to 2) 6
4437^3 CASUAL WATER (Ire) 9-0 M Birch (1) *steadied strt, shaken up and steady hdwy last 2 fs, nvr plcd to chal.* ....(6 to 1 op 5 to 1) 7
4326^9 PAVACINI 9-0 T Williams (10) *chsd alng in midfield, kpt on last 2 fs, no imprsn.* ....(50 to 1 op 33 to 1) 8
LITTLE BROWNIE 8-9 J Carroll (9) *sluggish strt, outpcd and wl beh till styd on fnl furlong.* ....(13 to 2 op 6 to 1 tchd 8 to 1) 9
4326^5 COURSE FISHING 9-0 A Mackay (7) *slight ld for 2 fs, styd hndy till fdd last two furlongs....* (16 to 1 op 14 to 1) 10
4316 REBECCAS SECRET (Ire) 9-0 J Lowe (4) *chsd alng in midfield, not pace of ldrs frm hfwy.* ....(50 to 1) 11
4220 CHELSEA LADY (Ire) 8-9 M Wood (5) *sn outpcd and drvn alng, nvr a factor.* ....(50 to 1 op 33 to 1) 12
MRS BIZZYBODY 8-9 A Munro (3) *al struggling, tld off frm hfwy.* ....(16 to 1 op 14 to 1) 13
4332^6 ANOTHER SOLOMON 8-9 (5*) K Rutter (11) *bolted one and a half fs gng to post, missed break, al tld off.* ....(25 to 1 op 20 to 1) 14

Dist: ½l, 6l, 5l, 1l, 1½l, 1½l, nk, 4l, ¾l, ¾l. 1m 20.80s. a 6.10s (14 Ran).

SR: 26/19/-/-/-/-/ (Tom Ford), Miss Jacqueline S Doyle

4528 Blackmires Claiming Stakes Class F (2-y-o) £3,248 6f................(3:00)

4358 STRAPPED 8-1 N Adams (17) *sluggish strt, last and wl outpcd aftr 2 fs, brght wide and rapid hdwy o'r one furlong out, led post.* ....(20 to 1 op 14 to 1) 1
3508^7 BET A PLAN (Ire) (bl) 7-12 F Norton (12) *al hndy, drvn ahead fnl furlong, rdn and ct post.* ....(14 to 1 op 12 to 1) 2
3554^6 PLAINSONG 8-7 N Connorton (5) *made most till hdd entering fnl furlong, kpt on same pace....* (7 to 1 op 8 to 1) 3
4163 NORTHERN STORM (Ire) 8-4 W Woods (10) *broke wl, feeling pace and lost grnd hfwy, rallied o'r one furlong out, kpt on.* ....(33 to 1 op 25 to 1) 4
4264^4 HADDIAH (bl) 8-2 A Munro (18) *shwd up wl on outsd, edgd lft o'r 2 fs out, rdn and not quicken appr fnl furlong.* ....(9 to 2 op 4 to 1 tchd 7 to 2) 5
4318^4 STEADFAST ELITE (Ire) 8-2 J Weaver (11) *nvr far away, hrd at work entering fnl furlong, no extr.* ....(7 to 2 fav op 5 to 1 tchd 11 to 2) 6
2917^5 CRUISING CHICK 7-7 (5*) Darren Moffatt (14) *bustled alng to go pace hfwy, styd on last 2 fs, nvr nrr.* ....(50 to 1 op 25 to 1) 7
4358 ELLARUTH (Ire) $7\text{-}12^6$ (7*) J Gotobed (8) *sluggish strt, imprvg on ins whn not much room inside fnl furlong, nvr nrr.* ....(25 to 1 op 14 to 1) 8
4342^5 LAUREL ROMEO (Ire) (bl) 8-5 J Carroll (3) *al pressing ldrs, hrd at work o'r 2 fs out, one pace...* (11 to 2 op 5 to 1) 9
4329 LITTLE HOOLIGAN (v) 8-3 C Rutter (9) *chsd alng in midfield, no imprsn last 2 fs.* ....(25 to 1 op 16 to 1) 10
4264^9 TUTU SIXTYSIX (v) 8-2 G Duffield (16) *wl plcd on outsd, bumped and checked o'r 2 fs out, nvr able to rcvr.* ....(8 to 1) 11
3686 ARIAN SPIRIT (Ire) 7-11 (5*) D McCabe (7) *bustled alng in midfield, no imprsn last 2 fs.....* (33 to 1 op 25 to 1) 12
4329 LEGAL TRAIN (bl) 8-2 J Lowe (2) *chsd alng beh ldg bunch, effrt o'r 2 fs out, not rch ldrs......* (14 to 1 op 12 to 1) 13
4500 QUEEN'S ADMIRAL 8-4 T Williams (1) *chsd ldrs, struggling to go pace o'r 2 fs out, nvr dngrs..* .(33 to 1 op 25 to 1) 14
4453 SECONDS AWAY 8-2 (3*) S Maloney (15) *bustled alng to keep up aftr 2 fs, nvr a threat.....* (20 to 1 op 12 to 1) 15
4165^9 PORTITE SOPHIE 7-8 (5*) D Wright (6) *broke wl to show gd speed in frnt rnk 4 fs, fdd.........* (50 to 1 op 25 to 1) 16
4264 FOXTOWNS GIRL 8-0 J Quinn (4) *chsd alng to go pace hfwy, nvr a factor.* ....(50 to 1 op 25 to 1) 17
SPACE-PERIL (Ire) $8\text{-}1^2$ P Robinson (13) *struggling to keep up hfwy, eased whn btn o'r one furlong out.* ....(12 to 1 op 7 to 1) 18

Dist: Hd, 2l, 2l, sht-hd, 1l, 1½l, ½l, 1½l, 1l, 1½l. 1m 20.40s. a 5.70s (18 Ran).

SR: 21/17/18/7/4/-/ (M J Watson), M R Channon

4529 Tote Silver Tankard Stakes Class A (Listed Race) (2-y-o) £13,190 1m 4yds ....(3:30)

4249^8 BARBAROJA 9-0 W R Swinburn (5) *dictated pace, quickened up o'r 3 fs out, styd on strly to go clr fnl furlong.* ....(3 to 1 op 5 to 2) 1
4015^5 THE FLYING PHANTOM 9-0 P Robinson (8) *rcd freely in frnt rnk, ev ch and pushed alng o'r 2 fs out, kpt on same pace.* ....(16 to 1) 2
3776^2 ALAFLAK (Ire) 9-0 R Hills (1) *trkd ldg 5, feeling pace and drvn alng o'r 3 fs out, rallied, fnshd strly.* ....(7 to 1 op 6 to 1 tchd 11 to 2) 3
4259* DARONNE 9-0 R Cochrane (3) *tucked away on ins, hrd at work o'r 3 fs out, rdn and btn 2 out.* ....(11 to 8 fav op 6 to 4 tchd 7 to 4 and 5 to 4) 4
4253* TWIN FALLS (Ire) 9-0 A Munro (6) *trkd ldg quartet, effrt and rdn o'r 2 fs out, no extr pace.* ....(3 to 1 op 5 to 2 tchd 7 to 2) 5
4249 FOURTH OF JUNE (USA) 8-11 B Doyle (7) *pressed ldg pair, struggling to hold pace o'r 2 fs out, sn btn.* ....(25 to 1 op 16 to 1) 6
4444^2 NORTHERN BAILIWICK (Ire) (bl) 8-11 G Duffield (2) *in tch, struggling to go pace hfwy, sn lost touch.* ....(33 to 1 op 25 to 1) 7
3698 VAYELLO (bl) 8-11 K Rutter (4) *missed break, al struggling, tld off frm hfwy.* ....(500 to 1) 8

Dist: 2l, hd, 3½l, 1l, 10l, 6l, 30l. 1m 48.20s. a 6.10s (8 Ran).

SR: 57/51/50/39/36/3/-/-/ (Marquesa de Moratalla), J G FitzGerald

4530 Bluff Cove Handicap Class E (0-70 3-y-o and up) £3,080 2m 1f 216yds.. (4:00)

4321* WORLD WITHOUT END (USA) [34] 4-8-7 J Quinn (8) *al wl plcd, led o'r 6 fs out, styd on gmely last 2 furlongs.* ....(11 to 8 fav op 5 to 4 tchd 6 to 4) 1
4321^4 AUTHORSHIP (USA) [45] 7-9-4 R Cochrane (6) *patiently rdn, improved to chal o'r 2 fs out, kpt on wl ins fnl furlong.* ....(8 to 1 op 7 to 1) 2
4321^5 MINGUS (USA) [37] 6-8-10 J Lowe (10) *steadied strt, patiently rdn, improved on ins to fitter o'r one furlong out, no extr towards finish.* ....(12 to 1) 3
4454^7 HELIOPSIS [44] 5-9-3 G Duffield (9) *nvr far away, rdn and ev ch last 3 fs, no extr ins last.......* (7 to 1 op 6 to 1) 4
4353^5 INTREPID LASS [43] 6-8-9 (7*) Antoinette Armes (1) *led till hdd o'r 6 fs out, rdn and outpcd appr strt, no imprsn.* ....(8 to 1 op 7 to 1) 5
2048^4 KOVALEVSKIA [33] 8-8-6 G Bardwell (2) *chsd ldg 5, struggling to keep up o'r 3 fs out, sn lost tch.* ....(12 to 1 tchd 14 to 1) 6
4321^3 DON'T CRY [27] 5-8-0 Kim Tinkler (5) *chsd ldrs to hfwy, struggling o'r 3 fs out, sn lost tch.* (12 to 1 op 10 to 1) 7
4102 GUESTWICK [63] 3-9-10 A Munro (7) *pressed ldg trio, ev ch and rdn o'r 3 fs out, wknd quickly...* (7 to 1 op 6 to 1) 8
DOVE GREY [30] 8-8-3 N Adams (4) *sluggish strt, beh and drvn alng half-way, nvr a factor.* ....(50 to 1) 9
3970 SATIN LAKE (USA) [30] (v) 6-8-3 A Mackay (3) *trkd ldg trio, struggling whn pace lifted o'r 4 fs out, sn lost tch.* ....(14 to 1 op 8 to 1 tchd 16 to 1) 10

Dist: ¾l, 2½l, 4l, 3l, 20l, hd, 12l, ½l, 1½l. 4m 16.00s. a 24.50s (10 Ran).

(Mrs Angela Norton), S G Norton

4531 Broomfield Nursery Class E (2-y-o) £3,782 1m 4yds................ (4:30)

4251^9 BE EXCITING (Ire) [73] 9-5 T Williams (6) *nvr far away, nosed ahead o'r one furlong out, ran on strly fnl furlong.* ....(16 to 1 op 12 to 1) 1
4418^2 MISTER BEAT [70] 9-2 W R Swinburn (14) *wth ldrs, led o'r 3 fs out till over one out, rallied, not quicken last 50 yards.* ....(7 to 1 jt-fav tchd 6 to 1) 2
4122^3 MEMORABLE [67] 8-13 P Robinson (16) *sn beh, drvn alng to improve on outsd last 3 fs, fnshd wl.* ....(9 to 1 op 7 to 1) 3
4215^5 BANG IN TROUBLE (Ire) [55] 8-1 Dale Gibson (12) *co'red up beh ldg bunch, weaved through last 2 fs, fnshd wl.* ....(12 to 1 tchd 14 to 1) 4
4236^9 GLENVALLY [60] 8-6 J Fortune (11) *chsd ldrs, effrt and bumped o'r 3 fs out, styd on fnl furlong.......* (25 to 1) 5
3819* MIDNIGHT LEGEND [75] 9-7 R Cochrane (22) *nvr far away, hrd at work o'r 2 fs out, no extr pace.* (9 to 1 op 7 to 1) 6
3597 SAWTID [67] 8-10 (3*) C Hodgson (17) *tucked away in midfield, shaken up to improve o'r 2 fs out, styd on finish.* ....(20 to 1) 7
4418 KOONOONA LADY [54] 8-0 N Adams (18) *beh and pushed alng, styd on wl last 2 fs, nvr nrr.* (25 to 1 op 20 to 1) 8
4444 NAWAFELL [70] 8-11 (5*) J Tate (21) *settled midfield, effrt and bustled alng 3 fs out, not pace of ldrs.* ....(12 to 1 op 10 to 1) 9
3865 HEATHYARDS CRUSADE (Ire) [57] 7-10 (7*) M Humphries (8) *broke wl to dispute ld for o'r 5 fs, fdd.* ....(33 to 1 op 25 to 1) 10
3997^4 CHANTRY BEATH [56] 8-2 J Fanning (20) *sluggish strt, swtchd lft to race on fence aftr a furlong, no imprsn last 3 fs.* ....(14 to 1) 11
4365^4 WINNING LINE [68] 9-0 M Birch (3) *co'red up on ins, effrt and drvn alng hfwy, no imprsn last 2 fs.* ....(10 to 1 tchd 12 to 1) 12
4342 WALWORTH LADY [53] 7-13 L Charnock (2) *chsd ldg bunch, feeling pace hfwy, no imprsn.........* (33 to 1) 13
4329 DYNAMIC DELUXE (USA) [72] 9-4 S O'Gorman (4) *chsd ldrs to hfwy, wknd quickly o'r 2 fs out.* (11 to 1 op 10 to 1) 14
3600^5 POTSCLOSE [67] 8-13 J Weaver (9) *broke wl to show gd speed in frnt rnk 5 fs, fdd.........* (20 to 1 op 16 to 1) 15
4349^8 DANIELLE HABIBI (Ire) [50] 7-10 J Quinn (19) *sluggish strt, nvr able to reco'r...* (25 to 1 tchd 33 to 1 and 20 to 1) 16
4266^7 SLASHER JACK (Ire) [74] 9-6 G Duffield (7) *drvn alng beh ldg bunch, nvr a threat.* ....(14 to 1) 17
2539^9 PARISIAN LOVER [60] 8-6 A Munro (10) *sluggish strt, drvn into midfield hfwy, btn o'r 2 fs out.* (20 to 1 op 16 to 1) 18
4215 DOUBLE SIXTEEN [55] 7-12 (3*) S Maloney (13) *settled midfield, struggling to go pace hfwy, nvr a threat.* ....(7 to 1 jt-fav op 10 to 1) 19
4427 TANFIRION CHIEF [60] 8-6 R P Elliott (15) *speed on outsd till wknd quickly o'r 2 fs out.* ....(50 to 1) 20

4033[9] FOOT TAPPER (Ire) [55] 8-1 F Norton (1) *chsd alng to keep up hfwy, sn btn*..............................(25 to 1) 21
4365[2] GLENLYON DUCHESS [60] 8-1 (5*) D Wright (5) *broke wl to ld till o'r 3 fs out, fdd*..............(12 to 1 op 10 to 1) 22
Dist: 1½l, 1l, sht-hd, 1½l, ¾l, 7l, ½l, 1½l, ½l, 3½l. 1m 49.70s. a 7.60s (22 Ran).
SR: 39/31/25/12/12/25/ (Stonethorn Stud Farms Limited), J L Dunlop

4532 Asta Hotel Barbados Handicap Class D (0-80 3-y-o and up) £5,049 5f.. (5:00)

4363 LOVE LEGEND [57] 8-8-5 A Munro (12) *rcd wide thrght, al hndy, rdn to ld fnl furlong, hld on grimly*.....(12 to 1) 1
4455[4] CHOIR PRACTICE [72] 6-9-6 C Rutter (14) *patiently rdn, weaved through frm midfield to draw level fnl furlong, jst hld*...............................(7 to 1 op 6 to 1) 2
4455 SADDLEHOME (USA) [61] 4-8-9 R Cochrane (18) *rcd wide thrght, nvr far away, ev ch o'r one furlong out, kpt on und pres*...............(9 to 1 op 12 to 1 tchd 8 to 1) 3
4487 VICTORIA HALL [64] 3-8-11 R Hills (8) *nvr far away, effrt and drvn alng o'r one furlong out, kpt on same pace.* ....(10 to 1) 4
4166 PALLIUM (Ire) [68] (v) 5-9-2 J Weaver (15) *al pressing ldrs, ev ch wl o'r one furlong out, styd on same pace.* ....(25 to 1) 5
4191[2] DESERT CHAMP (USA) [72] (bl) 4-9-6 W R Swinburn (9) *led or dsptd ld till hdd and no extr ins fnl furlong.* (7 to 1) 6
4487 NORDOORA (Ire) [53] 4-7-10 (5*) Darren Moffatt (10) *led or dsptd ld for o'r 3 fs, rdn and no extr*..........(33 to 1) 7
3955 WALK THE BEAT [74] 3-9-7 W Woods (2) *missed break, improved on ins last 2 fs, fnshd wl*............(16 to 1) 8
4487[7] SAVAHRA SOUND [62] 8-8-5[2] (7*) G Strange (1) *co'red up in midfield, effrt and rdn last 2 fs, no imprsn.* ....(14 to 1 op 12 to 1) 9+
4455* MAGIC PEARL [82] 3-9-8 (7*,7ex) S Knott (13) *al chasing ldrs, hrd at work o'r 2 fs out, kpt on same pace.* ....(11 to 2 fav op 4 to 1) 9+
3957 PANIKIN [75] 5-9-4 (5*) S Wynne (7) *struggling in rear to hfwy, styd on last 2 fs, nvr nrr*................(50 to 1) 11
4363 SONDERISE [64] 4-8-12 G Duffield (16) *pressed ldg bunch for o'r 3 fs, fdd*....................(20 to 1 op 16 to 1) 12
4455 DRUM SERGEANT [70] 6-9-4 N Connorton (4) *bustled alng in midfield, effrt o'r 2 fs out, no imprsn.* ....(12 to 1 tchd 14 to 1) 13
4393 DENSBEN [76] 9-9-10 P Robinson (17) *sluggish strt, chsd alng thrght, nvr dngrs*............(14 to 1 op 25 to 1) 14
4455 MILBANK CHALLENGER [62] 3-8-6 (3*) S Maloney (5) *chsd alng in midfield hfwy, nvr rchd chalg pos.* ....(12 to 1 tchd 14 to 1) 15
3877[8] LOCAL HEROINE [67] 3-9-0 J Carroll (11) *chsd ldrs, feeling pace o'r 2 fs out, fdd*..........................(16 to 1) 16
4180 BEAU VENTURE (USA) [75] (bl) 5-9-6 (3*) N Kennedy (3) *chsd ldg bunch for 3 fs, wknd quickly*..............(20 to 1) 17
Dist: Hd, 2l, 1l, sht-hd, ¾l, 1½l, nk, sht-hd, dd-ht, 3l. 1m 6.00s. a 4.80s (17 Ran).
SR: 35/49/30/28/32/33/8/27/15/ (George S Thompson), D W P Arbuthnot

4533 Pack Saddle Handicap Class E (0-70 3-y-o and up) £3,678 1¼m 6yds (5:30)

4101[2] SURREY DANCER [69] 5-9-7 (7*) S Copp (9) *patiently rdn, drvn through to ld entering fnl furlong, ran on strly.* ....(9 to 1 op 8 to 1) 1
4247[6] SANTANA LADY (Ire) [61] 4-9-1 (5*) D McCabe (4) *wth ldr, led wl o'r one furlong out till entering last, kpt on same pace*..............................(12 to 1 op 7 to 1) 2
3961[4] GROUND NUT (Ire) [62] 3-9-2 A Munro (6) *wtd wth, improved frm midfield to chal o'r 2 fs out, one pace fnl furlong*..........................(11 to 2 op 6 to 1) 3
4254[3] MYSILV [65] 3-9-5 P Robinson (11) *made most till hdd wl o'r one furlong out, rdn and one pace.* ....(8 to 1 op 5 to 1) 4
4470 MISTY GODDESS (Ire) [57] 5-8-11 (5*) K Rutter (17) *al pressing ldrs, styd on appr fnl furlong, nrst finish.* ....(20 to 1 op 14 to 1) 5
3831 GOLDEN TORQUE [58] 6-8-10 (7*) H Bastiman (18) *steadied strt, improved frm off the pace last 2 fs, fnshd wl.* ....(14 to 1 op 12 to 1 tchd 16 to 1) 6
3873[6] LEAR KING (USA) [64] 3-9-4 R Cochrane (16) *chsd ldg bunch, effrt and drvn alng o'r 2 fs out, kpt on same pace*...............................(14 to 1 op 12 to 1) 7
4391 EUROTWIST [62] 4-9-0 (7*) V Halliday (8) *settled off the pace, steady hdwy last 2 fs, nvr nrr*...........(33 to 1) 8
4101 ATHERTON GREEN (Ire) [65] 3-9-5 M Birch (2) *patiently rdn, improved on ins to fltter 2 fs out, ridden and no extr*..(20 to 1) 9
3873[9] STORM VENTURE (Ire) [68] 3-9-8 G Duffield (5) *chsd ldrs, hrd at work o'r 2 fs out, no imprsn*............(20 to 1) 10
4595a EL NIDO [60] 5-9-5 S Morris (15) *shwd up wl on outsd till fdd o'r 3 fs out*.................(7 to 2 fav op 12 to 1) 11
4254[2] MAHONG [57] 5-9-2 V Slattery (1) *nvr far away, feeling pace o'r 2 fs out, sn btn*............(10 to 1 op 8 to 1) 12
4213* IMPERIAL BID (Fr) [65] 5-9-10 N Connorton (3) *settled midfield, effrt and scrubbed alng o'r 2 fs out, nvr able to chal*..(14 to 1) 13
3783 FORTENSKY (USA) [70] 3-9-7 (3*) C Hodgson (10) *pressed ldrs, ev ch 3 fs out, fdd 2 out*.......(20 to 1 op 12 to 1) 14
4254* CASPIAN BELUGA [60] 5-9-5 J Quinn (7) *trkd ldg bunch, chsd alng 3 fs out, fdd.* (9 to 1 op 8 to 1 tchd 10 to 1) 15
3873[3] MITRAAS (USA) [68] (bl) 3-9-8 R Hills (13) *wth ldrs, hrd at work 3 fs out, sn btn*..........(12 to 1 op 10 to 1) 16
4133[7] NORTH ESK (USA) [60] 4-9-5 G Bardwell (12) *chsd alng in midfield hfwy, btn o'r 3 fs out*.....(16 to 1 op 10 to 1) 17
2598[3] QUARRELLING [66] 3-9-6 S Perks (14) *pressed ldrs till wknd rpdly o'r 4 fs out, tld off*.....(16 to 1 op 25 to 1) 18
4364[5] SONG OF SIXPENCE (USA) [62] 9-9-7 S O'Gorman (19) *chsd alng till pld up o'r 4 fs out, destroyed*.........(12 to 1) 0
Dist: 2½l, ½l, 2½l, 2l, 6l, 5l, nk, 6l, 2½l, 15l. 2m 19.00s. a 10.80s (19 Ran).
SR: 46/33/28/26/19/8/-/1/-/ (Laurel (Leisure) Limited), Mrs M Reveley

PUNCHESTOWN (IRE) (yielding)
Thursday October 21st

4534 Arthurstown Handicap (0-75 3-y-o and up) £2,760 7f 110yds............(2:30)

4408[5] BLUES COMPOSER (Ire) [-] 4-8-9 W J Supple (4)...(7 to 1) 1
4094[2] DARCY'S THATCHER [-] 9-9-5 (6*) J R Barry (5)....(8 to 1) 2
4057[7] NOBLE SAM (Ire) [-] 4-7-10 (4*) J J Behan (6).....(12 to 1) 3
4324[8] SOMERTON BOY (Ire) [-] 3-9-10 P Shanahan (12) ....(10 to 1) 4
2285 LHOTSE (Ire) [-] 3-9-0 (2*) P Carberry (1)..........(12 to 1) 5
4408 LUCKY PRINCE (Ire) [-] (bl) 3-9-3 (6*,7ex) D J O'Donohoe (18) ....(5 to 1) 6
4408[2] UNCLE BABY (Ire) [-] (bl) 5-7-5 (2*) D G O'Shea (9) ....(3 to 1 fav) 7
4001 BRACKLOON BOY (Ire) [-] 4-9-2 (4*) C Everard (17) (12 to 1) 8
4408[9] SUTTON CENTENARY (Ire) [-] 5-7-7[1] (4*) W J Smith (14) ....(10 to 1) 9
4370 LOVE OF ERIN (Ire) [-] (bl) 4-6-13 (8*) G M Moylan (3) ....(25 to 1) 10
3580 BONNIFER (Ire) [-] 4-8-9 (10*) A Ward (2).........(14 to 1) 11
4324[2] RAFFERTY'S INNER (Ire) [-] 3-9-1 S Craine (11).....(7 to 1) 12
EMPEROR GLEN (Ire) [-] 5-9-4 R Hughes (7).......(20 to 1) 13
1645[7] BELMARTIN [-] 7-9-4 (10*) A C O'Brien (8)..........(12 to 1) 14
3160[6] SALLUSTAR [-] (bl) 8-8-13 N G McCullagh (10).....(6 to 1) 15
4370[9] DAHAR'S LOVE (USA) [-] (bl) 4-7-9[1] Joanna Morgan (15) ....(10 to 1) 16
4162 PENNINE'S DAUGHTER [-] 3-9-0 (8*) G Coogan (13) ....(12 to 1) 17
3368[5] LADYS BID (Ire) [-] 3-8-0 J F Egan (16)...........(16 to 1) 18
Dist: 2l, ½l, 1½l, nk. 1m 41.70s. (18 Ran).
(Aidan Walsh), Kevin Prendergast

4535 Nine Tree Hill E.B.F. Maiden (2-y-o) £3,795 6f.......................(3:00)

4459 MISS PROVIDER (Ire) 8-11 S Craine (2)............(8 to 1) 1
4244[2] FLYING EAGLE 9-0 R Hughes (3)...................(5 to 2) 2
4369[2] LIMANDA (Ire) 8-11 P Shanahan (15)..........(5 to 4 on) 3
4460 CLASSIC PAL (USA) 9-0 C Roche (5)............(16 to 1) 4
4405[2] AINE'S PET (Ire) 8-9 (2*) P Carberry (11)...........(8 to 1) 5
4369 HI HANDSOME (Ire) 9-0 D Hogan (8).............(16 to 1) 6
4058[8] LESLEY'S ANGEL (Ire) 9-0 P Lowry (6)...........(20 to 1) 7
4460 MORE JUSTICE (Ire) 8-4 (10*) T M Finn (16).......(20 to 1) 8
YOU ARE MY HERO (Ire) 9-0 N G McCullagh (14) (16 to 1) 9
MIYOKO (Ire) 8-7 (4*) W J Smith (1)..............(20 to 1) 10
BALLYGUNNER LADY (Ire) 8-11 J F Egan (7).....(12 to 1) 11
FORNIDO 9-0 K J Manning (4)...................(16 to 1) 12
4388[8] BLACKDABRONZE (Ire) 8-11 W J Supple (12).....(16 to 1) 13
4405[4] BELLA SIGURA (USA) 8-3 (8*) J J Stack (18)......(12 to 1) 14
4405 ACRABOY LADY (Ire) 8-11 N Byrne (10)..........(33 to 1) 15
3073 SOCIAL GATHERING (Ire) 8-11 N T Egan (9)......(33 to 1) 16
4380 KILNOE (Ire) 8-1 (10*) S P Kelly (13)..............(33 to 1) 17
4388 CHANGED AROUND (Ire) 8-11 Joanna Morgan (17) (20 to 1) 18
Dist: 2l, 1l, 2l, ¾l. 1m 15.30s. (18 Ran).
(Park Racing Syndicate), Liam Browne

DONCASTER (good)
Friday October 22nd

Going Correction: PLUS 0.25 sec. per fur. (races 1,2,7,8), PLUS 0.30 (3,4,5,6)

4536 October Apprentice Handicap Class F (0-70 3-y-o) £3,493 7f........... (1:25)

4322[9] GLOWING JADE [56] 8-5 (3*) R Painter (17) *prmnt, effrt o'r 2 fs out, styd on wl to ld ins fnl furlong*....... (12 to 1) 1
4320[5] CLAIRIFICATION (Ire) [51] (bl) 8-3 B Russell (1) *rcd far side, led aftr 2 fs till hdd and no extr ins fnl furlong.* ....(12 to 1 op 10 to 1) 2
3100[8] MASTER BEVELED [46] 7-12 S Sanders (8) *swtchd rght strt, in tch, hrd rdn and drifted lft fnl 2 fs, nrst finish.* ....(33 to 1 op 25 to 1) 3
4164 DUKE OF DREAMS [58] 8-5 (5*) S Copp (22) *beh, styd on wl fnl 2 fs, nrst finish*...........................(12 to 1) 4
4181[8] DANCING DOMINO [69] 9-7 Mark Denaro (4) *chsd ldr far side frm hfwy, wknd fnl furlong*....(10 to 1 op 8 to 1) 5
4424[4] INFANTRY GLEN [50] (v) 8-2 N Varley (16) *prmnt, kpt on same pace fnl 2 fs*................(14 to 1 op 12 to 1) 6

4348[8] DAILY SPORT DON [65] 8-10 (7*) E Greehy (7) *prmnt far side, wknd o'r one furlong out.* ....(11 to 1 op 10 to 1 tchd 12 to 1) 7
3981[4] MISS FASCINATION [62] 9-0 P McCabe (18) *prmnt till wknd 2 fs out*....................(8 to 1 tchd 9 to 1) 8
3739[8] MURPHY'S HOPE (Ire) [48] 7-11 (3*) D Gibbs (14) *prmnt till wknd 2 fs out*....................(33 to 1) 9
4348[9] EGG [54] 7-13 (7*) Kimberley Hart (6) *chsd ldrs far side till wknd 2 fs out*....................(12 to 1 op 8 to 1) 10
4394 KARINSKA [64] 8-11 (5*) S Knott (12) *nvr dngrs.* ....(16 to 1 op 12 to 1) 11
4222[4] NOBLE MEASURE (Ire) [47] (bl) 7-8 (5*) M Baird (19) *nvr dngrs*....................(20 to 1 op 14 to 1) 12
4270[2] AHJAY [50] 8-2 J D Smith (21) *in tch, effrt o'r 2 fs out, no hdwy*.............(7 to 1 fav op 6 to 1 tchd 8 to 1) 13
3942[8] PENNY FAN [61] 8-13 Antoinette Armes (15) *cl up till wknd o'r 2 fs out*....................(16 to 1 op 14 to 1) 14
4333 TIME HONORED (USA) [57] 8-9 T G McLaughlin (20) *nvr dngrs*....................(16 to 1 op 14 to 1) 15
4317[9] BOLD SEVEN (Ire) [63] 9-1 H Bastiman (11) *dwlt, sn in tch, wknd o'r 2 fs out*....................(20 to 1) 16
4222* MELODIC DRIVE [58] 8-5 (5*) J Edmunds (2) *dwlt, sn in tch, wknd 3 fs out*....................(10 to 1 op 8 to 1) 17
4433[6] MASTER FIDDLER [48] 8-0 M Humphries (3) *rcd far side, led 2 fs, wknd hfwy*....................(33 to 1) 18
4458 LAMSONETTI [60] 8-9 (3*) G Parkin (9) *in tch till wknd 3 fs out*....................(25 to 1 op 20 to 1) 19
4131 KAPUCHKA (Ire) [52] 8-4 V Halliday (13) *in tch till wknd 3 fs out*....................(33 to 1) 20
4336 NYMPH ERRANT [50] 8-2 S Mulvey (5) *beh frm hfwy.* ....(20 to 1 op 16 to 1) 21
4333 VILAMAR (Ire) [50] 8-2 Claire Balding (10) *cl up till wknd 3 fs out*....................(25 to 1) 22

Dist: 1½l, ½l, 1½l, 1l, 3l, 1l, ½l, hd, dd-ht, nk. 1m 28.32s. a 4.92s (22 Ran).
SR: 46/36/29/36/44/16/28/23/8/ (Brian T Eastick), M R Channon

4537 Don Valley Claiming Stakes Class E (3,4,5-y-o) £3,548 7f............ (1:55)

4415[4] ALLINSON'S MATE (Ire) 5-9-6 W Ryan (20) *beh, hdwy to ld jst ins fnl furlong, ran on wl*.......(13 to 2 op 7 to 2) 1
3906 ASHGORE 3-8-11 M Roberts (19) *beh, ran on strly fnl 2 fs, not rch wnr*....................(10 to 1 op 14 to 1) 2
4394 DEAD CALM (v) 3-8-7 M Tebbutt (11) *sn prmnt, rdn to ld entering fnl furlong, soon hdd, no extr.* ....(25 to 1 op 20 to 1) 3
4187 HAWAYMYSON (Ire) 3-8-1 (3*) S Maloney (2) *rcd far side, chsd ldr, rdn 2 fs out, kpt on fnl furlong*.......(50 to 1) 4
4241[6] QUEEN OF THE QUORN 3-8-7 W Newnes (1) *rcd far side, led, rdn 2 fs out, hdd entering last, no extr.* ....(25 to 1 op 20 to 1) 5
4207[4] KNOCK TO ENTER (USA) 5-9-1 (5*) D Wright (10) *rcd centre, prmnt, kpt on same pace fnl 2 fs.* (13 to 8 fav op Evens) 6
4376[6] GRAND VITESSE (Ire) 4-8-13 (7*) D Gibbs (5) *led centre grp, no extr fnl 2 fs*.........(6 to 1 op 8 to 1 tchd 10 to 1) 7
4168 MINIZEN MUSIC (Ire) 5-8-9 M Wigham (22) *cl up, kpt on same pace fnl furlong*....................(50 to 1) 8
4394[6] SARTIGILA 4-8-12 L Dettori (6) *rcd centre, in tch, no extr fnl 2 fs*..............(14 to 1 op 12 to 1 tchd 16 to 1) 9
3744[9] COURTENAY BEE 4-8-11 R Price (16) *prmnt till wknd 2 fs out*....................(25 to 1) 10
4331 LARN FORT (v) 3-8-8 J Fanning (15) *chsd ldrs, no hdwy fnl 2 fs*....................(25 to 1) 11
4158 DEBSY DO (USA) 4-8-10 (3*) O Pears (21) *in tch, no hdwy fnl 2 fs*....................(15 to 2 op 6 to 1 tchd 8 to 1) 12
4016[9] PYTCHLEY DAWN 3-8-0 N Carlisle (18) *prmnt till wknd 2 fs out*....................(33 to 1) 13
4270 WESTERING 3-8-1 P Robinson (8) *rcd centre, in tch till wknd 2 fs out*....................(20 to 1) 14
4331 COLMAR 3-7-11 A Mackay (14) *chsd ldrs till wknd 2 fs out*....................(33 to 1) 15
4270[8] SEASON'S STAR 3-8-0 S Dawson (3) *rcd far side, chsd ldrs till wknd 2 fs out*....................(25 to 1) 16
4045[7] THROW AWAY LINE 4-7-12 (5*) J Tate (9) *dwlt, swtchd rght strt, in tch till wknd o'r 2 fs out*..............(50 to 1) 17
4348 BRIGADORE GOLD (bl) 3-7-10 (3*) N Kennedy (12) *cl up till wknd o'r 2 fs out*....................(33 to 1) 18
BITOUT THE MIDDLE 4-8-5 J Carroll (13) *in tch till wknd o'r 2 fs out*....................(33 to 1) 19
4317 FREDDIE JACK (bl) 3-8-9 J Fortune (4) *rcd centre, prmnt till wknd o'r 2 fs out*....................(50 to 1) 20
1101[5] BOLD PHILIP 3-7-11 (5*) A Garth (17) *sn beh, tld off.* ....(33 to 1) 21

Dist: 1l, ½l, ¾l, nk, 2l, sht-hd, 1½l, nk, hd, 3½l. 1m 28.66s. a 5.26s (21 Ran).
SR: 53/41/35/30/32/39/38/22/24/ (Peter Jones), T D Barron

4538 English Estates Handicap Class D (0-85 3-y-o and up) £4,142 1¾m 132yds ....(2:30)

4283 SHUJAN (USA) [72] 4-9-4 L Dettori (2) *made all, sn clr, rdn wl o'r one furlong out, hld on gmely fnl furlong.* ....(12 to 1) 1
4432[3] WHITE WILLOW [71] 4-9-3 R Cochrane (4) *in tch, hdwy to chase wnr fnl 2 fs, sn hrd rdn, ch final furlong, no extr.* ....(9 to 2 fav tchd 5 to 1) 2
4283[4] MARADONNA (USA) [72] 4-9-4 J Weaver (3) *chsd ldrs, pushed alng o'r 4 fs out, styd on same pace.* ....(5 to 1 op 4 to 1) 3
4344[7] CUMBRIAN RHAPSODY [72] 3-8-9 M Birch (13) *in tch, hdwy 6 fs out, rdn o'r 3 out, one pace.* ....(12 to 1 op 10 to 1) 4
4283[8] SUBSONIC (Ire) [75] 5-9-7 W Carson (6) *beh till styd on fnl 3 fs, nrst finish*....................(8 to 1 tchd 9 to 1) 5
4283[7] WINGS COVE [77] 3-9-0 J Williams (11) *chsd ldrs, effrt o'r 3 fs out, sn btn*....................(5 to 1 op 4 to 1) 6
4321 ADMINISTER [50] (bl) 5-7-10 J Quinn (10) *in tch, effrt o'r 4 fs out, no hdwy*....................(50 to 1) 7
4189[2] GOOD HAND (USA) [82] 7-10-0 N Connorton (5) *wl beh till styd on well fnl 3 fs, not trble ldrs.* ....(9 to 1 op 8 to 1 tchd 10 to 1) 8
4357[4] HIERARCH (USA) [65] (v) 4-8-11 W R Swinburn (9) *chsd ldrs till wknd o'r 2 fs out*....(13 to 2 op 7 to 1 tchd 8 to 1) 9
4188[4] SURE HAVEN (Ire) [72] 4-9-4 G Duffield (7) *chsd clr ldr till wknd o'r 3 fs out*....................(9 to 1 op 7 to 1) 10
4426[2] FAMOUS BEAUTY [47] 6-7-7[5] (5*) A Garth (8) *in tch, some hdwy 5 fs out, rdn o'r 3 out, sn wknd*.........(20 to 1) 11
4364 EXPO MONDIAL (Ire) [67] 3-8-1 (3*) N Kennedy (1) *in tch till outpcd 6 fs out, tld off*....................(33 to 1) 12
NONCOMMITAL [47] 6-7-3[1] (5*) Darren Moffatt (12) *al beh, lost tch 4 fs out, tld off*...........(100 to 1 op 50 to 1) 13

Dist: 1l, 7l, nk, 2l, 2½l, 2l, 1½l, nk, 2½l, 5l. 3m 13.95s. a 9.45s (13 Ran).
SR: 53/50/37/27/35/23/1/30/12/ (M J Polglase), R W Armstrong

4539 EBF Wheatley Park Fillies' Maiden Stakes Class D (2-y-o) £4,485 1m (3:00)

4121[2] COIGACH 8-11 W Ryan (8) *made all, hld on wl fnl furlong*....................(10 to 1 op 7 to 1) 1
3209[3] BRENTWOOD (Ire) 8-11 J Reid (3) *trkd ldrs, effrt 2 fs out, styd on wl fnl furlong, not rch wnr*..........(12 to 1) 2
QUANDARY (USA) 8-11 Pat Eddery (9) *hld up in tch, hdwy 3 fs out, ev ch frm 2 out, edgd lft and no extr fnl furlong*..................(2 to 1 fav op 11 to 10) 3
4190[3] REALIZE 8-11 L Dettori (2) *prmnt, ev ch 2 fs out, no extr fnl furlong*....................(6 to 1 tchd 13 to 2) 4
DANCING HEIGHTS (Ire) 8-11 S O'Gorman (14) *in tch, hdwy o'r 2 fs out, styd on same pace fnl furlong.* ....(12 to 1) 5
4396[3] AZHAAR (USA) 8-11 W Carson (12) *chsd ldrs till wknd o'r 2 fs out*..............(5 to 1 op 9 to 2 tchd 11 to 2) 6
3284[7] MILLIE'S DREAM 8-11 S Perks (1) *in tch, effrt 2 fs out, no hdwy*....................(33 to 1) 7
4276 SAMSONESQUE 8-11 W R Swinburn (4) *nvr dngrs.* ....(25 to 1) 8
4003[6] FRUSTRATION 8-11 J Williams (7) *nvr dngrs*....(20 to 1) 9
4121[4] SPRINGTIME AFFAIR 8-11 B Raymond (13) *in tch, effrt 3 fs out, wknd o'r one out*....................(33 to 1) 10
3738[4] IOLANI 8-11 R Cochrane (6) *in tch, pushed alng hfwy, sn btn*....................(12 to 1) 11
DUWON (Ire) 8-11 M Roberts (10) *dwlt, swshd tail thrght, nvr dngrs*....................(10 to 1 op 8 to 1) 12
4121[7] MY FIORE 8-4 (7*) C Hawksley (11) *chsd ldr till wknd 3 fs out*....................(50 to 1) 13
4422[4] MWAARED 8-11 R Hills (5) *chsd ldrs till wknd o'r 3 fs out.* ....(11 to 2 op 5 to 1 tchd 6 to 1) 14

Dist: 1l, hd, 1½l, 2l, 8l, sht-hd, nk, hd, ½l, hd. 1m 43.25s. a 6.55s (14 Ran).
SR: 35/32/31/26/20/-/ (Sir David Wills), H R A Cecil

4540 Doncaster Writers Conditions Stakes Class C (3-y-o and up) £4,166 2m 110yds........................ (3:30)

3405[3] ALLEGAN (USA) 4-9-11 Pat Eddery (1) *made all, quickened o'r 5 fs out, rdn and styd on wl fnl furlong.* ....(6 to 4 on op 7 to 4 on tchd 11 to 8 on) 1
4466 JACK BUTTON (Ire) 4-9-12 N Connorton (3) *trkd wnr, rdn wl o'r 2 fs out, ev ch entering last, no extr.* ....(7 to 4 tchd 15 to 8) 2
4366[3] CALIANDAK (Ire) 3-8-8 M Birch (2) *in tch, rdn 3 fs out, wknd*....................(8 to 1 tchd 9 to 1) 3
288[4] MRS JAWLEYFORD (USA) 5-8-4 (5*) K Rutter (4) *dwlt, sn cl up, rdn and wknd 4 fs out*....................(100 to 1) 4

Dist: 2½l, 15l, 5l. 3m 45.32s. a 15.32s (4 Ran).
SR: 7/5/-/-/ (K Abdulla), H R A Cecil

4541 'Harry Jones Memorial' Nursery Class D (2-y-o) £4,435 1m.......(4:00)

4365[3] NON VINTAGE (Ire) [71] (bl) 8-4 K Fallon (16) *hld up in midfield, hdwy to ld entering fnl furlong, edgd lft, styd on wl und pres*.....(14 to 1 op 12 to 1 tchd 16 to 1) 1
4249 STASH THE CASH (Ire) [74] 8-7 L Dettori (11) *trkd ldrs, led briefly o'r one furlong out, styd on und pres.* ....(7 to 2 fav op 3 to 1 tchd 11 to 4) 2
4208[2] ZUBOON (USA) [86] 9-5 W Carson (8) *mid-div, effrt o'r 2 fs out, styd on fnl furlong*............(5 to 1 tchd 7 to 1) 3
3997[3] HIT THE CANVAS (USA) [74] 8-7 W Ryan (6) *beh, hdwy fnl 3 fs, nrst finish*...........(7 to 1 op 8 to 1 tchd 9 to 1) 4
4338* KAITAK (Ire) [75] 8-8 S Morris (9) *prmnt, led 2 fs out till o'r one out, btn whn hmpd ins last.* ....(8 to 1 op 6 to 1 tchd 9 to 1) 5

4015* BENFLEET [72] 8-5 R Price (1) *hld up in midfield, not clr run o'r 3 fs out, swtchd rght over 2 out, not trble ldrs.* ....(12 to 1 op 10 to 1) 6
4365 NEW INN [75] 8-8 W Newnes (13) *chsd ldrs, wknd 2 fs out.* ....(25 to 1) 7
4375* LIME STREET BLUES (Ire) [86] 9-5 Pat Eddery (5) *beh, hdwy 3 fs out, wknd fnl furlong*.......... (7 to 1 op 6 to 1) 8
4251 CARAPELLE [66] 7-12² (3*) S Maloney (7) *nvr dngrs.* ....(20 to 1) 9
4240⁴ TO CROWN IT ALL (USA) [80] 8-13 S Perks (12) *trkd ldrs till wknd o'r 2 fs out*....................(20 to 1 op 14 to 1) 10
4106 DURHAM DRAPES [60] 7-7 J Lowe (4) *led to 2 fs out, wknd quickly*....................(20 to 1) 11
3389* PAT'S SPLENDOUR [69] 8-2 J Quinn (10) *prmnt, ev ch 2 fs out, wknd quickly*............... (14 to 1 op 12 to 1) 12
4342 GLORIETTE [67] 7-7 (7*) C Hawksley (3) *al beh*.... (16 to 1) 13
4423⁹ OCHOS RIOS (Ire) [88] 9-2 (5*) D Wright (2) *beh most of way.* ....(16 to 1) 14
4329 CARA CARLTON (USA) [62] 7-9² L Charnock (15) *prmnt till wknd 3 fs out*....................(25 to 1) 15
4365 CAPTAIN SCARLET (Ire) [74] 8-4 (3*) B Doyle (14) *sn beh.* ....(20 to 1) 16

Dist: 1½l, 3l, 1½l, 2l, 4l, 1½l, ½l, 2½l, sht-hd, 1½l. 1m 42.36s. a 5.66s (16 Ran).

SR: 41/39/42/25/20/5/3/12/-/ (H R Leetham), M H Easterby

4542 EBF Flaxton Maiden Stakes Class D (Div I) (2-y-o) £4,932 7f..........(4:30)

4276⁹ DANCE TURN 9-0 W Woods (2) *al prmnt, led one furlong out, hld on wl*....................(20 to 1 op 16 to 1) 1
EZZ ALSEBA (USA) 9-0 M Roberts (6) *made most to one furlong out, kpt on wl.* ....(11 to 1 op 10 to 1 tchd 12 to 1) 2
4249 WESTERN GENERAL 9-0 P Robinson (12) *trkd ldrs, effrt whn squeezed o'r one furlong out, swtchd and sn rdn, ev ch ins last, wknd nr finish.* ....(11 to 4 op 5 to 2 tchd 3 to 1) 3
4252⁴ PTOTO 9-0 R Cochrane (3) *prmnt, dsptd ld 3 fs out, rdn 2 out, wknd o'r one out.* ....(13 to 8 fav op 6 to 4 tchd 5 to 4 and 7 to 4) 4
CRACKHILL FARM 9-0 J Reid (14) *beh till styd on fnl 2 fs, nrst finish*....................(20 to 1 tchd 33 to 1) 5
4276 LUCAYAN CAY (Ire) 9-0 L Dettori (11) *in tch, bumped 4 fs out, not trble ldrs*................ (33 to 1 op 20 to 1) 6
IMPRECISE 8-9 R Hills (1) *prmnt till wknd fnl 2 fs.* ....(12 to 1 op 10 to 1) 7
LAUNCHSELECT 9-0 J Fanning (8) *in tch, wndrd 4 fs out, nvr dngrs*....................(50 to 1) 8
JABAROOT (Ire) 9-0 W R Swinburn (10) *nvr nr ldrs.* ....(10 to 1 op 5 to 1) 9
3990 MUCH TOO CLEVER 9-0 M Tebbutt (4) *in tch, bumped 4 fs out, nvr dngrs*....................(50 to 1) 10
2706⁵ NORTHWISE (Ire) 8-9 Dale Gibson (15) *in tch till wknd 3 fs out*....................(33 to 1) 11
4179⁴ WHISPERING LOCH (Ire) 9-0 M Birch (13) *chsd ldrs till wknd 3 fs out*....................(16 to 1 op 14 to 1) 12
4253⁸ RUN WITH JOY (Ire) 9-0 W Newnes (7) *beh most of way.* ....(33 to 1 op 25 to 1) 13
TEGUILA (Ire) 8-9 B Raymond (9) *dwlt, chsd ldrs till wknd hfwy*....................(14 to 1) 14
4419 ANIF (USA) 9-0 W Carson (5) *in tch, bumped 4 fs out, wknd 3 out*....................(10 to 1 op 6 to 1) 15

Dist: ½l, ½l, 2l, 3½l, 1½l, ¾l, sht-hd, nk, 1l, 2l. 1m 29.53s. a 6.13s (15 Ran).

SR: 34/32/30/24/13/8/1/5/4/ (George Ward), R W Armstrong

4543 EBF Flaxton Maiden Stakes Class D (Div II) (2-y-o) £4,932 7f.........(5:00)

GOLDEN NASHWAN (Ire) 9-0 J Reid (2) *trkd ldrs gng wl, led o'r 2 fs out, sn clr, easily.* ......(11 to 8 fav op 5 to 4 tchd 11 to 10 and 6 to 4) 1
3992² MOVING ARROW 9-0 N Connorton (4) *trkd ldrs, chlgd o'r 2 fs out, ran on wl, no ch wth wnr*... (4 to 1 tchd 9 to 2) 2
3259⁶ FAAL MARIO (USA) 9-0 M Roberts (15) *trkd ldrs, effrt o'r 2 fs out, styd on wl fnl furlong*........ (8 to 1 op 7 to 1) 3
4337³ ARTIC COURIER 9-0 L Dettori (13) *chsd ldrs, kpt on same pace fnl 2 fs*....................(20 to 1 op 16 to 1) 4
4099 CONIC HILL (Ire) 9-0 M Hills (14) *prmnt, effrt 3 fs out, one pace*....................(25 to 1) 5
3974 MILL CITY 9-0 D Harrison (1) *slight ld till o'r 2 fs out, fdd.* ....(50 to 1) 6
WANDESTA 8-9 Pat Eddery (8) *trkd ldrs, effrt 2 fs out, edgd lft o'r one out, one pace*...... (4 to 1 tchd 9 to 2) 6
3888⁷ THE LONE DANCER 9-0 S O'Gorman (12) *prmnt, effrt 3 fs out, fdd*....................(33 to 1 op 25 to 1) 8
3974⁶ RISING SPRAY 9-0 M Birch (9) *dwlt, nvr dngrs*...(20 to 1) 9
4167 DALERIVER 9-0 W Carson (5) *prmnt till wknd o'r 2 fs out.* ....(33 to 1 op 25 to 1) 10
3828⁹ WILLOW 8-9 W Ryan (6) *prmnt till wknd 2 fs out.* ....(25 to 1 tchd 20 to 1) 11
CHIMANIMANI 9-0 G Duffield (11) *al beh.* ....(20 to 1 op 16 to 1) 12
MYRRH 8-9 M Tebbutt (7) *sn beh*................(20 to 1) 13
BLESSED MEMORY (USA) 8-9 W R Swinburn (10) *dwlt, beh most of way*....................(12 to 1 op 10 to 1) 14
4356 BLUE DOMAIN 9-0 S Perks (3) *dwlt, in tch till outpcd hfwy*....................(50 to 1) 15

Dist: 3½l, 3l, 2½l, 1½l, 3½l, dd-ht, ½l, 1l, nk, 1l. 1m 28.80s. a 5.40s (15 Ran).

SR: 45/34/25/17/12/1/ (Scuderia Golden Horse S R L), P W Chapple-Hyam

DONCASTER (good)
Saturday October 23rd

Going Correction: PLUS 0.20 sec. per fur. (races 1,4,5), PLUS 0.10 (2,3,6,7)

4544 Variety Club Autumn Claiming Stakes Class D (3-y-o and up) £3,200 1¼m 60yds.......................... (1:40)

3722⁶ DEE RAFT (USA) 3-8-11 D Holland (21) *trkd ldrs, hdwy 4 fs out, led 2 out, clr fnl furlong*........ (8 to 1 op 6 to 1) 1
3588 COMPLETE MADNESS 3-8-7 C Asmussen (14) *al prmnt, rdn o'r 2 fs out, kpt on, no ch wth wnr.* ....(10 to 1 op 8 to 1) 2
4458⁸ QUEENS CONSUL (Ire) 3-7-12 S Wood (17) *prmnt, led 4 fs out to 2 out, kpt on same pace*..... (8 to 1 op 11 to 2) 3
4254⁹ JADE GREEN 4-8-6 W Ryan (16) *beh, hdwy 4 fs out, styd on wl frm 2 out, nrst finish*...... (14 to 1 tchd 16 to 1) 4
4374² LIGHT HAND 7-8-5 (7*) S Mulvey (15) *in tch, hdwy 4 fs out, kpt on same pace frm 2 out.* ....(5 to 2 fav op 3 to 1 tchd 2 to 1) 5
4644a COMSTOCK 6-8-8 J Fortune (2) *prmnt, rdn o'r 2 fs out, one pace*....................(10 to 1 op 8 to 1) 6
4457⁹ AUSTRAL JANE 3-7-8 (5*) B Russell (19) *beh, styd on fnl 2 fs, not trble ldrs.* ....(11 to 2 op 6 to 1 tchd 7 to 1 and 5 to 1) 7
4376⁷ SARAH HEIGHTS 3-7-12 D Harrison (10) *prmnt, effrt o'r 3 fs out, wknd*....................(50 to 1 op 25 to 1) 8
4016⁵ DARING KING 3-8-7 L Dettori (11) *in tch, no hdwy fnl 3 fs.* ....(16 to 1 op 14 to 1 tchd 20 to 1) 9
4206⁸ BOLD STAR 3-8-4 Paul Eddery (8) *nvr dngrs.* ....(33 to 1 op 25 to 1) 10
4279 REJECTS REPLY 3-7-12 (5*) D McCabe (7) *dwlt, mid-div, no hdwy fnl 3 fs*....................(33 to 1) 11
BLANCHLAND 4-9-2 M Birch (13) *prmnt till wknd o'r 2 fs out*....................(33 to 1 op 20 to 1) 12
4155⁹ SABERAGE 3-8-4 A Munro (6) *in tch, rdn 3 fs out, sn btn.* ....(25 to 1 op 16 to 1) 13
4234 MENA 3-7-10 J Lowe (9) *nvr dngrs.* (25 to 1 op 20 to 1) 14
4279⁸ SPARKY'S SONG 3-8-0 (3*) B Doyle (20) *slwly into strd, nvr dngrs*....................(25 to 1 op 16 to 1) 15
2860⁷ MALINDI BAY 5-8-7 M Wigham (3) *sn beh.* ....(50 to 1 op 33 to 1) 16
4343⁷ ROCK OPERA (Ire) (v) 5-8-12 K Fallon (4) *sn beh.* ....(25 to 1 op 16 to 1 tchd 33 to 1) 17
4364 FLASHMAN 3-8-7¹ S Perks (5) *prmnt till wknd quickly 4 fs out*....................(16 to 1 tchd 20 to 1) 18
3244a ONE FOR TONDY 3-7-12 L Charnock (18) *sn beh.* ....(33 to 1 op 25 to 1) 19
4191⁶ REMEESON 3-8-2 N Carlisle (12) *sn beh.* ....(33 to 1 op 20 to 1) 20
4327³ LITTLE OSBORNE (Ire) (bl) 3-7-13 A Mackay (1) *led to 4 fs out, wknd quickly*................ (16 to 1 op 12 to 1) 21

Dist: 7l, 1½l, 3l, nk, 1½l, sht-hd, 4l, 2l, sht-hd, 3l. 2m 13.15s. a 6.45s (21 Ran).

SR: 53/35/23/25/30/23/13/4/9/ (D O Pickering), B W Hills

4545 Teleconnection Conditions Stakes Class B (3-y-o and up) £5,700 7f (2:10)

4173⁷ HALF TERM (USA) 3-8-9 L Dettori (8) *trkd ldrs, effrt 2 fs out, sn rdn, kpt on wl to ld ins last.* ....(Evens fav op 11 to 8 on) 1
4428³ CELESTIAL KEY (USA) 3-9-7 K Fallon (3) *led till ins fnl furlong, kpt on wl*..............(10 to 1 tchd 11 to 1) 2
4153⁵ LACERTA (Ire) 3-8-4 D Holland (5) *trkd ldrs, effrt 3 fs out, sn rdn, ev ch ins last, no extr cl hme.* (8 to 1 op 7 to 1) 3
4139⁴ SERIOUS 3-8-9 Pat Eddery (7) *hld up, swtchd lft hfwy, ev ch 2 fs out, wknd entering last.* ....(5 to 1 op 8 to 1 tchd 10 to 1) 4
817* LOWER EGYPT (USA) 3-8-9 J Carroll (6) *trkd ldrs, effrt o'r 2 fs out, edgd lft and no hdwy.* ....(5 to 1 op 4 to 1 tchd 11 to 2) 5
4428² GREAT STEPS 3-8-6 A Munro (2) *cl up till wknd 3 fs out.* ....(20 to 1 op 16 to 1) 6
4441⁹ MR MARTINI (Ire) (v) 3-8-12 B Doyle (1) *cl up till rdn and wknd o'r 2 fs out*....................(20 to 1) 7
ROSSINGTON (Ire) 3-8-9 M Birch (4) *dwlt, al beh, lost tch 3 fs out, tld off*....................(33 to 1 op 20 to 1) 8

Dist: Hd, nk, 2l, ¾l, 6l, nk, 15l. 1m 27.65s. a 4.25s (8 Ran).

SR: 42/53/35/34/32/11/16/-/ (Sheikh Mohammed), J H M Gosden

4546 F Cross & Sons Doncaster Stakes Class A (Listed Race) (2-y-o) £8,357 6f ....(2:40)

4195⁶ ULTIMO IMPERATORE 8-12 L Piggott (8) *al prmnt, rdn to ld o'r one furlong out, ran on wl.* (16 to 1 op 14 to 1) 1
4154² MULTI NATIONAL 8-9 K Fallon (3) *in tch, pushed alng hfwy, hdwy 2 fs out, ch one out, no extr fnl furlong.* ....(4 to 1 co-fav op 9 to 2 tchd 5 to 1) 2

3898^{2} GREAT DEEDS 8-7 Paul Eddery (1) *chsd ldrs, ev ch o'r one furlong out, wknd fnl furlong*..............(4 to 1 co-fav op 3 to 1) 3
4440^{2} TABOOK (Ire) 8-9 C Asmussen (2) *steadied strt, beh, some hdwy fnl 2 fs, not trble ldrs*. ....(11 to 2 op 5 to 1 tchd 6 to 1) 4
4392* PALACEGATE JACK (Ire) 9-1 J Carroll (7) *slight ld till o'r one furlong out, sn btn*......................(4 to 1 co-fav tchd 7 to 2 and 9 to 2) 5
2335^{5} WAJIBA RIVA (Ire) 8-12 Pat Eddery (9) *prmnt till wknd 2 fs out*......................................(5 to 1 op 9 to 2) 6
4020^{3} RANDONNEUR (Ire) 8-4 A Munro (4) *sn pushed alng, beh hfwy*.............................. (16 to 1 op 14 to 1) 7
3510^{4} CLASSIC SKY (Ire) 8-12 W Ryan (6) *edgd lft strt, nvr on terms*.................................(20 to 1 op 16 to 1) 8
4273^{7} PINKERTON'S PAL 8-9 M Birch (5) *hmpd strt, al beh*. ....(9 to 1 op 10 to 1 tchd 8 to 1) 9

Dist: 2l, ½l, 6l, 1l, 7l, 2l, 3l, 10l. 1m 14.04s. a 2.64s (9 Ran).
SR: 57/46/42/20/22/-/ (Gerecon Italia), J L Dunlop

4547 Racing Post Trophy Class A (Group 1) (2-y-o) £86,779 1m............. (3:10)

4027* KING'S THEATRE (Ire) 9-0 W Ryan (3) *trkd ldr, led and quickened hfwy, rdn o'r one furlong out, styd on strly*. ....(9 to 2 op 3 to 1) 1
4171* FAIRY HEIGHTS (Ire) 8-9 C Asmussen (4) *hld up, hdwy to chase wnr 3 fs out, rdn entering last, kpt on, no imprsn*. ....(11 to 8 fav op 6 to 4 tchd 7 to 4) 2
2559* BUDE 9-0 Pat Eddery (7) *hld up, effrt hfwy, styd on wl und pres fnl 2 fs, nrst finish*. ....(4 to 1 op 5 to 1 tchd 7 to 2) 3
4259^{2} KHAMASEEN 9-0 L Piggott (6) *prmnt, effrt hfwy, styd on same pace*..........................(14 to 1 tchd 16 to 1) 4
4144^{4} CHICKAWICKA (Ire) 9-0 J Carroll (2) *beh, hdwy 3 fs out, kpt on same pace frm 2 out*........................(100 to 1) 5
4182* XYLEM (USA) 9-0 L Dettori (5) *in tch, effrt hfwy, no hdwy*. ....(6 to 1 tchd 13 to 2) 6
4174^{4} HAWKER HUNTER (USA) 9-0 A Munro (8) *in tch, shaken up hfwy, sn btn*. ....(13 to 2 op 7 to 1 tchd 8 to 1 and 6 to 1) 7
1975^{4} VENTA DE POSSA (USA) 9-0 D Harrison (9) *trkd ldrs, shaken up hfwy, sn btn*...................... (50 to 1) 8
4318^{2} CHIEF EXECUTIVE 9-0 A Mackay (1) *led to hfwy, wknd quickly, tld off*.............................. (100 to 1) 9

Dist: 1l, 3l, ¾l, 6l, 6l, 10l, 2½l, 15l. 1m 41.04s. a 4.34s (9 Ran).
SR: 59/51/47/45/27/9/ (Michael Poland), H R A Cecil

4548 Ladbroke Handicap Class C (0-95 3-y-o and up) £11,452 1½m......... (3:40)

4364^{6} IN THE MONEY (Ire) [55] 4-7-6 (5*) A Garth (3) *trkd ldrs gng wl, led on bit o'r 2 fs out, pushed out fnl furlong*. ....(14 to 1 op 20 to 1) 1
4319^{3} ADMIRALS SEAT [54] 5-7-10 J Fanning (9) *hld up, hdwy 3 fs out, rdn to chase wnr entering last, styd on strly nr finish*........................(5 to 1 co-fav op 4 to 1) 2
3466 CHATHAM ISLAND [69] 5-8-8 (3*) B Doyle (5) *in tch, effrt 3 fs out, styd on wl und pres fnl furlong*........(16 to 1) 3
4036* HIGH SUMMER [70] 3-8-5 D Harrison (11) *cl up, led o'r 4 fs out till over 2 out, wknd entering last*. ....(13 to 2 op 6 to 1) 4
4110* ELATIS (USA) [82] 3-9-3 L Dettori (10) *prmnt, effrt 3 fs out, kpt on same pace*..........(5 to 1 co-fav op 4 to 1) 5
4374^{4} HILLZAH (USA) [60] 5-8-2 L Charnock (1) *in tch, effrt 3 fs out, no hdwy*.........(7 to 1 op 12 to 1 tchd 14 to 1) 6
4175^{8} MILLION IN MIND (Ire) [79] 4-9-7 C Asmussen (7) *chsd ldrs, effrt 3 fs out, wknd*..............(10 to 1 tchd 12 to 1) 7
4424^{9} KIVETON TYCOON (Ire) [64] (bl) 4-8-6 J Lowe (4) *nvr on terms*................................(12 to 1 op 10 to 1) 8
4248^{7} PRINCE HANNIBAL [82] 6-9-10 Pat Eddery (2) *beh, effrt 3 fs out, sn btn*.........................(10 to 1 op 12 to 1) 9
4374 LIABILITY ORDER [59] 4-8-1 A Mackay (6) *beh most of way*. ....(25 to 1) 10
4188^{3} SHIRLEY ROSE [74] 3-8-9 Paul Eddery (8) *led till o'r 4 fs out, wknd*.................(5 to 1 co-fav tchd 9 to 2) 11

Dist: 1½l, 3l, 1½l, sht-hd, 2½l, 3l, 5l, 5l, 1½l, 1l. 2m 37.79s. a 7.29s (11 Ran).
SR: 34/30/39/30/41/21/34/9/17/ (J E Bigg), R Hollinshead

4549 Doncaster Racecourse Exhibition Centre Rated Class B Handicap (0-100 3-y-o and up) £6,639 5f......... (4:15)

4112^{2} INHERENT MAGIC (Ire) [82] 4-8-7 Pat Eddery (10) *chsd ldrs, effrt 2 fs out, led ins last, ran on wl*. ....(3 to 1 fav op 5 to 1 tchd 5 to 2) 1
4465^{8} GONE SAVAGE [83] 5-8-8 L Dettori (3) *prmnt, led o'r one furlong out till ins last, kpt on*.......(8 to 1 op 7 to 1) 2
4465^{6} PRESS THE BELL [83] 3-8-7 J Carroll (11) *led till o'r one furlong out, kpt on same pace*.......(7 to 1 op 9 to 2) 3
4465^{3} SIR JOEY (USA) [86] 4-8-6 (5*) S Drowne (6) *in tch, effrt hfwy, kpt on und pres fnl furlong*. (7 to 2 tchd 9 to 2) 4
3995^{2} CALL TO THE BAR (Ire) [82] 4-8-7 A Clark (1) *in tch, effrt hfwy, rdn entering fnl furlong, kpt on*. ....(9 to 1 op 8 to 1 tchd 10 to 1) 5
3877^{5} ALLTHRUTHENIGHT (Ire) [82] 4-8-7 A Munro (9) *beh, styd on und pres fnl 2 fs, not trble ldrs*. (12 to 1 op 10 to 1) 6
4465 ASHTINA [82] 8-8-4 (3*) N Kennedy (4) *cl up till wknd o'r one furlong out*......(14 to 1 op 12 to 1 tchd 16 to 1) 7
4455^{5} NEVER IN THE RED [82] (bl) 5-8-7 L Piggott (7) *nvr dngrs*. ....(10 to 1 op 8 to 1) 8
4465 BODARI [82] 4-8-7 D Harrison (5) *prmnt, pushed alng hfwy, wknd wl o'r one furlong out*. ....(12 to 1 op 10 to 1) 9
4465 EL YASAF (Ire) [96] (bl) 5-9-7 D Holland (8) *al beh*. (20 to 1) 10
3127^{9} BANGLES [82] 3-8-6 K Fallon (2) *prmnt till wknd o'r one furlong out*........................(20 to 1 op 16 to 1) 11

Dist: 1½l, 1l, ½l, nk, 3l, 1½l, nk, nk, 1½l, 2½l. 1m 0.67s. a 1.87s (11 Ran).
SR: 66/61/56/58/53/41/35/34/33/ (Mrs S J Stovold), M McCormack

4550 Levy Board Nursery Stakes Class C (2-y-o) £4,480 7f................(4:50)

4223^{2} DIESAN (USA) [99] 9-12 L Dettori (4) *rcd centre, in tch gng wl, hdwy to ld jst ins fnl furlong, ran on well*. ....(8 to 1 op 7 to 1 tchd 9 to 1) 1
3485^{5} THREE IN ONE [73] 8-0 D Harrison (1) *rcd centre, in tch, rdn to ld entering fnl furlong, sn hdd, kpt on*. ....(9 to 1 op 10 to 1) 2
4167^{2} TOWER GREEN [83] 8-10 W Ryan (16) *beh, effrt and swtchd lft o'r 2 fs out, ran on strly entering last, nrst finish*..... (5 to 1 op 4 to 1 tchd 7 to 2 and 11 to 2) 3
3836* GREATEST [78] 8-5 R Price (13) *al prmnt, no extr fnl furlong*.......................(10 to 1 tchd 11 to 1) 4
4444^{5} SANS ECOCIDE [73] (bl) 8-0 N Carlisle (11) *chsd ldrs, kpt on same pace fnl 2 fs*..............................(14 to 1) 5
4418* SLMAAT [67] 7-3 (5*) Darren Moffatt (10) *prmnt, rdn o'r 2 fs out, kpt on same pace*. ....(7 to 2 fav op 11 to 2 tchd 6 to 1) 6
4444 LUGANO [69] 7-10 A Mackay (12) *slwly into strd, sn in tch and pushed alng, nvr dngrs*.......(20 to 1 op 16 to 1) 7
4230^{6} DOWN D ISLANDS [72] (bl) 7-13 J Lowe (5) *led centre till entering fnl furlong, wknd quickly*............(16 to 1) 8
4051^{3} CLIFTON BEAT (USA) [72] 7-13 A Munro (9) *chsd ldrs till wknd o'r one furlong out*. ....(9 to 1 op 8 to 1 tchd 10 to 1) 9
4266^{3} LUNAR MISSION (Ire) [74] 7-11^{3} (7*) S Mulvey (2) *nvr dngrs*. ....(20 to 1 op 14 to 1) 10
4251^{6} TASHLA [75] (v) 8-2 J Carroll (14) *cl up till wknd o'r one furlong out*........................(16 to 1 op 14 to 1) 11
4453 BROCTUNE GOLD [80] 8-7 K Fallon (8) *beh, some hdwy fnl 2 fs, nvr nr to chal*............... (20 to 1 op 16 to 1) 12
4453 PRIZEFIGHTER [72] 7-11^{1} (3*) S Maloney (17) *nvr dngrs*. ....(14 to 1 op 16 to 1 tchd 10 to 1) 13
4427^{7} BARNPARK [68] 7-9^{2} L Charnock (15) *sn beh*.... (100 to 1) 14
4225 JASARI (Ire) [75] 8-2 Paul Eddery (3) *prmnt centre, rdn hfwy, sn wknd*..................................(14 to 1) 15
4418^{7} NIGHT SNOW [66] 7-2^{2} (7*) N Varley (6) *prmnt centre till wknd und pres fnl 2 fs*.............. (25 to 1 op 20 to 1) 16
4082* MISS MAH-JONG [85] 8-12 Pat Eddery (7) *sn rdn alng, beh hfwy*............................. (12 to 1 op 10 to 1) 17

Dist: 2l, 1l, 1l, sht-hd, sht-hd, 2l, 2l, 5l, ½l, sht-hd. 1m 28.49s. a 5.09s (17 Ran).
SR: 46/14/21/13/7/-/ (Sheikh Ahmed Al Maktoum), J H M Gosden

LEOPARDSTOWN (IRE) (good to yielding)
Saturday October 23rd
Going Correction: PLUS 0.10 sec. per fur.

4551 Autumn Nursery Handicap (2-y-o) £3,105 7f...................... (2:00)

4462* ZAVALETA (Ire) [-] 8-13 (8*,5ex) A P McCoy (18) (3 to 1 fav) 1
4462^{5} SOPHIE'S PET (Ire) [-] 8-8 J F Egan (7)...........(10 to 1) 2
3911^{7} EUPHORIC (Ire) [-] 8-8^{1} J P Murtagh (12)..........(6 to 1) 3
4285* JOIN FORCES (Ire) [-] 8-3 (4*) W J Smith (14)..... (12 to 1) 4
4382^{7} OUT IN THE SUN (USA) [-] 8-0 (6*) R V Skelly (9).. (12 to 1) 5
4462^{6} GO MILLIE (Ire) [-] 8-10 W J Supple (11)..........(10 to 1) 6
4462^{8} DON'T KNOW (Ire) [-] 9-4 K J Manning (2)........(10 to 1) 7
4183^{7} AVALIN (Ire) [-] 7-5^{1} (8*) R T Fitzpatrick (15)....... (33 to 1) 8
3730^{7} MEGLIO CHE POSSO (Ire) [-] 7-11 (2*) R M Burke (1) ....(33 to 1) 9
4360^{7} RAHAL (Ire) [-] (bl) 8-13 P Shanahan (10)...........(7 to 1) 10
3731^{6} KAKASHDA (Ire) [-] 7-10 (2*) D G O'Shea (16)..... (10 to 1) 11
4360^{3} BRIEF RESPITE (Ire) [-] 8-7 C Roche (6)...........(7 to 1) 12
4244^{7} NORTHERN FANCY (Ire) [-] 7-6 (8*) G M Moylan (8) (33 to 1) 13
4059^{5} FOOLISH FLIGHT (Ire) [-] 7-10 Joanna Morgan (5) (20 to 1) 14
4134^{7} FRIARY TOWN (Ire) [-] 7-5 (6*) P P Murphy (3)..... (33 to 1) 15
4000^{2} BRUGATTI (Ire) [-] 7-7 (4*) J J Behan (4)...........(7 to 1) 16
4000^{5} ROSE BUNCH [-] 7-12 (8*) J J Mullins (17)........(14 to 1) 17
4323^{5} SEE YOU (Ire) [-] (bl) 8-5 (6*) B J Walsh (13)........(16 to 1) 18

Dist: 2l, 1l, hd, 1½l. 1m 31.20s. a 5.80s (18 Ran).
SR: 31/12/9/7/1/-/ (Mrs Catherine Shubotham), J S Bolger

4552 Crofton E.B.F. Race (3-y-o and up) £3,795 7f..................... (2:30)

4386^{2} MYSTERIOUS WAYS (Ire) 3-9-2 J P Murtagh (4) (10 to 9 on) 1
4056 DIAMONDS GALORE (Can) 8-9-0 P Shanahan (3).. (5 to 1) 2
4463^{4} DASHING COLOURS (Ire) (bl) 4-8-11 C Roche (1)... (2 to 1) 3
4407* TALES OF HEARSAY (Ger) (bl) 3-9-2 N G McCullagh (5) ....(8 to 1) 4
4370^{8} TODDY MARK (Ire) 4-8-6 (8*) G M Moylan (2)..... (50 to 1) 5

Dist: 2½l, nk, 3½l, 9l. 1m 29.90s. a 4.50s (5 Ran).
SR: 45/35/31/25/-/ (Mrs A Manning), M V O'Brien

4553 J.R.A. E.B.F. Killavullan Stakes (Group 3) (2-y-o) £14,375 1m.... (3:00)

4261* BROADMARA (Ire) 8-7 R Hughes (1) *prog frm mid-div to track ldrs entering strt, rdn to ld one furlong out, ran on wl*......(10 to 1) 1
4406* TRAGIC POINT (Ire) 8-7 J A Heffernan (9) *led or dsptd ld till lost pl 2 fs out, styd on ins last*......(20 to 1) 2
4286^{2} RAZIDA (Ire) 8-7 K J Manning (6) *mid-div, rdn 3 fs out, kpt on fnl furlong*......(7 to 1) 3
4462 NEWPORT MADAM (Ire) 8-7 J F Egan (4) *mid-div, rdn 2 fs out, kpt on fnl furlong*......(20 to 1) 4
3527* DANCING ACTION (USA) 8-7 P Shanahan (5) *trkd ldrs into strt, not clr run 2 fs out, sn btn, eased cl hme.*......(5 to 4 on) 5
4286^{3} FAIRY WATER 8-7 W J Supple (8) *trkd ldrs till rdn and wknd one and a half fs out*......(7 to 1) 6
4134* ANSARIYA (USA) 8-8^{1} J P Murtagh (2) *dsptd ld 5 fs out, led 2 out, hdd and wknd one out*......(7 to 2) 7
COSSACK PRINCESS (Ire) 8-7 J J Behan (3) *al rear.*......(33 to 1) 8
4380^{5} ACROSS THE TRACKS (Ire) 8-7 D G O'Shea (7) *al rear.*......(20 to 1) 9
Dist: ¾l, ½l, nk, nk. 1m 45.10s. a 7.10s (9 Ran).
(Mrs Clodagh Kean), A J Maxwell

4554 Dargle Handicap (0-105 3-y-o and up) £6,900 1m...... (3:30)

4386^{3} KURDISTAN (Ire) [-] 3-8-13 P V Gilson (5)......(12 to 1) 1
4284 ELIZABETH'S PET (Ire) [-] 3-8-12 S Craine (10)......(12 to 1) 2
4384* WANDERING THOUGHTS (Ire) [-] 4-9-12 (7ex) C Roche (7)......(5 to 2 fav) 3
4185 JUST ONE CANALETTO [-] 5-7-5 (2*) D G O'Shea (1)......(20 to 1) 4
4384^{3} SHARP REVIEW (Ire) [-] 5-9-9 P Shanahan (3)......(11 to 2) 5
4136^{3} SEEK THE FAITH (USA) [-] (bl) 4-8-2 (6*) D J O'Donohoe (15)......(8 to 1) 6
4384^{8} RONDELLI (Ire) [-] 3-8-12 (8*) A P McCoy (13)......(14 to 1) 7
3926^{2} CLASSIC MATCH (Ire) [-] 5-9-12 (2*) P Carberry (11) (9 to 1) 8
4384^{4} SABAYA (USA) [-] 3-9-5 W J Supple (6)......(10 to 1) 9
3494^{8} OVERCAST (Ire) [-] 3-7-8 (4*) J J Behan (9)......(20 to 1) 10
4384 LOS ANGELES (Ire) [-] 4-7-13 (4*) J A Heffernan (8) (33 to 1) 11
3916^{4} SWEET NASHA (Ire) [-] 4-9-12 J P Murtagh (12)... (11 to 2) 12
4136^{2} STATE PRINCESS (Ire) [-] 3-8-8 R Hughes (14)......(7 to 1) 13
Dist: ½l, 1l, sht-hd, nk. 1m 43.80s. a 5.80s (13 Ran).
SR: 24/21/32/-/27/-/ (C S Gaisford-St Lawrence), Michael Kauntze

4555 October Handicap (0-90 3-y-o and up) £3,450 1¼m...... (4:00)

4136 SOUNDPROOF (Ire) [-] 3-8-5 (4*) J J Behan (12)... (20 to 1) 1
4284 LIMBO LADY (USA) [-] 3-8-11 C Roche (21)......(16 to 1) 2
3858* GREAT CABARET (Ire) [-] (bl) 3-8-7 (4*) W J Smith (6)......(20 to 1) 3
4368* MY KERRY DANCER (USA) [-] 3-8-8 K J Manning (5) (7 to 1) 4
4185^{4} FONTANAYS (Ire) [-] 5-7-7 (6*) P P Murphy (22)......(12 to 1) 5
4384^{7} GALLARDINI (Ire) [-] 4-8-10 (8*) A P McCoy (1)......(16 to 1) 6
4185* PHASE IN [-] 3-8-7 (6*) D J O'Donohoe (7)......(6 to 1 fav) 7
3275* CALL MY GUEST (Ire) [-] 3-8-5 W J Supple (15)... (12 to 1) 8
3770^{5} SIR SLAVES [-] 3-9-2 P Shanahan (8)......(14 to 1) 9
4408^{6} DEVIL'S HOLIDAY (USA) [-] 3-8-5 (2*) R M Burke (13)......(12 to 1) 10
4185^{5} MEJEVE [-] 5-8-11 S Craine (11)......(12 to 1) 11
4409 ALBONA [-] 5-7-12 (4*) J A Heffernan (4)......(20 to 1) 12
4501a GLENCLOUD (Ire) [-] 5-9-5 (2*) P Carberry (2)......(20 to 1) 13
4185^{3} ISLAND VISION (Ire) [-] 3-7-6 (8*) R T Fitzpatrick (17)......(10 to 1) 14
4384 LOUGHMOGUE (Ire) [-] 3-9-2 A J Nolan (3)......(33 to 1) 15
4461 SHARKASHKA (Ire) [-] 3-9-5 J P Murtagh (14)......(10 to 1) 16
3976* NORA ANN (Ire) [-] 4-7-12 D V Smith (9)......(25 to 1) 17
4409^{3} SHARASTAMINA (USA) [-] 4-7-13 (6*) R V Skelly (16)......(16 to 1) 18
4461^{5} ELIADE (Ire) [-] 4-9-4 N G McCullagh (18)......(7 to 1) 19
942^{3} ROMAN FORUM (Ire) [-] 5-8-0 (8*) P J Smullen (10) (20 to 1) 20
4383^{7} FLAME OF PERSIA (Ire) [-] 3-9-11 P V Gilson (20) (12 to 1) 21
4246^{6} RETURN AGAIN (Ire) [-] 3-8-13 R Hughes (19)......(10 to 1) 22
Dist: 3½l, ½l, 2½l, sht-hd. 2m 9.70s. a 5.00s (22 Ran).
SR: 55/50/49/41/31/-/ (Yoshiki Akazawa), Patrick Prendergast

4556 Merrion E.B.F. Maiden (3-y-o) £3,450 1¼m...... (4:30)

VANISHING PRAIRIE (USA) (bl) 8-11 J F Egan (18)..(5 to 1) 1
4429^{9} NANNAKA (USA) 8-7 (4*) J J Behan (4)......(10 to 1) 2
ASTER AWEKE (Ire) 8-11 N G McCullagh (17)......(14 to 1) 3
4383 ANDANTE (Ire) 8-9 (2*) R M Burke (3)......(8 to 1) 4
4407^{4} DAHLIA'S BEST (USA) 8-8 (6*) B J Walsh (7)......(10 to 1) 5
4410^{3} NA-AMMAH (Ire) 8-11 W J Supple (9)......(9 to 2) 6
4162^{9} NORDIC QUEEN (Ire) 8-11 K J Manning (13)......(8 to 1) 7
3768^{5} RENEWED DYNASTY (USA) (bl) 9-0 P Shanahan (10)......(9 to 2) 8
4060^{3} ARROGANT LADY 8-11 P V Gilson (5)......(10 to 1) 9
2095 BAEZA 8-6 (8*) P M Donohue (8)......(33 to 1) 10
3856^{3} CAPTURE THE MAGIC (Ire) 8-11 S Craine (2)......(14 to 1) 11
4407^{5} MERSADA (Ire) 8-7 (4*) J A Heffernan (12)......(7 to 2 fav) 12
3975^{7} CLANFLUTHER (Ire) 9-0 Joanna Morgan (6)......(33 to 1) 13
QUENIE TWO (Ire) 8-5 (6*) P P Murphy (1)......(20 to 1) 14
4407^{3} ANOTHER FIDDLE (Ire) 9-0 R Hughes (15)......(10 to 1) 15
4407 DANCING SEER 8-11 R Dolan (16)......(16 to 1) 16
NO POSSIBLE DOUBT (Ire) 8-11 J P Murtagh (19) (33 to 1) 17
4368 VAGUELY DREAM (Ger) 8-9 (2*) D G O'Shea (20)..(50 to 1) 18
Dist: 5l, 1l, 3l, 4l. 2m 10.10s. a 5.40s (18 Ran).
SR: 53/43/41/35/30/-/ (Mrs M J Grassick), M J Grassick

MARSEILLE (FR) (soft)
Saturday October 23rd

4557 Prix Andre Baboin (Group 3) (3-y-o and up) £23,895 1¼m...... (2:45)

4295^{3} MARILDO (Fr) 6-9-8 G Guignard, *trkd ldr till led 5 fs out, rdn 2 out, ran on wl*...... 1
5624 MATARUN (Ire) 5-8-9 O Peslier, *al in tch, 5th strt, hdwy 2 fs out, ran on one pace fnl furlong*...... 2
4219^{4} FUNNY BABY (Fr) 5-8-13 A Badel, *led 5 fs, second strt, ev ch o'r one furlong out, one pace*...... 3
SNOW HOUSE (Ire) 4-8-6 P Julien, *7th strt, gd hdwy wl o'r one furlong out, one pace fnl furlong*...... 4
3844^{4} SHOWGUM (Fr) 3-8-8^{2} G Dubroeucq, *last strt, hdwy fnl 2 fs, nrst at finish*...... 5
KAWA BOY (Fr) 5-8-9 J Leclet, *trkd ldrs, 4th strt, sn one pace*...... 6
SKY SWALLOW (Fr) 6-8-9 G Elorriaga-Santos, *8th strt, nvr a factor*...... 7
4219^{6} SHARPELA 3-9-0 O Poirier, *trkd ldrs, 3rd strt, ev ch 2 fs out, wknd*...... 8
NINI PRINCESSE (Ire) 4-8-6 F Sauret, *6th strt, sn btn*...... 9
Dist: 1½l, 1l, ½l, ½l, 2½l, nk. (Time not taken) (9 Ran).
(D Smaga), D Smaga

NEWBURY (good to soft)
Saturday October 23rd
Going Correction: PLUS 0.60 sec. per fur. (races 1,2,3,6,7), PLUS 0.40 (4,5,8)

4558 Radley Stakes Class A (Listed Race) (2-y-o) £9,260 7f 64yds...... (1:30)

4111* BEARALL (Ire) 8-8 B Rouse (6) *wth ldr, led appr 2 fs out, edgd rght and hdd briefly ins last, ran on wl.*......(10 to 1 op 8 to 1 tchd 11 to 1) 1
4251^{5} PALANA (USA) 8-8 M Hills (1) *trkd ldrs, ev ch whn crrd rght ins fnl furlong, ran on wl.*......(10 to 1 op 12 to 1 tchd 14 to 1) 2
4361* CLYDE GODDESS (Ire) 8-8 W Carson (5) *hld up and took gd hold in rear, hdwy on ins o'r 2 fs out led briefly inside last, no extr cl hme*......(10 to 1 tchd 12 to 1) 3
4302^{4} LEONOVA 8-8 J Weaver (10) *hld up in rear, hdwy 2 fs out, kpt on*......(5 to 2 fav op 9 to 4 tchd 11 to 4) 4
4232* QUEENBIRD 8-8 B Raymond (2) *sn led, hdd appr 2 fs out, ev ch wl o'r one out, one pace*......(8 to 1 op 9 to 2) 5
4396* SILVER HUT (USA) 8-8 M Roberts (3) *chsd ldrs, pushed alng and hdwy o'r 3 fs out, sn outpcd.*......(5 to 1 op 3 to 1) 6
4111^{3} OMNIA (USA) 8-8 C Rutter (4) *chsd ldrs, rdn alng o'r 4 fs out, sn btn*......(16 to 1 op 12 to 1 tchd 20 to 1) 7
4371* TAMAR'S BRIGADE 8-8 A Clark (8) *cl up, pushed alng and wknd 3 fs out*......(9 to 1 op 8 to 1 tchd 10 to 1) 8
4251* MANHATTAN SUNSET (USA) 8-8 J Reid (7) *sn rdn alng, nvr on terms*......(14 to 1 op 10 to 1 tchd 16 to 1) 9
4442^{4} THREATENING 8-11 G Bardwell (11) *mid-div, rdn 3 fs out, btn 2 out, wknd quickly.*......(10 to 1 op 8 to 1 tchd 12 to 1) 10
4220* SPARKLING LYRIC 8-8 W Woods (9) *al beh.*......(25 to 1 op 16 to 1 tchd 33 to 1) 11
Dist: Nk, hd, 1l, 2½l, 2½l, 3l, 8l, 1½l, nk, sht-hd. 1m 34.46s. a 7.16s (11 Ran).
SR: 52/51/50/47/39/31/22/-/-/ (Mr And Mrs M Winterford), R Hannon

4559 Burmah Handicap Class D (0-80 3-y-o and up) £6,515 1½m 5yds...... (2:00)

4157^{4} MIDYAN BLUE (Ire) [71] 3-9-3 B Raymond (2) *al prmnt led one and a half fs out, ran on strly.*......(11 to 1 op 10 to 1 tchd 12 to 1) 1
4502* WARM SPELL [79] 3-9-11 (5ex) B Rouse (18) *al prmnt, hrd rdn o'r 2 fs out, kpt on one pace*.... (10 to 1 op 8 to 1) 2
4414 WESTFIELD MOVES (Ire) [56] 5-8-9 J Quinn (15) *reared strt and beh, hdwy 4 fs out, kpt on wl und pres frm 2 out.*......(14 to 1 tchd 16 to 1) 3
4486 RAPPORTEUR (USA) [64] 7-9-3 W Newnes (9) *wth ldr, led o'r 8 fs out, hdd one and a half out, one pace.*......(25 to 1 op 20 to 1) 4
4374^{3} HIGHLAND SPIRIT [57] 5-8-10 J Reid (5) *trkd ldrs, hrd rdn o'r one furlong out, one pace*...(7 to 1 fav tchd 9 to 1) 5
4354^{4} HEAD TURNER [45] 5-7-12^{5} F Norton (4) *beh, hdwy on ins o'r 2 fs out, kpt on till eased cl hme.*......(16 to 1 tchd 20 to 1) 6

4283* ADDICTED TO LOVE [66] (bl) 4-9-5 T Sprake (6) *mid-div, hdwy 3 fs out, edgd lft and one pace frm o'r one out.* ....(11 to 1 op 10 to 1 tchd 12 to 1) 7
4254[7] SWIFT ROMANCE (Ire) [53] 5-8-6 S Whitworth (21) *strted slwly, rdn alng and hdwy o'r 3 fs out, no imprsn frm over one out*..........(16 to 1 tchd 20 to 1) 8
SEIZE THE DAY (Ire) [65] 5-9-1 (3*) M Fenton (11) *led til hdd o'r 8 fs out, cl up until wknd over 2 out.* ....(50 to 1 tchd 66 to 1) 9
2326[3] MEANT TO BE [68] 3-9-0 M Tebbutt (20) *al prmnt, hrd rdn and wknd wl o'r one furlong out.* (25 to 1 op 20 to 1) 10
2991[4] BOOKCASE [70] 6-9-9 J Williams (3) *beh, hdwy on ins o'r 5 fs out, outpcd over 2 out*.....................(16 to 1) 11
4064 SUPREME MASTER [72] 3-8-11 (7*) Mark Denaro (7) *nvr better than mid-div.* (11 to 1 op 10 to 1 tchd 12 to 1) 12
3893[3] ANORAK (USA) [66] 3-8-12 M Roberts (13) *nvr dfangerous.* ....(16 to 1 op 12 to 1) 13
4457* EURYTHMIC [55] 3-8-1 Dale Gibson (14) *chsd ldrs, rdn alng o'r 4 fs out, sn wknd*..........(9 to 1 op 8 to 1) 14
4352[5] CITY LINE [50] 4-8-3 A Tucker (12) *chsd ldrs till rdn alng and lost pl hfwy*.... (50 to 1 op 33 to 1 tchd 66 to 1) 15
4470 DUTOSKY [68] 3-9-0 G Bardwell (17) *mid-div, rdn alng o'r 4 fs out, no imprsn*............... (25 to 1 op 20 to 1) 16
4414[3] SEASONAL SPLENDOUR (Ire) [76] 3-9-8 D Biggs (16) *beh, effrt 4 fs out, no imprsn.* ....(11 to 1 op 10 to 1 tchd 12 to 1) 17
STATAJACK (Ire) [73] (bl) 5-9-7 (5*) D Wright (1) *al beh.* ....(33 to 1) 18
527* THINKING TWICE (USA) [66] 4-9-5 W Carson (10) *al beh.* ....(10 to 1 tchd 11 to 1) 19
4502 ALLESCA [71] 3-9-3 N Adams (8) *al beh.* .... (33 to 1 op 16 to 1) 20
4254[5] INCHCAILLOCH (Ire) [63] 4-8-11 (5*) A Procter (19) *chsd ldrs till wknd appr 3 fs out.* ....(20 to 1 op 16 to 1 tchd 25 to 1) 21
Dist: 3½l, 1½l, ¾l, ¾l, 2l, 4l, 5l, nk, sht-hd, 6l. 2m 41.57s. a 11.97s (21 Ran).
SR: 55/56/37/43/34/18/31/8/19/ (Keith H Palmer), J M P Eustace

4560 Castrol St Simon Stakes Class A (Group 3) (3-y-o and up) £20,940 1½m 5yds.......................... (2:30)

3467* KITHANGA (Ire) 3-8-4 J Weaver (2) *trkd ldrs, al gng wl, led 3 fs out, sn quickened clr, eased cl hme, imprsv.* ....(4 to 1 fav op 5 to 2) 1
3846* ANNA OF SAXONY 4-9-0 M Roberts (1) *hld up in mid-div, hdwy o'r 2 fs out, chsd wnr fnl furlong, no imprsn.* ....(9 to 2 op 4 to 1) 2
4055[8] LINPAC WEST 7-9-3 G Hind (5) *trkd ldrs, hrd rdn and wndrd und pres 2 fs out, one pace.* ....(16 to 1 op 14 to 1 tchd 20 to 1) 3
4301[4] SHAMBO 6-9-3 R Hills (7) *beh, rdn alng 3 fs out, plugged on one pace*.................................. (25 to 1) 4
1323[7] UP ANCHOR (Ire) 4-8-11 C Rutter (6) *sn led, hdd 3 fs out, wknd*..........(16 to 1 op 14 to 1 tchd 20 to 1) 5
4175* LEAGUE LEADER (Ire) 3-8-7 M Hills (4) *cl up, ev ch 3 fs out, wknd o'r 2 out*................... (12 to 1 op 10 to 1) 6
4467[6] BOBZAO (Ire) 4-9-0 J Reid (8) *hld up in rear, effrt o'r 4 fs out, btn over 2 out*....(9 to 2 op 4 to 1 tchd 5 to 1) 7
4300 LORD OF THE FIELD 6-9-3 W Newnes (9) *al beh.* ....(7 to 1 op 5 to 1) 8
3846[3] SPRING 4-8-11 W Carson (3) *mid-div, beh fnl 4 fs.* .... (7 to 1 op 10 to 1) 9
4271* MUHAYAA (USA) 4-9-0 B Raymond (10) *cl up til wknd quickly 3 fs out*..............(10 to 1 tchd 11 to 1) 10
4064[9] BRIGHT SPELLS 3-8-5[1] J Williams (11) *mid-div, drpd rear 4 fs out, tld off*................ (50 to 1 tchd 66 to 1) 11
Dist: 6l, 4l, 5l, ½l, 4l, 1l, 6l, 2½l, 2l, 25l. 2m 38.86s. a 9.26s (11 Ran).
SR: 69/67/62/52/45/33/38/29/18/ (Fittocks Stud Limited), L M Cumani

4561 Dick Dawson Nursery Class C (2-y-o) £5,526 6f 8yds................... (3:00)

4249[7] CANASKA DANCER (Ire) [90] 9-7 J Reid (5) *trkd ldrs gng wl, led appr fnl furlong, rdn and quickened clr.* .... (100 to 30 fav op 5 to 2 tchd 7 to 2) 1
3664* KERRIE-JO [70] 8-1 J Quinn (3) *strted slwly, sn chsd ldrs, not clr run o'r one furlong out, kpt on wl ins last.* ....(16 to 1 op 14 to 1) 2
4144[6] DANCING LAWYER [70] 8-1 A McGlone (13) *led til hdd appr fnl furlong, one pace*....... (16 to 1 op 12 to 1) 3
4416[3] QUEEN'S TRUST [62] 7-7 G Bardwell (10) *drvn alng o'r 3 fs out, swtchd rght over one out, kpt on.* ....(10 to 1 op 8 to 1 tchd 11 to 1) 4
4423 EVANRO (Ire) [67] 7-12 N Adams (11) *cl up, ev ch o'r one furlong out, one pace.* ....(20 to 1 op 16 to 1 tchd 25 to 1) 5
4225[4] JAREEF'S WAY (Ire) [75] (v) 8-6 W Carson (6) *strted slwly, rdn alng thrght, kpt on appr fnl furlong, nvr nr to chal*..................................(10 to 1 tchd 9 to 1) 6
4098[3] AWS (Ire) [70] 8-1[1] R Hills (1) *trkd ldrs, ev ch o'r 2 fs out, sn outpcd*..............(16 to 1 op 14 to 1 tchd 20 to 1) 7
3485* BALANDRA BAY (Ire) [86] 9-3 G Duffield (8) *cl up till outpcd hfwy*..................(11 to 2 op 6 to 1 tchd 5 to 1) 8
4444 MERLIN'S FIELD (Ire) [77] 8-8 M Roberts (12) *prmnt till wknd wl o'r one furlong out*.......(16 to 1 op 14 to 1) 9
3888[8] BERMUDA LADY (USA) [67] 7-12[2] F Norton (2) *outpcd.* ....(25 to 1) 10
4416* GADGE [69] 8-0 T Williams (9) *sn pushed alng to track ldrs, hrd rdn o'r 2 fs out, wknd*..... (11 to 2 op 5 to 1) 11
4299[7] MOCKINGBIRD [62] (v) 7-2 (5*) D Wright (4) *cl up, ev ch 2 fs out, sn wknd*..................(12 to 1 op 10 to 1) 12
4264[5] CHAMPAGNE GIRL [65] 7-10 Dale Gibson (7) *trkd ldrs till wknd appr 2 fs out*.......................... (12 to 1) 13
Dist: 4l, ¾l, 1l, nk, 3½l, 4l, nk, ½l, nk, ¾l. 1m 16.69s. a 4.99s (13 Ran).
SR: 55/19/16/4/8/2/ (Mrs June M Sifton), P W Chapple-Hyam

4562 Whatcombe Conditions Stakes Class C (2-y-o) £4,204 1m............ (3:30)

4249 STAR SELECTION 8-11 M Roberts (2) *trkd ldr, rdn o'r one furlong out, ran on to ld wl ins last.* ....(11 to 10 on op 5 to 4 tchd 11 to 8) 1
4365* IN LIKE FLYNN 9-1 J Reid (3) *led til hdd wl ins fnl furlong, no extr*..................(9 to 4 op 6 to 4) 2
4232[3] KUTBEYA (USA) 8-8 W Carson (5) *hld up in cl tch, reminders appr 2 fs out, sn outpcd.* ....(4 to 1 op 3 to 1 tchd 9 to 2) 3
3570[2] YOUNG AT HEART (Ire) 8-11 B Raymond (4) *hld up in tch, swtchd lft to hold ev ch 2 fs out, sn outpcd.* ....(14 to 1 op 8 to 1) 4
4356 RAVEN'S ROOST (Ire) 8-11 W Newnes (1) *in cl tch till outpcd fnl 2 fs*...... (33 to 1 op 20 to 1 tchd 40 to 1) 5
Dist: 1l, 6l, 1l, 20l. 1m 44.20s. a 7.10s (5 Ran).
SR: 39/40/15/15/-/ (M Arbib), P F I Cole

4563 Paddock Pavilions Rated Class B Handicap (0-100 3-y-o and up) £7,985 1m 1f.......................... (4:05)

4247 BOLD STROKE [77] 4-8-9 J Reid (5) *trkd ldrs, led 2 fs out, ran on strly*..................... (10 to 1 tchd 12 to 1) 1
4300 CONEYBURY (Ire) [86] (bl) 3-9-0 J Weaver (9) *mid-div, hdwy o'r 2 fs out, hng lft appr last, no extr.* ....(12 to 1 op 10 to 1 tchd 14 to 1) 2
4424* MISSED FLIGHT [91] 3-9-5 G Duffield (12) *hld up towards rear, cld 3 fs out, kpt on frm o'r one out.* ....(3 to 1 fav op 5 to 2) 3
4414[7] DEER HUNT [83] 4-9-1 B Raymond (14) *cl up, hrd rdn o'r one furlong out, one pace.* .... (15 to 2 op 8 to 1 tchd 9 to 1) 4
4468 WALKING THE PLANK [75] (v) 4-8-7 M Hills (6) *trkd ldrs, rdn 2 fs out, ran on ins last*...... (16 to 1 tchd 20 to 1) 5
4280 WUFUD (USA) [84] 3-8-12 W Carson (4) *beh, hrd rdn 2 fs out, ran on ins last*..............(33 to 1 op 25 to 1) 6
4247 PORT SUNLIGHT (Ire) [75] 5-8-7 A McGlone (2) *hld up, cld o'r 3 fs out, ch over one out, sn btn and eased.* ....(16 to 1 tchd 14 to 1) 7
4415[6] ISAIAH [83] 4-9-1 J Quinn (16) *led til hdd 2 fs out, wknd appr last*..................(10 to 1 tchd 12 to 1) 8
4300 KNOWTH (Ire) [78] 4-8-5 (5*) D Wright (3) *hld up in rear, hdwy und pres 3 fs out, btn 2 out*.... (9 to 1 op 8 to 1) 9
4274 LINDON LIME (USA) [93] 3-9-7 C Rutter (8) *chsd ldrs till rdn and wknd o'r 3 fs out*..........(14 to 1 tchd 16 to 1) 10
2941[7] ARUSHA (Ire) [78] 3-8-6 J Williams (15) *al beh, tld off aftr 3 fs*..................................(33 to 1 op 20 to 1) 11
4300[2] TALENT (USA) [89] (v) 5-9-7 M Roberts (11) *cl up till rdn and wknd o'r 2 fs out.* (6 to 1 op 5 to 1 tchd 13 to 2) 12
3757[4] LT WELSH (USA) [75] (v) 3-8-3 S O'Gorman (7) *al beh.* ....(16 to 1 tchd 20 to 1) 13
4300 CROSSILLION [83] 5-9-1 F Norton (13) *chsd ldrs, pushed alng and hdwy 4 fs out, btn 2 out.* (14 to 1 op 12 to 1) 14
2961 WALI (USA) [83] 3-8-11 R Hills (1) *mid-div, rdn alng o'r 4 fs out, sn lost pl*.................. (33 to 1 op 20 to 1) 15
1745[2] HOOCHIECOOCHIE MAN (Ire) [75] 3-7-12[2] (7*) D O'Neill (10) *trkd ldrs till wknd 3 fs out, tld off.* (25 to 1 op 33 to 1) 16
Dist: 4l, 1l, 2l, ¾l, 2l, ¾l, sht-hd, 4l, hd, 2l. 1m 58.48s. a 9.28s (16 Ran).
SR: 38/31/33/23/13/12/5/12/-/ (Tom Wilson), J L Dunlop

4564 Levy Board Nursery Class D (2-y-o) £3,933 7f 64yds.................. (4:35)

4418[3] MILLION LIGHTS (Ire) [66] (v) 8-12 M Roberts (19) *cl up, led o'r 2 fs out, ran on wl.* ....(4 to 1 fav op 6 to 1 tchd 13 to 2) 1
4329[8] AL JINN [60] 8-6 D Biggs (1) *strted slwly, rdn and hdwy o'r 3 fs out, kpt on*... (20 to 1 op 16 to 1 tchd 25 to 1) 2
4128* CANDI DAS (Ire) [54] 7-7 (7*) Antoinette Armes (7) *mid-div, swtchd lft 2 fs out, kpt on one pace.* ....(20 to 1 op 16 to 1) 3
4029* PLUNDER BAY (USA) [71] 9-3 B Raymond (11) *cl up, rdn alng hfwy, kpt on one pace und pres.* .... (10 to 1 op 8 to 1) 4
3145[4] STARICA (Ire) [52] (bl) 7-12 J Quinn (8) *chsd ldrs, hrd rdn 2 fs out, one pace*..................................(20 to 1) 5
4097[5] DOUCE MAISON (Ire) [59] 8-5 N Adams (6) *slwly into strd, beh, hdwy 3 fs out, not clr run wl o'r one out, kpt on ins last*..................(16 to 1 op 14 to 1 tchd 20 to 1) 6
4029[9] SANGARE (Ire) [60] 8-6 A McGlone (15) *beh, hdwy und pres o'r one furlong out, nrst finish*.... (20 to 1 op 16 to 1) 7
4299[5] MIDUSHI (USA) [75] 9-7 M Hills (4) *beh, hdwy hfwy, ev ch 2 fs out, swshd tail und pres and sn btn.* .... (11 to 1 op 12 to 1 tchd 14 to 1) 8

4003* ALASKAN HEIR [75] 9-7 C Rutter (18) *beh, kpt on und pres frm o'r 2 fs out*.................. (20 to 1 op 14 to 1) 9
4350* SUGAR TOWN (Ire) [68] 8-9 (5*) T G McLaughlin (14) *chsd ldrs, pushed alng o'r 4 fs out, btn appr 2 out*. .... (13 to 2 op 6 to 1 tchd 7 to 1) 10
3667[6] PERSIAN AFFAIR (Ire) [71] 9-0 (3*) M Fenton (9) *cl up till rdn and wknd o'r 2 fs out*............ (20 to 1 op 14 to 1) 11
4337[4] JEMIMA PUDDLEDUCK [55] 8-1 F Norton (2) *trkd ldrs, ev ch 2 fs out, sn btn*....(12 to 1 op 10 to 1 tchd 14 to 1) 12
4329 DULFORD LAD [66] 8-12 S Whitworth (16) *al beh*. ....(20 to 1 tchd 25 to 1) 13
3704[5] LEAR DANCER (USA) [72] 9-4 W Newnes (13) *al beh*. .... (16 to 1 op 14 to 1 tchd 20 to 1) 14
4251 HELLO IRELAND [74] 9-6 W Carson (5) *chsd ldrs till wknd 2 fs out*................(11 to 1 op 10 to 1 tchd 12 to 1) 15
4358 JOBISDUN [55] (bl) 8-1 G Bardwell (10) *trkd ldrs, ev ch 2 fs out, sn hrd rdn and edgd lft, eased whn btn ins last*. .... (33 to 1 op 25 to 1) 16
4365 VANESSA ROSE [69] 8-10 (5*) D Wright (3) *led til hdd o'r 2 fs out, wknd quickly*..... (13 to 2 op 7 to 1 tchd 5 to 1) 17
3940 ROBBY (Ire) [60] 8-6 G Duffield (17) *cl up till wknd hfwy*. .... (20 to 1 op 16 to 1) 18
4338[4] LADY SILK [69] 9-1 T Williams (12) *al beh*. .... (20 to 1 op 16 to 1 tchd 25 to 1) 19

Dist: 2½l, ¾l, 5l, hd, 2½l, ¾l, ¾l, hd, 1½l, nk. 1m 36.86s. a 9.56s (19 Ran).
SR: 20/6/-/-/-/ (Million In Mind Partnership (2)), R Hannon

4565 Sparsholt Maiden Stakes (Class D) (3-y-o) £3,435 1m................. (5:05)

1868[3] SIMAAT (USA) 8-9 M Hills (8) *trkd ldrs, squeezed through and ran on ld wl ins fnl furlong*. .... (8 to 1 op 6 to 1 tchd 10 to 1) 1
4322[7] FLOWING OCEAN 9-0 B Crossley (3) *trkd ldrs, led 2 fs out till hdd wl ins last*.....(12 to 1 op 6 to 1 tchd 14 to 1) 2
FORESHORE (Ire) 8-9 S Whitworth (1) *in cl tch, ev ch 2 fs out, one pace*......................(9 to 1 op 6 to 1) 3
TRIBECA 8-9 A McGlone (4) *trkd ldrs, led appr 3 fs out till hdd 2 out, one pace*..... (8 to 1 op 4 to 1 tchd 9 to 1) 4
3514[3] BADRAH (USA) 8-9 W Carson (9) *trkd ldrs, ev ch 2 fs out, one pace und pres*. (2 to 1 fav tchd 5 to 2 and 7 to 4) 5
4126[4] PRIME OF LIFE (Ire) 9-0 S Raymont (6) *beh till styd on ins fnl furlong*............(8 to 1 op 6 to 1 tchd 10 to 1) 6
4372[6] FIRE CARPET (USA) 9-0 J Reid (11) *in tch, pushed alng hfwy, no hdwy*....... (12 to 1 op 6 to 1 tchd 14 to 1) 7
SAMAH 9-0 R Hills (5) *slwly into strd, hdwy on ins o'r 2 fs out, ev ch over one out, wknd inside last, better for race*..................................(12 to 1 op 7 to 2) 8
WILLINGLY (Ire) 8-9 C Rutter (2) *in tch till outpcd fnl 2 fs*. .... (14 to 1 op 16 to 1 tchd 20 to 1) 9
4126 WEB OF STEEL 9-0 W Newnes (12) *trkd ldrs till wknd 3 fs out, tld off*..................(33 to 1 op 25 to 1) 10
4499 GARRALLAN 9-0 G Hind (7) *led till hdd appr 3 fs out, sn wknd, tld off*........ (33 to 1 op 25 to 1 tchd 50 to 1) 11

Dist: Nk, 2½l, 1½l, hd, 1l, sht-hd, ½l, 1½l, 25l, 10l. 1m 46.00s. a 8.90s (11 Ran).
SR: 10/14/1/-/-/-/ (Hamdan Al-Maktoum), J H M Gosden

DUSSELDORF (GER) (heavy)
Sunday October 24th

4566 Preis der Spielbanken des Landes Nordrhein-Westfalen (Group 3) (3-y-o and up) £20,408 1½m...........(2:45)

4201[5] PROTEKTOR (Ger) 4-9-6 T Hellier, *mid-div, str run to ld ins fnl furlong, ran on wl*.................................. 1
4306[6] CAPTAIN HORATIUS (Ire) 4-9-2 W Ryan, *3rd strt, ev ch one furlong out, ran on one pace*.......................... 2
4201[6] EMBARCADERO (Ger) 5-9-4 M Rimmer, *second strt, led 2 fs out till ins fnl furlong, no extr*....................... 3
2259[5] CONCEPCION (Ger) 3-8-8 A Boschert, *in tch, ev ch 2 fs out, kpt on fnl furlong*.................................. 4
IN DUBIO (Ger) 4-9-2 , *nvr nr to chal*.................... 5
3929[4] ELISHA (Ger) 4-8-7 A Bond, *nvr dngrs*..................... 6
KANUDOS (Ger) 4-9-2 A Tylicki, *prmnt for m*............. 7
4305[3] RACING BLUE 3-8-2 W J Supple, *al beh*................. 8
3929[3] SHINE SHARE (Ire) 3-8-4 N Grant, *al in rear*............. 9
4306[7] HONDO MONDO (Ire) 5-9-2 A Best, *al beh*................ 10
4196[4] BEDAVA (Fr) 3-8-8 N Jeanpierre, *led to 2 fs out, sn wknd*. 11

Dist: 1 ¾l, ½l, 2½l, 5l, 2½l, 1 ¾l, nk. 2m 43.89s. (11 Ran).
(D Joswich), A Lowe

LONGCHAMP (FR) (soft)
Sunday October 24th
Going Correction: PLUS 0.85 sec. per fur.

4567 Prix des Reservoirs (Group 3) 2yo Fillies £23,895 1m................ (1:25)

4399[2] THREE ANGELS (USA) 8-9 C Asmussen, *second strt, chlgd 2 fs out, led wl ins fnl furlong, ran on well*........... 1
PAPAGO (Ire) 8-9 S Guillot, *led till hdd wl ins fnl furlong, ran on*... 2
VALDARA 8-9 T Jarnet, *mid-div, 5th strt, outpcd 2 fs out, hdwy appr fnl furlong, fnshd wl*..................... 3
ZAPATA BEAUTY (USA) 8-9 D Boeuf, *4th strt, hdwy 2 fs out, ev ch o'r one furlong out, one pace fnl furlong*.... 4
TRULY A DREAM (Ire) 8-9 M Boutin, *3rd strt, ev ch 2 fs out, kpt on one pace*.................................. 5
4195[3] FILHA DO AR (USA) 8-9 O Peslier, *al in rear, last strt, rdn 2 fs out, kpt on one pace*............................. 6

Dist: Hd, sht-hd, ¾l, nk, 1½l. 1m 54.00s. a 18.00s (6 Ran).
(W Young), F Boutin

4568 Prix du Petit-Couvert (Group 3) (2-y-o and up) £23,895 5f..............(1:55)

4287[2] LAVINIA FONTANA (Ire) 4-9-8 L Dettori, *chsd ldr, sn rdn, hdwy to ld one furlong out, ran on wl*.............. 1
4304* PALACEGATE EPISODE (Ire) 3-9-8 J Carroll,............... 2
4312[4] ZIETEN (USA) 3-10-0 T Jarnet, *in rear, prog 2 and a half fs out on ins, nvr rchd ldrs*.......................... 3
4010 TENGA (USA) 3-9-8 C Asmussen, *last till hdwy 2 and a half fs out, kpt on fnl two furlongs*................. 4
4304[4] HATTA FORT 6-9-11 J Reid, *al mid-div, rdn 2 and a half fs out, one pace*....................................... 5
4413[5] ZELDA (Ire) 3-9-8 G Mosse, *prmnt early on outsd, wknd 3 fs out*.. 6
TIEN NGO (Fr) 3-9-8 M de Smyter, *prmnt till rdn and wknd o'r 3 fs out*....................................... 7
FLORIDA FLYER (Ire) 2-8-5 S Coerette, *al beh*............ 8

Dist: 2½l, 2½l, 2½l, 1½l, 4l, ¾l, 1½l. 1m 1.50s. a 6.00s (8 Ran).
SR: 73/63/59/43/40/21/18/-/ (Cyril Humphris), C Collins

4569 Prix Royal-Oak (Group 1) (3-y-o and up) £47,790 1m 7f 110yds....... (2:55)

4296[2] RAINTRAP 3-8-11 Pat Eddery, *hld up, last strt, not clr run one and a half fs out, gd hdwy one furlong out, led last strds*.. 1
4395* MASHAALLAH (USA) 5-9-3 L Dettori, *led, hrd rdn 2 fs out, ran on wl, ct last strds*.................................. 2
4294[3] SONUS (Ire) 4-9-3 C Asmussen, *mid-div, 6th strt, outpcd 2 fs out, ran on fnl furlong, fnshd wl*..................... 3
4292* HALESIA (USA) 4-9-0 D Boeuf, *prmnt, 4th strt, ev ch one and a half fs out, one pace fnl furlong*............... 4
4294* ASSESSOR (Ire) 4-9-3 J Reid, *prmnt, bumped and stumbled 5 fs out, 3rd strt, ev ch 2 furlongs out, one pace fnl furlong*... 5
4294[4] DOUBLE BLASH 4-9-3 O Peslier, *trkd ldr, second strt, ev ch 2 fs out, no extr fnl furlong*........................ 6
4296* SHAIYBARA (Ire) 3-8-8 G Mosse, *pld hrd in rear, 7th strt, rdn and hdwy 2 fs out, drpd back frm two furlongs out*. 7
4301* FURTHER FLIGHT 7-9-3 M Hills, *mid-div, 5th strt, rdn and wknd 2 fs out*... 8

Dist: Sht-nk, nose, 1l, nk, 1½l, 2½l, 1½l. 2m 45.80s. a 29.30s (8 Ran).
(K Abdulla), A Fabre

4570 Prix du Ranelagh (Listed) 3yo Colts & Geldings £14,337 1m........... (3:25)

4075[3] JACKDIDI (Fr) 9-2 D Boeuf,.............................. 1
HURON WARRIOR (USA) 8-12 O Peslier,................. 2
2803[9] LYNTON (USA) 9-2 Pat Eddery,.......................... 3
4076[3] NEVERNEYEV (USA) 8-12 O Doleuze,.................... 4
WOOD STAG (USA),.. 5
4196[6] IRISH PROSPECTOR (Fr),.................................. 6
4325[2] EMBROS (USA),.. 7
4401[2] LITTLE MUNCHKIN (Ire) 8-12 L Dettori, *prmnt o'r 5 fs*..... 8

Dist: ¾l, nk, 1½l, ½l, ½l, nk, 2l. 1m 45.90s. a 9.90s (8 Ran).
SR: 55/49/52/43/-/-/-/32/ (M Benillouche), E Lellouche

SAN SIRO (ITY) (heavy)
Sunday October 24th

4571 Premio Bagutta-Memorial S Cumani (Group 3) Fillies/Mares (3-y-o and up) £28,780 1m................... (1:50)

4300* PENNY DROPS 4-8-8 D Harrison, *rcd in 5th, drpd back to 7th on bend, gd hdwy 2 fs out, led ins fnl furlong, ran on*... 1
IMCO CHARMER (Ire) 3-8-6 Jacqueline Freda, *trkd ldrs, 3rd strt, chlgd 2 and a half fs out, ev ch one furlong out, one pace*... 2
3934[6] FOOLISH HEART (Ire) 3-8-6 L Sorrentino, *trkd ldr, second strt, ev ch o'r one furlong out, one pace*.............. 3
1222[8] PAESANELLA 3-8-6 G Forte, *led till ins fnl furlong, wknd cl hme*.. 4
3934* JULY GIRL 4-8-8 M Esposito, *al beh*..................... 5
4403[4] ROUQUETTE 3-8-9 A Badel, *6th strt, nvr able to chal*.... 6
3934[2] CIVIDALE (Ire) 4-8-8 M Planard, *al beh*.................. 7
4199[7] SEEING (USA) 3-8-6 M Vargiu, *4th strt, sn wknd, tld off*. 8

Dist: 2l, ½l, 1l, 14l, 12l, 7l, dist. 1m 52.50s. (8 Ran).
(Stanley J Sharp), Lord Huntingdon

4572 Gran Criterium (Group 1) 2yo Colts & Fillies £65,853 1m.............(3:10)

2649* TORRISMONDO (USA) 8-11 T Quinn, *made all, unchlgd.* 1
4281^{4} INNISHOWEN (USA) 8-11 B Raymond, *rced in 4th, lost grnd entering strt, ran on wl frm 2 fs out*.............. 2
4382* SHERIDAN (Ire) 8-11 D Holland, *rcd in 3rd, ran on one pace frm one and a half fs out*......................... 3
4314* CHOCOLUNE (Ity) 8-11 S Dettori,.......................... 4
4198* LEAR WHITE (USA) 8-11 V Mezzatesta,.................... 5
4249* FUMO DI LONDRA (Ire) 8-11 L Piggott,..................... 6
RAVIER (Fr) 8-11 B Jovine,.................................. 7
4198^{6} ISLAND MAGIC 8-11 Jacqueline Freda,.................. 8
Dist: 2l, 6l, ½l, 15l, 2l, 16l, 10l. 1m 50.70s. (8 Ran).
(Lord Portman), P F I Cole

GALWAY (IRE) (good to yielding)
Monday October 25th

4573 Bank Of Ireland Intern Div QR's Race (4-y-o and up) £3,750 2m....... (3:10)

3805^{8} AIYBAK (Ire) 5-11-3 (5*) Mr J A Nash (4)....... (2 to 1 fav) 1
4430* FOR REG (Ire) 4-11-3 Mr P Fenton (10)........ (100 to 30) 2
4411* NIGHTMAN 4-11-3 Mr A J Martin (11)............. (5 to 1) 3
4095* PADASHPAN (USA) 4-11-5 (3*) Mrs J M Mullins (2)..(9 to 2) 4
PRINCE OLE (Ire) 5-10-10 (7*) Mr E Norris (5)..... (14 to 1) 5
PERSIAN HALO (Ire) 5-10-10 (7*) Miss S Kauntze (3) .... (70 to 1) 6
KING OF THE GLEN 7-10-10 (7*) Mr J T McNamara (1) .... (20 to 1) 7
4411^{6} INDIANA GOLD (Ire) 5-10-7 (7*) Ms W Fox (8)..... (25 to 1) 8
ALICES RUN 6-10-10 (7*) Miss F M Crowley (7)... (10 to 1) 9
961^{6} VON CARTY (Ire) 4-10-10 (7*) Mrs F A O'Sullivan (6) (20 to 1) 10
MARYVILLE LADY (Ire) 4-10-7 (7*) Mr C B Hynes (9) (50 to 1) 11
Dist: 1½l, ½l, 8l, 1½l. 3m 45.10s. (11 Ran).
(Michael W J Smurfit), D K Weld

LEICESTER (good to soft)
Monday October 25th
Going Correction: PLUS 0.60 sec. per fur.

4574 Seagrave Apprentices' Claiming Handicap Class G (0-70 3-y-o and up) £2,679 1m 8yds................ (1:20)

3247^{5} TOCCO JEWEL [35] 3-7-11 (5*) M Baird (6) *patiently rdn, improved into midfield hfwy, led o'r one furlong out, styd on wl*........................ (8 to 1 op 12 to 1) 1
4104 FORMAESTRE (Ire) [38] 3-8-5 D Gibbs (4) *co'red up in midfield, rdn to draw level over one furlong out, styd on*..................................... (12 to 1 op 8 to 1) 2
4354^{2} MAI PEN RAI [44] 5-8-9 (5*) Ruth Coulter (15) *chsd alng to improve frm midfield last 2 fs, fnshd wl*.....(11 to 2 jt-fav op 5 to 1) 3
3536^{4} OVERPOWER [52] 9-9-3 (5*) J Gotobed (10) *reared strt, drvn alng to improve into midfield whn hmpd o'r 2 fs out, kpt on ins last*............ (11 to 2 jt-fav op 4 to 1) 4
4391^{8} RESOLUTE BAY [55] 7-9-11 G Parkin (11) *patiently rdn, hdwy last 2 fs, ran on finish*..................... (12 to 1) 5
4348 SPORTING SPIRIT [34] (bl) 3-7-12 (3*) C Teague (7) *nvr far away, feeling pace and rdn last 2 fs, one pace.* (33 to 1) 6
4431^{7} COBBS CROSS [38] 3-7-12 (7*) W Hollick (20) *tucked away, effrt and pushed alng o'r 2 fs out, kpt on same pace*.............................. (40 to 1 op 33 to 1) 7
4490 WOLF POWER (Ire) [53] 3-9-6 S Copp (1) *settled gng wl, led on bit o'r 3 fs out, hdd over one out, fdd.* .... (9 to 1 op 10 to 1 tchd 12 to 1) 8
4083^{5} HALL BANK COTTAGE [41] 3-8-3 (5*) J Dennis (18) *settled midfield, effrt and drvn alng o'r 2 fs out, not pace to chal*...(12 to 1) 9
4525 SHEFFORD [45] 3-8-7 (5*) C Adamson (5) *speed on outsd for o'r 5 fs*.....................(25 to 1 op 20 to 1) 10
3547^{2} DODGY [48] (v) 6-8-13 (5*) A Martinez (9) *trkd ldrs, effrt and rdn hfwy, fdd 2 fs out*.........(12 to 1 op 8 to 1) 11
4327 VICTORIAS PASSION [36] 3-8-3^{7} (7*) Sarah Senior (12) *chsd alng to keep up, nvr a factor*...... (40 to 1 op 33 to 1) 12
NAIL DON [50] 8-9-1 (5*) D O'Neill (19) *pressed ldrs, swrvd lft o'r 2 fs out, sn btn*.............(40 to 1 op 33 to 1) 13
3207a WATER DIVINER [48] 3-8-8 (7*) T Beaver (14) *chsd alng to go pace, nvr nr to chal*........... (20 to 1 op 14 to 1) 14
4104^{2} MALCESINE (Ire) [42] 4-8-12 P Roberts (3) *bustled alng in midfield hfwy, nvr a threat*..........(7 to 1 op 6 to 1) 15
4206^{7} MIM [34] 3-7-10 (5*) Iona Wands (8) *sn outpcd and drvn alng, nvr a factor*...................................(33 to 1) 16
4501 NOEPROB (USA) [56] 3-9-4 (5*) L Aspell (17) *shwd up wl till wknd quickly 2 fs out*............ (16 to 1 op 14 to 1) 17
3175 COOL COQUELIN (Ire) [33] 5-8-0^{4} (7*) Sally Wall (16) *clr ldr centre till o'r 3 fs out, wknd 2 out.* (40 to 1 op 33 to 1) 18
3124^{5} FOOLISH TOUCH [37] 11-8-0 (7*) G Faulkner (13) *rcd alone far side, struggling hfwy*.......... (12 to 1 op 8 to 1) 19
3820^{7} MISS KINGFISHER (USA) [42] 4-8-7 (5*) D Griffiths (2) *sluggish strt, not reco'r*..................... (33 to 1) 20
Dist: ¾l, 1½l, sht-hd, nk, 2½l, ¾l, 1½l, 4l, hd, 4l. 1m 46.30s. a 11.20s (20 Ran).
(Mrs M J Ryan), M J Ryan

4575 EBF Fleckney Maiden Fillies' Stakes Class D (2-y-o) £4,556 5f 218yds (1:50)

4303^{3} PRIMO STAMPARI 8-11 Pat Eddery (14) *made all, shaken up o'r one furlong out, styd on strly last 100 yards*. .... (6 to 1 tchd 4 to 1) 1
4142^{4} VERDIGRIS (Ire) 8-11 J Weaver (11) *tucked away on ins, ev ch and rdn o'r one furlong out, sn outpcd, kpt on nr finish*..................(11 to 8 fav op Evens tchd 6 to 4) 2
4345^{3} BINTALSHAATI 8-11 R Hills (10) *nvr far away, ev ch appr fnl furlong, kpt on same pace*.....(3 to 1 tchd 4 to 1) 3
LALINDI (Ire) 8-11 M Hills (13) *missed break, last hfwy, ran on strly appr fnl furlong, unlucky*...(8 to 1 op 4 to 1) 4
FUTURE OPTIONS 8-11 J Williams (7) *chsd ldrs, improved o'r one furlong out, styd on*..........................(33 to 1) 5
4350^{6} IT'S SO EASY 8-11 K Fallon (3) *chsd alng to improve frm midfield last 2 fs, nrst finish*.......(33 to 1 op 25 to 1) 6
HAD A GIRL 8-11 T Quinn (5) *nvr far away, feeling pace and rdn 2 fs out, no extr*..........(20 to 1 op 16 to 1) 7
NAIS (Ire) 8-8 (3*) M Fenton (4) *sluggish strt, hdwy on outsd last 2 fs, nvr plcd to chal*.... (20 to 1 op 10 to 1) 8
4345^{7} CHANTELYS 8-11 G Hind (2) *speed on outsd for o'r 4 fs, no extr*..(25 to 1) 9
RISQUE-TOUT 8-11 D Holland (6) *pressed ldrs, drvn alng whn pace quickened last 2 fs, fdd.* (20 to 1 op 10 to 1) 10
SUPERTURN 8-11 M Tebbutt (15) *bustled alng in midfield, nvr rch ldrs*......................(50 to 1 op 33 to 1) 11
4345 ELLASTYLE (Ire) 8-11 J Fortune (9) *bustled alng in midfield, nvr a factor*.................................. (100 to 1) 12
4257^{5} MARYKIRK 8-11 S Whitworth (12) *sn outpcd and drvn alng, al beh*.........................(66 to 1 op 50 to 1) 13
4452 BAIRN GLEN 8-11 M Birch (8) *wth ldrs, feeling pace and lost grnd o'r 2 fs out, eased whn btn.* .... (20 to 1 op 33 to 1) 14
4265^{4} INDIAN LAMENT 8-6 (5*) S Drowne (1) *reluctant to enter stalls, swrvd and uns rdr strt*.................. (20 to 1) ur
Dist: 1½l, ½l, 2l, 1½l, 1½l, nk, 3l, hd, 1½l, 3l. 1m 18.20s. a 7.80s (15 Ran).
SR: 13/7/5/-/-/-/ (Miss L J Vickers), R Hannon

4576 Squirrel Conditions Stakes Class C (3-y-o and up) £4,448 1m 3f 183yds (2:20)

4064^{8} SCOTTISH PEAK (Ire) 3-8-7 Pat Eddery (3) *set steady pace aftr 100 yards, quickened o'r 2 fs out, styd on strly nr finish*.................................(7 to 1 op 6 to 1) 1
4155* WAJIH (USA) 3-8-9 R Hills (2) *al hndy, rdn to chal o'r 2 fs out, kpt on nr finish*... (5 to 1 op 7 to 2 tchd 11 to 2) 2
4395^{2} PETER QUINCE 3-8-9 W Ryan (4) *led 100 yards, settled gng wl hfwy, outpcd and rdn o'r 2 fs out, styd on finish*...................... (15 to 8 on op 2 to 1 on) 3
4499^{3} WOODCHAT (USA) 3-8-10 A Munro (1) *trkd ldg trio, struggling whn pace quickened o'r 2 fs out, sn btn*. ....(9 to 2 op 7 to 2) 4
Dist: 1l, nk, 5l. 2m 46.20s. a 17.70s (4 Ran).
(Lord Weinstock), Lord Huntingdon

4577 John O'Gaunt Nursery Class E (2-y-o) £3,522 7f 9yds.................. (2:50)

4453^{4} ARCTIC DIAMOND [60] 9-0 K Fallon (4) *outpcdin midfield hfwy, swtchd outsd to improve o'r one furlong out, ran on und pres to ld last strds*......... (7 to 2 op 9 to 4) 1
4329^{7} WESTERN FLEET (USA) [67] 9-7 Pat Eddery (13) *tucked away in midfield, drvn to ld o'r one furlong out, rdn and hdd last strds*............... (5 to 1 tchd 6 to 1) 2
4358^{5} SUSELJA (Ire) [53] 8-7 S Whitworth (3) *struggling to go early pace, hdwy stands side last 2 fs, ran on finish*. .... (14 to 1 op 12 to 1) 3
4330^{7} TONE CONTROL [62] 9-2 W Woods (6) *al hndy, ev ch and rdn 2 fs out, kpt on same pace*...... (16 to 1 op 14 to 1) 4
3743^{5} DUBALL REMY [54] 8-8 A Munro (14) *settled midfield, effrt on outsd o'r 2 fs out, bumped over one out, one pace*. ....(10 to 1 tchd 11 to 1) 5
4338^{9} LITTLE LUKE (Ire) [45] 7-13 F Norton (12) *chsd alng in midfield, kpt on last 2 fs, nvr able to chal*. .... (33 to 1 op 16 to 1) 6
4329^{5} NORTHERN STARLIGHT [50] (v) 8-0^{1} (5*) S Drowne (11) *nvr far away, ev ch and rdn 2 fs out, no extr*. .... (15 to 2 op 7 to 1 tchd 8 to 1) 7
2588^{8} LONE RISK [50] 8-4 N Carlisle (1) *outpcd and drvn alng hfwy, no imprsn last 2 fs*...................(33 to 1) 8
4329 KENILWORTH FORD [50] 8-4 J Fanning (2) *tucked away beh ldrs, not clr run 2 fs out, barged through, styd on, nrst finish*...................... (50 to 1 op 33 to 1) 9
4342^{7} MISTY WISE [50] 8-1 (3*) M Fenton (10) *prmnt, ev ch and rdn alng 2 fs out, fdd*...........(10 to 1 tchd 12 to 1) 10
4349* FORGOTTEN LADY (Ire) [66] 9-6 T Quinn (5) *made most for o'r 5 fs, fdd*.........(3 to 1 fav op 7 to 2 tchd 4 to 1) 11
4356 CLUBS ARE TRUMPS (Ire) [50] 8-4 S Dawson (7) *chsd alng beh ldrs, nvr nr to chal*.......................... (33 to 1) 12
4342 TOOGOODFORYOU [45] (bl) 7-13 L Charnock (8) *rcd freely in frnt rnk, feeling pace whn hmpd o'r one furlong out, eased when btn*...................... (33 to 1 op 50 to 1) 13
4342 SEMAH'S DREAM [42] 7-10 J O'Reilly (15) *reared strt, al struggling*........................ (50 to 1 op 25 to 1) 14

4480 RICHARD'S ERROR [55] 8-4 (5*) D Wright (9) *settled beh ldrs, shaken up hfwy, nvr dngrs.* (33 to 1 op 16 to 1) 15
Dist: Hd, 3l, 2l, ½l, 1½l, nk, 2½l, 1½l, 2l, 2l. 1m 33.30s. a 11.40s (15 Ran).
(Mrs B D Southam), Mrs J R Ramsden

4578 Wysall Conditions Stakes Class D (3-y-o and up) £3,260 7f 9yds...... (3:20)

4499[4] ETOSHA (bl) 3-8-8 M Hills (5) *reluctant to enter stalls, sluggish strt, improved hfwy, led entering fnl furlong, styd on*.............................. (7 to 2 op 3 to 1) 1
4415 KAYVEE 4-9-0 Pat Eddery (1) *trkd ldg trio, effrt and rdn o'r 2 fs out, led briefly entering last, eased whn btn last 50 yards*........... (5 to 4 fav op Evens tchd 11 to 8) 2
4393 PETERSFORD GIRL (Ire) 3-8-8 T Quinn (4) *co'red up on ins, effrt and not much room over one furlong out, swtchd entering last, styd on*....(7 to 2 op 3 to 1 tchd 4 to 1) 3
4463[8] DAGNY JUEL (USA) 3-8-8 W Ryan (6) *set modest pace, quickened o'r 2 fs out, hdd and no extr entering last.* ....(5 to 1 op 4 to 1) 4
4125 MR PERKY 3-8-9 J Williams (2) *patiently rdn, effrt hfwy, struggling whn pace quickened o'r 2 fs out, sn lost tch.* ....(100 to 1 op 66 to 1) 5
SAGA BLUE 3-8-4 W Woods (3) *trkd ldr, struggling to hold pl o'r 2 fs out, tld off*........(100 to 1 op 66 to 1) 6
Dist: 2½l, hd, 2½l, 20l, 15l. 1m 32.30s. a 10.40s (6 Ran).
SR: 1/-/-/ (A E Oppenheimer), G Wragg

4579 EBF Widmerpool Maiden Stakes Class D (2-y-o) £5,343 7f 9yds...(3:50)

4303[2] NOBLE ROSE (Ire) 8-9 J Weaver (3) *steadied strt, last hfwy, quickened to ld appr fnl furlong, ran on wl.* ....(5 to 4 fav op 11 to 10 tchd 6 to 4) 1
4440 RED EARTH (USA) 9-0 Pat Eddery (10) *led gng wl, shaken up o'r 2 fs out, hdd appr last, kpt on same pace.* ....(7 to 2 op 9 to 2 tchd 3 to 1) 2
4480[2] DANGER POINT 9-0 A Munro (4) *tucked away in midfield, effrt and drvn alng o'r one furlong out, styd on.* ....(5 to 1 op 4 to 1) 3
JAAWIS 9-0 D Holland (12) *nvr far away, ran green o'r one furlong out, no extr, better for race.* .... (16 to 1 op 10 to 1) 4
DALLAI (Ire) 9-0 R Hills (2) *patiently rdn, effrt hfwy, drvn alng last 2 fs, no extr*.............(20 to 1 op 14 to 1) 5
INTERACT 9-0 S Raymont (6) *in tch, effrt on far side o'r 2 fs out, not rch ldrs*................ (25 to 1 op 12 to 1) 6
TEMPS PERDU 9-0 S Whitworth (5) *speed frnt rnk for o'r 5 fs*................................(50 to 1 op 33 to 1) 7
4434[5] EQUERRY 9-0 W Woods (1) *frnt rnk till wknd last 2 fs.* .... (25 to 1 op 14 to 1) 8
HAWKER'S NEWS (Ire) 9-0 K Fallon (8) *sluggish strt, drvn alng hfwy, nvr dngrs*..................(8 to 1 op 7 to 2) 9
4229 DAWN DEFENDER (Ire) 9-0 M Hills (7) *chsd alng beh ldrs hfwy, nvr nr to chal*............. (33 to 1 op 16 to 1) 10
4099 MARSH ARAB 9-0 J Williams (9) *pressed ldrs for o'r 4 fs, sn btn*...(50 to 1) 11
4397[4] ALCIAN BLUE 9-0 W Ryan (11) *chsd alng far side, feeling pace hfwy, sn btn*................................(25 to 1) 12
Dist: 2l, ¾l, 8l, ½l, 4l, 1½l, 1l, nk, ¾l, 7l. 1m 30.00s. a 8.10s (12 Ran).
SR: 37/36/34/10/8/-/ (Sheikh Mohammed), L M Cumani

4580 Thrussington Handicap Class E (0-70 3-y-o and up) £3,652 5f 218yds.. (4:20)

4168* BAYIN (USA) [52] 4-8-12 R Street (15) *nvr far away, led centre appr fnl furlong, kpt on wl.* (10 to 1 op 7 to 1) 1
4501* LEIGH CROFTER [60] (bl) 4-9-6 (8ex) G Hind (19) *al hndy, ev ch centre o'r one furlong out, kpt on wl.* ....(10 to 1 tchd 12 to 1) 2
4488[7] PANTHER (Ire) [57] (v) 3-9-1 W Woods (12) *clr stands side, hdd appr fnl furlong, one pace*....(20 to 1 op 33 to 1) 3
4217* CRAIGIE BOY [52] (bl) 3-8-3 (7*) S Copp (6) *trkd ldrs stands side, shaken up ins fnl furlong, ran on.* .... (14 to 1 op 12 to 1) 4
4123[8] BERNSTEIN BETTE [54] 7-9-0 J Williams (11) *chsd alng to improve frm midfield last 2 fs, fnshd wl.* ....(7 to 1 fav op 10 to 1) 5
4487[2] PATSY GRIMES [64] (bl) 3-9-1 (7*) Mark Denaro (22) *speed far side, kpt on same pace fnl furlong.* ....(10 to 1 tchd 12 to 1) 6
4156 FORTIS PAVIOR (Ire) [60] 3-9-4 A Culhane (10) *chsd alng to go pace, improved stands side last 2 fs, nvr nrr.* .... (14 to 1 op 12 to 1) 7
4468 NOBBY BARNES [55] 4-9-1 Pat Eddery (21) *bustled alng in midfield, styd on same pace last 2 fs.* .... (8 to 1 op 12 to 1 tchd 7 to 1) 8
4501[2] PALACEGATE GOLD (Ire) [54] 4-9-0 A Munro (3) *drvn alng to improve frm midfield last 2 fs, nrst finish.* .... (12 to 1 op 10 to 1) 9
3946[9] SYLVAN STARLIGHT [60] (bl) 3-9-4 K Fallon (7) *chsd alng to keep up, ran on last 2 fs, nvr nrr.* (16 to 1 op 14 to 1) 10
3906[7] HONEY SEEKER [62] 4-9-8 M Hills (5) *tucked away stands side, effrt and not much room o'r one furlong out, kpt on same pace*..................... (14 to 1 op 12 to 1) 11
3707* AGWA [50] 4-8-10 F Norton (18) *in tch, drvn into midfield 2 fs out, not pace to chal.* .... (8 to 1 op 7 to 1 tchd 10 to 1) 12
4333 CEE-EN-CEE [49] (bl) 9-8-9 A Tucker (17) *outpcd and drvn alng, some hdwy last 2 fs, nvr dngrs*.......... (20 to 1) 13
4485[3] MY RUBY RING [68] 6-9-7 (7*) P Bowe (20) *chsd alng far side, feeling pace hfwy, nvr dngrs.* (25 to 1 op 16 to 1) 14
4317[7] HICKORY BLUE [69] 3-9-6 (7*) C Teague (13) *speed centre 4 fs, fdd*...(25 to 1) 15
3995 OUR MICA [52] (v) 3-8-10 R Hills (9) *speed stands side till wknd 2 fs out*................(33 to 1 op 25 to 1) 16
9067 RESPECTABLE JONES [58] 7-9-4 W Ryan (4) *bustled alng in midfield hfwy, nvr rch ldrs*....(25 to 1 tchd 33 to 1) 17
4168[8] LETSBEONESTABOUTIT [64] (v) 7-9-10 D Holland (2) *wl plcd stands side 4 fs*.......................... (20 to 1) 18
117* SPEEDY CLASSIC (USA) [52] 4-8-7 (5*) D Wright (14) *speed centre till wknd 2 fs out*.......... (20 to 1 op 16 to 1) 19
4317[5] WESTERN VALLEY [53] 3-8-11 S Whitworth (16) *wl plcd stands side till wknd 2 fs out*...... (14 to 1 op 10 to 1) 20
4495[5] SOVIET EXPRESS [55] (bl) 3-8-13 T Quinn (8) *beh and drvn alng hfwy*........................ (16 to 1 op 12 to 1) 21
1230 BURISHKI [53] 3-8-8 (3*) Stephen Davies (1) *struggling stands side aftr 2 fs*............... (33 to 1 op 20 to 1) 22
Dist: Hd, 1½l, ¾l, 1l, nk, 1l, 1l, 1½l, sht-hd, hd. 1m 16.90s. a 6.50s (22 Ran).
SR: 40/47/36/28/28/35/27/20/13/ (Trevor Barker), M D I Usher

LEOPARDSTOWN (IRE) (good to yielding) Monday October 25th

4581 Laidlaw Perpetual Challenge Cup EBF Maiden (Div 1) (2-y-o) £5,244 1m (1:00)

2072[8] LAKE KARIBA 9-0 J A Heffernan (15)............ (10 to 1) 1
4460 BAYDUR (Ire) 8-8 (6*) D J O'Donohoe (18)........ (20 to 1) 2
AL MOHAAJIR (USA) 9-0 K J Manning (16).....(2 to 1 fav) 3
4323[2] ZARA'S BIRTHDAY (Ire) 8-10[1] (2*) P Carberry (3)....(6 to 1) 4
4261[6] INCHARDER (Ire) 8-11 P V Gilson (7)..............(8 to 1) 5
4058[9] MOOBAKKR (USA) 9-0 P Shanahan (17)......... (10 to 1) 6
SIMAFAR (Ire) 9-0 J P Murtagh (2)................ (3 to 1) 7
4380 DEEP IN SEPTEMBER (Ire) 8-5 (6*) R V Skelly (8).. (25 to 1) 8
4290[9] BLAKE'S HOTEL 9-0 J F Egan (4)................ (7 to 1) 9
SUBTLE BRIEF (Ire) 8-10 (4*) J J Behan (13)....... (8 to 1) 10
4460 EASY STEP (Ire) 9-0 W J Supple (12).............(16 to 1) 11
4244 BOLD ENCOUNTER (Ire) 8-11 R Hughes (6)...... (16 to 1) 12
3911 EMELIA'S PET (Ire) 9-0 R Dolan (11)............ (33 to 1) 13
CRIMSON CITY (Ire) 8-11 N Byrne (10)........... (25 to 1) 14
4406 DARK POET (Ire) 9-0 S Craine (1)................(12 to 1) 15
4323 ALKEN (Ire) 9-0 N G McCullagh (5)............... (16 to 1) 16
RIGHT ANGLE (Ire) 8-12 (2*) D G O'Shea (9)...... (25 to 1) 17
Dist: 1l, 1½l, 1l, sht-hd. 1m 43.30s. a 5.30s (17 Ran).
SR: 21/18/13/7/6/-/ (Mrs John Magnier), Charles O'Brien

4582 Laidlaw Perpetual Challenge Cup EBF Maiden (Div 2) (2-y-o) £5,244 1m (1:30)

ELUSIVE DOMAIN (USA) 9-0 P Shanahan (2)...... (7 to 1) 1
4388[3] ANTIQUITY (Ire) 8-11 K J Manning (1).............(8 to 1) 2
4058[2] FLAG FEN (USA) 9-0 J P Murtagh (15)......... (5 to 4 on) 3
CONTINUOUS (Ire) 8-5 (6*) D J O'Donohoe (12).... (8 to 1) 4
BAYARIYKA (Ire) 8-11 D Hogan (17).................(8 to 1) 5
MONKSTOWN MAJOR (Ire) 8-12 (2*) P Carberry (6) (10 to 1) 6
4290[8] REGAL DOMAIN (Ire) 9-0 W J Supple (9)......... (12 to 1) 7
4382[9] NEW TRIBE (Ire) 9-0 S Craine (4).................. (8 to 1) 8
4406[5] NORTHREEL 8-10 (4*) J J Behan (13)............(10 to 1) 9
4406 ACUMEN (Ire) 8-7 (4*) W J Smith (11)............. (20 to 1) 10
4135[6] GRACEFUL RESIGN 8-11 N G McCullagh (14).... (12 to 1) 11
4244 PHARDY (Ire) 9-0 N Byrne (7).................... (25 to 1) 12
4460[7] ROYAL CRIMSON 9-0 P V Gilson (18)............(14 to 1) 13
4460 LEO'S FRIEND (Ire) 8-10 (4*) J A Heffernan (3).... (16 to 1) 14
TALAHARI (Ire) 8-11 R Hughes (16)............... (14 to 1) 15
4261 CARANNA 8-11 J F Egan (5)......................(16 to 1) 16
4535 KILNOE (Ire) 8-5 (6*) R V Skelly (10)..............(20 to 1) 17
Dist: 1l, nk, 6l, 1½l. 1m 42.90s. a 4.90s (17 Ran).
SR: 27/21/23/2/-/-/ (Moyglare Stud Farms Ltd), D K Weld

4583 Kilmacud Handicap (0-90 3-y-o and up) £3,105 7f.................. (2:00)

4384 TOPOGRAPHE (Fr) [-] 3-9-0 (6*) D J O'Donohoe (6) (14 to 1) 1
4245[5] FOREST CONCERT (Ire) [-] 4-9-9 K J Manning (13) ....(11 to 4 fav) 2
4184 DOBIE (USA) [-] 5-9-3 P Shanahan (5)............(12 to 1) 3
4408[8] KENTUCKY BABY (Ire) [-] (bl) 3-7-12 (4*,6ex) J A Heffernan (3) ....(10 to 1) 4
4407[2] BRITANNIA BAY (Ire) [-] 3-9-0 P V Gilson (11)...... (8 to 1) 5
2608[2] DESERT CALM (Ire) [-] 4-9-5 (6*) B J Walsh (2).... (10 to 1) 6
4554* KURDISTAN (Ire) [-] 3-9-9 (4*,5ex) J J Behan (1).... (6 to 1) 7
4463 CORTIJA PARK (Ire) [-] 3-9-8 R Hughes (10)...... (12 to 1) 8
4385 BENE MERENTI (Ire) [-] (bl) 3-8-13 (6*) R V Skelly (7) (14 to 1) 9
4384[5] RAJAURA (Ire) [-] 3-9-6 J P Murtagh (17).......... (7 to 1) 10
3770[6] ROBERTOLOMY (USA) [-] 4-9-0 N G McCullagh (12) (9 to 1) 11
4118[6] RUNNING GUEST (Ire) [-] 3-7-12 (2*) D G O'Shea, (20 to 1) 12
4407[7] ADRIEN DE VRIES (Ire) [-] 3-9-2 S Craine (4)...... (14 to 1) 13
4284 WHAT A PLEASURE (Ire) [-] 3-7-13 (10*) I Browne (9) ....(20 to 1) 14

4384⁹ LA CENERENTOLA (Ire) [-] 3-8-11 (2*) P Carberry (16) ....(14 to 1) 15
4463 ROLANDS GIRL (Ire) [-] 3-8-1 W J Supple,........(20 to 1) 16
4385 MARY'S CASE (Ire) [-] (bl) 3-8-6 J F Egan (14).....(20 to 1) 17
1123⁹ FRIAR STREET (Ire) [-] 3-8-0 (6*) P P Murphy (8)....(14 to 1) 18
Dist: Nk, 2½l, hd, 1l. 1m 29.80s. a 4.40s (18 Ran).
SR: 40/42/28/12/21/-/ (Mrs A J F O'Reilly), D K Weld

4584 E.B.F. Leopardstown Stakes (Group 3) (2-y-o) £14,375 7f..............(2:30)

4369* CAJARIAN (USA) 8-10 J P Murtagh (8) *trkd ldrs into strt, quickened to ld one and a half fs out, ran on strly.* ....(5 to 2 fav) 1
4286⁴ INSTAMATIC 8-7 S Craine (5) *mid-div into strt, rdn and styd on fnl furlong without troubling wnr*.....(13 to 2) 2
4460* GUIDED TOUR (Ire) 8-10 J F Egan (1) *trkd ldrs into strt, rdn one and a half fs out, kpt on*..............(3 to 1) 3
4382³ BAWARDI (Ire) 8-10 R Hughes (2) *led till hdd one and a half fs out, kpt on till wknd cl hme*............(7 to 1) 4
4459* MARKET SLIDE (USA) 8-7 P Shanahan (7) *6th and rdn into strt, styd on und pres fnl furlong*..........(100 to 30) 5
4380 FLY THE CREST (USA) 8-10 W J Supple (6) *slwly into strd, last into strt, rdn and no imprsn fnl 2 fs*.......(25 to 1) 6
3922* REGAL ACCESS (USA) (bl) 8-10 P Carberry (3) *wl plcd till rdn and wknd 2 fs out*........................(7 to 1) 7
Dist: 3l, sht-hd, nk, ¾l. 1m 30.80s. a 5.40s (7 Ran).
SR: 15/3/5/4/ (H H Aga Khan), John M Oxx

4585 Leopardstown Golf Centre Trigo Stakes (Listed) (3-y-o and up) £8,625 1 ¼m.........................(4:00)

4053² PRE-EMINENT 6-9-8 P Shanahan (5) *trkd ldrs, rdn 3 fs out, styd on strly fnl furlong to ld 100 yards out.* ....(9 to 1) 1
4463⁶ CHEVIOT AMBLE (Ire) 5-9-0 J F Egan (4) *last till steady prog frm 3 fs out to chal ins last, styd on*......(16 to 1) 2
4289* IDRIS (Ire) 3-9-3 J P Murtagh (7) *trkd ldrs into strt, rdn to ld one furlong out, hdd and wknd 100 yards out.* ....(7 to 4 on) 3
4383* EUROSTORM (USA) (bl) 3-9-0 P V Gilson (1) *wl plcd, prog to ld 2 and a half fs out, hdd and wknd one out.* (6 to 1) 4
4383⁵ OENOTHERA (Ire) 3-8-9 S Craine (6) *led till hdd and wknd 2 and a half fs out, eased fnl furlong*.........(16 to 1) 5
4289² APPROACH THE BENCH (Ire) 5-9-8 W J Supple (3) *hld up in rear, rdn and wknd quickly entering strt*......(5 to 1) 6
4383² TRYARRA (Ire) 3-8-9 N G McCullagh (8) *rear, rdn and btn 3 fs out*....................(12 to 1) 7
Dist: 1l, 1l, 2l, 3½l. 2m 8.90s. a 4.20s (7 Ran).
SR: 66/56/57/50/38/-/-/ (Michael W J Smurfit), D K Weld

4586 Waterford Crystal Downs Synd. Private Stakes (3-y-o and up) £1 2m (4:40)

4095⁴ HACKETTS CROSS (Ire) 5-12-7 Robert Coonan (12) ....(6 to 4 fav) 1
2035⁹ LEGAL ADVISER 6-12-1 E M Kelly (7)............(9 to 2) 2
4185 ZORIA (Ire) 5-11-6 T Carberry (15)..............(4 to 1) 3
4387⁵ MIDNIGHT COURT (USA) 10-12-7 Majella Butler (23) ....(16 to 1) 4
RUNAWAY GOLD 6-12-1⁶ Pat O'Hagan (8)........(14 to 1) 5
TARTAN TAILOR 12-12-7 Tom Nevin (19)..........(12 to 1) 6
4387³ SARAKAYA 8-11-6 David Moloney (5)............(10 to 1) 7
3419 ABEREDW (Ire) 3-10-11 Siobhain McClafferty (13) (14 to 1) 8
4387⁷ PERCY LANE (Ire) 3-11-0 Colm Gainey (1)..........(12 to 1) 9
3853⁹ INNOCENT MAN (Ire) 3-11-0 John Tarrant (10)....(16 to 1) 10
KIZZY ROSE 6-11-6 William O'Doherty (18)..........(20 to 1) 11
CASTLE CELEBRITY (Ire) 4-11-8² Tony McInerney (16) ....(14 to 1) 12
JO-SU-KI 6-11-9 James Kelly (22)..................(20 to 1) 13
3682a NEVER BE GREAT 11-12-7 Mark Mortell (14).....(14 to 1) 14
3399 REASON TO BELIEVE (Ire) 4-11-6 Shona McDonagh (20) ....(20 to 1) 15
3396 BLENHEIM PALACE (USA) 6-12-2¹ Richard Ranaghan (21) ....(16 to 1) 16
SCREEN PRINTER (Ire) 4-11-10⁴ Thomas O'Doherty (3) ....(16 to 1) 17
SALINA BAY 7-11-6 Caroline Benson (17)..........(14 to 1) 18
NORDIC BLUE (Ire) 5-12-12²⁰ Bob Champion (11) (20 to 1) 19
4370² ICANSEEFORMILES (Ire) 5-12-2⁴ C Coldrick (24)..(10 to 1) 20
Dist: 2l, 3l, 3l. (Time not taken) (20 Ran).
(F Heffernan), Noel T Chance

LINGFIELD (good to soft)
Monday October 25th
Going Correction: PLUS 0.75 sec. per fur.

4587 EBF Willow Maiden Stakes Class D (Div I) (2-y-o) £4,020 7f..........(1:10)

DARKWOOD BAY (USA) 9-0 W Newnes (4) *slwly away and ran green, chsd ldrs, rdn 2 fs out, styd on wl to ld ins last*.....................(11 to 2 op 4 to 1) 1
INDIAN FLY 9-0 G Duffield (2) *led aftr 2 and a half fs, hdd and unbl to quicken ins last*... (7 to 2 jt-fav op 6 to 4) 2
4419 BONIFACCIO BANDIT (Ire) 9-0 B Rouse (3) *dwlt, sn reco'red, shaken up frm hfwy, ev ch one furlong out, kpt on*............(9 to 2 op 6 to 1 tchd 7 to 1) 3
ROYAL CREST 9-0 W Carson (5) *nvr far away, rdn and ev ch wl o'r one furlong out, not quicken.* ....(7 to 1 op 2 to 1 tchd 8 to 1) 4
3990⁶ PILIB (Ire) 9-0 M Wigham (8) *chsd ldrs, rdn hfwy, sn no imprsn*..........(7 to 1 op 8 to 1 tchd 6 to 1) 5
4326⁴ RED CLOUD (Ire) 8-2 (7*) S Mulvey (7) *led 2 and a half fs, lost pl fnl 3*....... (7 to 2 jt-fav op 7 to 4 tchd 4 to 1) 6
4339⁸ FOOD BROKER FELLA (Ire) 9-0 R Perham (1) *struggling frm hfwy*..........................(25 to 1 op 12 to 1) 7
LADY VALIENT 8-9 A McGlone (9) *slwly away, al beh.* ....(33 to 1 tchd 40 to 1) 8
4418 AILEENS GIRL 8-9 R Price (6) *al beh.* ....(33 to 1 op 25 to 1 tchd 40 to 1) 9
Dist: 1½l, ½l, 1½l, 8l, 2l, 7l, 8l, nk. 1m 30.02s. a 9.32s (9 Ran).
SR: 39/34/32/27/3/-/ (Raymond Tooth), D R C Elsworth

4588 EBF Willow Maiden Stakes Class D (Div II) (2-y-o) £4,449 7f.........(1:40)

2630⁸ BOLD SIXTEEN (USA) 8-9 Paul Eddery (4) *in tch, ev ch whn hmpd wl o'r 2 fs out, sn led, ran on well.* ....(8 to 1 op 12 to 1 tchd 14 to 1) 1
SHEPPARD'S CROSS 8-9 L Dettori (14) *al hndy, hdwy o'r 2 fs out and sn ev ch, not quicken ins last.* ....(10 to 1 op 7 to 1) 2
4067 FRED'S DELIGHT (Ire) 9-0 J Carroll (16) *chsd ldrs, rdn and styd on fnl one and a half fs*.........(8 to 1 op 6 to 1) 3
BID FOR A RAINBOW 9-0 C Rutter (8) *slwly into strd, sn reco'red to midfield, hdwy over 2 fs out, kpt on.* ....(33 to 1) 4
4440 SHARP REBUFF 9-0 T Sprake (1) *prmnt, rdn and ev ch 2 fs out, one pace*......... (10 to 1 op 8 to 1 tchd 12 to 1) 5
DOCTOR DEATH (Ire) 9-0 A Clark (12) *beh and outpcd till styd on fnl 2 fs, nvr nrr*....................(33 to 1) 6
3589 GOLD'N SHROUD (Ire) 9-0 W Newnes (2) *led till hdd o'r 2 fs out, sn btn*.....................(20 to 1 op 12 to 1) 7
PORTE BELLOCH 8-9 R Perham (7) *trkd ldrs, edgd lft wl o'r 2 fs out, sn no extr*..........................(33 to 1) 8
4489 ERIN'S LAD 9-0 D Biggs (13) *prmnt, rdn 3 fs out, sn wknd.* ....(33 to 1) 9
JOYS FIRST 9-0 J Quinn (3) *in tch, slightly hmpd wl o'r 2 fs out, no extr*....................(16 to 1 op 10 to 1) 10
4480⁶ PHIL'S TIME 9-0 B Rouse (15) *midfield, effrt wl o'r 2 fs out, eased whn btn ins last.* ....(100 to 30 op 11 to 4 tchd 7 to 2) 11
MR DIAMOND (USA) 9-0 B Raymond (10) *slwly into strd, nvr trbld ldrs*................(5 to 2 fav tchd 11 to 4) 12
4210 SPANISH DAWN 8-9 D Harrison (6) *beh frm hfwy.* ....(25 to 1 op 20 to 1) 13
1706 TAKHRIJ (USA) (v) 9-0 A McGlone (9) *prmnt till wknd wl o'r 2 fs out, sn in rear*................(25 to 1 op 20 to 1) 14
Dist: 1l, 2½l, 1l, 1l, sht-hd, ½l, ½l, 3½l, sht-hd, sht-hd. 1m 29.69s. a 8.99s (14 Ran).
SR: 39/36/33/30/27/26/24/17/11/ (Miss Donna E Dillard), Mrs J Cecil

4589 Burr Conditions Stakes Class D (2-y-o) £3,348 5f.................(2:40)

4456* MARY HINGE 9-0 Paul Eddery (5) *chsd ldg pair, hdwy to ld o'r one furlong out, sn clr, easily.* (Evens fav op 5 to 4) 1
4299⁴ ELEUTHERA 8-8 L Dettori (2) *wth ldr, hrd rdn and ev ch o'r one furlong out, not pace of wnr.* ....(15 to 8 op 5 to 4 tchd 2 to 1) 2
4332⁴ IVA'S FLYER (Ire) 8-10 J Carroll (3) *led till hdd o'r one furlong out, sn rdn and no extr.* ....(11 to 2 op 7 to 1 tchd 5 to 1) 3
3103⁸ JUST A SINGLE (Ire) 8-11 T Williams (1) *beh early, hdwy o'r 2 fs out, kpt on ins last*...........(66 to 1 op 20 to 1) 4
3869⁴ CHARISMA GIRL 8-6 G Bardwell (6) *speed one furlong, sn rdn alng and lost pl*..............(20 to 1 op 10 to 1) 5
TODAY'S STAR 8-6 (5*) B Russell (4) *slwly away, outpcd.* ....(66 to 1 op 50 to 1) 6
Dist: 4l, 1l, hd, 6l, 2l. 1m 2.87s. a 5.97s (6 Ran).
SR: 56/34/32/32/3/-/ (Mrs J Cecil), Mrs J Cecil

4590 Sycamore Maiden Stakes Class D (3-y-o) £3,523 1¾m..............(3:10)

4372² PURPLE SPLASH 9-0 L Dettori (1) *trkd ldrs, effrt o'r 3 fs out, led wl over one out, drvn clr*...(4 to 1 tchd 7 to 2) 1
4445² CUFF LINK (Ire) 9-0 L Piggott (2) *trkd ldrs, wnt second 5 fs out, led o'r 3 out, hdd wl over one out, eased whn btn.* ....(11 to 10 fav tchd 6 to 4) 2
4432⁹ ADMIRAL'S WELL (Ire) 9-0 W Carson (7) *niggled alng early, beh till hdwy frm 5 fs out, styd on wl fnl 2, not rch ldrs.* ....(14 to 1 op 8 to 1 tchd 16 to 1) 3
DOCTOOR (USA) 9-0 A Clark (5) *pld hrd, chsd ldrs, rdn o'r 4 fs out, no imprsn*... (12 to 1 op 10 to 1 tchd 14 to 1) 4
3980² GEORDIE SONG 8-9 A McGlone (11) *led till hdd o'r 3 fs out, sn btn*.........................(7 to 2 op 9 to 4) 5
4493⁶ SNOW DREAM 8-9 D Biggs (6) *in tch till rdn 4 fs out, sn wknd*...........(25 to 1 op 20 to 1 tchd 33 to 1) 6

3872[9] SEATTLE AFFAIR (Ire) (bl) 8-9 D Harrison (3) *slwly into strd, reco'red to track ldr till wknd 5 fs out.* .... (50 to 1 op 20 to 1) 7
GLISTENING DAWN 8-9 J Quinn (8) *slwly into strd, beh, rdn o'r 6 fs out, no hdwy*.........(50 to 1 op 33 to 1) 8
4322 CELESTIAL CHOIR 8-9 N Adams (9) *al beh.* .... (33 to 1 op 20 to 1) 9
IF IT SUITS 9-0 R Perham (4) *al beh, tld off.* .... (33 to 1 op 20 to 1) 10
DOUBLE-U-GEE (Ire) 9-0 W Newnes (10) *slwly into strd, sn beh and tld off frm hfwy.* ....(50 to 1 op 33 to 1 tchd 66 to 1) 11
Dist: 6l, 5l, 5l, 2l, 10l, 8l, 8l, 1l, 30l, dist. 3m 13.42s. a 18.42s (11 Ran).
SR: 21/9/-/-/-/-/ (Christopher Walford), P J Makin

LINGFIELD (A.W) (std)
Monday October 25th
Going Correction: MINUS 0.20 sec. per fur.

4591 Elm Handicap Class E (0-70 3-y-o and up) £3,313 1½m................ (2:10)

4247[4] DASHING FELLOW (Ire) [58] 5-9-3 J Quinn (16) *beh till steady hdwy frm hfwy, led one furlong out, hld on wl.* ....(9 to 2 op 3 to 1 tchd 5 to 1) 1
3907 RAGTIME SONG [41] 4-8-0 N Adams (5) *trkd ldrs, effrt 3 fs out, ev ch one out, kpt on*.........(12 to 1 op 10 to 1) 2
4486[3] YOUNG FREEMAN (USA) [69] 4-10-0 G Duffield (14) *led till hdd one furlong out, no extr*......(10 to 1 tchd 8 to 1) 3
3479[6] TOUCHING TIMES [43] 5-8-2 D Harrison (11) *pushed alng in midfield early, hdwy o'r 3 fs out, kpt on.* .... (12 to 1 op 10 to 1) 4
4006 YOUNG FACT [40] 8-7-8 (5*) B Russell (12) *wl beh till styd on fnl 3 fs, nvr nrr*............... (33 to 1 op 20 to 1) 5
3961 BRONZE MAQUETTE (Ire) [56] 3-8-8 B Raymond (7) *beh early, hdwy 5 fs out till no extr fnl 2.* .... (9 to 1 op 7 to 1 tchd 10 to 1) 6
2317[3] SWIFT SPRING (Fr) [52] 3-8-4 C Rutter (9) *trkd ldg bunch till rdn o'r 2 fs out, sn btn.* ....(14 to 1 op 10 to 1 tchd 16 to 1) 7
4486 DANCING YEARS (USA) [55] 4-9-0 A Morris (6) *beh and rdn alng till ran on fnl 3 fs, nrst finish.* (20 to 1 op 14 to 1) 8
4028 STRAT'S LEGACY [60] 6-9-5 R Price (4) *hld up and hehind, steady hdwy fnl 3 fs, nvr plcd to chal.* ....(8 to 1 op 5 to 1) 9
2847[2] WILD STRAWBERRY [61] 4-9-6 B Rouse (10) *midfield, reminders o'r 6 fs out, nvr trbld ldrs.* ....(6 to 1 tchd 7 to 1) 10
4234[2] GREEN KILT [70] (v) 3-9-8 L Dettori (8) *chsd ldr till rdn and wknd 2 fs out*.......(7 to 2 fav op 5 to 1 tchd 6 to 1) 11
MEDIATOR [44] 4-8-3 A Clark (3) *nvr a dngr.* .... (33 to 1 op 20 to 1) 12
3840* CRETOES DANCER (USA) [50] (bl) 4-8-9 Kim McDonnell (15) *chsd ldrs till rdn and wknd wl o'r 2 fs out.* ....(10 to 1 op 8 to 1 tchd 12 to 1) 13
4629a ALREEF [42] 7-8-1 D Biggs (13) *trkd ldrs till lost pl frm hfwy*...................(14 to 1 op 10 to 1 tchd 16 to 1) 14
4209 HARD EIGHT [50] 3-8-2 A McGlone (2) *rdn alng in midfield whn not clr run o'r 5 fs out, sn wknd.* .... (25 to 1 op 16 to 1) 15
4088[7] EXPRESS MARIECURIE (Ire) [52] (v) 3-7-11 (7*) Madeleine Smith (1) *trkd ldr early, lost pl frm hfwy.* .... (25 to 1 op 20 to 1) 16
Dist: Sht-hd, 3½l, 1½l, 3l, sht-hd, nk, hd, nk, 3½l, 1½l. 2m 34.62s. a 5.32s (16 Ran).
SR: 26/8/29/-/-/-/-/3/7/ (Mrs Val Rapkins), Mrs L Piggott

4592 Falling Leaf Limited Stakes Class F (3-y-o and up) £2,847 7f........... (3:40)

4156 COURTING NEWMARKET 5-8-9 (7*) Marie Plowright (9) *al hndy gng wl, led one furlong out, sn clr.* .... (20 to 1 op 16 to 1) 1
3118[4] MINDOMICA 4-8-8 (3*) Emma O'Gorman (4) *in tch, hdwy gng wl o'r 2 fs out, not much room appr last, ran on.* ....(7 to 1 op 6 to 1) 2
4231* NICHODOULA 3-8-8 G Duffield (6) *midfield, hdwy on outsd o'r 2 fs out, kpt on.* ....(5 to 2 fav op 9 to 4 tchd 3 to 1) 3
4455 PRINCE BELFORT 5-9-2 N Adams (15) *led till hdd one furlong out, no extr.* (16 to 1 op 14 to 1 tchd 20 to 1) 4
4092[2] MAID WELCOME (v) 6-8-4 (7*) Madeleine Smith (10) *broke wl, nvr far away, ran on same pace fnl one and a half fs*...................(12 to 1 op 10 to 1 tchd 14 to 1) 5
4333 GALLERY ARTIST (Ire) 5-8-9 (7*) S Eiffert (14) *midfield, rdn o'r 2 fs out, kpt on same pace clsg stages.* .... (20 to 1 op 14 to 1) 6
4123 WALK THAT WALK 4-8-6 (5*) P McCabe (3) *nvr trbld ldrs.* ....(20 to 1) 7
3266[5] KENSWORTH LADY 3-8-8 A McGlone (13) *beh till rdn and some hdwy hfwy, nvr able to chal*............(20 to 1) 8
4087 JULIASDARKINVADER 3-8-13 A Clark (7) *outpcd early, no dngr*.............................. (33 to 1) 9
4394[8] KISSAVOS (v) 7-9-2 W Newnes (16) *chsd ldrs, rdn o'r 2 fs out, sn wknd*.......................(8 to 1 op 6 to 1) 10

3447 FAIR ENCHANTRESS (bl) 5-8-11 J Quinn (12) *al rear div.* ....(33 to 1) 11
4221[4] SPLASH OF SALT (Ire) 3-8-3 (5*) A Garth (8) *al beh.* .... (10 to 1 op 8 to 1) 12
4481* BICHETTE 3-8-8 B Rouse (5) *prmnt till wknd o'r 2 fs out.* ....(100 to 30 op 4 to 1 tchd 5 to 1) 13
4221[6] MOVING IMAGE (Ire) 3-8-9[1] C Dwyer (11) *al hndy, ev ch o'r 2 fs out, wknd quickly and eased whn btn.* ....(12 to 1 op 10 to 1 tchd 14 to 1) 14
4168 SPRING HIGH (bl) 6-8-11 G Bardwell (1) *sn rdn alng, beh frm hfwy*...........(12 to 1 op 10 to 1 tchd 14 to 1) 15
Dist: 2½l, hd, 1½l, 4l, sht-hd, 1½l, 1l, ¾l, 1½l, 1½l. 1m 26.31s. a 2.91s (15 Ran).
SR: 37/24/20/23/6/10/ (Geo Taylor), Mrs A Knight

ST-CLOUD (FR) (heavy)
Monday October 25th
Going Correction: PLUS 0.80 sec. per fur.

4593 Prix Thomas Bryon (Group 3) (2-y-o) £23,895 1m.................... (2:00)

FADEYEV (USA) 8-9 T Jarnet (1) *rcd in 3rd till strt, chlgd one and a half fs out, led 100 yards out, ran on wl.* ....(14 to 10 fav) 1
4074[7] OCEAN INDIEN (Fr) 8-9 C Asmussen (4) *led, rdn one and a half fs out, hdd 100yds out, ran on*......... (108 to 10) 2
4242* DARE AND GO (USA) 8-9 O Doleuze (6) *trkd ldr, second strt, styd on one pace frm one and a half fs out.* ....(19 to 10) 3
4412[2] VOLOCHINE (Ire) 8-9 W Mongil (7) *hld up, 5th strt, hdwy o'r one furlong out, fnshd wl*................ (33 to 10) 4
BLUE KING (Fr) 8-9 S Guillot (2) *4th strt, chlgd 2 fs out, kpt on one pace*.............................. (19 to 1) 5
4242[2] TELLURIUM (USA) 8-9 F Head (5) *hld up, 6th strt, outpcd 2 out, ran on wl fnl furlong*.....................(8 to 1) 6
3851[4] ROBUR (Fr) 8-9 O Peslier (3) *last strt, sn drpd out.* ....(15 to 1) 7
Dist: 1½l, ¾l, nose, ¾l, sht-hd, 20l. 1m 47.90s. a 9.40s (7 Ran).
SR: 50/45/43/42/40/39/-/ (Maktoum Al-Maktoum), A Fabre

LEICESTER (good to soft)
Tuesday October 26th
Going Correction: PLUS 0.50 sec. per fur.

4594 Tugby Median Auction Maiden Stakes Class F (2-y-o) £3,468 5f 218yds (1:20)

4416[8] MR BERGERAC (Ire) 9-0 D Holland (20) *broke smartly centre, made all, clr frm hfwy, unchlgd.* (8 to 1 op 6 to 1) 1
4440[5] ST LOUIS LADY 8-9 M Tebbutt (21) *chsd alng centre, styd on last 2 fs, not rch wnr.* ....(2 to 1 fav op 5 to 4 tchd 9 to 4) 2
4098 THE WITCHBOY 9-0 W Hood (22) *chsd ldrs centre, wnt second hfwy, rdn and no extr fnl furlong*..... (33 to 1) 3
4342 CROFT POOL 9-0 S D Williams (18) *speed centre thrght, styd on same pace last 2 fs, nvr able to chal.* .... (33 to 1 op 25 to 1) 4
KARON BEACH 8-9 M Hills (6) *bustled alng to go pace, styd on frm midfield last 2 fs, nrst finish*...... (20 to 1) 5
4044[6] KATHYS RAINBOW 8-9 J Quinn (16) *chsd alng to show speed centre for 4 fs, no imprsn*............... (33 to 1) 6
4358[8] SKIPTAMALOO 8-4 (5*) D Wright (12) *chsd wnr to hfwy, drvn alng stands side 2 fs out, no extr.* .... (14 to 1 op 10 to 1) 7
4497[8] HIGH TYPHA 8-9 Pat Eddery (3) *chsd alng stands side, kpt on same pace last 2 fs, nvr dngrs.* (12 to 1 op 10 to 1) 8
4263[6] SUGAR RISK 8-9 T Quinn (17) *early speed, struggling to keep up hfwy, sn btn*..............(16 to 1 op 14 to 1) 9
3475 CURBRIDGE (Ire) 9-0 J Williams (4) *struggling to go pace in midfield hfwy, nvr dngrs*.................... (50 to 1) 10
3698 HOLLY ST GERMAINE (Ire) 8-9 G Bardwell (9) *taken slwly to post, missed break, nvr on terms*...(25 to 1 op 20 to 1) 11
4067 GALLANT SPIRIT (Ire) 9-0 L Dettori (8) *pushed alng in midfield, nvr able to rch chalg pos.* ....(3 to 1 op 5 to 2 tchd 7 to 2) 12
DARLIN'BUDS OF MAY 8-9 G Hind (19) *slow to break, struggling far side thrght*.....................(50 to 1) 13
3876 NAPOLEON STAR (Ire) 9-0 M Wigham (14) *sn struggling in rear, nvr a threat*................ (20 to 1 op 16 to 1) 14
BUCKLEY BOYS 8-9 A Mackay (13) *chsd alng in midfield, outpcd frm hfwy*.............................. (33 to 1) 15
MR SOX 9-0 R Price (15) *bustled alng to go pace aftr 2 fs, nvr on terms*..................................(50 to 1) 16
3711[8] COLONEL SINCLAIR (Ire) 9-0 S Perks (7) *outpcd and drvn alng thrght, nvr dngrs*.......... (33 to 1 op 14 to 1) 17
708[5] VIVS FUTURE (Ire) 8-9 N Carlisle (2) *struggling to go pace aftr 2 fs, al beh*...................(33 to 1 op 20 to 1) 18
SOUND OF THUNDER 9-0 W Carson (10) *sn outpcd and drvn alng, nvr on terms*.......... (14 to 1 op 25 to 1) 19
HORACE HALL 9-0 N Adams (5) *sluggish strt, tld off.* ....(50 to 1) 20
TANHOUSE LADY 8-9 A Munro (1) *sluggish strt, tld off.* ....(33 to 1) 21

Dist: 5l, hd, 5l, 2½l, 2l, ½l, 2½l, ¾l, 2½l, hd. 1m 16.70s. a 6.30s (21 Ran).
SR: 34/9/13/-/-/-/ (P R John), B Palling

4595 EBF Hoby Maiden Stakes Class D (2-y-o) £4,305 1m 8yds............(1:50)

COLZA (USA) 8-9 Pat Eddery (10) *tucked away gng wl, quickened through to ld o'r one furlong out, smoothly.* ....(5 to 1 op 7 to 2) 1
DUKE OF WARSAW (USA) 9-0 J Weaver (12) *steadied strt, improved into midfield hfwy, ev ch o'r one furlong out, can improve*...(3 to 1 jt-fav tchd 100 to 30 and 7 to 2) 2
4230[7] TANAH MERAH (Ire) 9-0 T Quinn (8) *rcd freely centre, swtchd outsd to improve hfwy, ev ch entering fnl furlong, kpt on same pace*.......................(33 to 1) 3
4252[7] SILVER HUNTER (USA) 9-0 A Munro (11) *al hndy, nosed ahead 3 fs out, hdd o'r one out, kpt on same pace.* ....(3 to 1 jt-fav op 6 to 4) 4
SERAPHIC 8-9 W Ryan (5) *steadied strt, improved into midfield and ran green o'r 2 fs out, styd on, prmsg.* ....(10 to 1 op 5 to 1) 5
4419 MESHED 9-0 L Dettori (4) *settled midfield, effrt and pushed alng last 2 fs, styd on*.......(10 to 1 op 5 to 1) 6
3979[5] SAKIC (USA) 9-0 S O'Gorman (1) *co'red up in midfield, effrt 2 fs out, styd on*..................(6 to 1 op 4 to 1) 7
4497[9] KARLINE KA (Fr) 8-9 C Rutter (7) *tucked away in midfield, feeling pace and drvn alng o'r 2 fs out, no imprsn.* ....(33 to 1 op 50 to 1) 8
QUEST AGAIN 9-0 R Price (2) *shwd up on outsd for o'r 5 fs, fdd*..........................(50 to 1) 9
4497 DAKOTA GIRL 8-9 J Williams (6) *settled off the pace, effrt and not much room hfwy, nvr able to chal*.... (50 to 1) 10
4446 IVANHOE 9-0 M Hills (14) *rcd freely towards far side, fdd und pres 2 fs out*..................(20 to 1 op 14 to 1) 11
4252 MATO 9-0 W Carson (13) *slight ld centre for 5 fs, fdd 2 furlongs out*..........................(25 to 1) 12
4356[8] GAY DEVIL 9-0 A McGlone (16) *wth ldrs centre, drw level o'r 2 fs out, wknd and eased over one out*..... (14 to 1) 13
4421[8] LIGHTNING QUEST (Ire) 9-0 J Quinn (15) *trkd ldrs, drvn 3 fs out, fdd*..........................(25 to 1) 14
4489 UNISON 9-0 D Holland (3) *wth ldrs, drvn o'r 2 fs out, sn btn*..........................(50 to 1) 15
Dist: 1½l, 1½l, ½l, 1l, ¾l, 2½l, 10l, ½l, 2½l, hd. 1m 44.40s. a 9.30s (15 Ran).
SR: 15/15/10/8/-/3/ (K Abdulla), H R A Cecil

4596 Fosse Way Claiming Stakes Class F (3-y-o) £3,346 1m 8yds..........(2:20)

4488[2] ALWAYS RISKY 8-0 J Quinn (14) *trkd ldrs gng wl, quickend ahead well o'r one furlong out, rdn last 100 yards, jst lasted*..............(11 to 2 op 7 to 2 tchd 6 to 1) 1
3681 BLOWEDIFIKNOW (bl) 8-13 J Williams (6) *co'red up midfield, swtchd outsd to improve entering fnl furlong, ran on, jst fld*..................(25 to 1 op 20 to 1) 2
4536[5] DANCING DOMINO 9-3 W Ryan (18) *settled gng wl, drvn alng 2 fs out, styd on same pace fnl furlong.* ....(9 to 4 fav op 11 to 4) 3
4016[7] DUBAI SUMMER (bl) 9-1 W Carson (4) *chsd alng to improve frm midfield last 2 fs, styd on, nvr nrr.* ....(11 to 1 op 10 to 1 tchd 12 to 1) 4
4481[2] NUTTY BROWN 8-10 (3*) O Pears (20) *clr ldr centre till hdd and no extr wl o'r one furlong out.* ....(10 to 1 op 8 to 1 tchd 11 to 1) 5
4479[4] TAUTEN (Ire) 8-6 B Rouse (12) *co'red up beh ldrs, effrt 2 fs out, styd on same pace*...........(12 to 1 op 14 to 1) 6
1859[7] LANZAMAR 8-4 A Munro (8) *settled midfield, drvn o'r 2 fs out, no imprsn*..................(50 to 1 op 33 to 1) 7
4537 COLMAR 7-5 (7*) L Suthern (15) *patiently rdn, steady hdwy last 2 fs, nvr plcd to chal*....(50 to 1 op 25 to 1) 8
3138[3] STAPLEFORD LASS (bl) 8-3[1] W Woods (19) *settled midfield, drvn alng o'r 2 fs out, not pace of ldrs.* ....(20 to 1 op 16 to 1) 9
RISKY VENTURE 8-9 M Tebbutt (13) *settled off the pace, styd on last 2 fs, nvr plcd to chal*..............(20 to 1) 10
4479 BERING ISLAND (USA) (bl) 8-13 L Dettori (1) *broke wl to show speed stands side till fdd o'r 2 fs out.* ....(12 to 1 op 10 to 1 tchd 14 to 1) 11
CLOVER JACK 9-3 C Rutter (3) *trkd ldrs stands side, drvn o'r 2 fs out, fdd*..........................(50 to 1) 12
3050[2] MRS DAWSON 8-6 Pat Eddery (7) *early speed, drvn alng hfwy, sn struggling*..................(7 to 1 op 5 to 1) 13
4233[4] CLELIA 8-6 N Carlisle (11) *chsd ldg bunch for o'r 5 fs, fdd.* ....(50 to 1 op 33 to 1) 14
KNIGHT SHEPHERD 8-9 G Hind (5) *sluggish strt, al struggling*..........................(33 to 1) 15
4125[6] MISS CHARLIE 8-5 (7*) W Hawksley (9) *rcd freely in frnt rnk to hfwy, wknd quickly*........(16 to 1 op 12 to 1) 16
PETITE LASS 7-7 (5*) D Wright (10) *settled midfield, drvn alng hfwy, sn btn*..........................(33 to 1) 17
4016[4] ASCOM PAGER TOO 8-6 B Crossley (17) *pressed ldrs centre, drvn o'r 2 fs out, sn btn*....... (20 to 1 op 16 to 1) 18
WILBURY WONDER 8-4 A Mackay (2) *sluggish strt, al struggling*..........................(33 to 1) 19
3948 TASSAGH BRIDGE (Ire) (bl) 7-12 G Bardwell (16) *pressed ldrs for o'r 5 fs, fdd*..........................(50 to 1) 20
Dist: Hd, 1½l, 8l, ½l, 2l, 2l, ¾l, hd, ¾l, ¾l. 1m 45.00s. a 9.90s (20 Ran).
SR: -/10/9/-/-/-/ (Donald Cooper), Mrs N Macauley

4597 Ermine Street Handicap Class C (0-90 3-y-o and up) £5,005 1m 8yds... (2:50)

4490[4] MISTY SILKS [70] 3-9-0 W Carson (6) *co'red up in midfield, swtchd outsd to ld wl over one furlong out, drvn out.* ....(5 to 1 tchd 9 to 2) 1
4470[7] AITCH N'BEE [75] 10-9-8 L Dettori (11) *tucked away, drvn through appr fnl furlong, styd on to take second last strds*..............(11 to 2 op 5 to 1 tchd 6 to 1) 2
4501 BLUE TOPAZE [72] 5-9-5 J Williams (8) *trkd ldg bunch, ev ch 2 fs out, rdn and not quicken towards finish.* ....(20 to 1 op 14 to 1) 3
4254 TIFFANY'S CASE (Ire) [53] 4-8-0 A Munro (10) *settled midfield, drw level o'r 2 fs out, kpt on same pace fnl furlong*..........................(8 to 1 op 6 to 1) 4
3766[7] FROSTY MORNING [62] 3-8-3 (3*) B Doyle (9) *patiently rdn, drvn up to chal o'r 2 fs out, no extr.* ....(14 to 1 op 12 to 1) 5
4300 TOP SHIEL [73] 5-9-6 J Weaver (5) *settled gng wl, led on bit hfwy, hdd and rdn well o'r one furlong out, no extr.* ....(5 to 1 op 4 to 1 tchd 11 to 2) 6
4490* TONY'S MIST [76] 3-9-6 (5ex) Pat Eddery (7) *flt out in midfield aftr 2 fs, nvr a threat*... (9 to 2 fav op 4 to 1) 7
4470 FABRIANA [80] 3-9-10 D Holland (1) *broke wl, struggling to hold pl hfwy, sn lost tch*.......... (16 to 1 op 14 to 1) 8
4116 DORAZINE [71] 3-8-10 (5*) D Wright (3) *broke smartly to ld to hfwy, wknd quickly 2 fs out.* ....(11 to 1 op 8 to 1 tchd 12 to 1) 9
4274 SHIRO [77] 3-9-7 T Quinn (12) *pressed ldrs, drvn o'r 2 fs out, sn btn*....................... (16 to 1 tchd 14 to 1) 10
4470 ELANMATINA (Ire) [65] 4-8-12 W Woods (2) *shwd up in frnt rnk, drvn o'r 2 fs out, sn btn*.......(25 to 1 op 20 to 1) 11
3956[3] GUSTAVIA (Ire) [80] (bl) 3-9-10 M Hills (4) *trkd ldg quartet, struggling o'r 2 fs out, sn btn*......(14 to 1 op 12 to 1) 12
Dist: 3l, hd, 1½l, 4l, 2l, 8l, 1½l, 2½l, nk, ½l. 1m 45.00s. a 9.90s (12 Ran).
SR: 12/11/7/-/-/-/ (P E Axon), M J Ryan

4598 Pytchley Conditions Stakes Class D (2-y-o) £3,289 7f 9yds...........(3:20)

4223[8] CAZZUTO (Ire) 9-3 W Carson (4) *took keen hold, made most, quickened up gng wl hfwy, sprinted clr fnl furlong*.......................... (7 to 2 op 5 to 2) 1
3422[3] SMART FAMILY (USA) 8-11 T Quinn (5) *trkd wnr, drvn o'r 2 fs out, unbl to quicken fnl furlong.* ....(7 to 2 on op 3 to 1 on tchd 5 to 2 on) 2
4098[8] PAB'S CHOICE 8-6 A Clark (2) *nvr far away, struggling to hold pl o'r 2 fs out, sn rdn and btn.* ....(16 to 1 op 20 to 1 tchd 22 to 1) 3
4303 MUTINIQUE 8-6 N Adams (1) *veered lft leaving stalls, reco'red aftr 2 fs, hng left frm hfwy, sn outpcd.* (50 to 1) 4
4452 MA FOLIE 8-1 (5*) D Wright (3) *dsptd ld, struggling to hold pl hfwy, sn lost tch*..............(50 to 1 op 33 to 1) 5
Dist: 12l, 8l, 3l, 12l. 1m 32.30s. a 10.40s (5 Ran).
(J L Dunlop), J L Dunlop

4599 Barsby Limited Stakes Class E (3-y-o) £3,132 1m 3f 183yds............(3:50)

4479[7] HOME FROM THE HILL (Ire) 8-6 (3*) M Fenton (2) *patiently rdn, improved to join issue o'r 2 fs out, kpt on wl to ld cl hme*..........................(16 to 1 op 14 to 1) 1
4129* SCORCHED AIR 8-9 M Hills (8) *nvr far away, drvn ahead o'r 2 fs out, hdd and no extr cl hme.* (9 to 2 op 7 to 2) 2
4479[2] PRESTON GUILD (Ire) 9-0 L Dettori (7) *co'red up on ins, drvn up to chal over one furlong out, styd on same pace*..........................(13 to 2 op 6 to 1) 3
3839[7] JOY OF FREEDOM 8-6 (3*) B Doyle (11) *led for one and a half fs, styd hndy till hrd rdn o'r 2 furlongs out, sn btn.* ....(33 to 1) 4
3211[8] RAFIF (USA) 8-9 W Carson (5) *settled to track ldg quartet, feeling pace o'r 2 fs out, fdd.* ....(11 to 2 op 5 to 1 tchd 6 to 1) 5
4247[3] SUNTARA (Ire) 8-9 Pat Eddery (1) *co'red up in midfield, effrt on far rls over 2 fs out, sn rdn and outpcd.* ....(85 to 40 fav op 2 to 1 tchd 5 to 2) 6
4322[4] VILLAGE GREEN (Fr) 9-0 D Holland (9) *led aftr one and a half fs, quickened 6 ls clr entering strt, wndrd and hdd o'r 2 out, sn btn*..................(14 to 1 op 10 to 1) 7
4155[7] SHILLELAGH BAY (Ire) 9-0 N Adams (10) *trkd ldg pair, drvn o'r 2 fs out, wknd rpdly*..... (33 to 1 op 20 to 1) 8
4426[5] CUTLASS (Ire) (bl) 8-9 W Ryan (6) *pressed ldg trio, struggling to hold pl o'r 2 fs out, sn lost tch.* ....(8 to 1 op 6 to 1) 9
4426[6] HEATHYARDS BOY (bl) 9-0 S Perks (3) *steadied strt, rcd freely for a m, sn lost tch*......... (20 to 1 op 16 to 1) 10
3945 FARANDOLE (bl) 9-0 J O'Reilly (4) *tubed, pressed ldrs till wknd rpdly entering strt, tld off.* (100 to 1 op 50 to 1) 11
Dist: Hd, 3l, 7l, 5l, 2l, 5l, 3½l, sht-hd, 1½l, dist. 2m 41.00s. a 12.50s (11 Ran).
SR: 29/28/27/8/-/-/ (Capt B W Bell), M Bell

4600 Castle Handicap Class E (0-70 3-y-o and up) £3,652 1m 1f 218yds.... (4:20)

4178[9] AEGAEN LADY [50] 4-8-9 J Weaver (8) *settled gng wl, improved frm midfield o'r one furlong out, styd on to ld last 50 yards*...................... (20 to 1 op 16 to 1) 1

4354* SKY BURST [46] 3-8-0 N Carlisle (4) *wth ldr, led on bit 3 fs out, rdn and hdd last 50 yards, one pace.* .... (10 to 1 op 8 to 1) 2
4490 MARIUS (Ire) [63] 3-9-3 Pat Eddery (13) *trkd ldrs gng wl, ev ch o'r 2 fs out, styd on und pres*.... (10 to 1 op 7 to 1) 3
4354^{8} ROCK THE BARNEY (Ire) [46] 4-8-5 B Rouse (15) *settled midfield, effrt and not clr run o'r 2 fs out, staying on finish*.............................(14 to 1 op 20 to 1) 4
2970^{4} ALTERMEERA [43] (bl) 5-7-11 (5*) D Wright (16) *trkd ldg bunch, improved wl o'r 2 fs out, styd on one pace fnl furlong*.......................................(16 to 1) 5
4486^{4} PERSIAN BUD (Ire) [43] 5-8-2 S Raymont (6) *settled midfield, drvn alng to improve last 2 fs, nrst finish.* ....(20 to 1) 6
3018^{6} OOZLEM (Ire) [45] 4-8-4 R Price (14) *beh and pushed alng hfwy, styd on last 2 fs, nvr nrr*.... (50 to 1 op 33 to 1) 7
4470 SWIFT SILVER [57] 6-9-2 A McGlone (17) *tucked away in midfield, effrt 3 fs out, rdn and no imprsn.* ....(3 to 1 fav op 9 to 2) 8
4533 CASPIAN BELUGA [60] 5-9-5 J Quinn (11) *made most till hdd 3 fs out, fdd*................... (12 to 1 op 10 to 1) 9
4335* SARAH-CLARE [67] 5-9-12 D Holland (3) *in tch, drvn into midfield o'r 2 fs out, no imprsn.* ....(9 to 1 op 7 to 1 tchd 10 to 1) 10
4391^{9} INFERRING [43] 5-7-9 (7*) M Humphries (9) *chsd alng in midfield, effrt o'r 3 fs out, nvr dngrs*......... (25 to 1) 11
4495 BLUE FLAG (USA) [67] 4-9-12 A Munro (18) *pressed ldg 5, drvn 3 fs out, fdd*...............................(12 to 1) 12
4125^{8} ARAMON [48] 3-7-11 (5*) B Russell (10) *pressed ldg bunch till fdd und pres last 3 fs*...........(10 to 1 op 7 to 1) 13
3961 HEART OF SPAIN [63] 3-8-10 (7*) C Hawksley (7) *chsd alng to keep up hfwy, nvr dngrs*.................... (14 to 1) 14
4155^{4} EVER SO LYRICAL [58] 3-8-12 W Ryan (12) *trkd ldg quartet, drvn o'r 3 fs out, fdd*........... (10 to 1 op 8 to 1) 15
2427^{5} ATLANTIC WAY [54] 5-8-13 N Adams (5) *in tch, effrt and swtchd outsd 3 fs out, nvr able to chal*........ (14 to 1) 16
4349a PEACE FORMULA (Ire) [52] 4-8-11 J Williams (2) *struggling to keep up appr strt, tld off*...... (33 to 1 tchd 50 to 1) 17
2270^{9} SYLVANIA (Ire) [51] 3-8-5 L Dettori (19) *dsptd ld early, lost tch entering strt, tld off*.......................(14 to 1) 18

Dist: ½l, 1½l, 1½l, hd, 3l, ½l, 5l, 1l, ½l, 1½l. 2m 13.40s. a 10.50s (18 Ran).
SR: 40/30/44/29/25/19/20/22/23/ (D H Blackwood), J Etherington

MAISONS-LAFFITTE (FR) (heavy)
Tuesday October 26th
Going Correction: PLUS 0.35 sec. per fur.

4601 Prix Scaramouche (Listed) (3-y-o and up) £14,337 1½m................(2:20)

4311 DARIYOUN (USA) 5-9-2 F Head,........................ 1
4674a^{3} BIKASAITE (Fr) 4-9-2 O Benoist,.......................... 2
4296^{5} HURTEVENT (Fr) 3-8-12 D Boeuf,........................ 3
4296^{4} DONDOOK (USA) 3-8-12 O Peslier,....................... 4

Dist: Nose, 4l, 4l, ½l, 6l, 20l. 2m 35.40s. a 7.40s (8 Ran).
SR: 70/69/57/49/ (Mme M S Vidal), C Laffon-Parias

REDCAR (good to soft)
Tuesday October 26th
Going Correction: PLUS 0.45 sec. per fur. (races 1,4,5,6,7), PLUS 0.70 (2,3)

4602 Levy Board Nursery Class E (2-y-o) £3,002 6f...................... (1:00)

4299^{2} BLURRED IMAGE (Ire) [73] 9-7 J Reid (8) *beh, hdwy hfwy, led ins fnl furlong, ran on wl.* ....(7 to 2 fav op 4 to 1 tchd 9 to 2) 1
4436^{9} RICH GLOW [48] (bl) 7-10 L Charnock (13) *led till heded ins fnl furlong, no extr*.............. (25 to 1 op 20 to 1) 2
4342* BENEFICIARY [60] 8-8 M Birch (9) *in tch, effrt o'r 2 out, styd on wl und pres fnl furlong, nrst finish.* ....(5 to 1 op 6 to 1) 3
4500* DANGEROUS SHADOW [75] 9-2 (7*,7ex) S Copp (11) *beh, styd on wl fnl 2 fs, not rch ldrs*....(6 to 1 tchd 13 to 2) 4
4318* JUST FLAMENCO [68] 8-13 (3*) C Hodgson (5) *in tch, sn pushed alng, styd on und pres fnl 2 fs, not trble ldrs.* ....(9 to 2 op 3 to 1) 5
4375^{2} DISTINCTIVE AIR [71] 9-5 W Newnes (6) *chsd ldrs, sn rdn alng, hdwy o'r 2 out, ev ch over one out, wknd fnl furlong*.......................................(10 to 1) 6
4453^{3} SPRING LOADED [66] 9-0 J Fanning (10) *nvr nr to chal.* ....(11 to 1 op 10 to 1 tchd 12 to 1) 7
4342^{3} NEVER SO TRUE [50] 7-12 T Williams (12) *slwly into strd, sn chasing ldrs, grad wknd fnl 2 fs.* ....(12 to 1 op 10 to 1) 8
4489^{8} MELODY DANCER [64] 8-7 (5*) A Garth (7) *nvr on terms.* ....(50 to 1) 9
4516* PALACEGATE JO (Ire) [67] 9-1 (7ex) J Carroll (2) *chsd ldrs, ev ch o'r one out, sn wknd*............ (8 to 1 op 7 to 1) 10
4484^{6} WARTHILL WHISPERS [47] 7-9 J Lowe (4) *cl up till wknd o'r one out*........................(20 to 1 op 16 to 1) 11
4434^{9} STEEL SOVEREIGN [46] 7-8^{6} (5*) Darren Moffatt (1) *chsd ldrs till wknd o'r one out*..........(50 to 1 op 33 to 1) 12
4332^{5} PLEASURE TRICK (USA) [60] 8-8 Paul Eddery (3) *cl up till wknd o'r 2 out*.................... (14 to 1 op 10 to 1) 13

Dist: 1l, hd, 1l, 3l, ¾l, 2½l, ¾l, nk, 1l, 1l. 1m 17.30s. a 7.60s (13 Ran).
SR: 9/-/-/2/-/-/ (N Ahamad), R Hannon

4603 Brass Castle Claiming Stakes Class F (3-y-o and up) £3,027 1m 3f..... (1:30)

3135* KAGRAM QUEEN 5-8-6 K Fallon (9) *hld up in tch, pushed alng hfwy, steady hdwy to ld entering fnl furlong, ran on wl*............................(9 to 4 fav op 2 to 1) 1
4538 FAMOUS BEAUTY 6-8-5 (5*) A Garth (3) *hld up in tch, hdwy 3 out, swtchd one out, styd on.* ....(9 to 1 op 8 to 1 tchd 10 to 1) 2
4432 ALKABAR 5-9-0 (5*) D Harrison (10) *prmnt, effrt o'r 2 out, dsptd ld over one out, no extr fnl furlong.* ....(33 to 1 op 25 to 1) 3
3788^{9} BARLEY CAKE 3-7-10 J Fanning (5) *beh, effrt o'r 3 out, styd on fnl 2 fs, nrst finish, fnshd 4th, disqualified, rdr failing to weigh in*.............(9 to 1 op 7 to 1) 4D
4049^{2} GYPSY CRYSTAL (USA) 3-8-0 Dale Gibson (2) *cl up, led 4 out, hdd entering fnl furlong, no extr, fnshd 5th, plcd fourth*.............................. (8 to 1 op 7 to 1) 4
3712 SEA-AYR (Ire) 3-8-0 J Lowe (12) *hld up, hdwy o'r 3 out, one pace fnl 2 fs, fnshd 6th, plcd 5th.* ....(33 to 1 op 50 to 1) 5
2520^{3} VALIANT WORDS (bl) 6-9-3 J Reid (4) *led till hdd 4 out, grad wknd*.................................(8 to 1 op 6 to 1) 7
4544^{6} COMSTOCK 6-8-13 J Fortune (11) *chsd ldrs, pushed alng 5 out, hrd rdn 3 out, wknd 2 out.* ....(11 to 4 op 2 to 1 tchd 3 to 1) 8
4319 SIR EDWARD HENRY (Ire) (v) 3-8-11 Paul Eddery (1) *chsd ldrs till wknd o'r 3 out*.............. (16 to 1 op 14 to 1) 9
3536 JOSEPH'S WINE (Ire) 4-8-10 (7*) H Bastiman (7) *al beh.* ....(25 to 1) 10
MASTER GLEN 5-9-7 M Birch (6) *al beh, tld off.* ....(20 to 1 op 12 to 1) 11

Dist: 1l, 2l, 1½l, nk, 5l, 12l, ¾l, 4l, ¾l, 15l. 2m 28.90s. a 13.50s (11 Ran).
SR: 34/36/41/15/18/8/1/-/-/ (Mrs E A Kettlewell), Mrs M Reveley

4604 Teleprompter Limited Stakes Class F (3-y-o) £2,924 1¼m.............(2:00)

4506^{5} PRINCESS TATEUM (Ire) 8-4^{2} (7*) R Painter (1) *made all, hld on wl fnl furlong, all out.* ....(4 to 1 op 7 to 2 tchd 9 to 2) 1
4343^{6} BILOELA 8-9 K Fallon (5) *trkd ldrs, effrt 3 out, ev ch fnl 2 fs, no extr und pres final furlong.* .... (11 to 2 op 5 to 1 tchd 6 to 1) 2
4533^{4} MYSILV 8-9 J Reid (9) *al prmnt, swtchd ins o'r one out, styd on und pres fnl furlong.* .... (11 to 10 on op Evens tchd 11 to 10) 3
4431^{4} MOONLIGHT ECLIPSE 8-7 (7*) S Knott (6) *beh till styd on und pres fnl 3 fs, nvr trbld ldrs*.... (16 to 1 op 14 to 1) 4
4234^{8} RUMPUS (Ire) 8-6 (3*) C Hodgson (2) *cl up till wknd o'r 2 out*.............. (11 to 2 op 9 to 2 tchd 6 to 1) 5
4431^{6} IJAB (Can) 8-9 (5*) Darren Moffatt (8) *chsd ldrs till wknd o'r 3 out*............................(25 to 1 op 20 to 1) 6
3355^{9} BARDIA 8-9 Kim Tinkler (7) *dwlt, nvr on terms.* (100 to 1) 7
4047 WARM TOES 8-9 J Carroll (11) *in tch, effrt 4 out, sn btn.* ....(25 to 1) 8
2594^{9} SABO SONG 8-9 S Webster (10) *sn beh*.......... (16 to 1) 9
4431 CITY LIGHTER (v) 8-9 J Fortune (4) *sn beh, tld off.* (66 to 1) 10
4234 MADAM CAPRICE (bl) 8-9 D Harrison (3) *chsd ldrs till wknd quickly o'r 3 out, tld off*........... (16 to 1 op 14 to 1) 11

Dist: Sht-hd, 1½l, 10l, 5l, 2½l, hd, 4l, 15l, 20l, 2l. 2m 13.40s. a 12.20s (11 Ran).
SR: 43/42/39/24/9/9/3/-/-/ (J R Good), M R Channon

4605 B.B.C. Radio Cleveland Handicap Class D (0-80 3-y-o and up) £3,611 1m ....(2:30)

4537^{9} SARTIGILA [58] 4-8-4 (5*) J Marshall (9) *dwlt, hld up, hdwy 2 out, styd on wl to ld ins fnl furlong.* .... (20 to 1 op 16 to 1) 1
4364^{4} COUREUR [45] 4-7-10 J Lowe (10) *trkd ldrs, led 2 out, hdd ins fnl furlong, no extr*........... (7 to 2 tchd 4 to 1) 2
4506^{7} NO COMEBACKS [55] 5-8-6 Paul Eddery (3) *beh till styd on fnl 3 fs, nrst finish*...............................(14 to 1) 3
4415 PARLIAMENT PIECE [75] 7-9-7 (5*) Darren Moffatt (1) *led till hdd 2 out, kpt on same pace*......... (9 to 1 op 8 to 1) 4
4424^{7} HARPOON LOUIE (USA) [74] 3-9-8 M Birch (7) *in tch, effrt 3 out, kpt on same pace*.............. (7 to 1 op 6 to 1) 5
4470^{4} RETENDER (USA) [58] 4-8-9 K Fallon (8) *chsd ldrs, pushed alng o'r 3 out, no hdwy.* ....(11 to 4 fav tchd 5 to 2 and 3 to 1) 6
4424 SPANISH VERDICT [65] 6-8-9 (7*) C Teague (13) *in tch, rdn o'r 3 out, no hdwy*................ (25 to 1 op 20 to 1) 7
4468^{9} SWEET MIGNONETTE [73] 5-9-3 (7*) S Copp (2) *in tch, shaken up o'r 2 out, no hdwy*...... (10 to 1 op 8 to 1) 8
4320^{6} TARNSIDE ROSAL [62] 3-8-10 J Carroll (4) *nvr dngrs.* ....(12 to 1) 9
4488 WATCH ME GO (Ire) [46] 4-7-11 L Charnock (11) *prmnt till wknd 3 out*.......................... (33 to 1 op 25 to 1) 10
2737 VENTURE FOURTH [42] 4-7-7 S Wood (14) *in tch till wknd 3 out*..........................(50 to 1 op 66 to 1) 11

4348 CAN CAN CHARLIE [53] 3-8-1 T Williams (5) *prmnt till wknd quickly o'r 2 out.* ....(10 to 1 op 9 to 1 tchd 11 to 1) 12
592 MAJOR MOUSE [72] 5-9-9 A Culhane (6) *beh frm hfwy.* ....(33 to 1) 13
4133³ LAKAB (USA) [72] 3-9-6 R Hills (12) *swtchd rght strt to race alone stands side, beh frm hfwy.* ....(17 to 2 op 9 to 1 tchd 11 to 1 and 8 to 1) 14
Dist: 1½l, 4l, 3½l, 4l, nk, 1½l, nk, 1½l, 3½l, hd. 1m 42.00s. a 7.10s (14 Ran).
SR: 43/25/23/32/16/2/4/11/-/ (John Lishman), M D Hammond

4606 Provideo Rated Class B Handicap (0-95 3-y-o and up) £6,338 7f.... (3:00)

4464⁸ CROFT VALLEY [95] 6-9-7 J Reid (1) *rcd alone far side, made all, rdn fnl 2 fs, jst hld on*......(4 to 1 op 7 to 2) 1
4415² JADE CITY [81] 3-8-1 (3*) S Maloney (5) *al prmnt, chsd wnr fnl 2 fs, kpt on und pres, jst fld*...... (4 to 1 op 7 to 2) 2
4532 PANIKIN [81] 5-8-7 M Birch (4) *cl up, led main grp hfwy, one pace fnl 2 fs*..................(25 to 1 op 14 to 1) 3
4532 DENSBEN [81] 9-8-7 K Fallon (10) *in tch, hdwy 3 out, kpt on same pace fnl 2 fs*........................(25 to 1) 4
4424⁶ FIELD OF VISION (Ire) [81] 3-8-4 T Williams (7) *prmnt till grad wknd fnl 2 fs*...........................(7 to 1) 5
4394 SEA DEVIL [81] 7-8-7 L Charnock (9) *hld up in tch, effrt 3 out, no hdwy*.......... (7 to 1 op 6 to 1 tchd 8 to 1) 6
4465⁷ BENZOE (Ire) [87] (bl) 3-8-10 R Hills (8) *prmnt, rdn o'r 2 out, sn btn*..............(2 to 1 fav op 9 to 4 tchd 5 to 2) 7
4393 NEITHER NOR [81] 4-8-4 (3*) C Hodgson (6) *sn pushed alng and beh*......................(14 to 1 tchd 16 to 1) 8
4038 RED ROSEIN [81] 7-8-7 J Carroll (3) *dwlt, nvr on terms.* ....(20 to 1 op 16 to 1) 9
3372⁶ PLAY HEVER GOLF [94] 3-9-3 Paul Eddery (2) *led main grp to hfwy, grad wknd.* (14 to 1 op 12 to 1 tchd 16 to 1) 10
Dist: Hd, 3l, 2½l, 4l, 3l, 2½l, 4l, nk, ½l. 1m 29.30s. a 7.50s (10 Ran).
SR: 42/24/18/10/-/-/ (Miss Vivian Pratt), R Akehurst

4607 Captain Cook Conditions Stakes Class C (2-y-o) £4,507 7f........(3:30)

4562² IN LIKE FLYNN 9-1 J Reid (3) *made all, shaken up o'r one out, drw clr.* (7 to 4 on op 2 to 1 on tchd 13 to 8 on) 1
4423⁴ TAKADOU (Ire) 8-13 D Harrison (2) *cl up, rdn 2 out, styd on, no ch wth wnr*......................(7 to 4 op 6 to 4) 2
4528³ PLAINSONG 8-6 N Connorton (1) *cl up, shaken up o'r 2 out, wknd over one out*..........(12 to 1 tchd 14 to 1) 3
Dist: 6l, 8l. 1m 29.80s. a 8.00s (3 Ran).
SR: 28/8/-/ (M M Matalon), R Hannon

4608 EBF Wilton Median Auction Maiden Stakes Class F (2-y-o) £3,002 5f (4:00)

4516³ RANKAIDADE 8-4 (5*) A Garth (5) *cl up, led 2 out, ran on wl fnl furlong*..............(5 to 1 op 7 to 2 tchd 11 to 2) 1
CAVERS YANGOUS 9-0 T Williams (7) *dwlt, beh, hdwy 2 out, ran on strly fnl furlong, nrst finish.* ....(10 to 1 op 6 to 1) 2
4124⁴ PAONIC (Ire) 8-11 (3*) C Hodgson (10) *cl up, effrt 2 out, edgd lft und pres one out, no extr.* ....(11 to 10 fav op Evens tchd 5 to 4) 3
4436³ LOCHON 9-0 S Webster (6) *prmnt, effrt 2 out, kpt on same pace*.................. (8 to 1 op 7 to 1 tchd 9 to 1) 4
3754 MUZZ (Ire) 9-0 R P Elliott (9) *chsd ldrs till wknd o'r one out*..................(11 to 1 op 8 to 1 tchd 12 to 1) 5
4452⁵ CELTIC GOVERNESS 8-9 J Fortune (2) *in tch, hdwy to chase ldrs hfwy, wknd o'r one out*............ (33 to 1) 6
3972⁹ IT MUST BE MILLIE 8-9 Dale Gibson (8) *slight ld, rdn hfwy, hdd 2 out, fdd*..................(50 to 1 op 25 to 1) 7
4436⁶ ARTA 9-0 A Culhane (3) *chsd ldrs till wknd hfwy.* ....(14 to 1 op 10 to 1) 8
2845⁵ ANOTHERONE TO NOTE 9-0 J Carroll (1) *chsd ldrs till wknd hfwy*..........................(6 to 1 tchd 7 to 1) 9
2659⁸ CALL ME GRAHAM 8-7 (7*) R Painter (4) *al beh.* ....(14 to 1 op 8 to 1) 10
Dist: 1l, nk, 3l, hd, 1½l, 1l, 6l, 2½l, ½l. 1m 2.10s. a 5.40s (10 Ran).
SR: 32/33/32/20/19/8/4/-/-/ (Mrs B Bell), R Hollinshead

NAVAN (IRE) (good)
Wednesday October 27th

4609 Skryne (C&G) EBF Race (2-y-o) £4,140 1m..........................(1:30)

4382⁴ CLIFDON FOG (Ire) (bl) 9-3 K J Manning (16) ... (7 to 2 fav) 1
3332³ ZIRAVELLO (Ire) 9-3 P Shanahan (12)............ (5 to 1) 2
3922⁸ SHOREWOOD (Ire) 8-10 R Hughes (4)............ (10 to 1) 3
4382⁶ MR RESPECTFULL 8-10 N G McCullagh (5)....... (5 to 1) 4
4323⁶ COLLECTOR GENERAL (Ire) (bl) 8-10 S Craine (14) (16 to 1) 5
MILE A MINUTE (Ire) 8-4 (6*) B J Walsh (11).......(16 to 1) 6
4581 SUBTLE BRIEF (Ire) 8-6 (4*) J J Behan (15)....... (14 to 1) 7
ZAITOON (Ire) 8-10 W J Supple (7)............... (10 to 1) 8
4380 CAPITAL GAIN 8-2 (8*) T E Durcan (8)...........(33 to 1) 9
4535⁹ YOU ARE MY HERO (Ire) 8-10 J F Egan (10)....... (16 to 1) 10
4380² AARDWOLF 8-10 P V Gilson (17)...................(4 to 1) 11
4535⁸ MORE JUSTICE (Ire) 8-0 (10*) T M Finn (2).........(20 to 1) 12
3416⁸ BUBBLY PROSPECT (USA) 8-6 (4*) J A Heffernan (13) ....(20 to 1) 13
NIYAMPOUR (Ire) 8-10 D Hogan (3)..............(6 to 1) 14
4380 STRANGFORD LOUGH (Ire) 8-10² (2*) P Carberry (6) ....(16 to 1) 15
AN GABH DUBH (Ire) 8-8 (2*) D G O'Shea (9)..... (14 to 1) 16
SUPER TRIG (Ire) 8-2 (8*) R T Fitzpatrick (1)...... (25 to 1) 17
Dist: 3½l, 5l, 2l, 1l. 1m 44.10s. (17 Ran).
(J P Hill), J S Bolger

4610 Kilcarn Stud Fillies Race (2-y-o) £4,140 1m.................... (2:30)

TANAKARA (Ire) 8-10 R Hughes (10).............. (4 to 1) 1
4553² TRAGIC POINT (Ire) 9-3 K J Manning (7)......(11 to 8 fav) 2
2294⁵ ORANGE PLEASURE (USA) 8-10 N G McCullagh (14) ....(16 to 1) 3
BIRD'S WING (Ire) 8-10 D Hogan (4)............. (10 to 1) 4
4462 LADY'S VISION (Ire) 9-3 J F Egan (15).............(5 to 1) 5
MINNIE TONKA (Ire) 8-10 W J Supple (1)......... (10 to 1) 6
4581 CRIMSON CITY (Ire) 8-10 P V Gilson (9)..........(25 to 1) 7
4135⁷ GLIMMERING GIRL (USA) 8-10 S Craine (11)..... (10 to 1) 8
4459 THISTLE HILL (Ire) 8-4 (6*) B J Walsh (13)........ (16 to 1) 9
QUICKSAND BAY (Ire) 8-0 (10*) I Browne (17)..... (20 to 1) 10
LATCH ON (Ire) 8-6 (4*) J J Behan (2)............. (10 to 1) 11
PERSIAN SYMPHONY (Ire) 8-11³ (2*) P Carberry (18) ....(10 to 1) 12
ELLE CARVOEIRO (Ire) 8-6 (4*) W J Smith (5)..... (33 to 1) 13
4388⁶ CNOCMA (Ire) 8-10 M G Cleary (3).............. (25 to 1) 14
LYRIC PLAYER (Ire) 8-4 (6*) R V Skelly (8)..........(12 to 1) 15
3954⁴ TINERANA ROSE (Ire) 8-2 (8*) P J Smullen (6).....(16 to 1) 16
4369⁸ GREENRIDGE COURT (Ire) 8-2 (8*) G M Moylan (12) ....(25 to 1) 17
4388 GESHA (Ire) 8-2 (8*) T E Durcan (16)............ (33 to 1) 18
Dist: Nk, hd, ¾l, ½l. 1m 46.10s. (18 Ran).
(H H Aga Khan), John M Oxx

YARMOUTH (good to soft)
Wednesday October 27th

Going Correction: PLUS 0.75 sec. per fur. (races 1,2), PLUS 0.30 (3,4,5,6)

4611 Hemsby Claiming Stakes Class F (3-y-o and up) £2,660 1¾m 17yds.. (1:20)

4357 STREPHON (Ire) 3-8-6 (7*) S Mulvey (3) *made all, drvn alng entering strt, kpt on wl last 2 fs*......(6 to 1 op 4 to 1) 1
4129⁷ BUSMAN (Ire) 4-9-4 M Roberts (2) *patiently rdn, improved entering strt, swtchd ins and hrd drvn last 2 fs, one pace*...............(7 to 2 op 2 to 1 tchd 4 to 1) 2
3344⁶ MICHAELA MIA (USA) (bl) 3-8-0 W Carson (1) *nvr far away, drvn alng last 3 fs, styd on same pace*.......(11 to 4 jt-fav op 3 to 1 tchd 5 to 2) 3
3694* EDGE OF DARKNESS 4-9-3 G Duffield (4) *trkd ldg trio, struggling to keep up o'r 3 fs out, sn rdn and btn.* ....(11 to 4 jt-fav op 3 to 1 tchd 4 to 1) 4
4486 ARMASHOCKER 5-9-4 V Smith (7) *last and pushed alng hfwy, effrt appr strt, sn lost tch*... (50 to 1 op 33 to 1) 5
4279⁹ SHINGLE PATH 3-8-4 W Woods (5) *pressed ldg 4, effrt entering strt, lost tch last 3 fs.* ....(16 to 1 op 10 to 1 tchd 20 to 1) 6
3945 BLACK BEAN 3-8-0 (3*) B Doyle (8) *in tch, struggling to hold pl appr strt, tld off last 3 fs*... (33 to 1 op 20 to 1) 7
4667a⁷ PLEASE PLEASE ME (Ire) 5-8-9 T Williams (6) *trkd wnr till lost grnd o'r 6 fs out, pld up lme in strt.* ....(40 to 1 op 25 to 1 tchd 50 to 1) pu
Dist: 1½l, 1½l, 12l, 10l, 2½l, 20l. 3m 15.20s. a 18.20s (8 Ran).
SR: 22/24/3/-/-/ (Mark Tompkins Elite), M H Tompkins

4612 Hopton Conditions Stakes Class D (3-y-o and up) £3,882 1¼m 21yds.. (1:50)

4298⁶ DEL DEYA (Ire) 3-8-10 L Dettori (5) *trkd ldg pair, led o'r 2 fs out, drvn out*..........................(4 to 1 op 5 to 2) 1
4282⁶ WAGON MASTER (Fr) 3-9-7 W Carson (2) *led till rdn and hdd o'r 2 fs out, rallied, no extr cl hme.* ....(4 to 1 op 3 to 1 tchd 9 to 2) 2
4420² JURA 5-9-2 W R Swinburn (3) *trkd ldg trio, feeling pace and rdn alng o'r 2 fs out, no extr.* ....(Evens fav op 5 to 4 tchd 11 to 8) 3
4100⁴ COUNT OF FLANDERS (Ire) 3-9-1 M Roberts (1) *trkd ldr, struggling whn pace lifted o'r 2 fs out, sn lost tch.* ....(5 to 1 op 7 to 2 tchd 11 to 2) 4
2758 NURYANDRA 3-8-6 M Hills (4) *last and hld up, feeling pace entering strt, sn btn*......(16 to 1 tchd 20 to 1) 5
Dist: 1½l, 6l, 10l, 1½l. 2m 15.50s. a 11.50s (5 Ran).
SR: 56/64/47/26/14/ (Sheikh Ahmed Al Maktoum), J H M Gosden

4613 Vauxhall Nursery Class E (2-y-o) £2,976 5f 43yds................ (2:20)

4516⁷ ROYALE FIGURINE (Ire) [75] 8-12 W R Swinburn (7) *tucked away, led wl o'r one furlong out, quickened clr last 100 yards*.................(4 to 1 op 11 to 4 tchd 9 to 2) 1

4416[5] HIGH HOLME [70] (v) 8-7 L Dettori (6) *al wl plcd, drvn alng o'r one furlong out, kpt on, not pace of wnr.* ....(5 to 1 op 3 to 1) 2
4484 INSIDER TRADER [60] 7-11 W Carson (4) *slight ld one furlong, hndy till rdn and not quicken appr fnl furlong*..................(11 to 1 op 8 to 1 tchd 12 to 1) 3
4500 CABCHARGE PRINCESS (Ire) [70] (v) 8-0 (7*) S Mulvey (5) *chsd ldrs, feeling pace and rdn 2 fs out, nvr able to chal*..................(20 to 1 op 12 to 1) 4
4272* NO MEAN CITY (Ire) [79] (bl) 9-2 A Mackay (3) *dashed up to ld aftr one furlong, rdn and hdd wl o'r one out, fdd.* ....(3 to 1 fav op 11 to 4 tchd 100 to 30) 5
4484 CRAFTY CRICKETER [56] (bl) 7-7 N Adams (8) *steadied strt, swtchd outsd and rdn hfwy, no imprsn.* ....(33 to 1 op 16 to 1) 6
3989[4] BASHFUL BRAVE [69] 8-6 M Hills (9) *co'red up in midfield, effrt and drvn alng hfwy, fdd*.......(6 to 1 op 9 to 2) 7
4483[3] CAZANOVE'S PET [57] 7-8[1] J Quinn (2) *drvn alng hfwy, sn struggling*..................(14 to 1 op 12 to 1) 8
2996 DANCE FOCUS [84] 9-7 R Cochrane (1) *chsd ldrs, struggling to go pace hfwy, nvr a threat.* (6 to 1 tchd 8 to 1) 9
Dist: 4l, 3l, nk, 1l, 1½l, 1½l, 2½l, nk. 1m 4.70s. a 4.00s (9 Ran).
SR: 50/29/7/16/21/-/-/-/3/ (Ms Christine Walker), M J Fetherston-Godley

4614 Ted Pillar Fillies' Conditions Stakes Class C (2-y-o) £5,048 6f 3yds...(2:50)

4546[7] RANDONNEUR (Ire) 8-13 G Hind (3) *made all, jnd and drifted rght appr fnl furlong, kpt on gmely.* ....(7 to 1 op 4 to 1) 1
3317[3] INGOZI 8-11 M Hills (1) *trkd ldg pair, swtchd ins to draw level whn crowded appr fnl furlong, kpt on same pace.* ....(85 to 40 op 6 to 4 tchd 9 to 4) 2
ASTE NAGUSIA (USA) 8-11 W Ryan (4) *sluggish strt, niggled alng and ran in snatches frm hfwy, one pace fnl furlong*..................(6 to 4 on op 5 to 4 on) 3
4442[9] CHOWPOR 8-11 M Roberts (2) *wth wnr, struggling to hold pl o'r 2 fs out, sn lost tch.* ....(16 to 1 op 10 to 1 tchd 20 to 1) 4
Dist: ½l, 3½l, 20l. 1m 15.90s. a 4.90s (4 Ran).
SR: 37/33/19/-/ (T A Scothern), E Weymes

4615 EBF Seashore Maiden Stakes Class D (2-y-o) £4,521 7f 3yds..........(3:25)

4229 GREEN CRUSADER 9-0 W R Swinburn (1) *nvr far away, ev ch o'r 2 fs out, feeling pace and rdn appr last, rallied to ld last strd*............(9 to 1 op 5 to 1 tchd 10 to 1) 1
4276 WINTER COAT (USA) 9-0 L Dettori (4) *trkd ldr, led o'r 2 fs out, rdn appr last, ct last strd.* ....(11 to 10 on op 6 to 4 tchd 2 to 1) 2
4421 SADLER'S WALK 9-0 M Hills (7) *steadied strt, impoved on ins to track ldrs hfwy, kpt on fnl furlong.* ....(9 to 2 op 3 to 1) 3
4149[6] AUGUSTAN 9-0 M Roberts (3) *steadied strt, effrt and shaken up o'r 2 fs out, eased whn btn ins last.* ....(5 to 1 op 7 to 2 tchd 11 to 2) 4
4266 CHARLIE CHARLIE 9-0 J Weaver (5) *led till o'r 2 fs out, rdn and one pace appr last*...........(10 to 1 op 14 to 1) 5
4480 FLEUR DE TAL 8-9 W Woods (6) *wnt rght strt, effrt aftr 2 fs, rdn and outpcd frm two out*....(66 to 1 op 33 to 1) 6
3592 RINGMASTER (Ire) 9-0 G Duffield (2) *steadied strt, struggling and lost action hfwy, tld off.* ....(9 to 2 op 5 to 1 tchd 6 to 1 and 4 to 1) 7
Dist: Sht-hd, 4l, ¾l, 1½l, 3½l, 25l. 1m 30.30s. a 7.10s (7 Ran).
SR: 25/24/12/10/5/-/-/ (Cheveley Park Stud), M R Stoute

4616 California Cliffs Handicap Class E (0-70 3-y-o and up) £3,106 7f 3yds ....(3:55)

4485[2] PENNY BANGER (Ire) [68] (bl) 3-10-0 M Roberts (3) *wnt lft strt, made most centre, hrd pressed fnl furlong, hld on wl*..................(7 to 1 op 6 to 1) 1
4495[3] KNOBBLEENEEZE [63] (v) 3-9-2 (7*) R Painter (10) *nvr far away, str chal appr fnl furlong, jst hld.* ....(10 to 1 tchd 12 to 1) 2
3323* HIGHBORN (Ire) [63] 4-9-12 G Hind (14) *chsd alng to go pace hfwy, styd on fnl furlong, nrst finish.* ....(7 to 1 op 6 to 1 tchd 15 to 2) 3
4514[6] KINGCHIP BOY [57] (v) 4-9-1 (5*) P McCabe (11) *speed stands side, one pace fnl furlong.* ....(7 to 1 tchd 8 to 1 and 13 to 2) 4
4518 TAKENHALL [52] 8-9-1 F Norton (8) *struggling aftr 2 fs, styd on wl appr fnl furlong, nrst finish.* ....(12 to 1 op 10 to 1 tchd 14 to 1) 5
4016[2] KALOKAGATHOS [31] 4-7-8[1] J Quinn (1) *in tch, struggling to go pace hfwy, styd on, nvr nrr*..........(12 to 1) 6
3946[7] BALLON [56] 3-8-13 (3*) B Doyle (6) *rdn alng to go pace, styd on last 2 fs, nrst finish*.......(20 to 1 op 16 to 1) 7
4415 LA BAMBA [64] 7-9-13 W Hood (5) *chsd alng to improve centre hfwy, no extr appr fnl furlong.* ....(13 to 2 fav op 6 to 1 tchd 7 to 1) 8
4458[2] ON Y VA (USA) [56] 6-8-12 (7*) Sarah Thompson (13) *chsd ldrs, feeling pace hfwy, fdd 2 fs out.* (10 to 1 op 8 to 1) 9
4340[8] VERRO (USA) [31] (bl) 6-7-8[1] G Bardwell (4) *pressed ldrs for o'r 4 fs, sn btn*....... (33 to 1 op 25 to 1 tchd 50 to 1) 10
4340[2] ZINBAQ [42] 7-8-5 T Williams (7) *chsd alng in midfield, nvr rch ldrs*..........(7 to 1 op 6 to 1 tchd 15 to 2) 11
4487 HARCLIFF [56] (bl) 4-9-0 (5*) K Rutter (2) *hmpd strt, swtchd to centre aftr 2 fs, nvr dngrs*.......(14 to 1 op 10 to 1) 12
4348[3] GLEN MILLER [60] 3-9-6 L Dettori (12) *pressed ldrs for o'r 4 fs, wknd quickly*..........(7 to 1 op 6 to 1) 13
4317 OUR SHADEE (USA) [52] (v) 3-8-12 M Wigham (15) *beh and drvn alng aftr 2 fs, nvr a factor*....(16 to 1 op 12 to 1) 14
4470 BRILLIANT [58] 5-9-7 M Hills (9) *tld off aftr 2 fs.* ....(20 to 1 op 12 to 1) 15
Dist: Hd, 5l, hd, 2l, sht-hd, 2½l, hd, 10l, hd, 3l. 1m 29.50s. a 6.30s (15 Ran).
SR: 51/45/33/26/15/-/7/17/-/ (R W Huggins), M Johnston

NOTTINGHAM (good)
Thursday October 28th

Going Correction: PLUS 0.45 sec. per fur. (races 1,2,3), PLUS 0.65 (4,5,6,7)

4617 Sneinton Conditions Stakes Class D (3-y-o and up) £3,363 6f 15yds...(1:20)

3782[3] GARAH 4-8-11 W Ryan (11) *in tch stands side, hdwy o'r 2 fs out, led entering last, ran on.* ....(13 to 8 fav op 11 to 10 tchd 2 to 1) 1
4172 MATILA (Ire) 3-8-10 W Carson (14) *led stands side grp, o'rall ldr appr fnl 2 fs, rdn and hdd ins last, kpt on wl.* ....(9 to 1 op 8 to 1 tchd 10 to 1) 2
4507[2] CARRANITA (Ire) 3-8-11 (3*) Stephen Davies (8) *prmnt stands side, ev ch 2 fs out, sn rdn, one pace appr last.* ....(10 to 1 op 7 to 1 tchd 12 to 1) 3
4464[6] HARD TO FIGURE 7-9-13 R Cochrane (2) *steadied strt, beh, swtchd to stands side hfwy, hdwy 2 fs out, rdn and kpt on entering last*............(7 to 1 op 7 to 2) 4
4415[5] WAFFLE ON (v) 3-8-10 W R Swinburn (12) *chsd ldrs stands side, effrt and rdn 2 fs out, kpt on one pace.* ....(6 to 1 tchd 7 to 1) 5
4507[3] ARABELLAJILL (bl) 4-8-10 Pat Eddery (4) *o'rall ldr centre, rdn and hdd over 2 fs out, wknd*....(10 to 1 op 7 to 1) 6
4532[8] WALK THE BEAT 3-8-11 W Woods (5) *chsd ldrs, rdn o'r 2 fs out, sn btn*..................(25 to 1 op 20 to 1) 7
4280[6] DUPLICITY (Ire) 5-8-13 J Reid (7) *nvr rch ldrs.* ....(6 to 1 op 8 to 1 tchd 11 to 2) 8
4168 CLASSIC STORM 3-8-6 J Carroll (1) *chsd ldr centre, rdn o'r 2 fs out, sn btn*..........(25 to 1 op 16 to 1) 9
4331[8] THE OLD CHAPEL 4-9-0[1] T Wall (13) *prmnt stands side, rdn alng hfwy, sn wknd*..................(20 to 1) 10
4317 MIGHTY WRATH 3-8-11 Dale Gibson (9) *slwly into strd, al rear*..................(50 to 1 op 33 to 1) 11
2469[5] GIRL NEXT DOOR 3-8-6 J O'Reilly (6) *chsd ldrs centre, rdn hfwy, sn wknd*..................(50 to 1 op 33 to 1) 12
4515[6] JARIN ROSE (Ire) 3-8-1 (5*) J Tate (3) *al beh*..... (100 to 1) 13
3006[7] SILVER STONE BOY 5-8-13 S Webster (10) *al rear, beh hfwy*..................(50 to 1 op 40 to 1) 14
Dist: Nk, 4l, ½l, hd, 7l, 1l, 5l, 3l, 1½l, 4l. 1m 15.90s. a 4.40s (14 Ran).
SR: 63/61/49/60/42/14/11/-/-/ (Prince A A Faisal), H R A Cecil

4618 Dennis Coxon Memorial Nursery Class E (0-75 2-y-o) £3,494 6f 15yds ....(1:50)

4453[5] MONKEY'S WEDDING [72] (bl) 9-5 J Carroll (15) *made all stands side, rdn o'r one furlong out, ran on wl.* ....(12 to 1 op 10 to 1) 1
4418[5] REMINISCENCE (Ire) [60] 8-7 M Roberts (6) *chsd ldrs centre, hdwy o'r 2 fs out, rdn and styd on ins last.* ....(6 to 1 op 5 to 1 tchd 13 to 2) 2
4561[3] DANCING LAWYER [70] 9-3 A McGlone (17) *chsd ldrs stands side, ev ch o'r one furlong out, sn rdn, kpt on ins last*..................(10 to 1 op 8 to 1) 3
4500[3] CHEERFUL GROOM (Ire) [57] 8-4 W Carson (21) *chsd ldrs stands side, rdn o'r one furlong out, one pace ins last.* ....(9 to 1 op 7 to 1 tchd 10 to 1) 4
4423 THE MULTIYORKER (Ire) [74] 9-0 (7*) S Mulvey (18) *hmpd strt, hdwy on stands side hfwy, rdn and ch o'r one furlong out, wknd ins last*........(12 to 1 op 10 to 1) 5
4528* STRAPPED [59] 8-6 (7ex) N Adams (19) *beh stands side, hdwy o'r one furlong out, styd on strly und pres ins last*..........(10 to 1 op 8 to 1 tchd 11 to 2) 6
4227 BEDAZZLE [49] 7-10 J Lowe (12) *mid-div, pushed alng hfwy, styd on fnl 2 fs, nvr dngrs*...(33 to 1 op 25 to 1) 7
4416 LA RESIDENCE [63] 8-10 J Quinn (9) *speed centre for o'r 3 fs*..................(20 to 1 op 14 to 1) 8
4500[8] EUROPHARM LASSIE [73] 9-6 B Rouse (20) *nvr rch ldrs.* ....(25 to 1) 9
900 GRANDEE [50] 7-11 A Mackay (14) *chsd ldrs stands side, rdn o'r 2 fs out, sn wknd*..................(33 to 1) 10
4358 CA IRA (Ire) [46] 7-4[2] (5*) Darren Moffatt (7) *nvr a factor.* ....(33 to 1) 11
4453[7] FEARLESS WONDER [58] 8-5 M Birch (13) *beh, some hdwy fnl 2 fs*..................(10 to 1 tchd 11 to 1) 12
4034[3] BOLD ARISTOCRAT (Ire) [69] 9-2 S Perks (4) *cl up centre, rdn 2 and a half fs out, sn wknd*...(16 to 1 op 20 to 1) 13
4577 TOOGOODFORYOU [48] (bl) 7-9[2] L Charnock (2) *led centre grp, rdn hfwy, sn hdd and wknd.* ....(33 to 1 tchd 50 to 1) 14

4528[2] BET A PLAN (Ire) [49] (bl) 7-5 (5*) D Wright (11) *slwly away, al beh*..............(11 to 2 fav op 5 to 1 tchd 6 to 1) 15
3545[9] SUN CHIEF (Ire) [59] 8-6 W Ryan (5) *al beh*. ....(16 to 1 op 14 to 1) 16
4367[7] THE ARDINGLY FAIR (Ire) [50] 7-11 G Bardwell (16) *speed stands side to hfwy, sn wknd*..................(33 to 1) 17
4416[4] AT THE SAVOY (Ire) [57] 8-4 K Fallon (10) *prmnt stands side, rdn alng hfwy, wknd 2 fs out*.......(12 to 1 op 8 to 1) 18
4496[3] MILLICENT NORTH [68] 8-10 (5*) S Drowne (8) *al beh*. ....(12 to 1 op 14 to 1) 19
4144[9] NOBLE SPIRIT (Ire) [70] 9-3 Pat Eddery (3) *al beh*. ....(10 to 1 tchd 12 to 1) 20

Dist: 1½l, sht-hd, ½l, ½l, sht-hd, 3½l, sht-hd, 5l, 8l, ¾l. 1m 17.40s. a 5.90s (20 Ran).
SR: 41/23/32/17/32/16/-/5/-/ (The Monkey Racing Club Limited), J Berry

4619 Roseland Conditions Stakes Class D (2-y-o) £2,992 6f 15yds..........(2:20)

4130[4] BLUE BOMBER 9-0 Pat Eddery (3) *made all, pushed clr appr fnl furlong, ran on*. ....(6 to 1 on op 9 to 2 on tchd 4 to 1 on) 1
1798 FAIREY FIREFLY 8-5 L Charnock (2) *trkd ldrs, hdwy 2 fs out, sn rdn, one pace appr last*...... (8 to 1 op 6 to 1) 2
LA REINA BLANCA (Spa) 8-5 S Whitworth (4) *trkd ldrs, effrt o'r 2 fs out, sn rdn, wknd wl over one out*. ....(9 to 1 op 6 to 1 tchd 10 to 1) 3
4504[3] NILEGUNNER 8-0 (5*) A Garth (1) *cl up, rdn o'r 2 fs out, sn wknd*..............................(25 to 1 op 20 to 1) 4

Dist: 3l, 5l, 8l. 1m 17.80s. a 6.30s (4 Ran).
SR: 28/7/-/-/ (Cheveley Park Stud), R Hannon

4620 EBF Netherfield Maiden Stakes Class D (2-y-o) £4,987 1m 54yds...... (2:50)

4099[5] SHERMAN (Ire) 9-0 R Hills (8) *al prmnt, hdwy to ld 3 fs out, rdn and ran on wl frm 2 out*. ....(9 to 2 op 5 to 1 tchd 6 to 1) 1
4419[2] TOM WALLER (Ire) 9-0 W Ryan (11) *trkd ldrs, effrt on outsd 3 fs out, sn chasing wnr, rdn 2 out, edgd lft, one pace appr last*.....(6 to 4 on op 5 to 4 on tchd Evens) 2
3352[7] GOLDEN ARROW (Ire) 9-0 R Cochrane (2) *chsd ldrs, rdn 3 fs out, kpt on frm 2 out*.............(10 to 1 op 6 to 1) 3
TURRET 8-9 W Carson (1) *in tch, hdwy o'r 3 fs out, rdn and one pace frm 2 out*..............(16 to 1 op 14 to 1) 4
MARSHALL NEY (USA) 9-0 Pat Eddery (10) *chsd ldrs, pushed alng hfwy, rdn 3 fs out, sn btn*. ....(9 to 1 op 6 to 1) 5
4377[4] SILENCE IN COURT (Ire) 9-0 A Mackay (16) *slwly into strd, beh till hdwy on outsd 3 fs out, kpt on, nvr dngrs*. ....(20 to 1 op 16 to 1) 6
4579[6] INTERACT 9-0 J Reid (9) *beh, styd on fnl 2 fs, nvr dngrs*. ....(20 to 1 op 14 to 1) 7
4182[4] MR TOWSER 8-11 (3*) C Hodgson (3) *led to 3 fs out, sn rdn, wknd wl o'r one out*..............(50 to 1 op 33 to 1) 8
PRINCERULLAH 9-0 M Wigham (5) *al rear*....... (33 to 1) 9
3990 JUNDI (Ire) (v) 9-0 W R Swinburn (14) *mid-div, pushed alng hfwy, sn btn*..................(20 to 1 op 14 to 1) 10
4491 SOTTISES (Ire) 8-2 (7*) N Varley (6) *slwly into strd, sn chasing ldrs, rdn and wknd 4 fs out*...........(50 to 1) 11
MY TIME 8-9 M Hills (4) *in tch, rdn 3 fs out, sn wknd*. ....(33 to 1) 12
4419 LITTLE BROOK 9-0 R Perham (12) *mid-div, hdwy on ins o'r 3 fs out, rdn and wknd quickly 2 out*.......(33 to 1) 13
4489[9] BURRINGHAM BOY 9-0 J Quinn (15) *al beh*. ....(50 to 1 op 33 to 1) 14
4179[8] NEEDWOOD JOKER 9-0 J Williams (7) *al rear*. ....(50 to 1 op 33 to 1) 15
4491[8] ADMIRAL ROUS 9-0 G Bardwell (13) *al rear*. ....(50 to 1 op 33 to 1) 16

Dist: 3l, hd, 3½l, 10l, ½l, nk, 1½l, 1½l, 2½l, 1½l. 1m 49.30s. a 9.30s (16 Ran).
SR: 41/32/31/15/-/-/ (Mrs H T Jones), H Thomson Jones

4621 Mapperley Handicap Class D (0-80 3-y-o and up) £3,669 1¾m 15yds (3:20)

4414[9] DREAMS END [77] 5-9-7 (5*) K Rutter (7) *mid-div, hdwy on outsd 3 fs out, led appr last, rdn and ran on*. ....(10 to 1 op 8 to 1) 1
4152[4] JONSALAN [66] 3-8-6 J Reid (5) *chsd ldr, led 3 fs out, rdn and hdd appr last, rallied und pres*. ....(12 to 1 op 10 to 1) 2
4559[2] WARM SPELL [79] 3-9-5 (5ex) B Rouse (2) *al prmnt, effrt 3 fs out, sn ev ch, rdn wl o'r one out, wknd ins last*. ....(7 to 1 op 5 to 1) 3
4538[2] WHITE WILLOW [73] 4-9-1 (7*) S Copp (13) *hld up beh, hdwy o'r 3 fs out, styd on frm 2 out, nrst finish*. ....(6 to 1 fav op 5 to 1) 4
4519[2] ENCORE UNE FOIS (Ire) [76] 4-9-11 M Roberts (1) *prmnt, ev ch 3 fs out, sn rdn, one pace frm 2 out*. ....(7 to 1 tchd 8 to 1) 5
4454[3] KEYLOCK (USA) [59] 3-7-13 W Carson (10) *chsd ldrs, rdn and lost pl 5 fs out, styd on und pres frm 2 out*. ....(7 to 1 op 6 to 1) 6
4494[8] ZEALOUS KITTEN (USA) [58] 5-8-4 (3*) Stephen Davies (3) *mid-div, hdwy hfwy, rdn 3 fs out, sn wknd*. ....(14 to 1 op 10 to 1) 7
4432[2] FUNNY HILARIOUS (USA) [72] 3-8-12 Pat Eddery (9) *mid-div, hdwy on ins 4 fs out, swtchd rght 2 out, sn rdn and btn*..................................(13 to 2 op 5 to 1) 8
427* AVRO ANSON [66] 5-9-1 L Charnock (8) *hld up, hdwy on outsd 4 fs out, sn rdn, wknd o'r 2 out*. (8 to 1 op 7 to 1) 9
4466 ISLAND BLADE (Ire) [57] 4-8-6 T Quinn (11) *mid-div, hdwy hfwy, rdn 3 fs out, sn wknd*.......(12 to 1 op 10 to 1) 10
4502 ELECTROLYTE [54] 3-7-8[1] J Lowe (4) *sn led, rdn and hdd 3 fs out, wknd*..................................(33 to 1) 11
4454* SALU [62] 4-8-11 J Carroll (6) *al rear*... (7 to 1 op 8 to 1) 12
LANDED GENTRY (USA) [60] 4-8-9 M Wigham (12) *mid-div, effrt and some hdwy 4 fs out, sn rdn, wknd quickly, tld off frm 2 out*..................................(33 to 1) 13

Dist: Nk, 2l, 3l, 1l, 1½l, 5l, 5l, ½l, ½l, sht-hd. 3m 12.40s. a 14.50s (13 Ran).
SR: 58/37/46/43/44/15/13/8/10/ (T G Price), Dr J D Scargill

4622 The Levy Board Maiden Stakes (Class D) (3-y-o) £3,523 1m 1f 213yds.. (3:50)

4524[5] CASCASSI (USA) 8-9 M Roberts (1) *dwlt, sn pushed alng in mid-div, hdwy on outsd 3 fs out, styd on wl und pres to ld appr last, ran on*. ....(13 to 8 fav op 5 to 4 tchd 7 to 4) 1
4525[6] PRINCESS SIOUX 8-9 R Price (7) *in tch, hdwy o'r 4 fs out, chlgd 2 out, rdn to ld briefly appr last, edgd lft, one pace*..............................(7 to 1 op 6 to 1) 2
RAMIYA 8-9 W Carson (5) *in tch, hdwy on ins o'r 4 fs out, rdn and one pace frm 3 out*..............(4 to 1 op 3 to 1) 3
4525[5] RYNAVEY 8-9 W Ryan (6) *prmnt, led aftr 2 fs, sn clr, rdn o'r two out, hrd drvn and hdd over one out, wknd*. ....(3 to 1) 4
4590[6] SNOW DREAM 8-9 D Biggs (9) *chsd ldrs, rdn 3 fs out, sn one pace*..................................(20 to 1) 5
HIGH FINISH 8-9 W Newnes (8) *prmnt, effrt 3 fs out, sn rdn, wknd 2 out*..................(12 to 1 op 10 to 1) 6
KING'S GOLD 9-0 R Perham (10) *nvr rch ldrs*. ....(33 to 1 op 25 to 1) 7
4524[7] LATHERON (Ire) 9-0 T Quinn (3) *al rear*. ....(4 to 1 op 7 to 2 tchd 5 to 1) 8
HOBBS (Ire) 9-0 D Harrison (4) *al rear*..............(14 to 1) 9
4155 VINTAGE RED 9-0 J Carroll (2) *prmnt till rdn and wknd o'r 4 fs out*..............................(33 to 1 op 25 to 1) 10

Dist: 2½l, 1½l, 1½l, 6l, 10l, ¾l, 2l, 5l, 5l. 2m 15.60s. a 12.60s (10 Ran).
SR: 34/29/26/23/11/-/ (Sheikh Mohammed), J H M Gosden

4623 Woodthorpe Handicap Class E (0-70 3-y-o and up) £3,753 1m 54yds.. (4:20)

3891[7] AFFA [40] 4-8-1 D Biggs (13) *al prmnt, effrt 2 fs out, rdn to ld and edgd lft one and a half out, sn clr, styd on ins last*..............................(11 to 1 op 10 to 1) 1
4468[5] PROUD BRIGADIER (Ire) [66] 5-9-13 T Quinn (5) *al prmnt, effrt 2 fs out, ev ch whn not much room one and a half out, kpt on und pres ins last*. ....(15 to 2 op 7 to 1 tchd 8 to 1) 2
4488[8] EAST BARNS (Ire) [37] (bl) 5-7-12 J Fanning (11) *beh, hdwy 3 fs out, rdn 2 out, styd on strly ins last, nrst finish*. ....(16 to 1 op 10 to 1) 3
3697[5] RED COTTON [62] 3-9-6 Paul Eddery (1) *sn led, rdn 3 fs out, hdd one and a half out, soon wknd*. ....(17 to 2 op 8 to 1 tchd 9 to 1) 4
4518[3] BUDDY'S FRIEND (Ire) [55] 5-8-9 (7*) Sarah Thompson (12) *mid-div, hdwy 3 fs out, rdn 2 out, sn one pace*. ....(11 to 1 op 10 to 1 tchd 12 to 1) 5
4533 MAHONG [57] 5-9-4 J Williams (4) *mid-div, hdwy o'r 2 fs out, sn rdn, kpt on, nrst finish*.... (16 to 1 op 14 to 1) 6
4490[7] BRESIL (USA) [50] 4-8-11 A Clark (10) *mid-div, hdwy and not clr run 2 and a half fs out, rdn and styd on appr last, nrst finish*..............(11 to 1 tchd 14 to 1) 7
4391[4] STOPROVERITATE [54] 4-9-1 N Connorton (6) *mid-div, rdn and styd on fnl 2 fs, nvr dngrs*.... (8 to 1 tchd 10 to 1) 8
1931[9] SHAHAADA (USA) [64] 3-9-8 W Carson (15) *mid-div, pushed alng hfwy, nvr dngrs*..............(14 to 1) 9
2869 RED KITE [40] 4-7-8 (7*) M Baird (14) *in tch till rdn and wknd o'r 3 fs out*..............(25 to 1 tchd 33 to 1) 10
4333 SIRTELIMAR (Ire) [52] 4-8-13 A Mackay (19) *chsd ldr, rdn and wknd o'r 3 fs out*...........(14 to 1 tchd 16 to 1) 11
4687a[8] COLFAX STARLIGHT [52] 3-8-10 S Wood (3) *in tch, wknd 3 fs out*..........................(33 to 1 tchd 50 to 1) 12
3591 RIVA ROCK [42] 3-8-0 A McGlone (7) *nvr rch ldrs*. ....(20 to 1 op 16 to 1 tchd 25 to 1) 13
4518 HARVEST ROSE [60] 4-9-7 V Slattery (16) *slwly into strd, al rear*..............(20 to 1 tchd 25 to 1) 14
1604 SAAHI (USA) [57] 4-8-13 (5*) K Rutter (9) *nvr a factor*. ....(25 to 1 op 20 to 1) 15
4133[9] PRECIOUS AIR (Ire) [54] 5-9-1 B Rouse (2) *chsd ldrs, hmpd and lost pl aftr 3 fs, nvr dngrs*.... (12 to 1 op 10 to 1) 16
4235 WILD PROSPECT [49] 5-8-10 M Birch (20) *chsd ldrs till rdn and wknd 3 fs out*..............................(20 to 1) 17
4394[5] HAWAII STORM (Fr) [43] 5-8-4 R Street (17) *dwlt, sn in tch, hdwy on outsd 4 fs out, rdn 3 out, soon wknd*. ....(7 to 1 fav op 6 to 1) 18
4490[8] SCOTTISH PARK [53] 4-9-0 J Quinn (18) *in tch, hdwy on outsd 4 fs out, rdn 3 out, sn wknd*..........(16 to 1) 19

Dist: 2½l, 2l, hd, ½l, nk, nk, 2½l, 10l, 2l, hd. 1m 49.10s. a 9.10s (19 Ran).
SR: 31/49/14/35/29/30/22/18/-/ (G Oliver), T Thomson Jones

TIPPERARY (IRE) (good (race 1), good to yielding (2))
Thursday October 28th

4624 **Kilmallock E.B.F. Maiden (2-y-o) £3,795 7f. . . . . (1:30)**

4535^{2} FLYING EAGLE 9-0 R Hughes (2). . . . . (5 to 4 fav) 1
1650^{5} COPPER MOUNTAIN (Ire) 9-0 P Shanahan (3). . . . . . (3 to 1) 2
4261^{5} SUBARASHII (USA) 8-11 N G McCullagh (8). . . . . . (5 to 1) 3
4459^{7} BLUE DOMINION (Ire) 8-10^{1} (2*) P Carberry (12). . .(10 to 1) 4
3954 FINAL EXHIBIT (Ire) 8-11 K J Manning (6). . . . .(10 to 1) 5
4406 WOLFIES RASCAL (Ire) (bl) 9-0 W J Supple (1). . . . (14 to 1) 6
MODEL SHOW (Ire) 8-7 (4*) J J Behan (7). . . . .(10 to 1) 7
4290^{6} BE GIVING (Ire) 8-11 Ann O'Rourke (5). . . . .(10 to 1) 8
4323 GRENNAN CLASSIC (Ire) 8-11 M G Cleary (9). . . . .(16 to 1) 9
2880^{9} JENNY JINGLE (Ire) 8-3 (8*) G M Moylan (16). . . . . (10 to 1) 10
4323 THE DREAM FACTORY (Ire) 8-11 J F Egan (11). . . (20 to 1) 11
4581 EMELIA'S PET (Ire) 9-0 R Dolan (14). . . . . (25 to 1) 12
4459 SECRET SENSATION (Ire) 8-11 S Craine (15). . . . . (20 to 1) 13
3922 PIPER ZERO (Ire) 9-0 P V Gilson (10). . . . .(8 to 1) 14
4459 CANGERAC (Ire) 8-3 (8*) P J Smullen (4). . . . . (25 to 1) 15
CAHERASS COURT (Ire) 8-5 (6*) P P Murphy (13) (14 to 1) 16
Dist: 1½l, sht-hd, 3l, sht-hd. 1m 39.90s. (16 Ran).
(Sheikh Mohammed), John M Oxx

4625 **Templemore Fillies Race (3-y-o and up) £2,760 1m 1f. . . . . (2:00)**

961* FORCE SEVEN 6-9-1^{1} (6*) T P Treacy (6). . . . . (10 to 1) 1
4463^{7} SAFAYN (USA) (bl) 3-9-1 P Shanahan (8). . . . . (6 to 1) 2
4554^{9} SABAYA (USA) 3-8-10 W J Supple (5). . . . . (7 to 4 fav) 3
4556^{7} NORDIC QUEEN (Ire) 3-8-10 K J Manning (10). . . . . (7 to 1) 4
3561^{5} COMMON BOND (Ire) 3-8-2 (8*) B Fenton (13). . . . . (8 to 1) 5
4118^{9} ESTAFETTE (Ire) 3-8-10 P V Gilson (9). . . . .(33 to 1) 6
4555 FLAME OF PERSIA (Ire) 3-9-5 R Hughes (11). . . . . . .(3 to 1) 7
3733^{4} DO-TELL-ME (Ire) 3-8-2 (8*) R T Fitzpatrick (1). . . . (20 to 1) 8
4409 TRANQUIL BEAUTY (Ire) 4-8-10 (10*) S P Cooke (7) (25 to 1) 9
4556 QUENIE TWO (Ire) 3-8-4 (6*) P P Murphy (4). . . . . . (33 to 1) 10
KELTIC OPTION (Ire) 3-8-6 (4*) J A Heffernan (12) (10 to 1) 11
4368 CATCHMENOT (Ire) 3-8-10 S Craine (14). . . . . (33 to 1) 12
4368 KERRYKEEL LADY (Ire) 3-8-10 M G Cleary (2). . . . (20 to 1) 13
4386^{5} WASSL'S NANNY (Ire) (bl) 4-9-1 N G McCullagh (15)
. . . .(14 to 1) 14
Dist: 2½l, 2l, 1l, 8l. 2m 1.60s. (14 Ran).
(Mrs C A Moore), P Mullins

MAISONS-LAFFITTE (FR) (soft)
Friday October 29th

4626 **Prix Niceas (Listed) (4-y-o and up) £14,337 1¼m. . . . . (2:20)**

3208^{6} PORTICO (USA) 4-9-2 F Head, ... 1
2979^{6} POLYTAIN (Fr) 4-9-2 O Peslier, ... 2
2771^{6} GRAND FLOTILLA (USA) 6-9-2 D Boeuf, ... 3
4711a STOP PRESS (USA) 5-8-13 F Sanchez, ... 4
Dist: Nose, 1½l, ¾l, ½l, ½l, 6l. (Time not taken) (7 Ran).
(Carlos Garcia Pardo), M V O'Brien

NEWMARKET (good)
Friday October 29th
Going Correction: PLUS 0.10 sec. per fur. (races 1,2,3,6), PLUS 0.05 (4,5,7)

4627 **EBF Red Lodge Maiden Stakes Class D (2-y-o) £4,581 6f. . . . .(1:10)**

GREEN GREEN DESERT (Fr) 9-0 W R Swinburn (4) *strted slwly, hld up beh, hdwy o'r one furlong out, quickened to ld wl ins last, imprsv.*
. . . . (3 to 1 op 5 to 4 tchd 100 to 30) 1
ALAZWAR (USA) 9-0 R Hills (1) *cl up, led hfwy till hdd and no extr wl ins fnl furlong*. . . . . . (11 to 4 fav op 3 to 1) 2
3979^{8} DANISH HEIGHTS (Ire) 9-0 R Price (8) *mid-div, hdwy 2 fs out, sn hrd rdn and one pace*. . . . . (4 to 1 tchd 5 to 1) 3
YAZEANHAA (USA) 8-9 Pat Eddery (3) *chsd ldrs, shaken up appr 2 fs out, one pace, better for race.*
. . . . (12 to 1 op 5 to 1) 4
4498^{7} TRADE WIND 9-0 J Williams (7) *beh, hdwy o'r one furlong out, styd on*. . . . .(14 to 1 op 8 to 1 tchd 16 to 1) 5
NEVER SO BLUE (Ire) 9-0 J Reid (9) *missed break, sn in tch, wknd o'r one furlong out, better for race.*
. . . . (12 to 1 op 8 to 1) 6
LAKE POET (USA) 9-0 M Roberts (12) *trkd ldrs, ch appr 2 fs out, wknd and eased ins last, improve.*
. . . . (10 to 1 op 7 to 1) 7
4350 TEN-TO-SIX GIRL (bl) 8-9 W Ryan (10) *took keen hold, chsd ldrs till wknd o'r one furlong out.*
. . . . (33 to 1 op 25 to 1 tchd 50 to 1) 8
3250^{4} MILLRIDGE (Ire) 8-9 W Woods (6) *trkd ldrs till rdn and wknd 2 fs out*. . . . . . . (33 to 1 op 25 to 1 tchd 50 to 1) 9
4011^{8} PRISCILLA ROSE 8-9 E Guest (2) *led till hdd hfwy, wknd.*
. . . .(33 to 1 tchd 50 to 1) 10
4496^{7} FAVILLA (Ire) 8-9 J Fortune (11) *mid-div till outpcd o'r 2 fs out*. . . . .(33 to 1 tchd 50 to 1) 11
ADDED DIMENSION (Ire) 9-0 R Cochrane (5) *missed break, al beh*. . . . .(14 to 1 op 7 to 1 tchd 16 to 1) 12
Dist: ½l, 2½l, 1½l, 2l, 1l, ½l, 2½l, 1½l, ½l, 3l. 1m 14.94s. a 3.54s (12 Ran).
SR: 41/39/29/18/15/11/9/-/-/ (Mana Al Maktoum), M R Stoute

4628 **Soham House Conditions Stakes Class C (2-y-o) £5,435 1m. . . . . . .(1:40)**

KING OF NAPLES (USA) 8-11 S Raymont (5) *chsd ldrs, took keen hold, hdwy o'r one furlong out, ran on und pres to ld wl ins last*. . . . (14 to 1 op 10 to 1 tchd 16 to 1) 1
4520^{5} BLUEGRASS PRINCE (Ire) 9-3 Pat Eddery (4) *cl up, rdn 2 fs out, ev ch und pres ins last, kpt on one pace.*
. . . .(7 to 2 op 5 to 2) 2
3695* PURSUIT OF GLORY 8-6 J Weaver (3) *set slow pace, rdn alng o'r 2 fs out, hdd and no extr wl ins last.*
. . . .(10 to 1 tchd 12 to 1) 3
SEA OF ROCKS 8-11 M Roberts (6) *strted slwly, beh, rdn and hdwy 2 fs out, not clr run o'r one out, ran on one pace*. . . . .(9 to 2 op 5 to 1 tchd 11 to 2) 4
4508* WAITING 8-13 A Munro (2) *trkd ldrs, rdn 2 fs out, wknd ins last*. . . . . (11 to 8 fav op Evens) 5
4498 DIGGERS WELL (USA) 8-11 G Duffield (7) *hld up beh, hdwy o'r one furlong out, ran on wl.*
. . . . (16 to 1 op 14 to 1 tchd 20 to 1) 6
4542^{9} JABAROOT (Ire) 8-11 W R Swinburn (9) *hld up, hdwy 3 fs out, hmpd and squeezed out 2 furlongs out, not reco'r.*
. . . . (10 to 1 op 7 to 1 tchd 12 to 1) 7
4421^{9} THUNDERHEART 8-11 M Marongiu (10) *chsd ldrs, rdn and hng lft 2 fs out, sn btn.*
. . . . (33 to 1 op 16 to 1 tchd 50 to 1) 8
4329* SHOOFK 8-11 L Piggott (8) *trkd ldrs, wkng whn hmpd 2 fs out*. . . . . (16 to 1 op 10 to 1 tchd 20 to 1) 9
Dist: ¾l, ½l, 1½l, nk, ½l, 3½l, hd, ¾l. 1m 45.15s. a 7.95s (9 Ran).
(Lord de La Warr And Mrs M Kerr-Dineen), R Charlton

4629 **James Seymour Stakes Class A (Listed Race) (3-y-o and up) £10,464 1¼m . . . .(2:10)**

4420* MEADOW PIPIT (Can) 4-8-9 W R Swinburn (1) *chsd ldrs, rdn alng and hdwy 2 fs out, led one out, ran on strly.*
. . . .(6 to 1 op 5 to 2) 1
4420^{3} YOUNG BUSTER (Ire) 5-9-0 Pat Eddery (9) *hld up in rear, smooth hdwy to ld one and a half fs out, hdd one out, no extr*. . . . . (2 to 1 fav op 9 to 4 tchd 11 to 4) 2
3402 RED BISHOP (USA) 5-9-7 M Roberts (4) *chsd ldrs, rdn alng 2 fs out, sn one pace*. . . . . (4 to 1 tchd 7 to 2) 3
4305^{6} FRENCHPARK 3-8-9 J Carroll (2) *trkd ldr, led appr 3 fs out, hdd one and a half out, one pace.*
. . . . (20 to 1 op 16 to 1 tchd 25 to 1) 4
4383^{3} KATIBA (USA) 3-8-4 W Carson (5) *chsd ldrs, pushed alng o'r 4 fs out, sn lost pl, styd on ins last.*
. . . . (11 to 1 op 10 to 1 tchd 12 to 1) 5
HALKOPOUS 7-9-0 A Clark (8) *hld up in rear, hdwy o'r one furlong out, nrst finish*. . . . . . (50 to 1 op 33 to 1) 6
1149^{9} FRET (USA) 3-8-9 A Munro (7) *al beh*. (20 to 1 op 16 to 1) 7
4499^{2} FAYFA (Ire) 3-8-4 W Ryan (10) *cl up, rdn and ev ch 2 fs out, sn wknd*. . . . . (11 to 2 op 7 to 1 tchd 8 to 1) 8
4300^{8} ROSE ALTO 5-8-9 G Duffield (3) *trkd ldrs, pushed alng o'r 3 fs out, sn lost pl*. . . . . (20 to 1 op 16 to 1) 9
4207^{2} GEISWAY (Can) (v) 3-8-12 J Reid (6) *led till hdd 3 fs out, sn wknd*. . . . .(14 to 1 op 10 to 1 tchd 16 to 1) 10
Dist: 3l, 3l, ½l, ¾l, nk, 4l, nk, 2½l, 3l. 2m 7.12s. a 4.42s (10 Ran).
SR: 61/60/61/48/41/50/37/31/31/ (Sheikh Mohammed), J H M Gosden

4630 **George Stubbs Rated Class A Handicap (Listed Race) (0-105 3-y-o and up) £9,820 2m. (2:45)**

4466^{6} MY PATRIARCH [99] 3-9-1 Pat Eddery (3) *hld up in rear, smooth hdwy frm 3 fs out, led on bit appr last, quickened clr*. . . . . (7 to 4 fav op 11 to 4 tchd 3 to 1) 1
4466^{2} RITTO [85] 3-8-1 M Roberts (8) *hld up in rear, pushed alng 7 fs out, hdwy o'r 3 out, led over 2 out till hdd and one pace appr last*. . . . . (7 to 2 tchd 4 to 1) 2
MORLEY STREET [95] 9-9-7 J Williams (1) *hld up in rear, hdwy und pres wl o'r one furlong out, styd on.*
. . . . (12 to 1 op 14 to 1) 3
4466 RODEO STAR (USA) [81] 7-8-7 L Piggott (12) *hld up beh ldrs, rdn and not quicken o'r 2 fs out, styd on ins last.*
. . . .(20 to 1 tchd 25 to 1) 4
4414* DERAB (USA) [81] 7-8-7 B Rouse (7) *al prmnt, led 3 fs out till hdd o'r 2 out, one pace.*
. . . . (12 to 1 op 8 to 1 tchd 14 to 1) 5
4466^{3} MY DESIRE [84] 5-8-10 T Quinn (4) *hld up, hdwy 4 fs out, ev ch appr 2 out, sn one pace*. . . . . . . (8 to 1 op 6 to 1) 6
4466 ROSINA MAE [81] 4-8-7 A Munro (11) *prmnt, rdn o'r 5 fs out, wknd over 3 out*. (16 to 1 op 14 to 1 tchd 25 to 1) 7
3846^{9} SOLARTICA (USA) [82] 3-7-12 W Carson (9) *cl up till drvn and wknd 2 fs out*. . . .(25 to 1 op 14 to 1 tchd 33 to 1) 8

4189[4] NOT IN DOUBT (USA) [91] (bl) 4-9-3 W Newnes (2) *led til hdd 3 fs out, wknd*.................(8 to 1 op 7 to 1) 9
4505[2] AUDE LA BELLE (Fr) [81] 5-8-7 A Mackay (5) *al beh*. ....(50 to 1 op 33 to 1) 10
4505[4] MALAMUTE SALOON (USA) [81] (v) 7-8-7 Paul Eddery (6) *al beh*.....................(25 to 1 tchd 33 to 1) 11
4292[6] NASSMA (Ire) [92] 3-8-8 W Ryan (10) *chsd ldrs till rdn and wknd appr 3 fs out*..................(9 to 1 op 5 to 1) 12
Dist: 4l, ¾l, nk, ½l, sht-hd, 7l, 2l, ½l, 10l, sht-hd. 3m 34.17s. a 10.17s (12 Ran).
SR: 7/-/7/-/-/-/ (Peter S Winfield), J L Dunlop

4631 Fitzroy House Handicap Class E (0-70 3-y-o and up) £5,020 1½m...... (3:15)

4176[8] RIZ BIZ (USA) [44] 3-7-4 (5*) Darren Moffatt (31) *trkd ldrs, led o'r 3 fs out, ran on wl*........(16 to 1 tchd 14 to 1) 1
3710[6] CAST THE LINE [66] 3-9-3 W Carson (26) *took keen hold, chsd ldrs, cld 2 fs out, drvn and kpt on one pace*. ....(16 to 1) 2
4432 BROUGHTON'S TANGO (Ire) [60] 4-8-13 (5*) D McCabe (30) *mid-div, hdwy and edgd lft 2 fs out, kpt on wl*. (20 to 1) 3
4559[6] HEAD TURNER [40] 5-7-12 D Biggs (35) *chsd ldg grp, ran on frm o'r 2 fs out, kpt on*........(12 to 1 tchd 14 to 1) 4
4283[2] LOOKINGFORARAINBOW (Ire) [67] 5-9-11 M Wigham (11) *mid-div, hdwy 3 fs out, fnshd wl*.............(16 to 1) 5
4279[6] RUFFLE [57] 3-8-8 D Harrison (29) *mid-div, hdwy 3 fs out, styd on one pace*................ (12 to 1 tchd 14 to 1) 6
4486 AMAZON EXPRESS [65] 4-9-9 T Quinn (6) *beh, hdwy o'r 2 fs out, btn over one out*. ....(12 to 1 op 14 to 1 tchd 16 to 1) 7
4486[5] CRACKLING [42] 4-8-0 S Dawson (27) *trkd ldrs, kpt on one pace fnl 2 fs*.......................(14 to 1 op 16 to 1) 8
4432* ABSALOM'S PILLAR [54] 3-8-5 L Charnock (28) *chsd ldrs till wknd o'r one furlong out*...... (16 to 1 op 14 to 1) 9
3699[2] ROSE NOBLE (USA) [56] 3-8-7 M Tebbutt (4) *hdwy 4 fs out, hrd rdn 2 out, no imprsn*.........(16 to 1 tchd 20 to 1) 10
4426[3] MERRY MERMAID [52] 3-7-10 (7*) M Humphries (16) *beh, hdwy 2 fs out, not rch ldrs*.......(12 to 1 tchd 10 to 1) 11
4502[2] KISMETIM [56] 3-8-7 K Fallon (25) *beh, hdwy 4 fs out, hrd rdn o'r one out, btn ins last*....(10 to 1 fav op 14 to 1) 12
4374[5] BEAUMONT (Ire) [59] 3-8-10 Pat Eddery (3) *hdwy frm rear 3 fs out, short of room o'r 2 out, sn no imprsn*. ....(20 to 1 op 14 to 1) 13
3943[4] ROMALITO [61] 3-8-12 R Cochrane (13) *mid-div, drvn o'r 2 fs out, no response*..............................(20 to 1) 14
1305 HIGHLAND FLAME [40] 4-7-12[1]2 (7*) S Mulvey (24) *mid-div, effrt 3 fs out, sn btn*................................(50 to 1) 15
3479[8] HALLOW FAIR [39] 8-7-11[4] T Williams (12) *mid-div, effrt o'r 3 fs out, btn over one out*.......... (33 to 1 op 25 to 1) 16
4432 ROUSITTO [49] 5-8-7 W Ryan (8) *stumbled strt, beh, hdwy o'r 2 fs out, nvr on terms*..........................(20 to 1) 17
3056 JULFAAR (USA) [46] 6-8-4 J McLaughlin (33) *chsd ldrs till wknd o'r 2 fs out*..................(33 to 1 op 25 to 1) 18
4432 RUSTY REEL [59] (v) 3-8-7 (3*) B Doyle (21) *trkd ldrs, ev ch appr 3 fs out, sn wknd*........................(33 to 1) 19
BOTTLES (USA) [70] 6-10-0 J Quinn (2) *al beh*.... (33 to 1) 20
4354 ROXY RIVER [46] 4-8-4 Paul Eddery (10) *chsd ldrs till wknd 3 fs out*.......................................(50 to 1) 21
VAIGLY BLAZED [37] 9-7-9[2] Dale Gibson (19) *al beh*. ....(66 to 1) 22
4374[7] EIRE LEATH-SCEAL [43] 6-8-1 J Lowe (7) *chsd ldrs, cld 3 fs out, sn btn*......................(25 to 1 op 20 to 1) 23
4502[5] SOOJAMA (Ire) [42] (bl) 3-7-7 N Adams (15) *hdwy to track ldrs 3 fs out, sn btn*..............(33 to 1 tchd 50 to 1) 24
3961 BROUGHTONS FORMULA [54] 3-8-5 A Mackay (5) *al beh*. ....(20 to 1) 25
4028[7] SCENIC DANCER [46] 5-7-13 (5*) J Tate (32) *chsd ldrs till wknd o'r 3 fs out*................................ (16 to 1) 26
4341[5] WHO'S THE BEST (Ire) [50] 3-7-10 (5*) D Wright (14) *al beh*. ....(25 to 1 op 20 to 1) 27
4391 BARBARY REEF (Ire) [38] 5-7-10[8] (5*) P McCabe (1) *nvr dngrs*.. (100 to 1) 28
4524[8] TIGHT FIST (Ire) [67] 3-9-4 B Rouse (17) *chsd ldrs till wknd wl o'r 2 fs out*......................(33 to 1 tchd 40 to 1) 29
2828[5] DESPERATE MAN [48] 4-8-6[10] S D Williams (18) *al beh*. ....(100 to 1) 30
3320[5] MELANCOLIA [35] 7-7-0 (7*) M Baird (9) *al beh*....(50 to 1) 31
3308[7] ENCHANTED FLYER [35] 6-7-5[5] (7*) C Hawksley (34) *strted slwly, al beh*... (100 to 1) 32
4319[8] QUESSONG [42] 3-7-7 N Carlisle (20) *cl up till wknd o'r 3 fs out*.. (100 to 1) 33
4233a FINAL ACTION [42] 3-7-3[3] (7*) N Varley (23) *led, sn clr, hdd o'r 3 fs out, wknd quickly*............................(66 to 1) 34
3108[5] SHARRO [58] 3-8-9 G Bardwell (22) *cl up till wknd o'r 3 fs out*...(50 to 1) 35
Dist: 1½l, hd, hd, ¾l, nk, 3½l, hd, ½l, hd, nk. 2m 35.50s. a 5.90s (35 Ran).
SR: 28/47/47/26/51/33/41/17/21/ (Anthony Rizzo), M Bell

4632 Potter Nursery Class D (2-y-o) £3,882 5f............................ (3:45)

4613[2] HIGH HOLME [70] 8-6 M Roberts (1) *wth ldr, led hfwy, ran on wl*.....................................(9 to 2 op 5 to 1) 1
4299 FEATHERSTONE LANE [65] 8-1 D Harrison (10) *sn rdn alng in rear, hdwy appr 2 fs out, ev ch one out, no extr*. ....(8 to 1 op 7 to 1 tchd 9 to 1) 2
4114[7] BRAVE EDGE [82] 9-4 Pat Eddery (9) *slwly into strd, rdn alng hfwy, hmpd 2 fs out, kpt on wl und pres ins last*. ....(9 to 2 op 4 to 1 tchd 5 to 1) 3
4193* ALLWIGHT THEN (Ire) [85] 9-7 Paul Eddery (5) *led to hfwy, ev ch one furlong out, one pace*...(5 to 1 tchd 11 to 2) 4
4265 BILLY CRUNCHEON [67] 8-3 W Woods (4) *chsd ldrs, no hdwy frm o'r one furlong out*....(16 to 1 tchd 20 to 1) 5
4456[2] RECAPTURED DAYS (Ire) [84] 9-6 W R Swinburn (2) *dwlt, sn cl up, rdn whn hmpd o'r one furlong out, no extr*. ....(15 to 8 fav op 2 to 1 tchd 7 to 4) 6
4114[6] RAISA POINT [66] 8-2 T Sprake (8) *outpcd frm hfwy*. ....(20 to 1 tchd 33 to 1) 7
4516[9] LEGATEE [80] 9-2 W Carson (6) *nvr on terms*. ....(25 to 1 op 20 to 1 tchd 33 to 1) 8
4263 HOLLINGTON SONG [57] 7-7 N Adams (7) *trkd ldrs till wknd 2 fs out*. ....(33 to 1 op 25 to 1 tchd 50 to 1 and 66 to 1) 9
Dist: 1l, 1½l, ½l, sht-hd, ½l, 2l, 1½l, 7l. 1m 1.26s. a 2.66s (9 Ran).
SR: 49/40/51/52/33/48/22/30/-/ (Jack Ashurst), D T Thom

4633 Avenue Apprentice Handicap Class E (0-70 3-y-o) £4,500 1m 1f........(4:15)

4536[3] MASTER BEVELED [46] 7-11 S Sanders (18) *in tch, cld on ldrs 3 fs out, led appr last, ran on wl*. (9 to 1 op 8 to 1) 1
4391 SILVER GROOM (Ire) [60] 8-8 (3*) D Gibbs (14) *chsd ldrs, led o'r 2 fs out till hdd appr last, ran on*. ....(14 to 1 op 12 to 1) 2+
4087[2] MO-ADDAB (Ire) [70] 9-0 (7*) C Dykes (21) *rcd centre, mid-div, hdwy o'r 3 fs out, ev ch ins last, no extr*. .... (11 to 1 op 10 to 1 tchd 12 to 1) 2+
2970 MOVE SMARTLY (Ire) [51] 8-2[1] T G McLaughlin (15) *al prmnt, ev ch o'r one furlong out, one pace und pres*. ....(16 to 1) 4
4536* GLOWING JADE [61] 8-12 (5ex) R Painter (3) *hld up in mid-div, styd on frm o'r 2 fs out*. ....(9 to 2 fav op 11 to 2 tchd 6 to 1) 5
3818* EXHIBIT AIR (Ire) [69] (v) 9-1 (5*) A Whelan (13) *al prmnt, ev ch 3 fs out, not much room and one pace frm o'r one out*..(9 to 1) 6
4596[2] BLOWEDIFIKNOW [53] (bl) 8-4 B Russell (10) *beh, styd on und str pres frm o'r one out*. ....(13 to 2 op 6 to 1 tchd 7 to 1) 7
4536[4] DUKE OF DREAMS [58] 8-6 (3*) S Copp (2) *trkd ldrs, led o'r 3 fs out till hdd over 2 out, wknd und pres*. ....(12 to 1 op 10 to 1) 8
4045[8] COMTEC'S LEGEND [46] 7-11 M Humphries (17) *chsd ldrs, no hdwy 5 2 fs*.................... (16 to 1 op 14 to 1) 9
4334[6] CANDARELA [42] 7-2 (5*) Sally Radford-Howes (20) *in tch till lost pl hfwy, some modest late prog*. ....(50 to 1 tchd 100 to 1) 10
4274 HOTSOCKS [55] 8-3 (3*) P Bowe (11) *nvr on terms*. ....(33 to 1 op 25 to 1) 11
1311 ARRASAS LADY [45] 7-5 (5*) Wendy Jones (4) *chsd ldrs o'r 5 fs*..........................(50 to 1 tchd 66 to 1) 12
4479[3] FRANCIA [50] 8-1 P McCabe (6) *hld up in tch, hdwy to ld o'r 3 fs out, hdd over 2 out, wknd quickly*. ....(8 to 1 op 9 to 1) 13
4499[7] MELISIO [50] 8-1 N Varley (16) *al beh*. ....(20 to 1 op 50 to 1 tchd 66 to 1) 14
4544[9] DARING KING [44] 7-9 C Hawksley (8) *al beh*. ....(20 to 1 op 16 to 1 tchd 25 to 1) 15
4536 AHJAY [50] 8-1 J D Smith (9) *cl up till wknd o'r 3 fs out*. ....(14 to 1 op 10 to 1) 16
4536 NYMPH ERRANT [50] 8-1 S Mulvey (19) *wth ldrs till wknd 4 fs out*............................(33 to 1 tchd 50 to 1) 17
4336[9] PONDICHERRY (USA) [56] 8-0 (7*) A Liggins (22) *rcd alone far side, led till hdd o'r 3 fs out, wknd quickly*. ....(50 to 1 op 40 to 1 tchd 66 to 1) 18
3530[5] CHILTERN HUNDREDS (USA) [42] 7-2 (5*) M Baird (5) *prmnt, ev ch 3 fs out, sn btn*. (50 to 1 op 25 to 1 tchd 66 to 1) 19
3887 MEDLAND (Ire) [43] 7-5[2] (5*) Sharon Millard (7) *prmnt till wknd hfwy*...............................(20 to 1 op 16 to 1) 20
2182[4] MAJOR TRIUMPH (Ire) [54] 8-5[1] Michael Denaro (12) *al beh, tld off*.............(20 to 1 op 16 to 1 tchd 25 to 1) 21
Dist: ½l, dd-ht, ½l, 1½l, 2l, ¾l, sht-hd, 4l, 2l, 2l. 1m 54.63s. a 4.93s (21 Ran).
SR: 16/28/38/17/22/24/6/10/-/ (Mrs E J Williams), P D Evans

DOWN ROYAL (IRE) (good)
Saturday October 30th

4634 Her Majesty's Plate (3-y-o and up) £1,725 1½m 68yds............ (3:45)

4556* VANISHING PRAIRIE (USA) (bl) 3-8-13 D Hogan (1) ....(11 to 8 on) 1
4461 SAIBOT (USA) (bl) 4-9-7 (4*) W J Smith (4)......... (5 to 2) 2
3368[3] JAZZY REFRAIN (Ire) 3-8-13[7] (2*) P Carberry (2).....(6 to 1) 3
4461 MAYFIELD PRINCE (Ire) 4-9-9 W J O'Connor (3).. (12 to 1) 4
JANESWOOD (Ire) 5-8-7 (8*) R T Fitzpatrick (5)....(40 to 1) 5
Dist: 3l, 5l, 7l, 10l. (Time not taken) (5 Ran).
(Mrs M J Grassick), M J Grassick

4635 Ballyclare Handicap (0-75 3-y-o and up) £1,207 5f...................(4:15)

4389^{2} HAWAIAN TASCA (Ire) [-] 4-7-0 (8*) B J Halligan (5) (4 to 1) 1
4385 MAGIC DON (Ire) [-] (bl) 4-9-6 (8*) R T Fitzpatrick (4) (10 to 1) 2
4389^{7} DUNSFORD [-] 7-7-7 L O'Shea (2)...............(10 to 1) 3
4385^{4} AURLIANO (Ire) [-] 3-8-13 (2*) P Carberry (7)......(11 to 2) 4
4552^{5} TODDY MARK (Ire) [-] 4-8-11 D Manning (1)......(16 to 1) 5
4385^{6} LADY PRESIDENT (Ire) [-] (bl) 4-9-10 W J O'Connor (6) ....(13 to 8 fav) 6
3417^{7} LOOK NONCHALANT (Ire) [-] 4-9-2 D Hogan (3)....(8 to 1) 7
4389^{5} FIVE LITTLE GIRLS (Ire) [-] 3-8-10 D V Smith (9)....(6 to 1) 8
4161 NORDIC RACE [-] 6-8-8 (4*) W J Smith (8)........(20 to 1) 9
Dist: 1l, ½l, ½l, 1½l. (Time not taken) (9 Ran).
(B J Caffrey), Edward P Mitchell

KEENELAND (USA) (yielding)
Saturday October 30th

4636 Queen Elizabeth II Challenge Cup (Grade 1) (3-y-o) £82,119 1m 1f..(8:40)

TRIBULATION (USA) 8-9 J-L Smayn,..........(214 to 10) 1
1200^{6} MIAMI SANDS (Ire) 8-9 L Pincay Jr,...............(77 to 10) 2
POSSIBLY PERFECT (USA) 8-9 P Day,.....(12 to 5 jt-fav) 3
4309^{5} MARILLETTE (USA) 8-9 C McCarron,..........(136 to 10) 4
665^{7} WEEKEND MADNESS (Ire) 8-9 C Woods,.......(94 to 10) 5
AMAL HAYATI (USA) 8-9 S Sellers,............(103 to 10) 6
4309^{4} AJFAN (USA) 8-9 W Martinez,.................(172 to 10) 7
3501^{5} KIROV PREMIERE 8-9 J D Bailey,..........(12 to 5 jt-fav) 8
4403^{3} NICER (Ire) 8-9 D Holland,...........................(6 to 1) 9
Dist: 2l, ½l, 3l, 2l, ½l, nk, 2l, 6l. 1m 53.60s. (9 Ran).
(G Seelbinder), J J Toner

NAAS (IRE) (good)
Saturday October 30th

4637 Rathbride E.B.F. Maiden (2-y-o) £3,795 6f......................(1:25)

4460^{9} QUINTILIANI (Ire) 9-0 J F Egan (15)...............(8 to 1) 1
4290^{4} RINJANI 9-0 R Hughes (12).................(2 to 1 jt-fav) 2
4462 FIONN DE COOL (Ire) (bl) 9-0 K J Manning (6).....(10 to 1) 3
4380 OPULENT 9-0 P V Gilson (4).......................(10 to 1) 4
4535^{7} LESLEY'S ANGEL (Ire) 9-0 P Lowry (11)...........(20 to 1) 5
4460^{3} IRISH ARMADA (USA) 8-8 (6*) D J O'Donohoe (3) (2 to 1 jt-fav) 6
4581^{9} BLAKE'S HOTEL 8-10 (4*) J J Behan (8)..........(12 to 1) 7
RULING LIGHT (Ire) 9-0 B Coogan (14)..............(8 to 1) 8
4460 HOW'S IT GOIN (Ire) 8-4 (10*) S P Cooke (13).....(16 to 1) 9
4323^{8} DAMERS DUKE (Ire) 9-0 W J Supple (10).........(12 to 1) 10
3911 IMPOSING TIME 9-0 S Craine (2)...................(16 to 1) 11
4582 PHARDY (Ire) 8-4 (10*) P P O'Grady (5)...........(20 to 1) 12
4582 ROYAL CRIMSON 9-0 C Roche (9)...................(14 to 1) 13
4405 CONTRASTING (Ire) 9-0 Joanna Morgan (16).....(25 to 1) 14
STRONG BOOST (USA) 9-0 P Shanahan (1)..........(11 to 2) 15
4146 THREE LEAVES (Ire) 9-0 N G McCullagh (7).......(25 to 1) 16
Dist: 5½l, 1l, sht-hd, ¾l. 1m 12.50s. a 3.00s (16 Ran).
SR: 40/18/14/13/10/-/ (M Borza), Peadar Matthews

4638 Maudlins Nursery (2-y-o) £2,760 5f ....(1:55)

4551^{4} JOIN FORCES (Ire) [-] 8-3 J F Egan (12)..........(8 to 1) 1
4285^{3} KING SANCHO (Ire) [-] 9-0 C Roche (5)...........(13 to 2) 2
4462^{3} MULMUS (Ire) [-] 8-13 R Hughes (1)..........(11 to 10 fav) 3
4462 PEACE TOKEN (Ire) [-] 8-13 (8*) G Coogan (10).....(8 to 1) 4
3683 PASTELLE [-] 7-1^{4} (10*) L Cummins (11)..........(14 to 1) 5
4462^{7} SMART ROSIE (Ire) [-] 7-9^{2} (6*) R V Skelly (3)........(7 to 1) 6
4405 BERGERACONHOLIDAY (Ire) [-] 7-7 A J Nolan (4) (25 to 1) 7
4285^{9} EASTROP DANCER (Ire) [-] 7-5 (2*) D G O'Shea (8) (20 to 1) 8
4183 LAXEY LEAP (Ire) [-] 7-1 (6*) P P Murphy (9).......(14 to 1) 9
3683^{9} THE MARDYKE (Ire) [-] (bl) 7-7^{2} (4*) J J Behan (7)...(20 to 1) 10
4244 SUN MARK (Ire) [-] (bl) 7-7 (8*) G M Moylan (2)....(16 to 1) 11
4535^{5} AINE'S PET (Ire) [-] (bl) 8-4 N G McCullagh (6).......(8 to 1) 12
Dist: 3½l, 1l, 1½l, ¾l. 1m 0.30s. a 2.30s (12 Ran).
SR: 43/40/35/37/6/-/ (Mrs M A O'Toole), M A O'Toole

4639 Sherlockstown Handicap (0-75 3-y-o and up) £5,520 1m 3f...........(3:25)

4555^{4} MY KERRY DANCER (USA) [-] 3-9-2 (6*) T P Treacy (16) ....(5 to 1 fav) 1
4555 SHARASTAMINA (USA) [-] 4-9-2 (4*) J J Behan (13) (12 to 1) 2
4409* WICKLOW WAY (Ire) [-] 3-8-12 (6*,9ex) B J Walsh (14) ....(8 to 1) 3
4555^{5} FONTANAYS (Ire) [-] 5-9-0 S Craine (15)............(8 to 1) 4
4288^{4} MORNING SARGE [-] 5-9-5 C Roche (18)...........(8 to 1) 5
4137^{5} DANCING VISION (Ire) [-] 3-8-12 P Shanahan (12) (14 to 1) 6
4409^{7} KAWA-KAWA [-] (bl) 6-7-5 (2*) D G O'Shea (2).....(33 to 1) 7
4119^{4} L-WAY FIRST (Ire) [-] 3-8-2 J F Egan (10).........(16 to 1) 8
4246 BOBADIL (Ire) [-] 3-8-1 (8*) P J Smullen (3).........(20 to 1) 9
4060* LOWLACK [-] (bl) 3-9-4 F Woods (9)...............(14 to 1) 10
4409 GRECIAN LADY (Ire) [-] (bl) 4-8-3 Joanna Morgan (6) ....(20 to 1) 11
4534^{2} DARCY'S THATCHER [-] 9-9-5 (6*) J R Barry (1)...(10 to 1) 12
4186^{8} KARABAKH (Ire) [-] 4-9-2 (4*) C Everard (4).......(12 to 1) 13
3854^{6} OPEN MARKET (USA) [-] (bl) 4-9-5 (6*) D J O'Donohoe (8) ....(8 to 1) 14
2143* KEPPOLS PRINCE [-] 6-8-8 A J Nolan (11).......(10 to 1) 15
4409^{2} MRS KEPPEL [-] 5-8-8 (4*) J A Heffernan (7)......(12 to 1) 16
4534 EMPEROR GLEN (Ire) [-] 5-9-4 R Hughes (5).......(8 to 1) 17
3720^{7} TOP DIVER (Ire) [-] (bl) 3-8-9 W J Supple (17).....(25 to 1) 18
Dist: 2l, sht-hd, 3l, 1l. 2m 25.20s. a 8.70s (18 Ran).
SR: 21/15/12/2/5/-/ (Hudson Valley Equine Inc), P Mullins

NEWCASTLE (soft)
Saturday October 30th

Going Correction: PLUS 0.35 sec. per fur. (races 1,2,3), PLUS 0.50 (4,5,6)

4640 'Moonglow' Handicap Class E (0-70 3-y-o and up) £3,235 7f.........(1:35)

4235^{9} CICERONE [46] 3-8-4 G Hind (1) *chsd ldr far side, effrt 2 fs out, rdn to ld ins last, ran on*..................(16 to 1) 1
4164^{4} ROAR ON TOUR [33] 4-7-8 J Fanning (4) *o'rall ldr far side, rdn 2 fs out, hdd and not quicken ins last.* ....(9 to 1 op 7 to 1) 2
4458^{3} MAM'ZELLE ANGOT [58] 3-9-2 J Fortune (5) *trkd ldrs far side, not clr run 2 fs out, swtchd rght appr fnl furlong, ran on und pres ins last*.............(8 to 1 op 6 to 1) 3
4348^{4} MUSTN'T GRUMBLE (Ire) [58] 3-9-2 J Carroll (13) *trkd ldrs stands side, hdwy and swtchd to far side 2 fs out, sn rdn, kpt on one pace appr last.* (6 to 1 fav tchd 7 to 1) 4
4394^{9} GENTLE HERO (USA) [46] 7-8-7 N Connorton (7) *chsd ldrs far side, rdn 2 fs out, sn one pace*............(20 to 1) 5
1865^{7} CLAUDIA MISS [55] 6-9-2 Dale Gibson (10) *in tch far side, hdwy o'r 2 fs out, sn rdn and no imprsn.* ....(25 to 1 op 20 to 1) 6
4164 PUBLIC WAY (Ire) [45] 3-7-10 (7*) C Teague (9) *prmnt far side, rdn 3 fs out, grad wknd*..................(20 to 1) 7
4518^{5} SPANISH LOVE [37] 7-7-11^{4} (5*) J Marshall (3) *rcd far side, styd on fnl 2 fs, nvr dngrs.* ....(9 to 1 op 8 to 1 tchd 10 to 1) 8
4123^{4} PETAL'S JARRED [35] 3-7-2 (5*) Darren Moffatt (6) *nvr rch ldrs*..(8 to 1 op 6 to 1) 9
4317* BECKYHANNAH [44] (bl) 3-7-9 (7*) M Humphries (16) *prmnt stands side, rdn 3 fs out, sn wknd.* (12 to 1 op 10 to 1) 10
2459 MISS HOSTESS [33] (bl) 6-7-8^{4} (3*) N Kennedy (15) *al rear.* ....(66 to 1 op 33 to 1) 11
4104^{6} COOL ENOUGH [36] 12-7-11 T Williams (2) *beh far side, hfwy, effrt and some hdwy o'r 2 fs out, sn wknd.* ....(12 to 1 op 10 to 1) 12
4488 TWILIGHT FALLS [42] 8-8-3 L Charnock (11) *in tch stands side, rdn hfwy, sn btn*.............(12 to 1 op 10 to 1) 13
1190 MARIETTE LARKIN [40] 4-8-1 M Wood (17) *in tch stands side to hfwy*.......................(40 to 1 op 33 to 1) 14
4468 PRIDE OF PENDLE [67] 4-9-7 (7*) H Bastiman (19) *cl up stands side, rdn wl o'r 2 fs out, sn wknd.* ....(12 to 1 tchd 14 to 1) 15
4458 WEE SARAH [53] 5-8-7 (7*) V Halliday (14) *al rear.* (12 to 1) 16
2269^{6} VALLEY OF TIME (Fr) [32] 5-7-3^{3} (7*) C Adamson (8) *chsd ldrs far side to hfwy, sn wknd*.....(40 to 1 op 33 to 1) 17
4391^{7} SALDA [57] 4-9-4 A Culhane (18) *led stands side, rdn 3 fs out and sn wknd*.................(14 to 1 op 12 to 1) 18
3712^{8} COASTAL EXPRESS [51] (bl) 4-8-12 M Birch (12) *cl up stands side, rdn o'r 2 fs out and wknd quickly.* ....(16 to 1 op 14 to 1) 19
Dist: 2l, 1l, 3l, 1l, 3½l, nk, ½l, 1½l, ¾l, 2l. 1m 30.20s. a 6.20s (19 Ran).
SR: 34/18/37/28/16/14/ (Miss S Moore), P Calver

4641 'Moon River' Maiden Stakes Class D (2-y-o) £3,289 7f................(2:05)

4543^{2} MOVING ARROW 9-0 N Connorton (5) *trkd ldr gng wl, shaken up to ld appr last, sn clr, easily.* ..(2 to 1 on op 5 to 4 on tchd 11 to 10 on and Evens) 1
4542^{8} LAUNCHSELECT 9-0 J Fanning (7) *led, rdn and edgd lft 2 fs out, hdd appr last, kpt on one pace.* ....(14 to 1 op 8 to 1) 2
4089^{3} SARIYAA 8-9 W Ryan (1) *cl up, pushed alng and outpcd o'r 2 fs out, kpt on one pace und pres ins last.* ....(9 to 4 op 6 to 4) 3
4489 KILERNAN 9-0 J Fortune (4) *sn beh, hdwy o'r 2 fs out, soon rdn and kpt on one pace*.................(25 to 1) 4
4503^{5} EL SALVADOR 9-0 J Carroll (2) *in tch, pushed alng 3 fs out, rdn and wknd 2 furlongs out.* (12 to 1 op 8 to 1) 5
ALNIK 8-9 S Perks (3) *in tch on outer, rdn wl o'r 2 fs out and sn wknd*.....................(14 to 1 op 8 to 1) 6
DISPOL DANCER 9-0 G Hind (6) *very slwly away, hdwy to join ldrs aftr 2 fs, rdn wl o'r two furlongs out and sn wknd*..(25 to 1) 7
Dist: 2½l, ½l, 4l, ½l, 2½l, 15l. 1m 32.17s. a 8.17s (7 Ran).
SR: 14/6/-/-/ (W G Barker), Miss S E Hall

4642 'Fly Me To The Moon' Nursery Class D (2-y-o) £3,201 6f................(2:35)

4602^{4} DANGEROUS SHADOW [74] 9-1 (5*) Darren Moffatt (5) *cl up, led o'r 2 fs out, rdn entering last, ran on gmely.* ....(11 to 8 fav tchd 6 to 4) 1

4230^{5} WIXI (Ire) [75] 9-7 Dale Gibson (7) *hld up, hdwy 2 and a half fs out, effrt to chal ins last and ev ch till no extr fnl 50 yards*..............................(8 to 1 op 7 to 1) 2
4516^{6} ORIENTAL AIR (Ire) [60] 8-6 G Hind (4) *led, rdn and hdd o'r 2 fs out, kpt on ins last*..........................(6 to 1) 3
4436^{8} BOLD ALEX [68] 9-0 N Connorton (1) *trkd ldrs, effrt and hdwy 3 fs out, rdn 2 furlongs out and sn one pace.* ....(5 to 1 op 4 to 1) 4
4427 DINOT (Ire) [56] 7-9 (7*) M Humphries (3) *chsd ldrs, rdn 3 fs out, wknd o'r 2 furlongs out*..................(16 to 1) 5
4416 MONKEY MUSIC [60] (v) 8-6 J Carroll (2) *rdn alng 3 fs out, sn wknd*..............................(6 to 1 op 5 to 1) 6
4526 BUSTLE'EM (Ire) [65] 8-8 (3*) S Maloney (6) *prmnt, rdn alng 3 fs out, sn wknd*..........................(10 to 1 op 9 to 1) 7

Dist: 2l, nk, 4l, 5l, 6l, ¾l. 1m 17.64s. a 5.64s (7 Ran).

SR: 35/28/12/4/ (Prime Maintenance), Mrs M Reveley

4643 'Moonman' Handicap Class D (0-80 3-y-o and up) £3,348 1¼m 32yds (3:05)

4604^{2} BILOELA [58] 3-8-7 W Ryan (5) *mid-div, hdwy o'r 4 fs out, quickened to ld one and a half out, rdn and styd on fnl furlong*..............................(7 to 2 op 4 to 1) 1
4533* SURREY DANCER [74] 5-9-7 (7*) S Copp (4) *hld up and beh, hdwy 3 fs out, swtchd rght one and a half out, styd on strly ins last.* ....(3 to 1 fav op 5 to 2 tchd 100 to 30) 2
4086^{5} CUTTHROAT KID (Ire) [48] (bl) 3-7-6 (5*) Darren Moffatt (9) *mid-div, jnd ldrs 6 fs out, effrt o'r 2 out, sn rdn and kpt on*..............................(20 to 1 op 16 to 1) 3
4187* ESSAYEFFSEE [55] 4-8-9 J Fanning (12) *in tch, hdwy to ld 2 fs out, sn rdn and hdd, wknd wl ins last.* ....(7 to 1 op 6 to 1) 4
4533 IMPERIAL BID (Fr) [62] 5-8-9 (7*) C Teague (3) *slwly into strd, sn in tch, effrt and rdn o'r 2 fs out, one pace.* ....(16 to 1 op 12 to 1) 5
4600* AEGAEN LADY [54] 4-8-8 (4ex) M Birch (7) *in tch, effrt and hdwy 2 fs out, rdn appr fnl furlong, sn wknd.* ....(5 to 1 op 6 to 1) 6
4374^{8} DOCTOR ROY [46] 5-8-0 L Charnock (1) *chsd ldrs, rdn 3 fs out, wknd o'r 2 out*..............................(20 to 1) 7
4468^{7} SELF EXPRESSION [62] 5-8-9 (7*) D Thomas (2) *hld up, effrt and some hdwy 3 fs out, no imprsn.* ....(6 to 1 op 7 to 1) 8
4364 PERSIAN FOUNTAIN (Ire) [50] (bl) 3-7-13 S Wood (6) *al rear.* ....(33 to 1) 9
2678^{4} RAPID MOVER [43] (bl) 6-7-11^{4} T Williams (8) *led and sn clr, rdn, hdd and wknd quickly 2 fs out.* ....(33 to 1 op 25 to 1) 10
INSPIRED GUESS (USA) [55] 6-8-9 J Fortune (11) *chsd ldr till rdn 3 fs out, sn wknd*.........(33 to 1 tchd 50 to 1) 11
FAMILY LINE [68] 5-9-8 J Carroll (10) *chsd ldr, rdn o'r 3 fs out, sn wknd*..............................(25 to 1) 12

Dist: 1l, ¾l, 2l, 2½l, 2l, 3½l, 1l, 5l, 9l, 5l. 2m 17.11s. a 10.61s (12 Ran).

SR: 38/57/24/32/34/22/7/21/-/ (R Brewis), J G FitzGerald

4644 'Moonlight Becomes You' Claiming Stakes Class E (2-y-o) £3,054 1m 1f 9yds. (3:35)

4439^{3} RESPONSE 8-13 G Hind (1) *hld up and beh, hdwy on outer o'r 2 fs out, sn rdn, styd on strly ins last to ld post.* ....(9 to 1 op 6 to 1) 1
4531^{3} MEMORABLE 9-3 W Ryan (10) *chsd ldrs, hdwy to ld one and a half fs out, sn rdn, ct on line.* ....(7 to 4 fav op 3 to 1 tchd 100 to 30) 2
4427^{2} MISS FREEBIE (Ire) 7-9 (3*) N Kennedy (13) *hld up and beh, hdwy 3 fs out, rdn and ev ch appr fnl furlong, kpt on.* ....(6 to 1 op 9 to 2 tchd 13 to 2) 3
4342^{9} DRAGON MAN 7-10 (7*) C Adamson (16) *al prmnt, effrt and ev ch 2 fs out, sn rdn, wknd entering last.* ....(10 to 1 op 8 to 1) 4
4602^{8} NEVER SO TRUE 7-12 T Williams (14) *mid-div, gd hdwy on outer o'r 2 fs out, sn rdn and one pace appr last.* ....(11 to 1 op 10 to 1 tchd 12 to 1) 5
4550 BARNPARK 8-12 (3*) S Maloney (4) *beh, hdwy o'r 2 fs out, kpt on und pres*..................(20 to 1 tchd 25 to 1) 6
4531^{5} GLENVALLY 8-4 J Fortune (9) *chsd ldrs, rdn 2 and a half fs out, sn one pace.* ....(9 to 2 op 5 to 1 tchd 6 to 1 and 7 to 1) 7
4528^{9} LAUREL ROMEO (Ire) (bl) 8-7 J Carroll (5) *cl up, effrt and ev ch 2 fs out, sn rdn and wknd.* ....(11 to 1 op 10 to 1 tchd 12 to 1) 8
4527 CHELSEA LADY (Ire) 7-12 S Wood (6) *nvr rchd ldrs.* ....(50 to 1 op 20 to 1) 9
4528 LEGAL TRAIN 8-3 A Culhane (15) *led, rdn and hdd appr fnl 2 fs, sn wknd*..................(14 to 1 op 10 to 1) 10
4342 BIRCHWOOD STAR 7-8^{1} (7*) M Humphries (12) *nvr dngrs.* ....(25 to 1 op 20 to 1) 11
4489^{7} RAINBOWS RHAPSODY 8-10 L Charnock (2) *in tch, effrt and hdwy on inner 3 fs out, rdn 2 out and sn btn, eased*..............(9 to 1 op 5 to 1 tchd 10 to 1) 12
4342 LADY GWEN (Ire) (bl) 7-12 Dale Gibson (11) *in tch till rdn o'r 2 fs out, grad wknd*..............(14 to 1 op 10 to 1) 13
4342 LITTLE SENOR (Ire) 7-12 (5*) J Marshall (8) *nvr a factor.* ....(20 to 1 op 16 to 1) 14
4427^{9} ASTROLOGY 8-4 Kim Tinkler (3) *al rear.* ....(50 to 1 op 25 to 1) 15
4577 SEMAH'S DREAM 8-4 J O'Reilly (7) *slwly into strd, gd hdwy on outer to join ldrs 5 fs out, rdn and wknd quickly 3 out*..................(50 to 1 op 25 to 1) 16

Dist: Sht-hd, 1½l, 3l, 2l, 1½l, 1½l, 2l, 2½l, ½l, 3½l. 2m 3.29s. a 11.29s (16 Ran).

(W B Leach), Dr J D Scargill

4645 'Blue Moon' Maiden Stakes Class D (3-y-o) £3,201 1m. (4:05)

4565^{2} FLOWING OCEAN 9-0 J Carroll (8) *beh, rdn alng hfwy, hdwy und pres o'r 2 fs out, styd on ins last to ld nr finish*..............................(6 to 4 fav) 1
4544^{3} QUEENS CONSUL (Ire) 8-9 S Wood (2) *cl up, led hfwy and quickened clr, wknd ins last, ct nr finish.* ....(12 to 1 tchd 14 to 1) 2
4565^{4} TRIBECA 8-9 W Ryan (4) *in tch, effrt 3 fs out, rdn and one pace o'r one out*..................(7 to 2 tchd 4 to 1) 3
4565^{3} FORESHORE (Ire) 8-9 S Whitworth (5) *chsd ldrs, effrt and hdwy o'r 2 fs out, sn rdn and one pace.* ....(4 to 1 op 3 to 1) 4
CRAMONA (Ire) 8-9 J Fortune (6) *hld up, hdwy hfwy, rdn 3 fs out, sn wknd*..........................(50 to 1 op 33 to 1) 5
4544 ONE FOR TONDY 8-9 L Charnock (9) *al beh.* ....(66 to 1 op 33 to 1) 6
HEJRAAN (USA) 8-9 M Birch (1) *cl up, rdn 3 fs out and sn btn, virtually pld up fnl furlong*.....(5 to 1 op 9 to 2) 7
2869 CLAR DUBH (Ire) 8-9 M Wood (3) *prmnt to hfwy, sn lost pl and beh*..............................(66 to 1 op 33 to 1) 8
4700a ROMEO OSCAR 9-0 Dale Gibson (7) *led to hfwy, sn wknd and beh*..............................(33 to 1 op 20 to 1) 9

Dist: ½l, 5l, 3l, 8l, 25l, 5l, hd, 10l. 1m 47.61s. a 8.61s (9 Ran).

SR: 31/24/9/-/-/-/ (Herbert Allen), J H M Gosden

NEWMARKET (good)
Saturday October 30th
Going Correction: PLUS 0.10 sec. per fur.

4646 Suffolk Selling Nursery Class E (2-y-o) £3,548 1m. (1:10)

4418^{8} ONCE MORE FOR LUCK (Ire) [65] 9-1 K Fallon (18) *hld up, str run 2 fs out, led one out, clr whn wndrd lft last 100 yards*..............(9 to 1 op 7 to 1 tchd 10 to 1) 1
4444^{6} SHERIFF [71] 9-4 (3*) B Doyle (24) *cld on ldrs hfwy, led 2 fs out to one out, ran on same pace*.... (8 to 1 op 6 to 1) 2
4531 CHANTRY BEATH [56] 8-6 G Duffield (21) *sn cl up, led 3 fs out to 2 out, no extr fnl furlong.* (12 to 1 tchd 14 to 1) 3
4531^{8} KOONOONA LADY [50] 7-9 (5*) D Wright (20) *trkd ldrs, rdn and styd on one pace last 2 fs*.... (14 to 1 op 20 to 1) 4
4492^{8} RIVER JUNCTION (Ire) [55] 8-0 (5*) D McCabe (14) *wl plcd, rdn and not quicken 3 fs out, styd on frm 2 out.* ....(14 to 1 op 16 to 1) 5
4418 MR MORIARTY (Ire) [47] 7-11 N Carlisle (23) *made most 5 fs, outpcd 2 out*..................(16 to 1 op 14 to 1) 6
4009^{7} KNIGHTRIDER [56] 8-6 T Quinn (11) *dsptd ld for o'r 5 fs, btn over one out*..............(14 to 1 tchd 16 to 1) 7
4122^{6} SHARONE [50] 8-0 G Bardwell (10) *hld up mid-div, rdn and no prog ins last 2 fs*..................(16 to 1) 8
4128^{6} FOREVER BLUSHING [51] 7-10 (5*) P McCabe (6) *nvr nrr.* ....(14 to 1) 9
4541 GLORIETTE [60] 8-10 R Cochrane (22) *pressed ldrs for o'r 5 fs, fdd*..................(10 to 1 op 12 to 1) 10
4528^{7} CRUISING CHICK [54] 7-11 (7*) D Gibbs (13) *wl plcd 5 fs.* ....(20 to 1) 11
4418 CLASSICAL (Ire) [60] 8-10 B Rouse (12) *handily plcd till rdn and btn o'r 2 fs out*..........(20 to 1 tchd 25 to 1) 12
3871^{8} SOUTHDOWN GIRL [43] 7-7^{5} (5*) A Garth (7) *rapid hdwy frm rear and swtchd rght hfwy, effrt shrtlvd.* (33 to 1) 13
4365 BURES (Ire) [70] 8-13 (7*) S Mulvey (5) *effrt und pres o'r 2 fs out, no imprsn*..................(9 to 1 op 8 to 1) 14
4082^{5} STORM HEIGHTS [49] 7-13 J Lowe (2) *cld on frnt rnk hfwy, no prog last 2 fs*..................(16 to 1) 15
4528 ARIAN SPIRIT (Ire) [47] 7-11^{2} A Mackay (16) *slwly into strd, nvr rch ldrs*..................(33 to 1 op 20 to 1) 16
4492 MY SONG OF SONGS [45] 7-9^{2} J Quinn (4) *speed for o'r 4 fs*..................(20 to 1 op 40 to 1) 17
3876 ZOES PET [60] 8-10 J Williams (3) *strted slwly, al rear.* ....(25 to 1) 18
4318^{6} BROUGHTONS PARTNER [45] 7-9 N Adams (1) *improved hfwy, lost pl und pres last 2 fs.* ....(14 to 1 op 12 to 1 tchd 16 to 1) 19
4351^{6} RED TAR [60] 8-10 A Munro (17) *sn wth ldrs, wknd 3 fs out.* ....(16 to 1 op 14 to 1 tchd 20 to 1) 20
4214^{3} DEER IN THE GLEN [65] 9-1 J Weaver (9) *chsd ldrs for o'r 4 fs*..................(14 to 1 tchd 16 to 1) 21
4009* HERR TRIGGER [53] (bl) 7-13^{1} (5*) K Rutter (15) *squeezed for room early, rdn alng in mid-div hfwy, tld off last 3 fs.* ....(5 to 1 fav op 4 to 1) 22

Dist: 4l, 3½l, 1½l, 5l, ½l, sht-hd, ¾l, ¾l, nk, 1l. 1m 41.83s. a 4.63s (22 Ran).

SR: 44/38/12/1/-/-/ (C C Buckley), Mrs M Reveley

4647 Sporting Life Zetland Stakes Class A (Listed Race) (2-y-o) £8,140 1¼m ....(1:40)

4192* DOUBLE TRIGGER (Ire) 8-9 J Weaver (5) *hld up, hdwy o'r 2 fs out, rdn to ld last 150 yards, styd on wl.* ....(3 to 1 op 9 to 4 tchd 100 to 30) 1
4529* BARBAROJA 9-0 W R Swinburn (4) *wl in tch, led 2 fs out, hdd and not quicken last 150 yards.* ....(5 to 2 fav op 9 to 4 tchd 11 to 4) 2
4539[2] BRENTWOOD (Ire) 8-4 R Hills (2) *cld on ldrs 4 fs out, ev ch 2 out, styd on one pace fnl furlong.* ....(8 to 1 op 7 to 1 tchd 9 to 1) 3
4252 MR ARTISTIC (USA) 8-9 M Roberts (3) *steadied strt, hld up, prog frm rear o'r 3 fs out, rdn and no extr appr last.* ....(33 to 1 op 25 to 1) 4
4529[2] THE FLYING PHANTOM 8-9 R Cochrane (9) *led to 2 fs out, wekened fnl furlong...* (15 to 2 op 5 to 1 tchd 8 to 1) 5
4106[3] PHYLIAN 8-4 K Fallon (7) *settled rear, rdn alng hfwy, effrt und pres 2 fs out, no imprsn.* ....(25 to 1 op 14 to 1 tchd 33 to 1) 6
4316* MUWAFIK 8-9 W Carson (10) *in tch till rdn and wknd o'r one furlong out..*.................. (4 to 1 op 6 to 1) 7
3704* PAMPERED GUEST (Ire) 8-9 T Quinn (1) *sn tracking ldr, ev ch 3 fs out till wknd o'r 2 out.* ....(8 to 1 op 6 to 1 tchd 9 to 1) 8
SAILS LEGEND 8-9 A Munro (8) *rdn alng in mid-div 5 fs out, wknd 3 out..*..................(66 to 1 op 50 to 1) 9
4419[9] ACERBUS DULCIS 8-9 M Hills (6) *pressed ldrs till lost pl quickly o'r 3 fs out, tld off.* ....(66 to 1 op 50 to 1 tchd 100 to 1) 10

Dist: 1½l, 1½l, 2½l, 3½l, 1½l, 3l, 5l, nk, 15l. 2m 7.84s. a 5.14s (10 Ran).
SR: 54/56/43/43/36/28/27/17/16/ (R W Huggins), M Johnston

4648 Ben Marshall Stakes Class A (Listed Race) (3-y-o and up) £9,768 1m (2:10)

4300[7] MELLOTTIE 8-9-1 J Lowe (8) *in tch, ran on o'r 2 fs out, shaken up to ld ins last, styd on*..................(3 to 1 jt-fav op 5 to 2) 1
4417[4] FRAAM 4-8-12 W R Swinburn (9) *pressed ldrs, rdn to ld o'r one furlong out, hdd and not quicken ins last.* ....(3 to 1 jt-fav op 5 to 2 tchd 7 to 2) 2
4474[5] GARDEN OF HEAVEN (USA) 4-8-12 T Quinn (5) *cld on ldrs frm rear o'r 2 fs out, rdn and one pace ins last.* ....(12 to 1 op 14 to 1 tchd 20 to 1) 3
4545[5] LOWER EGYPT (USA) 3-8-9 M Roberts (3) *hld up rear, improved o'r 2 fs out, not quicken appr last.* ....(11 to 2 op 9 to 2 tchd 6 to 1) 4
4545[4] SERIOUS 3-8-9 R Cochrane (2) *made most till o'r one furlong out, styd on same pace.* ....(11 to 1 op 10 to 1 tchd 12 to 1) 5
3477* LAP OF LUXURY 4-8-10 M Tebbutt (6) *hld up mid-div, effrt und pres o'r 2 fs out, no imprsn on ldrs.* ....(10 to 1 tchd 11 to 1) 6
4441[6] JETBEEAH (Ire) 3-8-4 G Duffield (1) *in tch, rdn hfwy, btn o'r 2 fs out..*..........(25 to 1 op 14 to 1 tchd 33 to 1) 7
4132[4] SPANISH STORM (Ire) (v) 4-8-12 W Woods (4) *chsd ldrs for o'r 5 fs*.................. (50 to 1 tchd 66 to 1) 8
4170[8] EUROLINK THUNDER 3-9-1 Pat Eddery (7) *wth ldr till rdn and wknd o'r 2 fs out..*..................(6 to 1 op 9 to 2) 9

Dist: 1½l, 1½l, 1½l, ½l, ½l, hd, 4l, 6l. 1m 40.10s. a 2.90s (9 Ran).
SR: 70/62/57/49/47/46/39/35/20/ (Mrs J G Fulton), Mrs M Reveley

4649 Royston Conditions Stakes Class C (2 & 3-y-o) £6,570 7f.............. (2:45)

4469[8] DUMAANI (USA) 2-8-5 W Carson (1) *handily plcd, shaken up to ld entering fnl furlong, pushed clr.* ....(3 to 1 op 9 to 4 tchd 100 to 30) 1
3987[2] MITHL AL HAWA 3-9-2 W R Swinburn (4) *dsptd ld till entering fnl furlong, kpt on same pace.* ....(2 to 1 fav op 7 to 4) 2
4545[3] LACERTA (Ire) 3-9-5 J Reid (2) *dsptd ld till entering fnl furlong, not quicken und pres.....* (3 to 1 tchd 7 to 2) 3
4277* SASEEDO (USA) 3-9-10 J Williams (6) *hld up, hdwy o'r 2 fs out, not quicken fnl furlong.* ....(5 to 1 op 9 to 2 tchd 11 to 2) 4
4565[9] WILLINGLY (Ire) 3-9-2 C Rutter (5) *outpcd, lost tch 3 fs out.* ....(50 to 1 op 25 to 1) 5
3428[2] NAKITA 2-8-0 N Carlisle (3) *lost several ls strt, sn tracking ldrs, rdn and lost pl o'r 2 fs out.* ....(16 to 1 op 12 to 1 tchd 20 to 1) 6

Dist: 2½l, nk, hd, 10l, 3½l. 1m 28.34s. a 4.84s (6 Ran).
SR: 29/32/34/38/-/-/ (Hamdan Al-Maktoum), J L Dunlop

4650 Ladbroke Autumn Handicap Class B (0-100 3-y-o and up) £23,677 1m (3:15)

4280[5] CAMBARA [90] 3-9-4 M Roberts (8) *hld up, made considerable grnd and swtchd lft o'r one furlong out, str brst to ld last strd..*..................(16 to 1 op 20 to 1) 1
4415 SHINTILLO (Ire) [91] 3-9-5 R Cochrane (5) *pressed ldrs stands side, rdn to ld 50 yards out, hdd last strd.* ....(4 to 1 fav op 7 to 1 tchd 8 to 1) 2
4468[2] SAND TABLE [79] 4-8-10 J Reid (26) *in tch far side, ran on o'r one furlong out, led ins last, hdd last 50 yards, rallied*..................(12 to 1 op 10 to 1) 3
4172 HOB GREEN [82] 4-8-13 K Fallon (22) *hld up far side, jnd ldrs o'r one furlong out, ev ch ins last, not quicken nr line..*..................(16 to 1 tchd 20 to 1) 4
4514 HIGHLAND MAGIC (Ire) [75] 5-8-6 F Norton (3) *hld up stands side, str run und pres appr fnl furlong, fnshd fst*..................(33 to 1 tchd 40 to 1) 5
4507[5] VELOCE (Ire) [73] 5-8-4 A Mackay (30) *hld up far side, ran on and swtchd lft o'r one furlong out, styd on ins last.* ....(33 to 1 op 25 to 1) 6
4470 ROSE ELEGANCE [65] 4-7-5 (5*) D Wright (29) *led far side for o'r 4 fs, kpt on clsg stages*..................(50 to 1) 7
4468* SAIFAN [83] (bl) 4-8-11 (3*) C Hodgson (19) *wl plcd centre, led o'r 2 fs out till hdd and wknd ins last.* ....(12 to 1 op 14 to 1) 8
4424 WAINWRIGHT (USA) [86] 4-9-3 W R Swinburn (28) *cl up far side, ev ch 2 fs out, btn fnl furlong*..................(33 to 1) 9
4415* NORFOLK HERO [83] (bl) 3-8-11 Pat Eddery (21) *hld up rear, improved o'r 3 fs out, one pace ins last 2.* ....(20 to 1 op 16 to 1) 10
3910* SET THE FASHION [72] (v) 4-8-3 D Harrison (13) *in tch, rdn and not quicken o'r 2 fs out, styd on nr finish.* ....(12 to 1 op 14 to 1) 11
4468[4] HI NOD [86] 3-9-0 Paul Eddery (9) *steadied strt, pld hrd to join ldrs aftr 2 fs, rdn and no extr frm two out.* ....(12 to 1 op 14 to 1 tchd 10 to 1) 12
4470[2] BUROOJ [85] 3-8-13 W Carson (23) *in tch far side 6 fs.* ....(12 to 1 op 10 to 1) 13
4605[8] SWEET MIGNONETTE [73] 5-8-4 J Lowe (11) *rcd stands side, nvr better than mid-div......* (33 to 1 op 25 to 1) 14
4468[3] TISSISAT (USA) [87] (v) 4-9-4 M Hills (25) *effrt far side o'r 2 fs out, not rch ldrs*..................(20 to 1) 15
4513[5] SHOW FAITH (Ire) [93] 3-9-7 L Piggott (12) *hld up rear, nvr on terms*..................(25 to 1) 16
4514* SAGEBRUSH ROLLER [83] 5-9-0 G Duffield (4) *trkd stands side ldrs 5 fs*..................(33 to 1 op 25 to 1) 17
4563[8] ISAIAH [82] 4-8-13 J Quinn (27) *mid-div, no prog last 2 fs.* ....(25 to 1) 18
4280[2] REALITIES (USA) [93] 3-9-7 R Hills (10) *hld up mid-div, rdn and no extr 2 fs out*.................. (20 to 1 op 16 to 1) 19
4514[3] ARANY [80] 6-8-4 (7*) S Mulvey (15) *handily plcd till wknd o'r 2 fs out*..................(33 to 1) 20
4470[3] ARAK (USA) [72] 5-8-3 J Weaver (6) *wl plcd stands side 5 fs.* ....(25 to 1 op 20 to 1) 21
3350 LAW COMMISSION [86] 3-9-0 W Newnes (16) *effrt 3 fs out, wknd 2 out*..................(33 to 1) 22
4490[6] BATTLE COLOURS (Ire) [71] 4-7-11 (5*) B Russell (17) *chsd frnt rnk 4 fs, sn wknd*..................(33 to 1 op 25 to 1) 23
4470* PRENONAMOSS [76] 5-8-7 J Williams (2) *al rear.* ....(20 to 1 tchd 25 to 1) 24
4300 HE'S A KING (USA) [85] 3-8-13 T Quinn (14) *wth ldr centre 5 fs*..................(33 to 1) 25
3350 COLOUR SERGEANT [86] 5-9-3 A Munro (7) *chsd stands side ldrs for o'r 6 fs*..................(20 to 1) 26
4470 DASWAKI (Can) [71] 5-7-13 (3*) M Fenton (18) *cl up centre, led o'r 3 fs out till over 2 out, wknd quickly.* ....(33 to 1 tchd 40 to 1) 27
4373[2] TAUFAN BLU (Ire) [96] (bl) 4-9-8 (5*) J Tate (24) *pressed far side grp for o'r 4 fs*..................(33 to 1) 28
4514[2] COMANCHE COMPANION [74] 3-7-11 (5*) A Garth (1) *in tch stands side to hfwy*.................. (20 to 1 op 25 to 1) 29
4275 ANONYMOUS [85] 3-8-10 (3*) B Doyle (20) *in tch to hfwy.* ....(66 to 1) 30

Dist: Sht-hd, hd, 1l, nk, ½l, hd, ½l, 1l, sht-hd, sht-hd. 1m 40.75s. a 3.55s (30 Ran).
SR: 63/63/53/53/45/41/32/48/48/ (Sheikh Mohammed), M R Stoute

4651 EBF Balaton Lodge Maiden Fillies' Stakes Class D (2-y-o) £5,205 7f (3:50)

4316[6] CRAZY FOR YOU (v) 8-11 T Quinn (5) *made all, drvn out fnl furlong, styd on strly.* ....(12 to 1 op 8 to 1 tchd 14 to 1) 1
INTERIM 8-11 Pat Eddery (12) *ldg grp, ev ch o'r one furlong out, one pace ins last.....* (7 to 2 jt-fav op 5 to 2) 2
4440 LADY VALENSINA (Ire) 8-11 J Williams (16) *chsd ldrs, kpt on one pace appr fnl furlong......* (33 to 1 op 20 to 1) 3
MUNNAYA (USA) 8-11 W R Swinburn (19) *hld up, hdwy frm rear o'r 2 fs out, styd on ins last.* ....(11 to 2 op 5 to 2 tchd 6 to 1) 4
LITTLE SISTER (Ire) 8-11 Paul Eddery (2) *mid-div, shaken up and ran on 2 fs out, no imprsn ins last.* ....(5 to 1 tchd 6 to 1) 5
ISCA 8-11 M Tebbutt (8) *chsd ldrs 5 fs, no extr.* ....(16 to 1 op 10 to 1 tchd 20 to 1) 6
ZORETTE (USA) 8-11 W Woods (17) *trkd frnt rnk, hmpd and lost pl o'r 2 fs out, rallied ins last.* - ....(20 to 1 tchd 25 to 1) 7
COSTLY 8-11 J Reid (14) *dwlt, rear till moderate late prog*..................(11 to 1 op 8 to 1 tchd 12 to 1) 8
RED OCTOBER 8-11 M Hills (10) *hdwy frm rear last 2 fs, not trble ldrs*.................. (7 to 2 jt-fav op 4 to 1) 9
4326[7] TRYPANIS (Ire) 8-11 G Duffield (15) *in tch on outsd till hmpd and crrd rght appr last 2 fs.* ....(20 to 1 op 14 to 1 tchd 25 to 1) 10

TELOPEA 8-11 W Newnes (18) *wl plcd till wndrd rght und pres o'r 2 fs out, sn btn*...........(33 to 1 op 25 to 1) 11
PHYLLODE 8-11 A McGlone (11) *speed 4 fs*. ....(20 to 1 op 14 to 1 tchd 25 to 1) 12
CHANSON D'AVRIL 8-11 A Clark (9) *dwlt, nvr on terms*. ....(50 to 1 op 33 to 1) 13
FOOLS TREASURE (Ire) 8-11 R Hills (4) *slwly into strd, al rear*..........(33 to 1 op 25 to 1 tchd 40 to 1) 14
DAILY SPORT CLUB 8-11 G Bardwell (7) *speed to hfwy*. ....(33 to 1 op 25 to 1 tchd 40 to 1) 15
CANDANE 8-4 (7*) S Mulvey (3) *sn rdn alng, outpcd hfwy*. ....(33 to 1 op 20 to 1) 16
MIRADOR 8-11 J Lowe (6) *outpcd*. ....(33 to 1 op 20 to 1 tchd 50 to 1) 17
COVEN STAR 8-8 (3*) C Hodgson (1) *chsd ldrs for o'r 4 fs, wknd quickly*.......(33 to 1 op 20 to 1 tchd 40 to 1) 18

Dist: 2½l, 2l, 1½l, sht-hd, 1l, sht-hd, 2½l, ½l, 1½l, 2l. 1m 29.31s. a 5.81s (18 Ran).
SR: 20/12/6/1/-/-/ (Club 7 Racing), M R Channon

4652 Burrough Green Handicap Class D (0-80 3-y-o and up) £4,532 7f.... (4:20)

4415 RISE UP SINGING [60] (bl) 5-8-8 Pat Eddery (24) *cl up centre, led hfwy, sn wl clr, eased nr finish*. ....(4 to 1 fav op 6 to 1 tchd 8 to 1) 1
4297 EURO FESTIVAL [74] 4-9-3 (5*) D McCabe (18) *in tch, outpcd hfwy, chsd wnr frm 2 fs out, no imprsn ins last*. ....(16 to 1 tchd 20 to 1) 2
4518⁶ GREAT HALL [69] 4-9-3 J Williams (17) *outpcd 3 fs out, hdwy o'r one out, fnshd wl*. ....(10 to 1 op 16 to 1 tchd 7 to 1) 3
4224⁴ LADY SABO [52] 4-7-9 (5*) A Garth (21) *wl plcd, rdn and outpcd o'r 2 fs out, kpt on und pres fnl furlong*. ....(33 to 1 op 25 to 1) 4
4518⁸ HELIOS [69] 5-9-3 W Carson (14) *ran on 2 fs out, hrd rdn and styd on ins last*..........(20 to 1 op 16 to 1) 5
4495⁸ LORD ALFIE [50] 4-7-12 N Carlisle (27) *chsd far side ldrs till outpcd o'r 2 fs out, ran on und pres ins last*. ....(33 to 1 op 25 to 1) 6
4518⁷ YOUNG DUKE (Ire) [64] 5-8-12 A Clark (16) *wl plcd till rdn and outpcd o'r 2 fs out, styd on fnl furlong*. ....(33 to 1 op 25 to 1) 7
4164 PERDITION (Ire) [60] 3-8-5 D Harrison (12) *mid-div, ran on one pace frm 2 fs out*..........(33 to 1 op 25 to 1) 8
4083* GUESSTIMATION (USA) [49] 4-7-11 G Bardwell (4) *improved frm rear hfwy, hrd rdn and ran on ins fnl furlong*. ....(16 to 1 op 20 to 1) 9
4470⁸ NITOUCHE [65] 3-8-10 K Fallon (19) *rdn and outpcd o'r 2 fs out, styd on ins last*. (20 to 1 op 16 to 1 tchd 25 to 1) 10
4490³ CHIEF OF STAFF [66] 4-9-0 M Wigham (2) *slwly into strd, beh till styd on strly ins last 2 fs*..........(20 to 1) 11
4468 LEGEND DULAC (Ire) [50] 4-7-12 J Quinn (11) *in tch till rdn and outpcd o'r 2 fs out*..........(33 to 1 op 25 to 1) 12
4525 TIMOTHY CASEY [63] 3-8-8 A Tucker (25) *wl plcd till outpcd o'r 2 fs out*..........(33 to 1) 13
4518² TEANARCO (Ire) [67] 5-8-10 (5*) S Drowne (23) *hld up, effrt hfwy, rdn and btn o'r one furlong out*. ....(7 to 1 op 12 to 1) 14
4415 AL MOULOUKI [80] 3-9-11 R Cochrane (7) *nvr rch chalg pos*..........(12 to 1 op 10 to 1 tchd 14 to 1) 15
3697⁴ CAPTAIN MARMALADE [51] 4-7-13 J Lowe (9) *rdn alng mid-div, not quicken 3 fs out, no further hdwy*. ....(14 to 1 op 16 to 1) 16
4470 BRAVEBOY [64] 5-8-9 (3*) B Doyle (5) *nvr rch ldrs*. ....(16 to 1 op 14 to 1) 17
SALISONG [65] 4-8-10 (3*) C Hodgson (22) *in tch 4 fs*. ....(33 to 1 op 25 to 1) 18
4495* WATERLORD (Ire) [59] 3-8-4 Paul Eddery (28) *wl plcd till rdn and outpcd o'r 2 fs out*..........(20 to 1 op 16 to 1) 19
3839⁶ POCKET PIECE (USA) [74] 3-9-5 M Roberts (13) *hld up mid-div, effrt hfwy, wknd and not much room ins last 2 fs*. ....(11 to 1 op 12 to 1) 20
4490 PETRACO (Ire) [71] 5-9-5 S D Williams (20) *led to hfwy, btn o'r 2 fs out*..........(33 to 1) 21
3839* BELFRY GREEN (Ire) [80] 3-9-11 R Hills (6) *chsd ldrs for o'r 5 fs*..........(14 to 1 op 12 to 1) 22
4470 ROCALITY [61] 4-8-9 W Woods (8) *in tch, rdn alng hfwy, sn drpd rear*..........(16 to 1 tchd 20 to 1) 23
4168 EASY LINE [78] 10-9-12 G Duffield (1) *in tch for o'r 4 fs*. ....(33 to 1) 24
4518 PRAIRIE GROVE [67] (bl) 3-8-12 J Reid (26) *handily plcd till outpcd o'r 2 fs out*..........(16 to 1 tchd 25 to 1) 25
3450 SURREY RACING [60] 5-8-8 B Rouse (10) *mid-div to hfwy*. ....(16 to 1 tchd 20 to 1) 26
3378⁴ ABIGAILS BOY (Hol) [48] 4-7-5 (5*) D Wright (15) *outpcd*. ....(33 to 1) 27
3973⁹ CAVATINA [72] 3-9-3 N Adams (3) *dwlt, al outpcd*. (33 to 1) 28

Dist: 2l, ¾l, ¾l, ¾l, sht-hd, sht-hd, nk, 1½l, 1l, 1l. 1m 28.73s. a 5.23s (28 Ran).
SR: 26/34/27/8/23/3/16/8/-/ (Mrs Rita Brown), W J Musson1.10-0.1

SAN SIRO (ITY) (heavy)
Sunday October 31st

4653 Premio Carlo Porta (Group 3) (3-y-o and up) £30,232 1¼m..........(3:10)

4073⁷ VINCENZO (Ger) 4-8-10 R Morse, *made all, rdn o'r 2 fs out, jst hld on*.......... 1
4441⁴ REVERE (Ire) 3-8-7 A Munro, *rcd in second, ev ch 2 fs out, ran on wl, jst fld*.......... 2
4557³ FUNNY BABY (Fr) 5-8-10 M Planard, *prmnt, ev ch fnl 2 fs, one pace*.......... 3
4306⁵ DREAM FOR FUTURE (Ire) 3-8-7 J Reid, *mid-div, kpt on one pace*.......... 4
4398⁴ LE JARDIN (Ger) 5-8-10 J Lowe, *mid-div, kpt on one pace*. 5
CHEYENNE FIRE (Ire) 4-8-10 N Mulas, *prmnt, 3rd strt, wknd 2 fs out*.......... 6
2439* PAY ME BACK (Ire) 4-8-10 S Dettori, *al mid-div*.......... 7
3921³ GUADO D'ANNIBALE (Ire) 4-8-10 L Sorrentino, *nvr plcd to chal*.......... 8
MALI PRINC 3-8-7 G Pretta, *outpcd*.......... 9
2083² CAPOLAGO (Ire) 6-8-10 G Scardino, *nvr seen wth ch*..... 0
4475 FORMATO UNI (Ire) 3-8-7 M Tellini, *al rear*.......... 0
4477⁵ PATRIK OF IRELAND (Ire) 5-8-10 M Esposito, *al beh*....... 0
1364 JOHNNY STECCHINO (USA) 3-8-10 S Soto, *al rear*...... 0
DUKE OF MARIE (Ity) 3-8-7 G Forte, *al beh*.......... 0

Dist: Sht-nk, 2l, 4l, 3l, 7l, ½l, 3l, 1½l, ¾l, 5l. 2m 13.50s. (14 Ran).
(Stall Nordpol), G Ording

ST-CLOUD (FR) (soft)
Sunday October 31st
Going Correction: PLUS 0.50 sec. per fur.

4654 Criterium de Saint-Cloud (Group 1) (2-y-o) £59,737 1¼m..............(1:55)

4399³ SUNSHACK 8-11 T Jarnet (2) *in rear, last strt, rdn and quickened 2 out, led jst ins fnl furlong, ran on wl*. ....(5 to 2 on) 1
4293⁴ ZINDARI (USA) 8-11 Pat Eddery (3) *led till jst ins fnl furlong*..........(5 to 2 on) 2
TIKKANEN (USA) 8-11 G Guignard (4) *prmnt, second strt, ev ch 2 out, one pace one and a half fs out*... (69 to 10) 3
3851² FAIR FABULOUS (Fr) 8-11 D Boeuf (5) *mid-div, 6th strt, rdn 2 fs out, one pace*..........(95 to 10) 4
BLUE PARADISE (Ire) 8-11 C Asmussen (1) *mid-div on ins, rdn o'r 2 out, no extr fnl furlong*..........(41 to 10) 5
4208* BLAAZIING JOE (Ire) 8-11 T Quinn (7) *prmnt, 3rd strt, ev ch 2 fs out, sn wknd*..........(41 to 10) 6
4443⁹ VILLAGE EAGLE (Fr) 8-11 M Roberts (6) *al beh*....(23 to 1) 7

Dist: 4l, 1½l, 1l, ½l, ¾l, 1l. 2m 15.20s. a 11.20s (7 Ran).
SR: 35/27/24/22/21/19/17/ (K Abdulla), A Fabre

4655 Prix de Flore (Group 3) (3-y-o and up) £23,895 1¼m 110yds.......... (2:50)

OXAVA (Fr) (bl) 3-8-9 O Peslier (3) *5th strt, chlgd one out, ran on ins fnl furlong, led nr finish*..........(76 to 10) 1
4201⁸ CHESA PLANA 4-8-11 G Guignard (7) *7th strt, quickened 2 fs out, chlgd one out, dsptd fnl furlong, no extr nr finish*..........(29 to 1) 2
1722⁶ ROYALE CHANTOU (Fr) 3-8-9 C Asmussen (10) *beh strt, quickened 2 fs out, chlgd one out, kpt on*.....(39 to 10) 3
3929⁵ ELACATA (Ger) 3-8-9 E Saint-Martin (4) *last strt, rdn and hdwy 2 fs out, nrst finish*..........(88 to 1) 4
4243* RING PINK (USA) 3-8-9 O Doleuze (9) *al prmnt, 3rd strt, chlgd 2 fs out, led one out, ct cl hme*..........(61 to 10) 5
4298³ FELAWNAH (USA) 3-8-9 W Carson (2) *8th strt, some prog 2 out, one pace one and a half fs out*........(8 to 5 fav) 6
4557⁵ SHOWGUM (Fr) 3-8-9 T Jarnet (8) *6th strt, one pace 2 fs out, nvr dngrs*..........(28 to 1) 7
4473* WAKRIA (Ire) 3-8-9 W Mongil (11) *beh strt, some prog 2 fs out, sn one pace*..........(39 to 10) 8
4243² ADORED SLEW (USA) 3-8-9 D Boeuf (13) *beh strt, rdn 2 out, wknd one and a half fs out*..........(13 to 1) 9
4199³ FORTHWITH 3-8-9 M Hills (6) *led till one and a half fs out, wknd quickly*..........(32 to 1) 0
4307* INSIJAAM (USA) 3-8-9 W R Swinburn (1) *prmnt early, second strt, led briefly one and a half fs out, wknd quickly*..........(46 to 10) 0
KARTABULA (Fr) 3-8-9 G Mosse (5) *prmnt, 4th strt, rdn and wknd 2 fs out*..........(24 to 1) 0
DIVI 3-8-9 F Sanchez (12) *al rear*..........(38 to 1) 0

Dist: ¾l, nk, ½l, sht-nk, 1½l, ¾l, sht-hd, 1l, 6l, 2½l. 2m 17.90s. a 7.40s (13 Ran).
SR: 74/74/71/70/69/66/64/63/61/ (C Maarek), E Lellouche

CLONMEL (IRE) (good)
Monday November 1st

4656 K.L.M. City Hopper Race (3-y-o and up) £2,760 1¼m...............(1:15)

3773³ PETOFI 3-8-11 (6*) D J O'Donohoe (5)..........(3 to 1) 1
4555³ GREAT CABARET (Ire) (bl) 3-8-13 (4*) W J Smith (1) ....(6 to 4 fav) 2
GRAND TOUR (NZ) 5-9-8 P V Gilson (2)..........(12 to 1) 3

4556^{5} DAHLIA'S BEST (USA) (bl) 3-8-10 W J Supple (7) . . . (6 to 1) 4
4409^{4} BLACK PIPER (Ire) 3-8-7 J F Egan (4) . . . . (7 to 1) 5
4430 BALLYTIGUE LORD 7-8-7 (8*) B Fenton (3) . . . . (14 to 1) 6
NISHIKI (USA) 4-8-12 N G McCullagh (8) . . . . (12 to 1) 7
4410 CARRICK PIKE (USA) (bl) 3-8-10 K J Manning (6) . . . (8 to 1) ref
Dist: 1½l, ¾l, ½l, 2½l. 2m 11.50s. (8 Ran).

(Mrs S Khan), D K Weld

4657 Aer Rianta Cork Airport Handicap (0-65 3-y-o and up) £2,760 1½m (1:45)

2841^{9} LIFE SAVER (Ire) [-] 4-9-12 (2*) P Carberry (1) . . . (6 to 4 fav) 1
4639^{7} KAWA-KAWA [-] (bl) 6-7-13 (6*) P P Murphy (7) . . . . (25 to 1) 2
3975^{4} WARREN STREET (Ire) [-] 3-9-6 S Craine (15) . . . . . (20 to 1) 3
4161^{2} TIME IS UP (Ire) [-] (bl) 4-9-4 P V Gilson (10) . . . . (7 to 1) 4
3975^{6} DARK HYACINTH (Ire) [-] 3-8-10 (8*) G M Moylan (9) (20 to 1) 5
4119* TREBLE BOB (Ire) [-] 3-9-1 (6*) D J O'Donohoe (6) . . (8 to 1) 6
1508^{3} SHARP INVITE [-] 6-8-12 K J Manning (3) . . . . (8 to 1) 7
4534^{7} UNCLE BABY (Ire) [-] 5-8-4 (2*) D G O'Shea (11) . . . (12 to 1) 8
4119^{5} RIYADH DANCER (Ire) [-] 3-8-9 J F Egan (12) . . . . . (12 to 1) 9
4534 LOVE OF ERIN (Ire) [-] (bl) 4-7-7 L O'Shea (14) . . . . . (25 to 1) 10
4429^{8} ARCH-T-GLEN (Ire) [-] (bl) 3-8-13 N G McCullagh (5) . . . . (16 to 1) 11
4185^{2} NORDIC MINE (Ire) [-] 3-8-6 (4*) J J Behan (2) . . . . . . (7 to 1) 12
4408 HAANEM [-] 3-9-3 W J Supple (18) . . . . (20 to 1) 13
NORTHERN BREGA [-] 6-7-8[1] Joanna Morgan (8) (50 to 1) 14
3074 VERIFIED (Ire) [-] 3-9-4 C Roche (17) . . . . (8 to 1) 15
4635^{9} NORDIC RACE [-] (bl) 6-9-1 (6*) B J Walsh, ... (14 to 1) 16
4534^{9} SUTTON CENTENARY (Ire) [-] (bl) 5-8-4 (4*) W J Smith (4) . . . . (16 to 1) 17
4184 EDENS LANDING (Ire) [-] 3-9-6 R Hughes (16) . . . . (20 to 1) ro
Dist: Nk, 2½l, ½l, 1l. 2m 53.40s. (18 Ran).

(Mrs H A Hegarty), Noel Meade

NEWCASTLE (soft)
Monday November 1st
Going Correction: PLUS 0.55 sec. per fur.

4658 'The Pirate' Claiming Handicap Class F (0-60 3-y-o and up) £2,959 1m (1:30)

4640^{7} PUBLIC WAY (Ire) [45] 3-8-10 (3*) M Fenton (3) *trkd ldrs, not much room 2 out, rdn to ld ins fnl furlong, all out.* . . . . (16 to 1) 1
4458^{4} ACROSS THE BAY [57] 6-10-0 J Fortune (14) *in tch, sn pushed alng, styd on wl und pres fnl 2 fs, not rch wnr.* . . . . (12 to 1 op 10 to 1) 2
4574 MALCESINE (Ire) [42] 4-8-8 (5*) Darren Moffatt (1) *in tch, effrt whn not clr run o'r 2 out, swtchd wl over one out, ran on well fnl furlong, nrst finish.* . . . . (12 to 1 op 10 to 1) 3
4424 SHANNON EXPRESS [41] (v) 6-8-12 K Fallon (18) *prmnt, led o'r 2 out till hdd ins fnl furlong, no extr.* . . . . (25 to 1) 4
4085^{6} PANIC BUTTON (Ire) [41] 3-8-9 J Quinn (12) *mid-div, hdwy 3 out, styd on fnl 2 fs.* . . . . (16 to 1 op 12 to 1) 5
4574 FOOLISH TOUCH [37] 11-8-3 (5*) D McCabe (10) *hld up, effrt o'r 3 out, styd on fnl 2 fs nrst finish.* . . . . . (14 to 1) 6
4537^{3} DEAD CALM [52] (v) 3-9-6 W Ryan (2) *prmnt, ev ch o'r one out, no extr.* . . . . (9 to 1 op 10 to 1) 7
4241 SPICE AND SUGAR [50] (bl) 3-9-4 A Munro (5) *trkd ldrs, effrt o'r 2 out, no hdwy.* . . . . (14 to 1) 8
4104^{5} VANART [42] 4-8-13 S Webster (13) *trkd ldrs, effrt o'r 2 out, wknd entering fnl furlong.* (12 to 1 tchd 14 to 1) 9
4391 MARY MACBLAIN [33] 4-7-13 (5*) D Wright (7) *slight ld till hdd o'r 2 out, grad wknd.* . . . . (12 to 1 tchd 14 to 1) 10
3006^{5} BLAKES BEAU [45] 3-8-13 M Birch (11) *wth ldrs, rdn 3 out, wknd 2 out.* . . . . (12 to 1) 11
4322 SAMANTHAS JOY [42] 3-8-5 (5*) P McCabe (19) *beh, some late hdwy, nvr nr to chal.* . . . . (50 to 1) 12
4574* TOCCO JEWEL [35] 3-7-10 (7*) M Baird (16) *beh, effrt 3 out, no hdwy.* . . . . (5 to 2 fav op 3 to 1 tchd 9 to 4) 13
4164^{9} ARABAT [57] 6-10-0 J Weaver (8) *dwlt, nvr dngrs.* (16 to 1) 14
4022^{8} PAULINUS [30] 5-7-8 (7*) C Teague (17) *nvr better than mid-div.* . . . . (20 to 1) 15
4574^{9} HALL BANK COTTAGE [41] 3-8-9 F Norton (6) *nvr better than mid-div.* . . . . (14 to 1 op 12 to 1) 16
4574^{5} RESOLUTE BAY [55] 7-9-12 A Culhane (9) *mid-div, effrt 3 out, sn btn.* . . . . (14 to 1) 17
2939^{7} DOCTOR-J (Ire) [47] 3-9-1 J Carroll (4) *trkd ldrs till wknd 2 out.* . . . . (25 to 1 op 20 to 1) 18
4043 SIE AMATO (Ire) [32] 4-8-3 J Fanning (15) *wth ldrs till wknd quickly o'r 2 out.* . . . . (25 to 1 op 20 to 1) 19
4045^{5} MISS OFFIE [36] 3-7-13 (5*) A Garth (20) *sn beh.* . . . . (20 to 1 op 16 to 1) 20
Dist: Nk, ½l, nk, ½l, 1l, nk, nk, 2½l, 1l, ½l. 1m 49.33s. a 10.33s (20 Ran).
SR: 10/24/7/5/-/-/7/4/-/ (N Chamberlain), N Chamberlain

4659 'Anything Goes' Conditions Stakes Class D (3-y-o and up) £3,451 1m 1f 9yds. . . . . (2:00)

3963^{7} CAMPANA (Ire) 3-8-9 J Carroll (3) *trkd ldr, led o'r 3 out, rdn over one out, styd on wl.* . . . . . (Evens tchd 11 to 10) 1
LORD PRESIDENT (USA) 3-8-12 A Munro (2) *in tch, trkd wnr frm o'r 2 out, shaken up over one out, rdn fnl furlong, no imprsn.* . . . . (5 to 4 on op 6 to 4 on tchd 6 to 5 on) 2
TOTAL UP (Ire) 4-9-0 C Dwyer (1) *led till hdd o'r 3 out, wknd quickly over 2 out, tld off.* (20 to 1 tchd 25 to 1) 3
Dist: 2½l, 25l. 2m 2.58s. a 10.58s (3 Ran).
SR: 11/9/-/ (Sheikh Mohammed), J H M Gosden

4660 'High Society' Rated Class B Handicap (0-100 3-y-o and up) £6,496 1¼m 32yds. . . . . (2:30)

4513* MAJED (Ire) [84] 5-8-2 (5*) Darren Moffatt (1) *hld up, effrt 2 out, sn rdn, styd on wl fnl furlong to ld post.* . . . . (11 to 8 fav op Evens tchd 7 to 4) 1
4175 MR CONFUSION (Ire) [88] 5-8-11 J Fortune (2) *chsd ldr, shaken up to ld wl o'r one out, sn rdn and quickened, styd on well, ct post.* . . . . (6 to 4 tchd 11 to 10) 2
4063 LUCKY GUEST [95] 6-9-4 W Ryan (3) *hld up, effrt 2 out, one pace fnl furlong.* . . . . (7 to 2 tchd 4 to 1) 3
4300 REPORTED (Ire) [98] 4-9-7 J Carroll (4) *led till hdd wl o'r one out, sn btn.* . . . . (16 to 1 op 12 to 1) 4
Dist: Sht-hd, 3½l, 3l. 2m 17.60s. a 11.10s (4 Ran).
SR: 38/41/41/38/ (Laurel (Leisure) Limited), Mrs M Reveley

4661 'Singing In The Saddle' Handicap Class D (0-80 3-y-o and up) £3,201 1½m 93yds. . . . . (3:00)

4538^{4} CUMBRIAN RHAPSODY [71] 3-9-0 M Birch (6) *in tch gng wl, led o'r one out, ran on strly.* . . . . . (5 to 1 op 4 to 1) 1
4559^{3} WESTFIELD MOVES (Ire) [57] 5-8-7 J Quinn (2) *trkd ldrs, pushed alng o'r 3 out, styd on wl und pres fnl furlong.* . . . . (7 to 2 op 4 to 1) 2
4548* IN THE MONEY (Ire) [63] 4-8-8 (5*) A Garth (5) *trkd ldrs, chlgd o'r one out, sn rdn and one pace.* . . . . (100 to 30 fav op 11 to 4 tchd 7 to 2) 3
4466 GREY POWER [74] 6-9-10 J Fanning (3) *hld up, effrt o'r 3 out, styd on und pres fnl 2 fs, not trble ldrs.* . . . . (7 to 2 op 3 to 1) 4
4506* SOBA UP [60] 3-8-3[2] A Culhane (1) *cl up, led 5 out till hdd o'r one out, wknd quickly.* . . . . (7 to 2 tchd 3 to 1 and 4 to 1) 5
PRECIOUS BOY [60] 7-8-10 J Fortune (4) *hld up, effrt o'r 3 out, rdn and wknd over 2 out.* . . . . (14 to 1 op 25 to 1) 6
MARLINGFORD [48] 6-7-12[3] A Morris (7) *led till hdd 5 out, wknd quickly and sn beh, tld off.* . . . . (33 to 1) 7
Dist: 2½l, ½l, 3½l, 5l, 12l, 30l. 2m 49.87s. a 12.17s (7 Ran).
SR: 47/35/40/44/13/-/-/ (Cumbrian Industrials Ltd), M H Easterby

4662 'You'll Never Get Rich' Handicap Class E (0-70 3-y-o) £2,742 2m 19yds . . . . (3:30)

4604^{4} MOONLIGHT ECLIPSE [52] 8-7 K Fallon (2) *beh, pushed alng frm hfwy, hdwy 3 out, led one out, edgd lft und pres fnl furlong, all out.* . . . . (10 to 1 op 9 to 1) 1
4493^{5} ARC BRIGHT (Ire) [48] 7-12 (5*) A Garth (1) *prmnt, led o'r 2 out, hdd over one out, edgd lft und pres and no extr fnl furlong.* . . . . (7 to 2 tchd 4 to 1) 2
4599* HOME FROM THE HILL (Ire) [69] 9-7 (3*,3ex) M Fenton (5) *hld up, hdwy o'r 4 out, chlgd 2 out, ev ch till no extr ins fnl furlong.* . . . . (7 to 4 fav op 5 to 4 tchd 2 to 1) 3
4433^{5} ROSMARINO [48] 8-3 J Fanning (6) *in tch, rdn to ld o'r one out, sn hdd, btn whn hmpd ins fnl furlong.* . . . . . (8 to 1) 4
4431^{5} TROY BOY [39] (v) 7-8 J Quinn (7) *cl up, led o'r 6 out, hdd over 2 out, wknd entering fnl furlong.* . . . . (10 to 1) 5
4218 MILNGAVIE (Ire) [45] 8-0 F Norton (3) *in tch, sddl slpd and hdwy to track ldr aftr 5 fs, outpcd five out, kpt on und pres fnl 3 furlongs.* . . . . (4 to 1 tchd 9 to 2) 6
4431^{8} GECKO ROUGE [45] 8-0[5] A Munro (4) *led till hdd o'r 6 out, sn wknd, tld off.* . . . . (16 to 1 op 14 to 1) 7
Dist: 1½l, sht-hd, 1½l, 1½l, 3½l, 25l. 3m 46.99s. a 20.99s (7 Ran).

(R Smalley), E J Alston

4663 EBF 'Something For The Boys' Maiden Stakes Class D (2-y-o) £3,687 6f. . . . . (4:00)

DESERT INVADER (Ire) 9-0 W R Swinburn (3) *dwlt, sn tracking ldrs, chlgd 2 out, kpt on wl to ld towards finish.* . . . . (11 to 10 fav op 6 to 4 on) 1
4503^{3} ASTRAC (Ire) 9-0 K Fallon (4) *in tch, rdn to ld entering fnl furlong, fdd and no extr towards finish.* . . . . (7 to 1 tchd 8 to 1) 2
4422^{6} WILD ROSE OF YORK 8-9 J Weaver (5) *prmnt, led o'r 2 out, hdd entering fnl furlong, one pace.* (11 to 2 op 5 to 1) 3
KALOU 8-9 J Quinn (8) *beh, effrt o'r 2 out, kpt on wl fnl furlong.* . . . . (33 to 1 op 20 to 1) 4
FORESTA VERDE (USA) 8-9 A Culhane (6) *in tch, kpt on fnl 2 fs, not trble ldrs.* . . . . (20 to 1 op 14 to 1) 5
4452 TARNSIDE TURBO 9-0 M Birch (2) *in tch, sn pushed alng, wknd 2 out.* . . . . (16 to 1 op 14 to 1) 6
4437^{7} BARRIER BOY 9-0 J Fortune (7) *led till hdd o'r 2 out, sn wknd.* . . . . (33 to 1 op 25 to 1) 7

3713[2] KILLY'S RAYNJA (Ire) 9-0 J Carroll (1) *prmnt till wknd o'r 2 out*............................. (7 to 2 tchd 100 to 30) 8

Dist: Nk, 2½l, nk, 6l, 3½l, 5l, 6l. 1m 18.34s. a 6.34s (8 Ran).
SR: 39/38/23/22/-/ (Maktoum Al Maktoum), A A Scott

SOUTHWELL (A.W) (std)
Monday November 1st
Going Correction: PLUS 0.15 sec. per fur.

4664 Charlecote Maiden Stakes Class D (Div I) (3-y-o) £3,289 1m....... (12:50)

MIDNIGHT JAZZ (Ire) 8-11 (3*) Emma O'Gorman (8) *cl up, led aftr 3 fs, clr three out, unchlgd*...(8 to 1 op 7 to 2) 1
4322 ABLE CHOICE (Ire) 9-0 R Price (1) *slwly into strd, hdwy on outer 3 fs out, styd on fnl 2 furlongs, no ch wth wnr*. ....(4 to 1 op 5 to 2 tchd 9 to 2) 2
4030[7] FLASHFEET 9-0 J Williams (5) *beh, styd on fnl 3 fs, nvr dngrs*.................................. (7 to 1 op 7 to 2) 3
4428[5] TATIKA 9-0 Paul Eddery (9) *chsd ldrs, effrt 3 fs out, sn rdn and wknd*.......(13 to 8 on op 5 to 4 tchd 7 to 4 on) 4
4596 CLOVER JACK 9-0 C Rutter (7) *chsd ldrs, rdn 3 fs out, sn wknd*.. (33 to 1) 5
4623 COLFAX STARLIGHT 8-9 S Wood (2) *led 3 fs, chsd wnr till rdn and wknd 2 out*................(33 to 1 op 20 to 1) 6
1943[5] BARSAL (Ire) 9-0 D Harrison (6) *in tch till hfwy, sn lost pl*. ....(20 to 1 op 16 to 1) 7
JOYCE E JACKSON 8-9 A McGlone (4) *slwly into strd, al beh*................................ (25 to 1 op 20 to 1) 8
SCOTTISH TEMPTRESS 8-6 (3*) Stephen Davies (3) *cl up 3 fs, sn lost pl and beh*..............................(50 to 1) 9

Dist: 8l, 1½l, 12l, 2l, 2½l, 2½l, 12l, 8l. 1m 43.50s. a 4.50s (9 Ran).
SR: 51/27/22/-/-/-/ (S Fustok), W A O'Gorman

4665 Pendeford Open Maiden Class D (Div I) (2-y-o) £3,260 6f..............(1:20)

4345[5] CHAMPAGNE ATEASTER 8-9 G Duffield (8) *chsd ldrs, rdn to chal one and a half fs out, sn hrd drvn, styd on ins last to ld nr finish*. (5 to 2 jt-fav op 9 to 4 tchd 3 to 1) 1
4229[5] FORT KNOX (Ire) 9-0 R Price (6) *chsd ldr, led o'r 2 fs out, sn rdn, hdd and no extr nr finish*..............(5 to 2 jt-fav op 11 to 4 tchd 3 to 1) 2
2718 DAME PROSPECT 8-9 S D Williams (5) *chsd ldrs, rdn 2 fs out, kpt on one pace*..............(33 to 1 op 25 to 1) 3
2916[2] CINNAMON SPRINGS (Ire) 8-2 (7*) S Mulvey (10) *beh, hdwy hfwy, rdn and kpt on one pace fnl 2 fs*. ....(7 to 2 op 5 to 2) 4
4339 ARCTIC SHREWD 8-9 M Wigham (4) *beh till styd on fnl 2 fs, nvr dngrs*.......................(50 to 1 op 25 to 1) 5
4480 TELEPHONE TAP 9-0 W Newnes (2) *led, rdn and hdd o'r 2 fs out, sn wknd*......................(14 to 1 op 10 to 1) 6
NORDIC MADAM (Ire) 8-9 L Charnock (1) *slwly away, al rear*...(50 to 1 op 33 to 1) 7
4456[5] JUST DUGGIE 9-0 A Mackay (7) *chsd ldrs, rdn hfwy, sn wknd*....................................... (8 to 1 op 5 to 1) 8
4594 DARLIN'BUDS OF MAY 8-9 G Hind (3) *al rear*. .... (50 to 1 op 33 to 1) 9

Dist: Hd, 7l, 8l, 2½l, sht-hd, 2l, 1½l, 15l. 1m 17.80s. a 4.40s (9 Ran).
SR: 25/29/-/-/-/-/ (Jem Racing), S G Norton

4666 Charlecote Maiden Stakes Class D (Div II) (3-y-o) £3,260 1m........(1:50)

4457 SAVINGS BANK 8-7 (7*) V Halliday (4) *trkd ldrs gng wl, swtchd outsd 3 furlons out, crrd wide strt, led 2 out, sn rdn clr*.................................. (14 to 1 tchd 16 to 1) 1
4524[4] LADY SABINA 8-9 A Clark (2) *led aftr 3 fs, rdn o'r 2 out, sn hdd and one pace*. ....(5 to 4 on tchd Evens and 11 to 8 on) 2
4596 RISKY VENTURE 9-0 M Tebbutt (5) *cl up, wide strt, ev ch o'r 2 fs out, sn rdn and one pace*.....(9 to 2 op 7 to 2) 3
3274[5] DANAMORE (Ire) 9-0 D Harrison (3) *slwly into strd and beh, styd on und pres fnl 2 fs, nvr dngrs*...... (10 to 1) 4
3896 MR JAZZ DANCER (Ire) 9-0 M Wigham (8) *outpcd and beh till some hdwy und pres fnl 2 fs*..................(20 to 1) 5
4537 PYTCHLEY DAWN 8-9 N Carlisle (6) *led 3 fs, cl up till rdn three out, sn wknd*......................(7 to 1 op 6 to 1) 6
3866 WESSHAUN 8-9 T Sprake (7) *prmnt till rdn and wknd 3 fs out*.....................................(8 to 1 op 5 to 1) 7
ALBERSTAN 9-0 S D Williams (1) *slwly into strd, al beh*. ....(33 to 1) 8

Dist: 10l, 1½l, 1½l, 7l, 1½l, 1½l, 25l. 1m 45.40s. a 6.40s (8 Ran).
SR: 22/-/-/-/-/ (J Baggott), T D Barron

4667 Castlecroft Handicap Class C (0-90 3-y-o and up) £5,047 7f......... (2:20)

4394 DREAM CARRIER (Ire) [63] 5-7-12 (7*) V Halliday (8) *beh, hdwy and swtchd wide strt, str run to ld appr fnl furlong, sn clr, easily*.............. (12 to 1 op 10 to 1) 1
4606[5] FIELD OF VISION (Ire) [79] 3-9-5 T Williams (7) *in tch, rdn alng hfwy, hdwy o'r 2 fs out, sn ridden, styd on ins last, no ch wth wnr*................ (10 to 1 op 8 to 1) 2
4616[3] HIGHBORN (Ire) [78] 4-9-6 G Hind (2) *prmnt, rdn alng hfwy, styd on fnl 2 fs*. .... (7 to 2 fav op 9 to 2 tchd 6 to 1 and 3 to 1) 3
4490 FIGHTER SQUADRON [61] (bl) 4-8-3 S D Williams (1) *al cl up, rdn to ld 2 fs out, hdd and wknd appr last*. ....(20 to 1 op 16 to 1) 4
2327[8] ROSEATE LODGE [80] 7-9-8 D Harrison (10) *beh till styd on fnl 2 fs, nrst finish*..............(10 to 1 tchd 11 to 1) 5
4235 GYMCRAK TYCOON [64] 4-8-6[1] J Williams (4) *mid-div, rdn o'r 2 fs out, styd on fnl furlong, not rch ldrs*. ....(20 to 1 op 25 to 1 tchd 16 to 1) 6
3324* CRECHE [85] (bl) 4-9-6 (7*) E Husband (15) *cl up, led aftr 2 fs, rdn and hdd two out, sn wknd*. (16 to 1 op 10 to 1) 7
4297[7] CALEMAN [86] 4-10-0 G Duffield (3) *chsd ldrs, rdn 3 fs out, sn btn*................................(10 to 1 op 6 to 1) 8
4514 HEART BROKEN [70] 3-8-10 Paul Eddery (12) *chsd ldrs, rdn 3 fs out, sn wknd*..................(16 to 1 op 14 to 1) 9
4297[8] HERORA (Ire) [72] (bl) 4-9-0 A McGlone (9) *chsd ldrs, rdn 3 fs out, sn wknd*........................ (12 to 1 op 5 to 1) 10
3447 JORDYWRATH [56] 3-7-10 S Wood (5) *nvr rch ldrs*. ....(33 to 1) 11
4458[7] SUPER BENZ [80] 7-9-1 (7*) L Aspell (14) *led for 2 fs, cl up till rdn and wknd two and a half out*. .... (16 to 1 op 14 to 1) 12
3458[9] MISS GORGEOUS (Ire) [76] 3-8-13 (3*) Emma O'Gorman (11) *very slwly away, al rear*...........................(14 to 1) 13
1808 GYMCRAK TIGER (Ire) [87] 3-9-13 A Clark (6) *slwly into strd, al beh*.................... (33 to 1 op 16 to 1) 14
4415 LEE ARTISTE [82] (bl) 5-9-10 T Quinn (16) *al rear*. ....(14 to 1 op 12 to 1) 15
4514[4] THORNTON GATE [71] 4-8-10 (3*) S Maloney (13) *al rear, wl beh 3 fs out, eased*.....(10 to 1 op 9 to 1 tchd 12 to 1) 16

Dist: 4l, 1l, nk, 2l, 2½l, 3l, ½l, 4l, ½l, 1l. 1m 31.10s. a 5.00s (16 Ran).
SR: 32/34/32/14/27/3/15/14/-/ (Stephen Woodall), T D Barron

4668 Pendeford Open Maiden Class D (Div II) (2-y-o) £3,231 6f............. (2:50)

4512[3] IN A MOMENT (USA) (v) 9-0 G Duffield (9) *cl up, rdn 2 fs out, styd on to ld entering last, ran on und pres*. ....(11 to 4 op 2 to 1 tchd 100 to 30) 1
4480[3] CLARION CALL (Ire) 9-0 T Quinn (4) *made most, rdn one and a half fs out, hdd entering last, eased whn btn nr finish*...............................(5 to 4 on op 5 to 4) 2
4437[6] CURIE CRUSADER (Ire) 9-0 J Williams (7) *chsd ldrs, rdn o'r 2 fs out, kpt on one pace*. ....(7 to 1 op 5 to 1 tchd 15 to 2) 3
4452[8] MYSTICAL MICKEY (Ire) 9-0 S D Williams (10) *chsd ldrs, rdn 3 fs out, sn one pace*..............(25 to 1 op 20 to 1) 4
3816 SKELTON PRINCESS (Ire) 8-9 S Perks (6) *chsd ldrs, rdn 3 fs out, no hdwy*.......................... (25 to 1 op 16 to 1) 5
3828 AVONDALE ROSE 8-9 S Wood (8) *al rear*. ....(33 to 1 op 25 to 1) 6
ANNABELLE ROSE 8-9 N Adams (5) *dwlt, al rear*. ....(20 to 1 op 33 to 1) 7
AMI PIAF 8-9 W Newnes (3) *al rear*..(20 to 1 op 10 to 1) 8
GARDNER DOUGLAS 9-0 A Clark (1) *in tch till rdn and wknd wl o'r 2 fs out*. (25 to 1 op 14 to 1 tchd 33 to 1) 9
4098 DEAR SILVERS 8-9 C Rutter (2) *slwly into strd and outpcd, sn beh, pld up o'r 2 fs out, broke leg, destroyed*. ....(25 to 1 op 20 to 1) pu

Dist: 3l, 7l, 4l, 1l, 3l, 3l, nk, 2½l. 1m 17.90s. a 4.50s (10 Ran).
SR: 28/16/-/-/-/-/ (David Scott), S G Norton

4669 Shifnal Claiming Stakes Class F (3-y-o and up) £2,735 1½m............(3:20)

4218[8] CLIBURNEL NEWS (Ire) 3-8-1 (7*) S Mulvey (2) *trkd ldrs, effrt 3 fs out, sn led, clr appr last*. ....(9 to 2 op 4 to 1 tchd 5 to 1) 1
4045 DON'T BE SAKI (Ire) 3-8-0 C Rutter (10) *al prmnt, effrt and ev ch 3 fs out, sn rdn, one pace appr last*...... (33 to 1) 2
4374 NANCY (Ire) (bl) 3-7-5 (7*) Claire Balding (7) *mid-div, steady hdwy hfwy, rdn o'r 3 fs out, styd on*......... (20 to 1) 3
4279[3] SAFFAAH (USA) 6-9-6 W Newnes (13) *in tch, jnd ldrs hfwy, effrt to chal 3 fs out, sn rdn and wknd 2 out*. ....(9 to 4 fav op 7 to 2 tchd 4 to 1) 4
4247 CLIFTON CHASE (bl) 4-9-10 Paul Eddery (8) *chsd ldr, rdn alng 4 fs out, ev ch 3 out, one pace 2 out*. .... (10 to 1 op 8 to 1) 5
4457[5] TRANQUIL LADY (Ire) 3-8-5 (3*) S Maloney (15) *beh, styd on fnl 2 fs, nvr dngrs*.............................. (33 to 1) 6
4031[8] MUMMYS ROCKET 4-8-5 A Mackay (17) *beh, hdwy hfwy, rdn 3 fs out, no imprsn*..............................(33 to 1) 7
4544 MALINDI BAY (bl) 5-8-8 T Williams (5) *prmnt to hfwy, wknd*.. (33 to 1) 8
CHAPEL HAVEN (Ire) 3-8-4 D Harrison (4) *al rear*. (50 to 1) 9
294 MILLIE (USA) 5-7-10 (7*) Antoinette Armes (16) *slwly into strd, al rear*........................(33 to 1 op 25 to 1) 10
709* TEMPERING 7-9-10 S Wood (1) *led, rdn o'r 3 fs out, sn hdd and wknd*.........(11 to 4 op 6 to 4 tchd 3 to 1) 11
3689 CLEAR LIGHT 6-8-13 M Wigham (14) *chsd ldrs, rdn alng hfwy, sn lost pl*..................(25 to 1 op 20 to 1) 12
4254 MYSTICAL GUEST 7-9-2 S Whitworth (6) *nvr a factor*. ....(50 to 1) 13
4457 FLORA LADY (bl) 3-8-4 J Lowe (3) *al rear*....... (50 to 1) 14
4574 VICTORIAS PASSION 3-7-11[1] D Biggs (11) *al rear*. (33 to 1) 15

4213 HIGHLAND PRINCESS 3-7-12 L Charnock (9) *in tch, rdn alng hfwy, sn lost pl and beh*................(50 to 1) 16
3021[6] MR WISHING WELL (e/s) 7-8-8 T Quinn (12) *al rear, tld off fnl 3 fs, virtually pld up final furlong*.........(14 to 1) 17
Dist: 10l, nk, 7l, 2½l, 2½l, 15l, 3½l, 5l, 15l, nk. 2m 43.50s. a 9.60s (17 Ran).
SR: 16/-/-/-/-/-/ (East Lancs Newspapers Readers Club), M H Tompkins

4670 West Midlands Apprentice Handicap Class E (0-70 3-y-o and up) £3,339 6f ....(3:50)

4501[7] PHARAOH'S DANCER [62] 6-9-7 D Gibbs (16) *chsd ldrs, chlgd 2 fs out, rdn to ld appr fnl furlong, ran on*. .... (9 to 1 op 10 to 1 tchd 12 to 1) 1
4331[2] AVRIL ETOILE [49] 3-8-2 (5*) Iona Wands (4) *chsd ldrs, hdwy 2 fs out, sn rdn, kpt on ins last*. .... (12 to 1 op 8 to 1) 2
4532[9] SAVAHRA SOUND [62] 8-9-4 (3*) G Strange (2) *in tch, effrt 2 fs out, sn rdn, styd on ins last, nrst finish*. .... (12 to 1 op 20 to 1) 3
3687[6] VERY DICEY [65] 5-9-5 (5*) Ruth Coulter (9) *led aftr one furlong, rdn 2 fs out, hdd and wknd appr last*. .... (12 to 1 op 8 to 1) 4
4532[4] VICTORIA HALL [62] 3-8-13 (7*) L Suthern (6) *led for one furlong, cl up, rdn 2 fs out, sn wknd*. .... (8 to 1 op 6 to 1 tchd 10 to 1) 5
4580[3] PANTHER (Ire) [52] (v) 3-8-10 S Copp (15) *mid-div, hdwy on outer o'r 2 fs out, styd on und pres ins last*. .... (8 to 1 op 7 to 1 tchd 12 to 1) 6
4536 EGG [52] 3-8-3 (7*) Kimberley Hart (13) *beh till some late hdwy*..........................(12 to 1 op 10 to 1) 7
4217[2] MU-ARRIK [50] 5-8-6[2] (5*) D Thomas (11) *cl up, effrt o'r 2 fs out, sn rdn and wknd*.........(7 to 1 fav tchd 10 to 1) 8
4592 SPLASH OF SALT (Ire) [64] (bl) 3-9-5 (3*) S McCarthy (3) *chsd ldrs, rdn o'r 2 fs out, wknd*..... (12 to 1 tchd 14 to 1) 9
4045 COLFAX CLASSIC [46] 3-8-0[1] (5*) C Scudder (5) *nvr rch ldrs*..............................(14 to 1 tchd 12 to 1) 10
4592[4] PRINCE BELFORT [52] 5-8-11 P Roberts (8) *cl up, rdn o'r 2 fs out, sn btn*.......................(9 to 1 op 14 to 1) 11
4507[6] GONDO [69] (v) 6-9-11 (3*) S Knott (10) *nvr a factor*. .... (12 to 1 op 8 to 1 tchd 14 to 1) 12
4168[4] INVIGILATE [55] 4-8-9 (5*) J Dennis (1) *nvr a factor*. ....(12 to 1 tchd 10 to 1) 13
4327 JOCKS JOKER [56] 3-8-9 (5*) D Griffiths (12) *chsd ldrs for 2 fs, sn lost pl and beh*..........................(20 to 1) 14
4458 HEATHYARDS GEM [57] 3-8-10 (5*) L Aspell (14) *slwly into strd, al rear*...................................(12 to 1) 15
4487 COALISLAND [55] 3-8-8 (5*) D Toole (7) *al rear*. .... (12 to 1 op 10 to 1) 16
Dist: 2l, 1½l, nk, 1½l, ¾l, ½l, 1l, nk, 4l, nk. 1m 17.80s. a 4.40s (16 Ran).
SR: 37/15/23/25/15/2/-/-/7/ (Pharaohs Computers Ltd), M McCormack

4671 Moseley Nursery Class D (0-85 2-y-o) £3,494 1m.....................(4:20)

4550[8] DOWN D ISLANDS [70] (bl) 8-11 W Newnes (3) *made all, quickened clr 2 fs out, eased nr finish*. ....(5 to 1 op 4 to 1) 1
4251 HIGHLY FASHIONABLE (Ire) [69] 8-10 T Quinn (11) *al prmnt, effrt to chase wnr 2 fs out, sn rdn and not quicken*. .... (11 to 2 op 5 to 1 tchd 6 to 1) 2
4531 WALWORTH LADY [54] 7-9[2] L Charnock (13) *mid-div, hdwy on outer 3 fs out, rdn 2 out, styd on ins last*. ....(33 to 1) 3
4577[4] TONE CONTROL [62] 8-3 D Biggs (4) *chsd wnr, rdn o'r 2 fs out, sn one pace*.......................(14 to 1 op 7 to 1) 4
4541* NON VINTAGE (Ire) [79] (bl) 9-3 (3*) S Maloney (7) *mid-div, hdwy o'r 3 fs out, rdn 2 out, sn one pace*. ....(9 to 4 fav op 5 to 2 tchd 7 to 2) 5
4122 SHARPISH WORDS [54] 7-9[2] J Lowe (10) *beh till styd on fnl 2 fs, nvr dngrs*...............................(20 to 1) 6
4531 HEATHYARDS CRUSADE (Ire) [61] 8-2[1] Paul Eddery (2) *chsd ldrs, rdn hfwy, sn wknd*..........(12 to 1 op 10 to 1) 7
3940 PETITJEAN (Ire) [57] 7-12 C Rutter (1) *chsd ldrs, rdn 2 and a half fs out, wknd*..................(8 to 1 op 12 to 1) 8
1983[4] ACCESS ADVANTAGE [62] 8-3[1] G Duffield (8) *cl up, hmpd and snatched up hfwy, sn beh*...(12 to 1 tchd 10 to 1) 9
4361[8] AUNTIE FAY (Ire) [52] 7-7 S Wood (12) *al rear*..... (33 to 1) 10
4564[5] STARICA (Ire) [52] (bl) 7-3[3] (7*) Claire Balding (9) *al rear*. .... (12 to 1 op 10 to 1) 11
4444 PAVAKA [80] (bl) 9-7 M Tebbutt (5) *outpcd*. .... (9 to 1 op 6 to 1 tchd 10 to 1) 12
4342 HOTCROFT [52] 7-0 (7*) Antoinette Armes (6) *al beh*. .... (33 to 1 op 25 to 1) 13
Dist: 4l, nk, ¾l, 1l, 5l, ½l, 3½l, 1½l, ½l, 1½l. 1m 45.30s. a 6.30s (13 Ran).
SR: 21/8/-/-/12/-/ (R J Shannon), R Hannon

FLEMINGTON (AUS) (good to firm)
Tuesday November 2nd

4672 Foster's Melbourne Cup (Group 1) (3-y-o and up) £590,909 2m........(5:20)

4055* VINTAGE CROP 6-8-10 M Kinane,.......................... 1
TE AKAU NICK (NZ) 5-8-11 R Vance,...................... 2
MERCATOR (NZ) 7-8-7 C Johnson,......................... 3
GREAT VINTAGE (NZ) 4-7-11 S King,...................... 4
Dist: 3l, hd. 3m 25.43s. (24 Ran).
(Michael W J Smurfit), D K Weld

REDCAR (good)
Tuesday November 2nd
Going Correction: PLUS 0.25 sec. per fur. (races 1,2,5,6), PLUS 0.50 (3,4)

4673 Ian Hird Conditions Stakes Class D (2-y-o) £3,201 6f..................(1:15)

4511[4] BRAILLE (Ire) 8-13 J Weaver (1) *cl up, effrt to dispute ld 2 fs out, rdn to lead entering last, ran on wl*. .... (5 to 2 op 2 to 1 tchd 11 to 4) 1
4512* AMBER VALLEY (USA) 9-1 W Carson (2) *led, pushed alng 2 fs out, rdn and hdd entering last, kpt on und pres*. .... (Evens fav op 11 to 10) 2
3898[8] CRAGGANMORE 8-13 M Hills (4) *cl up, rdn o'r 2 fs out, sn wknd*...............................(7 to 1 op 4 to 1) 3
4520[8] SERIOUS OPTION (Ire) 9-5 T Quinn (3) *cl up, pushed alng bef hfwy, sn rdn and wknd*. ....(7 to 2 op 5 to 2 tchd 4 to 1) 4
Dist: Sht-hd, 8l, hd. 1m 14.40s. a 4.70s (4 Ran).
SR: 35/36/2/7/ (L G McMullan), M Johnston

4674 Jon Charlton Nursery Class E (2-y-o) £3,494 7f.....................(1:45)

4602[3] BENEFICIARY [60] 7-10 W Carson (8) *cl up centre, effrt to ld 2 fs out, rdn and hdd briefly ins last, rallied and ran on wl nr finish*............. (3 to 1 fav op 2 to 1) 1
4541[5] KAITAK (Ire) [73] 8-2 (7*) G Parkin (9) *in tch centre, gd hdwy 2 and a half fs out, rdn to ld briefly ins last, no extr nr finish*..............................(10 to 1 op 8 to 1) 2
4541[7] NEW INN [70] 8-6 J Quinn (13) *trkd ldrs centre, hdwy 2 fs out, sn rdn and kpt on ins last*.... (16 to 1 op 20 to 1) 3
4516[4] SHARP FALCON (Ire) [65] 8-1 M Roberts (3) *prmnt far side, rdn o'r 2 fs out and ev ch till wknd appr last*. ....(7 to 1 op 5 to 1) 4
4531 DYNAMIC DELUXE (USA) [70] 8-6 K Fallon (14) *hld up centre, hdwy o'r 2 fs out, sn rdn and one pace*. .... (12 to 1 op 8 to 1) 5
4618[6] STRAPPED [65] 8-1 N Adams (7) *in tch far side, effrt and hdwy 2 fs out, sn rdn and one pace appr last*. ....(10 to 1 tchd 12 to 1) 6
4564[6] DOUCE MAISON (Ire) [57] 7-4[2] (5*) D Wright (5) *chsd ldrs, rdn 2 fs out, grad wknd*........... (6 to 1 op 12 to 1) 7
4021[2] CLOSE TO REALITY [85] 9-0 (7*) D Thomas (6) *made most centre till hdd 2 fs out and grad wknd*. .... (16 to 1 op 8 to 1) 8
4550 PRIZEFIGHTER [66] 7-13 (3*) S Maloney (11) *beh, hdwy o'r 2 fs out, not rch ldrs*. (16 to 1 op 12 to 1 tchd 20 to 1) 9
4550 BROCTUNE GOLD [77] 8-13 T Quinn (1) *lost many ls strt, beh till hdwy o'r 2 fs out, kpt on*...(14 to 1 op 20 to 1) 10
4512[9] FRUSTRATED POET (USA) [70] 8-6 L Charnock (12) *chsd ldrs till rdn 3 fs out and sn wknd*... (7 to 1 op 14 to 1) 11
4528 SECONDS AWAY [58] 7-8[1] J Lowe (10) *mid-div, sn rdn alng, nvr a factor*...............................(33 to 1) 12
4602[9] MELODY DANCER [60] 7-7[2] (5*) A Garth (4) *prmnt 4 fs, sn wknd*.. (33 to 1) 13
4435[7] GRETELS PET [58] 7-8[1] G Bardwell (15) *sn outpcd and wl beh frm hfwy*...................................(50 to 1) 14
Dist: Hd, 3l, 3½l, 1l, 2l, ¾l, ¾l, 2½l, ¾l, 1½l. 1m 27.60s. a 5.80s (14 Ran).
SR: 21/33/21/5/7/-/-/12/-/ (Reg Griffin), M H Easterby

4675 Beryl Berry Handicap Class D (0-80 3-y-o and up) £3,850 1m 3f......(2:15)

4522[9] TUDOR ISLAND [56] 4-8-9 M Birch (6) *trkd ldrs, hdwy to ld o'r 3 fs out, rdn 2 out, hdd appr fnl furlong, rallied to lead ins last, ran on wl*................(8 to 1 op 7 to 1) 1
3937[3] DARK DEN (USA) [77] 3-9-10 Paul Eddery (9) *trkd ldrs, hdwy 3 fs out, rdn to ld briefly appr fnl furlong, hdd ins last, kpt on*...................(9 to 2 op 5 to 1) 2
4188[2] GILDERDALE [75] 11-9-7 (7*) M Henry (11) *hld up and beh, hdwy 3 fs out, rdn 2 out, styd on*..............(6 to 1) 3
4631 ROUSITTO [49] 5-7-11 (5*) A Garth (7) *hld up in tch, hdwy 3 fs out, sn rdn, styd on ins last*... (14 to 1 op 10 to 1) 4
4643[2] SURREY DANCER [74] 5-9-6 (7*) S Copp (3) *hld up and beh, hdwy on inner 3 fs out, rdn 2 out, kpt on ins last*. ....(13 to 8 fav op 5 to 4 tchd 7 to 4) 5
4457[3] PRIMO FIGLIO [60] (bl) 3-8-7 D Harrison (10) *mid-div, hdwy on outer 3 fs out, sn rdn, kpt on one pace*. .... (10 to 1 op 8 to 1) 6
4604[7] BARDIA [46] 3-7-7 Kim Tinkler (1) *slwly into strd and beh till styd on fnl 2 fs, nvr dngrs*................(100 to 1) 7
4603* KAGRAM QUEEN [61] 5-9-0 (5ex) K Fallon (4) *trkd ldrs, effrt 3 fs out, rdn 2 out, wknd ins last*. ....(6 to 1 tchd 13 to 2) 8
4374 BOLD AMBITION [41] 6-7-8[1] J Lowe (5) *prmnt, chsd ldr hfwy till rdn and wknd o'r 3 fs out*............(25 to 1) 9
4432 UNFINISHEDBUSINESS [64] 3-8-11 N Connorton (8) *led, rdn and hdd o'r 3 fs out, sn wknd*. (20 to 1 op 14 to 1) 10
4045 HOTEL CALIFORNIA (Ire) [47] 3-7-8 S Wood (2) *prmnt till rdn and wknd o'r 3 fs out*.....................(50 to 1) 11

Dist: ½l, ¾l, ½l, 1l, ¾l, 3l, 1l, 8l, 8l, ¾l. 2m 27.40s. a 12.00s (11 Ran).
SR: 30/44/46/19/42/20/-/19/-/ (D Sieff), C E Brittain

4676 Dick Glarvey Handicap Class E (0-70 3-y-o and up) £3,340 1¼m...... (2:45)

4522 MR TATE (Ire) [66] 4-10-0 T Quinn (13) *trkd ldrs, wide strt, gd hdwy to ld appr fnl furlong, clr ins last.* ....(9 to 1 op 10 to 1 tchd 12 to 1) 1
4533[5] MISTY GODDESS (Ire) [55] 5-8-12 (5*) K Rutter (14) *mid-div, swtchd outsd and hdwy o'r 2 fs out, rdn and ran on ins last.* ....(10 to 1 tchd 11 to 1) 2
4603[3] ALKABAR [43] 5-8-5 D Harrison (10) *trkd ldrs, hdwy 4 fs out, led o'r 2 out, sn rdn, hdd appr fnl furlong, kpt on.* ....(11 to 1 op 8 to 1 tchd 12 to 1) 3
4522[3] WASSL THIS THEN (Ire) [60] 4-9-8 R Price (9) *chsd ldrs, effrt 2 fs out, sn rdn, kpt on.*........ (11 to 2 fav op 9 to 2) 4
4470 LET'S GET LOST [65] 4-9-13 J Carroll (15) *hld up and beh, gd hdwy o'r 2 fs out, kpt on ins last.* ....(16 to 1 op 14 to 1) 5
4506[2] LOMBARD SHIPS [58] (bl) 6-9-6 A Mackay (7) *chsd ldrs, rdn 2 fs out, kpt on.*......................(6 to 1 op 7 to 1) 6
4623[7] BRESIL (USA) [50] 4-8-12 A Clark (17) *hld up, gd hdwy 3 fs out, swtchd rght and rdn o'r one furlong out, kpt on.* ....(7 to 1 tchd 8 to 1) 7
4235 FLASHELLA (Ire) [46] 3-8-3 W Carson (6) *prmnt, effrt and rdn o'r 2 fs out, grad wknd.*.......(20 to 1 op 16 to 1) 8
4605* SARTIGILA [62] 4-9-5 (5*,5ex) J Marshall (11) *mid-div, effrt and some hdwy o'r 2 fs out, sn rdn and btn.* ....(10 to 1 op 8 to 1) 9
4605[3] NO COMEBACKS [52] 5-9-0 K Fallon (2) *hld up and beh, swtchd wide 2 fs out and styd on ins last.* ....(10 to 1 tchd 9 to 1) 10
4643[4] ESSAYEFFSEE [55] 4-8-12 (5*) Darren Moffatt (12) *hld up, effrt and hdwy 2 and a half fs out, sn rdn and wknd o'r one out.*.......................... (10 to 1 tchd 12 to 1) 11
4319 MODEST HOPE (USA) [46] 6-8-3 (5*) A Garth (4) *trkd ldr, led o'r 3 fs out till hdd over 2 furlongs out, sn wknd.* ....(33 to 1) 12
4424 MEDIA MESSENGER [51] 4-8-6 (7*) C Teague (3) *prmnt till rdn and wknd o'r 2 fs out.*........ (20 to 1 op 16 to 1) 13
4187[5] YOUNG JASON [40] 10-8-2 Paul Eddery (5) *mid-div, effrt and some hdwy o'r 4 fs out, sn wknd.*.........(20 to 1) 14
4533[8] EUROTWIST [52] 4-8-7 (7*) V Halliday (8) *al rear.* (12 to 1) 15
4107[9] ROYAL CITIZEN (Ire) [66] 4-9-11 (3*) S Maloney (16) *al rear.* ....(20 to 1 op 25 to 1) 16
4343[4] NO SUBMISSION (USA) [55] 7-9-3 S Wood (1) *led, rdn and hdd o'r 3 fs out, sn wknd.*.................... (20 to 1) 17

Dist: 2½l, nk, ¾l, ½l, nk, ¾l, ¾l, ½l, nk, hd. 2m 12.50s. a 11.30s (17 Ran).
SR: 51/35/22/37/41/33/23/12/32/ (John Falvey), R Akehurst

4677 EBF Harry Rudland Maiden Stakes Class D (2-y-o) £4,199 7f........(3:15)

4503[2] SOUTHERN POWER (Ire) 9-0 J Reid (1) *made all, shaken up appr fnl furlong and quickened clr.* ....(13 to 8 on op 2 to 1 on tchd 6 to 4 on) 1
BEDOON RESOOM (USA) 9-0 M Roberts (8) *trkd ldrs, hdwy 3 fs out, effrt and ch 2 out, sn rdn and not quicken appr last.*..... (9 to 4 op 5 to 2 tchd 11 to 4) 2
COLLIER ROW (Ire) 9-0 T Quinn (6) *cl up, rdn 2 fs out, sn one pace.*..........................(12 to 1 op 10 to 1) 3
SHELTERED COVE (Ire) 9-0 M Birch (3) *chsd ldrs, rdn 3 fs out, kpt on one pace.*........................(10 to 1) 4
3677[9] CULRAIN 9-0 N Connorton (2) *chsd ldrs, rdn 3 fs out, sn wknd.*............................(25 to 1 op 20 to 1) 5
4032[5] SUPERHOO 9-0 J Fanning (4) *in tch, rdn 3 fs out, sn wknd.*...........................(66 to 1 op 50 to 1) 6
BLACK ICE BOY (Ire) 8-9[2] (7*) H Bastiman (7) *slwly away, al outpcd and wl beh, tld off hfwy*... (25 to 1 op 20 to 1) 7
4452 EILEEN'S DARLING 8-9 J Lowe (5) *in tch, sn rdn alng, lost pl hfwy, tld off fnl 2 fs.*.......................(100 to 1) 8

Dist: 4l, 2l, 5l, 1½l, 2l, dist, 10l. 1m 27.90s. a 6.10s (8 Ran).
SR: 35/23/17/2/-/ (Lucayan Stud), R Hannon

4678 John Berry Conditions Stakes Class C (3-y-o and up) £4,157 5f.........(3:45)

4464[3] BLYTON LAD 7-9-10 S Webster (1) *cl up, shaken up to ld entering last, ran on.*..... (11 to 10 on op 13 to 8 on) 1
4521[8] CRADLE DAYS 4-8-13 M Roberts (5) *led, rdn appr fnl furlong, hdd entering last, kpt on.* ....(3 to 1 op 4 to 1 tchd 9 to 2) 2
4549* INHERENT MAGIC (Ire) 4-9-0 A Clark (7) *trkd ldrs, rdn 2 fs out, kpt on ins last.*....(11 to 2 op 6 to 1 tchd 7 to 1) 3
4465 MEDAILLE D'OR (bl) 5-9-2 A Munro (4) *cl up, rdn 2 fs out, wknd appr last.*........(7 to 1 op 6 to 1 tchd 8 to 1) 4
4487* CALAMANCO 3-8-7 M Birch (6) *outpcd till hdwy 2 fs out, sn rdn and kpt on.*............(16 to 1 tchd 25 to 1) 5
4521[9] ANSELLMAN 3-8-9 (7*) Mark Denaro (2) *cl up, pushed alng bef hfwy and sn lost pl.*........(25 to 1 op 16 to 1) 6
4532[9] MAGIC PEARL 3-8-6 (7*) S Knott (8) *cl up, rdn hfwy, sn wknd.*............................(16 to 1 op 14 to 1) 7

Dist: 1½l, 2½l, ½l, 1l, ¾l, nk. 59.30s. a 2.60s (7 Ran).
SR: 83/66/57/57/44/50/46/ (Mrs J Addleshaw), M J Camacho

BATH (good)

Wednesday November 3rd
Going Correction: PLUS 0.10 sec. per fur.

4679 Extra Ordinary Maiden Stakes Class D (Div I) (2-y-o) £3,535 1m 5yds... (1:15)

4469[7] BROADWAY FLYER (USA) 9-0 Paul Eddery (12) *sn prmnt, led o'r 2 fs out, clr one out, cmftbly.* ....(4 to 1 op 2 to 1 tchd 9 to 2) 1
4089[7] KIROV ROYALE 8-9 A McGlone (1) *prmnt, ran on one pace o'r one furlong out, no ch wth wnr.* ....(14 to 1 tchd 33 to 1) 2
4396[2] MICROLITE (USA) 8-9 T Quinn (13) *led aftr 2 fs, hrd rdn and hdd o'r two out, no extr.* ....(11 to 8 fav op 5 to 4 tchd 6 to 4) 3
MOOFAJI 9-0 J Williams (6) *beh, ran on o'r 2 fs out, nvr nrr.*................................(8 to 1 op 5 to 1) 4
HONEY MOUNT 9-0 S Whitworth (2) *slwly into strd, rear till rdn and styd on fnl 2 fs, nvr nrr.* .... (8 to 1 op 6 to 1 tchd 10 to 1) 5
GOLDENBERRY 8-9 D Holland (10) *pld hrd, trkd ldrs, effrt 2 fs out, wknd appr last.*..........(10 to 1 op 4 to 1) 6
4595 UNISON 8-11 (3*) Stephen Davies (4) *led for 2 fs, sn lost pl, no prog fnl two furlongs.*......... (50 to 1 op 14 to 1) 7
JACKS TO OPEN (USA) 9-0 R Perham (9) *sn prmnt, wth ldr aftr 3 fs till wknd three out.* ....(20 to 1 op 14 to 1 tchd 25 to 1) 8
SOPHIE MAY 8-9 A Clark (8) *mid-div, no ch fnl 2 fs.* .... (50 to 1 op 14 to 1) 9
4002[7] GINGER JIM 9-0 J Weaver (11) *strted slwly, al beh.* ....(20 to 1 op 8 to 1) 10
4498 CLIFTON SET 9-0 D Harrison (7) *al beh.* ....(50 to 1 op 14 to 1) 11
4497 SILKY MAGNA 8-9 R Price (5) *al beh.* (33 to 1 op 14 to 1) 12
4496 CRYSTAL HEART (Ire) 8-9 M Wigham (3) *al beh.* ....(33 to 1 op 16 to 1) 13

Dist: 4l, 2l, ¾l, nk, 2l, ¾l, 5l, hd, 1½l, nk. 1m 45.10s. a 6.10s (13 Ran).
SR: 21/4/-/1/-/-/ (Mrs S Bosher), J W Hills

4680 Extra Ordinary Maiden Stakes Class D (Div II) (2-y-o) £3,509 1m 5yds...(1:45)

4579[3] DANGER POINT 9-0 A Munro (7) *tracking ldrs gng easily 3 fs out, led appr last, drvn out.*......(7 to 1 op 5 to 1) 1
4498[3] YOUNG CLIFFORD (USA) 9-0 T Quinn (10) *in ld 3 fs out, sn hrd rdn, hdd appr last, ran on.* ....(5 to 4 fav tchd 6 to 4 and 6 to 5) 2
4208[3] ASTRAL INVASION (USA) 9-0 J Reid (2) *wth ldrs 3 fs out, sn rdn and outpcd, kpt on ins last.* ....(7 to 1 op 6 to 1 tchd 8 to 1) 3
CANARY BLUE (Ire) 8-9 T Sprake (5) *ran on o'r one furlong out, nvr nrr.*.........................(25 to 1 op 20 to 1) 4
4541[3] ZUBOON (USA) 9-0 Paul Eddery (6) *second and chalg 3 fs out, sn hrd rdn, wknd appr last.* ....(9 to 4 op 5 to 2 tchd 3 to 1) 5
ZEETARO 9-0 B Procter (11) *ran on o'r one furlong out, nrst finish.*.............. (16 to 1 op 10 to 1) 6
4498 DRIMARD (Ire) 9-0 C Rutter (13)..... (33 to 1 op 16 to 1) 7
3166[9] MASURI KABISA (USA) 8-9 J Quinn (14) .... (25 to 1 op 33 to 1) 8
4595 DAKOTA GIRL 8-9 J Williams (4)..... (25 to 1 op 20 to 1) 9
4264 SECRATORIUS (Ire) 9-0 R Perham (15) ....(50 to 1 op 20 to 1) 10
4523 BOLD-MAX 9-0 A McGlone (12)...... (50 to 1 op 33 to 1) 11
RINGSIDE TICKET (USA) 9-0 M Hills (3) ....(20 to 1 op 12 to 1) 12
4497 VITE ETOILE 8-4 (5*) S Drowne (8)... (50 to 1 op 20 to 1) 13
CASSIO'S BOY 9-0 R Price (1)...... (25 to 1 op 20 to 1) 14
CHAMPION REEF 9-0 M Wigham (9) *tld off.* ....(25 to 1 op 20 to 1) 15

Dist: 1½l, 5l, ½l, 2l, 1l, 6l, ½l, nk, 2½l, 2l. (Time not taken) (15 Ran).
(Fahd Salman), R Hannon

4681 Extra Raceday Handicap Class D (0-80 3-y-o and up) £3,561 5f 161yds.. (2:15)

4518[9] CHAMPAGNE GRANDY [75] 3-9-4 (7*) R Painter (19) *rear till gd prog 2 fs out, led wl ins fnl furlong, ran on well.* ....(14 to 1 op 10 to 1) 1
4597[3] BLUE TOPAZE [70] 5-9-7 J Williams (18) *rear till gd prog o'r 2 fs out, led briefly ins fnl furlong, ran on.* ....(8 to 1 op 10 to 1 tchd 7 to 1) 2
4501[6] JIGSAW BOY [73] (v) 4-9-5 (5*) S Drowne (7) *prog 2 fs out, ev ch ins last, ran on.*......(7 to 1 op 6 to 1 tchd 8 to 1) 3
4485[4] EFRA [74] 4-9-11 S Raymont (13) *prog o'r one furlong out, ran on ins last.*........ (8 to 1 op 6 to 1 tchd 10 to 1) 4
4580[6] PATSY GRIMES [64] (bl) 3-9-0 T Quinn (12) *prmnt, led 2 fs out till entering last, wknd.*.......(14 to 1 op 16 to 1) 5
4532[2] CHOIR PRACTICE [75] 6-9-12 C Rutter (1) *rear till styd on o'r one furlong out, nrst finish.*... (12 to 1 op 10 to 1) 6
4580[2] LEIGH CROFTER [57] (bl) 4-8-8 G Hind (2) *led, rdn and hdd 2 fs out, sn btn.*... (11 to 2 fav op 5 to 1 tchd 13 to 2) 7
4574 NOEPROB (USA) [53] 3-8-3 J Quinn (8) *nvr nrr.* ....(33 to 1 tchd 50 to 1) 8
4549[5] CALL TO THE BAR (Ire) [77] 4-10-0 A Clark (9) *towards rear hfwy, nvr dngrs.*..................(14 to 1 op 10 to 1) 9

4518 BELLSABANGING [72] 3-9-8 G Duffield (11) *prmnt for 4 fs.* ......(14 to 1 op 10 to 1) 10
4465 HOPE HALL (Ire) [73] 5-9-10 A Culhane (14) *chsd ldrs for 4 fs.*......(20 to 1 tchd 25 to 1) 11
4277[7] ARAGROVE [76] 3-9-12 J Reid (4) *in tch hfwy, sn btn.* ......(14 to 1 op 10 to 1) 12
4501 DOUBLE SHIFT [60] 4-8-11 D Holland (17) *made no show.* ......(20 to 1 op 16 to 1 tchd 25 to 1) 13
4532* LOVE LEGEND [63] 8-9-0 A Munro (16) *cl up to hfwy.* ......(12 to 1 tchd 14 to 1) 14
4507[8] SIMPLY SOOTY [78] 3-10-0 J Weaver (6) *made no show.* ......(20 to 1 op 14 to 1 tchd 25 to 1) 15
4580 LETSBEONESTABOUTIT [64] (bl) 7-9-1 Paul Eddery (10) *prmnt till hfwy*......(20 to 1 op 14 to 1) 16
3778 FOLLOWMEGIRLS [57] 4-8-8 S Perks (3) *made no show.* ......(20 to 1 op 14 to 1 tchd 25 to 1) 17
4501 FIVESEVENFIVEO [67] 5-9-4 M Hills (5) *wth ldr till hfwy, wknd rpdly*......(20 to 1 op 14 to 1) 18
4501 FINJAN [76] 6-9-6 (7*) S McCarthy (15) *al beh, tld off.* ......(25 to 1 op 20 to 1 tchd 33 to 1) 19
Dist: ½l, nk, 2l, ½l, 1l, ½l, 1½l, ½l, ½l, ½l. (Time not taken) (19 Ran).
(Grandy Girls), M R Channon

4682 Extra Special Median Auction Maiden Stakes Class E (2-y-o) £3,006 5f 161yds......(2:45)

4452[2] PURPLE FLING 9-0 G Duffield (8) *led till rdn and hdd one furlong out, rallied to ld wl ins last, drvn out.* ......(11 to 10 on op 6 to 4 tchd 7 to 4) 1
4523[7] HUMBERT'S LANDING (Ire) 9-0 T Quinn (6) *al prmnt, rdn to ld one furlong out, hdd and no extr wl ins last.* ......(5 to 1 op 5 to 2) 2
4211[5] PUELLA BONA 8-9 D Holland (9) *wth ldrs, hrd rdn 2 fs out, wknd appr last*......(5 to 1 op 4 to 1) 3
4594[8] HIGH TYPHA 8-9 W Newnes (2) *chsd ldrs, rdn and kpt on one pace fnl 2 fs*......(16 to 1 op 12 to 1) 4
GOVERNORS BELLE 8-9 T Sprake (4) *beh till styd on frm o'r one furlong out, nrst finish*.... (16 to 1 op 14 to 1) 5
4523 MINNIE NORTH 8-9 M Hills (11) *prmnt till wknd 2 fs out.* ......(25 to 1 op 20 to 1) 6
4497 COURT SERENADE (v) 8-9 J Williams (1) *outpcd, neaver nrr*......(33 to 1 op 20 to 1) 7
FOREST SILK 8-9 A Culhane (7) *al rear.* ......(33 to 1 op 20 to 1) 8
4561[5] EVANRO (Ire) 9-0 J Reid (3) *chsd ldrs for 4 fs, wknd.* ......(11 to 2 op 5 to 1 tchd 6 to 1) 9
4503[4] BRUZ 9-0 S Perks (5) *chsd ldrs till hfwy, sn wknd.* ......(16 to 1 op 10 to 1) 10
4543 BLUE DOMAIN 9-0 Paul Eddery (10) *al wl beh.* ......(20 to 1 op 16 to 1) 11
Dist: Nk, 6l, ½l, 3½l, 1½l, 3l, ¾l, 4l, ½l, 12l. (Time not taken) (11 Ran).
(Cheveley Park Stud), Sir Mark Prescott

4683 Extra Helping Handicap Class E (0-70 3-y-o and up) £3,447 1m 5yds... (3:15)

4490[2] QUANTITY SURVEYOR [58] 4-9-6 T Quinn (6) *mid-div, rdn and prog 3 fs out, ran on strly ins last to ld fnl strds.* ......(9 to 2 fav op 7 to 2) 1
4563 HOOCHIECOOCHIE MAN (Ire) [59] 3-9-4 R Price (2) *mid-div, effrt and prog 3 fs out, rdn to ld appr last, hdd fnl strds.* ......(12 to 1 tchd 14 to 1 and 10 to 1) 2
4258[8] CASTING SHADOWS [51] 4-8-13 D Holland (1) *in ld 4 fs out, rdn and hdd 2 out, sn led ag'n, headed appr last, ran on.*......(9 to 1 op 6 to 1) 3
4101 BOLD ACRE [65] 3-9-3 (7*) S Mulvey (16) *prmnt gng easily hfwy, one pace fnl 2 fs.* ......(16 to 1 op 14 to 1 tchd 20 to 1) 4
4495[2] PUSEY STREET BOY [57] 6-9-5 Paul Eddery (9) *nvr nrr.* ......(5 to 1 tchd 6 to 1) 5
4574[3] MAI PEN RAI [44] 5-8-6 A Munro (8) *nvr nrr.* ......(10 to 1 op 7 to 1) 6
4623 PRECIOUS AIR (Ire) [54] 5-9-2 B Rouse (7) *rear, brght wide and effrt 3 fs out, nvr rch ldrs*... (14 to 1 tchd 16 to 1) 7
4156 DONTDRESSFORDINNER [46] 3-8-5 R Perham (13) *mid-div, effrt and rdn 3 fs out, wknd o'r one out.* ......(50 to 1 op 20 to 1) 8
2330[8] SALBYNG [54] 5-9-2 M Hills (11) *prmnt till hrd rdn and wknd 2 fs out*......(10 to 1 tchd 8 to 1) 9
4524[9] CUCKMERE VENTURE [47] 3-8-6 N Adams (5) *nvr dngrs.* ......(50 to 1 op 33 to 1) 10
4616[2] KNOBBLEENEEZE [63] (v) 3-9-1 (7*) R Painter (17) *prog and rdn o'r 3 fs out, led 2 out, sn hdd and wknd, eased.* ......(6 to 1 tchd 13 to 2) 11
4479[9] PALACE PARADE (USA) [46] 3-8-5 N Carlisle (18) *chasing ldrs hfwy, sn btn*......(33 to 1) 12
4355[6] CHAPKA (Ire) [57] (bl) 3-9-2 J Williams (10) *prmnt till wknd o'r 2 fs out*......(14 to 1 op 12 to 1) 13
1280[8] HITCHIN A RIDE [43] 6-8-2 (3*) M Fenton (4) *made no show.* ......(33 to 1) 14
4254 BOMBLET [65] 3-9-10 J Reid (15) *second hfwy, wknd o'r 2 fs out*......(20 to 1 op 16 to 1) 15
4191[4] JASARAH (Ire) [67] 3-9-12 A Clark (3) *chasing ldrs hfwy, sn wknd*......(14 to 1 op 10 to 1 tchd 16 to 1) 16
4536 KAPUCHKA (Ire) [47] 3-8-6 S Whitworth (12) *made no show.* ......(50 to 1 op 16 to 1) 17

4481 APACHE MYTH [59] 3-9-4 W Newnes (14) *tld off.* ......(14 to 1 op 10 to 1 tchd 16 to 1) 18
Dist: ½l, ½l, 3l, 2½l, 2l, 2l, sht-hd, ½l, ¾l, ½l. 1m 44.30s. a 5.30s (18 Ran).
SR: 39/35/28/30/17/-/2/-/-/ (A D Spence), R Akehurst

4684 Extra Time Handicap Class E (0-70 3-y-o and up) £3,080 2m 1f 34yds (3:45)

4519[3] SWORD MASTER [70] 4-10-0 M Wigham (8) *mid-div, prog 2 fs out, hrd rdn and ran on to ld wl ins last.* ......(13 to 2 op 7 to 2 tchd 7 to 1) 1
4353 ACCESS SUN [46] 6-8-4 T Quinn (11) *set slow early pace, hrd rdn and strly pressed 2 fs out, hdd wl ins last.* ......(12 to 1 op 10 to 1) 2
4559[7] ADDICTED TO LOVE [66] (bl) 4-9-10 T Sprake (12) *prmnt, ev ch 2 fs out, ran on ins last.* ......(6 to 1 op 4 to 1 tchd 7 to 1) 3
4466[7] ALLMOSA [60] 4-9-4 D Holland (4) *prmnt, rdn to chal 2 fs out, btn ins last*....(4 to 1 jt-fav op 5 to 1 tchd 7 to 2) 4
4519* MONARDA [70] 6-9-9 (5*) T G McLaughlin (6) *hld up early, nrst finish*......(4 to 1 jt-fav op 3 to 1 tchd 9 to 2) 5
4621[7] ZEALOUS KITTEN (USA) [56] 5-8-11 (3*) Stephen Davies (1) *chsd ldrs, effrt and rdn o'r 2 fs out, no imprsn.* ......(8 to 1 op 12 to 1) 6
4176 AMILLIONMEMORIES [54] 3-8-2 R Price (13) *hld up early, rdn and ev ch 3 fs out, sn btn*......(33 to 1 op 20 to 1) 7
4559 CITY LINE [47] 4-8-5 A Tucker (10) *chsd ldrs, rdn and no prog fnl 2 fs*......(12 to 1 op 8 to 1) 8
4466[8] GO SOUTH [58] 9-9-2 S Whitworth (7) *mid-div, no prog fnl 2 fs*......(12 to 1 op 10 to 1 tchd 14 to 1) 9
4353[3] CHILD STAR (Fr) [41] 4-7-13 S Dawson (2) *no ch fnl 3 fs.* ......(8 to 1 op 7 to 1) 10
4321[7] PATROCLUS [36] 8-7-8[1] N Adams (5) *al beh.* ......(20 to 1 tchd 25 to 1) 11
4256 KILLSHANDRA (Ire) [35] (v) 4-7-4[2] (5*) D Wright (14) *al beh.* ......(33 to 1) 12
4591 MEDIATOR [45] 4-8-3[1] A Clark (3) *trkd ldr early, no ch fnl 3 fs*......(25 to 1 op 20 to 1 tchd 33 to 1) 13
Dist: Hd, 1l, 3l, nk, 2l, nk, nk, sht-hd, 8l, 5l. (Time not taken) (13 Ran).
(Ian A Vogt), Bob Jones

CURRAGH (IRE) (good to yielding)
Wednesday November 3rd
Going Correction: PLUS 0.80 sec. per fur.

4685 Morny Wing Memorial Apprentice Handicap (0-75 3-y-o and up) £3,105 6f ......(1:00)

3606[9] SOUTHERN REVIEW (Ire) [-] (bl) 3-8-12 (4*) I Browne (4) ......(16 to 1) 1
4407 MATCHLESS PRINCE (Ire) [-] 3-8-8 (4*) S P Cooke (22) ......(25 to 1) 2
4370 MASTER WORK [-] (bl) 5-7-7 P P Murphy (6)......(12 to 1) 3
4534[3] NOBLE SAM (Ire) [-] 4-7-13[1] (2*) T J Daly (20)......(10 to 1) 4
4245 ANOTHER SKY-LARK (Ire) [-] 5-9-0 (2*) A P McCoy (23) ......(25 to 1) 5
4245 BAVARIAN BALLAD (Ire) [-] 3-8-6 (4*) D O'Callaghan (18) ......(2 to 1 fav) 6
4385[9] SAMOT (Ire) [-] 3-9-6 (4*) W J Walsh (9)......(12 to 1) 7
4385[5] MACQUARIE RIDGE (USA) [-] 5-8-4 (2*) T E Durcan (17) ......(6 to 1) 8
4635* HAWAIAN TASCA (Ire) [-] 4-7-5 (2*,5ex) G M Moylan (2) ......(7 to 1) 9
4534[8] BRACKLOON BOY (Ire) [-] 4-9-4 (2*) P O Casey (1) (14 to 1) 10
4534 RAFFERTY'S INNER (Ire) [-] 3-9-1 (2*) R T Fitzpatrick (7) ......(12 to 1) 11
4534 BONNIFER (Ire) [-] 4-9-1 (4*) A Ward (15)......(20 to 1) 12
4625[5] COMMON BOND (Ire) [-] 3-9-10 (2*) B Fenton (13)..(8 to 1) 13
4586 ICANSEEFORMILES (Ire) [-] 5-7-3 (4*) D J Newman (5) ......(12 to 1) 14
4583 FRIAR STREET (Ire) [-] (bl) 3-9-4 (4*) J P Cornally (8) (20 to 1) 15
4370 SUNBED SUE (Ire) [-] 3-8-1[1] (2*) P J Smullen (14)...(8 to 1) 16
4389* DAIRINE'S DELIGHT (Ire) [-] 3-8-6 D J O'Donohoe (11) ......(6 to 1) 17
4386[7] SYDNEY SUSSEX (Ire) [-] (bl) 3-9-1 (2*) M W Martin (12) ......(25 to 1) 18
4534[5] LHOTSE (Ire) [-] 3-9-0 (4*) M Cornally (10)......(12 to 1) 19
4408 BARNAGEERA BOY (Ire) [-] 4-8-4 (2*) B J Halligan (19) ......(10 to 1) 20
3419[8] VERITABLE GALLERY (Ire) [-] 3-8-8 (2*) G Coogan (3) ......(12 to 1) 21
4370 NEWYORK CONNECTION (Ire) [-] 3-7-12 (4*) D Cullen (16) ......(33 to 1) 22
4635[8] FIVE LITTLE GIRLS (Ire) [-] 3-8-5 (2*) P M Donohue (21) ......(16 to 1) 23
Dist: Hd, sht-hd, nk, ½l. 1m 18.20s. a 7.70s (23 Ran).
SR: 44/39/19/25/39/-/ (Noel Carter), Kevin Prendergast

4686 Getting Out EBF Race (3-y-o and up) £3,795 7f...... (1:30)

4552[2] DIAMONDS GALORE (Can) 8-8-11 P Shanahan (9) (3 to 1) 1
4386* DINESEN 3-9-4 R Hughes (8)......(6 to 4 fav) 2
4287[3] HIGH TYCOON (Ire) 3-8-3 (6*) D J O'Donohoe (7)...(7 to 2) 3
MAJBOOR (Ire) 4-8-11 P V Gilson (6)......(14 to 1) 4

4410[4] BAJAN QUEEN (Ire) 3-8-6 W J Supple (4)..........(8 to 1) 5
2184[7] MADAME MINISTER (USA) 3-8-2 (4*) J J Behan (2) (20 to 1) 6
4583[8] CORTIJA PARK (Ire) 3-8-5 (6*) P P Murphy (5).....(10 to 1) 7
4384 DIFFERENT TIMES (Ire) 3-9-0 S Craine (1)........(10 to 1) 8
4554 OVERCAST (Ire) 3-8-11 W J O'Connor (3)........(20 to 1) 9
Dist: ¾l, 2½l, ¾l, 1l. 1m 31.90s. a 8.70s (9 Ran).
SR: 51/56/39/39/31/-/ (Frank Stronach), D K Weld

4687 Eyrefield EBF Race (Listed) (2-y-o) £8,625 1m 1f.................. (2:00)

4382[2] CITY NIGHTS (Ire) 8-10 P Shanahan (4) *mid-div, trkd ldrs entering strt, led one furlong out, easily*....(2 to 1 fav) 1
4582[8] NEW TRIBE (Ire) 8-10 S Craine (5) *last till hfwy, chsd ldrs 2 fs out, ran on und pres fnl furlong*............(20 to 1) 2
4360[6] METROELLA (Ire) 8-10 C Roche (6) *prog 2 fs out, styd on ins last*..................................(10 to 1) 3
4581* LAKE KARIBA 8-13 P V Gilson (12) *trkd ldrs, rdn one and a half fs out, styd on*..........................(8 to 1) 4
4553[7] ANSARIYA (USA) 8-10 R Hughes (11) *led till rdn and hdd one furlong out, no extr ins last*................(5 to 1) 5
4553[4] NEWPORT MADAM (Ire) 8-7 J F Egan (8) *prog frm mid-div to chase ldrs 3 fs out, sn rdn and btn*..........(6 to 1) 6
4093* SWIFT RIPOSTE (Ire) (bl) 9-1 K J Manning (3) *wl plcd till rdn and wknd 2 fs out*..............................(4 to 1) 7
4406[2] CLOUD INSPECTOR (Ire) 8-10 W J Supple (7) *rear, rdn and btn 2 fs out*....................................(8 to 1) 8
4553[8] COSSACK PRINCESS (Ire) 8-7 J J Behan (1) *nvr nr to chal.* ....(25 to 1) 9
4553[9] ACROSS THE TRACKS (Ire) 8-7 Joanna Morgan (10) *wl plcd till rdn and wknd 3 fs out*.....................(25 to 1) 10
4462 AVONDALE FOREST (Ire) 8-7 N G McCullagh (9) *mid-div till rdn and wknd 3 fs out*.........................(25 to 1) 11
Dist: 5½l, ¾l, hd, ¾l. 2m 0.70s. a 11.20s (11 Ran).
SR: 36/25/23/25/20/-/ (Rachid Damania), D K Weld

4688 End Of Season (C&G EBF) Maiden (2-y-o) £5,244 7f.................. (2:30)

4382[8] SHARP TRY (Ire) 8-10 (4*) J J Behan (22).........(8 to 1) 1
POETICAL JUSTICE (Ire) 9-0 P Shanahan (16).....(8 to 1) 2
3922[9] MUZRAK (Can) 9-0 W J Supple (12).............(12 to 1) 3
4406[3] NIYAZI (Ire) 9-0 D Hogan (19)...................(11 to 2) 4
4581[2] BAYDUR (Ire) 8-8 (6*) D J O'Donohoe (8).....(5 to 1 jt-fav) 5
4380[7] IXWORTH 9-0 P V Gilson (9)................(5 to 1 jt-fav) 6
4637[9] HOW'S IT GOIN (Ire) 8-8 (6*) R V Skelly (6)........(20 to 1) 7
4581[7] SIMAFAR (Ire) 9-0 R Hughes (14)..................(11 to 2) 8
4359[5] CAIRNBRAE (Ire) (bl) 9-0 J F Egan (13).............(8 to 1) 9
4380 KNIGHT OF VISION (Ire) 9-0 C Roche (17)........(12 to 1) 10
4535[6] HI HANDSOME (Ire) 9-0 N G McCullagh (18)......(10 to 1) 11
4609 STRANGFORD LOUGH (Ire) 8-13[3] (4*) C Everard (21) ....(33 to 1) 12
4380 BURKEAN MELODY (Ire) 9-0 Joanna Morgan (4)..(20 to 1) 13
4637[8] RULING LIGHT (Ire) 8-6 (8*) G Coogan (15).......(12 to 1) 14
4460[5] WOODY 9-0 S Craine (20)..........................(8 to 1) 15
4609[9] CAPITAL GAIN 9-0 K J Manning (1)...............(16 to 1) 16
4609[7] SUBTLE BRIEF (Ire) 8-8 (6*) P P Murphy (3)........(16 to 1) 17
4359[8] JINGLING SILVER (Ire) (bl) 8-6 (8*) J J Mullins (5)..(25 to 1) 18
4609 YOU ARE MY HERO (Ire) 9-0 D Manning (7)......(16 to 1) 19
JUMPCREST (Ire) 8-6 (8*) R T Fitzpatrick (11).....(25 to 1) 20
MASTER SHOWMAN (Ire) 9-0 W J O'Connor (10) (12 to 1) 21
4609 SUPER TRIG (Ire) 9-0 P Lowry (2)...................(33 to 1) 22
Dist: Nk, 1l, 1l, nk. 1m 31.80s. a 8.60s (22 Ran).
SR: 55/54/51/48/47/-/ (Marvin Malmuth), Liam Browne

4689 Newbridge Handicap (0-90 3-y-o and up) £3,105 6f.................. (3:00)

4408[3] THREE MUSKETEERS (Ire) [-] 4-7-13[2] N G McCullagh (13) ....(14 to 1) 1
4583 ROBERTOLOMY (USA) [-] 4-8-13[1] (4*) C Everard (9) ....(14 to 1) 2
4056[2] PEARL DAWN (Ire) [-] 3-9-0 (8*) R T Fitzpatrick (1)..(8 to 1) 3
4284 HANG A RIGHT [-] 6-8-12[1] (6*) T P Treacy (7).....(10 to 1) 4
4554[6] SEEK THE FAITH (USA) [-] (bl) 4-8-13 (6*) D J O'Donohoe (2) ....(8 to 1) 5
4583[2] FOREST CONCERT (Ire) [-] (bl) 4-9-7 (4*) J J Behan (18) ....(5 to 2 fav) 6
4583[9] BENE MERENTI (Ire) [-] (bl) 3-9-3 (6*) R V Skelly (5) (12 to 1) 7
4385[2] PETITE EPAULETTE [-] 3-8-10 (8*) G M Moylan (15) (10 to 1) 8
4635[4] AURLIANO (Ire) [-] 3-7-8 (6*) P P Murphy (14).....(14 to 1) 9
4635[2] MAGIC DON (Ire) [-] 4-9-0 P Lowry (3)............(14 to 1) 10
4635[5] TODDY MARK (Ire) [-] (bl) 4-7-2 (8*) B J Halligan (16) ....(25 to 1) 11
4534 BELMARTIN [-] 7-8-6 (10*) A C O'Brien (6)........(16 to 1) 12
4583[7] KURDISTAN (Ire) [-] 3-10-2 (4ex) W J O'Connor (11) (10 to 1) 13
3544[9] FAIRY BRIDE (Ire) [-] 3-7-12[5] Joanna Morgan (12) (20 to 1) 14
4245 JOSH'S BEN (Ire) [-] 4-8-6 W J Supple (10)........(5 to 1) 15
4583 MARY'S CASE (Ire) [-] (bl) 3-8-10 J F Egan (17)....(20 to 1) 16
4556[9] ARROGANT LADY [-] (bl) 3-7-10[1] (8*) P M Donohue (8) ....(20 to 1) 17
3497[9] ALASKAN GIRL (Ire) [-] 3-8-12 S Craine (4).......(20 to 1) pu
Dist: 1l, 1l, ¾l, ¾l. 1m 17.50s. a 7.00s (18 Ran).
SR: 41/54/56/48/47/-/ (D P Kelly), D P Kelly

4690 Last Chance (EBF) Maiden (3-y-o) £3,450 1½m.................. (3:30)

4556[4] ANDANTE (Ire) (bl) 8-11 P V Gilson (15)..............(8 to 1) 1
4429[2] KADASSA (Ire) 8-11 D Hogan (6)............(5 to 1 jt-fav) 2
4410[2] GLENSTAL FLAGSHIP (Ire) 9-0 C Roche (10) (5 to 1 jt-fav) 3
4429[5] DRUMS OF FREEDOM (USA) 8-11 R Hughes (17) (10 to 1) 4
4429 BISSTAMI (Ire) 9-0 B Coogan (18)...................(25 to 1) 5
4556[6] NA-AMMAH (Ire) 8-11 W J Supple (4)............(10 to 1) 6
4556[2] NANNAKA (USA) 8-7 (4*) J J Behan (8)............(6 to 1) 7
MUSCOVY DUCK (Ire) 8-11 S Craine (16)..........(8 to 1) 8
2810[4] KYRENIA 8-11 N G McCullagh (14)................(12 to 1) 9
944[3] POLITICAL DOMAIN (Ire) 9-0 P Shanahan (3)......(6 to 1) 10
4429[4] HERMES GOLD (Ire) 8-3 (8*) I Browne (7).........(10 to 1) 11
4429[6] SERANERA (Ire) 8-5 (6*) P P Murphy (11)..........(16 to 1) 12
4625 KERRYKEEL LADY (Ire) 8-3 (8*) G M Moylan (13)..(33 to 1) 13
4556 MERSADA (Ire) 8-11 K J Manning (1)...............(6 to 1) 14
4625[8] DO-TELL-ME (Ire) 8-3 (8*) R T Fitzpatrick (9).......(33 to 1) 15
4137[6] HAWTHORN ROSE (Ire) 8-3 (8*) P J Smullen (2)...(20 to 1) 16
4407 CHARTY (Ire) 8-8 (6*) B J Walsh (12)..............(33 to 1) 17
SIESTA TIME (USA) 8-11 W J O'Connor (5).......(10 to 1) 18
Dist: 3l, 2l, 1½l, hd. 2m 45.70s. a 16.20s (18 Ran).
SR: 31/25/24/18/20/-/ (Patrick O'Leary), Patrick O'Leary

ST-CLOUD (FR) (soft)
Wednesday November 3rd
Going Correction: PLUS 0.55 sec. per fur.

4691 Prix Amandine (Listed) (3-y-o) £14,337 1m............................ (1:50)

4473[2] SEATTLE VICTORY (USA) 8-9 G Guignard,............... 1
4169[2] LA GROUPIE (Fr) 8-9 O Doleuze,........................ 2
PROSPECTIVE PRINCE (USA) 8-9 F Sanchez,............ 3
4362* BASHAYER (USA) 8-9 W Carson, *led till jst und 2 fs out, ran on one pace*.................................... 4
Dist: ¾l, 4l, 1½l, 1½l, ¾l, 2l, dd-ht. 1m 44.50s. a 6.00s (8 Ran).
SR: 71/69/57/52/ (C Stelling), D Smaga

DONCASTER (good)
Thursday November 4th
Going Correction: PLUS 0.20 sec. per fur. (races 1,2,6,7), PLUS 0.10 (3,4,5)

4692 Have Your Wedding Here Maiden Fillies' Stakes Class D (Div I) (2-y-o) £3,465 7f..................... (1:05)

4539[4] REALIZE 8-11 R Cochrane (4) *nvr far away, quickened to ld one furlong out, ran on strly*......(7 to 1 op 9 to 2) 1
4453[2] HEATHYARDS LADY (USA) 8-11 S Perks (5) *tucked away in midfield, gng wl hfwy, swtchd wide o'r one furlong out, fnshd fst*..................(16 to 1 op 14 to 1) 2
LATIFOLIA 8-11 L Piggott (11) *made most, hdd and rdn one furlong out, kpt on same pace.* ....(11 to 4 fav op 7 to 2 tchd 5 to 2) 3
FABULOUS FAIRY (USA) 8-11 W Ryan (8) *tucked away, effrt and drvn alng on outsd o'r 2 fs out, styd on.* ....(5 to 1 op 7 to 2) 4
DALU (Ire) 8-11 S Whitworth (1) *al hndy, drvn alng whn pace quickened o'r 2 fs out, one pace.* ....(10 to 1 op 12 to 1) 5
2044[3] SAMHEH (USA) 8-11 W Carson (7) *wth ldr, ev ch and drvn alng o'r one furlong out, fdd*....... (7 to 2 op 2 to 1) 6
SALSIFIS (Ire) 8-11 W Newnes (2) *co'red up in midfield, outpcd hfwy, kpt on wl, prmsg*.... (25 to 1 op 16 to 1) 7
BLUE ISLE (Ire) 8-11 G Duffield (3) *outpcd and struggling hfwy, nvr able to rch ldrs*..........................(33 to 1) 8
SHALLOP 8-11 M Birch (13) *sn struggling to go pace, nvr nr to chal*..........................(16 to 1 op 14 to 1) 9
4523[6] PERICARDIA 8-11 J Reid (10) *co'red up on ins, not much room and swtchd wide over 2 fs out, sn outpcd.* .... (8 to 1 op 10 to 1 tchd 12 to 1) 10
GREEN JANNAT (USA) 8-11 D Harrison (9) *outpcd and drvn alng, nvr a factor*................ (8 to 1 op 6 to 1) 11
LINDY BELLE 8-11 Paul Eddery (6) *chsed alng in midfield hfwy, sn lost tch*................(33 to 1 op 25 to 1) 12
4446 MANATEE 8-11 M Tebbutt (12) *last and struggling thrght, tld off last 2 fs*.................. (33 to 1 op 25 to 1) 13
Dist: 2½l, nk, hd, 1½l, 3½l, ½l, 1½l, nk, hd, 4l. 1m 29.28s. a 5.88s (13 Ran).
SR: 30/22/21/20/15/4/2/-/-/ (Lord Hartington), J H M Gosden

4693 New Racecourse Banqueting Facilites Handicap Class D (0-80 3-y-o and up) £3,845 6f..................... (1:35)

3906 EDUCATED PET [69] 4-8-10 (7*) S Sanders (21) *tucked away stands side, brst through 2 fs out, kpt on wl to ld last 50 yards*......................(20 to 1 op 16 to 1) 1
4507[4] DOMICKSKY [72] 5-8-13 (7*) R Painter (10) *chsd alng to improve centre hfwy, effrt whn hmpd o'r one furlong out, rallied to ld ins last, ct last 50 yards.* .... (11 to 1 op 12 to 1 tchd 10 to 1) 2
4580[4] CRAIGIE BOY [52] (bl) 3-7-13 F Norton (2) *swtchd rght strt, led centre o'r 2 fs out till ins last, one pace.* ....(14 to 1 op 10 to 1) 3

4640 BECKYHANNAH [48] (bl) 3-7-9^{7} (5*) A Garth (14) *chsd alng to improve centre last 2 fs, fnshd wl.* ....(20 to 1 tchd 25 to 1) 4

4458 OBSIDIAN GREY [60] 6-8-3 (5*) D McCabe (8) *chsd alng centre, ran on last 2 fs, fnshd wl.* (20 to 1 tchd 25 to 1) 5

4606^{3} PANIKIN [69] (bl) 5-9-3 M Birch (6) *sluggish strt, reco'red to show speed centre for over 4 fs, no extr.* .... (8 to 1 op 10 to 1) 6

4507^{7} THE SHARP BIDDER (Ire) [68] 3-9-1 S Perks (17) *wth stands side ldrs 4 fs, no extr.*.... (20 to 1 op 16 to 1) 7

4455 METAL BOYS [80] 6-10-0 W Newnes (11) *settled stands side, effrt and pushed alng o'r 2 fs out, kpt on same pace*.... (25 to 1 op 20 to 1) 8+

4415 SHARP PROSPECT [73] 3-9-6 W Ryan (15) *beh, drvn alng stands side hfwy, styd on appr fnl furlong, nvr nrr.* .... (12 to 1 op 10 to 1) 8+

3896^{5} FAY'S SONG (Ire) [58] 5-8-6 D Harrison (13) *led centre till o'r 2 fs out, no extr*.... (8 to 1 op 7 to 1 tchd 10 to 1) 10

4532^{3} SADDLEHOME (USA) [60] 4-8-8 R Cochrane (1) *rcd alone far side, al wl plcd, not quicken appr fnl furlong.* .... (9 to 1 op 8 to 1) 11

4580* BAYIN (USA) [59] 4-8-7 (7ex) R Street (5) *beh and drvn alng hfwy, styd on last 2 fs, nrst finish.* .... (5 to 1 fav op 4 to 1 tchd 11 to 2) 12

4606^{4} DENSBEN [75] 9-9-9 L Piggott (20) *sluggish strt, improved into midfield hfwy, kpt on, nvr able to chal.* .... (14 to 1 op 12 to 1 tchd 20 to 1) 13

4681 LETSBEONESTABOUTIT [64] (bl) 7-8-12 Paul Eddery (16) *pressed ldrs centre, bustled alng o'r 2 fs out, fdd.* .... (25 to 1 op 20 to 1) 14

3404 SOUTHERN MEMORIES (Ire) [79] 3-9-12 J Reid (4) *settled wth centre grp, shaken up o'r 2 fs out, not rch ldrs.* .... (16 to 1 tchd 20 to 1) 15

4487^{9} JOE SUGDEN [45] 9-7-7 Kim McDonnell (18) *speed stands side till fdd o'r 2 fs out*.... (25 to 1 op 20 to 1) 16

4331^{9} STRIP CARTOON (Ire) [53] 5-8-1^{1} G Hind (9) *chsd alng to show speed centre for o'r 3 fs*.... (25 to 1 op 20 to 1) 17

USHBA (Fr) [55] 5-8-3 G Duffield (19) *speed stands side for o'r 3 fs*.... (33 to 1) 18

3988 WADERS DREAM (Ire) [62] 4-8-5 (5*) J Marshall (7) *in tch, struggling hfwy, fdd*.... (33 to 1) 19

4109 ORIENT AIR [54] 5-7-13 (3*) N Kennedy (3) *reared strt, reco'red aftr 2 fs to show speed centre, fdd.* .... (25 to 1 op 20 to 1) 20

ROUGH GUESS (Ire) [46] 3-7-5^{5} (7*) L Suthern (12) *unruly strt, missed break, al struggling*... (50 to 1 op 33 to 1) 21

Dist: Hd, 1½l, 1½l, hd, 2l, nk, hd, dd-ht, nk, hd. 1m 15.13s. a 3.73s (21 Ran).

SR: 52/54/27/17/29/30/27/39/31/ (Mrs E J Williams), P D Evans

4694 New St Leger Banqueting Suite Handicap Class D (0-75 3-y-o and up) £3,933 1m.... (2:05)

4600 EVER SO LYRICAL [58] 3-8-11 Paul Eddery (10) *settled off the pace, rapid hdwy last 2 fs, kpt on strly to ld last 50 yards*.... (20 to 1 op 16 to 1) 1

4633^{4} MOVE SMARTLY (Ire) [50] 3-8-0 (3*) N Kennedy (14) *al hndy, led wl o'r one furlong out, ran on und pres, ct last 50 yards*.... (14 to 1 op 12 to 1) 2

4633* MASTER BEVELED [47] 3-7-7 (7*) S Sanders (12) *pld hrd in midfield, effrt and rdn o'r 2 fs out, styd on wl fnl furlong*.... (7 to 1 tchd 10 to 1) 3

4536 KARINSKA [62] 3-9-1 L Piggott (4) *tucked away in midfield, swtchd lft and hmpd o'r 2 fs out, rallied fnl furlong*.... (14 to 1 op 16 to 1) 4

4600^{3} MARIUS (Ire) [61] 3-9-0 D Harrison (5) *pushed up frm midfield to chal last 2 fs, styd on same pace.* .... (10 to 1 op 7 to 1) 5

4633^{5} GLOWING JADE [61] 3-8-7 (7*) R Painter (6) *str hold, settled gng wl hfwy, ev ch till no extr o'r one furlong out.* .... (6 to 1 op 10 to 1) 6

4563^{7} PORT SUNLIGHT (Ire) [69] 5-9-11 J Reid (18) *settled on outsd, effrt o'r 2 fs out, styd on one pace.* .... (14 to 1 op 10 to 1) 7

4605^{6} RETENDER (USA) [58] 4-9-0 W Ryan (1) *patiently rdn, not clr run o'r 3 fs out, weaved through frm 2 out, nrst finish*.... (7 to 1 tchd 8 to 1) 8

4623^{5} BUDDY'S FRIEND (Ire) [56] 5-8-5 (7*) Sarah Thompson (13) *co'red up in midfield, effrt on ins over 2 fs out, one pace*.... (20 to 1 op 16 to 1) 9

4643^{8} SELF EXPRESSION [62] 5-8-11 (7*) D Thomas (8) *settled off the pace, effrt and drvn alng o'r 2 fs out, not pace to chal*.... (12 to 1 op 10 to 1) 10

3850^{7} WAHEM (Ire) [61] (bl) 3-9-0 R Cochrane (9) *slight ld till o'r one furlong out, fdd*.... (16 to 1 op 14 to 1) 11

4514^{7} KUMMEL KING [53] 5-8-2 (7*) S Knott (2) *wth ldrs, wkng whn squeezed for room o'r 2 fs out.* (20 to 1 op 16 to 1) 12

LAKE DOMINION [58] 4-9-0 M Birch (17) *prmnt on outsd till fdd o'r 2 fs out*.... (25 to 1) 13

4616^{5} TAKENHALL [50] 8-8-6 F Norton (16) *struggling to keep up entering strt, nvr a factor*.... (16 to 1) 14

4623 WILD PROSPECT [49] (v) 5-8-5 G Duffield (19) *dsptd ld to strt, fdd und pres o'r 2 fs out*.... (25 to 1) 15

4458^{5} FORT VALLY [50] 3-8-3 N Connorton (7) *tucked away on ins, not clr run o'r 3 fs out, not rcvr.* .... (20 to 1 op 16 to 1) 16

4565* SIMAAT (USA) [69] 3-9-8 W Carson (11) *sluggish strt, beh and drvn alng hfwy, nvr a threat.* .... (5 to 1 fav op 4 to 1) 17

4488* DON'T JUMP (Ire) [70] 3-9-2 (7*) S Mulvey (15) *sluggish strt, reco'red to press ldrs aftr 2 fs, fdd over two out.* .... (14 to 1) 18

4348 MONTONE (Ire) [48] (bl) 3-8-1^{1} G Hind (3) *beh, imprvg on ins whn not much room o'r 3 fs out, nvr dngrs.* (33 to 1) 19

Dist: ¾l, 2½l, hd, 1½l, ¾l, ½l, nk, 1½l, sht-hd, 5l. 1m 41.04s. a 4.34s (19 Ran).

SR: 44/34/23/37/31/29/38/26/19/ (The Pendley Punters), P W Harris

4695 New St Leger Bar Handicap Class E (0-70 3-y-o and up) £3,131 1¾m 132yds.... (2:35)

4631^{5} LOOKINGFORARAINBOW (Ire) [67] 5-10-0 M Wigham (6) *al gng wl, hdwy on ins to ld 2 fs out, pushed out.* .... (9 to 2 op 5 to 1) 1

4621^{6} KEYLOCK (USA) [59] 3-8-8 (3*) N Kennedy (3) *wth ldr, led entering strt to 2 fs out, styd on same pace.* .... (9 to 1 op 8 to 1) 2

4662^{6} MILNGAVIE (Ire) [45] 3-7-11 W Carson (10) *settled off the pace, improved into midfield entering strt, styd on und pres fnl furlong*.... (14 to 1 op 12 to 1 tchd 16 to 1) 3

4357^{5} LA MENORQUINA (USA) [61] 3-8-13 R Cochrane (11) *settled to track ldg trio, drvn alng last 2 fs, kpt on same pace.* .... (6 to 1 tchd 13 to 2) 4

4603^{2} FAMOUS BEAUTY [42] 6-7-12 (5*) A Garth (2) *nvr far away, feeling pace and drvn alng o'r 2 fs out, not quicken.* .... (9 to 1 op 8 to 1) 5

4445^{7} FOOLS ERRAND (Ire) [65] 3-9-3 J Reid (5) *trkd ldg 4, hrd drvn o'r 2 fs out, no extr*.... (6 to 1 tchd 13 to 2) 6

SWEET NOBLE (Ire) [48] 4-8-9 Paul Eddery (9) *chsd ldrs, struggling o'r 2 fs out, fdd*.... (20 to 1) 7

4426* BOLD ELECT [51] 5-8-12 A Culhane (7) *trkd ldrs, drvn alng o'r 2 fs out, sn btn*... (7 to 2 fav op 4 to 1 tchd 9 to 2) 8

4538^{7} ADMINISTER [49] (bl) 5-8-10 G Hind (8) *last and drvn alng entering strt, nvr a factor*.... (33 to 1) 9

1195^{9} NOTABLE EXCEPTION [44] 4-8-5 G Duffield (4) *chsd ldg 6, struggling 3 fs out, sn btn*.... (9 to 1 op 8 to 1) 10

4344^{6} BROCTUNE BAY [67] 4-10-0 M Birch (1) *led till entering strt, lost tch quickly last 2 fs*.... (13 to 2 op 6 to 1) 11

Dist: 1½l, ¾l, 3l, 4l, 2l, hd, 3l, 3l, 7l, 3l. 3m 13.75s. a 9.25s (11 Ran).

SR: 36/16/-/10/-/2/ (B M Saumtally), Bob Jones

4696 Have Your Christmas Party Here Maiden Stakes Class D (3-y-o) £3,435 1¼m 60yds.... (3:05)

4525^{3} FAIR SHIRLEY (Ire) 8-9 S Whitworth (4) *nvr far away, drvn to ld o'r one furlong out, styd on und pres.* .... (8 to 1 op 6 to 1) 1

4565^{7} FIRE CARPET (USA) 9-0 G Hind (1) *trkd ldrs, feeling pace and drvn alng o'r 3 fs out, styd on wl fnl furlong, nvr nrr*.... (8 to 1 tchd 9 to 1) 2

4590^{5} GEORDIE SONG 8-9 W Ryan (6) *al hndy, led 4 fs out till o'r one out, kpt on same pace last 100 yards.* .... (6 to 1 op 9 to 2) 3

4565^{8} SAMAH 9-0 F Norton (11) *patiently rdn, hdwy whn hng lft o'r 2 fs out, ran green, kpt on wl fnl furlong.* .... (10 to 1 op 8 to 1 tchd 11 to 1) 4

4209^{2} FAWARAN (USA) 9-0 W Carson (13) *ran in snatches, effrt and drvn alng o'r 2 fs out, styd on same pace fnl furlong*.... (3 to 1 fav op 2 to 1) 5

4493^{4} FIRM BUT FAIR 9-0 R Cochrane (5) *trkd ldrs gng wl, stumbled o'r 5 fs out, effrt whn not much room over 2 out, kpt on finish*.... (6 to 1 op 9 to 2) 6

4622^{3} RAMIYA 8-9 M Birch (8) *wl plcd on outsd, struggling o'r 3 fs out, sn btn*.... (7 to 1 op 6 to 1 tchd 8 to 1) 7

4490 HAYDON BRIDGE (Ire) 9-0 Paul Eddery (12) *wth ldr, led 5 fs out to 4 out, fdd o'r 2 out*.... (33 to 1) 8

4599^{7} VILLAGE GREEN (Fr) 9-0 J Reid (7) *pld hrd in midfield, effrt and hng lft und pres o'r 2 fs out, sn btn.* .... (8 to 1 op 10 to 1 tchd 16 to 1) 9

4525^{9} KATIE'S KID 9-0 D Harrison (9) *in tch, drvn alng to keep up o'r 3 fs out, sn lost touch*.... (33 to 1) 10

4544 REJECTS REPLY 8-9 (5*) D McCabe (3) *sluggish strt, last and drvn alng hfwy, nvr a factor*.... (33 to 1) 11

4493 HARQUIN 9-0 G Duffield (2) *slight ld to 5 fs out, fdd und pres frm 3 out*.... (25 to 1 op 33 to 1) 12

4622^{6} HIGH FINISH 8-9 W Newnes (10) *patiently rdn, improved entering strt, lost tch quickly o'r 2 fs out.* .... (11 to 1 op 10 to 1) 13

Dist: 1l, 1l, 1l, ½l, nk, 20l, 1½l, ½l, ¾l, 15l. 2m 13.55s. a 6.85s (13 Ran).

SR: 37/40/33/36/35/34/ (Sheikh Ahmed Al Maktoum), A C Stewart

4697 Have Your Wedding Here Maiden Fillies' Stakes Class D (Div II) (2-y-o) £3,435 7f.... (3:35)

RAWYA (USA) 8-11 D Harrison (10) *chsd alng to go pace hfwy, hdwy o'r one furlong out, ran on to ld last 100 yards*.... (8 to 1 op 7 to 1 tchd 9 to 1) 1

LADY LODGER 8-11 G Duffield (2) *patiently rdn, effrt and not clr run o'r one furlong out, swtchd lft, kpt on wl nr finish*.... (14 to 1 op 12 to 1) 2

4588[2] SHEPPARD'S CROSS 8-11 M Birch (9) *steadied strt, settled gng wl on ins hfwy, not clr run and swtchd o'r one furlong out, ran on, unlucky*........(6 to 1 op 7 to 2) 3
4614[3] ASTE NAGUSIA (USA) 8-11 W Ryan (12) *tucked away in midfield, effrt and swtchd lft hfwy, led o'r one furlong out, hdd and no extr last 100 yards.* .... (Evens fav op 6 to 5 tchd 5 to 4) 4
4440 DIABAIG 8-11 R Cochrane (4) *made most for o'r 5 fs, fdd.* ....(9 to 2 op 6 to 1 tchd 8 to 1) 5
DAME LORRAINE 8-11 J Reid (13) *nvr far away, edgd lft last 2 fs, no extr fnl furlong*..........(10 to 1 op 8 to 1) 6
COLIN'S PRIDE 8-11 M Tebbutt (5) *sluggish strt, improved hfwy, styd on, nvr nrr*............(33 to 1 op 20 to 1) 7
4594[6] KATHYS RAINBOW 8-11 G Hind (1) *dsptd ld, drvn alng 2 fs out, fdd*..........................(50 to 1 op 33 to 1) 8
4542 NORTHWISE (Ire) 8-11 W Newnes (6) *nvr far away, feeling pace o'r 2 fs out, fdd*................(50 to 1 op 20 to 1) 9
WHITE LODGE (USA) 8-11 Paul Eddery (8) *co'red up beh ldrs, hng lft und pres hfwy, sn btn*...(8 to 1 op 5 to 1) 10
GOOD EVANS 8-11 A Culhane (3) *sn struggling to go pace, lost tch hfwy*.....................(50 to 1 op 20 to 1) 11
3738[9] PIZZAZZ 8-11 F Norton (11) *wth ldrs, struggling to hold pl 2 fs out, tld off*...................(33 to 1 op 20 to 1) 12

Dist: ¾l, nk, 1½l, 5l, 2½l, 1½l, ½l, 3l, 1½l, 5l. 1m 29.83s. a 6.43s (12 Ran).

SR: 22/20/19/14/-/-/ (K Al-Said), B W Hills

4698 Book Early For Christmas Median Auction Maiden Stakes Class E (2-y-o) £3,624 1m..................... (4:05)

4252[5] EUROLINK CHIEFTAIN 9-0 W Ryan (10) *swtchd to stands side strt, in tch, effrt and rdn 2 fs out, sstnd run to ld ins last, kpt on wl.* (11 to 8 fav op 5 to 4 tchd 6 to 4) 1
4620[3] GOLDEN ARROW (Ire) 9-0 R Cochrane (19) *al prmnt stands side, led hfwy, quickened o'r one furlong out, hdd ins last, rallied*............ (5 to 2 op 4 to 1 tchd 9 to 4) 2
4421 WILCUMA 9-0 W Newnes (2) *dwlt, in tch far side, effrt hfwy, led grp ins fnl furlong, no ch wth stands side.* ....(33 to 1) 3
FARRINGDON HILL 9-0 B Procter (4) *prmnt, led far side grp o'r 4 fs out till ins last, no extr.* (33 to 1 op 25 to 1) 4
4526[4] LINCOLN TREASURE (Ire) 9-0 M Wigham (9) *cl up far side, effrt and rdn o'r 2 fs out, no extr ins last*..... (33 to 1) 5
FLAMINGO TIMES 8-9 D Harrison (22) *cl up stands side, outpcd and drvn alng o'r 2 fs out, kpt on same pace ins last*..................................(33 to 1 op 25 to 1) 6
4220[7] GINKA 8-9 M Birch (17) *in tch centre, shaken up 3 fs out, one pace frm 2 out*................ (33 to 1 op 20 to 1) 7
4421 ROMAN CAMP (Fr) 9-0 D Biggs (11) *in tch stands side, pushed alng o'r 3 fs out, one pace 2 out.* ....(20 to 1 op 16 to 1) 8
4543 CHIMANIMANI 9-0 S Whitworth (8) *swtchd rght strt, co'red up beh ldrs, shaken up 3 fs out, not rch frnt rnk.* ....(33 to 1 op 25 to 1) 9
4099[7] ELSDON (Ire) 8-7 (7*) S Mulvey (13) *beh stands side, sn pushed alng, improved o'r one furlong out, kpt on, nvr dngrs*...............................(20 to 1 op 16 to 1) 10
4595 IVANHOE 9-0 R Street (20) *beh stands side, rdn alng hfwy, no imprsn last 2 fs*.......................(33 to 1) 11
4240[9] DOCKMASTER 9-0 G Hind (21) *slwly into strd stands side, sn in tch, pushed alng hfwy, btn 2 fs out*..... (33 to 1) 12
4641[2] LAUNCHSELECT 9-0 Paul Eddery (15) *led stands side grp to hfwy, hng lft and no extr fnl 2 fs*........... (14 to 1) 13
DARK THOUGHTS 8-9 M Tebbutt (14) *pressed ldrs stands side, pushed alng o'r 3 fs out, wknd*..........(33 to 1) 14
PRUSSIA 9-0 G Duffield (16) *rear stands side, rdn alng hfwy, nvr able to chal*............(16 to 1 op 14 to 1) 15
4542[6] LUCAYAN CAY (Ire) 9-0 J Reid (18) *settled midfield stands side, shaken up o'r one furlong out, nvr nr to chal.* ....(14 to 1 op 12 to 1) 16
3969[5] YENGEMA 8-9 N Connorton (5) *chsd far side ldrs, effrt and rdn o'r 2 fs out, wknd*.......................(20 to 1) 17
SIR DICKIE COX (Ire) 8-11 (3*) N Kennedy (1) *led far side grp till o'r 4 fs out, sn lost pl*.......................(33 to 1) 18
JARAAB 9-0 W Carson (3) *slwly into strd, beh far side, drvn hfwy, nvr on terms*...........(7 to 1 tchd 9 to 1) 19
4437[8] SAN DIEGO CHARGER (Ire) 9-0 F Norton (12) *dwlt, beh stands side, rdn alng o'r 3 fs out, sn btn*.......(33 to 1) 20
3781 BROOKS MASQUERADE 8-2 (7*) Mark Denaro (6) *trkd far side ldrs, rdn alng o'r 3 fs out, fdd*........... (33 to 1) 21
4492[9] LADY TJONGER 8-4 (5*) K Rutter (7) *rcd far side, in tch on outsd, rdn and wknd quickly 3 fs out*.........(33 to 1) 22

Dist: Nk, 4l, 1l, 2l, sht-hd, 6l, hd, 1l, 1l, nk. 1m 42.90s. a 6.10s (22 Ran).

SR: 33/32/20/17/11/5/ (Eurolink Group Plc), J L Dunlop

EDINBURGH (good)
Thursday November 4th

Going Correction: PLUS 0.25 sec. per fur. (race 1), PLUS 0.35 (2,3,4,5,6)

4699 EBF Tennents 80 Shilling Ale Rating Related Maiden Stakes Class E (0-70 2-y-o) £3,046 5f................ (1:00)

4444[8] MAKE THE BREAK 9-0 T Quinn (2) *chsd ldrs, rdn and hdwy 2 fs out, styd on to ld ins last, ran on.* ....(9 to 4 fav op 6 to 4 tchd 5 to 2) 1
4642[3] ORIENTAL AIR (Ire) 8-9 J Quinn (1) *chaseed ldrs, rdn one and a half fs out, styd on ins last*....(5 to 2 op 7 to 2) 2
4512[6] MONKEY MAGIC (Ire) (bl) 9-0 J Carroll (7) *led to hfwy, sn rdn and kpt on one pace.* .... (11 to 4 op 9 to 4 tchd 3 to 1) 3
4452[7] RED GRIT (Ire) (bl) 8-9 J Weaver (5) *cl up, led hfwy, rdn and edgd lft entering last, sn hdd and wknd.* .... (33 to 1 op 25 to 1) 4
4358 MARBLE 8-4 (5*) Darren Moffatt (4) *sn outpcd and beh, styd on und pres fnl 2 fs, nvr dngrs.* ....(20 to 1 op 14 to 1) 5
4237[7] BEE DEE BEST (Ire) 9-0 Dale Gibson (6) *sn outpcd and beh.* .... (17 to 2 op 6 to 1 tchd 9 to 1) 6
4608[8] CELTIC GOVERNESS 8-9 J Fortune (3) *chsd ldrs, rdn 2 fs out and sn btn*..................(16 to 1 op 14 to 1) 7

Dist: 2½l, ½l, 1½l, 1½l, 2½l, 1½l. 1m 2.20s. a 4.40s (7 Ran).

SR: 37/22/25/14/8/3/-/ (Mrs J Reglar), R Hannon

4700 Tennents November Handicap Class E (0-70 3-y-o and up) £3,582 1m 7f 16yds........................... (1:30)

4530[3] MINGUS (USA) [37] 6-8-1 J Quinn (8) *hld up and beh, steady hdwy o'r 4 fs out, effrt 2 furlongs out, led entering last, pushed clr.* ....(9 to 2 op 5 to 1 tchd 6 to 1 and 4 to 1) 1
4086[6] AMERICAN HERO [60] 5-9-10 J Weaver (9) *led, rdn 2 fs out, hdd and not quicken entering last*...(8 to 1 op 7 to 1) 2
4218 GREAT ORATION (Ire) [33] (v) 4-7-11 L Charnock (5) *hld up and beh, hdwy hfwy, effrt 2 fs out and sn rdn, kpt on fnl furlong*..........................(14 to 1 tchd 16 to 1) 3
4433[3] MOONSHINE DANCER [43] 3-7-7 (5*) Darren Moffatt (4) *hld up, hdwy on outer 6 fs out, rdn o'r 2 furlongs out and sn one pace*......................(11 to 4 fav op 9 to 4) 4
4374 MUFID (USA) [45] 4-8-9 J Lowe (1) *prmnt, rdn alng and drpd rear 6 fs out, styd on und pres fnl 3 furlongs, nvr dngrs*..(33 to 1) 5
4433* FOLLINGWORTH GIRL (Ire) [57] 3-8-5 (7*) C Teague (10) *prmnt, effrt to chal and ev ch o'r 2 fs out, sn rdn and wknd wl over one furlong out.* ....(3 to 1 op 11 to 4 tchd 100 to 30) 6
4643 RAPID MOVER [37] (bl) 6-8-1 G Bardwell (11) *chsd ldrs, effrt and hdwy 3 fs out, rdn and wknd 2 furlongs out.* ....(16 to 1 op 14 to 1) 7
3056 CARA'S PRIDE [63] 3-9-4 Dale Gibson (3) *prmnt till lost pl and beh frm hfwy*.....................(14 to 1 op 12 to 1) 8
4432 J P MORGAN [40] (v) 5-8-4 J Fortune (6) *in tch, pushed alng 6 fs out, effrt and rdn 3 furlongs out, wknd 2 furlongs out*.......... (9 to 1 op 8 to 1 tchd 10 to 1) 9
2800[8] LORD ADVOCATE [37] (v) 5-7-8 (7*) C Adamson (2) *chsd ldrs, till wknd o'r 5 fs out, sn beh.* (20 to 1 op 16 to 1) 10

Dist: 3½l, hd, 2½l, 1l, ½l, 4l, 1l, 2½l, 8l. 3m 26.80s. a 14.80s (10 Ran).

SR: -/11/-/-/-/-/ (A Antonelli), R F Fisher

4701 EBF Tennents Lager Maiden Stakes Class D (2-y-o) £3,810 1m 16yds (2:00)

4541[2] STASH THE CASH (Ire) 9-0 S Raymont (7) *trkd ldrs, not clr run o'r 2 fs out, swtchd ins and hdwy to ld inside last, cmftbly*........ (11 to 10 fav op 6 to 4 on tchd 5 to 4) 1
AIR COMMODORE 9-0 T Quinn (6) *prmnt, effrt to ld 2 fs out, rdn appr fnl furlong, hdd and no extr ins last.* ....(2 to 1 op 3 to 1) 2
4480[5] FORENSIC EVIDENCE (Ire) 9-0 J Lowe (3) *hld up, hdwy and not clr run o'r 2 fs out, swtchd wide and rdn whn edgd rght entering last, kpt on*...... (6 to 1 op 4 to 1) 3
4365 ALL IN THE MIND 9-0 A Mackay (4) *in tch, hdwy on outer and ev ch o'r 2 fs out, sn rdn and one pace.* ....(14 to 1 op 10 to 1) 4
4427[3] CRISTAL SPRINGS 8-9 J Quinn (8) *al prmnt, effrt and ev ch o'r 2 fs out, sn rdn and wknd*...(33 to 1 op 25 to 1) 5
4491[4] GREETLAND HALL 9-0 J Weaver (9) *beh, effrt and some hdwy 3 fs out, nvr a factor*.......... (12 to 1 op 10 to 1) 6
4342 DENTON QUEEN 8-9 S Webster (5) *beh and pushed alng wide strt*...................................(100 to 1) 7
4215 STARSPORT (Ire) (v) 9-0 J Carroll (1) *chsd ldrs, effrt and ev ch o'r over 2 fs out, sn rdn and wknd.* ....(33 to 1 op 25 to 1) 8
4492[7] MONSIEUR BLEU 9-0 J Fortune (2) *sn led, rdn and hdd 2 fs out, soon wknd*.................... (33 to 1 op 25 to 1) 9

Dist: 1l, 1½l, 4l, 5l, 1½l, 2l, 3½l, 2½l. 1m 45.40s. a 6.90s (9 Ran).

SR: 38/35/30/18/-/-/ (J G Davis), R Hannon

4702 Tennents Special Handicap Class E (0-70 3-y-o and up) £2,905 1m 16yds ....(2:30)

4652[9] GUESSTIMATION (USA) [49] 4-8-9 G Bardwell (5) *hld up, gd hdwy o'r 2 fs out, rdn to ld wl ins last, ran on.* ....(8 to 1 op 7 to 1) 1
3812* BALLYRANTER [53] (v) 4-8-13 J Quinn (10) *al prmnt, effrt and rdn to ld one and a half fs out, hng rght, hdd and no extr wl ins last*...... (5 to 1 op 6 to 1 tchd 9 to 2) 2

3780[8] SPRING FLYER (Ire) [53] 3-8-10 J Carroll (2) *chsd ldrs, effrt and rdn 2 fs out, kpt on ins last.* (14 to 1 tchd 16 to 1) 3
4605[7] SPANISH VERDICT [65] 6-9-4 (7*) C Teague (12) *mid-div, gd hdwy on inner 2 fs out, styd on strly ins last, nrst finish*..........................(16 to 1 op 14 to 1) 4
3408 SKOLERN [35] 9-7-9[2] L Charnock (14) *led, rdn and hdd one and a half fs out, hmpd entering last, not reco'r.* ....(20 to 1) 5
4490[5] LAWNSWOOD JUNIOR [68] 6-10-0 T Quinn (6) *mid-div, gd hdwy o'r 3 fs out, rdn and wknd wl over one furlong out*.............................(4 to 1 fav op 7 to 2) 6
4536[6] INFANTRY GLEN [50] (v) 3-8-7 A Mackay (8) *al mid-div.* ....(9 to 1 op 7 to 1 tchd 10 to 1) 7
4623[3] EAST BARNS (Ire) [37] (bl) 5-7-11 Dale Gibson (11) *in tch, effrt o'r 2 fs out, sn rdn and btn*..... (5 to 1 op 3 to 1) 8
4241 MELODYS DAUGHTER [41] (bl) 3-7-8[3] (7*) M Humphries (3) *chsd ldrs, rdn 3 fs out, sn wknd*... (16 to 1 op 14 to 1) 9
4343 INVERTIEL [54] (bl) 9-9-0 S Webster (7) *nvr rch ldrs.* ....(14 to 1 op 12 to 1) 10
4085* THISONESFORALICE [37] 5-7-11 J Lowe (9) *al rear.* ....(8 to 1 op 7 to 1) 11
4640 MISS HOSTESS [33] (bl) 6-7-1[1] (7*) C Adamson (15) *in tch, effrt and hdwy 2 and a half fs out, rdn and wknd wl o'r one furlong out*..................................(50 to 1) 12
4640 VALLEY OF TIME (Fr) [33] 5-7-3[3] (7*) Claire Balding (13) *cl up till rdn and wknd o'r 2 fs out*.................(50 to 1) 13
4213 ANNE'S BAY (Ire) [36] 3-7-3[1] (5*) Darren Moffatt (16) *cl up till rdn and wknd 3 fs out*.......... (400 to 1 op 100 to 1) 14
4241 FRIENDLY KNIGHT [42] 3-7-6 (7*) F Savage (4) *slwly away, al beh*..(33 to 1) 15
Dist: 2l, 1l, 1l, 1½l, hd, 2l, hd, 3l, ½l, 1½l. 1m 45.20s. a 6.70s (15 Ran).
SR: 36/34/28/40/5/37/10/-/-/ (Quintet Partnership), J Pearce

4703 Tennents Aitkens Ale Maiden Auction Stakes Class F (2-y-o) £2,668 7f 15yds ....(3:00)

4577[2] WESTERN FLEET (USA) 9-0 S Raymont (7) *in tch, hdwy 2 fs out, edgd rght appr fnl furlong, rdn to ld wl ins last.* ....(3 to 1 op 9 to 4 tchd 2 to 1) 1
4480[4] UP IN FLAMES (Ire) 9-0 R Perham (8) *cl up, led hfwy, rdn appr fnl furlong, hdd and no extr wl ins last.* ....(5 to 1 op 4 to 1) 2
4526[3] KID ORY 9-0 Dale Gibson (1) *prmnt, rdn 2 fs out, hmpd appr fnl furlong, kpt on.* ....(5 to 1 op 4 to 1 tchd 11 to 2) 3
4587[4] ROYAL CREST 9-0 T Quinn (4) *led, hdd hfwy, rdn and wndrd appr fnl furlong, sn wknd.* ....(5 to 2 fav op 7 to 2 tchd 5 to 1) 4
4613[8] CAZANOVE'S PET 8-9 J Lowe (3) *beh, effrt and hdwy 2 fs out, kpt on one pace*.............. (33 to 1 op 25 to 1) 5
3993[3] ENCHANTEUR 8-9 J Weaver (6) *al rear.* ....(4 to 1 op 9 to 4 tchd 9 to 2) 6
4318[5] LEADING PRINCESS (Ire) 8-9 J Fortune (2) *in tch, rdn alng hfwy, sn wknd*....................(33 to 1 op 25 to 1) 7
4527[9] LITTLE BROWNIE 8-9 J Carroll (5) *chsd ldrs till rdn and wknd 2 and a half fs out.* ....(10 to 1 op 8 to 1 tchd 12 to 1) 8
Dist: ½l, 3l, 2l, ½l, 2½l, 1l, 10l. 1m 32.40s. a 7.20s (8 Ran).
SR: 29/27/18/12/5/ (Dr Susan Barnes), R Hannon

4704 Ladbrokes On-course Fillies' Handicap Class D (0-80 3-y-o and up) £3,078 1½m 31yds....................(3:30)

4486 MAHAASIN [40] 5-8-2 A Mackay (3) *hld up, hdwy o'r 3 fs out, led 2 and a half furlongs out, sn drvn clr.* ....(10 to 1 op 14 to 1 tchd 20 to 1) 1
4604* PRINCESS TATEUM (Ire) [65] 3-9-6 (5ex) T Quinn (4) *prmnt, effrt and ev ch o'r 2 fs out, sn rdn and one pace.* ....(6 to 4 fav op 5 to 4 tchd 7 to 4) 2
4548 SHIRLEY ROSE [73] 3-10-0 J Weaver (6) *led 4 fs, lost pl and beh hfwy, styd on wl fnl 2 furlongs.* ....(100 to 30 op 9 to 4 tchd 7 to 2) 3
4374 TRUBEN (USA) [66] 4-9-9 (5*) Darren Moffatt (1) *cl up, rdn 3 fs out, sn btn*..............(9 to 1 op 7 to 1 tchd 10 to 1) 4
2355[5] FOINERY [66] 3-9-7 J Carroll (5) *cl up, led aftr 4 fs, rdn 3 furlongs out, sn hdd and wknd*......(5 to 1 op 3 to 1) 5
4426 APACHE SQUAW [50] 3-8-5 J Quinn (2) *hld up, hdwy o'r 3 fs out, sn rdn and wknd 2 furlongs out.* ....(10 to 1 op 8 to 1) 6
Dist: 7l, nk, 2½l, 3½l, 6l. 2m 44.20s. a 11.40s (6 Ran).
SR: 17/21/28/23/9/-/ (Mrs Joan Cosgrove), A Bailey

GOWRAN PARK (IRE) (good to yielding)
Thursday November 4th

4705 Kilkenny E.B.F. Fillies Maiden (Div I) (2-y-o) £3,450 7f..............(12:50)

RUVOLINA (Ire) 9-0 P Shanahan (8)...............(5 to 2) 1
ALALIYA (Ire) 9-0 D Hogan (6)....................(10 to 1) 2
4582 GRACEFUL RESIGN 9-0 N G McCullagh (4)...... (10 to 1) 3
MARALIYKA (Ire) 9-0 R Hughes (7)............(9 to 4 fav) 4
LIFFEY'S SECRET (USA) 9-0 K J Manning (1)...... (4 to 1) 5
MOBILE MISS (Ire) 9-0 S Craine (11)..............(8 to 1) 6
ARDRESS (Ire) 8-6 (8*) R T Fitzpatrick,...........(33 to 1) 7
4406[8] DAY LIGHT (Ire) 9-0 P V Gilson (3)................(8 to 1) 8
4624[9] GRENNAN CLASSIC (Ire) 9-0 M G Cleary (14).....(25 to 1) 9
SIOG (Ire) 8-10 (4*) W J Smith (2)................(20 to 1) 10
4388[9] CAN'T AFFORD IT (Ire) 9-0 W J O'Connor (15).... (12 to 1) 11
4610 GESHA (Ire) 8-6 (8*) T E Durcan (13)............. (20 to 1) 12
4582 TALAHARI (Ire) 9-0 J F Egan (12)................ (20 to 1) 13
ILE VERTE (Ire) 9-0 R Dolan (9)...................(8 to 1) 14
3451 HELLS BELLS (Ire) (bl) 8-8 (6*) B J Walsh,........ (33 to 1) 15
Dist: ¾l, sht-hd, 6l, 2l. 1m 34.80s. (15 Ran).
(Andrea Schiavi), D K Weld

4706 Kilkenny E.B.F. Fillies Maiden (Div II) (2-y-o) £3,450 7f................(1:20)

4582[4] CONTINUOUS (Ire) 8-8 (6*) D J O'Donohoe (10).... (7 to 2) 1
DAFTIYNA (Ire) 9-0 R Hughes,................(6 to 4 fav) 2
SIREN (Ire) 9-0 S Craine (4)........................(3 to 1) 3
4135[2] ALMOST A LADY (Ire) 9-0 P V Gilson (3)..........(10 to 1) 4
3541[9] APPEARANCE MONEY (Ire) 9-0 W J Supple (2)... (20 to 1) 5
SEALAKE (Ire) 9-0 P Shanahan (5)..................(8 to 1) 6
4624[8] BE GIVING (Ire) 9-0 N G McCullagh (12)..........(10 to 1) 7
4535 ACRABOY LADY (Ire) 8-6 (8*) G M Moylan (11).....(8 to 1) 8
4610 LATCH ON (Ire) 9-0 W J O'Connor (1)............ (16 to 1) 9
4624[7] MODEL SHOW (Ire) 9-0 A O'Rourke,.............(20 to 1) 10
4610[7] CRIMSON CITY (Ire) 8-10 (4*) J J Behan (8).......(10 to 1) 11
4535 MIYOKO (Ire) 8-10 (4*) W J Smith (9).............(14 to 1) 12
4261 NOBODYS CHILD (Ire) 9-0 M G Cleary (13).......(25 to 1) 13
MOORFIELD DAISY (Ire) 9-0 J F Egan (7).........(25 to 1) 14
4388 FOUR DUSTY ROADS (Ire) 9-0 Yvonne Dillon (6).. (33 to 1) 15
Dist: Sht-hd, 1l, hd, 6l. 1m 35.80s. (15 Ran).
(Michael W J Smurfit), D K Weld

4707 Lower Grange Nursery (2-y-o) £2,760 1m...........................(1:50)

4146* ARTEMA (Ire) [-] 9-5 P Shanahan (3).............. (5 to 1) 1
4551[5] OUT IN THE SUN (USA) [-] 8-0 (6*) R V Skelly (6).... (9 to 2) 2
4551* ZAVALETA (Ire) [-] 9-7 (8*,8ex) A P McCoy (10)..(4 to 1 fav) 3
3922[5] SHANKAR (Ire) [-] 9-0 W J O'Connor (5)..........(10 to 1) 4
4551[3] EUPHORIC (Ire) [-] 8-7 P V Gilson (12)..............(6 to 1) 5
4262[7] JOMACOON (Ire) [-] 8-9 K J Manning (8)......... (12 to 1) 6
4609[5] COLLECTOR GENERAL (Ire) [-] 7-9 (6*) P P Murphy (16) ....(14 to 1) 7
4462 TRIMBLEMILL (Ire) [-] 8-3 (8*) R T Fitzpatrick (7)...(20 to 1) 8
4406[6] SCHONBEIN (Ire) [-] 8-1[2] W J Supple (1).........(10 to 1) 9
4262[3] MASCOT [-] 8-10 J F Egan (15)..................(10 to 1) 10
4405[9] NORDIC COLOURS (Ire) [-] 7-3 (10*) D Quirke,.....(25 to 1) 11
4360[4] RUDI'S PRIDE (Ire) [-] 8-3 N G McCullagh (9)......(10 to 1) 12
4551[9] MEGLIO CHE POSSO (Ire) [-] 7-5 (8*) B J Halligan (4) ....(20 to 1) 13
4551 KAKASHDA (Ire) [-] 7-10 (2*) D G O'Shea,........ (12 to 1) 14
4582[9] NORTHREEL [-] 8-0 (4*) J J Behan (13)...........(14 to 1) 15
Dist: 1l, sht-hd, 2l, sht-hd. 1m 45.50s. (15 Ran).
(Saleh Y Al-Homaisi), D K Weld

LINGFIELD (A.W) (std)
Thursday November 4th
Going Correction: MINUS 0.05 sec. per fur.

4708 Capricorn Rating Related Maiden Stakes Class F (2-y-o) £1,907 6f (1:15)

4416 PHONEAHOLIC (Ire) (bl) 9-0 B Rouse (7) *made virtually all, hrd rdn o'r one furlong out, hld on cl hme.* ....(6 to 1 tchd 4 to 1 and 13 to 2) 1
4251 BILLIE GREY 8-9 A Munro (13) *wl in tch, rdn and outpcd 2 fs out, ran on ins fnl furlong, fnshd well.* ....(5 to 1 tchd 6 to 1) 2
4210[5] VENUS VICTORIOUS (Ire) 8-9 M Hills (12) *pressed wnr most of way, ev ch 2 fs out, not quicken ins fnl furlong.* ....(7 to 2 op 4 to 1 tchd 5 to 1 and 3 to 1) 3
4269 SALTCORN (Ire) 9-0 D Holland (8) *ldg grp, rdn and styd on one pace ins fnl furlong*...........(25 to 1 op 16 to 1) 4
4350[3] SWITCH BLADE (Ire) (bl) 8-9 S O'Gorman (5) *in tch, not quicken appr fnl furlong, styd on nr finish.* ....(8 to 1 op 5 to 1) 5
4618[2] REMINISCENCE (Ire) 8-9 A McGlone (11) *mid-div, effrt und pres fnl furlong, eased whn btn last 50 yards.* ....(9 to 4 fav op 2 to 1 tchd 7 to 4 and 5 to 2) 6
4564 JOBISDUN (bl) 9-0 N Carlisle (1) *sn outpcd.* ....(25 to 1 op 14 to 1 tchd 33 to 1) 7
4482[5] ROYAL INTERPRETER (v) 8-9 (5*) D Wright (10) *rear most of way*................................ (20 to 1 op 12 to 1) 8
4484[4] KING BRUCE 8-11 (3*) Emma O'Gorman (3) *outpcd.* ....(12 to 1 op 7 to 1 tchd 14 to 1) 9
4264[7] GAELIC STAR (Ire) 8-7 (7*) L Aspell (2) *chsd ldg grp til rdn and wknd ins last 2 fs.* ....(20 to 1 op 14 to 1 tchd 25 to 1) 10
4577[8] LONE RISK 9-0 E Guest (6) *al outpcd.* ....(33 to 1 op 20 to 1) 11
4480 OUR STELLA 8-9 S Wood (4) *outpcd.* (33 to 1 op 20 to 1) 12
4594 CURBRIDGE (Ire) 9-0 N Adams (9) *missed break, al beh.* ....(33 to 1 op 20 to 1) 13
4484[8] MITSIS 9-0 C Rutter (14) *mid-div to hfwy, wknd quickly.* ....(20 to 1 op 16 to 1) 14

Dist: Nk, hd, 1l, nk, 2l, 3½l, hd, 4l, 1½l, 1l. 1m 15.87s. a 5.07s (14 Ran).
(K Higson), B J Meehan

4709 Scorpio Nursery Class E (2-y-o) £2,040 5f. . . . . (1:45)

4484² SULITELMA (USA) [59] 7-10¹ S O'Gorman (2) *handily plcd, bumped o'r one furlong out, ran on to ld last 100 yards.* . . . .(11 to 4 fav op 5 to 2 tchd 3 to 1) 1
4228⁸ RANDOM [56] 7-5⁵ (7*) C Hawksley (7) *slwly into strd, prog frm 2 fs out, str run fnl furlong, fnshd wl.* . . . . (25 to 1 op 20 to 1) 2
4613⁹ DANCE FOCUS [84] 9-4 (3*) Emma O'Gorman (3) *hld up towards rear, smooth run o'r one furlong out, led ins fnl furlong, sn hdd and one pace.* (8 to 1 tchd 7 to 1) 3
4528 TUTU SIXTYSIX [60] 7-6 (5*) D Wright (6) *hld up, ran on und pres fnl furlong, not quicken nr finish.* . . . .(4 to 1 tchd 5 to 1) 4
3871⁷ LOVESCAPE [71] 8-8 D Holland (9) *led, slightly hmpd o'r one furlong out, hdd and no extr ins fnl furlong.* . . . . (9 to 1 op 8 to 1 tchd 10 to 1) 5
4436 FLOATING TRIAL [67] (v) 8-4 A Munro (10) *ldg grp till rdn and edgd lft and rght o'r one furlong out, sn btn.* . . . . (11 to 2 op 6 to 1) 6
4632⁹ HOLLINGTON SONG [56] 7-0 (7*) Antoinette Armes (4) *chsd ldrs, rdn and ev ch wl o'r one furlong out, outpcd ins fnl furlong.* . . . . (33 to 1) 7
4416 TWICE IN BUNDORAN (Ire) [74] 8-11 M Hills (8) *chsd ldrs for o'r 3 fs, sn btn.* . . . .(6 to 1 op 5 to 1) 8
4339⁴ SMOOTH HOUND [61] 7-12¹ A McGlone (5) *sn rdn alng, beh hfwy, tld off.* . . . . (6 to 1 op 4 to 1) 9
Dist: ½l, nk, 1½l, nk, 2l, ½l, ¾l, 15l. 1m 1.44s. a 3.24s (9 Ran).
SR: 12/7/34/4/14/2/-/4/-/ (Miss K Rausing), I A Balding

4710 Richard E. Meyer Handicap Class D (0-75 3-y-o and up) £3,611 1m. . . (2:15)

4616⁴ KINGCHIP BOY [53] (v) 4-8-9 A Tucker (3) *wl plcd, led o'r 3 fs out, sn clr, rdn out.* . . . .(100 to 30 jt-fav op 3 to 1 tchd 7 to 2) 1
4164⁶ OUR EDDIE [52] (v) 4-8-3 (5*) B Russell (11) *hdwy hfwy, chsd wnr frm 2 fs out, kpt on one pace.* . . . . (14 to 1 op 12 to 1) 2
4007⁷ WAVE HILL [67] (v) 4-9-4 (5*) T G McLaughlin (8) *mid-div, ran on last 2 fs, not rch wnr.* . . . .(100 to 30 jt-fav op 3 to 1 tchd 7 to 2) 3
4518 CITY ROCKET [67] (v) 3-9-6 M Hills (12) *led aftr one furlong, hdd o'r 3 out, one pace last 2 fs.* . . . .(14 to 1) 4
4131 THE LITTLE FERRET [67] 3-9-6 B Rouse (5) *ldg grp, rdn and outpcd o'r 2 fs out.* . . . . (10 to 1 op 8 to 1 tchd 11 to 1) 5
1502⁵ QUINZII MARTIN [55] 5-8-11 T Williams (1) *hld up, moderate effrt 2 fs out, not rch ldrs.* . . . . . (14 to 1 op 12 to 1) 6
2382⁴ SARUM [51] 7-8-7 C Rutter (6) *wl in tch til outpcd o'r 3 fs out.* . . . . (7 to 1 op 10 to 1 tchd 6 to 1) 7
4092 SYLVAN SABRE (Ire) [72] (v) 4-10-0 A Munro (9) *strted slwly, al beh.* . . . .(10 to 1 op 8 to 1 tchd 12 to 1) 8
3325* GALLANT JACK (Ire) [58] 4-8-9 (5*) D Wright (7) *nvr on terms.* . . . . (13 to 2 op 5 to 1 tchd 7 to 1) 9
3887 PIGALLE WONDER [57] 5-8-13 A Clark (2) *led for one furlong, rdn and wknd o'r 3 out.* . . . . . .(16 to 1 op 12 to 1) 10
4164 APPEALING TIMES (USA) [62] 4-9-4 S Wood (4) *pressed ldrs till lost pl hfwy.* . . . .(14 to 1) 11
3102⁴ CALL ME BLUE [68] 3-9-7 D Holland (10) *slwly into strd, sn rdn to track ldg grp, wknd frm 3 fs out.* . . . .(10 to 1 tchd 12 to 1) 12
Dist: 5l, 4l, 1½l, 3½l, 3½l, 1½l, 2l, hd, hd, 1½l. 1m 41.16s. a 4.96s (12 Ran).
SR: 15/-/2/-/-/-/ (Four Jays Racing Partnership), M J Ryan

4711 Leo Claiming Stakes Class F (3-y-o and up) £1,553 1½m. . . . .(2:45)

4457⁷ DANCING DIAMOND (Ire) 3-7-9 (5*) B Russell (8) *hld up in tch, led o'r 3 fs out, rdn clr last 2 furlongs.* . . . .(4 to 1 op 3 to 1 tchd 9 to 2) 1
4611² BUSMAN (Ire) 4-8-12 D Holland (2) *hld up towards rear, hdwy o'r 3 fs out, styd on into second pl ins fnl furlong.* . . . .(7 to 2 jt-fav op 4 to 1 tchd 3 to 1) 2
1237² AWESOME POWER 7-9-10 M Hills (14) *hld up, hdwy o'r 4 fs out, chsd wnr 2 out till rdn and no extr ins fnl furlong.* . . . . (7 to 2 jt-fav tchd 5 to 1) 3
4603⁹ SIR EDWARD HENRY (Ire) (bl) 3-8-11 R Lappin (1) *led til hdd o'r 3 fs out, sn outpcd.* . . . . (16 to 1 op 12 to 1) 4
4506⁹ DONIA (USA) 4-8-8 (5*) D Wright (11) *improved frm rear on outsd 4 fs out, rdn and no imprsn last 2 furlongs.* . . . . (9 to 1 op 6 to 1 tchd 10 to 1) 5
4431⁹ PLAIN SAILING (Fr) 3-9-0 A Munro (10) *in tch, rdn alng hfwy, no hdwy last 3 fs.* . . . .(16 to 1 op 12 to 1 tchd 20 to 1) 6
3840⁵ SLEEPTITE (Fr) 3-8-8 A McGlone (9) *settled in mid-div, rdn and one pace 3 fs out.* . . . .(10 to 1 op 6 to 1) 7
4335⁹ CORDILLERO 7-8-9 B Rouse (12) *ldg grp til rdn and wknd appr last 3 fs.* . . . .(14 to 1 op 10 to 1) 8
4481⁸ KNYAZ 3-8-11 N Carlisle (4) *mid-div, no prog frm hfwy.* . . . .(14 to 1) 9
3957 KENESHA (Ire) (e/s) 3-8-6 T Williams (6) *nvr on terms.* . . . . (9 to 1 op 5 to 1 tchd 10 to 1) 10
3985⁸ APPLIANCEOFSCIENCE 6-8-10 (5*) P McCabe (15) *chsd ldrs aftr 2 fs, lost pl o'r 3 out.* . . . .(25 to 1 op 20 to 1 tchd 33 to 1) 11
DOCK OF THE BAY (Ire) 3-9-3 E Guest (5) *al in rear.* . . . . (33 to 1 op 20 to 1) 12
4256 MERRY MARIGOLD 7-8-8 (5*) S Drowne (16) *al towards rear.* . . . . (10 to 1 op 8 to 1 tchd 12 to 1) 13
4031 BLUE TRUMPET 3-8-2 R Price (13) *in tch til hrd rdn and lost pl o'r 4 fs out.* . . . . (33 to 1 op 20 to 1) 14
4110 BARNIEMEBOY 3-8-2 N Adams (3) *trkd ldrs for 4 fs, lost tch hfwy.* . . . .(33 to 1 op 20 to 1) 15
3866 DOUNHURST (bl) 6-8-10 A Clark (7) *beh most of way.* . . . . (33 to 1 op 20 to 1) 16
Dist: 10l, 1l, 4l, 2½l, ¾l, 3l, 2l, 1½l, 1l, 6l. 2m 36.58s. a 7.28s (16 Ran).
SR: 7/-/9/-/-/-/ (Geoff Lewis), G Lewis

4712 Taurus Handicap Class E (0-70 3-y-o and up) £1,900 5f. . . . .(3:15)

4363⁹ SAMSON-AGONISTES [67] 7-9-11 A Clark (7) *pressed ldr, shaken up to gain advantage o'r one furlong out, styd on wl.* . . . .(7 to 2 jt-fav op 4 to 1) 1
4670⁴ VERY DICEY [65] 5-9-2 (7*) Ruth Coulter (5) *slwly into strd, hdwy hfwy, chlgd o'r one furlong out, not quicken wl ins fnl furlong.* . . . .(7 to 2 jt-fav op 3 to 1 tchd 4 to 1) 2
2908⁹ JULIET BRAVO [61] 3-9-5 A Munro (8) *chsd ldrs, outpcd 2 fs out, styd on ag'n ins fnl furlong.* . . . .(6 to 1 op 13 to 5 on tchd 13 to 2) 3
3584 BANBURY FLYER [57] 5-9-1 M Hills (2) *wl plcd, rdn and not quicken well o'r one furlong out, ran on same pace nr finish.* . . . .(14 to 1 op 12 to 1) 4
4487 CHARITY EXPRESS (Ire) [64] 3-9-8 A McGlone (4) *hld up in rear, hdwy und pres appr fnl furlong, no ch wth wnr.* . . . .(7 to 1 tchd 6 to 1) 5
3995 SIGAMA (USA) [70] 7-10-0 R Lappin (3) *sn led, rdn and hdd o'r one furlong out, wknd quickly.* . . . . (8 to 1) 6
4363⁶ SIR TASKER [65] 5-9-4 (5*) D Wright (10) *in tch to hfwy, no prog last 2 fs.* . . . .(13 to 2 op 4 to 1 tchd 7 to 1) 7
4455 PALEY PRINCE (USA) [68] 7-9-12 N Adams (6) *al outpcd.* . . . . (10 to 1 op 8 to 1) 8
3739 SERIOUS HURRY [58] 5-9-2 B Rouse (9) *rdn and outpcd aftr 2 fs.* . . . .(8 to 1 op 7 to 1) 9
Dist: ¾l, 5l, sht-hd, sht-hd, 3l, nk, 1½l, 1½l. 1m 0.66s. a 2.46s (9 Ran).
SR: 57/52/28/23/29/23/17/14/-/ (J B Wilcox), B A McMahon

4713 Aries Amateur Riders' Handicap Class G (0-70 3-y-o and up) £1,730 1 ¼m. . . . . (3:45)

4234⁶ NIGHT EDITION [44] (e/s) 3-9-3 (5*) Mr T Cuff (8) *pressed ldr, led o'r 2 fs out, pushed out ins fnl furlong.* . . . . (5 to 1 op 16 to 1) 1
4652 CAPTAIN MARMALADE [53] 4-10-8 Miss Diana Jones (3) *hld up in rear, ran on frm 3 fs out, str run fnl furlong.* . . . . (10 to 1 op 7 to 1) 2
2315⁸ LOCH DUICH [50] 7-10-0 (5*) Miss A Sanders (7) *wl plcd, rdn and styd on one pace fnl furlong.* . . . . (20 to 1 op 16 to 1) 3
4591⁹ STRAT'S LEGACY [60] 6-11-1 Mrs D Arbuthnot (5) *hld up in mid-div, ran on and gng wl 2 fs out, not much room one out, styd on nr line.* . . . .(5 to 1 op 4 to 1) 4
4533² SANTANA LADY (Ire) [63] 4-10-13 (5*) Miss F Haynes (1) *led til hdd o'r 2 fs out, rdn and one pace fnl furlong.* . . . .(6 to 1 op 9 to 2) 5
4591* DASHING FELLOW (Ire) [64] 5-11-0 (5*,6ex) Mr C Appleby (4) *towards rear til cld on ldrs 4 fs out, rdn and no extr appr fnl furlong.* . . . . .(5 to 2 fav op 7 to 2 tchd 5 to 1) 6
4600⁶ PERSIAN BUD (Ire) [36] 5-9-0 (5*) Mrs S Bosley (6) *in tch, no imprsn on ldrs frm o'r 2 fs out.* . . . . . (20 to 1 op 16 to 1) 7
4515⁴ GRANACHE (Ire) [56] 4-10-11 Mr Raymond White (11) *improved frm rear hfwy, no extr ins last 2 fs.* . . . . (20 to 1 op 12 to 1) 8
4115³ DON'T GIVE UP [43] 5-9-12 Mrs M Cowdrey (10) *modest effrt frm rear o'r 3 fs out, not rch ldrs.* . . . . (10 to 1 op 6 to 1 tchd 12 to 1) 9
2822² FORGETFUL [47] 4-9-12¹ (5*) Mr S Blackwell (14) *ldg grp, rdn alng o'r 4 fs out, wknd 3 out.* (14 to 1 tchd 20 to 1) 10
4652 CHIEF OF STAFF [66] 4-11-7 Mrs L Pearce (9) *pressed ldrs til wknd 4 fs out.* . . . .(5 to 1 op 3 to 1 tchd 11 to 2) 11
4592⁹ JULIASDARKINVADER [50] 3-9-11² (5*) Mr T McCarthy (12) *mid-div for 6 fs, no further prog.* . . (14 to 1 op 12 to 1) 12
3910 LAMBOURN RAJA [40] 7-9-4 (5*) Mrs J Wilkinson (2) *lost many ls leaving stalls, al wl beh.* . .(33 to 1 op 25 to 1) 13
4486 STARLIGHT FLYER [38] 6-9-6⁴ (5*) Mr T Waters (13) *sn wl in rear.* . . . .(33 to 1 op 25 to 1) 14
Dist: ½l, 2½l, sht-hd, sht-hd, 1½l, 1½l, 4l, 2l, 8l, nk. 2m 11.28s. a 8.08s (14 Ran).
SR: 22/35/27/36/38/36/5/17/-/ (Ray Hawthorn), S Dow

DONCASTER (good)
Friday November 5th
Going Correction: PLUS 0.10 sec. per fur.

4714 EBF Flanders Maiden Stakes Class D (Div I) (2-y-o) £4,776 7f. . . . . . . (12:30)

RAMEAU (USA) 9-0 Paul Eddery (9) *in tch, sn pushed alng, gd hdwy to ld o'r one out, quickened and ran on wl.* ....(5 to 2 fav op 7 to 4) 1
MOKHTAR (Ire) 9-0 W Carson (5) *dwlt, sn in tch, effrt 2 out, soon rdn and swshd tail, kpt on fnl furlong, no imprsn on wnr*..........(3 to 1 op 6 to 4) 2
4489 SHARP THRILL 8-11 (3*) Stephen Davies (3) *made most till hdd o'r one out, kpt on wl fnl furlong.* ....(33 to 1 op 20 to 1) 3
BOWCLIFFE 9-0 N Connorton (6) *in tch, ran on wl fnl furlong, nrst finish*..........(25 to 1 op 12 to 1) 4
4263[9] ARAGON HOLLY 8-9 J Carroll (8) *hmpd aftr 2 fs, in tch, kpt on und pres fnl furlong.* ....(14 to 1 op 8 to 1 tchd 16 to 1) 5
MUSEUM (Ire) 9-0 A Munro (2) *prmnt till wknd o'r one out.* ....(14 to 1 op 10 to 1) 6
MAGICAL-MOU 9-0 A Culhane (4) *prmnt till wknd o'r one out*..........(16 to 1 op 10 to 1) 7
EFAAD (Ire) 9-0 B Raymond (1) *prmnt till wknd wl o'r one out*..........(7 to 1 op 5 to 1) 8
4526 NEEDWOOD SWIFT 8-9 S D Williams (7) *chsd ldrs till outpcd fnl 2 fs*..........(33 to 1 op 20 to 1) 9
MELANISTIC 9-0 W Ryan (12) *dwlt, beh whn hmpd aftr 2 fs, nvr dngrs*..........(6 to 1 op 3 to 1) 10
MOONAX (Ire) 9-0 T Quinn (10) *badly hmpd and uns rdr aftr 2 fs*..........(6 to 1 op 9 to 2 tchd 7 to 1) ur
Dist: 3l, ¾l, 2l, 2l, 1l, ¾l, 4l, 5l, 6l. 1m 30.21s. a 6.81s (11 Ran).
SR: 8/-/-/-/-/-/ (K Abdulla), J H M Gosden

4715 EBF Dunkirk Maiden Stakes Class D (2-y-o) £4,092 6f..........(1:00)

4523 OGGI 9-0 J Fortune (1) *beh, steady hdwy to ld 2 out, sn rdn, hld on wl fnl furlong*..........(50 to 1 op 33 to 1) 1
KILCOO 8-9 R Cochrane (3) *dwlt, trkd ldrs, effrt 2 out, kpt on wl fnl furlong, no extr towards finish.* ....(3 to 1 op 7 to 4) 2
1666[6] IRREPRESSIBLE (Ire) 9-0 J Reid (2) *prmnt, chlgd 2 out, sn rdn, no extr fnl furlong*..........(15 to 8 fav op 11 to 10) 3
4608[2] CAVERS YANGOUS 9-0 J Weaver (7) *in tch, outpcd hfwy, styd on fnl 2 fs, nvr dngrs*..........(2 to 1 tchd 5 to 2) 4
4512 ALPINE JOHNNY 9-0 S Perks (5) *led till hdd 2 out, fdd.* ....(14 to 1 op 10 to 1) 5
NEEDWOOD CUBE 9-0 S D Williams (4) *dwlt, beh, hdwy hfwy, rdn o'r 2 out, sn wknd*..........(33 to 1) 6
4575 SUPERTURN 8-9 W Ryan (6) *chsd ldr till wknd hfwy.* ....(25 to 1 op 20 to 1) 7
Dist: ½l, 1l, 4l, 3l, 6l, 1½l. 1m 15.46s. a 4.06s (7 Ran).
SR: 31/24/25/9/ (Skyline Racing Ltd), A G Foster

4716 Royal British Legion Conditions Stakes Class D (3-y-o and up) £3,055 1¾m 132yds..........(1:30)

4493[3] NAWAHIL 3-8-0 W Carson (4) *trkd ldr, led 7 out, hdd 4 out, led ag'n 2 out, styd on wl*..........(5 to 1 op 9 to 2) 1
4590* PURPLE SPLASH 3-8-9 R Cochrane (1) *chsd ldrs, led 4 out, hdd 2 out, kpt on same pace*... (11 to 10 fav op 5 to 4) 2
4414[8] CASPIAN TERN (USA) (bl) 4-8-9 A Munro (3) *hld up in tch, hdwy 7 out, chlgd 4 out, rdn 3 out, grad wknd.* ....(7 to 2 op 3 to 1) 3
4515[5] GRAEGOS (Ire) 3-8-9 W Ryan (5) *hld up in tch, effrt 4 out, sn btn*..........(5 to 1 op 4 to 1) 4
4160[4] KING UBAD (USA) 4-9-0 J Reid (2) *led till hdd 7 out, lost tch o'r 4 out*..........(20 to 1 op 16 to 1) 5
Dist: 4l, 7l, 15l, 12l. 3m 14.96s. a 10.46s (5 Ran).
(Hamdan Al-Maktoum), A C Stewart

4717 EBF Flanders Maiden Stakes Class D (Div II) (2-y-o) £4,737 7f..........(2:00)

3705[4] DONTFORGET INSIGHT (Ire) 9-0 A Munro (4) *trkd ldrs, led wl o'r one out, ran on strly fnl furlong.* ....(10 to 1 tchd 12 to 1) 1
OSATO (USA) 9-0 R Cochrane (6) *in tch, led o'r 2 out, sn hdd, one paced fnl furlong*..........(5 to 2 fav op 5 to 4) 2
4579[4] JAAWIS 9-0 B Raymond (11) *in tch, kpt on fnl 2 fs, not trble ldrs*..........(9 to 2 op 2 to 1 tchd 5 to 1) 3
RIPARIUS (USA) 9-0 W Newnes (7) *beh, effrt hfwy, rdn o'r 2 out, kpt on wl fnl furlong*..........(16 to 1 op 14 to 1) 4
4508[7] PRINCE DE BERRY 9-0 J Reid (8) *trkd ldrs, rdn 2 out, no hdwy*..........(14 to 1 op 12 to 1) 5
BIREQUEST 9-0 J Weaver (10) *hld up, hdwy 3 out, ch o'r one out, wknd fnl furlong*..........(33 to 1 op 20 to 1) 6
CAERLE LAD (Ire) 9-0 W Ryan (5) *dwlt, beh, hdwy 3 out, ch 2 out, sn wknd*..........(14 to 1 op 10 to 1) 7
4480[7] SWALLOWS DREAM (Ire) 9-0 L Piggott (1) *prmnt till wknd o'r 2 out*.......... (8 to 1 op 6 to 1 tchd 10 to 1) 8
4588[3] FRED'S DELIGHT (Ire) 9-0 J Carroll (2) *slight ld aftr one furlong till hdd o'r 2 out, sn wknd*... (8 to 1 op 5 to 1) 9
EBEN AL HABEEB (Ire) 9-0 W Carson (9) *sn beh.* ....(9 to 2 op 3 to 1 tchd 5 to 1) 10
ASCOT CONQUEROR (USA) 9-0 J Fortune (12) *dwlt, in tch, pushed alng hfwy, grad wknd.* ....(9 to 1 op 6 to 1 tchd 10 to 1) 11
NORD LYS (Ire) 9-0 S Perks (3) *slight ld one furlong, cl up till wknd quickly 2 out, tld off*.....(25 to 1 op 20 to 1) 12

Dist: 3l, 2l, nk, 1½l, hd, 2½l, nk, 1l, 1l, nk. 1m 29.40s. a 6.00s (12 Ran).
SR: 21/12/6/5/-/-/ (Insight Cartons Ltd), P F I Cole

4718 Unknown Soldier Fillies' Conditions Stakes Class D (3-y-o and up) £3,114 1¼m 60yds..........(2:30)

4515[2] INSTANT AFFAIR (USA) 3-8-11 W Carson (1) *trkd ldr, led 2 out, rdn and ran on wl fnl furlong, jst hld on.* ....(9 to 4 fav op 2 to 1 tchd 5 to 2) 1
4372[5] PIPERS POOL (Ire) 3-8-7 Paul Eddery (4) *hld up, hdwy 4 out, not much room o'r 2 out, swtchd and chsd wnr entering fnl furlong, ran on wl und pres, jst fld.* (8 to 1) 2
4629[8] FAYFA (Ire) 3-8-9 W Ryan (5) *chsd ldrs, chlgd 2 out, sn rdn, one pace fnl furlong*....(5 to 2 op 9 to 4 tchd 11 to 4) 3
4622* CASCASSI (USA) 3-8-11 R Cochrane (2) *trkd ldrs, pushed alng o'r 2 out, rdn over one out, kpt on same pace.* ....(11 to 4 op 9 to 4 tchd 3 to 1) 4
513[8] SLIGHT RISK (e/c) 4-8-12 D Harrison (3) *led till hdd 2 out, grad wknd*..........(20 to 1 op 14 to 1) 5
4578[3] PETERSFORD GIRL (Ire) 3-8-11 J Reid (7) *al beh, lost tch o'r 3 out, tld off*..........(8 to 1) 6
MY TREASURE 3-8-7 A Munro (6) *in tch till wknd quickly o'r 3 out, wl tld off*.......... (66 to 1 tchd 100 to 1) 7
Dist: Sht-hd, 3l, ½l, 6l, 20l, dist. 2m 14.32s. a 7.62s (7 Ran).
SR: 31/26/22/23/12/-/-/ (Athos Christodoulou), P F I Cole

4719 Normandy Beaches Nursery Class D (0-85 2-y-o) £3,289 5f..........(3:00)

4613* ROYALE FIGURINE (Ire) [82] 9-9 (7ex) J Reid (6) *hld up, hdwy 2 out, quickend to ld ins fnl furlong, ran on wl.* ....(6 to 4 fav op 5 to 4 tchd 7 to 4) 1
4632[5] BILLY CRUNCHEON [67] 8-8 B Raymond (2) *chsd ldrs, slight ld entering fnl furlong, sn hdd, no extr.* ....(14 to 1 op 10 to 1) 2
4632[2] FEATHERSTONE LANE [65] 8-6 D Harrison (5) *trkd ldrs, effrt 2 out, ev ch entering fnl furlong, one pace.* ....(11 to 2 op 4 to 1) 3
3894[3] ANN'S PEARL (Ire) [80] 9-7 W Ryan (3) *trkd ldrs, effrt and ev ch entering fnl furlong, one pace.* (6 to 1 op 5 to 1) 4
4613[3] INSIDER TRADER [58] 7-13 W Carson (8) *led to hfwy, cl up till wknd o'r one out*.......... (8 to 1 op 7 to 1) 5
4516[8] MY GALLERY (Ire) [69] (bl) 8-5 (5*) D Wright (7) *beh till some late hdwy, nvr dngrs*..........(9 to 1 op 7 to 1) 6
4416 MR B REASONABLE (Ire) [65] 8-1 (5*) D McCabe (1) *in tch, effrt 2 out, no hdwy*..........(9 to 1 op 6 to 1) 7
4436 NORDICO PRINCESS [70] 8-11 S Perks (4) *cl up, led hfwy till hdd and wknd entering fnl furlong.* ....(14 to 1 op 12 to 1) 8
4500[7] ADMIRALELLA [70] 8-4 (7*) M Humphries (9) *cl up till wknd 2 out*..........(12 to 1 tchd 14 to 1) 9
Dist: 1½l, 1l, 1l, ½l, nk, nk, hd, 2l. 1m 1.71s. a 2.91s (9 Ran).
SR: 61/40/34/45/21/31/26/30/22/ (Ms Christine Walker), M J Fetherston-Godley

4720 Western Desert Conditions Stakes Class D (2-y-o) £3,377 1m..........(3:30)

4421[5] TRUCKHAVEN SECRET 8-11 W Ryan (3) *dwlt, sn tracking ldrs pulling hrd, rdn to ld one out, styd on.* ....(11 to 8 on op 11 to 10) 1
4598* CAZZUTO (Ire) 9-5 W Carson (4) *led till hdd one out, kpt on same pace*..........(6 to 1 op 7 to 2) 2
4480* SUMMER HAIL (Ire) 9-1 A Munro (9) *trkd ldrs, slightly outpcd o'r 2 out, styd on und pres entering fnl furlong.* ....(7 to 1 op 5 to 1) 3
4498[2] LON ISA 8-6 D Harrison (1) *wth ldr, rdn 2 out, one paced entering fnl furlong*..........(9 to 1 op 10 to 1) 4
4223[5] ASKERN 9-1 J Lowe (5) *trkd ldrs, effrt 3 out, kpt on same pace*..........(12 to 1) 5
4498* WAYFARERS WAY (USA) 9-1 J Reid (2) *in tch, effrt 3 out, one paced*..........(7 to 1 op 4 to 1 tchd 8 to 1) 6
FOIL STONE 8-11 Paul Eddery (8) *strted slwly, beh, rdn o'r 2 out, no hdwy*..........(14 to 1 op 10 to 1) 7
4562[4] YOUNG AT HEART (Ire) 8-11 R Cochrane (6) *trkd ldrs, effrt 3 out, sn btn*..........(20 to 1 tchd 16 to 1) 8
BIENVENU 8-11 J Carroll (7) *sn pushed alng and beh, lost tch aftr 3 fs, wl tld off*..........(33 to 1 op 20 to 1) 9
Dist: 1l, 1½l, 1½l, ½l, 2½l, ½l, ½l, dist. 1m 42.50s. a 5.70s (9 Ran).
SR: 24/29/20/6/13/5/ (Truckhaven Limited), H R A Cecil

4721 Poppy Handicap Class D (0-80 3-y-o and up) £3,728 7f..........(4:00)

4652[2] EURO FESTIVAL [74] 4-9-5 (5*) D McCabe (1) *chsd ldrs, shaken up to ld one out, ran on wl.* ....(12 to 1 op 8 to 1 tchd 14 to 1) 1
4652[5] HELIOS [69] 5-9-5 B Raymond (3) *led till hdd one out, kpt on wl*..........(12 to 1) 2
4623[2] PROUD BRIGADIER (Ire) [66] 5-9-2 W Carson (8) *al chasing ldrs, kpt on wl fnl furlong*..........(13 to 2 op 6 to 1) 3
4640[6] CLAUDIA MISS [55] 6-8-2 (3*) N Kennedy (5) *in tch, effrt o'r 2 out, styd on wl fnl furlong*.......... (20 to 1) 4
4470 MULLITOVER [75] 3-9-9 A Munro (2) *al prmnt, kpt on same pace und pres fnl furlong*..........(25 to 1) 5

4591[3] YOUNG FREEMAN (USA) [69] 4-9-5 L Piggott (15) *beh till styd on wl fnl 2 fs, nrst finish*..... (12 to 1 op 11 to 1) 6
4652* RISE UP SINGING [66] (bl) 5-9-2 (6ex) J Reid (14) *wnt lft strt, beh, swtchd outsd aftr 3 fs, steady hdwy to chal o'r one out, wknd fnl furlong.* .... (3 to 1 fav op 11 to 4 tchd 5 to 2 and 7 to 2) 7
4652 TEANARCO (Ire) [67] 5-9-3 D Harrison (16) *nvr nr to chal.* .... (12 to 1 op 11 to 1) 8
4537[2] ASHGORE [64] 3-8-12 J Weaver (13) *bumped strt, in tch, kpt on fnl 2 fs, nvr dngrs*........ (10 to 1) 9
4537* ALLINSON'S MATE (Ire) [71] 5-9-7 W Ryan (9) *nvr nr to chal*........ (8 to 1) 10
4652[3] GREAT HALL [69] 4-9-5 R Cochrane (12) *dwlt, nvr dngrs.* .... (9 to 1 op 8 to 1) 11
4694 TAKENHALL [50] 8-8-0 F Norton (6) *chsd ldrs, sn pushed alng, rdn 3 out, grad wknd*........ (14 to 1) 12
4580[7] FORTIS PAVIOR (Ire) [60] 3-8-8 A Culhane (10) *al beh.* .... (16 to 1) 13
4495[4] GARTH [46] 5-7-10 J Lowe (7) *swtchd rght aftr strt, chsd ldrs till wknd o'r one out*........ (25 to 1) 14
4488[4] SHAKE TOWN (USA) [60] 5-8-10 W Newnes (4) *chsd ldrs till rdn and wknd 2 out*........ (16 to 1) 15
4394 AQUILETTA [60] 3-8-8 M Birch (11) *slightly hmpd strt, in tch till wknd 3 out*........ (12 to 1) 16
Dist: 1½l, 1½l, nk, 1l, 1l, ½l, nk, 1l, 1½l, ½l. 1m 28.11s. a 4.71s (16 Ran).
SR: 50/40/32/20/35/28/23/23/15/ (Christopher Price), Miss L C Siddall

YARMOUTH (good)
Friday November 5th
Going Correction: PLUS 0.30 sec. per fur. (races 1,6), PLUS 0.45 (2,3,4,5)

4722 Firework Handicap Class E (0-70 3-y-o and up) £2,924 1m 3f 101yds.... (1:15)

4631 ROSE NOBLE (USA) [56] 3-8-12 M Tebbutt (1) *led aftr one and a half fs, quickened appr strt, hrd pressed fnl furlong, hld on grimly.* (11 to 2 op 4 to 1 tchd 6 to 1) 1
2162[8] PRINCESS EVITA (Fr) [33] 4-7-9 J Quinn (4) *al hndy, rdn and ev ch appr fnl furlong, kpt on same pace.* .... (8 to 1 op 7 to 1) 2
4533[6] GOLDEN TORQUE [56] 6-8-13[2] (7*) H Bastiman (7) *patiently rdn, improved last 3 fs, ev ch ins last, not go passed*........ (4 to 1 op 11 to 4) 3
4599[3] PRESTON GUILD (Ire) [62] 3-9-4 G Duffield (3) *trkd ldr, niggled alng entering strt, wknd and lost tch last 2 fs.* .... (6 to 4 fav op 7 to 4 tchd 2 to 1) 4
4599[5] RAFIF (USA) [68] 3-9-10 S Whitworth (6) *wtd wth, shrtlvd effrt entering strt, fdd last 3 fs.* .... (14 to 1 op 8 to 1 tchd 16 to 1) 5
4599[4] JOY OF FREEDOM [57] 3-8-13 M Hills (5) *trkd ldg trio, hrd at work 3 fs out, fdd*..... (8 to 1 op 7 to 1 tchd 9 to 1) 6
4631 WHO'S THE BEST (Ire) [50] 3-8-6 D Holland (2) *led for one and a half fs, lost pl quickly appr strt, sn btn.* .... (12 to 1 op 8 to 1) 7
4493 HASTY SPARK [31] 5-7-4[4] (7*) N Varley (8) *co'red up beh ldrs, struggling to hold pl over 3 fs out, tld off.* .... (50 to 1 op 33 to 1) 8
Dist: ½l, 1l, 12l, 8l, 10l, 3½l, 15l. 2m 32.60s. a 9.10s (8 Ran).
SR: 42/24/45/21/11/ (Lady Howard de Walden), W Jarvis

4723 Jumping Jack Maiden Stakes Class D (2-y-o) £3,406 6f 3yds........... (1:45)

NIMPHIDIA (USA) 8-9 G Hind (4) *tucked away gng wl, quickened to ld o'r one furlong out, won going away.* .... (4 to 1 op 7 to 2 tchd 5 to 1) 1
4587[2] INDIAN FLY 9-0 M Hills (5) *patiently rdn, drvn up to chal appr fnl furlong, not pace of wnr last 100 yards.* .... (11 to 8 fav op 7 to 4 tchd 2 to 1) 2
3613 MUSIC OF DANCE (Ire) 8-4 (5*) J Tate (8) *made most aftr 2 fs, hdd and rdn o'r one furlong out, one pace.* .... (7 to 1 op 4 to 1) 3
4628[6] DIGGERS WELL (USA) 9-0 A McGlone (6) *steadied strt, effrt and shaken up 2 fs out, not pace to chal.* .... (3 to 1 op 2 to 1 tchd 7 to 2) 4
ULTIMATUM 9-0 G Duffield (2) *sluggish strt, reco'red to dispute ld centre for over 4 fs, fdd*.... (7 to 1 op 6 to 1) 5
4446 SAMBA SHARPLY 9-0 M Tebbutt (7) *nvr far away, effrt and drvn alng 2 fs out, sn outpcd.* (33 to 1 op 20 to 1) 6
3836 SOUTH EASTERN FRED 9-0 J Quinn (1) *pressed ldrs, hrd at work 2 fs out, fdd.* (40 to 1 op 25 to 1 tchd 50 to 1) 7
4227 CHARLYMOON 8-9 J McLaughlin (3) *led centre grp for 2 fs, drvn alng whn squeezed for room o'r two out, sn lost tch*........ (50 to 1 op 25 to 1) 8
Dist: 5l, 6l, 2l, 2½l, 1l, 8l, 1½l. 1m 16.10s. a 5.10s (8 Ran).
SR: 47/32/3/-/-/ (Sheikh Mohammed), J H M Gosden

4724 Penny For The Guy Claiming Stakes Class E (3-y-o and up) £2,898 1m 3yds ....(2:15)

4596* ALWAYS RISKY 3-8-9 J Quinn (6) *took str hold, settled till quickened up to ld wl o'r one furlong out, kpt on well.* .... (2 to 1 jt-fav op 7 to 4) 1
4658[7] DEAD CALM (v) 3-8-10 M Tebbutt (9) *settled gng wl, quickened up to draw level o'r one furlong out, ran on, jst hld*........ (11 to 4 op 2 to 1 tchd 3 to 1) 2
4652 SALISONG 4-8-9 Dale Gibson (7) *patiently rdn, shaken up to improve o'r 2 fs out, styd on finish*..... (2 to 1 jt-fav tchd 11 to 4) 3
4488 MEXICAN DANCER 4-8-7 (5*) S Drowne (8) *settled midfield, effrt and bustled alng o'r 2 fs out, not pace to chal.* .... (25 to 1 op 14 to 1) 4
4596 ASCOM PAGER TOO 3-8-5 T Williams (1) *led aftr 2 fs, quickened clr hfwy, hdd wl o'r one furlong out, fdd.* .... (16 to 1 op 12 to 1) 5
4524 GENERAL BUNCHING 3-9-4 R Price (2) *led for 2 fs, styd hndy till fdd und pres wl o'r one furlong out.* .... (12 to 1 op 14 to 1) 6
3744[4] CHAFF 6-8-6 (3*) C Hodgson (5) *chsd ldg pair, hrd at work o'r 2 fs out, sn btn*........ (12 to 1 tchd 16 to 1) 7
4544 REMEESON 3-8-12[1] (7*) H Bastiman (3) *sluggish strt, hrd at work and wndrd aftr 3 fs, sn lost tch.* .... (33 to 1 op 20 to 1) 8
4596 KNIGHT SHEPHERD 3-9-0 G Hind (4) *settled midfield, effrt and drvn alng hfwy, wknd quickly last 2 fs.* .... (33 to 1) 9
Dist: ½l, 3l, 8l, 1½l, 1½l, 3l, 12l, ½l. 1m 44.40s. a 8.60s (9 Ran).
SR: 20/19/9/-/-/-/ (Stephen Roots), Mrs N Macauley

4725 Sparkler Nursery Class D (2-y-o) £3,611 1m 3yds................ (2:45)

4427* ART TATUM (Ire) [70] 8-8 G Duffield (7) *pressed ldg pair, drvn alng whn pace quickened o'r 2 fs out, kpt on to ld entering fnl furlong, ran on wl.* .... (6 to 4 fav op 9 to 4 tchd 5 to 2) 1
4531* BE EXCITING (Ire) [78] 9-2 T Williams (2) *wth ldr, ev ch appr fnl furlong, kpt on same pace last 100 yards.* .... (4 to 1 op 11 to 4 tchd 9 to 2) 2
4215* MAKE A NOTE (USA) [83] 9-7 M Hills (5) *tried to make all, quickened o'r 2 fs out, hdd entering fnl furlong, one pace*........ (9 to 2 op 7 to 2 tchd 5 to 1) 3
4618[8] LA RESIDENCE [63] 8-1 J Quinn (3) *settled midfield, feeling pace and rdn hfwy, styd on, no imprsn.* .... (16 to 1 op 10 to 1 tchd 20 to 1) 4
4564[2] AL JINN [63] 8-1 D Biggs (4) *sluggish strt, improved into midfield hfwy, rdn and btn o'r 2 fs out.* .... (11 to 1 op 7 to 1 tchd 12 to 1) 5
4491[3] RISKY TU [57] 7-9 G Bardwell (6) *took keen hold, hmpd aftr 2 fs, rdn and btn o'r two out*.... (8 to 1 op 5 to 1) 6
4526[5] TU OPES [66] 8-4 Dale Gibson (1) *speed on outsd to hfwy, wknd quickly*........ (6 to 1 op 9 to 2 tchd 7 to 1) 7
4531[7] SAWTID [63] 8-1 A McGlone (8) *steadied strt, effrt and shaken up hfwy, fdd o'r 2 fs out.* .... (12 to 1 op 10 to 1 tchd 14 to 1) 8
Dist: 2l, nk, 6l, 5l, 1½l, 3l, 8l. 1m 43.00s. a 7.20s (8 Ran).
SR: 40/42/46/8/-/ (R Cohen & Mr A F Merritt), R Hannon

4726 Guy Fawkes Maiden Stakes Class D (2-y-o) £4,371 7f 3yds........... (3:15)

LINNEY HEAD (USA) 9-0 G Hind (18) *wl plcd stand side thrght, quickened ahead o'r 2 fs out, drvn out fnl furlong*..... (11 to 2 op 9 to 2 tchd 4 to 1 and 6 to 1) 1
TUKANO (Can) 9-0 S Raymont (2) *nvr far away, shaken up 2 fs out, ran on strly fnl furlong.* .... (16 to 1 op 14 to 1 tchd 20 to 1) 2
4497[5] CLASSIC LIGHT (Ire) 8-9 M Wigham (4) *tucked away beh ldrs, bustled alng to improve last 2 fs, fnshd wl.* .... (50 to 1 op 33 to 1) 3
MOKAAFI 9-0 R Price (8) *co'red up in midfield, effrt over 2 fs out, kpt on fnl furlong.* .... (8 to 1 op 6 to 1 tchd 9 to 1) 4
4252 ALWAYS ALOOF (USA) 9-0 D Holland (3) *pressed ldg bunch, effrt and drvn alng o'r 2 fs out, kpt on same pace*........ (7 to 1 op 5 to 1) 5
4421 ENVIRONMENTALIST (Ire) 9-0 A Mackay (1) *patiently rdn, steady hdwy frm midfield last 2 fs, prmsg.* .... (50 to 1 op 33 to 1) 6
4446[3] CALYPSO MONARCH (Ire) 9-0 R Perham (13) *co'red up in midfield, effrt and drvn alng over 2 fs out, not pace to chal*........ (8 to 1 op 6 to 1) 7
THUNDEROUS 9-0 A McGlone (6) *made most in centre till hdd o'r 2 fs out, better for race*... (4 to 1 fav op 5 to 2) 8
TANSEEQ 9-0 N Carlisle (10) *wth ldr gng wl, ev ch 2 fs out, fdd*........ (10 to 1 op 7 to 1) 9
JERMYN STREET (USA) 9-0 M Hills (5) *gd speed in frnt rnk for o'r 5 fs, fdd*........ (7 to 1 op 12 to 1) 10
KING OF THE HORSE (Ire) 9-0 M Tebbutt (15) *chsd alng to go pace hfwy, nvr rchd ldrs*....... (16 to 1 op 12 to 1) 11
KARTTIKEYA (Fr) 9-0 S Whitworth (9) *struggling to go pace hfwy, nvr able to chal*........ (14 to 1 op 12 to 1) 12
3592 CHILLY LAD 9-0 D Biggs (14) *outpcd and drvn alng hfwy, nvr a factor*........ (50 to 1 op 33 to 1) 13
4356 DIA GEORGY 8-7 (7*) S Eiffert (12) *chsd ldrs for o'r 4 fs, fdd*........ (50 to 1 op 33 to 1) 14
4276 LUCKY TUCKY 9-0 T Wilson (11) *broke wl to show speed for 5 fs, fdd*........ (33 to 1) 15
PORTOLANO (Fr) 9-0 G Bardwell (7) *early speed, drvn alng o'r 2 fs out, fdd*..... (25 to 1 op 16 to 1 tchd 33 to 1) 16

AJDAR 9-0 J Quinn (16) *chsd alng to keep up hfwy, nvr a threat*.............. (14 to 1 op 10 to 1 tchd 16 to 1) 17
SESTRIERE (USA) 8-9 G Duffield (17) *wth ldrs for o'r 4 fs, sn wknd*............ (16 to 1 op 14 to 1 tchd 20 to 1) 18
Dist: ¾l, ½l, 1½l, 7l, ½l, 3l, ¾l, ½l, sht-hd, hd. 1m 30.40s. a 7.20s (18 Ran).
SR: 39/37/30/30/9/7/ (Sheikh Mohammed), J H M Gosden

4727 Roman Candle Handicap Class E (0-70 3-y-o and up) £3,339 1¼m 21yds (3:45)

4548[6] HILLZAH (USA) [59] 5-8-13[2] (7*) H Bastiman (7) *settled gng wl, led 2 fs out, hld on grimly cl hme*. ....(8 to 1 op 5 to 1 tchd 9 to 1) 1
645 JOLI'S GREAT [36] (bl) 5-7-2 (7*) M Baird (11) *trkd ldg 6, improved to chal entering fnl furlong, ran on, jst fld*. ....(14 to 1 tchd 16 to 1) 2
4391[5] GOLD BLADE [51] 4-8-10 M Hills (10) *patiently rdn, improved frm midfield o'r 2 fs out, styd on, no imprsn*. ....(7 to 2 jt-fav op 9 to 2) 3
4623[9] SHAHAADA (USA) [64] 3-9-4 R Price (4) *chsd alng to improve frm midfield entering strt, kpt on same pace last 2 fs*........................ (16 to 1 tchd 20 to 1) 4
4600[7] OOZLEM (Ire) [45] (bl) 4-8-4 A McGlone (2) *sluggish strt, reco'red aftr 2 fs, led over 4 furlongs out till hdd two out, fdd*...........................(14 to 1 op 10 to 1) 5
4493[8] LADY CONFESS [41] 3-7-9[2] J Quinn (5) *led till hdd o'r 4 fs out, wknd quickly last 2 furlongs*.............(33 to 1) 6
4506[3] NEMEA (USA) [61] 3-9-1 D Biggs (9) *trkd ldg pair, ev ch o'r 2 fs out, sn rdn and btn*.............(5 to 1 op 4 to 1) 7
4514 AVENUE FOCH (Ire) [66] 4-9-11 M Wigham (1) *last and struggling hfwy, nvr a factor*....(16 to 1 tchd 20 to 1) 8
4499[8] FISIO SANDS [50] 4-8-4 (5*) B Russell (3) *chsd ldrs, hrd at work 3 fs out, sn btn*.............. (10 to 1 op 6 to 1) 9
4522 SON OF SHARP SHOT (Ire) [70] 3-9-10 G Duffield (6) *took str hold, wl plcd till wknd quickly o'r 2 fs out*. .... (8 to 1 op 7 to 1 tchd 10 to 1) 10
4633[2] SILVER GROOM (Ire) [60] 3-9-0 D Holland (12) *chsd ldrs to strt, tld off last 2 fs*.........................(7 to 2 jt-fav op 3 to 1 tchd 4 to 1) 11
4574[6] SPORTING SPIRIT [39] (bl) 3-7-7 S Wood (8) *wth ldrs to strt, tld off last 3 fs*...............(33 to 1 op 20 to 1) 12
Dist: Sht-hd, 7l, 1½l, 4l, 3½l, sht-hd, 5l, 2l, 3l, 20l. 2m 13.50s. a 9.50s (12 Ran).
SR: 39/15/16/21/-/-/2/2/-/ (Mrs P Churm), R Bastiman

DONCASTER (good)
Saturday November 6th
Going Correction: MINUS 0.10 sec. per fur. (races 1,2,6,7), PLUS 0.15 (3,4,5)

4728 Guinness 'Pure Genius' C.I.U. Macmillan Nurse Appeal Median Auction Maiden Stakes Class E (2-y-o) £3,626 6f............................(12:55)

4422[2] CO PILOT (Ire) 8-9 A Munro (13) *al prmnt, led o'r one furlong out, ran on strly*....(11 to 10 fav tchd 11 to 8) 1
TRIPLE JOY 8-9 G Duffield (4) *cl up, chlgd o'r one furlong out, kpt on fnl furlong, no ch wth wnr*. .... (12 to 1 op 5 to 1) 2
4543 DALERIVER 9-0 L Piggott (7) *in tch, effrt hfwy, styd on strly und pres fnl 2 fs, nrst finish*. (20 to 1 op 14 to 1) 3
4594[4] CROFT POOL 9-0 S D Williams (5) *led till o'r one furlong out, wknd fnl furlong*. .... (20 to 1 op 8 to 1 tchd 25 to 1) 4
4103 MUSICAL STAR 8-9 J Weaver (12) *prmnt, no extr fnl 2 fs*. .... (16 to 1 op 10 to 1 tchd 20 to 1) 5
4575[7] HAD A GIRL 8-9 T Quinn (16) *chsd ldrs, pushed alng o'r 2 fs out, kpt on same pace*...........(12 to 1 op 9 to 1) 6
3835[4] ANSELLADY 8-9 R Perham (17) *sn pushed alng, beh till styd on fnl 2 fs, nrst finish*...................(16 to 1) 7
BROUGHTON SINGER (Ire) 8-4 (5*) D McCabe (1) *nvr nr to chal*............................ (50 to 1 op 33 to 1) 8
4435[4] WACKY (Ire) 8-9 A Culhane (11) *chsd ldrs till wknd 2 fs out*.............................. (20 to 1 op 16 to 1) 9
4651[8] COSTLY 8-9 J Reid (15) *in tch, pushed alng hfwy, no hdwy*................(11 to 2 op 3 to 1 tchd 6 to 1) 10
4128 LEESON STREET LADY (Ire) 8-9 D Harrison (10) *prmnt, drvn alng hfwy, wknd*...........(50 to 1 op 33 to 1) 11
KINGSWOOD STAR (Ire) 9-0 M Tebbutt (3) *chsd ldrs till wknd 2 fs out*........(16 to 1 op 8 to 1 tchd 20 to 1) 12
4349[9] BIRD OF THE WIND 8-9 J Carroll (8) *prmnt till wknd o'r 2 fs out*.............................. (50 to 1 op 25 to 1) 13
4594 COLONEL SINCLAIR (Ire) 9-0 S Perks (14) *chsd ldrs, drvn alng o'r 2 fs out, sn wknd*....... (50 to 1 op 33 to 1) 14
BLACK DEED 9-0 S Whitworth (2) *dwlt, al beh*. .... (50 to 1 op 33 to 1) 15
4594 HOLLY ST GERMAINE (Ire) 8-9 G Bardwell (9) *sn beh*. ....(33 to 1) 16
MISS TIPSY 8-9 W Newnes (18) *al beh*. .... (50 to 1 op 33 to 1) 17
4598[5] MA FOLIE 8-9 L Charnock (6) *chsd ldrs to hfwy, wknd quickly, tld off*...................(50 to 1 op 33 to 1) 18
Dist: 5l, 2l, ½l, 2l, 1l, 1l, 1l, 1½l, 1½l, hd. 1m 14.62s. a 3.22s (18 Ran).
SR: 19/-/-/-/-/-/ (Denis J Larke), M A Jarvis

4729 Daily Star Remembrance Day Stakes Class A (Listed Race) (3-y-o and up) £9,942 6f..................... (1:25)

4678* BLYTON LAD 7-8-11 S Webster (11) *trkd ldrs, effrt 2 fs out, ran on wl to ld well ins last, all out*. ......(9 to 4 fav op 3 to 1 tchd 100 to 30 and 2 to 1) 1
4521* BRANSTON ABBY (Ire) 4-8-9 J Weaver (14) *beh, effrt 2 fs out, styd on strly fnl furlong, jst fld*. (6 to 1 op 9 to 2) 2
4617* GARAH 4-8-6 W Ryan (13) *hld up, effrt 2 fs out, styd on wl fnl furlong, nrst finish*............. (6 to 1 op 5 to 1) 3
4617[2] MATILA (Ire) 3-8-5 W Carson (4) *prmnt, chlgd o'r one furlong out, ev ch till no extr ins last*. (9 to 1 op 7 to 1) 4
4464* MONTENDRE 6-9-0 J Reid (1) *trkd ldrs, led o'r one furlong out till ins last, no extr*........(13 to 2 op 5 to 1) 5
4617[3] CARRANITA (Ire) 3-8-5 Stephen Davies (12) *in tch, kpt on fnl 2 fs, not trble ldrs*.............................. (25 to 1) 6
4415[9] GHOST TREE (Ire) 3-8-5 G Hind (3) *trkd ldrs, effrt 2 fs out, kpt on same pace*..................(25 to 1 op 20 to 1) 7
4521 MASSIBA (Ire) 4-8-6 D McCabe (5) *made most till o'r one furlong out, fdd*..................................(33 to 1) 8
4650 TAUFAN BLU (Ire) (bl) 4-8-6 A Munro (7) *dwlt, early reminders, beh till styd on fnl 2 fs, nvr dngrs*. ....(16 to 1 op 14 to 1 tchd 20 to 1) 9
4393[4] BORN TO BE 4-8-6 G Duffield (9) *chsd ldrs, no hdwy fnl 2 fs*...(50 to 1) 10
4040 CASTLEREA LAD 4-8-11 L Piggott (8) *in tch, effrt o'r 2 fs out, wknd entering fnl furlong*............... (25 to 1) 11
4464 FYLDE FLYER (bl) 4-8-11 J Carroll (15) *rcd alone stands side, beh fnl 2 fs*...............................(20 to 1) 12
4545[2] CELESTIAL KEY (USA) 3-8-13 K Fallon (6) *wth ldrs till wknd quickly o'r 2 fs out*...........(12 to 1 op 10 to 1) 13
4545[7] MR MARTINI (Ire) (bl) 3-8-10 M Birch (2) *wth ldrs till wknd quickly o'r 2 fs out*..............................(50 to 1) 14
4038 SAMSOLOM 5-8-11 J Quinn (10) *in tch, pushed alng hfwy, sn btn*.............................. (50 to 1) 15
Dist: Hd, hd, 1l, ½l, nk, 3½l, 2½l, nk, sht-hd, 5l. 1m 13.12s. a 1.72s (15 Ran).
SR: 51/48/44/39/46/36/22/13/12/ (Mrs J Addleshaw), M J Camacho

4730 Macmillan Nurse Appeal Serlby Stakes Class A (Listed Race) (3-y-o and up) £9,507 1½m............(1:55)

4566[2] CAPTAIN HORATIUS (Ire) 4-9-5 W Ryan (6) *trkd ldrs, led and quickened wl o'r 3 fs out, sn clr, styd on well*. ....(9 to 2 op 7 to 2) 1
4560[2] ANNA OF SAXONY 4-9-3 G Hind (2) *cl up, effrt o'r 3 fs out, styd on, no ch wth wnr*............(11 to 4 op 9 to 4) 2
4560[4] SHAMBO 6-9-8 M Hills (7) *hld up in tch, not much room o'r 4 fs out, effrt over 3 out, kpt on same pace*. .... (10 to 1 op 7 to 1) 3
4515* BALLET PRINCE (Ire) 3-8-7 R Cochrane (3) *trkd ldrs, effrt o'r 3 fs out, sn rdn and btn*. ....(11 to 8 fav op 5 to 4 tchd 6 to 4) 4
4629[7] FRET (USA) 3-8-7 A Munro (1) *led or dsptd ld till wl o'r 3 fs out, sn btn*......................(20 to 1 op 14 to 1) 5
4499 SPEAKER'S HOUSE (USA) (v) 4-9-0 T Quinn (5) *dwlt, hld up, effrt o'r 3 fs out, sn rdn and btn*. .... (50 to 1 op 33 to 1 tchd 66 to 1) 6
3914[2] KHALYANI (Ire) 3-8-7 J Reid (4) *pld hrd, hdwy to dispute ld 7 fs out, wknd quickly o'r 3 out, tld off*. .... (8 to 1 op 16 to 1) 7
Dist: 5l, 6l, 3½l, 2½l, 3l, 15l. 2m 36.71s. a 6.21s (7 Ran).
SR: 61/49/42/20/15/16/-/ (D R Hunnisett), J L Dunlop

4731 William Hill November Handicap Class B (3-y-o and up) £24,686 1½m ....(2:30)

4425[2] QUICK RANSOM [90] 5-8-10 J Weaver (9) *trakced ldrs, rdn to ld o'r one furlong out, styd on wl fnl furlong*. ....(6 to 1 fav op 8 to 1) 1
4695* LOOKINGFORARAINBOW (Ire) [73] 5-7-7 (4ex) L Charnock (14) *in tch gng wl, hdwy on bit whn not much room 2 fs out, swtchd entering fnl furlong, ran on well, not rch wnr*...................................(33 to 1 op 25 to 1) 2
4425[7] FLIGHT LIEUTENANT (USA) [82] 4-8-2 A McGlone (7) *hld up, hdwy 3 fs out, ch o'r one out, kpt on fnl furlong*. ....(33 to 1) 3
4425* SAFETY IN NUMBERS [90] 3-8-3 (4ex) J Quinn (23) *in tch, pushed alng 3 fs out, rdn wl o'r one out, styd on well fnl furlong*...........(10 to 1 op 8 to 1 tchd 11 to 1) 4
4548[5] ELATIS (USA) [82] 3-7-9 Dale Gibson (18) *in tch, hdwy and ev ch o'r one furlong out, one pace fnl furlong*. .... (25 to 1 op 20 to 1) 5
4660* MAJED (Ire) [81] 5-7-10 (5*,8ex) Darren Moffatt (19) *in tch, pushed alng o'r 3 fs out, styd on strly frm 2 out, nrst finish*..............(11 to 1 op 10 to 1 tchd 12 to 1) 6
4108* DARRERY [92] 3-8-5 R Cochrane (13) *prmnt, led wl o'r 2 fs out, swshd tail, hdd over one out, one pace*. ....(10 to 1 tchd 11 to 1) 7
4202* BLACKPATCH HILL [84] 4-8-4 T Quinn (10) *beh, effrt 3 fs out, styd on, nrst finish*......... (16 to 1 tchd 20 to 1) 8
4364[2] EXPRESS GIFT [75] 4-7-9[1] W Carson (6) *in tch, styd on fnl 2 fs, nrst finish*......(10 to 1 op 12 to 1 tchd 14 to 1) 9

4414[4] HIGHBROOK (USA) [82] 5-8-2 P Robinson (24) *in tch, hdwy 4 fs out, kpt on same pace frm 2 out.* (8 to 1 op 12 to 1) 10
4364* BIT ON THE SIDE (Ire) [73] 4-7-7 J Lowe (5) *nvr dngrs.* .... (25 to 1 op 20 to 1) 11
4513[2] DESERT POWER [73] 4-7-3[1] (5*) D Wright (17) *led till wl o'r 2 fs out, fdd.*........................ (25 to 1) 12
4621[5] ENCORE UNE FOIS (Ire) [77] 4-7-11[1] D Biggs (11) *nvr dngrs.* .... (40 to 1 op 33 to 1) 13
4414 GLIDE PATH (USA) [87] 4-8-7 M Hills (12) *in tch, effrt 3 fs out, no hdwy.*........................ (33 to 1 op 20 to 1) 14
4414 CASTORET [85] 7-8-5 D Harrison (1) *nvr dngrs.* .... (28 to 1 op 25 to 1 tchd 33 to 1) 15
4560[3] LINPAC WEST [104] 7-9-10 B Raymond (16) *prmnt, pushed alng o'r 3 fs out, wknd.*........................ (25 to 1) 16
4425[6] ROBERTY LEA [76] 5-7-10 F Norton (22) *prmnt till wknd o'r 2 fs out.*........................ (50 to 1 op 33 to 1) 17
4248[4] CAPTAIN'S GUEST (Ire) [96] 3-8-9 J Reid (25) *mid-div till wknd o'r 2 fs out.*........................ (20 to 1) 18
4283[6] FIRST BID [73] 6-7-6[2] (3*) N Kennedy (21) *prmnt, pushed alng 5 fs out, wknd o'r 3 out.*..... (25 to 1 tchd 33 to 1) 19
2925[8] DARU (USA) [98] (v) 4-9-4 G Hind (8) *al beh.* .... (20 to 1 tchd 25 to 1) 20
4037* EDEN'S CLOSE [75] 4-7-9[1] A Mackay (3) *nvr better than mid-div.*........................ (25 to 1) 21
4576* SCOTTISH PEAK (Ire) [87] 3-8-0 (4ex) A Munro (20) *prmnt, ev ch 3 fs out, wknd quickly.*...... (16 to 1 op 14 to 1) 22
4513[9] MAD MILITANT (Ire) [73] 4-7-7[5] (5*) A Garth (15) *al beh.* .... (50 to 1) 23
4425[5] MUCH SOUGHT AFTER [83] 4-8-3 G Duffield (2) *prmnt till wknd 4 fs out.*........................ (33 to 1) 24
4352* IVORY PALM (USA) [89] 3-8-2 Paul Eddery (4) *cl up, sn pushed alng, wknd quickly 4 fs out.*........... (16 to 1) 25
Dist: 1l, 1½l, ¾l, sht-hd, 1l, hd, 1l, sht-hd, 2l, 1l. 2m 34.53s. a 4.03s (25 Ran).
SR: 74/55/61/60/51/55/58/55/45/ (J S Morrison), M Johnston

4732 Coalite Dragon Handicap Class C (0-95 3-y-o and up) £5,572 2m 110yds .... (3:00)

4466 BARDOLPH (USA) [72] (bl) 6-8-7 T Quinn (4) *in tch, hdwy to track ldrs hfwy, led o'r 2 fs out, clr one out, rdn wl ins last, jst hld on.*........................(10 to 1 tchd 12 to 1) 1
4505[3] STAR PLAYER [75] 7-8-10 J Williams (1) *hld up, hdwy whn not much room 2 fs out, swtchd and effrt entering last, ran on strly, jst fld.*........................ (12 to 1) 2
4433[2] ELBURG (Ire) [74] 3-7-13 J Quinn (6) *prmnt, rdn 3 fs out, styd on wl frm 2 out.*............ (10 to 1 tchd 11 to 1) 3
4662[3] HOME FROM THE HILL (Ire) [68] 3-7-0 (7*) M Baird (12) *trkd ldrs, effrt 3 fs out, styd on wl frm 2 out.* ....(12 to 1 tchd 14 to 1) 4
4630[6] MY DESIRE [84] 5-9-0 (5*) Darren Moffatt (13) *beh till styd on strly und pres fnl 2 fs, nrst finish.*........... (8 to 1) 5
4466[5] DOYCE [67] 4-8-2 W Carson (5) *in tch, outpcd 4 fs out, styd on frm 2 out.*........................(8 to 1 op 7 to 1) 6
4540[2] JACK BUTTON (Ire) [93] 4-10-0 L Piggott (11) *in tch, pushed alng 6 fs out, rdn o'r 3 out, no hdwy.*.........(6 to 1 jt-fav op 7 to 1) 7
4466 TILTY (USA) [73] 3-7-12[1] A McGlone (7) *prmnt till outpcd o'r 3 fs out, kpt on und pres frm 2 out.* .... (10 to 1 op 8 to 1) 8
4143[7] IOTA [67] 4-8-2 G Duffield (10) *cl up, led wl o'r 3 fs out till over 2 out, wknd entering fnl furlong.* ....(14 to 1 tchd 16 to 1) 9
4494* SILLARS STALKER (Ire) [58] 5-7-7 N Carlisle (8) *in tch, effrt 3 fs out, rdn 2 out, sn btn.*..... (6 to 1 jt-fav op 9 to 2) 10
4661[4] GREY POWER [74] 6-8-9 A Munro (3) *beh, effrt 3 fs out, sn btn.*........................ (12 to 1 op 10 to 1) 11
4538[8] GOOD HAND (USA) [80] 7-9-1 N Connorton (9) *in tch, pushed alng hfwy, sn beh.*........ (7 to 1 tchd 8 to 1) 12
4538[5] SUBSONIC (Ire) [74] 5-8-9 J Weaver (2) *led till wl o'r 3 fs out, sn wknd and eased, tld off.*...(12 to 1 op 10 to 1) 13
Dist: ½l, 3l, ¾l, 1l, 1½l, 2l, 5l, nk, ½l, 4l. 3m 46.00s. a 16.00s (13 Ran).
(Sir George Meyrick), P F I Cole

4733 Wembley Nursery Class D (2-y-o) £3,947 7f........................ (3:35)

4427[5] SANDMOOR CHAMBRAY [65] (bl) 8-6 M Birch (11) *made most, quickened clr o'r 2 fs out, rdn ins last, jst hld on.* .... (16 to 1 op 14 to 1 tchd 20 to 1) 1
4526[2] WALSHAM WHISPER (Ire) [64] 8-5 P Robinson (12) *al chasing ldrs, rdn o'r one furlong out, styd on ins last, jst fld.*........................ (6 to 1 jt-fav op 10 to 1) 2
4674[2] KAITAK (Ire) [73] 8-7 (7*) G Parkin (1) *al cl up, effrt and ev ch ins fnl furlong, kpt on wl und pres.* .... (10 to 1 op 9 to 1) 3
4602* BLURRED IMAGE (Ire) [80] 9-7 J Reid (14) *in tch, hdwy 2 fs out, kpt on und pres fnl furlong.*.... (8 to 1 op 7 to 1) 4
4646* ONCE MORE FOR LUCK (Ire) [76] 9-3 W Newnes (3) *in tch, hdwy 2 fs out, rdn entering last, kpt on same pace.* .... (10 to 1 op 8 to 1) 5
4504[2] ROOFTOP FLYER (Ire) [80] 9-7 T Quinn (16) *in tch, hdwy 2 fs out, sn rdn and one pace.*..... (12 to 1 tchd 14 to 1) 6
4618[4] CHEERFUL GROOM (Ire) [58] 7-13 W Carson (7) *cl up, rdn 2 fs out, wknd.*........................(12 to 1) 7
4577* ARCTIC DIAMOND [65] 8-6 K Fallon (6) *nvr nr to chal.* ....(6 to 1 jt-fav op 7 to 1 tchd 8 to 1) 8
4423[8] SARMATIAN (USA) [68] 8-6 (3*) Stephen Davies (4) *mid-div, outpcd hfwy, styd on und pres entering fnl furlong.* ....(9 to 1 op 8 to 1) 9
4508[2] WINN'S PRIDE (Ire) [70] 8-11 S Perks (10) *cl up till rdn and wknd o'r 2 fs out.*............... (14 to 1 tchd 16 to 1) 10
1189* PRIVATE FIXTURE (Ire) [71] 8-12 M Tebbutt (15) *chsd ldrs, rdn o'r 2 fs out, sn wknd.*........................(20 to 1) 11
4561[2] KERRIE-JO [73] 9-0 B Raymond (8) *chsd ldrs till rdn and wknd o'r 2 fs out.*........................(10 to 1 op 7 to 1) 12
4649[6] NAKITA [77] 9-4 J Williams (13) *al beh.* ....(25 to 1 op 20 to 1 tchd 33 to 1) 13
4719[3] FEATHERSTONE LANE [68] 8-9 D Harrison (2) *mid-div, rdn o'r 2 fs out, sn wknd.*............ (14 to 1 op 10 to 1) 14
4542 MUCH TOO CLEVER [65] 8-6 G Duffield (5) *slwly into strd, al beh.*........................(25 to 1 op 20 to 1) 15
4527* RAFTER-J [69] 8-10 J Quinn (9) *beh hfwy.* .... (12 to 1 op 10 to 1) 16
Dist: Sht-hd, ¾l, 1½l, hd, 3l, 2½l, 1½l, ½l, nk, ¾l. 1m 28.44s. a 5.04s (16 Ran).
SR: 6/4/11/13/8/3/ (Sandmoor Textiles Co Ltd), M H Easterby

4734 C.I.U. Macmillan Nurse Appeal Handicap Class D (0-80 3-y-o and up) £4,370 5f........................ (4:10)

4363 LORD HIGH ADMIRAL (Can) [76] 5-9-10 R Perham (18) *made all stands side, clr entering fnl furlong, ran on wl.* .... (20 to 1 op 14 to 1) 1
4693[2] DOMICKSKY [72] 5-8-13 (7*) R Painter (11) *in tch centre, effrt 2 fs out, rdn and ran on ins last.* ....(3 to 1 fav op 7 to 1) 2
4681 BELLSABANGING [72] 3-9-6 G Duffield (2) *al cl up far side, rdn and ch appr fnl furlong, kpt on.* ....(14 to 1 tchd 16 to 1) 3
4681[6] CHOIR PRACTICE [75] 6-9-9 C Rutter (10) *in tch centre, hdwy o'r one furlong out, styd on und pres ins last.* .... (11 to 1 op 12 to 1 tchd 10 to 1) 4
4532[5] PALLIUM (Ire) [66] (v) 5-9-0 J Weaver (1) *chsd far side ldrs, rdn entering fnl furlong, styd on wl.*..........(16 to 1) 5
3348[6] CANTORIS [79] 7-9-13 D Holland (20) *mid-div, styd on wl fnl furlong, nrst finish.* .... (10 to 1 op 8 to 1 tchd 12 to 1) 6
4277[6] FIRST OPTION [69] 3-9-3 M Birch (4) *chsd far side ldrs, hdwy and ev ch 2 fs out, rdn entering last, fdd.* ....(14 to 1 op 12 to 1 tchd 16 to 1) 7
4277[8] DOMULLA [74] 3-9-8 T Quinn (17) *chsd ldrs stands side, rdn 2 fs out, kpt on same pace.*............... (14 to 1) 8
4455[8] SHADOW JURY [71] 3-9-5 S Wood (19) *chsd wnr, rdn 2 fs out, wknd.*........................ (16 to 1 op 14 to 1) 9
4532 SONDERISE [62] 4-8-10 W Newnes (14) *mid-div, rdn 2 fs out, kpt on same pace.*.......... (20 to 1 tchd 25 to 1) 10
3270 DAANIERA (Ire) [60] 3-8-8 J Quinn (21) *slwly into strd, beh stands side, some late hdwy, nvr dngrs.*.......(33 to 1) 11
4455[2] PRIMULA BAIRN [72] (v) 3-9-6 K Fallon (3) *prmnt far side till wknd 2 fs out.*........(9 to 1 op 8 to 1 tchd 10 to 1) 12
4670[5] VICTORIA HALL [62] 3-8-10 Paul Eddery (6) *prmnt far side till wknd 2 fs out.*................(16 to 1 op 12 to 1) 13
4532 DRUM SERGEANT [68] (bl) 6-9-2 S Whitworth (13) *nvr dngrs.*........................ (16 to 1 tchd 20 to 1) 14
4363 MY ABBEY [59] 4-8-0 (7*) S Knott (22) *sn beh.*.... (33 to 1) 15
3739[4] RHYTHMIC DANCER [72] 5-9-6 A Mackay (9) *nvr dngrs.* ....(16 to 1 op 14 to 1 tchd 20 to 1) 16
2794 LOUISVILLE BELLE (Ire) [61] 4-8-9 D Harrison (8) *in tch centre till wknd hfwy.*.............. (25 to 1 tchd 33 to 1) 17
4455[9] BREEZY DAY [61] (bl) 7-8-2 (7*) S Sanders (15) *chsd ldrs stands side till wknd 2 fs out.*..... (20 to 1 op 16 to 1) 18
4681 HOPE HALL (Ire) [73] 5-9-0 (7*) G Parkin (16) *prmnt stands side till wknd 2 fs out.*.................. (33 to 1 op 25 to 1) 19
4485[6] PEERAGE PRINCE [62] (bl) 4-8-10 A Munro (12) *nvr on terms.*........................ (20 to 1 op 16 to 1) 20
4487 SUPER ROCKY [63] 4-8-11 A Culhane (5) *nvr on terms.* ....(25 to 1 op 20 to 1) 21
4038 SLADES HILL [63] 6-8-11 A McGlone (7) *chsd far side ldrs, rdn 2 fs out, sn wknd.* .... (20 to 1 op 12 to 1 tchd 25 to 1) 22
Dist: 3l, ½l, ½l, ½l, 1l, ½l, nk, hd, 1l, ½l. 1m 0.80s. a 2.00s (22 Ran).
SR: 60/44/42/43/32/41/29/33/29/ (E J G Young), M J Heaton-Ellis

LEOPARDSTOWN (IRE) (good to yielding)
Saturday November 6th
Going Correction: PLUS 0.15 sec. per fur.

4735 Colibri Gold Cup (3-y-o and up) £5,520 1¼m........................ (1:45)

4585[2] CHEVIOT AMBLE (Ire) 5-8-13 J F Egan (3)..... (6 to 4 fav) 1
4639[2] SHARASTAMINA (USA) 4-8-6 (4*) J J Behan (1)... (16 to 1) 2
3577* MUBADIR (USA) 5-9-7 (2*) P Carberry (2).......... (9 to 4) 3
4461[7] LIFEWATCH VISION (bl) 6-9-2 P Shanahan (4)..... (7 to 2) 4
4461[2] NEVER BACK DOWN (Ire) 3-8-8 W J Supple (5)... (11 to 2) 5
Dist: 4l, 2l, 1½l, 3l. 2m 10.30s. a 5.60s (5 Ran).
SR: 58/47/56/46/32/ (Michael W J Smurfit), Patrick Joseph Flynn

4736 Knockaire Stakes (Listed) (3-y-o and up) £8,625 7f........................ (2:15)

4585* PRE-EMINENT (bl) 6-9-5 P Shanahan (1) *led, hdd briefly 2 fs out, rdn and ran on strly fnl furlong*....... (4 to 1) 1
4463^3 MILLIE'S CHOICE (Ire) 4-9-2 W J Supple (2) *rdn in mid-div 2 fs out, styd on fnl furlong*.................(6 to 1) 2
4552^3 DASHING COLOURS (Ire) 4-9-2 W J O'Connor (5) *rear, prog to track ldrs entering strt, short of room on ins 2 fs out, swtchd rght and ran on inside last*............(8 to 1) 3
4554^3 WANDERING THOUGHTS (Ire) 4-8-12 P V Gilson (6) *trkd ldrs, kpt on und pres fnl 2 fs*................. (9 to 2) 4
4689^6 FOREST CONCERT (Ire) 4-8-9 S Craine (4) *last strt, rdn and styd on frm one and a half fs out, not rch ldrs.* ....(20 to 1) 5
4463* THATCHING CRAFT (Ire) 4-9-2 J J Behan (3) *trkd ldr into strt, rdn to ld briefly 2 fs out, sn wknd*......... (8 to 1) 6
4585^3 IDRIS (Ire) 3-9-3 R Hughes (7) *4th strt, rdn and wknd quickly 2 fs out*........................... (6 to 4 fav) 7

Dist: 1l, 1l, ½l, ½l, 1l. 1m 30.80s. a 5.40s (7 Ran).
SR: 40/34/31/25/19/-/-/ (Michael W J Smurfit), D K Weld

4737 Leopardstown November Handicap (0-110 3-y-o and up) £13,000 2m (3:15)

4288* CLIVEDEN GAIL (Ire) [-] 4-9-0 (6*) D J O'Donohoe (28) ....(8 to 1) 1
4288^2 SHIRLEY'S DELIGHT (Ire) [-] 3-8-9 (2*) P Carberry (5) ....(5 to 1 fav) 2
4288^5 BITOFABANTER [-] 6-8-4^2 R Hughes (10) ....(7 to 1) 3
4288^7 CAMDEN BUZZ (Ire) [-] 5-7-11 (6*) R V Skelly (26) (10 to 1) 4
3824^3 JUDICIAL FIELD (Ire) [-] (bl) 4-9-10 P Shanahan (11) (20 to 1) 5
4057 TIME IT RIGHT (Ire) [-] 4-7-12 (4*) J J Behan (25) .. (33 to 1) 6
2408^4 GENERAL IDEA [-] 8-7-7 (4*) W J Smith (22) .... (8 to 1) 7
4461^4 TONY'S FEN [-] 4-9-2 (6*) B J Walsh (2) .... (16 to 1) 8
4625* FORCE SEVEN [-] 6-8-12 (8ex) C Roche (13) ......(10 to 1) 9
4461 VALONA (Ire) [-] 3-7-11^2 (4*) J A Heffernan (15).... (25 to 1) 10
4639^4 FONTANAYS (Ire) [-] 5-7-7 Joanna Morgan (20) .....(33 to 1) 11
4430 THATCH AND GOLD (Ire) [-] 5-8-0 W J Supple (1) (25 to 1) 12
4573^2 FOR REG (Ire) [-] 4-9-1 P V Gilson (7) .... (10 to 1) 13
3577^4 NORDIC SUN (Ire) [-] 5-8-10 K J Manning (21) .... (20 to 1) 14
3560 GARBONI (USA) [-] 4-9-1 D V Smith (3) ....(20 to 1) 15
4555 ELIADE (Ire) [-] 4-8-8 N G McCullagh (12) ....(25 to 1) 16
4639^5 MORNING SARGE [-] 5-7-0 (8*) G M Moylan (27) .. (14 to 1) 17
4586* HACKETTS CROSS (Ire) [-] 5-7-5 (8*) R T Fitzpatrick (16) ....(14 to 1) 18
4461^3 ENQELAAB (USA) [-] 5-8-2 J F Egan (6) .... (14 to 1) 19
4639 KEPPOLS PRINCE [-] 6-6-13 (8*) B J Halligan (14) (25 to 1) 20
4555 GLENCLOUD (Ire) [-] 5-8-11 S Craine (17) .... (20 to 1) 21
4389^3 BOLERO DANCER (Ire) [-] 5-7-7 A O'Rourke (18) .. (50 to 1) 22
3398^6 HEAD OF CHAMBERS (Ire) [-] 5-7-7 L O'Shea (24) (20 to 1) 23
4370 DARCARI ROSE (Ire) [-] 4-7-7 A J Nolan (29) ...... (50 to 1) 24
4573^5 PRINCE OLE (Ire) [-] 5-8-6 D Hogan (9) ....(20 to 1) 25
4461 OFTEN AHEAD (Ire) [-] 5-7-13^5 (8*) B Fenton (4) ... (16 to 1) 26
4685a GAMARA (Ire) [-] 5-7-5 (2*) D G O'Shea (19) ....(33 to 1) 27
3275^4 MAXWELTON BRAES (Ire) [-] (bl) 4-7-4 (6*) P P Murphy (23) ....(40 to 1) 28
LEGAL PROFESSION (Ire) [-] 5-7-11 (8*) P M Donohoe (8) ....(12 to 1) ro

Dist: Nk, 1l, 1l, nk. 3m 31.30s. a 6.30s (29 Ran).
SR: 67/57/49/47/67/-/ (Int Thoroughbred Breeders Inc), D K Weld

4738 Inter Varsity Cup Handicap (0-100 3-y-o and up) £3,105 1m 1f..........(3:45)

4555* SOUNDPROOF (Ire) [-] 3-8-7 (4*,7ex) J J Behan (2) (7 to 1) 1
4136* ALSHOU (Ire) [-] 4-7-7 A J Nolan (9) ....(12 to 1) 2
4408* BRAZEN ANGEL (Ire) [-] 3-8-0 J F Egan (6) .... (10 to 1) 3
4639^3 WICKLOW WAY (Ire) [-] 3-7-5 (8*) R T Fitzpatrick (13) ....(10 to 1) 4
4554 SWEET NASHA (Ire) [-] 4-10-0 P V Gilson (11) .....(10 to 1) 5
4686^8 DIFFERENT TIMES (Ire) [-] 3-8-10 S Craine (5) .... (20 to 1) 6
4583^6 DESERT CALM (Ire) [-] 4-8-12 (6*) B J Walsh (3) (13 to 2 fav) 7
4625^2 SAFAYN (USA) [-] (bl) 3-8-5 (6*) D J O'Donohoe (12) (10 to 1) 8
4686^4 MAJBOOR (Ire) [-] 4-9-2 W J O'Connor (7) ....(14 to 1) 9
2957^3 PRIVATE GUY (Ire) [-] (bl) 4-9-5 P Shanahan (21) ....(7 to 1) 10
4585^7 TRYARRA (Ire) [-] 3-9-7 C Roche (14) ....(9 to 1) 11
4689^4 HANG A RIGHT [-] 6-8-8 R Hughes (8) .... (8 to 1) 12
3544 ALBERTA ROSE (Ire) [-] 4-7-6 (6*) P P Murphy (16) (25 to 1) 13
4555 DEVIL'S HOLIDAY (USA) [-] 3-8-2 N G McCullagh (15) ....(14 to 1) 14
4408^4 ACCELL (Ire) [-] 4-6-13 (8*) G M Moylan (18) ...... (14 to 1) 15
4685 BRACKLOON BOY (Ire) [-] 4-7-13 L O'Shea (1) .....(20 to 1) 16
4639 LOWLACK [-] (bl) 3-7-8^1 (6*) R V Skelly (4) ....(25 to 1) 17
4556 CLANFLUTHER (Ire) [-] (bl) 3-7-7^4 (4*) W J Smith (20) ....(100 to 1) 18
789 BALLYSPARKLE (Ire) [-] (bl) 3-7-7 Joanna Morgan (17) ....(25 to 1) 19
4555 MEJEVE [-] 5-8-5 W J Supple (10) ....(16 to 1) 20
4583^4 KENTUCKY BABY (Ire) [-] (bl) 3-7-6 (2*) D G O'Shea (19) ....(14 to 1) 21

Dist: 4l, sht-hd, hd, 5½l. 1m 56.40s. a 5.90s (21 Ran).
SR: 29/3/9/7/25/-/ (Yoshiki Akazawa), Patrick Prendergast

SANTA ANITA (USA) (firm)
Saturday November 6th

4739 Breeders' Cup Sprint (Grade 1) (dirt) (3-y-o and up) £344,371 6f.......(6:55)

595^4 CARDMANIA (USA) 7-9-0 E Delahoussaye (5) *hdwy hfwy, pld out o'r 2 fs out, ran on to ld last strds*.... (53 to 10) 1
MEAFARA (USA) 4-8-11 G Stevens (8) *led till last strds.* ....(17 to 2) 2
GILDED TIME (USA) 3-8-12 C McCarron (2) *al prmnt, 3rd strt, kpt on one pace*...........................(54 to 10) 3
THIRTY SLEWS (USA) 6-9-0 K Desormeaux (14) *al cl up, 4th strt, kpt on one pace*...................... (102 to 10) 4
DEMALOOT DEMASHOOT (Can) 3-8-12 J Santos (4) *trkd ldr till wknd fnl furlong*..................... (35 to 1) 5
MUSIC MERCI (Can) 7-9-0 L Pincay Jr (1) *dwlt, beh till some prog fnl 2 fs, nrst finish*............... (30 to 1) 6
4312^3 MONDE BLEU (bl) 5-9-0 Pat Eddery (13) *hdwy hfwy, 6th strt, no extr*.................................. (17 to 1) 7
NOW LISTEN (USA) 6-9-0 P Day (6) *stumbled aftr strt, beh till some late prog*........................... (28 to 1) 8
FLY SO FREE (USA) 5-9-0 J Bailey (11) *outpcd*..... (8 to 1) 9
4275^5 SURPRISE OFFER (bl) 3-8-12 C Asmussen (7) *prmnt for o'r 3 fs*..(17 to 1) 0
4173^4 SAYYEDATI 3-8-9 W R Swinburn (9) *bumped strt, rear early, in tch hfwy, wknd 2 fs out*........ (17 to 1) 0
4379^5 ALYDEED (Can) 4-9-0 D Seymour (12) *prmnt for 3 fs.* ....(62 to 10) 0
3207^3 APELIA (Can) 4-8-11 H McCauley (10) *bumped strt, beh fnl 3 fs*..(21 to 1) 0
4379* BIRDONTHEWIRE (USA) 4-9-0 M Smith (3) *dwlt, al outpcd.* ....(32 to 10 fav) 0

Dist: Nk, ½l, 1 ¼l, nose, 1 ¾l, 1 ¼l, hd, 4 ¾l, hd, ½l. 1m 8.60s. (14 Ran).
(Jean Couvercelle), D Meredith

4740 Breeders' Cup Juvenile Fillies (Grade 1) (dirt) (2-y-o) £344,371 1m 110yds ....(7:30)

4390* PHONE CHATTER (USA) 8-7 L Pincay Jr (6) *hdwy 4 fs out, second strt, rdn to ld wl ins fnl furlong*...... (23 to 10) 1
4390^2 SARDULA (USA) 8-7 E Delahoussaye (1) *led till ins fnl furlong, ran on und pres*......................... (22 to 10) 2
4449* HEAVENLY PRIZE (USA) 8-7 M Smith (4) *al in tch, 3rd strt, ev ch o'r one furlong out, no extr*.........(19 to 10 fav) 3
4310^5 COUP DE GENIE (USA) 8-7 C Asmussen (7) *hld up, 5th strt, swtchd outsd appr fnl furlong, took 3rd whn broke blood vessel*....................................... (73 to 10) 4
STELLAR CAT (USA) 8-7 P Day (2) *trkd ldr, ev ch 2 fs out, wknd strt*...................................... (17 to 1) 5
4390^4 RHAPSODIC (USA) 8-7 C McCarron (8) *al rear*...(22 to 10) 6
4390^3 TRICKY CODE (USA) 8-7 G Stevens (5) *6th strt, nvr able to chal*..(32 to 1) 7
MEADOW RENDEZVOUS (USA) 8-7 J L Diaz (3) *prmnt for 6 fs*.. (29 to 1) 8

Dist: Hd, 3l, ½l, 2 ¾l, 6½l, 1 ¼l, 6½l. 1m 43.00s. (8 Ran).
(H Sarkowsky), R Mandella

4741 Breeders' Cup Distaff (Grade 1) (dirt) (3-y-o and up) £344,371 1m 1f... (8:05)

2441* HOLLYWOOD WILDCAT (USA) 3-8-8 E Delahoussaye (6) *trkd ldr, led o'r one furlong out, drvn out, jst hld on.* ....(13 to 10 fav) 1
4472* PASEANA (Arg) 6-8-11 C McCarron (3) *al cl up, second strt, rdn and ev ch fnl furlong, jst fld*.............. (5 to 2) 2
3150^4 RE TOSS (Arg) 6-8-11 C Nakatani (7) *nrst finish.* ....(184 to 10) 3
4450* DISPUTE (USA) 3-8-8 J Bailey (2) *trkd ldrs, rdn and 5th strt, kpt on one pace*.................................(9 to 2) 4
2440* SKY BEAUTY (USA) 3-8-8 M Smith (1) *hdwy o'r 2 fs out, 3rd and ev ch strt, sn one pace*................(43 to 10) 5
SUPAH GEM (USA) 3-8-8 A Solis (8) *led till o'r one furlong out*..(95 to 1) 6
MAGICAL MAIDEN (USA) 4-8-11 G Stevens (4) *swrvd strt, al rear*.. (48 to 1) 7
2085^3 PARTY CITED (USA) 4-8-11 K Desormeaux (5) *hld up, effrt hfwy, btn 2 fs out*.................................(42 to 1) 8

Dist: Nose, 2½l, 1l, ¾l, 3½l, 4l, 2l. 1m 48.20s. (8 Ran).
(I & Marjorie Cowan), N Drysdale

4742 Breeders' Cup Mile (Grade 1) (turf) (3-y-o and up) £344,371 1m........(8:40)

2084^2 LURE (USA) 4-9-0 M Smith (12) *crrd wide 1st bend, led 5 fs out, clr o'r one out, rdn out*............. (13 to 10 fav) 1
4400^2 SKI PARADISE (USA) 3-8-8 T Jarnet (1) *led and hng rght 1st bend, hdd aftr 3 fs, second strt, ran on.* (182 to 10) 2
FOURSTARS ALLSTAR (USA) 5-9-0 J Santos (2) *al cl up, 3rd strt, kpt on one pace*..............................(74 to 1) 3
TOUSSAUD (USA) 4-8-11 K Desormeaux (9) *bumped 1st bend, rear till hdwy o'r 2 fs out, 6th strt, nrst finish.* ....(11 to 1) 4
4173^2 BARATHEA (Ire) 3-8-11 G Stevens (3) *hng 1st bend, mid-div, 4th strt, one pace*..............................(19 to 2) 5
4173* BIGSTONE (Ire) 3-8-11 Pat Eddery (8) *rear and hng rght 1st bend, hdwy o'r 2 fs out, 5th strt, one pace*..... (12 to 1) 6
3654^3 JOHANN QUATZ (Fr) 4-9-0 E Delahoussaye (10) *rear till hdwy 3 fs out, 7th strt, no extr fnl furlong*.....(20 to 1) 7
PARADISE CREEK (USA) 4-9-0 P Day (6) *crrd wide 1st bend, prmnt 6 fs, wknd strt*.................. (82 to 10) 8

3609* FLAWLESSLY (USA) 5-8-11 C McCarron (4) *squeezed 1st bend, in tch till wknd 2 fs out*...............(31 to 10) 9
4312^{7} WOLFHOUND (USA) 4-9-0 L Dettori (13) *badly hmpd 1st bend, not reco'r*.......................(19 to 2) 0
4417* CATRAIL (USA) 3-8-11 C Asmussen (5) *hmpd 1st bend, prmnt o'r 4 fs out, hampered over 3 furlongs out, not rcvr*.......................................(19 to 2) 0
LECH (USA) 5-9-0 C Perret (7) *prmnt till hmpd 1st bend, beh fnl 3 fs*..................................(103 to 1) 0
BUCKHAR (USA) 5-9-0 J Cruguet (11) *hmpd 1st bend, al beh*...(28 to 1) 0
Dist: 2 ¼l, 1 ¾l, hd, hd, 1l, nk, 2½l, 2l, 5l, 3½l. 1m 33.40s. (13 Ran).
(Claiborne Farm), C McGaughey

4743 Breeders' Cup Juvenile (Grade 1) (2-y-o) £344,371 1m 110yds........(9:15)

BROCCO (USA) 8-10 G Stevens (5) *hld up in tch, 4th and hdwy strt, led ins fnl furlong, drvn clr*.........(3 to 1) 1
BLUMIN AFFAIR (USA) 8-10 J Bailey (11) *rear till hdwy o'r 2 fs out, 5th strt, hrd rdn, kpt on one pace.* (424 to 10) 2
TABASCO CAT (USA) 8-10 P Day (4) *cl up till o'r 2 fs out, drpd back strt, rallied nr near finish*.........(333 to 10) 3
FLYING SENSATION (USA) 8-10 L Pincay Jr (8) *nvr able to chal*...(64 to 10) 4
WINNING PACT (USA) 8-10 C Nakatani (10) *led till wknd quickly ins fnl furlong*..........................(41 to 1) 5
SHEPHERD'S FIELD (USA) 8-10 M Smith (3) *nvr dngrs.*
....(17 to 1) 6
RAMBLIN GUY (USA) 8-10 E Delahoussaye (6) *trkd ldr, second and ev ch strt, sn btn*.....................(15 to 1) 7
4448* DEHERE (USA) 8-10 C McCarron (7) *trkd ldr, second and ev ch strt, sn btn*.......................... (10 to 7 on) 8
FERRARA (USA) 8-10 K Desormeaux (2) *mid-div 6 fs.*
....(36 to 1) 9
CRESTON (USA) 8-10 C Black (1) *al beh*............. (95 to 1) 0
HOT NUMBER (USA) 8-10 A Solis (9) *beh fnl 3 fs*. (213 to 1) 0
Dist: 5l, 1½l, 3l, nk, hd, 2 ¼l, ½l, 1l, 3½l, 1½l. 1m 42.80s. (11 Ran).
(A Broccoli), R Winick

4744 Breeders' Cup Turf (Grade 1) (3-y-o and up) £688,742 1½m..........(9:50)

4404* KOTASHAAN (Fr) 5-9-0 K Desormeaux (13) *hld up, hdwy 3 fs out, 4th strt, ran on wl to ld cl hme*........(6 to 4 fav) 1
4071^{6} BIEN BIEN (USA) 4-9-0 C McCarron (12) *al in tch, 3rd strt, led one furlong out till ct cl hme*............. (43 to 10) 2
4404^{2} LUAZUR (Fr) 4-9-0 P Day (6) *led till one furlong out, kpt on one pace*................................(171 to 10) 3
4378^{5} FRAISE (USA) 5-9-0 P Valenzuela (1) *hld up, hdwy and not clr run o'r 3 fs out, fnshd wl*...................(14 to 1) 4
4467* HATOOF (USA) 4-8-11 W R Swinburn (8) *mid-div, hdwy and 5th strt, kpt on one pace*.....................(15 to 1) 5
4311^{3} OPERA HOUSE 5-9-0 M Roberts (4) *pld hrd tracking ldr, second and ev ch strt, wknd fnl furlong*........(41 to 10) 6
3890^{5} FAIRY GARDEN (USA) 5-8-11 L Pincay Jr (2) *hld up, some hdwy fnl 2 fs, nrst finish*.......................(60 to 1) 7
4311 WEMYSS BIGHT 3-8-7 Pat Eddery (3) *mid-div, cl up hfwy, 6th and rdn strt, no extr*.........................(41 to 1) 8
4378* APPLE TREE (Fr) (bl) 4-9-0 M Smith (10) *dwlt, al beh.*
....(11 to 1) 9
4467^{3} DERNIER EMPEREUR (USA) 3-8-10 T Jarnet (7) *in tch for one m*..(89 to 1) 0
4311 HERNANDO (Fr) 3-8-10 C Asmussen (5) *prmnt for 9 fs.*
....(15 to 1) 0
4071^{2} SERRANT (USA) 5-9-0 J Santos (9) *al rear*.........(31 to 1) 0
4311^{4} INTREPIDITY 3-8-7 G Stevens (14) *al beh*............ (41 to 10) 0
4378^{2} SOLAR SPLENDOUR (USA) 6-9-0 H McCauley (11) *prmnt for 9 fs*...(60 to 1) 0
Dist: ½l, 1 ¼l, ¾l, 1 ¼l, 1 ¼l, 2l, ½l, 1 ¼l, ¾l, 1 ¼l. 2m 25.00s. (14 Ran).
(S Okada), R Mandella

4745 Breeders' Cup Classic (Grade 1) (dirt) (3-y-o and up) £1,033,113 1¼m.......

4295^{4} ARCANGUES (USA) 5-9-0 J Bailey (13) *hdwy o'r 3 fs out, 5th strt, ran on wl to ld ins fnl furlong*.......(133 to 10) 1
4068* BERTRANDO (USA) 4-9-0 G Stevens (8) *led till ins fnl furlong*...................................(6 to 5 co-fav) 2
4291^{4} KISSIN KRIS (USA) 3-8-10 P Day (5) *rapid hdwy o'r 3 fs out, rcd wide, ev ch one out, one pace*.........(63 to 10) 3
4438* MARQUETRY (USA) 6-9-0 K Desormeaux (1) *trkd ldr, second strt, sn no extr*.........................(6 to 5 co-fav) 4
PLEASANT TANGO (USA) 3-8-11 A Solis (3) *hdwy o'r 2 fs out, ran on und pres, nrst finish*.................(74 to 1) 5
4447^{5} DIAZO (USA) 3-8-10 L Pincay Jr (12) *al in tch, 4th strt, one pace*...(23 to 1) 6
4467^{2} EZZOUD (Ire) 4-9-0 W R Swinburn (2) *rcd in 3rd to strt, wknd one furlong out*..............................(106 to 1) 7
4447^{4} DEVIL HIS DUE (USA) 4-9-0 M Smith (10) *hdwy 2 fs out, 6th strt, sn btn*......................................(21 to 1) 8
4291* WALLENDA (USA) 3-8-10 H McCauley (9) *sn beh.* (33 to 1) 9
4068^{4} MISSIONARY RIDGE 6-9-0 E Delahoussaye (7) *outpcd.*
.... (6 to 5 co-fav) 0
2243* BEST PAL (USA) 5-9-0 C Black (4) *prmnt for 7 fs*...(9 to 5) 0
4447^{2} COLONIAL AFFAIR (USA) 3-8-10 J Santos (11) *prmnt for o'r 6 fs*...(15 to 1) 0
4447* MINER'S MARK (USA) 3-8-10 C McCarron (14) *hdwy o'r 4 fs out, wknd over 2 out*..............................(19 to 1) 0
Dist: 2l, 1 ¾l, 1 ¼l, nk, nose, nk, 1 ¾l, 3l, nk, hd. 2m 0.80s. (13 Ran).
(D Wildenstein), A Fabre

CAPANNELLE (ITY) (heavy)
Sunday November 7th

4746 Premio Ribot (Group 2) (3-y-o and up) £34,219 1m.................... (2:10)

4403* ALHIJAZ 4-8-12 W Carson, *led, sn clr, unchlgd*.......... 1
2650^{4} ANOTHER BOB (USA) 5-8-12 Jacqueline Freda, *mid-div, hdwy 2 fs out, no ch wth wnr*.................................. 2
GLACIAL 4-8-12 A Luongo, *rear till prog und pres one and a half fs out, kpt on one pace*.......................... 3
2650^{2} TAFF'S ACRE (Ire) 4-8-12 F Jovine, *nvr plcd to chal*...... 4
4403^{6} GOLDEN BECHETT (Ire) 3-8-12 D Holland, *prmnt, rdn 2 fs out, sn wknd*.. 5
4648^{2} FRAAM 4-8-12 B Raymond, *in tch, rdn 2 fs out, sn btn*... 6
LANDOLFI 5-8-12 S Dettori, *al beh*........................ 7
Dist: 4l, 2½l, ¾l, 3½l, nk, 6l. 1m 41.70s. (7 Ran).
(Prince A A Faisal), J L Dunlop

SANTA ANITA (USA) (firm)
Sunday November 7th

4747 Carleton F Burke Handicap (Grade 2) (3-y-o and up) £63,576 1¼m..........

KNOW HEIGHTS (Ire) 4-8-5 K Desormeaux,................ 1
4295^{2} FANMORE (USA) 5-8-4 Pat Eddery,.......................... 2
MYRAKALU (Fr) 5-8-2 C Black,.............................. 3
Dist: 2½l, ¾l, 2 ¾l, 1l, 7l, 2l. 2m 0.07s. (7 Ran).
(Caulfield & Jeremys Stable),

4748 Sunny Slope Stakes (2-y-o) £30,397 7f ....(9:30)

SUBTLE TROUBLE (USA) 8-5 A Solis,...................... 1
TROYALTY (USA) 8-7 K Desormeaux,...................... 2
STATE CRAFT (USA) 8-4 E Delahoussaye,.................. 3
JUST A ROMAN (USA) 8-3 V Navarro,...................... 4
4195^{5} EAGLE EYED (USA) 8-5 Pat Eddery,........................ 5
Dist: Nose, 4l, hd, nk. 1m 22.80s. (5 Ran).
(Coelho & Valenti), M Stute

4749 Louis R Rowan Handicap (3-y-o and up) £33,543 1m.......................

1370^{6} MISS TURKANA (USA) 4-8-6 A Castanon,................ 1
4413* COX ORANGE (USA) 3-8-2 T Jarnet,.................... 2
1370^{5} WEDDING RING (Ire) 4-8-4 E Delahoussaye,............ 3
Dist: ¾l, ½l, nose, nose, 2 ¼l, 1 ¾l, ½l, ¾l, ½l. 1m 34.80s. (10 Ran).
(Fawn Leap Farm Inc), G Jones

FOLKESTONE (good to soft)
Monday November 8th

Going Correction: PLUS 0.95 sec. per fur. (races 1,2,4,6), PLUS 0.50 (3,5)

4750 Cutlass Nursery Class E (0-75 2-y-o) £3,157 6f 189yds.............. (1:00)

4483* FOLLY FINNESSE [67] 9-4 S Whitworth (7) *hld up towards rear, hdwy o'r 2 fs out, led appr last, sn clr.*
...................................(7 to 2 fav op 3 to 1) 1
4671 STARICA (Ire) [51] (bl) 8-2 Dale Gibson (4) *trkd ldr, led 2 fs out till appr last, one pace*.......(20 to 1 tchd 25 to 1) 2
4615^{5} CHARLIE CHARLIE [62] 8-13 A McGlone (3) *chsd ldrs, kpt on one pace fnl 2 fs.* (14 to 1 op 12 to 1 tchd 16 to 1) 3
3750^{7} SILVER SLIPPER [63] 9-0 L Dettori (2) *chsd ldrs, effrt o'r 2 fs out, one pace*........ (6 to 1 op 4 to 1 tchd 13 to 2) 4
4674^{6} STRAPPED [60] 8-11 N Adams (6) *outpcd, hdwy blw 2 fs out, kpt on, nrst finish.* (15 to 2 op 6 to 1 tchd 8 to 1) 5
4356^{4} PASSING PLAYER (USA) [70] 9-7 M Hills (1) *trkd ldg pair, rdn 2 fs out, one pace*.................(9 to 2 op 6 to 1) 6
4575^{9} CHANTELYS [57] 8-8 D Biggs (5) *chsd ldrs, no prog fnl 2 fs.*
.... (20 to 1 op 12 to 1) 7
3520* YO-CANDO (Ire) [70] 9-2 (5*) L Newton (8) *nvr nr to chal.*
....(5 to 1 op 5 to 2) 8
4618^{9} EUROPHARM LASSIE [70] 9-7 B Rouse (10) *broke wl, sn beh*...................................(33 to 1 op 20 to 1) 9
4497 SHIFTING MIST [55] 8-6 G Duffield (9) *outpcd.*
.............(20 to 1 op 14 to 1 tchd 25 to 1) 10
4351 KILLING TIME [60] (bl) 8-11 J Reid (11) *led to 2 fs out, wknd quickly*................................(14 to 1 op 12 to 1) 11
Dist: 3½l, 4l, sht-hd, sht-hd, hd, hd, 2½l, ¾l, ¾l. 1m 32.00s. a 11.10s (11 Ran).
SR: 37/10/9/9/5/14/ (Richard Withers), B R Millman

4751 Foil Selling Handicap Stakes Class G (0-60 3-y-o and up) £2,070 1½m (1:30)

3891^{6} IBSEN [42] 5-8-10 D Holland (2) *prmnt in chasing grp, rdn to ld ins fnl furlong, ran on*......(2 to 1 fav op 5 to 2) 1
4722^{2} PRINCESS EVITA (Fr) [33] 4-8-1 D Harrison (8) *led chasing grp, o'rall ldr 3 fs out, hdd ins last, no extr.* ....(5 to 1 op 3 to 1 tchd 11 to 2) 2
3066^{3} BY ARRANGEMENT (Ire) [41] 4-8-9 L Dettori (1) *mid-div, hdwy o'r 4 fs out, one pace 2 out.* ....(9 to 1 op 7 to 1 tchd 10 to 1) 3
4574 NAIL DON [46] 8-9-0 A McGlone (15) *cl up in chasing grp, rdn alng 2 fs out, wknd ins last*....(50 to 1 op 33 to 1) 4
MAJORITY HOLDING [39] 8-8-7 M Wigham (7) *beh, hdwy o'r one furlong out, nvr nrr*....... (25 to 1 op 20 to 1) 5
4600^{4} ROCK THE BARNEY (Ire) [43] 4-8-11 B Rouse (9) *hld up rear, hdwy o'r 4 fs out, rdn appr 2 out, eased whn btn.* ....(3 to 1 op 9 to 4 tchd 100 to 30) 6
4633 ARRASAS LADY [39] 3-7-7 (7*) Wendy Jones (16) *chsd ldrs till outpcd o'r 3 fs out.* ....(20 to 1 op 50 to 1 tchd 66 to 1) 7
2471 SHAMROCK DANCER (Ire) [39] 3-7-11^{2} (5*) B Russell (3) *pld hrd early, chsd ldrs, outpcd hfwy.* (20 to 1 op 33 to 1) 8
NATHIR (USA) [31] 7-7-13 N Adams (5) *strted slwly, al beh.* ....(50 to 1 op 33 to 1) 9
4574 WATER DIVINER [44] 3-7-12 (7*) M Baird (12) *trkd ldrs till lost pl o'r 4 fs out*..........(33 to 1 tchd 40 to 1) 10
4254 MYFONTAINE [52] 6-9-6 W Newnes (10) *beh, cld o'r 3 fs out, sn wknd*........ (10 to 1 op 8 to 1 tchd 12 to 1) 11
SHADOWLAND (Ire) [38] 5-8-6^{3} V Slattery (11) *mid-div, wknd o'r 4 fs out*.................(40 to 1 op 25 to 1) 12
4485^{7} PRINCE ROONEY (Ire) [60] 5-9-9 (5*) S Drowne (14) *al beh.* ....(14 to 1 op 10 to 1 tchd 16 to 1) 13
4008 DISTANT DYNASTY [32] 3-7-4^{4} (7*) N Varley (4) *rcd freely, led, sn wl clr, tired and hdd 3 fs out, wknd quickly.* ....(50 to 1 op 33 to 1) 14
4680a GRAND FELLOW (Ire) [46] (bl) 4-9-0 J Williams (6) *al beh, sn tld off*............................(25 to 1 op 16 to 1) 15

Dist: 1½l, 4l, 6l, 5l, 8l, sht-hd, 1l, 1½l, 2l, 10l. 2m 50.80s. a 20.30s (15 Ran).
SR: 7/-/-/-/-/-/ (R Akehurst), R Akehurst

4752 EBF Broadsword Median Auction Maiden Stakes Class E (2-y-o) £3,340 6f............................ (2:00)

4594 GALLANT SPIRIT (Ire) 9-0 L Dettori (5) *cl up, led appr 2 fs out, ran on wl*......................(5 to 1 op 9 to 2) 1
3642^{3} MATHANDAN 8-9 D Holland (3) *al prmnt, pushed alng hfwy, kpt on ins last*................ (4 to 1 op 5 to 2) 2
4594^{9} SUGAR RISK 8-9 S Whitworth (13) *chsd ldrs, swtchd rght one furlong out, kpt on.* ....(20 to 1 op 10 to 1 tchd 25 to 1) 3
4697^{6} DAME LORRAINE 8-9 J Reid (15) *led till appr 2 fs out, edgd lft and one pace*...........(7 to 2 fav op 2 to 1) 4
DALCROSS 8-2 (7*) C Hawksley (7) *chsd ldrs, no hdwy fnl 2 fs*.............................. (25 to 1 op 20 to 1) 5
4338^{7} DANDINI 9-0 N Adams (2) *outpcd, hdwy 2 fs out, swtchd rght o'r one out, ran on ins last*... (25 to 1 op 20 to 1) 6
4651 DAILY SPORT CLUB 8-9 G Bardwell (14) *trkd ldrs for o'r 4 fs*..............................(20 to 1 op 14 to 1) 7
GRAND SALT (Ire) 9-0 J Williams (9) *nvr on terms.* .... (25 to 1 op 16 to 1 tchd 33 to 1) 8
PREJON 8-4 (5*) B Russell (12) *sn pushed alng, nvr on terms*.................................. (33 to 1 op 20 to 1) 9
DEVILSDANCER 9-0 V Smith (1) *outpcd.* ....(25 to 1 op 20 to 1) 10
4594^{3} THE WITCHBOY 9-0 W Hood (4) *trkd ldrs till wknd o'r one furlong out*............ (5 to 1 op 7 to 2 tchd 6 to 1) 11
4594 VIVS FUTURE (Ire) 8-9 D Harrison (8) *cl up till wknd o'r 2 fs out*..............................(33 to 1 op 20 to 1) 12
TIMELYINTERVENTION (Ire) 9-0 G Duffield (10) *outpcd.* ....(8 to 1 tchd 10 to 1) 13
4527^{5} GROVE PRIMROSE (Ire) 8-9 P Robinson (6) *wth ldrs till wknd quickly appr 2 fs out*.........(8 to 1 op 10 to 1) 14
ONLY DREAMING 8-9 R Perham (11) *strted slwly, outpcd.* .... (8 to 1 op 7 to 1 tchd 10 to 1) 15

Dist: 3l, 4l, ¾l, ½l, hd, 1l, 2½l, 2½l, nk, 1½l. 1m 19.30s. a 8.30s (15 Ran).
(P B Adams), R Hannon

4753 Claymore Claiming Handicap Stakes Class F (0-65 3-y-o and up) £2,243 2m 93yds........................ (2:30)

4684^{9} GO SOUTH [58] 9-10-0 S Whitworth (5) *hld up, cld o'r 3 fs out, sstnd run to ld on line*.........(10 to 1 op 6 to 1) 1
3943^{8} MAD CASANOVA [54] (bl) 8-9-10 D Biggs (6) *hld up, hdwy o'r 4 fs out, led one and a half out till ct on line.* ....(7 to 2 jt-fav op 3 to 1 tchd 5 to 2) 2
4530^{6} KOVALEVSKIA [32] 8-8-2 G Bardwell (10) *chsd ldrs, pushed alng 7 fs out, styd on frm o'r one out.* ....(4 to 1 op 5 to 2 tchd 9 to 2) 3
4631 SOOJAMA (Ire) [40] (bl) 3-8-0 N Adams (3) *hld up rear, cld o'r 4 fs out, kpt on*................ (20 to 1 op 12 to 1) 4
4611^{5} ARMASHOCKER [37] 5-8-7^{2} M Wigham (1) *hld up last, hdwy o'r 3 fs out, sn one pace*..... (33 to 1 op 25 to 1) 5
4797a SMARTIE LEE [46] 6-9-2 W Newnes (4) *led to one and a half fs out, no extr*.... (10 to 1 op 6 to 1 tchd 12 to 1) 6
4486^{8} MATCHING GREEN [58] 4-10-0 J Williams (2) *cl up, pushed alng 3 fs out, wknd o'r one out.* (7 to 2 jt-fav op 5 to 2) 7
3985^{6} ALYVAIR [35] 3-7-2 (7*) M Baird (8) *hld up in tch, shrtlvd effrt 5 fs out, nvr dngrs*.................. (4 to 1 tchd 6 to 1) 8
4631 BARBARY REEF (Ire) [29] 5-7-13^{4} D Harrison (7) *al beh.* ....(33 to 1 op 20 to 1 tchd 50 to 1) 9
4092 THREEOFUS [36] (bl) 3-7-10^{1} Dale Gibson (9) *cl up, pushed alng 7 fs out, wknd 6 out, tld off*...(25 to 1 op 12 to 1) 10
KAURI [47] 6-9-3 G Duffield (11) *trkd ldrs, pushed alng 4 fs out, wknd quickly o'r 2 out, tld off.* ....(14 to 1 op 20 to 1 tchd 33 to 1) 11

Dist: Sht-hd, 4l, ½l, nk, 4l, 1l, 2½l, 6l, 20l, ¾l. 4m 0.30s. a 29.30s (11 Ran).
(Rex Joachim), J R Jenkins

4754 Epee Conditions Stakes Class D (2-y-o) £3,231 5f.................. (3:00)

4594* MR BERGERAC (Ire) 9-1 D Holland (2) *made virtually all, clr o'r one furlong out, ran on strly.* ....(100 to 30 op 5 to 2 tchd 7 to 2) 1
4272^{4} DOLLAR GAMBLE (Ire) 9-0 (7*) Mark Denaro (3) *wth wnr, ev ch 2 fs out, one pace.* ....(85 to 40 fav op 2 to 1 tchd 9 to 4) 2
4523 PERFECT BRAVE 8-11 J Williams (7) *mid-div till styd on ins fnl furlong*......... (5 to 1 op 7 to 1 tchd 10 to 1) 3
4436^{2} POST MISTRESS (Ire) 8-10 G Duffield (8) *niggled alng thrght, cl up till outpcd wl o'r one furlong out.* ....(100 to 30 op 3 to 1 tchd 7 to 2) 4
4627^{8} TEN-TO-SIX GIRL 8-6 B Procter (9) *hld up in mid-div, lost pl wl o'r one furlong out, kpt on ins last.* ....(20 to 1 op 12 to 1) 5
4598^{4} MUTINIQUE 8-6 D Harrison (6) *sn outpcd.* ....(33 to 1 op 20 to 1) 6
4709^{8} TWICE IN BUNDORAN (Ire) 8-5 (5*) L Newton (1) *cl up till wknd 2 fs out*......... (10 to 1 op 5 to 1 tchd 11 to 1) 7
4575^{6} IT'S SO EASY 8-6 L Dettori (4) *cl up, rdn o'r 2 fs out, sn btn*.................. (10 to 1 op 5 to 1 tchd 12 to 1) 8
3982 BATON BLEU 8-11 B Rouse (5) *strted slwly, al beh, sn tld off*............................(33 to 1 op 14 to 1) 9

Dist: 4l, 3l, 1½l, ¾l, 2l, 1l, 2l, 25l. 1m 4.00s. a 5.40s (9 Ran).
SR: 43/33/11/4/-/-/ (P R John), B Palling

4755 Sabre Handicap Class E (0-70 3-y-o) £2,976 1½m.................. (3:30)

4713* NIGHT EDITION [50] 8-3^{1} (5ex) G Duffield (7) *keen hold early, al prmnt, led appr 2 fs out, hld on wl.* ....(9 to 2 op 3 to 1 tchd 5 to 1) 1
4631 BROUGHTONS FORMULA [53] (bl) 8-6 D Biggs (4) *set steady pace, hdd appr 2 fs out, kpt on.* ....(12 to 1 op 8 to 1 tchd 14 to 1) 2
4524^{3} DILI (USA) [68] 9-7 L Dettori (2) *al prmnt, rdn 2 fs out, one pace o'r one out*............... (13 to 8 fav op 2 to 1) 3
4631 KISMETIM [56] 8-9 J Reid (6) *in tch, pushed alng 4 fs out, hdwy 2 out, one pace o'r one out.* ....(11 to 2 op 9 to 2 tchd 6 to 1) 4
4631* RIZ BIZ (USA) [49] 7-13 (3*) M Fenton (5) *wtd wth, cld appr 3 fs out, sn rdn and btn*...........(5 to 2 tchd 9 to 4) 5
4631 TIGHT FIST (Ire) [58] 8-11 B Rouse (3) *hld up rear, shrtlvd effrt o'r 2 fs out*....................(25 to 1 tchd 33 to 1) 6
4633 MELISIO [45] 7-12^{1} C Rutter (1) *cl up, rdn o'r 2 fs out, sn wknd*........................... (33 to 1 tchd 40 to 1) 7

Dist: 1½l, 3l, 1½l, 15l, ¾l, 7l. 2m 54.30s. a 23.80s (7 Ran).
(Ray Hawthorn), S Dow

SOUTHWELL (A.W) (std)
Monday November 8th

Going Correction: NIL (races 1,3), PLUS 0.30 (2,4,5,6,7)

4756 Silver Birch Claiming Stakes Class E (Div I) (2-y-o) £2,950 5f........ (12:40)

4618* MONKEY'S WEDDING (bl) 9-3 T Quinn (11) *made all, pushed alng hfwy, rdn clr ins fnl 2 fs, easily.* ....(7 to 4 on op 2 to 1 on) 1
4163 HENRY THE HAWK (v) 8-9 S Webster (4) *outpcd and beh till hdwy 2 fs out, styd on ins last, nrst finish.* ....(12 to 1 op 8 to 1) 2
4618 TOOGOODFORYOU (bl) 8-5 A Munro (8) *in tch, rdn hfwy, kpt on one pace und pres appr fnl furlong.* ....(16 to 1 op 33 to 1) 3
MARINERS GUIDE 8-6 J Quinn (9) *chsd ldrs, rdn and one pace fnl 2 fs*.............(10 to 1 op 8 to 1) 4
4436 CHINA ROBIN 8-1 (7*) S Sanders (2) *chsd ldrs, rdn hfwy, sn wknd*..................................(8 to 1) 5
4668^{9} GARDNER DOUGLAS 8-11 A Clark (10) *nvr a factor.* ....(33 to 1) 6
4269^{8} THEE AND ME 7-8^{1} (7*) M Humphries (7) *slwly into strd and beh, some hdwy fnl 2 fs.* ....(25 to 1 op 20 to 1 tchd 33 to 1) 7
4434^{8} HONG KONG FUTURE (Ire) (bl) 8-4 (5*) J Tate (6) *cl up, ev ch o'r 2 fs out, sn rdn and wknd wl over one furlong out.* ....(16 to 1 op 14 to 1) 8

4618 CA IRA (Ire) 7-11 (5*) A Garth (5) *sn outpcd and beh.* ....(16 to 1 op 14 to 1) 9
4594 BUCKLEY BOYS 8-3 (5*) D Wright (3) *al beh.*..... (20 to 1) 10
Dist: 8l, 1½l, 5l, ½l, hd, nk, ½l, 2l, sht-hd. 1m 0.90s. a 3.00s (10 Ran).
SR: 43/3/-/-/-/-/ (The Monkey Racing Club Limited), J Berry

4757 Rowan Limited Stakes Class F (0-65 3-y-o and up) £2,950 1m 3f...... (1:10)

4669^{5} CLIFTON CHASE (bl) 4-9-7 Paul Eddery (7) *made all, quickened clr 3 fs out, rdn fnl 2 furlongs, styd on gmely.* ....(11 to 1 op 14 to 1) 1
4713^{6} DASHING FELLOW (Ire) 5-9-7 J Quinn (6) *hld up in tch, gd hdwy 3 fs out and sn chasing wnr, rdn and ev ch appr last, kpt on*....................(15 to 8 fav op 3 to 1) 2
4107 SILVER SAMURAI 4-9-0 (7*) S Mulvey (5) *slwly into strd, hld up, gd hdwy 3 fs out, rdn 2 out, styd on.* ....(85 to 40 op 5 to 4 tchd 9 to 4) 3
4622^{2} PRINCESS SIOUX 3-8-10 R Price (2) *hld up in tch, hdwy 4 fs out, effrt and rdn one and a half out, kpt on one pace ins last*.......... (4 to 1 op 11 to 4 tchd 9 to 2) 4
4544^{8} SARAH HEIGHTS 3-8-5 (5*) D McCabe (8) *cl up, rdn 3 fs out, sn wknd, eased fnl furlong*...............(33 to 1) 5
3320^{6} IZITALLWORTHIT 4-9-2 A Clark (1) *hld up and beh, effrt and some hdwy 4 fs out, sn rdn, nvr dngrs*.... (20 to 1) 6
4457^{4} YOUNG TESS 3-8-10 N Connorton (3) *trkd ldrs, effrt and rdn 4 fs out, sn wknd*...............(8 to 1 op 6 to 1) 7
4544 BOLD STAR (v) 3-9-1 S Perks (4) *chsd ldrs, rdn o'r 4 fs out, sn wknd*..............................(33 to 1) 8
Dist: 1l, ½l, ¾l, 8l, 3l, hd, ½l. 2m 32.00s. a 10.20s (8 Ran).
SR: 38/36/35/22/6/6/-/3/ (David Cahal), J L Harris

4758 Silver Birch Claiming Stakes Class E (Div II) (2-y-o) £2,924 5f.......... (1:40)

4699^{4} RED GRIT (Ire) (bl) 8-5^{1} S Webster (8) *mid-div, hdwy on stands side 2 fs out, rdn to ld ins last, ran on.* ....(10 to 1 op 8 to 1) 1
3677^{7} CLARET BUMBLE 8-0 T Williams (4) *cl up centre, effrt and ev ch entering fnl furlong, kpt on und pres.* ....(3 to 1 tchd 5 to 2) 2
3781 LIVELY (Ire) 7-9 (5*) Darren Moffatt (7) *slwly into strd, hdwy centre 2 fs out, ev ch ins last, kpt on.* ....(9 to 2 op 4 to 1 tchd 5 to 1) 3
4709^{6} FLOATING TRIAL (v) 8-6 A Munro (2) *slwly into strd, sn chasing ldrs centre, rdn and led briefly appr fnl furlong, hdd ins last, wknd.* ....(9 to 4 fav op 7 to 4 tchd 11 to 4) 4
4668^{4} MYSTICAL MICKEY (Ire) 8-5 S D Williams (11) *o'rall ldr stands rail, rdn 2 fs out, sn hdd and wknd ins last.* ....(20 to 1 tchd 25 to 1) 5
4436 PASTURES NEW (Ire) 8-2 S Wood (5) *cl up centre, ev ch 2 fs out, sn rdn, wknd appr fnl furlong.* ....(14 to 1 op 12 to 1) 6
4483^{7} WILKS DREAM (Ire) (bl) 8-6 T Sprake (9) *prmnt, rdn hfwy, sn wknd*............(14 to 1 op 12 to 1 tchd 16 to 1) 7
4674 SECONDS AWAY (v) 8-9 K Fallon (1) *nvr rchd ldrs.* ....(16 to 1 op 14 to 1) 8
3755 GOVERNOR'S BAY 8-12^{1} T Wall (6) *cl up, rdn hfwy, sn wknd*....................................(33 to 1) 9
4663^{5} FORESTA VERDE (USA) 8-10 A Culhane (3) *nvr rchd ldrs.* ....(15 to 2 op 5 to 1 tchd 8 to 1) 10
299 KALAKAFU 7-9^{2} (7*) S Sanders (10) *slwly into strd, al rear.* ....(33 to 1) 11
Dist: ½l, ½l, 1l, nk, 7l, ½l, ½l, 3l, 1l, 1½l. 1m 1.80s. a 3.90s (11 Ran).
SR: 13/6/4/6/4/-/ (C Michael Wilson), M Dods

4759 Ash Handicap Class E (0-70 3-y-o and up) £3,106 1¾m................ (2:10)

1654 MALENOIR (USA) [45] (v) 5-8-5 A Clark (10) *al prmnt, hdwy 4 fs out, led 3 out, rdn and ran on wl fnl 2 furlongs.* .... (20 to 1 op 16 to 1 tchd 25 to 1) 1
4621 ELECTROLYTE [66] 3-9-1 (3*) Stephen Davies (13) *al prmnt, effrt 3 fs out, sn rdn, kpt on fnl 2 furlongs.* ....(9 to 1 op 14 to 1) 2
4669* CLIBURNEL NEWS (Ire) [58] 3-8-10 (5ex) Kim McDonnell (2) *hld up and beh, hdwy 2 fs out, styd on wl ins last, nrst finish*..............................(6 to 1 op 5 to 1) 3
4621 SALU [50] 4-8-10 T Quinn (4) *in tch, hdwy 5 fs out, effrt o'r 2 out, sn rdn, ev ch till wknd entering last.* ....(5 to 1 fav tchd 6 to 1) 4
AIDE MEMOIRE (Ire) [51] 4-8-4 (7*) V Halliday (3) *hld up and beh, hdwy 6 fs out, rdn o'r 2 out, kpt on one pace.* ....(20 to 1 op 14 to 1) 5
4505^{5} GOODBYE MILLIE [60] 3-8-5 (7*) D Gibbs (11) *mid-div, effrt 4 fs out, rdn 3 out, kpt on one pace.* (8 to 1 op 6 to 1) 6
4353^{8} BEAU QUEST [40] (bl) 6-7-9 (5*) Darren Moffatt (1) *hld up and beh, styd on fnl 2 fs, nvr dngrs*..........(33 to 1) 7
4669^{6} TRANQUIL LADY (Ire) [46] 3-7-7 (5*) D Wright (5) *hld up and beh, hdwy 5 fs out, rdn o'r 2 out, plugged on one pace.* ....(16 to 1 op 20 to 1) 8
3961 PROTON [64] 3-9-2 T Williams (8) *led, hdd 3 fs out, sn wknd*..............................(20 to 1 op 33 to 1) 9
4676 MODEST HOPE (USA) [63] 6-9-9 Alex Greaves (6) *hld up and beh, some hdwy fnl 3 fs, nvr dngrs.* ....(20 to 1 op 16 to 1) 10

4178^{6} TIGER SHOOT [54] 6-9-0 N Carlisle (14) *chsd ldr, rdn and wknd 3 fs out*.........................(10 to 1 tchd 14 to 1) 11
4494^{7} PRINCESS DAVID (USA) [54] 3-8-6 Paul Eddery (16) *chsd ldrs, rdn hfwy and sn lost pl*................(20 to 1) 12
4354 NORTHERN JUDY (Ire) [44] 3-7-7^{2} (5*) A Garth (7) *prmnt to hfwy, sn beh*.................................(25 to 1) 13
4631 BOTTLES (USA) [68] 6-9-9 (5*) K Rutter (17) *al rear.* ....(14 to 1 op 12 to 1) 14
4611^{3} MICHAELA MIA (USA) [50] 3-8-2 A Munro (9) *chsd ldrs, rdn and wknd hfwy*...............................(20 to 1) 15
4600 ATLANTIC WAY [54] 5-9-0 J Quinn (15) *al rear.* ....(7 to 1 op 4 to 1) 16
4631^{6} RUFFLE [57] 3-8-9 K Fallon (12) *chsd ldrs, rdn alng hfwy, wknd 4 fs out, eased*.....(7 to 1 op 4 to 1 tchd 8 to 1) 17
Dist: 2½l, 1l, nk, 3l, ¾l, ¾l, 3½l, 3½l, 1½l, 1l. 3m 13.10s. a 13.10s (17 Ran).
SR: 2/10/-/-/-/-/ (John Purcell), R C Spicer

4760 Oak Handicap Class D (0-80 3-y-o and up) £3,552 1m..................(2:40)

4490 RURAL LAD [54] 4-8-5 A Munro (16) *in tch, hdwy 3 fs out, rdn to ld one and a half out, styd on wl.* ....(20 to 1 op 10 to 1) 1
4623^{4} RED COTTON [65] 3-8-13 Paul Eddery (7) *cl up, effrt 2 and a half fs out, rdn and led briefly two out, sn hdd, kpt on*..................... (5 to 1 op 4 to 1 tchd 6 to 1) 2
4658 SIE AMATO (Ire) [47] 4-7-7 (5*) Darren Moffatt (14) *chsd ldrs, rdn and outpcd 3 fs out, styd on und pres ins last.* ....(20 to 1) 3
4623^{8} STOPROVERITATE [58] 4-8-2 (7*) D Gibbs (13) *chsd ldrs, hdwy and rdn 2 fs out, one pace appr last.* ....(9 to 1 op 10 to 1 tchd 12 to 1) 4
4640^{3} MAM'ZELLE ANGOT [58] 3-8-6 N Connorton (1) *al chasing ldrs, rdn and kpt on fnl 2 fs*........ (10 to 1 op 7 to 1) 5
4666* SAVINGS BANK [49] 3-7-11 (6ex) J Fanning (3) *mid-div and pushed alng, hdwy o'r 2 fs out, styd on ins last.* .... (3 to 1 fav op 2 to 1 tchd 100 to 30) 6
4172 ERTLON [80] 3-10-0 T Quinn (4) *led aftr 2 fs, rdn and hdd two out, grad wknd*...............(10 to 1 op 8 to 1) 7
4623 SIRTELIMAR (Ire) [70] 4-9-7 J McLaughlin (10) *led 2 fs, cl up till rdn and wknd 3 out.* ....(14 to 1 op 12 to 1 tchd 16 to 1) 8
40 GIRL AT THE GATE [58] 3-8-6 K Fallon (11) *mid-div and sn pushed alng, wide strt, styd on fnl 2 fs, nvr dngrs.* ....(20 to 1 tchd 33 to 1) 9
4676 NO COMEBACKS [48] (v) 5-7-13 T Williams (5) *slow into strd, al rear*....................(14 to 1 op 16 to 1) 10
2774^{9} TENDRESSE (Ire) [46] 5-7-11 J Quinn (15) *al rear.* ....(10 to 1 op 16 to 1) 11
4600 PEACE FORMULA (Ire) [47] 4-7-12 N Carlisle (12) *in tch till rdn and wknd hfwy*............................(33 to 1) 12
4101 AWESTRUCK [69] 3-9-3 T Wall (2) *nvr a factor.* ....(16 to 1 op 14 to 1) 13
245* ASHOVER [64] 3-8-5 (7*) V Halliday (8) *slwly into strd, al rear*.......................(16 to 1 op 10 to 1) 14
3211 ANNACURRAGH (Ire) [53] 4-8-4^{1} A Clark (6) *al rear.* ....(33 to 1) 15
3973 MOHICAN BRAVE (Ire) [71] 3-9-0 (5*) D McCabe (9) *al beh.* ....(14 to 1 op 10 to 1) 16
Dist: 2½l, ¾l, nk, 2l, sht-hd, 1l, ½l, 2l, 10l, ¾l. 1m 45.60s. a 6.60s (16 Ran).
SR: 28/28/11/21/12/2/30/21/-/ (John Purcell), R C Spicer

4761 Beech Maiden Stakes Class D (2-y-o) £3,699 7f...................... (3:10)

4598^{2} SMART FAMILY (USA) 9-0 T Quinn (3) *cl up, led hfwy, quickened wl clr 2 fs out, eased rght dwn ins last.* ....(11 to 10 on op 2 to 1 on tchd Evens) 1
4434^{6} BETABETCORBETT 9-0 K Fallon (9) *cl up, rdn and ev ch 2 fs out, kpt on und pres, no chance wth wnr.* .... (9 to 1 op 6 to 1 tchd 10 to 1) 2
4577^{5} DUBALL REMY 8-9 A Munro (8) *prmnt, effrt o'r 2 fs out, sn ev ch, rdn and one pace fnl two furlongs.* ....(7 to 1 tchd 9 to 1 and 10 to 1) 3
4618 GRANDEE 9-0 A Clark (4) *chsd ldrs, rdn o'r 2 fs out, sn one pace*.................................... (50 to 1) 4
LITTLE MINER (Ire) 8-6 (3*) Stephen Davies (2) *slwly into strd and beh, styd on fnl 2 fs*..... (25 to 1 op 20 to 1) 5
4698 PRUSSIA 9-0 C Nutter (6) *sn pushed alng, al rear.* ....(6 to 1 op 3 to 1) 6
4435 BECKENHAM LADY (Ire) (v) 8-9 N Connorton (1) *led to hfwy, sn wknd*...................(25 to 1 op 20 to 1) 7
T'NIEL 8-9 S Perks (7) *slwly into strd, al rear.* ....(11 to 2 op 14 to 1) 8
4098 WENLOCH LAD 9-0 T Wall (5) *beh frm hfwy*.....(50 to 1) 9
Dist: 2l, sht-hd, 2½l, 4l, 4l, 3½l, 15l, nk. 1m 33.40s. a 7.30s (9 Ran).
SR: 22/16/10/7/-/-/ (Alan C Elliot), P F I Cole

4762 Willow Handicap Class D (0-80 3-y-o and up) £3,552 6f...............(3:40)

4537 DEBSY DO (USA) [70] 4-9-0 (5*) Darren Moffatt (14) *in tch, wide strt, hdwy 2 fs out, rdn and styd on to ld ins last, ran on*.. (16 to 1) 1
4168^{3} MISS ARAGON [55] 5-7-13 (5*) D McCabe (9) *al prmnt, effrt 2 fs out, rdn to ld briefly ins last, sn hdd and no extr.* ....(12 to 1 op 7 to 1) 2

4670* PHARAOH'S DANCER [62] 6-8-4 (7*) D Gibbs (1) *cl up, effrt 2 fs out, rdn to ld briefly appr last, sn hdd and not quicken*.......... (9 to 4 fav tchd 5 to 2 and 11 to 4) 3
4667³ HIGHBORN (Ire) [78] 4-9-13 G Hind (16) *sn led, rdn 2 fs out, hdd appr last, no extr.*
............(13 to 2 op 6 to 1 tchd 7 to 1 and 8 to 1) 4
4221³ SECOND COLOURS (USA) [61] 3-8-9 T Quinn (2) *chsd ldrs, hmpd and lost pl aftr one furlong, hdwy on inner 2 out, styd on ins last, nrst finish.*
.... (9 to 1 op 7 to 1 tchd 10 to 1) 5
4640* CICERONE [52] 3-8-0 N Carlisle (6) *steadied strt and beh, wide strt, styd on fnl 2 fs, nvr dngrs.*
.................................(12 to 1 tchd 10 to 1) 6
4652⁴ LADY SABO [51] 4-8-0 A Munro (11) *beh till styd on fnl 2 fs, nvr dngrs*........................(10 to 1 op 12 to 1) 7
4224 FARMER JOCK [55] 11-8-4 J Quinn (10) *in tch, effrt and hdwy 2 fs out, sn rdn and wknd appr last*.....(20 to 1) 8
4617 GIRL NEXT DOOR [59] 3-8-7 J O'Reilly (15) *cl up, ev ch 2 fs out, sn rdn and wknd*.......... (16 to 1 tchd 20 to 1) 9
4670³ SAVAHRA SOUND [62] 8-8-5¹ (7*) G Strange (4) *nvr rchd ldrs*..............................(9 to 1 op 14 to 1) 10
4363 SO SUPERB [58] (bl) 4-8-7 S Webster (3) *chsd ldrs, rdn 2 fs out, sn wknd*................................(33 to 1) 11
4507⁹ SOBA GUEST (Ire) [75] 4-9-7 (3*) Emma O'Gorman (5) *al rear*..............................(14 to 1 op 10 to 1) 12
3410 ABSOLUTELY NUTS [61] 4-8-3 (7*) S Sanders (12) *in tch, hdwy on outer o'r 2 fs out, sn rdn and wknd.*
.... (11 to 1 op 6 to 1) 13
4168 GLENCROFT [55] 9-8-4 S Wood (7) *al rear.*
.... (40 to 1 op 33 to 1) 14
4109 ARC LAMP [53] 7-8-2 J Fanning (8) *nvr a factor.* (16 to 1) 15
4606⁹ RED ROSEIN [79] 7-10-0 K Fallon (13) *slwly into strd, al beh*.............................(16 to 1 op 14 to 1) 16

Dist: 1½l, ½l, nk, 1½l, ½l, sht-hd, 4l, sht-hd, ¾l, ¾l. 1m 18.00s. a 4.60s (16 Ran).
SR: 49/28/33/48/24/13/12/-/2/ (Lintscan Ltd (Corbett Bookmakers)), S G Norton

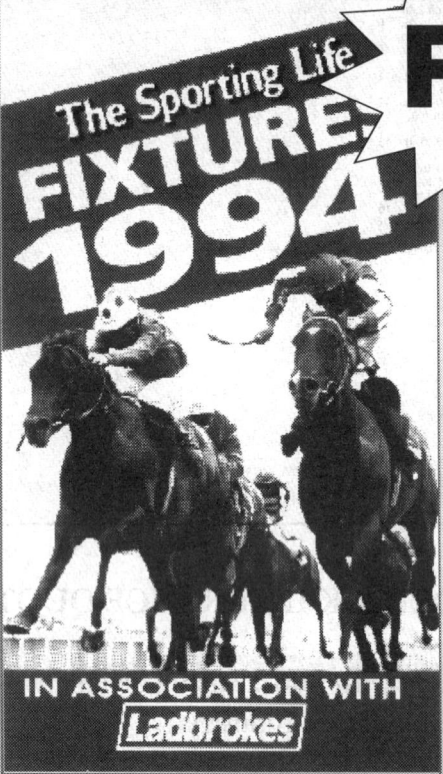

Index to Flat Race Results 1992-93

7 **A GENTLEMAN TWO,** b h All Systems Go - Solar Honey by Roi Soleil (J L Eyre) 2232[5] 2455[4] 2709[4] 3716 4321[6]
2 **AGGIES DREAM,** ch g Librate - Achnahuaigh by Known Fact (USA) (J M Bradley) 1245 1863 2176[4] 3098
3 **AGGRESSIVE CHIEF (USA),** 585
3 **AGHAR (Ire),** ch c Ahonoora - Foliage by Thatching (D R C Elsworth) 510[2] 691[6] 872 2580[5]
3 **AGIL'S PET,** b f Tina's Pet - High Voltage by Electrify (J Sutcliffe) 600[7] 927[7] 1059 1606[9]
4 **AGWA,** b c Local Suitor (USA) - Meissarah (USA) by Silver Hawk (USA) (R J O'Sullivan) 3011[6] 3292[1] 3707[1] 4580
3 **AHJAY,** br c Tina's Pet - City Link Rose by Lochnager (D A Wilson) 1714[6] 2011[8] 2560[7] 2719[7] 2912[3] 3070[1] 3783[6] 3830[8] 4270[2] 4536 4633
2 **AHSANT MTOTO,** b c Mtoto - Masarrah by Formidable (USA) (R W Armstrong) 3592 3819[6] 4113[6] 4316[9]
4 **AIDE MEMOIRE (Ire),** b f Don't Forget Me - Pharjoy (Fr) by Pharly (Fr) (T D Barron) 4759[5]
2 **AILEENS GIRL,** ch f Hubbly Bubbly (USA) - Remould by Reform (J E Long) 4004[5] 4339[5] 4418 4587[9]
2 **AINE'S PET (Ire),** b f Fayruz - Stellarevagh by Le Levanstell (Noel Meade) 2188[2] 2880 3911[3] 4405[2] 4535[5] 4638
6 **AIN'TLIFELIKETHAT,** gr h Godswalk (USA) - Blue Alicia by Wolver Hollow (T J Naughton) 4681a[5] 144[5] 249 2327 2524 3042[9]
3 **AIR COMMAND (Bar),** br c Concorde Hero (USA) - Hubbardair by Town And Country (R J Hodges) 4734a[6] 4791a[8] 31[4] 129[8] 602 720[1] 927 1095[7] 1233[5] 1627 3229[9]
2 **AIR COMMODORE,** b c Elegant Air - Belle Enfant by Beldale Flutter (USA) (P F I Cole) 4701[2]
2 **AIR RAID,** ch g Jalmood (USA) - Strawberry Song by Final Straw (B R Millman) 1265 1741 3264
3 **AIR REVEUSE (Ire),** ch f Niniski (USA) - Arriance by Gay Mecene (P Bary) 296[3]
2 **AIRSPEED FLYER (USA),** b c Explodent (USA) - Beau Mirage (USA) by To The Quick (USA) (R Akehurst) 2571 3387[9]
3 **AISLA (USA),** ch f Miswaki (USA) - Angela Serra by Arctic Tern (USA) (F Boutin) 694[5] 1753[3] 3534[3] 3844[1] 4413[4]
10 **AITCH N'BEE,** ch g Northfields (USA) - Hot Case by Upper Case (USA) (Lady Herries) 411[6] 771[3] 1207[1] 2022[6] 2330[4] 2622[9] 3155[9] 3257[5] 4133[2] 4470[7] 4597[2]
5 **AIYBAK (Ire),** b g Lashkari - Aytana (Fr) by Riverman (USA) (D K Weld) 807[5] 2035[1] 2841 3336[6] 3805[8] 4573[1]
3 **AJALAN (Ire),** ch c Be My Guest (USA) - Intensive (USA) by Sir Wiggle (USA) (M R Stoute) 1145[1] 1558[5] 2019[3] 2758[6] 3353[8] 3970[6]
2 **AJDAR,** b c Slip Anchor - Loucoum (Fr) by Iron Duke (Fr) (A C Stewart) 4726
3 **AJDAYT (USA),** b or br c Danzig (USA) - Barely Even (USA) by Creme Dela Creme (A C Stewart) 529 751 1330[2] 1597[1] 2156[1] 2421[1] 2961 3290[7]
3 **AJFAN (USA),** ch f Woodman (USA) - Misinskie (USA) by Nijinsky (Can) (H Thomson Jones) 472[2] 749[3] 1200 2941[4] 3519[1] 3882[1] 4309[4] 4636[7]
3 **AJMAAN (USA),** b or br c Arctic Tern (USA) - Melodina by Tudor Melody (A C Stewart) 825[7] 1746[5] 2293[2] 2663[3] 2995[2] 3507
2 **AJNAS (Ire),** b or br f Doyoun - Narjis (USA) by Blushing Groom (Fr) (H Thomson Jones) 1418 3001[8] 3627[8] 4318
4 **AJZEM (USA),** gr c Blushing Groom (Fr) - Nobiliare (USA) by Vaguely Noble (M R Stoute) 426[4] 824
2 **AKHIYAR (Ire),** gr c Doyoun - Akishka by Nishapour (Fr) (John M Oxx) 4380[1]
3 **AKHLAK (Ire),** b f Soviet Star (USA) - Pilot Bird by Blakeney (P T Walwyn) 583 1132[3] 1482[5] 1972[4] 3226 3981 4258 4506[8]
5 **AKKAZAO (Ire),** b or br m Alzao (USA) - Akka by Malacate (USA) (T G Mills) 4782a 315 756 978[1] 1414[9] 1800[2] 2328[2] 3017[8] 3269[9] 3623[6] 3883
6 **AKTIONAR (Fr),** 3582[8]
2 **ALACRITY,** b f Alzao (USA) - Hastening by Shirley Heights (W Jarvis) 1393[5] 3443[4] 3738[5] 3966[6] 4251 4427[4]
2 **ALAFLAK (Ire),** b c Caerleon (USA) - Safe Haven by Blakeney (J L Dunlop) 2990[2] 3423[1] 3776[2] 4529[3]
2 **ALALIYA (Ire),** b f Sadler's Wells (USA) - Alannya (Fr) by Relko (John M Oxx) 4705[2]
3 **ALALJA (Ire),** b f Entitled - Miss Turnberry by Mummy's Pet (Patrick Joseph Flynn) 787[9] 1201[9] 1823[1] 2039[9] 2245[4] 3926
2 **ALANEES,** b c Cadeaux Genereux - Dabaweyaa by Shareef Dancer (USA) (C E Brittain) 1828[6] 2335[6] 3435[4] 3679[2] 4062[2] 4443
3 **ALASAD,** ch c Kris - Midway Lady (USA) by Alleged (USA) (B Hanbury) 1176[3] 2332 2776[2] 3173[4] 4110
3 **ALASIB,** gr f Siberian Express (USA) - Fahrenheit by Mount Hagen (Fr) (W Jarvis) 1326[3] 1633[7] 2731[1] 3051[3] 3756[1] 4278[2] 4465[4]
3 **ALASKAN GIRL (Ire),** ch f Affirmed (USA) - Yukon Baby (USA) by Northern Dancer (Declan Gillespie) 847[4] 1164 3417[1] 3497[9] 4689
2 **ALASKAN HEIR,** b g Northern State (USA) - Royal Meeting by Dara Monarch (D J G Murray Smith) 3658[8] 4003[1] 4564[9]
3 **ALASKAN PRINCESS (Ire),** b f Prince Rupert (Fr) - Ivory North (USA) by Sir Ivor (P F I Cole) 821[3] 1911[5] 2227[4] 4355
2 **ALASTOR (Fr),** b c Fabulous Dancer (USA) - Anahita by Gay Mecene (G Verricelli) 4204[1]
2 **ALAZWAR (USA),** b c Gulch (USA) - Khwlah (USA) by Best Turn (USA) (H Thomson Jones) 4627[2]
2 **AL BATTAR (USA),** ch c Blushing John (USA) - Golden Way (USA) by Diplomat Way (L M Cumani) 3104[1] 4130[5]
3 **ALBEIT,** ch f Mandrake Major - Sioux Be It by Warpath (C W Thornton) 428[8] 728[7] 883 1852[9] 2104 2593[3] 2765[4] 2978[2] 3216[4] 4085[2]
4 **ALBEMINE (USA),** b g Al Nasr (Fr) - Lady Be Mine (USA) by Sir Ivor (Mrs J Cecil) 1069[3] 2156[9] 3269[4] 3863[3]
3 **ALBERSTAN,** b g Stanford - Afrabela by African Sky (R F Marvin) 4666[8]
6 **ALBERT,** b g Kings Lake (USA) - Darine by Nonoalco (USA) (D A Wilson) 13 67[2] 85 103[1] 158[1] 224 294[1] 387[1] 456[6] 731 964[4] 1120 1659[1] 1820[6] 2127[9] 2490[3] 2894[7] 3420[7] 3710 4028
2 **ALBERTA DIAMOND,** b f Dowsing (USA) - Hyatti by Habitat (D K Weld) 2037 2742 4323[9]
4 **ALBERTA ROSE (Ire),** b f Phardante (Fr) - Rathclare by Pontifex (Patrick Joseph Flynn) 1293[2] 1440 1644[5] 2142[2] 2322[3] 2901[8] 3294[7] 3544 4738
3 **ALBERTAZZI (Ire),** b c Ahonoora - For Going by Balidar (J S Bolger) 3025[2] 3616[2] 3733[1] 3916[8] 4245
6 **ALBERTITO (Fr),** b g Esprit Du Nord (USA) - Aranita by Arctic Tern (USA) (R Hollinshead) 179[3]
4 **ALBERTS LADY (Ire),** gr f Roselier (Fr) - Duilleog by Tarqogan (P Delaney) 309
4 **ALBERT THE BOLD,** b g Never So Bold - Alcassa (Fr) by Satingo (A L Forbes) 4757a[5] 12[7] 101[5] 157[6] 232[9] 276[6]
5 **AL BILLAL,** b h Enchantment - Liana Louise by Silly Season (J J Bridger) 4678a 4721a[7]
5 **ALBONA,** b m Neltino - Cry Of Truth by Town Crier (D G McArdle) 310 640 4001[6] 4136[8] 4409 4555
6 **ALBURY GREY,** gr m Petong - Infelice by Nishapour (Fr) (P M McEntee) 210
2 **ALCIAN BLUE,** b c Tina's Pet - Rhiannon by Welsh Pageant (R Hollinshead) 4397[4] 4579
2 **ALCOVE,** ch c Faustus (USA) - Cubby Hole by Town And Country (R Hannon) 687[5] 998[4] 1277[3] 3222[3] 3760[1] 3940[2] 4249
4 **ALCOY (Ire),** b g Glow (USA) - Organdy by Blakeney (P A Kelleway) 527
8 **ALDAHE,** ch g Dalsaan - Alanood by Northfields (USA) (B R Millman) 4673a[9]
3 **ALDENA (Ire),** ch f Heraldiste (USA) - Pollixena by Sexton Blake (Richard Lister) 870 1574 2556[6] 3076[9] 3294 3454[5] 3856[4]
4 **ALDERBROOK,** b c Ardross - Twine by Thatching (Mrs J Cecil) 416[1] 500[1] 731[1] 1346[1] 1845[1] 2581[6] 3437[2] 4063

2 **ATAARED (USA),** b or br c Danzig (USA) - Madame Secretary (USA) by Secretariat (USA) (A A Scott) 2994[2]

4 **ATHAR (Ire),** b f Master Willie - Walladah (USA) by Northern Dancer (R J Baker) 840[2] 1094[3] 1409[8] 1878[1] 2029[4] 2111[4] 2669

2 **ATHENE (Ire),** br f Rousillon (USA) - Gay Hellene by Ela-Mana-Mou (R Charlton) 4496

3 **ATHENS BELLE (Ire),** b f Groom Dancer (USA) - Greektown by Ela-Mana-Mou (R Charlton) 1030[1] 2238[6] 3149[5]

3 **ATHERTON GREEN (Ire),** ch c Shy Groom (USA) - Primacara by Rusticaro (Fr) (J A Glover) 801 2000[3] 2354[5] 2774[3] 3113[3] 3630[1] 3790[9] 4101 4533[9]

3 **ATLANTIC ADIOS (Ire),** ch c Don't Forget Me - Les Enfants by Try My Best (USA) (D K Weld) 788[5] 1609[5] 2092[4] 2485[6]

5 **ATLANTIC WAY,** gr m Bold Owl - Overseas by Sea Hawk II (C J Hill) 4715a[9] 4788a[2] 4813a[3] 18[1] 42[2] 53[1] 64[5] 148[6] 175[3] 229[1] 287[5] 373[1] 442[4] 879[8] 1094[2] 1305[1] 1586[5] 1840[7] 2427[5] 4600 4759

4 **A-TO-Z (Ire),** b f Ahonoora - Zenga by Try My Best (USA) (M Bell) 675[8] 1029[9]

7 **AT PEACE,** b g Habitat - Peace by Klairon (J White) 2585[4]

3 **ATSUKO (Ire),** b f Mtoto - Maresca by Mill Reef (USA) (T Stack) 943[7] 1507 2140

5 **ATTADALE,** b g Ardross - Marypark by Charlottown (L Lungo) 4321

2 **AT THE SAVOY (Ire),** gr c Exhibitioner - Hat And Gloves by Wolver Hollow (C B B Booth) 3642 3816[6] 4220[9] 4416[4] 4618

2 **ATTYMON (Ire),** b f Red Sunset - Grace de Bois by Tap On Wood (A J Maxwell) 2319

4 **AT YOUR SERVICE (Ire),** b g The Noble Player (USA) - Mazzola (Fr) by Val de Loir (Basil King) 753 2346[6] 2516[4] 2958[7] 3951 4162

3 **AUBE INDIENNE (Fr),** ch f Bluebird (USA) - Salvoro by Spectacular Bid (Mme C Head) 1290[1] 1722[9] 3149[4] 3801[4] 4307[5]

2 **AUCKLAND CASTLE,** b c Chilibang - Palace Tor by Dominion (Denys Smith) 2603[8] 2973[5]

4 **AUDACIOUS (Ire),** ch g Rhoman Rule (USA) - Glencoe Lights by Laser Light (Declan Gillespie) 1293

5 **AUDE LA BELLE (Fr),** ch m Ela-Mana-Mou - Arjona (Ger) by Caracol (Fr) (Mrs L Piggott) 53[6] 81[7] 122[5] 182[5] 303 539[5] 783[3] 857[9] 1840[8] 2026[6] 2337[8] 2467[2] 3473[2] 3690[1] 4013[7] 4212 4505[2] 4630

7 **AUGHFAD,** b h Millfontaine - Saulonika by Saulingo (T Casey) 659 796 1127[3] 1348 1485[6] 1806 2255[9] 2620[6] 2965[2] 3051[4] 3348[8] 3621 3947[7] 4090 4363

2 **AUGUSTAN,** b c Shareef Dancer (USA) - Krishnagar by Kris (C E Brittain) 3833[5] 4149[6] 4615[4]

3 **AULD STOCK (Ire),** b f Entitled - Obsession by Wolver Hollow (Patrick Joseph Flynn) 640[2] 789[4] 1123[6] 1513[4] 1922[1] 2297[3] 2675[4] 2922[6] 3327[2] 3454[2] 3732[8]

4 **AUNT ADA,** ch f Adonijah - Balidilemma by Balidar (R Rowe) 1311 1816[9] 2160[5] 2520 3007

2 **AUNTIE FAY (Ire),** ch f Fayruz - Auntie Ponny by Last Fandango (B S Rothwell) 1897 3792 3969 4361[8] 4671

3 **AUNTIE GINGER,** ch f Blushing Scribe (USA) - Soho by Camden Town (P Butler) 823[8] 1010[7] 1240[7]

4 **AUNTIE LORNA,** b f Uncle Pokey - Bronze Tango by Bronze Hill (M D Hammond) 1038[8]

2 **AUNT TATE,** b f Tate Gallery (USA) - Aunty (Fr) by Riverman (USA) (W R Muir) 4269

3 **AURLIANO (Ire),** b f Knesset (USA) - How True by Known Fact (USA) (D P Kelly) 2843[6] 3161[7] 3417 4385[4] 4635[4] 4689[9]

3 **AUSTRAL JANE,** b f Dominion - Dabbiana (Can) by Fappiano (USA) (G Thorner) 1256[6] 1818[5] 4120[2] 4457[9] 4544[7]

7 **AUTHORSHIP (USA),** b or br g Balzac (USA) - Piap (USA) by L'aiglon (USA) (W J Musson) 4102[4] 4321[4] 4530[2]

4 **AUTOCRACY (Ire),** b c Alzao (USA) - Addabub by Manado (G Ording) 1084[4] 2436[5] 3013[7] 4398[8]

3 **AUTUMNIS (USA),** ch c Diesis - Autumn Glory (USA) by Graustark (B W Hills) 538[2] 991[3] 3132[2] 3817[5]

5 **AUVILLAR (USA),** br g Temperence Hill (USA) - Exquisita (USA) by Cougar (Chi) (D Burchell) 4798a[8]

2 **AVALIN (Ire),** b f Cyrano de Bergerac - Lady Bidder by Auction Ring (USA) (J T Gorman) 1994[8] 2244[9] 2319[7] 3073[8] 3608[8] 3953[8] 4183[7] 4551[8]

3 **AVALONIA (Ire),** b f Colmore Row - Mary Mitsu by Carboosh (USA) (Patrick Joseph Flynn) 868 981[8] 1251

2 **AVANTI XIQUET,** gr c Mashhor Dancer (USA) - Mummy's Chick by Mummy's Pet (J White) 3387 3869[9]

4 **AVENUE FOCH (Ire),** gr g Saint Estephe (Fr) - Marie D'Irlande (Fr) by Kalamoun (J Pearce) 4005[9] 4132[8] 4362[5] 4514 4727[8]

2 **AVERTI (Ire),** b c Warning - Imperial Jade by Lochnager (W R Muir) 3016[1] 3223[1] 3611[3]

2 **AVERTI (USA),** b f Known Fact (USA) - Safe Play (USA) by Sham (USA) (H R A Cecil) 2887[1] 3248[2] 4171[9]

4 **AVIAN ASSEMBLY (USA),** 4450[5]

3 **AVIATOR'S DREAM,** b g Valiyar - Maputo Princess by Raga Navarro (Ity) (J F Bottomley) 3324[3] 3523 4376[8]

2 **AVIE'S FANCY (USA),** 4449[6]

3 **AVIE'S SHADOW (USA),** b or br f Lord Avie - Gold Shadow by Mr Prospector 570[2] 762[4]

2 **AVIRA,** b f Dancing Brave (USA) - Sephira by Luthier (B W Hills) 4361

6 **AVISHAYES (USA),** b g Al Nasr (Fr) - Rose Goddess by Sassafras (Fr) (Mrs M Reveley) 2816[1] 3058[6] 3523[7] 3714[5] 3812[9]

2 **AVONDALE FOREST (Ire),** b f Elegant Air - Chase Paperchase by Malinowski (USA) (Liam Browne) 269[4] 305[3] 896[3] 1045[4] 1571[5] 1854[9] 4462 4687

2 **AVONDALE ROSE,** br f Squill (USA) - Run Little Lady (USA) by J O Tobin (USA) (B S Rothwell) 2234[5] 2862 3828 4668[6]

3 **AVRIL ETOILE,** ch f Sharpo - Alsiba by Northfields (USA) (L J Holt) 716 871[4] 1312 2011 2288[4] 2476[2] 2967[2] 3383[5] 3661[8] 4008[6] 4331[2] 4670[2]

5 **AVRO ANSON,** b g Ardross - Tremellick by Mummy's Pet (M J Camacho) 303[4] 427[1] 4621[9]

3 **AWAD (USA),** b c Caveat (USA) - Dancer's Dandy by Noble Dancer 3653[1] 4478[8]

3 **AWAY GIRL,** b f Kalaglow - Miss Runaway by Runnett (T J Naughton) 2332 3012 3449[7] 3840

7 **AWESOME POWER,** b g Vision (USA) - Majestic Nurse by On Your Mark (J W Hills) 4678a[2] 4735a[1] 4759a[2] 9[2] 59[4] 171[2] 225[2] 234[2] 322[4] 918[5] 1146[6] 1237[2] 4711[3]

3 **AWESOME VENTURE,** b c Formidable (USA) - Pine Ridge by High Top (J A R Toller) 2749[6] 3132[1] 3697 4065

3 **AWESTRIKE (USA),** b c Imperial Falcon (Can) - Awe (USA) by Le Fabuleux (Mrs J Cecil) 2202[7] 2416[5] 2752[5] 3101[1] 3261[3] 3585[2] 4116

3 **AWESTRUCK,** b c Primo Dominie - Magic Kingdom by Kings Lake (USA) (B Preece) 764[2] 1204[8] 1357[1] 1780[2] 2379[3] 2551[6] 3192[4] 4101 4760

2 **AWFULLY RISKY,** b f Risk Me (Fr) - Gemma Kaye by Cure The Blues (USA) (G Lewis) 3446

2 **AWS (Ire),** b c Jareer (USA) - Ilsassa (Hol) by Sassafras (Fr) (T Thomson Jones) 1905 3009[9] 4098[3] 4561[7]

2 **AWTAAR (USA),** b f Lyphard (USA) - Magic Slipper by Habitat (P T Walwyn) 3317 4177[5] 4437[5]

2 **AXLENO (Ire),** ch f Bold Arrangement - Connaught Rose by Connaught (K O'Sullivan) 2880[4] 3071[8]

6 **AYIA NAPA,** b g Known Fact (USA) - Folgoet (Fr) by Pharly (Fr) (Mrs S C Bradburne) 4235[8] 4343

6 **AYR RAIDER,** ch h Claude Monet (USA) - Thimothea (Fr) by Timmy My Boy (Miss L A Perratt) 4673a 4690a[8] 700[7] 883[3] 1228[4] 2568[3] 2738[3]

2 **AZHAAR (USA),** ch f Nijinsky (Can) - Smart Heiress (USA) by Vaguely Noble (J L Dunlop) 2887 3659[3] 4396[3] 4539[6]

3 **AZHAR,** b c Night Shift (USA) - Aunt Jemima by Busted (M R Stoute) 388[4] 690[5] 989[3] 1328[1] 1717[1] 1958[1] 2393[3] 3488[2] 3904[1]

3 **AZILIAN (Ire),** b or br c Top Ville - D'Azy by Persian Bold (J H M Gosden) 3217[2] 3620[2] 3899[9]

3 **AZOLA (Ire),** b f Alzao (USA) - Carnival Dance by Welsh Pageant (D R Loder) 1171[5] 1595[4] 1851[3] 2163[5] 2953[1] 3460[1] 3780[3]

3 **AZRAG (Ire),** b c Bluebird (USA) - Red Val by Red God (T Thomson Jones) 761[9] 2191[6]

3 **AZTEC HILL (USA),** 762[7] 3767[6]

2 **BARNPARK,** b c Caerwent - Pride Of Paris by Troy (N Bycroft) 1998 3792 3969^{6} 4240^{8} 4427^{7} 4550 4644^{6}

2 **BARODET (USA),** b c Afleet (Can) - Endurable Heights by Graustark (A Fabre) 3048^{1} 4074^{4}

3 **BARON FERDINAND,** ch c Ferdinand (USA) - In Perpetuity by Great Nephew (R Charlton) 842^{2} 1093^{1} 1958^{2} 2433^{1} 3647^{2}

2 **BAROSKI,** b c Petoski - Gohar (USA) by Barachois (Can) (J L Harris) 2586^{8} 2826^{6}

2 **BAROSSA VALLEY (Ire),** b c Alzao (USA) - Night Of Wind by Tumble Wind (USA) (P W Chapple-Hyam) 2571^{1} 3289^{2} 3537^{5}

3 **BARRAAK,** b c El Gran Senor (USA) - Rosia Bay by High Top (Major W R Hern) 557 1005^{4} 1242^{3} 1423^{1} 1605^{2}

3 **BARRATRY,** ch c Caerleon (USA) - Tolmi by Great Nephew (H R A Cecil) 529^{6} 751^{8} 1154^{4} 2708^{4} 3211^{2} 3503^{3} 4414 4513^{7}

2 **BARRIER BOY,** ch g Jester - Finally by Final Straw (M G Meagher) 4437^{7} 4663^{7}

4 **BARRY'S PRINCESS (Ire),** b f Anita's Prince - Lady Ingrid by Taufan (USA) (Luke Comer) 806^{7} 1105^{7}

3 **BARSAL (Ire),** b g Absalom - La Bella Fontana by Lafontaine (USA) (J Parkes) 32 62^{5} 162^{3} 230^{2} 344^{4} 434^{9} 507^{2} 1161^{8} 1421^{6} 1459^{5} 1943^{5} 4664^{7}

3 **BARSLEY,** ch c Kalaglow - Mycenae Cherry by Troy (J R Jenkins) 602 980 1906^{7} 2523^{9} 2784^{7} 2943^{4} 3170^{6}

2 **BARTOK (Ire),** b c Fairy King (USA) - Euromill by Shirley Heights (C Collins) 571^{3} 938^{1} 2075^{3} 2807^{1} 3612^{4}

4 **BARTON PRIDE (Ire),** b g Phardante (Fr) - Ginosa by Kalamoun (M D Hammond) 727 910 1276^{9} 1564

5 **BARUD (Ire),** b g Persian Bold - Pale Moon by Jukebox (D J Wintle) 918^{7}

3 **BASHAYER (USA),** b f Mr Prospector (USA) - Height Of Fashion (Fr) by Bustino (Major W R Hern) 512^{7} 856^{2} 1525 1952^{7} 2961^{4} 3262^{6} 3645^{4} 3892^{4} 4207^{3} 4362^{1} 4691^{4}

2 **BASHFUL BRAVE,** ch c Indian Ridge - Shy Dolly by Cajun (M Bell) 2374^{7} 3528^{2} 3754^{3} 3989^{4} 4613^{7}

4 **BASIE NOBLE,** ch g Local Suitor (USA) - Prima Ballerina (Fr) by Nonoalco (USA) (John J McLoughlin) 666 787^{6} 1199^{5} 1645^{4} 1856^{8} 4057^{3} 4147 4461

3 **BASIM (USA),** b c Capote (USA) - Mer Belle (USA) by Far North (Can) (J S Bolger) 580^{5} 2362^{9}

2 **BASKERVILLE,** ch c Night Shift (USA) - Bay Bay by Bay Express (R F Johnson Houghton) 554^{3} 859^{3} 1131^{6} 2137^{1} 3448^{3} 3635^{7} 4272^{7}

4 **BASSETJA (Ire),** b f Lashkari - Belle Doche (Fr) by Riverman (USA) (J F C Maxwell) 1997 2512^{3} 3245^{4} 3662^{6} 3976^{5}

4 **BASSETLAW BELLE,** b f Lucky Wednesday - Delayed Action by Jolly Jet (S R Bowring) 4768a 4^{6}

4 **BASSIO (Bel),** b g Efisio - Batalya (Bel) by Boulou (Bel) (C N Allen) 4767a^{8} 4782a 8 38 329^{9} 440^{7} 700 771 861 1237^{6} 1453 1701^{5} 1874^{3} 2590^{2} 2747^{7} 2920^{7} 3140^{4} 3190^{6} 3550^{2} 3591

2 **BASSMAAT (USA),** b f Cadeaux Genereux - Mangayah (USA) by Spectacular Bid (USA) (J S Bolger) 1022^{2} 2037^{2} 2403^{5} 3541^{2}

4 **BATABANOO,** ch g Bairn (USA) - For Instance by Busted (Mrs M Reveley) 2678^{3} 2871^{1} 3373^{1} 3503^{4} 3565^{5}

4 **BATCHWORTH BOUND,** b f Ballacashtal (Can) - Treasurebound by Beldale Flutter (USA) (S Mellor) 837 1257^{7} 1903^{8} 2352^{1} 2549^{2} 2688^{1} 2910^{2} 3270^{3} 3383^{3} 3584^{3} 3739^{2} 3946^{2} 4363^{3} 4487^{5}

6 **BATEAU ROUGE,** b h Red Sunset - Last Gunboat by Dominion (I A Balding) 4682a

2 **BATIEN'S RIVER,** b f Risk Me (Fr) - Lady Chaser by Posse (USA) (P C Haslam) 381^{5} 449^{3} 564^{3} 767^{3} 3600^{7} 3815^{8}

2 **BATON BLEU,** b c Music Boy - Fair Eleanor by Saritamer (USA) (P Howling) 3982 4754^{9}

4 **BATTLE COLOURS (Ire),** b c Petorius - Streamertail by Shirley Heights (Mrs J R Ramsden) 274^{6} 403^{5} 2015^{2} 2989^{4} 3258^{1} 3623^{7} 3712^{5} 4022^{1} 4297 4394 4490^{6} 4650

6 **BATTLE STANDARD (Can),** b g Storm Bird (Can) - Hoist Emy's Flag (USA) by Hoist The Flag (USA) (Mrs S A Bramall) 831^{7}

4 **BATTLING BELLA (USA),** b f Fighting Fit (USA) - Belle Marina by Lochnager (G L Moore) 4501

2 **BATTLING BLUE,** b c Primo Dominie - Ethel Knight by Thatch (USA) (R Hannon) 2364^{4} 2519^{1} 3223^{3} 3596^{3} 3949^{5}

4 **BATTUTA,** ch f Ballacashtal (Can) - Valpolicella by Lorenzaccio (G R Oldroyd) 123^{5} 148 202^{6} 2104^{8} 2694^{5}

3 **BAULKING TOWERS,** b g Kala Shikari - Carrula by Palm Track (M McCormack) 483 1090^{6} 1316 1961

3 **BAVARIAN BALLAD (Ire),** ch f Ballad Rock - Alaria (Ger) by Kaiseradler (Joseph M Canty) 4245 4685^{6}

3 **BAWAETH (USA),** b f Blushing Groom (Fr) - Last Feather (USA) by Vaguely Noble (B W Hills) 842^{4} 2310^{2} 3491^{4} 4209^{4}

2 **BAWARDI (Ire),** br c Doyoun - Badedra by Kings Lake (USA) (John M Oxx) 3771^{1} 4382^{3} 4584^{4}

3 **BAYA (USA),** ch f Nureyev - Barger by Riverman (A Fabre) 697^{1} 1086^{4} 1722^{2} 2409^{7} 3650^{2} 4219^{2}

2 **BAYARIYKA (Ire),** b f Slip Anchor - Bayazida by Bustino (John M Oxx) 4582^{5}

6 **BAYBEEJAY,** b m Buzzards Bay - Peak Condition by Mountain Call (R Brotherton) 4494^{5}

2 **BAYBELLINA (Ire),** b f Robellino (USA) - Brosna (USA) by Irish River (Fr) (C J Benstead) 4497^{7}

3 **BAYDON BELLE (USA),** br f Al Nasr (Fr) - Vague Prospect (USA) by Vaguely Noble (G Lewis) 328^{7} 827^{5} 1586^{8} 1912^{9} 3710

2 **BAYDUR (Ire),** b c Danehill (USA) - Sutton Place by Tyrant (USA) (D K Weld) 4460 4581^{2} 4688^{5}

3 **BAYFAN (Ire),** b g Taufan (USA) - Laurel Express by Bay Express (J S Moore) 417 582 759 2938 3292^{8} 3449

4 **BAYIN (USA),** b c Caro - Regatela (USA) by Dr Fager (M D I Usher) 4814a^{5} 35^{9} 77^{3} 107^{6} 163^{4} 205^{7} 238^{9} 1007 1375^{8} 1681^{9} 1902 3747^{4} 3794^{1} 4168^{1} 4580^{1} 4693

3 **BAY QUEEN,** b f Damister (USA) - Be My Queen by Be My Guest (USA) (M Bell) 452^{1} 644^{1} 875^{2} 1111^{1} 1483^{6} 1958^{7} 2576^{8} 2708^{3} 3282^{1} 3431^{6} 4018^{7} 4414

3 **BAYRAK (USA),** b g Bering - Phydilla (Fr) by Lyphard (USA) (C R Egerton) 679^{9} 1092^{9} 1733^{3} 2091^{1}

5 **BAYROUGE (Ire),** br m Gorytus (USA) - Bay Tree (Fr) by Relko (Mrs A M O'Brien) 309^{9}

3 **BAY RUM,** br f Green Ruby (USA) - Cuba Libre by Rum (USA) (K O Cunningham-Brown) 4677a

7 **BAYSHAM (USA),** b g Raise A Native - Sunny Bay (USA) by Northern Bay (USA) (B R Millman) 479^{7} 756^{4} 1373^{7} 1584^{6} 1927^{3} 2418^{5} 2663^{6} 3261 3707^{3} 3896 4172

7 **BAY TERN (USA),** b h Arctic Tern (USA) - Unbiased (USA) by Foolish Pleasure (USA) (T Dyer) 1890^{7} 2091^{2} 2740^{7} 3147^{1}

3 **BAYYINAT (USA),** b c Woodman (USA) - Turn Of Joy by Lomond (USA) (C Weedon) 1793^{6} 3669 4091

3 **B B GLEN,** b f Hadeer - Damaska (USA) by Damascus (USA) (D Morris) 813 1627^{3} 1866 2095^{5} 2499^{2} 2784^{5} 3249^{4} 3311^{3}

4 **BEACHWOOD (Fr),** b c Script Ohio - Sass Go by Sassafras (Fr) (R Rossini) 2083^{2}

5 **BEACHY HEAD,** gr g Damister (USA) - No More Rosies by Warpath (J J O'Neill) 1056^{2}

3 **BEACON TOWERS,** b g Petoski - Final Thought by Final Straw (J A R Toller) 1344

2 **BEAMING,** b or br f Mtoto - Glancing by Grundy (J R Fanshawe) 4011^{7} 4345^{2} 4434^{1}

4 **BEAM ME UP SCOTTY (Ire),** br g Orchestra - Bright Path by He Loves Me (Mrs S D Williams) 35^{4} 82^{1} 115^{5} 182^{8} 210^{4} 322^{6}

2 **BEARALL (Ire),** b f Al Hareb (USA) - Soxoph by Hotfoot (R Hannon) 325^{4} 496^{2} 1009^{1} 2112^{3} 2473^{4} 3499^{6} 3845 4111^{1} 4558^{1}

5 **BEATLE SONG,** b m Song - Betyle (Fr) by Hardicanute (C J Hill) 134 330 458^{8} 1097 2327 3099^{5} 3459^{1} 3593^{6} 3830 4131^{6}

2 **BEAT OF DRUMS,** b c Warning - Nyoka by Raja Baba (G Botti) 3802^{1}

2 **BEATS WORKING,** b g Aragon - Relatively Easy by Relkino (Mrs J R Ramsden) 2766^{4} 3001^{1} 3309^{9} 3635^{3} 3865^{4} 3997^{1}

3 **BEAT THE BAGMAN (Ire),** b g Bob Back (USA) - Dacani by Polyfoto (J Akehurst) 334 519^{6} 733 1007^{7} 1349^{6} 1685^{6} 1902^{9} 2162^{2} 2471^{9}

6 **BEAU BEAUCHAMP,** b g Thatching - El Pina by Be My Guest (USA) (Noel Meade) 2664^{5} 2900^{8} 3853

3 **BEAUCHAMP HERO,** b c Midyan (USA) - Buss by Busted (J L Dunlop) 1092^{5} 1375^{2} 1808^{5} 2361^{1} 2627^{1} 3285^{8} 3897^{2} 4300^{9}

2 **BEAUCHAMP IMPERIAL,** b c Nishapour (Fr) - Afariya (Fr) by Silver Shark (J G Burns) 1824^{3} 2701^{4} 3771^{6}

3 **BEAUMAN,** b c Rainbow Quest (USA) - Gliding by Tudor Melody (B A McMahon) 947^{8} 1329^{4} 1785 2398^{5} 2696^{3} 3119^{5} 3476 3900^{4} 4158^{1} 4513^{6}

3 **BEAUMONT (Ire),** br c Be My Native (USA) - Say Yes by Junius (USA) (J Pearce) 803^{4} 1039^{6} 1306^{6} 1704^{1} 1976^{4} 2758 3256^{5} 4374^{5} 4631

4 **BEAUMONT HOUSE (Ire),** b c Where To Dance (USA) - Allorette by Ballymore (Robert Norris) 807^{6} 1202^{5} 1514^{5}

7 **BEAUMOOD,** b g Jalmood (USA) - Falcon Berry (Fr) by Bustino (E J Alston) 530 745^{4} 1054^{3} 1305^{3} 4426

6 **BEAU QUEST,** b h Rainbow Quest (USA) - Elegant Tern (USA) by Sea-Bird II (B R Cambidge) 453 1321 2152^{6} 2921^{3} 4102^{8} 4353^{6} 4759^{7}

2 **BEAUTETE,** b g Komaite (USA) - New Central by Remainder Man (S Dow) 2006^{1} 2924^{6} 3223^{5} 4230

5 **BEAU VENTURE (USA),** ch h Explodent (USA) - Old Westbury (USA) by Francis S (F H Lee) 436^{3} 750^{9} 1000 1215^{8} 1679^{8} 2392 2753^{5} 3034^{6} 3511 4180 4532

2 **BECCARI (USA),** b c Lyphard (USA) - Belle Pensee (USA) by Ribot (A Fabre) 3932^{5}

2 **BECKENHAM LADY (Ire),** ch f Al Hareb (USA) - Angel Divine by Ahonoora (S G Norton) 4190^{7} 4435 4761^{7}

3 **BECKY BOO,** b f White Mill - Aber Cothi by Dominion (R J Price) 518^{4} 614 1133 1319^{6}

3 **BECKYHANNAH,** b f Rambling River - Munequita by Marching On (R Bastiman) 829^{5} 1273 1463^{9} 4031 4317^{1} 4640 4693^{4}

3 **BECKY'S GIRL,** br f Sweet Monday - Bransford by Hallodri (Ata) (R Brotherton) 62^{8} 185^{9} 2464

3 **BEDAVA (Fr),** b g Double Bed (Fr) - Avanie by Avatar (F Doumen) 3583^{1} 4196^{4} 4566

2 **BEDAZZLE,** b g Formidable (USA) - Wasimah by Caerleon (USA) (M Brittain) 1135^{6} 1715^{8} 1897^{7} 2453^{4} 3816 3997^{9} 4227 4618^{7}

3 **BEDEVIL (USA),** b c Devil's Bag (USA) - Pailleron (USA) by Majestic Light (USA) (Mrs J Cecil) 1176 1429^{6} 1831^{6} 3757^{3}

2 **BEDOON RESOOM (USA),** b c Sovereign Dancer (USA) - Sans Supplement (USA) by Grey Dawn II (J H M Gosden) 4677^{2}

6 **BEDOUIN PRINCE (USA),** b h Danzig (USA) - Regal Heiress by English Prince (B Richmond) 25^{1} 42^{3} 64^{3} 81^{1} 122^{7} 137^{2} 165^{4} 175^{2} 226^{3} 254^{3} 279^{6} 303 973^{7}

2 **BEECHFIELD FLYER,** ch g Northern State (USA) - Djimbaran Bay by Le Levanstell (J Berry) 2542^{5} 3031^{5} 3470^{4}

2 **BEE DEE BEST (Ire),** b c Try My Best (USA) - Eloquent Charm (USA) by Private Account (USA) (Miss L A Perratt) 3809^{5} 4042^{3} 4237^{7} 4699^{6}

7 **BEEKMAN STREET,** b g Jalmood (USA) - Plato's Retreat by Brigadier Gerard (Mrs M Reveley) 3442^{2} 3567^{3}

2 **BE EXCITING (Ire),** ch f Be My Guest (USA) - Exciting by Mill Reef (USA) (J L Dunlop) 1916 3209^{7} 3625^{5} 3905^{2} 4251^{9} 4531^{1} 4725^{2}

2 **BEFUTO (Fr),** 4242^{4}

2 **BE GIVING (Ire),** b f Cyrano de Bergerac - Lady Huntingtower by Hard Fought (John J McLoughlin) 4290^{6} 4624^{8} 4706^{7}

6 **BEIJA FLOR,** gr g Busted - Rusticello by Rusticaro (Fr) (F Jordan) 50^{8} 1626

6 **BELAFONTE,** b g Derrylin - Ulla Laing by Mummy's Pet (Miss K M George) 1430 1840

4 **BELATED,** gr f Bellypha - Enchanted by Song (P C Haslam) 4739a^{4} 4796a^{7} 815^{7} 883

4 **BEL BARAKA (Ire),** ch g Bering - Typhoon Polly by Lord Gayle (USA) (D R C Elsworth) 4756a^{6} 4795a^{3}

6 **BELFORT PRINCE,** b g Belfort (Fr) - Turtle Dove by Gyr (USA) (Mrs S C Bradburne) 2455^{9}

6 **BELFORT RULER,** b g Belfort (Fr) - Call Me Kate by Firestreak (B Gubby) 1348 1527^{8} 1744^{4} 1953^{7}

3 **BELFRY GREEN (Ire),** ro c Doulab (USA) - Checkers by Habat (C A Horgan) 582 825 1114^{2} 1375^{6} 3080^{3} 3585^{5} 3839^{1} 4652

4 **BELGRAN (USA),** b g El Gran Senor (USA) - Belle Of Dodge Me (USA) by Creme Dela Creme (P D Evans) 3157^{7} 3353

4 **BELIEVE IN ME (Ire),** b c Don't Forget Me - Fast Bay by Bay Express (B A McMahon) 4696a^{8} 4705a 4767a^{4} 4777a^{2} 5^{3}

5 **BELJINSKI,** b m Myjinski (USA) - Lady Bedale by Comedy Star (USA) (B J McMath) 87

3 **BELLA BALLERINA,** b f Sadler's Wells (USA) - Bella Colora by Bellypha (M R Stoute) 662^{4} 992^{1} 1404^{6}

3 **BELLA BAMBOLA (Ire),** ch f Tate Gallery (USA) - Sciambola by Great Nephew (K O Cunningham-Brown) 2121 2728^{6} 3100

2 **BELLA PARKES,** b f Tina's Pet - Summerhill Spruce by Windjammer (USA) (J Berry) 325^{2} 889^{4} 1234^{3} 1580^{1} 2569^{1} 2996^{5} 3472^{1} 3845^{9}

2 **BELLA RAGAZZA,** b f Caerleon (USA) - Prima Domina (Fr) by Dominion (R Hannon) 3317 3625

2 **BELLAROY,** b f Gallic League - Crystal Pool by Taufan (USA) (B Palling) 1317^{5} 1583 2526^{9}

2 **BELLA SIGURA (USA),** b f El Gran Senor (USA) - Dae Julie (USA) by Taylor's Falls (USA) (T Stack) 4134^{8} 4405^{4} 4535

5 **BELLATRIX,** b m Persian Bold - Sorebelle by Prince Tenderfoot (USA) (C E Brittain) 333^{4} 1007^{5} 1612 2847

2 **BELLEMINETTE (Ire),** ch f Simply Great (Fr) - Kitty's Sister by Bustino (D Haydn Jones) 2147^{4} 2862^{3} 3352

5 **BELLE OF DREAMS (Ire),** b m Sarab - Bells Of Ireland by Northfield (USA) (M Brew) 868^{5} 1433^{5} 1620 2248 2511^{8}

4 **BELLE O' THE BAY (Ire),** br f Rowlandson - Slippery Bell by No Argument (J R Cox) 1295^{8} 1443 2512^{8} 3397 3663^{6}

3 **BELLE SOIREE,** ch f Night Shift (USA) - Party Game by Red Alert (R Akehurst) 4794a^{8} 21^{3} 44^{3} 116^{3} 156^{3} 250^{1} 379^{8} 1233^{7} 1714 3270^{8} 3707 3955

2 **BELLE VIVE (Ire),** ch f Exhibitioner - Court Bally by Barrons Court (P J Casserly) 3953 4135

6 **BELLEZZA,** b m Ardross - Bobo Ema by Auction Ring (USA) (A Moore) 1315

3 **BELLISSI (Ire),** b f Bluebird (USA) - Ingabelle by Taufan (USA) (T F Lacy) 1164^{4} 1568^{3} 1796^{2} 2184^{3} 2285^{3} 2779^{6} 3297^{4} 3579^{1} 4245^{7} 4463

3 **BELL LAD (Ire),** ch c Common Grounds - Quack Shot (USA) by Quack (USA) (C A Smith) 926 1233^{4} 1419 1480 3948

2 **BELLO GALLICO (Ire),** b c Gallic League - Jeewan by Touching Wood (USA) (R Hannon) 3421 3979

2 **BEL LORE (Ity),** ch c Adonijah - Beatrice Fellows by Prince Tady 1543^{3}

2 **BELLROI (Ire),** b g Roi Danzig (USA) - Balela by African Sky (M H Tompkins) 673 1324 1926^{5} 4215

3 **BELLSABANGING,** b c Chilibang - Bells Of St Martin by Martinmas (D R Laing) 491^{2} 721^{4} 871^{1} 993^{3} 1394^{5} 1687^{4} 1957^{6} 2728^{1} 3099^{2} 3266^{4} 3571^{6} 3739^{5} 4518 4681 4734^{3}

4 **BELLS OF LONGWICK,** b f Myjinski (USA) - Bells Of St Martin by Martinmas (D R Laing) 627^{3} 722^{4} 923^{8} 1127 1918^{7} 2524^{1} 2753^{9} 2846^{3} 3348 3739^{9} 3947 4501

5 **BELLTON,** gr g Bellypha - Celestial Air by Rheingold (J G FitzGerald) 589^{4} 831^{5}

7 **BELMARTIN,** gr g Bellypha - Martinova by Martinmas (C Collins) 640^{4} 787 1199^{9} 1645^{7} 4534 4689

3 **BELMONT PRINCESS (Ire),** b f Carmelite House (USA) - Silly Song by Silly Season (A P Jones) 1587 2032^{4} 2401^{7} 2661^{4} 2910^{4} 3229 3459^{2} 3584^{8}

8 **BELMOREDEAN,** ch g Be My Guest (USA) - Hanna Alta (Fr) by Busted (R J O'Sullivan) 4782a^{3} 4807a^{6} 9^{6} 59^{6} 184^{1} 232^{1} 603^{1} 3512

6 **BEL'S SCARLET (USA),** ro m Bel Bolide (USA) - Vigor's Star by Vigors (R Mandella) 1370^{3}

4 **BELTHORN,** ro f Belfort (Fr) - Blowing Bubbles by Native Admiral (USA) (J J Bridger) 421^{9} 721 916^{7} 1352^{6} 1925 2225^{5} 2620^{9} 3099^{7} 4008^{8}

4 **BE MY HABITAT,** ch g Be My Guest (USA) - Fur Hat by Habitat (Miss L C Siddall) 702

2 **BLUE SIREN,** ch f Bluebird (USA) - Manx Millenium by Habitat (I A Balding) 2754^{2} 3114^{1} 3448^{1} 3737^{2} 4302^{5}

3 **BLUES TRAVELLER (Ire),** b c Bluebird (USA) - Natuschka by Authi (B W Hills) 588^{4} 890^{2} 1448^{3} 2261^{4} 3402^{6} 3823^{5}

5 **BLUE TAIL,** gr m Petong - Glyn Rhosyn by Welsh Saint (P Butler) 2723^{8} 3011 4486

5 **BLUE TOPAZE,** ch m Fast Topaze (USA) - Forever Mary by Red Alert (M S Saunders) 758^{1} 1096^{3} 1267^{5} 1537^{1} 1806 2582^{2} 2987^{7} 3099^{4} 3450 4297 4501 4597^{3} 4681^{2}

3 **BLUE TRUMPET,** b g Respect - Sans Blague by Above Suspicion (D Burchell) 962 1175^{9} 1500^{4} 2023^{8} 2499 4031 4711

2 **BLUEY,** ch c Tobin Lad (USA) - Palvic Grey by Kampala (J Mooney) 3141^{6}

2 **BLUMIN AFFAIR (USA),** b c Dynaformer (USA) - Medical Affair (USA) by Dr Blum (USA) (J Van Berg) 4743^{2}

2 **BLURRED IMAGE (Ire),** ch c Exactly Sharp (USA) - Bear's Affair by Gay Fandango (USA) (R Hannon) 454 1857^{6} 2417^{2} 2687^{1} 3386^{4} 4029^{6} 4299^{2} 4602^{1} 4733^{4}

3 **BLUSHING BARADA (USA),** b f Blushing Groom (Fr) - Galletto (USA) by Nijinsky (Can) (A A Scott) 686^{5} 1077^{4} 2977^{4}

2 **BLUSHINGBIRD (Ire),** b f Shaadi (USA) - Rising Spirits by Cure The Blues (USA) (H R A Cecil) 4190^{4} 4422^{7}

7 **BLUSHING BUNNY,** b m Blushing Scribe (USA) - Blesseen by So Blessed (Bernard Lawlor) 3662

2 **BLUSHING FLAME (USA),** b c Blushing Groom (Fr) - Nearctic Flame by Sadler's Wells (USA) (M R Stoute) 4276

3 **BLUSH RAMBLER (USA),** b c Blushing Groom (Fr) - Romanette (USA) by Alleged (USA) (J E Hammond) 954^{7}

4 **BLYOSTKA (USA),** ch f Gone West (USA) - Calypsa (USA) by The Minstrel (Can) (M D Hammond) 645

3 **BLYTHE (Arg),** b f Forlitano (Arg) - Marginal Money (USA) by Plugged Nickle (USA) (Noel Meade) 2221^{8} 2879

7 **BLYTON LAD,** b g Skyliner - Ballinacurra by King's Troop (M J Camacho) 1019 2927^{6} 3464^{5} 4275^{3} 4464^{3} 4678^{1} 4729^{1}

5 **BLYTON STAR (Ire),** b g Horage - Saintly Angel by So Blessed (K R Burke) 4698a^{8} 4742a 134^{4} 163^{3} 217^{8} 326^{3} 492 837 882 2312^{8}

2 **BOARDWALKER (Ire),** ch f Waajib - Standing Ovation by Godswalk (USA) (B V Kelly) 1994^{7} 4134^{5} 4406^{9}

3 **BOBADIL (Ire),** br f Bob Back (USA) - Thyme Music by Tudor Music (T F Lacy) 258 280 959^{6} 1553^{9} 1794^{1} 1987^{8} 2186^{3} 2702^{9} 2842 4246 4639^{9}

2 **BOB BARNES (Ire),** b c Bob Back (USA) - Court Barns (USA) by Riva Ridge (USA) (A P O'Brien) 2840^{5} 2982^{6} 3416 4093 4360

3 **BOBBIE DEE,** b f Blakeney - Aldbury Girl by Galivanter (D R C Elsworth) 4703a 755^{2} 946^{6} 1525 1839^{5} 2563^{2} 2961^{8} 3286^{5} 3514^{9}

3 **BOBBYSOXER,** b f Valiyar - Beveridge (USA) by Spectacular Bid (USA) (J L Dunlop) 483^{7} 827 1111 1399^{2} 1993^{2} 2685^{1} 2899^{1} 3263^{1} 3572^{3} 3786^{7} 4226^{8}

3 **BOBROSS (Ire),** b g Bob Back (USA) - Testarossa (Fr) by Kenmare (Fr) (Peter McCreery) 268^{1} 307^{4} 789 1569^{6} 1995^{1} 2142 2957^{9} 3826^{9} 4136^{9}

4 **BOB'S GIRL (Ire),** ch f Bob Back (USA) - Norme (Fr) by Dark Tiger (P Hughes) 2321 2901^{3}

3 **BOB'S RETURN (Ire),** br c Bob Back (USA) - Quality Of Life by Auction Ring (USA) (M H Tompkins) 947^{1} 1448^{6} 3403^{1} 3899^{1} 4311^{6}

2 **BOBSTAR DANCER (Ire),** b g Bob Back (USA) - Saint Simbir by Simbir (T G McCourt) 2284^{8}

3 **BOB THE YANK (Ire),** b g Bar Dexter (USA) - Jambrel (USA) by Tropic King II (Patrick O'Leary) 311 1236^{9} 3329^{6}

4 **BOBZAO (Ire),** b c Alzao (USA) - Brilleaux by Manado (T G Mills) 390^{8} 1118^{2} 2070^{1} 2621^{1} 3784^{2} 4141^{2} 4467^{6} 4560^{7}

3 **BOCANDE (Ire),** ch c Fayruz - African Cousin by Kampala (T Stack) 704^{2} 960^{6}

2 **BODANTREE,** b c Rambo Dancer (Can) - Snow Tree by Welsh Pageant (J L Spearing) 3446 4208^{9} 4316

4 **BODARI,** b g Prince Sabo - City Link Rose by Lochnager (D A Wilson) 479^{4} 659^{2} 1066 1127^{8} 1449^{9} 1485^{7} 1957^{7} 2255^{5} 2524^{3} 2965^{1} 3153 3266^{3} 3481^{3} 3621 3739^{1} 3849^{9} 3955^{5} 4465 4549^{9}

2 **BODINIYEH (Ire),** 2648^{5}

3 **BODY LANGUAGE,** ch f Petoski - Whipp's Cross by Kris (Mrs J R Ramsden) 398 681

3 **BOHEMIAN CROWN (USA),** b g Danzig (USA) - Infantes (USA) by Exclusive Native (USA) (M R Stoute) 602^{4} 827^{3} 1115^{2} 1299^{2} 2158^{2} 3449^{3}

3 **BOHEMIAN QUEEN,** ch f Doulab (USA) - Tittlemouse by Castle Keep (J L Spearing) 2555^{6}

3 **BOISTEROUS,** b g Sizzling Melody - Balgreggan by Hallez (Fr) (W R Muir) 493^{7} 1005 1133

2 **BOJOLLY,** b f Absalom - String Of Beads by Ile de Bourbon (USA) (J Etherington) 2973^{3} 3186^{7} 3432 3743^{7} 4082^{8} 4215^{6}

7 **BOKARO (Fr),** b g Air Du Nord - Tzara by Night And Day (C P E Brooks) 783^{2} 1224^{3} 1533^{2} 1752 1809^{5}

4 **BO KNOWS BEST (Ire),** ch g Burslem - Do We Know by Derrylin (G L Moore) 3010^{6} 3388^{6} 3666^{1} 4064

2 **BO KNOWS NIGEL (Ire),** b g Taufan (USA) - Fais Vite (USA) by Sharpen Up (J Sutcliffe) 4339^{9} 4523

2 **BOLAS,** br f Unfuwain (USA) - Three Stars by Star Appeal (B W Hills) 4276

3 **BOLD ACRE,** ch g Never So Bold - Nicola Wynn by Nicholas Bill (D Burchell) 1686^{1} 2031^{3} 2551^{4} 2601^{3} 3957^{7} 4101 4683^{4}

2 **BOLD ALEX,** b g Full Extent (USA) - Gunner Girl by Gunner B (S G Norton) 2772^{4} 3792^{4} 4044^{1} 4225^{2} 4318^{3} 4436^{8} 4642^{4}

6 **BOLD AMBITION,** b g Ela-Mana-Mou - Queen Of The Dance by Dancer's Image (USA) (T Kersey) 1305^{2} 1476^{2} 2043^{7} 2891^{1} 3033^{7} 3970^{8} 4374 4675^{9}

3 **BOLD AMUSEMENT,** ch g Never So Bold - Hysterical by High Top (Mrs M Reveley) 1040^{4} 1402^{2} 2060^{9} 2351^{2} 3158^{3}

2 **BOLDANDPRETTY,** br f Balidar - Be Bold by Bustino (P A Kelleway) 730 2234^{6} 2826 3389 4124^{8}

6 **BOLD ANGEL,** b g Lochnager - Lobela by Lorenzaccio (M H Easterby) 2017^{3} 2106^{4} 2396^{1} 2657^{4} 3155^{3} 3487^{3} 3791^{6} 3901^{8} 4166

2 **BOLD ARISTOCRAT (Ire),** b c Bold Arrangement - Wyn Mipet by Welsh Saint (R Hollinshead) 312^{2} 374^{1} 1461^{5} 1565^{4} 1899^{5} 3122^{4} 3363^{3} 3657^{7} 4034^{3} 4618

4 **BOLD CAT (Ire),** b c Bold Arrangement - Le Chat by Burglar (Joseph Sheahan) 3605^{6}

3 **BOLD COUNTY,** b f Never So Bold - Hants by Exbury (M Johnston) 634^{6} 2024^{3} 2132^{4} 2305^{8} 2594^{7} 2829^{9} 3059^{6} 3995

2 **BOLD CYRANO (Ire),** b c Cyrano de Bergerac - Court Hussar by Queen's Hussar (B Palling) 469^{4}

2 **BOLD DEPUTY (USA),** ch c Bold Run (USA) - Surrogate Miss by Surreal 2438^{3}

5 **BOLD ELECT,** b g Electric - Famous Band (USA) by Banderilla (USA) (P Wigham) 1779^{4} 2235^{4} 2871^{6} 3724^{7} 4344^{5} 4426^{1} 4695^{8}

2 **BOLD EMIR,** b c Emarati (USA) - Monstrosa by Monsanto (Fr) (T Stack) 1442 2093^{5} 2284

2 **BOLD ENCOUNTER (Ire),** b f Persian Bold - Welshwyn by Welsh Saint (Michael Kauntze) 4244 4581

2 **BOLD FLAME,** ch c Never So Bold - Red Tapsi by Tap On Wood (J Pearce) 4014^{7} 4337^{9}

3 **BOLD FLASH,** ch g Flash Of Steel - Amenaide by Known Fact (USA) (P C Haslam) 4661a 1596^{2} 2353 3355

2 **BOLD GEM,** b f Never So Bold - Precious Jade by Northfields (USA) (B J Meehan) 1234^{4} 2137^{3} 2325^{7} 2689^{2} 2886^{3}

2 **BOLD GREEK,** b c Never So Bold - Thessaloniki by Julio Mariner (J M P Eustace) 3990

6 **BOLD HABIBTI,** b m Never So Bold - Cardinal Palace by Royal Palace (J S Bolger) 942^{8}

8 **BOLD HABIT,** ch g Homing - Our Mother by Bold Lad (Ire) (J Pearce) 4743a 4808a 28^{8} 39^{4} 101^{2} 140^{3} 292^{9} 401^{7} 475^{8} 677 1036 1207^{6} 2445^{7} 2944^{8}

2 **BOLD JOKER,** b c Jester - Bold Difference by Bold Owl (J P Leigh) 3279^{8}

6 **BOLD LEZ,** b h Never So Bold - Classy Nancy (USA) by Cutlass (USA) (M J Haynes) 481^1 675^7 993^1 1205^6 1680^5 2252^5 3571^3 3849 4151^3 4465 4521^5

4 **BOLD LILLIAN (Ire),** ch f Bold Arrangement - La Cita by Le Levanstell (Michael Cunningham) 937^4

3 **BOLD LINE,** br f Never So Bold - Known Line by Known Fact (USA) (P C Haslam) 304 907^6 2104^7 2593^5 2769^2 2934^7 2976^3 3216^6 3591

2 **BOLD-MAX,** ch c Bold Owl - Country-Inn by Town And Country (M P Muggeridge) 4263^7 4523 4680

4 **BOLD MELODY,** b f Never So Bold - Broken Melody by Busted (P C Haslam) 885 1634^6 2088^4 2680^6 2931^1 3088 3374^8 3812^6 4104

4 **BOLD MEMORY,** br g Never So Bold - Try To Remember by Music Boy (P C Haslam) 2008^5 2671^6 2989^3

2 **BOLD MICK,** b c Never So Bold - Purple Fan by Dalsaan (D J G Murray Smith) 4067 4263^3 4512^8

4 **BOLD MOLLY (Ire),** b or br f Treasure Kay - Ice Baby by Grundy (J C Harley) 599^2 868 1385 1923^5 2675^2 2879^3 3160^7 3827 4389

4 **BOLD N' FLASHY (Can),** b c Bold Ruckus (USA) - Flashy Chestnut (Can) by Briartic (Can) (Ms Deborah England) 3464^8

3 **BOLD NOT BEAT (Ire),** gr g Bold Arrangement - Disco Beat by No Mercy (J C Harley) 489^8 848^8 1995 3298^5 4119

3 **BOLD PHILIP,** b g King Of Spain - Our Mother by Bold Lad (Ire) (R T Juckes) 655^8 862^5 1101^5 4537

3 **BOLD PROSPECT,** b c Never So Bold - Petite Hester by Wollow (P Calver) 2643^7

4 **BOLD PURSUIT (Ire),** b g Thatching - Pursue by Auction Ring (USA) (J G FitzGerald) 1462^2 2376^4 3437 3722^5

4 **BOLD REINE (Fr),** b f Policeman (Fr) - Labold by Bold Lad (Ire) (R J Hodges) 1533 1816

5 **BOLD RESOLUTION (Ire),** b g Shardari - Valmarine (Fr) by Val de Loir (C A Cyzer) 420^6 682 857 1457^9 1669^7 2755^1 3125^1 3319^1 3595^2 3724^9 4143^4 4466

2 **BOLDROUS,** 3803^4

4 **BOLD SETKO (Ire),** b g Bold Arrangement - Ribamba by Ribocco (C T Nash) 1487

3 **BOLD SEVEN (Ire),** ch f Never So Bold - First Blush by Ela-Mana-Mou (F H Lee) 400 846^6 1017 2396^4 2651^1 3213^7 3756^9 4317^9 4536

2 **BOLD SIXTEEN (USA),** b f Diesis - Go For Bold (USA) by Bold Forbes (USA) (Mrs J Cecil) 2630^8 4588^1

5 **BOLD SPARK,** br g Electric - Boldie by Bold Lad (Ire) (J M Bradley) 108 150^4

3 **BOLD STAR,** b c Persian Bold - Star Arrangement by Star Appeal (R Hollinshead) 3489^4 3727^9 4022 4206^8 4544 4757^8

3 **BOLD STREET (Ire),** ch c Shy Groom (USA) - Ferry Lane by Dom Racine (Fr) (A Bailey) 57^1 109^5 187^7 3778^9 3906 4277^9 4490^9

4 **BOLD STROKE,** br g Persian Bold - Fariha by Mummy's Pet (J L Dunlop) 513^6 792^9 1064 2581^3 3883^4 4107^2 4247 4563^1

3 **BOLD THATCHER,** b or br c Thatching - Bold Apple by Bold Lad (Ire) (P W Harris) 476^2 803^2 1145^5 1330^6 1833^3 2522 3957^6

2 **BOLD TIME MONKEY,** ch f Bold Owl - Play For Time by Comedy Star (USA) (M Tate) 1475^4 2180^5 2586^7 3557^6 4084^2 4452^6

2 **BOLD TIMING,** b f Never So Bold - Brilliant Timing (USA) by The Minstrel (Can) (Mrs M Reveley) 2429^4 2759^1

3 **BOLD TREASURE (Ire),** b f Treasure Kay - Granny Stock by Imperial Fling (USA) (Mrs N Macauley) 455 713^5 1356^7

3 **BOLDVILLE BASH (Ire),** br c Bold Arrangement - Yashville by Top Ville (T D Barron) 3004 3219 3507

4 **BOLD WINDY (USA),** b f Bold Tropic (USA) - Windy Pj (USA) by Nevada (USA) (G Jones) 1695^2 2645^5

5 **BOLERO DANCER (Ire),** b g Shareef Dancer (USA) - Legend Of Arabia by Great Nephew (Thomas O'Neill) 1385^5 2320^5 2484 2901^6 3076^6 3296^2 3399^1 3721^8 4001 4370^4 4389^3 4737

3 **BOLLIN DUNCAN,** b c Petoski - Bollin Emily by Lochnager (M H Easterby) 1080^7

2 **BOLLIN MARY,** b f Chilibang - Bollin Zola by Alzao (USA) (M H Easterby) 544^4 1339^3 1739^7 3001^4 3715 4193

2 **BOLLIN NEIL,** b c Jalmood (USA) - Bollin Emily by Lochnager (M H Easterby) 2129^8 2630^5 3031^7

4 **BOLOARDO,** b g Persian Bold - Northshiel by Northfields (USA) (C E Brittain) 390^5 533^1 689^3 1085^5 1538^4 2070^5 2432^3 3434 4063^4 4175 4420^9

7 **BOLTON FLYER,** b m Aragon - Linda's Romance (USA) (O O'Neill) 4802a 42

3 **BOLTROSE,** b c Electric - Garnette Rose by Floribunda (K White) 872 1090^7 1534^4 2117^7 2773^5 3232^4

3 **BOMBLET,** b f Persian Bold - Buzzbomb by Bustino (R F Johnson Houghton) 3272^5 3590^8 3832^3 4254 4683

2 **BONAIGUA (Ire),** ch c Lomond (USA) - Watership (USA) by Foolish Pleasure (USA) (G Harwood) 1949^4 2419^5 3079^3 3259^3 3597^5 3974^2 4230 4444

3 **BONAR BRIDGE (USA),** b or br g Quadratic (USA) - Merririver (USA) by Taylor's Falls (USA) (R Hannon) 755^4 876^4 1067^5 1299^4 1769^7

2 **BONASH,** b f Rainbow Quest (USA) - Sky Love by Nijinsky (Can) (A Fabre) 3977^1

9 **BONDAID,** b g Main Reef - Regency Gold by Prince Regent (Fr) (J White) 2471^3 2684^1 2849^4

2 **BONIFACCIO BANDIT (Ire),** b c Dance Of Life (USA) - Smash by Busted (G L Moore) 4419 4587^3

3 **BONITA BEE,** b f King Of Spain - Lady Annie Laurie by Pitcairn (J C McConnochie) 606 872 1027 1487^6 1817^5 1977^8 2378^8

2 **BONNIE CRATHIE (Ire),** b f Common Grounds - Run Bonnie by Runnett (C Collins) 269^6 305^5 896^6 1104^1 1924^1 2704^5 2983^8 4285

4 **BONNIFER (Ire),** ch g Royal And Regal (USA) - Piper's Lady (Can) by Scotch Fool (USA) (Liam Browne) 3197^3 3580 4534 4685

2 **BONNY BRIDE (Ire),** ch f Lomond (USA) - Blue Wedding (USA) by Irish River (Fr) (D R Loder) 3186^2 3659^1 3884^4

2 **BONNY MELODY,** b f Sizzling Melody - Bonny Quiver by Gorytus (USA) (J R Fanshawe) 4210^7 4526^7

3 **BONNY PRINCESS,** br f Petoski - True Queen (USA) by Silver Hawk (USA) (W Storey) 4717a 642 976 1191^5 1702^6 1896^7 2340^3 2709^6 3090 3355^7 4048^5

3 **BON POINT,** b c Soviet Star (USA) - Twixt by Kings Lake (A Fabre) 3285^1 3618^1 4308^5

2 **BON TON,** ch f Beveled (USA) - Sweet Straw by Thatching (M R Channon) 1063 1234^5 1909^4 2718^8 2911^9 3103

3 **BONUS POINT,** ch g Don't Forget Me - Blue Aria by Cure The Blues (USA) (Mrs M Reveley) 3182^7

4 **BOOGIE BOPPER (Ire),** b or br g Taufan (USA) - Mey by Canisbay (M C Pipe) 709^7 1389^7

6 **BOOKCASE,** b g Siberian Express (USA) - Colourful (Fr) by Gay Mecene (USA) (D R C Elsworth) 4782a^6 225^3 389^1 473^6 663^4 874^4 1143^8 1409^6 1820^1 2029^2 2474^6 2795^5 2991^4 4559

2 **BOOKWORM,** b g Petoski - Beryl's Jewel by Siliconn (S Dow) 2325^9

5 **BOOMING (Fr),** b or br h Leading Counsel (USA) - Donche by Roi Dagobert (R Collett) 153^3

5 **BOOTIKIN,** ch m Relkino - Galosh by Pandofell (C W C Elsey) 1224^6 1533 1984^5 2166^6 3087

3 **BOOTS 'N JACKIE (USA),** 762^5

5 **BORAGE (Fr),** b g Carwhite - Balsamine by Gosport (G Lellouche) 4517^1

4 **BORING (USA),** ch g Foolish Pleasure (USA) - Arriya by Luthier (W Storey) 78 2678^7 3035^7 3240^9 3565^7 4457

4 **BORN TO BE,** b f Never So Bold - Beryl's Jewel by Siliconn (S Dow) 1473^1 1860^3 2255^6 2753^8 2965^3 3266^7 3906^2 4151^9 4393^4 4729

5 **BOROCAY,** b g Lochnager - Maybehandy by Some Hand (M J Camacho) 27^3 110^6 448^2 1075^3 1260^2

3 **BORODISLEW (USA),** b f Seattle Slew (USA) - Breath Taking (Fr) by Nureyev (USA) (Miss C Head) 638^3 853^2 1368^2 2055^1 3015^8 3717^6

3 **BORROWED AND BLUE,** b f Local Suitor (USA) - Abielle by Abwah (P J Hobbs) 1344 1746 2273^4 2828^7 3106^4 3412^8 3962^6

3 **BOSSY PATRICIA (Ire),** ch f Glenstal (USA) - Biddy Mulligan by Ballad Rock (Owen Weldon) 2700^{7} 3074^{6} 3419^{9}

6 **BOSTON TWO STEP (USA),** (A Fabre) 810^{8}

3 **BOSTON VIEW (Ire),** br f Simply Great (Fr) - Fingers by Lord Gayle (USA) (D J Barry) 3297^{6}

3 **BOTANIC VERSES (Ire),** ch f King Persian - Rose A Village by River Beauty (George Gracey) 4162

3 **BOTHSIDESNOW (Ire),** b g Exhibitioner - Caroline's Mark by On Your Mark (Noel Meade) 577 848^{7} 1026^{2} 1510^{3} 2877^{3} 2903^{2} 3300^{3} 3382^{1} 3805^{2}

6 **BOTTLES (USA),** b g North Pole (Can) - Fooling Around by Jaazeiro (USA) (J E Banks) 4631 4759

4 **BOULABAS (Ire),** ch f Nashamaa - Betty Bun by St Chad (J Pearce) 348^{8} 424^{4} 970 1232 1453 1696

3 **BOULMERKA,** ch f Farajullah - The Victor Girls by Crofthall (B R Cambidge) 16^{8} 80^{6} 162^{5} 378^{8}

6 **BOUNDER ROWE,** b g Henbit (USA) - Arita (Fr) by Kronzeuge (J Ffitch-Heyes) 4732a^{6}

3 **BOURBON JACK,** b c Robellino (USA) - Bushti Music by Bustino (J W Payne) 4704a

5 **BOURREE,** b h Nordance (USA) - Cerise Bouquet by Mummy's Pet (J E Mulhern) 3334^{8} 3928^{9} 4385

4 **BOURSIN (Ire),** b g Taufan (USA) - Cloven Dancer (USA) by Hurok (USA) (P Calver) 592 893^{5} 1177^{4} 1494^{3} 1835 3774 4166^{7} 4394

4 **BOUT EN BOUT (Fr),** b c Solicitor - Regnante by Habitat (P Marchand) 629^{3}

2 **BOWCLIFFE,** b c Petoski - Gwiffina by Welsh Saint (Miss S E Hall) 4714^{4}

5 **BOWDEN BOY (Ire),** b g Never So Bold - Glebehill by Northfields (USA) (B Preece) 133^{3} 188^{4}

3 **BOXBOY,** b c Kings Lake (USA) - Majan by Brigadier Gerard (K O Cunningham-Brown) 185^{8} 724^{2} 876 1906^{5} 2615^{4} 2669 2942 3170^{2} 4256 4341

2 **BOY IN BLACK (Ire),** b c Bob Back (USA) - Be My Dame by Be My Guest (USA) (J F Bailey Jun) 305 786 1104^{8} 4146

4 **BOY MARTIN,** ch g Local Suitor (USA) - Mary Martin by Be My Guest (USA) (S E Kettlewell) 4673a^{6} 28^{7} 39^{3} 79^{3} 134^{6} 147^{5} 176^{6} 1865 2106^{6} 2797^{4}

3 **BOY SOLDIER,** b g Governor General - London Fling by Jaazeiro (USA) (T G Mills) 1628^{7} 1992 2416

3 **BOZO BAILEY,** gr g Hadeer - Perceive (USA) by Nureyev (USA) (Victor Bowens) 2842

2 **BRAARI (USA),** b f Gulch (USA) - So Cozy (USA) by Lyphard (USA) (B W Hills) 1403^{3} 1916^{1} 2301^{6} 3751^{1} 4020^{1} 4442^{7}

3 **BRACKENTHWAITE,** ch g Faustus (USA) - Cosset by Comedy Star (USA) (T D Barron) 4717a^{8} 4790a^{6} 1^{1} 15^{1} 203^{1} 213^{1} 295 710^{1} 934^{5} 2597^{3} 2764^{3} 3256^{2} 3444^{4} 3812 4043

4 **BRACKLOON BOY (Ire),** ch g Lemhi Gold (USA) - Vibrant Hue (USA) by Exclusive Native (USA) (Ms E Cassidy) 1794^{4} 2345 2957^{4} 3076^{8} 3418^{1} 3826^{4} 4001 4534^{8} 4685 4738

4 **BRADAWN BREEVER (Ire),** b c Salmon Leap (USA) - Ozone by Auction Ring (USA) (Kevin Prendergast) 897^{2} 1201 1551^{2} 2073^{7} 2187^{4} 2407^{5} 2805^{9} 3162^{9} 3333^{7} 3496^{1} 3912^{6} 4056^{1} 4287^{1}

2 **BRADWELL (Ire),** b f Taufan (USA) - Tabriya by Nishapour (Fr) (M H Tompkins) 2535^{3} 3156^{7} 4011^{3}

2 **BRAILLE (Ire),** br c Vision (USA) - Winning Feature by Red Alert (M Johnston) 1053^{2} 1324^{2} 1598^{1} 2209^{2} 2906^{5} 3115^{2} 4423^{6} 4511^{4} 4673^{1}

4 **BRAMBLES WAY,** ch g Clantime - Streets Ahead by Ovid (W L Barker) 1436

2 **BRAMCOTE CENTURY,** gr f Absalom - Elaine Ann by Garda's Revenge (USA) (J Hetherton) 1590^{6} 1759^{5} 1889^{4} 2446^{6} 2705^{3} 2952^{5} 3235^{6} 3406^{7} 4342

2 **BRANDON COURT (Ire),** b c Law Society (USA) - Dance Date (Ire) by Sadler's Wells (USA) (I A Balding) 3316^{4} 4027^{5} 4316^{3}

5 **BRANDON GROVE,** b m Welsh Captain - Cottagers Lane by Farm Walk (T D Barron) 288^{5} 646^{8} 799 1307

3 **BRANDONHURST,** b g Elegant Air - Wolverina by Wolver Hollow (I A Balding) 397^{4} 690^{8} 1069 1670^{1} 2333 2758^{2} 3314 3883 4274

5 **BRANDON PRINCE (Ire),** b g Shernazar - Chanson de Paris (USA) by The Minstrel (Can) (I A Balding) 478^{5} 661^{6} 1155^{1} 1380^{6} 1840^{2} 2061^{3} 2432^{1} 2655^{1} 3434^{8}

3 **BRANSBY ROAD (Ire),** ch g Salt Dome (USA) - Ivory Smooth (USA) by Sir Ivor (R Akehurst) 838^{4} 1134^{7} 2124^{1} 2495^{6} 3044^{5} 3548

4 **BRANSTON ABBY (Ire),** ch f Risk Me (Fr) - Tuxford Hideaway by Cawston's Clown (M Johnston) 4666a^{6} 316 654^{1} 986^{1} 1205^{2} 1806^{8} 2252^{6} 3023^{1} 3468 3725^{2} 3936 4172 4278^{1} 4464 4521^{1} 4729^{2}

3 **BRASS BUTTON (Ire),** ch f Fools Holme (USA) - Nolnocan by Colum (B J Ryan) 258 297 1610 3040^{7}

3 **BRATA (USA),** br f Dixieland Band (USA) - Val's Girl (USA) by Sir Ivor (D K Weld) 2703^{1} 3380^{2} 3419^{4} 3852^{7}

5 **BRAVEBOY,** b g Never So Bold - Relkina (Fr) by Relkino (C E Brittain) 2431 2715^{8} 3017 3458^{2} 3697^{8} 4297^{1} 4470 4652

2 **BRAVE EDGE,** b c Beveled (USA) - Daring Ditty by Daring March (R Hannon) 1489^{7} 2030^{8} 3016^{2} 3250^{3} 3475^{1} 3688^{2} 4061^{2} 4114^{7} 4632^{3}

5 **BRAVEFOOT,** b h Dancing Brave (USA) - Swiftfoot by Run The Gantlet (USA) (J H Scott) 753^{1} 1514

5 **BRAVE HENRY,** br g Miner's Lamp - Miss Posey by Pitskelly (A J McNamara) 3295^{2}

3 **BRAVE HERO (USA),** b g Our Native (USA) - Decision (USA) by Resound (USA) (C A Cyzer) 825 1060 1212^{7} 1426 1701^{6} 2014^{3} 3325^{2} 3575^{5}

7 **BRAVE MELODY,** b g Heroic Air - Kaymay by Maystreak (Capt J Wilson) 1815^{5} 2264^{9} 2456^{7} 2682^{7} 3002 4164

2 **BRAVE NOTE (Ire),** b c Dancing Brave (USA) - Rensaler (USA) by Stop The Music (USA) (J E Hammond) 2144^{2} 2647^{4}

2 **BRAVE PATRIARCH (Ire),** gr c Alzao (USA) - Early Rising (USA) by Grey Dawn II (J L Dunlop) 2964^{7} 3592^{4} 3974^{3} 4365

3 **BRAVE RAIDER (Ire),** ch c Dixieland Band (USA) - Trusted Partner (USA) by Affirmed (USA) (D K Weld) 1568^{2} 1796^{3} 2743^{1} 3772^{2} 4246^{9}

7 **BRAVE STAR,** b g Glen Quaich - Accidental by Energist (Francis Berry) 753^{8} 1797^{6}

2 **BRAVE TORNADO,** ch c Dominion - Accuracy by Gunner B (G B Balding) 4113 4259^{8}

4 **BRAVURA,** b g Never So Bold - Avahra by Sahib (W J Haggas) 1830^{8} 2300^{2} 2794^{6} 3269 3697

3 **BRAXTON BRAGG (Ire),** ch c Glenstal (USA) - Chanting Music by Taufan (USA) (M D Hammond) 962^{9} 1178^{8} 1271^{6} 1891^{2} 2168^{4} 2338^{2} 2540^{7} 2932^{7}

3 **BRAZANY (USA),** b c Strawberry Road (Aus) - Waffle's Lake by Kings Lake (F Boutin) 266^{3} 696^{5} 1548^{4} 3653^{3} 4451^{7}

3 **BRAZEN ANGEL (Ire),** b f Nordico (USA) - Angel Passing by Kind Of Hush (Patrick Joseph Flynn) 1105 1441 1610^{4} 2556^{5} 3112 3827^{7} 4057^{1} 4136 4408^{1} 4738^{3}

4 **BREAK BREAD (USA),** b g Bering - Troyanna by Troy (P W Chapple-Hyam) 426^{2} 525^{9} 2654^{8} 4108^{4}

4 **BREAKDANCER (Ire),** b g Fabulous Dancer (USA) - Bennetta (Fr) by Top Ville (W R Muir) 4721a^{1} 4760a^{8} 8^{1} 46^{4} 102^{1} 126^{2} 171^{1} 199^{1} 225^{7}

3 **BREAKFAST BOOGIE,** b f Sizzling Melody - Bonne de Berry by Habitat (J R Fanshawe) 623^{2} 871^{2} 1160^{2} 1618^{4} 2504^{2} 2788^{5} 3459^{3} 3967^{1}

3 **BREAKING HEARTS (Ire),** ch f Broken Hearted - Rags To Riches by High Hat (A P Stringer) 590^{6} 2635^{6} 3311^{5} 3631 4164

6 **BRECKENBROUGH LAD,** b g Uncle Pokey - Fabulous Beauty by Royal Avenue (D T Turner) 340^{4} 645 740^{5} 1034 1305 1781 2354^{7} 2858^{5}

3 **BRECKLAND (Ire),** b c Trojan Fen - Rose Noir by Floribunda (K O Cunningham-Brown) 2410^{6}

4 **BREEZE AWAY,** b f Prince Sabo - Ballad Island by Ballad Rock (D Eddy) 568 655^{5} 837 1397^{6} 1606^{2} 1799^{9} 2165^{4}

7 **BREEZED WELL,** b g Wolverlife - Precious Baby by African Sky (B R Cambidge) 4771a^{5} 67^{9} 85^{6} 210^{7} 294^{9} 1316 1781 2232^{4} 2445^{8} 3090^{6} 3551^{9}

7 **BREEZY DAY,** ch m Day Is Done - Bedouin Dancer by Lorenzaccio (B A McMahon) 3481 3947 4363 4455^{9} 4734

4 **BRENDA HUNT (Ire),** gr f Huntingdale - Brenda by Sovereign Path (J S Moore) 294

2 **BRENSHAM FOLLY,** b g High Kicker (USA) - Sally Foxtrot by Music Boy (R Brotherton) 3691^2

2 **BRENTWOOD (Ire),** b f Waajib - Silent Sail by Aglojo (R Hannon) 1916^8 2394^2 3209^3 4539^2 4647^3

4 **BRESIL (USA),** b g Bering - Clever Bidder (USA) by Bold Bidder (A P Jarvis) 646^7 799^7 925^4 1120 1268 2108^5 2354 2597^5 2869^5 4490^7 4623^7 4676^7

3 **BRIARTIC STAR (Can),** 2442^9

6 **BRIDGE PLAYER,** ch m The Noble Player (USA) - Auction Bridge by Auction Ring (USA) (D Moffatt) 4714a^9 4742a^9 356^9 453^8 1847^4 2368^4 2683^5 3147^5 4321^8

4 **BRIDGE STREET BOY,** ch g Risk Me (Fr) - Bridge Street Lady by Decoy Boy (J R Bosley) 4667a 4488

2 **BRIDIE'S PRIDE,** b g Alleging (USA) - Miss Monte Carlo by Reform (G A Ham) 4099 4208

3 **BRIEF MERGER (Ire),** ch f Shernazar - Software (USA) by Lyphard (USA) (D K Weld) 4410^5

2 **BRIEF RESPITE (Ire),** b or br c Simply Great (Fr) - No Time To Dance by Shareef Dancer (USA) (Declan Gillespie) 3332^9 3562^6 4000^1 4360^3 4551

4 **BRIER CREEK (USA),** b c Blushing Groom (Fr) - Savannah Dancer (USA) by Northern Dancer (J H M Gosden) 773^1 1065^1 1405^1

2 **BRIERLEY,** br f Sharrood (USA) - Crystallize by Reliance II (B Smart) 2492^2 2887^7 3166^1 3537^4 4029 4453^9

4 **BRIGADE,** b c Sharpo - Matoa (USA) by Tom Rolfe (D R Loder) 497^3 604^3 1003^5 1402^1 1636^2 2194^6 2413^6 2854^5 3350 4040 4347^4

3 **BRIGADORE GOLD,** br f Petong - Brigado by Brigadier Gerard (F H Lee) 361^9 3794 4045 4348 4537

3 **BRIGANTE DI CIELO,** b c Robellino (USA) - Follow The Stars by Sparkler (R Hannon) 295^7 875^4 989^2 1204^1 1808^3 2961^9 3314^4 3680^3 4300

3 **BRIGENSER (Ire),** b g Digamist (USA) - Lady Anna Livia by Ahonoora (Declan Gillespie) 268 307 789^3 1046 1139^5 1574^4 1995^3 2677 2922^4

3 **BRIGG FAIR,** b c Aragon - Brig Of Ayr by Brigadier Gerard (R Hannon) 347^3 993^7 1174^5 1786 2303 2574^4 2698^4 3725^3 3889^3 3987^6

5 **BRIGGSMAID,** b m Elegant Air - Merry Yarn by Aggressor (J M P Eustace) 924^4 1288^5 1457^5 1984^4 2150^2 2251^8 2683^2 2735^3 2801^4 3252^4 3716^5 3821^1 4023^5 4321^9

3 **BRIGHT GEM,** b f Heraldiste (USA) - Spring Bride by Auction Ring (USA) (T Fairhurst) 4687a^1 4708a^4 4773a^4 532^3 883^9 1186^7 2338^3 2454^6 2769^6 4221

3 **BRIGHT GENERATION (Ire),** b f Rainbow Quest (USA) - New Generation by Young Generation (P F I Cole) 472^3 748^2 1222^1 1789^4 3931^6 4471^2

3 **BRIGHT MOON (USA),** ch f Alysheba (USA) - Bonshamile by Ile de Bourbon (USA) (A Fabre) 1033^2 1722^5 2690^1 3194^1 3931^3 4311

3 **BRIGHT MOUNTAIN (USA),** b f Time For A Change (USA) - Blue Tip (Fr) by Tip Moss (Fr) (E Lellouche) 2054^3 2690^3 3109^2

4 **BRIGHTNESS,** gr f Elegant Air - Jove's Voodoo (USA) by Northern Jove (Can) (Miss Gay Kelleway) 4680a

4 **BRIGHT PARAGON (Ire),** b or br g Treasure Kay - Shining Bright (USA) by Bold Bidder (H J Collingridge) 4725a^5 4789a^6 4816a^3 364 117^7 501^6 700^5 887^6 1249^9 1492^6 1881^1 2110^2 2305^3 2582^5 2788^2 3593 3745 4109^6 4487^6

3 **BRIGHTSIDE (Ire),** b f Last Tycoon - Wedgewood Blue (USA) by Sir Ivor (P F I Cole) 946^4 1222^6

3 **BRIGHT SPELLS,** ch f Salse (USA) - Scattered Showers by Ardross (D R C Elsworth) 734^3 1030^4 1638^9 3735^3 4064^9 4560

3 **BRIGHT STORM (Ire),** b g Wassl - Bridget O'Bird (USA) by Storm Bird (Can) (J S Bolger) 256^5

2 **BRIGHT VENUS,** gr f Petong - Fields Of Grain by Final Straw (M D I Usher) 1391 1741 1909

5 **BRIGTINA,** b g Tina's Pet - Bristle-Moss by Brigadier Gerard (J M Bradley) 4788a

5 **BRILLIANT,** ch m Never So Bold - Diamond Hill by High Top (J Pearce) 2232^3 2633^3 2874^4 2970^3 3356^9 4343 4470 4616

4 **BRILLIANT BLUE (USA),** 146^8

6 **BRISAS,** ch g Vaigly Great - Legal Sound by Legal Eagle (C W Fairhurst) 4666a 76^5 147 218^3 330^9 409^3 909 1589^8 2456^4 2682^8 3002^8 3032^2 3251^4 3603^6 3995

3 **BRITANNIA BAY (Ire),** ch c Waajib - Red Line Fever by Bay Express (Charles O'Brien) 311^6 1610^2 4407^2 4583^5

2 **BRITANNIA MILLS,** gr f Nordico (USA) - May Fox by Healaugh Fox (M C Chapman) 2199^3 2482^5 3432^8

5 **BROAD APPEAL,** ch m Star Appeal - Cinderwench by Crooner (R C Spicer) 38^6 84^6 152^8

2 **BROADMARA (Ire),** b f Thatching - Erzsi by Caerleon (USA) (A J Maxwell) 4261^1 4553^1

3 **BROADSTAIRS BEAUTY (Ire),** ch g Dominion Royale - Holy Water by Monseigneur (USA) (J J O'Neill) 4700a^2 4708a^1 29^5 361

2 **BROADWAY FLYER (USA),** b c Theatrical - Serena (Saf) by Jan Ekels (J W Hills) 4469^7 4679^1

4 **BROADWAY RUCKUS (Can),** br f Bold Ruckus (USA) - Broadway Beauty (USA) by Chompion (USA) (D R Laing) 756 2327 2577 2940 3310^5 4129 4486

2 **BROCCO (USA),** b c Kris S (USA) - Anytime Ms (USA) by Aurelius II (R Winick) 4743^1

3 **BROCKTON DANCER,** b f Fairy King (USA) - Susie's Baby by Balidar (R Hannon) 823^1 1031^3 1415^4 2971^7 3291^7

4 **BROCTUNE BAY,** b g Midyan (USA) - Sweet Colleen by Connaught (Mrs M Reveley) 1039 1275^7 1868^2 2501^3 3033^2 3881^4 4344^6 4695

2 **BROCTUNE GOLD,** b c Superpower - Golden Sunlight by Ile de Bourbon (USA) (Mrs M Reveley) 830^1 998^3 1168^1 1381^3 2016^2 2430^6 3903^3 4165^5 4453 4550 4674

7 **BRODESSA,** gr g Scallywag - Jeanne Du Barry by Dubassoff (USA) (Mrs M Reveley) 3521^4 4218

3 **BROKEN PEACE (Fr),** b or br f Devil's Bag (USA) - Bedside by Le Fabuleux (A Fabre) 1368^1

3 **BROKEN PEACE (USA),** f (E Lellouche) 809^3 1722

3 **BRONZE MAQUETTE (Ire),** b f Ahonoora - Working Model by Ile de Bourbon (USA) (B J McMath) 780^5 921^5 1161^4 1417^7 1961 2716^5 2859^1 2948^2 3394^5 3681^2 3734^6 3961 4591^6

9 **BRONZE RUNNER,** b g Gunner B - Petingalyn by Petingo (S Mellor) 332^8 1353 2012^3 2052^4 2353^1 2471^1 2684^9 3224^7 3518

2 **BROOKHEAD LADY,** b f Petong - Lewista by Mandrake Major (P D Evans) 886^6 1108^1 1590^2 1774^1 2119^1 2412^8 2772^5

3 **BROOKLANDS EXPRESS,** gr g Absalom - Lucy's Melody by On Your Mark (J D Bethell) 4668a^9 535^5 884^6 1735^5 2540^5 3216

4 **BROOKS EXPRESS (Fr),** b c Siberian Express (USA) - Brook's Dilemma by Known Fact (USA) (R Akehurst) 2256^6 2970 3228

2 **BROOKS MASQUERADE,** gr f Absalom - Miss Cindy by Mansingh (USA) (R Hannon) 3317 3781 4698

3 **BROOMHOUSE LADY,** b f General Wade - Dairy Queen by Queen's Hussar (M Johnston) 630^5 1356^6 2341^9

5 **BROOM ISLE,** b m Damister (USA) - Vynz Girl by Tower Walk (D Burchell) 478^9

5 **BROUGHTON BLUES (Ire),** ch g Tender King - Princess Galicia by Welsh Pageant (W J Musson) 4678a^8 4750a^8 4798a 35 1902 2127^5 2471 2860^5

3 **BROUGHTONS FORMULA,** b c Night Shift (USA) - Forward Rally by Formidable (USA) (W J Musson) 4676a 4724a 4790a^7 1 40^1 93^1 129^2 186^1 295^2 434^2 547^4 976 1180^6 1426^7 1906^4 2272^3 2669^7 2972^7 3078 3588^1 3757^5 3961 4631 4755^2

2 **BROUGHTON SINGER (Ire),** ch f Common Grounds - Unbidden Melody (USA) by Chieftain II (W J Musson) 4728^8

2 **BROUGHTONS PARTNER,** ch g Formidable (USA) - Elisa River (USA) by Irish River (Fr) (W J Musson) 933^6 1182^6 1535^2 3222^9 3508 3829 4318^6 4646

3 **BROUGHTON'S PORT,** b g Reesh - Tawnais by Artaius (USA) (W J Musson) 803^5 975^3 1817^4 2590^4 2715^2 3155^8

4 **BROUGHTON'S TANGO (Ire),** b g Tender King - Topless Dancer by Northfields (USA) (M J Heaton-Ellis) 290^9 520^1 628^2 739^1 1268^3 4432 4631^3

2 **CABCHARGE PRINCESS (Ire),** b f Rambo Dancer (Can) - Eiswave by Welsh Pageant (M H Tompkins) 1350[3] 1689[1] 2292[6] 2886[6] 3222[8] 4272[9] 4500 4613[4]
2 **CADEAUX PREMIERE,** b c Cadeaux Genereux - Clare Island by Connaught (N Bycroft) 3520
2 **CADENABBIA (USA),** ch f Ferdinand (USA) - Blink Naskra (USA) by Naskra (USA) (C C Elsey) 2754[6] 4232[5]
2 **CAERLE LAD (Ire),** b c Caerleon (USA) - Miss Zadig by Thatch (USA) (G Harwood) 4717[7]
3 **CAESOUR (USA),** br c Nureyev - Don't Sulk by Graustark (F Boutin) 656[1] 1367[7] 2298[2] 2803[8] 3618[9] 4219[7]
2 **CAFE SOLO,** b or br f Nomination - Piney Lake by Sassafras (Fr) (N Bycroft) 4237 4345[8] 4434[7]
2 **CAHERASS COURT (Ire),** b f Taufan (USA) - Grass Court by Thatch (USA) (M Quaid) 4624
8 **CAHERASS KATE,** b g Miner's Lamp - Moves Well by Green God (M Quaid) 309
2 **CA IRA (Ire),** b f Dancing Dissident (USA) - Silver Mantle by Bustino (R C Spicer) 1317[6] 1583 1741[9] 2493[2] 2668[7] 3052 4358 4618 4756[9]
2 **CAIRNBRAE (Ire),** b c Bluebird (USA) - Pitmarie by Pitskelly (M J Grassick) 2701 3243[4] 3492[4] 4359[5] 4688[9]
3 **CAIRO PRINCE (Ire),** b c Darshaan - Sphinx (Ger) by Alpenkonig (Ger) (P W Chapple-Hyam) 557[1] 843[4] 1448[4] 1751[7]
2 **CAJARIAN (USA),** b c Sharastani (USA) - Caraniya by Darshaan (John M Oxx) 4369[1] 4584[1]
2 **CAJUN CADET,** b c Cadeaux Genereux - Petty Purse by Petingo (R Charlton) 4263[2] 4523[1]
3 **CALAMANCO,** ch f Clantime - Laena by Roman Warrior (A Smith) 2231[5] 2698[6] 3132[4] 3359[3] 3789[3] 4487[1] 4678[5]
4 **CALCUTTA QUEEN,** ch f Night Shift (USA) - Happy Snap by Jalmood (USA) (R Simpson) 714
2 **CALDER KING,** ch c Rakaposhi King - Name The Game by Fair Season (J L Eyre) 3713[7] 4182[5] 4452
4 **CALEMAN,** b g Daring March - Lillemor by Connaught (R Boss) 436 605[3] 1066 2062[5] 2434 2969[6] 3105[7] 3531[1] 3774[1] 3885[8] 4297[7] 4667[8]
6 **CALGARY REDEYE,** gr h Kalaglow - River Call (Fr) by Riverman (USA) (Mrs J G Retter) 3231[7]
3 **CALIANDAK (Ire),** b g Darshaan - Cadisa by Top Ville (N Tinkler) 311 2185[4] 3524[1] 4366[3] 4540[3]
3 **CALIBRATE,** b g Blakeney - Vernair (USA) by Super Concorde (USA) (B J Meehan) 825 1068[9] 1309[7] 1704[4] 2669 4088
3 **CALISAR,** br g Mummy's Game - Maycrest by Imperial Fling (USA) (W G M Turner) 455 741[3] 878[3] 1038[1] 1186[1] 1628[3] 2160[3] 2724[8] 3447
2 **CALLABONNA,** b f Cadeaux Genereux - A Lyph (USA) by Lypheor (Sir Mark Prescott) 1988[2] 2541[2] 3339[4] 4265[9] 4484[3]
2 **CALLING (USA),** ch c Phone Trick (USA) - Sweet Singer (USA) by Sing Sing (USA) (J W Hills) 687 2250[5] 2785[4] 4427[8]
4 **CALLING COLLECT (USA),** ch c Phone Trick (USA) - My Little Guest by Be My Guest (USA) (L M Cumani) 1747[8] 2853[7]
3 **CALL ME BLUE,** gr c Kalaglow - Woodfold by Saritamer (USA) (T J Naughton) 1911[6] 2489[3] 2937[5] 3102[4] 4710
2 **CALL ME GRAHAM,** ro c Ballacashtal (Can) - Sylvan Song by Song (M R Channon) 2472[5] 2659[8] 4608
3 **CALL ME I'M BLUE (Ire),** b g Reasonable (Fr) - Bluebutton by Blue Cashmere (N Tinkler) 683 1273[8] 1478[1] 1740[1] 2024[1] 2375[3] 2660[2] 2908[1] 3438[2] 3849[3] 4151[1] 4275[4]
3 **CALL MY GUEST (Ire),** b g Be My Guest (USA) - Overcall by Bustino (Kevin Prendergast) 668[6] 1046[4] 1235[4] 1553[5] 1757[1] 2142 2517[2] 2842[2] 3275[1] 4555[8]
4 **CALL THE BUREAU,** ch g Gorytus (USA) - Mount Of Light by Sparkler (H E Haynes) 1487 1743[4] 2474[5] 2834
4 **CALL THE GUV'NOR,** b g Saint Estephe (Fr) - Gay Charlotte by Charlottown (H R A Cecil) 679[6] 799[4] 967[2] 1345[9] 1593[1] 3271[3] 3521[8] 3848
2 **CALL TO MIND (Ire),** b c Don't Forget Me - Pharjoy (Fr) by Pharly (Fr) (M H Easterby) 908[5] 1189[2] 1895[2] 2167[1] 3281[3] 3406[1]
4 **CALL TO THE BAR (Ire),** b g Kafu - Papun (USA) by Mount Hagen (Fr) (M McCormack) 421[3] 721 1096[2] 1352[5] 2050[2] 3099[1] 3348[3] 3638[5] 3995[2] 4549[5] 4681[9]
5 **CAL NORMA'S LADY (Ire),** ch m Lyphard's Special (USA) - June Darling by Junius (USA) (A Hide) 68[5] 141 678[8] 971[5] 1421[3] 1612[4] 1900[4]
4 **CALOUNIA (Ire),** b f Pharly (Fr) - Cadisa by Top Ville (John M Oxx) 4686a
4 **CAL'S BOY,** b g Green Ruby (USA) - Green Gypsy by Creetown (J P Smith) 4785a[7] 67[7] 108[6] 135[8] 227[6] 253 531 837
7 **CALVANNE MISS,** b m Martinmas - Blue Empress by Blue Cashmere (C J Hill) 4768a
2 **CALVA'S GLOW (Ire),** b f Glow (USA) - Bay Empress by Empery 3652[2]
7 **CALYMAR,** gr h Bay Express - Tula Singh by Mansingh (USA) (S G Norton) 646
2 **CALYPSO MONARCH (Ire),** b c Fairy King (USA) - Rebecca's Song by Artaius (USA) (R Hannon) 1131 2994[4] 3446[2] 3941[9] 4446[3] 4726[7]
3 **CAMBARA,** b f Dancing Brave (USA) - Cambretta (USA) by Roberto (USA) (M R Stoute) 2752 3225[3] 3506[1] 3680[1] 4153[3] 4280[5] 4650[1]
2 **CAMBREL (Ire),** b f Soviet Star (USA) - Cambretta (USA) by Roberto (USA) (H R A Cecil) 4496[2]
5 **CAMDEN BUZZ (Ire),** ch m Camden Town - Wild Bee by Hill Gail (P Mullins) 911[2] 1140[2] 1467[7] 2676[2] 4288[7] 4737[4]
6 **CAMDEN'S RANSOM (USA),** b g Hostage (USA) - Camden Court (USA) by Inverness Drive (USA) (D Marks) 211[3] 264[1] 329[5] 387[2] 663[1] 978[2] 1450 1711[7] 2211[6] 2930[3] 3290[3]
3 **CAMEO KIRBY (Fr),** b c Lead On Time (USA) - Nofret (Fr) by Meautry (Fr) (A A Scott) 507[3] 719[8] 1007[4] 1185[1] 1377[1] 1496[6]
6 **CAMEO SHADES,** b g King Of Spain - Sweet Ecstasy by Rarity (M McCormack) 4735a[8] 4795a[8]
3 **CAMEY'S CHOICE (Ire),** b f Digamist (USA) - Riverwave (USA) by Riverman (USA) (Edward Lynam) 280 1620[5] 2451[7] 3244[7] 4001[8] 4409
4 **CAMINO A RONDA,** ch f Hallgate - Viva Ronda by Kampala (Pat Mitchell) 4768a 6 916 1925 2215[8] 2747[8] 3020 3247[8] 3459
6 **CAMPAGNARDE (Arg),** 4729a[4] 4769a[5] 597[5]
3 **CAMPALTO (Ire),** ch c Fools Holme (USA) - Simply Gorgeous by Hello Gorgeous 4703a[6] 958[2] 1364[8]
3 **CAMPANA (Ire),** b f Sadler's Wells (USA) - Two Rings (USA) by Round Table (J H M Gosden) 3639[1] 3963[7] 4659[1]
5 **CAMPO MARZIO (Chi),** 2243[7]
4 **CANADIAN BOY (Ire),** b c Commanche Run - Canadian Guest by Be My Guest (USA) (Miss K M George) 626
4 **CANADIAN CAPERS,** ch f Ballacashtal (Can) - Carolynchristensen by Sweet Revenge (M R Channon) 4669a[5] 4731a[6] 2548 2940[9] 3139[5] 3261 3340[4] 3547[7]
3 **CANADIAN EAGLE,** ch f Risk Me (Fr) - Princess Lily by Blakeney (G Lewis) 334 443[7] 838[8] 1237
3 **CANADIAN SHIELD (Ire),** (A Fabre) 955[9]
2 **CANARY BLUE (Ire),** b f Bluebird (USA) - Norfolk Bonnet by Morston (Fr) (P J Makin) 4680[4]
2 **CANASKA DANCER (Ire),** b c Green Desert (USA) - Gay France (Fr) by Sir Gaylord (P W Chapple-Hyam) 1523[2] 1750[6] 3446[1] 4249[7] 4561[1]
3 **CANASKA STAR,** b c Doyoun - North Telstar by Sallust (P W Chapple-Hyam) 541[9] 797[6] 1116[5] 1448 1842[3] 3665[1] 4478
3 **CANAZEI,** b f Mazaad - Captain Bonnie by Captain James (Don Enrico Incisa) 1187[6] 1396[9] 1965[7] 3144[8] 3948
4 **CANBRACK (Ire),** b g Glenstal (USA) - Cottage Style by Thatch (USA) (J E Long) 4696a[5] 4716a 2471 2670
2 **CAN BUT DREAM (Ire),** br f Petorius - Praiseworthy by Known Fact (USA) (J C Harley) 1387[3] 2450[8] 4059[4]
3 **CAN CAN CHARLIE,** gr g Vaigly Great - Norton Princess by Wolver Hollow (M Johnston) 2308 2820[6] 3973[3] 4235[1] 4348 4605
2 **CANDANE,** b f Danehill (USA) - American Beauty by Mill Reef (USA) (M H Tompkins) 4651

3 **CATHERINEOFARAGON,** ch f Aragon - Edna by Shiny Tenth (W G R Wightman) 558^{7} 716^{5} 1348^{8} 1667^{7} 2560^{4} 2908^{7} 3348^{2} 3476^{7} 3906^{4} 4038 4501^{4}

10 **CATHERINES WELL,** ch m Junius (USA) - Restless Lady by Sandford Lad (M W Easterby) 436 591 800 1036 1379^{3} 1560^{2} 1679^{1} 2018^{9} 2230^{6} 2392 2594^{1} 2813^{8} 3504^{6} 3849

8 **CATHOS (Fr),** b g Bellman (Fr) - Charming Doll by Don (Ity) (D A Wilson) 25^{7} 1430 1781^{6} 2126^{9} 2256^{5} 2415^{3} 3078 3430^{6} 3548

3 **CATRAIL (USA),** b c Storm Cat (USA) - Tough As Nails (USA) by Majestic Light (USA) (J H M Gosden) 1412^{1} 1747^{5} 2206^{1} 2574^{1} 3777^{2} 4170^{1} 4417^{1} 4742

2 **CATTANO (Ger),** b c Homing - Carbonara by Windwurf (J Hartmann) 3581^{2}

5 **CATUNDRA (Ire),** ch m Far North (Can) - 'tis A Kitten (USA) by Tisab (USA) (Mrs A Knight) 970^{5}

2 **CATWALKER (Ire),** b g Reasonable (Fr) - Norse Lady by Viking (USA) (E J O'Grady) 1121^{5} 1608^{1} 3332^{7} 3613^{7} 4052^{5}

3 **CAUGHT REDHANDED (Ire),** gr f Standaan (Fr) - Chi-Chi by Sing Sing (R J R Williams) 1162^{6} 1577^{8} 1829 2033^{5}

4 **CAURSELLE (Ire),** b f Bob Back - Bodelle by Falcon (T F Lacy) 270^{6} 665 1201 2404^{8}

8 **CAUSLEY,** br g Swing Easy (USA) - Four Lawns by Forlorn River (B A McMahon) 818^{8} 1130 1304^{3} 1591^{1} 1777^{4} 1939^{2} 2198^{5} 2396^{3} 2775^{2} 3004^{2} 3257^{4} 3540^{4} 3712^{1} 3973^{8}

3 **CAVALIER PRINCE (Ire),** b g Prince Rupert (Fr) - Peace Princess by On Your Mark (A P Jarvis) 417 3007

3 **CAVATINA,** br f Chief Singer - Pennycuick by Celtic Ash (T W Donnelly) 1109^{1} 2572 3676^{4} 3973^{9} 4652

3 **CAVEAT'S IMAGE (USA),** 4451

2 **CAVERS YANGOUS,** b g Daring March - Rapid Lady by Rapid River (M Johnston) 4608^{2} 4715^{4}

2 **CAZANOVE'S PET,** ch f Tina's Pet - Echo Chamber by Music Boy (G C Bravery) 1456^{7} 3695^{4} 4220^{6} 4483^{3} 4613^{8} 4703^{5}

2 **CAZZUTO (Ire),** b c Kefaah (USA) - Hay Knot by Main Reef (J L Dunlop) 3172^{1} 4223^{8} 4598^{1} 4720^{2}

3 **C D SHAREPLAN (USA),** b g Lucky North (USA) - Lady Andromeda (USA) by Nordic Prince (USA) (M R Channon) 2317^{8} 2587^{4}

5 **CEDAR COURT (Ire),** b g Yashgan - Friendly Ann by Arteus (USA) (Patrick O'Leary) 298^{3} 598^{2} 852^{5} 1013^{2} 1141^{5} 1467^{6} 1996^{3} 2143^{9} 2693^{4} 3245^{3}

2 **CEDEZ LE PASSAGE (Fr),** br c Warning - Microcosme (USA) by Golden Fleece (USA) (C E Brittain) 2792^{4}

4 **CEE DEE,** ch g Grey Desire - Record Lady by Record Token (K G Wingrove) 3687

9 **CEE-EN-CEE,** b g Junius (USA) - Lady Red Rose by Pitskelly (Mrs M McCourt) 721^{7} 923 1096 1588^{5} 2121 2327 2868^{3} 3168^{8} 3447 4333 4580

6 **CEE-JAY-AY,** gr g Free State - Raffinrula by Raffingora (J Berry) 4663a^{7} 274^{9} 302^{1} 403^{3} 592 801^{2} 893^{1} 1079^{3} 1298^{2} 1530^{3} 1876^{2} 2060 2371^{5} 2926^{6} 3155^{5}

3 **CELESTIAL BLISS (USA),** gr f Relaunch (USA) - North Of Eden by Northfields (USA) (Michael Kauntze) 870^{7} 1048

3 **CELESTIAL CHOIR,** b f Celestial Storm (USA) - Choir by High Top (J L Eyre) 803^{3} 1039^{5} 1109^{5} 4181^{7} 4322 4590^{9}

3 **CELESTIAL CROWN (Ire),** b c Mazaad - Kimstar by Aureole (Noel Furlong) 848^{9}

2 **CELESTIAL DANCE,** b f Scottish Reel - Celeste by Sing Sing (J Berry) 1798^{9} 2668 2819^{2} 3235^{3} 3390^{8} 3829^{4} 4081^{2} 4342^{8} 4418

3 **CELESTIAL KEY (USA),** br g Star de Naskra (USA) - Casa Key (USA) by Cormorant (USA) (S G Norton) 218^{6} 277^{1} 289^{1} 846^{8} 1113^{6} 1337^{2} 1532^{1} 2237 4139^{2} 4428^{3} 4545^{2} 4729

2 **CELESTIAL PLAIN (Ire),** b f Thatching - Fighting Run by Runnett (J G Burns) 2804^{6} 3911^{6}

2 **CELESTIAL RUMOUR (Ire),** b g Astronef - Gossip by Sharp Edge (M H Easterby) 1401^{2} 1846^{1} 2552^{3} 2973^{2} 4342^{6} 4418^{4}

4 **CELESTINE,** b f Skyliner - Stellaris by Star Appeal (C W Fairhurst) 1286^{3} 2309 2434 2639^{2} 2680^{3} 3004^{6} 3182^{5} 3558 4045^{1} 4224^{2} 4333^{8} 4458

5 **CELIA BRADY,** b m Last Tycoon - Lucayan Princess by High Line (H Candy) 1120 1626^{5} 2149^{5} 3340^{3} 3655^{3} 3991^{1}

2 **CELLA (Ire),** 3014^{7}

4 **CELLITO (Ire),** b c Flash Of Steel - Apocalypse by Auction Ring (USA) (W A O'Gorman) 4699a 4810a

2 **CELTIC ARMS (Fr),** b c Comrade In Arms - Amour Celtique by Northfields (P Bary) 2980^{3} 3515^{4} 3932^{4} 4399^{1}

13 **CELTIC BOB,** ch g Celtic Cone - Quaife Sport by Quayside (O O'Neill) 64^{8} 1316

5 **CELTICCARO (Ire),** b g Rusticaro (Fr) - Celtic Match by Royal Match (Patrick G Kelly) 2497^{7} 2877^{6} 3395

2 **CELTIC CEILIDH,** ch f Scottish Reel - Show Home by Music Boy (J Wharton) 1580^{3} 3209^{5}

3 **CELTIC CHERRY,** br f Green Ruby (USA) - Celtic Bird by Celtic Cone (J Balding) 214^{8}

2 **CELTIC GOVERNESS,** b f Governor General - Celtic Bird by Celtic Cone (J Balding) 1158^{9} 1529 3411^{7} 3566^{5} 4452^{5} 4608^{6} 4699^{7}

3 **CELTIC RISING,** b g Primitive Rising (USA) - Cass Avon by Celtic Cone (P Beaumont) 3712

8 **CENTENARY STAR,** b g Broadsword (USA) - Tina's Gold by Goldhill (Mrs M Reveley) 4357

3 **CENTER MORICHES (Ire),** ch f Magical Wonder (USA) - Tumble Royal by Tumble Wind (USA) (J R Banahan) 2140^{1} 3038^{7} 3494^{9} 3615^{9} 3770

2 **CERIGNOLA (Ire),** 2648^{8}

4 **CERTAIN LADY,** ch f Absalom - Bold Duchess by Persian Bold (R T Juckes) 4756a

3 **CERTAIN PROSPECT,** b f Miswaki (USA) - Throw Away Line (USA) by Assert (John M Oxx) 3579^{2} 3808 4162^{6}

3 **CERTAIN WAY (Ire),** ch c Sure Blade (USA) - Ruffling Point by Gorytus (USA) (C Tinkler) 4697a^{2} 4717a^{3} 4770a^{5} 378^{1} 415^{1} 710^{2} 907^{8} 1247^{2} 1357^{2} 1812^{6}

2 **CERTIFICATE-X,** b f Never So Bold - Screenable (USA) by Silent Screen (USA) (Martyn Meade) 804^{2} 984^{6} 1475^{2} 1814^{2} 2342^{1} 3133^{5} 3677^{3} 3982^{3} 4272^{8} 4453^{1}

4 **CEZANNE,** b c Ajdal (USA) - Reprocolor by Jimmy Reppin (M R Stoute) 1064^{9} 3900^{6} 4107^{1} 4178^{2}

3 **CHADDLEWORTH (Ire),** b c Ahonoora - Perlita (Fr) by Baldric II (P W Chapple-Hyam) 541^{6} 794 1031^{2}

2 **CHADWELL HALL,** b c Kala Shikari - Cherrywood Blessin by Good Times (Ity) (L R Lloyd-James) 3673^{8} 3972^{7} 4237^{9} 4452

5 **CHADWICK'S GINGER,** ch m Crofthall - Knight Hunter by Skyliner (B C Morgan) 840 1781^{7} 2091^{7}

6 **CHAFF,** b g Final Straw - Silky (USA) by Nijinsky (Can) (D Morris) 4735a^{7} 1035^{5} 2670^{5} 3744^{4} 4724^{7}

3 **CHAIN DANCE,** b f Shareef Dancer (USA) - Historical Fact by Reform (C V Lines) 999^{3} 1719 1904^{3}

3 **CHAJOTHELYTBRIGADE (Ire),** b f Electric - Rampage by Busted (M Avison) 799 928

5 **CHAKALAK,** b g Damister (USA) - Wig And Gown by Mandamus (S Dow) 626^{9} 822^{6} 1321^{7} 1605^{3} 1752^{8} 1929^{2} 2477^{1} 2755^{3} 2904^{7} 3255^{3} 4143 4466

3 **CHALLENGER ROW (Ire),** b g Colmore Row - Tunguska by Busted (C W Thornton) 434^{5} 652^{3} 888^{2} 1600^{2} 1630^{4} 2091^{5} 2800^{3} 2870^{8}

6 **CHAMBROS,** ch g Krayyan - Chilcombe by Morston (Fr) (N A Twiston-Davies) 1064 1268^{5} 2115^{3}

2 **CHAMPAGNE ATEASTER,** b f Hubbly Bubbly (USA) - Eastern Ember by Indian King (USA) (S G Norton) 4103^{8} 4345^{5} 4665^{1}

2 **CHAMPAGNE GIRL,** b f Robellino (USA) - Babycham Sparkle by So Blessed (P J Makin) 1857^{1} 2845^{6} 3982^{4} 4264^{5} 4561

6 **CHAMPAGNE GOLD,** ch g Bairn (USA) - Halkissimo by Khalkis (J C McConnochie) 1041^{7} 1321^{3} 1430^{4} 1669^{2} 1840^{3}

3 **CHAMPAGNE GRANDY,** ch f Vaigly Great - Monstrosa by Monsanto (Fr) (M R Channon) 352 455^{1} 711 927^{3} 1095^{2} 1341^{2} 1528^{5} 1714^{1} 1977^{7} 2214^{7} 3343^{5} 4181^{2} 4458^{1} 4518^{9} 4681^{1}

3 **CHEROKEE RUN (USA),** (F Alexander) 1070[2] 1542[6]

5 **CHERRYWOOD LASS,** br m Belfort (Fr) - Rainbow Vision by Prince Tenderfoot (USA) (R Curtis) 4804a[4] 4815a[5] 76[7] 159[5]

4 **CHESA PLANA,** b f Niniski (USA) - Top Of The League by High Top (B Schutz) 695[6] 2079[3] 2837[2] 3206[2] 3582[7] 3929[9] 4201[8] 4655[2]

4 **CHESHIRE ANNIE (Ire),** br f Double Schwartz - So Valiant by So Blessed (R Simpson) 263[9] 600 990

4 **CHESNAO (Fr),** 145[2]

9 **CHESTER TERRACE,** ch g Crofter (USA) - Persian Mourne by Mourne (J L Spearing) 114

3 **CHEVALIER VERT,** b c Aragon - Little Mercy by No Mercy (C E Brittain) 1617

6 **CHEVEUX MITCHELL,** ch h Dunbeath (USA) - Hide Out by Habitat (M R Channon) 200[8] 222[2] 247 391 756 990[7] 1144[1] 1270[2] 1382[7] 1667

5 **CHEVIOT AMBLE (Ire),** ch m Pennine Walk - Miss Turnberry by Mummy's Pet (Patrick Joseph Flynn) 4684a[6] 270[5] 787[1] 1050[6] 1552 1823[4] 2078[6] 2606[5] 2878 4384[2] 4463[6] 4585[2] 4735[1]

3 **CHEVROTAIN,** b g Salse (USA) - Mary Mary Mouse (USA) by Valdez (USA) (J W Watts) 643[3] 844[3] 1153[3]

4 **CHEYENNE FIRE (Ire),** 4653[6]

3 **CHIAPPUCCI (Ire),** b g Doulab (USA) - Jenny's Child by Crash Course (J White) 744[1] 1165[3] 1417[2] 1827 2523[3] 2783[2]

3 **CHICAGO (Ire),** gr g Standaan (Fr) - Ruling Pride by Bold Lad (Ire) (C Tinkler) 380[5] 491[7] 974[2] 1273 1503[7]

4 **CHICARD,** b f Mashhor Dancer (USA) - Two Stroke by Malicious (T J Naughton) 2327[6] 2868 3447[8] 3670[7] 3938[4]

2 **CHICKAWICKA (Ire),** b c Dance Of Life (USA) - Shabby Doll by Northfields (USA) (B R Millman) 517[2] 922[4] 1446[3] 1790[7] 2546[1] 3406 3762[4] 4144[4] 4547[5]

3 **CHICKCHARNIE,** ch g Stanford - Lucky Angel by Lucky Wednesday (J P Leigh) 630[3] 803[1] 1113 1833[5] 3712

2 **CHIEF EXECUTIVE,** b c Unfuwain (USA) - Two Worlds (USA) by Diesis (W R Muir) 1131 1828[4] 2069[9] 2539[3] 2929[4] 3597 3815[4] 4114[4] 4228[2] 4318[2] 4547[9]

4 **CHIEF MINISTER (Ire),** br g Rainbow Quest (USA) - Riverlily (Fr) by Green Dancer (USA) (T Dyer) 365[6] 527[9] 785[4] 1173 1336[4] 2204[2] 2904[5] 3152[3] 3848[5] 4205[2]

4 **CHIEF OF STAFF,** ch c Caerleon (USA) - Fanny's Cove by Mill Reef (USA) (J Pearce) 294 425 4092[1] 4343 4490[3] 4652 4713

2 **CHIEF PRINTER,** ch c Indian Ridge - Arbor Lane by Wolverlife (R Harris) 1499

5 **CHIEFS BABU,** ch g Chief Singer - Nullah by Riverman (USA) (R O'Leary) 4391

3 **CHIEF'S SONG,** b g Chief Singer - Tizzy by Formidable (USA) (S Dow) 304 719[5] 4372[3]

2 **CHIEFTAIN'S CROWN (USA),** ch c Chief's Crown (USA) - Simple Taste (USA) by Sharpen Up (Mrs J Cecil) 3633 3974

2 **CHILDREN'S CHOICE (Ire),** b f Taufan (USA) - Alice Brackloon (USA) by Melyno (P J McBride) 2748[4]

4 **CHILD STAR (Fr),** gr f Bellypha - Miss Shirley (Fr) by Shirley Heights (D Marks) 4671a[4] 1094[9] 1318[7] 2048[8] 2755 3078[5] 3479 4102[3] 4353[3] 4684

2 **CHILIGRAY,** gr c Formidable (USA) - Chili Girl by Skymaster (J L Dunlop) 1350 2030[5] 2325 3421[7] 3762[9] 3989[5]

3 **CHILI HEIGHTS,** gr g Chilibang - Highest Tender by Prince Tenderfoot (USA) (G B Balding) 1066[7] 1348 1584[3] 1806 2522[3] 2928[4] 3313[5] 3637[1] 4024[7]

3 **CHILI LADY,** ch f Chilibang - Barbary Court by Grundy (P J Makin) 872 1132[8] 1470[5] 2711[4] 2939[5] 4008[5] 4327[5]

2 **CHILIOLA,** ch f Chilibang - Sisola (USA) by Coastal (USA) (M H Easterby) 804 1272[6] 1837[3] 2435[5] 3133[2] 3254[3] 3903[8]

3 **CHILLY BREEZE,** b or br f Ballad Rock - Chicobin (USA) by J O Tobin (USA) (Sir Mark Prescott) 3531[1] 1231 1633[2] 2011[2] 2276[3] 2821[3] 3251[2] 3343[4] 4096[4] 4485[5]

2 **CHILLY LAD,** ch c High Kicker (USA) - Miss Poll Flinders by Swing Easy (USA) (M J Ryan) 3592 4726

2 **CHILLY TIME,** ch f Chilibang - Leap In Time by Dance In Time (Can) (P G Murphy) 1955[5] 2316[8] 2659[4] 3009[6] 4500

3 **CHILTERN HUNDREDS (USA),** b g Premiership (USA) - Halo Lady (USA) by Halo (USA) (W J Musson) 183[3] 248[4] 440 1062[7] 1130 1488[8] 1861[7] 2520 2870[5] 3170[4] 3530[5] 4633

2 **CHILTERN SHOW,** b f Rambo Dancer (Can) - Susie's Baby by Balidar (A Bailey) 2044[6] 2274[9] 2610[4] 2796[4]

2 **CHIMANIMANI,** b c Petong - La Primavera by Northfields (USA) (J L Dunlop) 4543 4698[9]

2 **CHIMES BAND (USA),** b or br c Dixieland Band (USA) - Chimes (USA) by Mr Prospector (USA) (P Bary) 4074[1] 4293[5]

4 **CHINAMAN,** b g Noalto - Diorina by Manacle (W G R Wightman) 1007 1281[7] 2007 2162[4] 2471

2 **CHINA ROBIN,** ch f Night Shift (USA) - Portvasco by Sharpo (P D Evans) 1229[6] 1955[8] 3016[7] 3265[8] 4097[4] 4436 4756[5]

5 **CHINA SKY,** b g Tina's Pet - Buy G's by Blakeney (J S Moore) 232

3 **CHINESE GORDON (Ire),** b c Kahyasi - Abalvina by Abdos (J E Pease) 4510[4]

2 **CHINESE TREASURE (Ire),** b g Treasure Kay - Eclipse Bid by Rusticaro (Fr) (W Jarvis) 466 3742[8] 3969

3 **CHIPALA,** b g Efisio - Riva Renald by Try My Best (USA) (T W Donnelly) 3506[8] 3712

3 **CHIPPENDALE LADD (Can),** b g Commemorate (USA) - Jackie Pearl (USA) by Ruffled Feathers (C R Egerton) 439[7] 759[8] 1629[3]

6 **CHIRKPAR,** b g Shernazar - Callianire by Sir Gaylord (J S Bolger) 4288

2 **CHITA RIVERA,** b f Chief Singer - Shirley Superstar by Shirley Heights (P J Makin) 2866 4026[4] 4227[6]

2 **CHOCOLAT DE MEGURO (USA),** ch c Seattle Dancer (USA) - Clef En Or (USA) by Alydar (USA) (G Harwood) 4276[4]

2 **CHOCOLUNE (Ity),** ro c Nadjar (Fr) - Bloc Lait by Be My Guest (USA) (A Pandolfi) 2257[2] 4314[1] 4572[4]

6 **CHOICE LOT,** b h Auction Ring (USA) - More Candy by Ballad Rock (A W Jones) 4764a 4808a 76 138[2] 163[5] 177[4] 194[2] 218[4] 242[5] 330 909 1052[4] 1494[8] 1631[3] 2636

6 **CHOIR PRACTICE,** ch g Chief Singer - Good Try by Good Bond (W J Haggas) 1073[5] 1177[5] 1394[8] 2428[2] 2527[3] 2849[5] 3180[6] 3383[4] 3584[1] 3739[6] 3947[1] 4180[2] 4455[4] 4532[2] 4681[6] 4734[4]

2 **CHOPENDOZ (USA),** ch c Shadeed (USA) - Truly Graceful (Can) by It's True (USA) (W Jarvis) 3422 3686[8] 4113

6 **CHORUS LINE (Fr),** b h R B Chesne - Berguette by Philemon (J-C Napoli) 75[2]

3 **CHOUETTE,** b f Try My Best (USA) - Bugle Sound by Bustino (P Mitchell) 516[6] 685 1776[4] 2014[5] 2685 2847[9] 3142[8] 3301[9]

2 **CHOWPOR,** b f Nishapour (Fr) - Salchow by Niniski (USA) (C E Brittain) 4303[8] 4442[9] 4614[4]

4 **CHRIS'S GLEN,** ch g Librate - Misty Glen by Leander (J M Bradley) 1928 2858[9]

2 **CHRIS'S LAD,** b c Thowra (Fr) - Stockline by Capricorn Line (B J Meehan) 4259

3 **CHRISTIAN SPIRIT,** gr g Petong - Hidden Asset by Hello Gorgeous (USA) (K T Ivory) 4747a[4] 4755a[1] 4790a[5] 1604

4 **CHRISTIAN WARRIOR,** gr g Primo Dominie - Rashah by Blakeney (R E Peacock) 1097 1623 2004[5] 2350[7] 2638[4] 3006[6] 3313 3661 4031 4327

3 **CHRISTY MOORE (Ire),** ch c The Noble Player (USA) - Lisdoonvarna by Miami Springs (Peadar Matthews) 552 912 1251 1755

10 **CHUCKLESTONE,** b g Chukaroo - Czar's Diamond by Queen's Hussar (J S King) 618 924[8] 1564 1989[2] 2115[2] 2662[1] 2755[5] 3231[4] 3479 4212

4 **CHUCK'S TREASURE (Ire),** b or br g Treasure Kay - Wisdom To Know by Bay Express (Seamus Fahey) 3295

3 **CHUMMY'S FRIEND (Ire),** ch f Be My Guest (USA) - So Directed by Homing (B W Hills) 711 1377[5] 3938 4340

3 **CHUMMY'S IDEA (Ire),** b f Fayruz - Adivara by Tyrnavos (J Sutcliffe) 881

INDEX TO FLAT RACE RESULTS 1992-93

7 **CRAZY LADY,** b m Bulldozer - Purranna (Capt D G Swan) 961^{8}

2 **CRAZY PAVING (Ire),** b c Danehill (USA) - Clunk Click by Star Appeal (C A Cyzer) 1489^{1} 1750^{5}

3 **CREAGMHOR,** gr g Cragador - Cawstons Prejudice by Cawston's Clown (B J Llewellyn) 720^{7} 1095^{9} 1264^{7} 1287^{7} 1599^{8} 1631^{8} 2109^{6} 2353 2550^{4} 3007

3 **CREAKING BOARD,** ch f Night Shift (USA) - Happy Landing by Homing (R Frankel) 4792a^{1}

5 **CREAM OF THE CROP (Ire),** ch g Milk Of The Barley - Hua Hin by Night Star (J Wharton) 962 3055^{8}

2 **CREATIVE BLOOM (USA),** ch f Dixieland Band (USA) - Epicure's Garden (USA) by Affirmed (USA) (D K Weld) 4135^{1}

3 **CREATIVE CRAFT (USA),** ch f Affirmed (USA) - Final Figure (USA) by Super Concorde (USA) (D K Weld) 870^{2} 3025^{4} 3417^{3}

4 **CRECHE,** b c Bairn (USA) - Melody Park by Music Boy (Mrs N Macauley) 4666a 4706a^{1} 4743a^{8} 4779a^{3} 4804a^{2} 56^{5} 195^{3} 212^{1} 221^{1} 242^{1} 255^{5} 285^{2} 320^{3} 677 1560 1981^{9} 2380^{3} 3324^{1} 4667^{7}

3 **CREDIT SQUEEZE,** ch g Superlative - Money Supply by Brigadier Gerard (R F Johnson Houghton) 328^{3} 685^{2} 836^{2} 1097^{2} 1408^{6} 1991^{3} 2421^{7} 2789^{3} 3090^{2} 3509^{3} 3623^{3} 4065 4468

11 **CREEAGER,** b g Creetown - Teenager by Never Say Die (J Wharton) 303^{9} 427^{8} 702^{2} 1041^{5} 1276^{8} 1564

2 **CREEK VALLEY,** ch g Valiyar - Russell Creek by Sandy Creek (Mrs J R Ramsden) 1798 2180^{4} 2554 2974 3236^{8} 3815 4329

3 **CREHELP EXPRESS (Ire),** br f Strong Gale - Canute Villa by Hardicanute (Victor Bowens) 552 870 2287 2484 2984^{9}

4 **CREPT OUT (Ire),** ch c On Your Mark - Valbona (Fr) by Abdos (J L Harris) 4771a 123^{6} 133^{7} 962

6 **CRESELLY,** b m Superlative - Gwiffina by Welsh Saint (R Allan) 4663a^{1} 4696a^{4} 4744a^{8} 1849^{5} 2088^{3} 2269^{1} 2459^{4} 2954^{4} 3440^{2} 3553^{5}

3 **CRESTA TREMENDOUS (USA),** 4704a^{5}

2 **CRESTON (USA),** ch c Flying Paster (USA) - Cheyenne Birdsong (USA) by Restless Wind (Jenine Sahadi) 4743

4 **CRESTWOOD LAD (USA),** ch g Palace Music (USA) - Sweet Ellen (USA) by Vitriolic (Mrs M Reveley) 1866^{9} 2091^{6}

2 **CRETAN GIFT,** ch c Cadeaux Genereux - Caro's Niece (USA) by Caro (J L Dunlop) 1706 3016^{9} 3836

4 **CRETOES DANCER (USA),** br g Secreto (USA) - Mary Read (USA) by Graustark (W R Muir) 4667a^{2} 4723a 4735a^{5} 4795a^{1} 4817a^{3} 35^{2} 158^{9} 169 3420 3655^{8} 3840^{1} 4591

3 **CRIME OFTHECENTURY,** b f Pharly (Fr) - Crime Of Passion by Dragonara Palace (USA) (P F I Cole) 491^{1} 627^{1} 823^{5} 1231^{6} 1415^{5}

3 **CRIMINAL RECORD (USA),** b c Fighting Fit (USA) - Charlie's Angel (USA) by Halo (USA) (W Clay) 761 980 2529^{3} 2828^{1} 3193^{4} 3574^{3}

2 **CRIMSON CITY (Ire),** b f Posen (USA) - Crimson Royale by High Line (W P Mullins) 4581 4610^{7} 4706

4 **CRIMSON CONSORT (Ire),** b g Red Sunset - Purple Princess by Right Tack (C W Thornton) 161 205^{9} 650 962^{8} 1230 1397

3 **CRISSY (Ire),** ch f Entitled - Antipol by Polyfoto (R J Cotter) 1510^{6} 1796^{5} 2249 2743 3062

2 **CRISTAL SPRINGS,** b f Dance Of Life (USA) - Cristalga by High Top (A Harrison) 2603^{6} 2836^{3} 3760 4082^{4} 4215 4427^{3} 4701^{5}

3 **CRODARSHAAN (Ire),** b c Darshaan - Croda Alta by Caro (L M Cumani) 2146^{9}

2 **CROESO-I-CYMRU,** b f Welsh Captain - Bridge Of Gold by Balidar (B A McMahon) 4211^{3}

2 **CROFT POOL,** b c Crofthall - Blackpool Belle by The Brianstan (J A Glover) 4342 4594^{4} 4728^{4}

6 **CROFT VALLEY,** ch g Crofthall - Sannavally by Sagaro (R Akehurst) 1636^{1} 2363 2413^{1} 3350^{6} 3897 4280^{7} 4464^{8} 4606^{1}

3 **CROIRE (Ire),** b f Lomond (USA) - Fighting Run by Runnett (G Wragg) 428^{3} 854^{2} 1171^{4} 1931^{2} 2401^{1} 2697^{3} 3214^{2} 3637^{9} 4166^{9}

3 **CROMARTY,** b f Shareef Dancer (USA) - Forres by Thatch (USA) (H R A Cecil) 679^{5} 1077^{1} 1585^{2} 1958^{4} 3152^{5} 3587^{6} 4506^{6}

4 **CROMER'S EXPRESS,** ch c Mansingh (USA) - Sallusteno by Sallust (T Kersey) 646 1419^{9} 1866 2183^{7} 3057

3 **CROPTON,** b f Flash Of Steel - Crymlyn by Welsh Pageant (Mrs J Cecil) 3519^{4} 3956^{6} 4513

5 **CROSSILLION,** b h Rousillon (USA) - Croda Rossa (Ity) by Grey Sovereign (G Wragg) 3182^{1} 4300 4563

2 **CROSS SWORDS (USA),** b g Sword Dance - Falabella by Steel Heart (Charles O'Brien) 2037 3492^{7} 3731^{5} 4285^{8}

5 **CROWDED HOUSE (Ire),** b or br g Mazaad - Standing Ovation by Godswalk (B V Kelly) 4685a^{5}

2 **CRUISING CHICK,** b f Nordico (USA) - Beautiful Orchid by Hays (S G Norton) 374^{5} 708^{8} 2637^{8} 2917^{5} 4528^{7} 4646

2 **CRY OF THE DOLPHIN,** gr f Mazilier (USA) - Ashbocking by Dragonara Palace (USA) (P C Haslam) 381^{8} 886^{9} 1759^{9}

4 **CRYSTADO (Fr),** ch c Crystal Glitters (USA) - Kantado by Saulingo (D R C Elsworth) 792^{6} 1172^{8} 1407^{9}

4 **CRYSTAL CROSS (USA),** b f Roberto (USA) - Crystal Cup (USA) by Nijinsky (Can) (I A Balding) 473^{4} 757^{1} 1682^{6} 2395^{1} 2625^{2} 3067^{5} 3466 4064 4189^{5}

2 **CRYSTAL HEART (Ire),** ch f Broken Hearted - Arachosia by Persian Bold (C A Smith) 4496 4679

5 **CRYSTAL JACK (Fr),** b h Crystal Glitters (USA) - Cackle (USA) by Crow (Fr) (F H Lee) 891^{8} 1301^{5} 1680 1945^{8} 2106^{5} 2969^{8} 3280^{6} 3486^{3} 3778

2 **CRYSTAL LAKE (Ire),** b f Shirley Heights - Woodstream (USA) by Northern Dancer (Charles O'Brien) 3541^{3} 3729^{1} 4249^{9}

2 **CRYSTAL MAGIC,** b f Mazilier (USA) - Thulium by Mansingh (USA) (R Hannon) 776^{6} 3052^{3} 3387^{1} 3657^{1} 3737^{3} 4154^{6}

3 **CRYSTAL REAY,** br f Sovereign Dancer (USA) - Crystal Bright by Bold Lad (Ire) (L M Cumani) 752^{6} 1285^{3} 1816^{5} 2534^{4} 3780^{5} 4231^{5}

3 **CRYSTAL SHIP (Ire),** br f Caerleon (USA) - Inisfree (USA) by Hoist The Flag (USA) (Charles O'Brien) 2184^{6} 2609^{3} 3025^{1} 3497^{4} 3852^{3} 4245

6 **CRYSTAL SPIRIT,** b g Kris - Crown Treasure (USA) by Graustark (I A Balding) 462^{2} 4283

3 **CRYSTAL STONE,** b f Commanche Run - Bonnie Banks by Lomond (USA) (T Thomson Jones) 498^{9} 838^{7} 2034^{7} 2658

2 **CUANGO (Ire),** b or br c Mtoto - Barinia by Corvaro (USA) (R Hollinshead) 4252

3 **CUBIST (Ire),** b f Tate Gallery (USA) - Finalist by Star Appeal (D Morley) 685^{8} 1037^{4} 1399 1932 2151^{4} 2540^{1} 2724

3 **CUCKMERE VENTURE,** br f King Of Spain - Kala Nashan by Kala Shikari (R Voorspuy) 3225 4110 4524^{9} 4683

3 **CUDDLY DATE,** b f Nomination - Persane (Fr) by Persepolis (Fr) (D T Thom) 2157^{8} 2560^{8} 3002^{2} 3270 3459^{5} 3591 3745

3 **CUFF LINK (Ire),** ch g Caerleon (USA) - Corinth Canal by Troy (Major W R Hern) 2725^{4} 3225^{6} 3590^{3} 4110^{3} 4445^{2} 4590^{2}

2 **CULLENSTOWN LADY (Ire),** gr f Wood Chanter - Dawn Goddess by St Chad (P Hughes) 1994

2 **CULRAIN,** b g Hadeer - La Vie En Primrose by Henbit (USA) (Miss S E Hall) 3677^{9} 4677^{5}

2 **CULSYTH FLYER,** b c Nomination - Polly Worth by Wolver Hollow (R Hollinshead) 291^{3} 343^{2} 517^{1} 841^{4} 1381^{5} 2058^{5} 2356^{2} 2772^{1} 2988 3539^{2} 3755^{5} 3903^{4} 4106

2 **CULT HERO (Can),** b or br c Silver Deputy (Can) - Joyful Juliet (USA) by What A Pleasure (USA) (P W Chapple-Hyam) 2616^{2} 3400^{4} 3888^{4}

4 **CULTURE VULTURE (USA),** ch f Timeless Moment (USA) - Perfect Example (USA) by Far North (Can) (P F I Cole) 1029^{3} 1548^{1} 2074^{6} 2334^{3} 2905^{4} 3800^{9}

3 **CUMBRIAN CALYPSO,** gr g Absalom - Burglar Tip by Burglar (M H Easterby) 899^{7} 1039^{9} 1192^{5} 1760 2312

2 **DAME PROSPECT,** br f Damister (USA) - View by Shirley Heights (J A Glover) 2336 2718 4665^3

2 **DAMERS DUKE (Ire),** b g Cyrano de Bergerac - Ginosa by Kalamoon (G T Hourigan) 4323^8 4637

4 **DAMHSA (Den),** ch f Where To Dance (USA) - Choice Of Emblems by Milford (J S Bolger) 1295 3853

4 **DAMODAR,** gr g Damister (USA) - Obertura (USA) by Roberto (USA) (F Flood) 309

3 **DAMP (USA),** 594^7

5 **DAMPIERRE (USA),** b g Lear Fan (USA) - Danseuse Etoile by Buckpasser (A Fabre) 283^6

6 **DANAE DE BRULE (Fr),** b m Garde Royale - Belle de Brule by Sir Tor (USA) (A Fabre) 104^2 145^1

4 **DANAGROOM (USA),** b f Groom Dancer (USA) - Charmante Dame by Bellypha (Mme C Head) 4726a^5

3 **DANAKAL (USA),** b c Diesis - Danishkada by Thatch (A de Royer-Dupre) 613^3 1220^4 2488^3 3015^2 3717^8 4010^6 4400^5

3 **DANAMORE (Ire),** b g Lomond (USA) - Millieme by Mill Reef (USA) (R Guest) 944^6 2185^9 2609^9 2902^7 3274^5 4666^4

3 **DANA SPRINGS (Ire),** b f Aragon - Dance By Night by Northfields (USA) (R Hannon) 371^1 717^1 1638^3 2211^3 2907^1 3262^1 3501^1 3931^5 4175

3 **DANCEALOT (Ire),** b c Dance Of Life (USA) - Arburie by Exbury (P Aspell) 2185^6 2743^7 3526^6

3 **DANCE FEVER (Ire),** ch g Orchestra - Dance Away by Red God (J G FitzGerald) 3096^8

2 **DANCE FOCUS,** b c Aragon - Brassy Nell by Dunbeath (USA) (W A O'Gorman) 2370^2 2519^2 2720^1 2996 4613^9 4709^3

2 **DANCE OF THE SWANS (Ire),** ch f Try My Best (USA) - Arrapata by Thatching (Mrs M Reveley) 680^1 1078^1 1303^3 2435^3 2886 3715^6 4042^4

4 **DANCE OF WORDS (Ire),** b f Commanche Run - Mimicry by Thatch (USA) (J H Johnson) 1986^3 2900^3

5 **DANCE ON SIXPENCE,** b g Lidhame - Burning Ambition by Troy (D Eddy) 247^8 319^8 990^9 1436^5 1744^7 1898^6 2445 2863^7

3 **DANCES WITH GOLD,** b f Glint Of Gold - Northern Ballerina by Dance In Time (Can) (M Johnston) 452^2 642^5 744^2 928^4 1133 1578^5 2104^5 2480^4 2737^2 2932^6 3216^5 3374 3631^4 3788 4085^4

2 **DANCES WITH RISK,** ch f Risk Me (Fr) - Dancing Belle by Dance In Time (Can) (G Lewis) 1523^3 1773^1 2292^7 2610^1 2886^9 3103^4 3657^2 3871^1 4061^7 4416

4 **DANCE THIS TUNE (USA),** b g Palace Music (USA) - Leaping Lucy (USA) by Restless Native (John J McLoughlin) 598

3 **DANCE TO ORDER (Ire),** b g Somethingfabulous (USA) - Bloomsbarry (USA) by Apalachee (USA) (Sir Mark Prescott) 4766a^1 685^7 802^9 1037^7 1703^2 1875^3

2 **DANCE TO THE TOP,** b f Sadler's Wells (USA) - Aim For The Top (USA) by Irish River (Fr) (M R Stoute) 3248^1 3765^1 4171^2

2 **DANCE TURN,** b c Damister (USA) - Spin Turn by Homing (R W Armstrong) 4276^9 4542^1

3 **DANCIENNE (Fr),** b f Groom Dancer (USA) - Termienne by Armos (E Lellouche) 4693a^1 561^2 1218^2 1722^3 3501^2 3933^3 4311 4474^1

2 **DANCING ACTION (USA),** b f Danzatore (Can) - Ready For Action (USA) by Riverman (USA) (D K Weld) 3527^1 4553^5

2 **DANCING ANGEL,** ch f Adbass (USA) - Blue And White by Busted (A P Jarvis) 2044^7 2492

2 **DANCING AT LUNASA (Ire),** b f Dancing Dissident (USA) - In The Clover by Meadow Mint (USA) (A P O'Brien) 1022^5 1509^3 2742^2 3203^3 3451^4 3730^3 4093^3 4462^4

4 **DANCING BEAU (Ire),** b g Dance Of Life (USA) - Kentucky Belle by Glint Of Gold (S Dow) 4667a^3 4758a^4 4802a^3 4817a^5 332^3 603 840^6 1120^5 1474^4 1659^2 1707^2 1956^4 2289^4 2459^7 3257^1 3623^2 3973^2 4019^3 4164

3 **DANCING BLOOM (Ire),** b f Sadler's Wells (USA) - Dancing Shadow by Dancer's Image (USA) (M R Stoute) 2334^2 2986^6 3433^2 4467^8

4 **DANCING BOAT,** b g Shareef Dancer (USA) - Sauceboat by Connaught (J L Harris) 4748a^3 4759a^5 4793a^2 4817a^8 113^3 264^8 1035^6 3518

2 **DANCING BRIEF (Ire),** b c Nordico (USA) - Bold And Brief by Bold Lad (Ire) (N C Bell) 1550^8 1824^5 2037 3379^9 3806^5 3917^6 4360

2 **DANCING CLOWN,** b c Rambo Dancer (Can) - Lipreader (USA) by Mr Leader (USA) (N A Callaghan) 2968 3130

7 **DANCING DAYS,** ch g Glenstal (USA) - Royal Agnes by Royal Palace (J Parkes) 4788a^8 18^3 226^9 1873^1 2235^3 2455^1 2800^6

3 **DANCING DIAMOND (Ire),** b f Alzao (USA) - Shay Tien by Gunner B (G Lewis) 1408 2122^3 2832 3634^8 3887^5 4088^1 4247 4457^7 4711^1

3 **DANCING DOMINO,** ch g Primo Dominie - Waltz by Jimmy Reppin (M H Easterby) 1181^1 1496^2 1658^2 1893^1 2269^3 2764^1 2864^1 2915^2 3553^1 3726 4181^8 4536^5 4596^3

2 **DANCING HEIGHTS (Ire),** b f High Estate - Alpine Symphony by Northern Dancer (I A Balding) 4539^5

2 **DANCING LAWYER,** b c Thowra (Fr) - Miss Lawsuit by Neltino (B J Meehan) 1905^8 2250 2492^4 3009^1 3222^6 3386^3 4144^6 4561^3 4618^3

4 **DANCING MISS (Ire),** ch f Heraldiste (USA) - Tasmania Star by Captain James (P R Hedger) 2989^9 3425 3839^9 4335

3 **DANCING PRIZE (Ire),** b f Sadler's Wells (USA) - Aim For The Top (USA) by Irish River (Fr) (M R Stoute) 662^2 946^3 1311^2

2 **DANCING REBEL (Ire),** b c Dancing Dissident (USA) - Soucaro by Rusticaro (Fr) (M Bell) 2875^7

2 **DANCING ROSINA (Ire),** ch f Digamist (USA) - Sunblast by Roan Rocket (P Mitchell) 1708^6 2866 3888

3 **DANCING SEER,** b f Lead On Time (USA) - Ile de Danse by Ile de Bourbon (USA) (Peadar Matthews) 4407 4556

6 **DANCING SENSATION (USA),** b m Faliraki - Sweet Satina (USA) by Crimson Satan (R Akehurst) 4690a 4723a^9 4784a^5 48^4 91^5 881^1 1120^4 1474^2 1734^3 2004^1 2612^1 2882^4 3269^2 3425^2

3 **DANCING SPIRIT (Ire),** br f Ahonoora - Instinctive Move (USA) by Nijinsky (Can) (R Hannon) 523^4 752^4 872^9 1342^2 1587^6 1953^1 2418^7 3313^6

2 **DANCING SUCCESS (USA),** ch c Fred Astaire (USA) - Successfuly Yours (USA) by Successor (Liam Browne) 3159^3 3416^4 3608^2 3825^1

3 **DANCING TRALTHEE (Ire),** b f Dancing Brave (USA) - Tralthee (USA) by Tromos (L M Cumani) 1931^6 2332 3456^7 3873^1 4129^8

3 **DANCING VISION (Ire),** br g Vision (USA) - Dewan's Niece (USA) by Dewan (USA) (Augustine Leahy) 1122^9 2287 2902^6 3368^2 3524^6 4137^5 4639^6

4 **DANCING YEARS (USA),** b f Fred Astaire (USA) - Resembling (USA) by Nasty And Bold (USA) (G L Moore) 4486 4591^8

2 **DANDINI,** b g Reesh - Vent Du Soir by Main Reef (M Dixon) 3421 4338^7 4752^6

3 **DANDONG,** b c Doyoun - Danthonia (USA) by Northern Dancer (R Charlton) 3012 3272

4 **DANDY DESIRE,** ch g Grey Desire - Karsavina by Silly Season (B C Morgan) 815^8 1148 1799 1981^5 2354^8 2590^8 3591

3 **DANGER BABY,** ch g Bairn (USA) - Swordlestown Miss (USA) by Apalachee (USA) (R Dickin) 338^6 838^6 2340^2 2721^1 3097^3

2 **DANGEROUS SHADOW,** gr f Absalom - Golden Decoy by Decoy Boy (Mrs M Reveley) 1158^3 1418^9 1895^8 2569^5 2814^1 3279 3673^3 3755^4 4097^2 4251 4500^1 4602^4 4642^1

2 **DANGER POINT,** b g Danehill (USA) - Red Comes Up (USA) by Blushing Groom (Fr) (R Hannon) 1489^2 1828^7 2250^3 3992^3 4240^3 4480^2 4579^3 4680^1

2 **DANIELLE HABIBI (Ire),** b f Fools Holme (USA) - Zalazula by Lord Gayle (USA) (N A Graham) 3828 4121^6 4349^8 4531

2 **DANISH (Ire),** b f Danehill (USA) - Tea House by Sassafras (Fr) (Michael Kauntze) 1022^1 1571^2 2648^7 3335^4 3612^7

3 **DANISH FORT,** b c Danzig (USA) - I Want To Be (USA) by Roberto (USA) (H R A Cecil) 3012^3 3456^1 3645^1 3899^5

2 **DANISH HEIGHTS (Ire),** gr c Danehill (USA) - Chamonis (USA) by Affirmed (USA) (R W Armstrong) 3979^{8} 4627^{3}

2 **DANITA (Ire),** ch f Roi Danzig (USA) - Benita by Roan Rocket (J S Bolger) 2742^{6} 3527^{3} 3729 4134^{3} 4359^{1}

3 **DANNY BLUE (Ire),** ch c Bluebird (USA) - Bradan by Salmon Leap (USA) (Miss Gay Kelleway) 2164^{5} 2366^{5} 3068^{4} 3391

3 **DANNY BOY,** b or br c Damister (USA) - Irish Isle by Realm (R Hannon) 482 1090^{1} 1471^{5} 1670^{8} 2333 2757^{7} 3054^{4} 3710 3981^{2} 4241^{1} 4355^{4} 4424

3 **DANSE ROYALE (Ire),** b f Caerleon (USA) - Flame Of Tara by Artaius (USA) (M J Grassick) 576^{2} 943^{1} 1200^{3} 2038^{3} 2405^{5} 3149^{1} 3495^{3} 3913^{7}

2 **DANSEUSE DU NORD (Ire),** b f Kahyasi - Dance By Night by Northfields (USA) (E Lellouche) 4310^{7}

3 **DANSEUSE FRANCAISE (Ire),** b f Sicyos (USA) - Ninette de Valois (Fr) by Gay Mecene (USA) (M Bell) 672^{5} 826 1061^{6} 3088^{8} 3518

2 **DANTE'S RUBICON (Ire),** ch c Common Grounds - Dromorehill by Ballymore (J D Bethell) 1272 2063^{4} 2876^{8} 3539^{3} 4165^{3} 4375^{3} 4416^{9}

7 **DANZA HEIGHTS,** br g Head For Heights - Dankalia by Le Levanstell (Mrs M Reveley) 1438^{6} 1593^{4}

2 **DANZIG TOUCH (USA),** b c Danzig Connection (USA) - Touchy Lady (F Brogi) 2257^{4}

3 **DARAJAH (USA),** ch f Diesis - Whitethroat by Artaius (USA) (J H M Gosden) 3132

4 **DARBAWAN (Ire),** b c Lashkari - Darazina by Labus (A de Royer-Dupre) 1908^{8}

3 **DARBONNE (USA),** b c Danzig (USA) - Bon Debarras (Can) by Ruritania (USA) (G Harwood) 526^{5} 953^{4} 1084 3268^{3} 3519^{5}

4 **DARCARI ROSE (Ire),** b f Try My Best (USA) - Shikari Rose by Kala Shikari (F W Pennicott) 281 996^{9} 3398^{9} 4370 4737

9 **DARCY'S THATCHER,** b or br g Thatching - Lancette by Double Jump (W P Browne) 2782^{4} 3061^{2} 3328^{7} 4094^{2} 4534^{2} 4639

3 **DARDANELLE,** ch f Stanford - Tarte Aux Pommes by Song (W L Barker) 545^{5} 728^{5} 974^{3} 1159^{5} 1360^{4} 1516^{5}

2 **DARE AND GO (USA),** b c Alydar (USA) - Partygoer (USA) by Secretariat (USA) (Mrs C Head) 4242^{1} 4593^{3}

3 **DARECLIFF (USA),** ch c Diesis - Come On Sunshine (USA) by T V Lark (R Hannon) 825^{3} 1068^{1} 1637^{1} 2259 3401^{8} 3749^{2} 4150^{5}

4 **DARE TO DREAM (Ire),** b g Baillamont (USA) - Tears Of Allah (Fr) by Troy (P J Hobbs) 1268^{2} 1752

3 **DARE TO DUEL (USA),** 3823

5 **DARIKA LAD,** gr g Belfort (Fr) - Lindrake's Pride by Mandrake Major (A Harrison) 2733 3180

2 **DARING DESTINY,** b f Daring March - Raunchy Rita by Brigadier Gerard (K R Burke) 2069^{5} 4089^{1} 4371^{3}

3 **DARING KING,** b g King Of Spain - Annacando by Derrylin (G A Pritchard-Gordon) 2154^{7} 3007^{4} 3588^{4} 4016^{5} 4544^{9} 4633

4 **DARINGLY,** b c Daring March - Leylandia by Wolver Hollow (J C McConnochie) 3639

3 **DARING PAST,** b g Daring March - Better Buy Baileys by Sharpo (R Boss) 185^{2} 237^{1} 259^{2} 398^{6} 733^{2} 966^{8} 1238^{6} 1812^{2} 2948^{1} 3175^{5} 3507^{8} 3669^{4} 4336^{4}

5 **DARIYOUN (USA),** b h Shahrastani (USA) - Darara by Top Ville (C Laffon-Parias) 726^{2} 1291^{3} 1888^{4} 3930^{4} 4311 4601^{1}

3 **DARK AND STORMY,** b g Aragon - Spanish Chestnut by Philip Of Spain (M Dixon) 568 827

3 **DARK CANYON,** 2259

3 **DARK DEN (USA),** b c Val de L'orne (Fr) - Covert (USA) by Turn To Mars (USA) (Mrs J Cecil) 2776^{8} 3272^{8} 3590^{6} 3937^{3} 4675^{2}

3 **DARK EYED LADY (Ire),** b f Exhibitioner - Tribal Eye by Tribal Chief (D W P Arbuthnot) 2303 2661^{2} 3127^{4} 3313^{9} 3621^{9} 3947 4277^{2} 4465

3 **DARK HYACINTH (Ire),** b f Darshaan - Priddy Blue by Blue Cashmere (M J Grassick) 282 819^{2} 1250^{6} 1466^{4} 1963^{6} 3077^{3} 3274^{3} 3975^{6} 4657^{5}

2 **DARK POET (Ire),** br c Darshaan - Exclusive Fable (USA) by Exclusive Native (USA) (T Stack) 4406 4581

3 **DARK REEF,** gr c Fast Topaze (USA) - Lady Reef by Mill Reef (USA) (John M Oxx) 1646^{6} 2247^{5} 2606^{2}

3 **DARK STREET (Ire),** b or br c Darshaan - Bay Street by Grundy (L Camici) 4703a^{8} 1322^{3} 3796^{3}

3 **DARK SWAN (Ire),** br c Soughaan (USA) - Last Stop by Charlottown (T J O'Mara) 959^{1} 1139^{9} 2040^{6} 2517^{5} 2842 3294^{8} 3484^{6} 3576^{9} 4185

2 **DARK THOUGHTS,** b f Aragon - Fille de Fraise by Mr Fluorocarbon (Dr J D Scargill) 4698

4 **DARK VISION,** br f Noalto - Valeur by Val de Loir (J S King) 211^{9}

2 **DARKWOOD BAY (USA),** b or br c Green Dancer (USA) - Unyielding (USA) by Never Bend (D R C Elsworth) 4587^{1}

2 **DARLIN'BUDS OF MAY,** b f North Briton - Still Marching by Riboboy (USA) (P S Felgate) 4594 4665^{9}

3 **DARMSTADT (USA),** b or br c Manila (USA) - Frau Daruma (Arg) by Frari (Arg) (J H M Gosden) 751 1068 1275^{4} 1838^{1} 2019^{1} 2373^{5} 2632^{1} 2907 3401^{5} 3881^{9}

2 **DARNAY,** br c Darshaan - Flawless Image (USA) by The Minstrel (Can) (J H M Gosden) 4276^{1}

2 **DARONNE,** b c Darshaan - Pipina (USA) by Sir Gaylord (L M Cumani) 4014^{2} 4259^{1} 4529^{4}

4 **DAROS,** b g Damister (USA) - Tikanova (USA) by Northern Dancer (M Puhich) 146^{5}

2 **DARREN BOY (Ire),** ch g Ballad Rock - Trojan Relation by Trojan Fen (P F I Cole) 1985^{1} 2616^{5} 3386^{2} 3539^{1}

3 **DARRERY,** b f Darshaan - Flamenco (USA) by Dance Spell (USA) (M R Stoute) 3590^{2} 3909^{1} 4108^{1} 4731^{7}

4 **D'ARROS (Ire),** b c Baillamont (USA) - Bella Senora (USA) by Northern Dancer (F Boutin) 1411^{3} 1971^{1} 3187^{7} 4404^{4}

3 **DARSING,** b g Chief Singer - Alydear (USA) by Alydar (USA) (G A Pritchard-Gordon) 3740^{9}

4 **DARU (USA),** gr g Caro - Frau Daruma (Arg) by Frari (Arg) (J H M Gosden) 438^{1} 735^{5} 1018^{7} 1405^{4} 1787^{7} 2925^{8} 4731

3 **DARUBENA (Ity),** bl f Chief Singer - Dora Horn by Gren Dancer 1727^{7}

6 **DARUSSALAM,** ch m Tina's Pet - Chinese Falcon by Skymaster (R Lee) 1066 1267 1394^{9} 1494^{5} 1953 2548^{6} 2734^{5} 3011^{7} 3155^{7} 3896^{2} 3946^{3} 4123

3 **DARZEE,** b c Darshaan - Royal Lorna (USA) by Val de L'orne (Fr) (L M Cumani) 1176^{4} 1603^{2} 1864^{2}

4 **DASHING COLOURS (Ire),** b or br f Be My Native (USA) - Near The End by Shirley Heights (Daniel J Murphy) 4684a^{1} 897^{3} 1201 1551^{4} 1646^{2} 2805^{3} 3029^{3} 3162^{4} 3559^{5} 4053^{3} 4463^{4} 4552^{3} 4736^{3}

2 **DASHING DANCER (Ire),** ch c Conquering Hero (USA) - Santa Maria (Ger) by Literat (J G Coogan) 1121^{6} 1608^{5} 1792^{4} 2294

5 **DASHING FELLOW (Ire),** b g Sure Blade (USA) - Belle Viking (Fr) by Riverman (USA) (Mrs L Piggott) 709^{8} 973 2827^{3} 3193^{1} 3346^{1} 3714^{1} 4036 4247^{4} 4591^{1} 4713^{6} 4757^{2}

4 **DASHING MARCH,** b f Daring March - Miss Casanova by Galivanter (M S Saunders) 1315^{9} 2351^{4} 2580^{4} 3088 3445^{6}

5 **DASWAKI (Can),** b g Miswaki (USA) - Nice Manners (Can) by Barachois (Can) (G L Moore) 4680a^{3} 4722a^{1} 4781a^{1} 4803a^{4} 247 315 475 756^{8} 1130^{3} 1474^{8} 1604^{9} 3269 3887^{1} 3957^{1} 4024^{8} 4116 4470 4650

4 **DAUBERVAL (USA),** b c Danzig (USA) - Dancealot (USA) by Round Table (A Fabre) 637^{1} 795^{2}

2 **DAUNTLESS FORT,** gr f Belfort (Fr) - Dauntless Flight by Golden Mallard (B W Murray) 1272 2595^{5} 3183^{4} 4193

4 **DAVAMAL,** ch f Little Wolf - Princess Glory by Prince de Galles (J M Bradley) 1925

2 **DAVANNE,** ch f Indian Ridge - Fair And Wise by High Line (P F I Cole) 1916^{4}

4 **DAVE'S LASS,** ch f Crever - Monagram by Mon Fetiche (D Burchell) 3007

2 **DAVID BLUE (Ire),** b g Colmore Row - Royal Aunt by Martinmas (J White) 1602

2 **DAVIDS DIAMOND,** b f Sizzling Melody - Jeedamaya by Taufan (USA) (J R Jenkins) 2137^{8} 2668 2946^{6} 3641

2 **DAVID'S DREAM (Hol),** gr f Superlative - Heartbreaker by Steel Heart (Dr J D Scargill) 3166

2 **DURABLE,** b c Caerleon (USA) - Colorvista by Shirley Heights (J H M Gosden) 4113[7] 4377[2]
2 **DURANDETTE,** ch f Durandal - Siblette by Persepolis (Fr) (J J Bridger) 913 1131 1403
2 **DURANO,** b g Dunbeath (USA) - Norapa by Ahonoora (M H Easterby) 1798[8]
2 **DURHAM,** ch c Caerleon (USA) - Sanctuary by Welsh Pageant (P F I Cole) 4498[9]
2 **DURHAM DRAPES,** b f Taufan (USA) - Miss Bali Beach by Nonoalco (USA) (M H Easterby) 1418[8] 2021[7] 2603[2] 3627[7] 4106 4541
4 **DURSHAN (USA),** ch c Shahrastani (USA) - Dukayna by Northfields (USA) (J R Jenkins) 390[7] 601[2] 757[4] 822[2] 1129[2] 1770[5] 2617 3067[4] 3434 4143
3 **DUSKY DUCHESS (Ire),** b f Entitled - June Darling by Junius (USA) (Miss L A Perratt) 1629[5] 1737 2087[6] 3144[5] 3355
9 **DUSTSCREEN (USA),** gr g Grey Dawn II - Slip Screen (USA) by Silent Screen (USA) (Wilbert Tolerton) 2484
3 **DUSTY POINT (Ire),** b c Reference Point - Noble Dust (USA) by Dust Commander (USA) (B Hanbury) 1170[1] 1372[1] 1582[1] 1917[1] 2239[6] 2561[1] 2907 3401 3724
5 **DUSTY SCREEN (USA),** 4438[8]
3 **DUSTY'S DARLING,** b f Doyoun - Proserpina (Fr) by Shafaraz (Fr) (M A Jarvis) 992 1278[7]
3 **DUTCH DEBUTANTE,** ch f Nicholas Bill - Dutch Princess by Royalty (Miss B Sanders) 662 980[7] 1255[3] 1605[6] 1906[6]
2 **DUTCH MISS,** b f Dutch Treat - Mini Maid by Fair Hunter (W G Turner) 3641
3 **DUTOSKY,** b f Doulab (USA) - Butosky by Busted (R J R Williams) 295[1] 684[3] 875[6] 1338[7] 2333[5] 2576[1] 2961 3181[2] 3585 3850[8] 4470 4559
4 **DUTY SERGEANT (Ire),** b g Pennine Walk - Plainsong (Fr) by Amen (Fr) (M P Muggeridge) 333[6] 603 881[8] 1490[7] 1743 2113 4007
2 **DUTY TIME,** b c Night Shift (USA) - Moorish Idol by Aragon (J L Dunlop) 1131[9] 1489[8] 2419[2] 2988[6] 3351[1] 3597[9] 3865[1] 4444
3 **DUVEEN (Ire),** b g Tate Gallery (USA) - Wish You Were Here (USA) by Secretariat (USA) (M Bell) 250[3] 378[2] 437[1] 530[8] 976[2] 1309[1] 1488[1] 1976[1] 2333 2537[1] 2961 3507[4] 3555[4] 4247
2 **DUWON (Ire),** b f Polish Precedent (USA) - Moon Parade by Welsh Pageant (A C Stewart) 4539
3 **DYAB (USA),** b c Diesis - Petrava (NZ) by Imposing (Aus) (C N Williams) 494[6] 875[5] 1204[6] 1483[5] 4522
5 **DYD,** b m Sulaafah (USA) - Wrekin Belle by Dance In Time (Can) (F Jordan) 498
4 **DYEGETME (Ire),** b f Prince Tenderfoot (USA) - Alizarina (Ity) by Ragusa (Patrick Martin) 1295 1986 4368
2 **DYHIM (USA),** b or br c Polish Navy (USA) - Savage Bunny by Never Bend (A Wohler) 3701[1]
2 **DYNAMIC DELUXE (USA),** ch c Sir Ivor - Shanameg (USA) by Rise Jim (USA) (Mrs J R Ramsden) 2626[4] 3091[3] 3704[3] 4113[1] 4329 4531 4674[5]
3 **DYNAMIC GEORGE,** b g Jupiter Island - Truly Blest by So Blessed (N A Callaghan) 1060 1239[9] 2219
2 **DYNAMIS (Ire),** b f Dancing Brave (USA) - Diasprina (Ger) by Aspros (Ger) (N A Graham) 1393[8]
6 **EAGER DEVA,** b h Lochnager - Deva Rose by Chestergate (R Hollinshead) 292[2] 355[2] 1000 1215[2] 1301[6] 1420[1] 2018 2620[7] 2813[6] 3638 3692[1] 3834[5]
2 **EAGLE EYED (USA),** b c Danzig (USA) - Razyana (USA) by His Majesty (USA) (A Fabre) 3799[2] 4195[5] 4748[5]
4 **EARLY GALES,** b f Precocious - Galesa by Welsh Pageant (J Pearce) 4780a[7]
4 **EARLY STAR,** b c Precocious - Staritsa (USA) by Alleged (USA) (K Bishop) 4490
3 **EARLY TO RISE,** b g Don't Forget Me - Foreno by Formidable (USA) (Miss L C Siddall) 338[3] 628[6] 976[9] 1266[8] 1627[7] 2007[4] 2536[4] 2850[2] 3049[3] 3170[1] 3361[2] 3574[6] 3694[4]
5 **EARTH AND FIRE (Bel),** b g Balkan Prince - Tumble Star by Tumble Wind 3372[1]
2 **EARTH CHARTER,** b f Slip Anchor - Docklands by On Your Mark (C E Brittain) 2394[3] 4089[6]
2 **EAS GEIPTINE,** b g Fast Topaze (USA) - Yarzah (USA) by Silver Hawk (USA) (E McNamara) 1567[6] 2840[4] 2982[7] 3607[8] 4093 4360
5 **EAST BARNS (Ire),** gr g Godswalk (USA) - Rocket Lass by Touch Paper (T D Barron) 4690a[4] 4710a[6] 4744a[1] 4764a[1] 13[4] 27[2] 120[4] 4488[8] 4623[3] 4702[8]
3 **EASTERN CHARLY (Bel),** br g Ishamo - Sarah Bear by Mansingh (USA) (P C Ritchens) 2578[8] 3174[7] 3550[8] 3634 3840
8 **EASTERN EVENING,** gr g Runnett - Sacola by Busted (J C Poulton) 3509
3 **EASTERN GLOW,** ch f Hadeer - Turtle Dove by Gyr (USA) (S P C Woods) 334[6] 410[4] 813 962[4] 1453 1829[5] 2154[3] 2993[6] 3213[3] 3744[5]
5 **EASTERN MAGIC,** b g Faustus (USA) - Hithermoor Lass by Red Alert (G Barnett) 520 994[8] 1268 1880[4] 2353[6]
3 **EASTERN MEMORIES (Ire),** b c Don't Forget Me - East River (Fr) by Arctic Tern (USA) (R Hannon) 4730a[1] 328[1] 400[5] 558[1] 690[1]
7 **EASTER SIXTEEN,** b g Prince Bee - Hidden Hand (USA) by Ribocco (Patrick Prendergast) 3077[2] 3857[6]
5 **EASTER TERM,** b m Welsh Term - Silly Woman by Silly Season (M R Channon) 141[9]
4 **EASTLEIGH,** b c Efisio - Blue Jane by Blue Cashmere (R Hollinshead) 4739a[6] 4765a[4] 4802a[1] 13 43[1] 69[1] 130[4] 155[2] 200[1] 327[4] 403[6]
3 **EAST LIBERTY (USA),** ch f Halo (USA) - Pennsylvania (USA) by Northjet (I A Balding) 400[7] 1016[9] 1950[3] 2361 2697[1] 3476[8] 3736
2 **EASTROP DANCER (Ire),** b c Jareer (USA) - Benicia (USA) by Sir Ivor (J P Kavanagh) 786 896[4] 1104[9] 1608[4] 3110[4] 4285[9] 4638[8]
3 **EASY ACCESS (Ire),** b c Thatching - Savannah Song (USA) by Riverman (USA) (R Hannon) 747[1] 1017[9] 1808 2361[4] 2622[4]
2 **EASY D'OR,** b g Glint Of Gold - Eastern Command (USA) by Far Out East (USA) (M Bell) 2331 3126[7] 4128
2 **EASY FOR ME,** b g Mandrake Major - Beads by Noalcoholic (Fr) (C W Thornton) 886[7] 1413[5]
10 **EASY LINE,** ch g Swing Easy (USA) - Impromptu by My Swanee (P J Feilden) 1348[9] 2329[2] 2969[9] 4168 4652
2 **EASY STEP (Ire),** ch g Digamist (USA) - Up To You by Sallust (Kevin Prendergast) 1121[8] 4323[4] 4460 4581
5 **EASY TOOMEY,** br h Swing Easy (USA) - Miss Twomey by Will Somers (J R Jenkins) 1951[7] 2178 2751[8]
3 **EASY TOUCH,** b f Bairn (USA) - Lappet by Kampala (D Haydn Jones) 1675[9] 2425[7] 2859 3233 3693 3893[6] 4209[9]
3 **EATON ROW (USA),** b c Alydar (USA) - Royal Entrance (USA) by Tim Tam (P W Chapple-Hyam) 357[2] 1004[1]
2 **EBEN AL HABEEB (Ire),** ch c Nashwan (USA) - Family Style (USA) by State Dinner (USA) (Major W R Hern) 4717
4 **EBONY AND IVORY (Ire),** br f Bob Back (USA) - Geraldville by Lord Gayle (USA) (Kevin Prendergast) 895[7] 1511[7] 2461[3] 2841[3] 3577[6] 3915[7] 4186[5] 4383 4430[3]
2 **EBONY BLAZE,** b g Aragon - Velvet Pigeon by Homing (G Lewis) 3941[6] 4523
2 **ECHARDE,** ch f Cadeaux Genereux - Splintering by Sharpo (P T Walwyn) 3781[8] 4067
4 **ECHO-LOGICAL,** gr c Belfort (Fr) - North Pine by Import (R Hannon) 465[6] 737 1806[7] 2136[1] 3906 4040 4280[4] 4415 4521[2]
2 **ECHO WOOD,** ch g Woodman (USA) - Resonation (Can) by Coastal (USA) (P G Murphy) 4113 4498
3 **ECU DE FRANCE (Ire),** ch c Groom Dancer (USA) - Racing Connection (USA) by Sharpen Up (M Madgwick) 558[5] 875[7] 1483[2] 2485[5] 3909[4] 4110[6] 4267 4519[6]
3 **EDBAYSAAN (Ire),** b c Slip Anchor - Legend Of Arabia by Great Nephew (H R A Cecil) 1314[5] 1603[1] 2174[3] 2907[6] 3401[1] 3735[2] 3899[3] 4301[2]
8 **EDDIE WALSHE,** b g Smackover - Ashmore Lady by Ashmore (Fr) (R F Stone) 650
4 **EDEN'S CLOSE,** ch g Green Dancer (USA) - Royal Agreement (USA) by Vaguely Noble (M H Tompkins) 2624[3] 2882[5] 3179[2] 3512[3] 4037[1] 4731

3 **EDENS LANDING (Ire),** b f Kafu - Madeira Lady by On Your Mark (E J O'Grady) 1611 3419^7 3720^6 4184 4657

4 **EDGE OF DARKNESS,** br f Vaigly Great - Atoka by March Past (J W Hills) 678^2 994 1392^5 1832^2 2149^3 2669^5 3288^7 3694^1 4611^4

5 **EDGE OF THE GLEN,** b g Alleging (USA) - Scotch Bonnet by Supreme Sovereign (R J Hodges) 49

5 **EDIREPUS,** b g Lightning Dealer - Pentland Beauty by Remainder Man (Mrs M Reveley) 3185^2 3461^7

3 **EDITHMEAD (Ire),** b f Shardari - Bless The Match by So Blessed (N J Henderson) 1802^8 2776^4 3272 3682^4 4267^3

4 **EDUCATED PET,** gr g Petong - School Road by Great Nephew (P D Evans) 1835^7 1953^8 2062^2 2173^5 2434^8 2628^5 2777^9 2987 3481^1 3638 3778 3906 4693^1

3 **EDUCATED RISK (USA),** b f Mr Prospector (USA) - Pure Profit (USA) by Key To The Mint (USA) (C R McGaughey III) 935^2 2999^3

2 **EDWINA (Ire),** b f Caerleon (USA) - Indian Jubilee by Indian King (USA) (M Bell) 2583^5 3317^7 3713^3 3966^9

2 **EFAAD (Ire),** b c Shaadi (USA) - Krismas River by Kris (A A Scott) 4714^8

2 **EFFICACY,** b f Efisio - Lady Killane by Reform (A P Jarvis) 3781 4098 4339

3 **EFFICIENT FUNDING (Ire),** ch f Entitled - Late Summer by Habitat (Noel O'Callaghan) 552 790^9 850^7 1574 4094

4 **EFHARISTO,** b c Dominion - Excellent Alibi (USA) by Exceller (USA) (C E Brittain) 315 581^9 737^5 1002^3 1407^6 1768 2884^5 3437^8 3897^8 4300^5 4415^7

3 **EFIZIA,** b f Efisio - Millie Grey by Grey Ghost (Mrs M Reveley) 507^1 2130^6 2341^2 2551^3 2856^1 3113^1 3256^1 3630^4 4188^9 4343^1

4 **EFRA,** b g Efisio - Ra Ra by Lord Gayle (USA) (R Hannon) 479^1 677^4 1209^7 4340^1 4485^4 4681^4

3 **EGALITE (Ire),** b f Fools Holme (USA) - Firefly Night by Salmon Leap (USA) (Declan Gillespie) 1466^6 2142^8 2221^7 2496^8

3 **EGG,** gr g Another Realm - Slick Chick by Shiny Tenth (T D Barron) 341^6 1801 2594^8 3148^2 3778^7 4038 4181^3 4348^9 4536 4670^7

3 **EGOISTE (USA),** b c Sicyos (USA) - Reine Des Fleurs by Sharpman 3024^2

4 **EGYPTOWN (Fr),** b f Top Ville - Reine D'Egypte by Val de L'orne (Mme C Head) 4694a^1 1088^2 1754^1 3801^2 4292^5

2 **EHTEFAAL (USA),** b c Alysheba (USA) - Bolt From The Blue (USA) by Blue Times (USA) (P T Walwyn) 3908^3

2 **EHTFAAL (Ire),** b f Soviet Star (USA) - Bashush (USA) by Caro (H Thomson Jones) 3230^1 3679^1 3994^4 4392^3

2 **EICHTERCUA (Ire),** b f Petorius - Night Of Gaiety by What A Guest (K O'Sullivan) 1022^7 1442^2 1567^1 2403^1

4 **EIGHTANDAHALF (Ire),** b c Be My Guest (USA) - Nancy Chere (USA) by Gallant Man (B Beasley) 520 674 1161 2306^1 2729^8 3056^1 3252^3 3848

2 **EIGHTEEN TWELVE,** b g Music Boy - Glowing Report by Kalaglow (R Hannon) 1640^4 2049^1 2389^4

2 **EILEEN'S DARLING,** b or br f Belfort (Fr) - Captain Bonnie by Captain James (T Kersey) 4452 4677^8

3 **EILEENS HOPE (Ire),** br f Treasure Kay - Dunfern by Wolver Hollow (M Halford) 550 806 1105 2248 2295^6

2 **EILIEHUSH,** b f Kind Of Hush - Silver Susan by Ampney Prince (J P Leigh) 3677

4 **EIRAS MOOD,** b or br f Jalmood (USA) - Pure Perfection by So Blessed (B Palling) 4678a 2353 2673 3043^4 3655^1 3891 4488^9

6 **EIRE LEATH-SCEAL,** b g Legend Of France (USA) - Killarney Belle (USA) by Irish Castle (USA) (M Brittain) 189^3 219^9 290^6 349^3 495^8 727^7 894^3 988^4 1112^1 1305^5 1439^1 1593^6 2201^4 2506^6 3790 4037^6 4218^1 4374^7 4631

3 **EISHRELA,** b f Night Shift (USA) - Red Laser by Red God (B R Millman) 1132 1470^6 2032^9 2504^6 3233

3 **EITLEAN ALAINN (Ire),** b f Waajib - Stealth by Strong Gale (T F Lacy) 3526^8

3 **ELA BILLANTE,** ch f Ela-Mana-Mou - Billante (USA) by Graustark (J R Fanshawe) 679^8 1176^5 1625^6 1936^1 2158^3 3255^7 3521^3 3761^8

4 **ELABJER (USA),** b g Shadeed (USA) - Glamour Girl (Fr) by Riverman (USA) (P D Evans) 50^7 161^5

3 **ELACATA (Ger),** f (B Schutz) 805 1395^4 2259 3206^5 3929^5 4655^4

5 **ELAINE TULLY (Ire),** b m Persian Bold - Hanna Alta (Fr) by Busted (M J Heaton-Ellis) 1094^1 1586^2 2002^4 2755 3263^5 4101 4226

4 **ELA-MANA-SUE (Ire),** b f Soughaan (USA) - Ela Minnie Mou by Ela-Mana-Mou (F Lennon) 870 997^5 3916 4370

4 **ELANMATINA (Ire),** ch f Burslem - Sally St Clair by Sallust (C F Wall) 2025^6 4470 4597

3 **EL ARZ,** b c Primo Dominie - Zinzi by Song (J W Payne) 1396^4 1655^7 2231^1 2560^9

3 **ELATIS (USA),** ch f El Gran Senor (USA) - Summer Review (USA) by Graustark (J H M Gosden) 3491^3 3682^2 4110^1 4548^5 4731^5

2 **EL BAILADOR (Ire),** b c Dance Of Life (USA) - Sharp Ego (USA) by Sharpen Up (J D Bethell) 2990 3728^3

3 **EL BAKAN (USA),** (A Callejas) 779 1070^3 4291

6 **ELBIO,** b h Precocious - Maganyos (Hun) by Pioneer (USA) (P J Makin) 1807^1 2362^7 3464^4

3 **ELBURG (Ire),** b c Ela-Mana-Mou - Iosifa by Top Ville (R P C Hoad) 1603^4 1935^3 3304^1 3907^5 4212^2 4433^2 4732^3

2 **ELBURZ (Ity),** b c Jurado - Elear by Ela Man Mou 1885^3

2 **EL COHETE,** ch c Beveled (USA) - Donosa by Posse (USA) (A P Jarvis) 949 1135^8 1933^7 2493^4 3098

4 **EL CORTES (USA),** b c El Gran Senor (USA) - Millingdale Lillie by Tumble Wind (USA) (M J Haynes) 1207 1348

5 **EL DINERO (Ire),** b h Last Tycoon - Eltisley (USA) by Grey Sovereign (W Jarvis) 593^2 1548^9

5 **EL DOMINIO,** b h King Of Spain - Domicile by Dominion (K O Cunningham-Brown) 4760a^4 4782a 4798a^7 58^2 73^4 115^2 141^3 182^3 235^7 420 628^9 757^5 1268 1605^9

3 **EL DUCO (USA),** b c El Gran Senor (USA) - Most Honourable (USA) by Exclusive Native (USA) (R Charlton) 1027^3 2725^1 3268^6 3519^2 3889^1 4417^3

2 **ELECTION SPECIAL,** b or br f Chief Singer - Electo by Julio Mariner (J M P Eustace) 1418^1 1683^4 2473^3

2 **ELECTRIFY (USA),** b c Warning - Dokki (USA) by Northern Dancer (H R A Cecil) 2909^1 3436^4 3949^3

5 **ELECTROJET,** b m Electric - Shy Talk by Sharpen Up (A W Jones) 210^5 279 1702 2353

3 **ELECTROLYTE,** b g Electric - This Sensation by Balidar (B Palling) 755^6 980 1244^1 4502 4621 4759^2

3 **ELEGANT BLOOM (Ire),** b f Be My Guest (USA) - Honey Bend (USA) by Never Bend (D K Weld) 258^2 573^4 1513^3 2078^7 2604^6

3 **ELEGANT ELLIE,** b f Alleging (USA) - Highly Polished by High Top (Mrs L Piggott) 4697a 4761a^7 23^7

5 **ELEGANT FRIEND,** ch g Music Boy - Cardinal Palace by Royal Palace (M H Tompkins) 3523 4319^9

3 **ELEGANT HUSSAR,** b c Shareef Dancer (USA) - Brigata by Brigadier Gerard (C E Brittain) 529 950^6 1068 2773^6 3053^5 3258^5 3741^2 3945^6

9 **ELEGANT ISLE,** br g Ile de Bourbon (USA) - Elegant Tern (USA) by Sea Bird II (Wilbert Tolerton) 3076

3 **ELEGANT JADE,** b f Elegant Air - Jade Ring by Auction Ring (USA) (J A R Toller) 3012 3272

4 **ELEGANT KING (Ire),** b g Tender King - Malvern Beauty by Shirley Heights (A P Jarvis) 1669^8 1840 2115^6 2386^3 3479^4

3 **ELEGANT NORA (Ire),** ch f Ahonoora - Elegant Act (USA) by Shecky Greene (USA) (P Henley) 3074 3417 3605^7 3768^6 4118 4408

4 **ELEGANT TOUCH,** b or br f Elegant Air - Teye by Mummy's Pet (M C Pipe) 1130 1237^8 1373^8 1696^5 1956 2109^7 2384

2 **ELEUTHERA,** b f Mazilier (USA) - So It Goes by Free State (D R Loder) 1229^3 3557^1 4034^2 4299^4 4589^2

2 **ELEVATOR SHAFT (Ire),** b g Double Schwartz - Silk Trade by Auction Ring (USA) (D W P Arbuthnot)

1063[6] 1602 2866[4] 3432[5] 3657[5] 3867[1] 3982[1] 4264[2] 4416

2 **ELFLAA (Ire),** b or br c Sure Blade (USA) - Miss Gris (USA) by Hail The Pirates (USA) (D Morley) 2875[4]

3 **EL GAHAR,** b c Green Desert (USA) - Dafinah (USA) by Graustark (H R A Cecil) 459[2] 646[4] 1039[4] 1617[3] 2046[2] 3005[1] 3476[3]

3 **EL GRANDO,** b g King Of Spain - Easterly Wind by Windjammer (USA) (K O Cunningham-Brown) 4676a 3838[3]

4 **ELIADE (Ire),** b f Flash Of Steel - Diva Encore by Star Appeal (J G Burns) 4461[5] 4555 4737

3 **ELIMINATOR,** 2643

4 **ELISHA (Ger),** b f Konigsstuhl (Ger) - Elke by Authi (P Lautner) 3929[4] 4566[6]

3 **ELITE GUEST (Ire),** ch f Be My Guest (USA) - Elevate by Ela-Mana-Mou (P Bary) 1290[3] 1506[3] 3944

4 **ELITE REG,** b g Electric - Coppice by Pardao (M C Pipe) 1654[5] 1984[3]

3 **ELIZA (USA),** b f Mt Livermore (USA) - Daring Bidder by Bold Bidder (A Hassinger Jr) 762[2]

4 **ELIZABETHAN AIR,** b f Elegant Air - Lizabeth Chudleigh by Imperial Fling (USA) (A J Chamberlain) 128

3 **ELIZABETH BAY (USA),** b f Mr Prospector (USA) - Life At The Top (USA) by Seattle Slew (USA) (A Fabre) 432[2] 749[8] 1767[2] 2981[3] 3369[4] 4309[3]

3 **ELIZABETH'S PET (Ire),** b f Vision (USA) - Persian Royale by Persian Bold (E P Harty) 666[5] 1855[3] 2078[3] 2483[1] 2741[1] 3029[6] 3610 3926[7] 4284 4554[2]

5 **ELIZA WOODING,** b m Faustus (USA) - Red Gloves by Red God (C J Hill) 4763a[8] 14[4] 65[4] 165[6] 226[5] 278[3] 2162[9] 3656[6]

3 **EL JUBAIL (Ire),** b c Shirley Heights - Abha by Thatching (H R A Cecil) 1671[5] 2117[1] 3318[3]

2 **ELLARUTH (Ire),** b f Kefaah (USA) - Gaelic Jewel by Scottish Rifle (M H Tompkins) 1135[3] 1418[5] 2102[3] 2502[9] 4358 4528[8]

2 **ELLASTYLE (Ire),** b f Waajib - Grecian Hill by Ela-Mana-Mou (B S Rothwell) 4182[8] 4345 4575

3 **ELLE A TED (Ire),** b f Glenstal (USA) - Elle Va Bon by Tanfirion (Patrick Martin) 705[2] 2667[4] 3074 4060[7] 4324[5]

2 **ELLE CARVOEIRO (Ire),** ch f Al Hareb (USA) - Elle Va Bon by Tanfirion (Patrick Martin) 4610

3 **ELLE SHAPED (Ire),** b g Treasure Kay - Mamie's Joy by Prince Tenderfoot (USA) (S G Norton) 858[1] 1337[8] 1718 2206[4] 2399[7] 3438[8] 3571[7] 4238[5]

11 **ELLE VA BON,** b m Tanfirion - Mall's Star by Pall Mall (Patrick Martin) 1293

5 **EL NIDO,** ch g Adonijah - Seleter by Hotfoot (M J Camacho) 4533

2 **ELRAFA AH (USA),** b f Storm Cat (USA) - Bubbles Darlene (USA) by Fappiano (USA) (H Thomson Jones) 1393[1] 1766[3] 2210[1]

2 **EL RASHID (Ire),** b c Jareer (USA) - Sheer Audacity by Troy 3802[3]

4 **ELSA,** gr f Green Ruby (USA) - Classey by Dubassoff (USA) (P G Murphy) 331[8]

2 **EL SALVADOR,** b c Efisio - San Salvador (Ger) by Klairon (J Berry) 4503[5] 4641[5]

2 **ELSDON (Ire),** b g Taufan (USA) - Goldwyn Princess by Native Prince (M H Tompkins) 3130 4099[7] 4698

3 **ELSKA DIG,** b f Sayf El Arab (USA) - Galetzky by Radetzky (W Jarvis) 4791a 16[9]

3 **ELTARA,** b f Ela-Mana-Mou - Zepha by Great Nephew (W Jarvis) 2670[8] 3012 3506[5] 3988[6] 4206[6]

2 **EL TEL (Fr),** b c Midyan (USA) - Elka (USA) by Val de L'orne (Fr) (P F I Cole) 1725[2] 2257[6] 4229

4 **ELTON LEDGER (Ire),** b g Cyrano de Bergerac - Princess Of Nashua by Crowned Prince (USA) (A A Scott) 391[9] 492[6] 771 1096[9] 2191[1] 2276[7] 2636[8] 2945[5] 3229 3593[5] 3745

2 **ELUNED MAY,** ch f Clantime - Arroganza by Crofthall (R M Whitaker) 1798[5] 2370[5] 3505[2] 3715[7] 4105[5]

2 **ELUSIVE DOMAIN (USA),** b c Lyphard's Wish (Fr) - Anya Ylina (USA) by Bold Reasoning (USA) (D K Weld) 4582[1]

6 **EL VOLADOR,** br h Beldale Flutter (USA) - Pharjoy (Fr) by Pharly (Fr) (R J O'Sullivan) 4760a[1] 4798a[1] 4819a[1] 58[1] 115[1] 402[4] 2673 3263[3] 3587[7] 3873[2] 4152

5 **EL YASAF (Ire),** b h Sayf El Arab (USA) - Winsong Melody by Music Maestro (T J Naughton) 923[2] 1449[1] 1807[5] 2399[4] 2927[7] 3849 4040 4465 4549

3 **EL ZORRO DORADO (Ire),** b c Tate Gallery (USA) - Tough Lady by Bay Express (T Stack) 897[7] 2606[9] 3027[4] 3542[2] 3912[8] 4053[8]

4 **EMAURA,** ch f Dominion - Klaire by Klairon (K O Cunningham-Brown) 12 87 114

3 **EMBANKMENT (Ire),** b or br c Tate Gallery (USA) - Great Leighs by Vaigly Great (R Hannon) 346[1] 514[6] 690[3] 1016[4] 1451[2] 1808 2928[8] 3350[8] 3791[3] 4116[1] 4300 4522[2]

5 **EMBARCADERO (Ger),** b h Vacarme (USA) - Escadrille by Frontal (B Schutz) 406[3] 695[4] 1042[1] 2079[4] 3516[5] 4201[6] 4566[3]

3 **EMBROS (USA),** b c L'emigrant (USA) - Lady Rebecca by Sir Ivor (F Boutin) 4753a[2] 853[4] 2208[3] 4196[3] 4325[2] 4570[7]

2 **EMELIA'S PET (Ire),** b g Conquering Hero (USA) - Gay's Flutter by Beldale Flutter (USA) (Peadar Matthews) 3030 3683 3911 4581 4624

2 **EMERALD COLONY (USA),** 4390[5]

4 **EMERALD EARS,** ch f Dublin Lad - Impish Ears by Import (P M McEntee) 4783a 4802a[7] 50[4] 96[4] 138[7] 621[5] 975 1230[9] 1902[5] 2127 2670[7] 2847 3551

3 **EMERALD SANDS,** b f Green Desert (USA) - Bold Flawless (USA) by Bold Bidder (M D Hammond) 1039

4 **EMILY ALLAN (Ire),** b f Shirley Heights - St Louis Sue (Fr) by Nonoalco (USA) (K O Cunningham-Brown) 4670a

2 **EMMA GRIMES (Ire),** b f Nordico (USA) - Keep The Faith by Furry Glen (M P Muggeridge) 922[8] 1142[7] 1949 2844[4] 4122 4266

3 **EMMA WOODFORD,** ch f Master Willie - Kindjal by Kris (P W Harris) 2277[3] 2937[9] 3514

4 **EMPEEKA (USA),** b g At The Threshold (USA) - Laughing Ruler (USA) by Iron Ruler (USA) (W A O'Gorman) 4664a[8]

5 **EMPEROR ALEXANDER (Ire),** b g Tender King - Persian Apple (USA) by No Robbery (J Barclay) 4707a[2] 4806a[5] 3 78[2] 1307 1460[8] 1900 2218[4] 2426[5]

5 **EMPEROR GLEN (Ire),** b g Glenstal (USA) - Cooliney Princess by Bruni (E J O'Grady) 4534 4639

3 **EMPEROR JONES (USA),** b c Danzig (USA) - Qui Royalty (USA) by Native Royalty (USA) (J H M Gosden) 541[1] 794[8] 1748[3] 2081[5] 2803[2] 3622[3] 3862[2] 4308[6]

3 **EMPIRE POOL,** ch g Sharrood (USA) - Reflection by Mill Reef (USA) (Lord Huntingdon) 558 1006[1] 1526[2] 1785[9]

5 **EN ATTENDANT (Fr),** ch g Bairn (USA) - Vizenia by Vitiges (Fr) (B Hanbury) 605[5] 818[3] 1144[3] 1382[2] 1830[1] 2060[3] 2363[1] 3177[1] 3468[3] 3618[3] 4172 4282[3] 4464[5]

2 **EN CACHETTE (Ire),** b f Danehill (USA) - Clandestina (USA) by Secretariat (USA) (P W Chapple-Hyam) 2336[4] 2909[4] 3443[1]

2 **EN-CEE-TEE,** b c Risk Me (Fr) - Kentucky Tears (USA) by Cougar (Chi) (C W Fairhurst) 395 607[3] 708[1]

6 **ENCHANTED FLYER,** b g Doulab (USA) - Enchanted by Song (T W Donnelly) 3089[4] 3308[7] 4631

2 **ENCHANTEUR,** b f Damister (USA) - Brown Maid (Uru) by Admirals Launch (J Etherington) 3993[3] 4703[6]

2 **ENCORE M'LADY (Ire),** b f Dancing Dissident (USA) - Diva Encore by Star Appeal (F H Lee) 1536[2] 1846[3]

3 **ENCOREMOI (USA),** b f Assert - Encorelle (Fr) by Arctic Tern (USA) (F Boutin) 770[3] 1033[8] 3801[1] 4292[4] 4474[6]

2 **ENCORE SENOR (USA),** b c El Gran Senor (USA) - Still Waving (USA) by Star Spangled (USA) (N A Callaghan) 3990[9] 4149[7]

4 **ENCORE UNE FOIS (Ire),** b f Shirley Heights - Guest Performer by Be My Guest (USA) (M Johnston) 1041[1] 1380[5] 3434 3538[4] 3907[3] 4143 4466 4519[2] 4621[5] 4731

3 **ENDSONG (USA),** b f El Gran Senor (USA) - Mystical River (USA) by Riverman (USA) (Charles O'Brien) 2247[4] 2743[3] 3198[2] 3616[3] 3952[4] 4368

6 **FAILAND,** b m Kala Shikari - What A Mint by Meadow Mint (USA) (R Brotherton) 714 2121^5 2548 3007^1 3216

2 **FAIR AND FANCY (Fr),** b c Always Fair (USA) - Fancy Star (Fr) by Bellypha (B Hanbury) 3979^7 4229^3 4489^2

2 **FAIR COURT,** b c Shareef Dancer (USA) - Sangala (Fr) by Jim French (USA) (M R Stoute) 3836^9 4099^8 4356^7

5 **FAIR ENCHANTRESS,** b m Enchantment - Pts Fairway by Runnymede (J A Bennett) 4716a^8 1059 1487^5 1696^4 2004^4 2747^4 3340^7 3447 4592

2 **FAIREY FIREFLY,** b f Hallgate - Tremellick by Mummy's Pet (M J Camacho) 1798 4619^2

2 **FAIR FABULOUS (Fr),** b c Fabulous Dancer (USA) - Fairolan by Olantengy (E Lellouche) 3851^2 4654^4

2 **FAIRFIELD CHOICE,** b f Nomination - Beaufort Star by Great Nephew (C R Barwell) 1624^6 2030

2 **FAIRFIELD DANCER,** ch f Dominion - Young May Moon by Hopeful Venture (C R Barwell) 1877^8 2417^4

10 **FAIRFIELDS CONE,** ch m Celtic Cone - Bond's Best by Good Bond (R Dickin) 522^6 616^4 910^7

4 **FAIR FLYER (Ire),** b g Tilt Up (USA) - Fair Siobahn by Petingo (P J Bevan) 632^2 739 988 1260^3 1593^2 1764^2 1967^4 2871^2 3033^1 3282^2 3565^4 4374 4457^6

4 **FAIRFORD,** br g Forzando - Fuddled by Malacate (USA) (L J Barratt) 834 1035^4 1316 2047 2310^6 2544^8 3758

5 **FAIRGROUNDPRINCESS,** ch m Kalaglow - Hide Out by Habitat (M R Channon) 3479 3572^5 3821 4188

3 **FAIRLEAD,** b f Slip Anchor - St Isadora by Lyphard (USA) (M Bell) 4372^7

3 **FAIR SHIRLEY (Ire),** b f Shirley Heights - Fairy Dancer (USA) by Nijinsky (Can) (A C Stewart) 4525^3 4696^1

4 **FAIRSPEAR,** b g Faustus (USA) - Emma's Star by Comedy Star (USA) (J White) 5^6

2 **FAIR SWOP (Ire),** b f Cyrano de Bergerac - Eight Mile Rock by Dominion (M H Easterby) 1082^4 3711^5 3969^9 4163

3 **FAIR TO THE WIND (USA),** b f Nijinsky (Can) - Promising Times (USA) by Olden Times (M R Stoute) 780^4 1077^8 1625^9 3431^9

7 **FAIRWAYS ON TARGET,** b g Billion (USA) - Aileen's Belle by The Parson (Mrs M Reveley) 799^9 1224^5 1533^5 1772^6 2729 3056^4 3412^3

3 **FAIRY BRIDE (Ire),** b f Fairy King (USA) - Swift Linnet by Wolver Hollow (Hugh McMahon) 311 648^8 847^9 1105^9 1619^7 2248^5 2556^7 3419^5 3544^9 4689

3 **FAIRYDEL (Ire),** b c Fairy King (USA) - Bodelle by Falcon (T F Lacy) 572^7 868 1023^5 1569^9 1793^1 1995^4 2141^6 2451 3160 4136

3 **FAIRY FANTASY (Ire),** b f Fairy King (USA) - Perfect Choice by Bold Lad (Ire) (Declan Gillespie) 2406^9 2516^5 3769^9 3856^5

4 **FAIRY FREE,** b f Rousillon (USA) - Fairy Fans by Petingo (C E Brittain) 3461 3734^9 4101

5 **FAIRY GARDEN (USA),** b m Lyphard (USA) - Possible Mate (USA) by King's Bishop (USA) (R Attfield) 3890^5 4744^7

2 **FAIRY HEIGHTS (Ire),** b f Fairy King (USA) - Commanche Belle by Shirley Heights (N A Callaghan) 2364^7 2583^1 3176^1 4171^1 4547^2

3 **FAIRY LORE (Ire),** b f Fairy King (USA) - Gentle Freedom by Wolver Hollow (Charles O'Brien) 1796^1 3165^4 3916^5 4383

2 **FAIRY MUSIC (Ire),** b f Tate Gallery (USA) - Ture Rocket by Roan Rocket (Neil S McGrath) 3453^6 3729^6 4135

3 **FAIRY STORY (Ire),** ch f Persian Bold - Certain Story by Known Fact (USA) (J W Hills) 995^2 1528^1 1947^1 2212 2926 3624^7 4518

2 **FAIRY TRYST (Ire),** br c Fairy King (USA) - Intensive (USA) by Sir Wiggle (USA) (D Hanley) 3562^5

2 **FAIRY WATER,** b f Warning - Istiska (Fr) by Irish River (Fr) (Liam Browne) 4286^3 4553^6

4 **FAIRY WISHER (Ire),** b f Fairy King (USA) - Valediction by Town Crier (M F Barraclough) 456 719^9 837^6 1320^6 1537 1743 2859^8 3142^1 3479^7 3821^7 4028^4

3 **FALCARRAGH (Ire),** b g Common Grounds - Tatra by Niniski (USA) (B V Kelly) 1236^7 2185^7

7 **FALCON FLIGHT,** ch g Tampero (Fr) - Kemoening by Falcon (R Simpson) 4816a^7 103^2

6 **FALCONS DAWN,** b g Exhibitioner - African Bloom by African Sky (M G Meagher) 4689a^3 4723a^5 4732a^3 254^6 302^7 350^4 425^9 530^4 801^6 845^5 1307^7 1498 2308^8 2444^5 2889^6

2 **FALLING IN LOVE (Ire),** b f Sadler's Wells (USA) - Ivy (USA) by Sir Ivor (Michael Kauntze) 4388

4 **FALUCHO (Ire),** 3208

2 **FAMILIAR ART,** b f Faustus (USA) - Mill D'Art by Artaius (USA) (J R Fanshawe) 4227^7 4435^8

3 **FAMILY FORTUNE (Ire),** b g Prince Rupert (Fr) - Fashion Parade by Mount Hagen (Fr) (Charles O'Brien) 1510^1 2092^1

5 **FAMILY LINE,** b g High Line - Princess Dina by Huntercombe (Miss L A Perratt) 4643

4 **FAMILY ROSE,** gr g Absalom - Greenhill Lass by Upper Case (USA) (Pat Mitchell) 1320 1618^5 1874^2 2215^3 2428^4 2584^5 3020^3 4031^1

6 **FAMOUS BEAUTY,** br m Vision (USA) - Relfo by Relko (R Hollinshead) 618 727 1056^7 1929^3 2207^3 2306^3 2544^3 2871^5 3283^4 3407^1 3552^7 3814 4226^5 4319^5 4426^2 4538 4603^2 4695^5

5 **FAMOUS DANCER,** b g Top Ville - Dancing Place (Fr) by Green Dancer (USA) (Victor Bowens) 298

7 **FANATICAL (USA),** b h Lear Fan (USA) - Gal A Tic (USA) by Assagai (R J Baker) 366^6 723^6 894^4 1281^2 1702^8 2043^8 2347^4 2658^1 3066^2 3288^6 3479^9 3761 4256

6 **FANATIC BOY (Arg),** 2262^4

2 **FANCY BOOTS (Ire),** ch f Salt Dome (USA) - Jolly Widow by Busted (F Dunne) 1550^9 1650 1994^2 2319 3917^7

3 **FANFOLD (Ire),** gr f Siberian Express (USA) - Broken Melody by Busted (R Akehurst) 878^1 1528^8 2726^2 2898^2 3480^5 3547^4

4 **FANGIO,** b g Nordance (USA) - Verily Jane by Royben (W G M Turner) 3410^8 3511^2 3849 4112^5

5 **FANLIGHT,** b h Beldale Flutter (USA) - Carib Flash by Mill Reef (USA) (A Moore) 2007

5 **FANMORE (USA),** b g Lear Fan (USA) - Lady Blackfoot by Prince Tenderfoot (USA) (A Fabre) 2298^1 4295^2 4747^2

4 **FANTANTE (Ire),** b g Taufan (USA) - La Tante by Bold Lad (Ire) (C Collins) 310^4 599 868 1251^6 2323^7 2511^1 3244^4 3330

3 **FANTASTIC DREAM (Ire),** b c Dreams To Reality (USA) - Khloud by Pitskelly (E Lellouche) 266^1 536^5 954^5 1546^6 4219^9

5 **FANTOMAS (Ger),** b h Ahonoora - Flunkerei by Luciano 3023^2 3717 4304

4 **FARAGHAN (Ire),** b g Darshaan - Fair Fight by Fine Blade (USA) (Noel Meade) 2461

3 **FARAGINGO,** b g Farajullah - Ming Ho Gold by Homing (M R Leach) 4125^9

3 **FARANDOLE,** b g Shareef Dancer (USA) - Greenhill Lass by Upper Case (USA) (A A Hambly) 423 686^9 3817^9 3945 4599

2 **FARAS ELNAAS,** b c Mtoto - Summer Impressions (USA) by Lyphard (USA) (C F Wall) 3130 3979^6 4237^2

7 **FAR DARA,** ch m Pharly (Fr) - Sardara by Alcide (N Bycroft) 25 175

6 **FARFELU,** b h Lyphard's Special (USA) - Spring Azure by Mountain Call (W R Muir) 722^5 1449^8 2062^3 2628^7 3105^3 3511^5 4040

3 **FARMAAN (Ire),** b c Shareef Dancer (USA) - Fair Fight by Fine Blade (USA) (John M Oxx) 257^1 306^2 576^6 1514^3

11 **FARMER JOCK,** ch h Crofter (USA) - Some Dame by Will Somers (Mrs N Macauley) 1096 1282^2 1560^6 1728^2 1914^3 2225^3 2723^1 2910^8 3229^7 3481^9 3707^5 4224 4762^8

9 **FARMER'S CROSS,** br g Derring Rose - Kylogue Daisy by Little Buskins (P Beaumont) 1467

4 **FARMER'S PET,** ch f Sharrood (USA) - Rectitude by Runnymede (G A Pritchard-Gordon) 527 967^6 1380^9 1929^1 2337^4 2729^1 3252^1 3666^7

2 **FAR MIST (Fr),** b f River Mist (USA) - Sandie Far (Fr) by Faraway Son (USA) (F Flachi) 2647^3 3515^8 3651^1

6 **FARM STREET,** b g Henbit (USA) - Mill Hill (USA) by Riva Ridge (USA) (C D Broad) 19^2 176^1 227 327

3 **FIELD OF VISION (Ire),** b g Vision (USA) - Bold Meadows by Persian Bold (M Johnston) 1058^{1} 1408^{4} 1697^{2} 1833^{1} 2212^{1} 2363 2479^{2} 2928^{2} 3017^{2} 3637^{5} 3885^{4} 3996^{3} 4424^{6} 4606^{5} 4667^{2}

4 **FIELDRIDGE,** ch g Rousillon (USA) - Final Thought by Final Straw (C P E Brooks) 663 1093^{2} 1450^{1} 2239 3067^{7}

5 **FIERCE,** ch g Carwhite - Nosey by Nebbiolo (J R Jenkins) 994^{5} 1173

4 **FIGHTER SQUADRON,** ch g Primo Dominie - Formidable Dancer by Formidable (USA) (J A Glover) 4743a^{6} 4768a 796^{5} 1081^{8} 1177^{5} 1382^{1} 1658^{6} 2060 2969^{4} 3127^{6} 3177 3638 4038 4490 4667^{4}

3 **FIGHTING JET (USA),** 2999^{5}

2 **FIGHTING SPIRIT,** ch c Adbass (USA) - Broadway Stomp (USA) by Broadway Forli (USA) (A P Jarvis) 1666 4099

4 **FIGHTING TALK (USA),** b g Fighting Fit (USA) - Nanna's Joy (USA) by Tentam (USA) (A L T Moore) 3295^{6}

4 **FIGHTING TEMERAIRE (Ire),** b c Tate Gallery (USA) - Maid Of Erin (USA) by Irish River (Fr) (P F I Cole) 1011^{6}

5 **FIGHT TO WIN (USA),** b g Fit To Fight (USA) - Spark Of Life (USA) by Key To The Mint (USA) (R J Manning) 924

2 **FILCH,** ch f Precocious - Pilfer by Vaigly Great (Mrs L Piggott) 1933^{8} 2533^{3} 2718 3210^{8}

2 **FILHA DO AR (USA),** b f Trempolino (USA) - Buckeye Gal by Good Counsel (C Lerner) 2144^{5} 3014^{6} 4195^{3} 4567^{6}

7 **FILICAIA,** ro m Sallust - Fine Flame by Le Prince (Don Enrico Incisa) 800 1287 1537 2230^{8} 2434 2553^{7} 2707^{7} 3747

3 **FILL,** ch f Soviet Star (USA) - Aldhabyih by General Assembly (USA) (A C Stewart) 3178^{6} 3789^{9}

9 **FILL MY GLASS,** b h Try My Best (USA) - Wineglass by Wolver Hollow (Wilbert Tolerton) 868^{6} 1385^{3} 1923 2511^{2} 3330 4389^{6}

7 **FILM LIGHTING GIRL,** ch m Persian Bold - Mey by Canisbay (J L Harris) 3552^{9}

3 **FILOU FILANT (Fr),** b g In Fijar (USA) - First Appeal by Star Appeal (J R Jenkins) 975^{5} 1175^{4} 2499^{6} 2898^{7} 3249^{3} 3384^{7} 3744^{7}

3 **FINAL ACTION,** ch f Nicholas Bill - Strathclair by Klairon (G C Bravery) 4631

2 **FINAL EXHIBIT (Ire),** ch f Exhibitioner - Stativa by Don (J S Bolger) 3039^{9} 3243^{6} 3954 4624^{5}

4 **FINAL FAVOUR (Ire),** b g Drumalis - Please Oblige by Le Levanstell (Daniel J Murphy) 298^{4} 852

3 **FINAL FRONTIER (Ire),** b g Common Grounds - Last Gunboat by Dominion (R Akehurst) 444^{2} 836^{1} 1058^{4} 1408^{3} 1859^{4} 3070^{5} 3863^{1} 4514^{9}

3 **FINAL OAK,** b f Nicholas Bill - Final Rush by Final Straw (B A McMahon) 428 614^{6} 899 1740^{5} 2425^{3} 2824^{3} 3311 4333

2 **FINAL OPERA (Ire),** ch f Bold Arrangement - Opera Star (Fr) by Appiani II (J R Cox) 1650^{7} 1994^{9} 2450^{7}

2 **FINAL REMINDER (Ire),** ch c Don't Forget Me - Pleasant Review (USA) by The Minstrel (Can) (J G Burns) 2778^{8} 3731

8 **FINDER'S CHOICE (USA),** b or br h Buckfinder (USA) - Trail Landing (USA) by Solo Landing (C Hadry) 2084^{3}

3 **FINDON ACADEMY (Ire),** ch g Glenstal (USA) - Rashana by Sharpen Up (G L Moore) 951^{6} 1060^{9} 1911^{9} 3168 3766^{8} 3938^{6}

2 **FINGER OF LIGHT,** b f Green Desert (USA) - Circus Ring by High Top (M R Stoute) 4303^{1}

3 **FINIR EN BEAUTE (Fr),** b f Groom Dancer (USA) - The Bean Sidhe by Corvaro (A Fabre) 561^{4} 1290^{2}

2 **FINISHING KIND,** b f Kind Of Hush - Print Finisher by Mandrake Major (Bob Jones) 1253^{6} 1774^{5} 2588^{5} 2973^{7} 3303^{9} 3829

6 **FINJAN,** b g Thatching - Capriconia by Try My Best (USA) (A G Foster) 750^{8} 891^{5} 1348^{7} 1680 1835^{9} 2106^{3} 2172^{6} 2975^{1} 3034^{4} 3504 4168 4331^{1} 4501 4681

2 **FIONN DE COOL (Ire),** b c Mazaad - Pink Fondant by Northfields (USA) (J S Bolger) 820^{4} 1567^{3} 1824^{8} 3911^{8} 4285 4369^{3} 4462 4637^{3}

3 **FIR COPSE,** b f Aragon - New Pastures by Formidable (USA) (D R Laing) 927 1487

5 **FIREBIRD LAD,** ch g Electric - Arbatina by Sallust (R Curtis) 4279

3 **FIRE CARPET (USA),** b c Blushing Groom (Fr) - Mystical Mood (USA) by Roberto (USA) (J H M Gosden) 4030^{4} 4372^{6} 4565^{7} 4696^{2}

4 **FIREFIGHTER,** ch c Sharpo - Courtesy Call by Northfields (USA) (B P J Baugh) 4662a

2 **FIRE MUSIC,** ch c Squill (USA) - Misfire by Gunner B (K R Burke) 586^{7} 3362

4 **FIRING LINE (Ire),** b or br c Slip Anchor - Red Partridge by Solinus (L Brogi) 1323^{6}

3 **FIRM BUT FAIR,** b c Shirley Heights - Free Guest by Be My Guest (USA) (L M Cumani) 515^{6} 791^{4} 4493^{4} 4696^{6}

3 **FIRM FRIEND (Ire),** ch f Affirmed (USA) - Chere Amie (Fr) by Gay Mecene (USA) (A Renzoni) 694^{2} 1086^{7} 3920^{6} 4199^{6}

3 **FIRM PLEDGE (USA),** b c Affirmed (USA) - Rutledge Place (USA) by Caro (P F I Cole) 580^{6} 746^{1} 954 1347^{5} 1765

4 **FIRST AMENDMENT (Fr),** 1908^{7}

6 **FIRST BID,** ch h Crofthall - Redgrave Design by Nebbiolo (R M Whitaker) 384^{2} 645^{2} 831^{3} 988^{2} 1143 1439^{3} 3003^{4} 3240^{2} 3503^{1} 3724^{2} 3881^{1} 4037^{4} 4283^{6} 4731

4 **FIRST CENTURY (Ire),** b g Petorius - Parima by Pardao (B J Llewellyn) 4172

4 **FIRST FLING (Ire),** b f Last Tycoon - Flamme D'Amour by Gift Card (Fr) (Dr J D Scargill) 4679a^{4} 4793a^{3} 8^{3} 61^{7} 126^{4} 495 2585^{1} 2827^{4} 3320^{2} 3761^{3} 4035^{5} 4357^{8}

4 **FIRST GOLD,** gr g Absalom - Cindys Gold by Sonnen Gold (J Wharton) 292 677 814^{4} 1081^{4} 1563^{6} 3425 3687^{5} 3946^{8}

4 **FIRST HEIRESS (Ire),** b f Last Tycoon - Age Of Elegance by Troy (Lady Herries) 498

6 **FIRST HOME,** b g Homing - Mill Wind by Blakeney (Pat Mitchell) 238^{6} 2747 2921^{5}

3 **FIRST OPTION,** ch g Primo Dominie - Merrywren by Julio Mariner (M H Easterby) 716 1083^{2} 1187^{2} 1478^{2} 1801^{4} 2214^{3} 3095^{1} 3343^{3} 3687^{1} 3955^{9} 4277^{6} 4734^{7}

3 **FIRST PLAY,** b f Primo Dominie - School Concert by Music Boy (J Berry) 1396^{1} 1801^{6} 2132^{6} 3603

2 **FIRST SHOT,** b c Emarati (USA) - First Time Over by Derrylin (P R Hedger) 1119 1640^{8} 2610^{3}

2 **FIRST TRUMP,** ch c Primo Dominie - Valika by Valiyar (G Wragg) 1456^{1} 1920^{1} 2335^{1} 2906^{1} 4062^{3} 4273^{1}

3 **FIRST VEIL,** b f Primo Dominie - Valika by Valiyar (D R C Elsworth) 2202^{1} 2572^{5} 3227^{3} 4040

4 **FISIO SANDS,** b f Efisio - Sayida-Shahira by Record Run (F J O'Mahony) 672 4441 4499^{8} 4727^{9}

5 **FIT THE BILL,** b g Nicholas Bill - Golden Windlass by Princely Gift (C Tinkler) 4810a^{8} 20^{5} 78^{5}

3 **FIT TO LEAD (USA),** b or br f Fit To Fight (USA) - Islands by Forli (R Mandella) 4792a^{7} 2441^{2}

3 **FITZCARRALDO (USA),** ch c Riverman (USA) - Quest (USA) by The Minstrel (Can) (L M Cumani) 658^{4} 1047^{4} 1347^{4} 1952^{4} 2579^{4} 2985^{4} 3468^{7} 3800^{8} 4132^{2}

2 **FITZROVIAN (Ire),** b c Miller's Mate - Nuravia by Nureyev (USA) (D R Loder) 2756^{3}

3 **FITZROY LAD,** b g Grey Desire - My-Elane by Welsh Saint (M R Channon) 519^{4} 719 836 966 4256

2 **FIVE AND UP FIVE,** b f Reprimand - Five Farthings by Busted (Mrs M Reveley) 3627^{9} 4342

3 **FIVE CLUBS (Ire),** ch f King Of Clubs - Tristan Du Cunha (USA) by Sir Ivor (D T Thom) 4745a^{6}

3 **FIVE ISLANDS,** b f Bairn (USA) - Melody Park by Music Boy (Mrs N Macauley) 716 1010^{8} 1233^{3} 3046^{4} 3948

3 **FIVE LITTLE GIRLS (Ire),** ch f Knesset (USA) - Wall Street Blues by Ahonoora (J F Bailey Jun) 1105^{3} 1333 1649^{9} 1795 2295^{3} 2511^{9} 3395 3606^{6} 4389^{5} 4635^{8} 4685

3 **FIVEOFIVE (Ire),** b f Fairy King (USA) - North Hut by Northfields (USA) (N A Callaghan) 881^{6} 1058^{5} 1257^{1} 1524 2023^{9} 3068^{5} 3447^{9} 3591 4131^{8}

3 **FOLLY VISION (Ire),** b f Vision (USA) - Folle Remont by Prince Tenderfoot (USA) (B J Meehan) 313^{6} 418^{8} 563^{2} 871^{5} 1341^{6} 2967^{6} 3942 4133

3 **FONDLY REMEMBERED (USA),** 2441^{9}

5 **FONTANAYS (Ire),** b g Wassl - Mombones by Lord Gayle (USA) (B V Kelly) $4686a^{3}$ 487^{1} 598^{1} 912^{3} 2842^{1} 3275^{2} 3560^{4} 3854^{3} 4185^{4} 4555^{5} 4639^{4} 4737

2 **FOOD BROKER FELLA (Ire),** b c Simply Great (Fr) - Social Butterfly (USA) by Sir Ivor (R Akehurst) 4339^{8} 4587^{7}

5 **FOOD OF LOVE,** ch m Music Boy - Shortbread by Crisp And Even (J Wharton) 1835^{7} 2255^{8} 2392 2829^{5} 3085^{1} 3348^{9} 3571^{5} 3638^{8} 3877^{7}

2 **FOOLISH FLIGHT (Ire),** ch f Fools Holme (USA) - Black Crow by Sea Hawk II (C Collins) 2880^{6} 3527^{7} 4059^{5} 4551

3 **FOOLISH HEART (Ire),** ch f Fools Holme (USA) - Honorine (USA) by Blushing Groom (Fr) (N A Graham) 694 3934^{6} 4571^{3}

11 **FOOLISH TOUCH,** b g Hot Spark - Nushka by Tom Fool (W J Musson) 391^{8} 565 676 990^{4} 1453^{9} 1743^{6} 2300 2920^{9} 3124^{5} 4574 4658^{6}

3 **FOOLS ERRAND (Ire),** b g Fools Holme (USA) - Zalazula by Lord Gayle (USA) (R Hannon) 1469^{7} 1661^{5} 1946^{2} 2135^{2} 2991^{3} 3344^{2} 3706^{2} 4006^{3} 4267^{2} 4445^{7} 4695^{6}

2 **FOOLS TREASURE (Ire),** ch f Fools Holme (USA) - Gender Gap (USA) by Shecky Greene (USA) (P J McBride) 4651

3 **FOOT-BEAT,** ch f Infantry - Milford Moss by Record Token (H Candy) 2410^{5}

2 **FOOTING (USA),** b or br f Forty-Niner (USA) - Footy (USA) by Topsider (USA) (W Mott) 3700^{4} 4449^{3}

2 **FOOTSTEPS (Ire),** br f Broken Hearted - Remoosh by Glint Of Gold (P F I Cole) 657^{8} 1009^{2} 1418^{3} 2492^{1} 3129^{1} 3351^{6} 3966^{7}

2 **FOOT TAPPER (Ire),** b g Hotfoot - Silver Stone by Derrylin (D W P Arbuthnot) 3287 3658^{7} 4033^{9} 4531

2 **FORBIDDEN MONKEY,** br f Gabitat - State Romance by Free State (J Berry) 1739^{4} 2103^{2} 2271^{3} 2946^{7}

6 **FORCE SEVEN,** b m Strong Gale - Dorcetta by Condorcet (Fr) (P Mullins) 309^{3} 961^{1} 4625^{1} 4737^{9}

3 **FORDALLIA,** ch f Stanford - Alligata by Vilgora (J Hetherton) 1396^{8} 1577^{7} 1762^{7} 2699^{7} 4123 4277

2 **FOREMMA,** b f Formidable (USA) - Great Dilemma by Vaigly Great (M R Channon) 715

2 **FORENSIC EVIDENCE (Ire),** b c Danehill (USA) - Daring Grey by Bold Lad (Ire) (G C Bravery) 4067^{8} 4480^{5} 4701^{3}

3 **FORENZA,** ch f Formidable (USA) - Rexana by Relko (Mrs J R Ramsden) 2064 2307^{6}

3 **FORESEE,** b c Vision (USA) - Sovereign Dona by Sovereign Path (John M Oxx) 941^{3} 1751^{4} 2076^{3} 3403^{2} 4055^{3} 4381^{1}

3 **FORESHORE (Ire),** b f Don't Forget Me - Krismas River by Kris (A C Stewart) 4565^{3} 4645^{4}

3 **FOREST,** br g Forzando - Tomard by Thatching (T Stack) 486 868^{2} 1570^{9} 1619^{1} 1825^{1} 2248 2463^{9} 2675^{5}

2 **FORESTA VERDE (USA),** ch f Green Forest (USA) - Diffusion (Fr) by Habitat (C B B Booth) 4663^{5} 4758

4 **FOREST CONCERT (Ire),** ch f Thatching - Sense Of Rhythm by Cure The Blues (USA) (Patrick Prendergast) 308 787^{4} 4245^{5} 4583^{2} 4689^{6} 4736^{5}

3 **FOREST FLYER,** ch f Indian Forest (USA) - Fine A Leau (USA) by Youth (USA) (M W Eckley) 196^{3} 214^{9} 361^{7} 634

2 **FOREST GAZELLE (USA),** ch c Green Forest (USA) - Nimble Feet (USA) by Danzig (USA) (R Charlton) 2994^{1} 3596^{1} 4062^{5}

2 **FOREST LOCH,** ch f Lomond (USA) - Arbour (USA) by Graustark (G A Pritchard-Gordon) 1403 1660^{5} 2331^{5} 3546^{8} 4483^{6}

2 **FOREST SILK,** b f Elegant Air - Little Bittern (USA) by Riva Ridge (USA) (R M Whitaker) 4682^{8}

3 **FOREST SONG,** b f Forzando - Persian Air by Persian Bold (R Charlton) $4695a^{5}$ $4724a^{6}$

4 **FOREST STAR (USA),** b c Green Forest (USA) - Al Madina (USA) by Round Table (Miss Gay Kelleway) 1816^{7} 2235^{7} 2470^{3} 2815^{2} 3102^{1} 3308

2 **FOREVER BLUSHING,** b f Blushing Scribe (USA) - Rheinza by Rheingold (P Butler) 337^{6} 625^{6} 949^{5} 1254^{4} 1624^{7} 1909^{2} 2271 3390^{1} 3546^{5} 4128^{6} 4646^{9}

6 **FOREVER DIAMONDS,** ch g Good Times (Ity) - Mel Mira by Roi Soleil (M H Easterby) 592^{4} 676^{4} 801^{1} 1079^{2} 1298^{5} 1530^{2} 1768^{8} 2391^{1} 2926 3680^{7} 3901^{4}

3 **FOREVER SHINEING,** b f Glint Of Gold - Patosky by Skymaster (R J R Williams) 422^{1} 584^{6} 2272^{6} 2758 2963^{9} 3252^{5} 3392^{4} 3759^{6} 3962^{7} 4091^{6}

5 **FORGE,** ch g Formidable (USA) - Red Shoes by Dance In Time (Can) (K O Cunningham-Brown) 626^{5} 924^{9}

6 **FORGE BAY,** b g Buzzards Bay - Korresia by Derring-Do (H J Collingridge) 4328^{3}

3 **FORGE GOLD,** b g Buzzards Bay - Korresia by Derring-Do (H J Collingridge) 1746 2529^{7} 2914^{6}

4 **FORGETFUL,** br f Don't Forget Me - Peak Squaw (USA) by Icecapade (USA) (D Burchell) 2822^{2} 4713

3 **FOR GOLD,** b f Tina's Pet - Golden Decoy by Decoy Boy (Mrs M Reveley) 3180 3744

2 **FORGOTTEN DANCER (Ire),** ch c Don't Forget Me - Dancing Diana by Raga Navarro (Ity) (R Hannon) 1706^{7} 3422^{5} 3982^{2} 4339^{1} 4511^{3}

2 **FORGOTTEN LADY (Ire),** ch f Don't Forget Me - Lady Vivienne by Golden Fleece (USA) (P F I Cole) 715^{7} 4349^{1} 4577

3 **FORMAESTRE (Ire),** b f Formidable (USA) - Maestrette by Manado (G L Humphrey) 228^{6} 362^{9} 410^{1} 612^{4} 883^{8} 1101^{2} 1358^{3} 1562^{5} 1943^{3} 2371^{3} 2550^{4} 3324^{4} 3788^{6} 4104 4574^{2}

3 **FORMAL AFFAIR,** b f Rousillon (USA) - Muznah by Royal And Regal (USA) (C A Cyzer) 514^{9} 1058^{8} 1313^{5} 1771^{3} 2523^{7} 2726^{1} 2898^{1} 3460^{3} 3669^{6} 4354^{7} 4481^{4}

3 **FORMATO UNI (Ire),** b c Mtoto - Martinova by Martinmas (J L Dunlop) 679^{3} 903^{3} 1178^{3} 4203^{1} 4475 4653

2 **FORMIDABLE LASS,** ch f Formidable (USA) - Stock Hill Lass by Air Trooper (L G Cottrell) 325^{5} 2030

3 **FORMIDABLE LIZ,** ch f Formidable (USA) - Areej by Rusticaro (Fr) (M D Hammond) 907 1160^{4} 1273^{2} 1419^{4} 1760^{1} 1938^{4} 2309^{1} 2861^{3} 2919^{2} 3504 3747

2 **FORNIDO,** ch c Forzando - Minne Love by Homeric (C Collins) 4535

4 **FOR REG (Ire),** b g Theatrical - Swalthee (Fr) by Sword Dancer (USA) (Patrick Joseph Flynn) 308 3852^{5} 4260^{2} 4430^{1} 4573^{2} 4737

2 **FORREST MASTER (Ire),** b g Runnett - Fine Form (USA) by Fachendon (Miss L A Perratt) 865^{5} 1051^{3} 1598^{5} 1889^{8} 3281^{9} 3600^{9} 4042^{7}

3 **FORTENSKY (USA),** b c Blushing Groom (Fr) - Casey by Caerleon (USA) (L M Cumani) 684 3314 3783 4533

2 **FORT ERIE,** gr c Lochnager - Olibanum by Frankincense (J F Bottomley) 1561^{2} 1814^{1}

3 **FOR THE PRESENT,** b g Then Again - Axe Valley by Royben (T D Barron) 683^{5} 1273^{1} 1718^{7} 1801^{1} 2600^{2} 3504^{5} 3906 4038

4 **FORT HOPE,** gr g Belfort (Fr) - Hopeful Katie by Full Of Hope (T J Naughton) 4752a $4779a^{8}$

3 **FORTHWITH,** b f Midyan (USA) - Top Society by High Top (J W Hills) 915^{6} 1524^{2} 1839^{2} 2333 2997^{1} 3674^{2} 3963^{1} 4199^{3} 4655

3 **FORTIS PAVIOR (Ire),** b g Salt Dome (USA) - Heather Lil by Ballymore (R M Whitaker) 1396^{6} 1577^{2} 1760^{6} 1937^{1} 2280^{5} 2765^{2} 3180^{2} 3535^{9} 3946^{1} 4156 4580^{7} 4721

2 **FORT KNOX (Ire),** b g Treasure Kay - Single Viking by Viking (USA) (R W Armstrong) 3958^{4} 4229^{5} 4665^{2}

3 **FORTROSE (USA),** ch f Forty Niner (USA) - Danseur Fabuleux (USA) by Northern Dancer (F Boutin) 1290^{4} 1753^{2}

3 **FORTUNATE FAITH (USA),** 2802^{4} 3767^{7}

5 **FORTUNE'S GIRL,** b m Ardross - Heaven High by High Line (M D Hammond) 3684^{3} 3854^{1}

4 **FORTUNE STAR (Ire),** b c Glow (USA) - Lucky For Me by Appiani II (J J Bridger) 2422^{9} 2789 2992 3221^{4} 3509^{8} 3689 4028 4268^{7}

3 **FORT VALLY,** gr f Belfort (Fr) - Hivally by High Line (B W Murray) 644^{5} 963^{8} 1852^{2} 2597^{8} 2978^{8} 3631^{6} 4458^{5} 4694

4 **FROMTHEGETGO (Ire),** ro g Salmon Leap (USA) - Stapara by Mill Reef (USA) (B S Rothwell) 852 3398^7

2 **FROM THE LEFT (Ire),** br c Ela-Mana-Mou - Autumn Tint (USA) by Roberto (USA) (M Johnston) 4192^5 4316^4

3 **FRONTIER FLIGHT (USA),** b c Flying Paster (USA) - Sly Charmer (USA) by Valdez (USA) (R Charlton) 2116^4 2941^8 3314^9 4101 4335^4

6 **FRONT PAGE,** ch h Adonijah - Recent Events by Stanford (J Akehurst) 387

3 **FROSTY MORNING,** b f Be My Guest (USA) - Romantic Age by Mill Reef (USA) (C E Brittain) 999^5 1931^4 2697^4 3247^3 3766^7 4597^5

10 **FROZEN FRIEND,** br g Scorpio (Fr) - Run Wardasha by Run The Gantlet (USA) (M J Corbett) 2094

4 **FRUITFUL AFFAIR (Ire),** b f Taufan (USA) - Lucky Engagement (USA) by What Luck (USA) (T Thomson Jones) 978 1384^5

2 **FRUSTRATED POET (USA),** b c Meadowlake (USA) - Queen Arete (USA) by Riva Ridge (USA) (J Etherington) 3779^9 4179^3 4512^9 4674

2 **FRUSTRATION,** b f Salse (USA) - Baffle by Petingo (Lady Herries) 4003^6 4539^9

3 **FUCHU,** ch f Jupiter Island - Dalchroy by Hotfoot (C E Brittain) 1616^6 2202 2563 2749^1 2912^5 3634^1 3988^5 4394

3 **FULL FEATHER (USA),** ch g Storm Bird (Can) - Carolina Moon (USA) by Grey Dawn II (J H M Gosden) 538 951^1 1412^6 3837 4221^2

2 **FULL OF SPARKLE (Ire),** ch f Persian Heights - Diamond Shine by Kings Lake (USA) (Michael Kauntze) 4406

8 **FULL QUIVER,** br g Gorytus (USA) - Much Pleasure by Morston (Fr) (Mrs Barbara Waring) 495^6 879^4 994 1414^7 1712^3 2101^1 2669^4 2942^4 3388^2

4 **FULL SHILLING (USA),** b c Sovereign Dancer (USA) - Full Virtue (USA) by Full Out (USA) (K R Burke) 1007^9 1409 1743 1961 2226^5 2849^2 3102

4 **FULL SIGHT (Ire),** b g Vision (USA) - Peaches And Cream (Fr) by Rusticaro (Fr) (I Campbell) 975 1075

2 **FUMO DI LONDRA (Ire),** ch c Indian Ridge - Fettle by Relkino (J L Dunlop) 1886^1 2260^2 2906^3 3753^2 4249^1 4572^6

5 **FUNAMBULE (Ire),** ch h Be My Guest (USA) - Flushing Meadow by Raise A Native (K Schafflutzel) 2083^4

4 **FUNDEGHE (USA),** b g Rainbow Quest (USA) - Les Biches (Can) by Northern Dancer (J E Banks) 4780a^4 4814a^6 49^8

2 **FUN'N'FORTUNE,** b f Nomination - More Fun by Malicious (M Brittain) 1561^8

5 **FUNNY BABY (Fr),** b h Baby Turk - Funny Reef by Mill Reef (Mme M Bollack-Badel) 283^3 407 692^2 1411^1 1971^5 2437^3 2979^8 4219^4 4557^3 4653^3

3 **FUNNY CHOICE (Ire),** b f Commanche Run - Best Of Fun by Blakeney (P Monteith) 1283^1 1847^1 2599^1

3 **FUNNY HILARIOUS (USA),** ch f Sir Ivor - Polestar by Northfields (USA) (J R Fanshawe) 1344^8 2563^5 3431^4 3759^3 4129^3 4432^2 4621^8

3 **FUNNY ROSE,** b f Belfort (Fr) - Scottish Rose by Warpath (P Monteith) 2550^7

5 **FURIELLA,** ch m Formidable (USA) - Palmella (USA) by Grundy (P C Haslam) 4681a^6

3 **FURIETTO (Ire),** b g Lafontaine (USA) - Sesetta by Lucky Brief (Capt D G Swan) 4137^4 4368^3

4 **FURIOUSLY (USA),** b or br c Danzig - Whirl Series by Roberto (C R McGaughey III) 4071^5

7 **FURTHER FLIGHT,** gr g Pharly (Fr) - Flying Nelly by Nelcius (B W Hills) 892^4 1405^7 1787^8 3405^1 3861^2 4301^1 4569^8

4 **FURTHER NOTICE (Ire),** gr g Standaan (Fr) - Raffaela (Ger) by Neckar (V T O'Brien) 1621^2 2556 3277^7

2 **FUSSY HEN,** b f Risk Me (Fr) - Chapel Cottage by Homing (M W Easterby) 1672^3

2 **FUSSY SIOUX,** ch f Indian Ridge - Spring Water (USA) by Effervescing (USA) (M W Easterby) 812^6 1082^5 3215^9 3432 3755

3 **FUTURBALLA,** b c Taufan (USA) - Raja Moulana by Raja Baba (USA) (J L Dunlop) 4703a 1887 3151^2

4 **FUTURE FAME (USA),** b c Stately Don (USA) - Hooplah (USA) by Hillary (USA) (Mrs S M Austin) 284^7 531^2 714 964^7 1421^5 1866

2 **FUTURE OPTIONS,** ch f Lomond (USA) - Hemline by Sharpo (J W Hills) 4575^5

2 **FUTURE PLAN (Ire),** b f Common Grounds - Future Shock by Full Out (USA) (F Dunne) 3954^9

3 **FUTURE PRETENSE (USA),** b f Fappiano (USA) - Pretty Pretender by Quack (J Pierce) 570^4 2440^2 3767^4 4472^5

4 **FUTURES GIFT (Ire),** b g Try My Best (USA) - Plum Cordial (USA) by Proudest Roman (USA) (A W Potts) 92^4 120^9 531^8 861

3 **FUTURE STORM (USA),** ch f Storm Cat (USA) - Sea Sands by Sea-Bird II (A Renzoni) 4704a^8 3823^2 4291^6

5 **FUTURIST (USA),** 3187^5

4 **FYLDE FLYER,** ch c Music Boy - Djimbaran Bay by Le Levanstell (J Berry) 316^8 511^5 587^1 986 1205^4 1786^9 2362^6 3427^2 3936^5 4040 4373^7 4464 4729

3 **GABHADERA,** ch f Gabitat - Hadera by Northfields (USA) (B Gubby) 821 1008^9

3 **GABR,** b c Green Desert (USA) - Ardassine by Ahonoora (R W Armstrong) 2572^2 2985^1 3315^4 3622^5 3886^3 4282^1 4441^7

2 **GADGE,** br g Nomination - Queenstyle by Moorestyle (J Sutcliffe) 3642^9 3958^3 4127^4 4416^1 4561

2 **GAELIC HEATHER (Ire),** b f Cyrano de Bergerac - Dancing Heather by Gay Fandango (USA) (D P Kelly) 896 1442

6 **GAELIC MYTH (USA),** b g Nijinsky (Can) - Irish Valley (USA) by Irish River (Fr) (T Stack) 670^5

2 **GAELIC RISK,** b c Risk Me (Fr) - Protected (Fr) by Blakeney (Pat Mitchell) 1877

2 **GAELIC STAR (Ire),** b c Gallic League - Derring Dee by Derrylin (R Hollinshead) 395^2 454^4 776^8 1561^3 2500^6 3086^3 3279^4 3598^4 4105^4 4264^7 4708

5 **GAILY DANCE,** b m Monsanto (Fr) - Step You Gaily by King's Company (J Hetherton) 1600^5 2427^7

2 **GAINSBOROUGH'S BOY (Ire),** b c Tate Gallery (USA) - Pallas's Blue by Pitskelly (John M Oxx) 2037 2402^2 2778^2 3064^1 3335^8

3 **GAIRSIC (Fr),** (Mme M Bollack-Badel) 1545^7 1722 2409 2981

3 **GALACTIC FURY,** ch g Celestial Storm (USA) - Mother Brown by Candy Cane (B Stevens) 1266^4 1491^5 1819^2 2124 4256

4 **GALAVOTTI (Ire),** b g Vision (USA) - Fauchee by Busted (J S Bolger) 309 851^2

2 **GALAXY RAIN,** ch c Smackover - Little Tich by Great Nephew (B A McMahon) 2818^7

3 **GALEJADE,** b f Sharrood (USA) - Sans Blague (USA) by The Minstrel (Can) (D Haydn Jones) 707^5 1690^5 2228^5 3049^5 3232^1 3518^7 3873^7 4036

11 **GALLANT HOPE,** ch g Ahonoora - Amiga Mia by Be Friendly (L G Cottrell) 948 1096 1473^5 1914^7 2327 2549^6 3292^9 3425 3707^6

4 **GALLANT JACK (Ire),** b g Flash Of Steel - Milveagh by Milesian (D Haydn Jones) 1307 1626 2920^5 3325^1 4710^9

2 **GALLANT SPIRIT (Ire),** br c Gallic League - So Valiant by So Blessed (R Hannon) 2909^6 3746^4 4067 4594 4752^1

4 **GALLARDINI (Ire),** b c Nordico (USA) - Sweet by Pitkelly (J S Bolger) 787 1199^8 2608^6 2878 2957^7 3494 3615^6 3770^7 3924^5 4284^9 4384^7 4555^6

5 **GALLERY ARTIST (Ire),** ch h Tate Gallery (USA) - Avec L'amour by Realm (R Guest) 376^2 610^1 828^7 2639^3 4333 4592^6

4 **GALLERY OF ZURICH (Ire),** b c Tate Gallery (USA) - Dear Lorraine (Fr) by Nonoalco (USA) (Kevin Prendergast) 3703

3 **GALLETINA (Ire),** gr f Persian Heights - Grafton Street (Ger) by Pentathlon (D Hanley) 4410^6

4 **GALLEY GOSSIP,** b g Dunbeath (USA) - Mother Brown by Candy Cane (R Brotherton) 4739a 77^8

2 **GALLIC FLAIR (Ire),** b or br c Gallic League - Serriyya by Tap On Wood (J C Hayden) 1197^7

2 **GALLIC GENT,** b g Gallic League - Gentalyn by Henbit (USA) (C Tinkler) 395^3 968 1561 1798 2772 3792

3 **GLEN ECHO (Ire),** b c Taufan (USA) - Addabub by Manado (G Harwood) 538[8] 825[4] 1375[1] 1785 3623[5]
5 **GLENFIELD GRETA,** ch m Gabitat - Glenfield Portion by Mummy's Pet (P S Felgate) 636 1194[4] 1981[6] 2193[4] 2426[3] 2590[1] 2919[3] 3190[3] 3365[7] 3774 3988[3] 4224
3 **GLENGARRY BONNET (Ire),** ch f Hateem (USA) - Fiodoir by Weavers' Hall (James O'Haire) 2449[3] 2781
6 **GLEN KATE,** b m Glenstal (USA) - Miss Kate (Fr) by Nonoalco (USA) (W Shoemaker) 595[1]
5 **GLENLIVET (Swe),** ch g Grant's - Skyline by Jimmy Reppin (L Kelp) 3936[3] 4304[7] 4401[3]
2 **GLENLYON DUCHESS,** b f Risk Me (Fr) - Ma Famille by Welsh Saint (Miss L A Perratt) 2278[8] 2554 3598[6] 4082[2] 4215[2] 4365[2] 4531
3 **GLEN MILLER,** b c Music Boy - Blakeney Sound by Blakeney (J W Payne) 444[4] 683 1697[9] 1991[5] 2421 2710[1] 2944[7] 3213[1] 4348[3] 4616
7 **GLENSCAR,** gr g Glenstal (USA) - Caranina (USA) by Caro (J L Spearing) 1316[3] 1743
3 **GLENSTAL FLAGSHIP (Ire),** b g Glenstal (USA) - Fourth Degree by Oats (A P O'Brien) 2956[5] 3526[7] 4118[4] 4162[4] 4410[2] 4690[3]
6 **GLENSTAL PRIORY,** b m Glenstal (USA) - Jumbolia by Wolver Hollow (S B Avery) 4688a[5]
2 **GLENUGIE,** b g Insan (USA) - Excavator Lady by Most Secret (R M Whitaker) 3432 3746[6] 4050[2] 4375[4] 4437[4]
2 **GLENVALLY,** gr f Belfort (Fr) - Hivally by High Line (B W Murray) 968[8] 1758[2] 2695[6] 3281[8] 4236[9] 4531[5] 4644[7]
4 **GLIDE PATH (USA),** ch c Stalwart (USA) - Jolly Polka (USA) by Nice Dancer (Can) (J W Hills) 350[5] 620[6] 1143[1] 1398[8] 1770 2239[1] 3067[1] 3434 3775[2] 4414 4731
2 **GLIDINGONBY (Ire),** b f Alzao (USA) - Tremulous (USA) by Gregorian (USA) (B W Hills) 1810[7] 2394[5]
2 **GLIMMERING GIRL (USA),** b f Spectacular Bid (USA) - Glimmering by Troy (T Stack) 4135[7] 4610[8]
2 **GLIMPSE,** b f Night Shift (USA) - Lovers Light by Grundy (L M Cumani) 4011[1] 4232[4]
3 **GLIMPSE OF HEAVEN,** b f Vision (USA) - Adriya by Vayrann (R M Whitaker) 1271[9] 1891[5] 2366[6] 3311 3948 4085[8]
3 **GLINT OF AYR,** b f Glint Of Gold - Iyamski (USA) by Baldski (USA) (R H Goldie) 821 1315[5] 1732[4] 2101[7] 2388[8] 3144[7]
3 **GLISSO (Ire),** ch c Digamist (USA) - Gulf Bird by Gulf Pearl (M C Pipe) 829 2930 3233
3 **GLISTENING DAWN,** ch f Beveled (USA) - Andrea Dawn by Run The Gantlet (USA) (R E Peacock) 4590[8]
2 **GLITTERAZZI,** b c Midyan (USA) - Burnt Amber by Balidar (D R C Elsworth) 2325[5] 2571[4] 4276 4446[6]
3 **GLOIRE DE ROSE,** gr f Mtoto - Hold Dear by Caro (F Doumen) 3944[2] 4307[6]
6 **GLORIA MUNDI (Fr),** b h Saint Cyrien (Fr) - Chester County by Realm (F Doumen) 4754a[4] 461[4] 798[5]
2 **GLORIETTE,** br f Petoski - Reflected Glory (Swe) by Relko (R Guest) 1350[4] 1763[7] 2603[3] 3126[8] 3968[1] 4342 4541 4646
3 **GLORIEUX DANCER (Fr),** b c Le Glorieux - Teree by Kaldoun (R Collet) 613[4] 953[5] 2803[7] 3022[6]
6 **GLOSSY,** ch g Derrylin - Floor Show by Galivanter (B A McMahon) 82[9]
2 **GLOWING ACCOUNT (Ire),** b g Glow (USA) - Redeem Herself by General Assembly (USA) (Gerard Stack) 4405[7]
3 **GLOWING JADE,** b f Kalaglow - Precious Jade by Northfields (USA) (M R Channon) 4155[8] 4322[9] 4536[1] 4633[5] 4694[6]
3 **GLOWING LINES (Ire),** br f Glow (USA) - Eyeliner (USA) by Raise A Native (T Stack) 3524[9] 3856[9] 4118[7]
3 **GLOWING PATH,** b g Kalaglow - Top Tina by High Top (R J Hodges) 80 162[2] 204[5] 725[8] 1074[5] 2095[2] 2775[1] 3101[9] 3311[1] 4479
3 **GLOWING VALUE (Ire),** b c Glow (USA) - Party Piece by Thatch (USA) (F Dunne) 666 1549[3] 2039[6] 2247[8] 2452[3] 2779[7] 3380[3] 3610[8] 3852[1]
4 **GLYER (USA),** ch c Seattle Dancer (USA) - Tea And Roses (USA) by Fleet Nasrullah (T Stack) 895[4] 1024[7] 1552[5]
2 **GNEISS (USA),** ch c Diesis - Rangoon Ruby by Sallust (Mrs J Cecil) 3746[2] 4098[1] 4273[6]
2 **GOBSMACKED (USA),** b c Explodent (USA) - Starry Eyed (USA) by Star de Naskra (USA) (W J Haggas) 2792[6]
6 **GO DEAS,** ch m King Persian - St Louisan by St Chad (A P O'Brien) 1508[8] 1757 1962 2094[7] 2143[6] 2557[3] 2693
5 **GODS EXPRESS (Ire),** gr g Godswalk (USA) - Monetary Wish by Wishing Star (Victor Bowens) 2878
2 **GOFFREDO GORI,** b c Celestial Storm (USA) - Brisky Of Gold by Glint Of Gold 4313[2]
2 **GOFFREDO GORI (Ire),** 3803[5]
3 **GO FLIGHTLINE (Ire),** ch f Common Grounds - Whilst by Dalsaan (D A Wilson) 342[2] 450[4] 977[8] 1226[2] 1505[4] 1714[3] 1826[2] 2011[4] 2280[3] 2560[6] 2908[8] 3220 3584[4] 3707[8]
8 **GO FORUM,** ch g Tumble Wind (USA) - Devine Lady by The Parson (G L Moore) 1858[5] 1951[5] 2126[7] 2415[7] 3066[9]
3 **GOLD AND BLUE (Ire),** b f Bluebird (USA) - Golden Grundy by Grundy (D K Weld) 1236
4 **GOLD BELT (Ire),** gr f Bellypha - Golden Braid by Glint Of Gold (R Hollinshead) 4696a 4786a[1]
4 **GOLD BLADE,** ch g Rousillon (USA) - Sharp Girl (Fr) by Sharpman (N A Graham) 4735a[4] 4777a[4] 68[2] 159[1] 224[2] 321[1] 402[2] 845 1414 1712[6] 3831[1] 4101[4] 4391[5] 4727[3]
3 **GOLD BRAISIM (Ire),** b f Jareer (USA) - Mashmoon (USA) by Habitat (J S Bolger) 280[4] 486[4] 806[1] 939[2] 1023[6] 1513[9] 1825[6] 3496[6] 3610[6]
3 **GOLD DESIRE,** b g Grey Desire - Glory Gold by Hittite Glory (M Brittain) 437[4] 608[6] 764[3] 966 1181[3] 1852[1] 2341[5] 2764[5] 3440[4] 3632[5] 4022 4241
10 **GOLDEN ANCONA,** ch g London Bells (Can) - Golden Darling by Darling Boy (M Brittain) 1284 3216[8] 3536
2 **GOLDEN ARROW (Ire),** ch c Glint Of Gold - Sheer Luck by Shergar (I A Balding) 3352[7] 4620[3] 4698[2]
2 **GOLDEN BALL (Ire),** b c Sadler's Wells (USA) - Sun Princess by English Prince (M R Stoute) 3833
3 **GOLDEN BECHETT (Ire),** b c Green Forest (USA) - Assertive Lady by Assert (G Fratini) 1363[1] 1548[8] 4403[6] 4746[5]
2 **GOLDEN BENGAL (USA),** 1647[6] 4198[3]
2 **GOLDENBERRY,** ch f Sharrood (USA) - Moberry by Mossberry (B W Hills) 4679[6]
2 **GOLDEN BULLION,** b f Glint Of Gold - National Dress by Welsh Pageant (S Dow) 4002 4229[9] 4337[7]
5 **GOLDEN CHIP (Ire),** ch g M Double M (USA) - Kimangao by Garda's Revenge (USA) (A P Stringer) 315 383[1] 592[2] 801 930[7] 1520[6] 1777[7] 2045[5] 2391[3] 2633[1] 2762[2] 3019[9] 3364[1]
2 **GOLDEN COMPLIANCE (USA),** ch c Compliance - Bunnys Wedding by Crash Course 3875[2]
2 **GOLDEN FERN,** ch f Glint Of Gold - Icefern by Moorestyle (P T Walwyn) 3389[7] 3659[7] 4220[5]
4 **GOLDEN FORZANDO,** 2650[7]
2 **GOLDEN GRAND,** b c Sayf El Arab (USA) - Lavenham Blue by Streetfighter (R J R Williams) 1355[2] 1499[1] 2058[9] 3428[5] 3667[4] 4032[1] 4266[4]
3 **GOLDEN GUEST,** ch f Rainbow Quest (USA) - Intimate Guest by Be My Guest (USA) (Mrs J Cecil) 823[3] 1171[3] 1278[3] 1931[1] 2361 3036[3] 3477[9]
3 **GOLDEN HAWK,** ch c Cock Robin - Hale by Gairloch (Y Kara) 2839[3]
2 **GOLDEN HELLO,** b g Glint Of Gold - Waltz by Jimmy Reppin (M H Easterby) 3554[4] 4192[2] 4316[2]
9 **GOLDEN ISLE,** b h Golden Fleece (USA) - Dunette (Fr) by Hard To Beat (J I A Charlton) 1654 2059
3 **GOLDEN KABBUBY (USA),** ch c Green Forest (USA) - Assertive Lass by Asset (G Fratini) 1887[2]
3 **GOLDEN KLAIR,** b f Damister (USA) - Woolpack by Golden Fleece (USA) (C J Hill) 4697a[1] 4717a[1] 4770a[1] 4811a[1] 109[1] 203[4] 239[2] 252[1] 472 875
2 **GOLDEN MEMORIES (Ire),** ch c Shernazar - Buz Kashi by Bold Lad (Ire) (M J Heaton-Ellis) 4489[1]
5 **GOLDEN MINTAGE (USA),** b h The Minstrel (Can) - Golden Bowl (USA) by Vaguely Noble (M Ciciarelli) 692[4] 1089[2] 1548[6] 4403[7]

INDEX TO FLAT RACE RESULTS 1992-93

3 **GRAEGOS (Ire),** b c Shareef Dancer (USA) - Trikymia by Final Straw (H R A Cecil) 1581[2] 1901[1] 4515[5] 4716[4]

4 **GRANACHE (Ire),** br c Rousillon (USA) - Mpani by Habitat (M R Channon) 4420 4515[4] 4713[8]

2 **GRANBY BELL,** b c Ballacashtal (Can) - Betbellof by Averof (M P Muggeridge) 1489 1959[6] 2419 3264 4356 4484

3 **GRAND APPLAUSE (Ire),** gr c Mazaad - Standing Ovation by Godswalk (USA) (R Simpson) 725[2] 827[2] 1068[5] 1115[5] 1976[6] 4064

2 **GRANDEE,** b c Aragon - Bourbon Queen by Ile de Bourbon (USA) (B A McMahon) 454 673 900 4618 4761[4]

3 **GRANDERISE (Ire),** b g Digamist (USA) - Miss Morgan by Native Prince (D G Swindlehurst) 712[5] 842 1566 2596[7] 2737[9]

3 **GRANDEUR (Ire),** b c Prince Rupert (Fr) - Isla Bonita by Kings Lake (USA) (Joseph M Canty) 3397 3684[8] 4429

4 **GRAND FELLOW (Ire),** br g Thatching - Concave by Connaught (A M Forte) 4680a 4751

6 **GRAND FLOTILLA (USA),** ro h Caro - Maurita by Harbor Prince (E Lellouche) 4674a[4] 798[4] 1291[2] 2771[6] 4626[3]

5 **GRAND GUIGNOL,** ch g Superlative - Boule de Suif by Major Portion (G Wragg) 952[3]

4 **GRAND HONDA (Ire),** b g Lomond (USA) - Braneakins by Sallust (C E Brittain) 211[7] 235

2 **GRAND LODGE (USA),** ch c Chief's Crown (USA) - La Papagena by Habitat (W Jarvis) 2792[1] 3400[3] 4281[1] 4443[1]

2 **GRANDMAN (Ire),** b g Executive Perk - Gerise by Nishapour (Fr) (D Moffatt) 354[5] 433[7] 698[9] 4318[9] 4491[9]

4 **GRAND PLAISIR (Ire),** b c Darshaan - Tapage Nocturne by Irish River (J-C Cunnington) 1694[5]

5 **GRAND PRINCESS (Ire),** b m Fayruz - Princess Grand by Kashiwa (David J McGrath) 640

2 **GRAND SALT (Ire),** b c Salt Dome (USA) - Fifty Grand by Ballad Rock (M J Haynes) 4752[8]

4 **GRAND TIME,** ch c Clantime - Panay by Arch Sculptor (C J Hill) 4719a[7] 4768a 147[3] 195[5] 236[9] 409[7] 1096 2352[9]

5 **GRAND TOUR (NZ),** b g Gold Blend (USA) - Alrua (Aus) by Ruantallan (Michael Robinson) 4656[3]

4 **GRAND VITESSE (Ire),** br c Alzao (USA) - Au Revoir by Ballymoss (R Hannon) 350[8] 756[6] 1130 1768 2475[5] 2989[1] 3450[3] 3722[2] 4376[6] 4537[7]

2 **GRANGE DANCER (Ire),** ch f The Noble Player (USA) - Ballinagale by Dunphy (T A K Cuthbert) 2370[6] 3443[7] 3755

2 **GRANGE VENTURE,** ch g Never So Bold - North Page (Fr) by Northfields (USA) (T A K Cuthbert) 3754

6 **GRANITTON BAY,** b g Prince Tenderfoot (USA) - Miss Redmarshall by Most Secret (R M Whitaker) 1530 1721[9] 1865[2] 1939[4] 2550[3]

2 **GRANMAS DELIGHT,** b f Hadeer - Miss Caro Star by Rusticaro (Fr) (K T Ivory) 496[8] 949[2] 1265[8] 1523[6] 2946[3]

3 **GRAN SENORUM (USA),** ch c El Gran Senor (USA) - Sanctum Sanctorum (USA) by Secretariat (USA) (P F I Cole) 313[2] 582 784[2] 950[2] 1060[2] 1424[2] 1729[1] 2220[1] 2479[5] 3234[3] 3783[3] 4181[9] 4518

3 **GRANSE OAKS (USA),** b f Nureyev (USA) - Dry Fly (Fr) by Mill Reef (USA) (F Boutin) 697[5] 1545[6]

3 **GRANVILLE CORNER,** ch g Formidable (USA) - Zilda (Fr) by Zino (J A R Toller) 1308[5] 2749[8] 3174[6] 3747

8 **GRANVILLE GRILL,** b g Furry Glen - Glamorous Night by Sir Herbert (Francis Berry) 753

4 **GRAY CASHMERE (USA),** gr f Relaunch (USA) - Feature Price (USA) by Quack (USA) (P Vestal) 4472[2]

2 **GREAC,** ch f Risk Me (Fr) - Rosinante (Fr) by Busted (A P O'Brien) 3453 3953 4261 4359

4 **GREAT ABSALOM,** gr c Absalom - Sallytude by Tudor Music (J S Wainwright) 4707a

3 **GREAT CABARET (Ire),** ch c The Minstrel (Can) - Tremulous (USA) by Gregorian (USA) (D K Weld) 1649[2] 3161[2] 3544 3858[1] 4555[3] 4656[2]

2 **GREAT DEEDS,** b f Forzando - Deed by Derring-Do (M R Channon) 1583[1] 1804[1] 2210[3] 2790[4] 3463[4] 3898[2] 4546[3]

2 **GREATEST,** b c Superlative - Pillowing by Good Times (Ity) (R W Armstrong) 543[3] 998[9] 3836[1] 4550[4]

2 **GREATEST HOPES,** ch c Aragon - Singora by Blue Cashmere (C J Benstead) 3589 4067 4265 4500

5 **GREATEST OF ALL (Ire),** ch m Ela-Mana-Mou - Red Jade by Red God (D J S Cosgrove) 4817a 24[7]

4 **GREAT HALL,** gr g Hallgate - Lily Of France by Monsanto (Fr) (P D Cundell) 348[4] 492[3] 760[5] 948[9] 1232[1] 1394[1] 1658[5] 1903[1] 2110[5] 2276[2] 3051[5] 3169[3] 3313[1] 3593[2] 3778 4038 4518[6] 4652[3] 4721

7 **GREAT HAND,** b g Tumble Wind (USA) - Great Aunt by Great Nephew (R Rowe) 2548[4] 2869[4] 3550[4] 3887 4268[8]

6 **GREAT HEIGHTS,** b g Shirley Heights - As You Desire Me by Kalamoun (J J O'Neill) 831

3 **GREAT INDY,** ch f Vaigly Great - Indian Flower by Mansingh (USA) (A A Hambly) 4222

7 **GREAT LAKES,** b h Lomond (USA) - Costly Wave (Fr) by Caro (M V O'Brien) 4401[7]

4 **GREAT MAX (Ire),** b or br g Simply Great (Fr) - Lockwood Girl by Prince Tenderfoot (USA) (C Parker) 290[7] 769[2]

4 **GREAT NORTH ROAD,** ch g Night Shift (USA) - Tactless by Romulus (Pat Mitchell) 4715a

4 **GREAT ORATION (Ire),** b or br c Simply Great (Fr) - Spun Gold by Thatch (USA) (F Watson) 910 1676[6] 1832 2530[2] 2740[4] 3373[7] 4218 4700[3]

4 **GREAT PALM (USA),** gr c Manila (USA) - Hat Tab Girl (USA) by Al Hattab (USA) (P F I Cole) 689[2] 1085[1] 2253[8]

3 **GREAT PLOVER,** b g Prince Of Peace - Avec Amour by Jolly Jet (Mrs A Knight) 2351[6] 2670 2937 3893[9]

3 **GREAT STEPS,** ch f Vaigly Great - Step You Gaily by King's Company (E Weymes) 1016 1153[5] 4158 4428[2] 4545[6]

2 **GREAT TRIVIALITY,** ch f Hadeer - Royal Yacht (USA) by Riverman (USA) (C E Brittain) 3176[7] 3586[6] 4011[4]

4 **GREAT VINTAGE (NZ),** 4672[4]

2 **GRECIAN GARDEN,** b f Sharrood (USA) - Greek Goddess by Young Generation (A A Hambly) 715[9] 1254[1] 1413[2] 1590[7] 1964[8] 3345[7] 3566 3815

4 **GRECIAN LADY (Ire),** b f Be My Guest (USA) - Grecian Sky by African Sky (P J Molloy) 1962[7] 2286 2513[2] 2923[3] 3326[4] 3854[9] 4409 4639

4 **GREEK CHIME (Ire),** gr g Bellypha - Corinth Canal by Troy (M A O'Toole) 912[7] 1987 2693[2] 2842[7] 3063[8] 3277[9] 3367[3] 3397[3] 4161

4 **GREEK GOLD (Ire),** b g Rainbow Quest (USA) - Gay Hellene by Ela-Mana-Mou (J A Glover) 389[6] 845 1720[8] 2211 3487 3973

2 **GREEK NIGHT OUT (Ire),** b f Ela-Mana-Mou - Ce Soir by Northern Baby (Can) (M Johnston) 1863[3] 2044[4] 2331[6] 3235[4] 3829

3 **GREENACRES STAR,** ch f Seymour Hicks (Fr) - Greenacres Girl by Tycoon II (B A McMahon) 2858[3] 3117

3 **GREENBANK (USA),** b g Trempolino (USA) - Green Boundary (USA) by Robellino (USA) (I A Balding) 1027[4] 1469[3] 1901[3] 3722[8] 3981[3] 4191[3]

2 **GREENCASTLE ROSE (Ire),** b f Cyrano de Bergerac - Hill's Realm (USA) by Key To The Kingdom (USA) (Augustine Leahy) 1121[4] 1571[8] 4117[6] 4290 4459

3 **GREEN CHILI,** ch f Chilibang - Deja Vu (Fr) by Be My Guest (USA) (J W Hills) 582[6] 835[7] 1312 3053[4] 3783 3887

2 **GREEN CRUSADER,** b c Green Desert (USA) - Hysterical by High Top (M R Stoute) 4229 4615[1]

10 **GREEN DOLLAR,** b g Tickled Pink - Burglars Girl by Burglar (P Howling) 750[7] 986 1066 1172[5] 1485 3906 4040 4280 4393 4518

2 **GREENFINCH (Can),** gr g Green Dancer (USA) - Princess Verna (USA) by Al Hattab (USA) (M P Naughton) 1020[8] 1324[7] 1949 2714[7] 4377[5] 4489

4 **GREEN GLEN (USA),** b g Green Dancer (USA) - Red Red Rose (USA) by Blushing Groom (Fr) (Neil S McGrath) 4685a[6] 575 959 2035 2498[2] 2842[5]

2 **GREEN GOLIGHTLY (USA),** b c Green Dancer (USA) - Polly Daniels (USA) by Clever Trick (USA) (M A Jarvis) 1131[4] 1706[1]

3 **GUV'S JOY (Ire),** b f Thatching - Joanne's Joy by Ballymore (B W Hills) 556^{6} 1231 3956^{5} 4320

2 **GUYLAIN,** b c Fairy King (USA) - Karonga by Main Reef (P Calver) 2167^{7} 2505^{9}

3 **GWEEK (Ire),** ch f Common Grounds - Do We Know by Derrylin (M H Tompkins) 907^{3} 1306^{9} 1932^{5} 2086^{3} 2529^{2} 3193^{9} 3304^{2} 3962^{1} 4213^{2} 4457^{2}

2 **GWERNYMYNYDD,** b f Dreams To Reality (USA) - My Valentine Card (USA) by Forli (Arg) (B W Hills) 1916 2862^{9} 4227 4483^{8}

3 **GYMCRAK DIAMOND (Ire),** b g Taufan (USA) - Down The Line by Brigadier Gerard (G Holmes) 4191 4322 4431

5 **GYMCRAK FORTUNE (Ire),** b g Kafu - Forlorn Chance by Fighting Don (P D Cundell) 10^{4} 67

5 **GYMCRAK PREMIERE,** ch g Primo Dominie - Oraston by Morston (Fr) (G Holmes) 792 1002^{2} 1768 2254^{3} 3465 3897 4373^{8}

3 **GYMCRAK TIGER (Ire),** b g Colmore Row - Gossip by Sharp Edge (G Holmes) 1808 4667

4 **GYMCRAK TYCOON,** b g Last Tycoon - Brazen Faced by Bold And Free (G Holmes) 4692a^{5} 4744a^{6} 4781a^{5} 4808a^{9} 54^{8} 3948 4235 4667^{6}

2 **GYPSOPHILA,** b f Good Times (Ity) - Romany Home by Gabitat (Miss L A Perratt) 3598

3 **GYPSY CRYSTAL (USA),** gr f Flying Saucer - U R Grounded (USA) by Grounded (R M Whitaker) 813^{7} 1133^{5} 1566^{6} 3185^{3} 3669^{3} 4049^{2} 4603^{4}

3 **HAANEM,** b f Mtoto - Nobly Born (USA) by The Minstrel (Can) (Kevin Prendergast) 790^{6} 1997^{7} 2702^{8} 3329^{2} 3732^{6} 3975^{5} 4408 4657

2 **HABBI (Ire),** b f Runnett - Atropine by Beldale Flutter (USA) (E P Harty) 2701

3 **HABEEBITTI NADIA,** b f Night Shift (USA) - Mrs Feathers by Pyjama Hunt (J D Bethell) 4695a 2631 3681 3814

7 **HABETA (USA),** ch h Habitat - Prise by Busted (J W Watts) 302 425^{5} 885^{2} 1274^{1} 1520^{5} 2057 2283^{4} 2816 3358^{7} 3540^{5} 3901 4019^{9} 4343 4468

5 **HACKETTS CROSS (Ire),** b g Rusticaro (Fr) - Anglesea Market by Sea Hawk II (Noel T Chance) 937^{1} 1576^{3} 1996^{8} 2035^{6} 2324^{1} 2841 3398^{2} 3915^{6} 4095^{4} 4586^{1} 4737

2 **HAD A GIRL,** b f Hadeer - Lady Of Itatiba (Bel) by King Of Macedon (B A McMahon) 4575^{7} 4728^{6}

3 **HADDAAJ (Ire),** ch c Ela-Mana-Mou - Sweet Pleasure by Sweet Revenge (B Hanbury) 529 646^{9} 1802^{5} 2005^{1} 2177^{1} 2713^{1}

2 **HADDIAH,** b f Persian Bold - Ashshama (USA) by Arctic Tern (USA) (J L Dunlop) 1142^{2} 2316^{4} 4089^{5} 4264^{4} 4528^{5}

3 **HADEER'S DANCE,** b c Hadeer - Harvest Dance by Mill Reef (USA) (R W Armstrong) 1390^{3} 1697^{4} 1808 2672^{5} 2930 3364^{2} 3575^{1}

2 **HADI (Ire),** b c Robellino (USA) - Java Jive by Hotfoot (D R Loder) 2964^{8} 3259 3755^{9}

6 **HADLEIGHS CHOICE,** b g Fairy King (USA) - Jillette by Fine Blade (USA) (J Mooney) 67

3 **HAIL TO HOME (Ire),** b f Soughaan (USA) - Run Swift by Run The Gauntlet (USA) (M O Cullinane) 982^{7} 2676^{6} 2956^{8} 3062^{8} 3951^{9}

4 **HALBERT,** b g Song - Stoneydale by Tickled Pink (T Casey) 301 401^{8} 659^{9} 1144 1729^{2} 2121 2686^{6} 3046^{2} 3233^{8}

6 **HALEIM,** ch g Formidable (USA) - Miss Reasoning (USA) by Bold Reasoning (USA) (J E Long) 2127^{8} 2371^{8} 2673

4 **HALESIA (USA),** b f Chief's Crown (USA) - Hurry Harriet by Yrrah Jr (E Lellouche) 4711a^{1} 1088^{4} 3194^{5} 3649^{5} 4292^{1} 4569^{4}

3 **HALF A DOZEN (USA),** ch f Saratoga Six (USA) - Exotic Source (USA) by The Minstrel (Can) (J R Fanshawe) 371^{3}

5 **HALF A TICK (USA),** b g Timeless Moment (USA) - Moon Star Miss (USA) by Star Envoy (USA) (P F I Cole) 390^{2} 596 1269^{6} 1427^{3} 2083^{1} 2437^{2} 2962^{6} 3154^{3} 3500^{6}

3 **HALF TERM (USA),** b c Mr Prospector (USA) - Six Months Long (USA) by Northern Dancer (J H M Gosden) 1117^{1} 2853^{2} 3622^{6} 4173^{7} 4545^{1}

3 **HALHAM TARN (Ire),** b c Pennine Walk - Nouniya by Vayrann (D R C Elsworth) 4677a^{9} 4761a^{4} 72^{3} 129^{4} 185^{3} 209^{3} 245^{3} 509^{2} 717^{4} 926^{5} 1976^{5} 2134^{1} 2615^{1} 3078^{9}

2 **HALI (Ire),** b c Rousillon (USA) - Hocus by High Top (Mrs N Macauley) 673^{3} 933^{3} 1672^{1} 1999^{5} 2974^{8} 3490^{9} 3815^{5}

7 **HALKOPOUS,** b g Beldale Flutter (USA) - Salamina by Welsh Pageant (M H Tompkins) 4629^{6}

3 **HALL BANK COTTAGE,** br f Tina's Pet - Cresta Leap by Piaffer (USA) (M Johnston) 323^{2} 428^{9} 491^{3} 1760^{5} 2276^{8} 2503^{2} 2719 3006^{9} 3789^{5} 4083^{5} 4574^{9} 4658

2 **HALLIARD,** b c Hallgate - Princess Blanco by Prince Regent (Fr) (T M Jones) 4127

2 **HALL OF PEARLS,** b f Crofthall - Purrlea Atoll by Gulf Pearl (Mrs N Macauley) 3209 4220

3 **HALLORINA,** b f Hallgate - Diorina by Manacle (W G R Wightman) 927^{1} 1095^{1} 1744^{3} 2011^{9} 2476^{7} 2928^{7} 3450 3549^{4} 3946 4038 4501

8 **HALLOW FAIR,** b h Wolver Hollow - Fingers by Lord Gayle (USA) (C A Horgan) 1607^{8} 1951 2834^{4} 3078^{3} 3479^{8} 4631

3 **HALMANERROR,** gr g Lochnager - Counter Coup by Busted (C W C Elsey) 4691a 534^{5} 686^{6} 985^{6}

5 **HAMADRYAD (Ire),** b h Fairy King (USA) - Clifden Bottoms by Wolver Hollow (S G Norton) 651^{4} 801^{4} 1398 1940 3093^{5}

4 **HAMANAKA (USA),** b f Conquistador Cielo (USA) - Tastefully (USA) by Hail To Reason (M D Hammond) 3716

4 **HAMAS (Ire),** b or br c Danzig (USA) - Fall Aspen (USA) by Pretense (P T Walwyn) 511^{6} 1019^{1} 1406^{8} 1786^{8} 2362^{1} 3777^{7} 4170^{9}

2 **HAM N'EGGS,** b c Robellino (USA) - Rose And The Ring by Welsh Pageant (R Hannon) 1602 2274^{1} 3281^{1} 3865 4223^{3}

7 **HAND IN GLOVE,** b g Star Appeal - Cash Limit by High Top (R Brotherton) 65

4 **HAND ON HEART (Ire),** b f Taufan (USA) - Pichincha by Pharly (Fr) (P Monteith) 885 1286 1634^{8} 1811^{6} 1970^{3} 2550^{6} 2656^{8} 2799^{3} 3058^{5} 3258^{4} 3408^{5} 3630^{6}

6 **HANG A RIGHT,** b g Enchantment - Martina's Magic by Martinmas (P Mullins) 1986^{1} 2324^{2} 2841 3076^{4} 3327^{6} 3544^{1} 3826^{1} 4094^{4} 4284 4689^{4} 4738

2 **HANKYPANKYMANKI,** ch f Risk Me (Fr) - Vaisigano (USA) by Vaguely Noble (R Hannon) 1403 1583^{2}

2 **HANNAH'S MUSIC,** b f Music Boy - Pink Mex by Tickled Pink (P C Haslam) 2876^{1} 3357^{1} 3679^{4} 3751^{5}

10 **HANSOM LAD,** b g Dublin Taxi - Trackalady by Track Spare (W W Haigh) 147^{7} 194^{4} 568

7 **HANTAYO YO (Ity),** ch h Rissoso - Cara Donna by Pipino 4702a^{4} 1365^{6}

8 **HAPPY ROVER,** b g Bold Lad (Ire) - Topping Girl by Sea Hawk II (F Dunne) 2297^{1} 2345^{2} 3202^{5} 3928

3 **HAPPY TUPPENCE,** b or br f Valiyar - Happy Donna by Huntercombe (C J Hill) 2098^{5} 3083^{5} 3228

4 **HARARE SUN (Ire),** b f Sun Valley - Mafiosa by Miami Springs (Eamon O'Connell) 598

4 **HARCLIFF,** b g Never So Bold - Mrs Danvers by Balidar (C V Lines) 4673a^{8} 4680a^{8} 710^{5} 970^{3} 1246^{4} 1696^{3} 2047^{2} 4487 4616

3 **HARD EIGHT,** b c Primo Dominie - Faisalah by Gay Mecene (USA) (A C Stewart) 459 825 4209 4591

2 **HARDING,** b c Dowsing (USA) - Orange Hill by High Top (J L Dunlop) 1998^{2} 2862 3421^{6} 3678^{2} 4444

4 **HARDLINER,** b or br c Sizzling Melody - Miss Trilli by Ardoon (C F Wall) 11^{7} 87 677 948^{3} 1059 1352^{7} 1560

6 **HARD ROCK (Aus),** 596

3 **HARD ROCK MINER,** b c Alleging (USA) - Illiney Girl by Lochnager (T P McGovern) 759 950 1147^{9} 1352 2476 3047 4008^{3} 4340^{7}

6 **HARD SELL,** ch g Hard Fought - Misoptimist by Blakeney (J G FitzGerald) 4690a^{7} 4710a^{9}

3 **HARD TASK,** b f Formidable (USA) - Myth by Troy (R F Johnson Houghton) 835^{3} 1145^{4} 1383^{5} 1586^{3} 2272^{4} 3356^{1} 3587^{8} 4064 4283 4432

7 **HARD TO FIGURE,** gr h Telsmoss - Count On Me by No Mercy (R J Hodges) 465^{4} 604^{2} 750^{3} 986 1003^{4} 1348 1806^{6} 2363 2987^{2} 3504^{1} 3725^{6} 4040^{1} 4170^{4} 4464^{6} 4617^{4}

INDEX TO FLAT RACE RESULTS 1992-93

3 **HEATHYARDS BOY,** b c Sayf El Arab (USA) - French Cooking by Royal And Regal (USA) (R Hollinshead) 468^{9} 684^{8} 1579^{7} 3488^{4} 3757 3961 4357^{7} 4426^{6} 4599

2 **HEATHYARDS CRUSADE (Ire),** ch c Digamist (USA) - Theda by Mummy's Pet (R Hollinshead) 466^{5} 730 1758^{5} 2274^{7} 2586^{1} 3490^{4} 3865 4531 4671^{7}

3 **HEATHYARDS GEM,** b f Governor General - Quenlyn by Welsh Pageant (R Hollinshead) 398^{4} 532^{4} 644^{7} 934^{6} 1341^{5} 2001^{8} 2318^{5} 2425^{4} 2919^{1} 3190^{8} 4123^{6} 4458 4670

2 **HEATHYARDS LADY (USA),** b f Mining (USA) - Dubiously (USA) by Jolie Jo (USA) (R Hollinshead) 1897^{5} 2102^{4} 4177^{4} 4375^{5} 4453^{2} 4692^{2}

5 **HEAVEN-LIEGH-GREY,** gr m Grey Desire - North Pine by Import (J Berry) 4672a^{7} 1679^{4} 1835^{6} 2230^{7} 2392^{7} 3105^{1} 3348^{1} 3638

2 **HEAVENLY PRIZE (USA),** b f Seeking The Gold (USA) - What A Dance (USA) by Nijinsky (Can) (C R McGaughey) 4449^{1} 4740^{3}

3 **HEAVENLY RISK,** gr g Risk Me (Fr) - Halo by Godswalk (USA) (R Hannon) 923^{1} 1718^{6} 2303^{9} 2620^{2} 3105^{4} 3511^{4} 4040 4280^{9}

4 **HEAVENLY WATERS,** b f Celestial Storm (USA) - Idle Waters by Mill Reef (USA) (R F Johnson Houghton) 1430^{8}

4 **HEAVY ROCK (Ire),** ch f Ballad Rock - Asian Princess by Native Prince (D J S Cosgrove) 2104^{1} 2195^{4} 2457^{3} 2847^{8} 3420

4 **HEAVYWEIGHT (Ire),** gr g Bellypha - Pennyweight by Troy (Major D N Chappell) 756 994 1268

3 **HEBER SPRING (Ire),** br g Cyrano de Bergerac - Naval Artiste by Captain's Gig (USA) (J Ffitch-Heyes) 419

3 **HEDGEHOG,** b f Electric - Demderise by Vaigly Great (J O'Donoghue) 1746

3 **HEGAR (USA),** (P Lewis) 1070^{9} 4291^{8}

2 **HEIGHT OF DECORUM,** b c Heights Of Gold - Ribogirl by Riboboy (USA) (P D Cundell) 2502 2836^{8} 3009

8 **HEIR OF EXCITEMENT,** b g Krayyan - Merry Choice by Yankee Gold (A P Stringer) 78 135^{1} 165^{5} 349 1075^{5} 1676^{7} 1941^{8}

3 **HEJRAAN (USA),** b f Alydar (USA) - Top Socialite (USA) by Topsider (USA) (M R Stoute) 4645^{7}

4 **HELENE STAR (NZ),** 595^{2}

5 **HELENSVILLE (Ire),** ch m Horage - Calaloo Sioux (USA) by Our Native (USA) (M A Jarvis) 1042^{8}

5 **HELIOPSIS,** b g Shirley Heights - If (Fr) by Kashmir II (M D Hammond) 4454^{7} 4530^{4}

5 **HELIOS,** br g Blazing Saddles (Aus) - Mary Sunley by Known Fact (USA) (R Simpson) 605 1144^{2} 1527^{7} 1730^{4} 2136^{5} 2363 2413^{7} 3837^{5} 4518^{8} 4652^{5} 4721^{2}

2 **HELLABY,** b c Jester - Yahalom (USA) by Diamond Prospect (USA) (S G Norton) 1135^{9} 1556^{5} 1798^{6} 2370^{3} 2818^{4} 3086^{6} 3279^{5} 3563^{6} 3903^{5} 4081

7 **HELL DRIVER (Fr),** b g Piling (USA) - Hatra by Dubassoff (Frau E Mader) 406^{5}

3 **HELLO EXCUSE ME (USA),** b c Storm Bird (Can) - Dream Play (USA) by Blushing Groom (Fr) (J E Mulhern) 669^{9} 1444 4408^{7}

3 **HELLO HOBSON'S (Ire),** b f Fayruz - Castleforbes by Thatching (R Bastiman) 1160^{5} 1760 2105^{9} 3060 3830 4123

2 **HELLO IRELAND,** b f Reference Point - Select Sale by Auction Ring (USA) (R Charlton) 2316^{5} 2818^{3} 3209^{4} 3667^{1} 4251 4564

2 **HELLO MAMA,** ch f Most Welcome - Ask Mama by Mummy's Pet (J L Dunlop) 2844 3389^{8} 4121^{9}

2 **HELLO MISTER,** b c Efisio - Ginnies Petong by Petong (J O'Donoghue) 1241^{3} 1428^{5} 3041^{4} 3762^{8} 3835^{3} 3978^{1} 4061^{3} 4144 4423

5 **HELLO MY DARLING (Ire),** b g Law Society (USA) - Helaplane (USA) by Super Concorde (USA) (W R Muir) 527^{6} 826^{2} 1173

10 **HELLO SAM,** ch g Hello Gorgeous (USA) - Samra by Welsh Saint (J A Bennett) 2347

2 **HELLS BELLS (Ire),** ch f Heraldiste (USA) - Ring Dem Bells by Simply Great (Fr) (D Carroll) 3451 4705

3 **HELVELLYN (USA),** b f Gone West (USA) - Accredited (USA) by Alleged (USA) (H R A Cecil) 472^{8} 999^{2} 1950^{7}

5 **HENBURY HALL (Ire),** gr g Bellypha - Rustic Stile by Rusticaro (Fr) (K F Clutterbuck) 681 2291^{5} 2520 2873 3258^{7} 3535^{7} 3744 4115

4 **HENIU (USA),** b c Danzig Connection (USA) - Arianne Mon Amour (USA) by Bold Bidder (Lord Huntingdon) 4705a^{3} 4751a^{1} 12^{4} 144^{1} 249^{1} 302^{2} 801^{8}

2 **HENRY'S LUCK,** b c Bold Owl - Rahesh by Raffingora (M R Channon) 2224^{6} 2417^{3} 2668 3104^{4} 3287 3532^{3} 3546^{1} 3696^{1} 3750^{6}

2 **HENRY THE HAWK,** b g Doulab (USA) - Plum Blossom (USA) by Gallant Romeo (USA) (M Dods) 2103^{4} 2739^{4} 2933^{3} 3363^{6} 4163 4756^{2}

4 **HERBERT LODGE (Ire),** b g Montelimar (USA) - Mindyourbusiness by Run The Gantlet (USA) (J C Hayden) 2324^{9}

4 **HERBRAND (Ire),** b g Petorius - Peace Princess by On Your Mark (M H Easterby) 1038^{5} 1159^{7} 1304 1591 2525^{6}

5 **HERE COMES A STAR,** b g Night Shift (USA) - Rapidus by Sharpen Up (J M Carr) 800 1420^{9} 1589^{6} 2230^{5} 2813^{3} 2910^{1} 3280^{2} 3410^{5} 3603^{3} 3947^{3} 4168 4363

7 **HERE HE COMES,** b g Alzao (USA) - Nanette by Worden II (R Akehurst) 332^{1} 416^{2} 620^{4} 840^{1} 1238^{2} 1626^{3}

3 **HERETICAL MISS,** br f Sayf El Arab (USA) - Silent Prayer by Queen's Hussar (J Ffitch-Heyes) 4708a^{3} 771 1207^{5} 1316 1733^{5} 1969^{7} 2195^{5} 3551 3910^{5} 3938^{5} 4164^{7} 4481^{6} 4518

3 **HERMES GOLD (Ire),** b f Dance Of Life (USA) - Carange by Known Fact (USA) (Kevin Prendergast) 1107^{5} 1513^{8} 1645^{2} 1923^{7} 1995^{2} 2516^{2} 2903^{4} 3061^{3} 3769^{5} 3856^{2} 4429^{4} 4690

3 **HERNANDO (Fr),** b c Niniski (USA) - Whakilyric (USA) by Miswaki (USA) (F Boutin) 811^{1} 1087^{1} 1544^{1} 2076^{2} 3933^{1} 4311 4744

4 **HERORA (Ire),** b f Heraldiste (USA) - Kilfenora by Tribal Chief (N A Graham) 524^{3} 1172^{3} 1527^{4} 1830 2363^{5} 2854^{6} 3531^{8} 4297^{8} 4667

4 **HERO'S LIGHT (USA),** ch c Hero's Honor (USA) - I Love You Baby (USA) by Damascus (USA) (P F I Cole) 406

5 **HERO'S LOVE (USA),** 3609^{4}

2 **HERR TRIGGER,** gr g Sharrood (USA) - Four-Legged Friend by Aragon (Dr J D Scargill) 2535^{4} 2720^{5} 3009 3743^{9} 4009^{1} 4646

3 **HERSHEBAR,** ch c Stanford - Sugar Token by Record Token (S R Bowring) 4708a^{9} 4741a^{6} 4773a^{5} 4811a^{6} 16^{6} 51^{2} 121^{4} 151^{2} 206^{1} 214^{1} 255^{3} 535^{2} 683^{6} 1137^{4} 1273^{5} 1982^{6} 2469^{3} 3365^{5} 3553^{2} 3780^{6} 3948^{6}

9 **HE'S A FLYER,** ch g Whistling Deer - Bluemore (E P Harty) 2808^{6} 3028

3 **HE'S A KING (USA),** b c Key To The Kingdom (USA) - She's A Jay (USA) by Honey Jay (USA) (J L Dunlop) 439^{2} 644^{2} 932^{6} 1642^{3} 2421^{9} 2912^{1} 3214^{1} 4140^{2} 4300 4650

2 **HE'S BIZZI (Ire),** b g Roi Danzig (USA) - Local Belle by Ballymore (G L Moore) 4113

2 **HESELL STREET (Ire),** b c Dancing Dissident (USA) - Soyata by Bustino (L M Cumani) 3990^{7} 4229^{2}

2 **HESFINMENTALTOO,** b g Never So Bold - Nativity (USA) by Native Royalty (USA) (A Bailey) 3377^{7} 3470 3810^{6} 3992^{7} 4503^{6}

2 **HE SHALL REIGN,** b g Dominion - It's Terrific by Vaguely Noble (J Ffitch-Heyes) 776 1119^{7} 1959^{2} 2216^{2} 2652^{4} 3362^{8}

2 **HEVER GOLF ROSE,** b f Efisio - Sweet Rosina by Sweet Revenge (T J Naughton) 1229^{4} 2546^{2} 2695^{1} 2996^{1}

3 **HEY HAZEL (Can),** 570^{6}

2 **HICKLETON LADY (Ire),** br f Kala Shikari - Honest Opinion by Free State (Mrs M Reveley) 2342^{2} 2814^{4} 2933^{2} 3598^{2}

3 **HICKORY BLUE,** ch c Clantime - Blueit (Fr) by Bold Lad (Ire) (S G Norton) 2698^{5} 3153^{8} 3220^{5} 3687^{7} 4317^{7} 4580

4 **HIDDEN LIGHT (Ire),** ch g High Line - Beach Light by Bustino (C Collins) 575 807

4 **HIERARCH (USA),** ch c Diesis - Highclere by Queen's Hussar (Lord Huntingdon) 90[3] 118 288[1] 559[3] 1840[6] 2061 2857[2] 3271[6] 3848[8] 4143 4357[4] 4538[9]

2 **HIGH ACCOUNT (USA),** b c El Gran Senor (USA) - Good Economics (USA) by Damascus (USA) (P W Chapple-Hyam) 4421[7]

4 **HIGHBORN (Ire),** b or br g Double Schwartz - High State by Free State (P S Felgate) 492[4] 710 837[2] 970[2] 1073[1] 1502[1] 1871[1] 2527[4] 3323[1] 4616[3] 4667[3] 4762[4]

5 **HIGHBROOK (USA),** b m Alphabatim (USA) - Tell-spot (USA) by Tell (USA) (M H Tompkins) 1845[3] 2433[9] 3466[3] 4039[5] 4175[5] 4414[4] 4731

3 **HIGH CHAIR,** b f Precocious - Camp Chair by Ela-Mana-Mou (P C Haslam) 215[5] 1275 1802 2107[9] 3049[9] 4049[8]

2 **HIGH DOMAIN (Ire),** b c Dominion Royale - Recline by Wollow (M McCormack) 913[1] 1310[1] 1461[3] 1788[6] 2618 3448[4] 3723[5]

10 **HIGHEST PRAISE (USA),** ch g Topsider (USA) - Prides Promise (USA) by Crozier (USA) (J W Hills) 771 1144 1453 1696 2109[9]

3 **HIGHEST SWEEP (Fr),** br c Highest Honor (Fr) - Sweep On by Sharpen Up (P Bary) 2531[9]

2 **HIGHFIELD LAD,** ch c Hard Fought - Jendor by Condorcet (Fr) (C W Fairhurst) 1272[8] 2505 2705[1] 4215

8 **HIGH FINANCE,** ch g Billion (USA) - Miss Plumes by Prince de Galles (R J Weaver) 4714a[7] 967

3 **HIGH FINISH,** ch f High Line - Oatfield by Great Nephew (H Candy) 4622[6] 4696

7 **HIGHFLYING,** br g Shirley Heights - Nomadic Plea-sure by Habitat (G M Moore) 988[9] 1336[6] 1681[1] 1779[1] 2061[1] 2239[2] 3675[2]

5 **HIGH GRADE,** b g High Top - Bright Sun by Mill Reef (USA) (Miss S J Wilton) 618[9]

2 **HIGH HOLME,** ch c Fools Holme (USA) - Corn Seed by Nicholas Bill (D T Thom) 2866 3120[4] 3633[2] 4210[4] 4416[5] 4613[2] 4632[1]

3 **HIGHLAND ARK (Ire),** b g Architect (USA) - High-lands Babe (USA) by Pappa Steve (USA) (Daniel J Murphy) 639 850 1014[7]

2 **HIGHLAND BONNIE,** ch f Dreams To Reality (USA) - Highland Rossie by Pablond (R Brotherton) 2659

4 **HIGHLAND DRESS,** b c Lomond (USA) - Colorspin (Fr) by High Top (M R Stoute) 925[1] 1427[2] 1805[3] 2211 3784[9]

4 **HIGHLAND FANTASY (USA),** b f Alleged (USA) - Sheer Fantasy (USA) by Damascus (USA) (B W Hills) 4714a[1]

4 **HIGHLAND FLAME,** ch g Dunbeath (USA) - Blakesware Saint by Welsh Saint (M H Tompkins) 731 919 1305 4631

2 **HIGHLAND LEGEND (USA),** ch f Storm Bird (Can) - Santella (USA) by Coastal (USA) (H R A Cecil) 2447[1] 3939[1]

5 **HIGHLAND MAGIC (Ire),** b g Stalker - Magic Picture by Deep Diver (M J Fetherston-Godley) 581 737[9] 824[2] 1721[1] 1830[5] 2363[8] 3155[6] 3471[6] 4172 4514 4650[5]

3 **HIGHLAND PRINCESS,** b f Northern State (USA) - Gay Princess by Lord Gayle (USA) (B Beasley) 1077[9] 4213 4669

5 **HIGHLAND SPIRIT,** ch m Scottish Reel - Sala-cious by Sallust (M C Pipe) 3891[3] 4226[2] 4374[3] 4559[5]

2 **HIGHLAND WARNING,** b f Warning - Tarvie by Swing Easy (USA) (M J Fetherston-Godley) 839[8] 1063 3317

5 **HIGH LOW (USA),** b g Clever Trick (USA) - En Tiempo (USA) by Bold Hour (Sir Mark Prescott) 824[9] 2567[3] 2930[6] 3358[2] 4065 4300

2 **HIGHLY FASHIONABLE (Ire),** b f Polish Prece-dent (USA) - Circulate by High Top (P F I Cole) 715[3] 2528[1] 3386[5] 3750[5] 4251 4671[2]

6 **HIGHLY SECURE,** b g Shirley Heights - Caring by Crowned Prince (USA) (M C Pipe) 498[3] 840 919[9]

5 **HIGH PREMIUM,** b g Forzando - High Halo by High Top (Mrs J R Ramsden) 315[1] 513[9] 1768 2060[5] 2363 2601[2]

3 **HIGH ROMANCE,** b or br f Today And Tomorrow - Nahawand by High Top (D Moffatt) 341[4] 451[1] 742[3] 766[3] 1160[8] 1852 4317 4487

3 **HIGH SUMMER,** b g Green Desert (USA) - Beacon Hill by Bustino (Lord Huntingdon) 4800a[5] 32[2] 72[1] 584[2] 1426[8] 2422[1] 3288[2] 3521[2] 4036[1] 4548[4]

2 **HIGH SWINGER,** b g Rambo Dancer (Can) - Top Wallah by High Top (H J Collingridge) 3009 3264[8] 3390[3] 3743[8] 3870[7]

5 **HIGHTOWN-PRINCESS (Ire),** gr m King Persian - Ambient by Amber Rama (USA) (M P Muggeridge) 321[9]

3 **HIGH TYCOON (Ire),** br c Last Tycoon - Nyama (USA) by Pretense (D K Weld) 1050 4287[3] 4686[3]

2 **HIGH TYPHA,** b f Dowsing (USA) - Zepha by Great Nephew (R Hannon) 3738 4497[8] 4594[8] 4682[4]

2 **HI HANDSOME (Ire),** b c High Estate - Bonnie Bess by Ardoon (M J Grassick) 4369 4535[6] 4688

2 **HI KIKI,** b f Rambo Dancer (Can) - Hachimitsu by Vaigly Great (Mrs M McCourt) 4350[8] 4523[8]

3 **HILARY GERRARD (USA),** ch c Naevus (USA) - Firm Lady (USA) by Grey Dawn II (Mrs J Cecil) 470[1] 658[9] 1329[5] 3080 3983[3] 4158[5]

2 **HILL FARM DANCER,** ch f Gunner B - Loadplan Lass by Nicholas Bill (P D Evans) 2465[4] 2679[5] 2917[7]

2 **HILL FARM KATIE,** b f Derrylin - Kate Brook by Nicholas Bill (P D Evans) 312[3] 364[2] 466[7] 730[7] 886[1] 3490

3 **HILL OF DREAMS,** b g Shirley Heights - Forest Flower (USA) by Green Forest (USA) (I A Balding) 557[7] 876[6] 1224[7] 1603[6] 2228[1] 2963[8] 3513[6] 4344[8] 4445[6]

2 **HILL REEF (Fr),** b g Danehill (USA) - Green Reef by Mill Reef (USA) (Mrs J R Ramsden) 2630[9] 3001[5] 3377[4] 3750[4] 4236[3]

3 **HILLSDOWN BOY (Ire),** ch c Dominion Royale - Lady Mary by Sallust (S Dow) 4675a[3] 4709a[5] 825 1073 1316 1642[4] 1861[1] 2347[8] 2712[9] 3346[4]

2 **HILLSWICK,** ch c Norwick (USA) - Quite Lucky by Precipice Wood (J S King) 3979 4259[7] 4489[3]

4 **HILLTOWN BLUES,** gr g Le Solaret (Fr) - Herminda by King Of Spain (T Dyer) 1737

5 **HILLZAH (USA),** ch g Blushing Groom (Fr) - Glam-our Girl (Arg) by Mysolo (R Bastiman) 279[8] 620 681 910[5] 1190[3] 1392[4] 2108[3] 2544[2] 2750[4] 3307[3] 4152[1] 4374[4] 4548[6] 4727[1]

2 **HILTONS TRAVEL (Ire),** b g Red Sunset - Free Rein by Sagaro (E J Alston) 291 466[8] 743[1] 998[7] 1461[7] 2400[6] 4034[7] 4159[8] 4223[7] 4423

8 **HINARI VIDEO,** b g Sallust - Little Cynthia by Wolver Hollow (M Johnston) 4701a 4736a[4] 4768a[2] 6[1] 99[9] 144[9] 180 212[5] 236[6] 263[2] 348[7] 548[4] 610[3] 909 1076[8] 1167[6]

3 **HIND VISION (Ire),** b f Vision (USA) - Pitiless Pan-ther by No Mercy (Patrick Joseph Flynn) 1106[9] 1140[3] 1335[7] 2842 3543[8] 3951[8] 4246 4409[9]

3 **HI NOD,** b c Valiyar - Vikris by Viking (USA) (M J Camacho) 397[2] 802[1] 1017[1] 3901[2] 3996[1] 4468[4] 4650

6 **HINTERLAND,** ch g The Noble Player (USA) - Sev-ens Wild by Malinowski (USA) (Noel Meade) 1295[4]

4 **HINTON HARRY (Ire),** b g Kafu - Rosy O'Leary by Majetta (S Mellor) 4758a 4819a

2 **HIPS'N HAWS (Ire),** ch f Thatching - Broadway Rosie by Absalom (M Bell) 528[6] 715[6]

7 **HIRAM B BIRDBATH,** b g Ragapan - At The King's Side (USA) by Kauai King (J A Glover) 3087

2 **HI-RUBY,** b f Green Ruby (USA) - Hitravelscene by Mansingh (USA) (W G M Turner) 325

4 **HISHI MASARU (Jpn),** 4728a[5]

4 **HISTOIRE VRAI (Fr),** b f Zino - Night Favour by Nadjar 118[3]

6 **HITCHIN A RIDE,** b g Dublin Taxi - Farmers Daugh-ter by Red Slipper (M P Muggeridge) 138[9] 330[2] 501[2] 760 837[9] 1280[8] 4683

2 **HIT THE CANVAS (USA),** ch c At The Threshold (USA) - Also Royal (USA) by Native Royalty (USA) (Mrs M Reveley) 1381 1998[3] 2826[2] 3129[2] 3997[3] 4541[4]

4 **HIT THE FAN,** b or br g Lear Fan (USA) - Embroglio (USA) by Empery (USA) (N A Twiston-Davies) 350 495[7]

7 **HIZEEM,** b g Alzao (USA) - Good Member by Man-singh (USA) (Martyn Wane) 964 1421 2459

2 **HOBART,** b c Reprimand - Constant Companion by Pas de Seul (G C Bravery) 2756[4] 3143[1]

3 **HOBBS (Ire),** b g Phardante (Fr) - Merry Watt by Last Fandango (G A Pritchard-Gordon) 4622[9]

1584[8] 2008[1] 2434[2] 2987[3] 3404[1] 3621[8] 4040[6] 4393 4521

3 **HOY-LIEGH-RAG,** b g Glow (USA) - Wuthering Falls by Wind And Wuthering (USA) (J Berry) 1196[3] 1869[3]

3 **HUDO (USA),** (F Boutin) 954[3] 1546[7] 3369[8] 3800 3933[5]

3 **HUFFA (USA),** b g Ziggy's Boy (USA) - Science Hill (USA) by Cox's Ridge (USA) (W J Haggas) 2746[3] 3474[9] 3834[6]

5 **HUGH DANIELS,** b g Adonijah - Golden Realm by Red Regent (A L T Moore) 1987 2498[5] 3397 3663[7]

4 **HULLO MARY DOLL,** br f Lidhame - Princess Story by Prince de Galles (S Mellor) 1977 2350[9] 3661[9]

3 **HUMAM (Ire),** ch c Nijinsky (Can) - Passamaquoddy (USA) by Drone (H Thomson Jones) 1174[3] 1447[4] 1765[8] 2572[3] 3468[5] 4139[3]

3 **HUMBER'S SUPREME (Ire),** b f Digamist (USA) - Raise A Princess (USA) by Raise A Native (B S Rothwell) 899[2] 1157[5] 1463[7] 1655[4] 2231[8] 3603 3794 4348

2 **HUMBERT'S LANDING (Ire),** b c Cyrano de Bergerac - Bilander by High Line (P F I Cole) 4523[7] 4682[2]

2 **HUMMINBIRDPRINCESS,** b f Interrex (Can) - Under The Wing by Aragon (A Moore) 877[8] 1350[5] 2112[5] 2492 3103[9] 3345[6] 3546

4 **HUNDREDFOLD (USA),** b c Magesterial (USA) - Hundred Times by Olden Times (Mlle I Turc) 153[1]

6 **HUNTED,** ch g Busted - Madam Cody by Hot Spark (Miss S L Gallie) 826

3 **HUNTERS OF BRORA (Ire),** b f Sharpo - Nihad by Alleged (USA) (J D Bethell) 1285[6] 1850[1] 2390[6] 2928[3] 3487[1] 3901[3]

5 **HUNTING GROUND,** b g Dancing Brave (USA) - Ack's Secret (USA) by Ack Ack (USA) (A Bailey) 4797a 4819a[5] 34[4] 73[2] 141[4] 182[2] 495 626[4] 702[6] 857[7] 1041[9] 1345 2397[5] 2683[1] 2950[1] 3087[1] 3231[5] 3473[7] 3716[7] 3872[1] 4023[1]

3 **HUNTING HAWK (Ire),** b c Sadler's Wells (USA) - High Hawk by Shirley Heights (A Fabre) 408[3] 696[1] 1544[3]

3 **HURON WARRIOR (USA),** b c Sagace (Fr) - Heiress (Fr) by Habitat (E Lellouche) 4570[2]

3 **HURTEVENT (Fr),** gr c Highest Honor (Fr) - La Bucaille (Fr) by Labus (Fr) (E Lellouche) 867[7] 2208[4] 3617[3] 4296[5] 4601[3]

3 **HUSBAND (USA),** b c Diesis - Beaming Bride by King Emperor (J Fellows) 1149[6] 2082[5] 3241[1] 3649[3] 4478[1]

3 **HUSHANG (Ire),** b c Shernazar - Highest Hopes by Hethersett (John M Oxx) 669[1] 941[4] 1198[1] 1512[2]

3 **HUSH BABY (Ire),** b f Ballacashtal (Can) - Kind Lady by Kind Of Hush (C N Allen) 4675a[4] 1[6] 40[6] 72[2] 185[7] 213[5] 230[1] 339[6] 699 973 1006[3]

8 **HYDEONIUS,** b g Crystal Palace (Fr) - Razannda (Fr) by Labus (Fr) (C Tinkler) 495 863[9]

3 **HYDE'S HAPPY HOUR,** b g Primo Dominie - Ixia by I Say (N Tinkler) 567[6] 833[2] 1812[1] 2182[3] 2551[7]

4 **HYDRO CALIDO (USA),** b f Nureyev (USA) - Coup de Folie (USA) by Halo (USA) (F Boutin) 4729a[5]

6 **HYDROPIC,** b g Kabour - Hydrangea by Warpath (D W Chapman) 1284[9] 1498[8] 1866 2183[2] 2388[5] 2737[5] 2859[7] 3240[3] 3430 3552[5] 3821

4 **HYLANDRA (USA),** ro f Bering - Aphilandra (Mme C Head) 3618

2 **HYMIE HALL,** ch c Hallgate - Sussarando by Music Boy (M R Channon) 3098 3264

4 **HYMN BOOK (Ire),** b f Darshaan - Divina (Ger) by Alpenkonig (Ger) (R J Manning) 331 520 924

5 **HYMNE D'AMOUR (USA),** b m Dixieland Band (USA) - La Francaise (USA) by Jim French (USA) (Miss H C Knight) 994

3 **HYPHENATE (USA),** b or br c Lyphard (USA) - Unite by Kris (M R Stoute) 4525[7]

3 **HY WILMA,** b f Jalmood (USA) - Hymettus by Blakeney (R J Hodges) 614[2] 720[2] 878

2 **IAN MY BOY (Ire),** ch c Digamist (USA) - Ballysnip by Ballymore (P J Lally) 3159[7] 3771

3 **IBDA,** b f Mtoto - Abhaaj by Kris (Kevin Prendergast) 307 1825[7] 2780[5] 3075[5] 3614[7] 4324[9]

2 **IBERIAN MAGIC (Ire),** b g Toca Madera - Magic Picture by Deep Diver (Denys Smith) 1098[4] 1598[6] 1889[5] 3411[9] 3793[6]

6 **IBERO (Arg),** b or br h Conco Grande (Arg) - Iberienne by Treviglio (R McAnally) 4379[4]

4 **IBIANO (Ire),** 1042[7] 3718[4]

5 **IBSEN,** b g Gorytus (USA) - State Of Mind by Mill Reef (USA) (R Akehurst) 531 754 2109 2353[8] 3891[6] 4751[1]

3 **IBTIKAR (USA),** b f Private Account (USA) - Anne Campbell (USA) by Never Bend (P T Walwyn) 532[9] 977 1257[8] 1776[5] 2207[6] 2640[2] 3392[8] 3821 4341[7]

5 **ICANSEEFORMILES (Ire),** gr g Godswalk (USA) - Saintly Tune by Welsh Saint (J T Gorman) 2322[6] 2556[9] 3296[8] 3395 4161 4370[2] 4586 4685

2 **ICANSPELL,** b g Petoski - Bewitched by African Sky (T D Barron) 3792

3 **ICEFLOW (Fr),** b f Siberian Express (USA) - Yarzah (USA) by Silver Hawk (USA) (A Redmond) 847[8] 1386[3] 2041 2513[4] 2703[8] 2903[5] 3075[7] 3278[3] 3576[8] 4060[5] 4408

6 **ICE MAGIC,** ch g Red Sunset - Free Rein by Sagaro (F J Yardley) 382[9] 495 826 1156[8] 1321 4268[9]

3 **ICE POOL (USA),** b f Diesis - Skating by Mill Reef (USA) (H R A Cecil) 3117[2] 3727[1] 4352[4]

3 **ICE REBEL,** br g Robellino (USA) - Ice Chocolate (USA) by Icecapade (USA) (Miss B Sanders) 1058 1256[2] 1469[4] 2134[7] 3306[4] 3533[1] 4087[7]

4 **ICE STRIKE (USA),** b c Eskimo (USA) - Gama Tres (USA) by El Pitirre (USA) (J W Hills) 470[8] 678 1120 1686[6] 1930[1] 2201[7]

3 **ICTERINA (USA),** b f Secreto (USA) - Sugar And Spice (USA) by Key To The Mint (USA) (P W Chapple-Hyam) 204[4]

2 **ICY HOT (Ire),** b c Superlative - Damia by Vision (USA) (H R A Cecil) 1456[3] 3833

3 **ICY SOUTH (USA),** b or br c Alleged (USA) - Arctic Eclipse (USA) by Northern Dancer (J H M Gosden) 2290[2] 2654 3385[1] 3878[3] 4100[1] 4420[7]

2 **ICY TUNDRA,** b f Shaadi (USA) - Tundra Goose by Habitat (John M Oxx) 3071[4] 3527[2] 3730[1]

2 **IDLE HOUND (USA),** b c Lear Fan (USA) - French Poem (USA) by Sharpen Up (Sir Mark Prescott) 2714[6]

3 **IDRIS (Ire),** b c Ahonoora - Idara by Top Ville (John M Oxx) 788[2] 3916[1] 4289[1] 4585[3] 4736[7]

2 **I FEAR NOTHING,** gr f Kalaglow - Noirmont Girl by Skymaster (D R Loder) 2785[3] 3627[4] 3960[2] 4249

3 **IF IT SUITS,** b c Local Suitor (USA) - If (Fr) by Kashmir II (R Akehurst) 4590

5 **IF YOU SAY YES (Ire),** b m Ya Zaman (USA) - Saulest by Saulingo (W P Mullins) 4430[2]

3 **IGNITED,** b c Colmore Row - Flame Up by Bustino (K A Morgan) 4773a[9] 2183[8]

2 **IGUASSU (Fr),** b f Fabulous Dancer (USA) - Irish Sea by Irish River (M Papoin) 3048[3]

2 **I HAVE A DREAM (Ire),** b g Vision (USA) - Danger Signal by Red God (E P Harty) 896 2701 3073

3 **I HAVE TO SAY (Ire),** b f Jareer (USA) - Say Something by Reform (J C Harley) 573[6]

3 **IHTIRAZ,** ch c Soviet Star (USA) - Azyaa by Kris (H Thomson Jones) 400[1] 643[7] 1153[4] 2060[6] 2854[1] 3350[1] 3764[6] 4172[8]

3 **IJAB (Can),** b c Ascot Knight (Can) - Renounce (USA) by Buckpasser (J Parkes) 602[7] 836 2181[2] 2635[3] 2820[7] 3233 4431[6] 4604[6]

2 **IJLAL (Ire),** ch c Unfuwain (USA) - Shurooq (USA) by Affirmed (USA) (H Thomson Jones) 2153

3 **IKHTIRAA (USA),** b c Imperial Falcon (Can) - True Native (USA) by Raise A Native (P Mitchell) 441[8] 717[7] 813 1037[1] 1274 1858[6]

2 **IKIS GIRL,** ch f Silver Hawk (USA) - Jealous One (USA) by Raise A Native (M Bell) 4421[4]

6 **IKUNO DICTUS (Jpn),** 4728a[9]

2 **IL CARAVAGGIO (Ire),** gr c Tate Gallery (USA) - Phazania by Tap On Wood (D K Weld) 664[1] 1045[5] 1886[2] 2745[1] 3436[5]

6 **ILDERTON ROAD,** br m Noalto - Mac's Melody by Wollow (Mrs Barbara Waring) 34[7] 628[8] 978[3]

2 **ILE VERTE (Ire),** b f Glenstal (USA) - Isola (Ger) by Konigsstuhl (Ger) (D K Weld) 4705

3 **I'LLEAVEITOYOU (Ire),** b g Supreme Leader - Bally by Balidar (S Dow) 4800a^1 97^5 153^2 181^6 481^5 729^6 945^3 1058

6 **ILLOGICAL,** br m Ile de Bourbon (USA) - Modern Romance by Dance In Time (Can) (J A Glover) 904^6

3 **IMAD (USA),** b or br c Al Nasr (Fr) - Blue Grass Field by Top Ville (J White) 552^1 1292^3 1554^3 2077^6 2408^7 3037^4 3525^7 3805 4147^8 4288 4387^1

3 **I'M A DREAMER (Ire),** b g Mister Majestic - Lady Wise by Lord Gayle (USA) (W W Haigh) 4665a^1 4811a^2 40^3 378^6 546^4 813^2 966^1 1422^1 1867^5 2551^2 3134^4 3256^3 3555^7 4101

3 **IMAGERY,** br f Vision (USA) - Petty Purse by Petingo (R J Baker) 732 980 2023^7 2615^5

3 **IMAGINARY (Ire),** b f Dancing Brave (USA) - Bold Fantasy by Bold Lad (Ire) (H R A Cecil) 1831^1 2623^3 2985^3

4 **IMA RED NECK (USA),** b g Dixieland Band (USA) - Bright Reply (USA) by Gleaming (USA) (J S Moore) 1663^7 2029^6 2353^4 2470^1 2713^4 3263

3 **IMCO ACE (Ity),** 4703a^7

3 **IMCO CHARMER (Ire),** b f Last Tycoon - Maiden Concert by Condorcet (A Renzoni) 4571^2

5 **IMCO DOUBLE (Ire),** ch g Double Schwartz - Cupids Hill by Sallust (R Harris) 4701a 4736a^8 4775a^8 96^8 180^7

4 **I'M CURIOUS,** b f Kirchner - The Dupecat by Javelot (R Thompson) 4671a^9 229^7 420

2 **IMEME (Ity),** 4077^6

3 **I'M NO LADY (Ire),** b f Common Grounds - Impressive Lady by Mr Fluorocarbon (Thomas O'Neill) 1164 2700^8 3074 3395^3 3733^7

2 **IMNOTAKROOK (Ire),** b c Common Grounds - Les Enfants by Try My Best (USA) (J C Hayden) 1197^9

3 **IMPECCABLE TASTE,** b f Slip Anchor - Spring Triple (USA) by Spring Double (C A Cyzer) 662 2416^4 2752^8 3106^1 3473 3706^7 3761 4256^8

2 **IMPERIAL BAILIWICK (Ire),** b f Imperial Frontier (USA) - Syndikos (USA) by Nashua (M D I Usher) 625^5 657^4 839^1 1009^4 1253^1 1590^3 1804^3 2960^2 3898^1 4250^5

4 **IMPERIAL BALLET (Ire),** b c Sadler's Wells (USA) - Amaranda (USA) by Bold Lad (Ire) (H R A Cecil) 619^1 1002^5 1768^1

3 **IMPERIAL BANDIT (Can),** 2442

5 **IMPERIAL BID (Fr),** b g No Pass No Sale - Tzaritsa (USA) by Young Emperor (Denys Smith) 315 425^7 1634^3 1811^3 2086^1 2459^2 2816^5 3035^1 3444^5 3812^5 4019^8 4213^1 4533 4643^5

3 **IMPERIAL FORTE,** b f Midyan (USA) - Sunfleet by Red Sunset (S N Cole) 1349^8 1829

3 **IMPERIAL TOKAY (USA),** gr g Caro - Chaudennay (USA) by Assert (A L Forbes) 300^5 582 825 1255^8

2 **IMPERIAL TREATMENT,** ch c Master Willie - Regent Miss (Can) by Vice Regent (Can) (H Candy) 1640 2096^6

2 **IMPLICIT VIEW,** b f Persian Bold - Arvel by Thatching (John J McLoughlin) 3729^9

4 **IMPORTANT DECISION,** b g Import - Three Terns by Seaepic (USA) (D W Chapman) 285^7 376^8 531 1421

2 **IMPOSING GROOM (Ire),** b c Posen (USA) - Beechwood (USA) by Blushing Groom (Fr) (J L Dunlop) 730 1189^6 1763^1 2539^7 3532^6

2 **IMPOSING TIME,** b c Music Boy - Jandell (NZ) by Shifnal (Thomas Kinane) 2804 3911 4637

2 **IMPRECISE,** b f Polish Precedent (USA) - Vaguely by Bold Lad (Ire) (R Charlton) 4542^7

2 **IMPRESSIVE,** ch g Formidable (USA) - Ritsurin by Mount Hagen (Fr) (C Tinkler) 3259

3 **IMPREVEDIBILE (Ire),** b c Bluebird (USA) - Corozal by Corvaro (P Ceriotti) 1365^2 3874^1 4476^6

4 **IMPRIMATUR,** b g Midyan (USA) - Archaic by Relic (M A O'Toole) 1293^5 1444^2 1611^6

3 **IMSHI,** gr f Petong - Lexia by Sharpo (D J G Murray Smith) 4720a

2 **I'M YOUR LADY,** ch f Risk Me (Fr) - Impala Lass by Kampala (B A McMahon) 1944^3 2336^5 2575^2 3463^9

3 **I'M YOURS,** b or br f Forzando - Welsh Jane by Bold Lad (Ire) (R Hannon) 921^9 1171^8 4123

2 **IN A MOMENT (USA),** ch c Moment Of Hope (USA) - Teenage Fling (USA) by Laomedonte (USA) (S G Norton) 3091^5 4167 4512^3 4668^1

2 **INAMORATA,** b f Adbass (USA) - Key To Enchantment by Key To Content (USA) (A P Jarvis) 2103^7 2356^5

4 **IN A TIFF (Ire),** b c Caerleon (USA) - Tiftrums by Thatch (USA) (D K Weld) 4682a^8

4 **INAUGURATION (Ire),** b g Ela Mana Mou - Crimson Robes by Artaius (USA) (P Aspell) 849 1235 1569 2806^6 3684^7 3854 4185

2 **IN BEHIND (Ire),** b f Entitled - Murroe Star by Glenstal (USA) (G L Moore) 3908^9

3 **IN CASE (USA),** b c Storm Cat (USA) - In Essence (USA) by In Reality (R Charlton) 1213^7 3438^1 3668^4 4465^1

2 **INCHARDER (Ire),** b f Slip Anchor - Inch by English Prince (C Collins) 4261^6 4581^5

4 **INCHCAILLOCH (Ire),** b c Lomond (USA) - Glowing With Pride by Ile de Bourbon (USA) (J S King) 1129^5 1430^7 2111^2 2420^3 2913^5 3388^3 3646^4 4254^5 4559

3 **INCHINOR,** ch c Ahonoora - Inchmurrin by Lomond (USA) (R Charlton) 580^1 794^6 2068^1 2905^3 3315^1 3622^4

2 **INCHINTAGGART,** b c Thatching - Lariston Gale by Pas de Seul (C Collins) 2701 3492^9 3922^6

7 **INCOLA,** b g Liboi (USA) - Sdenka (Fr) by Habitat (H Candy) 674^7 1607^4 2152^4 2669^9 2942^9 3394^4 3706^5

4 **INCREDIBLE JOHN (Ire),** b g Vision (USA) - Ramich John by Kampala (K O'Sullivan) 851

2 **INDEFENCE (Ire),** b c Conquering Hero (USA) - Cathryn's Song by Prince Tenderfoot (USA) (M R Channon) 1877^4 2274^2 2502^3 2785^2 3362^1 3490^2 3671^1 3841^3

3 **INDERAPUTERI,** b f Bold Fort - Hello Cuddles by He Loves Me (Miss Gay Kelleway) 797^5 1057^5 1239^1 1697^6 1947^3 2491^4 2816^7 3302^4

2 **INDHAR,** b c Warning - Clarista (USA) by Riva Ridge (USA) (J E Banks) 3990^1 4469^1

4 **INDIA DANCER (Fr),** 104^3

2 **INDIAHRA,** b f Indian Ridge - Mavahra by Mummy's Pet (R Hollinshead) 528^2 1296^2 1944^2 2695^9 3000^4 3215^1 3309^1 3472^2 3894^6 4211^6 4423

5 **INDIANA GOLD (Ire),** b m Commanche Run - Golden Carrier by Homing (Mrs Ian Fox) 309 852^7 1141 3276^8 3773^6 4186^7 4411^6 4573^8

2 **INDIAN CASTLE (Ire),** ch g Nashamaa - Tuckers Witch by Junius (USA) (B J Meehan) 730 949 1959^9 2331 3546^7

2 **INDIAN CRYSTAL,** gr f Petong - Gentle Gypsy by Junius (USA) (M Johnston) 433^6 812^3 1071^3 1561^1 2200^5 2435^7 3254 3566^6

2 **INDIAN DREAMER,** b g Midyan (USA) - Cool Combination by Indian King (USA) (M Bell) 291^2 364^1 446^3 1778^6 2500^8 3475^9 3871^6 4436^1

4 **INDIAN ENDEAVOUR,** b f Green Desert (USA) - Swanilda (Fr) by Habitat (R Guest) 4672a^1 4752a^1 4768a^1 4796a^3 11^3

2 **INDIAN EXPRESS,** ch f Indian Ridge - Bazaar Promise by Native Bazaar (J G Coogan) 3039 3911 4117^8

3 **INDIAN FIRE,** ch g Indian Forest (USA) - Saintly Game by Welsh Saint (K O Cunningham-Brown) 2724

3 **INDIAN FLASH (Ire),** b f Chief's Crown (USA) - Sovereign Flash (Fr) by Busted (R Guest) 672 1005^3 1161^6 1732^1 2118^1 2555^1 2783^5 3212^5 3873^5 4268^5

2 **INDIAN FLY,** b c Indian Ridge - Tinas Image by He Loves Me (R Hannon) 4587^2 4723^2

4 **INDIAN LAKE,** b c Kings Lake (USA) - Imperial Jade by Lochnager 3013^6 4304

2 **INDIAN LAMENT,** b f Indian Ridge - Miss Swansong by Young Generation (R J Hodges) 4265^4 4575

7 **INDIAN MAESTRO,** b g Music Maestro - Indian Wells by Reliance II (G F Edwards) 4705a 4739a^9 4771a^8

5 **INDIAN MOHAWK (Ire),** ch h Ahonoora - Joshua's Daughter by Joshua (M P Muggeridge) 48^9

3 **INDIAN SECRET (Ire),** ch g Indian Forest (USA) - Pendle's Secret by Le Johnstan (S E Kettlewell) 367^6 590 962^6

2 **INDIAN SERENADE,** ch c Mansingh (USA) - La Melodie by Silly Season (P W Harris) 3779 4527^6

5 **INDIAN SLAVE (Ire),** ch h Commanche Run - Commanche Belle by Shirley Heights (R Guest) 302[4] 737[3] 1177[1] 1768 2601[8] 3177[2] 4065 4468

2 **INDIAN TEMPLE,** ch c Minster Son - Indian Flower by Mansingh (USA) (M Williams) 3260[9] 4253[4] 4498

4 **INDIAN TERRITORY,** ch g Dominion - Lady Capilano by Nebbiolo (D Haydn Jones) 4707a 4806a[4] 158[4] 199[4] 1075[7] 1305

3 **INDIGENT (Ire),** b f Superlative - Needy by High Top (Kevin Prendergast) 669[7] 1441 2810[5]

5 **INDIGO,** ch m Primo Dominie - Blueit (Fr) by Bold Lad (Ire) (R M Whitaker) 1036[6] 1215[9]

4 **IN DUBIO (Ger),** 4566[5]

3 **INFANTRY GLEN,** gr g Infantry - Rage Glen by Grey Mirage (G R Oldroyd) 519[8] 719 3035[5] 3355[1] 3722[9] 4424[4] 4536[6] 4702[7]

5 **INFERRING,** b g Alleging (USA) - Be My Darling by Windjammer (USA) (J S Wainwright) 1460[7] 1781[9] 2183[1] 2354[9] 4391[9] 4600

3 **INFORMANT,** ch c Kris - Infanta Real by Formidable (USA) (F Boutin) 1289[6] 3703

3 **INFORMATRICE (USA),** ch f Trempolino (USA) - Informatique (USA) by Quack (USA) (H R A Cecil) 2334[5] 2623[7]

2 **INFRA BLUE (Ire),** b f Bluebird (USA) - In For More by Don (G Lewis) 2895[7] 3287 4263 4483

3 **INFRASONIC,** b c Dancing Brave (USA) - Infra Green by Laser Light (A Fabre) 1012[2] 1364[4] 1769[1] 2082[2]

2 **INGOZI,** b f Warning - Inchmurrin by Lomond (USA) (G Wragg) 2720[2] 3317[3] 4614[2]

4 **INHERENT MAGIC (Ire),** ch f Magical Wonder (USA) - Flo Kelly by Florescence (M McCormack) 555[2] 891[4] 1000 3291[8] 3511[7] 4112[2] 4549[1] 4678[3]

3 **IN HER GLORY (USA),** b or br f Miswaki (USA) - Forever Waving by Hoist The Flag (F Schulhofer) 935[3] 3767[3]

5 **INHERITANCE (Ire),** b h Last Tycoon - Unknown Lady (USA) by Hoist The Flag (USA) (G Harwood) 406

2 **INISHMANN (Ire),** ch c Soughaan (USA) - Danova (Fr) by Dan Cupid (M Halford) 2319 3073 3332[6] 3917[3] 4093

3 **INISHMOT (Ire),** b f Glenstal (USA) - Taling Shop by General Assembly (USA) (Daniel J Murphy) 282 488[6] 936[4] 959[5] 1139 1622[8] 2295[4] 2879 3328[5] 3399 3769[6]

5 **INK BY THE DRUM (USA),** ch h Salutely (USA) - Sharp Pencil (USA) by Olden Times (E J O'Grady) 3037[3] 3336

5 **INKOGNITO (Ger),** b h Nebos (Ger) - Iracema by Konigsstuhl 2079[7] 2644[7]

2 **IN LIKE FLYNN,** b c Handsome Sailor - Thevetia by Mummy's Pet (R Hannon) 2027[2] 2472[2] 3633[3] 4167[1] 4365[1] 4562[2] 4607[1]

2 **IN MY LEAGUE (Ire),** b g Gallic League - Polynesian Charm (USA) by What A Pleasure (USA) (Denys Smith) 1556[4] 2021

4 **INNER CITY (Ire),** ch c Bob Back (USA) - Heartland by Northfields (USA) (L M Cumani) 1089[1] 1747[2] 2068[3] 2905 3862[4] 4173[9]

2 **INNISHOWEN (USA),** b or br c Arctic Tern (USA) - Skeeb (USA) by Topsider (USA) (R Hannon) 2792[5] 3130[2] 3592[1] 3884[1] 4281[4] 4572[2]

3 **INNOCENT ABROAD (Den),** b f Viking (USA) - Police Girl (Fr) by Kashmir II (C B B Booth) 344[6] 437 609[4] 1074[7] 1399[8] 2104 2443[5]

4 **INNOCENT GEORGE,** b g Hallgate - Are You Guilty by Runnett (C B B Booth) 4739a[8] 4789a 4[1] 49[5] 91 207[9]

3 **INNOCENT MAN (Ire),** gr c Neltino - Cry Of Truth by Town Crier (B V Kelly) 819[5] 3853[9] 4586

4 **INNOCENT PARTY (Ire),** b g Nashamaa - Holernzaye by Sallust (M J Grassick) 1107 1443

2 **INNOVATIVE (Ire),** br g Posen (USA) - Innate by Be My Native (USA) (J G Burns) 2701 3771[9]

3 **INONDER,** bl f Belfort (Fr) - Rainfall by Relko (Lady Herries) 519 797[9] 927[8] 1147[7] 1376[6] 1714[9] 4336

3 **INOVAR,** b g Midyan (USA) - Princess Cinders by King Of Spain (C B B Booth) 784[5] 1185[5] 2057 2823[4] 3239[8] 3536[6] 3985[4] 4213

4 **IN QUARTO,** ch c Shahrastani (USA) - Imperial Dancer by Tudor Music (E Lellouche) 392[4] 3500[7]

2 **INSIDER TRADER,** b c Dowsing (USA) - Careless Whisper by Homing (R J R Williams) 2542[6] 2817[6] 4265[6] 4484 4613[3] 4719[5]

3 **INSIJAAM (USA),** b f Secretariat (USA) - Cadeaux D'Amie (USA) by Lyphard (USA) (Mrs C Head) 484[4] 770[2] 1033[4] 3944[1] 4307[1] 4655

2 **INSPIRATION POINT,** ch f Indian Ridge - Low Line by High Line (H Candy) 4263[4]

6 **INSPIRED GUESS (USA),** b g Robellino (USA) - Inspire (USA) by Tell (USA) (D A Nolan) 4643

2 **INSTAMATIC,** b f Night Shift (USA) - Camera Girl by Kalaglow (T Stack) 4286[4] 4584[2]

3 **INSTANT AFFAIR (USA),** br f Lyphard (USA) - Asiram (USA) by Sharpen Up (P F I Cole) 1404[3] 2623[1] 2986[7] 3262[5] 3477[7] 4515[2] 4718[1]

2 **INSUPERABLE (Ire),** b f Cyrano de Bergerac - Souveniers by Relko (J G Burns) 2188[5] 2666[3] 3807[5]

7 **INSWINGER,** br g Swing Easy (USA) - Cheri Berry by Air Trooper (W G R Wightman) 4672a[6] 4701a 4736a[9] 4815a[4] 117[6] 131 224

3 **INTENTION (USA),** b c Shahrastani (USA) - Mimi Baker (USA) by What Luck (USA) (Mrs J Cecil) 1429[8] 2752

2 **INTERACT,** gr c Interrex (Can) - Cestrefeld by Capistrano (R Hannon) 4579[6] 4620[7]

2 **INTERIM,** b f Sadler's Wells (USA) - Intermission by Stage Door Johnny (R Charlton) 4651[2]

2 **INTERNATIONAL STAR (Ire),** b f Astronef - Brave Ivy by Decoy Boy (W A O'Gorman) 1211[4] 1303[1] 1565[2] 2292[2]

3 **INTERVALLO (USA),** ch c Miswaki (USA) - Spadina (USA) by Sharpen Up (F Boutin) 2171[3] 3208 4076[7]

3 **INTERVIEW,** ch f Interrex (Can) - Rest Hill Dolly by Balinger (T M Jones) 878 1817

4 **IN THE MONEY (Ire),** b c Top Ville - Rensaler (USA) by Stop The Music (USA) (R Hollinshead) 456[4] 589[1] 845 988 1764[8] 1967[8] 3790[3] 4364[6] 4548[1] 4661[3]

3 **INTIMACY (USA),** b or br f Al Nasr (Fr) - Apalachee Princess (USA) by Apalachee (USA) (D Hanley) 3605[2] 4053[7] 4463[9]

6 **INTO THE FUTURE,** b g Mummy's Game - Valley Farm by Red God (A P Stringer) 1161[5] 1832

4 **INTREPID FORT,** gr g Belfort (Fr) - Dauntless Flight by Golden Mallard (B W Murray) 4787a[5] 4810a 3788[8] 4374 4457

3 **INTREPIDITY,** b f Sadler's Wells (USA) - Intrepid Lady (USA) by Bold Ruler (A Fabre) 484[1] 1218[1] 1525[1] 2405[4] 3931[1] 4311[4] 4744

6 **INTREPID LASS,** b m Wassl - Risk All by Run The Gantlet (USA) (H Candy) 727 1321[2] 2034[4] 2573[2] 3412[7] 4353[5] 4530[5]

5 **INTRICACY,** b m Formidable (USA) - Baffle by Petingo (C C Elsey) 279[4] 420 559[6] 727 822[7] 1075[6] 1353[3] 1669[9] 1809 2218[3]

5 **IN TRUTH,** ch g Dreams To Reality (USA) - Persian Express by Persian Bold (M D Hammond) 1112[2] 1305[8]

9 **INVERTIEL,** b g Sparkling Boy - Phyl's Pet by Aberdeen (R Allan) 769[5] 861[2] 1101[4] 1520[4] 4343 4702

4 **INVIGILATE,** ch g Viking (USA) - Maria Da Gloria by St Chad (Martyn Wane) 1938[3] 2173[9] 2276[5] 2434[7] 2594[5] 2707[4] 3365[3] 3535 4168[4] 4670

4 **INVISIBLE ARMOUR,** gr g Precocious - Haunting by Lord Gayle (USA) (P C Haslam) 18[8] 745[7] 1600 2823[3] 3239[6] 3412[6]

11 **INVITE D'HONNEUR (NZ),** ch g Guest Of Honour (NZ) - Jillion's Joy (NZ) by Khan Sahib (C D Broad) 4488

6 **INVOCATION,** ch g Kris - Royal Saint (USA) by Crimson Satan (A Moore) 4796a[2] 12[5] 144[3] 197[1] 222[3] 249[2] 369[4] 475[3] 581 1207 1527[5] 1744[6] 2136 2382[2] 2848[4] 2987 3302[9] 3575[6]

2 **INZAR,** b c Warning - Star Face by African Sky (D R Loder) 2419[6] 3573[4] 4480[8]

2 **IOLANI,** b f Alzao (USA) - Sans Blague (USA) by The Minstrel (Can) (R Charlton) 2571 3738[4] 4539

3 **IOLITE,** b or br f Forzando - Thulium by Mansingh (USA) (M A Jarvis) 4734a[1] 4773a[1] 977 1455[7] 1966[7] 2378

3 **IOMMELLI (Ire),** ch c Don't Forget Me - Inner Pearl by Gulf Pearl (P A Kelleway) 540[5] 688[5] 958[3] 1887[3]

INDEX TO FLAT RACE RESULTS 1992-93

3 **JAAZIM,** ch c Night Shift (USA) - Mesmerize by Mill Reef (USA) (Major W R Hern) 872[2] 1114[4] 1424[3] 1698[4] 2202[3] 2379[6] 2787[4] 3343[1] 3756[5]

2 **JABAROOT (Ire),** b c Sadler's Wells (USA) - Arctic Heroine (USA) by Arctic Tern (USA) (M R Stoute) 4542[9] 4628[7]

3 **JACKAREW BOY,** ch c Brotherly (USA) - Lady Peggy by Young Nelson (M J Heaton-Ellis) 2313[5] 2849[8]

4 **JACK BUTTON (Ire),** b g Kings Lake (USA) - Tallantire (USA) by Icecapade (USA) (Bob Jones) 303[3] 462[1] 682[3] 783[1] 857[2] 1752[3] 1809[2] 2925[6] 3319[6] 3538[2] 3861[3] 4013[2] 4466 4540[2] 4732[7]

3 **JACKDIDI (Fr),** ch c Ti King - Luth Commander by Dust Commander (E Lellouche) 1648[2] 2171[1] 2803[6] 4075[3] 4570[1]

5 **JACK GRAY,** b g Sallust - Alice Parry by Kampala (J L Spearing) 1992[9] 2329[6] 2639[9] 3002 3896 4164

5 **JACK LANG,** b h Damister (USA) - Jilt (Ity) by Bolkonski (L Camici) 1323[5] 3921[2]

3 **JACKPOT STAR,** ch c Pharly (Fr) - Claironcita by Don Carlos (R Hannon) 578[5] 1524[5] 1719[2] 1958[5] 2941[5] 3636[5] 4063[2] 4300 4414

2 **JACKSON HOUSE,** b g Absalom - Vynz Girl by Tower Walk (J G FitzGerald) 968 1245[2] 2129 2453[5]

4 **JACKSONPORT (USA),** 2262[5] 3640[5]

3 **JACKSONS BAY,** b g Creetown - Siblette by Persepolis (Fr) (R Rowe) 2410[9]

2 **JACKS TO OPEN (USA),** ch g The Minstrel (Can) - Sublime Mime (USA) by His Majesty (J W Hills) 4679[8]

2 **JACOB BOGDANI,** ch g Night Shift (USA) - Green's Collection by High Top (P F I Cole) 1091[2] 2096[2] 2316[1]

3 **JACODY (USA),** b or br f Lost Code (USA) - Jacolina (USA) by Smiling Jack (W Donovan) 4472[3]

2 **JACQUIMO (Ire),** b c Dancing Dissident (USA) - Rhein Honey by Rheingold (John M Oxx) 3030[7] 3492 4380

2 **JACQUI'S STAR (Ire),** ch c Mulhollande (USA) - Stomata (USA) by Storm Bird (Can) (B S Rothwell) 1413 1590 2229

3 **JADE CITY,** gr g Belfort (Fr) - Dear Glenda by Gold Song (J G FitzGerald) 899[1] 1302[6] 2206[5] 2527[5] 2975[6] 3220[6] 3410[4] 4038 4415[2] 4606[2]

4 **JADE GREEN,** b f Midyan (USA) - Pilley Green by Porto Bello (P J Makin) 4678a 4715a[1] 55[6] 1712[4] 2564[2] 3119[6] 3734[7] 3985[2] 4254[9] 4544[4]

2 **JADE PET,** b or br f Petong - Pea Green by Try My Best (USA) (R Hannon) 657[2] 889[3] 1032[3] 1804[8] 1955[1] 2886[7] 3167[1]

4 **JADE VALE,** b f Petorius - Deja Vu (Fr) by Be My Guest (USA) (J W Hills) 676[2] 1069[1] 1374[1] 1768[7] 2300[5] 2794 3234[2] 3722[1]

5 **JADIDH,** b m Touching Wood (USA) - Petrol by Troy (Mrs J C Dawe) 925[5] 1094[7] 1345[5] 1688[3] 1840 2034[6]

3 **JADIRAH (USA),** b f Deputy Minister (Can) - Sharmila (Fr) by Blakeney (J L Dunlop) 1008[1] 1225[8] 2100[4] 2834 3088 3734

2 **JADY'S DREAM (Ire),** b f Dreams To Reality (USA) - Lemon Balm by High Top (B Palling) 3422 3659

2 **JAFEICA (Ire),** b c Dance Of Life (USA) - Moretta by Artaius (USA) (R Hannon) 2069[7] 2419[4] 3836[2] 4099[1]

3 **JAFETICA,** gr f Kalaglow - Rashah by Blakeney (D R Laing) 880 1315 1627 2013[7] 3221[5]

4 **JAHANGIR (Ire),** ch g Ballad Rock - Marsh Benham by Dragonara Palace (USA) (B Hanbury) 676 930[7] 1274[2] 1434[2] 1777[6] 2025[5] 2391[5] 2717[2] 2944[3] 2989[8] 3408[1] 3623[8] 3957[5] 4158[6] 4376[3] 4424

2 **JAKDUL (Ire),** b c Nordance (USA) - Melika Iran by Fine Blade (USA) (Edward Lynam) 4460[6]

3 **JAKE THE PAKE (Ire),** b g Double Schwartz - Traminer by Status Seeker (K R Burke) 614[4] 1358[1] 2065[6] 2525[9] 2824[9]

3 **JALCANTO,** ch g Jalmood (USA) - Bella Canto by Crooner (Mrs M Reveley) 439[1] 1016 1579[5] 2019[4] 3831 4164[8]

3 **JALIB (Ire),** b c Lomond (USA) - Crown Godiva by Godswalk (USA) (C J Benstead) 1344 1698[7] 2122[1] 2938 3226[9] 3981[7]

7 **JALMUSIQUE,** ch g Jalmood (USA) - Rose Music by Luthier (M H Easterby) 425 1721[5] 2022[5] 2391 2601[4] 2816[4]

4 **JALORE,** gr g Jalmood (USA) - Lorelene (Fr) by Lorenzaccio (S Coathup) 4688a[3] 4714a[5] 4742a[5] 4776a[7] 122 1248[5] 1702[1] 1880[1] 2007[3] 2178[6] 2282[1]

3 **JAMAICA BRIDGE,** b g Doulab (USA) - Mill Hill (USA) by Riva Ridge (USA) (J G FitzGerald) 4718a[3] 1464[8]

3 **JAMANE,** b c Forzando - Mellow Girl by Mountain Call (J Mackie) 1109[6] 1271[8] 1416 2641

5 **JAMES IS SPECIAL (Ire),** b g Lyphard's Special (USA) - High Explosive by Mount Hagen (Fr) (H J Collingridge) 4689a[9] 589[5] 785[3] 1143[6] 1305 1531[1] 2043 2521[5] 2735[4] 3147[3]

2 **JANE HERRING,** gr f Nishapour (Fr) - Langton Herring by Nearly A Hand (R J Hodges) 839 3230 3738

5 **JANESWOOD (Ire),** b m Henbit (USA) - Stipa by Silver Shark (M V Manning) 4634[5]

2 **JANGADA,** b f Chief Singer - Nuggar by Posse (USA) (B W Hills) 2583[4] 3939[3]

2 **JANGLE (Ire),** b c Danehill (USA) - Soleiade by Posse (USA) (B W Hills) 4067[4]

10 **JANISKI,** b g Niniski (USA) - Seasurf by Seaepic (USA) (Mrs Barbara Waring) 331[4] 495[4] 924[2] 1173

3 **JANROFFOLE (Can),** b or br c Le Danseur (Can) - La Bourrasque by Victoria Park (J Dumas) 2442[3]

4 **JAPE (USA),** b c Alleged (USA) - Northern Blossom (Can) by Snow Knight (P F I Cole) 579[7]

2 **JARAAB,** b c Sure Blade (USA) - Ostora (USA) by Blushing Groom (Fr) (R W Armstrong) 4698

2 **JAREEF'S WAY (Ire),** b g Jareer (USA) - Honagh Lee by Main Reef (R Charlton) 2030[2] 2571[2] 3470[3] 3705[2] 4225[4] 4561[6]

3 **JARGONEL (Ire),** b f Jareer (USA) - Native Flower by Tumble Wind (USA) (A J Maxwell) 1513 1645[8] 2323[8] 2604[7] 2780

3 **JARIN ROSE (Ire),** b f Jareer (USA) - Turin Rose by Martinmas (W M Brisbourne) 2464 4191 4515[6] 4617

2 **JARRE BOVE (Ire),** b f Jareer (USA) - Star Above by Formidable (G Verricelli) 4077[3]

4 **J'ARRIVE,** ch f Aragon - Balatina by Balidar (D Morris) 4688a 610[4] 861[5] 1453[7] 1696 2190[6]

2 **JARZELA,** ch f Jareer (USA) - Soie Gentille by Shantung (M Brittain) 1413

5 **JARZON DANCER,** br g Lidhame - Long Valley by Ribero (D A Wilson) 332 1281[5]

3 **JASARAH (Ire),** b or br f Green Desert (USA) - Raise A Memory (USA) by Raise A Native (Major W R Hern) 3286[2] 3489[5] 3839[2] 4191[4] 4683

2 **JASARI (Ire),** b g Ajraas (USA) - Rue Del Peru by Linacre (R Hannon) 312[4] 399[4] 2546[5] 2988[3] 3597[8] 3809[1] 4225 4550

2 **JASDAN,** b or br c Dancing Brave (USA) - Kajall (USA) by Vaguely Noble (G Harwood) 4167[9]

3 **JASPER ONE,** b g Jalmood (USA) - First Pleasure by Dominion (R D E Woodhouse) 2775 3092[4] 3506[9] 3689[8] 3945[3] 4049[4]

3 **JAVA QUEEN (USA),** ch f Java Gold (USA) - Two For The Show (USA) by Stage Door Johnny (I A Balding) 423[9] 3514[1] 3889[4]

3 **JAWAAL,** ch g Soviet Star (USA) - Pencil Sharpener (USA) by Sharpen Up (A A Scott) 3178[4] 3359[5]

5 **JAWANI (Ire),** b g Last Tycoon - Fabled Lady by Bold Lad (Ire) (Dr J D Scargill) 2386[2] 3021[3] 3716[2] 4023[7]

3 **JAWLENSKY (Fr),** ch c Caerleon (USA) - Bold Lady (Fr) by Bold Lad (USA) (F Boutin) 4510[2]

2 **JAYANNPEE,** ch g Doulab (USA) - Amina by Brigadier Gerard (I A Balding) 3287[3] 3958[2] 4210 4416[7]

2 **JAZEEL (USA),** b c Topsider (USA) - Secretarial Queen (USA) by Secretariat (USA) (J L Dunlop) 1324[3] 1715[2] 2909[2] 3462[3] 3992[1]

5 **JAZILAH (Fr),** br g Persian Bold - Muznah by Royal And Regal (USA) (R Akehurst) 358[2] 620[1] 931[4] 1521[3] 1894[2] 2311[3] 2433[3] 3512[1] 3900[2] 4414[6]

3 **JAZZY REFRAIN (Ire),** b f Jareer (USA) - Gay Refrain by Furry Glen (Noel Meade) 3368[3] 4634[3]

4 **JDAAYEL,** b f Ajdal (USA) - Vaguely by Bold Lad (Ire) (A C Stewart) 4711a

3 **JEAN BRODIE,** b f Governor General - Lochmar by Lochnager (H S Howe) 1698 1990[9] 2661[5]

INDEX TO FLAT RACE RESULTS 1992-93

5 **KABELIA,** b m Kabour - Belhill by Beldale Flutter (USA) (S Coathup) 906

8 **KACHINA MAID,** b m Anfield - Grey Twig by Godswalk (USA) (Mrs A Knight) 190^{8} 227 241 264

3 **KADASSA (Ire),** b f Shardari - Kadissya (USA) by Blushing Groom (Fr) (John M Oxx) 2036^{3} 2449^{2} 4368^{5} 4429^{2} 4690^{2}

3 **KADASTROF (Fr),** ch c Port Etienne (Fr) - Kadastra (Fr) by Stradavinsky (R Dickin) 989 1204 1372^{2} 2547^{2} 2755 3307^{5} 3521^{1} 3724^{4} 4064 4212

5 **KADBRIDGE (NZ),** 595^{5}

3 **KADOUNOR (Fr),** b c Kaldoun (Fr) - Ticarock (Fr) by Baly Rockette (J Laumain) 536^{6} 696^{4} 1367^{6} 1546^{4}

3 **KAFIOCA (Ire),** b f Fairy King (USA) - Secret Montague by Tumble Wind (USA) (B J Meehan) 4778a^{9} 4805a^{6} 1^{5} 882^{5} 927^{9}

5 **KAGRAM QUEEN,** b m Prince Ragusa - Arodstown Alice by Sahib (Mrs M Reveley) 1832^{3} 2369^{8} 3135^{1} 4603^{1} 4675^{8}

3 **KAHILI GINGER,** b f Top Ville - Kamisha (Fr) by Lyphard (USA) (N A Graham) 2227^{7}

3 **KAHLO,** b f Jalmood (USA) - Five Farthings by Busted (M W Easterby) 1784 2275^{7} 2598^{5} 3256^{7} 3556 3759

4 **KAISER WILHELM,** b c Slip Anchor - Kaisersage (Fr) by Exbury (H R A Cecil) 674^{1} 1041^{2} 1682^{3} 2061 2432^{2} 3319^{3} 3538^{1} 4189^{6}

2 **KAITAK (Ire),** ch g Broken Hearted - Klairelle by Klairon (J M Carr) 4167^{6} 4338^{1} 4541^{5} 4674^{2} 4733^{3}

2 **KAKASHDA (Ire),** b c Darshaan - Kashka (USA) by The Minstrel (Can) (John M Oxx) 3416 3562^{4} 3731^{6} 4551 4707

2 **KALAKAFU,** b f Street Kafu - Peaconpala by Kampala (P D Evans) 299 4758

4 **KALAMOSS,** ch f Kalaglow - Moss Pink (USA) by Levmoss (N R Mitchell) 4028

4 **KALAR,** b g Kabour - Wind And Reign by Tumble Wind (USA) (D W Chapman) 4719a 96^{2} 134^{8} 207^{5} 218^{7} 236^{5} 548^{9} 887^{9} 1036^{2} 1148^{3} 1589^{7} 2215^{1} 2264^{5} 3032^{7} 3603^{1} 3877^{4} 4109 4168 4363^{8}

5 **KALITA MELODY,** b m Chief Singer - Belle Reef by Mill Reef 3150^{5}

2 **KALKABRINO (USA),** b c El Gran Senor (USA) - Golden Screen (USA) by Silent Screen (USA) (P W Chapple-Hyam) 4440^{4} 4523^{5}

4 **KALKO,** b g Kalaglow - Salchow by Niniski (USA) (M D Hammond) 290^{4} 365^{5} 3090

4 **KALOKAGATHOS,** b c King Of Spain - Kip's Sister by Cawston's Clown (Mrs S D Williams) 4780a^{9} 914^{8} 1316^{7} 2127 2350^{5} 3102^{9} 4016^{2} 4616^{6}

2 **KALOU,** b f K-Battery - Louise Moulton by Moulton (C W C Elsey) 4663^{4}

3 **KAMAATERA (Ire),** ch g Night Shift (USA) - La Tuerta by Hot Spark (A A Scott) 336^{2} 464^{8}

3 **KAMIKAZE,** gr c Kris - Infamy by Shirley Heights (J White) 3832 4110^{7} 4267^{1}

2 **KANGRA VALLEY,** ch f Indian Ridge - Thorner Lane by Tina's Pet (J Wharton) 708^{2} 1082^{1} 2200^{6} 3309^{7} 3715^{5} 4034^{4}

4 **KANUDOS (Ger),** 4566^{7}

3 **KAPUCHKA (Ire),** b f Soviet Star (USA) - Proskona (USA) by Mr Prospector (USA) (K O Cunningham-Brown) 1482^{6} 2032^{5} 3178^{7} 4131 4536 4683

4 **KARABAKH (Ire),** b g Bob Back (USA) - Such Moor by Santa Claus (W P Mullins) 1295 1467 1573^{7} 1797^{1} 4119^{9} 4186^{6} 4639

3 **KARACHI,** b g Nishapour (Fr) - Lady Dacre by Queen's Hussar (C E Brittain) 2023^{1} 2783^{1} 3314 3759^{5} 4366^{4}

6 **KARAMID (USA),** b g Caro - Kamisha (USA) by Lyphard (USA) (Patrick Phelan) 3769^{7}

4 **KARAMOJA,** b g Auction Ring (USA) - Cadasi by Persian Bold (N A Graham) 4715a^{3} 4763a^{4} 92^{3} 192^{1} 229^{2} 287^{2} 420^{8} 3521 4035^{7}

3 **KARAR (Ire),** b c Shadari - Karaserya by Green Dancer (R Rowe) 3524^{4} 3773^{5} 3999^{1}

3 **KARAYOR (Fr),** b c Esprit Du Nord (USA) - Karaya by Shakapour (E Lellouche) 1012^{3} 1410^{2} 2082^{6}

3 **KARDELLE,** b f Kalaglow - Arderelle (Fr) by Pharly (Fr) (M J Charles) 1311^{5} 3491^{2} 3682^{3} 4110

3 **KARIB,** b f K-Battery - Bonny's Pet by Mummy's Pet (R F Stone) 357^{4} 653^{2} 864^{6} 2107 2448^{6}

6 **KARINGA BAY,** ch h Ardross - Handy Dancer by Green God (G L Moore) 293^{3} 1084^{1} 1217^{3} 1882^{1} 2253^{4} 3582^{1} 3703^{7}

3 **KARINIYD (Ire),** ch c Blushing Groom (Fr) - Katiyfa by Auction Ring (USA) (John M Oxx) 940^{4} 1853^{2} 2485^{3} 2808^{5}

3 **KARINSKA,** b f Master Willie - Kaiserchronik (Ger) by Cortez (Ger) (M C Chapman) 1102^{2} 1225^{5} 1453^{1} 2066^{5} 2270^{7} 2480^{7} 3535^{1} 3747^{1} 3988^{2} 4320^{7} 4394 4536 4694^{4}

2 **KARLINE KA (Fr),** ch f Franc Parler - Kadastra (Fr) by Stradavinsky (R Dickin) 4497^{9} 4595^{8}

4 **KARMISYK (Fr),** b c Bikala - Karmisyn by Baldric II (F Boutin) 461^{2}

3 **KARMOUSIL (USA),** br c Private Account (USA) - Karmiska (Fr) by Bikala (F Boutin) 1648^{3} 2082^{3}

2 **KARON BEACH,** ch f Handsome Sailor - Winter Resort by Miami Springs (J W Hills) 4594^{5}

3 **KAR OR,** br c Doyoun - Cape Race (USA) by Northern Dancer (Edward Lynam) 3075^{9} 3494^{7} 3914^{4} 4147^{9} 4246^{5} 4461^{1}

2 **KARPACKA (Ire),** b f Rousillon (USA) - Lutoviska by Glenstal (G Verricelli) 2258^{2} 4402

2 **KARSEAM (Ire),** ch c Mon Tresor - Northern Amber by Shack (USA) (J S Wainwright) 812^{5} 968^{3} 1227^{3} 1602^{6} 3259 3563^{8} 3671^{3} 3969^{7} 4236^{5}

3 **KARSHI,** b g Persian Bold - Kashmiri Snow by Shirley Heights (J R Fanshawe) 529^{3} 751^{9} 3012^{8} 3512^{2} 3832^{2}

3 **KARTABULA (Fr),** (F Boutin) 4655

3 **KARTHAGO (Ire),** ch c Salt Dome (USA) - Kobrin by Bruni 1884^{3}

2 **KARTTIKEYA (Fr),** br c Darshaan - Karosa (Fr) by Caro (A C Stewart) 4726

3 **KARUKERA,** ch f Hallgate - Water Folly by Sharpo (B R Millman) 721 1376^{1} 1977 2711^{6} 3213^{4} 3896^{8} 4131^{4} 4270^{7}

3 **KASALTO (Ger),** 1369^{9}

5 **KASHAN (Ire),** b g Darshaan - Kamanika (Fr) by Amber Rama (USA) (J M Bradley) 1041^{8} 1392^{8} 2942

3 **KASHANI (USA),** b c Danzig (USA) - Kashan (USA) by Damascus (USA) (A Fabre) 431^{3} 3619^{1} 4010^{5}

4 **KASKAZI,** b f Dancing Brave (USA) - Fly Me (Fr) by Luthier (John M Oxx) 4686a^{9}

3 **KASSAB,** b c Caerleon (USA) - Red Comes Up (USA) by Blushing Groom (Fr) (J L Dunlop) 457^{2} 567^{1} 985^{1} 1585^{1} 1769^{3} 2360^{8}

3 **KASSBAAN (USA),** b g Alydar (USA) - Ma Biche (USA) by Key To The Kingdom (USA) (A A Scott) 459^{5} 686 1212^{4} 1408^{1} 1808 2066^{9} 2333^{8} 2757^{2} 2995^{1} 3177^{7} 3476^{1} 3637^{4} 3885^{7}

3 **KASSERHOM (USA),** ch c Woodman (USA) - Kesarini (USA) by Singh (USA) (J H M Gosden) 463^{3}

4 **KATEB (Ire),** ch c Pennine Walk - Ridge The Times (USA) by Riva Ridge (USA) (S Jensen) 4205^{1}

2 **KATHANNA,** gr f Bold Owl - Moon Charter by Runnymede (B Palling) 2911^{1} 3570^{7}

4 **KATHY FAIR (Ire),** b f Nicholas Bill - Fair Flutter by Beldale Flutter (USA) (C J Hill) 4758a 3518^{2} 3787^{3} 3943^{6}

2 **KATHY FAIRUZ (Ire),** b f Fayruz - Isa by Dance In Time (A Peraino) 3875^{1} 4197^{7}

2 **KATHYS RAINBOW,** b f Handsome Sailor - Rainbow Lady by Jaazeiro (USA) (M G Meagher) 4044^{6} 4594^{6} 4697^{8}

3 **KATIBA (USA),** b f Gulch (USA) - Schematic (USA) by Upper Nile (USA) (J L Dunlop) 472^{9} 734^{5} 1415^{3} 1950^{5} 3312^{1} 3660^{2} 3882^{2} 4153^{4} 4383^{3} 4629^{5}

4 **KATIE-A (Ire),** b f Cyrano de Bergerac - Que Tranquila by Dominion (Mrs A Swinbank) 655^{6} 866^{5} 1397

3 **KATIE EILEEN (USA),** ch f Bering - Katrina (Fr) by Anne's Pretender (USA) (R J R Williams) 516^{7} 724 2104

3 **KATIE'S KID,** br g Balidar - Khahmens Delight by Come On Grey (T Casey) 4030^{6} 4525^{9} 4696

3 **KATIES VISION (Ire),** b f Vision (USA) - Brigadina by Brigadier Gerard (Noel Meade) 550^{8} 849^{9} 1139

6 **KATY'S LAD,** b g Camden Town - Cathryn's Song by Prince Tenderfoot (USA) (B A McMahon) 189^{4} 274^{5} 425^{6} 500^{3} 645 1307^{7} 1566^{8}

6 **KAURI,** b g Ela-Mana-Mou - Crannog by Habitat (C Weedon) 4753

6 **KAUSAR (USA),** b h Vaguely Noble - Kozana by Kris (G M Moore) 4102 4357
5 **KAWA BOY (Fr),** 4557^6
6 **KAWA-KAWA,** b m Niniski (USA) - Kaweah Maid (Mrs P Collier) 3077 3295 4370^7 4409^7 4639^7 4657^2
3 **KAWASIR (Can),** b or br g Gulch (USA) - Madame Treasurer (Can) by Key To The Mint (USA) (P C Haslam) 813^5 1238 1703^4 2163^9 4115 4374
4 **KAYARTIS,** b f Kaytu - Polyartis by Artaius (USA) (Mrs M Reveley) 1195^2 1654^1 1890^3 2166^2 3473^8 3599^3
2 **KAYDARAJ,** b f Domynsky - Uptown Girl by Caruso (R A Fahey) 1082^6 1272^3 1475^3 3183^6 3566 3673^9 4193
4 **KAYFA (Ire),** b f Shernazar - Kaysama (Fr) by Kenmare (Fr) (Noel Meade) $4684a^5$ 308 787^3 942^1 1199^2 2078^5 2606^1 2878 3072^1 3923^4
5 **KAYMONT,** b m Germont - Kaymay by Maystreak (Capt J Wilson) 5^8 67 294
5 **KAYRUZ,** b g Fayruz - Rheinbloom by Rheingold (Graham Richards) $4774a^8$
4 **KAYVEE,** gr g Kaldoun (Fr) - Secret Life (USA) by Elocutionist (USA) (G Harwood) 737^2 1172 2363^9 2854^3 3350^2 3624^6 4172^3 4280^3 4415 4578^2
5 **KAZKAR (Ire),** b g Darshaan - Kashka (USA) by The Minstrel (Can) (J F Bailey Jun) 272 308 1576^9 3336^8
3 **KEATING (Aus),** ch g Keen - Artistic Princess (Aus) by Luskin Star (Aus) (Mrs A Swinbank) 62^7 93^7
3 **KEDGE,** b c Slip Anchor - Bercheba by Bellypha (R F Johnson Houghton) 842^9 1068 1690^3 1948^2 3087 3759 3943^5 4256^9 4457
4 **KEDWICK (Ire),** b g Be My Guest (USA) - Lady Pavlova by Ballymore (J G Burns) 2041 2346^4 3858^6
3 **KEEN AND CLEAN (Ire),** b f Taufan (USA) - Weavers' Tack by Weavers' Hall (D Moffatt) 1851^6 2202 2651^5
2 **KEEN BID (Ire),** b c Alzao (USA) - Gaychimes by Steel Heart (W Jarvis) 4419
6 **KEEN HUNTER (USA),** ch h Diesis - Love's Reward by Nonoalco (USA) (J H M Gosden) 1786^2 2362^4 2927^3 3464^6
5 **KEEN VISION (Ire),** b g Vision (USA) - Calvino by Relkino (D W P Arbuthnot) $4798a^2$
3 **KEEP BATTLING,** b g Hard Fought - Keep Mum by Mummy's Pet (A Harrison) 1595^5 2064^9 2338^4 2953^6 3564 4217^7 4348
3 **KEEP BREATHING,** b g Northern Tempest (USA) - Stolen-Secret by Burglar (S Gollings) $4766a^8$ $4772a^8$
4 **KEEP ME IN MIND (Ire),** b g Don't Forget Me - Gold Trinket by Golden Fleece (USA) (N R Mitchell) 719^7 994 1143^9
3 **KEEP SAFE,** b f Superlative - Jem Jen by Great Nephew (C A Cyzer) 443^6 821 1175^8
3 **KEEP YOUR DISTANCE,** b g Elegant Air - Normanby Lass by Bustino (Mrs M Reveley) 318^9 966 1426
2 **KEFAHI (Ire),** ch g Kefaah (USA) - Shomoose by Habitat (A A Scott) 3589^5 3809^2 3990^3 4167 4427^6
4 **KELIMUTU,** br f Top Ville - Soemba by General Assembly (USA) (J Pearce) 2127^1 2873^6 3308^6 3551^1 3710^1 3831^2 4086^1 4271^6 4336
3 **KELLSBORO LASS (Ire),** ch f Glenstal (USA) - Secret Meeting by Pas de Seul (J G Burns) 268^7 307^6 647^5
3 **KELLY MAC,** b c Precocious - Ridalia by Ridan (USA) (M R Channon) 491^5 2212 2686^4 3080^6 3311^2 3712^4 3766^3 3938^8
2 **KELLYSI,** b g Primo Dominie - Formidable Dancer by Formidable (USA) (P F I Cole) 793^8 3836^3 4033^7 4356 4500^4
5 **KELLY'S KITE,** br m Buzzards Bay - Bold Kelly by Pitskelly (H J Collingridge) 1209 1453 2001^2 2520^8 2747 3057^7 3643^7 4164
3 **KELTIC OPTION (Ire),** ch f Doulab (USA) - Break Of Day by On Your Mark (J S Bolger) 4625
4 **KENBU (Fr),** gr f Kenmare (Fr) - Tarlace by Targowice (F Boutin) 273^3 2981^8 3414^6
3 **KENESHA (Ire),** br f Don't Forget Me - Calvino by Relkino (S Dow) 821^5 992^7 3670 3863^6 3957 4711
2 **KENILWORTH FORD,** b f Merdon Melody - Earles-Field by Wolverlife (Capt J Wilson) 3520 3754 3972 4329 4577^9
3 **KENNEDYS PRIMA,** b or br f Primo Dominie - Double Finesse by Double Jump (A A Scott) 683 2697 3006^2 3343^8 3459 4222^5 4346^3
2 **KENNET BOY,** b c Nomination - Helewise by Dance In Time (Can) (P F I Cole) 399^3 554^5 877^7 3688^3 3841^7 4418
3 **KENNINGTON PROTON,** br f Interrex (Can) - Supper Party by He Loves Me (R T Juckes) 1266 1685 2151^9 2481
3 **KENSWORTH LADY,** b f Formidable (USA) - Icefern by Moorestyle (M Blanshard) 418 927 1137^5 1352^3 1728^1 2214 2352^6 2728^2 2910^9 3266^5 4592^8
2 **KENTAVRUS WAY (Ire),** b g Thatching - Phantom Row by Adonijah (R Charlton) 2990 3260^3 4067
3 **KENTUCKY BABY (Ire),** ch f Shy Groom (USA) - Ice Baby by Grundy (Edward Lynam) 258^9 281 307^5 1574^8 1995 2702 2922^7 3399^2 3544^3 3576^4 4136^7 4370^1 4408^8 4583^4 4738
5 **KENTUCKY COFFEE (Fr),** ch h Kenmare (Fr) - Marie de Fontenoy (Fr) by Lightning (Fr) (R Collett) 4010
3 **KENTUCKY DREAMS,** b g Dreams To Reality (USA) - Kentucky Tears (USA) by Cougar (Chi) (Ronald Thompson) 275^7 362^7 928 1074 1896^8 2095
2 **KENTUCKY FLYER,** ch f Bairn (USA) - Kentucky Air (USA) by Czaravich (USA) (J F Bottomley) 2102 3183^5 3321^2 3903 4358 4436
4 **KENYATTA (USA),** b g Mogambo (USA) - Caranga (USA) by Caro (A Moore) $4806a^3$ 61^5 159^3 2162 2822^5
3 **KEPPOLS HARRIER (Ire),** b or br g Phardante (Fr) - Keppols by Furry Glen (John Houghton) 2249^9 2902^3 3578^7 3772^8 4137^7 4368
6 **KEPPOLS PRINCE,** b or br h Kampala - Keppols by Furry Glen (John Houghton) 2035^5 2143^1 4639 4737
2 **KERAKA (USA),** b f Storm Bird (Can) - Kerita by Formidable (USA) (John M Oxx) 3039^1 3200^4 3611^1 3925^5
2 **KERAMIC,** b f Efisio - Branston Express by Bay Express (D Haydn Jones) 1071^4 1241^2 1583^8 2472^4
3 **KERB CRAWLER,** b g Tina's Pet - Sovereign Love by He Loves Me (T Stack) 256^3 280^1 572^6
3 **KERKI (USA),** b c Shareef Dancer (USA) - Sophonisbe by Wollow (F Boutin) 2646^6
3 **KERKURA (USA),** ch f Riverman (USA) - Kenanga by Kris (H R A Cecil) 2464^2 3173^2 3491^1
3 **KERMIS (Fr),** b g Honest Pleasure (USA) - Kiri by Kris (Patrick Woods) 577 788^7 3380^9 4246
3 **KERRIA,** b f Celestial Storm (USA) - Tree Mallow by Malicious (R Earnshaw) 712^7
2 **KERRIE-JO,** b f Merdon Melody - Whipalash by Stephen George (M J Haynes) 399^2 477^3 657^5 1009^3 1279^6 2137^5 2500^4 3167^3 3664^1 4561^2 4733
3 **KERRYKEEL LADY (Ire),** b f Vision (USA) - Persian Caprice by Persian Bold (D T Hughes) 4368 4625 4690
3 **KESANTA,** b f The Dissident - Nicaline by High Line (W G M Turner) 351^6 499^8
4 **KESS (Ire),** b f Kafu - Joanns Goddess by Godswalk (USA) (W T Bourke) 851 1295^5 1507 1822^8 3614^8 4408
3 **KESTON POND (Ire),** b g Taufan (USA) - Maria Renata by Jaazeiro (USA) (G C Bravery) 2752^4 3272^7 3817^2 4125^2
3 **KEYLOCK (USA),** b f Diesis - Sure Locked (USA) by Lyphard (USA) (W Jarvis) 1452^4 3514^6 3639^9 3961^9 4176^1 4353^2 4454^3 4621^6 4695^2
2 **KEY OF LUCK (USA),** b c Chief's Crown (USA) - Balbonela by Gay Mecene (Mrs C Head) 2980^2 3413^2 3799^1 4195^1
2 **KEYS OF SILCA,** b c Hallgate - Princess Silca Key by Grundy (M R Channon) 4523
3 **KEY TO MY HEART (Ire),** b c Broken Hearted - Originality by Godswalk (USA) (D Moffatt) 468^2 855^2 1338^3 1719^3 2393^1 3434^4 3879^2 4039^3
3 **KEYWAY (USA),** ch c Groovy (USA) - Maui Manor (USA) by Hawaii (Sir Mark Prescott) 284^1 370^1 474^4 1780^6 2066^7 2220^2 2680^5 2995^5 4241^3 4335^3 4481^5
2 **KEZIO RUFO (Ire),** gr c Persian Heights - Kashapour by Nishapour (Fr) (P A Kelleway) 1810^1 2438^2 2998^6
6 **KFAAF (Ire),** 2644^9 3023^4

4 **KHALIDI (Ire)**, b g Shernazar - Khaiyla by Mill Reef (USA) (D R Gandolfo) 2992 3307 3646^{3}

4 **KHALLOOF (Ire)**, b g Ballad Rock - Tapiola by Tap On Wood (Denys Smith) 358^{8} 505^{5} 610 887^{5} 1052 1186^{3} 1436 1578^{3} 1736^{7} 2017^{2} 4104 4217^{6}

3 **KHALYANI (Ire)**, b c Akarad (Fr) - Khaiyla by Mill Reef (USA) (R Rowe) 2249^{2} 2460^{1} 3494^{1} 3914^{2} 4730^{7}

2 **KHAMASEEN**, b c Slip Anchor - Tanouma (USA) by Miswaki (USA) (J L Dunlop) 2250^{6} 4027^{3} 4259^{2} 4547^{4}

3 **KHARASAR (Ire)**, b c Standaan (Fr) - Khatima by Relko (John M Oxx) 256^{4} 311^{3} 551^{1} 1050^{3}

3 **KHASI HILLS (Ire)**, br f Kafu - Tower Bank by Tower Walk (Patrick Martin) 1333 1649

2 **KHATIR (Can)**, gr c Alwasmi (USA) - Perfect Poppy (USA) by Poppy Jay (D Morley) 3742^{7} 4014^{4} 4316^{5} 4492^{1}

3 **KHATTAT (USA)**, ch c El Gran Senor (USA) - Don't Joke (USA) by Shecky Greene (USA) (J L Dunlop) 470^{6} 1060^{3}

2 **KHAYA**, br f Mazilier (USA) - Always A Lady by Dominion (M McCormack) 3317 3781^{9} 4269^{6}

5 **KHAZARI (USA)**, ch g Shahrastani (USA) - Kozana by Kris (W Rock) 2808^{7} 4288

3 **KHISAL (Can)**, ch c Deputy Minister (Can) - Karenja (USA) by Raja Baba (USA) (D Morley) 459^{6} 567^{3} 799^{3} 1165^{5} 1591^{5} 1907

5 **KHOJOHN**, ch g Chief Singer - Pirate Lass (USA) by Cutlass (USA) (Mrs V A Aconley) 4742a

3 **KHORAZ (USA)**, b c The Minstrel (Can) - Kozana by Kris (John M Oxx) 574^{4} 1364 3618^{7}

3 **KHRAUSS (Fr)**, (J de Roualle) 1410^{6}

4 **KHRISMA**, ch f Kris - Sancta by So Blessed (Mrs J Cecil) 4670a^{3} 4749a^{1} 4782a^{2} 9^{4}

3 **KHUBZA**, b f Green Desert (USA) - Breadcrumb by Final Straw (H R A Cecil) 752^{1} 1231^{2} 1950

3 **KIAWAH**, ch f Master Willie - Polly Packer by Reform (C C Elsey) 499^{9} 1005^{8} 1133^{1} 1389 1771^{2} 3221^{1} 3689^{2} 4152^{8} 4279^{5}

4 **KICK ON MAJESTIC (Ire)**, b g Mister Majestic - Avebury Ring by Auction Ring (USA) (N Bycroft) 1286^{2} 1578 1938^{8} 2217^{8} 2369^{7} 2768^{6} 3002 3057

3 **KIDAMIYA (Ire)**, b f Darshaan - Kimiya (USA) by Sir Ivor (A P O'Brien) 552^{7} 1014^{2} 2287 2881 3293

2 **KID ORY**, ch g Rich Charlie - Woomargama by Creetown (P Calver) 3520^{6} 3972^{4} 4526^{3} 4703^{3}

2 **KIERCHEM (Ire)**, b c Mazaad - Smashing Gale by Lord Gayle (USA) (R F Fisher) 433^{1} 1168^{2} 1381^{7}

4 **KILADANTE (Ire)**, b f Phardante (Fr) - Marble Cloud by Hard Tack (A P O'Brien) 3382^{2}

2 **KILCOO**, b f Green Desert (USA) - Kiliniski by Niniski (USA) (J H M Gosden) 4715^{2}

4 **KILCSEM EILE (Ire)**, b f Commanche Run - Senane by Vitiges (Fr) (James O'Haire) 3295^{8} 3854

3 **KILDEE LAD**, b c Presidium - National Time (USA) by Lord Avie (USA) (A P Jones) 455^{2} 600 1232^{6} 1505^{2} 1655^{2} 1874^{5} 2033^{4} 2967^{3} 3253^{4} 3709^{4} 3942^{1} 4090^{3} 4277

3 **KILDERRY (Ire)**, b f Nordico (USA) - Affordalot by Forham (USA) (A J McNamara) 2677

2 **KILERNAN**, ch c K-Battery - Lekuti by Le Coq D'Or (T D Barron) 3974^{9} 4489 4641^{4}

3 **KILLEEN STAR (Ire)**, b c Wolverlife - Movement by Daring Display (USA) (M J Grassick) 1105^{2} 1386^{2} 1515^{5} 2295^{1} 3244^{8} 3561^{9} 3928^{6} 4057

5 **KILLICK**, b m Slip Anchor - Enthralment (USA) by Sir Ivor (A Bailey) 4688a^{6} 4748a^{1} 4758a^{1} 4799a^{3} 48^{2} 87^{2} 142^{2} 169^{2} 198^{7} 403^{2} 628^{7} 845^{2} 894^{1} 1398 1593^{5} 1681^{8} 1946^{3} 2149^{6} 2373^{8}

5 **KILLIGO (Swe)**, 3936^{6}

2 **KILLING TIME**, b c Good Times (Ity) - Kelly's Bid by Pitskelly (R Hannon) 1063^{9} 1497^{7} 2419^{7} 3989^{3} 4351 4750

4 **KILLSHANDRA (Ire)**, b f Heraldiste (USA) - Gulistan by Sharpen Up (Mrs Barbara Waring) 4256 4684

4 **KILLY**, ch c Dominion - Figini by Glint Of Gold (F H Lee) 232^{4} 302

3 **KILLY'S FILLY**, b f Lochnager - May Kells by Artaius (USA) (J Berry) 353^{2} 451^{2} 611^{2} 884^{1} 1167^{2} 1480^{1} 1760^{9} 1891^{4} 2707^{2} 2934^{4} 3118^{3} 3354^{4} 3378^{3} 3564^{4}

2 **KILLY'S RAYNJA (Ire)**, gr c Petong - Home In Pasadena by Home Guard (USA) (J Berry) 3114^{7} 3713^{2} 4663^{8}

2 **KILMOOD LASS (Ire)**, ch f Tout Ensemble - Exburys Rose by Viking (USA) (Daniel J Murphy) 4388^{1}

2 **KILNOE (Ire)**, b or br f Rhoman Rule (USA) - Paddock Princess by Dragonara Palace (USA) (A P O'Brien) 4380 4535 4582

3 **KILTIMAGH (Ire)**, b f Imperial Frontier (USA) - Star Above (Fr) by Formidable (USA) (Edward Lynam) 790^{5} 1107^{3} 1507^{3} 1755^{4}

3 **KILTIMONY**, b f Sharpo - Epithet by Mill Reef (USA) (C Collins) 280 486^{6} 639^{7} 2674^{2} 3161^{1} 3497^{3} 3544^{8} 3928^{2} 4056^{5}

4 **KILTROUM (Fr)**, gr g Courtroom (Fr) - Kiltie by Habat (C Tinkler) 4743a^{2} 3409^{7} 3535 3758^{8} 3794^{2} 4031^{6} 4085^{3}

3 **KIMBERLEY BOY**, b c Mtoto - Diamond House by Habitat (G F H Charles-Jones) 2135^{5} 2758^{5} 3587

5 **KIMBERLEY PARK**, b m Try My Best (USA) - Georgina Park by Silly Season (D W P Arbuthnot) 2821^{5} 2987 3504 3747^{5} 3957^{4} 4024^{1}

3 **KIMBOLTON KORKER**, ch f Interrex (Can) - One Sharper by Dublin Taxi (J Balding) 1157^{6} 1360^{3} 1516^{1} 1714^{4} 1966^{3} 2934^{6} 4109

3 **KIMMY'S PRINCESS**, ch f Prince Sabo - Miss Kimmy by Tower Walk (J L Harris) 367^{5} 428 1990^{5} 2365^{5} 3967^{5}

4 **KINCARDINE BRIDGE (USA)**, b g Tiffany Ice (USA) - Priestess (USA) by Time To Explode (USA) (Mrs S C Bradburne) 1517^{6} 1736^{9}

3 **KINCHENJUNGA**, b f Darshaan - Konigsalpen (Ger) by Priamos (Ger) (W R Muir) 1176^{8} 1603 2977^{3} 3320^{8}

3 **KINDERGARTEN**, b f Trempolino (USA) - Children's Corner (Fr) by Top Ville (A Fabre) 2690^{6} 3149^{8}

2 **KINDERGARTEN BOY (Ire)**, b c Mon Tresor - High Profile by High Top (R Boss) 3592

3 **KINDNESS ITSELF (Ire)**, ch f Ahonoora - Redeem Herself by General Assembly (USA) (John M Oxx) 806^{2} 1333^{1} 1575^{2} 2078^{4} 2604^{4} 3928^{3} 4056^{3} 4287^{9}

3 **KINEMA RED (USA)**, ch c Diesis - Kinema (USA) by Graustark (J H M Gosden) 304^{2} 441^{3}

2 **KING ACRYLIC (Ire)**, b c King Of Clubs - Maynooth Belle by Busted (R F Fisher) 767^{4} 1051^{4}

5 **KING ATHELSTAN (USA)**, b h Sovereign Dancer (USA) - Wimbledon Star (USA) by Hoist The Flag (USA) (J H M Gosden) 581^{6} 1768 2433^{2} 2884

2 **KING BRUCE**, b c Clantime - Miss Spinney by Uncle Pokey (W A O'Gorman) 3746^{8} 3958^{6} 4339^{6} 4484^{4} 4708^{9}

4 **KINGCHIP BOY**, b g Petong - Silk St James by Pas de Seul (M J Ryan) 4680a^{2} 4758a^{3} 676 1130^{1} 1474^{9} 2161 2327^{7} 2882^{2} 3042^{2} 3269^{3} 3726^{5} 4133^{1} 4514^{6} 4616^{4} 4710^{1}

2 **KING CURAN (USA)**, b c Lear Fan (USA) - Runaway Lady (USA) by Caucasus (USA) (M Bell) 2968 3470^{1} 3813^{1} 4365

3 **KINGDOM OF SHADES (USA)**, ch c Risen Star (USA) - Dancers Countess (USA) by Northern Dancer (J H M Gosden) 1176^{7}

2 **KINGFISHER GREY**, gr c Belfort (Fr) - Lady Ever-So-Sure by Malicious (R F Fisher) 395^{4} 865^{8} 1598^{9}

3 **KINGMAMBO (USA)**, b c Mr Prospector (USA) - Miesque (USA) by Nureyev (USA) (F Boutin) 431^{1} 954^{1} 1749^{1} 3369^{3} 3800^{1} 4173^{3}

2 **KING OF NAPLES (USA)**, b c Ferdinand (USA) - Processional (USA) by Reviewer (USA) (R Charlton) 4628^{1}

4 **KING OF NORMANDY (Ire)**, ch g King Of Clubs - Miss Deauville by Sovereign Path (S G Chadwick) 4795a^{4} 918^{6} 1242

7 **KING OF THE GLEN**, b g King's Ride - Anabore by Darantus (A J McNamara) 4573^{7}

2 **KING OF THE HORSE (Ire)**, ch g Hatim (USA) - Milly Whiteway by Great White Way (USA) (D R Loder) 4726

3 **KING PARIS (Ire)**, ch g King Of Clubs - Alkis (USA) by Roberto (USA) (M Bell) 736^{4} 1125^{5} 1720^{7} 2065^{1} 2279^{4} 2578^{5} 2995^{6} 3174^{2} 3476^{6} 3634^{2} 3811^{1} 3991^{5} 4470

2 **LADY FAIRFAX,** b f Sharrood (USA) - Rathvindon by Realm (R Boss) 3760^{3} 4302^{2} 4422^{3}

2 **LADY FEATHERS,** ch f Kabour - Miss Plumes by Prince de Galles (D W Chapman) 3321

3 **LADY GAIL,** ch f Sharrood (USA) - Martian Princess by Cure The Blues (USA) (L J Barratt) 522 719

3 **LADY GLOW (Ire),** b f Glow (USA) - Splendid Chance by Random Shot (John M Oxx) 488^{8} 1649 2140

2 **LADY GREY (Swe),** gr f Diaghlyphard (USA) - Lady Victoria by Northfields (USA) (D W P Arbuthnot) 3362^{7} 3792^{6} 4003^{8}

2 **LADY GWEN (Ire),** b f Taufan (USA) - Special Meeting by Persian Bold (J J O'Neill) 3554^{9} 3760 4342 4644

2 **LADY HAWK,** ch f Infantry - Wanracine by Dom Racine (Fr) (J White) 3387

2 **LADY HIGHFIELD,** br f High Kicker (USA) - Judy Burton by Mummy's Pet (M J Ryan) 673^{2} 2542^{7}

3 **LADY HONDA (Ire),** ch f Adonijah - Wolverhants by Wolver Hollow (C E Brittain) 2787^{5} 3178^{8} 4087

4 **LADY HOSTESS (Ire),** b f M Double M (USA) - Sunny Eyes by Reliance II (Francis Berry) 4245 4386^{8}

2 **LADY HUNTER (USA),** 4070^{6}

6 **LADY LACEY,** b m Kampala - Cecily by Prince Regent (Fr) (G B Balding) 4723a^{4} 4760a^{3} 521 834^{2} 1120 1316^{6} 1626^{7} 1878^{4} 2520^{1} 2757^{3} 2930^{2} 3290^{6} 3787^{1} 4116^{5} 4254^{6} 4522

2 **LADY LODGER,** ch f Be My Guest (USA) - Eversince (USA) by Foolish Pleasure (USA) (Sir Mark Prescott) 4697^{2}

3 **LADY MAGADI,** b f Mtoto - Lady Of The Land by Wollow (B Richmond) 80 3138^{4} 3361^{6}

3 **LADY MAVIS,** ch f Nearly A Hand - Pullandese by Kinglet (A M Forte) 3660^{5} 3937

3 **LADY NOBLE (Ire),** b f The Noble Player (USA) - Racy Lady by Continuation (Patrick Joseph Flynn) 1610^{6} 1796^{7} 2140^{3} 2518^{3} 3062^{7} 4324^{4}

6 **LADY OF PERSIA (USA),** ch m Persian Bold - Tants by Vitiges (Fr) (T Clout) 4754a^{1} 693^{7}

3 **LADY OF SHADOWS,** ch f Ballacashtal (Can) - Little Madam by Habat (S Dow) 4677a^{8} 4708a 600 720 1095 2445^{5} 2724 3047^{4}

5 **LADY OLEIN (Ire),** b m Alzao (USA) - Katie Cecil by Princely Gift (Mrs John Harrington) 4245^{4}

3 **LADY OUNAVARRA (Ire),** br f Simply Great (Fr) - Hostess by Be My Guest (USA) (Liam Browne) 4704a

2 **LADY PHYL,** b f Northiam (USA) - Phyl by Ballad Rock (B J Meehan) 2096^{4} 2292^{8} 2357^{7} 2895^{4} 3082^{1} 3406^{6} 3635^{8}

5 **LADY POLY,** b m Dunbeath (USA) - First Temptation (USA) by Mr Leader (USA) (R F Stone) 1861

4 **LADY PRESIDENT (Ire),** b or br f Dominion - Mrs McArdy by Tribal Chief (Patrick Prendergast) 310^{5} 599^{6} 1515^{3} 1620^{2} 1795^{3} 1923^{2} 2323^{2} 2675^{1} 3244^{6} 3606^{2} 4385^{6} 4635^{6}

4 **LADY RANDOLPH,** b f Elegant Air - Cara Rose by Rheingold (B Ellison) 1562 1873^{7}

3 **LADY RELKO,** b f Sizzling Melody - Rosalka (Ity) by Relko (R Voorspuy) 519 758 1313 1488^{9} 3634^{9} 3766 3955 4088

2 **LADY RISKY,** ch f Risk Me (Fr) - First Fastnet by Ahonoora (R Hannon) 1082^{8} 1555^{2} 1741^{7} 2125^{4}

4 **LADY ROXANNE,** br f Cyrano de Bergerac - Red Lory by Bay Express (Lord Huntingdon) 206^{3} 217^{5} 319^{3} 1246^{5}

3 **LADY SABINA,** ch f Bairn (USA) - Calibina by Caliban (O O'Neill) 2032^{3} 3693^{9} 3893^{5} 4125^{3} 4524^{4} 4666^{2}

4 **LADY SABO,** br f Prince Sabo - Nice Lady by Connaught (R C Spicer) 4669a^{4} 421^{4} 568 948^{4} 1537^{7} 1977^{4} 2466^{1} 3020^{8} 3593 3788^{3} 4224^{4} 4652^{4} 4762^{7}

2 **LADY SAPIEN (Ire),** b f Homo Sapien - Sarmonia (Fr) by Armos (A J McNamara) 2742 3453^{9} 3527^{5} 4360^{8}

3 **LADYS BID (Ire),** b f Auction Ring (USA) - Miss Spencer by Imperial Fling (USA) (M A O'Toole) 2743^{8} 2903^{7} 3074^{8} 3368^{5} 4534

2 **LADY SHERIFF,** b f Taufan (USA) - Midaan by Sallust (M W Easterby) 1837^{5} 2128^{1} 2446^{2} 2814^{2} 3133^{4} 3279^{1} 3629^{2} 3845 4193^{7} 4436^{7}

6 **LADY SHIRL (USA),** b m That's A Nice - Canonization by Bold Native 4729a^{8}

2 **LADY SILK,** ch f Prince Sabo - Adduce (USA) by Alleged (USA) (J L Dunlop) 3209 3446^{5} 4338^{4} 4564

6 **LADY SNOOBLE,** b m King Of Clubs - Ides Of March by Mummy's Pet (K O Cunningham-Brown) 4673a^{7} 113^{8}

2 **LADY'S VISION (Ire),** b f Vision (USA) - Ladys Prerogative by General Assembly (USA) (Patrick Joseph Flynn) 3954^{1} 4462 4610^{5}

2 **LADY SWIFT,** ch f Jalmood (USA) - Appealing by Star Appeal (K W Hogg) 299 395^{9} 2447^{4} 2505^{8}

2 **LADY TETRUS,** b f Music Boy - Belaka by Beldale Flutter (USA) (I A Balding) 4496

2 **LADY TJONGER,** b f Sharrood (USA) - Indian Pink (USA) by Seattle Slew (USA) (Dr J D Scargill) 4492^{9} 4698

3 **LADY TYONE (Ire),** b f Jareer (USA) - True Colour (Fr) by Known Fact (USA) (A P O'Brien) 789^{2} 1046^{2} 3038^{4} 3163^{6}

2 **LADY VALENSINA (Ire),** ch f Jareer (USA) - Coshlea by Red Alert (D R C Elsworth) 4127 4440 4651^{3}

2 **LADY VALIENT,** b f Handsome Sailor - Polola by Aragon (Mark Campion) 4587^{8}

2 **LADY VENDETTA (USA),** ch f Explosive Bid (USA) - Shredaline (USA) by Shredder (USA) (N A Callaghan) 3041^{5}

2 **LADY WESTBURY (Ire),** b f Superpower - Fleur-De-Luce by Tumble Wind (USA) (K R Burke) 1555^{6} 2526^{4} 2825^{6} 4264^{8}

9 **LADY WESTGATE,** b m Welsh Chanter - Church Bay by Reliance II (G B Balding) 4760a

2 **LADY WILLIAMS (Ire),** ch f Roi Danzig (USA) - Apple Rings by Godswalk (USA) (Lord Huntingdon) 3009^{5} 3642^{2} 3958^{5} 4251

6 **LAFKADIO,** b g Gay Mecene (USA) - Lakonia by Kris (M C Chapman) 4742a^{7} 4813a^{4} 53^{2} 137^{4} 175^{5} 226^{7} 303 427^{5} 702^{4} 901^{3} 1564

5 **LA FRANCESA (Arg),** ch m Fort de France (Arg) - La Endiablada (Arg) by Right Of Way (Mme C Head) 3801^{6} 4309^{2}

2 **LAFTAH (USA),** ch c Affirmed (USA) - Norette by Northfields (USA) (B Hanbury) 2364^{3} 4003^{5} 4440^{7}

2 **LA GRANDE CASCADE (USA),** b f Beaudelaire (USA) - Sandy Baby by Al Hattab (R Collet) 2980^{4} 4402^{6}

4 **LAGRION (USA),** ch f Diesis - Wrap It Up by Mount Hagen (Fr) (A J Maxwell) 959^{4} 1202^{9} 1962^{9} 3038^{6} 3326^{8}

3 **LA GROUPIE (Fr),** ch f Groom Dancer (USA) - L'irlandaise by Irish River (Mme C Head) 359^{2} 983^{2} 1545^{5} 4169^{2} 4691^{2}

4 **LAHOOB (USA),** b g Miswaki (USA) - Sure Locked (USA) by Lyphard (USA) (B Hanbury) 475 651^{3}

3 **LAID BACK BEN,** ch g Starch Reduced - Mrs Dumbfounded by Adropejo (B Palling) 4668a^{8} 326^{9} 418^{5} 713^{3} 871^{9} 1376^{7} 2424^{6} 3188^{7} 3391^{7} 3734

3 **L'AIGLE D'OR (USA),** ch c Believe It (USA) - Thirst For Gold (USA) by Mr Prospector (USA) (R M Flower) 300

3 **LAILATI (USA),** ch f Mr Prospector (USA) - Carduel (USA) by Buckpasser (M R Stoute) 1671^{3} 1911^{4} 3866^{3} 4188

4 **LAJADHAL (Fr),** gr g Bellypha - Rose D'Amour (USA) by Lines Of Power (USA) (J A Bennett) 4721a^{8} 4780a^{5} 8^{8} 61^{9} 179^{7} 826^{9} 1321

3 **LAKAB (USA),** ch f Manila (USA) - River Lullaby (USA) by Riverman (USA) (H Thomson Jones) 444^{3} 725 1181^{4} 3341^{1} 3736 4133^{3} 4605

2 **LAKE COUNTRY (Ire),** b f Fairy King (USA) - Fantasy Land by Nonoalco (USA) (M V O'Brien) 1509^{1} 2075^{4} 2647^{2}

4 **LAKE DOMINION,** b g Primo Dominie - Piney Lake by Sassafras (Fr) (P W Harris) 4694

4 **LAKE HOTEL (Ire),** br g Nashamaa - Killyhevlin by Green God (W M Roper) 959^{7} 1163^{7} 3028^{7}

2 **LAKE KARIBA,** b c Persian Bold - Gold Bracelet by Golden Fleece (USA) (Charles O'Brien) 2072^{8} 4581^{1} 4687^{4}

3 **LAKE OF LOUGHREA (Ire),** ch g Kings Lake (USA) - Polynesian Charm (USA) by What A Pleasure (USA) (Kevin Prendergast) 789 1025 1139^{6} 2186^{5} 2296^{4} 3277^{1} 3367^{1} 3484^{2} 3604^{5} 4246

2 **LAKE PARVA,** ch c Thatching - Laugharne by Known Fact (USA) (P F I Cole) 2250[9] 3260[7] 3888

2 **LAKE POET (USA),** b c Danzig (USA) - Lake Valley (USA) by Mr Prospector (USA) (M R Stoute) 4627[7]

3 **LAKE POOPO (Ire),** b f Persian Heights - Bolivia (Ger) by Windwurf (Ger) (B W Hills) 352[3] 534[2] 1256[4] 1813[1] 2152[2] 3513[2] 3998[1] 4283

4 **LALA,** 2839[5]

2 **LALA MUSA,** b f Kris - Laluche (USA) by Alleged (USA) (C E Brittain) 4026[2]

2 **LALINDI (Ire),** b f Cadeaux Genereux - Soemba by General Assembly (USA) (G Wragg) 4575[4]

4 **LA MAJA (Ire),** b f Lafontaine (USA) - Eiger Sanctions by St Alphage (Capt D G Swan) 309 4162

4 **LAMASTRE,** b f Jalmood (USA) - Daring Lass by Bold Lad (Ire) (C Weedon) 211

3 **LAMBADA (Ger),** 2259 3647[7]

3 **LAMBAST,** b f Relkino - Lambay by Lorenzaccio (D Nicholson) 1746[2] 2937[3] 3708[2] 3980[4] 4279[2]

2 **LAMBENT,** b f Rambo Dancer (Can) - Nafla (Fr) by Arctic Tern (USA) (E Weymes) 544[1] 841[6] 1303[2] 2234[2] 2592[3] 3145[1]

7 **LAMBOURN RAJA,** b g Indian King (USA) - Take A Chance (Fr) by Baldric II (J O'Donoghue) 2789 2992 3509 3551 3910 4713

6 **LAMBSON,** b g Petorius - Julie Be Quick (USA) by Selari (R M Whitaker) 1112[6] 1781

3 **LA MENORQUINA (USA),** b f Woodman (USA) - Hail The Lady (USA) by Hail The Pirates (USA) (L M Cumani) 1656[4] 1919[8] 3212[3] 3461 3943[2] 4357[5] 4695[4]

4 **LAMORE RITORNA,** br f Lidhame - Arbor Lane by Wolverlife (K O Cunningham-Brown) 43[7] 114

3 **LAMSONETTI,** b f Never So Bold - Orient by Bay Express (R M Whitaker) 428[5] 742[2] 963[4] 1136 1761[4] 2133[5] 2760[5] 3378[2] 3439[1] 3564[7] 3747 4458 4536

3 **LAMU LADY (Ire),** b f Lomond (USA) - Noble Mark by On Your Mark (P W Chapple-Hyam) 855[6] 1919 2315[4] 2685[7] 4152[9] 4506

2 **LANCASHIRE LIFE (Ire),** b c Petorius - Parlais by Pardao (E J Alston) 1296[4] 2374[6] 2630[7] 4021[5] 4193[9]

3 **LANCASTER PILOT,** ch g Crofthall - Spinner by Blue Cashmere (R M Whitaker) 397[6] 836 1869[4] 2602[4]

6 **LAND AFAR,** b g Dominion - Jouvencelle by Rusticaro (Fr) (J Webber) 3761[5] 4157[2]

4 **LANDED GENTRY (USA),** b c Vaguely Noble - Phydilla (Fr) by Lyphard (USA) (C D Broad) 4621

3 **LANDO (Ger),** b c Acatenango (Ger) - Laurea by Sharpman (H Jentzsch) 953[6] 1724[7] 2259[1] 3371[2] 3795[1]

3 **LAND O'LAKES (Ire),** b c Kings Lake (USA) - Amboselli by Raga Navarro (Ity) (Sir Mark Prescott) 4691a[3] 4718a[2] 1500[1] 1701[9] 1892[4]

5 **LANDOLFI,** 4746[7]

3 **LANDRAIL (USA),** ch f Storm Bird (Can) - Vaguely Sensitive (USA) by Sensitive Prince (USA) (B W Hills) 854[5] 1464[2] 2087[4] 3533[4] 4087[4] 4454[5]

4 **LANGTONIAN,** br g Primo Dominie - Yankee Special by Bold Lad (Ire) (J L Eyre) 379[4] 429[4] 866[4] 1052 1183[3] 1631[2] 1815[2] 1937[6] 2215[6] 2456[5] 2682[5] 3568[2] 3758 3995

7 **LANGTRY LADY,** b m Pas de Seul - Arianna Aldini by Habitat (M J Ryan) 990[2] 1110[6] 1346[5] 1530[4] 1730[5] 2045[2] 2198[6]

6 **LANGUEDOC,** b g Rousillon (USA) - Can Can Girl by Gay Fandango (USA) (Martyn Wane) 677[1] 796 1081[3] 1228[3] 1397[3] 1494[4] 2241[4] 2392[8] 2600 3184[7] 3354[3] 3440[3] 3676[9] 4217[3] 4458[9]

3 **LANKRIDGE,** b c Alzao (USA) - Free Dance (Fr) by Green Dancer (USA) (Major W R Hern) 2117[5] 2563[3] 2907[9] 3850[4] 4209[5] 4470

5 **LANTERN LUCK (Ire),** b or br m The Parson - Cahernane Girl by Bargello (Michael Hourigan) 753

3 **LANZAMAR,** b f Buzzards Bay - Maravista by Swing Easy (USA) (R T Phillips) 624[8] 761 1192[7] 1496[9] 1859[7] 4596[7]

4 **LAP OF LUXURY,** gr f Sharrood (USA) - Lap Of Honour by Final Straw (W Jarvis) 2211 2794 3093[1] 3477[1] 4648[6]

4 **LA POINTE,** 1219[6]

3 **LA POSADA,** b f Procida (USA) - Chepstow Vale (USA) by Key To The Mint (USA) (J S Moore) 1713[9] 3708[4]

2 **LA QUICA,** b f Reference Point - Flamenco (USA) by Dance Spell (USA) (P F I Cole) 2583[2]

5 **LARA'S BABY (Ire),** ch m Valiyar - Tapiola by Tap On Wood (P D Evans) 123[4] 164[4] 3121[5] 3407[6]

2 **LA REINA BLANCA (Spa),** b f Glauco (Spa) - Ribaka (USA) by Ribot (T Thomson Jones) 4619[3]

5 **LA REINE ROUGE (Ire),** ch m Red Sunset - Free Rein by Sagaro (Mrs A Knight) 55[7] 78 141[6] 189[2] 229[6] 235[4] 265[1] 322[1] 601[3] 723[5] 1075[9] 1346

2 **LA RESIDENCE,** b c Doulab (USA) - Ideal Home by Home Guard (USA) (Mrs N Macauley) 3520[5] 3816[2] 4210 4416 4618[8] 4725[4]

3 **LARGO KEY (Ire),** b f Taufan (USA) - Dance On Lady by Grundy (Kevin Prendergast) 280 486

2 **LA RIVERAINE (USA),** b f Riverman (USA) - La Romaria (USA) by Vaguely Noble (J W Hills) 3352[5] 3659[4] 4249

3 **LARKSPUR LEGEND,** ch g Legend Of France (USA) - Remainder Tip by Remainder Man (J Mackie) 3092[5] 3361[5]

6 **LARNACA,** b g Shernazar - Checkers by Habat (B V Kelly) 4686a[5]

3 **LARN FORT,** gr g Belfort (Fr) - Larnem by Meldrum (C W Fairhurst) 4770a[3] 40[8] 63[3] 106[4] 275[1] 398[8] 568[7] 907[4] 1160[1] 1356[5] 2105[4] 2469[2] 2651[3] 3184[8] 3628[5] 4331 4537

4 **LARRIKIN (USA),** b f Slew O'Gold (USA) - For The Flag (USA) by Forli (Arg) (Lord Huntingdon) 4188[5] 4364

3 **LASKO (Ger),** b c Caerwent - La Salina by Kronzeuge (B Schutz) 594[3] 1125[2] 1882[7] 4194[3] 4398[5]

2 **LAS MENINAS (Ire),** b f Glenstal (USA) - Spanish Habit by Habitat (T Stack) 1571[1] 3200[2]

3 **LA SPEZIA,** b f Last Tycoon - Helenetta by Troy (J H M Gosden) 3117[5] 3514[2] 3708[1] 3963[4] 4274[4] 4502

4 **LA SPIA (USA),** f (R Winick) 1695[7]

4 **LAST APPEARANCE,** b f Slip Anchor - Thespian by Ile de Bourbon (USA) (R T Phillips) 1238 2869 3171[5] 4048[7]

3 **LAST ATTEMPT (Nor),** b c Jalmood (USA) - Catechism by Mummy's Pet 3517[2]

4 **LAST CONQUEST (Ire),** b g Slip Anchor - Migiyas by Kings Lake (USA) (R J O'Sullivan) 3288[5]

4 **LAST EMBRACE (Ire),** b f Shernazar - Melodramatic by Tudor Melody (Lord Huntingdon) 1064[2] 1770[4] 2433 4107[5] 4425[4]

6 **LAST EMPEROR (USA),** b h Forli (Arg) - Image Intensifier (USA) by Dancer's Image (USA) (J G Burns) 2345[7] 2692[6] 3826[6] 3951[6]

7 **LAST GOODBYE,** ch g Deep Run - Anaglogs Daughter by Above Suspicion (S J Treacy) 1467[2] 1756[7]

3 **LASTING GRACE (Ire),** (R Collet) 613[6]

2 **LASTOTHEBRADFIELDS,** b f Risk Me (Fr) - Crimpsall by Vaigly Great (M W Easterby) 564[7] 900 1245[9]

5 **LAST STRAW,** b g Blushing Scribe (USA) - Straw Reef by Final Straw (A W Jones) 4719a 4783a[6] 107[2] 138[1] 180[1] 207[7] 236[3] 548[5] 1249[3] 1379[4] 1982[5] 2241[8] 2481[3] 2829[7]

3 **LAST TYPHOON,** b or br f Dowsing (USA) - Song Grove by Song (T H Caldwell) 206 238[8]

2 **LATCH ON (Ire),** b f Dance Of Life (USA) - Latch String by Thatch (USA) (P Aspell) 4610 4706[9]

2 **LATE PARADE (Ire),** b c Astronef - Skisette by Malinowski (A Renzoni) 2260[4] 4197[1]

3 **LATEST FLAME (Ire),** b or br f Last Tycoon - Vagrant Maid (USA) by Honest Pleasure (USA) (D R C Elsworth) 875[8] 1111[8] 1351[6] 1656[7] 1991[2] 2181[3]

3 **LATHERON (Ire),** b c Reference Point - La Romance (USA) by Lyphard (USA) (R Akehurst) 515[8] 4524[7] 4622[8]

2 **LATIFOLIA,** b f Dancing Brave (USA) - Lastcomer (USA) by Kris (D R Loder) 4692[3]

5 **LATIN AMERICAN (USA),** b h Riverman (Fr) - Clever Dance by Mr Prospector (A Fabre) 671[1] 2243[6]

3 **LATIN LEADER,** b c Primo Dominie - Ravaro by Raga Navarro (Ity) (C R Egerton) 397[3] 644[6] 4028

2 **LITTLE SISTER (Ire),** b f Kris - Happy Kin (USA) by Bold Hitter (USA) (M R Stoute) 4651^5
3 **LITTLE TOO MUCH (Ire),** b c Storm Bird (Can) - Begonia (USA) by Plugged Nickle (USA) (G Harwood) 3013^3
4 **LITTLE WASSL (Fr),** 3583^4
4 **LITTLEWICK (Ire),** b f Green Desert (USA) - Loralane by Habitat (G Wragg) 4696a
4 **LIVE AND LET FLY,** gr g Import - Glendyne by Precipice Wood (W S Cunningham) 92^8 133^8
2 **LIVELY (Ire),** b f Digamist (USA) - Georgian Melody by Hello Gorgeous (USA) (G Lewis) 3446 3781 4758^3
2 **LIVELY STREAM,** b c Dance Of Life (USA) - Birch Creek by Carwhite (J M P Eustace) 469^7 687^3
3 **LIVONIAN,** b g Kris - Air Distingue (USA) by Sir Ivor (O Sherwood) 515 825 1212^5 2291^7 2635^1 4181
3 **LIWAN (USA),** b c Lear Fan (USA) - Dual Blessing (USA) by Danzig (USA) (H Thomson Jones) 529
5 **LIYOUN (Ire),** b h Shernazar - Lisana by Alleged (USA) (A Royer Dupre) 1291^4 1754^4
4 **LIZEALITY (USA),** 3207^7
4 **LIZZIE DRIPPIN (Can),** b f Artichoke (USA) - Adieu (Fr) by Tompion (USA) (M D I Usher) 4689a^8 68^6 78^9 164^7
4 **LLOYDS DREAM,** b g Lidhame - Christines Lady by Roman Warrior (D Shaw) 349 416^4 626
5 **LOACH (USA),** 4379^6
3 **LOBELIA (Ire),** ch f Digamist (USA) - Gaylom by Lord Gayle (USA) (T J Naughton) 23^6 62^9 220^7 1237 1861 3068^7
4 **LOBILIO (USA),** b c Robellino (USA) - Nabila (USA) by Foolish Pleasure (USA) (C E Brittain) 350^2 513^3 739 1064 1827 2256^1 2521^4 3018^5 3512 3706^1 4143^8 4364^7
5 **LOCAL DEALER,** ch g Scottish Reel - Green Pool by Whistlefield (J F Bottomley) 745^8
3 **LOCAL HEROINE,** ch f Clantime - Hollia by Touch Boy (J Berry) 866^3 1151^2 1478^6 3136^5 3877^8 4532
2 **LOCHBELLE,** b f Robellino (USA) - Peckitts Well by Lochnager (I A Balding) 1916 2887^4 3939^4
7 **LOCH DUICH,** ch h Kris - Sleat by Santa Claus (R J Hodges) 826^5 1097^8 1237^4 1880^8 1928^2 2315^8 4713^3
5 **LOCH GARANNE,** br m Lochnager - Raperon by Rapid River (M J Camacho) 288^9 453^6
3 **LOCHNAU LADY (Fr),** (J Hammond) 3149^6 3844^8
2 **LOCHON,** br g Lochnager - Sky Mariner by Julio Mariner (W L Barker) 2129 2706 3411^6 3566^3 4044^2 4163^2 4436^3 4608^4
3 **LOCHORE,** b c Nordico (USA) - Hound Song by Jukebox (R Ingram) 4717a^7 4770a^8 813 1524^9 1818^1 2009^6 2311^5 2712^3 3226^3 3588 4231^3 4490
3 **LOCH PATRICK,** b g Beveled (USA) - Daisy Loch by Lochnager (L J Holt) 872^7 1057^1 1841^1 2303^5 2908^2 3438^7 4151^6
5 **LOCHSONG,** b m Song - Peckitts Well by Lochnager (I A Balding) 795^3 1019^4 1406^4 1465^3 2252^1 2927^1 3464^1 3777^3 4312^1
7 **LOCK KEEPER (USA),** b g Riverman (USA) - Jamila by Sir Gaylord (R J Hodges) 4705a^4 4744a^2 4764a^3 4785a^1 13^3 38^3 50^1 108^5 150^1 188^2 202^2 229^8 4115^8 4391
3 **LOCK'S HEATH (Can),** b f Topsider (USA) - Lock's Dream (USA) by Youth (USA) (John M Oxx) 1445^1 2606^8 2779^2 3300^1 3542^9
3 **LOCK TIGHT (USA),** b g Key To The Kingdom (USA) - Parissaul by Saulingo (R M Whitaker) 642^1 817^5 1146 2130^9
5 **LODESTAR (Ire),** b h Rainbow Quest (USA) - Air Distingue (USA) by Sir Ivor (N Tinkler) 681
6 **LODGING,** ch g Longleat (USA) - Mollified by Lombard (Ger) (B Ellison) 4662a 1900 2178^5
10 **LOFT BOY,** b g Cawston's Clown - Burglar Tip by Burglar (J D Bethell) 887^3 1036 1287 1815^3 2215^5 2935^5 3995
3 **LOFTY DEED (USA),** b g Shadeed (USA) - Soar Aloft (USA) by Avatar (USA) (W J Musson) 834
3 **LOGAN'S LUCK (USA),** b c Believe It (USA) - Fancy Wings (USA) by Wing Out (USA) (Lady Herries) 1150^5
5 **LOKI (Ire),** ch g Thatching - Sigym by Lord Gayle (USA) (D K Weld) 513^1 663^3 1021^5 1717^3 2878^4 3494^6 3752^2 4300^4
3 **LOLA WANTS,** br f Lidhame - Plain Tree by Wolver Hollow (C F Wall) 3118^6
2 **LOMAS (Ire),** b c Ela-Mana-Mou - Bold Miss by Bold Lad (Ire) (R Hannon) 1949^1 2209^1 2924^3
4 **LOMBARD OCEAN,** ch g Ballacashtal (Can) - Realm Gift by Realm (A Bailey) 4689a
6 **LOMBARD SHIPS,** ch m Orchestra - Tina's Star by Simbir (A Bailey) 565^7 650^2 893 1186^4 1316^5 1591^3 1811^1 1849^3 2175^1 2371^2 2656^2 2762^5 3175^2 3258^2 3712^3 3780 4022^3 4506^2 4676^6
2 **LOMOND MIST (Ire),** b c Lomond (USA) - Miss Allowed (USA) by Alleged (USA) (R M Whitaker) 3400^6 4099
2 **LONDON KID (Ire),** b c Glow (USA) - Fancy Dress by Local Suitor 1221^3 1886^3
7 **LONELY LASS,** b m Headin' Up - Lonely Dawn (USA) by Plenty Old (USA) (A W Jones) 4706a^9 131 206^8
2 **LONE RISK,** b c Risk Me (Fr) - Madam de Seul by Pas de Seul (C N Allen) 1828 2229 2588^8 4577^8 4708
5 **LONESOME DOVE (Ire),** br m Fast Topaze (USA) - Magic In The Air (USA) by Home Guard (USA) (J White) 4795a^7
5 **LONG FURLONG,** b g Castle Keep - Myrtlegrove by Scottish Rifle (R Akehurst) 350^9 456^8 1238^8 1902^6 2149^9 2315^6
2 **LONG GALLERY (Ire),** ch g Tate Gallery (USA) - My Therape by Jimmy Reppin (M J Grassick) 820^1 1045^3 1788^4 2403^2
7 **LONG LANE LADY,** ch m Longleat (USA) - Teresa Way by Great White Way (USA) (J Mackie) 4789a
4 **LONG LAST,** b f Kabour - Final Cast by Saulingo (D W Chapman) 138 180 231 866^8
4 **LONG SILENCE (USA),** b f Alleged (USA) - Mystical Mood (USA) by Roberto (USA) (Mrs J Cecil) 617^3 822^1 1268^7
2 **LON ISA,** ch f Grey Desire - Stripanoora by Ahonoora (B Palling) 4498^2 4720^4
4 **LOOIE CAPOTE (USA),** 560^2 2802^2
5 **LOOKINGFORARAINBOW (Ire),** ch g Godswalk (USA) - Bridget Folly by Crofter (USA) (Bob Jones) 4670a^1 4705a^2 4776a^1 9^3 81^6 128^1 169^6 200^6 254^5 302 402^6 727^2 967^4 1041^4 1173 2343^3 2727^1 3067^3 3430^5 3548^2 3790^2 4036^8 4283^2 4631^5 4695^1 4731^2
2 **LOOKIN' ROSIE,** b f Mazilier (USA) - Shadow Play by Busted (Dr J D Scargill) 3695^5 4032 4265
4 **LOOK NONCHALANT (Ire),** ch f Fayruz - Gobolino by Don (C P Magnier) 2843^4 3074^7 3417^7 4635^7
3 **LOOK WHO'S HERE (Ire),** b g Heraldiste (USA) - House Call by Artaius (USA) (B A McMahon) 1017^5 1337^1 1718^4 2237^1 2574^7 3315^6 4170^5 4521^4
5 **LOON,** ch g Bairn (USA) - Patois by I Say (R J O'Sullivan) 320^4 416 600^5 882
2 **LOOSE CHANGE,** br f Spin Of A Coin - Lirchur by Lir (G L Moore) 2559^7 2909 4089
4 **LOOSE ZEUS (USA),** b g Double Zeus (USA) - Dareing Driver (USA) by Sadair (C F Wall) 771 1961 2466^6
7 **LOOTING (USA),** b or br g Pirate's Bounty (USA) - Bank Examiner (USA) by Buckfinder (USA) (R J O'Sullivan) 4736a^6 4756a^4 4783a 4803a^5 4816a^2 19^3 48^8 241^7 319^9 501^8 760 1059 1903
5 **LORD ADVOCATE,** br g Law Society (USA) - Kereolle by Riverman (USA) (D A Nolan) 4662a 4698a^2 4742a^4 4788a^7 65^2 94^5 122^6 164^5 863 1054^8 1517^1 1890^6 1941^3 2265^1 2455^8 2800^8 4700
4 **LORD ALFIE,** ch g Beveled (USA) - Fair Nic by Romancero (B J Meehan) 1270^3 1490^5 1707^5 1954^7 2121^1 2270 3261^2 3450^1 3676^3 3747 4258 4495^8 4652^6
4 **LORD BELMONTE (Ire),** b g Cyrano de Bergerac - Noble Nancy by Royal And Regal (USA) (P M McEntee) 225^5 288^8
3 **LORD BENTLEY,** b c Rousillon (USA) - Lady Bentley by Bellypha (J S Bolger) 1572^3 2076 3163^4
3 **LORD BOTHWELL (USA),** b or br c El Gran Senor (USA) - Mary Queenofscots (USA) by Royal Gunner (USA) (P W Chapple-Hyam) 510^5 761^4 1784^3 1992^8

2 **LUCIUS LOCKET (Ire),** b g Mazaad - Pocket by Tumble Wind (USA) (J Berry) 1053[3] 1837[2] 2199[2] 2554[5] 2814[7] 3279[2] 3441[5] 3673

5 **LUCKNAM DREAMER,** b g Macmillion - River Damsel by Forlorn River (Mrs Barbara Waring) 1177[9]

5 **LUCKNAM STYLE,** b g Macmillion - Mrs Currie by He Loves Me (Mrs Barbara Waring) 4681a[9] 4725a[6] 4751a[5] 4758a[6] 24[6]

4 **LUCK OF A LADY (Ire),** b f Trojan Fen - Ounovarra by Homeric (Peter McCreery) 2512[5] 2958[8] 3077 3245[6] 3663[4] 3976[7]

3 **LUCKY BOSS (Ire),** b c Taufan (USA) - Line Of Reason by High Line (F Carnevali) 2439[4]

2 **LUCKY FOURTEEN,** b c Nomination - Lucky Saran by Lucky Wednesday (D W Chapman) 1759[2] 1889[1] 2058 2180[3] 2435[8] 2974[9] 4021[8] 4358

6 **LUCKY GUEST,** bl h Be My Guest (USA) - Gay Fantasy by Troy (J L Dunlop) 480[1] 1021[2] 1398[4] 1883[1] 2830[2] 3636[4] 3752[1] 4063 4660[3]

2 **LUCKY HELEN,** b f Faustus (USA) - Lismore by Relkino (S Dow) 1959 2465[8] 3264 3546[9] 4009[9]

4 **LUCKY LINDY (Ire),** b c Trojan Fen - Excruciating (Can) by Bold Forbes (USA) (R Hannon) 525[4] 660[6] 1029 1748 2644[4] 3022[7] 3500[3] 3784[7] 4141[4] 4420[4]

2 **LUCKY LIZZY,** b f Thatching - Hawaiian Song by Henbit (USA) (M Brittain) 1082[7] 1158[8] 1759

2 **LUCKY MESSAGE (USA),** b f Phone Trick (USA) - How Fortunate (USA) by What Luck (USA) (J Etherington) 2199[5] 2482[2] 2706[2] 3115[3] 3671[4] 4105[1] 4193[3]

3 **LUCKY MILL,** b f Midyan (USA) - Frasquita by Song (F H Lee) 361[4] 634[8] 1463[6] 1740[6] 2707[5] 2760[2] 3032 3603 3794[3] 4222[7]

5 **LUCKY NOIRE,** b m Aragon - Noire Small (USA) by Elocutionist (USA) (G Harwood) 387 603 914 1120 1498 1659[7] 2126[8] 2544[7] 2685[9] 2847[4] 3090[1]

3 **LUCKY OWL,** ch f Indian Forest (USA) - Heldigvis by Hot Grove (M Johnston) 608[8]

3 **LUCKY PARKES,** b f Full Extent (USA) - Summerhill Spruce by Windjammer (USA) (J Berry) 464[3] 858[2] 1113[1] 1614[1] 2252[3] 2661[1] 2855[1] 3291[2] 3912[5] 4112[1] 4238[1]

3 **LUCKY PRINCE (Ire),** b or br g Prince Rupert (Fr) - Lucky Realm by Realm (D K Weld) 256[8] 649[3] 848[6] 1922[4] 3112[3] 3399[4] 3576 3827[2] 4324[1] 4408 4534[6]

2 **LUCKY TUCKY,** b c Alleging (USA) - Romana by Roman Warrior (J R Jenkins) 3990[8] 4276 4726

4 **LUCY BELLE (Ire),** b or br f Nashamaa - Bella Lucia by Camden Town (E A Wheeler) 260[8]

2 **LUCY'S GOLD,** b f Efisio - Hinton Rose by Frimley Park (M J Ryan) 776 1211 1536[6] 1933[2] 2377[9] 3210[6] 3426[3] 4338[8]

2 **LUDDEN LADY (Ire),** b f Alzao (USA) - Noblanna (USA) by Vaguely Noble (Edward P Mitchell) 786 938[4] 1442[3] 1854[3] 2462[3] 2983[6] 3200[9] 3379[1] 3925

2 **LUGANO,** b c Rousillon (USA) - Arita (Fr) by Kronzeuge (N A Callaghan) 1666[8] 1959[1] 2592[4] 4444 4550[7]

2 **LUHUK (USA),** ch c Forty-Niner (USA) - Royal Stance (USA) by Dr Fager (J L Dunlop) 3979[1] 4469[6]

2 **LUKES BROTHER (Ire),** ch g Kirchner - Golden Baby by Sharpen Up (A Hide) 3086[8]

5 **LUKS AKURA,** b g Dominion - Pacificus (USA) by Northern Dancer (M Johnston) 18[6] 58[6] 382[4] 904[5] 1112[5] 1564[6] 2201[2] 3056[3]

2 **LUNAFAIRY (Fr),** gr f Always Fair (USA) - Luna Blue by Cure The Blues (A Fabre) 3338[2]

2 **LUNAR MISSION (Ire),** b g Waajib - Lunulae by Tumble Wind (USA) (M H Tompkins) 730 2818[2] 3091[6] 3743[3] 4266[3] 4550

3 **LUNAR PRINCE,** b c Mansingh (USA) - Lunate by Faraway Times (USA) (P J McBride) 4030[9]

2 **LUNAR RHAPSODY,** br f Merdon Melody - Silvery Moon by Lorenzaccio (P S Felgate) 900[4] 1078[4] 1355[6] 1863[8] 3816 4097[8] 4318[8]

3 **LUNAR RISK,** b c Risk Me (Fr) - Moonlight Princess by Alias Smith (USA) (W R Muir) 483[5] 827 1126[1] 1266[5] 1662[1] 2228[3] 2783[6] 3881[7] 4341 4395[3]

3 **LUNAR SPOOK (USA),** gr f Silver Ghost (USA) - Rafael Luna by Idle Minds 570[1] 762[9]

6 **L'UOMO CLASSICS,** b g Indian King (USA) - Sperrin Mist by Camden Town (R Rowe) 189[5] 416[3] 628

5 **LUPESCU,** ch m Dixieland Band (USA) - Keep Me Posted (USA) by Stage Door Johnny (D R Loder) 4711a[3] 426[3] 2070[2] 2238[4] 2793[4] 3609[6]

3 **LUPULINA (USA),** 3196

4 **LURE (USA),** b c Danzig - Endear by Alydar (C McGaughey) 2084[2] 4742[1]

2 **LUROCC (Ity),** 2260[5]

3 **LUSTRINO (USA),** b g Irish River (Fr) - Sequins by Be My Guest (USA) (D K Weld) 850[3] 2040 2287[6] 2902[1]

8 **LUSTY LAD,** b g Decoy Boy - Gluhwein by Ballymoss (M J Haynes) 4750a[7]

4 **LUTE AND LYRE (Ire),** b f The Noble Player (USA) - Kool For Kats by Malinowski (USA) (E J O'Grady) 310 572 1515 2078[8] 2404 2780[9]

4 **LUV ME LUV ME NOT (USA),** b f It's Freezing (USA) - Reason With Me by Bold Reason (G Wismer) 560[3]

2 **LUZARCHES (Ire),** b f Alzao (USA) - Assya by Double Form (T Stack) 3611[2]

3 **L-WAY FIRST (Ire),** b or br f Vision (USA) - Lacey Brief (USA) by Roi Dagobert (M J Grassick) 936[5] 1122[6] 1431[3] 2496[3] 3063[7] 3275[3] 4119[4] 4639[8]

2 **LYDIA MC (Ire),** b f Fairy King (USA) - La Petrushka by Ballad Rock (Kevin Prendergast) 2294[4] 2745[3] 3073

3 **LYFORD CAY (Ire),** ch g Waajib - Island Goddess by Godswalk (USA) (C R Egerton) 558[2] 844[4] 1785[6] 2333 2961[7] 3282 4063[9]

2 **LYING EYES,** ch f Interrex (Can) - Lysithea by Imperial Fling (USA) (W G M Turner) 299[6] 449[2] 768[1] 1391[8] 1909[3] 2229[5] 2505[2]

5 **LYNDON'S LINNET,** b g Prince Sabo - Miss Rossi by Artaius (USA) (R Ingram) 4716a[9] 4768a[6] 86[2] 131[9] 2225[7] 2910[6] 3081[4] 3270[1] 3739[7]

4 **LYN'S RETURN (Ire),** b g Nordico (USA) - Salmas (Fr) by Right Royal V (R Simpson) 59[3] 115[6] 539[7] 2161[4] 2727[7] 3887[4] 3985[3] 4115[2] 4335[5]

3 **LYNTON (USA),** b c Lyphard (USA) - Nashmeel by Blushing Groom (A Fabre) 2208[1] 2803[9] 4570[3]

7 **LYPH (USA),** b g Lypheor - Scottish Lass by Scotland (P R Hedger) 4793a[4] 8[2] 46[2] 82[3] 126[1] 182[6] 331[9] 420[9]

4 **LYPHANTASTIC (USA),** b c Lyphard's Wish (Fr) - Tango Five Juliet (USA) by Fappiano (USA) (C J Mann) 527[8] 988 1129[4] 1770 2059[7] 4247

5 **LYPHARD ABU (Ire),** b m Lyphard's Special (USA) - Ishtar Abu by St Chad (J S Bolger) 298 575[1] 706[4] 1757[2] 2186[1] 2461[4] 2702[3] 3038[3] 3525[2] 3604[6] 3805[5] 4461

3 **LYPHARD'S DELTA (USA),** b f Lyphard (USA) - Proud Delta (USA) by Delta Judge (H R A Cecil) 1212[2] 1587[1] 1879[1] 2333[1] 2986[1] 3886[4] 4298[4]

2 **LYPHARD'S FABLE (USA),** b c Al Nasr (Fr) - Affirmative Fable (USA) by Affirmed (USA) (W J Haggas) 4113[8] 4498

2 **LYPHARD STREET (USA),** b f Lyphard (USA) - Hotel Street (USA) by Alleged (USA) (P F I Cole) 3317[5] 3659[2] 3960[3]

3 **LYRIC FANTASY (Ire),** b f Tate Gallery (USA) - Flying Melody by Auction Ring (USA) (R Hannon) 749[6] 1214[1] 1807[7] 3464

2 **LYRIC PLAYER (Ire),** ch f Astronef - Marlova (Fr) by Salvo (Patrick O'Leary) 4610

5 **MAAMUR (USA),** gr g Robellino (USA) - Tiger Trap (USA) by Al Hattab (USA) (D Burchell) 4714a[3] 4466

3 **MAASHAI LAWM (Ire),** b g Lomond (USA) - Gay Apparel (Can) by Up Spirits (USA) (M A Jarvis) 529 751 3590 3740[8]

3 **MAASTRICHT,** b g Common Grounds - Awatef by Ela-Mana-Mou (D Burchell) 4697a[7] 609[2] 763[3] 928 1271 2120[1] 4258

2 **MAASTRICHT (USA),** ch f Mining (USA) - Raja Jewel by Raja Baba (L Brogi) 1361[1]

4 **MA BELLA LUNA,** b f Jalmood (USA) - Macarte (Fr) by Gift Card (Fr) (J L Dunlop) 458[6] 676[9] 1490[8] 2113[3] 3107[3]

5 **MABTHUL (USA),** b g Northern Baby (Can) - Persuadable (USA) by What A Pleasure (USA) (R T Juckes) 2471 2670

2 **MACAROON LADY,** b f Prince Sabo - Cookie Time by Posse (USA) (N Bycroft) 1158^6 1519^2 3235^9 4097 4375^8

2 **MACE EL REEM,** b f Thatching - Mists Of Avalon (USA) by Nureyev (USA) (P Howling) 337^8 708 1203^8 3103^6 3573^5 3870^9

5 **MACFARLANE,** br g Kala Shikari - Tarvie by Swing Easy (USA) (M J Fetherston-Godley) 501 760 1000^1 1066^2 1188^2 1679^3 1806 1918^3 3153^3 3404 3486^1 3877^2 4180^9 4465

4 **MACGILLYCUDDY (Ire),** b or br g Petorius - My Bonnie by Highland Melody (Patrick Prendergast) 280^2 486^1 868^7 1050^2 1569^5 2073^5 2780^1 2879^6 3561^1 4184^4

2 **MACIZO,** b g Aragon - Free On Board by Free State (L J Holt) 1905^6 2096^5 2472^3 2929^9

4 **MACK THE KNIFE,** b g Kris - The Dancer (Fr) by Green Dancer (USA) (Major W R Hern) 2349^1 2579^3 2835^1 3644^7 4039^2

5 **MACQUARIE RIDGE (USA),** ch m Cox's Ridge (USA) - Ocean's Answer (USA) by Northern Answer (USA) (D P Kelly) 1444^1 1611^3 3330^2 3928^5 4184^6 4370^3 4385^5 4685^8

9 **MACROBIAN,** b g Bay Express - White Domino by Sharpen Up (M H Easterby) 1680

8 **MAC'S FIGHTER,** ch h Hard Fought - Geoffrey's Sister by Sparkler (R J O'Sullivan) 56^4 101^6 140^4 197^4 222^6 244^6 260^1 990 1267 1641^9 3305

6 **MACS MAHARANEE,** b m Indian King (USA) - High State by Free State (P S Felgate) 436 591 800^9 1036^7 1537^2 1835^1 1982^1 2628^2 3051^6 3404^9 3638^3 3964^7

3 **MAC TOMB,** b g Valiyar - Elaine Ann by Garda's Revenge (USA) (R J Price) 2411^6 2833^4 3049^7

2 **MAD ABOUT MEN,** b f Roaring Riva - Old Silver by Bold Lad (Ire) (J Berry) 343^3 449^4 2949^1 3254^8 3566 4193 4436^4

5 **MADAGANS GREY,** gr g Carwhite - Cheri Berry by Air Trooper (R Boss) 4725a^8 87^4 184^5 200^5 302 2506^7 2992 3522^7 4131^5

3 **MADAM CAPRICE,** b f Salse (USA) - Maiden Pool by Sharpen Up (R Guest) 3523 4234 4604

2 **MADAME GREGOIRE,** b f Presidium - Laleston by Junius (USA) (H J Collingridge) 337^1 446^2 625^3 1742^5 2689^4 3264^3 3532^5 4193^8

3 **MADAME L'ENJOLEUR (USA),** b f L'ensorceleur - Lady Blackfoot by Prince Tenderfoot (USA) 4792a^3

3 **MADAME MINISTER (USA),** ch f Deputy Minister (Can) - Kauai Princess by General Assembly (USA) (P Aspell) 1855 2184^7 4686^6

2 **MADAM FRASCATI (Ire),** ch f Tate Gallery (USA) - Ahonita by Ahonoora (C N Allen) 2377

3 **MADAM GYMCRAK,** b f Celestial Storm (USA) - Finlandaise (Fr) by Arctic Tern (USA) (G Holmes) 1642^1 2131^2 3970^9 4226^6

3 **MADANIYYA (USA),** ch f Shahrastani (USA) - Meadow Glen Lady (USA) by Believe It (USA) (John M Oxx) 1573^4 1822^1 2092^2 2702^1 3164^1 3770^3 3924^3

8 **MAD CASANOVA,** b g Scorpio (Fr) - Parveen (Fr) by Kouban (Fr) (R J O'Sullivan) 1533^8 1816^3 1911^7 2521^6 3306^3 3513 3943^8 4753^2

3 **MADELEINE'S DREAM (USA),** b or br f Theatrical - L'attrayante by Tyrant (F Boutin) 4738a^1 484^3 1086^1

4 **MADE OF GOLD (USA),** ch c Green Forest (USA) - Vindaria (USA) by Roi Dagobert (M Moubarak) 2084^6

2 **MADLY SHARP,** ch c Sharpo - Madison Girl by Last Fandango (J W Watts) 3031^2

3 **MAD MARTIGAN,** b c Alleging (USA) - Be My Lady by Be My Guest 4703a^3 1364^7 3796^4

4 **MAD MILITANT (Ire),** b c Vision (USA) - Ullapool by Dominion (R Hollinshead) 358^5 500^5 894^6 1328^4 1946^1 2373^3 3121^2 3308^5 3900^3 4175^7 4513^9 4731

3 **MAD MYTTON,** b g Crowning Honors (Can) - Vynz Girl by Tower Walk (A Bailey) 437^5 609^8 1005

5 **MADRAJ (Ire),** b or br h Double Schwartz - Poka Poka (Fr) by King Of Macedon (R J Hodges) 327^6 456

2 **MADURAI,** b f Chilibang - Macarte (Fr) by Gift Card (Fr) (J L Dunlop) 1032^6

3 **M A EL-SAHN,** b c Presidium - Hoonah (Fr) by Luthier (R Hannon) 4720a^8 4747a^6 3661

4 **MAESTROSO (Ire),** b g Mister Majestic - That's Easy by Swing Easy (USA) (R F Johnson Houghton) 3319^8

2 **MA FOLIE,** br f Tragic Role (USA) - Frivole by Comedy Star (USA) (J S Wainwright) 4452 4598^5 4728

4 **MAGADEER (USA),** b f Mogambo (USA) - Star Silhouette (USA) by Dancer's Profile (USA) (J L Dunlop) 4750a^9

4 **MAGICAL MAIDEN (USA),** b or br f Lord Avie - Gils Magic by Magesterial (W Stute) 4741^7

2 **MAGICAL-MOU,** b c Bustino - Magic Vision by Shergar (R Boss) 4714^7

3 **MAGICAL RETREAT (USA),** b f Sir Ivor - Known Charter by Known Fact (USA) (C A Cyzer) 482^1 684^6 748^1 856^3 1030^7 1789^6 2360^3 2925^7 3262^3 3846^4 3929^2

3 **MAGICAL RIVER (USA),** 2259

5 **MAGIC ARTS (Ire),** b m Fairy King (USA) - Maura Paul by Bonne Noel (T J O'Mara) 308^9 849^3 996^5 1235^1 1440^9 1794

3 **MAGICATION,** b f Nomination - Gundreda by Gunner B (J Balding) 151^6 193^5 313^8 455^3 614^7 884^2 1186^5 1577^1 1965^3 2602^5 3535 3758^6 3946 4221^5

4 **MAGIC DON (Ire),** b g Dominion - Simple Magic (USA) by Taylor's Falls (USA) (J T Gorman) 310^8 572^1 939^6 1023^2 1444^8 1515^4 1795^1 2073 2404^7 2780^2 3201^7 3330 4385 4635^2 4689

3 **MAGIC FAN (Ire),** b g Taufan (USA) - Magic Gold by Sallust (Mrs A Swinbank) 759 1007^8 1278^8 2538^3 3355^8 3811

3 **MAGIC FEELING (Ire),** ch f Magical Wonder (USA) - Papsie's Pet by Busted (A P O'Brien) 2781^3 2956^4 4162^3 4410^1

2 **MAGIC JUNCTION (USA),** b c Danzig Connection (USA) - Sleeping Beauty by Mill Reef (USA) (Lord Huntingdon) 4523

2 **MAGIC MAGGIE,** b f Beveled (USA) - Miss Solo by Runnymede (M R Channon) 3421 3529^4 3869^5 4128 4342

3 **MAGIC ORB,** b f Primo Dominie - Tricky by Song (J L Spearing) 460^1 691^1 1083^6 1478^3 2255^1 2969^7 3511^8 3756^3 4393

3 **MAGIC PEARL,** gr f Belfort (Fr) - Oyster Gray by Tanfirion (E J Alston) 974^4 3094^5 3359^2 4180 4222^2 4327^1 4455^1 4532^9 4678^7

4 **MAGIC RING (Ire),** b c Green Desert (USA) - Emaline (Fr) by Empery (USA) (P F I Cole) 1205^9

3 **MAGIC ROYALE (Ire),** ch f Dominion Royale - Magic Miss by Mandrake Major (Peadar Matthews) 639^4 1164^6 1619^8

4 **MAGIC SPIRIT (Ire),** b c Magical Wonder (USA) - Inis Ealga by Sallust (Noel Furlong) 3495^7

3 **MAGIQUE ROND POINT (USA),** b f Greinton - Petit Rond Point (USA) by Round Table (H R A Cecil) 512^6 823^6 1404^2 1978^4 2885^8 4100^5

2 **MAGNASONIC (USA),** b c Known Fact (USA) - Itsamazing (USA) by The Minstrel (Can) (R Charlton) 2364^1

4 **MAGNETIC POINT (USA),** ch f Bering - Nonoalca (Fr) by Nonoalco (USA) (A Hide) 4690a 2737^3 3461^6 3631

2 **MAGNETIC REEL,** ch g Scottish Reel - Miss Magnetism by Baptism (J Berry) 3457^3 3760^4 3876^6

4 **MAGNUM STAR (Ire),** b g Damister (USA) - North Telstar by Sallust (J E Mulhern) 1440 3494 3580^5 4161

8 **MAGNUS PYM,** b g Al Nasr (Fr) - Full Of Reason (USA) by Bold Reason (G B Balding) 46^7

8 **MAGSOOD,** ch g Mill Reef (USA) - Shark Song by Song (S Mellor) 3078

5 **MAHAASIN,** b m Bellypha - Dame Ashfield by Grundy (A Bailey) 4234^3 4279^4 4457 4486 4704^1

2 **MAHASEAL (USA),** b f Ferdinand (USA) - Naqiyah (USA) by In Reality (Kevin Prendergast) 938^9 1197^8 2188^1 3110^2 4285

5 **MAHONG,** gr g Petong - Balearica by Bustino (Mrs H Parrott) 3891^9 4254^2 4533 4623^6

4 **MAHOOL (USA),** b c Alydar (USA) - Tax Dodge (USA) by Seattle Slew (USA) (A A Scott) 513^7 731 3991^2

3 **MAM'ZELLE ANGOT,** b f Balidar - Ragirl by Ragusa (Miss S E Hall) 3036[9] 3354 4458[3] 4640[3] 4760[5]
2 **MANAAFIS (Ire),** gr c High Estate - Negligence by Roan Rocket (Kevin Prendergast) 2037[9] 2402[3] 2804[4] 3039[4] 3683[1] 3806[1] 4382[5]
3 **MANAARAH (USA),** ch f Slew O' Gold (USA) - Edgewater (USA) by Verbatim (USA) (A A Scott) 4189[8]
3 **MANADEL,** b f Governor General - Manabel by Manado (S R Bowring) 4700a 4741a 1505[7] 3190 3946 4327
2 **MANATEE,** b f Taufan (USA) - Vitalise by Vitiges (Fr) (C F Wall) 4269[9] 4446 4692
3 **MANDE MERCHANT (Ire),** b g Digamist (USA) - Ghana's Daughter by Sallust (John M Oxx) 577[1]
2 **MANDEVILLE GEORGE,** b c Emarati (USA) - Stately Gala by Gala Performance (USA) (R Hannon) 3009 3264 3867[2] 4128[7]
2 **MANFATH (Ire),** br f Last Tycoon - Pilot Bird by Blakeney (D Morley) 3990
3 **MANGANS HILL (Ire),** br f Glint Of Gold - Baddaweeya by Formidable (USA) (Miss I T Oakes) 257 2679 790 936[1] 1163[4] 1292[6] 2286 2496[2] 2517[7] 3326 3397 3662[5]
8 **MANGO MANILA,** b h Martinmas - Trigamy by Tribal Chief (C A Horgan) 1172 1768
3 **MANHATTAN PROJECT,** 2643[2]
5 **MANHATTAN RIVER (Fr),** 2056[2]
2 **MANHATTAN SUNSET (USA),** ch f El Gran Senor (USA) - Mezimica (USA) by Dewan (USA) (P W Chapple-Hyam) 2240[3] 2595[2] 2759[2] 3865 4251[1] 4558[9]
4 **MANIANA (Ire),** b c Try My Best (USA) - Dinalina (Fr) by Top Ville (R Collett) 2263[3]
3 **MANILA BAY (USA),** b c Manila (USA) - Betty Money (USA) by Our Native (USA) (M Bell) 547[3] 926[1] 2820[2] 3179[8] 3444[6]
2 **MANNTARI (Ire),** br c Doyoun - Manntika by Kalamoun (John M Oxx) 3203[1] 4054[1]
3 **MANNY'S PROSPECT (USA),** 3823[9]
3 **MAN OF ARRAN (Ire),** ch g Be My Native (USA) - Raregirl by Rarity (Patrick O'Leary) 297[1] 850[6] 997[4] 1292[4] 2984[8]
2 **MAN OF KASHMIR (Ire),** b g Mansooj - Dame Brisene (Fr) by Kashmir II (M D I Usher) 1741
7 **MAN OF STRAW,** ch g Ela-Mana-Mou - House Of Straw by Thatch (USA) (P J Lally) 1163 1293[3] 1385[9] 1987[6] 2094
4 **MAN OF THE SEASON (USA),** ch g Naked Sky (USA) - Kizzie (USA) by Naskra (USA) (J Akehurst) 2109 2670 3228[5] 3591
2 **MANOLETE,** b c Hard Fought - Andalucia by Rheingold (C W C Elsey) 3218[6] 3672[7]
3 **MANON LESCAUT,** b f Then Again - Rather Warm by Tribal Chief (J White) 483 976[7] 1266[9] 1372[5] 1491[4] 1936[6] 2007[2] 2495[2] 2611
3 **MANOR ADVENTURE,** ch f Smackover - Klairove by Averof (P T Dalton) 1136[4] 1537[8] 1881[4] 1925[1] 2777[2] 3051 3438[6] 4180[6]
6 **MANSE KEY GOLD,** ch m Vaigly Great - Carafran by Stanford (J Dooler) 41[7] 67
4 **MANULEADER,** b g King Of Spain - Balnerino by Rolfe (USA) (J Norton) 96 177[7] 383[6] 531 1498 1799 1979[4] 2178
4 **MANULIFE,** b g King Of Spain - Try G's by Hotfoot (R Brotherton) 2694[8]
3 **MANX MONARCH,** ch f Dara Monarch - Solemn Occasion (USA) by Secreto (USA) (K W Hogg) 642 733 1416[3] 1480[4] 1578 1937 1965[2] 2106[2] 2478[4] 2540[2] 2593[2] 2889[2] 2978[5] 3002[9] 3216[2] 3237[5]
3 **MANZALA (USA),** b f Irish River (Fr) - Marazika by Great Nephew (John M Oxx) 282[8] 1649[1] 4057[9] 4136 4324[6]
5 **MANZOOR SAYADAN (USA),** b g Shahrastani (USA) - Icing by Prince Tenderfoot (USA) (Mrs J Pitman) 559[5] 674
3 **MAORI (Ity),** b c Alex Nureyev - Speedy Reef by Mill Reef (USA) (F Gnesi) 1363[3] 1887[4] 3151[3]
2 **MAPENGO,** b c Salse (USA) - Premiere Cuvee by Formidable (USA) (G Harwood) 4149[3] 4356
4 **MAPLE BAY (Ire),** b c Bold Arrangement - Cannon Boy (USA) by Canonero II (USA) (K White) 4689a[4] 4767a[3] 500[8] 620[9] 1034 1414 1956
3 **MAP OF STARS (USA),** b c Danzig (USA) - Luminaire (USA) by Al Hattab (USA) (M R Stoute) 459 1617[4] 2022[3] 2333[3] 2545[3] 3036[4] 3512
3 **MARAAN (Ity),** b c Dalsaan - Marina Di Giola by Gay Fandango 778[2]
4 **MARACAIBO (Den),** 3936[9]
4 **MARADONNA (USA),** b g Alleged (USA) - Kiss by Habitat (L M Cumani) 3555[5] 3970[1] 4283[4] 4538[3]
2 **MARAGON,** ch f Aragon - Mana (Ger) by Windwurf (Ger) (R J R Williams) 1393[2] 1844[1] 4250[6]
2 **MARALIYKA (Ire),** b f Affirmed (USA) - Marazika by Great Nephew (John M Oxx) 4705[4]
6 **MARANDISA,** ch m Pharly (Fr) - Marissiya by Nishapour (Fr) (Martyn Wane) 3240
3 **MARASTANI (USA),** ch g Shahrastani (USA) - Marianna's Girl (USA) by Dewan (USA) (G Harwood) 304[1] 663[5] 1407[2] 1973[2] 2361[7] 3476[4] 4415
3 **MARAT (USA),** ch c Meadowlake (USA) - Affection Affirmed (USA) by Affirmed (USA) (J R Jenkins) 417[8] 623[4] 950[8] 1697 2098[3] 2712 3384[5]
3 **MARATHIA,** ch f Blushing Scribe (USA) - Nonpareil (Fr) by Pharly (Fr) (S P C Woods) 712[3] 1099[3] 1504[3] 1907[7] 2613[3] 3533[5] 3945[9] 4335
2 **MARBLE,** b f Petong - Hymettus by Blakeney (D Moffatt) 343 743[5] 1158 2541[9] 3131[2] 3377[3] 3598[5] 4163[5] 4358 4699[5]
3 **MARCHAND DE SABLE (USA),** b or br c Theatrical - Mercantile by Kenmare (E Lellouche) 485[2] 955[2]
3 **MARCHMAIN,** b g Midyan (USA) - Misty Arch by Starch Reduced (J Berry) 872[8] 1320 2711[5] 3628[2] 4222[3] 4327[9]
8 **MARCHMAN,** b g Daring March - Saltation by Sallust (J S King) 620[3] 994[9] 1242[6] 2029[1] 2506[5] 3089[2] 3891
2 **MARCH OF TIME,** b g Dowsing (USA) - Triple Bar by Jimmy Reppin (D T Thom) 374[6] 543[8] 776[2] 1481[5] 1828[9] 2618 3001 3267[8] 3508
3 **MARCO BAY (USA),** 569[5]
3 **MARCO CLAUDIO (Ire),** br c Standaan (Fr) - Mandy Girl by Manado (P A Kelleway) 1074[3] 1416 1813[4]
3 **MARCO MAGNIFICO (USA),** b or br g Bering - Viscosity (USA) by Sir Ivor (B W Hills) 185[1] 578[4] 929[5] 4274[8] 4445[1]
2 **MARCONI (Ire),** b c Sadler's Wells (USA) - Lisadell (USA) by Forli (Arg) (M V O'Brien) 2402[4]
4 **MARCOVALDO (Ire),** b g Supreme Leader - Ahadoon by Gulf Pearl (E J O'Grady) 895[9]
5 **MARDIOR,** b m Martinmas - Diorina by Manacle (W G R Wightman) 4817a 85 914
8 **MARDOOD,** b g Ela-Mana-Mou - Tigeen by Habitat (P Leach) 1195[1] 1564[1] 1752[7] 2115[1] 2422[2] 4466
2 **MAREMMA MIA (Ity),** 2648[6]
5 **MARGANCE (Fr),** (A Rossio) 90[1]
3 **MARGARET'S GIFT,** ch f Beveled (USA) - Persiandale by Persian Bold (J Berry) 683[1] 802[3] 1214[3] 1338[8] 2028[3] 2304[6] 2885[7] 3404[3] 3621[1] 4040 4278
2 **MARGOT'S BOY,** ch g Gypsy Castle - Rosinka by Raga Navarro (Ity) (D McCune) 3809[7] 3992[6]
6 **MARIAN EVANS,** b m Dominion - Kindjal by Kris (T Craig) 1261[4] 1597[7] 1969[9]
7 **MARIAN YEAR,** b or br m Creative Plan (USA) - Callula by Crash Course (Thomas Walker) 298[7] 2693[5] 3276[9] 3483[4] 3580 4119[7]
3 **MARIBELLA,** b f Robellino (USA) - Infanta Maria by King Of Spain (S Gollings) 532[5] 711[6] 963[6] 1133
3 **MARIBEN (Ity),** b c Welnor - Machine Gun by Manado (G Benetti) 4476[3]
4 **MARIETTE LARKIN,** b f Elegant Air - Straw Boater by Thatch (USA) (J Hetherton) 152[9] 188[5] 231[5] 1190 4640
6 **MARILDO (Fr),** br h Romildo - Marike by Nasram (D Smaga) 4737a[1] 4754a[3] 104[1] 145[3] 283[2] 407[1] 810[5] 1366[6] 1971[2] 2979[1] 3500[5] 3649[6] 4075[2] 4295[3] 4557[1]
3 **MARILLETTE (USA),** b f Diesis - Stormette (USA) by Assert (J H M Gosden) 987[1] 1525[8] 2038[9] 2986[5] 4309[5] 4636[4]
4 **MARILYN (Ire),** ch f Kings Lake (USA) - Welshwyn by Welsh Saint (M A O'Toole) 575[7] 1962[1] 2881[7] 3560
2 **MARINA GRIMALDI (Ire),** (P W Chapple-Hyam) 3918

INDEX TO FLAT RACE RESULTS 1992-93

3 **MISS CHARLIE,** ch f Pharly (Fr) - Close To You by Nebbiolo (A Bailey) 3439^{4} 4125^{6} 4596

3 **MISS COPYFORCE,** ch f Aragon - Sharper Still by Sharpen Up (Miss B Sanders) 951^{7} 1522^{6} 2138^{6} 3341^{7} 3669^{9}

5 **MISS CRUSTY,** gr m Belfort (Fr) - Blue Empress by Blue Cashmere (O O'Neill) 3233^{1} 3523 3896

5 **MISS DARCY (Ire),** b m Glow (USA) - Lancette by Double Jump (W P Browne) 1757^{8} 1987^{5} 2513^{5} 2692^{9} 3038^{8}

3 **MISS DELIVERY,** bl f Durandal - Paphidia by Mansingh (USA) (P Howling) 4695a^{6} 21^{4} 98^{4} 168^{6}

2 **MISS DENBIGH,** br f Handsome Sailor - Springle by Le Johnstan (M Bell) 1905 2492

3 **MISSED FLIGHT,** b c Dominion - Loveskate (USA) by Overskate (Can) (C F Wall) 1884 4126^{6} 4322^{1} 4424^{1} 4563^{3}

5 **MISSED OPPORTUNITY (Ire),** b m Exhibitioner - Good Opportunity (USA) (Miss I T Oakes) 1797^{5} 2512^{6}

3 **MISSED THE BOAT (Ire),** b g Cyrano de Bergerac - Lady Portobello by Porto Bello (Miss S J Wilton) 4762a^{3} 29^{3} 106^{5} 1160^{6} 1735^{2} 1893^{3} 2168^{3} 2602^{3} 3002^{7} 3237^{6} 3628^{4} 3811^{4} 4104^{8}

3 **MISSED THE STORM (USA),** b or br f Storm Cat (USA) - Missed The Wedding (USA) by Blushing Groom (Fr) (W Mott) 2999^{1} 3207^{5}

5 **MISS EL ARAB (Ire),** ch m Sayf El Arab (USA) - Shining Bright (USA) by Bold Bidder (Mrs V A Aconley) 147 231 292 2775^{9} 3002 3374^{9}

3 **MISS ELODIE (Fr),** b f The Wonder (Fr) - Kawsara by Akarad (J Bertran de Balanda) 432^{3}

3 **MISS FASCINATION,** b f Damister (USA) - Tantalizing Song (Can) by The Minstrel (Can) (M A Jarvis) 4778a^{3} 1005^{2} 1242^{5} 1656^{2} 1912^{6} 2712^{2} 3088^{2} 3670^{1} 3981^{4} 4536^{8}

2 **MISS FREEBIE (Ire),** b f Satco (Fr) - Masina by Current Coin (R M Whitaker) 2278^{6} 2465^{2} 2819^{3} 3235^{5} 3563 3829 4427^{2} 4644^{3}

3 **MISS GORGEOUS (Ire),** b f Damister (USA) - Rocket Alert by Red Alert (W A O'Gorman) 4700a^{5} 4720a^{2} 4791a^{1} 4811a^{4} 29^{1} 60^{1} 71^{2} 747^{5} 836 1455^{2} 1859^{3} 1982^{2} 2193^{1} 2382^{3} 2770^{1} 3070^{4} 3458^{9} 4667

4 **MISS HAGGIS,** b f Scottish Reel - Bambolona by Bustino (R Boss) 824 1069 1382^{6} 1830^{7} 2060 2309^{2} 2861^{1} 3034^{7}

5 **MISS HIGH BLADE (USA),** 2645^{4}

6 **MISS HOSTESS,** gr m Petong - Rosalina by Porto Bello (D A Nolan) 610 862^{3} 1103^{5} 1264^{6} 1520 1938^{7} 2269^{5} 2459 4640 4702

2 **MISS IGLOO,** ch f Beveled (USA) - Northern Scene by Habitat (C James) 949^{6} 2911 3345^{8}

3 **MISS IN-A-BIT,** b f Ayyabaan - Miss Moritz by Majority Blue (N A Smith) 80^{9} 4493

3 **MISS INDY ANNA (Can),** ch f Apalachee (USA) - Savanna Anna by Vice Regent (E Allard) 2999^{2}

6 **MISSIONARY RIDGE,** ch h Caerleon (USA) - Shellshock by Salvo (R Frankel) 671^{2} 1541^{5} 2243^{5} 4068^{4} 4745

3 **MISS KADROU (Fr),** (P Demercastel) 4753a^{3} 561^{3} 1033^{9} 1506^{6}

2 **MISS KATIE LOUISE,** b f Monsanto (Fr) - Shari Louise by Radetzky (J L Spearing) 2554 3120^{7} 4163^{6} 4358 4483^{9}

3 **MISS KINABALU,** b f Shirley Heights - Miss Kuta Beach by Bold Lad (Ire) (G Wragg) 522^{3} 821 2749^{9} 3431^{7} 3693^{6} 4031^{3} 4348^{6} 4506

4 **MISS KINGFISHER (USA),** b f Temperence Hill (USA) - Glory Street (USA) by The Pruner (USA) (J Dooler) 3820^{7} 4574

2 **MISS KRISTIN (Ire),** b f Alzao (USA) - Catos Ridge (USA) by Cox's Ridge (USA) (J S Bolger) 3039^{2} 3451^{1} 3611^{4} 3927^{3}

5 **MISS LAWN (Fr),** ch m Lashkari - Miss Jonquiere (Fr) by Dictus (Fr) (D Burchell) 179^{5} 229^{4}

4 **MISS LIMELIGHT,** ch f Crofthall - Floral Light by Florescence (A Smith) 2481^{9} 2872^{9}

6 **MISS MAC,** ch m Smackover - Stewart's Rise by Good Bond (E J Alston) 50^{9}

5 **MISS MAGENTA (Ire),** b m Tate Gallery (USA) - Crimson Crown by Lord Gayle (USA) (R Thompson) 610^{7} 861^{9} 1453 2127^{4} 2684^{6}

2 **MISS MAH-JONG,** b f Absalom - Brookfield Miss by Welsh Pageant (M Johnston) 968^{4} 1098^{1} 1381^{6} 1899^{2} 2200^{3} 2569^{3} 3236^{2} 3563^{1} 3966^{3} 4082^{1} 4550

3 **MISS MARESE (Ire),** b f Cyrano de Bergerac - Card Queen by Lord Gayle (USA) (Neil S McGrath) 847^{6} 1333^{9} 2140 3075^{6} 3294 3721

4 **MISS MARIGOLD,** b f Norwick (USA) - Kiki Star by Some Hand (R J Hodges) 4102^{9}

3 **MISS MAYTHORN (Ire),** br f Cyrano de Bergerac - Thornbeam by Beldale Flutter (USA) (M Halford) 2781^{9} 2923^{7} 3454^{9}

3 **MISS MICHELLE,** ch f Jalmood (USA) - Southern Dynasty by Gunner B (S Mellor) 583 951^{8} 1092 1746 2685^{5} 3106^{5} 3384^{3} 3572 3945

2 **MISS MILLIPEDE,** b f Primitive Rising (USA) - Ramilie by Rambah (J Etherington) 1418 1998^{6} 3760

3 **MISS MISTLETOES (Ire),** br f The Minstrel (Can) - December Blossom by Condorcet (Fr) (T Stack) 550^{1} 1046^{9} 1549^{4} 1856^{3} 2406^{3} 2741^{5} 3380^{1} 4136^{6} 4386^{4} 4463^{2}

7 **MISS MOODY,** ch m Jalmood (USA) - Ice Galaxie (USA) by Icecapade (USA) (J M Bradley) 147

4 **MISS MOVIE WORLD,** b f Slim Jim - Regal Artist by Breakspear II (N Bycroft) 292^{7} 355^{6} 591^{6} 700 796^{7} 1036

6 **MISS MUSKY,** b m Muscatite - Fiona's Wish by Wishing Star (W J Martin) 3276

2 **MISS NANUSHKA,** b f Governor General - Not So Shy by Star Appeal (A L Forbes) 4098

2 **MISS NUTWOOD (Ire),** b f Prince Rupert (Fr) - Merry Twinkle by Martinmas (Joseph G Murphy) 2462^{2} 2982^{1} 4093^{2}

3 **MISS OFFIE,** b f Presidium - Off The Mark by On Your Mark (R Hollinshead) 4665a^{9} 4745a^{7} 124^{6} 346^{6} 733 1577^{3} 2047^{9} 2151^{5} 4045^{5} 4658

2 **MISS PARAMOUNT,** b f Dominion - Glebehill by Northfields (USA) (Martyn Wane) 528^{9}

2 **MISS PIGALLE,** b f Good Times (Ity) - Panayr by Faraway Times (USA) (Miss L A Perratt) 1846 2759^{3} 2949^{2} 3284^{8} 3754^{7} 4042^{8}

3 **MISS PIGLET (Ire),** ch f Double Schwartz - Miss Bagatelle by Mummy's Pet (R Ingram) 4761a

3 **MISS PIMPERNEL,** b f Blakeney - New Edition by Great Nephew (J J Birkett) 992 1359^{2} 1732^{5} 2218^{6}

4 **MISS PIN UP,** gr f Kalaglow - Allander Girl by Miralgo (Pat Mitchell) 527^{3} 727^{6} 994^{1} 1173^{1} 1345^{6} 1827^{4} 2026^{2} 2256^{4} 3252^{7} 3881^{6} 4283^{5} 4466

3 **MISS PITTYPAT (Ire),** ch f Seclude (USA) - Ladysin by Paddy's Stream (Victor Bowens) 944^{9}

4 **MISS PLUM,** b f Ardross - Heaven High by High Line (D R Loder) 1028^{6} 1336 1809^{3} 2061 2397^{1} 2904^{4} 3538^{3} 4013^{3}

2 **MISS POTTER (Ire),** b f Dancing Dissident (USA) - Biddy Mulligan by Ballad Rock (T A Regan) 4459^{4}

5 **MISS PRECOCIOUS,** b m Precocious - Hissy Missy by Bold Lad (Ire) (D Shaw) 333^{7} 501^{5} 600 2110^{9} 2352^{7}

2 **MISS PROVIDER (Ire),** b f Dancing Dissident (USA) - Park Lady by Tap On Wood (Liam Browne) 4459 4535^{1}

3 **MISS RIBBONS,** br f Nomination - New Ribbons by Ribero (Pat Mitchell) 1134 1500^{5} 1642^{7} 2411^{9} 2578^{7} 3430^{7} 3551 4017^{8}

2 **MISS RINJANI,** b f Shirley Heights - Miss Kuta Beach by Bold Lad (Ire) (G Wragg) 2748^{2} 3186^{1} 3765^{5}

2 **MISS RISKY,** b f Risk Me (Fr) - Merle by Gunner B (R Hannon) 490^{3} 625^{8} 4349

4 **MISS RITA,** ch f Master Willie - Florita by Lord Gayle (USA) (J Pearce) 1594^{4} 2328^{8} 2751^{9} 3342^{7}

3 **MISS RITZ,** b f Robellino (USA) - Gold Market by Hotfoot (W W Haigh) 2596^{3} 3132^{8} 3359^{9}

2 **MISS SACHA (Ire),** b f Last Tycoon - Heaven High by High Line (C Collins) 4058^{3}

3 **MISS SHAGRA (USA),** b f Danzig (USA) - Dusty Dollar by Kris (M R Stoute) 662 1178^{2} 1816^{1} 2398^{6} 2722^{1} 2991^{5} 3757^{8}

4 **MISS SIHAM (Ire),** ch f Green Forest (USA) - Miss Derby (USA) by Master Derby (USA) (J Balding) 1397 1631^{1} 2481^{2} 2682^{1} 3032^{5} 3568^{7}

2 **MISS SPRINGTIME,** b f Bluebird (USA) - Spring Lane by Forlorn River (Sir Mark Prescott) 2203^{3}

2 **MISS TEMERITY,** b f Sharrood (USA) - Humble Pie by Known Fact (USA) (M Blanshard) 2492^{9} 2695 3659

2 **MISS TIPSY,** b f Reprimand - Miss Alkie by Noalcoholic (Fr) (W W Haigh) 4728

2 **MISS TRIANGLE,** gr f Grey Desire - My-Elane by Welsh Saint (M R Channon) 922 1413

4 **MISS TURKANA (USA),** b f Turkoman - Reigning Countess by Far North (G Jones) 1370^{6} 4749^{1}

2 **MISS TUT (Ire),** br f Phardante (Fr) - Lady Tut by Fine Blade (USA) (T T Bill) 2917^{6} 3828 4121^{8}

3 **MISS TWIN PEAKS (Ire),** b f Persian Heights - Monterana by Sallust (Michael Kauntze) 267^{1} 1574 2451 2513^{3} 3326^{9}

2 **MISSUS MURHILL (Ire),** ch f Mon Tresor - Decoy Duck by Decoy Boy (D K Weld) 4000^{7} 4183^{1}

4 **MISS VAXETTE,** b f Norwick (USA) - Langton Herring by Nearly A Hand (J L Spearing) 401^{2} 659 1036^{8} 1473^{2} 1560^{3} 1860^{1} 2018^{5} 2392^{1} 2628^{1} 2753 3291^{6} 3668^{5} 3849^{8} 4040

3 **MISS WHITTINGHAM (Ire),** b f Fayruz - Windini by Windjammer (USA) (J Berry) 250^{2} 275^{6} 367^{3} 631^{1} 742^{5} 1264^{2} 1503^{1} 1677^{3} 1874^{4} 1966^{1} 2170^{3} 2469^{1} 2553^{2} 2738^{1} 2861^{6} 3323^{2} 3393^{2} 3964^{2} 4217^{5}

4 **MISSY-S (Ire),** b f Sarab - Monaco Lady by Manado (B J Llewellyn) 458^{5} 952^{4} 1210 2550^{1} 3050^{1}

2 **MISTER BAILEYS,** b c Robellino (USA) - Thimblerigger by Sharpen Up (M Johnston) 2021^{1} 2616^{3} 2924^{1} 3435^{6} 4174^{1}

2 **MISTER BEAT,** b g Brustolon - Miss May (Fr) by Northern Treat (USA) (J G FitzGerald) 1499^{4} 2331^{3} 2554^{4} 2916^{1} 3236^{3} 3502^{6} 4165 4418^{2} 4531^{2}

3 **MISTER BLAKE,** b g Damister (USA) - Larive by Blakeney (I Campbell) 4675a^{2} 4717a^{4} 4745a^{1} 4772a^{3} 4790a^{1} 4809a^{2} 15^{3} 52^{2} 80^{2} 143^{2} 167^{1} 183^{4} 233^{1} 252^{5} 378^{3} 410^{2} 1074^{4} 1306^{5} 1566^{7} 2537^{5} 2717^{7} 2863^{6} 3140^{7} 3364^{5}

2 **MISTER BLOY,** b g Dowsing (USA) - Casbah Girl by Native Bazaar (J Berry) 687^{8} 1182^{1} 1461^{4} 2200^{4} 2500^{3} 3502^{4}

3 **MISTER FORUM,** b g Damister (USA) - Ballad Island by Ballad Rock (B J Meehan) 2578 2726^{8}

4 **MISTERIOSO,** b f Forzando - Ragged Moon by Raga Navarro (Ity) (Lord Huntingdon) 1370^{8}

4 **MISTER JOLSON,** br g Latest Model - Impromptu by My Swanee (R J Hodges) 99^{1} 170^{6} 223^{4} 292^{4} 421^{1} 659^{5} 721^{2} 916^{3} 1000^{4} 1240^{4} 1492^{2} 1687^{1} 1957^{4} 2524 2868 3168

7 **MISTER LAWSON,** ch g Blushing Scribe (USA) - Nonpareil (Fr) by Pharly (Fr) (B Forsey) 4756a 4798a^{6} 4817a^{9} 3171^{3}

2 **MISTER MAYBE,** b c Damister (USA) - Maybe So by So Blessed (R Hannon) 4067 4208^{8} 4491^{6}

3 **MISTER NAIF (USA),** b c Danzig Connection (USA) - Fly It Betsy by Hoist The Flag (USA) (L Brogi) 1363^{4}

2 **MISTER O'GRADY (Ire),** b c Mister Majestic - Judy O'Grady by Whistler (Pat Mitchell) 2720^{6} 3130 3421 3520 4416 4484

2 **MISTER PISTE (Ire),** b c Fayruz - Gluhwein by Ballymoss (Miss L A Perratt) 1227^{7} 1798^{1} 2400^{9} 3441^{2} 3994^{6}

3 **MISTERTOPOGIGO (Ire),** b c Thatching - Decadence by Vaigly Great (B Beasley) 591^{3} 858^{4} 1083^{3} 3153^{5} 3438^{4} 3638^{2} 3849^{4} 4151^{2} 4465^{9}

4 **MISTIC GLEN (Ire),** b f Mister Majestic - Northern Glen by Northfields (USA) (J Parkes) 1156^{9}

3 **MISTLE CAT (USA),** gr c Storm Cat (USA) - Mistle Toe (USA) by Maribeau (S P C Woods) 751^{2} 1027^{1} 1347^{1} 2068^{2} 2803^{4} 3622^{2} 3862^{3} 4173^{8}

4 **MISTRESS BEE (USA),** b f Grub (USA) - Golden Regent (Can) by Vice Regent (Can) (S Coathup) 679 799 1004^{6} 2536^{1} 2709^{5}

3 **MISTROY,** gr f Damister (USA) - Troja by Troy (M D Hammond) 1642^{5} 2010^{7} 2310^{4} 2767^{6} 3461^{3}

5 **MISTY GODDESS (Ire),** gr m Godswalk (USA) - Silent Sail by Aglojo (M A Jarvis) 1612^{9} 1900^{8} 2354^{1} 2641^{1} 2894^{2} 3308^{9} 4470 4533^{5} 4676^{2}

3 **MISTY JENNI (Ire),** b f Night Shift (USA) - Mousil by Moulton (R Akehurst) 1606 1906^{8} 2421

3 **MISTY SILKS,** b f Scottish Reel - Silk St James by Pas de Seul (M J Ryan) 483 995^{8} 1390^{1} 2156^{7} 2421^{4} 2874^{2} 3088^{1} 3431^{2} 4320^{1} 4490^{4} 4597^{1}

4 **MISTY VIEW,** gr f Absalom - Long View by Persian Bold (J White) 1120 1586 2113^{9} 2273^{1} 3734^{5}

2 **MISTY WISE,** b f Rambo Dancer (Can) - Gigiolina by King Emperor (USA) (M Bell) 3659 4033 4342^{7} 4577

3 **MISWAKI DANCER (USA),** ch g Miswaki (USA) - Simply Divine (USA) by Danzig (USA) (M R Stoute) 2563^{7} 3117^{9} 3268^{7} 4047^{4} 4241^{4}

5 **MITAH (Ire),** ch m Hatim (USA) - Pearl Reef by Main Reef (A J McNamara) 2186^{6} 2881^{9} 3163^{3} 3326^{3}

3 **MITHI AL GAMAR (USA),** ch f Blushing Groom (Fr) - Raahia (Can) by Vice Regent (Can) (M R Stoute) 797^{4} 1060^{1} 1697^{8} 2136 3054^{5}

3 **MITHL AL HAWA,** b f Salse (USA) - Moon Drop by Dominion (J R Fanshawe) 1214^{2} 1765^{6} 2304^{2} 2885^{9} 3987^{2} 4649^{2}

3 **MITRAAS (USA),** br c Chief's Crown (USA) - Khwlah (USA) by Best Turn (USA) (H Thomson Jones) 1617^{2} 2064^{3} 2563^{6} 3314 3873^{3} 4533

2 **MITSIS,** b c Picea - Edith Piaf by Thatch (USA) (W J Musson) 1798^{7} 1999^{3} 3426^{2} 3743 4351 4484^{8} 4708

3 **MIXMATCH (Ire),** ch f Woodman (USA) - Our Duckling (USA) by Quack (USA) (Mrs C Head) 1218^{7}

2 **MIYOKO (Ire),** b f Prince Rupert (Fr) - Etoile Grise by Sea Hawk II (Patrick Martin) 4535 4706

4 **MIZAAYA,** ch c Riverman (USA) - Exclusive Order (USA) by Exclusive Native (USA) (M R Stoute) 315^{2} 675^{2} 1002^{8} 2413^{3} 3437^{6} 3636^{2} 3764^{4}

4 **MIZRAHI (USA),** ch f Fit To Fight (USA) - Jo Dan (USA) by Buckpasser (J S Bolger) 3685

5 **MIZYAN (Ire),** b g Melyno - Maid Of Erin (USA) by Irish River (Fr) (J E Banks) 61^{2} 495^{2} 857 1173^{7} 1457^{1} 1764^{4}

2 **MLOUKIAH (Fr),** gr f Teenoso (USA) - Money Moon by Auction Ring (USA) (P Howling) 1602

2 **MNAAFA (Ire),** b f Darshaan - Nahilah by Habitat (P T Walwyn) 3781

3 **MO-ADDAB (Ire),** b g Waajib - Tissue Paper by Touch Paper (A C Stewart) 2097^{4} 2596^{2} 3456^{5} 3820^{3} 4087^{2} 4633^{2}

2 **MOBILE MISS (Ire),** br f Classic Secret (USA) - Ellaline by Corvaro (USA) (Noel Meade) 4705^{6}

2 **MOCCASIN RUN (USA),** b c Topsider (USA) - Regal Heights (USA) by Forli (Arg) (I A Balding) 1446^{1}

2 **MOCKINGBIRD,** ch f Sharpo - Mountain Bluebird (USA) by Clever Trick (USA) (Lord Huntingdon) 1032 1265^{5} 1624^{5} 2528^{4} 3082^{4} 4163^{1} 4299^{7} 4561

3 **MODAAYIN,** b c Doyoun - Summer Impressions (USA) by Lyphard (USA) (B Hanbury) 1212 1340^{6}

2 **MODEL SHOW (Ire),** b f Dominion - Lomond's Breeze by Lomond (USA) (John J McLoughlin) 4624^{7} 4706

6 **MODEST HOPE (USA),** b h Blushing Groom (Fr) - Key Dancer (USA) by Nijinsky (Can) (B Richmond) 4707a^{1} 4788a^{3} 3^{3} 42^{1} 115^{7} 141^{1} 199^{3} 243^{1} 314^{3} 456 2530^{3} 2774^{1} 2948^{4} 3193^{5} 3595^{9} 3831^{8} 4036^{7} 4319 4676 4759

5 **MODESTO (USA),** b g Al Nasr (Fr) - Modena (USA) by Roberto (USA) (K O Cunningham-Brown) 20^{6} 59^{8} 84^{7} 128^{9} 234^{6} 321^{5} 402^{1} 500^{7} 1699^{7} 2381^{2} 3019^{7}

4 **MODHISH (Ire),** b c Sadler's Wells (USA) - Arctique Royale by Royal And Regal (USA) (A Fabre) 407^{7} 695^{3} 1124^{1} 1694^{2} 2261^{3} 3649^{4} 3930^{2} 4478^{4}

3 **MODI (USA),** b f Deputy Minister (Can) - Katie Cochran (USA) by Roberto (USA) (Lord Huntingdon) 2010^{4} 3272 3706^{6}

4 **MOGILNY (USA),** 4517^{7}

4 **MOGWAI (Ire),** b c Alzao (USA) - Maltese Pet by Dragonara Palace (USA) (S Dow) 4681a^{8} 4781a^{4} 101^{7} 1209 1664^{4} 1903^{2} 2139^{5} 3305^{7} 3447^{2} 3591^{5} 3938^{1} 4424^{5}

2 **MOHAAJIR (USA),** b c Saddler's Wells (USA) - Very Charming (USA) by Vaguely Noble (J S Bolger) 2072^{6} 3203^{4}

3 **MOHAYA (USA),** b g Cox's Ridge (USA) - Mazyoun (USA) by Blushing Groom (Fr) (J C McConnochie) 1617 1802 1935^{5} 4267 4353

3 **MOHICAN BRAVE (Ire),** ch g Salt Dome (USA) - Mrs Tittlemouse by Nonoalco (USA) (J G FitzGerald) 1247^{3} 1501^{1} 1940^{9} 2220^{4} 2816^{9} 3192^{1} 3364^{3} 3973 4760

2 **MOIANA (Ire),** 1361^{3}

3 **MOIDART,** b f Electric - Marypark by Charlottown (J R Fanshawe) 534^{6} 980^{9} 1099^{1} 1613^{2} 2458^{4} 3087^{3} 3479^{2} 3907^{1} 4143^{9}

4 **MOJAVE,** b c Green Desert (USA) - Out Of Shot by Shirley Heights (M R Stoute) 660^{7} 1532^{3} 3315^{9}

2 **MOKAAFI,** b c Green Desert (USA) - Peace Girl by Dominion (R W Armstrong) 4726^{4}

2 **MOKAITE,** b f Komaite (USA) - Manhunt by Posse (USA) (M D Hammond) 968^{2} 1182^{4} 2129^{1} 2268^{2} 2569^{6} 2679^{2} 2952^{1} 3363^{8} 3677

2 **MOKHTAR (Ire),** b c Sadler's Wells (USA) - Flame Of Tara by Artaius (USA) (J L Dunlop) 4714^{2}

7 **MOLDAVIA,** ch m Glenstal (USA) - Sooner Or Later by Sheshoon (T Stack) 487

3 **MOLESNES (USA),** (M Rolland) 561^{6} 1915

2 **MOLLINSBURN (Ire),** br g Tender King - Roundstone Lass by Montekin (T Craig) 1598^{8} 2429^{9} 2796^{7} 3143^{8}

3 **MOLLY BRAZEN,** ch f Risk Me (Fr) - Polly Peachum by Singing Strand (J Etherington) 899^{6} 1136^{5} 1396^{3} 2366^{7} 3789 4031

6 **MOLLY SPLASH,** b m Dunbeath (USA) - Nelly Do Da by Derring-Do (C A Cyzer) 440^{1} 990 1820 2048^{9} 3066^{6}

2 **MOMENT OF GLORY (Ire),** ch c Harp Islet (USA) - No Distractions by Tap On Wood (R J R Williams) 1350^{6} 1602^{5} 1870^{2} 2718^{2} 3597^{6} 4418

2 **MOMENTS TO CARE (Ire),** ch f Mon Tresor - Choral Park by Music Boy (John J McLoughlin) 1197^{6} 2037^{8} 3613^{8} 3953^{3} 4093^{6} 4323^{3}

2 **MONAASSABAAT (USA),** ch f Zilzal (USA) - It's In The Air (USA) by Mr Prospector (USA) (M R Stoute) 1403^{9} 2357^{3} 3091^{1} 3845^{3} 4020^{5}

6 **MONARDA,** ch g Pharly (Fr) - Emaline (Fr) by Empery (USA) (P F I Cole) 520^{4} 723 1731^{4} 1984^{1} 2386^{1} 2422^{3} 3231^{3} 3690^{3} 4519^{1} 4684^{5}

3 **MONASTIC FLIGHT (Ire),** ch g Carmelite House (USA) - Short Stay by Be My Guest (USA) (B S Rothwell) 1737^{6} 1875^{4} 2130^{4} 2859 3681^{9}

3 **MONAZITE,** b c Damister (USA) - Princely Maid by King's Troop (J C McConnochie) 1671^{8} 2097^{7} 3522^{8} 3694^{3} 3943

5 **MONDE BLEU,** b h Last Tycoon - Make Plans (USA) by Go Marching (USA) (A Fabre) 1011^{2} 1465^{2} 1786 3414^{1} 4312^{3} 4739^{7}

3 **MONDRAGON,** b c Niniski (USA) - La Lutine by My Swallow (Mrs M Reveley) 295^{4} 468^{7} 932^{5} 1180^{5} 1423^{2} 2196^{1} 3056^{2} 3556^{1} 3998^{2} 4344^{3} 4445^{3}

3 **MONDSEE,** b f Caerleon (USA) - Papermoon by Troy (D Smaga) 1368^{4}

3 **MONET MONET MONET,** ch f Claude Monet (USA) - Delta Wind by Tumble Wind (USA) (T G Mills) 1501^{6} 2095

2 **MONEYBROKER (Ire),** gr c Petorius - Pete's Money (USA) by Caucasus (USA) (W M Roper) 1332 3416 3608^{6} 4146^{4} 4380^{6}

2 **MONICA'S CHOICE (Ire),** b c Shaadi (USA) - Tendermark by Prince Tenderfoot (USA) (P Burke) 1197 1442^{6} 2745^{6} 3379^{4} 3607^{9} 4052

2 **MONIS (Ire),** ch c Waajib - Gratify by Grundy (T Thomson Jones) 2766^{5} 3528^{1} 3902^{3} 4130^{3}

2 **MONKEY BOY (Ire),** b g Mazaad - Zareeta by Free State (J Berry) 2342^{7} 3754^{8}

2 **MONKEY FACE,** gr f Clantime - Charming View by Workboy (J Hetherton) 3183 3810^{4} 3972^{8} 4342

2 **MONKEY MAGIC (Ire),** b g Fayruz - Charo by Mariacci (Fr) (J Berry) 312^{5} 433^{3} 908 3490^{7} 4044^{4} 4159^{2} 4326^{2} 4512^{6} 4699^{3}

2 **MONKEY MONEY (Ire),** b f Classic Secret (USA) - Mystery Bid by Auction Ring (USA) (J Berry) 496^{6} 886^{5} 1254^{6} 1555^{9}

2 **MONKEY MUSIC,** ch g Music Boy - Low Dalby by Longleat (USA) (J Berry) 466^{9} 1098^{2} 1899^{3} 2659^{1} 3133^{3} 3428^{6} 4165 4351^{7} 4416 4642^{6}

2 **MONKEY'S WEDDING,** b g Skyliner - Munequita by Marching On (J Berry) 743^{2} 1263^{2} 1561^{5} 2021 2876^{2} 3215^{4} 3432^{4} 3569^{2} 4042^{6} 4358^{1} 4453^{5} 4618^{1} 4756^{1}

2 **MONKEY WENCH (Ire),** b f Taufan (USA) - Northern Valkyrie by Glenstal (USA) (J Berry) 3186^{5} 3598^{3} 3792^{9} 4082^{6} 4435

2 **MONKSTOWN MAJOR (Ire),** b g Classic Secret (USA) - Little Min by Nebbiolo (Noel Meade) 4582^{6}

2 **MONMOUTH PARK,** b c Faustus (USA) - Femme Formidable by Formidable (USA) (J C Harley) 938^{8} 2319^{5}

3 **MONOPOLY MONEY (Ire),** b g Taufan (USA) - Pickety Place by Prince Tenderfoot (USA) (C Collins) 669^{5} 1510^{5} 2185^{2} 2877^{2} 3605^{1}

2 **MON PANACHE (Ire),** b f Classic Secret (USA) - Be Nimble by Wattlefield (Noel Meade) 571 896^{8} 2244^{5} 2450^{2} 2983^{4} 3273^{4}

4 **MON PETITNAMOUR (Ire),** b f Darshaan - Headin' Home by Habitat (K O Cunningham-Brown) 46^{6} 69^{4} 229 246^{6} 458^{7} 622^{5} 739^{9} 1242 2757^{4} 2847^{5} 2989^{5} 3787^{7} 3984^{3} 4152 4336^{6}

2 **MON ROUGE (Ire),** b g Mon Tresor - Another Tune by Red God (R Boss) 2167^{6} 2502^{7} 3505^{3}

2 **MONRUSH (Ire),** b c Shirley Heights - Switched On by Known Fact (USA) (S Dow) 2990^{9}

5 **MONSCOMA (Ire),** b h Montelimar (USA) - Scoma by Lord Gayle (USA) (R Ingram) 4699a 4760a 4795a^{5}

2 **MONSIEUR BLEU,** ch g Jalmood (USA) - Misowni by Niniski (USA) (Miss L A Perratt) 2554^{8} 2952^{3} 3235^{7} 3563^{7} 3829^{2} 4215^{4} 4492^{7} 4701^{9}

3 **MONSIEUR DUPONT (Ire),** b g Alzao (USA) - Katie Koo by Persian Bold (B W Hills) 459 2130^{3} 2751^{1} 3097^{2} 3556

2 **MONSIEUR PETONG,** b c Petong - Little Madam by Habat (M R Channon) 1091 1241^{5} 3098^{4} 3279^{9} 3641^{3} 3815^{2} 3978^{5} 4061^{9}

3 **MONSIGNOR PAT (USA),** b c Irish Tower (USA) - Song To Remember by Song (H R A Cecil) 880^{6} 1068 1330^{4} 1703^{1} 2989^{7} 3246^{8} 4188^{6}

3 **MONSUN (Ger),** b c Konigsstuhl (Ger) - Mosella by Surumu (H Jentzsch) 594^{1} 1369^{1} 2259^{2} 3370^{1} 4201^{1}

4 **MONTAGNE,** br f Midyan (USA) - La Masse by High Top (M W Eckley) 3689^{9} 3938

2 **MONTAYA,** b c Taufan (USA) - Kellys Reef by Pitskelly (J M Troy) 543^{2} 687^{1} 1381^{4} 1804^{4}

8 **MONTEFIORE,** b h Corvaro (USA) - Distant Bells (Fr) (J E Mulhern) 272 308

2 **MONTEGO BAY (Ire),** b f Be My Guest (USA) - Susan's Way by Red God (Declan Gillespie) 3071 3451

3 **MONTEJUSTICE (Ire),** br f Montelimar (USA) - Wild Justice by Sweet Revenge (P J Casserly) 552^{8} 1014^{6} 1139 2287

2 **MONTE MARIO (USA),** b g Imp Society (USA) - Ditdad (USA) by Tudor Grey (D K Weld) 1197^{4} 1550^{1} 2075^{7} 3200^{8}

6 **MONTENDRE,** b g Longleat (USA) - La Lutine by My Swallow (M McCormack) 316^{4} 511^{2} 1019^{3} 1786^{4} 2574^{3} 3162^{2} 3594^{5} 4170^{6} 4464^{1} 4729^{5}

4 **MONTEPULCIANO (USA),** ch c General Assembly (USA) - Mocambique by Frontal 2242^{4} 3717^{9} 4200^{3} 4304^{2}

2 **MONTICINO (Ire),** ch c Dominion - Fantoccini by Taufan (USA) (R Charlton) 3446^{7} 3888^{5} 4269^{3} 4452^{1}

3 **MONTONE (Ire),** b c Pennine Walk - Aztec Princess by Indian King (USA) (C B B Booth) 1833^{6} 2011 2993^{9} 4022 4235 4348 4694

6 **MONTPELIER LAD,** br g Elegant Air - Leg Glance by Home Guard (USA) (G Richards) 910^{8}

2 **MOOBAKKR (USA),** b or br c Mr Prospector (USA) - Without Feathers (USA) by Brave Shot (D K Weld) 3771^{4} 4058^{9} 4581^{6}

2 **MOOFAJI,** b c Night Shift (USA) - Three Piece by Jaazeiro (USA) (Major W R Hern) 4679^{4}

2 **MOONAX (Ire),** ch c Caerleon (USA) - Moonsilk by Solinus (B W Hills) 4714

3 **MOON CARNIVAL,** b f Be My Guest (USA) - Castle Moon by Kalamoun (Lady Herries) 295 502^{1} 717^{3} 976^{1} 1426^{3}

3 **MOON FLASK (Ire),** b c Common Grounds - Flaxen Hair by Thatch (USA) (P J Makin) 784^{4} 1114^{5}

3 **MOONLIGHT ECLIPSE,** ch c Jupiter Island - Moonlight Bay by Palm Track (E J Alston) 344^{3} 534^{4} 1055^{4} 1423^{7} 4431^{4} 4604^{4} 4662^{1}

3 **MOONLIGHT PARTNER (Ire),** b f Red Sunset - Dance Partner (USA) by Graustark (Declan Gillespie) 790 870 2285^{6} 2604^{2} 2843^{8} 3455^{1} 3912^{7} 4056 4287

3 **MUSTAKIM (Ire),** ch c Persian Bold - Majestic Amber (USA) by Majestic Light (USA) (R W Armstrong) 1330^{5} 1617^{8} 3456 3726^{4} 4016 4320

5 **MUST BE MAGICAL (USA),** ch g Temperence Hill (USA) - Honorine (USA) by Blushing Groom (Fr) (J Mackie) 709^{2} 973^{6} 1702^{5} 2178^{3} 2585^{2} 3087^{8} 4035^{1}

3 **MUSTN'T GRUMBLE (Ire),** b g Orchestra - Gentle Heiress by Prince Tenderfoot (USA) (B Beasley) 1424^{5} 2064 2202 2764^{2} 2953^{3} 4348^{4} 4640^{4}

3 **MUSWELL BROOK (Ire),** br c Nashamaa - Motus by Anfield (J S Bolger) 550 848^{3} 1164^{5} 1856^{7} 3381 3498^{4} 3576^{3} 3605^{3} 3769^{4} 4094^{9}

3 **MUTAKALLAM (USA),** b c Fappiano (USA) - Stark Drama (USA) by Graustark (H Thomson Jones) 1080^{3} 1459^{1} 2233^{5} 3540^{2} 3783 4116^{8} 4320

2 **MUTAKDDIM (USA),** ch c Seeking The Gold (USA) - Oscillate (USA) by Seattle Slew (USA) (J H M Gosden) 3779^{2} 4149^{1} 4443^{8}

3 **MUTAMANNI,** b c Sadler's Wells (USA) - Betty's Secret (USA) by Secretariat (USA) (Major W R Hern) 529^{8} 672 842^{6} 1176^{9} 3263^{6} 3655^{2} 3820^{2} 4043^{5} 4148^{5}

5 **MUTARJJAM (USA),** b or br h Stop The Music (USA) - So Smooth (USA) by Third Martini (Kevin Prendergast) 1084^{6}

3 **MUTAWALI (Ire),** ch c Exactly Sharp (USA) - Ludovica by Bustino (D Morley) 980^{4} 1154^{3} 1581^{5} 1934^{5} 2281^{2} 2751^{6} 3306^{5} 3699^{8} 4320^{9} 4479^{5}

3 **MUTHAHB (Ire),** br c Mtoto - Coven by Sassafras (Fr) (A C Stewart) 1831^{8}

2 **MUTIARA,** b f Never So Bold - Hello Cuddles by He Loves Me (Miss Gay Kelleway) 4303^{7}

2 **MUTINIQUE,** br f General Wade - Little Visitor by Tina's Pet (J E Long) 4142^{8} 4303 4598^{4} 4754^{6}

2 **MUWAFIK,** ch c Nashwan (USA) - Ashayer (USA) by Lomond (USA) (J L Dunlop) 2756^{5} 3728^{2} 4316^{1} 4647^{7}

2 **MUZRAK (Can),** ch c Forty Niner (USA) - Linda North (USA) by Northern Dancer (Kevin Prendergast) 3922^{9} 4688^{3}

2 **MUZZ (Ire),** br c Gallic League - Cartier Bijoux by Ahonoora (M Johnston) 395^{7} 3754 4608^{5}

2 **MWAARED,** b f Unfuwain (USA) - Nouvelle Star (Aus) by Luskin Star (Aus) (Major W R Hern) 4422^{4} 4539

4 **MY ABBEY,** b f Hadeer - Rose Barton by Pas de Seul (E J Alston) 887 1287^{9} 1925^{3} 2777^{1} 3486^{9} 4109 4363 4734

4 **MYASHA (USA),** b g Imp Society (USA) - Mauna Loa (USA) by Hawaii (Mrs L Piggott) 3372^{2}

3 **MY BALLYBOY,** ch g Ballacashtal (Can) - Pink N' Perky by Tickled Pink (A Bailey) 4691a^{9} 4717a 742^{6} 1674 2555^{4} 2736^{5} 2763^{2} 3374

3 **MY BEST VALENTINE,** b c Try My Best (USA) - Pas de Calais by Pas de Seul (P W Harris) 398^{1} 801 1058^{9} 1436^{1} 1721^{2} 1954^{4} 2212^{4} 2431^{3} 3017^{4} 3450^{9} 3774^{2} 4166^{1}

3 **MY BONUS,** b f Cyrano de Bergerac - Dress In Spring by Northfields (USA) (D J S Cosgrove) 460^{5} 716^{3} 1010^{4} 1213^{9} 1826^{1} 2024^{4} 2660^{5} 2940 3220^{7} 3955 4317

4 **MY BOY BUSTER,** b c Kind Of Hush - Happy Donna by Huntercombe (C J Hill) 3007 3661

7 **MY CHIARA,** b m Ardross - My Tootsie by Tap On Wood (P J Bevan) 1155^{5} 3473

5 **MY DESIRE,** ch m Grey Desire - Another Move by Farm Walk (Mrs M Reveley) 967^{1} 1155^{4} 2235^{1} 2477^{2} 3255^{2} 4466^{3} 4630^{6} 4732^{5}

3 **MY FABULEUSE (Fr),** b f Fabulous Dancer (USA) - Bonicarielle by Bourbon (J-M Beguigne) 296^{4}

2 **MY FIORE,** b f Midyan (USA) - My Tootsie by Tap On Wood (P J Bevan) 4121^{7} 4539

6 **MYFONTAINE,** b h Persepolis (Fr) - Mortefontaine (Fr) by Polic (K T Ivory) 329^{2} 500^{4} 1318^{6} 4091^{4} 4254 4751

3 **MY FOXY LADY,** b f Jalmood (USA) - La Petite Noblesse by Thatching (D Haydn Jones) 4687a^{9} 491^{6} 927^{5} 1240^{8} 1925

2 **MY GALLERY (Ire),** ch f Tate Gallery (USA) - Sententious by Kautokeino (Fr) (A Bailey) 2240^{9} 2400^{5} 3156^{6} 3284^{6} 3754^{5} 4114^{1} 4272^{5} 4516^{8} 4719^{6}

4 **MY GIRL FRIDAY,** b f Scorpio (Fr) - Nikancy by Castlenik (D W Chapman) 2427^{9}

3 **MY GODSON,** br g Valiyar - Blessit by So Blessed (B Beasley) 535^{1} 683^{7} 1160^{9} 1589^{5} 1760^{4} 2170^{2} 2553^{5} 3094^{7} 3564^{6} 4317

3 **MY GOSSIP (Ire),** ch f Camden Town - Hard Sweet by Hard Fought (Joseph M Canty) 1995^{7} 2496^{5} 3112^{1} 3298^{2} 3732^{4} 4001^{7}

4 **MY GRAIN,** ch f Ballacashtal (Can) - Sequoia by Sassafras (Fr) (T Thomson Jones) 1930 2289^{6} 3185^{7}

3 **MY HARVINSKI,** b g Myjinski (USA) - Autumn Harvest by Martinmas (P R Hedger) 372^{6} 725^{3} 864^{2} 1255^{7} 1504^{2} 1907^{4} 2291^{2} 2663^{9}

3 **MYJINKA,** gr f Myjinski (USA) - Royal Bat by Crowned Prince (USA) (J O'Donoghue) 3286 3509 3665^{6} 3910

3 **MYKERINA (USA),** 89^{2} 154^{3}

3 **MY KERRY DANCER (USA),** ch c Seattle Dancer (USA) - Mumble Peg by General Assembly (USA) (P Mullins) 1855^{4} 2249^{5} 2743^{2} 2903^{6} 3297^{5} 3579^{5} 3733^{2} 4246^{7} 4368^{1} 4555^{4} 4639^{1}

9 **MYLIEGE,** b g Lord Gayle (USA) - My Natalie by Rheingold (P Leach) 1562

2 **MY LIFETIME LADY (Ire),** ch f Indian Ridge - Liffey Reef by Main Reef (R Hollinshead) 680^{3} 1158^{1} 2119^{2} 2446^{1} 2974^{2} 3115^{5} 3845 4299^{8}

6 **MY LINDIANNE,** gr m Alias Smith (USA) - Lindrick Passion by Silly Season (J Dooler) 2631^{6} 3536^{5}

3 **MY MINNIE,** b f Kind Of Hush - Miami Mouse by Miami Springs (R J Hodges) 921^{8} 1311^{7} 1587 1993^{6} 2358^{4} 2938^{3} 3233^{3} 4206^{1} 4270^{9}

2 **MY MOONA,** b f Ballacashtal (Can) - Salala by Connaught (P J Hobbs) 3166 4227 4496^{9}

3 **MYNYOSS,** b g Domynsky - Cross Your Heart by Busted (J Berry) 2464^{8} 2763^{3} 2888^{5} 3442^{4}

3 **MY-O-MY (Ire),** b f Waajib - Maimiti by Goldhill (T Stack) 1105^{1} 1575^{4} 2073 2780^{3} 3201^{1} 3496^{5} 3561^{2} 4275^{1}

3 **MY PATRIARCH,** ch c Be My Guest (USA) - Early Rising (USA) by Grey Dawn II (J L Dunlop) 514^{7} 772^{5} 1426^{6} 1827^{3} 2158^{1} 2355^{1} 2963^{3} 3595^{1} 4239^{1} 4466^{6} 4630^{1}

2 **MY RAGAMUFFIN (Ire),** b f Common Grounds - Golden Rhythm by Cure The Blues (USA) (F Dunne) 1442^{7} 1650^{8} 1792^{1} 2246^{4} 2487^{5} 2704^{6} 3379^{3} 3806^{4} 4093^{7} 4262^{4}

5 **MYRAKALU (Fr),** gr h Kaldoun (Fr) - Muravera (USA) by L'enjoleur (Can) (F Boutin) 4747^{3}

3 **MYRO BALANNE (Ire),** b f Glenstal (USA) - Raise A Plum (USA) by Raise A Cup (USA) (F X Doyle) 847 1610^{9} 1822^{5} 2667^{6} 3294^{6} 3498

4 **MY ROSSINI,** b g Ardross - My Tootsie by Tap On Wood (P J Bevan) 2071^{1} 2376^{5} 2835^{3} 3152^{8} 3690^{8} 4212

2 **MYRRH,** b f Salse (USA) - Hot Spice by Hotfoot (D Morley) 4543

6 **MY RUBY RING,** b m Blushing Scribe (USA) - Bells Of St Martin by Martinmas (D R Laing) 760^{9} 1059^{3} 1209^{8} 1537^{4} 1744 1977 2378^{1} 2494^{3} 2723^{2} 3168^{1} 3393^{1} 3621 3896^{9} 4096^{8} 4485^{3} 4580

4 **MY SENOR,** b g Jalmood (USA) - San Marguerite by Blakeney (M Madgwick) 3984^{4}

3 **MY SET PEACE,** ch f Prince Of Peace - Spreading Sunset by Amber Rama (USA) (M P Muggeridge) 1625 2005^{2} 2313^{4} 2611^{5}

3 **MYSILV,** ch f Bustino - Miss By Miles by Milesian (D Nicholson) 732^{5} 1109^{3} 1705^{1} 2220^{5} 3358 3540^{9} 3961^{3} 4101^{1} 4254^{3} 4533^{4} 4604^{3}

2 **MY SIN (Ire),** (C Laffon-Parias) 2144^{6} 3413^{6}

3 **MY SISTER LUCY,** b f Farajullah - Woven Gold by No Lute (Fr) (A P Jarvis) 422 905^{5} 1138 1309 3102

2 **MY SONG OF SONGS,** b f Norwick (USA) - Pas de Chat by Relko (R P C Hoad) 1253^{7} 1933 4128^{9} 4492 4646

7 **MY SPARKLING RING,** b g Sparkling Boy - Bells Of St Martin by Martinmas (C T Nash) 1699^{4} 1862^{5} 2381^{6}

3 **MY SPECIAL GUEST (Ire),** b f Be My Guest (USA) - Venecia (Fr) by Luthier (J G Coogan) 870 1997 2743

6 **MYSTERIOUS MAID (USA),** ch m L'emigrant (USA) - Body Heat (USA) by Sir Ivor (J Pearce) 994 1414 1781^{2} 2347^{6} 2729 3430^{1} 4218 4268^{3} 4486^{2}

3 **MYSTERIOUS WAYS (Ire),** b c Fairy King (USA) - Sronica by Midsummer Night II (M V O'Brien) 667^4 1047^9 2805^5 3027^7 3334^1 4056^4 4386^2 4552^1

2 **MYSTERY MOON,** b f Reprimand - Ragged Moon by Raga Navarro (Ity) (N A Graham) 1211 2417^7

3 **MYSTICAL CITY (Ire),** ch f The Noble Player (USA) - Felicitas by Mr Fluoracarbon (Adrian Taylor) 1507^5 3497^8 3616^6 4246 4383

7 **MYSTICAL GUEST,** b h Be My Guest (USA) - Saygood (USA) by Royal Ascot (J R Bostock) 4102 4254 4669

2 **MYSTICAL MICKEY (Ire),** b c Anita's Prince - Mooned by Fair Season (W W Haigh) 2042^5 3972 4163 4452^8 4668^4 4758^5

3 **MYSTIC GODDESS (USA),** ch f Storm Bird (Can) - Rose Goddess by Sassafras (Fr) (M R Stoute) 746^5 1404^5 2334^6 2885^5 3465

2 **MYSTIC HILL,** b c Shirley Heights - Nuryana by Nureyev (USA) (R Charlton) 4253^2 4498^6

4 **MYSTIC MEMORY,** b f Ela-Mana-Mou - Mountain Memory by High Top (Mrs M Reveley) 427^6 1847^7 2343^1 2506^2 2857^3 3848 4454^2

2 **MYSTIC MOMENT (Ire),** ch f Entitled - Rusty Goddess by Hard Fought (Declan Gillespie) 4380

8 **MY SWAN SONG,** b g Soul Singer - Palmaria by Be Friendly (J P Smith) 702^8

2 **MYTILENE (Ire),** b f Soviet Star (USA) - Dancing Meg (USA) by Marshua's Dancer (USA) (J H M Gosden) 3833^1 4171^7

2 **MY TIME,** b f Cigar - Rowan Ville by Sexton Blake (J W Hills) 4620

4 **MY TOMBOLA (USA),** 4471^5

3 **MY TREASURE,** b f Petrizzo - Mandrake Madam by Mandrake Major (Mrs M J Bennett) 4718^7

3 **MY TRELAWNY (Ire),** b f Dowsing (USA) - Taniokey by Grundy (J C Harley) 257^6 488^3 847^1

2 **MY TRIVET (Ire),** b c Thatching - Blue Scholar by Hotfoot (J T Gorman) 2037 4369 4405^5

5 **MY TURN NEXT,** b m King Of Spain - Its My Turn by Palm Track (K W Hogg) 4357

3 **MYZA (USA),** b f Danzig - My Darling One by Exclusive Native (A Fabre) 3619^3

3 **NA-AMMAH (Ire),** b f Ela-Mana-Mou - Adrana by Bold Lad (Ire) (Kevin Prendergast) 1048^6 1335^2 2609^6 4410^3 4556^6 4690^6

3 **NAAWY,** b c Reference Point - Strike Home by Be My Guest (USA) (C Smith) 1772^4 2943^3 4353

3 **NA-AYIM (Ire),** b f Shirley Heights - Christabelle (USA) by Northern Dancer (A A Scott) 734^7 1789^8

7 **NABEEL (USA),** ch g Nodouble (USA) - Abeer (USA) by Dewan (USA) (Wilbert Tolerton) 2514^8 3395^6

3 **NABJELSEDR,** b c Never So Bold - Klewraye by Lord Gayle (USA) (C J Benstead) 471^6 747^7 2672^6

3 **NAFIHA (USA),** ch f Riverman (USA) - Azayim by Be My Guest (USA) (R W Armstrong) 1212 4191^5

3 **NAFUTH (USA),** b or br c Nureyev (USA) - Costly Array (USA) by Riverman (USA) (P T Walwyn) 510^3 951^2 1595^1 2066^3 2333 2758^4 3158^8 3476 4133^8 4320

4 **NAGIDA,** b f Skyliner - Kept In Style by Castle Keep (J A R Toller) 796^9 1066^3 1806^1 2987 3504 4278^3 4393

3 **NAHLATI (Ire),** b f Mtoto - Formido by Formidable (USA) (C E Brittain) 1005^1 2398 3045^4 3460^7 3699^5

3 **NAIF (USA),** b c Storm Bird (Can) - Benguela (USA) by Little Current (USA) (L M Cumani) 825^9 1330^1 1867^3 3219^1 3585^3 3883

8 **NAIL DON,** b h Don - Vivungi (USA) by Exbury (J S Moore) 4574 4751^4

2 **NAIS (Ire),** b f Fairy King (USA) - Alkis (USA) by Roberto (USA) (M Bell) 4575^8

4 **NAIVITY (Ire),** b f Auction Ring (USA) - Futility by Tower Walk (Liam Browne) 665^8 4056 4287^6 4385^7

5 **NAIYSARI (Ire),** gr g Mouktar - Naiymat by Troy (Mrs A M O'Brien) 575^3

4 **NAJEB (USA),** b g Chief's Crown (USA) - Modiste (USA) by Sir Ivor (P D Evans) 3

2 **NAJM ALMAYDAAN (USA),** b or br c Nureyev (USA) - Teacher's Joy (USA) by Daryl's Joy (NZ) (J H M Gosden) 2299^8

2 **NAKITA,** ch f Efisio - Ra Ra by Lord Gayle (USA) (C N Allen) 528^3 657^6 1277^2 2027^3 2067^9 2417^1 3428^2 4649^6 4733

4 **NAKUPITA (Ire),** ch f Formidable (USA) - Bassita by Bustino (A C Stewart) 537^3

9 **NAMELOC,** ch g Deep Run - Kitty Cullen by Pollerton (J E Kiely) 2557^6

2 **NAME THE TUNE,** b c Chief Singer - Try To Remember by Music Boy (P Howling) 2325 2866 3167^4 3475^6

9 **NANARCH (USA),** ch g Dara Monarch - Natuschka by Authi (Kevin Prendergast) 4685a 1468^6 2143^7 3063^4 3276^1 3398^1 3663^1

3 **NANCY (Ire),** b f Vision (USA) - Splendidly Gay by Lord Gayle (USA) (D J Wintle) 4697a^5 203^5 434^3 652^5 1112 1283^4 1477^5 1896^4 2178^8 2800^4 3239^5 3552 4048^2 4374 4669^3

2 **NANCYS WOOD (Ire),** br f Doubletour (USA) - Sarsenet by Saritamer (USA) (F W Pennicott) 1854 2701 3073 4244

2 **NANDURA,** b f Nordico (USA) - The Ranee by Royal Palace (M J Heaton-Ellis) 4498

3 **NANNAKA (USA),** b f Exceller (USA) - Najidiya (USA) by Riverman (USA) (P Mullins) 3382^3 3733^5 4429^9 4556^2 4690^7

6 **NANNERL (USA),** ch m Valid Appeal (USA) - Allouette by Proud Birdie (F Schulhofer) 1184^6 3207^4 3804^2

3 **NANNY MARGARET (Ire),** b f Prince Rupert (Fr) - Ferjima's Gem (USA) by Wajima (USA) (P A Kelleway) 4677a^7 4709a^4 4778a^4 32^4 83^7

3 **NANQUIDNO,** ch f Krayyan - Nancherrow by Scallywag (Mrs J G Retter) 1057^8 1628 2151^7 2504^7 3305^8 3661

2 **NAPOLEON STAR (Ire),** ch g Mulhollande (USA) - Lady Portobello by Porto Bello (M S Saunders) 3086^4 3505^6 3876 4594

4 **NASEER (USA),** b g Hero's Honor (USA) - Sweet Delilah (USA) by Super Concorde (USA) (B Forsey) 4760a 4807a^4 4819a^8 46^1 103^3 141^5 1242^8 1731^3 1862^2 2007^9

4 **NASHOON (Ire),** b c Nashamaa - Nistona by Will Somers (T Kersey) 1038^9 1479^7

4 **NASHVILLE BLUES (Ire),** ch f Try My Best (USA) - Requena by Dom Racine (Fr) (J W Hills) 1471^4 1768 2254^9 3093^4 3512 4470

3 **NASR ALLAH (USA),** ch c Mogambo (USA) - Quick Blush by Blushing Groom (F Scheffer) 953^2 2436^3 3196^2 3717^3 4194^1

6 **NASSAU,** b g Cure The Blues (USA) - Nanticious by Northfield (USA) (D K Weld) 1025^2 2245^1 2461^5

3 **NASSMA (Ire),** b f Sadler's Wells (USA) - Pretoria by Habitat (J R Fanshawe) 992^2 1383^2 2328^1 2795^2 3488^1 4292^6 4630

3 **NATASHA NORTH,** ch f Northern State (USA) - Pilley Green by Porto Bello (T Casey) 1635^9 2313^6

4 **NATCHEZ TRACE,** b f Commanche Run - Lighted Lamp (USA) by Sir Gaylord (I A Balding) 522^5 679 1730^8 2358^7 2710^3 3301^8

7 **NATHIR (USA),** b g Diesis - As You Would (USA) by Fleet Nasrullah (P Butler) 4751^9

3 **NATIONAL FLAG (Fr),** b c Sure Blade (USA) - On The Staff (USA) by Master Willie (John M Oxx) 1443^6

4 **NATIVE CHAMPION (Ire),** ch g Be My Native (USA) - Dedham Vale by Dike (USA) (M J Corbett) 851

4 **NATIVE CHIEFTAN,** b g Trojan Fen - Habituee by Habitat (S Dow) 4748a^4 4782a^8 4802a^5 8^5 224^1 321^8 440^8 663 822^4 1129^6 1862^6 2127 4268^6

5 **NATIVE CROWN (Ire),** b g Be My Native (USA) - Crystal Halo by St Chad (Mrs S C Bradburne) 2059^8 2267^3 2565^4 2683^4 2950^3

6 **NATIVE HIGH LINE,** br m Be My Native (USA) - Line Of Reason by High Line (G O'Hagan) 4685a

6 **NATIVE MISSION,** ch g Be My Native (USA) - Sister Ida by Bustino (J G FitzGerald) 857^8 1112^8

3 **NATIVE NOBLE,** gr f Bold Arrangement - Zedative (Fr) by Zeddaan (K O Cunningham-Brown) 522

6 **NATIVE PORTRAIT,** ch g Be My Native (USA) - Dedham Vale by Dike (USA) (M J Corbett) 2039 2461^1 2841^5 3525^4 3805^6

4 **NATIVE WOODFIRE (Ire),** b f Mister Majestic - Larch by Busted (M J Corbett) 3579

8 **NATURAL ABILITY,** ch g Billion (USA) - Confident Girl by Quorum (Noel Meade) 575^9

3 **OK BERTIE,** b g Interrex (Can) - Rockery by Track Spare (R A Fahey) 995^4 1239^6 2212^5 2522^4 2993^1 3219^4 3558^3 3778^1 3906

6 **OK CORRAL (USA),** gr g Malinowski (USA) - Tiger Trap (USA) by Al Hattab (USA) (D Nicholson) 2317^5

3 **OKEEDOKEE (Fr),** gr c Kaldoun - Multitude by Lyphard (Mme C Head) 811^2 1149^7 4196^8

6 **OLD COMRADES,** ch g Music Boy - Miss Candine by King Emperor (USA) (L G Cottrell) 521^4 754^3 1207^4 1588^2 1876^5 2121^6 2757^6 3042^4 3447^4 3887

4 **OLD FOX (Fr),** b g In Fijar (USA) - Warning Bell by Bustino (D Sasse) 4678a 4710a

2 **OLD HOOK (Ire),** b or br c Digamist (USA) - Day Dress by Ashmore (Fr) (Allan Smith) 1279^5 2125^1 3086^7 4193 4228

8 **OLD MAN RIVER,** ch g Artaius (USA) - Running Brook by Run The Gantlet (USA) (D K Weld) 3604

3 **OLD PROVENCE,** b c Rainbow Quest (USA) - Orange Hill by High Top (L M Cumani) 1539^1 2003^1

3 **OLD RED (Ire),** ch c Ela-Mana-Mou - Sea Port by Averof (P F I Cole) 509^8 1004^3 3590 3937^7 4267^7

5 **OLD STEINE,** b g Elegant Air - Brightelmstone by Prince Regent (Fr) (P J Hobbs) 924 1075

2 **OLD SUNSHINE (Ire),** b or br c Sula Bula - The Burden by Kafu (F W Pennicott) 3492

6 **OLD TALKA RIVER,** b h Dunphy - Day In Town by Pall Mall (F W Pennicott) 4686a 272 281 575 942^7

3 **OLICANA (Ire),** ch g Persian Bold - Maniusha by Sallust (M D Hammond) 1900 2736^1 2769^4 2931^5 3536^8 3712^7

5 **OLIFANTSFONTEIN,** b h Thatching - Taplow by Tap On Wood (P Calver) 555^1 659 722^8 1449 2255 3511

3 **OLIVADI (Ire),** b c Prince Rupert (Fr) - So Stylish by Great Nephew (L M Cumani) 880^8 3759

2 **OLIVER-J,** b g Almushmmir - Olymena by Royalty (R Lee) 3760 4227^9

2 **OLIVER MESSEL (Ire),** b c Common Grounds - Boldabsa by Persian Bold (Kevin Prendergast) 269^3 305^6 1824^2 2072^2 2344^1

3 **OLIVIA VAL,** b f Valiyar - Traditional Miss by Traditionalist (USA) (C J Hill) 499 1074^6 1266 1627 3233 3896 4016

3 **OLLI STAR (Ire),** ch f Glenstal (USA) - Water Khet by Wittgenstein (C Ferrari) 1727^4 3920^4

4 **OLLIVER DUCKETT,** b g Bustino - Tatiana by Habitat (P Calver) 366^8 589^8

3 **OLYMPIA,** ch f Music Boy - Stepping Gaily by Gay Fandango (USA) (J L Spearing) 1655^3 2787^6 4331

2 **OLYMPIC BID,** gr f Absalom - Seven Seas (Fr) by Riverman (USA) (J Berry) 812 1189^4 1895 2216^5 2588^7 2679^4 3563^9 3968^4 4215^3 4492^5

3 **OMESMACJOY (Ire),** b g Corvaro (USA) - Mrs Baggins by English Prince (M McDonagh) 2674^7 2902 2956 3951

3 **OMIDJOY (Ire),** ch f Nishapour (Fr) - Fancy Finish by Final Straw (J R Jenkins) 385^4 816^3 1244^2 1935^6 2213^5 2684^8 3384

2 **OMNIA (USA),** b f Green Dancer (USA) - Rutledge Place (USA) by Caro (P F I Cole) 1393^3 3765^3 4111^3 4558^7

3 **ON BROADWAY,** b g Nomination - Formidable Dancer by Formidable (USA) (Mrs A Swinbank) 1039^7 1275 1477^4 2107^7

2 **ONCE MORE FOR LUCK (Ire),** b g Petorius - Mrs Lucky by Royal Match (Mrs M Reveley) 1401^7 2554^1 3950^5 4163^3 4358^7 4418^8 4646^1 4733^5

5 **ON CREDIT (Fr),** ch m No Pass No Sale (Ire) - Noble Tiara (USA) by Vaguely Noble (Ire) (P Bary) 4711a^2

2 **ONE DAY LATE,** b f Nishapour (Fr) - Pro Scania by Niniski (USA) (J G Burns) 2344^3 3807^7

2 **ONE FALSE MOVE (Ire),** b f Don't Forget Me - Ninette de Valois (Fr) by Gay Mecene (USA) (C Collins) 4244^9

5 **ONE FOR LUCK (Ire),** b g Trojan Fen - Gratify by Grundy (J J O'Neill) 753

5 **ONE FOR THE CHIEF,** b g Chief Singer - Action Belle by Auction Ring (USA) (R M Whitaker) 122^4 175^6

2 **ONE FOR THE LADIES,** b g Crofthall - Perma Fina by Nonoalco (USA) (J Balding) 4342 4452

8 **ONE FOR THE POT,** ch g Nicholas Bill - Tea-Pot by Ragstone (M P Naughton) 356^7 1056^8 4017^5 4374

3 **ONE FOR TONDY,** b f Local Suitor (USA) - Transcendence (USA) by Sham (USA) (N Bycroft) 4544 4645^6

3 **ONE MORE POUND,** b g Northern State (USA) - Malise by Royal Palace (M Dixon) 4761a 4801a 557^9 976 1319^3 1709^4 1951 2834 3171^6

3 **ONE-O-EIGHT,** b f Sweet Monday - Bloffa by Derrylin (P D Cundell) 2109 2499 4335^7

3 **ONE OFF THE RAIL (USA),** b c Rampage (USA) - Catty Queen (USA) by Tom Cat (A Moore) 4761a^3 4778a^2 4801a^2 880^9 1062^1 1238^4 1699^1 1862^3 2014^1 2381^1 2614^3 3019^6 3752 4086^9

2 **ONE ON ONE,** b f Primo Dominie - Number One Lady by Shernazar (W J Haggas) 2866^2 3052^1 3428^1 4020^4 4456^4

5 **ONESIXNINE (Ire),** b m Trojan Fen - Finoon Caroline (USA) by Sauce Boat (USA) (D K Weld) 4727a^5 553^4 957^2

3 **ONE VOICE (USA),** ch c Affirmed (USA) - Elk's Ellie (USA) by Vaguely Noble (Sir Mark Prescott) 338^1 1134^4

2 **ONE WILD OAT,** b f Shareef Dancer (USA) - Short Rations by Lorenzaccio (M R Stoute) 2250^7 2796^2 3698^4 4015^7

3 **ON GOLDEN POND (Ire),** b f Bluebird (USA) - Art Age by Artaius (USA) (G M Moore) 516^3 732 1058 1875 2183^3 2313^3

3 **ONLY ALPHA (USA),** 1542

3 **ONLY A MIRAGE,** b c Damister (USA) - Magic Vision by Shergar (W R Muir) 1429 1746^9

4 **ONLY A ROSE,** br f Glint Of Gold - No More Rosies by Warpath (C W Thornton) 356^6

2 **ONLY DREAMING,** b f Dominion - Welsh Jane by Bold Lad (Ire) (R Hannon) 4752

2 **ONLY FOOLS,** b g Midyan (USA) - Dame Scarlet by Blakeney (G B Balding) 2866 3642 3958^8 4418

4 **ONLY ROYALE (Ire),** b f Caerleon (USA) - Etoile de Paris by Crowned Prince (USA) (L M Cumani) 1538^2 2654^2 2986^2 3433^1 3930^1 4311^5 4477^4

3 **ONODI (Ire),** b f Glenstal (USA) - Empress Kim by Formidable (USA) (W J Martin) 257 282 790 2693 4429

3 **ONOMATOPOEIA (Ire),** ch g Theatrical - Sealy by Filiberto (USA) (Patrick Joseph Flynn) 487^4 2664^3 3580^7 3854 3951^2 4119

5 **ON THE BEACH (NZ),** 596

3 **ON THE LEDGE (USA),** b c Alleged (USA) - Field Dancer by Northfields (USA) (A C Stewart) 3225 3456^9

2 **ONTHEOTHEREND (Ire),** b c Satco (Fr) - Miysam by Supreme Sovereign (Miss A M Winters) 820^7 896

2 **ON THE WING AGAIN,** b f Mazilier (USA) - Midnight Flit by Bold Lad (Ire) (Mark Campion) 2377^7 2610^6

3 **ON YOUR MARK (Ger),** 1125^4

4 **ON Y REVIENT,** 4754a^2

6 **ON Y VA (USA),** ch m Victorious (USA) - Golden Moony by Northfields (USA) (R J R Williams) 4757a^2 4803a^3 54^2 91^2 134^2 197^5 253^2 391^3 521^3 754^8 970^1 1246^7 1701^3 1876^1 2031^7 2426^2 2824^4 3124^7 3325^6 4333^3 4458^2 4616^9

2 **OOH AH CANTONA,** b g Crofthall - Chablisse by Radetzky (R M Whitaker) 1863^1 2430^5 2973^1 3406^4 4051^4

4 **OOZLEM (Ire),** b g Burslem - Fingers by Lord Gayle (USA) (R M Flower) 2669 3018^6 4600^7 4727^5

4 **OPEN AGENDA (Ire),** b c Ajdal (USA) - Metair by Laser Light (K White) 975^9 1284^8 1588^7

4 **OPEN MARKET (USA),** b g Northern Baby (Can) - Spiranthes (USA) by Vaguely Noble (D K Weld) 807 1025^7 1794^8 2900^5 3604^3 3684^2 3854^6 4639

8 **OPEN THE GATE,** gr g The Parson - Etrenne by Happy New Year (D T Hughes) 309

7 **OPERA GHOST,** b h Caerleon (USA) - Premier Rose by Sharp Edge (P W Harris) 1711^4 1974^2 2395^4 3152 3434 3786^3 4248^3

5 **OPERA HOUSE,** b h Sadler's Wells (USA) - Colorspin (Fr) by High Top (M R Stoute) 810^2 1472^1 2253^1 2791^1 3913^2 4311^3 4744^6

7 **OPERATION WOLF,** ch g Adonijah - Sesta by Artaius (USA) (N Tinkler) 1720^9 1832^6

3 **PADDINGTON GIRL (Ire)**, b f Alzao (USA) - Bear's Affair by Gay Fandango (USA) (J L Dunlop) 1587 2097

7 **PADDY CHALK**, gr h Tina's Pet - Guiletta by Runnymede (L J Holt) 659[3] 1066[9] 1348[2] 1584[7] 2255[2] 2987 3348 3621

3 **PADDYS COCKTAIL (Ire)**, b f Tremblant - Melungeon by Ardoon (Noel Meade) 1333

2 **PADDY'S RICE**, ch g Hadeer - Requiem by Song (L J Holt) 2049[4] 2866[8]

3 **PAESANELLA**, b f Seattle Song (USA) - Excitable by Nijinsky (G Botti) 1222[8] 4571[4]

3 **PAETRO (Ger)**, 2259[7]

4 **PAGEBOY**, b g Tina's Pet - Edwins' Princess by Owen Dudley (P C Haslam) 436 591 700[8] 1000 2305[2] 2532[5] 2935[1] 3085[8] 3378[7] 3410 3638 4217[4] 4455

6 **PAGET**, b g Taufan (USA) - Haco by Trible Chief (A Redmond) 309[8] 2693[1] 3276[4]

2 **PAGODA**, gr f Petong - Priors Dean by Monsanto (Fr) (W Jarvis) 2668[8] 3279[6] 3673[4] 4084[5]

3 **PAINT THE WIND (Ire)**, b f Fayruz - Pink Fondant by Northfields (USA) (R F Fisher) 4741a[7] 4772a[7] 109[6] 138

3 **PAIR OF JACKS (Ire)**, ch c Music Boy - Lobbino by Bustino (W R Muir) 542[3] 945[7] 1137 1408[2] 2212 2379[4] 2758 3745[5] 3946 4131

4 **PAIX BLANCHE (Fr)**, b or br f Fabulous Dancer (USA) - Alma Ata (Fr) by Rheffic (Fr) (M Zilber) 693[3]

3 **PAKED (Ire)**, b f Treasure Kay - Sales Talk by Auction Ring (USA) (A D Evans) 2452[5] 2810[6] 3074[9] 3662[7] 3914 4246

4 **PAKOL (Ire)**, b f Martin John - Tamen John by African Sky (A D Evans) 2879[4] 3395[2] 3561[4] 3606[3] 3928 4184[7]

3 **PALACEGATE EPISODE (Ire)**, b f Drumalis - Pasadena Lady by Captain James (J Berry) 566[2] 781[1] 1551[3] 2399[2] 3571[2] 3912[3] 4200[1] 4304[1] 4568[2]

3 **PALACEGATE GIRL**, ch f Music Boy - Long Girl by Longleat (USA) (J Berry) 4700a[7] 51[5] 116[5] 151[9] 214[3]

4 **PALACEGATE GOLD (Ire)**, b c Sarab - Habilite by Habitat (R J Hodges) 187[5] 236[4] 263[8] 501[3] 600[1] 760[6] 1209[3] 1282[6] 1664[1] 1903[3] 2548[3] 2897 3168[7] 4394[4] 4501[2] 4580[9]

2 **PALACEGATE JACK (Ire)**, gr c Neshad (USA) - Pasadena Lady by Captain James (J Berry) 730[2] 859[2] 1556[6] 3001[3] 3411[1] 3613[1] 3994[1] 4392[1] 4546[5]

2 **PALACEGATE JO (Ire)**, b f Drumalis - Welsh Rhyme by Welsh Term (J Berry) 564[2] 900[2] 1108[2] 1519[1] 2377[2] 3363[1] 3539[6] 4163[4] 4516[1] 4602

3 **PALACEGATE SUNSET**, gr g Skyliner - Grey Morley by Pongee (J Berry) 339[1] 608[3] 642[3] 928[9] 1191[3] 1283[3] 1493[4] 2566[5] 2761[4]

3 **PALACEGATE TOUCH**, gr g Petong - Dancing Chimes by London Bells (Can) (J Berry) 347[6] 1326[5] 1801 2106[1] 2303[7] 2651[2] 2892[2] 3123[1] 3376[1] 3474[1] 3906 4040 4393 4521[6]

6 **PALACE GEM**, b g Horage - Angela's Gem by My Swallow (Peter Casey) 1508[9] 3276[7]

5 **PALACE MAN (USA)**, ch g Island Kingdom (USA) - Palace Maid (USA) by Golden Palace (USA) (P G Murphy) 3656 4022 4328[4]

3 **PALACE OF GOLD**, b g Slip Anchor - Salacious by Sallust (C A Cyzer) 515[9] 4525[2]

3 **PALACE PAGEANT (USA)**, b c Nijinsky (Can) - Crown Treasure (USA) by Graustark (I A Balding) 388[6] 736[5] 1558[1]

3 **PALACE PARADE (USA)**, ch g Cure The Blues (USA) - Parasail (USA) by In Reality (B R Millman) 489[9] 669[6] 960[5] 4256 4479[9] 4683

5 **PALACE REVOLT (USA)**, b Fast Gold (USA) - Palace Gate (USA) by Soy Numero Uno (M Goswell) 4471[4]

2 **PALACIOS (Ity)**, 4313[6]

3 **PALAIROS (Fr)**, (D Smaga) 1410[7] 4196

3 **PALAIYTA (Ire)**, b f Shardari - Palitana by Nonoalco (USA) (John M Oxx) 1441[6] 3299[4]

2 **PALANA (USA)**, b f Gulch (USA) - Cor Anglais (USA) by Nijinsky (Can) (I A Balding) 1660[1] 2112[1] 2562[4] 3765[7] 4251[5] 4558[2]

3 **PALATE**, ch g Luskin Star - Julep 1331[3]

7 **PALEY PRINCE (USA)**, b h Tilt Up (USA) - Apalachee Princess (USA) by Apalachee (USA) (M D I Usher) 4752a[3] 659 923[7] 1560[5] 1668[3] 1957[9] 4455 4712[8]

5 **PALLIUM (Ire)**, b g Try My Best (USA) - Jungle Gardenia by Nonoalco (USA) (M P Naughton) 1113 1679[9] 2018 2230[4] 2600[6] 2813[7] 2935[2] 3280[8] 3410[1] 3638 3834[7] 3995 4166 4532[5] 4734[5]

3 **PALMETTO EXPRESS**, br c Glint Of Gold - Justine by Luciano (Frau E Mader) 4305[4]

4 **PALM LAGOON (Ire)**, ch g Thatching - Deepwater Blues by Gulf Pearl (C Tinkler) 531 828[8]

2 **PAMPERED GUEST (Ire)**, b c Be My Guest (USA) - Miss Garuda by Persian Bold (M Bell) 3352 3704[1] 4647[8]

3 **PAMZIG (USA)**, b f Danzig (USA) - Burst Of Colors (USA) by Crimson Satan (B W Hills) 748[3] 987[5] 2333

8 **PANATHINAIKOS (USA)**, b g Nodouble (USA) - Faisana (Arg) by Yata Nahuel (G A Ham) 4797a[7]

4 **PANCHELLITA (USA)**, b f Pancho Villa (USA) - Counselor's Pride (USA) by Good Counsel (USA) (G L Moore) 1606[3] 1912[3] 2327[1] 2824[1] 3302[1] 3425[3] 3837[3] 4131

2 **PANDROP**, b f Sharrood (USA) - Trying For Gold (USA) by Northern Baby (Can) (I A Balding) 2325

7 **PANDY**, b g Thatching - Hot Stone by Hotfoot (G Thorner) 3479

3 **PANIC BUTTON (Ire)**, br f Simply Great (Fr) - Hysteria by Prince Bee (M H Easterby) 3256[8] 4085[6] 4658[5]

5 **PANIKIN**, gr g Red Sunset - Haunting by Lord Gayle (USA) (J Wharton) 4692a[3] 4765a[2] 4796a[1] 17[6] 3404 3774 3957 4532 4606[3] 4693[6]

3 **PANTHER (Ire)**, ch g Primo Dominie - High Profile by High Top (J Hetherton) 467[2] 549[3] 630[2] 685[4] 907[2] 1080[5] 1247[9] 2371[9] 4022[5] 4083[3] 4241[5] 4343[5] 4488[7] 4580[3] 4670[6]

2 **PAONIC (Ire)**, ch c Exactly Sharp (USA) - Robinia (USA) by Roberto (USA) (L M Cumani) 2626[2] 3215[3] 3457[2] 4124[4] 4608[3]

2 **PAPAGAYOS (Ire)**, ch c Salt Dome (USA) - Sun Bed by Habitat (C E Brittain) 1804 2359[5] 2618 3613 3905

2 **PAPAGO (Ire)**, gr f Sadler's Wells (USA) - Passamaquoddy (USA) by Drone (A Fabre) 4567[2]

2 **PAPARAZZO**, b c Posen (USA) - Royale Warning (USA) by Sir Ivor (J D Bethell) 4237

3 **PAPER DAYS**, b c Teenoso (USA) - April Days by Silly Season (P G Murphy) 502[6] 717[5] 838[3] 1134[1] 1495[7] 2150[6] 2547[4]

2 **PAPPA'S PET**, br g Petong - What A Pet by Mummy's Pet (J L Dunlop) 2096[9] 3589 3833 4269

4 **PARADISE CREEK (USA)**, b or br c Irish River (Fr) - North Of Eden by Northfields (W Mott) 4742[8]

4 **PARADISE NAVY**, b g Slip Anchor - Ivory Waltz (USA) by Sir Ivor (N C Wright) 290

2 **PARADISE NEWS**, b f Sure Blade (USA) - Monaiya by Shareef Dancer (USA) (G C Bravery) 325[3] 454[5] 886[4] 1317[2] 1870[1]

3 **PARANGO (USA)**, gr c Manila (USA) - Sureya by Sharpen Up (C E Brittain) 1344[7] 2752[7]

2 **PARCACURRY PETE (Ire)**, b c Vision (USA) - Effortless by Try My Best (USA) (Noel Meade) 1442[9] 1650[6] 1824[6]

6 **PAR DE LUXE**, b m Superlative - Parbold by Sassafras (Fr) (Miss S J Wilton) 409[5] 837 970[9]

4 **PARFAIT AMOUR**, ch f Clantime - Chablisse by Radetzky (R M Whitaker) 348[6] 436 1230[2] 1480[5] 1898[4] 2001[3] 2197[1] 2431[4] 2656[3] 2915[3] 3088[4] 3788[1] 4045[2] 4470[9]

5 **PARIOS (Fr)**, ch h Sicyos (USA) - Parga (Fr) by Gay Mecene (USA) (J W Payne) 3936 4200[6] 4304[9]

3 **PARIS BY NIGHT (Ire)**, b f Slew O' Gold (USA) - I'll Take Paris (USA) by Vaguely Noble (C J Hill) 63[5] 95[4]

4 **PARIS HOUSE**, gr c Petong - Foudroyer by Artaius (USA) (J Berry) 795[1] 1406[1] 1807[3] 2927[2] 3464[2]

2 **PARISH WALK (Ire)**, ch g Pennine Walk - Baby Caroline by Martin John (K W Hogg) 673 730[5] 1998[5] 2129[4] 3218 3281

8 **PARISIAN**, b h Shirley Heights - Miss Paris by Sovereign Path (J A Bennett) 82[7] 210 2617

2 **PARISIAN LOVER**, b g Gallic League - Dear Heart by Blakeney (T D Barron) 1227[9] 1758[4] 1998[7] 2539[9] 4531

5 **PEGGOTTY,** gr m Capricorn Line - Silver Empress by Octavo (USA) (P Hayward) 1961 2831^{3} 3047 4340

3 **PELAGIC,** b f Rainbow Quest (USA) - Fleet Girl by Habitat (F Boutin) 2080^{3} 3944^{6}

2 **PELAMIS,** ch g Handsome Sailor - Snake Song by Mansingh (USA) (J A Glover) 3114^{4} 3321^{4} 3673^{7}

3 **PELDER (Ire),** b c Be My Guest (USA) - Sheer Audacity by Troy (L D'Auria) 4403^{2}

8 **PELORUS,** b g High Top - St Isabel by Saint Crespin III (D R C Elsworth) 480^{7} 792^{4} 1064^{5} 2211^{9}

2 **PEMBRIDGE PLACE,** b c Niniski (USA) - Rose D'Amour (USA) by Lines Of Power (USA) (J L Dunlop) 4113^{5} 4377^{1}

3 **PEMBROKE (USA),** b c Gone West (USA) - College Bold (USA) by Boldnesian (J H M Gosden) 540^{6} 794 1765 2194^{1} 2572^{7} 3065^{2}

2 **PENCADER (Ire),** ch c Caerleon (USA) - Jackie Berry by Connaught (P W Chapple-Hyam) 3352^{1} 3859^{2}

3 **PENCOMBE (USA),** b c Nureyev (USA) - Mrs Penny (USA) by Great Nephew (F Boutin) 4075^{4}

10 **PENDOR DANCER,** b g Piaffer (USA) - Bounding by Forlorn River (B Forsey) 4672a^{8} 4752a^{5} 4783a^{9} 4818a^{5}

3 **PENNINE LAD (Ire),** ch g Pennine Walk - Dominica (Ger) by Zank (B Gubby) 826^{3} 1067^{7} 1417^{6} 1491^{6}

3 **PENNINE MIST (Ire),** gr f Pennine Walk - Panserina by Sovereign Path (D K Weld) 267^{2} 488^{4} 705^{1} 1569

4 **PENNINE PASS (Ire),** b g Pennine Walk - Red Realm by Realm (D L Williams) 308

2 **PENNINE PINK (Ire),** gr f Pennine Walk - Alpine Spring by Head For Heights (Sir Mark Prescott) 2785^{5}

3 **PENNINE PRINCE (Ire),** b g Pennine Walk - Mouette (Fr) by Fabulous Dancer (USA) (Daniel J Murphy) 1107

3 **PENNINE'S DAUGHTER,** b f Pennine Walk - Inesdela by Wolver Hollow (J G Coogan) 639^{2} 847^{3} 1106^{6} 4057^{8} 4162 4534

4 **PENNINE TUNE (Ire),** ch g Pennine Walk - Jazz Tune (Fr) by Lyphard (USA) (J S Bolger) 2408^{8}

3 **PENNY A DAY (Ire),** b g Supreme Leader - Mursuma by Rarity (Mrs M Reveley) 311 669 848^{5} 2249 3381^{1} 3576^{1} 3610^{5}

3 **PENNY BANGER (Ire),** b f Pennine Walk - High Explosive by Mount Hagen (Fr) (M Johnston) 711^{2} 862^{7} 972^{1} 1247^{6} 1696^{1} 2217^{2} 2425^{1} 2811^{5} 2897^{9} 3190^{2} 3365^{2} 3564^{5} 4270^{1} 4333^{2} 4485^{2} 4616^{1}

4 **PENNY DROPS,** b f Sharpo - Darine by Nonoalco (USA) (Lord Huntingdon) 4749a^{5} 676^{3} 1604^{1} 2328^{3} 2794^{2} 4065^{1} 4172^{2} 4300^{1} 4571^{1}

3 **PENNY FAN,** b f Nomination - Trwyn Cilan by Import (H Candy) 2231^{2} 2580^{7} 3178^{5} 3942^{8} 4536

5 **PENNY HASSET,** b m Lochnager - Bad Payer by Tanfirion (M W Easterby) 355^{1} 429^{1} 700^{9} 1000^{7} 1494^{6} 1835 2018 3136^{2} 3354^{8} 3486^{5} 3906 4123^{7} 4180^{4}

3 **PENOL (Ger),** 3647^{5}

2 **PENZAAD (Ire),** ch g Mazaad - Miss Weeber by On Your Mark (D Carroll) 3719^{7} 3911 4059^{9} 4290 4406

3 **PEPERONATA (Ire),** b f Cyrano de Bergerac - Good Game by Mummy's Game (P W Chapple-Hyam) 2399^{8}

5 **PEPPERS PET (Ire),** b m Soughaan (USA) - Pampered Rose (P Mullins) 912^{9} 1013^{9} 1251^{9}

3 **PERCY LANE (Ire),** b g Prince Rupert (Fr) - Miss Merryweather by Sexton Blake (Victor Bowens) 1385^{8} 2141 2514 4387^{7} 4586^{9}

3 **PERDITION (Ire),** b f Red Sunset - Free Rein by Sagaro (J W Hills) 719 1058^{2} 1388^{4} 1635^{2} 1972^{1} 2503^{4} 2864^{3} 3634^{3} 4164 4652^{8}

5 **PERFAY (USA),** ch h Nodouble (USA) - Perfect Example (USA) by Far North (Can) (D A Wilson) 525 1021 2794^{9} 4247 4415

2 **PERFECT BRAVE,** b c Indian Ridge - Perfect Timing by Comedy Star (USA) (D R C Elsworth) 4523 4754^{3}

2 **PERFECT CADENCE (Ire),** b f Nordance (USA) - Perfect Choice by Bold Lad (Ire) (N C Bell) 3073 3332 3729 4117^{5} 4285^{7}

3 **PERFECT IMPOSTER (Ire),** b c Persian Bold - Tifrums by Thatch (USA) (J S Bolger) 306^{3} 941^{1} 3913

3 **PERFECTLY ENTITLED (Ire),** ch f Entitled - Little Red Hut by Habitat (J Pearce) 4700a

3 **PERFECT PASSION,** b f Clantime - Charming View by Workboy (J J Bridger) 871^{7} 991^{8} 1376^{4} 1714^{8} 2288^{5} 2504^{4} 2967^{1} 3383^{6} 3709^{5} 3782^{4}

3 **PERFECT POET (Ire),** b g Jareer (USA) - Seta Pura by Sallust (T Stack) 550^{6} 649^{5} 1107^{4} 1621^{7}

3 **PERFECT VINTAGE,** b c Shirley Heights - Fair Salinia by Petingo (M R Stoute) 3456^{2} 3727^{2}

4 **PERFORATE,** b g Teenoso (USA) - Bag Lady by Be My Guest (USA) (R J Baker) 331 420^{3} 559^{9} 783^{4} 924^{6} 1321 1688^{7} 2115^{4} 2386^{6}

2 **PERHAPS,** gr c Hadeer - April Wind by Windjammer (USA) (N C Wright) 1828 4252 4419

2 **PERICARDIA,** gr f Petong - Greensward Blaze by Sagaro (R Hannon) 3738 4523^{6} 4692

6 **PERKNAPP,** b g King Persian - Knapping by Busted (R Donoghue) 1576^{4}

7 **PERMANENTLY PINK,** b g Auction Ring (USA) - Hawaiian Joss (USA) by Hawaii (R T Phillips) 1659 1873^{9}

3 **PERNILLA (Ire),** b f Tate Gallery (USA) - Clonsella Lady by High Top (J S Bolger) 258^{6} 573 665^{4} 1201^{2} 1646^{1} 2078^{1} 2187^{5} 2805^{4} 4053^{5}

3 **PERO,** b c Reference Point - Pelf (USA) by Al Nasr (Fr) (B W Hills) 482^{5} 1802^{7} 2148^{5}

5 **PERPENDICULAR,** b h Shirley Heights - Pris by Priamos (Ger) (H R A Cecil) 4420^{8}

2 **PERSIAN AFFAIR (Ire),** b c Persian Heights - Lady Chesterfield (USA) by In Reality (M Bell) 687^{6} 1211^{8} 2862^{1} 3667^{6} 4564

2 **PERSIAN BLOOM (Ire),** b f Pennine Walk - Divine Bloom by Yashgan (Patrick Joseph Flynn) 4183^{9} 4323^{7} 4406^{7} 4459

3 **PERSIAN BRAVE (Ire),** b c Persian Heights - Commanche Belle by Shirley Heights (M Bell) 468^{1} 843^{3} 989^{1} 1364^{9} 3879^{3} 4063 4271^{3}

5 **PERSIAN BUD (Ire),** b or br g Persian Bold - Awakening Rose by Le Levanstell (J R Bosley) 4333^{7} 4486^{4} 4600^{6} 4713^{7}

3 **PERSIAN CHARMER (Ire),** b c Persian Heights - Merlins Charm (USA) by Bold Bidder (Miss L A Perratt) 1178^{4} 1540^{3} 1597^{2} 1869^{2} 3439^{3} 3630^{8} 3900^{7}

3 **PERSIAN CHIMES (Ire),** b g Persian Heights - Ring The Changes by Auction Ring (USA) (G A Pritchard-Gordon) 797^{7} 1057^{9}

4 **PERSIAN CREEK (Ire),** br c Treasure Kay - Evangola by Persian Bold (J S Bolger) 270^{4} 2073 2606^{7} 2805^{2} 3027^{6} 3542^{6} 4056^{9}

2 **PERSIAN ELITE (Ire),** ch c Persian Heights - Late Sally by Sallust (P F I Cole) 2785^{1} 3145^{3}

4 **PERSIAN EMPRESS (Ire),** br f Persian Bold - Route Royale by Roi Soleil (Owen Weldon) 912

4 **PERSIAN FLEECE,** ch f Bold Arrangement - Microcosme by Golden Fleece (USA) (N Tinkler) 4797a^{6} 8^{6} 42^{9} 92^{6}

3 **PERSIAN FOUNTAIN (Ire),** ch f Persian Heights - Misty Lady by Habitat (B S Rothwell) 1111^{6} 1566^{2} 1900^{9} 3970 4178 4364 4643^{9}

3 **PERSIAN GEM (Ire),** b f Persian Heights - Nancy Shere (USA) by Gallant Man (Ms Rosemary Rooney) 311 847^{5} 1333^{3} 1610^{5} 2140

6 **PERSIAN GLEN,** b g Glenstal (USA) - Persian's Glory by Prince Tenderfoot (USA) (T G McCourt) 2512^{7}

3 **PERSIAN GUSHER (Ire),** gr g King Persian - Magnanimous by Runnymede (S Dow) 4724a^{2} 4794a^{1} 22^{4} 143^{5} 208^{2} 262^{1} 370^{2} 606^{6} 2139^{6} 2379^{5} 3020^{6} 3575^{2} 4270

5 **PERSIAN HALO (Ire),** b or br g Sunny's Halo (Can) - Persian Susan (USA) by Herbager (Michael Kauntze) 4573^{6}

4 **PERSIAN HAZE (Ire),** ch g Bold Arrangement - Crufty Wood by Sweet Revenge (P R Lenihan) 753^{4} 1576^{7} 2143^{3}

2 **PERSIAN HERITAGE,** ch c Persian Bold - Middleham Jewel by Swing Easy (USA) (J W Payne) 469^{8} 698^{2} 908^{2} 2866^{6} 3129^{3} 3428^{4} 4266

4 **PERSIAN HILL (Ire),** b g King Persian - Northern Joy by Northern Value (USA) (Victor Bowens) 3721

6 **PHARAOH'S DANCER,** b g Fairy King (USA) - Marie Louise by King Emperor (USA) (M McCormack) 475^{5} 700 1066 1270^{7} 1664^{3} 1744^{5} 2110^{8} 4168^{7} 4501^{7} 4670^{1} 4762^{3}

2 **PHARDY (Ire),** b g Phardante (Fr) - Enchanted Lady by Bold Lad (Ire) (T J O'Mara) 4244 4582 4637

5 **PHARELLA,** ch m Pharly (Fr) - Shindella by Furry Glen (M Quaid) 648^{5} 1202 2142^{9} 2463^{4} 2957

4 **PHARFETCHED,** br f Phardante (Fr) - Rust Free by Free State (A P O'Brien) $4685a^{1}$ 807^{1} 1025^{4} 1511^{2} 1770^{7} 2077^{9}

4 **PHARGOLD (Ire),** ch g Phardante (Fr) - Mallee by Malinowski (USA) (J L Harris) $4688a^{7}$

3 **PHARLING,** ch f Pharly (Fr) - Sibley by Northfields (USA) (B J Curley) 1320^{8} 1698^{8} 2032^{7} 3394^{7}

4 **PHARLY DANCER,** b g Pharly (Fr) - Martin-Lavell Mail by Dominion (W W Haigh) 426^{5} 1075^{2} 1248^{2} 1531^{5} 1676^{1} 2427^{2} 2591^{2} 2827^{5} 4036^{3} 4218^{4}

5 **PHARLY STORY,** b h Pharly (Fr) - Certain Story by Known Fact (USA) (M C Pipe) 1146^{3} 1450^{5} 1717^{6} 2793^{7}

3 **PHARNAS,** 953

6 **PHAROAH'S GUEST,** ch g Pharly (Fr) - Exuberine (Fr) by Be My Guest (USA) (N A Twiston-Davies) 331^{1} 924^{7} 1156

3 **PHARUZAL,** b f Pharly (Fr) - Lightning Gem (Fr) by African Song (T Stack) 981 1444^{9}

3 **PHASE IN,** ch c Pharly (Fr) - Lone Galaxie (USA) by Nodouble (USA) (D K Weld) 256 311 898^{3} 981^{2} 2901^{2} 3028^{1} 3298^{1} 3543^{4} 3826^{8} 4185^{1} 4555^{7}

3 **PHASE ONE (Ire),** b f Horage - Fayes Ben by Don (A A Hambly) 835^{9} 1136^{8} 1192^{7} 1503^{8}

6 **PHIL-BLAKE,** br g Blakeney - Philogyny by Philip Of Spain (S Mellor) 210 265^{7}

4 **PHILCO'S ANGEL,** gr f Habs Lad - Regal Whim by Lord Of Arabia (Mrs A L M King) 1035^{8}

4 **PHILGUN,** b g K-Battery - Andalucia by Rheingold (C W C Elsey) 358^{7} 453^{1} 745^{3} 894^{2} 1260^{5} 1531^{2} 1681^{2} 1946^{6} 2617^{7} 3152^{7} 3473^{5} 3599^{4} 4037 4218^{7} 4357^{1} 4454^{6}

4 **PHILIDOR,** b c Forzando - Philgwyn by Milford (J M P Eustace) 1021^{7} 1398^{2} 1768^{3} 2211^{4} 2926^{1} 3465^{2} 4300

3 **PHILIP PATRICK (Ire),** ch g Hadeer - Hollow Candle by Wolver Hollow (B V Kelly) 268^{8} 981^{5} 2141 2297 3028

3 **PHILNIC,** b c Waajib - The Silver Darling by John Splendid (M D Hammond) 1762^{3} 2064^{4} 2598^{4} 2918^{2} 3191^{5}

2 **PHIL'S TIME,** b c Damister (USA) - Coca by Levmoss (T G Mills) 4338^{3} 4480^{6} 4588

2 **PHIL THE TILL,** b g Jalmood (USA) - Cut It Fine (USA) by Big Spruce (USA) (W W Haigh) 1758 1863 2917

2 **PHONEAHOLIC (Ire),** ch g Heraldiste (USA) - Clonross Lady by Red Alert (B J Meehan) 3387^{2} 3528^{4} 3941^{3} 4210 4330^{2} 4416 4708^{1}

2 **PHONE CHATTER (USA),** ch f Phone Trick (USA) - Passing My Way (USA) by Pass The Glass (USA) (R Mandella) 4390^{1} 4740^{1}

2 **PHONE ME UP,** b c Aragon - Persian Air by Persian Bold (A A Scott) 386^{8} 730

3 **PHROSE,** b g Pharly (Fr) - Rose Chanelle by Welsh Pageant (C Weedon) 372^{3} 422^{2} 1028^{8} 1349^{2} 1910^{3} 2272^{5} 2963 3961

2 **PHYLIAN,** b f Glint Of Gold - Phylae by Habitat (A Hide) 1580^{4} 2234^{3} 3389^{3} 3865 4106^{3} 4647^{6}

2 **PHYLLODE,** ch f Pharly (Fr) - Catalpa by Reform (W Jarvis) 4651

2 **PICCOLO,** b c Warning - Woodwind (Fr) by Whistling Wind (M R Channon) 1063^{7} 1324^{8} 3352^{3} 3672^{3} 3902^{1} 4249^{3}

5 **PICKLES,** b g Petoski - Kashmiri Snow by Shirley Heights (R Lee) 845^{4} 1981^{7} 2236^{3} 2733^{9} 3078^{4} 3656^{1}

5 **PICK'N HILL (Ire),** b g Kind Of Hush - Shagra by Sallust (T G McCourt) 1163^{6} 1385 1651^{9} 2322 2451

4 **PIE HATCH (Ire),** b f Huntingdale - Small Is Beautiful by Condorcet (Fr) (B J McMath) 1731^{7} 2052^{3} 2282^{3} 2658^{4} 2800^{2} 3066^{1} 3342^{5} 3565^{2}

7 **PIER THIRTY NINE,** br g Torus - Mrs Optimist by African Sky (Noel T Chance) 753^{7}

5 **PIGALLE WONDER,** br h Chief Singer - Hi-Tech Girl by Homeboy (R J O'Sullivan) $4681a^{7}$ $4736a^{3}$ $4783a^{1}$ $4816a^{1}$ 24^{2} 87^{8} 113^{2} 157^{1} 198^{4} 234^{1} 264^{7} 321^{7} 3224 3887 4710

3 **PILGRIM BAY (Ire),** b g Treasure Kay - Lala by Welsh Saint (E J O'Grady) 868 1570^{1} 1825^{2} 1923^{1} 2248^{3} 2323^{5} 2604^{1} 3027^{8} 3614^{3} 3928^{4} 4184^{2} 4385

2 **PILIB (Ire),** b g Salt Dome (USA) - Princess Elinor by Captain James (J Pearce) 3592 3990^{6} 4587^{5}

6 **PIMSBOY,** b g Tender King - Hitopah by Bustino (B S Rothwell) 1591 1898^{8} 2197 3518^{5} 3712

5 **PIMS CLASSIC,** gr g Absalom - Musical Maiden by Record Token (J L Harris) 278^{4} 287^{7} 1702^{7}

2 **PINATUBO,** ch g Nicholas Bill - Hi-Hunsley by Swing Easy (USA) (H Candy) 3303 3641^{7} 4032^{8} 4418 4482^{9}

3 **PINEAPPLE PRINCE,** br c Beveled (USA) - Pineapple's Pride by John de Coombe (R J Hodges) 3687 3893 4125

3 **PINE RIDGE LAD (Ire),** gr g Taufan (USA) - Rosserk by Roan Rocket (B Beasley) 16^{3} 37^{5} 66^{2} 121^{1} 149^{1} 178^{1} 191^{2} 262^{4} 429^{5} 906^{8} 1273^{3} 1563^{4} 2105^{3} 2280^{1} 2468^{5} 2731^{4} 3354 4168

8 **PINISI,** ch g Final Straw - Bireme by Grundy (J Wharton) 331^{5} 901^{4} 2729^{5} 3087

3 **PINK CITY,** br g Green Ruby (USA) - Hitravelscene by Mansingh (USA) (J Balding) 4809a 16 3506 3628

2 **PINKERTON'S PAL,** ch c Dominion - White Domino by Sharpen Up (C E Brittain) 3462^{2} 3746^{1} 3994^{2} 4273^{7} 4546^{9}

3 **PINKERTON'S SILVER,** gr g Northern State (USA) - Real Silver by Silly Season (M H Easterby) 2341^{8} 3142^{3} 3408^{6} 3631^{8} 4083^{8}

4 **PINK'N BLACK (Ire),** b f Double Schwartz - Miss Pinkerton by Above Suspicion (G Blum) 4774a $4815a^{6}$ 47^{9}

3 **PINOT (Ger),** b c Nebos (Ger) - Prairie Art by Prince Tenderfoot (B Schutz) 4305^{1}

3 **PINTA (Ire),** ch f Ahonoora - Heaven High by High Line (A Renzoni) 1222^{7}

7 **PINTAIL BAY,** b g Buzzards Bay - Pin Hole by Parthia (C P E Brooks) 1316

3 **PIPERS POOL (Ire),** b f Mtoto - Pipina (USA) by Sir Gaylord (G Wragg) 1931^{5} 4372^{5} 4718^{2}

3 **PIPERS REEL,** ch f Palace Music (USA) - Fair Country by Town And Country (G W Davies) $4668a^{2}$ $4740a^{1}$ $4805a^{8}$ 2673 3042^{6} 3518 3840^{6}

2 **PIPER ZERO (Ire),** ch g Tate Gallery (USA) - Truely Thankful (Can) by Groustark (Charles O'Brien) 3922 4624

2 **PIP'S DREAM,** b f Glint Of Gold - Arabian Rose (USA) by Lyphard (USA) (M J Ryan) 477^{6}

4 **PIP'S OPTIMIST,** b g Primo Dominie - Great Optimist by Great Nephew (P J Feilden) $4763a^{6}$ $4793a^{6}$

3 **PIPS PRIDE,** ch c Efisio - Elkie Brooks by Relkino (R Hannon) 1205^{1} 1786 3196^{1} 3777^{5}

6 **PIQUANT,** b or br g Sharpo - Asnoura (Mor) by Asandre (Fr) (Lord Huntingdon) 1069^{2} 1298^{7} 1768 2060^{2} 2854^{4} 3512^{8} 3680^{9} 4166 4297

3 **PIRANGA (Ire),** b f Surumu - Princess D'Espoir by Sensitive Prince (A Wohler) 3929^{1} 4305^{7}

3 **PIRATES GOLD (Ire),** ch g Vaigly Great - Hemline by Sharpo (J White) 21^{2} 44^{2} 116^{1} 178^{3} 233^{3} 878^{4} 1486^{2} 2013^{2} 2476^{4}

3 **PISH KESH,** b or br f Sure Blade (USA) - Gift Wrapped by Wolver Hollow (W R Muir) 1671^{4} 2117^{3} 2314^{3} 2716^{9} 2937 4267^{5} 4445^{4}

3 **PISONE (Ity),** 2146^{2}

3 **PISTOL (Ire),** ch c Glenstal (USA) - First Wind by Windjammer (USA) (C A Horgan) $4747a^{5}$ 2522 3012 3585

3 **PISTOL RIVER (Ire),** b c Simply Great (Fr) - Pampala by Bold Lad (Ire) (N J H Walker) 875^{3} 1115^{1} 1785^{2} 2907^{8} 3434 3881^{2} 4248^{2} 4414

4 **PISTOLS AND ROSES (USA),** 2838^{7}

3 **PISTOLS AT DAWN (USA),** b g Al Nasr (Fr) - Cannon Run (USA) by Cannonade (USA) (R Hannon) 717 976^{5} 1309^{3} 1493^{2} 1961^{8} 2523^{1} 2669^{1} 2867^{1} 3212^{1}

3 **PISTON (Ire),** b g Common Grounds - Domino's Nurse by Dom Racine (Fr) (B Hanbury) 2580^{8} 2787^{3} 3070^{7} 3439^{5} 3634^{6}

2 **PITIARA,** b f Doctor Wall - Honiara by Pitcairn (M F Barraclough) 3303 3677

3 **PIXTON (Ire),** b c Common Grounds - Sallywell by Manado (Mrs J Cecil) 1344[5] 2596[1] 3358 4181

3 **PIZZA CONNECTION,** b c Chilibang - Glen Na Smole by Ballymore (J L Dunlop) 4702a[8]

2 **PIZZAZZ,** ch f Unfuwain (USA) - Pushoff (USA) by Sauce Boat (USA) (N A Graham) 2754[8] 3738[9] 4697

3 **PLACERVILLE (USA),** b c Mr Prospector (USA) - Classy Cathy (USA) by Private Account (USA) (H R A Cecil) 540[1] 688[2] 1367[5] 1748[1]

2 **PLACITANA (USA),** ch f Topsider (USA) - Placer Queen by Habitat (P W Harris) 2357[2] 2887[3]

8 **PLAIN FACT,** b g Known Fact (USA) - Plain Tree by Wolver Hollow (J W Hills) 555[4] 891[2] 1000 1668[5] 1806

3 **PLAIN SAILING (Fr),** b g Slip Anchor - Lassalia by Sallust (D Morley) 3740[7] 4110 4431[9] 4711[6]

2 **PLAINSONG,** b f Ballad Rock - No Jargon by Nonoalco (USA) (Denys Smith) 1739[1] 2400[4] 3000[2] 3554[6] 4528[3] 4607[3]

3 **PLANETARY ASPECT (USA),** b or br c Risen Star (USA) - Santiki by Be My Guest (USA) (P W Chapple-Hyam) 582[1] 775[2] 1001[2] 1448 2621[4] 3268[5] 3519[3]

4 **PLATINI (Ger),** ch c Surumu (Ger) - Prairie Darling by Stanford (Bruno Schuetz) 1217[1] 1888[1] 2791 3795[2] 4311

2 **PLATINI (Ire),** b c Gallic League - Tardy (USA) by Tom Rolfe (R Hannon) 2571[9] 3287[4] 3589 4029

3 **PLATINUM EMPIRE (USA),** b g Nijinsky (Can) - Kelley's Day (USA) by Graustark (Charles O'Brien) 2249[3] 2449[1] 3924[4] 4288

3 **PLATINUM VENTURE,** ch g Legend Of France (USA) - Ceramic (USA) by Raja Baba (USA) (S P C Woods) 1875[8] 2311[4] 2948[3] 3461[4] 3669[8] 4279[7]

3 **PLAY HEVER GOLF,** b g Alleging (USA) - Sweet Rosina by Sweet Revenge (T J Naughton) 4730a[4] 4791a[2] 21[1] 66[1] 106[1] 144[6] 191[4] 846[1] 1258[1] 1841[6] 3080[1] 3372[6] 4606

2 **PLAYING TRICKS,** b f Elegant Air - Magic Kingdom by Kings Lake (USA) (W J Haggas) 2240[6] 2492[6]

3 **PLAY WITH ME (Ire),** b or br f Alzao (USA) - Strike It Rich (Fr) by Rheingold (J L Dunlop) 761[5] 1223[1] 1586[9] 1912[2] 2576[2] 3121[6] 3670[8] 4254

4 **PLEASANT BABY (USA),** 3150[7]

3 **PLEASANT TANGO (USA),** b c Pleasant Colony (USA) - Dancer's Saga (USA) by Northern Dancer (C Speckert) 4745[5]

5 **PLEASE PLEASE ME (Ire),** b m Tender King - Tacama by Daring Display (USA) (J J Bridger) 4667a[7] 4611

3 **PLEASE SAY YES (Ire),** b g Nordance (USA) - That's Swiss by Thatching (J Ffitch-Heyes) 2065[5] 2154[2] 2454[4] 2736[2] 2953[5]

3 **PLEASE WIDD (Ire),** b f Thatching - Gold Piece by Golden Fleece (USA) (J S Bolger) 311

6 **PLEASURE AHEAD,** b g Taufan (USA) - Nan's Mill by Milford (A Moore) 4671a[3] 4750a[5] 4760a[6] 4776a 46[3] 126[6]

4 **PLEASURE QUEST,** b f Efisio - Eagle's Quest by Legal Eagle (D W P Arbuthnot) 4663a

2 **PLEASURE TRICK (USA),** br c Clever Trick (USA) - Pleasure Garden (USA) by Foolish Pleasure (USA) (F H Lee) 2021[5] 3537[7] 4332[5] 4602

3 **PLUCK,** b f Never So Bold - Tahilla by Moorestyle (R Charlton) 2522[5] 3051[1] 3736[6]

4 **PLUMBOB (Ire),** br g Bob Back (USA) - Naujella by Malinowski (USA) (T F Lacy) 852 4119[6] 4161

2 **PLUM DENNIS,** b g Robellino (USA) - Kaleidophone by Kalaglow (N Bycroft) 2973[9] 3218[9] 3592 3865 4215[7] 4365[7]

3 **PLUM FIRST,** b c Nomination - Plum Bold by Be My Guest (USA) (N Bycroft) 535[3] 829[2] 1083[1] 1341[4] 1518[3] 1760[2] 1841 2264[6] 2434 2594[4] 2797[3] 3438 3603[7] 3747 4096[9]

3 **PLUM LICK (Ire),** b f Commanche Run - Lady Chesterfield (USA) by In Reality (J S Bolger) 577[9] 1140[5] 1507[2] 1963[3] 2460[2] 2557[2]

2 **PLUNDER BAY (USA),** b g Cutlass (USA) - La Ninouchka (USA) by Bombay Duck (USA) (G Lewis) 1949[8] 2419[9] 2964[5] 3704 4029[1] 4564[4]

3 **POCKET PIECE (USA),** ch f Diesis - Secret Asset (USA) by Graustark (M R Stoute) 3514[4] 3639[2] 3839[6] 4652

3 **POCONO KNIGHT,** gr g Petong - Avahra by Sahib (C H Jones) 991[6] 1212 1817[6] 2160[6] 2411[7] 2726[7]

2 **POETICAL JUSTICE (Ire),** ch c Kris - Love For Poetry by Lord Gayle (USA) (D K Weld) 4688[2]

2 **POETIC FANCY,** ch f Then Again - Massawa (Fr) by Tennyson (Fr) (N A Twiston-Davies) 3084[8] 3264 3659

3 **POETIC FORM (Ire),** gr c Ballad Rock - Bobs by Warpath (C Weedon) 980 1145[7] 1746 2048[5] 2495[5] 3322[1] 3556[6] 4036

5 **POETS COVE,** b g Bay Express - Miss Milton by Young Christopher (M McCormack) 1079[9] 1744 2008[7] 3261 4024

4 **POINCIANA,** b c Big Spruce (USA) - Andrushka (USA) by Giboulee (Can) (R Hannon) 389[5] 559[7] 874[7] 1336[5] 2263[1]

3 **POINT THE WAY (Ire),** b f Reference Point - Tender Loving Care by Final Straw (M R Stoute) 799[2] 1533[3] 1935[4] 2615[3] 3320[3] 3556[7]

3 **POKER CHIP,** ch f Bluebird (USA) - Timely Raise (USA) by Raise A Man (USA) (I A Balding) 2885 3196[7] 3504 3725[5] 3849 4278

2 **POLAR CAP,** b g Nordico (USA) - Golden Crown by Main Reef (J M P Eustace) 2274 3686

3 **POLAR MOON,** b f Damister (USA) - Almitra by Targowice (USA) (B A McMahon) 3286[6] 4126[9]

2 **POLAR QUEST,** b c Merdon Melody - Basin Street by Tudor Melody (M McCormack) 3287[8] 3686[2] 4167[8]

3 **POLAR STORM (Ire),** b f Law Society (USA) - Arctic Winter (Can) by Briartic (Can) (Lady Herries) 758[3] 977[7] 1312[1] 1604[7] 2940[4] 3290[1] 3585[7] 3956[7] 4297

7 **POLDER,** b g Lochnager - Dutch Girl by Workboy (D L Williams) 2282[5] 2662

3 **POLEDEN (USA),** b c Danzig (USA) - Paradise (Fr) by Brigadier Gerard (R C Spicer) 4691a[1] 4745a[2] 3017 3540[7]

2 **POLHYMNIA,** br f Chief Singer - Six Ashes by Bruni (B W Hills) 2472[8] 3598

3 **POLICY MATTER (USA),** ch c Topsider (USA) - With A Twist by Fappiano 3208[3]

2 **POLISH ADMIRAL,** b c Roi Danzig (USA) - Strapless by Bustino (C F Wall) 2535[1] 2845[2] 3753[4] 4223[4]

2 **POLISH CONSUL,** ch c Polish Precedent (USA) - Consolation by Troy (Major W R Hern) 4067

2 **POLISH LAUGHTER (USA),** b c Danzig Connection (USA) - Chuckle (USA) by Shecky Greene (USA) (B Hanbury) 1324[1] 1750[2] 2075[1] 4062[1] 4443[4]

3 **POLITICAL DOMAIN (Ire),** b c Shernazar - Irish Green by Ragusa (D K Weld) 257 944[3] 4690

3 **POLITICAL SURGE (USA),** ch c Shahrastani (USA) - Starushka (USA) by Sham (USA) (D K Weld) 1026[3] 1573[1] 3525[8] 3924[2]

2 **POLIUTO (Ire),** b c Last Tycoon - Ploy by Posse (L Brogi) 2257[3]

3 **POLKA DANCER,** b f Dancing Brave (USA) - Pretty Pol by Final Straw (J R Fanshawe) 734[1] 1404[1]

3 **POLLY LEACH,** b f Pollerton - Come On Gracie by Hardiran (G A Ham) 3693 3937[9]

4 **POLLYS GLOW (Ire),** b f Glow (USA) - Suspicious Polly by Above Suspicion (John W Nicholson) 895[5] 1202 2607[4]

3 **POLLY'S WIKA (USA),** ch f Miswaki (USA) - Polly's Harde (Fr) by Lyphard (USA) (F Boutin) 983[3] 1368[3] 2409[5]

2 **POLO KIT (Ire),** b c Trempolino (USA) - Nikitina by Nijinsky (Can) (J R Fanshawe) 4252 4419

2 **POLY SCREEN,** ch c Ballacashtal (Can) - Scenic Villa by Top Ville (M R Channon) 3642 3979[9] 4253[7]

4 **POLYTAIN (Fr),** ch c Bikala - Paulistana (USA) by Pretense (A Spanu) 407[3] 810[6] 1694[4] 2261[8] 2979[6] 4626[2]

3 **POLY VISION (Ire),** b c Vision (USA) - Beechwood (USA) by Blushing Groom (Fr) (M Tate) 4675a[7]

4 **POLYXENA (USA),** b f Lyphard (USA) - Minstrel Girl (Fr) by Luthier (Mrs C Head) 4711a

2 **POMMES FRITES (Ire),** b f Cyrano de Bergerac - Shannon Lady by Monsanto (Fr) (R Hannon) 528[1] 979[2] 1766 2618[2] 3347[5]

3 **POM POM GIRL (Fr),** b f Caerleon (USA) - In A Dream by Bolkonski 4510[5]

9 **PONDERED BID,** b or br g Auction Ring (USA) - Ponca by Jim French (USA) (J Dooler) 4662a 287[4] 495[9] 709 826 4319[6]

3 **PONDERING,** br g Another Realm - Fishpond by Homing (M C Pipe) 4665a[3] 4717a 422[3] 499[6] 691[1] 826[4] 1075[8] 1305[4] 1491[1] 1929[7] 2547[1] 2721[3] 4486[1]

3 **PONDICHERRY (USA),** b f Sir Wimborne (USA) - Perceptive Lady (USA) by Damascus (USA) (S P C Woods) 1454[1] 1950[8] 3458[7] 3986[6] 4336[9] 4633

4 **PONDORO,** ch c Don't Forget Me - Pampa Bella (Fr) by Armos (E Lellouche) 407[8]

3 **PONTEVECCHIO MODA,** b f Jalmood (USA) - Pontevecchio Due by Welsh Pageant (W Jarvis) 1175[7] 1528[9] 2724[4] 3068[2] 3249[9]

5 **PONTYNYSWEN,** b g Ballacashtal (Can) - Tropingay by Cawston's Clown (D Burchell) 288[6]

2 **POOR PRINTER (Ire),** ch f Digamist (USA) - No Reproach by Northfields (USA) (D P Kelly) 4388

2 **POOR WILLY,** b g Rich Charlie - Julia Mawe by Dominion (W Jarvis) 2946[8] 3321

6 **POPSI'S LEGACY,** ch m Little Wolf - Popsi's Poppet by Hill Clown (USA) (M J Haynes) 1816[4] 2071[2] 2729 3761[1] 3907 4466

4 **POP TO STANS,** b g Gold Crest (USA) - Lady Of Camelot (Fr) by Bolkonski (J Pearce) 4765a[5] 4803a[7] 39[8] 150[2] 190[3] 227 709[5] 1035[2] 1453 2190[3] 2915[8] 3174[5] 3591

2 **PORPHYRIOS,** b c Mtoto - Tamassos by Dance In Time (Can) (G Harwood) 4276[3]

2 **PORTE BELLOCH,** br f Belfort (Fr) - Keyanloch by Lochnager (C T Nash) 4588[8]

4 **PORT ERIN (USA),** b f Diesis - Caitanya (USA) by Roberto (USA) (T Stack) 937[2]

3 **PORTERSTOWN BOY (Ire),** b c Shernazar - Bean Siamsa by Solinus (N Tinkler) 1122[1] 1292[1] 2076[9] 2607[5] 3331[4]

2 **PORTESHAM (USA),** ch c Riverman (USA) - Umaimah (USA) by Halo (USA) (C E Brittain) 3776[3]

4 **PORTICO (USA),** ch c El Gran Senor (USA) - Thorough by Thatch (USA) (C Laffon-Parias) 629[4] 1908[4] 3208[6] 4626[1]

4 **PORT IN A STORM,** b c Blakeney - Crusader's Dream by St Paddy (N Tinkler) 18[9]

2 **PORTITE SOPHIE,** b f Doulab (USA) - Impropriety by Law Society (USA) (M Brittain) 381[2] 466[2] 743[7] 841[7] 933[7] 1263[6] 2766[7] 3993[6] 4165[9] 4528

3 **PORT LUCAYA,** ch c Sharpo - Sister Sophie (USA) by Effervescing (USA) (R Hannon) 388[3] 658[1] 1125[1] 1347[2] 1952[2] 2621[2] 3337[4] 3644[5] 3748[2] 3886[5] 4398[1]

5 **PORTOFERRAIO (Arg),** 671[6]

2 **PORTOLANO (Fr),** b c Reference Point - Kottna (USA) by Lyphard (USA) (R J R Williams) 4726

2 **PORTO VARAS (USA),** ch c Miswaki (USA) - Angela Serra by Arctic Tern (F Boutin) 2144[1] 2647[5]

2 **PORT QUEEN (Ire),** b f Nashamaa - Cereal Queen by Oats (Richard O'Donovan) 3453

3 **PORTRAIT GALLERY (Ire),** gr c Sadler's Wells (USA) - Lady Capulet (USA) by Sir Ivor (Charles O'Brien) 808[4] 1198[8] 4260[1] 4381[2]

5 **PORT SUNLIGHT (Ire),** ch g Tate Gallery (USA) - Nana's Girl by Tin Whistle (R Hannon) 581[8] 824[8] 1064 1409[5] 1770[9] 2025[3] 2564[1] 2884[4] 3224[3] 3986[2] 4247 4563[7] 4694[7]

2 **POSCIMUR (Ire),** b f Prince Rupert (Fr) - Song Beam by Song (W P Mullins) 3954 4135 4369

2 **POSE AND CAMPAIGN (Ire),** br g Posen (USA) - Cailin D'Oir by Roi Soleil (J G Burns) 2778[9]

2 **POSENZEE (Ire),** b f Posen (USA) - Dolphin Bay by Rarity (R Hannon) 3389[5] 3613

3 **POSITIVE VIEW (Ire),** b g Fools Holme (USA) - Royal Cloak by Hardicanute (Patrick O'Leary) 552 1139

2 **POSITIVO,** br c Robellino (USA) - Primetta by Precocious (Lord Huntingdon) 4263[5]

2 **POSSIBILITY,** b f Robellino (USA) - Bentinck Hotel by Red God (Mrs L Piggott) 3422 3698[6] 3836[6] 4097[6] 4330[3] 4484

3 **POSSIBLY PERFECT (USA),** b f Northern Baby (Can) - Avasand by Avatar (R Frankel) 4636[3]

6 **POSTAGE STAMP,** ch g The Noble Player (USA) - Takealetter by Wolver Hollow (J Pearce) 25[6] 303

4 **POST IMPRESSIONIST (Ire),** b f Ahonoora - Roblanna by Roberto (USA) (J L Harris) 4698a[7] 290 456 628 863[2] 1034[2] 1156[2] 1517[3] 2124[3] 2265[2] 2536[2] 2694[1] 2891[2] 3283[1] 3405[6] 3599[7] 3861[5]

7 **POST MASTER,** ch g Ovac (Ity) - Late Post VI by Paddy's Birthday (Mrs Sarah Treacy) 4387[9]

2 **POST MISTRESS (Ire),** b or br f Cyrano de Bergerac - Postie by Sharpo (Sir Mark Prescott) 3529[1] 3723[3] 3894[4] 4436[2] 4754[4]

2 **POSTPONE (Ire),** b f Nordico (USA) - Postscript by Final Straw (J S Bolger) 1442[5] 3730[5]

2 **POTENTATE (USA),** b or br c Capote (USA) - Gay Fantastic by Ela-Mana-Mou (P F I Cole) 1666[2] 2299[2]

2 **POT LEEK LADY,** br f Squill (USA) - Normanby Lass by Bustino (W Bentley) 968 1158 1798

5 **POTRILLON (Arg),** 2243

2 **POTSCLOSE,** ch f Miswaki (USA) - Starr Danias (USA) by Sensitive Prince (USA) (M Johnston) 2595[1] 2890[6] 3600[5] 4531

3 **POUNDWORLD (Ire),** b f Orchestra - Maun by Red Alert (T F Lacy) 1757 3484[7] 3604[9] 3951 4162

4 **POWERFUL EDGE,** ch g Primo Dominie - Sharp Castan by Sharpen Up (I A Balding) 497[2] 675 1029[8] 1471[2] 1747[9] 2363[9] 2732[1] 3065[1] 3350

3 **POWER OF POLLY (USA),** br c Green Dancer (USA) - Polly Daniels (USA) by Clever Trick (USA) (P F I Cole) 4315[4]

2 **POWER SHARE,** ch g Superpower - Collegian by Stanford (R M Whitaker) 3505[8]

5 **POWER SOURCE (Ire),** b g Red Sunset - Lovely Kate by Le Levanstell (T F Lacy) 281 487[9]

4 **POYLE AMBER,** ch f Sharrood (USA) - Hithermoor Lass by Red Alert (M Blanshard) 4673a 1977[2] 2378[2] 2549[4] 2868[2] 3108[2] 3305[3] 3661[2] 3830 4123[5] 4340[9]

8 **POYLE GEORGE,** br h Sharpo - Hithermoor Lass by Red Alert (D R C Elsworth) 993[5] 1215[3] 1449[5] 2392[3] 2620[1] 3153

3 **PRACER (USA),** gr f Lyphard (USA) - Shindy by Roberto (A de Royer Dupre) 1915[4] 2646[5] 3206[7] 4199[1]

3 **PRAIRIE BAYOU (USA),** ch g Little Missouri (USA) - Whiffling by Wavering Monarch (T Bohannan) 779[2] 1070[1] 1542

4 **PRAIRIE DAWN,** b f Valiyar - Tibouchina by Runnymede (K White) 1668[6] 2219[6]

3 **PRAIRIE GROVE,** b g Primo Dominie - Fairy Fans by Petingo (R Hannon) 623[1] 827[9] 1697[3] 1859[1] 2421 2715[5] 2995[3] 3269[7] 3637[3] 3957 4518 4652

7 **PRECENTOR,** ro g Music Boy - La Magna by Runnymede (J D Bethell) 800 1215 1589 2309[9] 3707

5 **PRECIOUS AIR (Ire),** ch m Precocious - Astra Adastra by Mount Hagen (Fr) (A Moore) 4733a[3] 4759a[4] 4799a[6] 260[2] 603[4] 1257[2] 1686[7] 2161[2] 2869[3] 3042[4] 3643[2] 4133[9] 4623 4683[7]

7 **PRECIOUS BOY,** b g Taufan (USA) - Carrigeen Moss by Red God (M G Meagher) 4661[6]

5 **PRECIOUS CAROLINE (Ire),** b m The Noble Player (USA) - What A Breeze by Whistling Wind (P D Cundell) 48[7] 2174 253 327 1685[9] 2012[1] 2149[8] 2347[9] 2847[7]

8 **PRECIOUS MEMORIES,** br g Kabour - Kings Fillet by King's Bench (M P Naughton) 702[9]

4 **PRECIOUS WONDER,** b g Precocious - B M Wonder by Junius (USA) (P Butler) 4783a[5] 4803a[8] 333[3] 440[3] 475[2] 604[4] 737 917 1954 2670

5 **PRECISE TIMING,** ch g Shardari - Going Digital by Northern Baby (Can) (D K Weld) 309 1611 2286

2 **PRECISION EDGE (Ire),** b f Exactly Sharp (USA) - War Ballad (Fr) by Green Dancer (USA) (R F Fisher) 354[3] 607[6]

3 **PRECUSSION,** b g Dominion - Cymbal by Ribero (R W Armstrong) 4676a[8] 4709a[1] 1501[4] 1872[5] 2669[8] 2948[6] 3430[8]

7 **PREDICTABLE,** ch g Music Boy - Piccadilly Etta by Floribunda (Mrs A Knight) 4680a[6] 4746a[7] 4802a[9] 54[4] 771

6 **PRE-EMINENT,** b g Local Suitor (USA) - Fluella by Welsh Pageant (D K Weld) 1552[8] 2245[6] 2608[1] 2809[1] 3559[7] 4053[2] 4585[1] 4736[1]

2 **PREJON,** ch f Precocious - Johnkeina (Fr) by Johnny O'Day (USA) (G Lewis) 4752^9

3 **PREMIATA (Ire),** b f Sadler's Wells (USA) - Cormorant Wood by Home Guard (USA) (P W Chapple-Hyam) 529 3433^8 3693^4

3 **PREMIER BLUES (Fr),** b f Law Society (USA) - Etoile D'Ocean (USA) by Northern Dancer (R J R Williams) 167^4 183^5 826 1133 1244^3 1557^5 1702^4 1873^8 1980^5 2340^4

3 **PREMIER CHEER (USA),** 4291

6 **PREMIER DANCE,** ch g Bairn (USA) - Gigiolina by King Emperor (USA) (D Haydn Jones) 4662a^7 4807a^7 4817a^2 20^3 114^3 198^8 264^3 321^4 1304^8 2109^5 2273^8 2471^2 2860^2 3193^2 3656^1 4036^2 4354^6

4 **PREMIER ENVELOPE (Ire),** b g King Persian - Kellys Risc by Pitskelly (Mrs P A Barker) 54 91 3628^9 3948

3 **PREMIER LEAGUE (Ire),** gr c Don't Forget Me - Kilmara (USA) by Caro (J E Banks) 672^1 890^5 1302^1

4 **PREMIER LEAP (Ire),** ch f Salmon Leap (USA) - Faapette by Runnett (Augustine Leahy) 1013^6 1962^5 2517^6 2842^4 3277^3 3543^3 3604^4 3853^3 4161^7

4 **PREMIER MAJOR (Ire),** b g Bluebird (USA) - Calvino by Relkino (P R Rodford) 962 1421 1578 2283^7 2445^9 2761^3

3 **PREMIER STAR,** ch g Precocious - Grove Star by Upper Case (USA) (M Dods) 1388^6 1642^6 1771^4 2181^6 2638^5 3310^2 3523^4 3631^2 4019 4258

4 **PREMONITORY DREAM (Can),** 4517^6

5 **PRENONAMOSS,** b g Precocious - Nonabella by Nonoalco (USA) (D W P Arbuthnot) 1636^8 2136^4 2431^6 2926 3358^3 3540^8 3863^2 4172^9 4297^9 4470^1 4650

2 **PRENUP (USA),** 4069^3

3 **PREPONDERANCE (Ire),** br f Cyrano de Bergerac - Mitsubishi Style by Try My Best (USA) (J G Burns) 573^8 2187^8

3 **PREROGATIVE,** ch g Dominion - Nettle by Kris (M C Pipe) 582^4 825^8 1092^4 2989^6 3480^2

2 **PRESENTLY,** b f Cadeaux Genereux - Mrs Bacon by Balliol (M Bell) 2990 4440

7 **PRESENT TIMES,** b g Sayf El Arab (USA) - Coins And Art (USA) by Mississipian (USA) (A J Taylor) 84^2 128^7 171^3 402^5 1353^8

2 **PRESS BARON (USA),** b c Private Account (USA) - Zaizafon (USA) by The Minstrel (Can) (A Fabre) 4242^3

3 **PRESS CARD (USA),** b c Fappiano (USA) - Courtly Dee by Never Bend (F S Schulhofer) 4438^9

3 **PRESS GALLERY,** ch c Carmelite House (USA) - Mixed Applause (USA) by Nijinsky (Can) (Mrs J Cecil) 380^4 624^1 915^5 1213 1584^4 1835^4 2237^9 2746^1 3427^5 3964^9

3 **PRESS ONWARD,** ch f Presidium - Ondine by Ballacashtal (Can) (M Johnston) 1396^7 1698^9 1937^9 2089^4 2593^7

3 **PRESS THE BELL,** br g Belfort (Fr) - Northern Empress by Northfields (USA) (J Berry) 324^1 361^1 634^2 716^7 1010^3 2050^1 2375^6 2908^4 3266^1 3668^2 4465^6 4549^3

3 **PRESSURE OFF,** gr c Petong - Arch Sculptress by Arch Sculptor (J H Johnson) 361

3 **PRESTON GUILD (Ire),** b g Mazaad - Dying Craft by Thatching (R J R Williams) 338^2 434^1 628^5 976^6 1309^2 1858^1 2641^2 2820^1 3139^8 3757 4479^2 4599^3 4722^4

5 **PRETONIC,** b m Precocious - Northern Ballerina by Dance In Time (Can) (M Johnston) 4660a^1 4692a^1 4739a^2 4808a^1 28^1 70^1 505^2 677 814^3 930^5 1348 1563^5

3 **PRETTY BABY,** b f Celestial Storm (USA) - Pretty Thing by Star Appeal (M S Saunders) 1388^2 1642^2 2189^8 3106^6 3461 3741^6 3945^2 4088^5

4 **PRETTY CHIC,** b g Kabour - Boom Shanty by Dragonara Palace (USA) (D W Chapman) 206^6 217^9 253 1937 2312^9 2584^9 3006^8 3794^5 4031

5 **PRETTY NICE (Ire),** br m Dalsaan - Princess Kofiyah by High Line (M J Grassick) 911^1

3 **PREVENE (Ire),** b c Alzao (USA) - Assya by Double Form (P F I Cole) 3636^9

4 **PRIDE OF BRITAIN (Can),** ch f Linkage (USA) - Witches Alibhai (USA) by Your Alibhai (L G Cottrell) 626^3 973^3 1586^4 1840^1

4 **PRIDE OF PENDLE,** ro f Grey Desire - Pendle's Secret by Le Johnstan (R Bastiman) 366^5 530^7 645^8 964^2 1284^6 1578^1 1799^2 2057^1 2283^2 2445^1 2816^2 3004^3 3182^4 3358^1 3540^1 3680^4 3901^9 4468 4640

3 **PRIDE'S DESIRE,** gr f Grey Desire - Lindrake's Pride by Mandrake Major (T D Barron) 4346^4

3 **PRIDWELL,** b g Sadler's Wells (USA) - Glowing With Pride by Ile de Bourbon (USA) (M C Pipe) 557^8 4110^9 4267^8

2 **PRIMA SILK,** b f Primo Dominie - Silk St James by Pas de Seul (M J Ryan) 776 1583^3 2067^7 2224^1 2473^5 3428^3 3688^1 3845^7 4165^2 4516

3 **PRIMA SINFONIA,** b f Fairy King (USA) - Bourbon Queen by Ile de Bourbon (USA) (P W Chapple-Hyam) 4125^4

5 **PRIME MOVER,** b g Mummy's Game - Feast-Rite by Reform (I Campbell) 4771a^3 17^1 76^1 170^5 218^1 253

3 **PRIME OF LIFE (Ire),** b g Midyan (USA) - Ominous by Dominion (R Charlton) 1713^2 1992^6 2752 4126^4 4565^6

3 **PRIME PAINTER,** b c Robellino (USA) - Sharp Lady by Sharpen Up (R F Fisher) 437 609^5 763^6 905^1 1180^2 1259^1 1781^3 1894^5 2177^4

3 **PRIMITIVE GIFT,** b f Primitive Rising (USA) - Annes Gift by Ballymoss (M D Hammond) 803

3 **PRIMOCELLE,** br f Primo Dominie - Jouvencelle by Rusticaro (Fr) (H Candy) 2580 2939 3302

3 **PRIMO FIGLIO,** b g Assert - Prima Domina (Fr) by Dominion (Miss L C Siddall) 827^8 990 4115 4335^2 4457^3 4675^6

2 **PRIMOST,** b g Most Welcome - Primulette by Mummy's Pet (M Williams) 517^8 1689^3 1959 2271^1 2911^2 3264^6 4264^6 4500^6

2 **PRIMO STAMPARI,** ch f Primo Dominie - Balatina by Balidar (R Hannon) 839^4 984^4 1229^7 3870^4 4303^3 4575^1

3 **PRIMULA BAIRN,** b f Bairn (USA) - Miss Primula by Dominion (Mrs J R Ramsden) 367^1 634^1 846 1157^4 2001^7 2699^4 3220^2 3877^1 4038 4455^2 4734

2 **PRIMUM TEMPUS,** br f Primo Dominie - Baggin Time by Pinsun (M H Easterby) 2706^9 3754 4044^5 4163

2 **PRINCE AZZAAN (Ire),** b c Rousillon (USA) - Victory Kingdom (Can) by Viceregal (Can) (N A Callaghan) 1020^4 1241^1 1446^8 2689^1 2996^9 3222^2 3435^7 3898^6

2 **PRINCE BABAR,** b g Fairy King (USA) - Bell Toll by High Line (G A Pritchard-Gordon) 687 1063^1 1639^2 2335^3 2924^2 3499^1

5 **PRINCE BELFORT,** b g Belfort (Fr) - Princess Sharpenup by Lochnager (J L Eyre) 800 1036^3 1215 1420^4 1589 1782^7 1865^3 2309^5 2434^5 2653^3 2734^3 2935^4 3877^9 4038 4224^9 4455 4592^4 4670

2 **PRINCE DANZIG (Ire),** ch g Roi Danzig (USA) - Veldt by High Top (D J G Murray Smith) 913^7 1131^7 1877 2274^5 2546^3 2988^7 3351^7 3532^2 3841^2 4033^4 4122

2 **PRINCE DE BERRY,** ch c Ballacashtal (Can) - Hoonah (Fr) by Luthier (R Hannon) 4508^7 4717^5

3 **PRINCE DIANON (Fr),** br c Solicitor - Miss Dianon by Iron Duke 173^2 201^1 4196

6 **PRINCE HANNIBAL,** b h High Top - Fluctuate by Sharpen Up (J L Dunlop) 442^3 618 1143^3 1764^1 2152^1 3587^3 4248^7 4548^9

3 **PRINCELY FAVOUR (Ire),** b g Anita's Prince - Kiss The Bride by Sweet Revenge (R Hannon) 317^5 471^4 772^9 1312^2 1584^5 1818^4 2212^6 2832^4 2939^2 2993^5 3445^1 3756^4 3983^1 4415

2 **PRINCELY GAIT,** b c Darshaan - Roussalka by Habitat (C A Cyzer) 2964

3 **PRINCE OF ANDROS (USA),** b c Al Nasr (Fr) - Her Radiance (USA) by Halo (USA) (D R Loder) 2189^2 2464^1 2941^1 3318^1 3879^1 4141^1

2 **PRINCE OF ANITA (Ire),** b c Anita's Prince - Take More (Ger) by Frontal (B Palling) 3287^5

2 **PRINCE OF GAELS,** b c Gallic League - Last Note by Welsh Pageant (M McCormack) 3265^5 3528^3 3755^7 3867^8

3 **PRINCE OF SOUL,** ch c Faustus (USA) - Casa Rosada by Known Fact (USA) (R Harris) 4691a^8 4730a 95^2 193^3 237^4 437

5 **PRINCE OLE (Ire),** b g Montelimar (USA) - Port-O-Call by Import (Patrick Joseph Flynn) 4573^5 4737

INDEX TO FLAT RACE RESULTS 1992-93

3 **RED WHIRLWIND,** b c Shadeed (USA) - Red Red Rose (USA) by Blushing Groom (Fr) (B J McMath) 538 1093[4] 1349[5] 1597[5]

2 **REED MY LIPS (Ire),** br c Thatching - Taunsa by Nishapour (Fr) (P T Walwyn) 1203[4] 1489[5] 3422[9] 4029[5] 4356 4500[5]

4 **REEL OF TULLOCH (Ire),** b g Salmon Leap (USA) - Miss Sandman by Manacle (P C Haslam) 1389 1601[7] 1900[3] 2162[3] 2455[2] 2800[1] 2888[2] 2950[4] 3442[6]

6 **REFERENCE LIGHT (USA),** b h Diesis - Lulworth Cove by Averof (M R Stoute) 3874[2]

5 **REFINED HEIR,** b g Elegant Air - Pearlesque by Gulf Pearl (Noel Meade) 1141[8]

4 **REFLECTING (Ire),** b c Ahonoora - Shining Water by Kalaglow (J H M Gosden) 4678a[9] 4817a[4] 20[1] 58[3] 169[4] 1120[1]

3 **REFUGIO,** b c Reference Point - Fatah Flare (USA) by Alydar (USA) (H R A Cecil) 1275[1] 2003[4] 4283

2 **REGAL ACCESS (USA),** br c Lear Fan (USA) - Low Approach by Artaius (USA) (Noel Meade) 2402[9] 3492[3] 3922[1] 4584[7]

3 **REGAL AURA (Ire),** ch g Glow (USA) - Dignified Air (Fr) by Wolver Hollow (G M Moore) 690[6] 875 1346 2867[4] 3101[6] 3540

4 **REGAL CHIMES,** gr c Another Realm - London Cries (Fr) by Bellman (Fr) (B A McMahon) 316[1] 555[3] 795[7] 1019[9] 2018[4] 2399[6] 2753[1] 3725 4040 4275[9]

2 **REGAL DOMAIN (Ire),** gr c Dominion Royale - Adaraya (Fr) by Zeddaan (Kevin Prendergast) 4290[8] 4582[7]

3 **REGAL JEST,** gr f Jester - Royal Huntress by Royal Avenue (B W Murray) 4155

9 **REGAL PARADE,** br h Hello Gorgeous (USA) - Danseuse Classique (Can) by Northern Dancer (D K Weld) 4205[3]

3 **REGAL PRETENDER (Ire),** ch g Simply Great (Fr) - Frances Jordan by Prince Regent (Fr) (Edward Lynam) 311 639 1139[8] 2484[5] 2692 2842 3367[2] 3397[7] 3721 3856 3975[2]

2 **REGAL PURSUIT (Ire),** b f Roi Danzig (USA) - Pursue by Auction Ring (USA) (C A Horgan) 3625[9] 4259[6] 4421

2 **REGAL RAMBLER (Can),** ch g Regal Classic (Can) - Rushing Rachel (USA) by Breezing On (USA) (L J Barratt) 1523[9] 2006[7] 2493[6] 4512

3 **REGALSETT,** b c Blakeney - Sleepline Princess by Royal Palace (M C Pipe) 836 1425[2] 1641[7] 2065[4] 2138[4] 2663[7] 3083[2] 3480[1]

3 **REGENCY,** b c Dancing Brave (USA) - Regal Lady by Will Hays (Mme C Head) 408[2] 955[1] 1544[5] 2076[4] 3337[5] 4478[3]

3 **REGENT RUNNER (Can),** 2442[7]

8 **REGGAE BEAT,** b g Be My Native (USA) - Invery Lady by Sharpen Up (I Campbell) 840

2 **REGINA ALICIA,** b f Dowsing (USA) - Kissagram Queen by Song (M Johnston) 3215[8] 3566

2 **REHLAT FARAH (USA),** b c Pleasant Colony (USA) - Venus Bound (USA) by Conquistador Cielo (USA) (L M Cumani) 4113[3] 4276[8] 4419[8]

2 **REIGNING ROYAL,** ch f Tina's Pet - Regency Brighton by Royal Palace (R J Hodges) 839 1091 1254[7]

5 **REIGN ROAD (USA),** b h Sovereign Dancer (USA) - Road Princess by Gallant Man (J Robbins) 671[5]

3 **REINE DE NEIGE,** b f Kris - Don't Rush (USA) by Alleged (USA) (A A Scott) 662[3] 856[5] 1789[7] 3012[4] 3225[1] 3477[2] 3844[6] 4153[8]

4 **REINE KAMI (Fr),** 90[2]

3 **REJECTS REPLY,** b g Balliol - Fair Dino by Thatch (USA) (W J Musson) 4279 4544 4696

6 **REKLAW,** b g Hard Fought - Rubina Park by Ashmore (Fr) (S G Chadwick) 4786a[3] 64[7]

3 **REKORD (Ger),** 3717

2 **RELATIVELY SPECIAL,** b f Alzao (USA) - Someone Special by Habitat (L M Cumani) 3317[4] 3781[1] 4171[4] 4442[1]

3 **RELENTLESS BOY (Ire),** gr g Sizzling Melody - Spinnaker Lady by Windjammer (USA) (Edward Lynam) 551[2] 787[5] 1853[3] 2452[1] 2878

5 **RELENTLESS PURSUIT (Ire),** b h Thatching - Daring Way (USA) by Alydar (USA) (P W Chapple-Hyam) 771[8] 1207 1623 2264[2] 3313[3] 4092[5]

2 **REMAIN ANONYMOUS (Ire),** ch f Shy Groom (USA) - Inishannagh by St Alphage (Edward Lynam) 3071 3273[5] 4000

4 **REMANY,** gr f Bellypha - Moonscape by Ribero (J R Fanshawe) 645[5] 1120 1712[1]

3 **REMBO (Su),** 2643[6]

3 **REMEESON,** b g Alleging (USA) - Iron Lass by Thatch (USA) (R Bastiman) 4191[6] 4544 4724[8]

3 **REMEMBER THE NIGHT,** b c Petong - Free On Board by Free State (M McCormack) 482

3 **REMEMBER THIS (Ire),** b g Don't Forget Me - Regal Twin (USA) by Majestic Prince (C A Cyzer) 3225 3456 3639[8] 3988[9] 4270

2 **REMINISCENCE (Ire),** ch f Thatching - Measuring by Moorestyle (R Hannon) 3573[8] 4264[3] 4418[5] 4618[2] 4708[6]

4 **RENASHAAN (Fr),** b f Darshaan - Gerbera by Lyphard (Mme C Head) 4711a[9]

3 **RENEWED DYNASTY (USA),** ch c Arctic Tern (USA) - Sweetened Offer by General Assembly (USA) (D K Weld) 2810[2] 3768[5] 4556[8]

2 **RENNYHOLME,** ch c Rich Charlie - Jacqui Joy by Music Boy (M W Ellerby) 1499[8] 1798 4452

5 **RENOMEE (Ger),** 1084[7]

4 **REPORTED (Ire),** ch c Heraldiste (USA) - Peach Melba by So Blessed (M J Heaton-Ellis) 3764[7] 4300 4660[4]

2 **REPREHEND,** br g Reprimand - Lake Ormond by Kings Lake (USA) (R Hannon) 1640[1] 1920[2] 3289[3] 3510[5]

6 **REQUESTED,** b g Rainbow Quest (USA) - Melody Hour by Sing Sing (R Akehurst) 478 661[4] 874[1] 1752 1809 2617 2755[2] 3595[5]

3 **RESARIO (Fr),** 97[3]

5 **RESISTING (USA),** b g Desert Wine (USA) - Fool's Miss (USA) by Saltville (M C Chapman) 67 94[7] 122[8] 152[6] 179[6] 202[8] 278[7] 973[8] 1453 1873[4]

3 **RESIST THE FORCE (USA),** br g Shadeed (USA) - Countess Tully by Hotfoot (C A Cyzer) 510[4] 658[7] 3511 3665[2] 3906

7 **RESOLUTE BAY,** b g Crofthall - Spinner by Blue Cashmere (R M Whitaker) 1680[6] 2062[9] 2173[6] 2434 2639[3] 2897[4] 3057 4038 4235 4391[8] 4574[5] 4658

2 **RESONANT,** ch c Forzando - Madam Cody by Hot Spark (Sir Mark Prescott) 1773[2] 2049[2] 2370[4] 3426[1] 3871[3] 4042[1] 4193[4]

4 **RESOUNDING SUCCESS (Ire),** b f Law Society (USA) - Dawn Echo by Don (Ity) (B W Hills) 4679a

7 **RESPECTABLE JONES,** ch g Tina's Pet - Jonesee by Dublin Taxi (R Hollinshead) 4779a[2] 4804a[1] 4815a[1] 19[1] 56[3] 112[1] 140[2] 197 244[3] 260[3] 320[2] 521 650[4] 828[6] 906[7] 4580

2 **RESPONSE,** b c Most Welcome - Knavesmire by Runnymede (Dr J D Scargill) 4227[3] 4439[3] 4644[1]

4 **RESTLESS MINSTREL (USA),** b g The Minstrel (Can) - Dismasted (USA) by Restless Native (J E Banks) 288 1979[6] 2694[6]

10 **RESTORE,** ch g Habitat - Never So Lovely by Realm (R M Flower) 2723[9] 3593 3745[2] 4012[6]

3 **RESTRAINT,** b f Bustino - Queens Message by Town Crier (P Calver) 1077[7] 1275 2107 3142[6]

4 **RETENDER (USA),** br g Storm Bird (Can) - Dandy Bury (Fr) by Exbury (Mrs J R Ramsden) 3973[6] 4247[7] 4470[4] 4605[6] 4694[8]

3 **RETICENT BRIDE (Ire),** b f Shy Groom (USA) - Larosterna by Busted (D K Weld) 258[8] 1793[2] 2285[8] 2483[2] 2674[5] 3242[2] 3720[1]

6 **RE TOSS (Arg),** b m Egg Toss (USA) - Rezagante by Practicante (H Moreno) 4729a[7] 1695[3] 2645[1] 3150[4] 4741[3]

3 **RETURN AGAIN (Ire),** b f Top Ville - Perfect Guest by What A Guest (D T Hughes) 2956[2] 3299[2] 3616[5] 3773[1] 4246[6] 4555

4 **RETURN JOURNEY (Ire),** b f Pennine Walk - Carhue Lady by Tap On Wood (Patrick O'Leary) 868[9] 1235[9] 1440[4] 2141 2782[6]

4 **REVASSER (USA),** br f Riverman (USA) - Nijinsky's Star by Nijinsky 4769a[4] 1370[4] 3187[4]

3 **REVELATION (Ire),** b c Thatching - Angelus Chimes by Northfields (USA) (R Hannon) 526[2] 794 1367[4] 1765[5] 2531[1] 3402[4] 3913[8] 4073[3] 4467

3 **REVERE (Ire),** b c Dancing Brave (USA) - Bint Pasha (USA) by Affirmed (USA) (P F I Cole) 2174[4] 2390[3] 2907 4441[4] 4653[2]

5 **REVIF (Fr),** gr h Kenmare (Fr) - Reverente (Fr) by Riverman (USA) (A C Stewart) 4674a[1]

6 **REXY BOY,** b g Dunbeath (USA) - Coca by Levmoss (W L Barker) 901[7] 1195[7] 1276[7]

5 **REZA,** gr g Superlative - Moon Charter by Runnymede (J L Eyre) 4710a 294 530

5 **REZON (Su),** b h Neman - Razmashka by Montcontour 1084 1883[3]

2 **RHAPSODIC (USA),** b f Dixieland Band (USA) - Tamanaco Day by Naskra (B Mayberry) 4390[4] 4740[6]

5 **RHAZYA,** b m Rousillon (USA) - Destina (USA) by Youth (USA) (J J Bridger) 3693

3 **RHODE ISLAND (Ger),** ch f Waajib - Reduced by Irish River 805[4]

5 **RHYTHMIC DANCER,** b g Music Boy - Stepping Gaily by Gay Fandango (USA) (J L Spearing) 4818a[1] 11[2] 70[3] 99[4] 212[6] 2387[1] 3099[6] 3739[4] 4734

3 **RIBBOLD,** b c Bustino - Water Woo (USA) by Tom Rolfe (C E Brittain) 515 3727[4]

3 **RIBBONWOOD (USA),** b f Diesis - Ribbon (USA) by His Majesty (USA) (J H M Gosden) 556[2] 1030[3] 3864[5]

3 **RIBHI (USA),** b c Riverman (USA) - Antartica (Fr) by Arctic Tern (USA) (D Morley) 397[1] 684[4] 1524[1] 1808[6] 2233[2] 2794[4] 3465[5] 3900[1] 4063

2 **RICHARD'S ERROR,** ch c Risk Me (Fr) - Bocas Rose by Jalmood (USA) (G Lewis) 687 913 1279[4] 4480 4577

5 **RICHARD'S LASS (USA),** m (A Callejas) 560[9] 1184[9]

3 **RICH ASSET (Ire),** b c Treasure Kay - Pride And Joy (Fr) by Miami Springs (C B B Booth) 300[8] 832[3] 1224[9] 1836 3757[9] 4176

4 **RICHER SPIRIT,** b f Grey Desire - Pokey's Pet by Uncle Pokey (B Beasley) 3005[7] 3628

2 **RICH GLOW,** b g Rich Charlie - Mayglow by Sparkling Boy (N Bycroft) 3259 3746[9] 3972 4163 4318 4436[9] 4602[2]

2 **RICH HARMONY,** ch g Rich Charlie - Out Of Harmony by Song (E Weymes) 364[5] 908[9] 2342[4] 2541[7] 3133 3321

4 **RICH HEIRESS (Ire),** b f Last Tycoon - Lamya (USA) by Alydar (USA) (V Thompson) 4780a[6] 4814a[2] 43 82[8] 139[6]

3 **RICH LIFE (Ire),** b g Dance Of Life (USA) - Ringawoody by Auction Ring (USA) (C Weedon) 486 806[9] 1574[6] 1995 2484[3] 3396[5] 3482[2] 3951[7]

2 **RICH MISS,** ch f Rich Charlie - Miss Never Hyde by Alias Smith (USA) (Miss B Sanders) 2559[5] 3016[3] 3166[7] 3704

4 **RICH PICKINGS,** b f Dominion - Miss By Miles by Milesian (D R Tucker) 757[7] 2034[1] 2662[6] 2729 3231[8]

4 **RICKY'S TORNADO (Ire),** ch g Night Shift (USA) - Fodens Eve by Dike (USA) (J Parkes) 326[7] 479[9] 659 2110[4] 2318[2] 2494[7] 3100[6] 3794[7] 3948[1] 4096

2 **RIDGE POOL (Ire),** ch f Bluebird (USA) - Casting Couch by Thatching (M J Grassick) 1022[8] 2037[3] 2244[1] 2605

2 **RIDGEWOOD BEN,** b c Indian Ridge - Ben's Pearl by Tap On Wood (John M Oxx) 4405[1]

4 **RIENROE (Ire),** b f Caerleon (USA) - Flying Bid by Auction Ring (USA) (D K Weld) 851[5] 1235[2] 1295[1] 1644[1] 2141[2] 2463[2] 2879[1] 3029[8]

9 **RIENZI,** ch g Busted - Mortice by Morston (Fr) (C Collins) 281 298 1013[8] 1508

3 **RIFLEBIRD (Ire),** b f Runnett - Sacred Ibis by Red God (J G Burns) 2700[4] 3040[6] 3827

2 **RIGHT ANGLE (Ire),** b c Shy Groom (USA) - Mamie's Joy by Prince Tenderfoot (USA) (W M Roper) 4581

3 **RIGHT WIN (Ire),** br c Law Society (USA) - Popular Win by Lorenzaccio (R Hannon) 474[1] 794 1364[5] 1843[2] 2883[1] 3403[6] 4078[1]

5 **RIMOUSKI,** b h Sure Blade (USA) - Rimosa's Pet by Petingo (B R Cambidge) 290 1276[4] 1840 2544[1] 3078

2 **RING-A-RUAN (Ire),** b g Classic Secret (USA) - Castleforbes by Thatching (M A O'Toole) 2840[8] 3073 4369

5 **RINGLAND (USA),** b h Gate Dancer (USA) - Tinnitus (USA) by Restless Wind (T A K Cuthbert) 4744a[3] 315[4] 425[4] 1940[7] 2433 2601[7]

2 **RINGMASTER (Ire),** b c Taufan (USA) - Salustrina by Sallust (M H Tompkins) 3592 4615[7]

3 **RING PINK (USA),** b f Bering - Pink Valley by Never Bend (Mrs C Head) 4243[1] 4655[5]

2 **RINGSIDE TICKET (USA),** ch c Phone Trick (USA) - The Old Maryann (USA) by Well Mannered (USA) (J W Hills) 4680

2 **RINJANI,** ch c Salse (USA) - Chasing Moonbeams by Final Straw (John M Oxx) 4290[4] 4637[2]

2 **RINUS MAJOR (Ire),** b g Don't Forget Me - Needy by High Top (D McCain) 3602[4] 3779 4508[6]

2 **RINUS MANOR (Ire),** b c Ballad Rock - Never Never Land by Habitat (D McCain) 4512

2 **RINUS MASTER (Ire),** ch g Jareer (USA) - Prodical Daughter by Faraway Son (USA) (D McCain) 2836[9] 3362

4 **RIO TRUSKY,** b g Ballacashtal (Can) - Polly's Song by Song (D M Grissell) 4748a[6] 68[7]

2 **RIPARIUS (USA),** b c Riverman (USA) - Sweet Simone (Fr) by Green Dancer (USA) (H Candy) 4717[4]

4 **RIPSNORTER (Ire),** ch c Rousillon (USA) - Formulate by Reform (J A Bennett) 67[1] 85[2] 152[7] 169 224[4] 247[5] 274[2] 294[8] 771 971[7] 1207 1316

5 **RISE UP SINGING,** ch g Noalto - Incarnadine by Hot Spark (W J Musson) 391 475 771[1] 914[9] 1172[2] 1316[4] 1604[2] 1830[3] 2363[6] 2624[8] 3358 4415 4652[1] 4721[7]

2 **RISING SPRAY,** ch c Waajib - Rose Bouquet by General Assembly (USA) (P W Harris) 3592 3974[6] 4543[9]

5 **RISING TEMPO (Ire),** b g Lomond (USA) - May Hill by Hill Clown (USA) (B P J Baugh) 1034[6] 1438[1] 1979[2] 2373[4] 2767[7]

5 **RISING WATERS (Ire),** b g Sure Blade (USA) - Over The Waves by Main Reef (Desmond McDonogh) 1576[5] 2035 2841[4] 4288[9] 4430[9]

3 **RISING WOLF,** b c Shirley Heights - Bustara by Busted (R J O'Sullivan) 423[5] 686[7] 1176 1838[5]

2 **RISK A PICTURE,** b f Risk Me (Fr) - Happy Snap by Jalmood (USA) (R Simpson) 1254[9]

2 **RISKIE THINGS,** ch f Risk Me (Fr) - Foolish Things by Song (J S Moore) 299[2] 386[2] 445[6] 715 949[1] 1119[5] 1391[2] 2689[3] 2929[8] 3432 4228

4 **RISK MASTER,** b c Risk Me (Fr) - Trigamy by Tribal Chief (C A Horgan) 581[2] 737 1002[1] 1450 1845[4] 2793[5] 3158[5] 4063 4140[3] 4467

4 **RISKMEMAY,** ch f Risk Me (Fr) - Dutch May by Maystreak (A A Hambly) 615 800 970 1072[8]

2 **RISK OF FIRE,** br c Risk Me (Fr) - Grey Twig by Godswalk (USA) (G Lewis) 3573[9] 3816 3958[7] 4351[4] 4418

3 **RISK PROOF,** b c Risk Me (Fr) - Queen's Piper by Song (K O Cunningham-Brown) 4675a 754 1237[5] 1607 2712 2898

3 **RISK THE WITCH,** b f Risk Me (Fr) - Singing Witch by Sing Sing (R J R Williams) 1454[7] 3514 3789 4016

2 **RISKY,** b f Risk Me (Fr) - Dona Krista by King Of Spain (R Hannon) 477[1] 841[1] 1428[2] 1766[1] 2618[1] 2960[1] 3463[2] 4250[2] 4423[2]

2 **RISKY AFFAIR,** b g Risk Me (Fr) - Farras by Song (G Lewis) 386[3] 445[4] 625[4] 776 1119[8] 1959[5] 2689[5] 3210[3]

3 **RISKY GALORE,** ch c Risk Me (Fr) - Esta Bonita (USA) by To-Agori-Mou (A P O'Brien) 2902 4162 4260[6] 4368

2 **RISKY GIFT,** b c Risk Me (Fr) - Sir Tangs Gift by Runnett (J G FitzGerald) 2766[8] 3131[7] 4032

2 **RISKY PRINCESS,** ch f Risk Me (Fr) - Princess Lily by Blakeney (N Bycroft) 3972 4167

3 **RISKY ROSIE,** ch f Risk Me (Fr) - Star Rose (Fr) by Star Appeal (R Voorspuy) 880

2 **RISKY TU,** ch f Risk Me (Fr) - Sarah Gillian (USA) by Zen (USA) (P A Kelleway) 2990[6] 3462[8] 4491[3] 4725[6]

3 **RISKY TUESDAY,** ch f Risk Me (Fr) - Give Me A Day by Lucky Wednesday (G H Yardley) 1628[8] 2151 2499

3 **RISKY VENTURE,** b g Bluebird (USA) - Fire Risk by Thatch (USA) (W Jarvis) 4596 4666^{3}

3 **RISPOTO,** b f Mtoto - River Spey by Mill Reef (USA) (Sir Mark Prescott) 352^{7} 1111^{7} 3106^{3} 3301^{3} 3461^{2} 3699^{3} 4048^{1} 4268^{2} 4454^{8}

2 **RISQUE-TOUT,** ch f Risk Me (Fr) - Valldemosa by Music Boy (B W Hills) 4575

3 **RISTON LADY (Ire),** b f Salt Dome (USA) - Trompe D'Oeil by Longleat (USA) (B S Rothwell) 566^{3} 858^{5} 1258^{4} 1449 2018 3849^{6} 4180^{8} 4363^{4} 4455

4 **RISZARD (USA),** ch g Danzig Connection (USA) - Tendresse (USA) by Secretariat (USA) (J S Bolger) 309^{2} 553^{1} 895^{3} 961^{2} 1576^{1} 1809^{1} 2841 3434

2 **RITA'S JOY,** ch f Jalmood (USA) - Cash Limit by High Top (W G M Turner) 922^{9} 1108^{3} 1254^{2} 1774^{3} 2216^{3} 3829^{7} 3968^{5} 4208

3 **RITTO,** b c Arctic Tern (USA) - Melodrama by Busted (B W Hills) 476^{3} 1154^{1} 1960^{4} 2655^{3} 4143^{2} 4466^{2} 4630^{2}

3 **RITZY,** gr f Sharrood (USA) - Ritsurin by Mount Hagen (Fr) (Miss C Johnsey) 557 672 876 3384^{4} 3840^{3}

5 **RIVAL BID (USA),** b g Cannonade (USA) - Love Triangle (USA) by Nodouble (USA) (M A Jarvis) 919^{8} 1414^{6} 1934^{2} 2311^{2} 2884^{8} 3139^{1} 3424^{3} 4107^{7} 4470

3 **RIVA ROCK,** b g Roaring Riva - Kivulini by Hotfoot (W J Musson) 2065^{7} 2578^{6} 2775^{8} 3591 4623

2 **RIVA'S BOOK (USA),** b c Mari's Book (USA) - Riva's Revenge (USA) by Riva Ridge (USA) (J D Bethell) 804 1227^{8} 3259^{9} 3678^{4} 3997^{7} 4365^{6}

3 **RIVE (USA),** b f Riverman (USA) - Arewehavingfunyet (USA) by Sham (USA) (F Boutin) 2690^{4} 3929^{7}

5 **RIVE-JUMELLE (Ire),** b m M Double M (USA) - Riverwave (USA) by Riverman (USA) (M Bell) 2948^{7} 3224^{9}

2 **RIVER ARLY (Fr),** b c River Mist - Sacadu by Tyrant (N Clement) 3339^{2}

3 **RIVER BOARD,** b c Dominion - Miss Thames by Tower Walk (W J Haggas) 1027^{2}

3 **RIVER BOYNE (USA),** ch c Irish River (Fr) - Bethamane (USA) by Wajima (USA) (G Harwood) 2275^{1} 2941^{2} 3509^{1} 3636^{7}

2 **RIVER DEEP (USA),** ch c Riverman (USA) - Affection Affirmed (USA) by Affirmed (USA) (P F I Cole) 738^{2} 1975^{3} 4276^{2} 4443^{7}

4 **RIVER DEFENCES (USA),** b c Riverman (USA) - Durtal by Lyphard (USA) (P W Chapple-Hyam) 1365

3 **RIVERETTE,** b f Caerleon (USA) - Riviere Bleue by Riverman (USA) (B W Hills) 1587

3 **RIVER FIRE (Ire),** br f Petong - River Maiden (Fr) by Riverman (USA) (J Wharton) 1705^{6} 2425^{8} 2859 3088^{6} 3591 4016

5 **RIVER ISLAND (USA),** b g Spend A Buck (USA) - Promising Risk (USA) by Exclusive Native (USA) (J A B Old) 64^{6}

2 **RIVER JUNCTION (Ire),** b g Cyrano de Bergerac - Lovestream by Sandy Creek (P C Haslam) 3592 3990^{5} 4492^{8} 4646^{5}

3 **RIVER LIFE,** b c Irish River (Fr) - Exclusive Life (USA) by Exclusive Native (USA) (P F I Cole) 463^{1}

3 **RIVER NORTH (Ire),** ch g Lomond (USA) - Petillante (USA) by Riverman (USA) (Lady Herries) 318^{3} 441^{1} 684^{1} 1398^{1} 1719^{1} 2211^{2} 2654^{1} 3371^{3} 3886^{2}

4 **RIVER NYMPH (USA),** b f Riverman (USA) - Fourteen by Bellypha (J de Roualle) 4711a^{8} 693^{4}

3 **RIVER REFUGE,** gr c Belfort (Fr) - Rhodabourne by Aragon (J A R Toller) 2711^{7} 3095^{7} 3938^{9}

7 **RIVER TEST (USA),** b h Critique (USA) - River Valley by Riverman (USA) (D Mercier) 4294

6 **RIVER VERDON,** b h Be My Native (USA) - Tuyenu by Welsh Pageant (D Hill) 596^{5}

3 **RIVIERE ACTOR (USA),** b or br c Theatrical - Riviere Salee (Fr) by Luthier (J L Dunlop) 1068 1429^{9} 1961^{2} 2326^{2} 2751^{3} 3271^{9} 3971^{1} 4212^{8} 4433^{4}

3 **RIYADH DANCER (Ire),** b g Montelimar (USA) - Rebel's Lyric (USA) by Mutineer (USA) (Patrick Joseph Flynn) 849 1251^{8} 1621^{6} 1987 2693^{3} 3277^{5} 3580 3853^{7} 4119^{5} 4657^{9}

8 **RIYADH LIGHTS,** b g Formidable (USA) - Rivers Maid by Rarity (M D I Usher) 4750a^{4} 4797a^{3}

5 **RIYASHA (Ire),** ch f Commanche Run - Riyda by Be My Guest (USA) (P J Lally) 851 1295 2958^{9} 3853

3 **RIYOOM (USA),** br f Vaguely Noble - Lt Snoopy (USA) by Lt Stevens (J S Bolger) 1511^{4} 2038 3560^{5}

3 **RIZ BIZ (USA),** ch f El Gran Senor (USA) - Dictina (Fr) by Dictus (Fr) (M Bell) 2752 3012 3225 3759 3943^{3} 4176^{8} 4631^{1} 4755^{5}

3 **ROADRUNNER,** ch g Sunley Builds - Derraleena by Derrylin (W G R Wightman) 1344 1746 3839

3 **ROAMIN RACHEL (USA),** b f Mining (USA) - One Smart Lady by Clever Trick 570^{3}

4 **ROAR ON TOUR,** b g Dunbeath (USA) - Tickled Trout by Red Alert (Mrs M Reveley) 1865 2057 2591^{7} 3134^{9} 4164^{4} 4640^{2}

2 **ROBBY (Ire),** b c Bob Back (USA) - Allberry by Alzao (USA) (W R Muir) 2123^{5} 2502 2718^{4} 3362^{2} 3940 4564

2 **ROBELLION,** b c Robellino (USA) - Tickled Trout by Red Alert (D W P Arbuthnot) 922^{1} 1639^{3}

4 **ROBENKO (USA),** b c Roberto (USA) - Kendra Road (USA) by Kennedy Road (USA) (C E Brittain) 2696 3179^{6} 3587 3831^{6} 4426

2 **ROBERO,** b c Robellino (USA) - Copt Hall Princess by Crowned Prince (USA) (R Lee) 1265 2030^{6} 2502^{8} 3352

4 **ROBERTOLOMY (USA),** ch g Roberto (USA) - Respectfully (USA) by The Minstrel (Can) (John J McLoughlin) 3542^{4} 3770^{6} 4583 4689^{2}

5 **ROBERTY LEA,** b h Alleging (USA) - Rosy Lee (Fr) by Le Haar (Mrs M Reveley) 2857^{4} 3121^{1} 3466^{2} 3848^{2} 4064^{6} 4425^{6} 4731

5 **ROBIN DES PINS (USA),** b h Nureyev (USA) - Rare Mint (USA) by Key To The Mint (USA) (F Boutin) 430^{5} 1011^{1} 1465^{4} 2242^{1} 3015^{7} 3717^{1} 4417^{2}

4 **ROBINGO (Ire),** b g Bob Back (USA) - Mill's Girl by Le Levanstell (M C Pipe) 478^{2} 661^{1} 857^{5} 1345^{1}

2 **ROBIN LAKE (Ire),** b f Thatching - Circo by High Top (I A Balding) 1708^{2} 1955^{2} 3754^{2}

3 **ROBIX (Ire),** b g Glenstal (USA) - Pocket by Tumble Wind (USA) (D W Chapman) 51^{7} 93^{4} 503^{7} 862 3216 3568 3758 4348

3 **ROBLEU,** b g Robellino (USA) - Blue Flower (Fr) by Carwhite (G Harwood) 797^{3} 991^{1} 1382^{8} 1808

3 **ROBRO,** ch g Rich Charlie - Cresta (Fr) by Ribero (W M Brisbourne) 2769

2 **ROBSERA (Ire),** b g Robellino (USA) - Que Sera by Music Boy (G Lewis) 2990^{7} 3387^{4} 3705^{3} 3940^{3} 4122^{5} 4444^{7}

2 **ROBUR (Fr),** ch c Tropular - Reggae by New Chapter (B Vanheeghe) 3851^{4} 4593^{7}

4 **ROCALITY,** b f Dreams To Reality (USA) - Rocas by Ile de Bourbon (USA) (M R Channon) 1447^{8} 1730^{7} 4007^{2} 4297 4470 4652

4 **ROCA MURADA (Ire),** br g Cyrano de Bergerac - Keppols by Furry Glen (D Nicholson) 677 881 1932^{8} 2582^{1} 2717^{1} 2944^{1} 3127^{2} 3593 3863 4096^{2} 4415

2 **ROCHE ABBEY (Ire),** br f Satco (Fr) - Lyphalla by Lyphard's Special (USA) (M Johnston) 2103^{1} 3755^{6} 3903 4081^{6} 4358^{4}

3 **ROCHESSON (Fr),** b c Garde Royale - Armee D'Afrique by Armadou (G Philippeau) 119^{1}

2 **ROCKABYE BAILEYS,** ch f Midyan (USA) - Council Rock by General Assembly (USA) (B J McMath) 299^{5} 374^{4} 490^{6} 1615^{5} 3345^{4} 3641 4009

3 **ROCKAMUNDO (USA),** b c Key To The Mint (USA) - Crystal Cup by Nijinsky (O Glass Jr) 585^{1} 779 1070^{7}

4 **ROCKAWHILE (Ire),** b f Dancing Brave (USA) - Melody (USA) by Lord Gayle (USA) (H R A Cecil) 616^{3} 1021^{4} 1845^{6} 2941^{3}

4 **ROCK BAND (Ire),** b c Ballad Rock - Bobs by Warpath (T M Jones) 4817a

4 **ROCKBOURNE,** b f Midyan (USA) - River Music by Riverman (USA) (Mrs J Cecil) 47^{7} 138^{4} 177^{5}

2 **ROCKETEER (Ire),** ch c Bluebird (USA) - Chive by St Chad (W R Muir) 1857^{4} 3446^{6} 3569^{7} 4114 4351^{9}

6 **ROCKET FUEL (USA),** 2084^{5}

5 **ROCK LEGEND,** ch h Legend Of France (USA) - Two Rock by Mill Reef (USA) (D Shaw) 135^{5}

5 **ROCK OPERA (Ire),** ch g Ballad Rock - Time For Romance by Cure The Blues (USA) (M P Naughton) 4701a^{9} 4716a^{3} 1287^{8} 1589 1782^{5} 2707^{3} 2975^{9} 3057 3409^{2} 3747 4022^{4} 4343^{7} 4544

4 **ROCK SONG (Ire),** ch g Ballad Rock - Mrs Tittlemouse by Nonoalco (USA) (J Mackie) 710 893^{9} 1073^{7} 1560 2106^{7} 2590^{7}

5 **SARAH-CLARE,** b m Reach - Northern Dynasty by Breeders Dream (R Akehurst) 4759a^{6} 678^{6} 1146^{1} 1663^{2} 1912^{1} 2291 4335^{1} 4600

3 **SARAH HEIGHTS,** b f Sayyaf - Temple Heights by Shirley Heights (Miss L C Siddall) 1300^{4} 1656^{6} 3601^{5} 4376^{7} 4544^{8} 4757^{5}

2 **SARAH'S OPERA (Ire),** ch f Salt Dome (USA) - Opera Guest by Be My Guest (USA) (K R Burke) 3363^{5} 3867^{6}

3 **SARAKARTA (USA),** ch f Trempolino (USA) - Sarshara by Habitat (John M Oxx) 3025^{5}

8 **SARAKAYA,** gr m Dalsaan - Safaya (Fr) by Zeddaan (Francis Berry) 911^{5} 4368 4387^{3} 4586^{7}

3 **SARA MAURETTE (Ire),** b f Heraldiste (USA) - Valdora by High Hat (Edward Lynam) 311 1123^{4} 1251^{1} 1433^{3} 1923^{6} 2321^{8} 2514^{5} 3328^{4} 3419^{6}

3 **SARAMY (Ire),** ch f Orchestra - Saceili by Saher (Edward Lynam) 3856^{6} 3975

2 **SARANGA (Ire),** ch f Sharastani (USA) - Sarshara by Habitat (John M Oxx) 2742^{3} 3451^{3} 3807^{3} 4262^{8}

3 **SARANGANI BAY (USA),** b c Manila (USA) - Homespun (USA) by Round Table (P W Chapple-Hyam) 563^{3} 1597^{3} 2326^{4} 3325^{7}

2 **SARASONIA,** b f Dunbeath (USA) - La Graciosa by Comedy Star (USA) (R J Baker) 1317^{9}

4 **SARATOGA SOURCE (USA),** ch f Saratoga Six (USA) - Exotic Source (USA) by The Minstrel (Can) (I A Balding) 3890^{7}

5 **SARAWAT,** b g Slip Anchor - Eljazzi by Artaius (USA) (R Akehurst) 682^{8} 1682^{4} 2061^{8} 2655^{7} 3434^{1} 3513^{3} 3848

4 **SARAZAR (USA),** ch g Shahrastani (USA) - Sarshara by Habitat (R Akehurst) 442 994 1430^{5} 1669 2415^{9}

2 **SARDULA (USA),** b f Storm Cat (USA) - Honor An Offer (USA) by Hoist The Flag (USA) (B Mayberry) 4390^{2} 4740^{2}

5 **SAREEN EXPRESS (Ire),** gr g Siberian Express (USA) - Three Waves by Cure The Blues (USA) (C P Wildman) 4680a^{1} 4722a^{6} 4733a^{6} 48^{5} 69^{3} 113^{7} 152 232^{5} 327 754^{1} 1097^{4} 1686^{4} 1956^{8} 2226^{7} 2548^{8} 2715^{7}

3 **SARENA LADY (Ire),** b f Auction Ring (USA) - Parima by Pardao (P F I Cole) 2032^{2}

4 **SARISAKA,** 2839^{6}

2 **SARIYAA,** b f Persian Bold - Bedouin Veil (USA) by Shareef Dancer (USA) (M R Stoute) 3248^{6} 4089^{3} 4641^{3}

3 **SARLIYA (Ire),** gr f Doyoun - Safita by Habitat (A de Royer-Dupre) 2080^{4} 3944^{4}

2 **SARMATIAN (USA),** br c Northern Flagship (USA) - Tracy L (USA) by Bold Favorite (USA) (C F Wall) 2659^{7} 3267^{4} 3421 3978^{4} 4193 4423^{8} 4733^{9}

4 **SAROS ON THE TOWN (USA),** 2645

4 **SARTIGILA,** b f Efisio - Ichnusa by Bay Express (M D Hammond) 436^{2} 591 909^{3} 1081^{1} 1193^{5} 1865^{5} 1939^{3} 2172^{4} 2915^{4} 3354^{7} 4156^{6} 4394^{6} 4537^{9} 4605^{1} 4676^{9}

7 **SARUM,** b g Tina's Pet - Contessa (Hun) by Peleid (C P Wildman) 4722a^{5} 4781a^{6} 12 33^{3} 48^{3} 87^{3} 101^{3} 130^{2} 157^{5} 249^{6} 319^{2} 403^{8} 754 952^{2} 1097^{7} 1701^{4} 2382^{4} 4710^{7}

3 **SASEEDO (USA),** ch g Afleet (Can) - Barbara's Moment (USA) by Super Moment (USA) (W A O'Gorman) 4724a^{5} 22^{2} 66^{3} 4277^{1} 4649^{4}

6 **SASKIA'S HERO,** ch g Bairn (USA) - Comtec Princess by Gulf Pearl (J F Bottomley) 1979^{5}

9 **SASKIA'S REPRIEVE,** ch g Giacometti - Anjamadi by Buff's Own (J F Bottomley) 1984^{7}

3 **SASSAMOUSE,** b f Bairn (USA) - Westminster Waltz by Dance In Time (Can) (R Guest) 905^{3} 1061^{4}

3 **SASSIVER (USA),** b c Riverman (USA) - Sassabunda by Sassafras (Fr) (R Hollinshead) 1340^{4} 2046^{4} 2776

3 **SATANK (USA),** b c Victory Stride (USA) - Iron Franco (USA) by Barrera (USA) (J W Watts) 566^{5} 795 2018^{3} 2206^{3}

3 **SATELLITE GLINT,** b c Glint Of Gold - Satellite by Busted 1547^{3}

3 **SATIN DANCER,** b g Rousillon (USA) - Sequin Lady by Star Appeal (G Harwood) 772^{3} 1204^{5} 1827^{2} 2135^{4} 2907^{7} 3353^{7} 3666^{3}

6 **SATIN LAKE (USA),** b m Well Decorated (USA) - Bunny Lake by Northern Baby (Can) (G R Oldroyd) 3970 4530

5 **SATIN LOVER,** ch g Tina's Pet - Canoodle by Warpath (N Tinkler) 1682^{7} 2061

2 **SATIN VELVET (USA),** ch f El Gran Senor (USA) - Sateen (USA) by Round Table (J H M Gosden) 4367^{3}

2 **SATLEY LASS,** br f Gallic League - Fleet Fact by Known Fact (USA) (P C Haslam) 1632^{6} 4345

5 **SATRAP (Ire),** ch g Persian Bold - Zedative (Fr) by Zeddaan (N J H Walker) 1830 2363

3 **SAUKARA (Fr),** b f Arokar - Sauhatz by Alpenkonig (M Pimbonnet) 174^{1}

8 **SAVAHRA SOUND,** b h Song - Savahra by Free State (S R Bowring) 195^{4} 253^{7} 289^{9} 545^{4} 906^{3} 1382^{9} 1520 1898^{5} 2309^{6} 2428^{6} 2863^{2} 3004^{7} 3280^{3} 3558^{8} 3778 4394 4487^{7} 4532^{9} 4670^{3} 4762

4 **SAVALARO,** b f Tinoco - Miss Shifter by Realm (J Ffitch-Heyes) 4815a^{3} 47

2 **SAVE THE WEST (Ire),** b f Bold Arrangement - Crystal Halo by St Chad (Patrick G Kelly) 3453^{7} 3527^{6} 3807 4134^{9}

3 **SAVINGS BANK,** b c Shernazar - Yen (Aus) by Biscay (Aus) (T D Barron) 434 652^{6} 4457 4666^{1} 4760^{6}

4 **SAVINIEN (Ire),** b g Cyrano de Bergerac - Golden Tears by Rheingold (P J Feilden) 4716a 4796a^{9} 147

3 **SAVOY TRUFFLE (Fr),** b f Law Society (USA) - Light Of Hope (USA) by Lyphard (USA) (H R A Cecil) 686^{3} 1383^{1} 2290^{4} 3036^{7} 4157^{5} 4502

3 **SAWASDEE (Fr),** b c Nikos - Tkisam by Olantengy (J P Pelat) 4753a^{1} 266^{2} 485^{3} 955^{3} 2531^{6} 2979^{4} 4219^{3}

2 **SAWDUST (Ire),** ch f Heraldiste (USA) - Persian Palm by Tamerlane (Edward Lynam) 2487^{6} 3073

2 **SAWLAJAN (USA),** ch c Woodman (USA) - Crafty Satin (USA) by Crimson Satan (J L Dunlop) 2299^{5} 2964^{3} 3570^{1} 4174^{9}

2 **SAWTID,** b f Chief Singer - Bourgeonette by Mummy's Pet (D Morris) 1615^{1} 1899^{1} 2629^{4} 2996 3597 4531^{7} 4725^{8}

3 **SAXON MAGIC,** ch f Faustus (USA) - Wessex Kingdom by Vaigly Great (J A Bennett) 414^{2} 707^{3} 951 2918^{3} 3301^{5} 3811 4088^{6} 4481

3 **SAXON SHORE (USA),** ch f Halo (USA) - Sweeping View (USA) by Reviewer (USA) (Lord Huntingdon) 204^{6} 248^{6}

7 **SAYMORE,** ch g Seymour Hicks (Fr) - Huahinee (Fr) by Riverman (USA) (R Hollinshead) 3193^{8}

6 **SAYSANA,** b m Sayf El Arab (USA) - Rosana Park by Music Boy (A Moore) 264 368^{5}

3 **SAY SUNPAK,** b f Sayf El Arab (USA) - Melindra by Gold Form (Mrs V A Aconley) 3095^{6} 3758

3 **SAYYEDATI,** b f Shadeed (USA) - Dubian by High Line (C E Brittain) 512^{3} 749^{1} 2905^{2} 3369^{1} 4173^{4} 4739

7 **SCALES OF JUSTICE,** br m Final Straw - Foiled Again by Bold Lad (Ire) (J W Hills) 4749a^{6} 4782a^{4} 20^{7}

3 **SCALP (Ire),** b g Thatching - Tribal Rite by Be My Native (USA) (V Kennedy) 1164 1445^{4} 1649^{4} 1922^{2} 2285^{4} 2674^{3} 3242^{6} 3808^{6} 4136^{4}

3 **SCALPEL (Ire),** b f Exactly Sharp (USA) - Vivi by Welsh Saint (D Thomas Sheridan) 3579 4118

5 **SCALP 'EM (Ire),** b g Commanche Run - Supremely Royal by Crowned Prince (USA) (P D Evans) 2871^{3} 3239^{2} 3412^{1} 4357

3 **SCANNO'S CHOICE (Ire),** br f Pennine Walk - Spring Snow by Reliance II (M Halford) 647^{2} 912 1139^{7}

2 **SCARLET DIVA,** ch f Soviet Star (USA) - Soprano by Kris (I A Balding) 1844^{5} 2571^{3} 3260^{4} 3940^{6}

5 **SCARLET PRINCESS,** b m Daring March - Noble Mistress by Lord Gayle (USA) (R J Hodges) 837 1096^{6} 1373^{5} 1977^{9} 2549^{3} 2723^{4} 4123

3 **SCARLET TUNIC (USA),** b c Blushing Groom (Fr) - Highclere by Queen's Hussar (Lord Huntingdon) 582^{7} 876 2071^{4} 2326^{1}

3 **SCATTERED STEPS (USA),** b g Fred Astaire (USA) - Cloud Castle (USA) by Graustark (USA) (R Reinacher) 4451^{2}

5 **SCENIC DANCER,** b g Shareef Dancer (USA) - Bridestones by Jan Ekels (A Hide) 500^{6} 879^{5} 1143 1781^{1} 2232^{2} 2347^{7} 2992^{3} 3430^{2} 3761^{9} 4028^{7} 4631

3 **SCENT JAR (Ire),** ch f Jareer (USA) - Sericana Run by Run The Gantlet (USA) (B V Kelly) 3524

4 **SENSE OF VALUE,** br f Trojan Fen - War Ballad (Fr) by Green Dancer (USA) (F Dunne) 912¹ 1013 2035⁷ 2484¹ 2842³ 3580³ 3684¹ 4288 4409
5 **SENSITIVE KING (Ire),** b g Tender King - Jumana by Windjammer (J C Harley) 706 1013 3483¹ 3580² 3853¹
3 **SENTIMENTALDIAMOND (USA),** 570⁷
3 **SENTIMENTAL MOI (USA),** 4451⁸
3 **SERANERA (Ire),** b f Doyoun - Hardi Hostess by Be My Guest (USA) (D T Hughes) 3975 4368⁸ 4429⁶ 4690
2 **SERAPHIC,** b f Slip Anchor - Cephira (Fr) by Abdos (H R A Cecil) 4595⁵
4 **SERAPHIM (Fr),** b f Lashkari - Sassika (Ger) by Arratos (Fr) (A Harrison) 3821⁹ 4023² 4321
3 **SEREN QUEST,** b f Rainbow Quest (USA) - Serenesse by Habat (R Akehurst) 482² 842 1911¹ 2333² 2907⁴ 4298⁷
3 **SERIOUS,** b g Shadeed (USA) - Azallya (Fr) by Habitat (M R Stoute) 658⁶ 4139⁴ 4545⁴ 4648⁵
4 **SERIOUS ACTION,** b g Slip Anchor - Silly Woman by Silly Season (R J O'Sullivan) 4733a 4764a 4807a 13 165³ 182¹ 210³ 3171⁴
5 **SERIOUS HURRY,** ch g Forzando - Lady Bequick by Sharpen Up (C C Elsey) 4672a³ 4752a² 4779a⁴ 4818a³ 86⁸ 99⁸ 170² 187¹ 236¹ 401⁴ 600⁸ 916¹ 1148⁸ 1352 1492 1728³ 2050⁹ 2305⁷ 3584 3739 4712⁹
2 **SERIOUS OPTION (Ire),** b c Reprimand - Top Bloom by Thatch (USA) (P F I Cole) 1063² 1296¹ 1565¹ 4520⁸ 4673⁴
6 **SERJITAK,** b m Saher - Parijatak by Pardao (P Mullins) 852³ 1508⁵ 1962⁸ 2498⁸ 2693⁹ 3277
3 **SEROTINA (Ire),** b f Mtoto - Northshiel by Northfields (USA) (W Jarvis) 732² 1285⁵ 1482³ 2697² 3185¹ 4018⁶ 4178⁵
5 **SERRANT (USA),** b g Bering - Saison by L'enjoleur (A Fabre) 562¹ 1291¹ 1694¹ 2771¹ 4071² 4744
2 **SE SOUVENIR (Fr),** b f Always Fair (USA) - Catherine Schratt by General Assembly (D Smaga) 3499²
2 **SESTRIERE (USA),** b f Sir Ivor - Havana Moon (USA) by Cox's Ridge (USA) (Sir Mark Prescott) 4726
4 **SET TABLE (USA),** gr g Caro - Room For The Sauce (USA) by Sauce Boat (USA) (J H M Gosden) 1830
4 **SET THE FASHION,** br g Green Desert (USA) - Prelude by Troy (Lord Huntingdon) 139² 261² 321³ 1007² 1434⁴ 1730¹ 1940³ 2475³ 2920¹ 3234¹ 3364⁴ 3460² 3780¹ 3910¹ 4650
2 **SE VENDE (Ire),** b g Maelstrom Lake - Giddy Lyn (USA) by Relko (J Berry) 708
2 **SEVEN UP CYD,** ch f Handsome Sailor - Bloffa by Derrylin (P D Cundell) 1253⁴ 1602 1905 3210⁷
3 **SEVERE STORM,** ch g Fort Nayef - Able Abbe by Absalom (Miss J L Rae) 611⁴ 860⁵ 1099⁶ 1630⁷ 1852⁸
4 **SEVERINE (USA),** b f Trempolino (USA) - Sharmila (Fr) by Blakeney (R Guest) 3394⁶
6 **SEXY MOVER,** ch g Coquelin (USA) - Princess Sinna by Sun Prince (W Storey) 2683⁷ 3599⁶ 3716⁹ 4023⁸
8 **SHABANAZ,** b g Imperial Fling (USA) - Claironcita by Don Carlos (W R Muir) 2236⁴ 2433⁶ 2884³ 3119⁴
6 **SHABRA CONNECTION,** b or br g New Express - Italian Connection by Communication (Patrick O Brady) 4411
4 **SHADANZA (Ire),** b g Shardari - Amanzi by African Sky (A P Stringer) 508⁷ 645 1930
5 **SHADES OF JADE,** gr m General Wade - Gellifawr by Saulingo (J J Bridger) 1352 1492 1860⁴ 2050⁶ 2671 2896⁵ 3081⁸ 3229 3420 3571⁹
3 **SHADOW JURY,** ch g Doulab (USA) - Texita by Young Generation (D W Chapman) 317⁸ 450⁵ 591⁵ 742⁴ 766¹ 1151³ 1157² 1226¹ 1518¹ 1848² 2132³ 3220 3947⁴ 3995⁶ 4317⁸ 4455⁸ 4734⁹
5 **SHADOWLAND (Ire),** ch g Be My Native (USA) - Sunland Park by Baragoi (M J Charles) 4751
3 **SHADOWPLAY (Fr),** b c Shareef Dancer (USA) - Sunset Dawn (USA) by Alleged (USA) (J R Fanshawe) 965⁵ 1176
5 **SHADOWS OF SILVER,** gr m Carwhite - Mimika by Lorenzaccio (B A McMahon) 1206² 1538⁵ 1770 2207² 3003³ 3353⁶ 3666²
3 **SHADY BANK (USA),** b f Alleged (USA) - Bank On Love (USA) by Gallant Romeo (USA) (R W Armstrong) 3980³
6 **SHAFFIC (Fr),** b g Auction Ring (USA) - Tavella (Fr) by Petingo (Mrs M Reveley) 1601⁴ 2043² 2467⁴ 4426⁴
3 **SHAHAADA (USA),** b f Private Account (USA) - Linda's Magic (USA) by Far North (Can) (R W Armstrong) 1212 1452³ 1931⁹ 4623⁹ 4727⁴
3 **SHAHIK (USA),** b c Spectacular Bid (USA) - Sham Street (USA) by Sham (USA) (Kevin Prendergast) 940³ 1201⁸ 2074⁸ 2247³ 2606
2 **SHAHNAAD (Ire),** ch g Neshad (USA) - Flower Dell by Wolver Hollow (Noel T Chance) 4059
9 **SHAHNIZAM (USA),** b g Youth (USA) - Shahneez by St Paddy (B R Cambidge) 294 396 1419
3 **SHAHZADI (Ire),** ch c Pharly (Fr) - Shahdiza (USA) by Blushing Groom (Fr) (John M Oxx) 306¹ 668⁹ 808³ 1046³ 1553²
3 **SHAIBA (USA),** ch c Alysheba (USA) - Stage Luck (USA) by Stage Door Johnny (M R Stoute) 775⁴ 1001³ 1751⁸ 3318⁴ 3620¹
3 **SHAIKALA (Ire),** b f Doyoun - Shaiyra by Relko (John M Oxx) 258⁴ 787⁷ 1199 2040⁹
3 **SHAIYBARA (Ire),** gr f Kahyasi - Shamiyda (USA) by Sir Ivor (John M Oxx) 1507¹ 2408¹ 2744¹ 3718³ 4296¹ 4569⁷
4 **SHAKANDA (Ire),** b f Shernazar - Safiah (Fr) by St Paddy (John M Oxx) 4685a⁷
5 **SHAKE TOWN (USA),** b g Caro - All Dance (USA) by Northern Dancer (J Mackie) 4343⁹ 4488⁴ 4721
4 **SHAKINSKI,** gr f Niniski (USA) - Shakana by Grundy (M J Ryan) 4776a³ 4813a⁶ 53³ 81⁵
4 **SHALABIA,** ch f Fast Topaze (USA) - Mangala (USA) by Sharpen Up (C Parker) 650⁶ 906² 1285⁹ 1736⁴ 1969¹ 2656⁵ 3057⁸
3 **SHALAKO,** b g Nomination - Straffan Girl by Sallust (K W Hogg) 1327⁷ 1416 1464⁹ 2481⁵ 2510⁷ 2634⁹
2 **SHALBOURNE (USA),** ch f Nureyev (USA) - Copperama (Aus) by Comeram (Fr) (P W Chapple-Hyam) 1403⁷ 1632⁴ 3230⁴ 4503¹
3 **SHALHOLME,** ch f Fools Holme (USA) - Shalati (Fr) by High Line (P G Murphy) 921 1377⁴ 1745⁵ 1991⁷ 2384 2833¹ 3232⁶ 3734⁴ 4354
2 **SHALLOP,** b f Salse (USA) - Boathouse by Habitat (Major W R Hern) 4692⁹
4 **SHALOU,** b c Forzando - Axe Valley by Royben (R J Hodges) 327² 440⁵ 754 1487⁷ 1696⁹ 2109² 2291⁶ 2747 3007³ 3228 3938
3 **SHAMAM (USA),** ch c Shadeed (USA) - Goodbye Shelley (Fr) by Home Guard (USA) (P T Walwyn) 400² 772¹ 1016 1524³ 2361² 2926 4132⁵
2 **SHAMARDAL (Ire),** b c Taufan (USA) - Red Line Fever by Bay Express (B Hanbury) 3633
6 **SHAMBO,** b h Lafontaine (USA) - Lucky Appeal by Star Appeal (C E Brittain) 314¹ 579⁶ 892¹ 1018⁴ 3349⁵ 4301⁴ 4560⁴ 4730³
3 **SHAMGAAN (USA),** b or br c Nureyev (USA) - Fine Spirit (USA) by Secretariat (USA) (B Hanbury) 463⁵ 630⁴ 1204 2099⁸ 3631³ 3991⁸
2 **SHAMINA,** b f Governor General - Alzamina by Alzao (USA) (J White) 1741
3 **SHAMISEN,** ch f Diesis - Contralto by Busted (C E Brittain) 556⁵ 856⁶ 1231⁸ 2732⁴ 2961
3 **SHAMROCK DANCER (Ire),** b f Dance Of Life (USA) - Practical by Ballymore (R J Baker) 1705³ 2057 2471 4751⁸
5 **SHAMSHOM AL ARAB (Ire),** gr h Glenstal (USA) - Love Locket by Levmoss (S G Norton) 745¹ 904¹ 1056¹ 1190⁴ 1521² 1781⁵ 3116⁴ 3373⁸ 4432
3 **SHAMSIYA (USA),** b f The Minstrel (Can) - Sharaniya by Alleged (USA) (A de Royer-Dupre) 2409⁸ 3195⁴ 4169³ 4413³
6 **SHANAKEE,** b g Wassl - Sheeog by Reform (K S Bridgwater) 4699a 4705a⁹
3 **SHANDON LAKE (Ire),** b or br c Darshaan - Lake Mist by Kings Lake (USA) (J S Bolger) 576¹ 955⁴ 1544⁹
3 **SHANGANOIR (Ire),** br f Prince Rupert (Fr) - All Pink by Hello Gorgeous (USA) (Noel Meade) 3417⁹ 3808⁵ 3999³

4 **SHANGHAI (USA),** b c Procida (USA) - Korveya (USA) by Riverman (USA) (F Boutin) 430² 920² 1366³ 1723² 2055³
4 **SHANGOL DE PERSE (Fr),** 1908⁹
2 **SHANKAR (Ire),** gr c Shareef Dancer (USA) - Sibelle D'Oa (Fr) by Kenmare (Fr) (Michael Kauntze) 3159⁴ 3416³ 3922⁵ 4707⁴
6 **SHANKORAK,** b g Darshaan - Shanjarina (USA) by Blushing Groom (Fr) (Francis Berry) 281⁵ 1468¹ 2841¹ 3560⁷ 4095⁵
2 **SHANNARA (Ire),** b f Treasure Kay - Elegant Owl by Tumble Wind (USA) (M W Ellerby) 968⁹ 3183⁹
6 **SHANNON EXPRESS,** gr g Magic Mirror - Tatisha by Habitat (E J Alston) 4705a 4786a⁶ 13 27⁴ 205⁶ 340¹ 592⁷ 902⁴ 1284 2283¹ 2799⁹ 3310 3535 3812 4104 4424 4658⁴
6 **SHANTALLA BAY,** b m Pollerton - Break The Bank by Gala Performance (USA) (T F Lacy) 4685a⁴ 807³
3 **SHARAAR (USA),** ch c Bering - Trasimeno by Kings Lake (USA) (W J Haggas) 529⁵ 825⁵ 991² 1349¹ 1808 2118³ 3146¹ 3585
2 **SHARADA,** b f Shareef Dancer (USA) - Casa Rosada by Known Fact (USA) (N A Graham) 4032
4 **SHARASTAMINA (USA),** b f Shahrastani (USA) - Naxos (USA) by Big Spruce (USA) (John J McLoughlin) 942⁴ 1202⁸ 1514⁴ 1794⁶ 2186⁷ 3773² 4147 4288 4409³ 4555 4639² 4735²
2 **SHARE A DREAM (Ire),** b f Bluebird (USA) - Verette by Posse (USA) (J C Harley) 896⁹ 1432¹ 3607⁵
3 **SHARE A MOMENT (Can),** b g Timeless Moment (USA) - Silver Slippers (USA) by Silver Series (USA) (R Hollinshead) 679 1055² 1259⁴ 1479⁵ 1942³ 2443² 2529⁶ 3138² 3240 3840⁸ 4048⁴
5 **SHARED INTEREST (USA),** b m Pleasant Colony (USA) - Surgery (USA) by Dr Fager (USA) (F S Schulhofer) 1184² 2802³ 4079¹ 4450²
4 **SHAREEF ALLIANCE (Ire),** b g Shareef Dancer (USA) - In The Clover by Meadow Mint (USA) (Michael Hourigan) 851³ 1467⁴
3 **SHAREEK (USA),** b c Alysheba (USA) - All Rainbows (USA) by Bold Hour (M R Stoute) 679¹ 947³ 1448 2883² 3403⁴ 3899⁴
3 **SHARJAH (USA),** b c Nijinsky (Can) - Office Wife (USA) by Secretariat (USA) (M A Jarvis) 494⁴ 985⁴ 2066⁸ 2333⁴ 2997³ 3314³ 3636¹ 4300
3 **SHARKASHKA (Ire),** ch f Shardari - Kashka (USA) by The Minstrel (Can) (John M Oxx) 2609⁴ 2781¹ 3197⁴ 3578¹ 3915 4461 4555
3 **SHARMAN (USA),** b c Blushing Groom (Fr) - Sonic Lady (USA) by Nureyev (USA) (A Fabre) 656² 1546¹ 2081⁷ 3618²
2 **SHARONE,** ch f Sharrood (USA) - Ward One by Mr Fluorocarbon (M J Camacho) 2429 2875⁶ 3627 3968⁷ 4122⁶ 4646⁸
3 **SHARP AT SIX (Ire),** ch g Sure Blade (USA) - Sixpenny by English Prince (D K Weld) 1652⁶ 2221⁶ 2516⁸ 3381⁵
4 **SHARP COUNSEL (Fr),** b c Leading Counsel (USA) - Dosha by Sharpman (E Lellouche) 461¹ 726¹ 1124⁴ 1888⁷
4 **SHARP DANCE,** b f Dance Of Life (USA) - Sharp Jose (USA) by Sharpen Up (B Smart) 4667a⁵ 4723a⁸ 102² 126⁸
3 **SHARPELA,** 105³ 3647⁴ 4219⁶ 4557⁸
2 **SHARPENING,** ch f Sharpo - False Lift by Grundy (Lord Huntingdon) 4264¹ 4511⁶
2 **SHARP FALCON (Ire),** gr f Shaadi (USA) - Honey Buzzard by Sea Hawk II (J Wharton) 3779⁸ 4098⁷ 4349² 4516⁴ 4674⁴
3 **SHARP GAZELLE,** ch f Beveled (USA) - Shadha by Shirley Heights (B Smart) 223⁸ 405⁷ 917⁹ 1377⁸ 2164⁶ 2724⁷ 3046¹ 3547¹ 4231
3 **SHARP GEM,** br f Elegant Air - Brightelmstone by Prince Regent (Fr) (B Smart) 3693 4524
3 **SHARP IMP,** b g Sharpo - Implore by Ile de Bourbon (USA) (R M Flower) 518⁵ 721 1240⁵ 1913⁶ 2384 3233⁴
6 **SHARP INVITE,** ch m Sharpo - Invitation by Faberge II (W P Mullins) 298² 1013¹ 1508³ 4657⁷
2 **SHARPISH WORDS,** b g Reprimand - Tabeeba by Diesis (W W Haigh) 395 1759⁷ 1964⁵ 2229⁷ 2705⁶ 4122 4671⁶
5 **SHARP ISSUE (USA),** ch g Diesis - Concentrate (USA) by Broadway Forli (USA) (M C Chapman) 4812a
2 **SHARP PHASE (Ire),** ch c Sharp Victor (USA) - Faye by Monsanto (Fr) (Liam Browne) 571⁷ 786¹ 1750⁴ 2605⁴
3 **SHARP PROD (USA),** ch c Sharpo - Gentle Persuasion by Bustino (Lord Huntingdon) 580² 3196⁴ 3777⁶ 4076¹ 4401¹
3 **SHARP PROSPECT,** ch c Sharpo - Sabatina (USA) by Verbatim (USA) (P W Harris) 624 1162¹ 1614⁴ 2237⁶ 4024⁵ 4415 4693⁸
2 **SHARP REBUFF,** b c Reprimand - Kukri by Kris (P J Makin) 4440 4588⁵
5 **SHARP REVIEW (Ire),** b g Sharpen Up - Pleasant Review (USA) by The Minstrel (Can) (D K Weld) 1199³ 4245² 4384³ 4554⁵
3 **SHARP SENSATION,** ch g Crofthall - Pink Sensation by Sagaro (M D Hammond) 3096⁷ 3407⁴
3 **SHARP SILK,** b f Sharpo - Temple Row by Ardross (H Candy) 732
2 **SHARP SPRING,** ch g Beveled (USA) - Sea Farer Lake by Gairloch (J White) 2316⁷ 3103⁵
2 **SHARP SUMMIT (Ire),** b f Exactly Sharp (USA) - Yashville by Top Ville (B S Rothwell) 1082 1499⁶ 1672⁴ 3505⁹ 3557⁷ 4032
7 **SHARP THISTLE,** b m Sharpo - Marphousha (Fr) by Shirley Heights (W J Musson) 4784a⁴ 30⁵ 114⁴ 198
2 **SHARP THRILL,** ch c Squill (USA) - Brightelmstone by Prince Regent (Fr) (B Smart) 1640 4489 4714³
4 **SHARPTINO,** ch c Bustino - Sharper Still by Sharpen Up (S Dow) 4781a⁷ 1352 1527 2329⁸
5 **SHARP TOP,** b m Sharpo - Two High by High Top (M J Ryan) 4760a⁹ 2501⁶ 2713³
2 **SHARP TRY (Ire),** ch c Sharp Victor (USA) - Aspire by Nebbiolo (Liam Browne) 4244⁵ 4382⁸ 4688¹
2 **SHARP TYCOON (Ire),** ch c Exactly Sharp (USA) - Typhoon Polly by Lord Gayle (USA) (B J Meehan) 1666³ 1949⁷ 2274⁴ 2988⁴ 3597² 3865⁹ 4230⁴ 4444⁹
6 **SHARQUIN,** b h Indian King (USA) - Lady Of The Land by Wollow (M Brittain) 198⁹ 366² 396² 931⁷ 1414¹ 1460⁶ 1566⁵ 2354² 2444³ 2591⁶ 3630³ 3714⁸ 4043⁹ 4086⁷ 4319
3 **SHARRO,** gr g Sharrood (USA) - Sarah Gillian (USA) by Zen (USA) (P A Kelleway) 4665a⁵ 4717a 1733⁴ 2613⁷ 3108⁵ 4631
5 **SHAURNI GIRL,** ch m Precocious - Crockfords Green by Roan Rocket (R Harris) 2195⁸
3 **SHAWGATNY (USA),** ch f Danzig Connection (USA) - Star Empress (USA) by Disciplinarian (J S Bolger) 1609³ 3037² 3197² 3578² 3773⁴
2 **SHAWN CUDDY,** ch c Hubbly Bubbly (USA) - Quick Kick by Saritamer (USA) (J L Harris) 3833 3974⁸ 4223⁶
8 **SHAYISTA,** b m Tap On Wood - Shayina by Run The Gantlet (USA) (Ronald O'Neill) 1467⁸ 1756³ 1986² 2693⁸ 2841⁷ 3276⁶
2 **SHAYNES DOMAIN,** b c Dominion - Glen Na Smole by Ballymore (J Sutcliffe) 3387 4330⁵ 4440
4 **SHEBA DANCER (Fr),** b f Fabulous Dancer (USA) - Elisheba by Nonoalco (E Lellouche) 283⁸ 693⁶
6 **SHEBA'S PAL,** b m Claude Monet (USA) - Bread 'n Honey by Goldhills Pride (P Delaney) 3242⁸ 3296 3614
2 **SHEEN FALLS (Ire),** b f Prince Rupert (Fr) - Ishtar Abu by St Chad (D K Weld) 1994³ 2344⁵ 3243
3 **SHEER ECSTASY,** b g Sure Blade (USA) - Height Of Passion by Shirley Heights (P M McEntee) 724 1353
3 **SHEER OPULANCE (Ire),** b c Shernazar - Speciality Package (USA) by Blushing Groom (Fr) (D K Weld) 1441⁴ 2185³ 2903³ 4162⁸
4 **SHEER POWER (Ire),** b g Exhibitioner - Quality Blake by Blakeney (R Rowe) 1146
2 **SHEER STYLE (Ire),** ch f Jareer (USA) - Shirotae by Florescence (Noel Meade) 3071⁶ 3807⁹ 4000 4406
3 **SHEFFORD,** b f Jupiter Island - Channing Girl by Song (M D I Usher) 583⁹ 752 1313³ 1628⁵ 1771⁸ 4115 4525 4574
6 **SHEIKH DANCER,** b h Shareef Dancer (USA) - Viole D'Amour by Luthier 283⁵
3 **SHEILA'S SECRET (Ire),** b f Bluebird (USA) - Exemplary by Sovereign Lord (T G Mills) 542⁸ 729⁴ 1214⁵ 1415² 2028² 2303² 2971² 3291³ 4275⁷

2 **SHREWD ALIBI**, gr g Sharrood (USA) - Alsiba by Northfields (USA) (I A Balding) 3658[9]
3 **SHREWD IDEA**, b c Alleged (USA) - Domludge (USA) by Lyphard (USA) (Michael Kauntze) 668[3] 843[2] 1369[3] 2076[6] 2839[1] 3370[3] 4055[7] 4381[4]
4 **SHREWD MOVE**, b g Majestic Light (USA) - Detecting (USA) by Seattle Slew (USA) (E McNamara) 3328[9]
3 **SHROPSHIRE BLUE**, gr f Risk Me (Fr) - Six Ashes by Bruni (B W Hills) 2670 2858
4 **SHUAILAAN (USA)**, ch c Roberto (USA) - Lassie's Lady (USA) by Alydar (USA) (A C Stewart) 525[8] 774[4] 1065[2] 1538[3] 2654[5]
7 **SHUIL AR AGHAIDH**, b m The Parson - Shuil Eile by Deep Run (P Kiely) 553[5]
4 **SHUJAN (USA)**, b c Diesis - Linda's Magic (USA) by Far North (Can) (R Akehurst) 241[4] 274[4] 315 456 618[7] 1075[1] 1276[2] 1676[2] 1840[4] 2427[1] 2530[1] 2713[1] 3152[6] 3666[9] 4283 4538[1]
2 **SHUTTLECOCK**, ch g Pharly (Fr) - Upper Sister by Upper Case (USA) (P C Haslam) 395[8] 998[5] 1051[2] 2331 2952[2] 3189[3] 3696[4] 3968 4081[1] 4418
2 **SHUTTLINGSLOW**, b f Celestial Storm (USA) - Sharanella by Shareef Dancer (USA) (M Bell) 4349[6] 4489[5]
5 **SHY GAL (Ire)**, b m Shy Groom (USA) - Sandfords Gal by Sandford Lad (Oliver Finnegan) 911[9] 1797[4] 1987[7] 2484[6] 4387[6]
3 **SHYNON**, gr g Nishapour (Fr) - Sunset Ray by Hotfoot (M H Tompkins) 502[2] 652[1] 910[2] 1180[1] 1495[1] 2963[4]
3 **SHY TEACHER (Ire)**, b f Shy Groom (USA) - Atlantic Passage (USA) by Buckfinder (USA) (Owen Weldon) 2843[5] 3417 4407[9]
3 **SHY WIN (Ire)**, ch f Shy Groom (USA) - Winning Feature by Red Alert (J C Hayden) 311 550 789
3 **SIAM (USA)**, b c Nureyev (USA) - Pasadoble (USA) by Prove Out (USA) (F Boutin) 2081[3] 2531[3] 3369[6]
4 **SIANISKI**, b f Niniski (USA) - Pagan Queen by Vaguely Noble (N A Graham) 3173 3449[8]
3 **SIAN WYN**, ch f Hotfoot - Curzon House by Green God (K R Burke) 1993[7] 2358[9] 2859[9]
2 **SIBELIAN SOUND**, b c Kahyasi - Samata (Fr) by Rheffic (Fr) (G Wragg) 4419
5 **SIBERIAN BREEZE**, gr g Siberian Express (USA) - Zepha by Great Nephew (J A Glover) 731
4 **SIBERIAN SUMMER (USA)**, gr c Siberian Express (USA) - Mia Karina by Icecapade (R McAnally) 146[1] 4438[7]
3 **SICILY OAK**, b f Ballacashtal (Can) - Martyrdom (USA) by Exceller (USA) (D McCain) 2504[5] 3032 3780
6 **SICUTERAT**, b f Sadler's Wells (USA) - Smeralda by Dschingis Khan (G Botti) 4475[4]
5 **SIDDHARTA (USA)**, b m Chief's Crown (USA) - Do Designs by Vaguely Noble (G Verricelli) 3934[7]
3 **SIDE BAR**, b g Mummy's Game - Joli's Girl by Mansingh (USA) (M J Ryan) 880 1936[4] 2850[5] 3049[1] 3556[3] 4102 4321
5 **SIDE OUT FRONT (USA)**, 560[8]
5 **SIDE WINGER (USA)**, b g Topsider (USA) - Fancy Wings (USA) by Wing Out (USA) (T Stack) 3936[8]
4 **SIE AMATO (Ire)**, ch g Soughaan (USA) - Wolviston by Wolverlife (Capt J Wilson) 251[6] 498 645 964 2057 2525[1] 2920[4] 3325 3840 4043 4658 4760[3]
3 **SIENNA SOUND (Ire)**, ch f Carmelite House (USA) - Sweet Chimes by Orchestra (J G Coogan) 789[6] 1046 1252[6]
2 **SIERRA MADRE (Fr)**, ro f Baillamont (USA) - Marie D'Irlande by Kalamoun (P Bary) 3977[3] 4310[1]
3 **SIESTA TIME (USA)**, ch f Cure The Blues (USA) - Villa Rose (USA) by Key To The Mint (USA) (P Aspell) 4690
7 **SIGAMA (USA)**, ch g Stop The Music (USA) - Lady Speedwell (USA) by Secretariat (USA) (F H Lee) 292 1449[4] 1679 2018 2392 2846[4] 3238[5] 3709[2] 3995 4712[6]
2 **SIGANCA**, br f Dowsing (USA) - Gipping by Vision (USA) (M Bell) 1169[1] 2845[9] 3539[7] 4358
4 **SIGHTSEER (Ire)**, b f Vision (USA) - Grand Duchy by Prince Tenderfoot (USA) (D G McArdle) 598 911[6] 1163[9] 1569 2041[8] 2297[6] 2345[8] 2514[7]
2 **SIGNE DIVIN (USA)**, b c Bering - Lumen Dei by Raise A Native (A Fabre) 3338[1] 4293[2]
4 **SIGNORE DE ANGLES**, b g Sizzling Melody - Lady Lorelei by Derring-Do (J M Bradley) 3893
6 **SIGNORETTO (Fr)**, b h Milles Balles - Sardagnola by Bon Mot (E Castela) 4325[3] 4517[3]
5 **SIGNOR SASSIE (USA)**, ch h The Minstrel (Can) - Sahsie (USA) by Forli (Arg) (N Tinkler) 53[5] 1400[9]
4 **SILCA-CISA**, ch f Hallgate - Princess Silca Key by Grundy (M R Channon) 316[2] 511[7] 2399[5]
2 **SILENCE IN COURT (Ire)**, b c Law Society (USA) - Fair Flutter by Beldale Flutter (USA) (B A McMahon) 3876[9] 4377[4] 4620[6]
3 **SILENT EXPRESSION**, gr f Siberian Express (USA) - Silent Sun by Blakeney (D Morris) 963[3] 1175[2] 1416[2] 1628[1] 1829[1] 3736[1] 3983[6] 4297
12 **SILENT JET**, b or br g Mugatpura - Chilita by Tarqogan (M Dunne) 2094[3]
3 **SILENT PRINCE**, b c Prince Sabo - Queensbury Star by Wishing Star (Miss B Sanders) 4805a 32[6]
6 **SILICON BAVARIA (Fr)**, br m Procida (USA) - Siliciana by Silly Season (USA) (R Collett) 345[2] 595
7 **SILK DYNASTY**, b g Prince Tenderfoot (USA) - Mountain Chase by Mount Hagen (Fr) (J Carden) 67[6]
4 **SILKEN WORDS (USA)**, b f Alleged (USA) - Tie A Bow (USA) by Dance Spell (USA) (W R Muir) 4671a[2]
3 **SILK ISLAND**, ch c Ela-Mana-Mou - Silky (USA) by Nijinsky (Can) (J H M Gosden) 3012 3225[9] 3506[4] 3734
3 **SILKY FEATHER (USA)**, b or br f Personal Flag (USA) - Fleur de Soie (USA) by Graustasrk (USA) (R Violette) 935[4] 2440[3] 3767[2]
3 **SILKY HEIGHTS (Ire)**, b f Head For Heights - Silk Trade by Auction Ring (USA) (M J Camacho) 493[8] 1836[1] 2207[4] 2899[4] 3320[1]
2 **SILKY MAGNA**, b f Farajullah - Bella Magna by Mister Flurocarbon (D R Laing) 4497 4679
4 **SILKY SIREN**, b f Formidable (USA) - Smooth Siren (USA) by Sea Bird II (M C Pipe) 190[1] 227[2] 327[1] 458[3] 893[3] 1097[5] 1527[1] 1734[1] 2172[2] 2577[9] 2966[3] 3531[2] 3957[8] 4514
5 **SILLARS STALKER (Ire)**, b g Stalker - Mittens by Run The Gantlet (USA) (Mrs J R Ramsden) 303[6] 427 702[5] 4357[9] 4494[1] 4732
7 **SILLY HABIT (USA)**, b m Assert - Habitassa by Habitat (H J Collingridge) 4670a 4742a 4797a[9] 2658
2 **SILVER BRIEF**, gr g Sulaafah (USA) - Briefing by Rusticaro (Fr) (R J Hodges) 1091 1959 2610[5]
3 **SILVERDALE (USA)**, ch g Silver Hawk (USA) - Norene's Nemesis (Can) by King Emperor (USA) (J H M Gosden) 515[2] 842[3] 1176[1] 1539[2] 1769[2] 2082[4] 2360[5] 3405[2] 3899[7]
6 **SILVERDALE FOX**, ch g Sweet Monday - Its My Turn by Palm Track (K W Hogg) 4454[9]
7 **SILVER GIPSEY**, gr m Belfalas - Silver Doll by Sovereign Gleam (M J Grassick) 309
3 **SILVER GROOM (Ire)**, gr g Shy Groom (USA) - Rustic Lawn by Rusticaro (Fr) (A P Jarvis) 335[3] 503[8] 1312[5] 1487[2] 1661[4] 2358[1] 2489[2] 2882[6] 3101[3] 3476 3783 3981[1] 4258[2] 4391 4633[2] 4727
2 **SILVER HUNTER (USA)**, b c Silver Hawk (USA) - Martha Queen (USA) by Nijinsky (Can) (P F I Cole) 4252[7] 4595[4]
2 **SILVER HUT (USA)**, ch f Silver Hawk (USA) - Ice House by Northfields (USA) (R Charlton) 4002[2] 4396[1] 4558[6]
2 **SILVERISTE (Ire)**, gr c Heraldiste (USA) - God's Kiss by Godswalk (USA) (C A Smith) 1317 1555 2176[6] 3940 4223
3 **SILVER JAR (Ire)**, gr f Jareer (USA) - Galerida by Silver Shark (P Mullins) 2140 2497[6] 2843[3] 3111[4] 3294 3417
3 **SILVERLOCKS**, gr f Sharrood (USA) - Philgwyn by Milford (Miss S E Hall) 643[6] 1016[8] 1780[3] 2279[1] 2478[1] 2789[5] 3036[1] 3674[4] 4018[4] 4274[5]
3 **SILVER MAPLE (USA)**, b f Silver Hawk (USA) - Dead Letter (USA) by Kirtling (J H M Gosden) 4126[3] 4372[1]
4 **SILVERNESIAN (USA)**, b or br c Alleged (USA) - Loot (USA) by Boldnesian (J L Dunlop) 774[8] 1405[8] 1787[9] 3405[9] 3718[5] 4477[6]
3 **SILVER OF SILVER (USA)**, 779[8] 1542[4]
4 **SILVER SAMURAI**, b c Alleging (USA) - Be My Lady by Be My Guest (USA) (Mrs V A Aconley) 4689a[2]

2 **SOUTH EASTERN FRED,** b c Primo Dominie - Soheir by Track Spare (H J Collingridge) 2968 3836 4723^{7}

6 **SOUTHERN DANCER,** b h Gerald Martin - Petona by Mummy's Pet (O Kandur) 2830^{1}

3 **SOUTHERN MEMORIES (Ire),** b g Don't Forget Me - Our Pet by Mummy's Pet (R Hannon) 846^{7} 977^{1} 1337^{3} 1718^{8} 2237^{4} 2431^{5} 3080^{8} 3404 4693

2 **SOUTHERN POWER (Ire),** b c Midyan (USA) - Tap The Line by Tap On Wood (R Hannon) 2299^{3} 2756^{2} 3352^{4} 3876^{5} 4503^{2} 4677^{1}

3 **SOUTHERN REVIEW (Ire),** ch g Magical Wonder (USA) - Showing Style by Pas de Seul (Kevin Prendergast) 2185^{8} 2497^{4} 2700^{2} 3161^{8} 3395^{7} 3606^{9} 4685^{1}

2 **SOUTHERN RIDGE,** b c Indian Ridge - Southern Sky by Comedy Star (USA) (D R C Elsworth) 1640^{6} 2137^{7} 3589^{7} 4067^{1} 4281^{9}

6 **SOUTHERN RULE,** b g Law Society (USA) - Isobelline (USA) by Pronto (Malachy McKenna) 281 599^{5} 868^{1} 1293 1923^{8} 2323^{3} 2511^{5} 2879^{8} 3330^{9} 3614^{9} 4184^{8} 4389^{4}

5 **SOUTHERN TRUCE (USA),** 560^{7} 2645^{6}

4 **SOVEREIGN GRACE (Ire),** gr f Standaan (Fr) - Gay Nocturne by Lord Gayle (USA) (J G Burns) 1023^{7} 2187^{2} 2927^{9} 3912^{9}

2 **SOVEREIGN KITTY (USA),** 4070^{3} 4449^{4}

5 **SOVEREIGN NICHE (Ire),** gr g Nishapour (Fr) - Sovereign Flash (Fr) by Busted (M C Pipe) 4705a^{7} 42^{7}

4 **SOVEREIGN PAGE (USA),** ch g Caro - Tashinsky (USA) by Nijinsky (Can) (B Hanbury) 527 845^{3} 1260^{6} 1612^{1} 1783^{1} 1800^{1} 2198^{3} 2722^{4} 3211^{3} 3507^{2} 4247^{5}

2 **SOVETSKY,** ch c Soviet Star (USA) - Helen Street by Troy (A Fabre) 4196^{2}

3 **SOVIET CHOICE (Ire),** b f Soviet Star (USA) - Miracle Drug (USA) by Seattle Slew (USA) (D K Weld) 2036^{1} 2702^{2} 3038^{2} 4147^{2} 4383^{9}

3 **SOVIET EXPRESS,** br c Siberian Express (USA) - Our Shirley by Shirley Heights (P F I Cole) 370^{5} 836^{5} 1356^{1} 1686^{8} 2182^{8} 3783^{9} 4495^{5} 4580

3 **SOVIET LINE (Ire),** b g Soviet Star (USA) - Shore Line by High Line (M R Stoute) 459^{1} 755^{1} 1329^{3} 4063^{6} 4282^{4} 4441^{3}

2 **SOVINISTA,** b f Soviet Star (USA) - Princess Genista by Ile de Bourbon (USA) (G A Pritchard-Gordon) 3352

2 **SOZZLED,** gr c Absalom - The High Dancer by High Line (B W Hills) 2792^{7}

2 **SPACE-PERIL (Ire),** b f Astronef - Farriers Slipper by Prince Tenderfoot (USA) (M H Tompkins) 4528

2 **SPAGHETTI WESTERN (Ire),** ch c Chilibang - Presentable by Sharpen Up (J L Dunlop) 1221^{5} 1543^{1} 2257^{1} 3798^{1} 4314^{4}

2 **SPAIN LANE (USA),** b f Seeking The Gold (USA) - Regent's Walk (Can) by Vice Regent (Can) (A Fabre) 3515^{3} 3925^{2}

5 **SPANIARDS CLOSE,** b g King Of Spain - Avon Belle by Balidar (P J Makin) 795^{9} 1011^{4} 1406^{7} 1551^{5} 4025^{7} 4151^{7} 4465 4521

2 **SPANISH DAWN,** b f Aragon - Shaft Of Sunlight by Sparkler (C R Egerton) 3816 4210 4588

7 **SPANISH LOVE,** b or br m Precocious - San Marguerite by Blakeney (Mrs S D Williams) 1623 1954 2548^{2} 2940 4518^{5} 4640^{8}

4 **SPANISH PERFORMER,** br f King Of Spain - Dauphiness by Supreme Sovereign (M J Camacho) 3747 4045^{9} 4187

3 **SPANISH REFUGE,** b g King Of Spain - Base Camp by Derring-Do (Lord Huntingdon) 57^{2} 209^{2} 237^{3} 415^{4} 2669^{6} 3078^{6} 3412^{4}

3 **SPANISH SAHARA (Ire),** b c Sadler's Wells (USA) - Melody (USA) by Lord Gayle (USA) (P W Chapple-Hyam) 1068 3937^{6} 4212^{9}

4 **SPANISH STORM (Ire),** b g King Of Spain - Storm Crest by Lord Gayle (USA) (S P C Woods) 316 1412^{4} 1768 2194^{3} 2363 3008^{2} 3268^{4} 3748^{4} 4066^{4} 4132^{4} 4648^{8}

2 **SPANISH STRIPPER (USA),** b c El Gran Senor (USA) - Gourmet Dinner (USA) by Raise A Cup (USA) (J A R Toller) 3698^{5}

6 **SPANISH VERDICT,** b g King Of Spain - Counsel's Verdict by Firestreak (Denys Smith) 302 651^{9} 801^{3} 1434^{3} 1591^{4} 1940^{4} 2308^{1} 2567^{5} 2811^{1} 3058^{2} 3358 3553^{4} 3747^{7} 4019^{6} 4166^{8} 4424 4605^{7} 4702^{4}

6 **SPANISH WHISPER,** b g Aragon - Whisper Gently by Pitskelly (J R Bostock) 4776a^{9} 1873^{6} 2585^{6}

3 **SPARK (Ire),** ch f Flash Of Steel - Sperrin Mist by Camden Town (C W C Elsey) 999^{4} 1338^{6} 1780^{8} 2304^{4} 2657^{9} 3474^{5} 3637 4018 4464

7 **SPARKLER GEBE,** b g Be My Native (USA) - Siliferous by Sandy Creek (R J O'Sullivan) 3548^{8}

2 **SPARKLING LYRIC,** b f Damister (USA) - Tantalizing Song (Can) by The Minstrel (Can) (M A Jarvis) 3633^{8} 3895^{3} 4220^{1} 4558

2 **SPARKLING ROBERTA,** b f Kind Of Hush - Hitesca by Tesco Boy (M D I Usher) 2571 2836^{6} 4002^{4} 4251

3 **SPARKY'S GIRL,** ch f Doulab (USA) - Romantic Overture (USA) by Stop The Music (USA) (R J Baker) 4499

3 **SPARKY'S SONG,** b or br f Electric - Daring Ditty by Daring March (J W Hills) 724 980 1126^{2} 1266^{7} 1993^{1} 2523^{6} 2914^{2} 3246^{5} 3669^{5} 4028 4279^{8} 4544

4 **SPARTAN SHAREEF (Ire),** b c Shareef Dancer (USA) - Spartan Helen by Troy (C E Brittain) 1748^{9} 1952^{1} 2650^{1} 3402^{3} 3784^{1} 4073^{6}

4 **SPEAKER'S HOUSE (USA),** b c Lear Fan (USA) - Bring Me Flowers (Fr) by Dancer's Image (USA) (P F I Cole) 4100^{6} 4499 4730^{6}

5 **SPECIAL CORNER (Ire),** b g Millfontaine - Ellette by Le Levanstell (D T Hughes) 2665^{8}

3 **SPECIAL DAWN (Ire),** ch g Be My Guest (USA) - Dawn Star by High Line (J L Dunlop) 459 602^{8} 1080^{1} 1488^{3} 3850^{5} 4129^{5} 4486

3 **SPECIAL OFFER (Ire),** b f Shy Groom (USA) - Big Bugs Bomb by Skymaster (F Dunne) 790 870^{4} 1441^{3} 1822 2035 3684

3 **SPECIAL ONE,** b f Aragon - Special Guest by Be My Guest (USA) (J W Hills) 683^{8} 977^{2} 1213^{5} 1718 2522^{6} 2832^{5}

3 **SPECIAL PAGEANT (Ire),** br f Ahonoora - Special Display by Welsh Pageant (J S Bolger) 282^{1} 576^{4} 668^{2} 1024^{6} 1198^{6} 2038^{4} 2405^{7} 2789^{2} 3029^{2} 3199^{5}

6 **SPECIAL POWER (Ire),** b h Lyphard's Special (USA) - Angevin by English Prince (L D'Auria) 1365^{4}

3 **SPECIAL RISK (Ire),** br g Simply Great (Fr) - Ahonita by Ahonoora (R Akehurst) 1^{3} 29^{2} 57^{4} 129 1540^{7} 2130^{8} 2411 2859^{4} 3249^{5}

5 **SPECIAL SECRET (Ire),** b g Lyphard's Special (USA) - Sarahcee by Prominer (Peter Casey) 1163 1385 2141 3395

3 **SPECIFIED (USA),** ch c Known Fact (USA) - Scierpan (USA) by Sharpen Up (J H M Gosden) 729^{1} 1031^{1} 1786

2 **SPECS APPEAL (Ire),** b c Last Tycoon - Beparoejojo by Lord Gayle (USA) (J S Bolger) 2072^{3} 2402^{1} 2807

4 **SPECTACLE JIM,** b g Mummy's Game - Welsh Blossom by Welsh Saint (J O'Donoghue) 330 521^{9} 636^{7} 1267 2110^{3} 2524^{6} 2671^{7} 2868^{1} 3168 3393^{6} 4090^{5}

4 **SPECTACULAR DAWN,** gr f Spectacular Bid (USA) - Early Rising (USA) by Grey Dawn II (J L Dunlop) 478^{7} 1094^{5} 1688^{2} 2251^{6} 2477^{4} 3231^{1} 3690^{4} 4212

4 **SPECTACULAR TIDE (USA),** b or br c Tsunami Slew (USA) - Bid Me Adieu by Spectacular Bid (S Hough) 3187^{1} 4071^{7}

3 **SPEED DEMON,** b g Hadeer - Lunar Shamal-Gal by Tumble Wind (USA) (J T Gorman) 848 1106 1570^{8} 2323 2514

4 **SPEED OIL,** br c Java Tiger - Maydrum by Meldrum (R Bastiman) 161^{4} 217^{3} 279^{9} 531^{7} 1035^{3} 1674

2 **SPEEDWELL BLUE (USA),** b f In Fijar (USA) - April Blues by Cure The Blues (D K Weld) 2093^{6} 2450^{1}

4 **SPEEDY CLASSIC (USA),** br g Storm Cat (USA) - Shadows Lengthen by Star Appeal (M J Heaton-Ellis) 4680a^{9} 4817a 47^{3} 117^{1} 4580

2 **SPEEDY SNAPS IMAGE,** ch c Ballacashtal (Can) - Lillicara (Fr) by Caracolero (USA) (M P Muggeridge) 1624 2030^{7} 3009 3658 3867^{3} 4127^{8} 4482^{6}

4 **SPENCER'S REVENGE,** ch g Bay Express - Armour Of Light by Hot Spark (Lord Huntingdon) 4803a^{2} 38^{2} 101^{1} 222^{1} 315^{9}

STEEL SOVEREIGN, gr g Nishapour (Fr) - Periscope by Legend Of France (USA) (Mrs M Reveley) 4103 4220 4434^9 4602

STEFF GRAF (Brz), ch m Executioner (USA) - Lessel Loo (USA) by Lunard (USA) (J Feld) 1695^6 2085^4

STELFOX (Ire), b c Conquering Hero (USA) - Mary's Dream by Midsummer Night II (E J O'Grady) 2840^6 3243^3 3541 4093^4

STELLA MYSTIKA (USA), ch f Diesis - Share The Fantasy (USA) by Exclusive Native (USA) (L M Cumani) 523^1 749 3227^1 3864^4 4153

STELLAR CAT (USA), b f Storm Cat (USA) - Sweet Valentine (USA) by Honey Jay (USA) (D W Lukas) 4740^5

STELLOSO, ch c Midyan (USA) - Follow The Stars by Sparkler (D R Loder) 1773^3 2063^3 2374^3 2817^1

STEPANOV (USA), br c Nureyev (USA) - Sigy (Fr) by Habitat (J H M Gosden) 1614^3 2628^8 3153^2 3438

STEPHENS GUEST (Ire), b or br f Don't Forget Me - Guestaway by Be My Guest (USA) (Michael Cunningham) 936

STEPHENSONS ROCKET, ch g Music Boy - Martian Princess by Cure The Blues (USA) (J Berry) 1324 1870^3 2203^4 2766^3 3120^1 3309^6

STEP ON IT, ch f Music Boy - Quick As A Wink by Glint Of Gold (C P Wildman) 2032^8

STEPPE CLOSER, gr f Nishapour (Fr) - Red Shoes by Dance In Time (Can) (M D I Usher) 4709a^8 2834^7 3102^5 3461

STEPPEY LANE, b m Tachypous - Alpine Alice by Abwah (W W Haigh) 125^4 219^5 279^1

STEPPIN HIGH, gr g Siberian Express (USA) - Moogie by Young Generation (Lord Huntingdon) 2577 3766

STERLING PRINCESS, b or br f Sayf El Arab (USA) - Make Or Mar by Daring March (P Howling) 3707 3839

STERNKONIG (Ire), gr c Kalaglow - Sternwappen by Wauthi (T Grieper) 1724^2 2259^3 3370^6 3647^1 4201^3

STERRETJIE (Ire), b f Thatching - Massive Powder by Caerleon (USA) (R Simpson) 4127

STETTIN, b c Polish Navy (USA) - Blonde Prospect (USA) by Mr Prospector (USA) (R Hannon) 3908^8 4419^6

STEVE CURTIS (Ity), b c Dominion - Annamaria Pacifico by Niniski 4704a^3

STEVE LUCKY (Ire), gr c Law Society (USA) - Stapara by Mill Reef (A Mattei) 958^4 2650^8 4475^1

STEVEN'S DREAM (Ire), ch f Heraldiste (USA) - Battle Queen by Kind Of Hush (J White) 4668a^7

STEVIE'S WONDER (Ire), ch g Don't Forget Me - Azurai by Dance In Time (Can) (T G Mills) 4801a^3 32 172^1 228^3 405^2 733 1417^8 1991^4 2163^3 2489^4 2726^4 2898^3 3325^8 4231^7

STIMULANT, b f Sharpo - Anodyne by Dominion (J W Watts) 544^2 889^1 1437^3 2400^1 3347^2 3898^7

STING IN THE TAIL, b f Scorpio (Fr) - Polola by Aragon (P R Hedger) 4667a^9

STINGRAY CITY (USA), b g Raft (USA) - Out Of This World by High Top (L Lungo) 1400^4 1517^2 1834^2

ST JOHN'S HILL, ch g Norwick (USA) - Dame Nellie by Dominion (W G M Turner) 82^6

ST KITTS, b f Tragic Role (USA) - T Catty (USA) by Sensitive Prince (USA) (W G M Turner) 3828 4208

ST LOUIS LADY, gr f Absalom - Pearl Cove by Town And Country (W Jarvis) 4440^5 4594^2

ST MARTHA (Ire), b f Double Schwartz - Miss Moat by Dike (USA) (M H Tompkins) 1575^5 1853^4 4385

ST NINIAN, ch h Ardross - Caergwrle by Crepello (M H Easterby) 1559^1 1952^5 2376^3 3465^6 3775^6

STOCKFORCE, ch g Infantry - Stockline by Capricorn Line (B J Meehan) 459 624 872 2095 2288

STOCKTINA, ch m Tina's Pet - Mrewa by Runnymede (B J Meehan) 1148^7 1240 1352^2 1473^3 1728^6 2050^7 2305^9 2549^8 2846^6 2896^8

STOLLER (USA), ch c El Gran Senor (USA) - Carolglen Jo (Can) by Victoria Park (Mrs J Cecil) 3592 3990^2 4356^1

STOMPIN, b c Alzao (USA) - Celebrity by Troy (C E Brittain) 738 1949 3704^8

STONECROP, br g Kefaah (USA) - Sweet Pleasure by Sweet Revenge (J White) 3908^6 4113

2 **STONEHATCH (USA),** ch c Storm Bird (Can) - Lively Living (USA) by Key To The Mint (USA) (P W Chapple-Hyam) 998^1 1750^1 2906^2 4443^2

3 **STONEY VALLEY,** b c Caerleon (USA) - Startino by Bustino (P W Chapple-Hyam) 538^4 842^1 1015^4 2926 3437^1 3878^6

2 **STONY BEST (Ire),** 2649^8 3798^4 4198^4

5 **STOP PRESS (USA),** b m Sharpen Up - Glad Tidings (Fr) by Pharly (Fr) (M R Stoute) 4711a 4626^4

4 **STOPROVERITATE,** ch f Scorpio (Fr) - Luscinia by Sing Sing (S G Norton) 376^1 448^1 650^3 710^8 885 3469 3722^4 4101^6 4391^4 4623^8 4760^4

5 **STORAIA (Aus),** 595

2 **STOREY'S GATE (Ire),** b c Red Sunset - Crimbourne by Mummy's Pet (J R Fanshawe) 2179^9 3816^3 4167^3 4416^2

3 **STORITHS (Ire),** b c Double Schwartz - Atlantic Dream (USA) by Muscovite (USA) (J W Watts) 591^4 846^4 1326^1 2060^4 2303^1

2 **STORM,** gr c Celestial Storm (USA) - Musical Maiden by Record Token (N A Callaghan) 469 1119^9 1245^6 2216^6 2465^7 2718^9

3 **STORM CANYON (Ire),** ch c Storm Bird (Can) - Diamond Field (USA) by Mr Prospector (USA) (J H M Gosden) 3005^2 3178^1 3427^1 3987^1 4172^6

4 **STORM DUST,** b g Celestial Storm (USA) - Mary Sunley by Known Fact (USA) (J R Fanshawe) 520^5

7 **STORM FREE (USA),** b g Storm Bird (Can) - No Designs (USA) by Vaguely Noble (L G Cottrell) 155^4 211^5 261^1 327^3 621^2 918^1 1146^2 1699^3 3734^8 3891

2 **STORM HEIGHTS,** br f Squill (USA) - Travel Storm by Lord Gayle (USA) (M Brittain) 1245^4 1391^9 2825^5 3563 3968^2 4082^5 4646

2 **STORM LEADER,** br g Squill (USA) - African Dash by African Sky (M Brittain) 1324 1758^8 2229

2 **STORM NYMPH (USA),** b f Storm Bird (Can) - Secret Obsession (USA) by Secretariat (USA) (J R Fanshawe) 3633^6

2 **STORM REGENT,** b or br c Prince Sabo - Bread 'n Honey by Goldhills Pride (S P C Woods) 730 1098^3 1456^8 2364 2652^1 3082^9 3236^6 3436^6 4061 4264

4 **STORM RISK,** ch c Risk Me (Fr) - Lightning Legend by Lord Gayle (USA) (Mrs A Knight) 603

2 **STORM SHIP (Ire),** b g Petorius - Selham by Derring-Do (A A Scott) 2994^5 3421^5 3589^2 3810^1 4144^2 4423

3 **STORM TOWER (USA),** b c Irish Tower (USA) - Storm Doll by Storm Bird (B Perkins Jr) 569^1 779

3 **STORM VENTURE (Ire),** b g Taufan (USA) - Crimson Crest by Pampapaul (W Jarvis) 719^6 1080^2 1338 1907^2 2311^1 2474^2 2961 3507 3873^9 4533

4 **STORM VIXEN,** ch f Jester - Double Duchess by Connaught (L R Lloyd-James) 1562 3359 3506 3758

3 **STORMY HEIGHTS,** b or br f Golden Heights - Brown Taw by Whistlefield (J R Jenkins) 606^5 711^7 1528 1606 2214^1 2560^5 3188^6 3251^3 3638 3707

2 **STRADISHALL,** ch c Squill (USA) - Zilda (Fr) by Zino (G C Bravery) 793^7 1561 1985^5 2844^6 3137^4 3362^6 3597 3968^8 4122^1

3 **STRAIGHT APPROACH (USA),** gr g Caro - Point With Pride (USA) by Halo (USA) (J W Hills) 1266 1819^5

2 **STRAIGHT ARROW,** ch c Indian Ridge - Harmonical (USA) by Lyphard's Wish (Fr) (Lord Huntingdon) 913^3 1203^1 2618^7 2996^2 3339^1 3803^1 4520^7

2 **STRANGERSARDANGERS (Ire),** b f Classic Secret (USA) - Bally by Balidar (A Bailey) 3443^5 3755 3993^7 4358 4435^9 4508^5

4 **STRANGERSINTHENITE,** ch g Legend Of France (USA) - Angail by Northfields (USA) (J S Wainwright) 531 740^7

2 **STRANGFORD LOUGH (Ire),** b c Cyrano de Bergerac - Firdaunt by Tanfirion (Noel T Chance) 3064^4 3541 4380 4609 4688

2 **STRAPPED,** b f Reprimand - Marista by Mansingh (USA) (M R Channon) 979^6 1203^3 1339^4 1665^4 2058^7 2316^9 2786^8 2988^5 3508^5 3626^2 3688^4 4358 4528^1 4618^6 4674^6 4750^5

3 **STRATAGEM,** ch g Jalmood (USA) - Strathoykel by Aberdeen (Sir Mark Prescott) 4770a^9

2 **STRATEGIC MANEUVER (USA),** b f Cryptoclearance (USA) - Prayer Wheel (USA) by Conquistador Cielo (USA) (F S Shulhofer) 3700^{1} 4070^{1} 4449^{7}

3 **STRATEGIC TIMING (Ire),** b f Chief Singer - Going Digital (USA) by Northern Baby (Can) (D K Weld) 1855^{2} 3074^{1} 3497^{1} 3855^{2} 4057

4 **STRATFORD LADY,** b f Touching Wood (USA) - Hawks Nest by Moulton (J A Glover) 4662a

6 **STRATHELLA,** gr m Ela-Mana-Mou - Strathdearn by Saritamer (USA) (J L Eyre) 681

2 **STRATH KITTEN,** ch f Scottish Reel - Elemis (USA) by Sir Ivor (K O Cunningham-Brown) 4253^{9}

2 **STRATHTORE DREAM (Ire),** b or br f Jareer (USA) - Beyond Words by Ballad Rock (Miss L A Perratt) 1846 2603^{5} 3613^{5} 4237^{5}

6 **STRAT'S LEGACY,** b g Chukaroo - State Romance by Free State (D W P Arbuthnot) 4760a^{2} 4819a^{2} 73^{1} 141^{2} 210^{1} 235^{1} 265^{2} 402 3551^{8} 4028 4591^{9} 4713^{4}

3 **STRATTON FLYER,** b f Mas Media - Empress Valley by Gay Fandango (USA) (H S Howe) 1090 1371^{6}

8 **STRAWBERRY DOLLAR,** b h Red Regent - Buck's Fairy (D Carroll) 298

5 **STRAWTALDI (Ire),** b g Cataldi - Stramenta (Eamon O'Connell) 2324

4 **STRAW THATCH,** b g Thatching - Lashing (USA) by Storm Bird (Can) (R Allan) 448^{9} 651^{7} 885^{9} 1260^{9} 2057^{2} 2283^{3} 2567^{4} 3146 3375^{7} 4043^{8}

5 **STREET REBEL (Can),** b h Robellino (USA) - Street Ballet (USA) by Nijinsky (Can) (Noel Meade) 4684a^{2} 1201^{3} 1552^{6} 1646^{3} 1786^{7} 4401

2 **STREISAND,** 1726^{3} 4402

3 **STREPHON (Ire),** b g Fairy King (USA) - Madame Fair by Monseigneur (USA) (J J O'Neill) 4740a^{6} 83 3741^{4} 4049^{1} 4256^{3} 4357 4611^{1}

3 **STRICTLY PERSONAL (USA),** b or br g Secreto (USA) - Tash (USA) by Never Bend (M J Wilkinson) 4730a^{3} 4755a^{2} 4778a^{1} 328^{2} 468^{5}

3 **STRIKE-A-POSE,** ch f Blushing Scribe (USA) - My Bushbaby by Hul A Hul (B J Llewellyn) 1453^{4} 1829^{2} 2190^{2} 2578^{2} 2898^{4} 3249^{8} 4187

5 **STRIKE THE GOLD (USA),** ch h Alydar (USA) - Majestic Gold (USA) by Hatchet Man (USA) (N Zito) 1541^{3}

4 **STRIKING IMAGE (Ire),** ch f Flash Of Steel - Sister Sala by Double-U-Jay (J S Moore) 416 520^{7} 626 723 3420^{6} 3655^{9} 3814^{7}

5 **STRIP CARTOON (Ire),** ch g Tate Gallery (USA) - Reveal by Pitskelly (S R Bowring) 4664a^{6} 4699a^{7} 4716a^{5} 6^{7} 96^{6} 138^{5} 180^{2} 207^{4} 231^{1} 289^{5} 379^{3} 492^{2} 568^{2} 655^{1} 887^{2} 1076^{6} 1589 2466^{3} 2636^{5} 2829^{1} 3188^{3} 3360^{6} 3535^{6} 3946 4224^{8} 4331^{9} 4693

4 **STRIPPED CLEAN,** ch f Be My Native (USA) - White's Ferry by Northfields (USA) (Kevin Prendergast) 4684a^{7}

3 **STROLLING ALONG (USA),** b or br c Danzig (USA) - Cadillacing (USA) by Alydar (USA) (C R McGaughey III) 4451^{1}

2 **STROLLING MINSTREL (Ire),** b c Fayruz - Airy Queen (USA) by Sadair (B S Rothwell) 3969

2 **STRONG BOOST (USA),** b c Topsider (USA) - Final Figure (USA) by Super Concorde (USA) (D K Weld) 4637

5 **STRONG CASE (Ire),** gr g Strong Gale - Sunshot by Candy Cane (Liam Browne) 2077^{6} 2515^{2} 3405^{8} 3857^{1}

5 **STRONG LIFE (Ire),** b h Fire Of Life (USA) - Strong On The Sly by On The Sly (G Favretto) 4727a^{4} 4475^{2}

2 **STRUMPET CITY,** b f Emarati (USA) - Double Touch (Fr) by Nonoalco (USA) (R Charlton) 3642^{1} 4257^{2}

4 **STUBASS (Ire),** b c Alzao (USA) - St Louisan by St Chad (L M Cumani) 660^{4} 1029^{5} 1447^{5}

2 **STUDFORD GIRL,** b f Midyan (USA) - Calder Hall by Grundy (M W Easterby) 812^{8} 1078^{3} 1158^{4} 1561^{6} 1870^{4} 2167^{5} 2637^{4}

4 **STYLE AND CLASS,** ch g Local Suitor (USA) - Shindella by Furry Glen (R Rowe) 298^{6}

6 **STYLISH GENT,** br g Vitiges (Fr) - Squire's Daughter by Bay Express (P C Clarke) 4104 4187

3 **STYLISH ROSE (Ire),** b f Don't Forget Me - Cottage Style by Thatch (USA) (P Cheesbrough) 304^{7} 1080^{8} 1459^{6} 1656^{1} 3219^{7}

2 **SUAAD (Ire),** ch f Fools Holme (USA) - Tootle by Main Reef (H Thomson Jones) 2240^{2} 2748^{1} 4004^{2} 4456^{3}

3 **SUAVE GROOM (Ire),** ch c Shy Groom (USA) - Croglin Water by Monsanto (Fr) (D K Weld) 311^{5} 489^{4} 704^{1} 1549^{2} 3075^{1}

2 **SUAVE REDSKIN (Ire),** ch c Persian Bold - Richman Sisters by Captain James (Kevin Prendergast) 2093^{3} 2319 2450^{4} 3379^{7} 4262^{5} 4360

2 **SUBARASHII (USA),** b f Danzig Connection (USA) - David's Tobin (USA) by Tobin Bronze (Michael Kauntze) 3527 3730^{2} 4261^{5} 4624^{3}

5 **SUBSONIC (Ire),** b h Be My Guest (USA) - Broken Wide by Busted (Martyn Wane) 3724^{8} 4283^{8} 4538^{5} 4732

2 **SUBTLE BRIEF (Ire),** b c Law Society (USA) - Pig Tail by Habitat (Liam Browne) 4581 4609^{7} 4688

2 **SUBTLE TROUBLE (USA),** b g Native Prospector (USA) - The Babe by Fleet Mel (M Stute) 4748^{1}

2 **SUCCESS STORY,** gr f Sharrood (USA) - Starlet by Teenoso (USA) (Lord Huntingdon) 4220^{4}

3 **SUDAH (USA),** br f Rainbow Quest (USA) - Sledge by Young Generation 4738a^{2}

4 **SUDANOR (Ire),** b g Khartoum (USA) - Alencon by Northfields (USA) (B R Millman) 754 975 1930^{7} 2317^{2} 2662 3288

3 **SUDDEN SPIN,** b g Doulab (USA) - Lightning Legacy (USA) by Super Concorde (USA) (J Berry) 447^{4} 860^{3} 1185^{3} 1866^{4} 2366^{4} 2634^{1} 2851^{4} 4156^{7} 4317

3 **SUEBOOG (Ire),** b f Darshaan - Nordica by Northfields (USA) (C E Brittain) 556^{1} 987^{3} 1525^{4} 2986^{3}

3 **SUEENA,** b f Presidium - Meads Lass by Saritamer (USA) (R J Hodges) 921 1278^{9} 2351^{8} 3011

3 **SUEKAR (Ire),** b f Don't Forget Me - Honey Buzzard by Sea Hawk II (John M Oxx) 577 1443^{3} 1796^{4} 2497^{1} 2703^{5}

4 **SUEZ CANAL (Ire),** b g Commanche Run - Sphinx (Ger) by Alpenkonig (Ger) (F Jordan) 3690

2 **SUGARLAND EXPRESS (Ire),** 2649^{5} 4198^{2}

2 **SUGAR RISK,** b f Risk Me (Fr) - Sugar Loch by Lochnager (C R Egerton) 4263^{6} 4594^{9} 4752^{3}

2 **SUGAR TOWN (Ire),** b f Tate Gallery (USA) - Skhiza by Targowice (USA) (P F I Cole) 3828 4089^{4} 4350^{1} 4564

7 **SUGEMAR,** ch g Young Generation - Jade Ring by Auction Ring (USA) (M C Chapman) 4696a^{3} 4710a 4744a 4764a^{7} 4771a^{7} 3^{4} 25^{2} 55^{1} 81^{3} 125^{5} 148^{2} 189 219^{4} 254^{2} 279^{2} 290^{3} 396^{3} 645^{9} 931^{8} 1075^{4} 1676 2195^{2} 2427^{3} 2641^{3} 3503

5 **SUGUNAS (Ger),** b h Lagunas - Sumba by Tudor Melody (A Wohler) 406^{2} 692^{1} 1217^{7} 2079^{2} 3370^{5} 3582 4073^{5} 4306^{3}

3 **SUI GENERIS (Ire),** ch f Doulab (USA) - Markon by On Your Mark (Mrs S D Williams) 927 1233^{6} 1696 3100 3661

3 **SUIVEZ,** b c Persian Bold - Butterfly Kiss by Beldale Flutter (USA) (P C Haslam) 404^{4} 2622 3487^{6} 3740 3900^{9} 4428^{4}

7 **SUKEY TAWDRY,** gr m Wassl - Jenny Diver (USA) by Hatchet Man (USA) (Mrs M J Bennett) 2109 286

3 **SULA MOON,** bl f Sulaafah (USA) - Moonstream Belle by John de Coombe (C C Elsey) 582 2563 3065 3420^{8} 3787 4267

5 **SULDA,** 593^{8}

2 **SULFORICH (USA),** 4313^{5}

2 **SULITELMA (USA),** b f The Minstrel (Can) - Sharmila (Fr) by Blakeney (I A Balding) 3781^{5} 4067^{5} 4265 4484^{2} 4709^{1}

2 **SULLAMELL,** b g Sulaafah (USA) - Melody Lane by Horage (R J Hodges) 949 1555^{8} 1741^{6}

12 **SULLY'S CHOICE (USA),** b g King Pellinor (USA) - Salute The Coates (USA) by Solar Salute (USA) (D W Chapman) 147^{6} 176^{7} 568^{4} 1249^{7} 1494 1898^{2} 2173^{4} 2309^{7} 2594^{3} 2975^{7} 3002 3778

7 **SULTAN'S SON,** b g Kings Lake (USA) - Get Ahead by Silly Season (K S Bridgwater) 4354

8 **SULUK (USA),** b h Lypheor - Cheerful Heart by Petingo (R Hollinshead) 4698a^{4} 4813a^{8} 973^{5} 1873 2530^{5} 2585^{8}

6 **SUM MEDE,** b g King Persian - Brun's Toy (Fr) by Bruni (B S Rothwell) 382

2 **TARTHOOTH (Ire),** ch c Bob Back (USA) - Zoly (USA) by Val de L'orne (Fr) (C J Benstead) 4498

3 **TARTIB (Ire),** b c Fayruz - June Lady by Junius (USA) (C J Benstead) 510[6] 797[8] 1057[4] 1470[7] 3343[9] 4270[3] 4394

2 **TASHLA,** b f Reprimand - Tarsa by Ballad Rock (D R Loder) 2695[2] 3218[4] 3389[2] 3966[2] 4251[6] 4550

3 **TASHTIYANA (Ire),** b or br f Doyoun - Tashtiya by Shergar (A de Royer-Dupre) 266[4]

3 **TASSAGH BRIDGE (Ire),** b f Double Schwartz - Kasarose by Owen Dudley (J W Payne) 950[9] 1060 2338[7] 2719[9] 3948 4596

3 **TASSET (Can),** ch c Tasso (USA) - While I'm Away (USA) by Buckpasser (P F I Cole) 602[6] 761 880[4] 1216[3] 1594[1] 1960[3] 2963 3263[4]

2 **TATAMI (USA),** b c Lyphard (USA) - Tash (USA) by Never Bend (L M Cumani) 3633[5] 3974[1] 4255[1] 4520[1]

3 **TATIKA,** ch c Tate Gallery (USA) - Independentia by Home Guard (USA) (G Wragg) 4428[5] 4664[4]

9 **TAUBER,** b g Taufan (USA) - Our Bernie by Continuation (Pat Mitchell) 4672a[4] 4752a[7] 796

4 **TAUFAN BLU (Ire),** b f Taufan (USA) - Engage by Whistling Wind (B Beasley) 316[6] 675 1079[1] 1636[7] 2060[8] 3465[9] 3680[5] 3864[3] 3996[5] 4216[2] 4373[2] 4650 4729[9]

2 **TAUFELIANE,** b f Taufan (USA) - Sweet Eliane by Birdbrook (J L Harris) 1303[6] 1556[7] 2695[8] 3815

3 **TAUM GO LEOR (Ire),** b or br c Mister Majestic - Walnut Lass by Tap On Wood (P Henley) 4407

5 **TAUNTING (Ire),** b g Taufan (USA) - Dancing Decoy by Troy (S Coathup) 4759a[1] 4784a[3] 35[3] 58[4] 114[5] 199[5] 294 440[2] 603[5] 834 1138 1902[1] 2289[7] 2398 2858[2] 3043[3] 3469[4] 3840[2] 4036[6]

4 **TAURIAN PRINCESS,** b f Electric - Facetious by Malicious (W Clay) 1305

3 **TAUTEN (Ire),** br f Taufan (USA) - Pitaka by Pitskelly (P Burgoyne) 599[3] 705[8] 1622[4] 2141[7] 2322 2497[5] 3831 4110 4354[3] 4479[4] 4596[6]

4 **TAWAFIJ (USA),** ch g Diesis - Dancing Brownie (USA) by Nijinsky (Can) (R Allan) 438[3] 655[4] 862[2] 1193[1] 1325[3] 2060[1] 2363[4] 2657[3] 3791[4] 4038[6]

3 **TAWAR (Ire),** b c Doyoun - Tafaana (Fr) by Top Ville (John M Oxx) 960[1] 1609[1] 2039[5]

6 **TAYLORS PRINCE,** ch g Sandhurst Prince - Maiden's Dance by Hotfoot (H J Collingridge) 994[3] 1384[2] 1712[8] 2126[6] 2948[8] 3551

3 **TBAAREEH (USA),** ch f Chief's Crown (USA) - Eye Drop (USA) by Irish River (Fr) (J S Bolger) 943[5] 2035[2] 2245[2] 3336[2] 3560[9]

3 **TEACHER (Ire),** b g Caerleon (USA) - Clunk Click by Star Appeal (A A Scott) 423[6] 679 1068[8] 1417 1582[5]

5 **TE AKAU NICK (NZ),** 4672[2]

3 **TEAK ROAD (Ire),** b g Jareer (USA) - Great Dora by Great Nephew (D J Barry) 2703 2877[7]

5 **TEANARCO (Ire),** b m Kafu - Lady Kasbah by Lord Gayle (USA) (P G Murphy) 1623[5] 1977[6] 2577[2] 2940[3] 3425[1] 3736[2] 4024 4518[2] 4652 4721[8]

3 **TEAZEL BOY,** b c Forzando - Emma's Whisper by Kind Of Hush (C Collins) 256[2] 848[1] 1609[2]

3 **TEBRE (USA),** b f Sir Ivor - Ignition (Chi) by Damascus Silver (USA) (Kevin Prendergast) 258 550[7] 1140[4] 1466[3] 2140[5] 2702[7] 3038[5] 3274[2] 3482[3] 3662[1] 3854[8] 4409[6]

2 **TECHNICOLORED,** b f Unfuwain (USA) - Oh So Bold (USA) by Better Bee (J L Dunlop) 2836[7] 4204[3]

4 **TEDDY'S PLAY (USA),** b g Theatrical - Stricly (Arg) by Dancing Moss (C J Mann) 967

4 **TEDDY'S TOP TEN (USA),** ch f Gate Dancer (USA) - Anchorwoman by Iron Ruler (B Barnett) 3804[4]

3 **TEE-EMM,** b g Lidhame - Tower Glades by Tower Walk (P Howling) 4747a[1] 4762a[8] 7[3] 31[2] 117[8] 156[5] 236[7] 606[7] 720[3] 1010[5] 1148[5] 1473 1728[5] 1990[4] 2728[5] 3584[5]

3 **TEE GEE JAY,** b f Northern Tempest (USA) - Immaculate Girl by Habat (C N Williams) 1175 1416[6] 1903[6] 2476[3] 2717[6] 2993[4] 3459[8] 3591 3965[4] 4481

2 **TEE JAY BABY,** b f Rambling River - Megan's Move by Move Off (W Storey) 3131[9]

3 **TEEN JAY,** b c Teenoso (USA) - Spoilt Again by Mummy's Pet (S E Sherwood) 1746[1] 2579[5] 3217[4]

2 **TEETOTALLER (Ire),** gr c Taufan (USA) - Mainly Dry by The Brianstan (J Berry) 364[6] 1632[2] 2090[3] 3950[1]

3 **TEGEMEZA (Ire),** b f Cyrano de Bergerac - Overstay by Be My Guest (USA) (J C Harley) 258 2667[7] 3074[5] 4060[8] 4370

2 **TEGUILA (Ire),** ch f Salse (USA) - Free Touch by Kris (A A Scott) 4542

3 **TEJANO GOLD (USA),** ch g Tejano (USA) - Nelli Forli (USA) by Broadway Forli (USA) (P Bradley) 284[4] 405[4] 724[4] 1005[7] 1673[2] 2358[5] 3689[3] 3945[8]

3 **TEJ SINGH (USA),** b g Tejano (USA) - Deep River Woman (USA) by Miswaki (USA) (L M Cumani) 529[7] 784[3] 1239[2] 1868[1] 2066 2873[3] 3107[1]

2 **TELEPHONE TAP,** b c Night Shift (USA) - Princess Lieven by Royal Palace (R Hannon) 4263[8] 4480 4665[6]

3 **TELEPHONIC (USA),** b g Phone Trick (USA) - Sound Of Summer (USA) by Drone (Sir Mark Prescott) 4791a[9] 284[5] 346 503[5] 699

4 **TELEPHUS,** b g Efisio - Mrs Bizz by Status Seeker (B J McMath) 1307[2] 1521[4] 1900[2] 2354[3] 2633[7] 3655[4] 3831[4]

6 **TEL E THON,** b g Ela-Mana-Mou - Costa Rossa (Ity) by Welsh Pageant (P J Jones) 924 3473

3 **TELL ME WHY (Fr),** 74[3]

2 **TELLURIUM (USA),** b c Timeless Moment (USA) - Chinguetti by Green Dancer (J-C Cunnington) 2144[4] 3014[5] 4242[2] 4593[6]

2 **TELOPEA,** b f Teenoso (USA) - Orlaith by Final Straw (H Candy) 4651

5 **TEL QUEL (Fr),** b h Akarad (Fr) - Best Girl by Birdbrook (A Fabre) 4769a[6]

4 **TEMPELHOF (Ire),** b c Alzao (USA) - Konigin Kate (Ger) by Authi (Miss Jacqueline S Doyle) 628

7 **TEMPERING,** b g Kris - Mixed Applause (USA) by Nijinsky (Can) (D W Chapman) 4662a[6] 4688a[2] 4707a[3] 4715a[5] 4767a[1] 4771a[4] 4812a[1] 14[1] 55[2] 65[1] 81[2] 94[1] 202[1] 243[2] 254[1] 278[1] 366[4] 645 709[1] 4669

4 **TEMPLE FORTUNE (USA),** br f Ziggy's Boy (USA) - Our Feast (USA) by Banquet Table (USA) (B J Meehan) 796 1127 1492 3081[9]

3 **TEMPLE HILL,** br f Another Realm - Gay Patricia by Gay Fandango (USA) (J M Carr) 4665a 62 204[7]

4 **TEMPLE KNIGHT,** b g Never So Bold - Nelly Do Da by Derring-Do (Miss C Johnsey) 874[8] 1146[9] 2727[3] 2970[6] 3128[2] 3656[4] 4006

5 **TEMPLERAINEY (Ire),** b g Welsh Term - Saharan by Tarboosh (USA) (A P O'Brien) 4186[4] 4411[3]

2 **TEMPS PERDU,** b g Don't Forget Me - Res Nova (USA) by Blushing Groom (Fr) (C R Egerton) 4579[7]

5 **TENAYESTELIGN,** gr m Bellypha - Opale by Busted (D Marks) 158[3] 199[7] 210[6] 332[2] 387[9] 498[1] 628[3]

3 **TENBY,** b c Caerleon (USA) - Shining Water by Kalaglow (H R A Cecil) 775[1] 1001[1] 1448 2253[3] 2791[8] 3402[7] 4467[4]

3 **TENCA (Ire),** ch g Tender King - Baby Clair by Gulf Pearl (E J O'Grady) 959 1139[4] 1757[6] 2141 2484[8]

5 **TENDER MOMENT (Ire),** b m Caerleon (USA) - Cannon Boy (USA) by Canonero II (USA) (C E Brittain) 4757a 475[1] 737[1] 1172 1768[6] 2334[7] 2885 3315

2 **TENDER NORTH,** ch f Sure Blade (USA) - Shillay by Lomond (USA) (P C Haslam) 607[4] 743[6]

5 **TENDRESSE (Ire),** b m Tender King - Velinowski by Malinowski (USA) (C J Hill) 4696a[1] 4705a[6] 30[3] 78 840[8] 1307[1] 1626[1] 1919[9] 2348[4] 2774[9] 4760

3 **TENET (Fr),** b c Private Account (USA) - Karmiska by Bikala (E Bartholomew) 1648[4] 1915[8]

3 **TENGA (USA),** b f Mr Prospector (USA) - Royal Strait Flush (USA) by Seattle Slew (USA) (F Boutin) 1086[6] 3619[2] 4010 4568[4]

4 **TEN HIGH (Ire),** b f Leap High (USA) - Another Decade by Daring Display (USA) (J Dooler) 4662a 349 1305[9] 2694[9]

2 **TENPIN PROPHET (Ire),** ch f Salt Dome (USA) - Finesse by Miralgo (M Tate) 680[6] 812 1158[5] 1561 1759[3] 3968

2 **TEN TIMES TANGO,** ch f Grey Desire - Tango Lady by Gorytus (USA) (M Brittain) 1108[8] 1189 1499[7] 1863

2 **TEN-TO-SIX GIRL,** b f Night Shift (USA) - Nasty Niece (Can) by Great Nephew (Major W R Hern) 4350 4627[8] 4754[5]

3 **TEOROMA,** ch c Teofane - Poppy Kelly by Netherkelly (Dr J D Scargill) 3012 3173

INDEX TO FLAT RACE RESULTS 1992-93

3 **TIRIZI (Ire),** ch c Shernazar - Tibrizaby by Nighapour (John M Oxx) 271[3]

5 **TIR NA NOLLAIG (Ire),** b m Le Johnstan - Rosabuskins by Little Buskins (Norman Cassidy) 3395

2 **TISA WASITEEN (Ire),** b f Taufan (USA) - Evanna's Pride by Main Reef (J E Banks) 1897[9] 2385[6]

4 **TISSISAT (USA),** ch g Green Forest (USA) - Expansive by Exbury (I A Balding) 581[1] 1002[4] 1407[5] 1973[5] 2794[8] 3158[7] 3487[2] 4065[5] 4468[3] 4650

3 **TISZA,** ch f Kris - Twyla by Habitat (J H M Gosden) 992 1383[6]

2 **TITANIA'S DANCE (Ire),** br f Fairy King (USA) - Camden Dancer by Camden Town (M Bell) 680 1091[8] 1391[1]

2 **TITANIUM HONDA (Ire),** gr c Doulab (USA) - Cumbrian Melody by Petong (C E Brittain) 2027[6]

2 **TITCH ON TIME,** b f Absalom - Fast Asleep by Hotfoot (M H Tompkins) 1555[7] 1933

4 **TITI STATILIO (Ire),** 593

3 **TITLED GIRL (Ire),** b f Alzao (USA) - Sweet Goodbye by Petorius (P F I Cole) 4677a 4778a[5] 4809a[7]

5 **TITLE ROLL (Ire),** ch m Tate Gallery (USA) - Tough Lady by Bay Express (M Bell) 3847[7]

3 **TI ZINO (Fr),** 594[6] 2242[5] 4304[5]

2 **T'NIEL,** ch f Librate - Classy Colleen by St Paddy (R Hollinshead) 4761[8]

4 **TOAST AND HONEY (Ire),** br f Glow (USA) - Bees Nest by Scorpio (Fr) (Patrick Martin) 1996 2692[7] 3061[1] 3397 3604[7]

3 **TOCCATELLA,** b f Chief Singer - Woodwind (Fr) by Whistling Wind (B J Meehan) 417[9] 614 975 1232

3 **TOCCO JEWEL,** br f Reesh - Blackpool Belle by The Brianstan (M J Ryan) 1931 2154[9] 2499[7] 2912[4] 3247[5] 4574[1] 4658

3 **TOCHAR BAN (USA),** b f Assert - Guest Night by Sir Ivor (D R C Elsworth) 821[2] 992[3] 1311[3] 1842[2] 3012[1] 3620[4] 4153[7]

2 **TO CROWN IT ALL (USA),** b or br c Chief's Crown (USA) - Bamesian (USA) by Buckpasser (F H Lee) 1497[3] 1778[5] 3779[4] 4240[4] 4541

5 **TODAY'S FANCY,** b g Today And Tomorrow - Fancy Pages by Touch Paper (P Burgoyne) 3228

2 **TODAY'S STAR,** b c Today And Tomorrow - Lady Henham by Breakspear II (J Ffitch-Heyes) 4589[6]

3 **TODDEN,** b g Aragon - Marguerite Gerard by Rheingold (J A Hellens) 1390[7] 2151[8]

4 **TODDY MARK (Ire),** b c Sovereign Don (USA) - Marietta Meagher (USA) by Solford (USA) (Ms E Cassidy) 3198[6] 3382[8] 3616[8] 3951 4370[8] 4552[5] 4635[5] 4689

3 **TODESCHINA,** 1727[5]

3 **TOFF SUNDAE,** b g Risk Me (Fr) - Rose Sundae by Dominion (P M McEntee) 418 714[5] 771 1147[5] 1313 1502[6] 3270

5 **TOKAI TEIO (Jpn),** (S Matsumoto) 4728a[1]

3 **TOKYO,** b f Mtoto - Rosetta Stone by Guillaume Tell (USA) (M R Stoute) 3012 3491[5] 3682[5] 4046[4]

3 **TOLEDO QUEEN (Ire),** gr f El Gran Senor (USA) - Grey Dream by Auction Ring (USA) (P W Chapple-Hyam) 1016 1225[1] 1761[2] 2304[1] 2657[7]

4 **TOLL BOOTH,** b f Import - Little Hut by Royal Palace (J W Hope) 3216 4213

4 **TOMASHENKO,** ch g Efisio - Stockingful by Santa Claus (T W Donnelly) 1900 3089[8]

5 **TOMBARA (Ire),** ch g Reasonable (Fr) - Nejwah by Morston (Fr) (J G Coogan) 2141[8] 2321[2] 2556 3397[8]

2 **TOM MORGAN,** b c Faustus (USA) - Pirate Maid by Auction Ring (USA) (P T Walwyn) 2792[3] 3143[2] 3421[8] 4124[2] 4339[3] 4439[1]

2 **TOMMY COOPER,** br c Macmillion - My Charade by Cawston's Clown (Mrs Barbara Waring) 3079 3760[8] 4208[6]

4 **TOMMY TEMPEST,** ch g Northern Tempest (USA) - Silently Yours (USA) by Silent Screen (USA) (K R Burke) 4672a[5] 4719a[9] 4818a[2] 86[5] 348[3] 548[1] 721 1052[9] 1881[5] 2352[5] 2549[7] 3032[3] 3383[7]

3 **TOMMY TRUNGLE,** b g Jalmood (USA) - Lossiewells by Bustino (T H Caldwell) 2175 2205[3] 2443[6]

3 **TOMOS,** b c Sure Blade (USA) - Princess Genista by Ile de Bourbon (USA) (D Morley) 736[3] 2793[3] 3217[1] 3401 4150[4] 4352[2]

3 **TOM PARKER,** b g Today And Tomorrow - Winding Street by Pitskelly (P Howling) 4676a

3 **TOM PIPER,** b g Music Boy - Run For Love by Runnett (J Norton) 535[7] 1157[8] 1226[4] 1740[9]

3 **TOMSK,** ro c Siberian Express (USA) - Matoa (USA) by Tom Rolfe (N A Twiston-Davies) 3096[3] 3480[4]

2 **TOM WALLER (Ire),** b c Rainbow Quest (USA) - Alligatrix (USA) by Alleged (USA) (H R A Cecil) 4419[2] 4620[2]

2 **TONDRES (USA),** br c Chief's Crown (USA) - Icing by Prince Tenderfoot (USA) (C E Brittain) 793 2720[4] 2998[5]

2 **TONE CONTROL,** b c Sizzling Melody - Bold Duchess by Persian Bold (S P C Woods) 2720[7] 4127[5] 4330[7] 4577[4] 4671[4]

2 **TONGABEZI (Ire),** b f Shernazar - Hostellerie by Be My Guest (USA) (J C Harley) 3332[2] 3608[3] 4183[2] 4323[1] 4462

3 **TONI BUIO (Ire),** 1363[5]

5 **TONY'S DELIGHT (Ire),** b g Krayyan - Tinas Image by He Loves Me (G B Balding) 4686a[1]

4 **TONY'S FEN,** b c Trojan Fen - Ladyfish by Pampapaul (Kevin Prendergast) 4685a[2] 272[1] 308[1] 942[6] 1202[1] 2035[8] 2245[3] 2608[5] 3336[7] 3926[6] 4288[6] 4461[4] 4737[8]

3 **TONY'S MIST,** b g Digamist (USA) - Tinas Image by He Loves Me (R Hannon) 4675a[5] 1313[2] 1470[3] 1907[1] 2291 2712[5] 2864[2] 3837[8] 4024[2] 4120[1] 4490[1] 4597[7]

3 **TOOCANDO (Ire),** b f Nordance (USA) - Romantic Air by He Loves Me (C N Allen) 512[4] 823[2] 2068

2 **TOOGOODFORYOU,** b c Doc Marten - Lady Carol by Lord Gayle (USA) (N Bycroft) 1759 2817[8] 3321[8] 4032[9] 4342 4577 4618 4756[3]

4 **TOOLITTLE TOOLATE (Ire),** ch g Be My Guest (USA) - Star Of India by General Assembly (USA) (J C Harley) 1025[8] 3398[5] 3663[2] 4119

2 **T O O MAMMA'S (Ire),** ch f Classic Secret (USA) - Bohemian Rhapsody by On Your Mark (J Berry) 969[5] 1189[5] 1391[7] 1964

3 **TOO WILD (USA),** (N Zito) 1070

3 **TOP CEES,** b c Shirley Heights - Sing Softly by Luthier (P W Harris) 459 761[1] 1204[2] 2025[2] 2393[2] 2907

3 **TOP DIVER (Ire),** br g Primo Dominie - Jenny Diver (USA) by Hatchet Man (USA) (Francis M O'Brien) 3395 3720[7] 4639

3 **TOPESKI,** b f Petoski - Top Of The League by High Top (P J Makin) 2097[3]

4 **TOP GENERATION,** b f High Top - Likeness by Young Generation (Michael Cunningham) 1651[4] 1962[6] 2512[2] 2881 3685[2] 3773[9]

2 **TOP GUIDE (USA),** ch c Diesis - Raahia (Can) by Vice Regent (Can) (A A Scott) 4421[2]

3 **TOP GUNNER (Ire),** b g Lomond (USA) - Top Mouse by High Top (Mrs M E Long) 323[5] 441[9] 1061[5]

2 **TOPNOTCH,** ch f Indian Ridge - Serration by Kris (R M Whitaker) 4103[5] 4345[6] 4423

3 **TOPOGRAPHE (Fr),** b g Doyoun - Tirana (USA) by Fappiano (USA) (D K Weld) 307[1] 576[9] 4384 4583[1]

8 **TOP ONE,** ch g Sallust - Light Diamond by Florescence (C J Hill) 39[6] 133[4] 163 837[1] 1097 1588 3460 3758[7] 3896

2 **TOP PERFORMER (Ire),** br f Chief Singer - Star Of India by General Assembly (USA) (P Aspell) 4459

3 **TOP PET (Ire),** br g Petong - Pounelta by Tachypous (R Akehurst) 690 945[9] 1483[7] 2212[7] 2715 3450 3837 4092[4] 4341

3 **TOP RANK,** b c Law Society (USA) - On The Top by High Top (M C Pipe) 459 875 1526[5] 1910[1] 2135[3] 4502[4]

4 **TOP REGISTER (USA),** b c Dixieland Band (USA) - Contralto by Busted (Lord Huntingdon) 293[8] 4420[6]

3 **TOP SALSE (Fr),** b g Salse (USA) - Justicia by Nonoalco (M Rolland) 637[4]

3 **TOPSEYS TIPPLE (Ire),** br f Hatim (USA) - Gradille by Home Guard (USA) (Daniel J Murphy) 1106[1] 1511[9] 1553 2286[8]

5 **TOP SHIEL,** b h Top Ville - Gelder Shiel by Grundy (L M Cumani) 1720[2] 2581 3986[3] 4300 4597[6]

3 **WARSPITE,** b g Slip Anchor - Valkyrie by Bold Lad (Ire) (J Joseph) 515^5 842^7 1067^6 1469^8

2 **WARTHILL WHISPERS,** ch f Grey Desire - Dunesian by Dunbeath (USA) (M Brittain) 1182^2 1461^9 2199^6 3629^8 4484^6 4602

2 **WARWICK WARRIOR (Ire),** b g Reasonable (Fr) - Almost Heaven by Corvaro (USA) (P C Haslam) 2819^5 3084^5 3126^4 3815^3

2 **WARWICK WHISPER (Ire),** ch g Classic Secret (USA) - Enaam by Shirley Heights (P C Haslam) 2917

4 **WASHINGTON RED,** ch g Tickled Pink - Apple Queen by Behistoun (R Lee) 2729

4 **WASSL'S NANNY (Ire),** b f Wassl - Granny's Bank by Music Boy (John J McLoughlin) 1513 4057 4386^5 4625

4 **WASSL THIS THEN (Ire),** b f Wassl - Dancing Decoy by Troy (D W P Arbuthnot) 674 894^8 1268^8 2113^1 2474^4 3010^5 3282^8 3891^1 4364^8 4522^3 4676^4

2 **WATANI (USA),** ch c Riverman (USA) - Azayim by Be My Guest (USA) (R W Armstrong) 3633^1 3785^1 4273^8

4 **WATCH ME GO (Ire),** b g On Your Mark - Nighty Night by Sassafras (Fr) (M Dods) 120^3 4488 4605

2 **WATER BARON (USA),** b or br g Greinton - Rosey Ramble (USA) by Chieftain II (M J Heaton-Ellis) 3079^7

3 **WATER DIVINER,** b g Dowsing (USA) - Prudence by Grundy (K G Wingrove) 4574 4751

3 **WATER GYPSY,** b f Dowsing (USA) - Fortune Teller by Troy (M J Heaton-Ellis) 2578^1 2898^9 4254

3 **WATERLORD (Ire),** b g Bob Back (USA) - Ringtail by Auction Ring (USA) (M J Heaton-Ellis) 44^5 172^2 220^5 328^4 519^2 836^4 3140^2 3302^3 3487^9 3766 4333 4495^1 4652

3 **WATER SKIER,** b c Nishapour (Fr) - Wave Dancer by Dance In Time (Can) (M C Chapman) 4322^5 4525^8

3 **WATHIK (USA),** ch c Ogygian (USA) - Copper Creek by Habitat (H Thomson Jones) 1806 2206^6 3177 3791^2 4166^6

4 **WAVE HILL,** b g Sizzling Melody - Trikymia by Final Straw (P R Hedger) 663 1069^8 1346^4 1641^1 1973^6 2156^4 2622^6 3269 3531^3 3883^6 4007^7 4710^3

2 **WAVELET,** ch f Sharrood (USA) - Wave Dancer by Dance In Time (Can) (B W Hills) 2357^6 4033^3

6 **WAVE MASTER,** b g Chief Singer - Sea Fret by Habat (R J Hodges) 4115

2 **WAVE THE WAND (Ire),** b c Fairy King (USA) - Blasted Heath by Thatching (M Halford) 1608^2 1643^1 2403^7 2745^5 4052

5 **WAWEEWAWOO (Ire),** b m Rusticaro (Fr) - Ceduna (Fr) by Right Tack (D Moffatt) 3005^6 3135^6 3536^9 4217^9

6 **WAXING LYRICAL,** b m Noalto - Honey To Spare by Track Spare (J L Eyre) 531

2 **WAYFARERS WAY (USA),** ch c Manastash Ridge (USA) - Miss Daytona (USA) by Nashua (R Hannon) 3130^5 3422^4 4498^1 4720^6

4 **WAYWARD SON,** ro g Risk Me (Fr) - Mummy's Chick by Mummy's Pet (J J Bridger) 4806a^9 85 224^9 771

3 **WAZEERAH (USA),** b f The Minstrel (Can) - Gramy (Fr) by Tapioca II (J H M Gosden) 2401^8

2 **WAZIN (USA),** b c Afleet (Can) - On To Royalty (USA) by On To Glory (USA) (H Thomson Jones) 2875^2 3470

3 **WEALTHYWOO,** ch f Rich Charlie - Woomargama by Creetown (H J Collingridge) 4734a^4 4805a 7^6 31^5 167^6 240^6 455^6 614^9 1148 2052^9 2288^8

3 **WEAVER BIRD,** b f Master Willie - Sweet Snow (USA) by Lyphard (USA) (H Candy) 2290^5 4320^3 4522

3 **WEAVER GEORGE (Ire),** b g Flash Of Steel - Nephrite by Godswalk (USA) (N Chamberlain) 608^4 888^4 1271 1832^5 3090^9 3374^7

3 **WEB OF STEEL,** gr g Regal Steel - Wenreb Vii (T Casey) 4126 4565

4 **WEDDING RING (Ire),** ch f Never So Bold - Fleur D'Oranger by Northfields (USA) (R Collett) 1370^5 4749^3

5 **WEDNESDAYS AUCTION (Ire),** b g Mazaad - Happy Always by Lucky Wednesday (P R Rodford) 2865^6 3066^5 3513^9

5 **WEEKDAY CROSS (Ire),** b g Taufan (USA) - Isoldes Tower by Balliol (J R Jenkins) 2869

4 **WEEKEND GIRL,** b f Vorvados - Mrs Scattercash by Northfields (USA) (W M Brisbourne) 227 837 1038^7 1230 1537

3 **WEEKEND MADNESS (Ire),** b f Dance Of Life (USA) - Spring Break by Cure The Blues (USA) (P Aspell) 258^1 573^2 665^7 4636^5

5 **WEE SARAH,** ch m Electric - Playtex by Be Friendly (T D Barron) 107^3 161^3 253^4 383^4 592^3 818^7 4031^2 4458 4640

3 **WEFY (USA),** b c Danzig (USA) - Harbor Flag (USA) by Hoist The Flag (USA) (A A Scott) 3117^6 3590^7 4126^7

2 **WEIGH ANCHOR,** b c Slip Anchor - Argon Laser by Kris (I A Balding) 4259^3 4419^1

6 **WELL AND TRULY,** b m Rousillon (USA) - Altana by Grundy (B A McMahon) 3^2 30^1 55^4 111^3 165^2 219^3 279^3 290

4 **WELL APPOINTED (Ire),** b g Petorius - So Stylish by Great Nephew (A A Hambly) 315 480^5 533^4 619^5 2020^2 2367^4 2670^3 3986^4

4 **WELL BOUGHT (Ire),** b f Auction Ring (USA) - Knighton House by Pall Mall (C V Lines) 127^2 492^5 882^6 1354^8

4 **WELLINGTON ROCK (USA),** ch g Lyphard's Wish (Fr) - Cuz's Star (USA) by Galaxy Libra (J A R Toller) 771^6 2816^3 3290^5 3714^9

3 **WELL SUITED,** b g Elegant Air - Gay Appeal by Star Appeal (B J McMath) 951^3 1027 1713^8 2289^2 2758^8 3053^2 3263^8 3787^6 4129^9

6 **WELLSY LAD (USA),** ch g El Baba (USA) - Iwishiknew (USA) by Damascus (USA) (D W Chapman) 4692a^2 4716a^7 4808a^8 17^7 77^6 144^2 177^6 200^7 249 409^9 565^3 700^6 914 1073^4 3323^8

3 **WELL TRIED (Ire),** b f Thatching - Good Effort by Try My Best (USA) (R Hollinshead) 4773a^6 1 121^5 428

7 **WELLWOTDOUTHINK,** b m Rymer - Doubly Royal by Royal Buck (Mrs M Reveley) 3832^5 3971^6

3 **WELSH HERITAGE (Ire),** b f Slip Anchor - Mohibbah (USA) by Conquistador Cielo (USA) (Lord Huntingdon) 2563^8 3225^8 4254

7 **WELSHMAN,** ch g Final Straw - Joie de Galles by Welsh Pageant (M Blanshard) 857^3 1752 2101^4 2397^3 2662^3 3473^1 3675^1 3907^7 4505^1

4 **WELSH MILL (Ire),** b c Caerleon (USA) - Gay Milly (Fr) by Mill Reef (USA) (N Tinkler) 792 1484^1 2061 2395^3 2962

2 **WELSH MIST,** b f Damister (USA) - Welwyn by Welsh Saint (R Boss) 1814^5 2114^1 2618^4 3472^4 3723^1

3 **WEMYSS BIGHT,** b f Dancing Brave (USA) - Bahamian by Mill Reef (A Fabre) 561^1 1033^1 1525^5 2054^1 2405^1 3931^2 4311 4744^8

2 **WENLOCH LAD,** b g Royal Match - Remainder Lady by Connaught (J H Peacock) 3084 4098 4761^9

2 **WENLOCK LADY,** b f Lochnager - Be Serious (USA) by Laugh Aloud (J H Peacock) 2423^8

4 **WE'RE ALL GAME,** b f Mummy's Game - Swynford's Pride by Rapid River (B C Morgan) 421^5 548 837 1052^8 1982^7 2215^9 2584

9 **WE'RE IN THE MONEY,** ch m Billion (USA) - Fandance by Gay Fandango (USA) (J Wharton) 3689^6

4 **WESBEST (Ire),** b or br g Balboa - Rose Of Carlow Vii (Michael McCullagh) 1468 1996^6 2296^2 2461^9 2842 3805^6

8 **WESSEX MILORD,** ch g Stanford - Miss Osprey by Sea Hawk II (J A Bennett) 4746a^5 43^6 114^6 235^8 1701^8 2012^5 2350^8 4206

7 **WESSEX WARRIOR,** b g Anfield - Achiever by Tarqogan (A A Hambly) 244^9 826 1146 1696^7 1961

3 **WESSHAUN,** b f Shaunicken - Wessex Flyer by Pony Express (W G M Turner) 4700a^6 4720a^6 3693^5 3866 4666^7

2 **WEST BUOYANT (USA),** b or br c Gone West (USA) - Mrs Beeton (USA) by Temperence Hill (USA) (J L Dunlop) 3130^9 3704^2 4182^2

4 **WEST BY WEST (USA),** b c Gone West (USA) - West Turn by Cox's Ridge (George Arnold) 1541^1 2262^3 3640^2 4068^6

3 **WEST COAST,** b f Forty-Niner (USA) - Harifa by Green Dancer (A Fabre) 4169^4 4473^4

2 **WESTCOAST,** b g Handsome Sailor - Pichon by Formidable (USA) (M Tate) 908^8 1108^6 1519^3 2539 2705^8 3131^8 4050^3 4453

3 **WHO'S TOM (Ire),** b g Tate Gallery (USA) - Clover Princess by Right Tack (W J Musson) 934 1496[8] 1902 3249

3 **WHYALLA RAIN,** br f Chief Singer - Nullah by Riverman (USA) (D R Laing) 4740a[8] 516[9] 1300[5] 1419 1627 2120[9] 4481

4 **WHY ME LINDA (Ire),** ch f Nashamaa - Last Act by Gala Performance (USA) (Richard O'Donovan) 790 1386[5] 1619[6] 2295[5] 2511[4] 3296[9] 3395

2 **WICKLOW BOY (Ire),** b c Roi Danzig (USA) - Pickety Place by Prince Tenderfoot (USA) (R Hannon) 687[7] 1241[4] 1624[4] 2412[5] 3129[8] 3704[4]

3 **WICKLOW WAY (Ire),** b f Pennine Walk - Faraway Places by Flair Path (Kevin Prendergast) 2827 870[3] 1122[3] 1431[2] 1755[8] 2496[4] 2923[6] 3164[4] 3368[1] 3684[5] 4246[4] 4409[1] 4639[3] 4738[4]

7 **WICK POUND,** b g Niniski (USA) - Hors Serie (USA) by Vaguely Noble (J A B Old) 73[3]

2 **WIDE OUTSIDE (Ire),** b f Don't Forget Me - East River (Fr) by Arctic Tern (USA) (G L Moore) 1955 2364 2817[5] 4127[9] 4339[7] 4483[5]

8 **WIDE SUPPORT,** br g Be My Guest (USA) - Riva Ring by Riva Ridge (USA) (A Moore) 4336

2 **WIJDAN (USA),** ch f Mr Prospector (USA) - Height Of Fashion (Fr) by Bustino (Major W R Hern) 4421[3]

3 **WILBURY WONDER,** ch f Precious Metal - Bridgett Ann by Keep The Peace (R Brotherton) 4596

2 **WILCUMA,** b c Most Welcome - Miss Top Ville (Fr) by Top Ville (P J Makin) 3760[6] 4421 4698[3]

5 **WILD AND LOOSE,** b g Precocious - Regain by Relko (D R C Elsworth) 259[5] 327[8] 475 3020[2] 3292[7] 4007[8]

3 **WILDE (Ire),** b g Commanche Run - Brews Bridge by Thatching (F Dunne) 267[4] 1822

5 **WILDERNESS SONG (Can),** (J Day) 4472[8]

3 **WILD EXPRESSION,** ch g Then Again - Pleasure Island by Dalsaan (C Tinkler) 699 928

5 **WILD FANTASY (Ire),** b m Cataldi - Sea Shrub by Ballymore (A P O'Brien) 3524[5] 3577[9] 3857[2] 4137[2]

2 **WILDFIRE (Swi),** br c Beldale Flutter (USA) - Little White Star by Mill Reef (USA) (R Akehurst) 1640 2571[6]

3 **WILD GALE (USA),** 779[3] 1070[8] 1542[3]

2 **WILD INVADER (USA),** b c Seattle Slew (USA) - Double Axle (USA) by The Axe II (H R A Cecil) 2299[4] 2964[6]

3 **WILD JEWEL (Can),** b or br f Wild Again (USA) - Jewel Of The Mile (USA) by Spectacular Bid (USA) (J Hammond) 4413[2]

2 **WILD PLANET (USA),** b f Nureyev (USA) - Ivory Wings (USA) by Sir Ivor (R Charlton) 2240[5] 2909[3] 3265[1] 3586[2] 3925[6]

4 **WILD POPPY,** br f Norwick (USA) - Brandon Creek by Be My Guest (USA) (P M McEntee) 605 723[9] 1425

5 **WILD PROSPECT,** b g Homing - Cappuccilli by Lorenzaccio (C Tinkler) 363[5] 565[2] 1194 1436 3523 4235 4623 4694

2 **WILD ROSE OF YORK,** gr f Unfuwain (USA) - Chepstow Vale (USA) by Key To The Mint (USA) (M Johnston) 3992[5] 4422[6] 4663[3]

4 **WILD STRAWBERRY,** ro f Ballacashtal (Can) - Pts Fairway by Runnymede (Miss B Sanders) 1059[9] 1588[4] 1956[1] 2291[1] 2475[7] 2847[2] 4591

5 **WILD SURPRISE (Ire),** ch g Coquelin (USA) - Passeggiata (USA) by Elocutionist (USA) (John J McLoughlin) 2039

2 **WILD TRUFFES (Ire),** b f Danehill (USA) - Wild Abandon (USA) by Graustark (N A Graham) 3422 3836

4 **WILKINS,** b g Master Willie - Segos by Runnymede (Miss H C Knight) 349[4] 1041[3] 1380 2026[5]

2 **WILKS DREAM (Ire),** ch f Ballacashtal (Can) - Indy by Indigenous (W G M Turner) 325[9] 708[4] 886 4483[7] 4758[7]

2 **WILL GLOW,** b c Glow (USA) - Radiant (USA) by Foolish Pleasure (USA) (T G Mills) 2123 3520

3 **WILL HYDE,** b c Coquelin (USA) - Debutante Ball by Cut Above (C Weedon) 1126[3] 1662[7] 2213[6]

3 **WILLIAMSTOWN (USA),** b or br c Seattle Slew (USA) - Winter Sparkle (USA) by Northjet (USA) (P Vestal) 3822[2]

2 **WILLIAM TELL,** gr c Chief Singer - Aim To Please by Gunner B (R F Johnson Houghton) 3979[2] 4276[6] 4423

3 **WILLINGLY (Ire),** ch f Master Willie - Soon To Be by Hot Spark (H Candy) 4565[9] 4649[5]

4 **WILL OF STEEL,** ch g Master Willie - Collapse by Busted (Mrs J R Ramsden) 315[3] 524[1] 581[5] 737 1298 1530[9] 2045[7] 2601[6] 2854

4 **WILL OF STEEL (Fr),** 4194[7] 4398[7]

2 **WILLOW,** br f Kind Of Hush - Pickwood Sue by Right Boy (Lady Herries) 3828[9] 4543

3 **WILLOW RIVER (Can),** b f Vice Regent (Can) - Barkerville Belle (USA) by Ruthie's Native (USA) (J H M Gosden) 522[4] 3132[6] 3489[3] 3818[4]

3 **WILLSHE GAN,** b f Precocious - Quisissanno by Be My Guest (USA) (Denys Smith) 633[1] 1017 1780[5] 2731[6] 3220[4] 3410 3995 4166

3 **WILL'S LEGACY,** ch c Northern Tempest (USA) - Crosby Triangle by Windjammer (USA) (G Lewis) 326[8] 1470[8] 1991 2291

4 **WILL SOON,** ch g Nicholas Bill - Henceforth by Full Of Hope (H Candy) 1069 1318[5] 1604[4] 2121[7] 2371[1] 3830[4] 4024 4355

2 **WILLWIN,** gr f Belfort (Fr) - Harem Queen by Prince Regent (Fr) (J L Harris) 1182[5] 1598[4] 1863[4] 2268[3] 2637[2] 2949[8] 4097 4264 4489

3 **WILLY THE WEAVER (Ire),** b f Petorius - We've Just Begun (USA) by Huguenot (USA) (Michael Cunningham) 1649 2322

4 **WILSONIC,** b f Damister (USA) - Cape Chestnut by Bustino (M Johnston) 651[5] 824 1178[7] 1398 2059[3] 2091[4] 2239[9] 2457[2] 2735[2]

5 **WILTOSKI,** b g Petoski - Cojean (USA) by Prince John (R R Ledger) 1880

2 **WIND IN HER HAIR (Ire),** b f Alzao (USA) - Burghclere by Busted (J W Hills) 3625[2] 4249

2 **WINDOW DISPLAY,** gr c Chilibang - Stubble by Balidar (Mrs N Macauley) 399[8] 625[1] 738[8] 979[4] 1168[5] 1343[3] 1741[3] 2125[2] 2377[6] 2588[2] 2825[2] 3475[4] 3688[5] 3950[4] 4034[8]

3 **WINDRUSH BOY,** br g Dowsing (USA) - Bridge Street Lady by Decoy Boy (M McCormack) 367[7] 1095[6]

3 **WINDRUSH LADY,** ch f Risk Me (Fr) - Pusey Street by Native Bazaar (M McCormack) 1713[4] 4030[1] 4499[6]

8 **WINE BROKER,** b g Corvaro (USA) - Peak Time by Exdirectory (D T Hughes) 819[8]

3 **WINGED VICTORY (Ire),** b f Dancing Brave (USA) - Mighty Fly by Comedy Star (USA) (I A Balding) 583[1] 746[4] 915[1] 3312[4] 3474[4] 3660[3] 4145[2] 4280

3 **WINGED VICTORY (USA),** b c Nijinsky (Can) - Wedding Picture (USA) by Blushing Groom (Fr) (J H M Gosden) 751[6] 1429[2] 1751[2] 2174[1] 3784[8] 3899[8]

4 **WINGED WHISPER (USA),** ch g Air Forbes Won (USA) - Soft Reply (USA) by Personality (USA) (J A Pickering) 264 375[7] 521 678[9] 834 1034[9] 1389[3] 1562[6] 1880 2149 2353[5] 2729

2 **WINGS AHEAD,** b c Precocious - Pakpao by Mansingh (USA) (T Fairhurst) 564[4] 1189[7] 1391[6] 1759 1863[6] 1964[6] 2229[6] 2453[3] 2679[3] 3598[8] 3671[5] 3968[3] 4081[4] 4215[8] 4491[5]

3 **WINGS COVE,** b g Elegant Air - Bel Esprit by Sagaro (Lady Herries) 318[5] 3224[4] 3513[1] 3646[2] 4283[7] 4538[6]

5 **WINGS OF FREEDOM (Ire),** b g Fairy King (USA) - Wingau (Fr) by Hard To Beat (J R Jenkins) 3010[7]

2 **WINGS OF HORAGE (Ire),** b c Horage - Villars by Home Guard (USA) (R Champion) 2325 2687[6] 3362[9] 4526[8]

2 **WINNER RUSH (Ire),** 3803[6]

3 **WINNING APPEAL (Fr),** b f Law Society (USA) - Bella Senora (USA) by Northern Dancer (R Hannon) 582 1315[4] 1469[9]

6 **WINNING HEART,** ch m Horage - Silver Heart by Yankee Gold (A P O'Brien) 272[5] 308 895[6] 1552[9] 3029

2 **WINNING LINE,** ch g Master Willie - Buckhurst by Gulf Pearl (M H Easterby) 3091[4] 3362[3] 3598[1] 4122[4] 4365[4] 4531

2 **WINNING PACT (USA),** b c Alydar (USA) - Six Months Long (USA) by Northern Dancer (G Jones) 4743[5]

NOTES

Speed Ratings Flat 1993

● THIS list derived from Sporting Life Average Times, represents the optimum time-rating of a horse after taking into account varying ground conditions, adjusted to 9st. To qualify for inclusion a horse must earn a speed rating of over 39.(Two-year-olds 35). Supplementary information after the name, figure, and finishing position indicates the distance, course, going based on time, date and type of race the rating was achieved in.

A Prayer For Wings 44[2] (6f, Kemp, S, Apr 12)
Abbey's Gal 59[1] (6f 209yds, Brig, F, Apr 8, *H*)
Abbraak (USA) 49[1] (1m, Ayr, Y, Jun 19, *M*)
Abergele 46[3] (6f, York, Y, Jun 12, *H*)
Able Choice (IRE) 40[2] (7f 16yds, Sand, Y, Sep 15)
Absolute Magic 49[3] (6f 212yds, Sali, F, Jun 24)
Absolutely Nuts 41[6] (5f, Folk, F, May 25, *H*)
Absolution 40[1] (5f, Edin, F, Jul 12, *H*)
Abury (IRE) 51 (1m 4f 10yds, Epso, F, Jun 5, *G*)
Acanthus (IRE) 44[1] (1m 6f 132yds, Donc, G, May 3, *H*)
Accommodating (USA) 65[3] (1m 2f, Long, G, May 23, *G*)
Acrobate (USA) 43[3] (1m 4f, Sali, G, Jul 29, *H*)
Acteur Francais (USA) 74[2] (7f, Long, Y, Sep 19, *L*)
Addicted To Love 40[1] (1m 6f, Newm, G, Oct 1, *H*)
Admirals Realm 44[1] (5f, Beve, G, Aug 12, *H*)
Adolescence (IRE) 46[2] (1m, Naas, G, Jul 21)
Adored Slew (USA) 68[5] (1m 2f, Deau, G, Aug 29, *G*)
Advocat (GER) 54[2] (1m 2f, Leop, G, May 8, *G*)
Aegaen Lady 40[1] (1m 1f 218yds, Leic, Y, Oct 26, *H*)
Air Reveuse (IRE) 42[3] (1m 2f 110yds, Stcl, G, Mar 25, *L*)
Aisla (USA) 61[4] (7f, Long, S, Oct 14, *L*)
Aitch N'bee 56[2] (7f 214yds, Brig, F, Sep 22, *H*)
Aiybak (IRE) 48[1] (1m 4f, Curr, F, Jun 26)
Ajdayt (USA) 48[1] (1m, Sali, G, Jul 10, *H*)
Ajfan (USA) 77[3] (1m, Newm, F, Apr 29, *G*)
Akkazao (IRE) 49[2] (1m 2f, Ripo, F, Jun 17, *H*)
Al Moulouki 49[1] (7f, Good, Y, Jul 29, *H*)
Al Senafi (IRE) 62[2] (1m 2f, Asco, Y, Sep 24, *H*)
Alasad 49[2] (1m 4f 8yds, Pont, F, Jul 23, *M*)
Alasib 58[4] (5f, Newm, G, Oct 16, *H*)
Albemine (USA) 41[4] (1m 14yds, Sand, G, Aug 11, *H*)
Albertazzi (IRE) 43[2] (1m 2f, Curr, F, Aug 28, *M*)
Alderbrook 63[2] (1m 2f 85yds, York, G, Aug 18, *H*)
Alderney Prince (USA) 44[1] (1m 1f 209yds, Brig, F, Jul 1, *H*)
Alflora (IRE) 78[2] (1m, Long, Y, Oct 3, *G*)
Alhijaz 72[5] (1m, Good, G, Jul 28, *G*)
Alice Springs (USA) 62[3] (1m 2f 110yds, Stcl, G, May 14, *G*)
Alinova (USA) 41[5] (1m 6f, Good, Y, Jul 30, *H*)
Aljaz 41[3] (5f 11yds, Bath, G, Jul 19)
Aljazzaf 61[1] (1m 2f 36yds, Chep, F, Jun 29)
Alkabar 41[3] (1m 3f, Redc, Y, Oct 26, *C*)
Alkhafji 59[1] (1m 4f, Sali, G, Jul 29, *M*)
Allegan (USA) 68[3] (1m 7f 195yds, York, G, Aug 17, *L*)
Alleged Saron (USA) 54[6] (1m 2f 110yds, Stcl, G, May 14, *G*)
Allinson's Mate (IRE) 53[1] (7f, Donc, G, Oct 22, *C*)
Allmosa 43[3] (1m 6f, Sali, G, Aug 12, *H*)
Allthruthenight (IRE) 53[1] (5f, Epso, F, Jul 28, *H*)
Almamzar (USA) 48[2] (1m 4f 66yds, Ches, G, Jul 9, *H*)
Alouette 48[1] (1m 4f, Leop, G, Aug 7, *H*)
Always Friendly 74[1] (1m 4f, Newj, G, Jul 16)
Amaze 66[3] (1m 2f 6yds, Pont, G, Sep 20, *H*)
Amazing Feat (IRE) 78[2] (1m 1f, Newm, G, Oct 15, *L*)
Amazon Express 50[1] (1m 4f, Newj, G, Jun 25, *H*)
Ambiguously Regal (USA) 57[3] (1m 4f, Thir, F, Jun 15, *H*)
Amenable 47 (1m, Ripo, G, May 26, *H*)
American Hero 47[1] (1m 4f 17yds, Hami, F, Sep 6, *H*)
American Swinger (USA) 49[2] (1m 14yds, Sand, G, Aug 20, *H*)
Amron 68[1] (5f 140yds, Donc, G, Sep 8, *H*)
Ancestral Dancer 55 (1m, Deau, G, Jul 31, *G*)
Andromaque (USA) 62[1] (1m, Kemp, G, Jun 23)
Aneesati 42[1] (1m, Kemp, G, May 3, *M*)
Anna Of Saxony 73[4] (1m 4f, Good, Y, Jul 30, *L*)
Anne Bonny 64[4] (2m, Good, Y, Jul 29, *G*)
Another Episode (IRE) 50[3] (5f, Donc, F, May 3, *C*)
Another Jade 53[1] (6f, Hayd, G, May 29, *H*)
Another Lane 47[1] (5f, Beve, G, Jul 27, *C*)
Ansellman 50[6] (5f, Redc, G, Nov 2)
Apogee 67[1] (1m 4f, Stcl, G, Jun 4, *G*)
Apple Tree (FR) 85[3] (1m 4f 10yds, Epso, F, Jun 3, *G*)
Appledorn 56[3] (6f, Donc, F, Mar 27, *L*)
Appliance 46[2] (1m 2f 110yds, Stcl, G, Mar 25, *L*)
Approach The Bench (IRE) 62[5] (1m 2f, Leop, F, Sep 11)
Arabat 45[1] (7f, Redc, F, Jun 19, *H*)
Arabellajill 70[3] (6f, Asco, Y, Jun 18, *H*)
Aradanza 57[1] (6f, York, Y, Jun 12, *H*)
Aragrove 46 (5f, Newm, G, Sep 30, *H*)
Arak (USA) 51[2] (1m, Ayr, F, Sep 17, *H*)
Arany 53[5] (1m, Newm, G, Oct 16, *H*)
Arbusha (USA) 76[3] (1m 4f, Curr, G, Aug 14, *G*)
Arcadian Heights 72[3] (2m, Good, Y, Jul 29, *G*)
Arcangues (USA) 76[6] (1m 2f 7yds, Sand, G, Jul 3, *G*)
Archange (USA) 65[4] (1m 2f, Deau, G, Aug 21, *G*)
Ardkinglass 71[3] (1m, Kemp, F, Sep 3, *L*)
Aremef (USA) 41[2] (1m 3f 106yds, Ling, F, Aug 14, *H*)
Argyle Cavalier (IRE) 43[3] (1m 3f 16yds, Hami, G, Jun 10, *H*)
Arjuzah (IRE) 57[1] (7f, Donc, G, Sep 9, *L*)
Arkaan (USA) 53[4] (1m 4f, Kemp, F, Sep 4, *H*)
Armiger 74[2] (1m 6f 132yds, Donc, G, Sep 11, *G*)
Aroom 44[1] (5f, Donc, G, May 29)
Artistic Reef 70[3] (6f, Newm, G, Apr 13, *L*)
Asema (USA) 72[1] (1m, Curr, G, Jul 10, *L*)
Ashgore 44[1] (6f, Newc, G, Jul 26, *H*)
Ashtina 63[2] (5f, Asco, F, Jul 23, *H*)
Aspect (USA) 40[4] (1m 2f, Newj, F, Jul 7, *M*)
Assessor (IRE) 82[2] (1m 6f, Curr, Y, Sep 18, *G*)
Astair (FR) 71[1] (1m 1f, Evry, F, Jul 24, *G*)
Aster Aweke (IRE) 41[3] (1m 2f, Leop, G, Oct 23, *M*)
Asterix 42[3] (6f 16yds, Chep, G, Sep 11, *H*)
Astudillo (IRE) 64[3] (7f, Long, Y, May 4, *L*)
Athens Belle (IRE) 58[5] (1m 2f, Deau, G, Aug 7, *G*)
Atherton Green (IRE) 45[1] (1m 2f 32yds, Newc, F, Aug 28, *H*)
Aube Indienne (FR) 60[4] (1m 2f, Deau, G, Aug 7, *G*)
Aughfad 64[3] (6f, Good, F, May 19, *H*)
Autumnis (USA) 45[2] (7f, Newm, F, Apr 15, *M*)
Awesome Venture 41[1] (7f, Redc, G, Aug 6, *M*)
Awestrike (USA) 47[3] (6f 212yds, Sali, F, Aug 11, *H*)
Azhar 68[1] (1m 4f, Sali, G, Jun 23, *H*)
Azilian (IRE) 57[2] (1m 4f, Thir, G, Aug 9)
Azureus (IRE) 52[2] (1m 2f, Ripo, F, Aug 2, *C*)
Azzilfi 71[3] (1m 4f, Asco, G, Jun 15, *G*)
Badie (USA) 48[4] (1m 2f 7yds, Wind, G, Aug 16)
Badolato (USA) 69[6] (1m 4f, Chan, F, Jun 6, *G*)
Bag Of Tricks (IRE) 42[1] (1m 2f 18yds, Epso, F, Aug 30, *C*)
Bagalino (USA) 40[1] (1m 3f 135yds, Wind, G, Jul 31, *H*)
Baladiya 43[1] (1m 3f 101yds, Yarm, F, Jul 22, *C*)
Balawhar (IRE) 44[3] (1m 4f, Curr, S, Oct 9, *G*)
Baligay 54[1] (5f, Sali, F, Jun 23, *H*)
Ballad Dancer 46[2] (6f 15yds, Nott, G, Aug 3, *H*)
Ballasecret 70[1] (6f, Good, G, Sep 11, *H*)
Ballerina Bay 48[4] (1m, Asco, G, Jul 24)
Ballet Shoes (IRE) 42[1] (5f, Ripo, G, Aug 14, *M*)
Ballinamallard (USA) 77[5] (1m, Deau, G, Jul 31, *G*)
Ballykett Prince (IRE) 49[5] (1m, Curr, S, Mar 27, *H*)
Ballykett Lady (USA) 60[6] (1m 4f, Curr, G, Jul 10, *G*)
Band On The Run 55[5] (7f, Asco, G, Sep 25, *H*)
Barathea (IRE) 86[2] (1m, Asco, G, Sep 25, *G*)
Barboukh 59[6] (1m 2f, Good, Y, Jul 30, *H*)
Bardolph (USA) 47[3] (2m 1f 34yds, Bath, F, Sep 27, *H*)
Barford Lad 51[3] (1m 2f 6yds, Newb, F, May 15, *H*)
Baron Ferdinand 64[1] (1m 2f 85yds, York, F, Jul 10, *H*)
Barratry 41[2] (1m 1f 218yds, Leic, F, Aug 9, *H*)
Bashayer (USA) 75[4] (1m 2f, Good, Y, Jul 30, *H*)
Batabanoo 54[1] (1m 4f 17yds, Hami, F, Aug 16, *H*)
Battle Colours (IRE) 49[6] (1m 54yds, Nott, Y, Oct 18, *H*)
Bay Queen 52[1] (1m 1f 207yds, Beve, G, Aug 12, *H*)
Baya (USA) 75[2] (1m 2f, Mais, Y, Sep 27, *G*)
Bayin (USA) 40[1] (5f 218yds, Leic, Y, Oct 25, *H*)

Baysham (USA) 41[6] (6f, Sali, G, Jun 8, *H*)
Beau Venture (USA) 57[3] (6f, Ripo, Y, Apr 7, *H*)
Beauchamp Hero 59[1] (1m, Newj, G, Jul 17, *H*)
Bedava (FR) 65[4] (1m 2f, Evry, Y, Sep 25, *L*)
Bellissi (IRE) 44[2] (1m, Naas, S, Jun 17, *M*)
Bells Of Longwick 46[1] (5f 6yds, Sand, G, Jul 14, *H*)
Bellsabanging 47[6] (5f, Ling, F, Aug 26)
Belmoredean 44[1] (7f 214yds, Brig, G, Apr 19, *H*)
Bene Merenti (IRE) 56[1] (6f, Curr, G, Sep 12, *H*)
Beneficial 73[1] (1m 4f, Asco, G, Jun 15, *G*)
Bentico 41[1] (1m 2f 7yds, Wind, G, Jul 12, *H*)
Benzoe (IRE) 64[1] (6f, York, S, Oct 9, *H*)
Berinsfield 57[6] (1m, Long, G, May 9, *G*)
Bernstein Bette 42[2] (7f 100yds, Beve, F, Jun 2, *H*)
Bertie Wooster 47[3] (6f, Newj, F, Jul 30, *H*)
Bescaby Boy 41[2] (1m 4f, Donc, F, Mar 25, *H*)
Beware Of Agents 64[3] (7f, Newj, F, Aug 7, *H*)
Big Blue 42[3] (1m 2f 21yds, Yarm, F, Jul 21, *H*)
Big Pat 40[4] (1m 4f 93yds, Newc, F, Jun 26, *H*)
Bigstone (IRE) 91[1] (1m, Asco, G, Sep 25, *G*)
Bikasaite (FR) 69[2] (1m 4f, Mais, G, Oct 26, *L*)
Biljan (USA) 40[2] (1m 2f 46yds, Bath, F, May 8)
Biloela 42[2] (1m 2f, Redc, Y, Oct 26)
Bin Ajwaad (IRE) 73[2] (1m, Long, G, May 9, *G*)
Bint Lariaaf (USA) 57[2] (1m, Long, G, Sep 7, *L*)
Bint Lariaff (USA) 59[1] (1m, Mais, G, May 11, *L*)
Bit On The Side (IRE) 57[1] (1m 2f 85yds, York, S, Oct 6, *H*)
Bitofabanter 49[3] (2m, Leop, G, Nov 6, *H*)
Bitter's End (IRE) 52[1] (7f, Epso, F, Jun 5, *M*)
Bizana (IRE) 47[1] (1m, Curr, G, Jul 10, *H*)
Black Dragon (IRE) 45 (1m 2f, Asco, Y, Sep 24, *H*)
Blackpatch Hill 58[3] (1m 4f, Asco, Y, Jun 16, *H*)
Blockade (USA) 57[2] (1m, Newc, G, Jun 25, *H*)
Blow Dry (IRE) 46[4] (6f 214yds, York, Y, Jun 12, *H*)
Blue Blazer 52[2] (1m 1f, Sand, G, Jun 11, *H*)
Blue Grit 43[2] (6f, Pont, F, Jun 7, *H*)
Blue Grotto (IRE) 48[2] (1m 2f, Ayr, F, Sep 18, *H*)
Blue Judge (IRE) 79[2] (1m 4f 10yds, Epso, F, Jun 2, *G*)
Blue Lion 60[3] (7f 202yds, York, S, Oct 6)
Blue Topaze 55[1] (5f 218yds, Leic, F, Jun 5, *H*)
Blues Traveller (IRE) 74[3] (1m 4f 10yds, Epso, F, Jun 2, *G*)
Blush Rambler (USA) 55 (1m, Long, G, May 9, *G*)
Blyton Lad 83[1] (5f, Redc, G, Nov 2)
Bo Knows Best (IRE) 50[1] (1m 4f 10yds, Epso, F, Aug 30, *H*)
Bob's Return (IRE) 84[1] (1m 3f 195yds, York, G, Aug 17, *G*)
Bobbie Dee 47 (1m 2f, Good, Y, Jul 30, *H*)
Bobbysoxer 46[1] (1m 4f, Sali, F, Aug 11, *H*)
Bobzao (IRE) 78[1] (1m 2f 6yds, Newb, G, Jul 17, *L*)
Bodari 59[1] (5f, Sali, F, Sep 2, *H*)
Bold Angel 48[4] (6f, Ripo, F, Jun 28, *C*)
Bold Lez 72[1] (5f, Kemp, G, May 12)
Bold Memory 40[3] (1m, Good, G, Jul 31, *C*)
Bold N' Flashy (CAN) 56 (5f, York, G, Aug 19, *G*)
Bold Pursuit (IRE) 58[4] (1m 2f 75yds, Ches, G, Jul 9)
Bold Resolution (IRE) 51[4] (2m 45yds, Asco, Y, Sep 23, *H*)
Bold Stroke 58[2] (1m 2f 6yds, Pont, G, Sep 20, *H*)
Boloardo 69[4] (1m 3f 183yds, Leic, F, Jun 5, *L*)
Bon Point 64[1] (1m, Deau, G, Aug 28, *G*)
Bookcase 46[1] (1m 2f, Good, Y, Jun 18, *H*)
Borage (FR) 60[1] (1m, Mais, Y, Oct 21, *L*)
Born To Be 57[2] (6f, Good, G, Sep 11, *H*)
Borodislew (USA) 63 (6f 110yds, Deau, G, Aug 1, *G*)
Boursin (IRE) 45[5] (7f 122yds, Ches, F, May 6, *H*)
Bout En Bout (FR) 57[3] (1m, Mais, G, Apr 20, *L*)
Bradawn Breever (IRE) 72[2] (5f, Leop, G, Jun 7, *G*)
Brandon Prince (IRE) 54[2] (2m 45yds, Asco, G, Jun 19, *H*)
Brandonhurst 52[1] (1m 1f, Sand, G, Jun 11, *H*)
Branston Abby (IRE) 78[1] (6f, York, Y, May 11, *H*)
Brata (USA) 48[1] (1m, Naas, G, Jul 21)
Brave Raider (IRE) 46[3] (1m, Naas, S, Jun 17, *M*)
Bravura 58[2] (1m, Newj, F, Jul 6, *H*)
Brazany (USA) 50[5] (1m 2f 110yds, Long, Y, Apr 25, *G*)
Break Bread (USA) 59 (1m 2f, Ayr, G, Jul 19, *G*)
Breakfast Boogie 46[1] (5f 43yds, Yarm, G, Sep 14, *M*)
Brigade 63[2] (7f, Newb, F, Jun 10, *H*)
Brigante Di Cielo 62[1] (1m 2f, Ling, G, May 22, *H*)
Brigg Fair 66[4] (6f 8yds, Newb, G, Jul 16, *L*)
Bright Generation (IRE) 72[6] (1m 4f, Long, Y, Sep 12, *G*)
Bright Moon (USA) 81[3] (1m 4f, Long, Y, Sep 12, *G*)
Bright Mountain (USA) 58[3] (1m 4f, Long, F, Jun 26, *G*)
Brilliant 46[3] (1m 2f, Newj, F, Jul 30, *H*)
Broctune Bay 41 (1m 2f, Ripo, G, May 26, *M*)
Brodessa 42[4] (1m 6f 15yds, Nott, G, Aug 23, *H*)
Broughtons Turmoil 43[2] (7f, Kemp, F, Sep 3, *H*)
Broughton's Tango (IRE) 47[3] (1m 4f, Newm, G, Oct 29, *H*)
Brown's (FR) 53[1] (1m, Ripo, G, Jun 16, *H*)
Bunty Boo 69[1] (5f, Sali, G, Aug 12)
Burdur 60[1] (1m, Mais, G, May 25, *L*)
Burooj 61[2] (1m, Newm, G, Oct 16, *H*)
Bustinetta 51[3] (1m 6f, Hayd, G, May 29, *H*)
Buzzards Bellbuoy 54[2] (7f 202yds, York, F, Jul 9, *H*)
Caesour (USA) 62[2] (1m, Mais, G, Jul 6, *G*)
Cairo Prince (IRE) 68[4] (1m 4f 10yds, Epso, F, Jun 2, *G*)
Calamanco 46[1] (5f 13yds, Nott, Y, Oct 18)
Caleman 56[1] (6f 209yds, Brig, F, Aug 24, *H*)
Call Me I'm Blue (IRE) 65[1] (5f, Asco, G, Sep 24, *H*)
Call The Guv'nor 45[3] (1m 6f, Sand, G, Aug 11, *H*)
Call To The Bar (IRE) 56[2] (5f, Ayr, Hrd, Sep 16, *H*)
Cambara 63[1] (1m, Newm, G, Oct 30, *H*)
Camden Buzz (IRE) 47[4] (2m, Leop, G, Nov 6, *H*)
Camden's Ransom (USA) 49[1] (1m 2f 7yds, Sand, G, Apr 23, *H*)
Canny Chronicle 46[2] (1m 4f, Asco, Y, Sep 24, *H*)
Cantoris 54[6] (5f 34yds, Newb, F, Aug 14, *H*)
Cape Pigeon (USA) 47[3] (7f, Epso, F, Jun 5, *H*)
Captain Horatius (IRE) 61[1] (1m 4f, Donc, G, Nov 6, *L*)
Captain's Guest (IRE) 56[2] (1m 4f, Sali, G, May 28)
Cardoun (FR) 76[3] (5f, Long, G, May 13, *G*)
Carelaman 63[3] (1m 2f 75yds, Ches, S, Oct 20, *H*)
Caromish (USA) 42[1] (6f, Good, G, Jun 18, *H*)
Carranita (IRE) 49[3] (6f 15yds, Nott, Y, Oct 28)
Case Law 53[1] (5f 11yds, Bath, Y, Apr 27)
Caspian Beluga 45[1] (1m 1f 209yds, Sali, G, Sep 29, *H*)
Caspian Tern (USA) 42 (1m 4f, Good, Y, Jul 30, *L*)
Cast The Line 47[2] (1m 4f, Newm, G, Oct 29, *H*)
Casteddu 52[1] (6f 214yds, York, Y, May 12)
Casting Shadows 44[1] (7f, Kemp, F, Sep 3, *H*)
Castle Courageous 63[1] (1m 6f 19yds, Redc, G, Sep 25, *H*)
Castlerea Lad 67[1] (6f, Newc, G, Jun 26, *H*)
Castoret 53[6] (1m 4f 10yds, Epso, F, Aug 30, *H*)
Catherines Well 64[1] (5f, York, Y, Jun 11, *H*)
Catherineofaragon 52[4] (6f 16yds, Chep, Y, Oct 19, *H*)
Catrail (USA) 90[2] (6f, Hayd, F, Sep 4, *G*)
Causley 48[2] (6f 206yds, Carl, F, Jun 23, *H*)
Cee-Jay-Ay 50[2] (7f, Warw, G, Jun 19, *H*)
Celestial Key (USA) 53[2] (7f, Donc, G, Oct 23)
Cezanne 59[1] (1m 2f 6yds, Pont, G, Sep 20, *H*)
Chaddleworth (IRE) 57[6] (1m, Newm, F, Apr 15, *G*)
Champagne Grandy 49[1] (7f, Catt, Y, Oct 16, *H*)
Chanzi (USA) 56[1] (1m, Curr, G, Sep 12, *G*)
Charme Slave (FR) 64[4] (6f, Evry, G, Jul 13, *G*)
Charmed Knave 44[2] (7f, Ling, F, Aug 7)
Chatham Island 44[2] (1m 4f 5yds, Newb, F, Aug 14, *H*)
Chatoyant 58[1] (1m 2f, Newm, G, Sep 30, *H*)
Chef Supreme (USA) 66[5] (1m 2f, Mais, Y, Sep 27, *G*)
Chesa Plana 74[2] (1m 2f 110yds, Stcl, Y, Oct 31, *G*)
Cheveux Mitchell 47[2] (7f 64yds, Newb, Y, May 26, *H*)
Cheviot Amble (IRE) 59[1] (7f, Naas, G, May 1, *H*)
Chief Minister (IRE) 41[4] (1m 6f, Hayd, G, May 29, *H*)
Chief Of Staff 47[3] (1m 54yds, Nott, Y, Oct 18, *H*)
Chili Heights 45[3] (6f, Sali, G, Jun 8, *H*)
Chilly Breeze 46[2] (5f 43yds, Yarm, F, Aug 10, *H*)
Choir Practice 50[1] (5f 2yds, Leic, G, Sep 13, *H*)
Ciseaux (USA) 59[1] (6f, Curr, Y, Aug 14, *H*)
Civil Law (IRE) 42[3] (1m 2f, Ripo, G, May 26, *M*)
Clandolly (IRE) 62[1] (5f, Leop, S, May 14, *H*)
Classic Match (IRE) 57[2] (1m, Curr, G, Sep 12, *H*)
Classical Affair (IRE) 65[2] (5f, Leop, G, Aug 8, *H*)
Claudia Miss 40[1] (6f 206yds, Carl, G, May 7, *C*)
Cliveden Gail (IRE) 67[1] (2m, Leop, G, Nov 6, *H*)
Cloud Of Dust 73[2] (1m, Kemp, F, Sep 3, *L*)
Clouded Elegance 42[4] (1m 2f 85yds, York, G, May 11, *H*)
College Chapel 86[1] (6f 110yds, Deau, G, Aug 1, *G*)
Collier Bay 51[2] (1m 6f 19yds, Redc, Y, Oct 5, *H*)
Coltrane 45[1] (1m 1f 149yds, Folk, S, Oct 5)

Comanche Companion 46^{1} (1m 14yds, Sand, G, Jul 21, *H*)
Command 'n Control 45^{4} (1m 2f, Leop, G, Aug 2, *H*)
Commander In Chief 86^{1} (1m 4f 10yds, Epso, F, Jun 2, *G*)
Commendable (IRE) 51 (1m 6f 110yds, Stcl, S, May 1, *G*)
Common Council 49^{3} (1m 2f 32yds, Newc, G, Mar 30, *H*)
Common Law (IRE) 51^{1} (6f, Redc, G, Oct 5, *M*)
Complete Madness 43^{2} (1m 2f 36yds, Chep, S, Jul 15)
Compota (FR) 62^{2} (1m 2f 110yds, Stcl, G, Apr 24, *G*)
Coneybury (IRE) 54^{5} (1m 14yds, Sand, G, Aug 20, *H*)
Confronter 47 (7f, Asco, G, Apr 28, *H*)
Conspicuous (IRE) 44^{2} (1m 1f 218yds, Leic, G, Apr 24, *M*)
Cool Luke (IRE) 45^{5} (7f 214yds, Carl, F, Jun 23, *H*)
Coolrain Lady (IRE) 43^{3} (1m 2f, Leop, F, Sep 11, *H*)
Corals Dream (IRE) 69^{2} (1m, Kemp, Y, Sep 21, *H*)
Corona Gold 40^{1} (7f, Sout, F, Aug 6, *H*)
Corrazona (USA) 71 (1m 4f, Long, Y, Sep 12, *G*)
Corrouge (USA) 56^{3} (1m 7f, Chan, Y, Jun 15, *L*)
Count Of Flanders (IRE) 48^{1} (1m 1f 218yds, Leic, F, Sep 7, *M*)
Courageous Knight 47^{3} (1m 2f 36yds, Chep, G, Jul 8, *H*)
Court Minstrel 41^{1} (6f 212yds, Sali, F, Aug 11, *H*)
Cox Orange (USA) 66^{1} (7f, Long, S, Oct 14, *L*)
Crack Regiment (USA) 78^{6} (6f 110yds, Deau, G, Aug 1, *G*)
Cradle Days 66^{2} (5f, Redc, G, Nov 2)
Credit Squeeze 50^{3} (1m, Asco, G, Jul 24)
Crime Ofthecentury 47^{1} (5f, Folk, F, Apr 20)
Croft Valley 63^{1} (7f, Newb, F, Jun 10, *H*)
Croire (IRE) 50^{2} (7f 2yds, Ches, F, May 5, *M*)
Cromarty 43^{6} (1m 2f 75yds, Ches, Y, Oct 19, *H*)
Crossillion 51^{1} (1m, Redc, F, Aug 7, *H*)
Crystado (FR) 52^{6} (1m 2f, Newm, F, May 1, *H*)
Crystal Jack (FR) 42^{6} (5f, Beve, G, Aug 12, *H*)
Cuff Link (IRE) 49^{3} (1m 4f, Kemp, Y, Sep 21, *M*)
Culture Vulture (USA) 75^{3} (1m, Newj, F, Jul 7, *G*)
Cumbrian Waltzer 70^{2} (6f, Asco, Y, Jun 18, *H*)
Cumbrian Rhapsody 47^{1} (1m 4f 93yds, Newc, Y, Nov 1, *H*)
Cumbrian Challenge (IRE) 61^{3} (1m 2f 85yds, York, G, Aug 18, *H*)
Cutting Reef (IRE) 41^{1} (1m 7f 110yds, Mais, Y, Apr 2, *L*)
Cynic 41^{2} (6f 214yds, York, G, May 13, *H*)
D'Arros (IRE) 42^{1} (1m 2f, Long, G, Jun 24, *G*)
Dadarissime (FR) 76 (1m 4f, Stcl, F, Jul 4, *G*)
Daftari (IRE) 43^{2} (1m, Curr, S, Jun 2, *M*)
Dagny Juel (USA) 44^{1} (7f, Ling, G, Jul 10, *M*)
Dahlia's Best (USA) 47^{5} (1m 2f, Leop, G, Apr 17, *L*)
Dajraan (IRE) 67^{6} (1m 6f 110yds, Stcl, S, May 1, *G*)
Dana Springs (IRE) 73^{5} (1m 4f, Long, Y, Sep 12, *G*)
Danakal (USA) 77^{2} (6f 110yds, Deau, G, Aug 1, *G*)
Dancienne (FR) 77^{3} (1m 4f, Long, Y, Sep 12, *G*)
Dancing Bloom (IRE) 69^{2} (1m, Newj, F, Jul 7, *G*)
Dancing Domino 44^{5} (7f, Donc, G, Oct 22, *H*)
Dancing Spirit (IRE) 40^{1} (6f, Kemp, G, Jun 23, *H*)
Dancing Sensation (USA) 40^{2} (7f, Kemp, F, Aug 18, *H*)
Danish Fort 59^{1} (1m 3f 135yds, Wind, F, Aug 28)
Danny Boy 51^{1} (1m, Newc, G, Sep 28, *C*)
Danse Royale (IRE) 69^{1} (1m 2f, Deau, G, Aug 7, *G*)
Darbonne (USA) 49^{5} (7f, Newm, G, Apr 14, *L*)
Darecliff (USA) 59^{5} (1m 2f, Asco, Y, Sep 24, *H*)
Dariyoun (USA) 70^{1} (1m 4f, Mais, G, Oct 26, *L*)
Dark Den (USA) 44^{2} (1m 3f, Redc, Y, Nov 2, *H*)
Dark Eyed Lady (IRE) 57^{2} (5f, Newm, G, Sep 30, *H*)
Darmstadt (USA) 41^{5} (1m 5f 194yds, York, G, Aug 17, *H*)
Darrery 58 (1m 4f, Donc, G, Nov 6, *H*)
Daru (USA) 61 (2m, Good, Y, Jul 29, *G*)
Darussalam 40^{2} (6f 16yds, Chep, G, Sep 11, *H*)
Dashing Colours (IRE) 72^{4} (6f, Leop, G, Aug 7, *G*)
Dashing Fellow (IRE) 40^{1} (1m 2f, Ripo, F, Aug 31, *H*)
Daswaki (CAN) 52^{1} (7f 16yds, Sand, Y, Sep 14, *H*)
Dauberval (USA) 63^{1} (6f, Evry, F, Apr 21, *L*)
Dawning Street (IRE) 72^{1} (7f 202yds, York, G, Aug 19, *H*)
Dayflower (USA) 70^{5} (1m, Newm, F, Apr 29, *G*)
Dayjuz (IRE) 41^{1} (5f, Pont, F, Jul 6, *H*)
Dear Doctor (FR) 80^{5} (1m 4f, Stcl, F, Jul 4, *G*)
Deb's Ball 41^{1} (1m 4f 44yds, Catt, G, Mar 31, *H*)
Debsy Do (USA) 52^{1} (6f 206yds, Carl, F, Jun 23, *H*)
Declassified (USA) 69^{3} (1m 3f 195yds, York, G, Aug 17, *G*)
Deduce 56^{2} (1m 6f, Newm, G, May 21, *H*)
Dee Raft (USA) 53^{1} (1m 2f 60yds, Donc, G, Oct 23, *C*)
Deer Hunt 44^{4} (1m 4f, Asco, G, Sep 25, *H*)
Deevee 42^{1} (1m, Newj, G, Jul 17, *H*)
Del Deya (IRE) 56^{1} (1m 2f 21yds, Yarm, Y, Oct 27)
Delpiombo 46^{1} (1m 4yds, Pont, G, May 28, *C*)
Delve (IRE) 42^{1} (1m 1f 213yds, Nott, F, Apr 19)
Densben 59^{1} (6f, Ayr, F, Jul 24, *H*)
Derab (USA) 44^{1} (1m 4f, Newm, G, Oct 14, *H*)
Dernier Empereur (USA) 83^{2} (1m 4f, Long, Y, Sep 12, *G*)
Desert Calm (IRE) 49^{5} (1m 1f, Curr, G, Jun 26, *H*)
Desert Champ (USA) 50^{2} (7f, Redc, G, Sep 25, *M*)
Desert Power 53^{2} (1m 2f 75yds, Ches, S, Oct 20, *H*)
Desert Secret (IRE) 43^{6} (1m 2f 75yds, Ches, F, May 6, *L*)
Desert Shot 47^{6} (7f, Ling, G, Sep 16)
Desert Team (USA) 54^{1} (1m 4f, Newj, F, Jul 6, *G*)
Desert Thunder (IRE) 64^{3} (5f, Leop, G, Apr 17, *H*)
Desert Zone (USA) 52 (1m 2f 75yds, Ches, F, May 4, *H*)
Devilry 40^{1} (1m 2f 6yds, Newb, F, May 15, *H*)
Devils Den (IRE) 49^{2} (1m, Newc, G, Sep 28, *C*)
Diaco 50^{3} (1m 54yds, Nott, Y, Oct 18, *C*)
Diaco (USA) 41^{4} (1m 4f 110yds, Deau, G, Aug 28, *L*)
Diamonaka (FR) 63^{2} (1m 4f, Stcl, G, Jun 4, *G*)
Diamonds Galore (CAN) 70^{3} (6f, Leop, G, Aug 2, *H*)
Diese (USA) 65^{1} (1m 2f 110yds, Stcl, G, Apr 24, *G*)
Diet 47^{2} (6f, York, G, Aug 17, *H*)
Digpast (IRE) 42^{3} (6f 209yds, Brig, F, Sep 22, *H*)
Dili (USA) 49^{2} (1m 2f 120yds, Hayd, Y, Sep 24, *M*)
Dinesen 56^{2} (7f, Curr, S, Nov 3)
Diplomatist 40^{2} (1m 2f 7yds, Sand, G, Jul 21)
Dis Moi Tout (FR) 58^{4} (1m, Evry, G, Jul 10, *G*)
Discord 59^{1} (1m 5f 61yds, Newb, G, Jul 17, *H*)
Dittisham (USA) 41^{3} (7f 2yds, Ches, F, May 5, *M*)
Dixie Favor (USA) 44^{2} (7f, Curr, G, Jun 5, *H*)
Dixieland Melody (USA) 47^{2} (7f, Newj, F, Aug 28, *H*)
Djais (FR) 57^{2} (1m 7f, Chan, Y, Jun 15, *L*)
Dokkha Oyston (IRE) 55^{1} (5f, Edin, F, Jul 5, *H*)
Dolphin Street (FR) 83^{1} (7f, Long, S, Oct 10, *G*)
Domicksky 54^{2} (6f, Donc, G, Nov 4, *H*)
Dominuet 69^{1} (6f, York, Y, Jun 11, *H*)
Domulla 48^{2} (6f 8yds, Newb, F, Aug 13, *H*)
Don't Jump (IRE) 52^{1} (1m 54yds, Nott, Y, Oct 18, *C*)
Dondook (USA) 54^{2} (1m 4f 110yds, Mais, F, Jun 22, *L*)
Donnasoo (IRE) 52^{2} (5f, Leop, G, Apr 17, *H*)
Double Bass (USA) 57^{2} (1m 2f 36yds, Chep, F, Jun 29)
Double Blue 61^{2} (6f, Newm, F, Apr 29, *H*)
Double Blash 42^{1} (1m 7f 110yds, Long, F, Jun 26)
Double Bounce 42^{1} (6f, Folk, F, Aug 17)
Double Flutter 51 (1m, Good, Y, Jul 29, *H*)
Double Shift 41^{2} (6f, Folk, G, Sep 20, *H*)
Down The Flag (USA) 51^{5} (1m 4f, Long, Y, Apr 27, *G*)
Doyce 43^{3} (1m 4f, Donc, G, Sep 10, *H*)
Dramanice (USA) 51^{2} (6f 212yds, Sali, F, Jun 24)
Dream Talk 75^{5} (5f, Long, G, May 13, *G*)
Dreams End 59^{3} (1m 5f 194yds, York, G, Aug 18, *H*)
Dress Sense (IRE) 68^{3} (7f, Newj, F, Jul 8, *H*)
Drum Sergeant 56^{2} (5f, York, Y, May 12, *H*)
Drum Taps (USA) 73^{5} (1m 4f, Asco, G, Jul 24, *G*)
Drummer Hicks 59^{1} (1m 205yds, York, S, Oct 9, *H*)
Duckey Fuzz 47^{1} (7f, Newb, Y, Oct 21, *H*)
Duke Of Eurolink 65^{5} (1m 4f, Good, Y, Jul 30, *L*)
Dune River 45^{3} (7f 100yds, Beve, F, May 8, *H*)
Duplicity (IRE) 75^{2} (6f, York, Y, May 11, *H*)
Durshan (USA) 44^{5} (1m 4f, Asco, Y, Jun 16, *H*)
Dutosky 41^{5} (1m 2f, Newj, F, Jul 7, *H*)
Duveen (IRE) 41^{1} (1m 2f 21yds, Yarm, F, Jul 14, *H*)
Dyab (USA) 54^{6} (1m 2f, Ling, G, May 22, *H*)
Eager Deva 63^{1} (5f, Redc, F, Jun 1, *H*)
East Liberty (USA) 42^{3} (1m, Kemp, G, Jun 23)
Eastern Memories (IRE) 65^{1} (1m 14yds, Sand, Y, Apr 24, *H*)
Easy Access (IRE) 49^{4} (1m, Newb, G, Jul 17, *H*)
Easy Line 52^{2} (6f, Kemp, G, Jul 7, *C*)
Echo-Logical 55^{1} (7f, Epso, F, Jun 30, *H*)
Ecu de France (IRE) 56^{2} (1m 2f 18yds, Epso, F, Jun 4, *H*)
Edbaysaan (IRE) 71^{3} (1m 6f 132yds, Donc, G, Sep 11, *G*)
Eden's Close 47^{3} (1m 2f 7yds, Sand, G, Aug 21, *H*)
Educated Pet 52^{1} (6f, Donc, G, Nov 4, *H*)

Efharisto 62[5] (1m 2f, Good, Y, Jul 27, *H*)
Efizia 43[4] (1m 2f 32yds, Newc, F, Aug 28, *H*)
Efra 50[1] (6f, Folk, Y, Oct 5, *H*)
Egyptown (FR) 67[2] (1m 4f, Long, F, Sep 5, *L*)
El Duco (USA) 58[3] (7f, Newm, G, Oct 14)
El Gahar 52[3] (1m 14yds, Sand, G, Aug 20, *H*)
El Jubail (IRE) 48[1] (1m 2f 36yds, Chep, F, Jun 29, *M*)
El Volador 42[3] (1m 4f, Sali, F, Aug 11, *H*)
El Yasaf (IRE) 65[1] (5f, Epso, G, Jun 2, *H*)
El Zorro Dorado (IRE) 49[4] (6f, Leop, G, Aug 2, *H*)
Elacata (GER) 70[4] (1m 2f 110yds, Stcl, Y, Oct 31, *G*)
Elaine Tully (IRE) 53[2] (1m 4f, Sali, F, Jun 8, *H*)
Elatis (USA) 51[5] (1m 4f, Donc, G, Nov 6, *H*)
Elbio 82[1] (5f, Asco, G, Jun 18, *G*)
Elite Guest (IRE) 55[3] (1m 4f, Stcl, G, Jun 4, *G*)
Elizabeth Bay (USA) 72[3] (1m, Deau, G, Jul 31, *G*)
Elle Shaped (IRE) 62[1] (5f 16yds, Ches, F, May 5, *H*)
Embankment (IRE) 64[1] (1m, Kemp, Y, Sep 21, *H*)
Embros (USA) 64[3] (1m 2f, Evry, Y, Sep 25, *L*)
Emperor Jones (USA) 72[2] (1m 1f, Evry, F, Jul 24, *G*)
Empire Pool 44[2] (1m 4f 10yds, Epso, F, Jun 5, *H*)
En Attendant (FR) 82[1] (7f, Newj, F, Aug 7, *H*)
Encore Une Fois (IRE) 46[3] (2m, Good, G, Sep 11, *H*)
Encoremoi (USA) 56[1] (1m 4f, Long, F, Sep 5, *L*)
Enharmonic (USA) 76[5] (1m 2f, Asco, G, Jun 15, *G*)
Enjoy Plan (USA) 44[4] (1m 2f, Long, Y, May 20, *G*)
Environment Friend 84[2] (1m 4f 10yds, Epso, F, Jun 3, *G*)
Epaphos (GER) 64[1] (1m 6f, Stcl, G, May 31, *G*)
Erdiya (USA) 54[3] (1m 4f, Long, F, Sep 5, *L*)
Ertlon 53[1] (7f 202yds, York, F, Sep 1, *H*)
Etosha 51[2] (1m, Kemp, G, Jun 23)
Euro Festival 59[4] (7f, Thir, S, May 15, *H*)
Eurolink Thunder 64[1] (7f, Newc, G, Jul 26, *G*)
Eurostorm (USA) 57[6] (1m 2f, Curr, G, Jun 26, *G*)
Ever So Lyrical 44[1] (1m, Donc, G, Nov 4, *H*)
Everglades (IRE) 71[1] (6f, York, G, Jul 10, *H*)
Ewald (IRE) 48[4] (5f, York, G, Jul 9, *H*)
Express Gift 63[2] (1m 2f 85yds, York, S, Oct 6, *H*)
Extra Point 58 (1m 2f, Evry, Y, Sep 25, *L*)
Eye Witness (IRE) 44[3] (1m 1f 213yds, Nott, Y, Jun 16, *H*)
Ezzoud (IRE) 85[1] (1m 2f 85yds, York, G, Aug 17, *G*)
Face North (IRE) 49[1] (6f, Folk, F, Jul 13)
Face The Future 52[1] (6f 3yds, Yarm, G, Sep 16, *H*)
Factual (USA) 56[4] (6f, Good, G, May 18)
Fairy Lore (IRE) 46[1] (1m, Naas, S, Jun 17, *M*)
Fairy Story (IRE) 47[1] (7f 2yds, Ches, F, Jun 23, *H*)
Fairydel (IRE) 41[1] (7f, Naas, S, Jun 17)
Fangio 58[2] (5f 6yds, Sand, G, Aug 21, *H*)
Fanmore (USA) 72[1] (1m, Mais, G, Jul 6, *G*)
Fantastic Dream (IRE) 58[5] (1m, Long, G, May 9, *G*)
Farfelu 66[3] (6f, Newc, G, Jun 26, *H*)
Farmaan (IRE) 49[2] (1m, Curr, S, Mar 27)
Farmer's Pet 50 (1m 4f 10yds, Epso, F, Aug 30, *H*)
Fascination Waltz 52[4] (6f, Good, F, Aug 28, *H*)
Fastness (IRE) 68[3] (1m 1f, Evry, F, Jul 24, *G*)
Fatherland (IRE) 69[2] (1m, Curr, Y, May 15, *G*)
Fawz (IRE) 47[1] (7f 16yds, Sand, G, Jun 11, *H*)
Fay's Song (IRE) 42[5] (6f 16yds, Chep, G, Sep 11, *H*)
Faydini (IRE) 57[2] (1m 2f, Curr, G, Jun 5, *H*)
Fayfa (IRE) 44[2] (1m 2f 6yds, Newb, G, May 14, *L*)
Felawnah (USA) 72[4] (1m, Newm, F, Apr 29, *G*)
Feminine Wiles (IRE) 68[4] (1m, Newj, F, Jul 7, *G*)
Ferrycarrig Hotel (IRE) 55[2] (1m 2f, Leop, G, Aug 2, *H*)
Field Of Vision (IRE) 49[2] (7f 140yds, Ling, F, Aug 1, *H*)
Fieldridge 44[1] (1m 2f 18yds, Epso, F, Jun 2, *H*)
Fighter Squadron 40[6] (6f, Newj, F, Aug 6, *H*)
Fighting Temeraire (IRE) 45[6] (5f, Long, G, May 13, *G*)
Final Frontier (IRE) 49[1] (7f, Donc, G, Sep 9, *H*)
Finir En Beaute (FR) 49[4] (1m 2f 110yds, Stcl, Y, Apr 16, *G*)
Finjan 54[1] (6f, Thir, F, Jul 30, *H*)
Fire Carpet (USA) 40[2] (1m 2f 60yds, Donc, G, Nov 4, *M*)
Firm But Fair 43[6] (1m 2f, Newm, G, Apr 13, *M*)
Firm Pledge (USA) 46[1] (7f, Newm, F, Apr 29)
First Bid 54[1] (1m 4f, Donc, G, Sep 10, *H*)
First Gold 40[5] (5f, Warw, F, Aug 30, *C*)
First Option 51[1] (5f, Warw, F, Aug 30, *C*)
Fitzcarraldo (USA) 65[4] (1m, Curr, Y, May 15, *G*)
Fivesevenfiveo 55[2] (5f 161yds, Bath, G, Jun 12, *H*)
Flight Lieutenant (USA) 61[3] (1m 4f, Donc, G, Nov 6, *H*)
Fluvial (IRE) 42[1] (1m, Newm, G, Apr 14)
Food Of Love 52[1] (5f 13yds, Nott, F, Aug 4, *H*)
For The Present 49[2] (6f, Ayr, G, Jul 17, *H*)
Foresee 75[3] (1m 4f, Curr, G, Jun 27, *G*)
Forest Concert (IRE) 42[2] (7f, Leop, G, Oct 25, *H*)
Forever Diamonds 64[1] (7f 202yds, York, F, Jul 9, *H*)
Fort Wood (USA) 77[1] (1m 2f, Long, F, Jun 27, *G*)
Forthwith 62[2] (1m 2f 32yds, Newc, F, Aug 30, *L*)
Fourforfun 56[1] (7f 16yds, Sand, Y, Jul 14, *H*)
Fox Sparrow 50[2] (1m 205yds, York, S, Oct 9, *H*)
Fraam 65[1] (7f, Newm, G, Oct 1, *H*)
Freddie Lloyd (USA) 59[4] (5f, Asco, G, Jun 18, *G*)
Free Mover (IRE) 55[3] (1m 4f, Newj, G, Jun 25, *H*)
Freezing Bird (USA) 64 (1m 4f, Chan, F, Jun 6, *G*)
Frenchpark 48[4] (1m 2f, Newm, G, Oct 29, *L*)
Frescade (USA) 54 (1m 2f, Ling, G, May 22, *H*)
Fresher 73[2] (1m, Deau, G, Jul 31, *G*)
Fret (USA) 54[4] (1m 2f 75yds, Ches, F, May 6, *L*)
Friendly Brave (USA) 47[3] (7f 64yds, Newb, G, Sep 17, *H*)
Frogmarch (USA) 60[4] (1m, Good, Y, Jul 29, *H*)
Frontier Flight (USA) 46[4] (1m 2f 36yds, Chep, F, Jun 29)
Frosty Morning 45 (7f, Kemp, F, Sep 3, *H*)
Funny Baby (FR) 69[4] (1m 2f, Mais, Y, Sep 27, *G*)
Funny Hilarious (USA) 45[3] (1m 3f 200yds, Hayd, G, Sep 3, *H*)
Further Flight 81[1] (1m 7f 195yds, York, G, Aug 17, *L*)
Fylde Flyer 64[5] (6f, Newm, G, Apr 13, *L*)
Gabr 67[4] (7f 64yds, Newb, F, Aug 13, *G*)
Gant Bleu (FR) 43[1] (7f, Thir, G, Apr 16, *H*)
Garah 71[3] (5f 6yds, Sand, G, May 31, *G*)
Garden Of Heaven (USA) 57[3] (1m, Newm, G, Oct 30, *L*)
Garnock Valley 60[1] (6f, Kemp, S, Apr 10, *H*)
General Chaos (IRE) 47[5] (1m 2f, Curr, F, Aug 28, *H*)
General John (IRE) 42[1] (6f, Newj, F, Aug 27, *H*)
General Mouktar 56[2] (1m 4f, Kemp, F, Sep 4, *H*)
George Augustus (USA) 82[4] (1m 2f, Asco, G, Jun 15, *G*)
George Dillingham 50 (1m 2f, Newj, F, Jul 7, *H*)
Ghost Tree (IRE) 57[4] (7f 64yds, Newb, G, Sep 17, *H*)
Gilderdale 61[2] (1m 3f, Redc, G, Sep 25)
Gilt Throne 54[3] (6f 16yds, Chep, Y, Oct 19, *H*)
Gipsy Fiddler 59[2] (7f, Redc, F, Sep 24, *H*)
Gisarne (USA) 59 (1m 2f 32yds, Newc, F, Aug 30, *L*)
Glacial Arctic (USA) 63[1] (7f, Curr, G, Aug 28, *H*)
Glanville (USA) 45 (1m 4f 110yds, Deau, G, Aug 29, *G*)
Glide Path (USA) 59[1] (1m 3f 200yds, Hayd, G, Jul 3, *H*)
Gloire de Rose 40[2] (1m 2f, Evry, Y, Sep 13, *L*)
Gloria Mundi (FR) 60[5] (1m 6f 110yds, Stcl, S, May 1, *G*)
Glorieux Dancer (FR) 66 (1m 1f, Evry, F, Jul 24, *G*)
Glowing Jade 46[1] (7f, Donc, G, Oct 22, *H*)
Glowing Value (IRE) 54[3] (7f, Leop, G, Jun 7, *H*)
Gold Blade 43[1] (1m 1f 218yds, Leic, F, Sep 7, *H*)
Gold Braisim (IRE) 47[2] (6f, Leop, G, May 8, *H*)
Gold Script (FR) 42[2] (1m 7f 110yds, Mais, Y, Apr 2, *L*)
Gold Splash (USA) 69[3] (1m, Long, F, May 16, *G*)
Golden Chip (IRE) 54[1] (1m 2f, Ripo, F, Jul 17, *H*)
Golden Guest 40[3] (6f, Newm, G, May 21, *M*)
Golden Torque 46[3] (1m 3f 16yds, Hami, G, Apr 30)
Gondo 49[1] (5f, Ayr, F, Jul 19, *H*)
Gone For A Burton (IRE) 62[3] (1m 2f, Asco, Y, Sep 24, *H*)
Gone Savage 66[1] (5f 6yds, Sand, G, Jun 11, *C*)
Gone Troppo 43[2] (1m 2f, Ripo, G, Jun 16, *M*)
Good Hand (USA) 54[3] (2m 19yds, Newc, F, Aug 30, *H*)
Goodnight Kiss 64[2] (1m, Curr, Y, May 22, *G*)
Googly 56[1] (1m 2f 6yds, Newb, Y, Oct 21, *H*)
Gorinsky (IRE) 76[2] (5f 34yds, Newb, G, Sep 17)
Gothland (FR) 73[4] (7f, Long, Y, Sep 19, *L*)
Gran Senorum (USA) 46[1] (1m, Sout, G, Jul 2, *H*)
Grand Flotilla (USA) 63[4] (1m 6f 110yds, Stcl, S, May 1, *G*)
Grand Vitesse (IRE) 54[1] (1m, Good, G, Jul 31, *C*)
Granitton Bay 46[2] (7f, Redc, F, Jun 19, *H*)
Granse Oaks (USA) 54[5] (1m, Long, Y, Apr 25, *G*)
Great Cabaret (IRE) 49[3] (1m 2f, Leop, G, Oct 23, *H*)
Great Hall 50[2] (6f, Newj, F, Aug 27, *H*)
Great Max (IRE) 51[2] (1m 3f 16yds, Hami, G, Apr 30)
Great Palm (USA) 78[2] (1m 2f 7yds, Sand, Y, Apr 24, *G*)
Green Dollar 45[5] (7f, Newm, G, May 21, *H*)
Green Lane (USA) 54[1] (2m 1f 34yds, Bath, F, Sep 27, *H*)
Greenbank (USA) 42[4] (1m, Newb, G, May 14, *M*)
Greenlet (IRE) 50[2] (6f, Donc, G, May 29, *H*)
Grey Charmer (IRE) 44[1] (5f 217yds, Wind, G, Jun 14, *H*)
Grey Power 52[1] (1m 4f 8yds, Pont, Y, Oct 4, *H*)

Ground Nut (IRE) 40[4] (1m 2f 7yds, Sand, Y, Sep 14, *H*)
Grove Daffodil (IRE) 45 (1m 2f 85yds, York, F, Jul 10, *H*)
Guado D'Annibale (IRE) 57 (1m 2f 85yds, York, G, Aug 17, *G*)
Guest Of Honor (FR) 48[4] (1m, Mais, G, Apr 23, *L*)
Guide (FR) 55[1] (1m, Long, G, May 23, *L*)
Gussie Fink-Nottle (IRE) 41[1] (5f, Catt, G, Jul 28, *H*)
Gustavia (IRE) 46[3] (7f 9yds, Leic, F, May 24)
Gymcrak Premiere 72[3] (1m 14yds, Sand, G, Jul 3, *H*)
Habeta (USA) 44[1] (1m, Ripo, G, May 26, *H*)
Halesia (USA) 63[1] (1m 4f 110yds, Long, S, Oct 2, *G*)
Half A Tick (USA) 71[6] (1m 4f, Good, Y, Jul 30, *L*)
Half Term (USA) 63[2] (7f, Newc, G, Jul 26, *G*)
Halkopous 50[6] (1m 2f, Newm, G, Oct 29, *L*)
Hamadryad (IRE) 45[4] (1m, Thir, G, May 1, *H*)
Hamas (IRE) 74[1] (6f, York, G, May 13, *G*)
Hang A Right 48[4] (6f, Curr, S, Nov 3, *H*)
Hard Task 42[1] (1m 4f 60yds, Ripo, F, Aug 14, *H*)
Hard To Figure 78[1] (6f, Ripo, G, Aug 21, *H*)
Haroldon (IRE) 41[1] (1m 1f 213yds, Nott, F, Sep 6)
Harpoon Louie (USA) 42[4] (1m, Ayr, F, Sep 17, *H*)
Harry's Coming 41[1] (5f 217yds, Wind, G, Jun 28, *H*)
Hasten To Add (USA) 43[2] (1m 3f 195yds, York, G, Jun 12)
Hatoof (USA) 87[1] (1m 2f, Mais, Y, Sep 27, *G*)
Hatta Fort 40[5] (5f, Long, S, Oct 24, *G*)
Hawk Beauty (USA) 62[3] (1m, Long, Y, Apr 25, *G*)
Hazaam (USA) 70[3] (1m, Asco, G, Jun 15, *G*)
Hazard A Guess (IRE) 43[1] (1m 3f 200yds, Hayd, G, Sep 3, *H*)
He's A King (USA) 52[1] (1m 8yds, Leic, F, Aug 9, *H*)
Heaven-Liegh-Grey 53[1] (5f 34yds, Newb, F, Aug 14, *H*)
Heavenly Risk 60[4] (5f 6yds, Sand, G, Aug 21, *H*)
Helios 51[2] (7f, Good, F, May 20, *H*)
Here Comes A Star 52[3] (5f, Thir, G, Aug 27, *H*)
Hernando (FR) 86[1] (1m 4f, Long, Y, Sep 12, *G*)
Herora (IRE) 55[4] (7f, Epso, F, Jun 5, *H*)
Hi Nod 65[4] (1m, Newm, G, Oct 16, *H*)
Hickory Blue 43[5] (5f, Thir, G, Aug 9, *H*)
Hierarch (USA) 45[2] (1m 4f 93yds, Newc, F, Jul 26, *H*)
High Low (USA) 52[2] (1m, Ripo, F, Aug 14, *H*)
High Premium 64[2] (1m, Ayr, G, Jul 17, *H*)
High Summer 51[1] (1m 4f, Sout, G, Sep 17, *H*)
High Tycoon (IRE) 47[3] (6f, Curr, S, Oct 2, *L*)
Highbrook (USA) 67[3] (1m 3f 195yds, York, G, Aug 19, *H*)
Highest Sweep (FR) 49 (1m 2f, Stcl, G, Jul 14, *G*)
Highflying 66[2] (1m 3f 200yds, Hayd, G, Jul 3, *H*)
Highland Dress 47[3] (1m 4f, Asco, Y, Jun 18, *G*)
Highland Magic (IRE) 63[1] (6f 214yds, York, Y, Jun 12, *H*)
Hob Green 62[4] (6f, Ayr, Hrd, Sep 18, *H*)
Holly Golightly 71[4] (1m, Deau, G, Jul 31, *G*)
Home Park (IRE) 41[2] (1m 4f 8yds, Pont, F, Aug 4)
Homme de Loi (IRE) 55[2] (1m, Mais, Y, Oct 21, *L*)
Hopeful Bid (IRE) 47[2] (7f 140yds, Ling, F, May 7)
Hopesville (IRE) 52[5] (1m 2f, Leop, G, Aug 2, *H*)
Host (IRE) 50[4] (1m 14yds, Sand, G, Jul 3, *H*)
Hotaria 42[1] (6f 15yds, Nott, G, May 19, *H*)
How's Yer Father 65[1] (6f, York, G, Aug 17, *H*)
Hudo (USA) 61[3] (1m, Long, G, May 9, *G*)
Humam (IRE) 61[3] (7f 64yds, Newb, G, Jul 16)
Hunting Hawk (IRE) 75[3] (1m 4f, Chan, F, Jun 6, *G*)
Huron Warrior (USA) 49[2] (1m, Long, S, Oct 24, *G*)
Hurtevent (FR) 57[3] (1m 4f, Mais, G, Oct 26, *L*)
Husband (USA) 49[5] (1m 7f, Long, F, Jun 27, *G*)
Hushang (IRE) 61[1] (1m 2f, Curr, G, May 22, *L*)
Hyde's Happy Hour 40[1] (1m 2f, Ayr, Y, Jun 18, *H*)
Ice Pool (USA) 44[2] (1m 4yds, Pont, G, Aug 5, *M*)
Icy South (USA) 49[2] (1m 2f 7yds, Wind, F, Jul 5)
Idris (IRE) 57[3] (1m 2f, Leop, G, Oct 25, *L*)
Ihtiraz 67[1] (7f, Newb, F, Aug 14, *H*)
Imaginary (IRE) 60[3] (1m 2f, Newj, G, Jul 17)
Imperial Bid (FR) 48[1] (1m 2f, Ripo, F, Aug 2, *C*)
Imperial Ballet (IRE) 80[1] (1m, Asco, S, Jun 16, *H*)
Imprimatur 55[2] (6f, Curr, S, Jun 2, *H*)
In Case (USA) 73[1] (5f, Newm, G, Oct 16, *H*)
In The Money (IRE) 46[1] (1m 4f, Thir, G, Apr 17)
Inchcailloch (IRE) 45[3] (1m 4f, Sali, G, Jul 10, *H*)
Inchinor 79[1] (7f 64yds, Newb, F, Aug 13, *G*)
Indian Slave (IRE) 47[3] (7f, Asco, G, Apr 28, *H*)
Indigo 48[6] (5f, Thir, Y, May 14, *H*)
Informant 43[6] (7f, Long, G, May 27, *G*)
Informatrice (USA) 44[5] (1m, Newj, F, Jul 7, *G*)
Infrasonic 57[2] (1m 7f, Long, F, Jun 27, *G*)
Inherent Magic (IRE) 66[1] (5f, Donc, G, Oct 23, *H*)
Inner City (IRE) 82[3] (7f, Newj, F, Jun 26, *G*)
Insijaam (USA) 58[2] (1m 2f 110yds, Mais, G, Apr 30, *L*)
Instant Affair (USA) 58[1] (1m 2f, Newj, G, Jul 17)
Intervallo (USA) 60 (7f, Long, Y, Sep 19, *L*)
Intrepidity 85[1] (1m 4f, Long, Y, Sep 12, *G*)
Invocation 51[2] (7f, Ling, F, Jul 9, *H*)
Iommelli (IRE) 46[5] (1m 1f, Newm, F, Apr 15, *L*)
Iota 41 (2m 45yds, Asco, Y, Sep 23, *H*)
Irish Memory 69[4] (1m, Curr, G, Jul 10, *L*)
Irish Prospector (FR) 59[6] (1m 2f, Evry, Y, Sep 25, *L*)
Irish Source 54[5] (1m 2f 110yds, Stcl, G, Apr 24, *G*)
Irish Stamp (IRE) 47[2] (2m 9yds, Nott, F, Sep 6, *H*)
Is Me (CAN) 50[3] (1m 6f, Stcl, G, May 31, *G*)
Isaiah 55[6] (7f, Newm, G, Oct 14, *H*)
Island Heather (IRE) 62[3] (6f, Curr, S, Jun 2, *H*)
Island Knight (IRE) 44[2] (6f, Redc, F, May 31, *C*)
Iviza (IRE) 54[2] (1m 4f, Asco, Y, Jun 17, *G*)
Ivory Frontier (IRE) 66[5] (1m, Newm, F, Apr 15, *G*)
Jaazim 45[1] (6f, Ling, F, Aug 14)
Jack Button (IRE) 64[6] (2m, Good, Y, Jul 29, *G*)
Jackdidi (FR) 64[6] (1m 1f, Evry, F, Jul 24, *G*)
Jackpot Star 61[2] (1m 2f 85yds, York, G, Jun 12, *L*)
Jade City 51[4] (5f, Carl, F, Aug 18, *H*)
Jade Vale 53[1] (1m 7yds, Newb, F, May 15, *H*)
Jahangir (IRE) 52[2] (1m, Ripo, G, May 26, *H*)
Jalmusique 52[5] (6f 214yds, York, Y, Jun 12, *H*)
Jasarah (IRE) 52[2] (6f 212yds, Sali, G, Aug 12, *M*)
Jazilah (FR) 63[2] (1m 2f 60yds, Donc, G, Sep 11, *H*)
Jervia 52[4] (1m, Newc, G, Jun 25, *H*)
Jetbeeah (IRE) 60[2] (1m, Kemp, G, Jun 23)
Jeune 63[4] (1m 4f, Newj, F, Jul 6, *G*)
Jeune Homme (USA) 53[1] (1m 2f, Long, G, Sep 7, *L*)
Jigsaw Boy 50[4] (6f, Kemp, G, Jun 23, *H*)
Jimlil 48[3] (1m 1f 213yds, Nott, G, Apr 27, *H*)
Jobie 42[1] (6f 3yds, Yarm, G, Jul 29, *H*)
John Balliol (USA) 59[4] (1m 4f, Newm, G, Sep 30, *L*)
Johns Act (USA) 48[2] (1m 2f 6yds, Newb, F, Aug 13, *H*)
Jubran (USA) 56[3] (1m 2f, Ripo, F, Aug 31, *H*)
Judicial Field (IRE) 67[5] (2m, Leop, G, Nov 6, *H*)
Jura 63[2] (1m 2f, Newm, G, Oct 14)
Jura Forest 46[3] (1m, Newj, G, Jul 17, *H*)
Just Bob 53[1] (5f, Ayr, Y, Jun 18, *H*)
Just You Dare (IRE) 57[2] (1m, Good, G, Jun 25, *H*)
Kadastrof (FR) 44[1] (1m 6f 15yds, Nott, G, Aug 23, *H*)
Kadounor (FR) 58[4] (1m 2f 110yds, Long, Y, Apr 25, *G*)
Kaiser Wilhelm 43[1] (1m 3f 183yds, Leic, G, Apr 24, *H*)
Kar Or 50[4] (1m 2f, Leop, F, Sep 11, *H*)
Karachi 41[5] (1m 3f 200yds, Hayd, G, Sep 3, *H*)
Karayor (FR) 54[2] (1m 6f, Stcl, G, May 31, *G*)
Karinga Bay 79[4] (1m 2f 7yds, Sand, G, Jul 3, *G*)
Kariniyd (IRE) 40[5] (1m 2f, Leop, G, Jul 24, *H*)
Karinska 45[1] (6f 214yds, York, G, Sep 2, *H*)
Karmisyk (FR) 52[2] (1m 4f, Long, Y, Apr 8, *L*)
Karmousil (USA) 56[3] (1m 7f, Long, F, Jun 27, *G*)
Karshi 53[2] (1m 2f 7yds, Sand, G, Aug 21, *H*)
Kashani (USA) 68[1] (5f, Deau, G, Aug 28, *L*)
Kassab 43[1] (1m 5f 194yds, York, G, May 11)
Kassbaan (USA) 62[1] (1m 14yds, Sand, G, Aug 20, *H*)
Kasserhom (USA) 40[3] (7f 30yds, Hayd, Y, Apr 10, *M*)
Katiba (USA) 62[2] (7f 16yds, Chep, F, Aug 30)
Kayfa (IRE) 67[2] (1m, Curr, Y, May 22, *H*)
Kayvee 73[2] (7f, Asco, G, Apr 28, *H*)
Keen Hunter (USA) 90[3] (5f, Good, Y, Jul 29, *G*)
Kelimutu 40[2] (1m 1f 218yds, Leic, F, Sep 7, *H*)
Kelly Mac 42[3] (7f, Kemp, F, Sep 3, *H*)
Kenbu (FR) 70 (1m, Deau, G, Jul 31, *G*)
Kerkura (USA) 42[2] (1m 4f, Newj, F, Aug 7, *M*)
Keston Pond (IRE) 43[4] (1m 2f, Asco, G, Jul 23, *M*)
Key To My Heart (IRE) 68[2] (1m 4f, Donc, G, Sep 10, *L*)
Khalyani (IRE) 70[2] (1m 2f, Leop, F, Sep 11, *H*)
Khoraz (USA) 55 (1m, Deau, G, Aug 28, *G*)
Khubza 50[1] (7f, Newm, F, Apr 29, *M*)
Kiltimony 43[2] (6f, Curr, G, Sep 12, *H*)
Kimberley Park 43[1] (7f 64yds, Newb, G, Sep 17, *H*)
Kindergarten 53 (1m 2f, Deau, G, Aug 7, *G*)
Kindness Itself (IRE) 53[3] (6f, Curr, G, Sep 12, *H*)
Kinema Red (USA) 46[2] (1m, Donc, F, Mar 26, *M*)

King Athelstan (USA) 76[2] (1m 2f 85yds, York, F, Jul 10, *H*)
King's Signet (USA) 78[1] (6f, Good, Y, Jul 31, *H*)
Kingmambo (USA) 78[3] (1m, Asco, G, Sep 25, *G*)
Kinoko 43[2] (1m 4f, Carl, F, Jun 24, *H*)
Kirov Premiere 43[1] (1m 2f, Curr, G, Jun 5, *H*)
Kiruna (USA) 60[4] (1m, Long, Y, Apr 25, *G*)
Kithanga (IRE) 69[1] (1m 4f 5yds, Newb, Y, Oct 23, *G*)
Kitwood (USA) 64[3] (1m, Stcl, Y, Apr 6, *G*)
Kiveton Kabooz 44 (1m 4f, Donc, F, May 29, *H*)
Knifebox (USA) 87[1] (1m 1f 165yds, Long, S, Oct 2, *G*)
Knight Of Shalot (IRE) 46[3] (1m 100yds, Beve, G, Jul 3, *H*)
Knobbleeneeze 45[2] (7f 3yds, Yarm, G, Oct 27, *H*)
Knock Knock 62[1] (1m 3f, Redc, G, Sep 25)
Knock To Enter (USA) 66[1] (6f, Kemp, G, Jul 7, *C*)
Knowth (IRE) 54[2] (1m 2f 18yds, Epso, F, Aug 31, *H*)
Kristianstad 60[3] (1m 1f 213yds, Nott, G, Jun 7)
Kurdistan (IRE) 60[3] (7f, Curr, G, Aug 28, *H*)
Kusamba (USA) 56[4] (1m 4f, Donc, G, Sep 10, *L*)
La Barberina (USA) 45[4] (1m 4f, Evry, G, Sep 29, *L*)
La Francesa (ARG) 67[2] (1m 1f 55yds, Long, Y, Oct 3, *G*)
La Groupie (FR) 69[2] (1m, Stcl, Y, Nov 3, *L*)
Labudd (USA) 46[1] (1m 14yds, Chep, G, Sep 11, *M*)
Laburnum 43[3] (1m 4f, Donc, F, May 29, *H*)
Lacerta (IRE) 58[4] (6f 212yds, Sali, F, Sep 2, *H*)
Lackel (GER) 61[4] (1m 2f, Curr, G, Aug 21, *H*)
Lacotte (IRE) 57[2] (1m 2f, Asco, G, Jul 23, *M*)
Lady Of Persia (USA) 49 (1m 2f 110yds, Stcl, G, Apr 24, *G*)
Lady President (IRE) 41[3] (5f, Curr, G, Jun 5, *H*)
Lakab (USA) 47[3] (7f 214yds, Brig, F, Sep 22, *H*)
Langtry Lady 53[2] (1m, Kemp, G, May 12, *H*)
Languedoc 43[3] (6f, Thir, G, May 15, *H*)
Lap Of Luxury 66[1] (1m 14yds, Sand, G, Aug 20, *L*)
Last Embrace (IRE) 58[2] (1m 2f 6yds, Newb, F, May 15, *H*)
Latvian 51[4] (1m 4f, Thir, G, Sep 4, *H*)
Laurel Delight 61[2] (5f, Asco, Y, Jun 19, *H*)
Laurel Queen (IRE) 54[1] (7f 140yds, Ling, G, Sep 16)
Lavinia Fontana (IRE) 73[1] (5f, Long, S, Oct 24, *G*)
Law Commission 48[6] (7f, Newb, F, Jun 10, *H*)
Lawnswood Junior 47[5] (1m 54yds, Nott, Y, Oct 18, *H*)
Le Balafre (FR) 62 (1m 2f, Long, F, Jun 27, *G*)
League Leader (IRE) 55[2] (1m 5f 194yds, York, G, Aug 17, *H*)
Lear King (USA) 42[3] (1m 1f 213yds, Nott, F, Aug 3)
Learmont (USA) 63[1] (1m 4f, Asco, Y, Jun 17, *H*)
Leave It To Lib 43[1] (1m 16yds, Edin, G, Jul 30, *H*)
Lee Artiste 59[3] (7f 140yds, Ling, G, May 22)
Legal Flair (IRE) 54[1] (7f, Leop, G, Jun 7, *H*)
Legend Dulac (IRE) 43[2] (7f, Donc, F, Jul 22, *H*)
Leif The Lucky (USA) 48[4] (1m 2f 6yds, Pont, G, Sep 20, *H*)
Leigh Crofter 47[2] (5f 218yds, Leic, Y, Oct 25, *H*)
Let's Get Lost 44[4] (1m 1f 218yds, Leic, F, Aug 9, *H*)
Letsbeonestaboutit 48[2] (5f 161yds, Bath, G, Sep 13, *H*)
Licorne 64[1] (1m 2f 32yds, Newc, F, Aug 30, *L*)
Lida's Delight (IRE) 41[1] (5f, Beve, F, Jun 9, *H*)
Lifewatch Vision 46[4] (1m 2f, Leop, G, Nov 6)
Like The Sun (USA) 44[4] (1m 2f 7yds, Sand, G, Aug 11, *M*)
Lille Hammer 58[1] (1m 6f, Good, Y, Jul 30, *H*)
Limbo Lady (USA) 50[2] (1m 2f, Leop, G, Oct 23, *H*)
Lindon Lime (USA) 69[5] (1m 4f, Asco, G, Jun 15, *G*)
Link River (USA) 49[1] (1m 3yds, Yarm, G, Jun 2, *M*)
Linpac West 62[3] (1m 4f 5yds, Newb, Y, Oct 23, *G*)
Little Bean 60[2] (7f, Newm, G, Apr 14, *H*)
Little Munchkin (IRE) 52[4] (7f 64yds, Newb, G, Jul 16)
Little Rousillon 42[4] (7f, Asco, G, Apr 28, *H*)
Little Saboteur 44[1] (5f, Good, F, Jun 4, *H*)
Liyoun (IRE) 53[4] (1m 7f, Chan, Y, Jun 15, *L*)
Lobilio (USA) 45[1] (1m 4f 10yds, Epso, F, Aug 31)
Loch Patrick 58[1] (5f, Asco, Y, Jun 19, *H*)
Lochnau Lady (FR) 57[6] (1m 2f, Deau, G, Aug 7, *G*)
Lochsong 104[1] (5f, Long, S, Oct 3, *G*)
Loki (IRE) 62[3] (1m 2f 7yds, Sand, G, Apr 23, *H*)
Lombard Ships 41[2] (1m 2f 75yds, Ches, Y, Oct 19, *H*)
Look Who's Here (IRE) 62[1] (6f, Hayd, G, Jul 3, *H*)
Lookingforarainbow (IRE) 55[2] (1m 4f, Donc, G, Nov 6, *H*)
Lord Chickney (USA) 45[3] (7f, York, S, Oct 7, *H*)
Lord High Admiral (CAN) 60[1] (5f, Donc, G, Nov 6, *H*)
Lord Oberon (IRE) 48[1] (1m, Newb, G, Jul 17, *H*)
Lord Of The Field 69[3] (1m 2f, Leop, F, Sep 11)
Lord Olivier (IRE) 59[2] (6f, Good, G, May 18)
Lost Prairie (USA) 54[1] (1m, Deau, Y, Aug 24, *L*)
Lost Soldier (USA) 75[2] (1m, Good, Y, Jul 29, *H*)
Louisville Belle (IRE) 41[3] (6f 8yds, Newb, G, May 26, *H*)
Love Legend 41[6] (5f 6yds, Sand, G, Apr 23, *H*)
Love Returned 60[1] (5f, Redc, G, Aug 6, *H*)
Lower Egypt (USA) 49[4] (1m, Newm, G, Oct 30, *L*)
Lt Welsh (USA) 47[1] (1m 1f 213yds, Nott, F, Aug 3)
Luazur (FR) 69[2] (1m 4f, Stcl, G, May 18, *G*)
Lucedeo 44[5] (5f, Hayd, G, Jul 3, *H*)
Lucio (IRE) 42[4] (1m 6f, Stcl, G, May 31, *G*)
Lucky Guest 61[4] (1m 2f, Redc, G, May 31, *H*)
Lucky Parkes 75[1] (5f, Newc, F, Sep 28)
Lupescu 51[4] (1m 2f, Asco, G, Jul 24, *H*)
Lyford Cay (IRE) 54 (1m 2f, Good, Y, Jul 30, *H*)
Lyndon's Linnet 48[1] (5f 6yds, Sand, G, Aug 11, *H*)
Lynton (USA) 56 (1m 1f, Evry, F, Jul 24, *G*)
Lyphantastic (USA) 43 (1m 4f 93yds, Newc, F, Jun 26, *H*)
Lyphard's Delta (USA) 56[1] (1m 2f, Newj, F, Jul 7, *H*)
Lyric Fantasy (IRE) 71[1] (6f, Newm, G, May 22, *L*)
Macfarlane 62[2] (5f, Donc, G, Sep 10, *H*)
Mack The Knife 66[1] (1m 4f 115yds, Warw, G, Jul 24)
Macs Maharanee 60[2] (5f, Newj, G, Jul 17, *H*)
Mad Militant (IRE) 50[5] (1m 2f 32yds, Newc, G, Mar 30, *H*)
Madeleine's Dream (USA) 72[1] (1m, Long, F, May 16, *G*)
Magic Don (IRE) 50[1] (5f, Naas, Y, Jun 17, *H*)
Magic Orb 45 (5f 6yds, Sand, G, Aug 21, *H*)
Magic Pearl 58[1] (5f, Catt, Y, Oct 16, *H*)
Magical Retreat (USA) 60[3] (1m 1f 209yds, Sali, F, Aug 11, *L*)
Magique Rond Point (USA) 43[4] (6f 212yds, Sali, F, Jun 24)
Mahong 40[2] (1m 1f 209yds, Sali, G, Sep 29, *H*)
Mahrajan 42[2] (1m 3f 135yds, Wind, G, Jul 19, *H*)
Majed (IRE) 59[2] (1m, Redc, S, Oct 14, *H*)
Majority (IRE) 61[5] (1m 3f 195yds, York, G, Aug 17, *G*)
Makin (USA) 44[3] (1m 4yds, Pont, G, Aug 5, *M*)
Malvernico (IRE) 75[2] (1m, Curr, G, Jul 10, *L*)
Mamoura (IRE) 69[2] (1m 2f, Curr, F, Aug 28, *H*)
Manhattan River (FR) 42[2] (1m 7f 110yds, Long, F, Jun 26)
Manila Bay (USA) 42[1] (1m 2f 46yds, Bath, F, May 8)
Manor Adventure 41[1] (5f, Warw, F, Jun 22, *H*)
Map Of Stars (USA) 50[3] (1m 2f, Newj, F, Jul 7, *H*)
Maradonna (USA) 42[5] (1m 2f, Redc, G, Aug 25)
Marastani (USA) 61[4] (1m 14yds, Sand, G, Aug 20, *H*)
Marchand de Sable (USA) 44[2] (1m 4f, Long, G, May 9, *G*)
Mardood 41[2] (1m 6f, Sali, F, Jul 10)
Margaret's Gift 62[1] (6f, Good, F, Aug 28, *H*)
Marildo (FR) 77[5] (1m 2f 110yds, Long, S, May 2, *G*)
Marillette (USA) 54[5] (1m 1f 55yds, Long, Y, Oct 3, *G*)
Marina Park 75[2] (6f, Newm, G, Oct 16, *L*)
Marine Diver 45[3] (7f 2yds, Ches, G, Aug 20, *H*)
Marius (IRE) 44[3] (1m 1f 218yds, Leic, Y, Oct 26, *H*)
Market Booster (USA) 78[2] (1m 2f, Curr, G, Jun 26, *G*)
Markievicz (IRE) 41[3] (1m, Naas, G, Jul 21)
Maroof (USA) 68[3] (1m, Long, Y, Oct 3, *G*)
Martina 48[1] (5f, Ripo, F, Aug 2, *H*)
Masad (IRE) 69[6] (1m 2f 7yds, Sand, Y, Apr 24, *G*)
Masai Warrior 42[2] (1m 4f, Leop, G, Apr 17, *H*)
Mashaallah (USA) 55[5] (1m 4f, Newm, G, Apr 30, *G*)
Mashair (USA) 54[2] (1m 2f 6yds, Newb, F, Jun 10, *L*)
Masnun (USA) 53[2] (6f, Good, F, May 19, *H*)
Massiba (IRE) 64[1] (6f, Kemp, F, May 29, *H*)
Massyar (IRE) 66[3] (1m, Curr, Y, May 15, *G*)
Master Charlie 66[3] (1m 4f, Asco, Y, Jun 17, *H*)
Master Foodbroker (IRE) 48[4] (1m 6f, Newm, G, May 21, *H*)
Master Hyde (USA) 43[2] (1m, Donc, G, May 3, *H*)
Master Of Passion 60[4] (6f, Good, Y, Jul 31, *H*)
Master Planner 68[2] (6f, Good, F, Aug 28, *H*)
Master Pokey 45[1] (5f 207yds, Carl, F, Jun 23, *H*)
Master Tribe (IRE) 63[5] (1m, Curr, Y, May 15, *G*)
Matelot (USA) 76[3] (6f 110yds, Deau, G, Aug 1, *G*)
Matila (IRE) 61[2] (6f 15yds, Nott, Y, Oct 28)

Meadow Pipit (CAN) 61^{1} (1m 2f, Newm, G, Oct 29, *L*)

Meavy 45^{3} (1m 3f 195yds, York, G, Sep 2, *H*)

Mecklenburg (IRE) 61^{1} (1m 2f 32yds, Newc, F, Jul 24, *H*)

Medaille D'Or 73^{6} (5f, York, Y, Jun 11, *H*)

Mellaby (USA) 51^{4} (1m 3f 195yds, York, G, Jun 11, *H*)

Mellottie 70^{1} (1m, Newm, G, Oct 30, *L*)

Memsahb 59^{2} (5f, Curr, G, Jun 5, *H*)

Mentalasanythin 47^{1} (1m, Ayr, G, Jul 17, *H*)

Merlins Wish (USA) 47^{4} (6f, Kemp, G, Jul 7, *C*)

Merryhill Maid (IRE) 49^{1} (6f, Ling, G, May 15, *H*)

Mesleh 61^{3} (1m 2f 85yds, York, G, May 13, *H*)

Metal Boys 60^{1} (5f 6yds, Sand, G, Sep 14, *C*)

Mhemeanles 44^{2} (7f, Redc, G, Oct 5, *H*)

Midhish 71^{3} (6f, Leop, G, Aug 7, *G*)

Midnight Heights 62^{2} (1m 2f, Good, Y, Jul 30, *H*)

Midyan Blue (IRE) 55^{1} (1m 4f 5yds, Newb, Y, Oct 23, *H*)

Millie's Choice (IRE) 66^{3} (7f, Naas, G, Oct 16, *L*)

Million In Mind (IRE) 51^{5} (1m 4f 5yds, Newb, G, May 14, *H*)

Millsolin (IRE) 53^{6} (7f, Asco, G, Apr 28, *H*)

Mindomica 40^{2} (6f, Sout, F, Jul 17, *H*)

Minydoun (IRE) 59^{4} (1m 2f 110yds, Long, F, May 16, *G*)

Misbelief 52^{1} (1m 4f, Thir, G, Sep 4, *H*)

Misil (USA) 88^{2} (1m 2f 7yds, Sand, G, Jul 3, *G*)

Mislemani (IRE) 40^{2} (1m 14yds, Chep, G, Sep 11, *M*)

Miss Anita (IRE) 44^{1} (5f, Naas, G, Jul 21, *M*)

Miss Gorgeous (IRE) 45^{1} (7f 3yds, Yarm, Hrd, Jul 1, *H*)

Miss Haggis 57^{2} (6f, Pont, F, Jul 6, *H*)

Miss Kadrou (FR) 51^{3} (1m 2f 110yds, Stcl, Y, Apr 16, *G*)

Miss Mistletoes (IRE) 60^{2} (7f, Naas, G, Oct 16, *L*)

Miss Pin Up 59^{2} (1m 4f, Newj, G, Jun 25, *H*)

Miss Plum 46^{3} (2m 2f 51yds, Yarm, G, Sep 16, *H*)

Miss Vaxette 68^{1} (5f, Newj, G, Jul 17, *H*)

Miss Whittingham (IRE) 43^{2} (6f 3yds, Yarm, G, Sep 14, *H*)

Missed Flight 69^{1} (1m, Redc, S, Oct 14, *H*)

Mister Jolson 51^{1} (5f 161yds, Bath, G, Jun 12, *H*)

Mistertopogigo (IRE) 54^{4} (5f 140yds, Donc, G, Sep 8, *H*)

Mistle Cat (USA) 69^{2} (7f, Newj, F, Jun 26, *G*)

Misty Silks 48^{4} (1m 54yds, Nott, Y, Oct 18, *H*)

Mithi Al Gamar (USA) 41^{1} (7f, Ling, G, May 15, *M*)

Mithl Al Hawa 61^{2} (6f, Newm, G, May 22, *L*)

Mizaaya 74^{2} (1m, Donc, F, Mar 27, *H*)

Mizyan (IRE) 43^{4} (1m 4f, Thir, F, Jun 15, *H*)

Modhish (IRE) 83^{3} (1m 4f, Stcl, F, Jul 4, *G*)

Mojave 48 (7f 64yds, Newb, F, Aug 13, *G*)

Monarda 42^{1} (1m 6f 194yds, Warw, G, Jul 9, *H*)

Monde Bleu 85^{2} (5f, Long, G, May 13, *G*)

Mondragon 48^{3} (1m 6f 19yds, Redc, Y, Oct 5, *H*)

Montendre 82^{1} (6f, Newm, G, Oct 16, *L*)

Moon Carnival 49^{3} (1m 3f 91yds, Sand, G, Jun 1, *H*)

Moon Over Miami 56^{1} (7f, Good, Y, Jul 27, *L*)

Moon Spin 55^{1} (1m 5yds, Bath, F, Jul 19, *H*)

Moonlight Quest 57^{1} (1m 4f 66yds, Ches, G, Jul 9, *H*)

Moonlight Partner (IRE) 48^{2} (6f, Leop, G, Jul 17, *H*)

Moonshine Lake 47^{3} (1m 5f 194yds, York, G, Aug 17, *H*)

Moorish 46^{1} (1m 30yds, Hayd, G, May 29, *H*)

Morocco (IRE) 50^{1} (7f 64yds, Newb, Y, May 26, *H*)

Moscow Sea (USA) 46^{1} (1m 2f, Asco, G, Jul 23, *H*)

Mot de France (FR) 66^{4} (5f, Deau, G, Aug 28, *L*)

Mougins (IRE) 43^{1} (1m 14yds, Sand, G, Jun 1, *C*)

Mouloudya (IRE) 52^{6} (1m 2f, Deau, G, Aug 29, *G*)

Mr Confusion (IRE) 57^{5} (1m 2f 85yds, York, G, Aug 18, *H*)

Mr Martini (IRE) 58^{4} (7f 202yds, York, S, Oct 6)

Mr Nevermind (IRE) 43^{2} (6f 209yds, Brig, F, Aug 4, *H*)

Mr Tate (IRE) 51^{1} (1m 2f, Redc, Y, Nov 2, *H*)

Mr Woodcock 45^{3} (1m 3f 16yds, Hami, F, Jul 22, *H*)

Mt Templeman (USA) 41^{2} (1m, Newm, G, Apr 14)

Mu-Arrik 41^{2} (6f 5yds, Hami, G, Sep 27, *H*)

Mubadir (USA) 70^{1} (1m 4f, Leop, F, Jul 17)

Much Sought After 57^{1} (1m 3f 183yds, Leic, G, Jul 28, *H*)

Mugnano 41^{2} (5f, Naas, Y, Jun 17, *H*)

Muhayaa (USA) 70^{2} (1m 4f, Good, Y, Jul 30, *L*)

Muhtarram (USA) 75^{1} (1m 2f, Leop, F, Sep 11)

Mujaazafah (USA) 54^{1} (1m 4yds, Pont, G, Aug 5, *M*)

Mujawab 46^{4} (1m 5f 194yds, York, G, Aug 17, *H*)

Mulciber 42^{5} (1m 1f 209yds, Brig, F, Aug 25, *H*)

Mull House 50^{2} (2m 24yds, Newj, F, Jul 7, *H*)

Mullitover 55^{2} (7f, Newm, G, Apr 13, *H*)

Murray's Mazda (IRE) 41^{2} (6f, Ayr, F, May 24, *H*)

Mutakallam (USA) 44^{2} (1m 4yds, Pont, F, Aug 24, *H*)

My Abbey 40^{1} (5f, Pont, F, Jul 23, *H*)

My Best Valentine 51^{1} (7f, Redc, F, Sep 24, *H*)

My Bonus 53^{1} (5f, Newj, G, Jun 18, *H*)

My Desire 40^{1} (2m 4yds, Redc, G, May 10, *H*)

My Kerry Dancer (USA) 41^{4} (1m 2f, Leop, G, Oct 23, *H*)

My Patriarch 56^{3} (1m 6f, Good, Y, Jul 30, *H*)

My Rossini 47^{5} (1m 2f 75yds, Ches, G, Jul 9)

My Ruby Ring 46 (6f 16yds, Chep, G, Sep 11, *H*)

My-O-My (IRE) 61^{1} (5f, Newm, G, Sep 30, *L*)

Mysilv 44^{1} (1m 1f 213yds, Nott, Y, Sep 20, *H*)

Mysterious Ways (IRE) 50^{1} (7f, Curr, Y, Aug 14, *H*)

Myza (USA) 62^{3} (5f, Deau, G, Aug 28, *L*)

Nafuth (USA) 40^{3} (1m, Newj, F, Jun 26, *H*)

Nagida 68^{1} (6f, Asco, Y, Jun 18, *H*)

Naif (USA) 47^{1} (1m, Thir, G, Aug 9, *H*)

Nannaka (USA) 43^{2} (1m 2f, Leop, G, Oct 23, *M*)

Nashville Blues (IRE) 44^{4} (1m 114yds, Epso, F, Jun 3)

Nassau 51^{2} (1m 2f, Leop, S, May 14, *H*)

Nassma (IRE) 48^{2} (1m 2f 60yds, Donc, G, May 31, *M*)

Natural Lad 41^{3} (1m 2f, Good, G, Jun 11, *C*)

Ned's Bonanza 55^{1} (5f, Newj, Hrd, Jul 6, *H*)

Needle Gun (IRE) 63^{2} (1m, Asco, G, Jun 15, *G*)

Neither Nor 55^{5} (6f, Good, G, Sep 11, *H*)

Neptune's Pet 55^{5} (1m, Kemp, G, May 3, *H*)

Nessun Dorma 51^{2} (1m 2f, Newj, F, Jul 31, *H*)

Never In The Red 68^{2} (5f, York, Y, Jun 11, *H*)

Neverneyev (USA) 69^{3} (7f, Long, Y, Sep 19, *L*)

New Capricorn (USA) 61^{2} (1m 14yds, Sand, Y, Apr 24, *H*)

New Cyberian (USA) 49^{3} (1m, Mais, G, Apr 23, *L*)

New Europe 61^{2} (6f, Evry, G, Jul 13, *G*)

Newton's Law (IRE) 74^{4} (1m 4f, Chan, F, Jun 6, *G*)

Nicer (IRE) 70^{1} (1m, Curr, Y, May 22, *G*)

Niche 80^{1} (1m, Newj, F, Jul 7, *G*)

Nidd (USA) 57^{1} (7f, Long, F, Jun 26, *G*)

Night Clubbing (IRE) 65^{3} (1m 4f, Sali, F, Jun 24, *H*)

Night Jar 56^{4} (6f, Curr, Y, May 22, *G*)

Night Melody (IRE) 64^{2} (5f, Newc, F, Sep 28)

Nitouche 47^{1} (7f, Redc, G, Oct 5, *H*)

No Extras (IRE) 52^{2} (5f, Sali, F, Aug 11, *H*)

No Reservations (IRE) 55^{1} (7f 30yds, Hayd, G, Aug 7, *H*)

No Submission (USA) 45^{2} (1m 4yds, Pont, G, May 28, *C*)

Noble Pet 59^{2} (7f, Good, F, Aug 28, *H*)

Nominator 56^{2} (1m, Kemp, Y, Apr 2)

Non Partisan (USA) 63^{3} (1m 4f, Long, Y, Apr 27, *G*)

Nordan Raider 51^{1} (6f 15yds, Nott, G, Sep 20)

Nordic Fox (IRE) 66^{5} (6f, Leop, G, Aug 7, *G*)

Nordic Oak (IRE) 53^{2} (6f, Leop, G, Aug 2, *H*)

Norfolk Hero 57^{1} (7f, Newm, G, Oct 14, *H*)

Northern Crystal 77^{3} (1m, Stcl, Y, May 7, *G*)

Northern Bird 54^{5} (1m, Good, Y, Jul 29, *H*)

Northern Chief 40^{1} (7f 15yds, Edin, F, Aug 26, *H*)

Northern Bound (IRE) 54^{2} (1m 4f, Sali, F, Aug 11, *H*)

Northern Bred (IRE) 48^{3} (1m 4yds, Pont, F, Aug 24, *H*)

Northern Park (USA) 45^{3} (1m 7f 110yds, Mais, Y, Apr 2, *L*)

Northern Graduate (USA) 55^{1} (1m 4f, Carl, F, Jun 24, *H*)

Not In Doubt (USA) 66^{5} (2m, Good, Y, Jul 29, *G*)

Number One Spot 46^{1} (7f, Redc, G, Sep 25, *M*)

Nunivak (USA) 55^{2} (6f, Naas, G, Jul 3, *H*)

Nutty Brown 41^{2} (6f 189yds, Folk, S, Oct 18, *C*)

Oakmead (IRE) 70^{3} (1m 4f, Curr, G, Jul 10, *G*)

Oenothera (IRE) 57^{3} (1m 2f, Curr, F, Aug 28, *H*)

Oh So Risky 76^{2} (1m 5f 194yds, York, G, Aug 18, *H*)

Oiche Mhaith 46^{1} (6f, Naas, G, Jul 3, *H*)

Oiseau de Feu (USA) 49^{5} (1m 2f, Curr, G, May 22, *L*)

Ok Bertie 41^{1} (6f, Hayd, F, Sep 4, *H*)

Okeedokee (FR) 50 (1m 2f, Evry, Y, Sep 25, *L*)

Old Provence 63^{1} (1m 4f, Donc, G, Jun 25)

Olifantsfontein 64^{1} (5f 34yds, Newb, Y, Apr 16, *H*)

On Y Va (USA) 40^{1} (7f, Warw, G, Jun 19, *H*)

Only Royale (IRE) 85^{5} (1m 4f, Long, Y, Oct 3, *G*)

Opera Ghost 64^{3} (1m 4f, Kemp, F, Sep 4, *H*)

Opera House 98^{1} (1m 4f, Asco, G, Jul 24, *G*)

Ormsby (IRE) 61^{6} (1m 2f, Ayr, G, Jul 19, *G*)

Oubava (FR) 51^{5} (1m 4f, Stcl, G, Jun 4, *G*)

Oumnaz (FR) 60^{6} (1m 4f, Stcl, G, May 18, *G*)

Our Rita 50^{1} (6f 214yds, York, S, Oct 9, *H*)

Overcast (IRE) 41^{1} (1m, Curr, S, Jun 2, *M*)

Overpower 40³ (1m 2f 21yds, Yarm, F, Jul 14, *H*)
Oxava (FR) 74¹ (1m 2f 110yds, Stcl, Y, Oct 31, *G*)
Paddy Chalk 59² (5f 6yds, Sand, G, Jul 3, *H*)
Pageboy 42¹ (5f 4yds, Hami, F, Jul 29, *H*)
Paix Blanche (FR) 61³ (1m 2f 110yds, Stcl, G, Apr 24, *G*)
Palacegate Touch 52¹ (6f, Hayd, G, Aug 6, *C*)
Palacegate Gold (IRE) 40² (6f 16yds, Chep, Y, Oct 19, *H*)
Palacegate Episode (IRE) 66² (5f, Ling, F, Aug 26)
Paley Prince (USA) 51³ (5f 6yds, Sand, G, Jun 11, *C*)
Pallium (IRE) 52¹ (5f, Carl, F, Aug 18, *H*)
Panchellita (USA) 41¹ (6f 189yds, Folk, F, Aug 13, *H*)
Parfait Amour 45¹ (7f 100yds, Beve, F, Jul 2, *H*)
Paris House 89² (5f, Good, Y, Jul 29, *G*)
Parliament Piece 48² (7f, Ayr, G, Jul 19, *H*)
Pater Noster (USA) 68¹ (7f, Redc, G, Oct 5)
Patience Please 42³ (7f, Donc, F, Jul 22, *H*)
Patsy Grimes 43² (5f 13yds, Nott, Y, Oct 18)
Pay Homage 71¹ (1m, Kemp, G, May 3, *H*)
Peaches Polly 45³ (1m 2f, Newj, F, Jul 7, *M*)
Pearl Dawn (IRE) 56³ (6f, Curr, S, Nov 3, *H*)
Pearly Mist (IRE) 54¹ (1m 2f 21yds, Yarm, F, Aug 18, *H*)
Peerage Prince 44² (5f, Kemp, F, Aug 4, *H*)
Pelagic 51³ (1m 2f, Long, F, Jun 27, *L*)
Pelorus 51⁵ (1m 2f 6yds, Newb, F, May 15, *H*)
Pembroke (USA) 60² (6f 209yds, Brig, F, Aug 4)
Penny A Day (IRE) 40⁵ (7f, Curr, G, Aug 28, *H*)
Penny Banger (IRE) 51¹ (7f 3yds, Yarm, G, Oct 27, *H*)
Penny Drops 70¹ (1m 1f, Newm, G, Oct 2, *H*)
Penny Hasset 42¹ (5f, Newc, G, Mar 30, *H*)
Perfect Imposter (IRE) 55¹ (1m 2f, Leop, G, May 8, *G*)
Pernilla (IRE) 59² (6f, Curr, Y, May 22, *G*)
Persian Brave (IRE) 71¹ (1m 2f 85yds, York, G, May 11, *H*)
Persian Creek (IRE) 59² (6f, Leop, G, Jul 24, *L*)
Persiansky (IRE) 41¹ (1m, Good, G, Jun 25, *H*)
Persuasive 41¹ (1m 3f 16yds, Hami, G, May 26, *H*)
Petardia 67⁴ (1m, Newm, F, May 1, *G*)
Peter Davies (USA) 80¹ (1m 14yds, Sand, G, Jul 3, *H*)
Peter Quince 63¹ (1m 2f, Asco, G, Jul 23, *M*)
Petersford Girl (IRE) 57⁴ (5f 34yds, Newb, G, Sep 17)
Petit Loup (USA) 61² (1m 4f 110yds, Deau, G, Aug 29, *G*)
Petite-D-Argent 65³ (6f, Good, G, Sep 11, *H*)
Peto 61² (1m 1f 213yds, Nott, G, Jun 7)
Petonellajill 40² (7f, Epso, F, Jun 5, *H*)
Petraco (IRE) 49⁶ (6f, Good, G, Sep 11, *H*)
Pharaoh's Dancer 49³ (6f, Good, G, Jun 11, *H*)
Pharfetched 42 (1m 4f, Asco, Y, Jun 16, *H*)
Pharly Story 48⁵ (1m 2f 18yds, Epso, F, Jun 2, *H*)
Phase In 48¹ (1m 2f, Leop, G, Aug 2, *H*)
Philgun 48² (1m 4f 66yds, Ches, F, May 6, *H*)
Philidor 72¹ (1m, Good, Y, Jul 29, *H*)
Pilgrim Bay (IRE) 45¹ (6f, Leop, G, Jul 17, *H*)
Pips Pride 71⁵ (6f, Hayd, F, Sep 4, *G*)
Piquant 59² (1m 7yds, Newb, F, May 15, *H*)
Pistol River (IRE) 69² (1m 4f, Asco, Y, Jun 17, *H*)
Placerville (USA) 71¹ (1m 2f, Asco, G, Jun 15, *G*)
Plain Fact 59² (5f 16yds, Ches, F, May 6, *H*)
Planetary Aspect (USA) 61² (1m 2f 85yds, York, G, May 12, *G*)
Play Hever Golf 53¹ (6f 18yds, Ches, F, May 4, *H*)
Pluck 51¹ (6f 15yds, Nott, G, Aug 3, *H*)
Plum First 41² (6f, Thir, G, Jun 15, *H*)
Poker Chip 47⁵ (6f, York, G, Sep 1, *H*)
Political Surge (USA) 42¹ (1m 2f, Leop, F, Jun 8, *M*)
Polly's Wika (USA) 57⁵ (1m, Evry, G, Jul 10, *G*)
Pollys Glow (IRE) 52⁴ (1m 4f, Leop, F, Jul 17)
Polytain (FR) 76⁶ (1m 2f 110yds, Long, S, May 2, *G*)
Pondicherry (USA) 40¹ (7f 3yds, Yarm, G, Jun 2)
Pondoro 56 (1m 2f, Long, G, Apr 4, *G*)
Port Lucaya 67² (1m 205yds, York, G, Sep 2, *L*)
Port Sunlight (IRE) 47⁴ (1m 2f, Good, Y, Jul 27, *H*)
Porterstown Boy (IRE) 53 (1m 4f, Curr, G, Jun 27, *G*)
Portico (USA) 61⁴ (1m, Mais, G, Apr 20, *L*)
Portrait Gallery (IRE) 59² (1m 4f, Curr, S, Oct 9, *G*)
Powerful Edge 64¹ (7f, Donc, F, Jul 22)
Poyle George 69¹ (5f 34yds, Newb, G, Jul 17, *H*)
Pre-Eminent 66¹ (1m 2f, Leop, G, Oct 25, *L*)
Precious Wonder 45² (7f, Kemp, Y, Apr 10, *H*)
Precious Air (IRE) 40² (7f 214yds, Brig, Hrd, May 26, *H*)
Premier League (IRE) 50¹ (1m 1f 218yds, Leic, G, Apr 24, *M*)
Prenonamoss 57² (7f, Donc, G, Sep 9, *H*)
Press Gallery 49⁴ (6f, Sali, G, Jun 8, *H*)
Press The Bell 56³ (5f, Donc, G, Oct 23, *H*)
Pride Of Pendle 49¹ (1m 4yds, Pont, F, Aug 24, *H*)
Prime Of Life (IRE) 42² (7f 16yds, Sand, Y, Jun 12, *M*)
Primula Bairn 50² (5f, Catt, Y, Oct 16, *H*)
Prince Belfort 41³ (7f, Redc, F, Jun 19, *H*)
Prince Hannibal 58¹ (1m 4f, Thir, F, Jun 15, *H*)
Prince Of Andros (USA) 69¹ (1m 4f, Donc, G, Sep 10, *L*)
Prince Rodney 44¹ (7f 16yds, Chep, Y, Jul 15, *H*)
Princely Favour (IRE) 49¹ (7f 16yds, Sand, Y, Sep 15)
Princess Kris 51⁴ (7f, Newj, F, Aug 7, *H*)
Princess Maxine (IRE) 42³ (7f, Redc, F, Aug 3, *H*)
Princess Tateum (IRE) 43¹ (1m 2f, Redc, Y, Oct 26)
Princess Borghese (USA) 40¹ (1m 2f 120yds, Hayd, G, May 29, *M*)
Prosequendo (USA) 41⁴ (1m 5f 61yds, Newb, Y, May 26, *H*)
Prospective Prince (USA) 57³ (1m, Stcl, Y, Nov 3, *L*)
Protektor (GER) 57 (1m 4f, Stcl, G, May 18, *G*)
Proud Brigadier (IRE) 49² (1m 54yds, Nott, Y, Oct 28, *H*)
Provence 49² (2m, Thir, G, Aug 27, *H*)
Purple Splash 50² (1m 4f, Kemp, Y, Sep 21, *M*)
Quadrireme 52⁴ (1m 4f, Sali, F, Jun 24, *H*)
Quantity Surveyor 41² (1m 54yds, Nott, Y, Oct 18, *H*)
Quartannier (FR) 56 (7f, Long, Y, Sep 19, *L*)
Quaver (USA) 45² (7f 3yds, Yarm, Hrd, Jul 1, *H*)
Queen Of Love (GER) 54 (1m 2f, Deau, G, Aug 7, *G*)
Queen Of Shannon (IRE) 42⁴ (7f 64yds, Newb, Y, May 26, *H*)
Queen Warrior 49³ (1m 2f, Ayr, F, Sep 17, *H*)
Queen's View (FR) 67² (7f, Ling, G, Sep 16)
Quick Ransom 74¹ (1m 4f, Donc, G, Nov 6, *H*)
Quillon 48³ (1m 4f 8yds, Pont, F, Jul 23, *M*)
Quinsigimond 40¹ (6f, Redc, F, Aug 3)
Quinta Royale 46³ (6f 209yds, Brig, Hrd, May 6, *H*)
Rafif (USA) 41¹ (1m 2f 7yds, Sand, G, Jul 21)
Rafters 54² (1m 1f 218yds, Leic, G, Apr 24, *M*)
Ragamuffin Romeo 42² (1m 6f 194yds, Warw, F, Mar 27, *H*)
Rahil (IRE) 52¹ (1m 2f, Asco, G, Sep 24, *H*)
Rain Brother (USA) 52⁶ (6f 8yds, Newb, G, Jul 16, *L*)
Rainbow Lake 56¹ (1m 2f 6yds, Newb, F, Jun 10, *L*)
Raintrap 59¹ (1m 4f 110yds, Mais, F, Jun 22, *L*)
Rajaura (IRE) 58² (7f, Curr, G, Aug 28, *H*)
Rakis (IRE) 47⁶ (7f 64yds, Newb, G, Sep 17, *H*)
Rambo's Hall 72³ (1m 1f, Newm, G, Oct 2, *H*)
Raneen Alwatar 40¹ (1m 4f, Sali, F, Jun 8, *H*)
Range Rider (IRE) 48² (1m 4f 110yds, Deau, G, Aug 28, *L*)
Ranger (FR) 68⁶ (7f, Long, Y, Sep 19, *L*)
Rapid Repeat (IRE) 54⁴ (1m 4f, Stcl, G, Jun 4, *G*)
Rapid Success (USA) 57⁵ (1m 2f 6yds, Newb, F, Aug 13, *H*)
Rapporteur (USA) 53¹ (1m 3f 106yds, Ling, S, Sep 30)
Rayseka (IRE) 74¹ (1m 4f, Curr, G, Aug 14, *G*)
Ready (IRE) 54³ (6f, Leop, G, May 8, *H*)
Realities (USA) 48² (7f, Newm, G, Oct 1, *H*)
Red Admiral 41² (6f, Folk, F, Aug 17)
Red Bishop (USA) 62³ (1m 4f, Newj, F, Jul 6, *G*)
Red Rosein 59³ (5f 218yds, Leic, G, May 31, *H*)
Redenham (USA) 66² (7f 202yds, York, S, Oct 6)
Redstella (USA) 57⁵ (1m 4f, Donc, F, May 29, *H*)
Refugio 47¹ (1m 2f, Ripo, G, May 26, *M*)
Regal Chimes 79¹ (5f, Asco, F, Jul 23, *H*)
Regency 71⁵ (1m 4f, Chan, F, Jun 6, *G*)
Reine de Neige 57² (1m 14yds, Sand, G, Aug 20, *L*)
Relentless Pursuit (IRE) 43² (5f, Edin, F, Jul 5, *H*)
Remany 41⁵ (1m 1f 207yds, Beve, G, Apr 22, *H*)
Requested 46¹ (1m 6f, Sali, F, May 5, *H*)
Revelation (IRE) 76¹ (1m 2f, Stcl, G, Jul 14, *G*)
Revere (IRE) 62⁴ (1m 1f, Newm, G, Oct 15, *L*)
Rhythmic Dancer 49¹ (5f, Warw, F, Jul 9, *H*)
Ribhi (USA) 73¹ (1m 2f 60yds, Donc, G, Sep 11, *H*)
Ricky's Tornado (IRE) 45⁴ (5f 217yds, Wind, G, Jun 28, *H*)
Right Win (IRE) 57¹ (1m 4f, Good, Y, Jul 27, *G*)
Ring Pink (USA) 69⁵ (1m 2f 110yds, Stcl, Y, Oct 31, *G*)
Ringland (USA) 50⁴ (1m, Donc, F, Mar 27, *H*)
Rise Up Singing 45⁴ (1m, Warw, G, May 28, *H*)
Risk Master 65¹ (7f 202yds, York, G, May 12, *L*)

Riston Lady (IRE) 55^{3} (5f, Thir, G, Apr 16)
Ritto 47^{2} (2m 45yds, Asco, Y, Sep 23, *H*)
Rival Bid (USA) 48^{2} (1m 2f 21yds, Yarm, F, Jun 22, *H*)
Rive (USA) 41^{4} (1m 4f, Stcl, G, Jul 20, *G*)
River Board 59^{2} (1m, Newb, G, May 14, *M*)
River Boyne (USA) 45^{2} (1m 1f 209yds, Sali, G, Jul 29)
River Life 44^{1} (7f 30yds, Hayd, Y, Apr 10, *M*)
River North (IRE) 74^{1} (1m 2f 85yds, York, G, Jun 12, *L*)
River Nymph (USA) 61^{4} (1m 2f 110yds, Stcl, G, Apr 24, *G*)
Riviere Actor (USA) 41^{2} (1m 1f 209yds, Sali, G, Jun 23, *H*)
Robenko (USA) 41^{6} (1m 1f 218yds, Leic, F, Sep 7, *H*)
Robertolomy (USA) 54^{2} (6f, Curr, S, Nov 3, *H*)
Roberty Lea 54^{2} (1m 3f 195yds, York, G, Aug 19, *H*)
Robin Des Pins (USA) 80^{1} (5f, Long, G, May 13, *G*)
Robingo (IRE) 61^{1} (2m, Kemp, F, May 29, *H*)
Roca Murada (IRE) 50^{2} (6f 15yds, Nott, G, Sep 20)
Rock Symphony 61^{3} (6f 3yds, Yarm, G, Sep 15)
Rockawhile (IRE) 53^{4} (1m 2f 85yds, York, G, May 13, *H*)
Rocky Waters (USA) 63^{2} (7f, Epso, F, Jun 30, *H*)
Roger The Butler (IRE) 40^{2} (5f 218yds, Leic, F, Mar 30)
Roi Des Champs 49^{1} (1m, Evry, G, Sep 18, *L*)
Roll A Dollar 63^{3} (1m 5f 194yds, York, G, May 13, *G*)
Romola Nijinsky 40^{1} (1m 1f 207yds, Beve, G, Apr 22, *H*)
Romoosh 43^{3} (1m 54yds, Nott, G, Jun 28, *H*)
Rondelli (IRE) 46^{3} (1m, Curr, G, Sep 12, *H*)
Rose Alto 72^{1} (1m 2f, Good, Y, Jul 27, *H*)
Rose Noble (USA) 42^{1} (1m 3f 101yds, Yarm, G, Nov 5, *H*)
Rosina Mae 54^{2} (2m 24yds, Newj, G, Aug 6, *H*)
Rouquette 65^{1} (1m, Evry, G, Jul 10, *G*)
Rousitto 41^{3} (1m 1f 218yds, Leic, F, Sep 7, *H*)
Royal Ballerina (IRE) 78^{2} (1m 4f, Curr, G, Jul 10, *G*)
Royal Chantou 42^{3} (1m 2f, Long, Y, Oct 3, *L*)
Royal Citizen (IRE) 40^{2} (1m 2f, Redc, F, Jun 19, *H*)
Royal Girl 40^{1} (7f, Donc, G, Jun 25, *H*)
Royal Interval 48^{1} (1m 100yds, Beve, G, Jul 3, *H*)
Royal Roller (IRE) 42^{1} (1m, Thir, F, Jul 30, *H*)
Royal Seaton 62^{5} (1m 2f 7yds, Sand, G, Jul 2, *H*)
Royal Vision (IRE) 64^{4} (1m 2f, Curr, F, Aug 28, *H*)
Royale Chantou (FR) 71^{3} (1m 2f 110yds, Stcl, Y, Oct 31, *G*)
Ruby Tiger 76^{1} (1m 2f 7yds, Sand, Y, Apr 24, *G*)
Rue Rembrandt (USA) 47^{2} (1m 5yds, Bath, F, Jul 19, *H*)
Rumpus (IRE) 41^{2} (1m 3f 101yds, Yarm, F, Sep 2, *M*)
Runaway Pete (USA) 49^{1} (1m 3f 196yds, Brig, F, Aug 3, *H*)
Running Glimpse (IRE) 57^{1} (6f, Epso, F, Jun 4, *H*)
Rural Lad 40^{1} (7f 100yds, Beve, F, May 8, *H*)
Rustic Craft (IRE) 60 (6f 110yds, Deau, G, Aug 1, *G*)
Rutland Water (USA) 43^{2} (1m 2f 7yds, Sand, G, Apr 23, *H*)
Saafend 50^{1} (1m 14yds, Sand, G, Aug 11, *H*)
Sabre Rattler 71^{1} (5f, Epso, F, Aug 30, *H*)
Sabrehill (USA) 74^{2} (1m 2f 85yds, York, G, Aug 17, *G*)
Saddlehome (USA) 46^{2} (5f, York, Y, Oct 6, *H*)
Safayn (USA) 49^{2} (1m, Curr, G, Jul 10, *H*)
Safety In Numbers 60^{4} (1m 4f, Donc, G, Nov 6, *H*)
Safir (USA) 44^{5} (1m 2f 46yds, Bath, F, Jul 7, *H*)
Sagebrush Roller 55^{2} (6f, Pont, G, Apr 26, *H*)
Sahara Sun (USA) 58^{3} (1m 1f, Long, S, Oct 17, *L*)
Saibot (USA) 67^{1} (1m 2f, Leop, F, Sep 11, *H*)
Saifan 67^{1} (1m, Newm, G, Oct 16, *H*)
Saint Ciel (USA) 45^{3} (1m 1f 218yds, Leic, G, Apr 8, *H*)
Saint Express 63^{3} (5f 2yds, Leic, F, Sep 7)
Saint Keyne 45 (1m 6f 175yds, Newj, F, Jul 8, *L*)
Salatin (USA) 67^{4} (1m 2f 85yds, York, G, Aug 18, *H*)
Salda 43^{2} (1m 65yds, Hami, Y, Mar 29, *H*)
Salmon Eile (IRE) 56^{1} (1m 2f, Curr, S, Apr 24, *L*)
Samsolom 58^{3} (6f, Good, F, Aug 28, *H*)
Samson-Agonistes 57^{1} (5f, Ling, G, Nov 4, *H*)
Sand Table 63^{2} (1m, Newm, G, Oct 16, *H*)
Sandcreek (IRE) 60^{2} (1m, Deau, Y, Aug 12, *L*)
Sapience 58^{5} (1m 4f, Newj, F, Jul 6, *G*)
Sarah-Clare 44^{1} (7f 214yds, Brig, F, Jun 22, *H*)
Sarawat 60^{1} (1m 5f 194yds, York, G, Aug 18, *H*)
Sarliya (IRE) 46^{4} (1m 2f, Long, F, Jun 27, *L*)
Sartigila 45^{1} (6f, Thir, G, May 15, *H*)
Saseedo (USA) 64^{1} (5f, Newm, G, Sep 30, *H*)
Satank (USA) 73^{3} (5f, Newc, F, Jun 25, *H*)
Satin Dancer 54^{5} (1m 2f, Ling, G, May 22, *H*)
Savahra Sound 47^{3} (6f 206yds, Carl, G, May 7, *C*)
Savoy Truffle (FR) 51^{1} (1m 2f 60yds, Donc, G, May 31, *M*)
Sawasdee (FR) 72^{3} (1m 2f, Mais, Y, Sep 27, *G*)
Sayyedati 80^{1} (1m, Newm, F, Apr 29, *G*)
Scorpius 49^{1} (1m 3f 101yds, Yarm, F, Sep 2, *M*)
Scottish Bambi 56^{1} (1m 1f 218yds, Leic, F, Aug 9, *H*)
Sculler (USA) 55^{1} (1m 2f 18yds, Epso, F, Jun 4, *H*)
Sea Devil 55^{2} (6f, Redc, F, Jun 18, *H*)
Sea Gazer (IRE) 68^{1} (5f, Leop, G, Jun 7, *G*)
Sea Siren 41^{2} (1m, Newb, G, Jul 17, *H*)
Sea-Deer 40^{1} (5f 34yds, Newb, F, Jun 22, *H*)
Seama (USA) 44^{2} (1m 3f 101yds, Yarm, Y, Sep 14, *C*)
Seasonal Splendour (IRE) 40^{4} (1m 2f 6yds, Newb, F, Jun 10, *L*)
Seaton Delaval (USA) 59^{3} (1m, Stcl, G, Mar 30, *L*)
Seattle Victory (USA) 71^{1} (1m, Stcl, Y, Nov 3, *L*)
Seba Le Rouge (FR) 44^{4} (1m, Evry, G, Sep 18, *L*)
Second Chance (IRE) 40^{3} (7f 16yds, Sand, G, Jul 2, *H*)
Second Revolution (IRE) 40^{4} (1m 2f, Leop, G, Jul 24, *H*)
Secrage (USA) 62 (1m, Newm, F, Apr 29, *G*)
Seek The Pearl 51^{2} (1m 2f 21yds, Yarm, Y, Sep 14, *L*)
Seek The Faith (USA) 47^{5} (6f, Curr, S, Nov 3, *H*)
Semillon 66^{6} (1m 2f, Long, F, Jun 27, *G*)
Semple Stadium (IRE) 57^{3} (1m 4f, Leop, F, Jul 17)
Sense Of Priority 44^{1} (5f, Beve, G, Aug 11, *S*)
Seren Quest 53^{2} (1m 2f, Newj, F, Jul 7, *H*)
Serious 47^{5} (1m, Newm, G, Oct 30, *L*)
Serrant (USA) 45^{1} (1m 4f, Evry, G, Jun 12, *G*)
Set The Fashion 49^{1} (1m 30yds, Hayd, G, Sep 4)
Shabanaz 56^{3} (1m 2f, Good, Y, Jul 27, *H*)
Shadow Jury 48^{4} (5f 2yds, Leic, G, Sep 13, *H*)
Shadows Of Silver 59^{2} (1m 4f 10yds, Epso, F, Aug 30, *H*)
Shahik (USA) 43^{3} (1m, Naas, F, Jul 3)
Shahzadi (IRE) 47^{1} (1m, Curr, S, Mar 27)
Shaiba (USA) 58^{3} (1m 2f 85yds, York, G, May 12, *G*)
Shamam (USA) 54^{1} (1m, Newm, G, Apr 30, *H*)
Shambo 65^{4} (1m 5f 194yds, York, G, May 13, *G*)
Shamsiya (USA) 62^{3} (7f, Long, S, Oct 14, *L*)
Shandon Lake (IRE) 62^{1} (1m 2f, Leop, G, Apr 17, *L*)
Shanghai (USA) 83^{2} (1m, Stcl, Y, May 7, *G*)
Sharaar (USA) 42^{1} (1m 2f, Ayr, S, Aug 7, *H*)
Sharastamina (USA) 47^{2} (1m 2f, Leop, G, Nov 6)
Shareek (USA) 70^{4} (1m 6f 132yds, Donc, G, Sep 11, *G*)
Sharjah (USA) 56^{3} (1m 2f, Newj, F, Jul 31, *H*)
Sharman (USA) 67^{2} (1m, Deau, G, Aug 28, *G*)
Sharp Counsel (FR) 66^{4} (1m 4f, Stcl, G, May 18, *G*)
Sharp Prospect 45^{5} (7f 64yds, Newb, G, Sep 17, *H*)
Sharp Prod (USA) 75^{1} (7f, Long, Y, Sep 19, *L*)
Sharp Review (IRE) 58^{3} (1m, Curr, Y, May 22, *H*)
Sharpela 60^{6} (1m 2f, Mais, Y, Sep 27, *G*)
She's Smart 52^{2} (5f 212yds, Catt, G, Jul 14, *H*)
Sheba Dancer (FR) 58^{6} (1m 2f 110yds, Stcl, G, Apr 24, *G*)
Sheila's Secret (IRE) 62^{3} (5f, Sali, G, Aug 12)
Shemaka (IRE) 76^{1} (1m 2f, Deau, G, Aug 29, *G*)
Shikari's Son 57^{2} (6f, Epso, F, Jun 30, *H*)
Shining Jewel 53^{3} (1m 3yds, Yarm, F, Aug 30, *H*)
Shintillo (IRE) 66^{1} (7f, Newm, G, Oct 14, *H*)
Shir Dar (FR) 53^{4} (1m, Mais, G, May 11, *L*)
Shirley Rose 48^{3} (1m 3f, Redc, G, Sep 25)
Shirley's Delight (IRE) 57^{2} (2m, Leop, G, Nov 6, *H*)
Shivaree (FR) 49^{3} (7f, Long, G, May 9, *L*)
Shoot The Dealer (IRE) 49^{1} (5f, Curr, G, Jun 5, *H*)
Show Faith (IRE) 68^{3} (1m, Good, Y, Jul 29, *H*)
Showgum (FR) 64 (1m 2f 110yds, Stcl, Y, Oct 31, *G*)
Shrewd Idea 60^{6} (1m 4f, Curr, G, Jun 27, *G*)
Shuailaan (USA) 76^{3} (1m 3f 183yds, Leic, F, Jun 5, *L*)
Shujan (USA) 53^{1} (1m 6f 132yds, Donc, G, Oct 22, *H*)
Siam (USA) 74^{3} (1m 2f, Long, F, Jun 27, *G*)
Sigama (USA) 51^{2} (5f, Epso, F, Aug 31, *S*)
Signoretto (FR) 47^{3} (1m, Mais, Y, Oct 21, *L*)
Silca-Cisa 58^{2} (6f, Donc, F, Mar 27, *L*)
Silent Expression 48^{1} (6f 212yds, Sali, F, Sep 2, *H*)
Silicon Bavaria (FR) 59^{2} (6f, Mais, F, Mar 29, *L*)
Silky Siren 45^{3} (7f 122yds, Ches, F, May 6, *H*)
Silver Maple (USA) 42^{1} (1m 2f 85yds, York, S, Oct 7, *M*)
Silver Samurai 50^{5} (1m 2f 60yds, Donc, G, Sep 11, *H*)
Silver Wisp (USA) 67^{4} (1m 2f 7yds, Sand, Y, Apr 24, *G*)
Silver Wizard (USA) 66^{5} (1m, Newm, F, May 1, *G*)
Silverdale (USA) 60^{2} (1m 7f 195yds, York, G, Aug 17, *L*)

Silverlocks 52[4] (1m 2f, Ayr, F, Sep 17, *H*)
Silvernesian (USA) 41 (1m 7f 195yds, York, G, Aug 17, *L*)
Simmie's Special 44[1] (5f, York, Y, Oct 6, *H*)
Simply Finesse 51[2] (7f 16yds, Sand, Y, Jul 14, *H*)
Simply Sooty 41[3] (5f 6yds, Sand, G, Apr 24, *H*)
Sin Kiang (FR) 65[5] (1m 2f, Stcl, G, Jul 14, *G*)
Singing Star 50[3] (5f, Carl, F, Aug 18, *H*)
Sinissipi (USA) 63[3] (1m 2f, Leop, G, Apr 17, *L*)
Sir Harry Hardman 68[2] (6f, York, Y, Jun 11, *H*)
Sir Joey (USA) 60[1] (5f, Ayr, Hrd, Sep 16, *H*)
Sir Tasker 51[2] (5f, Donc, F, May 3, *C*)
Sismart (FR) 60 (1m 2f, Stcl, G, Jul 14, *G*)
Siwaayib 49 (7f 64yds, Newb, F, Aug 13, *G*)
Sizzling Saga (IRE) 59[3] (6f, Kemp, G, Jul 7, *C*)
Ski Paradise (USA) 79[2] (7f, Long, S, Oct 10, *G*)
Skipo (USA) 53[1] (1m 2f, Leop, G, Jul 24, *H*)
Slades Hill 45[1] (5f, Carl, G, May 27)
Smarginato (IRE) 76[1] (1m 2f 7yds, Sand, G, Jul 2, *H*)
Snow Board 42[5] (1m 6f, Newm, G, May 21, *H*)
Snurge 68[1] (1m 4f 110yds, Deau, G, Aug 29, *G*)
So Factual (USA) 65[1] (7f, Newm, G, Apr 14, *L*)
So Intrepid (IRE) 49[1] (6f, Newj, Y, Jul 16, *M*)
So Rhythmical 51[2] (7f, Epso, F, Jun 5, *H*)
So So 54[1] (1m, Newc, G, Jun 25, *H*)
So Superb 46[3] (5f, Sout, G, Aug 14, *H*)
Sober Lad (IRE) 42[3] (5f 13yds, Nott, Y, Oct 18)
Sobering Thoughts 54[1] (6f, Ayr, Hrd, Sep 18, *H*)
Solartica (USA) 49[2] (1m 6f, Good, Y, Jul 30, *H*)
Solas Abu (IRE) 51[5] (1m 2f, Curr, G, Aug 21, *H*)
Solomon's Dancer (USA) 44[1] (1m 2f, Redc, G, Jul 21)
Somersham (USA) 53[5] (6f, Evry, G, Jul 13, *G*)
Son Pardo 69[3] (7f, Good, F, Aug 28, *H*)
Sonderise 46[1] (5f, Thir, G, May 1, *H*)
Song Of Sixpence (USA) 45[1] (1m 2f, Newm, G, Sep 29, *H*)
Sonus (IRE) 79[2] (1m 4f, Newj, G, Jul 16)
Sought Out (IRE) 75[2] (1m 6f 110yds, Stcl, S, May 1, *G*)
Soul Emperor 48[2] (1m 4f 5yds, Newb, F, Jun 10, *H*)
Soundproof (IRE) 55[1] (1m 2f, Leop, G, Oct 23, *H*)
Souplesse (USA) 65[3] (1m 2f, Deau, G, Aug 7, *G*)
Source Of Light 80[1] (1m 4f, Sali, F, Jun 24, *H*)
Southern Memories (IRE) 52[1] (5f 217yds, Wind, F, May 10, *H*)
Southern Review (IRE) 44[1] (6f, Curr, S, Nov 3, *H*)
Sovereign Grace (IRE) 52 (5f, Good, Y, Jul 29, *G*)
Sovereign Page (USA) 59[2] (1m 2f, Ripo, F, Aug 21, *H*)
Soviet Line (IRE) 63[3] (1m 1f, Newm, G, Oct 15, *L*)
Spaniards Close 73[4] (5f, Long, G, May 13, *G*)
Spanish Storm (IRE) 46[3] (7f 3yds, Yarm, Hrd, Jul 1)
Spanish Verdict 42 (6f 214yds, York, G, Sep 2, *H*)
Spartan Shareef (IRE) 72[3] (1m 2f 85yds, York, G, Aug 17, *G*)
Special Dawn (IRE) 43[1] (1m, Thir, S, May 15, *M*)
Special Pageant (IRE) 59 (1m 4f, Curr, G, Jul 10, *G*)
Specified (USA) 52[1] (6f 8yds, Newb, G, May 14)
Spin Doctor (IRE) 52[6] (1m 2f, Newj, F, Jul 7, *H*)
Splash Of Salt (IRE) 42[2] (5f, Folk, F, Jul 20, *H*)
Splice 73[1] (6f, Newm, F, Apr 29, *H*)
Spring 71[4] (1m 3f 195yds, York, G, Aug 18, *G*)
Spring To Action 58[1] (1m 6f 175yds, Newj, F, Jul 8, *L*)
St Ninian 65[3] (1m 2f 75yds, Ches, G, Jul 9)
Stack Rock 80[2] (5f, Long, S, Oct 3, *G*)
Star Family Friend (IRE) 56 (5f, Hayd, G, Aug 7, *H*)
Star Goddess (USA) 49[3] (6f, Epso, F, Jun 30, *H*)
Star Manager (USA) 45[5] (1m 2f, Newm, G, Apr 30, *L*)
Star Player 51[6] (2m 45yds, Asco, Y, Sep 23, *H*)
Star Quest 47[4] (2m 24yds, Newj, G, Aug 6, *H*)
State Flyer 40[3] (6f 214yds, York, G, Sep 2, *H*)
Stella Mystika (USA) 42[1] (7f, Newm, G, Apr 14, *M*)
Stepanov (USA) 59[2] (5f, Hayd, G, Aug 7, *H*)
Stoney Valley 59[1] (1m 2f 85yds, York, G, Aug 18, *H*)
Storiths (IRE) 58[1] (6f, Donc, G, May 29, *H*)
Storm Canyon (IRE) 75[1] (6f 3yds, Yarm, G, Sep 15)
Storm Venture (IRE) 42[2] (1m 2f 7yds, Wind, G, Jul 12, *H*)
Street Rebel (CAN) 64[3] (6f, Curr, Y, May 22, *G*)
Stubass (IRE) 61[5] (1m, Newb, G, May 14, *G*)
Suave Groom (IRE) 46[2] (7f, Leop, G, Jun 7, *H*)
Sueboog (IRE) 58[4] (1m 4f 10yds, Epso, F, Jun 5, *G*)
Suivez 40[3] (1m 3f 101yds, Yarm, F, Sep 2, *M*)
Summer Pageant 47[1] (1m 3f 106yds, Ling, F, Aug 26, *H*)
Summer Wind (IRE) 48[1] (1m 6f, Sali, G, Aug 12, *H*)
Sumoto 59[1] (7f, Ling, G, Sep 16)
Sun Of Spring 50[1] (1m 4f, Kemp, F, Aug 18, *H*)
Sunday's Hill 54[3] (7f, Ling, G, Sep 16)
Sunderland Echo 54[1] (1m 4f, Carl, G, Jul 23, *H*)
Suntara (IRE) 45[3] (1m 2f, Newm, G, Sep 29, *H*)
Super Blues 41[1] (1m 4f, Thir, F, Jul 30, *H*)
Super Rocky 47[1] (5f, Edin, F, Jul 30, *H*)
Superoo 48[1] (7f 9yds, Leic, G, Jul 5, *H*)
Supertop 47[2] (1m 1f 207yds, Beve, G, Jun 3, *H*)
Supreme Master 48[1] (1m 4f, Kemp, F, Sep 4, *H*)
Sure Haven (IRE) 57[4] (1m 3f, Redc, G, Sep 25)
Sure Lord (IRE) 48[2] (5f 213yds, Brig, F, Jun 22, *H*)
Surprise Offer 72[1] (5f 34yds, Newb, G, Sep 17)
Surprise Surprise 57[2] (1m 2f, Newj, G, Jul 17)
Surrey Dancer 57[2] (1m 2f 32yds, Newc, Y, Oct 30, *H*)
Surrey Racing 42[4] (6f 212yds, Sali, F, Aug 11, *H*)
Sweet Glow (FR) 44 (1m 7f 110yds, Long, F, Jun 26)
Sweet Mignonette 51[3] (7f 202yds, York, F, Sep 1, *H*)
Sweet Nasha (IRE) 53[1] (1m 1f, Leop, G, Aug 8, *H*)
Swift Silver 46[3] (1m 2f 85yds, York, S, Oct 6, *H*)
Swing Low 80[3] (7f 64yds, Newb, F, Aug 13, *G*)
Sword Master 52[1] (1m 3f 144yds, Bath, Y, Apr 27, *H*)
Sylvan (IRE) 44[3] (7f 16yds, Sand, G, Jun 11, *H*)
Sylvan Breeze 45[2] (6f, Ling, F, May 8, *H*)
Tahdid 55[1] (7f 140yds, Ling, F, Aug 1, *H*)
Tajdif (USA) 48[2] (7f, Newc, G, Jul 24, *H*)
Tajhiz (USA) 46[2] (6f, Redc, G, Oct 5, *M*)
Takarouna (USA) 62[1] (1m 2f, Curr, G, Jun 26, *G*)
Take By Storm (IRE) 42[4] (1m 3f 16yds, Hami, G, Apr 30)
Take Risks (FR) 75[4] (1m, Stcl, Y, May 7, *G*)
Talent (USA) 60[2] (1m 14yds, Sand, G, Jul 3, *H*)
Talented 74[3] (1m 2f, Deau, G, Aug 29, *G*)
Talented Ting (IRE) 43[1] (1m 1f 213yds, Nott, F, Aug 4, *H*)
Tales Of Hearsay (GER) 41[4] (1m 2f, Curr, F, Aug 28, *M*)
Talloires (USA) 75 (1m 4f, Long, Y, Oct 3, *G*)
Talos (IRE) 45[4] (1m 4f, Newj, G, Jun 25, *H*)
Taos (IRE) 50[3] (1m 7yds, Newb, G, Sep 18)
Tap On Air 62[1] (1m 2f, Asco, Y, Sep 24, *H*)
Tapatch (IRE) 44[2] (1m 2f, Ripo, F, Aug 31, *H*)
Tapis Rouge (IRE) 74[4] (1m, Kemp, G, May 3, *H*)
Tarakana (USA) 54 (1m 2f, Curr, G, Jun 26, *G*)
Taroudant 49[1] (2m, Ripo, G, May 26, *H*)
Tasset (CAN) 45[4] (1m 4f, Sali, F, Aug 11, *H*)
Taufan Blu (IRE) 75[1] (7f, Thir, S, May 15, *H*)
Tawafij (USA) 51[4] (7f, Newj, F, Jul 8, *H*)
Tbaareeh (USA) 40[2] (1m 4f, Curr, F, Jun 26)
Teanarco (IRE) 50[2] (7f, Newb, Y, Oct 21, *H*)
Tej Singh (USA) 46[3] (1m 1f 207yds, Beve, F, Jul 27, *H*)
Tenby 74[3] (1m 2f 7yds, Sand, G, Jul 3, *G*)
Tender Moment (IRE) 51[1] (7f, Asco, G, Apr 28, *H*)
Tenet (FR) 43[4] (1m 2f 110yds, Chan, G, Jun 11, *L*)
Tenga (USA) 64[2] (5f, Deau, G, Aug 28, *L*)
Terrhars (IRE) 59[4] (5f 34yds, Newb, F, Aug 14, *H*)
Teshami (USA) 63[5] (1m 2f, Good, Y, Jul 30, *H*)
Thaleros 48[3] (1m 2f 46yds, Bath, F, Jul 7, *H*)
Thatching Craft (IRE) 69[1] (7f, Naas, G, Oct 16, *L*)
Thawakib (IRE) 57[1] (1m 4f, Asco, Y, Jun 17, *G*)
The Auction Bidder 53[1] (6f, Hayd, G, Jun 4, *H*)
The Burser 64[3] (1m 2f, Leop, G, Aug 2, *H*)
The Executor 42[1] (1m 114yds, Epso, F, Jun 30, *C*)
The Little Ferret 47[2] (7f, Ling, G, Jul 10, *M*)
The Noble Oak (IRE) 48[2] (5f, Good, G, May 20, *H*)
The Sharp Bidder (IRE) 49[2] (5f 16yds, Ches, G, Jul 9, *H*)
Theatrician (USA) 57[3] (1m 110yds, Long, F, Jun 21, *L*)
Thornton Gate 50[2] (7f 2yds, Ches, G, Aug 20, *H*)
Thourios 79[1] (7f 64yds, Newb, G, Jul 16)
Thousla Rock (IRE) 78[2] (5f 140yds, Donc, G, Sep 8, *H*)
Three For Fantasy (IRE) 62[1] (6f, Evry, G, Jul 13, *G*)
Three Musketeers (IRE) 41[1] (6f, Curr, S, Nov 3, *H*)
Tickerty's Gift 50[1] (1m 2f 60yds, Donc, G, Sep 8)
Tik Fa (USA) 68[2] (7f 202yds, York, F, Jul 9)
Time Again 46[3] (7f, Newm, G, Oct 2, *H*)
Tinerana (IRE) 43[3] (1m 1f, Curr, G, Jun 26, *H*)
Tinners Way (USA) 80[3] (7f, Long, S, Oct 10, *G*)
Tioman Island 65[2] (1m 3f 106yds, Ling, F, May 8, *G*)
Tissisat (USA) 70[3] (1m, Newm, G, Oct 16, *H*)
Tochar Ban (USA) 48[1] (1m 2f 7yds, Wind, G, Jul 31, *M*)
Tomos 66[4] (1m 2f, Asco, Y, Sep 24, *H*)
Tony's Fen 52[1] (1m 2f, Curr, G, May 22, *H*)
Tony's Mist 55[1] (1m 54yds, Nott, Y, Oct 18, *H*)
Toocando (IRE) 40[4] (7f, Newm, G, Apr 13, *G*)

Top Cees 57[2] (1m 2f, Ling, G, May 22, *H*)
Top Salse (FR) 40[4] (6f, Evry, F, Apr 21, *L*)
Top Spin 49[3] (2m, Kemp, S, Apr 12, *H*)
Topographe (FR) 40[1] (7f, Leop, G, Oct 25, *H*)
Tot Ou Tard (IRE) 68[1] (1m 2f, Evry, Y, Sep 25, *L*)
Trammel 51[1] (1m 4f 8yds, Pont, F, Jul 23, *M*)
Trapezium 64[2] (6f, Kemp, G, Sep 4)
Treasure Time (IRE) 42[1] (5f 43yds, Yarm, Hrd, Jun 30)
Tree Of Life 44[3] (1m 2f, Asco, G, Jul 23, *M*)
Tremolando (USA) 60[2] (1m 4f, Donc, G, Jun 25)
Trentesimo (IRE) 44[1] (6f, Sout, G, Sep 27, *S*)
Tresor Du Mesnil (FR) 50 (1m, Deau, G, Aug 28, *G*)
Trevorsninepoints 41[1] (5f, Edin, F, Aug 26, *H*)
Triarius (USA) 50[1] (1m 4f 110yds, Deau, G, Aug 28, *L*)
Troon 50[2] (6f, York, Y, Jun 12, *H*)
Trooping (IRE) 51[2] (1m, Good, F, May 19, *H*)
Tropical 80[1] (5f, Leop, F, Sep 11)
Truben (USA) 54[5] (1m 4f 93yds, Newc, F, Jun 26, *H*)
True Bearing (USA) 62[5] (7f, Long, Y, Sep 19, *L*)
True Hero (USA) 58[2] (1m 1f, Ripo, Y, Apr 7)
True Precision 46[1] (6f, Newm, G, May 22, *H*)
Truthful Image 60[1] (5f 212yds, Catt, G, Jul 14, *H*)
Tryarra (IRE) 63[1] (1m 2f, Curr, F, Aug 28, *H*)
Turgenev (IRE) 74[3] (1m 3f 200yds, Hayd, G, Jul 3, *H*)
Turgeon (USA) 71[3] (1m 6f 110yds, Stcl, S, May 1, *G*)
Turners Hill 79[4] (1m 4f, Long, Y, Sep 12, *G*)
Tuscan Dawn 65[3] (5f 34yds, Newb, G, Sep 17)
Two Moves In Front (IRE) 49[3] (6f, Hayd, G, May 29, *H*)
Tychonic 50[3] (7f 202yds, York, G, May 13, *H*)
Tyrian Purple (IRE) 43[4] (7f 122yds, Ches, F, May 6, *H*)
Ukud (USA) 55[4] (7f, Curr, G, Aug 28, *H*)
Um Algowain (USA) 51[1] (1m 2f 36yds, Chep, G, Sep 11)
Underwater (USA) 51[2] (1m 7yds, Newb, F, Jun 22)
Unforgiving Minute 57[2] (1m 2f, Newm, F, May 1, *H*)
Up Anchor (IRE) 45[5] (1m 4f 5yds, Newb, Y, Oct 23, *G*)
Up And At 'em 71[2] (5f, Hayd, G, Apr 10, *L*)
Up She Flew (USA) 43[3] (1m 2f, Curr, G, Aug 21, *H*)
Urban Sea (USA) 91[1] (1m 4f, Long, Y, Oct 3, *G*)
Urgent Request (IRE) 57[1] (1m 3f 144yds, Bath, F, Jul 7)
Usaidit 78[1] (1m 2f 7yds, Wind, F, Aug 28, *L*)
User Friendly 84[1] (1m 4f, Stcl, F, Jul 4, *G*)
Utrillo (USA) 40[1] (1m 3f 101yds, Yarm, F, Aug 19, *H*)
Val Sauvage 53[3] (1m 4f 110yds, Mais, F, Jun 22, *L*)
Vallance 52[1] (1m 2f, Redc, F, Jun 19, *H*)
Valley Quest 48[3] (1m 4f, Evry, G, Sep 29, *L*)
Valona (IRE) 40[3] (1m 2f, Leop, G, Jun 7, *H*)
Vanishing Prairie (USA) 53[1] (1m 2f, Leop, G, Oct 23, *M*)
Vasiliev 41[4] (1m 3f 216yds, Beve, G, May 7, *H*)
Velasco (IRE) 46[2] (1m 3yds, Yarm, F, Aug 30, *H*)
Veloce (IRE) 57[2] (6f, Ayr, F, Jul 24, *H*)
Ventiquattrofogli (IRE) 65[3] (1m, Newm, F, Apr 15, *G*)
Venture Capitalist 70[4] (6f, York, Y, May 11, *H*)
Verde Alitalia (IRE) 57[2] (5f, Newc, F, Jun 25, *H*)
Versainville (FR) 48 (1m 2f, Evry, Y, Sep 25, *L*)
Vert Amande (FR) 86[1] (1m 2f 110yds, Long, S, May 2, *G*)
Verveine (USA) 79[1] (1m 1f 55yds, Long, Y, Oct 3, *G*)
Very Dicey 52[2] (5f, Ling, G, Nov 4, *H*)
Via Parigi (IRE) 61[3] (1m, Curr, G, Jul 10, *L*)
Village Green (FR) 44[2] (1m 67yds, Wind, G, Aug 9, *M*)
Vintage Crop 87[1] (1m 6f, Curr, Y, Sep 18, *G*)
Vishnu (USA) 47[3] (1m 4f, Thir, G, Aug 9)
Visto Si Stampi (IRE) 59[2] (1m, Good, G, Jul 31)
Viviana (USA) 69[4] (1m 2f, Deau, G, Aug 29, *G*)
Voleris (FR) 81[1] (1m, Long, Y, Oct 3, *G*)
Vratislav (USA) 47[3] (1m 3f 135yds, Wind, F, Aug 28)
Waffle On 57[5] (7f, Newm, G, Oct 14, *H*)
Wagon Master (FR) 64[2] (1m 2f 21yds, Yarm, Y, Oct 27)
Wahem (IRE) 41[2] (1m, Newm, G, Apr 30, *H*)
Wainwright (USA) 65[1] (1m, Ayr, F, Sep 17, *H*)
Wajih (USA) 55[1] (1m 2f 120yds, Hayd, Y, Sep 24, *M*)
Wakil (IRE) 47[2] (1m 67yds, Wind, G, Jul 12, *H*)
Wakria (IRE) 64[1] (1m 1f, Long, S, Oct 17, *L*)
Wali (USA) 48[3] (1m, Newb, G, Jul 17, *H*)
Walk The Beat 49[3] (5f, Asco, Y, Jun 19, *H*)
Walking The Plank 53[2] (1m 7yds, Newb, G, Sep 18, *H*)
Wandering Thoughts (IRE) 60[3] (1m 2f, Curr, Y, Oct 2, *H*)
Wannabe 43[1] (1m, Warw, F, Aug 30, *M*)
Warm Spell 56[2] (1m 4f 5yds, Newb, Y, Oct 23, *H*)
Warspite 44[5] (1m 2f, Newm, G, Apr 13, *M*)
Wathik (USA) 49[6] (7f, Redc, F, Sep 24, *H*)
Wave Hill 42[4] (1m 2f, Kemp, F, May 29, *H*)
Weaver Bird 42[3] (1m 4yds, Pont, Y, Oct 4, *H*)
Well Suited 43[2] (1m 1f 213yds, Nott, F, Aug 3)
Wellington Rock (USA) 44[3] (1m, Newc, F, Jul 24, *H*)
Welsh Mill (IRE) 52[1] (1m 4f 10yds, Epso, F, Jun 4, *H*)
Welshman 42[1] (2m 19yds, Newc, F, Aug 30, *H*)
Wemyss Bight 84[2] (1m 4f, Long, Y, Sep 12, *G*)
West Coast 50[4] (1m, Stcl, G, Sep 24, *L*)
Western Cape (USA) 70[1] (1m 2f, Good, Y, Jul 30, *H*)
Western Dynasty 49[1] (1m 5f 61yds, Newb, Y, May 26, *H*)
Westholme (USA) 42 (1m 2f 6yds, Pont, G, May 28, *H*)
Wharf (USA) 77[1] (1m 1f, Newm, G, Oct 15, *L*)
What Katy Did (USA) 49[3] (1m, Mais, G, May 25, *L*)
What Kay Did (USA) 42[3] (1m, Evry, G, Sep 18, *L*)
White Muzzle 86[2] (1m 4f, Long, Y, Oct 3, *G*)
White Shadow (IRE) 49 (6f, Good, G, Sep 11, *H*)
White Willow 56[1] (1m 3f 16yds, Hami, G, Apr 30)
Whitechapel (USA) 50[2] (1m 4f, Newm, G, Oct 14, *H*)
Wild Jewel (CAN) 65[2] (7f, Long, S, Oct 14, *L*)
Will Of Steel 55[1] (7f, Newm, G, Apr 14, *H*)
Willshe Gan 43[4] (5f, Thir, G, Aug 9, *H*)
Wilsonic 48[3] (1m 4f 93yds, Newc, F, Jun 26, *H*)
Winged Victory (IRE) 58[3] (7f 16yds, Chep, F, Aug 30)
Winged Victory (USA) 72[2] (1m 4f, Asco, G, Jun 15, *G*)
Winter Forest (USA) 58[1] (1m 2f, Good, F, Aug 27, *M*)
Witness Box (USA) 56[4] (1m 7f 195yds, York, G, Aug 17, *L*)
Wolf Prince (USA) 42 (1m 4f 10yds, Epso, F, Jun 2, *G*)
Wolfhound (USA) 97[1] (6f, Hayd, F, Sep 4, *G*)
Wootton Rivers (USA) 60[5] (1m 2f, Evry, Y, Sep 25, *L*)
Wrets 46[4] (1m 1f 213yds, Nott, G, Jun 7)
Yahmi (IRE) 49[2] (1m 4f, Sali, F, May 5, *M*)
Yajeed (USA) 54[3] (1m, Kemp, Y, Sep 21, *H*)
Yakin (USA) 53[4] (5f, Sali, G, Aug 12)
Yaqthan (IRE) 40[1] (7f, Kemp, Y, Apr 10, *M*)
Yawl 41[2] (1m 2f, Good, F, May 19, *L*)
Yeltsin 66[6] (1m 4f, Asco, G, Jun 15, *G*)
Yildiz 59[1] (1m 3f 195yds, York, G, Aug 19, *H*)
Young Buster (IRE) 75[6] (1m 2f, Asco, G, Jun 15, *G*)
Young Ern 74[1] (7f, Asco, G, Sep 25, *H*)
Young Freeman (USA) 45 (1m 2f 6yds, Newb, F, May 15, *H*)
Young Senor (USA) 70[2] (1m 2f 75yds, Ches, G, Jul 9)
Yours By Right 53[2] (5f 218yds, Leic, G, May 31, *H*)
Yukon Gold (IRE) 53[3] (1m 2f, Curr, S, Apr 24, *L*)
Zaahi (USA) 56 (1m, Curr, G, Jun 27, *G*)
Zabar 69[3] (1m, Mais, G, Jul 6, *G*)
Zaffera (USA) 40[5] (1m 4f, Stcl, G, Jul 20, *G*)
Zafonic (USA) 92[1] (1m, Newm, F, May 1, *G*)
Zarani Sidi Anna (USA) 73[6] (5f, Long, S, Oct 3, *G*)
Zeboim 44[4] (6f, Folk, F, Aug 13, *H*)
Zieten (USA) 80[4] (5f, Long, S, Oct 3, *G*)
Zigreen (FR) 61[1] (1m, Stcl, G, Sep 24, *L*)
Zimzalabim 40[2] (1m 1f 207yds, Beve, G, Apr 3)
Zinaad 70[3] (2m, Newm, G, Oct 2, *G*)
Zind (IRE) 53[6] (1m 3f 106yds, Ling, F, May 8, *G*)

Two year olds

A Smooth One (IRE) 45[1] (6f, Asco, G, Jul 24, *G*)
Air Commodore 35[2] (1m 16yds, Edin, G, Nov 4, *M*)
Alaflak (IRE) 50[3] (1m 4yds, Pont, G, Oct 21, *L*)
Alanees 55[2] (6f, Ripo, G, Aug 30, *L*)
Alazwar (USA) 39[2] (6f, Newm, G, Oct 29, *M*)
Aljawza (USA) 51[2] (6f, Naas, G, Oct 16, *H*)
Allez Cyrano (IRE) 36[2] (7f, Newc, F, Aug 30, *M*)
Allwight Then (IRE) 52[4] (5f, Newm, G, Oct 29, *H*)
Alzianah 51[1] (6f, Asco, G, Sep 23, *H*)
Amber Valley (USA) 47[1] (6f 18yds, Ches, S, Oct 20, *M*)
Amidst 42[1] (6f, Kemp, F, Sep 3, *H*)
Amoret (IRE) 35[1] (6f, Ripo, G, Aug 30, *S*)
Angel Of The Night (USA) 36 (5f 110yds, Mais, G, Jul 18, *G*)
Ann's Pearl (IRE) 45[4] (5f, Donc, G, Nov 5, *H*)
Areciba (USA) 48[1] (6f 8yds, Newb, F, Aug 13, *M*)
Art Tatum (IRE) 40[1] (1m 3yds, Yarm, Y, Nov 5, *H*)
Arz (USA) 42[2] (5f, Donc, G, May 31, *M*)
Arzina (USA) 36[1] (5f, Ling, G, Sep 30, *M*)
Askern 44[1] (7f, Redc, G, Aug 25)

Astrac (IRE) 38^{2} (6f, Newc, Y, Nov 1, *M*)
Averti (IRE) 48^{1} (5f 217yds, Wind, F, Aug 9)
Averti (USA) 36^{1} (7f, Good, Y, Jul 27, *M*)
Back From Heaven (IRE) 40^{1} (7f, Naas, G, Jul 21, *M*)
Bagshot 35^{2} (6f 16yds, Chep, Y, Oct 19, *H*)
Balanchine (USA) 43^{1} (6f 212yds, Sali, F, Sep 2, *M*)
Bali Warrior (IRE) 36^{2} (1m, Donc, G, Sep 9, *H*)
Ballard Ring (IRE) 41^{2} (7f, Newm, G, Oct 15, *G*)
Ballykett Nancy (IRE) 35 (1m, Asco, G, Sep 25, *G*)
Barbaroja 57^{1} (1m 4yds, Pont, G, Oct 21, *L*)
Barodet (USA) 51^{1} (7f, Deau, G, Aug 3, *L*)
Barossa Valley (IRE) 35^{1} (6f 8yds, Newb, G, Jul 16, *M*)
Bashful Brave 36^{2} (5f 59yds, Brig, F, Aug 24, *M*)
Baskerville 42^{3} (5f, Sali, F, Aug 19)
Bassmaat (USA) 42^{2} (6f, Curr, G, Jun 26, *M*)
Battling Blue 39^{1} (5f 6yds, Sand, G, Jul 14)
Bawardi (IRE) 36^{3} (1m, Curr, S, Oct 9, *G*)
Baydur (IRE) 47^{5} (7f, Curr, S, Nov 3, *M*)
Be Exciting (IRE) 42^{2} (1m 3yds, Yarm, Y, Nov 5, *H*)
Beaming 39^{1} (5f 212yds, Catt, Y, Oct 15, *M*)
Bearall (IRE) 52^{1} (7f 64yds, Newb, Y, Oct 23, *L*)
Beats Working 44^{4} (1m, Donc, G, Sep 9, *H*)
Beccari (USA) 58^{5} (7f, Long, G, Sep 12, *G*)
Best Kept Secret 35^{2} (6f, Ripo, G, Jun 16)
Bid For Blue 55^{1} (5f, York, G, Aug 18)
Billy Cruncheon 40^{2} (5f, Donc, G, Nov 5, *H*)
Bintalshaati 36^{3} (6f, Redc, G, Oct 5, *M*)
Blair Castle (IRE) 36^{4} (7f, Good, Y, Jul 30, *M*)
Blaze Away (USA) 46^{1} (7f, Sout, F, Aug 6, *M*)
Blue Bomber 53^{1} (5f, Hayd, G, Sep 3, *M*)
Blue Burgee (USA) 50^{3} (7f, Deau, G, Aug 29, *G*)
Blue King (FR) 40^{5} (1m, Stcl, S, Oct 25, *G*)
Blue Siren 46^{1} (5f, Sali, F, Aug 19)
Bluegrass Prince (IRE) 48^{3} (6f 212yds, Sali, G, Sep 29)
Bold Alex 36^{1} (5f 212yds, Catt, G, Sep 18, *M*)
Bold Sixteen (USA) 39^{1} (7f, Ling, Y, Oct 25, *M*)
Braari (USA) 46^{1} (6f, Ayr, F, Sep 17, *L*)
Braille (IRE) 35^{1} (6f, Redc, G, Nov 2)
Brave Edge 51^{3} (5f, Newm, G, Oct 29, *H*)
Brave Note (IRE) 53^{4} (5f 110yds, Mais, G, Jul 18, *G*)
Brentwood (IRE) 43^{3} (1m 2f, Newm, G, Oct 30, *L*)
Broctune Gold 37^{1} (5f, Newc, G, May 3, *M*)
Bude 47^{3} (1m, Donc, G, Oct 23, *G*)
Bures (IRE) 40^{3} (7f 100yds, Beve, G, Sep 15, *M*)
Cajun Cadet 36^{1} (6f 8yds, Newb, Y, Oct 21, *M*)
Canaska Dancer (IRE) 55^{1} (6f 8yds, Newb, G, Oct 23, *H*)
Cape Merino 45^{2} (5f, York, G, Sep 1)
Carmot 43^{1} (7f, Newj, F, Jul 31)
Caspian Gold 36^{1} (5f 4yds, Hami, F, Jun 28)
Castle Gardens (IRE) 48^{2} (6f, Naas, G, Oct 16, *M*)
Cella (IRE) 38 (6f, Deau, G, Aug 1, *G*)
Celtic Arms (FR) 59^{4} (7f, Long, G, Sep 12, *G*)
Charity Crusader 46^{1} (1m 30yds, Hayd, G, Sep 4)
Cherokee Rose (IRE) 55^{2} (7f, Deau, G, Aug 29, *G*)
Chickawicka (IRE) 40^{4} (6f, Kemp, F, Sep 3, *H*)
Chimes Band (USA) 54^{5} (1m, Long, S, Oct 2, *G*)
City Nights (IRE) 51^{2} (1m, Curr, S, Oct 9, *G*)
Clarinda (IRE) 38^{1} (5f, Donc, G, May 31, *M*)
Classic Sky (IRE) 37^{3} (6f, York, G, May 13, *M*)
Close To Reality 48^{2} (6f, Ayr, F, Sep 17, *H*)
Clyde Goddess (IRE) 50^{3} (7f 64yds, Newb, Y, Oct 23, *L*)
Coigach 35^{1} (1m, Donc, G, Oct 22, *M*)
Cois Na Tine (IRE) 56^{1} (6f, Leop, G, Jul 17, *L*)
Colonel Collins (USA) 61^{2} (7f, Newm, G, Oct 1, *L*)
Comeonup 40^{1} (6f, Folk, S, Oct 18)
Common Rumpus (IRE) 52^{2} (6f, Leop, G, Jul 17, *L*)
Concordial (USA) 56^{1} (6f 214yds, York, G, Aug 17)
Cotteir Chief (IRE) 47^{1} (7f 2yds, Ches, S, Oct 20)
Coup de Genie (USA) 72^{1} (7f, Long, G, Sep 12, *G*)
Cragganmore 44^{2} (5f, Ripo, G, Aug 14)
Crazy Paving (IRE) 37^{1} (6f, Good, F, Jun 4, *M*)
Crystal Lake (IRE) 40 (7f, Newm, G, Sep 29)
Crystal Magic 35^{1} (5f 10yds, Wind, F, Aug 16, *M*)
Cult Hero (CAN) 37^{4} (6f 214yds, York, G, Aug 17)
Daily Star 35^{2} (5f 6yds, Sand, G, Sep 15, *H*)
Dance Focus 43^{1} (5f 43yds, Yarm, F, Jul 21, *M*)
Dance To The Top 59^{2} (1m, Asco, G, Sep 25, *G*)
Danger Point 36^{3} (7f, Ayr, F, Sep 16, *M*)
Dangerous Shadow 39^{1} (6f 16yds, Chep, Y, Oct 19, *H*)
Danish (IRE) 40^{2} (6f, Leop, G, Jun 8, *L*)
Danseuse Du Nord (IRE) 35 (1m, Long, Y, Oct 3, *G*)
Dare And Go (USA) 43^{3} (1m, Stcl, S, Oct 25, *G*)
Darkwood Bay (USA) 39^{1} (7f, Ling, Y, Oct 25, *M*)
Daronne 39^{4} (1m 4yds, Pont, G, Oct 21, *L*)
Darren Boy (IRE) 44^{2} (5f 217yds, Wind, F, Aug 16, *H*)
Desert Invader (IRE) 39^{1} (6f, Newc, Y, Nov 1, *M*)
Devotee 39^{3} (5f 11yds, Bath, G, Aug 10, *M*)
Diamond Park (IRE) 39^{2} (7f, Kemp, F, Sep 3)
Diesan (USA) 50^{1} (7f, Good, G, Sep 11, *H*)
Diligent Dodger (IRE) 40^{1} (6f, Curr, S, Jun 2, *M*)
Dirigeante (FR) 50^{4} (7f, Deau, G, Aug 21, *L*)
Dollar Gamble (IRE) 49^{1} (5f 16yds, Chep, G, Sep 11)
Dominion King 35^{1} (5f 11yds, Bath, F, Sep 27, *M*)
Domino Queen (IRE) 43^{1} (5f 6yds, Sand, G, Sep 14)
Double Trigger (IRE) 54^{1} (1m 2f, Newm, G, Oct 30, *L*)
Dover Straits (USA) 38^{2} (1m, Newm, G, Sep 29, *M*)
Duty Time 50^{1} (1m, Donc, G, Sep 9, *H*)
Dynamic Deluxe (USA) 43^{1} (1m, Kemp, G, Sep 21, *M*)
Ehtfaal (IRE) 52^{1} (6f, Ripo, G, Aug 30, *L*)
Eichtercua (IRE) 55^{1} (5f, Curr, G, Jul 10, *G*)
Electrify (USA) 42^{1} (6f, Good, G, Jul 28, *M*)
Eleuthera 43^{4} (6f, Newm, G, Oct 2, *H*)
Elrafa Ah (USA) 46^{1} (5f 6yds, Sand, G, Jul 2, *L*)
Ensorcelles Moi (USA) 45^{5} (7f, Deau, G, Aug 29, *G*)
ERHaab (USA) 59^{2} (6f 212yds, Sali, G, Sep 29)
Escarpment (USA) 51^{1} (7f, Good, Y, Jul 30, *M*)
Eternal Reve (USA) 51^{2} (6f, Evry, G, Sep 25, *L*)
Fadeyev (USA) 50^{1} (1m, Stcl, S, Oct 25, *G*)
Fairy Heights (IRE) 64^{1} (1m, Asco, G, Sep 25, *G*)
Fairy Water 54^{3} (7f, Curr, S, Oct 2, *G*)
Far Mist (FR) 56^{1} (7f, Deau, G, Aug 29, *G*)
Fast Eddy 49^{3} (7f, Newm, G, Oct 1, *L*)
Fawaakeh (USA) 44^{2} (7f, Newm, G, Sep 29, *H*)
Fawlty Towers (IRE) 47^{3} (1m, Newm, G, Oct 15, *H*)
Fawran (USA) 41^{1} (6f 209yds, Brig, G, Sep 28, *M*)
Featherstone Lane 40^{2} (5f, Newm, G, Oct 29, *H*)
Filha Do Ar (USA) 46^{6} (6f, Deau, G, Aug 1, *G*)
First Trump 71^{1} (6f, Newm, G, Sep 30, *G*)
Flagbird (USA) 49^{2} (1m, Long, Y, Oct 3, *G*)
Flagny (FR) 36^{4} (7f, Deau, G, Aug 3, *L*)
Folly Finnesse 37^{1} (6f 189yds, Folk, S, Nov 8, *H*)
Footsteps (IRE) 39^{1} (7f, Newj, F, Aug 6, *H*)
Forest Gazelle (USA) 40^{1} (6f, Newj, F, Aug 27)
Foxhound (USA) 57^{2} (6f, Deau, G, Aug 1, *G*)
Fred Bongusto (IRE) 59^{4} (6f, Deau, G, Aug 1, *G*)
French Gift 46^{4} (7f, Newm, G, Sep 29)
Friendly Champ (IRE) 47^{1} (7f, Kemp, F, Sep 3)
Fumo Di Londra (IRE) 58^{1} (7f, Newm, G, Sep 29)
General Gubbins 36^{2} (5f, Ripo, G, Jul 17, *M*)
Glatisant 40^{1} (7f, Good, F, Aug 27, *G*)
Gneiss (USA) 46^{1} (6f 15yds, Nott, G, Sep 20, *M*)
Gold Land (USA) 59^{2} (5f 16yds, Chep, G, Sep 11)
Golden Nashwan (IRE) 45^{1} (7f, Donc, G, Oct 22, *M*)
Gothic Dream (IRE) 54^{4} (7f, Curr, G, Sep 12, *G*)
Governor George (USA) 42^{1} (5f 34yds, Newb, G, May 26, *M*)
Grand Lodge (USA) 68^{1} (7f, Newm, G, Oct 1, *L*)
Great Deeds 58^{2} (5f, Donc, G, Sep 11, *G*)
Green Green Desert (FR) 41^{1} (6f, Newm, G, Oct 29, *M*)
Green Tune (USA) 56^{3} (6f, Deau, G, Aug 1, *G*)

Guided Tour (IRE) 58[1] (6f, Naas, G, Oct 16, *M*)
Hannah's Music 42[1] (5f, Ripo, G, Aug 14)
Harvest Mouse 35[1] (6f 212yds, Sali, G, Jul 10, *M*)
Hawajiss 65[1] (1m, Donc, G, Sep 9, *G*)
Hawker Hunter (USA) 42[4] (1m, Asco, G, Sep 25, *G*)
Hello Mister 41[1] (5f 6yds, Sand, G, Sep 15, *H*)
Hever Golf Rose 41[1] (6f, Newj, F, Jul 31, *H*)
High Domain (IRE) 46[1] (5f, Sali, G, May 28)
High Holme 49[1] (5f, Newm, G, Oct 29, *H*)
Iguassu (FR) 38[3] (7f, Deau, G, Aug 3, *L*)
Il Caravaggio (IRE) 41[1] (5f, Curr, S, Apr 24)
Imperial Bailiwick (IRE) 59[1] (5f, Donc, G, Sep 11, *G*)
In Like Flynn 40[2] (1m, Newb, G, Oct 23)
Indhar 39[1] (7f, Newm, G, Oct 16)
Indiahra 42[1] (5f, Hayd, G, Aug 13, *H*)
Ingozi 44[3] (6f 8yds, Newb, F, Aug 13, *M*)
Innishowen (USA) 45[4] (7f, Newm, G, Oct 1, *L*)
Instamatic 46[4] (7f, Curr, S, Oct 2, *G*)
Iradah (USA) 36[3] (5f 43yds, Yarm, F, Jul 21, *M*)
Iron Gent (USA) 43[2] (7f 100yds, Beve, G, Sep 15, *M*)
Isabella Sharp 42[5] (5f, Donc, G, Sep 11, *G*)
Island Magic 35[1] (5f, Carl, F, Jul 23, *M*)
Jade Pet 41[1] (5f, Ling, F, Aug 7)
Jasari (IRE) 40[1] (6f 5yds, Hami, F, Sep 6)
Jayannpee 44[2] (5f 6yds, Sand, G, Sep 14)
Jazeel (USA) 43[1] (7f, Ayr, F, Sep 16, *M*)
Join Forces (IRE) 43[1] (5f, Naas, G, Oct 30, *H*)
Just Happy (USA) 55[2] (6f 214yds, York, G, Aug 17)
Kalkabrino (USA) 47[4] (6f, Newm, G, Oct 15, *M*)
Kefahi (IRE) 35[3] (7f 3yds, Yarm, G, Sep 15, *M*)
Keraka (USA) 53[5] (7f, Curr, G, Sep 12, *G*)
Key Of Luck (USA) 58[1] (6f, Evry, G, Sep 25, *L*)
Khamaseen 45[4] (1m, Donc, G, Oct 23, *G*)
King Rat (IRE) 43[1] (5f 59yds, Brig, G, Sep 28, *S*)
King Sancho (IRE) 40[2] (5f, Naas, G, Oct 30, *H*)
King's Theatre (IRE) 59[1] (1m, Donc, G, Oct 23, *G*)
Kissing Cousin (IRE) 59[2] (1m, Donc, G, Sep 9, *G*)
Knayton Lass 45[2] (6f, Ayr, F, Sep 17, *L*)
Lady Sheriff 37[2] (5f, Newc, G, Aug 28, *H*)
Lady Williams (IRE) 39[2] (5f 217yds, Wind, G, Aug 28, *M*)
Lake Country (IRE) 53[2] (5f 110yds, Mais, G, Jul 18, *G*)
Las Meninas (IRE) 44[1] (6f, Leop, G, Jun 8, *L*)
Legatee 36[3] (5f, Hayd, G, Aug 13, *H*)
Lemon Souffle 69[1] (7f, Curr, G, Sep 12, *G*)
Leonova 47[4] (7f 64yds, Newb, Y, Oct 23, *L*)
Lime Street Blues (IRE) 40[1] (6f, York, S, Oct 7, *H*)
Link Miles 47[1] (7f, Warw, Y, Oct 5, *H*)
Linney Head (USA) 39[1] (7f 3yds, Yarm, Y, Nov 5, *M*)
Lomas (IRE) 56[1] (7f, Kemp, G, Jun 23, *M*)
Long Gallery (IRE) 48[2] (5f, Curr, G, Jul 10, *G*)
Lord Sky 35[1] (5f, Folk, S, Oct 18)
Lost World (IRE) 67[1] (1m, Long, S, Oct 2, *G*)
Low Key Affair (USA) 55[3] (7f, Curr, G, Sep 12, *G*)
Luana 55[1] (6f, Newm, G, Oct 15, *M*)
Luhuk (USA) 36[1] (7f 16yds, Sand, Y, Sep 15, *M*)
Lunafairy (FR) 58[2] (7f, Deau, G, Aug 14, *L*)
Majestic Role (FR) 63[2] (7f, Long, G, Sep 12, *G*)
Majestic Eagle (IRE) 43[2] (6f, Kemp, G, Sep 4, *L*)
Major Success (IRE) 44[1] (5f 217yds, Wind, F, Aug 16, *H*)
Make A Note (USA) 46[3] (1m 3yds, Yarm, Y, Nov 5, *H*)
Make A Stand 49[1] (1m, Newm, G, Oct 15, *H*)
Make The Break 37[1] (5f, Edin, G, Nov 4)
Manhattan Sunset (USA) 37[1] (7f, Newm, G, Sep 29, *H*)
Manntari (IRE) 70[1] (7f, Curr, Y, Sep 18, *G*)
Marjorie's Memory (IRE) 39[1] (5f 2yds, Leic, F, Jul 13, *H*)
Market Slide (USA) 50[1] (6f, Naas, G, Oct 16, *M*)
Mary Hinge 56[1] (5f, Ling, Y, Oct 25)
Masawa (IRE) 47[3] (6f, Naas, G, Oct 16, *M*)
Mazentre Forward (IRE) 52[1] (6f, Sali, G, Sep 29)
Mehthaaf (USA) 61[1] (6f, Hayd, G, Aug 7, *M*)
Memorable 37[3] (1m 1f 213yds, Nott, S, Sep 21, *H*)
Michelle Hicks 40[3] (6f, Newj, F, Jun 26, *L*)
Midushi (USA) 35[2] (7f 64yds, Newb, F, Aug 14, *H*)
Mild Rebuke 42[2] (6f, Asco, G, Jul 24, *G*)
Millicent North 36[2] (6f, Good, Y, Jul 29, *H*)
Miss Potter (IRE) 46[4] (6f, Naas, G, Oct 16, *M*)
Mister Baileys 53[1] (1m, Asco, G, Sep 25, *G*)
Mister Beat 41[2] (7f, Newm, G, Oct 14, *S*)
Mister Piste (IRE) 35[2] (5f, Ayr, G, Aug 19, *H*)
Monis (IRE) 37[1] (5f 59yds, Brig, F, Aug 24, *M*)
Monkey's Wedding 43[1] (5f, Sout, G, Nov 8, *C*)
Montaya 41[1] (5f 6yds, Sand, G, Apr 24, *M*)
Monticino (IRE) 45[1] (5f, Catt, Y, Oct 16, *M*)
Morcote (IRE) 63[1] (7f, Curr, S, Oct 2, *G*)
Moscow Road 47[1] (5f, Newj, G, Jul 17)
Moving Arrow 42[2] (7f, Ayr, F, Sep 16, *M*)
Mr Artistic (USA) 43[4] (1m 2f, Newm, G, Oct 30, *L*)
Mr Bergerac (IRE) 43[1] (5f, Folk, Y, Nov 8)
Mr Eubanks (USA) 39[5] (7f, Newm, G, Oct 1, *L*)
Mr M-E-N (IRE) 39[4] (5f, Ripo, G, Aug 14)
Mulmus (IRE) 50[3] (6f, Naas, G, Oct 16, *H*)
Multi National 51[2] (5f, Asco, G, Sep 24)
Mutakddim (USA) 36 (7f, Newm, G, Oct 15, *G*)
Muzrak (CAN) 51[3] (7f, Curr, S, Nov 3, *M*)
Mytilene (IRE) 53 (1m, Asco, G, Sep 25, *G*)
Nec Plus Ultra (FR) 49[2] (7f, Deau, G, Aug 3, *L*)
Nera 40[1] (5f 2yds, Leic, G, Apr 24)
Nice Welcome 49[3] (7f, Newm, G, Sep 29, *H*)
Nicolotte 57[2] (7f, Newm, G, Sep 29)
Night City 42[2] (6f, Naas, G, Oct 16, *M*)
Nightitude 39[1] (5f, York, G, Jul 10, *H*)
Nijo 42[1] (7f 16yds, Sand, G, Jul 21, *M*)
Nimphidia (USA) 47[1] (6f 3yds, Yarm, Y, Nov 5, *M*)
Niyazi (IRE) 48[4] (7f, Curr, S, Nov 3, *M*)
Nizaal (USA) 38[1] (6f, Pont, G, Sep 20, *M*)
No Mean City (IRE) 42[1] (6f, Ayr, F, Sep 17, *H*)
Noble Rose (IRE) 37[1] (7f 9yds, Leic, Y, Oct 25, *M*)
Non Vintage (IRE) 41[1] (1m, Donc, G, Oct 22, *H*)
Nordico Princess 36[2] (5f, Ripo, F, Aug 31, *H*)
North Reef (IRE) 40[1] (5f 212yds, Catt, Y, Oct 15, *M*)
Northern Bailiwick (IRE) 36[2] (1m, Newm, G, Oct 15, *H*)
Numbered Account 49[3] (6f, Newm, G, Oct 15, *M*)
Ocean Indien (FR) 45[2] (1m, Stcl, S, Oct 25, *G*)
Omnia (USA) 37[3] (7f, Kemp, F, Sep 3)
Once More For Luck (IRE) 44[1] (1m, Newm, G, Oct 30, *H*)
Overbury (IRE) 50[3] (1m, Asco, G, Sep 25, *G*)
Owington 70[2] (6f, Newm, G, Sep 30, *G*)
Palacegate Jack (IRE) 45[1] (6f, York, S, Oct 9, *L*)
Palana (USA) 51[2] (7f 64yds, Newb, Y, Oct 23, *L*)
Paonic (IRE) 43[2] (6f, Newj, G, Jul 17, *M*)
Party Season 42[4] (1m, Asco, G, Sep 25, *G*)
Peace Token (IRE) 42[4] (5f, Curr, G, Jul 10, *G*)
Pencader (IRE) 43[1] (7f, Newb, F, Aug 14, *M*)
Persian Heritage 35[2] (5f, Carl, F, May 7, *M*)
Perusal 46[5] (7f 64yds, Newb, F, Aug 14, *H*)
Peter Rowley 38[1] (6f, Kemp, G, Jul 7)
Petula 56[1] (5f 34yds, Newb, F, Aug 14, *L*)
Phoneaholic (IRE) 36[2] (5f 10yds, Wind, F, Aug 16, *M*)
Piccolo 52[3] (7f, Newm, G, Sep 29)
Pinkerton's Pal 41[2] (6f, York, G, Aug 19, *M*)
Poetical Justice (IRE) 54[2] (7f, Curr, S, Nov 3, *M*)
Polish Laughter (USA) 49[4] (7f, Newm, G, Oct 15, *G*)
Pommes Frites (IRE) 47[1] (5f, Newm, G, Apr 14)
Porto Varas (USA) 55[1] (5f, Long, G, Jun 30, *G*)
Post Mistress (IRE) 38[2] (5f, Catt, Y, Oct 15, *H*)
Prima Silk 35[2] (6f, Redc, F, Sep 24, *H*)
Prince Azzaan (IRE) 41[6] (5f, Donc, G, Sep 11, *G*)
Prince Babar 58[1] (7f, Deau, G, Aug 21, *L*)
Prophecy (IRE) 67[1] (6f, Newm, G, Sep 29, *G*)
Psychobabble (IRE) 63[1] (5f 110yds, Mais, G, Jul 18, *G*)

Ptoto 35[4] (1m, Newm, G, Sep 29, *M*)
Purple Fling 39[2] (5f, Catt, Y, Oct 16, *M*)
Quasimodo (IRE) 35[2] (7f, Naas, G, Jul 21, *M*)
Queenbird 49[1] (5f, York, Y, May 11, *M*)
Quintiliani (IRE) 40[1] (6f, Naas, G, Oct 30)
Rafferty's Rules (IRE) 61[1] (6f, Newm, G, Oct 2, *H*)
Ragsat Al Omor (IRE) 43[4] (1m, Newm, G, Oct 15, *H*)
Rakli 47[2] (6f 8yds, Newb, F, Aug 13, *M*)
Ramani (USA) 46[2] (6f, Newm, G, Oct 15, *M*)
Randonneur (IRE) 39[3] (6f, Ayr, F, Sep 17, *L*)
Razida (IRE) 55[2] (7f, Curr, S, Oct 2, *G*)
Reason To Dance 41[1] (5f 161yds, Bath, G, Sep 13, *M*)
Recaptured Days (IRE) 48[6] (5f, Newm, G, Oct 29, *H*)
Red Earth (USA) 36[2] (7f 9yds, Leic, Y, Oct 25, *M*)
Red Rita (IRE) 42[2] (6f, Asco, G, Jul 24, *G*)
Redoubtable (USA) 67[3] (6f, Newm, G, Sep 30, *G*)
Redress (USA) 46[2] (6f, Kemp, G, Sep 4, *M*)
Rehlat Farah (USA) 40[3] (1m, Kemp, G, Sep 21, *M*)
Relatively Special 56[1] (7f, Newm, G, Oct 15, *G*)
Reprehend 37[2] (6f 8yds, Newb, F, Jun 22)
Resonant 45[1] (5f 43yds, Yarm, G, Aug 18, *C*)
Risky 65[2] (6f, Newm, G, Sep 29, *G*)
River Deep (USA) 41 (7f, Newm, G, Oct 15, *G*)
Robellion 39[1] (5f 11yds, Bath, F, May 8, *M*)
Rohita (IRE) 48[2] (6f, Newj, F, Jun 26, *L*)
Rose Ciel (IRE) 37[3] (7f 64yds, Newb, F, Aug 14, *H*)
Roxanian (IRE) 46[1] (6f, Redc, F, Sep 24, *H*)
Royal Insignia 39[1] (6f, Newj, F, Aug 28, *H*)
Royale Figurine (IRE) 61[1] (5f, Donc, G, Nov 5, *H*)
Rupan 36[2] (6f 209yds, Brig, G, Sep 28, *H*)
Sail Storm (USA) 43[6] (1m, Long, Y, Oct 3, *G*)
Sawlajan (USA) 45[3] (7f, Good, Y, Jul 30, *M*)
Se Souvenir (FR) 52[2] (7f, Deau, G, Aug 21, *L*)
Second Sight (IRE) 38[1] (6f 16yds, Chep, G, Jun 10)
Segala (IRE) 42[1] (6f 189yds, Folk, S, Oct 5)
Selhurstpark Flyer (IRE) 63[1] (5f, Asco, G, Sep 24)
Sensazione 40[6] (7f, Deau, G, Aug 29, *G*)
Serious Option (IRE) 44[1] (5f, Hayd, G, May 28)
Shalbourne (USA) 35[4] (5f 11yds, Bath, G, Aug 10, *M*)
Sharp Phase (IRE) 41[4] (6f, Leop, G, Jul 17, *L*)
Sharp Try (IRE) 55[1] (7f, Curr, S, Nov 3, *M*)
Shepherd Market (IRE) 38[1] (5f 213yds, Brig, F, Sep 22, *M*)
Sheppard's Cross 36[2] (7f, Ling, Y, Oct 25, *M*)
Sheridan (IRE) 63[1] (1m, Curr, S, Oct 9, *G*)
Sheriff 38[2] (1m, Newm, G, Oct 30, *H*)
Sherman (IRE) 41[1] (1m 54yds, Nott, Y, Oct 28, *M*)
Shoalhaven (USA) 52[1] (5f, Deau, G, Aug 18, *L*)
Sierra Madre (FR) 50[1] (1m, Long, Y, Oct 3, *G*)
Signe Divin (USA) 65[2] (1m, Long, S, Oct 2, *G*)
Silver Wedge (USA) 40[2] (5f 6yds, Sand, G, Apr 24, *M*)
Simply Tricky (USA) 62[2] (7f, Deau, G, Aug 14, *L*)
Sinners Reprieve 41[2] (5f, Beve, G, Jun 2)
Sixpees 42[1] (6f, Good, G, Sep 10, *M*)
Smart Pet 47[1] (5f, Newc, G, Aug 28, *H*)
Snipe Hall 49[1] (6f, Newj, F, Jun 26, *L*)
So Sedulous (USA) 40[2] (5f 11yds, Bath, G, Aug 10, *M*)
Solid Illusion (USA) 36 (1m, Long, S, Oct 2, *G*)
Southern Ridge 37[1] (6f 8yds, Newb, G, Sep 18, *M*)
Southern Power (IRE) 35[1] (7f, Redc, G, Nov 2, *M*)
Sovetsky 66[2] (1m 2f, Evry, Y, Sep 25, *L*)
Spain Lane (USA) 57[2] (7f, Curr, G, Sep 12, *G*)
Spot Prize (USA) 55[5] (1m, Asco, G, Sep 25, *G*)
Star Carnival (USA) 37[6] (7f, Newm, G, Oct 1, *L*)
Star Jazz (IRE) 39[1] (7f 100yds, Beve, G, Sep 15, *M*)
Star Selection 40[2] (6f, York, G, May 13, *M*)
Star Speeder (IRE) 38[4] (6f, Newj, F, Jul 31, *H*)
Star Talent (USA) 55[1] (6f, Good, Y, Jul 31, *M*)
Stash The Cash (IRE) 42[2] (1m, Kemp, G, Sep 21, *M*)
State Crystal (IRE) 43[1] (7f 16yds, Chep, Y, Oct 19, *M*)
State Performer (USA) 57[1] (6f, Asco, S, Jun 17, *L*)
Stimulant 50[2] (5f 34yds, Newb, F, Aug 14, *L*)
Stoller (USA) 36[2] (7f 3yds, Yarm, G, Sep 15, *M*)
Stonehatch (USA) 67[2] (6f, Good, G, Jul 28, *G*)
Storm Ship (IRE) 47[2] (6f, Asco, G, Sep 23, *H*)
Straight Arrow 52[2] (6f, Newj, F, Jul 31, *H*)
Strumpet City 45[1] (5f 217yds, Wind, G, Aug 28, *M*)
Sunshack 35[1] (1m 2f, Stcl, Y, Oct 31, *G*)
Suplizi (IRE) 38[2] (7f, Newm, G, Oct 16)
Suris (IRE) 43[2] (7f, Redc, G, Aug 25)
Sweetings Pisces 36[2] (5f, Beve, F, May 8)
Tablah (USA) 36[5] (7f, Newm, G, Oct 15, *G*)
Tabook (IRE) 57[2] (6f, Newm, G, Oct 15, *M*)
Taghareed (USA) 37[1] (6f, Redc, F, Jul 21, *M*)
Tailcoat (USA) 36[2] (5f 161yds, Bath, G, Sep 13, *M*)
Takadou (IRE) 39[2] (5f, Newm, G, Sep 30, *H*)
Tamar's Brigade 45[1] (6f 214yds, York, S, Oct 7)
Tango Trio (IRE) 48[1] (6f, Curr, G, Jun 26, *M*)
Tansy 43[1] (6f, Redc, G, Oct 5, *M*)
Tatami (USA) 58[1] (6f 212yds, Sali, G, Sep 29)
Tellurium (USA) 51[5] (6f, Deau, G, Aug 1, *G*)
Thabit (USA) 42[2] (7f, Newb, F, Aug 13, *L*)
The Deep (IRE) 43[1] (1m, Newm, G, Sep 29, *M*)
The Flying Phantom 51[2] (1m 4yds, Pont, G, Oct 21, *L*)
The Puzzler (IRE) 46[3] (5f, Curr, G, Jul 10, *G*)
Threatening 37[4] (7f, Newm, G, Oct 15, *G*)
Time Star (USA) 41[2] (6f, Asco, S, Jun 17, *L*)
Timiniya (IRE) 40[5] (7f, Curr, S, Oct 2, *G*)
Tinker Osmaston 40[1] (5f, Donc, G, Jun 25)
Tom Waller (IRE) 42[2] (1m, Newm, G, Oct 14, *M*)
Top Guide (USA) 47[2] (1m, Newm, G, Oct 14, *M*)
Torch Rouge 49[6] (7f, Newm, G, Sep 29)
Tricorne 44[3] (5f 34yds, Newb, F, Aug 14, *L*)
Triple Tie (USA) 41[2] (7f 16yds, Chep, Y, Oct 19, *M*)
Tukano (CAN) 37[2] (7f 3yds, Yarm, Y, Nov 5, *M*)
Turtle Island (IRE) 66[1] (5f, Asco, S, Jun 17, *G*)
Twice In Bundoran (IRE) 36[1] (5f, Ripo, F, Jul 5, *M*)
Twin Falls (IRE) 36[5] (1m 4yds, Pont, G, Oct 21, *L*)
Tzu'mu 53[1] (6f, Newm, G, Oct 15, *M*)
Ultimo Imperatore 57[1] (6f, Donc, G, Oct 23, *L*)
Unblest 47[2] (6f, York, G, Aug 18, *G*)
Velvet Moon (IRE) 61[1] (6f, York, G, Aug 19, *G*)
Vercingetorix (IRE) 43[1] (6f, Good, Y, Jul 29, *H*)
Village Eagle (FR) 35 (7f, Newm, G, Oct 15, *G*)
Volochine (IRE) 60[3] (7f, Long, G, Sep 12, *G*)
Waafed (USA) 38[3] (6f, Kemp, F, Sep 3, *H*)
Waiting 36[3] (1m, Newm, G, Sep 29, *M*)
Wajiba Riva (IRE) 50[1] (5f, Asco, F, Apr 28)
Watani (USA) 57[1] (6f, Kemp, G, Sep 4, *L*)
Weigh Anchor 54[1] (1m, Newm, G, Oct 14, *M*)
Welsh Mist 49[1] (5f, York, G, Sep 1)
West Man (USA) 55[3] (7f, Deau, G, Aug 14, *L*)
Wezzo (USA) 38[3] (5f, Deau, G, Aug 18, *L*)
Wild Planet (USA) 39[2] (7f, Good, F, Aug 27, *G*)
Winning Line 35[4] (1m 1f 213yds, Nott, S, Sep 21, *H*)
Wishing (USA) 50[2] (7f, Good, Y, Jul 30, *M*)
Ya Malak 53[4] (5f, Donc, G, Sep 11, *G*)
Yet More Roses 38[6] (6f, Newm, G, Oct 15, *M*)
Zavaleta (IRE) 52[1] (6f, Naas, G, Oct 16, *H*)
Zindari (USA) 55[4] (1m, Long, S, Oct 2, *G*)
Zuboon (USA) 42[3] (1m, Donc, G, Oct 22, *H*)
Zuno Star (USA) 37[2] (6f, Kemp, F, May 29)

Speed Ratings Flat (A.W.) 1993

● THIS list derived from Sporting Life Average Times, represents the optimum time-rating of a horse after taking into account varying ground conditions, adjusted to 9st. To qualify for inclusion a horse must earn a speed rating of over 25. Supplementary information after the name, figure, and finishing position indicates the distance, course, going based on time, date and type of race the rating was achieved in.

Abalene 40^{3} (1m 4f, Sout, Std, Aug 7, *H*)
Abbey Strand (USA) 43^{3} (1m, Ling, Fast, Nov 28 1992, *H*)
Aberdeen Heather 41^{4} (1m 2f, Ling, Fast, Aug 1, *H*)
Aberlady 34^{5} (5f, Ling, Std, Nov 13, *H*)
Able Choice (IRE) 27^{2} (1m, Sout, Std, Nov 1, *M*)
Absolutely Fact (USA) 39^{1} (1m 2f, Ling, Std, Jan 14, *H*)
Absolution 43^{5} (5f, Sout, Fast, Nov 27 1992, *H*)
Absonal 47^{1} (1m, Ling, Fast, Jan 2, *H*)
Admirals Secret (USA) 45^{2} (1m, Sout, Std, Jan 29, *H*)
African Chimes 49^{1} (6f, Sout, Fast, Dec 2 1992, *C*)
Aitch N'bee 26^{6} (7f, Sout, Std, Apr 5, *H*)
Albert 29^{1} (1m 4f, Ling, Fast, Feb 11, *H*)
Albert The Bold 34^{5} (7f, Ling, Fast, Dec 9 1992, *H*)
Aljaz 42^{1} (6f, Sout, Std, Jul 2, *M*)
Allinson's Mate (IRE) 59^{4} (7f, Ling, Fast, Feb 27, *H*)
Amenable 34^{3} (1m, Sout, Std, Apr 26, *H*)
Amour Royal 25^{2} (1m 4f, Sout, Std, Feb 12, *C*)
Anar (IRE) 26^{3} (1m 4f, Sout, Std, Jul 16, *H*)
Annacurragh (IRE) 32^{1} (1m 2f, Ling, Fast, Nov 30 1992, *C*)
Another Episode (IRE) 62^{2} (5f, Ling, Fast, Feb 20, *C*)
Appealing Times (USA) 50^{2} (6f, Sout, Std, Mar 5, *H*)
Appledorn 57^{1} (6f, Sout, Std, Mar 24, *C*)
Arc Lamp 42^{1} (5f, Sout, Std, Aug 14, *H*)
Arctic Guest (IRE) 31^{1} (1m 2f, Ling, Fast, Feb 4, *H*)
Ashdren 38^{4} (7f, Sout, Std, Apr 5, *H*)
Ashgore 50^{1} (7f, Sout, Std, Nov 16, *H*)
Ashover 25^{1} (1m 2f, Ling, Fast, Mar 6, *H*)
Assignment 46^{3} (5f, Ling, Fast, Feb 13, *H*)
Atlantic Way 37^{2} (1m 4f, Sout, Std, Jan 11, *H*)
Aude La Belle (FR) 28^{5} (2m, Sout, Std, Feb 1, *H*)
Awesome Power 58^{2} (1m 2f, Ling, Fast, Jan 2, *H*)
Awestruck 33^{1} (1m, Sout, Std, May 29)
Backstabber 34^{2} (1m, Sout, Std, Nov 16, *C*)
Bag Of Tricks (IRE) 37^{2} (1m 2f, Ling, Fast, Nov 10, *H*)
Ballyranter 34^{2} (1m 2f, Ling, Std, Mar 16, *H*)
Banbury Flyer 37^{1} (6f, Ling, Fast, Nov 30 1992, *H*)
Barahin (IRE) 35^{1} (1m 2f, Ling, Fast, Jul 26, *S*)
Battle Colours (IRE) 38^{2} (1m, Ling, Fast, Jun 25)
Bedouin Prince (USA) 30^{3} (1m 4f, Sout, Std, Jan 11, *H*)
Belated 28^{4} (6f, Sout, Fast, Dec 2 1992, *C*)
Believe In Me (IRE) 41^{2} (1m, Sout, Std, Dec 15 1992, *M*)
Belmoredean 49^{1} (1m, Ling, Std, Mar 4, *H*)
Bescaby Boy 51^{2} (1m, Sout, Std, Mar 8, *C*)
Beverly Knight 29^{1} (1m 2f, Ling, Std, Nov 13, *M*)
Biljan (USA) 36^{3} (1m 2f, Ling, Fast, Jun 19, *H*)
Black Boy (IRE) 34^{2} (7f, Sout, Std, Feb 26, *M*)
Blanchland 33^{1} (1m 2f, Ling, Std, Nov 13, *M*)
Boy Martin 38^{6} (7f, Sout, Slow, Feb 5, *H*)
Brackenthwaite 45^{1} (1m, Sout, Std, Apr 26, *H*)
Breakdancer (IRE) 30^{1} (1m 4f, Ling, Fast, Feb 20, *H*)
Brisas 29^{3} (6f, Sout, Std, Feb 26, *H*)
Broughtons Formula 43^{2} (1m 2f, Ling, Fast, Feb 4, *H*)
Buddy's Friend (IRE) 37^{1} (1m, Ling, Std, Jan 14, *H*)
Buzbour 32^{1} (6f, Sout, Std, Jan 29, *M*)
Calamanco 25^{5} (5f, Sout, Fast, Nov 16, *H*)
Camden's Ransom (USA) 63^{1} (1m 2f, Ling, Std, Mar 16, *H*)
Cantoris 31 (5f, Sout, Fast, Nov 16, *H*)
Captain Marmalade 35^{2} (1m 2f, Ling, Std, Nov 4, *H*)
Carlowitz (USA) 44^{2} (1m 2f, Ling, Std, Jan 30, *H*)
Caspian Beluga 44^{1} (1m 4f, Ling, Std, Nov 13, *H*)
Celestial Key (USA) 59^{1} (5f, Sout, Fast, Mar 24, *H*)
Certain Way (IRE) 36^{2} (1m, Sout, Std, Apr 26, *H*)
Charity Express (IRE) 29^{5} (5f, Ling, Std, Nov 4, *H*)
Charlie Bigtime 30^{3} (1m, Sout, Std, Jul 2, *H*)
Chatham Island 49^{2} (1m 2f, Ling, Fast, Aug 1, *H*)
Cheat (USA) 27^{3} (6f, Sout, Std, Jul 2, *M*)
Cheveux Mitchell 51^{2} (7f, Ling, Fast, Feb 27, *H*)
Choice Lot 30^{2} (6f, Sout, Slow, Feb 5, *H*)
Choir Practice 36^{5} (7f, Sout, Std, May 15, *H*)
Christian Spirit 25^{1} (1m, Ling, Fast, Dec 9 1992, *M*)
Clanrock 30^{6} (5f, Ling, Std, Nov 13, *H*)
Classic Account 39^{2} (1m 4f, Sout, Std, Dec 28 1992, *C*)
Claudia Miss 37^{1} (7f, Sout, Slow, Mar 1, *C*)
Cliburnel News (IRE) 26^{1} (1m 3f, Sout, Std, Aug 14, *C*)
Clifton Chase 38^{1} (1m 3f, Sout, Std, Nov 8)
Coleridge 40^{1} (2m, Ling, Fast, Jan 16, *H*)
Coltrane 49^{1} (1m 2f, Ling, Fast, Nov 30 1992, *H*)
Comet Whirlpool (IRE) 38^{2} (5f, Ling, Std, Nov 13, *H*)
Common Council 33^{2} (1m 2f, Ling, Fast, Nov 30 1992, *C*)
Continuity 33^{6} (1m 4f, Sout, Std, Jan 1, *H*)
Convenient Moment 29^{3} (5f, Sout, Fast, Jul 16, *H*)
Convoy 27^{6} (1m 2f, Ling, Std, May 15, *H*)
Courting Newmarket 37^{1} (7f, Ling, Fast, Oct 25)
Covent Garden Girl 42^{2} (6f, Sout, Std, Aug 7, *H*)
Creche 73^{1} (6f, Sout, Std, Mar 5, *H*)
Cretoes Dancer (USA) 32^{1} (1m 2f, Ling, Fast, Sep 7, *H*)
Criminal Record (USA) 30^{4} (1m 4f, Sout, Std, Aug 7, *H*)
Croft Imperial 30^{4} (5f, Sout, Fast, Nov 16, *H*)
Daaniera (IRE) 50^{1} (5f, Ling, Fast, Feb 11, *H*)
Daily Sport Don 37^{3} (7f, Ling, Fast, Jun 25, *C*)
Dam Certain (IRE) 26^{4} (1m, Ling, Fast, Feb 11, *H*)
Dance To Order (IRE) 36^{1} (7f, Sout, Std, Dec 10 1992, *M*)
Dashing Fellow (IRE) 36^{2} (1m 3f, Sout, Std, Nov 8)
Daswaki (CAN) 57^{1} (1m, Ling, Fast, Nov 28 1992, *H*)
Day Of History (IRE) 36^{2} (1m 2f, Ling, Fast, Jun 12, *H*)
Debacle (USA) 36^{3} (1m 2f, Ling, Fast, Jan 19, *H*)
Debsy Do (USA) 51^{1} (7f, Sout, Std, Mar 5, *H*)
Deduce 30^{3} (1m 4f, Sout, Std, Mar 24, *M*)
Devious Dancer 40^{1} (7f, Ling, Fast, Jun 25, *C*)
Diamond Inthe Dark (USA) 36^{2} (7f, Sout, Std, Feb 22, *H*)
Diamond Lucy 28^{5} (1m 2f, Ling, Fast, Feb 4, *H*)
Diamond Point 28^{2} (7f, Sout, Std, Dec 15 1992, *C*)
Digger Doyle 36^{1} (1m, Sout, Std, Feb 1, *C*)
Disputed Call (USA) 30^{2} (1m 4f, Ling, Fast, Nov 28 1992, *C*)
Doc's Coat 37^{2} (1m 4f, Sout, Std, Mar 24, *M*)
Doesyoudoes 36^{3} (5f, Sout, Fast, Nov 27 1992, *H*)
Donia (USA) 43^{2} (1m 2f, Ling, Fast, Nov 28 1992, *H*)
Dorazine 38^{1} (7f, Sout, Std, Feb 1, *H*)
Dream Carrier (IRE) 56^{1} (7f, Sout, Std, Feb 22, *H*)
Drummer's Dream (IRE) 28^{1} (5f, Sout, Std, Dec 15 1992, *H*)
Dune River 49^{1} (7f, Sout, Std, Apr 5, *H*)
Early To Rise 32^{2} (1m 3f, Sout, Std, Aug 14, *C*)
East Barns (IRE) 32^{1} (1m, Sout, Std, Dec 10 1992, *H*)
Eastern Memories (IRE) 28^{1} (7f, Ling, Fast, Nov 30 1992, *M*)
Eastleigh 35^{1} (1m, Ling, Fast, Jan 19, *C*)
Educated Pet 51^{3} (5f, Ling, Std, Nov 13, *H*)
El Dominio 36^{4} (1m 4f, Ling, Fast, Dec 9 1992, *H*)
El Volador 58^{4} (1m 2f, Ling, Fast, Apr 3, *H*)
Emperor Alexander (IRE) 41^{2} (1m 4f, Sout, Slow, Jan 22, *H*)
Erlking (IRE) 27^{2} (7f, Sout, Std, Dec 17 1992, *H*)
Ertlon 30 (1m, Sout, Std, Nov 8, *H*)
Etiquette 32^{2} (2m, Sout, Std, Feb 1, *H*)
Eurotwist 31^{3} (1m 4f, Sout, Std, Jan 15, *H*)
Ewald (IRE) 47^{4} (5f, Sout, Std, Mar 1, *H*)
Excess Baggage (IRE) 38^{2} (1m 2f, Ling, Std, Jan 14, *H*)
Express Service 46^{3} (1m 2f, Ling, Std, May 7, *C*)
Falcons Dawn 32^{3} (1m 2f, Ling, Fast, Nov 30 1992, *H*)
Family Rose 27^{1} (7f, Sout, Std, Sep 17, *H*)
Farm Street 26^{1} (7f, Sout, Std, Feb 15, *C*)
Fen Dance (IRE) 29^{5} (1m 2f, Ling, Fast, Jan 16, *H*)
Ferdia (IRE) 57^{1} (1m 2f, Ling, Std, Jan 30, *H*)
Field Of Vision (IRE) 34^{2} (7f, Sout, Std, Nov 1, *H*)
First Fling (IRE) 33^{2} (1m 4f, Sout, Std, Aug 13, *H*)
First Option 44^{4} (5f, Ling, Std, Nov 13, *H*)

Five To Seven (USA) 37^{3} (1m 4f, Sout, Std, Mar 5, *H*)
Food Of Love 33^{5} (5f, Sout, Std, Jul 24, *H*)
Formidable Liz 30^{2} (6f, Sout, Std, Jul 28, *H*)
Frescade (USA) 39^{4} (1m 2f, Ling, Fast, Nov 10, *H*)
Gallant Jack (IRE) 30^{1} (1m, Sout, Std, Aug 13, *H*)
Gilderdale 53^{1} (1m 2f, Ling, Fast, Nov 10, *H*)
Girl Next Door 29^{4} (6f, Sout, Std, Jan 4, *C*)
Glenfield Greta 29^{1} (7f, Sout, Std, Jul 16, *H*)
Gold Blade 44^{2} (1m 2f, Ling, Fast, Apr 3, *H*)
Golden Chip (IRE) 47^{1} (1m, Sout, Std, Aug 14, *H*)
Golden Klair 64^{1} (7f, Sout, Std, Mar 8, *H*)
Gran Senorum (USA) 46^{1} (1m, Sout, Std, Jul 2, *H*)
Grand Guignol 28^{3} (1m, Ling, Std, May 8, *H*)
Grand Time 30 (5f, Sout, Fast, Nov 27 1992, *H*)
Green's Fair (IRE) 45^{2} (7f, Sout, Std, Mar 8, *H*)
Greenwich Chalenge 29^{1} (7f, Sout, Std, Jan 1, *C*)
Guesstimation (USA) 34^{2} (1m, Ling, Fast, Dec 22 1992, *C*)
Gussie Fink-Nottle (IRE) 31^{5} (5f, Sout, Std, Aug 14, *H*)
Hadeer's Dance 49^{1} (7f, Ling, Fast, Aug 26, *H*)
Harcliff 31^{4} (7f, Sout, Std, May 25, *H*)
Hasten To Add (USA) 25^{1} (1m 4f, Sout, Std, Jun 4, *M*)
Hawaii Storm (FR) 31^{2} (1m, Sout, Std, Dec 15 1992, *H*)
Hazy Kay (IRE) 26^{2} (6f, Ling, Fast, Nov 10)
Heart Broken 41^{1} (6f, Sout, Std, Jul 10)
Heniu (USA) 61^{1} (7f, Ling, Fast, Mar 6, *H*)
Hershebar 30^{1} (5f, Sout, Fast, Feb 26, *C*)
Hierarch (USA) 38^{1} (1m 4f, Sout, Std, Mar 24, *M*)
High Summer 51^{1} (1m 4f, Sout, Std, Sep 17, *H*)
Highborn (IRE) 56^{1} (7f, Sout, Std, Jun 4, *H*)
Hinari Video 41^{1} (5f, Sout, Fast, Jan 1, *H*)
Honey Vision 41^{2} (6f, Ling, Std, Jan 14, *H*)
Horizon (IRE) 56^{1} (1m 6f, Sout, Std, Mar 24, *H*)
Indian Endeavour 56^{1} (5f, Sout, Fast, Dec 10 1992, *H*)
Intricacy 31^{3} (2m, Ling, Std, May 29, *H*)
Invocation 55^{2} (7f, Ling, Fast, Mar 6, *H*)
Iolite 51^{1} (5f, Sout, Std, Dec 15 1992, *H*)
Island Knight (IRE) 28^{1} (7f, Sout, Std, Jul 28)
Jake The Pake (IRE) 25^{1} (7f, Sout, Std, May 29, *C*)
Jess Rebec 26^{6} (5f, Sout, Fast, Jul 16, *H*)
Johnston's Express (IRE) 55^{1} (6f, Sout, Std, Feb 19, *H*)
Jordywrath 36^{2} (7f, Sout, Std, Feb 8, *H*)
Jovial Kate (USA) 26^{4} (6f, Ling, Std, Jan 14, *H*)
Juliet Bravo 28^{3} (5f, Ling, Std, Nov 4, *H*)
Juvenara 31^{2} (7f, Sout, Std, Dec 28 1992, *H*)
Kalar 28^{1} (5f, Sout, Fast, Jul 2, *H*)
Karinska 41^{2} (7f, Sout, Std, Nov 16, *H*)
Keyway (USA) 45^{2} (1m, Sout, Std, Jul 2, *H*)
Khrisma 44^{4} (1m 2f, Ling, Fast, Jan 2, *H*)
Killick 33^{2} (1m 2f, Ling, Fast, Feb 13, *H*)
Killy 30^{4} (1m, Ling, Std, Mar 4, *H*)
King Parrot (IRE) 28^{4} (1m, Sout, Std, Apr 1, *H*)
Kingston Brown 35^{3} (7f, Sout, Std, May 29, *H*)
Kissavos 28^{1} (7f, Ling, Fast, Nov 28 1992, *H*)
Klairover 27^{3} (7f, Sout, Std, Nov 24 1992, *H*)
Knock To Enter (USA) 63^{1} (7f, Ling, Fast, Mar 6, *C*)
Lady Dundee (USA) 36^{1} (1m 2f, Ling, Fast, Dec 22 1992, *H*)
Lady Lacey 32^{3} (1m 4f, Ling, Fast, Dec 9 1992, *H*)
Lady Roxanne 37^{3} (7f, Ling, Fast, Mar 27, *H*)
Langtonian 29^{4} (5f, Sout, Fast, Apr 1, *H*)
Last Straw 36^{3} (5f, Ling, Std, Mar 4, *H*)
Le Chic 39^{2} (5f, Ling, Fast, Feb 18, *H*)
Lily's Lover (USA) 25^{5} (7f, Sout, Slow, Mar 1, *C*)
Lincstone Boy (IRE) 39^{4} (5f, Sout, Std, Feb 15, *H*)
Little Saboteur 50^{2} (5f, Sout, Fast, Nov 27 1992, *H*)
Loch Duich 27^{3} (1m 2f, Ling, Std, Nov 4, *H*)
Lock Keeper (USA) 47^{1} (1m, Sout, Std, Dec 17 1992, *C*)
Lookingforarainbow (IRE) 47^{6} (1m 2f, Ling, Fast, Feb 13, *H*)
Lord Naskra (USA) 50^{2} (6f, Sout, Std, Feb 22, *H*)
Lord Nitrogen (USA) 41^{1} (1m 4f, Sout, Std, Apr 5, *M*)
Love Legend 55^{1} (5f, Sout, Std, Mar 8, *H*)
Lowawatha 46^{1} (1m 2f, Ling, Fast, Aug 1, *H*)
Lucayan Treasure 52^{2} (6f, Sout, Std, Mar 18, *H*)
Lyndon's Linnet 37^{2} (5f, Ling, Fast, Jan 23, *H*)
Mac's Fighter 42^{6} (7f, Ling, Fast, Feb 27, *H*)
Maid Welcome 42^{2} (5f, Sout, Std, May 15, *H*)
Majal (IRE) 31^{2} (1m 2f, Ling, Fast, Feb 4, *H*)
Major Triumph (IRE) 30^{2} (7f, Sout, Std, Dec 10 1992, *M*)
Marine Diver 28 (7f, Ling, Fast, Aug 26, *H*)
Marowins 35^{1} (7f, Sout, Std, Feb 26, *M*)
Martina 44^{4} (5f, Sout, Fast, Jan 1, *H*)
Martini Executive 30^{2} (1m, Sout, Slow, Jan 22, *H*)
Masnun (USA) 32 (1m, Ling, Fast, Mar 6, *H*)
Master Hyde (USA) 40^{1} (1m, Ling, Std, Jan 30, *H*)
Meeson Times 41^{2} (5f, Sout, Std, Aug 14, *H*)
Mel's Rose 29 (1m 2f, Ling, Fast, Jan 2, *H*)
Mentalasanythin 44^{2} (1m, Sout, Std, Feb 8, *H*)
Merlins Wish (USA) 54^{5} (7f, Ling, Fast, Feb 27, *H*)
Midnight Jazz (IRE) 51^{1} (1m, Sout, Std, Nov 1, *M*)
Mingus (USA) 36^{5} (1m 4f, Sout, Std, Jan 1, *H*)
Miss Aragon 28^{2} (6f, Sout, Std, Nov 8, *H*)
Miss Calculate 33^{2} (6f, Sout, Std, Jan 8, *C*)
Miss Gorgeous (IRE) 45^{1} (7f, Sout, Std, Jan 8, *H*)
Miss Whittingham (IRE) 27^{3} (5f, Sout, Fast, Jun 11, *H*)
Missed The Boat (IRE) 28^{3} (7f, Sout, Std, Jan 8, *H*)
Mister Blake 29^{1} (7f, Ling, Std, Mar 4, *C*)
Mister Jolson 45^{1} (5f, Ling, Fast, Jan 28, *H*)
Mizyan (IRE) 42^{2} (2m, Ling, Fast, Jan 16, *H*)
Modest Hope (USA) 47^{1} (1m 4f, Sout, Std, Jan 11, *H*)
Modesto (USA) 26^{1} (1m 2f, Ling, Fast, Apr 3, *H*)
Mohican Brave (IRE) 37^{4} (1m, Sout, Std, Jul 2, *H*)
Moonstruck Bard 33^{1} (7f, Sout, Std, Dec 15 1992, *C*)
Moot Point (USA) 29^{3} (2m, Sout, Std, Feb 1, *H*)
Morpick 29^{4} (7f, Sout, Slow, Mar 1, *C*)
Moscow Dynamo 43^{3} (7f, Sout, Std, Mar 5, *H*)
Most Surprising (IRE) 28^{3} (7f, Sout, Slow, Mar 1, *C*)
Mr Nevermind (IRE) 30^{3} (7f, Ling, Fast, Nov 10, *H*)
Mr Poppleton 41^{1} (1m 4f, Sout, Std, Feb 15, *M*)
Mulawih (USA) 34^{2} (1m 4f, Sout, Std, Feb 15, *M*)
Mulciber 54^{1} (1m 2f, Ling, Fast, Feb 13, *H*)
Music Dancer 36^{1} (7f, Sout, Std, Jul 2, *H*)
Must Be Magical (USA) 28^{2} (1m 4f, Sout, Std, Jul 16, *H*)
Mustn't Grumble (IRE) 33^{1} (6f, Ling, Fast, Nov 10)
Native Chieftan 36^{1} (1m 2f, Ling, Fast, Feb 27, *H*)
Nellie's Gamble 30^{3} (7f, Sout, Std, Jul 16, *H*)
Night Clubbing (IRE) 41^{5} (1m 2f, Ling, Fast, Dec 22 1992, *H*)
Nikki Noo Noo 39^{1} (6f, Sout, Std, Jan 4, *C*)
Nilu (IRE) 27^{4} (5f, Sout, Fast, Jul 16, *H*)
No More The Fool 35 (1m 4f, Sout, Std, Jan 1, *H*)
No Submission (USA) 60^{1} (1m, Sout, Std, Mar 8, *C*)
Nobby Barnes 40^{1} (6f, Ling, Fast, Feb 4, *H*)
North Esk (USA) 40^{5} (6f, Ling, Std, Jan 14, *H*)
On Y Va (USA) 46^{2} (7f, Sout, Slow, Feb 5, *H*)
One Off The Rail (USA) 51^{1} (1m 2f, Ling, Fast, Jun 12, *H*)
Our Eddie 32^{2} (1m 2f, Ling, Std, Nov 13, *M*)
Our Mica 28^{2} (5f, Sout, Std, May 25, *H*)
Palacegate Gold (IRE) 31^{4} (5f, Ling, Std, Mar 4, *H*)
Paley Prince (USA) 46^{3} (5f, Ling, Fast, Dec 3 1992, *H*)
Pallium (IRE) 30^{2} (5f, Sout, Fast, Nov 16, *H*)
Panchellita (USA) 35^{1} (7f, Sout, Std, Jul 24, *H*)
Panikin 45^{2} (7f, Sout, Std, Dec 10 1992, *H*)
Pay Homage 50^{4} (1m, Ling, Fast, Mar 6, *H*)
Peerage Prince 56^{1} (5f, Sout, Std, May 15, *H*)
Penny Banger (IRE) 31^{2} (7f, Sout, Std, Jul 2, *H*)
Persian Gusher (IRE) 41^{2} (7f, Ling, Fast, Aug 26, *H*)
Pesidanamich (IRE) 36^{2} (6f, Sout, Std, Dec 28 1992, *H*)
Pharaoh's Dancer 37^{1} (6f, Sout, Std, Nov 1, *H*)
Pharly Dancer 53^{3} (1m 4f, Sout, Std, Sep 17, *H*)
Pigalle Wonder 33^{1} (1m, Ling, Fast, Feb 11, *H*)
Pine Ridge Lad (IRE) 50^{1} (7f, Sout, Std, Feb 8, *H*)
Pirates Gold (IRE) 38^{2} (7f, Ling, Fast, Jun 25, *C*)
Play Hever Golf 52^{1} (6f, Sout, Std, Jan 29, *H*)
Point The Way (IRE) 33^{3} (1m 4f, Sout, Std, Aug 13, *H*)
Predictable 42^{1} (7f, Sout, Slow, Jan 22, *H*)
Premier Dance 34^{2} (1m 4f, Sout, Std, Sep 17, *H*)
Press The Bell 28^{1} (5f, Ling, Fast, Mar 27, *H*)
Pretonic 49^{1} (6f, Ling, Fast, Jan 19, *H*)
Prime Mover 54^{1} (6f, Sout, Std, Feb 26, *H*)
Purbeck Centenary 31^{3} (5f, Ling, Fast, Jan 9, *C*)
Quantity Surveyor 29^{6} (1m, Sout, Std, Jul 28, *H*)
Quatre Femme 46^{1} (6f, Sout, Std, Feb 22, *H*)
Quinsigimond 31^{2} (6f, Sout, Fast, Jun 19)
Quinzii Martin 43^{1} (7f, Sout, Slow, Feb 5, *H*)
Raging Thunder 41^{1} (7f, Ling, Std, May 29, *H*)
Rapporteur (USA) 63^{1} (1m 2f, Ling, Fast, Jan 2, *H*)
Record Lover (IRE) 35^{2} (1m 4f, Sout, Std, Jul 24, *H*)
Red Cotton 35^{2} (7f, Sout, Std, Jul 24, *H*)
Reflecting (IRE) 50^{1} (1m 2f, Ling, Fast, Jan 7, *H*)
Respectable Jones 48^{2} (5f, Ling, Fast, Dec 16 1992, *C*)

Rhythmic Dancer 57^{1} (5f, Ling, Fast, Dec 31 1992, *H*)
Ringland (USA) 32^{3} (1m, Sout, Fast, Dec 2 1992, *H*)
Ripsnorter (IRE) 31^{4} (1m 2f, Ling, Fast, Feb 27, *H*)
Rocality 30^{1} (7f, Ling, Fast, Nov 10, *H*)
Rock Opera (IRE) 30^{3} (6f, Sout, Std, Nov 27 1992, *H*)
Rockbourne 41^{4} (6f, Sout, Slow, Feb 5, *H*)
Rose Elegance 33^{3} (1m 2f, Ling, Fast, Nov 10, *H*)
Rose Flyer (IRE) 33^{3} (7f, Sout, Std, Jul 2, *H*)
Roseate Lodge 56^{3} (6f, Sout, Std, Mar 5, *H*)
Roveredo (USA) 35^{1} (1m 4f, Sout, Std, Apr 1, *M*)
Runaway Pete (USA) 53^{1} (1m 4f, Sout, Fast, Jun 19, *H*)
Running Glimpse (IRE) 55^{2} (6f, Ling, Fast, Jan 19, *H*)
Rural Lad 42^{1} (7f, Sout, Std, Feb 12, *H*)
Rushanes 33^{4} (7f, Ling, Fast, Mar 6, *C*)
Saahi (USA) 49^{1} (1m, Ling, Std, Mar 16, *C*)
Sabo The Hero 42^{1} (5f, Sout, Std, May 29, *H*)
Sakharov 38^{1} (6f, Sout, Std, Aug 7, *H*)
Salbus 30^{2} (1m 2f, Ling, Fast, Apr 3)
Salbyng 34^{4} (1m 2f, Ling, Std, Mar 16, *H*)
Sally's Son 30^{1} (7f, Sout, Std, Mar 8, *C*)
Samsolom 30^{4} (6f, Sout, Std, Nov 27 1992, *H*)
Samson-Agonistes 57^{1} (5f, Ling, Std, Nov 4, *H*)
Sandmoor Denim 47^{2} (7f, Sout, Std, Jun 4, *H*)
Santana Lady (IRE) 38^{5} (1m 2f, Ling, Std, Nov 4, *H*)
Sarum 42^{3} (1m, Ling, Std, Jan 14, *H*)
Scots Law 42^{1} (7f, Ling, Fast, Mar 27, *H*)
Serious Hurry 52^{1} (5f, Ling, Std, Mar 4, *H*)
Set The Fashion 53^{1} (1m, Sout, Std, Jul 28, *H*)
Shujan (USA) 57^{1} (1m 4f, Sout, Std, May 15, *H*)
Silky Heights (IRE) 38^{1} (1m 4f, Sout, Std, Aug 13, *H*)
Silky Siren 35^{2} (7f, Sout, Slow, Mar 1, *C*)
Silver Samurai 39^{3} (1m 4f, Sout, Slow, Jan 22, *H*)
Sinclair Lad (IRE) 29^{2} (1m 4f, Ling, Std, Mar 4, *H*)
Sir Norman Holt (IRE) 44^{1} (7f, Ling, Fast, Dec 9 1992, *H*)
Sir Tasker 47^{1} (5f, Sout, Fast, Apr 1, *H*)
Sir Thomas Beecham 35^{1} (2m, Ling, Fast, Aug 26, *H*)
Sirtelimar (IRE) 53^{1} (1m, Sout, Std, Feb 8, *H*)
Slades Hill 30 (5f, Sout, Std, Mar 1, *H*)
Slight Risk 36^{2} (1m 2f, Ling, Fast, Jan 7, *H*)
Smiles Ahead 29^{1} (1m 4f, Sout, Std, Jul 2, *S*)
So Superb 46^{3} (5f, Sout, Std, Aug 14, *H*)
Soba Guest (IRE) 56^{1} (5f, Ling, Fast, Jan 23, *H*)
Soviet Express 42^{1} (7f, Sout, Std, May 29, *H*)
Special Risk (IRE) 26^{2} (7f, Sout, Std, Jan 8, *H*)
Speed Oil 29^{3} (7f, Sout, Std, Feb 26, *M*)
Spencer's Revenge 60^{1} (7f, Ling, Fast, Feb 27, *H*)
Spender 30^{1} (6f, Ling, Std, Mar 16, *H*)
Splash Of Salt (IRE) 29^{1} (5f, Ling, Fast, Jan 9, *C*)
Spring High 41^{2} (5f, Sout, Fast, Jul 16, *H*)
Stalled (IRE) 36^{2} (1m 2f, Ling, Std, May 15, *H*)
Star Goddess (USA) 43^{1} (7f, Ling, Fast, Jul 9, *H*)
Stardust Express 38^{2} (6f, Sout, Std, Jul 14, *H*)
Steppey Lane 27^{1} (1m 6f, Sout, Std, Mar 18, *H*)
Stoproveritate 33^{1} (1m, Sout, Std, Nov 16, *C*)
Storm Free (USA) 55^{1} (1m 2f, Ling, Std, May 7, *C*)
Strat's Legacy 41^{1} (1m 4f, Ling, Std, Mar 4, *H*)
Strip Cartoon (IRE) 43^{1} (5f, Sout, Std, Mar 1, *H*)
Sugemar 43^{3} (1m 4f, Sout, Fast, Jun 11)
Sunset Street (IRE) 30^{4} (7f, Ling, Fast, Mar 27, *H*)
Super Lunar 38^{2} (1m 4f, Ling, Fast, Feb 11, *H*)
Super Summit 39^{1} (1m, Sout, Std, Dec 17 1992, *C*)
Superlativemaximus (IRE) 48^{2} (5f, Sout, Fast, Jul 2, *H*)
Suragon 28^{2} (6f, Sout, Std, Jul 2, *M*)
Sure Haven (IRE) 41^{4} (1m 4f, Sout, Std, Sep 17, *H*)
Sweet Romeo 41^{1} (6f, Sout, Std, Jul 14, *H*)
Sword Master 51^{1} (1m 4f, Sout, Std, Jan 18, *H*)
Sylvan Breeze 31^{4} (7f, Ling, Std, May 29, *H*)
Sylvan Sabre (IRE) 46^{1} (1m 2f, Ling, Fast, Jul 17)
Tacit Mac (USA) 59^{1} (7f, Sout, Std, Jan 15, *H*)
Tadora (IRE) 28^{2} (1m, Ling, Fast, Dec 9 1992, *H*)
Take Your Partner (IRE) 25^{5} (1m 2f, Ling, Std, May 15, *H*)
Talented Ting (IRE) 40^{6} (1m 2f, Ling, Fast, Nov 28 1992, *H*)
Tanagome (USA) 25^{2} (6f, Sout, Std, Mar 18, *C*)
Taunting (IRE) 27^{5} (1m 2f, Ling, Std, Jan 30, *H*)
Tee-Emm 30^{2} (5f, Ling, Fast, Jan 9, *C*)
Telephus 29^{2} (1m 4f, Ling, Std, Nov 13, *H*)
Tempering 58^{2} (1m 4f, Sout, Std, Jan 15, *H*)
The Dream Maker (IRE) 30^{3} (7f, Sout, Slow, Feb 5, *H*)
The Institute Boy 36^{4} (5f, Ling, Fast, Feb 11, *H*)
Themaam 41^{4} (7f, Sout, Std, Feb 22, *H*)
Tiger Shoot 46^{1} (1m 4f, Sout, Std, May 25)
Tino Tere 48^{2} (5f, Sout, Fast, Mar 24, *H*)
Tony's Mist 36^{5} (1m 2f, Ling, Fast, Nov 10, *H*)
Toshiba Comet 28^{6} (6f, Sout, Slow, Feb 5, *H*)
Trial Times (USA) 45^{2} (1m, Ling, Fast, Nov 28 1992, *H*)
Trioming 35^{2} (5f, Sout, Fast, Jun 11, *H*)
Tropical Jungle (USA) 36^{2} (1m 2f, Ling, Fast, Aug 14, *H*)
Trove 27 (1m 2f, Ling, Fast, Dec 31 1992, *H*)
Try Leguard (IRE) 28^{2} (1m, Ling, Fast, Jan 19, *C*)
Twilight Secret 36^{1} (1m 2f, Ling, Fast, Nov 28 1992, *H*)
Tyrian Purple (IRE) 39^{3} (6f, Ling, Fast, Feb 4, *H*)
Tyrone Flyer 49^{3} (7f, Sout, Std, Dec 28 1992, *H*)
Ulladulla 30^{3} (7f, Ling, Fast, Dec 9 1992, *C*)
Umhambi 28^{3} (1m 2f, Ling, Fast, Feb 4, *H*)
Usk The Way 40^{2} (2m, Ling, Fast, Aug 26, *H*)
Veloce (IRE) 40^{3} (6f, Sout, Std, Feb 22, *H*)
Very Dicey 52^{2} (5f, Ling, Std, Nov 4, *H*)
Vintage 29^{2} (1m 5f, Ling, Fast, Dec 22 1992, *H*)
Vuchterbacher 33^{4} (7f, Sout, Std, Dec 28 1992, *H*)
Waki Gold (USA) 45^{2} (1m 2f, Ling, Fast, Jul 17)
Watch Me Go (IRE) 28^{3} (1m, Sout, Std, Feb 1, *H*)
Wave Hill 30 (1m 2f, Ling, Fast, Nov 10, *H*)
Wee Sarah 41^{2} (7f, Sout, Std, Sep 17, *H*)
Well And Truly 32^{2} (1m 6f, Sout, Std, Feb 12, *H*)
Who's That Lady 26^{6} (7f, Sout, Std, Dec 28 1992, *H*)
Wild And Loose 30^{2} (7f, Ling, Fast, Aug 1, *S*)
Wintering (IRE) 39^{3} (5f, Sout, Fast, Mar 24, *H*)
Without A Flag (USA) 37^{2} (7f, Ling, Std, May 29, *H*)
Young Freeman (USA) 29^{3} (1m 4f, Ling, Fast, Oct 25, *H*)
Zeboim 30^{2} (7f, Ling, Std, Nov 13, *C*)

Two year olds

Astrac (IRE) 34^{1} (6f, Sout, Std, Nov 16, *M*)
Bold Aristocrat (IRE) 30^{3} (5f, Sout, Std, Sep 17)
Champagne Ateaster 25^{1} (6f, Sout, Std, Nov 1, *M*)
Convoy Point (IRE) 33^{1} (1m, Sout, Std, Sep 17, *M*)
Dance Focus 34^{3} (5f, Ling, Std, Nov 4, *H*)
Demi-Plie 28^{1} (7f, Sout, Std, Jul 16, *C*)
Eleuthera 29^{2} (5f, Sout, Std, Sep 17)
Fawlty Towers (IRE) 27^{1} (1m, Ling, Std, Nov 13, *H*)
Floating Trial 31^{1} (5f, Sout, Std, Aug 13, *S*)
Fort Knox (IRE) 29^{2} (6f, Sout, Std, Nov 1, *M*)
Golden Grand 36^{1} (7f, Sout, Std, Sep 17, *S*)
In A Moment (USA) 28^{1} (6f, Sout, Std, Nov 1, *M*)
Indefence (IRE) 26^{1} (7f, Sout, Std, Aug 14)
Make A Note (USA) 27^{3} (1m, Ling, Std, Nov 13, *H*)
Mister Beat 30^{1} (6f, Sout, Std, Jul 28, *M*)
Monkey's Wedding 43^{1} (5f, Sout, Std, Nov 8, *C*)
Royal Crest 30^{2} (6f, Sout, Std, Nov 16, *M*)
The Fernhill Flyer (IRE) 39^{1} (5f, Sout, Std, Sep 17)
Trendy Dancer (IRE) 36^{1} (5f, Sout, Std, Jul 10, *C*)

NOTES

NOTES

NOTES

NOTES

NOTES

NOTES

NOTES

NOTES

NOTES

NOTES

NOTES

NOTES

NOTES

NOTES

NOTES

NOTES

NOTES

NOTES

NOTES

NOTES

NOTES

NOTES

NOTES

NOTES

NOTES

NOTES

NOTES